Campbell Biology
with Additional Chapters of *A Short Guide to Writing about Biology*

Custom Ninth Edition for University of Southern California

Taken from:
Campbell Biology, Ninth Edition by Jane B. Reece, Lisa A. Urry, Michael L. Cain,
Steven A. Wasserman, Peter V. Minorsky, and Robert B. Jackson

A Short Guide to Writing about Biology, Seventh Edition by Jan A. Pechenik

Cover Art: Courtesy of PhotoDisc/Getty Images

Taken from:

Campbell Biology, Ninth Edition
by Jane B. Reece, Lisa A. Urry, Michael L. Cain, Steven A. Wasserman, Peter V. Minorsky, and Robert B. Jackson
Copyright © 2011, 2008, 2005 by Pearson Education, Inc.
Published by Benjamin Cummings
San Francisco, California 94111

A Short Guide To Writing About Biology, Seventh Edition
by Jan A. Pechenik
Copyright © 2010, 2007, 2004 by Pearson Education, Inc.
Published by Longman
New York, New York 10019

This special edition published in cooperation with Pearson Learning Solutions.

All trademarks, service marks, registered trademarks, and registered service marks are the property of their respective owners and are used herein for identification purposes only.

Pearson Learning Solutions, 501 Boylston Street, Suite 900,
Boston, MA 02116
A Pearson Education Company
www.pearsoned.com

Printed in the United States of America

3 4 5 6 7 8 9 10 0BRV 16 15 14 13 12

000200010270746458

CB

EARSON   ISBN 10: 1-256-27643-X
                ISBN 13: 978-1-256-27643-2

Dear USC Student:

In this course you will be using MasteringBiology®, an online tutorial and homework program that accompanies your textbook. *If you have joined a MasteringBiology course before and can still log in:* Save time by following the guide for joining another course (available from www.masteringbiology.com > Tours & Training > Getting Started) instead of this page.

What You Need:

- ✓ **A valid email address**
- ✓ **A student access code**
  (Comes in the Student Access Code Card/Kit that may have been packaged with your new textbook or that may be available separately in your school's bookstore. Otherwise, you can purchase access online at www.masteringbiology.com.)
- ✓ **The ZIP or other postal code for your school: 90089**
- ✓ **A Course ID:** _____ (May be provided by your instructor)

1. Register

- Go to www.masteringbiology.com and click **Students** under **Register**.
- To register using the student access code inside the MasteringBiology Student Access Code Card/Kit, select **Yes, I have an access code.** Click **Continue**.

  –OR– *Purchase access online:* Select **No, I need to purchase access online now.** Select your textbook, whether you want access to the eText, and click **Continue**. Follow the on-screen instructions to purchase access using a credit card. The purchase path includes registration, but the process is a bit different from the steps printed here.

- **License Agreement and Privacy Policy:** Click **I Accept** to indicate that you have read and agree to the license agreement and privacy policy.

- Select the appropriate option under "Do you have a Pearson Education account?" Continue to give the requested information until you complete the process. The **Confirmation & Summary** page confirms your registration. This information will also be emailed to you for your records.

- **Did you receive multiple access codes for MasteringBiology and/or Virtual Biology Labs?** Sometimes new books come with more than one student access code card. If you have more than one code, register using all of your codes BEFORE clicking Log In Now. For each additional code that you have, return to http://www.masteringbiology.com/ and click the **Students** button under Register again. *Important:* Identify the SAME student account each time you register. To do this, answer **Yes** to "Do you have a Pearson account?" Then enter your existing login name and password.

2. Log In

- Go to www.masteringbiology.com.
- Enter your Login Name and Password that you specified during registration and click **Log In**.

3. Join Your Instructor's Course and/or Open Self-Study Resources

Upon first login, you'll be asked to do one or more of the following:

- **Join a Course** by entering the **MasteringBiology Course ID** provided by your instructor. If you don't have a Course ID now, you can return to join the MasteringBiology course later. When you join a course, you may also be asked for a Student ID (follow on-screen instructions).

- **Explore the Study Area** or **Launch Your eText**, if these resources are available for your textbook.

To Access MasteringBiology Again Later

Simply go to www.masteringbiology.com, enter your Login Name and Password, and click **Log In**.

After you have joined a course: You can open any assignments from the **Assignments Due Soon** area or from the **Assignments** page. For self-study, click **eText** or **Study Area**, if these options are available.

Support

Access Customer Support at www.masteringbiology.com/support, where you will find:

- System Requirements
- Answers to Frequently Asked Questions
- Registration Tips & Tricks video
- Additional contact information for Customer Support, including Live Chat

Brief Contents

1 Introduction: Themes in the Study of Life 1

UNIT 1 The Chemistry of Life 28

2 The Chemical Context of Life 30
3 Water and Life 46
4 Carbon and the Molecular Diversity of Life 58
5 The Structure and Function of Large Biological Molecules 68

UNIT 2 The Cell 92

6 A Tour of the Cell 94
7 Membrane Structure and Function 125
8 An Introduction to Metabolism 142
9 Cellular Respiration and Fermentation 163
10 Photosynthesis 184
11 Cell Communication 206
12 The Cell Cycle 228

UNIT 3 Genetics 246

13 Meiosis and Sexual Life Cycles 248
14 Mendel and the Gene Idea 262
15 The Chromosomal Basis of Inheritance 286
16 The Molecular Basis of Inheritance 305
17 From Gene to Protein 325
18 Regulation of Gene Expression 351
19 Viruses 381
20 Biotechnology 396
21 Genomes and Their Evolution 426

UNIT 4 Mechanisms of Evolution 450

22 Descent with Modification: A Darwinian View of Life 452
23 The Evolution of Populations 469
24 The Origin of Species 488
25 The History of Life on Earth 507

UNIT 5 The Evolutionary History of Biological Diversity 534

26 Phylogeny and the Tree of Life 536
27 Bacteria and Archaea 556
28 Protists 575

29 Plant Diversity I: How Plants Colonized Land 600
30 Plant Diversity II: The Evolution of Seed Plants 618
31 Fungi 636
32 An Overview of Animal Diversity 654
33 An Introduction to Invertebrates 666
34 The Origin and Evolution of Vertebrates 697

UNIT 6 Plant Form and Function 736

35 Plant Structure, Growth, and Development 738
36 Resource Acquisition and Transport in Vascular Plants 764
37 Soil and Plant Nutrition 785
38 Angiosperm Reproduction and Biotechnology 801
39 Plant Responses to Internal and External Signals 821

UNIT 7 Animal Form and Function 850

40 Basic Principles of Animal Form and Function 852
41 Animal Nutrition 875
42 Circulation and Gas Exchange 897
43 The Immune System 929
44 Osmoregulation and Excretion 953
45 Hormones and the Endocrine System 974
46 Animal Reproduction 996
47 Animal Development 1021
48 Neurons, Synapses, and Signaling 1045
49 Nervous Systems 1062
50 Sensory and Motor Mechanisms 1085
51 Animal Behavior 1118

UNIT 8 Ecology 1142

52 An Introduction to Ecology and the Biosphere 1144
53 Population Ecology 1170
54 Community Ecology 1194
55 Ecosystems and Restoration Ecology 1218
56 Conservation Biology and Global Change 1238

About the Authors

The Ninth Edition author team's contributions reflect their biological expertise as researchers and teaching sensibilities gained from years of experience as instructors at diverse institutions. The team's highly collaborative style continues to be evident in the cohesiveness and consistency of the Ninth Edition.

Jane B. Reece

The head of the Ninth Edition author team, Jane Reece was Neil Campbell's longtime collaborator. She has participated in every edition of *BIOLOGY*. Earlier, Jane taught biology at Middlesex County College and Queensborough Community College. She holds an A.B. in Biology from Harvard University, an M.S. in Microbiology from Rutgers University, and a Ph.D. in Bacteriology from the University of California, Berkeley. Jane's research as a doctoral student and postdoctoral fellow focused on genetic recombination in bacteria. Besides her work on *CAMPBELL BIOLOGY*, she has been a coauthor of *Biology: Concepts & Connections*, *Essential Biology*, and *The World of the Cell*.

Lisa A. Urry

Lisa Urry (Chapter 1 and Units 1–3) is a professor and developmental biologist and recent Chair of the Biology Department at Mills College. After graduating from Tufts University with a double major in Biology and French, Lisa completed her Ph.D. in molecular and developmental biology at Massachusetts Institute of Technology (MIT). She has published a number of research papers, most of them focused on gene expression during embryonic and larval development in sea urchins. Lisa is also deeply committed to promoting opportunities for women in science education and research.

Michael L. Cain

Michael Cain (Units 4 and 5) is an ecologist and evolutionary biologist who is now writing full-time. Michael earned a joint degree in Biology and Math at Bowdoin College, an M.Sc. from Brown University, and a Ph.D. in Ecology and Evolutionary Biology from Cornell University. As a faculty member at New Mexico State University and Rose-Hulman Institute of Technology, he taught a wide range of courses, including introductory biology, ecology, evolution, botany, and conservation biology. Michael is the author of dozens of scientific papers on topics that include foraging behavior in insects and plants, long-distance seed dispersal, and speciation in crickets. In addition to his work on *CAMPBELL BIOLOGY*, Michael is also the lead author of an ecology textbook.

Steven A. Wasserman

Steve Wasserman (Unit 7) is a professor at the University of California, San Diego (UCSD). He earned his A.B. in Biology from Harvard University and his Ph.D. in Biological Sciences from MIT. Through his research on regulatory pathway mechanisms in the fruit fly *Drosophila*, Steve has contributed to the fields of developmental biology, reproduction, and immunity. As a faculty member at the University of Texas Southwestern Medical Center and UCSD, he has taught genetics, development, and physiology to undergraduate, graduate, and medical students. He has also served as the research mentor for more than a dozen doctoral students and more than 50 aspiring scientists at the undergraduate and high school levels. Steve has been the recipient of distinguished scholar awards from both the Markey Charitable Trust and the David and Lucille Packard Foundation. In 2007, he received UCSD's Distinguished Teaching Award for undergraduate teaching.

Peter V. Minorsky

Peter Minorsky (Unit 6) is a professor at Mercy College in New York, where he teaches evolution, ecology, botany, and introductory biology. He received his B.A. in Biology from Vassar College and his Ph.D. in Plant Physiology from Cornell University. He is also the science writer for the journal *Plant Physiology*. After a postdoctoral fellowship at the University of Wisconsin at Madison, Peter taught at Kenyon College, Union College, Western Connecticut State University, and Vassar College. He is an electrophysiologist who studies responses of plants to stress. Peter received the 2008 Award for Teaching Excellence at Mercy College.

Robert B. Jackson

Rob Jackson (Unit 8) is a professor of biology and Nicholas Chair of Environmental Sciences at Duke University. Rob holds a B.S. in Chemical Engineering from Rice University, as well as M.S. degrees in Ecology and Statistics and a Ph.D. in Ecology from Utah State University. Rob directed Duke's Program in Ecology for many years and just finished a term as the Vice President of Science for the Ecological Society of America. Rob has received numerous awards, including a Presidential Early Career Award in Science and Engineering from the National Science Foundation. He also enjoys popular writing, having published a trade book about the environment, *The Earth Remains Forever*, and two books of poetry for children, *Animal Mischief* and *Weekend Mischief.*

Neil A. Campbell

Neil Campbell combined the investigative nature of a research scientist with the soul of an experienced and caring teacher. He earned his M.A. in Zoology from UCLA and his Ph.D. in Plant Biology from the University of California, Riverside, where he received the Distinguished Alumnus Award in 2001. Neil published numerous research articles on desert and coastal plants and how the sensitive plant (*Mimosa*) and other legumes move their leaves. His 30 years of teaching in diverse environments included general biology courses at Cornell University, Pomona College, and San Bernardino Valley College, where he received the college's first Outstanding Professor Award in 1986. Neil was a visiting scholar in the Department of Botany and Plant Sciences at the University of California, Riverside. In addition to his authorship of this book, he coauthored *Biology: Concepts & Connections* and *Essential Biology* with Jane Reece. For the Ninth Edition of this book, we honor Neil's contributions to biology education by adopting the title CAMPBELL BIOLOGY.

Preface

Biology is an enormous subject, one that can seem overwhelming to students and scientists alike. Moreover, discoveries are being made at an unprecedented pace—from new kinds of small RNA molecules to the Neanderthal genome, from new biofuels to communities of organisms thriving beneath vast glaciers, from emerging infectious diseases to cancer vaccines. As a result, a general biology course faces a daunting challenge: to keep students from suffocating under an avalanche of information. CAMPBELL BIOLOGY addresses this challenge by providing a strong foundation for understanding both current knowledge and new developments in the context of underlying biological concepts.

Key Concepts and Unifying Themes

In each chapter of this textbook, a framework of three to six carefully chosen **Key Concepts** provide context for supporting details, helping students distinguish the "forest" from the "trees." The numbered Key Concepts are presented at the beginning of the chapter and then serve as headings for each chapter section. Concept Check Questions at the end of each section provide a hierarchical framework for self-assessment that builds students' confidence and then challenges them to push the limits of their understanding with several types of critical thinking questions. The Summary of Key Concepts at the end of the chapter refocuses students on the main points. CAMPBELL BIOLOGY also helps students organize and make sense of what they learn on a grander scale by emphasizing **evolution and other unifying themes** that pervade biology. These themes are introduced in Chapter 1 and integrated throughout the book.

New to This Edition: An Emphasis on Making Connections

In addition to Key Concepts and themes, we've created new features for the Ninth Edition that help students see the big picture by *making connections*. These include the following:

New Make Connections Questions: Making connections across chapters

New **Make Connections Questions** help students see how different areas of biology tie together, helping them overcome the tendency to compartmentalize information. Each question challenges students to move beyond memorization and gain a deeper understanding of biological principles by asking them to relate chapter content to material they learned earlier in the course. For example, we ask students to connect

- DNA replication (Chapter 16, see p. 319) to the cell cycle (Chapter 12);
- Soil formation (Chapter 37, see p. 789) to the properties of water (Chapter 3); and
- Aquatic biomes (Chapter 52, see p. 1163) to osmoregulation (Chapter 44).

At least three Make Connections Questions appear in each chapter. In addition, online *Make Connections Tutorials* in MasteringBiology® (see p. xi) connect content from two different chapters using figures from the book.

Expanded Evolution Coverage: Making connections to evolution in every chapter

Evolution is the core theme of biology, and in this edition it is more evident than ever. At least one **Evolution section in every chapter** focuses on evolutionary aspects of the chapter material, highlighted by a new Evolution banner. See, for example, the new discussions of enzyme evolution (p. 157), coevolution of flowers and pollinators (p. 806), and evolution of hormone function in animals (pp. 988–989).

New Impact Figures: Making connections between scientific advances and the real world

Our new **Impact Figures** motivate students by highlighting the dramatic impact of recent discoveries in biology. These figures feature high-interest topics such as induced pluripotent stem cells and regenerative medicine (Chapter 20, p. 417), the discovery of *Tiktaalik* (Chapter 34, p. 710), and the use of forensic ecology to track elephant poaching (Chapter 56, p. 1243). The *Why It Matters* section of each figure explains the relevance of the research to students' lives, global problems, or the field of biology itself. Each Impact Figure ends with a suggestion for *Further Reading* and a *What If?* or *Make Connections Question* to develop critical thinking skills.

New Visual Organizers and 3-D Art: Making connections visually

The new **Visual Organizer** format highlights the main parts of a figure, helping students see the key categories at a glance. See, for instance, Figure 17.24 on types of small-scale mutations (p. 345) or Figure 27.3, Gram staining (p. 557). Throughout the book, selected figures have been rendered in a more **3-D art style** while keeping an appropriate balance between realism and teaching effectiveness. Figure 52.3, Exploring Global Climate Patterns (p. 1146), is one example.

Restructured Chapter Reviews:
Making connections at a higher level

In the chapter summaries, each concept section now concludes with a new **Summary of Key Concepts Question** that is tied to a major learning goal. Also, this edition increases student awareness of different levels of thinking by organizing the end-of-chapter questions into three levels based on **Bloom's taxonomy**, which classifies types of thinking that are important in learning. Our levels are (1) Knowledge/Comprehension, (2) Application/Analysis, and (3) Synthesis/Evaluation. (These same levels are used in the Campbell Test Bank.) The range of question types helps students develop critical thinking skills and prepare for the kinds of questions they'll encounter on exams. New **Write About a Theme Questions** give students practice writing short, coherent essays that connect the chapter's content to one of the book's themes. (A suggested grading rubric can be found on p. xv, and sample answers are provided for instructors in the MasteringBiology Instructor Resources area.) A new **MasteringBiology preview section** at the end of each chapter lists *Assignments*—tutorials, activities, and questions that instructors can assign. This section also directs students to the *eText* and *Study Area* for online self study.

New Content:
Making connections to advances in science

As in each new edition, the Ninth Edition incorporates **new scientific content** and **organizational improvements**. These are summarized on pp. viii–ix, following this Preface.

MasteringBiology®:
Making connections outside of class

MasteringBiology, the most widely used online assessment and tutorial program for biology, provides an extensive library of homework assignments that are graded automatically. In addition to BioFlix® Tutorials, other Tutorials, Activities, Reading Quiz Questions in every chapter, and 4,500 Test Bank Questions, MasteringBiology for the Ninth Edition features an **improved user interface** and the following **new Tutorials and Questions**: *Make Connections Tutorials, Student Misconceptions Questions* for every chapter, *Data Analysis Tutorials, Experimental Inquiry Tutorials, Video Tutor Sessions,* and *MasteringBiology: Virtual Biology Labs*. For more information, see pp. xvi–xix and www.masteringbiology.com.

Our Hallmark Features

Besides our Key Concepts and unifying themes, several other features have contributed to the success of CAMPBELL BIOLOGY. Because text and illustrations are equally important for learning biology, **integration of figures and text** has been a hallmark of this book since its inception. Our popular *Exploring Figures* on selected topics epitomize this approach:

Each is a learning unit of core content that brings together related illustrations and text. Another example is our *Guided Tour Figures*, which use descriptions in blue type to walk students through complex figures like an instructor would, pointing out key structures, functions, and steps of processes.

To encourage **active learning**, recent editions have incorporated new types of questions: *What If? Questions, Figure Legend Questions,* and *Draw It Questions* that ask students to sketch a structure, annotate a figure, or graph data. In the Ninth Edition, these questions are augmented by the new *Make Connections Questions*. Online, the highly interactive *MasteringBiology tutorials* are sophisticated active-learning tools.

Finally, CAMPBELL BIOLOGY features **scientific inquiry**, an essential component of any biology course. Complementing stories of scientific discovery in the text narrative and the unit-opening interviews, *Inquiry Figures* help students understand "how we know what we know" and provide a model of how to think like a scientist. Each one begins with a research question and then describes how researchers designed an experiment, interpreted their results, and drew conclusions. The source article is referenced, and a What If? Question asks students to consider an alternative scenario. Selected Inquiry Figures invite students to read and analyze the original research article in the supplement *Inquiry in Action: Interpreting Scientific Papers* (see p. xxi). At the end of each chapter, *Scientific Inquiry Questions* give students additional opportunities to practice critical thinking by developing hypotheses, designing experiments, and analyzing real research data. Beyond the book, activities involving scientific inquiry are featured in MasteringBiology and other supplements, both print and electronic (see pp. xviii–xxi).

Our Partnership with Instructors

A core value underlying all our work as authors is our belief in the importance of our partnership with instructors. Our primary way of serving instructors, of course, is providing a textbook, supplements, and media resources that serve their students well. In addition, Benjamin Cummings makes available a rich variety of instructor resources, in both print and electronic form (see p. xx). In our continuing efforts to improve the book and its supplements, we benefit tremendously from instructor feedback, not only in formal reviews from hundreds of scientists, but also via informal communication, often by e-mail.

The real test of any textbook is how well it helps instructors teach and students learn. We welcome comments from the students and instructors who use CAMPBELL BIOLOGY. Please address your suggestions to any of us:

Jane Reece at janereece@cal.berkeley.edu
Lisa Urry (Chapter 1 and Units 1–3) at lurry@mills.edu
Michael Cain (Units 4 and 5) at mcain@bowdoin.edu
Peter Minorsky (Unit 6) at pminorsky@mercy.edu
Steve Wasserman (Unit 7) at stevenw@ucsd.edu
Rob Jackson (Unit 8) at jackson@duke.edu

New Content

This section provides just a few highlights of new content and organizational improvements in *CAMPBELL BIOLOGY*, Ninth Edition.

CHAPTER 1 Introduction: Themes in the Study of Life

We have added a separate new theme on energy flow while retaining a theme on environmental interactions. Concept 1.3, on the scientific method, has been reframed to more accurately reflect the scientific process, with a focus on observations and hypotheses. A new Concept 1.4 discusses the value of technology to society while emphasizing the cooperative nature of science and the value of diversity among scientists.

UNIT ONE The Chemistry of Life

For this edition, the basic chemistry is enlivened by new content connecting it to evolution, ecology, and other areas of biology. Examples of new material include omega-3 fatty acids, the isomeric forms of methamphetamine, arsenic contamination of groundwater, and the basis of mad cow disease. The burgeoning importance of nucleic acids throughout biology has prompted us to expand our coverage of DNA and RNA structures in this first unit. In fact, a general aim for the first two units is to infuse the chapters with more detail about nucleic acids, genes, and related topics. Another enhancement, in this and the next two units, is the inclusion of more computer models of important proteins in contexts where they support students' understanding of molecular function.

UNIT TWO The Cell

For Chapter 6, we developed an Exploring Figure on microscopy, which includes new types of microscopy, and we added micrographs of various cell types to the Exploring Figure on eukaryotic cells. We also expanded our description of chromosome composition, with the goal of preempting some common student misconceptions about chromosomes and DNA. New connections to evolution include an introduction to the endosymbiont theory in Chapter 6 and some interesting evolutionary adaptations of cell membranes in Chapter 7. We've added a new section to Chapter 8 on the evolution of enzymes with new functions, which not only strengthens enzyme coverage but also provides an early introduction to the concept that mutations contribute to molecular evolution. In Chapter 9, we simplified the glycolysis figure and emphasized pyruvate oxidation as a separate step to help students focus on the main ideas. In keeping with our increased focus on global

issues in the Ninth Edition, Chapter 10 has an Impact Figure on biofuels and a discussion of the possible effect of climate change on the distribution of C_3 and C_4 plants. In Chapter 11, we have added an Impact Figure to highlight the importance and medical relevance of G protein-coupled receptors.

UNIT THREE Genetics

In Chapters 13–17, we have added material to stimulate student interest—for example, a new Impact Figure on genetic testing for disease-associated mutations. As done throughout the Ninth Edition, we ask students to make connections between chapters so that they avoid the trap of compartmentalizing the information in each chapter. For instance, Chapter 15 discusses the Philadelphia chromosome associated with chronic myelogenous leukemia and asks students to connect this information to what they learned about signaling in the cell cycle in Chapter 12. Also, we encourage students to connect what they learn about DNA replication and chromosome structure in Chapter 16 to the material on chromosome behavior during the cell cycle in Chapter 12. Chapter 16 has a new figure showing a current 3-D model of the DNA replication complex, with the lagging strand looping back through it.

Chapters 18–21 are extensively updated, with the changes dominated by new genomic sequence data and discoveries about the regulation of gene expression. (The introduction to genes, genomes, and gene expression in Units One and Two should help prepare students for these revisions.) Chapter 18 includes a new section on nuclear architecture, which describes the organization of chromatin in the nucleus in relation to gene expression. The roles of various types of RNA molecules in regulation also receive special attention. In the section on cancer, we describe how technical advances can contribute to personalized cancer treatments based on the molecular characteristics of an individual's tumor. Chapter 19 discusses the 2009 H1N1 flu pandemic. Chapter 20 includes advances in techniques for DNA sequencing and for obtaining induced pluripotent stem (iPS) cells. Finally, the heavily revised Chapter 21 describes what has been learned from the sequencing of many genomes, including those of a number of human individuals.

UNIT FOUR Mechanisms of Evolution

For this edition, we have continued to bolster our presentation of the vast evidence for evolution by adding new examples and figures that illustrate key conceptual points throughout the unit. For example, Chapter 22 now presents research data on adaptive evolution in soapberry bugs, fossil findings that shed light on the origins of cetaceans, and an Impact Figure on the rise of methicillin-resistant *Staphylococcus aureus*. Chapter 23 examines gene flow and adaptation in songbird populations. Chapter 24 incorporates several new examples of speciation research, including reproductive isolation in mosquitofish, speciation in shrimp, and hybridization of bear species. Other changes strengthen the storyline of the unit, ensuring that the chapters flow smoothly and build to a clear overall picture of what evolution is and how it works. For instance, new connections between Chapters 24 and 25 illustrate how differences in speciation and extinction rates shape the broad patterns in the history of life. We've also added earlier and more discussion of "tree thinking," the interpretation and application of phylogenetic trees, beginning in Chapter 22.

UNIT FIVE The Evolutionary History of Biological Diversity

One of our goals for the diversity unit was to expand the coverage of the scientific evidence underlying the evolutionary story told in the chapters. So, for example, Chapter 27 now presents new findings on the evolutionary origin of bacterial flagella. In keeping with our increased emphasis on big-picture "tree thinking," we've added an "evogram" on tetrapod evolution in Chapter 34. (An evogram is a diagram illustrating the multiple lines of evidence that support the hypothesis shown in an evolutionary tree.) In addition, to help engage students, we've included new applications and woven more ecological information into our discussions of groups of organisms. Examples include new material on global growth of photosynthetic protists (Chapter 28), endangered molluscs (Chapter 33), and the impact of a pathogenic chytrid fungus on amphibian population declines (Chapters 31 and 34).

UNIT SIX Plant Form and Function

Plant biology is in a transitional phase; some professors prefer strong coverage of classical botany while others seek more in-depth coverage of the molecular biology of plants. In developing the Ninth Edition, we have continued to balance the old and the new to provide students with a basic understanding of plant anatomy and function while highlighting dynamic areas of plant research and the many important connections between plants and other organisms. One major revision goal was to provide more explicit discussion of the evolutionary aspects of plant biology, such as the coevolution of flowering plants and pollinators (Chapter 38). Updates include new findings in plant development in Concept 35.5 and new material on the dynamism of plant architecture as it relates to resource acquisition in Chapter 36.

UNIT SEVEN Animal Form and Function

In revising this unit, we strove to introduce physiological systems through a comparative approach that underscores how adaptations are linked to shared physiological challenges. In particular, we have highlighted the interrelationship of the endocrine and nervous systems at multiple points in the unit, helping students appreciate how these two forms of communication link tissues, organs, and individuals. Other revisions aim to keep students focused on fundamental concepts amid the details of complex systems. For example, many figures have been reconceived to emphasize key information, including new figures comparing single and double circulation (Chapter 42) and examining the function of antigen receptors (Chapter 43), as well as new Exploring Figures on the vertebrate kidney (Chapter 44) and the structure and function of the human eye (Chapter 50). Chapter 43 has been significantly revised to support students' conceptual understanding of basic immunological responses and the key cellular players. Throughout the unit, new state-of-the-art images and material on current and compelling topics—such as circadian rhythms (Chapter 40), novel strains of influenza (Chapter 43), the effects of climate change on animal reproductive cycles (Chapter 46), and advances in understanding brain plasticity and function (Chapter 49)—will help engage students and encourage them to make connections beyond the text.

UNIT EIGHT Ecology

Our revision was informed by the fact that biologists are increasingly asked to apply their knowledge to help solve global problems, such as climate change, that already are profoundly affecting life on Earth. As part of our increased emphasis on global ecology in this edition, we have made significant changes to Unit Eight's organization and content. The organizational changes begin with the introductory chapter of the unit (Chapter 52), which includes a new Key Concept 52.1: "Earth's climate varies by latitude and season and is changing rapidly." Introducing the global nature of climate and its effects on life at the beginning of the chapter provides a logical foundation for the rest of the material. New content in Chapters 53 and 54 highlights factors that limit population growth, the ecological importance of disease, positive interactions among organisms, and biodiversity. Chapter 55 now explores restoration ecology together with ecosystem ecology because successful restoration efforts depend on understanding ecosystem structure and function. Finally, the new title of the unit's capstone, Chapter 56, reflects its emphasis on the combined importance of conservation and our changing Earth: "Conservation Biology and Global Change." Several new Impact Figures in the unit show students how ecologists apply biological knowledge and ecological theory at all scales to understand and solve problems in the world around them.

Focus on the Key Concepts.

Each chapter is organized around a framework of 3 to 6 **Key Concepts** that will help you stay focused on the big picture and give you a context for the supporting details.

52

An Introduction to Ecology and the Biosphere

▲ Figure 52.1 **What threatens this amphibian's survival?**

KEY CONCEPTS

52.1 Earth's climate varies by latitude and season and is changing rapidly

52.2 The structure and distribution of terrestrial biomes are controlled by climate and disturbance

52.3 Aquatic biomes are diverse and dynamic systems that cover most of Earth

52.4 Interactions between organisms and the environment limit the distribution of species

OVERVIEW

Discovering Ecology

When University of Delaware undergraduate Justin Yeager spent his summer abroad in Costa Rica, all he wanted was to see the tropical rain forest and to practice his Spanish. Instead, he rediscovered the variable harlequin toad (*Atelopus varius*), a species thought to be extinct in the mountain slopes of Costa

Rica and Panama where it once lived (Figure 52.1). During the 1980s and 1990s, roughly two-thirds of the 82 known species of harlequin toads vanished. Scientists think that a disease-causing chytrid fungus, *Batrachochytrium dendrobatidis* (see Figure 31.26), contributed to many of these extinctions. Why was the fungus suddenly thriving in the rain forest? Cloudier days and warmer nights associated with global warming appear to have created an environment ideal for its success. As of 2009, the species that Yeager found was surviving as a single known population of fewer than 100 individuals.

What environmental factors limit the geographic distribution of harlequin toads? How do variations in their food supply or interactions with other species, such as pathogens, affect the size of their population? Questions like these are the subject of **ecology** (from the Greek *oikos*, home, and *logos*, study), the scientific study of the interactions between organisms and the environment. Ecological interactions occur at a hierarchy of scales that ecologists study, from single organisms to the globe (Figure 52.2).

Ecology's roots are in our basic human interest in observing other organisms. Naturalists, including Aristotle and Darwin, have long studied the living world and systematically recorded their observations. However, modern ecology involves more than observation. It is a rigorous experimental science that requires a breadth of biological knowledge. Ecologists generate hypotheses, manipulate environmental variables, and observe the outcome. In this unit, you will encounter many examples of ecological experiments, whose complex challenges have made ecologists innovators in experimental design and statistical inference.

In addition to providing a conceptual framework for understanding the field of ecology, Figure 52.2 provides the organizational framework for our final unit. In this chapter, we first describe Earth's climate and the importance of climate and other physical factors in determining the location of major life zones on land and in the oceans. We then examine how ecologists determine what controls the distribution and abundance of individual species. The next three chapters investigate population, community, and ecosystem ecology in detail, including approaches for restoring degraded ecosystems. The final chapter explores conservation biology and global ecology as we consider how ecologists apply biological knowledge to predict the global consequences of human activities and to conserve Earth's biodiversity.

concept 52.1

Earth's climate varies by latitude and season and is changing rapidly

The most significant influence on the distribution of organisms on land and in the oceans is **climate**, the long-term, prevailing weather conditions in a given area. Four physical

Before you begin reading the chapter, get oriented by reading the **list of Key Concepts,** which introduces the big ideas covered in the chapter.

Each **Key Concept** serves as the heading for a major section of the chapter.

After reading a concept section, check your understanding using the **Concept Check Questions** at the end of the section. Work through these questions on your own or in a study group—they're good practice for the kinds of questions you might be asked on an exam.

What If? Questions ask you to apply what you've learned. New **Make Connections Questions** ask you to relate content in the chapter to a concept you learned earlier in the course.

If you can answer these questions (see Appendix A to check your work), you're ready to move on. ▶

CONCEPT CHECK 52.1

1. Explain how the sun's unequal heating of Earth's surface leads to the development of deserts around 30° north and south of the equator.

2. What are some of the differences in microclimate between an unplanted agricultural field and a nearby stream corridor with trees?

3. **WHAT IF?** Changes in Earth's climate at the end of the last ice age happened gradually, taking centuries to thousands of years. If the current global warming happens very quickly, as predicted, how may this rapid climate change affect the ability of long-lived trees to evolve, compared with annual plants, which have much shorter generation times?

4. **MAKE CONNECTIONS** In Concept 10.4 (pp. 199–201), you learned about the important differences between C_3 and C_4 plants. Focusing just on the effects of temperature, would you expect the global distribution of C_4 plants to expand or contract as Earth becomes warmer? Why?

For suggested answers, see Appendix A.

Make connections across biology.

By relating the content of a chapter to material you learned earlier in the course, new **Make Connections Questions** help you develop a deeper understanding of biological principles.

CONCEPT CHECK **41.1**

2. **MAKE CONNECTIONS** Review the discussion of enzymes in metabolic reactions in Concept 8.4 (pp. 152–156). Then explain why vitamins are required in very small amounts in the diet.

Enzymes
(Chapter 8)

Animal nutrition
(Chapter 41)

CONCEPT CHECK **16.2**

3. **MAKE CONNECTIONS** What is the relationship between DNA replication and the S phase of the cell cycle? See Figure 12.6, page 231.

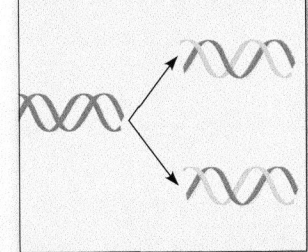

Cell cycle
(Chapter 12)

DNA replication
(Chapter 16)

CONCEPT CHECK **31.2**

1. **MAKE CONNECTIONS** Compare Figure 31.5 with Figure 13.6 (p. 252). In terms of haploidy versus diploidy, how do the life cycles of fungi and animals differ?

Meiosis
(Chapter 13)

Fungi
(Chapter 31)

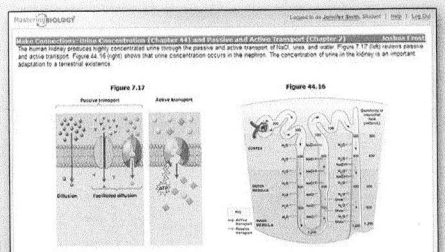

New **Make Connections Tutorials** help you connect biological concepts across chapters in an interactive way.

Make connections to **evolution,** the fundamental theme of biology.

Look for new **Evolution banners** highlighting sections in each chapter that focus on evolutionary aspects of the topic.

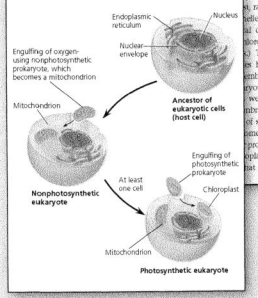

The Evolutionary Origins of Mitochondria and Chloroplasts

EVOLUTION Mitochondria and chloroplasts display similarities with bacteria that led to the **endosymbiont theory**, illustrated in Figure 6.16. This theory states that an early ancestor of eukaryotic cells engulfed an oxygen-using nonphotosynthetic prokaryotic cell. Eventually, the engulfed cell formed a relationship with the host cell in which it was enclosed, becoming an *endosymbiont* (a cell living within another cell). Indeed, over the course of evolution, the host cell and its endosymbiont merged into a single organism, a eukaryotic cell with a mitochondrion. At least one of these cells may have then taken up a photosynthetic prokaryote, becoming the ancestor of eukaryotic cells that contain chloroplasts.

This is a widely accepted theory, which we will discuss in more detail in Chapter 25. The model it proposes is consistent with many structural features of mitochondria and chloroplasts, rather than being bounded by a single membrane like the organelles of the endomembrane system, mitochondria and chloroplasts have two membranes surrounding them. Mitochondria and chloroplasts also have an internal system of membranes as well. There is evidence that the ancestral engulfed prokaryotes had two outer membranes, which became the double membranes of mitochondria and chloroplasts. Second, like prokaryotes, mitochondria and chloroplasts contain ribosomes, as well as circular DNA molecules attached to their inner membranes. The DNA in these organelles programs the synthesis of some of their own proteins, which are made on and completed on ribosomes inside the organelles. Third, also consistent with their probable evolutionary origins as cells, mitochondria and chloroplasts are autonomous (somewhat independent) organelles that grow and reproduce within the cell.

Practice thinking like a scientist.

New **Impact Figures** demonstrate the ▶
dramatic impact of recent discoveries in biology
and show that biology is constantly changing
as new discoveries add to our understanding.

Inquiry Figures reveal "how we know what
we know" by highlighting how researchers
designed an experiment, interpreted their
results, and drew conclusions.
▼

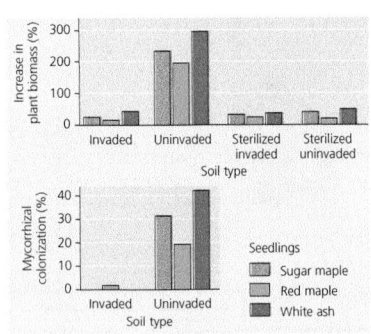

▽ Figure 37.14   **INQUIRY**

**Does the invasive weed garlic mustard disrupt
mutualistic associations between native tree
seedlings and arbuscular mycorrhizal fungi?**

EXPERIMENT Kristina Stinson, of Harvard
University, and colleagues investigated the effect of invasive garlic mustard on the growth of
native tree seedlings and associated mycorrhizal
fungi. In one experiment, they grew seedlings of three North American trees—sugar
maple, red maple, and white ash—in four
different soils. Two of the soil samples were
collected from a location where garlic mustard was growing, and one of these samples
was sterilized. The other two soil samples
were collected from a location devoid of garlic mustard, and one was then sterilized.
After four months of growth, the researchers harvested the shoots and
roots and determined the dried biomass. The roots were also analyzed
for percent colonization by arbuscular mycorrhizal fungi.

RESULTS Native tree seedlings grew more slowly and were less able to
form mycorrhizal associations when grown either in sterilized soil or in
unsterilized soil collected from a location that had been invaded by garlic mustard.

CONCLUSION The data support the hypothesis that garlic mustard
suppresses growth of native trees by affecting the soil in a way that disrupts mutualistic associations between the trees and arbuscular mycorrhizal fungi.

SOURCE K. A. Stinson et al., Invasive plant suppresses the growth of
native tree seedlings by disrupting belowground mutualisms, *PLoS Biol
(Public Library of Science: Biology)* 4(5): e140 (2006).

INQUIRY IN ACTION Read and analyze the original paper in *Inquiry in
Action: Interpreting Scientific Papers.*

WHAT IF? What effect would applying inorganic phosphate to soil
invaded by garlic mustard have on the plant's ability to outcompete native species?

▲
After exploring the featured experiment,
test your analytical skills by answering the
What If? Question. Suggested answers are
provided in Appendix A to help you gauge
your understanding.

Why It Matters explains the ▶
relevance of the research.

Further Reading directs you ▶
to articles to explore.

A **Make Connections** or ▶
What If? Question
encourages critical thinking.

Some **Inquiry Figures**
invite you to read and
analyze the original research
paper in its complete form.
You can find the journal
article, along with a worksheet
guiding you through it, in
◀ the separate book *Inquiry
in Action: Interpreting
Scientific Papers.*

▽ Figure 56.9
IMPACT

Forensic Ecology and Elephant Poaching

This array of severed tusks is part of an illegal shipment of 6,000 kg
of ivory intercepted on its way from Africa to Singapore in 2002.
Investigators wondered whether the elephants slaughtered for the
ivory—perhaps as many as 6,500—were killed in the area where the
shipment originated, primarily Zambia, or instead were killed across
Africa, indicating a broader smuggling ring. Samuel Wasser, of the
University of Washington, and colleagues amplified specific segments
of DNA from the tusks using the polymerase chain reaction (PCR).
These segments included stretches of DNA containing short tandem
repeats (STRs; see Concept 20.4, pp. 420–421), the number of which
varies among different elephant populations. The researchers then
compared alleles at seven or more loci with a reference DNA database
they had generated for elephants of known geographic origin. Their
results showed conclusively that the elephants came from a narrow
east-west band centered on Zambia rather than from across Africa.

WHY IT MATTERS The DNA analyses suggested that poaching
rates were 30 times higher in Zambia than previously estimated.
This news led to improved antipoaching efforts by the Zambian
government. Techniques like those used in this study are being employed by conservation biologists to track the harvesting of many
endangered species, including whales, sharks, and orchids.

FURTHER READING S. K. Wasser et al., Forensic tools battle ivory
poachers, *Scientific American* 399:68–76 (2009); S. K. Wasser et al.,
Using DNA to track the origin of the largest ivory seizure since the
1989 trade ban, *Proceedings of the National Academy of Sciences USA*
104:4228–4233 (2007).

MAKE CONNECTIONS Figure 26.6 (p. 539) describes another example in which conservation biologists used DNA analyses to compare harvested samples with a reference DNA database. How are
these examples similar, and how are they different? What limitations might there be to using such forensic methods in other suspected cases of poaching?

Mastering**BIOLOGY**
www.masteringbiology.com

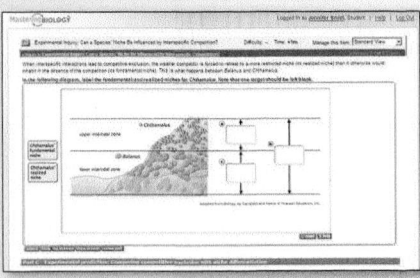

New **Experimental Inquiry Tutorials**
give you practice analyzing experimental
design and data and drawing conclusions.

Study the figures as you read the text.

▼ Figure 5.15 **An overview of protein functions.**

Enzymatic proteins

Function: Selective acceleration of chemical reactions
Example: Digestive enzymes catalyze the hydrolysis of bonds in food molecules.

Enzyme

Storage proteins

Function: Storage of amino acids
Examples: Casein, the protein of milk, is the major source of amino acids for baby mammals. Plants have storage proteins in their seeds. Ovalbumin is the protein of egg white, used as an amino acid source for the developing embryo.

Ovalbumin → Amino acids for embryo

Hormonal proteins

Function: Coordination of an organism's activities
Example: Insulin, a hormone secreted by the pancreas, causes other tissues to take up glucose, thus regulating blood sugar concentration.

High blood sugar → Insulin secreted → Normal blood sugar

Contractile and motor proteins

Function: Movement
Examples: Motor proteins are responsible for the undulations of cilia and flagella. Actin and myosin proteins are responsible for the contraction of muscles.

Actin   Myosin

Muscle tissue   100 μm

Defensive proteins

Function: Protection against disease
Example: Antibodies inactivate and help destroy viruses and bacteria.

Antibodies
Virus   Bacterium

Transport proteins

Function: Transport of substances
Examples: Hemoglobin, the iron-containing protein of vertebrate blood, transports oxygen from the lungs to other parts of the body. Other proteins transport molecules across cell membranes.

Transport protein
Cell membrane

Hormonal proteins

Receptor proteins

Function: Response of cell to chemical stimuli
Example: Receptors built into the membrane of a nerve cell detect signaling molecules released by other nerve cells.

Receptor protein
Signaling molecules

Structural proteins

Function: Support
Examples: Keratin is the protein of hair, horns, feathers, and other skin appendages. Insects and spiders use silk fibers to make their cocoons and webs, respectively. Collagen and elastin proteins provide a fibrous framework in animal connective tissues.

Connective tissue   60 μm

◄ New **Visual Organizers** help you to see important categories at a glance.

By integrating text and visuals, **Exploring Figures** help you learn more efficiently.
▼

In selected illustrations, **a three-dimensional art style** ► helps you visualize biological structures.

Mastering BIOLOGY
www.masteringbiology.com

Many **Tutorials** and **Activities** integrate art from the textbook, providing a unified learning experience.

▼ Figure 7.22

Exploring Endocytosis in Animal Cells

| Phagocytosis | Pinocytosis | Receptor-Mediated Endocytosis |

EXTRACELLULAR FLUID
Solutes
Pseudopodium
Plasma membrane
Receptor
Ligand
Coat proteins
"Food" or other particle
Vesicle
Coated pit
Coated vesicle

Food vacuole

CYTOPLASM

In **phagocytosis,** a cell engulfs a particle by wrapping pseudopodia (singular, *pseudopodium*) around it and packaging it within a membranous sac called a food vacuole. The particle will be digested after the food vacuole fuses with a lysosome containing hydrolytic enzymes (see Figure 6.13a).

In **pinocytosis,** the cell "gulps" droplets of extracellular fluid into tiny vesicles. It is not the fluid itself that is needed by the cell, but the molecules dissolved in the droplets. Because any and all included solutes are taken into the cell, pinocytosis is nonspecific in the substances it transports.

Receptor-mediated endocytosis enables the cell to acquire bulk quantities of specific substances, even though those substances may not be very concentrated in the extracellular fluid. Embedded in the membrane are proteins with specific receptor sites exposed to the extracellular fluid, to which specific substances (ligands) bind. The receptor proteins then cluster in regions of the membrane called coated pits, which are lined on their cytoplasmic side by a fuzzy layer of coat proteins. Next, each coated pit forms a vesicle containing the ligand molecules. Notice that there are relatively more bound molecules (purple) inside the vesicle, but other molecules (green) are also present. After the ingested material is liberated from the vesicle, the emptied receptors are recycled to the plasma membrane by the same vesicle.

Pseudopodium of amoeba
Bacterium
Food vacuole

An amoeba engulfing a bacterium via phagocytosis (TEM).

Pinocytosis vesicles forming (indicated by arrows) in a cell lining a small blood vessel (TEM).   0.5 μm

Plasma membrane
Coat proteins

Top: A coated pit. Bottom: A coated vesicle forming during receptor-mediated endocytosis (TEMs).   0.25 μm

ANIMATION **BioFlix** Visit the Study Area at www.masteringbiology.com for the BioFlix® 3-D Animation on Membrane Transport.

CHAPTER 7 Membrane Structure and Function **139**

▲

BioFlix® icons direct you to high-impact 3-D animations in the Study Area at www.masteringbiology.com.

Review what you've learned.

Chapter Reviews help you efficiently master the chapter content by focusing on the main points of the chapter and offering opportunities to practice for exams.

Summary Figures present key information in a visual way.

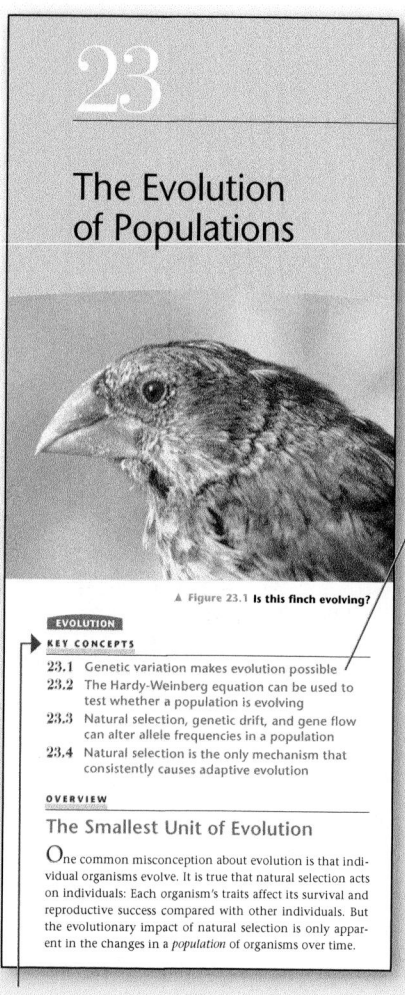

23

The Evolution of Populations

▲ Figure 23.1 **Is this finch evolving?**

EVOLUTION

KEY CONCEPTS

23.1 Genetic variation makes evolution possible
23.2 The Hardy-Weinberg equation can be used to test whether a population is evolving
23.3 Natural selection, genetic drift, and gene flow can alter allele frequencies in a population
23.4 Natural selection is the only mechanism that consistently causes adaptive evolution

OVERVIEW

The Smallest Unit of Evolution

One common misconception about evolution is that individual organisms evolve. It is true that natural selection acts on individuals: Each organism's traits affect its survival and reproductive success compared with other individuals. But the evolutionary impact of natural selection is only apparent in the changes in a *population* of organisms over time.

Key Concepts, which were introduced in the beginning of the chapter and developed in the text, are summarized in the Chapter Review.

New **Summary of Key Concepts Questions** appear at the end of each concept summary. Check your answers using Appendix A.

---

23 CHAPTER REVIEW

SUMMARY OF KEY CONCEPTS

CONCEPT 23.1

Genetic variation makes evolution possible (pp. 469–473)

- **Genetic variation** refers to genetic differences among individuals within a population.
- The nucleotide differences that provide the basis of genetic variation arise by mutation and other processes that produce new alleles and new genes.
- New genetic variants are produced rapidly in organisms with short generation times. In sexually reproducing organisms, most of the genetic differences among individuals result from crossing over, the independent assortment of chromosomes, and fertilization.

? *Why do biologists estimate gene variability and nucleotide variability, and what do these estimates represent?*

CONCEPT 23.2

The Hardy-Weinberg equation can be used to test whether a population is evolving (pp. 473–476)

- A **population**, a localized group of organisms belonging to one species, is united by its **gene pool**, the aggregate of all the alleles in the population.
- The **Hardy-Weinberg principle** states that the allele and genotype frequencies of a population will remain constant if the population is large, mating is random, mutation is negligible, there is no gene flow, and there is no natural selection. For such a population, if p and q represent the frequencies of the only two possible alleles at a particular locus, then p^2 is the frequency of one kind of homozygote, q^2 is the frequency of the other kind of homozygote, and $2pq$ is the frequency of the heterozygous genotype.

? *Is it circular reasoning to calculate p and q from observed genotype frequencies and then use those values of p and q to test if the population is in Hardy-Weinberg equilibrium? Explain your answer. (Hint: Consider a specific case, such as a population with 195 individuals of genotype AA, 10 of genotype Aa, and 195 of genotype aa.)*

CONCEPT 23.3

Natural selection, genetic drift, and gene flow can alter allele frequencies in a population (pp. 476–480)

- In natural selection, individuals that have certain inherited traits tend to survive and reproduce at higher rates than other individuals *because of* those traits.
- In **genetic drift**, chance fluctuations in allele frequencies over generations tend to reduce genetic variation.
- **Gene flow**, the transfer of alleles between populations, tends to reduce genetic differences between populations over time.

? *Would two small, geographically isolated populations in very different environments be likely to evolve in similar ways? Explain.*

CONCEPT 23.4

Natural selection is the only mechanism that consistently causes adaptive evolution (pp. 480–485)

- One organism has greater **relative fitness** than a second organism if it leaves more fertile descendants than the second

organism. The modes of natural selection differ in how selection acts on phenotype (the white arrows in the summary diagram below represent selective pressure on a population).

Original population   Evolved population

Directional selection   Disruptive selection   Stabilizing selection

- Unlike genetic drift and gene flow, natural selection consistently increases the frequencies of alleles that enhance survival and reproduction, thus improving the match between organisms and their environment.
- **Sexual selection** influences evolutionary change in secondary sex characteristics that can give individuals advantages in mating.
- Despite the winnowing effects of selection, populations have considerable genetic variation. Some of this variation represents **neutral variation**; additional variation can be maintained by diploidy and balancing selection.
- There are constraints to evolution: Natural selection can act only on available variation; structures result from modified ancestral anatomy; adaptations are often compromises; and chance, natural selection, and the environment interact.

? *How might secondary sex characteristics differ between males and females in a species in which females compete for mates?*

TEST YOUR UNDERSTANDING

LEVEL 1: KNOWLEDGE/COMPREHENSION

1. Natural selection changes allele frequencies because some _____ survive and reproduce more successfully than others.
   a. alleles   c. gene pools   e. individuals
   b. loci   d. species

2. No two people are genetically identical, except for identical twins. The main source of genetic variation among human individuals is
   a. new mutations that occurred in the preceding generation.
   b. genetic drift due to the small size of the population.
   c. the reshuffling of alleles in sexual reproduction.
   d. geographic variation within the population.
   e. environmental effects.

3. Sparrows with average-sized wings survive severe storms better than those with longer or shorter wings, illustrating
   a. the bottleneck effect.
   b. disruptive selection.
   c. frequency-dependent selection.
   d. neutral variation.
   e. stabilizing selection.

To help you prepare for the various kinds of questions that may appear on a test, the end-of-chapter questions are now organized into three levels based on Bloom's Taxonomy:

Level 1: Knowledge/Comprehension
Level 2: Application/Analysis
Level 3: Synthesis/Evaluation

Evolution Connection Questions in the Chapter Review ask you to think critically about how an aspect of the chapter relates to evolution. ▶

Scientific Inquiry Questions ▶ at the end of each chapter give you opportunities to practice scientific thinking by developing hypotheses, designing experiments, and analyzing real research data.

Draw It Exercises in each chapter ask you to put pencil to paper and draw a structure, annotate a figure, or graph experimental data.

LEVEL 2: APPLICATION/ANALYSIS

4. If the nucleotide variability of a locus equals 0%, what is the gene variability and number of alleles at that locus?
   a. gene variability = 0%; number of alleles = 0
   b. gene variability = 0%; number of alleles = 1
   c. gene variability = 0%; number of alleles = 2
   d. gene variability > 0%; number of alleles = 2
   e. Without more information, gene variability and number of alleles cannot be determined.

5. There are 40 individuals in population 1, all with genotype *A1A1*, and there are 25 individuals in population 2, all with genotype *A2A2*. Assume that these populations are located far from each other and that their environmental conditions are very similar. Based on the information given here, the observed genetic variation is most likely an example of
   a. genetic drift.   d. discrete variation.
   b. gene flow.   e. directional selection.
   c. disruptive selection.

6. A fruit fly population has a gene with two alleles, *A1* and *A2*. Tests show that 70% of the gametes produced in the population contain the *A1* allele. If the population is in Hardy-Weinberg equilibrium, what proportion of the flies carry both *A1* and *A2*?
   a. 0.7   b. 0.49   c. 0.21   d. 0.42   e. 0.09

LEVEL 3: SYNTHESIS/EVALUATION

7. **EVOLUTION CONNECTION**
   How is the process of evolution revealed by the imperfections of living organisms?

8. **SCIENTIFIC INQUIRY**
   DRAW IT   Richard Koehn, of the State University of New York, Stony Brook, and Thomas Hilbish, of the University of South Carolina, studied genetic variation in the marine mussel *Mytilus edulis* around Long Island, New York. They measured the frequency of a particular allele (*lap⁹⁴*) for an enzyme involved in regulating the mussel's internal saltwater balance. The researchers presented their data as a series of pie charts linked to sampling sites within Long Island Sound, where the salinity is highly variable, and along the coast of the open ocean, where salinity is constant:

Data from R. K. Koehn and T. J. Hilbish, The adaptive importance of genetic variation, *American Scientist* 75:134–141 (1987).

(Question 8, continued)

Create a data table for the 11 sampling sites by estimating the frequency of *lap⁹⁴* from the pie charts. (*Hint:* Think of each pie chart as a clock face to help you estimate the proportion of the shaded area.) Then graph the frequencies for sites 1–8 to show how the frequency of this allele changes with increasing salinity in Long Island Sound (from southwest to northeast). How do the data from sites 9–11 compare with the data from the sites within the Sound?

Construct a hypothesis that explains the patterns you observe in the data and that accounts for the following observations: (1) the *lap⁹⁴* allele helps mussels maintain osmotic balance in water with a high salt concentration but is costly to use in less salty water; and (2) mussels produce larvae that can disperse long distances before they settle on rocks and grow into adults.

9. **WRITE ABOUT A THEME**
   Emergent Properties Heterozygotes at the sickle-cell locus produce both normal and abnormal (sickle-cell) hemoglobin (see Concept 14.4). When hemoglobin molecules are packed into a heterozygote's red blood cells, some cells receive relatively large quantities of abnormal hemoglobin, making these cells prone to sickling. In a short essay (approximately 100–150 words), explain how these molecular and cellular events lead to emergent properties at the individual and population levels of biological organization.

For selected answers, see Appendix A.

MasteringBIOLOGY   www.masteringbiology.com

1. MasteringBiology® Assignments
   Make Connections Tutorial Hardy-Weinberg Principle (Chapter 23) and Inheritance of Alleles (Chapter 14)
   Experimental Inquiry Tutorial Did Natural Selection of Ground Finches Occur When the Environment Changed?
   BioFlix Tutorial Mechanisms of Evolution
   Tutorial Hardy-Weinberg Principle
   Activities Genetic Variation from Sexual Recombination • The Hardy-Weinberg Principle • Causes of Evolutionary Change • Three Modes of Natural Selection
   Questions Student Misconceptions • Reading Quiz • Multiple Choice • End-of-Chapter

2. eText
   Read your book online, search, take notes, highlight text, and more.

3. The Study Area
   Practice Tests • Cumulative Test • **BioFlix** 3-D Animations • MP3 Tutor Sessions • Videos • Activities • Investigations • Lab Media • Audio Glossary • Word Study Tools • Art

---

▶ New **Write About a Theme Questions** give you practice writing a short essay that connects the chapter's content to one of the bookwide themes introduced in Chapter 1.

◀ Each chapter now ends with a preview of the **MasteringBiology®** resources that can help you succeed in the course.

◀ This **Writing Rubric** explains criteria on which your writing may be graded. The rubric and tips for writing good short-answer essays can be found in the Study Area at www.masteringbiology.com.

Suggested Grading Rubric for "Write About a Theme" Short-Answer Essays

	Understanding of Theme and Relationship to Topic	Use of Supporting Examples or Details	Appropriate Use of Terminology	Quality of Writing
4	Evidence of full and complete understanding	Examples well chosen, details accurate and applied to theme	Accurate scientific terminology enhances the essay	Excellent organization, sentence structure, and grammar
3	Evidence of good understanding	Examples or details are generally well applied to theme	Terminology is correctly used	Good sentence flow, sentence structure, and grammar
2	Evidence of a basic understanding	Supporting examples and details are adequate	Terminology used is not totally accurate or appropriate	Some organizational and grammatical problems
1	Evidence of limited understanding	Examples and details are minimal	Appropriate terminology is not present	Poorly organized. Grammatical and spelling errors detract from essay
0	Essay shows no understanding of theme	Examples lacking or incorrect	Terminology lacking or incorrect	Essay is very poorly written

The Mastering system empowers you to take charge of your learning—at your convenience, 24/7.

Use the Study Area on your own or in a study group.

BioFlix

▲ **BioFlix® 3-D animations** explore the most difficult biology topics, reinforced with tutorials, quizzes, and more.

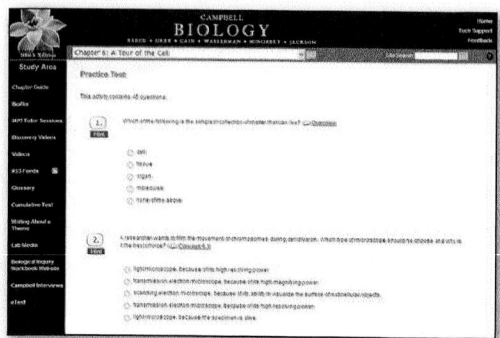

▲ **Practice Tests** help you assess your understanding of each chapter, providing feedback for right and wrong answers.

▲ The **Cumulative Test** allows you to build a practice test with questions from multiple chapters.

Access your book online.

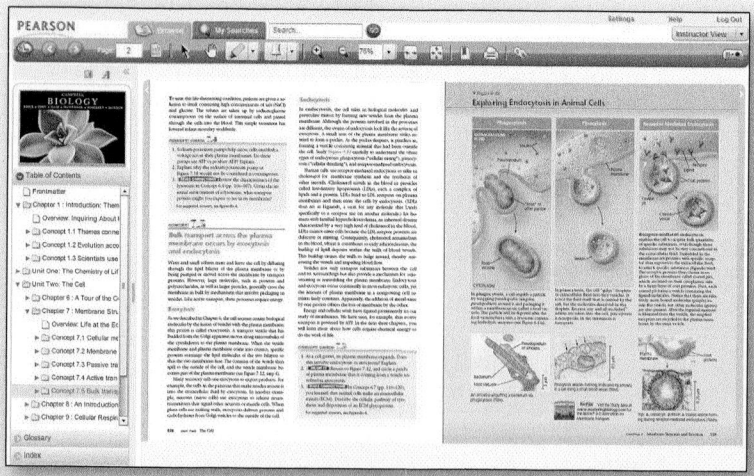

◄ The **Pearson eText** gives you access to the text whenever and wherever you can access the Internet. The eText includes powerful interactive and customization functions:

- write notes
- highlight text
- bookmark pages
- zoom
- click hyperlinked words to view definitions
- search
- link to media activities and quizzes

Your professor can also write notes for the class and highlight important material using a new tool that works like an electronic pen on a whiteboard.

Use MasteringBiology®

Get personalized coaching & feedback.

Your instructor may assign self-paced **MasteringBiology®** tutorials that provide individualized coaching with specific hints and feedback on the toughest topics in the course.

1 If you get stuck...

2 Specific wrong-answer **feedback** appears in the purple feedback box.

3 You are offered **hints** to coach you to the correct response.

MasteringBiology is the most effective and widely used online science tutorial, homework, and assessment system available.

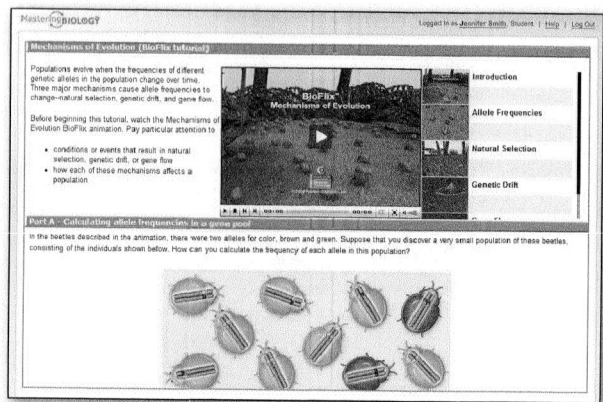

BioFlix® Tutorials use 3-D, movie-quality animations and coaching exercises to help students master tough topics outside of class. Tutorials and animations include:

- A Tour of the Animal Cell
- A Tour of the Plant Cell
- Membrane Transport
- Cellular Respiration
- Photosynthesis
- Mitosis
- Meiosis
- DNA Replication
- Protein Synthesis
- Mechanisms of Evolution
- Water Transport in Plants
- Homeostasis: Regulating Blood Sugar
- Gas Exchange
- How Neurons Work
- How Synapses Work
- Muscle Contraction
- Population Ecology
- The Carbon Cycle

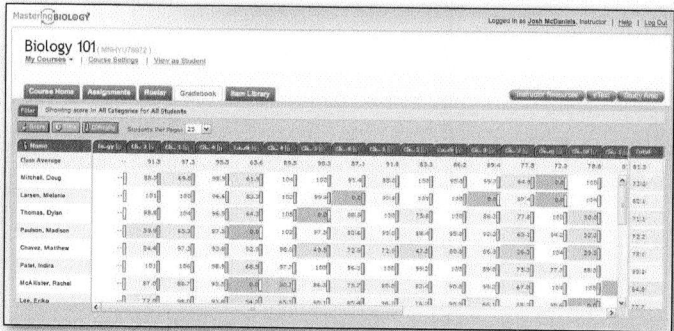

The MasteringBiology **gradebook** provides you with quick results and easy-to-interpret insights into student performance. Every assignment is **automatically graded** and shades of red highlight vulnerable students and challenging assignments.

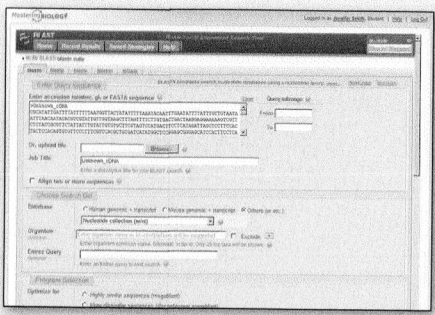

New **Data Analysis Tutorials** allow students to analyze real data from online databases.

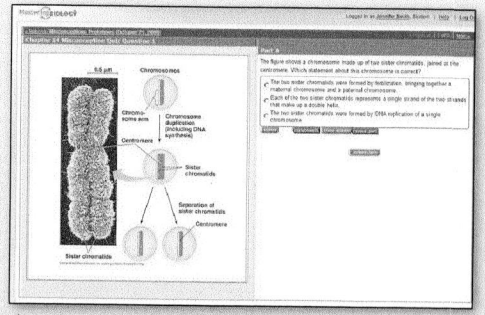

New **Student Misconceptions Questions** provide assignable quizzes for each chapter based on common student misconceptions. Students are provided with feedback, and the instructor is provided with in-class strategies for overcoming these misconceptions.

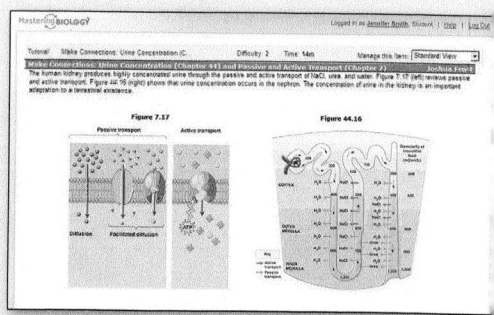

New **Make Connections Tutorials** help students connect what they are learning in one chapter with material they learned in an earlier chapter.

MasteringBiology®

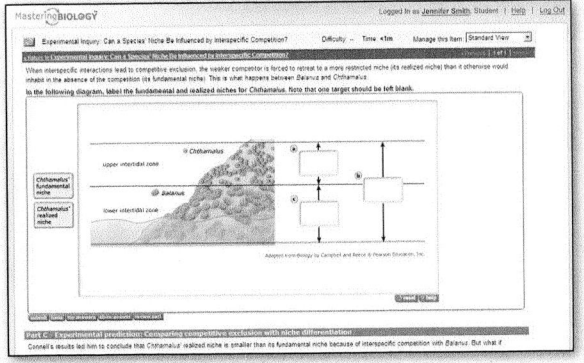

◄ New **Experimental Inquiry Tutorials,** based on some of biology's most influential experiments, give students practice analyzing experimental design and data, and help students understand how to reach conclusions based on collected data. Topics include:

- What Can You Learn About the Process of Science from Investigating a Cricket's Chirp?
- Which Wavelengths of Light Drive Photosynthesis?
- What Is the Inheritance Pattern of Sex-Linked Traits?
- Does DNA Replication Follow the Conservative, Semiconservative, or Dispersive Model?
- Did Natural Selection of Ground Finches Occur When the Environment Changed?
- What Effect Does Auxin Have on Coleoptile Growth?
- What Role Do Genes Play in Appetite Regulation?
- How Do Calcium Ions Help to Prevent Polyspermy During Egg Fertilization?
- Can a Species' Niche Be Influenced by Interspecific Competition?
- What Factors Influence the Loss of Nutrients from a Forest Ecosystem?

◄ The New **Video Tutor Sessions** walk students through tough topics with clearly explained visuals and demonstrations. Topics include:

- Mitosis and Meiosis
- Sex-Linked Pedigrees
- DNA Structure
- DNA Profiling Techniques
- Biodiversity
- Phylogenetic Trees

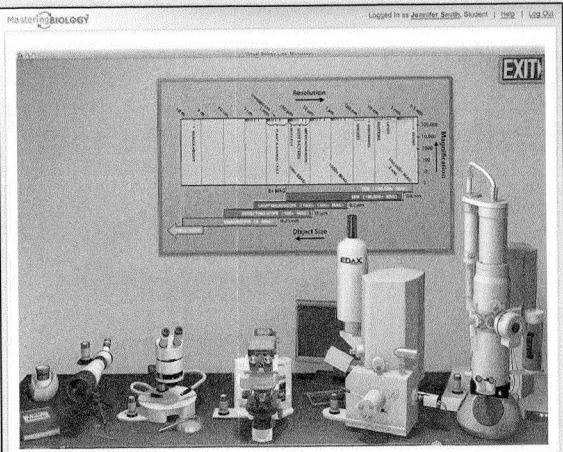

◄ The new **MasteringBiology: Virtual Biology Labs** online environment promotes critical thinking skills using virtual experiments and explorations that may be difficult to perform in a wet lab environment due to time, cost, or safety concerns.

- MasteringBiology: Virtual Biology Labs offer unique learning experiences in microscopy, molecular biology, genetics, ecology, and systematics.
- Choose from 20–30 automatically graded, "pre-set" lab activities that are ready to assign to students, or create your own from scratch.
- Each "pre-set" lab provides an assignable lab report with questions that are automatically graded and recorded in the MasteringBiology gradebook.
- Student subscriptions are available standalone or packaged with the CAMPBELL *BIOLOGY* textbook.

Supplements

For Instructors

Instructor Resource DVD
978-0-321-67786-0 • 0-321-67786-2

Assets for each chapter include:

- All figures, photos, and tables in JPEG and PowerPoint®
- Prepared PowerPoint Presentations for each chapter, with lecture notes, editable figures from the text, and links to animations and videos
- Clicker Questions in PowerPoint
- 250+ Instructor Animations, including 3-D BioFlix®
- Discovery Channel™ Videos
- Test Bank questions in TestGen® software and Microsoft® Word

BioFlix® animations invigorate classroom lectures with 3-minute "movie quality" 3-D graphics (see list on p. xviii).

Customizable PowerPoints provide a jumpstart for each lecture.

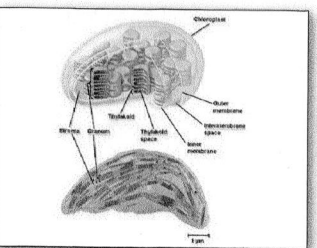

Clicker Questions can be used to stimulate effective classroom discussions (for use with or without clickers).

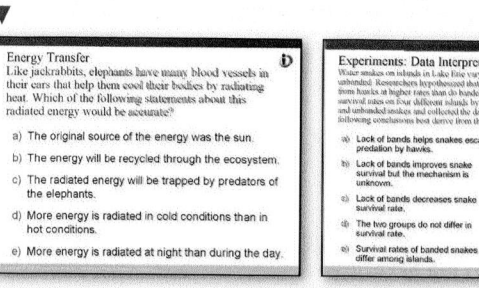

All of the art and photos from the book are provided with customizable labels. More than 1,600 photos from the text and other sources are included.

Printed Test Bank
by Louise Paquin, *McDaniel College*, Michael Dini, *Texas Tech University*, John Lepri, *University of North Carolina, Greensboro*, Jung Choi, *Georgia Institute of Technology*, John Zarnetske, *Hoosick Falls Central School*, and Ronald Balsamo, *Villanova University*
978-0-321-69729-5 • 0-321-69729-4

For the Ninth Edition, the Test Bank authors have increased the number of high-level application and synthesis questions.

Transparency Acetates
978-0-321-69708-0 • 0-321-69708-1

Course Management Systems

Test Bank questions, quizzes, and selected content from the Study Area of MasteringBiology are available in these popular course management systems:

CourseCompass™ (www.pearsonhighered.com)

Blackboard (www.pearsonhighered.com)

Instructor Resources Area in MasteringBiology

This area includes:

- PowerPoint® Lectures
- Clicker Questions
- JPEG Images
- Animations
- Videos
- Lecture Outlines
- Learning Objectives
- Strategies for Overcoming Common Student Misconceptions
- Instructor Guides for Supplements
- Write About a Theme: Tips for Grading Short-Answer Essays
- Suggested Answers for Essay Questions
- Test Bank Files
- Lab Media

For Students

Study Guide, Ninth Edition
by Martha R. Taylor, *Cornell University*
978-0-321-62992-0 • 0-321-62992-2

This popular study guide helps students extract key ideas from the textbook and organize their knowledge of biology. Exercises include concept maps, chapter summaries, word roots, chapter tests, and a variety of interactive questions in various formats.

Inquiry in Action: Interpreting Scientific Papers, Second Edition*
by Ruth Buskirk, *University of Texas at Austin*, and Christopher M. Gillen, *Kenyon College*
978-0-321-68336-6 • 0-321-68336-6

Selected Inquiry Figures in the Ninth Edition direct students to read and analyze the complete original research paper. In this supplement, those articles are reprinted and accompanied by questions that help students analyze the article. The Inquiry Figures from the book are reprinted in the supplement.

Practicing Biology: A Student Workbook, Fourth Edition*
by Jean Heitz and Cynthia Giffen, *University of Wisconsin, Madison*
978-0-321-68328-1 • 0-321-68328-5

This workbook offers a variety of activities to suit different learning styles. Activities such as modeling and mapping allow students to visualize and understand biological processes. Other activities focus on basic skills, such as reading and drawing graphs.

Biological Inquiry: A Workbook of Investigative Cases, Third Edition*
by Margaret Waterman, *Southeast Missouri State University*, and Ethel Stanley, *BioQUEST Curriculum Consortium and Beloit College*
978-0-321-68320-5 • 0-321-68320-X

This workbook offers ten investigative cases. A student website is in the Study Area at **www.masteringbiology.com.**

Study Card, Ninth Edition
978-0-321-68322-9 • 0-321-68322-6

This quick-reference card provides an overview of the entire field of biology and helps students see the connections between topics.

Spanish Glossary, Ninth Edition
by Laura P. Zanello, *University of California, Riverside*
978-0-321-68321-2 • 0-321-68321-8

This resource provides definitions in Spanish for all the glossary terms.

Into the Jungle: Great Adventures in the Search for Evolution
by Sean B. Carroll, *University of Wisconsin, Madison*
978-0-321-55671-4 • 0-321-55671-2

These nine short tales vividly depict key discoveries in evolutionary biology and the excitement of the scientific process. Online resources available at www.aw-bc.com/carroll.

Get Ready for Biology
978-0-321-50057-1 • 0-321-50057-1

This engaging workbook helps students brush up on important math and study skills and get up to speed on biological terminology and the basics of chemistry and cell biology.

A Short Guide to Writing About Biology, Seventh Edition
by Jan A. Pechenik, *Tufts University*
978-0-321-66838-7 • 0-321-66838-3

This best-selling writing guide teaches students to think as biologists and to express ideas clearly and concisely through their writing.

An Introduction to Chemistry for Biology Students, Ninth Edition
by George I. Sackheim, *University of Illinois, Chicago*
978-0- 8053-9571-6 • 0-8053-9571-7

This text/workbook helps students review and master all the basic facts, concepts, and terminology of chemistry that they need for their life science course.

The Chemistry of Life CD-ROM, Biology Version, Second Edition
by Robert M. Thornton, *University of California, Davis*
978-0-8053-3063-2 • 0-8053-3063-1

This CD-ROM uses animations, interactive simulations, and quizzes with feedback to help students learn or review the chemistry needed to succeed in introductory biology.

For Lab

Investigating Biology Laboratory Manual, Seventh Edition
by Judith G. Morgan, *Emory University*, and M. Eloise Brown Carter, *Oxford College of Emory University*
978-0-321-66821-9 • 0-321-66821-9

The Seventh Edition emphasizes connections to recurring themes in biology, including structure and function, unity and diversity, and the overarching theme of evolution.

Annotated Instructor Edition for Investigating Biology Laboratory Manual, Seventh Edition
by Judith G. Morgan, *Emory University*, and M. Eloise Brown Carter, *Oxford College of Emory University*
978-0-321-67668-9 • 0-321-67668-8

Preparation Guide for Investigating Biology Laboratory Manual, Seventh Edition
by Judith G. Morgan, *Emory University*, and M. Eloise Brown Carter, *Oxford College of Emory University*
978-0-321-67669-6 • 0-321-67669-6

Symbiosis: The Benjamin Cummings Custom Laboratory Program for the Biological Sciences
www.pearsoncustom.com/database/symbiosis/bc.html

MasteringBiology®: Virtual Biology Labs
www.masteringbiology.com
This online environment promotes critical thinking skills using virtual experiments and explorations that may be difficult to perform in a wet lab environment due to time, cost, or safety concerns. Designed to supplement or substitute for existing wet labs, this product offers students unique learning experiences and critical thinking exercises in the areas of microscopy, molecular biology, genetics, ecology, and systematics.

* An Instructor Guide is available for download in the Instructor Resources Area at www.masteringbiology.com.

Featured Figures

Impact Figures

3.12 The Threat of Ocean Acidification to Coral Reef Ecosystems 55
7.11 Blocking HIV Entry into Cells as a Treatment for HIV Infections 130
10.3 Alternative Fuels from Plants and Algae 185
11.8 Determining the Structure of a G Protein-Coupled Receptor (GPCR) 213
12.21 Advances in Treatment of Breast Cancer 243
14.18 Genetic Testing 280
16.23 Painting Chromosomes 322
20.22 The Impact of Induced Pluripotent Stem (iPS) Cells on Regenerative Medicine 417
22.14 The Rise of MRSA 462
28.28 Marine Protists in a Warmer World 597
30.16 Clear-Cutting of Tropical Forests 633
31.26 Amphibians Under Attack 651
33.22 Molluscs: The Silent Extinction 681
34.20 Discovery of a "Fishapod": *Tiktaalik* 710
38.17 Fighting World Hunger with Transgenic Cassava 817
43.26 Vaccinating Against Cervical Cancer 950
49.14 Using Functional Brain Imaging to Map Activity in the Working Brain 1072
50.21 Gene Therapy for Vision 1100
54.29 Identifying Lyme Disease Host Species 1214
55.7 Ocean Production Revealed 1222
56.9 Forensic Ecology and Elephant Poaching 1243

Exploring Figures

1.4 Levels of Biological Organization 4
4.9 Some Biologically Important Chemical Groups 64
5.20 Levels of Protein Structure 82
6.3 Microscopy 96
6.8 Eukaryotic Cells 100
6.32 Cell Junctions in Animal Tissues 121
7.22 Endocytosis in Animal Cells 139
11.7 Cell-Surface Transmembrane Receptors 211
12.7 Mitosis in an Animal Cell 232
13.8 Meiosis in an Animal Cell 254
16.22 Chromatin Packing in a Eukaryotic Chromosome 320
24.3 Reproductive Barriers 490
25.6 The Origin of Mammals 513
27.17 Major Groups of Bacteria 568
28.3 Protistan Diversity 578
29.5 Derived Traits of Land Plants 602
29.9 Bryophyte Diversity 608
29.15 Seedless Vascular Plant Diversity 614
30.5 Gymnosperm Diversity 622
30.13 Angiosperm Diversity 630
31.11 Fungal Diversity 642
33.3 Invertebrate Diversity 667
33.38 Insect Diversity 690
34.41 Mammalian Diversity 724
35.10 Examples of Differentiated Plant Cells 744
37.15 Unusual Nutritional Adaptations in Plants 798
38.4 Flower Pollination 804

38.11 Fruit and Seed Dispersal 811
40.5 Structure and Function in Animal Tissues 856
41.6 Four Main Feeding Mechanisms of Animals 881
42.5 Double Circulation in Vertebrates 901
44.14 The Mammalian Excretory System 962
46.12 Human Gametogenesis 1006
49.9 The Organization of the Human Brain 1068
50.10 The Structure of the Human Ear 1091
50.17 The Structure of the Human Eye 1096
50.30 The Regulation of Skeletal Muscle Contraction 1107
52.2 The Scope of Ecological Research 1145
52.3 Global Climate Patterns 1146
52.12 Terrestrial Biomes 1153
52.16 Aquatic Biomes 1159
53.17 Mechanisms of Density-Dependent Regulation 1183
55.14 Water and Nutrient Cycling 1228
55.19 Restoration Ecology Worldwide 1234

Inquiry Figures

*†1.27 Does the presence of venomous coral snakes affect predation rates on their mimics, kingsnakes? 22
*2.2 What creates "devil's gardens" in the rain forest? 31
4.2 Can organic molecules form under conditions estimated to simulate those on the early Earth? 59
5.24 What can the 3-D shape of the enzyme RNA polymerase II tell us about its function? 86
6.29 What role do microtubules play in orienting deposition of cellulose in cell walls? 119
7.7 Do membrane proteins move? 128
8.20 Are there allosteric inhibitors of caspase enzymes? 159
†10.10 Which wavelengths of light are most effective in driving photosynthesis? 191
11.17 How do signals induce directional cell growth during mating in yeast? 221
12.9 At which end do kinetochore microtubules shorten during anaphase? 235
12.14 Do molecular signals in the cytoplasm regulate the cell cycle? 238
14.3 When F_1 hybrid pea plants self- or cross-pollinate, which traits appear in the F_2 generation? 264
14.8 Do the alleles for one character assort into gametes dependently or independently of the alleles for a different character? 268
†15.4 In a cross between a wild-type female fruit fly and a mutant white-eyed male, what color eyes will the F_1 and F_2 offspring have? 289
15.9 How does linkage between two genes affect inheritance of characters? 293
16.2 Can a genetic trait be transferred between different bacterial strains? 306
16.4 Is protein or DNA the genetic material of phage T2? 307
*†16.11 Does DNA replication follow the conservative, semiconservative, or dispersive model? 312
17.2 Do individual genes specify the enzymes that function in a biochemical pathway? 327
18.22 Is Bicoid a morphogen that determines the anterior end of a fruit fly? 372

* The Inquiry Figure, original research paper, and a worksheet to guide you through the paper are provided in *Inquiry in Action: Interpreting Scientific Papers*, Second Edition.
† See the related Experimental Inquiry Tutorial in MasteringBiology® (www.masteringbiology.com).

19.2 What causes tobacco mosaic disease? *382*

20.18 Can the nucleus from a differentiated animal cell direct development of an organism? *413*

21.17 What is the function of a gene (*FOXP2*) that is rapidly evolving in the human lineage? *444*

22.13 Can a change in a population's food source result in evolution by natural selection? *461*

*23.16 Do females select mates based on traits indicative of "good genes"? *483*

24.10 Can divergence of allopatric populations lead to reproductive isolation? *495*

24.12 Does sexual selection in cichlids result in reproductive isolation? *497*

24.19 How does hybridization lead to speciation in sunflowers? *503*

25.25 What causes the loss of spines in lake stickleback fish? *528*

26.6 What is the species identity of food being sold as whale meat? *539*

27.10 Can prokaryotes evolve rapidly in response to environmental change? *561*

28.23 What is the root of the eukaryotic tree? *593*

29.10 Can bryophytes reduce the rate at which key nutrients are lost from soils? *609*

31.21 Do endophytes benefit a woody plant? *648*

32.6 Did β-catenin play an ancient role in the molecular control of gastrulation? *659*

33.29 Did the arthropod body plan result from new *Hox* genes? *685*

34.50 Did Neanderthals give rise to European humans? *732*

35.9 Do soybean pod trichomes deter herbivores? *743*

36.19 Does phloem sap contain more sugar near sources than sinks? *781*

*37.14 Does the invasive weed garlic mustard disrupt mutualistic associations between native tree seedlings and arbuscular mycorrhizal fungi? *797*

39.5 What part of a grass coleoptile senses light, and how is the signal transmitted? *825*

†39.6 Does asymmetrical distribution of a growth-promoting chemical cause a coleoptile to grow toward the light? *826*

39.7 What causes polar movement of auxin from shoot tip to base? *828*

39.17 How does the order of red and far-red illumination affect seed germination? *836*

40.14 How does a Burmese python generate heat while incubating eggs? *867*

40.21 What happens to the circadian clock during hibernation? *872*

*41.4 Can diet influence the frequency of birth defects? *879*

†41.22 What are the roles of the *ob* and *db* genes in appetite regulation? *894*

42.21 Can inactivating a liver enzyme lower plasma LDL levels? *914*

42.26 What causes respiratory distress syndrome? *920*

43.5 Can a single antimicrobial peptide protect fruit flies against infection? *931*

44.21 Can aquaporin mutations cause diabetes insipidus? *970*

45.22 What role do hormones play in making a mammal male or female? *992*

46.9 Why is sperm usage biased when female fruit flies mate twice? *1002*

†47.4 Does the distribution of Ca^{2+} in an egg correlate with formation of the fertilization envelope? *1024*

47.22 How does distribution of the gray crescent affect the developmental potential of the first two daughter cells? *1038*

47.23 Can the dorsal lip of the blastopore induce cells in another part of the amphibian embryo to change their developmental fate? *1039*

47.25 What role does the zone of polarizing activity (ZPA) play in limb pattern formation in vertebrates? *1041*

48.18 Does the brain have a specific protein receptor for opiates? *1059*

49.12 Which cells control the circadian rhythm in mammals? *1071*

50.23 How do mammals detect different tastes? *1102*

50.40 What are the energy costs of locomotion? *1114*

51.8 Does a digger wasp use landmarks to find her nest? *1125*

51.23 Are the songs of green lacewing species under the control of multiple genes? *1134*

51.26 Are differences in migratory orientation within a species genetically determined? *1136*

52.20 Does feeding by sea urchins limit seaweed distribution? *1165*

53.13 How does caring for offspring affect parental survival in kestrels? *1180*

53.20 How does food availability affect emigration and foraging in a cellular slime mold? *1186*

†54.3 Can a species' niche be influenced by interspecific competition? *1196*

54.17 Is *Pisaster ochraceus* a keystone predator? *1205*

54.28 How does species richness relate to area? *1213*

55.8 Which nutrient limits phytoplankton production along the coast of Long Island? *1223*

55.15 How does temperature affect litter decomposition in an ecosystem? *123*

*56.13 What caused the drastic decline of the Illinois greater prairie chicken population? *1246*

Research Method Figures

2.6 Radioactive Tracers *34*

6.4 Cell Fractionation *97*

7.4 Freeze-fracture *126*

10.9 Determining an Absorption Spectrum *190*

13.3 Preparing a Karyotype *250*

14.2 Crossing Pea Plants *263*

14.7 The Testcross *267*

15.11 Constructing a Linkage Map *296*

20.4 Cloning Genes in Bacterial Plasmids *399*

20.7 Detecting a Specific DNA Sequence by Hybridization with a Nucleic Acid Probe *402*

20.8 The Polymerase Chain Reaction (PCR) *404*

20.9 Gel Electrophoresis *405*

20.11 Southern Blotting of DNA Fragments *407*

20.12 Dideoxy Chain Termination Method for Sequencing DNA *408*

20.13 RT-PCR Analysis of the Expression of Single Genes *409*

20.15 DNA Microarray Assay of Gene Expression Levels *411*

20.19 Reproductive Cloning of a Mammal by Nuclear Transplantation *414*

20.26 Using the Ti Plasmid to Produce Transgenic Plants *422*

26.15 Applying Parsimony to a Problem in Molecular Systematics *546*

35.21 Using Dendrochronology to Study Climate *753*

37.7 Hydroponic Culture *790*

48.9 Intracellular Recording *1050*

53.2 Determining Population Size Using the Mark-Recapture Method *1171*

54.11 Determining Microbial Diversity Using Molecular Tools *1201*

55.5 Determining Primary Production with Satellites *1221*

Interviews

UNIT 1

The Chemistry of Life 28

Susan Solomon

National Oceanic and Atmospheric Administration, Boulder, Colorado

UNIT 2

The Cell 92

Bonnie L. Bassler

Princeton University

UNIT 3

Genetics 246

Joan A. Steitz

Yale University

UNIT 4

Mechanisms of Evolution 450

Geerat J. Vermeij

University of California, Davis

UNIT 5

The Evolutionary History of Biological Diversity 534

W. Ford Doolittle

Dalhousie University, Canada

UNIT 6

Plant Form and Function 736

Luis Herrera-Estrella

National Polytechnic Institute, Mexico

UNIT 7

Animal Form and Function 850

Baldomero M. Olivera

University of Utah

UNIT 8

Ecology 1142

Camille Parmesan

University of Texas, Austin

Acknowledgments

The authors wish to express their gratitude to the global community of instructors, researchers, students, and publishing professionals who have contributed to this edition.

As authors of this text, we are mindful of the daunting challenge of keeping up to date in all areas of our rapidly expanding subject. We are grateful to the many scientists who helped shape this edition by discussing their research fields with us, answering specific questions in their areas of expertise, and sharing their ideas about biology education. We are especially grateful to the following, listed alphabetically: John Archibald, John Armour, Kristian Axelsen, Scott Bowling, Barbara Bowman, Andy Cameron, Scott Carroll, Amy Cheng-Vollmer, Michele Clamp, David DeRosier, Doug DeSimone, Binh An Diep, David Ehrhardt, Robert Fowler, Peter Fraser, Matt Friedman, Tom Gingeras, Anita Gondor, Ken Halanych, Jeff Hardin, Catherine Hurlbut, Adam Johnson, Dale Kaiser, Patrick Keeling, Emir Khatipov, Chris Killian, Andrew Knoll, Nikos Kyrpides, Teri Liegler, Zhe-Xi Luo, Kent MacDonald, Nick Matzke, Melissa Michael, Nadia Naffakh, Rolf Ohlsson, Aharon Oren, Tom Owens, Kevin Padian, Nathalie Pardigon, Bruce Pavlik, Kevin J. Peterson, Michael Pollock, Rebekah Rasooly, Andrew Roger, Ole Seehausen, Alastair Simpson, Betty Smocovitis, Frank Solomon, Pam Soltis, Hans Thewissen, Mark Uhen, Vance Vredenburg, Elisabeth Wade, Phil Zamore, and Christine Zardecki. In addition, a total of 168 biologists, listed on pages xxvi–xxvii, provided detailed reviews of chapters for this edition, helping us ensure the book's scientific accuracy and improve its pedagogical effectiveness. And finally, we thank Marty Taylor, author of all nine editions of the *Student Study Guide*, for her many contributions to the accuracy, clarity, and consistency of the book.

Thanks also to the other professors and students, from all over the world, who offered suggestions directly to the authors. We alone bear the responsibility for any errors that remain in the text, but the dedication of our consultants, reviewers, and other correspondents makes us confident in the accuracy and effectiveness of this edition.

Interviews with prominent scientists have been a hallmark of *CAMPBELL BIOLOGY* since its inception, and conducting these interviews was again one of the great pleasures of revising the book. To open the eight units of this edition, we are proud to include interviews with Susan Solomon, Bonnie Bassler, Joan Steitz, Geerat Vermeij, Ford Doolittle, Luis Herrera-Estrella, Toto Olivera, and Camille Parmesan.

The value of *CAMPBELL BIOLOGY* as a learning tool is greatly enhanced by the supplementary materials that have been created for instructors and students. We recognize that the dedicated authors of these materials are essentially writing mini (and not so mini) books. We much appreciate the hard work and creativity of all the authors listed, with their creations, on pages xx–xxi. In addition, we are grateful to Joan Sharp (*Lecture Outlines, Learning Objectives*, and *Student Misconceptions*) and Erin Barley and Kathleen Fitzpatrick (*PowerPoint® Lectures*).

The electronic media for this text are invaluable teaching and learning aids. We thank the hardworking and creative authors of the new material for this edition: Tom Owens, Joan Sharp, and Jennifer Yeh (*MasteringBiology®*); Richard Cowlishaw, Tod Duncan, and Stephanie Pandolfi (*Study Area Practice Tests*); and Eric Simon (*VideoTutors*). And we thank Brian White for his work. Also, we are grateful to the many other people—biology instructors, editors, artists, production experts, and narrators—who are listed in the credits for these and other elements of the electronic media that accompany the book. And we thank the reviewers and class testers of BioFlix® and MasteringBiology.

CAMPBELL BIOLOGY, Ninth Edition, results from an unusually strong synergy between a team of scientists and a team of publishing professionals. Our editorial team at Benjamin Cummings again demonstrated unmatched talents, commitment, and pedagogical insights. Our new Acquisitions Editor, Josh Frost, brought publishing savvy, intelligence, and a much appreciated level head to leading the whole team. The clarity and effectiveness of every page owe much to our extraordinary Supervising Editors Pat Burner and Beth Winickoff, who headed the top-notch development team: Developmental Editors John Burner, Matt Lee, and Mary Catherine Hager; and Developmental Artists Hilair Chism, Carla Simmons, Andrew Recher, and Jay McElroy. Our unsurpassed Senior Editorial Manager Ginnie Simione Jutson, Executive Director of Development Deborah Gale, Assistant Editor Logan Triglia, and Editor-in-Chief Beth Wilbur were indispensable in moving the project in the right direction. We also want to thank Robin Heyden for organizing the annual Biology Leadership Conferences and keeping us in touch with the world of AP Biology.

You would not have this beautiful book in your hands today if not for the work of the book production team: Executive Managing Editor Erin Gregg; Managing Editor Michael Early; Senior Production Project Manager Shannon Tozier; Senior Photo Editor Donna Kalal; Photo Researcher Maureen Spuhler; Copy Editor Janet Greenblatt; Art Editor Laura Murray; Proofreaders Joanna Dinsmore and Pete Shanks; Permissions Editors Sue Ewing and Beth Keister; Senior Project Editor Emily Bush, S4Carlisle; Composition Manager Holly Paige, S4Carlisle; Art Production Manager Kristina Seymour, Precision Graphics; Design Director Mark Ong; Designer Gary Hespenheide; and Manufacturing Buyer Michael Penne. We also thank those who worked on the book's supplements: Susan Berge, Nina Lewallen Hufford, Brady Golden, Jane Brundage, James Bruce, and John Hammett. And for creating the wonderful package of electronic media that accompanies the book, we are grateful to Tania Mlawer, Director of Editorial Content for MasteringBiology, and Jonathan Ballard, Deb Greco, Sarah Jensen, Mary Catherine Hager, Alice Fugate, Juliana Tringali, Josh Gentry, Steve Wright, Kristen Sutton, Katie Foley, Karen Sheh, and David Kokorowski, as well as Director of Media Development Lauren Fogel and Director of Media Strategy Stacy Treco.

For their important roles in marketing the book, we thank Christy Lawrence, Lauren Harp, Scott Dustan, Lillian Carr, Jane Campbell, Jessica Perry, Nora Massuda, and Jessica Tree.

We are grateful to Linda Davis, President of Pearson Math and Science, who has shared our commitment to excellence and provided strong support for five editions now. Moreover, we thank Paul Corey, President of Pearson Benjamin Cummings, and Editorial Director Frank Ruggirello for their enthusiasm, encouragement, and support.

The Pearson sales team, which represents *CAMPBELL BIOLOGY* on campus, is an essential link to the users of the text. They tell us what you like and don't like about the book, communicate the features of the book, and provide prompt service. We thank them for their hard work and professionalism. For representing our book to our international audience, we thank our sales and marketing partners throughout the world. They are all strong allies in biology education.

Finally, we wish to thank our families and friends for their encouragement and patience throughout this long project. Our special thanks to Paul, Dan, Maria, Armelle, and Sean (J.B.R.); Lily, Ross, Lily-too, and Alex (L.A.U.); Debra and Hannah (M.L.C.); Harry, Elga, Aaron, Sophie, Noah, and Gabriele (S.A.W.); Natalie (P.V.M.); and Sally, Robert, David, and Will (R.B.J.). And, as always, thanks to Rochelle, Allison, Jason, and McKay.

Jane Reece, Lisa Urry, Michael Cain,
Steve Wasserman, Peter Minorsky, and Rob Jackson

Reviewers

Ninth Edition Reviewers

Ann Aguanno, *Marymount Manhattan College*
Marc Albrecht, *University of Nebraska*
John Alcock, *Arizona State University*
Eric Alcorn, *Acadia University*
Terry Austin, *Temple College*
Brian Bagatto, *University of Akron*
Virginia Baker, *Chipola College*
Bonnie Baxter, *Westminster College*
Marilee Benore, *University of Michigan, Dearborn*
Catherine Black, *Idaho State University*
William Blaker, *Furman University*
Edward Blumenthal, *Marquette University*
David Bos, *Purdue University*
Scott Bowling, *Auburn University*
Beth Burch, *Huntington University*
Ragan Callaway, *The University of Montana*
Kenneth M. Cameron, *University of Wisconsin, Madison*
Patrick Canary, *Northland Pioneer College*
Cheryl Keller Capone, *Pennsylvania State University*
Karen I. Champ, *Central Florida Community College*
David Champlin, *University of Southern Maine*
Brad Chandler, *Palo Alto College*
Wei-Jen Chang, *Hamilton College*
Jung Choi, *Georgia Institute of Technology*
Steve Christensen, *Brigham Young University, Idaho*
James T. Colbert, *Iowa State University*
William Cushwa, *Clark College*
Shannon Datwyler, *California State University, Sacramento*
Eugene Delay, *University of Vermont*
Daniel DerVartanian, *University of Georgia*
Janet De Souza-Hart, *Massachusetts College of Pharmacy & Health Sciences*
Kathryn A. Durham, *Lorain Community College*
Curt Elderkin, *College of New Jersey*
Mary Ellard-Ivey, *Pacific Lutheran University*
George Ellmore, *Tufts University*
Robert C. Evans, *Rutgers University, Camden*
Sam Fan, *Bradley University*
Paul Farnsworth, *University of New Mexico*
Myriam Alhadeff Feldman, *Cascadia Community College*
Teresa Fischer, *Indian River Community College*
David Fitch, *New York University*
T. Fleming, *Bradley University*
Robert Fowler, *San Jose State University*
Robert Franklin, *College of Charleston*
Art Fredeen, *University of Northern British Columbia*
Matt Friedman, *University of Chicago*
Cynthia M. Galloway, *Texas A&M University, Kingsville*
Simon Gilroy, *University of Wisconsin, Madison*
Jim Goetze, *Laredo Community College*
Lynda Goff, *University of California, Santa Cruz*
Roy Golsteyn, *University of Lethbridge*
Barbara E. Goodman, *University of South Dakota*
David Grise, *Texas A&M University, Corpus Christi*
Devney Hamilton, *Stanford University (student)*
Matthew B. Hamilton, *Georgetown University*
Jeanne M. Harris, *University of Vermont*
Stephanie Harvey, *Georgia Southwestern State University*
Bernard Hauser, *University of Florida*
Andreas Hejnol, *Sars International Centre for Marine Molecular Biology*
Jason Hodin, *Stanford University*
Sara Huang, *Los Angeles Valley College*
Catherine Hurlbut, *Florida State College, Jacksonville*
Diane Husic, *Moravian College*
Thomas Jacobs, *University of Illinois*
Mark Jaffe, *Nova Southeastern University*
Douglas Jensen, *Converse College*
Lance Johnson, *Midland Lutheran College*
Cheryl Jorcyk, *Boise State University*
Caroline Kane, *University of California, Berkeley*
Jennifer Katcher, *Pima Community College*
Eric G. Keeling, *Cary Institute of Ecosystem Studies*
Chris Kennedy, *Simon Fraser University*
Hillar Klandorf, *West Virginia University*
Mark Knauss, *Georgia Highlands College*

Roger Koeppe, *University of Arkansas*
Peter Kourtev, *Central Michigan University*
Eliot Krause, *Seton Hall University*
Steven Kristoff, *Ivy Tech Community College*
William Kroll, *Loyola University*
Rukmani Kuppuswami, *Laredo Community College*
Lee Kurtz, *Georgia Gwinnett College*
Michael P. Labare, *United States Military Academy, West Point*
Ellen Lamb, *University of North Carolina, Greensboro*
William Lamberts, *College of St Benedict and St John's University*
Tali D. Lee, *University of Wisconsin, Eau Claire*
Hugh Lefcort, *Gonzaga University*
Alcinda Lewis, *University of Colorado, Boulder*
Graeme Lindbeck, *Valenica Community College*
Hannah Lui, *University of California, Irvine*
Cindy Malone, *California State University, Northridge*
Julia Marrs, *Barnard College (student)*
Kathleen Marrs, *Indiana University-Purdue University, Indianapolis*
Mike Mayfield, *Ball State University*
Kamau Mbuthia, *Bowling Green State University*
Tanya McGhee, *Craven Community College*
Darcy Medica, *Pennsylvania State University*
Susan Meiers, *Western Illinois University*
Alex Mills, *University of Windsor*
Eli Minkoff, *Bates College*
Subhash Minocha, *University of New Hampshire*
Ivona Mladenovic, *Simon Fraser University*
Courtney Murren, *College of Charleston*
Kimberlyn Nelson, *Pennsylvania State University*
Jacalyn Newman, *University of Pittsburgh*
Kathleen Nolta, *University of Michigan*
Aharon Oren, *The Hebrew University*
Henry R. Owen, *Eastern Illinois University*
Stephanie Pandolfi, *Michigan State University*
Nathalie Pardigon, *Institut Pasteur*
Cindy Paszkowski, *University of Alberta*
Andrew Pease, *Stevenson University*
Nancy Pelaez, *Purdue University*
Irene Perry, *University of Texas of the Permian Basin*
Roger Persell, *Hunter College*
Mark Pilgrim, *College of Coastal Georgia*
Vera M. Piper, *Shenadoah University*
Crima Pogge, *City College of San Francisco*
Michael Pollock, *Mount Royal University*
Roberta Pollock, *Occidental College*
Therese M. Poole, *Georgia State University*
Angela R. Porta, *Kean University*
Robert Powell, *Avila University*
Elena Pravosudova, *University of Nevada, Reno*
Terrell Pritts, *University of Arkansas, Little Rock*
Monica Ranes-Goldberg, *University of California, Berkeley*
Robert S. Rawding, *Gannon University*
Sarah Richart, *Azusa Pacific University*
Kenneth Robinson, *Purdue University*
Heather Roffey, *Marianopolis College*
Patricia Rugaber, *College of Coastal Georgia*
Scott Russell, *University of Oklahoma*
Louis Santiago, *University of California, Riverside*
Tom Sawicki, *Spartanburg Community College*
Thomas W. Schoener, *University of California, Davis*
Patricia Schulte, *University of British Colombia*
Brenda Schumpert, *Valencia Community College*
David Schwartz, *Houston Community College*
Brent Selinger, *University of Lethbridge*
Alison M. Shakarian, *Salve Regina University*
Robin L. Sherman, *Nova Southeastern University*
Sedonia Sipes, *Southern Illinois University, Carbondale*
Joel Stafstrom, *Northern Illinois University*
Alam Stam, *Capital University*
Judy Stone, *Colby College*
Cynthia Surmacz, *Bloomsburg University*
David Tam, *University of North Texas*
Yves Tan, *Cabrillo College*
Emily Taylor, *California Polytechnic State University*
Franklyn Tan Te, *Miami Dade College*
Kent Thomas, *Wichita State University*

Saba Valadkhan, *Center for RNA Molecular Biology*
Sarah VanVickle-Chavez, *Washington University, St. Louis*
William Velhagen, *New York University*
Janice Voltzow, *University of Scranton*
Margaret Voss, *Penn State Erie*
Charles Wade, *C.S. Mott Community College*
Claire Walczak, *Indiana University*
Jerry Waldvogel, *Clemson University*
Robert Lee Wallace, *Ripon College*
Fred Wasserman, *Boston University*
John Weishampel, *University of Central Florida*
Susan Whittemore, *Keene State College*
Janet Wolkenstein, *Hudson Valley Community College*
Grace Wyngaard, *James Madison University*
Paul Yancey, *Whitman College*
Anne D. Yoder, *Duke University*
Nina Zanetti, *Siena College*
Sam Zeveloff, *Weber State University*
Theresa Zucchero, *Methodist University*

Reviewers of Previous Editions

Kenneth Able (*State University of New York, Albany*)
Thomas Adams (*Michigan State University*)
Martin Adamson (*University of British Columbia*)
Dominique Adriaens (*Ghent University*)
Shylaja Akkaraju (*Bronx Community College of CUNY*)
John Alcock (*Arizona State University*)
George R. Aliaga (*Tarrant County College*)
Richard Almon (*State University of New York, Buffalo*)
Bonnie Amos (*Angelo State University*)
Katherine Anderson (*University of California, Berkeley*)
Richard J. Andren (*Montgomery County Community College*)
Estry Ang (*University of Pittsburgh, Greensburg*)
Jeff Appling (*Clemson University*)
J. David Archibald (*San Diego State University*)
David Armstrong (*University of Colorado, Boulder*)
Howard J. Arnott (*University of Texas, Arlington*)
Mary Ashley (*University of Illinois, Chicago*)
Angela S. Aspbury (*Texas State University*)
Robert Atherton (*University of Wyoming*)
Karl Aufderheide (*Texas A&M University*)
Leigh Auleb (*San Francisco State University*)
P. Stephen Baenziger (*University of Nebraska*)
Ellen Baker (*Santa Monica College*)
Katherine Baker (*Millersville University*)
William Barklow (*Framingham State College*)
Susan Barman (*Michigan State University*)
Steven Barnhart (*Santa Rosa Junior College*)
Andrew Barton (*University of Maine Farmington*)
Rebecca A. Bartow (*Western Kentucky University*)
Ron Basmajian (*Merced College*)
David Bass (*University of Central Oklahoma*)
Bonnie Baxter (*Hobart & William Smith Colleges*)
Tim Beagley (*Salt Lake Community College*)
Margaret E. Beard (*College of the Holy Cross*)
Tom Beatty (*University of British Columbia*)
Chris Beck (*Emory University*)
Wayne Becker (*University of Wisconsin, Madison*)
Patricia Bedinger (*Colorado State University*)
Jane Beiswenger (*University of Wyoming*)
Anne Bekoff (*University of Colorado, Boulder*)
Marc Bekoff (*University of Colorado, Boulder*)
Tania Beliz (*College of San Mateo*)
Adrianne Bendich (*Hoffman-La Roche, Inc.*)
Barbara Bentley (*State University of New York, Stony Brook*)
Darwin Berg (*University of California, San Diego*)
Werner Bergen (*Michigan State University*)
Gerald Bergstrom (*University of Wisconsin, Milwaukee*)
Anna W. Berkovitz (*Purdue University*)
Dorothy Berner (*Temple University*)
Annalisa Berta (*San Diego State University*)
Paulette Bierzychudek (*Pomona College*)
Charles Biggers (*Memphis State University*)
Kenneth Birnbaum (*New York University*)
Michael W. Black (*California Polytechnic State University, San Luis Obispo*)
Robert Blanchard (*University of New Hampshire*)
Andrew R. Blaustein (*Oregon State University*)
Judy Bluemer (*Morton College*)
Edward Blumenthal (*Marquette University*)
Robert Blystone (*Trinity University*)
Robert Boley (*University of Texas, Arlington*)
Jason E. Bond (*East Carolina University*)

Eric Bonde (*University of Colorado, Boulder*)
Cornelius Bondzi (*Hampton University*)
Richard Boohar (*University of Nebraska, Omaha*)
Carey L. Booth (*Reed College*)
Allan Bornstein (*Southeast Missouri State University*)
Oliver Bossdorf (*State University of New York, Stony Book*)
James L. Botsford (*New Mexico State University*)
Lisa Boucher (*University of Nebraska, Omaha*)
J. Michael Bowes (*Humboldt State University*)
Richard Bowker (*Alma College*)
Robert Bowker (*Glendale Community College, Arizona*)
Barbara Bowman (*Mills College*)
Barry Bowman (*University of California, Santa Cruz*)
Deric Bownds (*University of Wisconsin, Madison*)
Robert Boyd (*Auburn University*)
Sunny Boyd (*University of Notre Dame*)
Jerry Brand (*University of Texas, Austin*)
Edward Braun (*Iowa State University*)
Theodore A. Bremner (*Howard University*)
James Brenneman (*University of Evansville*)
Charles H. Brenner (*Berkeley, California*)
Lawrence Brewer (*University of Kentucky*)
Donald P. Briskin (*University of Illinois, Urbana*)
Paul Broady (*University of Canterbury*)
Chad Brommer (*Emory University*)
Judith L. Bronstein (*University of Arizona*)
Danny Brower (*University of Arizona*)
Carole Browne (*Wake Forest University*)
Mark Browning (*Purdue University*)
David Bruck (*San Jose State University*)
Robb T. Brumfield (*Louisiana State University*)
Herbert Bruneau (*Oklahoma State University*)
Gary Brusca (*Humboldt State University*)
Richard C. Brusca (*University of Arizona, Arizona-Sonora Desert Museum*)
Alan H. Brush (*University of Connecticut, Storrs*)
Howard Buhse (*University of Illinois, Chicago*)
Arthur Buikema (*Virginia Tech*)
Al Burchsted (*College of Staten Island*)
Meg Burke (*University of North Dakota*)
Edwin Burling (*De Anza College*)
William Busa (*Johns Hopkins University*)
Jorge Busciglio (*University of California, Irvine*)
John Bushnell (*University of Colorado*)
Linda Butler (*University of Texas, Austin*)
David Byres (*Florida Community College, Jacksonville*)
Guy A. Caldwell (*University of Alabama*)
Jane Caldwell (*West Virginia University*)
Kim A. Caldwell (*University of Alabama*)
R. Andrew Cameron (*California Institute of Technology*)
Alison Campbell (*University of Waikato*)
Iain Campbell (*University of Pittsburgh*)
W. Zacheus Cande (*University of California, Berkeley*)
Robert E. Cannon (*University of North Carolina, Greensboro*)
Deborah Canington (*University of California, Davis*)
Frank Cantelmo (*St. John's University*)
John Capeheart (*University of Houston, Downtown*)
Gregory Capelli (*College of William and Mary*)
Richard Cardullo (*University of California, Riverside*)
Nina Caris (*Texas A&M University*)
Jeffrey Carmichael (*University of North Dakota*)
Robert Carroll (*East Carolina University*)
Laura L. Carruth (*Georgia State University*)
J. Aaron Cassill (*University of Texas, San Antonio*)
David Champlin (*University of Southern Maine*)
Bruce Chase (*University of Nebraska, Omaha*)
P. Bryant Chase (*Florida State University*)
Doug Cheeseman (*De Anza College*)
Shepley Chen (*University of Illinois, Chicago*)
Giovina Chinchar (*Tougaloo College*)
Joseph P. Chinnici (*Virginia Commonwealth University*)
Jung H. Choi (*Georgia Institute of Technology*)
Geoffrey Church (*Fairfield University*)
Henry Claman (*University of Colorado Health Science Center*)
Anne Clark (*Binghamton University*)
Greg Clark (*University of Texas*)
Patricia J. Clark (*Indiana University-Purdue University, Indianapolis*)
Ross C. Clark (*Eastern Kentucky University*)
Lynwood Clemens (*Michigan State University*)
Janice J. Clymer (*San Diego Mesa College*)
William P. Coffman (*University of Pittsburgh*)
Austin Randy Cohen (*California State University, Northridge*)
J. John Cohen (*University of Colorado Health Science Center*)
Jim Colbert (*Iowa State University*)
Jan Colpaert (*Hasselt University*)

Robert Colvin *(Ohio University)*
Jay Comeaux *(McNeese State University)*
David Cone *(Saint Mary's University)*
Elizabeth Connor *(University of Massachusetts)*
Joanne Conover *(University of Connecticut)*
Gregory Copenhaver *(University of North Carolina, Chapel Hill)*
John Corliss *(University of Maryland)*
James T. Costa *(Western Carolina University)*
Stuart J. Coward *(University of Georgia)*
Charles Creutz *(University of Toledo)*
Bruce Criley *(Illinois Wesleyan University)*
Norma Criley *(Illinois Wesleyan University)*
Joe W. Crim *(University of Georgia)*
Greg Crowther *(University of Washington)*
Karen Curto *(University of Pittsburgh)*
Anne Cusic *(University of Alabama, Birmingham)*
Richard Cyr *(Pennsylvania State University)*
Marymegan Daly *(The Ohio State University)*
W. Marshall Darley *(University of Georgia)*
Cynthia Dassler *(The Ohio State University)*
Marianne Dauwalder *(University of Texas, Austin)*
Larry Davenport *(Samford University)*
Bonnie J. Davis *(San Francisco State University)*
Jerry Davis *(University of Wisconsin, La Crosse)*
Michael A. Davis *(Central Connecticut State University)*
Thomas Davis *(University of New Hampshire)*
John Dearn *(University of Canberra)*
Maria E. de Bellard *(California State University, Northridge)*
Teresa DeGolier *(Bethel College)*
James Dekloe *(University of California, Santa Cruz)*
Patricia A. DeLeon *(University of Delaware)*
Veronique Delesalle *(Gettysburg College)*
T. Delevoryas *(University of Texas, Austin)*
Roger Del Moral *(University of Washington)*
Charles F. Delwiche *(University of Maryland)*
Diane C. DeNagel *(Northwestern University)*
William L. Dentler *(University of Kansas)*
Daniel Dervartanian *(University of Georgia)*
Jean DeSaix *(University of North Carolina, Chapel Hill)*
Biao Ding *(Ohio State University)*
Michael Dini *(Texas Tech University)*
Andrew Dobson *(Princeton University)*
Stanley Dodson *(University of Wisconsin, Madison)*
Mark Drapeau *(University of California, Irvine)*
John Drees *(Temple University School of Medicine)*
Charles Drewes *(Iowa State University)*
Marvin Druger *(Syracuse University)*
Gary Dudley *(University of Georgia)*
Susan Dunford *(University of Cincinnati)*
Betsey Dyer *(Wheaton College)*
Robert Eaton *(University of Colorado)*
Robert S. Edgar *(University of California, Santa Cruz)*
Douglas J. Eernisse *(California State University, Fullerton)*
Betty J. Eidemiller *(Lamar University)*
Brad Elder *(Doane College)*
William D. Eldred *(Boston University)*
Michelle Elekonich *(University of Nevada, Las Vegas)*
Mary Ellard-Ivey *(Pacific Lutheran University)*
Norman Ellstrand *(University of California, Riverside)*
Johnny El-Rady *(University of South Florida)*
Dennis Emery *(Iowa State University)*
John Endler *(University of California, Santa Barbara)*
Margaret T. Erskine *(Lansing Community College)*
Gerald Esch *(Wake Forest University)*
Frederick B. Essig *(University of South Florida)*
Mary Eubanks *(Duke University)*
David Evans *(University of Florida)*
Robert C. Evans *(Rutgers University, Camden)*
Sharon Eversman *(Montana State University)*
Olukemi Fadayomi *(Ferris State University)*
Lincoln Fairchild *(Ohio State University)*
Peter Fajer *(Florida State University)*
Bruce Fall *(University of Minnesota)*
Lynn Fancher *(College of DuPage)*
Ellen H. Fanning *(Vanderbilt University)*
Paul Farnsworth *(University of Texas, San Antonio)*
Larry Farrell *(Idaho State University)*
Jerry F. Feldman *(University of California, Santa Cruz)*
Lewis Feldman *(University of California, Berkeley)*
Eugene Fenster *(Longview Community College)*
Russell Fernald *(University of Oregon)*
Rebecca Ferrell *(Metropolitan State College of Denver)*
Kim Finer *(Kent State University)*

Milton Fingerman *(Tulane University)*
Barbara Finney *(Regis College)*
Frank Fish *(West Chester University)*
David Fisher *(University of Hawaii, Manoa)*
Jonathan S. Fisher *(St. Louis University)*
Steven Fisher *(University of California, Santa Barbara)*
Kirk Fitzhugh *(Natural History Museum of Los Angeles County)*
Lloyd Fitzpatrick *(University of North Texas)*
William Fixsen *(Harvard University)*
Abraham Flexer *(Manuscript Consultant, Boulder, Colorado)*
Kerry Foresman *(University of Montana)*
Norma Fowler *(University of Texas, Austin)*
Robert G. Fowler *(San Jose State University)*
David Fox *(University of Tennessee, Knoxville)*
Carl Frankel *(Pennsylvania State University, Hazleton)*
James Franzen *(University of Pittsburgh)*
Bill Freedman *(Dalhousie University)*
Otto Friesen *(University of Virginia)*
Frank Frisch *(Chapman University)*
Virginia Fry *(Monterey Peninsula College)*
Bernard Frye *(University of Texas, Arlington)*
Jed Fuhrman *(University of Southern California)*
Alice Fulton *(University of Iowa)*
Chandler Fulton *(Brandeis University)*
Sara Fultz *(Stanford University)*
Berdell Funke *(North Dakota State University)*
Anne Funkhouser *(University of the Pacific)*
Zofia E. Gagnon *(Marist College)*
Michael Gaines *(University of Miami)*
Arthur W. Galston *(Yale University)*
Stephen Gammie *(University of Wisconsin, Madison)*
Carl Gans *(University of Michigan)*
John Gapter *(University of Northern Colorado)*
Andrea Gargas *(University of Wisconsin, Madison)*
Lauren Garner *(California Polytechnic State University, San Luis Obispo)*
Reginald Garrett *(University of Virginia)*
Patricia Gensel *(University of North Carolina)*
Chris George *(California Polytechnic State University, San Luis Obispo)*
Robert George *(University of Wyoming)*
J. Whitfield Gibbons *(University of Georgia)*
J. Phil Gibson *(Agnes Scott College)*
Frank Gilliam *(Marshall University)*
Simon Gilroy *(Pennsylvania State University)*
Alan D. Gishlick *(Gustavus Adolphus College)*
Todd Gleeson *(University of Colorado)*
Jessica Gleffe *(University of California, Irvine)*
John Glendinning *(Barnard College)*
David Glenn-Lewin *(Wichita State University)*
William Glider *(University of Nebraska)*
Tricia Glidewell *(Marist School)*
Elizabeth A. Godrick *(Boston University)*
Lynda Goff *(University of California, Santa Cruz)*
Elliott Goldstein *(Arizona State University)*
Paul Goldstein *(University of Texas, El Paso)*
Sandra Gollnick *(State University of New York, Buffalo)*
Anne Good *(University of California, Berkeley)*
Judith Goodenough *(University of Massachusetts, Amherst)*
Wayne Goodey *(University of British Columbia)*
Robert Goodman *(University of Wisconsin, Madison)*
Ester Goudsmit *(Oakland University)*
Linda Graham *(University of Wisconsin, Madison)*
Robert Grammer *(Belmont University)*
Joseph Graves *(Arizona State University)*
Phyllis Griffard *(University of Houston, Downtown)*
A. J. F. Griffiths *(University of British Columbia)*
William Grimes *(University of Arizona)*
Mark Gromko *(Bowling Green State University)*
Serine Gropper *(Auburn University)*
Katherine L. Gross *(Ohio State University)*
Gary Gussin *(University of Iowa)*
Mark Guyer *(National Human Genome Research Institute)*
Ruth Levy Guyer *(Bethesda, Maryland)*
R. Wayne Habermehl *(Montgomery County Community College)*
Mac Hadley *(University of Arizona)*
Joel Hagen *(Radford University)*
Jack P. Hailman *(University of Wisconsin)*
Leah Haimo *(University of California, Riverside)*
Ken Halanych *(Auburn University)*
Jody Hall *(Brown University)*
Douglas Hallett, *(Northern Arizona University)*
Rebecca Halyard *(Clayton State College)*
E. William Hamilton *(Washington and Lee University)*
Sam Hammer *(Boston University)*
Penny Hanchey-Bauer *(Colorado State University)*

William F. Hanna (*Massasoit Community College*)
Laszlo Hanzely (*Northern Illinois University*)
Jeff Hardin (*University of Wisconsin, Madison*)
Lisa Harper (*University of California, Berkeley*)
Richard Harrison (*Cornell University*)
Carla Hass (*Pennsylvania State University*)
Chris Haufler (*University of Kansas*)
Bernard A. Hauser (*University of Florida*)
Chris Haynes (*Shelton State Community College*)
Evan B. Hazard (*Bemidji State University, Emeritus*)
H. D. Heath (*California State University, East Bay*)
George Hechtel (*State University of New York, Stony Brook*)
S. Blair Hedges (*Pennsylvania State University*)
Brian Hedlund (*University of Nevada, Las Vegas*)
David Heins (*Tulane University*)
Jean Heitz (*University of Wisconsin, Madison*)
John D. Helmann (*Cornell University*)
Colin Henderson (*University of Montana*)
Susan Hengeveld (*Indiana University*)
Michelle Henricks (*University of California, Los Angeles*)
Caroll Henry (*Chicago State University*)
Frank Heppner (*University of Rhode Island*)
Albert Herrera (*University of Southern California*)
Scott Herrick (*Missouri Western State College*)
Ira Herskowitz (*University of California, San Francisco*)
Paul E. Hertz (*Barnard College*)
David Hibbett (*Clark University*)
R. James Hickey (*Miami University*)
William Hillenius (*College of Charleston*)
Kenneth Hillers (*California Polytechnic State University, San Luis Obispo*)
Ralph Hinegardner (*University of California, Santa Cruz*)
William Hines (*Foothill College*)
Robert Hinrichsen (*Indiana University of Pennsylvania*)
Helmut Hirsch (*State University of New York, Albany*)
Tuan-hua David Ho (*Washington University*)
Carl Hoagstrom (*Ohio Northern University*)
James Hoffman (*University of Vermont*)
A. Scott Holaday (*Texas Tech University*)
N. Michele Holbrook (*Harvard University*)
James Holland (*Indiana State University, Bloomington*)
Charles Holliday (*Lafayette College*)
Lubbock Karl Holte (*Idaho State University*)
Alan R. Holyoak (*Brigham Young University, Idaho*)
Laura Hoopes (*Occidental College*)
Nancy Hopkins (*Massachusetts Institute of Technology*)
Sandra Horikami (*Daytona Beach Community College*)
Kathy Hornberger (*Widener University*)
Pius F. Horner (*San Bernardino Valley College*)
Becky Houck (*University of Portland*)
Margaret Houk (*Ripon College*)
Daniel J. Howard (*New Mexico State University*)
Ronald R. Hoy (*Cornell University*)
Cristin Hulslander (*University of Oregon*)
Donald Humphrey (*Emory University School of Medicine*)
Robert J. Huskey (*University of Virginia*)
Steven Hutcheson (*University of Maryland, College Park*)
Sandra Hsu (*Skyline College*)
Linda L. Hyde (*Gordon College*)
Bradley Hyman (*University of California, Riverside*)
Mark Iked (*San Bernardino Valley College*)
Jeffrey Ihara (*Mira Costa College*)
Cheryl Ingram-Smith (*Clemson University*)
Alice Jacklet (*State University of New York, Albany*)
John Jackson (*North Hennepin Community College*)
John C. Jahoda (*Bridgewater State College*)
Dan Johnson (*East Tennessee State University*)
Lee Johnson (*The Ohio State University*)
Randall Johnson (*University of California, San Diego*)
Stephen Johnson (*William Penn University*)
Wayne Johnson (*Ohio State University*)
Kenneth C. Jones (*California State University, Northridge*)
Russell Jones (*University of California, Berkeley*)
Chad Jordan (*North Carolina State University*)
Alan Journet (*Southeast Missouri State University*)
Walter Judd (*University of Florida*)
Thomas W. Jurik (*Iowa State University*)
Caroline M. Kane (*University of California, Berkeley*)
Thomas C. Kane (*University of Cincinnati*)
Tamos Kapros (*University of Missouri*)
E. L. Karlstrom (*University of Puget Sound*)
Jennifer Katcher (*Pima Community College*)
Laura A. Katz (*Smith College*)
Maureen Kearney (*Field Museum of Natural History*)
Patrick Keeling (*University of British Columbia*)

Elizabeth A. Kellogg (*University of Missouri, St. Louis*)
Norm Kenkel (*University of Manitoba*)
Chris Kennedy (*Simon Fraser University*)
George Khoury (*National Cancer Institute*)
Rebecca T. Kimball (*University of Florida*)
Mark Kirk (*University of Missouri, Columbia*)
Robert Kitchin (*University of Wyoming*)
Attila O. Klein (*Brandeis University*)
Daniel Klionsky (*University of Michigan*)
Jennifer Knight (*University of Colorado*)
Ned Knight (*Linfield College*)
David Kohl (*University of California, Santa Barbara*)
Greg Kopf (*University of Pennsylvania School of Medicine*)
Thomas Koppenheffer (*Trinity University*)
Margareta Krabbe (*Uppsala University*)
Anselm Kratochwil (*Universität Osnabrück*)
Deborah M. Kristan (*California State University, San Marcos*)
William Kroll (*Loyola University, Chicago*)
Janis Kuby (*San Francisco State University*)
Justin P. Kumar (*Indiana University*)
David Kurijaka (*Ohio University*)
Marc-André Lachance (*University of Western Ontario*)
J. A. Lackey (*State University of New York, Oswego*)
Elaine Lai (*Brandeis University*)
Mohamed Lakrim (*Kingsborough Community College*)
Lynn Lamoreux (*Texas A&M University*)
William L'Amoreaux (*College of Staten Island*)
Carmine A. Lanciani (*University of Florida*)
Kenneth Lang (*Humboldt State University*)
Dominic Lannutti (*El Paso Community College*)
Allan Larson (*Washington University*)
John Latto (*University of California, Santa Barbara*)
Diane K. Lavett (*State University of New York, Cortland, and Emory University*)
Charles Leavell (*Fullerton College*)
C. S. Lee (*University of Texas*)
Daewoo Lee (*Ohio University*)
Robert Leonard (*University of California, Riverside*)
Michael R. Leonardo (*Coe College*)
John Lepri (*University of North Carolina, Greensboro*)
Donald Levin (*University of Texas, Austin*)
Mike Levine (*University of California, Berkeley*)
Joseph Levine (*Boston College*)
Bill Lewis (*Shoreline Community College*)
John Lewis (*Loma Linda University*)
Lorraine Lica (*California State University, East Bay*)
Harvey Liftin (*Broward Community College*)
Harvey Lillywhite (*University of Florida, Gainesville*)
Graeme Lindbeck (*Valencia Community College*)
Clark Lindgren (*Grinnell College*)
Diana Lipscomb (*George Washington University*)
Christopher Little (*The University of Texas, Pan American*)
Kevin D. Livingstone (*Trinity University*)
Andrea Lloyd (*Middlebury College*)
Sam Loker (*University of New Mexico*)
Christopher A. Loretz (*State University of New York, Buffalo*)
Jane Lubchenco (*Oregon State University*)
Douglas B. Luckie (*Michigan State University*)
Margaret A. Lynch (*Tufts University*)
Steven Lynch (*Louisiana State University, Shreveport*)
Richard Machemer Jr. (*St. John Fisher College*)
Elizabeth Machunis-Masuoka (*University of Virginia*)
James MacMahon (*Utah State University*)
Christine R. Maher (*University of Southern Maine*)
Linda Maier (*University of Alabama, Huntsville*)
Jose Maldonado (*El Paso Community College*)
Richard Malkin (*University of California, Berkeley*)
Charles Mallery (*University of Miami*)
Keith Malmos (*Valencia Community College, East Campus*)
Cindy Malone (*California State University, Northridge*)
Carol Mapes (*Kutztown University of Pennsylvania*)
William Margolin (*University of Texas Medical School*)
Lynn Margulis (*Boston University*)
Kathleen A. Marrs (*Indiana University-Purdue University, Indianapolis*)
Edith Marsh (*Angelo State University*)
Diane L. Marshall (*University of New Mexico*)
Linda Martin Morris (*University of Washington*)
Karl Mattox (*Miami University of Ohio*)
Joyce Maxwell (*California State University, Northridge*)
Jeffrey D. May (*Marshall University*)
Lee McClenaghan (*San Diego State University*)
Richard McCracken (*Purdue University*)
Andrew McCubbin (*Washington State University*)
Kerry McDonald (*University of Missouri, Columbia*)
Jacqueline McLaughlin (*Pennsylvania State University, Lehigh Valley*)

Neal McReynolds (Texas A&M International)
Lisa Marie Meffert (Rice University)
Michael Meighan (University of California, Berkeley)
Scott Meissner (Cornell University)
Paul Melchior (North Hennepin Community College)
Phillip Meneely (Haverford College)
John Merrill (Michigan State University)
Brian Metscher (University of California, Irvine)
Ralph Meyer (University of Cincinnati)
James Mickle (North Carolina State University)
Roger Milkman (University of Iowa)
Helen Miller (Oklahoma State University)
John Miller (University of California, Berkeley)
Kenneth R. Miller (Brown University)
John E. Minnich (University of Wisconsin, Milwaukee)
Michael J. Misamore (Texas Christian University)
Kenneth Mitchell (Tulane University School of Medicine)
Alan Molumby (University of Illinois, Chicago)
Nicholas Money (Miami University)
Russell Monson (University of Colorado, Boulder)
Joseph P. Montoya (Georgia Institute of Technology)
Frank Moore (Oregon State University)
Janice Moore (Colorado State University)
Randy Moore (Wright State University)
William Moore (Wayne State University)
Carl Moos (Veterans Administration Hospital, Albany, New York)
Michael Mote (Temple University)
Alex Motten (Duke University)
Jeanette Mowery (Madison Area Technical College)
Deborah Mowshowitz (Columbia University)
Rita Moyes (Texas A&M College Station)
Darrel L. Murray (University of Illinois, Chicago)
John Mutchmor (Iowa State University)
Elliot Myerowitz (California Institute of Technology)
Gavin Naylor (Iowa State University)
John Neess (University of Wisconsin, Madison)
Tom Neils (Grand Rapids Community College)
Raymond Neubauer (University of Texas, Austin)
Todd Newbury (University of California, Santa Cruz)
James Newcomb (New England College)
Harvey Nichols (University of Colorado, Boulder)
Deborah Nickerson (University of South Florida)
Bette Nicotri (University of Washington)
Caroline Niederman (Tomball College)
Maria Nieto (California State University, East Bay)
Anders Nilsson (University of Umeå)
Greg Nishiyama (College of the Canyons)
Charles R. Noback (College of Physicians and Surgeons, Columbia University)
Jane Noble-Harvey (Delaware University)
Mary C. Nolan (Irvine Valley College)
Peter Nonacs (University of California, Los Angeles)
Mohamed A. F. Noor (Duke University)
Shawn Nordell (St. Louis University)
Richard S. Norman (University of Michigan, Dearborn, Emeritus)
David O. Norris (University of Colorado, Boulder)
Steven Norris (California State University, Channel Islands)
Gretchen North (Occidental College)
Cynthia Norton (University of Maine, Augusta)
Steve Norton (East Carolina University)
Steve Nowicki (Duke University)
Bette H. Nybakken (Hartnell College)
Brian O'Conner (University of Massachusetts, Amherst)
Gerard O'Donovan (University of North Texas)
Eugene Odum (University of Georgia)
Mark P. Oemke (Alma College)
Linda Ogren (University of California, Santa Cruz)
Patricia O'Hern (Emory University)
Nathan O. Okia (Auburn University, Montgomery)
Jeanette Oliver (St. Louis Community College, Florissant Valley)
Gary P. Olivetti (University of Vermont)
John Olsen (Rhodes College)
Laura J. Olsen (University of Michigan)
Sharman O'Neill (University of California, Davis)
Wan Ooi (Houston Community College)
John Oross (University of California, Riverside)
Gay Ostarello (Diablo Valley College)
Catherine Ortega (Fort Lewis College)
Charissa Osborne (Butler University)
Thomas G. Owens (Cornell University)
Penny Padgett (University of North Carolina, Chapel Hill)
Kevin Padian (University of California, Berkeley)
Dianna Padilla (State University of New York, Stony Brook)
Anthony T. Paganini (Michigan State University)
Barry Palevitz (University of Georgia)

Michael A. Palladino (Monmouth University)
Daniel Papaj (University of Arizona)
Peter Pappas (County College of Morris)
Bulah Parker (North Carolina State University)
Stanton Parmeter (Chemeketa Community College)
Robert Patterson (San Francisco State University)
Ronald Patterson (Michigan State University)
Crellin Pauling (San Francisco State University)
Kay Pauling (Foothill Community College)
Daniel Pavuk (Bowling Green State University)
Debra Pearce (Northern Kentucky University)
Patricia Pearson (Western Kentucky University)
Shelley Penrod (North Harris College)
Imara Y. Perera (North Carolina State University)
Beverly Perry (Houston Community College)
David Pfennig (University of North Carolina, Chapel Hill)
David S. Pilliod (California Polytechnic State University, San Luis Obispo)
J. Chris Pires (University of Missouri, Columbia)
Bob Pittman (Michigan State University)
James Platt (University of Denver)
Martin Poenie (University of Texas, Austin)
Scott Poethig (University of Pennsylvania)
Jeffrey Pommerville (Texas A&M University)
Angela R. Porta (Kean University)
Warren Porter (University of Wisconsin)
Daniel Potter (University of California, Davis)
Donald Potts (University of California, Santa Cruz)
Andy Pratt (University of Canterbury)
David Pratt (University of California, Davis)
Halina Presley (University of Illinois, Chicago)
Mary V. Price (University of California, Riverside)
Mitch Price (Pennsylvania State University)
Rong Sun Pu (Kean University)
Rebecca Pyles (East Tennessee State University)
Scott Quackenbush (Florida International University)
Ralph Quatrano (Oregon State University)
Peter Quinby (University of Pittsburgh)
Val Raghavan (Ohio State University)
Deanna Raineri (University of Illinois, Champaign-Urbana)
Talitha Rajah (Indiana University Southeast)
Charles Ralph (Colorado State University)
Thomas Rand (Saint Mary's University)
Robert H. Reavis (Glendale Community College)
Kurt Redborg (Coe College)
Ahnya Redman (Pennsylvania State University)
Brian Reeder (Morehead State University)
Bruce Reid (Kean University)
David Reid (Blackburn College)
C. Gary Reiness (Lewis & Clark College)
Charles Remington (Yale University)
Erin Rempala (San Diego Mesa College)
David Reznick (University of California, Riverside)
Douglas Rhoads (University of Arkansas)
Fred Rhoades (Western Washington State University)
Eric Ribbens (Western Illinois University)
Christina Richards (New York University)
Christopher Riegle (Irvine Valley College)
Loren Rieseberg (University of British Columbia)
Bruce B. Riley (Texas A&M University)
Donna Ritch (Pennsylvania State University)
Carol Rivin (Oregon State University East)
Laurel Roberts (University of Pittsburgh)
Thomas Rodella (Merced College)
Rodney Rogers (Drake University)
William Roosenburg (Ohio University)
Mike Rosenzweig (Virginia Polytechnic Institute and State University)
Wayne Rosing (Middle Tennessee State University)
Thomas Rost (University of California, Davis)
Stephen I. Rothstein (University of California, Santa Barbara)
John Ruben (Oregon State University)
Albert Ruesink (Indiana University)
Neil Sabine (Indiana University)
Tyson Sacco (Cornell University)
Rowan F. Sage (University of Toronto)
Tammy Lynn Sage (University of Toronto)
Don Sakaguchi (Iowa State University)
Walter Sakai (Santa Monica College)
Mark F. Sanders (University of California, Davis)
Ted Sargent (University of Massachusetts, Amherst)
K. Sathasivan (University of Texas, Austin)
Gary Saunders (University of New Brunswick)
Thomas R. Sawicki (Spartanburg Community College)
Inder Saxena (University of Texas, Austin)
Carl Schaefer (University of Connecticut)

Maynard H. Schaus (*Virginia Wesleyan College*)
Renate Scheibe (*University of Osnabrück*)
David Schimpf (*University of Minnesota, Duluth*)
William H. Schlesinger (*Duke University*)
Mark Schlissel (*University of California, Berkeley*)
Christopher J. Schneider (*Boston University*)
Thomas W. Schoener (*University of California, Davis*)
Robert Schorr (*Colorado State University*)
Patricia M. Schulte (*University of British Columbia*)
Karen S. Schumaker (*University of Arizona*)
David J. Schwartz (*Houston Community College*)
Christa Schwintzer (*University of Maine*)
Erik P. Scully (*Towson State University*)
Robert W. Seagull (*Hofstra University*)
Edna Seaman (*Northeastern University*)
Duane Sears (*University of California, Santa Barbara*)
Orono Shukdeb Sen (*Bethune-Cookman College*)
Wendy Sera (*Seton Hill University*)
Timothy E. Shannon (*Francis Marion University*)
Joan Sharp (*Simon Fraser University*)
Victoria C. Sharpe (*Blinn College*)
Elaine Shea (*Loyola College, Maryland*)
Stephen Sheckler (*Virginia Polytechnic Institute and State University*)
Richard Sherwin (*University of Pittsburgh*)
Lisa Shimeld (*Crafton Hills College*)
James Shinkle (*Trinity University*)
Barbara Shipes (*Hampton University*)
Richard M. Showman (*University of South Carolina*)
Peter Shugarman (*University of Southern California*)
Alice Shuttey (*DeKalb Community College*)
James Sidie (*Ursinus College*)
Daniel Simberloff (*Florida State University*)
Rebecca Simmons (*University of North Dakota*)
Anne Simon (*University of Maryland, College Park*)
Robert Simons (*University of California, Los Angeles*)
Alastair Simpson (*Dalhousie University*)
Susan Singer (*Carleton College*)
Roger Sloboda (*Dartmouth University*)
John Smarrelli (*Le Moyne College*)
Andrew T. Smith (*Arizona State University*)
Kelly Smith (*University of North Florida*)
Nancy Smith-Huerta (*Miami Ohio University*)
John Smol (*Queen's University*)
Andrew J. Snope (*Essex Community College*)
Julio G. Soto (*San Jose State University*)
Mitchell Sogin (*Woods Hole Marine Biological Laboratory*)
Susan Sovonick-Dunford (*University of Cincinnati*)
Frederick W. Spiegel (*University of Arkansas*)
John Stachowicz (*University of California, Davis*)
Amanda Starnes (*Emory University*)
Karen Steudel (*University of Wisconsin*)
Barbara Stewart (*Swarthmore College*)
Gail A. Stewart (*Camden County College*)
Cecil Still (*Rutgers University, New Brunswick*)
Margery Stinson (*Southwestern College*)
James Stockand (*University of Texas Health Science Center, San Antonio*)
John Stolz (*California Institute of Technology*)
Richard D. Storey (*Colorado College*)
Stephen Strand (*University of California, Los Angeles*)
Eric Strauss (*University of Massachusetts, Boston*)
Antony Stretton (*University of Wisconsin, Madison*)
Russell Stullken (*Augusta College*)
Mark Sturtevant (*University of Michigan, Flint*)
John Sullivan (*Southern Oregon State University*)
Gerald Summers (*University of Missouri*)
Judith Sumner (*Assumption College*)
Marshall D. Sundberg (*Emporia State University*)
Lucinda Swatzell (*Southeast Missouri State University*)
Daryl Sweeney (*University of Illinois, Champaign-Urbana*)
Samuel S. Sweet (*University of California, Santa Barbara*)
Janice Swenson (*University of North Florida*)
Michael A. Sypes (*Pennsylvania State University*)
Lincoln Taiz (*University of California, Santa Cruz*)
Samuel Tarsitano (*Southwest Texas State University*)
David Tauck (*Santa Clara University*)
Emily Taylor (*California Polytechnic State University, San Luis Obispo*)
James Taylor (*University of New Hampshire*)
John W. Taylor (*University of California, Berkeley*)
Martha R. Taylor (*Cornell University*)
Thomas Terry (*University of Connecticut*)
Roger Thibault (*Bowling Green State University*)
William Thomas (*Colby-Sawyer College*)
Cyril Thong (*Simon Fraser University*)
John Thornton (*Oklahoma State University*)

Robert Thornton (*University of California, Davis*)
William Thwaites (*Tillamook Bay Community College*)
Stephen Timme (*Pittsburg State University*)
Eric Toolson (*University of New Mexico*)
Leslie Towill (*Arizona State University*)
James Traniello (*Boston University*)
Paul Q. Trombley (*Florida State University*)
Nancy J. Trun (*Duquesne University*)
Constantine Tsoukas (*San Diego State University*)
Marsha Turell (*Houston Community College*)
Robert Tuveson (*University of Illinois, Urbana*)
Maura G. Tyrrell (*Stonehill College*)
Catherine Uekert (*Northern Arizona University*)
Claudia Uhde-Stone (*California State University, East Bay*)
Gordon Uno (*University of Oklahoma*)
Lisa A. Urry (*Mills College*)
Saba Valadkhan (*Case Western Reserve University School of Medicine*)
James W. Valentine (*University of California, Santa Barbara*)
Joseph Vanable (*Purdue University*)
Theodore Van Bruggen (*University of South Dakota*)
Kathryn VandenBosch (*Texas A&M University*)
Gerald Van Dyke (*North Carolina State University*)
Brandi Van Roo (*Framingham State College*)
Moira Van Staaden (*Bowling Green State University*)
Steven D. Verhey (*Central Washington University*)
Kathleen Verville (*Washington College*)
Sara Via (*University of Maryland*)
Frank Visco (*Orange Coast College*)
Laurie Vitt (*University of California, Los Angeles*)
Neal Voelz (*St. Cloud State University*)
Thomas J. Volk (*University of Wisconsin, La Crosse*)
Leif Asbjørn Vøllestad (*University of Oslo*)
Susan D. Waaland (*University of Washington*)
William Wade (*Dartmouth Medical College*)
D. Alexander Wait (*Southwest Missouri State University*)
John Waggoner (*Loyola Marymount University*)
Jyoti Wagle (*Houston Community College*)
Edward Wagner (*University of California, Irvine*)
Dan Walker (*San Jose State University*)
Robert L. Wallace (*Ripon College*)
Jeffrey Walters (*North Carolina State University*)
Linda Walters (*University of Central Florida*)
Nickolas M. Waser (*University of California, Riverside*)
Margaret Waterman (*University of Pittsburgh*)
Charles Webber (*Loyola University of Chicago*)
Peter Webster (*University of Massachusetts, Amherst*)
Terry Webster (*University of Connecticut, Storrs*)
Beth Wee (*Tulane University*)
Andrea Weeks (*George Mason University*)
Peter Wejksnora (*University of Wisconsin, Milwaukee*)
Kentwood Wells (*University of Connecticut*)
David J. Westenberg, (*University of Missouri, Rolla*)
Richard Wetts (*University of California, Irvine*)
Matt White (*Ohio University*)
Ernest H. Williams (*Hamilton College*)
Kathy Williams (*San Diego State University*)
Stephen Williams (*Glendale Community College*)
Elizabeth Willott (*University of Arizona*)
Christopher Wills (*University of California, San Diego*)
Paul Wilson (*California State University, Northridge*)
Fred Wilt (*University of California, Berkeley*)
Peter Wimberger (*University of Puget Sound*)
Robert Winning (*Eastern Michigan University*)
E. William Wischusen (*Louisiana State University*)
Susan Whittemore (*Keene State College*)
Clarence Wolfe (*Northern Virginia Community College*)
Vickie L. Wolfe (*Marshall University*)
Robert T. Woodland (*University of Massachusetts Medical School*)
Joseph Woodring (*Louisiana State University*)
Denise Woodward (*Pennsylvania State University*)
Patrick Woolley (*East Central College*)
Sarah E. Wyatt (*Ohio University*)
Ramin Yadegari (*University of Arizona*)
Paul Yancey (*Whitman College*)
Philip Yant (*University of Michigan*)
Linda Yasui (*Northern Illinois University*)
Hideo Yonenaka (*San Francisco State University*)
Gina M. Zainelli (*Loyola University, Chicago*)
Edward Zalisko (*Blackburn College*)
Zai Ming Zhao (*University of Texas, Austin*)
John Zimmerman (*Kansas State University*)
Miriam Zolan (*Indiana University*)
Uko Zylstra (*Calvin College*)

Detailed Contents

Campbell Biology, Ninth Edition by Jane B. Reece, Lisa A. Urry, Michael L. Cain, Steven A. Wasserman, Peter V. Minorsky, and Robert B. Jackson

1 Introduction: Themes in the Study of Life 1

OVERVIEW Inquiring About Life 1
CONCEPT 1.1 The themes of this book make connections across different areas of biology 2
   Theme: New Properties Emerge at Each Level in the Biological Hierarchy 3
   Theme: Organisms Interact with Other Organisms and the Physical Environment 6
   Theme: Life Requires Energy Transfer and Transformation 6
   Theme: Structure and Function Are Correlated at All Levels of Biological Organization 7
   Theme: The Cell Is an Organism's Basic Unit of Structure and Function 8
   Theme: The Continuity of Life Is Based on Heritable Information in the Form of DNA 8
   Theme: Feedback Mechanisms Regulate Biological Systems 10
   Evolution, the Overarching Theme of Biology 11
CONCEPT 1.2 The Core Theme: Evolution accounts for the unity and diversity of life 11
   Classifying the Diversity of Life 12
   Charles Darwin and the Theory of Natural Selection 14
   The Tree of Life 16
CONCEPT 1.3 In studying nature, scientists make observations and then form and test hypotheses 18
   Making Observations 18
   Forming and Testing Hypotheses 19
   The Flexibility of the Scientific Method 20
   A Case Study in Scientific Inquiry: Investigating Mimicry in Snake Populations 20
   Theories in Science 23
CONCEPT 1.4 Science benefits from a cooperative approach and diverse viewpoints 23
   Building on the Work of Others 23
   Science, Technology, and Society 24
   The Value of Diverse Viewpoints in Science 25

UNIT 1 The Chemistry of Life 28

Interview: Susan Solomon

2 The Chemical Context of Life 30

OVERVIEW A Chemical Connection to Biology 30
CONCEPT 2.1 Matter consists of chemical elements in pure form and in combinations called compounds 31
   Elements and Compounds 31
   The Elements of Life 32
   Case Study: Evolution of Tolerance to Toxic Elements 32

CONCEPT 2.2 An element's properties depend on the structure of its atoms 33
   Subatomic Particles 33
   Atomic Number and Atomic Mass 33
   Isotopes 34
   The Energy Levels of Electrons 35
   Electron Distribution and Chemical Properties 36
   Electron Orbitals 37
CONCEPT 2.3 The formation and function of molecules depend on chemical bonding between atoms 38
   Covalent Bonds 38
   Ionic Bonds 39
   Weak Chemical Bonds 40
   Molecular Shape and Function 41
CONCEPT 2.4 Chemical reactions make and break chemical bonds 42

3 Water and Life 46

OVERVIEW The Molecule That Supports All of Life 46
CONCEPT 3.1 Polar covalent bonds in water molecules result in hydrogen bonding 46
CONCEPT 3.2 Four emergent properties of water contribute to Earth's suitability for life 47
   Cohesion of Water Molecules 47
   Moderation of Temperature by Water 48
   Floating of Ice on Liquid Water 49
   Water: The Solvent of Life 50
   Possible Evolution of Life on Other Planets with Water 52
CONCEPT 3.3 Acidic and basic conditions affect living organisms 52
   Acids and Bases 53
   The pH Scale 53
   Buffers 54
   Acidification: A Threat to Water Quality 55

4 Carbon and the Molecular Diversity of Life 58

OVERVIEW Carbon: The Backbone of Life 58
CONCEPT 4.1 Organic chemistry is the study of carbon compounds 58
   Organic Molecules and the Origin of Life on Earth 59
CONCEPT 4.2 Carbon atoms can form diverse molecules by bonding to four other atoms 60
   The Formation of Bonds with Carbon 60
   Molecular Diversity Arising from Carbon Skeleton Variation 61
CONCEPT 4.3 A few chemical groups are key to the functioning of biological molecules 63
   The Chemical Groups Most Important in the Processes of Life 63
   ATP: An Important Source of Energy for Cellular Processes 66
   The Chemical Elements of Life: *A Review* 66

5 The Structure and Function of Large Biological Molecules 68

OVERVIEW The Molecules of Life 68
CONCEPT 5.1 Macromolecules are polymers, built from monomers 68
    The Synthesis and Breakdown of Polymers 68
    The Diversity of Polymers 69
CONCEPT 5.2 Carbohydrates serve as fuel and building material 69
    Sugars 69
    Polysaccharides 70
CONCEPT 5.3 Lipids are a diverse group of hydrophobic molecules 74
    Fats 74
    Phospholipids 76
    Steroids 77
CONCEPT 5.4 Proteins include a diversity of structures, resulting in a wide range of functions 77
    Polypeptides 77
    Protein Structure and Function 80
CONCEPT 5.5 Nucleic acids store, transmit, and help express hereditary information 86
    The Roles of Nucleic Acids 86
    The Components of Nucleic Acids 87
    Nucleotide Polymers 88
    The Structures of DNA and RNA Molecules 88
    DNA and Proteins as Tape Measures of Evolution 89
    The Theme of Emergent Properties in the Chemistry of Life: *A Review* 89

UNIT 2 The Cell 92

 Interview: Bonnie L. Bassler

6 A Tour of the Cell 94

OVERVIEW The Fundamental Units of Life 94
CONCEPT 6.1 Biologists use microscopes and the tools of biochemistry to study cells 94
    Microscopy 94
    Cell Fractionation 97
CONCEPT 6.2 Eukaryotic cells have internal membranes that compartmentalize their functions 98
    Comparing Prokaryotic and Eukaryotic Cells 98
    A Panoramic View of the Eukaryotic Cell 99

CONCEPT 6.3 The eukaryotic cell's genetic instructions are housed in the nucleus and carried out by the ribosomes 102
    The Nucleus: Information Central 102
    Ribosomes: Protein Factories 102
CONCEPT 6.4 The endomembrane system regulates protein traffic and performs metabolic functions in the cell 104
    The Endoplasmic Reticulum: Biosynthetic Factory 104
    The Golgi Apparatus: Shipping and Receiving Center 105
    Lysosomes: Digestive Compartments 106
    Vacuoles: Diverse Maintenance Compartments 107
    The Endomembrane System: *A Review* 108
CONCEPT 6.5 Mitochondria and chloroplasts change energy from one form to another 109
    The Evolutionary Origins of Mitochondria and Chloroplasts 109
    Mitochondria: Chemical Energy Conversion 110
    Chloroplasts: Capture of Light Energy 110
    Peroxisomes: Oxidation 111
CONCEPT 6.6 The cytoskeleton is a network of fibers that organizes structures and activities in the cell 112
    Roles of the Cytoskeleton: Support and Motility 112
    Components of the Cytoskeleton 113
CONCEPT 6.7 Extracellular components and connections between cells help coordinate cellular activities 118
    Cell Walls of Plants 118
    The Extracellular Matrix (ECM) of Animal Cells 119
    Cell Junctions 120
    The Cell: A Living Unit Greater Than the Sum of Its Parts 122

7 Membrane Structure and Function 125

OVERVIEW Life at the Edge 125
CONCEPT 7.1 Cellular membranes are fluid mosaics of lipids and proteins 125
    Membrane Models: *Scientific Inquiry* 125
    The Fluidity of Membranes 127
    Evolution of Differences in Membrane Lipid Composition 128
    Membrane Proteins and Their Functions 129
    The Role of Membrane Carbohydrates in Cell-Cell Recognition 130
    Synthesis and Sidedness of Membranes 130
CONCEPT 7.2 Membrane structure results in selective permeability 131
    The Permeability of the Lipid Bilayer 131
    Transport Proteins 131
CONCEPT 7.3 Passive transport is diffusion of a substance across a membrane with no energy investment 132
    Effects of Osmosis on Water Balance 133
    Facilitated Diffusion: Passive Transport Aided by Proteins 134
CONCEPT 7.4 Active transport uses energy to move solutes against their gradients 135
    The Need for Energy in Active Transport 135
    How Ion Pumps Maintain Membrane Potential 136
    Cotransport: Coupled Transport by a Membrane Protein 137
CONCEPT 7.5 Bulk transport across the plasma membrane occurs by exocytosis and endocytosis 138
    Exocytosis 138
    Endocytosis 138

8 An Introduction to Metabolism 142

OVERVIEW The Energy of Life 142
CONCEPT 8.1 An organism's metabolism transforms matter and energy, subject to the laws of thermodynamics 142
Organization of the Chemistry of Life into Metabolic Pathways 142
Forms of Energy 143
The Laws of Energy Transformation 144
CONCEPT 8.2 The free-energy change of a reaction tells us whether or not the reaction occurs spontaneously 146
Free-Energy Change, ΔG 146
Free Energy, Stability, and Equilibrium 146
Free Energy and Metabolism 147
CONCEPT 8.3 ATP powers cellular work by coupling exergonic reactions to endergonic reactions 149
The Structure and Hydrolysis of ATP 149
How the Hydrolysis of ATP Performs Work 150
The Regeneration of ATP 151
CONCEPT 8.4 Enzymes speed up metabolic reactions by lowering energy barriers 152
The Activation Energy Barrier 152
How Enzymes Lower the E_A Barrier 153
Substrate Specificity of Enzymes 153
Catalysis in the Enzyme's Active Site 154
Effects of Local Conditions on Enzyme Activity 155
The Evolution of Enzymes 157
CONCEPT 8.5 Regulation of enzyme activity helps control metabolism 158
Allosteric Regulation of Enzymes 158
Specific Localization of Enzymes Within the Cell 160

9 Cellular Respiration and Fermentation 163

OVERVIEW Life Is Work 163
CONCEPT 9.1 Catabolic pathways yield energy by oxidizing organic fuels 164
Catabolic Pathways and Production of ATP 164
Redox Reactions: Oxidation and Reduction 164
The Stages of Cellular Respiration: A Preview 167
CONCEPT 9.2 Glycolysis harvests chemical energy by oxidizing glucose to pyruvate 168
CONCEPT 9.3 After pyruvate is oxidized, the citric acid cycle completes the energy-yielding oxidation of organic molecules 170
Oxidation of Pyruvate to Acetyl CoA 170
The Citric Acid Cycle 170
CONCEPT 9.4 During oxidative phosphorylation, chemiosmosis couples electron transport to ATP synthesis 172
The Pathway of Electron Transport 172
Chemiosmosis: The Energy-Coupling Mechanism 173
An Accounting of ATP Production by Cellular Respiration 174
CONCEPT 9.5 Fermentation and anaerobic respiration enable cells to produce ATP without the use of oxygen 177
Types of Fermentation 177
Comparing Fermentation with Anaerobic and Aerobic Respiration 178
The Evolutionary Significance of Glycolysis 179
CONCEPT 9.6 Glycolysis and the citric acid cycle connect to many other metabolic pathways 179
The Versatility of Catabolism 179
Biosynthesis (Anabolic Pathways) 180
Regulation of Cellular Respiration via Feedback Mechanisms 181

10 Photosynthesis 184

OVERVIEW The Process That Feeds the Biosphere 184
CONCEPT 10.1 Photosynthesis converts light energy to the chemical energy of food 186
Chloroplasts: The Sites of Photosynthesis in Plants 186
Tracking Atoms Through Photosynthesis: Scientific Inquiry 187
The Two Stages of Photosynthesis: A Preview 188
CONCEPT 10.2 The light reactions convert solar energy to the chemical energy of ATP and NADPH 189
The Nature of Sunlight 189
Photosynthetic Pigments: The Light Receptors 190
Excitation of Chlorophyll by Light 192
A Photosystem: A Reaction-Center Complex Associated with Light-Harvesting Complexes 192
Linear Electron Flow 193
Cyclic Electron Flow 195
A Comparison of Chemiosmosis in Chloroplasts and Mitochondria 196
CONCEPT 10.3 The Calvin cycle uses the chemical energy of ATP and NADPH to reduce CO_2 to sugar 198
CONCEPT 10.4 Alternative mechanisms of carbon fixation have evolved in hot, arid climates 199
Photorespiration: An Evolutionary Relic? 199
C_4 Plants 200
CAM Plants 201
The Importance of Photosynthesis: A Review 203

11 Cell Communication 206

OVERVIEW Cellular Messaging 206
CONCEPT 11.1 External signals are converted to responses within the cell 206
    Evolution of Cell Signaling 206
    Local and Long-Distance Signaling 208
    The Three Stages of Cell Signaling: *A Preview* 209
CONCEPT 11.2 Reception: A signaling molecule binds to a receptor protein, causing it to change shape 210
    Receptors in the Plasma Membrane 210
    Intracellular Receptors 214
CONCEPT 11.3 Transduction: Cascades of molecular interactions relay signals from receptors to target molecules in the cell 214
    Signal Transduction Pathways 215
    Protein Phosphorylation and Dephosphorylation 215
    Small Molecules and Ions as Second Messengers 216
CONCEPT 11.4 Response: Cell signaling leads to regulation of transcription or cytoplasmic activities 219
    Nuclear and Cytoplasmic Responses 219
    Fine-Tuning of the Response 220
CONCEPT 11.5 Apoptosis integrates multiple cell-signaling pathways 223
    Apoptosis in the Soil Worm *Caenorhabditis elegans* 224
    Apoptotic Pathways and the Signals That Trigger Them 224

12 The Cell Cycle 228

OVERVIEW The Key Roles of Cell Division 228
CONCEPT 12.1 Most cell division results in genetically identical daughter cells 229
    Cellular Organization of the Genetic Material 229
    Distribution of Chromosomes During Eukaryotic Cell Division 229
CONCEPT 12.2 The mitotic phase alternates with interphase in the cell cycle 230
    Phases of the Cell Cycle 231
    The Mitotic Spindle: *A Closer Look* 231
    Cytokinesis: *A Closer Look* 234
    Binary Fission in Bacteria 236
    The Evolution of Mitosis 237
CONCEPT 12.3 The eukaryotic cell cycle is regulated by a molecular control system 238
    Evidence for Cytoplasmic Signals 238
    The Cell Cycle Control System 238
    Loss of Cell Cycle Controls in Cancer Cells 242

UNIT

3 Genetics 246

Interview: Joan A. Steitz

13 Meiosis and Sexual Life Cycles 248

OVERVIEW Variations on a Theme 248
CONCEPT 13.1 Offspring acquire genes from parents by inheriting chromosomes 248
    Inheritance of Genes 249
    Comparison of Asexual and Sexual Reproduction 249

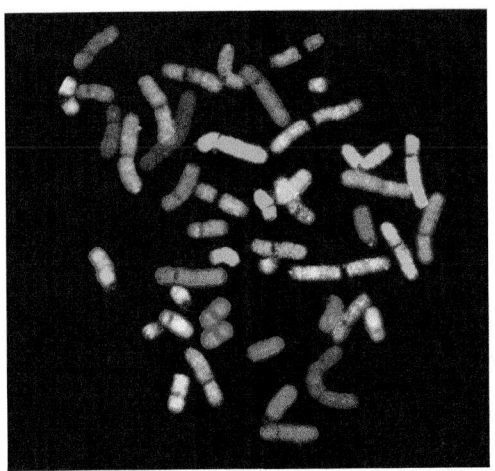

CONCEPT 13.2 Fertilization and meiosis alternate in sexual life cycles 250
    Sets of Chromosomes in Human Cells 250
    Behavior of Chromosome Sets in the Human Life Cycle 251
    The Variety of Sexual Life Cycles 252
CONCEPT 13.3 Meiosis reduces the number of chromosome sets from diploid to haploid 253
    The Stages of Meiosis 253
    A Comparison of Mitosis and Meiosis 257
CONCEPT 13.4 Genetic variation produced in sexual life cycles contributes to evolution 257
    Origins of Genetic Variation Among Offspring 257
    The Evolutionary Significance of Genetic Variation Within Populations 259

14 Mendel and the Gene Idea 262

OVERVIEW Drawing from the Deck of Genes 262
CONCEPT 14.1 Mendel used the scientific approach to identify two laws of inheritance 262
    Mendel's Experimental, Quantitative Approach 262
    The Law of Segregation 264
    The Law of Independent Assortment 267
CONCEPT 14.2 The laws of probability govern Mendelian inheritance 269
    The Multiplication and Addition Rules Applied to Monohybrid Crosses 269
    Solving Complex Genetics Problems with the Rules of Probability 270
CONCEPT 14.3 Inheritance patterns are often more complex than predicted by simple Mendelian genetics 271
    Extending Mendelian Genetics for a Single Gene 271
    Extending Mendelian Genetics for Two or More Genes 273
    Nature and Nurture: The Environmental Impact on Phenotype 274
    Integrating a Mendelian View of Heredity and Variation 275
CONCEPT 14.4 Many human traits follow Mendelian patterns of inheritance 275
    Pedigree Analysis 275
    Recessively Inherited Disorders 276
    Dominantly Inherited Disorders 278
    Multifactorial Disorders 279
    Genetic Testing and Counseling 279

15 The Chromosomal Basis of Inheritance 286

OVERVIEW Locating Genes Along Chromosomes 286
CONCEPT 15.1 Mendelian inheritance has its physical basis in the behavior of chromosomes 286
Morgan's Experimental Evidence: *Scientific Inquiry* 288
CONCEPT 15.2 Sex-linked genes exhibit unique patterns of inheritance 289
The Chromosomal Basis of Sex 289
Inheritance of X-Linked Genes 290
X Inactivation in Female Mammals 291
CONCEPT 15.3 Linked genes tend to be inherited together because they are located near each other on the same chromosome 292
How Linkage Affects Inheritance 292
Genetic Recombination and Linkage 294
Mapping the Distance Between Genes Using Recombination Data: *Scientific Inquiry* 296
CONCEPT 15.4 Alterations of chromosome number or structure cause some genetic disorders 297
Abnormal Chromosome Number 297
Alterations of Chromosome Structure 298
Human Disorders Due to Chromosomal Alterations 299
CONCEPT 15.5 Some inheritance patterns are exceptions to standard Mendelian inheritance 300
Genomic Imprinting 300
Inheritance of Organelle Genes 301

16 The Molecular Basis of Inheritance 305

OVERVIEW Life's Operating Instructions 305
CONCEPT 16.1 DNA is the genetic material 305
The Search for the Genetic Material: *Scientific Inquiry* 305
Building a Structural Model of DNA: *Scientific Inquiry* 308
CONCEPT 16.2 Many proteins work together in DNA replication and repair 311
The Basic Principle: Base Pairing to a Template Strand 311
DNA Replication: *A Closer Look* 312
Proofreading and Repairing DNA 316
Evolutionary Significance of Altered DNA Nucleotides 318
Replicating the Ends of DNA Molecules 318
CONCEPT 16.3 A chromosome consists of a DNA molecule packed together with proteins 320

17 From Gene to Protein 325

OVERVIEW The Flow of Genetic Information 325
CONCEPT 17.1 Genes specify proteins via transcription and translation 325
Evidence from the Study of Metabolic Defects 326
Basic Principles of Transcription and Translation 328
The Genetic Code 328
CONCEPT 17.2 Transcription is the DNA-directed synthesis of RNA: *a closer look* 331
Molecular Components of Transcription 331
Synthesis of an RNA Transcript 332
CONCEPT 17.3 Eukaryotic cells modify RNA after transcription 334
Alteration of mRNA Ends 334
Split Genes and RNA Splicing 334

CONCEPT 17.4 Translation is the RNA-directed synthesis of a polypeptide: *a closer look* 337
Molecular Components of Translation 337
Building a Polypeptide 340
Completing and Targeting the Functional Protein 342
CONCEPT 17.5 Mutations of one or a few nucleotides can affect protein structure and function 344
Types of Small-Scale Mutations 344
Mutagens 346
CONCEPT 17.6 While gene expression differs among the domains of life, the concept of a gene is universal 346
Comparing Gene Expression in Bacteria, Archaea, and Eukarya 346
What Is a Gene? *Revisiting the Question* 347

18 Regulation of Gene Expression 351

OVERVIEW Conducting the Genetic Orchestra 351
CONCEPT 18.1 Bacteria often respond to environmental change by regulating transcription 351
Operons: The Basic Concept 352
Repressible and Inducible Operons: Two Types of Negative Gene Regulation 353
Positive Gene Regulation 355
CONCEPT 18.2 Eukaryotic gene expression is regulated at many stages 356
Differential Gene Expression 356
Regulation of Chromatin Structure 357
Regulation of Transcription Initiation 358
Mechanisms of Post-Transcriptional Regulation 362
CONCEPT 18.3 Noncoding RNAs play multiple roles in controlling gene expression 364
Effects on mRNAs by MicroRNAs and Small Interfering RNAs 365
Chromatin Remodeling and Effects on Transcription by ncRNAs 366
The Evolutionary Significance of Small ncRNAs 366
CONCEPT 18.4 A program of differential gene expression leads to the different cell types in a multicellular organism 366
A Genetic Program for Embryonic Development 366
Cytoplasmic Determinants and Inductive Signals 367
Sequential Regulation of Gene Expression During Cellular Differentiation 367
Pattern Formation: Setting Up the Body Plan 369
CONCEPT 18.5 Cancer results from genetic changes that affect cell cycle control 373
Types of Genes Associated with Cancer 373
Interference with Normal Cell-Signaling Pathways 374
The Multistep Model of Cancer Development 376
Inherited Predisposition and Other Factors Contributing to Cancer 376

19 Viruses 381

OVERVIEW A Borrowed Life 381
CONCEPT 19.1 A virus consists of a nucleic acid surrounded by a protein coat 381
The Discovery of Viruses: *Scientific Inquiry* 381
Structure of Viruses 382

CONCEPT 19.2 Viruses replicate only in host cells 384

General Features of Viral Replicative Cycles 384
Replicative Cycles of Phages 385
Replicative Cycles of Animal Viruses 387
Evolution of Viruses 390

CONCEPT 19.3 Viruses, viroids, and prions are formidable pathogens in animals and plants 390

Viral Diseases in Animals 391
Emerging Viruses 391
Viral Diseases in Plants 393
Viroids and Prions: The Simplest Infectious Agents 393

20 Biotechnology 396

OVERVIEW The DNA Toolbox 396

CONCEPT 20.1 DNA cloning yields multiple copies of a gene or other DNA segment 396

DNA Cloning and Its Applications: *A Preview* 397
Using Restriction Enzymes to Make Recombinant DNA 398
Cloning a Eukaryotic Gene in a Bacterial Plasmid 398
Expressing Cloned Eukaryotic Genes 402
Amplifying DNA *in Vitro*: The Polymerase Chain Reaction (PCR) 403

CONCEPT 20.2 DNA technology allows us to study the sequence, expression, and function of a gene 405

Gel Electrophoresis and Southern Blotting 405
DNA Sequencing 407
Analyzing Gene Expression 409
Determining Gene Function 410

CONCEPT 20.3 Cloning organisms may lead to production of stem cells for research and other applications 412

Cloning Plants: Single-Cell Cultures 412
Cloning Animals: Nuclear Transplantation 413
Stem Cells of Animals 415

CONCEPT 20.4 The practical applications of DNA technology affect our lives in many ways 417

Medical Applications 417
Forensic Evidence and Genetic Profiles 420
Environmental Cleanup 421
Agricultural Applications 421
Safety and Ethical Questions Raised by DNA Technology 422

21 Genomes and Their Evolution 426

OVERVIEW Reading the Leaves from the Tree of Life 426

CONCEPT 21.1 New approaches have accelerated the pace of genome sequencing 427

Three-Stage Approach to Genome Sequencing 427
Whole-Genome Shotgun Approach to Genome Sequencing 428

CONCEPT 21.2 Scientists use bioinformatics to analyze genomes and their functions 429

Centralized Resources for Analyzing Genome Sequences 429
Identifying Protein-Coding Genes and Understanding Their Functions 429
Understanding Genes and Gene Expression at the Systems Level 430

CONCEPT 21.3 Genomes vary in size, number of genes, and gene density 432

Genome Size 432
Number of Genes 433
Gene Density and Noncoding DNA 434

CONCEPT 21.4 Multicellular eukaryotes have much noncoding DNA and many multigene families 434

Transposable Elements and Related Sequences 434
Other Repetitive DNA, Including Simple Sequence DNA 436
Genes and Multigene Families 437

CONCEPT 21.5 Duplication, rearrangement, and mutation of DNA contribute to genome evolution 438

Duplication of Entire Chromosome Sets 438
Alterations of Chromosome Structure 438
Duplication and Divergence of Gene-Sized Regions of DNA 439
Rearrangements of Parts of Genes: Exon Duplication and Exon Shuffling 441
How Transposable Elements Contribute to Genome Evolution 441

CONCEPT 21.6 Comparing genome sequences provides clues to evolution and development 442

Comparing Genomes 442
Comparing Developmental Processes 445

UNIT 4 Mechanisms of Evolution 450

Interview: Geerat J. Vermeij

22 Descent with Modification: A Darwinian View of Life 452

OVERVIEW Endless Forms Most Beautiful 452

CONCEPT 22.1 The Darwinian revolution challenged traditional views of a young Earth inhabited by unchanging species 453

Scala Naturae and Classification of Species 453
Ideas About Change over Time 454
Lamarck's Hypothesis of Evolution 454

CONCEPT 22.2 Descent with modification by natural selection explains the adaptations of organisms and the unity and diversity of life 455

Darwin's Research 455
The Origin of Species 457

CONCEPT 22.3 Evolution is supported by an overwhelming amount of scientific evidence 460

Direct Observations of Evolutionary Change 460
Homology 462
The Fossil Record 465
Biogeography 466
What Is Theoretical About Darwin's View of Life? 467

23 The Evolution of Populations 469

OVERVIEW The Smallest Unit of Evolution 469
CONCEPT 23.1 Genetic variation makes evolution possible 469
  Genetic Variation 470
  Sources of Genetic Variation 471
CONCEPT 23.2 The Hardy-Weinberg equation can be used to test whether a population is evolving 473
  Gene Pools and Allele Frequencies 473
  The Hardy-Weinberg Principle 473
CONCEPT 23.3 Natural selection, genetic drift, and gene flow can alter allele frequencies in a population 476
  Natural Selection 476
  Genetic Drift 477
  Gene Flow 479
CONCEPT 23.4 Natural selection is the only mechanism that consistently causes adaptive evolution 480
  A Closer Look at Natural Selection 480
  The Key Role of Natural Selection in Adaptive Evolution 482
  Sexual Selection 482
  The Preservation of Genetic Variation 483
  Why Natural Selection Cannot Fashion Perfect Organisms 484

24 The Origin of Species 488

OVERVIEW That "Mystery of Mysteries" 488
CONCEPT 24.1 The biological species concept emphasizes reproductive isolation 488
  The Biological Species Concept 489
  Other Definitions of Species 492
CONCEPT 24.2 Speciation can take place with or without geographic separation 493
  Allopatric ("Other Country") Speciation 493
  Sympatric ("Same Country") Speciation 495
  Allopatric and Sympatric Speciation: A Review 497
CONCEPT 24.3 Hybrid zones reveal factors that cause reproductive isolation 498
  Patterns Within Hybrid Zones 498
  Hybrid Zones over Time 499
CONCEPT 24.4 Speciation can occur rapidly or slowly and can result from changes in few or many genes 501
  The Time Course of Speciation 501
  Studying the Genetics of Speciation 503
  From Speciation to Macroevolution 504

25 The History of Life on Earth 507

OVERVIEW Lost Worlds 507
CONCEPT 25.1 Conditions on early Earth made the origin of life possible 507
  Synthesis of Organic Compounds on Early Earth 508
  Abiotic Synthesis of Macromolecules 509
  Protocells 509
  Self-Replicating RNA and the Dawn of Natural Selection 509
CONCEPT 25.2 The fossil record documents the history of life 510
  The Fossil Record 510
  How Rocks and Fossils Are Dated 512
  The Origin of New Groups of Organisms 512

CONCEPT 25.3 Key events in life's history include the origins of single-celled and multicelled organisms and the colonization of land 514
  The First Single-Celled Organisms 514
  The Origin of Multicellularity 517
  The Colonization of Land 518
CONCEPT 25.4 The rise and fall of groups of organisms reflect differences in speciation and extinction rates 519
  Plate Tectonics 519
  Mass Extinctions 521
  Adaptive Radiations 524
CONCEPT 25.5 Major changes in body form can result from changes in the sequences and regulation of developmental genes 525
  Effects of Developmental Genes 525
  The Evolution of Development 526
CONCEPT 25.6 Evolution is not goal oriented 529
  Evolutionary Novelties 529
  Evolutionary Trends 530

UNIT

5

The Evolutionary History of Biological Diversity 534

Interview: W. Ford Doolittle

26 Phylogeny and the Tree of Life 536

OVERVIEW Investigating the Tree of Life 536
CONCEPT 26.1 Phylogenies show evolutionary relationships 537
  Binomial Nomenclature 537
  Hierarchical Classification 537
  Linking Classification and Phylogeny 538
  What We Can and Cannot Learn from Phylogenetic Trees 539
  Applying Phylogenies 539
CONCEPT 26.2 Phylogenies are inferred from morphological and molecular data 540
  Morphological and Molecular Homologies 540
  Sorting Homology from Analogy 540
  Evaluating Molecular Homologies 541
CONCEPT 26.3 Shared characters are used to construct phylogenetic trees 542
  Cladistics 542
  Phylogenetic Trees with Proportional Branch Lengths 544
  Maximum Parsimony and Maximum Likelihood 544
  Phylogenetic Trees as Hypotheses 547
CONCEPT 26.4 An organism's evolutionary history is documented in its genome 548
  Gene Duplications and Gene Families 548
  Genome Evolution 548
CONCEPT 26.5 Molecular clocks help track evolutionary time 549
  Molecular Clocks 549
  Applying a Molecular Clock: The Origin of HIV 550
CONCEPT 26.6 New information continues to revise our understanding of the tree of life 551
  From Two Kingdoms to Three Domains 551
  A Simple Tree of All Life 552
  Is the Tree of Life Really a Ring? 553

27 Bacteria and Archaea 556

OVERVIEW Masters of Adaptation 556
CONCEPT 27.1 Structural and functional adaptations contribute to prokaryotic success 556
    Cell-Surface Structures 557
    Motility 558
    Internal Organization and DNA 559
    Reproduction and Adaptation 560
CONCEPT 27.2 Rapid reproduction, mutation, and genetic recombination promote genetic diversity in prokaryotes 561
    Rapid Reproduction and Mutation 561
    Genetic Recombination 561
CONCEPT 27.3 Diverse nutritional and metabolic adaptations have evolved in prokaryotes 564
    The Role of Oxygen in Metabolism 564
    Nitrogen Metabolism 564
    Metabolic Cooperation 565
CONCEPT 27.4 Molecular systematics is illuminating prokaryotic phylogeny 565
    Lessons from Molecular Systematics 566
    Archaea 566
    Bacteria 567
CONCEPT 27.5 Prokaryotes play crucial roles in the biosphere 570
    Chemical Recycling 570
    Ecological Interactions 570
CONCEPT 27.6 Prokaryotes have both beneficial and harmful impacts on humans 571
    Mutualistic Bacteria 571
    Pathogenic Bacteria 571
    Prokaryotes in Research and Technology 572

28 Protists 575

OVERVIEW Living Small 575
CONCEPT 28.1 Most eukaryotes are single-celled organisms 575
    Structural and Functional Diversity in Protists 576
    Endosymbiosis in Eukaryotic Evolution 576
    Five Supergroups of Eukaryotes 576
CONCEPT 28.2 Excavates include protists with modified mitochondria and protists with unique flagella 580
    Diplomonads and Parabasalids 580
    Euglenozoans 580
CONCEPT 28.3 Chromalveolates may have originated by secondary endosymbiosis 582
    Alveolates 582
    Stramenopiles 585
CONCEPT 28.4 Rhizarians are a diverse group of protists defined by DNA similarities 589
    Radiolarians 589
    Forams 589
    Cercozoans 590
CONCEPT 28.5 Red algae and green algae are the closest relatives of land plants 590
    Red Algae 590
    Green Algae 591
CONCEPT 28.6 Unikonts include protists that are closely related to fungi and animals 593
    Amoebozoans 593
    Opisthokonts 596

CONCEPT 28.7 Protists play key roles in ecological communities 596
    Symbiotic Protists 596
    Photosynthetic Protists 597

29 Plant Diversity I: How Plants Colonized Land 600

OVERVIEW The Greening of Earth 600
CONCEPT 29.1 Land plants evolved from green algae 600
    Morphological and Molecular Evidence 600
    Adaptations Enabling the Move to Land 601
    Derived Traits of Plants 601
    The Origin and Diversification of Plants 604
CONCEPT 29.2 Mosses and other nonvascular plants have life cycles dominated by gametophytes 606
    Bryophyte Gametophytes 606
    Bryophyte Sporophytes 609
    The Ecological and Economic Importance of Mosses 609
CONCEPT 29.3 Ferns and other seedless vascular plants were the first plants to grow tall 610
    Origins and Traits of Vascular Plants 610
    Classification of Seedless Vascular Plants 613
    The Significance of Seedless Vascular Plants 615

30 Plant Diversity II: The Evolution of Seed Plants 618

OVERVIEW Transforming the World 618
CONCEPT 30.1 Seeds and pollen grains are key adaptations for life on land 618
    Advantages of Reduced Gametophytes 618
    Heterospory: The Rule Among Seed Plants 619
    Ovules and Production of Eggs 619
    Pollen and Production of Sperm 620
    The Evolutionary Advantage of Seeds 620
CONCEPT 30.2 Gymnosperms bear "naked" seeds, typically on cones 621
    Gymnosperm Evolution 621
    The Life Cycle of a Pine: *A Closer Look* 625
CONCEPT 30.3 The reproductive adaptations of angiosperms include flowers and fruits 625
    Characteristics of Angiosperms 625
    Angiosperm Evolution 628
    Angiosperm Diversity 630
    Evolutionary Links Between Angiosperms and Animals 632
CONCEPT 30.4 Human welfare depends greatly on seed plants 632
    Products from Seed Plants 633
    Threats to Plant Diversity 633

31 Fungi 636

OVERVIEW Mighty Mushrooms 636
CONCEPT 31.1 Fungi are heterotrophs that feed by absorption 636
    Nutrition and Ecology 636
    Body Structure 637
    Specialized Hyphae in Mycorrhizal Fungi 638

CONCEPT 31.2 Fungi produce spores through sexual or asexual life cycles 638
    Sexual Reproduction 639
    Asexual Reproduction 639
CONCEPT 31.3 The ancestor of fungi was an aquatic, single-celled, flagellated protist 640
    The Origin of Fungi 640
    Are Microsporidia Fungi? 641
    The Move to Land 641
CONCEPT 31.4 Fungi have radiated into a diverse set of lineages 641
    Chytrids 641
    Zygomycetes 643
    Glomeromycetes 644
    Ascomycetes 644
    Basidiomycetes 646
CONCEPT 31.5 Fungi play key roles in nutrient cycling, ecological interactions, and human welfare 648
    Fungi as Decomposers 648
    Fungi as Mutualists 648
    Fungi as Pathogens 650
    Practical Uses of Fungi 651

32 An Overview of Animal Diversity 654

OVERVIEW Welcome to Your Kingdom 654
CONCEPT 32.1 Animals are multicellular, heterotrophic eukaryotes with tissues that develop from embryonic layers 654
    Nutritional Mode 654
    Cell Structure and Specialization 654
    Reproduction and Development 655
CONCEPT 32.2 The history of animals spans more than half a billion years 656
    Neoproterozoic Era (1 Billion–542 Million Years Ago) 656
    Paleozoic Era (542–251 Million Years Ago) 657
    Mesozoic Era (251–65.5 Million Years Ago) 658
    Cenozoic Era (65.5 Million Years Ago to the Present) 658
CONCEPT 32.3 Animals can be characterized by "body plans" 658
    Symmetry 658
    Tissues 659
    Body Cavities 660
    Protostome and Deuterostome Development 660
CONCEPT 32.4 New views of animal phylogeny are emerging from molecular data 662
    Points of Agreement 662
    Progress in Resolving Bilaterian Relationships 663
    Future Directions in Animal Systematics 664

33 An Introduction to Invertebrates 666

OVERVIEW Life Without a Backbone 666
CONCEPT 33.1 Sponges are basal animals that lack true tissues 670
CONCEPT 33.2 Cnidarians are an ancient phylum of eumetazoans 671
    Hydrozoans 672
    Scyphozoans 672
    Cubozoans 672
    Anthozoans 673
CONCEPT 33.3 Lophotrochozoans, a clade identified by molecular data, have the widest range of animal body forms 674
    Flatworms 674
    Rotifers 676
    Lophophorates: Ectoprocts and Brachiopods 677
    Molluscs 677
    Annelids 681
CONCEPT 33.4 Ecdysozoans are the most species-rich animal group 683
    Nematodes 683
    Arthropods 684
CONCEPT 33.5 Echinoderms and chordates are deuterostomes 692
    Echinoderms 692
    Chordates 694

34 The Origin and Evolution of Vertebrates 697

OVERVIEW Half a Billion Years of Backbones 697
CONCEPT 34.1 Chordates have a notochord and a dorsal, hollow nerve cord 697
    Derived Characters of Chordates 698
    Lancelets 699
    Tunicates 700
    Early Chordate Evolution 700
CONCEPT 34.2 Craniates are chordates that have a head 701
    Derived Characters of Craniates 701
    The Origin of Craniates 702
    Hagfishes 702
CONCEPT 34.3 Vertebrates are craniates that have a backbone 703
    Derived Characters of Vertebrates 703
    Lampreys 703
    Fossils of Early Vertebrates 703
    Origins of Bone and Teeth 704
CONCEPT 34.4 Gnathostomes are vertebrates that have jaws 704
    Derived Characters of Gnathostomes 704
    Fossil Gnathostomes 705
    Chondrichthyans (Sharks, Rays, and Their Relatives) 705
    Ray-Finned Fishes and Lobe-Fins 707
CONCEPT 34.5 Tetrapods are gnathostomes that have limbs 709
    Derived Characters of Tetrapods 709
    The Origin of Tetrapods 709
    Amphibians 710
CONCEPT 34.6 Amniotes are tetrapods that have a terrestrially adapted egg 713
    Derived Characters of Amniotes 713
    Early Amniotes 714
    Reptiles 715
CONCEPT 34.7 Mammals are amniotes that have hair and produce milk 720
    Derived Characters of Mammals 720
    Early Evolution of Mammals 721
    Monotremes 721
    Marsupials 722
    Eutherians (Placental Mammals) 723
CONCEPT 34.8 Humans are mammals that have a large brain and bipedal locomotion 728
    Derived Characters of Humans 728
    The Earliest Hominins 728
    Australopiths 729
    Bipedalism 730
    Tool Use 730
    Early *Homo* 731
    Neanderthals 731
    Homo sapiens 732

UNIT 6 — Plant Form and Function 736

Interview: Luis Herrera-Estrella

35 Plant Structure, Growth, and Development 738

OVERVIEW Are Plants Computers? 738
CONCEPT 35.1 Plants have a hierarchical organization consisting of organs, tissues, and cells 738
    The Three Basic Plant Organs: Roots, Stems, and Leaves 739
    Dermal, Vascular, and Ground Tissues 742
    Common Types of Plant Cells 743
CONCEPT 35.2 Meristems generate cells for primary and secondary growth 746
CONCEPT 35.3 Primary growth lengthens roots and shoots 747
    Primary Growth of Roots 747
    Primary Growth of Shoots 749
CONCEPT 35.4 Secondary growth increases the diameter of stems and roots in woody plants 751
    The Vascular Cambium and Secondary Vascular Tissue 751
    The Cork Cambium and the Production of Periderm 754
    Evolution of Secondary Growth 754
CONCEPT 35.5 Growth, morphogenesis, and cell differentiation produce the plant body 755
    Model Organisms: Revolutionizing the Study of Plants 755
    Growth: Cell Division and Cell Expansion 756
    Morphogenesis and Pattern Formation 758
    Gene Expression and Control of Cell Differentiation 759
    Shifts in Development: Phase Changes 759
    Genetic Control of Flowering 760

36 Resource Acquisition and Transport in Vascular Plants 764

OVERVIEW Underground Plants 764
CONCEPT 36.1 Adaptations for acquiring resources were key steps in the evolution of vascular plants 764
    Shoot Architecture and Light Capture 765
    Root Architecture and Acquisition of Water and Minerals 766
CONCEPT 36.2 Different mechanisms transport substances over short or long distances 767
    The Apoplast and Symplast: Transport Continuums 767
    Short-Distance Transport of Solutes Across Plasma Membranes 768
    Short-Distance Transport of Water Across Plasma Membranes 768
    Long-Distance Transport: The Role of Bulk Flow 771
CONCEPT 36.3 Transpiration drives the transport of water and minerals from roots to shoots via the xylem 772
    Absorption of Water and Minerals by Root Cells 772
    Transport of Water and Minerals into the Xylem 772
    Bulk Flow Transport via the Xylem 772
    Xylem Sap Ascent by Bulk Flow: *A Review* 776

CONCEPT 36.4 The rate of transpiration is regulated by stomata 776
    Stomata: Major Pathways for Water Loss 776
    Mechanisms of Stomatal Opening and Closing 777
    Stimuli for Stomatal Opening and Closing 777
    Effects of Transpiration on Wilting and Leaf Temperature 778
    Adaptations That Reduce Evaporative Water Loss 778
CONCEPT 36.5 Sugars are transported from sources to sinks via the phloem 779
    Movement from Sugar Sources to Sugar Sinks 779
    Bulk Flow by Positive Pressure: The Mechanism of Translocation in Angiosperms 780
CONCEPT 36.6 The symplast is highly dynamic 781
    Changes in Plasmodesmata 782
    Phloem: An Information Superhighway 782
    Electrical Signaling in the Phloem 782

37 Soil and Plant Nutrition 785

OVERVIEW A Horrifying Discovery 785
CONCEPT 37.1 Soil contains a living, complex ecosystem 785
    Soil Texture 786
    Topsoil Composition 786
    Soil Conservation and Sustainable Agriculture 787
CONCEPT 37.2 Plants require essential elements to complete their life cycle 789
    Macronutrients and Micronutrients 790
    Symptoms of Mineral Deficiency 790
    Improving Plant Nutrition by Genetic Modification: Some Examples 792
CONCEPT 37.3 Plant nutrition often involves relationships with other organisms 792
    Soil Bacteria and Plant Nutrition 793
    Fungi and Plant Nutrition 795
    Epiphytes, Parasitic Plants, and Carnivorous Plants 797

38 Angiosperm Reproduction and Biotechnology 801

OVERVIEW Flowers of Deceit 801
CONCEPT 38.1 Flowers, double fertilization, and fruits are unique features of the angiosperm life cycle 801
    Flower Structure and Function 802
    Double Fertilization 806
    Seed Development, Form, and Function 807
    Fruit Form and Function 809
CONCEPT 38.2 Flowering plants reproduce sexually, asexually, or both 812
    Mechanisms of Asexual Reproduction 812
    Advantages and Disadvantages of Asexual Versus Sexual Reproduction 812
    Mechanisms That Prevent Self-Fertilization 813
    Vegetative Propagation and Agriculture 814
CONCEPT 38.3 Humans modify crops by breeding and genetic engineering 815
    Plant Breeding 815
    Plant Biotechnology and Genetic Engineering 816
    The Debate over Plant Biotechnology 817

39 Plant Responses to Internal and External Signals 821

OVERVIEW Stimuli and a Stationary Life 821
CONCEPT 39.1 Signal transduction pathways link signal reception to response 821
  Reception 822
  Transduction 822
  Response 823
CONCEPT 39.2 Plant hormones help coordinate growth, development, and responses to stimuli 824
  The Discovery of Plant Hormones 825
  A Survey of Plant Hormones 826
  Systems Biology and Hormone Interactions 834
CONCEPT 39.3 Responses to light are critical for plant success 835
  Blue-Light Photoreceptors 836
  Phytochromes as Photoreceptors 836
  Biological Clocks and Circadian Rhythms 838
  The Effect of Light on the Biological Clock 838
  Photoperiodism and Responses to Seasons 839
CONCEPT 39.4 Plants respond to a wide variety of stimuli other than light 841
  Gravity 841
  Mechanical Stimuli 842
  Environmental Stresses 843
CONCEPT 39.5 Plants respond to attacks by herbivores and pathogens 845
  Defenses Against Herbivores 845
  Defenses Against Pathogens 846

UNIT

Animal Form and Function 850

Interview: Baldomero M. Olivera

40 Basic Principles of Animal Form and Function 852

OVERVIEW Diverse Forms, Common Challenges 852
CONCEPT 40.1 Animal form and function are correlated at all levels of organization 852
  Evolution of Animal Size and Shape 853
  Exchange with the Environment 853
  Hierarchical Organization of Body Plans 855
  Coordination and Control 859
CONCEPT 40.2 Feedback control maintains the internal environment in many animals 860
  Regulating and Conforming 860
  Homeostasis 860
CONCEPT 40.3 Homeostatic processes for thermoregulation involve form, function, and behavior 862
  Endothermy and Ectothermy 863
  Variation in Body Temperature 863
  Balancing Heat Loss and Gain 864
  Acclimatization in Thermoregulation 867
  Physiological Thermostats and Fever 867
CONCEPT 40.4 Energy requirements are related to animal size, activity, and environment 868
  Energy Allocation and Use 868
  Quantifying Energy Use 869
  Minimum Metabolic Rate and Thermoregulation 869
  Influences on Metabolic Rate 870
  Energy Budgets 871
  Torpor and Energy Conservation 871

41 Animal Nutrition 875

OVERVIEW The Need to Feed 875
CONCEPT 41.1 An animal's diet must supply chemical energy, organic molecules, and essential nutrients 875
  Essential Nutrients 876
  Dietary Deficiencies 878
  Assessing Nutritional Needs 879
CONCEPT 41.2 The main stages of food processing are ingestion, digestion, absorption, and elimination 880
  Digestive Compartments 880
CONCEPT 41.3 Organs specialized for sequential stages of food processing form the mammalian digestive system 883
  The Oral Cavity, Pharynx, and Esophagus 883
  Digestion in the Stomach 885
  Digestion in the Small Intestine 887
  Absorption in the Small Intestine 887
  Absorption in the Large Intestine 888
CONCEPT 41.4 Evolutionary adaptations of vertebrate digestive systems correlate with diet 889
  Dental Adaptations 889
  Stomach and Intestinal Adaptations 890
  Mutualistic Adaptations 890
CONCEPT 41.5 Feedback circuits regulate digestion, energy storage, and appetite 891
  Regulation of Digestion 891
  Regulation of Energy Storage 892
  Regulation of Appetite and Consumption 893
  Obesity and Evolution 894

42 Circulation and Gas Exchange 897

OVERVIEW Trading Places 897
CONCEPT 42.1 Circulatory systems link exchange surfaces with cells throughout the body 897
  Gastrovascular Cavities 898
  Evolutionary Variation in Circulatory Systems 898
  Organization of Vertebrate Circulatory Systems 899
CONCEPT 42.2 Coordinated cycles of heart contraction drive double circulation in mammals 902
  Mammalian Circulation 902
  The Mammalian Heart: A Closer Look 902
  Maintaining the Heart's Rhythmic Beat 904
CONCEPT 42.3 Patterns of blood pressure and flow reflect the structure and arrangement of blood vessels 905
  Blood Vessel Structure and Function 905
  Blood Flow Velocity 905
  Blood Pressure 906
  Capillary Function 908
  Fluid Return by the Lymphatic System 909
CONCEPT 42.4 Blood components function in exchange, transport, and defense 910
  Blood Composition and Function 910
  Cardiovascular Disease 913

CONCEPT 42.5 Gas exchange occurs across specialized respiratory surfaces 915
    Partial Pressure Gradients in Gas Exchange 915
    Respiratory Media 915
    Respiratory Surfaces 916
    Gills in Aquatic Animals 916
    Tracheal Systems in Insects 917
    Lungs 918
CONCEPT 42.6 Breathing ventilates the lungs 920
    How an Amphibian Breathes 920
    How a Bird Breathes 920
    How a Mammal Breathes 921
    Control of Breathing in Humans 922
CONCEPT 42.7 Adaptations for gas exchange include pigments that bind and transport gases 923
    Coordination of Circulation and Gas Exchange 923
    Respiratory Pigments 923
    Respiratory Adaptations of Diving Mammals 925

43 The Immune System 929

OVERVIEW Recognition and Response 929
CONCEPT 43.1 In innate immunity, recognition and response rely on traits common to groups of pathogens 930
    Innate Immunity of Invertebrates 930
    Innate Immunity of Vertebrates 932
    Evasion of Innate Immunity by Pathogens 934
CONCEPT 43.2 In adaptive immunity, receptors provide pathogen-specific recognition 935
    Antigen Recognition by B Cells and Antibodies 935
    Antigen Recognition by T Cells 936
    B Cell and T Cell Development 937
CONCEPT 43.3 Adaptive immunity defends against infection of body fluids and body cells 940
    Helper T Cells: A Response to Nearly All Antigens 940
    Cytotoxic T Cells: A Response to Infected Cells 941
    B Cells and Antibodies: A Response to Extracellular Pathogens 942
    Summary of the Humoral and Cell-Mediated Immune Responses 944
    Active and Passive Immunization 944
    Antibodies as Tools 945
    Immune Rejection 945
CONCEPT 43.4 Disruptions in immune system function can elicit or exacerbate disease 946
    Exaggerated, Self-Directed, and Diminished Immune Responses 946
    Evolutionary Adaptations of Pathogens That Underlie Immune System Avoidance 948
    Cancer and Immunity 950

44 Osmoregulation and Excretion 953

OVERVIEW A Balancing Act 953
CONCEPT 44.1 Osmoregulation balances the uptake and loss of water and solutes 953
    Osmosis and Osmolarity 953
    Osmotic Challenges 954
    Energetics of Osmoregulation 956
    Transport Epithelia in Osmoregulation 957

CONCEPT 44.2 An animal's nitrogenous wastes reflect its phylogeny and habitat 958
    Forms of Nitrogenous Waste 958
    The Influence of Evolution and Environment on Nitrogenous Wastes 959
CONCEPT 44.3 Diverse excretory systems are variations on a tubular theme 960
    Excretory Processes 960
    Survey of Excretory Systems 960
CONCEPT 44.4 The nephron is organized for stepwise processing of blood filtrate 963
    From Blood Filtrate to Urine: *A Closer Look* 964
    Solute Gradients and Water Conservation 965
    Adaptations of the Vertebrate Kidney to Diverse Environments 967
CONCEPT 44.5 Hormonal circuits link kidney function, water balance, and blood pressure 968
    Antidiuretic Hormone 969
    The Renin-Angiotensin-Aldosterone System 970
    Homeostatic Regulation of the Kidney 971

45 Hormones and the Endocrine System 974

OVERVIEW The Body's Long-Distance Regulators 974
CONCEPT 45.1 Hormones and other signaling molecules bind to target receptors, triggering specific response pathways 975
    Intercellular Communication 975
    Endocrine Tissues and Organs 976
    Chemical Classes of Hormones 976
    Cellular Response Pathways 977
    Multiple Effects of Hormones 978
    Signaling by Local Regulators 979
    Coordination of Neuroendocrine and Endocrine Signaling 980
CONCEPT 45.2 Feedback regulation and antagonistic hormone pairs are common in endocrine systems 981
    Simple Hormone Pathways 981
    Feedback Regulation 982
    Insulin and Glucagon: Control of Blood Glucose 982
CONCEPT 45.3 The hypothalamus and pituitary are central to endocrine regulation 984
    Coordination of Endocrine and Nervous Systems in Vertebrates 984
    Thyroid Regulation: A Hormone Cascade Pathway 987
    Evolution of Hormone Function 988
    Tropic and Nontropic Hormones 989
CONCEPT 45.4 Endocrine glands respond to diverse stimuli in regulating homeostasis, development, and behavior 989
    Parathyroid Hormone and Vitamin D: Control of Blood Calcium 989
    Adrenal Hormones: Response to Stress 990
    Gonadal Sex Hormones 992
    Melatonin and Biorhythms 993

CONCEPT 47.3 Cytoplasmic determinants and inductive signals contribute to cell fate specification 1035
  Fate Mapping 1035
  Cell Fate Determination and Pattern Formation by Inductive Signals 1039

48 Neurons, Synapses, and Signaling 1045

OVERVIEW Lines of Communication 1045
CONCEPT 48.1 Neuron organization and structure reflect function in information transfer 1045
  Introduction to Information Processing 1046
  Neuron Structure and Function 1046
CONCEPT 48.2 Ion pumps and ion channels establish the resting potential of a neuron 1048
  Formation of the Resting Potential 1048
  Modeling the Resting Potential 1049
CONCEPT 48.3 Action potentials are the signals conducted by axons 1050
  Hyperpolarization and Depolarization 1050
  Graded Potentials and Action Potentials 1050
  Generation of Action Potentials: *A Closer Look* 1051
  Conduction of Action Potentials 1053
CONCEPT 48.4 Neurons communicate with other cells at synapses 1055
  Generation of Postsynaptic Potentials 1056
  Summation of Postsynaptic Potentials 1056
  Modulated Signaling at Synapses 1057
  Neurotransmitters 1057

49 Nervous Systems 1062

OVERVIEW Command and Control Center 1062
CONCEPT 49.1 Nervous systems consist of circuits of neurons and supporting cells 1062
  Organization of the Vertebrate Nervous System 1063
  Glia 1065
  The Peripheral Nervous System 1066
CONCEPT 49.2 The vertebrate brain is regionally specialized 1067
  Arousal and Sleep 1067
  Biological Clock Regulation 1070
  Emotions 1071
CONCEPT 49.3 The cerebral cortex controls voluntary movement and cognitive functions 1072
  Language and Speech 1072
  Lateralization of Cortical Function 1073
  Information Processing 1074
  Frontal Lobe Function 1075
  Evolution of Cognition in Vertebrates 1075
CONCEPT 49.4 Changes in synaptic connections underlie memory and learning 1076
  Neural Plasticity 1076
  Memory and Learning 1077
  Long-Term Potentiation 1077
  Stem Cells in the Brain 1078
CONCEPT 49.5 Many nervous system disorders can be explained in molecular terms 1079
  Schizophrenia 1079
  Depression 1080
  Drug Addiction and the Brain's Reward System 1080
  Alzheimer's Disease 1081
  Parkinson's Disease 1081

46 Animal Reproduction 996

OVERVIEW Pairing Up for Sexual Reproduction 996
CONCEPT 46.1 Both asexual and sexual reproduction occur in the animal kingdom 996
  Mechanisms of Asexual Reproduction 996
  Sexual Reproduction: An Evolutionary Enigma 997
  Reproductive Cycles 998
  Variation in Patterns of Sexual Reproduction 998
CONCEPT 46.2 Fertilization depends on mechanisms that bring together sperm and eggs of the same species 999
  Ensuring the Survival of Offspring 1000
  Gamete Production and Delivery 1000
CONCEPT 46.3 Reproductive organs produce and transport gametes 1002
  Female Reproductive Anatomy 1002
  Male Reproductive Anatomy 1004
  Gametogenesis 1005
CONCEPT 46.4 The interplay of tropic and sex hormones regulates mammalian reproduction 1008
  Hormonal Control of Female Reproductive Cycles 1008
  Hormonal Control of the Male Reproductive System 1010
  Human Sexual Response 1011
CONCEPT 46.5 In placental mammals, an embryo develops fully within the mother's uterus 1011
  Conception, Embryonic Development, and Birth 1012
  Maternal Immune Tolerance of the Embryo and Fetus 1015
  Contraception and Abortion 1015
  Modern Reproductive Technologies 1017

47 Animal Development 1021

OVERVIEW A Body-Building Plan 1021
CONCEPT 47.1 Fertilization and cleavage initiate embryonic development 1022
  Fertilization 1022
  Cleavage 1025
CONCEPT 47.2 Morphogenesis in animals involves specific changes in cell shape, position, and survival 1027
  Gastrulation 1027
  Developmental Adaptations of Amniotes 1031
  Organogenesis 1031
  Mechanisms of Morphogenesis 1033

50 Sensory and Motor Mechanisms 1085

OVERVIEW Sensing and Acting 1085
CONCEPT 50.1 Sensory receptors transduce stimulus energy and transmit signals to the central nervous system 1085
 Sensory Pathways 1086
 Types of Sensory Receptors 1088
CONCEPT 50.2 The mechanoreceptors responsible for hearing and equilibrium detect moving fluid or settling particles 1090
 Sensing of Gravity and Sound in Invertebrates 1090
 Hearing and Equilibrium in Mammals 1090
 Hearing and Equilibrium in Other Vertebrates 1094
CONCEPT 50.3 Visual receptors in diverse animals depend on light-absorbing pigments 1095
 Evolution of Visual Perception 1095
 The Vertebrate Visual System 1097
CONCEPT 50.4 The senses of taste and smell rely on similar sets of sensory receptors 1101
 Taste in Mammals 1101
 Smell in Humans 1102
CONCEPT 50.5 The physical interaction of protein filaments is required for muscle function 1103
 Vertebrate Skeletal Muscle 1104
 Other Types of Muscle 1109
CONCEPT 50.6 Skeletal systems transform muscle contraction into locomotion 1110
 Types of Skeletal Systems 1111
 Types of Locomotion 1113
 Energy Costs of Locomotion 1114

51 Animal Behavior 1118

OVERVIEW The How and Why of Animal Activity 1118
CONCEPT 51.1 Discrete sensory inputs can stimulate both simple and complex behaviors 1118
 Fixed Action Patterns 1119
 Migration 1119
 Behavioral Rhythms 1120
 Animal Signals and Communication 1120
CONCEPT 51.2 Learning establishes specific links between experience and behavior 1123
 Experience and Behavior 1123
 Learning 1123
CONCEPT 51.3 Selection for individual survival and reproductive success can explain most behaviors 1128
 Foraging Behavior 1128
 Mating Behavior and Mate Choice 1129
CONCEPT 51.4 Inclusive fitness can account for the evolution of behavior, including altruism 1134
 Genetic Basis of Behavior 1134
 Genetic Variation and the Evolution of Behavior 1135
 Altruism 1137
 Inclusive Fitness 1137
 Evolution and Human Culture 1139

UNIT 8 Ecology 1142
Interview: Camille Parmesan

52 An Introduction to Ecology and the Biosphere 1144

OVERVIEW Discovering Ecology 1144
CONCEPT 52.1 Earth's climate varies by latitude and season and is changing rapidly 1144
 Global Climate Patterns 1147
 Regional and Local Effects on Climate 1147
 Microclimate 1149
 Global Climate Change 1149
CONCEPT 52.2 The structure and distribution of terrestrial biomes are controlled by climate and disturbance 1150
 Climate and Terrestrial Biomes 1151
 General Features of Terrestrial Biomes 1151
 Disturbance and Terrestrial Biomes 1152
CONCEPT 52.3 Aquatic biomes are diverse and dynamic systems that cover most of Earth 1157
 Zonation in Aquatic Biomes 1157
CONCEPT 52.4 Interactions between organisms and the environment limit the distribution of species 1163
 Dispersal and Distribution 1164
 Behavior and Habitat Selection 1165
 Biotic Factors 1165
 Abiotic Factors 1166

53 Population Ecology 1170

OVERVIEW Counting Sheep 1170
CONCEPT 53.1 Dynamic biological processes influence population density, dispersion, and demographics 1170
 Density and Dispersion 1171
 Demographics 1173
CONCEPT 53.2 The exponential model describes population growth in an idealized, unlimited environment 1175
 Per Capita Rate of Increase 1175
 Exponential Growth 1176

CONCEPT 53.3 The logistic model describes how a population grows more slowly as it nears its carrying capacity 1177
 The Logistic Growth Model 1177
 The Logistic Model and Real Populations 1178
CONCEPT 53.4 Life history traits are products of natural selection 1179
 Evolution and Life History Diversity 1180
 "Trade-offs" and Life Histories 1180
CONCEPT 53.5 Many factors that regulate population growth are density dependent 1182
 Population Change and Population Density 1182
 Mechanisms of Density-Dependent Population Regulation 1182
 Population Dynamics 1184
CONCEPT 53.6 The human population is no longer growing exponentially but is still increasing rapidly 1187
 The Global Human Population 1187
 Global Carrying Capacity 1190

54 Community Ecology 1194

OVERVIEW Communities in Motion 1194
CONCEPT 54.1 Community interactions are classified by whether they help, harm, or have no effect on the species involved 1194
 Competition 1195
 Predation 1197
 Herbivory 1198
 Symbiosis 1198
 Facilitation 1200
CONCEPT 54.2 Diversity and trophic structure characterize biological communities 1200
 Species Diversity 1200
 Diversity and Community Stability 1201
 Trophic Structure 1202
 Species with a Large Impact 1204
 Bottom-Up and Top-Down Controls 1206
CONCEPT 54.3 Disturbance influences species diversity and composition 1207
 Characterizing Disturbance 1207
 Ecological Succession 1208

Human Disturbance 1210
CONCEPT 54.4 Biogeographic factors affect community diversity 1211
 Latitudinal Gradients 1211
 Area Effects 1211
 Island Equilibrium Model 1212
CONCEPT 54.5 Pathogens alter community structure locally and globally 1213
 Pathogens and Community Structure 1214
 Community Ecology and Zoonotic Diseases 1214

55 Ecosystems and Restoration Ecology 1218

OVERVIEW Cool Ecosystem 1218
CONCEPT 55.1 Physical laws govern energy flow and chemical cycling in ecosystems 1219
 Conservation of Energy 1219
 Conservation of Mass 1219
 Energy, Mass, and Trophic Levels 1219
CONCEPT 55.2 Energy and other limiting factors control primary production in ecosystems 1220
 Ecosystem Energy Budgets 1221
 Primary Production in Aquatic Ecosystems 1223
 Primary Production in Terrestrial Ecosystems 1224
CONCEPT 55.3 Energy transfer between trophic levels is typically only 10% efficient 1225
 Production Efficiency 1225
 Trophic Efficiency and Ecological Pyramids 1225
CONCEPT 55.4 Biological and geochemical processes cycle nutrients and water in ecosystems 1227
 Biogeochemical Cycles 1227
 Decomposition and Nutrient Cycling Rates 1230
 Case Study: Nutrient Cycling in the Hubbard Brook Experimental Forest 1231
CONCEPT 55.5 Restoration ecologists help return degraded ecosystems to a more natural state 1232
 Bioremediation 1232
 Biological Augmentation 1233
 Restoration Projects Worldwide 1233

56 Conservation Biology and Global Change 1238

OVERVIEW Striking Gold 1238

CONCEPT 56.1 Human activities threaten Earth's biodiversity 1239
Three Levels of Biodiversity 1239
Biodiversity and Human Welfare 1240
Threats to Biodiversity 1241

CONCEPT 56.2 Population conservation focuses on population size, genetic diversity, and critical habitat 1244
Small-Population Approach 1245
Declining-Population Approach 1247
Weighing Conflicting Demands 1249

CONCEPT 56.3 Landscape and regional conservation help sustain biodiversity 1249
Landscape Structure and Biodiversity 1249
Establishing Protected Areas 1251

CONCEPT 56.4 Earth is changing rapidly as a result of human actions 1254
Nutrient Enrichment 1254
Toxins in the Environment 1255
Greenhouse Gases and Global Warming 1256
Depletion of Atmospheric Ozone 1258

CONCEPT 56.5 Sustainable development can improve human lives while conserving biodiversity 1260
Sustainable Biosphere Initiative 1260
The Future of the Biosphere 1261

A Short Guide to Writing about Biology, Seventh Edition
by Jan A. Pechenik
Chapter 1: General Advice on Reading and Note–Taking 1267
Chapter 2: Citing Sources and Listing References 1277
Chapter 3: Writing Laboratory and Other Research Reports 1283

Campbell Biology, Ninth Edition by Jane B. Reece, Lisa A. Urry, Michael L. Cain, Steven A. Wasserman, Peter V. Minorsky, and Robert B. Jackson

Appendix A   Answers A–1
Appendix B   Periodic Table of the Elements B–1
Appendix C   The Metric System C–1
Appendix D   A Comparison of the Light Microscope and the Electron Microscope D–1
Appendix E   Classification of Life E–1
Credits CR–1
Glossary G–1
Index I–1

1

Introduction: Themes in the Study of Life

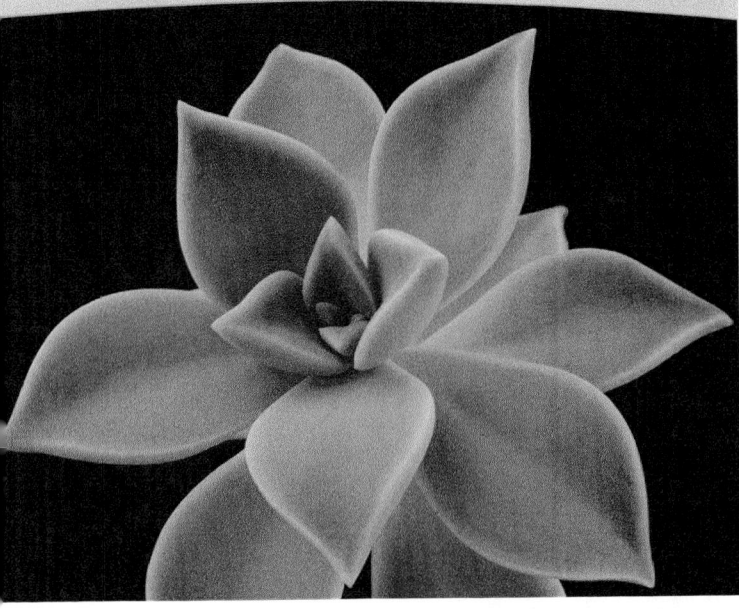

▲ **Figure 1.1 How is the mother-of-pearl plant adapted to its environment?**

KEY CONCEPTS

1.1 The themes of this book make connections across different areas of biology

1.2 The Core Theme: Evolution accounts for the unity and diversity of life

1.3 In studying nature, scientists make observations and then form and test hypotheses

1.4 Science benefits from a cooperative approach and diverse viewpoints

OVERVIEW

Inquiring About Life

The mother-of-pearl plant, or ghost plant (**Figure 1.1** and cover), is native to a single mountain in northeastern Mexico. Its fleshy, succulent leaves and other features allow this plant to store and conserve water. Even when rain falls, the plant's access to water is limited because it grows in crevices

of vertical rock walls, where little soil is present to hold rainwater (**Figure 1.2**). The plant's water-conserving characteristics help it survive and thrive in these nooks and crannies. Similar features are found in many plants that live in dry environments, allowing them to eke out a living where rain is unpredictable.

An organism's adaptations to its environment, such as adaptations for conserving water, are the result of **evolution**, the process of change that has transformed life on Earth from its earliest beginnings to the diversity of organisms living today. Evolution is the fundamental organizing principle of biology and the core theme of this book.

Although biologists know a great deal about life on Earth, many mysteries remain. For instance, what exactly led to the origin of flowering among plants such as the one pictured here? Posing questions about the living world and seeking science-based answers—scientific inquiry—are the central activities of **biology**, the scientific study of life. Biologists' questions can be ambitious. They may ask how a single tiny cell becomes a tree or a dog, how the human mind works, or how the different forms of life in a forest interact. Most people wonder about the organisms living around them, and many interesting questions probably occur to you when you are out-of-doors, surrounded by the natural world. When they do, you are already thinking like a biologist. More than anything else, biology is a quest, an ongoing inquiry about the nature of life.

What is life? Even a small child realizes that a dog or a plant is alive, while a rock or a lawn mower is not. Yet the phenomenon we call life defies a simple, one-sentence definition. We recognize life by what living things do. **Figure 1.3**, on the next page, highlights some of the properties and processes we associate with life.

While limited to a handful of images, Figure 1.3 reminds us that the living world is wondrously varied. How do biologists

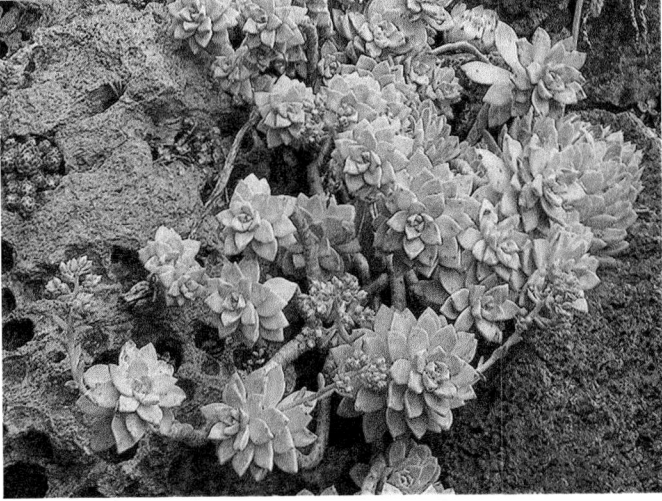

▲ **Figure 1.2 The mother-of-pearl plant (*Graptopetalum paraguayense*).** This plant's thick leaves hold water, enabling it to live where soil is scarce. The leaves vary in color, as seen here.

▼ **Order.** This close-up of a sunflower illustrates the highly ordered structure that characterizes life.

▲ **Response to the environment.** This Venus flytrap closed its trap rapidly in response to the environmental stimulus of a damselfly landing on the open trap.

▲ **Evolutionary adaptation.** The appearance of this pygmy sea horse camouflages the animal in its environment. Such adaptations evolve over many generations by the reproductive success of those individuals with heritable traits that are best suited to their environments.

▶ **Reproduction.** Organisms (living things) reproduce their own kind. Here, a baby giraffe stands close to its mother.

▲ **Regulation.** The regulation of blood flow through the blood vessels of this jackrabbit's ears helps maintain a constant body temperature by adjusting heat exchange with the surrounding air.

▲ **Energy processing.** This hummingbird obtains fuel in the form of nectar from flowers. The hummingbird will use chemical energy stored in its food to power flight and other work.

◀ **Growth and development.** Inherited information carried by genes controls the pattern of growth and development of organisms, such as this Nile crocodile.

▲ **Figure 1.3 Some properties of life.**

make sense of this diversity and complexity? This opening chapter sets up a framework for answering this question. The first part of the chapter provides a panoramic view of the biological "landscape," organized around some unifying themes. We then focus on biology's core theme, evolution, with an introduction to the reasoning that led Charles Darwin to his explanatory theory. Next, we look at scientific inquiry—how scientists raise and attempt to answer questions about the natural world. Finally, we address the culture of science and its effects on society.

CONCEPT 1.1

The themes of this book make connections across different areas of biology

Biology is a subject of enormous scope, and news reports reveal exciting new biological discoveries being made every day. Simply memorizing the factual details of this huge subject is most likely not the best way to develop a coherent view of life. A better approach is to take a more active role by connecting the many things you learn to a set of themes that pervade all of biology. Focusing on a few big ideas—ways of thinking about life that will still hold true decades from now—will help you organize and make sense of all the information you'll encounter as you study biology. To help you, we have selected eight unifying themes to serve as touchstones as you proceed through this book.

Theme: New Properties Emerge at Each Level in the Biological Hierarchy

The study of life extends from the microscopic scale of the molecules and cells that make up organisms to the global scale of the entire living planet. We can divide this enormous range into different levels of biological organization.

Imagine zooming in from space to take a closer and closer look at life on Earth. It is spring in Ontario, Canada, and our destination is a local forest, where we will eventually explore a maple leaf right down to the molecular level. **Figure 1.4**, on the next two pages, narrates this journey into life, with the numbers leading you through the levels of biological organization illustrated by the photographs.

Emergent Properties

If we now zoom back out from the molecular level in Figure 1.4, we can see that novel properties emerge at each step, properties that are not present at the preceding level. These **emergent properties** are due to the arrangement and interactions of parts as complexity increases. For example, although photosynthesis occurs in an intact chloroplast, it will not take place in a disorganized test-tube mixture of chlorophyll and other chloroplast molecules. Photosynthesis requires a specific organization of these molecules in the chloroplast. To take another example, if a blow to the head disrupts the intricate architecture of a human brain, the mind may cease to function properly even though all of the brain tissues are still present. Our thoughts and memories are emergent properties of a complex network of nerve cells. At a much higher level of biological organization—at the ecosystem level—the recycling of chemical elements essential to life, such as carbon, depends on a network of diverse organisms interacting with each other and with the soil, water, and air.

Emergent properties are not unique to life. A box of bicycle parts won't take you anywhere, but if they are arranged in a certain way, you can pedal to your chosen destination. And while the graphite in a pencil "lead" and the diamond in a wedding ring are both pure carbon, they have very different appearances and properties due to the different arrangements of their carbon atoms. Both of these examples point out the importance of arrangement. Compared to such nonliving examples, however, the unrivaled complexity of biological systems makes the emergent properties of life especially challenging to study.

The Power and Limitations of Reductionism

Because the properties of life emerge from complex organization, scientists seeking to understand biological systems confront a dilemma. On the one hand, we cannot fully explain a higher level of order by breaking it down into its parts. A dissected animal no longer functions; a cell reduced to its chemical ingredients is no longer a cell. Disrupting a living system interferes with its functioning. On the other hand, something as complex as an organism or a cell cannot be analyzed without taking it apart.

Reductionism—the approach of reducing complex systems to simpler components that are more manageable to study—is a powerful strategy in biology. For example, by studying the molecular structure of DNA that had been extracted from cells, James Watson and Francis Crick inferred, in 1953, how this molecule could serve as the chemical basis of inheritance. The central role of DNA in cells and organisms became better understood, however, when scientists were able to study the interactions of DNA with other molecules. Biologists must balance the reductionist strategy with the larger-scale, holistic objective of understanding emergent properties—how the parts of cells, organisms, and higher levels of order, such as ecosystems, work together. This is the goal of an approach developed over the last 50 years called systems biology.

Systems Biology

A system is simply a combination of components that function together. A biologist can study a system at any level of organization. A single leaf cell can be considered a system, as can a frog, an ant colony, or a desert ecosytem. To understand how such systems work, it is not enough to have a "parts list," even a complete one. Realizing this, many researchers are now complementing the reductionist approach with new strategies for studying whole systems. This change in perspective is analogous to moving from ground level on a street corner, where you can observe local traffic, to a helicopter high above a city, from which you can see how variables such as time of day, construction projects, accidents, and traffic-signal malfunctions affect traffic throughout the city.

Systems biology is an approach that attempts to model the dynamic behavior of whole biological systems based on a study of the interactions among the system's parts. Successful models enable biologists to predict how a change in one or more variables will affect other components and the whole system. Thus, the systems approach enables us to pose new kinds of questions. How might a drug that lowers blood pressure affect the functioning of organs throughout the human body? How might increasing a crop's water supply affect processes in the plants, such as the storage of molecules essential for human nutrition? How might a gradual increase in atmospheric carbon dioxide alter ecosystems and the entire biosphere? The ultimate aim of systems biology is to answer large-scale questions like the last one.

Exploring Levels of Biological Organization

◄1 The Biosphere

As soon as we are near enough to Earth to make out its continents and oceans, we begin to see signs of life—in the green mosaic of the planet's forests, for example. This is our first view of the biosphere, which consists of all life on Earth and all the places where life exists—most regions of land, most bodies of water, the atmosphere to an altitude of several kilometers, and even sediments far below the ocean floor and rocks many kilometers below Earth's surface.

◄2 Ecosystems

As we approach Earth's surface for an imaginary landing in Ontario, we can begin to make out a forest with an abundance of trees that lose their leaves in one season and grow new ones in another (deciduous trees). Such a deciduous forest is an example of an ecosystem. Grasslands, deserts, and the ocean's coral reefs are other types of ecosystems. An ecosystem consists of all the living things in a particular area, along with all the nonliving components of the environment with which life interacts, such as soil, water, atmospheric gases, and light. All of Earth's ecosystems combined make up the biosphere.

►3 Communities

The entire array of organisms inhabiting a particular ecosystem is called a biological community. The community in our forest ecosystem includes many kinds of trees and other plants, a diversity of animals, various mushrooms and other fungi, and enormous numbers of diverse microorganisms, which are living forms, such as bacteria, that are too small to see without a microscope. Each of these forms of life is called a *species*.

►4 Populations

A population consists of all the individuals of a species living within the bounds of a specified area. For example, our Ontario forest includes a population of sugar maple trees and a population of white-tailed deer. We can now refine our definition of a community as the set of populations that inhabit a particular area.

▲5 Organisms

Individual living things are called organisms. Each of the maple trees and other plants in the forest is an organism, and so is each forest animal—whether deer, squirrel, frog, or beetle. The soil teems with microorganisms such as bacteria.

▼ 6 Organs and Organ Systems

The structural hierarchy of life continues to unfold as we explore the architecture of the more complex organisms. A maple leaf is an example of an organ, a body part that carries out a particular function in the body. Stems and roots are the other major organs of plants. Examples of human organs are the brain, heart, and kidney. The organs of humans, other complex animals, and plants are organized into organ systems, each a team of organs that cooperate in a larger function. For example, the human digestive system includes such organs as the tongue, stomach, and intestines. Organs consist of multiple tissues.

50 μm

◄ 7 Tissues

Our next scale change—to see the tissues of a leaf—requires a microscope. Each tissue is made up of a group of cells that work together, performing a specialized function. The leaf shown here has been cut on an angle. The honeycombed tissue in the interior of the leaf (left portion of photo) is the main location of photosynthesis, the process that converts light energy to the chemical energy of sugar and other food. We are viewing the sliced leaf from a perspective that also enables us to see the jigsaw puzzle–like "skin" on the surface of the leaf, a tissue called epidermis (right part of photo). The pores through the epidermis allow the gas carbon dioxide, a raw material for sugar production, to reach the photosynthetic tissue inside the leaf. At this scale, we can also see that each tissue has a distinct cellular structure.

Cell   10 μm

▶ 9 Organelles

Chloroplasts are examples of organelles, the various functional components present in cells. In this image, a very powerful tool called an electron microscope brings a single chloroplast into sharp focus.

Chloroplast

1 μm

◄ 8 Cells

The cell is life's fundamental unit of structure and function. Some organisms, such as amoebas and most bacteria, are single cells. Other organisms, including plants and animals, are multicellular. Instead of a single cell performing all the functions of life, a multicellular organism has a division of labor among specialized cells. A human body consists of trillions of microscopic cells of many different kinds, such as muscle cells and nerve cells, which are organized into the various specialized tissues. For example, muscle tissue consists of bundles of muscle cells. In the photo at the upper left, we see a more highly magnified view of some cells in a leaf tissue. One cell is only about 40 micrometers (μm) across. It would take about 500 of these cells to reach across a small coin. As tiny as these cells are, you can see that each contains numerous green structures called chloroplasts, which are responsible for photosynthesis.

▶ 10 Molecules

Our last scale change drops us into a chloroplast for a view of life at the molecular level. A molecule is a chemical structure consisting of two or more small chemical units called atoms, which are represented as balls in this computer graphic of a chlorophyll molecule. Chlorophyll is the pigment molecule that makes a maple leaf green. One of the most important molecules on Earth, chlorophyll absorbs sunlight during the first step of photosynthesis. Within each chloroplast, millions of chlorophyll molecules, together with accessory molecules, are organized into the equipment that converts light energy to the chemical energy of food.

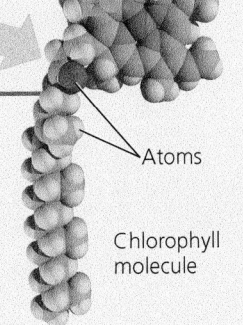

Atoms

Chlorophyll molecule

Systems biology is relevant to the study of life at all levels. During the early years of the 20th century, biologists studying how animal bodies function (animal physiology) began integrating data on how multiple organs coordinate processes such as the regulation of sugar concentration in the blood. And in the 1960s, scientists investigating ecosystems pioneered a more mathematically sophisticated systems approach with elaborate models diagramming the network of interactions between organisms and nonliving components of ecosystems, such as salt marshes. More recently, with the sequencing of DNA from many species, systems biology has taken hold at the cellular and molecular levels, as we'll describe later when we discuss DNA.

Theme: Organisms Interact with Other Organisms and the Physical Environment

Turn back again to Figure 1.4, this time focusing on the forest. In an ecosystem, each organism interacts continuously with its environment, which includes both other organisms and physical factors. The leaves of a tree, for example, absorb light from the sun, take in carbon dioxide from the air, and release oxygen to the air (Figure 1.5). Both the organism and the environment are affected by the interactions between them. For example, a plant takes up water and minerals from the soil through its roots, and its roots help form soil by breaking up rocks. On a global scale, plants and other photosynthetic organisms have generated all the oxygen in the air.

A tree also interacts with other organisms, such as soil microorganisms associated with its roots, insects that live in the tree, and animals that eat its leaves and fruit. Interactions between organisms ultimately result in the cycling of nutrients in ecosystems. For example, minerals acquired by a tree will eventually be returned to the soil by other organisms that decompose leaf litter, dead roots, and other organic debris. The minerals are then available to be taken up by plants again.

Like all organisms, we humans interact with our environment. Unfortunately, our interactions sometimes have drastic consequences. For example, since the Industrial Revolution in the 1800s, the burning of fossil fuels (coal, oil, and gas) has been increasing at an ever-accelerating pace. This practice releases gaseous compounds into the atmosphere, including prodigious amounts of carbon dioxide (CO_2). About half the human-generated CO_2 stays in the atmosphere, acting like a layer of glass around the planet that admits radiation that warms the Earth but prevents heat from radiating into outer space. Scientists estimate that the average temperature of the planet has risen 1°C since 1900 due to this "greenhouse effect," and they project an additional rise in average global temperature of at least 3°C over the course of the 21st century.

This global warming, a major aspect of **global climate change**, has already had dire effects on life-forms and their habitats all over planet Earth. Polar bears have lost a significant portion of the ice platform from which they hunt, and there are examples of small rodents and plant species that have shifted their ranges to higher altitudes, as well as bird populations that have altered their migration schedules. Only time will reveal the consequences of these changes. Scientists predict that even if we stopped burning fossil fuels today, it would take several centuries to return to preindustrial CO_2 levels. That scenario is highly improbable, so it is imperative that we learn all we can about the effects of global climate change on Earth and its populations. Acting as the stewards of our planet, we must strive to find ways to address this problem.

Theme: Life Requires Energy Transfer and Transformation

As you saw in Figure 1.5, a tree's leaves absorb sunlight. The input of energy from the sun makes life possible: A fundamental characteristic of living organisms is their use of energy to carry out life's activities. Moving, growing, reproducing, and the other activities of life are work, and work requires energy. In the business of living, organisms often

▲ Figure 1.5 **Interactions of an African acacia tree with other organisms and the physical environment.**

Sunlight

Leaves absorb light energy from the sun.

Leaves take in carbon dioxide from the air and release oxygen.

CO_2

O_2

Cycling of chemical nutrients

Leaves fall to the ground and are decomposed by organisms that return minerals to the soil.

Water and minerals in the soil are taken up by the tree through its roots.

Animals eat leaves and fruit from the tree.

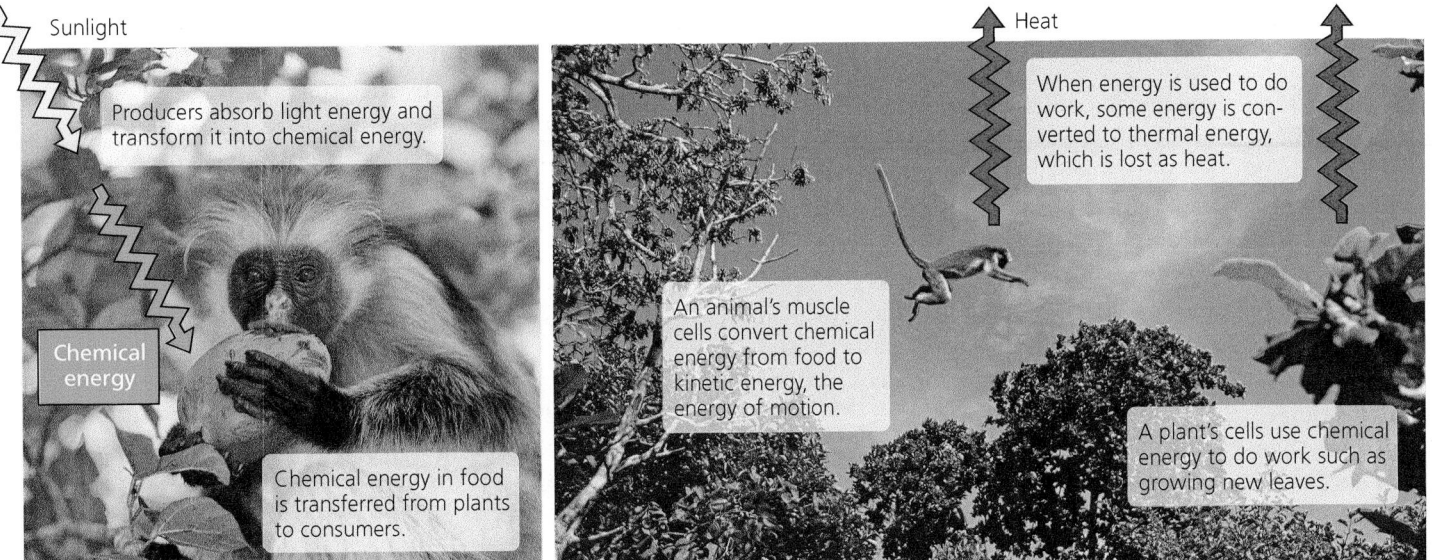

Sunlight

Producers absorb light energy and transform it into chemical energy.

Chemical energy

Chemical energy in food is transferred from plants to consumers.

(a) Energy flow from sunlight to producers to consumers

Heat

When energy is used to do work, some energy is converted to thermal energy, which is lost as heat.

An animal's muscle cells convert chemical energy from food to kinetic energy, the energy of motion.

A plant's cells use chemical energy to do work such as growing new leaves.

(b) Using energy to do work

▲ Figure 1.6 **Energy flow in an ecosystem.** This endangered Red Colobus monkey lives in Tanzania.

transform one form of energy to another. Chlorophyll molecules within the tree's leaves harness the energy of sunlight and use it to drive photosynthesis, converting carbon dioxide and water to sugar and oxygen. The chemical energy in sugar is then passed along by plants and other photosynthetic organisms (producers) to consumers. Consumers are organisms, such as animals, that feed on producers and other consumers **(Figure 1.6a)**.

An animal's muscle cells use sugar as fuel to power movements, converting chemical energy to kinetic energy, the energy of motion **(Figure 1.6b)**. The cells in a leaf use sugar to drive the process of cell proliferation during leaf growth, transforming stored chemical energy into cellular work. In both cases, some of the energy is converted to thermal energy, which dissipates to the surroundings as heat. In contrast to chemical nutrients, which recycle within an ecosystem, energy flows through an ecosystem, usually entering as light and exiting as heat.

Theme: Structure and Function Are Correlated at All Levels of Biological Organization

Another theme evident in Figure 1.4 is the idea that form fits function, which you'll recognize from everyday life. For example, a screwdriver is suited to tighten or loosen screws, a hammer to pound nails. How a device works is correlated with its structure. Applied to biology, this theme is a guide to the anatomy of life at all its structural levels. An example from Figure 1.4 is seen in the leaf: Its thin, flat shape maximizes the amount of sunlight that can be captured by its chloroplasts. Analyzing a biological structure gives us clues about what it does and how it works. Conversely, knowing the function of something provides insight into its construction. An example from the animal kingdom, the wing of a bird, provides additional instances of the structure-function theme **(Figure 1.7)**. In exploring life on its different structural levels, we discover functional beauty at every turn.

(a) A bird's wings have an aerodynamically efficient shape.

(b) Wing bones have a honeycombed internal structure that is strong but lightweight.

▲ Figure 1.7 **Form fits function in a gull's wing. (a)** The shape of a bird's wings and **(b)** the structure of its bones make flight possible.

? *How does form fit function in a human hand?*

Theme: The Cell Is an Organism's Basic Unit of Structure and Function

In life's structural hierarchy, the cell has a special place as the lowest level of organization that can perform all activities required for life. Moreover, the activities of organisms are all based on the activities of cells. For instance, the movement of your eyes as you read this line is based on activities of muscle and nerve cells. Even a global process such as the recycling of carbon is the cumulative product of cellular activities, including the photosynthesis that occurs in the chloroplasts of leaf cells. Understanding how cells work is a major focus of biological research.

All cells share certain characteristics. For example, every cell is enclosed by a membrane that regulates the passage of materials between the cell and its surroundings. And every cell uses DNA as its genetic information. However, we can distinguish between two main forms of cells: prokaryotic cells and eukaryotic cells. The cells of two groups of microorganisms, called bacteria (singular, *bacterium*) and archaea (singular, *archaean*), are prokaryotic. All other forms of life, including plants and animals, are composed of eukaryotic cells.

A **eukaryotic cell** is subdivided by internal membranes into various membrane-enclosed organelles (**Figure 1.8**). In most eukaryotic cells, the largest organelle is the nucleus, which contains the cell's DNA. The other organelles are located in the cytoplasm, the entire region between the nucleus and outer membrane of the cell. The chloroplast you saw in Figure 1.4 is an organelle found in eukaryotic cells that carry out photosynthesis. Prokaryotic cells are much simpler and generally smaller than eukaryotic cells, as seen clearly in Figure 1.8. In a **prokaryotic cell**, the DNA is not separated from the rest of the cell by enclosure in a membrane-bounded nucleus. Prokaryotic cells also lack the other kinds of membrane-enclosed organelles that characterize eukaryotic cells. The properties of all organisms, whether prokaryotic or eukaryotic, are based in the structure and function of cells.

Theme: The Continuity of Life Is Based on Heritable Information in the Form of DNA

The division of cells to form new cells is the foundation for all reproduction and for the growth and repair of multicellular organisms. Inside the dividing cell in **Figure 1.9**, you can see structures called chromosomes, which are stained with a blue-glowing dye. The chromosomes have almost all of the cell's genetic material, its **DNA** (short for deoxyribonucleic acid). DNA is the substance of **genes**, the units of inheritance that transmit information from parents to offspring. Your blood group (A, B, AB, or O), for example, is the result of certain genes that you inherited from your parents.

DNA Structure and Function

Each chromosome contains one very long DNA molecule, with hundreds or thousands of genes arranged along its length. The genes encode the information necessary to build other molecules in the cell, most notably proteins. Proteins play structural roles and are also responsible for carrying out cellular work. They thus establish a cell's identity.

The DNA of chromosomes replicates as a cell prepares to divide, and each of the two cellular offspring inherits a complete set of genes, identical to that of the parent cell. Each of us began life as a single cell stocked with DNA inherited from our parents. Replication of that DNA with each round of cell division transmitted copies of the DNA to our trillions of cells. The DNA controls the development and maintenance of the entire organism and, indirectly, everything the organism does (**Figure 1.10**). The DNA serves as a central database.

Eukaryotic cell

Membrane

Cytoplasm

Membrane-enclosed organelles

DNA (throughout nucleus)

Nucleus (membrane-enclosed)

Prokaryotic cell

DNA (no nucleus)

Membrane

1 μm

▲ Figure 1.8 **Contrasting eukaryotic and prokaryotic cells in size and complexity.**

25 μm

▲ Figure 1.9 **A lung cell from a newt divides into two smaller cells that will grow and divide again.**

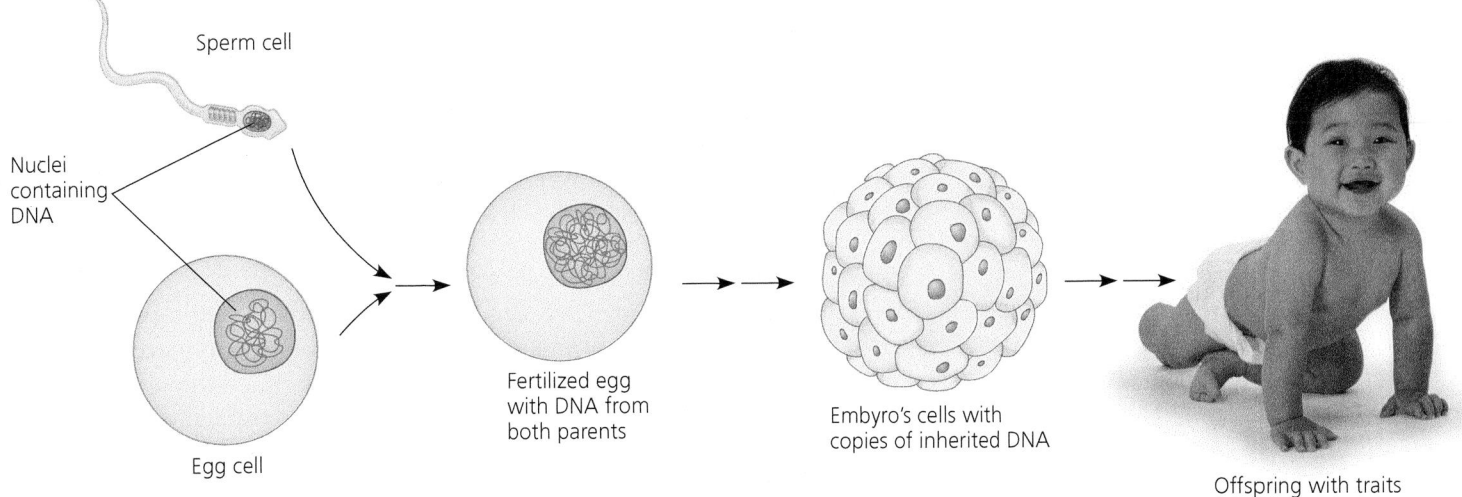

▲ Figure 1.10 **Inherited DNA directs development of an organism.**

The molecular structure of DNA accounts for its ability to store information. Each DNA molecule is made up of two long chains, called strands, arranged in a double helix. Each chain is made up of four kinds of chemical building blocks called nucleotides, abbreviated A, T, C, and G (Figure 1.11). The way DNA encodes information is analogous to how we arrange the letters of the alphabet into precise sequences with specific meanings. The word *rat*, for example, evokes a rodent; the words *tar* and *art*, which contain the same letters, mean very different things. We can think of nucleotides as a four-letter alphabet of inheritance. Specific sequential arrangements of these four nucleotide letters encode the information in genes, which are typically hundreds or thousands of nucleotides long.

DNA provides the blueprints for making proteins, and proteins are the main players in building and maintaining the cell and carrying out its activities. For instance, the information carried in a bacterial gene may specify a certain protein in a bacterial cell membrane, while the information in a human gene may denote a protein hormone that stimulates growth. Other human proteins include proteins in a muscle cell that drive contraction and the defensive proteins called antibodies. Enzymes, which catalyze (speed up) specific chemical reactions, are mostly proteins and are crucial to all cells.

The DNA of genes controls protein production indirectly, using a related kind of molecule called RNA as an intermediary. The sequence of nucleotides along a gene is transcribed into RNA, which is then translated into a specific protein with a unique shape and function. This entire process, by which the information in a gene directs the production of a cellular product, is called **gene expression**. In translating genes into proteins, all forms of life employ essentially the same genetic code. A particular sequence of nucleotides says the same thing in one organism as it does in another. Differences between organisms reflect differences between their nucleotide sequences rather than between their genetic codes.

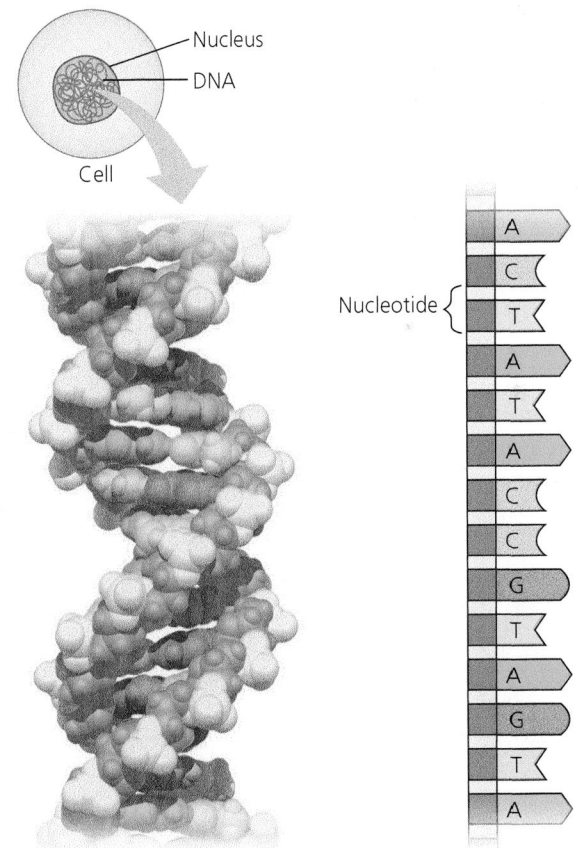

(a) DNA double helix. This model shows each atom in a segment of DNA. Made up of two long chains of building blocks called nucleotides, a DNA molecule takes the three-dimensional form of a double helix.

(b) Single strand of DNA. These geometric shapes and letters are simple symbols for the nucleotides in a small section of one chain of a DNA molecule. Genetic information is encoded in specific sequences of the four types of nucleotides. (Their names are abbreviated A, T, C, and G.)

▲ Figure 1.11 **DNA: The genetic material.**

Not all RNA molecules in the cell are translated into protein; some RNAs carry out other important tasks. We have known for decades that some types of RNA are actually components of the cellular machinery that manufactures proteins. Recently, scientists have discovered whole new classes of RNA that play other roles in the cell, such as regulating the functioning of protein-coding genes. All these RNAs are specified by genes, and the process of their transcription is also referred to as gene expression. By carrying the instructions for making proteins and RNAs and by replicating with each cell division, DNA ensures faithful inheritance of genetic information from generation to generation.

Genomics: Large-Scale Analysis of DNA Sequences

The entire "library" of genetic instructions that an organism inherits is called its **genome**. A typical human cell has two similar sets of chromosomes, and each set has DNA totaling about 3 billion nucleotide pairs. If the one-letter abbreviations for the nucleotides of one strand were written in letters the size of those you are now reading, the genetic text would fill about 600 books the size of this one. Within this genomic library of nucleotide sequences are genes for about 75,000 kinds of proteins and an as yet unknown number of RNA molecules that do not code for proteins.

Since the early 1990s, the pace at which we can sequence genomes has accelerated at an almost unbelievable rate, enabled by a revolution in technology. The development of new methods and DNA-sequencing machines, such as those shown in **Figure 1.12**, have led the charge. The entire sequence of nucleotides in the human genome is now known, along with the genome sequences of many other organisms, including bacteria, archaea, fungi, plants, and other animals.

The sequencing of the human genome was heralded as a scientific and technological achievement comparable to landing the *Apollo* astronauts on the moon in 1969. But it

▲ **Figure 1.12 Biology as an information science.** Automatic DNA-sequencing machines and abundant computing power make the sequencing of genomes possible. This facility in Walnut Creek, California, is part of the Joint Genome Institute.

was only the beginning of an even bigger research endeavor, an effort to learn how the activities of the myriad proteins encoded by the DNA are coordinated in cells and whole organisms. To make sense of the deluge of data from genome-sequencing projects and the growing catalog of known protein functions, scientists are applying a systems approach at the cellular and molecular levels. Rather than investigating a single gene at a time, these researchers have shifted to studying whole sets of genes of a species as well as comparing genomes between species—an approach called **genomics**.

Three important research developments have made the genomic approach possible. One is "high-throughput" technology, tools that can analyze biological materials very rapidly and produce enormous amounts of data. The automatic DNA-sequencing machines that made the sequencing of the human genome possible are examples of high-throughput devices (see Figure 1.12). The second major development is **bioinformatics**, the use of computational tools to store, organize, and analyze the huge volume of data that result from high-throughput methods. The third key development is the formation of interdisciplinary research teams—melting pots of diverse specialists that may include computer scientists, mathematicians, engineers, chemists, physicists, and, of course, biologists from a variety of fields.

Theme: Feedback Mechanisms Regulate Biological Systems

Just as a coordinated control of traffic flow is necessary for a city to function smoothly, regulation of biological processes is crucial to the operation of living systems. Consider your muscles, for instance. When your muscle cells require more energy during exercise, they increase their consumption of the sugar molecules that serve as fuel. In contrast, when you rest, a different set of chemical reactions converts surplus sugar to storage molecules.

Like most of the cell's chemical processes, those that either decompose or store sugar are accelerated, or catalyzed, by proteins called enzymes. Each type of enzyme catalyzes a specific chemical reaction. In many cases, these reactions are linked into chemical pathways, each step with its own enzyme. How does the cell coordinate its various chemical pathways? In our example of sugar management, how does the cell match fuel supply to demand, regulating its opposing pathways of sugar consumption and storage? The key is the ability of many biological processes to self-regulate by a mechanism called feedback.

In feedback regulation, the output, or product, of a process regulates that very process. The most common form of regulation in living systems is **negative feedback**, in which accumulation of an end product of a process slows that process. For example, the cell's breakdown of sugar generates chemical energy in the form of a substance called ATP. When a cell makes more ATP than it can use, the excess ATP "feeds back"

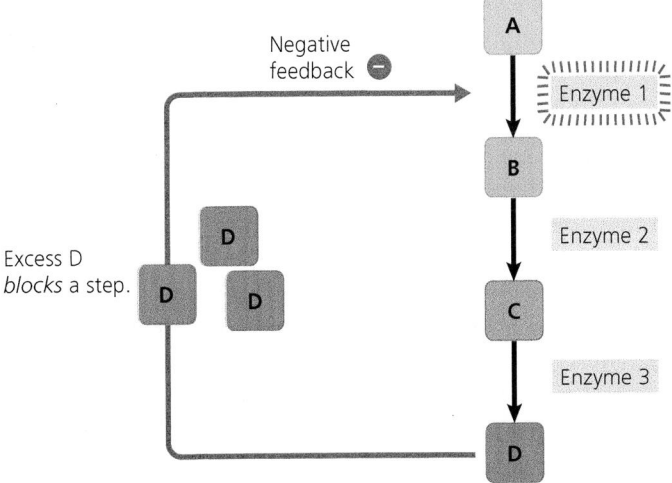

(a) Negative feedback. This three-step chemical pathway converts substance A to substance D. A specific enzyme catalyzes each chemical reaction. Accumulation of the final product (D) inhibits the first enzyme in the sequence, thus slowing down production of more D.

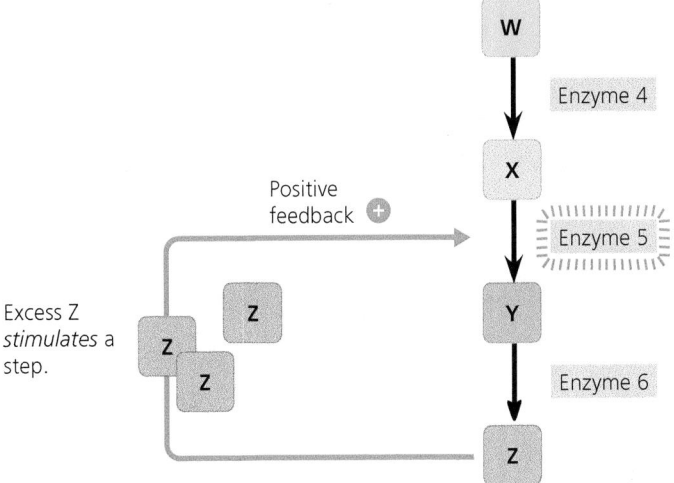

(b) Positive feedback. In a biochemical pathway regulated by positive feedback, a product stimulates an enzyme in the reaction sequence, increasing the rate of production of the product.

▲ **Figure 1.13 Regulation by feedback mechanisms.**

? *What would happen to the feedback system if enzyme 2 were missing?*

and inhibits an enzyme near the beginning of the pathway (Figure 1.13a).

Though less common than processes regulated by negative feedback, there are also many biological processes regulated by **positive feedback**, in which an end product *speeds up* its own production (Figure 1.13b). The clotting of your blood in response to injury is an example. When a blood vessel is damaged, structures in the blood called platelets begin to aggregate at the site. Positive feedback occurs as chemicals released by the platelets attract *more* platelets. The platelet pileup then initiates a complex process that seals the wound with a clot.

Feedback is a regulatory motif common to life at all levels, from the molecular level to ecosystems and the biosphere.

Such regulation is an example of the integration that makes living systems much greater than the sum of their parts.

Evolution, the Overarching Theme of Biology

Having considered all the other themes that run through this book, let's now turn to biology's core theme—evolution. Evolution is the one idea that makes sense of everything we know about living organisms. Life has been evolving on Earth for billions of years, resulting in a vast diversity of past and present organisms. But along with the diversity we find many shared features. For example, while the sea horse, jackrabbit, hummingbird, crocodile, and giraffes in Figure 1.3 look very different, their skeletons are basically similar. The scientific explanation for this unity and diversity—and for the suitability of organisms for their environments—is evolution: the idea that the organisms living on Earth today are the modified descendants of common ancestors. In other words, we can explain traits shared by two organisms with the idea that they have descended from a common ancestor, and we can account for differences with the idea that heritable changes have occurred along the way. Many kinds of evidence support the occurrence of evolution and the theory that describes how it takes place. In the next section, we'll consider the fundamental concept of evolution in greater detail.

CONCEPT CHECK **1.1**

1. For each biological level in Figure 1.4, write a sentence that includes the next "lower" level. Example: "A community consists of *populations* of the various species inhabiting a specific area."
2. What theme or themes are exemplified by (a) the sharp spines of a porcupine, (b) the cloning of a plant from a single cell, and (c) a hummingbird using sugar to power its flight?
3. **WHAT IF?** For each theme discussed in this section, give an example not mentioned in the book.

For suggested answers, see Appendix A.

CONCEPT **1.2**

The Core Theme: Evolution accounts for the unity and diversity of life

EVOLUTION The list of biological themes discussed in Concept 1.1 is not absolute; some people might find a shorter or longer list more useful. There is consensus among biologists, however, as to the core theme of biology: It is evolution. To quote one of the founders of modern evolutionary theory, Theodosius Dobzhansky, "Nothing in biology makes sense except in the light of evolution."

In addition to encompassing a hierarchy of size scales from molecules to the biosphere, biology extends across the great diversity of species that have ever lived on Earth. To understand Dobzhansky's statement, we need to discuss how biologists think about this vast diversity.

Classifying the Diversity of Life

Diversity is a hallmark of life. Biologists have so far identified and named about 1.8 million species. To date, this diversity of life is known to include at least 100,000 species of fungi, 290,000 plant species, 52,000 vertebrate species (animals with backbones), and 1 million insect species (more than half of all known forms of life)—not to mention the myriad types of single-celled organisms. Researchers identify thousands of additional species each year. Estimates of the total number of species range from about 10 million to over 100 million. Whatever the actual number, the enormous variety of life

gives biology a very broad scope. Biologists face a major challenge in attempting to make sense of this variety.

Grouping Species: The Basic Idea

There is a human tendency to group diverse items according to their similarities and their relationships to each other. For instance, we may speak of "squirrels" and "butterflies," though we recognize that many different species belong to each group. We may even sort groups into broader categories, such as rodents (which include squirrels) and insects (which include butterflies). Taxonomy, the branch of biology that names and classifies species, formalizes this ordering of species into groups of increasing breadth, based on the degree to which they share characteristics (**Figure 1.14**). You will learn more about the details of this taxonomic scheme in Chapter 26. For

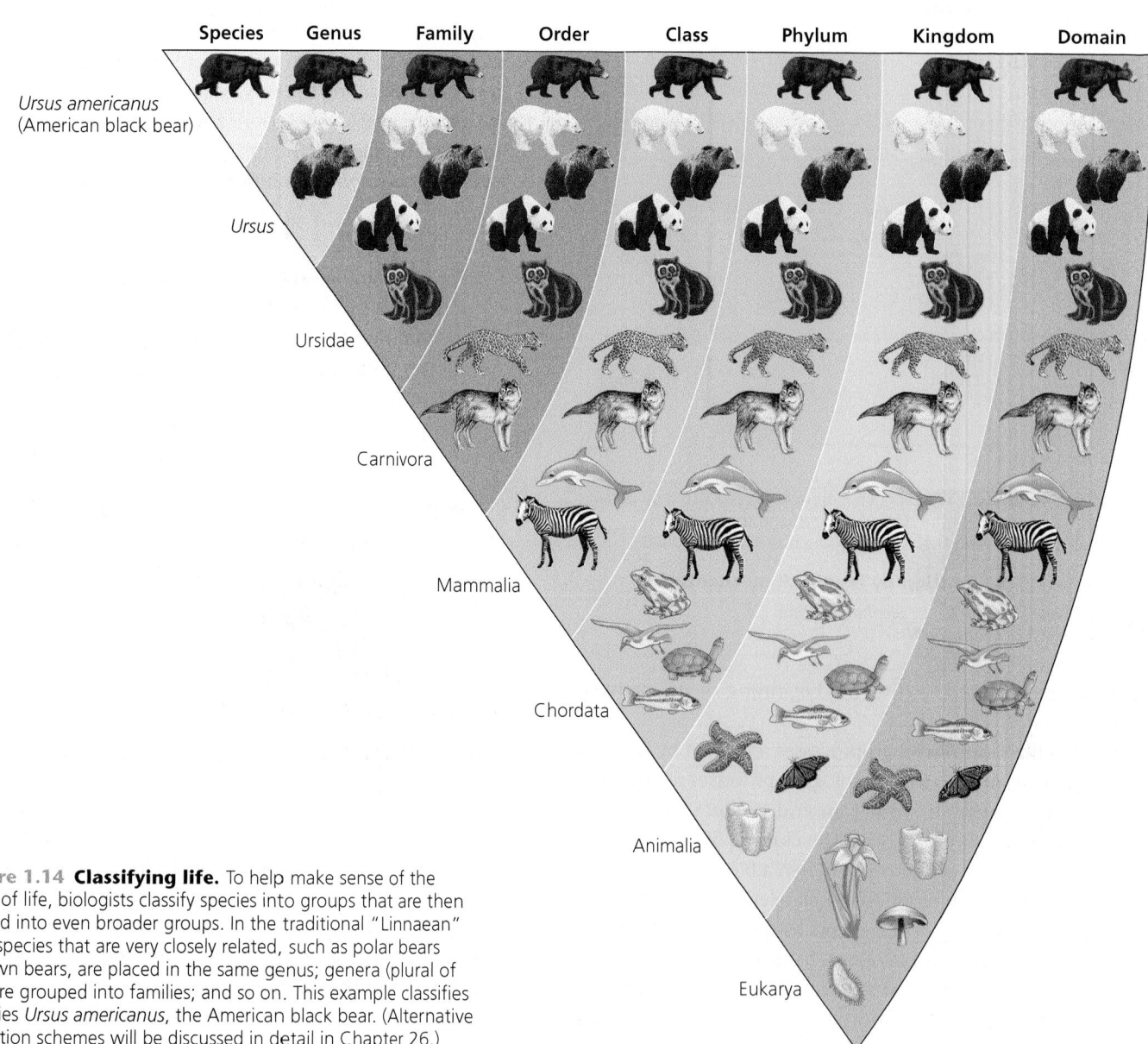

▲ **Figure 1.14 Classifying life.** To help make sense of the diversity of life, biologists classify species into groups that are then combined into even broader groups. In the traditional "Linnaean" system, species that are very closely related, such as polar bears and brown bears, are placed in the same genus; genera (plural of genus) are grouped into families; and so on. This example classifies the species *Ursus americanus*, the American black bear. (Alternative classification schemes will be discussed in detail in Chapter 26.)

now, we will focus on the big picture by considering the broadest units of classification, kingdoms and domains.

The Three Domains of Life

Historically, scientists have classified the diversity of life-forms into kingdoms and finer groupings by careful comparisons of structure, function, and other obvious features. In the last few decades, new methods of assessing species relationships, such as comparisons of DNA sequences, have led to an ongoing reevaluation of the number and boundaries of kingdoms. Researchers have proposed anywhere from six kingdoms to dozens of kingdoms. While debate continues at the kingdom level, there is consensus among biologists that the kingdoms of life can be grouped into three even higher levels of classification called domains. The three domains are named Bacteria, Archaea, and Eukarya (**Figure 1.15**).

The organisms making up two of the three domains—domain **Bacteria** and domain **Archaea**—are all prokaryotic. Most prokaryotes are single-celled and microscopic. Previously, bacteria and archaea were combined in a single kingdom because they shared the prokaryotic form of cell structure. But much evidence now supports the view that bacteria and archaea represent two very distinct branches of prokaryotic life, different in key ways that you'll learn about in Chapter 27. There is also evidence that archaea are at least as closely related to eukaryotic organisms as they are to bacteria.

All the eukaryotes (organisms with eukaryotic cells) are now grouped in domain **Eukarya**. This domain includes three kingdoms of multicellular eukaryotes: kingdoms Plantae,

▼ Figure 1.15 **The three domains of life.**

(a) Domain Bacteria

Bacteria are the most diverse and widespread prokaryotes and are now classified into multiple kingdoms. Each rod-shaped structure in this photo is a bacterial cell.

(b) Domain Archaea

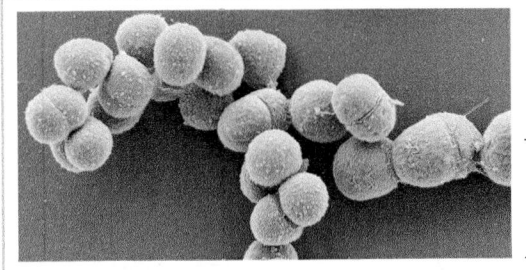

Many of the prokaryotes known as **archaea** live in Earth's extreme environments, such as salty lakes and boiling hot springs. Domain Archaea includes multiple kingdoms. Each round structure in this photo is an archaeal cell.

(c) Domain Eukarya

▲ **Kingdom Plantae** consists of terrestrial multicellular eukaryotes (land plants) that carry out photosynthesis, the conversion of light energy to the chemical energy in food.

▶ **Kingdom Fungi** is defined in part by the nutritional mode of its members (such as this mushroom), which absorb nutrients from outside their bodies.

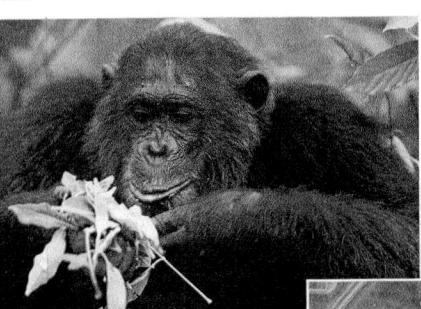

◀ **Kingdom Animalia** consists of multicellular eukaryotes that ingest other organisms.

▶ **Protists** are mostly unicellular eukaryotes and some relatively simple multicellular relatives. Pictured here is an assortment of protists inhabiting pond water. Scientists are currently debating how to classify protists in a way that accurately reflects their evolutionary relationships.

Fungi, and Animalia. These three kingdoms are distinguished partly by their modes of nutrition. Plants produce their own sugars and other food molecules by photosynthesis. Fungi absorb dissolved nutrients from their surroundings; many decompose dead organisms and organic wastes (such as leaf litter and animal feces) and absorb nutrients from these sources. Animals obtain food by ingestion, which is the eating and digesting of other organisms. Animalia is, of course, the kingdom to which we belong. But neither animals, plants, nor fungi are as numerous or diverse as the single-celled eukaryotes we call protists. Although protists were once placed in a single kingdom, biologists now realize that they do not form a single natural group of species. And recent evidence shows that some protist groups are more closely related to multicellular eukaryotes such as animals and fungi than they are to each other. Thus, the recent taxonomic trend has been to split the protists into several groups.

Unity in the Diversity of Life

As diverse as life is, it also displays remarkable unity. Earlier we mentioned both the similar skeletons of different vertebrate animals and the universal genetic language of DNA (the genetic code). In fact, similarities between organisms are evident at all levels of the biological hierarchy. For example, unity is obvious in many features of cell structure (Figure 1.16).

How can we account for life's dual nature of unity and diversity? The process of evolution, explained next, illuminates both the similarities and differences in the world of life and introduces another dimension of biology: historical time.

Charles Darwin and the Theory of Natural Selection

The history of life, as documented by fossils and other evidence, is the saga of a changing Earth billions of years old, inhabited by an evolving cast of living forms (Figure 1.17). This evolutionary view of life came into sharp focus in November 1859, when Charles Robert Darwin published one of the most important and influential books ever written. Entitled *On the Origin of Species by Means of Natural Selection*, Darwin's book was an immediate bestseller and soon made "Darwinism," as it was dubbed at the time, almost synonymous with the concept of evolution (Figure 1.18).

The Origin of Species articulated two main points. The first point was that contemporary species arose from a succession of ancestors, an idea that Darwin supported with a large amount of evidence. (We will discuss the evidence for evolution in detail in Chapter 22.) Darwin called this evolutionary history of species "descent with modification." It was an insightful phrase, as it captured the duality of life's unity and diversity—unity in the kinship among species that descended

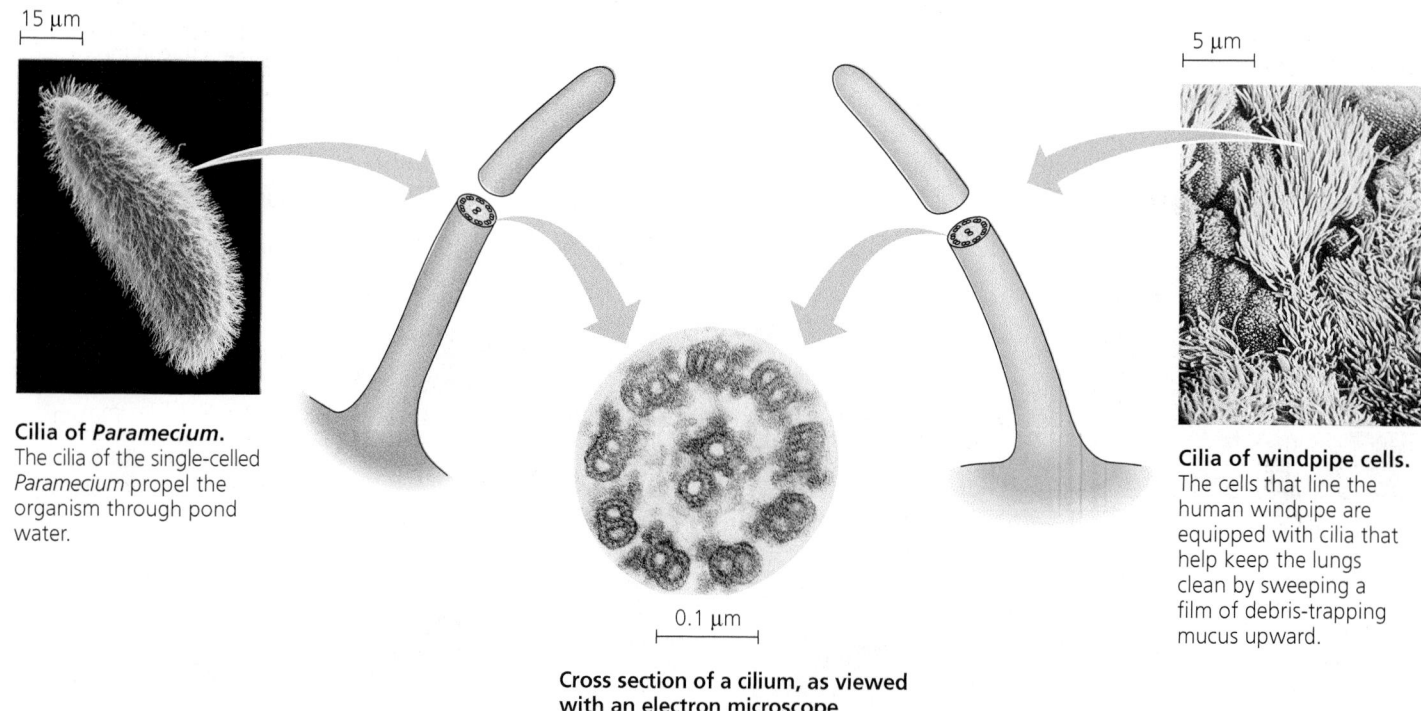

Cilia of *Paramecium*.
The cilia of the single-celled *Paramecium* propel the organism through pond water.

15 µm

0.1 µm

Cross section of a cilium, as viewed with an electron microscope

5 µm

Cilia of windpipe cells.
The cells that line the human windpipe are equipped with cilia that help keep the lungs clean by sweeping a film of debris-trapping mucus upward.

▲ Figure 1.16 **An example of unity underlying the diversity of life: the architecture of cilia in eukaryotes.** Cilia (singular, *cilium*) are extensions of cells that function in locomotion. They occur in eukaryotes as diverse as *Paramecium* and humans. Even organisms so different share a common architecture for their cilia, which have an elaborate system of tubules that is striking in cross-sectional views.

▲ Figure 1.17 **Digging into the past.** Paleontologists carefully excavate the hind leg of a long-necked dinosaur (*Rapetosaurus krausei*) from rocks in Madagascar.

from common ancestors, diversity in the modifications that evolved as species branched from their common ancestors (Figure 1.19). Darwin's second main point was a proposed mechanism for descent with modification. He called this evolutionary mechanism "natural selection."

Darwin synthesized his theory of natural selection from observations that by themselves were neither new nor profound. Others had the pieces of the puzzle, but Darwin saw how they fit together. He started with the following three observations from nature: First, individuals in a population vary in their traits, many of which seem to be heritable (passed on from parents to offspring). Second, a population can produce far more offspring than can survive to produce offspring of their own. With more individuals than the environment is able to support, competition is inevitable. Third, species generally suit their environments—in other words, they

▲ Figure 1.18 **Charles Darwin as a young man.**

are adapted to their environments. For instance, a common adaptation among birds with tough seeds as their major food source is that they have especially strong beaks.

Darwin made inferences from these observations to arrive at his theory of evolution. He reasoned that individuals with inherited traits that are best suited to the local environment are more likely to survive and reproduce than less suited individuals. Over many generations, a higher and higher proportion of individuals in a population will have the advantageous traits. Evolution occurs as the unequal reproductive success of individuals ultimately leads to adaptation to their environment, as long as the environment remains the same.

Darwin called this mechanism of evolutionary adaptation **natural selection** because the natural environment "selects" for the propagation of certain traits among naturally occurring variant traits in the population. The example

◀ Figure 1.19 **Unity and diversity in the orchid family.** These three orchids are variations on a common floral theme. For example, each of these flowers has a liplike petal that helps attract pollinating insects and provides a landing platform for the pollinators.

① Population with varied inherited traits

② Elimination of individuals with certain traits

③ Reproduction of survivors

④ Increasing frequency of traits that enhance survival and reproductive success

▲ **Figure 1.20 Natural selection.** This imaginary beetle population has colonized a locale where the soil has been blackened by a recent brush fire. Initially, the population varies extensively in the inherited coloration of the individuals, from very light gray to charcoal. For hungry birds that prey on the beetles, it is easiest to spot the beetles that are lightest in color.

in **Figure 1.20** illustrates the ability of natural selection to "edit" a population's heritable variations in color. We see the products of natural selection in the exquisite adaptations of various organisms to the special circumstances of their way of life and their environment. The wings of the bat shown in **Figure 1.21** are an excellent example of adaptation.

The Tree of Life

Take another look at the skeletal architecture of the bat's wings in Figure 1.21. These forelimbs, though adapted for flight, actually have all the same bones, joints, nerves, and blood vessels found in other limbs as diverse as the human arm, the horse's foreleg, and the whale's flipper. Indeed, all mammalian forelimbs are anatomical variations of a common architecture, much as the flowers in Figure 1.19 are variations on an underlying "orchid" theme. Such examples of kinship connect life's unity in diversity to the Darwinian

concept of descent with modification. In this view, the unity of mammalian limb anatomy reflects inheritance of that structure from a common ancestor—the "prototype" mammal from which all other mammals descended. The diversity of mammalian forelimbs results from modification by natural selection operating over millions of generations in different environmental contexts. Fossils and other evidence corroborate anatomical unity in supporting this view of mammalian descent from a common ancestor.

Darwin proposed that natural selection, by its cumulative effects over long periods of time, could cause an ancestral species to give rise to two or more descendant species. This could occur, for example, if one population fragmented into several subpopulations isolated in different environments. In these separate arenas of natural selection, one species could gradually radiate into multiple species as the geographically isolated populations adapted over many generations to different sets of environmental factors.

The "family tree" of 14 finches in **Figure 1.22** illustrates a famous example of adaptive radiation of new species from a common ancestor. Darwin collected specimens of these birds during his 1835 visit to the remote Galápagos Islands, 900 kilometers (km) off the Pacific coast of South America. These relatively young, volcanic islands are home to many species of plants and animals found nowhere else in the world, though most Galápagos organisms are clearly related to species on the South American mainland. After volcanism built the Galápagos several million years ago, finches probably diversified on the various islands from an ancestral finch species that by chance reached the archipelago from elsewhere. (Once thought to have originated on the mainland of South America like many Galápagos organisms, the ancestral finches are now thought to have come from the West Indies—islands of the Caribbean that were once much closer to the Galápagos than they are now.)

▲ **Figure 1.21 Evolutionary adaptation.** Bats, the only mammals capable of active flight, have wings with webbing between extended "fingers." In the Darwinian view of life, such adaptations are refined over time by natural selection.

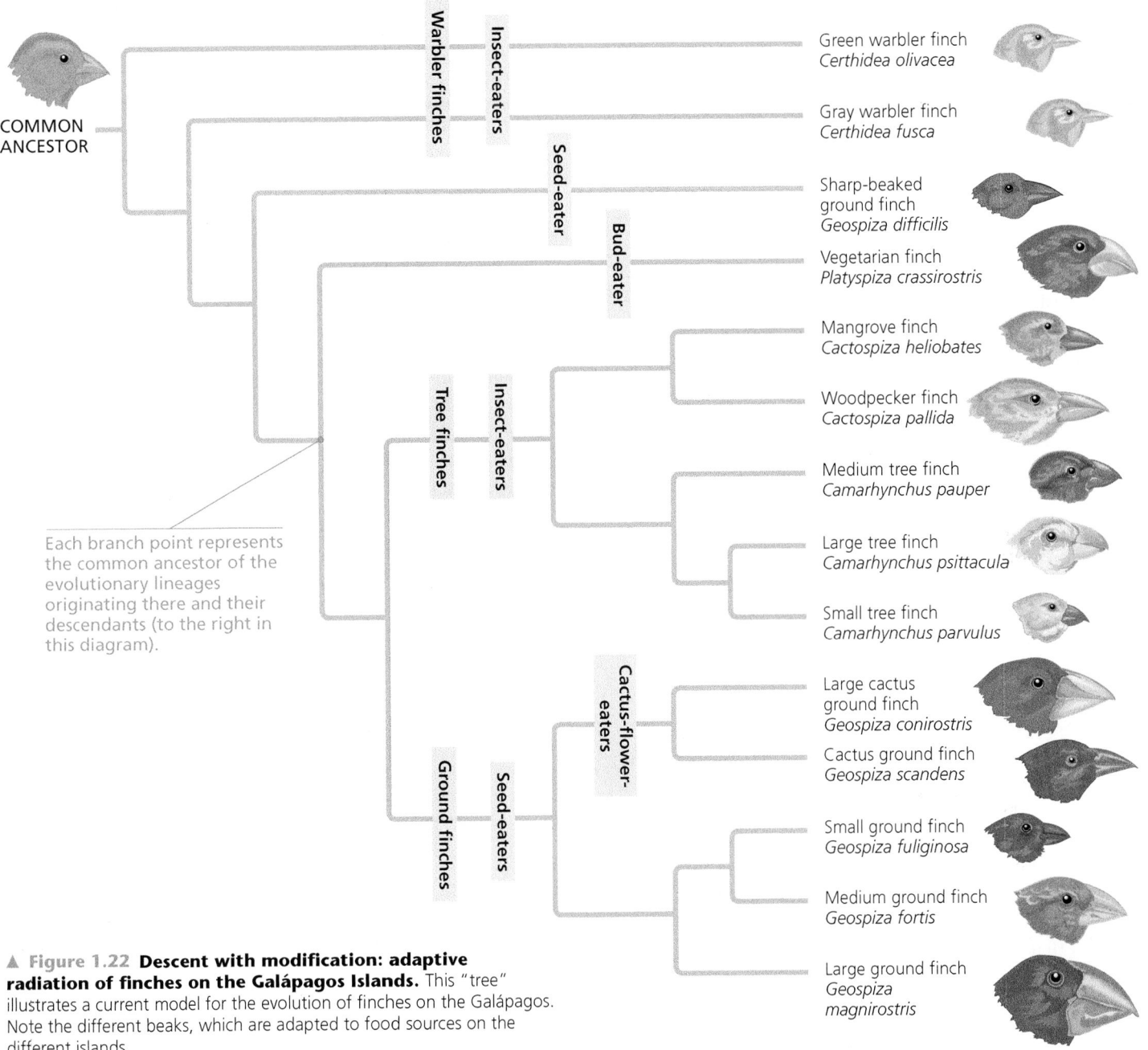

▲ **Figure 1.22 Descent with modification: adaptive radiation of finches on the Galápagos Islands.** This "tree" illustrates a current model for the evolution of finches on the Galápagos. Note the different beaks, which are adapted to food sources on the different islands.

Years after Darwin's collection of Galápagos finches, researchers began to sort out the relationships among the finch species, first from anatomical and geographic data and more recently with the help of DNA sequence comparisons.

Biologists' diagrams of evolutionary relationships generally take treelike forms, though today biologists usually turn the trees sideways as in Figure 1.22. Tree diagrams make sense: Just as an individual has a genealogy that can be diagrammed as a family tree, each species is one twig of a branching tree of life extending back in time through ancestral species more and more remote. Species that are very similar, such as the Galápagos finches, share a common ancestor at a relatively recent branch point on the tree of life. But through an ancestor that lived much farther back in time, finches are related to sparrows, hawks, penguins, and all other birds. And birds, mammals, and all other vertebrates share a common ancestor even more ancient. We find evidence of still broader relationships in such similarities as the identical construction of all eukaryotic cilia (see Figure 1.16). Trace life back far enough, and there are only fossils of the primeval prokaryotes that inhabited Earth over 3.5 billion years ago. We can recognize their vestiges in our own cells—in the universal genetic code, for example. All of life is connected through its long evolutionary history.

1. How is a mailing address analogous to biology's hierarchical taxonomic system?
2. Explain why "editing" is an appropriate metaphor for how natural selection acts on a population's heritable variation.
3. **WHAT IF?** The three domains you learned about in Concept 1.2 can be represented in the tree of life as the three main branches, with three subbranches on the eukaryotic branch being the kingdoms Plantae, Fungi, and Animalia. What if fungi and animals are more closely related to each other than either of these kingdoms is to plants—as recent evidence strongly suggests? Draw a simple branching pattern that symbolizes the proposed relationship between these three eukaryotic kingdoms.

For suggested answers, see Appendix A.

CONCEPT 1.3

In studying nature, scientists make observations and then form and test hypotheses

The word *science* is derived from a Latin verb meaning "to know." **Science** is a way of knowing—an approach to understanding the natural world. It developed out of our curiosity about ourselves, other life-forms, our planet, and the universe. Striving to understand seems to be one of our basic urges.

At the heart of science is **inquiry**, a search for information and explanation, often focusing on specific questions. Inquiry drove Darwin to seek answers in nature for how species adapt to their environments. And today inquiry drives the genomic analyses that are helping us understand biological unity and diversity at the molecular level. In fact, the inquisitive mind is the engine that drives all progress in biology.

There is no formula for successful scientific inquiry, no single scientific method with a rule book that researchers must rigidly follow. As in all quests, science includes elements of challenge, adventure, and luck, along with careful planning, reasoning, creativity, cooperation, competition, patience, and the persistence to overcome setbacks. Such diverse elements of inquiry make science far less structured than most people realize. That said, it is possible to distill certain characteristics that help to distinguish science from other ways of describing and explaining nature.

Scientists attempt to understand how natural phenomena work using a process of inquiry that includes making observations, forming logical hypotheses, and testing them. The process is necessarily repetitive: In testing a hypothesis, more observations may force formation of a new hypothesis or revision of the original one, and further testing. In this way,

scientists circle closer and closer to their best estimation of the laws governing nature.

Making Observations

In the course of their work, scientists describe natural structures and processes as accurately as possible through careful observation and analysis of data. The observations are often valuable in their own right. For example, a series of detailed observations have shaped our understanding of cell structure, and another set of observations are currently expanding our databases of genomes of diverse species.

Types of Data

Observation is the use of the senses to gather information, either directly or indirectly with the help of tools such as microscopes that extend our senses. Recorded observations are called **data**. Put another way, data are items of information on which scientific inquiry is based.

The term *data* implies numbers to many people. But some data are *qualitative*, often in the form of recorded descriptions rather than numerical measurements. For example, Jane Goodall spent decades recording her observations of chimpanzee behavior during field research in a Tanzanian jungle (**Figure 1.23**). She also documented her observations with photographs and movies. Along with these qualitative data, Goodall also enriched the field of animal behavior with volumes of *quantitative* data, which are generally recorded as

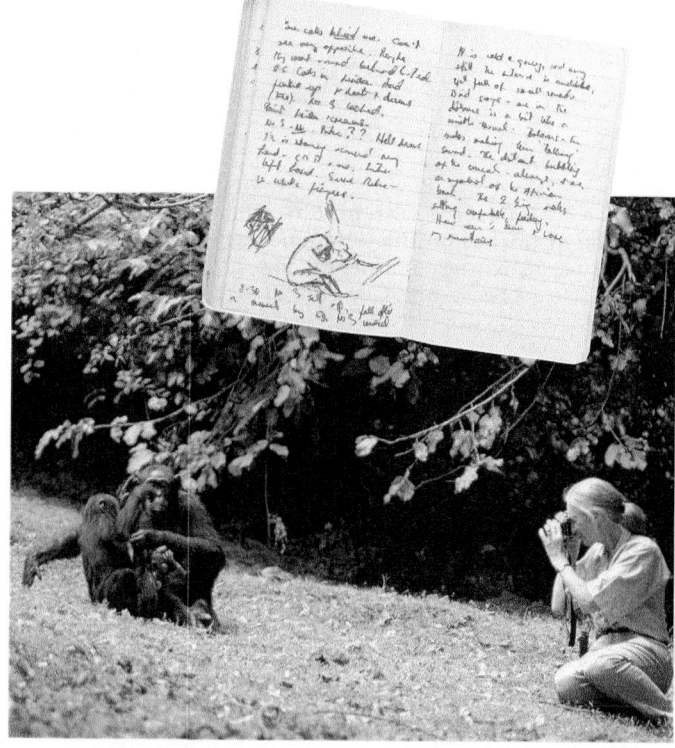

▲ Figure 1.23 **Jane Goodall collecting qualitative data on chimpanzee behavior.** Goodall recorded her observations in field notebooks, often with sketches of the animals' behavior.

measurements. Skim through any of the scientific journals in your college library, and you'll see many examples of quantitative data organized into tables and graphs.

Inductive Reasoning

Collecting and analyzing observations can lead to important conclusions based on a type of logic called **inductive reasoning**. Through induction, we derive generalizations from a large number of specific observations. "The sun always rises in the east" is an example. And so is "All organisms are made of cells." The latter generalization, part of the so-called cell theory, was based on two centuries of microscopic observations by biologists of cells in diverse biological specimens. Careful observations and data analyses, along with the generalizations reached by induction, are fundamental to our understanding of nature.

Forming and Testing Hypotheses

Observations and inductive reasoning stimulate us to seek natural causes and explanations for those observations. What *caused* the diversification of finches on the Galápagos Islands? What *causes* the roots of a plant seedling to grow downward and the leaf-bearing shoot to grow upward? What *explains* the generalization that the sun always rises in the east? In science, such inquiry usually involves the proposing and testing of hypothetical explanations—that is, hypotheses.

The Role of Hypotheses in Inquiry

In science, a **hypothesis** is a tentative answer to a well-framed question—an explanation on trial. It is usually a rational accounting for a set of observations, based on the available data and guided by inductive reasoning. A scientific hypothesis leads to predictions that can be tested by making additional observations or by performing experiments.

We all use hypotheses in solving everyday problems. Let's say, for example, that your flashlight fails during a camp-out. That's an observation. The question is obvious: Why doesn't the flashlight work? Two reasonable hypotheses based on your experience are that (1) the batteries in the flashlight are dead or (2) the bulb is burnt out. Each of these alternative hypotheses leads to predictions you can test with experiments. For example, the dead-battery hypothesis predicts that replacing the batteries will fix the problem. **Figure 1.24** diagrams this campground inquiry. Of course, we rarely dissect our thought processes this way when we are solving a problem using hypotheses, predictions, and experiments. But the hypothesis-based nature of science clearly has its origins in the human tendency to figure things out by trial and error.

Deductive Reasoning and Hypothesis Testing

A type of logic called deduction is built into the use of hypotheses in science. Deduction contrasts with induction,

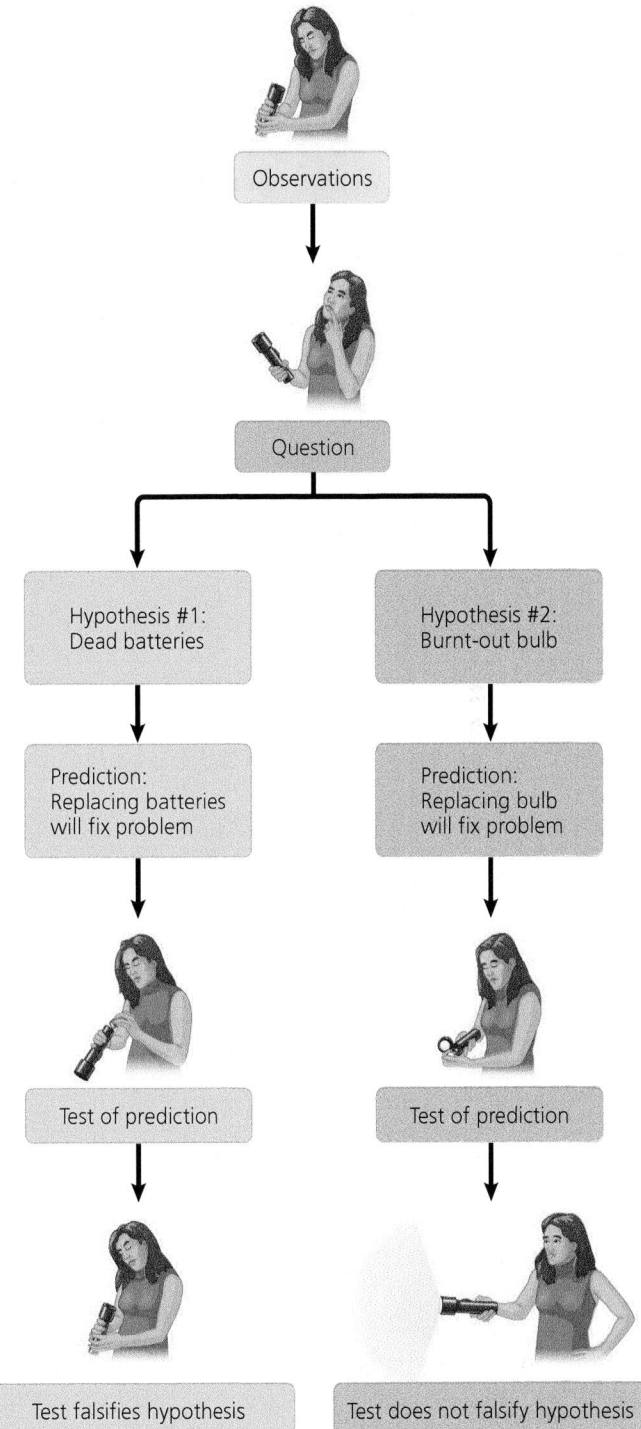

▲ Figure 1.24 **A campground example of hypothesis-based inquiry.**

which, remember, is reasoning from a set of specific observations to reach a general conclusion—a process that feeds into hypothesis formation. **Deductive reasoning** is generally used after the hypothesis has been developed and involves logic that flows in the opposite direction, from the general to the specific. From general premises, we extrapolate to the specific results we should expect if the premises are true. If all organisms are made of cells (premise 1), and humans are organisms (premise 2), then humans are composed of cells (deductive prediction about a specific case).

When using hypotheses in the scientific process, deductions usually take the form of predictions of experimental or observational results that will be found if a particular hypothesis (premise) is correct. We then test the hypothesis by carrying out the experiments or observations to see whether or not the results are as predicted. This deductive testing takes the form of "*If . . . then*" logic. In the case of the flashlight example: *If* the dead-battery hypothesis is correct and you replace the batteries with new ones, *then* the flashlight should work.

The flashlight inquiry demonstrates a key point about the use of hypotheses in science: that the initial observations may give rise to multiple hypotheses. The ideal is to design experiments to test all these candidate explanations. In addition to the two explanations tested in Figure 1.24, for instance, another of the many possible alternative hypotheses is that *both* the batteries *and* the bulb are bad. What does this hypothesis predict about the outcome of the experiments in Figure 1.24? What additional experiment would you design to test this hypothesis of multiple malfunctions?

We can mine the flashlight scenario for yet another important lesson about the scientific inquiry process. The burnt-out bulb hypothesis stands out as the most likely explanation, but notice that the testing supports that hypothesis *not* by proving that it is correct, but rather by not eliminating it through falsification (proving it false). Perhaps the first bulb was simply loose, so it wasn't making electrical contact, and the new bulb was inserted correctly. We could attempt to falsify the burnt-out bulb hypothesis by trying another experiment—removing the original bulb and carefully reinstalling it. If the flashlight still doesn't work, the burnt-out bulb hypothesis can stand. But no amount of experimental testing can *prove* a hypothesis beyond a shadow of doubt, because it is impossible to test *all* alternative hypotheses. A hypothesis gains credibility by surviving multiple attempts to falsify it while alternative hypotheses are eliminated (falsified) by testing.

Questions That Can and Cannot Be Addressed by Science

Scientific inquiry is a powerful way to learn about nature, but there are limitations to the kinds of questions it can answer. The flashlight example illustrates two important qualities of scientific hypotheses. First, a hypothesis must be *testable*; there must be some way to check the validity of the idea. Second, a hypothesis must be *falsifiable*; there must be some observation or experiment that could reveal if such an idea is actually *not* true. The hypothesis that dead batteries are the sole cause of the broken flashlight could be falsified by replacing the old batteries with new ones and finding that the flashlight still doesn't work.

Not all hypotheses meet the criteria of science: You wouldn't be able to devise a test to falsify the hypothesis that invisible campground ghosts are fooling with your flashlight! Because science requires natural explanations for natural phenomena, it can neither support nor falsify hypotheses that angels, ghosts, or spirits, whether benevolent or evil, cause storms, rainbows, illnesses, and cures. Such supernatural explanations are simply outside the bounds of science, as are religious matters, which are issues of personal faith.

The Flexibility of the Scientific Method

The flashlight example of Figure 1.24 traces an idealized process of inquiry called *the scientific method*. We can recognize the elements of this process in most of the research articles published by scientists, but rarely in such structured form. Very few scientific inquiries adhere rigidly to the sequence of steps prescribed by the "textbook" scientific method. For example, a scientist may start to design an experiment, but then backtrack upon realizing that more preliminary observations are necessary. In other cases, puzzling observations simply don't prompt well-defined questions until other research places those observations in a new context. For example, Darwin collected specimens of the Galápagos finches, but it wasn't until years later, as the idea of natural selection began to gel, that biologists began asking key questions about the history of those birds.

Moreover, scientists sometimes redirect their research when they realize they have been asking the wrong question. For example, in the early 20th century, much research on schizophrenia and manic-depressive disorder (now called bipolar disorder) got sidetracked by focusing too much on the question of how life experiences might cause these serious maladies. Research on the causes and potential treatments became more productive when it was refocused on questions of how certain chemical imbalances in the brain contribute to mental illness. To be fair, we acknowledge that such twists and turns in scientific inquiry become more evident with the advantage of historical perspective.

It is important for you to get some experience with the power of the scientific method—by using it for some of the laboratory inquiries in your biology course, for example. But it is also important to avoid stereotyping science as a lock-step adherence to this method.

A Case Study in Scientific Inquiry: Investigating Mimicry in Snake Populations

Now that we have highlighted the key features of scientific inquiry—making observations and forming and testing hypotheses—you should be able to recognize these features in a case study of actual scientific research.

The story begins with a set of observations and inductive generalizations. Many poisonous animals are brightly colored, often with distinctive patterns that stand out against the background. This is called *warning coloration* because it apparently signals "dangerous species" to potential predators. But there are also mimics. These imposters look like poisonous species but are actually harmless. A question that follows from these observations is: What is the function of such mimicry? A reasonable hypothesis is that the "deception" is an evolutionary adaptation that reduces the harmless animal's risk of being eaten because predators mistake it for the poisonous species. This hypothesis was first formulated by British scientist Henry Bates in 1862.

As obvious as this hypothesis may seem, it has been relatively difficult to test, especially with field experiments. But in 2001, biologists David and Karin Pfennig, of the University of North Carolina, along with William Harcombe, an undergraduate, designed a simple but elegant set of field experiments to test Bates's mimicry hypothesis.

The team investigated a case of mimicry among snakes that live in North and South Carolina (Figure 1.25). A venomous snake called the eastern coral snake has warning coloration: bold, alternating rings of red, yellow (or white), and black. (The word *venomous* is used when a poisonous species delivers their poison actively, by stinging, stabbing, or biting.) Predators rarely attack these coral snakes. It is unlikely that the predators learn this avoidance behavior by trial and

error, as a first encounter with a coral snake is usually deadly. In areas where coral snakes live, natural selection has apparently increased the frequency of predators that have inherited an instinctive avoidance of the coral snake's coloration. A nonvenomous snake named the scarlet kingsnake mimics the ringed coloration of the coral snake.

Both types of snakes live in the Carolinas, but the kingsnakes' geographic range also extends into regions where no coral snakes are found (see Figure 1.25). The geographic distribution of the snakes made it possible to test the key prediction of the mimicry hypothesis. Avoiding snakes with warning coloration is an adaptation we expect to be present only in predator populations that evolved in areas where the venomous coral snakes are present. Therefore, mimicry should help protect kingsnakes from predators *only in regions where coral snakes also live*. The mimicry hypothesis predicts that predators adapted to the warning coloration of coral snakes will attack kingsnakes less frequently than will predators in areas where coral snakes are absent.

Field Experiments with Artificial Snakes

To test the prediction, Harcombe made hundreds of artificial snakes out of wire covered with plasticine. He fashioned two versions of fake snakes: an *experimental group* with the red, black, and white ring pattern of kingsnakes and a *control group* of plain brown artificial snakes as a basis of comparison (Figure 1.26).

The researchers placed equal numbers of the two types of artificial snakes in field sites throughout North and South

Scarlet kingsnake (nonvenomous)

Key	
	Range of scarlet kingsnake only
	Overlapping ranges of scarlet kingsnake and eastern coral snake

North Carolina

South Carolina

Eastern coral snake (venomous)

Scarlet kingsnake (nonvenomous)

▲ **Figure 1.25 The geographic ranges of a venomous snake and its mimic.** The scarlet kingsnake (*Lampropeltis triangulum*) mimics the warning coloration of the venomous eastern coral snake (*Micrurus fulvius*).

(a) Artificial kingsnake

(b) Brown artificial snake that has been attacked

▲ **Figure 1.26 Artificial snakes used in field experiments to test the mimicry hypothesis.** A bear has chewed on the brown artificial snake in **(b)**.

Carolina, including the region where coral snakes are absent. After four weeks, the scientists retrieved the fake snakes and recorded how many had been attacked by looking for bite or claw marks. The most common predators were foxes, coyotes, and raccoons, but black bears also attacked some of the artificial snakes (see Figure 1.26b).

The data fit the key prediction of the mimicry hypothesis. Compared to the brown artificial snakes, the ringed artificial snakes were attacked by predators less frequently only in field sites within the geographic range of the venomous coral snakes. **Figure 1.27** summarizes the field experiments that the researchers carried out. This figure also introduces a format we will use throughout the book for other examples of biological inquiry.

Experimental Controls and Repeatability

The snake mimicry experiment is an example of a **controlled experiment**, one that is designed to compare an experimental group (the artificial kingsnakes, in this case) with a control group (the brown artificial snakes). Ideally, the experimental and control groups differ only in the one factor the experiment is designed to test—in our example, the effect of the snakes' coloration on the behavior of predators. Without the control group, the researchers would not have been able to rule out other factors as causes of the more frequent attacks on the artificial kingsnakes—such as different numbers of predators or different temperatures in the different test areas. The clever experimental design left coloration as the only factor that could account for the low predation rate on the artificial kingsnakes placed within the range of coral snakes. It was not the absolute number of attacks on the artificial kingsnakes that counted, but the difference between that number and the number of attacks on the brown snakes.

A common misconception is that the term *controlled experiment* means that scientists control the experimental environment to keep everything constant except the one variable being tested. But that's impossible in field research and not realistic even in highly regulated laboratory environments. Researchers usually "control" unwanted variables not by *eliminating* them through environmental regulation, but by *canceling out* their effects by using control groups.

Another hallmark of science is that the observations and experimental results must be repeatable. Observations that can't be verified may be interesting or even entertaining, but they cannot count as evidence in scientific inquiry. The headlines of supermarket tabloids would have you believe that humans are occasionally born with the head of a dog and that some of your classmates are extraterrestrials. The unconfirmed eyewitness accounts and the computer-rigged photos are amusing but unconvincing. In science, evidence from observations and experiments is only convincing if it stands up to the criterion of repeatability. The scientists who investigated snake mimicry in the Carolinas obtained similar data when they

▼ **Figure 1.27** | **INQUIRY**

Does the presence of venomous coral snakes affect predation rates on their mimics, kingsnakes?

EXPERIMENT David Pfennig and his colleagues made artificial snakes to test a prediction of the mimicry hypothesis: that kingsnakes benefit from mimicking the warning coloration of venomous coral snakes only in regions where coral snakes are present. The researchers placed equal numbers of artificial kingsnakes (experimental group) and brown artificial snakes (control group) at 14 field sites, half in the area the two snakes cohabit and half in the area where coral snakes are absent. The researchers recovered the artificial snakes after four weeks and tabulated predation data based on teeth and claw marks on the snakes.

RESULTS In field sites where coral snakes are absent, most attacks were on artificial kingsnakes. Where coral snakes were present, most attacks were on brown artificial snakes.

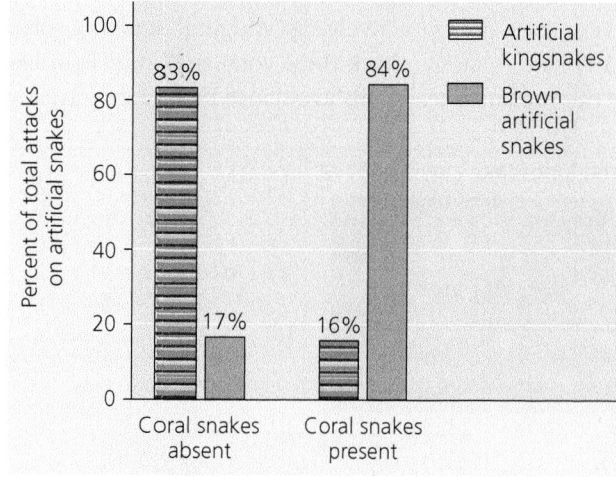

CONCLUSION The field experiments support the mimicry hypothesis by not falsifying the prediction, which was that mimicking coral snakes is effective only in areas where coral snakes are present. The experiments also tested an alternative hypothesis: that predators generally avoid all snakes with brightly colored rings. That hypothesis was falsified by the data showing that in areas without coral snakes, the ringed coloration failed to repel predators. (The fake kingsnakes may have been attacked more often in those areas because their bright pattern made them easier to spot than the brown fakes.)

SOURCE D. W. Pfennig, W. R. Harcombe, and K. S. Pfennig, Frequency-dependent Batesian mimicry, *Nature* 410:323 (2001).

INQUIRY IN ACTION Read and analyze the original paper in *Inquiry in Action: Interpreting Scientific Papers*.

(MB) See the related Experimental Inquiry Tutorial in MasteringBiology.

WHAT IF? What experimental results would you predict if predators throughout the Carolinas avoided all snakes with brightly colored ring patterns?

repeated their experiments with different species of coral snakes and kingsnakes in Arizona. And *you* should be able to obtain similar results if you were to repeat the snake experiments.

Theories in Science

"It's just a theory!" Our everyday use of the term *theory* often implies an untested speculation. But the term *theory* has a different meaning in science. What is a scientific theory, and how is it different from a hypothesis or from mere speculation?

First, a scientific **theory** is much broader in scope than a hypothesis. *This* is a hypothesis: "Mimicking the coloration of venomous snakes is an adaptation that protects nonvenomous snakes from predators." But *this* is a theory: "Evolutionary adaptations arise by natural selection." Darwin's theory of natural selection accounts for an enormous diversity of adaptations, including mimicry.

Second, a theory is general enough to spin off many new, specific hypotheses that can be tested. For example, two researchers at Princeton University, Peter and Rosemary Grant, were motivated by the theory of natural selection to test the specific hypothesis that the beaks of Galápagos finches evolve in response to changes in the types of available food. (Their results supported their hypothesis; see p. 469.)

And third, compared to any one hypothesis, a theory is generally supported by a much greater body of evidence. Those theories that become widely adopted in science (such as the theory of natural selection) explain a great diversity of observations and are supported by a vast accumulation of evidence. In fact, scrutiny of theories continues through testing of the specific, falsifiable hypotheses they spawn.

In spite of the body of evidence supporting a widely accepted theory, scientists must sometimes modify or even reject theories when new research methods produce results that don't fit. For example, the theory of biological diversity that lumped bacteria and archaea together as a kingdom of prokaryotes began to erode when new methods for comparing cells and molecules made it possible to test some of the hypothetical relationships between organisms that were based on the theory. If there is "truth" in science, it is conditional, based on the preponderance of available evidence.

CONCEPT CHECK 1.3

1. Contrast inductive reasoning with deductive reasoning.
2. In the snake mimicry experiment, what is the variable?
3. Why is natural selection called a theory?
4. **WHAT IF?** Suppose you extended the snake mimicry experiment to an area of Virginia where neither type of snake is known to live. What results would you predict at your field site?

For suggested answers, see Appendix A.

CONCEPT 1.4

Science benefits from a cooperative approach and diverse viewpoints

Movies and cartoons sometimes portray scientists as loners working in isolated labs. In reality, science is an intensely social activity. Most scientists work in teams, which often include both graduate and undergraduate students **(Figure 1.28)**. And to succeed in science, it helps to be a good communicator. Research results have no impact until shared with a community of peers through seminars, publications, and websites.

Building on the Work of Others

The great scientist Sir Isaac Newton once said: "To explain all nature is too difficult a task for any one man or even for any one age. 'Tis much better to do a little with certainty, and leave the rest for others that come after you. . . ." Anyone who becomes a scientist, driven by curiosity about how nature works, is sure to benefit greatly from the rich storehouse of discoveries by others who have come before.

Scientists working in the same research field often check one another's claims by attempting to confirm observations or repeat experiments. If experimental results cannot be repeated by scientific colleagues, this failure may reflect some underlying weakness in the original claim, which will then have to be revised. In this sense, science polices itself. Integrity and adherence to high professional standards in reporting results are central to the scientific endeavor. After all, the validity of experimental data is key to designing further lines of inquiry.

It is not unusual for several scientists to converge on the same research question. Some scientists enjoy the challenge of being first with an important discovery or key experiment, while others derive more satisfaction from cooperating with fellow scientists working on the same problem.

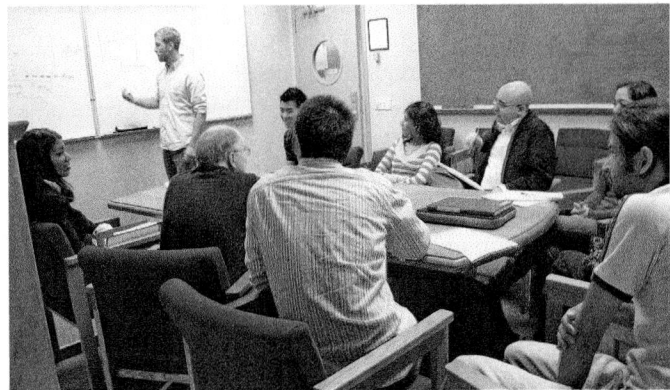

▲ **Figure 1.28 Science as a social process.** In laboratory meetings, lab members help each other interpret data, troubleshoot experiments, and plan future lines of inquiry.

Cooperation is facilitated when scientists use the same organism. Often it is a widely used **model organism**—a species that is easy to grow in the lab and lends itself particularly well to the questions being investigated. Because all organisms are evolutionarily related, lessons learned from a model organism are often widely applicable. For example, genetic studies of the fruit fly *Drosophila melanogaster* have taught us a lot about how genes work in other species, including humans. Some other popular model organisms are the mustard plant *Arabidopsis thaliana*, the soil worm *Caenorhabditis elegans*, the zebrafish *Danio rerio*, the mouse *Mus musculus*, and the bacterium *Escherichia coli*. As you read through this book, note the many contributions that these and other model organisms have made to the study of life.

Biologists may come at interesting questions from different angles. Some biologists focus on ecosystems, while others study natural phenomena at the level of organisms or cells. This book is divided into units that look at biology from different levels. Yet any given problem can be addressed from many perspectives, which in fact complement each other.

As a beginning biology student, you can benefit from making connections between the different levels of biology. You can begin to develop this skill by noticing when certain topics crop up again and again in different units. One such topic is sickle-cell disease, a well-understood genetic condition that is prevalent among native inhabitants of Africa and other warm regions and their descendants. Another topic viewed at different levels in this book is global climate change, mentioned earlier in this chapter. Sickle-cell disease and global climate change will appear in several units of the book, each time addressed at a new level. We hope these recurring topics will help you integrate the material you're learning and enhance your enjoyment of biology by helping you keep the "big picture" in mind.

Science, Technology, and Society

The biology community is part of society at large, embedded in the cultural milieu of the times. Some philosophers of science argue that scientists are so influenced by cultural and political values that science is no more objective than other ways of understanding nature. At the other extreme are people who speak of scientific theories as though they were natural laws instead of human interpretations of nature. The reality of science is probably somewhere in between—rarely perfectly objective, but continuously vetted through the expectation that observations and experiments be repeatable and hypotheses be testable and falsifiable.

The relationship of science to society becomes clearer when we add technology to the picture. Though science and technology sometimes employ similar inquiry patterns, their basic goals differ. The goal of science is to understand natural phenomena. In contrast, **technology** generally *applies* scientific knowledge for some specific purpose. Biologists and

▲ **Figure 1.29 DNA technology and crime scene investigation.** In 2008, forensic analysis of DNA samples from a crime scene led to the release of Charles Chatman from prison after he had served nearly 27 years for a rape he didn't commit. The photo shows Judge John Creuzot hugging Mr. Chatman after his conviction was overturned. The details of forensic analysis of DNA will be described in Chapter 20.

other scientists usually speak of "discoveries," while engineers and other technologists more usually speak of "inventions." And the beneficiaries of those inventions include scientists, who put new technology to work in their research. Thus, science and technology are interdependent.

The potent combination of science and technology can have dramatic effects on society. Sometimes, the applications of basic research that turn out to be the most beneficial come out of the blue, from completely unanticipated observations in the course of scientific exploration. For example, discovery of the structure of DNA by Watson and Crick 60 years ago and subsequent achievements in DNA science led to the technologies of DNA manipulation that are transforming applied fields such as medicine, agriculture, and forensics **(Figure 1.29)**. Perhaps Watson and Crick envisioned that their discovery would someday lead to important applications, but it is unlikely that they could have predicted exactly what all those applications would be.

The directions that technology takes depend less on the curiosity that drives basic science than on the current needs and wants of people and on the social environment of the times. Debates about technology center more on "*should* we do it" than "*can* we do it." With advances in technology come difficult choices. For example, under what circumstances is it acceptable to use DNA technology to find out if particular people have genes for hereditary diseases? Should such tests always be voluntary, or are there circumstances when genetic testing should be mandatory? Should insurance companies or employers have access to the information, as they do for many other types of personal health data? These questions are becoming much more urgent as the sequencing of individual genomes becomes quicker and cheaper.

Such ethical issues have as much to do with politics, economics, and cultural values as with science and technology. All citizens—not only professional scientists—have a responsibility to be informed about how science works and about the potential benefits and risks of technology. The relationship between science, technology, and society increases the significance and value of any biology course.

The Value of Diverse Viewpoints in Science

Many of the technological innovations with the most profound impact on human society originated in settlements along trade routes, where a rich mix of different cultures ignited new ideas. For example, the printing press, which helped spread knowledge to all social classes and ultimately led to the book in your hands, was invented by the German Johannes Gutenberg around 1440. This invention relied on several innovations from China, including paper and ink. Paper traveled along trade routes from China to Baghdad, where technology was developed for its mass production. This technology then migrated to Europe, as did water-based ink from China, which was modified by Gutenberg to become oil-based ink. We have the cross-fertilization of diverse cultures to thank for the printing press, and the same can be said for other important inventions.

Along similar lines, science stands to gain much from embracing a diversity of backgrounds and viewpoints among its practitioners. But just how diverse a population are scientists in relation to gender, race, ethnicity, and other attributes?

The scientific community reflects the cultural standards and behaviors of society at large. It is therefore not surprising that until recently, women and certain minorities have faced huge obstacles in their pursuit to become professional scientists in many countries around the world. Over the past 50 years, changing attitudes about career choices have increased the proportion of women in biology and some other sciences, so that now women constitute roughly half of undergraduate biology majors and biology Ph.D. students. The pace has been slow at higher levels in the profession, however, and women and many racial and ethnic groups are still significantly underrepresented in many branches of science. This lack of diversity hampers the progress of science. The more voices that are heard at the table, the more robust, valuable, and productive the scientific interchange will be. The authors of this textbook welcome all students to the community of biologists, wishing you the joys and satisfactions of this very exciting and satisfying field of science—biology.

CONCEPT CHECK 1.4

1. How does science differ from technology?
2. **WHAT IF?** The gene that causes sickle-cell disease is present in a higher percentage of residents of sub-Saharan Africa than it is among those of African descent living in the United States. The presence of this gene provides some protection from malaria, a serious disease that is widespread in sub-Saharan Africa. Discuss an evolutionary process that could account for the different percentages among residents of the two regions.

For suggested answers, see Appendix A.

1 CHAPTER REVIEW

SUMMARY OF KEY CONCEPTS

CONCEPT 1.1

The themes of this book make connections across different areas of biology (pp. 2–11)

- **Theme: New properties emerge at each level in the biological hierarchy**
The hierarchy of life unfolds as follows: biosphere > ecosystem > community > population > organism > organ system > organ > tissue > cell > organelle > molecule > atom. With each step upward from atoms, new properties emerge as a result of interactions among components at the lower levels. In an approach called reductionism, complex systems are broken down to simpler components that are more manageable to study. In **systems biology**, scientists attempt to model the dynamic behavior of whole biological systems based on a study of the interactions among the system's parts.

- **Theme: Organisms interact with other organisms and the physical environment**
Plants take up nutrients from the soil and chemicals from the air and use energy from the sun. Interactions between plants and other organisms result in cycling of chemical nutrients within an ecosystem. One harmful outcome of human interactions with the environment has been global climate change, caused by burning of fossil fuels and increasing atmospheric CO_2.

- **Theme: Life requires energy transfer and transformation**
Energy flows through an ecosystem. All organisms must perform work, which requires energy. Energy from sunlight is converted to chemical energy by producers, which is then passed on to consumers.

- **Theme: Structure and function are correlated at all levels of biological organization**
  The form of a biological structure suits its function and vice versa.

- **Theme: The cell is an organism's basic unit of structure and function**
  The cell is the lowest level of organization that can perform all activities required for life. Cells are either prokaryotic or eukaryotic. **Eukaryotic cells** contain membrane-enclosed organelles, including a DNA-containing nucleus. **Prokaryotic cells** lack such organelles.

- **Theme: The continuity of life is based on heritable information in the form of DNA**
  Genetic information is encoded in the nucleotide sequences of **DNA**. It is DNA that transmits heritable information from parents to offspring. DNA sequences program a cell's protein production by being transcribed into RNA and then translated into specific proteins, a process called **gene expression**. Gene expression also results in RNAs that are not translated into protein but serve other important functions. **Genomics** is the large-scale analysis of the DNA sequences within a species as well as the comparison of sequences between species.

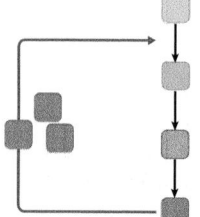

- **Theme: Feedback mechanisms regulate biological systems**
  In **negative feedback**, accumulation of an end product slows the process that makes that product. In **positive feedback**, the end product stimulates the production of more product. Feedback is a type of regulation common to life at all levels, from molecules to ecosystems.

- **Evolution, the Overarching Theme of Biology**
  Evolution accounts for the unity and diversity of life and also for the match of organisms to their environments.

? *Why is evolution considered the core theme of biology?*

CONCEPT 1.2

The Core Theme: Evolution accounts for the unity and diversity of life (pp. 11–18)

- Biologists classify species according to a system of broader and broader groups. Domain **Bacteria** and domain **Archaea** consist of prokaryotes. Domain **Eukarya**, the eukaryotes, includes various groups of protists and the kingdoms Plantae, Fungi, and Animalia. As diverse as life is, there is also evidence of remarkable unity, which is revealed in the similarities between different kinds of organisms.

- Darwin proposed **natural selection** as the mechanism for evolutionary adaptation of populations to their environments.

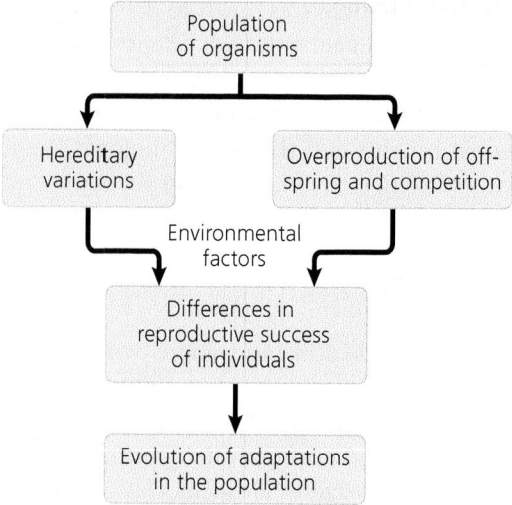

- Each species is one twig of a branching tree of life extending back in time through ancestral species more and more remote. All of life is connected through its long evolutionary history.

? *How could natural selection have led to the evolution of adaptations such as the thick, water-conserving leaves of the mother-of-pearl plant on the cover of this book?*

CONCEPT 1.3

In studying nature, scientists make observations and then form and test hypotheses (pp. 18–23)

- In scientific **inquiry**, scientists make observations (collect **data**) and use **inductive reasoning** to draw a general conclusion, which can be developed into a testable **hypothesis**. **Deductive reasoning** makes predictions that can be used to test hypotheses: If a hypothesis is correct, and we test it, then we can expect the predictions to come true. Hypotheses must be testable and falsifiable; science can address neither the possibility of supernatural phenomena nor the validity of religious beliefs.
- **Controlled experiments**, such as the study investigating mimicry in snake populations, are designed to demonstrate the effect of one variable by testing control groups and experimental groups that differ in only that one variable.
- A scientific **theory** is broad in scope, generates new hypotheses, and is supported by a large body of evidence.

? *What are the roles of inductive and deductive reasoning in the process of scientific inquiry?*

CONCEPT 1.4

Science benefits from a cooperative approach and diverse viewpoints (pp. 23–25)

- Science is a social activity. The work of each scientist builds on the work of others that have come before. Scientists must be able to repeat each other's results, so integrity is key. Biologists approach questions at different levels; their approaches complement each other.
- **Technology** is a method or device that applies scientific knowledge for some specific purpose that affects society. The ultimate impact of basic research is not always immediately obvious.
- Diversity among scientists promotes progress in science.

? *Explain why different approaches and diverse backgrounds among scientists are important.*

LEVEL 1: KNOWLEDGE/COMPREHENSION

1. All the organisms on your campus make up
   a. an ecosystem.
   b. a community.
   c. a population.
   d. an experimental group.
   e. a taxonomic domain.

2. Which of the following is a correct sequence of levels in life's hierarchy, proceeding downward from an individual animal?
   a. brain, organ system, nerve cell, nervous tissue
   b. organ system, nervous tissue, brain
   c. organism, organ system, tissue, cell, organ
   d. nervous system, brain, nervous tissue, nerve cell
   e. organ system, tissue, molecule, cell

3. Which of the following is *not* an observation or inference on which Darwin's theory of natural selection is based?
   a. Poorly adapted individuals never produce offspring.
   b. There is heritable variation among individuals.
   c. Because of overproduction of offspring, there is competition for limited resources.
   d. Individuals whose inherited characteristics best fit them to the environment will generally produce more offspring.
   e. A population can become adapted to its environment over time.

4. Systems biology is mainly an attempt to
   a. analyze genomes from different species.
   b. simplify complex problems by reducing the system into smaller, less complex units.
   c. understand the behavior of entire biological systems.
   d. build high-throughput machines for the rapid acquisition of biological data.
   e. speed up the technological application of scientific knowledge.

5. Protists and bacteria are grouped into different domains because
   a. protists eat bacteria.
   b. bacteria are not made of cells.
   c. protists have a membrane-bounded nucleus, which bacterial cells lack.
   d. bacteria decompose protists.
   e. protists are photosynthetic.

6. Which of the following best demonstrates the unity among all organisms?
   a. matching DNA nucleotide sequences
   b. descent with modification
   c. the structure and function of DNA
   d. natural selection
   e. emergent properties

7. A controlled experiment is one that
   a. proceeds slowly enough that a scientist can make careful records of the results.
   b. tests experimental and control groups in parallel.
   c. is repeated many times to make sure the results are accurate.
   d. keeps all variables constant.
   e. is supervised by an experienced scientist.

8. Which of the following statements best distinguishes hypotheses from theories in science?
   a. Theories are hypotheses that have been proved.
   b. Hypotheses are guesses; theories are correct answers.
   c. Hypotheses usually are relatively narrow in scope; theories have broad explanatory power.
   d. Hypotheses and theories are essentially the same thing.
   e. Theories are proved true; hypotheses are often falsified.

LEVEL 2: APPLICATION/ANALYSIS

9. Which of the following is an example of qualitative data?
   a. The temperature decreased from 20°C to 15°C.
   b. The plant's height is 25 centimeters (cm).
   c. The fish swam in a zigzag motion.
   d. The six pairs of robins hatched an average of three chicks.
   e. The contents of the stomach are mixed every 20 seconds.

10. Which of the following best describes the logic of scientific inquiry?
    a. If I generate a testable hypothesis, tests and observations will support it.
    b. If my prediction is correct, it will lead to a testable hypothesis.
    c. If my observations are accurate, they will support my hypothesis.
    d. If my hypothesis is correct, I can expect certain test results.
    e. If my experiments are set up right, they will lead to a testable hypothesis.

11. **DRAW IT** With rough sketches, draw a biological hierarchy similar to the one in Figure 1.4 but using a coral reef as the ecosystem, a fish as the organism, its stomach as the organ, and DNA as the molecule. Include all levels in the hierarchy.

LEVEL 3: SYNTHESIS/EVALUATION

12. **EVOLUTION CONNECTION**
    A typical prokaryotic cell has about 3,000 genes in its DNA, while a human cell has about 20,500 genes. About 1,000 of these genes are present in both types of cells. Based on your understanding of evolution, explain how such different organisms could have this same subset of genes. What sorts of functions might these shared genes have?

13. **SCIENTIFIC INQUIRY**
    Based on the results of the snake mimicry case study, suggest another hypothesis researchers might use to extend the investigation.

14. **WRITE ABOUT A THEME**
    Evolution In a short essay (100–150 words), discuss Darwin's view of how natural selection resulted in both unity and diversity of life on Earth. Include in your discussion some of his evidence. (See p. xv for a suggested grading rubric. The rubric and tips for writing good essays can also be found in the Study Area of MasteringBiology.)

For selected answers, see Appendix A.

Mastering **BIOLOGY**   www.masteringbiology.com

1. MasteringBiology® Assignments
Experimental Inquiry Tutorial What Can You Learn About the Process of Science from Investigating a Cricket's Chirp?
Tutorial The Scientific Method
Activities The Levels of Life Card Game • Form Fits Function: Cells • Heritable Information: DNA • Introduction to Experimental Design • GraphIt!: An Introduction to Graphing
Questions Student Misconceptions • Reading Quiz • Multiple Choice • End-of-Chapter

2. eText
Read your book online, search, take notes, highlight text, and more.

3. The Study Area
Practice Tests • Cumulative Test • *BioFlix* 3-D Animations • MP3 Tutor Sessions • Videos • Activities • Investigations • Lab Media • Audio Glossary • Word Study Tools • Art

An Interview with

Susan Solomon

Although Susan Solomon is not a biologist, her research as an atmospheric chemist has profound implications for life on Earth. Since earning degrees from the Illinois Institute of Technology and the University of California, Berkeley, Dr. Solomon has been a leader in determining the cause of the Antarctic ozone hole and in producing the 2007 report of the United Nations Intergovernmental Panel on Climate Change (IPCC), which concluded that warming of Earth's climate is unequivocal. These activities have given her a public role in communicating science to policymakers and society at large. In recognition of her scientific accomplishments, she has been awarded the U.S. National Medal of Science, the Blue Planet Prize, and, with Al Gore and the other IPCC members, the Nobel Peace Prize. A member of the U.S. National Academy of Sciences, the European Academy of Sciences, the Academy of Sciences of France, and the Royal Society of the United Kingdom, she works for the National Oceanic and Atmospheric Administration in Boulder, Colorado.

How is Earth's atmosphere important to life?

Life on Earth today could not have evolved without an atmosphere. We all know that we and many other organisms require oxygen (O_2) from the atmosphere, and plants use carbon dioxide (CO_2) to grow. The atmosphere also contains a form of oxygen called ozone that has three oxygen atoms (O_3) instead of two. Organisms would never have been able to leave the ocean and survive on land without the development of an ozone layer in the upper atmosphere. Ozone has the important property of absorbing ultraviolet (UV) light, which would otherwise cause DNA damage. Damage from UV can lead to skin cancer and cataracts; it can also harm many crops and even phytoplankton [small photosynthetic aquatic organisms].

Early in your career, you led an expedition to make measurements of the atmosphere in Antarctica. Tell us about that.

In 1985, the British Antarctic Survey reported a surprising discovery: that the springtime ozone at their station in Antarctica had fallen by 30–50% since the late 1970s, resulting in an "ozone hole"! Peo-

ple had begun to be worried about whether the ozone layer might be vulnerable to changes caused by human activity, but only very minor changes had been expected. In 1986, I had the chance to lead a new Antarctic expedition to help confirm the British data and to study the problem further. We didn't just measure ozone; we measured about a dozen other atmospheric molecules that allowed us to tell *why* the ozone was being destroyed.

What did you find out?

It turns out that the ozone chemistry in Antarctica is extremely different from what it is anywhere else. That's because Antarctica is very cold—it really is the coldest place on Earth. It's so cold that clouds form in its upper stratosphere, about 10–30 kilometers above sea level, and those clouds help convert chemicals from chlorofluorocarbons (CFCs) to ozone-damaging substances.

CFCs are synthetic compounds, made only by humans. They were used back then for a variety of purposes—for example, in refrigeration, as solvents, and as propellants for sprays. Many tons of CFCs were emitted every year. I came up with the idea that the reason an ozone hole developed in Antarctica had to do with chemical reactions that happen between a gas and a surface and that the surface in this case was the small particles that make up those stratospheric clouds. Our data supported this hypothesis. The reactions on those particles make the CFCs hundreds of times more damaging than they would be otherwise. The absence of such clouds in most other parts of the world is why we don't have ozone holes elsewhere, although stratospheric clouds form occasionally in the Arctic and there is significant ozone loss there. Scientists had been concerned since the mid-1970s that human use of CFCs might cause some ozone depletion, but they had expected a loss of only about 3–5% in 100 years.

How do CFCs destroy ozone?

When CFCs arrive at the stratosphere, which typically takes a few years, high-energy radiation up there can break them down, releasing chlorine atoms. The chlorine atoms destroy the ozone catalytically, which means that the atoms don't get used up in the process. So even if only a small amount of CFC is broken down, the tiny bit of chlorine produced can destroy an enormous amount of ozone.

In the U.N. Montreal Protocol of 1987, the nations of the world agreed to stop producing CFCs. However, the CFCs in the atmosphere disappear only very slowly; typically they hang around for 50 to 100 years. What that means is that the CFCs we've already put in the atmosphere will continue to produce an ozone hole for many decades to come, even though we're not using these substances any more. Global emissions are very near zero now, and we're beginning to see the ozone hole slowly diminish. But it will probably not go away completely until around 2060.

While the ozone hole remains, it continues to cause damage. For example, there is evidence that the phytoplankton in the Antarctic Ocean are being affected by increased UV, and the phytoplankton are the base of the main Antarctic food chain: They feed the krill, which feed the fish, which feed the penguins, seals, and whales.

Let's talk about an effect that other atmospheric changes are having—climate change.

There's no question that the planet is getting warmer. We know that, on average, our planet is about 1.4°F (0.8°C) warmer than it was 100 years ago, and this past decade has been the warmest decade in at least the last 100 years. We also know that glaciers worldwide are retreating and that sea level is rising. There's a breadth of scientific data, acquired by different techniques, that tells us that global warming really is unequivocal.

The warming has to do with the greenhouse effect, right?

We're lucky that this planet has a greenhouse effect, because if it didn't, we would be very cold indeed! Our planet is heated by the sun, and much of the infrared radiation (heat) that would otherwise be released back into space is trapped by "greenhouse gases" in the atmosphere. This makes the planet about 30°C hotter than it would be otherwise. But of course anything can be bad if you have too much of it, and what we're doing now is increasing the greenhouse effect of our atmosphere beyond its natural state. If we keep emitting the greenhouse gases that are causing the warming, then we will see some very significant warming in the coming century.

The main greenhouse gas we're adding to the atmosphere is CO_2, from burning fossil fuel and to a lesser extent deforestation. We have increased the atmospheric concentration of CO_2 by about 30% compared to any value that has been found for the last 800,000 years. This has been determined by digging up ice cores in Antarctica and measuring the gases in the air bubbles trapped in the ice. So we know that we have perturbed the atmosphere in a way that the planet hasn't seen in at least 800,000 years.

The CFCs we discussed earlier are actually the third most important greenhouse gas at present, after CO_2 and methane. Pound for pound, CFCs are much more potent as greenhouse gases than CO_2. The phase-out of CFCs since the signing of the Montreal Protocol has not only avoided a lot of ozone destruction that would otherwise have happened, but has also reduced our input of gases that cause climate change.

How is life on Earth being affected by climate change?

There are some things that we can already begin to see and talk about, but there's an enormous amount that we still don't know. We do know that the oceans are getting more acidic because CO_2 is taken up by the ocean and converted to carbonic acid, which can affect the ability of shellfish to make their shells. Other ocean life is also likely to be harmed by the increased acidity, such as the organisms of coral reefs. But there's also emerging evidence that some other marine organisms may do better—lobsters, perhaps.

As a westerner I'm extremely concerned about the greatly increased population of pine beetles in the western United States. These beetles are killing pine trees in unprecedented numbers. There's good evidence that a contributing factor to this explosion of pine beetles is global warming. I think we're going to see more of this kind of thing. Also, it is clear that bird migration is already being affected by global warming. Whether global warming will lead to extinction of some animals is an important question. The signature extinction issue is the polar bear; as the sea ice of the Arctic decreases, the polar bear could become extinct. We don't really know yet how much biological adaptation is possible in the time available. We'll probably find out that there are some winner species out there and some loser species. In agriculture, many crops are sensitive to increasing temperatures. One of the relevant findings about corn is that for every degree of warming, about 10% of crop production is lost—a big change.

Does less precipitation always go along with higher temperatures?

In some places there will probably be less precipitation and in other places more. There's a band of subtropical and tropical regions where we are pretty confident that it will get drier—for example, Mexico, the Mediterranean region, parts of Australia. In the higher latitudes, places like Canada and Norway will likely get wetter. In between, it's harder to predict.

Tell us about the IPCC and your work on it.

The IPCC is fundamentally a mechanism for the communication of information about climate change from the science community to the policy community. It was set up in 1988 when people were beginning to recognize that climate change was a real possibility. Policymakers decided that they needed to get reliable scientific information so they could begin to talk about what to do, if anything. Every six or seven years, scientists are asked by their governments to get together and assess what we know and don't know on the basis of the published scientific literature.

I have been involved in the IPCC since 1992, and in 2001 I was elected by the panel, representing over 100 governments, to co-chair the scientific assessment team. In a process lasting several years, we generated a detailed report summarizing the state of climate science. Our report was then reviewed by dozens of governments and more than 600 scientists. The report itself and every one of their 30,000 comments are available on the Internet. We refined and refined the draft in consideration of those comments and finalized the document in 2007.

What were the main conclusions of your 2007 report?

The first conclusion, based on many independent lines of evidence, was that the Earth is warming. There's no doubt we are now living on a planet that is warmer than a century ago. The second main conclusion was that most—more than half—of the warming is very likely due to increases in greenhouse gases, primarily CO_2. We did a careful analysis of the uncertainties: When we say "very likely," we mean that there's a 90% chance or greater that most of the warming is due to emissions of greenhouse gases by human activity.

What have you learned about working at the interface of science and policy?

It's one of the most difficult things a scientist can do. Science normally takes us into a laboratory or out into the field or into scholarly discussions with colleagues. Getting involved with policy is quite different: It takes us out of the lab and makes us much more aware of the strong emotions around many issues. In that sense, it's a bit daunting. But it's uplifting to see how valuable science can be in helping society make more informed choices. Scientists can help make sure that whatever it is we choose to do as a society we're doing knowingly, not in ignorance. I appreciate all the reasons why people ask tough questions about the science. How much do we know? What really are the uncertainties? Yes, there's a lot at stake here, all the more reason why there has to be really good science going into it.

"There's a breadth of scientific data, acquired by different techniques, that tells us that global warming really is unequivocal."

Susan Solomon (right) with Jane Reece

2

The Chemical Context of Life

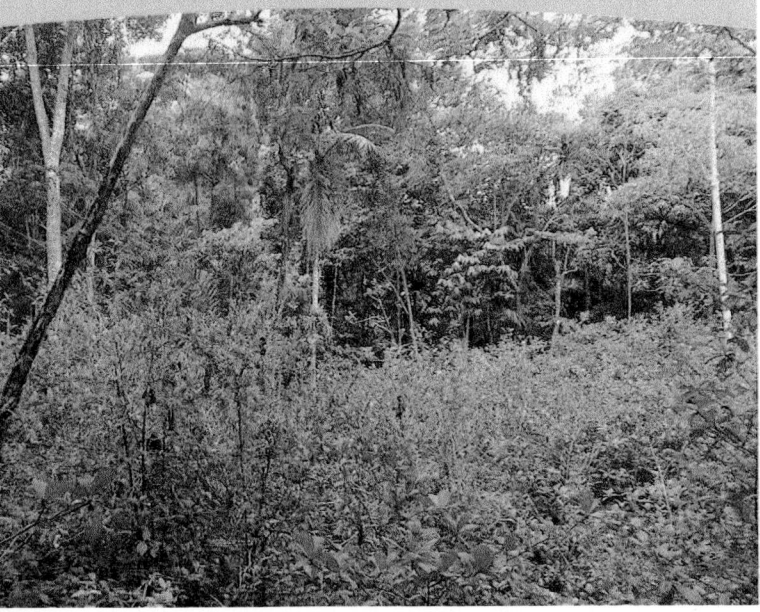

▲ Figure 2.1 **Who tends this "garden"?**

KEY CONCEPTS

2.1 Matter consists of chemical elements in pure form and in combinations called compounds

2.2 An element's properties depend on the structure of its atoms

2.3 The formation and function of molecules depend on chemical bonding between atoms

2.4 Chemical reactions make and break chemical bonds

OVERVIEW

A Chemical Connection to Biology

The Amazon rain forest in South America is a showcase for the diversity of life on Earth. Colorful birds, insects, and other animals live in a densely-packed environment of trees, shrubs, vines, and wildflowers, and an excursion along a waterway or a forest path typically reveals a lush variety of plant life. Visitors traveling near the Amazon's headwaters in Peru are therefore surprised to come across tracts of forest like that seen in the foreground of the photo in **Figure 2.1**. This patch is almost completely dominated by a single plant species—a small flowering tree called *Duroia hirsuta*. Travelers may wonder if the plot of land is planted and maintained by local people, but the indigenous people are as mystified as the visitors. They call these stands of *Duroia* trees "devil's gardens," from a legend attributing them to an evil forest spirit.

Seeking a scientific explanation, a research team at Stanford University recently solved the "devil's garden" mystery. **Figure 2.2** describes their main experiment. The researchers showed that the "farmers" who create and maintain these gardens are actually ants that live in the hollow stems of the *Duroia* trees. The ants do not plant the *Duroia* trees, but they prevent other plant species from growing in the garden by injecting intruders with a poisonous chemical. In this way, the ants create space for the growth of the *Duroia* trees that serve as their home. With the ability to maintain and expand its habitat, a single colony of devil's garden ants can live for hundreds of years.

The chemical used by the ants to weed their garden turns out to be formic acid. This substance is produced by many species of ants and in fact got its name from the Latin word for ant, *formica*. For many ant species, the formic acid probably serves as a disinfectant that protects the ants against microbial parasites. The devil's garden ant is the first ant species found to use formic acid as an herbicide, an important addition to the list of functions mediated by chemicals in the insect world. Scientists have long known that chemicals play a major role in insect communication, attraction of mates, and defense against predators.

Research on devil's gardens is only one example of the relevance of chemistry to the study of life. Unlike a list of college courses, nature is not neatly packaged into the individual natural sciences—biology, chemistry, physics, and so forth. Biologists specialize in the study of life, but organisms and their environments are natural systems to which the concepts of chemistry and physics apply. Biology is a multidisciplinary science.

This unit of chapters introduces some basic concepts of chemistry that apply to the study of life. We will make many connections to the themes introduced in Chapter 1. One of these themes is the organization of life into a hierarchy of structural levels, with additional properties emerging at each successive level. In this unit, we will see how emergent properties are apparent at the lowest levels of biological organization—such as the ordering of atoms into molecules and the interactions of those molecules within cells. Somewhere in the transition from molecules to cells, we will cross the blurry boundary between nonlife and life. This chapter focuses on the chemical components that make up all matter.

INQUIRY

What creates "devil's gardens" in the rain forest?

EXPERIMENT Working under Deborah Gordon and with Michael Greene, graduate student Megan Frederickson sought the cause of "devil's gardens," stands of a single species of tree, *Duroia hirsuta*. One hypothesis was that ants living in these trees, *Myrmelachista schumanni*, produce a poisonous chemical that kills trees of other species; another was that the *Duroia* trees themselves kill competing trees, perhaps by means of a chemical.

To test these hypotheses, Frederickson did field experiments in Peru. Two saplings of a local nonhost tree species, *Cedrela odorata*, were planted inside each of ten devil's gardens. At the base of one sapling, a sticky insect barrier was applied; the other was unprotected. Two more *Cedrela* saplings, with and without barriers, were planted about 50 meters outside each garden.

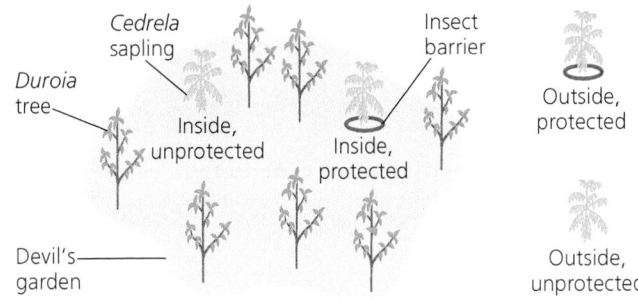

The researchers observed ant activity on the *Cedrela* leaves and measured areas of dead leaf tissue after one day. They also chemically analyzed contents of the ants' poison glands.

RESULTS The ants made injections from the tips of their abdomens into leaves of unprotected saplings in their gardens (see photo). Within one day, these leaves developed dead areas (see graph). The protected saplings were uninjured, as were the saplings planted outside the gardens. Formic acid was the only chemical detected in the poison glands of the ants.

Cedrela saplings, inside and outside devil's gardens

CONCLUSION Ants of the species *Myrmelachista schumanni* kill nonhost trees by injecting the leaves with formic acid, thus creating hospitable habitats (devil's gardens) for the ant colony.

SOURCE M. E. Frederickson, M. J. Greene, and D. M. Gordon, "Devil's gardens" bedevilled by ants, *Nature* 437:495–496 (2005).

INQUIRY IN ACTION Read and analyze the original paper in *Inquiry in Action: Interpreting Scientific Papers*.

WHAT IF? What would be the results if the unprotected saplings' inability to grow in the devil's gardens was caused by a chemical released by the *Duroia* trees rather than by the ants?

Matter consists of chemical elements in pure form and in combinations called compounds

Organisms are composed of **matter**, which is defined as anything that takes up space and has mass.* Matter exists in many diverse forms. Rocks, metals, oils, gases, and humans are just a few examples of what seems an endless assortment of matter.

Elements and Compounds

Matter is made up of elements. An **element** is a substance that cannot be broken down to other substances by chemical reactions. Today, chemists recognize 92 elements occurring in nature; gold, copper, carbon, and oxygen are examples. Each element has a symbol, usually the first letter or two of its name. Some symbols are derived from Latin or German; for instance, the symbol for sodium is Na, from the Latin word *natrium*.

A **compound** is a substance consisting of two or more different elements combined in a fixed ratio. Table salt, for example, is sodium chloride (NaCl), a compound composed of the elements sodium (Na) and chlorine (Cl) in a 1:1 ratio. Pure sodium is a metal, and pure chlorine is a poisonous gas. When chemically combined, however, sodium and chlorine form an edible compound. Water (H_2O), another compound, consists of the elements hydrogen (H) and oxygen (O) in a 2:1 ratio. These are simple examples of organized matter having emergent properties: A compound has characteristics different from those of its elements (Figure 2.3).

Sodium   **Chlorine**   **Sodium chloride**

▲ Figure 2.3 **The emergent properties of a compound.** The metal sodium combines with the poisonous gas chlorine, forming the edible compound sodium chloride, or table salt.

---

*Sometimes we substitute the term weight for mass, although the two are not identical. Mass is the amount of matter in an object, whereas the weight of an object is how strongly that mass is pulled by gravity. The weight of an astronaut walking on the moon is approximately 1/6 the astronaut's weight on Earth, but his or her mass is the same. However, as long as we are earthbound, the weight of an object is a measure of its mass; in everyday language, therefore, we tend to use the terms interchangeably.

The Elements of Life

Of the 92 natural elements, about 20–25% are **essential elements** that an organism needs to live a healthy life and reproduce. The essential elements are similar among organisms, but there is some variation—for example, humans need 25 elements, but plants need only 17.

Just four elements—oxygen (O), carbon (C), hydrogen (H), and nitrogen (N)—make up 96% of living matter. Calcium (Ca), phosphorus (P), potassium (K), sulfur (S), and a few other elements account for most of the remaining 4% of an organism's mass. **Trace elements** are required by an organism in only minute quantities. Some trace elements, such as iron (Fe), are needed by all forms of life; others are required only by certain species. For example, in vertebrates (animals with backbones), the element iodine (I) is an essential ingredient of a hormone produced by the thyroid gland. A daily intake of only 0.15 milligram (mg) of iodine is adequate for normal activity of the human thyroid. An iodine deficiency in the diet causes the thyroid gland to grow to abnormal size, a condition called goiter. Where it is available, eating seafood or iodized salt reduces the incidence of goiter. All the elements needed by the human body are listed in Table 2.1.

Some naturally occurring elements are toxic to organisms. In humans, for instance, the element arsenic has been linked to numerous diseases and can be lethal. In some areas of the world, arsenic occurs naturally and can make its way into the groundwater. As a result of using water from drilled wells in southern Asia, millions of people have been inadvertently exposed to arsenic-laden water. Efforts are under way to reduce arsenic levels in their water supply.

▲ **Figure 2.4 Serpentine plant community.** The plants in the large photo are growing on serpentine soil, which contains elements that are usually toxic to plants. The insets show a close-up of serpentine rock and one of the plants, a Tiburon Mariposa lily.

Case Study: Evolution of Tolerance to Toxic Elements

EVOLUTION Some species have become adapted to environments containing elements that are usually toxic. A compelling example is found in serpentine plant communities. Serpentine is a jade-like mineral that contains toxic elements such as chromium, nickel, and cobalt. Although most plants cannot survive in soil that forms from serpentine rock, a small number of plant species have adaptations that allow them to do so (Figure 2.4). Presumably, variants of ancestral, nonserpentine species arose that could survive in serpentine soils, and subsequent natural selection resulted in the distinctive array of species we see in these areas today.

CONCEPT CHECK 2.1

1. **MAKE CONNECTIONS** Review the discussion of emergent properties in Chapter 1 (p. 3). Explain how table salt has emergent properties.
2. Is a trace element an essential element? Explain.
3. In humans, iron is a trace element required for the proper functioning of hemoglobin, the molecule that carries oxygen in red blood cells. What might be the effects of an iron deficiency?
4. **MAKE CONNECTIONS** Review the discussion of natural selection in Chapter 1 (pp. 14–16) and explain how natural selection might have played a role in the evolution of species that are tolerant of serpentine soils.

For suggested answers, see Appendix A.

Table 2.1 Elements in the Human Body		
Element	Symbol	Percentage of Body Mass (including water)
Oxygen	O	65.0%
Carbon	C	18.5%
Hydrogen	H	9.5%
Nitrogen	N	3.3%
Calcium	Ca	1.5%
Phosphorus	P	1.0%
Potassium	K	0.4%
Sulfur	S	0.3%
Sodium	Na	0.2%
Chlorine	Cl	0.2%
Magnesium	Mg	0.1%

96.3% (for O, C, H, N); 3.7% (for Ca, P, K, S, Na, Cl, Mg)

Trace elements (less than 0.01% of mass): Boron (B), chromium (Cr), cobalt (Co), copper (Cu), fluorine (F), iodine (I), iron (Fe), manganese (Mn), molybdenum (Mo), selenium (Se), silicon (Si), tin (Sn), vanadium (V), zinc (Zn)

CONCEPT 2.2

An element's properties depend on the structure of its atoms

Each element consists of a certain type of atom that is different from the atoms of any other element. An **atom** is the smallest unit of matter that still retains the properties of an element. Atoms are so small that it would take about a million of them to stretch across the period printed at the end of this sentence. We symbolize atoms with the same abbreviation used for the element that is made up of those atoms. For example, the symbol C stands for both the element carbon and a single carbon atom.

Subatomic Particles

Although the atom is the smallest unit having the properties of an element, these tiny bits of matter are composed of even smaller parts, called *subatomic particles*. Physicists have split the atom into more than a hundred types of particles, but only three kinds of particles are relevant here: **neutrons**, **protons**, and **electrons**. Protons and electrons are electrically charged. Each proton has one unit of positive charge, and each electron has one unit of negative charge. A neutron, as its name implies, is electrically neutral.

Protons and neutrons are packed together tightly in a dense core, or **atomic nucleus**, at the center of an atom; protons give the nucleus a positive charge. The electrons form a sort of cloud of negative charge around the nucleus, and it is the attraction between opposite charges that keeps the electrons in the vicinity of the nucleus. **Figure 2.5** shows two commonly used models of the structure of the helium atom as an example.

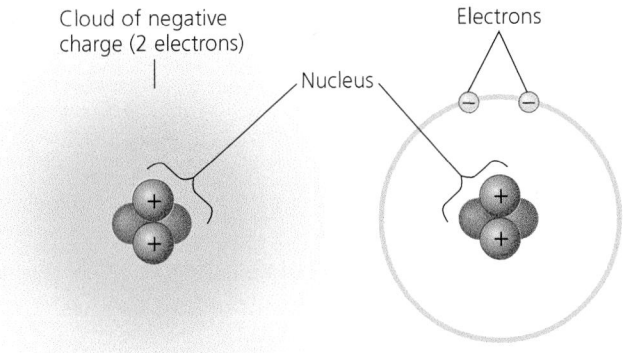

(a) This model represents the two electrons as a cloud of negative charge.

(b) In this more simplified model, the electrons are shown as two small yellow spheres on a circle around the nucleus.

▲ **Figure 2.5 Simplified models of a helium (He) atom.** The helium nucleus consists of 2 neutrons (brown) and 2 protons (pink). Two electrons (yellow) exist outside the nucleus. These models are not to scale; they greatly overestimate the size of the nucleus in relation to the electron cloud.

The neutron and proton are almost identical in mass, each about 1.7×10^{-24} gram (g). Grams and other conventional units are not very useful for describing the mass of objects so minuscule. Thus, for atoms and subatomic particles (and for molecules, too), we use a unit of measurement called the **dalton**, in honor of John Dalton, the British scientist who helped develop atomic theory around 1800. (The dalton is the same as the *atomic mass unit*, or *amu*, a unit you may have encountered elsewhere.) Neutrons and protons have masses close to 1 dalton. Because the mass of an electron is only about 1/2,000 that of a neutron or proton, we can ignore electrons when computing the total mass of an atom.

Atomic Number and Atomic Mass

Atoms of the various elements differ in their number of subatomic particles. All atoms of a particular element have the same number of protons in their nuclei. This number of protons, which is unique to that element, is called the **atomic number** and is written as a subscript to the left of the symbol for the element. The abbreviation $_2$He, for example, tells us that an atom of the element helium has 2 protons in its nucleus. Unless otherwise indicated, an atom is neutral in electrical charge, which means that its protons must be balanced by an equal number of electrons. Therefore, the atomic number tells us the number of protons and also the number of electrons in an electrically neutral atom.

We can deduce the number of neutrons from a second quantity, the **mass number**, which is the sum of protons plus neutrons in the nucleus of an atom. The mass number is written as a superscript to the left of an element's symbol. For example, we can use this shorthand to write an atom of helium as $_2^4$He. Because the atomic number indicates how many protons there are, we can determine the number of neutrons by subtracting the atomic number from the mass number: The helium atom, $_2^4$He, has 2 neutrons. For sodium (Na):

$_{11}^{23}$Na

Mass number = number of protons + neutrons
= 23 for sodium

Atomic number = number of protons
= number of electrons in a neutral atom
= 11 for sodium

Number of neutrons = mass number – atomic number
= 23 − 11 = 12 for sodium

The simplest atom is hydrogen, $_1^1$H, which has no neutrons; it consists of a single proton with a single electron.

As mentioned earlier, the contribution of electrons to mass is negligible. Therefore, almost all of an atom's mass is concentrated in its nucleus. Because neutrons and protons each have a mass very close to 1 dalton, the mass number is an approximation of the total mass of an atom, called its **atomic mass**. So we might say that the atomic mass of sodium ($_{11}^{23}$Na) is 23 daltons, although more precisely it is 22.9898 daltons.

Isotopes

All atoms of a given element have the same number of protons, but some atoms have more neutrons than other atoms of the same element and therefore have greater mass. These different atomic forms of the same element are called **isotopes** of the element. In nature, an element occurs as a mixture of its isotopes. For example, consider the three isotopes of the element carbon, which has the atomic number 6. The most common isotope is carbon-12, $^{12}_6C$, which accounts for about 99% of the carbon in nature. The isotope $^{12}_6C$ has 6 neutrons. Most of the remaining 1% of carbon consists of atoms of the isotope $^{13}_6C$, with 7 neutrons. A third, even rarer isotope, $^{14}_6C$, has 8 neutrons. Notice that all three isotopes of carbon have 6 protons; otherwise, they would not be carbon. Although the isotopes of an element have slightly different masses, they behave identically in chemical reactions. (The number usually given as the atomic mass of an element, such as 22.9898 daltons for sodium, is actually an average of the atomic masses of all the element's naturally occurring isotopes.)

Both ^{12}C and ^{13}C are stable isotopes, meaning that their nuclei do not have a tendency to lose particles. The isotope ^{14}C, however, is unstable, or radioactive. A **radioactive isotope** is one in which the nucleus decays spontaneously, giving off particles and energy. When the decay leads to a change in the number of protons, it transforms the atom to an atom of a different element. For example, when a radioactive carbon atom decays, it becomes an atom of nitrogen.

Radioactive isotopes have many useful applications in biology. In Chapter 25, you will learn how researchers use measurements of radioactivity in fossils to date these relics of past life. As shown in **Figure 2.6**, radioactive isotopes are also useful as tracers to follow atoms through metabolism, the chemical processes of an organism. Cells use the radioactive atoms as they would use nonradioactive isotopes of the same element, but the radioactive tracers can be readily detected.

Radioactive tracers are important diagnostic tools in medicine. For example, certain kidney disorders can be diagnosed by injecting small doses of substances containing radioactive isotopes into the blood and then measuring the amount of tracer excreted in the urine. Radioactive tracers are also used in combination with sophisticated imaging instruments. PET scanners, for instance, can monitor chemical processes, such as those involved in cancerous growth, as they actually occur in the body (**Figure 2.7**).

Although radioactive isotopes are very useful in biological research and medicine, radiation from decaying isotopes also poses a hazard to life by damaging cellular molecules. The severity of this damage depends on the type and amount of radiation an organism absorbs. One of the most serious environmental threats is radioactive fallout from nuclear accidents. The doses of most isotopes used in medical diagnosis, however, are relatively safe.

▼ Figure 2.6

RESEARCH METHOD

Radioactive Tracers

APPLICATION Scientists use radioactive isotopes to label certain chemical compounds, creating tracers that allow them to follow a metabolic process or locate the compound within an organism. In this example, radioactive tracers are utilized to determine the effect of temperature on the rate at which cells make copies of their DNA.

TECHNIQUE

Compounds including radioactive tracer (bright blue)

Human cells

Incubators

10°C 15°C 20°C
25°C 30°C 35°C
40°C 45°C 50°C

❶ Compounds used by cells to make DNA are added to human cells. One ingredient is labeled with ^3H, a radioactive isotope of hydrogen. Nine dishes of cells are incubated at different temperatures. The cells make new DNA, incorporating the radioactive tracer.

❷ Cells from each incubator are placed in tubes; their DNA is isolated; and unused labeled compounds are removed.

10° 15° 20° 25° 30° 35° 40° 45° 50°

DNA (old and new)

❸ A solution called scintillation fluid is added to the samples, which are then placed in a scintillation counter. As the ^3H in the newly made DNA decays, it emits radiation that excites chemicals in the scintillation fluid, causing them to give off light. Flashes of light are recorded by the scintillation counter.

RESULTS The frequency of flashes, which is recorded as counts per minute, is proportional to the amount of the radioactive tracer present, indicating the amount of new DNA. In this experiment, when the counts per minute are plotted against temperature, it is clear that temperature affects the rate of DNA synthesis; the most DNA was made at 35°C.

Optimum temperature for DNA synthesis

◀ **Figure 2.7 A PET scan, a medical use for radioactive isotopes.** PET, an acronym for positron-emission tomography, detects locations of intense chemical activity in the body. The bright yellow spot marks an area with an elevated level of radioactively labeled glucose, which in turn indicates high metabolic activity, a hallmark of cancerous tissue.

The Energy Levels of Electrons

The simplified models of the atom in Figure 2.5 greatly exaggerate the size of the nucleus relative to the volume of the whole atom. If an atom of helium were the size of a typical football stadium, the nucleus would be the size of a pencil eraser in the center of the field. Moreover, the electrons would be like two tiny gnats buzzing around the stadium. Atoms are mostly empty space.

When two atoms approach each other during a chemical reaction, their nuclei do not come close enough to interact. Of the three kinds of subatomic particles we have discussed, only electrons are directly involved in the chemical reactions between atoms.

An atom's electrons vary in the amount of energy they possess. **Energy** is defined as the capacity to cause change—for instance, by doing work. **Potential energy** is the energy that matter possesses because of its location or structure. For example, water in a reservoir on a hill has potential energy because of its altitude. When the gates of the reservoir's dam are opened and the water runs downhill, the energy can be used to do work, such as turning generators. Because energy has been expended, the water has less energy at the bottom of the hill than it did in the reservoir. Matter has a natural tendency to move to the lowest possible state of potential energy; in this example, the water runs downhill. To restore the potential energy of a reservoir, work must be done to elevate the water against gravity.

The electrons of an atom have potential energy because of how they are arranged in relation to the nucleus. The negatively charged electrons are attracted to the positively charged nucleus. It takes work to move a given electron farther away from the nucleus, so the more distant an electron is from the nucleus, the greater its potential energy. Unlike the continuous flow of water downhill, changes in the potential energy of electrons can occur only in steps of fixed amounts. An electron having a certain amount of energy is something like a ball on a staircase (Figure 2.8a). The ball can have different amounts of potential energy, depending on which step it is

(a) A ball bouncing down a flight of stairs provides an analogy for energy levels of electrons, because the ball can come to rest only on each step, not between steps.

Third shell (highest energy level in this model)

Second shell (higher energy level)

First shell (lowest energy level)

Atomic nucleus

Energy absorbed

Energy lost

(b) An electron can move from one shell to another only if the energy it gains or loses is exactly equal to the difference in energy between the energy levels of the two shells. Arrows in this model indicate some of the stepwise changes in potential energy that are possible.

▲ **Figure 2.8 Energy levels of an atom's electrons.** Electrons exist only at fixed levels of potential energy called electron shells.

on, but it cannot spend much time between the steps. Similarly, an electron's potential energy is determined by its energy level. An electron cannot exist between energy levels.

An electron's energy level is correlated with its average distance from the nucleus. Electrons are found in different **electron shells**, each with a characteristic average distance and energy level. In diagrams, shells can be represented by concentric circles (Figure 2.8b). The first shell is closest to the nucleus, and electrons in this shell have the lowest potential energy. Electrons in the second shell have more energy, and electrons in the third shell even more energy. An electron can change the shell it occupies, but only by absorbing or losing an amount of energy equal to the difference in potential energy between its position in the old shell and that in the new shell. When an electron absorbs energy, it moves to a shell farther out from the nucleus. For example, light energy can excite an electron to a higher energy level. (Indeed, this is the first step taken when plants harness the energy of sunlight for photosynthesis, the process that produces food from carbon dioxide and water.) When an electron loses energy, it "falls back" to a shell closer to the nucleus, and the lost energy is usually released to the environment as heat. For example, sunlight excites electrons in the surface of a car to higher energy levels. When the electrons fall back to their original levels, the car's surface heats up. This thermal energy can be transferred to the air or to your hand if you touch the car.

Electron Distribution and Chemical Properties

The chemical behavior of an atom is determined by the distribution of electrons in the atom's electron shells. Beginning with hydrogen, the simplest atom, we can imagine building the atoms of the other elements by adding 1 proton and 1 electron at a time (along with an appropriate number of neutrons). **Figure 2.9**, an abbreviated version of what is called the *periodic table of the elements*, shows this distribution of electrons for the first 18 elements, from hydrogen ($_1$H) to argon ($_{18}$Ar). The elements are arranged in three rows, or periods, corresponding to the number of electron shells in their atoms. The left-to-right sequence of elements in each row corresponds to the sequential addition of electrons and protons. (See Appendix B for the complete periodic table.)

Hydrogen's 1 electron and helium's 2 electrons are located in the first shell. Electrons, like all matter, tend to exist in the lowest available state of potential energy. In an atom, this state is in the first shell. However, the first shell can hold no more than 2 electrons; thus, hydrogen and helium are the only elements in the first row of the table. An atom with more than 2 electrons must use higher shells because the first shell

is full. The next element, lithium, has 3 electrons. Two of these electrons fill the first shell, while the third electron occupies the second shell. The second shell holds a maximum of 8 electrons. Neon, at the end of the second row, has 8 electrons in the second shell, giving it a total of 10 electrons.

The chemical behavior of an atom depends mostly on the number of electrons in its *outermost* shell. We call those outer electrons **valence electrons** and the outermost electron shell the **valence shell**. In the case of lithium, there is only 1 valence electron, and the second shell is the valence shell. Atoms with the same number of electrons in their valence shells exhibit similar chemical behavior. For example, fluorine (F) and chlorine (Cl) both have 7 valence electrons, and both form compounds when combined with the element sodium (see Figure 2.3). An atom with a completed valence shell is unreactive; that is, it will not interact readily with other atoms. At the far right of the periodic table are helium, neon, and argon, the only three elements shown in Figure 2.9 that have full valence shells. These elements are said to be *inert*, meaning chemically unreactive. All the other atoms in Figure 2.9 are chemically reactive because they have incomplete valence shells.

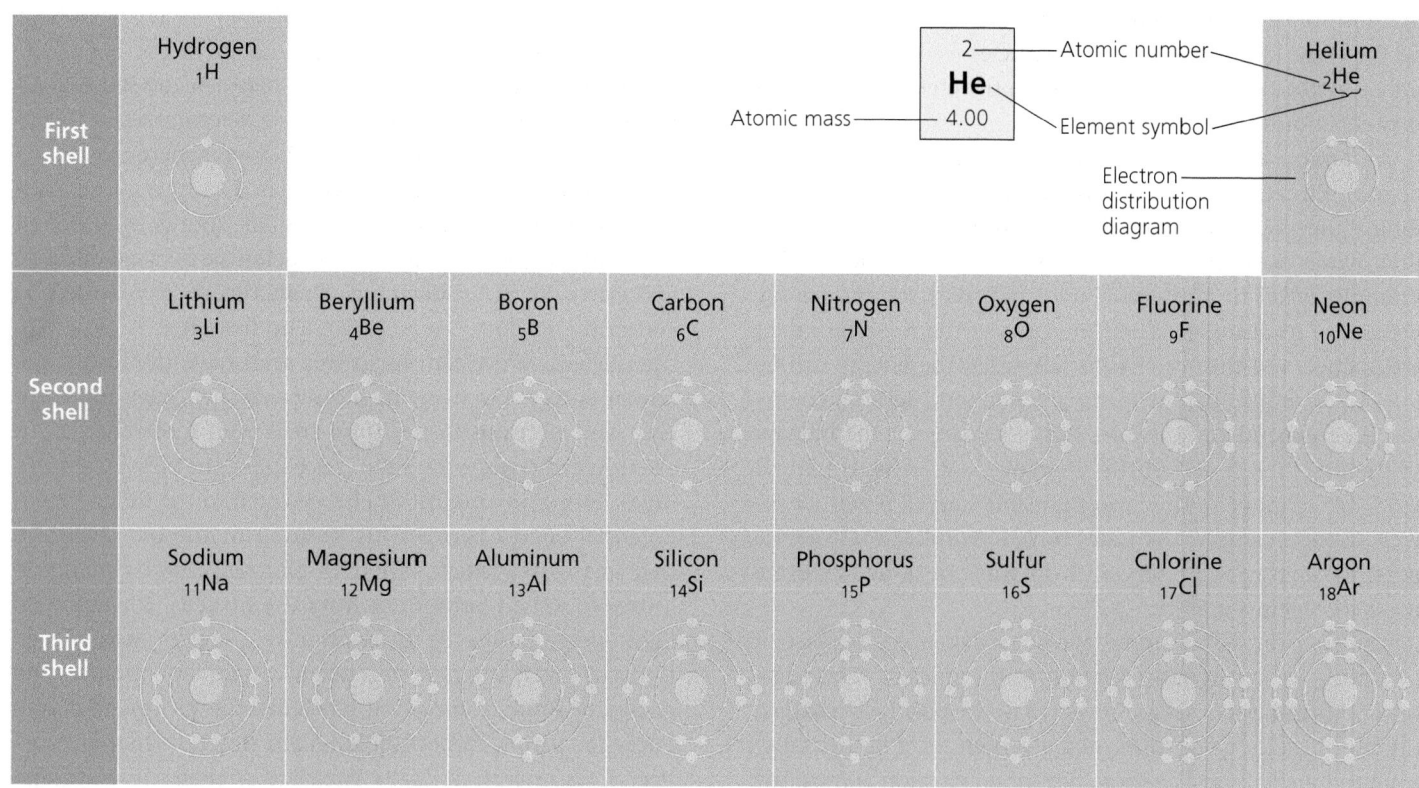

▲ **Figure 2.9 Electron distribution diagrams for the first 18 elements in the periodic table.** In a standard periodic table (see Appendix B), information for each element is presented as shown for helium in the inset. In the diagrams in this table, electrons are represented as yellow dots and electron shells as concentric circles. These diagrams are a convenient way to picture the distribution of an atom's electrons among its electron shells, but these simplified models do not accurately represent the shape of the atom or the location of its electrons. The elements are arranged in rows, each representing the filling of an electron shell. As electrons are added, they occupy the lowest available shell.

? *What is the atomic number of magnesium? How many protons and electrons does it have? How many electron shells? How many valence electrons?*

Electron Orbitals

In the early 1900s, the electron shells of an atom were visualized as concentric paths of electrons orbiting the nucleus, somewhat like planets orbiting the sun. It is still convenient to use two-dimensional concentric-circle diagrams, as in Figure 2.9, to symbolize three-dimensional electron

Neon, with two filled shells (10 electrons)

First shell

Second shell

(a) Electron distribution diagram. An electron distribution diagram is shown here for a neon atom, which has a total of 10 electrons. Each concentric circle represents an electron shell, which can be subdivided into electron orbitals.

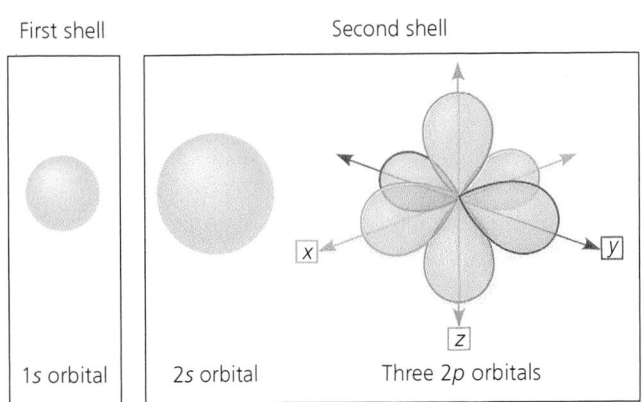

First shell   Second shell

x   *y*

z

1s orbital   2s orbital   Three 2p orbitals

(b) Separate electron orbitals. The three-dimensional shapes represent electron orbitals—the volumes of space where the electrons of an atom are most likely to be found. Each orbital holds a maximum of 2 electrons. The first electron shell, on the left, has one spherical (*s*) orbital, designated 1*s*. The second shell, on the right, has one larger *s* orbital (designated 2*s* for the second shell) plus three dumbbell-shaped orbitals called *p* orbitals (2*p* for the second shell). The three 2*p* orbitals lie at right angles to one another along imaginary *x*-, *y*-, and *z*-axes of the atom. Each 2*p* orbital is outlined here in a different color.

1s, 2s, and 2p orbitals

(c) Superimposed electron orbitals. To reveal the complete picture of the electron orbitals of neon, we superimpose the 1*s* orbital of the first shell and the 2*s* and three 2*p* orbitals of the second shell.

▲ Figure 2.10 **Electron orbitals.**

shells. However, you need to remember that each concentric circle represents only the *average* distance between an electron in that shell and the nucleus. Accordingly, the concentric-circle diagrams do not give a real picture of an atom. In reality, we can never know the exact location of an electron. What we can do instead is describe the space in which an electron spends most of its time. The three-dimensional space where an electron is found 90% of the time is called an **orbital**.

Each electron shell contains electrons at a particular energy level, distributed among a specific number of orbitals of distinctive shapes and orientations. **Figure 2.10** shows the orbitals of neon as an example, with its electron distribution diagram for reference. You can think of an orbital as a component of an electron shell. The first electron shell has only one spherical *s* orbital (called 1*s*), but the second shell has four orbitals: one large spherical *s* orbital (called 2*s*) and three dumbbell-shaped *p* orbitals (called 2*p* orbitals). (The third shell and other higher electron shells also have *s* and *p* orbitals, as well as orbitals of more complex shapes.)

No more than 2 electrons can occupy a single orbital. The first electron shell can therefore accommodate up to 2 electrons in its *s* orbital. The lone electron of a hydrogen atom occupies the 1*s* orbital, as do the 2 electrons of a helium atom. The four orbitals of the second electron shell can hold up to 8 electrons, 2 in each orbital. Electrons in each of the four orbitals have nearly the same energy, but they move in different volumes of space.

The reactivity of atoms arises from the presence of unpaired electrons in one or more orbitals of their valence shells. As you will see in the next section, atoms interact in a way that completes their valence shells. When they do so, it is the *unpaired* electrons that are involved.

CONCEPT CHECK 2.2

1. A lithium atom has 3 protons and 4 neutrons. What is its atomic mass in daltons?
2. A nitrogen atom has 7 protons, and the most common isotope of nitrogen has 7 neutrons. A radioactive isotope of nitrogen has 8 neutrons. Write the atomic number and mass number of this radioactive nitrogen as a chemical symbol with a subscript and superscript.
3. How many electrons does fluorine have? How many electron shells? Name the orbitals that are occupied. How many electrons are needed to fill the valence shell?
4. **WHAT IF?** In Figure 2.9, if two or more elements are in the same row, what do they have in common? If two or more elements are in the same column, what do they have in common?

For suggested answers, see Appendix A.

The formation and function of molecules depend on chemical bonding between atoms

Now that we have looked at the structure of atoms, we can move up the hierarchy of organization and see how atoms combine to form molecules and ionic compounds. Atoms with incomplete valence shells can interact with certain other atoms in such a way that each partner completes its valence shell: The atoms either share or transfer valence electrons. These interactions usually result in atoms staying close together, held by attractions called **chemical bonds**. The strongest kinds of chemical bonds are covalent bonds and ionic bonds.

Covalent Bonds

A **covalent bond** is the sharing of a pair of valence electrons by two atoms. For example, let's consider what happens when two hydrogen atoms approach each other. Recall that hydrogen has 1 valence electron in the first shell, but the shell's capacity is 2 electrons. When the two hydrogen atoms come close enough for their 1s orbitals to overlap, they can share their electrons (**Figure 2.11**). Each hydrogen atom is now associated with 2 electrons in what amounts

to a completed valence shell. Two or more atoms held together by covalent bonds constitute a **molecule**, in this case a hydrogen molecule.

Figure 2.12a shows several ways of representing a hydrogen molecule. Its *molecular formula*, H_2, simply indicates that the molecule consists of two atoms of hydrogen. Electron sharing can be depicted by an electron distribution diagram or by a *Lewis dot structure*, in which element symbols are surrounded by dots that represent the valence electrons (H:H). We can also use a *structural formula*, H—H, where the line represents a **single bond**, a pair of shared electrons. A space-filling model comes closest to representing the actual shape of the molecule.

Oxygen has 6 electrons in its second electron shell and therefore needs 2 more electrons to complete its valence shell. Two oxygen atoms form a molecule by sharing *two* pairs of valence electrons (**Figure 2.12b**). The atoms are thus joined by a **double bond** ($O=O$).

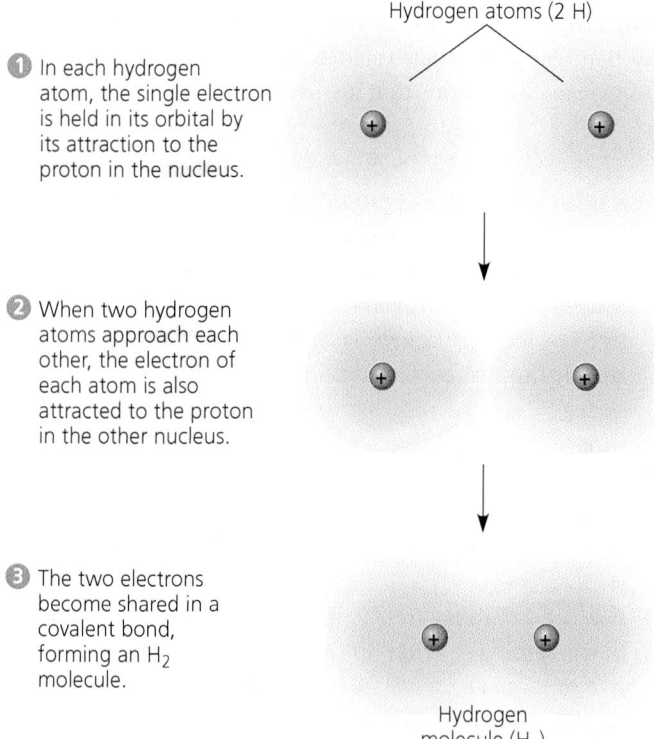

① In each hydrogen atom, the single electron is held in its orbital by its attraction to the proton in the nucleus.

② When two hydrogen atoms approach each other, the electron of each atom is also attracted to the proton in the other nucleus.

③ The two electrons become shared in a covalent bond, forming an H_2 molecule.

Hydrogen molecule (H_2)

▲ **Figure 2.11 Formation of a covalent bond.**

Name and Molecular Formula	Electron Distribution Diagram	Lewis Dot Structure and Structural Formula	Space-Filling Model
(a) Hydrogen (H_2). Two hydrogen atoms share one pair of electrons, forming a single bond.		H:H H—H	
(b) Oxygen (O_2). Two oxygen atoms share two pairs of electrons, forming a double bond.		$\ddot{O}::\ddot{O}$ $O=O$	
(c) Water (H_2O). Two hydrogen atoms and one oxygen atom are joined by single bonds, forming a molecule of water.		$:\ddot{O}:H$ H O—H | H	
(d) Methane (CH_4). Four hydrogen atoms can satisfy the valence of one carbon atom, forming methane.		H H:C:H H H | H—C—H | H	

▲ **Figure 2.12 Covalent bonding in four molecules.** The number of electrons required to complete an atom's valence shell generally determines how many covalent bonds that atom will form. This figure shows several ways of indicating covalent bonds.

Each atom that can share valence electrons has a bonding capacity corresponding to the number of covalent bonds the atom can form. When the bonds form, they give the atom a full complement of electrons in the valence shell. The bonding capacity of oxygen, for example, is 2. This bonding capacity is called the atom's **valence** and usually equals the number of unpaired electrons required to complete the atom's outermost (valence) shell. See if you can determine the valences of hydrogen, oxygen, nitrogen, and carbon by studying the electron distribution diagrams in Figure 2.9. You can see that the valence of hydrogen is 1; oxygen, 2; nitrogen, 3; and carbon, 4. However, the situation is more complicated for elements in the third row of the periodic table. Phosphorus, for example, can have a valence of 3, as we would predict from the presence of 3 unpaired electrons in its valence shell. In some molecules that are biologically important, however, phosphorus can form three single bonds and one double bond. Therefore, it can also have a valence of 5.

The molecules H_2 and O_2 are pure elements rather than compounds because a compound is a combination of two or more *different* elements. Water, with the molecular formula H_2O, is a compound. Two atoms of hydrogen are needed to satisfy the valence of one oxygen atom. **Figure 2.12c** shows the structure of a water molecule. Water is so important to life that Chapter 3 is devoted entirely to its structure and behavior.

Methane, the main component of natural gas, is a compound with the molecular formula CH_4. It takes four hydrogen atoms, each with a valence of 1, to complement one atom of carbon, with its valence of 4 **(Figure 2.12d)**. We will look at many other compounds of carbon in Chapter 4.

Atoms in a molecule attract shared electrons to varying degrees, depending on the element. The attraction of a particular atom for the electrons of a covalent bond is called its **electronegativity**. The more electronegative an atom is, the more strongly it pulls shared electrons toward itself. In a covalent bond between two atoms of the same element, the electrons are shared equally because the two atoms have the same electronegativity—the tug-of-war is at a standoff. Such a bond is called a **nonpolar covalent bond**. For example, the single bond of H_2 is nonpolar, as is the double bond of O_2. However, when one atom is bonded to a more electronegative atom, the electrons of the bond are not shared equally. This type of bond is called a **polar covalent bond**. Such bonds vary in their polarity, depending on the relative electronegativity of the two atoms. For example, the bonds between the oxygen and hydrogen atoms of a water molecule are quite polar **(Figure 2.13)**.

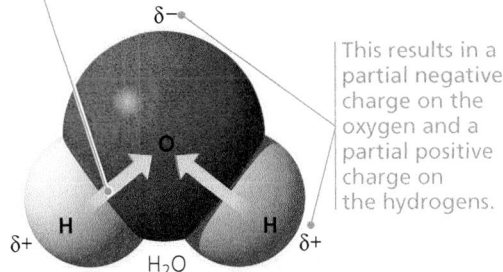

Because oxygen (O) is more electronegative than hydrogen (H), shared electrons are pulled more toward oxygen.

This results in a partial negative charge on the oxygen and a partial positive charge on the hydrogens.

▲ **Figure 2.13 Polar covalent bonds in a water molecule.**

Oxygen is one of the most electronegative of all the elements, attracting shared electrons much more strongly than hydrogen does. In a covalent bond between oxygen and hydrogen, the electrons spend more time near the oxygen nucleus than they do near the hydrogen nucleus. Because electrons have a negative charge and are pulled toward oxygen in a water molecule, the oxygen atom has a partial negative charge (indicated by the Greek letter δ with a minus sign, $\delta-$, or "delta minus"), and each hydrogen atom has a partial positive charge ($\delta+$, or "delta plus"). In contrast, the individual bonds of methane (CH_4) are much less polar because the electronegativities of carbon and hydrogen are similar.

Ionic Bonds

In some cases, two atoms are so unequal in their attraction for valence electrons that the more electronegative atom strips an electron completely away from its partner. This is what happens when an atom of sodium ($_{11}Na$) encounters an atom of chlorine ($_{17}Cl$) **(Figure 2.14)**. A sodium atom has a total of 11 electrons, with its single valence electron in the third electron shell. A chlorine atom has a total of 17 electrons,

1 The lone valence electron of a sodium atom is transferred to join the 7 valence electrons of a chlorine atom.

2 Each resulting ion has a completed valence shell. An ionic bond can form between the oppositely charged ions.

Na
Sodium atom

Cl
Chlorine atom

Na⁺
Sodium ion (a cation)

Cl⁻
Chloride ion (an anion)

Sodium chloride (NaCl)

▲ **Figure 2.14 Electron transfer and ionic bonding.** The attraction between oppositely charged atoms, or ions, is an ionic bond. An ionic bond can form between any two oppositely charged ions, even if they have not been formed by transfer of an electron from one to the other.

with 7 electrons in its valence shell. When these two atoms meet, the lone valence electron of sodium is transferred to the chlorine atom, and both atoms end up with their valence shells complete. (Because sodium no longer has an electron in the third shell, the second shell is now the valence shell.)

The electron transfer between the two atoms moves one unit of negative charge from sodium to chlorine. Sodium, now with 11 protons but only 10 electrons, has a net electrical charge of 1+. A charged atom (or molecule) is called an **ion**. When the charge is positive, the ion is specifically called a **cation**; the sodium atom has become a cation. Conversely, the chlorine atom, having gained an extra electron, now has 17 protons and 18 electrons, giving it a net electrical charge of 1–. It has become a chloride ion—an **anion**, or negatively charged ion. Because of their opposite charges, cations and anions attract each other; this attraction is called an **ionic bond**. The transfer of an electron is not the formation of a bond; rather, it allows a bond to form because it results in two ions of opposite charge. Any two ions of opposite charge can form an ionic bond. The ions do not need to have acquired their charge by an electron transfer with each other.

Compounds formed by ionic bonds are called **ionic compounds**, or **salts**. We know the ionic compound sodium chloride (NaCl) as table salt (**Figure 2.15**). Salts are often found in nature as crystals of various sizes and shapes. Each salt crystal is an aggregate of vast numbers of cations and anions bonded by their electrical attraction and arranged in a three-dimensional lattice. Unlike a covalent compound, which consists of molecules having a definite size and number of atoms, an ionic compound does not consist of molecules. The formula for an ionic compound, such as NaCl, indicates only the ratio of elements in a crystal of the salt. "NaCl" by itself is not a molecule.

Not all salts have equal numbers of cations and anions. For example, the ionic compound magnesium chloride ($MgCl_2$) has two chloride ions for each magnesium ion. Magnesium ($_{12}Mg$) must lose 2 outer electrons if the atom is to have a complete valence shell, so it tends to become a cation with a net charge of 2+ (Mg^{2+}). One magnesium cation can therefore form ionic bonds with two chloride anions.

The term *ion* also applies to entire molecules that are electrically charged. In the salt ammonium chloride (NH_4Cl), for instance, the anion is a single chloride ion (Cl^-), but the cation is ammonium (NH_4^+), a nitrogen atom with four covalently bonded hydrogen atoms. The whole ammonium ion has an electrical charge of 1+ because it is 1 electron short.

Environment affects the strength of ionic bonds. In a dry salt crystal, the bonds are so strong that it takes a hammer and chisel to break enough of them to crack the crystal in two. If the same salt crystal is dissolved in water, however, the ionic bonds are much weaker because each ion is partially shielded by its interactions with water molecules. Most drugs are manufactured as salts because they are quite stable when dry but can dissociate (come apart) easily in water. In the next chapter, you will learn how water dissolves salts.

Weak Chemical Bonds

In organisms, most of the strongest chemical bonds are covalent bonds, which link atoms to form a cell's molecules. But weaker bonding within and between molecules is also indispensable in the cell, contributing greatly to the emergent properties of life. Many large biological molecules are held in their functional form by weak bonds. In addition, when two molecules in the cell make contact, they may adhere temporarily by weak bonds. The reversibility of weak bonding can be an advantage: Two molecules can come together, respond to one another in some way, and then separate.

Several types of weak chemical bonds are important in organisms. One is the ionic bond as it exists between ions dissociated in water, which we just discussed. Hydrogen bonds and van der Waals interactions are also crucial to life.

Hydrogen Bonds

Among the various kinds of weak chemical bonds, hydrogen bonds are so important in the chemistry of life that they deserve special attention. The partial positive charge on a hydrogen atom that is covalently bonded to an electronegative atom allows the hydrogen to be attracted to a different electronegative atom nearby. This noncovalent attraction between a hydrogen and an electronegative atom is called a **hydrogen bond**. In living cells, the electronegative partners are usually oxygen or nitrogen atoms. Refer to **Figure 2.16** to examine the simple case of hydrogen bonding between water (H_2O) and ammonia (NH_3).

Van der Waals Interactions

Even a molecule with nonpolar covalent bonds may have positively and negatively charged regions. Electrons are not always symmetrically distributed in such a molecule; at any

▲ **Figure 2.15 A sodium chloride (NaCl) crystal.** The sodium ions (Na^+) and chloride ions (Cl^-) are held together by ionic bonds. The formula NaCl tells us that the ratio of Na^+ to Cl^- is 1:1.

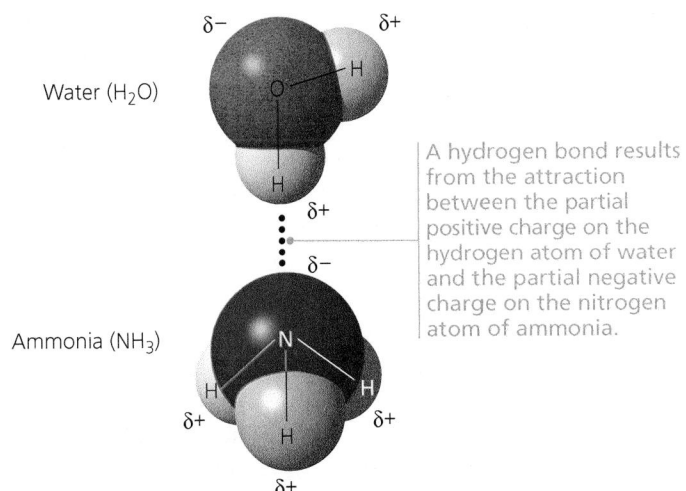

Water (H₂O)

Ammonia (NH₃)

A hydrogen bond results from the attraction between the partial positive charge on the hydrogen atom of water and the partial negative charge on the nitrogen atom of ammonia.

▲ Figure 2.16 **A hydrogen bond.**

DRAW IT *Draw five water molecules using structural formulas and indicating partial charges, and show how they can make hydrogen bonds with each other.*

instant, they may accumulate by chance in one part of the molecule or another. The results are ever-changing regions of positive and negative charge that enable all atoms and molecules to stick to one another. These **van der Waals interactions** are individually weak and occur only when atoms and molecules are very close together. When many such interactions occur simultaneously, however, they can be powerful: Van der Waals interactions are the reason a gecko lizard (right) can walk straight up a wall! Each gecko toe has hundreds of thousands of tiny hairs, with multiple projections at each hair's tip that increase surface area. Apparently, the van der Waals interactions between the hair tip molecules and the molecules of the wall's surface are so numerous that despite their individual weakness, together they can support the gecko's body weight.

Van der Waals interactions, hydrogen bonds, ionic bonds in water, and other weak bonds may form not only between molecules but also between parts of a large molecule, such as a protein. The cumulative effect of weak bonds is to reinforce the three-dimensional shape of the molecule. You will learn more about the very important biological roles of weak bonds in Chapter 5.

Molecular Shape and Function

A molecule has a characteristic size and shape. The precise shape of a molecule is usually very important to its function in the living cell.

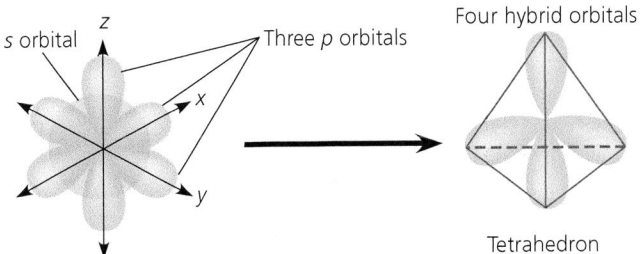

(a) Hybridization of orbitals. The single *s* and three *p* orbitals of a valence shell involved in covalent bonding combine to form four teardrop-shaped hybrid orbitals. These orbitals extend to the four corners of an imaginary tetrahedron (outlined in pink).

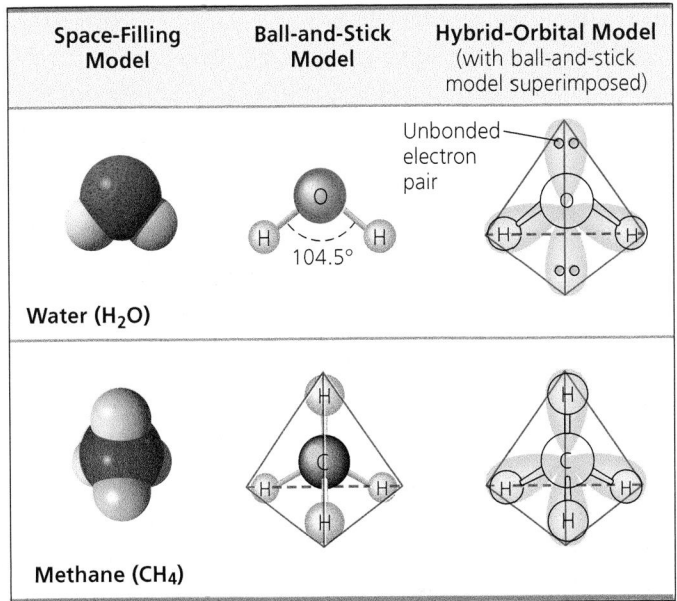

(b) Molecular-shape models. Three models representing molecular shape are shown for water and methane. The positions of the hybrid orbitals determine the shapes of the molecules.

▲ Figure 2.17 **Molecular shapes due to hybrid orbitals.**

A molecule consisting of two atoms, such as H₂ or O₂, is always linear, but most molecules with more than two atoms have more complicated shapes. These shapes are determined by the positions of the atoms' orbitals. When an atom forms covalent bonds, the orbitals in its valence shell undergo rearrangement. For atoms with valence electrons in both *s* and *p* orbitals (review Figure 2.10), the single *s* and three *p* orbitals form four new hybrid orbitals shaped like identical teardrops extending from the region of the atomic nucleus (Figure 2.17a). If we connect the larger ends of the teardrops with lines, we have the outline of a geometric shape called a tetrahedron, a pyramid with a triangular base.

For the water molecule (H₂O), two of the hybrid orbitals in the oxygen atom's valence shell are shared with hydrogen atoms (Figure 2.17b). The result is a molecule shaped roughly like a V, with its two covalent bonds spread apart at an angle of 104.5°.

The methane molecule (CH_4) has the shape of a completed tetrahedron because all four hybrid orbitals of the carbon atom are shared with hydrogen atoms (see Figure 2.17b). The carbon nucleus is at the center, with its four covalent bonds radiating to hydrogen nuclei at the corners of the tetrahedron. Larger molecules containing multiple carbon atoms, including many of the molecules that make up living matter, have more complex overall shapes. However, the tetrahedral shape of a carbon atom bonded to four other atoms is often a repeating motif within such molecules.

Molecular shape is crucial in biology because it determines how biological molecules recognize and respond to one another with specificity. Biological molecules often bind temporarily to each other by forming weak bonds, but this can happen only if their shapes are complementary. We can see this specificity in the effects of opiates, drugs derived from opium. Opiates, such as morphine and heroin, relieve pain and alter mood by weakly binding to specific receptor molecules on the surfaces of brain cells. Why would brain cells carry receptors for opiates, compounds that are not made by our bodies? The discovery of endorphins in 1975 answered this question. Endorphins are signaling molecules made by the pituitary gland that bind to the receptors, relieving pain and producing euphoria during times of stress, such as intense exercise. It turns out that opiates have shapes similar to endorphins and mimic them by binding to endorphin receptors in the brain. That is why opiates (such as morphine) and endorphins have similar effects (Figure 2.18). The role of molecular shape in brain chemistry illustrates the relationship between structure and function, one of biology's unifying themes.

CONCEPT CHECK 2.3

1. Why does the structure H—C=C—H fail to make sense chemically?
2. What holds the atoms together in a crystal of magnesium chloride ($MgCl_2$)?
3. **WHAT IF?** If you were a pharmaceutical researcher, why would you want to learn the three-dimensional shapes of naturally occurring signaling molecules?

For suggested answers, see Appendix A.

CONCEPT 2.4

Chemical reactions make and break chemical bonds

The making and breaking of chemical bonds, leading to changes in the composition of matter, are called **chemical reactions**. An example is the reaction between hydrogen and oxygen molecules that forms water:

Key

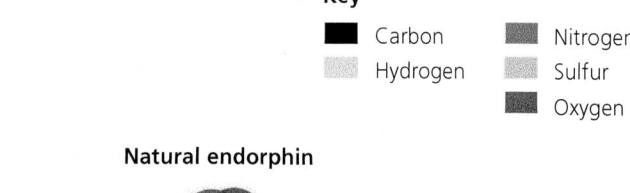

Carbon   Nitrogen
Hydrogen   Sulfur
   Oxygen

Natural endorphin

Morphine

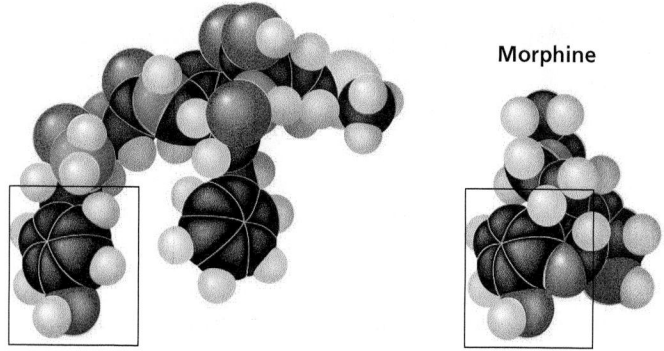

(a) Structures of endorphin and morphine. The boxed portion of the endorphin molecule (left) binds to receptor molecules on target cells in the brain. The boxed portion of the morphine molecule (right) is a close match.

Natural endorphin

Morphine

Endorphin receptors

Brain cell

(b) Binding to endorphin receptors. Both endorphin and morphine can bind to endorphin receptors on the surface of a brain cell.

▲ **Figure 2.18 A molecular mimic.** Morphine affects pain perception and emotional state by mimicking the brain's natural endorphins.

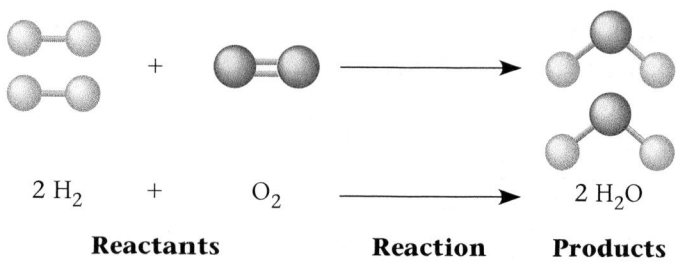

$$2\ H_2 \quad + \quad O_2 \quad \longrightarrow \quad 2\ H_2O$$

Reactants   **Reaction**   **Products**

This reaction breaks the covalent bonds of H_2 and O_2 and forms the new bonds of H_2O. When we write a chemical reaction, we use an arrow to indicate the conversion of the starting materials, called the **reactants**, to the **products**. The coefficients indicate the number of molecules involved; for example, the coefficient 2 in front of the H_2 means that

▲ **Figure 2.19 Photosynthesis: a solar-powered rearrangement of matter.** *Elodea*, a freshwater plant, produces sugar by rearranging the atoms of carbon dioxide and water in the chemical process known as photosynthesis, which is powered by sunlight. Much of the sugar is then converted to other food molecules. Oxygen gas (O_2) is a by-product of photosynthesis; notice the bubbles of oxygen escaping from the leaves in the photo.

? *Explain how this photo relates to the reactants and products in the equation for photosynthesis given in the text. (You will learn more about photosynthesis in Chapter 10.)*

the reaction starts with two molecules of hydrogen. Notice that all atoms of the reactants must be accounted for in the products. Matter is conserved in a chemical reaction: Reactions cannot create or destroy matter but can only rearrange it.

Photosynthesis, which takes place within the cells of green plant tissues, is a particularly important example of how chemical reactions rearrange matter. Humans and other animals ultimately depend on photosynthesis for food and oxygen, and this process is at the foundation of almost all ecosystems. The following chemical shorthand summarizes the process of photosynthesis:

$$6 \, CO_2 + 6 \, H_2O \rightarrow C_6H_{12}O_6 + 6 \, O_2$$

The raw materials of photosynthesis are carbon dioxide (CO_2), which is taken from the air, and water (H_2O), which is absorbed from the soil. Within the plant cells, sunlight powers the conversion of these ingredients to a sugar called glucose ($C_6H_{12}O_6$) and oxygen molecules (O_2), a by-product that the plant releases into the surroundings **(Figure 2.19)**. Although photosynthesis is actually a sequence of many chemical reactions, we still end up with the same number and types of atoms that we had when we started. Matter has simply been rearranged, with an input of energy provided by sunlight.

All chemical reactions are reversible, with the products of the forward reaction becoming the reactants for the reverse reaction. For example, hydrogen and nitrogen molecules can combine to form ammonia, but ammonia can also decompose to regenerate hydrogen and nitrogen:

$$3 \, H_2 + N_2 \rightleftharpoons 2 \, NH_3$$

The two opposite-headed arrows indicate that the reaction is reversible.

One of the factors affecting the rate of a reaction is the concentration of reactants. The greater the concentration of reactant molecules, the more frequently they collide with one another and have an opportunity to react and form products. The same holds true for products. As products accumulate, collisions resulting in the reverse reaction become more frequent. Eventually, the forward and reverse reactions occur at the same rate, and the relative concentrations of products and reactants stop changing. The point at which the reactions offset one another exactly is called **chemical equilibrium**. This is a dynamic equilibrium; reactions are still going on, but with no net effect on the concentrations of reactants and products. Equilibrium does *not* mean that the reactants and products are equal in concentration, but only that their concentrations have stabilized at a particular ratio. The reaction involving ammonia reaches equilibrium when ammonia decomposes as rapidly as it forms. In some chemical reactions, the equilibrium point may lie so far to the right that these reactions go essentially to completion; that is, virtually all the reactants are converted to products.

We will return to the subject of chemical reactions after more detailed study of the various types of molecules that are important to life. In the next chapter, we focus on water, the substance in which all the chemical processes of organisms occur.

CONCEPT CHECK 2.4

1. **MAKE CONNECTIONS** Consider the reaction between hydrogen and oxygen that forms water, shown with ball-and-stick models on page 42. Study Figure 2.12 and draw the Lewis dot structures representing this reaction.
2. Which type of chemical reaction occurs faster at equilibrium, the formation of products from reactants or reactants from products?
3. **WHAT IF?** Write an equation that uses the products of photosynthesis as reactants and the reactants of photosynthesis as products. Add energy as another product. This new equation describes a process that occurs in your cells. Describe this equation in words. How does this equation relate to breathing?

For suggested answers, see Appendix A.

SUMMARY OF KEY CONCEPTS

CONCEPT 2.1

Matter consists of chemical elements in pure form and in combinations called compounds (pp. 31–32)

- **Elements** cannot be broken down chemically to other substances. A **compound** contains two or more different elements in a fixed ratio. Oxygen, carbon, hydrogen, and nitrogen make up approximately 96% of living matter.

> **?** *In what way does the need for iodine or iron in your diet differ from your need for calcium or phosphorus?*

CONCEPT 2.2

An element's properties depend on the structure of its atoms (pp. 33–37)

- An **atom**, the smallest unit of an element, has the following components:

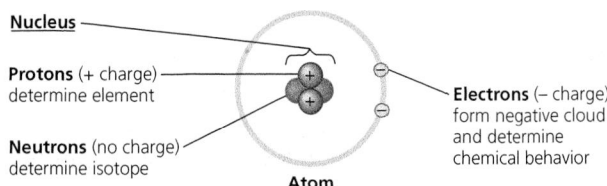

Nucleus
Protons (+ charge) determine element
Neutrons (no charge) determine isotope
Electrons (– charge) form negative cloud and determine chemical behavior
Atom

- An electrically neutral atom has equal numbers of electrons and protons; the number of protons determines the **atomic number**. The **atomic mass** is measured in **daltons** and is roughly equal to the sum of protons plus neutrons. **Isotopes** of an element differ from each other in neutron number and therefore mass. Unstable isotopes give off particles and energy as radioactivity.
- In an atom, electrons occupy specific **electron shells**; the electrons in a shell have a characteristic energy level. Electron distribution in shells determines the chemical behavior of an atom. An atom that has an incomplete outer shell, the **valence shell**, is reactive.
- Electrons exist in **orbitals**, three-dimensional spaces with specific shapes that are components of electron shells.

Electron orbitals

> **DRAW IT** *Draw the electron distribution diagrams for neon ($_{10}$Ne) and argon ($_{18}$Ar). Use these diagrams to explain why these elements are chemically unreactive.*

CONCEPT 2.3

The formation and function of molecules depend on chemical bonding between atoms (pp. 38–42)

- **Chemical bonds** form when atoms interact and complete their valence shells. **Covalent bonds** form when pairs of electrons are shared.

$$H\cdot + H\cdot \longrightarrow H:H$$
Single covalent bond

$$:\ddot{O}: + \cdot\ddot{O}: \longrightarrow \ddot{O}::\ddot{O}:$$
Double covalent bond

- **Molecules** consist of two or more covalently bonded atoms. The attraction of an atom for the electrons of a covalent bond is its **electronegativity**. If both atoms are the same, they have the same electronegativity and share a **nonpolar covalent bond**. Electrons of a **polar covalent bond** are pulled closer to the more electronegative atom.
- An **ion** forms when an atom or molecule gains or loses an electron and becomes charged. An **ionic bond** is the attraction between two oppositely charged ions.

Ionic bond

Electron transfer forms ions

Na
Sodium atom

Cl
Chlorine atom

Na⁺
Sodium ion (a cation)

Cl⁻
Chloride ion (an anion)

- Weak bonds reinforce the shapes of large molecules and help molecules adhere to each other. A **hydrogen bond** is an attraction between a hydrogen atom carrying a partial positive charge ($\delta+$) and an electronegative atom ($\delta-$). **Van der Waals interactions** occur between transiently positive and negative regions of molecules.
- A molecule's shape is determined by the positions of its atoms' valence orbitals. Covalent bonds result in hybrid orbitals, which are responsible for the shapes of H_2O, CH_4, and many more complex biological molecules. Shape is usually the basis for the recognition of one biological molecule by another.

> **?** *In terms of electron sharing between atoms, compare nonpolar covalent bonds, polar covalent bonds, and the formation of ions.*

CONCEPT 2.4

Chemical reactions make and break chemical bonds (pp. 42–43)

- **Chemical reactions** change **reactants** into **products** while conserving matter. All chemical reactions are theoretically reversible. **Chemical equilibrium** is reached when the forward and reverse reaction rates are equal.

> **?** *What would happen to the concentration of products if more reactants were added to a reaction that was in chemical equilibrium? How would this addition affect the equilibrium?*

TEST YOUR UNDERSTANDING

LEVEL 1: KNOWLEDGE/COMPREHENSION

1. In the term *trace element*, the adjective *trace* means that
   a. the element is required in very small amounts.
   b. the element can be used as a label to trace atoms through an organism's metabolism.
   c. the element is very rare on Earth.
   d. the element enhances health but is not essential for the organism's long-term survival.
   e. the element passes rapidly through the organism.

2. Compared with ^{31}P, the radioactive isotope ^{32}P has
   a. a different atomic number.
   b. a different charge.
   c. one more proton.
   d. one more electron.
   e. one more neutron.

3. The reactivity of an atom arises from
   a. the average distance of the outermost electron shell from the nucleus.
   b. the existence of unpaired electrons in the valence shell.
   c. the sum of the potential energies of all the electron shells.
   d. the potential energy of the valence shell.
   e. the energy difference between the s and p orbitals.

4. Which statement is true of all atoms that are anions?
   a. The atom has more electrons than protons.
   b. The atom has more protons than electrons.
   c. The atom has fewer protons than does a neutral atom of the same element.
   d. The atom has more neutrons than protons.
   e. The net charge is $1-$.

5. Which of the following statements correctly describes any chemical reaction that has reached equilibrium?
   a. The concentrations of products and reactants are equal.
   b. The reaction is now irreversible.
   c. Both forward and reverse reactions have halted.
   d. The rates of the forward and reverse reactions are equal.
   e. No reactants remain.

LEVEL 2: APPLICATION/ANALYSIS

6. We can represent atoms by listing the number of protons, neutrons, and electrons—for example, $2p^+$, $2n^0$, $2e^-$ for helium. Which of the following represents the ^{18}O isotope of oxygen?
   a. $6p^+$, $8n^0$, $6e^-$
   b. $8p^+$, $10n^0$, $8e^-$
   c. $9p^+$, $9n^0$, $9e^-$
   d. $7p^+$, $2n^0$, $9e^-$
   e. $10p^+$, $8n^0$, $9e^-$

7. The atomic number of sulfur is 16. Sulfur combines with hydrogen by covalent bonding to form a compound, hydrogen sulfide. Based on the number of valence electrons in a sulfur atom, predict the molecular formula of the compound.
   a. HS   b. HS_2 c. H_2S d. H_3S_2 e. H_4S

8. What coefficients must be placed in the following blanks so that all atoms are accounted for in the products?

   $C_6H_{12}O_6 \rightarrow$ _____ $C_2H_6O +$ _____ CO_2

   a. 1; 2   b. 3; 1   c. 1; 3   d. 1; 1   e. 2; 2

9. **DRAW IT** Draw Lewis dot structures for each hypothetical molecule shown below, using the correct number of valence electrons for each atom. Determine which molecule makes sense because each atom has a complete valence shell and each bond has the correct number of electrons. Explain what makes the other molecules nonsensical, considering the number of bonds each type of atom can make.

   (a) $O{=}C{-}H$

   (b)
   ```
        H   H
        |   |
   H—O—C—C=O
        |
        H
   ```

   (c)
   ```
        H       H
        |       |
   H—C—H—C=O
        |
        H
   ```

   (d) $H{-}N{=}H$

LEVEL 3: SYNTHESIS/EVALUATION

10. **EVOLUTION CONNECTION**

    The percentages of naturally occurring elements making up the human body (see Table 2.1) are similar to the percentages of these elements found in other organisms. How could you account for this similarity among organisms?

11. **SCIENTIFIC INQUIRY**

    Female silkworm moths (*Bombyx mori*) attract males by emitting chemical signals that spread through the air. A male hundreds of meters away can detect these molecules and fly toward their source. The sensory organs responsible for this behavior are the comblike antennae visible in the photograph shown here. Each filament of an antenna is equipped with thousands of receptor cells that detect the sex attractant. Based on what you learned in this chapter, propose a hypothesis to account for the ability of the male moth to detect a specific molecule in the presence of many other molecules in the air. What predictions does your hypothesis make? Design an experiment to test one of these predictions.

12. **WRITE ABOUT A THEME**

    Emergent Properties While waiting at an airport, Neil Campbell once overheard this claim: "It's paranoid and ignorant to worry about industry or agriculture contaminating the environment with their chemical wastes. After all, this stuff is just made of the same atoms that were already present in our environment." Drawing on your knowledge of electron distribution, bonding, and the theme of emergent properties (pp. 3–5), write a short essay (100–150 words) countering this argument.

For selected answers, see Appendix A.

MasteringBIOLOGY   www.masteringbiology.com

1. MasteringBiology® Assignments

Tutorials The Anatomy of Atoms • Atomic Number and Mass Number

Activities Structure of the Atomic Nucleus • Electron Arrangement • Covalent Bonds • Nonpolar and Polar Molecules • Ionic Bonds • Hydrogen Bonds

Questions Student Misconceptions • Reading Quiz • Multiple Choice • End-of-Chapter

2. eText

Read your book online, search, take notes, highlight text, and more.

3. The Study Area

Practice Tests • Cumulative Test • **BioFlix** 3-D Animations • MP3 Tutor Sessions • Videos • Activities • Investigations • Lab Media • Audio Glossary • Word Study Tools • Art

3

Water and Life

▲ **Figure 3.1 How does the habitat of a polar bear depend on the chemistry of water?**

KEY CONCEPTS

3.1 Polar covalent bonds in water molecules result in hydrogen bonding

3.2 Four emergent properties of water contribute to Earth's suitability for life

3.3 Acidic and basic conditions affect living organisms

OVERVIEW

The Molecule That Supports All of Life

As astronomers study newly discovered planets orbiting distant stars, they hope to find evidence of water on these far-off celestial bodies, for water is the substance that makes possible life as we know it here on Earth. All organisms familiar to us are made mostly of water and live in an environment dominated by water. Water is the biological medium here on Earth, and possibly on other planets as well.

Three-quarters of Earth's surface is covered by water. Although most of this water is in liquid form, water is also present on Earth as a solid (ice) and a gas (water vapor). Water is the only common substance to exist in the natural environment in all three physical states of matter. Furthermore, the solid state of water floats on the liquid, a rare property emerging from the chemistry of the water molecule. Ice can thus provide a hunting platform for the polar bear in **Figure 3.1**.

The abundance of water is a major reason Earth is habitable. In a classic book called *The Fitness of the Environment*, ecologist Lawrence Henderson highlighted the importance of water to life. While acknowledging that life adapts to its environment through natural selection, Henderson emphasized that for life to exist at all, the environment must first be suitable.

Life on Earth began in water and evolved there for 3 billion years before spreading onto land. Modern life, even terrestrial (land-dwelling) life, remains tied to water. All living organisms require water more than any other substance. Human beings, for example, can survive for quite a few weeks without food, but only a week or so without water. Molecules of water participate in many chemical reactions necessary to sustain life. Most cells are surrounded by water, and cells themselves are about 70–95% water.

What properties of the simple water molecule make it so indispensable to life on Earth? In this chapter, you will learn how the structure of a water molecule allows it to interact with other molecules, including other water molecules. This ability leads to water's unique emergent properties that help make Earth suitable for life.

CONCEPT 3.1

Polar covalent bonds in water molecules result in hydrogen bonding

Water is so common that it is easy to overlook the fact that it is an exceptional substance with many extraordinary qualities. Following the theme of emergent properties, we can trace water's unique behavior to the structure and interactions of its molecules.

Studied on its own, the water molecule is deceptively simple. It is shaped like a wide V, with its two hydrogen atoms joined to the oxygen atom by single covalent bonds. Oxygen is more electronegative than hydrogen, so the electrons of the covalent bonds spend more time closer to oxygen than to hydrogen; these are **polar covalent bonds** (see Figure 2.13). This unequal sharing of electrons and water's V-like shape make it a **polar molecule**, meaning that its overall charge is unevenly distributed: The oxygen region of the molecule has a partial negative charge ($\delta-$), and each hydrogen has a partial positive charge ($\delta+$).

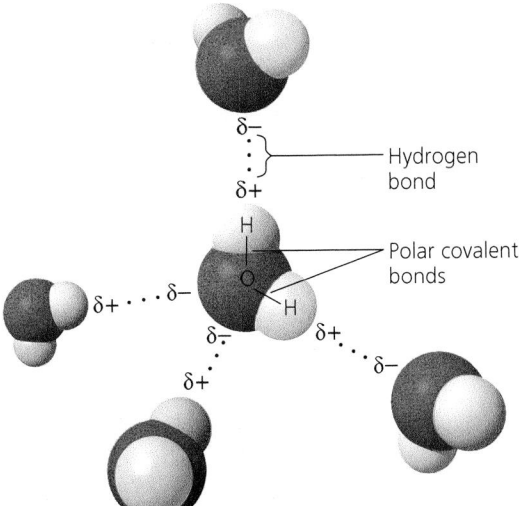

▲ **Figure 3.2 Hydrogen bonds between water molecules.**
The charged regions in a water molecule are due to its polar covalent bonds. Oppositely charged regions of neighboring water molecules are attracted to each other, forming hydrogen bonds. Each molecule can hydrogen-bond to multiple partners, and these associations are constantly changing.

DRAW IT *Draw partial charges on all the atoms of the water molecule on the far left above, and draw two more water molecules hydrogen-bonded to it.*

The properties of water arise from attractions between oppositely charged atoms of different water molecules: The slightly positive hydrogen of one molecule is attracted to the slightly negative oxygen of a nearby molecule. The two molecules are thus held together by a hydrogen bond (**Figure 3.2**). When water is in its liquid form, its hydrogen bonds are very fragile, each about 1/20 as strong as a covalent bond. The hydrogen bonds form, break, and re-form with great frequency. Each lasts only a few trillionths of a second, but the molecules are constantly forming new hydrogen bonds with a succession of partners. Therefore, at any instant, a substantial percentage of all the water molecules are hydrogen-bonded to their neighbors. The extraordinary qualities of water are emergent properties resulting in large part from the hydrogen bonding that organizes water molecules into a higher level of structural order.

CONCEPT CHECK 3.1

1. **MAKE CONNECTIONS** What is electronegativity, and how does it affect interactions between water molecules? Review p. 39 and Figure 2.13.
2. Why is it unlikely that two neighboring water molecules would be arranged like this?

$$O \diagdown_{H\ H}^{H\ H} \diagup O$$

3. **WHAT IF?** What would be the effect on the properties of the water molecule if oxygen and hydrogen had equal electronegativity?

For suggested answers, see Appendix A.

Four emergent properties of water contribute to Earth's suitability for life

We will examine four emergent properties of water that contribute to Earth's suitability as an environment for life: cohesive behavior, ability to moderate temperature, expansion upon freezing, and versatility as a solvent.

Cohesion of Water Molecules

Water molecules stay close to each other as a result of hydrogen bonding. Although the arrangement of molecules in a sample of liquid water is constantly changing, at any given moment many of the molecules are linked by multiple hydrogen bonds. These linkages make water more structured than most other liquids. Collectively, the hydrogen bonds hold the substance together, a phenomenon called **cohesion**.

Cohesion due to hydrogen bonding contributes to the transport of water and dissolved nutrients against gravity in plants (**Figure 3.3**). Water from the roots reaches the leaves through a network of water-conducting cells. As water evaporates from a

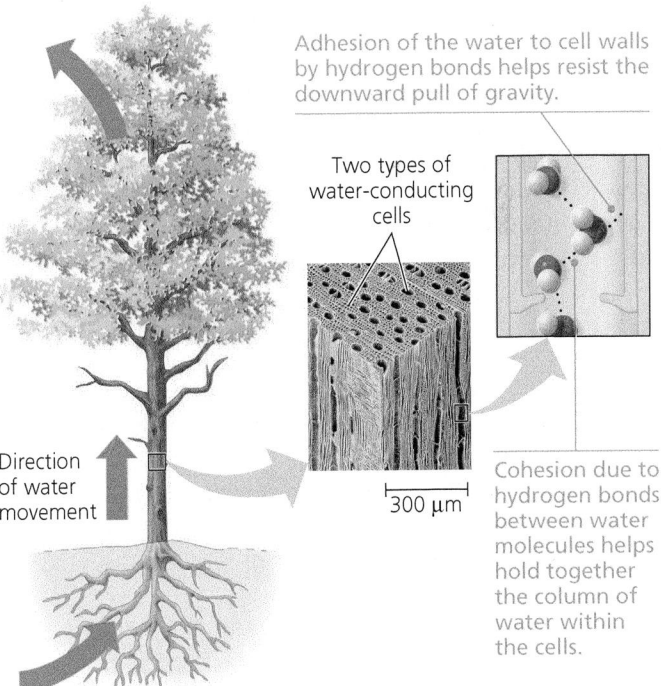

Adhesion of the water to cell walls by hydrogen bonds helps resist the downward pull of gravity.

Two types of water-conducting cells

Direction of water movement

300 μm

Cohesion due to hydrogen bonds between water molecules helps hold together the column of water within the cells.

▲ **Figure 3.3 Water transport in plants.** Evaporation from leaves pulls water upward from the roots through water-conducting cells. Because of the properties of cohesion and adhesion, the tallest trees can transport water more than 100 m upward—approximately one-quarter the height of the Empire State Building in New York City.

ANIMATION **BioFlix** Visit the Study Area at **www.masteringbiology.com** for the BioFlix® 3-D Animation on Water Transport in Plants.

▲ **Figure 3.4 Walking on water.** The high surface tension of water, resulting from the collective strength of its hydrogen bonds, allows this raft spider to walk on the surface of a pond.

leaf, hydrogen bonds cause water molecules leaving the veins to tug on molecules farther down, and the upward pull is transmitted through the water-conducting cells all the way to the roots. **Adhesion**, the clinging of one substance to another, also plays a role. Adhesion of water to cell walls by hydrogen bonds helps counter the downward pull of gravity (see Figure 3.3).

Related to cohesion is **surface tension**, a measure of how difficult it is to stretch or break the surface of a liquid. Water has a greater surface tension than most other liquids. At the interface between water and air is an ordered arrangement of water molecules, hydrogen-bonded to one another and to the water below. This makes the water behave as though coated with an invisible film. You can observe the surface tension of water by slightly overfilling a drinking glass; the water will stand above the rim. In a more biological example, some animals can stand, walk, or run on water without breaking the surface **(Figure 3.4)**.

Moderation of Temperature by Water

Water moderates air temperature by absorbing heat from air that is warmer and releasing the stored heat to air that is cooler. Water is effective as a heat bank because it can absorb or release a relatively large amount of heat with only a slight change in its own temperature. To understand this capability of water, we must first look briefly at heat and temperature.

Heat and Temperature

Anything that moves has **kinetic energy**, the energy of motion. Atoms and molecules have kinetic energy because they are always moving, although not necessarily in any particular direction. The faster a molecule moves, the greater its kinetic energy. **Heat** is a form of energy. For a given body of matter, the amount of heat is a measure of the matter's *total* kinetic energy due to motion of its molecules; thus, heat depends in part on the matter's volume. Although heat is related to temperature, they are not the same thing. **Temperature** is a

measure of heat intensity that represents the *average* kinetic energy of the molecules, regardless of volume. When water is heated in a coffeemaker, the average speed of the molecules increases, and the thermometer records this as a rise in temperature of the liquid. The amount of heat also increases in this case. Note, however, that although the pot of coffee has a much higher temperature than, say, the water in a swimming pool, the swimming pool contains more heat because of its much greater volume.

Whenever two objects of different temperature are brought together, heat passes from the warmer to the cooler object until the two are the same temperature. Molecules in the cooler object speed up at the expense of the kinetic energy of the warmer object. An ice cube cools a drink not by adding coldness to the liquid, but by absorbing heat from the liquid as the ice itself melts.

In general, we will use the **Celsius scale** to indicate temperature. (Celsius degrees are abbreviated °C; Appendix C shows how to convert between Celsius and Fahrenheit.) At sea level, water freezes at 0°C and boils at 100°C. The temperature of the human body averages 37°C, and comfortable room temperature is about 20–25°C.

One convenient unit of heat used in this book is the **calorie (cal)**. A calorie is the amount of heat it takes to raise the temperature of 1 g of water by 1°C. Conversely, a calorie is also the amount of heat that 1 g of water releases when it cools by 1°C. A **kilocalorie (kcal)**, 1,000 cal, is the quantity of heat required to raise the temperature of 1 kilogram (kg) of water by 1°C. (The "calories" on food packages are actually kilocalories.) Another energy unit used in this book is the **joule (J)**. One joule equals 0.239 cal; one calorie equals 4.184 J.

Water's High Specific Heat

The ability of water to stabilize temperature stems from its relatively high specific heat. The **specific heat** of a substance is defined as the amount of heat that must be absorbed or lost for 1 g of that substance to change its temperature by 1°C. We already know water's specific heat because we have defined a calorie as the amount of heat that causes 1 g of water to change its temperature by 1°C. Therefore, the specific heat of water is 1 calorie per gram and per degree Celsius, abbreviated as 1 cal/g·°C. Compared with most other substances, water has an unusually high specific heat. For example, ethyl alcohol, the type of alcohol in alcoholic beverages, has a specific heat of 0.6 cal/g·°C; that is, only 0.6 cal is required to raise the temperature of 1 g of ethyl alcohol by 1°C.

Because of the high specific heat of water relative to other materials, water will change its temperature less when it absorbs or loses a given amount of heat. The reason you can burn your fingers by touching the side of an iron pot on the stove when the water in the pot is still lukewarm is that the specific heat of water is ten times greater than that of iron.

▲ **Figure 3.5 Effect of a large body of water on climate.** By absorbing or releasing heat, oceans moderate coastal climates. In this example from an August day in Southern California, the relatively cool ocean reduces coastal air temperatures by absorbing heat.

In other words, the same amount of heat will raise the temperature of 1 g of the iron much faster than it will raise the temperature of 1 g of the water. Specific heat can be thought of as a measure of how well a substance resists changing its temperature when it absorbs or releases heat. Water resists changing its temperature; when it does change its temperature, it absorbs or loses a relatively large quantity of heat for each degree of change.

We can trace water's high specific heat, like many of its other properties, to hydrogen bonding. Heat must be absorbed in order to break hydrogen bonds; by the same token, heat is released when hydrogen bonds form. A calorie of heat causes a relatively small change in the temperature of water because much of the heat is used to disrupt hydrogen bonds before the water molecules can begin moving faster. And when the temperature of water drops slightly, many additional hydrogen bonds form, releasing a considerable amount of energy in the form of heat.

What is the relevance of water's high specific heat to life on Earth? A large body of water can absorb and store a huge amount of heat from the sun in the daytime and during summer while warming up only a few degrees. At night and during winter, the gradually cooling water can warm the air. This is the reason coastal areas generally have milder climates than inland regions (Figure 3.5). The high specific heat of water also tends to stabilize ocean temperatures, creating a favorable environment for marine life. Thus, because of its high specific heat, the water that covers most of Earth keeps temperature fluctuations on land and in water within limits that permit life. Also, because organisms are made primarily of water, they are better able to resist changes in their own temperature than if they were made of a liquid with a lower specific heat.

Evaporative Cooling

Molecules of any liquid stay close together because they are attracted to one another. Molecules moving fast enough to overcome these attractions can depart the liquid and enter the air as a gas. This transformation from a liquid to a gas is called vaporization, or *evaporation*. Recall that the speed of molecular movement varies and that temperature is the *average* kinetic energy of molecules. Even at low temperatures, the speediest molecules can escape into the air. Some evaporation occurs at any temperature; a glass of water at room temperature, for example, will eventually evaporate completely. If a liquid is heated, the average kinetic energy of molecules increases and the liquid evaporates more rapidly.

Heat of vaporization is the quantity of heat a liquid must absorb for 1 g of it to be converted from the liquid to the gaseous state. For the same reason that water has a high specific heat, it also has a high heat of vaporization relative to most other liquids. To evaporate 1 g of water at 25°C, about 580 cal of heat is needed—nearly double the amount needed to vaporize a gram of alcohol or ammonia. Water's high heat of vaporization is another emergent property resulting from the strength of its hydrogen bonds, which must be broken before the molecules can make their exodus from the liquid.

The high amount of energy required to vaporize water has a wide range of effects. On a global scale, for example, it helps moderate Earth's climate. A considerable amount of solar heat absorbed by tropical seas is consumed during the evaporation of surface water. Then, as moist tropical air circulates poleward, it releases heat as it condenses and forms rain. On an organismal level, water's high heat of vaporization accounts for the severity of steam burns. These burns are caused by the heat energy released when steam condenses into liquid on the skin.

As a liquid evaporates, the surface of the liquid that remains behind cools down. This **evaporative cooling** occurs because the "hottest" molecules, those with the greatest kinetic energy, are the most likely to leave as gas. It is as if the hundred fastest runners at a college transferred to another school; the average speed of the remaining students would decline.

Evaporative cooling of water contributes to the stability of temperature in lakes and ponds and also provides a mechanism that prevents terrestrial organisms from overheating. For example, evaporation of water from the leaves of a plant helps keep the tissues in the leaves from becoming too warm in the sunlight. Evaporation of sweat from human skin dissipates body heat and helps prevent overheating on a hot day or when excess heat is generated by strenuous activity. High humidity on a hot day increases discomfort because the high concentration of water vapor in the air inhibits the evaporation of sweat from the body.

Floating of Ice on Liquid Water

Water is one of the few substances that are less dense as a solid than as a liquid. In other words, ice floats on liquid water. While other materials contract and become denser when they solidify, water expands. The cause of this exotic behavior is, once again, hydrogen bonding. At temperatures above

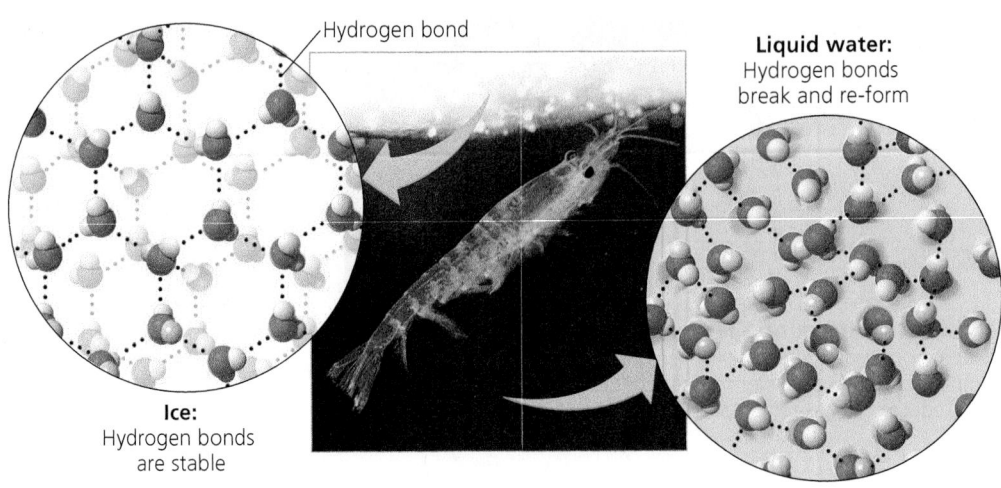

▶ Figure 3.6 **Ice: crystalline structure and floating barrier.** In ice, each molecule is hydrogen-bonded to four neighbors in a three-dimensional crystal. Because the crystal is spacious, ice has fewer molecules than an equal volume of liquid water. In other words, ice is less dense than liquid water. Floating ice becomes a barrier that protects the liquid water below from the colder air. The marine organism shown here is a type of shrimp called krill; it was photographed beneath floating ice in the Southern Ocean near Antarctica.

WHAT IF? *If water did not form hydrogen bonds, what would happen to the shrimp's environment?*

Hydrogen bond

Ice: Hydrogen bonds are stable

Liquid water: Hydrogen bonds break and re-form

4°C, water behaves like other liquids, expanding as it warms and contracting as it cools. As the temperature falls from 4°C to 0°C, water begins to freeze because more and more of its molecules are moving too slowly to break hydrogen bonds. At 0°C, the molecules become locked into a crystalline lattice, each water molecule hydrogen-bonded to four partners **(Figure 3.6)**. The hydrogen bonds keep the molecules at "arm's length," far enough apart to make ice about 10% less dense (10% fewer molecules for the same volume) than liquid water at 4°C. When ice absorbs enough heat for its temperature to rise above 0°C, hydrogen bonds between molecules are disrupted. As the crystal collapses, the ice melts, and molecules are free to slip closer together. Water reaches its greatest density at 4°C and then begins to expand as the molecules move faster. Even in liquid water, many of the molecules are connected by hydrogen bonds, though only transiently: The hydrogen bonds are constantly breaking and re-forming.

The ability of ice to float due to its lower density is an important factor in the suitability of the environment for life. If ice sank, then eventually all ponds, lakes, and even oceans would freeze solid, making life as we know it impossible on Earth. During summer, only the upper few inches of the ocean would thaw. Instead, when a deep body of water cools, the floating ice insulates the liquid water below, preventing it from freezing and allowing life to exist under the frozen surface, as shown in the photo in Figure 3.6. Besides insulating the water below, ice also provides solid habitat for some animals, such as polar bears and seals (see Figure 3.1).

Along with many other scientists, Susan Solomon, the interviewee for this unit (see pp. 28–29), is worried that these bodies of ice are at risk of disappearing. Global warming, which is caused by carbon dioxide and other "greenhouse" gases in the atmosphere, is having a profound effect on icy environments around the globe. In the Arctic, the average air temperature has risen 1.4°C just since 1961. This temperature increase has affected the seasonal balance between Arctic sea ice and liquid water, causing ice to form later in the year, to melt earlier, and to cover a smaller area. The alarming rate at which glaciers and Arctic sea ice are disappearing is posing an extreme challenge to animals that depend on ice for their survival.

Water: The Solvent of Life

A sugar cube placed in a glass of water will dissolve. The glass will then contain a uniform mixture of sugar and water; the concentration of dissolved sugar will be the same everywhere in the mixture. A liquid that is a completely homogeneous mixture of two or more substances is called a **solution**. The dissolving agent of a solution is the **solvent**, and the substance that is dissolved is the **solute**. In this case, water is the solvent and sugar is the solute. An **aqueous solution** is one in which water is the solvent.

The medieval alchemists tried to find a universal solvent, one that would dissolve anything. They learned that nothing works better than water. Yet, water is not a universal solvent; if it were, it would dissolve any container in which it was stored, including our cells. Water is a very versatile solvent, however, a quality we can trace to the polarity of the water molecule.

Suppose, for example, that a spoonful of table salt, the ionic compound sodium chloride (NaCl), is placed in water **(Figure 3.7)**. At the surface of each grain, or crystal, of salt, the sodium and chloride ions are exposed to the solvent. These ions and the water molecules have a mutual affinity owing to the attraction between opposite charges. The oxygen regions of the water molecules are negatively charged and are attracted to sodium cations. The hydrogen regions are positively charged and are attracted to chloride anions. As a result, water molecules surround the individual sodium and chloride ions, separating and shielding them from one another. The sphere of water molecules around each dissolved ion is called a **hydration shell**. Working inward from the surface of each salt crystal, water eventually dissolves all the ions. The result is a solution of two solutes, sodium cations and chloride anions, homogeneously mixed with water, the solvent. Other ionic compounds also dissolve in water. Seawater, for instance, contains a great variety of dissolved ions, as do living cells.

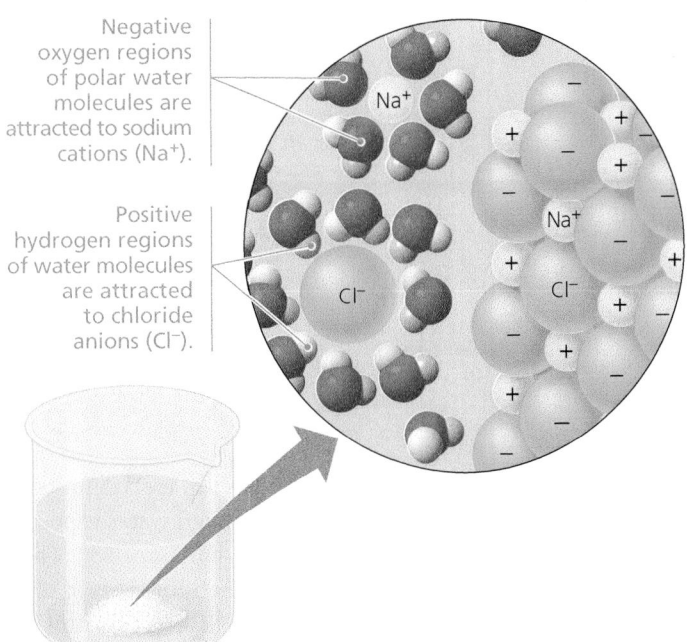

Negative oxygen regions of polar water molecules are attracted to sodium cations (Na^+).

Positive hydrogen regions of water molecules are attracted to chloride anions (Cl^-).

▲ **Figure 3.7 Table salt dissolving in water.** A sphere of water molecules, called a hydration shell, surrounds each solute ion.

WHAT IF? *What would happen if you heated this solution for a long time?*

A compound does not need to be ionic to dissolve in water; many compounds made up of nonionic polar molecules, such as sugars, are also water-soluble. Such compounds dissolve when water molecules surround each of the solute molecules, forming hydrogen bonds with them. Even molecules as large as proteins can dissolve in water if they have ionic and polar regions on their surface **(Figure 3.8)**. Many different kinds of polar compounds are dissolved (along with ions) in the water of such biological fluids as blood, the sap of plants, and the liquid within all cells. Water is the solvent of life.

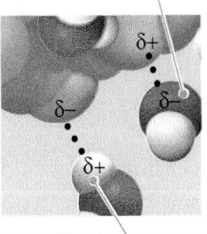

This oxygen is attracted to a slight positive charge on the lysozyme molecule.

This hydrogen is attracted to a slight negative charge on the lysozyme molecule.

▲ **Figure 3.8 A water-soluble protein.** Human lysozyme is a protein found in tears and saliva that has antibacterial action. This model shows the lysozyme molecule (purple) in an aqueous environment. Ionic and polar regions on the protein's surface attract water molecules.

Hydrophilic and Hydrophobic Substances

Any substance that has an affinity for water is said to be **hydrophilic** (from the Greek *hydro*, water, and *philios*, loving). In some cases, substances can be hydrophilic without actually dissolving. For example, some molecules in cells are so large that they do not dissolve. Instead, they remain suspended in the aqueous liquid of the cell. Such a mixture is an example of a **colloid**, a stable suspension of fine particles in a liquid. Another example of a hydrophilic substance that does not dissolve is cotton, a plant product. Cotton consists of giant molecules of cellulose, a compound with numerous regions of partial positive and partial negative charges that can form hydrogen bonds with water. Water adheres to the cellulose fibers. Thus, a cotton towel does a great job of drying the body, yet it does not dissolve in the washing machine. Cellulose is also present in the walls of water-conducting cells in a plant; you read earlier how the adhesion of water to these hydrophilic walls allows water transport to occur.

There are, of course, substances that do not have an affinity for water. Substances that are nonionic and nonpolar (or otherwise cannot form hydrogen bonds) actually seem to repel water; these substances are said to be **hydrophobic** (from the Greek *phobos*, fearing). An example from the kitchen is vegetable oil, which, as you know, does not mix stably with water-based substances such as vinegar. The hydrophobic behavior of the oil molecules results from a prevalence of relatively nonpolar covalent bonds, in this case bonds between carbon and hydrogen, which share electrons almost equally. Hydrophobic molecules related to oils are major ingredients of cell membranes. (Imagine what would happen to a cell if its membrane dissolved!)

Solute Concentration in Aqueous Solutions

Biological chemistry is "wet" chemistry. Most of the chemical reactions in organisms involve solutes dissolved in water. To understand such reactions, we must know how many atoms and molecules are involved and be able to calculate the concentration of solutes in an aqueous solution (the number of solute molecules in a volume of solution).

When carrying out experiments, we use mass to calculate the number of molecules. We know the mass of each atom in a given molecule, so we can calculate the **molecular mass**, which is simply the sum of the masses of all the atoms in a molecule. As an example, let's calculate the molecular mass of table sugar (sucrose), which has the molecular formula $C_{12}H_{22}O_{11}$. In round numbers of daltons, the mass of a carbon atom is 12, the mass of a hydrogen atom is 1, and the mass of an oxygen atom is 16. Thus, sucrose has a molecular mass of $(12 \times 12) + (22 \times 1) + (11 \times 16) = 342$ daltons. Of course, weighing out small numbers of molecules is not practical. For this reason, we usually measure substances in units called moles. Just as a dozen always means 12 objects, a **mole (mol)** represents an exact number of objects: 6.02×10^{23}, which is called Avogadro's number. Because of the way in which Avogadro's number and the unit *dalton* were originally defined, there are 6.02×10^{23} daltons in 1 g. This is significant because once we determine the molecular mass of a molecule such as sucrose, we can use the same number (342), but with the unit *gram*, to represent the mass of 6.02×10^{23} molecules of sucrose, or 1 mol of sucrose (this is sometimes called the *molar mass*). To obtain 1 mol of sucrose in the lab, therefore, we weigh out 342 g.

The practical advantage of measuring a quantity of chemicals in moles is that a mole of one substance has exactly the same number of molecules as a mole of any other substance. If the molecular mass of substance A is 342 daltons and that of substance B is 10 daltons, then 342 g of A will have the same number of molecules as 10 g of B. A mole of ethyl alcohol (C_2H_6O) also contains 6.02×10^{23} molecules, but its mass is only 46 g because the mass of a molecule of ethyl alcohol is less than that of a molecule of sucrose. Measuring in moles makes it convenient for scientists working in the laboratory to combine substances in fixed ratios of molecules.

How would we make a liter (L) of solution consisting of 1 mol of sucrose dissolved in water? We would measure out 342 g of sucrose and then gradually add water, while stirring, until the sugar was completely dissolved. We would then add enough water to bring the total volume of the solution up to 1 L. At that point, we would have a 1-molar (1 *M*) solution of sucrose. **Molarity**—the number of moles of solute per liter of solution—is the unit of concentration most often used by biologists for aqueous solutions.

Water's capacity as a versatile solvent complements the other properties discussed in this chapter. Since these remarkable properties allow water to support life on Earth so well, scientists who seek life elsewhere in the universe look for water as a sign that a planet might sustain life.

Possible Evolution of Life on Other Planets with Water

EVOLUTION Humans have probably always gazed skyward, wondering whether other living beings exist beyond Earth. And if life has arisen on other planets, into what form or forms has it evolved? Biologists who look for life elsewhere in the universe (known as *astrobiologists*) have concentrated their search on planets that might have water. To date, more than 200 planets have been found outside our solar system, and there is evidence for the presence of water vapor on one or two of them. In our own solar system, Mars has been most compelling to astrobiologists as a focus of study.

Like Earth, Mars has an ice cap at both poles. And in the decades since the age of space exploration began, scientists have found intriguing signs that water may exist elsewhere on Mars. Finally, in 2008, the robotic spacecraft *Phoenix* landed on Mars and began to sample its surface. Years of debate were

◀ **Figure 3.9 Subsurface ice and morning frost on Mars.** This photograph was taken by the Mars lander *Phoenix* in 2008. The trench was scraped by a robotic arm, uncovering ice (white in rectangle near bottom) below the surface material. Frost also appears as a white coating in several places in the upper half of the image. This photograph was colorized by NASA to highlight the ice.

resolved by the images sent back from *Phoenix*: Ice is definitely present just under Mars's surface, and enough water vapor is in the Martian atmosphere for frost to form (**Figure 3.9**). This exciting finding has reinvigorated the search for signs of life, past or present, on Mars and other planets. If any life-forms or fossils are found, their study will shed light on the process of evolution from an entirely new perspective.

CONCEPT CHECK 3.2

1. Describe how properties of water contribute to the upward movement of water in a tree.
2. Explain the saying "It's not the heat; it's the humidity."
3. How can the freezing of water crack boulders?
4. The concentration of the appetite-regulating hormone ghrelin is about $1.3 \times 10^{-10} M$ in a fasting person. How many molecules of ghrelin are in 1 L of blood?
5. **WHAT IF?** A water strider (which can walk on water) has legs that are coated with a hydrophobic substance. What might be the benefit? What would happen if the substance were hydrophilic?

For suggested answers, see Appendix A.

CONCEPT 3.3

Acidic and basic conditions affect living organisms

Occasionally, a hydrogen atom participating in a hydrogen bond between two water molecules shifts from one molecule to the other. When this happens, the hydrogen atom leaves its electron behind, and what is actually transferred is a **hydrogen ion** (H^+), a single proton with a charge of 1+. The water molecule that lost a proton is now a **hydroxide ion** (OH^-), which has a charge of 1−. The proton binds to the other water molecule, making that molecule a **hydronium ion** (H_3O^+). We can picture the chemical reaction as shown at the top of the next page.

2 H₂O   Hydronium   Hydroxide
                ion (H_3O^+)   ion (OH^-)

By convention, H^+ (the hydrogen ion) is used to represent H_3O^+ (the hydronium ion), and we follow that practice here. Keep in mind, though, that H^+ does not exist on its own in an aqueous solution. It is always associated with another water molecule in the form of H_3O^+.

As indicated by the double arrows, this is a reversible reaction that reaches a state of dynamic equilibrium when water molecules dissociate at the same rate that they are being re-formed from H^+ and OH^-. At this equilibrium point, the concentration of water molecules greatly exceeds the concentrations of H^+ and OH^-. In pure water, only one water molecule in every 554 million is dissociated; the concentration of each ion in pure water is 10^{-7} M (at 25°C). This means there is only one ten-millionth of a mole of hydrogen ions per liter of pure water and an equal number of hydroxide ions.

Although the dissociation of water is reversible and statistically rare, it is exceedingly important in the chemistry of life. H^+ and OH^- are very reactive. Changes in their concentrations can drastically affect a cell's proteins and other complex molecules. As we have seen, the concentrations of H^+ and OH^- are equal in pure water, but adding certain kinds of solutes, called acids and bases, disrupts this balance. Biologists use something called the pH scale to describe how acidic or basic (the opposite of acidic) a solution is. In the remainder of this chapter, you will learn about acids, bases, and pH and why changes in pH can adversely affect organisms.

Acids and Bases

What would cause an aqueous solution to have an imbalance in H^+ and OH^- concentrations? When acids dissolve in water, they donate additional H^+ to the solution. An **acid** is a substance that increases the hydrogen ion concentration of a solution. For example, when hydrochloric acid (HCl) is added to water, hydrogen ions dissociate from chloride ions:

$$HCl \rightarrow H^+ + Cl^-$$

This source of H^+ (dissociation of water is the other source) results in an acidic solution—one having more H^+ than OH^-.

A substance that reduces the hydrogen ion concentration of a solution is called a **base**. Some bases reduce the H^+ concentration directly by accepting hydrogen ions. Ammonia (NH_3), for instance, acts as a base when the unshared electron pair in nitrogen's valence shell attracts a hydrogen ion from the solution, resulting in an ammonium ion (NH_4^+):

$$NH_3 + H^+ \rightleftharpoons NH_4^+$$

Other bases reduce the H^+ concentration indirectly by dissociating to form hydroxide ions, which combine with hydrogen ions and form water. One such base is sodium hydroxide (NaOH), which in water dissociates into its ions:

$$NaOH \rightarrow Na^+ + OH^-$$

In either case, the base reduces the H^+ concentration. Solutions with a higher concentration of OH^- than H^+ are known as basic solutions. A solution in which the H^+ and OH^- concentrations are equal is said to be neutral.

Notice that single arrows were used in the reactions for HCl and NaOH. These compounds dissociate completely when mixed with water, so hydrochloric acid is called a strong acid and sodium hydroxide a strong base. In contrast, ammonia is a relatively weak base. The double arrows in the reaction for ammonia indicate that the binding and release of hydrogen ions are reversible reactions, although at equilibrium there will be a fixed ratio of NH_4^+ to NH_3.

There are also weak acids, which reversibly release and accept back hydrogen ions. An example is carbonic acid:

$$H_2CO_3 \rightleftharpoons HCO_3^- + H^+$$

  Carbonic   Bicarbonate   Hydrogen
    acid   ion   ion

Here the equilibrium so favors the reaction in the left direction that when carbonic acid is added to pure water, only 1% of the molecules are dissociated at any particular time. Still, that is enough to shift the balance of H^+ and OH^- from neutrality.

The pH Scale

In any aqueous solution at 25°C, the *product* of the H^+ and OH^- concentrations is constant at 10^{-14}. This can be written

$$[H^+][OH^-] = 10^{-14}$$

In such an equation, brackets indicate molar concentration. In a neutral solution at room temperature (25°C), $[H^+] = 10^{-7}$ and $[OH^-] = 10^{-7}$, so in this case, 10^{-14} is the product of $10^{-7} \times 10^{-7}$. If enough acid is added to a solution to increase $[H^+]$ to 10^{-5} M, then $[OH^-]$ will decline by an equivalent amount to 10^{-9} M (note that $10^{-5} \times 10^{-9} = 10^{-14}$). This constant relationship expresses the behavior of acids and bases in an aqueous solution. An acid not only adds hydrogen ions to a solution, but also removes hydroxide ions because of the tendency for H^+ to combine with OH^-, forming water. A base has the opposite effect, increasing OH^- concentration but also reducing H^+ concentration by the formation of water. If enough of a base is added to raise the OH^- concentration to 10^{-4} M, it will cause the H^+ concentration to drop to 10^{-10} M. Whenever we know the concentration of either H^+ or OH^- in an aqueous solution, we can deduce the concentration of the other ion.

Because the H^+ and OH^- concentrations of solutions can vary by a factor of 100 trillion or more, scientists have

pH Scale

- 0
- 1 Battery acid
- 2 Gastric juice, lemon juice
- 3 Vinegar, wine, cola
- 4 Tomato juice
      Beer
- 5 Black coffee
      Rainwater
- 6 Urine
      Saliva
- 7 **Pure water**
      Human blood, tears
- 8 Seawater
      Inside of small intestine
- 9
- 10
      Milk of magnesia
- 11
      Household ammonia
- 12
      Household bleach
- 13
      Oven cleaner
- 14

Increasingly Acidic [H⁺] > [OH⁻]

Neutral [H⁺] = [OH⁻]

Increasingly Basic [H⁺] < [OH⁻]

Acidic solution

Neutral solution

Basic solution

▲ **Figure 3.10 The pH scale and pH values of some aqueous solutions.**

developed a way to express this variation more conveniently than in moles per liter. The pH scale (**Figure 3.10**) compresses the range of H⁺ and OH⁻ concentrations by employing logarithms. The **pH** of a solution is defined as the negative logarithm (base 10) of the hydrogen ion concentration:

$$pH = -\log [H^+]$$

For a neutral aqueous solution, [H⁺] is 10^{-7} *M*, giving us

$$-\log 10^{-7} = -(-7) = 7$$

Notice that pH *declines* as H⁺ concentration *increases*. Notice, too, that although the pH scale is based on H⁺ concentration, it also implies OH⁻ concentration. A solution of pH 10 has a hydrogen ion concentration of 10^{-10} *M* and a hydroxide ion concentration of 10^{-4} *M*.

The pH of a neutral aqueous solution at 25°C is 7, the midpoint of the pH scale. A pH value less than 7 denotes an acidic solution; the lower the number, the more acidic the solution. The pH for basic solutions is above 7. Most biological fluids are within the range pH 6–8. There are a few exceptions, however,

including the strongly acidic digestive juice of the human stomach, which has a pH of about 2.

Remember that each pH unit represents a tenfold difference in H⁺ and OH⁻ concentrations. It is this mathematical feature that makes the pH scale so compact. A solution of pH 3 is not twice as acidic as a solution of pH 6, but a thousand times ($10 \times 10 \times 10$) more acidic. When the pH of a solution changes slightly, the actual concentrations of H⁺ and OH⁻ in the solution change substantially.

Buffers

The internal pH of most living cells is close to 7. Even a slight change in pH can be harmful, because the chemical processes of the cell are very sensitive to the concentrations of hydrogen and hydroxide ions. The pH of human blood is very close to 7.4, or slightly basic. A person cannot survive for more than a few minutes if the blood pH drops to 7 or rises to 7.8, and a chemical system exists in the blood that maintains a stable pH. If you add 0.01 mol of a strong acid to a liter of pure water, the pH drops from 7.0 to 2.0. If the same amount of acid is added to a liter of blood, however, the pH decrease is only from 7.4 to 7.3. Why does the addition of acid have so much less of an effect on the pH of blood than it does on the pH of water?

The presence of substances called buffers allows biological fluids to maintain a relatively constant pH despite the addition of acids or bases. A **buffer** is a substance that minimizes changes in the concentrations of H⁺ and OH⁻ in a solution. It does so by accepting hydrogen ions from the solution when they are in excess and donating hydrogen ions to the solution when they have been depleted. Most buffer solutions contain a weak acid and its corresponding base, which combine reversibly with hydrogen ions.

There are several buffers that contribute to pH stability in human blood and many other biological solutions. One of these is carbonic acid (H_2CO_3), formed when CO_2 reacts with water in blood plasma. As mentioned earlier, carbonic acid dissociates to yield a bicarbonate ion (HCO_3^-) and a hydrogen ion (H^+):

	Response to a rise in pH			
H_2CO_3	⇌	HCO_3^-	+	H^+
H⁺ donor (acid)	Response to a drop in pH	H⁺ acceptor (base)		Hydrogen ion

The chemical equilibrium between carbonic acid and bicarbonate acts as a pH regulator, the reaction shifting left or right as other processes in the solution add or remove hydrogen ions. If the H⁺ concentration in blood begins to fall (that is, if pH rises), the reaction proceeds to the right and more carbonic acid dissociates, replenishing hydrogen ions. But when H⁺ concentration in blood begins to rise (when pH drops), the reaction proceeds to the left, with HCO_3^- (the base) removing the hydrogen ions from the solution and forming H_2CO_3. Thus, the carbonic acid–bicarbonate buffering system consists of an acid and a base in equilibrium with each other. Most other buffers are also acid-base pairs.

Acidification: A Threat to Water Quality

Among the many threats to water quality posed by human activities is the burning of fossil fuels, which releases gaseous compounds into the atmosphere. When certain of these compounds react with water, the water becomes more acidic, altering the delicate balance of conditions for life on Earth.

Carbon dioxide is the main product of fossil fuel combustion. About 25% of human-generated CO_2 is absorbed by the oceans. In spite of the huge volume of water in the oceans, scientists worry that the absorption of so much CO_2 will harm marine ecosystems.

Recent data have shown that such fears are well founded. When CO_2 dissolves in seawater, it reacts with water to form carbonic acid, which lowers ocean pH, a process known as **ocean acidification**. Based on measurements of CO_2 levels in air bubbles trapped in ice over thousands of years, scientists calculate that the pH of the oceans is 0.1 pH unit lower now than at any time in the past 420,000 years. Recent studies predict that it will drop another 0.3–0.5 pH unit by the end of this century.

As seawater acidifies, the extra hydrogen ions combine with carbonate ions (CO_3^{2-}) to form bicarbonate ions (HCO_3^-), thereby reducing the carbonate concentration **(Figure 3.11)**.

Some carbon dioxide (CO_2) in the atmosphere dissolves in the ocean, where it reacts with water to form carbonic acid (H_2CO_3).

$$CO_2 + H_2O \rightarrow H_2CO_3$$

Carbonic acid dissociates into hydrogen ions (H^+) and bicarbonate ions (HCO_3^-).

$$H_2CO_3 \rightarrow H^+ + HCO_3^-$$

$$H^+ + CO_3^{2-} \rightarrow HCO_3^-$$

The added H^+ combines with carbonate ions (CO_3^{2-}), forming more HCO_3^-.

$$CO_3^{2-} + Ca^{2+} \rightarrow CaCO_3$$

Less CO_3^{2-} is available for calcification — the formation of calcium carbonate ($CaCO_3$)— by marine organisms such as corals.

▲ **Figure 3.11 Atmospheric CO_2 from human activities and its fate in the ocean.**

▼ **Figure 3.12**
IMPACT

The Threat of Ocean Acidification to Coral Reef Ecosystems

Recently, scientists have sounded the alarm about the effects of ocean acidification, the process in which oceans become more acidic due to increased atmospheric carbon dioxide levels (see Figure 3.11). They predict that the resulting decrease in the concentration of carbonate ion (CO_3^{2-}) will take a serious toll on coral reef calcification. Taking many studies into account, and including the effects of ocean warming as well, one group of scientists defined three scenarios for coral reefs during this century, depending on whether the concentration of atmospheric CO_2 (a) stays at today's level, (b) increases at the current rate, or (c) increases more rapidly. The photographs below show coral reefs resembling those predicted under each scenario.

(a)   **(b)**   **(c)**

The healthy coral reef in (a) supports a highly diverse group of species and bears little resemblance to the damaged coral reef in (c).

WHY IT MATTERS The disappearance of coral reef ecosystems would be a tragic loss of biological diversity. In addition, coral reefs provide shoreline protection, a feeding ground for many commercial fishery species, and a popular tourist draw, so coastal human communities would suffer from greater wave damage, collapsed fisheries, and reduced tourism.

FURTHER READING O. Hoegh-Guldberg et al., Coral reefs under rapid climate change and ocean acidification, *Science* 318:1737–1742 (2007). S. C. Doney, The dangers of ocean acidification, *Scientific American*, March 2006, 58–65.

WHAT IF? Would lowering the ocean's carbonate concentration have any effect, even indirectly, on organisms that don't form $CaCO_3$? Explain.

Scientists predict that ocean acidification will cause the carbonate concentration to decrease by 40% by the year 2100. This is of great concern because carbonate is required for calcification, the production of calcium carbonate ($CaCO_3$) by many marine organisms, including reef-building corals and animals that build shells. Coral reefs are sensitive ecosystems that act as havens for a great diversity of marine life **(Figure 3.12)**.

The burning of fossil fuels is also a major source of sulfur oxides and nitrogen oxides. These compounds react with water in the air to form strong acids, which fall to Earth with rain or snow. **Acid precipitation** refers to rain, snow, or fog with a pH lower (more acidic) than 5.2. (Uncontaminated rain has a pH of about 5.6, which is slightly acidic due to the formation of carbonic acid from CO_2 and water.) Acid precipitation can damage life in lakes and streams, and it adversely affects plants on land by changing soil chemistry. To address this problem, the U.S. Congress amended the Clean Air Act in 1990, and the mandated improvements in industrial technologies have been largely responsible for improving the health of most North American lakes and forests.

If there is any reason for optimism about the future quality of water resources on our planet, it is that we have made progress in learning about the delicate chemical balances in oceans, lakes, and rivers. Continued progress can come only from the actions of informed individuals, like yourselves, who are concerned about environmental quality. This requires understanding the crucial role that water plays in the suitability of the environment for continued life on Earth.

3 CHAPTER REVIEW

SUMMARY OF KEY CONCEPTS

CONCEPT 3.1

Polar covalent bonds in water molecules result in hydrogen bonding (pp. 46–47)

- A hydrogen bond forms when the slightly negatively charged oxygen of one water molecule is attracted to the slightly positively charged hydrogen of a nearby water molecule. Hydrogen bonding between water molecules is the basis for water's properties.

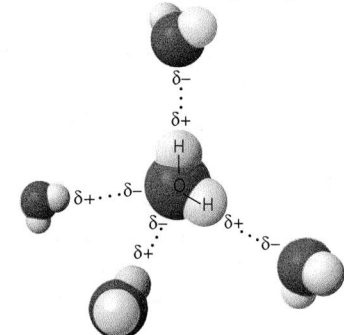

DRAW IT Label a hydrogen bond and a polar covalent bond in this figure. How many hydrogen bonds can each water molecule make?

CONCEPT 3.2

Four emergent properties of water contribute to Earth's suitability for life (pp. 47–52)

- Hydrogen bonding keeps water molecules close to each other, and this **cohesion** helps pull water upward in the microscopic water-conducting cells of plants. Hydrogen bonding is also responsible for water's **surface tension**.
- Water has a high **specific heat**: Heat is absorbed when hydrogen bonds break and is released when hydrogen bonds form. This helps keep temperatures relatively steady, within limits that permit life. **Evaporative cooling** is based on water's high **heat of vaporization**. The evaporative loss of the most energetic water molecules cools a surface.
- Ice floats because it is less dense than liquid water. This allows life to exist under the frozen surfaces of lakes and polar seas.

Ice: stable hydrogen bonds

Liquid water: transient hydrogen bonds

- Water is an unusually versatile **solvent** because its polar molecules are attracted to charged and polar substances capable of forming hydrogen bonds. **Hydrophilic** substances have an affinity for water; **hydrophobic** substances do not. **Molarity**, the number of moles of **solute** per liter of **solution**, is used as a measure of solute concentration in solutions. A **mole** is a certain number of molecules of a substance. The mass of a mole of a substance in grams is the same as the **molecular mass** in daltons.
- The emergent properties of water support life on Earth and may contribute to the potential for life to have evolved on other planets.

? *Describe how different types of solutes dissolve in water. Explain the difference between a solution and a colloid.*

CONCEPT 3.3

Acidic and basic conditions affect living organisms (pp. 52–56)

- A water molecule can transfer an H^+ to another water molecule to form H_3O^+ (represented simply by H^+) and OH^-.
- The concentration of H^+ is expressed as **pH**; $pH = -\log [H^+]$. **Buffers** in biological fluids resist changes in pH. A buffer consists of an acid-base pair that combines reversibly with hydrogen ions.
- The burning of fossil fuels increases the amount of CO_2 in the atmosphere. Some CO_2 dissolves in the oceans, causing **ocean acidification**, which has potentially grave consequences for coral reefs. The burning of fossil fuels also releases oxides of sulfur and nitrogen, leading to **acid precipitation**.

Acidic $[H^+] > [OH^-]$

Neutral $[H^+] = [OH^-]$

Basic $[H^+] < [OH^-]$

Acids donate H^+ in aqueous solutions.

Bases donate OH^- or accept H^+ in aqueous solutions.

0

7

14

? *Explain how increasing amounts of CO_2 dissolving in the ocean leads to ocean acidification. How does this change in pH affect carbonate ion concentration and the rate of calcification?*

LEVEL 1: KNOWLEDGE/COMPREHENSION

1. Many mammals control their body temperature by sweating. Which property of water is most directly responsible for the ability of sweat to lower body temperature?
   a. water's change in density when it condenses
   b. water's ability to dissolve molecules in the air
   c. the release of heat by the formation of hydrogen bonds
   d. the absorption of heat by the breaking of hydrogen bonds
   e. water's high surface tension

2. The bonds that are broken when water vaporizes are
   a. ionic bonds.
   b. hydrogen bonds between water molecules.
   c. covalent bonds between atoms within water molecules.
   d. polar covalent bonds.
   e. nonpolar covalent bonds.

3. Which of the following is a hydrophobic material?
   a. paper   d. sugar
   b. table salt   e. pasta
   c. wax

4. We can be sure that a mole of table sugar and a mole of vitamin C are equal in their
   a. mass in daltons.   d. number of atoms.
   b. mass in grams.   e. number of molecules.
   c. volume.

5. Measurements show that the pH of a particular lake is 4.0. What is the hydrogen ion concentration of the lake?
   a. $4.0 \, M$ b. $10^{-10} \, M$ c. $10^{-4} \, M$ d. $10^4 \, M$ e. 4%

6. What is the *hydroxide* ion concentration of the lake described in question 5?
   a. $10^{-10} \, M$ b. $10^{-4} \, M$ c. $10^{-7} \, M$ d. $10^{-14} M$ e. $10 \, M$

LEVEL 2: APPLICATION/ANALYSIS

7. A slice of pizza has 500 kcal. If we could burn the pizza and use all the heat to warm a 50-L container of cold water, what would be the approximate increase in the temperature of the water? (*Note*: A liter of cold water weighs about 1 kg.)
   a. 50°C   b. 5°C   c. 1°C   d. 100°C   e. 10°C

8. How many grams of acetic acid ($C_2H_4O_2$) would you use to make 10 L of a 0.1 M aqueous solution of acetic acid? (*Note*: The atomic masses, in daltons, are approximately 12 for carbon, 1 for hydrogen, and 16 for oxygen.)
   a. 10 g   b. 0.1 g   c. 6.0 g   d. 60 g   e. 0.6 g

9. **DRAW IT** Draw the hydration shells that form around a potassium ion and a chloride ion when potassium chloride (KCl) dissolves in water. Label the positive, negative, and partial charges on the atoms.

10. **MAKE CONNECTIONS** What do global warming (see Chapter 1, p. 6) and ocean acidification have in common?

LEVEL 3: SYNTHESIS/EVALUATION

11. In agricultural areas, farmers pay close attention to the weather forecast. Right before a predicted overnight freeze, farmers spray water on crops to protect the plants. Use the properties of water to explain how this method works. Be sure to mention why hydrogen bonds are responsible for this phenomenon.

12. **EVOLUTION CONNECTION**
   This chapter explains how the emergent properties of water contribute to the suitability of the environment for life. Until fairly recently, scientists assumed that other physical requirements for life included a moderate range of temperature, pH, atmospheric pressure, and salinity, as well as low levels of toxic chemicals. That view has changed with the discovery of organisms known as extremophiles, which have been found flourishing in hot, acidic sulfur springs, around hydrothermal vents deep in the ocean, and in soils with high levels of toxic metals. Why would astrobiologists be interested in studying extremophiles? What does the existence of life in such extreme environments say about the possibility of life on other planets?

13. **SCIENTIFIC INQUIRY**
   Design a controlled experiment to test the hypothesis that acid precipitation inhibits the growth of *Elodea*, a common freshwater plant (see Figure 2.19, p. 43).

14. **SCIENTIFIC INQUIRY**
   In a study reported in 2000, C. Langdon and colleagues used an artificial coral reef system to test the effect of carbonate concentration on the rate of calcification by reef organisms. The graph on the right presents one set of their results. Describe what these data show. How do these results relate to the ocean acidification that is associated with increasing atmospheric CO_2 levels?

15. **SCIENCE, TECHNOLOGY, AND SOCIETY**
   Agriculture, industry, and the growing populations of cities all compete, through political influence, for water. If you were in charge of water resources in an arid region, what would your priorities be for allocating the limited water supply for various uses? How would you try to build consensus among the different special-interest groups?

16. **WRITE ABOUT A THEME**
   Emergent Properties Several emergent properties of water contribute to the suitability of the environment for life. In a short essay (100–150 words), describe how the ability of water to function as a versatile solvent arises from the structure of water molecules.

For selected answers, see Appendix A.

 www.masteringbiology.com

1. MasteringBiology® Assignments
Tutorials Hydrogen Bonding and Water • The pH Scale
Activities The Polarity of Water • Cohesion of Water • Dissociation of Water Molecules • Acids, Bases, and pH
Questions Student Misconceptions • Reading Quiz • Multiple Choice • End-of-Chapter

2. eText
Read your book online, search, take notes, highlight text, and more.

3. The Study Area
Practice Tests • Cumulative Test • **BioFlix** 3-D Animations • MP3 Tutor Sessions • Videos • Activities • Investigations • Lab Media • Audio Glossary • Word Study Tools • Art

4

Carbon and the Molecular Diversity of Life

▲ **Figure 4.1 What properties make carbon the basis of all life?**

KEY CONCEPTS

4.1 Organic chemistry is the study of carbon compounds

4.2 Carbon atoms can form diverse molecules by bonding to four other atoms

4.3 A few chemical groups are key to the functioning of biological molecules

OVERVIEW

Carbon: The Backbone of Life

Water is the universal medium for life on Earth, but living organisms, such as the plants and Roosevelt elk in Figure 4.1, are made up of chemicals based mostly on the element carbon. Carbon enters the biosphere through the action of plants. Plants use solar energy to transform atmospheric CO_2 into the molecules of life, which are then taken in by plant-eating animals.

Of all chemical elements, carbon is unparalleled in its ability to form molecules that are large, complex, and varied, making possible the diversity of organisms that have evolved on Earth. Proteins, DNA, carbohydrates, and other molecules that distinguish living matter from inanimate material are all composed of carbon atoms bonded to one another and to atoms of other elements. Hydrogen (H), oxygen (O), nitrogen (N), sulfur (S), and phosphorus (P) are other common ingredients of these compounds, but it is the element carbon (C) that accounts for the enormous variety of biological molecules.

Large biological molecules, such as proteins, are the main focus of Chapter 5. In this chapter, we investigate the properties of smaller molecules. We will use these small molecules to illustrate concepts of molecular architecture that will help explain why carbon is so important to life, at the same time highlighting the theme that emergent properties arise from the organization of matter in living organisms.

CONCEPT 4.1

Organic chemistry is the study of carbon compounds

For historical reasons, compounds containing carbon are said to be organic, and the branch of chemistry that specializes in the study of carbon compounds is called **organic chemistry**. Organic compounds range from simple molecules, such as methane (CH_4), to colossal ones, such as proteins, with thousands of atoms. Most organic compounds contain hydrogen atoms in addition to carbon atoms.

The overall percentages of the major elements of life—C, H, O, N, S, and P—are quite uniform from one organism to another. Because of carbon's versatility, however, this limited assortment of atomic building blocks can be used to build an inexhaustible variety of organic molecules. Different species of organisms, and different individuals within a species, are distinguished by variations in their organic molecules.

Since the dawn of human history, people have used other organisms as sources of valued substances—from foods and medicines to fabrics. The science of organic chemistry originated in attempts to purify and improve the yield of such products. By the early 1800s, chemists had learned to make many simple compounds in the laboratory by combining elements under the right conditions. Artificial synthesis of the complex molecules extracted from living matter seemed impossible, however. At that time, the Swedish chemist Jöns Jakob Berzelius made the distinction between organic compounds, those thought to arise only in living organisms, and inorganic compounds, those found only in the nonliving world. *Vitalism*, the belief in a life force outside the jurisdiction of physical and chemical laws, provided the foundation for the new discipline of organic chemistry.

Chemists began to chip away at the support for vitalism when they finally learned to synthesize organic compounds in the laboratory. In 1828, Friedrich Wöhler, a German chemist who had studied with Berzelius, tried to make an "inorganic" salt, ammonium cyanate, by mixing solutions of ammonium ions (NH_4^+) and cyanate ions (CNO^-). Wöhler was astonished to find that instead he had made urea, an organic compound present in the urine of animals. Wöhler challenged the vitalists when he wrote, "I must tell you that I can prepare urea without requiring a kidney or an animal, either man or dog." However, one of the ingredients used in the synthesis, the cyanate, had been extracted from animal blood, and the vitalists were not swayed by Wöhler's discovery. A few years later, however, Hermann Kolbe, a student of Wöhler's, made the organic compound acetic acid from inorganic substances that could be prepared directly from pure elements. Vitalism crumbled completely after several decades of laboratory synthesis of increasingly complex organic compounds.

Organic Molecules and the Origin of Life on Earth

EVOLUTION In 1953, Stanley Miller, a graduate student of Harold Urey's at the University of Chicago, helped bring the abiotic (nonliving) synthesis of organic compounds into the context of evolution. Study **Figure 4.2** to learn about his classic experiment. From his results, Miller concluded that complex organic molecules could arise spontaneously under conditions thought to have existed on the early Earth. Miller also performed experiments designed to mimic volcanic conditions, with roughly similar results. In 2008, a former graduate student of Miller's discovered some samples from these experiments. Reanalyzing them using modern equipment, he identified additional organic compounds that had not been found by Miller. Although the jury is still out, these experiments support the idea that abiotic synthesis of organic compounds, perhaps near volcanoes, could have been an early stage in the origin of life (see Chapter 25).

The pioneers of organic chemistry helped shift the mainstream of biological thought from vitalism to *mechanism*, the view that physical and chemical laws govern all natural phenomena, including the processes of life. Organic chemistry was redefined as the study of carbon compounds, regardless of origin. Organisms produce most of the naturally occurring organic compounds, and these molecules represent a diversity and range of complexity unrivaled by inorganic compounds. However, the rules of chemistry apply to all molecules. The foundation of organic chemistry is not some intangible life force, but the unique chemical versatility of the element carbon.

CONCEPT CHECK 4.1

1. Why was Wöhler astonished to find he had made urea?
2. **WHAT IF?** When Miller tried his experiment without the electrical discharge, no organic compounds were found. What might explain this result?

For suggested answers, see Appendix A.

Can organic molecules form under conditions estimated to simulate those on the early Earth?

EXPERIMENT In 1953, Stanley Miller set up a closed system to mimic conditions thought to have existed on the early Earth. A flask of water simulated the primeval sea. The water was heated so that some vaporized and moved into a second, higher flask containing the "atmosphere"—a mixture of gases. Sparks were discharged in the synthetic atmosphere to mimic lightning.

❷ The "atmosphere" contained a mixture of hydrogen gas (H_2), methane (CH_4), ammonia (NH_3), and water vapor.

❸ Sparks were discharged to mimic lightning.

"Atmosphere"

CH_4

Water vapor

Electrode

❶ The water mixture in the "sea" flask was heated; vapor entered the "atmosphere" flask.

NH_3 H_2

Condenser

Cooled "rain" containing organic molecules

Cold water

H_2O "sea"

Sample for chemical analysis

❺ As material cycled through the apparatus, Miller periodically collected samples for analysis.

❹ A condenser cooled the atmosphere, raining water and any dissolved molecules down into the sea flask.

RESULTS Miller identified a variety of organic molecules that are common in organisms. These included simple compounds, such as formaldehyde (CH_2O) and hydrogen cyanide (HCN), and more complex molecules, such as amino acids and long chains of carbon and hydrogen known as hydrocarbons.

CONCLUSION Organic molecules, a first step in the origin of life, may have been synthesized abiotically on the early Earth. (We will explore this hypothesis in more detail in Chapter 25.)

SOURCE S. L. Miller, A production of amino acids under possible primitive Earth conditions, *Science* 117:528–529 (1953).

WHAT IF? If Miller had increased the concentration of NH_3 in his experiment, how might the relative amounts of the products HCN and CH_2O have differed?

Carbon atoms can form diverse molecules by bonding to four other atoms

The key to an atom's chemical characteristics is its electron configuration. This configuration determines the kinds and number of bonds an atom will form with other atoms.

The Formation of Bonds with Carbon

Carbon has 6 electrons, with 2 in the first electron shell and 4 in the second shell; thus, it has 4 valence electrons in a shell that holds 8 electrons. A carbon atom usually completes its valence shell by sharing its 4 electrons with other atoms so that 8 electrons are present. Each pair of shared electrons constitutes a covalent bond (see Figure 2.12d). In organic molecules, carbon usually forms single or double covalent bonds. Each carbon atom acts as an intersection point from which a molecule can branch off in as many as four directions. This ability is one facet of carbon's versatility that makes large, complex molecules possible.

When a carbon atom forms four single covalent bonds, the arrangement of its four hybrid orbitals causes the bonds to angle toward the corners of an imaginary tetrahedron (see Figure 2.17b). The bond angles in methane (CH_4) are 109.5° (Figure 4.3a), and they are roughly the same in any group of atoms where carbon has four single bonds. For example,

ethane (C_2H_6) is shaped like two overlapping tetrahedrons (Figure 4.3b). In molecules with more carbons, every grouping of a carbon bonded to four other atoms has a tetrahedral shape. But when two carbon atoms are joined by a double bond, as in ethene (C_2H_4), the atoms joined to those carbons are in the same plane as the carbons (Figure 4.3c). We find it convenient to write molecules as structural formulas, as if the molecules being represented are two-dimensional, but keep in mind that molecules are three-dimensional and that the shape of a molecule often determines its function.

The electron configuration of carbon gives it covalent compatibility with many different elements. Figure 4.4 shows the valences of carbon and its most frequent partners—hydrogen, oxygen, and nitrogen. These are the four major atomic components of organic molecules. These valences are the basis for the rules of covalent bonding in organic chemistry—the building code for the architecture of organic molecules.

Let's consider how the rules of covalent bonding apply to carbon atoms with partners other than hydrogen. We'll look at two examples, the simple molecules carbon dioxide and urea.

In the carbon dioxide molecule (CO_2), a single carbon atom is joined to two atoms of oxygen by double covalent bonds. The structural formula for CO_2 is shown here:

$$O=C=O$$

Each line in a structural formula represents a pair of shared electrons. Thus, the two double bonds in CO_2 have the same number of shared electrons as four single bonds. The arrangement completes the valence shells of all atoms in the molecule.

Name and Comment	Molecular Formula	Structural Formula	Ball-and-Stick Model (molecular shape in pink)	Space-Filling Model
(a) Methane. When a carbon atom has four single bonds to other atoms, the molecule is tetrahedral.	CH_4	H │ H─C─H │ H		
(b) Ethane. A molecule may have more than one tetrahedral group of single-bonded atoms. (Ethane consists of two such groups.)	C_2H_6	H H │ │ H─C─C─H │ │ H H		
(c) Ethene (ethylene). When two carbon atoms are joined by a double bond, all atoms attached to those carbons are in the same plane; the molecule is flat.	C_2H_4	H H \ C=C / H H		

▲ Figure 4.3 **The shapes of three simple organic molecules.**

Hydrogen (valence = 1)   **Oxygen** (valence = 2)   **Nitrogen** (valence = 3)   **Carbon** (valence = 4)

H·   ·Ö: ·N̈·   ·C̈·

▲ **Figure 4.4 Valences of the major elements of organic molecules.** Valence is the number of covalent bonds an atom can form. It is generally equal to the number of electrons required to complete the valence (outermost) shell (see Figure 2.9). All the electrons are shown for each atom in the electron distribution diagrams (top). Only the valence shell electrons are shown in the Lewis dot structures (bottom). Note that carbon can form four bonds.

MAKE CONNECTIONS *Refer to Figure 2.9 (p. 36) and draw the Lewis dot structures for sodium, phosphorus, sulfur, and chlorine.*

Because CO_2 is a very simple molecule and lacks hydrogen, it is often considered inorganic, even though it contains carbon. Whether we call CO_2 organic or inorganic, however, it is clearly important to the living world as the source of carbon for all organic molecules in organisms.

Urea, $CO(NH_2)_2$, is the organic compound found in urine that Wöhler synthesized in the early 1800s. Again, each atom has the required number of covalent bonds. In this case, one carbon atom participates in both single and double bonds.

Urea

Urea and carbon dioxide are molecules with only one carbon atom. But as Figure 4.3 shows, a carbon atom can also use one or more valence electrons to form covalent bonds to other carbon atoms, linking the atoms into chains of seemingly infinite variety.

Molecular Diversity Arising from Carbon Skeleton Variation

Carbon chains form the skeletons of most organic molecules. The skeletons vary in length and may be straight, branched, or arranged in closed rings **(Figure 4.5)**. Some carbon skeletons have double bonds, which vary in number and location. Such variation in carbon skeletons is one important source of the molecular complexity and diversity that characterize living matter. In addition, atoms of other elements can be bonded to the skeletons at available sites.

Hydrocarbons

All of the molecules shown in Figures 4.3 and 4.5 are **hydrocarbons**, organic molecules consisting of only carbon and hydrogen. Atoms of hydrogen are attached to the carbon skeleton wherever electrons are available for covalent bonding. Hydrocarbons are the major components of petroleum, which is called a fossil fuel because it consists of the partially decomposed remains of organisms that lived millions of years ago.

▼ **Figure 4.5 Four ways that carbon skeletons can vary.**

(a) Length

Ethane   Propane

Carbon skeletons vary in length.

(b) Branching

Butane   2-Methylpropane (commonly called isobutane)

Skeletons may be unbranched or branched.

(c) Double bond position

1-Butene   2-Butene

The skeleton may have double bonds, which can vary in location.

(d) Presence of rings

Cyclohexane   Benzene

Some carbon skeletons are arranged in rings. In the abbreviated structural formula for each compound (at the right), each corner represents a carbon and its attached hydrogens.

Although hydrocarbons are not prevalent in most living organisms, many of a cell's organic molecules have regions consisting of only carbon and hydrogen. For example, the molecules known as fats have long hydrocarbon tails attached to a nonhydrocarbon component **(Figure 4.6**, on the next page). Neither petroleum nor fat dissolves in water; both are hydrophobic compounds because the great majority of their bonds are relatively nonpolar carbon-to-hydrogen linkages. Another characteristic of hydrocarbons is that they can undergo reactions that release a relatively large amount of energy. The gasoline that fuels a car consists of hydrocarbons, and the hydrocarbon tails of fats serve as stored fuel for animals.

Nucleus

Fat droplets

10 µm

(a) Part of a human adipose cell   **(b) A fat molecule**

▲ **Figure 4.6 The role of hydrocarbons in fats.** (a) Mammalian adipose cells stockpile fat molecules as a fuel reserve. This colorized micrograph shows part of a human adipose cell with many fat droplets, each containing a large number of fat molecules. (b) A fat molecule consists of a small, nonhydrocarbon component joined to three hydrocarbon tails that account for the hydrophobic behavior of fats. The tails can be broken down to provide energy. (Black = carbon; gray = hydrogen; red = oxygen.)

MAKE CONNECTIONS *How do the tails account for the hydrophobic nature of fats? (See Concept 3.2, p. 51.)*

Isomers

Variation in the architecture of organic molecules can be seen in **isomers**, compounds that have the same numbers of atoms of the same elements but different structures and hence different properties. We will examine three types of isomers: structural isomers, *cis-trans* isomers, and enantiomers.

Structural isomers differ in the covalent arrangements of their atoms. Compare, for example, the two five-carbon compounds in **Figure 4.7a**. Both have the molecular formula C_5H_{12}, but they differ in the covalent arrangement of their carbon skeletons. The skeleton is straight in one compound but branched in the other. The number of possible isomers increases tremendously as carbon skeletons increase in size. There are only three forms of C_5H_{12} (two of which are shown in Figure 4.7a), but there are 18 variations of C_8H_{18} and 366,319 possible structural isomers of $C_{20}H_{42}$. Structural isomers may also differ in the location of double bonds.

In **cis-trans** isomers (formerly called *geometric isomers*), carbons have covalent bonds to the same atoms, but these atoms differ in their spatial arrangements due to the inflexibility of double bonds. Single bonds allow the atoms they join to rotate freely about the bond axis without changing the compound. In contrast, double bonds do not permit such rotation. If a double bond joins two carbon atoms, and each C also has two different atoms (or groups of atoms) attached to it, then two distinct *cis-trans* isomers are possible. Consider a simple molecule with two double-bonded carbons, each of which has an H and an X attached to it (**Figure 4.7b**). The arrangement with both Xs on the same side of the double bond is called a *cis isomer*, and that with the Xs on opposite sides is called a *trans* isomer. The subtle difference in shape between such isomers can dramatically affect the biological activities of organic molecules. For example, the biochem-

▼ **Figure 4.7 Three types of isomers, compounds with the same molecular formula but different structures.**

(a) Structural isomers

Structural isomers differ in covalent partners, as shown in this example of two isomers of C_5H_{12}: pentane (left) and 2-methyl butane (right).

(b) Cis-trans isomers

cis isomer: The two Xs are on the same side.   *trans* isomer: The two Xs are on opposite sides.

Cis-trans isomers differ in arrangement about a double bond. In these diagrams, X represents an atom or group of atoms attached to a double-bonded carbon.

(c) Enantiomers

CO_2H CO_2H

H   C NH_2 NH_2 H

CH_3 CH_3

L isomer   D isomer

Enantiomers differ in spatial arrangement around an asymmetric carbon, resulting in molecules that are mirror images, like left and right hands. The two isomers are designated the L and D isomers from the Latin for "left" and "right" (*levo* and *dextro*). Enantiomers cannot be superimposed on each other.

DRAW IT *There are three structural isomers of C_5H_{12}; draw the one not shown in (a).*

istry of vision involves a light-induced change of retinal, a chemical compound in the eye, from the *cis* isomer to the *trans* isomer (see Figure 50.17). Another example involves *trans* fats, which are discussed in Chapter 5.

Enantiomers are isomers that are mirror images of each other and that differ in shape due to the presence of an *asymmetric carbon*, one that is attached to four different atoms or groups of atoms. (See the middle carbon in the ball-and-stick models shown in **Figure 4.7c**.) The four groups can be arranged in space around the asymmetric carbon in two different ways that are mirror images. Enantiomers are, in a way, left-handed and right-handed versions of the molecule. Just as your right hand won't fit into a left-handed glove, a "right-handed" molecule won't fit into the same space as the "left-handed" version.

Drug	Condition	Effective Enantiomer	Ineffective Enantiomer
Ibuprofen	Pain; inflammation	S-Ibuprofen	R-Ibuprofen
Albuterol	Asthma	R-Albuterol	S-Albuterol

▲ Figure 4.8 **The pharmacological importance of enantiomers.** Ibuprofen and albuterol are examples of drugs whose enantiomers have different effects. (S and R are letters used in one system to distinguish between enantiomers.) Ibuprofen reduces inflammation and pain. It is commonly sold as a mixture of the two enantiomers. The S enantiomer is 100 times more effective than the other. Albuterol is used to relax bronchial muscles, improving airflow in asthma patients. Only R-albuterol is synthesized and sold as a drug; the S form counteracts the active R form.

Usually, only one isomer is biologically active because only that form can bind to specific molecules in an organism.

The concept of enantiomers is important in the pharmaceutical industry because the two enantiomers of a drug may not be equally effective, as is the case for both ibuprofen and the asthma medication albuterol (Figure 4.8). Methamphetamine also occurs in two enantiomers that have very different effects. One enantiomer is the highly addictive stimulant drug known as "crank," sold illegally in the street drug trade. The other has a much weaker effect and is even found as an ingredient in an over-the-counter vapor inhaler for treatment of nasal congestion! The differing effects of enantiomers in the body demonstrate that organisms are sensitive to even the most subtle variations in molecular architecture. Once again, we see that molecules have emergent properties that depend on the specific arrangement of their atoms.

CONCEPT CHECK 4.2

1. **DRAW IT** Draw a structural formula for C_2H_4.
2. Which molecules in Figure 4.5 are isomers? For each pair, identify the type of isomer.
3. How are gasoline and fat chemically similar?
4. **WHAT IF?** Can propane (C_3H_8) form isomers?

For suggested answers, see Appendix A.

CONCEPT 4.3

A few chemical groups are key to the functioning of biological molecules

The distinctive properties of an organic molecule depend not only on the arrangement of its carbon skeleton but also on

the chemical groups attached to that skeleton. We can think of hydrocarbons, the simplest organic molecules, as the underlying framework for more complex organic molecules. A number of chemical groups can replace one or more of the hydrogens bonded to the carbon skeleton of the hydrocarbon. (Some groups include atoms of the carbon skeleton, as we will see.) These groups may participate in chemical reactions or may contribute to function indirectly by their effects on molecular shape. The number and arrangement of the groups help give each molecule its unique properties.

The Chemical Groups Most Important in the Processes of Life

Consider the differences between estradiol (a type of estrogen) and testosterone. These compounds are female and male sex hormones, respectively, in humans and other vertebrates. Both are steroids, organic molecules with a common carbon skeleton in the form of four fused rings. These sex hormones differ only in the chemical groups attached to the rings (shown here in abbreviated form); the distinctions in molecular architecture are shaded in blue:

The different actions of these two molecules on many targets throughout the body help produce the contrasting anatomical and physiological features of male and female vertebrates. Thus, even our sexuality has its biological basis in variations of molecular architecture.

In the example of sex hormones, different chemical groups contribute to function by affecting the molecule's shape. In other cases, the chemical groups affect molecular function by being directly involved in chemical reactions; these important chemical groups are known as **functional groups**. Each functional group participates in chemical reactions in a characteristic way from one organic molecule to another.

The seven chemical groups most important in biological processes are the hydroxyl, carbonyl, carboxyl, amino, sulfhydryl, phosphate, and methyl groups. The first six groups can act as functional groups; they are also hydrophilic and thus increase the solubility of organic compounds in water. The methyl group is not reactive, but instead often serves as a recognizable tag on biological molecules. Before reading further, study Figure 4.9 on the next two pages to familiarize yourself with these biologically important chemical groups.

Exploring Some Biologically Important Chemical Groups

CHEMICAL GROUP	Hydroxyl	Carbonyl	Carboxyl
STRUCTURE	—OH (may be written HO—) In a **hydroxyl group** (—OH), a hydrogen atom is bonded to an oxygen atom, which in turn is bonded to the carbon skeleton of the organic molecule. (Do not confuse this functional group with the hydroxide ion, OH⁻.)	The **carbonyl group** (>CO) consists of a carbon atom joined to an oxygen atom by a double bond.	When an oxygen atom is double-bonded to a carbon atom that is also bonded to an —OH group, the entire assembly of atoms is called a **carboxyl group** (—COOH).
NAME OF COMPOUND	**Alcohols** (Their specific names usually end in -*ol*.)	**Ketones** if the carbonyl group is within a carbon skeleton **Aldehydes** if the carbonyl group is at the end of the carbon skeleton	**Carboxylic acids**, or organic acids
EXAMPLE	**Ethanol**, the alcohol present in alcoholic beverages	**Acetone**, the simplest ketone **Propanal**, an aldehyde	**Acetic acid**, which gives vinegar its sour taste
FUNCTIONAL PROPERTIES	• Is polar as a result of the electrons spending more time near the electronegative oxygen atom. • Can form hydrogen bonds with water molecules, helping dissolve organic compounds such as sugars. (Sugars are shown in Figure 5.3.)	• A ketone and an aldehyde may be structural isomers with different properties, as is the case for acetone and propanal. • Ketone and aldehyde groups are also found in sugars, giving rise to two major groups of sugars: ketoses (containing ketone groups) and aldoses (containing aldehyde groups).	• Acts as an acid; can donate an H⁺ because the covalent bond between oxygen and hydrogen is so polar: Nonionized ⇌ Ionized + H⁺ • Found in cells in the ionized form with a charge of 1− and called a carboxylate ion.

Amino	Sulfhydryl	Phosphate	Methyl

The **amino group** (—NH₂) consists of a nitrogen atom bonded to two hydrogen atoms and to the carbon skeleton.

The **sulfhydryl group** (—SH) consists of a sulfur atom bonded to an atom of hydrogen; it resembles a hydroxyl group in shape.

(may be written HS —)

In the **phosphate group** shown here, a phosphorus atom is bonded to four oxygen atoms; one oxygen is bonded to the carbon skeleton; two oxygens carry negative charges (—OPO₃²⁻). In this text, Ⓟ represents an attached phosphate group.

A **methyl group** (—CH₃) consists of a carbon bonded to three hydrogen atoms. The carbon of a methyl group may be attached to a carbon or to a different atom.

Amines

Thiols

Organic phosphates

Methylated compounds

Glycine, a compound that is both an amine and a carboxylic acid because it has both an amino group and a carboxyl group; compounds with both groups are called **amino acids**

Cysteine, an important sulfur-containing amino acid

Glycerol phosphate, which takes part in many important chemical reactions in cells; glycerol phosphate also provides the backbone for phospholipids, the most prevalent molecules in cell membranes

5-Methyl cytidine, a component of DNA that has been modified by addition of a methyl group

---

- Acts as a base; can pick up an H⁺ from the surrounding solution (water, in living organisms):

$$H^+ + \quad —N\overset{H}{\underset{H}{|}} \rightleftharpoons \quad —\overset{+}{N}\overset{H}{\underset{H}{|}}—H$$

Nonionized   Ionized

- Found in cells in the ionized form with a charge of 1+.

- Two sulfhydryl groups can react, forming a covalent bond. This "cross-linking" helps stabilize protein structure (see Figure 5.20, Tertiary Structure).
- Cross-linking of cysteines in hair proteins maintains the curliness or straightness of hair. Straight hair can be "permanently" curled by shaping it around curlers and then breaking and re-forming the cross-linking bonds.

- Contributes negative charge to the molecule of which it is a part (2− when at the end of a molecule, as above; 1− when located internally in a chain of phosphates).
- Molecules containing phosphate groups have the potential to react with water, releasing energy.

- Addition of a methyl group to DNA, or to molecules bound to DNA, affects the expression of genes.
- Arrangement of methyl groups in male and female sex hormones affects their shape and function (see p. 63).

MAKE CONNECTIONS *Given the information in this figure and what you know about the electronegativity of oxygen (see Concept 2.3, p. 39), predict which of the following molecules would be the stronger acid (see Concept 3.3, p. 53). Explain your answer.*

a.

$$H—\overset{H}{\underset{H}{\overset{|}{C}}}—\overset{H}{\underset{H}{\overset{|}{C}}}—C\overset{\displaystyle O}{\underset{\displaystyle OH}{}}$$

b.

$$H—\overset{H}{\underset{H}{\overset{|}{C}}}—C\overset{\displaystyle O}{}—C\overset{\displaystyle O}{\underset{\displaystyle OH}{}}$$

ATP: An Important Source of Energy for Cellular Processes

The "Phosphate" column in Figure 4.9 shows a simple example of an organic phosphate molecule. A more complicated organic phosphate, **adenosine triphosphate**, or **ATP**, is worth mentioning here because its function in the cell is so important. ATP consists of an organic molecule called adenosine attached to a string of three phosphate groups:

Where three phosphates are present in series, as in ATP, one phosphate may be split off as a result of a reaction with water. This inorganic phosphate ion, $HOPO_3^{2-}$, is often abbreviated P_i in this book. Having lost one phosphate, ATP becomes adenosine *di*phosphate, or ADP. Although ATP is sometimes said to store energy, it is more accurate to think of it as storing the potential to react with water. This reaction releases energy that can be used by the cell. You will learn about this in more detail in Chapter 8.

CONCEPT CHECK 4.3

1. What does the term *amino acid* signify about the structure of such a molecule?
2. What chemical change occurs to ATP when it reacts with water and releases energy?
3. **WHAT IF?** Suppose you had an organic molecule such as cysteine (see Figure 4.9, sulfhydryl group example), and you chemically removed the —NH₂ group and replaced it with —COOH. Draw the structural formula for this molecule and speculate about its chemical properties. Is the central carbon asymmetric before the change? After?

For suggested answers, see Appendix A.

The Chemical Elements of Life: *A Review*

Living matter, as you have learned, consists mainly of carbon, oxygen, hydrogen, and nitrogen, with smaller amounts of sulfur and phosphorus. These elements all form strong covalent bonds, an essential characteristic in the architecture of complex organic molecules. Of all these elements, carbon is the virtuoso of the covalent bond. The versatility of carbon makes possible the great diversity of organic molecules, each with particular properties that emerge from the unique arrangement of its carbon skeleton and the chemical groups appended to that skeleton. At the foundation of all biological diversity lies this variation at the molecular level.

4 CHAPTER REVIEW

SUMMARY OF KEY CONCEPTS

CONCEPT 4.1

Organic chemistry is the study of carbon compounds (pp. 58–59)

- Living matter is made mostly of carbon, oxygen, hydrogen, and nitrogen, with some sulfur and phosphorus. Biological diversity has its molecular basis in carbon's ability to form a huge number of molecules with particular shapes and chemical properties.
- Organic compounds were once thought to arise only within living organisms, but this idea (vitalism) was disproved when chemists were able to synthesize organic compounds in the laboratory.

? *How did Stanley Miller's experiments extend the idea of mechanism to the origin of life?*

CONCEPT 4.2

Carbon atoms can form diverse molecules by bonding to four other atoms (pp. 60–63)

- Carbon, with a valence of 4, can bond to various other atoms, including O, H, and N. Carbon can also bond to other carbon atoms, forming the carbon skeletons of organic compounds.

These skeletons vary in length and shape and have bonding sites for atoms of other elements. **Hydrocarbons** consist only of carbon and hydrogen.

- **Isomers** are compounds with the same molecular formula but different structures and properties. Three types of isomers are **structural isomers**, *cis-trans* isomers, and **enantiomers**.

? *Refer back to Figure 4.9. What type of isomers are acetone and propanal? How many asymmetric carbons are present in acetic acid, glycine, and glycerol phosphate? Can these three molecules exist as forms that are enantiomers?*

CONCEPT 4.3

A few chemical groups are key to the functioning of biological molecules (pp. 63–66)

- Chemical groups attached to the carbon skeletons of organic molecules participate in chemical reactions (**functional groups**) or contribute to function by affecting molecular shape (see Figure 4.9).
- **ATP (adenosine triphosphate)** consists of adenosine attached to three phosphate groups. ATP can react with water, forming inorganic phosphate and ADP (adenosine diphosphate). This reaction releases energy that can be used by the cell (see the equation at the top of the next page).

ATP reaction diagram:

$$P-P-P-\boxed{Adenosine} \xrightarrow[\text{with } H_2O]{\text{Reacts}} P_i + P-P-\boxed{Adenosine} + Energy$$

ATP   Inorganic   ADP
            phosphate

? *In what ways does a methyl group differ chemically from the other six important chemical groups shown in Figure 4.9?*

TEST YOUR UNDERSTANDING

LEVEL 1: KNOWLEDGE/COMPREHENSION

1. Organic chemistry is currently defined as
   a. the study of compounds made only by living cells.
   b. the study of carbon compounds.
   c. the study of vital forces.
   d. the study of natural (as opposed to synthetic) compounds.
   e. the study of hydrocarbons.

2. Which functional group is *not* present in this molecule?
   a. carboxyl
   b. sulfhydryl
   c. hydroxyl
   d. amino

3. **MAKE CONNECTIONS** Which chemical group is most likely to be responsible for an organic molecule behaving as a base (see Concept 3.3, p. 53)?
   a. hydroxyl   c. carboxyl   e. phosphate
   b. carbonyl   d. amino

LEVEL 2: APPLICATION/ANALYSIS

4. Which of the following hydrocarbons has a double bond in its carbon skeleton?
   a. C_3H_8 b. C_2H_6 c. CH_4 d. C_2H_4 e. C_2H_2

5. Choose the term that correctly describes the relationship between these two sugar molecules:
   a. structural isomers
   b. *cis-trans* isomers
   c. enantiomers
   d. isotopes

6. Identify the asymmetric carbon in this molecule:

7. Which action could produce a carbonyl group?
   a. the replacement of the —OH of a carboxyl group with hydrogen
   b. the addition of a thiol to a hydroxyl
   c. the addition of a hydroxyl to a phosphate
   d. the replacement of the nitrogen of an amine with oxygen
   e. the addition of a sulfhydryl to a carboxyl

8. Which of the molecules shown in question 5 has an asymmetric carbon? Which carbon is asymmetric?

LEVEL 3: SYNTHESIS/EVALUATION

9. **EVOLUTION CONNECTION**
   DRAW IT Some scientists think that life elsewhere in the universe might be based on the element silicon, rather than on carbon, as on Earth. Look at the electron distribution diagram for silicon in Figure 2.9 and draw the Lewis dot structure for silicon. What properties does silicon share with carbon that would make silicon-based life more likely than, say, neon-based life or aluminum-based life?

10. **SCIENTIFIC INQUIRY**
    Thalidomide achieved notoriety 50 years ago because of a wave of birth defects among children born to women who took this drug during pregnancy as a treatment for morning sickness. Thalidomide is a mixture of two enantiomers; one reduces morning sickness, but the other causes severe birth defects. (Although the beneficial enantiomer can be synthesized and given to patients, it is converted in the body to the harmful enantiomer.) The U.S. Food and Drug Administration (FDA) withheld approval of thalidomide in 1960. Since then, however, the FDA has approved this drug for the treatment of conditions associated with Hansen's disease (leprosy) and newly diagnosed multiple myeloma, a blood and bone marrow cancer. In clinical trials, thalidomide also shows promise as a treatment for AIDS, tuberculosis, inflammatory diseases, and some other types of cancer. Assuming that molecules related to thalidomide could be synthesized in the laboratory, describe in a broad way the type of experiments you would do to improve the benefits of this drug and minimize its harmful effects.

11. **WRITE ABOUT A THEME**
    Structure and Function In 1918, an epidemic of sleeping sickness caused an unusual rigid paralysis in some survivors, similar to symptoms of advanced Parkinson's disease. Years later, L-dopa (below, left), a chemical used to treat Parkinson's disease, was given to some of these patients, as dramatized in the movie *Awakenings*, starring Robin Williams. L-dopa was remarkably effective at eliminating the paralysis, at least temporarily. However, its enantiomer, D-dopa (right), was subsequently shown to have no effect at all, as is the case for Parkinson's disease. In a short essay (100–150 words), discuss how the effectiveness of one enantiomer and not the other illustrates the theme of structure and function.

L-dopa   **D-dopa**

For selected answers, see Appendix A.

Mastering BIOLOGY   www.masteringbiology.com

1. MasteringBiology® Assignments
Tutorial Carbon Bonding and Functional Groups
Activities Diversity of Carbon-Based Molecules • Isomers • Functional Groups
Questions Student Misconceptions • Reading Quiz • Multiple Choice • End-of-Chapter

2. eText
Read your book online, search, take notes, highlight text, and more.

3. The Study Area
Practice Tests • Cumulative Test • **BioFlix** 3-D Animations • MP3 Tutor Sessions • Videos • Activities • Investigations • Lab Media • Audio Glossary • Word Study Tools • Art

5

The Structure and Function of Large Biological Molecules

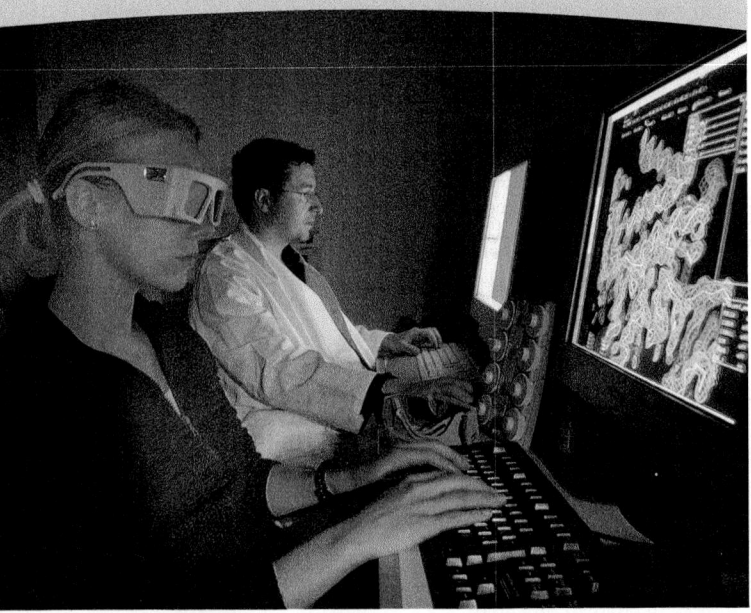

▲ **Figure 5.1 Why do scientists study the structures of macromolecules?**

KEY CONCEPTS

5.1 Macromolecules are polymers, built from monomers
5.2 Carbohydrates serve as fuel and building material
5.3 Lipids are a diverse group of hydrophobic molecules
5.4 Proteins include a diversity of structures, resulting in a wide range of functions
5.5 Nucleic acids store, transmit, and help express hereditary information

OVERVIEW

The Molecules of Life

Given the rich complexity of life on Earth, we might expect organisms to have an enormous diversity of molecules. Remarkably, however, the critically important large molecules of all living things—from bacteria to elephants—fall into just four main classes: carbohydrates, lipids, proteins, and nucleic

acids. On the molecular scale, members of three of these classes—carbohydrates, proteins, and nucleic acids—are huge and are therefore called **macromolecules**. For example, a protein may consist of thousands of atoms that form a molecular colossus with a mass well over 100,000 daltons. Considering the size and complexity of macromolecules, it is noteworthy that biochemists have determined the detailed structure of so many of them. The scientist in the foreground of **Figure 5.1** is using 3-D glasses to help her visualize the structure of the protein displayed on her screen.

The architecture of a large biological molecule helps explain how that molecule works. Like water and simple organic molecules, large biological molecules exhibit unique emergent properties arising from the orderly arrangement of their atoms. In this chapter, we'll first consider how macromolecules are built. Then we'll examine the structure and function of all four classes of large biological molecules: carbohydrates, lipids, proteins, and nucleic acids.

CONCEPT **5.1**

Macromolecules are polymers, built from monomers

The macromolecules in three of the four classes of life's organic compounds—carbohydrates, proteins, and nucleic acids—are chain-like molecules called polymers (from the Greek *polys*, many, and *meros*, part). A **polymer** is a long molecule consisting of many similar or identical building blocks linked by covalent bonds, much as a train consists of a chain of cars. The repeating units that serve as the building blocks of a polymer are smaller molecules called **monomers** (from the Greek *monos*, single). Some of the molecules that serve as monomers also have other functions of their own.

The Synthesis and Breakdown of Polymers

Although each class of polymer is made up of a different type of monomer, the chemical mechanisms by which cells make and break down polymers are basically the same in all cases. In cells, these processes are facilitated by **enzymes**, specialized macromolecules that speed up chemical reactions. Monomers are connected by a reaction in which two molecules are covalently bonded to each other, with the loss of a water molecule; this is known as a **dehydration reaction** (Figure 5.2a). When a bond forms between two monomers, each monomer contributes part of the water molecule that is released during the reaction: One monomer provides a hydroxyl group (—OH), while the other provides a hydrogen (—H). This reaction is repeated as monomers are added to the chain one by one, making a polymer.

Polymers are disassembled to monomers by **hydrolysis**, a process that is essentially the reverse of the dehydration reac-

(a) Dehydration reaction: synthesizing a polymer

(b) Hydrolysis: breaking down a polymer

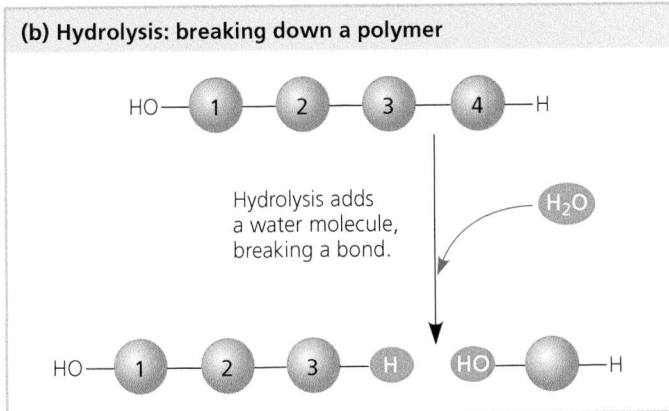

tion **(Figure 5.2b)**. Hydrolysis means to break using water (from the Greek *hydro*, water, and *lysis*, break). The bond between the monomers is broken by the addition of a water molecule, with the hydrogen from the water attaching to one monomer and the hydroxyl group attaching to the adjacent monomer. An example of hydrolysis working within our bodies is the process of digestion. The bulk of the organic material in our food is in the form of polymers that are much too large to enter our cells. Within the digestive tract, various enzymes attack the polymers, speeding up hydrolysis. The released monomers are then absorbed into the bloodstream for distribution to all body cells. Those cells can then use dehydration reactions to assemble the monomers into new, different polymers that can perform specific functions required by the cell.

The Diversity of Polymers

Each cell has thousands of different macromolecules; the collection varies from one type of cell to another even in the same organism. The inherent differences between human siblings reflect small variations in polymers, particularly DNA and proteins. Molecular differences between unrelated individuals are more extensive and those between species greater still. The diversity of macromolecules in the living world is vast, and the possible variety is effectively limitless.

What is the basis for such diversity in life's polymers? These molecules are constructed from only 40 to 50 common monomers and some others that occur rarely. Building a huge variety of polymers from such a limited number of monomers is analogous to constructing hundreds of thousands of words from only 26 letters of the alphabet. The key is arrangement—the particular linear sequence that the units follow. However, this analogy falls far short of describing the great diversity of macromolecules because most biological polymers have many more monomers than the number of letters in the longest word. Proteins, for example, are built from 20 kinds of amino acids arranged in chains that are typically hundreds of amino acids long. The molecular logic of life is simple but elegant: Small molecules common to all organisms are ordered into unique macromolecules.

Despite this immense diversity, molecular structure and function can still be grouped roughly by class. Let's examine each of the four major classes of large biological molecules. For each class, the large molecules have emergent properties not found in their individual building blocks.

CONCEPT CHECK 5.1

1. What are the four main classes of large biological molecules? Which class does not consist of polymers?
2. How many molecules of water are needed to completely hydrolyze a polymer that is ten monomers long?
3. **WHAT IF?** Suppose you eat a serving of fish. What reactions must occur for the amino acid monomers in the protein of the fish to be converted to new proteins in your body?

For suggested answers, see Appendix A.

CONCEPT 5.2

Carbohydrates serve as fuel and building material

Carbohydrates include both sugars and polymers of sugars. The simplest carbohydrates are the monosaccharides, or simple sugars; these are the monomers from which more complex carbohydrates are constructed. Disaccharides are double sugars, consisting of two monosaccharides joined by a covalent bond. Carbohydrates also include macromolecules called polysaccharides, polymers composed of many sugar building blocks.

Sugars

Monosaccharides (from the Greek *monos*, single, and *sacchar*, sugar) generally have molecular formulas that are some multiple of the unit CH_2O. Glucose ($C_6H_{12}O_6$), the most common monosaccharide, is of central importance in the chemistry

Aldoses (Aldehyde Sugars) Carbonyl group at end of carbon skeleton	Ketoses (Ketone Sugars) Carbonyl group within carbon skeleton
Trioses: 3-carbon sugars (C₃H₆O₃)	
Glyceraldehyde An initial breakdown product of glucose	**Dihydroxyacetone** An initial breakdown product of glucose
Pentoses: 5-carbon sugars (C₅H₁₀O₅)	
Ribose A component of RNA	**Ribulose** An intermediate in photosynthesis
Hexoses: 6-carbon sugars (C₆H₁₂O₆)	
Glucose Galactose Energy sources for organisms	**Fructose** An energy source for organisms

▲ **Figure 5.3 The structure and classification of some monosaccharides.** Sugars vary in the location of their carbonyl groups (orange), the length of their carbon skeletons, and the spatial arrangement around asymmetric carbons (compare, for example, the purple portions of glucose and galactose).

MAKE CONNECTIONS *In the 1970s, a process was developed that converts the glucose in corn syrup to its sweeter isomer, fructose. High-fructose corn syrup, a common ingredient in soft drinks and processed food, is a mixture of glucose and fructose. What type of isomers are glucose and fructose? See Figure 4.7, p. 62.*

of life. In the structure of glucose, we can see the trademarks of a sugar: The molecule has a carbonyl group (C=O) and multiple hydroxyl groups (—OH) (**Figure 5.3**). Depending on the location of the carbonyl group, a sugar is either an aldose (aldehyde sugar) or a ketose (ketone sugar). Glucose, for example, is an aldose; fructose, an isomer of glucose, is a ketose. (Most names for sugars end in *-ose*.) Another criterion for classifying sugars is the size of the carbon skeleton, which ranges from three to seven carbons long. Glucose, fructose, and other sugars that have six carbons are called hexoses. Trioses (three-carbon sugars) and pentoses (five-carbon sugars) are also common.

Still another source of diversity for simple sugars is in the spatial arrangement of their parts around asymmetric carbons. (Recall that an asymmetric carbon is a carbon attached to four different atoms or groups of atoms.) Glucose and galactose, for example, differ only in the placement of parts around one asymmetric carbon (see the purple boxes in Figure 5.3). What seems like a small difference is significant enough to give the two sugars distinctive shapes and behaviors.

Although it is convenient to draw glucose with a linear carbon skeleton, this representation is not completely accurate. In aqueous solutions, glucose molecules, as well as most other five- and six-carbon sugars, form rings (**Figure 5.4**).

Monosaccharides, particularly glucose, are major nutrients for cells. In the process known as cellular respiration, cells extract energy in a series of reactions starting with glucose molecules. Simple-sugar molecules are not only a major fuel for cellular work, but their carbon skeletons also serve as raw material for the synthesis of other types of small organic molecules, such as amino acids and fatty acids. Sugar molecules that are not immediately used in these ways are generally incorporated as monomers into disaccharides or polysaccharides.

A **disaccharide** consists of two monosaccharides joined by a **glycosidic linkage**, a covalent bond formed between two monosaccharides by a dehydration reaction. For example, maltose is a disaccharide formed by the linking of two molecules of glucose (**Figure 5.5a**). Also known as malt sugar, maltose is an ingredient used in brewing beer. The most prevalent disaccharide is sucrose, which is table sugar. Its two monomers are glucose and fructose (**Figure 5.5b**). Plants generally transport carbohydrates from leaves to roots and other nonphotosynthetic organs in the form of sucrose. Lactose, the sugar present in milk, is another disaccharide, in this case a glucose molecule joined to a galactose molecule.

Polysaccharides

Polysaccharides are macromolecules, polymers with a few hundred to a few thousand monosaccharides joined by glycosidic linkages. Some polysaccharides serve as storage material, hydrolyzed as needed to provide sugar for cells. Other polysaccharides serve as building material for structures that

(a) **Linear and ring forms.** Chemical equilibrium between the linear and ring structures greatly favors the formation of rings. The carbons of the sugar are numbered 1 to 6, as shown. To form the glucose ring, carbon 1 bonds to the oxygen attached to carbon 5.

(b) **Abbreviated ring structure.** Each corner represents a carbon. The ring's thicker edge indicates that you are looking at the ring edge-on; the components attached to the ring lie above or below the plane of the ring.

▲ **Figure 5.4 Linear and ring forms of glucose.**

DRAW IT *Start with the linear form of fructose (see Figure 5.3) and draw the formation of the fructose ring in two steps. First, number the carbons starting at the top of the linear structure. Then attach carbon 5 via its oxygen to carbon 2. Compare the number of carbons in the fructose and glucose rings.*

(a) **Dehydration reaction in the synthesis of maltose.**
The bonding of two glucose units forms maltose. The glycosidic linkage joins the number 1 carbon of one glucose to the number 4 carbon of the second glucose. Joining the glucose monomers in a different way would result in a different disaccharide.

Glucose   Glucose   Maltose

1–4 glycosidic linkage

(b) **Dehydration reaction in the synthesis of sucrose.**
Sucrose is a disaccharide formed from glucose and fructose. Notice that fructose, though a hexose like glucose, forms a five-sided ring.

Glucose   Fructose   Sucrose

1–2 glycosidic linkage

▲ **Figure 5.5 Examples of disaccharide synthesis.**

DRAW IT *Referring to Figure 5.4, number the carbons in each sugar in this figure. Show how the numbering is consistent with the name of the glycosidic linkage in each disaccharide.*

protect the cell or the whole organism. The architecture and function of a polysaccharide are determined by its sugar monomers and by the positions of its glycosidic linkages.

Storage Polysaccharides

Both plants and animals store sugars for later use in the form of storage polysaccharides. Plants store **starch**, a polymer of glucose monomers, as granules within cellular structures known as plastids, which include chloroplasts. Synthesizing starch enables the plant to stockpile surplus glucose. Because glucose is a major cellular fuel, starch represents stored en-

ergy. The sugar can later be withdrawn from this carbohydrate "bank" by hydrolysis, which breaks the bonds between the glucose monomers. Most animals, including humans, also have enzymes that can hydrolyze plant starch, making glucose available as a nutrient for cells. Potato tubers and grains—the fruits of wheat, maize (corn), rice, and other grasses—are the major sources of starch in the human diet.

Most of the glucose monomers in starch are joined by 1–4 linkages (number 1 carbon to number 4 carbon), like the glucose units in maltose (see Figure 5.5a). The simplest form of starch, amylose, is unbranched. Amylopectin, a more complex

(a) Starch: a plant polysaccharide. This micrograph shows part of a plant cell with a chloroplast, the cellular organelle where glucose is made and then stored as starch granules. Amylose (unbranched) and amylopectin (branched) are two forms of starch.

Chloroplast   Starch granules

Amylopectin

Amylose

1 μm

(b) Glycogen: an animal polysaccharide. Animal cells stockpile glycogen as dense clusters of granules within liver and muscle cells, as shown in this micrograph of part of a liver cell. Mitochondria are cellular organelles that help break down glucose released from glycogen. Note that glycogen is more branched than amylopectin starch.

Mitochondria   Glycogen granules

Glycogen

0.5 μm

▲ Figure 5.6 **Storage polysaccharides of plants and animals.** These examples, starch and glycogen, are composed entirely of glucose monomers, represented here by hexagons. Because of the angle of the 1–4 linkages, the polymer chains tend to form helices in unbranched regions.

starch, is a branched polymer with 1–6 linkages at the branch points. Both of these starches are shown in **Figure 5.6a**.

Animals store a polysaccharide called **glycogen**, a polymer of glucose that is like amylopectin but more extensively branched (**Figure 5.6b**). Humans and other vertebrates store glycogen mainly in liver and muscle cells. Hydrolysis of glycogen in these cells releases glucose when the demand for sugar increases. This stored fuel cannot sustain an animal for long, however. In humans, for example, glycogen stores are depleted in about a day unless they are replenished by consumption of food. This is an issue of concern in low-carbohydrate diets.

Structural Polysaccharides

Organisms build strong materials from structural polysaccharides. For example, the polysaccharide called **cellulose** is a major component of the tough walls that enclose plant cells. On a global scale, plants produce almost 10^{14} kg (100 billion tons) of cellulose per year; it is the most abundant organic compound on Earth. Like starch, cellulose is a polymer of glucose, but the glycosidic linkages in these two polymers differ. The difference is based on the fact that there are actually two slightly different ring structures for glucose (**Figure 5.7a**). When glucose forms a ring, the hydroxyl group attached to the number 1 carbon is positioned either below or above the plane of the ring. These two ring forms for glucose are called alpha (α) and beta (β), respectively. In starch, all the glucose monomers are in the α configuration (**Figure 5.7b**), the arrangement we saw in Figures 5.4 and 5.5. In contrast, the glucose monomers of cellulose are all in the β configuration, making every glucose monomer "upside down" with respect to its neighbors (**Figure 5.7c**).

The differing glycosidic linkages in starch and cellulose give the two molecules distinct three-dimensional shapes. Whereas certain starch molecules are largely helical, a cellulose molecule is straight. Cellulose is never branched, and some hydroxyl groups on its glucose monomers are free to hydrogen-bond with the hydroxyls of other cellulose molecules lying parallel to it. In plant cell walls, parallel cellulose molecules held together in this way are grouped into units called microfibrils (**Figure 5.8**). These cable-like microfibrils are a strong building material for plants and an important substance for humans because cellulose is the major constituent of paper and the only component of cotton.

Enzymes that digest starch by hydrolyzing its α linkages are unable to hydrolyze the β linkages of cellulose because of the distinctly different shapes of these two molecules. In fact, few organisms possess enzymes that can digest cellulose. Animals, including humans, do not; the cellulose in our food passes through the digestive tract and is eliminated with the feces. Along the way, the cellulose abrades the wall of the digestive tract and stimulates the lining to secrete mucus, which aids in the smooth passage of food through the tract. Thus, although cellulose is not a nutrient for humans, it is an important part of a healthful diet. Most fresh fruits, vegetables, and whole grains are rich in cellulose. On food packages, "insoluble fiber" refers mainly to cellulose.

(a) α and β glucose ring structures. These two interconvertible forms of glucose differ in the placement of the hydroxyl group (highlighted in blue) attached to the number 1 carbon.

α Glucose

β Glucose

(b) Starch: 1–4 linkage of α glucose monomers. All monomers are in the same orientation. Compare the positions of the —OH groups highlighted in yellow with those in cellulose (c).

(c) Cellulose: 1–4 linkage of β glucose monomers. In cellulose, every β glucose monomer is upside down with respect to its neighbors.

▲ **Figure 5.7 Starch and cellulose structures.**

Cell wall

10 μm

Cellulose microfibrils in a plant cell wall

Microfibril

0.5 μm

About 80 cellulose molecules associate to form a microfibril, the main architectural unit of the plant cell wall.

Cellulose molecules

Parallel cellulose molecules are held together by hydrogen bonds between hydroxyl groups attached to carbon atoms 3 and 6.

A cellulose molecule is an unbranched β glucose polymer.

β Glucose monomer

▲ **Figure 5.8 The arrangement of cellulose in plant cell walls.**

Some microorganisms can digest cellulose, breaking it down into glucose monomers. A cow harbors cellulose-digesting prokaryotes and protists in its stomach. These microbes hydrolyze the cellulose of hay and grass and convert the glucose to other compounds that nourish the cow. Similarly, a termite, which is unable to digest cellulose by itself, has prokaryotes or protists living in its gut that can make a meal of wood. Some fungi can also digest cellulose, thereby helping recycle chemical elements within Earth's ecosystems.

Another important structural polysaccharide is **chitin**, the carbohydrate used by arthropods (insects, spiders, crustaceans, and related animals) to build their exoskeletons (**Figure 5.9**). An exoskeleton is a hard case that surrounds the soft parts of an animal. Pure chitin is leathery and flexible, but it becomes hardened when encrusted with calcium carbonate, a salt. Chitin is also found in many fungi, which use this polysaccharide rather than cellulose as the building material for their cell walls. Chitin is similar to cellulose, with β linkages, except that the glucose monomer of chitin has a nitrogen-containing appendage (see Figure 5.9, top right).

◀ The structure of the chitin monomer

◀ Chitin forms the exoskeleton of arthropods. This cicada is molting, shedding its old exoskeleton and emerging in adult form.

▲ Chitin is used to make a strong and flexible surgical thread that decomposes after the wound or incision heals.

▲ **Figure 5.9 Chitin, a structural polysaccharide.**

CONCEPT CHECK 5.2

1. Write the formula for a monosaccharide that has three carbons.
2. A dehydration reaction joins two glucose molecules to form maltose. The formula for glucose is $C_6H_{12}O_6$. What is the formula for maltose?
3. **WHAT IF?** After a cow is given antibiotics to treat an infection, a vet gives the animal a drink of "gut culture" containing various prokaryotes. Why is this necessary?

For suggested answers, see Appendix A.

CONCEPT 5.3

Lipids are a diverse group of hydrophobic molecules

Lipids are the one class of large biological molecules that does not include true polymers, and they are generally not big enough to be considered macromolecules. The compounds called **lipids** are grouped together because they share one important trait: They mix poorly, if at all, with water. The hydrophobic behavior of lipids is based on their molecular structure. Although they may have some polar bonds associated with oxygen, lipids consist mostly of hydrocarbon regions. Lipids are varied in form and function. They include waxes and certain pigments, but we will focus on the most biologically important types of lipids: fats, phospholipids, and steroids.

Fats

Although fats are not polymers, they are large molecules assembled from smaller molecules by dehydration reactions. A **fat** is constructed from two kinds of smaller molecules: glycerol and fatty acids (**Figure 5.10a**). Glycerol is an alcohol; each of its three carbons bears a hydroxyl group. A **fatty acid** has a long carbon skeleton, usually 16 or 18 carbon atoms in length. The carbon at one end of the skeleton is part of a carboxyl group, the functional group that gives these molecules the name fatty *acid*. The rest of the skeleton consists of a hydrocarbon chain. The relatively nonpolar C—H bonds in the hydrocarbon chains of fatty acids are the reason fats are hydrophobic. Fats separate from water because the water molecules hydrogen-bond to one another and exclude the fats. This is the reason that vegetable oil (a liquid fat) separates from the aqueous vinegar solution in a bottle of salad dressing.

In making a fat, three fatty acid molecules are each joined to glycerol by an ester linkage, a bond between a hydroxyl group and a carboxyl group. The resulting fat, also called a **triacylglycerol**, thus consists of three fatty acids linked to one glycerol molecule. (Still another name for a fat is

Fatty acid
(in this case, palmitic acid)

Glycerol

(a) One of three dehydration reactions in the synthesis of a fat

Ester linkage

(b) Fat molecule (triacylglycerol)

▲ **Figure 5.10 The synthesis and structure of a fat, or triacylglycerol.** The molecular building blocks of a fat are one molecule of glycerol and three molecules of fatty acids. **(a)** One water molecule is removed for each fatty acid joined to the glycerol. **(b)** A fat molecule with three fatty acid units, two of them identical. The carbons of the fatty acids are arranged zigzag to suggest the actual orientations of the four single bonds extending from each carbon (see Figure 4.3a).

triglyceride, a word often found in the list of ingredients on packaged foods.) The fatty acids in a fat can be the same, or they can be of two or three different kinds, as in **Figure 5.10b**.

The terms *saturated fats* and *unsaturated fats* are commonly used in the context of nutrition (**Figure 5.11**). These terms refer to the structure of the hydrocarbon chains of the fatty acids. If there are no double bonds between carbon atoms composing a chain, then as many hydrogen atoms as possible are bonded to the carbon skeleton. Such a structure is said to be *saturated* with hydrogen, and the resulting fatty acid therefore called a **saturated fatty acid** (**Figure 5.11a**). An **unsaturated fatty acid** has one or more double bonds, with one fewer hydrogen atom on each double-bonded carbon. Nearly all double bonds in naturally occurring fatty acids are *cis* double bonds, which cause a kink in the hydrocarbon chain wherever they occur (**Figure 5.11b**). (See Figure 4.7 to remind yourself about *cis* and *trans* double bonds.)

A fat made from saturated fatty acids is called a saturated fat. Most animal fats are saturated: The hydrocarbon chains of their fatty acids—the "tails" of the fat molecules—lack double bonds, and their flexibility allows the fat molecules to pack together tightly. Saturated animal fats—such as lard and butter—are solid at room temperature. In contrast, the fats of plants

▼ **Figure 5.11 Saturated and unsaturated fats and fatty acids.**

(a) Saturated fat

At room temperature, the molecules of a saturated fat, such as the fat in butter, are packed closely together, forming a solid.

Structural formula of a saturated fat molecule (Each hydrocarbon chain is represented as a zigzag line, where each bend represents a carbon atom and hydrogens are not shown.)

Space-filling model of stearic acid, a saturated fatty acid (red = oxygen, black = carbon, gray = hydrogen)

(b) Unsaturated fat

At room temperature, the molecules of an unsaturated fat such as olive oil cannot pack together closely enough to solidify because of the kinks in some of their fatty acid hydrocarbon chains.

Structural formula of an unsaturated fat molecule

Space-filling model of oleic acid, an unsaturated fatty acid

Cis double bond causes bending.

and fishes are generally unsaturated, meaning that they are built of one or more types of unsaturated fatty acids. Usually liquid at room temperature, plant and fish fats are referred to as oils—olive oil and cod liver oil are examples. The kinks where the *cis* double bonds are located prevent the molecules from packing together closely enough to solidify at room temperature. The phrase "hydrogenated vegetable oils" on food labels means that unsaturated fats have been synthetically converted to saturated fats by adding hydrogen. Peanut butter, margarine, and many other products are hydrogenated to prevent lipids from separating out in liquid (oil) form.

A diet rich in saturated fats is one of several factors that may contribute to the cardiovascular disease known as atherosclerosis. In this condition, deposits called plaques develop within the walls of blood vessels, causing inward bulges that impede blood flow and reduce the resilience of the vessels. Recent studies have shown that the process of hydrogenating vegetable oils produces not only saturated fats but also unsaturated fats with *trans* double bonds. These **trans fats** may contribute more than saturated fats to atherosclerosis (see Chapter 42) and other problems. Because trans fats are especially common in baked goods and processed foods, the U.S. Department of Agriculture requires nutritional labels to include information on trans fat content. Some U.S. cities and at least one country—Denmark—have even banned the use of trans fats in restaurants.

Certain unsaturated fatty acids must be supplied in the human diet because they cannot be synthesized in the body. These essential fatty acids include the omega-3 fatty acids, which are required for normal growth in children and appear to protect against cardiovascular disease in adults. Fatty fish and certain nuts and vegetable oils are rich in omega-3 fatty acids (so named because they have a double bond at the third carbon-carbon bond from the end of the hydrocarbon chain).

The major function of fats is energy storage. The hydrocarbon chains of fats are similar to gasoline molecules and just as rich in energy. A gram of fat stores more than twice as much energy as a gram of a polysaccharide, such as starch. Because plants are relatively immobile, they can function with bulky energy storage in the form of starch. (Vegetable oils are gener-ally obtained from seeds, where more compact storage is an asset to the plant.) Animals, however, must carry their energy stores with them, so there is an advantage to having a more compact reservoir of fuel—fat. Humans and other mammals stock their long-term food reserves in adipose cells (see Figure 4.6a), which swell and shrink as fat is deposited and withdrawn from storage. In addition to storing energy, adipose tissue also cushions such vital organs as the kidneys, and a layer of fat beneath the skin insulates the body. This subcutaneous layer is especially thick in whales, seals, and most other marine mammals, protecting them from cold ocean water.

Phospholipids

Cells could not exist without another type of lipid—**phospholipids** (Figure 5.12). Phospholipids are essential for cells because they make up cell membranes. Their structure provides a classic example of how form fits function at the molecular level. As shown in Figure 5.12, a phospholipid is similar to a fat molecule but has only two fatty acids attached to glycerol rather than three. The third hydroxyl group of glycerol is joined to a phosphate group, which has a negative electrical charge in the cell. Additional small molecules, which are usually charged or polar, can be linked to the phosphate group to form a variety of phospholipids.

The two ends of phospholipids show different behavior toward water. The hydrocarbon tails are hydrophobic and are excluded from water. However, the phosphate group and its attachments form a hydrophilic head that has an affinity for water. When phospholipids are added to water, they self-assemble into double-layered structures called "bilayers," shielding their hydrophobic portions from water (Figure 5.13).

◀ **Figure 5.12 The structure of a phospholipid.** A phospholipid has a hydrophilic (polar) head and two hydrophobic (nonpolar) tails. Phospholipid diversity is based on differences in the two fatty acids and in the groups attached to the phosphate group of the head. This particular phospholipid, called a phosphatidylcholine, has an attached choline group. The kink in one of its tails is due to a *cis* double bond. Shown here are **(a)** the structural formula, **(b)** the space-filling model (yellow = phosphorus, blue = nitrogen), and **(c)** the symbol for a phospholipid that will appear throughout this book. (In most figures, this symbol will be used to represent a phospholipid with either saturated or unsaturated tails.)

DRAW IT *Draw an oval around the hydrophilic head of the space-filling model.*

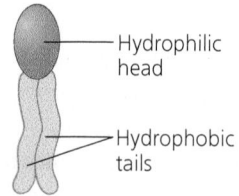

Hydrophilic head

Hydrophobic tails

Hydrophilic head

CH₂ — N(CH₃)₃⁺

CH₂

O

O = P — O⁻

O

CH₂ — CH — CH₂

O   O

C = O C = O

Choline

Phosphate

Glycerol

Hydrophobic tails

Fatty acids

(a) Structural formula

(b) Space-filling model

(c) Phospholipid symbol

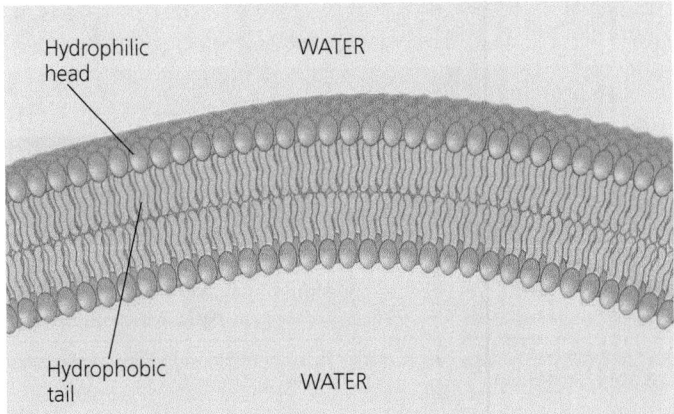

Hydrophilic head

WATER

Hydrophobic tail

WATER

▲ **Figure 5.13 Bilayer structure formed by self-assembly of phospholipids in an aqueous environment.** The phospholipid bilayer shown here is the main fabric of biological membranes. Note that the hydrophilic heads of the phospholipids are in contact with water in this structure, whereas the hydrophobic tails are in contact with each other and remote from water.

At the surface of a cell, phospholipids are arranged in a similar bilayer. The hydrophilic heads of the molecules are on the outside of the bilayer, in contact with the aqueous solutions inside and outside of the cell. The hydrophobic tails point toward the interior of the bilayer, away from the water. The phospholipid bilayer forms a boundary between the cell and its external environment; in fact, cells could not exist without phospholipids.

Steroids

Steroids are lipids characterized by a carbon skeleton consisting of four fused rings. Different steroids, such as cholesterol and the vertebrate sex hormones, are distinguished by the particular chemical groups attached to this ensemble of rings (**Figure 5.14**). **Cholesterol** is a crucial molecule in animals. It is a common component of animal cell membranes and is also the precursor from which other steroids are synthesized. In vertebrates, cholesterol is synthesized in the liver

▲ **Figure 5.14 Cholesterol, a steroid.** Cholesterol is the molecule from which other steroids, including the sex hormones, are synthesized. Steroids vary in the chemical groups attached to their four interconnected rings (shown in gold).

MAKE CONNECTIONS *Compare cholesterol with the sex hormones shown in Concept 4.3 on p. 63. Circle the chemical groups that cholesterol has in common with estradiol; put a square around the chemical groups that cholesterol has in common with testosterone.*

and obtained from the diet. A high level of cholesterol in the blood may contribute to atherosclerosis. In fact, both saturated fats and trans fats exert their negative impact on health by affecting cholesterol levels.

CONCEPT CHECK 5.3

1. Compare the structure of a fat (triglyceride) with that of a phospholipid.
2. Why are human sex hormones considered lipids?
3. **WHAT IF?** Suppose a membrane surrounded an oil droplet, as it does in the cells of plant seeds. Describe and explain the form it might take.

For suggested answers, see Appendix A.

CONCEPT 5.4

Proteins include a diversity of structures, resulting in a wide range of functions

Nearly every dynamic function of a living being depends on proteins. In fact, the importance of proteins is underscored by their name, which comes from the Greek word *proteios*, meaning "first," or "primary." Proteins account for more than 50% of the dry mass of most cells, and they are instrumental in almost everything organisms do. Some proteins speed up chemical reactions, while others play a role in defense, storage, transport, cellular communication, movement, or structural support. **Figure 5.15**, on the next page, shows examples of proteins with these functions, which you'll learn more about in later chapters.

Life would not be possible without enzymes, most of which are proteins. Enzymatic proteins regulate metabolism by acting as **catalysts**, chemical agents that selectively speed up chemical reactions without being consumed by the reaction. Because an enzyme can perform its function over and over again, these molecules can be thought of as workhorses that keep cells running by carrying out the processes of life.

A human has tens of thousands of different proteins, each with a specific structure and function; proteins, in fact, are the most structurally sophisticated molecules known. Consistent with their diverse functions, they vary extensively in structure, each type of protein having a unique three-dimensional shape.

Polypeptides

Diverse as proteins are, they are all unbranched polymers constructed from the same set of 20 amino acids. Polymers of amino acids are called **polypeptides**. A **protein** is a biologically functional molecule that consists of one or more polypeptides, each folded and coiled into a specific three-dimensional structure.

Enzymatic proteins

Function: Selective acceleration of chemical reactions

Example: Digestive enzymes catalyze the hydrolysis of bonds in food molecules.

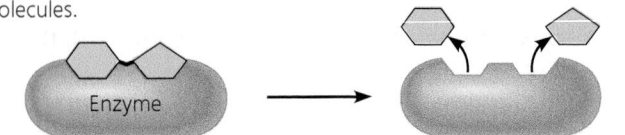

Enzyme

Defensive proteins

Function: Protection against disease

Example: Antibodies inactivate and help destroy viruses and bacteria.

Antibodies

Virus   Bacterium

Storage proteins

Function: Storage of amino acids

Examples: Casein, the protein of milk, is the major source of amino acids for baby mammals. Plants have storage proteins in their seeds. Ovalbumin is the protein of egg white, used as an amino acid source for the developing embryo.

Ovalbumin   Amino acids for embryo

Transport proteins

Function: Transport of substances

Examples: Hemoglobin, the iron-containing protein of vertebrate blood, transports oxygen from the lungs to other parts of the body. Other proteins transport molecules across cell membranes.

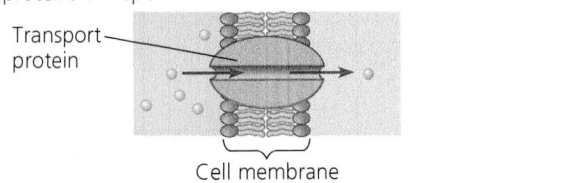

Transport protein

Cell membrane

Hormonal proteins

Function: Coordination of an organism's activities

Example: Insulin, a hormone secreted by the pancreas, causes other tissues to take up glucose, thus regulating blood sugar concentration.

High blood sugar

Insulin secreted

Normal blood sugar

Receptor proteins

Function: Response of cell to chemical stimuli

Example: Receptors built into the membrane of a nerve cell detect signaling molecules released by other nerve cells.

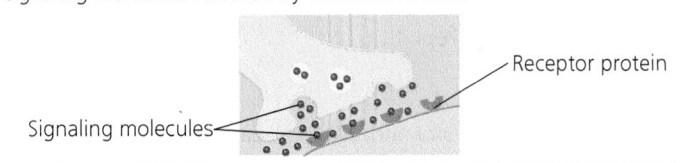

Receptor protein

Signaling molecules

Contractile and motor proteins

Function: Movement

Examples: Motor proteins are responsible for the undulations of cilia and flagella. Actin and myosin proteins are responsible for the contraction of muscles.

Actin   Myosin

Muscle tissue   100 μm

Structural proteins

Function: Support

Examples: Keratin is the protein of hair, horns, feathers, and other skin appendages. Insects and spiders use silk fibers to make their cocoons and webs, respectively. Collagen and elastin proteins provide a fibrous framework in animal connective tissues.

Collagen

Connective tissue   60 μm

Amino Acid Monomers

All amino acids share a common structure. An **amino acid** is an organic molecule possessing both an amino group and a carboxyl group (see Figure 4.9). The illustration at the right shows the general formula for an amino acid. At the center of the amino acid is an asymmetric carbon atom called the *alpha (α) carbon*. Its four different partners are an amino group, a car-

Side chain (R group)

R

α carbon

Amino group   Carboxyl group

boxyl group, a hydrogen atom, and a variable group symbolized by R. The R group, also called the side chain, differs with each amino acid.

Figure 5.16 shows the 20 amino acids that cells use to build their thousands of proteins. Here the amino groups and carboxyl groups are all depicted in ionized form, the way they usually exist at the pH found in a cell. The side chain (R group) may be as simple as a hydrogen atom, as in the amino acid glycine, or it may be a carbon skeleton with various functional groups attached, as in glutamine.

▼ **Figure 5.16** **The 20 amino acids of proteins.** The amino acids are grouped here according to the properties of their side chains (R groups) and shown in their prevailing ionic forms at pH 7.2, the pH within a cell. The three-letter and one-letter abbreviations for the amino acids are in parentheses. All amino acids used in proteins are L enantiomers, the form shown here (see Figure 4.7).

Nonpolar side chains; hydrophobic

Polar side chains; hydrophilic

Electrically charged side chains; hydrophilic

The physical and chemical properties of the side chain determine the unique characteristics of a particular amino acid, thus affecting its functional role in a polypeptide. In Figure 5.16, the amino acids are grouped according to the properties of their side chains. One group consists of amino acids with nonpolar side chains, which are hydrophobic. Another group consists of amino acids with polar side chains, which are hydrophilic. Acidic amino acids are those with side chains that are generally negative in charge owing to the presence of a carboxyl group, which is usually dissociated (ionized) at cellular pH. Basic amino acids have amino groups in their side chains that are generally positive in charge. (Notice that *all* amino acids have carboxyl groups and amino groups; the terms *acidic* and *basic* in this context refer only to groups on the side chains.) Because they are charged, acidic and basic side chains are also hydrophilic.

Amino Acid Polymers

Now that we have examined amino acids, let's see how they are linked to form polymers (**Figure 5.17**). When two amino acids are positioned so that the carboxyl group of one is adjacent to the amino group of the other, they can become joined by a dehydration reaction, with the removal of a water molecule. The resulting covalent bond is called a **peptide bond**. Repeated over and over, this process yields a polypeptide, a polymer of many amino acids linked by peptide bonds.

The repeating sequence of atoms highlighted in purple in Figure 5.17 is called the polypeptide backbone. Extending from this backbone are the different side chains (R groups) of the amino acids. Polypeptides range in length from a few amino acids to a thousand or more. Each specific polypeptide has a unique linear sequence of amino acids. Note that one end of the polypeptide chain has a free amino group, while the opposite end has a free carboxyl group. Thus, a polypeptide of any length has a single amino end (N-terminus) and a single carboxyl end (C-terminus). In a polypeptide of any significant size, the side chains far outnumber the terminal groups, so the chemical nature of the molecule as a whole is determined by the kind and sequence of the side chains. The immense variety of polypeptides in nature illustrates an important concept introduced earlier—that cells can make many different polymers by linking a limited set of monomers into diverse sequences.

Protein Structure and Function

The specific activities of proteins result from their intricate three-dimensional architecture, the simplest level of which is the sequence of their amino acids. The pioneer in determining the amino acid sequence of proteins was Frederick Sanger, who, with his colleagues at Cambridge University in England, worked on the hormone insulin in the late 1940s and early 1950s. He used agents that break polypeptides at

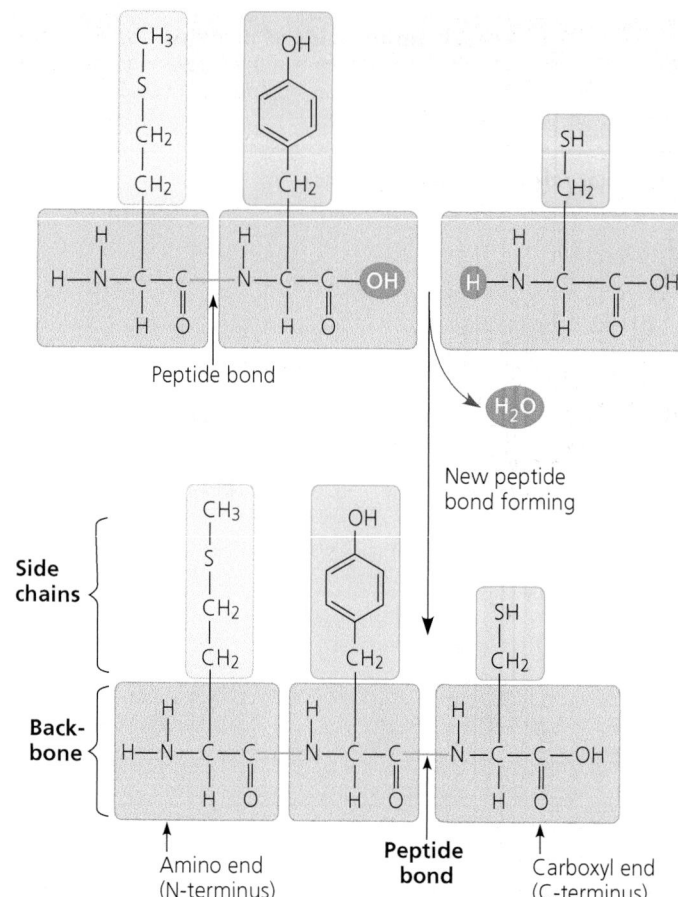

▲ Figure 5.17 Making a polypeptide chain. Peptide bonds are formed by dehydration reactions, which link the carboxyl group of one amino acid to the amino group of the next. The peptide bonds are formed one at a time, starting with the amino acid at the amino end (N-terminus). The polypeptide has a repetitive backbone (purple) to which the amino acid side chains (yellow and green) are attached.

DRAW IT *Circle and label the carboxyl and amino groups that will form the new peptide bond.*

specific places, followed by chemical methods to determine the amino acid sequence in these small fragments. Sanger and his co-workers were able, after years of effort, to reconstruct the complete amino acid sequence of insulin. Since then, most of the steps involved in sequencing a polypeptide have been automated.

Once we have learned the amino acid sequence of a polypeptide, what can it tell us about the three-dimensional structure (commonly referred to simply as the "structure") of the protein and its function? The term *polypeptide* is not synonymous with the term *protein*. Even for a protein consisting of a single polypeptide, the relationship is somewhat analogous to that between a long strand of yarn and a sweater of particular size and shape that can be knit from the yarn. A functional protein is not *just* a polypeptide chain, but one or more polypeptides precisely twisted, folded, and coiled into a molecule of unique shape (**Figure 5.18**). And it is the amino acid sequence of each polypeptide that determines what

(a) A **ribbon model** shows how the single polypeptide chain folds and coils to form the functional protein. (The yellow lines represent disulfide bridges that stabilize the protein's shape; see Figure 5.20.)

(b) A **space-filling model** shows more clearly the globular shape seen in many proteins, as well as the specific three-dimensional structure unique to lysozyme.

▲ **Figure 5.18 Structure of a protein, the enzyme lysozyme.** Present in our sweat, tears, and saliva, lysozyme is an enzyme that helps prevent infection by binding to and destroying specific molecules on the surface of many kinds of bacteria. The groove is the part of the protein that recognizes and binds to the target molecules on bacterial walls.

three-dimensional structure the protein will have under normal cellular conditions.

When a cell synthesizes a polypeptide, the chain generally folds spontaneously, assuming the functional structure for that protein. This folding is driven and reinforced by the formation of a variety of bonds between parts of the chain, which in turn depends on the sequence of amino acids. Many proteins are roughly spherical (*globular proteins*), while others are shaped like long fibers (*fibrous proteins*). Even within these broad categories, countless variations exist.

A protein's specific structure determines how it works. In almost every case, the function of a protein depends on its ability to recognize and bind to some other molecule. In an especially striking example of the marriage of form and function, **Figure 5.19** shows the exact match of shape between an antibody (a protein in the body) and the particular foreign substance on a flu virus that the antibody binds to and marks for destruction. In Chapter 43, you'll learn more about how the immune system generates antibodies that match the shapes of specific foreign molecules so well. Also, you may recall from Chapter 2 that natural signaling molecules called endorphins bind to specific receptor proteins on the surface of brain cells in humans, producing euphoria and relieving pain. Morphine, heroin, and other opiate drugs are able to mimic endorphins because they all share a similar shape with endorphins and can thus fit into and bind to endorphin receptors in the brain. This fit is very specific, something like a lock and key (see Figure 2.18). Thus, the function of a protein—for instance, the ability of a receptor protein to bind to a particular pain-relieving signaling molecule—is an emergent property resulting from exquisite molecular order.

Antibody protein   Protein from flu virus

▲ **Figure 5.19 An antibody binding to a protein from a flu virus.** A technique called X-ray crystallography was used to generate a computer model of an antibody protein (blue and orange, left) bound to a flu virus protein (green and yellow, right). Computer software was then used to back the images away from each other, revealing the exact complementarity of shape between the two protein surfaces.

Four Levels of Protein Structure

With the goal of understanding the function of a protein, learning about its structure is often productive. In spite of their great diversity, all proteins share three superimposed levels of structure, known as primary, secondary, and tertiary structure. A fourth level, quaternary structure, arises when a protein consists of two or more polypeptide chains. **Figure 5.20**, on the following two pages, describes these four levels of protein structure. Be sure to study this figure thoroughly before going on to the next section.

Exploring Levels of Protein Structure

Primary Structure

Linear chain of amino acids

Amino acids

$+H_3N$ — Gly Pro Thr Gly Thr Gly Glu Ser Lys Cys
Amino end
1 ... 5 ... 10

Pro
Leu
Met
Val
15
Lys
Val His Val Ala Val Asn Ile Ala Pro Ser Gly Arg Val Ala Asp Leu Val
30 ... 25 ... 20

Val
Phe
Arg
Lys
35 ... 40 ... 45 ... 50
Ala Ala Asp Asp Thr Trp Glu Pro Phe Ala Ser Gly Lys Thr Ser Glu Ser

Primary structure of transthyretin

Gly
Glu
55 Leu
70 ... 65 ... 60 His
Asp Ile Glu Val Lys Tyr Ile Gly Glu Val Phe Glu Glu Glu Thr Thr Leu Gly
Thr 75
Lys
80 ... 85 ... 90
Ser Tyr Trp Lys Ala Leu Gly Ile Ser Pro Phe His Glu His Ala Glu Val Val
Phe
95
Thr
Ala
115 ... 110 ... 105 ... 100 Asn
Tyr Ser Tyr Pro Ser Leu Leu Ala Ala Ile Thr Tyr Arg Arg Pro Gly Ser Asp
Ser
Thr
Thr 120 ... 125
Ala Val Val Thr Asn Pro Lys Glu — C
Carboxyl end

The **primary structure** of a protein is a linked series of amino acids with a unique sequence. As an example, let's consider transthyretin, a globular blood protein that transports vitamin A and one of the thyroid hormones throughout the body. Transthyretin is made up of four identical polypeptide chains, each composed of 127 amino acids. Shown here is one of these chains unraveled for a closer look at its primary structure. Each of the 127 positions along the chain is occupied by one of the 20 amino acids, indicated here by its three-letter abbreviation.

The primary structure is like the order of letters in a very long word. If left to chance, there would be 20^{127} different ways of making a polypeptide chain 127 amino acids long. However, the precise primary structure of a protein is determined not by the random linking of amino acids, but by inherited genetic information. The primary structure in turn dictates secondary and tertiary structure, due to the chemical nature of the backbone and the side chains (R groups) of the amino acids positioned along the chain.

Secondary Structure

Regions stabilized by hydrogen bonds between atoms of the polypeptide backbone

α helix

Hydrogen bond

β pleated sheet

β strand, shown as a flat arrow pointing toward the carboxyl end

Hydrogen bond

Most proteins have segments of their polypeptide chains repeatedly coiled or folded in patterns that contribute to the protein's overall shape. These coils and folds, collectively referred to as **secondary structure**, are the result of hydrogen bonds between the repeating constituents of the polypeptide backbone (not the amino acid side chains). Within the backbone, the oxygen atoms have a partial negative charge, and the hydrogen atoms attached to the nitrogens have a partial positive charge (see Figure 2.16); therefore, hydrogen bonds can form between these atoms. Individually, these hydrogen bonds are weak, but because they are repeated many times over a relatively long region of the polypeptide chain, they can support a particular shape for that part of the protein.

One such secondary structure is the α **helix**, a delicate coil held together by hydrogen bonding between every fourth amino acid, shown above. Although each transthyretin polypeptide has only one α helix region (see tertiary structure on the next page), other globular proteins have multiple stretches of α helix separated by nonhelical regions (see hemoglobin on the next page). Some fibrous proteins, such as α-keratin, the structural protein of hair, have the α helix formation over most of their length.

The other main type of secondary structure is the β **pleated sheet**. As shown above, in this structure two or more strands of the polypeptide chain lying side by side (called β strands) are connected by hydrogen bonds between parts of the two parallel polypeptide backbones. β pleated sheets make up the core of many globular proteins, as is the case for transthyretin (see tertiary structure on the next page), and dominate some fibrous proteins, including the silk protein of a spider's web. The teamwork of so many hydrogen bonds makes each spider silk fiber stronger than a steel strand of the same weight.

▼ Spiders secrete silk fibers made of a structural protein containing β pleated sheets, which allow the spider web to stretch and recoil.

Tertiary Structure

Three-dimensional shape stabilized by interactions between side chains

Transthyretin polypeptide

Quaternary Structure

Association of multiple polypeptides, forming a functional protein

Transthyretin protein (four identical polypeptides)

Superimposed on the patterns of secondary structure is a protein's tertiary structure, shown above in a ribbon model of the transthyretin polypeptide. While secondary structure involves interactions between backbone constituents, **tertiary structure** is the overall shape of a polypeptide resulting from interactions between the side chains (R groups) of the various amino acids. One type of interaction that contributes to tertiary structure is—somewhat misleadingly—called a **hydrophobic interaction**. As a polypeptide folds into its functional shape, amino acids with hydrophobic (nonpolar) side chains usually end up in clusters at the core of the protein, out of contact with water. Thus, a "hydrophobic interaction" is actually caused by the exclusion of nonpolar substances by water molecules. Once nonpolar amino acid side chains are close together, van der Waals interactions help hold them together. Meanwhile, hydrogen bonds between polar side chains and ionic bonds between positively and negatively charged side chains also help stabilize tertiary structure. These are all weak interactions in the aqueous cellular environment, but their cumulative effect helps give the protein a unique shape.

Covalent bonds called **disulfide bridges** may further reinforce the shape of a protein. Disulfide bridges form where two cysteine monomers, which have sulfhydryl groups (—SH) on their side chains (see Figure 4.9), are brought close together by the folding of the protein. The sulfur of one cysteine bonds to the sulfur of the second, and the disulfide bridge (—S—S—) rivets parts of the protein together (see yellow lines in Figure 5.18a). All of these different kinds of interactions can contribute to the tertiary structure of a protein, as shown here in a small part of a hypothetical protein:

Some proteins consist of two or more polypeptide chains aggregated into one functional macromolecule. **Quaternary structure** is the overall protein structure that results from the aggregation of these polypeptide subunits. For example, shown above is the complete globular transthyretin protein, made up of its four polypeptides.

Another example is collagen, shown below, which is a fibrous protein that has three identical helical polypeptides intertwined into a larger triple helix, giving the long fibers great strength. This suits collagen fibers to their function as the girders of connective tissue in skin, bone, tendons, ligaments, and other body parts. (Collagen accounts for 40% of the protein in a human body.)

Collagen

Hemoglobin, the oxygen-binding protein of red blood cells shown below, is another example of a globular protein with quaternary structure. It consists of four polypeptide subunits, two of one kind (α) and two of another kind (β). Both α and β subunits consist primarily of α-helical secondary structure. Each subunit has a nonpolypeptide component, called heme, with an iron atom that binds oxygen.

Heme
Iron
β subunit
α subunit
α subunit
β subunit

Hemoglobin

Hydrogen bond

Hydrophobic interactions and van der Waals interactions

Disulfide bridge

Ionic bond

Polypeptide backbone

	Primary Structure	Secondary and Tertiary Structures	Quaternary Structure	Function	Red Blood Cell Shape
Normal hemoglobin	1 Val 2 His 3 Leu 4 Thr 5 Pro 6 Glu 7 Glu	β subunit	Normal hemoglobin α β α β	Molecules do not associate with one another; each carries oxygen.	Normal red blood cells are full of individual hemoglobin molecules, each carrying oxygen. 10 μm
Sickle-cell hemoglobin	1 Val 2 His 3 Leu 4 Thr 5 Pro 6 Val 7 Glu	Exposed hydrophobic region β subunit	Sickle-cell hemoglobin α β α β	Molecules interact with one another and crystallize into a fiber; capacity to carry oxygen is greatly reduced.	Fibers of abnormal hemoglobin deform red blood cell into sickle shape. 10 μm

▲ Figure 5.21 **A single amino acid substitution in a protein causes sickle-cell disease.**

MAKE CONNECTIONS *Considering the chemical characteristics of the amino acids valine and glutamic acid (see Figure 5.16), propose a possible explanation for the dramatic effect on protein function that occurs when valine is substituted for glutamic acid.*

Sickle-Cell Disease: A Change in Primary Structure

Even a slight change in primary structure can affect a protein's shape and ability to function. For instance, **sickle-cell disease**, an inherited blood disorder, is caused by the substitution of one amino acid (valine) for the normal one (glutamic acid) at a particular position in the primary structure of hemoglobin, the protein that carries oxygen in red blood cells. Normal red blood cells are disk-shaped, but in sickle-cell disease, the abnormal hemoglobin molecules tend to crystallize, deforming some of the cells into a sickle shape (Figure 5.21). A person with the disease has periodic "sickle-cell crises" when the angular cells clog tiny blood vessels, impeding blood flow. The toll taken on such patients is a dramatic example of how a simple change in protein structure can have devastating effects on protein function.

What Determines Protein Structure?

You've learned that a unique shape endows each protein with a specific function. But what are the key factors determining protein structure? You already know most of the answer: A polypeptide chain of a given amino acid sequence can spontaneously arrange itself into a three-dimensional shape determined and maintained by the interactions responsible for secondary and tertiary structure. This folding normally occurs as the protein is being synthesized in the crowded environment within a cell, aided by other proteins. However, protein structure also depends on the physical and chemical conditions of the protein's environment. If the pH, salt concentration, temperature, or other aspects of its environment are altered, the weak chemical bonds and interactions within a protein may be destroyed, causing the protein to unravel and lose its native shape, a change called **denaturation** (Figure 5.22). Because it is misshapen, the denatured protein is biologically inactive.

Most proteins become denatured if they are transferred from an aqueous environment to a nonpolar solvent, such as

Denaturation

Renaturation

Normal protein   Denatured protein

▲ Figure 5.22 **Denaturation and renaturation of a protein.** High temperatures or various chemical treatments will denature a protein, causing it to lose its shape and hence its ability to function. If the denatured protein remains dissolved, it can often renature when the chemical and physical aspects of its environment are restored to normal.

ether or chloroform; the polypeptide chain refolds so that its hydrophobic regions face outward toward the solvent. Other denaturation agents include chemicals that disrupt the hydrogen bonds, ionic bonds, and disulfide bridges that maintain a protein's shape. Denaturation can also result from excessive heat, which agitates the polypeptide chain enough to overpower the weak interactions that stabilize the structure. The white of an egg becomes opaque during cooking because the denatured proteins are insoluble and solidify. This also explains why excessively high fevers can be fatal: Proteins in the blood can denature at very high body temperatures.

When a protein in a test-tube solution has been denatured by heat or chemicals, it can sometimes return to its functional shape when the denaturing agent is removed. We can conclude that the information for building specific shape is intrinsic to the protein's primary structure. The sequence of amino acids determines the protein's shape—where an α helix can form, where β pleated sheets can exist, where disulfide bridges are located, where ionic bonds can form, and so on. But how does protein folding occur in the cell?

Protein Folding in the Cell

Biochemists now know the amino acid sequence for more than 10 million proteins and the three-dimensional shape for more than 20,000. Researchers have tried to correlate the primary structure of many proteins with their three-dimensional structure to discover the rules of protein folding. Unfortunately, however, the protein-folding process is not that simple. Most proteins probably go through several intermediate structures on their way to a stable shape, and looking at the mature structure does not reveal the stages of folding required to achieve that form. However, biochemists have developed methods for tracking a protein through such stages.

Crucial to the folding process are **chaperonins** (also called chaperone proteins), protein molecules that assist in the proper folding of other proteins (**Figure 5.23**). Chaperonins do not specify the final structure of a polypeptide. Instead, they keep the new polypeptide segregated from "bad influences" in the cytoplasmic environment while it folds spontaneously. The chaperonin shown in Figure 5.23, from the bacterium *E. coli*, is a giant multiprotein complex shaped like a hollow cylinder. The cavity provides a shelter for folding polypeptides. In the past decade, researchers have discovered molecular systems that interact with chaperonins and check whether proper folding has occurred. Such systems either refold the misfolded proteins correctly or mark them for destruction.

Misfolding of polypeptides is a serious problem in cells. Many diseases, such as Alzheimer's, Parkinson's, and mad cow disease, are associated with an accumulation of misfolded proteins. In fact, misfolded versions of the transthyretin protein featured in Figure 5.20 have been implicated in several diseases, including one form of senile dementia.

Even when scientists have a correctly folded protein in hand, determining its exact three-dimensional structure is not simple, for a single protein molecule has thousands of atoms. The first 3-D structures were worked out in 1959 for hemoglobin and a related protein. The method that made these feats possible was **X-ray crystallography**, which has since been used to determine the 3-D structure of many other proteins. In a recent example, Roger Kornberg and his colleagues at Stanford University used this method to elucidate the structure of RNA polymerase, an enzyme that plays a crucial role in the expression of genes (**Figure 5.24**, on the next page). Another method for analyzing protein structure is nuclear magnetic resonance (NMR) spectroscopy, which does not require protein crystallization. A still newer approach employs bioinformatics (see Chapter 1) to predict the 3-D structure of polypeptides from their amino acid sequence. X-ray crystallography, NMR spectroscopy, and bioinformatics are complementary approaches to understanding protein structure and function.

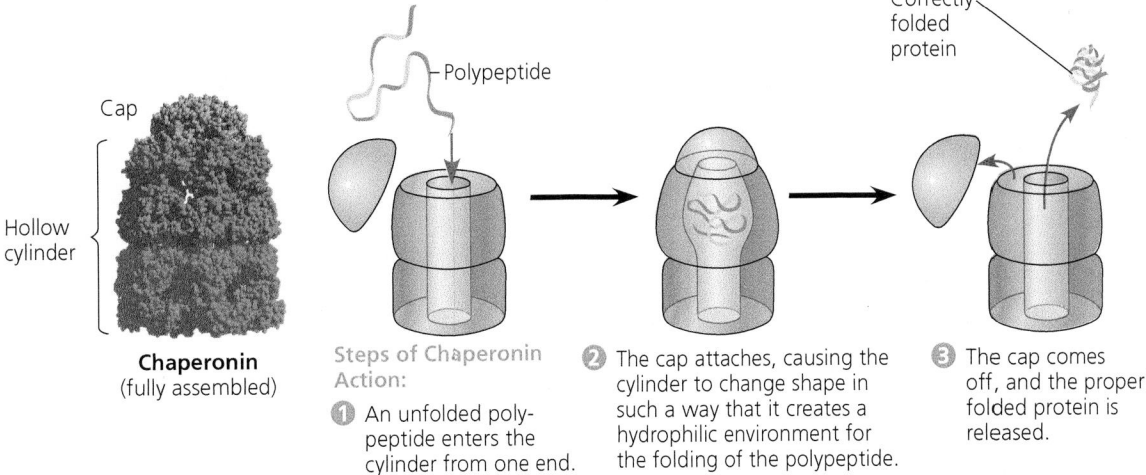

▶ **Figure 5.23 A chaperonin in action.** The computer graphic (left) shows a large chaperonin protein complex from the bacterium *E. coli*. It has an interior space that provides a shelter for the proper folding of newly made polypeptides. The complex consists of two proteins: One protein is a hollow cylinder; the other is a cap that can fit on either end.

Cap

Hollow cylinder

Chaperonin (fully assembled)

Polypeptide

Correctly folded protein

Steps of Chaperonin Action:

❶ An unfolded polypeptide enters the cylinder from one end.

❷ The cap attaches, causing the cylinder to change shape in such a way that it creates a hydrophilic environment for the folding of the polypeptide.

❸ The cap comes off, and the properly folded protein is released.

INQUIRY

What can the 3-D shape of the enzyme RNA polymerase II tell us about its function?

EXPERIMENT In 2006, Roger Kornberg was awarded the Nobel Prize in Chemistry for using X-ray crystallography to determine the 3-D shape of RNA polymerase II, which binds to the DNA double helix and synthesizes RNA. After crystallizing a complex of all three components, Kornberg and his colleagues aimed an X-ray beam through the crystal. The atoms of the crystal diffracted (bent) the X-rays into an orderly array that a digital detector recorded as a pattern of spots called an X-ray diffraction pattern.

RESULTS Using data from X-ray diffraction patterns, as well as the amino acid sequence determined by chemical methods, Kornberg and colleagues built a 3-D model of the complex with the help of computer software.

CONCLUSION By analyzing their model, the researchers developed a hypothesis about the functions of different regions of RNA polymerase II. For example, the region above the DNA may act as a clamp that holds the nucleic acids in place. (You'll learn more about this enzyme in Chapter 17.)

SOURCE A. L. Gnatt et al., Structural basis of transcription: an RNA polymerase II elongation complex at 3.3Å, *Science* 292:1876–1882 (2001).

WHAT IF? If you were an author of the paper and were describing the model, what type of protein structure would you call the small polypeptide spirals in RNA polymerase II?

CONCEPT CHECK 5.4

1. Why does a denatured protein no longer function normally?
2. What parts of a polypeptide participate in the bonds that hold together secondary structure? Tertiary structure?
3. **WHAT IF?** Where would you expect a polypeptide region that is rich in the amino acids valine, leucine, and isoleucine to be located in the folded polypeptide? Explain.

For suggested answers, see Appendix A.

CONCEPT 5.5

Nucleic acids store, transmit, and help express hereditary information

If the primary structure of polypeptides determines a protein's shape, what determines primary structure? The amino acid sequence of a polypeptide is programmed by a discrete unit of inheritance known as a **gene**. Genes consist of DNA, which belongs to the class of compounds called nucleic acids. **Nucleic acids** are polymers made of monomers called *nucleotides*.

The Roles of Nucleic Acids

The two types of nucleic acids, **deoxyribonucleic acid (DNA)** and **ribonucleic acid (RNA)**, enable living organisms to reproduce their complex components from one generation to the next. Unique among molecules, DNA provides directions for its own replication. DNA also directs RNA synthesis and, through RNA, controls protein synthesis **(Figure 5.25)**.

DNA is the genetic material that organisms inherit from their parents. Each chromosome contains one long DNA molecule, usually carrying several hundred or more genes. When a cell reproduces itself by dividing, its DNA molecules are copied and passed along from one generation of cells to the next. Encoded in the structure of DNA is the information that

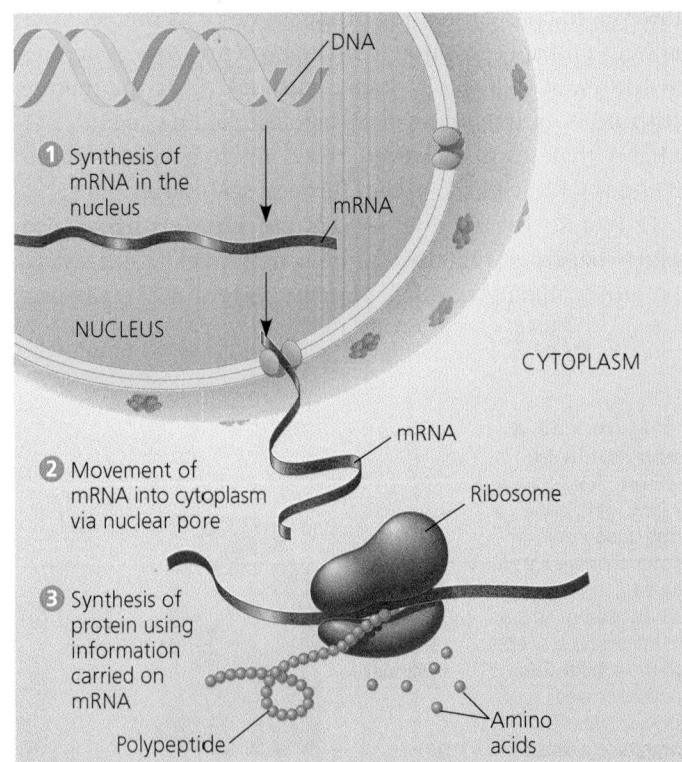

▲ **Figure 5.25 DNA → RNA → protein.** In a eukaryotic cell, DNA in the nucleus programs protein production in the cytoplasm by dictating synthesis of messenger RNA (mRNA). (The cell nucleus is actually much larger relative to the other elements of this figure.)

programs all the cell's activities. The DNA, however, is not directly involved in running the operations of the cell, any more than computer software by itself can print a bank statement or read the bar code on a box of cereal. Just as a printer is needed to print out a statement and a scanner is needed to read a bar code, proteins are required to implement genetic programs. The molecular hardware of the cell—the tools for biological functions—consists mostly of proteins. For example, the oxygen carrier in red blood cells is the protein hemoglobin, not the DNA that specifies its structure.

How does RNA, the other type of nucleic acid, fit into gene expression, the flow of genetic information from DNA to proteins? Each gene along a DNA molecule directs synthesis of a type of RNA called *messenger RNA* (*mRNA*). The mRNA molecule interacts with the cell's protein-synthesizing machinery to direct production of a polypeptide, which folds into all or part of a protein. We can summarize the flow of genetic information as DNA → RNA → protein (see Figure 5.25). The sites of protein synthesis are tiny structures called ribosomes. In a eukaryotic cell, ribosomes are in the cytoplasm, but DNA resides in the nucleus. Messenger RNA conveys genetic instructions for building proteins from the nucleus to the cytoplasm. Prokaryotic cells lack nuclei but still use mRNA to convey a

message from the DNA to ribosomes and other cellular equipment that translate the coded information into amino acid sequences. In recent years, the spotlight has been turned on other, previously unknown types of RNA that play many other roles in the cell. As is so often true in biology, the story is still being written! You'll hear more about the newly discovered functions of RNA molecules in Chapter 18.

The Components of Nucleic Acids

Nucleic acids are macromolecules that exist as polymers called **polynucleotides** (**Figure 5.26a**). As indicated by the name, each polynucleotide consists of monomers called **nucleotides**. A nucleotide, in general, is composed of three parts: a nitrogen-containing (nitrogenous) base, a five-carbon sugar (a pentose), and one or more phosphate groups (**Figure 5.26b**). In a polynucleotide, each monomer has only one phosphate group. The portion of a nucleotide without any phosphate groups is called a *nucleoside*.

To build a nucleotide, let's first consider the nitrogenous bases (**Figure 5.26c**). Each nitrogenous base has one or two rings that include nitrogen atoms. (They are called nitrogenous *bases* because the nitrogen atoms tend to take up H^+

▲ **Figure 5.26 Components of nucleic acids.** **(a)** A polynucleotide has a sugar-phosphate backbone with variable appendages, the nitrogenous bases. **(b)** A nucleotide monomer includes a nitrogenous base, a sugar, and a phosphate group. Without the phosphate group, the structure is called a nucleoside. **(c)** A nucleoside includes a nitrogenous base (purine or pyrimidine) and a five-carbon sugar (deoxyribose or ribose).

from solution, thus acting as bases.) There are two families of nitrogenous bases: pyrimidines and purines. A **pyrimidine** has one six-membered ring of carbon and nitrogen atoms. The members of the pyrimidine family are cytosine (C), thymine (T), and uracil (U). **Purines** are larger, with a six-membered ring fused to a five-membered ring. The purines are adenine (A) and guanine (G). The specific pyrimidines and purines differ in the chemical groups attached to the rings. Adenine, guanine, and cytosine are found in both DNA and RNA; thymine is found only in DNA and uracil only in RNA.

Now let's add a sugar to the nitrogenous base. In DNA the sugar is **deoxyribose**; in RNA it is **ribose** (see Figure 5.26c). The only difference between these two sugars is that deoxyribose lacks an oxygen atom on the second carbon in the ring; hence the name *deoxy*ribose. To distinguish the numbers of the sugar carbons from those used for the ring atoms of the attached nitrogenous base, the sugar carbon numbers of a nucleoside or nucleotide have a prime (') after them. Thus, the second carbon in the sugar ring is the 2' ("2 prime") carbon, and the carbon that sticks up from the ring is called the 5' carbon.

So far, we have built a nucleoside (nitrogenous base plus sugar). To complete the construction of a nucleotide, we attach a phosphate group to the 5' carbon of the sugar (see Figure 5.26b). The molecule is now a nucleoside monophosphate, better known as a nucleotide.

Nucleotide Polymers

Now we can see how these nucleotides are linked together to build a polynucleotide. Adjacent nucleotides are joined by a phosphodiester linkage, which consists of a phosphate group that links the sugars of two nucleotides. This bonding results in a backbone with a repeating pattern of sugar-phosphate units (see Figure 5.26a). (Note that the nitrogenous bases are not part of the backbone.) The two free ends of the polymer are distinctly different from each other. One end has a phosphate attached to a 5' carbon, and the other end has a hydroxyl group on a 3' carbon; we refer to these as the 5' end and the 3' end, respectively. We can say that a polynucleotide has a built-in directionality along its sugar-phosphate backbone, from 5' to 3', somewhat like a one-way street. All along this sugar-phosphate backbone are appendages consisting of the nitrogenous bases.

The sequence of bases along a DNA (or mRNA) polymer is unique for each gene and provides very specific information to the cell. Because genes are hundreds to thousands of nucleotides long, the number of possible base sequences is effectively limitless. A gene's meaning to the cell is encoded in its specific sequence of the four DNA bases. For example, the sequence 5'-AGGTAACTT-3' means one thing, whereas the sequence 5'-CGCTTTAAC-3' has a different meaning. (Entire genes, of course, are much longer.) The linear order of bases in a gene specifies the amino acid sequence—the primary structure—of a protein, which in turn specifies that protein's three-dimensional structure and its function in the cell.

The Structures of DNA and RNA Molecules

RNA molecules usually exist as single polynucleotide chains like the one shown in Figure 5.26a. In contrast, DNA molecules have two polynucleotides, or "strands," that spiral around an imaginary axis, forming a **double helix** (Figure 5.27a). The two sugar-phosphate backbones run in opposite 5' → 3' directions from each other; this arrangement is referred to as **antiparallel**, somewhat like a divided highway. The sugar-phosphate backbones are on the outside of the helix, and the nitrogenous bases are paired in the interior of the helix. The two strands are held together by hydrogen bonds between the paired bases (see Figure 5.27a). Most DNA molecules are very long, with thousands or even millions of base pairs. One long DNA double helix includes many genes, each one a particular segment of the molecule.

Only certain bases in the double helix are compatible with each other. Adenine (A) always pairs with thymine (T), and guanine (G) always pairs with cytosine (C). If we were to read the sequence of bases along one strand of the double helix, we would know the sequence of bases along the other strand. If a stretch of one strand has the base sequence 5'-AGGTCCG-3', then the base-pairing rules tell us that the same stretch of the other strand must have the sequence 3'-TCCAGGC-5'. The two strands of the double helix are *complementary*, each the predictable counterpart of the other. It is this feature of DNA that makes it possible to generate two identical copies of each DNA molecule in a cell that is preparing to divide. When the cell divides, the copies are distributed to the daughter cells, making them genetically identical to the parent cell. Thus, the structure of DNA accounts for its function of transmitting genetic information whenever a cell reproduces.

Complementary base pairing can also occur between parts of two RNA molecules or even between two stretches of nucleotides in the *same* RNA molecule. In fact, base pairing within an RNA molecule allows it to take on the particular three-dimensional shape necessary for its function. Consider, for example, the type of RNA called *transfer RNA* (*tRNA*), which brings amino acids to the ribosome during the synthesis of a polypeptide. A tRNA molecule is about 80 nucleotides in length. Its functional shape results from base pairing between nucleotides where complementary stretches of the molecule run antiparallel to each other (Figure 5.27b).

Note that in RNA, adenine (A) pairs with uracil (U); thymine (T) is not present in RNA. Another difference between RNA and DNA is that DNA almost always exists as a double helix, whereas RNA molecules are more variable in shape. This variability arises because the extent and location of complementary base pairing within an RNA molecule differs in different types of RNA, as you will see in Chapter 17.

► **Figure 5.27 The structures of DNA and tRNA molecules. (a)** The DNA molecule is usually a double helix, with the sugar-phosphate backbones of the antiparallel polynucleotide strands (symbolized here by blue ribbons) on the outside of the helix. Holding the two strands together are pairs of nitrogenous bases attached to each other by hydrogen bonds. As illustrated here with symbolic shapes for the bases, adenine (A) can pair only with thymine (T), and guanine (G) can pair only with cytosine (C). Each DNA strand in this figure is the structural equivalent of the polynucleotide diagrammed in Figure 5.26a. **(b)** A tRNA molecule has a roughly L-shaped structure, with complementary base pairing of antiparallel stretches of RNA. In RNA, A pairs with U.

DNA and Proteins as Tape Measures of Evolution

EVOLUTION We are accustomed to thinking of shared traits, such as hair and milk production in mammals, as evidence of shared ancestors. Because we now understand that DNA carries heritable information in the form of genes, we can see that genes and their products (proteins) document the hereditary background of an organism. The linear sequences of nucleotides in DNA molecules are passed from parents to offspring; these sequences determine the amino acid sequences of proteins. Siblings have greater similarity in their DNA and proteins than do unrelated individuals of the same species. If the evolutionary view of life is valid, we should be able to extend this concept of "molecular genealogy" to relationships between species: We should expect two species that appear to be closely related based on fossil and anatomical evidence to also share a greater proportion of their DNA and protein sequences than do more distantly related species. In fact, that is the case. An example is the comparison of the β polypeptide chain of human hemoglobin with the corresponding hemoglobin polypeptide in other vertebrates. In this chain of 146 amino acids, humans and gorillas differ in just 1 amino acid, while humans and frogs differ in 67 amino acids. Molecular biology has added a new tape measure to the toolkit biologists use to assess evolutionary kinship.

The Theme of Emergent Properties in the Chemistry of Life: *A Review*

Recall that life is organized along a hierarchy of structural levels (see Figure 1.4). With each increasing level of order, new properties emerge. In Chapters 2–5, we have dissected the chemistry of life. But we have also begun to develop a more integrated view of life, exploring how properties emerge with increasing order.

We have seen that water's behavior results from the interactions of its molecules, each an ordered arrangement of hydrogen and oxygen atoms. We reduced the complexity and diversity of organic compounds to carbon skeletons and appended chemical groups. We saw that macromolecules are assembled from small organic molecules, taking on new properties. By completing our overview with an introduction to macromolecules and lipids, we have built a bridge to Unit Two, where we will study cell structure and function. We will keep a balance between the need to reduce life to simpler processes and the ultimate satisfaction of viewing those processes in their integrated context.

CONCEPT CHECK 5.5

1. **DRAW IT** Go to Figure 5.26a and, for the top three nucleotides, number all the carbons in the sugars, circle the nitrogenous bases, and star the phosphates.
2. **DRAW IT** In a DNA double helix, a region along one DNA strand has this sequence of nitrogenous bases: 5'-TAGGCCT-3'. Copy this sequence, and write down its complementary strand, clearly indicating the 5' and 3' ends of the complementary strand.
3. **WHAT IF?** (a) Suppose a substitution occurred in one DNA strand of the double helix in question 2, resulting in

   5'-TAAGCCT-3'
   3'-ATCCGGA-5'

   Copy these two strands, and circle and label the mismatched bases. (b) If the modified top strand is used by the cell to construct a complementary strand, what would that matching strand be?

   For suggested answers, see Appendix A.

5 CHAPTER REVIEW

SUMMARY OF KEY CONCEPTS

CONCEPT 5.1

Macromolecules are polymers, built from monomers
(pp. 68–69)

• Carbohydrates, proteins, and nucleic acids are **polymers**, chains of **monomers**. The components of lipids vary.

Monomers form larger molecules by **dehydration reactions**, in which water molecules are released. Polymers can disassemble by the reverse process, **hydrolysis**. An immense variety of polymers can be built from a small set of monomers.

? *What is the fundamental basis for the differences between carbohydrates, proteins, and nucleic acids?*

Large Biological Molecules	Components	Examples	Functions
CONCEPT 5.2 Carbohydrates serve as fuel and building material (pp. 69–74) ? *Compare the composition, structure, and function of starch and cellulose. What role do starch and cellulose play in the human body?*	CH₂OH (Monosaccharide monomer)	**Monosaccharides:** glucose, fructose	Fuel; carbon sources that can be converted to other molecules or combined into polymers
		Disaccharides: lactose, sucrose	
		Polysaccharides: • Cellulose (plants) • Starch (plants) • Glycogen (animals) • Chitin (animals and fungi)	• Strengthens plant cell walls • Stores glucose for energy • Stores glucose for energy • Strengthens exoskeletons and fungal cell walls
CONCEPT 5.3 Lipids are a diverse group of hydrophobic molecules (pp. 74–77) ? *Why are lipids not considered to be macromolecules or polymers?*	Glycerol 3 fatty acids	**Triacylglycerols** (fats or oils): glycerol + 3 fatty acids	Important energy source
	Head with Ⓟ 2 fatty acids	**Phospholipids:** phosphate group + 2 fatty acids	Lipid bilayers of membranes Hydrophobic tails Hydrophilic heads
	Steroid backbone	**Steroids:** four fused rings with attached chemical groups	• Component of cell membranes (cholesterol) • Signaling molecules that travel through the body (hormones)
CONCEPT 5.4 Proteins include a diversity of structures, resulting in a wide range of functions (pp. 77–86) ? *Proteins are the most structurally and functionally diverse class of biological molecules. Explain the basis for this diversity.*	R (Amino acid monomer (20 types))	• Enzymes • Structural proteins • Storage proteins • Transport proteins • Hormones • Receptor proteins • Motor proteins • Defensive proteins	• Catalyze chemical reactions • Provide structural support • Store amino acids • Transport substances • Coordinate organismal responses • Receive signals from outside cell • Function in cell movement • Protect against disease
CONCEPT 5.5 Nucleic acids store, transmit, and help express hereditary information (pp. 86–89) ? *What role does complementary base pairing play in the functions of nucleic acids?*	Nitrogenous base Phosphate group Ⓟ—CH₂ Sugar	**DNA:** • Sugar = deoxyribose • Nitrogenous bases = C, G, A, T • Usually double-stranded	Stores hereditary information
		RNA: • Sugar = ribose • Nitrogenous bases = C, G, A, U • Usually single-stranded	Various functions during gene expression, including carrying instructions from DNA to ribosomes

TEST YOUR UNDERSTANDING

LEVEL 1: KNOWLEDGE/COMPREHENSION

1. Which of the following categories includes all others in the list?
   - a. monosaccharide
   - b. disaccharide
   - c. starch
   - d. carbohydrate
   - e. polysaccharide

2. The enzyme amylase can break glycosidic linkages between glucose monomers only if the monomers are in the α form. Which of the following could amylase break down?
   - a. glycogen, starch, and amylopectin
   - b. glycogen and cellulose
   - c. cellulose and chitin
   - d. starch and chitin
   - e. starch, amylopectin, and cellulose

3. Which of the following statements concerning *unsaturated* fats is true?
   - a. They are more common in animals than in plants.
   - b. They have double bonds in the carbon chains of their fatty acids.
   - c. They generally solidify at room temperature.
   - d. They contain more hydrogen than do saturated fats having the same number of carbon atoms.
   - e. They have fewer fatty acid molecules per fat molecule.

4. The structural level of a protein *least* affected by a disruption in hydrogen bonding is the
   - a. primary level.
   - b. secondary level.
   - c. tertiary level
   - d. quaternary level.
   - e. All structural levels are equally affected.

5. Enzymes that break down DNA catalyze the hydrolysis of the covalent bonds that join nucleotides together. What would happen to DNA molecules treated with these enzymes?
   - a. The two strands of the double helix would separate.
   - b. The phosphodiester linkages of the polynucleotide backbone would be broken.
   - c. The purines would be separated from the deoxyribose sugars.
   - d. The pyrimidines would be separated from the deoxyribose sugars.
   - e. All bases would be separated from the deoxyribose sugars.

LEVEL 2: APPLICATION/ANALYSIS

6. The molecular formula for glucose is $C_6H_{12}O_6$. What would be the molecular formula for a polymer made by linking ten glucose molecules together by dehydration reactions?
   - a. $C_{60}H_{120}O_{60}$
   - b. $C_6H_{12}O_6$
   - c. $C_{60}H_{102}O_{51}$
   - d. $C_{60}H_{100}O_{50}$
   - e. $C_{60}H_{111}O_{51}$

7. Which of the following pairs of base sequences could form a short stretch of a normal double helix of DNA?
   - a. 5'-purine-pyrimidine-purine-pyrimidine-3' with 3'-purine-pyrimidine-purine-pyrimidine-5'
   - b. 5'-AGCT-3' with 5'-TCGA-3'
   - c. 5'-GCGC-3' with 5'-TATA-3'
   - d. 5'-ATGC-3' with 5'-GCAT-3'
   - e. All of these pairs are correct.

8. Construct a table that organizes the following terms, and label the columns and rows.

phosphodiester linkages	polypeptides	monosaccharides
peptide bonds	triacylglycerols	nucleotides
glycosidic linkages	polynucleotides	amino acids
ester linkages	polysaccharides	fatty acids

9. **DRAW IT** Copy the polynucleotide strand in Figure 5.26a and label the bases G, T, C, and T, starting from the 5' end. Assuming this is a DNA polynucleotide, now draw the complementary strand, using the same symbols for phosphates (circles), sugars (pentagons), and bases. Label the bases. Draw arrows showing the 5'→39' direction of each strand. Use the arrows to make sure the second strand is antiparallel to the first. *Hint*: After you draw the first strand vertically, turn the paper upside down; it is easier to draw the second strand from the 5' toward the 3' direction as you go from top to bottom.

LEVEL 3: SYNTHESIS/EVALUATION

10. **EVOLUTION CONNECTION**
    Comparisons of amino acid sequences can shed light on the evolutionary divergence of related species. If you were comparing two living species, would you expect all proteins to show the same degree of divergence? Why or why not?

11. **SCIENTIFIC INQUIRY**
    Suppose you are a research assistant in a lab studying DNA-binding proteins. You have been given the amino acid sequences of all the proteins encoded by the genome of a certain species and have been asked to find candidate proteins that could bind DNA. What type of amino acids would you expect to see in such proteins? Why?

12. **SCIENCE, TECHNOLOGY, AND SOCIETY**
    Some amateur and professional athletes take anabolic steroids to help them "bulk up" or build strength. The health risks of this practice are extensively documented. Apart from health considerations, how do you feel about the use of chemicals to enhance athletic performance? Is an athlete who takes anabolic steroids cheating, or is such use part of the preparation required to succeed in competition? Explain.

13. **WRITE ABOUT A THEME**

    Structure and Function Proteins, which have diverse functions in a cell, are all polymers of the same subunits—amino acids. Write a short essay (100–150 words) that discusses how the structure of amino acids allows this one type of polymer to perform so many functions.

For selected answers, see Appendix A.

 www.masteringbiology.com

1. MasteringBiology® Assignments
Tutorials Types of Carbohydrates • Amino Acid Functional Groups • Levels of Structure in Proteins • Nucleic Acid Building Blocks • The Double Helix
Activities Condensation and Hydrolysis Reactions • Making and Breaking Polymers • Carbohydrate Structure and Function • Carbohydrates • Lipids • Protein Functions • Protein Structure • Nucleic Acid Structure • Structure of RNA and DNA
Questions Student Misconceptions • Reading Quiz • Multiple Choice • End-of-Chapter

2. eText
Read your book online, search, take notes, highlight text, and more.

3. The Study Area
Practice Tests • Cumulative Test • *BioFlix* 3-D Animations • MP3 Tutor Sessions • Videos • Activities • Investigations • Lab Media • Audio Glossary • Word Study Tools • Art

An Interview with
Bonnie L. Bassler

Bonnie Bassler loves her life as a biologist scrutinizing the secret lives of bacteria. For the past 20 years or so, Bonnie and her lab (her "gang," as she calls them) have made momentous discoveries about how bacterial cells use chemicals to communicate with each other in a process called quorum sensing. Dr. Bassler has a B.S. in Biochemistry from the University of California at Davis and a Ph.D. in Biochemistry from The Johns Hopkins University. Among her many awards and honors, she has received a MacArthur Foundation Fellowship and is a member of the National Academy of Sciences. She is the 2010–2011 President of the American Society for Microbiology, the largest specialized life science organization in the world. At Princeton University since 1994, she is currently the Squibb Professor in Molecular Biology and an Investigator of the Howard Hughes Medical Institute.

How did you get started in science?
I've always been interested in nature and animals, and in puzzles and mystery books—I really like figuring things out. As an undergraduate at UC Davis, I worked in a lab on a bacterial project while taking courses in both biochemistry and genetics. Then, as a graduate student at Johns Hopkins, I learned a lot of biochemistry while studying marine bacteria. The bacteria belong to the genus *Vibrio*, and I was working on chemotaxis, movement by cells toward food or away from noxious chemicals in the environment.

What are the advantages of using bacteria for research in cell biology?
Bacteria have been the foundation of molecular biology for the last 100 years because they're accessible. They grow fast, they form clones of identical cells, and they're amenable to biochemical and genetic analyses. Most of what we initially learned about molecular biology—about genes and proteins and other biomolecules—came from work done on bacteria. Because of evolutionary history, the most basic and ancient life processes that happen in bacteria also happen in humans and other higher organisms. Humans have more

bells and whistles, more proteins, more sophistication, more complexity. But if you want to understand the basic components of a process, very often you can use bacteria to do that. Also, working with bacteria fits my personality. I prefer having 10 billion bacterial offspring the day after an experiment to having to wait weeks or months for a small number of baby mice. Every morning there's a surprise waiting for me in the incubator!

What is quorum sensing, and how did you first hear about it?
When I was finishing my graduate work, I heard a talk by Mike Silverman, a scientist with the Agouron Institute in San Diego, about how bacteria "talk" to each other, "count" their own numbers, and coordinate their behavior. Mike had been working on a light-producing (bioluminescent) marine bacterium called *Vibrio fischeri* that lives symbiotically inside a variety of marine animals. The animal provides nutrients for the bacteria, which live in an enclosed space within the animal's body. In return, the bacteria provide light that benefits the animal—by scaring away predators or attracting prey or a mate. But if only a small number of bacteria are present, they do not make light—producing light would waste energy because the light wouldn't be visible. The word "quorum" means "the number needed to do something," and bacteria can sense whether there is a quorum or not and act accordingly.

The way quorum sensing works is that bacteria release certain signaling chemicals into the environment. As the bacterial cells increase in number, the molecules reach a concentration at which many of them bind to receptor proteins on the surface of or inside the bacteria. The signaling molecule fits together with the receptor like a key in a lock. In the case of the surface receptors, each receptor molecule has a part on the outside of the cell and a part on the inside. The signaling chemical binds to the outer part of the receptor, "tickling" the protein so that it makes something happen inside the cell. For instance, in *Vibrio fischeri*, binding of signaling molecules ultimately turns on genes that code for enzymes that make light. Mike had worked out this mechanism of how cells of *Vibrio fischeri* turn on light in synchrony.

It's important to understand that back then, we just didn't think about bacteria like that—we thought bacteria ignored each other and did their own thing as solitary cells. I was totally fascinated. I thought, "He's either crazy or he's brilliant—but I just have to work on that." I went up to the podium after his talk and begged him to let me be his postdoc. Finally he said yes, even though he was a geneticist and I was a biochemist! He took a chance on me.

How does a genetic approach differ from a biochemical one?
Geneticists make lots of mutant organisms, then think up clever strategies to find the ones with mutations in the genes they're interested in. In the case of quorum sensing in bioluminescent bacteria, you look for cells that remain dark. If you have mutated genes involved in quorum sensing, you would expect the bacteria not to make light because light emission depends on the cells communicating with each other. Eventually, you would hope to identify the components that function in normal light-emitting bacteria but not in the mutants. Biochemists, on the other hand, start by isolating molecules and studying their properties directly. Genetics and biochemistry are complementary approaches. I'm glad I know both because the combination is more effective than either approach by itself.

What did you learn about quorum sensing as a postdoc?
In Mike's lab, I worked on another species of bioluminescent *Vibrio* called *Vibrio harveyi*. Because these bacteria are free-living in the ocean, we thought their quorum-sensing molecular circuitry might be more complicated than that of *Vibrio fischeri*. What I found was that *Vibrio harveyi* has two parallel systems for quorum sensing, one that senses cells of the same species and one that counts bacteria of other species. Fast-forwarding a decade or so, this second system

seems to be present in *many* bacteria, and the second signaling molecule appears to be universal. So, apparently bacteria can measure the ratios of these two signals, and they're saying, "How many of us and how many of you are there?" Then they do different things, depending on who is in the majority. And this isn't just restricted to bioluminescence. Other bacterial behaviors are also controlled by quorum sensing, such as forming an organized thin layer (called a biofilm) on your teeth or coordinating a virulent infection.

Tell us more about biofilms.

We used to think that most bacteria lived as individual cells suspended in liquid environments. But we now understand that in the wild, they live attached to surfaces in biofilms, and they secrete carbohydrates and other molecules that form a protective slime on the biofilm surface. Most of us have noticed the biofilm coating our teeth every morning. Believe it or not, there are about 600 bacterial species in that biofilm just trying to make a living, getting nutrients from us, but the side effect is that we get cavities. And when someone has a lung infection or an implant or heart valve that harbors an infection, the bacteria are growing as a biofilm in the lungs or on the introduced device. So we now understand why these infections are so hard to treat: It's because the slime on the biofilm is providing a protective shield that antibiotics can't penetrate.

What questions are you and your lab asking now?

My group is interested in how information outside an organism gets inside so that the organism does the right thing at the right time. We work on bacteria because they're simple, but we hope that we will have insights for people working on higher organisms. And we're curious about how collective behaviors first evolved on Earth. How did multicellularity come about? We know that the first organisms were bacteria, but how did they begin to do things together? How did groups of cells in your body come to act like a liver or a heart? We're very interested in how the flow of information through networks facilitates multicellularity.

Are there applications for the basic research you do?

When you're asking fundamental questions, you hope that surprises, things you never thought of, will come out of it. Now that we know that bacteria talk to each other and perform group activities, the question is whether we could interfere with these conversations for therapeutic purposes. Could we make molecules that keep bacteria from "talking" or "hearing"? Maybe these would be new antibiotics. Biofilms are a terrible problem in medicine and dental health, and now that we are starting to know the molecular basis for their formation, maybe we can learn how to prevent them from forming.

Bacteria get a lot of bad press for the negative things they do. On the other hand, bacteria also do many miraculous things that keep us alive; they are working for us every instant of our lives. You are covered with a bacterial biofilm that acts as invisible body armor—these good bacteria occupy all the spaces on your skin, preventing invading bacteria from attaching. Throughout your gut you have a huge mass of bacteria, and they're making vitamins for you and helping you digest your food. So all biofilms aren't bad—and for the good biofilms, what if we could find a molecule to make quorum sensing better? Rather than an antibiotic, this would be a probiotic.

Where do you think this field is going?

I think we'll be turning our attention to the possibility of communication between organisms from different kingdoms and different domains. Bacteria have been around for over 4 billion years and have probably been living with multicellular eukaryotic hosts for hundreds of millions of years. So why wouldn't these hosts have evolved strategies to listen in, say, to the conversation being carried out by a group of pathogenic bacteria? Does our immune system "hear" bacterial signaling molecules? Do hosts actively prevent quorum sensing among pathogenic bacteria? Do they tune in and help the good bacteria? I think this is going to be a dialogue, not a monologue.

What do you enjoy most about your life as a scientist?

I love what I work on. I figured out as a postdoc how much fun this life in science is—that it is not about me against other scientists or who is going to discover something first. Instead, it's me against this bacterium, and we are in it head-to-head for the rest of our lives, in a contest of wills between bacteria trying to keep their secrets and me trying to discover them. Also, the basic question of how groups work together fascinates me. I work with a fantastic group of students and we share everything—everybody gives everybody everything, and then we all get more. That's quorum sensing! Both my molecular and nonmolecular lives involve getting the group to do more than the individual. I love that parallelism! My gang of students show me their data, and it's my job to help them figure out the science and get on with their careers. I'm so lucky—having 24 hands and 12 brains is so much better than two hands and one brain. The science is always changing, and trying to keep up with these young and tireless people is hugely challenging and rewarding.

What is your advice to an undergraduate who is considering a career in biology?

For undergraduates who are considering a life in science, my advice is to work on something that you are passionate about. Don't be limited by thinking that bench science is the only thing a scientist can do. There are so many potential careers for a biologist. You could work on Capitol Hill as a scientific advisor or policymaker. You could teach. You could be a lawyer. You could be a writer who helps the public understand science. You could work on science education at the kindergarten level. Figure out your particular combination of personality traits and what you really love doing as a scientist; then make that niche for yourself and bring science to that career. The sky's the limit for biologists because biology is the science of the 21st century and it touches every part of our lives.

"The sky's the limit for biologists because biology is the science of the 21st century and it touches every part of our lives."

Bonnie Bassler (left) with Lisa Urry (center) and Jane Reece

6

A Tour of the Cell

▲ Figure 6.1 **How do your brain cells help you learn about biology?**

KEY CONCEPTS

6.1 Biologists use microscopes and the tools of biochemistry to study cells

6.2 Eukaryotic cells have internal membranes that compartmentalize their functions

6.3 The eukaryotic cell's genetic instructions are housed in the nucleus and carried out by the ribosomes

6.4 The endomembrane system regulates protein traffic and performs metabolic functions in the cell

6.5 Mitochondria and chloroplasts change energy from one form to another

6.6 The cytoskeleton is a network of fibers that organizes structures and activities in the cell

6.7 Extracellular components and connections between cells help coordinate cellular activities

The Fundamental Units of Life

Given the scope of biology, you may wonder sometimes how you will ever learn all the material in this course! The answer involves cells, which are as fundamental to the living systems of biology as the atom is to chemistry. The contraction of muscle cells moves your eyes as you read this sentence. The words on the page are translated into signals that nerve cells carry to your brain. **Figure 6.1** shows extensions from one nerve cell (purple) making contact with another nerve cell (orange) in the brain. As you study, your goal is to make connections like these that solidify memories and permit learning to occur.

All organisms are made of cells. In the hierarchy of biological organization, the cell is the simplest collection of matter that can be alive. Indeed, many forms of life exist as single-celled organisms. More complex organisms, including plants and animals, are multicellular; their bodies are cooperatives of many kinds of specialized cells that could not survive for long on their own. Even when cells are arranged into higher levels of organization, such as tissues and organs, the cell remains the organism's basic unit of structure and function.

All cells are related by their descent from earlier cells. However, they have been modified in many different ways during the long evolutionary history of life on Earth. But although cells can differ substantially from one another, they share common features. In this chapter, we'll first examine the tools and techniques that allow us to understand cells, then tour the cell and become acquainted with its components.

CONCEPT 6.1

Biologists use microscopes and the tools of biochemistry to study cells

How can cell biologists investigate the inner workings of a cell, usually too small to be seen by the unaided eye? Before we tour the cell, it will be helpful to learn how cells are studied.

Microscopy

The development of instruments that extend the human senses has gone hand in hand with the advance of science. The discovery and early study of cells progressed with the invention of microscopes in 1590 and their refinement during the 1600s. Cell walls were first seen by Robert Hooke in 1665 as he looked through a microscope at dead cells from the bark of an oak tree. But it took the wonderfully crafted lenses of Antoni van Leeuwenhoek to visualize living cells. Imagine Hooke's awe when he visited van Leeuwenhoek in 1674 and the world of microorganisms—what his host called "very little animalcules"—was revealed to him.

The microscopes first used by Renaissance scientists, as well as the microscopes you are likely to use in the laboratory, are all light microscopes. In a **light microscope (LM)**, visible light is passed through the specimen and then through glass lenses. The lenses refract (bend) the light in such a way that the image of the specimen is magnified as it is projected into the eye or into a camera (see Appendix D).

Three important parameters in microscopy are magnification, resolution, and contrast. *Magnification* is the ratio of an object's image size to its real size. Light microscopes can magnify effectively to about 1,000 times the actual size of the specimen; at greater magnifications, additional details cannot be seen clearly. *Resolution* is a measure of the clarity of the image; it is the minimum distance two points can be separated and still be distinguished as two points. For example, what appears to the unaided eye as one star in the sky may be resolved as twin stars with a telescope, which has a higher resolving ability than the eye. Similarly, using standard techniques, the light microscope cannot resolve detail finer than about 0.2 micrometer (µm), or 200 nanometers (nm), regardless of the magnification (**Figure 6.2**). The third parameter, *contrast*, accentuates differences in parts of the sample. Improvements in light microscopy have included new methods for enhancing contrast, such as staining or labeling cell components to stand out visually. **Figure 6.3**, on the next page, shows different types of microscopy; study this figure as you read the rest of this section.

Until recently, the resolution barrier prevented cell biologists from using standard light microscopy to study **organelles**, the membrane-enclosed structures within eukaryotic cells. To see these structures in any detail required the development of a new instrument. In the 1950s, the electron microscope was introduced to biology. Rather than light, the **electron microscope (EM)** focuses a beam of electrons through the specimen or onto its surface (see Appendix D). Resolution is inversely related to the wavelength of the radiation a microscope uses for imaging, and electron beams have much shorter wavelengths than visible light. Modern electron microscopes can theoretically achieve a resolution of about 0.002 nm, though in practice they usually cannot resolve structures smaller than about 2 nm across. Still, this is a hundredfold improvement over the standard light microscope.

The **scanning electron microscope (SEM)** is especially useful for detailed study of the topography of a specimen (see Figure 6.3). The electron beam scans the surface of the sample, usually coated with a thin film of gold. The beam excites electrons on the surface, and these secondary electrons are detected by a device that translates the pattern of electrons into an electronic signal to a video screen. The result is an image of the specimen's surface that appears three-dimensional.

The **transmission electron microscope (TEM)** is used to study the internal structure of cells (see Figure 6.3). The TEM aims an electron beam through a very thin section of the specimen, similar to the way a light microscope transmits light through a slide. The specimen has been stained with

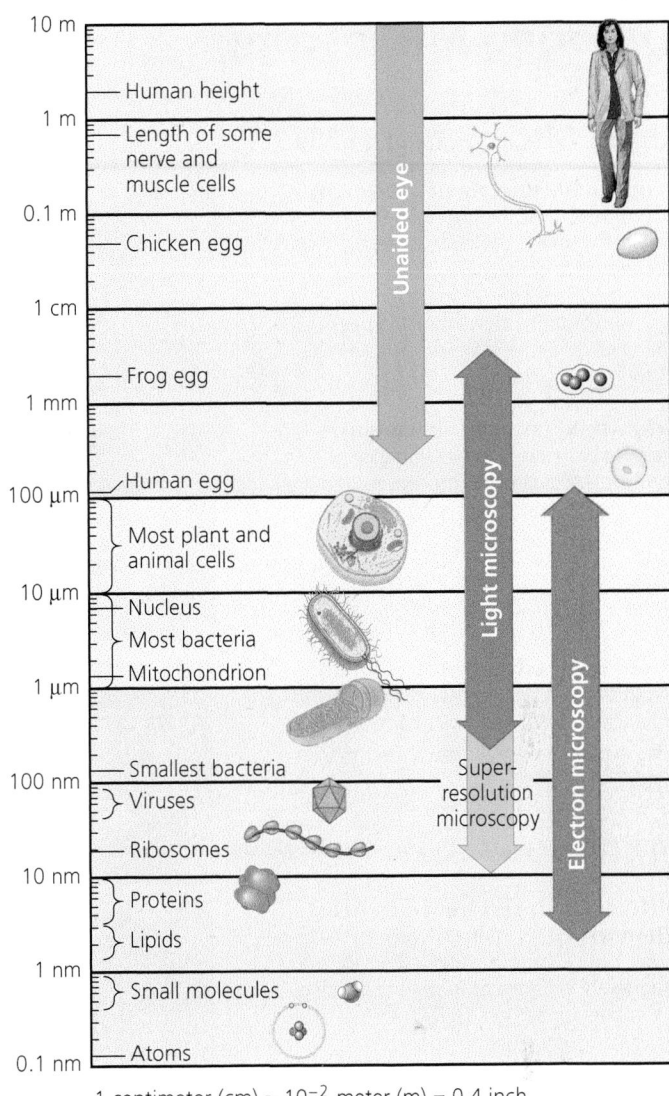

1 centimeter (cm) = 10^{-2} meter (m) = 0.4 inch
1 millimeter (mm) = 10^{-3} m
1 micrometer (µm) = 10^{-3} mm = 10^{-6} m
1 nanometer (nm) = 10^{-3} µm = 10^{-9} m

▲ **Figure 6.2 The size range of cells.** Most cells are between 1 and 100 µm in diameter (yellow region of chart) and are therefore visible only under a microscope. Notice that the scale along the left side is logarithmic to accommodate the range of sizes shown. Starting at the top of the scale with 10 m and going down, each reference measurement marks a tenfold decrease in diameter or length. For a complete table of the metric system, see Appendix C.

atoms of heavy metals, which attach to certain cellular structures, thus enhancing the electron density of some parts of the cell more than others. The electrons passing through the specimen are scattered more in the denser regions, so fewer are transmitted. The image displays the pattern of transmitted electrons. Instead of using glass lenses, the TEM uses electromagnets as lenses to bend the paths of the electrons, ultimately focusing the image onto a monitor for viewing.

Electron microscopes have revealed many organelles and other subcellular structures that were impossible to resolve with the light microscope. But the light microscope offers advantages, especially in studying living cells. A disadvantage of

Exploring Microscopy

Light Microscopy (LM)

Brightfield (unstained specimen). Light passes directly through the specimen. Unless the cell is naturally pigmented or artificially stained, the image has little contrast. (The first four light micrographs show human cheek epithelial cells; the scale bar pertains to all four micrographs.)

Brightfield (stained specimen). Staining with various dyes enhances contrast. Most staining procedures require that cells be fixed (preserved).

Phase-contrast. Variations in density within the specimen are amplified to enhance contrast in unstained cells, which is especially useful for examining living, unpigmented cells.

Differential-interference-contrast (Nomarski). As in phase-contrast microscopy, optical modifications are used to exaggerate differences in density, making the image appear almost 3-D.

Fluorescence. The locations of specific molecules in the cell can be revealed by labeling the molecules with fluorescent dyes or antibodies; some cells have molecules that fluoresce on their own. Fluorescent substances absorb ultraviolet radiation and emit visible light. In this fluorescently labeled uterine cell, nuclear material is blue, organelles called mitochondria are orange, and the cell's "skeleton" is green.

10 μm

Confocal. The top image is a standard fluorescence micrograph of fluorescently labeled nervous tissue (nerve cells are green, support cells are orange, and regions of overlap are yellow); below it is a confocal image of the same tissue. Using a laser, this "optical sectioning" technique eliminates out-of-focus light from a thick sample, creating a single plane of fluorescence in the image. By capturing sharp images at many different planes, a 3-D reconstruction can be created. The standard image is blurry because out-of-focus light is not excluded.

50 μm

Deconvolution. The top of this split image is a compilation of standard fluorescence micrographs through the depth of a white blood cell. Below is an image of the same cell reconstructed from many blurry images at different planes, each of which was processed using deconvolution software. This process digitally removes out-of-focus light and reassigns it to its source, creating a much sharper 3-D image.

10 μm

Super-resolution. On the top is a confocal image of part of a nerve cell, using a fluorescent label that binds to a molecule clustered in small sacs in the cell (vesicles) that are 40 nm in diameter. The greenish-yellow spots are blurry because 40 nm is below the 200-nm limit of resolution for standard light microscopy. Below is an image of the same part of the cell, seen using a new "super-resolution" technique. Sophisticated equipment is used to light up individual fluorescent molecules and record their position. Combining information from many molecules in different places "breaks" the limit of resolution, resulting in the sharp greenish-yellow dots seen here. (Each dot is a 40-nm vesicle.)

1 μm

Electron Microscopy (EM)

Scanning electron microscopy (SEM). Micrographs taken with a scanning electron microscope show a 3-D image of the surface of a specimen. This SEM shows the surface of a cell from a trachea (windpipe) covered with cilia. Beating of the cilia helps move inhaled debris upward toward the throat. The SEM and TEM shown here have been artificially colorized. (Electron micrographs are black and white, but are often artificially colorized to highlight particular structures.)

Abbreviations used in this book:
LM = Light Micrograph
SEM = Scanning Electron Micrograph
TEM = Transmission Electron Micrograph

Cilia

Longitudinal section of cilium   Cross section of cilium

2 μm

2 μm

Transmission electron microscopy (TEM). A transmission electron microscope profiles a thin section of a specimen. Here we see a section through a tracheal cell, revealing its internal structure. In preparing the TEM, some cilia were cut along their lengths, creating longitudinal sections, while other cilia were cut straight across, creating cross sections.

electron microscopy is that the methods used to prepare the specimen kill the cells. For all microscopy techniques, in fact, specimen preparation can introduce artifacts, structural features seen in micrographs that do not exist in the living cell.

In the past several decades, light microscopy has been revitalized by major technical advances (see Figure 6.3). Labeling individual cellular molecules or structures with fluorescent markers has made it possible to see such structures with increasing detail. In addition, both confocal and deconvolution microscopy have sharpened images of three-dimensional tissues and cells. Finally, over the past ten years, a group of new techniques and labeling molecules have allowed researchers to "break" the resolution barrier and distinguish subcellular structures as small as 10–20 nm across. As this "super-resolution microscopy" becomes more widespread, the images we'll see of living cells may well be as awe-inspiring to us as van Leeuwenhoek's were to Robert Hooke 350 years ago.

Microscopes are the most important tools of *cytology*, the study of cell structure. To understand the function of each structure, however, required the integration of cytology and *biochemistry*, the study of the chemical processes (metabolism) of cells.

Cell Fractionation

A useful technique for studying cell structure and function is **cell fractionation**, which takes cells apart and separates major organelles and other subcellular structures from one another **(Figure 6.4)**. The instrument used is the centrifuge, which spins test tubes holding mixtures of disrupted cells at a series of increasing speeds. At each speed, the resulting force causes a fraction of the cell components to settle to the bottom of the tube, forming a pellet. At lower speeds, the pellet consists of larger components, and higher speeds yield a pellet with smaller components.

Cell fractionation enables researchers to prepare specific cell components in bulk and identify their functions, a task not usually possible with intact cells. For example, on one of the cell fractions, biochemical tests showed the presence of enzymes involved in cellular respiration, while electron microscopy revealed large numbers of the organelles called mitochondria. Together, these data helped biologists determine that mitochondria are the sites of cellular respiration. Biochemistry and cytology thus complement each other in correlating cell function with structure.

CONCEPT CHECK 6.1

1. How do stains used for light microscopy compare with those used for electron microscopy?
2. **WHAT IF?** Which type of microscope would you use to study (a) the changes in shape of a living white blood cell and (b) the details of surface texture of a hair?

For suggested answers, see Appendix A.

▼ Figure 6.4 **RESEARCH METHOD**

Cell Fractionation

APPLICATION Cell fractionation is used to isolate (fractionate) cell components based on size and density.

TECHNIQUE Cells are homogenized in a blender to break them up. The resulting mixture (homogenate) is centrifuged. The supernatant (liquid) is poured into another tube and centrifuged at a higher speed for a longer time. This process is repeated several times. This "differential centrifugation" results in a series of pellets, each containing different cell components.

Homogenization

Tissue cells

Homogenate

Centrifugation

Centrifuged at 1,000 *g* (1,000 times the force of gravity) for 10 min

Supernatant poured into next tube

Differential centrifugation

20,000 *g* 20 min

Pellet rich in nuclei and cellular debris

80,000 *g* 60 min

Pellet rich in mitochondria (and chloroplasts if cells are from a plant)

150,000 *g* 3 hr

Pellet rich in "microsomes" (pieces of plasma membranes and cells' internal membranes)

Pellet rich in ribosomes

RESULTS In early experiments, researchers used microscopy to identify the organelles in each pellet and biochemical methods to determine their metabolic functions. These identifications established a baseline for this method, enabling today's researchers to know which cell fraction they should collect in order to isolate and study particular organelles.

Eukaryotic cells have internal membranes that compartmentalize their functions

Cells—the basic structural and functional units of every organism—are of two distinct types: prokaryotic and eukaryotic. Organisms of the domains Bacteria and Archaea consist of prokaryotic cells. Protists, fungi, animals, and plants all consist of eukaryotic cells.

Comparing Prokaryotic and Eukaryotic Cells

All cells share certain basic features: They are all bounded by a selective barrier, called the *plasma membrane*. Inside all cells is a semifluid, jellylike substance called **cytosol**, in which subcellular components are suspended. All cells contain *chromosomes*, which carry genes in the form of DNA. And all cells have *ribosomes*, tiny complexes that make proteins according to instructions from the genes.

A major difference between prokaryotic and eukaryotic cells is the location of their DNA. In a **eukaryotic cell**, most of the DNA is in an organelle called the *nucleus*, which is bounded by a double membrane (see Figure 6.8, on pp. 100–101). In a **prokaryotic cell**, the DNA is concentrated in a region that is not membrane-enclosed, called the **nucleoid** (**Figure 6.5**). The word *eukaryotic* means "true nucleus" (from the Greek *eu*, true, and *karyon*, kernel, here referring to the nucleus), and

the word *prokaryotic* means "before nucleus" (from the Greek *pro*, before), reflecting the fact that prokaryotic cells evolved before eukaryotic cells.

The interior of either type of cell is called the **cytoplasm**; in eukaryotic cells, this term refers only to the region between the nucleus and the plasma membrane. Within the cytoplasm of a eukaryotic cell, suspended in cytosol, are a variety of organelles of specialized form and function. These membrane-bounded structures are absent in prokaryotic cells. Thus, the presence or absence of a true nucleus is just one aspect of the disparity in structural complexity between the two types of cells.

Eukaryotic cells are generally much larger than prokaryotic cells (see Figure 6.2). Size is a general feature of cell structure that relates to function. The logistics of carrying out cellular metabolism sets limits on cell size. At the lower limit, the smallest cells known are bacteria called mycoplasmas, which have diameters between 0.1 and 1.0 μm. These are perhaps the smallest packages with enough DNA to program metabolism and enough enzymes and other cellular equipment to carry out the activities necessary for a cell to sustain itself and reproduce. Typical bacteria are 1–5 μm in diameter, about ten times the size of mycoplasmas. Eukaryotic cells are typically 10–100 μm in diameter.

Metabolic requirements also impose theoretical upper limits on the size that is practical for a single cell. At the boundary of every cell, the **plasma membrane** functions as a selective barrier that allows passage of enough oxygen, nutrients, and wastes to service the entire cell (**Figure 6.6**). For each square micrometer of membrane, only a limited amount of a particular

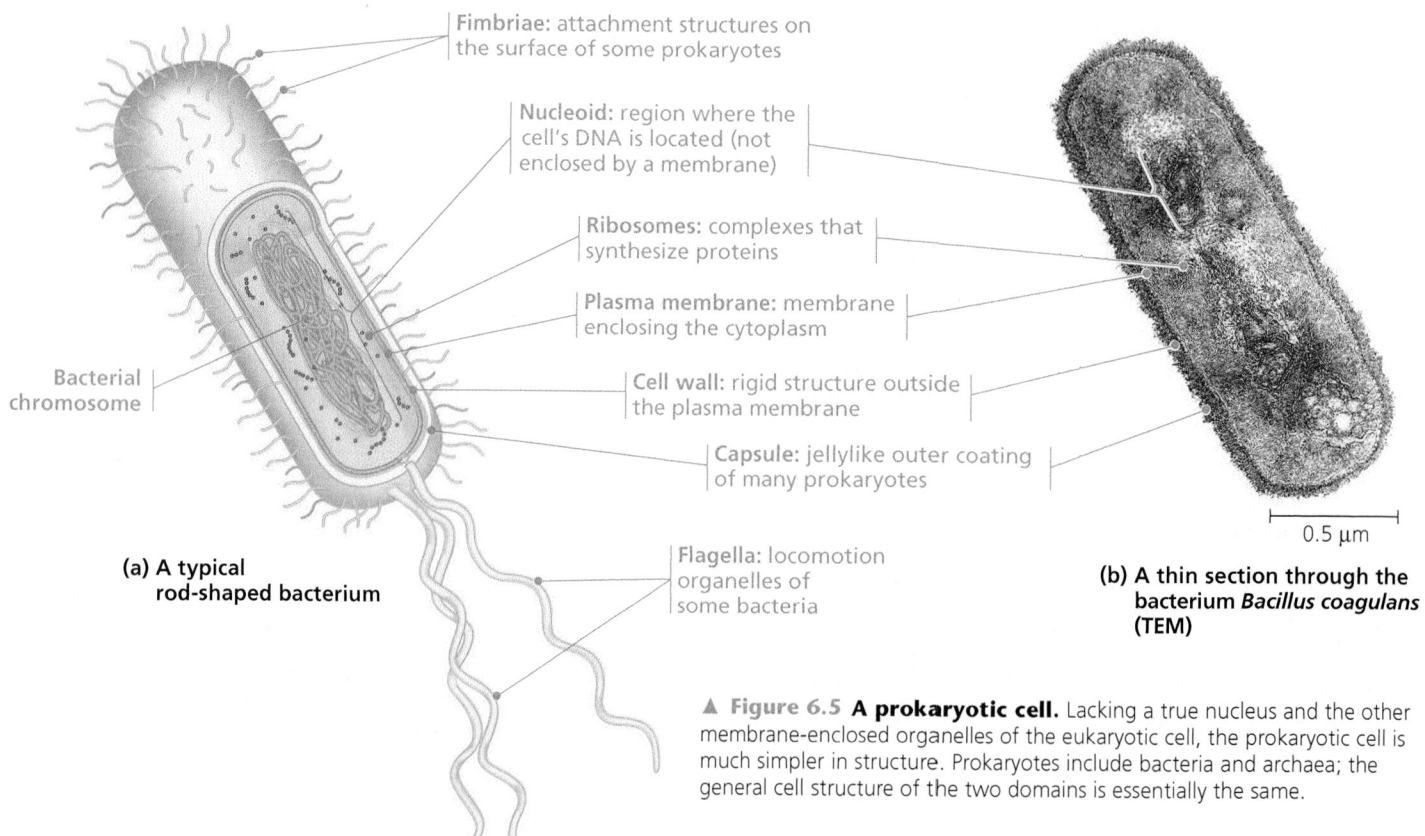

Fimbriae: attachment structures on the surface of some prokaryotes

Nucleoid: region where the cell's DNA is located (not enclosed by a membrane)

Ribosomes: complexes that synthesize proteins

Plasma membrane: membrane enclosing the cytoplasm

Cell wall: rigid structure outside the plasma membrane

Capsule: jellylike outer coating of many prokaryotes

Bacterial chromosome

Flagella: locomotion organelles of some bacteria

(a) A typical rod-shaped bacterium

0.5 μm

(b) A thin section through the bacterium *Bacillus coagulans* (TEM)

▲ **Figure 6.5 A prokaryotic cell.** Lacking a true nucleus and the other membrane-enclosed organelles of the eukaryotic cell, the prokaryotic cell is much simpler in structure. Prokaryotes include bacteria and archaea; the general cell structure of the two domains is essentially the same.

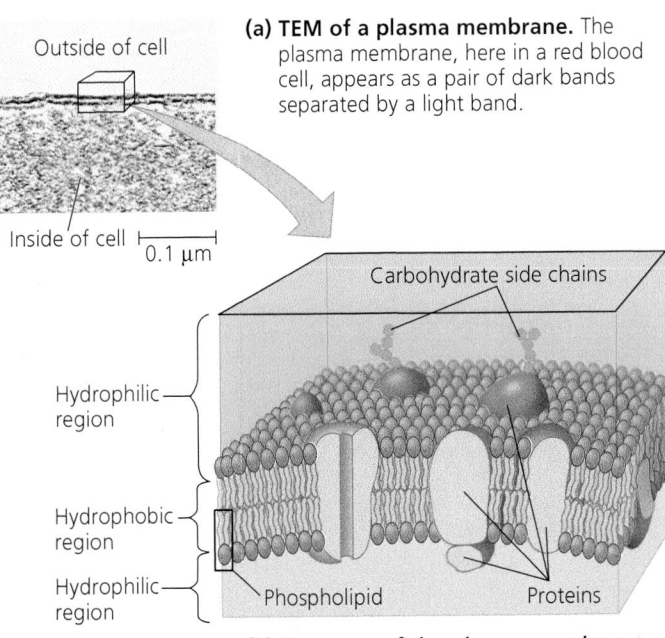

Outside of cell

(a) TEM of a plasma membrane. The plasma membrane, here in a red blood cell, appears as a pair of dark bands separated by a light band.

Inside of cell ├── 0.1 μm ──┤

Carbohydrate side chains

Hydrophilic region

Hydrophobic region

Hydrophilic region

Phospholipid

Proteins

(b) Structure of the plasma membrane

▲ **Figure 6.6 The plasma membrane.** The plasma membrane and the membranes of organelles consist of a double layer (bilayer) of phospholipids with various proteins attached to or embedded in it. The hydrophobic parts, including phospholipid tails and interior portions of membrane proteins, are found in the interior of the membrane. The hydrophilic parts, including phospholipid heads, exterior portions of proteins, and channels of proteins, are in contact with the aqueous solution. Carbohydrate side chains may be attached to proteins or lipids on the outer surface of the plasma membrane.

MAKE CONNECTIONS *Review Figure 5.12 (p. 76) and describe the characteristics of a phospholipid that allow it to function as the major component in the plasma membrane.*

substance can cross per second, so the ratio of surface area to volume is critical. As a cell (or any other object) increases in size, its volume grows proportionately more than its surface area. (Area is proportional to a linear dimension squared, whereas volume is proportional to the linear dimension cubed.) Thus, a smaller object has a greater ratio of surface area to volume **(Figure 6.7)**.

The need for a surface area sufficiently large to accommodate the volume helps explain the microscopic size of most cells and the narrow, elongated shapes of others, such as nerve cells. Larger organisms do not generally have *larger* cells than smaller organisms—they simply have *more* cells (see Figure 6.7). A sufficiently high ratio of surface area to volume is especially important in cells that exchange a lot of material with their surroundings, such as intestinal cells. Such cells may have many long, thin projections from their surface called *microvilli*, which increase surface area without an appreciable increase in volume.

The evolutionary relationships between prokaryotic and eukaryotic cells will be discussed later in this chapter, and prokaryotic cells will be described in detail in Chapter 27. Most of the discussion of cell structure that follows in this chapter applies to eukaryotic cells.

Surface area increases while total volume remains constant →

	1	5	1
Total surface area [sum of the surface areas (height × width) of all box sides × number of boxes]	6	150	750
Total volume [height × width × length × number of boxes]	1	125	125
Surface-to-volume (S-to-V) ratio [surface area ÷ volume]	6	1.2	6

▲ **Figure 6.7 Geometric relationships between surface area and volume.** In this diagram, cells are represented as boxes. Using arbitrary units of length, we can calculate the cell's surface area (in square units, or units^2), volume (in cubic units, or units^3), and ratio of surface area to volume. A high surface-to-volume ratio facilitates the exchange of materials between a cell and its environment.

A Panoramic View of the Eukaryotic Cell

In addition to the plasma membrane at its outer surface, a eukaryotic cell has extensive and elaborately arranged internal membranes that divide the cell into compartments—the organelles mentioned earlier. The cell's compartments provide different local environments that facilitate specific metabolic functions, so incompatible processes can go on simultaneously inside a single cell. The plasma membrane and organelle membranes also participate directly in the cell's metabolism, because many enzymes are built right into the membranes.

Because membranes are so fundamental to the organization of the cell, Chapter 7 will discuss them in detail. The basic fabric of most biological membranes is a double layer of phospholipids and other lipids. Embedded in this lipid bilayer or attached to its surfaces are diverse proteins (see Figure 6.6). However, each type of membrane has a unique composition of lipids and proteins suited to that membrane's specific functions. For example, enzymes embedded in the membranes of the organelles called mitochondria function in cellular respiration.

Before continuing with this chapter, examine the eukaryotic cells in **Figure 6.8**, on the next two pages. The generalized diagrams of an animal cell and a plant cell introduce the various organelles and highlight the key differences between animal and plant cells. The micrographs at the bottom of the figure give you a glimpse of cells from different types of eukaryotic organisms.

Exploring Eukaryotic Cells

Animal Cell (cutaway view of generalized cell)

Flagellum: motility structure present in some animal cells, composed of a cluster of microtubules within an extension of the plasma membrane

Centrosome: region where the cell's microtubules are initiated; contains a pair of centrioles

ENDOPLASMIC RETICULUM (ER): network of membranous sacs and tubes; active in membrane synthesis and other synthetic and metabolic processes; has rough (ribosome-studded) and smooth regions

Rough ER   Smooth ER

Nuclear envelope: double membrane enclosing the nucleus; perforated by pores; continuous with ER

Nucleolus: nonmembranous structure involved in production of ribosomes; a nucleus has one or more nucleoli

Chromatin: material consisting of DNA and proteins; visible in a dividing cell as individual condensed chromosomes

NUCLEUS

Plasma membrane: membrane enclosing the cell

CYTOSKELETON: reinforces cell's shape; functions in cell movement; components are made of protein. Includes:

Microfilaments

Intermediate filaments

Microtubules

Microvilli: projections that increase the cell's surface area

Ribosomes (small brown dots): complexes that make proteins; free in cytosol or bound to rough ER or nuclear envelope

Golgi apparatus: organelle active in synthesis, modification, sorting, and secretion of cell products

Peroxisome: organelle with various specialized metabolic functions; produces hydrogen peroxide as a by-product, then converts it to water

Mitochondrion: organelle where cellular respiration occurs and most ATP is generated

Lysosome: digestive organelle where macromolecules are hydrolyzed

In animal cells but not plant cells:
Lysosomes
Centrosomes, with centrioles
Flagella (but present in some plant sperm)

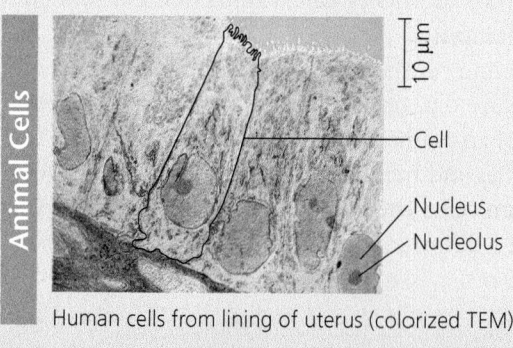

Animal Cells

Cell

Nucleus
Nucleolus

Human cells from lining of uterus (colorized TEM)

Fungal Cells

Parent cell

Buds

Yeast cells: reproducing by budding (above, colorized SEM) and a single cell (right, colorized TEM)

Cell wall

Vacuole

Nucleus

Mitochondrion

Plant Cell (cutaway view of generalized cell)

NUCLEUS
- Nuclear envelope
- Nucleolus
- Chromatin

Rough endoplasmic reticulum

Smooth endoplasmic reticulum

ANIMATION

BioFlix Visit the Study Area at **www.masteringbiology.com** for the BioFlix® 3-D Animations Tour of an Animal Cell and Tour of a Plant Cell.

Ribosomes (small brown dots)

Central vacuole: prominent organelle in older plant cells; functions include storage, breakdown of waste products, hydrolysis of macromolecules; enlargement of vacuole is a major mechanism of plant growth

Golgi apparatus

CYTOSKELETON
- Microfilaments
- Intermediate filaments
- Microtubules

Mitochondrion

Peroxisome

Plasma membrane

Chloroplast: photosynthetic organelle; converts energy of sunlight to chemical energy stored in sugar molecules

Cell wall: outer layer that maintains cell's shape and protects cell from mechanical damage; made of cellulose, other polysaccharides, and protein

Wall of adjacent cell

Plasmodesmata: cytoplasmic channels through cell walls that connect the cytoplasms of adjacent cells

In plant cells but not animal cells:
Chloroplasts
Central vacuole
Cell wall
Plasmodesmata

Plant Cells

- Cell
- Cell wall
- Chloroplast
- Mitochondrion
- Nucleus
- Nucleolus

5 μm

Cells from duckweed (*Spirodela oligorrhiza*), a floating plant (colorized TEM)

Protistan Cells

8 μm

Unicellular green alga *Chlamydomonas* (above, colorized SEM; right, colorized TEM)

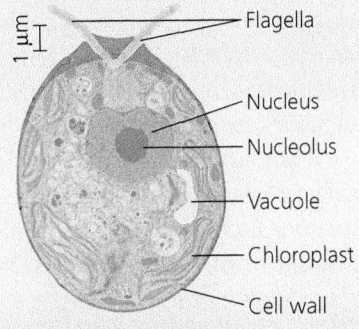

1 μm

- Flagella
- Nucleus
- Nucleolus
- Vacuole
- Chloroplast
- Cell wall

1. After carefully reviewing Figure 6.8, briefly describe the structure and function of the nucleus, the mitochondrion, the chloroplast, and the endoplasmic reticulum.
2. **WHAT IF?** Imagine an elongated cell (such as a nerve cell) that measures $125 \times 1 \times 1$ arbitrary units. Predict how its surface-to-volume ratio would compare with those in Figure 6.7. Then calculate the ratio and check your prediction.

For suggested answers, see Appendix A.

CONCEPT **6.3**

The eukaryotic cell's genetic instructions are housed in the nucleus and carried out by the ribosomes

On the first stop of our detailed tour of the cell, let's look at two cellular components involved in the genetic control of the cell: the nucleus, which houses most of the cell's DNA, and the ribosomes, which use information from the DNA to make proteins.

The Nucleus: Information Central

The **nucleus** contains most of the genes in the eukaryotic cell. (Some genes are located in mitochondria and chloroplasts.) It is generally the most conspicuous organelle in a eukaryotic cell, averaging about 5 µm in diameter. The **nuclear envelope** encloses the nucleus **(Figure 6.9)**, separating its contents from the cytoplasm.

The nuclear envelope is a *double* membrane. The two membranes, each a lipid bilayer with associated proteins, are separated by a space of 20–40 nm. The envelope is perforated by pore structures that are about 100 nm in diameter. At the lip of each pore, the inner and outer membranes of the nuclear envelope are continuous. An intricate protein structure called a *pore complex* lines each pore and plays an important role in the cell by regulating the entry and exit of proteins and RNAs, as well as large complexes of macromolecules. Except at the pores, the nuclear side of the envelope is lined by the **nuclear lamina**, a netlike array of protein filaments that maintains the shape of the nucleus by mechanically supporting the nuclear envelope. There is also much evidence for a *nuclear matrix*, a framework of protein fibers extending throughout the nuclear interior. The nuclear lamina and matrix may help organize the genetic material so it functions efficiently.

Within the nucleus, the DNA is organized into discrete units called **chromosomes**, structures that carry the genetic information. Each chromosome contains one long DNA molecule associated with many proteins. Some of the proteins help coil the DNA molecule of each chromosome, reducing its length and allowing it to fit into the nucleus. The complex of DNA and proteins making up chromosomes is called **chromatin**. When a cell is not dividing, stained chromatin appears as a diffuse mass in micrographs, and the chromosomes cannot be distinguished from one another, even though discrete chromosomes are present. As a cell prepares to divide, however, the chromosomes coil (condense) further, becoming thick enough to be distinguished as separate structures. Each eukaryotic species has a characteristic number of chromosomes. For example, a typical human cell has 46 chromosomes in its nucleus; the exceptions are the sex cells (eggs and sperm), which have only 23 chromosomes in humans. A fruit fly cell has 8 chromosomes in most cells and 4 in the sex cells.

A prominent structure within the nondividing nucleus is the **nucleolus** (plural, *nucleoli*), which appears through the electron microscope as a mass of densely stained granules and fibers adjoining part of the chromatin. Here a type of RNA called *ribosomal RNA* (rRNA) is synthesized from instructions in the DNA. Also in the nucleolus, proteins imported from the cytoplasm are assembled with rRNA into large and small subunits of ribosomes. These subunits then exit the nucleus through the nuclear pores to the cytoplasm, where a large and a small subunit can assemble into a ribosome. Sometimes there are two or more nucleoli; the number depends on the species and the stage in the cell's reproductive cycle.

As we saw in Figure 5.25, the nucleus directs protein synthesis by synthesizing messenger RNA (mRNA) according to instructions provided by the DNA. The mRNA is then transported to the cytoplasm via the nuclear pores. Once an mRNA molecule reaches the cytoplasm, ribosomes translate the mRNA's genetic message into the primary structure of a specific polypeptide. This process of transcribing and translating genetic information is described in detail in Chapter 17.

Ribosomes: Protein Factories

Ribosomes, which are complexes made of ribosomal RNA and protein, are the cellular components that carry out protein synthesis **(Figure 6.10)**. Cells that have high rates of protein synthesis have particularly large numbers of ribosomes. For example, a human pancreas cell has a few million ribosomes. Not surprisingly, cells active in protein synthesis also have prominent nucleoli.

Ribosomes build proteins in two cytoplasmic locales. At any given time, *free ribosomes* are suspended in the cytosol, while *bound ribosomes* are attached to the outside of the endoplasmic reticulum or nuclear envelope (see Figure 6.10). Bound and free ribosomes are structurally identical, and ribosomes can alternate between the two roles. Most of the proteins made on free ribosomes function within the cytosol; examples are enzymes that catalyze the first steps of sugar breakdown. Bound ribosomes generally make proteins that are destined for insertion into membranes, for packaging

1 μm

▲ Surface of nuclear envelope. TEM of a specimen prepared by a technique known as freeze-fracture.

Nucleus

Nucleolus

Chromatin

Nuclear envelope:
Inner membrane
Outer membrane
Nuclear pore

Nucleus

Rough ER

Pore complex

Ribosome

0.25 μm

▲ Pore complexes (TEM). Each pore is ringed by protein particles.

◄ Close-up of nuclear envelope

1 μm

▲ Chromatin. Part of a chromosome from a non-dividing cell shows two states of coiling of the DNA (blue) and protein (purple) complex. The thicker form is sometimes also organized into long loops.

◄ Nuclear lamina (TEM). The netlike lamina lines the inner surface of the nuclear envelope.

▲ Figure 6.9 The nucleus and its envelope. Within the nucleus are the chromosomes, which appear as a mass of chromatin (DNA and associated proteins), and one or more nucleoli (singular, *nucleolus*),

which function in ribosome synthesis. The nuclear envelope, which consists of two membranes separated by a narrow space, is perforated with pores and lined by the nuclear lamina.

MAKE CONNECTIONS *Since the chromosomes contain the genetic material and reside in the nucleus, how does the rest of the cell get access to the information they carry? See Figure 5.25, page 86.*

▶ Figure 6.10 Ribosomes. This electron micrograph of part of a pancreas cell shows many ribosomes, both free (in the cytosol) and bound (to the endoplasmic reticulum). The simplified diagram of a ribosome shows its two subunits.

DRAW IT *After you have read the section on ribosomes, circle a ribosome in the micrograph that might be making a protein that will be secreted.*

Ribosomes

ER

0.25 μm

Free ribosomes in cytosol

Endoplasmic reticulum (ER)

Ribosomes bound to ER

Large subunit

Small subunit

TEM showing ER and ribosomes

Diagram of a ribosome

within certain organelles such as lysosomes (see Figure 6.8), or for export from the cell (secretion). Cells that specialize in protein secretion—for instance, the cells of the pancreas that secrete digestive enzymes—frequently have a high proportion of bound ribosomes. You will learn more about ribosome structure and function in Chapter 17.

CONCEPT CHECK 6.3

1. What role do ribosomes play in carrying out genetic instructions?
2. Describe the molecular composition of nucleoli and explain their function.
3. **WHAT IF?** As a cell begins the process of dividing, its chromatin becomes more and more condensed. Does the number of chromosomes change during this process? Explain.

For suggested answers, see Appendix A.

CONCEPT 6.4

The endomembrane system regulates protein traffic and performs metabolic functions in the cell

Many of the different membranes of the eukaryotic cell are part of the **endomembrane system**, which includes the nuclear envelope, the endoplasmic reticulum, the Golgi apparatus, lysosomes, various kinds of vesicles and vacuoles, and the plasma membrane. This system carries out a variety of tasks in the cell, including synthesis of proteins, transport of proteins into membranes and organelles or out of the cell, metabolism and movement of lipids, and detoxification of poisons. The membranes of this system are related either through direct physical continuity or by the transfer of membrane segments as tiny **vesicles** (sacs made of membrane). Despite these relationships, the various membranes are not identical in structure and function. Moreover, the thickness, molecular composition, and types of chemical reactions carried out in a given membrane are not fixed, but may be modified several times during the membrane's life. Having already discussed the nuclear envelope, we will now focus on the endoplasmic reticulum and the other endomembranes to which the endoplasmic reticulum gives rise.

The Endoplasmic Reticulum: Biosynthetic Factory

The **endoplasmic reticulum (ER)** is such an extensive network of membranes that it accounts for more than half the total membrane in many eukaryotic cells. (The word *endoplasmic* means "within the cytoplasm," and *reticulum* is

Latin for "little net.") The ER consists of a network of membranous tubules and sacs called cisternae (from the Latin *cisterna*, a reservoir for a liquid). The ER membrane separates the internal compartment of the ER, called the ER lumen (cavity) or cisternal space, from the cytosol. And because the ER membrane is continuous with the nuclear envelope, the space between the two membranes of the envelope is continuous with the lumen of the ER (**Figure 6.11**).

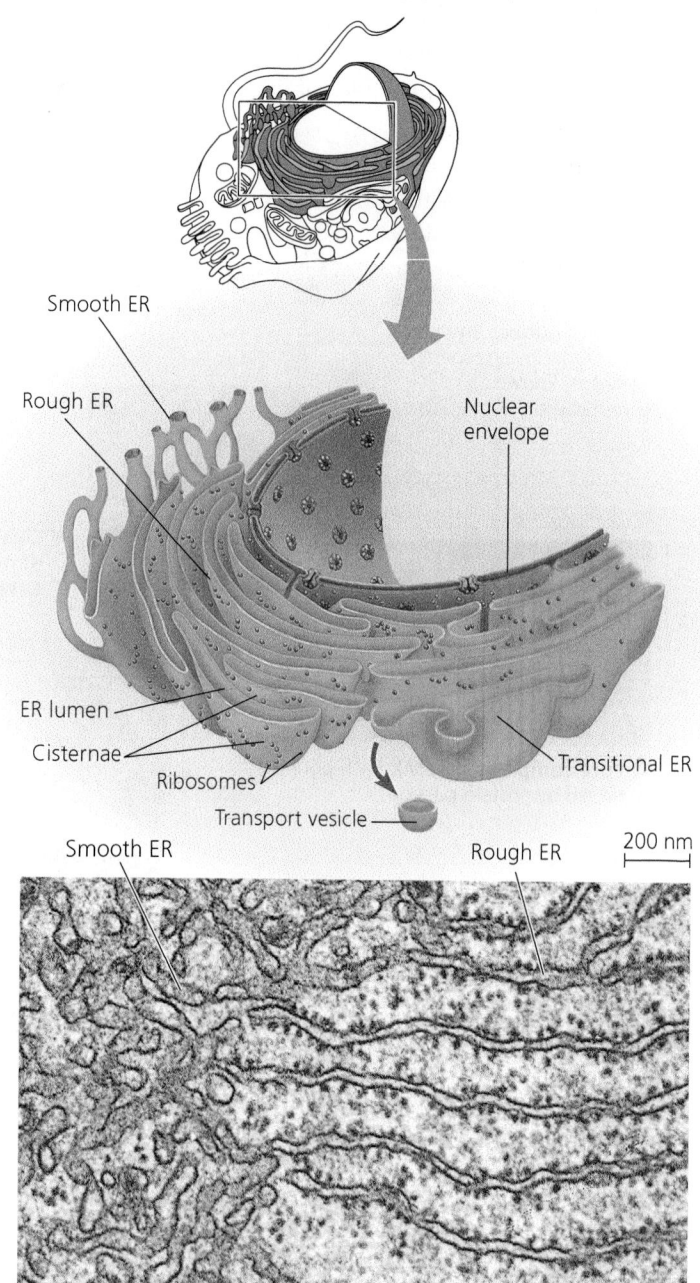

▲ **Figure 6.11 Endoplasmic reticulum (ER).** A membranous system of interconnected tubules and flattened sacs called cisternae, the ER is also continuous with the nuclear envelope. (The drawing is a cutaway view.) The membrane of the ER encloses a continuous compartment called the ER lumen (or cisternal space). Rough ER, which is studded on its outer surface with ribosomes, can be distinguished from smooth ER in the electron micrograph (TEM). Transport vesicles bud off from a region of the rough ER called transitional ER and travel to the Golgi apparatus and other destinations.

There are two distinct, though connected, regions of the ER that differ in structure and function: smooth ER and rough ER. **Smooth ER** is so named because its outer surface lacks ribosomes. **Rough ER** is studded with ribosomes on the outer surface of the membrane and thus appears rough through the electron microscope. As already mentioned, ribosomes are also attached to the cytoplasmic side of the nuclear envelope's outer membrane, which is continuous with rough ER.

Functions of Smooth ER

The smooth ER functions in diverse metabolic processes, which vary with cell type. These processes include synthesis of lipids, metabolism of carbohydrates, detoxification of drugs and poisons, and storage of calcium ions.

Enzymes of the smooth ER are important in the synthesis of lipids, including oils, phospholipids, and steroids. Among the steroids produced by the smooth ER in animal cells are the sex hormones of vertebrates and the various steroid hormones secreted by the adrenal glands. The cells that synthesize and secrete these hormones—in the testes and ovaries, for example—are rich in smooth ER, a structural feature that fits the function of these cells.

Other enzymes of the smooth ER help detoxify drugs and poisons, especially in liver cells. Detoxification usually involves adding hydroxyl groups to drug molecules, making them more soluble and easier to flush from the body. The sedative phenobarbital and other barbiturates are examples of drugs metabolized in this manner by smooth ER in liver cells. In fact, barbiturates, alcohol, and many other drugs induce the proliferation of smooth ER and its associated detoxification enzymes, thus increasing the rate of detoxification. This, in turn, increases tolerance to the drugs, meaning that higher doses are required to achieve a particular effect, such as sedation. Also, because some of the detoxification enzymes have relatively broad action, the proliferation of smooth ER in response to one drug can increase tolerance to other drugs as well. Barbiturate abuse, for example, can decrease the effectiveness of certain antibiotics and other useful drugs.

The smooth ER also stores calcium ions. In muscle cells, for example, the smooth ER membrane pumps calcium ions from the cytosol into the ER lumen. When a muscle cell is stimulated by a nerve impulse, calcium ions rush back across the ER membrane into the cytosol and trigger contraction of the muscle cell. In other cell types, calcium ion release from the smooth ER triggers different responses, such as secretion of vesicles carrying newly synthesized proteins.

Functions of Rough ER

Many types of cells secrete proteins produced by ribosomes attached to rough ER. For example, certain pancreatic cells synthesize the protein insulin in the ER and secrete this hormone into the bloodstream. As a polypeptide chain grows from a bound ribosome, the chain is threaded into the ER lumen through a pore formed by a protein complex in the ER membrane. As the new polypeptide enters the ER lumen, it folds into its native shape. Most secretory proteins are **glycoproteins**, proteins that have carbohydrates covalently bonded to them. The carbohydrates are attached to the proteins in the ER by enzymes built into the ER membrane.

After secretory proteins are formed, the ER membrane keeps them separate from proteins that are produced by free ribosomes and that will remain in the cytosol. Secretory proteins depart from the ER wrapped in the membranes of vesicles that bud like bubbles from a specialized region called transitional ER (see Figure 6.11). Vesicles in transit from one part of the cell to another are called **transport vesicles**; we will discuss their fate shortly.

In addition to making secretory proteins, rough ER is a membrane factory for the cell; it grows in place by adding membrane proteins and phospholipids to its own membrane. As polypeptides destined to be membrane proteins grow from the ribosomes, they are inserted into the ER membrane itself and anchored there by their hydrophobic portions. Like the smooth ER, the rough ER also makes membrane phospholipids; enzymes built into the ER membrane assemble phospholipids from precursors in the cytosol. The ER membrane expands and portions of it are transferred in the form of transport vesicles to other components of the endomembrane system.

The Golgi Apparatus: Shipping and Receiving Center

After leaving the ER, many transport vesicles travel to the **Golgi apparatus**. We can think of the Golgi as a warehouse for receiving, sorting, shipping, and even some manufacturing. Here, products of the ER, such as proteins, are modified and stored and then sent to other destinations. Not surprisingly, the Golgi apparatus is especially extensive in cells specialized for secretion.

The Golgi apparatus consists of flattened membranous sacs—cisternae—looking like a stack of pita bread (**Figure 6.12**, on the next page). A cell may have many, even hundreds, of these stacks. The membrane of each cisterna in a stack separates its internal space from the cytosol. Vesicles concentrated in the vicinity of the Golgi apparatus are engaged in the transfer of material between parts of the Golgi and other structures.

A Golgi stack has a distinct structural directionality, with the membranes of cisternae on opposite sides of the stack differing in thickness and molecular composition. The two sides of a Golgi stack are referred to as the *cis* face and the *trans* face; these act, respectively, as the receiving and shipping departments of the Golgi apparatus. The *cis* face is usually located near the ER. Transport vesicles move material from the ER to the Golgi apparatus. A vesicle that buds from the ER can add its membrane and the contents of its lumen to the *cis* face by fusing with a Golgi membrane. The *trans* face gives rise to vesicles that pinch off and travel to other sites.

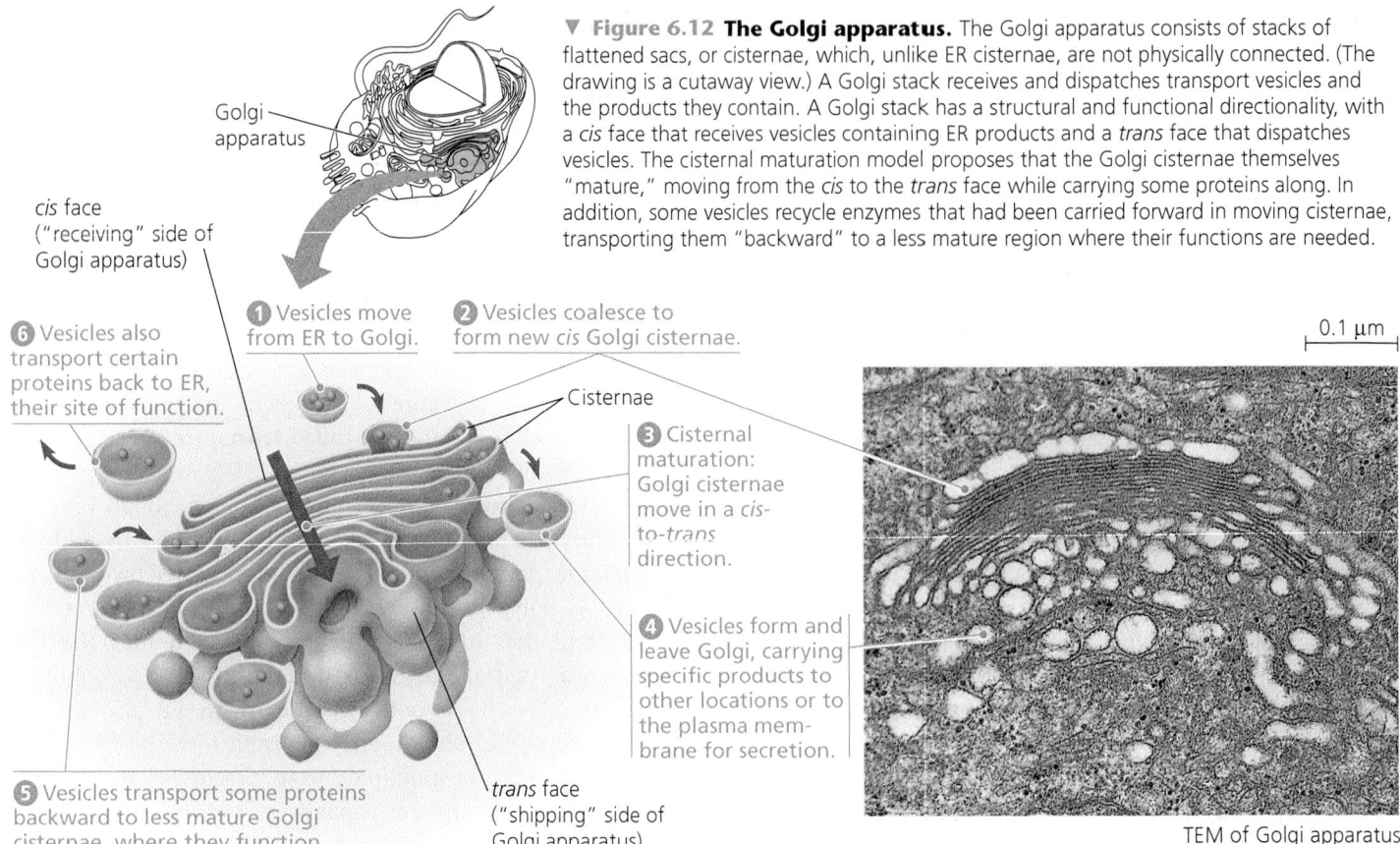

▼ **Figure 6.12 The Golgi apparatus.** The Golgi apparatus consists of stacks of flattened sacs, or cisternae, which, unlike ER cisternae, are not physically connected. (The drawing is a cutaway view.) A Golgi stack receives and dispatches transport vesicles and the products they contain. A Golgi stack has a structural and functional directionality, with a *cis* face that receives vesicles containing ER products and a *trans* face that dispatches vesicles. The cisternal maturation model proposes that the Golgi cisternae themselves "mature," moving from the *cis* to the *trans* face while carrying some proteins along. In addition, some vesicles recycle enzymes that had been carried forward in moving cisternae, transporting them "backward" to a less mature region where their functions are needed.

Golgi apparatus

cis face ("receiving" side of Golgi apparatus)

6 Vesicles also transport certain proteins back to ER, their site of function.

1 Vesicles move from ER to Golgi.

2 Vesicles coalesce to form new *cis* Golgi cisternae.

Cisternae

3 Cisternal maturation: Golgi cisternae move in a *cis*-to-*trans* direction.

4 Vesicles form and leave Golgi, carrying specific products to other locations or to the plasma membrane for secretion.

5 Vesicles transport some proteins backward to less mature Golgi cisternae, where they function.

trans face ("shipping" side of Golgi apparatus)

0.1 μm

TEM of Golgi apparatus

Products of the endoplasmic reticulum are usually modified during their transit from the *cis* region to the *trans* region of the Golgi apparatus. For example, glycoproteins formed in the ER have their carbohydrates modified, first in the ER itself, then as they pass through the Golgi. The Golgi removes some sugar monomers and substitutes others, producing a large variety of carbohydrates. Membrane phospholipids may also be altered in the Golgi.

In addition to its finishing work, the Golgi apparatus also manufactures some macromolecules. Many polysaccharides secreted by cells are Golgi products. For example, pectins and certain other noncellulose polysaccharides are made in the Golgi of plant cells and then incorporated along with cellulose into their cell walls. Like secretory proteins, nonprotein Golgi products that will be secreted depart from the *trans* face of the Golgi inside transport vesicles that eventually fuse with the plasma membrane.

The Golgi manufactures and refines its products in stages, with different cisternae containing unique teams of enzymes. Until recently, biologists viewed the Golgi as a static structure, with products in various stages of processing transferred from one cisterna to the next by vesicles. While this may occur, recent research has given rise to a new model of the Golgi as a more dynamic structure. According to the *cisternal maturation model*, the cisternae of the Golgi actually progress forward from the *cis* to the *trans* face, carrying and modifying their cargo as they move. Figure 6.12 shows the details of this model.

Before a Golgi stack dispatches its products by budding vesicles from the *trans* face, it sorts these products and targets them for various parts of the cell. Molecular identification tags, such as phosphate groups added to the Golgi products, aid in sorting by acting like ZIP codes on mailing labels. Finally, transport vesicles budded from the Golgi may have external molecules on their membranes that recognize "docking sites" on the surface of specific organelles or on the plasma membrane, thus targeting the vesicles appropriately.

Lysosomes: Digestive Compartments

A **lysosome** is a membranous sac of hydrolytic enzymes that an animal cell uses to digest (hydrolyze) macromolecules. Lysosomal enzymes work best in the acidic environment found in lysosomes. If a lysosome breaks open or leaks its contents, the released enzymes are not very active because the cytosol has a neutral pH. However, excessive leakage from a large number of lysosomes can destroy a cell by self-digestion.

Hydrolytic enzymes and lysosomal membrane are made by rough ER and then transferred to the Golgi apparatus for further processing. At least some lysosomes probably arise by budding from the *trans* face of the Golgi apparatus (see Figure 6.12). How are the proteins of the inner surface of the lysosomal membrane and the digestive enzymes themselves spared from destruction? Apparently, the three-dimensional shapes of these proteins protect vulnerable bonds from enzymatic attack.

Lysosomes carry out intracellular digestion in a variety of circumstances. Amoebas and many other protists eat by engulfing smaller organisms or food particles, a process called **phagocytosis** (from the Greek *phagein*, to eat, and *kytos*, vessel, referring here to the cell). The *food vacuole* formed in this way then fuses with a lysosome, whose enzymes digest the food (Figure 6.13a, bottom). Digestion products, including simple sugars, amino acids, and other monomers, pass into the cytosol and become nutrients for the cell. Some human cells also carry out phagocytosis. Among them are macrophages, a type of white blood cell that helps defend the body by engulfing and destroying bacteria and other invaders (see Figure 6.13a, top, and Figure 6.33).

Lysosomes also use their hydrolytic enzymes to recycle the cell's own organic material, a process called *autophagy*. During autophagy, a damaged organelle or small amount of cytosol becomes surrounded by a double membrane (of unknown origin), and a lysosome fuses with the outer membrane of this vesicle (Figure 6.13b). The lysosomal enzymes dismantle the enclosed material, and the organic monomers are returned to the cytosol for reuse. With the help of lysosomes, the cell continually renews itself. A human liver cell, for example, recycles half of its macromolecules each week.

The cells of people with inherited lysosomal storage diseases lack a functioning hydrolytic enzyme normally present in lysosomes. The lysosomes become engorged with indigestible substrates, which begin to interfere with other cellular activities. In Tay-Sachs disease, for example, a lipid-digesting enzyme is missing or inactive, and the brain becomes impaired by an accumulation of lipids in the cells. Fortunately, lysosomal storage diseases are rare in the general population.

Vacuoles: Diverse Maintenance Compartments

Vacuoles are large vesicles derived from the endoplasmic reticulum and Golgi apparatus. Thus, vacuoles are an integral part of a cell's endomembrane system. Like all cellular membranes, the vacuolar membrane is selective in transporting solutes; as a result, the solution inside a vacuole differs in composition from the cytosol.

Nucleus — 1 µm

Lysosome

Vesicle containing two damaged organelles — 1 µm

Mitochondrion fragment

Peroxisome fragment

① Lysosome contains active hydrolytic enzymes.
② Food vacuole fuses with lysosome.
③ Hydrolytic enzymes digest food particles.

Digestive enzymes

Lysosome

Plasma membrane

Food vacuole

Digestion

(a) Phagocytosis: lysosome digesting food

① Lysosome fuses with vesicle containing damaged organelles.
② Hydrolytic enzymes digest organelle components.

Lysosome

Peroxisome

Vesicle

Mitochondrion

Digestion

(b) Autophagy: lysosome breaking down damaged organelles

▲ **Figure 6.13 Lysosomes.** Lysosomes digest (hydrolyze) materials taken into the cell and recycle intracellular materials. **(a)** *Top:* In this macrophage (a type of white blood cell) from a rat, the lysosomes are very dark because of a stain that reacts with one of the products of digestion within the lysosome (TEM).

Macrophages ingest bacteria and viruses and destroy them using lysosomes. *Bottom:* This diagram shows one lysosome fusing with a food vacuole during the process of phagocytosis by a protist. **(b)** *Top:* In the cytoplasm of this rat liver cell is a vesicle containing two disabled organelles; the vesicle

will fuse with a lysosome in the process of autophagy (TEM). *Bottom:* This diagram shows fusion of such a vesicle with a lysosome. This type of vesicle has a double membrane of unknown origin. The outer membrane fuses with the lysosome, and the inner membrane is degraded along with the damaged organelles.

Vacuoles perform a variety of functions in different kinds of cells. **Food vacuoles**, formed by phagocytosis, have already been mentioned (see Figure 6.13a). Many freshwater protists have **contractile vacuoles** that pump excess water out of the cell, thereby maintaining a suitable concentration of ions and molecules inside the cell (see Figure 7.16). In plants and fungi, certain vacuoles carry out enzymatic hydrolysis, a function shared by lysosomes in animal cells. (In fact, some biologists consider these hydrolytic vacuoles to be a type of lysosome.) In plants, smaller vacuoles can hold reserves of important organic compounds, such as the proteins stockpiled in the storage cells in seeds. Vacuoles may also help protect the plant against herbivores by storing compounds that are poisonous or unpalatable to animals. Some plant vacuoles contain pigments, such as the red and blue pigments of petals that help attract pollinating insects to flowers.

Mature plant cells generally contain a large **central vacuole** (**Figure 6.14**), which develops by the coalescence of smaller vacuoles. The solution inside the central vacuole, called cell sap, is the plant cell's main repository of inorganic ions, including potassium and chloride. The central vacuole plays a major role in the growth of plant cells, which enlarge as the vacuole absorbs water, enabling the cell to become larger with a minimal investment in new cytoplasm. The cytosol often occupies only a thin layer between the central vacuole and the plasma membrane, so the ratio of plasma membrane surface to cytosolic volume is sufficient, even for a large plant cell.

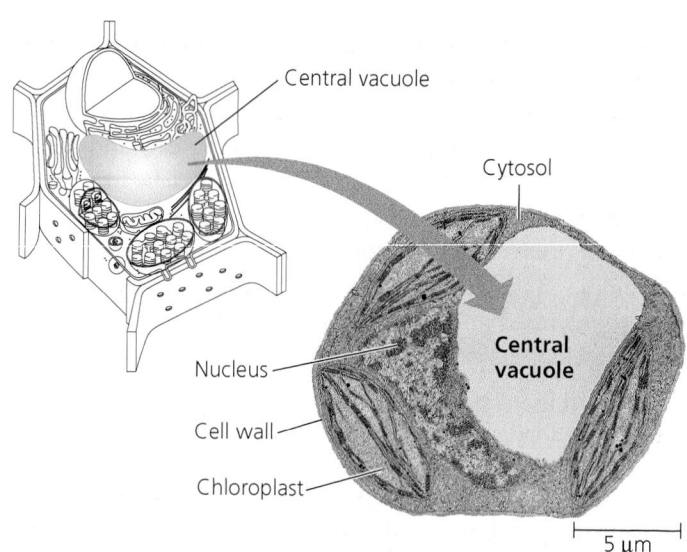

▲ **Figure 6.14 The plant cell vacuole.** The central vacuole is usually the largest compartment in a plant cell; the rest of the cytoplasm is often confined to a narrow zone between the vacuolar membrane and the plasma membrane (TEM).

The Endomembrane System: *A Review*

Figure 6.15 reviews the endomembrane system, showing the flow of membrane lipids and proteins through the various organelles. As the membrane moves from the ER to the Golgi and then elsewhere, its molecular composition and metabolic functions are modified, along with those of its contents. The

❶ Nuclear envelope is connected to rough ER, which is also continuous with smooth ER.

❷ Membranes and proteins produced by the ER flow in the form of transport vesicles to the Golgi.

❸ Golgi pinches off transport vesicles and other vesicles that give rise to lysosomes, other types of specialized vesicles, and vacuoles.

❹ Lysosome is available for fusion with another vesicle for digestion.

❺ Transport vesicle carries proteins to plasma membrane for secretion.

❻ Plasma membrane expands by fusion of vesicles; proteins are secreted from cell.

▲ **Figure 6.15 Review: relationships among organelles of the endomembrane system.** The red arrows show some of the migration pathways for membranes and the materials they enclose.

endomembrane system is a complex and dynamic player in the cell's compartmental organization.

We'll continue our tour of the cell with some organelles that are not closely related to the endomembrane system but play crucial roles in the energy transformations carried out by cells.

CONCEPT CHECK 6.4

1. Describe the structural and functional distinctions between rough and smooth ER.
2. Describe how transport vesicles integrate the endomembrane system.
3. **WHAT IF?** Imagine a protein that functions in the ER but requires modification in the Golgi apparatus before it can achieve that function. Describe the protein's path through the cell, starting with the mRNA molecule that specifies the protein.

For suggested answers, see Appendix A.

CONCEPT 6.5

Mitochondria and chloroplasts change energy from one form to another

Organisms transform the energy they acquire from their surroundings. In eukaryotic cells, mitochondria and chloroplasts are the organelles that convert energy to forms that cells can use for work. **Mitochondria** (singular, *mitochondrion*) are the sites of cellular respiration, the metabolic process that uses oxygen to generate ATP by extracting energy from sugars, fats, and other fuels. **Chloroplasts**, found in plants and algae, are the sites of photosynthesis. These organelles convert solar energy to chemical energy by absorbing sunlight and using it to drive the synthesis of organic compounds such as sugars from carbon dioxide and water.

In addition to having related functions, mitochondria and chloroplasts share a similar evolutionary origin, something we'll discuss briefly before describing their structure. In this section, we will also consider the peroxisome, an oxidative organelle. The evolutionary origin of the peroxisome, as well as its relation to other organelles, is still under debate.

The Evolutionary Origins of Mitochondria and Chloroplasts

EVOLUTION Mitochondria and chloroplasts display similarities with bacteria that led to the **endosymbiont theory**, illustrated in **Figure 6.16**. This theory states that an early ancestor of eukaryotic cells engulfed an oxygen-using nonphotosynthetic prokaryotic cell. Eventually, the engulfed cell formed a relationship with the host cell in which it was enclosed, becoming an *endosymbiont* (a cell living within an-

▲ **Figure 6.16 The endosymbiont theory of the origin of mitochondria and chloroplasts in eukaryotic cells.** According to this theory, the proposed ancestors of mitochondria were oxygen-using nonphotosynthetic prokaryotes, while the proposed ancestors of chloroplasts were photosynthetic prokaryotes. The large arrows represent change over evolutionary time; the small arrows inside the cells show the process of the endosymbiont becoming an organelle.

other cell). Indeed, over the course of evolution, the host cell and its endosymbiont merged into a single organism, a eukaryotic cell with a mitochondrion. At least one of these cells may have then taken up a photosynthetic prokaryote, becoming the ancestor of eukaryotic cells that contain chloroplasts.

This is a widely accepted theory, which we will discuss in more detail in Chapter 25. The model it proposes is consistent with many structural features of mitochondria and chloroplasts. First, rather than being bounded by a single membrane like organelles of the endomembrane system, mitochondria and typical chloroplasts have two membranes surrounding them. (Chloroplasts also have an internal system of membranous sacs.) There is evidence that the ancestral engulfed prokaryotes had two outer membranes, which became the double membranes of mitochondria and chloroplasts. Second, like prokaryotes, mitochondria and chloroplasts contain ribosomes, as well as circular DNA molecules attached to their inner membranes. The DNA in these organelles programs the synthesis of some of their own proteins, which are made on the ribosomes inside the organelles. Third, also consistent with their probable evolutionary origins as cells, mitochondria and chloroplasts are autonomous (somewhat independent) organelles that grow and reproduce within the cell.

In Chapters 9 and 10, we will focus on how mitochondria and chloroplasts function as energy transformers. Here we are concerned mainly with their structures and their roles.

Mitochondria: Chemical Energy Conversion

Mitochondria are found in nearly all eukaryotic cells, including those of plants, animals, fungi, and most protists. Some cells have a single large mitochondrion, but more often a cell has hundreds or even thousands of mitochondria; the number correlates with the cell's level of metabolic activity. For example, cells that move or contract have proportionally more mitochondria per volume than less active cells.

The mitochondrion is enclosed by two membranes, each a phospholipid bilayer with a unique collection of embedded proteins **(Figure 6.17)**. The outer membrane is smooth, but the inner membrane is convoluted, with infoldings called **cristae**. The inner membrane divides the mitochondrion into two internal compartments. The first is the intermembrane space, the narrow region between the inner and outer membranes. The second compartment, the **mitochondrial matrix**, is enclosed by the inner membrane. The matrix contains many different enzymes as well as the mitochondrial DNA and ribosomes. Enzymes in the matrix catalyze some of the steps of cellular respiration. Other proteins that function in respiration, including the enzyme that makes ATP, are built into the inner membrane. As highly folded surfaces, the cristae give the inner mitochondrial membrane a large surface area, thus enhancing the productivity of cellular respiration. This is another example of structure fitting function.

Mitochondria are generally in the range of 1–10 μm long. Time-lapse films of living cells reveal mitochondria moving around, changing their shapes, and fusing or dividing in two, unlike the static structures seen in electron micrographs of dead cells. These observations helped cell biologists understand that mitochondria in a living cell form a branched tubular network, seen in a whole cell in Figure 6.17.

Chloroplasts: Capture of Light Energy

Chloroplasts contain the green pigment chlorophyll, along with enzymes and other molecules that function in the photosynthetic production of sugar. These lens-shaped organelles, about 3–6 μm in length, are found in leaves and other green organs of plants and in algae **(Figure 6.18** and Figure 6.27c).

The contents of a chloroplast are partitioned from the cytosol by an envelope consisting of two membranes separated by a very narrow intermembrane space. Inside the chloroplast is another membranous system in the form of flattened, interconnected sacs called **thylakoids**. In some regions, thylakoids are stacked like poker chips; each stack is called a **granum** (plural, *grana*). The fluid outside the thylakoids is the **stroma**, which contains the chloroplast DNA and ribosomes as well as many enzymes. The membranes of the chloroplast divide the chloroplast space into three compartments: the intermembrane space, the stroma, and the thylakoid space. In Chapter 10, you will learn how this compartmental organization enables the chloroplast to convert light energy to chemical energy during photosynthesis.

As with mitochondria, the static and rigid appearance of chloroplasts in micrographs or schematic diagrams is not true

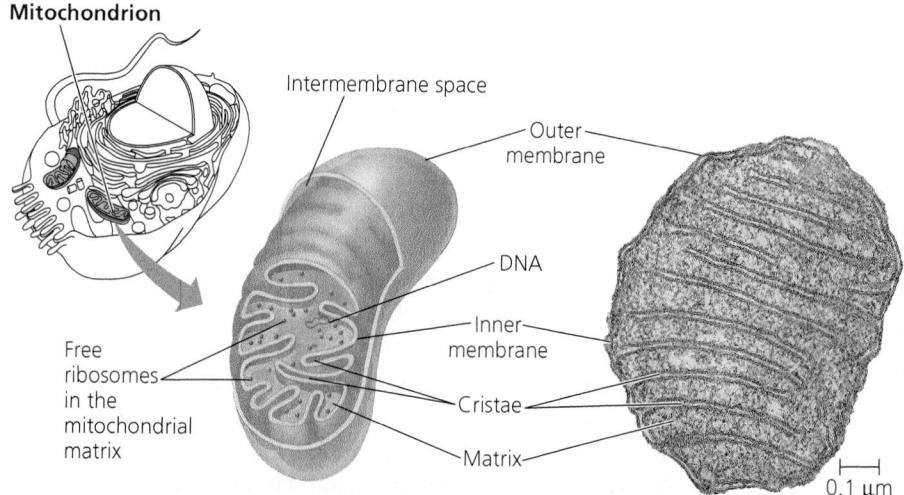

Mitochondrion

Intermembrane space

Outer membrane

DNA

Inner membrane

Free ribosomes in the mitochondrial matrix

Cristae

Matrix

0.1 μm

(a) Diagram and TEM of mitochondrion

10 μm

Mitochondria

Mitochondrial DNA

Nuclear DNA

(b) Network of mitochondria in a protist cell (LM)

▲ **Figure 6.17 The mitochondrion, site of cellular respiration. (a)** The inner and outer membranes of the mitochondrion are evident in the drawing and electron micrograph (TEM). The cristae are infoldings of the inner membrane, which increase its surface area. The cutaway drawing shows the two compartments bounded by the membranes: the intermembrane space and the mitochondrial matrix. Many respiratory enzymes are found in the inner membrane and the matrix. Free ribosomes are also present in the matrix. The DNA molecules are usually circular and are attached to the inner mitochondrial membrane.

(b) The light micrograph shows an entire unicellular protist (*Euglena gracilis*) at a much lower magnification than the TEM. The mitochondrial matrix has been stained green. The mitochondria form a branched tubular network. The nuclear DNA is stained red, and the molecules of mitochondrial DNA appear as bright yellow spots.

Figure 6.18 The chloroplast, site of photosynthesis. (a) Many plants have disk-shaped choloroplasts, as shown here. A typical chloroplast has three compartments: the intermembrane space, the stroma, and the thylakoid space. Free ribosomes are present in the stroma, as are copies of chloroplast DNA molecules. **(b)** This fluorescence micrograph shows a cell of the green alga *Spirogyra crassa*, which is named for its spiral chloroplasts. Under natural light the chloroplasts appear green, but under ultraviolet light they naturally fluoresce red, as shown here.

Chloroplast

Ribosomes
Stroma
Inner and outer membranes
Granum
DNA
Thylakoid
Intermembrane space

(a) Diagram and TEM of chloroplast

50 µm

Chloroplasts (red)

1 µm

(b) Chloroplasts in an algal cell

to their dynamic behavior in the living cell. Their shape is changeable, and they grow and occasionally pinch in two, reproducing themselves. They are mobile and, with mitochondria and other organelles, move around the cell along tracks of the cytoskeleton, a structural network we will consider later in this chapter.

The chloroplast is a specialized member of a family of closely related plant organelles called **plastids**. One type of plastid, the *amyloplast*, is a colorless organelle that stores starch (amylose), particularly in roots and tubers. Another is the *chromoplast*, which has pigments that give fruits and flowers their orange and yellow hues.

Peroxisomes: Oxidation

The **peroxisome** is a specialized metabolic compartment bounded by a single membrane (**Figure 6.19**). Peroxisomes contain enzymes that remove hydrogen atoms from various substrates and transfer them to oxygen (O_2), thus producing hydrogen peroxide (H_2O_2) as a by-product (from which the organelle derives its name). These reactions have many different functions. Some peroxisomes use oxygen to break fatty acids down into smaller molecules that are transported to mitochondria and used as fuel for cellular respiration. Peroxisomes in the liver detoxify alcohol and other harmful compounds by transferring hydrogen from the poisons to oxygen. The H_2O_2 formed by peroxisomes is itself toxic, but the organelle also contains an enzyme that converts H_2O_2 to water. This is an excellent example of how the cell's compartmental structure is crucial to its functions: The enzymes that produce hydrogen peroxide and those that dispose of this toxic compound are sequestered away from other cellular components that could be damaged.

Specialized peroxisomes called *glyoxysomes* are found in the fat-storing tissues of plant seeds. These organelles contain

enzymes that initiate the conversion of fatty acids to sugar, which the emerging seedling uses as a source of energy and carbon until it can produce its own sugar by photosynthesis.

How peroxisomes are related to other organelles is still an open question. They grow larger by incorporating proteins made in the cytosol and ER, as well as lipids made in the ER and within the peroxisome itself. Peroxisomes may increase in number by splitting in two when they reach a certain size, sparking the suggestion of an endosymbiotic evolutionary origin, but others argue against this scenario. The debate continues.

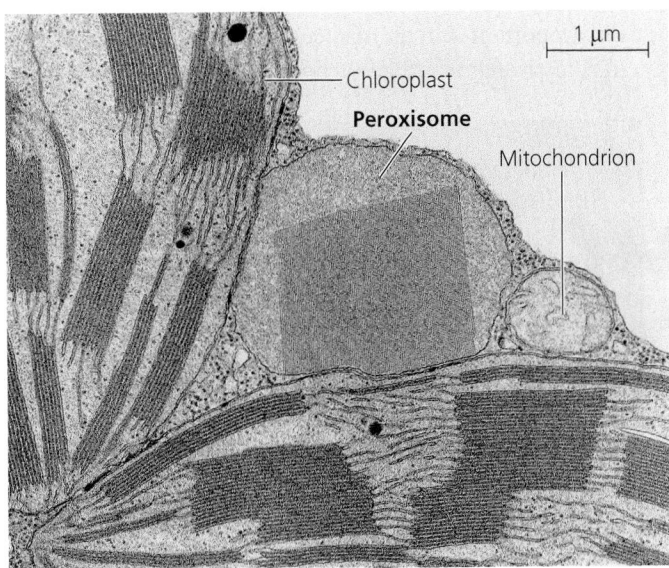

1 µm

Chloroplast
Peroxisome
Mitochondrion

▲ Figure 6.19 **A peroxisome.** Peroxisomes are roughly spherical and often have a granular or crystalline core that is thought to be a dense collection of enzyme molecules. This peroxisome is in a leaf cell (TEM). Notice its proximity to two chloroplasts and a mitochondrion. These organelles cooperate with peroxisomes in certain metabolic functions.

1. Describe two common characteristics of chloroplasts and mitochondria. Consider both function and membrane structure.
2. Do plant cells have mitochondria? Explain.
3. **WHAT IF?** A classmate proposes that mitochondria and chloroplasts should be classified in the endomembrane system. Argue against the proposal.

For suggested answers, see Appendix A.

CONCEPT **6.6**

The cytoskeleton is a network of fibers that organizes structures and activities in the cell

In the early days of electron microscopy, biologists thought that the organelles of a eukaryotic cell floated freely in the cytosol. But improvements in both light microscopy and electron microscopy have revealed the **cytoskeleton**, a network of fibers extending throughout the cytoplasm (**Figure 6.20**). The cytoskeleton, which plays a major role in organizing the structures and activities of the cell, is composed of three types of molecular structures: microtubules, microfilaments, and intermediate filaments.

Roles of the Cytoskeleton: Support and Motility

The most obvious function of the cytoskeleton is to give mechanical support to the cell and maintain its shape. This is especially important for animal cells, which lack walls. The remarkable strength and resilience of the cytoskeleton as a

whole is based on its architecture. Like a dome tent, the cytoskeleton is stabilized by a balance between opposing forces exerted by its elements. And just as the skeleton of an animal helps fix the positions of other body parts, the cytoskeleton provides anchorage for many organelles and even cytosolic enzyme molecules. The cytoskeleton is more dynamic than an animal skeleton, however. It can be quickly dismantled in one part of the cell and reassembled in a new location, changing the shape of the cell.

Several types of cell motility (movement) also involve the cytoskeleton. The term *cell motility* encompasses both changes in cell location and more limited movements of parts of the cell. Cell motility generally requires the interaction of the cytoskeleton with **motor proteins**. Examples of such cell motility abound. Cytoskeletal elements and motor proteins work together with plasma membrane molecules to allow whole cells to move along fibers outside the cell. Motor proteins bring about the bending of cilia and flagella by gripping microtubules within those organelles and sliding them against each other. A similar mechanism involving microfilaments causes muscle cells to contract. Inside the cell, vesicles and other organelles often use motor protein "feet" to "walk" to their destinations along a track provided by the cytoskeleton. For example, this is how vesicles containing neurotransmitter molecules migrate to the tips of axons, the long extensions of nerve cells that release these molecules as chemical signals to adjacent nerve cells (**Figure 6.21**). The vesicles that bud off

(a) Motor proteins that attach to receptors on vesicles can "walk" the vesicles along microtubules or, in some cases, microfilaments.

(b) In this SEM of a squid giant axon (a nerve cell extension), two vesicles containing neurotransmitters migrate toward the tip of the axon via the mechanism shown in (a).

▲ **Figure 6.21 Motor proteins and the cytoskeleton.**

▲ **Figure 6.20 The cytoskeleton.** As shown in this fluorescence micrograph, the cytoskeleton extends throughout the cell. The cytoskeletal elements have been tagged with different fluorescent molecules: green for microtubules and red for microfilaments. A third component of the cytoskeleton, intermediate filaments, is not evident here. (The DNA in the nucleus is blue.)

Table 6.1 The Structure and Function of the Cytoskeleton

Property	Microtubules (Tubulin Polymers)	Microfilaments (Actin Filaments)	Intermediate Filaments
Structure	Hollow tubes; wall consists of 13 columns of tubulin molecules	Two intertwined strands of actin, each a polymer of actin subunits	Fibrous proteins supercoiled into thicker cables
Diameter	25 nm with 15-nm lumen	7 nm	8–12 nm
Protein subunits	Tubulin, a dimer consisting of α-tubulin and β-tubulin	Actin	One of several different proteins (such as keratins), depending on cell type
Main functions	Maintenance of cell shape (compression-resisting "girders") Cell motility (as in cilia or flagella) Chromosome movements in cell division Organelle movements	Maintenance of cell shape (tension-bearing elements) Changes in cell shape Muscle contraction Cytoplasmic streaming Cell motility (as in pseudopodia) Cell division (cleavage furrow formation)	Maintenance of cell shape (tension-bearing elements) Anchorage of nucleus and certain other organelles Formation of nuclear lamina

Fluorescence micrographs of fibroblasts, a favorite cell type for cell biology studies. In each, the structure of interest has been tagged with fluorescent molecules. In the first and third micrographs, the DNA in the nucleus has also been tagged (blue or orange).

from the ER travel to the Golgi along cytoskeletal tracks. The cytoskeleton also manipulates the plasma membrane, making it bend inward to form food vacuoles or other phagocytic vesicles. And the streaming of cytoplasm that circulates materials within many large plant cells is yet another kind of cellular movement brought about by the cytoskeleton.

Components of the Cytoskeleton

Now let's look more closely at the three main types of fibers that make up the cytoskeleton: *Microtubules* are the thickest of the three types; *microfilaments* (also called actin filaments)

are the thinnest; and *intermediate filaments* are fibers with diameters in a middle range (Table 6.1).

Microtubules

All eukaryotic cells have **microtubules**, hollow rods measuring about 25 nm in diameter and from 200 nm to 25 μm in length. The wall of the hollow tube is constructed from a globular protein called tubulin. Each tubulin protein is a *dimer*, a molecule made up of two subunits. A tubulin dimer consists of two slightly different polypeptides, α-tubulin and β-tubulin. Microtubules grow in length by adding tubulin dimers; they can also be disassembled and their tubulin used to build microtubules elsewhere in the cell. Because of the orientation of tubulin dimers, the two ends of a microtubule are slightly different. One end can accumulate or release tubulin dimers at a much higher rate than the other, thus growing and shrinking significantly during cellular activities. (This is called the "plus end," not because it can only add tubulin proteins but because it's the end where both "on" and "off" rates are much higher.)

Microtubules shape and support the cell and also serve as tracks along which organelles equipped with motor proteins can move. In addition to the example in Figure 6.21, microtubules guide secretory vesicles from the Golgi apparatus to the plasma membrane. Microtubules are also involved in the separation of chromosomes during cell division, which will be discussed in Chapter 12.

Centrosomes and Centrioles In animal cells, microtubules grow out from a **centrosome**, a region that is often located near the nucleus and is considered a "microtubule-organizing center." These microtubules function as compression-resisting girders of the cytoskeleton. Within the centrosome is a pair of **centrioles**, each composed of nine sets of triplet microtubules arranged in a ring (**Figure 6.22**). Before an animal cell divides, the centrioles replicate. Although centrosomes with centrioles may help organize microtubule assembly in animal cells, they are not essential for this function in all eukaryotes; fungi and almost all plant cells lack centrosomes with centrioles but have well-organized microtubules. Apparently, other microtubule-organizing centers play the role of centrosomes in these cells.

Cilia and Flagella In eukaryotes, a specialized arrangement of microtubules is responsible for the beating of **flagella** (singular, *flagellum*) and **cilia** (singular, *cilium*), microtubule-containing extensions that project from some cells. (The bacterial flagellum, shown in Figure 6.5, has a completely different structure.) Many unicellular eukaryotes are propelled through water by cilia or flagella that act as locomotor appendages, and the sperm of animals, algae, and some plants have flagella. When cilia or flagella extend from cells that are held in place as part of a tissue layer, they can move fluid over the surface of the tissue. For example, the ciliated lining of the trachea (windpipe) sweeps mucus containing trapped debris out of the lungs (see the EMs in Figure 6.3). In a woman's reproductive tract, the cilia lining the oviducts help move an egg toward the uterus.

Motile cilia usually occur in large numbers on the cell surface. They are about 0.25 μm in diameter and about 2–20 μm long. Flagella are the same diameter but longer, 10–200 μm. Also, flagella are usually limited to just one or a few per cell.

Flagella and cilia differ in their beating patterns (**Figure 6.23**). A flagellum has an undulating motion that generates force in the same direction as the flagellum's axis, like the tail of a fish. In contrast, cilia work more like oars, with alternating power and

▲ **Figure 6.22 Centrosome containing a pair of centrioles.** Most animal cells have a centrosome, a region near the nucleus where the cell's microtubules are initiated. Within the centrosome is a pair of centrioles, each about 250 nm (0.25 μm) in diameter. The two centrioles are at right angles to each other, and each is made up of nine sets of three microtubules. The blue portions of the drawing represent nontubulin proteins that connect the microtubule triplets (TEM).

? *How many microtubules are in a centrosome? In the drawing, circle and label one microtubule and describe its structure. Circle and label a triplet.*

recovery strokes generating force in a direction perpendicular to the cilium's axis, much as the oars of a racing crew boat extend outward at a right angle to the boat's forward movement.

A cilium may also act as a signal-receiving "antenna" for the cell. Cilia that have this function are generally nonmotile, and there is only one per cell. (In fact, in vertebrate animals, it appears that almost all cells have such a cilium, which is called a *primary cilium*.) Membrane proteins on this kind of cilium transmit molecular signals from the cell's environment to its interior, triggering signaling pathways that may lead to changes in the cell's activities. Cilium-based signaling appears to be crucial to brain function and to embryonic development.

Though different in length, number per cell, and beating pattern, motile cilia and flagella share a common structure. Each motile cilium and flagellum has a group of microtubules sheathed in an extension of the plasma membrane (**Figure 6.24**). Nine doublets of microtubules are arranged in a ring; in the center of the ring are two single microtubules.

▶ **Figure 6.23**
A comparison of the beating of flagella and motile cilia.

(a) Motion of flagella. A flagellum usually undulates, its snakelike motion driving a cell in the same direction as the axis of the flagellum. Propulsion of a human sperm cell is an example of flagellate locomotion (LM).

Direction of swimming

5 μm

(b) Motion of cilia. Cilia have a back-and-forth motion. The rapid power stroke moves the cell in a direction perpendicular to the axis of the cilium. Then, during the slower recovery stroke, the cilium bends and sweeps sideways, closer to the cell surface. A dense nap of cilia, beating at a rate of about 40 to 60 strokes a second, covers this *Colpidium*, a freshwater protist (colorized SEM).

Direction of organism's movement

Power stroke   Recovery stroke

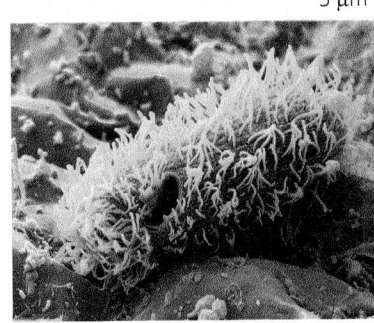

15 μm

0.1 μm

Outer microtubule doublet

Plasma membrane

Dynein proteins

Central microtubule

Radial spoke

Cross-linking proteins between outer doublets

Microtubules

Plasma membrane

Basal body

0.5 μm

(a) A longitudinal section of a motile cilium shows microtubules running the length of the structure (TEM).

(b) A cross section through a motile cilium shows the "9 + 2" arrangement of microtubules (TEM). The outer microtubule doublets and the two central microtubules are held together by flexible cross-linking proteins (blue in art), including the radial spokes. The doublets also have attached motor proteins called dyneins (red in art).

0.1 μm

Triplet

(c) Basal body: The nine outer doublets of a cilium or flagellum extend into the basal body, where each doublet joins another microtubule to form a ring of nine triplets. Each triplet is connected to the next by nontubulin proteins (thinner blue lines in diagram). This is a "9 + 0" arrangement: the two central microtubules are not present because they terminate above the basal body (TEM).

Cross section of basal body

▲ **Figure 6.24 Structure of a flagellum or motile cilium.**

DRAW IT *In (a), circle the central pair of microtubules. Show where they terminate, and explain why they aren't seen in the cross section of the basal body in (c).*

This arrangement, referred to as the "9 + 2" pattern, is found in nearly all eukaryotic flagella and motile cilia. (Nonmotile primary cilia have a "9 + 0" pattern, lacking the central pair of microtubules.) The microtubule assembly of a cilium or flagellum is anchored in the cell by a **basal body**, which is structurally very similar to a centriole, with microtubule triplets in a "9 + 0" pattern. In fact, in many animals (including humans), the basal body of the fertilizing sperm's flagellum enters the egg and becomes a centriole.

In flagella and motile cilia, flexible cross-linking proteins, evenly spaced along the length of the cilium or flagellum, connect the outer doublets to each other and to the two central microtubules. Each outer doublet also has pairs of protruding proteins spaced along its length and reaching toward the neighboring doublet; these are large motor proteins called **dyneins**, each composed of several polypeptides. Dyneins are responsible for the bending movements of the organelle. A dynein molecule performs a complex cycle of movements caused by changes in the shape of the protein, with ATP providing the energy for these changes (**Figure 6.25**).

The mechanics of dynein-based bending involve a process that resembles walking. A typical dynein protein has two "feet" that "walk" along the microtubule of the adjacent doublet, one foot maintaining contact while the other releases and reattaches one step farther along the microtubule. Without any restraints on the movement of the microtubule doublets, one doublet would continue to "walk" along and slide past the surface of the other, elongating the cilium or flagellum rather than bending it (see Figure 6.25a). For lateral movement of a cilium or flagellum, the dynein "walking" must have something to pull against, as when the muscles in your leg pull against your bones to move your knee. In cilia and flagella, the microtubule doublets seem to be held in place by the cross-linking proteins just inside the outer doublets and by the radial spokes and other structural elements. Thus, neighboring doublets cannot slide past each other very far. Instead, the forces exerted by dynein "walking" cause the doublets to curve, bending the cilium or flagellum (see Figure 6.25b and c).

Microfilaments (Actin Filaments)

Microfilaments are solid rods about 7 nm in diameter. They are also called actin filaments because they are built from molecules of **actin**, a globular protein. A microfilament is a twisted double chain of actin subunits (see Table 6.1). Besides occurring as linear filaments, microfilaments can form structural networks when certain proteins bind along the side of an actin filament and allow a new filament to extend as a branch. Like microtubules, microfilaments seem to be present in all eukaryotic cells.

In contrast to the compression-resisting role of microtubules, the structural role of microfilaments in the cytoskeleton is to bear tension (pulling forces). A three-dimensional network formed by microfilaments just inside the plasma

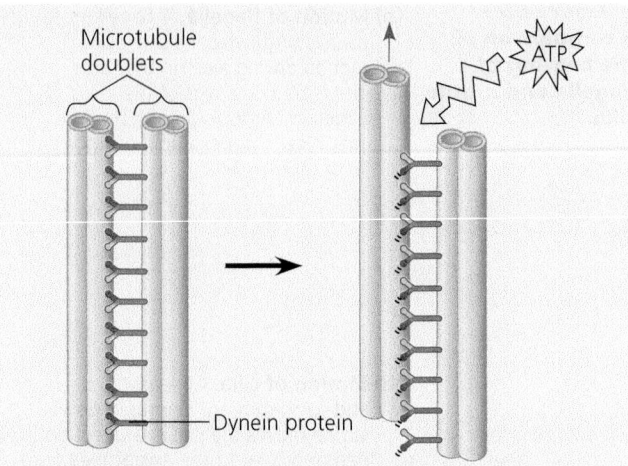

(a) Effect of unrestrained dynein movement. If a cilium or flagellum had no cross-linking proteins, the two feet of each dynein along one doublet (powered by ATP) would alternately grip and release the adjacent doublet. This "walking" motion would push the adjacent doublet up. Instead of bending, the doublets would slide past each other.

(b) Effect of cross-linking proteins. In a cilium or flagellum, two adjacent doublets cannot slide far because they are physically restrained by proteins, so they bend. (Only two of the nine outer doublets in Figure 6.24b are shown here.)

(c) Wavelike motion. Synchronized cycles of movement of many dyneins probably cause a bend to begin at the base of the cilium or flagellum and move outward toward the tip. Many successive bends, such as the ones shown here to the left and right, result in a wavelike motion. In this diagram, the two central microtubules and the cross-linking proteins are not shown.

▲ **Figure 6.25 How dynein "walking" moves flagella and cilia.**

Microvillus

Plasma membrane

Microfilaments (actin filaments)

Intermediate filaments

0.25 μm

▲ **Figure 6.26 A structural role of microfilaments.** The surface area of this nutrient-absorbing intestinal cell is increased by its many microvilli (singular, *microvillus*), cellular extensions reinforced by bundles of microfilaments. These actin filaments are anchored to a network of intermediate filaments (TEM).

membrane (*cortical microfilaments*) helps support the cell's shape (see Figure 6.8). This network gives the outer cytoplasmic layer of a cell, called the **cortex**, the semisolid consistency of a gel, in contrast with the more fluid (*sol*) state of the interior cytoplasm. In animal cells specialized for transporting materials across the plasma membrane, such as intestinal cells, bundles of microfilaments make up the core of microvilli, delicate projections that increase the cell's surface area (**Figure 6.26**).

Microfilaments are well known for their role in cell motility, particularly as part of the contractile apparatus of muscle cells. Thousands of actin filaments are arranged parallel to one another along the length of a muscle cell, interdigitated with thicker filaments made of a protein called **myosin** (**Figure 6.27a**). Like dynein when it interacts with microtubules, myosin acts as a motor protein by means of projections that "walk" along the actin filaments. Contraction of the muscle cell results from the actin and myosin filaments sliding past one another in this way, shortening the cell. In other kinds of cells, actin filaments are associated with myosin in miniature and less elaborate versions of the arrangement in muscle cells. These actin-myosin aggregates are responsible for

Muscle cell

0.5 μm

Actin filament

Myosin filament

Myosin head

(a) Myosin motors in muscle cell contraction. The "walking" of myosin projections (the so-called heads) drives the parallel myosin and actin filaments past each other so that the actin filaments approach each other in the middle (red arrows). This shortens the muscle cell. Muscle contraction involves the shortening of many muscle cells at the same time (TEM).

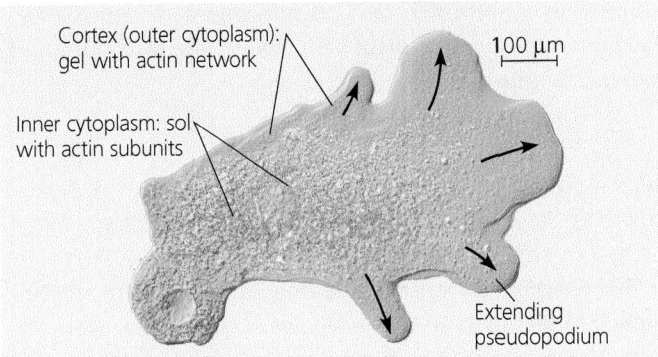

Cortex (outer cytoplasm): gel with actin network

100 μm

Inner cytoplasm: sol with actin subunits

Extending pseudopodium

(b) Amoeboid movement. Interaction of actin filaments with myosin causes contraction of the cell, pulling the cell's trailing end (at left) forward (to the right) (LM).

Chloroplast

30 μm

(c) Cytoplasmic streaming in plant cells. A layer of cytoplasm cycles around the cell, moving over a carpet of parallel actin filaments. Myosin motors attached to organelles in the fluid cytosol may drive the streaming by interacting with the actin (LM).

▲ **Figure 6.27 Microfilaments and motility.** In these three examples, interactions between actin filaments and motor proteins bring about cell movement.

localized contractions of cells. For example, a contracting belt of microfilaments forms a cleavage furrow that pinches a dividing animal cell into two daughter cells.

Localized contraction brought about by actin and myosin also plays a role in amoeboid movement (**Figure 6.27b**). A cell such as an amoeba crawls along a surface by extending cellular extensions called **pseudopodia** (from the Greek *pseudes*, false, and *pod*, foot), and moving toward them. Pseudopodia extend by assembly of actin subunits into microfilament networks that convert cytoplasm from a sol to a gel inside these cell projections. Cell surface proteins on the pseudopodium make strong attachments to the "road." Next, the interaction of microfilaments with myosin near the cell's trailing end causes contraction of that region, loosening its cell-surface attachments and pulling it forward toward the pseudopodia. Amoebae lacking myosin can still form pseudopodia, but forward movement is greatly slowed. Amoebas are not the only cells that move by crawling; so do many cells in the animal body, including some white blood cells.

In plant cells, both actin-myosin interactions and sol-gel transformations brought about by actin may be involved in **cytoplasmic streaming**, a circular flow of cytoplasm within cells (**Figure 6.27c**). This movement, which is especially common in large plant cells, speeds the distribution of materials within the cell.

Intermediate Filaments

Intermediate filaments are named for their diameter, which, at 8–12 nm, is larger than the diameter of microfilaments but smaller than that of microtubules (see Table 6.1, p. 113). Specialized for bearing tension (like microfilaments), intermediate filaments are a diverse class of cytoskeletal elements. Each type is constructed from a particular molecular subunit belonging to a family of proteins whose members include the keratins. Microtubules and microfilaments, in contrast, are consistent in diameter and composition in all eukaryotic cells.

Intermediate filaments are more permanent fixtures of cells than are microfilaments and microtubules, which are often disassembled and reassembled in various parts of a cell. Even after cells die, intermediate filament networks often persist; for example, the outer layer of our skin consists of dead skin cells full of keratin proteins. Chemical treatments that remove microfilaments and microtubules from the cytoplasm of living cells leave a web of intermediate filaments that retains its original shape. Such experiments suggest that intermediate filaments are especially sturdy and that they play an important role in reinforcing the shape of a cell and fixing the position of certain organelles. For instance, the nucleus typically sits within a cage made of intermediate filaments, fixed in location by branches of the filaments that extend into the cytoplasm. Other intermediate filaments make up the nuclear lamina, which lines the interior of the nuclear envelope (see Figure 6.9). By supporting a cell's shape, intermediate filaments help the cell carry out its specific function. For example, the long extensions (axons) of nerve cells that transmit impulses are strengthened by intermediate filaments. Thus, the various kinds of intermediate filaments may function together as the permanent framework of the entire cell.

CONCEPT 6.7

Extracellular components and connections between cells help coordinate cellular activities

Having crisscrossed the cell to explore its interior components, we complete our tour of the cell by returning to the surface of this microscopic world, where there are additional structures with important functions. The plasma membrane is usually regarded as the boundary of the living cell, but most cells synthesize and secrete materials that are extracellular, or external to the plasma membrane. Although these materials and the structures they form are outside the cell, their study is important to cell biology because they are involved in a great many cellular functions.

Cell Walls of Plants

The **cell wall** is an extracellular structure of plant cells that distinguishes them from animal cells (see Figure 6.8). The wall protects the plant cell, maintains its shape, and prevents excessive uptake of water. On the level of the whole plant, the strong walls of specialized cells hold the plant up against the force of gravity. Prokaryotes, fungi, and some protists also have cell walls, as you saw in Figures 6.5 and 6.8, but we will postpone discussion of them until Unit Five.

Plant cell walls are much thicker than the plasma membrane, ranging from 0.1 μm to several micrometers. The exact chemical composition of the wall varies from species to species and even from one cell type to another in the same plant, but the basic design of the wall is consistent. Microfibrils made of the polysaccharide cellulose (see Figure 5.8) are synthesized by an enzyme called cellulose synthase and secreted to the extracellular space, where they become embedded in a matrix of other polysaccharides and proteins. This combination of materials, strong fibers in a "ground substance" (matrix), is the same basic architectural design found in steel-reinforced concrete and in fiberglass.

A young plant cell first secretes a relatively thin and flexible wall called the **primary cell wall** (**Figure 6.28**). In actively

▲ **Figure 6.28 Plant cell walls.** The drawing shows several cells, each with a large vacuole, a nucleus, and several chloroplasts and mitochondria. The transmission electron micrograph shows the cell walls where two cells come together. The multilayered partition between plant cells consists of adjoining walls individually secreted by the cells.

growing cells, the cellulose fibrils are oriented at right angles to the direction of cell expansion. Researchers investigated the role of microtubules in orienting these cellulose fibrils (Figure 6.29). Their observations strongly support the idea that microtubules in the cell cortex guide cellulose synthase as it synthesizes and deposits cellulose fibrils. By orienting cellulose deposition, microtubules thus affect the growth pattern of the cells.

Between primary walls of adjacent cells is the **middle lamella**, a thin layer rich in sticky polysaccharides called pectins. The middle lamella glues adjacent cells together (see Figure 6.28). (Pectin is used as a thickening agent in jams and jellies.) When the cell matures and stops growing, it strengthens its wall. Some plant cells do this simply by secreting hardening substances into the primary wall. Other cells add a **secondary cell wall** between the plasma membrane and the primary wall. The secondary wall, often deposited in several laminated layers, has a strong and durable matrix that affords the cell protection and support. Wood, for example, consists mainly of secondary walls. Plant cell walls are usually perforated by channels between adjacent cells called plasmodesmata (see Figure 6.28), which will be discussed shortly.

▼ Figure 6.29

INQUIRY

What role do microtubules play in orienting deposition of cellulose in cell walls?

EXPERIMENT Previous experiments on preserved plant tissues had shown alignment of microtubules in the cell cortex with cellulose fibrils in the cell wall. Also, drugs that disrupted microtubules were observed to cause disoriented cellulose fibrils. To further investigate the possible role of cortical microtubules in guiding cellulose fibril deposition, David Ehrhardt and colleagues at Stanford University used a type of confocal microscopy to study cell wall deposition in living cells. In these cells, they labeled both cellulose synthase and microtubules with fluorescent markers and observed them over time.

RESULTS Each fluorescence image below represents a combination of 30 images taken over a 5-minute period to detect the movement of cellulose synthase and microtubules. These two coincided highly over time. The labeling molecules caused cellulose synthase to fluoresce green and the microtubules to fluoresce red. The arrowheads indicate prominent areas where the two are seen to align.

Distribution of cellulose synthase over time

Distribution of microtubules over time

CONCLUSION The organization of microtubules appears to directly guide the path of cellulose synthase as it lays down cellulose, thus determining the orientation of cellulose fibrils.

SOURCE A. R. Paradez et al., Visualization of cellulose synthase demonstrates functional association with microtubules, *Science* 312:1491–1495 (2006).

WHAT IF? In a second experiment, the researchers exposed the plant cells to blue light, previously shown to cause reorientation of microtubules. What events would you predict would follow blue light exposure?

The Extracellular Matrix (ECM) of Animal Cells

Although animal cells lack walls akin to those of plant cells, they do have an elaborate **extracellular matrix (ECM)**. The main ingredients of the ECM are glycoproteins and other carbohydrate-containing molecules secreted by the cells. (Recall that glycoproteins are proteins with covalently bonded carbohydrate, usually short chains of sugars.) The most abundant glycoprotein in the ECM of most animal cells is **collagen**, which forms strong fibers outside the cells (see Figure 5.20). In fact, collagen accounts for about 40% of the total protein in the human body. The collagen fibers are embedded in a network woven out of **proteoglycans** secreted

Collagen fibers are embedded in a web of proteoglycan complexes.

Fibronectin attaches the ECM to integrins embedded in the plasma membrane.

Plasma membrane

EXTRACELLULAR FLUID

Micro-filaments

CYTOPLASM

A **proteoglycan complex** consists of hundreds of proteoglycan molecules attached noncovalently to a single long polysaccharide molecule.

Integrins, membrane proteins with two subunits, bind to the ECM on one side and to associated proteins attached to microfilaments on the other. This linkage can transmit signals between the cell's external environment and its interior and can result in changes in cell behavior.

Polysaccharide molecule

Carbo-hydrates

Core protein

Proteoglycan molecule

Proteoglycan complex

▲ **Figure 6.30 Extracellular matrix (ECM) of an animal cell.** The molecular composition and structure of the ECM vary from one cell type to another. In this example, three different types of ECM molecules are present: proteoglycans, collagen, and fibronectin.

by cells (**Figure 6.30**). A proteoglycan molecule consists of a small core protein with many carbohydrate chains covalently attached, so that it may be up to 95% carbohydrate. Large proteoglycan complexes can form when hundreds of proteoglycan molecules become noncovalently attached to a single long polysaccharide molecule, as shown in Figure 6.30. Some cells are attached to the ECM by ECM glycoproteins such as **fibronectin**. Fibronectin and other ECM proteins bind to cell-surface receptor proteins called **integrins** that are built into the plasma membrane. Integrins span the membrane and bind on their cytoplasmic side to associated proteins attached to microfilaments of the cytoskeleton. The name *integrin* is based on the word *integrate*: Integrins are in a position to transmit signals between the ECM and the cytoskeleton and thus to integrate changes occurring outside and inside the cell.

Current research on fibronectin, other ECM molecules, and integrins is revealing the influential role of the extracellular matrix in the lives of cells. By communicating with a cell through integrins, the ECM can regulate a cell's behavior. For example, some cells in a developing embryo migrate along specific pathways by matching the orientation of their microfilaments to the "grain" of fibers in the extracellular matrix. Researchers have also learned that the extracellular matrix around a cell can influence the activity of genes in the nucleus. Information about the ECM probably reaches the nucleus by a combination of mechanical and chemical signaling pathways. Mechanical signaling involves fibronectin, integrins, and microfilaments of the cytoskeleton. Changes in the cytoskeleton may in turn trigger chemical signaling

pathways inside the cell, leading to changes in the set of proteins being made by the cell and therefore changes in the cell's function. In this way, the extracellular matrix of a particular tissue may help coordinate the behavior of all the cells of that tissue. Direct connections between cells also function in this coordination, as we discuss next.

Cell Junctions

Cells in an animal or plant are organized into tissues, organs, and organ systems. Neighboring cells often adhere, interact, and communicate via sites of direct physical contact.

Plasmodesmata in Plant Cells

It might seem that the nonliving cell walls of plants would isolate plant cells from one another. But in fact, as shown in **Figure 6.31**, cell walls are perforated with **plasmodesmata** (singular, *plasmodesma*; from the Greek *desmos*, to bind),

Cell walls

Interior of cell

Interior of cell

0.5 μm

Plasmodesmata   Plasma membranes

▲ **Figure 6.31 Plasmodesmata between plant cells.** The cytoplasm of one plant cell is continuous with the cytoplasm of its neighbors via plasmodesmata, cytoplasmic channels through the cell walls (TEM).

membrane-lined channels filled with cytoplasm. Cytosol passes through the plasmodesmata and joins the internal chemical environments of adjacent cells. These connections unify most of the plant into one living continuum. The plasma membranes of adjacent cells line the channel of each plasmodesma and thus are continuous. Water and small solutes can pass freely from cell to cell, and recent experiments have shown that in some circumstances, certain proteins and RNA molecules can also do this (see Concept 36.6). The macromolecules transported to neighboring cells appear to reach the plasmodesmata by moving along fibers of the cytoskeleton.

Tight Junctions, Desmosomes, and Gap Junctions in Animal Cells

In animals, there are three main types of cell junctions: *tight junctions*, *desmosomes*, and *gap junctions*. (Gap junctions are most like the plasmodesmata of plants, although gap junction pores are not lined with membrane.) All three types of cell junctions are especially common in epithelial tissue, which lines the external and internal surfaces of the body. **Figure 6.32** uses epithelial cells of the intestinal lining to illustrate these junctions.

▼ Figure 6.32

Exploring Cell Junctions in Animal Tissues

Tight junctions prevent fluid from moving across a layer of cells

Tight junction

Tight junction

Intermediate filaments

Desmosome

Gap junction

Ions or small molecules

Space between cells

Plasma membranes of adjacent cells

Extracellular matrix

Tight Junctions

Tight junction

TEM   0.5 µm

At **tight junctions**, the plasma membranes of neighboring cells are very tightly pressed against each other, bound together by specific proteins (purple). Forming continuous seals around the cells, tight junctions prevent leakage of extracellular fluid across a layer of epithelial cells. For example, tight junctions between skin cells make us watertight by preventing leakage between cells in our sweat glands.

Desmosomes

TEM   1 µm

Desmosomes (also called *anchoring junctions*) function like rivets, fastening cells together into strong sheets. Intermediate filaments made of sturdy keratin proteins anchor desmosomes in the cytoplasm. Desmosomes attach muscle cells to each other in a muscle. Some "muscle tears" involve the rupture of desmosomes.

Gap Junctions

TEM   0.1 µm

Gap junctions (also called *communicating junctions*) provide cytoplasmic channels from one cell to an adjacent cell and in this way are similar in their function to the plasmodesmata in plants. Gap junctions consist of membrane proteins that surround a pore through which ions, sugars, amino acids, and other small molecules may pass. Gap junctions are necessary for communication between cells in many types of tissues, such as heart muscle, and in animal embryos.

1. In what way are the cells of plants and animals structurally different from single-celled eukaryotes?
2. **WHAT IF?** If the plant cell wall or the animal extracellular matrix were impermeable, what effect would this have on cell function?
3. **MAKE CONNECTIONS** The polypeptide chain that makes up a tight junction weaves back and forth through the membrane four times, with two extracellular loops, and one loop plus short C-terminal and N-terminal tails in the cytoplasm. Looking at Figure 5.16 (p. 79), what would you predict about the amino acid sequence of the tight-junction protein?

For suggested answers, see Appendix A.

5 µm

▲ **Figure 6.33 The emergence of cellular functions.** The ability of this macrophage (brown) to recognize, apprehend, and destroy bacteria (yellow) is a coordinated activity of the whole cell. Its cytoskeleton, lysosomes, and plasma membrane are among the components that function in phagocytosis (colorized SEM).

The Cell: A Living Unit Greater Than the Sum of Its Parts

From our panoramic view of the cell's compartmental organization to our close-up inspection of each organelle's architecture, this tour of the cell has provided many opportunities to correlate structure with function. (This would be a good time to review cell structure by returning to Figure 6.8, on pp. 100 and 101.) But even as we dissect the cell, remember that none of its components works alone. As an example of cellular integration, consider the microscopic scene in **Figure 6.33**. The large cell is a macrophage (see Figure 6.13a). It helps defend the mammalian body against infections by ingesting bacteria (the smaller cells) into phagocytic vesicles. The macrophage crawls along a surface and reaches out to the bacteria with thin pseudopodia (called filopodia). Actin filaments interact with other elements of the cytoskeleton in these movements. After the macrophage engulfs the bacteria, they are destroyed by lysosomes. The elaborate endomembrane system produces the lysosomes. The digestive enzymes of the lysosomes and the proteins of the cytoskeleton are all made on ribosomes. And the synthesis of these proteins is programmed by genetic messages dispatched from the DNA in the nucleus. All these processes require energy, which mitochondria supply in the form of ATP. Cellular functions arise from cellular order: The cell is a living unit greater than the sum of its parts.

6 CHAPTER REVIEW

SUMMARY OF KEY CONCEPTS

CONCEPT 6.1

Biologists use microscopes and the tools of biochemistry to study cells (pp. 94–97)

- Improvements in microscopy that affect the parameters of magnification, resolution, and contrast have catalyzed progress in the study of cell structure. **Light microscopy** (LM) and **electron microscopy** (EM), as well as other types, remain important tools.
- Cell biologists can obtain pellets enriched in particular cellular components by centrifuging disrupted cells at sequential speeds, a process known as **cell fractionation**. Larger cellular components are in the pellet after lower-speed centrifugation, and smaller components are in the pellet after higher-speed centrifugation.

? *How do microscopy and biochemistry complement each other to reveal cell structure and function?*

CONCEPT 6.2

Eukaryotic cells have internal membranes that compartmentalize their functions (pp. 98–102)

- All cells are bounded by a **plasma membrane**.
- **Prokaryotic cells** lack nuclei and other membrane-enclosed **organelles**, while **eukaryotic cells** have internal membranes that compartmentalize cellular functions.
- The surface-to-volume ratio is an important parameter affecting cell size and shape.
- Plant and animal cells have most of the same organelles: a nucleus, endoplasmic reticulum, Golgi apparatus, and mitochondria. Some organelles are found only in plant or in animal cells. Chloroplasts are present only in cells of photosynthetic eukaryotes.

? *Explain how the compartmental organization of a eukaryotic cell contributes to its biochemical functioning.*

	Cell Component	Structure	Function
CONCEPT 6.3 The eukaryotic cell's genetic instructions are housed in the nucleus and carried out by the ribosomes (pp. 102–104) **?** *Describe the relationship between the nucleus and ribosomes.*	Nucleus (ER)	Surrounded by nuclear envelope (double membrane) perforated by nuclear pores; nuclear envelope continuous with endoplasmic reticulum (ER)	Houses chromosomes, which are made of chromatin (DNA and proteins); contains nucleoli, where ribosomal subunits are made; pores regulate entry and exit of materials
	Ribosome	Two subunits made of ribosomal RNA and proteins; can be free in cytosol or bound to ER	Protein synthesis
CONCEPT 6.4 The endomembrane system regulates protein traffic and performs metabolic functions in the cell (pp. 104–109) **?** *Describe the key role played by transport vesicles in the endomembrane system.*	Endoplasmic reticulum (Nuclear envelope)	Extensive network of membrane-bounded tubules and sacs; membrane separates lumen from cytosol; continuous with nuclear envelope	Smooth ER: synthesis of lipids, metabolism of carbohydrates, Ca^{2+} storage, detoxification of drugs and poisons Rough ER: aids in synthesis of secretory and other proteins from bound ribosomes; adds carbohydrates to proteins to make glycoproteins; produces new membrane
	Golgi apparatus	Stacks of flattened membranous sacs; has polarity (*cis* and *trans* faces)	Modification of proteins, carbohydrates on proteins, and phospholipids; synthesis of many polysaccharides; sorting of Golgi products, which are then released in vesicles
	Lysosome	Membranous sac of hydrolytic enzymes (in animal cells)	Breakdown of ingested substances, cell macromolecules, and damaged organelles for recycling
	Vacuole	Large membrane-bounded vesicle	Digestion, storage, waste disposal, water balance, cell growth, and protection
CONCEPT 6.5 Mitochondria and chloroplasts change energy from one form to another (pp. 109–112) **?** *What is the endosymbiont theory?*	Mitochondrion	Bounded by double membrane; inner membrane has infoldings (cristae)	Cellular respiration
	Chloroplast	Typically two membranes around fluid stroma, which contains thylakoids stacked into grana (in cells of photosynthetic eukaryotes, including plants)	Photosynthesis
	Peroxisome	Specialized metabolic compartment bounded by a single membrane	Contains enzymes that transfer hydrogen atoms from substrates to oxygen, producing hydrogen peroxide (H_2O_2) as a by-product; H_2O_2 is converted to water by another enzyme

CONCEPT 6.6

The cytoskeleton is a network of fibers that organizes structures and activities in the cell (pp. 112–118)

- The **cytoskeleton** functions in structural support for the cell and in motility and signal transmission.
- **Microtubules** shape the cell, guide organelle movement, and separate chromosomes in dividing cells. **Cilia** and **flagella** are motile appendages containing microtubules. Primary cilia also play sensory and signaling roles. **Microfilaments** are thin rods functioning in muscle contraction, amoeboid movement, **cytoplasmic streaming**, and microvillus support. **Intermediate filaments** support cell shape and fix organelles in place.

 Describe the role of motor proteins inside the eukaryotic cell and in whole-cell movement.

CONCEPT 6.7

Extracellular components and connections between cells help coordinate cellular activities (pp. 118–122)

- Plant **cell walls** are made of cellulose fibers embedded in other polysaccharides and proteins. Cellulose deposition is oriented along microtubules.
- Animal cells secrete glycoproteins and proteoglycans that form the **extracellular matrix (ECM)**, which functions in support, adhesion, movement, and regulation.
- Cell junctions connect neighboring cells in plants and animals. Plants have **plasmodesmata** that pass through adjoining cell walls. Animal cells have **tight junctions**, **desmosomes**, and **gap junctions**.

Compare the composition and functions of a plant cell wall and the extracellular matrix of an animal cell.

TEST YOUR UNDERSTANDING

LEVEL 1: KNOWLEDGE/COMPREHENSION

1. Which structure is *not* part of the endomembrane system?
   a. nuclear envelope
   b. chloroplast
   c. Golgi apparatus
   d. plasma membrane
   e. ER

2. Which structure is common to plant *and* animal cells?
   a. chloroplast
   b. wall made of cellulose
   c. central vacuole
   d. mitochondrion
   e. centriole

3. Which of the following is present in a prokaryotic cell?
   a. mitochondrion
   b. ribosome
   c. nuclear envelope
   d. chloroplast
   e. ER

4. Which structure-function pair is *mismatched*?
   a. nucleolus; production of ribosomal subunits
   b. lysosome; intracellular digestion
   c. ribosome; protein synthesis
   d. Golgi; protein trafficking
   e. microtubule; muscle contraction

LEVEL 2: APPLICATION/ANALYSIS

5. Cyanide binds to at least one molecule involved in producing ATP. If a cell is exposed to cyanide, most of the cyanide will be found within the
   a. mitochondria.
   b. ribosomes.
   c. peroxisomes.
   d. lysosomes.
   e. endoplasmic reticulum.

6. What is the most likely pathway taken by a newly synthesized protein that will be secreted by a cell?
   a. ER → Golgi → nucleus
   b. Golgi → ER → lysosome
   c. nucleus → ER → Golgi
   d. ER → Golgi → vesicles that fuse with plasma membrane
   e. ER → lysosomes → vesicles that fuse with plasma membrane

7. Which cell would be best for studying lysosomes?
   a. muscle cell
   b. nerve cell
   c. phagocytic white blood cell
   d. leaf cell of a plant
   e. bacterial cell

8. **DRAW IT** From memory, draw two eukaryotic cells, labeling the structures listed here and showing any physical connections between the internal structures of each cell: nucleus, rough ER, smooth ER, mitochondrion, centrosome, chloroplast, vacuole, lysosome, microtubule, cell wall, ECM, microfilament, Golgi apparatus, intermediate filament, plasma membrane, peroxisome, ribosome, nucleolus, nuclear pore, vesicle, flagellum, microvilli, plasmodesma.

LEVEL 3: SYNTHESIS/EVALUATION

9. **EVOLUTION CONNECTION**
   Which aspects of cell structure best reveal evolutionary unity? What are some examples of specialized modifications?

10. **SCIENTIFIC INQUIRY**
    Imagine protein X, destined to span the plasma membrane. Assume that the mRNA carrying the genetic message for protein X has already been translated by ribosomes in a cell culture. If you fractionate the cells (see Figure 6.4), in which fraction would you find protein X? Explain by describing its transit through the cell.

11. **WRITE ABOUT A THEME**
    Emergent Properties Considering some of the characteristics that define life and drawing on your new knowledge of cellular structures and functions, write a short essay (100–150 words) that discusses this statement: Life is an emergent property that appears at the level of the cell. (Review pp. 3–5 in Chapter 1.)

For selected answers, see Appendix A.

Mastering BIOLOGY   www.masteringbiology.com

1. **MasteringBiology® Assignments**
   BioFlix Tutorials Tour of an Animal Cell: The Endomembrane System • Structures and Functions; Tour of a Plant Cell: Structures and Functions
   Tutorial Connections Between Cells
   Activities Metric System Review • Prokaryotic Cell Structure and Function • Discovery Channel Video: Cells • Role of the Nucleus and Ribosomes in Protein Synthesis • Transport into the Nucleus • A Pulse Chase Experiment • The Endomembrane System • Cilia and Flagella • Cell Junctions • Review: Animal Cell Structure and Function
   Questions Student Misconceptions • Reading Quiz • Multiple Choice • End-of-Chapter

2. **eText**
   Read your book online, search, take notes, highlight text, and more.

3. **The Study Area**
   Practice Tests • Cumulative Test • **BioFlix** 3-D Animations • MP3 Tutor Sessions • Videos • Activities • Investigations • Lab Media • Audio Glossary • Word Study Tools • Art

7
Membrane Structure and Function

▲ Figure 7.1 **How do cell membrane proteins help regulate chemical traffic?**

KEY CONCEPTS

7.1 Cellular membranes are fluid mosaics of lipids and proteins

7.2 Membrane structure results in selective permeability

7.3 Passive transport is diffusion of a substance across a membrane with no energy investment

7.4 Active transport uses energy to move solutes against their gradients

7.5 Bulk transport across the plasma membrane occurs by exocytosis and endocytosis

OVERVIEW

Life at the Edge

The plasma membrane is the edge of life, the boundary that separates the living cell from its surroundings. A remarkable film only about 8 nm thick—it would take over 8,000 plasma membranes to equal the thickness of this page—the plasma membrane controls traffic into and out of the cell it surrounds. Like all biological membranes, the plasma membrane exhibits **selective permeability**; that is, it allows some substances to cross it more easily than others. One of the earliest episodes in the evolution of life may have been the formation of a membrane that enclosed a solution different from the surrounding solution while still permitting the uptake of nutrients and elimination of waste products. The ability of the cell to discriminate in its chemical exchanges with its environment is fundamental to life, and it is the plasma membrane and its component molecules that make this selectivity possible.

In this chapter, you will learn how cellular membranes control the passage of substances. The image in **Figure 7.1** shows the elegant structure of a eukaryotic plasma membrane protein that plays a crucial role in nerve cell signaling. This protein provides a channel for a stream of potassium ions (K^+) to exit a nerve cell at a precise moment after nerve stimulation, restoring the cell's ability to fire again. (The orange ball in the center represents one potassium ion moving through the channel.) In this way, the plasma membrane and its proteins not only act as an outer boundary but also enable the cell to carry out its functions. The same applies to the many varieties of internal membranes that partition the eukaryotic cell: The molecular makeup of each membrane allows compartmentalized specialization in cells. To understand how membranes work, we'll begin by examining their architecture.

CONCEPT 7.1

Cellular membranes are fluid mosaics of lipids and proteins

Lipids and proteins are the staple ingredients of membranes, although carbohydrates are also important. The most abundant lipids in most membranes are phospholipids. The ability of phospholipids to form membranes is inherent in their molecular structure. A phospholipid is an **amphipathic** molecule, meaning it has both a hydrophilic region and a hydrophobic region (see Figure 5.12). Other types of membrane lipids are also amphipathic. Furthermore, most of the proteins within membranes have both hydrophobic and hydrophilic regions.

How are phospholipids and proteins arranged in the membranes of cells? In the **fluid mosaic model**, the membrane is a fluid structure with a "mosaic" of various proteins embedded in or attached to a double layer (bilayer) of phospholipids. Scientists propose models as hypotheses, ways of organizing and explaining existing information. Let's explore how the fluid mosaic model was developed.

Membrane Models: *Scientific Inquiry*

Scientists began building molecular models of the membrane decades before membranes were first seen with the electron microscope (in the 1950s). In 1915, membranes isolated from red blood cells were chemically analyzed and found to be composed of lipids and proteins. Ten years later, two Dutch scientists reasoned that cell membranes must be phospholipid bilayers. Such a double layer of molecules could exist as a stable boundary between two aqueous compartments because the molecular arrangement shelters the hydrophobic tails of the phospholipids from water while exposing the hydrophilic heads to water (Figure 7.2).

If a phospholipid bilayer was the main fabric of a membrane, where were the proteins located? Although the heads of phospholipids are hydrophilic, the surface of a pure phospholipid bilayer adheres less strongly to water than does the surface of a biological membrane. Given this difference, Hugh Davson and James Danielli suggested in 1935 that the membrane might be coated on both sides with hydrophilic proteins. They proposed a sandwich model: a phospholipid bilayer between two layers of proteins.

When researchers first used electron microscopes to study cells in the 1950s, the pictures seemed to support the Davson-Danielli model. By the late 1960s, however, many cell biologists recognized two problems with the model. First, inspection of a variety of membranes revealed that membranes with different functions differ in structure and chemical composition. A second, more serious problem became apparent once membrane proteins were better characterized. Unlike proteins dissolved in the cytosol, membrane proteins are not very soluble in water because they are amphipathic. If such proteins were layered on the surface of the membrane, their hydrophobic parts would be in aqueous surroundings.

Taking these observations into account, S. J. Singer and G. Nicolson proposed in 1972 that membrane proteins reside in the phospholipid bilayer with their hydrophilic regions protruding (Figure 7.3). This molecular arrangement would maximize contact of hydrophilic regions of proteins and

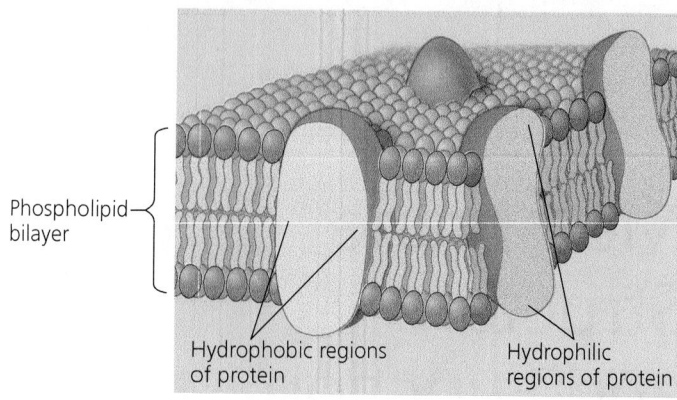

Phospholipid bilayer

Hydrophobic regions of protein

Hydrophilic regions of protein

▲ Figure 7.3 **The original fluid mosaic model for membranes.**

phospholipids with water in the cytosol and extracellular fluid, while providing their hydrophobic parts with a non-aqueous environment. In this fluid mosaic model, the membrane is a mosaic of protein molecules bobbing in a fluid bilayer of phospholipids.

A method of preparing cells for electron microscopy called freeze-fracture has demonstrated visually that proteins are indeed embedded in the phospholipid bilayer of the membrane (Figure 7.4). Freeze-fracture splits a membrane along the middle of the bilayer, somewhat like pulling apart a chunky peanut butter sandwich. When the membrane layers are viewed in the electron microscope, the interior of the

▼ Figure 7.4 **RESEARCH METHOD**

Freeze-fracture

APPLICATION A cell membrane can be split into its two layers, revealing the structure of the membrane's interior.

TECHNIQUE A cell is frozen and fractured with a knife. The fracture plane often follows the hydrophobic interior of a membrane, splitting the phospholipid bilayer into two separated layers. Each membrane protein goes wholly with one of the layers.

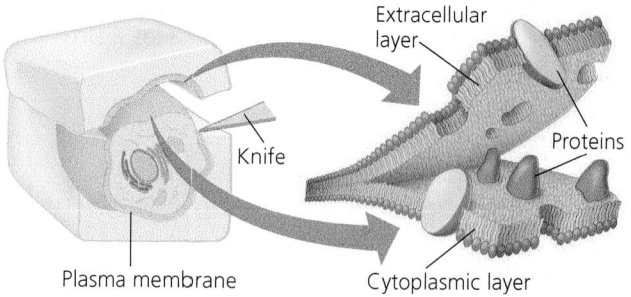

Extracellular layer

Proteins

Knife

Plasma membrane

Cytoplasmic layer

RESULTS These SEMs show membrane proteins (the "bumps") in the two layers, demonstrating that proteins are embedded in the phospholipid bilayer.

Inside of extracellular layer

Inside of cytoplasmic layer

▼ Figure 7.2 **Phospholipid bilayer (cross section).**

WATER

Hydrophilic head

Hydrophobic tail

WATER

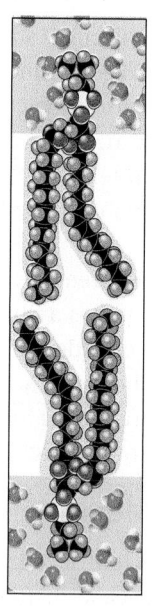

MAKE CONNECTIONS *Consulting Figure 5.12 (p. 76), circle the hydrophilic and hydrophobic portions of the enlarged phospholipids on the right. Explain what each portion contacts when the phospholipids are in the plasma membrane.*

Fibers of extra-
cellular matrix (ECM)

Glyco-
protein

Carbohydrate

Glycolipid

EXTRACELLULAR
SIDE OF
MEMBRANE

Cholesterol

Microfilaments
of cytoskeleton

Peripheral
proteins

Integral
protein

CYTOPLASMIC SIDE
OF MEMBRANE

▲ **Figure 7.5 Updated model of an animal cell's plasma membrane (cutaway view).**

bilayer appears cobblestoned, with protein particles interspersed in a smooth matrix, in agreement with the fluid mosaic model. Some proteins remain attached to one layer or the other, like the peanut chunks in the sandwich.

Because models are hypotheses, replacing one model of membrane structure with another does not imply that the original model was worthless. The acceptance or rejection of a model depends on how well it fits observations and explains experimental results. New findings may make a model obsolete; even then, it may not be totally scrapped, but revised to incorporate the new observations. The fluid mosaic model is continually being refined. For example, groups of proteins are often found associated in long-lasting, specialized patches, where they carry out common functions. The lipids themselves appear to form defined regions as well. Also, the membrane may be much more packed with proteins than imagined in the classic fluid mosaic model—compare the updated model in **Figure 7.5** with the original model in Figure 7.3. Let's now take a closer look at membrane structure.

The Fluidity of Membranes

Membranes are not static sheets of molecules locked rigidly in place. A membrane is held together primarily by hydrophobic interactions, which are much weaker than covalent bonds (see Figure 5.20). Most of the lipids and some of

the proteins can shift about laterally—that is, in the plane of the membrane, like partygoers elbowing their way through a crowded room **(Figure 7.6)**. It is quite rare, however, for a molecule to flip-flop transversely across the membrane, switching from one phospholipid layer to the other; to do so, the hydrophilic part of the molecule must cross the hydrophobic interior of the membrane.

The lateral movement of phospholipids within the membrane is rapid. Adjacent phospholipids switch positions about 10^7 times per second, which means that a phospholipid can travel about 2 μm—the length of many bacterial cells—in 1 second. Proteins are much larger than lipids and move more slowly, but some membrane proteins do drift, as shown in a classic experiment described in **Figure 7.7**, on the next page.

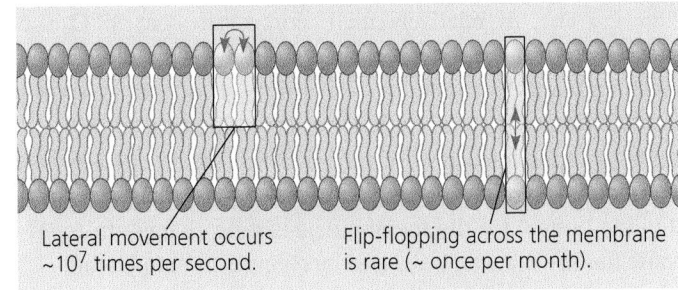

Lateral movement occurs
~10^7 times per second.

Flip-flopping across the membrane
is rare (~ once per month).

▲ **Figure 7.6 The movement of phospholipids.**

INQUIRY

Do membrane proteins move?

EXPERIMENT Larry Frye and Michael Edidin, at Johns Hopkins University, labeled the plasma membrane proteins of a mouse cell and a human cell with two different markers and fused the cells. Using a microscope, they observed the markers on the hybrid cell.

RESULTS

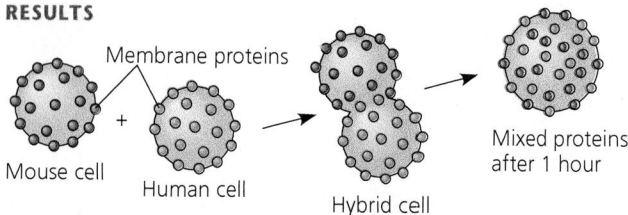

Membrane proteins

Mouse cell + Human cell → Hybrid cell → Mixed proteins after 1 hour

CONCLUSION The mixing of the mouse and human membrane proteins indicates that at least some membrane proteins move sideways within the plane of the plasma membrane.

SOURCE L. D. Frye and M. Edidin, The rapid intermixing of cell surface antigens after formation of mouse-human heterokaryons, *Journal of Cell Science* 7:319 (1970).

WHAT IF? Suppose the proteins did not mix in the hybrid cell, even many hours after fusion. Would you be able to conclude that proteins don't move within the membrane? What other explanation could there be?

And some membrane proteins seem to move in a highly directed manner, perhaps driven along cytoskeletal fibers by motor proteins connected to the membrane proteins' cytoplasmic regions. However, many other membrane proteins seem to be held immobile by their attachment to the cytoskeleton or to the extracellular matrix (see Figure 7.5).

A membrane remains fluid as temperature decreases until finally the phospholipids settle into a closely packed arrangement and the membrane solidifies, much as bacon grease forms lard when it cools. The temperature at which a membrane solidifies depends on the types of lipids it is made of. The membrane remains fluid to a lower temperature if it is rich in phospholipids with unsaturated hydrocarbon tails (see Figures 5.11 and 5.12). Because of kinks in the tails where double bonds are located, unsaturated hydrocarbon tails cannot pack together as closely as saturated hydrocarbon tails, and this makes the membrane more fluid (Figure 7.8a).

The steroid cholesterol, which is wedged between phospholipid molecules in the plasma membranes of animal cells, has different effects on membrane fluidity at different temperatures (Figure 7.8b). At relatively high temperatures—at 37°C, the body temperature of humans, for example—cholesterol makes the membrane less fluid by restraining phospholipid movement. However, because cholesterol also hinders the close packing of phospholipids, it lowers the temperature required for the membrane to solidify. Thus, cholesterol can be thought of as a "fluidity buffer" for the membrane, resisting changes in membrane fluidity that can be caused by changes in temperature.

Membranes must be fluid to work properly; they are usually about as fluid as salad oil. When a membrane solidifies,

its permeability changes, and enzymatic proteins in the membrane may become inactive if their activity requires them to be able to move within the membrane. However, membranes that are too fluid cannot support protein function either. Therefore, extreme environments pose a challenge for life, resulting in evolutionary adaptations that include differences in membrane lipid composition.

Evolution of Differences in Membrane Lipid Composition

EVOLUTION Variations in the cell membrane lipid compositions of many species appear to be evolutionary adaptations that maintain the appropriate membrane fluidity under specific environmental conditions. For instance, fishes that live in extreme cold have membranes with a high proportion of unsaturated hydrocarbon tails, enabling their membranes to remain fluid (see Figure 7.8a). At the other extreme, some bacteria and archaea thrive at temperatures greater than 90°C (194°F) in thermal hot springs and geysers. Their membranes include unusual lipids that may prevent excessive fluidity at such high temperatures.

The ability to change the lipid composition of cell membranes in response to changing temperatures has evolved in organisms that live where temperatures vary. In many plants that tolerate extreme cold, such as winter wheat, the percentage of unsaturated phospholipids increases in autumn, an adjustment that keeps the membranes from solidifying during winter. Certain bacteria and archaea can also change the proportion of unsaturated phospholipids in their cell membranes, depending on the temperature at which they are growing. Overall, natural selection has apparently favored organisms whose mix of membrane lipids ensures an appropriate level of membrane fluidity for their environment.

Fluid — Unsaturated hydrocarbon tails (kinked) prevent packing, enhancing membrane fluidity.

Viscous — Saturated hydrocarbon tails pack together, increasing membrane viscosity.

(a) Unsaturated versus saturated hydrocarbon tails.

(b) Cholesterol within the animal cell membrane. Cholesterol reduces membrane fluidity at moderate temperatures by reducing phospholipid movement, but at low temperatures it hinders solidification by disrupting the regular packing of phospholipids.

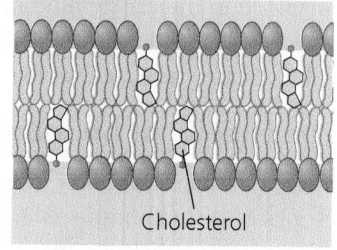

Cholesterol

▲ **Figure 7.8 Factors that affect membrane fluidity.**

Membrane Proteins and Their Functions

Now we come to the *mosaic* aspect of the fluid mosaic model. Somewhat like a tile mosaic, a membrane is a collage of different proteins, often clustered together in groups, embedded in the fluid matrix of the lipid bilayer (see Figure 7.5). More than 50 kinds of proteins have been found so far in the plasma membrane of red blood cells, for example. Phospholipids form the main fabric of the membrane, but proteins determine most of the membrane's functions. Different types of cells contain different sets of membrane proteins, and the various membranes within a cell each have a unique collection of proteins.

Notice in Figure 7.5 that there are two major populations of membrane proteins: integral proteins and peripheral proteins. **Integral proteins** penetrate the hydrophobic interior of the lipid bilayer. The majority are *transmembrane proteins*, which span the membrane; other integral proteins extend only partway into the hydrophobic interior. The hydrophobic regions of an integral protein consist of one or more stretches of nonpolar amino acids (see Figure 5.16), usually coiled into α helices (**Figure 7.9**). The hydrophilic parts of the molecule are exposed to the aqueous solutions on either side of the membrane. Some proteins also have a hydrophilic channel through their center that allows passage of hydrophilic substances (see Figure 7.1). **Peripheral proteins** are not embedded in the lipid bilayer at all; they are appendages loosely bound to the surface of the membrane, often to exposed parts of integral proteins (see Figure 7.5).

On the cytoplasmic side of the plasma membrane, some membrane proteins are held in place by attachment to the cytoskeleton. And on the extracellular side, certain membrane proteins are attached to fibers of the extracellular matrix (see Figure 6.30; *integrins* are one type of integral protein). These attachments combine to give animal cells a stronger framework than the plasma membrane alone could provide.

Figure 7.10 gives an overview of six major functions performed by proteins of the plasma membrane. A single cell

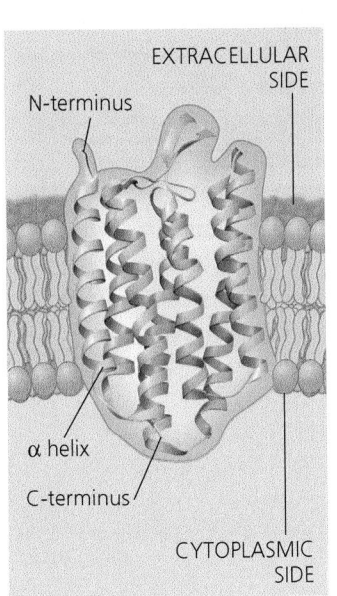

Figure 7.9 The structure of a transmembrane protein. Bacteriorhodopsin (a bacterial transport protein) has a distinct orientation in the membrane, with its N-terminus outside the cell and its C-terminus inside. This ribbon model highlights the α-helical secondary structure of the hydrophobic parts, which lie mostly within the hydrophobic interior of the membrane. The protein includes seven transmembrane helices. The nonhelical hydrophilic segments are in contact with the aqueous solutions on the extracellular and cytoplasmic sides of the membrane.

EXTRACELLULAR SIDE
N-terminus
α helix
C-terminus
CYTOPLASMIC SIDE

(a) Transport. *Left:* A protein that spans the membrane may provide a hydrophilic channel across the membrane that is selective for a particular solute. *Right:* Other transport proteins shuttle a substance from one side to the other by changing shape (see Figure 7.17). Some of these proteins hydrolyze ATP as an energy source to actively pump substances across the membrane.

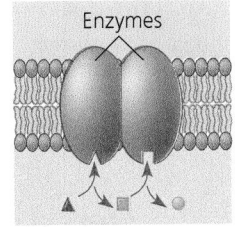

(b) Enzymatic activity. A protein built into the membrane may be an enzyme with its active site exposed to substances in the adjacent solution. In some cases, several enzymes in a membrane are organized as a team that carries out sequential steps of a metabolic pathway.

Enzymes

(c) Signal transduction. A membrane protein (receptor) may have a binding site with a specific shape that fits the shape of a chemical messenger, such as a hormone. The external messenger (signaling molecule) may cause the protein to change shape, allowing it to relay the message to the inside of the cell, usually by binding to a cytoplasmic protein (see Figure 11.6).

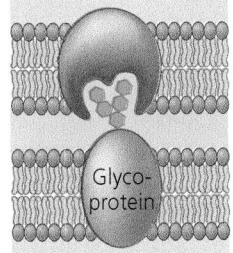

Signaling molecule
Receptor
Signal transduction

(d) Cell-cell recognition. Some glycoproteins serve as identification tags that are specifically recognized by membrane proteins of other cells. This type of cell-cell binding is usually short-lived compared to that shown in (e).

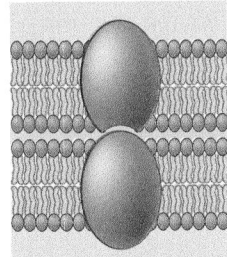

Glycoprotein

(e) Intercellular joining. Membrane proteins of adjacent cells may hook together in various kinds of junctions, such as gap junctions or tight junctions (see Figure 6.32). This type of binding is more long-lasting than that shown in (d).

(f) Attachment to the cytoskeleton and extracellular matrix (ECM). Microfilaments or other elements of the cytoskeleton may be noncovalently bound to membrane proteins, a function that helps maintain cell shape and stabilizes the location of certain membrane proteins. Proteins that can bind to ECM molecules can coordinate extracellular and intracellular changes (see Figure 6.30).

Figure 7.10 Some functions of membrane proteins. In many cases, a single protein performs multiple tasks.

? *Some transmembrane proteins can bind to a particular ECM molecule and, when bound, transmit a signal into the cell. Use the proteins shown here to explain how this might occur.*

IMPACT

Blocking HIV Entry into Cells as a Treatment for HIV Infections

Despite multiple exposures to HIV, a small number of people do not develop AIDS and show no evidence of HIV-infected cells. Comparing their genes with the genes of infected individuals, researchers discovered that resistant individuals have an unusual form of a gene that codes for an immune cell-surface protein called CCR5. Further work showed that HIV binds to a main protein receptor (CD4) on an immune cell, but on most cell types, HIV also needs to bind to CCR5 as a "co-receptor" to infect the cell (below, left). An absence of CCR5 on the cells of resistant individuals, due to the gene alteration, prevents the virus from entering the cells (below, right).

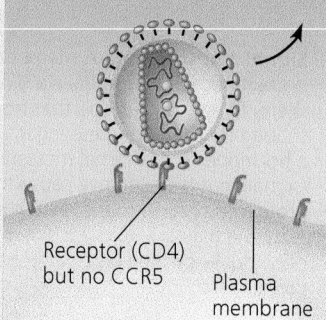

HIV can infect a cell that has CCR5 on its surface, as in most people.

HIV cannot infect a cell lacking CCR5 on its surface, as in resistant individuals.

WHY IT MATTERS Researchers have been searching for drugs to block cell-surface receptors involved in HIV infection. The main receptor protein, CD4, performs many important functions for cells, so interfering with it could cause dangerous side effects. Discovery of the CCR5 co-receptor provided a safer target for development of drugs that mask CCR5 and block HIV entry. One such drug, maraviroc (brand name Selzentry), was approved for treatment of HIV infection in 2007.

FURTHER READING T. Kenakin, New bull's-eyes for drugs, *Scientific American* 293(4):50–57 (2005).

MAKE CONNECTIONS Study Figures 2.18 (p. 42) and 5.19 (p. 81), both of which show pairs of molecules binding to each other. What would you predict about CCR5 that would allow HIV to bind to it? How could a drug molecule interfere with this binding?

---

may have membrane proteins carrying out several of these functions, and a single membrane protein may have multiple functions. In this way, the membrane is a functional mosaic as well as a structural one.

Proteins on the surface of a cell are important in the medical field because some proteins can help outside agents invade the cell. For example, cell-surface proteins help the human immunodeficiency virus (HIV) infect immune system cells, leading to acquired immune deficiency syndrome (AIDS). (You'll read more about HIV in Chapter 19.) Learning about the proteins that HIV binds to on immune cells has been central to developing a treatment for HIV infection (Figure 7.11).

The Role of Membrane Carbohydrates in Cell-Cell Recognition

Cell-cell recognition, a cell's ability to distinguish one type of neighboring cell from another, is crucial to the functioning of an organism. It is important, for example, in the sorting of cells into tissues and organs in an animal embryo. It is also the basis for the rejection of foreign cells by the immune system, an important line of defense in vertebrate animals (see Chapter 43). Cells recognize other cells by binding to molecules, often containing carbohydrates, on the extracellular surface of the plasma membrane (see Figure 7.10d).

Membrane carbohydrates are usually short, branched chains of fewer than 15 sugar units. Some are covalently bonded to lipids, forming molecules called **glycolipids**. (Recall that *glyco* refers to the presence of carbohydrate.) However, most are covalently bonded to proteins, which are thereby **glycoproteins** (see Figure 7.5).

The carbohydrates on the extracellular side of the plasma membrane vary from species to species, among individuals of the same species, and even from one cell type to another in a single individual. The diversity of the molecules and their location on the cell's surface enable membrane carbohydrates to function as markers that distinguish one cell from another. For example, the four human blood types designated A, B, AB, and O reflect variation in the carbohydrate part of glycoproteins on the surface of red blood cells.

Synthesis and Sidedness of Membranes

Membranes have distinct inside and outside faces. The two lipid layers may differ in specific lipid composition, and each protein has directional orientation in the membrane (see Figure 7.9). **Figure 7.12** shows how membrane sidedness arises: The asymmetrical arrangement of proteins, lipids, and their associated carbohydrates in the plasma membrane is determined as the membrane is being built by the endoplasmic reticulum (ER) and Golgi apparatus.

CONCEPT CHECK 7.1

1. The carbohydrates attached to some proteins and lipids of the plasma membrane are added as the membrane is made and refined in the ER and Golgi apparatus. The new membrane then forms transport vesicles that travel to the cell surface. On which side of the vesicle membrane are the carbohydrates?

2. **WHAT IF?** The soil immediately around hot springs is much warmer than that in neighboring regions. Two closely related species of native grasses are found, one in the warmer region and one in the cooler region. If you analyzed their membrane lipid compositions, what would you expect to find? Explain.

For suggested answers, see Appendix A.

❶ Membrane proteins and lipids are synthesized in the endoplasmic reticulum (ER). Carbohydrates (green) are added to the transmembrane proteins (purple dumbbells), making them glycoproteins. The carbohydrate portions may then be modified.

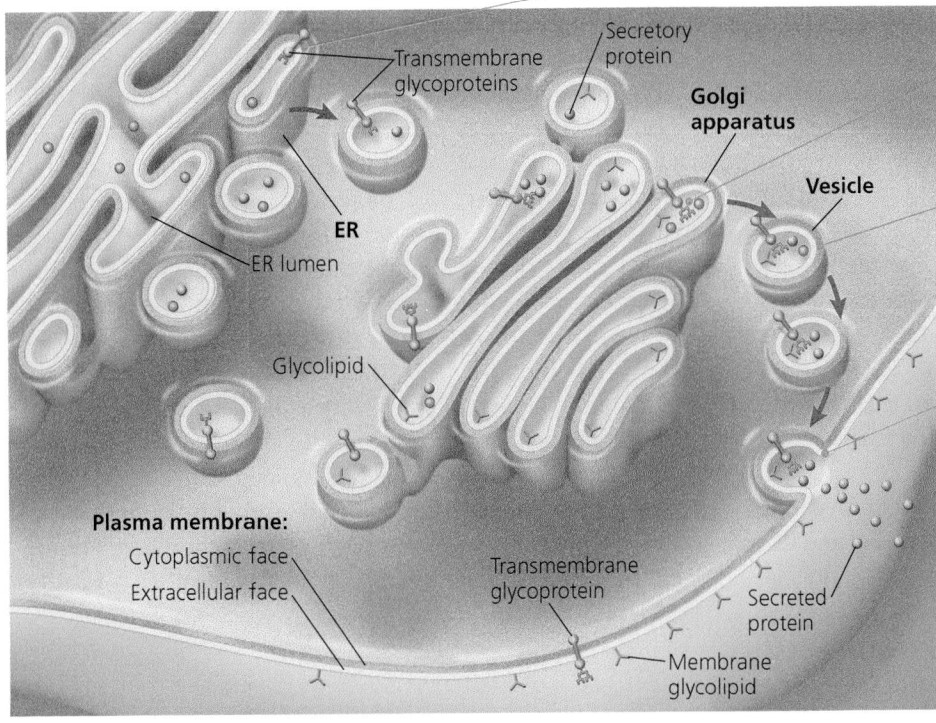

❷ Inside the Golgi apparatus, the glycoproteins undergo further carbo-hydrate modification, and lipids acquire carbohydrates, becoming glycolipids.

❸ The glycoproteins, glycolipids, and secretory proteins (purple spheres) are transported in vesicles to the plasma membrane.

❹ As vesicles fuse with the plasma membrane, the outside face of the vesicle becomes continuous with the inside (cytoplasmic) face of the plasma membrane. This releases the secretory proteins from the cell, a process called *exocytosis*, and positions the carbohydrates of membrane glycoproteins and glycolipids on the outside (extracellular) face of the plasma membrane.

DRAW IT *Draw an integral membrane protein extending from partway through the ER membrane into the ER lumen. Next, draw the protein where it would be located in a series of numbered steps ending at the plasma membrane. Would the protein contact the cytoplasm or the extracellular fluid?*

CONCEPT 7.2

Membrane structure results in selective permeability

The biological membrane is an exquisite example of a supramolecular structure—many molecules ordered into a higher level of organization—with emergent properties beyond those of the individual molecules. The remainder of this chapter focuses on one of the most important of those properties: the ability to regulate transport across cellular boundaries, a function essential to the cell's existence. We will see once again that form fits function: The fluid mosaic model helps explain how membranes regulate the cell's molecular traffic.

A steady traffic of small molecules and ions moves across the plasma membrane in both directions. Consider the chemical exchanges between a muscle cell and the extracellular fluid that bathes it. Sugars, amino acids, and other nutrients enter the cell, and metabolic waste products leave it. The cell takes in O_2 for use in cellular respiration and expels CO_2. Also, the cell regulates its concentrations of inorganic ions, such as Na^+, K^+, Ca^{2+}, and Cl^-, by shuttling them one way or the other across the plasma membrane. In spite of heavy traffic through them, cell membranes are selectively permeable, and substances do not cross the barrier indiscriminately. The cell is able to take up some small molecules and ions and exclude others. Also, substances that move through the membrane do so at different rates.

The Permeability of the Lipid Bilayer

Nonpolar molecules, such as hydrocarbons, carbon dioxide, and oxygen, are hydrophobic and can therefore dissolve in the lipid bilayer of the membrane and cross it easily, without the aid of membrane proteins. However, the hydrophobic interior of the membrane impedes the direct passage of ions and polar molecules, which are hydrophilic, through the membrane. Polar molecules such as glucose and other sugars pass only slowly through a lipid bilayer, and even water, an extremely small polar molecule, does not cross very rapidly. A charged atom or molecule and its surrounding shell of water (see Figure 3.7) find the hydrophobic interior of the membrane even more difficult to penetrate. Furthermore, the lipid bilayer is only one aspect of the gatekeeper system responsible for the selective permeability of a cell. Proteins built into the membrane play key roles in regulating transport.

Transport Proteins

Cell membranes *are* permeable to specific ions and a variety of polar molecules. These hydrophilic substances can avoid contact with the lipid bilayer by passing through **transport proteins** that span the membrane.

Some transport proteins, called *channel proteins*, function by having a hydrophilic channel that certain molecules or atomic ions use as a tunnel through the membrane (see Figure 7.10a, left). For example, the passage of water molecules through the membrane in certain cells is greatly facilitated by channel proteins known as **aquaporins**. Each aquaporin allows entry of up to *3 billion* (3×10^9) water molecules per second, passing single file through its central channel, which fits ten at a time. Without aquaporins, only a tiny fraction of these water molecules would pass through the same area of the cell membrane in a second, so the channel protein brings about a tremendous increase in rate. Other transport proteins, called *carrier proteins*, hold onto their passengers and change shape in a way that shuttles them across the membrane (see Figure 7.10a, right). A transport protein is specific for the substance it translocates (moves), allowing only a certain substance (or a small group of related substances) to cross the membrane. For example, a specific carrier protein in the plasma membrane of red blood cells transports glucose across the membrane 50,000 times faster than glucose can pass through on its own. This "glucose transporter" is so selective that it even rejects fructose, a structural isomer of glucose.

Thus, the selective permeability of a membrane depends on both the discriminating barrier of the lipid bilayer and the specific transport proteins built into the membrane. But what establishes the *direction* of traffic across a membrane? At a given time, what determines whether a particular substance will enter the cell or leave the cell? And what mechanisms actually drive molecules across membranes? We will address these questions next as we explore two modes of membrane traffic: passive transport and active transport.

CONCEPT CHECK 7.2

1. Two molecules that can cross a lipid bilayer without help from membrane proteins are O_2 and CO_2. What property allows this to occur?
2. Why is a transport protein needed to move water molecules rapidly and in large quantities across a membrane?
3. **MAKE CONNECTIONS** Aquaporins exclude passage of hydronium ions (H_3O^+; see pp. 52–53). Recent research on fat metabolism has shown that some aquaporins allow passage of glycerol, a three-carbon alcohol (see Figure 5.10, p. 75), as well as H_2O. Since H_3O^+ is much closer in size to water than is glycerol, what do you suppose is the basis of this selectivity?

For suggested answers, see Appendix A.

CONCEPT 7.3

Passive transport is diffusion of a substance across a membrane with no energy investment

Molecules have a type of energy called thermal energy (heat), due to their constant motion. One result of this motion is **diffusion**, the movement of molecules of any substance so that they spread out evenly into the available space. Each molecule moves randomly, yet diffusion of a *population* of molecules may be directional. To understand this process, let's imagine a synthetic membrane separating pure water from a solution of a dye in water. Study Figure 7.13a carefully to appreciate how diffusion would result in both solutions having equal concentrations of the dye molecules. Once that point is reached, there will be a dynamic equilibrium, with as many dye molecules crossing the membrane each second in one direction as in the other.

We can now state a simple rule of diffusion: In the absence of other forces, a substance will diffuse from where it is more concentrated to where it is less concentrated. Put another way, any substance will diffuse down its **concentration gradient**, the region along which the density of a chemical substance increases or decreases (in this case, decreases). No work must be done to make this happen; diffusion is a spontaneous process, needing no input of energy. Note that each substance diffuses down its *own* concentration gradient, unaffected by the concentration gradients of other substances (Figure 7.13b).

(a) **Diffusion of one solute.** The membrane has pores large enough for molecules of dye to pass through. Random movement of dye molecules will cause some to pass through the pores; this will happen more often on the side with more dye molecules. The dye diffuses from where it is more concentrated to where it is less concentrated (called diffusing down a concentration gradient). This leads to a dynamic equilibrium: The solute molecules continue to cross the membrane, but at equal rates in both directions.

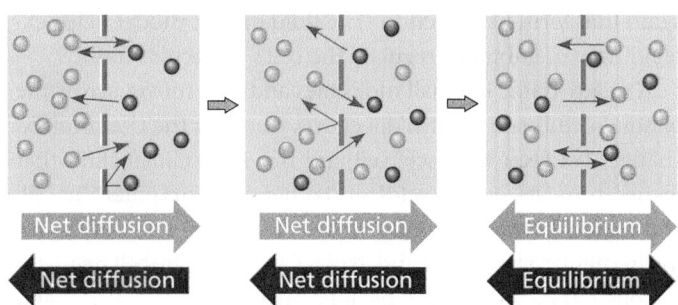

(b) **Diffusion of two solutes.** Solutions of two different dyes are separated by a membrane that is permeable to both. Each dye diffuses down its own concentration gradient. There will be a net diffusion of the purple dye toward the left, even though the *total* solute concentration was initially greater on the left side.

▲ **Figure 7.13 The diffusion of solutes across a synthetic membrane.** Each of the large arrows under the diagrams shows the net diffusion of the dye molecules of that color.

Much of the traffic across cell membranes occurs by diffusion. When a substance is more concentrated on one side of a membrane than on the other, there is a tendency for the substance to diffuse across the membrane down its concentration gradient (assuming that the membrane is permeable to that substance). One important example is the uptake of oxygen by a cell performing cellular respiration. Dissolved oxygen diffuses into the cell across the plasma membrane. As long as cellular respiration consumes the O_2 as it enters, diffusion into the cell will continue because the concentration gradient favors movement in that direction.

The diffusion of a substance across a biological membrane is called **passive transport** because the cell does not have to expend energy to make it happen. The concentration gradient itself represents potential energy (see Chapter 2, p. 35) and drives diffusion. Remember, however, that membranes are selectively permeable and therefore have different effects on the rates of diffusion of various molecules. In the case of water, aquaporins allow water to diffuse very rapidly across the membranes of certain cells. As we'll see next, the movement of water across the plasma membrane has important consequences for cells.

Effects of Osmosis on Water Balance

To see how two solutions with different solute concentrations interact, picture a U-shaped glass tube with a selectively permeable artificial membrane separating two sugar solutions (Figure 7.14). Pores in this synthetic membrane are too small for sugar molecules to pass through but large enough for water molecules. How does this affect the *water* concentration? It seems logical that the solution with the higher concentration of solute would have the lower concentration of water and that water would diffuse into it from the other side for that reason. However, for a dilute solution like most biological fluids, solutes do not affect the water concentration significantly. Instead, tight clustering of water molecules around the hydrophilic solute molecules makes some of the water unavailable to cross the membrane. It is the difference in *free* water concentration that is important. In the end, the effect is the same: Water diffuses across the membrane from the region of lower solute concentration (higher free water concentration) to that of higher solute concentration (lower free water concentration) until the solute concentrations on both sides of the membrane are equal. The diffusion of free water across a selectively permeable membrane, whether artificial or cellular, is called **osmosis**. The movement of water across cell membranes and the balance of water between the cell and its environment are crucial to organisms. Let's now apply to living cells what we have learned about osmosis in artificial systems.

Water Balance of Cells Without Walls

To explain the behavior of a cell in a solution, we must consider both solute concentration and membrane permeability.

▲ **Figure 7.14** **Osmosis.** Two sugar solutions of different concentrations are separated by a membrane that the solvent (water) can pass through but the solute (sugar) cannot. Water molecules move randomly and may cross in either direction, but overall, water diffuses from the solution with less concentrated solute to that with more concentrated solute. This diffusion of water, or osmosis, equalizes the sugar concentrations on both sides.

WHAT IF? *If an orange dye capable of passing through the membrane was added to the left side of the tube above, how would it be distributed at the end of the experiment? (See Figure 7.13.) Would the final solution levels in the tube be affected?*

Both factors are taken into account in the concept of **tonicity**, the ability of a surrounding solution to cause a cell to gain or lose water. The tonicity of a solution depends in part on its concentration of solutes that cannot cross the membrane (nonpenetrating solutes) relative to that inside the cell. If there is a higher concentration of nonpenetrating solutes in the surrounding solution, water will tend to leave the cell, and vice versa.

If a cell without a wall, such as an animal cell, is immersed in an environment that is **isotonic** to the cell (*iso* means "same"), there will be no *net* movement of water across the plasma membrane. Water diffuses across the membrane, but at the same rate in both directions. In an isotonic environment, the volume of an animal cell is stable (**Figure 7.15a**, on the next page).

Now let's transfer the cell to a solution that is **hypertonic** to the cell (*hyper* means "more," in this case referring to nonpenetrating solutes). The cell will lose water, shrivel, and probably die. This is one way an increase in the salinity (saltiness) of a lake can kill animals there; if the lake water becomes hypertonic to the animals' cells, the cells might shrivel and

(a) Animal cell. An animal cell fares best in an isotonic environment unless it has special adaptations that offset the osmotic uptake or loss of water.

Hypotonic solution	Isotonic solution	Hypertonic solution

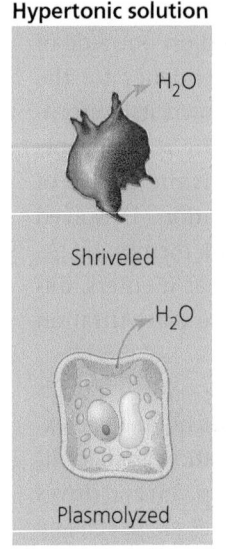

(b) Plant cell. Plant cells are turgid (firm) and generally healthiest in a hypotonic environment, where the uptake of water is eventually balanced by the wall pushing back on the cell.

▲ **Figure 7.15** **The water balance of living cells.** How living cells react to changes in the solute concentration of their environment depends on whether or not they have cell walls. **(a)** Animal cells, such as this red blood cell, do not have cell walls. **(b)** Plant cells do. (Arrows indicate net water movement after the cells were first placed in these solutions.)

die. However, taking up too much water can be just as hazardous to an animal cell as losing water. If we place the cell in a solution that is **hypotonic** to the cell (*hypo* means "less"), water will enter the cell faster than it leaves, and the cell will swell and lyse (burst) like an overfilled water balloon.

A cell without rigid walls can tolerate neither excessive uptake nor excessive loss of water. This problem of water balance is automatically solved if such a cell lives in isotonic surroundings. Seawater is isotonic to many marine invertebrates. The cells of most terrestrial (land-dwelling) animals are bathed in an extracellular fluid that is isotonic to the cells. In hypertonic or hypotonic environments, however, organisms that lack rigid cell walls must have other adaptations for **osmoregulation**, the control of solute concentrations and water balance. For example, the unicellular protist *Paramecium caudatum* lives in pond water, which is hypotonic to the cell. *P. caudatum* has a plasma membrane that is much less permeable to water than the membranes of most other cells, but this only slows the uptake of water, which continually enters the cell. The *P. caudatum*

Contractile vacuole   50 μm

▲ **Figure 7.16** **The contractile vacuole of *Paramecium caudatum*.** The vacuole collects fluid from a system of canals in the cytoplasm. When full, the vacuole and canals contract, expelling fluid from the cell (LM).

cell doesn't burst because it is also equipped with a contractile vacuole, an organelle that functions as a bilge pump to force water out of the cell as fast as it enters by osmosis **(Figure 7.16)**. We will examine other evolutionary adaptations for osmoregulation in Chapter 44.

Water Balance of Cells with Walls

The cells of plants, prokaryotes, fungi, and some protists are surrounded by walls (see Figure 6.28). When such a cell is immersed in a hypotonic solution— bathed in rainwater, for example—the wall helps maintain the cell's water balance. Consider a plant cell. Like an animal cell, the plant cell swells as water enters by osmosis **(Figure 7.15b)**. However, the relatively inelastic wall will expand only so much before it exerts a back pressure on the cell, called *turgor pressure*, that opposes further water uptake. At this point, the cell is **turgid** (very firm), which is the healthy state for most plant cells. Plants that are not woody, such as most houseplants, depend for mechanical support on cells kept turgid by a surrounding hypotonic solution. If a plant's cells and their surroundings are isotonic, there is no net tendency for water to enter, and the cells become **flaccid** (limp).

However, a wall is of no advantage if the cell is immersed in a hypertonic environment. In this case, a plant cell, like an animal cell, will lose water to its surroundings and shrink. As the plant cell shrivels, its plasma membrane pulls away from the wall. This phenomenon, called **plasmolysis**, causes the plant to wilt and can lead to plant death. The walled cells of bacteria and fungi also plasmolyze in hypertonic environments.

Facilitated Diffusion: Passive Transport Aided by Proteins

Let's look more closely at how water and certain hydrophilic solutes cross a membrane. As mentioned earlier, many polar molecules and ions impeded by the lipid bilayer of the membrane diffuse passively with the help of transport proteins that span the membrane. This phenomenon is called **facilitated diffusion**. Cell biologists are still trying to learn exactly how various transport proteins facilitate diffusion. Most transport proteins are very specific: They transport some substances but not others.

As described earlier, the two types of transport proteins are channel proteins and carrier proteins. Channel proteins simply provide corridors that allow specific molecules or ions to cross the membrane **(Figure 7.17a)**. The hydrophilic passageways

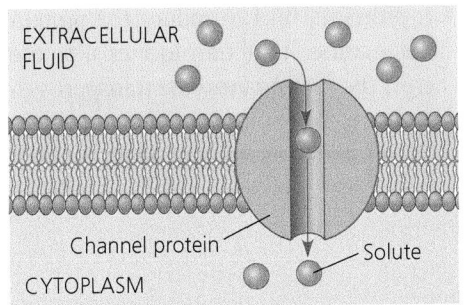

EXTRACELLULAR FLUID

Channel protein

CYTOPLASM

Solute

(a) A channel protein (purple) has a channel through which water molecules or a specific solute can pass.

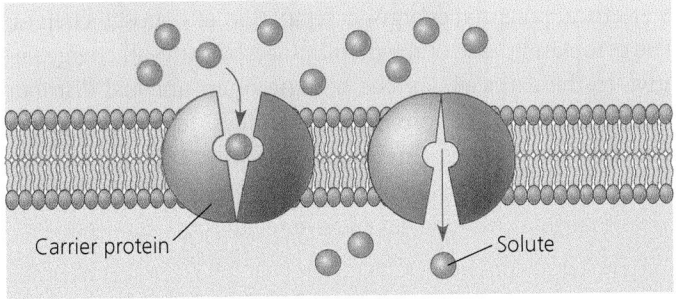

Carrier protein

Solute

(b) A carrier protein alternates between two shapes, moving a solute across the membrane during the shape change.

▲ **Figure 7.17 Two types of transport proteins that carry out facilitated diffusion.** In both cases, the protein can transport the solute in either direction, but the net movement is down the concentration gradient of the solute.

provided by these proteins can allow water molecules or small ions to diffuse very quickly from one side of the membrane to the other. Aquaporins, the water channel proteins, facilitate the massive amounts of diffusion that occur in plant cells and in animal cells such as red blood cells (see Figure 7.15). Certain kidney cells also have a high number of aquaporins, allowing them to reclaim water from urine before it is excreted. If the kidneys did not perform this function, you would excrete about 180 L of urine per day—and have to drink an equal volume of water!

Channel proteins that transport ions are called **ion channels**. Many ion channels function as **gated channels**, which open or close in response to a stimulus. For some gated channels, the stimulus is electrical. The ion channel shown in Figure 7.1, for example, opens in response to an electrical stimulus, allowing potassium ions to leave the cell. Other gated channels open or close when a specific substance other than the one to be transported binds to the channel. Both types of gated channels are important in the functioning of the nervous system, as you'll learn in Chapter 48.

Carrier proteins, such as the glucose transporter mentioned earlier, seem to undergo a subtle change in shape that somehow translocates the solute-binding site across the membrane **(Figure 7.17b)**. Such a change in shape may be triggered by the binding and release of the transported molecule. Like ion channels, carrier proteins involved in facilitated diffusion result in the net movement of a substance down its concentration gradient. No energy input is thus required: This is passive transport.

In certain inherited diseases, specific transport systems are either defective or missing altogether. An example is cystinuria, a human disease characterized by the absence of a carrier protein that transports cysteine and some other amino acids across the membranes of kidney cells. Kidney cells normally reabsorb these amino acids from the urine and return them to the blood, but an individual afflicted with cystinuria develops painful stones from amino acids that accumulate and crystallize in the kidneys.

CONCEPT CHECK 7.3

1. How do you think a cell performing cellular respiration rids itself of the resulting CO_2?
2. In the supermarket, produce is often sprayed with water. Explain why this makes vegetables look crisp.
3. **WHAT IF?** If a *Paramecium caudatum* swims from a hypotonic to an isotonic environment, will its contractile vacuole become more active or less? Why?

For suggested answers, see Appendix A.

CONCEPT 7.4

Active transport uses energy to move solutes against their gradients

Despite the help of transport proteins, facilitated diffusion is considered passive transport because the solute is moving down its concentration gradient, a process that requires no energy. Facilitated diffusion speeds transport of a solute by providing efficient passage through the membrane, but it does not alter the direction of transport. Some transport proteins, however, can move solutes against their concentration gradients, across the plasma membrane from the side where they are less concentrated (whether inside or outside) to the side where they are more concentrated.

The Need for Energy in Active Transport

To pump a solute across a membrane against its gradient requires work; the cell must expend energy. Therefore, this type of membrane traffic is called **active transport**. The transport proteins that move solutes against their concentration gradients are all carrier proteins rather than channel proteins. This makes sense because when channel proteins are open, they merely allow solutes to diffuse down their concentration gradients rather than picking them up and transporting them against their gradients.

Active transport enables a cell to maintain internal concentrations of small solutes that differ from concentrations in its environment. For example, compared with its surroundings,

① Cytoplasmic Na⁺ binds to the sodium-potassium pump. The affinity for Na⁺ is high when the protein has this shape.

② Na⁺ binding stimulates phosphorylation by ATP.

⑥ K⁺ is released; affinity for Na⁺ is high again, and the cycle repeats.

③ Phosphorylation leads to a change in protein shape, reducing its affinity for Na⁺, which is released outside.

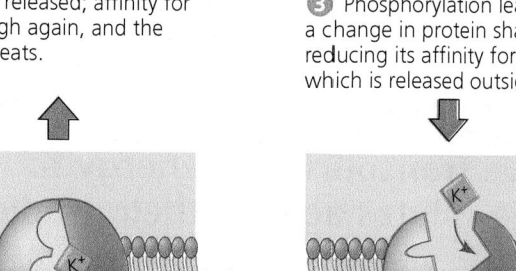

⑤ Loss of the phosphate group restores the protein's original shape, which has a lower affinity for K⁺.

④ The new shape has a high affinity for K⁺, which binds on the extracellular side and triggers release of the phosphate group.

▲ **Figure 7.18 The sodium-potassium pump: a specific case of active transport.** This transport system pumps ions against steep concentration gradients: Sodium ion concentration ([Na⁺]) is high outside the cell and low inside, while potassium ion concentration ([K⁺]) is low outside the cell and high inside. The pump oscillates between two shapes in a cycle that moves 3 Na⁺ out of the cell for every 2 K⁺ pumped into the cell. The two shapes have different affinities for Na⁺ and K⁺. ATP powers the shape change by transferring a phosphate group to the transport protein (phosphorylating the protein).

an animal cell has a much higher concentration of potassium ions (K⁺) and a much lower concentration of sodium ions (Na⁺). The plasma membrane helps maintain these steep gradients by pumping Na⁺ out of the cell and K⁺ into the cell.

As in other types of cellular work, ATP supplies the energy for most active transport. One way ATP can power active transport is by transferring its terminal phosphate group

directly to the transport protein. This can induce the protein to change its shape in a manner that translocates a solute bound to the protein across the membrane. One transport system that works this way is the **sodium-potassium pump**, which exchanges Na⁺ for K⁺ across the plasma membrane of animal cells (**Figure 7.18**). The distinction between passive transport and active transport is reviewed in **Figure 7.19**.

How Ion Pumps Maintain Membrane Potential

All cells have voltages across their plasma membranes. Voltage is electrical potential energy—a separation of opposite charges. The cytoplasmic side of the membrane is negative in charge relative to the extracellular side because of an unequal distribution of anions and cations on the two sides. The voltage across a membrane, called a **membrane potential**, ranges from about −50 to −200 millivolts (mV). (The minus sign indicates that the inside of the cell is negative relative to the outside.)

The membrane potential acts like a battery, an energy source that affects the traffic of all charged substances across the membrane. Because the inside of the cell is negative compared with the outside, the membrane potential favors the passive transport of cations into the cell and anions out of the cell. Thus, *two* forces drive the diffusion of ions across a membrane: a chemical force (the ion's concentration gradient) and an electrical force (the effect of the membrane potential on

▼ **Figure 7.19 Review: passive and active transport.**

Passive transport. Substances diffuse spontaneously down their concentration gradients, crossing a membrane with no expenditure of energy by the cell. The rate of diffusion can be greatly increased by transport proteins in the membrane.

Active transport. Some transport proteins act as pumps, moving substances across a membrane against their concentration (or electrochemical) gradients. Energy for this work is usually supplied by ATP.

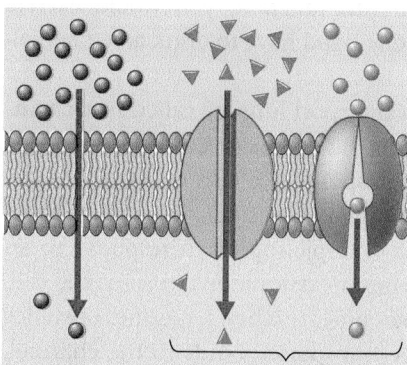

Diffusion. Hydrophobic molecules and (at a slow rate) very small uncharged polar molecules can diffuse through the lipid bilayer.

Facilitated diffusion. Many hydrophilic substances diffuse through membranes with the assistance of transport proteins, either channel proteins (left) or carrier proteins (right).

? *For each solute in the right panel, describe its direction of movement, and state whether it is going with or against its concentration gradient.*

the ion's movement). This combination of forces acting on an ion is called the **electrochemical gradient.**

In the case of ions, then, we must refine our concept of passive transport: An ion diffuses not simply down its *concentration* gradient but, more exactly, down its *electrochemical* gradient. For example, the concentration of Na^+ inside a resting nerve cell is much lower than outside it. When the cell is stimulated, gated channels open that facilitate Na^+ diffusion. Sodium ions then "fall" down their electrochemical gradient, driven by the concentration gradient of Na^+ and by the attraction of these cations to the negative side (inside) of the membrane. In this example, both electrical and chemical contributions to the electrochemical gradient act in the same direction across the membrane, but this is not always so. In cases where electrical forces due to the membrane potential oppose the simple diffusion of an ion down its concentration gradient, active transport may be necessary. In Chapter 48, you'll learn about the importance of electrochemical gradients and membrane potentials in the transmission of nerve impulses.

Some membrane proteins that actively transport ions contribute to the membrane potential. An example is the sodium-potassium pump. Notice in Figure 7.18 that the pump does not translocate Na^+ and K^+ one for one, but pumps three sodium ions out of the cell for every two potassium ions it pumps into the cell. With each "crank" of the pump, there is a net transfer of one positive charge from the cytoplasm to the extracellular fluid, a process that stores energy as voltage. A transport protein that generates voltage across a membrane is called an **electrogenic pump.** The sodium-potassium pump appears to be the major electrogenic pump of animal cells. The main electrogenic pump of plants, fungi, and bacteria is a **proton pump**, which actively transports protons (hydrogen ions, H^+) out of the cell. The pumping of H^+ transfers positive charge from the cytoplasm to the extracellular solution (**Figure 7.20**). By generating voltage across membranes, electrogenic pumps help store energy that can be tapped for cellular work. One important use of proton gradients in the cell is for ATP synthesis during cellular respiration, as you will see in Chapter 9. Another is a type of membrane traffic called cotransport.

Cotransport: Coupled Transport by a Membrane Protein

A single ATP-powered pump that transports a specific solute can indirectly drive the active transport of several other solutes in a mechanism called **cotransport**. A substance that has been pumped across a membrane can do work as it moves back across the membrane by diffusion, analogous to water that has been pumped uphill and performs work as it flows back down. Another transport protein, a cotransporter separate from the pump, can couple the "downhill" diffusion of this substance to the "uphill" transport of a second substance against its own concentration (or electrochemical) gradient. For example, a plant cell uses the gradient of H^+ generated by its proton pumps to drive the active transport of amino acids, sugars, and several other nutrients into the cell. One transport protein couples the return of H^+ to the transport of sucrose into the cell (**Figure 7.21**). This protein can translocate sucrose into the cell against a concentration gradient, but only if the sucrose molecule travels in the company of a hydrogen ion. The hydrogen ion uses the transport protein as an avenue to diffuse down the electrochemical gradient maintained by the proton pump. Plants use sucrose-H^+ cotransport to load sucrose produced by photosynthesis into cells in the veins of leaves. The vascular tissue of the plant can then distribute the sugar to nonphotosynthetic organs, such as roots.

What we know about cotransport proteins in animal cells has helped us find more effective treatments for diarrhea, a serious problem in developing countries. Normally, sodium in waste is reabsorbed in the colon, maintaining constant levels in the body, but diarrhea expels waste so rapidly that reabsorption is not possible, and sodium levels fall precipitously.

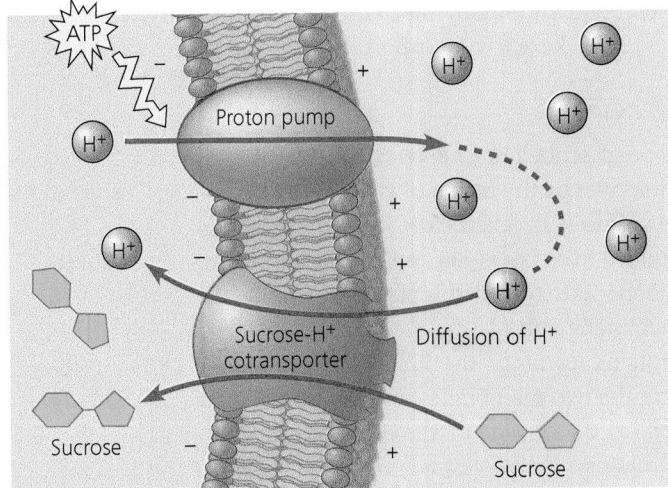

▲ Figure 7.21 **Cotransport: active transport driven by a concentration gradient.** A carrier protein, such as this sucrose-H^+ cotransporter in a plant cell, is able to use the diffusion of H^+ down its electrochemical gradient into the cell to drive the uptake of sucrose. The H^+ gradient is maintained by an ATP-driven proton pump that concentrates H^+ outside the cell, thus storing potential energy that can be used for active transport, in this case of sucrose. Thus, ATP indirectly provides the energy necessary for cotransport. (The cell wall is not shown.)

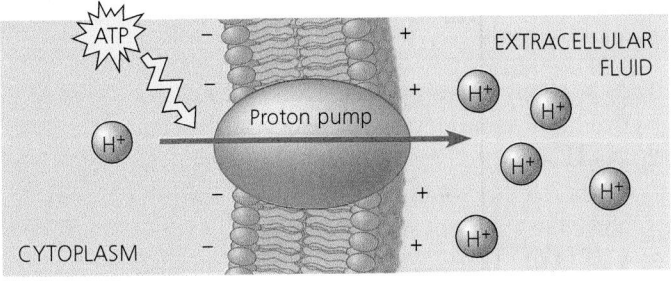

▲ Figure 7.20 **A proton pump.** Proton pumps are electrogenic pumps that store energy by generating voltage (charge separation) across membranes. A proton pump translocates positive charge in the form of hydrogen ions. The voltage and H^+ concentration gradient represent a dual energy source that can drive other processes, such as the uptake of nutrients. Most proton pumps are powered by ATP.

To treat this life-threatening condition, patients are given a solution to drink containing high concentrations of salt (NaCl) and glucose. The solutes are taken up by sodium-glucose cotransporters on the surface of intestinal cells and passed through the cells into the blood. This simple treatment has lowered infant mortality worldwide.

CONCEPT 7.5

Bulk transport across the plasma membrane occurs by exocytosis and endocytosis

Water and small solutes enter and leave the cell by diffusing through the lipid bilayer of the plasma membrane or by being pumped or moved across the membrane by transport proteins. However, large molecules, such as proteins and polysaccharides, as well as larger particles, generally cross the membrane in bulk by mechanisms that involve packaging in vesicles. Like active transport, these processes require energy.

Exocytosis

As we described in Chapter 6, the cell secretes certain biological molecules by the fusion of vesicles with the plasma membrane; this process is called **exocytosis**. A transport vesicle that has budded from the Golgi apparatus moves along microtubules of the cytoskeleton to the plasma membrane. When the vesicle membrane and plasma membrane come into contact, specific proteins rearrange the lipid molecules of the two bilayers so that the two membranes fuse. The contents of the vesicle then spill to the outside of the cell, and the vesicle membrane becomes part of the plasma membrane (see Figure 7.12, step 4).

Many secretory cells use exocytosis to export products. For example, the cells in the pancreas that make insulin secrete it into the extracellular fluid by exocytosis. In another example, neurons (nerve cells) use exocytosis to release neurotransmitters that signal other neurons or muscle cells. When plant cells are making walls, exocytosis delivers proteins and carbohydrates from Golgi vesicles to the outside of the cell.

Endocytosis

In **endocytosis**, the cell takes in biological molecules and particulate matter by forming new vesicles from the plasma membrane. Although the proteins involved in the processes are different, the events of endocytosis look like the reverse of exocytosis. A small area of the plasma membrane sinks inward to form a pocket. As the pocket deepens, it pinches in, forming a vesicle containing material that had been outside the cell. Study **Figure 7.22** carefully to understand the three types of endocytosis: phagocytosis ("cellular eating"), pinocytosis ("cellular drinking"), and receptor-mediated endocytosis.

Human cells use receptor-mediated endocytosis to take in cholesterol for membrane synthesis and the synthesis of other steroids. Cholesterol travels in the blood in particles called low-density lipoproteins (LDLs), each a complex of lipids and a protein. LDLs bind to LDL receptors on plasma membranes and then enter the cells by endocytosis. (LDLs thus act as **ligands**, a term for any molecule that binds specifically to a receptor site on another molecule.) In humans with familial hypercholesterolemia, an inherited disease characterized by a very high level of cholesterol in the blood, LDLs cannot enter cells because the LDL receptor proteins are defective or missing. Consequently, cholesterol accumulates in the blood, where it contributes to early atherosclerosis, the buildup of lipid deposits within the walls of blood vessels. This buildup causes the walls to bulge inward, thereby narrowing the vessels and impeding blood flow.

Vesicles not only transport substances between the cell and its surroundings but also provide a mechanism for rejuvenating or remodeling the plasma membrane. Endocytosis and exocytosis occur continually in most eukaryotic cells, yet the amount of plasma membrane in a nongrowing cell remains fairly constant. Apparently, the addition of membrane by one process offsets the loss of membrane by the other.

Energy and cellular work have figured prominently in our study of membranes. We have seen, for example, that active transport is powered by ATP. In the next three chapters, you will learn more about how cells acquire chemical energy to do the work of life.

Exploring Endocytosis in Animal Cells

Phagocytosis

EXTRACELLULAR FLUID

Solutes

Pseudopodium

"Food" or other particle

Food vacuole

CYTOPLASM

In **phagocytosis,** a cell engulfs a particle by wrapping pseudopodia (singular, *pseudopodium*) around it and packaging it within a membranous sac called a food vacuole. The particle will be digested after the food vacuole fuses with a lysosome containing hydrolytic enzymes (see Figure 6.13a).

Pseudopodium of amoeba

Bacterium

Food vacuole

1 μm

An amoeba engulfing a bacterium via phagocytosis (TEM).

Pinocytosis

Plasma membrane

Vesicle

In **pinocytosis,** the cell "gulps" droplets of extracellular fluid into tiny vesicles. It is not the fluid itself that is needed by the cell, but the molecules dissolved in the droplets. Because any and all included solutes are taken into the cell, pinocytosis is nonspecific in the substances it transports.

0.5 μm

Pinocytosis vesicles forming (indicated by arrows) in a cell lining a small blood vessel (TEM).

ANIMATION **BioFlix** Visit the Study Area at **www.masteringbiology.com** for the BioFlix® 3-D Animation on Membrane Transport.

Receptor-Mediated Endocytosis

Receptor

Ligand

Coat proteins

Coated pit

Coated vesicle

Receptor-mediated endocytosis enables the cell to acquire bulk quantities of specific substances, even though those substances may not be very concentrated in the extracellular fluid. Embedded in the membrane are proteins with specific receptor sites exposed to the extracellular fluid, to which specific substances (ligands) bind. The receptor proteins then cluster in regions of the membrane called coated pits, which are lined on their cytoplasmic side by a fuzzy layer of coat proteins. Next, each coated pit forms a vesicle containing the ligand molecules. Notice that there are relatively more bound molecules (purple) inside the vesicle, but other molecules (green) are also present. After the ingested material is liberated from the vesicle, the emptied receptors are recycled to the plasma membrane by the same vesicle.

Plasma membrane

Coat proteins

0.25 μm

Top: A coated pit. *Bottom:* A coated vesicle forming during receptor-mediated endocytosis (TEMs).

SUMMARY OF KEY CONCEPTS

CONCEPT 7.1

Cellular membranes are fluid mosaics of lipids and proteins (pp. 125–131)

- The Davson-Danielli sandwich model of the membrane has been replaced by the **fluid mosaic model**, in which **amphipathic** proteins are embedded in the phospholipid bilayer. Proteins with related functions often cluster in patches.
- Phospholipids and some proteins move laterally within the membrane. The unsaturated hydrocarbon tails of some phospholipids keep membranes fluid at lower temperatures, while cholesterol helps membranes resist changes in fluidity caused by temperature changes. Differences in membrane lipid composition, as well as the ability to change lipid composition, are evolutionary adaptations that ensure membrane fluidity.
- **Integral proteins** are embedded in the lipid bilayer; **peripheral proteins** are attached to the membrane surface. The functions of membrane proteins include transport, enzymatic activity, signal transduction, cell-cell recognition, intercellular joining, and attachment to the cytoskeleton and extracellular matrix. Short chains of sugars linked to proteins (in **glycoproteins**) and lipids (in **glycolipids**) on the exterior side of the plasma membrane interact with surface molecules of other cells.
- Membrane proteins and lipids are synthesized in the ER and modified in the ER and Golgi apparatus. The inside and outside faces of membranes differ in molecular composition.

? *In what ways are membranes crucial to life?*

CONCEPT 7.2

Membrane structure results in selective permeability (pp. 131–132)

- A cell must exchange molecules and ions with its surroundings, a process controlled by the **selective permeability** of the plasma membrane. Hydrophobic substances are soluble in lipid and pass through membranes rapidly, whereas polar molecules and ions generally require specific **transport proteins** to cross the membrane.

? *How do **aquaporins** affect the permeability of a membrane?*

CONCEPT 7.3

Passive transport is diffusion of a substance across a membrane with no energy investment (pp. 132–135)

- **Diffusion** is the spontaneous movement of a substance down its **concentration gradient**. Water diffuses out through the permeable membrane of a cell (**osmosis**) if the solution outside has a higher solute concentration (**hypertonic**) than the cytosol; water enters the cell if the solution has a lower solute concentration (**hypotonic**). If the concentrations are equal (**isotonic**), no net osmosis occurs. Cell survival depends on balancing water uptake and loss. Cells lacking walls (as in animals and some protists) are isotonic with their environments or have adaptations for **osmoregulation**. Plants, prokaryotes, fungi, and some protists have relatively inelastic cell walls, so the cells don't burst in a hypotonic environment.
- In a type of **passive transport** called **facilitated diffusion**, a transport protein speeds the movement of water or a solute across a membrane down its concentration gradient. **Ion channels**, some of which are **gated channels**, facilitate the diffusion of ions across a membrane. Carrier proteins can undergo changes in shape that translocate bound solutes across the membrane.

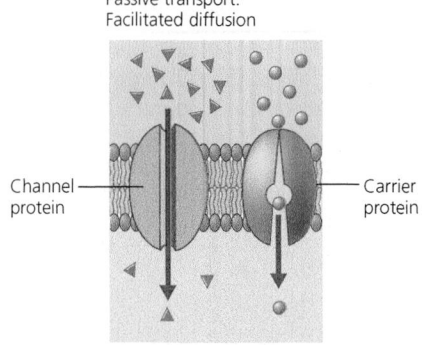

Passive transport:
Facilitated diffusion

Channel protein — Carrier protein

? *What happens to a cell placed in a hypertonic solution? Describe the free water concentration inside and out.*

CONCEPT 7.4

Active transport uses energy to move solutes against their gradients (pp. 135–138)

Active transport

- Specific membrane proteins use energy, usually in the form of ATP, to do the work of **active transport**. The **sodium-potassium pump** is an example.
- Ions can have both a concentration (chemical) gradient and an electrical gradient (voltage). These gradients combine in the **electrochemical gradient**, which determines the net direction of ionic diffusion. **Electrogenic pumps**, such as the sodium-potassium pump and **proton pumps**, are transport proteins that contribute to electrochemical gradients.
- **Cotransport** of two solutes occurs when a membrane protein enables the "downhill" diffusion of one solute to drive the "uphill" transport of the other.

? *ATP is not directly involved in the functioning of a cotransporter. Why, then, is cotransport considered active transport?*

CONCEPT 7.5

Bulk transport across the plasma membrane occurs by exocytosis and endocytosis (p. 138)

- In **exocytosis**, transport vesicles migrate to the plasma membrane, fuse with it, and release their contents. In **endocytosis**, molecules enter cells within vesicles that pinch inward from the plasma membrane. The three types of endocytosis are **phagocytosis**, **pinocytosis**, and **receptor-mediated endocytosis**.

? *Which type of endocytosis involves ligands? What does this type of transport enable a cell to do?*

TEST YOUR UNDERSTANDING

LEVEL 1: KNOWLEDGE/COMPREHENSION

1. In what way do the membranes of a eukaryotic cell vary?
   a. Phospholipids are found only in certain membranes.
   b. Certain proteins are unique to each membrane.

c. Only certain membranes of the cell are selectively permeable.

d. Only certain membranes are constructed from amphipathic molecules.

e. Some membranes have hydrophobic surfaces exposed to the cytoplasm, while others have hydrophilic surfaces facing the cytoplasm.

2. According to the fluid mosaic model of membrane structure, proteins of the membrane are mostly
   a. spread in a continuous layer over the inner and outer surfaces of the membrane.
   b. confined to the hydrophobic interior of the membrane.
   c. embedded in a lipid bilayer.
   d. randomly oriented in the membrane, with no fixed inside-outside polarity.
   e. free to depart from the fluid membrane and dissolve in the surrounding solution.

3. Which of the following factors would tend to increase membrane fluidity?
   a. a greater proportion of unsaturated phospholipids
   b. a greater proportion of saturated phospholipids
   c. a lower temperature
   d. a relatively high protein content in the membrane
   e. a greater proportion of relatively large glycolipids compared with lipids having smaller molecular masses

LEVEL 2: APPLICATION/ANALYSIS

4. Which of the following processes includes all others?
   a. osmosis
   b. diffusion of a solute across a membrane
   c. facilitated diffusion
   d. passive transport
   e. transport of an ion down its electrochemical gradient

5. Based on Figure 7.21, which of these experimental treatments would increase the rate of sucrose transport into the cell?
   a. decreasing extracellular sucrose concentration
   b. decreasing extracellular pH
   c. decreasing cytoplasmic pH
   d. adding an inhibitor that blocks the regeneration of ATP
   e. adding a substance that makes the membrane more permeable to hydrogen ions

6. **DRAW IT** An artificial "cell" consisting of an aqueous solution enclosed in a selectively permeable membrane is immersed in a beaker containing a different solution, the "environment," as shown below. The membrane is permeable to water and to the simple sugars glucose and fructose but impermeable to the disaccharide sucrose.
   a. Draw solid arrows to indicate the net movement of solutes into and/or out of the cell.
   b. Is the solution outside the cell isotonic, hypotonic, or hypertonic?

"Cell"
0.03 M sucrose
0.02 M glucose

"Environment"
0.01 M sucrose
0.01 M glucose
0.01 M fructose

   c. Draw a dashed arrow to show the net osmosis, if any.
   d. Will the artificial cell become more flaccid, more turgid, or stay the same?
   e. Eventually, will the two solutions have the same or different solute concentrations?

LEVEL 3: SYNTHESIS/EVALUATION

7. **EVOLUTION CONNECTION**
   Paramecium and other protists that live in hypotonic environments have cell membranes that limit water uptake, while those living in isotonic environments have membranes that are more permeable to water. What water regulation adaptations might have evolved in protists in hypertonic habitats such as Great Salt Lake? In habitats with changing salt concentration?

8. **SCIENTIFIC INQUIRY**
   An experiment is designed to study the mechanism of sucrose uptake by plant cells. Cells are immersed in a sucrose solution, and the pH of the solution is monitored. Samples of the cells are taken at intervals, and their sucrose concentration is measured. After a decrease in the pH of the solution to a steady, slightly acidic level, sucrose uptake begins. Propose a hypothesis for these results. What do you think would happen if an inhibitor of ATP regeneration by the cell were added to the beaker once the pH is at a steady level? Explain.

9. **SCIENCE, TECHNOLOGY, AND SOCIETY**
   Extensive irrigation in arid regions causes salts to accumulate in the soil. (When water evaporates, salts that were dissolved in the water are left behind in the soil.) Based on what you learned about water balance in plant cells, explain why increased soil salinity (saltiness) might be harmful to crops. Suggest ways to minimize damage. What costs are attached to your solutions?

10.

Environmental Interactions A human pancreatic cell obtains O_2, fuel molecules such as glucose, and building materials such as amino acids and cholesterol from its environment, and it releases CO_2 as a waste product of cellular respiration. In response to hormonal signals, the cell secretes digestive enzymes. It also regulates its ion concentrations by exchange with its environment. Based on what you have just learned about the structure and function of cellular membranes, write a short essay (100–150 words) that describes how such a cell accomplishes these interactions with its environment.

For selected answers, see Appendix A.

MasteringBIOLOGY® www.masteringbiology.com

1. MasteringBiology® Assignments
Make Connections Tutorial Plasma Membranes (Chapter 7) and Phospholipid Structure (Chapter 5)
BioFlix **Tutorials** Membrane Transport: Diffusion and Passive Transport • The Sodium-Potassium Pump • Cotransport • Bulk Transport
Tutorial Osmosis
Activities Membrane Structure • Selective Permeability of Membranes • Diffusion • Diffusion and Osmosis • Facilitated Diffusion • Membrane Transport Proteins • Osmosis and Water Balance in Cells • Active Transport • Exocytosis and Endocytosis
Questions Student Misconceptions • Reading Quiz • Multiple Choice • End-of-Chapter

2. eText
Read your book online, search, take notes, highlight text, and more.

3. The Study Area
Practice Tests • Cumulative Test • *BioFlix* 3-D Animations • MP3 Tutor Sessions • Videos • Activities • Investigations • Lab Media • Audio Glossary • Word Study Tools • Art

8

An Introduction to Metabolism

▲ **Figure 8.1 What causes these two squid to glow?**

KEY CONCEPTS

8.1 An organism's metabolism transforms matter and energy, subject to the laws of thermodynamics

8.2 The free-energy change of a reaction tells us whether or not the reaction occurs spontaneously

8.3 ATP powers cellular work by coupling exergonic reactions to endergonic reactions

8.4 Enzymes speed up metabolic reactions by lowering energy barriers

8.5 Regulation of enzyme activity helps control metabolism

OVERVIEW

The Energy of Life

The living cell is a chemical factory in miniature, where thousands of reactions occur within a microscopic space. Sugars can be converted to amino acids that are linked together into proteins when needed, and when food is digested, pro-

teins are dismantled into amino acids that can be converted to sugars. Small molecules are assembled into polymers, which may be hydrolyzed later as the needs of the cell change. In multicellular organisms, many cells export chemical products that are used in other parts of the organism. The process called cellular respiration drives the cellular economy by extracting the energy stored in sugars and other fuels. Cells apply this energy to perform various types of work, such as the transport of solutes across the plasma membrane, which we discussed in Chapter 7. In a more exotic example, cells of the two firefly squid (*Watasenia scintillans*) shown mating in **Figure 8.1** convert the energy stored in certain organic molecules to light, a process called bioluminescence. (The light pattern aids in mate recognition and protection from predators lurking below.) Bioluminescence and other metabolic activities carried out by a cell are precisely coordinated and controlled. In its complexity, its efficiency, and its responsiveness to subtle changes, the cell is peerless as a chemical factory. The concepts of metabolism that you learn in this chapter will help you understand how matter and energy flow during life's processes and how that flow is regulated.

CONCEPT 8.1

An organism's metabolism transforms matter and energy, subject to the laws of thermodynamics

The totality of an organism's chemical reactions is called **metabolism** (from the Greek *metabole*, change). Metabolism is an emergent property of life that arises from orderly interactions between molecules.

Organization of the Chemistry of Life into Metabolic Pathways

We can picture a cell's metabolism as an elaborate road map of the thousands of chemical reactions that occur in a cell, arranged as intersecting metabolic pathways. A **metabolic pathway** begins with a specific molecule, which is then altered in a series of defined steps, resulting in a certain product. Each step of the pathway is catalyzed by a specific enzyme:

Analogous to the red, yellow, and green stoplights that control the flow of automobile traffic, mechanisms that regulate enzymes balance metabolic supply and demand.

Metabolism as a whole manages the material and energy resources of the cell. Some metabolic pathways release energy by breaking down complex molecules to simpler compounds. These degradative processes are called **catabolic pathways**, or breakdown pathways. A major pathway of catabolism is cellular respiration, in which the sugar glucose and other organic fuels are broken down in the presence of oxygen to carbon dioxide and water. (Pathways can have more than one starting molecule and/or product.) Energy that was stored in the organic molecules becomes available to do the work of the cell, such as ciliary beating or membrane transport. **Anabolic pathways**, in contrast, consume energy to build complicated molecules from simpler ones; they are sometimes called biosynthetic pathways. Examples of anabolism are the synthesis of an amino acid from simpler molecules and the synthesis of a protein from amino acids. Catabolic and anabolic pathways are the "downhill" and "uphill" avenues of the metabolic landscape. Energy released from the downhill reactions of catabolic pathways can be stored and then used to drive the uphill reactions of anabolic pathways.

In this chapter, we will focus on mechanisms common to metabolic pathways. Because energy is fundamental to all metabolic processes, a basic knowledge of energy is necessary to understand how the living cell works. Although we will use some nonliving examples to study energy, the concepts demonstrated by these examples also apply to **bioenergetics**, the study of how energy flows through living organisms.

Forms of Energy

Energy is the capacity to cause change. In everyday life, energy is important because some forms of energy can be used to do work—that is, to move matter against opposing forces, such as gravity and friction. Put another way, energy is the ability to rearrange a collection of matter. For example, you expend energy to turn the pages of this book, and your cells expend energy in transporting certain substances across membranes. Energy exists in various forms, and the work of life depends on the ability of cells to transform energy from one form to another.

Energy can be associated with the relative motion of objects; this energy is called **kinetic energy**. Moving objects can perform work by imparting motion to other matter: A pool player uses the motion of the cue stick to push the cue ball, which in turn moves the other balls; water gushing through a dam turns turbines; and the contraction of leg muscles pushes bicycle pedals. **Heat**, or **thermal energy**, is kinetic energy associated with the random movement of atoms or molecules. Light is also a type of energy that can be harnessed to perform work, such as powering photosynthesis in green plants.

An object not presently moving may still possess energy. Energy that is not kinetic is called **potential energy**; it is energy that matter possesses because of its location or struc-ture. Water behind a dam, for instance, possesses energy because of its altitude above sea level. Molecules possess energy because of the arrangement of electrons in the bonds between their atoms. **Chemical energy** is a term used by biologists to refer to the potential energy available for release in a chemical reaction. Recall that catabolic pathways release energy by breaking down complex molecules. Biologists say that these complex molecules, such as glucose, are high in chemical energy. During a catabolic reaction, some bonds are broken and others formed, releasing energy and resulting in lower-energy breakdown products. This transformation also occurs, for example, in the engine of a car when the hydrocarbons of gasoline react explosively with oxygen, releasing the energy that pushes the pistons and producing exhaust. Although less explosive, a similar reaction of food molecules with oxygen provides chemical energy in biological systems, producing carbon dioxide and water as waste products. Biochemical pathways, carried out in the context of cellular structures, enable cells to release chemical energy from food molecules and use the energy to power life processes.

How is energy converted from one form to another? Consider the divers in **Figure 8.2**. The young woman climbing the ladder to the diving platform is releasing chemical energy from the food she ate for lunch and using some of that energy to perform the work of climbing. The kinetic energy of muscle movement is thus being transformed into potential energy due to her increasing height above the water. The young man diving is converting his potential energy to kinetic energy, which is then transferred to the water as he enters it. A small amount of energy is lost as heat due to friction.

A diver has more potential energy on the platform than in the water.

Diving converts potential energy to kinetic energy.

Climbing up converts the kinetic energy of muscle movement to potential energy.

A diver has less potential energy in the water than on the platform.

▲ **Figure 8.2 Transformations between potential and kinetic energy.**

Now let's go back one step and consider the original source of the organic food molecules that provided the necessary chemical energy for the diver to climb the steps. This chemical energy was itself derived from light energy by plants during photosynthesis. Organisms are energy transformers.

The Laws of Energy Transformation

The study of the energy transformations that occur in a collection of matter is called **thermodynamics**. Scientists use the word *system* to denote the matter under study; they refer to the rest of the universe—everything outside the system—as the *surroundings*. An *isolated system,* such as that approximated by liquid in a thermos bottle, is unable to exchange either energy or matter with its surroundings. In an *open system*, energy and matter can be transferred between the system and its surroundings. Organisms are open systems. They absorb energy—for instance, light energy or chemical energy in the form of organic molecules—and release heat and metabolic waste products, such as carbon dioxide, to the surroundings. Two laws of thermodynamics govern energy transformations in organisms and all other collections of matter.

The First Law of Thermodynamics

According to the **first law of thermodynamics**, the energy of the universe is constant: *Energy can be transferred and transformed, but it cannot be created or destroyed.* The first law is also known as the *principle of conservation of energy.* The electric company does not make energy, but merely converts it to a form that is convenient for us to use. By converting sunlight to chemical energy, a plant acts as an energy transformer, not an energy producer.

The brown bear in **Figure 8.3a** will convert the chemical energy of the organic molecules in its food to kinetic and other forms of energy as it carries out biological processes. What happens to this energy after it has performed work? The second law of thermodynamics helps to answer this question.

The Second Law of Thermodynamics

If energy cannot be destroyed, why can't organisms simply recycle their energy over and over again? It turns out that during every energy transfer or transformation, some energy becomes unavailable to do work. In most energy transformations, more usable forms of energy are at least partly converted to heat, which is the energy associated with the random motion of atoms or molecules. Only a small fraction of the chemical energy from the food in Figure 8.3a is transformed into the motion of the brown bear shown in **Figure 8.3b**; most is lost as heat, which dissipates rapidly through the surroundings.

In the process of carrying out chemical reactions that perform various kinds of work, living cells unavoidably convert other forms of energy to heat. A system can put heat to work only when there is a temperature difference that results in the heat flowing from a warmer location to a cooler one. If temperature is uniform, as it is in a living cell, then the only use for heat energy generated during a chemical reaction is to warm a body of matter, such as the organism. (This can make a room crowded with people uncomfortably warm, as each person is carrying out a multitude of chemical reactions!)

A logical consequence of the loss of usable energy during energy transfer or transformation is that each such event makes the universe more disordered. Scientists use a quantity called **entropy** as a measure of disorder, or randomness.

(a) First law of thermodynamics: Energy can be transferred or transformed but neither created nor destroyed. For example, chemical reactions in this brown bear (*Ursus arctos*) will convert the chemical (potential) energy in the fish into the kinetic energy of running, shown in (b).

(b) Second law of thermodynamics: Every energy transfer or transformation increases the disorder (entropy) of the universe. For example, as it runs, disorder is increased around the bear by the release of heat and small molecules that are the by-products of metabolism. A brown bear can run at speeds up to 35 miles per hour (56 km/hr)—as fast as a racehorse.

▲ **Figure 8.3** **The two laws of thermodynamics.**

The more randomly arranged a collection of matter is, the greater its entropy. We can now state the **second law of thermodynamics**: *Every energy transfer or transformation increases the entropy of the universe.* Although order can increase locally, there is an unstoppable trend toward randomization of the universe as a whole.

In many cases, increased entropy is evident in the physical disintegration of a system's organized structure. For example, you can observe increasing entropy in the gradual decay of an unmaintained building. Much of the increasing entropy of the universe is less apparent, however, because it appears as increasing amounts of heat and less ordered forms of matter. As the bear in Figure 8.3b converts chemical energy to kinetic energy, it is also increasing the disorder of its surroundings by producing heat and small molecules, such as the CO_2 it exhales, that are the breakdown products of food.

The concept of entropy helps us understand why certain processes occur without any input of energy. It turns out that for a process to occur on its own, without outside help, it must increase the entropy of the universe. A process that can occur without an input of energy is called a **spontaneous process**. Note that as we're using it here, the word *spontaneous* does not imply that such a process would occur quickly; rather, the word signifies that the process is energetically favorable. (In fact, it may be helpful for you to think of the phrase "energetically favorable" when you read the formal term "spontaneous.") Some spontaneous processes, such as an explosion, may be virtually instantaneous, while others, such as the rusting of an old car over time, are much slower. A process that cannot occur on its own is said to be nonspontaneous; it will happen only if energy is added to the system. We know from experience that certain events occur spontaneously and others do not. For instance, we know that water flows downhill spontaneously but moves uphill only with an input of energy, such as when a machine pumps the water against gravity. This understanding gives us another way to state the second law: *For a process to occur spontaneously, it must increase the entropy of the universe.*

Biological Order and Disorder

Living systems increase the entropy of their surroundings, as predicted by thermodynamic law. It is true that cells create ordered structures from less organized starting materials. For example, simpler molecules are ordered into the more complex structure of an amino acid, and amino acids are ordered into polypeptide chains. At the organismal level as well, complex and beautifully ordered structures result from biological processes that use simpler starting materials (Figure 8.4). However, an organism also takes in organized forms of matter and energy from the surroundings and replaces them with less ordered forms. For example, an animal obtains starch, proteins, and other complex molecules from the food it eats. As catabolic pathways break these molecules down,

▲ Figure 8.4 **Order as a characteristic of life.** Order is evident in the detailed structures of the sea urchin skeleton and the succulent plant shown here. As open systems, organisms can increase their order as long as the order of their surroundings decreases.

the animal releases carbon dioxide and water—small molecules that possess less chemical energy than the food did. The depletion of chemical energy is accounted for by heat generated during metabolism. On a larger scale, energy flows into most ecosystems in the form of light and exits in the form of heat (see Figure 1.6).

During the early history of life, complex organisms evolved from simpler ancestors. For example, we can trace the ancestry of the plant kingdom from much simpler organisms called green algae to more complex flowering plants. However, this increase in organization over time in no way violates the second law. The entropy of a particular system, such as an organism, may actually decrease as long as the total entropy of the *universe*—the system plus its surroundings—increases. Thus, organisms are islands of low entropy in an increasingly random universe. The evolution of biological order is perfectly consistent with the laws of thermodynamics.

CONCEPT CHECK 8.1

1. **MAKE CONNECTIONS** How does the second law of thermodynamics help explain the diffusion of a substance across a membrane? See Figure 7.13 on page 132.
2. Describe the forms of energy found in an apple as it grows on a tree, then falls, then is digested by someone who eats it.
3. **WHAT IF?** If you place a teaspoon of sugar in the bottom of a glass of water, it will dissolve completely over time. Left longer, eventually the water will disappear and the sugar crystals will reappear. Explain these observations in terms of entropy.

For suggested answers, see Appendix A.

The free-energy change of a reaction tells us whether or not the reaction occurs spontaneously

The laws of thermodynamics that we've just discussed apply to the universe as a whole. As biologists, we want to understand the chemical reactions of life—for example, which reactions occur spontaneously and which ones require some input of energy from outside. But how can we know this without assessing the energy and entropy changes in the entire universe for each separate reaction?

Free-Energy Change, ΔG

Recall that the universe is really equivalent to "the system" plus "the surroundings." In 1878, J. Willard Gibbs, a professor at Yale, defined a very useful function called the Gibbs free energy of a system (without considering its surroundings), symbolized by the letter G. We'll refer to the Gibbs free energy simply as free energy. **Free energy** is the portion of a system's energy that can perform work when temperature and pressure are uniform throughout the system, as in a living cell. Let's consider how we determine the free-energy change that occurs when a system changes—for example, during a chemical reaction.

The change in free energy, ΔG, can be calculated for a chemical reaction by applying the following equation:

$$\Delta G = \Delta H - T\Delta S$$

This equation uses only properties of the system (the reaction) itself: ΔH symbolizes the change in the system's *enthalpy* (in biological systems, equivalent to total energy); ΔS is the change in the system's entropy; and T is the absolute temperature in Kelvin (K) units (K = °C + 273; see Appendix C).

Once we know the value of ΔG for a process, we can use it to predict whether the process will be spontaneous (that is, whether it is energetically favorable and will occur without an input of energy). More than a century of experiments has shown that only processes with a negative ΔG are spontaneous. For ΔG to be negative, either ΔH must be negative (the system gives up enthalpy and H decreases) or $T\Delta S$ must be positive (the system gives up order and S increases), or both: When ΔH and $T\Delta S$ are tallied, ΔG has a negative value ($\Delta G < 0$) for all spontaneous processes. In other words, every spontaneous process decreases the system's free energy, and processes that have a positive or zero ΔG are never spontaneous.

This information is immensely interesting to biologists, for it gives us the power to predict which kinds of change can happen without help. Such spontaneous changes can be harnessed to perform work. This principle is very important in the study of metabolism, where a major goal is to determine which reactions can supply energy for cellular work.

Free Energy, Stability, and Equilibrium

As we saw in the previous section, when a process occurs spontaneously in a system, we can be sure that ΔG is negative. Another way to think of ΔG is to realize that it represents the difference between the free energy of the final state and the free energy of the initial state:

$$\Delta G = G_{\text{final state}} - G_{\text{initial state}}$$

Thus, ΔG can be negative only when the process involves a loss of free energy during the change from initial state to final state. Because it has less free energy, the system in its final state is less likely to change and is therefore more stable than it was previously.

We can think of free energy as a measure of a system's instability—its tendency to change to a more stable state. Unstable systems (higher G) tend to change in such a way that they become more stable (lower G). For example, a diver on top of a platform is less stable (more likely to fall) than when floating in the water; a drop of concentrated dye is less stable (more likely to disperse) than when the dye is spread randomly through the liquid; and a glucose molecule is less stable (more likely to break down) than the simpler molecules into which it can be split (Figure 8.5). Unless something prevents it, each of these systems will move toward greater stability: The diver falls, the solution becomes uniformly colored, and the glucose molecule is broken down.

Another term that describes a state of maximum stability is *equilibrium*, which you learned about in Chapter 2 in connection with chemical reactions. There is an important relationship between free energy and equilibrium, including chemical equilibrium. Recall that most chemical reactions are reversible and proceed to a point at which the forward and backward reactions occur at the same rate. The reaction is then said to be at chemical equilibrium, and there is no further net change in the relative concentration of products and reactants.

As a reaction proceeds toward equilibrium, the free energy of the mixture of reactants and products decreases. Free energy increases when a reaction is somehow pushed away from equilibrium, perhaps by removing some of the products (and thus changing their concentration relative to that of the reactants). For a system at equilibrium, G is at its lowest possible value in that system. We can think of the equilibrium state as a free-energy valley. Any change from the equilibrium position will have a positive ΔG and will not be spontaneous. For this reason, systems never spontaneously move away from equilibrium. Because a system at equilibrium cannot spontaneously change, it can do no work. *A process is spontaneous and can perform work only when it is moving toward equilibrium.*

- More free energy (higher G)
- Less stable
- Greater work capacity

In a **spontaneous change**
- The free energy of the system decreases ($\Delta G < 0$)
- The system becomes more stable
- The released free energy can be harnessed to do work

- Less free energy (lower G)
- More stable
- Less work capacity

(a) Gravitational motion. Objects move spontaneously from a higher altitude to a lower one.

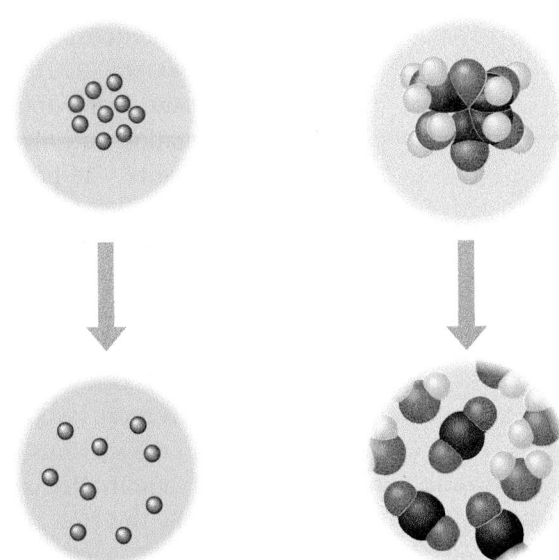

(b) Diffusion. Molecules in a drop of dye diffuse until they are randomly dispersed.

(c) Chemical reaction. In a cell, a glucose molecule is broken down into simpler molecules.

▲ Figure 8.5 **The relationship of free energy to stability, work capacity, and spontaneous change.** Unstable systems (top) are rich in free energy, G. They have a tendency to change spontaneously to a more stable state (bottom), and it is possible to harness this "downhill" change to perform work.

Free Energy and Metabolism

We can now apply the free-energy concept more specifically to the chemistry of life's processes.

Exergonic and Endergonic Reactions in Metabolism

Based on their free-energy changes, chemical reactions can be classified as either exergonic ("energy outward") or endergonic ("energy inward"). An **exergonic reaction** proceeds with a net release of free energy (**Figure 8.6a**). Because the chemical mixture loses free energy (G decreases), ΔG is negative for an exergonic reaction. Using ΔG as a standard for spontaneity, exergonic reactions are those that occur spontaneously. (Remember, the word *spontaneous* implies that it is energetically favorable, not that it will occur rapidly.) The magnitude of ΔG for an exergonic reaction represents the maximum amount of work the reaction can perform.* The greater the decrease in free energy, the greater the amount of work that can be done.

We can use the overall reaction for cellular respiration as an example:

$$C_6H_{12}O_6 + 6\ O_2 \rightarrow 6\ CO_2 + 6\ H_2O$$
$$\Delta G = -686\ \text{kcal/mol}\ (-2{,}870\ \text{kJ/mol})$$

*The word *maximum* qualifies this statement, because some of the free energy is released as heat and cannot do work. Therefore, ΔG represents a theoretical upper limit of available energy.

▼ Figure 8.6 **Free energy changes (ΔG) in exergonic and endergonic reactions.**

(a) Exergonic reaction: energy released, spontaneous

Reactants

Free energy

Energy

Products

Amount of energy released ($\Delta G < 0$)

Progress of the reaction

(b) Endergonic reaction: energy required, nonspontaneous

Products

Free energy

Energy

Reactants

Amount of energy required ($\Delta G > 0$)

Progress of the reaction

For each mole (180 g) of glucose broken down by respiration under what are called "standard conditions" (1 *M* of each reactant and product, 25°C, pH 7), 686 kcal (2,870 kJ) of energy are made available for work. Because energy must be conserved, the chemical products of respiration store 686 kcal less free energy per mole than the reactants. The products are, in a sense, the spent exhaust of a process that tapped the free energy stored in the bonds of the sugar molecules.

It is important to realize that the breaking of bonds does not release energy; on the contrary, as you will soon see, it requires energy. The phrase "energy stored in bonds" is shorthand for the potential energy that can be released when new bonds are formed after the original bonds break, as long as the products are of lower free energy than the reactants.

An **endergonic reaction** is one that absorbs free energy from its surroundings (**Figure 8.6b**). Because this kind of reaction essentially *stores* free energy in molecules (*G* increases), ΔG is positive. Such reactions are nonspontaneous, and the magnitude of ΔG is the quantity of energy required to drive the reaction. If a chemical process is exergonic (downhill), releasing energy in one direction, then the reverse process must be endergonic (uphill), using energy. A reversible process cannot be downhill in both directions. If $\Delta G = -686$ kcal/mol for respiration, which converts glucose and oxygen to carbon dioxide and water, then the reverse process—the conversion of carbon dioxide and water to glucose and oxygen—must be strongly endergonic, with $\Delta G = +686$ kcal/mol. Such a reaction would never happen by itself.

How, then, do plants make the sugar that organisms use for energy? Plants get the required energy—686 kcal to make a mole of glucose—from the environment by capturing light and converting its energy to chemical energy. Next, in a long series of exergonic steps, they gradually spend that chemical energy to assemble glucose molecules.

Equilibrium and Metabolism

Reactions in an isolated system eventually reach equilibrium and can then do no work, as illustrated by the isolated hydroelectric system in **Figure 8.7a**. The chemical reactions of metabolism are reversible, and they, too, would reach equilibrium if they occurred in the isolation of a test tube. Because systems at equilibrium are at a minimum of *G* and can do no work, a cell that has reached metabolic equilibrium is dead! The fact that metabolism as a whole is never at equilibrium is one of the defining features of life.

Like most systems, a living cell is not in equilibrium. The constant flow of materials in and out of the cell keeps the metabolic pathways from ever reaching equilibrium, and the cell continues to do work throughout its life. This principle is illustrated by the open (and more realistic) hydroelectric system in **Figure 8.7b**. However, unlike this simple single-step system, a catabolic pathway in a cell releases free energy in a series of re-

(a) An isolated hydroelectric system. Water flowing downhill turns a turbine that drives a generator providing electricity to a lightbulb, but only until the system reaches equilibrium.

(b) An open hydroelectric system. Flowing water keeps driving the generator because intake and outflow of water keep the system from reaching equilibrium.

(c) A multistep open hydroelectric system. Cellular respiration is analogous to this system: Glucose is broken down in a series of exergonic reactions that power the work of the cell. The product of each reaction becomes the reactant for the next, so no reaction reaches equilibrium.

▲ **Figure 8.7 Equilibrium and work in isolated and open systems.**

actions. An example is cellular respiration, illustrated by analogy in **Figure 8.7c**. Some of the reversible reactions of respiration are constantly "pulled" in one direction—that is, they are kept out of equilibrium. The key to maintaining this lack of equilibrium is that the product of a reaction does not accumulate but instead becomes a reactant in the next step; finally, waste products are expelled from the cell. The overall sequence of reactions is kept going by the huge free-energy difference between glucose and oxygen at the top of the energy "hill" and carbon dioxide and water at the "downhill" end. As long as our cells have a steady supply of glucose or other fuels and oxygen and are able to expel waste products to the surroundings, their metabolic pathways never reach equilibrium and can continue to do the work of life.

We see once again how important it is to think of organisms as open systems. Sunlight provides a daily source of free energy for an ecosystem's plants and other photosynthetic organisms. Animals and other nonphotosynthetic organisms in an ecosystem must have a source of free energy in the form of the organic products of photosynthesis. Now that we have applied the free-energy concept to metabolism, we are ready to see how a cell actually performs the work of life.

CONCEPT 8.3

ATP powers cellular work by coupling exergonic reactions to endergonic reactions

A cell does three main kinds of work:

- *Chemical work*, the pushing of endergonic reactions that would not occur spontaneously, such as the synthesis of polymers from monomers (chemical work will be discussed further here and in Chapters 9 and 10)
- *Transport work*, the pumping of substances across membranes against the direction of spontaneous movement (see Chapter 7)
- *Mechanical work*, such as the beating of cilia (see Chapter 6), the contraction of muscle cells, and the movement of chromosomes during cellular reproduction

A key feature in the way cells manage their energy resources to do this work is **energy coupling**, the use of an exergonic process to drive an endergonic one. ATP is responsible for mediating most energy coupling in cells, and in most cases it acts as the immediate source of energy that powers cellular work.

The Structure and Hydrolysis of ATP

ATP (adenosine triphosphate) was introduced in Chapter 4 when we discussed the phosphate group as a functional group. ATP contains the sugar ribose, with the nitrogenous base adenine and a chain of three phosphate groups bonded to it **(Figure 8.8a)**. In addition to its role in energy coupling, ATP is also one of the nucleoside triphosphates used to make RNA (see Figure 5.26).

The bonds between the phosphate groups of ATP can be broken by hydrolysis. When the terminal phosphate bond is broken by addition of a water molecule, a molecule of inorganic phosphate ($HOPO_3^{2-}$, abbreviated (P)_i throughout this book) leaves the ATP, which becomes adenosine diphosphate,

(a) **The structure of ATP.** In the cell, most hydroxyl groups of phosphates are ionized ($-O^-$).

(b) **The hydrolysis of ATP.** The reaction of ATP and water yields inorganic phosphate ((P)_i) and ADP and releases energy.

▲ **Figure 8.8 The structure and hydrolysis of adenosine triphosphate (ATP).**

or ADP (**Figure 8.8b**). The reaction is exergonic and releases 7.3 kcal of energy per mole of ATP hydrolyzed:

$$ATP + H_2O \rightarrow ADP + ⓟ_i$$
$$\Delta G = -7.3 \text{ kcal/mol} (-30.5 \text{ kJ/mol})$$

This is the free-energy change measured under standard conditions. In the cell, conditions do not conform to standard conditions, primarily because reactant and product concentrations differ from 1 M. For example, when ATP hydrolysis occurs under cellular conditions, the actual ΔG is about -13 kcal/mol, 78% greater than the energy released by ATP hydrolysis under standard conditions.

Because their hydrolysis releases energy, the phosphate bonds of ATP are sometimes referred to as high-energy phosphate bonds, but the term is misleading. The phosphate bonds of ATP are not unusually strong bonds, as "high-energy" may imply; rather, the reactants (ATP and water) themselves have high energy relative to the energy of the products (ADP and ⓟ_i). The release of energy during the hydrolysis of ATP comes from the chemical change to a state of lower free energy, not from the phosphate bonds themselves.

ATP is useful to the cell because the energy it releases on losing a phosphate group is somewhat greater than the energy most other molecules could deliver. But why does this hydrolysis release so much energy? If we reexamine the ATP molecule in Figure 8.8a, we can see that all three phosphate groups are negatively charged. These like charges are crowded together, and their mutual repulsion contributes to the instability of this region of the ATP molecule. The triphosphate tail of ATP is the chemical equivalent of a compressed spring.

How the Hydrolysis of ATP Performs Work

When ATP is hydrolyzed in a test tube, the release of free energy merely heats the surrounding water. In an organism, this same generation of heat can sometimes be beneficial. For instance, the process of shivering uses ATP hydrolysis during muscle contraction to generate heat and warm the body. In most cases in the cell, however, the generation of heat alone would be an inefficient (and potentially dangerous) use of a valuable energy resource. Instead, the cell's proteins harness the energy released during ATP hydrolysis in several ways to perform the three types of cellular work—chemical, transport, and mechanical.

For example, with the help of specific enzymes, the cell is able to use the energy released by ATP hydrolysis directly to drive chemical reactions that, by themselves, are endergonic. If the ΔG of an endergonic reaction is less than the amount of energy released by ATP hydrolysis, then the two reactions can be coupled so that, overall, the coupled reactions are exergonic (**Figure 8.9**). This usually involves the transfer of a phosphate

(a) Glutamic acid conversion to glutamine. Glutamine synthesis from glutamic acid (Glu) by itself is endergonic (ΔG is positive), so it is not spontaneous.

(b) Conversion reaction coupled with ATP hydrolysis. In the cell, glutamine synthesis occurs in two steps, coupled by a phosphorylated intermediate. ❶ ATP phosphorylates glutamic acid, making it less stable. ❷ Ammonia displaces the phosphate group, forming glutamine.

(c) Free-energy change for coupled reaction. ΔG for the glutamic acid conversion to glutamine (+3.4 kcal/mol) plus ΔG for ATP hydrolysis (–7.3 kcal/mol) gives the free-energy change for the overall reaction (–3.9 kcal/mol). Because the overall process is exergonic (net ΔG is negative), it occurs spontaneously.

ΔG_{Glu} = +3.4 kcal/mol
+ ΔG_{ATP} = –7.3 kcal/mol
Net ΔG = –3.9 kcal/mol

▲ **Figure 8.9 How ATP drives chemical work: Energy coupling using ATP hydrolysis.** In this example, the exergonic process of ATP hydrolysis is used to drive an endergonic process—the cellular synthesis of the amino acid glutamine from glutamic acid and ammonia.

(a) **Transport work:** ATP phosphorylates transport proteins.

(b) **Mechanical work:** ATP binds noncovalently to motor proteins and then is hydrolyzed.

▲ **Figure 8.10 How ATP drives transport and mechanical work.** ATP hydrolysis causes changes in the shapes and binding affinities of proteins. This can occur either **(a)** directly, by phosphorylation, as shown for a membrane protein carrying out active transport of a solute (see also Figure 7.18), or **(b)** indirectly, via noncovalent binding of ATP and its hydrolytic products, as is the case for motor proteins that move vesicles (and other organelles) along cytoskeletal "tracks" in the cell (see also Figure 6.21).

group from ATP to some other molecule, such as the reactant. The recipient with the phosphate group covalently bonded to it is then called a **phosphorylated intermediate**. The key to coupling exergonic and endergonic reactions is the formation of this phosphorylated intermediate, which is more reactive (less stable) than the original unphosphorylated molecule.

Transport and mechanical work in the cell are also nearly always powered by the hydrolysis of ATP. In these cases, ATP hydrolysis leads to a change in a protein's shape and often its ability to bind another molecule. Sometimes this occurs via a phosphorylated intermediate, as seen for the transport protein in **Figure 8.10a**. In most instances of mechanical work involving motor proteins "walking" along cytoskeletal elements (**Figure 8.10b**), a cycle occurs in which ATP is first bound noncovalently to the motor protein. Next, ATP is hydrolyzed, releasing ADP and $\text{\textcircled{P}}_i$. Another ATP molecule can then bind. At each stage, the motor protein changes its shape and ability to bind the cytoskeleton, resulting in movement of the protein along the cytoskeletal track.

The Regeneration of ATP

An organism at work uses ATP continuously, but ATP is a renewable resource that can be regenerated by the addition of phosphate to ADP (**Figure 8.11**). The free energy required to

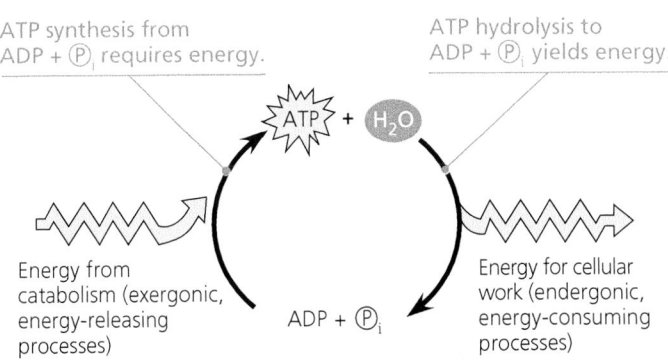

▲ **Figure 8.11 The ATP cycle.** Energy released by breakdown reactions (catabolism) in the cell is used to phosphorylate ADP, regenerating ATP. Chemical potential energy stored in ATP drives most cellular work.

phosphorylate ADP comes from exergonic breakdown reactions (catabolism) in the cell. This shuttling of inorganic phosphate and energy is called the ATP cycle, and it couples the cell's energy-yielding (exergonic) processes to the energy-consuming (endergonic) ones. The ATP cycle proceeds at an astonishing pace. For example, a working muscle cell recycles its entire pool of ATP in less than a minute. That turnover represents 10 million molecules of ATP consumed and regenerated per second per cell. If ATP could not be regenerated by the phosphorylation of ADP, humans would use up nearly their body weight in ATP each day.

Because both directions of a reversible process cannot be downhill, the regeneration of ATP from ADP and $\text{\textcircled{P}}_i$ is necessarily endergonic:

$$ADP + \text{\textcircled{P}}_i \rightarrow ATP + H_2O$$
$$\Delta G = +7.3 \text{ kcal/mol } (+30.5 \text{ kJ/mol}) \text{ (standard conditions)}$$

Since ATP formation from ADP and $\text{\textcircled{P}}_i$ is not spontaneous, free energy must be spent to make it occur. Catabolic (exergonic) pathways, especially cellular respiration, provide the energy for the endergonic process of making ATP. Plants also use light energy to produce ATP. Thus, the ATP cycle is a revolving door through which energy passes during its transfer from catabolic to anabolic pathways.

CONCEPT CHECK **8.3**

1. How does ATP typically transfer energy from exergonic to endergonic reactions in the cell?
2. Which of the following combinations has more free energy: glutamic acid + ammonia + ATP, or glutamine + ADP + $\text{\textcircled{P}}_i$? Explain your answer.
3. **MAKE CONNECTIONS** Considering what you learned in Concepts 7.3 and 7.4 (pp. 134–136), does Figure 8.10a show passive or active transport? Explain.

For suggested answers, see Appendix A.

Enzymes speed up metabolic reactions by lowering energy barriers

The laws of thermodynamics tell us what will and will not happen under given conditions but say nothing about the rate of these processes. A spontaneous chemical reaction occurs without any requirement for outside energy, but it may occur so slowly that it is imperceptible. For example, even though the hydrolysis of sucrose (table sugar) to glucose and fructose is exergonic, occurring spontaneously with a release of free energy ($\Delta G = -7$ kcal/mol), a solution of sucrose dissolved in sterile water will sit for years at room temperature with no appreciable hydrolysis. However, if we add a small amount of the enzyme sucrase to the solution, then all the sucrose may be hydrolyzed within seconds, as shown below:

Sucrase

Sucrose
($C_{12}H_{22}O_{11}$)

Glucose
($C_6H_{12}O_6$)

Fructose
($C_6H_{12}O_6$)

How does the enzyme do this?

An **enzyme** is a macromolecule that acts as a **catalyst**, a chemical agent that speeds up a reaction without being consumed by the reaction. (In this chapter, we are focusing on enzymes that are proteins. RNA enzymes, also called ribozymes, are discussed in Chapters 17 and 25.) Without regulation by enzymes, chemical traffic through the pathways of metabolism would become terribly congested because many chemical reactions would take such a long time. In the next two sections, we will see what prevents a spontaneous reaction from occurring faster and how an enzyme changes the situation.

The Activation Energy Barrier

Every chemical reaction between molecules involves both bond breaking and bond forming. For example, the hydrolysis of sucrose involves breaking the bond between glucose and fructose and one of the bonds of a water molecule and then forming two new bonds, as shown above. Changing one molecule into another generally involves contorting the starting molecule into a highly unstable state before the reaction can proceed. This contortion can be compared to the bending of a metal key ring when you pry it open to add a new key. The key ring is highly unstable in its opened form but returns to a stable state once the key is threaded all the way onto the ring. To reach the contorted state where bonds can change, reactant molecules must absorb energy from their surroundings. When the new bonds of the product molecules form, energy

is released as heat, and the molecules return to stable shapes with lower energy than the contorted state.

The initial investment of energy for starting a reaction—the energy required to contort the reactant molecules so the bonds can break—is known as the *free energy of activation*, or **activation energy**, abbreviated E_A in this book. We can think of activation energy as the amount of energy needed to push the reactants to the top of an energy barrier, or uphill, so that the "downhill" part of the reaction can begin. Activation energy is often supplied in the form of thermal energy (heat) that the reactant molecules absorb from the surroundings. The absorption of thermal energy accelerates the reactant molecules, so they collide more often and more forcefully. It also agitates the atoms within the molecules, making the breakage of bonds more likely. When the molecules have absorbed enough energy for the bonds to break, the reactants are in an unstable condition known as the *transition state*.

Figure 8.12 graphs the energy changes for a hypothetical exergonic reaction that swaps portions of two reactant molecules:

$$AB + CD \rightarrow AC + BD$$
Reactants   Products

The activation of the reactants is represented by the uphill portion of the graph, in which the free-energy content of the

The reactants AB and CD must absorb enough energy from the surroundings to reach the unstable transition state, where bonds can break.

After bonds have broken, new bonds form, releasing energy to the surroundings.

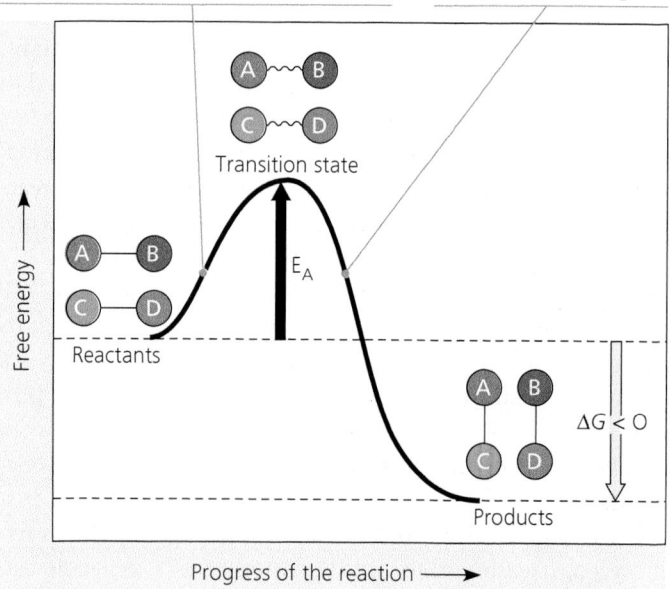

▲ **Figure 8.12 Energy profile of an exergonic reaction.** The "molecules" are hypothetical, with A, B, C, and D representing portions of the molecules. Thermodynamically, this is an exergonic reaction, with a negative ΔG, and the reaction occurs spontaneously. However, the activation energy (E_A) provides a barrier that determines the rate of the reaction.

DRAW IT *Graph the progress of an endergonic reaction in which EF and GH form products EG and FH, assuming that the reactants must pass through a transition state.*

reactant molecules is increasing. At the summit, when energy equivalent to E_A has been absorbed, the reactants are in the transition state: They are activated, and their bonds can be broken. As the atoms then settle into their new, more stable bonding arrangements, energy is released to the surroundings. This corresponds to the downhill part of the curve, which shows the loss of free energy by the molecules. The overall decrease in free energy means that E_A is repaid with interest, as the formation of new bonds releases more energy than was invested in the breaking of old bonds..

The reaction shown in Figure 8.12 is exergonic and occurs spontaneously ($\Delta G < 0$). However, the activation energy provides a barrier that determines the rate of the reaction. The reactants must absorb enough energy to reach the top of the activation energy barrier before the reaction can occur. For some reactions, E_A is modest enough that even at room temperature there is sufficient thermal energy for many of the reactant molecules to reach the transition state in a short time. In most cases, however, E_A is so high and the transition state is reached so rarely that the reaction will hardly proceed at all. In these cases, the reaction will occur at a noticeable rate only if the reactants are heated. For example, the reaction of gasoline and oxygen is exergonic and will occur spontaneously, but energy is required for the molecules to reach the transition state and react. Only when the spark plugs fire in an automobile engine can there be the explosive release of energy that pushes the pistons. Without a spark, a mixture of gasoline hydrocarbons and oxygen will not react because the E_A barrier is too high.

How Enzymes Lower the E_A Barrier

Proteins, DNA, and other complex molecules of the cell are rich in free energy and have the potential to decompose spontaneously; that is, the laws of thermodynamics favor their breakdown. These molecules persist only because at temperatures typical for cells, few molecules can make it over the hump of activation energy. However, the barriers for selected reactions must occasionally be surmounted for cells to carry out the processes needed for life. Heat speeds a reaction by allowing reactants to attain the transition state more often, but this solution would be inappropriate for biological systems. First, high temperature denatures proteins and kills cells. Second, heat would speed up *all* reactions, not just those that are needed. Instead of heat, organisms use catalysis to speed up reactions.

An enzyme catalyzes a reaction by lowering the E_A barrier (Figure 8.13), enabling the reactant molecules to absorb enough energy to reach the transition state even at moderate temperatures. An enzyme cannot change the ΔG for a reaction; it cannot make an endergonic reaction exergonic. Enzymes can only hasten reactions that would eventually occur anyway, but this function makes it possible for the cell to have a dynamic

▲ **Figure 8.13 The effect of an enzyme on activation energy.** Without affecting the free-energy change (ΔG) for a reaction, an enzyme speeds the reaction by reducing its activation energy (E_A).

metabolism, routing chemicals smoothly through the cell's metabolic pathways. And because enzymes are very specific for the reactions they catalyze, they determine which chemical processes will be going on in the cell at any particular time.

Substrate Specificity of Enzymes

The reactant an enzyme acts on is referred to as the enzyme's **substrate**. The enzyme binds to its substrate (or substrates, when there are two or more reactants), forming an **enzyme-substrate complex**. While enzyme and substrate are joined, the catalytic action of the enzyme converts the substrate to the product (or products) of the reaction. The overall process can be summarized as follows:

$$\text{Enzyme + } \atop \text{Substrate(s)} \rightleftharpoons \text{Enzyme-} \atop \text{substrate} \atop \text{complex} \rightleftharpoons \text{Enzyme + } \atop \text{Product(s)}$$

For example, the enzyme sucrase (most enzyme names end in -*ase*) catalyzes the hydrolysis of the disaccharide sucrose into its two monosaccharides, glucose and fructose (see p. 152):

$$\text{Sucrase + } \atop \text{Sucrose + } \atop H_2O \rightleftharpoons \text{Sucrase-} \atop \text{sucrose-}H_2O \atop \text{complex} \rightleftharpoons \text{Sucrase + } \atop \text{Glucose + } \atop \text{Fructose}$$

The reaction catalyzed by each enzyme is very specific; an enzyme can recognize its specific substrate even among closely related compounds. For instance, sucrase will act only on sucrose and will not bind to other disaccharides, such as maltose. What accounts for this molecular recognition? Recall that most enzymes are proteins, and proteins are macromolecules with unique three-dimensional configurations. The specificity of an enzyme results from its shape, which is a consequence of its amino acid sequence.

Only a restricted region of the enzyme molecule actually binds to the substrate. This region, called the **active site**, is typically a pocket or groove on the surface of the enzyme where catalysis occurs (Figure 8.14a). Usually, the active site is formed by only a few of the enzyme's amino acids, with the rest of the protein molecule providing a framework that determines the configuration of the active site. The specificity of an enzyme is attributed to a compatible fit between the shape of its active site and the shape of the substrate.

An enzyme is not a stiff structure locked into a given shape. In fact, recent work by biochemists has shown clearly that enzymes (and other proteins as well) seem to "dance" between subtly different shapes in a dynamic equilibrium, with slight differences in free energy for each "pose." The shape that best fits the substrate isn't necessarily the one with the lowest energy, but during the very short time the enzyme takes on this shape, its active site can bind to the substrate. It has been known for more than 50 years that the active site itself is also not a rigid receptacle for the substrate. As the substrate enters the active site, the enzyme changes shape slightly due to interactions between the substrate's chemical groups and chemical groups on the side chains of the amino acids that form the active site. This shape change makes the active site fit even more snugly around the substrate (Figure 8.14b). This **induced fit** is like a clasping handshake. Induced fit brings chemical groups of the active site into positions that enhance their ability to catalyze the chemical reaction.

Catalysis in the Enzyme's Active Site

In most enzymatic reactions, the substrate is held in the active site by so-called weak interactions, such as hydrogen bonds and ionic bonds. R groups of a few of the amino acids that make up the active site catalyze the conversion of substrate to product, and the product departs from the active site. The enzyme is then free to take another substrate molecule into its active site. The entire cycle happens so fast that a single enzyme molecule typically acts on about a thousand substrate molecules per second. Some enzymes are much faster. Enzymes, like other catalysts, emerge from the reaction in their original form. Therefore, very small amounts of enzyme can have a huge metabolic impact by functioning over and over again in catalytic cycles. Figure 8.15 shows a catalytic cycle involving two substrates and two products.

Substrate

Active site

Enzyme

Enzyme-substrate complex

(a) In this computer graphic model, the active site of this enzyme (hexokinase, shown in blue) forms a groove on its surface. Its substrate is glucose (red).

(b) When the substrate enters the active site, it forms weak bonds with the enzyme, inducing a change in the shape of the protein. This change allows additional weak bonds to form, causing the active site to enfold the substrate and hold it in place.

▲ Figure 8.14 **Induced fit between an enzyme and its substrate.**

Most metabolic reactions are reversible, and an enzyme can catalyze either the forward or the reverse reaction, depending on which direction has a negative ΔG. This in turn depends mainly on the relative concentrations of reactants and products. The net effect is always in the direction of equilibrium.

Enzymes use a variety of mechanisms that lower activation energy and speed up a reaction (see Figure 8.15, step ❸). First, in reactions involving two or more reactants, the active site provides a template on which the substrates can come together in the proper orientation for a reaction to occur between them. Second, as the active site of an enzyme clutches the bound substrates, the enzyme may stretch the substrate molecules toward their transition-state form, stressing and bending critical chemical bonds that must be broken during the reaction. Because E_A is proportional to the difficulty of breaking the bonds, distorting the substrate helps it approach the transition state and thus reduces the amount of free energy that must be absorbed to achieve that state.

Third, the active site may also provide a microenvironment that is more conducive to a particular type of reaction than the solution itself would be without the enzyme. For example, if the active site has amino acids with acidic R groups, the active site may be a pocket of low pH in an otherwise neutral cell. In such cases, an acidic amino acid may facilitate H^+ transfer to the substrate as a key step in catalyzing the reaction.

A fourth mechanism of catalysis is the direct participation of the active site in the chemical reaction. Sometimes this process even involves brief covalent bonding between the substrate and the side chain of an amino acid of the enzyme. Subsequent steps of the reaction restore the side chains to their original states, so that the active site is the same after the reaction as it was before.

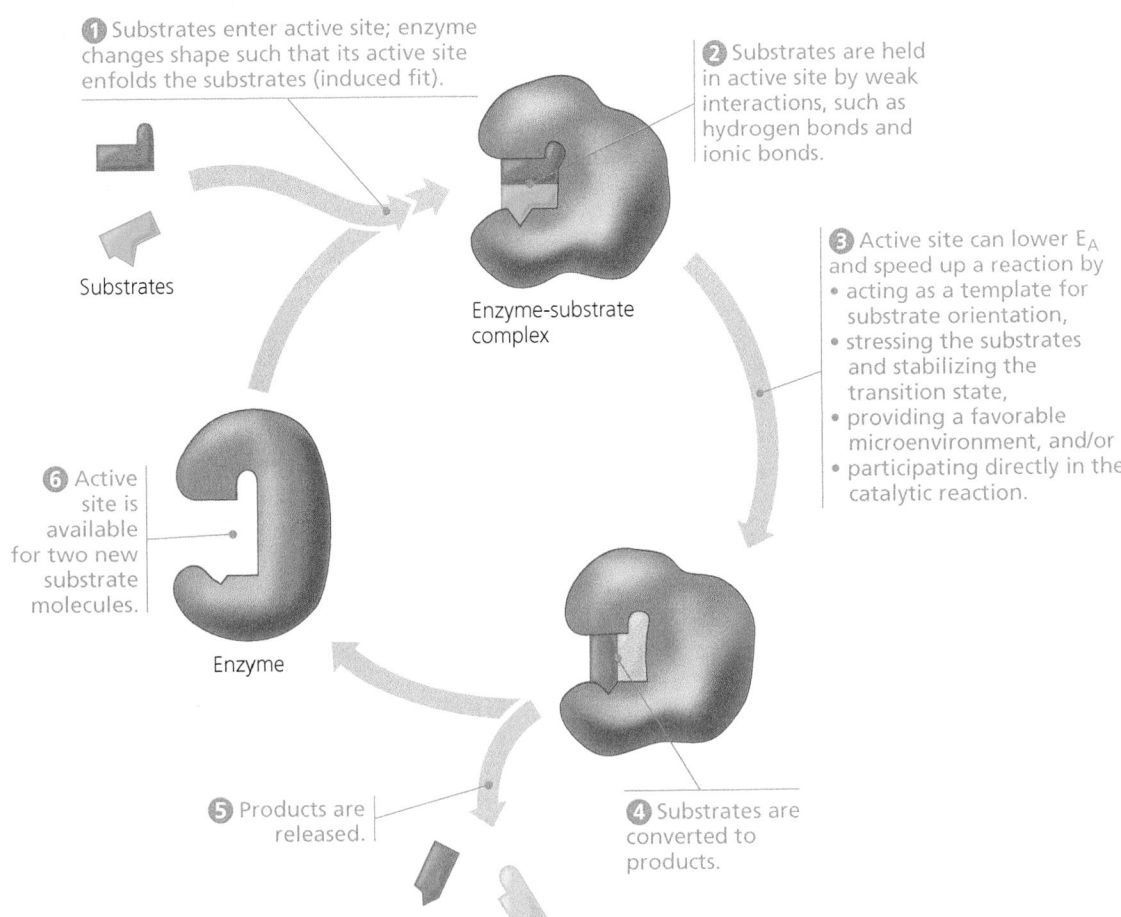

① Substrates enter active site; enzyme changes shape such that its active site enfolds the substrates (induced fit).

Substrates

② Substrates are held in active site by weak interactions, such as hydrogen bonds and ionic bonds.

Enzyme-substrate complex

③ Active site can lower E_A and speed up a reaction by
• acting as a template for substrate orientation,
• stressing the substrates and stabilizing the transition state,
• providing a favorable microenvironment, and/or
• participating directly in the catalytic reaction.

⑥ Active site is available for two new substrate molecules.

Enzyme

⑤ Products are released.

④ Substrates are converted to products.

Products

▲ **Figure 8.15 The active site and catalytic cycle of an enzyme.** An enzyme can convert one or more reactant molecules to one or more product molecules. The enzyme shown here converts two substrate molecules to two product molecules.

The rate at which a particular amount of enzyme converts substrate to product is partly a function of the initial concentration of the substrate: The more substrate molecules that are available, the more frequently they access the active sites of the enzyme molecules. However, there is a limit to how fast the reaction can be pushed by adding more substrate to a fixed concentration of enzyme. At some point, the concentration of substrate will be high enough that all enzyme molecules have their active sites engaged. As soon as the product exits an active site, another substrate molecule enters. At this substrate concentration, the enzyme is said to be *saturated*, and the rate of the reaction is determined by the speed at which the active site converts substrate to product. When an enzyme population is saturated, the only way to increase the rate of product formation is to add more enzyme. Cells often increase the rate of a reaction by producing more enzyme molecules.

Effects of Local Conditions on Enzyme Activity

The activity of an enzyme—how efficiently the enzyme functions—is affected by general environmental factors, such as temperature and pH. It can also be affected by chemicals that specifically influence that enzyme. In fact, researchers have learned much about enzyme function by employing such chemicals.

Effects of Temperature and pH

Recall from Chapter 5 that the three-dimensional structures of proteins are sensitive to their environment. As a consequence, each enzyme works better under some conditions than under other conditions, because these *optimal conditions* favor the most active shape for the enzyme molecule.

Temperature and pH are environmental factors important in the activity of an enzyme. Up to a point, the rate of an enzymatic reaction increases with increasing temperature, partly because substrates collide with active sites more frequently when the molecules move rapidly. Above that temperature, however, the speed of the enzymatic reaction drops sharply. The thermal agitation of the enzyme molecule disrupts the hydrogen bonds, ionic bonds, and other weak interactions that stabilize the active shape of the enzyme, and the protein molecule eventually denatures. Each enzyme has an optimal temperature at which its reaction rate is greatest. Without denaturing the enzyme, this temperature allows the greatest number of molecular collisions and the fastest conversion of the reactants to product molecules. Most human enzymes have optimal temperatures of about 35–40°C (close to human body temperature). The thermophilic bacteria that live in hot springs contain enzymes with optimal temperatures of 70°C or higher (**Figure 8.16a** on the next page).

(a) Optimal temperature for two enzymes

Optimal temperature for typical human enzyme (37°C)

Optimal temperature for enzyme of thermophilic (heat-tolerant) bacteria (77°C)

(b) Optimal pH for two enzymes

Optimal pH for pepsin (stomach enzyme)

Optimal pH for trypsin (intestinal enzyme)

▲ **Figure 8.16 Environmental factors affecting enzyme activity.** Each enzyme has an optimal **(a)** temperature and **(b)** pH that favor the most active shape of the protein molecule.

DRAW IT *Given that a mature lysosome has an internal pH of around 4.5, draw a curve in (b) showing what you would predict for a lysosomal enzyme, labeling its optimal pH.*

Just as each enzyme has an optimal temperature, it also has a pH at which it is most active. The optimal pH values for most enzymes fall in the range of pH 6–8, but there are exceptions. For example, pepsin, a digestive enzyme in the human stomach, works best at pH 2. Such an acidic environment denatures most enzymes, but pepsin is adapted to maintain its functional three-dimensional structure in the acidic environment of the stomach. In contrast, trypsin, a digestive enzyme residing in the alkaline environment of the human intestine, has an optimal pH of 8 and would be denatured in the stomach **(Figure 8.16b)**.

Cofactors

Many enzymes require nonprotein helpers for catalytic activity. These adjuncts, called **cofactors**, may be bound tightly to the enzyme as permanent residents, or they may bind loosely and reversibly along with the substrate. The cofactors of some enzymes are inorganic, such as the metal atoms zinc, iron, and copper in ionic form. If the cofactor is an organic molecule, it is more specifically called a **coenzyme**. Most vitamins are important in nutrition because they act as coenzymes or raw materials from which coenzymes are made. Cofactors function in various ways, but in all cases where they

are used, they perform a crucial chemical function in catalysis. You'll encounter examples of cofactors later in the book.

Enzyme Inhibitors

Certain chemicals selectively inhibit the action of specific enzymes, and we have learned a lot about enzyme function by studying the effects of these molecules. If the inhibitor attaches to the enzyme by covalent bonds, inhibition is usually irreversible.

Many enzyme inhibitors, however, bind to the enzyme by weak interactions, in which case inhibition is reversible. Some reversible inhibitors resemble the normal substrate molecule and compete for admission into the active site **(Figure 8.17a and b)**. These mimics, called **competitive inhibitors**, reduce

▼ **Figure 8.17 Inhibition of enzyme activity.**

(a) Normal binding

A substrate can bind normally to the active site of an enzyme.

Substrate

Active site

Enzyme

(b) Competitive inhibition

A competitive inhibitor mimics the substrate, competing for the active site.

Competitive inhibitor

(c) Noncompetitive inhibition

A noncompetitive inhibitor binds to the enzyme away from the active site, altering the shape of the enzyme so that even if the substrate can bind, the active site functions less effectively.

Noncompetitive inhibitor

the productivity of enzymes by blocking substrates from entering active sites. This kind of inhibition can be overcome by increasing the concentration of substrate so that as active sites become available, more substrate molecules than inhibitor molecules are around to gain entry to the sites.

In contrast, **noncompetitive inhibitors** do not directly compete with the substrate to bind to the enzyme at the active site (Figure 8.17c). Instead, they impede enzymatic reactions by binding to another part of the enzyme. This interaction causes the enzyme molecule to change its shape in such a way that the active site becomes less effective at catalyzing the conversion of substrate to product.

Toxins and poisons are often irreversible enzyme inhibitors. An example is sarin, a nerve gas that caused the death of several people and injury to many others when it was released by terrorists in the Tokyo subway in 1995. This small molecule binds covalently to the R group on the amino acid serine, which is found in the active site of acetylcholinesterase, an enzyme important in the nervous system. Other examples include the pesticides DDT and parathion, inhibitors of key enzymes in the nervous system. Finally, many antibiotics are inhibitors of specific enzymes in bacteria. For instance, penicillin blocks the active site of an enzyme that many bacteria use to make their cell walls.

Citing enzyme inhibitors that are metabolic poisons may give the impression that enzyme inhibition is generally abnormal and harmful. In fact, molecules naturally present in the cell often regulate enzyme activity by acting as inhibitors. Such regulation—selective inhibition—is essential to the control of cellular metabolism, as we will discuss in Concept 8.5.

The Evolution of Enzymes

EVOLUTION Thus far, biochemists have discovered and named more than 4,000 different enzymes in various species, and this list probably represents the tip of the proverbial iceberg. How did this grand profusion of enzymes arise? Recall that most enzymes are proteins, and proteins are encoded by genes. A permanent change in a gene, known as a *mutation*, can result in a protein with one or more changed amino acids. In the case of an enzyme, if the changed amino acids are in the active site or some other crucial region, the altered enzyme might have a novel activity or might bind to a different substrate. Under environmental conditions where the new function benefits the organism, natural selection would tend to favor the mutated form of the gene, causing it to persist in the population. This simplified model is generally accepted as the main way in which the multitude of different enzymes arose over the past few billion years of life's history.

Data supporting this model have been collected by researchers using a lab procedure that mimics evolution in natural populations. One group tested whether the function of an enzyme called β-galactosidase could change over time in populations of the bacterium *Escherichia coli* (*E. coli*). β-galactosidase

Two changed amino acids were found near the active site.

Active site

Two changed amino acids were found in the active site.

Two changed amino acids were found on the surface.

▲ **Figure 8.18 Mimicking evolution of an enzyme with a new function.** After seven rounds of mutation and selection in a lab, the enzyme β-galactosidase evolved into an enzyme specialized for breaking down a sugar different from lactose. This ribbon model shows one subunit of the altered enzyme; six amino acids were different.

breaks down the disaccharide lactose into the simple sugars glucose and galactose. Using molecular techniques, the researchers introduced random mutations into *E. coli* genes and then tested the bacteria for their ability to break down a slightly different disaccharide (one that has the sugar fucose in place of galactose). They selected the mutant bacteria that could do this best and exposed them to another round of mutation and selection. After seven rounds, the "evolved" enzyme bound the new substrate several hundred times more strongly, and broke it down 10 to 20 times more quickly, than did the original enzyme.

The researchers found that six amino acids had changed in the enzyme altered in this experiment. Two of these changed amino acids were in the active site, two were nearby, and two were on the surface of the protein (Figure 8.18). This experiment and others like it strengthen the notion that a few changes can indeed alter enzyme function.

CONCEPT CHECK 8.4

1. Many spontaneous reactions occur very slowly. Why don't all spontaneous reactions occur instantly?
2. Why do enzymes act only on very specific substrates?
3. **WHAT IF?** Malonate is an inhibitor of the enzyme succinate dehydrogenase. How would you determine whether malonate is a competitive or noncompetitive inhibitor?
4. **MAKE CONNECTIONS** In nature, what conditions could lead to natural selection favoring bacteria with enzymes that could break down the fucose-containing disaccharide discussed above? See the discussion of natural selection in Concept 1.2, pages 14–16.

For suggested answers, see Appendix A.

Regulation of enzyme activity helps control metabolism

Chemical chaos would result if all of a cell's metabolic pathways were operating simultaneously. Intrinsic to life's processes is a cell's ability to tightly regulate its metabolic pathways by controlling when and where its various enzymes are active. It does this either by switching on and off the genes that encode specific enzymes (as we will discuss in Unit Three) or, as we discuss here, by regulating the activity of enzymes once they are made.

Allosteric Regulation of Enzymes

In many cases, the molecules that naturally regulate enzyme activity in a cell behave something like reversible noncompetitive inhibitors (see Figure 8.17c): These regulatory molecules change an enzyme's shape and the functioning of its active site by binding to a site elsewhere on the molecule, via noncovalent interactions. **Allosteric regulation** is the term used to describe any case in which a protein's function at one site is affected by the binding of a regulatory molecule to a separate site. It may result in either inhibition or stimulation of an enzyme's activity.

Allosteric Activation and Inhibition

Most enzymes known to be allosterically regulated are constructed from two or more subunits, each composed of a polypeptide chain with its own active site. The entire complex oscillates between two different shapes, one catalytically active and the other inactive (**Figure 8.19a**). In the simplest kind of allosteric regulation, an activating or inhibiting regulatory molecule binds to a regulatory site (sometimes called an allosteric site), often located where subunits join. The binding of an *activator* to a regulatory site stabilizes the shape that has functional active sites, whereas the binding of an *inhibitor* stabilizes the inactive form of the enzyme. The subunits of an allosteric enzyme fit together in such a way that a shape change in one subunit is transmitted to all others. Through this interaction of subunits, a single activator or inhibitor molecule that binds to one regulatory site will affect the active sites of all subunits.

Fluctuating concentrations of regulators can cause a sophisticated pattern of response in the activity of cellular enzymes. The products of ATP hydrolysis (ADP and ⓟᵢ), for example, play a complex role in balancing the flow of traffic between anabolic and catabolic pathways by their effects on key enzymes. ATP binds to several catabolic enzymes allosterically, lowering their affinity for substrate and thus inhibiting their activity. ADP, however, functions as an activator of the same enzymes. This is logical because catabolism functions

▼ Figure 8.19 **Allosteric regulation of enzyme activity.**

(a) Allosteric activators and inhibitors

Allosteric enzyme with four subunits

Active site (one of four)

Allosteric activator stabilizes active form.

Regulatory site (one of four)

Activator

Active form

Stabilized active form

Oscillation

Allosteric inhibitor stabilizes inactive form.

Non-functional active site

Inactive form

Inhibitor

Stabilized inactive form

At low concentrations, activators and inhibitors dissociate from the enzyme. The enzyme can then oscillate again.

(b) Cooperativity: another type of allosteric activation

Binding of one substrate molecule to active site of one subunit locks all subunits in active conformation.

Substrate

Inactive form

Stabilized active form

The inactive form shown on the left oscillates with the active form when the active form is not stabilized by substrate.

in regenerating ATP. If ATP production lags behind its use, ADP accumulates and activates the enzymes that speed up catabolism, producing more ATP. If the supply of ATP exceeds demand, then catabolism slows down as ATP molecules accumulate and bind to the same enzymes, inhibiting them. (You'll see specific examples of this type of regulation when you learn about cellular respiration in the next chapter.) ATP, ADP, and other related molecules also affect key enzymes in anabolic pathways. In this way, allosteric enzymes control the rates of important reactions in both sorts of metabolic pathways.

In another kind of allosteric activation, a *substrate* molecule binding to one active site in a multisubunit enzyme triggers a shape change in all the subunits, thereby increasing catalytic activity at the other active sites (Figure 8.19b). Called **cooperativity**, this mechanism amplifies the response of enzymes to substrates: One substrate molecule primes an enzyme to act on additional substrate molecules more readily. Cooperativity is considered "allosteric" regulation because binding of the substrate to one active site affects catalysis in another active site.

Although the vertebrate oxygen transport protein hemoglobin is not an enzyme, classic studies of cooperative binding in this protein have elucidated the principle of cooperativity. Hemoglobin is made up of four subunits, each of which has an oxygen-binding site (see Figure 5.20). The binding of an oxygen molecule to one binding site increases the affinity for oxygen of the remaining binding sites. Thus, where oxygen is at high levels, such as in the lungs or gills, hemoglobin's affinity for oxygen increases as more binding sites are filled. In oxygen-deprived tissues, however, the release of each oxygen molecule decreases the oxygen affinity of the other binding sites, resulting in the release of oxygen where it is most needed. Cooperativity works similarly in multisubunit enzymes that have been studied.

Identification of Allosteric Regulators

Although allosteric regulation is probably quite widespread, relatively few of the many known metabolic enzymes have been shown to be regulated in this way. Allosteric regulatory molecules are hard to characterize, in part because they tend to bind the enzyme at low affinity and are therefore hard to isolate. Recently, however, pharmaceutical companies have turned their attention to allosteric regulators. These molecules are attractive drug candidates for enzyme regulation because they exhibit higher specificity for particular enzymes than do inhibitors that bind to the active site. (An active site may be similar to the active site in another, related enzyme, whereas allosteric regulatory sites appear to be quite distinct between enzymes.)

Figure 8.20 describes a search for allosteric regulators, carried out as a collaboration between researchers at the University of California at San Francisco and a company called Sunesis Pharmaceuticals. The study was designed to find allosteric inhibitors of *caspases*, protein-digesting enzymes that play an active role in inflammation and cell death. (You'll learn more about caspases and cell death in Chapter 11.) By specifically regulating these enzymes, we may be able to better manage inappropriate inflammatory responses, such as those commonly seen in vascular and neurodegenerative diseases.

▼ Figure 8.20

INQUIRY

Are there allosteric inhibitors of caspase enzymes?

EXPERIMENT In an effort to identify allosteric inhibitors of caspases, Justin Scheer and co-workers screened close to 8,000 compounds for their ability to bind to a possible allosteric binding site in caspase 1 and inhibit the enzyme's activity. Each compound was designed to form a disulfide bond with a cysteine near the site in order to stabilize the low-affinity interaction that is expected of an allosteric inhibitor. As the caspases are known to exist in both active and inactive forms, the researchers hypothesized that this linkage might lock the enzyme in the inactive form.

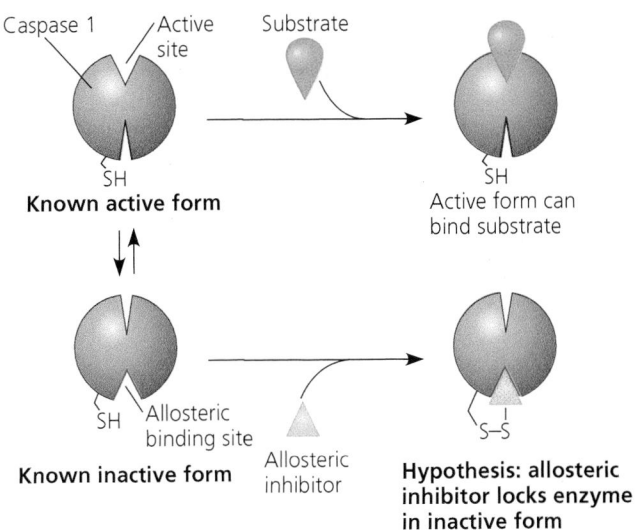

To test this model, X-ray diffraction analysis was used to determine the structure of caspase 1 when bound to one of the inhibitors and to compare it with the active and inactive structures.

RESULTS Fourteen compounds were identified that could bind to the proposed allosteric site (red) of caspase 1 and block enzymatic activity. The enzyme's shape when one such inhibitor was bound resembled the inactive caspase 1 more than the active form.

CONCLUSION That particular inhibitory compound apparently locks the enzyme in its inactive form, as expected for a true allosteric regulator. The data therefore support the existence of an allosteric inhibitory site on caspase 1 that can be used to control enzymatic activity.

SOURCE J. M. Scheer et al., A common allosteric site and mechanism in caspases, *Proceedings of the National Academy of Sciences* 103: 7595–7600 (2006).

WHAT IF? As a control, the researchers broke the disulfide linkage between one of the inhibitors and the caspase. Assuming that the experimental solution contains no other inhibitors, how would you expect the caspase 1 activity to be affected?

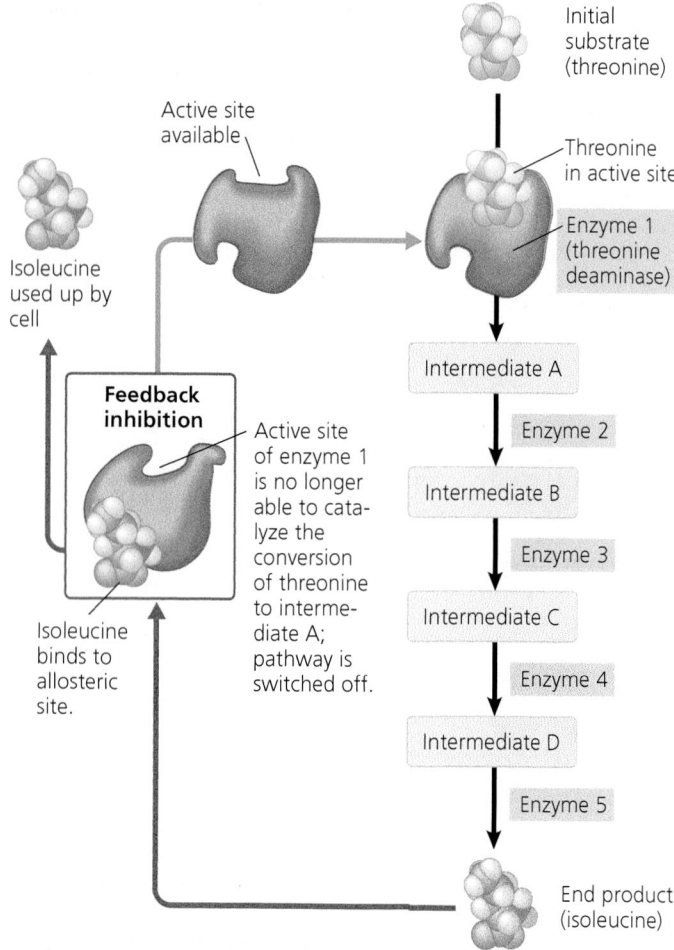

▲ **Figure 8.21 Feedback inhibition in isoleucine synthesis.**

Labels in figure:

Initial substrate (threonine)

Active site available

Threonine in active site

Enzyme 1 (threonine deaminase)

Isoleucine used up by cell

Feedback inhibition

Active site of enzyme 1 is no longer able to catalyze the conversion of threonine to intermediate A; pathway is switched off.

Isoleucine binds to allosteric site.

Intermediate A

Enzyme 2

Intermediate B

Enzyme 3

Intermediate C

Enzyme 4

Intermediate D

Enzyme 5

End product (isoleucine)

Feedback Inhibition

When ATP allosterically inhibits an enzyme in an ATP-generating pathway, as we discussed earlier, the result is feedback inhibition, a common mode of metabolic control. In **feedback inhibition**, a metabolic pathway is switched off by the inhibitory binding of its end product to an enzyme that acts early in the pathway. **Figure 8.21** shows an example of this control mechanism operating on an anabolic pathway. Certain cells use this five-step pathway to synthesize the amino acid isoleucine from threonine, another amino acid. As isoleucine accumulates, it slows down its own synthesis by allosterically inhibiting the enzyme for the first step of the pathway. Feedback inhibition thereby prevents the cell from wasting chemical resources by making more isoleucine than is necessary.

Specific Localization of Enzymes Within the Cell

The cell is not just a bag of chemicals with thousands of different kinds of enzymes and substrates in a random mix. The cell is compartmentalized, and cellular structures help bring order to metabolic pathways. In some cases, a team of enzymes for several steps of a metabolic pathway are assembled into a multienzyme complex. The arrangement facilitates the

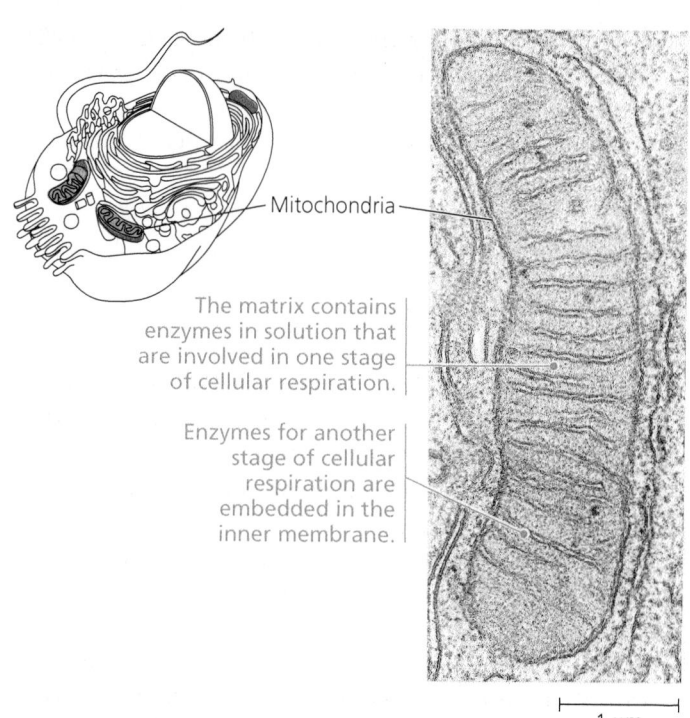

Mitochondria

The matrix contains enzymes in solution that are involved in one stage of cellular respiration.

Enzymes for another stage of cellular respiration are embedded in the inner membrane.

1 µm

▲ **Figure 8.22 Organelles and structural order in metabolism.** Organelles such as the mitochondrion (TEM) contain enzymes that carry out specific functions, in this case cellular respiration.

sequence of reactions, with the product from the first enzyme becoming the substrate for an adjacent enzyme in the complex, and so on, until the end product is released. Some enzymes and enzyme complexes have fixed locations within the cell and act as structural components of particular membranes. Others are in solution within particular membrane-enclosed eukaryotic organelles, each with its own internal chemical environment. For example, in eukaryotic cells, the enzymes for cellular respiration reside in specific locations within mitochondria **(Figure 8.22)**.

In this chapter, you have learned that metabolism, the intersecting set of chemical pathways characteristic of life, is a choreographed interplay of thousands of different kinds of cellular molecules. In the next chapter, we explore cellular respiration, the major catabolic pathway that breaks down organic molecules, releasing energy for the crucial processes of life.

CONCEPT CHECK 8.5

1. How do an activator and an inhibitor have different effects on an allosterically regulated enzyme?

2. **WHAT IF?** Imagine you are a pharmacological researcher who wants to design a drug that inhibits a particular enzyme. Upon reading the scientific literature, you find that the enzyme's active site is similar to that of several other enzymes. What might be a good approach to developing your inhibitor drug?

For suggested answers, see Appendix A.

8 CHAPTER REVIEW

SUMMARY OF KEY CONCEPTS

CONCEPT 8.1

An organism's metabolism transforms matter and energy, subject to the laws of thermodynamics (pp. 142–145)

- **Metabolism** is the collection of chemical reactions that occur in an organism. **Enzymes** catalyze reactions in intersecting **metabolic pathways**, which may be **catabolic** (breaking down molecules, releasing energy) or **anabolic** (building molecules, consuming energy).
- **Energy** is the capacity to cause change; some forms of energy do work by moving matter. **Kinetic energy** is associated with motion and includes **thermal energy (heat)** associated with random motion of atoms or molecules. **Potential energy** is related to the location or structure of matter and includes **chemical energy** possessed by a molecule due to its structure.
- **The first law of thermodynamics**, conservation of energy, states that energy cannot be created or destroyed, only transferred or transformed. The **second law of thermodynamics** states that **spontaneous processes**, those requiring no outside input of energy, increase the **entropy** (disorder) of the universe.

> ? Explain how the highly ordered structure of a cell does not conflict with the second law of thermodynamics.

CONCEPT 8.2

The free-energy change of a reaction tells us whether or not the reaction occurs spontaneously (pp. 146–149)

- A living system's **free energy** is energy that can do work under cellular conditions. The change in free energy (ΔG) during a biological process is related directly to enthalpy change (ΔH) and to the change in entropy (ΔS): $\Delta G = \Delta H - T\Delta S$. Organisms live at the expense of free energy. During a spontaneous change, free energy decreases and the stability of a system increases. At maximum stability, the system is at equilibrium and can do no work.
- In an **exergonic** (spontaneous) chemical reaction, the products have less free energy than the reactants ($-\Delta G$). **Endergonic** (nonspontaneous) reactions require an input of energy ($+\Delta G$). The addition of starting materials and the removal of end products prevent metabolism from reaching equilibrium.

> ? Explain the meaning of each component in the equation for the change in free energy of a spontaneous chemical reaction. Why are spontaneous reactions important in the metabolism of a cell?

CONCEPT 8.3

ATP powers cellular work by coupling exergonic reactions to endergonic reactions (pp. 149–151)

- **ATP** is the cell's energy shuttle. Hydrolysis of its terminal phosphate yields ADP and Ⓟi and releases free energy.
- Through **energy coupling**, the exergonic process of ATP hydrolysis drives endergonic reactions by transfer of a phosphate group to specific reactants, forming a **phosphorylated intermediate** that is more reactive. ATP hydrolysis (sometimes with protein phosphorylation) also causes changes in the shape and binding affinities of transport and motor proteins.
- Catabolic pathways drive regeneration of ATP from ADP + Ⓟi.

> ? Describe the ATP cycle: How is ATP used and regenerated in a cell?

CONCEPT 8.4

Enzymes speed up metabolic reactions by lowering energy barriers (pp. 152–157)

- In a chemical reaction, the energy necessary to break the bonds of the reactants is the **activation energy**, E_A.
- **Enzymes** lower the E_A barrier:

- Each type of enzyme has a unique **active site** that combines specifically with its **substrate(s)**, the reactant molecule(s) on which it acts. The enzyme changes shape slightly when it binds the substrate(s) (**induced fit**).
- The active site can lower an E_A barrier by orienting substrates correctly, straining their bonds, providing a favorable microenvironment, or even covalently bonding with the substrate.
- Each enzyme has an optimal temperature and pH. Inhibitors reduce enzyme function. A **competitive inhibitor** binds to the active site, whereas a **noncompetitive inhibitor** binds to a different site on the enzyme.
- Natural selection, acting on organisms with mutant genes encoding altered enzymes, is a major evolutionary force responsible for the diverse array of enzymes found in organisms.

> ? How do both activation energy barriers and enzymes help maintain the structural and metabolic order of life?

CONCEPT 8.5

Regulation of enzyme activity helps control metabolism (pp. 158–160)

- Many enzymes are subject to **allosteric regulation**: Regulatory molecules, either activators or inhibitors, bind to specific regulatory sites, affecting the shape and function of the enzyme. In **cooperativity**, binding of one substrate molecule can stimulate binding or activity at other active sites. In **feedback inhibition**, the end product of a metabolic pathway allosterically inhibits the enzyme for a previous step in the pathway.
- Some enzymes are grouped into complexes, some are incorporated into membranes, and some are contained inside organelles, increasing the efficiency of metabolic processes.

> ? What roles do allosteric regulation and feedback inhibition play in the metabolism of a cell?

LEVEL 1: KNOWLEDGE/COMPREHENSION

1. Choose the pair of terms that correctly completes this sentence: Catabolism is to anabolism as _____ is to _____.
   a. exergonic; spontaneous
   d. work; energy
   b. exergonic; endergonic
   e. entropy; enthalpy
   c. free energy; entropy

2. Most cells cannot harness heat to perform work because
   a. heat is not a form of energy.
   b. cells do not have much heat; they are relatively cool.
   c. temperature is usually uniform throughout a cell.
   d. heat can never be used to do work.
   e. heat must remain constant during work.

3. Which of the following metabolic processes can occur without a net influx of energy from some other process?
   a. $ADP + ℗_i → ATP + H_2O$
   b. $C_6H_{12}O_6 + 6 O_2 → 6 CO_2 + 6 H_2O$
   c. $6 CO_2 + 6 H_2O → C_6H_{12}O_6 + 6 O_2$
   d. amino acids → protein
   e. glucose + fructose → sucrose

4. If an enzyme in solution is saturated with substrate, the most effective way to obtain a faster yield of products is to
   a. add more of the enzyme.
   b. heat the solution to 90°C.
   c. add more substrate.
   d. add an allosteric inhibitor.
   e. add a noncompetitive inhibitor.

5. Some bacteria are metabolically active in hot springs because
   a. they are able to maintain a lower internal temperature.
   b. high temperatures make catalysis unnecessary.
   c. their enzymes have high optimal temperatures.
   d. their enzymes are completely insensitive to temperature.
   e. they use molecules other than proteins or RNAs as their main catalysts.

LEVEL 2: APPLICATION/ANALYSIS

6. If an enzyme is added to a solution where its substrate and product are in equilibrium, what will occur?
   a. Additional product will be formed.
   b. Additional substrate will be formed.
   c. The reaction will change from endergonic to exergonic.
   d. The free energy of the system will change.
   e. Nothing; the reaction will stay at equilibrium.

LEVEL 3: SYNTHESIS/EVALUATION

7. **DRAW IT** Using a series of arrows, draw the branched metabolic reaction pathway described by the following statements, and then answer the question at the end. Use red arrows and minus signs to indicate inhibition.

   L can form either M or N.
   M can form O.
   O can form either P or R.
   P can form Q.
   R can form S.
   O inhibits the reaction of L to form M.
   Q inhibits the reaction of O to form P.
   S inhibits the reaction of O to form R.

   Which reaction would prevail if both Q and S were present in the cell in high concentrations?
   a. L → M
   c. L → N
   e. R → S
   b. M → O
   d. O → P

8. **EVOLUTION CONNECTION**
   A recent revival of the antievolutionary "intelligent design" argument holds that biochemical pathways are too complex to have evolved, because all intermediate steps in a given pathway must be present to produce the final product. Critique this argument. How could you use the diversity of metabolic pathways that produce the same or similar products to support your case?

9. **SCIENTIFIC INQUIRY**
   DRAW IT A researcher has developed an assay to measure the activity of an important enzyme present in liver cells growing in culture. She adds the enzyme's substrate to a dish of cells and then measures the appearance of reaction products. The results are graphed as the amount of product on the *y*-axis versus time on the *x*-axis. The researcher notes four sections of the graph. For a short period of time, no products appear (section A). Then (section B) the reaction rate is quite high (the slope of the line is steep). Next, the reaction gradually slows down (section C). Finally, the graph line becomes flat (section D). Draw and label the graph, and propose a model to explain the molecular events occurring at each stage of this reaction profile.

10. **SCIENCE, TECHNOLOGY, AND SOCIETY**
    Organophosphates (organic compounds containing phosphate groups) are commonly used as insecticides to improve crop yield. Organophosphates typically interfere with nerve signal transmission by inhibiting the enzymes that degrade transmitter molecules. They affect humans and other vertebrates as well as insects. Thus, the use of organophosphate pesticides poses some health risks. On the other hand, these molecules break down rapidly upon exposure to air and sunlight. As a consumer, what level of risk are you willing to accept in exchange for an abundant and affordable food supply?

11. **WRITE ABOUT A THEME**
    Energy Transfer Life requires energy. In a short essay (100–150 words), describe the basic principles of bioenergetics in an animal cell. How is the flow and transformation of energy different in a photosynthesizing cell? Include the role of ATP and enzymes in your discussion.

For selected answers, see Appendix A.

Mastering BIOLOGY   www.masteringbiology.com

1. MasteringBiology® Assignments

Tutorials ATP and Energy • How Enzymes Function • Enzyme and Substrate Concentrations • Factors That Affect Reaction Rate • Enzyme Inhibition • Regulating Enzyme Action
Activities Energy Transformations • The Structure of ATP • Chemical Reactions and ATP • How Enzymes Work
Questions Student Misconceptions • Reading Quiz • Multiple Choice • End-of-Chapter

2. eText

Read your book online, search, take notes, highlight text, and more.

3. The Study Area

Practice Tests • Cumulative Test • *BioFlix* 3-D Animations • MP3 Tutor Sessions • Videos • Activities • Investigations • Lab Media • Audio Glossary • Word Study Tools • Art

9

Cellular Respiration and Fermentation

▲ **Figure 9.1 How do these leaves power the work of life for this chimpanzee?**

KEY CONCEPTS

9.1 Catabolic pathways yield energy by oxidizing organic fuels

9.2 Glycolysis harvests chemical energy by oxidizing glucose to pyruvate

9.3 After pyruvate is oxidized, the citric acid cycle completes the energy-yielding oxidation of organic molecules

9.4 During oxidative phosphorylation, chemiosmosis couples electron transport to ATP synthesis

9.5 Fermentation and anaerobic respiration enable cells to produce ATP without the use of oxygen

9.6 Glycolysis and the citric acid cycle connect to many other metabolic pathways

Life Is Work

Living cells require transfusions of energy from outside sources to perform their many tasks—for example, assembling polymers, pumping substances across membranes, moving, and reproducing. The chimpanzee in **Figure 9.1** obtains energy for its cells by eating plants; some animals feed on other organisms that eat plants. The energy stored in the organic molecules of food ultimately comes from the sun. Energy flows into an ecosystem as sunlight and exits as heat; in contrast, the chemical elements essential to life are recycled **(Figure 9.2)**. Photosynthesis generates oxygen and organic molecules used by the mitochondria of eukaryotes (including plants and algae) as fuel for cellular respiration. Respiration breaks this fuel down, generating ATP. The waste products of this type of respiration, carbon dioxide and water, are the raw materials for photosynthesis. In this chapter, we consider how cells harvest the chemical energy stored in organic molecules and use it to generate ATP, the molecule that drives most cellular work. After presenting some basics about respiration, we will focus on three key pathways of respiration: glycolysis, the citric acid cycle, and oxidative phosphorylation. We'll also consider fermentation, a somewhat simpler pathway coupled to glycolysis that has deep evolutionary roots.

▲ **Figure 9.2 Energy flow and chemical recycling in ecosystems.** Energy flows into an ecosystem as sunlight and ultimately leaves as heat, while the chemical elements essential to life are recycled.

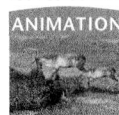 **ANIMATION** **BioFlix** Visit the Study Area at **www.masteringbiology.com** for the BioFlix® 3-D Animation on The Carbon Cycle.

Catabolic pathways yield energy by oxidizing organic fuels

As you learned in Chapter 8, metabolic pathways that release stored energy by breaking down complex molecules are called catabolic pathways. Electron transfer plays a major role in these pathways. In this section, we consider these processes, which are central to cellular respiration.

Catabolic Pathways and Production of ATP

Organic compounds possess potential energy as a result of the arrangement of electrons in the bonds between their atoms. Compounds that can participate in exergonic reactions can act as fuels. With the help of enzymes, a cell systematically degrades complex organic molecules that are rich in potential energy to simpler waste products that have less energy. Some of the energy taken out of chemical storage can be used to do work; the rest is dissipated as heat.

One catabolic process, **fermentation**, is a partial degradation of sugars or other organic fuel that occurs without the use of oxygen. However, the most prevalent and efficient catabolic pathway is **aerobic respiration**, in which oxygen is consumed as a reactant along with the organic fuel (*aerobic* is from the Greek *aer*, air, and *bios*, life). The cells of most eukaryotic and many prokaryotic organisms can carry out aerobic respiration. Some prokaryotes use substances other than oxygen as reactants in a similar process that harvests chemical energy without oxygen; this process is called *anaerobic respiration* (the prefix *an-* means "without"). Technically, the term **cellular respiration** includes both aerobic and anaerobic processes. However, it originated as a synonym for aerobic respiration because of the relationship of that process to organismal respiration, in which an animal breathes in oxygen. Thus, *cellular respiration* is often used to refer to the aerobic process, a practice we follow in most of this chapter.

Although very different in mechanism, aerobic respiration is in principle similar to the combustion of gasoline in an automobile engine after oxygen is mixed with the fuel (hydrocarbons). Food provides the fuel for respiration, and the exhaust is carbon dioxide and water. The overall process can be summarized as follows:

$$\text{Organic compounds} + \text{Oxygen} \rightarrow \text{Carbon dioxide} + \text{Water} + \text{Energy}$$

Although carbohydrates, fats, and proteins can all be processed and consumed as fuel, it is helpful to learn the steps of cellular respiration by tracking the degradation of the sugar glucose ($C_6H_{12}O_6$):

$$C_6H_{12}O_6 + 6\,O_2 \rightarrow 6\,CO_2 + 6\,H_2O + \text{Energy (ATP + heat)}$$

Glucose is the fuel that cells most often use; we will discuss other organic molecules contained in foods later in the chapter.

This breakdown of glucose is exergonic, having a free-energy change of −686 kcal (2,870 kJ) per mole of glucose decomposed ($\Delta G = -686$ kcal/mol). Recall that a negative ΔG indicates that the products of the chemical process store less energy than the reactants and that the reaction can happen spontaneously—in other words, without an input of energy.

Catabolic pathways do not directly move flagella, pump solutes across membranes, polymerize monomers, or perform other cellular work. Catabolism is linked to work by a chemical drive shaft—ATP, which you learned about in Chapter 8. To keep working, the cell must regenerate its supply of ATP from ADP and P_i (see Figure 8.11). To understand how cellular respiration accomplishes this, let's examine the fundamental chemical processes known as oxidation and reduction.

Redox Reactions: Oxidation and Reduction

How do the catabolic pathways that decompose glucose and other organic fuels yield energy? The answer is based on the transfer of electrons during the chemical reactions. The relocation of electrons releases energy stored in organic molecules, and this energy ultimately is used to synthesize ATP.

The Principle of Redox

In many chemical reactions, there is a transfer of one or more electrons (e^-) from one reactant to another. These electron transfers are called oxidation-reduction reactions, or **redox reactions** for short. In a redox reaction, the loss of electrons from one substance is called **oxidation**, and the addition of electrons to another substance is known as **reduction**. (Note that *adding* electrons is called *reduction*; negatively charged electrons added to an atom *reduce* the amount of positive charge of that atom.) To take a simple, nonbiological example, consider the reaction between the elements sodium (Na) and chlorine (Cl) that forms table salt:

$$\overbrace{Na + Cl \longrightarrow Na^+ + Cl^-}$$

becomes oxidized (loses electron)
becomes reduced (gains electron)

We could generalize a redox reaction this way:

$$Xe^- + Y \longrightarrow X + Ye^-$$

becomes oxidized
becomes reduced

In the generalized reaction, substance Xe^-, the electron donor, is called the **reducing agent**; it reduces Y, which accepts the donated electron. Substance Y, the electron acceptor, is the **oxidizing agent**; it oxidizes Xe^- by removing its electron. Because an electron transfer requires both a donor and an acceptor, oxidation and reduction always go together.

Not all redox reactions involve the complete transfer of electrons from one substance to another; some change the degree of electron sharing in covalent bonds. The reaction

Reactants   **Products**

$CH_4 + 2 O_2 \longrightarrow CO_2 + Energy + 2 H_2O$

becomes oxidized

becomes reduced

Methane (reducing agent)   Oxygen (oxidizing agent)   Carbon dioxide   Water

▲ **Figure 9.3 Methane combustion as an energy-yielding redox reaction.** The reaction releases energy to the surroundings because the electrons lose potential energy when they end up being shared unequally, spending more time near electronegative atoms such as oxygen.

between methane and oxygen, shown in **Figure 9.3**, is an example. As explained in Chapter 2, the covalent electrons in methane are shared nearly equally between the bonded atoms because carbon and hydrogen have about the same affinity for valence electrons; they are about equally electronegative. But when methane reacts with oxygen, forming carbon dioxide, electrons end up shared less equally between the carbon atom and its new covalent partners, the oxygen atoms, which are very electronegative. In effect, the carbon atom has partially "lost" its shared electrons; thus, methane has been oxidized.

Now let's examine the fate of the reactant O_2. The two atoms of the oxygen molecule (O_2) share their electrons equally. But when oxygen reacts with the hydrogen from methane, forming water, the electrons of the covalent bonds spend more time near the oxygen (see Figure 9.3). In effect, each oxygen atom has partially "gained" electrons, so the oxygen molecule has been reduced. Because oxygen is so electronegative, it is one of the most potent of all oxidizing agents.

Energy must be added to pull an electron away from an atom, just as energy is required to push a ball uphill. The more electronegative the atom (the stronger its pull on electrons), the more energy is required to take an electron away from it. An electron loses potential energy when it shifts from a less electronegative atom toward a more electronegative one, just as a ball loses potential energy when it rolls downhill. A redox reaction that moves electrons closer to oxygen, such as the burning (oxidation) of methane, therefore releases chemical energy that can be put to work.

Oxidation of Organic Fuel Molecules During Cellular Respiration

The oxidation of methane by oxygen is the main combustion reaction that occurs at the burner of a gas stove. The combustion of gasoline in an automobile engine is also a redox reaction; the energy released pushes the pistons. But the energy-yielding redox process of greatest interest to biologists

is respiration: the oxidation of glucose and other molecules in food. Examine again the summary equation for cellular respiration, but this time think of it as a redox process:

$$C_6H_{12}O_6 + 6 O_2 \longrightarrow 6 CO_2 + 6 H_2O + Energy$$

becomes oxidized

becomes reduced

As in the combustion of methane or gasoline, the fuel (glucose) is oxidized and oxygen is reduced. The electrons lose potential energy along the way, and energy is released.

In general, organic molecules that have an abundance of hydrogen are excellent fuels because their bonds are a source of "hilltop" electrons, whose energy may be released as these electrons "fall" down an energy gradient when they are transferred to oxygen. The summary equation for respiration indicates that hydrogen is transferred from glucose to oxygen. But the important point, not visible in the summary equation, is that the energy state of the electron changes as hydrogen (with its electron) is transferred to oxygen. In respiration, the oxidation of glucose transfers electrons to a lower energy state, liberating energy that becomes available for ATP synthesis.

The main energy-yielding foods, carbohydrates and fats, are reservoirs of electrons associated with hydrogen. Only the barrier of activation energy holds back the flood of electrons to a lower energy state (see Figure 8.12). Without this barrier, a food substance like glucose would combine almost instantaneously with O_2. If we supply the activation energy by igniting glucose, it burns in air, releasing 686 kcal (2,870 kJ) of heat per mole of glucose (about 180 g). Body temperature is not high enough to initiate burning, of course. Instead, if you swallow some glucose, enzymes in your cells will lower the barrier of activation energy, allowing the sugar to be oxidized in a series of steps.

Stepwise Energy Harvest via NAD⁺ and the Electron Transport Chain

If energy is released from a fuel all at once, it cannot be harnessed efficiently for constructive work. For example, if a gasoline tank explodes, it cannot drive a car very far. Cellular respiration does not oxidize glucose in a single explosive step either. Rather, glucose and other organic fuels are broken down in a series of steps, each one catalyzed by an enzyme. At key steps, electrons are stripped from the glucose. As is often the case in oxidation reactions, each electron travels with a proton—thus, as a hydrogen atom. The hydrogen atoms are not transferred directly to oxygen, but instead are usually passed first to an electron carrier, a coenzyme called **NAD⁺** (nicotinamide adenine dinucleotide, a derivative of the vitamin niacin). NAD⁺ is well suited as an electron carrier because it can cycle easily between oxidized (NAD⁺) and reduced (NADH) states. As an electron acceptor, NAD⁺ functions as an oxidizing agent during respiration.

How does NAD⁺ trap electrons from glucose and other organic molecules? Enzymes called dehydrogenases remove a

NAD⁺

Nicotinamide
(oxidized form)

Dehydrogenase
Reduction of NAD⁺
Oxidation of NADH

NADH

Nicotinamide
(reduced form)

◀ **Figure 9.4 NAD⁺ as an electron shuttle.** The full name for NAD⁺, nicotinamide adenine dinucleotide, describes its structure: The molecule consists of two nucleotides joined together at their phosphate groups (shown in yellow). (Nicotinamide is a nitrogenous base, although not one that is present in DNA or RNA; see Figure 5.26.) The enzymatic transfer of 2 electrons and 1 proton (H⁺) from an organic molecule in food to NAD⁺ reduces the NAD⁺ to NADH; the second proton (H⁺) is released. Most of the electrons removed from food are transferred initially to NAD⁺.

pair of hydrogen atoms (2 electrons and 2 protons) from the substrate (glucose, in this example), thereby oxidizing it. The enzyme delivers the 2 electrons along with 1 proton to its coenzyme, NAD⁺ (**Figure 9.4**). The other proton is released as a hydrogen ion (H⁺) into the surrounding solution:

$$H-\overset{|}{\underset{|}{C}}-OH + NAD^+ \xrightarrow{\text{Dehydrogenase}} \overset{|}{\underset{|}{C}}=O + NADH + H^+$$

By receiving 2 negatively charged electrons but only 1 positively charged proton, NAD⁺ has its charge neutralized when it is reduced to NADH. The name NADH shows the hydrogen that has been received in the reaction. NAD⁺ is the most versatile electron acceptor in cellular respiration and functions in several of the redox steps during the breakdown of glucose.

Electrons lose very little of their potential energy when they are transferred from glucose to NAD⁺. Each NADH molecule formed during respiration represents stored energy that can be tapped to make ATP when the electrons complete their "fall" down an energy gradient from NADH to oxygen.

How do electrons that are extracted from glucose and stored as potential energy in NADH finally reach oxygen? It will help to compare the redox chemistry of cellular respiration to a much simpler reaction: the reaction between hydrogen and oxygen to form water (**Figure 9.5a**). Mix H₂ and O₂, provide a spark for activation energy, and the

gases combine explosively. In fact, combustion of liquid H₂ and O₂ is harnessed to power the main engines of the space shuttle after it is launched, boosting it into orbit. The explosion represents a release of energy as the electrons of hydrogen "fall" closer to the electronegative oxygen atoms. Cellular respiration also brings hydrogen and oxygen together to form water, but there are two important differences. First, in cellular respiration, the hydrogen that reacts with oxygen is derived from organic molecules rather than H₂. Second, instead of occurring in one explosive reaction, respiration uses an

(a) Uncontrolled reaction

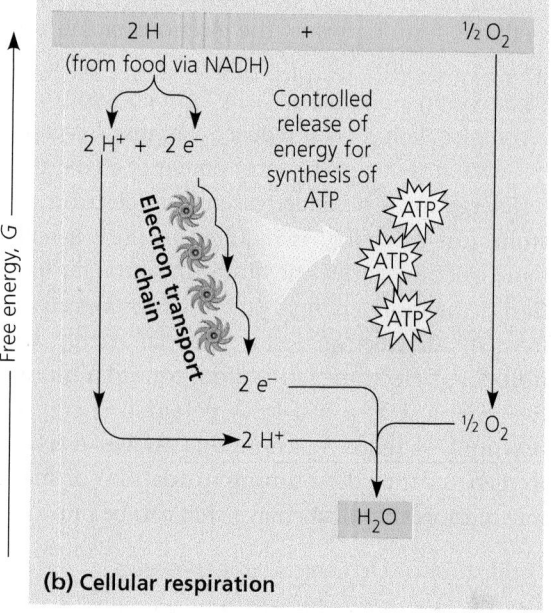

(b) Cellular respiration

▲ **Figure 9.5 An introduction to electron transport chains. (a)** The one-step exergonic reaction of hydrogen with oxygen to form water releases a large amount of energy in the form of heat and light: an explosion. **(b)** In cellular respiration, the same reaction occurs in stages: An electron transport chain breaks the "fall" of electrons in this reaction into a series of smaller steps and stores some of the released energy in a form that can be used to make ATP. (The rest of the energy is released as heat.)

electron transport chain to break the fall of electrons to oxygen into several energy-releasing steps (**Figure 9.5b**). An **electron transport chain** consists of a number of molecules, mostly proteins, built into the inner membrane of the mitochondria of eukaryotic cells and the plasma membrane of aerobically respiring prokaryotes. Electrons removed from glucose are shuttled by NADH to the "top," higher-energy end of the chain. At the "bottom," lower-energy end, O_2 captures these electrons along with hydrogen nuclei (H^+), forming water.

Electron transfer from NADH to oxygen is an exergonic reaction with a free-energy change of −53 kcal/mol (−222 kJ/mol). Instead of this energy being released and wasted in a single explosive step, electrons cascade down the chain from one carrier molecule to the next in a series of redox reactions, losing a small amount of energy with each step until they finally reach oxygen, the terminal electron acceptor, which has a very great affinity for electrons. Each "downhill" carrier is more electronegative than, and thus capable of oxidizing, its "uphill" neighbor, with oxygen at the bottom of the chain. Therefore, the electrons removed from glucose by NAD^+ fall down an energy gradient in the electron transport chain to a far more stable location in the electronegative oxygen atom. Put another way, oxygen pulls electrons down the chain in an energy-yielding tumble analogous to gravity pulling objects downhill.

In summary, during cellular respiration, most electrons travel the following "downhill" route: glucose → NADH → electron transport chain → oxygen. Later in this chapter, you will learn more about how the cell uses the energy released from this exergonic electron fall to regenerate its supply of ATP. For now, having covered the basic redox mechanisms of cellular respiration, let's look at the entire process by which energy is harvested from organic fuels.

The Stages of Cellular Respiration: *A Preview*

The harvesting of energy from glucose by cellular respiration is a cumulative function of three metabolic stages:

1. Glycolysis (color-coded teal throughout the chapter)
2. Pyruvate oxidation and the citric acid cycle (color-coded salmon)
3. Oxidative phosphorylation: electron transport and chemiosmosis (color-coded violet)

Biochemists usually reserve the term *cellular respiration* for stages 2 and 3. We include glycolysis, however, because most respiring cells deriving energy from glucose use glycolysis to produce the starting material for the citric acid cycle.

As diagrammed in **Figure 9.6**, glycolysis and pyruvate oxidation followed by the citric acid cycle are the catabolic pathways that break down glucose and other organic fuels. **Glycolysis**, which occurs in the cytosol, begins the degradation process by breaking glucose into two molecules of a compound called pyruvate. In eukaryotes, pyruvate enters the mitochondrion and is oxidized to a compound called acetyl CoA, which enters the **citric acid cycle**. There, the breakdown of glucose to carbon dioxide is completed. (In prokaryotes, these processes take place in the cytosol.) Thus, the carbon dioxide produced by respiration represents fragments of oxidized organic molecules.

Some of the steps of glycolysis and the citric acid cycle are redox reactions in which dehydrogenases transfer electrons from substrates to NAD^+, forming NADH. In the third stage of respiration, the electron transport chain accepts electrons from the breakdown products of the first two stages (most often via NADH) and passes these electrons from one molecule to another. At the end of the chain, the electrons are combined with molecular oxygen and hydrogen ions (H^+), forming water (see

▶ Figure 9.6 **An overview of cellular respiration.** During glycolysis, each glucose molecule is broken down into two molecules of the compound pyruvate. In eukaryotic cells, as shown here, the pyruvate enters the mitochondrion. There it is oxidized to acetyl CoA, which is further oxidized to CO_2 in the citric acid cycle. NADH and a similar electron carrier, a coenzyme called $FADH_2$, transfer electrons derived from glucose to electron transport chains, which are built into the inner mitochondrial membrane. (In prokaryotes, the electron transport chains are located in the plasma membrane.) During oxidative phosphorylation, electron transport chains convert the chemical energy to a form used for ATP synthesis in the process called chemiosmosis.

 BioFlix Visit the Study Area at **www.masteringbiology.com** for the BioFlix® 3-D Animation on Cellular Respiration.

Figure 9.5b). The energy released at each step of the chain is stored in a form the mitochondrion (or prokaryotic cell) can use to make ATP from ADP. This mode of ATP synthesis is called **oxidative phosphorylation** because it is powered by the redox reactions of the electron transport chain.

In eukaryotic cells, the inner membrane of the mitochondrion is the site of electron transport and chemiosmosis, the processes that together constitute oxidative phosphorylation. (In prokaryotes, these processes take place in the plasma membrane.) Oxidative phosphorylation accounts for almost 90% of the ATP generated by respiration. A smaller amount of ATP is formed directly in a few reactions of glycolysis and the citric acid cycle by a mechanism called **substrate-level phosphorylation** (**Figure 9.7**). This mode of ATP synthesis occurs when an enzyme transfers a phosphate group from a substrate molecule to ADP, rather than adding an inorganic phosphate to ADP as in oxidative phosphorylation. "Substrate molecule" here refers to an organic molecule generated as an intermediate during the catabolism of glucose.

For each molecule of glucose degraded to carbon dioxide and water by respiration, the cell makes up to about 32 molecules of ATP, each with 7.3 kcal/mol of free energy. Respiration cashes in the large denomination of energy banked in a single molecule of glucose (686 kcal/mol) for the small change of many molecules of ATP, which is more practical for the cell to spend on its work.

This preview has introduced you to how glycolysis, the citric acid cycle, and oxidative phosphorylation fit into the process of cellular respiration. We are now ready to take a closer look at each of these three stages of respiration.

CONCEPT CHECK 9.1

1. Compare and contrast aerobic and anaerobic respiration.
2. **WHAT IF?** If the following redox reaction occurred, which compound would be oxidized? Which reduced?

$$C_4H_6O_5 + NAD^+ \longrightarrow C_4H_4O_5 + NADH + H^+$$

For suggested answers, see Appendix A.

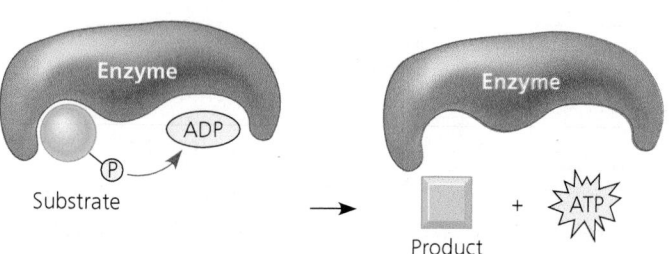

▲ **Figure 9.7 Substrate-level phosphorylation.** Some ATP is made by direct transfer of a phosphate group from an organic substrate to ADP by an enzyme. (For examples in glycolysis, see Figure 9.9, steps 7 and 10.)

MAKE CONNECTIONS *Review Figure 8.8 on page 149. Do you think the potential energy is higher for the reactants or the products in the reaction shown above? Explain.*

CONCEPT 9.2

Glycolysis harvests chemical energy by oxidizing glucose to pyruvate

The word *glycolysis* means "sugar splitting," and that is exactly what happens during this pathway. Glucose, a six-carbon sugar, is split into two three-carbon sugars. These smaller sugars are then oxidized and their remaining atoms rearranged to form two molecules of pyruvate. (Pyruvate is the ionized form of pyruvic acid.)

As summarized in **Figure 9.8**, glycolysis can be divided into two phases: energy investment and energy payoff. During the energy investment phase, the cell actually spends ATP. This investment is repaid with interest during the energy payoff phase, when ATP is produced by substrate-level phosphorylation and NAD^+ is reduced to NADH by electrons released from the oxidation of glucose. The net energy yield from glycolysis, per glucose molecule, is 2 ATP plus 2 NADH. The ten steps of the glycolytic pathway are shown in **Figure 9.9**.

All of the carbon originally present in glucose is accounted for in the two molecules of pyruvate; no carbon is released as CO_2 during glycolysis. Glycolysis occurs whether or not O_2 is present. However, if O_2 *is* present, the chemical energy stored in pyruvate and NADH can be extracted by pyruvate oxidation, the citric acid cycle, and oxidative phosphorylation.

▲ **Figure 9.8 The energy input and output of glycolysis.**

▼ **Figure 9.9 A closer look at glycolysis.** The orientation diagram on the left relates glycolysis to the entire process of respiration. Note that glycolysis is a source of ATP and NADH.

WHAT IF? *What would happen if you removed the dihydroxyacetone phosphate generated in step ④ as fast as it was produced?*

Glycolysis: Energy Investment Phase

Glucose → **Glucose 6-phosphate** → **Fructose 6-phosphate** → **Fructose 1,6-bisphosphate**

① Hexokinase

Hexokinase transfers a phosphate group from ATP to glucose, making it more chemically reactive. The charge on the phosphate also traps the sugar in the cell.

② Phosphogluco-isomerase

Glucose 6-phosphate is converted to its isomer, fructose 6-phosphate.

③ Phospho-fructokinase

Phosphofructokinase transfers a phosphate group from ATP to the opposite end of the sugar, investing a second molecule of ATP. This is a key step for regulation of glycolysis.

④ Aldolase

Aldolase cleaves the sugar molecule into two different three-carbon sugars (isomers).

Dihydroxyacetone phosphate ⇄ **Glyceraldehyde 3-phosphate**

⑤ Isomerase → To step 6

Isomerase catalyzes the reversible conversion between the two isomers. This reaction never reaches equilibrium: Glyceraldehyde 3-phosphate is used as the substrate of the next reaction (step 6) as fast as it forms.

The energy payoff phase occurs after glucose is split into two three-carbon sugars. Thus, the coefficient 2 precedes all molecules in this phase.

Glycolysis: Energy Payoff Phase

⑥ Triose phosphate dehydrogenase → **1,3-Bisphospho-glycerate** → **⑦ Phospho-glycerokinase** → **3-Phospho-glycerate** → **⑧ Phospho-glyceromutase** → **2-Phospho-glycerate** → **⑨ Enolase** → **Phosphoenol-pyruvate (PEP)** → **⑩ Pyruvate kinase** → **Pyruvate**

⑥ This enzyme catalyzes two sequential reactions. First, the sugar is oxidized by the transfer of electrons to NAD⁺, forming NADH. Second, the energy released from this exergonic redox reaction is used to attach a phosphate group to the oxidized substrate, making a product of very high potential energy.

⑦ The phosphate group added in the previous step is transferred to ADP (substrate-level phosphorylation) in an exergonic reaction. The carbonyl group of a sugar has been oxidized to the carboxyl group (—COO⁻) of an organic acid (3-phosphoglycerate).

⑧ This enzyme relocates the remaining phosphate group.

⑨ Enolase causes a double bond to form in the substrate by extracting a water molecule, yielding phosphoenolpyruvate (PEP), a compound with a very high potential energy.

⑩ The phosphate group is transferred from PEP to ADP (a second example of substrate-level phosphorylation), forming pyruvate.

CONCEPT CHECK 9.2

1. During the redox reaction in glycolysis (step 6 in Figure 9.9), which molecule acts as the oxidizing agent? The reducing agent?

2. **MAKE CONNECTIONS** Step 3 in Figure 9.9 is a major point of regulation of glycolysis. The enzyme phosphofructokinase is allosterically regulated by ATP and related molecules (see Concept 8.5, p. 158). Considering the overall result of glycolysis, would you expect ATP to inhibit or stimulate activity of this enzyme? (*Hint*: Make sure you consider the role of ATP as an allosteric regulator, not as a substrate of the enzyme.)

For suggested answers, see Appendix A.

After pyruvate is oxidized, the citric acid cycle completes the energy-yielding oxidation of organic molecules

Glycolysis releases less than a quarter of the chemical energy in glucose that can be released by cells; most of the energy remains stockpiled in the two molecules of pyruvate. If molecular oxygen is present, the pyruvate enters a mitochondrion (in eukaryotic cells), where the oxidation of glucose is completed. (In prokaryotic cells, this process occurs in the cytosol.)

Oxidation of Pyruvate to Acetyl CoA

Upon entering the mitochondrion via active transport, pyruvate is first converted to a compound called acetyl coenzyme A, or **acetyl CoA** (Figure 9.10). This step, linking glycolysis and the citric acid cycle, is carried out by a multienzyme complex that catalyzes three reactions: ❶ Pyruvate's carboxyl group ($-COO^-$), which is already fully oxidized and thus has little chemical energy, is removed and given off as a molecule of CO_2. (This is the first step in which CO_2 is released during respiration.) ❷ The remaining two-carbon fragment is oxidized, forming acetate (CH_3COO^-, the ionized form of acetic acid). The extracted electrons are transferred to NAD^+,

▲ **Figure 9.10 Oxidation of pyruvate to acetyl CoA, the step before the citric acid cycle.** Pyruvate is a charged molecule, so in eukaryotic cells it must enter the mitochondrion via active transport, with the help of a transport protein. Next, a complex of several enzymes (the pyruvate dehydrogenase complex) catalyzes the three numbered steps, which are described in the text. The acetyl group of acetyl CoA will enter the citric acid cycle. The CO_2 molecule will diffuse out of the cell. By convention, coenzyme A is abbreviated S-CoA when it is attached to a molecule, emphasizing the sulfur atom (S).

storing energy in the form of NADH. ❸ Finally, coenzyme A (CoA), a sulfur-containing compound derived from a B vitamin, is attached via its sulfur atom to the acetate, forming acetyl CoA, which has a high potential energy; in other words, the reaction of acetyl CoA to yield lower-energy products is highly exergonic. This molecule will now feed its acetyl group into the citric acid cycle for further oxidation.

The Citric Acid Cycle

The citric acid cycle is also called the tricarboxylic acid cycle or the Krebs cycle, the latter honoring Hans Krebs, the German-British scientist who was largely responsible for working out the pathway in the 1930s. The cycle functions as a metabolic furnace that oxidizes organic fuel derived from pyruvate. Figure 9.11 summarizes the inputs and outputs as pyruvate is broken down to three CO_2 molecules, including the molecule of CO_2 released during the conversion of pyruvate to acetyl CoA. The cycle generates 1 ATP per turn by

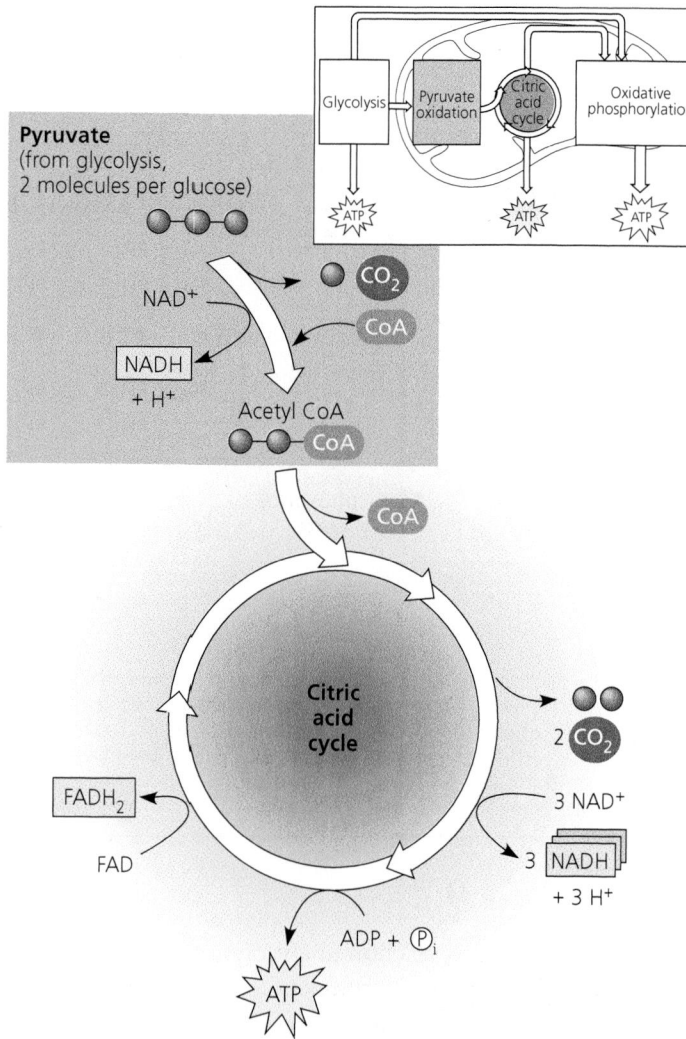

▲ **Figure 9.11 An overview of pyruvate oxidation and the citric acid cycle.** The inputs and outputs per pyruvate molecule are shown. To calculate on a per-glucose basis, multiply by 2, because each glucose molecule is split during glycolysis into two pyruvate molecules.

substrate-level phosphorylation, but most of the chemical energy is transferred to NAD^+ and a related electron carrier, the coenzyme FAD (flavin adenine dinucleotide, derived from riboflavin, a B vitamin), during the redox reactions. The reduced coenzymes, NADH and $FADH_2$, shuttle their cargo of high-energy electrons into the electron transport chain.

Now let's look at the citric acid cycle in more detail. The cycle has eight steps, each catalyzed by a specific enzyme. You can see in **Figure 9.12** that for each turn of the citric acid cycle, two carbons (red) enter in the relatively reduced form of an acetyl group (step 1), and two different carbons (blue) leave in the completely oxidized form of CO_2 molecules

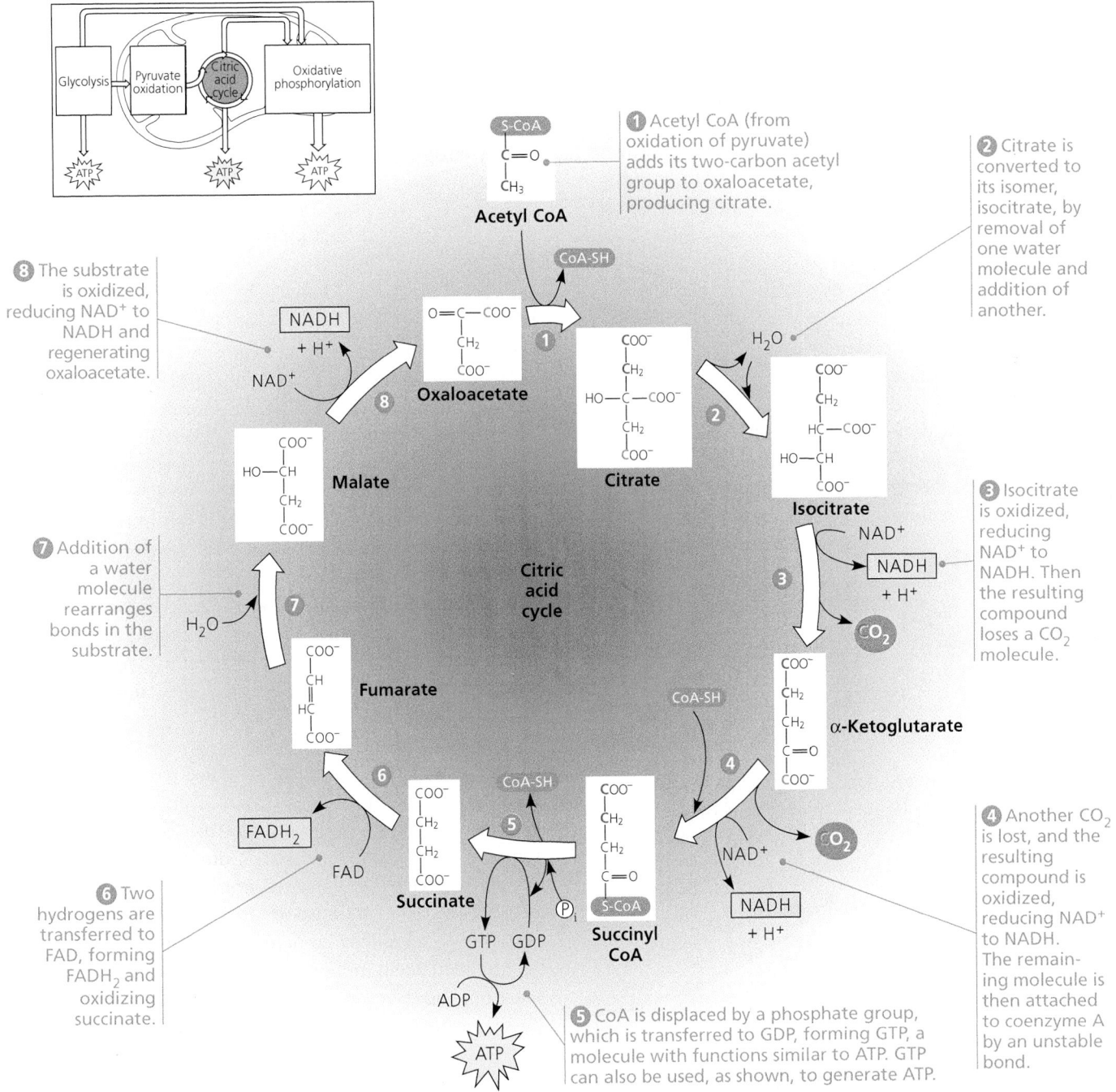

1 Acetyl CoA (from oxidation of pyruvate) adds its two-carbon acetyl group to oxaloacetate, producing citrate.

2 Citrate is converted to its isomer, isocitrate, by removal of one water molecule and addition of another.

3 Isocitrate is oxidized, reducing NAD^+ to NADH. Then the resulting compound loses a CO_2 molecule.

4 Another CO_2 is lost, and the resulting compound is oxidized, reducing NAD^+ to NADH. The remaining molecule is then attached to coenzyme A by an unstable bond.

5 CoA is displaced by a phosphate group, which is transferred to GDP, forming GTP, a molecule with functions similar to ATP. GTP can also be used, as shown, to generate ATP.

6 Two hydrogens are transferred to FAD, forming $FADH_2$ and oxidizing succinate.

7 Addition of a water molecule rearranges bonds in the substrate.

8 The substrate is oxidized, reducing NAD^+ to NADH and regenerating oxaloacetate.

▲ **Figure 9.12 A closer look at the citric acid cycle.** In the chemical structures, red type traces the fate of the two carbon atoms that enter the cycle via acetyl CoA (step 1), and blue type indicates the two carbons that exit the cycle as CO_2 in steps 3 and 4. (The red labeling goes only through step 5 because the succinate molecule is symmetrical; the two ends cannot be distinguished from each other.) Notice that the carbon atoms that enter the cycle from acetyl CoA do not leave the cycle in the same turn. They remain in the cycle, occupying a different location in the molecules on their next turn, after another acetyl group is added. As a consequence, the oxaloacetate that is regenerated at step 8 is composed of different carbon atoms each time around. In eukaryotic cells, all the citric acid cycle enzymes are located in the mitochondrial matrix except for the enzyme that catalyzes step 6, which resides in the inner mitochondrial membrane. Carboxylic acids are represented in their ionized forms, as $—COO^-$, because the ionized forms prevail at the pH within the mitochondrion. For example, citrate is the ionized form of citric acid.

(steps 3 and 4). The acetyl group of acetyl CoA joins the cycle by combining with the compound oxaloacetate, forming citrate (step 1). (Citrate is the ionized form of citric acid, for which the cycle is named.) The next seven steps decompose the citrate back to oxaloacetate. It is this regeneration of oxaloacetate that makes this process a *cycle*.

Now let's tally the energy-rich molecules produced by the citric acid cycle. For each acetyl group entering the cycle, 3 NAD^+ are reduced to NADH (steps 3, 4, and 8). In step 6, electrons are transferred not to NAD^+, but to FAD, which accepts 2 electrons and 2 protons to become $FADH_2$. In many animal tissue cells, step 5 produces a guanosine triphosphate (GTP) molecule by substrate-level phosphorylation, as shown in Figure 9.12. GTP is a molecule similar to ATP in its structure and cellular function. This GTP may be used to make an ATP molecule (as shown) or directly power work in the cell. In the cells of plants, bacteria, and some animal tissues, step 5 forms an ATP molecule directly by substrate-level phosphorylation. The output from step 5 represents the only ATP generated during the citric acid cycle.

Most of the ATP produced by respiration results from oxidative phosphorylation, when the NADH and $FADH_2$ produced by the citric acid cycle relay the electrons extracted from food to the electron transport chain. In the process, they supply the necessary energy for the phosphorylation of ADP to ATP. We will explore this process in the next section.

CONCEPT CHECK 9.3

1. Name the molecules that conserve most of the energy from the citric acid cycle's redox reactions. How is this energy converted to a form that can be used to make ATP?

2. What processes in your cells produce the CO_2 that you exhale?

3. **WHAT IF?** The conversions shown in Figure 9.10 and step 4 of Figure 9.12 are each catalyzed by a large multienzyme complex. What similarities are there in the reactions that occur in these two cases?

For suggested answers, see Appendix A.

CONCEPT 9.4

During oxidative phosphorylation, chemiosmosis couples electron transport to ATP synthesis

Our main objective in this chapter is to learn how cells harvest the energy of glucose and other nutrients in food to make ATP. But the metabolic components of respiration we have dissected so far, glycolysis and the citric acid cycle, produce only 4 ATP molecules per glucose molecule, all by substrate-level phosphorylation: 2 net ATP from glycolysis and 2 ATP from the citric acid cycle. At this point, molecules of NADH (and $FADH_2$) account for most of the energy extracted from the glucose. These electron escorts link glycolysis and the citric acid cycle to the machinery of oxidative phosphorylation, which uses energy released by the electron transport chain to power ATP synthesis. In this section, you will learn first how the electron transport chain works and then how electron flow down the chain is coupled to ATP synthesis.

The Pathway of Electron Transport

The electron transport chain is a collection of molecules embedded in the inner membrane of the mitochondrion in eukaryotic cells. (In prokaryotes, these molecules reside in the plasma membrane.) The folding of the inner membrane to form cristae increases its surface area, providing space for thousands of copies of the chain in each mitochondrion. (Once again, we see that structure fits function.) Most components of the chain are proteins, which exist in multiprotein complexes numbered I through IV. Tightly bound to these proteins are *prosthetic groups*, nonprotein components essential for the catalytic functions of certain enzymes.

Figure 9.13 shows the sequence of electron carriers in the electron transport chain and the drop in free energy as electrons travel down the chain. During electron transport along the chain, electron carriers alternate between reduced and oxidized states as they accept and donate electrons. Each component of the chain becomes reduced when it accepts electrons from its "uphill" neighbor, which has a lower affinity for electrons (is less electronegative). It then returns to its oxidized form as it passes electrons to its "downhill," more electronegative neighbor.

Now let's take a closer look at the electron transport chain in Figure 9.13. We'll first describe the passage of electrons through complex I in some detail, as an illustration of the general principles involved in electron transport. Electrons removed from glucose by NAD^+, during glycolysis and the citric acid cycle, are transferred from NADH to the first molecule of the electron transport chain in complex I. This molecule is a flavoprotein, so named because it has a prosthetic group called flavin mononucleotide (FMN). In the next redox reaction, the flavoprotein returns to its oxidized form as it passes electrons to an iron-sulfur protein (Fe·S in complex I), one of a family of proteins with both iron and sulfur tightly bound. The iron-sulfur protein then passes the electrons to a compound called ubiquinone (Q in Figure 9.13). This electron carrier is a small hydrophobic molecule, the only member of the electron transport chain that is not a protein. Ubiquinone is individually mobile within the membrane rather than residing in a particular complex. (Another name for ubiquinone is coenzyme Q, or CoQ; you may have seen it sold as a nutritional supplement.)

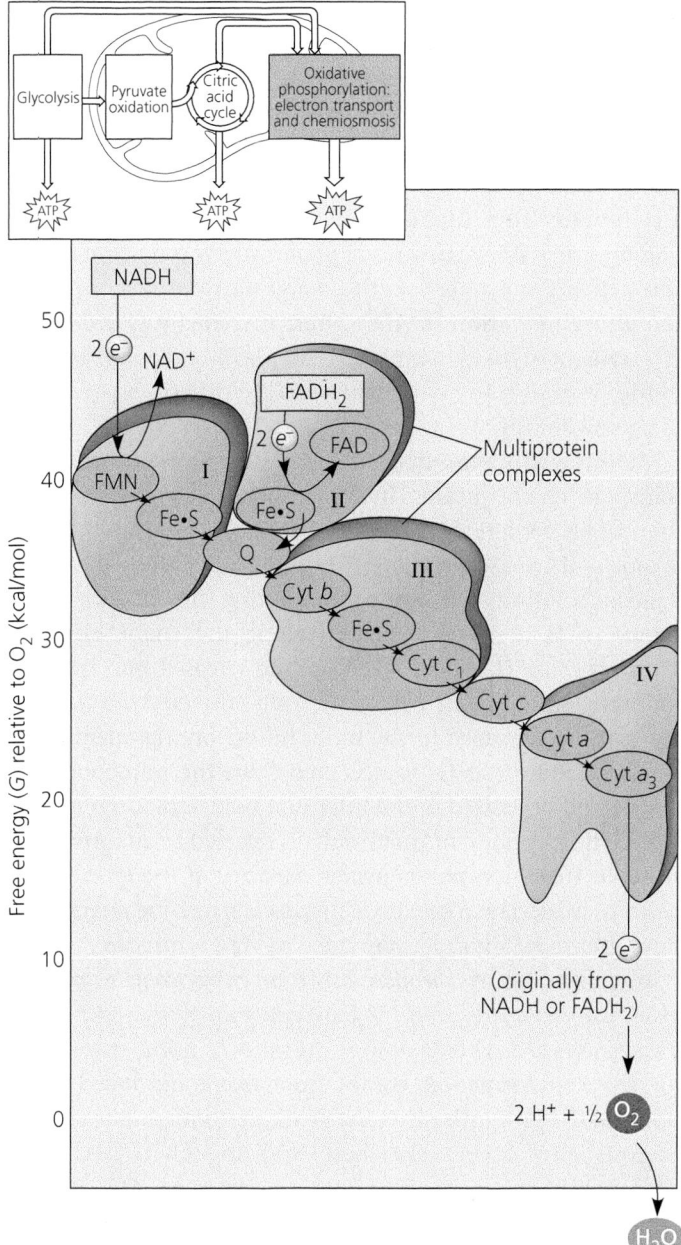

▲ **Figure 9.13 Free-energy change during electron transport.** The overall energy drop (ΔG) for electrons traveling from NADH to oxygen is 53 kcal/mol, but this "fall" is broken up into a series of smaller steps by the electron transport chain. (An oxygen atom is represented here as ½ O_2 to emphasize that the electron transport chain reduces molecular oxygen, O_2, not individual oxygen atoms.)

Most of the remaining electron carriers between ubiquinone and oxygen are proteins called **cytochromes**. Their prosthetic group, called a heme group, has an iron atom that accepts and donates electrons. (It is similar to the heme group in hemoglobin, the protein of red blood cells, except that the iron in hemoglobin carries oxygen, not electrons.) The electron transport chain has several types of cytochromes,

each a different protein with a slightly different electron-carrying heme group. The last cytochrome of the chain, cyt a_3, passes its electrons to oxygen, which is *very* electronegative. Each oxygen atom also picks up a pair of hydrogen ions from the aqueous solution, forming water.

Another source of electrons for the transport chain is $FADH_2$, the other reduced product of the citric acid cycle. Notice in Figure 9.13 that $FADH_2$ adds its electrons to the electron transport chain from within complex II, at a lower energy level than NADH does. Consequently, although NADH and $FADH_2$ each donate an equivalent number of electrons (2) for oxygen reduction, the electron transport chain provides about one-third less energy for ATP synthesis when the electron donor is $FADH_2$ rather than NADH. We'll see why in the next section.

The electron transport chain makes no ATP directly. Instead, it eases the fall of electrons from food to oxygen, breaking a large free-energy drop into a series of smaller steps that release energy in manageable amounts. How does the mitochondrion (or the prokaryotic plasma membrane) couple this electron transport and energy release to ATP synthesis? The answer is a mechanism called chemiosmosis.

Chemiosmosis: The Energy-Coupling Mechanism

Populating the inner membrane of the mitochondrion or the prokaryotic plasma membrane are many copies of a protein complex called **ATP synthase**, the enzyme that actually makes ATP from ADP and inorganic phosphate. ATP synthase works like an ion pump running in reverse. Recall from Chapter 7 that ion pumps usually use ATP as an energy source to transport ions against their gradients. In fact, the proton pump shown in Figure 7.20 is an ATP synthase. As we mentioned in Chapter 8, enzymes can catalyze a reaction in either direction, depending on the ΔG for the reaction, which is affected by the local concentrations of reactants and products. Rather than hydrolyzing ATP to pump protons against their concentration gradient, under the conditions of cellular respiration ATP synthase uses the energy of an existing ion gradient to power ATP synthesis. The power source for the ATP synthase is a difference in the concentration of H^+ on opposite sides of the inner mitochondrial membrane. (We can also think of this gradient as a difference in pH, since pH is a measure of H^+ concentration.) This process, in which energy stored in the form of a hydrogen ion gradient across a membrane is used to drive cellular work such as the synthesis of ATP, is called **chemiosmosis** (from the Greek *osmos*, push). We have previously used the word *osmosis* in discussing water transport, but here it refers to the flow of H^+ across a membrane.

From studying the structure of ATP synthase, scientists have learned how the flow of H^+ through this large enzyme powers ATP generation. ATP synthase is a multisubunit complex with four main parts, each made up of multiple polypeptides. Protons move one by one into binding sites on one of the parts (the rotor), causing it to spin in a way that catalyzes ATP production from ADP and inorganic phosphate (**Figure 9.14**). The flow of protons thus behaves somewhat like a rushing stream that turns a waterwheel. ATP synthase is the smallest molecular rotary motor known in nature.

How does the inner mitochondrial membrane or the prokaryotic plasma membrane generate and maintain the H^+ gradient that drives ATP synthesis by the ATP synthase protein complex? Establishing the H^+ gradient is a major function of the electron transport chain, which is shown in

its mitochondrial location in **Figure 9.15**. The chain is an energy converter that uses the exergonic flow of electrons from NADH and $FADH_2$ to pump H^+ across the membrane, from the mitochondrial matrix into the intermembrane space. The H^+ has a tendency to move back across the membrane, diffusing down its gradient. And the ATP synthases are the only sites that provide a route through the membrane for H^+. As we described previously, the passage of H^+ through ATP synthase uses the exergonic flow of H^+ to drive the phosphorylation of ADP. Thus, the energy stored in an H^+ gradient across a membrane couples the redox reactions of the electron transport chain to ATP synthesis, an example of chemiosmosis.

At this point, you may be wondering how the electron transport chain pumps hydrogen ions. Researchers have found that certain members of the electron transport chain accept and release protons (H^+) along with electrons. (The aqueous solutions inside and surrounding the cell are a ready source of H^+.) At certain steps along the chain, electron transfers cause H^+ to be taken up and released into the surrounding solution. In eukaryotic cells, the electron carriers are spatially arranged in the inner mitochondrial membrane in such a way that H^+ is accepted from the mitochondrial matrix and deposited in the intermembrane space (see Figure 9.15). The H^+ gradient that results is referred to as a **proton-motive force**, emphasizing the capacity of the gradient to perform work. The force drives H^+ back across the membrane through the H^+ channels provided by ATP synthases.

In general terms, *chemiosmosis is an energy-coupling mechanism that uses energy stored in the form of an H^+ gradient across a membrane to drive cellular work.* In mitochondria, the energy for gradient formation comes from exergonic redox reactions, and ATP synthesis is the work performed. But chemiosmosis also occurs elsewhere and in other variations. Chloroplasts use chemiosmosis to generate ATP during photosynthesis; in these organelles, light (rather than chemical energy) drives both electron flow down an electron transport chain and the resulting H^+ gradient formation. Prokaryotes, as already mentioned, generate H^+ gradients across their plasma membranes. They then tap the proton-motive force not only to make ATP inside the cell but also to rotate their flagella and to pump nutrients and waste products across the membrane. Because of its central importance to energy conversions in prokaryotes and eukaryotes, chemiosmosis has helped unify the study of bioenergetics. Peter Mitchell was awarded the Nobel Prize in 1978 for originally proposing the chemiosmotic model.

INTERMEMBRANE SPACE

❶ H^+ ions flowing down their gradient enter a half channel in a **stator**, which is anchored in the membrane.

❷ H^+ ions enter binding sites within a **rotor**, changing the shape of each subunit so that the rotor spins within the membrane.

❸ Each H^+ ion makes one complete turn before leaving the rotor and passing through a second half channel in the stator into the mitochondrial matrix.

❹ Spinning of the rotor causes an internal **rod** to spin as well. This rod extends like a stalk into the **knob** below it, which is held stationary by part of the stator.

❺ Turning of the rod activates catalytic sites in the knob that produce ATP from ADP and $(P)_i$.

H^+
Stator
Rotor
Internal rod
Catalytic knob
ADP + $(P)_i$
ATP
MITOCHONDRIAL MATRIX

▲ **Figure 9.14 ATP synthase, a molecular mill.** The ATP synthase protein complex functions as a mill, powered by the flow of hydrogen ions. Multiple copies of this complex reside in mitochondrial and chloroplast membranes of eukaryotes and in the plasma membranes of prokaryotes. Each of the four parts of ATP synthase consists of a number of polypeptide subunits.

An Accounting of ATP Production by Cellular Respiration

In the last few sections, we have looked rather closely at the key processes of cellular respiration. Now let's take a step

Intermembrane space

Inner mitochondrial membrane

Mitochondrial matrix

Protein complex of electron carriers

Cyt c

I

Q

II

III

IV

FADH₂   FAD

NADH   NAD⁺

(carrying electrons from food)

$2 H^+ + \frac{1}{2} O_2$ H_2O

ATP synthase

$ADP + P_i$ ATP

① Electron transport chain
Electron transport and pumping of protons (H⁺), which create an H⁺ gradient across the membrane

② Chemiosmosis
ATP synthesis powered by the flow of H⁺ back across the membrane

Oxidative phosphorylation

▲ **Figure 9.15 Chemiosmosis couples the electron transport chain to ATP synthesis.** ① NADH and FADH₂ shuttle high-energy electrons extracted from food during glycolysis and the citric acid cycle into an electron transport chain built into the inner mitochondrial membrane. The gold arrows trace the transport of electrons, which finally pass to oxygen at the "downhill" end of the chain, forming water. As Figure 9.13 showed, most of the electron carriers of the chain are grouped into four complexes. Two mobile carriers, ubiquinone (Q)

and cytochrome c (Cyt c), move rapidly, ferrying electrons between the large complexes. As complexes I, III, and IV accept and then donate electrons, they pump protons from the mitochondrial matrix into the intermembrane space. (In prokaryotes, protons are pumped outside the plasma membrane.) Note that FADH₂ deposits its electrons via complex II and so results in fewer protons being pumped into the intermembrane space than occurs with NADH. Chemical energy originally harvested from food is transformed into a proton-motive

force, a gradient of H⁺ across the membrane. ② During chemiosmosis, the protons flow back down their gradient via ATP synthase, which is built into the membrane nearby. The ATP synthase harnesses the proton-motive force to phosphorylate ADP, forming ATP. Together, electron transport and chemiosmosis make up oxidative phosphorylation.

WHAT IF? *If complex IV were nonfunctional, could chemiosmosis produce any ATP, and if so, how would the rate of synthesis differ?*

back and remind ourselves of its overall function: harvesting the energy of glucose for ATP synthesis.

During respiration, most energy flows in this sequence: glucose → NADH → electron transport chain → proton-motive force → ATP. We can do some bookkeeping to calculate the ATP profit when cellular respiration oxidizes a molecule of glucose to six molecules of carbon dioxide. The three main departments of this metabolic enterprise are glycolysis, the citric acid cycle, and the electron transport chain, which drives oxidative phosphorylation. **Figure 9.16**, on the next page, gives a detailed accounting of the ATP yield per glucose molecule oxidized. The tally adds

the 4 ATP produced directly by substrate-level phosphorylation during glycolysis and the citric acid cycle to the many more molecules of ATP generated by oxidative phosphorylation. Each NADH that transfers a pair of electrons from glucose to the electron transport chain contributes enough to the proton-motive force to generate a maximum of about 3 ATP.

Why are the numbers in Figure 9.16 inexact? There are three reasons we cannot state an exact number of ATP molecules generated by the breakdown of one molecule of glucose. First, phosphorylation and the redox reactions are not directly coupled to each other, so the ratio of the number of

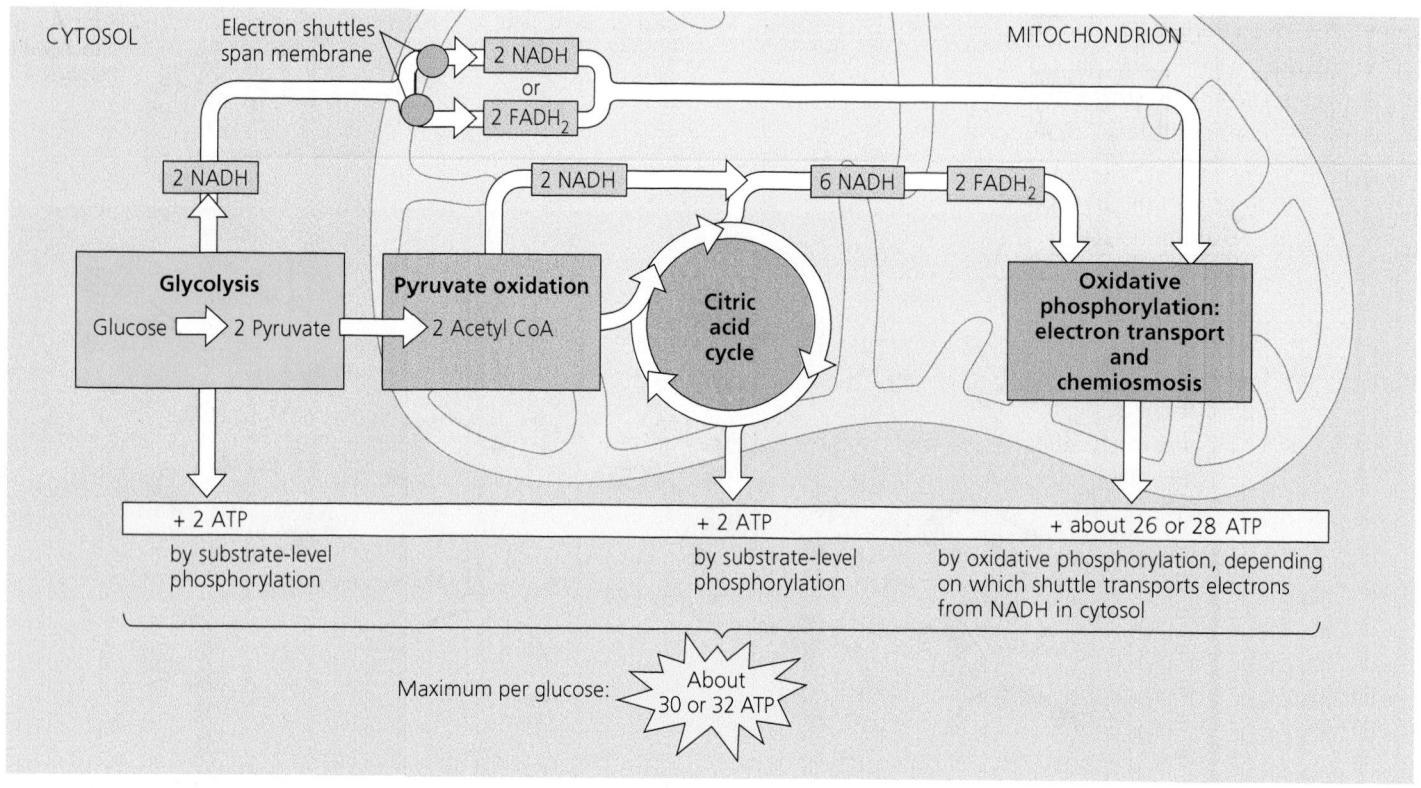

▲ **Figure 9.16 ATP yield per molecule of glucose at each stage of cellular respiration.**

? *Explain exactly how the numbers "26 or 28" were calculated.*

NADH molecules to the number of ATP molecules is not a whole number. We know that 1 NADH results in 10 H^+ being transported out across the inner mitochondrial membrane, but the exact number of H^+ that must reenter the mitochondrial matrix via ATP synthase to generate 1 ATP has long been debated. Based on experimental data, however, most biochemists now agree that the most accurate number is 4 H^+. Therefore, a single molecule of NADH generates enough proton-motive force for the synthesis of 2.5 ATP. The citric acid cycle also supplies electrons to the electron transport chain via $FADH_2$, but since its electrons enter later in the chain, each molecule of this electron carrier is responsible for transport of only enough H^+ for the synthesis of 1.5 ATP. These numbers also take into account the slight energetic cost of moving the ATP formed in the mitochondrion out into the cytosol, where it will be used.

Second, the ATP yield varies slightly depending on the type of shuttle used to transport electrons from the cytosol into the mitochondrion. The mitochondrial inner membrane is impermeable to NADH, so NADH in the cytosol is segregated from the machinery of oxidative phosphorylation. The 2 electrons of NADH captured in glycolysis must be conveyed into the mitochondrion by one of several electron shuttle systems. Depending on the kind of shuttle in a particular cell type, the electrons are passed either to NAD^+ or to FAD in the mitochondrial matrix (see Figure 9.16). If the electrons are passed to FAD, as in brain cells, only about 1.5 ATP can result from each NADH that was originally generated in the cytosol. If the

electrons are passed to mitochondrial NAD^+, as in liver cells and heart cells, the yield is about 2.5 ATP per NADH.

A third variable that reduces the yield of ATP is the use of the proton-motive force generated by the redox reactions of respiration to drive other kinds of work. For example, the proton-motive force powers the mitochondrion's uptake of pyruvate from the cytosol. However, if *all* the proton-motive force generated by the electron transport chain were used to drive ATP synthesis, one glucose molecule could generate a maximum of 28 ATP produced by oxidative phosphorylation plus 4 ATP (net) from substrate-level phosphorylation to give a total yield of about 32 ATP (or only about 30 ATP if the less efficient shuttle were functioning).

We can now roughly estimate the efficiency of respiration—that is, the percentage of chemical energy in glucose that has been transferred to ATP. Recall that the complete oxidation of a mole of glucose releases 686 kcal of energy under standard conditions ($\Delta G = -686$ kcal/mol). Phosphorylation of ADP to form ATP stores at least 7.3 kcal per mole of ATP. Therefore, the efficiency of respiration is 7.3 kcal per mole of ATP times 32 moles of ATP per mole of glucose divided by 686 kcal per mole of glucose, which equals 0.34. Thus, about 34% of the potential chemical energy in glucose has been transferred to ATP; the actual percentage is bound to vary as ΔG varies under different cellular conditions. Cellular respiration is remarkably efficient in its energy conversion. By comparison, the most efficient automobile converts only about 25% of the energy stored in gasoline to energy that moves the car.

The rest of the energy stored in glucose is lost as heat. We humans use some of this heat to maintain our relatively high body temperature (37°C), and we dissipate the rest through sweating and other cooling mechanisms.

Under certain conditions, it may be beneficial to reduce the efficiency of cellular respiration. A remarkable adaptation is shown by hibernating mammals, which overwinter in a state of inactivity and lowered metabolism. Although their internal body temperature is lower than normal, it still must be kept significantly higher than the external air temperature. One type of tissue, called brown fat, is made up of cells packed full of mitochondria. The inner mitochondrial membrane contains a channel protein called the uncoupling protein, which allows protons to flow back down their concentration gradient without generating ATP. Activation of these proteins in hibernating mammals results in ongoing oxidation of stored fuel stores (fats), generating heat without any ATP production. In the absence of such an adaptation, the ATP level would build up to a point that cellular respiration would be shut down due to regulatory mechanisms to be discussed later.

CONCEPT CHECK 9.4

1. What effect would an absence of O_2 have on the process shown in Figure 9.15?
2. **WHAT IF?** In the absence of O_2, as in question 1, what do you think would happen if you decreased the pH of the intermembrane space of the mitochondrion? Explain your answer.
3. **MAKE CONNECTIONS** In Concept 7.1 (pp. 127–128), you learned that membranes must be fluid to function properly. How does the operation of the electron transport chain support that assertion?

For suggested answers, see Appendix A.

CONCEPT 9.5

Fermentation and anaerobic respiration enable cells to produce ATP without the use of oxygen

Because most of the ATP generated by cellular respiration is due to the work of oxidative phosphorylation, our estimate of ATP yield from aerobic respiration is contingent on an adequate supply of oxygen to the cell. Without the electronegative oxygen to pull electrons down the transport chain, oxidative phosphorylation eventually ceases. However, there are two general mechanisms by which certain cells can oxidize organic fuel and generate ATP *without* the use of oxygen: anaerobic respiration and fermentation. The distinction between these two is that an electron transport chain is used in anaerobic respiration but not in fermentation. (The electron transport chain is also called the respiratory chain because of its role in both types of cellular respiration.)

We have already mentioned anaerobic respiration, which takes place in certain prokaryotic organisms that live in environments without oxygen. These organisms have an electron transport chain but do not use oxygen as a final electron acceptor at the end of the chain. Oxygen performs this function very well because it is extremely electronegative, but other, less electronegative substances can also serve as final electron acceptors. Some "sulfate-reducing" marine bacteria, for instance, use the sulfate ion (SO_4^{2-}) at the end of their respiratory chain. Operation of the chain builds up a proton-motive force used to produce ATP, but H_2S (hydrogen sulfide) is produced as a by-product rather than water. The rotten-egg odor you may have smelled while walking through a salt marsh or a mudflat signals the presence of sulfate-reducing bacteria.

Fermentation is a way of harvesting chemical energy without using either oxygen or any electron transport chain—in other words, without cellular respiration. How can food be oxidized without cellular respiration? Remember, oxidation simply refers to the loss of electrons to an electron acceptor, so it does not need to involve oxygen. Glycolysis oxidizes glucose to two molecules of pyruvate. The oxidizing agent of glycolysis is NAD^+, and neither oxygen nor any electron transfer chain is involved. Overall, glycolysis is exergonic, and some of the energy made available is used to produce 2 ATP (net) by substrate-level phosphorylation. If oxygen *is* present, then additional ATP is made by oxidative phosphorylation when NADH passes electrons removed from glucose to the electron transport chain. But glycolysis generates 2 ATP whether oxygen is present or not—that is, whether conditions are aerobic or anaerobic.

As an alternative to respiratory oxidation of organic nutrients, fermentation is an extension of glycolysis that allows continuous generation of ATP by the substrate-level phosphorylation of glycolysis. For this to occur, there must be a sufficient supply of NAD^+ to accept electrons during the oxidation step of glycolysis. Without some mechanism to recycle NAD^+ from NADH, glycolysis would soon deplete the cell's pool of NAD^+ by reducing it all to NADH and would shut itself down for lack of an oxidizing agent. Under aerobic conditions, NAD^+ is recycled from NADH by the transfer of electrons to the electron transport chain. An anaerobic alternative is to transfer electrons from NADH to pyruvate, the end product of glycolysis.

Types of Fermentation

Fermentation consists of glycolysis plus reactions that regenerate NAD^+ by transferring electrons from NADH to pyruvate or derivatives of pyruvate. The NAD^+ can then be reused to oxidize sugar by glycolysis, which nets two molecules of ATP by substrate-level phosphorylation. There are many types of fermentation, differing in the end products formed from pyruvate. Two common types are alcohol fermentation and lactic acid fermentation.

In **alcohol fermentation** (**Figure 9.17a**), pyruvate is converted to ethanol (ethyl alcohol) in two steps. The first step releases carbon dioxide from the pyruvate, which is converted to the two-carbon compound acetaldehyde. In the second step, acetaldehyde is reduced by NADH to ethanol. This regenerates the supply of NAD⁺ needed for the continuation of glycolysis. Many bacteria carry out alcohol fermentation under anaerobic conditions. Yeast (a fungus) also carries out alcohol fermentation. For thousands of years, humans have used yeast in brewing, winemaking, and baking. The CO_2 bubbles generated by baker's yeast during alcohol fermentation allow bread to rise.

During **lactic acid fermentation** (**Figure 9.17b**), pyruvate is reduced directly by NADH to form lactate as an end product, with no release of CO_2. (Lactate is the ionized form of lactic acid.) Lactic acid fermentation by certain fungi and bacteria is used in the dairy industry to make cheese and yogurt.

Human muscle cells make ATP by lactic acid fermentation when oxygen is scarce. This occurs during strenuous exercise, when sugar catabolism for ATP production outpaces the muscle's supply of oxygen from the blood. Under these conditions, the cells switch from aerobic respiration to fermentation. The lactate that accumulates was previously thought to cause muscle fatigue and pain, but recent research suggests instead that increased levels of potassium ions (K^+) may be to blame, while lactate appears to enhance muscle performance. In any case, the excess lactate is gradually carried away by the blood to the liver, where it is converted back to pyruvate by liver cells. Because oxygen is available, this pyruvate can then enter the mitochondria in liver cells and complete cellular respiration.

Comparing Fermentation with Anaerobic and Aerobic Respiration

Fermentation, anaerobic respiration, and aerobic respiration are three alternative cellular pathways for producing ATP by harvesting the chemical energy of food. All three use glycolysis to oxidize glucose and other organic fuels to pyruvate, with a net production of 2 ATP by substrate-level phosphorylation. And in all three pathways, NAD⁺ is the oxidizing agent that accepts electrons from food during glycolysis.

A key difference among the three pathways is the contrasting mechanisms for oxidizing NADH back to NAD⁺, which is required to sustain glycolysis. In fermentation, the final electron acceptor is an organic molecule such as pyruvate (lactic acid fermentation) or acetaldehyde (alcohol fermentation). In cellular respiration, by contrast, electrons carried by NADH are transferred to an electron transport chain, where they move stepwise down a series of redox reactions to a final electron acceptor. In aerobic respiration, the final electron acceptor is oxygen; in anaerobic respiration, the final acceptor is another molecule that is electronegative (although invariably less so than oxygen). Passage of electrons from NADH to the electron transport chain not only regenerates the NAD⁺ required for glycolysis but pays an ATP bonus when the stepwise electron transport from this NADH to oxygen drives oxidative phosphorylation. An even bigger ATP payoff comes from the oxidation of pyruvate in the mitochondrion, which is unique to respiration. Without an electron transport chain, the energy still stored in pyruvate is unavailable to most cells. Thus, cellular respiration harvests much more energy from

(a) Alcohol fermentation

(b) Lactic acid fermentation

▲ **Figure 9.17 Fermentation.** In the absence of oxygen, many cells use fermentation to produce ATP by substrate-level phosphorylation. Pyruvate, the end product of glycolysis, serves as an electron acceptor for oxidizing NADH back to NAD⁺, which can then be reused in glycolysis. Two of the common end products formed from fermentation are **(a)** ethanol and **(b)** lactate, the ionized form of lactic acid.

each sugar molecule than fermentation can. In fact, aerobic respiration yields up to 16 times as much ATP per glucose molecule as does fermentation—up to 32 molecules of ATP for respiration, compared with 2 molecules of ATP produced by substrate-level phosphorylation in fermentation.

Some organisms, called **obligate anaerobes**, carry out only fermentation or anaerobic respiration. In fact, these organisms cannot survive in the presence of oxygen, some forms of which can actually be toxic if protective systems are not present in the cell. A few cell types, such as cells of the vertebrate brain, can carry out only aerobic oxidation of pyruvate, not fermentation. Other organisms, including yeasts and many bacteria, can make enough ATP to survive using either fermentation or respiration. Such species are called **facultative anaerobes**. On the cellular level, our muscle cells behave as facultative anaerobes. In such cells, pyruvate is a fork in the metabolic road that leads to two alternative catabolic routes (**Figure 9.18**). Under aerobic conditions, pyruvate can be converted to acetyl CoA, and oxidation continues in the citric acid cycle via aerobic respiration. Under anaerobic conditions, lactic acid fermentation occurs: Pyruvate is diverted from the citric acid cycle, serving instead as an electron acceptor to recycle NAD⁺. To make the same amount of ATP, a facultative anaerobe has to consume sugar at a much faster rate when fermenting than when respiring.

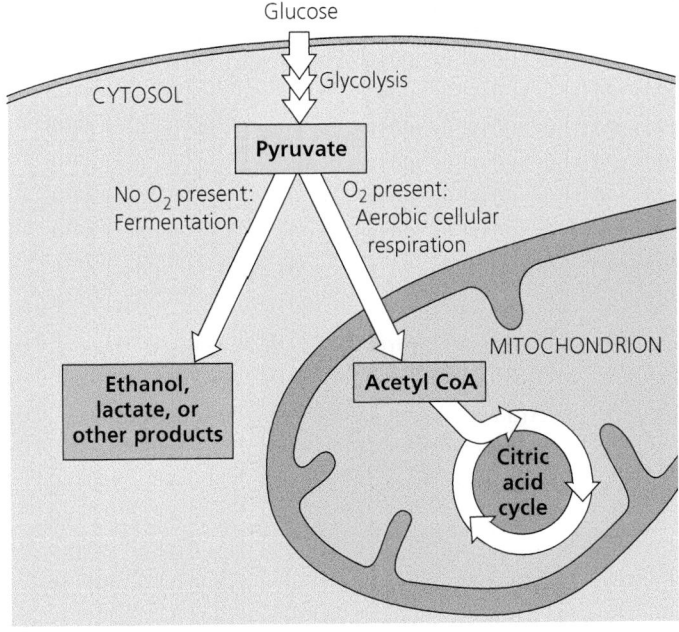

▲ **Figure 9.18 Pyruvate as a key juncture in catabolism.** Glycolysis is common to fermentation and cellular respiration. The end product of glycolysis, pyruvate, represents a fork in the catabolic pathways of glucose oxidation. In a facultative anaerobe or a muscle cell, which are capable of both aerobic cellular respiration and fermentation, pyruvate is committed to one of those two pathways, usually depending on whether or not oxygen is present.

The Evolutionary Significance of Glycolysis

EVOLUTION The role of glycolysis in both fermentation and respiration has an evolutionary basis. Ancient prokaryotes are thought to have used glycolysis to make ATP long before oxygen was present in Earth's atmosphere. The oldest known fossils of bacteria date back 3.5 billion years, but appreciable quantities of oxygen probably did not begin to accumulate in the atmosphere until about 2.7 billion years ago. Cyanobacteria produced this O_2 as a by-product of photosynthesis. Therefore, early prokaryotes may have generated ATP exclusively from glycolysis. The fact that glycolysis is today the most widespread metabolic pathway among Earth's organisms suggests that it evolved very early in the history of life. The cytosolic location of glycolysis also implies great antiquity; the pathway does not require any of the membrane-bounded organelles of the eukaryotic cell, which evolved approximately 1 billion years after the prokaryotic cell. Glycolysis is a metabolic heirloom from early cells that continues to function in fermentation and as the first stage in the breakdown of organic molecules by respiration.

CONCEPT CHECK 9.5

1. Consider the NADH formed during glycolysis. What is the final acceptor for its electrons during fermentation? What is the final acceptor for its electrons during aerobic respiration?
2. **WHAT IF?** A glucose-fed yeast cell is moved from an aerobic environment to an anaerobic one. How would its rate of glucose consumption change if ATP were to be generated at the same rate?

For suggested answers, see Appendix A.

CONCEPT 9.6

Glycolysis and the citric acid cycle connect to many other metabolic pathways

So far, we have treated the oxidative breakdown of glucose in isolation from the cell's overall metabolic economy. In this section, you will learn that glycolysis and the citric acid cycle are major intersections of the cell's catabolic and anabolic (biosynthetic) pathways.

The Versatility of Catabolism

Throughout this chapter, we have used glucose as the fuel for cellular respiration. But free glucose molecules are not common in the diets of humans and other animals. We obtain most of our calories in the form of fats, proteins, sucrose and other disaccharides, and starch, a polysaccharide. All these

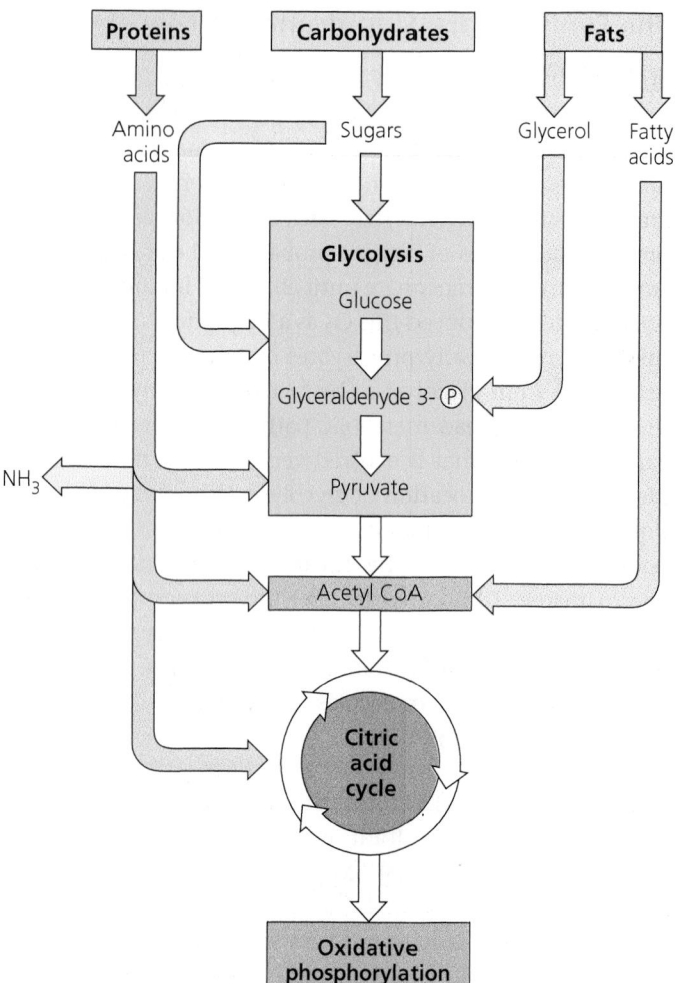

▲ **Figure 9.19 The catabolism of various molecules from food.** Carbohydrates, fats, and proteins can all be used as fuel for cellular respiration. Monomers of these molecules enter glycolysis or the citric acid cycle at various points. Glycolysis and the citric acid cycle are catabolic funnels through which electrons from all kinds of organic molecules flow on their exergonic fall to oxygen.

organic molecules in food can be used by cellular respiration to make ATP (Figure 9.19).

Glycolysis can accept a wide range of carbohydrates for catabolism. In the digestive tract, starch is hydrolyzed to glucose, which can then be broken down in the cells by glycolysis and the citric acid cycle. Similarly, glycogen, the polysaccharide that humans and many other animals store in their liver and muscle cells, can be hydrolyzed to glucose between meals as fuel for respiration. The digestion of disaccharides, including sucrose, provides glucose and other monosaccharides as fuel for respiration.

Proteins can also be used for fuel, but first they must be digested to their constituent amino acids. Many of the amino acids are used by the organism to build new proteins. Amino acids present in excess are converted by enzymes to intermediates of glycolysis and the citric acid cycle. Before amino acids can feed into glycolysis or the citric acid cycle, their amino groups must be removed, a process called *deamination*. The nitrogenous refuse is excreted from the animal in the form of ammonia (NH_3), urea, or other waste products.

Catabolism can also harvest energy stored in fats obtained either from food or from storage cells in the body. After fats are digested to glycerol and fatty acids, the glycerol is converted to glyceraldehyde 3-phosphate, an intermediate of glycolysis. Most of the energy of a fat is stored in the fatty acids. A metabolic sequence called **beta oxidation** breaks the fatty acids down to two-carbon fragments, which enter the citric acid cycle as acetyl CoA. NADH and $FADH_2$ are also generated during beta oxidation; they can enter the electron transport chain, leading to further ATP production. Fats make excellent fuel, in large part due to their chemical structure and the high energy level of their electrons (equally shared between carbon and hydrogen) compared to those of carbohydrates. A gram of fat oxidized by respiration produces more than twice as much ATP as a gram of carbohydrate. Unfortunately, this also means that a person trying to lose weight must work hard to use up fat stored in the body because so many calories are stockpiled in each gram of fat.

Biosynthesis (Anabolic Pathways)

Cells need substance as well as energy. Not all the organic molecules of food are destined to be oxidized as fuel to make ATP. In addition to calories, food must also provide the carbon skeletons that cells require to make their own molecules. Some organic monomers obtained from digestion can be used directly. For example, as previously mentioned, amino acids from the hydrolysis of proteins in food can be incorporated into the organism's own proteins. Often, however, the body needs specific molecules that are not present as such in food. Compounds formed as intermediates of glycolysis and the citric acid cycle can be diverted into anabolic pathways as precursors from which the cell can synthesize the molecules it requires. For example, humans can make about half of the 20 amino acids in proteins by modifying compounds siphoned away from the citric acid cycle; the rest are "essential amino acids" that must be obtained in the diet. Also, glucose can be made from pyruvate, and fatty acids can be synthesized from acetyl CoA. Of course, these anabolic, or biosynthetic, pathways do not generate ATP, but instead consume it.

In addition, glycolysis and the citric acid cycle function as metabolic interchanges that enable our cells to convert some kinds of molecules to others as we need them. For example, an intermediate compound generated during glycolysis, dihydroxyacetone phosphate (see Figure 9.9, step 5), can be converted to one of the major precursors of fats. If we eat more food than we need, we store fat even if our diet is fat-free. Metabolism is remarkably versatile and adaptable.

Regulation of Cellular Respiration via Feedback Mechanisms

Basic principles of supply and demand regulate the metabolic economy. The cell does not waste energy making more of a particular substance than it needs. If there is a glut of a certain amino acid, for example, the anabolic pathway that synthesizes that amino acid from an intermediate of the citric acid cycle is switched off. The most common mechanism for this control is feedback inhibition: The end product of the anabolic pathway inhibits the enzyme that catalyzes an early step of the pathway (see Figure 8.21). This prevents the needless diversion of key metabolic intermediates from uses that are more urgent.

The cell also controls its catabolism. If the cell is working hard and its ATP concentration begins to drop, respiration speeds up. When there is plenty of ATP to meet demand, respiration slows down, sparing valuable organic molecules for other functions. Again, control is based mainly on regulating the activity of enzymes at strategic points in the catabolic pathway. As shown in **Figure 9.20**, one important switch is phosphofructokinase, the enzyme that catalyzes step 3 of glycolysis (see Figure 9.9). That is the first step that commits the substrate irreversibly to the glycolytic pathway. By controlling the rate of this step, the cell can speed up or slow down the entire catabolic process. Phosphofructokinase can thus be considered the pacemaker of respiration.

Phosphofructokinase is an allosteric enzyme with receptor sites for specific inhibitors and activators. It is inhibited by ATP and stimulated by AMP (adenosine monophosphate), which the cell derives from ADP. As ATP accumulates, inhibition of the enzyme slows down glycolysis. The enzyme becomes active again as cellular work converts ATP to ADP (and AMP) faster than ATP is being regenerated. Phosphofructokinase is also sensitive to citrate, the first product of the citric acid cycle. If citrate accumulates in mitochondria, some of it passes into the cytosol and inhibits phosphofructokinase. This mechanism helps synchronize the rates of glycolysis and the citric acid cycle. As citrate accumulates, glycolysis slows down, and the supply of acetyl groups to the citric acid cycle decreases. If citrate consumption increases, either because of a demand for more ATP or because anabolic pathways are draining off intermediates of the citric acid cycle, glycolysis accelerates and meets the demand. Metabolic balance is augmented by the control of enzymes that catalyze other key steps of glycolysis and the citric acid cycle. Cells are thrifty, expedient, and responsive in their metabolism.

Cellular respiration and metabolic pathways play a role of central importance in organisms. Examine Figure 9.2 again to put cellular respiration into the broader context of energy flow and chemical cycling in ecosystems. The energy that keeps us alive is *released*, not *produced*, by cellular respiration. We are tapping energy that was stored in food by photosynthesis. In the next chapter, you will learn how photosynthesis captures light and converts it to chemical energy.

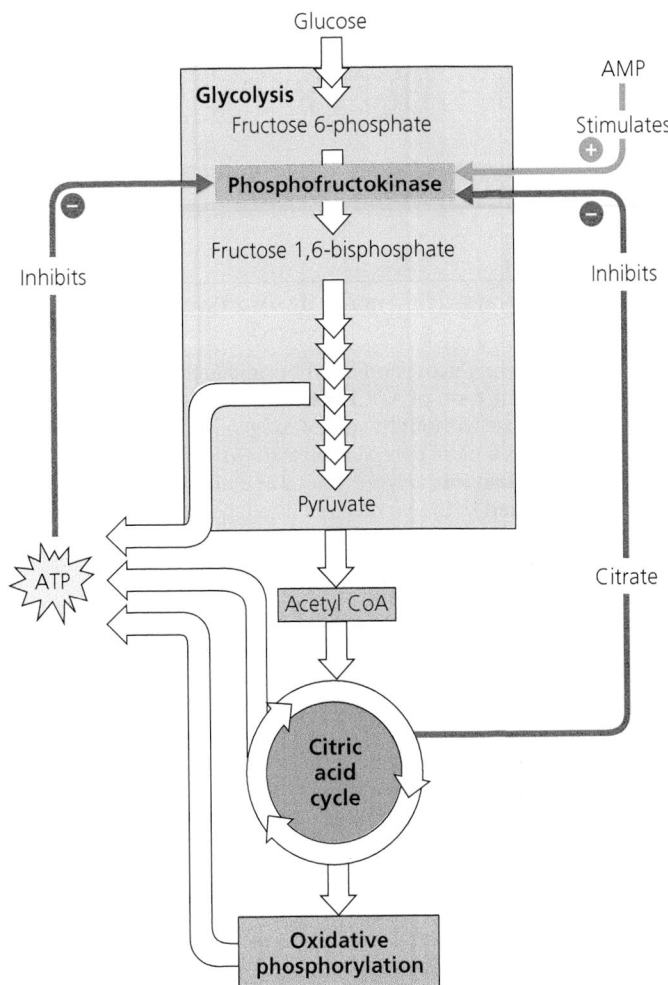

▲ **Figure 9.20 The control of cellular respiration.** Allosteric enzymes at certain points in the respiratory pathway respond to inhibitors and activators that help set the pace of glycolysis and the citric acid cycle. Phosphofructokinase, which catalyzes an early step in glycolysis (see Figure 9.9), is one such enzyme. It is stimulated by AMP (derived from ADP) but is inhibited by ATP and by citrate. This feedback regulation adjusts the rate of respiration as the cell's catabolic and anabolic demands change.

CONCEPT CHECK 9.6

1. **MAKE CONNECTIONS** Compare the structure of a fat (see Figure 5.10, p. 75) with that of a carbohydrate (see Figure 5.3, p. 70). What features of their structures make fat a much better fuel?

2. Under what circumstances might your body synthesize fat molecules?

3. **MAKE CONNECTIONS** Return to Figure 5.6b on page 72 and look at the arrangement of glycogen and mitochondria in the micrograph. What is the connection between glycogen and mitochondria?

4. **WHAT IF?** What will happen in a muscle cell that has used up its supply of oxygen and ATP? (Review Figures 9.18 and 9.20.)

5. **WHAT IF?** During intense exercise, can a muscle cell use fat as a concentrated source of chemical energy? Explain. (Review Figures 9.18 and 9.19.)

For suggested answers, see Appendix A.

SUMMARY OF KEY CONCEPTS

CONCEPT 9.1

Catabolic pathways yield energy by oxidizing organic fuels (pp. 164–168)

- Cells break down glucose and other organic fuels to yield chemical energy in the form of ATP. **Fermentation** is a partial degradation of glucose without the use of oxygen. **Cellular respiration** is a more complete breakdown of glucose; in **aerobic respiration**, oxygen is used as a reactant. The cell taps the energy stored in food molecules through **redox reactions**, in which one substance partially or totally shifts electrons to another. **Oxidation** is the loss of electrons from one substance, while **reduction** is the addition of electrons to the other.
- During aerobic respiration, glucose ($C_6H_{12}O_6$) is oxidized to CO_2, and O_2 is reduced to H_2O. Electrons lose potential energy during their transfer from glucose or other organic compounds to oxygen. Electrons are usually passed first to **NAD$^+$**, reducing it to NADH, and then from NADH to an **electron transport chain**, which conducts them to O_2 in energy-releasing steps. The energy is used to make ATP.
- Aerobic respiration occurs in three stages: (1) **glycolysis**, (2) pyruvate oxidation and the **citric acid cycle**, and (3) **oxidative phosphorylation** (electron transport and chemiosmosis).

? *Describe the difference between the two processes in cellular respiration that produce ATP: oxidative phosphorylation and substrate-level phosphorylation.*

CONCEPT 9.2

Glycolysis harvests chemical energy by oxidizing glucose to pyruvate (pp. 168–169)

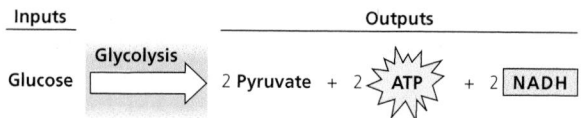

Inputs | Outputs

Glucose — Glycolysis → 2 Pyruvate + 2 ATP + 2 NADH

? *What is the source of energy for the formation of ATP and NADH in glycolysis?*

CONCEPT 9.3

After pyruvate is oxidized, the citric acid cycle completes the energy-yielding oxidation of organic molecules (pp. 170–172)

- In eukaryotic cells, pyruvate enters the mitochondrion and is oxidized to **acetyl CoA**, which is further oxidized in the citric acid cycle.

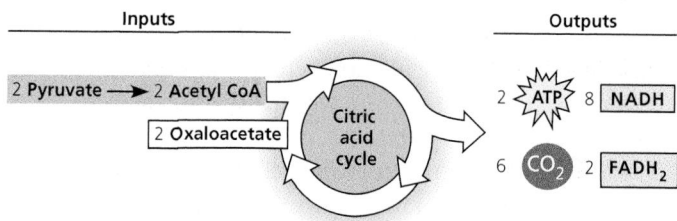

Inputs | Outputs

2 Pyruvate → 2 Acetyl CoA | 2 Oxaloacetate | Citric acid cycle | 2 ATP 8 NADH | 6 CO_2 2 FADH$_2$

? *What molecular products indicate the complete oxidation of glucose during cellular respiration?*

CONCEPT 9.4

During oxidative phosphorylation, chemiosmosis couples electron transport to ATP synthesis (pp. 172–177)

- NADH and FADH$_2$ transfer electrons to the electron transport chain. Electrons move down the chain, losing energy in several energy-releasing steps. Finally, electrons are passed to O_2, reducing it to H_2O.

- At certain steps along the electron transport chain, electron transfer causes protein complexes to move H$^+$ from the mitochondrial matrix (in eukaryotes) to the intermembrane space, storing energy as a **proton-motive force** (H$^+$ gradient). As H$^+$ diffuses back into the matrix through **ATP synthase**, its passage drives the phosphorylation of ADP, a process called **chemiosmosis**.

- About 34% of the energy stored in a glucose molecule is transferred to ATP during cellular respiration, producing a maximum of about 32 ATP.

? *Briefly explain the mechanism by which ATP synthase produces ATP. List three locations in which ATP synthases are found.*

CONCEPT 9.5

Fermentation and anaerobic respiration enable cells to produce ATP without the use of oxygen (pp. 177–179)

- Glycolysis nets 2 ATP by substrate-level phosphorylation, whether oxygen is present or not. Under anaerobic conditions, either anaerobic respiration or fermentation can take place. In anaerobic respiration, an electron transport chain is present with a final electron acceptor other than oxygen. In fermentation, the electrons from NADH are passed to pyruvate or a derivative of pyruvate, regenerating the NAD$^+$ required to oxidize more glucose. Two common types of fermentation are **alcohol fermentation** and **lactic acid fermentation**.
- Fermentation and anaerobic or aerobic respiration all use glycolysis to oxidize glucose, but they differ in their final electron acceptor and whether an electron transport chain is used (respiration) or not (fermentation). Respiration yields more ATP;

aerobic respiration, with O_2 as the final electron acceptor, yields about 16 times as much ATP as does fermentation.

- Glycolysis occurs in nearly all organisms and is thought to have evolved in ancient prokaryotes before there was O_2 in the atmosphere.

? *Which process yields more ATP, fermentation or anaerobic respiration? Explain.*

CONCEPT 9.6

Glycolysis and the citric acid cycle connect to many other metabolic pathways (pp. 179–181)

- Catabolic pathways funnel electrons from many kinds of organic molecules into cellular respiration. Many carbohydrates can enter glycolysis, most often after conversion to glucose. Amino acids of proteins must be deaminated before being oxidized. The fatty acids of fats undergo **beta oxidation** to two-carbon fragments and then enter the citric acid cycle as acetyl CoA. Anabolic pathways can use small molecules from food directly or build other substances using intermediates of glycolysis or the citric acid cycle.
- Cellular respiration is controlled by allosteric enzymes at key points in glycolysis and the citric acid cycle.

? *Describe how the catabolic pathways of glycolysis and the citric acid cycle intersect with anabolic pathways in the metabolism of a cell.*

TEST YOUR UNDERSTANDING

LEVEL 1: KNOWLEDGE/COMPREHENSION

1. The *immediate* energy source that drives ATP synthesis by ATP synthase during oxidative phosphorylation is the
   a. oxidation of glucose and other organic compounds.
   b. flow of electrons down the electron transport chain.
   c. affinity of oxygen for electrons.
   d. H^+ concentration across the membrane holding ATP synthase.
   e. transfer of phosphate to ADP.

2. Which metabolic pathway is common to both fermentation and cellular respiration of a glucose molecule?
   a. the citric acid cycle
   b. the electron transport chain
   c. glycolysis
   d. synthesis of acetyl CoA from pyruvate
   e. reduction of pyruvate to lactate

3. In mitochondria, exergonic redox reactions
   a. are the source of energy driving prokaryotic ATP synthesis.
   b. are directly coupled to substrate-level phosphorylation.
   c. provide the energy that establishes the proton gradient.
   d. reduce carbon atoms to carbon dioxide.
   e. are coupled via phosphorylated intermediates to endergonic processes.

4. The final electron acceptor of the electron transport chain that functions in aerobic oxidative phosphorylation is
   a. oxygen.   b. water.   c. NAD^+.   d. pyruvate.   e. ADP.

LEVEL 2: APPLICATION/ANALYSIS

5. What is the oxidizing agent in the following reaction?

   Pyruvate + NADH + H^+ → Lactate + NAD^+
   a. oxygen   b. NADH   c. NAD^+ d. lactate   e. pyruvate

6. When electrons flow along the electron transport chains of mitochondria, which of the following changes occurs?
   a. The pH of the matrix increases.
   b. ATP synthase pumps protons by active transport.
   c. The electrons gain free energy.
   d. The cytochromes phosphorylate ADP to form ATP.
   e. NAD^+ is oxidized.

7. Most CO_2 from catabolism is released during
   a. glycolysis.
   b. the citric acid cycle.
   c. lactate fermentation.
   d. electron transport.
   e. oxidative phosphorylation.

LEVEL 3: SYNTHESIS/EVALUATION

8. **DRAW IT** The graph here shows the pH difference across the inner mitochondrial membrane over time in an actively respiring cell. At the time indicated by the vertical arrow, a metabolic poison is added that specifically and completely inhibits all function of mitochondrial ATP synthase. Draw what you would expect to see for the rest of the graphed line.

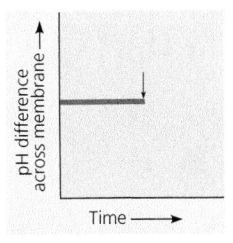

9. **EVOLUTION CONNECTION**
   ATP synthases are found in the prokaryotic plasma membrane and in mitochondria and chloroplasts. What does this suggest about the evolutionary relationship of these eukaryotic organelles to prokaryotes? How might the amino acid sequences of the ATP synthases from the different sources support or refute your hypothesis?

10. **SCIENTIFIC INQUIRY**
    In the 1930s, some physicians prescribed low doses of a compound called dinitrophenol (DNP) to help patients lose weight. This unsafe method was abandoned after some patients died. DNP uncouples the chemiosmotic machinery by making the lipid bilayer of the inner mitochondrial membrane leaky to H^+. Explain how this could cause weight loss and death.

11. **WRITE ABOUT A THEME**
    Emergent Properties In a short essay (100–150 words), explain how oxidative phosphorylation—the production of ATP using energy derived from the redox reactions of a spatially organized electron transport chain followed by chemiosmosis—is an example of how new properties emerge at each level of the biological hierarchy.

For selected answers, see Appendix A.

Mastering BIOLOGY®   www.masteringbiology.com

1. MasteringBiology® Assignments
BioFlix Tutorials Cellular Respiration: Inputs and Outputs • Glycolysis • Acetyl CoA Formation and the Citric Acid Cycle • Oxidative Phosphorylation • Summary
Tutorial Pathways for Pyruvate
Activities Build a Chemical Cycling System • Overview of Cellular Respiration • Redox Reactions • Glycolysis • The Citric Acid Cycle • Electron Transport • Fermentation • Glucose Metabolism • Discovery Channel Video: Space Plants
Questions Student Misconceptions • Reading Quiz • Multiple Choice • End-of-Chapter

2. eText
Read your book online, search, take notes, highlight text, and more.

3. The Study Area
Practice Tests • Cumulative Test • **BioFlix** 3-D Animations • MP3 Tutor Sessions • Videos • Activities • Investigations • Lab Media • Audio Glossary • Word Study Tools • Art

10

Photosynthesis

▲ Figure 10.1 **How can sunlight, seen here as a spectrum of colors in a rainbow, power the synthesis of organic substances?**

KEY CONCEPTS

10.1 Photosynthesis converts light energy to the chemical energy of food

10.2 The light reactions convert solar energy to the chemical energy of ATP and NADPH

10.3 The Calvin cycle uses the chemical energy of ATP and NADPH to reduce CO_2 to sugar

10.4 Alternative mechanisms of carbon fixation have evolved in hot, arid climates

The Process That Feeds the Biosphere

Life on Earth is solar powered. The chloroplasts of plants capture light energy that has traveled 150 million kilometers from the sun and convert it to chemical energy that is stored in sugar and other organic molecules. This conversion process is called **photosynthesis**. Let's begin by placing photosynthesis in its ecological context.

Photosynthesis nourishes almost the entire living world directly or indirectly. An organism acquires the organic compounds it uses for energy and carbon skeletons by one of two major modes: autotrophic nutrition or heterotrophic nutrition. **Autotrophs** are "self-feeders" (*auto-* means "self," and *trophos* means "feeder"); they sustain themselves without eating anything derived from other living beings. Autotrophs produce their organic molecules from CO_2 and other inorganic raw materials obtained from the environment. They are the ultimate sources of organic compounds for all nonautotrophic organisms, and for this reason, biologists refer to autotrophs as the *producers* of the biosphere.

Almost all plants are autotrophs; the only nutrients they require are water and minerals from the soil and carbon dioxide from the air. Specifically, plants are *photo*autotrophs, organisms that use light as a source of energy to synthesize organic substances **(Figure 10.1)**. Photosynthesis also occurs in algae, certain other protists, and some prokaryotes **(Figure 10.2)**. In this chapter, we will touch on these other groups in passing, but our emphasis will be on plants. Variations in autotrophic nutrition that occur in prokaryotes and algae will be described in Chapters 27 and 28.

Heterotrophs obtain their organic material by the second major mode of nutrition. Unable to make their own food, they live on compounds produced by other organisms (*hetero-* means "other"). Heterotrophs are the biosphere's *consumers*. The most obvious form of this "other-feeding" occurs when an animal eats plants or other animals. But heterotrophic nutrition may be more subtle. Some heterotrophs consume the remains of dead organisms by decomposing and feeding on organic litter such as carcasses, feces, and fallen leaves; they are known as decomposers. Most fungi and many types of prokaryotes get their nourishment this way. Almost all heterotrophs, including humans, are completely dependent, either directly or indirectly, on photoautotrophs for food—and also for oxygen, a by-product of photosynthesis.

The Earth's supply of fossil fuels was formed from remains of organisms that died hundreds of millions of years ago. In a sense, then, fossil fuels represent stores of the sun's energy from the distant past. Because these resources are being used at a much higher rate than they are replenished, researchers

(a) Plants

(b) Multicellular alga

(c) Unicellular protists

10 μm

(d) Cyanobacteria

40 μm

(e) Purple sulfur bacteria

1 μm

▲ **Figure 10.2 Photoautotrophs.** These organisms use light energy to drive the synthesis of organic molecules from carbon dioxide and (in most cases) water. They feed themselves and the entire living world. **(a)** On land, plants are the predominant producers of food. In aquatic environments, photoautotrophs include unicellular and **(b)** multicellular algae, such as this kelp; **(c)** some non-algal unicellular protists, such as *Euglena*; **(d)** the prokaryotes called cyanobacteria; and **(e)** other photosynthetic prokaryotes, such as these purple sulfur bacteria, which produce sulfur (the yellow globules within the cells) (c–e, LMs).

▼ **Figure 10.3**

IMPACT

Alternative Fuels from Plants and Algae

Biofuels from crops such as corn, soybeans, and cassava have been proposed as a supplement or even replacement for fossil fuels. To produce "bioethanol," the starch made naturally by the plants is simply converted to glucose and then fermented to ethanol by microorganisms. Alternatively, a simple chemical process can yield "biodiesel" from plant oils. Either product can be mixed with gasoline or used alone to power vehicles. Some species of unicellular algae are especially prolific oil producers, and they can be easily cultured in containers such as the tubular plastic bags shown below.

WHY IT MATTERS The rate of fossil fuel use by humans far outpaces its formation in the earth: Fossil fuels are a nonrenewable source of energy. Tapping the power of sunlight by using products of photosynthesis to generate energy is a sustainable alternative if cost-effective techniques can be developed. It is generally agreed that using algae is preferable to growing crops for this purpose because this use of cropland diminishes the food supply and drives up food prices.

FURTHER READING A. L. Haag, Algae bloom again, *Nature* 447:520–521 (2007).

WHAT IF? The main product of fossil fuel combustion is CO_2, and this combustion is the source of the increase in atmospheric CO_2 concentration. Scientists have proposed strategically situating containers of these algae near industrial plants, as shown above, or near highly congested city streets. Why does this arrangement make sense?

are exploring methods of capitalizing on the photosynthetic process to provide alternative fuels **(Figure 10.3)**.

In this chapter, you will learn how photosynthesis works. After a discussion of the general principles of photosynthesis, we will consider the two stages of photosynthesis: the light reactions, in which solar energy is captured and transformed into chemical energy; and the Calvin cycle, in which the chemical energy is used to make organic molecules of food. Finally, we will consider a few aspects of photosynthesis from an evolutionary perspective.

CONCEPT 10.1

Photosynthesis converts light energy to the chemical energy of food

The remarkable ability of an organism to harness light energy and use it to drive the synthesis of organic compounds emerges from structural organization in the cell: Photosynthetic enzymes and other molecules are grouped together in a biological membrane, enabling the necessary series of chemical reactions to be carried out efficiently. The process of photosynthesis most likely originated in a group of bacteria that had infolded regions of the plasma membrane containing clusters of such molecules. In existing photosynthetic bacteria, infolded photosynthetic membranes function similarly to the internal membranes of the chloroplast, a eukaryotic organelle. According to the endosymbiont theory, the original chloroplast was a photosynthetic prokaryote that lived inside an ancestor of eukaryotic cells. (You learned about this theory in Chapter 6 and it will be described more fully in Chapter 25.) Chloroplasts are present in a variety of photosynthesizing organisms (see Figure 10.2), but here we will focus on plants.

Chloroplasts: The Sites of Photosynthesis in Plants

All green parts of a plant, including green stems and unripened fruit, have chloroplasts, but the leaves are the major sites of photosynthesis in most plants (Figure 10.4). There are about half a million chloroplasts in a chunk of leaf with a top surface area of 1 mm^2. Chloroplasts are found mainly in the cells of the **mesophyll**, the tissue in the interior of the leaf. Carbon dioxide enters the leaf, and oxygen exits, by way of microscopic pores called **stomata** (singular, *stoma*; from the Greek, meaning "mouth"). Water absorbed by the roots is delivered to the leaves in veins. Leaves also use veins to export sugar to roots and other nonphotosynthetic parts of the plant.

A typical mesophyll cell has about 30–40 chloroplasts, each organelle measuring about 2–4 μm by 4–7 μm. A chloroplast has an envelope of two membranes surrounding a dense fluid called the **stroma**. Suspended within the stroma is a third membrane system, made up of sacs called **thylakoids**, which segregates the stroma from the *thylakoid space* inside these sacs. In some places, thylakoid sacs are stacked in columns called *grana* (singular, *granum*). **Chlorophyll**, the green pigment that gives leaves their color, resides in the thylakoid membranes of the chloroplast. (The internal photosynthetic membranes of some prokaryotes are also called thylakoid membranes; see Figure 27.7b.) It is the light energy absorbed

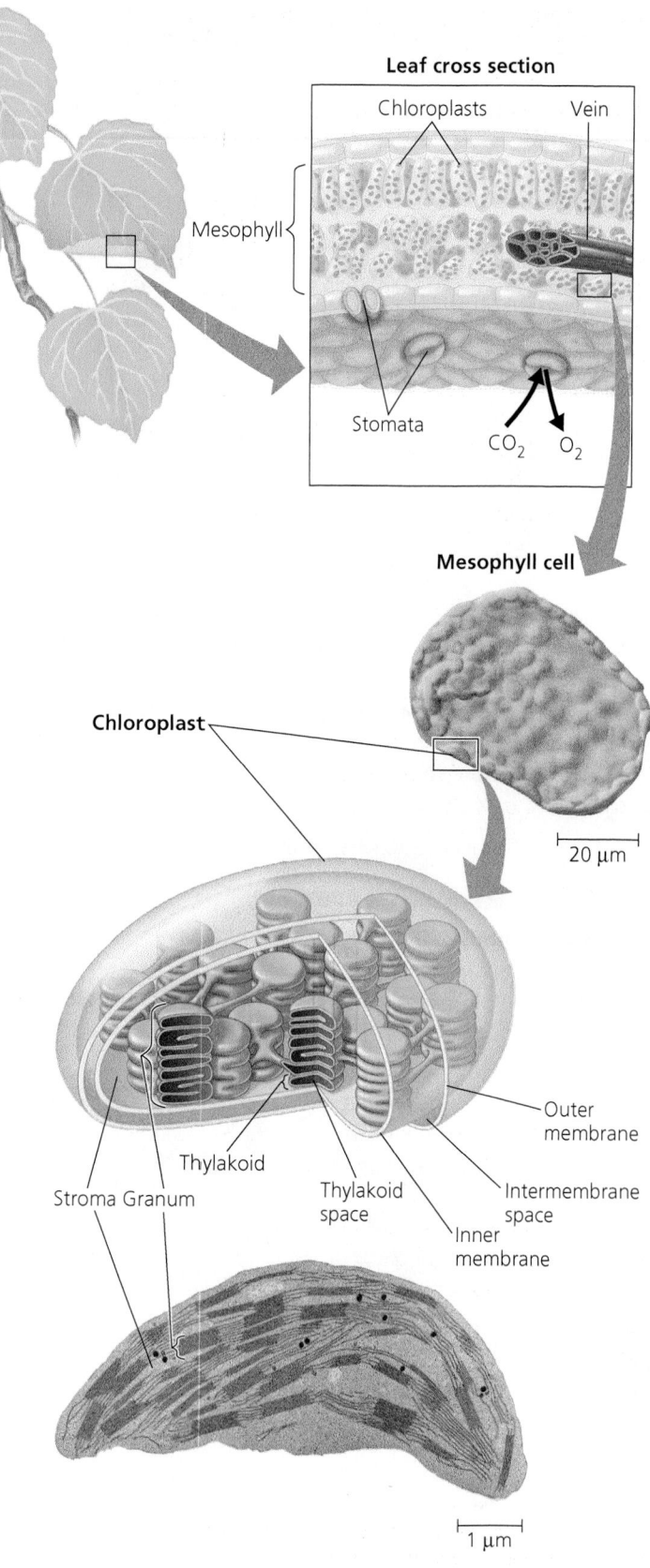

▲ Figure 10.4 **Zooming in on the location of photosynthesis in a plant.** Leaves are the major organs of photosynthesis in plants. These pictures take you into a leaf, then into a cell, and finally into a chloroplast, the organelle where photosynthesis occurs (middle, LM; bottom, TEM).

by chlorophyll that drives the synthesis of organic molecules in the chloroplast. Now that we have looked at the sites of photosynthesis in plants, we are ready to look more closely at the process of photosynthesis.

Tracking Atoms Through Photosynthesis: *Scientific Inquiry*

Scientists have tried for centuries to piece together the process by which plants make food. Although some of the steps are still not completely understood, the overall photosynthetic equation has been known since the 1800s: In the presence of light, the green parts of plants produce organic compounds and oxygen from carbon dioxide and water. Using molecular formulas, we can summarize the complex series of chemical reactions in photosynthesis with this chemical equation:

$$6 CO_2 + 12 H_2O + \text{Light energy} \rightarrow C_6H_{12}O_6 + 6 O_2 + 6 H_2O$$

We use glucose ($C_6H_{12}O_6$) here to simplify the relationship between photosynthesis and respiration, but the direct product of photosynthesis is actually a three-carbon sugar that can be used to make glucose. Water appears on both sides of the equation because 12 molecules are consumed and 6 molecules are newly formed during photosynthesis. We can simplify the equation by indicating only the net consumption of water:

$$6 CO_2 + 6 H_2O + \text{Light energy} \rightarrow C_6H_{12}O_6 + 6 O_2$$

Writing the equation in this form, we can see that the overall chemical change during photosynthesis is the reverse of the one that occurs during cellular respiration. Both of these metabolic processes occur in plant cells. However, as you will soon learn, chloroplasts do not synthesize sugars by simply reversing the steps of respiration.

Now let's divide the photosynthetic equation by 6 to put it in its simplest possible form:

$$CO_2 + H_2O \rightarrow [CH_2O] + O_2$$

Here, the brackets indicate that CH_2O is not an actual sugar but represents the general formula for a carbohydrate. In other words, we are imagining the synthesis of a sugar molecule one carbon at a time. Six repetitions would theoretically produce a glucose molecule. Let's now use this simplified formula to see how researchers tracked the elements C, H, and O from the reactants of photosynthesis to the products.

The Splitting of Water

One of the first clues to the mechanism of photosynthesis came from the discovery that the O_2 given off by plants is derived from H_2O and not from CO_2. The chloroplast splits water into hydrogen and oxygen. Before this discovery, the prevailing hypothesis was that photosynthesis split carbon dioxide ($CO_2 \rightarrow C + O_2$) and then added water to the carbon

($C + H_2O \rightarrow [CH_2O]$). This hypothesis predicted that the O_2 released during photosynthesis came from CO_2. This idea was challenged in the 1930s by C. B. van Niel, of Stanford University. Van Niel was investigating photosynthesis in bacteria that make their carbohydrate from CO_2 but do not release O_2. He concluded that, at least in these bacteria, CO_2 is not split into carbon and oxygen. One group of bacteria used hydrogen sulfide (H_2S) rather than water for photosynthesis, forming yellow globules of sulfur as a waste product (these globules are visible in Figure 10.2e). Here is the chemical equation for photosynthesis in these sulfur bacteria:

$$CO_2 + 2 H_2S \rightarrow [CH_2O] + H_2O + 2 S$$

Van Niel reasoned that the bacteria split H_2S and used the hydrogen atoms to make sugar. He then generalized that idea, proposing that all photosynthetic organisms require a hydrogen source but that the source varies:

Sulfur bacteria: $CO_2 + 2 H_2S \rightarrow [CH_2O] + H_2O + 2 S$
Plants: $CO_2 + 2 H_2O \rightarrow [CH_2O] + H_2O + O_2$
General: $CO_2 + 2 H_2X \rightarrow [CH_2O] + H_2O + 2 X$

Thus, van Niel hypothesized that plants split H_2O as a source of electrons from hydrogen atoms, releasing O_2 as a by-product.

Nearly 20 years later, scientists confirmed van Niel's hypothesis by using oxygen-18 (^{18}O), a heavy isotope, as a tracer to follow the fate of oxygen atoms during photosynthesis. The experiments showed that the O_2 from plants was labeled with ^{18}O *only* if water was the source of the tracer (experiment 1). If the ^{18}O was introduced to the plant in the form of CO_2, the label did not turn up in the released O_2 (experiment 2). In the following summary, red denotes labeled atoms of oxygen (^{18}O):

Experiment 1: $CO_2 + 2 H_2O \rightarrow [CH_2O] + H_2O + O_2$
Experiment 2: $CO_2 + 2 H_2O \rightarrow [CH_2O] + H_2O + O_2$

A significant result of the shuffling of atoms during photosynthesis is the extraction of hydrogen from water and its incorporation into sugar. The waste product of photosynthesis, O_2, is released to the atmosphere. **Figure 10.5** shows the fates of all atoms in photosynthesis.

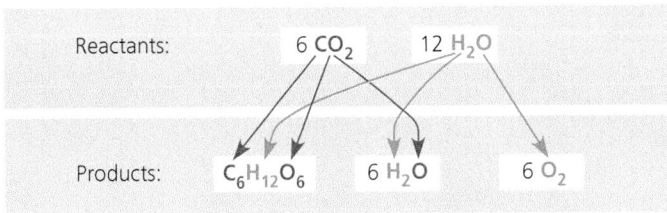

Reactants: $6 CO_2$ $12 H_2O$

Products: $C_6H_{12}O_6$ $6 H_2O$ $6 O_2$

▲ **Figure 10.5 Tracking atoms through photosynthesis.** The atoms from CO_2 are shown in magenta, and the atoms from H_2O are shown in blue.

Photosynthesis as a Redox Process

Let's briefly compare photosynthesis with cellular respiration. Both processes involve redox reactions. During cellular respiration, energy is released from sugar when electrons associated with hydrogen are transported by carriers to oxygen, forming water as a by-product (see p. 164). The electrons lose potential energy as they "fall" down the electron transport chain toward electronegative oxygen, and the mitochondrion harnesses that energy to synthesize ATP (see Figure 9.15). Photosynthesis reverses the direction of electron flow. Water is split, and electrons are transferred along with hydrogen ions from the water to carbon dioxide, reducing it to sugar.

$$\text{Energy} + 6\,CO_2 + 6\,H_2O \longrightarrow C_6H_{12}O_6 + 6\,O_2$$

becomes reduced

becomes oxidized

Because the electrons increase in potential energy as they move from water to sugar, this process requires energy—in other words is endergonic. This energy boost is provided by light.

The Two Stages of Photosynthesis: *A Preview*

The equation for photosynthesis is a deceptively simple summary of a very complex process. Actually, photosynthesis is not a single process, but two processes, each with multiple steps. These two stages of photosynthesis are known as the **light reactions** (the *photo* part of photosynthesis) and the **Calvin cycle** (the *synthesis* part) (Figure 10.6).

The light reactions are the steps of photosynthesis that convert solar energy to chemical energy. Water is split, providing a source of electrons and protons (hydrogen ions, H^+) and giving off O_2 as a by-product. Light absorbed by chlorophyll drives a transfer of the electrons and hydrogen ions from water to an acceptor called **NADP$^+$** (nicotinamide adenine dinucleotide phosphate), where they are temporarily stored. The electron acceptor NADP$^+$ is first cousin to NAD$^+$, which functions as an electron carrier in cellular respiration; the two molecules differ only by the presence of an extra phosphate group in the NADP$^+$ molecule. The light reactions use solar power to reduce NADP$^+$ to NADPH by adding a pair of electrons along with an H$^+$. The light reactions also generate ATP, using chemiosmosis to power the addition of a phosphate group to ADP, a process called **photophosphorylation**. Thus, light energy is initially converted to chemical energy in the form of two compounds: NADPH, a source of electrons as "reducing power" that can be passed along to an electron acceptor, reducing it, and ATP, the versatile energy currency of cells. Notice that the light reactions produce no sugar; that happens in the second stage of photosynthesis, the Calvin cycle.

The Calvin cycle is named for Melvin Calvin, who, along with his colleagues, began to elucidate its steps in the late 1940s. The cycle begins by incorporating CO_2 from the air

▶ **Figure 10.6 An overview of photosynthesis: cooperation of the light reactions and the Calvin cycle.** In the chloroplast, the thylakoid membranes are the sites of the light reactions, whereas the Calvin cycle occurs in the stroma. The light reactions use solar energy to make ATP and NADPH, which supply chemical energy and reducing power, respectively, to the Calvin cycle. The Calvin cycle incorporates CO_2 into organic molecules, which are converted to sugar. (Recall that most simple sugars have formulas that are some multiple of CH_2O.)

 ANIMATION *BioFlix* Visit the Study Area at **www.masteringbiology.com** for the BioFlix® 3-D Animation on Photosynthesis.

into organic molecules already present in the chloroplast. This initial incorporation of carbon into organic compounds is known as **carbon fixation**. The Calvin cycle then reduces the fixed carbon to carbohydrate by the addition of electrons. The reducing power is provided by NADPH, which acquired its cargo of electrons in the light reactions. To convert CO_2 to carbohydrate, the Calvin cycle also requires chemical energy in the form of ATP, which is also generated by the light reactions. Thus, it is the Calvin cycle that makes sugar, but it can do so only with the help of the NADPH and ATP produced by the light reactions. The metabolic steps of the Calvin cycle are sometimes referred to as the dark reactions, or light-independent reactions, because none of the steps requires light *directly*. Nevertheless, the Calvin cycle in most plants occurs during daylight, for only then can the light reactions provide the NADPH and ATP that the Calvin cycle requires. In essence, the chloroplast uses light energy to make sugar by coordinating the two stages of photosynthesis.

As Figure 10.6 indicates, the thylakoids of the chloroplast are the sites of the light reactions, while the Calvin cycle occurs in the stroma. On the outside of the thylakoids, molecules of $NADP^+$ and ADP pick up electrons and phosphate, respectively, and NADPH and ATP are then released to the stroma, where they play crucial roles in the Calvin cycle. The two stages of photosynthesis are treated in this figure as metabolic modules that take in ingredients and crank out products. In the next two sections, we'll look more closely at how the two stages work, beginning with the light reactions.

CONCEPT CHECK 10.1

1. How do the reactant molecules of photosynthesis reach the chloroplasts in leaves?
2. How did the use of an oxygen isotope help elucidate the chemistry of photosynthesis?
3. **WHAT IF?** The Calvin cycle requires ATP and NADPH, products of the light reactions. If a classmate asserted that the light reactions don't depend on the Calvin cycle and, with continual light, could just keep on producing ATP and NADPH, how would you respond?

For suggested answers, see Appendix A.

CONCEPT 10.2

The light reactions convert solar energy to the chemical energy of ATP and NADPH

Chloroplasts are chemical factories powered by the sun. Their thylakoids transform light energy into the chemical energy of ATP and NADPH. To understand this conversion better, we need to know about some important properties of light.

The Nature of Sunlight

Light is a form of energy known as electromagnetic energy, also called electromagnetic radiation. Electromagnetic energy travels in rhythmic waves analogous to those created by dropping a pebble into a pond. Electromagnetic waves, however, are disturbances of electric and magnetic fields rather than disturbances of a material medium such as water.

The distance between the crests of electromagnetic waves is called the **wavelength**. Wavelengths range from less than a nanometer (for gamma rays) to more than a kilometer (for radio waves). This entire range of radiation is known as the **electromagnetic spectrum** (Figure 10.7). The segment most important to life is the narrow band from about 380 nm to 750 nm in wavelength. This radiation is known as **visible light** because it can be detected as various colors by the human eye.

The model of light as waves explains many of light's properties, but in certain respects light behaves as though it consists of discrete particles, called **photons**. Photons are not tangible objects, but they act like objects in that each of them has a fixed quantity of energy. The amount of energy is inversely related to the wavelength of the light: the shorter the wavelength, the greater the energy of each photon of that light. Thus, a photon of violet light packs nearly twice as much energy as a photon of red light.

Although the sun radiates the full spectrum of electromagnetic energy, the atmosphere acts like a selective window, allowing visible light to pass through while screening out a substantial fraction of other radiation. The part of the spectrum we can see—visible light—is also the radiation that drives photosynthesis.

▲ **Figure 10.7 The electromagnetic spectrum.** White light is a mixture of all wavelengths of visible light. A prism can sort white light into its component colors by bending light of different wavelengths at different angles. (Droplets of water in the atmosphere can act as prisms, forming a rainbow; see Figure 10.1.) Visible light drives photosynthesis.

Photosynthetic Pigments: The Light Receptors

When light meets matter, it may be reflected, transmitted, or absorbed. Substances that absorb visible light are known as *pigments*. Different pigments absorb light of different wavelengths, and the wavelengths that are absorbed disappear. If a pigment is illuminated with white light, the color we see is the color most reflected or transmitted by the pigment. (If a pigment absorbs all wavelengths, it appears black.) We see green when we look at a leaf because chlorophyll absorbs violet-blue and red light while transmitting and reflecting green light (Figure 10.8). The ability of a pigment to absorb various wavelengths of light can be measured with an instrument called a **spectrophotometer**. This machine directs beams of light of different wavelengths through a solution of the pigment and measures the fraction of the light transmitted at each wavelength. A graph plotting a pigment's light absorption versus wavelength is called an **absorption spectrum** (Figure 10.9).

The absorption spectra of chloroplast pigments provide clues to the relative effectiveness of different wavelengths for driving photosynthesis, since light can perform work in chloroplasts only if it is absorbed. Figure 10.10a shows the absorption spectra of three types of pigments in chloroplasts: **chlorophyll *a***, which participates directly in the light reactions; the accessory pigment *chlorophyll b*; and a group of accessory pigments called carotenoids. The spectrum of chlorophyll *a* suggests that violet-blue and red light work best for photosynthesis, since they are absorbed, while green is the least effective

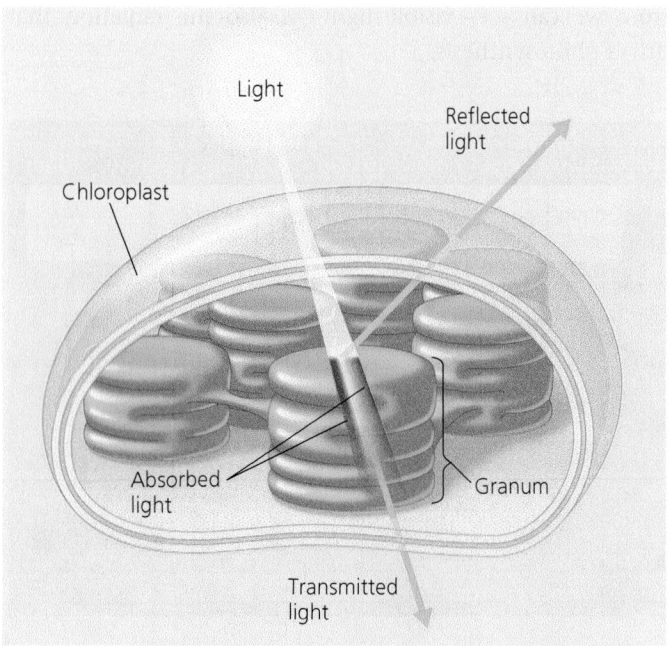

▲ **Figure 10.8 Why leaves are green: interaction of light with chloroplasts.** The chlorophyll molecules of chloroplasts absorb violet-blue and red light (the colors most effective in driving photosynthesis) and reflect or transmit green light. This is why leaves appear green.

▼ Figure 10.9

RESEARCH METHOD

Determining an Absorption Spectrum

APPLICATION An absorption spectrum is a visual representation of how well a particular pigment absorbs different wavelengths of visible light. Absorption spectra of various chloroplast pigments help scientists decipher each pigment's role in a plant.

TECHNIQUE A spectrophotometer measures the relative amounts of light of different wavelengths absorbed and transmitted by a pigment solution.

❶ White light is separated into colors (wavelengths) by a prism.

❷ One by one, the different colors of light are passed through the sample (chlorophyll in this example). Green light and blue light are shown here.

❸ The transmitted light strikes a photoelectric tube, which converts the light energy to electricity.

❹ The electric current is measured by a galvanometer. The meter indicates the fraction of light transmitted through the sample, from which we can determine the amount of light absorbed.

RESULTS See Figure 10.10a for absorption spectra of three types of chloroplast pigments.

color. This is confirmed by an **action spectrum** for photosynthesis (Figure 10.10b), which profiles the relative effectiveness of different wavelengths of radiation in driving the process. An action spectrum is prepared by illuminating chloroplasts with light of different colors and then plotting wavelength against some measure of photosynthetic rate, such as CO_2 consumption or O_2 release. The action spectrum for photosynthesis was first demonstrated by Theodor W. Engelmann, a German botanist, in 1883. Before equipment for measuring O_2 levels had even been invented, Engelmann performed a

INQUIRY

Which wavelengths of light are most effective in driving photosynthesis?

EXPERIMENT Absorption and action spectra, along with a classic experiment by Theodor W. Engelmann, reveal which wavelengths of light are photosynthetically important.

RESULTS

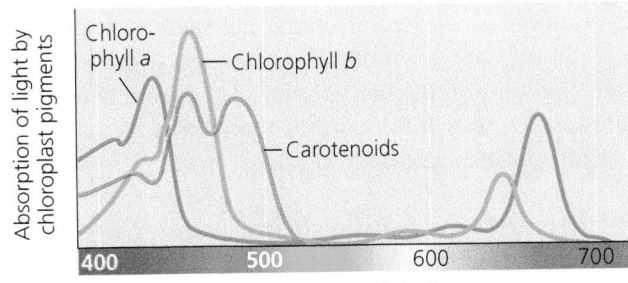

(a) Absorption spectra. The three curves show the wavelengths of light best absorbed by three types of chloroplast pigments.

(b) Action spectrum. This graph plots the rate of photosynthesis versus wavelength. The resulting action spectrum resembles the absorption spectrum for chlorophyll *a* but does not match exactly (see part a). This is partly due to the absorption of light by accessory pigments such as chlorophyll *b* and carotenoids.

(c) Engelmann's experiment. In 1883, Theodor W. Engelmann illuminated a filamentous alga with light that had been passed through a prism, exposing different segments of the alga to different wavelengths. He used aerobic bacteria, which concentrate near an oxygen source, to determine which segments of the alga were releasing the most O_2 and thus photosynthesizing most. Bacteria congregated in greatest numbers around the parts of the alga illuminated with violet-blue or red light.

CONCLUSION Light in the violet-blue and red portions of the spectrum is most effective in driving photosynthesis.

SOURCE T. W. Engelmann, *Bacterium photometricum. Ein Betrag zur vergleichenden Physiologie des Licht- und farbensinnes, Archiv. für Physiologie* 30:95–124 (1883).

(MB) See the related Experimental Inquiry Tutorial in MasteringBiology.

WHAT IF? If Engelmann had used a filter that allowed only red light to pass through, how would the results have differed?

clever experiment in which he used bacteria to measure rates of photosynthesis in filamentous algae (**Figure 10.10c**). His results are a striking match to the modern action spectrum shown in Figure 10.10b.

Notice by comparing Figures 10.10a and 10.10b that the action spectrum for photosynthesis does not exactly match the absorption spectrum of chlorophyll *a*. The absorption spectrum of chlorophyll *a* alone underestimates the effectiveness of certain wavelengths in driving photosynthesis. This is partly because accessory pigments with different absorption spectra are also photosynthetically important in chloroplasts and broaden the spectrum of colors that can be used for photosynthesis. **Figure 10.11** shows the structure of chlorophyll *a* compared with that of **chlorophyll *b***. A slight structural difference between them is enough to cause the two pigments to absorb at slightly different wavelengths in the red and blue parts of the spectrum (see Figure 10.10a). As a result, chlorophyll *a* is blue green and chlorophyll *b* is olive green.

Other accessory pigments include **carotenoids**, hydrocarbons that are various shades of yellow and orange because they absorb violet and blue-green light (see Figure 10.10a). Carotenoids may broaden the spectrum of colors that can drive photosynthesis. However, a more important function of at least some carotenoids seems to be *photoprotection*: These

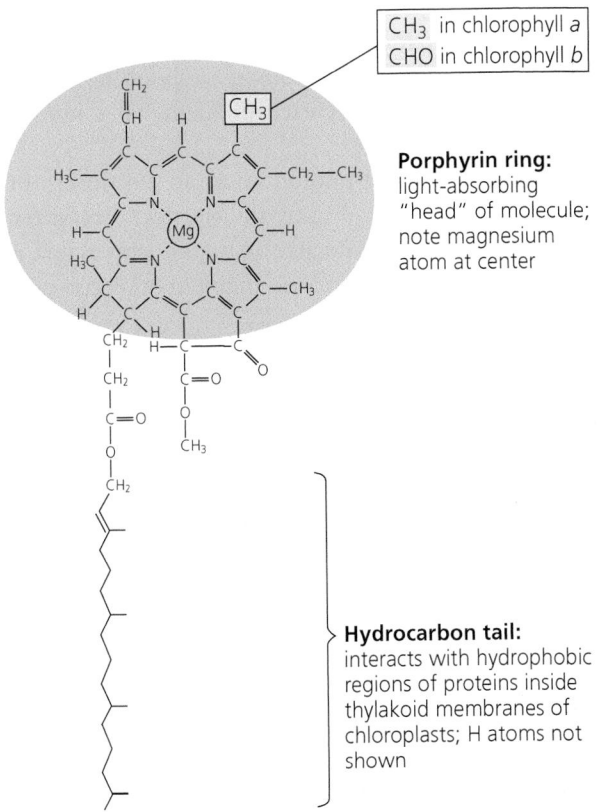

▲ Figure 10.11 Structure of chlorophyll molecules in chloroplasts of plants. Chlorophyll *a* and chlorophyll *b* differ only in one of the functional groups bonded to the porphyrin ring. (Also see the space-filling model of chlorophyll in Figure 1.4, p. 5.)

compounds absorb and dissipate excessive light energy that would otherwise damage chlorophyll or interact with oxygen, forming reactive oxidative molecules that are dangerous to the cell. Interestingly, carotenoids similar to the photoprotective ones in chloroplasts have a photoprotective role in the human eye. These and related molecules, often found in health food products, are valued as "phytochemicals" (from the Greek *phyton*, plant), compounds with antioxidant properties. Plants can synthesize all the antioxidants they require, but humans and other animals must obtain some of them from their diets.

Excitation of Chlorophyll by Light

What exactly happens when chlorophyll and other pigments absorb light? The colors corresponding to the absorbed wavelengths disappear from the spectrum of the transmitted and reflected light, but energy cannot disappear. When a molecule absorbs a photon of light, one of the molecule's electrons is elevated to an orbital where it has more potential energy. When the electron is in its normal orbital, the pigment molecule is said to be in its ground state. Absorption of a photon boosts an electron to an orbital of higher energy, and the pigment molecule is then said to be in an excited state. The only photons absorbed are those whose energy is exactly equal to the energy difference between the ground state and an excited state, and this energy difference varies from one kind of molecule to another. Thus, a particular compound absorbs only photons corresponding to specific wavelengths, which is why each pigment has a unique absorption spectrum.

Once absorption of a photon raises an electron from the ground state to an excited state, the electron cannot remain there long. The excited state, like all high-energy states, is unstable. Generally, when isolated pigment molecules absorb light, their excited electrons drop back down to the ground-state orbital in a billionth of a second, releasing their excess energy as heat. This conversion of light energy to heat is what makes the top of an automobile so hot on a sunny day. (White cars are coolest because their paint reflects all wavelengths of visible light, although it may absorb ultraviolet and other invisible radiation.) In isolation, some pigments, including chlorophyll, emit light as well as heat after absorbing photons. As excited electrons fall back to the ground state, photons are given off. This afterglow is called fluorescence. If a solution of chlorophyll isolated from chloroplasts is illuminated, it will fluoresce in the red-orange part of the spectrum and also give off heat (Figure 10.12).

A Photosystem: A Reaction-Center Complex Associated with Light-Harvesting Complexes

Chlorophyll molecules excited by the absorption of light energy produce very different results in an intact chloroplast than they do in isolation (see Figure 10.12). In their native environment of the thylakoid membrane, chlorophyll molecules are organized along with other small organic molecules and proteins into complexes called photosystems.

A **photosystem** is composed of a **reaction-center complex** surrounded by several light-harvesting complexes (Figure 10.13). The reaction-center complex is an organized association of proteins holding a special pair of chlorophyll *a* molecules. Each **light-harvesting complex** consists of various pigment molecules (which may include chlorophyll *a*, chlorophyll *b*, and carotenoids) bound to proteins. The number and variety of pigment molecules enable a photosystem to harvest light over a larger surface area and a larger portion of the spectrum than could any single pigment molecule alone. Together, these light-harvesting complexes act as an antenna for the reaction-center complex. When a pigment molecule

▶ **Figure 10.12 Excitation of isolated chlorophyll by light. (a)** Absorption of a photon causes a transition of the chlorophyll molecule from its ground state to its excited state. The photon boosts an electron to an orbital where it has more potential energy. If the illuminated molecule exists in isolation, its excited electron immediately drops back down to the ground-state orbital, and its excess energy is given off as heat and fluorescence (light). **(b)** A chlorophyll solution excited with ultraviolet light fluoresces with a red-orange glow.

WHAT IF? *If a leaf containing a similar concentration of chlorophyll as the solution was exposed to the same ultraviolet light, no fluorescence would be seen. Explain the difference in fluorescence emission between the solution and the leaf.*

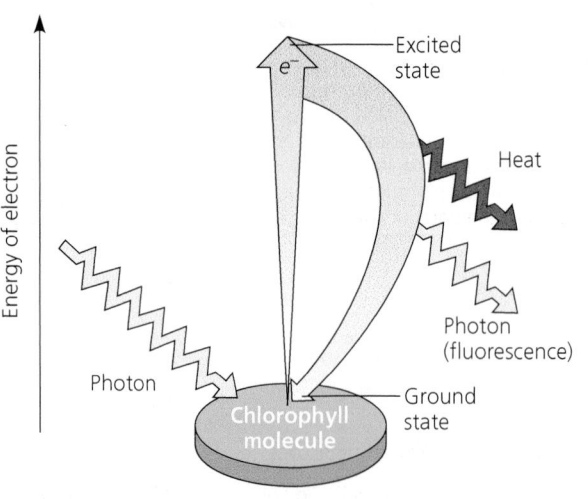

(a) Excitation of isolated chlorophyll molecule

(b) Fluorescence

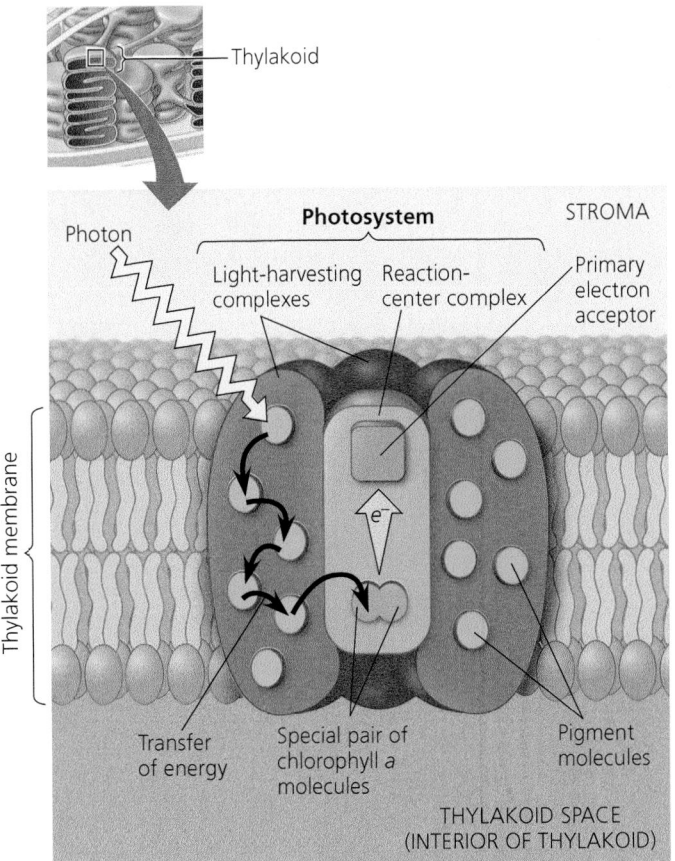

(a) **How a photosystem harvests light.** When a photon strikes a pigment molecule in a light-harvesting complex, the energy is passed from molecule to molecule until it reaches the reaction-center complex. Here, an excited electron from the special pair of chlorophyll *a* molecules is transferred to the primary electron acceptor.

(b) **Structure of photosystem II.** This computer model of photosystem II, based on X-ray crystallography, shows two photosystem complexes side by side. Chlorophyll molecules (small green ball-and-stick models) are interspersed with protein subunits (cylinders and ribbons). For simplicity, photosystem II will be shown as a single complex in the rest of the chapter.

▲ **Figure 10.13 The structure and function of a photosystem.**

absorbs a photon, the energy is transferred from pigment molecule to pigment molecule within a light-harvesting complex, somewhat like a human "wave" at a sports arena, until it is passed into the reaction-center complex. The reaction-center complex also contains a molecule capable of accepting electrons and becoming reduced; this is called the **primary electron acceptor**. The pair of chlorophyll *a* molecules in the reaction-center complex are special because their molecular environment—their location and the other molecules with which they are associated—enables them to use the energy from light not only to boost one of their electrons to a higher energy level, but also to transfer it to a different molecule—the primary electron acceptor.

The solar-powered transfer of an electron from the reaction-center chlorophyll *a* pair to the primary electron acceptor is the first step of the light reactions. As soon as the chlorophyll electron is excited to a higher energy level, the primary electron acceptor captures it; this is a redox reaction. In the flask shown in Figure 10.12, isolated chlorophyll fluoresces because there is no electron acceptor, so electrons of photoexcited chlorophyll drop right back to the ground state. In the structured environment of a chloroplast, however, an electron acceptor is readily available, and the potential energy represented by the excited electron is not dissipated as light and heat. Thus, each photosystem—a reaction-center complex surrounded by light-harvesting complexes—functions in the chloroplast as a unit. It converts light energy to chemical energy, which will ultimately be used for the synthesis of sugar.

The thylakoid membrane is populated by two types of photosystems that cooperate in the light reactions of photosynthesis. They are called **photosystem II (PS II)** and **photosystem I (PS I)**. (They were named in order of their discovery, but photosystem II functions first in the light reactions.) Each has a characteristic reaction-center complex—a particular kind of primary electron acceptor next to a special pair of chlorophyll *a* molecules associated with specific proteins. The reaction-center chlorophyll *a* of photosystem II is known as P680 because this pigment is best at absorbing light having a wavelength of 680 nm (in the red part of the spectrum). The chlorophyll *a* at the reaction-center complex of photosystem I is called P700 because it most effectively absorbs light of wavelength 700 nm (in the far-red part of the spectrum). These two pigments, P680 and P700, are nearly identical chlorophyll *a* molecules. However, their association with different proteins in the thylakoid membrane affects the electron distribution in the two pigments and accounts for the slight differences in their light-absorbing properties. Now let's see how the two photosystems work together in using light energy to generate ATP and NADPH, the two main products of the light reactions.

Linear Electron Flow

Light drives the synthesis of ATP and NADPH by energizing the two photosystems embedded in the thylakoid membranes of chloroplasts. The key to this energy transformation is a flow of electrons through the photosystems and other molecular components built into the thylakoid membrane. This is called

▼ **Figure 10.14 How linear electron flow during the light reactions generates ATP and NADPH.** The gold arrows trace the current of light-driven electrons from water to NADPH.

linear electron flow, and it occurs during the light reactions of photosynthesis, as shown in **Figure 10.14**. The following steps correspond to the numbered steps in the figure.

① A photon of light strikes a pigment molecule in a light-harvesting complex of PS II, boosting one of its electrons to a higher energy level. As this electron falls back to its ground state, an electron in a nearby pigment molecule is simultaneously raised to an excited state. The process continues, with the energy being relayed to other pigment molecules until it reaches the P680 pair of chlorophyll *a* molecules in the PS II reaction-center complex. It excites an electron in this pair of chlorophylls to a higher energy state.

② This electron is transferred from the excited P680 to the primary electron acceptor. We can refer to the resulting form of P680, missing an electron, as P680$^+$.

③ An enzyme catalyzes the splitting of a water molecule into two electrons, two hydrogen ions (H$^+$), and an oxygen atom. The electrons are supplied one by one to the P680$^+$ pair, each electron replacing one transferred to the primary electron acceptor. (P680$^+$ is the strongest biological oxidizing agent known; its electron "hole" must be filled. This greatly facilitates the transfer of electrons from the

split water molecule.) The H$^+$ are released into the thylakoid lumen. The oxygen atom immediately combines with an oxygen atom generated by the splitting of another water molecule, forming O$_2$.

④ Each photoexcited electron passes from the primary electron acceptor of PS II to PS I via an electron transport chain, the components of which are similar to those of the electron transport chain that functions in cellular respiration. The electron transport chain between PS II and PS I is made up of the electron carrier plastoquinone (Pq), a cytochrome complex, and a protein called plastocyanin (Pc).

⑤ The exergonic "fall" of electrons to a lower energy level provides energy for the synthesis of ATP. As electrons pass through the cytochrome complex, H$^+$ are pumped into the thylakoid lumen, contributing to the proton gradient that is subsequently used in chemiosmosis.

⑥ Meanwhile, light energy has been transferred via light-harvesting complex pigments to the PS I reaction-center complex, exciting an electron of the P700 pair of chlorophyll *a* molecules located there. The photoexcited electron was then transferred to PS I's primary electron acceptor, creating an electron "hole" in the P700—which we now can call P700$^+$. In other words, P700$^+$ can now act as an electron acceptor, accepting an electron that reaches the bottom of the electron transport chain from PS II.

7 Photoexcited electrons are passed in a series of redox reactions from the primary electron acceptor of PS I down a second electron transport chain through the protein ferredoxin (Fd). (This chain does not create a proton gradient and thus does not produce ATP.)

8 The enzyme NADP$^+$ reductase catalyzes the transfer of electrons from Fd to NADP$^+$. Two electrons are required for its reduction to NADPH. This molecule is at a higher energy level than water, and its electrons are more readily available for the reactions of the Calvin cycle than were those of water. This process also removes an H$^+$ from the stroma.

As complicated as the scheme shown in Figure 10.14 is, do not lose track of its functions. The light reactions use solar power to generate ATP and NADPH, which provide chemical energy and reducing power, respectively, to the carbohydrate-synthesizing reactions of the Calvin cycle. The energy changes of electrons during their linear flow through the light reactions are shown in a mechanical analogy in **Figure 10.15**.

Cyclic Electron Flow

In certain cases, photoexcited electrons can take an alternative path called **cyclic electron flow**, which uses photosystem I but not photosystem II. You can see in **Figure 10.16** that cyclic flow is a short circuit: The electrons cycle back from ferredoxin (Fd) to the cytochrome complex and from there continue on to a P700 chlorophyll in the PS I reaction-center complex. There is no production of NADPH and no release of oxygen. Cyclic flow does, however, generate ATP.

Several of the currently existing groups of photosynthetic bacteria are known to have photosystem I but not photosystem II; for these species, which include the purple sulfur bacteria (see Figure 10.2e), cyclic electron flow is the sole means of generating ATP in photosynthesis. Evolutionary biologists hypothesize that these bacterial groups are descendants of

▲ Figure 10.15 **A mechanical analogy for linear electron flow during the light reactions.**

the bacteria in which photosynthesis first evolved, in a form similar to cyclic electron flow.

Cyclic electron flow can also occur in photosynthetic species that possess both photosystems; this includes some prokaryotes, such as the cyanobacteria shown in Figure 10.2d, as well as the eukaryotic photosynthetic species that have been tested so far. Although the process is probably in part an "evolutionary leftover," it clearly plays at least one beneficial role for these organisms. Mutant plants that are not able to carry out cyclic electron flow are capable of growing well in low light, but do not grow well where light is intense. This is evidence for the idea that cyclic electron flow may be photoprotective. Later you'll learn more about cyclic electron flow as it relates to a particular adaptation of photosynthesis (C$_4$ plants; see Concept 10.4).

Whether ATP synthesis is driven by linear or cyclic electron flow, the actual mechanism is the same. Before we move on to consider the Calvin cycle, let's review chemiosmosis, the process that uses membranes to couple redox reactions to ATP production.

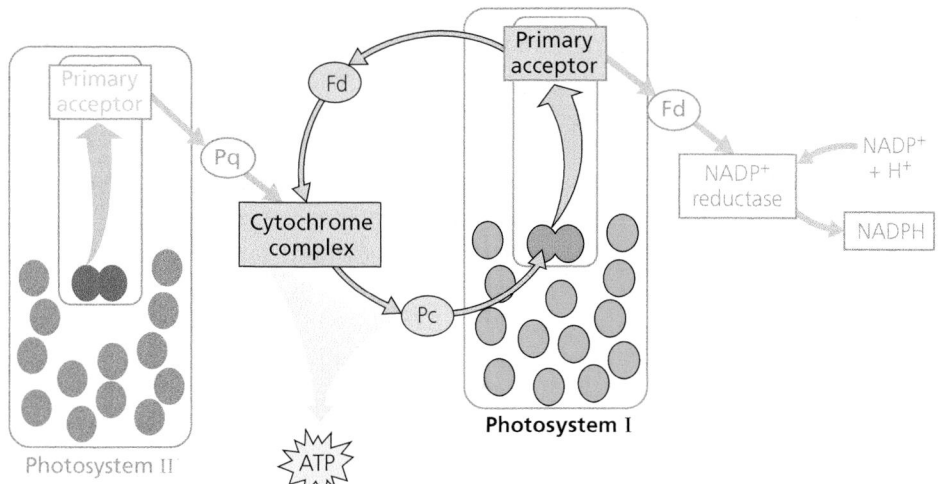

◄ Figure 10.16 **Cyclic electron flow.** Photoexcited electrons from PS I are occasionally shunted back from ferredoxin (Fd) to chlorophyll via the cytochrome complex and plastocyanin (Pc). This electron shunt supplements the supply of ATP (via chemiosmosis) but produces no NADPH. The "shadow" of linear electron flow is included in the diagram for comparison with the cyclic route. The two ferredoxin molecules shown in this diagram are actually one and the same—the final electron carrier in the electron transport chain of PS I.

? *Look at Figure 10.15, and explain how you would alter it to show a mechanical analogy for cyclic electron flow.*

A Comparison of Chemiosmosis in Chloroplasts and Mitochondria

Chloroplasts and mitochondria generate ATP by the same basic mechanism: chemiosmosis. An electron transport chain assembled in a membrane pumps protons across the membrane as electrons are passed through a series of carriers that are progressively more electronegative. In this way, electron transport chains transform redox energy to a proton-motive force, potential energy stored in the form of an H^+ gradient across a membrane. Built into the same membrane is an ATP synthase complex that couples the diffusion of hydrogen ions down their gradient to the phosphorylation of ADP. Some of the electron carriers, including the iron-containing proteins called cytochromes, are very similar in chloroplasts and mitochondria. The ATP synthase complexes of the two organelles are also very much alike. But there are noteworthy differences between oxidative phosphorylation in mitochondria and photophosphorylation in chloroplasts. In mitochondria, the high-energy electrons dropped down the transport chain are extracted from organic molecules (which are thus oxidized), while in chloroplasts, the source of electrons is water. Chloroplasts do not need molecules from food to make ATP; their photosystems capture light energy and use it to drive the electrons from water to the top of the transport chain. In other words, mitochondria use chemiosmosis to transfer chemical energy from food molecules to ATP, whereas chloroplasts transform light energy into chemical energy in ATP.

Although the spatial organization of chemiosmosis differs slightly between chloroplasts and mitochondria, it is easy to see similarities in the two **(Figure 10.17)**. The inner membrane of the mitochondrion pumps protons from the mitochondrial matrix out to the intermembrane space, which then serves as a reservoir of hydrogen ions. The thylakoid membrane of the chloroplast pumps protons from the stroma into the thylakoid space (interior of the thylakoid), which functions as the H^+ reservoir. If you imagine the cristae of mitochondria pinching off from the inner membrane, this may help you see how the thylakoid space and the intermembrane space are comparable spaces in the two organelles, while the mitochondrial matrix is analogous to the stroma of the chloroplast. In the mitochondrion, protons diffuse down their concentration gradient from the intermembrane space through ATP synthase to the matrix, driving ATP synthesis. In the chloroplast, ATP is synthesized as the hydrogen ions diffuse from the thylakoid space back to the stroma through ATP synthase complexes, whose catalytic knobs are on the stroma side of the membrane. Thus, ATP forms in the stroma, where it is used to help drive sugar synthesis during the Calvin cycle **(Figure 10.18)**.

The proton (H^+) gradient, or pH gradient, across the thylakoid membrane is substantial. When chloroplasts in an

Key ▪ Higher [H^+] ▪ Lower [H^+]

Mitochondrion   **Chloroplast**

MITOCHONDRION STRUCTURE   CHLOROPLAST STRUCTURE

Intermembrane space — Thylakoid space

Inner membrane — Thylakoid membrane

Electron transport chain

H^+ Diffusion

ATP synthase

Matrix — Stroma

ADP + (P)$_i$

H^+

ATP

▲ **Figure 10.17 Comparison of chemiosmosis in mitochondria and chloroplasts.** In both kinds of organelles, electron transport chains pump protons (H^+) across a membrane from a region of low H^+ concentration (light gray in this diagram) to one of high H^+ concentration (dark gray). The protons then diffuse back across the membrane through ATP synthase, driving the synthesis of ATP.

experimental setting are illuminated, the pH in the thylakoid space drops to about 5 (the H^+ concentration increases), and the pH in the stroma increases to about 8 (the H^+ concentration decreases). This gradient of three pH units corresponds to a thousandfold difference in H^+ concentration. If in the laboratory the lights are turned off, the pH gradient is abolished, but it can quickly be restored by turning the lights back on. Experiments such as this provided strong evidence in support of the chemiosmotic model.

Based on studies in several laboratories, Figure 10.18 shows a current model for the organization of the light-reaction "machinery" within the thylakoid membrane. Each of the molecules and molecular complexes in the figure is present in numerous copies in each thylakoid. Notice that NADPH, like ATP, is produced on the side of the membrane facing the stroma, where the Calvin cycle reactions take place.

Let's summarize the light reactions. Electron flow pushes electrons from water, where they are at a low state of potential energy, ultimately to NADPH, where they are stored at a high state of potential energy. The light-driven electron current also generates ATP. Thus, the equipment of the thylakoid membrane converts light energy to chemical energy stored in ATP and NADPH. (Oxygen is a by-product.) Let's now see how the Calvin cycle uses the products of the light reactions to synthesize sugar from CO_2.

▲ **Figure 10.18 The light reactions and chemiosmosis: the organization of the thylakoid membrane.** This diagram shows a current model for the organization of the thylakoid membrane. The gold arrows track the linear electron flow outlined in Figure 10.14. As electrons pass from carrier to carrier in redox reactions, hydrogen ions removed from the stroma are deposited in the thylakoid space, storing energy as a proton-motive force (H^+ gradient). At least three steps in the light reactions contribute to the proton gradient: **1** Water is split by photosystem II on the side of the membrane facing the thylakoid space; **2** as plastoquinone (Pq), a mobile carrier, transfers electrons to the cytochrome complex, four protons are translocated across the membrane into the thylakoid space; and **3** a hydrogen ion is removed from the stroma when it is taken up by $NADP^+$. Notice that in step 2, hydrogen ions are being pumped from the stroma into the thylakoid space, as in Figure 10.17. The diffusion of H^+ from the thylakoid space back to the stroma (along the H^+ concentration gradient) powers the ATP synthase. These light-driven reactions store chemical energy in NADPH and ATP, which shuttle the energy to the carbohydrate-producing Calvin cycle.

CONCEPT CHECK 10.2

1. What color of light is *least* effective in driving photosynthesis? Explain.
2. Compared to a solution of isolated chlorophyll, why do intact chloroplasts release less heat and fluorescence when illuminated?
3. In the light reactions, what is the initial electron donor? Where do the electrons finally end up?
4. **WHAT IF?** In an experiment, isolated chloroplasts placed in an illuminated solution with the appropriate chemicals can carry out ATP synthesis. Predict what would happen to the rate of synthesis if a compound is added to the solution that makes membranes freely permeable to hydrogen ions.

For suggested answers, see Appendix A.

CONCEPT 10.3

The Calvin cycle uses the chemical energy of ATP and NADPH to reduce CO₂ to sugar

The Calvin cycle is similar to the citric acid cycle in that a starting material is regenerated after molecules enter and leave the cycle. However, while the citric acid cycle is catabolic, oxidizing acetyl CoA and using the energy to synthesize ATP, the Calvin cycle is anabolic, building carbohydrates from smaller molecules and consuming energy. Carbon

enters the Calvin cycle in the form of CO_2 and leaves in the form of sugar. The cycle spends ATP as an energy source and consumes NADPH as reducing power for adding high-energy electrons to make the sugar.

As we mentioned previously, the carbohydrate produced directly from the Calvin cycle is actually not glucose, but a three-carbon sugar; the name of this sugar is **glyceraldehyde 3-phosphate (G3P)**. For the net synthesis of one molecule of G3P, the cycle must take place three times, fixing three molecules of CO_2. (Recall that carbon fixation refers to the initial incorporation of CO_2 into organic material.) As we trace the steps of the cycle, keep in mind that we are following three molecules of CO_2 through the reactions. **Figure 10.19** divides

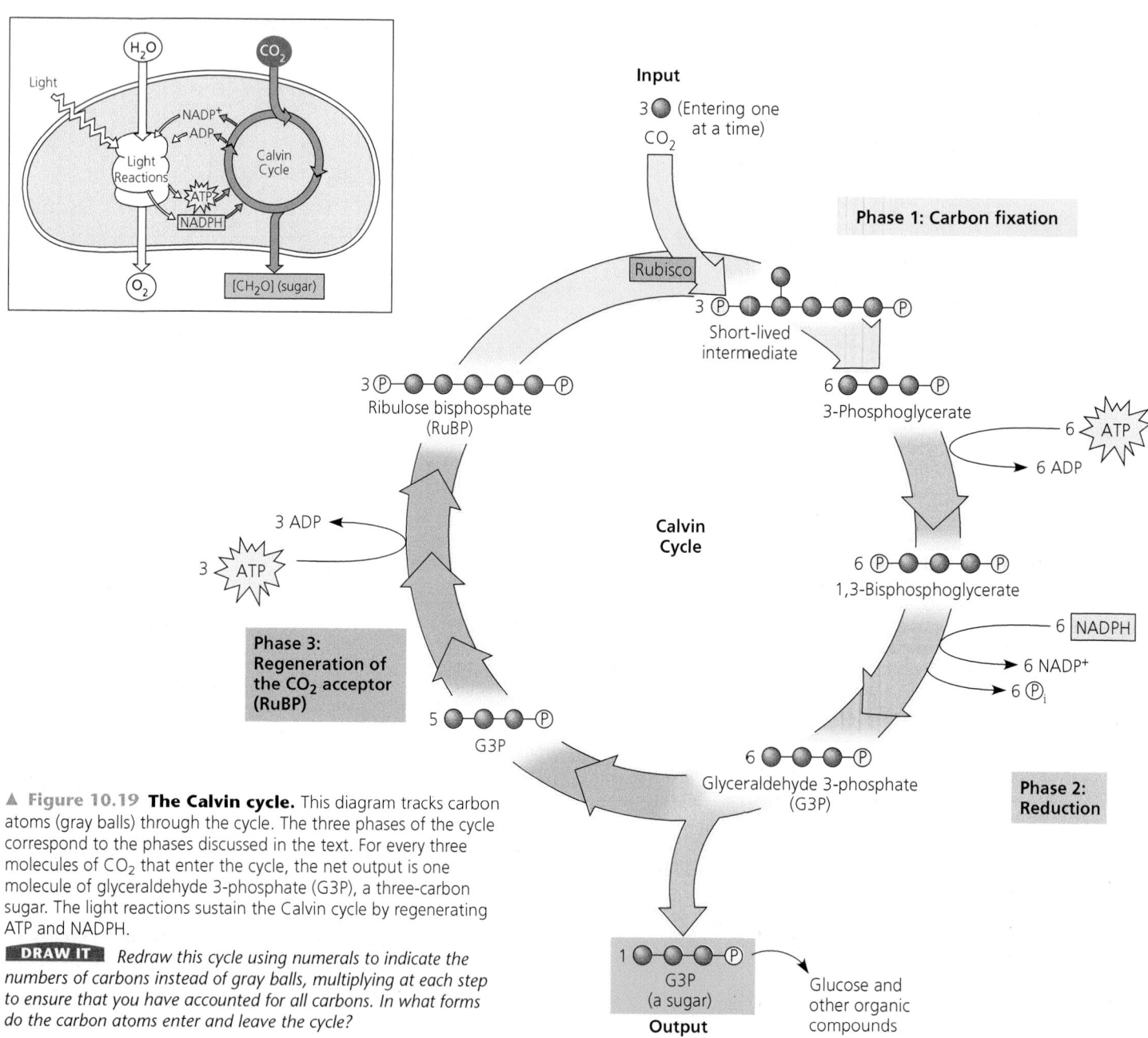

▲ **Figure 10.19 The Calvin cycle.** This diagram tracks carbon atoms (gray balls) through the cycle. The three phases of the cycle correspond to the phases discussed in the text. For every three molecules of CO_2 that enter the cycle, the net output is one molecule of glyceraldehyde 3-phosphate (G3P), a three-carbon sugar. The light reactions sustain the Calvin cycle by regenerating ATP and NADPH.

DRAW IT *Redraw this cycle using numerals to indicate the numbers of carbons instead of gray balls, multiplying at each step to ensure that you have accounted for all carbons. In what forms do the carbon atoms enter and leave the cycle?*

the Calvin cycle into three phases: carbon fixation, reduction, and regeneration of the CO_2 acceptor.

Phase 1: Carbon fixation. The Calvin cycle incorporates each CO_2 molecule, one at a time, by attaching it to a five-carbon sugar named ribulose bisphosphate (abbreviated RuBP). The enzyme that catalyzes this first step is RuBP carboxylase, or **rubisco**. (This is the most abundant protein in chloroplasts and is also thought to be the most abundant protein on Earth.) The product of the reaction is a six-carbon intermediate so unstable that it immediately splits in half, forming two molecules of 3-phosphoglycerate (for each CO_2 fixed).

Phase 2: Reduction. Each molecule of 3-phosphoglycerate receives an additional phosphate group from ATP, becoming 1,3-bisphosphoglycerate. Next, a pair of electrons donated from NADPH reduces 1,3-bisphosphoglycerate, which also loses a phosphate group, becoming G3P. Specifically, the electrons from NADPH reduce a carboxyl group on 1,3-bisphosphoglycerate to the aldehyde group of G3P, which stores more potential energy. G3P is a sugar—the same three-carbon sugar formed in glycolysis by the splitting of glucose (see Figure 9.9). Notice in Figure 10.19 that for every *three* molecules of CO_2 that enter the cycle, there are *six* molecules of G3P formed. But only one molecule of this three-carbon sugar can be counted as a net gain of carbohydrate. The cycle began with 15 carbons' worth of carbohydrate in the form of three molecules of the five-carbon sugar RuBP. Now there are 18 carbons' worth of carbohydrate in the form of six molecules of G3P. One molecule exits the cycle to be used by the plant cell, but the other five molecules must be recycled to regenerate the three molecules of RuBP.

Phase 3: Regeneration of the CO_2 acceptor (RuBP). In a complex series of reactions, the carbon skeletons of five molecules of G3P are rearranged by the last steps of the Calvin cycle into three molecules of RuBP. To accomplish this, the cycle spends three more molecules of ATP. The RuBP is now prepared to receive CO_2 again, and the cycle continues.

For the net synthesis of one G3P molecule, the Calvin cycle consumes a total of nine molecules of ATP and six molecules of NADPH. The light reactions regenerate the ATP and NADPH. The G3P spun off from the Calvin cycle becomes the starting material for metabolic pathways that synthesize other organic compounds, including glucose and other carbohydrates. Neither the light reactions nor the Calvin cycle alone can make sugar from CO_2. Photosynthesis is an emergent property of the intact chloroplast, which integrates the two stages of photosynthesis.

CONCEPT CHECK 10.3

1. To synthesize one glucose molecule, the Calvin cycle uses _____ molecules of CO_2, _____ molecules of ATP, and _____ molecules of NADPH.
2. Explain why the large numbers of ATP and NADPH molecules used during the Calvin cycle are consistent with the high value of glucose as an energy source.
3. **WHAT IF?** Explain why a poison that inhibits an enzyme of the Calvin cycle will also inhibit the light reactions.
4. **MAKE CONNECTIONS** Review Figures 9.9 (p. 169) and 10.19. Discuss the roles of intermediate and product played by glyceraldehyde 3-phosphate (G3P) in the two processes shown in these figures.

For suggested answers, see Appendix A.

CONCEPT 10.4

Alternative mechanisms of carbon fixation have evolved in hot, arid climates

EVOLUTION Ever since plants first moved onto land about 475 million years ago, they have been adapting to the problems of terrestrial life, particularly the problem of dehydration. In Chapters 29 and 36, we will consider anatomical adaptations that help plants conserve water, while in this chapter we are concerned with metabolic adaptations. The solutions often involve trade-offs. An important example is the compromise between photosynthesis and the prevention of excessive water loss from the plant. The CO_2 required for photosynthesis enters a leaf via stomata, the pores on the leaf surface (see Figure 10.4). However, stomata are also the main avenues of transpiration, the evaporative loss of water from leaves. On a hot, dry day, most plants close their stomata, a response that conserves water. This response also reduces photosynthetic yield by limiting access to CO_2. With stomata even partially closed, CO_2 concentrations begin to decrease in the air spaces within the leaf, and the concentration of O_2 released from the light reactions begins to increase. These conditions within the leaf favor an apparently wasteful process called photorespiration.

Photorespiration: An Evolutionary Relic?

In most plants, initial fixation of carbon occurs via rubisco, the Calvin cycle enzyme that adds CO_2 to ribulose bisphosphate. Such plants are called **C_3 plants** because the first organic product of carbon fixation is a three-carbon compound,

3-phosphoglycerate (see Figure 10.19). Rice, wheat, and soybeans are C_3 plants that are important in agriculture. When their stomata partially close on hot, dry days, C_3 plants produce less sugar because the declining level of CO_2 in the leaf starves the Calvin cycle. In addition, rubisco can bind O_2 in place of CO_2. As CO_2 becomes scarce within the air spaces of the leaf, rubisco adds O_2 to the Calvin cycle instead of CO_2. The product splits, and a two-carbon compound leaves the chloroplast. Peroxisomes and mitochondria rearrange and split this compound, releasing CO_2. The process is called **photorespiration** because it occurs in the light (*photo*) and consumes O_2 while producing CO_2 (*respiration*). However, unlike normal cellular respiration, photorespiration generates no ATP; in fact, photorespiration consumes ATP. And unlike photosynthesis, photorespiration produces no sugar. In fact, photorespiration *decreases* photosynthetic output by siphoning organic material from the Calvin cycle and releasing CO_2 that would otherwise be fixed.

How can we explain the existence of a metabolic process that seems to be counterproductive for the plant? According to one hypothesis, photorespiration is evolutionary baggage—a metabolic relic from a much earlier time when the atmosphere had less O_2 and more CO_2 than it does today. In the ancient atmosphere that prevailed when rubisco first evolved, the inability of the enzyme's active site to exclude O_2 would have made little difference. The hypothesis suggests that modern rubisco retains some of its chance affinity for O_2, which is now so concentrated in the atmosphere that a certain amount of photorespiration is inevitable.

We now know that, at least in some cases, photorespiration plays a protective role in plants. Plants that are impaired in their ability to carry out photorespiration (due to defective genes) are more susceptible to damage induced by excess light. Researchers consider this clear evidence that photorespiration acts to neutralize the otherwise damaging products of the light reactions, which build up when a low CO_2 concentration limits the progress of the Calvin cycle. Whether there are other benefits of photorespiration is still unknown. In many types of plants—including a significant number of crop plants—photorespiration drains away as much as 50% of the carbon fixed by the Calvin cycle. As heterotrophs that depend on carbon fixation in chloroplasts for our food, we naturally view photorespiration as wasteful. Indeed, if photorespiration could be reduced in certain plant species without otherwise affecting photosynthetic productivity, crop yields and food supplies might increase.

In some plant species, alternate modes of carbon fixation have evolved that minimize photorespiration and optimize the Calvin cycle—even in hot, arid climates. The two most important of these photosynthetic adaptations are C_4 photosynthesis and crassulacean acid metabolism (CAM).

C_4 Plants

The **C_4 plants** are so named because they preface the Calvin cycle with an alternate mode of carbon fixation that forms a four-carbon compound as its first product. Several thousand species in at least 19 plant families use the C_4 pathway. Among the C_4 plants important to agriculture are sugarcane and corn, members of the grass family.

A unique leaf anatomy is correlated with the mechanism of C_4 photosynthesis (Figure 10.20; compare with Figure 10.4). In C_4 plants, there are two distinct types of photosynthetic cells: bundle-sheath cells and mesophyll cells. **Bundle-sheath cells** are arranged into tightly packed sheaths around the veins of the leaf. Between the bundle sheath and the leaf surface are the more loosely arranged mesophyll cells. The Calvin cycle is confined to the chloroplasts of the bundle-sheath cells. However, the Calvin cycle is preceded by incorporation of CO_2 into organic compounds in the mesophyll cells. See the numbered steps in Figure 10.20, which are also described here:

❶ The first step is carried out by an enzyme present only in mesophyll cells called **PEP carboxylase**. This enzyme adds CO_2 to phosphoenolpyruvate (PEP), forming the four-carbon product oxaloacetate. PEP carboxylase has a much higher affinity for CO_2 than does rubisco and no affinity for O_2. Therefore, PEP carboxylase can fix carbon efficiently when rubisco cannot—that is, when it is hot and dry and stomata are partially closed, causing CO_2 concentration in the leaf to fall and O_2 concentration to rise.

❷ After the C_4 plant fixes carbon from CO_2, the mesophyll cells export their four-carbon products (malate in the example shown in Figure 10.20) to bundle-sheath cells through plasmodesmata (see Figure 6.31).

❸ Within the bundle-sheath cells, the four-carbon compounds release CO_2, which is reassimilated into organic material by rubisco and the Calvin cycle. The same reaction regenerates pyruvate, which is transported to mesophyll cells. There, ATP is used to convert pyruvate to PEP, allowing the reaction cycle to continue; this ATP can be thought of as the "price" of concentrating CO_2 in the bundle-sheath cells. To generate this extra ATP, bundle-sheath cells carry out cyclic electron flow, the process described earlier in this chapter (see Figure 10.16). In fact, these cells contain PS I but no PS II, so cyclic electron flow is their only photosynthetic mode of generating ATP.

In effect, the mesophyll cells of a C_4 plant pump CO_2 into the bundle sheath, keeping the CO_2 concentration in the bundle-sheath cells high enough for rubisco to bind carbon

Photosynthetic cells of C$_4$ plant leaf
- Mesophyll cell
- Bundle-sheath cell

Vein (vascular tissue)

C$_4$ leaf anatomy

Stoma

Mesophyll cell

PEP carboxylase

CO$_2$

The C$_4$ pathway

Oxaloacetate (4C) PEP (3C)

Malate (4C)

ADP

ATP

Pyruvate (3C)

Bundle-sheath cell

CO$_2$

Calvin Cycle

Sugar

Vascular tissue

❶ In mesophyll cells, the enzyme PEP carboxylase adds carbon dioxide to PEP.

❷ A four-carbon compound conveys the atoms of the CO$_2$ into a bundle-sheath cell via plasmodesmata.

❸ In bundle-sheath cells, CO$_2$ is released and enters the Calvin cycle.

▲ **Figure 10.20 C$_4$ leaf anatomy and the C$_4$ pathway.** The structure and biochemical functions of the leaves of C$_4$ plants are an evolutionary adaptation to hot, dry climates. This adaptation maintains a CO$_2$ concentration in the bundle sheath that favors photosynthesis over photorespiration.

dioxide rather than oxygen. The cyclic series of reactions involving PEP carboxylase and the regeneration of PEP can be thought of as a CO$_2$-concentrating pump that is powered by ATP. In this way, C$_4$ photosynthesis minimizes photorespiration and enhances sugar production. This adaptation is especially advantageous in hot regions with intense sunlight, where stomata partially close during the day, and it is in such environments that C$_4$ plants evolved and thrive today.

Since the Industrial Revolution began in the 1800s, human activities such as the burning of fossil fuels have drastically increased the concentration of CO$_2$ in the atmosphere. The resulting global climate change, including an increase in average temperatures around the planet, may have far-reaching effects on plant species. Scientists are concerned that increasing CO$_2$ concentration and temperature may affect C$_3$ and C$_4$ plants differently, thus changing the relative abundance of these species in a given plant community.

Which type of plant would stand to gain more from increasing CO$_2$ levels? Recall that in C$_3$ plants, the binding of O$_2$ rather than CO$_2$ by rubisco leads to photorespiration, lowering the efficiency of photosynthesis. C$_4$ plants overcome this problem by concentrating CO$_2$ in the bundle-sheath cells

at the cost of ATP. Rising CO$_2$ levels should benefit C$_3$ plants by lowering the amount of photorespiration that occurs. At the same time, rising temperatures have the opposite effect, increasing photorespiration. (Other factors such as water availability may also come into play.) In contrast, many C$_4$ plants could be largely unaffected by increasing CO$_2$ levels or temperature. In different regions, the particular combination of these two factors is likely to alter the balance of C$_3$ and C$_4$ plants in varying ways. The effects of such a widespread and variable change in community structure are unpredictable and thus a cause of legitimate concern.

CAM Plants

A second photosynthetic adaptation to arid conditions has evolved in many succulent (water-storing) plants, numerous cacti, pineapples, and representatives of several other plant families. These plants open their stomata during the night and close them during the day, just the reverse of how other plants behave. Closing stomata during the day helps desert plants conserve water, but it also prevents CO$_2$ from entering the leaves. During the night, when their stomata are open, these plants take up CO$_2$ and incorporate it into a variety

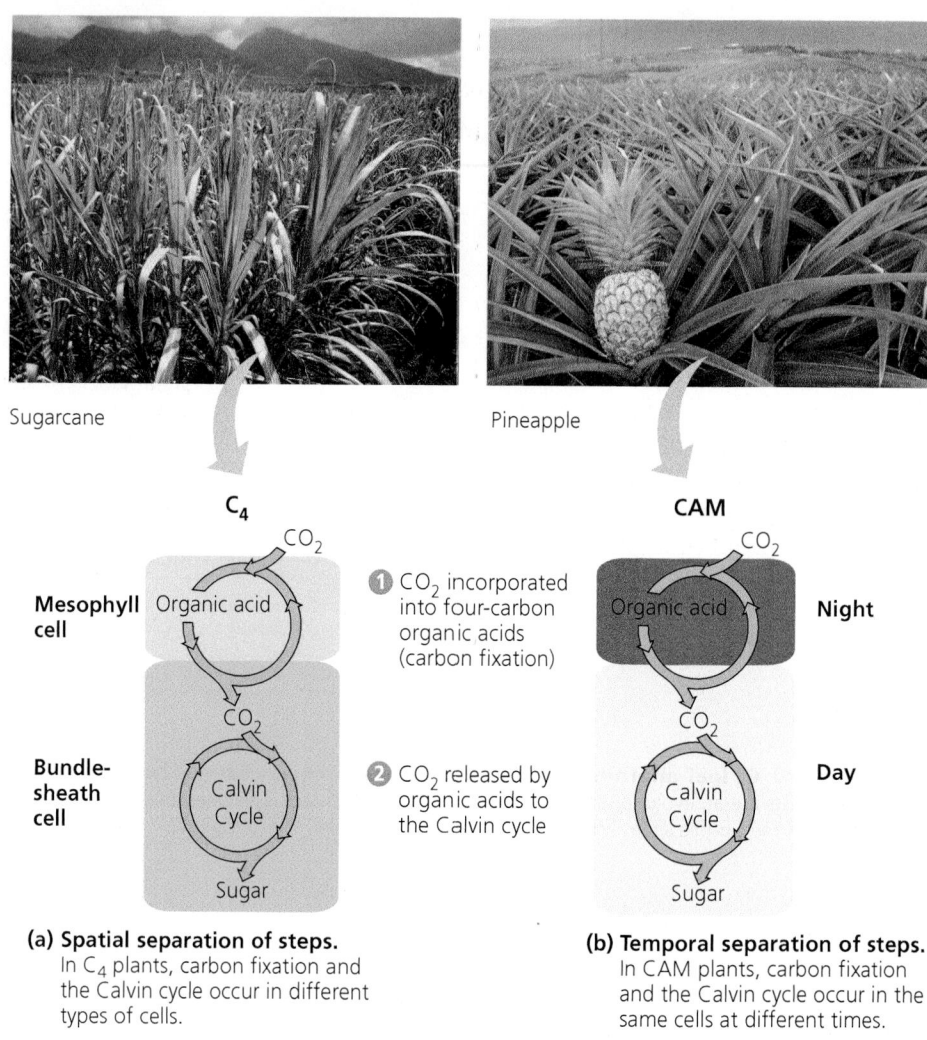

► **Figure 10.21 C₄ and CAM photosynthesis compared.** Both adaptations are characterized by ❶ preliminary incorporation of CO₂ into organic acids, followed by ❷ transfer of CO₂ to the Calvin cycle. The C₄ and CAM pathways are two evolutionary solutions to the problem of maintaining photosynthesis with stomata partially or completely closed on hot, dry days.

Sugarcane

Pineapple

C₄

Mesophyll cell — Organic acid

CO₂

❶ CO₂ incorporated into four-carbon organic acids (carbon fixation)

CO₂

Bundle-sheath cell — Calvin Cycle

❷ CO₂ released by organic acids to the Calvin cycle

Sugar

(a) Spatial separation of steps.
In C₄ plants, carbon fixation and the Calvin cycle occur in different types of cells.

CAM

Organic acid — Night

CO₂

CO₂

Calvin Cycle — Day

Sugar

(b) Temporal separation of steps.
In CAM plants, carbon fixation and the Calvin cycle occur in the same cells at different times.

of organic acids. This mode of carbon fixation is called **crassulacean acid metabolism**, or **CAM**, after the plant family Crassulaceae, the succulents in which the process was first discovered. The mesophyll cells of **CAM plants** store the organic acids they make during the night in their vacuoles until morning, when the stomata close. During the day, when the light reactions can supply ATP and NADPH for the Calvin cycle, CO₂ is released from the organic acids made the night before to become incorporated into sugar in the chloroplasts.

Notice in **Figure 10.21** that the CAM pathway is similar to the C₄ pathway in that carbon dioxide is first incorporated into organic intermediates before it enters the Calvin cycle. The difference is that in C₄ plants, the initial steps of carbon fixation are separated structurally from the Calvin cycle, whereas in CAM plants, the two steps occur at separate times but within the same cell. (Keep in mind that CAM, C₄, and C₃ plants all eventually use the Calvin cycle to make sugar from carbon dioxide.)

CONCEPT CHECK 10.4

1. Explain why photorespiration lowers photosynthetic output for plants.
2. The presence of only PS I, not PS II, in the bundle-sheath cells of C₄ plants has an effect on O₂ concentration. What is that effect, and how might that benefit the plant?
3. **MAKE CONNECTIONS** Refer to the discussion of ocean acidification in Concept 3.3 (p. 55). Ocean acidification and changes in the distribution of C₃ and C₄ plants may seem to be two very different problems, but what do they have in common? Explain.
4. **WHAT IF?** How would you expect the relative abundance of C₃ versus C₄ and CAM species to change in a geographic region whose climate becomes much hotter and drier, with no change in CO₂ concentration?

For suggested answers, see Appendix A.

The Importance of Photosynthesis: *A Review*

In this chapter, we have followed photosynthesis from photons to food. The light reactions capture solar energy and use it to make ATP and transfer electrons from water to NADP+, forming NADPH. The Calvin cycle uses the ATP and NADPH to produce sugar from carbon dioxide. The energy that enters the chloroplasts as sunlight becomes stored as chemical energy in organic compounds. See **Figure 10.22** for a review of the entire process.

What are the fates of photosynthetic products? The sugar made in the chloroplasts supplies the entire plant with chemical energy and carbon skeletons for the synthesis of all the major organic molecules of plant cells. About 50% of the organic material made by photosynthesis is consumed as fuel for cellular respiration in the mitochondria of the plant cells. Sometimes there is a loss of photosynthetic products to photorespiration.

Technically, green cells are the only autotrophic parts of the plant. The rest of the plant depends on organic molecules exported from leaves via veins. In most plants, carbohydrate is transported out of the leaves in the form of sucrose, a disaccharide. After arriving at nonphotosynthetic cells, the sucrose provides raw material for cellular respiration and a multitude of anabolic pathways that synthesize proteins, lipids, and other products. A considerable amount of sugar in the form of glucose is linked together to make the polysaccharide cellulose, especially in plant cells that are still growing and maturing. Cellulose, the main ingredient of cell walls, is the most abundant organic molecule in the plant—and probably on the surface of the planet.

Most plants manage to make more organic material each day than they need to use as respiratory fuel and precursors for biosynthesis. They stockpile the extra sugar by synthesizing starch, storing some in the chloroplasts themselves and some in storage cells of roots, tubers, seeds, and fruits. In accounting for the consumption of the food molecules produced by photosynthesis, let's not forget that most plants lose leaves, roots, stems, fruits, and sometimes their entire bodies to heterotrophs, including humans.

On a global scale, photosynthesis is the process responsible for the presence of oxygen in our atmosphere. Furthermore, in terms of food production, the collective productivity of the minuscule chloroplasts is prodigious: Photosynthesis makes an estimated 160 billion metric tons of carbohydrate per year (a metric ton is 1,000 kg, about 1.1 tons). That's organic matter equivalent in mass to a stack of about 60 trillion copies of this textbook—17 stacks of books reaching from Earth to the sun! No other chemical process on the planet can match the output of photosynthesis. And as we mentioned earlier, researchers are seeking ways to capitalize on photosynthetic production to produce alternative fuels. No process is more important than photosynthesis to the welfare of life on Earth.

▶ **Figure 10.22 A review of photosynthesis.** This diagram outlines the main reactants and products of the light reactions and the Calvin cycle as they occur in the chloroplasts of plant cells. The entire ordered operation depends on the structural integrity of the chloroplast and its membranes. Enzymes in the chloroplast and cytosol convert glyceraldehyde 3-phosphate (G3P), the direct product of the Calvin cycle, to many other organic compounds.

MAKE CONNECTIONS *Return to the micrograph in Figure 5.6a, on page 72. Label and describe where the light reactions and the Calvin cycle take place. Also explain where the starch granules in the micrograph came from.*

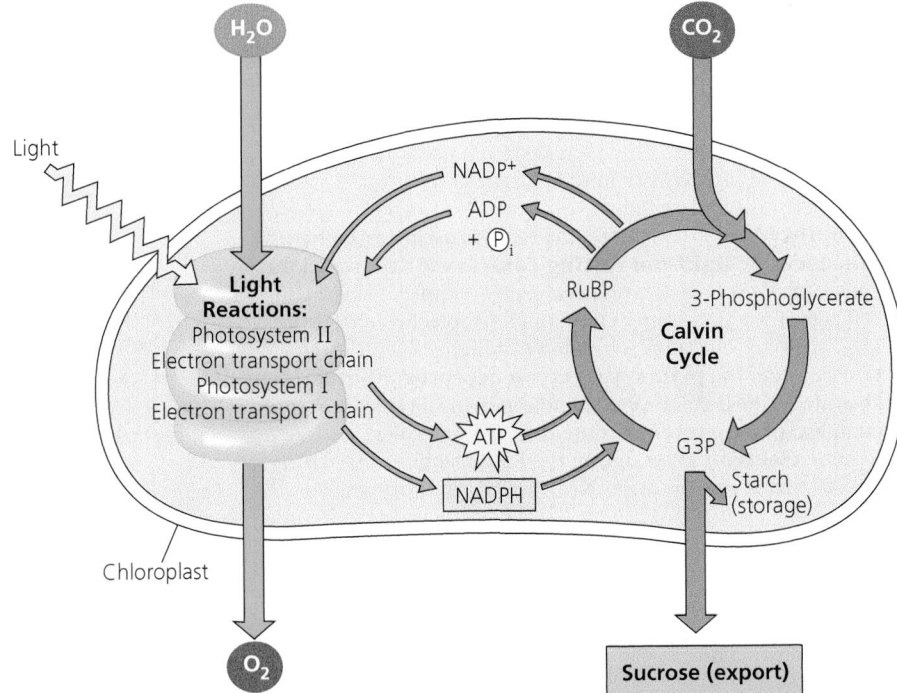

Light Reactions:
- Are carried out by molecules in the thylakoid membranes
- Convert light energy to the chemical energy of ATP and NADPH
- Split H_2O and release O_2 to the atmosphere

Calvin Cycle Reactions:
- Take place in the stroma
- Use ATP and NADPH to convert CO_2 to the sugar G3P
- Return ADP, inorganic phosphate, and NADP+ to the light reactions

SUMMARY OF KEY CONCEPTS

CONCEPT 10.1

Photosynthesis converts light energy to the chemical energy of food (pp. 186–189)

- In **autotrophic** eukaryotes, photosynthesis occurs in **chloroplasts**, organelles containing **thylakoids**. Stacks of thylakoids form grana. **Photosynthesis** is summarized as

$$6 CO_2 + 12 H_2O + \text{Light energy} \rightarrow C_6H_{12}O_6 + 6 O_2 + 6 H_2O.$$

Chloroplasts split water into hydrogen and oxygen, incorporating the electrons of hydrogen into sugar molecules. Photosynthesis is a redox process: H_2O is oxidized, and CO_2 is reduced. The **light reactions** in the thylakoid membranes split water, releasing O_2, producing ATP, and forming **NADPH**. The **Calvin cycle** in the **stroma** forms sugar from CO_2, using ATP for energy and NADPH for reducing power.

? *Compare and describe the roles of CO_2 and H_2O in respiration and photosynthesis.*

CONCEPT 10.2

The light reactions convert solar energy to the chemical energy of ATP and NADPH (pp. 189–197)

- Light is a form of electromagnetic energy. The colors we see as **visible light** include those **wavelengths** that drive photosynthesis. A pigment absorbs light of specific wavelengths; **chlorophyll *a*** is the main photosynthetic pigment in plants. Other accessory pigments absorb different wavelengths of light and pass the energy on to chlorophyll *a*.
- A pigment goes from a ground state to an excited state when a **photon** of light boosts one of the pigment's electrons to a higher-energy orbital. This excited state is unstable. Electrons from isolated pigments tend to fall back to the ground state, giving off heat and/or light.
- A **photosystem** is composed of a **reaction-center complex** surrounded by **light-harvesting complexes** that funnel the energy of photons to the reaction-center complex. When a special pair of reaction-center chlorophyll *a* molecules absorbs energy, one of its electrons is boosted to a higher energy level and transferred to the **primary electron acceptor**. **Photosystem II** contains P680 chlorophyll *a* molecules in the reaction-center complex; **photosystem I** contains P700 molecules.
- **Linear electron flow** during the light reactions uses both photosystems and produces NADPH, ATP, and oxygen:

- **Cyclic electron flow** employs only photosystem I, producing ATP but no NADPH or O_2.
- During chemiosmosis in both mitochondria and chloroplasts, electron transport chains generate an H^+ gradient across a membrane. ATP synthase uses this proton-motive force to make ATP.

? *The absorption spectrum of chlorophyll a differs from the action spectrum of photosynthesis. Explain this observation.*

CONCEPT 10.3

The Calvin cycle uses the chemical energy of ATP and NADPH to reduce CO_2 to sugar (pp. 198–199)

- The Calvin cycle occurs in the stroma, using electrons from NADPH and energy from ATP. One molecule of **G3P** exits the cycle per three CO_2 molecules fixed and is converted to glucose and other organic molecules.

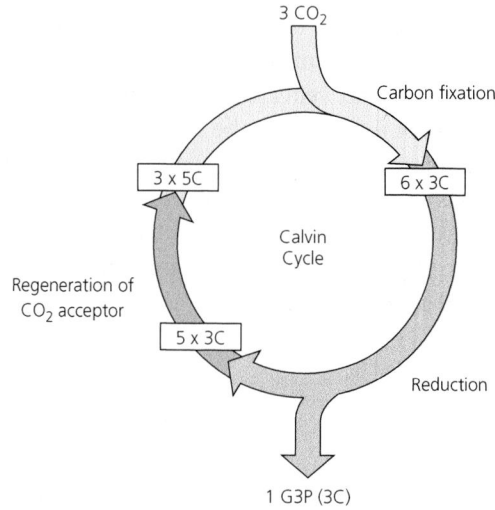

DRAW IT *On the diagram above, draw where ATP and NADPH are used and where rubisco functions. Describe these steps.*

CONCEPT 10.4

Alternative mechanisms of carbon fixation have evolved in hot, arid climates (pp. 199–202)

- On dry, hot days, **C₃ plants** close their stomata, conserving water. Oxygen from the light reactions builds up. In **photorespiration**, O_2 substitutes for CO_2 in the active site of rubisco. This process consumes organic fuel and releases CO_2 without producing ATP or carbohydrate. Photorespiration may be an evolutionary relic, and it may play a photoprotective role.
- **C₄ plants** minimize the cost of photorespiration by incorporating CO_2 into four-carbon compounds in mesophyll cells. These compounds are exported to **bundle-sheath cells**, where they release carbon dioxide for use in the Calvin cycle.
- **CAM plants** open their stomata at night, incorporating CO_2 into organic acids, which are stored in mesophyll cells. During the day, the stomata close, and the CO_2 is released from the organic acids for use in the Calvin cycle.
- Organic compounds produced by photosynthesis provide the energy and building material for ecosystems.

? *Why are C₄ and CAM photosynthesis more energetically expensive than C₃ photosynthesis? What climate conditions would favor C₄ and CAM plants?*

LEVEL 1: KNOWLEDGE/COMPREHENSION

1. The light reactions of photosynthesis supply the Calvin cycle with
   a. light energy.
   b. CO_2 and ATP.
   c. H_2O and NADPH.
   d. ATP and NADPH.
   e. sugar and O_2.

2. Which of the following sequences correctly represents the flow of electrons during photosynthesis?
   a. NADPH → O_2 → CO_2
   b. H_2O → NADPH → Calvin cycle
   c. NADPH → chlorophyll → Calvin cycle
   d. H_2O → photosystem I → photosystem II
   e. NADPH → electron transport chain → O_2

3. How is photosynthesis similar in C_4 plants and CAM plants?
   a. In both cases, only photosystem I is used.
   b. Both types of plants make sugar without the Calvin cycle.
   c. In both cases, rubisco is not used to fix carbon initially.
   d. Both types of plants make most of their sugar in the dark.
   e. In both cases, thylakoids are not involved in photosynthesis.

4. Which of the following statements is a correct distinction between autotrophs and heterotrophs?
   a. Only heterotrophs require chemical compounds from the environment.
   b. Cellular respiration is unique to heterotrophs.
   c. Only heterotrophs have mitochondria.
   d. Autotrophs, but not heterotrophs, can nourish themselves beginning with CO_2 and other nutrients that are inorganic.
   e. Only heterotrophs require oxygen.

5. Which of the following does *not* occur during the Calvin cycle?
   a. carbon fixation
   b. oxidation of NADPH
   c. release of oxygen
   d. regeneration of the CO_2 acceptor
   e. consumption of ATP

LEVEL 2: APPLICATION/ANALYSIS

6. In mechanism, photophosphorylation is most similar to
   a. substrate-level phosphorylation in glycolysis.
   b. oxidative phosphorylation in cellular respiration.
   c. the Calvin cycle.
   d. carbon fixation.
   e. reduction of $NADP^+$.

7. Which process is most directly driven by light energy?
   a. creation of a pH gradient by pumping protons across the thylakoid membrane
   b. carbon fixation in the stroma
   c. reduction of $NADP^+$ molecules
   d. removal of electrons from chlorophyll molecules
   e. ATP synthesis

LEVEL 3: SYNTHESIS/EVALUATION

8. **EVOLUTION CONNECTION**
   Photorespiration can decrease soybeans' photosynthetic output by about 50%. Would you expect this figure to be higher or lower in wild relatives of soybeans? Why?

9. **SCIENTIFIC INQUIRY**
   MAKE CONNECTIONS **DRAW IT** The following diagram represents an experiment with isolated thylakoids. The thylakoids were first made acidic by soaking them in a solution at pH 4. After the thylakoid space reached pH 4, the thylakoids were transferred to a basic solution at pH 8. The thylakoids then made ATP in the dark. (See Concept 3.3, pp. 53–54, to review pH).

Draw an enlargement of part of the thylakoid membrane in the beaker with the solution at pH 8. Draw ATP synthase. Label the areas of high H^+ concentration and low H^+ concentration. Show the direction protons flow through the enzyme, and show the reaction where ATP is synthesized. Would ATP end up in the thylakoid or outside of it? Explain why the thylakoids in the experiment were able to make ATP in the dark.

10. **SCIENCE, TECHNOLOGY, AND SOCIETY**
    Scientific evidence indicates that the CO_2 added to the air by the burning of wood and fossil fuels is contributing to global warming, a rise in global temperature. Tropical rain forests are estimated to be responsible for approximately 20% of global photosynthesis, yet the consumption of large amounts of CO_2 by living trees is thought to make little or no *net* contribution to reduction of global warming. Why might this be? (*Hint*: What processes in both living and dead trees produce CO_2?)

11. **WRITE ABOUT A THEME**
    Energy Transfer Life is solar powered. Almost all the producers of the biosphere depend on energy from the sun to produce the organic molecules that supply the energy and carbon skeletons needed for life. In a short essay (100–150 words), describe how the process of photosynthesis in the chloroplasts of plants transforms the energy of sunlight into the chemical energy of sugar molecules.

For selected answers, see Appendix A.

 www.masteringbiology.com

1. MasteringBiology® Assignments
Experimental Inquiry Tutorial Which Wavelengths of Light Drive Photosynthesis?
BioFlix Tutorials Photosynthesis: Inputs, Outputs, and Chloroplast Structure • The Light Reactions • The Calvin Cycle
Tutorial Energy Flow in Plants—Concept Map
Activities Overview of Photosynthesis • The Sites of Photosynthesis • Chemiosmosis • Light Energy and Pigments • Photosynthesis • The Light Reactions • The Calvin Cycle • Photosynthesis in Dry Climates
Questions Student Misconceptions • Reading Quiz • Multiple Choice • End-of-Chapter

2. eText
Read your book online, search, take notes, highlight text, and more.

3. The Study Area
Practice Tests • Cumulative Test • **BioFlix** 3-D Animations • MP3 Tutor Sessions • Videos • Activities • Investigations • Lab Media • Audio Glossary • Word Study Tools • Art

11

Cell Communication

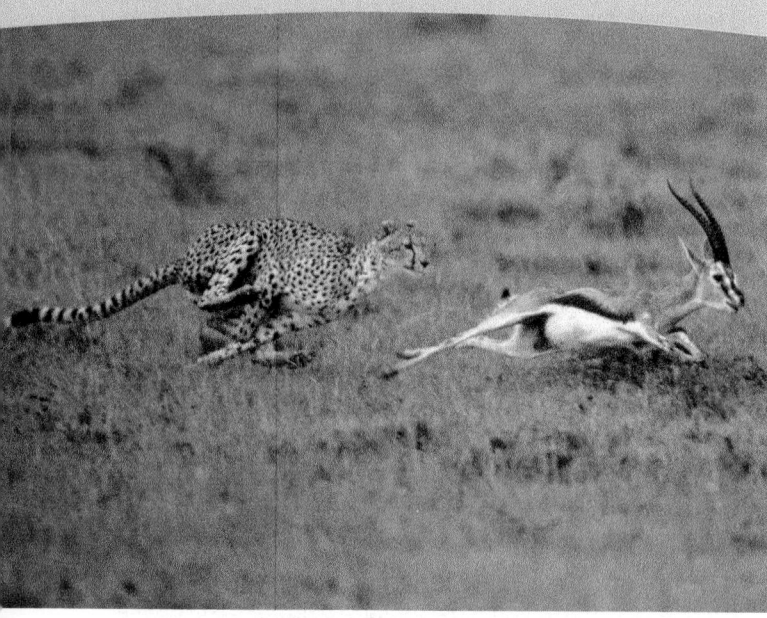

▲ **Figure 11.1 How does cell signaling trigger the desperate flight of this gazelle?**

KEY CONCEPTS

11.1 External signals are converted to responses within the cell

11.2 Reception: A signaling molecule binds to a receptor protein, causing it to change shape

11.3 Transduction: Cascades of molecular interactions relay signals from receptors to target molecules in the cell

11.4 Response: Cell signaling leads to regulation of transcription or cytoplasmic activities

11.5 Apoptosis integrates multiple cell-signaling pathways

Cellular Messaging

The Thomson's gazelle in **Figure 11.1** is fleeing for its life, seeking to escape the predatory cheetah nipping at its heels. The gazelle's heart is racing, its breathing accelerated and its muscles performing at their highest level. These physiological functions are all part of the "fight-or-flight" response, driven by hormones released from the adrenal glands at times of stress—in this case, when the gazelle first sensed the cheetah. Hormonal signaling and the subsequent response by cells and tissues throughout the gazelle's body illustrate how cell-to-cell communication allows the trillions of cells in a multicellular organism to "talk" to each other, coordinating their activities. Communication between cells is essential not only for multicellular organisms such as gazelles and oak trees but for many unicellular organisms as well.

In studying how cells signal to each other and how they interpret the signals they receive, biologists have discovered some universal mechanisms of cellular regulation, additional evidence for the evolutionary relatedness of all life. The same small set of cell-signaling mechanisms shows up again and again in diverse species, in biological processes ranging from hormone action to embryonic development to cancer. The signals received by cells, whether originating from other cells or from changes in the physical environment, take various forms, including light and touch. However, cells most often communicate with each other by chemical signals. For instance, the fight-or-flight response is triggered by a signaling molecule called epinephrine. In this chapter, we focus on the main mechanisms by which cells receive, process, and respond to chemical signals sent from other cells. We will also take a look at *apoptosis*, a type of programmed cell death that integrates input from multiple signaling pathways.

CONCEPT 11.1

External signals are converted to responses within the cell

What does a "talking" cell say to a "listening" cell, and how does the latter cell respond to the message? Let's approach these questions by first looking at communication among microorganisms, for microbes living today provide a glimpse into the role of cell signaling in the evolution of life on Earth.

Evolution of Cell Signaling

EVOLUTION One topic of cell "conversation" is sex—at least for the yeast *Saccharomyces cerevisiae*, which people have used for millennia to make bread, wine, and beer. Researchers have learned that cells of this yeast identify their mates by chemical signaling. There are two sexes, or mating types, called **a** and α (Figure 11.2). Cells of mating type **a** secrete a signaling

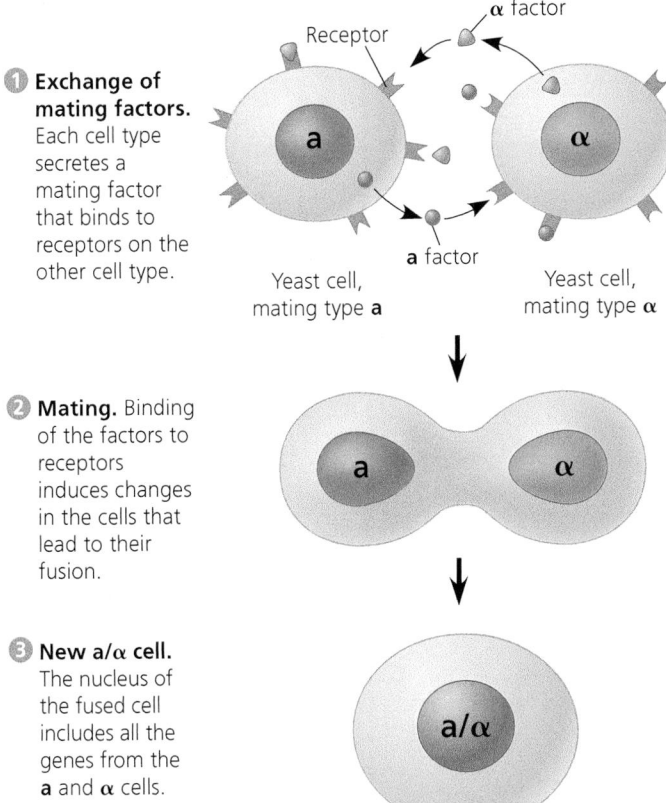

① Exchange of mating factors. Each cell type secretes a mating factor that binds to receptors on the other cell type.

α factor

Receptor

a

α

Yeast cell, mating type **a**

Yeast cell, mating type α

a factor

② Mating. Binding of the factors to receptors induces changes in the cells that lead to their fusion.

a

α

③ New a/α cell. The nucleus of the fused cell includes all the genes from the **a** and α cells.

a/α

▲ **Figure 11.2 Communication between mating yeast cells.** *Saccharomyces cerevisiae* cells use chemical signaling to identify cells of opposite mating type and initiate the mating process. The two mating types and their corresponding chemical signaling molecules, or mating factors, are called **a** and α.

molecule called **a** factor, which can bind to specific receptor proteins on nearby α cells. At the same time, α cells secrete α factor, which binds to receptors on **a** cells. Without actually entering the cells, the two mating factors cause the cells to grow toward each other and also bring about other cellular changes. The result is the fusion, or mating, of two cells of opposite type. The new **a/**α cell contains all the genes of both original cells, a combination of genetic resources that provides advantages to the cell's descendants, which arise by subsequent cell divisions.

Once received at the yeast cell surface, how is the mating signal changed, or *transduced*, into a form that brings about the cellular response of mating? The received signal is converted to a specific cellular response in a series of steps called a **signal transduction pathway**. Many such pathways have been extensively studied in both yeast and animal cells. Amazingly, the molecular details of signal transduction in yeast and mammals are strikingly similar, even though the last common ancestor of these two groups of organisms lived over a billion years ago. These similarities—and others more recently uncovered between signaling systems in bacteria and plants—suggest that early versions of today's cell-signaling mechanisms evolved well before the first multicellular creatures appeared on Earth.

Scientists such as Bonnie Bassler, the interviewee for Unit 2 (see pp. 92–93), think that signaling mechanisms first evolved in ancient prokaryotes and single-celled eukaryotes, then were adopted for new uses by their multicellular descendants. Cell signaling is critical in the microbial world; a classic example in one bacterial species is shown in **Figure 11.3**. Bacterial cells secrete small molecules that can be detected by other bacterial cells. The concentration of such signaling molecules, sensed by the bacteria, allows them to monitor the local density of cells, a phenomenon called *quorum sensing*. Quorum sensing allows bacterial populations to coordinate their behaviors so they can carry out activities that are only productive when performed by a given number of cells in synchrony. One example is formation of a *biofilm*, an aggregation of bacterial cells adhered to a surface; the cells in the biofilm generally derive nutrition from the surface they are on. You have probably encountered biofilms many times, perhaps without realizing it. The slimy coating on a fallen log or on leaves lying on a forest path, or on your teeth each morning, are examples of bacterial biofilms. Biofilms are responsible for cavities—a good argument for daily tooth brushing and flossing to disrupt them!

① Individual rod-shaped cells

0.5 mm

② Aggregation in progress

2.5 mm

③ Spore-forming structure (fruiting body)

Fruiting bodies

▲ **Figure 11.3 Communication among bacteria.** Soil-dwelling bacteria called myxobacteria ("slime bacteria") use chemical signals to share information about nutrient availability. When food is scarce, starving cells secrete a molecule that stimulates neighboring cells to aggregate. The cells form a structure, called a fruiting body, that produces thick-walled spores capable of surviving until the environment improves. The bacteria shown here are *Myxococcus xanthus* (steps 1–3, SEMs; lower photo, LM).

Local and Long-Distance Signaling

Like bacteria or yeast cells, cells in a multicellular organism usually communicate via chemical messengers targeted for cells that may or may not be immediately adjacent. As we saw in Chapters 6 and 7, eukaryotic cells may communicate by direct contact (**Figure 11.4**), one type of local signaling. Both animals and plants have cell junctions that, where present, directly connect the cytoplasms of adjacent cells (**Figure 11.4a**). In these cases, signaling substances dissolved in the cytosol can pass freely between adjacent cells. Moreover, animal cells may communicate via direct contact between membrane-bound cell-surface molecules in a process called cell-cell recognition (**Figure 11.4b**). This sort of local signaling is important in embryonic development and the immune response.

In many other cases of local signaling, messenger molecules are secreted by the signaling cell. Some of these travel only short distances; such **local regulators** influence cells in the vicinity. One class of local regulators in animals, *growth factors*, consists of compounds that stimulate nearby target cells to grow and divide. Numerous cells can simultaneously receive and respond to the molecules of growth factor produced by a single cell in their vicinity. This type of local signaling in animals is called *paracrine signaling* (**Figure 11.5a**).

Another, more specialized type of local signaling called *synaptic signaling* occurs in the animal nervous system (**Figure 11.5b**). An electrical signal along a nerve cell triggers the secretion of neurotransmitter molecules carrying a chemical signal. These molecules diffuse across the synapse, the

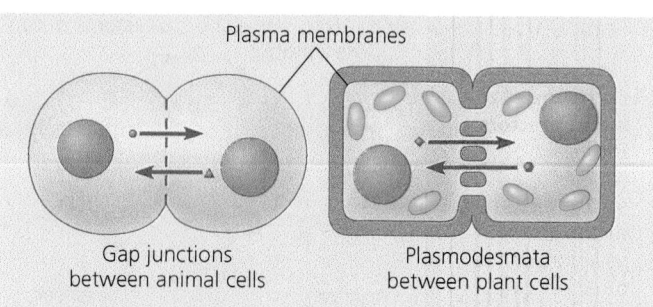

(a) **Cell junctions.** Both animals and plants have cell junctions that allow molecules to pass readily between adjacent cells without crossing plasma membranes.

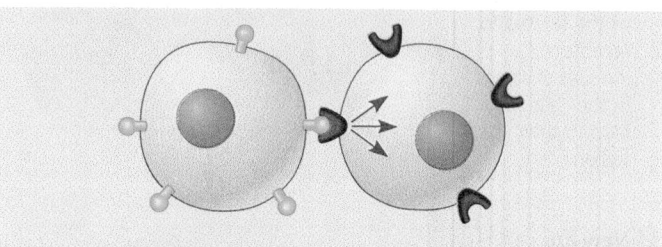

(b) **Cell-cell recognition.** Two cells in an animal may communicate by interaction between molecules protruding from their surfaces.

▲ Figure 11.4 **Communication by direct contact between cells.**

narrow space between the nerve cell and its target cell (often another nerve cell), triggering a response in the target cell.

Beyond communication through plasmodesmata (plant cell junctions), local signaling in plants is not as well understood. Because of their cell walls, plants use mechanisms somewhat different from those operating locally in animals.

(a) **Paracrine signaling.** A secreting cell acts on nearby target cells by discharging molecules of a local regulator (a growth factor, for example) into the extracellular fluid.

(b) **Synaptic signaling.** A nerve cell releases neurotransmitter molecules into a synapse, stimulating the target cell.

▲ Figure 11.5 **Local and long-distance cell signaling by secreted molecules in animals.** In both local and long-distance signaling, only specific target cells that can recognize a given signaling molecule will respond to it.

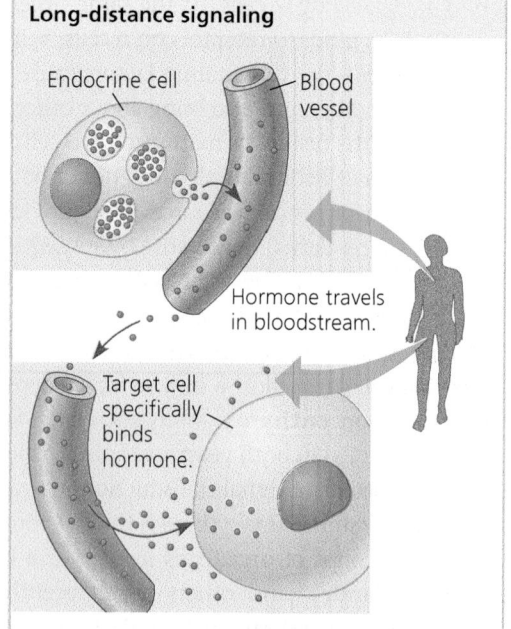

(c) **Endocrine (hormonal) signaling.** Specialized endocrine cells secrete hormones into body fluids, often blood. Hormones reach virtually all body cells, but are bound only by some cells.

Both animals and plants use chemicals called **hormones** for long-distance signaling. In hormonal signaling in animals, also known as *endocrine signaling*, specialized cells release hormone molecules, which travel via the circulatory system to other parts of the body, where they reach target cells that can recognize and respond to the hormones (**Figure 11.5c**). Plant hormones (often called *plant growth regulators*) sometimes travel in vessels but more often reach their targets by moving through cells or by diffusing through the air as a gas (see Chapter 39). Hormones vary widely in molecular size and type, as do local regulators. For instance, the plant hormone ethylene, a gas that promotes fruit ripening and helps regulate growth, is a hydrocarbon of only six atoms (C_2H_4), small enough to pass through cell walls. In contrast, the mammalian hormone insulin, which regulates sugar levels in the blood, is a protein with thousands of atoms.

The transmission of a signal through the nervous system can also be considered an example of long-distance signaling. An electrical signal travels the length of a nerve cell and is then converted back to a chemical signal when a signaling molecule is released and crosses the synapse to another nerve cell. Here it is converted back to an electrical signal. In this way, a nerve signal can travel along a series of nerve cells. Because some nerve cells are quite long, the nerve signal can quickly travel great distances—from your brain to your big toe, for example. This type of long-distance signaling will be covered in detail in Chapter 48.

What happens when a cell encounters a secreted signaling molecule? The ability of a cell to respond is determined by whether it has a specific receptor molecule that can bind to the signaling molecule. The information conveyed by this binding, the signal, must then be changed into another form—transduced—inside the cell before the cell can respond. The remainder of the chapter discusses this process, primarily as it occurs in animal cells.

The Three Stages of Cell Signaling: *A Preview*

Our current understanding of how chemical messengers act via signal transduction pathways had its origins in the pioneering work of Earl W. Sutherland, whose research led to a Nobel Prize in 1971. Sutherland and his colleagues at Vanderbilt University were investigating how the animal hormone epinephrine (also called adrenaline) stimulates the breakdown of the storage polysaccharide glycogen within liver cells and skeletal muscle cells. Glycogen breakdown releases the sugar glucose 1-phosphate, which the cell converts to glucose 6-phosphate. The cell (a liver cell, for example) can then use this compound, an early intermediate in glycolysis, for energy production. Alternatively, the compound can be stripped of phosphate and released from the liver cell into the blood as glucose, which can fuel cells throughout the body. Thus, one effect of epinephrine is the mobilization of fuel reserves, which can be used by the animal to either defend itself (fight) or escape whatever elicited a scare (flight). (The gazelle in Figure 11.1 is clearly engaged in the latter.)

Sutherland's research team discovered that epinephrine stimulates glycogen breakdown by somehow activating a cytosolic enzyme, glycogen phosphorylase. However, when epinephrine was added to a test-tube mixture containing the enzyme and its substrate, glycogen, no breakdown occurred. Epinephrine could activate glycogen phosphorylase only when the hormone was added to a solution containing *intact* cells. This result told Sutherland two things. First, epinephrine does not interact directly with the enzyme responsible for glycogen breakdown; an intermediate step or series of steps must be occurring inside the cell. Second, the plasma membrane is somehow involved in transmitting the signal.

Sutherland's early work suggested that the process going on at the receiving end of a cellular conversation can be dissected into three stages: reception, transduction, and response (**Figure 11.6**):

1. **Reception.** Reception is the target cell's detection of a signaling molecule coming from outside the cell. A chemical signal is "detected" when the signaling molecule binds to a receptor protein located at the cell's surface or inside the cell.

▶ **Figure 11.6 Overview of cell signaling.** From the perspective of the cell receiving the message, cell signaling can be divided into three stages: signal reception, signal transduction, and cellular response. When reception occurs at the plasma membrane, as shown here, the transduction stage is usually a pathway of several steps, with each relay molecule in the pathway bringing about a change in the next molecule. The final molecule in the pathway triggers the cell's response. The three stages are explained in more detail in the text.

? *How does the epinephrine in Sutherland's experiment fit into this diagram of cell signaling?*

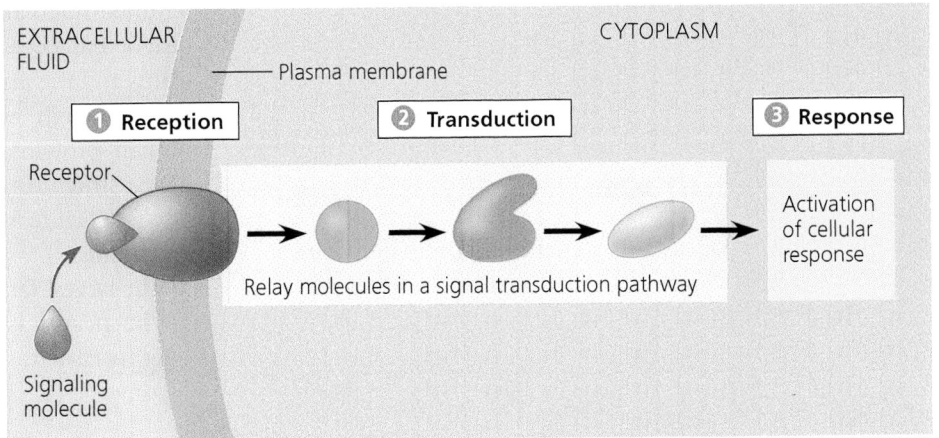

② **Transduction.** The binding of the signaling molecule changes the receptor protein in some way, initiating the process of transduction. The transduction stage converts the signal to a form that can bring about a specific cellular response. In Sutherland's system, the binding of epinephrine to a receptor protein in a liver cell's plasma membrane leads to activation of glycogen phosphorylase. Transduction sometimes occurs in a single step but more often requires a sequence of changes in a series of different molecules—a *signal transduction pathway*. The molecules in the pathway are often called relay molecules.

③ **Response.** In the third stage of cell signaling, the transduced signal finally triggers a specific cellular response. The response may be almost any imaginable cellular activity—such as catalysis by an enzyme (for example, glycogen phosphorylase), rearrangement of the cytoskeleton, or activation of specific genes in the nucleus. The cell-signaling process helps ensure that crucial activities like these occur in the right cells, at the right time, and in proper coordination with the activities of other cells of the organism. We'll now explore the mechanisms of cell signaling in more detail, including a discussion of fine-tuning and termination of the process.

CONCEPT CHECK 11.1

1. Explain how signaling is involved in ensuring that yeast cells fuse only with cells of the opposite mating type.
2. Explain how nerve cells provide examples of both local and long-distance signaling.
3. **WHAT IF?** When epinephrine is mixed with glycogen phosphorylase and glycogen in a test tube, is glucose 1-phosphate generated? Why or why not?
4. In liver cells, glycogen phosphorylase acts in which of the three stages of the signaling pathway associated with an epinephrine-initiated signal?

For suggested answers, see Appendix A.

CONCEPT 11.2

Reception: A signaling molecule binds to a receptor protein, causing it to change shape

A radio station broadcasts its signal indiscriminately, but it can only be picked up by radios tuned to the right wavelength: Reception of the signal depends on the receiver. Similarly, the signals emitted by an **a** yeast cell are "heard" only by its prospective mates, **α** cells. In the case of epinephrine, the hormone encounters many types of cells as it circulates in the blood, but only certain target cells detect and react to the hormone molecule. A receptor protein on or in the target cell allows the cell to "hear" the signal and respond to it. The signaling molecule is complementary in shape to a specific site on the receptor and attaches there, like a key in a lock or a substrate in the catalytic site of an enzyme. The signaling molecule behaves as a **ligand**, the term for a molecule that specifically binds to another molecule, often a larger one. Ligand binding generally causes a receptor protein to undergo a change in shape. For many receptors, this shape change directly activates the receptor, enabling it to interact with other cellular molecules. For other kinds of receptors, the immediate effect of ligand binding is to cause the aggregation of two or more receptor molecules, which leads to further molecular events inside the cell.

Most signal receptors are plasma membrane proteins. Their ligands are water-soluble and generally too large to pass freely through the plasma membrane. Other signal receptors, however, are located inside the cell. We discuss both of these types next.

Receptors in the Plasma Membrane

Most water-soluble signaling molecules bind to specific sites on receptor proteins that span the cell's plasma membrane. Such a transmembrane receptor transmits information from the extracellular environment to the inside of the cell by changing shape or aggregating when a specific ligand binds to it. We can see how cell-surface transmembrane receptors work by looking at three major types: G protein-coupled receptors, receptor tyrosine kinases, and ion channel receptors. These receptors are discussed and illustrated in **Figure 11.7**, on the next three pages; study this figure before going on.

Cell-surface receptor molecules play crucial roles in the biological systems of animals, and not surprisingly, their malfunctions are associated with many human diseases, including cancer, heart disease, and asthma. Working out the structure and function of these receptors will allow us to better understand and treat these conditions. Therefore, this endeavor has been a major focus of both university research teams and the pharmaceutical industry. In spite of this effort, and although cell-surface receptors make up 30% of all human proteins, they make up only 1% of the proteins whose structures have been determined by X-ray crystallography (see Figure 5.24): Their structures are very challenging to determine.

The largest family of human cell-surface receptors consists of the nearly 1,000 G protein-coupled receptors (GPCRs). After persistent efforts, researchers have made significant

Exploring Cell-Surface Transmembrane Receptors

G Protein-Coupled Receptors

Signaling molecule binding site

Segment that interacts with G proteins

G protein-coupled receptor

A **G protein-coupled receptor** (GPCR) is a cell-surface transmembrane receptor that works with the help of a **G protein**, a protein that binds the energy-rich molecule GTP. Many different signaling molecules, including yeast mating factors, epinephrine and many other hormones, and neurotransmitters, use G protein-coupled receptors. These receptors vary in the binding sites for their signaling molecules (often referred to as their ligands) and also for different types of G proteins inside the cell. Nevertheless, G protein-coupled receptor proteins are all remarkably similar in structure.

In fact, they make up a large family of eukaryotic receptor proteins with a secondary structure in which the single polypeptide, represented here as a ribbon, has seven transmembrane α helices, outlined with cylinders and depicted in a row for clarity. Specific loops

between the helices form binding sites for signaling and G protein molecules.

G protein-coupled receptor systems are extremely widespread and diverse in their functions, including roles in embryonic development and sensory reception. In humans, for example, vision, smell, and taste depend on such systems. Similarities in structure in G proteins and G protein-coupled receptors in diverse organisms suggest that G proteins and associated receptors evolved very early.

G protein systems are involved in many human diseases, including bacterial infections. The bacteria that cause cholera, pertussis (whooping cough), and botulism, among others, make their victims ill by producing toxins that interfere with G protein function. Pharmacologists now realize that up to 60% of all medicines used today exert their effects by influencing G protein pathways.

① Loosely attached to the cytoplasmic side of the membrane, the G protein functions as a molecular switch that is either on or off, depending on which of two guanine nucleotides is attached, GDP or GTP—hence the term *G protein*. (GTP, or guanosine triphosphate, is similar to ATP.) When GDP is bound to the G protein, as shown above, the G protein is inactive. The receptor and G protein work together with another protein, usually an enzyme.

② When the appropriate signaling molecule binds to the extracellular side of the receptor, the receptor is activated and changes shape. Its cytoplasmic side then binds an inactive G protein, causing a GTP to displace the GDP. This activates the G protein.

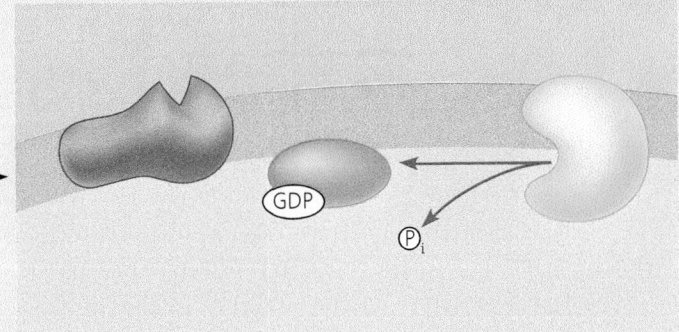

③ The activated G protein dissociates from the receptor, diffuses along the membrane, and then binds to an enzyme, altering the enzyme's shape and activity. Once activated, the enzyme can trigger the next step leading to a cellular response. (Binding of signaling molecules is reversible: Like other ligands, they bind and dissociate many times. The ligand concentration outside the cell determines how often a ligand is bound and causes signaling.)

④ The changes in the enzyme and G protein are only temporary because the G protein also functions as a GTPase enzyme—in other words, it then hydrolyzes its bound GTP to GDP. Now inactive again, the G protein leaves the enzyme, which returns to its original state. The G protein is now available for reuse. The GTPase function of the G protein allows the pathway to shut down rapidly when the signaling molecule is no longer present.

Continued on next page

Exploring Cell-Surface Transmembrane Receptors

Receptor Tyrosine Kinases

Receptor tyrosine kinases (RTKs) belong to a major class of plasma membrane receptors characterized by having enzymatic activity. A *kinase* is an enzyme that catalyzes the transfer of phosphate groups. The part of the receptor protein extending into the cytoplasm functions as a tyrosine kinase, an enzyme that catalyzes the transfer of a phosphate group from ATP to the amino acid tyrosine on a substrate protein. Thus, receptor tyrosine kinases are membrane receptors that attach phosphates to tyrosines.

One receptor tyrosine kinase complex may activate ten or more different transduction pathways and cellular responses. Often, more than one signal transduction pathway can be triggered at once, helping the cell regulate and coordinate many aspects of cell growth and cell reproduction. The ability of a single ligand-binding event to trigger so many pathways is a key difference between receptor tyrosine kinases and G protein-coupled receptors. Abnormal receptor tyrosine kinases that function even in the absence of signaling molecules are associated with many kinds of cancer.

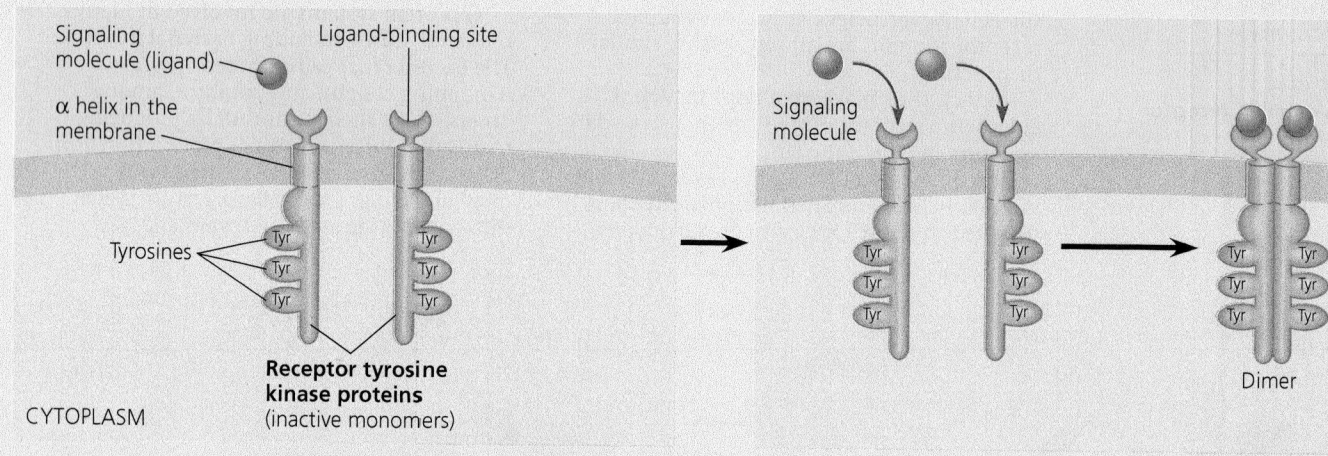

❶ Many receptor tyrosine kinases have the structure depicted schematically here. Before the signaling molecule binds, the receptors exist as individual units referred to as monomers. Notice that each has an extracellular ligand-binding site, an α helix spanning the membrane, and an intracellular tail containing multiple tyrosines.

❷ The binding of a signaling molecule (such as a growth factor) causes two receptor monomers to associate closely with each other, forming a complex known as a dimer (dimerization).

❸ Dimerization activates the tyrosine kinase region of each monomer; each tyrosine kinase adds a phosphate from an ATP molecule to a tyrosine on the tail of the other monomer.

❹ Now that the receptor is fully activated, it is recognized by specific relay proteins inside the cell. Each such protein binds to a specific phosphorylated tyrosine, undergoing a resulting structural change that activates the bound protein. Each activated protein triggers a transduction pathway, leading to a cellular response.

Ion Channel Receptors

A **ligand-gated ion channel** is a type of membrane receptor containing a region that can act as a "gate" when the receptor changes shape. When a signaling molecule binds as a ligand to the receptor protein, the gate opens or closes, allowing or blocking the flow of specific ions, such as Na⁺ or Ca²⁺, through a channel in the receptor. Like the other receptors we have discussed, these proteins bind the ligand at a specific site on their extracellular sides.

1 Here we show a ligand-gated ion channel receptor in which the gate remains closed until a ligand binds to the receptor.

2 When the ligand binds to the receptor and the gate opens, specific ions can flow through the channel and rapidly change the concentration of that particular ion inside the cell. This change may directly affect the activity of the cell in some way.

3 When the ligand dissociates from this receptor, the gate closes and ions no longer enter the cell.

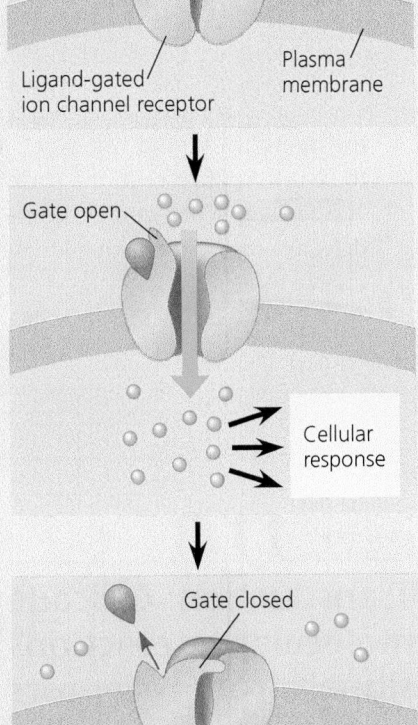

Ligand-gated ion channels are very important in the nervous system. For example, the neurotransmitter molecules released at a synapse between two nerve cells (see Figure 11.5b) bind as ligands to ion channels on the receiving cell, causing the channels to open. Ions flow in (or, in some cases, out), triggering an electrical signal that propagates down the length of the receiving cell. Some gated ion channels are controlled by electrical signals instead of ligands; these *voltage-gated ion channels* are also crucial to the functioning of the nervous system, as we will discuss in Chapter 48.

> **MAKE CONNECTIONS** *Examine the ion channel protein in Figure 7.1 (p. 125) and the discussion of it on page 135. What type of stimulus opens that ion channel? According to the information given above, what type of ion channel is described?*

▼ Figure 11.8
IMPACT

Determining the Structure of a G Protein-Coupled Receptor (GPCR)

GPCRs are flexible and inherently unstable, so they have been difficult to crystallize, a required step in determining their structure by X-ray crystallography. Recently, however, researchers have crystallized the human β₂-adrenergic receptor in the presence of a ligand similar to the natural one (green in the model below) and cholesterol (orange), which stabilized the receptor enough for its structure to be determined. Two receptor molecules (blue) are shown here as ribbon models in a side view within the plasma membrane.

WHY IT MATTERS The β₂-adrenergic receptor is found on smooth muscle cells throughout the body, and abnormal forms of it are associated with diseases such as asthma, hypertension, and heart failure. Current drugs used for these conditions produce unwanted side effects, and further research may yield better drugs. Also, since GPCRs share structural similarities, this work on the β₂-adrenergic receptor will aid development of treatments for diseases associated with other GPCRs.

FURTHER READING R. Ranganathan, Signaling across the cell membrane, *Science* 318:1253–1254 (2007).

WHAT IF? The model shown above represents the receptor in an inactive state, not bound to a G protein. Can you suggest conditions for crystallizing the protein that would reveal the structure of the receptor while it is actively signaling to the inside of the cell?

breakthroughs in elucidating the structure of several G protein-coupled receptors over the past few years **(Figure 11.8)**.

Abnormal functioning of receptor tyrosine kinases (RTKs) is associated with many types of cancers. For example, patients with breast cancer cells that have excessive levels of a receptor tyrosine kinase called HER2 have a poor prognosis. Using molecular biological techniques, researchers have developed a protein called Herceptin that binds to HER2 on cells and inhibits their growth, thus thwarting further tumor development. In some clinical studies, treatment with Herceptin improved patient survival rates by more than one-third. One goal of ongoing research into these cell-surface receptors and other cell-signaling proteins is development of additional successful treatments.

Intracellular Receptors

Intracellular receptor proteins are found in either the cytoplasm or nucleus of target cells. To reach such a receptor, a chemical messenger passes through the target cell's plasma membrane. A number of important signaling molecules can do this because they are either hydrophobic enough or small enough to cross the hydrophobic interior of the membrane. Such hydrophobic chemical messengers include the steroid hormones and thyroid hormones of animals. Another chemical signaling molecule with an intracellular receptor is nitric oxide (NO), a gas; its very small molecules readily pass between the membrane phospholipids.

The behavior of testosterone is representative of steroid hormones. In males, the hormone is secreted by cells of the testes. It then travels through the blood and enters cells all over the body. However, only cells that contain receptor molecules for testosterone respond. In these cells, the hormone binds to the receptor protein, activating it (**Figure 11.9**). With the hormone attached, the active form of the receptor protein then enters the nucleus and turns on specific genes that control male sex characteristics.

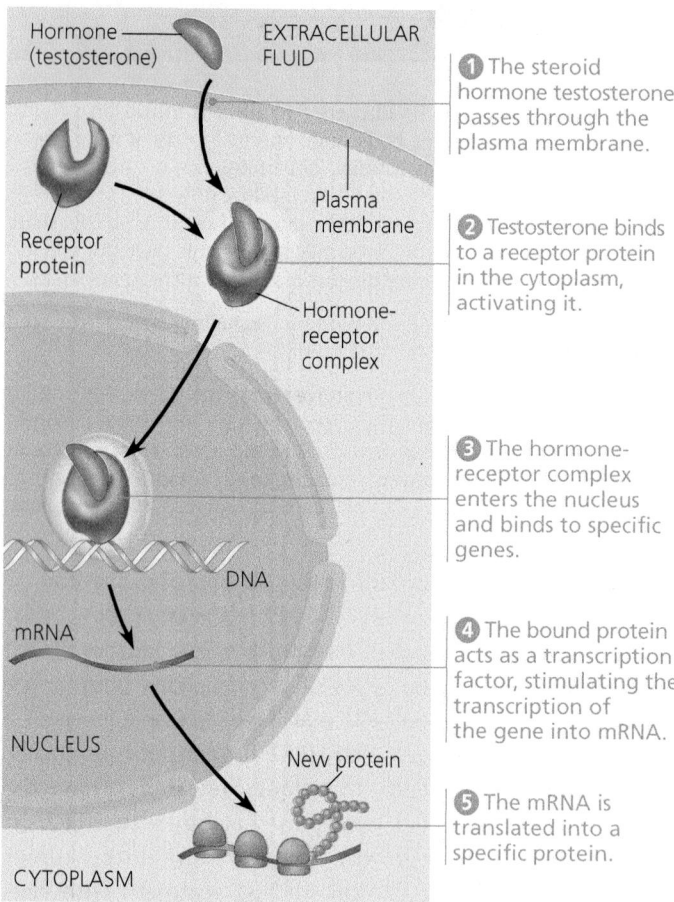

▲ **Figure 11.9 Steroid hormone interacting with an intracellular receptor.**

? *Why is a cell-surface receptor protein not required for this steroid hormone to enter the cell?*

Hormone (testosterone)
EXTRACELLULAR FLUID

1 The steroid hormone testosterone passes through the plasma membrane.

Receptor protein

Plasma membrane

2 Testosterone binds to a receptor protein in the cytoplasm, activating it.

Hormone-receptor complex

3 The hormone-receptor complex enters the nucleus and binds to specific genes.

DNA

mRNA

4 The bound protein acts as a transcription factor, stimulating the transcription of the gene into mRNA.

NUCLEUS

New protein

5 The mRNA is translated into a specific protein.

CYTOPLASM

How does the activated hormone-receptor complex turn on genes? Recall that the genes in a cell's DNA function by being transcribed and processed into messenger RNA (mRNA), which leaves the nucleus and is translated into a specific protein by ribosomes in the cytoplasm (see Figure 5.25). Special proteins called *transcription factors* control which genes are turned on—that is, which genes are transcribed into mRNA—in a particular cell at a particular time. The testosterone receptor, when activated, acts as a transcription factor that turns on specific genes.

By acting as a transcription factor, the testosterone receptor itself carries out the complete transduction of the signal. Most other intracellular receptors function in the same way, although many of them, such as the thyroid hormone receptor, are already in the nucleus before the signaling molecule reaches them. Interestingly, many of these intracellular receptor proteins are structurally similar, suggesting an evolutionary kinship.

CONCEPT CHECK 11.2

1. Nerve growth factor (NGF) is a water-soluble signaling molecule. Would you expect the receptor for NGF to be intracellular or in the plasma membrane? Why?
2. **WHAT IF?** What would the effect be if a cell made defective receptor tyrosine kinase proteins that were unable to dimerize?
3. **MAKE CONNECTIONS** How is ligand binding similar to the process of allosteric regulation of enzymes? See Figure 8.19 on page 158.

For suggested answers, see Appendix A.

CONCEPT 11.3

Transduction: Cascades of molecular interactions relay signals from receptors to target molecules in the cell

When receptors for signaling molecules are plasma membrane proteins, like most of those we have discussed, the transduction stage of cell signaling is usually a multistep pathway. Steps often include activation of proteins by addition or removal of phosphate groups or release of other small molecules or ions that act as messengers. One benefit of multiple steps is the possibility of greatly amplifying a signal. If some of the molecules in a pathway transmit the signal to numerous molecules at the next step in the series, the result can be a large number of activated molecules at the end of the pathway. Moreover, multistep pathways provide more opportunities for coordination and regulation than simpler systems do. This allows fine-tuning of the response, in both unicellular and multicellular organisms, as we'll discuss later in the chapter.

Signal Transduction Pathways

The binding of a specific signaling molecule to a receptor in the plasma membrane triggers the first step in the chain of molecular interactions—the signal transduction pathway—that leads to a particular response within the cell. Like falling dominoes, the signal-activated receptor activates another molecule, which activates yet another molecule, and so on, until the protein that produces the final cellular response is activated. The molecules that relay a signal from receptor to response, which we call relay molecules in this book, are often proteins. The interaction of proteins is a major theme of cell signaling. Indeed, protein interaction is a unifying theme of all regulation at the cellular level.

Keep in mind that the original signaling molecule is not physically passed along a signaling pathway; in most cases, it never even enters the cell. When we say that the signal is relayed along a pathway, we mean that certain information is passed on. At each step, the signal is transduced into a different form, commonly a shape change in a protein. Very often, the shape change is brought about by phosphorylation.

Protein Phosphorylation and Dephosphorylation

Previous chapters introduced the concept of activating a protein by adding one or more phosphate groups to it (see Figure 8.10a). In Figure 11.7, we have already seen how phosphorylation is involved in the activation of receptor tyrosine kinases. In fact, the phosphorylation and dephosphorylation of proteins is a widespread cellular mechanism for regulating protein activity. An enzyme that transfers phosphate groups from ATP to a protein is generally known as a **protein kinase**. Recall that a receptor tyrosine kinase phosphorylates tyrosines on the other receptor tyrosine kinase in a dimer. Most cytoplasmic protein kinases, however, act on proteins different from themselves. Another distinction is that most cytoplasmic protein kinases phosphorylate either of two other amino acids, serine or threonine, rather than tyrosine. Such serine/threonine kinases are widely involved in signaling pathways in animals, plants, and fungi.

Many of the relay molecules in signal transduction pathways are protein kinases, and they often act on other protein kinases in the pathway. **Figure 11.10** depicts a hypothetical

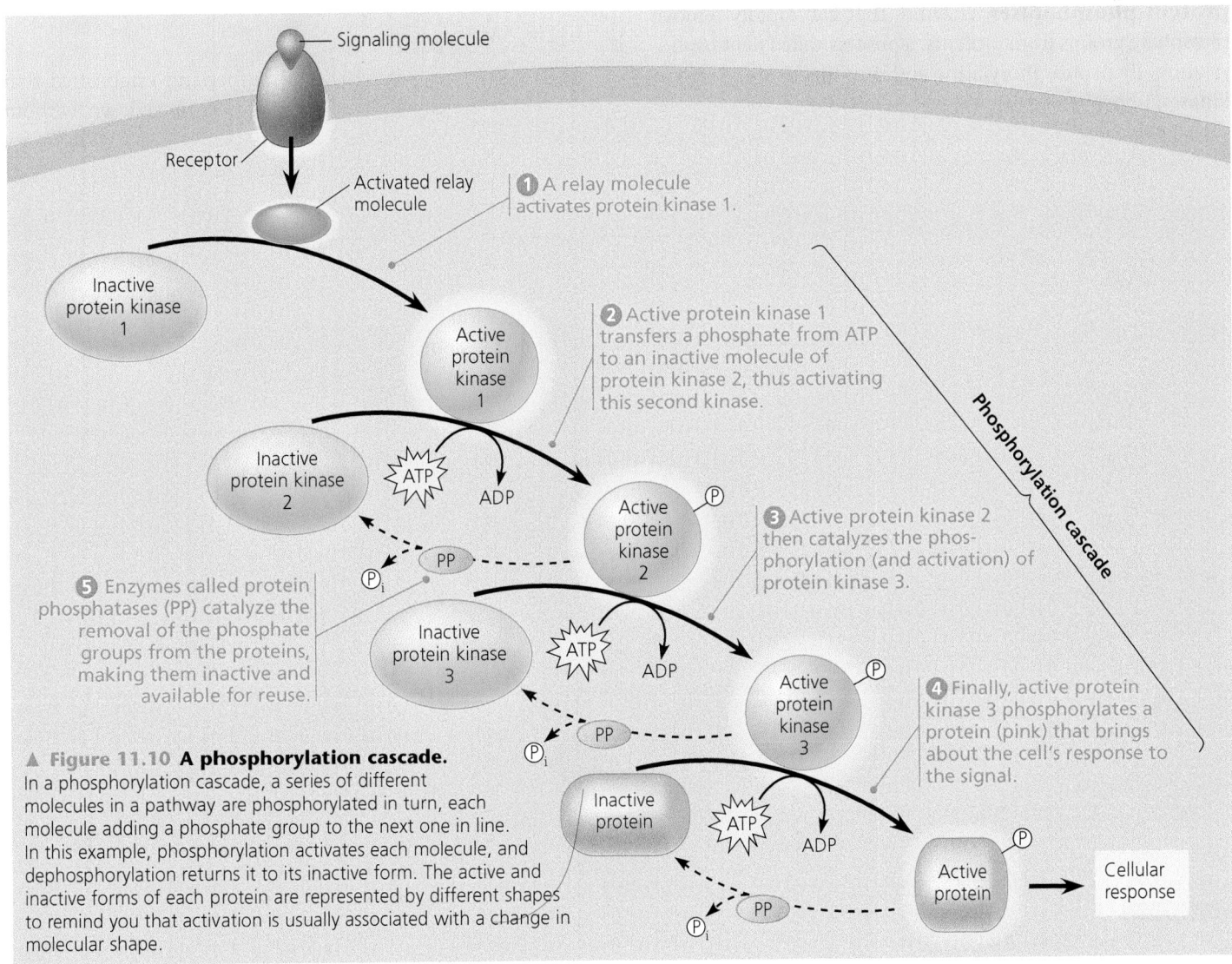

▲ **Figure 11.10 A phosphorylation cascade.** In a phosphorylation cascade, a series of different molecules in a pathway are phosphorylated in turn, each molecule adding a phosphate group to the next one in line. In this example, phosphorylation activates each molecule, and dephosphorylation returns it to its inactive form. The active and inactive forms of each protein are represented by different shapes to remind you that activation is usually associated with a change in molecular shape.

? *Which protein is responsible for activation of protein kinase 3?*

pathway containing three different protein kinases that create a "phosphorylation cascade." The sequence shown is similar to many known pathways, including those triggered in yeast by mating factors and in animal cells by many growth factors. The signal is transmitted by a cascade of protein phosphorylations, each bringing with it a shape change. Each such shape change results from the interaction of the newly added phosphate groups with charged or polar amino acids (see Figure 5.16). The addition of phosphate groups often changes a protein from an inactive form to an active form. In other cases, though, phosphorylation *decreases* the activity of the protein.

The importance of protein kinases can hardly be overstated. About 2% of our own genes are thought to code for protein kinases. A single cell may have hundreds of different kinds, each specific for a different substrate protein. Together, they probably regulate a large proportion of the thousands of proteins in a cell. Among these are most of the proteins that, in turn, regulate cell reproduction. Abnormal activity of such a kinase can cause abnormal cell growth and contribute to the development of cancer.

Equally important in the phosphorylation cascade are the **protein phosphatases**, enzymes that can rapidly remove phosphate groups from proteins, a process called dephosphorylation. By dephosphorylating and thus inactivating protein kinases, phosphatases provide the mechanism for turning off the signal transduction pathway when the initial signal is no longer present. Phosphatases also make the protein kinases available for reuse, enabling the cell to respond again to an extracellular signal. The phosphorylation-dephosphorylation system acts as a molecular switch in the cell, turning activities on or off, or up or down, as required. At any given moment, the activity of a protein regulated by phosphorylation depends on the balance in the cell between active kinase molecules and active phosphatase molecules.

Small Molecules and Ions as Second Messengers

Not all components of signal transduction pathways are proteins. Many signaling pathways also involve small, nonprotein, water-soluble molecules or ions called **second messengers**. (This term is used because the pathway's "first messenger" is considered to be the extracellular signaling molecule—the ligand—that binds to the membrane receptor.) Because second messengers are small and water-soluble, they can readily spread throughout the cell by diffusion. For example, as we'll see shortly, a second messenger called cyclic AMP carries the signal initiated by epinephrine from the plasma membrane of a liver or muscle cell into the cell's interior, where the signal eventually brings about glycogen breakdown. Second messengers participate in pathways that are initiated by both G protein-coupled receptors and receptor tyrosine kinases. The two most widely used second messengers are cyclic AMP and calcium ions, Ca^{2+}. A large variety of relay proteins are sensitive to the cytosolic concentration of one or the other of these second messengers.

Cyclic AMP

As discussed on page 209, Earl Sutherland established that epinephrine somehow causes glycogen breakdown without passing through the plasma membrane. This discovery prompted him to search for a second messenger that transmits the signal from the plasma membrane to the metabolic machinery in the cytoplasm.

Sutherland found that the binding of epinephrine to the plasma membrane of a liver cell elevates the cytosolic concentration of a compound called cyclic adenosine monophosphate, abbreviated as either **cyclic AMP** or **cAMP** (Figure 11.11). An enzyme embedded in the plasma

▲ **Figure 11.11 Cyclic AMP.** The second messenger cyclic AMP (cAMP) is made from ATP by adenylyl cyclase, an enzyme embedded in the plasma membrane. Cyclic AMP is inactivated by phosphodiesterase, an enzyme that converts it to AMP.

WHAT IF? *What would happen if a molecule that inactivated phosphodiesterase were introduced into the cell?*

membrane, **adenylyl cyclase**, converts ATP to cAMP in response to an extracellular signal—in this case, provided by epinephrine. But epinephrine doesn't stimulate adenylyl cyclase directly. When epinephrine outside the cell binds to a specific receptor protein, the protein activates adenylyl cyclase, which in turn can catalyze the synthesis of many molecules of cAMP. In this way, the normal cellular concentration of cAMP can be boosted 20-fold in a matter of seconds. The cAMP broadcasts the signal to the cytoplasm. It does not persist for long in the absence of the hormone because another enzyme, called phosphodiesterase, converts cAMP to AMP. Another surge of epinephrine is needed to boost the cytosolic concentration of cAMP again.

Subsequent research has revealed that epinephrine is only one of many hormones and other signaling molecules that trigger the formation of cAMP. It has also brought to light the other components of cAMP pathways, including G proteins, G protein-coupled receptors, and protein kinases (**Figure 11.12**). The immediate effect of cAMP is usually the activation of a serine/threonine kinase called *protein kinase A*. The activated protein kinase A then phosphorylates various other proteins, depending on the cell type. (The complete pathway for epinephrine's stimulation of glycogen breakdown is shown later, in Figure 11.16.)

Further regulation of cell metabolism is provided by other G protein systems that *inhibit* adenylyl cyclase. In these systems, a different signaling molecule activates a different receptor, which in turn activates an *inhibitory* G protein.

Now that we know about the role of cAMP in G protein signaling pathways, we can explain in molecular detail how certain microbes cause disease. Consider cholera, a disease that is frequently epidemic in places where the water supply is contaminated with human feces. People acquire the cholera bacterium, *Vibrio cholerae*, by drinking contaminated water. The bacteria form a biofilm on the lining of the small intestine and produce a toxin. The cholera toxin is an enzyme that chemically modifies a G protein involved in regulating salt and water secretion. Because the modified G protein is unable to hydrolyze GTP to GDP, it remains stuck in its active form, continuously stimulating adenylyl cyclase to make cAMP. The resulting high concentration of cAMP causes the intestinal cells to secrete large amounts of salts into the intestines, with water following by osmosis. An infected person quickly develops profuse diarrhea and if left untreated can soon die from the loss of water and salts.

Our understanding of signaling pathways involving cyclic AMP or related messengers has allowed us to develop treatments for certain conditions in humans. In one pathway, *cyclic GMP*, or *cGMP*, acts as a signaling molecule whose effects include relaxation of smooth muscle cells in artery walls. A compound that inhibits the hydrolysis of cGMP to GMP, thus prolonging the signal, was originally prescribed for chest pains because it increased blood flow to the heart muscle. Under the trade name Viagra, this compound is now widely used as a treatment for erectile dysfunction in human males. Because Viagra leads to dilation of blood vessels, it also allows increased blood flow to the penis, optimizing physiological conditions for penile erections.

Calcium Ions and Inositol Trisphosphate (IP₃)

Many signaling molecules in animals, including neurotransmitters, growth factors, and some hormones, induce responses in their target cells via signal transduction pathways that increase the cytosolic concentration of calcium ions (Ca^{2+}). Calcium is even more widely used than cAMP as a second messenger. Increasing the cytosolic concentration of Ca^{2+} causes many responses in animal cells, including muscle cell contraction, secretion of certain substances, and cell division. In plant cells, a wide range of hormonal and environmental stimuli can cause brief increases in cytosolic Ca^{2+} concentration, triggering various signaling pathways, such as the pathway for greening in response to light (see Figure 39.4). Cells use Ca^{2+} as a second messenger in both G protein and receptor tyrosine kinase pathways.

Although cells always contain some Ca^{2+}, this ion can function as a second messenger because its concentration in the cytosol is normally much lower than the concentration

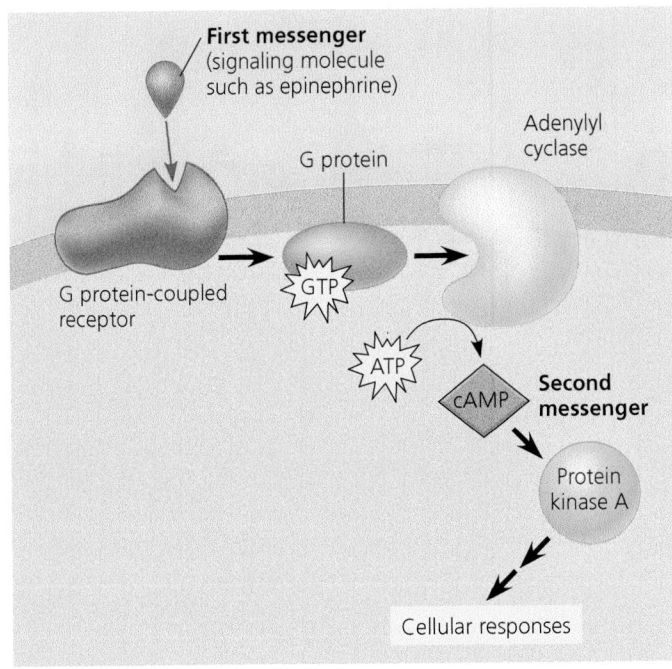

▲ **Figure 11.12 cAMP as a second messenger in a G protein signaling pathway.** The first messenger activates a G protein-coupled receptor, which activates a specific G protein. In turn, the G protein activates adenylyl cyclase, which catalyzes the conversion of ATP to cAMP. The cAMP then acts as a second messenger and activates another protein, usually protein kinase A, leading to cellular responses.

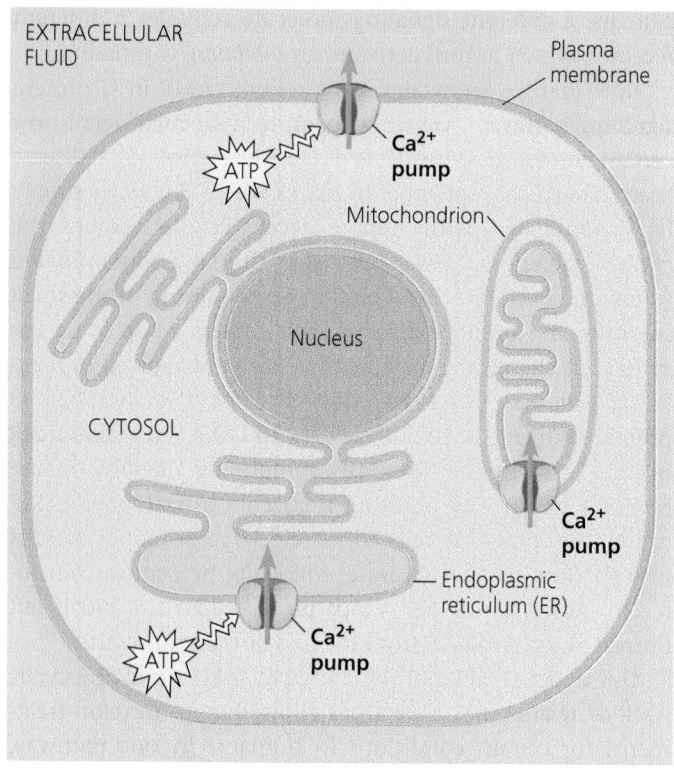

Key ▨ High [Ca²⁺] ▨ Low [Ca²⁺]

▲ **Figure 11.13 The maintenance of calcium ion concentrations in an animal cell.** The Ca²⁺ concentration in the cytosol is usually much lower (beige) than in the extracellular fluid and ER (blue). Protein pumps in the plasma membrane and the ER membrane, driven by ATP, move Ca²⁺ from the cytosol into the extracellular fluid and into the lumen of the ER. Mitochondrial pumps, driven by chemiosmosis (see Chapter 9), move Ca²⁺ into mitochondria when the calcium level in the cytosol rises significantly.

outside the cell (**Figure 11.13**). In fact, the level of Ca²⁺ in the blood and extracellular fluid of an animal is often more than 10,000 times higher than that in the cytosol. Calcium ions are actively transported out of the cell and are actively imported from the cytosol into the endoplasmic reticulum (and, under some conditions, into mitochondria and chloroplasts) by various protein pumps. As a result, the calcium concentration in the ER is usually much higher than that in the cytosol. Because the cytosolic calcium level is low, a small change in absolute numbers of ions represents a relatively large percentage change in calcium concentration.

In response to a signal relayed by a signal transduction pathway, the cytosolic calcium level may rise, usually by a mechanism that releases Ca²⁺ from the cell's ER. The pathways leading to calcium release involve still other second messengers, **inositol trisphosphate (IP₃)** and **diacylglycerol (DAG)**. These two messengers are produced by cleavage of a certain kind of phospholipid in the plasma membrane. **Figure 11.14** shows how this occurs and how IP₃ stimulates the release of calcium from the ER. Because IP₃ acts before calcium in these pathways, calcium could be considered a "*third* messenger." However, scientists use the term *second messenger* for all small, nonprotein components of signal transduction pathways.

❶ A signaling molecule binds to a receptor, leading to activation of phospholipase C.

❷ Phospholipase C cleaves a plasma membrane phospholipid called PIP₂ into DAG and IP₃.

❸ DAG functions as a second messenger in other pathways.

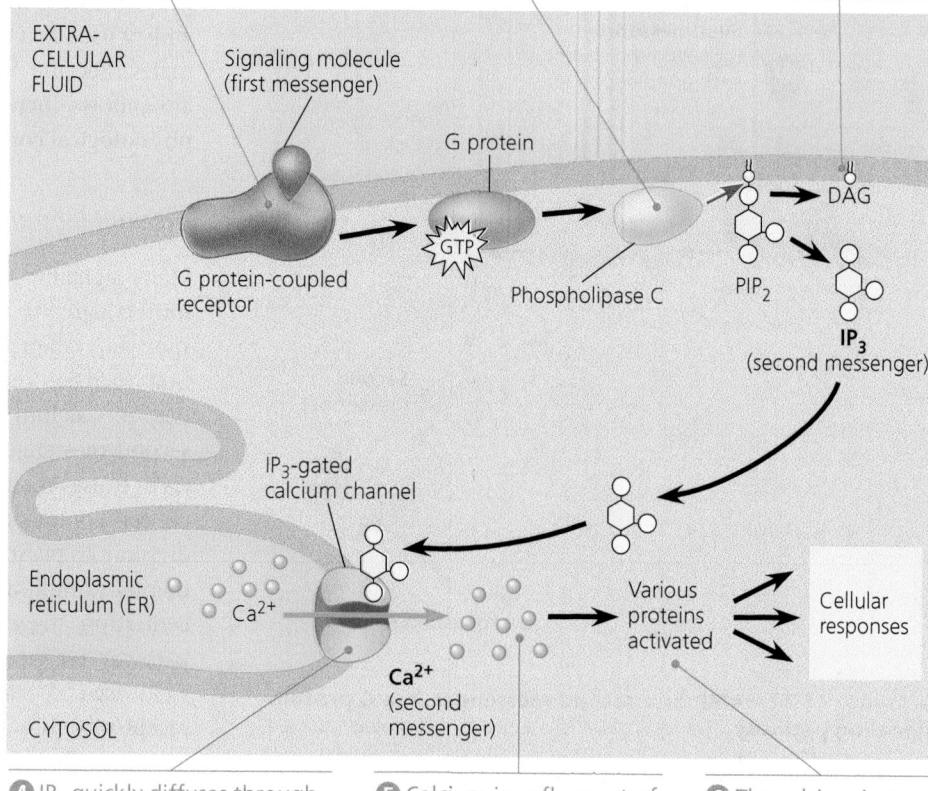

▶ **Figure 11.14 Calcium and IP₃ in signaling pathways.** Calcium ions (Ca²⁺) and inositol trisphosphate (IP₃) function as second messengers in many signal transduction pathways. In this figure, the process is initiated by the binding of a signaling molecule to a G protein-coupled receptor. A receptor tyrosine kinase could also initiate this pathway by activating phospholipase C.

❹ IP₃ quickly diffuses through the cytosol and binds to an IP₃-gated calcium channel in the ER membrane, causing it to open.

❺ Calcium ions flow out of the ER (down their concentration gradient), raising the Ca²⁺ level in the cytosol.

❻ The calcium ions activate the next protein in one or more signaling pathways.

1. What is a protein kinase, and what is its role in a signal transduction pathway?
2. When a signal transduction pathway involves a phosphorylation cascade, how does the cell's response get turned off?
3. What is the actual "signal" that is being transduced in any signal transduction pathway, such as those shown in Figures 11.6 and 11.10? In what way is this information being passed from the exterior to the interior of the cell?
4. **WHAT IF?** Upon activation of phospholipase C by the binding of a ligand to a receptor, what effect does the IP$_3$-gated calcium channel have on Ca^{2+} concentration in the cytosol?

For suggested answers, see Appendix A.

CONCEPT 11.4

Response: Cell signaling leads to regulation of transcription or cytoplasmic activities

We now take a closer look at the cell's subsequent response to an extracellular signal—what some researchers call the "output response." What is the nature of the final step in a signaling pathway?

Nuclear and Cytoplasmic Responses

Ultimately, a signal transduction pathway leads to the regulation of one or more cellular activities. The response at the end of the pathway may occur in the nucleus of the cell or in the cytoplasm.

Many signaling pathways ultimately regulate protein synthesis, usually by turning specific genes on or off in the nucleus. Like an activated steroid receptor (see Figure 11.9), the final activated molecule in a signaling pathway may function as a transcription factor. **Figure 11.15** shows an example in which a signaling pathway activates a transcription factor that turns a gene on: The response to the growth factor signal is transcription, the synthesis of mRNA, which will be translated in the cytoplasm into a specific protein. In other cases, the transcription factor might regulate a gene by turning it off. Often a transcription factor regulates several different genes.

Sometimes a signaling pathway may regulate the *activity* of proteins rather than their *synthesis*, directly affecting proteins that function outside the nucleus. For example, a signal may cause the opening or closing of an ion channel in the plasma membrane or a change in cell metabolism. As we

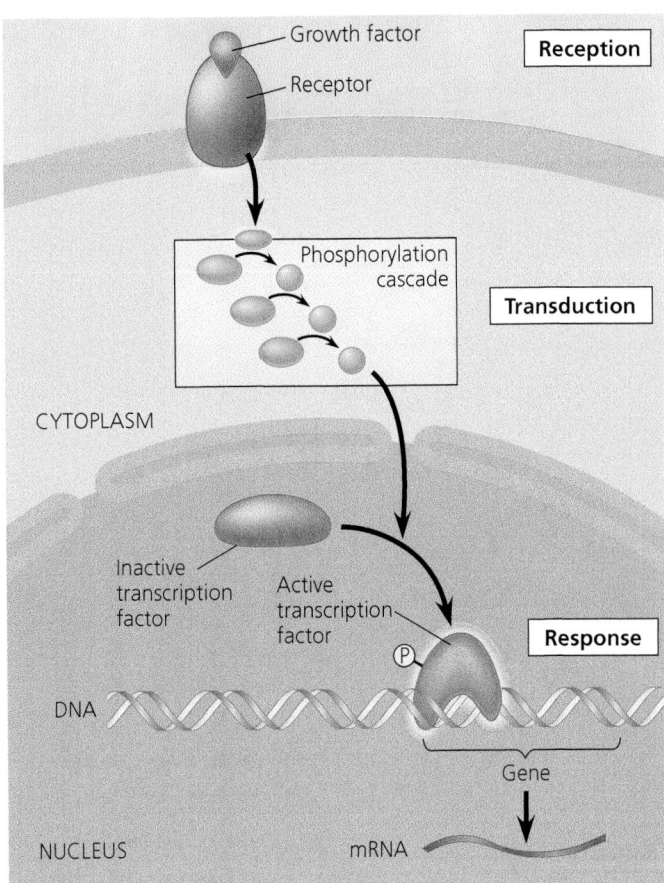

▲ Figure 11.15 **Nuclear responses to a signal: the activation of a specific gene by a growth factor.** This diagram is a simplified representation of a typical signaling pathway that leads to the regulation of gene activity in the cell nucleus. The initial signaling molecule, a local regulator called a growth factor, triggers a phosphorylation cascade, as in Figure 11.10. (The ATP molecules and phosphate groups are not shown.) Once phosphorylated, the last kinase in the sequence enters the nucleus and there activates a gene-regulating protein, a transcription factor. This protein stimulates transcription of a specific gene (or genes). The resulting mRNA then directs the synthesis of a particular protein in the cytoplasm.

have seen, the response of liver cells to the hormone epinephrine helps regulate cellular energy metabolism by affecting the activity of an enzyme. The final step in the signaling pathway that begins with epinephrine binding activates the enzyme that catalyzes the breakdown of glycogen. Figure 11.16, on the next page, shows the complete pathway leading to the release of glucose 1-phosphate molecules from glycogen. Notice that as each molecule is activated, the response is amplified, a subject we'll return to shortly.

In addition to controlling enzymes, signaling events may regulate other cellular attributes, even activities of the cell as a whole. An example of the latter can be found in the processes leading to the mating of yeast cells (see Figure 11.2). Yeast cells are not motile; their mating process depends on the growth of localized projections of one cell toward a cell of the

Reception

Binding of epinephrine to G protein-coupled receptor (1 molecule)

Transduction

Inactive G protein

Active G protein (10^2 molecules)

Inactive adenylyl cyclase

Active adenylyl cyclase (10^2)

ATP

Cyclic AMP (10^4)

Inactive protein kinase A

Active protein kinase A (10^4)

Inactive phosphorylase kinase

Active phosphorylase kinase (10^5)

Inactive glycogen phosphorylase

Active glycogen phosphorylase (10^6)

Response

Glycogen

Glucose 1-phosphate
(10^8 molecules)

▲ **Figure 11.16 Cytoplasmic response to a signal: the stimulation of glycogen breakdown by epinephrine.** In this signaling system, the hormone epinephrine acts through a G protein-coupled receptor to activate a succession of relay molecules, including cAMP and two protein kinases (see also Figure 11.12). The final protein activated is the enzyme glycogen phosphorylase, which uses inorganic phosphate to release glucose monomers from glycogen in the form of glucose 1-phosphate molecules. This pathway amplifies the hormonal signal: One receptor protein can activate about 100 molecules of G protein, and each enzyme in the pathway, once activated, can act on many molecules of its substrate, the next molecule in the cascade. The number of activated molecules given for each step is approximate.

opposite mating type. As shown in **Figure 11.17**, binding of the mating factor causes this directional growth. When the mating factor binds, it activates signaling pathway kinases that affect the growth and orientation of cytoskeletal microfilaments. Because activation of signaling kinases is coupled in this way to cytoskeletal dynamics, cell projections emerge from regions of the plasma membrane exposed to the highest concentration of the mating factor. As a result, these projections are oriented toward the cell of the opposite mating type, which is the source of the signaling molecule.

The signal receptors, relay molecules, and second messengers introduced so far in this chapter participate in a variety of pathways, leading to both nuclear and cytoplasmic responses. Some of these pathways lead to cell division. The

molecular messengers that initiate cell division pathways include growth factors and certain plant and animal hormones. Malfunctioning of growth factor pathways like the one in Figure 11.15 can contribute to the development of cancer, as we will see in Chapter 18.

Fine-Tuning of the Response

Regardless of whether the response occurs in the nucleus or in the cytoplasm, it is fine-tuned at multiple points rather than simply being turned "on" or "off." Here we'll consider four aspects of fine-tuning. First, as mentioned earlier, a signaling pathway with numerous steps between the initial signaling event at the cell surface and the cell's response results in amplification of the signal and thus the response. Second, such a multistep pathway has many different points at which the cell's response can be regulated, contributing to the specificity of the response and allowing coordination with other signaling pathways. Third, the overall efficiency of the response is enhanced by the presence of proteins known as scaffolding proteins. Finally, a crucial point in fine-tuning the response is the termination of the signal.

Signal Amplification

Elaborate enzyme cascades amplify the cell's response to a signal. At each catalytic step in the cascade, the number of activated products is much greater than in the preceding step. For example, in the epinephrine-triggered pathway in Figure 11.16, each adenylyl cyclase molecule catalyzes the formation of many cAMP molecules, each molecule of protein kinase A phosphorylates many molecules of the next kinase in the pathway, and so on. The amplification effect stems from the fact that these proteins persist in the active form long enough to process numerous molecules of substrate before they become inactive again. As a result of the signal's amplification, a small number of epinephrine molecules binding to receptors on the surface of a liver cell or muscle cell can lead to the release of hundreds of millions of glucose molecules from glycogen.

The Specificity of Cell Signaling and Coordination of the Response

Consider two different cells in your body—a liver cell and a heart muscle cell, for example. Both are in contact with your bloodstream and are therefore constantly exposed to many different hormone molecules, as well as to local regulators secreted by nearby cells. Yet the liver cell responds to some signals but ignores others, and the same is true for the heart cell. And some kinds of signals trigger responses in both cells—but different responses. For instance, epinephrine stimulates the liver cell to break down glycogen, but the main response of the heart cell to epinephrine is contraction, leading to a more rapid heartbeat. How do we account for this difference?

▼ Figure 11.17

INQUIRY

How do signals induce directional cell growth during mating in yeast?

EXPERIMENT When a yeast cell binds mating factor molecules from a cell of the opposite mating type, a signaling pathway causes it to grow a projection toward the potential mate. The cell with the projection is called a "shmoo" because it resembles a 1950s cartoon character by that name. Dina Matheos and colleagues in Mark Rose's lab at Princeton University sought to determine how mating factor signaling is linked to this asymmetrical growth. Previous work had shown that activation of Fus3, one of the kinases in the signaling cascade, caused it to move to the membrane near where the factor bound. Preliminary experiments by these researchers identified formin, a protein that directs the construction of microfilaments, as a phosphorylation target of Fus3 kinase. To examine the role of Fus3 and formin in shmoo formation, the researchers generated two mutant yeast strains: one that no longer had the kinase (this strain is called ΔFus3) and one that lacked the formin (Δformin). To observe the effects of these mutations on cell growth induced by the mating factor, the cell walls of each strain were first stained with a green fluorescent dye. These green-stained cells were then exposed to mating factor and stained with a red fluorescent dye that labeled new cell wall growth. Images taken of the cells after the staining procedure were then compared with a similarly treated strain that expressed Fus3 and formin (the wild type).

RESULTS The cells of the wild-type strain showed shmoo projections, whose walls were stained red, while the rest of their cell walls were green, indicating asymmetrical growth. Cells of both the ΔFus3 and Δformin strains showed no shmoo formation, and their cell walls were stained almost uniformly yellow. This color resulted from merged green and red stains, indicating symmetrical growth, characteristic of cells not exposed to mating factor.

Wild type (with shmoos)   ΔFus3   Δformin

CONCLUSION The similar defect (lack of ability to form shmoos) in strains lacking either Fus3 or formin suggests that both proteins are required for shmoo formation. These results led the investigators to propose the model shown here for the induction of asymmetrical growth in the receiving cell directed toward the cell of the opposite mating type.

SOURCE D. Matheos et al., Pheromone-induced polarization is dependent on the Fus3p MAPK acting through the formin Bni1p, *Journal of Cell Biology* 165:99–109 (2004).

WHAT IF? Based on these results and the proposed model from this work, what would happen to a cell if its Fus3 kinase were not able to associate with the membrane upon activation?

The explanation for the specificity exhibited in cellular responses to signals is the same as the basic explanation for virtually all differences between cells: Because different kinds of cells turn on different sets of genes, *different kinds of cells have different collections of proteins* (**Figure 11.18**, on the next page). The response of a particular cell to a signal depends on its particular collection of signal receptor proteins, relay proteins, and proteins needed to carry out the response. A liver cell, for example, is poised to respond appropriately to epinephrine by having the proteins listed in Figure 11.16 as well as those needed to manufacture glycogen.

Thus, two cells that respond differently to the same signal differ in one or more of the proteins that handle and respond

to the signal. Notice in Figure 11.18 that different pathways may have some molecules in common. For example, cells A, B, and C all use the same receptor protein for the red signaling molecule; differences in other proteins account for their differing responses. In cell D, a different receptor protein is used for the same signaling molecule, leading to yet another response. In cell B, a pathway that is triggered by a single kind of signal diverges to produce two responses; such branched pathways often involve receptor tyrosine kinases (which can activate multiple relay proteins) or second messengers (which can regulate numerous proteins). In cell C, two pathways triggered by separate signals converge to modulate a single response. Branching of pathways and "cross-talk" (interaction)

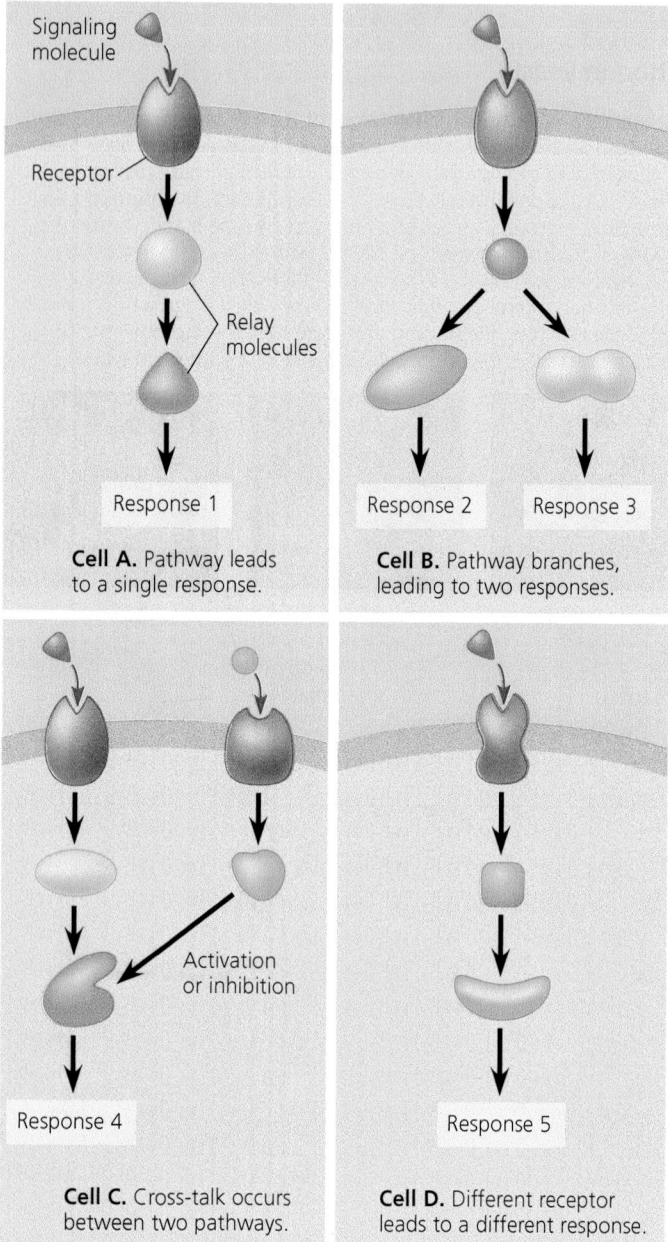

Signaling molecule

Receptor

Relay molecules

Response 1

Cell A. Pathway leads to a single response.

Response 2   Response 3

Cell B. Pathway branches, leading to two responses.

Activation or inhibition

Response 4

Cell C. Cross-talk occurs between two pathways.

Response 5

Cell D. Different receptor leads to a different response.

▲ **Figure 11.18 The specificity of cell signaling.** The particular proteins a cell possesses determine what signaling molecules it responds to and the nature of the response. The four cells in these diagrams respond to the same signaling molecule (red) in different ways because each has a different set of proteins (purple and teal). Note, however, that the same kinds of molecules can participate in more than one pathway.

MAKE CONNECTIONS *Study the signaling pathway shown in Figure 11.14 (p. 218), and explain how the situation pictured for cell B above could apply to that pathway.*

between pathways are important in regulating and coordinating a cell's responses to information coming in from different sources in the body. (You'll learn more about this coordination in Concept 11.5.) Moreover, the use of some of the same proteins in more than one pathway allows the cell to economize on the number of different proteins it must make.

Signaling Efficiency: Scaffolding Proteins and Signaling Complexes

The illustrations of signaling pathways in Figure 11.18 (as well as diagrams of other pathways in this chapter) are greatly simplified. The diagrams show only a few relay molecules and, for clarity's sake, display these molecules spread out in the cytosol. If this were true in the cell, signaling pathways would operate very inefficiently because most relay molecules are proteins, and proteins are too large to diffuse quickly through the viscous cytosol. How does a particular protein kinase, for instance, find its substrate?

In many cases, the efficiency of signal transduction is apparently increased by the presence of **scaffolding proteins**, large relay proteins to which several other relay proteins are simultaneously attached. For example, one scaffolding protein isolated from mouse brain cells holds three protein kinases and carries these kinases with it when it binds to an appropriately activated membrane receptor; it thus facilitates a specific phosphorylation cascade (**Figure 11.19**). Researchers have found scaffolding proteins in brain cells that *permanently* hold together networks of signaling pathway proteins at synapses. This hardwiring enhances the speed and accuracy of signal transfer between cells, because the rate of protein-protein interaction is not limited by diffusion. Furthermore, in addition to this indirect role in activation of relay proteins, the scaffolding proteins themselves may more directly activate some of the other relay proteins.

When signaling pathways were first discovered, they were thought to be linear, independent pathways. Our understanding of cellular communication has benefited from the realization that signaling-pathway components interact with each other in various ways. As seen in Figure 11.18, some proteins may participate in more than one pathway, either in different cell types or in the same cell at different times or under different conditions. These observations underscore

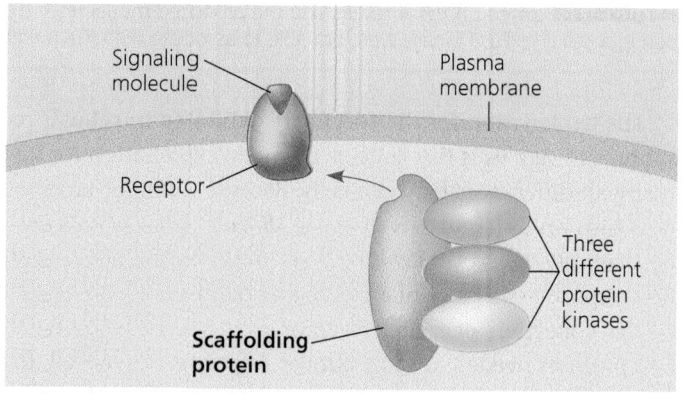

Signaling molecule

Plasma membrane

Receptor

Three different protein kinases

Scaffolding protein

▲ **Figure 11.19 A scaffolding protein.** The scaffolding protein shown here (pink) simultaneously binds to a specific activated membrane receptor and three different protein kinases. This physical arrangement facilitates signal transduction by these molecules and may directly activate relay molecules in some cases.

the importance of transient—or, in some cases, permanent—protein complexes in the process of cell signaling.

The importance of the relay proteins that serve as points of branching or intersection in signaling pathways is highlighted by the problems arising when these proteins are defective or missing. For instance, in an inherited disorder called Wiskott-Aldrich syndrome (WAS), the absence of a single relay protein leads to such diverse effects as abnormal bleeding, eczema, and a predisposition to infections and leukemia. These symptoms are thought to arise primarily from the absence of the protein in cells of the immune system. By studying normal cells, scientists found that the WAS protein is located just beneath the cell surface. The protein interacts both with microfilaments of the cytoskeleton and with several different components of signaling pathways that relay information from the cell surface, including pathways regulating immune cell proliferation. This multifunctional relay protein is thus both a branch point and an important intersection point in a complex signal transduction network that controls immune cell behavior. When the WAS protein is absent, the cytoskeleton is not properly organized and signaling pathways are disrupted, leading to the WAS symptoms.

Termination of the Signal

To keep Figure 11.18 simple, we did not indicate the *inactivation* mechanisms that are an essential aspect of cell signaling. For a cell of a multicellular organism to remain capable of responding to incoming signals, each molecular change in its signaling pathways must last only a short time. As we saw in the cholera example, if a signaling pathway component becomes locked into one state, whether active or inactive, consequences for the organism can be dire.

The ability of a cell to receive new signals depends on reversibility of the changes produced by prior signals. The binding of signaling molecules to receptors is reversible. As the external concentration of signaling molecules falls, fewer receptors are bound at any given moment, and the unbound receptors revert to their inactive form. The cellular response occurs only when the concentration of receptors with bound signaling molecules is above a certain threshold. When the number of active receptors falls below that threshold, the cellular response ceases. Then, by a variety of means, the relay molecules return to their inactive forms: The GTPase activity intrinsic to a G protein hydrolyzes its bound GTP; the enzyme phosphodiesterase converts cAMP to AMP; protein phosphatases inactivate phosphorylated kinases and other proteins; and so forth. As a result, the cell is soon ready to respond to a fresh signal.

In this section, we explored the complexity of signaling initiation and termination in a single pathway, and we saw the potential for pathways to intersect with each other. In the next section, we'll consider one especially important network of interacting pathways in the cell.

CONCEPT 11.5

Apoptosis integrates multiple cell-signaling pathways

To be or not to be? One of the most elaborate networks of signaling pathways in the cell seems to ask and answer this question posed by Hamlet. Cells that are infected, damaged, or have reached the end of their functional life span often undergo "programmed cell death." The best-understood type of this controlled cell suicide is **apoptosis** (from the Greek, meaning "falling off," and used in a classic Greek poem to refer to leaves falling from a tree). During this process, cellular agents chop up the DNA and fragment the organelles and other cytoplasmic components. The cell shrinks and becomes lobed (a change called "blebbing"; **Figure 11.20**), and the cell's parts are packaged up in vesicles that are engulfed and digested by specialized scavenger cells, leaving no trace. Apoptosis protects neighboring cells from damage that they would otherwise suffer if a dying cell merely leaked out all its contents, including its many digestive enzymes.

▲ **Figure 11.20 Apoptosis of a human white blood cell.** We can compare a normal white blood cell (left) with a white blood cell undergoing apoptosis (right). The apoptotic cell is shrinking and forming lobes ("blebs"), which eventually are shed as membrane-bounded cell fragments (colorized SEMs).

Apoptosis in the Soil Worm
Caenorhabditis elegans

Embryonic development is a period during which apoptosis is widespread and plays a crucial role. The molecular mechanisms underlying apoptosis were worked out in detail by researchers studying embryonic development of a small soil worm, a nematode called *Caenorhabditis elegans*. Because the adult worm has only about a thousand cells, the researchers were able to work out the entire ancestry of each cell. The timely suicide of cells occurs exactly 131 times during normal development of *C. elegans*, at precisely the same points in the cell lineage of each worm. In worms and other species, apoptosis is triggered by signals that activate a cascade of "suicide" proteins in the cells destined to die.

Genetic research on *C. elegans* has revealed two key apoptosis genes, called *ced-3* and *ced-4* (*ced* stands for "cell death"), which encode proteins essential for apoptosis. The proteins are called Ced-3 and Ced-4, respectively. These and most other proteins involved in apoptosis are continually present in cells, but in inactive form; thus, regulation occurs at the level of protein activity rather than through gene activity and protein synthesis. In *C. elegans*, a protein in the outer mitochondrial membrane, called Ced-9 (the product of the *ced-9* gene), serves as a master regulator of apoptosis, acting as a brake in the absence of a signal promoting apoptosis (**Figure 11.21**). When a death signal is received by the cell, it overrides the brake, and the apoptotic pathway activates proteases and nucleases, enzymes that cut up the proteins and DNA of the cell. The main proteases of apoptosis are called *caspases*; in the nematode, the chief caspase is Ced-3.

Apoptotic Pathways and the Signals That Trigger Them

In humans and other mammals, several different pathways, involving about 15 different caspases, can carry out apoptosis. The pathway that is used depends on the type of cell and on the particular signal that initiates apoptosis. One major pathway involves certain mitochondrial proteins that are triggered to form molecular pores in the mitochondrial outer membrane, causing it to leak and release other proteins that promote apoptosis. Surprisingly, these latter include cytochrome *c*, which functions in mitochondrial electron transport in healthy cells (see Figure 9.15) but acts as a cell death factor when released from mitochondria. The process of mitochondrial apoptosis in mammals uses proteins similar to the nematode proteins Ced-3, Ced-4, and Ced-9. These can be thought of as relay proteins capable of transducing the apoptotic signal.

At key gateways into the apoptotic program, relay proteins integrate signals from several different sources and can send a cell down an apoptotic pathway. Often, the signal originates outside the cell, like the death-signaling molecule depicted in

(a) No death signal. As long as Ced-9, located in the outer mitochondrial membrane, is active, apoptosis is inhibited, and the cell remains alive.

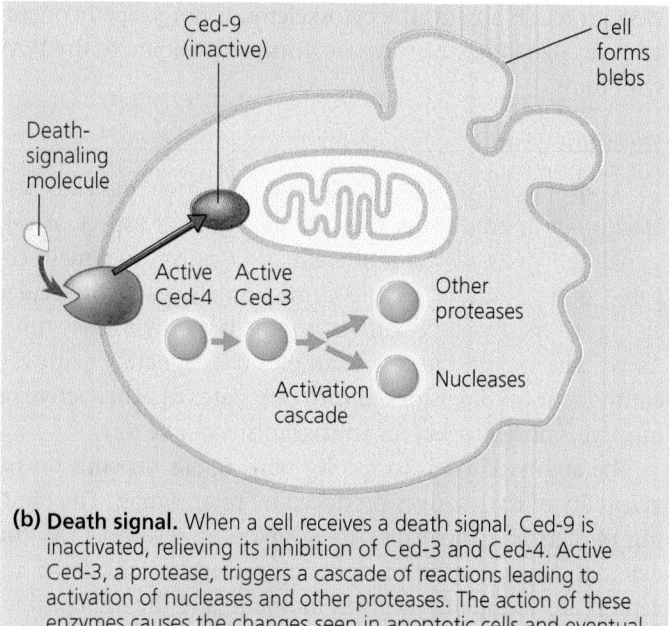

(b) Death signal. When a cell receives a death signal, Ced-9 is inactivated, relieving its inhibition of Ced-3 and Ced-4. Active Ced-3, a protease, triggers a cascade of reactions leading to activation of nucleases and other proteases. The action of these enzymes causes the changes seen in apoptotic cells and eventual cell death.

▲ **Figure 11.21 Molecular basis of apoptosis in C. *elegans*.** Three proteins, Ced-3, Ced-4, and Ced-9, are critical to apoptosis and its regulation in the nematode. Apoptosis is more complicated in mammals but involves proteins similar to those in the nematode.

Figure 11.21b, which presumably was released by a neighboring cell. When a death-signaling ligand occupies a cell-surface receptor, this binding leads to activation of caspases and other enzymes that carry out apoptosis, without involving the mitochondrial pathway. This process of signal reception, transduction, and response is similar to what we discussed earlier in this chapter. In a twist on the classic scenario, two other types of alarm signals that can lead to apoptosis originate from *inside* the cell rather than from a cell-surface receptor.

Interdigital tissue · Cells undergoing apoptosis · 1 mm · Space between digits

▲ **Figure 11.22 Effect of apoptosis during paw development in the mouse.** In mice, humans, other mammals, and land birds, the embryonic region that develops into feet or hands initially has a solid, platelike structure. Apoptosis eliminates the cells in the interdigital regions, thus forming the digits. The embryonic mouse paws shown in these fluorescence light micrographs are stained so that cells undergoing apoptosis appear a bright yellowish green. Apoptosis of cells begins at the margin of each interdigital region (left), peaks as the tissue in these regions is reduced (middle), and is no longer visible when the interdigital tissue has been eliminated (right).

One signal comes from the nucleus, generated when the DNA has suffered irreparable damage, and a second comes from the endoplasmic reticulum when excessive protein misfolding occurs. Mammalian cells make life-or-death "decisions" by somehow integrating the death signals and life signals they receive from these external and internal sources.

A built-in cell suicide mechanism is essential to development and maintenance in all animals. The similarities between apoptosis genes in nematodes and mammals, as well as the observation that apoptosis occurs in multicellular fungi and even in single-celled yeasts, indicate that the basic mechanism evolved early in the evolution of eukaryotes. In vertebrates, apoptosis is essential for normal development of the nervous system, for normal operation of the immune system, and for normal morphogenesis of hands and feet in humans and paws in other mammals (Figure 11.22). The level of apoptosis between the developing digits is lower in the webbed feet of ducks and other water birds than in the nonwebbed feet of land birds, such as chickens. In the case of humans, the failure of appropriate apoptosis can result in webbed fingers and toes.

Significant evidence points to the involvement of apoptosis in certain degenerative diseases of the nervous system, such as Parkinson's disease and Alzheimer's disease. Also, cancer can result from a failure of cell suicide; some cases of human melanoma, for example, have been linked to faulty forms of the human version of the *C. elegans* Ced-4 protein. It is not surprising, therefore, that the signaling pathways feeding into apoptosis are quite elaborate. After all, the life-or-death question is the most fundamental one imaginable for a cell.

This chapter has introduced you to many of the general mechanisms of cell communication, such as ligand binding, protein-protein interactions and shape changes, cascades of interactions, and protein phosphorylation. As you continue through the text, you will encounter numerous examples of cell signaling.

CONCEPT CHECK 11.5

1. Give an example of apoptosis during embryonic development, and explain its function in the developing embryo.
2. **WHAT IF?** What types of protein defects could result in apoptosis occurring when it should not? What types could result in apoptosis not occurring when it should?

For suggested answers, see Appendix A.

11 CHAPTER REVIEW

SUMMARY OF KEY CONCEPTS

CONCEPT 11.1

External signals are converted to responses within the cell (pp. 206–210)

- **Signal transduction pathways** are crucial for many processes, including the mating of yeast cells. In fact, signaling in microbes has much in common with processes in multicellular organisms, suggesting an early evolutionary origin of signaling mechanisms. Bacterial cells can sense the local density of bacterial cells (quorum sensing) by binding molecules secreted by other cells. In some cases, such signals lead to aggregation of these cells into biofilms.
- In local signaling, animal cells may communicate by direct contact or by secreting **local regulators**, such as growth factors or neurotransmitters. For long-distance signaling, both animals and plants use **hormones**; animals also pass signals electrically.

- Earl Sutherland discovered how the hormone epinephrine acts on cells. Like other hormones that bind to membrane receptors, it triggers a three-stage cell-signaling pathway:

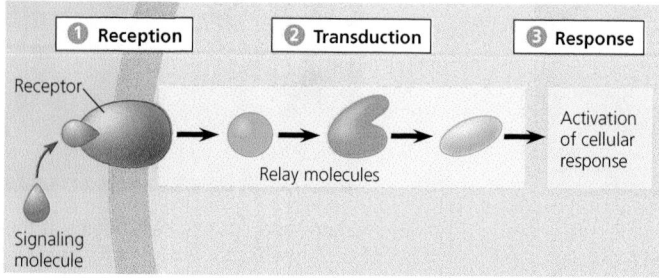

1 Reception   2 Transduction   3 Response

Receptor

Relay molecules

Activation of cellular response

Signaling molecule

? *What determines whether a cell responds to a hormone such as epinephrine? What determines how a cell responds to such a hormone?*

CONCEPT 11.2

Reception: A signaling molecule binds to a receptor protein, causing it to change shape (pp. 210–214)

- The binding between signaling molecule (**ligand**) and receptor is highly specific. A specific shape change in a receptor is often the initial transduction of the signal.
- There are three major types of cell-surface transmembrane receptors: (1) **G protein-coupled receptors (GPCRs)** work with the help of cytoplasmic **G proteins**. Ligand binding activates the receptor, which then activates a specific G protein, which activates yet another protein, thus propagating the signal along a signal transduction pathway. (2) **Receptor tyrosine kinases (RTKs)** react to the binding of signaling molecules by forming dimers and then adding phosphate groups to tyrosines on the cytoplasmic part of the other monomer making up the dimer. Relay proteins in the cell can then be activated by binding to different phosphorylated tyrosines, allowing this receptor to trigger several pathways at once. (3) **Ligand-gated ion channels** open or close in response to binding by specific signaling molecules, regulating the flow of specific ions across the membrane.
- The activity of all three types of receptors is crucial to proper cell functioning, and abnormal GPCRs and RTKs are associated with many human diseases.
- Intracellular receptors are cytoplasmic or nuclear proteins. Signaling molecules that are hydrophobic or small enough to cross the plasma membrane bind to these receptors inside the cell.

? *How are the structures of a G protein-coupled receptor and a receptor tyrosine kinase similar? In what key way does the triggering of signal transduction pathways differ for these two types of receptors?*

CONCEPT 11.3

Transduction: Cascades of molecular interactions relay signals from receptors to target molecules in the cell (pp. 214–219)

- At each step in a signal transduction pathway, the signal is transduced into a different form, which commonly involves a shape change in a protein. Many signal transduction pathways include phosphorylation cascades, in which a series of **protein kinases** each add a phosphate group to the next one in line, activating it. Enzymes called **protein phosphatases** remove the phosphate groups. The balance between phosphorylation and dephosphorylation regulates the activity of proteins involved in the sequential steps of a signal transduction pathway.
- **Second messengers**, such as the small molecule **cyclic AMP (cAMP)** and the ion Ca^{2+}, diffuse readily through the cytosol and thus help broadcast signals quickly. Many G proteins activate **adenylyl cyclase**, which makes cAMP from ATP. Cells use

Ca^{2+} as a second messenger in both G protein and tyrosine kinase pathways. The tyrosine kinase pathways can also involve two other second messengers, **diacylglycerol (DAG)** and **inositol trisphosphate (IP₃)**. IP$_3$ can trigger a subsequent increase in Ca^{2+} levels.

? *What is the difference between a protein kinase and a second messenger? Can both types of molecules operate in the same signal transduction pathway?*

CONCEPT 11.4

Response: Cell signaling leads to regulation of transcription or cytoplasmic activities (pp. 219–223)

- Some pathways lead to a nuclear response: Specific genes are turned on or off by activation of proteins called transcription factors. In other pathways, the response involves cytoplasmic regulation, including cytoskeletal rearrangement (which can lead to cell shape changes) or changes in enzyme activity.
- Cellular responses are not simply on or off; they are fine-tuned at many steps in the process. Each catalytic protein in a signaling pathway amplifies the signal by activating multiple copies of the next component of the pathway; for long pathways, the total amplification may be a millionfold or more. The particular combination of proteins in a cell gives the cell great specificity in both the signals it detects and the responses it carries out. **Scaffolding proteins** can increase signal transduction efficiency. Pathway branching and cross-talk further help the cell coordinate incoming signals and responses. Signal response is terminated quickly by the reversal of ligand binding.

? *What mechanisms in the cell terminate its response to a signal and maintain its ability to respond to new signals?*

CONCEPT 11.5

Apoptosis integrates multiple cell-signaling pathways (pp. 223–225)

- **Apoptosis** is a type of programmed cell death in which cell components are disposed of in an orderly fashion, without damage to neighboring cells. Studies of the soil worm *Caenorhabditis elegans* showed that apoptosis occurs at defined times during embryonic development and clarified molecular details of the signaling pathway involved in the process. A protein (Ced-9) in the mitochondrial membrane acts as a brake; when released by a death signal, it allows activation of caspases, the main proteases that carry out apoptosis, and nucleases.
- Several apoptotic signaling pathways exist in the cells of humans and other mammals, and these pathways may be triggered in several ways. A major pathway involves pore formation in the outer mitochondrial membrane, which leads to release of factors that activate caspases. Signals eliciting the apoptotic response can originate from outside or inside the cell.

? *What is an explanation for the similarities between genes in yeasts, nematodes, and mammals that control apoptosis?*

TEST YOUR UNDERSTANDING

LEVEL 1: KNOWLEDGE/COMPREHENSION

1. Phosphorylation cascades involving a series of protein kinases are useful for cellular signal transduction because
   a. they are species specific.
   b. they always lead to the same cellular response.
   c. they amplify the original signal manyfold.
   d. they counter the harmful effects of phosphatases.
   e. the number of molecules used is small and fixed.

2. Binding of a signaling molecule to which type of receptor leads directly to a change in the distribution of ions on opposite sides of the membrane?
   a. receptor tyrosine kinase
   b. G protein-coupled receptor
   c. phosphorylated receptor tyrosine kinase dimer
   d. ligand-gated ion channel
   e. intracellular receptor

3. The activation of receptor tyrosine kinases is characterized by
   a. dimerization and phosphorylation.
   b. dimerization and IP_3 binding.
   c. a phosphorylation cascade.
   d. GTP hydrolysis.
   e. channel protein shape change.

4. Lipid-soluble signaling molecules, such as testosterone, cross the membranes of all cells but affect only target cells because
   a. only target cells retain the appropriate DNA segments.
   b. intracellular receptors are present only in target cells.
   c. most cells lack the Y chromosome required.
   d. only target cells possess the cytosolic enzymes that transduce the testosterone.
   e. only in target cells is testosterone able to initiate the phosphorylation cascade leading to activated transcription factor.

5. Consider this pathway: epinephrine → G protein-coupled receptor → G protein → adenylyl cyclase → cAMP. Identify the second messenger.
   a. cAMP
   b. G protein
   c. GTP
   d. adenylyl cyclase
   e. G protein-coupled receptor

6. Apoptosis involves all but which of the following?
   a. fragmentation of the DNA
   b. cell-signaling pathways
   c. activation of cellular enzymes
   d. lysis of the cell
   e. digestion of cellular contents by scavenger cells

LEVEL 2: APPLICATION/ANALYSIS

7. Which observation suggested to Sutherland the involvement of a second messenger in epinephrine's effect on liver cells?
   a. Enzymatic activity was proportional to the amount of calcium added to a cell-free extract.
   b. Receptor studies indicated that epinephrine was a ligand.
   c. Glycogen breakdown was observed only when epinephrine was administered to intact cells.
   d. Glycogen breakdown was observed when epinephrine and glycogen phosphorylase were combined.
   e. Epinephrine was known to have different effects on different types of cells.

8. Protein phosphorylation is commonly involved with all of the following *except*
   a. regulation of transcription by extracellular signaling molecules.
   b. enzyme activation.
   c. activation of G protein-coupled receptors.
   d. activation of receptor tyrosine kinases.
   e. activation of protein kinase molecules.

LEVEL 3: SYNTHESIS/EVALUATION

9. **DRAW IT** Draw the following apoptotic pathway, which operates in human immune cells. A death signal is received when a molecule called Fas binds its cell-surface receptor. The binding of many Fas molecules to receptors causes receptor clustering. The intracellular regions of the receptors, when together, bind proteins called adaptor proteins. These in turn bind to inactive molecules of caspase-8, which become activated and then activate caspase-3. Once activated, caspase-3 initiates apoptosis.

10. **EVOLUTION CONNECTION**
    What evolutionary mechanisms might account for the origin and persistence of cell-to-cell signaling systems in unicellular prokaryotes?

11. **SCIENTIFIC INQUIRY**
    Epinephrine initiates a signal transduction pathway that involves production of cyclic AMP (cAMP) and leads to the breakdown of glycogen to glucose, a major energy source for cells. But glycogen breakdown is actually only part of the fight-or-flight response that epinephrine brings about; the overall effect on the body includes increased heart rate and alertness, as well as a burst of energy. Given that caffeine blocks the activity of cAMP phosphodiesterase, propose a mechanism by which caffeine ingestion leads to heightened alertness and sleeplessness.

12. **SCIENCE, TECHNOLOGY, AND SOCIETY**
    The aging process is thought to be initiated at the cellular level. Among the changes that can occur after a certain number of cell divisions is the loss of a cell's ability to respond to growth factors and other chemical signals. Much research into aging is aimed at understanding such losses, with the ultimate goal of significantly extending the human life span. Not everyone, however, agrees that this is a desirable goal. If life expectancy were greatly increased, what might be the social and ecological consequences?

13. **WRITE ABOUT A THEME**
    Emergent Properties The property of life emerges at the biological level of the cell. The highly regulated process of apoptosis is not simply the destruction of a cell; it is also an emergent property. Write a short essay (about 100–150 words) that briefly explains the role of apoptosis in the development and proper functioning of an animal and then describes how this form of programmed cell death is a process that emerges from the orderly integration of signaling pathways.

For selected answers, see Appendix A.

MasteringBIOLOGY®   www.masteringbiology.com

1. MasteringBiology® Assignments
Tutorials Cell Signaling: Reception • Cell Signaling: Transduction and Response
Activities Overview of Cell Signaling • Reception • Signal Transduction Pathways • Cellular Responses • Build a Signaling Pathway
Questions Student Misconceptions • Reading Quiz • Multiple Choice • End-of-Chapter

2. eText
Read your book online, search, take notes, highlight text, and more.

3. The Study Area
Practice Tests • Cumulative Test • *BioFlix* 3-D Animations • MP3 Tutor Sessions • Videos • Activities • Investigations • Lab Media • Audio Glossary • Word Study Tools • Art

12

The Cell Cycle

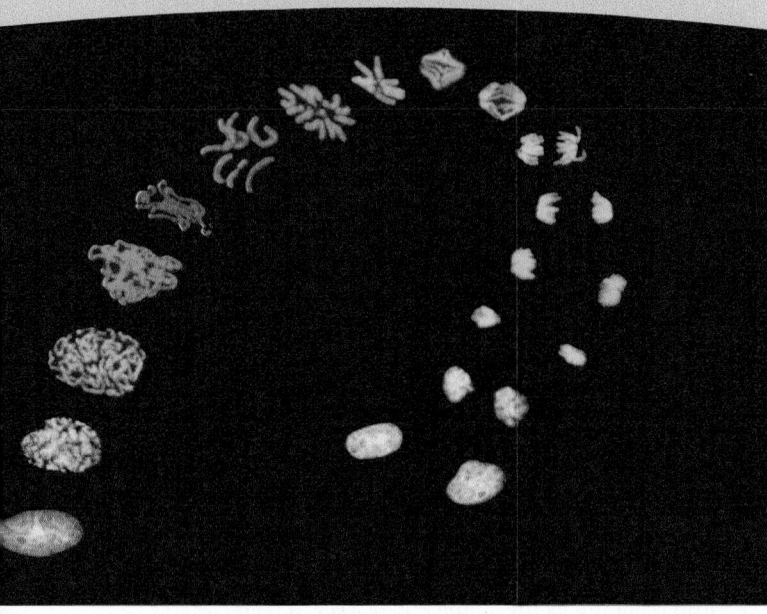

▲ Figure 12.1 **How do a cell's chromosomes change during cell division?**

KEY CONCEPTS

12.1 Most cell division results in genetically identical daughter cells

12.2 The mitotic phase alternates with interphase in the cell cycle

12.3 The eukaryotic cell cycle is regulated by a molecular control system

OVERVIEW

The Key Roles of Cell Division

The ability of organisms to produce more of their own kind is the one characteristic that best distinguishes living things from nonliving matter. This unique capacity to procreate, like all biological functions, has a cellular basis. Rudolf Virchow, a German physician, put it this way in 1855: "Where a cell exists, there must have been a preexisting cell, just as the animal arises only from an animal and the plant

only from a plant." He summarized this concept with the Latin axiom "*Omnis cellula e cellula*," meaning "Every cell from a cell." The continuity of life is based on the reproduction of cells, or **cell division**. The series of fluorescence micrographs in **Figure 12.1** follows an animal cell's chromosomes, from lower left to lower right, as one cell divides into two.

Cell division plays several important roles in life. The division of one prokaryotic cell reproduces an entire organism. The same is true of a unicellular eukaryote (**Figure 12.2a**). Cell division also enables multicellular eukaryotes to develop from a single cell, like the fertilized egg that gave rise to the two-celled embryo in **Figure 12.2b**. And after such an organism is fully grown, cell division continues to function in renewal and repair, replacing cells that die from normal wear and tear or accidents. For example, dividing cells in your bone marrow continuously make new blood cells (**Figure 12.2c**).

The cell division process is an integral part of the **cell cycle**, the life of a cell from the time it is first formed from a dividing parent cell until its own division into two daughter cells. (Our use of the words *daughter* or *sister* in relation to cells is not meant to imply gender.) Passing identical genetic material to cellular offspring is a crucial function of cell division. In this chapter, you will learn how this process occurs. After studying the cellular mechanics of cell division in eukaryotes and bacteria, you will learn about the molecular control system that regulates progress through the eukaryotic cell cycle and what happens when the control system malfunctions. Because a breakdown in cell cycle control plays a major role in cancer development, this aspect of cell biology is an active area of research.

◀ **(a) Reproduction.** An amoeba, a single-celled eukaryote, is dividing into two cells. Each new cell will be an individual organism (LM).

▶ **(b) Growth and development.** This micrograph shows a sand dollar embryo shortly after the fertilized egg divided, forming two cells (LM).

◀ **(c) Tissue renewal.** These dividing bone marrow cells will give rise to new blood cells (LM).

▲ Figure 12.2 **The functions of cell division.**

Most cell division results in genetically identical daughter cells

The reproduction of an assembly as complex as a cell cannot occur by a mere pinching in half; a cell is not like a soap bubble that simply enlarges and splits in two. In both prokaryotes and eukaryotes, most cell division involves the distribution of identical genetic material—DNA—to two daughter cells. (The exception is meiosis, the special type of eukaryotic cell division that can produce sperm and eggs.) What is most remarkable about cell division is the fidelity with which the DNA is passed along from one generation of cells to the next. A dividing cell duplicates its DNA, allocates the two copies to opposite ends of the cell, and only then splits into daughter cells. After we describe the distribution of DNA during cell division in animal and plant cells, we'll consider the process in other eukaryotes as well as in bacteria.

Cellular Organization of the Genetic Material

A cell's endowment of DNA, its genetic information, is called its **genome**. Although a prokaryotic genome is often a single DNA molecule, eukaryotic genomes usually consist of a number of DNA molecules. The overall length of DNA in a eukaryotic cell is enormous. A typical human cell, for example, has about 2 m of DNA—a length about 250,000 times greater than the cell's diameter. Yet before the cell can divide to form genetically identical daughter cells, all of this DNA must be copied, or replicated, and then the two copies must be separated so that each daughter cell ends up with a complete genome.

The replication and distribution of so much DNA is manageable because the DNA molecules are packaged into structures called **chromosomes**, so named because they take up certain dyes used in microscopy (from the Greek *chroma*, color, and *soma*, body) (Figure 12.3). Each eukaryotic chromosome consists of one very long, linear DNA molecule associated with many proteins (see Figure 6.9). The DNA molecule carries several hundred to a few thousand genes, the units of information that specify an organism's inherited traits. The associated proteins maintain the structure of the chromosome and help control the activity of the genes. Together, the entire complex of DNA and proteins that is the building material of chromosomes is referred to as **chromatin**. As you will soon see, the chromatin of a chromosome varies in its degree of condensation during the process of cell division.

Every eukaryotic species has a characteristic number of chromosomes in each cell nucleus. For example, the nuclei of human **somatic cells** (all body cells except the reproductive cells) each contain 46 chromosomes, made up of two sets of 23, one set inherited from each parent. Reproductive cells, or **gametes**—sperm and eggs—have half as many chromosomes as somatic cells, or one set of 23 chromosomes in humans. The

▲ Figure 12.3 **Eukaryotic chromosomes.** Chromosomes (stained purple) are visible within the nucleus of this cell from an African blood lily. The thinner red threads in the surrounding cytoplasm are the cytoskeleton. The cell is preparing to divide (LM).

number of chromosomes in somatic cells varies widely among species: 18 in cabbage plants, 48 in chimpanzees, 56 in elephants, 90 in hedgehogs, and 148 in one species of alga. We'll now consider how these chromosomes behave during cell division.

Distribution of Chromosomes During Eukaryotic Cell Division

When a cell is not dividing, and even as it replicates its DNA in preparation for cell division, each chromosome is in the form of a long, thin chromatin fiber. After DNA replication, however, the chromosomes condense as a part of cell division: Each chromatin fiber becomes densely coiled and folded, making the chromosomes much shorter and so thick that we can see them with a light microscope.

Each duplicated chromosome has two **sister chromatids**, which are joined copies of the original chromosome (Figure 12.4). The two chromatids, each containing an identical DNA molecule, are initially attached all along their lengths by protein complexes called *cohesins*; this attachment is known as *sister chromatid cohesion*. Each sister chromatid has a **centromere**, a region containing specific DNA sequences

Sister chromatids

Centromere   0.5 μm

▲ Figure 12.4 **A highly condensed, duplicated human chromosome (SEM).**

DRAW IT *Circle one sister chromatid of the chromosome in this micrograph.*

? *How many chromatid arms does the chromosome in* ❷ *have?*

❶ One of the multiple chromosomes in a eukaryotic cell is represented here, not yet duplicated. Normally it would be a long, thin chromatin fiber containing one DNA molecule and associated proteins; here its condensed form is shown for illustration purposes only.

Chromosomes

Chromosomal DNA molecules

Centromere

Chromosome arm

Chromosome duplication (including DNA replication) and condensation

❷ Once duplicated, a chromosome consists of two sister chromatids connected along their entire lengths by sister chromatid cohesion. Each chromatid contains a copy of the DNA molecule.

Sister chromatids

Separation of sister chromatids into two chromosomes

❸ Molecular and mechanical processes separate the sister chromatids into two chromosomes and distribute them to two daughter cells.

where the chromatid is attached most closely to its sister chromatid. This attachment is mediated by proteins bound to the centromeric DNA sequences and gives the condensed, duplicated chromosome a narrow "waist." The part of a chromatid on either side of the centromere is referred to as an *arm* of the chromatid. (An uncondensed, unduplicated chromosome has a single centromere and two arms.)

Later in the cell division process, the two sister chromatids of each duplicated chromosome separate and move into two new nuclei, one forming at each end of the cell. Once the sister chromatids separate, they are no longer called sister chromatids but are considered individual chromosomes. Thus, each new nucleus receives a collection of chromosomes identical to that of the parent cell (**Figure 12.5**). **Mitosis**, the division of the genetic material in the nucleus, is usually followed immediately by **cytokinesis**, the division of the cytoplasm. One cell has become two, each the genetic equivalent of the parent cell.

What happens to the chromosome number as we follow the human life cycle through the generations? You inherited 46 chromosomes, one set of 23 from each parent. They were combined in the nucleus of a single cell when a sperm from your father united with an egg from your mother, forming a fertilized egg, or zygote. Mitosis and cytokinesis produced the 200 trillion somatic cells that now make up your body, and the same processes continue to generate new cells to replace dead and damaged ones. In contrast, you produce gametes—eggs or sperm—by a variation of cell division called *meiosis*, which yields nonidentical daughter cells that have only one set of chromosomes, half as many chromosomes as the parent cell. Meiosis in humans occurs only in the gonads (ovaries or testes). In each generation, meiosis reduces the chromosome number from 46 (two sets of chromosomes) to 23 (one set). Fertilization fuses two gametes together and returns the chromosome number to 46, and mitosis conserves that number in every somatic cell nucleus of the new individual. In Chapter 13, we will examine the role of meiosis in reproduction and inheritance in more detail. In the remainder of this chapter, we focus on mitosis and the rest of the cell cycle in eukaryotes.

CONCEPT CHECK 12.1

1. How many chromatids are in a duplicated chromosome?

2. **WHAT IF?** A chicken has 78 chromosomes in its somatic cells. How many chromosomes did the chicken inherit from each parent? How many chromosomes are in each of the chicken's gametes? How many chromosomes will be in each somatic cell of the chicken's offspring?

For suggested answers, see Appendix A.

CONCEPT 12.2

The mitotic phase alternates with interphase in the cell cycle

In 1882, a German anatomist named Walther Flemming developed dyes that allowed him to observe, for the first time, the behavior of chromosomes during mitosis and cytokinesis. (In fact, Flemming coined the terms *mitosis* and *chromatin*.) During the period between one cell division and the next, it appeared to Flemming that the cell was simply growing larger. But we now know that many critical events occur during this stage in the life of a cell.

Phases of the Cell Cycle

Mitosis is just one part of the cell cycle (Figure 12.6). In fact, the **mitotic (M) phase**, which includes both mitosis and cytokinesis, is usually the shortest part of the cell cycle. Mitotic cell division alternates with a much longer stage called **interphase**, which often accounts for about 90% of the cycle. During interphase, a cell that is about to divide grows and copies its chromosomes in preparation for cell division. Interphase can be divided into subphases: the G_1 **phase** ("first gap"), the **S phase** ("synthesis"), and the G_2 **phase** ("second gap"). During all three subphases, a cell that will eventually divide grows by producing proteins and cytoplasmic organelles such as mitochondria and endoplasmic reticulum. However, chromosomes are duplicated only during the S phase. (We will discuss synthesis of DNA in Chapter 16.) Thus, a cell grows (G_1), continues to grow as it copies its chromosomes (S), grows more as it completes preparations for cell division (G_2), and divides (M). The daughter cells may then repeat the cycle.

A particular human cell might undergo one division in 24 hours. Of this time, the M phase would occupy less than 1 hour, while the S phase might occupy about 10–12 hours, or about half the cycle. The rest of the time would be apportioned between the G_1 and G_2 phases. The G_2 phase usually takes 4–6 hours; in our example, G_1 would occupy about 5–6 hours. G_1 is the most variable in length in different types of cells. Some cells in a multicellular organism divide very infrequently or not at all. These cells spend their time in G_1 (or a related phase called G_0) doing their job in the organism—a nerve cell carries impulses, for example.

Mitosis is conventionally broken down into five stages: **prophase**, **prometaphase**, **metaphase**, **anaphase**, and

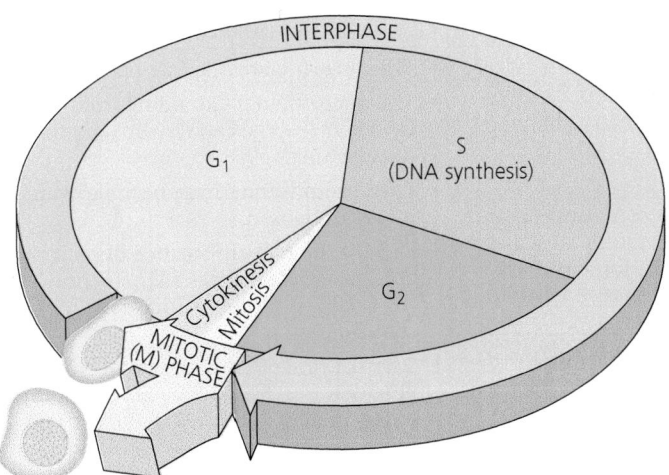

▲ **Figure 12.6 The cell cycle.** In a dividing cell, the mitotic (M) phase alternates with interphase, a growth period. The first part of interphase (G_1) is followed by the S phase, when the chromosomes duplicate; G_2 is the last part of interphase. In the M phase, mitosis distributes the daughter chromosomes to daughter nuclei, and cytokinesis divides the cytoplasm, producing two daughter cells. The relative durations of G_1, S, and G_2 may vary.

telophase. Overlapping with the latter stages of mitosis, cytokinesis completes the mitotic phase. Figure 12.7, on the next two pages, describes these stages in an animal cell. Study this figure thoroughly before progressing to the next two sections, which examine mitosis and cytokinesis more closely.

The Mitotic Spindle: *A Closer Look*

Many of the events of mitosis depend on the **mitotic spindle**, which begins to form in the cytoplasm during prophase. This structure consists of fibers made of microtubules and associated proteins. While the mitotic spindle assembles, the other microtubules of the cytoskeleton partially disassemble, providing the material used to construct the spindle. The spindle microtubules elongate (polymerize) by incorporating more subunits of the protein tubulin (see Table 6.1) and shorten (depolymerize) by losing subunits.

In animal cells, the assembly of spindle microtubules starts at the **centrosome**, a subcellular region containing material that functions throughout the cell cycle to organize the cell's microtubules. (It is also called the *microtubule-organizing center*.) A pair of centrioles is located at the center of the centrosome, but they are not essential for cell division: If the centrioles are destroyed with a laser microbeam, a spindle nevertheless forms during mitosis. In fact, centrioles are not even present in plant cells, which do form mitotic spindles.

During interphase in animal cells, the single centrosome duplicates, forming two centrosomes, which remain together near the nucleus. The two centrosomes move apart during prophase and prometaphase of mitosis as spindle microtubules grow out from them. By the end of prometaphase, the two centrosomes, one at each pole of the spindle, are at opposite ends of the cell. An **aster**, a radial array of short microtubules, extends from each centrosome. The spindle includes the centrosomes, the spindle microtubules, and the asters.

Each of the two sister chromatids of a duplicated chromosome has a **kinetochore**, a structure of proteins associated with specific sections of chromosomal DNA at each centromere. The chromosome's two kinetochores face in opposite directions. During prometaphase, some of the spindle microtubules attach to the kinetochores; these are called kinetochore microtubules. (The number of microtubules attached to a kinetochore varies among species, from one microtubule in yeast cells to 40 or so in some mammalian cells.) When one of a chromosome's kinetochores is "captured" by microtubules, the chromosome begins to move toward the pole from which those microtubules extend. However, this movement is checked as soon as microtubules from the opposite pole attach to the other kinetochore. What happens next is like a tug-of-war that ends in a draw. The chromosome moves first in one direction, then the other, back and forth, finally settling midway between the two ends of the cell. At metaphase, the centromeres of all the duplicated chromosomes are on a plane midway between the spindle's

Exploring Mitosis in an Animal Cell

G₂ of Interphase

Centrosomes (with centriole pairs)

Chromosomes (duplicated, uncondensed)

Nucleolus

Nuclear envelope

Plasma membrane

Prophase

Early mitotic spindle

Aster

Centromere

Chromosome, consisting of two sister chromatids

Prometaphase

Fragments of nuclear envelope

Nonkinetochore microtubules

Kinetochore

Kinetochore microtubule

G₂ of Interphase

- A nuclear envelope encloses the nucleus.
- The nucleus contains one or more nucleoli (singular, *nucleolus*).
- Two centrosomes have formed by duplication of a single centrosome. Centrosomes are regions in animal cells that organize the microtubules of the spindle. Each centrosome contains two centrioles.
- Chromosomes, duplicated during S phase, cannot be seen individually because they have not yet condensed.

The light micrographs show dividing lung cells from a newt, which has 22 chromosomes in its somatic cells. Chromosomes appear blue, microtubules green, and intermediate filaments red. For simplicity, the drawings show only 6 chromosomes.

Prophase

- The chromatin fibers become more tightly coiled, condensing into discrete chromosomes observable with a light microscope.
- The nucleoli disappear.
- Each duplicated chromosome appears as two identical sister chromatids joined at their centromeres and, in some species, all along their arms by cohesins (sister chromatid cohesion).
- The mitotic spindle (named for its shape) begins to form. It is composed of the centrosomes and the microtubules that extend from them. The radial arrays of shorter microtubules that extend from the centrosomes are called asters ("stars").
- The centrosomes move away from each other, propelled partly by the lengthening microtubules between them.

Prometaphase

- The nuclear envelope fragments.
- The microtubules extending from each centrosome can now invade the nuclear area.
- The chromosomes have become even more condensed.
- Each of the two chromatids of each chromosome now has a kinetochore, a specialized protein structure at the centromere.
- Some of the microtubules attach to the kinetochores, becoming "kinetochore microtubules," which jerk the chromosomes back and forth.
- Nonkinetochore microtubules interact with those from the opposite pole of the spindle.

? *How many molecules of DNA are in the prometaphase drawing? How many molecules per chromosome? How many double helices are there per chromosome? Per chromatid?*

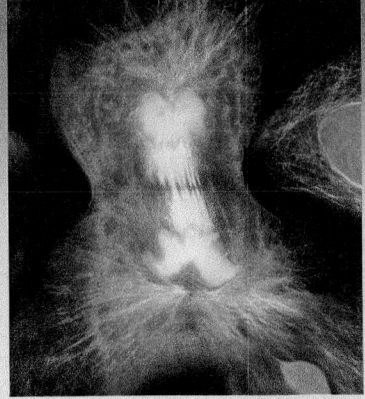

10 μm

Metaphase

Anaphase

Telophase and Cytokinesis

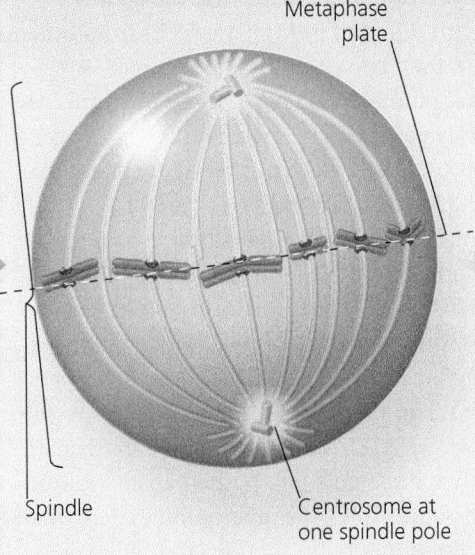

Metaphase plate

Spindle

Centrosome at one spindle pole

Daughter chromosomes

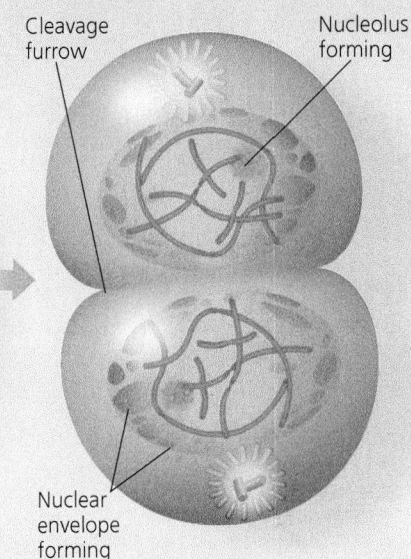

Cleavage furrow

Nucleolus forming

Nuclear envelope forming

Metaphase

- The centrosomes are now at opposite poles of the cell.

- The chromosomes convene at the *metaphase plate*, a plane that is equidistant between the spindle's two poles. The chromosomes' centromeres lie at the metaphase plate.

- For each chromosome, the kinetochores of the sister chromatids are attached to kinetochore microtubules coming from opposite poles.

Anaphase

- Anaphase is the shortest stage of mitosis, often lasting only a few minutes.

- Anaphase begins when the cohesin proteins are cleaved. This allows the two sister chromatids of each pair to part suddenly. Each chromatid thus becomes a full-fledged chromosome.

- The two liberated daughter chromosomes begin moving toward opposite ends of the cell as their kinetochore microtubules shorten. Because these microtubules are attached at the centromere region, the chromosomes move centromere first (at about 1 μm/min).

- The cell elongates as the nonkinetochore microtubules lengthen.

- By the end of anaphase, the two ends of the cell have equivalent—and complete—collections of chromosomes.

Telophase

- Two daughter nuclei form in the cell. Nuclear envelopes arise from the fragments of the parent cell's nuclear envelope and other portions of the endomembrane system.

- Nucleoli reappear.

- The chromosomes become less condensed.

- Any remaining spindle microtubules are depolymerized.

- Mitosis, the division of one nucleus into two genetically identical nuclei, is now complete.

Cytokinesis

- The division of the cytoplasm is usually well under way by late telophase, so the two daughter cells appear shortly after the end of mitosis.

- In animal cells, cytokinesis involves the formation of a cleavage furrow, which pinches the cell in two.

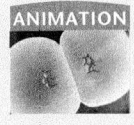

ANIMATION **BioFlix** Visit the Study Area at **www.masteringbiology.com** for the BioFlix® 3-D Animation on Mitosis.

two poles. This plane is called the **metaphase plate**, which is an imaginary rather than an actual cellular structure (Figure 12.8). Meanwhile, microtubules that do not attach to kinetochores have been elongating, and by metaphase they overlap and interact with other nonkinetochore microtubules from the opposite pole of the spindle. (These are sometimes called "polar" microtubules.) By metaphase, the microtubules of the asters have also grown and are in contact with the plasma membrane. The spindle is now complete.

Aster

Centrosome

Sister chromatids

Metaphase plate (imaginary)

Kineto-chores

Overlapping nonkinetochore microtubules

Kinetochore microtubules

Microtubules

Kinetochores

0.5 µm

Chromosomes

Centrosome

1 µm

▲ **Figure 12.8 The mitotic spindle at metaphase.** The kinetochores of each chromosome's two sister chromatids face in opposite directions. Here, each kinetochore is attached to a *cluster* of kinetochore microtubules extending from the nearest centrosome. Nonkinetochore microtubules overlap at the metaphase plate (TEMs).

DRAW IT *On the lower micrograph, draw a line indicating the position of the metaphase plate. Circle an aster. Draw arrows indicating the directions of chromosome movement once anaphase begins.*

The structure of the completed spindle correlates well with its function during anaphase. Anaphase commences suddenly when the cohesins holding together the sister chromatids of each chromosome are cleaved by an enzyme called *separase*. Once the chromatids become separate, full-fledged chromosomes, they move toward opposite ends of the cell.

How do the kinetochore microtubules function in this poleward movement of chromosomes? Apparently, two mechanisms are in play, both involving motor proteins. (To review how motor proteins move an object along a microtubule, see Figure 6.21.) A clever experiment carried out in 1987 suggested that motor proteins on the kinetochores "walk" the chromosomes along the microtubules, which depolymerize at their kinetochore ends after the motor proteins have passed (Figure 12.9). (This is referred to as the "Pacman" mechanism because of its resemblance to the arcade game character that moves by eating all the dots in its path.) However, other researchers, working with different cell types or cells from other species, have shown that chromosomes are "reeled in" by motor proteins at the spindle poles and that the microtubules depolymerize after they pass by these motor proteins. The general consensus now is that both mechanisms are used and that their relative contributions vary among cell types.

In a dividing animal cell, the nonkinetochore microtubules are responsible for elongating the whole cell during anaphase. Nonkinetochore microtubules from opposite poles overlap each other extensively during metaphase (see Figure 12.8). During anaphase, the region of overlap is reduced as motor proteins attached to the microtubules walk them away from one another, using energy from ATP. As the microtubules push apart from each other, their spindle poles are pushed apart, elongating the cell. At the same time, the microtubules lengthen somewhat by the addition of tubulin subunits to their overlapping ends. As a result, the microtubules continue to overlap.

At the end of anaphase, duplicate groups of chromosomes have arrived at opposite ends of the elongated parent cell. Nuclei re-form during telophase. Cytokinesis generally begins during anaphase or telophase, and the spindle eventually disassembles by depolymerization of microtubules.

Cytokinesis: *A Closer Look*

In animal cells, cytokinesis occurs by a process known as **cleavage**. The first sign of cleavage is the appearance of a **cleavage furrow**, a shallow groove in the cell surface near the old metaphase plate (Figure 12.10a). On the cytoplasmic side of the furrow is a contractile ring of actin microfilaments associated with molecules of the protein myosin. The actin microfilaments interact with the myosin molecules, causing the ring to contract. The contraction of the dividing cell's ring of microfilaments is like the pulling of a drawstring. The cleavage furrow deepens until the parent cell is pinched in two, producing two completely separated cells, each with its own nucleus and share of cytosol, organelles, and other subcellular structures.

INQUIRY

At which end do kinetochore microtubules shorten during anaphase?

EXPERIMENT Gary Borisy and colleagues at the University of Wisconsin wanted to determine whether kinetochore microtubules depolymerize at the kinetochore end or the pole end as chromosomes move toward the poles during mitosis. First they labeled the microtubules of a pig kidney cell in early anaphase with a yellow fluorescent dye.

Then they marked a region of the kinetochore microtubules between one spindle pole and the chromosomes by using a laser to eliminate the fluorescence from that region, while leaving the microtubules intact (see below). As anaphase proceeded, they monitored the changes in microtubule length on either side of the mark.

RESULTS As the chromosomes moved poleward, the microtubule segments on the kinetochore side of the mark shortened, while those on the spindle pole side stayed the same length.

CONCLUSION During anaphase in this cell type, chromosome movement is correlated with kinetochore microtubules shortening at their kinetochore ends and not at their spindle pole ends. This experiment supports the hypothesis that during anaphase, a chromosome is walked along a microtubule as the microtubule depolymerizes at its kinetochore end, releasing tubulin subunits.

SOURCE G. J. Gorbsky, P. J. Sammak, and G. G. Borisy, Chromosomes move poleward in anaphase along stationary microtubules that coordinately disassemble from their kinetochore ends, *Journal of Cell Biology* 104:9–18 (1987).

WHAT IF? If this experiment had been done on a cell type in which "reeling in" at the poles was the main cause of chromosome movement, how would the mark have moved relative to the poles? How would the microtubule lengths have changed?

(a) Cleavage of an animal cell (SEM)

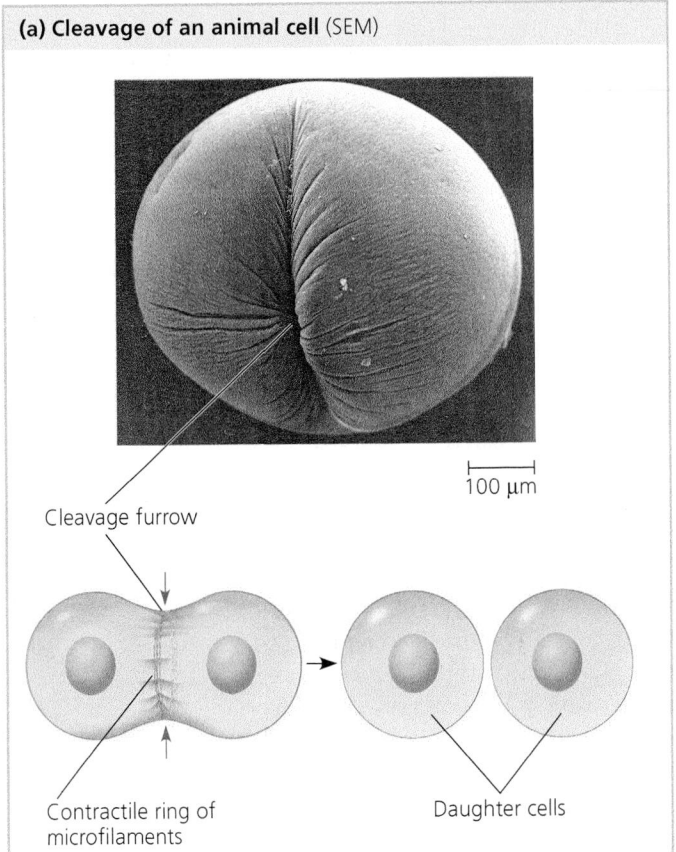

(b) Cell plate formation in a plant cell (TEM)

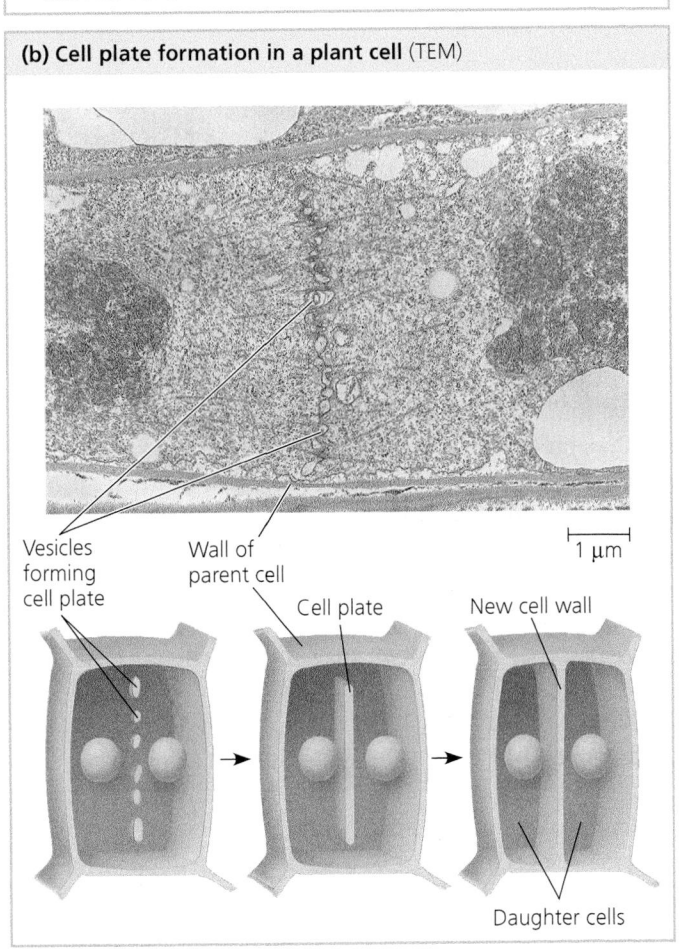

Nucleus   Chromosomes
   Nucleolus   condensing   Chromosomes   Cell plate   10 μm

1 Prophase. The chromosomes are condensing and the nucleolus is beginning to disappear. Although not yet visible in the micrograph, the mitotic spindle is starting to form.

2 Prometaphase. Discrete chromosomes are now visible; each consists of two aligned, identical sister chromatids. Later in prometaphase, the nuclear envelope will fragment.

3 Metaphase. The spindle is complete, and the chromosomes, attached to microtubules at their kinetochores, are all at the metaphase plate.

4 Anaphase. The chromatids of each chromosome have separated, and the daughter chromosomes are moving to the ends of the cell as their kinetochore microtubules shorten.

5 Telophase. Daughter nuclei are forming. Meanwhile, cytokinesis has started: The cell plate, which will divide the cytoplasm in two, is growing toward the perimeter of the parent cell.

▲ **Figure 12.11 Mitosis in a plant cell.** These light micrographs show mitosis in cells of an onion root.

Cytokinesis in plant cells, which have cell walls, is markedly different. There is no cleavage furrow. Instead, during telophase, vesicles derived from the Golgi apparatus move along microtubules to the middle of the cell, where they coalesce, producing a **cell plate** (Figure 12.10b). Cell wall materials carried in the vesicles collect in the cell plate as it grows. The cell plate enlarges until its surrounding membrane fuses with the plasma membrane along the perimeter of the cell. Two daughter cells result, each with its own plasma membrane. Meanwhile, a new cell wall arising from the contents of the cell plate has formed between the daughter cells.

Figure 12.11 is a series of micrographs of a dividing plant cell. Examining this figure will help you review mitosis and cytokinesis.

Binary Fission in Bacteria

Prokaryotes (bacteria and archaea) can undergo a type of reproduction in which the cell grows to roughly double its size and then divides to form two cells. The term **binary fission**, meaning "division in half," refers to this process and to the asexual reproduction of single-celled eukaryotes, such as the amoeba in Figure 12.2a. However, the process in eukaryotes involves mitosis, while that in prokaryotes does not.

In bacteria, most genes are carried on a single *bacterial chromosome* that consists of a circular DNA molecule and associated proteins. Although bacteria are smaller and simpler than eukaryotic cells, the challenge of replicating their genomes in an orderly fashion and distributing the copies equally to two daughter cells is still formidable. The chromosome of the bacterium *Escherichia coli*, for example, when it is fully stretched out, is about 500 times as long as the cell. For

such a long chromosome to fit within the cell requires that it be highly coiled and folded.

In *E. coli*, the process of cell division is initiated when the DNA of the bacterial chromosome begins to replicate at a specific place on the chromosome called the **origin of replication**, producing two origins. As the chromosome continues to replicate, one origin moves rapidly toward the opposite end of the cell (Figure 12.12). While the chromosome is replicating, the cell elongates. When replication is complete and the bacterium has reached about twice its initial size, its plasma membrane pinches inward, dividing the parent *E. coli* cell into two daughter cells. In this way, each cell inherits a complete genome.

Using the techniques of modern DNA technology to tag the origins of replication with molecules that glow green in fluorescence microscopy (see Figure 6.3), researchers have directly observed the movement of bacterial chromosomes. This movement is reminiscent of the poleward movements of the centromere regions of eukaryotic chromosomes during anaphase of mitosis, but bacteria don't have visible mitotic spindles or even microtubules. In most bacterial species studied, the two origins of replication end up at opposite ends of the cell or in some other very specific location, possibly anchored there by one or more proteins. How bacterial chromosomes move and how their specific location is established and maintained are still not fully understood. However, several proteins have been identified that play important roles: One resembling eukaryotic actin apparently functions in bacterial chromosome movement during cell division, and another that is related to tubulin seems to help pinch the plasma membrane inward, separating the two bacterial daughter cells.

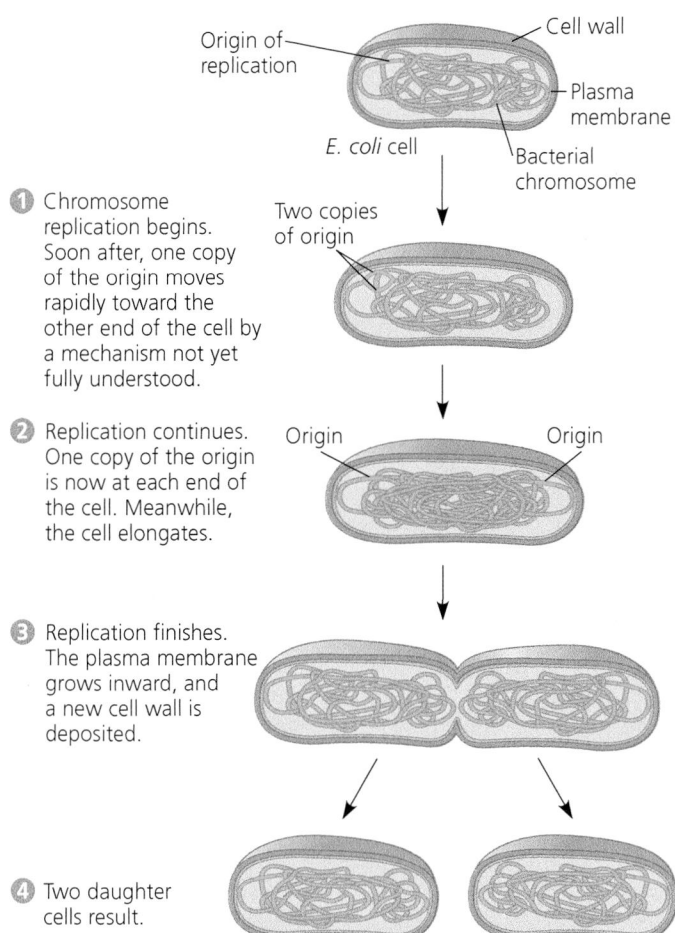

Origin of replication — Cell wall
— Plasma membrane
E. coli cell
—Bacterial chromosome

1 Chromosome replication begins. Soon after, one copy of the origin moves rapidly toward the other end of the cell by a mechanism not yet fully understood.

Two copies of origin

2 Replication continues. One copy of the origin is now at each end of the cell. Meanwhile, the cell elongates.

Origin   Origin

3 Replication finishes. The plasma membrane grows inward, and a new cell wall is deposited.

4 Two daughter cells result.

▲ **Figure 12.12 Bacterial cell division by binary fission.** The bacterium *E. coli*, shown here, has a single, circular chromosome.

The Evolution of Mitosis

EVOLUTION Given that prokaryotes preceded eukaryotes on Earth by more than a billion years, we might hypothesize that mitosis evolved from simpler prokaryotic mechanisms of cell reproduction. The fact that some of the proteins involved in bacterial binary fission are related to eukaryotic proteins that function in mitosis supports that hypothesis.

As eukaryotes evolved, along with their larger genomes and nuclear envelopes, the ancestral process of binary fission, seen today in bacteria, somehow gave rise to mitosis. **Figure 12.13** shows some variations on cell division in different groups of organisms. These processes may be similar to mechanisms used by ancestral species and thus may resemble steps in the evolution of mitosis from a binary fission-like process presumably carried out by very early bacteria. Possible intermediate stages are suggested by two unusual types of nuclear division found today in certain unicellular eukaryotes—dinoflagellates, diatoms, and some yeasts. These two modes of nuclear division are thought to be cases where ancestral mechanisms have remained relatively unchanged over evolutionary time. In both types, the nuclear envelope remains intact, in contrast to what happens in most eukaryotic cells.

Bacterial chromosome

(a) Bacteria. During binary fission in bacteria, the origins of the daughter chromosomes move to opposite ends of the cell. The mechanism is not fully understood, but proteins may anchor the daughter chromosomes to specific sites on the plasma membrane.

Chromosomes
Microtubules
Intact nuclear envelope

(b) Dinoflagellates. In unicellular protists called dinoflagellates, the chromosomes attach to the nuclear envelope, which remains intact during cell division. Microtubules pass through the nucleus inside cytoplasmic tunnels, reinforcing the spatial orientation of the nucleus, which then divides in a process reminiscent of bacterial binary fission.

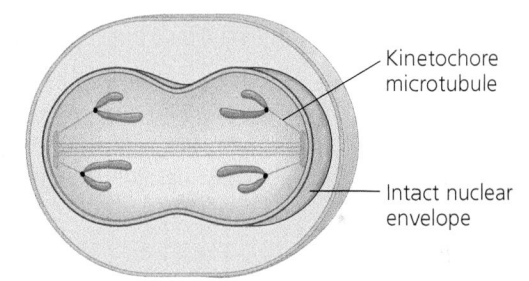

Kinetochore microtubule
Intact nuclear envelope

(c) Diatoms and some yeasts. In two other groups of unicellular protists, diatoms and some yeasts, the nuclear envelope also remains intact during cell division. In these organisms, the microtubules form a spindle *within* the nucleus. Microtubules separate the chromosomes, and the nucleus splits into two daughter nuclei.

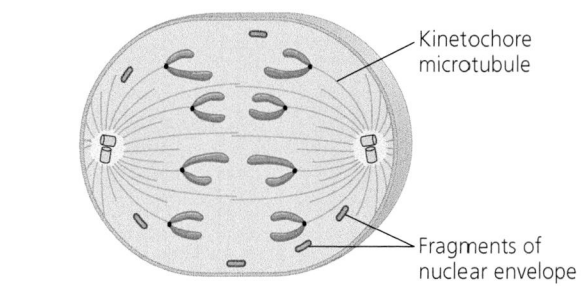

Kinetochore microtubule
Fragments of nuclear envelope

(d) Most eukaryotes. In most other eukaryotes, including plants and animals, the spindle forms outside the nucleus, and the nuclear envelope breaks down during mitosis. Microtubules separate the chromosomes, and two nuclear envelopes then form.

▲ **Figure 12.13 Mechanisms of cell division in several groups of organisms.** Some unicellular eukaryotes existing today have mechanisms of cell division that may resemble intermediate steps in the evolution of mitosis. Except for (a), these schematic diagrams do not show cell walls.

1. How many chromosomes are shown in the diagram in Figure 12.8? Are they duplicated? How many chromatids are shown?
2. Compare cytokinesis in animal cells and plant cells.
3. What is the function of nonkinetochore microtubules?
4. Compare the roles of tubulin and actin during eukaryotic cell division with the roles of tubulin-like and actin-like proteins during bacterial binary fission.
5. **MAKE CONNECTIONS** What other functions do actin and tubulin carry out? Name the proteins they interact with to do so. (Review Figures 6.21a and 6.27a.)
6. **WHAT IF?** During which stages of the cell cycle does a chromosome consist of two identical chromatids?

For suggested answers, see Appendix A.

CONCEPT 12.3

The eukaryotic cell cycle is regulated by a molecular control system

The timing and rate of cell division in different parts of a plant or animal are crucial to normal growth, development, and maintenance. The frequency of cell division varies with the type of cell. For example, human skin cells divide frequently throughout life, whereas liver cells maintain the ability to divide but keep it in reserve until an appropriate need arises—say, to repair a wound. Some of the most specialized cells, such as fully formed nerve cells and muscle cells, do not divide at all in a mature human. These cell cycle differences result from regulation at the molecular level. The mechanisms of this regulation are of intense interest, not only for understanding the life cycles of normal cells but also for understanding how cancer cells manage to escape the usual controls.

Evidence for Cytoplasmic Signals

What controls the cell cycle? One reasonable hypothesis might be that each event in the cell cycle merely leads to the next, as in a simple metabolic pathway. According to this hypothesis, the replication of chromosomes in the S phase, for example, might cause cell growth during the G_2 phase, which might in turn lead inevitably to the onset of mitosis. However, this hypothesis, which proposes a pathway that is not subject to either internal or external regulation, turns out to be incorrect.

In the early 1970s, a variety of experiments led to an alternative hypothesis: that the cell cycle is driven by specific signaling molecules present in the cytoplasm. Some of the first strong evidence for this hypothesis came from experiments with mammalian cells grown in culture. In these experiments, two cells in different phases of the cell cycle were fused to form

▼ Figure 12.14 | **INQUIRY**

Do molecular signals in the cytoplasm regulate the cell cycle?

EXPERIMENT Researchers at the University of Colorado wondered whether a cell's progression through the cell cycle is controlled by cytoplasmic molecules. To investigate this, they selected cultured mammalian cells that were at different phases of the cell cycle and induced them to fuse. Two such experiments are shown here.

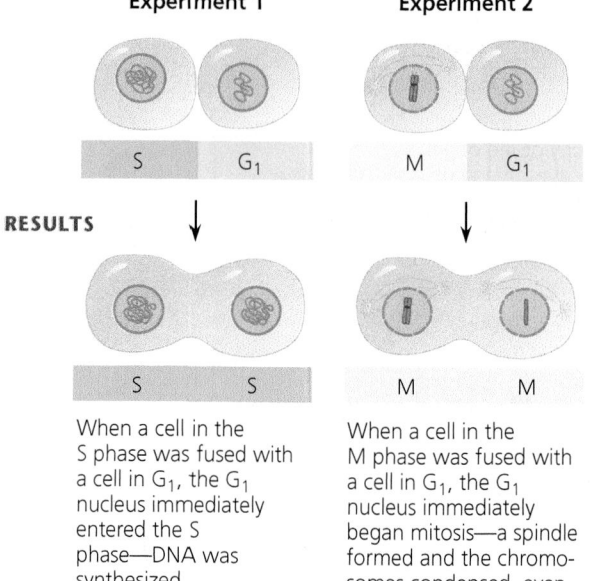

When a cell in the S phase was fused with a cell in G_1, the G_1 nucleus immediately entered the S phase—DNA was synthesized.

When a cell in the M phase was fused with a cell in G_1, the G_1 nucleus immediately began mitosis—a spindle formed and the chromosomes condensed, even though the chromosomes had not been duplicated.

CONCLUSION The results of fusing a G_1 cell with a cell in the S or M phase of the cell cycle suggest that molecules present in the cytoplasm during the S or M phase control the progression to those phases.

SOURCE R. T. Johnson and P. N. Rao, Mammalian cell fusion: Induction of premature chromosome condensation in interphase nuclei, *Nature* 226:717–722 (1970).

WHAT IF? If the progression of phases did not depend on cytoplasmic molecules and each phase began when the previous one was complete, how would the results have differed?

a single cell with two nuclei. If one of the original cells was in the S phase and the other was in G_1, the G_1 nucleus immediately entered the S phase, as though stimulated by signaling molecules present in the cytoplasm of the first cell. Similarly, if a cell undergoing mitosis (M phase) was fused with another cell in any stage of its cell cycle, even G_1, the second nucleus immediately entered mitosis, with condensation of the chromatin and formation of a mitotic spindle (Figure 12.14).

The Cell Cycle Control System

The experiment shown in Figure 12.14 and other experiments on animal cells and yeasts demonstrated that the sequential events of the cell cycle are directed by a distinct **cell cycle control system**, a cyclically operating set of molecules in the cell that both triggers and coordinates key events

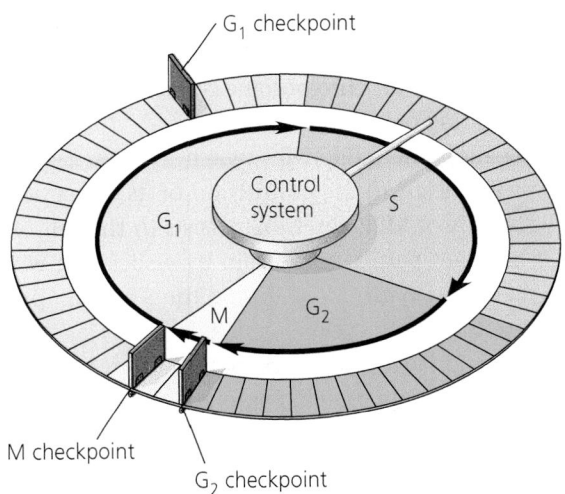

▲ **Figure 12.15 Mechanical analogy for the cell cycle control system.** In this diagram of the cell cycle, the flat "stepping stones" around the perimeter represent sequential events. Like the control device of an automatic washer, the cell cycle control system proceeds on its own, driven by a built-in clock. However, the system is subject to internal and external regulation at various checkpoints, of which three are shown (red).

in the cell cycle. The cell cycle control system has been compared to the control device of an automatic washing machine (Figure 12.15). Like the washer's timing device, the cell cycle control system proceeds on its own, according to a built-in clock. However, just as a washer's cycle is subject to both internal control (such as the sensor that detects when the tub is filled with water) and external adjustment (such as activation of the start mechanism), the cell cycle is regulated at certain checkpoints by both internal and external signals.

A **checkpoint** in the cell cycle is a control point where stop and go-ahead signals can regulate the cycle. (The signals are transmitted within the cell by the kinds of signal transduction pathways discussed in Chapter 11.) Animal cells generally have built-in stop signals that halt the cell cycle at checkpoints until overridden by go-ahead signals. Many signals registered at checkpoints come from cellular surveillance mechanisms inside the cell. These signals report whether crucial cellular processes that should have occurred by that point have in fact been completed correctly and thus whether or not the cell cycle should proceed. Checkpoints also register signals from outside the cell, as we will discuss later. Three major checkpoints are found in the G_1, G_2, and M phases (see Figure 12.15).

For many cells, the G_1 checkpoint—dubbed the "restriction point" in mammalian cells—seems to be the most important. If a cell receives a go-ahead signal at the G_1 checkpoint, it will usually complete the G_1, S, G_2, and M phases and divide. If it does not receive a go-ahead signal at that point, it will exit the cycle, switching into a nondividing state called the **G_0 phase** (Figure 12.16). Most cells of the human body are actually in the G_0 phase. As mentioned earlier, mature nerve cells and muscle cells never divide. Other cells, such as liver cells, can be "called back" from the G_0 phase to the

(a) If a cell receives a go-ahead signal at the G_1 checkpoint, the cell continues on in the cell cycle.

(b) If a cell does not receive a go-ahead signal at the G_1 checkpoint, the cell exits the cell cycle and goes into G_0, a nondividing state.

▲ **Figure 12.16 The G_1 checkpoint.**

WHAT IF? *What might be the result if the cell ignored the checkpoint and progressed through the cell cycle?*

cell cycle by external cues, such as growth factors released during injury.

To understand how cell cycle checkpoints work, we first need to see what kinds of molecules make up the cell cycle control system (the molecular basis for the cell cycle clock) and how a cell progresses through the cycle. Then we will consider the internal and external checkpoint signals that can make the clock pause or continue.

The Cell Cycle Clock: Cyclins and Cyclin-Dependent Kinases

Rhythmic fluctuations in the abundance and activity of cell cycle control molecules pace the sequential events of the cell cycle. These regulatory molecules are mainly proteins of two types: protein kinases and cyclins. Protein kinases are enzymes that activate or inactivate other proteins by phosphorylating them (see Chapter 11). Particular protein kinases give the go-ahead signals at the G_1 and G_2 checkpoints.

Many of the kinases that drive the cell cycle are actually present at a constant concentration in the growing cell, but much of the time they are in an inactive form. To be active, such a kinase must be attached to a **cyclin**, a protein that gets its name from its cyclically fluctuating concentration in the cell. Because of this requirement, these kinases are called **cyclin-dependent kinases**, or **Cdks**. The activity of a Cdk rises and falls with changes in the concentration of its cyclin partner. Figure 12.17a, on the next page, shows the fluctuating activity of **MPF**, the cyclin-Cdk complex that was discovered first (in frog eggs). Note that the peaks of MPF activity correspond to the peaks of cyclin concentration. The cyclin level rises during the S and G_2 phases and then falls abruptly during M phase.

The initials MPF stand for "maturation-promoting factor," but we can think of MPF as "M-phase-promoting factor" because it triggers the cell's passage past the G_2 checkpoint into

(a) Fluctuation of MPF activity and cyclin concentration during the cell cycle

① Synthesis of cyclin begins in late S phase and continues through G_2. Because cyclin is protected from degradation during this stage, it accumulates.

⑤ During G_1, the degradation of cyclin continues, and the Cdk component of MPF is recycled.

④ During anaphase, the cyclin component of MPF is degraded, terminating the M phase. The cell enters the G_1 phase.

③ MPF promotes mitosis by phosphorylating various proteins. MPF's activity peaks during metaphase.

② Cyclin combines with Cdk, producing MPF. When enough MPF molecules accumulate, the cell passes the G_2 checkpoint and begins mitosis.

(b) Molecular mechanisms that help regulate the cell cycle

▲ **Figure 12.17 Molecular control of the cell cycle at the G_2 checkpoint.** The steps of the cell cycle are timed by rhythmic fluctuations in the activity of cyclin-dependent kinases (Cdks). Here we focus on a cyclin-Cdk complex in animal cells called MPF, which acts at the G_2 checkpoint as a go-ahead signal, triggering the events of mitosis.

? *Explain how the events in the diagram in (b) are related to the "Time" axis of the graph in (a).*

M phase **(Figure 12.17b).** When cyclins that accumulate during G_2 associate with Cdk molecules, the resulting MPF complex phosphorylates a variety of proteins, initiating mitosis. MPF acts both directly as a kinase and indirectly by activating other kinases. For example, MPF causes phosphorylation of various proteins of the nuclear lamina (see Figure 6.9), which promotes

fragmentation of the nuclear envelope during prometaphase of mitosis. There is also evidence that MPF contributes to molecular events required for chromosome condensation and spindle formation during prophase.

During anaphase, MPF helps switch itself off by initiating a process that leads to the destruction of its own cyclin. The noncyclin part of MPF, the Cdk, persists in the cell, inactive until it becomes part of MPF again by associating with new cyclin molecules synthesized during the S and G_2 phases of the next round of the cycle.

Cell behavior at the G_1 checkpoint is also regulated by the activity of cyclin-Cdk protein complexes. Animal cells appear to have at least three Cdk proteins and several different cyclins that operate at this checkpoint. The fluctuating activities of different cyclin-Cdk complexes are of major importance in controlling all the stages of the cell cycle.

Stop and Go Signs: Internal and External Signals at the Checkpoints

Research scientists are currently working out the pathways that link signals originating inside and outside the cell with the responses by cyclin-dependent kinases and other proteins. An example of an internal signal occurs at the third important checkpoint, the M phase checkpoint. Anaphase, the separation of sister chromatids, does not begin until all the chromosomes are properly attached to the spindle at the metaphase plate. Researchers have learned that as long as some kinetochores are unattached to spindle microtubules, the sister chromatids remain together, delaying anaphase. Only when the kinetochores of all the chromosomes are properly attached to the spindle does the appropriate regulatory protein complex become activated. (In this case, the regulatory molecule is not a cyclin-Cdk complex but, instead, a different complex made up of several proteins.) Once activated, the complex sets off a chain of molecular events that activates the enzyme separase, which cleaves the cohesins, allowing the sister chromatids to separate. This mechanism ensures that daughter cells do not end up with missing or extra chromosomes.

Studies using animal cells in culture have led to the identification of many external factors, both chemical and physical, that can influence cell division. For example, cells fail to divide if an essential nutrient is lacking in the culture medium. (This is analogous to trying to run an automatic washing machine without the water supply hooked up; an internal sensor won't allow the machine to continue past the point where water is needed.) And even if all other conditions are favorable, most types of mammalian cells divide in culture only if the growth medium includes specific growth factors. As mentioned in Chapter 11, a **growth factor** is a protein released by certain cells that stimulates other cells to divide. Researchers have discovered more than 50 growth factors. Different cell types respond specifically to different growth factors or combinations of growth factors.

① A sample of human connective tissue is cut up into small pieces.

Scalpels

◀ **Figure 12.18 The effect of platelet-derived growth factor (PDGF) on cell division.**

Petri dish

② Enzymes are used to digest the extracellular matrix in the tissue pieces, resulting in a suspension of free fibroblasts.

③ Cells are transferred to culture vessels containing a basic growth medium consisting of glucose, amino acids, salts, and antibiotics (to prevent bacterial growth).

④ PDGF is added to half the vessels. The culture vessels are incubated at 37°C for 24 hours.

Without PDGF

In the basic growth medium without PDGF (the control), the cells fail to divide.

With PDGF

In the basic growth medium plus PDGF, the cells proliferate. The SEM shows cultured fibroblasts.

MAKE CONNECTIONS

PDGF signals cells by binding to a cell-surface receptor tyrosine kinase. If you added a chemical that blocked phosphorylation, how would the results differ? (See Figure 11.7.)

10 μm

Cells anchor to dish surface and divide (anchorage dependence).

When cells have formed a complete single layer, they stop dividing (density-dependent inhibition).

If some cells are scraped away, the remaining cells divide to fill the gap and then stop once they contact each other (density-dependent inhibition).

20 μm

(a) Normal mammalian cells. Contact with neighboring cells and the availability of nutrients, growth factors, and a substratum for attachment limit cell density to a single layer.

20 μm

(b) Cancer cells. Cancer cells usually continue to divide well beyond a single layer, forming a clump of overlapping cells. They do not exhibit anchorage dependence or density-dependent inhibition.

▲ **Figure 12.19 Density-dependent inhibition and anchorage dependence of cell division.** Individual cells are shown disproportionately large in the drawings.

Consider, for example, *platelet-derived growth factor (PDGF)*, which is made by blood cell fragments called platelets. The experiment illustrated in **Figure 12.18** demonstrates that PDGF is required for the division of cultured fibroblasts, a type of connective tissue cell. Fibroblasts have PDGF receptors on their plasma membranes. The binding of PDGF molecules to these receptors (which are receptor tyrosine kinases; see Chapter 11) triggers a signal transduction pathway that allows the cells to pass the G_1 checkpoint and divide. PDGF stimulates fibroblast division not only in the artificial conditions of cell culture, but also in an animal's body. When an injury occurs, platelets release PDGF in the vicinity. The resulting proliferation of fibroblasts helps heal the wound.

The effect of an external physical factor on cell division is clearly seen in **density-dependent inhibition**, a phenomenon in which crowded cells stop dividing (**Figure 12.19a**). As first observed many years ago, cultured cells normally divide until they form a single layer of cells on the inner surface of the culture container, at which point the cells stop dividing. If some cells are removed, those bordering the open space begin dividing again and continue until the vacancy is filled. Follow-up studies revealed that the binding of a cell-surface protein to its counterpart on an adjoining cell sends a growth-inhibiting signal to both cells, preventing them from moving forward in the cell cycle, even in the presence of growth factors.

Most animal cells also exhibit **anchorage dependence** (see Figure 12.19a). To divide, they must be attached to a substratum, such as the inside of a culture jar or the extracellular matrix of a tissue. Experiments suggest that like cell density, anchorage is signaled to the cell cycle control system via pathways involving plasma membrane proteins and elements of the cytoskeleton linked to them.

Density-dependent inhibition and anchorage dependence appear to function in the body's tissues as well as in cell culture, checking the growth of cells at some optimal density and location. Cancer cells, which we discuss next, exhibit neither density-dependent inhibition nor anchorage dependence (Figure 12.19b).

Loss of Cell Cycle Controls in Cancer Cells

Cancer cells do not heed the normal signals that regulate the cell cycle. They divide excessively and invade other tissues. If unchecked, they can kill the organism.

Cancer cells in culture do not stop dividing when growth factors are depleted. A logical hypothesis is that cancer cells do not need growth factors in their culture medium to grow and divide. They may make a required growth factor themselves, or they may have an abnormality in the signaling pathway that conveys the growth factor's signal to the cell cycle control system even in the absence of that factor. Another possibility is an abnormal cell cycle control system. In all of these scenarios, the underlying basis of the abnormality is almost always a change in one or more genes that alters the function of their protein products, resulting in faulty cell cycle control. You will learn more in Chapter 18 about the genetic bases of these changes and how these conditions may lead to cancer.

There are other important differences between normal cells and cancer cells that reflect derangements of the cell cycle. If and when they stop dividing, cancer cells do so at random points in the cycle, rather than at the normal checkpoints. Moreover, cancer cells can go on dividing indefinitely in culture if they are given a continual supply of nutrients; in essence, they are "immortal." A striking example is a cell line that has been reproducing in culture since 1951. Cells of this line are called HeLa cells because their original source was a tumor removed from a woman named Henrietta Lacks. By contrast, nearly all normal mammalian cells growing in culture divide only about 20 to 50 times before they stop dividing, age, and die. (We'll see a possible reason for this phenomenon when we discuss DNA replication in Chapter 16.) Finally, cancer cells evade the normal controls that trigger a cell to undergo apoptosis when something is wrong—for example, when an irreparable mistake has occurred during DNA replication preceding mitosis.

The abnormal behavior of cancer cells can be catastrophic when it occurs in the body. The problem begins when a single cell in a tissue undergoes **transformation**, the process that converts a normal cell to a cancer cell. The body's immune system normally recognizes a transformed cell as an insurgent and destroys it. However, if the cell evades destruction, it may proliferate and form a tumor, a mass of abnormal cells within otherwise normal tissue. The abnormal cells may remain at the original site if they have too few genetic and cellular changes to survive at another site. In that case, the tumor is called a **benign tumor**. Most benign tumors do not cause serious problems and can be completely removed by surgery. In contrast, a **malignant tumor** includes cells whose genetic and cellular changes enable them to spread to new tissues and impair the functions of one or more organs. An individual with a malignant tumor is said to have cancer; Figure 12.20 shows the development of breast cancer.

The changes that have occurred in cells of malignant tumors show up in many ways besides excessive proliferation. These cells may have unusual numbers of chromosomes,

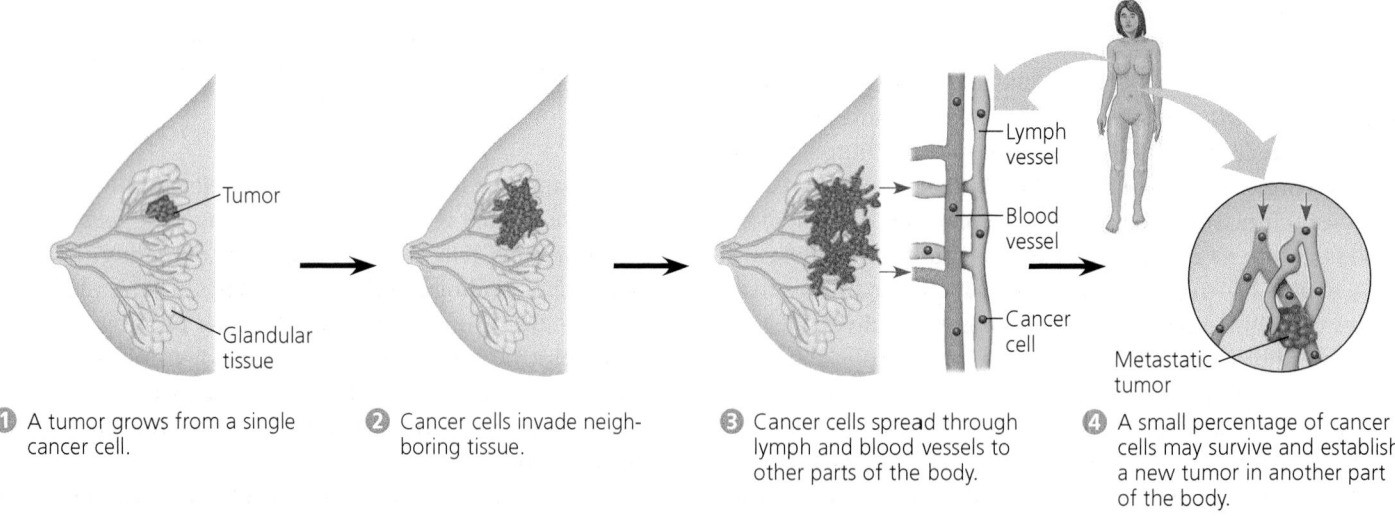

① A tumor grows from a single cancer cell.

② Cancer cells invade neighboring tissue.

③ Cancer cells spread through lymph and blood vessels to other parts of the body.

④ A small percentage of cancer cells may survive and establish a new tumor in another part of the body.

▲ Figure 12.20 **The growth and metastasis of a malignant breast tumor.** The cells of malignant (cancerous) tumors grow in an uncontrolled way and can spread to neighboring tissues and, via lymph and blood vessels, to other parts of the body. The spread of cancer cells beyond their original site is called metastasis.

though whether this is a cause or an effect of transformation is a current topic of debate. Their metabolism may be disabled, and they may cease to function in any constructive way. Abnormal changes on the cell surface cause cancer cells to lose attachments to neighboring cells and the extracellular matrix, allowing them to spread into nearby tissues. Cancer cells may also secrete signaling molecules that cause blood vessels to grow toward the tumor. A few tumor cells may separate from the original tumor, enter blood vessels and lymph vessels, and travel to other parts of the body. There, they may proliferate and form a new tumor. This spread of cancer cells to locations distant from their original site is called **metastasis** (see Figure 12.20).

A tumor that appears to be localized may be treated with high-energy radiation, which damages DNA in cancer cells much more than it does in normal cells, apparently because the majority of cancer cells have lost the ability to repair such damage. To treat known or suspected metastatic tumors, chemotherapy is used, in which drugs that are toxic to actively dividing cells are administered through the circulatory system. As you might expect, chemotherapeutic drugs interfere with specific steps in the cell cycle. For example, the drug Taxol freezes the mitotic spindle by preventing microtubule depolymerization, which stops actively dividing cells from proceeding past metaphase. The side effects of chemotherapy are due to the drugs' effects on normal cells that divide often. For example, nausea results from chemotherapy's effects on intestinal cells, hair loss from effects on hair follicle cells, and susceptibility to infection from effects on immune system cells.

Over the past several decades, researchers have produced a flood of valuable information about cell-signaling pathways and how their malfunction contributes to the development of cancer through effects on the cell cycle. Coupled with new molecular techniques, such as the ability to rapidly sequence the DNA of cells in a particular tumor, medical treatments for cancer are beginning to become more "personalized" to a particular patient's tumor. Breast cancer provides a good example. Basic research on the processes described in Chapters 11 and 12 has augmented our understanding of the molecular events underlying development of breast cancer. Proteins functioning in cell signaling pathways that affect the cell cycle are often found to be altered in breast cancer cells. Analyzing the level and sequences of such proteins has allowed physicians to better tailor the treatment to the cancers of some individuals, as shown in Figure 12.21.

One of the big lessons we've learned about the development of cancer, though, is how very complex the process is. There are many areas that remain to be explored. Perhaps the reason we have so many unanswered questions about cancer cells is that there is still so much to learn about how normal cells function. The cell, life's basic unit of structure and function, holds enough secrets to engage researchers well into the future.

▼ Figure 12.21

IMPACT

Advances in Treatment of Breast Cancer

Cancer cells, such as the breast cancer cell shown below, are analyzed by DNA sequencing and other molecular techniques to look for alterations in the level or sequence of specific proteins associated with cancer. For example, the cells of roughly 20–25% of breast cancer tumors show abnormally high amounts of a cell-surface receptor tyrosine kinase called HER2, and many show an increase in the number of estrogen receptor (ER) molecules, intracellular receptors that can trigger cell division. Based on lab findings, a physician can prescribe chemotherapy with a molecule that blocks the function of the specific protein (Herceptin for HER2 and tamoxifen for ERs). Treatment using these agents, when appropriate, has led to increased survival rates and fewer cancer recurrences.

WHY IT MATTERS Approximately one out of every eight women will develop breast cancer, the most common cancer among women. Worldwide, the incidence of breast cancer has been increasing annually. However, the mortality rate from this disease is falling in the United States and elsewhere, probably a result of earlier detection and improved treatment. Furthermore, what we are learning from the study of breast cancer also enhances our understanding of the development and treatment of other types of cancer.

FURTHER READING F. J. Esteva and G. N. Hortobagyi, Gaining ground on breast cancer, *Scientific American* 298:58–65 (2008).

MAKE CONNECTIONS Review the material in Chapter 11 on receptor tyrosine kinases and intracellular receptors (Figures 11.7 and 11.9 on pp. 212–214). Explain in general how these receptors might function in triggering cell division.

CONCEPT CHECK 12.3

1. In Figure 12.14, why do the nuclei resulting from experiment 2 contain different amounts of DNA?
2. How does MPF allow a cell to pass the G_2 phase checkpoint and enter mitosis? (See Figure 12.17.)
3. What phase are most of your body cells in?
4. Compare and contrast a benign tumor and a malignant tumor.
5. **WHAT IF?** What would happen if you performed the experiment in Figure 12.18 with cancer cells?

For suggested answers, see Appendix A.

SUMMARY OF KEY CONCEPTS

- Unicellular organisms reproduce by **cell division**; multicellular organisms depend on cell division for their development from a fertilized egg and for growth and repair. Cell division is part of the **cell cycle**, an ordered sequence of events in the life of a cell from its origin until it divides into daughter cells.

CONCEPT 12.1

Most cell division results in genetically identical daughter cells (pp. 229–230)

- The genetic material (DNA) of a cell—its **genome**—is partitioned among **chromosomes**. Each eukaryotic chromosome consists of one DNA molecule associated with many proteins that maintain chromosome structure and help control the activity of genes. Together, the complex of DNA and associated proteins is called **chromatin**. The chromatin of a chromosome exists in different states of condensation at different times. In animals, **gametes** have one set of chromosomes and **somatic cells** have two sets.
- Cells replicate their genetic material before they divide, ensuring that each daughter cell can receive a copy of the DNA. In preparation for cell division, chromosomes are duplicated, each one then consisting of two identical **sister chromatids** joined along their lengths by sister chromatid cohesion and held most tightly together at a constricted region at the **centromeres** of the chromatids. When this cohesion is broken, the chromatids separate during cell division, becoming the chromosomes of the new daughter cells. Eukaryotic cell division consists of **mitosis** (division of the nucleus) and **cytokinesis** (division of the cytoplasm).

? *Differentiate between these terms: chromosome, chromatin, and chromatid.*

CONCEPT 12.2

The mitotic phase alternates with interphase in the cell cycle (pp. 230–238)

- Between divisions, a cell is in **interphase**: the G_1, **S**, and G_2 phases. The cell grows throughout interphase, but DNA is replicated only during the synthesis (S) phase. Mitosis and cytokinesis make up the **mitotic (M) phase** of the cell cycle.

INTERPHASE
G_1
S
G_2

Cytokinesis
Mitosis
MITOTIC (M) PHASE

Telophase and Cytokinesis

Anaphase

Metaphase

Prometaphase

Prophase

- The **mitotic spindle** is an apparatus of microtubules that controls chromosome movement during mitosis. In animal cells, the spindle arises from the **centrosomes** and includes spindle microtubules and **asters**. Some spindle microtubules attach to the **kinetochores** of chromosomes and move the chromosomes to the **metaphase plate**. In anaphase, sister chromatids separate, and motor proteins move them along the kinetochore microtubules toward opposite ends of the cell. Meanwhile, motor proteins push nonkinetochore microtubules from opposite poles away from each other, elongating the cell. In telophase, genetically identical daughter nuclei form at opposite ends of the cell.
- Mitosis is usually followed by cytokinesis. Animal cells carry out cytokinesis by **cleavage**, and plant cells form a **cell plate**.
- During **binary fission** in bacteria, the chromosome replicates and the two daughter chromosomes actively move apart. Some of the proteins involved in bacterial binary fission are related to eukaryotic actin and tubulin.
- Since prokaryotes preceded eukaryotes by more than a billion years, it is likely that mitosis evolved from prokaryotic cell division. Certain unicellular eukaryotes exhibit mechanisms of cell division that may be similar to those of ancestors of existing eukaryotes. Such mechanisms might have been intermediate steps in the evolution of mitosis from bacterial binary fission.

? *In which of the three subphases of interphase and the stages of mitosis do chromosomes exist as single DNA molecules?*

CONCEPT 12.3

The eukaryotic cell cycle is regulated by a molecular control system (pp. 238–243)

- Signaling molecules present in the cytoplasm regulate progress through the cell cycle.
- The **cell cycle control system** is molecularly based. Cyclic changes in regulatory proteins work as a cell cycle clock. The key molecules are **cyclins** and **cyclin-dependent kinases (Cdks)**. The clock has specific **checkpoints** where the cell cycle stops until a go-ahead signal is received. Cell culture has enabled researchers to study the molecular details of cell division. Both internal signals and external signals control the cell cycle checkpoints via signal transduction pathways. Most cells exhibit **density-dependent inhibition** of cell division as well as **anchorage dependence**.
- Cancer cells elude normal cell cycle regulation and divide out of control, forming tumors. **Malignant tumors** invade surrounding tissues and can undergo **metastasis**, exporting cancer cells to other parts of the body, where they may form secondary tumors. Recent advances in understanding the cell cycle and cell signaling, as well as techniques for sequencing DNA, have allowed improvements in cancer treatment.

? *Explain the significance of the G_1, G_2, and M checkpoints and the go-ahead signals involved in the cell cycle control system.*

TEST YOUR UNDERSTANDING

LEVEL 1: KNOWLEDGE/COMPREHENSION

1. Through a microscope, you can see a cell plate beginning to develop across the middle of a cell and nuclei forming on either side of the cell plate. This cell is most likely
   a. an animal cell in the process of cytokinesis.
   b. a plant cell in the process of cytokinesis.

c. an animal cell in the S phase of the cell cycle.
d. a bacterial cell dividing.
e. a plant cell in metaphase.

2. Vinblastine is a standard chemotherapeutic drug used to treat cancer. Because it interferes with the assembly of microtubules, its effectiveness must be related to
   a. disruption of mitotic spindle formation.
   b. inhibition of regulatory protein phosphorylation.
   c. suppression of cyclin production.
   d. myosin denaturation and inhibition of cleavage furrow formation.
   e. inhibition of DNA synthesis.

3. One difference between cancer cells and normal cells is that cancer cells
   a. are unable to synthesize DNA.
   b. are arrested at the S phase of the cell cycle.
   c. continue to divide even when they are tightly packed together.
   d. cannot function properly because they are affected by density-dependent inhibition.
   e. are always in the M phase of the cell cycle.

4. The decline of MPF activity at the end of mitosis is due to
   a. the destruction of the protein kinase Cdk.
   b. decreased synthesis of Cdk.
   c. the degradation of cyclin.
   d. the accumulation of cyclin.
   e. synthesis of DNA.

5. In the cells of some organisms, mitosis occurs without cytokinesis. This will result in
   a. cells with more than one nucleus.
   b. cells that are unusually small.
   c. cells lacking nuclei.
   d. destruction of chromosomes.
   e. cell cycles lacking an S phase.

6. Which of the following does *not* occur during mitosis?
   a. condensation of the chromosomes
   b. replication of the DNA
   c. separation of sister chromatids
   d. spindle formation
   e. separation of the spindle poles

LEVEL 2: APPLICATION/ANALYSIS

7. In the light micrograph below of dividing cells near the tip of an onion root, identify a cell in each of the following stages: prophase, prometaphase, metaphase, anaphase, and telophase. Describe the major events occurring at each stage.

8. A particular cell has half as much DNA as some other cells in a mitotically active tissue. The cell in question is most likely in
   a. G$_1$.   c. prophase.   e. anaphase.
   b. G$_2$.   d. metaphase.

9. The drug cytochalasin B blocks the function of actin. Which of the following aspects of the animal cell cycle would be most disrupted by cytochalasin B?
   a. spindle formation
   b. spindle attachment to kinetochores
   c. DNA synthesis
   d. cell elongation during anaphase
   e. cleavage furrow formation and cytokinesis

10. **DRAW IT** Draw one eukaryotic chromosome as it would appear during interphase, during each of the stages of mitosis, and during cytokinesis. Also draw and label the nuclear envelope and any microtubules attached to the chromosome(s).

LEVEL 3: SYNTHESIS/EVALUATION

11. **EVOLUTION CONNECTION**
    The result of mitosis is that the daughter cells end up with the same number of chromosomes that the parent cell had. Another way to maintain the number of chromosomes would be to carry out cell division first and then duplicate the chromosomes in each daughter cell. Do you think this would be an equally good way of organizing the cell cycle? Why do you suppose that evolution has not led to this alternative?

12. **SCIENTIFIC INQUIRY**
    Although both ends of a microtubule can gain or lose subunits, one end (called the plus end) polymerizes and depolymerizes at a higher rate than the other end (the minus end). For spindle microtubules, the plus ends are in the center of the spindle, and the minus ends are at the poles. Motor proteins that move along microtubules specialize in walking either toward the plus end or toward the minus end; the two types are called plus end–directed and minus end–directed motor proteins, respectively. Given what you know about chromosome movement and spindle changes during anaphase, predict which type of motor proteins would be present on (a) kinetochore microtubules and (b) nonkinetochore microtubules.

13. **WRITE ABOUT A THEME**
    The Genetic Basis of Life The continuity of life is based on heritable information in the form of DNA. In a short essay (100–150 words), explain how the process of mitosis faithfully parcels out exact copies of this heritable information in the production of genetically identical daughter cells.

For selected answers, see Appendix A.

  www.masteringbiology.com

1. MasteringBiology® Assignments
BioFlix Tutorials Mitosis: Mitosis and the Cell Cycle • Mechanism of Mitosis • Comparing Cell Division in Animals, Plants, and Bacteria
Activities The Cell Cycle • Mitosis and Cytokinesis Animation • Four Phases of the Cell Cycle • Causes of Cancer • Discovery Channel Video: Fighting Cancer
Questions Student Misconceptions • Reading Quiz • Multiple Choice • End-of-Chapter

2. eText
Read your book online, search, take notes, highlight text, and more.

3. The Study Area
Practice Tests • Cumulative Test • **BioFlix** 3-D Animations • MP3 Tutor Sessions • Videos · Activities • Investigations • Lab Media • Audio Glossary • Word Study Tools • Art

UNIT 3

Genetics

An Interview with
Joan A. Steitz

RNA is Joan Steitz's favorite molecule, and her research into its structures and functions has made contributions of enormous importance to our understanding of genetics at the molecular level. Raised in Minnesota, Dr. Steitz has a B.S. in Chemistry from Antioch College and a Ph.D. in Biochemistry and Molecular Biology from Harvard, where she worked in the laboratory of James D. Watson. Among her many awards and honors are the National Medal of Science, the Gairdner International Award, and 12 honorary doctorates. She is a member of the National Academy of Sciences and the Institute of Medicine. A teacher and researcher at Yale University since 1970, she is now Sterling Professor of Molecular Biophysics and Biochemistry and an Investigator of the Howard Hughes Medical Institute.

How did you get started in molecular genetics?
I first learned about the structure of DNA in my third year of college, during a co-op job at MIT. I was enthralled with the idea that DNA might be the molecular basis for all of the genetics—red hair, wrinkled peas, and so forth—that I had learned about in high school. After that, I worked in a molecular biology lab in Germany as a student abroad. Nevertheless, I decided to go to medical school.

I didn't apply to a Ph.D. program because I'd never seen a woman heading up a research lab, and it didn't enter my mind that I could do that. But I did know some women physicians, so I applied to medical school and was admitted to Harvard. However, the summer before I was supposed to enter, I ended up working in the lab of cell biologist Joe Gall, then at the University of Minnesota. For the first time, I had my own project, and I loved it. By August 1st, I decided that I didn't care if I would never be the head of a lab; I just wanted to do research. Luckily, I was able to switch from the medical school to a graduate program at Harvard.

How did you end up as a graduate student of Jim Watson?
I was interested in the question of whether all cellular organelles have DNA, like mitochondria do. So I first approached a cell biolo-

gist, a famous microscopist who nevertheless reserved a bench in the corner of his lab for biochemistry. He conceded that his lab might be suitable, then gave me an unencouraging look and said, "But you're a woman. What are you going to do when you get married and have kids?" I barely made it out of his office before bursting into tears. Then I went to my second-choice thesis advisor, Jim Watson. I had done very well in his course, and he accepted me into his lab. So I became his first female graduate student, something I didn't discover until months later.

What was it like being in Watson's lab?
The Watson lab was a very exciting place at that time, in 1964. We knew that genes in DNA were transcribed into complementary RNA (a process called transcription) and that RNA called messenger RNA (mRNA) was translated into protein by ribosomes (translation). Besides mRNA, the only kinds of cellular RNA that were known were transfer RNA (tRNA) and ribosomal RNA (rRNA), although it was also known that some viruses had RNA instead of DNA as their genomes. But when I started grad school, we didn't yet know the genetic code—how the nucleotide sequence in mRNA corresponds to the amino acid sequence in protein—or much of anything about how transcription or translation occurred.

Jim would go off to meetings, and when he came back, everybody would crowd around him in the hall to find out what was new. Imagine the excitement when we heard, at an international biochemistry congress I actually attended, that the genetic code had been figured out! Or when someone in our lab discovered that a special kind of tRNA initiated protein synthesis. Things were happening very, very rapidly! The atmosphere was fiercely competitive but paradoxically collegial—the three or four labs that were working on the mechanisms of transcription and translation were all in contact with each other.

What was your research as a graduate student?
I worked on a newly discovered virus, R17, that infects the bacterium *E. coli*. Like other simple viruses, R17 is just a small amount of nucleic acid inside a protein coat. Throughout that era, molecular biologists fervently believed that unless you worked on something really simple, you would never figure out the molecular basis of life. So a virus that had only three genes (later found to be four) was the perfect thing to study.

The nucleic acid of R17, its genome, is RNA. This RNA gets into bacterial cells, and about an hour later out come 10,000 copies of the virus. So lots of things are happening in those cells. I studied a viral protein called the A-protein. For my thesis, I characterized the A-protein and what happened if there were mutations in its gene: You got virus particles that looked normal in the electron microscope but couldn't infect a bacterium. It turned out that the A-protein was needed for the virus to attach to the cell.

What did you do after graduate school?
I was married by then, and my husband had arranged to do a postdoc at the Medical Research Council (MRC) at Cambridge University, a mecca for structural and molecular biology. Jim Watson had written to Francis Crick asking him to find a place for me, but when I arrived at Cambridge, Francis suggested I do library research. Eventually, however, I found a bit of bench space for a lab project.

Fred Sanger's lab was nearby, and he was just working out his method for sequencing RNA. There was a lot of interchange with the people in Fred's lab, and they were very interested in the sequence of the R17 genome. Since it was very small, it was a really good molecule to work on. Previously, a paper had been published describing a method for isolating the particular stretches of mRNA bound to a functioning ribosome: You treated the mRNA-ribosome complex with ribonuclease, an enzyme that breaks down unprotected RNA, and you ended up with the part of the mRNA that had been bound and therefore protected by the ribosome, about 30 nucleotides long. The project I took on was to make ribosomes bind to R17 RNA (which functions as mRNA in normal virus infection) under conditions where they start but do not elongate proteins, and then isolate the ribosome-bound RNA segments. I would then determine the sequence of the parts of this RNA where translation started. Other people had considered and rejected this project. They were all male postdocs with wives and children who knew that in two years they would have to interview for tenure-track jobs, and this project had little chance of quick success. But since I thought I couldn't aim higher than a research position in somebody else's lab, I felt free to take on a risky project. (So, being a woman determined the two most important decisions of my early scientific career: ending up in Watson's lab and choosing my project at Cambridge.)

I determined the RNA nucleotide sequences at the beginning of the three R17 genes known at the time. These sequences included AUG, already known to be the "start codon" in mRNA (the first nucleotide triplet translated). And the sequences that followed AUG fit what was already known about the protein sequences, according to the genetic code. We also established that there were spaces between genes in the viral genome. And we figured out that sometimes the virus RNA folded into secondary structures that were important in regulating how many ribosomes would get on at a particular start site. This work at Cambridge—and better academic opportunities for women in the United States—led to my faculty position at Yale.

When you arrived at Yale, what was your first big discovery?
I found out how ribosomes locate the regions on mRNA where they attach and start translation. At Cambridge I had worked out the three 30-nucleotide sequences where ribosomes bind to R17 RNA, but it still wasn't clear how ribosomes homed in on these sequences out of the virus's 3,500 nucleotides. One idea was that a stretch of mRNA rich in purines, just upstream of where translation actually starts, would base-pair with the 3′ end of the rRNA molecule in the small ribosomal subunit of bacteria. So I went to work testing that hypothesis. I soon had direct evidence that there actually is a physical interaction between the end of the "16S" rRNA molecule and the regions of mRNA that are bound by ribosomes. So this RNA-RNA base pairing, along with RNA-RNA base pairing between tRNA and mRNA, is the basis of polypeptide initiation.

You then turned to eukaryotic mRNA. What is different about mRNA production in eukaryotic cells, compared with bacteria?
The main difference comes from the fact that the genes of humans and other eukaryotes have interruptions in them, stretches of nucleic acid that are not translated. These interruptions, called *introns*, have to be removed from the RNA transcript before it is translated. But we didn't know this when I got interested in the subject. At that time, all we knew was that only 5–10% of the RNA transcribed from eukaryotic genes got out of the nucleus as mRNA. I was intrigued by this mystery and decided to switch from prokaryotes to eukaryotes to try to study it. Then, when introns were discovered, the reason for the loss of RNA became clear—though not how the extra RNA was removed. To make mRNA, somehow the introns have to be precisely removed and the coding bits have to be glued back together—a process called RNA splicing.

What have you learned since then about RNA splicing?
The most important molecular players are small RNA molecules that base-pair with sequences at the ends of RNA introns. This base pairing initiates the assembly of a ribosome-sized machine called a *spliceosome* made of RNA-protein subunits called snRNPs (pronounced "snurps") and other proteins. A spliceosome removes introns and joins together the protein-coding pieces. So RNA-RNA base pairing is the basis of the whole splicing process, just like it's the basis of the initiation of translation. Now there is more and more evidence that the RNAs are the catalytic components of the spliceosome, with the proteins playing supporting roles.

Does your research have any medical relevance?
We learned early on that people with lupus, an autoimmune disease, make antibodies to snRNPs, the RNA-protein subunits of spliceosomes. This discovery has been useful for the diagnosis of a number of autoimmune diseases and even for the prognosis of individual patients—although it hasn't led to cures. What we do in my lab, however, is very basic research. Somebody's got to figure out the basics in order for somebody else to figure out how to apply it.

What's going on now in the RNA field?
Lots of new classes of small RNA molecules have been discovered that, like rRNA, tRNA, and the RNAs in snRNPs, do not themselves code for protein. All these RNAs are important in getting information out of the DNA and into the functioning proteins of the cell. For instance, tiny RNAs called microRNAs, which associate with particular proteins, are involved in regulating translation. Again, it's RNA-RNA base pairing that determines the specificity. The theme of my research over my entire career has been finding out how RNAs interact with other RNAs to provide specificity along the pathway of gene expression. Proteins play important auxiliary roles, but it's basically been one RNA interacting with another RNA. I started working on RNA while I was a student, and it has continued to be my favorite molecule! There's enough to learn to last for many more lifetimes.

What do the discoveries about RNA suggest about the early stages of life on Earth?
Most biologists think that RNA was the first and most important genetic material, probably serving the first cells as both genome and the means by which the information in the genome directed cellular functions. Over time, cells have replaced the RNA genome with DNA, and many of the other RNA molecules with proteins. But the crucial processes of gene expression and its regulation are still dependent on various RNAs— 4 billion years after life first arose!

> "I started working on RNA while I was a student, and it has continued to be my favorite molecule!"

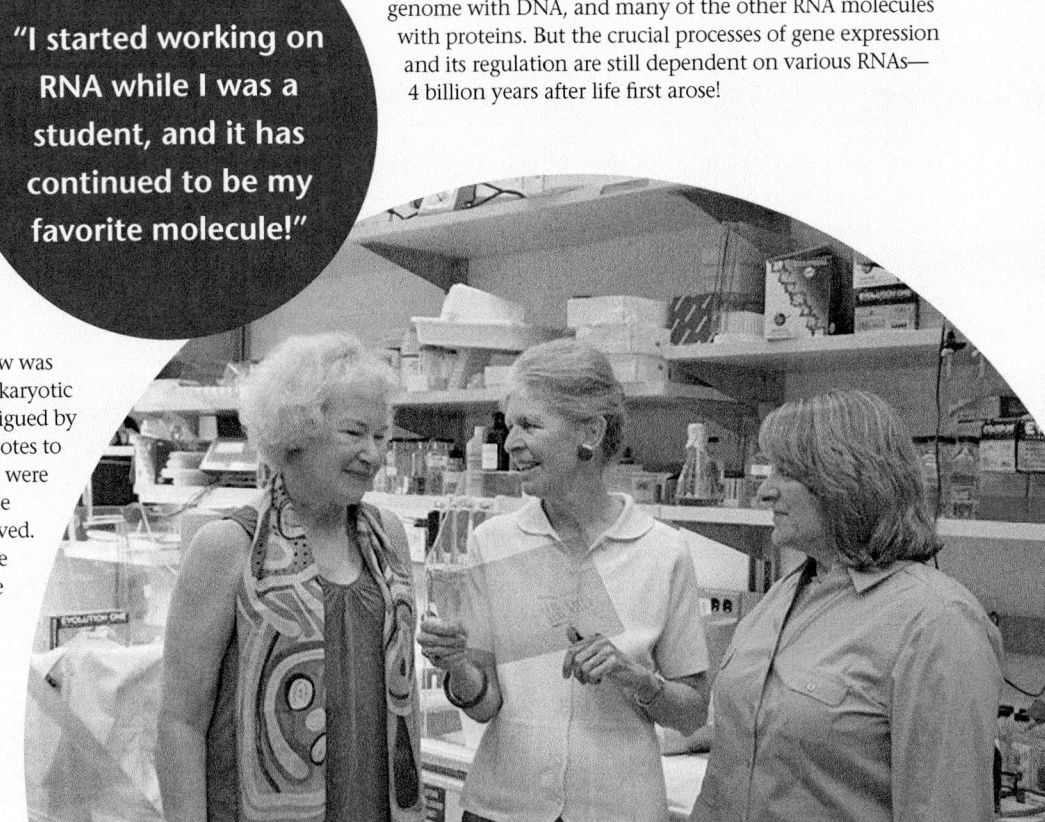

13

Meiosis and Sexual Life Cycles

▲ Figure 13.1 **What accounts for family resemblance?**

KEY CONCEPTS

13.1 Offspring acquire genes from parents by inheriting chromosomes

13.2 Fertilization and meiosis alternate in sexual life cycles

13.3 Meiosis reduces the number of chromosome sets from diploid to haploid

13.4 Genetic variation produced in sexual life cycles contributes to evolution

OVERVIEW

Variations on a Theme

Most people who send out birth announcements mention the sex of the baby, but they don't feel the need to specify that their offspring is a human being! One of the characteristics of life is the ability of organisms to reproduce their own kind—elephants produce little elephants, and oak trees gen-

erate oak saplings. Exceptions to this rule show up only as sensational but highly suspect stories in tabloid newspapers.

Another rule often taken for granted is that offspring resemble their parents more than they do unrelated individuals. If you examine the family members shown in **Figure 13.1**—actress Sissy Spacek and her husband Jack Fisk with daughters Madison and Schuyler Fisk—you can pick out some similar features among them. The transmission of traits from one generation to the next is called inheritance, or **heredity** (from the Latin *heres*, heir). However, sons and daughters are not identical copies of either parent or of their siblings. Along with inherited similarity, there is also **variation**. Farmers have exploited the principles of heredity and variation for thousands of years, breeding plants and animals for desired traits. But what are the biological mechanisms leading to the hereditary similarity and variation that we call a "family resemblance"? The answer to this question eluded biologists until the advance of genetics in the 20th century.

Genetics is the scientific study of heredity and hereditary variation. In this unit, you will learn about genetics at multiple levels, from organisms to cells to molecules. On the practical side, you will see how genetics continues to revolutionize medicine and agriculture, and you will be asked to consider some social and ethical questions raised by our ability to manipulate DNA, the genetic material. At the end of the unit, you will be able to stand back and consider the whole genome, an organism's entire complement of DNA. Rapid acquisition and analysis of the genome sequences of many species, including our own, have taught us a great deal about evolution on the molecular level—in other words, evolution of the genome itself. In fact, genetic methods and discoveries are catalyzing progress in all areas of biology, from cell biology to physiology, developmental biology, behavior, and even ecology.

We begin our study of genetics in this chapter by examining how chromosomes pass from parents to offspring in sexually reproducing organisms. The processes of meiosis (a special type of cell division) and fertilization (the fusion of sperm and egg) maintain a species' chromosome count during the sexual life cycle. We will describe the cellular mechanics of meiosis and explain how this process differs from mitosis. Finally, we will consider how both meiosis and fertilization contribute to genetic variation, such as the variation obvious in the family shown in Figure 13.1.

CONCEPT 13.1

Offspring acquire genes from parents by inheriting chromosomes

Family friends may tell you that you have your mother's freckles or your father's eyes. Of course, parents do not, in any literal sense, give their children freckles, eyes, hair, or any other traits. What, then, *is* actually inherited?

Inheritance of Genes

Parents endow their offspring with coded information in the form of hereditary units called **genes**. The genes we inherit from our mothers and fathers are our genetic link to our parents, and they account for family resemblances such as shared eye color or freckles. Our genes program the specific traits that emerge as we develop from fertilized eggs into adults.

The genetic program is written in the language of DNA, the polymer of four different nucleotides you learned about in Chapters 1 and 5. Inherited information is passed on in the form of each gene's specific sequence of DNA nucleotides, much as printed information is communicated in the form of meaningful sequences of letters. In both cases, the language is symbolic. Just as your brain translates the word *apple* into a mental image of the fruit, cells translate genes into freckles and other features. Most genes program cells to synthesize specific enzymes and other proteins, whose cumulative action produces an organism's inherited traits. The programming of these traits in the form of DNA is one of the unifying themes of biology.

The transmission of hereditary traits has its molecular basis in the precise replication of DNA, which produces copies of genes that can be passed from parents to offspring. In animals and plants, reproductive cells called **gametes** are the vehicles that transmit genes from one generation to the next. During fertilization, male and female gametes (sperm and eggs) unite, thereby passing on genes of both parents to their offspring.

Except for small amounts of DNA in mitochondria and chloroplasts, the DNA of a eukaryotic cell is packaged into chromosomes within the nucleus. Every species has a characteristic number of chromosomes. For example, humans have 46 chromosomes in their **somatic cells**—all cells of the body except the gametes and their precursors. Each chromosome consists of a single long DNA molecule elaborately coiled in association with various proteins. One chromosome includes several hundred to a few thousand genes, each of which is a specific sequence of nucleotides within the DNA molecule. A gene's specific location along the length of a chromosome is called the gene's **locus** (plural, *loci*; from the Latin, meaning "place"). Our genetic endowment consists of the genes that are part of the chromosomes we inherited from our parents.

Comparison of Asexual and Sexual Reproduction

Only organisms that reproduce asexually have offspring that are exact genetic copies of themselves. In **asexual reproduction**, a single individual is the sole parent and passes copies of all its genes to its offspring without the fusion of gametes. For example, single-celled eukaryotic organisms can reproduce asexually by mitotic cell division, in which DNA is copied and allocated equally to two daughter cells. The genomes of the offspring are virtually exact copies of the parent's genome. Some multicellular organisms are also capable of reproducing

 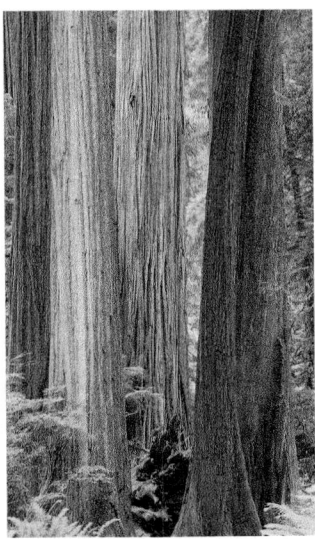

(a) Hydra   **(b) Redwoods**

▲ **Figure 13.2 Asexual reproduction in two multicellular organisms. (a)** This relatively simple animal, a hydra, reproduces by budding. The bud, a localized mass of mitotically dividing cells, develops into a small hydra, which detaches from the parent (LM). **(b)** All the trees in this circle of redwoods arose asexually from a single parent tree, whose stump is in the center of the circle.

asexually (**Figure 13.2**). Because the cells of the offspring are derived by mitosis in the parent, the "chip off the old block" is usually genetically identical to its parent. An individual that reproduces asexually gives rise to a **clone**, a group of genetically identical individuals. Genetic differences occasionally arise in asexually reproducing organisms as a result of changes in the DNA called mutations, which we will discuss in Chapter 17.

In **sexual reproduction**, two parents give rise to offspring that have unique combinations of genes inherited from the two parents. In contrast to a clone, offspring of sexual reproduction vary genetically from their siblings and both parents: They are variations on a common theme of family resemblance, not exact replicas. Genetic variation like that shown in Figure 13.1 is an important consequence of sexual reproduction. What mechanisms generate this genetic variation? The key is the behavior of chromosomes during the sexual life cycle.

CONCEPT CHECK 13.1

1. Explain what causes the traits of parents (such as hair color) to show up in their offspring.
2. How do asexually reproducing organisms produce offspring that are genetically identical to each other and to their parents?
3. **WHAT IF?** A horticulturalist breeds orchids, trying to obtain a plant with a unique combination of desirable traits. After many years, she finally succeeds. To produce more plants like this one, should she cross-breed it with another plant or clone it? Why?

For suggested answers, see Appendix A.

Fertilization and meiosis alternate in sexual life cycles

A **life cycle** is the generation-to-generation sequence of stages in the reproductive history of an organism, from conception to production of its own offspring. In this section, we use humans as an example to track the behavior of chromosomes through the sexual life cycle. We begin by considering the chromosome count in human somatic cells and gametes. We will then explore how the behavior of chromosomes relates to the human life cycle and other types of sexual life cycles.

Sets of Chromosomes in Human Cells

In humans, each somatic cell has 46 chromosomes. During mitosis, the chromosomes become condensed enough to be visible under a light microscope. At this point, they can be distinguished from one another by their size, the positions of their centromeres, and the pattern of colored bands produced by certain stains.

Careful examination of a micrograph of the 46 human chromosomes from a single cell in mitosis reveals that there are two chromosomes of each of 23 types. This becomes clear when images of the chromosomes are arranged in pairs, starting with the longest chromosomes. The resulting ordered display is called a **karyotype** (Figure 13.3). The two chromosomes composing a pair have the same length, centromere position, and staining pattern: These are called **homologous chromosomes**, or homologs. Both chromosomes of each pair carry genes controlling the same inherited characters. For example, if a gene for eye color is situated at a particular locus on a certain chromosome, then the homolog of that chromosome will also have a version of the same gene specifying eye color at the equivalent locus.

The two distinct chromosomes referred to as X and Y are an important exception to the general pattern of homologous chromosomes in human somatic cells. Human females have a homologous pair of X chromosomes (XX), but males have one X and one Y chromosome (XY). Only small parts of the X and Y are homologous. Most of the genes carried on the X chromosome do not have counterparts on the tiny Y, and the Y chromosome has genes lacking on the X. Because they determine an individual's sex, the X and Y chromosomes are called **sex chromosomes**. The other chromosomes are called **autosomes**.

The occurrence of pairs of homologous chromosomes in each human somatic cell is a consequence of our sexual origins. We inherit one chromosome of each pair from each parent. Thus, the 46 chromosomes in our somatic cells are actually two sets of 23 chromosomes—a maternal set (from our mother) and a paternal set (from our father). The number of chromosomes in

▼ **Figure 13.3**

RESEARCH METHOD

Preparing a Karyotype

APPLICATION A karyotype is a display of condensed chromosomes arranged in pairs. Karyotyping can be used to screen for defective chromosomes or abnormal numbers of chromosomes associated with certain congenital disorders, such as Down syndrome.

TECHNIQUE Karyotypes are prepared from isolated somatic cells, which are treated with a drug to stimulate mitosis and then grown in culture for several days. Cells arrested in metaphase, when chromosomes are most highly condensed, are stained and then viewed with a microscope equipped with a digital camera. A photograph of the chromosomes is displayed on a computer monitor, and the images of the chromosomes are arranged into pairs according to their appearance.

Pair of homologous duplicated chromosomes

Centromere

5 μm

Sister chromatids

Metaphase chromosome

RESULTS This karyotype shows the chromosomes from a normal human male. The size of the chromosome, position of the centromere, and pattern of stained bands help identify specific chromosomes. Although difficult to discern in the karyotype, each metaphase chromosome consists of two closely attached sister chromatids (see the diagram of a pair of homologous duplicated chromosomes).

a single set is represented by n. Any cell with two chromosome sets is called a **diploid cell** and has a diploid number of chromosomes, abbreviated $2n$. For humans, the diploid number is 46 ($2n = 46$), the number of chromosomes in our somatic cells. In a cell in which DNA synthesis has occurred, all the chromosomes are duplicated, and therefore each consists of two identical sister chromatids, associated closely at the centromere and along the arms. **Figure 13.4** helps clarify the various terms that we use to describe duplicated chromosomes in a diploid cell. Study this figure so that you understand the differences between homologous chromosomes, sister chromatids, nonsister chromatids, and chromosome sets.

Unlike somatic cells, gametes contain a single set of chromosomes. Such cells are called **haploid cells**, and each has a haploid number of chromosomes (n). For humans, the haploid number is 23 ($n = 23$). The set of 23 consists of the 22 autosomes plus a single sex chromosome. An unfertilized egg contains an X chromosome, but a sperm may contain an X or a Y chromosome.

Note that each sexually reproducing species has a characteristic diploid number and haploid number. For example, the fruit fly, *Drosophila melanogaster*, has a diploid number ($2n$) of 8 and a haploid number (n) of 4, while dogs have a diploid number of 78 and a haploid number of 39.

Now that you have learned the concepts of diploid and haploid numbers of chromosomes, let's consider chromosome behavior during sexual life cycles. We'll use the human life cycle as an example.

Key

$2n = 6$
- ▪ Maternal set of chromosomes ($n = 3$)
- ▪ Paternal set of chromosomes ($n = 3$)

Sister chromatids of one duplicated chromosome

Centromere

Two nonsister chromatids in a homologous pair

Pair of homologous chromosomes (one from each set)

▲ **Figure 13.4 Describing chromosomes.** A cell from an organism with a diploid number of 6 ($2n = 6$) is depicted here following chromosome duplication and condensation. Each of the six duplicated chromosomes consists of two sister chromatids associated closely along their lengths. Each homologous pair is composed of one chromosome from the maternal set (red) and one from the paternal set (blue). Each set is made up of three chromosomes in this example. Nonsister chromatids are any two chromatids in a pair of homologous chromosomes that are not sister chromatids—in other words, one maternal and one paternal chromatid.

? *What is the haploid number of this cell? Is a "set" of chromosomes haploid or diploid?*

Behavior of Chromosome Sets in the Human Life Cycle

The human life cycle begins when a haploid sperm from the father fuses with a haploid egg from the mother. This union of gametes, culminating in fusion of their nuclei, is called **fertilization**. The resulting fertilized egg, or **zygote**, is diploid because it contains two haploid sets of chromosomes bearing genes representing the maternal and paternal family lines. As a human develops into a sexually mature adult, mitosis of the zygote and its descendant cells generates all the somatic cells of the body. Both chromosome sets in the zygote and all the genes they carry are passed with precision to the somatic cells.

The only cells of the human body not produced by mitosis are the gametes, which develop from specialized cells called *germ cells* in the gonads—ovaries in females and testes in males **(Figure 13.5)**. Imagine what would happen if human gametes were made by mitosis: They would be diploid like the somatic cells. At the next round of fertilization, when two gametes fused, the normal chromosome number of 46 would

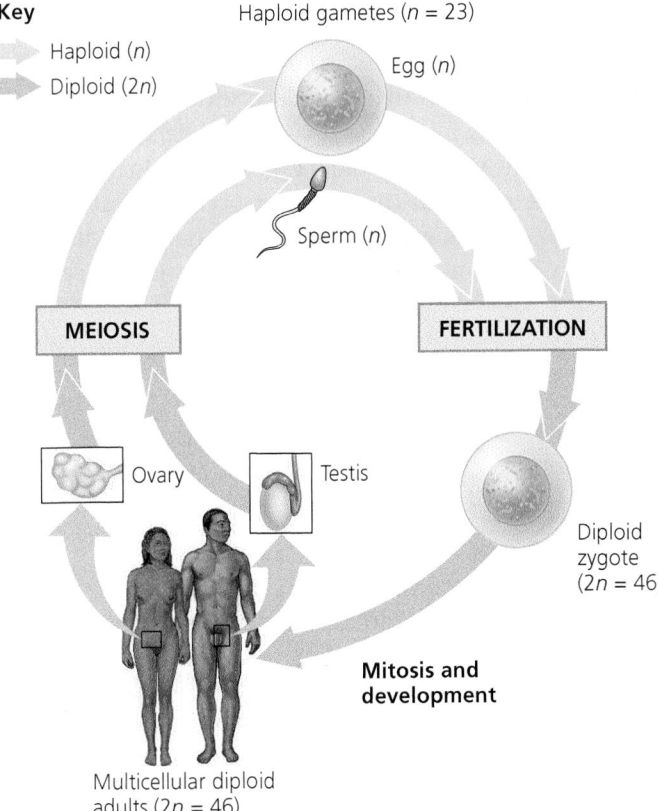

Key
- ▷ Haploid (n)
- ▷ Diploid ($2n$)

Haploid gametes ($n = 23$)

Egg (n)

Sperm (n)

MEIOSIS

FERTILIZATION

Ovary

Testis

Diploid zygote ($2n = 46$)

Mitosis and development

Multicellular diploid adults ($2n = 46$)

▲ **Figure 13.5 The human life cycle.** In each generation, the number of chromosome sets doubles at fertilization but is halved during meiosis. For humans, the number of chromosomes in a haploid cell is 23, consisting of one set ($n = 23$); the number of chromosomes in the diploid zygote and all somatic cells arising from it is 46, consisting of two sets ($2n = 46$).

This figure introduces a color code that will be used for other life cycles later in this book. The aqua arrows identify haploid stages of a life cycle, and the tan arrows identify diploid stages.

double to 92, and each subsequent generation would double the number of chromosomes yet again. This does not happen, however, because in sexually reproducing organisms, gamete formation involves a type of cell division called **meiosis**. This type of cell division reduces the number of sets of chromosomes from two to one in the gametes, counterbalancing the doubling that occurs at fertilization. In animals, meiosis occurs only in germ cells, which are in the ovaries or testes. As a result of meiosis, each human sperm and egg is haploid ($n = 23$). Fertilization restores the diploid condition by combining two haploid sets of chromosomes, and the human life cycle is repeated, generation after generation (see Figure 13.5). You will learn more about the production of sperm and eggs in Chapter 46.

In general, the steps of the human life cycle are typical of many sexually reproducing animals. Indeed, the processes of fertilization and meiosis are the hallmarks of sexual reproduction in plants, fungi, and protists as well as in animals. Fertilization and meiosis alternate in sexual life cycles, maintaining a constant number of chromosomes in each species from one generation to the next.

The Variety of Sexual Life Cycles

Although the alternation of meiosis and fertilization is common to all organisms that reproduce sexually, the timing of these two events in the life cycle varies, depending on the species. These variations can be grouped into three main types of life cycles. In the type that occurs in humans and most other animals, gametes are the only haploid cells. Meiosis occurs in germ cells during the production of gametes,

which undergo no further cell division prior to fertilization. After fertilization, the diploid zygote divides by mitosis, producing a multicellular organism that is diploid (**Figure 13.6a**).

Plants and some species of algae exhibit a second type of life cycle called **alternation of generations**. This type includes both diploid and haploid stages that are multicellular. The multicellular diploid stage is called the *sporophyte*. Meiosis in the sporophyte produces haploid cells called *spores*. Unlike a gamete, a haploid spore doesn't fuse with another cell but divides mitotically, generating a multicellular haploid stage called the *gametophyte*. Cells of the gametophyte give rise to gametes by mitosis. Fusion of two haploid gametes at fertilization results in a diploid zygote, which develops into the next sporophyte generation. Therefore, in this type of life cycle, the sporophyte generation produces a gametophyte as its offspring, and the gametophyte generation produces the next sporophyte generation (**Figure 13.6b**). Clearly, the term *alternation of generations* is a fitting name for this type of life cycle.

A third type of life cycle occurs in most fungi and some protists, including some algae. After gametes fuse and form a diploid zygote, meiosis occurs without a multicellular diploid offspring developing. Meiosis produces not gametes but haploid cells that then divide by mitosis and give rise to either unicellular descendants or a haploid multicellular adult organism. Subsequently, the haploid organism carries out further mitoses, producing the cells that develop into gametes. The only diploid stage found in these species is the single-celled zygote (**Figure 13.6c**).

Note that *either* haploid or diploid cells can divide by mitosis, depending on the type of life cycle. Only diploid cells,

Key

➤ Haploid (*n*)
➤ Diploid (2*n*)

(a) Animals

(b) Plants and some algae

(c) Most fungi and some protists

▲ **Figure 13.6 Three types of sexual life cycles.** The common feature of all three cycles is the alternation of meiosis and fertilization, key events that contribute to genetic variation among offspring. The cycles differ in the timing of these two key events.

however, can undergo meiosis because haploid cells have a single set of chromosomes that cannot be further reduced. Though the three types of sexual life cycles differ in the timing of meiosis and fertilization, they share a fundamental result: genetic variation among offspring. A closer look at meiosis will reveal the sources of this variation.

CONCEPT 13.3

Meiosis reduces the number of chromosome sets from diploid to haploid

Many of the steps of meiosis closely resemble corresponding steps in mitosis. Meiosis, like mitosis, is preceded by the duplication of chromosomes. However, this single duplication is followed by not one but two consecutive cell divisions, called **meiosis I** and **meiosis II**. These two divisions result in four daughter cells (rather than the two daughter cells of mitosis), each with only half as many chromosomes as the parent cell.

The Stages of Meiosis

The overview of meiosis in **Figure 13.7** shows, for a single pair of homologous chromosomes in a diploid cell, that both members of the pair are duplicated and the copies sorted into four haploid daughter cells. Recall that sister chromatids are two copies of *one* chromosome, closely associated all along their lengths; this association is called *sister chromatid cohesion*. Together, the sister chromatids make up one duplicated chromosome (see Figure 13.4). In contrast, the two chromosomes of a homologous pair are individual chromosomes that were inherited from different parents. Homologs appear alike in the microscope, but they may have different versions of genes, each called an *allele*, at corresponding loci (for example, an allele for freckles on one chromosome and an

▲ Figure 13.7 **Overview of meiosis: how meiosis reduces chromosome number.** After the chromosomes duplicate in interphase, the diploid cell divides *twice*, yielding four haploid daughter cells. This overview tracks just one pair of homologous chromosomes, which for the sake of simplicity are drawn in the condensed state throughout. (They would not normally be condensed during interphase.) The red chromosome was inherited from the female parent, the blue chromosome from the male parent.

DRAW IT *Redraw the cells in this figure using a simple double helix to represent each DNA molecule.*

allele for the absence of freckles at the same locus on the homolog). Homologs are not associated with each other in any obvious way except during meiosis, as you will soon see.

Figure 13.8, on the next two pages, describes in detail the stages of the two divisions of meiosis for an animal cell whose diploid number is 6. Meiosis halves the total number of chromosomes in a very specific way, reducing the number of sets from two to one, with each daughter cell receiving one set of chromosomes. Study Figure 13.8 thoroughly before going on.

▼ Figure 13.8

Exploring Meiosis in an Animal Cell

MEIOSIS I: Separates homologous chromosomes

Prophase I	Metaphase I	Anaphase I	Telophase I and Cytokinesis

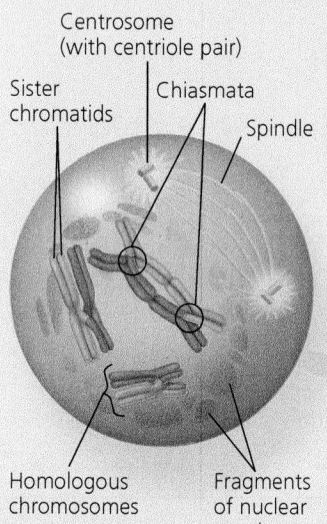

Centrosome (with centriole pair)

Sister chromatids

Chiasmata

Spindle

Homologous chromosomes

Fragments of nuclear envelope

Duplicated homologous chromosomes (red and blue) pair and exchange segments; 2n = 6 in this example.

Centromere (with kinetochore)

Metaphase plate

Microtubule attached to kinetochore

Chromosomes line up by homologous pairs.

Sister chromatids remain attached

Homologous chromosomes separate

Each pair of homologous chromosomes separates.

Cleavage furrow

Two haploid cells form; each chromosome still consists of two sister chromatids.

Prophase I

During early prophase I, before the stage shown above:

- Chromosomes begin to condense, and homologs loosely pair along their lengths, aligned gene by gene.

- Paired homologs become physically connected to each other along their lengths by a zipper-like protein structure, the *synaptonemal complex;* this state is called **synapsis.**

- **Crossing over**, a genetic rearrangement between non-sister chromatids involving the exchange of corresponding segments of DNA molecules, begins during pairing and synaptonemal complex formation, and is completed while homologs are in synapsis.

At the stage shown above:

- Synapsis has ended with the disassembly of the synaptonemal complex in mid-prophase, and the

chromosomes in each pair have moved apart slightly.

- Each homologous pair has one or more X-shaped regions called **chiasmata** (singular, *chiasma*). A chiasma exists at the point where a crossover has occurred. It appears as a cross because sister chromatid cohesion still holds the two original sister chromatids together, even in regions beyond the crossover point, where one chromatid is now part of the other homolog.

- Centrosome movement, spindle formation, and nuclear envelope breakdown occur as in mitosis.

Later in prophase I, after the stage shown above:

- Microtubules from one pole or the other attach to the two kinetochores, protein structures at the centromeres of the two homologs. The homologous pairs then move toward the metaphase plate.

Metaphase I

- Pairs of homologous chromosomes are now arranged at the metaphase plate, with one chromosome in each pair facing each pole.

- Both chromatids of one homolog are attached to kinetochore microtubules from one pole; those of the other homolog are attached to microtubules from the opposite pole.

Anaphase I

- Breakdown of proteins responsible for sister chromatid cohesion along chromatid arms allows homologs to separate.

- The homologs move toward opposite poles, guided by the spindle apparatus.

- Sister chromatid cohesion persists at the centromere, causing chromatids to move as a unit toward the same pole.

Telophase I and Cytokinesis

- At the beginning of telophase I, each half of the cell has a complete haploid set of duplicated chromosomes. Each chromosome is composed of two sister chromatids; one or both chromatids include regions of nonsister chromatid DNA.

- Cytokinesis (division of the cytoplasm) usually occurs simultaneously with telophase I, forming two haploid daughter cells.

- In animal cells like these, a cleavage furrow forms. (In plant cells, a cell plate forms.)

- In some species, chromosomes decondense and nuclear envelopes form.

- No chromosome duplication occurs between meiosis I and meiosis II.

MEIOSIS II: Separates sister chromatids

Prophase II	Metaphase II	Anaphase II	Telophase II and Cytokinesis

During another round of cell division, the sister chromatids finally separate; four haploid daughter cells result, containing unduplicated chromosomes.

Sister chromatids separate

Haploid daughter cells forming

Prophase II

- A spindle apparatus forms.
- In late prophase II (not shown here), chromosomes, each still composed of two chromatids associated at the centromere, move toward the metaphase II plate.

Metaphase II

- The chromosomes are positioned at the metaphase plate as in mitosis.
- Because of crossing over in meiosis I, the two sister chromatids of each chromosome are *not* genetically identical.
- The kinetochores of sister chromatids are attached to microtubules extending from opposite poles.

Anaphase II

- Breakdown of proteins holding the sister chromatids together at the centromere allows the chromatids to separate. The chromatids move toward opposite poles as individual chromosomes.

Telophase II and Cytokinesis

- Nuclei form, the chromosomes begin decondensing, and cytokinesis occurs.
- The meiotic division of one parent cell produces four daughter cells, each with a haploid set of (unduplicated) chromosomes.
- The four daughter cells are genetically distinct from one another and from the parent cell.

MAKE CONNECTIONS *Look at Figure 12.7 and imagine the two daughter cells undergoing another round of mitosis, yielding four cells. Compare the number of chromosomes in each of those four cells, after mitosis, with the number in each cell in Figure 13.8, after meiosis. What is it about the process of meiosis that accounts for this difference, even though meiosis also includes two cell divisions?*

ANIMATION **BioFlix** Visit the Study Area at **www.masteringbiology.com** for the BioFlix® 3-D Animation on Meiosis.

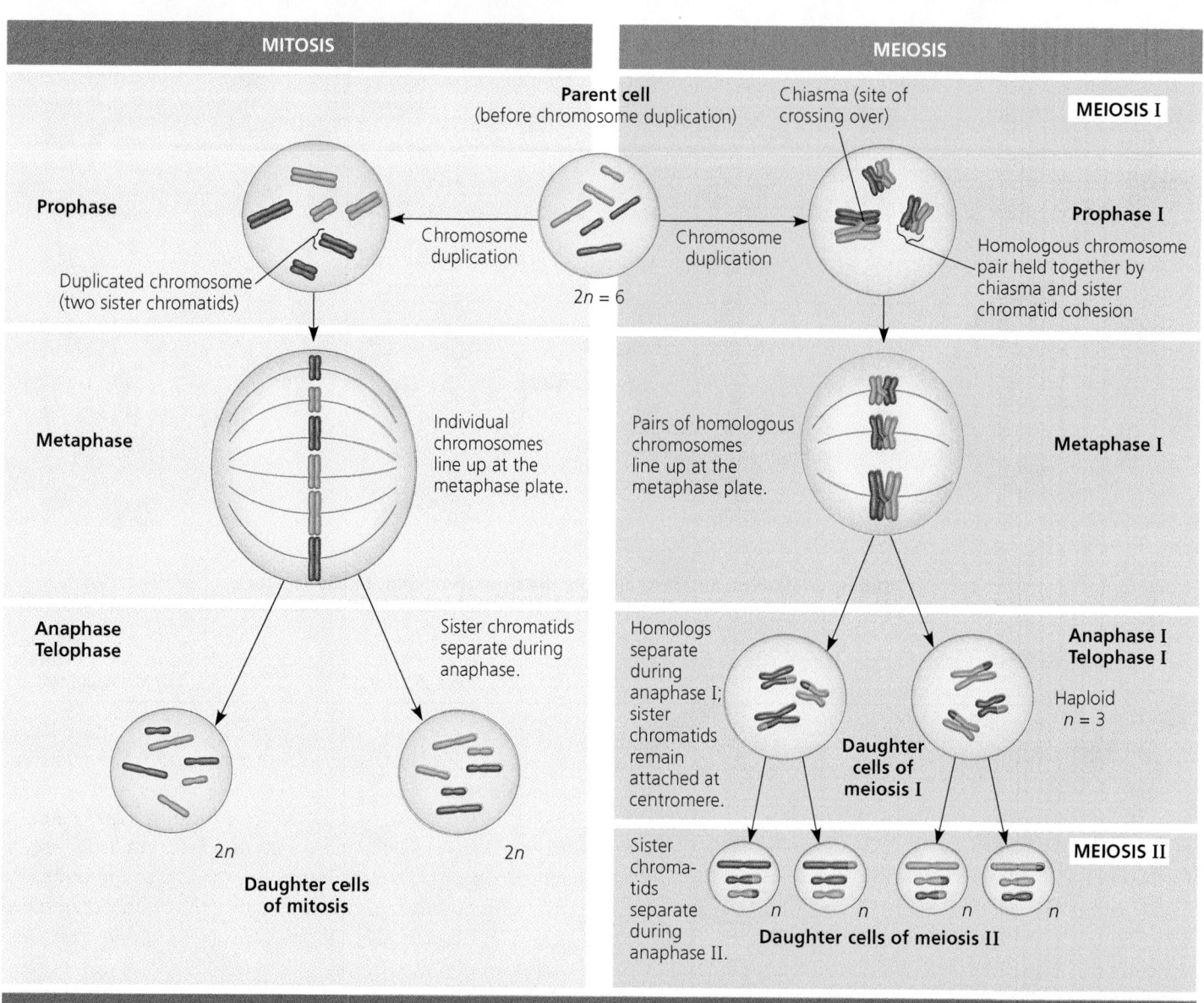

MITOSIS		MEIOSIS

Parent cell (before chromosome duplication)

Chiasma (site of crossing over)

MEIOSIS I

Prophase

Chromosome duplication

$2n = 6$

Chromosome duplication

Prophase I

Duplicated chromosome (two sister chromatids)

Homologous chromosome pair held together by chiasma and sister chromatid cohesion

Metaphase

Individual chromosomes line up at the metaphase plate.

Pairs of homologous chromosomes line up at the metaphase plate.

Metaphase I

Anaphase Telophase

Sister chromatids separate during anaphase.

Homologs separate during anaphase I; sister chromatids remain attached at centromere.

Anaphase I Telophase I

Haploid $n = 3$

Daughter cells of meiosis I

$2n$ $2n$

Daughter cells of mitosis

Sister chromatids separate during anaphase II.

n n n n

MEIOSIS II

Daughter cells of meiosis II

SUMMARY

Property	Mitosis	Meiosis
DNA replication	Occurs during interphase before mitosis begins	Occurs during interphase before meiosis I begins
Number of divisions	One, including prophase, prometaphase, metaphase, anaphase, and telophase	Two, each including prophase, metaphase, anaphase, and telophase
Synapsis of homologous chromosomes	Does not occur	Occurs during prophase I along with crossing over between nonsister chromatids; resulting chiasmata hold pairs together due to sister chromatid cohesion
Number of daughter cells and genetic composition	Two, each diploid ($2n$) and genetically identical to the parent cell	Four, each haploid (n), containing half as many chromosomes as the parent cell; genetically different from the parent cell and from each other
Role in the animal body	Enables multicellular adult to arise from zygote; produces cells for growth, repair, and, in some species, asexual reproduction	Produces gametes; reduces number of chromosome sets by half and introduces genetic variability among the gametes

▲ Figure 13.9 **A comparison of mitosis and meiosis in diploid cells.**

DRAW IT *Could any other combinations of chromosomes be generated during meiosis II from the specific cells shown in telophase I? Explain. (Hint: Draw the cells as they would appear in metaphase II.)*

A Comparison of Mitosis and Meiosis

Figure 13.9 summarizes the key differences between meiosis and mitosis in diploid cells. Basically, meiosis reduces the number of chromosome sets from two (diploid) to one (haploid), whereas mitosis conserves the number of chromosome sets. Therefore, meiosis produces cells that differ genetically from their parent cell and from each other, whereas mitosis produces daughter cells that are genetically identical to their parent cell and to each other.

Three events unique to meiosis occur during meiosis I:

1. **Synapsis and crossing over.** During prophase I, duplicated homologs pair up, and the formation of the synaptonemal complex between them holds them in synapsis. Crossing over also occurs during prophase I. Synapsis and crossing over normally do not occur during prophase of mitosis.

2. **Homologous pairs at the metaphase plate.** At metaphase I of meiosis, chromosomes are positioned at the metaphase plate as pairs of homologs, rather than individual chromosomes, as in metaphase of mitosis.

3. **Separation of homologs.** At anaphase I of meiosis, the duplicated chromosomes of each homologous pair move toward opposite poles, but the sister chromatids of each duplicated chromosome remain attached. In anaphase of mitosis, by contrast, sister chromatids separate.

How do sister chromatids stay together through meiosis I but separate from each other in meiosis II and mitosis? Sister chromatids are attached along their lengths by protein complexes called *cohesins*. In mitosis, this attachment lasts until the end of metaphase, when enzymes cleave the cohesins, freeing the sister chromatids to move to opposite poles of the cell. In meiosis, sister chromatid cohesion is released in two steps, one at the start of anaphase I and one at anaphase II. In metaphase I, homologs are held together by cohesion between sister chromatid arms in regions beyond points of crossing over, where stretches of sister chromatids now belong to different chromosomes. As shown in Figure 13.8, the combination of crossing over and sister chromatid cohesion along the arms results in the formation of a chiasma. Chiasmata hold homologs together as the spindle forms for the first meiotic division. At the onset of anaphase I, the release of cohesion along sister chromatid arms allows homologs to separate. At anaphase II, the release of sister chromatid cohesion at the centromeres allows the sister chromatids to separate. Thus, sister chromatid cohesion and crossing over, acting together, play an essential role in the lining up of chromosomes by homologous pairs at metaphase I.

Meiosis I is called the *reductional division* because it halves the number of chromosome sets per cell—a reduction from two sets (the diploid state) to one set (the haploid state). During the second meiotic division, meiosis II (sometimes called the *equational division*), the sister chromatids separate, pro-ducing haploid daughter cells. The mechanism for separating sister chromatids is virtually identical in meiosis II and mitosis. The molecular basis of chromosome behavior during meiosis continues to be a focus of intense research.

CONCEPT CHECK 13.3

1. **MAKE CONNECTIONS** How are the chromosomes in a cell at metaphase of mitosis similar to and different from the chromosomes in a cell at metaphase of meiosis II? (Compare Figures 12.7 and 13.8.)

2. **WHAT IF?** Given that the synaptonemal complex disappears by the end of prophase, how would the two homologs be associated if crossing over did not occur? What effect might this ultimately have on gamete formation?

For suggested answers, see Appendix A.

CONCEPT 13.4

Genetic variation produced in sexual life cycles contributes to evolution

How do we account for the genetic variation illustrated in Figure 13.1? As you will learn in more detail in later chapters, mutations are the original source of genetic diversity. These changes in an organism's DNA create the different versions of genes known as *alleles*. Once these differences arise, reshuffling of the alleles during sexual reproduction produces the variation that results in each member of a sexually reproducing population having a unique combination of traits.

Origins of Genetic Variation Among Offspring

In species that reproduce sexually, the behavior of chromosomes during meiosis and fertilization is responsible for most of the variation that arises in each generation. Let's examine three mechanisms that contribute to the genetic variation arising from sexual reproduction: independent assortment of chromosomes, crossing over, and random fertilization.

Independent Assortment of Chromosomes

One aspect of sexual reproduction that generates genetic variation is the random orientation of pairs of homologous chromosomes at metaphase of meiosis I. At metaphase I, the homologous pairs, each consisting of one maternal and one paternal chromosome, are situated at the metaphase plate. (Note that the terms *maternal* and *paternal* refer, respectively, to the mother and father of the individual whose cells are undergoing meiosis.) Each pair may orient with either its maternal or paternal homolog closer to a given pole—its orientation is as random as the flip of a coin. Thus, there is a 50% chance that a particular daughter cell of meiosis I will get the maternal chromosome of a certain homologous pair and a 50% chance that it will get the paternal chromosome.

Because each pair of homologous chromosomes is positioned independently of the other pairs at metaphase I, the first meiotic division results in each pair sorting its maternal and paternal homologs into daughter cells independently of every other pair. This is called *independent assortment*. Each daughter cell represents one outcome of all possible combinations of maternal and paternal chromosomes. As shown in **Figure 13.10**, the number of combinations possible for daughter cells formed by meiosis of a diploid cell with $n = 2$ (two pairs of homologous chromosomes) is four: two possible arrangements for the first pair times two possible arrangements for the second pair. Note that only two of the four combinations of daughter cells shown in the figure would result from meiosis of a *single* diploid cell, because a single parent cell would have one or the other possible chromosomal arrangement at metaphase I, but not both. However, the population of daughter cells resulting from meiosis of a large number of diploid cells contains all four types in approximately equal numbers. In the case of $n = 3$, eight combinations of chromosomes are possible for daughter cells. More generally, the number of possible combinations when chromosomes sort independently during meiosis is 2^n, where n is the haploid number of the organism.

In the case of humans ($n = 23$), the number of possible combinations of maternal and paternal chromosomes in the resulting gametes is 2^{23}, or about 8.4 million. Each gamete that you produce in your lifetime contains one of roughly 8.4 million possible combinations of chromosomes.

Crossing Over

As a consequence of the independent assortment of chromosomes during meiosis, each of us produces a collection of gametes differing greatly in their combinations of the chromosomes we inherited from our two parents. Figure 13.10 suggests that each chromosome in a gamete is exclusively maternal or paternal in origin. In fact, this is *not* the case, because crossing over produces **recombinant chromosomes**, individual chromosomes that carry genes (DNA) derived

from two different parents (**Figure 13.11**). In meiosis in humans, an average of one to three crossover events occur per chromosome pair, depending on the size of the chromosomes and the position of their centromeres.

Crossing over begins very early in prophase I as homologous chromosomes pair loosely along their lengths. Each gene on one homolog is aligned precisely with the corresponding gene on the other homolog. In a single crossover event, the DNA of two *nonsister* chromatids—one maternal and one paternal chromatid of a homologous pair—is broken by specific proteins at precisely corresponding points, and the two segments beyond the crossover point are each joined to the other chromatid. Thus, a paternal chromatid is joined to a piece of maternal chromatid beyond the crossover point, and vice versa. In this way, crossing over produces chromosomes with new combinations of maternal and paternal alleles (see Figure 13.11).

At metaphase II, chromosomes that contain one or more recombinant chromatids can be oriented in two alternative, nonequivalent ways with respect to other chromosomes, because their sister chromatids are no longer identical. The different possible arrangements of nonidentical sister chromatids during meiosis II further increase the number of genetic types of daughter cells that can result from meiosis.

You will learn more about crossing over in Chapter 15. The important point for now is that crossing over, by combining DNA inherited from two parents into a single chromosome, is an important source of genetic variation in sexual life cycles.

Random Fertilization

The random nature of fertilization adds to the genetic variation arising from meiosis. In humans, each male and female gamete represents one of about 8.4 million (2^{23}) possible chromosome combinations due to independent assortment. The fusion of a male gamete with a female gamete during

Possibility 1

Possibility 2

Two equally probable arrangements of chromosomes at metaphase I

Metaphase II

Daughter cells

Combination 1   Combination 2   Combination 3   Combination 4

▶ **Figure 13.10 The independent assortment of homologous chromosomes in meiosis.**

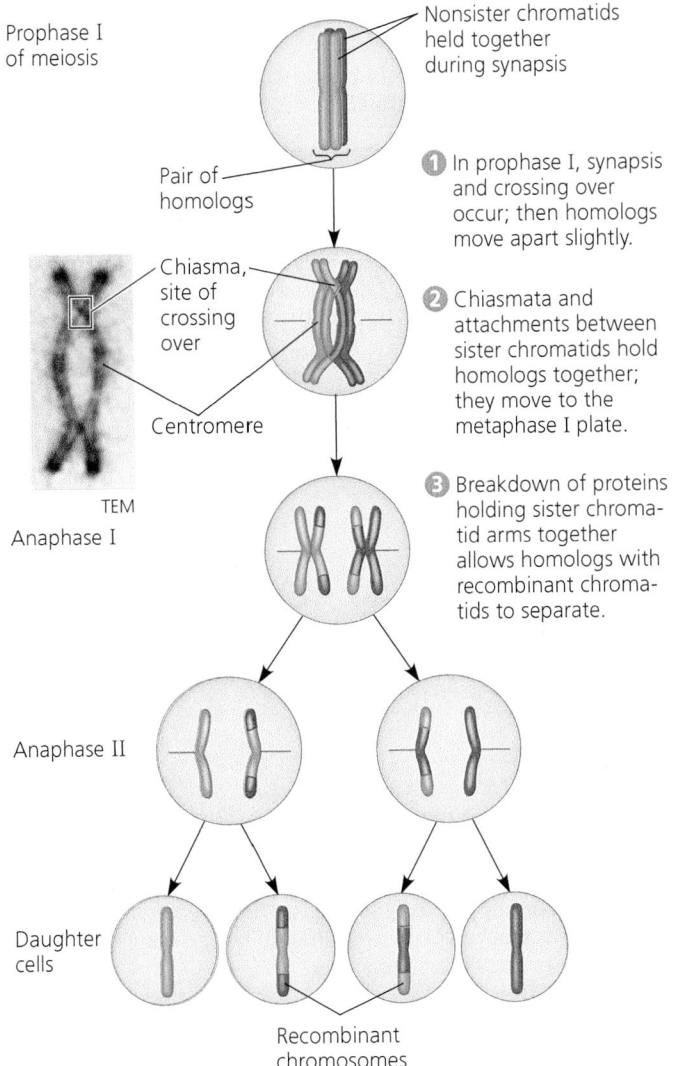

Prophase I
of meiosis

Nonsister chromatids
held together
during synapsis

Pair of
homologs

1 In prophase I, synapsis
and crossing over
occur; then homologs
move apart slightly.

Chiasma,
site of
crossing
over

2 Chiasmata and
attachments between
sister chromatids hold
homologs together;
they move to the
metaphase I plate.

Centromere

TEM

Anaphase I

3 Breakdown of proteins
holding sister chroma-
tid arms together
allows homologs with
recombinant chroma-
tids to separate.

Anaphase II

Daughter
cells

Recombinant
chromosomes

▲ **Figure 13.11 The results of crossing over during meiosis.**

fertilization will produce a zygote with any of about 70 trillion ($2^{23} \times 2^{23}$) diploid combinations. If we factor in the variation brought about by crossing over, the number of possibilities is truly astronomical. It may sound trite, but you really *are* unique.

The Evolutionary Significance of Genetic Variation Within Populations

EVOLUTION Now that you've learned how new combinations of genes arise among offspring in a sexually reproducing population, let's see how the genetic variation in a population relates to evolution. Darwin recognized that a population evolves through the differential reproductive success of its variant members. On average, those individuals best suited to the local environment leave the most offspring, thereby transmitting their genes. Thus, natural selection results in the accumulation of genetic variations favored by the environment. As the environment changes, the population may survive if,

in each generation, at least some of its members can cope effectively with the new conditions. Mutations are the original source of different alleles, which are then mixed and matched during meiosis. New and different combinations of alleles may work better than those that previously prevailed. The ability of sexual reproduction to generate genetic diversity is one of the most commonly proposed explanations for the evolutionary persistence of this process.

On the other hand, in a stable environment, asexual reproduction would seem to be more advantageous, because it ensures perpetuation of successful combinations of alleles. Furthermore, asexual reproduction is less expensive; its energy costs to the organism are lower than those of sexual reproduction, for reasons that will be discussed in Chapter 46.

In spite of these apparent disadvantages, sexual reproduction is almost universal among animals as far as we know. While a few species are capable of reproducing asexually under unusual circumstances, animals that always reproduce asexually are quite rare. The best-established example, to date, is a group of microscopic animals called bdelloid rotifers (the "b" in "bdelloid" is silent), shown in **Figure 13.12**. This group includes about 400 species that live in a great variety of environments around the world. They inhabit streams, lake bottoms, puddles, lichens, tree bark, and masses of decaying vegetation. Recent studies have provided convincing evidence that these animals reproduce only asexually and probably haven't engaged in sex in the 40 million years since their evolutionary origins!

Does the discovery of the evolutionarily successful, asexually reproducing bdelloid rotifer cast doubt on the advantage of genetic variation arising from sexual reproduction? On the contrary, this group may be considered an exception that proves the rule. In studies of bdelloid rotifers, biologists have found mechanisms other than sexual reproduction that increase genetic diversity in these organisms. For example, they live in environments that can dry up for long periods of time, during which they can enter a state of suspended animation. In this state, their cell membranes may crack in places, allowing entry of DNA from other rotifers and even other species. Evidence suggests that this DNA can become incorporated into the genome of the rotifer, leading to increased genetic diversity. (You'll learn more about this process, called *horizontal gene transfer*, in Chapter 26.) Taken as a whole, these studies support the idea that genetic variation is evolutionarily advantageous and that a

▲ **Figure 13.12 A bdelloid rotifer, an animal that reproduces only asexually.**

different mechanism to generate genetic variation has evolved in bdelloid rotifers.

In this chapter, we have seen how sexual reproduction greatly increases the genetic variation present in a population. Although Darwin realized that heritable variation is what makes evolution possible, he could not explain why offspring resemble—but are not identical to—their parents. Ironically, Gregor Mendel, a contemporary of Darwin, published a theory of inheritance that helps explain genetic variation, but his discoveries had no impact on biologists until 1900, more than 15 years after Darwin (1809–1882) and Mendel (1822–1884) had died. In the next chapter, you will learn how Mendel discovered the basic rules governing the inheritance of specific traits.

CONCEPT CHECK 13.4

1. What is the original source of variation among the different alleles of a gene?
2. The diploid number for fruit flies is 8, and the diploid number for grasshoppers is 46. If no crossing over took place, would the genetic variation among offspring from a given pair of parents be greater in fruit flies or grasshoppers? Explain.
3. **WHAT IF?** Under what circumstances would crossing over during meiosis *not* contribute to genetic variation among daughter cells?

For suggested answers, see Appendix A.

13 CHAPTER REVIEW

SUMMARY OF KEY CONCEPTS

CONCEPT 13.1

Offspring acquire genes from parents by inheriting chromosomes (pp. 248–249)

- Each **gene** in an organism's DNA exists at a specific **locus** on a certain chromosome. We inherit one set of chromosomes from our mother and one set from our father.
- In **asexual reproduction**, a single parent produces genetically identical offspring by mitosis. **Sexual reproduction** combines sets of genes from two different parents, leading to genetically diverse offspring.

? *Explain why human offspring resemble their parents but are not identical to them.*

CONCEPT 13.2

Fertilization and meiosis alternate in sexual life cycles (pp. 250–253)

- As seen in a **karyotype**, normal human **somatic cells** are **diploid**. They have 46 chromosomes made up of two sets of 23—one set from each parent. In human diploid cells, there are 22 **homologous** pairs of **autosomes**, each with a maternal and a paternal homolog. The 23rd pair, the **sex chromosomes**, determines whether the person is female (XX) or male (XY).
- At sexual maturity in the human **life cycle**, ovaries and testes (the gonads) produce **haploid gametes** by **meiosis**, each gamete containing a single set of 23 chromosomes ($n = 23$). During **fertilization**, an egg and sperm unite, forming a diploid ($2n = 46$) single-celled **zygote**, which develops into a multicellular organism by mitosis.
- Sexual life cycles differ in the timing of meiosis relative to fertilization and in the point(s) of the cycle at which a multicellular organism is produced by mitosis.

? *Compare the life cycles of animals and plants, mentioning their similarities and differences.*

CONCEPT 13.3

Meiosis reduces the number of chromosome sets from diploid to haploid (pp. 253–257)

- The two cell divisions of meiosis, **meiosis I** and **meiosis II**, produce four haploid daughter cells. The number of chromosome sets is reduced from two (diploid) to one (haploid) during meiosis I, the reductional division.
- Meiosis is distinguished from mitosis by three events of meiosis I:

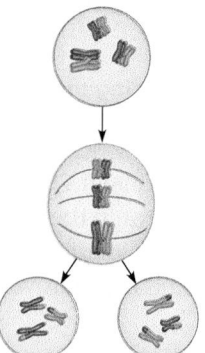

Prophase I: Each homologous pair undergoes **synapsis** and **crossing over** between nonsister chromatids with the subsequent appearance of **chiasmata**.

Metaphase I: Chromosomes line up as homologous pairs on the metaphase plate.

Anaphase I: Homologs separate from each other; sister chromatids remain joined at the centromere.

Meiosis II separates the sister chromatids.

- The combination of sister chromatid cohesion and crossing over leads to chiasmata, which hold homologs together until anaphase I. Cohesins are cleaved along the chromatid arms at anaphase I, allowing the homologs to separate, and at the centromeres in anaphase II, allowing sister chromatids to separate.

? *During prophase I, homologous chromosomes pair up and undergo synapsis and crossing over. Explain why this cannot also occur during prophase II.*

CONCEPT 13.4

Genetic variation produced in sexual life cycles contributes to evolution (pp. 257–260)

- Three events in sexual reproduction contribute to genetic variation in a population: independent assortment of chromosomes during meiosis, crossing over during meiosis I, and random fertilization of egg cells by sperm. Crossing over involves breakage and rejoining of the DNA of nonsister chromatids in a homologous pair, resulting in recombinant chromatids that will become **recombinant chromosomes**.

- Genetic variation is the raw material for evolution by natural selection. Mutations are the original source of this variation; the production of new combinations of variant genes in sexual reproduction generates additional genetic diversity. Animals that reproduce only asexually are quite rare, underscoring the apparently great advantage of genetic diversity.

? *Explain how three processes unique to meiosis generate a great deal of genetic variation.*

TEST YOUR UNDERSTANDING

LEVEL 1: KNOWLEDGE/COMPREHENSION

1. A human cell containing 22 autosomes and a Y chromosome is
   a. a sperm.
   b. an egg.
   c. a zygote.
   d. a somatic cell of a male.
   e. a somatic cell of a female.

2. Which life cycle stage is found in plants but not animals?
   a. gamete
   b. zygote
   c. multicellular diploid
   d. multicellular haploid
   e. unicellular diploid

3. Homologous chromosomes move toward opposite poles of a dividing cell during
   a. mitosis.
   b. meiosis I.
   c. meiosis II.
   d. fertilization.
   e. binary fission.

LEVEL 2: APPLICATION/ANALYSIS

4. Meiosis II is similar to mitosis in that
   a. sister chromatids separate during anaphase.
   b. DNA replicates before the division.
   c. the daughter cells are diploid.
   d. homologous chromosomes synapse.
   e. the chromosome number is reduced.

5. If the DNA content of a diploid cell in the G_1 phase of the cell cycle is x, then the DNA content of the same cell at metaphase of meiosis I would be
   a. $0.25x$.
   b. $0.5x$.
   c. x.
   d. $2x$.
   e. $4x$.

6. If we continued to follow the cell lineage from question 5, then the DNA content of a single cell at metaphase of meiosis II would be
   a. $0.25x$.
   b. $0.5x$.
   c. x.
   d. $2x$.
   e. $4x$.

7. How many different combinations of maternal and paternal chromosomes can be packaged in gametes made by an organism with a diploid number of 8 ($2n = 8$)?
   a. 2
   b. 4
   c. 8
   d. 16
   e. 32

8. **DRAW IT** The diagram at right shows a cell in meiosis.
   (a) Copy the drawing to a separate sheet of paper and label appropriate structures with these terms, drawing lines or brackets as needed: chromosome (label as duplicated or unduplicated), centromere, kinetochore, sister chromatids, nonsister chromatids, homologous pair, homologs, chiasma, sister chromatid cohesion.
   (b) Describe the makeup of a haploid set and a diploid set.
   (c) Identify the stage of meiosis shown.

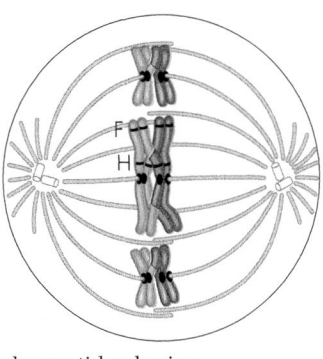

LEVEL 3: SYNTHESIS/EVALUATION

9. How can you tell the cell in question 8 is undergoing meiosis, not mitosis?

10. **EVOLUTION CONNECTION**
    Many species can reproduce either asexually or sexually. What might be the evolutionary significance of the switch from asexual to sexual reproduction that occurs in some organisms when the environment becomes unfavorable?

11. **SCIENTIFIC INQUIRY**
    The diagram above represents a meiotic cell in a certain individual. A previous study has shown that the freckles gene is located at the locus marked F, and the hair-color gene is located at the locus marked H, both on the long chromosome. The individual from whom this cell was taken has inherited different alleles for each gene ("freckles" and "black hair" from one parent, and "no freckles" and "blond hair" from the other). Predict allele combinations in the gametes resulting from this meiotic event. (It will help if you draw out the rest of meiosis, labeling alleles by name.) List other possible combinations of these alleles in this individual's gametes.

12. **WRITE ABOUT A THEME**
    The Genetic Basis of Life The continuity of life is based on heritable information in the form of DNA. In a short essay (100–150 words), explain how chromosome behavior during sexual reproduction in animals ensures perpetuation of parental traits in offspring and, at the same time, genetic variation among offspring.

For selected answers, see Appendix A.

  www.masteringbiology.com

1. MasteringBiology® Assignments
Video Tutor Session Mitosis vs. Meiosis
BioFlix **Tutorials** Meiosis: Genes, Chromosomes, and Sexual Reproduction • The Mechanism • Determinants of Heredity and Genetic Variation
Activities Asexual and Sexual Life Cycles • Meiosis Animation • Origins of Genetic Variation
Questions Student Misconceptions • Reading Quiz • Multiple Choice • End-of-Chapter

2. eText
Read your book online, search, take notes, highlight text, and more.

3. The Study Area
Practice Tests • Cumulative Test • *BioFlix* 3-D Animations • MP3 Tutor Sessions • Videos • Activities • Investigations • Lab Media • Audio Glossary • Word Study Tools • Art

14

Mendel and the Gene Idea

▲ **Figure 14.1 What principles of inheritance did Gregor Mendel discover by breeding garden pea plants?**

KEY CONCEPTS

14.1 Mendel used the scientific approach to identify two laws of inheritance

14.2 The laws of probability govern Mendelian inheritance

14.3 Inheritance patterns are often more complex than predicted by simple Mendelian genetics

14.4 Many human traits follow Mendelian patterns of inheritance

OVERVIEW

Drawing from the Deck of Genes

If you spotted a woman with bright purple hair walking down the street, you would probably deduce that she hadn't inherited her striking hair color from either parent. Consciously or not, you have transformed a lifetime of observations of hair

color and other features into a list of possible variations that occur naturally among people. Brown, blue, green, or gray eyes; black, brown, blond, or red hair—these are just a few examples of heritable variations that we may observe among individuals in a population. What are the genetic principles that account for the transmission of such traits from parents to offspring in humans and other organisms?

The explanation of heredity most widely in favor during the 1800s was the "blending" hypothesis, the idea that genetic material contributed by the two parents mixes in a manner analogous to the way blue and yellow paints blend to make green. This hypothesis predicts that over many generations, a freely mating population will give rise to a uniform population of individuals. However, our everyday observations and the results of breeding experiments with animals and plants contradict that prediction. The blending hypothesis also fails to explain other phenomena of inheritance, such as traits reappearing after skipping a generation.

An alternative to the blending model is a "particulate" hypothesis of inheritance: the gene idea. According to this model, parents pass on discrete heritable units—genes—that retain their separate identities in offspring. An organism's collection of genes is more like a deck of cards than a pail of paint. Like playing cards, genes can be shuffled and passed along, generation after generation, in undiluted form.

Modern genetics had its genesis in an abbey garden, where a monk named Gregor Mendel documented a particulate mechanism for inheritance. **Figure 14.1** shows Mendel (back row, holding a sprig of fuchsia) with his fellow monks. Mendel developed his theory of inheritance several decades before chromosomes were observed under the microscope and the significance of their behavior was understood. In this chapter, we will step into Mendel's garden to re-create his experiments and explain how he arrived at his theory of inheritance. We will also explore inheritance patterns more complex than those observed by Mendel in garden peas. Finally, we will see how the Mendelian model applies to the inheritance of human variations, including hereditary disorders such as sickle-cell disease.

CONCEPT **14.1**

Mendel used the scientific approach to identify two laws of inheritance

Mendel discovered the basic principles of heredity by breeding garden peas in carefully planned experiments. As we retrace his work, you will recognize the key elements of the scientific process that were introduced in Chapter 1.

Mendel's Experimental, Quantitative Approach

Mendel grew up on his parents' small farm in a region of Austria that is now part of the Czech Republic. In this agricultural area, Mendel and the other children received agricultural training in school along with their basic education. As an adolescent, Mendel overcame financial hardship and illness to excel in high school and, later, at the Olmutz Philosophical Institute.

In 1843, at the age of 21, Mendel entered an Augustinian monastery, a reasonable choice at that time for someone who valued the life of the mind. He considered becoming a teacher but failed the necessary examination. In 1851, he left the monastery to pursue two years of study in physics and chemistry at the University of Vienna. These were very important years for Mendel's development as a scientist, in large part due to the strong influence of two professors. One was the physicist Christian Doppler, who encouraged his students to learn science through experimentation and trained Mendel to use mathematics to help explain natural phenomena. The other was a botanist named Franz Unger, who aroused Mendel's interest in the causes of variation in plants. The instruction Mendel received from these two mentors later played a critical role in his experiments with garden peas.

After attending the university, Mendel returned to the monastery and was assigned to teach at a local school, where several other instructors were enthusiastic about scientific research. In addition, his fellow monks shared a long-standing fascination with the breeding of plants. The monastery therefore provided fertile soil in more ways than one for Mendel's scientific endeavors. Around 1857, Mendel began breeding garden peas in the abbey garden to study inheritance. Although the question of heredity had long been a focus of curiosity at the monastery, Mendel's fresh approach allowed him to deduce principles that had remained elusive to others.

One reason Mendel probably chose to work with peas is that they are available in many varieties. For example, one variety has purple flowers, while another variety has white flowers. A heritable feature that varies among individuals, such as flower color, is called a **character**. Each variant for a character, such as purple or white color for flowers, is called a **trait**.

Other advantages of using peas are their short generation time and the large number of offspring from each mating. Furthermore, Mendel could strictly control mating between plants. The reproductive organs of a pea plant are in its flowers, and each pea flower has both pollen-producing organs (stamens) and an egg-bearing organ (carpel).* In nature, pea plants usually self-fertilize: Pollen grains from the stamens land on the carpel of the same flower, and sperm released from the pollen grains fertilize eggs present in the carpel. To achieve cross-pollination (fertilization between different plants), Mendel removed the immature stamens of a plant before they produced pollen and then dusted pollen from another plant onto the

*As you learned in Figure 13.6b, meiosis in plants produces spores, not gametes. In flowering plants like the pea, each spore develops into a microscopic haploid gametophyte that contains only a few cells and is located on the parent plant. The gametophyte produces sperm, in pollen grains, and eggs, in the carpel. For simplicity, we will not include the gametophyte stage in our discussion of fertilization in plants.

▼ Figure 14.2   **RESEARCH METHOD**

Crossing Pea Plants

APPLICATION By crossing (mating) two true-breeding varieties of an organism, scientists can study patterns of inheritance. In this example, Mendel crossed pea plants that varied in flower color.

TECHNIQUE

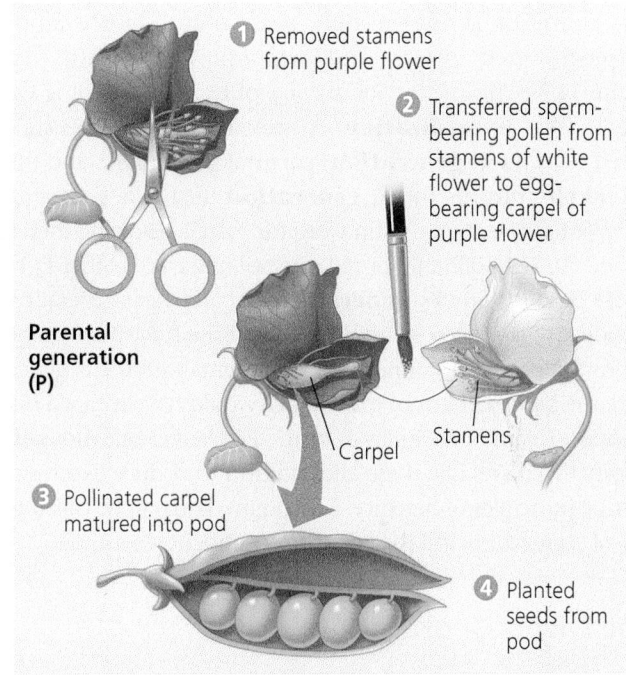

1 Removed stamens from purple flower

2 Transferred sperm-bearing pollen from stamens of white flower to egg-bearing carpel of purple flower

Parental generation (P)

Carpel   Stamens

3 Pollinated carpel matured into pod

4 Planted seeds from pod

RESULTS When pollen from a white flower was transferred to a purple flower, the first-generation hybrids all had purple flowers. The result was the same for the reciprocal cross, which involved the transfer of pollen from purple flowers to white flowers.

First filial generation offspring (F_1)

5 Examined offspring: all purple flowers

altered flowers (**Figure 14.2**). Each resulting zygote then developed into a plant embryo encased in a seed (pea). Mendel could thus always be sure of the parentage of new seeds.

Mendel chose to track only those characters that occurred in two distinct, alternative forms. For example, his plants had either purple flowers or white flowers; there were no colors intermediate between these two varieties. Had Mendel focused instead on characters that varied in a continuum among individuals—seed weight, for example—he would not have discovered the particulate nature of inheritance. (You'll learn why later.)

Mendel also made sure that he started his experiments with varieties that, over many generations of self-pollination, had produced only the same variety as the parent plant. Such plants are said to be **true-breeding**. For example, a plant with purple flowers is true-breeding if the seeds produced by self-pollination in successive generations all give rise to plants that also have purple flowers.

In a typical breeding experiment, Mendel cross-pollinated two contrasting, true-breeding pea varieties—for example, purple-flowered plants and white-flowered plants (see Figure 14.2). This mating, or *crossing*, of two true-breeding varieties is called **hybridization**. The true-breeding parents are referred to as the **P generation** (parental generation), and their hybrid offspring are the **F₁ generation** (first filial generation, the word *filial* from the Latin word for "son"). Allowing these F₁ hybrids to self-pollinate (or to cross-pollinate with other F₁ hybrids) produces an **F₂ generation** (second filial generation). Mendel usually followed traits for at least the P, F₁, and F₂ generations. Had Mendel stopped his experiments with the F₁ generation, the basic patterns of inheritance would have escaped him. Mendel's quantitative analysis of the F₂ plants from thousands of genetic crosses like these allowed him to deduce two fundamental principles of heredity, which have come to be called the law of segregation and the law of independent assortment.

The Law of Segregation

If the blending model of inheritance were correct, the F₁ hybrids from a cross between purple-flowered and white-flowered pea plants would have pale purple flowers, a trait intermediate between those of the P generation. Notice in Figure 14.2 that the experiment produced a very different result: All the F₁ offspring had flowers just as purple as the purple-flowered parents. What happened to the white-flowered plants' genetic contribution to the hybrids? If it were lost, then the F₁ plants could produce only purple-flowered offspring in the F₂ generation. But when Mendel allowed the F₁ plants to self-pollinate and planted their seeds, the white-flower trait reappeared in the F₂ generation.

Mendel used very large sample sizes and kept accurate records of his results: 705 of the F₂ plants had purple flowers, and 224 had white flowers. These data fit a ratio of approximately three purple to one white (Figure 14.3). Mendel reasoned that the heritable factor for white flowers did not disappear in the F₁ plants, but was somehow hidden, or masked, when the purple-flower factor was present. In Mendel's terminology, purple flower color is a *dominant* trait, and white flower color is a *recessive* trait. The reappearance of white-flowered plants in the F₂ generation was evidence that the heritable factor causing white flowers had not been diluted or destroyed by coexisting with the purple-flower factor in the F₁ hybrids.

Mendel observed the same pattern of inheritance in six other characters, each represented by two distinctly different

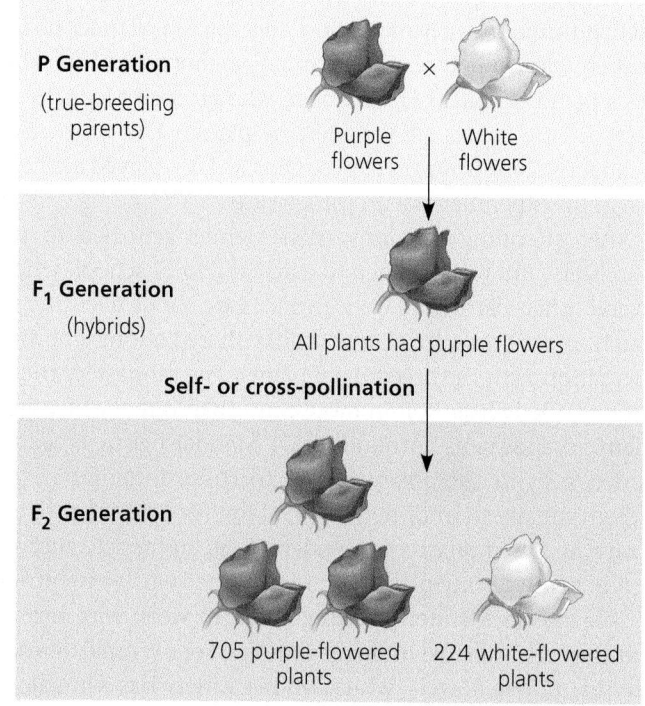

▼ **Figure 14.3** **INQUIRY**

When F₁ hybrid pea plants self- or cross-pollinate, which traits appear in the F₂ generation?

EXPERIMENT Around 1860, in a monastery garden in Brünn, Austria, Gregor Mendel used the character of flower color in pea plants to follow traits through two generations. He crossed true-breeding purple-flowered plants and white-flowered plants (crosses are symbolized by ✕). The resulting F₁ hybrids were allowed to self-pollinate or were cross-pollinated with other F₁ hybrids. The F₂ generation plants were then observed for flower color.

P Generation
(true-breeding parents)

Purple flowers ✕ White flowers

F₁ Generation
(hybrids)

All plants had purple flowers

Self- or cross-pollination

F₂ Generation

705 purple-flowered plants   224 white-flowered plants

RESULTS Both purple-flowered and white-flowered plants appeared in the F₂ generation, in a ratio of approximately 3:1.

CONCLUSION The "heritable factor" for the recessive trait (white flowers) had not been destroyed, deleted, or "blended" in the F₁ generation but was merely masked by the presence of the factor for purple flowers, which is the dominant trait.

SOURCE G. Mendel, Experiments in plant hybridization, *Proceedings of the Natural History Society of Brünn* 4:3–47 (1866).

WHAT IF? If you mated two purple-flowered plants from the P generation, what ratio of traits would you expect to observe in the offspring? Explain.

traits (Table 14.1). For example, when Mendel crossed a true-breeding variety that produced smooth, round pea seeds with one that produced wrinkled seeds, all the F₁ hybrids produced round seeds; this is the dominant trait for seed shape. In the F₂ generation, approximately 75% of the seeds were round and 25% were wrinkled—a 3:1 ratio, as in Figure 14.3. Now let's see how Mendel deduced the law of

Table 14.1 The Results of Mendel's F₁ Crosses for Seven Characters in Pea Plants

Character	Dominant Trait	×	Recessive Trait	F₂ Generation Dominant: Recessive	Ratio
Flower color	Purple	×	White	705:224	3.15:1
Flower position	Axial	×	Terminal	651:207	3.14:1
Seed color	Yellow	×	Green	6,022:2,001	3.01:1
Seed shape	Round	×	Wrinkled	5,474:1,850	2.96:1
Pod shape	Inflated	×	Constricted	882:299	2.95:1
Pod color	Green	×	Yellow	428:152	2.82:1
Stem length	Tall	×	Dwarf	787:277	2.84:1

▲ **Figure 14.4 Alleles, alternative versions of a gene.** A somatic cell has two copies of each chromosome (forming a homologous pair) and thus two copies of each gene; the alleles may be identical or different. This figure depicts a pair of homologous chromosomes in an F₁ hybrid pea plant. The paternally inherited chromosome (blue), which was present in the sperm within a pollen grain, has an allele for purple flowers, and the maternally inherited chromosome (red), which was present in an egg within a carpel, has an allele for white flowers.

segregation from his experimental results. In the discussion that follows, we will use modern terms instead of some of the terms used by Mendel. (For example, we'll use "gene" instead of Mendel's "heritable factor.")

Mendel's Model

Mendel developed a model to explain the 3:1 inheritance pattern that he consistently observed among the F₂ offspring in his pea experiments. We describe four related concepts making up this model, the fourth of which is the law of segregation.

First, *alternative versions of genes account for variations in inherited characters.* The gene for flower color in pea plants, for example, exists in two versions, one for purple flowers and the other for white flowers. These alternative versions of a gene are

called **alleles** (Figure 14.4). Today, we can relate this concept to chromosomes and DNA. As noted in Chapter 13, each gene is a sequence of nucleotides at a specific place, or locus, along a particular chromosome. The DNA at that locus, however, can vary slightly in its nucleotide sequence and hence in its information content. The purple-flower allele and the white-flower allele are two DNA sequence variations possible at the flower-color locus on one of a pea plant's chromosomes.

Second, *for each character, an organism inherits two copies of a gene, one from each parent.* (These are also called alleles of that gene.) Remarkably, Mendel made this deduction without knowing about the role, or even the existence, of chromosomes. Recall from Chapter 13 that each somatic cell in a diploid organism has two sets of chromosomes, one set inherited from each parent. Thus, a genetic locus is actually represented twice in a diploid cell, once on each homolog of a specific pair of chromosomes. The two alleles at a particular locus may be identical, as in the true-breeding plants of Mendel's P generation. Or the alleles may differ, as in the F₁ hybrids (see Figure 14.4).

Third, *if the two alleles at a locus differ, then one, the* **dominant allele**, *determines the organism's appearance; the other, the* **recessive allele**, *has no noticeable effect on the organism's appearance.* Accordingly, Mendel's F₁ plants had purple flowers because the allele for that trait is dominant and the allele for white flowers is recessive.

The fourth and final part of Mendel's model, the **law of segregation**, states that *the two alleles for a heritable character segregate (separate from each other) during gamete formation and end up in different gametes.* Thus, an egg or a sperm gets only one of the two alleles that are present in the somatic cells of the organism making the gamete. In terms of chromosomes, this segregation corresponds to the distribution of the two members of a pair of homologous chromosomes to different gametes in meiosis (see Figure 13.7). Note that if an organism has identical alleles for a particular character—that is, the organism is true-breeding for that character—then that allele is present in all gametes. But if different alleles are present, as in the F₁ hybrids, then 50% of the gametes receive the dominant allele and 50% receive the recessive allele.

Does Mendel's segregation model account for the 3:1 ratio he observed in the F₂ generation of his numerous crosses? For the flower-color character, the model predicts that the two different alleles present in an F₁ individual will segregate into gametes such that half the gametes will have the purple-flower allele and half will have the white-flower allele. During self-pollination, gametes of each class unite randomly. An egg with a purple-flower allele has an equal chance of being fertilized by a sperm with a purple-flower allele or one with a white-flower allele. Since the same is true for an egg with a white-flower allele, there are four equally likely combinations of sperm and egg. **Figure 14.5** illustrates these combinations using a **Punnett square**, a handy diagrammatic device for predicting the allele composition of offspring from a cross between individuals of known genetic makeup. Notice that we use a capital letter to symbolize a dominant allele and a lowercase letter for a recessive allele. In our example, P is the purple-flower allele, and p is the white-flower allele; the gene itself is sometimes referred to as the P/p gene.

In the F₂ offspring, what color will the flowers be? One-fourth of the plants have inherited two purple-flower alleles; clearly, these plants will have purple flowers. One-half of the F₂ offspring have inherited one purple-flower allele and one white-flower allele; these plants will also have purple flowers, the dominant trait. Finally, one-fourth of the F₂ plants have inherited two white-flower alleles and will express the recessive trait. Thus, Mendel's model accounts for the 3:1 ratio of traits that he observed in the F₂ generation.

Useful Genetic Vocabulary

An organism that has a pair of identical alleles for a character is said to be **homozygous** for the gene controlling that character. In the parental generation in Figure 14.5, the purple pea plant is homozygous for the dominant allele (PP), while the white plant is homozygous for the recessive allele (pp). Homozygous plants "breed true" because all of their gametes contain the same allele—either P or p in this example. If we cross dominant homozygotes with recessive homozygotes, every offspring will have two different alleles—Pp in the case of the F₁ hybrids of our flower-color experiment (see Figure 14.5). An organism that has two different alleles for a gene is said to be **heterozygous** for that gene. Unlike homozygotes, heterozygotes produce gametes with different alleles, so they are not true-breeding. For example, P- and p-containing gametes are both produced by our F₁ hybrids. Self-pollination of the F₁ hybrids thus produces both purple-flowered and white-flowered offspring.

Because of the different effects of dominant and recessive alleles, an organism's traits do not always reveal its genetic composition. Therefore, we distinguish between an organism's appearance or observable traits, called its **phenotype**, and its genetic makeup, its **genotype**. In the case of flower color in pea plants, PP and Pp plants have the same phenotype (purple) but different genotypes. **Figure 14.6** reviews these terms. Note that "phenotype" refers to physiological traits as well as traits that relate directly to appearance.

Each true-breeding plant of the parental generation has two identical alleles, denoted as either PP or pp.

Gametes (circles) each contain only one allele for the flower-color gene. In this case, every gamete produced by one parent has the same allele.

P Generation

Appearance: Purple flowers   White flowers
Genetic makeup: PP pp

Gametes: P p

Union of parental gametes produces F₁ hybrids having a Pp combination. Because the purple-flower allele is dominant, all these hybrids have purple flowers.

When the hybrid plants produce gametes, the two alleles segregate. Half of the gametes receive the P allele and the other half the p allele.

F₁ Generation

Appearance: Purple flowers
Genetic makeup: Pp

Gametes: ½ P ½ p

This box, a Punnett square, shows all possible combinations of alleles in offspring that result from an F₁ × F₁ (Pp × Pp) cross. Each square represents an equally probable product of fertilization. For example, the bottom left box shows the genetic combination resulting from a p egg fertilized by a P sperm.

F₂ Generation

Sperm from F₁ (Pp) plant
P p

Eggs from F₁ (Pp) plant
P: PP Pp
p: Pp pp

Random combination of the gametes results in the 3:1 ratio that Mendel observed in the F₂ generation.

3 : 1

▲ **Figure 14.5 Mendel's law of segregation.** This diagram shows the genetic makeup of the generations in Figure 14.3. It illustrates Mendel's model for inheritance of the alleles of a single gene. Each plant has two alleles for the gene controlling flower color, one allele inherited from each of the plant's parents. To construct a Punnett square that predicts the F₂ generation offspring, we list all the possible gametes from one parent (here, the F₁ female) along the left side of the square and all the possible gametes from the other parent (here, the F₁ male) along the top. The boxes represent the offspring resulting from all the possible unions of male and female gametes.

Phenotype		Genotype	
Purple		PP (homozygous)	1
Purple		Pp (heterozygous)	
Purple		Pp (heterozygous)	2
White		pp (homozygous)	1

Ratio 3:1   Ratio 1:2:1

▲ Figure 14.6 **Phenotype versus genotype.** Grouping F₂ offspring from a cross for flower color according to phenotype results in the typical 3:1 phenotypic ratio. In terms of genotype, however, there are actually two categories of purple-flowered plants, *PP* (homozygous) and *Pp* (heterozygous), giving a 1:2:1 genotypic ratio.

For example, there is a pea variety that lacks the normal ability to self-pollinate. This physiological variation (non-self-pollination) is a phenotypic trait.

The Testcross

Suppose we have a "mystery" pea plant that has purple flowers. We cannot tell from its flower color if this plant is homozygous (*PP*) or heterozygous (*Pp*) because both genotypes result in the same purple phenotype. To determine the genotype, we can cross this plant with a white-flowered plant (*pp*), which will make only gametes with the recessive allele (*p*). The allele in the gamete contributed by the mystery plant will therefore determine the appearance of the offspring (Figure 14.7). If all the offspring of the cross have purple flowers, then the purple-flowered mystery plant must be homozygous for the dominant allele, because a *PP* × *pp* cross produces all *Pp* offspring. But if both the purple and the white phenotypes appear among the offspring, then the purple-flowered parent must be heterozygous. The offspring of a *Pp* × *pp* cross will be expected to have a 1:1 phenotypic ratio. Breeding an organism of unknown genotype with a recessive homozygote is called a **testcross** because it can reveal the genotype of that organism. The testcross was devised by Mendel and continues to be an important tool of geneticists.

The Law of Independent Assortment

Mendel derived the law of segregation from experiments in which he followed only a *single* character, such as flower color. All the F₁ progeny produced in his crosses of true-breeding parents were **monohybrids**, meaning that they were

▼ Figure 14.7 **RESEARCH METHOD**

The Testcross

APPLICATION An organism that exhibits a dominant trait, such as purple flowers in pea plants, can be either homozygous for the dominant allele or heterozygous. To determine the organism's genotype, geneticists can perform a testcross.

TECHNIQUE In a testcross, the individual with the unknown genotype is crossed with a homozygous individual expressing the recessive trait (white flowers in this example), and Punnett squares are used to predict the possible outcomes.

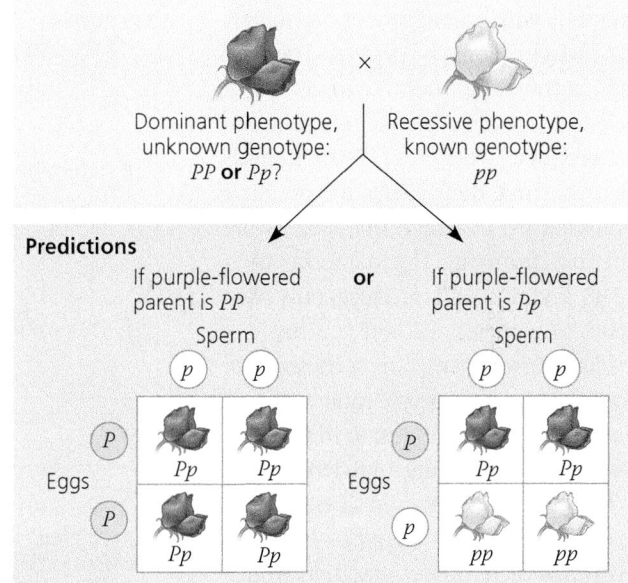

RESULTS Matching the results to either prediction identifies the unknown parental genotype (either *PP* or *Pp* in this example). In this testcross, we transferred pollen from a white-flowered plant to the carpels of a purple-flowered plant; the opposite (reciprocal) cross would have led to the same results.

All offspring purple   or   ½ offspring purple and ½ offspring white

heterozygous for the one particular character being followed in the cross. We refer to a cross between such heterozygotes as a **monohybrid cross**.

Mendel identified his second law of inheritance by following *two* characters at the same time, such as seed color and seed shape. Seeds (peas) may be either yellow or green. They also may be either round (smooth) or wrinkled. From single-character crosses, Mendel knew that the allele for yellow seeds is dominant (*Y*), and the allele for green seeds is recessive (*y*). For the seed-shape character, the allele for round is dominant (*R*), and the allele for wrinkled is recessive (*r*).

Imagine crossing two true-breeding pea varieties that differ in *both* of these characters—a cross between a plant with yellow-round seeds (*YYRR*) and a plant with green-wrinkled seeds (*yyrr*).

The F_1 plants will be **dihybrids**, individuals heterozygous for the two characters being followed in the cross ($YyRr$). But are these two characters transmitted from parents to offspring as a package? That is, will the Y and R alleles always stay together, generation after generation? Or are seed color and seed shape inherited independently? **Figure 14.8** shows how a **dihybrid cross**, a cross between F_1 dihybrids, can determine which of these two hypotheses is correct.

The F_1 plants, of genotype $YyRr$, exhibit both dominant phenotypes, yellow seeds with round shapes, no matter which hypothesis is correct. The key step in the experiment is to see what happens when F_1 plants self-pollinate and produce F_2 offspring. If the hybrids must transmit their alleles in the same combinations in which the alleles were inherited from the P generation, then the F_1 hybrids will produce only two classes of gametes: YR and yr. This "dependent assortment" hypothesis predicts that the phenotypic ratio of the F_2 generation will be 3:1, just as in a monohybrid cross (see Figure 14.8, left side).

The alternative hypothesis is that the two pairs of alleles segregate independently of each other. In other words, genes are packaged into gametes in all possible allelic combinations, as long as each gamete has one allele for each gene. In our example, an F_1 plant will produce four classes of gametes in equal quantities: YR, Yr, yR, and yr. If sperm of the four classes fertilize eggs of the four classes, there will be 16 (4 × 4) equally probable ways in which the alleles can combine in the F_2 generation, as shown in Figure 14.8, right side. These combinations result in four phenotypic categories with a ratio of 9:3:3:1 (nine yellow-round to three green-round to three yellow-wrinkled to one green-wrinkled). When Mendel did the experiment and classified the F_2 offspring, his results were close to the predicted 9:3:3:1 phenotypic ratio, supporting the hypothesis that the alleles for one gene—controlling seed color or seed shape, in this example—are sorted into gametes independently of the alleles of other genes.

Mendel tested his seven pea characters in various dihybrid combinations

and always observed a 9:3:3:1 phenotypic ratio in the F_2 generation. However, notice in Figure 14.8 that there is a 3:1 phenotypic ratio for each one of the two characters if you consider them separately: three yellow to one green, and three round to one wrinkled. As far as a single character is concerned, the alleles segregate as if this were a monohybrid cross. The results of

▼ **Figure 14.8**

INQUIRY

Do the alleles for one character assort into gametes dependently or independently of the alleles for a different character?

EXPERIMENT Gregor Mendel followed the characters of seed color and seed shape through the F_2 generation. He crossed a true-breeding plant with yellow-round seeds with a true-breeding plant with green-wrinkled seeds, producing dihybrid F_1 plants. Self-pollination of the F_1 dihybrids produced the F_2 generation. The two hypotheses (dependent and independent assortment) predict different phenotypic ratios.

RESULTS

315 ◯ 108 ◯ 101 ▨ 32 ▨   Phenotypic ratio approximately 9:3:3:1

CONCLUSION Only the hypothesis of independent assortment predicts the appearance of two of the observed phenotypes: green-round seeds and yellow-wrinkled seeds (see the right-hand Punnett square). The alleles for seed color and seed shape sort into gametes independently of each other.

SOURCE G. Mendel, Experiments in plant hybridization, *Proceedings of the Natural History Society of Brünn* 4:3–47 (1866).

WHAT IF? Suppose Mendel had transferred pollen from an F_1 plant to the carpel of a plant that was homozygous recessive for both genes. Set up the cross and draw Punnett squares that predict the offspring for both hypotheses. Would this cross have supported the hypothesis of independent assortment equally well?

Mendel's dihybrid experiments are the basis for what we now call the **law of independent assortment**, which states that *each pair of alleles segregates independently of each other pair of alleles during gamete formation.*

This law applies only to genes (allele pairs) located on different chromosomes—that is, on chromosomes that are not homologous—or very far apart on the same chromosome. (The latter case will be explained in Chapter 15, along with the more complex inheritance patterns of genes located near each other, which tend to be inherited together.) All the pea characters Mendel chose for analysis were controlled by genes on different chromosomes (or far apart on one chromosome); this situation greatly simplified interpretation of his multicharacter pea crosses. All the examples we consider in the rest of this chapter involve genes located on different chromosomes.

CONCEPT CHECK 14.1

1. **DRAW IT** Pea plants heterozygous for flower position and stem length ($AaTt$) are allowed to self-pollinate, and 400 of the resulting seeds are planted. Draw a Punnett square for this cross. How many offspring would be predicted to have terminal flowers and be dwarf? (See Table 14.1.)
2. **WHAT IF?** List all gametes that could be made by a pea plant heterozygous for seed color, seed shape, and pod shape ($YyRrIi$; see Table 14.1). How large a Punnett square would you need to draw to predict the offspring of a self-pollination of this "trihybrid"?
3. **MAKE CONNECTIONS** In some pea plant crosses, the plants are self-pollinated. Refer back to Concept 13.1 (pp. 248–249) and explain whether self-pollination is considered asexual or sexual reproduction.

For suggested answers, see Appendix A.

CONCEPT 14.2

The laws of probability govern Mendelian inheritance

Mendel's laws of segregation and independent assortment reflect the same rules of probability that apply to tossing coins, rolling dice, and drawing cards from a deck. The probability scale ranges from 0 to 1. An event that is certain to occur has a probability of 1, while an event that is certain *not* to occur has a probability of 0. With a coin that has heads on both sides, the probability of tossing heads is 1, and the probability of tossing tails is 0. With a normal coin, the chance of tossing heads is ½, and the chance of tossing tails is ½. The probability of drawing the ace of spades from a 52-card deck is $\frac{1}{52}$. The probabilities of all possible outcomes for an event must add up to 1. With a deck of cards, the chance of picking a card other than the ace of spades is $\frac{51}{52}$.

Tossing a coin illustrates an important lesson about probability. For every toss, the probability of heads is ½. The outcome of any particular toss is unaffected by what has happened on previous trials. We refer to phenomena such as coin tosses as independent events. Each toss of a coin, whether done sequentially with one coin or simultaneously with many, is independent of every other toss. And like two separate coin tosses, the alleles of one gene segregate into gametes independently of another gene's alleles (the law of independent assortment). Two basic rules of probability can help us predict the outcome of the fusion of such gametes in simple monohybrid crosses and more complicated crosses.

The Multiplication and Addition Rules Applied to Monohybrid Crosses

How do we determine the probability that two or more independent events will occur together in some specific combination? For example, what is the chance that two coins tossed simultaneously will both land heads up? The **multiplication rule** states that to determine this probability, we multiply the probability of one event (one coin coming up heads) by the probability of the other event (the other coin coming up heads). By the multiplication rule, then, the probability that both coins will land heads up is ½ × ½ = ¼.

We can apply the same reasoning to an F_1 monohybrid cross. With seed shape in pea plants as the heritable character, the genotype of F_1 plants is Rr. Segregation in a heterozygous plant is like flipping a coin in terms of calculating the probability of each outcome: Each egg produced has a ½ chance of carrying the dominant allele (R) and a ½ chance of carrying the recessive allele (r). The same odds apply to each sperm cell produced. For a particular F_2 plant to have wrinkled seeds, the recessive trait, both the egg and the sperm that come together must carry the r allele. The probability that an r allele will be present in both gametes at fertilization is found by multiplying ½ (the probability that the egg will have an r) × ½ (the probability that the sperm will have an r). Thus, the multiplication rule tells us that the probability of an F_2 plant having wrinkled seeds (rr) is ¼ (**Figure 14.9**, on the next page). Likewise, the probability of an F_2 plant carrying both dominant alleles for seed shape (RR) is ¼.

To figure out the probability that an F_2 plant from a monohybrid cross will be heterozygous rather than homozygous, we need to invoke a second rule. Notice in Figure 14.9 that the dominant allele can come from the egg and the recessive allele from the sperm, or vice versa. That is, F_1 gametes can combine to produce Rr offspring in two *mutually exclusive* ways: For any particular heterozygous F_2 plant, the dominant allele can come from the egg *or* the sperm, but not from both. According to the **addition rule**, the probability that any one of two or more mutually exclusive events will occur is calculated by adding their individual probabilities. As we have just seen, the multiplication rule gives us the individual

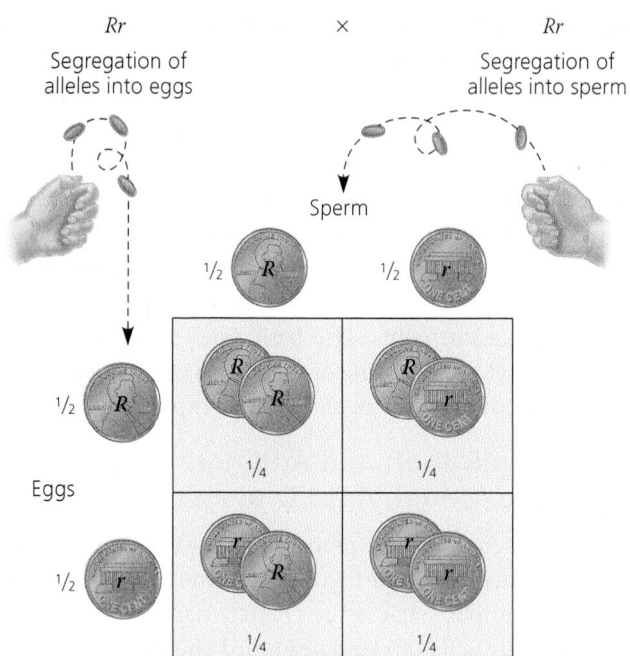

Rr × Rr

Segregation of alleles into eggs   Segregation of alleles into sperm

Sperm

Eggs

▲ Figure 14.9 Segregation of alleles and fertilization as chance events. When a heterozygote (Rr) forms gametes, whether a particular gamete ends up with an R or an r is like the toss of a coin. We can determine the probability for any genotype among the offspring of two heterozygotes by multiplying together the individual probabilities of an egg and sperm having a particular allele (R or r in this example).

probabilities that we will now add together. The probability for one possible way of obtaining an F_2 heterozygote—the dominant allele from the egg and the recessive allele from the sperm—is ¼. The probability for the other possible way—the recessive allele from the egg and the dominant allele from the sperm—is also ¼ (see Figure 14.9). Using the rule of addition, then, we can calculate the probability of an F_2 heterozygote as ¼ + ¼ = ½.

Solving Complex Genetics Problems with the Rules of Probability

We can also apply the rules of probability to predict the outcome of crosses involving multiple characters. Recall that each allelic pair segregates independently during gamete formation (the law of independent assortment). Thus, a dihybrid or other multicharacter cross is equivalent to two or more independent monohybrid crosses occurring simultaneously. By applying what we have learned about monohybrid crosses, we can determine the probability of specific genotypes occurring in the F_2 generation without having to construct unwieldy Punnett squares.

Consider the dihybrid cross between $YyRr$ heterozygotes shown in Figure 14.8. We will focus first on the seed-color character. For a monohybrid cross of Yy plants, we can use a simple Punnett square to determine that the probabilities of the offspring genotypes are ¼ for YY, ½ for Yy, and ¼ for yy. We can draw a second Punnett square to determine that the same

probabilities apply to the offspring genotypes for seed shape: ¼ RR, ½ Rr, and ¼ rr. Knowing these probabilities, we can simply use the multiplication rule to determine the probability of each of the genotypes in the F_2 generation. To give two examples, the calculations for finding the probabilities of two of the possible F_2 genotypes ($YYRR$ and $YyRR$) are shown below:

Probability of $YYRR$ = ¼ (probability of YY) × ¼ (RR) = $\frac{1}{16}$

Probability of $YyRR$ = ½ (Yy)   × ¼ (RR) = ⅛

The $YYRR$ genotype corresponds to the upper left box in the larger Punnett square in Figure 14.8 (one box = $\frac{1}{16}$). Looking closely at the larger Punnett square in Figure 14.8, you will see that 2 of the 16 boxes (⅛) correspond to the $YyRR$ genotype.

Now let's see how we can combine the multiplication and addition rules to solve even more complex problems in Mendelian genetics. Imagine a cross of two pea varieties in which we track the inheritance of three characters. Let's cross a trihybrid with purple flowers and yellow, round seeds (heterozygous for all three genes) with a plant with purple flowers and green, wrinkled seeds (heterozygous for flower color but homozygous recessive for the other two characters). Using Mendelian symbols, our cross is $PpYyRr$ × $Ppyyrr$. What fraction of offspring from this cross are predicted to exhibit the recessive phenotypes for *at least two* of the three characters?

To answer this question, we can start by listing all genotypes we could get that fulfill this condition: $ppyyRr$, $ppYyrr$, $Ppyyrr$, $PPyyrr$, and $ppyyrr$. (Because the condition is *at least two* recessive traits, it includes the last genotype, which shows all three recessive traits.) Next, we calculate the probability for each of these genotypes resulting from our $PpYyRr$ × $Ppyyrr$ cross by multiplying together the individual probabilities for the allele pairs, just as we did in our dihybrid example. Note that in a cross involving heterozygous and homozygous allele pairs (for example, Yy × yy), the probability of heterozygous offspring is ½ and the probability of homozygous offspring is ½. Finally, we use the addition rule to add the probabilities for all the different genotypes that fulfill the condition of at least two recessive traits, as shown below:

$ppyyRr$	¼ (probability of pp) × ½ (yy) × ½ (Rr)	= $\frac{1}{16}$
$ppYyrr$	¼ × ½ × ½	= $\frac{1}{16}$
$Ppyyrr$	½ × ½ × ½	= $\frac{2}{16}$
$PPyyrr$	¼ × ½ × ½	= $\frac{1}{16}$
$ppyyrr$	¼ × ½ × ½	= $\frac{1}{16}$
Chance of *at least two* recessive traits		= $\frac{6}{16}$ or $\frac{3}{8}$

In time, you'll be able to solve genetics problems faster by using the rules of probability than by filling in Punnett squares.

We cannot predict with certainty the exact numbers of progeny of different genotypes resulting from a genetic cross. But the rules of probability give us the *chance* of various outcomes. Usually, the larger the sample size, the closer the results will conform to our predictions. The reason Mendel counted so many offspring from his crosses is that he understood this statistical feature of inheritance and had a keen sense of the rules of chance.

CONCEPT 14.3

Inheritance patterns are often more complex than predicted by simple Mendelian genetics

In the 20th century, geneticists extended Mendelian principles not only to diverse organisms, but also to patterns of inheritance more complex than those described by Mendel. For the work that led to his two laws of inheritance, Mendel chose pea plant characters that turn out to have a relatively simple genetic basis: Each character is determined by one gene, for which there are only two alleles, one completely dominant and the other completely recessive. (There is one exception: Mendel's pod-shape character is actually determined by two genes.) Not all heritable characters are determined so simply, and the relationship between genotype and phenotype is rarely so straightforward. Mendel himself realized that he could not explain the more complicated patterns he observed in crosses involving other pea characters or other plant species. This does not diminish the utility of Mendelian genetics (also called Mendelism), however, because the basic principles of segregation and independent assortment apply even to more complex patterns of inheritance. In this section, we will extend Mendelian genetics to hereditary patterns that were not reported by Mendel.

Extending Mendelian Genetics for a Single Gene

The inheritance of characters determined by a single gene deviates from simple Mendelian patterns when alleles are not completely dominant or recessive, when a particular gene has more than two alleles, or when a single gene produces multiple phenotypes. We will describe examples of each of these situations in this section.

Degrees of Dominance

Alleles can show different degrees of dominance and recessiveness in relation to each other. In Mendel's classic pea crosses, the F$_1$ offspring always looked like one of the two parental varieties because one allele in a pair showed **complete dominance** over the other. In such situations, the phenotypes of the heterozygote and the dominant homozygote are indistinguishable.

For some genes, however, neither allele is completely dominant, and the F$_1$ hybrids have a phenotype somewhere between those of the two parental varieties. This phenomenon, called **incomplete dominance**, is seen when red snapdragons are crossed with white snapdragons: All the F$_1$ hybrids have pink flowers (**Figure 14.10**). This third, intermediate phenotype results from flowers of the heterozygotes having

▲ **Figure 14.10 Incomplete dominance in snapdragon color.** When red snapdragons are crossed with white ones, the F$_1$ hybrids have pink flowers. Segregation of alleles into gametes of the F$_1$ plants results in an F$_2$ generation with a 1:2:1 ratio for both genotype and phenotype. Neither allele is dominant, so rather than using upper- and lowercase letters, we use the letter *C* with a superscript to indicate an allele for flower color: C^R for red and C^W for white.

? *Suppose a classmate argues that this figure supports the blending hypothesis for inheritance. What might your classmate say, and how would you respond?*

less red pigment than the red homozygotes. (This is unlike the case of Mendel's pea plants, where the *Pp* heterozygotes make enough pigment for the flowers to be purple, indistinguishable from those of *PP* plants.)

At first glance, incomplete dominance of either allele seems to provide evidence for the blending hypothesis of inheritance, which would predict that the red or white trait could never be retrieved from the pink hybrids. In fact, interbreeding F_1 hybrids produces F_2 offspring with a phenotypic ratio of one red to two pink to one white. (Because heterozygotes have a separate phenotype, the genotypic and phenotypic ratios for the F_2 generation are the same, 1:2:1.) The segregation of the red-flower and white-flower alleles in the gametes produced by the pink-flowered plants confirms that the alleles for flower color are heritable factors that maintain their identity in the hybrids; that is, inheritance is particulate.

Another variation on dominance relationships between alleles is called **codominance**; in this variation, the two alleles each affect the phenotype in separate, distinguishable ways. For example, the human MN blood group is determined by codominant alleles for two specific molecules located on the surface of red blood cells, the M and N molecules. A single gene locus, at which two allelic variations are possible, determines the phenotype of this blood group. Individuals homozygous for the *M* allele (*MM*) have red blood cells with only M molecules; individuals homozygous for the *N* allele (*NN*) have red blood cells with only N molecules. But *both* M and N molecules are present on the red blood cells of individuals heterozygous for the *M* and *N* alleles (*MN*). Note that the MN phenotype is *not* intermediate between the M and N phenotypes, which distinguishes codominance from incomplete dominance. Rather, *both* M and N phenotypes are exhibited by heterozygotes, since both molecules are present.

The Relationship Between Dominance and Phenotype We've now seen that the relative effects of two alleles range from complete dominance of one allele, through incomplete dominance of either allele, to codominance of both alleles. It is important to understand that an allele is called *dominant* because it is seen in the phenotype, not because it somehow subdues a recessive allele. Alleles are simply variations in a gene's nucleotide sequence. When a dominant allele coexists with a recessive allele in a heterozygote, they do not actually interact at all. It is in the pathway from genotype to phenotype that dominance and recessiveness come into play.

To illustrate the relationship between dominance and phenotype, we can use one of the characters Mendel studied—round versus wrinkled pea seed shape. The dominant allele (round) codes for an enzyme that helps convert an unbranched form of starch to a branched form in the seed. The recessive allele (wrinkled) codes for a defective form of this enzyme, leading to an accumulation of unbranched starch, which causes excess water to enter the seed by osmosis. Later, when the seed dries, it wrinkles. If a dominant allele is present, no excess water enters the seed and it does not wrinkle when it dries. One dominant allele results in enough of the enzyme to synthesize adequate amounts of branched starch, which means that dominant homozygotes and heterozygotes have the same phenotype: round seeds.

A closer look at the relationship between dominance and phenotype reveals an intriguing fact: For any character, the observed dominant/recessive relationship of alleles depends on the level at which we examine phenotype. **Tay-Sachs disease**, an inherited disorder in humans, provides an example. The brain cells of a child with Tay-Sachs disease cannot metabolize certain lipids because a crucial enzyme does not work properly. As these lipids accumulate in brain cells, the child begins to suffer seizures, blindness, and degeneration of motor and mental performance and dies within a few years.

Only children who inherit two copies of the Tay-Sachs allele (homozygotes) have the disease. Thus, at the *organismal* level, the Tay-Sachs allele qualifies as recessive. However, the activity level of the lipid-metabolizing enzyme in heterozygotes is intermediate between that in individuals homozygous for the normal allele and that in individuals with Tay-Sachs disease. The intermediate phenotype observed at the *biochemical* level is characteristic of incomplete dominance of either allele. Fortunately, the heterozygote condition does not lead to disease symptoms, apparently because half the normal enzyme activity is sufficient to prevent lipid accumulation in the brain. Extending our analysis to yet another level, we find that heterozygous individuals produce equal numbers of normal and dysfunctional enzyme molecules. Thus, at the *molecular* level, the normal allele and the Tay-Sachs allele are codominant. As you can see, whether alleles appear to be completely dominant, incompletely dominant, or codominant depends on the level at which the phenotype is analyzed.

Frequency of Dominant Alleles Although you might assume that the dominant allele for a particular character would be more common in a population than the recessive allele, this is not a given. For example, about one baby out of 400 in the United States is born with extra fingers or toes, a condition known as polydactyly. Some cases are caused by the presence of a dominant allele. The low frequency of polydactyly indicates that the recessive allele, which results in five digits per appendage, is far more prevalent than the dominant allele in the population. In Chapter 23, you will learn how relative frequencies of alleles in a population are affected by natural selection.

Multiple Alleles

Only two alleles exist for the pea characters that Mendel studied, but most genes exist in more than two allelic forms. The ABO blood groups in humans, for instance, are determined by three alleles of a single gene: I^A, I^B, and i. A person's blood

(a) The three alleles for the ABO blood groups and their carbohydrates. Each allele codes for an enzyme that may add a specific carbohydrate (designated by the superscript on the allele and shown as a triangle or circle) to red blood cells.

Allele	I^A	I^B	i
Carbohydrate	A △	B ○	none

(b) Blood group genotypes and phenotypes. There are six possible genotypes, resulting in four different phenotypes.

Genotype	$I^A I^A$ or $I^A i$	$I^B I^B$ or $I^B i$	$I^A I^B$	ii
Red blood cell appearance				
Phenotype (blood group)	A	B	AB	O

▲ **Figure 14.11 Multiple alleles for the ABO blood groups.** The four blood groups result from different combinations of three alleles.

❓ *Based on the surface carbohydrate phenotype in (b), what are the dominance relationships among the alleles?*

group (phenotype) may be one of four types: A, B, AB, or O. These letters refer to two carbohydrates—A and B—that may be found on the surface of red blood cells. A person's blood cells may have carbohydrate A (type A blood), carbohydrate B (type B), both (type AB), or neither (type O), as shown schematically in **Figure 14.11**. Matching compatible blood groups is critical for safe blood transfusions (see Chapter 43).

Pleiotropy

So far, we have treated Mendelian inheritance as though each gene affects only one phenotypic character. Most genes, however, have multiple phenotypic effects, a property called **pleiotropy** (from the Greek *pleion*, more). In humans, for example, pleiotropic alleles are responsible for the multiple symptoms associated with certain hereditary diseases, such as cystic fibrosis and sickle-cell disease, discussed later in this chapter. In the garden pea, the gene that determines flower color also affects the color of the coating on the outer surface of the seed, which can be gray or white. Given the intricate molecular and cellular interactions responsible for an organism's development and physiology, it isn't surprising that a single gene can affect a number of characteristics in an organism.

Extending Mendelian Genetics for Two or More Genes

Dominance relationships, multiple alleles, and pleiotropy all have to do with the effects of the alleles of a single gene. We now consider two situations in which two or more genes are involved in determining a particular phenotype.

Epistasis

In **epistasis** (from the Greek for "standing upon"), the phenotypic expression of a gene at one locus alters that of a gene at a second locus. An example will help clarify this concept. In Labrador retrievers (commonly called "Labs"), black coat color is dominant to brown. Let's designate *B* and *b* as the two alleles for this character. For a Lab to have brown fur, its genotype must be *bb*; these dogs are called chocolate Labs. But there is more to the story. A second gene determines whether or not pigment will be deposited in the hair. The dominant allele, symbolized by *E*, results in the deposition of either black or brown pigment, depending on the genotype at the first locus. But if the Lab is homozygous recessive for the second locus (*ee*), then the coat is yellow, regardless of the genotype at the black/brown locus. In this case, the gene for pigment deposition (*E/e*) is said to be epistatic to the gene that codes for black or brown pigment (*B/b*).

What happens if we mate black Labs that are heterozygous for both genes (*BbEe*)? Although the two genes affect the same phenotypic character (coat color), they follow the law of independent assortment. Thus, our breeding experiment represents an F$_1$ dihybrid cross, like those that produced a 9:3:3:1 ratio in Mendel's experiments. We can use a Punnett square to represent the genotypes of the F$_2$ offspring (**Figure 14.12**). As a result

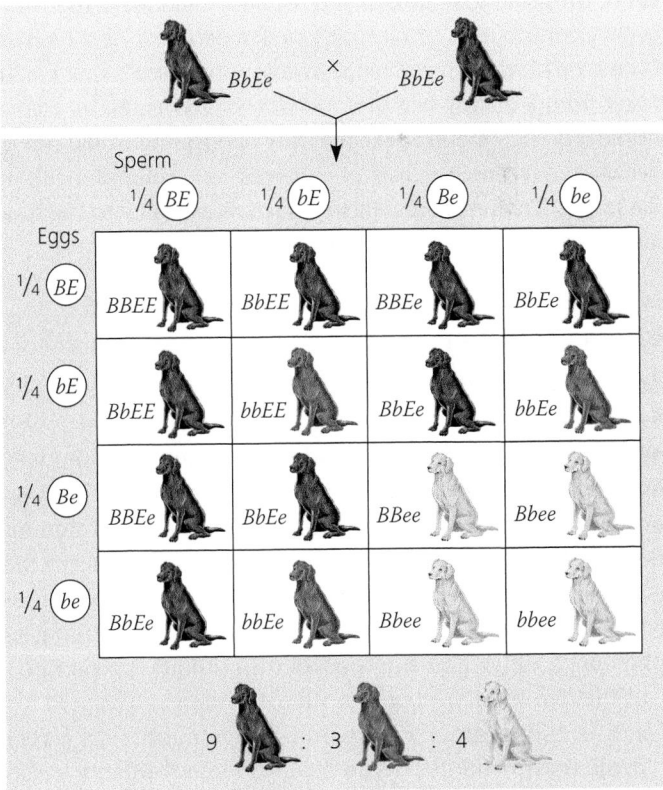

▲ **Figure 14.12 An example of epistasis.** This Punnett square illustrates the genotypes and phenotypes predicted for offspring of matings between two black Labrador retrievers of genotype *BbEe*. The *E/e* gene, which is epistatic to the *B/b* gene coding for hair pigment, controls whether or not pigment of any color will be deposited in the hair.

of epistasis, the phenotypic ratio among the F₂ offspring is nine black to three chocolate (brown) to four yellow. Other types of epistatic interactions produce different ratios, but all are modified versions of 9:3:3:1.

Polygenic Inheritance

Mendel studied characters that could be classified on an either-or basis, such as purple versus white flower color. But for many characters, such as human skin color and height, an either-or classification is impossible because the characters vary in the population in gradations along a continuum. These are called **quantitative characters**. Quantitative variation usually indicates **polygenic inheritance**, an additive effect of two or more genes on a single phenotypic character (the converse of pleiotropy, where a single gene affects several phenotypic characters).

There is evidence, for instance, that skin pigmentation in humans is controlled by at least three separately inherited genes (probably more, but we will simplify). Let's consider three genes, with a dark-skin allele for each gene (*A*, *B*, or *C*) contributing one "unit" of darkness (also a simplification) to the phenotype and being incompletely dominant to the other allele (*a*, *b*, or *c*). An *AABBCC* person would be very dark, while an *aabbcc* individual would be very light. An *AaBbCc* person would have skin of an intermediate shade. Because the alleles have a cumulative effect, the genotypes *AaBbCc* and *AABbcc* would make the same genetic contribution (three units) to skin darkness. As shown in **Figure 14.13**, there are seven skin-color phenotypes that could result from a mating between *AaBbCc* heterozygotes. In a large number of such matings, the majority of offspring would be expected to have intermediate phenotypes (skin color in the middle range). Environmental factors, such as exposure to the sun, also affect the skin-color phenotype.

Nature and Nurture: The Environmental Impact on Phenotype

Another departure from simple Mendelian genetics arises when the phenotype for a character depends on environment as well as genotype. A single tree, locked into its inherited genotype, has leaves that vary in size, shape, and greenness, depending on their exposure to wind and sun. For humans, nutrition influences height, exercise alters build, sun-tanning darkens the skin, and experience improves performance on intelligence tests. Even identical twins, who are genetic equals, accumulate phenotypic differences as a result of their unique experiences.

Whether human characteristics are more influenced by genes or the environment—nature versus nurture—is a very old and hotly contested debate that we will not attempt to settle here. We can say, however, that a genotype generally is not associated with a rigidly defined phenotype, but rather with a range of phenotypic possibilities due to environmental influences. This phenotypic range is called the **norm of reaction** for a genotype **(Figure 14.14)**. For some characters, such as the

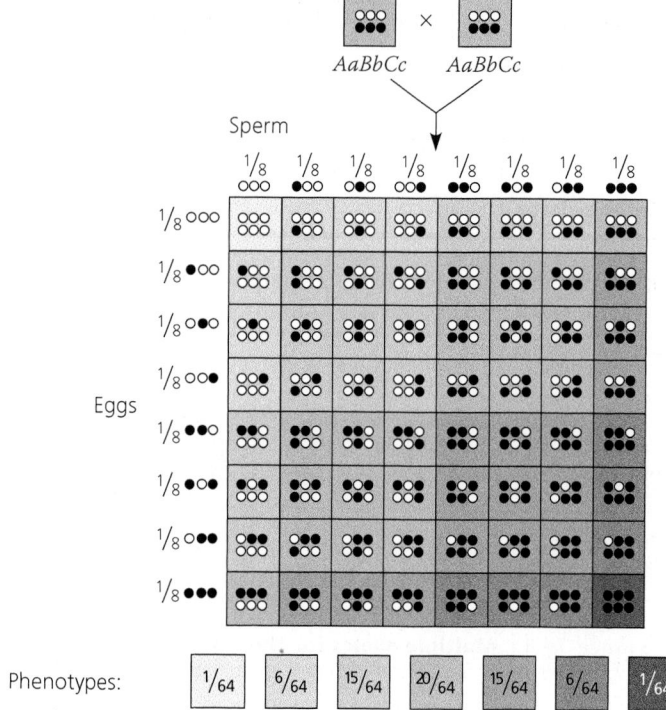

▲ **Figure 14.13 A simplified model for polygenic inheritance of skin color.** According to this model, three separately inherited genes affect the darkness of skin. The heterozygous individuals (*AaBbCc*) represented by the two rectangles at the top of this figure each carry three dark-skin alleles (black circles, which represent *A*, *B*, or *C*) and three light-skin alleles (white circles, which represent *a*, *b*, or *c*). The Punnett square shows all the possible genetic combinations in gametes and in offspring of a large number of hypothetical matings between these heterozygotes. The results are summarized by the phenotypic ratios under the Punnett square.

DRAW IT *Make a bar graph of the results, with skin color (number of dark-skin alleles) along the x-axis and fraction of offspring along the y-axis. Draw a rough curve corresponding to the results and discuss what it shows about the relative proportions of different phenotypes among the offspring.*

▲ **Figure 14.14 The effect of environment on phenotype.** The outcome of a genotype lies within its norm of reaction, a phenotypic range that depends on the environment in which the genotype is expressed. For example, hydrangea flowers of the same genetic variety range in color from blue-violet to pink, with the shade and intensity of color depending on the acidity and aluminum content of the soil.

ABO blood group system, the norm of reaction has no breadth whatsoever; that is, a given genotype mandates a very specific phenotype. Other characteristics, such as a person's blood count of red and white cells, vary quite a bit, depending on such factors as the altitude, the customary level of physical activity, and the presence of infectious agents.

Generally, norms of reaction are broadest for polygenic characters. Environment contributes to the quantitative nature of these characters, as we have seen in the continuous variation of skin color. Geneticists refer to such characters as **multifactorial**, meaning that many factors, both genetic and environmental, collectively influence phenotype.

Integrating a Mendelian View of Heredity and Variation

We have now broadened our view of Mendelian inheritance by exploring degrees of dominance as well as multiple alleles, pleiotropy, epistasis, polygenic inheritance, and the phenotypic impact of the environment. How can we integrate these refinements into a comprehensive theory of Mendelian genetics? The key is to make the transition from the reductionist emphasis on single genes and phenotypic characters to the emergent properties of the organism as a whole, one of the themes of this book.

The term *phenotype* can refer not only to specific characters, such as flower color and blood group, but also to an organism in its entirety—*all* aspects of its physical appearance, internal anatomy, physiology, and behavior. Similarly, the term *genotype* can refer to an organism's entire genetic makeup, not just its alleles for a single genetic locus. In most cases, a gene's impact on phenotype is affected by other genes and by the environment. In this integrated view of heredity and variation, an organism's phenotype reflects its overall genotype and unique environmental history.

Considering all that can occur in the pathway from genotype to phenotype, it is indeed impressive that Mendel could uncover the fundamental principles governing the transmission of individual genes from parents to offspring. Mendel's two laws, segregation and independent assortment, explain heritable variations in terms of alternative forms of genes (hereditary "particles," now known as the alleles of genes) that are passed along, generation after generation, according to simple rules of probability. This theory of inheritance is equally valid for peas, flies, fishes, birds, and human beings—indeed, for any organism with a sexual life cycle. Furthermore, by extending the principles of segregation and independent assortment to help explain such hereditary patterns as epistasis and quantitative characters, we begin to see how broadly Mendelism applies. From Mendel's abbey garden came a theory of particulate inheritance that anchors modern genetics. In the last section of this chapter, we will apply Mendelian genetics to human inheritance, with emphasis on the transmission of hereditary diseases.

CONCEPT CHECK 14.3

1. *Incomplete dominance* and *epistasis* are both terms that define genetic relationships. What is the most basic distinction between these terms?
2. If a man with type AB blood marries a woman with type O, what blood types would you expect in their children? What fraction would you expect of each type?
3. **WHAT IF?** A rooster with gray feathers and a hen of the same phenotype produce 15 gray, 6 black, and 8 white chicks. What is the simplest explanation for the inheritance of these colors in chickens? What phenotypes would you expect in the offspring of a cross between a gray rooster and a black hen?

For suggested answers, see Appendix A.

CONCEPT 14.4

Many human traits follow Mendelian patterns of inheritance

Peas are convenient subjects for genetic research, but humans are not. The human generation span is long—about 20 years—and human parents produce many fewer offspring than peas and most other species. Even more important, it wouldn't be ethical to ask pairs of humans to breed so that the phenotypes of their offspring could be analyzed! In spite of these constraints, the study of human genetics continues, spurred on by our desire to understand our own inheritance. New molecular biological techniques have led to many breakthrough discoveries, as we will see in Chapter 20, but basic Mendelism endures as the foundation of human genetics.

Pedigree Analysis

Unable to manipulate the mating patterns of people, geneticists must analyze the results of matings that have already occurred. They do so by collecting information about a family's history for a particular trait and assembling this information into a family tree describing the traits of parents and children across the generations—the family **pedigree**.

Figure 14.15a, on the next page, shows a three-generation pedigree that traces the occurrence of a pointed contour of the hairline on the forehead. This trait, called a widow's peak, is due to a dominant allele, *W*. Because the widow's-peak allele is dominant, all individuals who lack a widow's peak must be homozygous recessive (*ww*). The two grandparents with widow's peaks must have the *Ww* genotype, since some of their offspring are homozygous recessive. The offspring in the second generation who *do* have widow's peaks must also be heterozygous, because they are the products of *Ww* × *ww* matings. The third generation in this pedigree consists of two sisters. The one

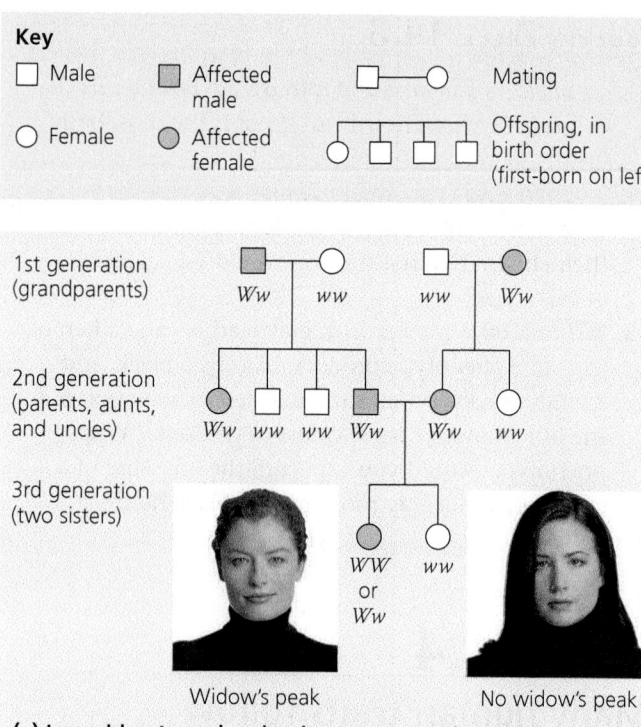

Key

☐ Male ▨ Affected male ☐—○ Mating

○ Female ⬤ Affected female Offspring, in birth order (first-born on left)

1st generation (grandparents) — ▨ *Ww* ○ *ww* ☐ *ww* ⬤ *Ww*

2nd generation (parents, aunts, and uncles) — ⬤ *Ww* ☐ *ww* ☐ *ww* ▨ *Ww* ⬤ *Ww* ○ *ww*

3rd generation (two sisters) — ⬤ *WW* or *Ww* ○ *ww*

Widow's peak   No widow's peak

(a) Is a widow's peak a dominant or recessive trait?
Tips for pedigree analysis: Notice in the third generation that the second-born daughter lacks a widow's peak, although both of her parents had the trait. Such a pattern of inheritance supports the hypothesis that the trait is due to a dominant allele. If the trait were due to a *recessive* allele, and both parents had the recessive phenotype, then *all* of their offspring would also have the recessive phenotype.

1st generation (grandparents) — ☐—○ *Ff Ff* ▨—○ *ff Ff*

2nd generation (parents, aunts, and uncles) — ○ *FF* or *Ff* ▨ *ff* ▨ *ff* ☐ *Ff* ○ *Ff* ⬤ *ff*

3rd generation (two sisters) — ⬤ *ff* ○ *FF* or *Ff*

Attached earlobe   Free earlobe

(b) Is an attached earlobe a dominant or recessive trait?
Tips for pedigree analysis: Notice that the first-born daughter in the third generation has attached earlobes, although both of her parents lack that trait (they have free earlobes). Such a pattern is easily explained if the attached-lobe phenotype is due to a recessive allele. If it were due to a *dominant* allele, then at least one parent would also have had the trait.

▲ **Figure 14.15 Pedigree analysis.** Each of these pedigrees traces a trait through three generations of the same family. The two traits have different inheritance patterns, as seen by analysis of the pedigrees.

who has a widow's peak could be either homozygous (*WW*) or heterozygous (*Ww*), given what we know about the genotypes of her parents (both *Ww*).

Figure 14.15b is a pedigree of the same family, but this time we focus on a recessive trait, attached earlobes. We'll use *f* for the recessive allele and *F* for the dominant allele, which results in free earlobes. As you work your way through the pedigree, notice once again that you can apply what you have learned about Mendelian inheritance to understand the genotypes shown for the family members.

An important application of a pedigree is to help us calculate the probability that a future child will have a particular genotype and phenotype. Suppose that the couple represented in the second generation of Figure 14.15 decides to have one more child. What is the probability that the child will have a widow's peak? This is equivalent to a Mendelian F_1 monohybrid cross (*Ww* × *Ww*), and thus the probability that a child will inherit a dominant allele and have a widow's peak is ¾ (¼ *WW* + ½ *Ww*). What is the probability that the child will have attached earlobes? Again, we can treat this as a monohybrid cross (*Ff* × *Ff*), but this time we want to know the chance that the offspring will be homozygous recessive (*ff*). That probability is ¼. Finally, what is the chance that the child will have a widow's peak *and* attached earlobes? Assuming that the genes for these two characters are on different chromosomes, the two pairs of alleles will assort independently in this dihybrid cross (*WwFf* × *WwFf*). Thus, we can use the multiplication rule: ¾ (chance of widow's peak) × ¼ (chance of attached earlobes) = ³⁄₁₆ (chance of widow's peak and attached earlobes).

Pedigrees are a more serious matter when the alleles in question cause disabling or deadly diseases instead of innocuous human variations such as hairline or earlobe configuration. However, for disorders inherited as simple Mendelian traits, the same techniques of pedigree analysis apply.

Recessively Inherited Disorders

Thousands of genetic disorders are known to be inherited as simple recessive traits. These disorders range in severity from relatively mild, such as albinism (lack of pigmentation, which results in susceptibility to skin cancers and vision problems), to life-threatening, such as cystic fibrosis.

The Behavior of Recessive Alleles

How can we account for the behavior of alleles that cause recessively inherited disorders? Recall that genes code for proteins of specific function. An allele that causes a genetic disorder (let's call it allele *a*) codes for either a malfunctioning protein or no protein at all. In the case of disorders classified as recessive, heterozygotes (*Aa*) are typically normal in phenotype because one copy of the normal allele (*A*) produces a sufficient amount of the specific protein. Thus, a recessively inherited disorder shows up only in the homozygous individuals (*aa*)

Parents

Normal
Aa × Normal *Aa*

Sperm

A a

Eggs

A

	A	a
A	*AA* Normal	*Aa* Normal (carrier)
a	*Aa* Normal (carrier)	*aa* Albino

▲ **Figure 14.16 Albinism: a recessive trait.** One of the two sisters shown here has normal coloration; the other is albino. Most recessive homozygotes are born to parents who are carriers of the disorder but themselves have a normal phenotype, the case shown in the Punnett square.

? *What is the probability that the sister with normal coloration is a carrier of the albinism allele?*

who inherit one recessive allele from each parent. Although phenotypically normal with regard to the disorder, heterozygotes may transmit the recessive allele to their offspring and thus are called **carriers**. Figure 14.16 illustrates these ideas using albinism as an example.

Most people who have recessive disorders are born to parents who are carriers of the disorder but have a normal phenotype, as is the case shown in the Punnett square in Figure 14.16. A mating between two carriers corresponds to a Mendelian F₁ monohybrid cross, so the predicted genotypic ratio for the offspring is 1 *AA* : 2 *Aa* : 1 *aa*. Thus, each child has a ¼ chance of inheriting a double dose of the recessive allele; in the case of albinism, such a child will be albino. From the genotypic ratio, we also can see that out of three offspring with the *normal* phenotype (one *AA* plus two *Aa*), two are predicted to be heterozygous carriers, a ⅔ chance. Recessive homozygotes could also result from *Aa* × *aa* and *aa* × *aa* matings, but if the disorder is lethal before reproductive age or results in sterility (neither of which is true for albinism), no *aa* individuals will reproduce. Even if recessive homozygotes are able to reproduce, such individuals will still account for a much smaller percentage of the population than heterozygous carriers (for reasons we will examine in Chapter 23).

In general, genetic disorders are not evenly distributed among all groups of people. For example, the incidence of Tay-Sachs disease, which we described earlier in this chapter, is disproportionately high among Ashkenazic Jews, Jewish people whose ancestors lived in central Europe. In that population, Tay-Sachs disease occurs in one out of 3,600 births, an incidence about 100 times greater than that among non-Jews or Mediterranean (Sephardic) Jews. This uneven distribution results from the different genetic histories of the world's peoples during less technological times, when populations were more geographically (and hence genetically) isolated.

When a disease-causing recessive allele is rare, it is relatively unlikely that two carriers of the same harmful allele will meet and mate. However, if the man and woman are close relatives (for example, siblings or first cousins), the probability of passing on recessive traits increases greatly. These are called consanguineous ("same blood") matings, and they are indicated in pedigrees by double lines. Because people with recent common ancestors are more likely to carry the same recessive alleles than are unrelated people, it is more likely that a mating of close relatives will produce offspring homozygous for recessive traits—including harmful ones. Such effects can be observed in many types of domesticated and zoo animals that have become inbred.

There is debate among geneticists about the extent to which human consanguinity increases the risk of inherited diseases. Many deleterious alleles have such severe effects that a homozygous embryo spontaneously aborts long before birth. Still, most societies and cultures have laws or taboos forbidding marriages between close relatives. These rules may have evolved out of empirical observation that in most populations, stillbirths and birth defects are more common when parents are closely related. Social and economic factors have also influenced the development of customs and laws against consanguineous marriages.

Cystic Fibrosis

The most common lethal genetic disease in the United States is **cystic fibrosis**, which strikes one out of every 2,500 people of European descent but is much rarer in other groups. Among people of European descent, one out of 25 (4%) are carriers of the cystic fibrosis allele. The normal allele for this gene codes for a membrane protein that functions in the transport of chloride ions between certain cells and the extracellular fluid. These chloride transport channels are defective or absent in the plasma membranes of children who inherit two recessive alleles for cystic fibrosis. The result is an abnormally high concentration of extracellular chloride, which causes the mucus that coats certain cells to become thicker and stickier than normal. The mucus builds up in the pancreas, lungs, digestive tract, and other organs, leading to multiple (pleiotropic) effects, including poor absorption of nutrients from the intestines, chronic bronchitis, and recurrent bacterial infections.

If untreated, most children with cystic fibrosis die before their 5th birthday. But daily doses of antibiotics to prevent infection, gentle pounding on the chest to clear mucus from clogged airways, and other preventive treatments can prolong life. In the United States, more than half of those with cystic fibrosis now survive into their late 20s or even 30s and beyond.

Sickle-Cell Disease: A Genetic Disorder with Evolutionary Implications

EVOLUTION The most common inherited disorder among people of African descent is **sickle-cell disease**, which affects one out of 400 African-Americans. Sickle-cell disease is caused by the substitution of a single amino acid in the hemoglobin protein of red blood cells; in homozygous individuals, all hemoglobin is of the sickle-cell (abnormal) variety. When the oxygen content of an affected individual's blood is low (at high altitudes or under physical stress, for instance), the sickle-cell hemoglobin molecules aggregate into long rods that deform the red cells into a sickle shape (see Figure 5.21). Sickled cells may clump and clog small blood vessels, often leading to other symptoms throughout the body, including physical weakness, pain, organ damage, and even paralysis. Regular blood transfusions can ward off brain damage in children with sickle-cell disease, and new drugs can help prevent or treat other problems, but there is no cure.

Although two sickle-cell alleles are necessary for an individual to manifest full-blown sickle-cell disease, the presence of one sickle-cell allele can affect the phenotype. Thus, at the organismal level, the normal allele is incompletely dominant to the sickle-cell allele. Heterozygotes (carriers), said to have *sickle-cell trait*, are usually healthy, but they may suffer some sickle-cell symptoms during prolonged periods of reduced blood oxygen. At the molecular level, the two alleles are codominant; both normal and abnormal (sickle-cell) hemoglobins are made in heterozygotes.

About one out of ten African-Americans have sickle-cell trait, an unusually high frequency of heterozygotes for an allele with severe detrimental effects in homozygotes. Why haven't evolutionary processes resulted in the disappearance of this allele among this population? One explanation is that having a single copy of the sickle-cell allele reduces the frequency and severity of malaria attacks, especially among young children. The malaria parasite spends part of its life cycle in red blood cells (see Figure 28.10), and the presence of even heterozygous amounts of sickle-cell hemoglobin results in lower parasite densities and hence reduced malaria symptoms. Thus, in tropical Africa, where infection with the malaria parasite is common, the sickle-cell allele confers an advantage to heterozygotes even though it is harmful in the homozygous state. (The balance between these two effects will be discussed in Chapter 23, p. 484.) The relatively high frequency of African-Americans with sickle-cell trait is a vestige of their African roots.

Dominantly Inherited Disorders

Although many harmful alleles are recessive, a number of human disorders are due to dominant alleles. One example is *achondroplasia*, a form of dwarfism that occurs in one of every 25,000 people. Heterozygous individuals have the dwarf phenotype (**Figure 14.17**). Therefore, all people who are not achondroplastic dwarfs—99.99% of the population—are homozygous for the recessive allele. Like the presence of extra fingers or toes mentioned earlier, achondroplasia is a trait for which the recessive allele is much more prevalent than the corresponding dominant allele.

▲ **Figure 14.17 Achondroplasia: a dominant trait.** Dr. Michael C. Ain has achondroplasia, a form of dwarfism caused by a dominant allele. This has inspired his work: He is a specialist in the repair of bone defects caused by achondroplasia and other disorders. The dominant allele (*D*) might have arisen as a mutation in the egg or sperm of a parent or could have been inherited from an affected parent, as shown for an affected father in the Punnett square.

Dominant alleles that cause a lethal disease are much less common than recessive alleles that have lethal effects. All lethal alleles arise by mutations (changes to the DNA) in cells that produce sperm or eggs; presumably, such mutations are equally likely to be recessive or dominant. A lethal recessive allele can be passed from one generation to the next by heterozygous carriers because the carriers themselves have normal phenotypes. A lethal dominant allele, however, often causes the death of afflicted individuals before they can mature and reproduce, so the allele is not passed on to future generations.

Huntington's Disease: A Late-Onset Lethal Disease

The timing of onset of a disease significantly affects its inheritance. A lethal dominant allele is able to be passed on if it causes death at a relatively advanced age. By the time symptoms are evident, the individual with the allele may have already transmitted it to his or her children. For example, **Huntington's disease**, a degenerative disease of the nervous system, is caused by a lethal dominant allele that has no obvious phenotypic effect until the individual is about 35 to 45 years old. Once the deterioration of the nervous system begins, it is irreversible and inevitably fatal. As with other dominant traits, a child born to a parent with the Huntington's disease allele has a 50% chance of inheriting the allele and the disorder (see the Punnett square in Figure 14.17). In the United States, this devastating disease afflicts about one in 10,000 people.

At one time, the onset of symptoms was the only way to know if a person had inherited the Huntington's allele, but this is no longer the case. By analyzing DNA samples from a large family with a high incidence of the disorder, geneticists tracked the Huntington's allele to a locus near the tip of chromosome 4, and the gene was sequenced in 1993. This information led to the development of a test that could detect the presence of the Huntington's allele in an individual's genome. (The methods that make such tests possible are discussed in Chapter 20.) The availability of this test poses an agonizing dilemma for those with a family history of Huntington's disease. Some individuals may want to be tested for this disease before planning a family, whereas others may decide it would be too stressful to find out. Clearly, this is a highly personal decision.

Multifactorial Disorders

The hereditary diseases we have discussed so far are sometimes described as simple Mendelian disorders because they result from abnormality of one or both alleles at a single genetic locus. Many more people are susceptible to diseases that have a multifactorial basis—a genetic component plus a significant environmental influence. Heart disease, diabetes, cancer, alcoholism, certain mental illnesses such as schizophrenia and bipolar disorder, and many other diseases are multifactorial. In many cases, the hereditary component is polygenic. For example, many genes affect cardiovascular health, making some of us more prone than others to heart attacks and strokes. No matter what our genotype, however, our lifestyle has a tremendous effect on phenotype for cardiovascular health and other multifactorial characters. Exercise, a healthful diet, abstinence from smoking, and an ability to handle stressful situations all reduce our risk of heart disease and some types of cancer.

At present, so little is understood about the genetic contributions to most multifactorial diseases that the best public health strategy is to educate people about the importance of environmental factors and to promote healthful behavior.

Genetic Testing and Counseling

Avoiding simple Mendelian disorders is possible when the risk of a particular genetic disorder can be assessed before a child is conceived or during the early stages of the pregnancy. Many hospitals have genetic counselors who can provide information to prospective parents concerned about a family history for a specific disease.

Counseling Based on Mendelian Genetics and Probability Rules

Consider the case of a hypothetical couple, John and Carol. Each had a brother who died from the same recessively inherited lethal disease. Before conceiving their first child, John and Carol seek genetic counseling to determine the risk of having a child with the disease. From the information about their brothers, we know that both parents of John and both parents of Carol must have been carriers of the recessive allele. Thus, John and Carol are both products of $Aa \times Aa$ crosses, where a symbolizes the allele that causes this particular disease. We also know that John and Carol are not homozygous recessive

(aa), because they do not have the disease. Therefore, their genotypes are either AA or Aa.

Given a genotypic ratio of $1\ AA : 2\ Aa : 1\ aa$ for offspring of an $Aa \times Aa$ cross, John and Carol each have a ⅔ chance of being carriers (Aa). According to the rule of multiplication, the overall probability of their firstborn having the disorder is ⅔ (the chance that John is a carrier) times ⅔ (the chance that Carol is a carrier) times ¼ (the chance of two carriers having a child with the disease), which equals ⅑. Suppose that Carol and John decide to have a child—after all, there is an ⅛ chance that their baby will not have the disorder. If, despite these odds, their child is born with the disease, then we would know that *both* John and Carol are, in fact, carriers (Aa genotype). If both John and Carol are carriers, there is a ¼ chance that any subsequent child this couple has will have the disease. The probability is higher for subsequent children because the diagnosis of the disease in the first child established that both parents are carriers, not because the genotype of the first child affects in any way that of future children.

When we use Mendel's laws to predict possible outcomes of matings, it is important to remember that each child represents an independent event in the sense that its genotype is unaffected by the genotypes of older siblings. Suppose that John and Carol have three more children, and *all three* have the hypothetical hereditary disease. There is only one chance in 64 ($\frac{1}{4} \times \frac{1}{4} \times \frac{1}{4}$) that such an outcome will occur. Despite this run of misfortune, the chance that still another child of this couple will have the disease remains ¼.

Tests for Identifying Carriers

Most children with recessive disorders are born to parents with normal phenotypes. The key to accurately assessing the genetic risk for a particular disease is therefore to find out whether the prospective parents are heterozygous carriers of the recessive allele. For an increasing number of heritable disorders, tests are available that can distinguish individuals of normal phenotype who are dominant homozygotes from those who are heterozygous carriers (**Figure 14.18**, on the next page). There are now tests that can identify carriers of the alleles for Tay-Sachs disease, sickle-cell disease, and the most common form of cystic fibrosis.

These tests for identifying carriers enable people with family histories of genetic disorders to make informed decisions about having children, but raise other issues. Could carriers be denied health or life insurance or lose the jobs providing those benefits, even though they themselves are healthy? The Genetic Information Nondiscrimination Act, signed into law in the United States in 2008, allays these concerns by prohibiting discrimination in employment or insurance coverage based on genetic test results. A question that remains is whether sufficient genetic counseling is available to help large numbers of individuals understand their genetic test results. Even when test results are clearly understood, affected individuals may still face difficult decisions. Advances in biotechnology offer

IMPACT

Genetic Testing

Since the sequencing of the human genome was completed in 2003, there has been a virtual explosion in the number and kinds of DNA-based genetic tests. As of 2010, genetic testing for over 2,000 different disease-causing alleles is available.

WHY IT MATTERS For prospective parents with a family history of a recessive or late-onset dominant disorder, deciding whether to have children can be a difficult decision. Genetic testing can eliminate some of the uncertainty and allow better predictions of the probabilities and risks involved.

FURTHER READING Designing rules for designer babies, *Scientific American* 300:29 (2009).

WHAT IF? If one parent tests positive and the other tests negative for a recessive allele associated with a disorder, what is the probability that their first child will have the disorder? That their first child will be a carrier? That, if their first child is a carrier, the second will also be a carrier?

the potential to reduce human suffering, but along with them come ethical issues that require conscientious deliberation.

Fetal Testing

Suppose a couple expecting a child learns that they are both carriers of the Tay-Sachs allele. In the 14th–16th week of pregnancy, tests performed along with a technique called **amniocentesis** can determine whether the developing fetus has Tay-Sachs disease (Figure 14.19a). In this procedure, a physician inserts a needle into the uterus and extracts about 10 mL of amniotic fluid, the liquid that bathes the fetus. Some genetic disorders can be detected from the presence of certain molecules in the amniotic fluid itself. Tests for other disorders, including Tay-Sachs disease, are performed on the DNA of cells cultured in the laboratory, descendants of fetal cells sloughed off into the amniotic fluid. A karyotype of these cultured cells can also identify certain chromosomal defects (see Figure 13.3).

In an alternative technique called **chorionic villus sampling (CVS)**, a physician inserts a narrow tube through the cervix into the uterus and suctions out a tiny sample of tissue from the placenta, the organ that transmits nutrients and fetal wastes between the fetus and the mother (Figure 14.19b). The cells of the chorionic villi of the placenta, the portion sampled, are derived from the fetus and have the same genotype and DNA sequence as the new individual. These cells are proliferating rapidly enough to allow karyotyping to be carried out immediately. This rapid analysis represents an advantage over amniocentesis, in which the cells must be cultured for several weeks before karyotyping. Another advantage of CVS is that it can be performed as early as the 8th–10th week of pregnancy.

Recently, medical scientists have developed methods for isolating fetal cells, or even fetal DNA, that have escaped into the mother's blood. Although very few are present, the cells can be cultured and tested, and the fetal DNA can also be analyzed.

Imaging techniques allow a physician to examine a fetus directly for major anatomical abnormalities that might not show up in genetic tests. In the *ultrasound* technique, reflected sound waves are used to produce an image of the fetus by a simple noninvasive procedure. In *fetoscopy*, a needle-thin tube containing a viewing scope and fiber optics (to transmit light) is inserted into the uterus.

Ultrasound and isolation of fetal cells or DNA from maternal blood pose no known risk to either mother or fetus, while the other procedures can cause complications in a small percentage of cases. Amniocentesis or CVS for diagnostic testing is generally offered to women over age 35, due to their increased risk of bearing a child with Down syndrome, and may also be offered to younger women if there are known concerns. If the fetal tests reveal a serious disorder, the parents face the difficult choice of either terminating the pregnancy or preparing to care for a child with a genetic disorder.

Newborn Screening

Some genetic disorders can be detected at birth by simple biochemical tests that are now routinely performed in most hospitals in the United States. One common screening program is for phenylketonuria (PKU), a recessively inherited disorder that occurs in about one out of every 10,000–15,000 births in the United States. Children with this disease cannot properly metabolize the amino acid phenylalanine. This compound and its by-product, phenylpyruvate, can accumulate to toxic levels in the blood, causing severe intellectual disability (mental retardation). However, if PKU is detected in the newborn, a special diet low in phenylalanine will usually allow normal development. (Among many other substances, this diet excludes the artificial sweetener aspartame, which contains phenylalanine.) Unfortunately, few other genetic disorders are treatable at present.

Fetal and newborn screening for serious inherited diseases, tests for identifying carriers, and genetic counseling all rely on the Mendelian model of inheritance. We owe the "gene idea"—the concept of heritable factors transmitted according

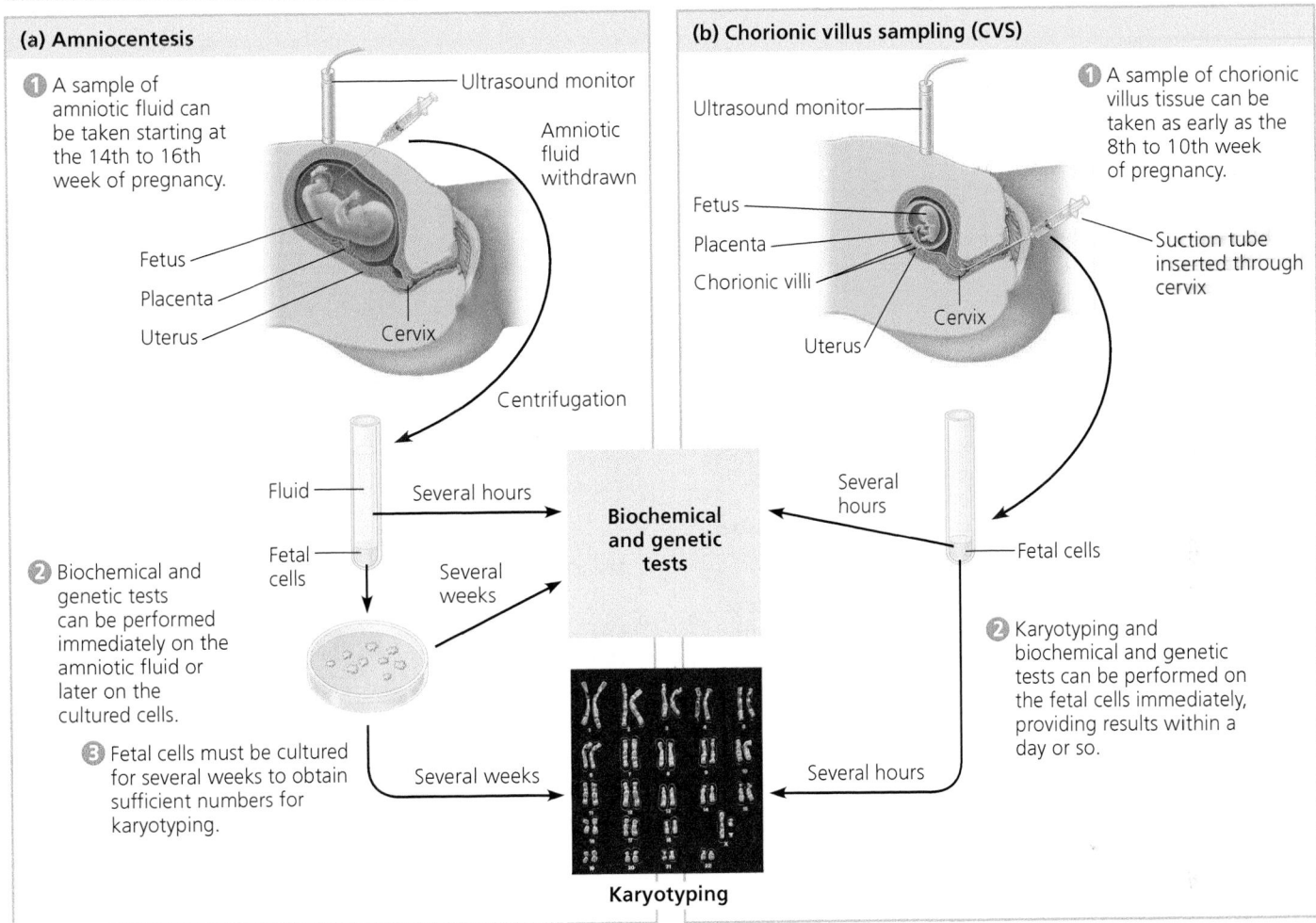

▼ Figure 14.19 Testing a fetus for genetic disorders. Biochemical tests may detect substances associated with particular disorders, and genetic testing can detect many genetic abnormalities. Karyotyping shows whether the chromosomes of the fetus are normal in number and appearance.

(a) Amniocentesis

1 A sample of amniotic fluid can be taken starting at the 14th to 16th week of pregnancy.

Ultrasound monitor

Amniotic fluid withdrawn

Fetus

Placenta

Uterus

Cervix

Centrifugation

Fluid

Several hours

Fetal cells

Several weeks

2 Biochemical and genetic tests can be performed immediately on the amniotic fluid or later on the cultured cells.

3 Fetal cells must be cultured for several weeks to obtain sufficient numbers for karyotyping.

Several weeks

Biochemical and genetic tests

Karyotyping

(b) Chorionic villus sampling (CVS)

Ultrasound monitor

1 A sample of chorionic villus tissue can be taken as early as the 8th to 10th week of pregnancy.

Fetus

Placenta

Chorionic villi

Cervix

Uterus

Suction tube inserted through cervix

Several hours

Fetal cells

2 Karyotyping and biochemical and genetic tests can be performed on the fetal cells immediately, providing results within a day or so.

Several hours

to simple rules of chance—to the elegant quantitative experiments of Gregor Mendel. The importance of his discoveries was overlooked by most biologists until early in the 20th century, decades after he reported his findings. In the next chapter, you will learn how Mendel's laws have their physical basis in the behavior of chromosomes during sexual life cycles and how the synthesis of Mendelism and a chromosome theory of inheritance catalyzed progress in genetics.

CONCEPT CHECK 14.4

1. Beth and Tom each have a sibling with cystic fibrosis, but neither Beth nor Tom nor any of their parents have the disease. Calculate the probability that if this couple has a child, the child will have cystic fibrosis. What would be the probability if a test revealed that Tom is a carrier but Beth is not? Explain your answers.

2. **MAKE CONNECTIONS** Review Figures 5.16, 5.20, and 5.21 (pp. 79 and 82–84). Explain how the change of a single amino acid in hemoglobin leads to the aggregation of hemoglobin into long rods.

3. Joan was born with six toes on each foot, a dominant trait called polydactyly. Two of her five siblings and her mother, but not her father, also have extra digits. What is Joan's genotype for the number-of-digits character? Explain your answer. Use D and d to symbolize the alleles for this character.

4. **MAKE CONNECTIONS** In Table 14.1 (p. 265), note the phenotypic ratio of the dominant to recessive trait in the F_2 generation for the monohybrid cross involving flower color. Then determine the phenotypic ratio for the offspring of the second-generation couple in Figure 14.15b. What accounts for the difference in the two ratios?

For suggested answers, see Appendix A.

14 CHAPTER REVIEW

SUMMARY OF KEY CONCEPTS

CONCEPT 14.1

Mendel used the scientific approach to identify two laws of inheritance (pp. 262–269)

- In the 1860s, Gregor Mendel formulated a theory of inheritance based on experiments with garden peas, proposing that parents pass on to their offspring discrete genes that retain their identity through generations. This theory includes two "laws."
- The **law of segregation** states that genes have alternative forms, or **alleles**. In a diploid organism, the two alleles of a gene segregate (separate) during meiosis and gamete formation; each sperm or egg carries only one allele of each pair. This law explains the 3:1 ratio of F_2 phenotypes observed when **monohybrids** self-pollinate. Each organism inherits one allele for each gene from each parent. In **heterozygotes**, the two alleles are different, and expression of one (the **dominant allele**) masks the phenotypic effect of the other (the **recessive allele**). **Homozygotes** have identical alleles of a given gene and are **true-breeding**.
- The **law of independent assortment** states that the pair of alleles for a given gene segregates into gametes independently of the pair of alleles for any other gene. In a cross between **dihybrids** (individuals heterozygous for two genes), the offspring have four phenotypes in a 9:3:3:1 ratio.

> **?** When Mendel crossed true-breeding purple- and white-flowered pea plants, the white-flowered trait disappeared from the F_1 generation but reappeared in the F_2 generation. Use genetic terms to explain why that happened.

CONCEPT 14.2

The laws of probability govern Mendelian inheritance (pp. 269–271)

- The **multiplication rule** states that the probability of two or more events occurring together is equal to the product of the individual probabilities of the independent single events. The **addition rule** states that the probability of an event that can occur in two or more independent, mutually exclusive ways is the sum of the individual probabilities.
- The rules of probability can be used to solve complex genetics problems. A dihybrid or other multicharacter cross is equivalent to two or more independent monohybrid crosses occurring simultaneously. In calculating the chances of the various offspring genotypes from such crosses, each character is first considered separately and then the individual probabilities are multiplied.

> **DRAW IT** Redraw the Punnett square on the right side of Figure 14.8 as two smaller monohybrid Punnett squares, one for each gene. Below each square, list the fractions of each phenotype produced. Use the rule of multiplication to compute the overall fraction of each possible dihybrid phenotype. What is the phenotypic ratio?

CONCEPT 14.3

Inheritance patterns are often more complex than predicted by simple Mendelian genetics (pp. 271–275)

- Extensions of Mendelian genetics for a single gene:

Relationship among alleles of a single gene	Description	Example
Complete dominance of one allele	Heterozygous phenotype same as that of homozygous dominant	PP Pp
Incomplete dominance of either allele	Heterozygous phenotype intermediate between the two homozygous phenotypes	$C^R C^R$ $C^R C^W$ $C^W C^W$
Codominance	Both phenotypes expressed in heterozygotes	$I^A I^B$
Multiple alleles	In the whole population, some genes have more than two alleles	ABO blood group alleles I^A, I^B, i
Pleiotropy	One gene is able to affect multiple phenotypic characters	Sickle-cell disease

- Extensions of Mendelian genetics for two or more genes:

Relationship among two or more genes	Description	Example
Epistasis	The phenotypic expression of one gene affects that of another	$BbEe \times BbEe$ 9 : 3 : 4
Polygenic inheritance	A single phenotypic character is affected by two or more genes	$AaBbCc \times AaBbCc$

- The expression of a genotype can be affected by environmental influences, the "nurture" in nature versus nurture. The phenotypic range of a particular genotype is called its **norm of reaction**.

Polygenic characters that are also influenced by the environment are called **multifactorial** characters.

- An organism's overall phenotype, including its physical appearance, internal anatomy, physiology, and behavior, reflects its overall genotype and unique environmental history. Even in more complex inheritance patterns, Mendel's fundamental laws of segregation and independent assortment still apply.

? *Which of the following are demonstrated by the inheritance patterns of the ABO blood group alleles: complete dominance, incomplete dominance, codominance, multiple alleles, pleiotropy, epistasis, and/or polygenic inheritance? Explain how, for each of your answers.*

CONCEPT 14.4

Many human traits follow Mendelian patterns of inheritance (pp. 275–281)

- Analysis of family **pedigrees** can be used to deduce the possible genotypes of individuals and make predictions about future offspring. Predictions are statistical probabilities rather than certainties.
- Many genetic disorders are inherited as simple recessive traits. Most affected (homozygous recessive) individuals are children of phenotypically normal, heterozygous **carriers**.

- Lethal dominant alleles are eliminated from the population if affected people die before reproducing. Nonlethal dominant alleles and lethal ones that strike relatively late in life can be inherited in a Mendelian way.
- Many human diseases are multifactorial—that is, they have both genetic and environmental components and do not follow simple Mendelian inheritance patterns.
- Using family histories, genetic counselors help couples determine the probability that their children will have genetic disorders. Genetic testing of prospective parents to reveal whether they are carriers of recessive alleles associated with specific disorders has become widely available. **Amniocentesis** and **chorionic villus sampling** can indicate whether a suspected genetic disorder is present in a fetus. Other genetic tests can be performed after birth.

? *Both members of a couple know that they are carriers of the cystic fibrosis allele. None of their three children has cystic fibrosis, but any one of them might be a carrier. They would like to have a fourth child but are worried that it would very likely have the disease, since the first three do not. What would you tell the couple? Would it remove some more uncertainty in their prediction if they could find out from genetic tests whether the three children are carriers?*

TIPS FOR GENETICS PROBLEMS

1. Write down symbols for the alleles. (These may be given in the problem.) When represented by single letters, the dominant allele is uppercase and the recessive is lowercase.

2. Write down the possible genotypes, as determined by the phenotype.
   a. If the phenotype is that of the dominant trait (for example, purple flowers), then the genotype is either homozygous dominant or heterozygous (PP or Pp, in this example).
   b. If the phenotype is that of the recessive trait, the genotype must be homozygous recessive (for example, pp).
   c. If the problem says "true-breeding," the genotype is homozygous.

3. Determine what the problem is asking for. If asked to do a cross, write it out in the form [Genotype] × [Genotype], using the alleles you've decided on.

4. To figure out the outcome of a cross, set up a Punnett square.
   a. Put the gametes of one parent at the top and those of the other on the left. To determine the allele(s) in each gamete for a given genotype, set up a systematic way to list all the possibilities. (Remember, each gamete has one allele of each gene.) Note that there are 2^n possible types of gametes, where n is the number of gene loci that are heterozygous. For example, an individual with genotype $AaBbCc$ would produce $2^3 = 8$ types of gametes. Write the genotypes of the gametes in circles above the columns and to the left of the rows.
   b. Fill in the Punnett square as if each possible sperm were fertilizing each possible egg, making all of the possible offspring. In a cross of $AaBbCc \times AaBbCc$, for example, the Punnett square would have 8 columns and 8 rows, so there are 64 different offspring; you would know the genotype of each and thus the phenotype. Count genotypes and phenotypes to obtain the genotypic and phenotypic ratios. Because the Punnett square is so large, this method is not the most efficient. Instead, see tip 5.

5. You can use the rules of probability if the Punnett square would be too big. (For example, see the question at the end of the summary for Concept 14.2 and question 7 on the next page.) You can consider each gene separately (see pp. 270–271).

6. If, instead, the problem gives you the phenotypic ratios of offspring, but not the genotypes of the parents in a given cross, the phenotypes can help you deduce the parents' unknown genotypes.
   a. For example, if ½ of the offspring have the recessive phenotype and ½ the dominant, you know that the cross was between a heterozygote and a homozygous recessive.
   b. If the ratio is 3:1, the cross was between two heterozygotes.
   c. If two genes are involved and you see a 9:3:3:1 ratio in the offspring, you know that each parent is heterozygous for both genes. Caution: Don't assume that the reported numbers will exactly equal the predicted ratios. For example, if there are 13 offspring with the dominant trait and 11 with the recessive, assume that the ratio is one dominant to one recessive.

7. For pedigree problems, use the tips in Figure 14.15 and below to determine what kind of trait is involved.
   a. If parents without the trait have offspring with the trait, the trait must be recessive and the parents both carriers.
   b. If the trait is seen in every generation, it is most likely dominant (see the next possibility, though).
   c. If both parents have the trait, then in order for it to be recessive, all offspring must show the trait.
   d. To determine the likely genotype of a certain individual in a pedigree, first label the genotypes of all the family members you can. Even if some of the genotypes are incomplete, label what you do know. For example, if an individual has the dominant phenotype, the genotype must be AA or Aa; you can write this as A-. Try different possibilities to see which fits the results. Use the rules of probability to calculate the probability of each possible genotype being the correct one.

LEVEL 1: KNOWLEDGE/COMPREHENSION

1. Match each term on the left with a statement on the right.

Term	Statement
__ Gene	a. Has no effect on phenotype in a
__ Allele	heterozygote
__ Character	b. A variant for a character
__ Trait	c. Having two identical alleles for a gene
__ Dominant allele	d. A cross between individuals
__ Recessive allele	heterozygous for a single character
__ Genotype	e. An alternative version of a gene
__ Phenotype	f. Having two different alleles for a gene
__ Homozygous	g. A heritable feature that varies
__ Heterozygous	among individuals
__ Testcross	h. An organism's appearance or
__ Monohybrid	observable traits
cross	i. A cross between an individual with an
	unknown genotype and a homozy-
	gous recessive individual
	j. Determines phenotype in a
	heterozygote
	k. The genetic makeup of an individual
	l. A heritable unit that determines a
	character; can exist in different forms

2. **DRAW IT** Two pea plants heterozygous for the characters of pod color and pod shape are crossed. Draw a Punnett square to determine the phenotypic ratios of the offspring.

3. In some plants, a true-breeding, red-flowered strain gives all pink flowers when crossed with a white-flowered strain: $C^R C^R$ (red) × $C^W C^W$ (white) → $C^R C^W$ (pink). If flower position (axial or terminal) is inherited as it is in peas (see Table 14.1), what will be the ratios of genotypes and phenotypes of the F_1 generation resulting from the following cross: axial-red (true-breeding) × terminal-white? What will be the ratios in the F_2 generation?

4. A man with type A blood marries a woman with type B blood. Their child has type O blood. What are the genotypes of these three individuals? What genotypes, and in what frequencies, would you expect in future offspring from this marriage?

5. A man has six fingers on each hand and six toes on each foot. His wife and their daughter have the normal number of digits. Remember that extra digits is a dominant trait. What fraction of this couple's children would be expected to have extra digits?

6. **DRAW IT** A pea plant heterozygous for inflated pods (*Ii*) is crossed with a plant homozygous for constricted pods (*ii*). Draw a Punnett square for this cross. Assume that pollen comes from the *ii* plant.

LEVEL 2: APPLICATION/ANALYSIS

7. Flower position, stem length, and seed shape are three characters that Mendel studied. Each is controlled by an independently assorting gene and has dominant and recessive expression as follows:

Character	Dominant	Recessive
Flower position	Axial (*A*)	Terminal (*a*)
Stem length	Tall (*T*)	Dwarf (*t*)
Seed shape	Round (*R*)	Wrinkled (*r*)

If a plant that is heterozygous for all three characters is allowed to self-fertilize, what proportion of the offspring would

you expect to be as follows? (*Note*: Use the rules of probability instead of a huge Punnett square.)

(a) homozygous for the three dominant traits
(b) homozygous for the three recessive traits
(c) heterozygous for all three characters
(d) homozygous for axial and tall, heterozygous for seed shape

8. A black guinea pig crossed with an albino guinea pig produces 12 black offspring. When the albino is crossed with a second black one, 7 blacks and 5 albinos are obtained. What is the best explanation for this genetic outcome? Write genotypes for the parents, gametes, and offspring.

9. In sesame plants, the one-pod condition (*P*) is dominant to the three-pod condition (*p*), and normal leaf (*L*) is dominant to wrinkled leaf (*l*). Pod type and leaf type are inherited independently. Determine the genotypes for the two parents for all possible matings producing the following offspring:

(a) 318 one-pod, normal leaf and 98 one-pod, wrinkled leaf
(b) 323 three-pod, normal leaf and 106 three-pod, wrinkled leaf
(c) 401 one-pod, normal leaf
(d) 150 one-pod, normal leaf, 147 one-pod, wrinkled leaf, 51 three-pod, normal leaf, and 48 three-pod, wrinkled leaf
(e) 223 one-pod, normal leaf, 72 one-pod, wrinkled leaf, 76 three-pod, normal leaf, and 27 three-pod, wrinkled leaf

10. Phenylketonuria (PKU) is an inherited disease caused by a recessive allele. If a woman and her husband, who are both carriers, have three children, what is the probability of each of the following?

(a) All three children are of normal phenotype.
(b) One or more of the three children have the disease.
(c) All three children have the disease.
(d) At least one child is phenotypically normal.
(*Note*: It will help to remember that the probabilities of all possible outcomes always add up to 1.)

11. The genotype of F_1 individuals in a tetrahybrid cross is *AaBbCcDd*. Assuming independent assortment of these four genes, what are the probabilities that F_2 offspring will have the following genotypes?

(a) *aabbccdd*
(b) *AaBbCcDd*
(c) *AABBCCDD*
(d) *AaBBccDd*
(e) *AaBBCCdd*

12. What is the probability that each of the following pairs of parents will produce the indicated offspring? (Assume independent assortment of all gene pairs.)

(a) *AABBCC* × *aabbcc* → *AaBbCc*
(b) *AABbCc* × *AaBbCc* → *AAbbCC*
(c) *AaBbCc* × *AaBbCc* → *AaBbCc*
(d) *aaBbCC* × *AABbcc* → *AaBbCc*

13. Karen and Steve each have a sibling with sickle-cell disease. Neither Karen nor Steve nor any of their parents have the disease, and none of them have been tested to see if they have the sickle-cell trait. Based on this incomplete information, calculate the probability that if this couple has a child, the child will have sickle-cell disease.

14. In 1981, a stray black cat with unusual rounded, curled-back ears was adopted by a family in California. Hundreds of descendants of the cat have since been born, and cat fanciers hope to develop the curl cat into a show breed. Suppose you

owned the first curl cat and wanted to develop a true-breeding variety. How would you determine whether the curl allele is dominant or recessive? How would you obtain true-breeding curl cats? How could you be sure they are true-breeding?

15. Imagine that a newly discovered, recessively inherited disease is expressed only in individuals with type O blood, although the disease and blood group are independently inherited. A normal man with type A blood and a normal woman with type B blood have already had one child with the disease. The woman is now pregnant for a second time. What is the probability that the second child will also have the disease? Assume that both parents are heterozygous for the gene that causes the disease.

16. In tigers, a recessive allele causes an absence of fur pigmentation (a white tiger) and a cross-eyed condition. If two phenotypically normal tigers that are heterozygous at this locus are mated, what percentage of their offspring will be cross-eyed? What percentage of cross-eyed tigers will be white?

17. In maize (corn) plants, a dominant allele *I* inhibits kernel color, while the recessive allele *i* permits color when homozygous. At a different locus, the dominant allele *P* causes purple kernel color, while the homozygous recessive genotype *pp* causes red kernels. If plants heterozygous at both loci are crossed, what will be the phenotypic ratio of the offspring?

18. The pedigree below traces the inheritance of alkaptonuria, a biochemical disorder. Affected individuals, indicated here by the colored circles and squares, are unable to metabolize a substance called alkapton, which colors the urine and stains body tissues. Does alkaptonuria appear to be caused by a dominant allele or by a recessive allele? Fill in the genotypes of the individuals whose genotypes can be deduced. What genotypes are possible for each of the other individuals?

19. Imagine that you are a genetic counselor, and a couple planning to start a family comes to you for information. Charles was married once before, and he and his first wife had a child with cystic fibrosis. The brother of his current wife, Elaine, died of cystic fibrosis. What is the probability that Charles and Elaine will have a baby with cystic fibrosis? (Neither Charles, Elaine, nor their parents have cystic fibrosis.)

20. In mice, black fur (*B*) is dominant to white (*b*). At a different locus, a dominant allele (*A*) produces a band of yellow just below the tip of each hair in mice with black fur. This gives a frosted appearance known as agouti. Expression of the recessive allele (*a*) results in a solid coat color. If mice that are heterozygous at both loci are crossed, what is the expected phenotypic ratio of their offspring?

LEVEL 3: SYNTHESIS/EVALUATION

21. **EVOLUTION CONNECTION**
Over the past half century, there has been a trend in the United States and other developed countries for people to marry and start families later in life than did their parents and grandparents. What effects might this trend have on the incidence (frequency) of late-acting dominant lethal alleles in the population?

22. **SCIENTIFIC INQUIRY**
You are handed a mystery pea plant with tall stems and axial flowers and asked to determine its genotype as quickly as possible. You know that the allele for tall stems (*T*) is dominant to that for dwarf stems (*t*) and that the allele for axial flowers (*A*) is dominant to that for terminal flowers (*a*).

   (a) What are *all* the possible genotypes for your mystery plant?
   (b) Describe the *one* cross you would do, out in your garden, to determine the exact genotype of your mystery plant.
   (c) While waiting for the results of your cross, you predict the results for each possible genotype listed in part a. How do you do this? Why is this not called "performing a cross"?
   (d) Explain how the results of your cross and your predictions will help you learn the genotype of your mystery plant.

23. **SCIENCE, TECHNOLOGY, AND SOCIETY**
Imagine that one of your parents has Huntington's disease. What is the probability that you, too, will someday manifest the disease? There is no cure for Huntington's. Would you want to be tested for the Huntington's allele? Why or why not?

24.

The Genetic Basis of Life The continuity of life is based on heritable information in the form of DNA. In a short essay (100–150 words), explain how the passage of genes from parents to offspring, in the form of particular alleles, ensures perpetuation of parental traits in offspring and, at the same time, genetic variation among offspring. Use genetic terms in your explanation.

For selected answers, see Appendix A.

Mastering**BIOLOGY**   www.masteringbiology.com

1. MasteringBiology® Assignments
Tutorials Determining Genotype: Pea Pod Color • Mendel's Law of Independent Assortment • Mendel's Law of Segregation • Inheritance of Fur Color in Mice • Pedigree Analysis: Dominant and Recessive Autosomal Conditions • Pedigree Analysis: Galactosemia
Activities Monohybrid Cross • Dihybrid Cross • Mendel's Experiments • The Principle of Independent Assortment • Gregor's Garden • Incomplete Dominance
Questions Student Misconceptions • Reading Quiz • Multiple Choice • End-of-Chapter

2. eText
Read your book online, search, take notes, highlight text, and more.

3. The Study Area
Practice Tests • Cumulative Test • *BioFlix* 3-D Animations • MP3 Tutor Sessions • Videos • Activities • Investigations • Lab Media • Audio Glossary • Word Study Tools • Art

15

The Chromosomal Basis of Inheritance

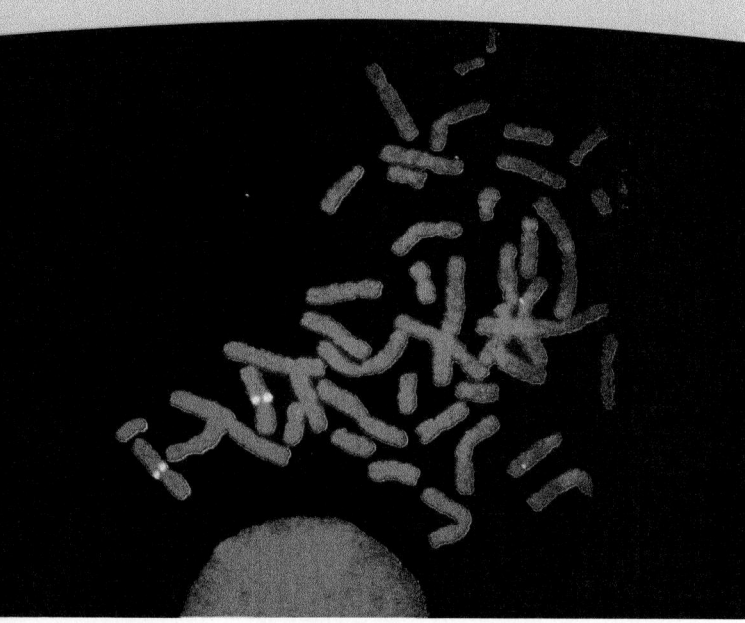

▲ Figure 15.1 **Where are Mendel's hereditary factors located in the cell?**

KEY CONCEPTS

15.1 Mendelian inheritance has its physical basis in the behavior of chromosomes

15.2 Sex-linked genes exhibit unique patterns of inheritance

15.3 Linked genes tend to be inherited together because they are located near each other on the same chromosome

15.4 Alterations of chromosome number or structure cause some genetic disorders

15.5 Some inheritance patterns are exceptions to standard Mendelian inheritance

Locating Genes Along Chromosomes

Gregor Mendel's "hereditary factors" were purely an abstract concept when he proposed their existence in 1860. At that time, no cellular structures were known that could house these imaginary units. Even after chromosomes were first observed, many biologists remained skeptical about Mendel's laws of segregation and independent assortment until there was sufficient evidence that these principles of heredity had a physical basis in chromosomal behavior.

Today, we know that genes—Mendel's "factors"—are located along chromosomes. We can see the location of a particular gene by tagging chromosomes with a fluorescent dye that highlights that gene. For example, the four yellow dots in **Figure 15.1** mark the locus of a specific gene on the sister chromatids of a homologous pair of replicated human chromosomes. This chapter extends what you learned in the past two chapters: We describe the chromosomal basis for the transmission of genes from parents to offspring, along with some important exceptions to the standard mode of inheritance.

CONCEPT 15.1

Mendelian inheritance has its physical basis in the behavior of chromosomes

Using improved techniques of microscopy, cytologists worked out the process of mitosis in 1875 and meiosis in the 1890s. Cytology and genetics converged when biologists began to see parallels between the behavior of chromosomes and the behavior of Mendel's proposed hereditary factors during sexual life cycles: Chromosomes and genes are both present in pairs in diploid cells; homologous chromosomes separate and alleles segregate during the process of meiosis; and fertilization restores the paired condition for both chromosomes and genes. Around 1902, Walter S. Sutton, Theodor Boveri, and others independently noted these parallels, and the **chromosome theory of inheritance** began to take form. According to this theory, Mendelian genes have specific loci (positions) along chromosomes, and it is the chromosomes that undergo segregation and independent assortment.

Figure 15.2 shows that the behavior of homologous chromosomes during meiosis can account for the segregation of the alleles at each genetic locus to different gametes. The figure also shows that the behavior of nonhomologous chromosomes can account for the independent assortment of the alleles for two or more genes located on different chromosomes. By carefully studying this figure, which traces the same dihybrid pea cross you learned about in Figure 14.8, you can see how the behavior of chromosomes during meiosis in the F_1 generation and subsequent random fertilization give rise to the F_2 phenotypic ratio observed by Mendel.

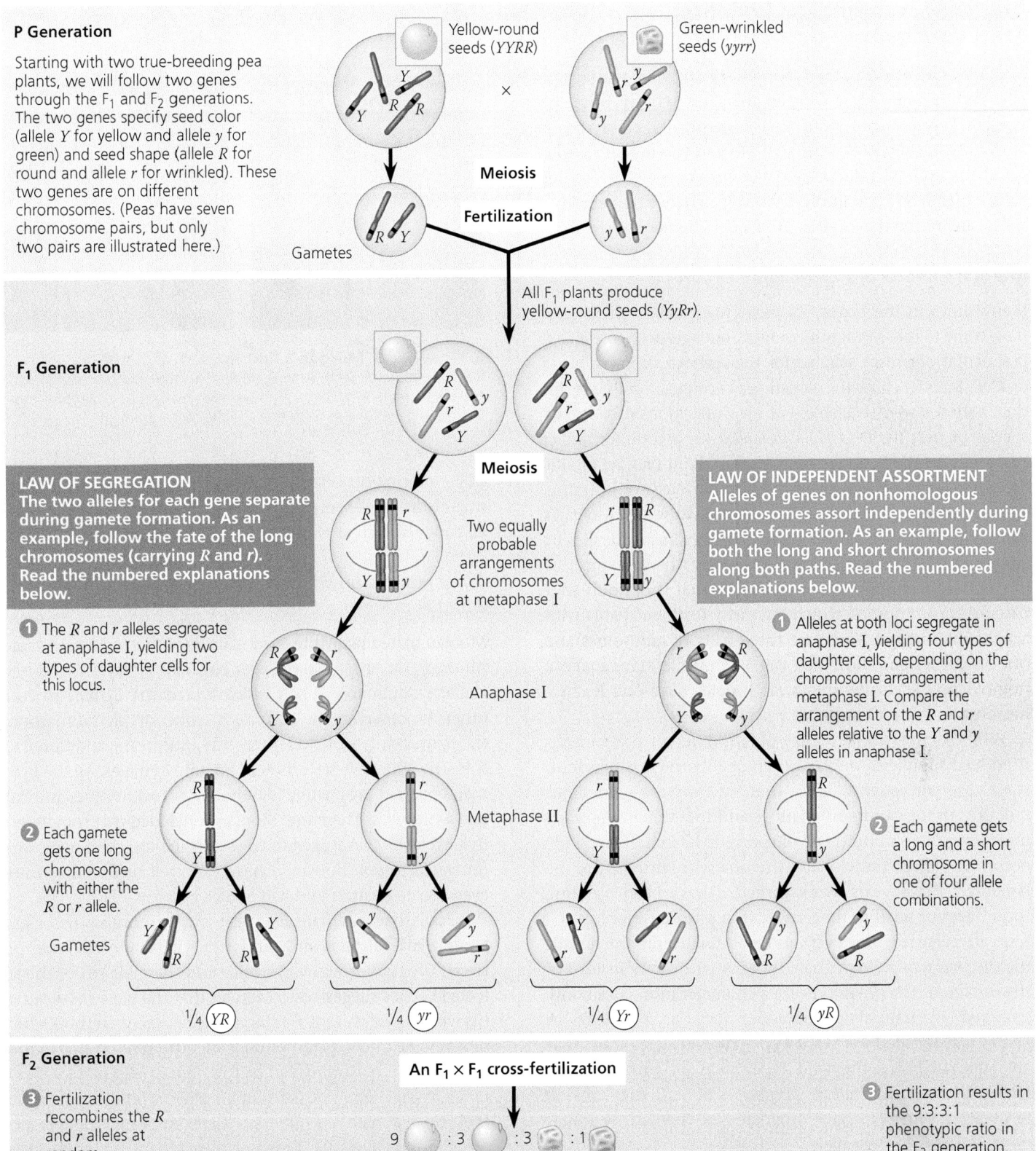

P Generation

Starting with two true-breeding pea plants, we will follow two genes through the F₁ and F₂ generations. The two genes specify seed color (allele *Y* for yellow and allele *y* for green) and seed shape (allele *R* for round and allele *r* for wrinkled). These two genes are on different chromosomes. (Peas have seven chromosome pairs, but only two pairs are illustrated here.)

Yellow-round seeds (*YYRR*)

Green-wrinkled seeds (*yyrr*)

×

Meiosis

Fertilization

Gametes

All F₁ plants produce yellow-round seeds (*YyRr*).

F₁ Generation

Meiosis

Two equally probable arrangements of chromosomes at metaphase I

LAW OF SEGREGATION
The two alleles for each gene separate during gamete formation. As an example, follow the fate of the long chromosomes (carrying *R* and *r*). Read the numbered explanations below.

LAW OF INDEPENDENT ASSORTMENT
Alleles of genes on nonhomologous chromosomes assort independently during gamete formation. As an example, follow both the long and short chromosomes along both paths. Read the numbered explanations below.

① The *R* and *r* alleles segregate at anaphase I, yielding two types of daughter cells for this locus.

Anaphase I

① Alleles at both loci segregate in anaphase I, yielding four types of daughter cells, depending on the chromosome arrangement at metaphase I. Compare the arrangement of the *R* and *r* alleles relative to the *Y* and *y* alleles in anaphase I.

Metaphase II

② Each gamete gets one long chromosome with either the *R* or *r* allele.

② Each gamete gets a long and a short chromosome in one of four allele combinations.

Gametes

¼ (*YR*)   ¼ (*yr*)   ¼ (*Yr*)   ¼ (*yR*)

F₂ Generation

An F₁ × F₁ cross-fertilization

③ Fertilization recombines the *R* and *r* alleles at random.

9 ⃝ : 3 ⃝ : 3 ⃝ : 1 ⃝

③ Fertilization results in the 9:3:3:1 phenotypic ratio in the F₂ generation.

▲ **Figure 15.2 The chromosomal basis of Mendel's laws.** Here we correlate the results of one of Mendel's dihybrid crosses (see Figure 14.8) with the behavior of chromosomes during meiosis (see Figure 13.8). The arrangement of chromosomes at metaphase I of meiosis and their movement during anaphase I account for the segregation and independent assortment of the alleles for seed color and shape. Each cell that undergoes meiosis in an F₁ plant produces two kinds of gametes. If we count the results for all cells, however, each F₁ plant produces equal numbers of all four kinds of gametes because the alternative chromosome arrangements at metaphase I are equally likely.

? *If you crossed an F₁ plant with a plant that was homozygous recessive for both genes (yyrr), how would the phenotypic ratio of the offspring compare with the 9:3:3:1 ratio seen here?*

Morgan's Experimental Evidence: Scientific Inquiry

The first solid evidence associating a specific gene with a specific chromosome came early in the 20th century from the work of Thomas Hunt Morgan, an experimental embryologist at Columbia University. Although Morgan was initially skeptical about both Mendelism and the chromosome theory, his early experiments provided convincing evidence that chromosomes are indeed the location of Mendel's heritable factors.

Morgan's Choice of Experimental Organism

Many times in the history of biology, important discoveries have come to those insightful or lucky enough to choose an experimental organism suitable for the research problem being tackled. Mendel chose the garden pea because a number of distinct varieties were available. For his work, Morgan selected a species of fruit fly, *Drosophila melanogaster*, a common insect that feeds on the fungi growing on fruit. Fruit flies are prolific breeders; a single mating will produce hundreds of offspring, and a new generation can be bred every two weeks. Morgan's laboratory began using this convenient organism for genetic studies in 1907 and soon became known as "the fly room."

Another advantage of the fruit fly is that it has only four pairs of chromosomes, which are easily distinguishable with a light microscope. There are three pairs of autosomes and one pair of sex chromosomes. Female fruit flies have a pair of homologous X chromosomes, and males have one X chromosome and one Y chromosome.

While Mendel could readily obtain different pea varieties from seed suppliers, Morgan was probably the first person to want different varieties of the fruit fly. He faced the tedious task of carrying out many matings and then microscopically inspecting large numbers of offspring in search of naturally occurring variant individuals. After many months of this, he lamented, "Two years' work wasted. I have been breeding those flies for all that time and I've got nothing out of it." Morgan persisted, however, and was finally rewarded with the discovery of a single male fly with white eyes instead of the usual red. The phenotype for a character most commonly observed in natural populations, such as red eyes in *Drosophila*, is called the **wild type** (**Figure 15.3**). Traits that are alternatives to the wild type, such as white eyes in *Drosophila*, are called *mutant phenotypes* because they are due to alleles assumed to have originated as changes, or mutations, in the wild-type allele.

Morgan and his students invented a notation for symbolizing alleles in *Drosophila* that is still widely used for fruit flies. For a given character in flies, the gene takes its symbol from the first mutant (non–wild type) discovered. Thus, the allele for white eyes in *Drosophila* is symbolized by *w*. A superscript + identifies the allele for the wild-type trait—w^+ for the allele for red eyes, for example. Over the years, a variety

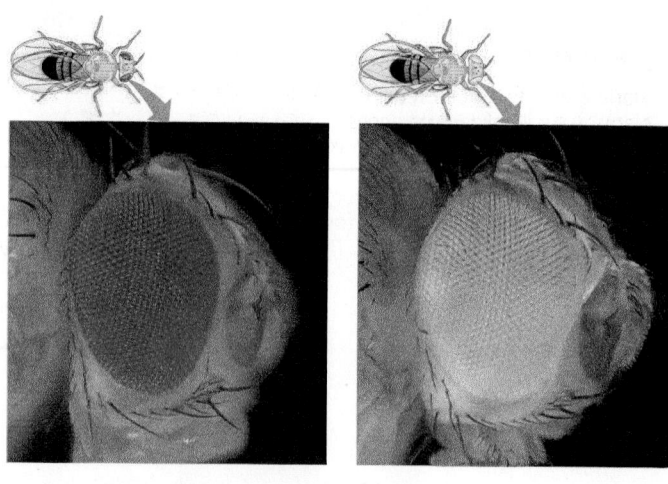

▲ **Figure 15.3 Morgan's first mutant.** Wild-type *Drosophila* flies have red eyes (left). Among his flies, Morgan discovered a mutant male with white eyes (right). This variation made it possible for Morgan to trace a gene for eye color to a specific chromosome (LMs).

of gene notation systems have been developed for different organisms. For example, human genes are usually written in all capitals, such as *HD* for the allele for Huntington's disease.

Correlating Behavior of a Gene's Alleles with Behavior of a Chromosome Pair

Morgan mated his white-eyed male fly with a red-eyed female. All the F_1 offspring had red eyes, suggesting that the wild-type allele is dominant. When Morgan bred the F_1 flies to each other, he observed the classical 3:1 phenotypic ratio among the F_2 offspring. However, there was a surprising additional result: The white-eye trait showed up only in males. All the F_2 females had red eyes, while half the males had red eyes and half had white eyes. Therefore, Morgan concluded that somehow a fly's eye color was linked to its sex. (If the eye-color gene were unrelated to sex, he would have expected half of the white-eyed flies to be male and half female.)

Recall that a female fly has two X chromosomes (XX), while a male fly has an X and a Y (XY). The correlation between the trait of white eye color and the male sex of the affected F_2 flies suggested to Morgan that the gene involved in his white-eyed mutant was located exclusively on the X chromosome, with no corresponding allele present on the Y chromosome. His reasoning can be followed in **Figure 15.4**. For a male, a single copy of the mutant allele would confer white eyes; since a male has only one X chromosome, there can be no wild-type allele (w^+) present to mask the recessive allele. On the other hand, a female could have white eyes only if both her X chromosomes carried the recessive mutant allele (*w*). This was impossible for the F_2 females in Morgan's experiment because all the F_1 fathers had red eyes.

Morgan's finding of the correlation between a particular trait and an individual's sex provided support for the chromosome theory of inheritance: namely, that a specific gene is

INQUIRY

In a cross between a wild-type female fruit fly and a mutant white-eyed male, what color eyes will the F₁ and F₂ offspring have?

EXPERIMENT Thomas Hunt Morgan wanted to analyze the behavior of two alleles of a fruit fly eye-color gene. In crosses similar to those done by Mendel with pea plants, Morgan and his colleagues mated a wild-type (red-eyed) female with a mutant white-eyed male.

Morgan then bred an F₁ red-eyed female to an F₁ red-eyed male to produce the F₂ generation.

RESULTS The F₂ generation showed a typical Mendelian ratio of 3 red-eyed flies : 1 white-eyed fly. However, no females displayed the white-eye trait; all white-eyed flies were males.

CONCLUSION All F₁ offspring had red eyes, so the mutant white-eye trait (w) must be recessive to the wild-type red-eye trait (w^+). Since the recessive trait—white eyes—was expressed only in males in the F₂ generation, Morgan deduced that this eye-color gene is located on the X chromosome and that there is no corresponding locus on the Y chromosome.

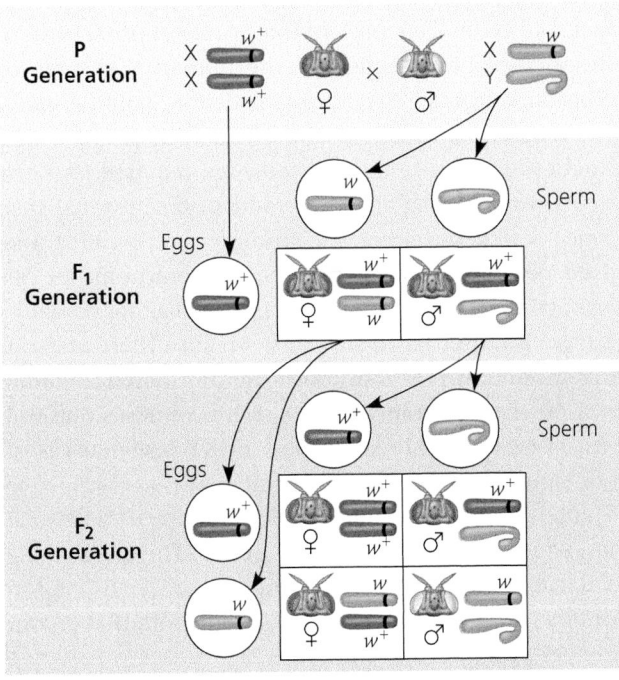

SOURCE: T. H. Morgan, Sex-limited inheritance in *Drosophila, Science* 32:120–122 (1910).

(MB) See the related Experimental Inquiry Tutorial in MasteringBiology.

WHAT IF? Suppose this eye-color gene were located on an autosome. Predict the phenotypes (including gender) of the F₂ flies in this hypothetical cross. (*Hint*: Draw a Punnett square.)

---

carried on a specific chromosome (in this case, an eye-color gene on the X chromosome). In addition, Morgan's work indicated that genes located on a sex chromosome exhibit unique inheritance patterns, which we will discuss in the next section. Recognizing the importance of Morgan's early work, many bright students were attracted to his fly room.

CONCEPT CHECK 15.1

1. Which one of Mendel's laws relates to the inheritance of alleles for a single character? Which law relates to the inheritance of alleles for two characters in a dihybrid cross?
2. **MAKE CONNECTIONS** Review the description of meiosis in Figure 13.8 (pp. 254–255) and Mendel's two laws in Concept 14.1 (pp. 264–269). What is the physical basis for each of Mendel's laws?
3. **WHAT IF?** Propose a possible reason that the first naturally occurring mutant fruit fly Morgan saw involved a gene on a sex chromosome.

For suggested answers, see Appendix A.

CONCEPT 15.2

Sex-linked genes exhibit unique patterns of inheritance

As you just learned, Morgan's discovery of a trait (white eyes) that correlated with the sex of flies was a key episode in the development of the chromosome theory of inheritance. Because the identity of the sex chromosomes in an individual could be inferred by observing the sex of the fly, the behavior of the two members of the pair of sex chromosomes could be correlated with the behavior of the two alleles of the eye-color gene. In this section, we consider the role of sex chromosomes in inheritance in more detail. We begin by reviewing the chromosomal basis of sex determination in humans and some other animals.

The Chromosomal Basis of Sex

Whether we are male or female is one of our more obvious phenotypic characters. Although the anatomical and physiological differences between women and men are numerous, the chromosomal basis for determining sex is rather simple. In humans and other mammals, there are two varieties of sex chromosomes, designated X and Y. The Y chromosome is much smaller than the X chromosome (Figure 15.5). A person who inherits two

▲ Figure 15.5 **Human sex chromosomes.**

X chromosomes, one from each parent, usually develops as a female. A male develops from a zygote containing one X chromosome and one Y chromosome (Figure 15.6a). Short segments at either end of the Y chromosome are the only regions that are homologous with corresponding regions of the X.

(a) The X-Y system. In mammals, the sex of an offspring depends on whether the sperm cell contains an X chromosome or a Y.

(b) The X-0 system. In grasshoppers, cockroaches, and some other insects, there is only one type of sex chromosome, the X. Females are XX; males have only one sex chromosome (X0). Sex of the offspring is determined by whether the sperm cell contains an X chromosome or no sex chromosome.

(c) The Z-W system. In birds, some fishes, and some insects, the sex chromosomes present in the egg (not the sperm) determine the sex of offspring. The sex chromosomes are designated Z and W. Females are ZW and males are ZZ.

(d) The haplo-diploid system. There are no sex chromosomes in most species of bees and ants. Females develop from fertilized eggs and are thus diploid. Males develop from unfertilized eggs and are haploid; they have no fathers.

▲ **Figure 15.6 Some chromosomal systems of sex determination.** Numerals indicate the number of autosomes in the species pictured. In *Drosophila*, males are XY, but sex depends on the ratio between the number of X chromosomes and the number of autosome sets, not simply on the presence of a Y chromosome.

These homologous regions allow the X and Y chromosomes in males to pair and behave like homologous chromosomes during meiosis in the testes.

In mammalian testes and ovaries, the two sex chromosomes segregate during meiosis, and each gamete receives one. Each egg contains one X chromosome. In contrast, sperm fall into two categories: Half the sperm cells a male produces contain an X chromosome, and half contain a Y chromosome. We can trace the sex of each offspring to the events of conception: If a sperm cell bearing an X chromosome happens to fertilize an egg, the zygote is XX, a female; if a sperm cell containing a Y chromosome fertilizes an egg, the zygote is XY, a male (see Figure 15.6a). Thus, sex determination is a matter of chance—a fifty-fifty chance. Note that the mammalian X-Y system isn't the only chromosomal system for determining sex. Figure 15.6b–d illustrates three other systems.

In humans, the anatomical signs of sex begin to emerge when the embryo is about 2 months old. Before then, the rudiments of the gonads are generic—they can develop into either testes or ovaries, depending on whether or not a Y chromosome is present. In 1990, a British research team identified a gene on the Y chromosome required for the development of testes. They named the gene *SRY*, for *s*ex-*d*etermining *r*egion of *Y*. In the absence of *SRY*, the gonads develop into ovaries. The biochemical, physiological, and anatomical features that distinguish males and females are complex, and many genes are involved in their development. In fact, *SRY* codes for a protein that regulates other genes.

Researchers have sequenced the human Y chromosome and have identified 78 genes that code for about 25 proteins (some genes are duplicates). About half of these genes are expressed only in the testis, and some are required for normal testicular functioning and the production of normal sperm. A gene located on either sex chromosome is called a **sex-linked gene**; those located on the Y chromosome are called *Y-linked genes*. The Y chromosome is passed along virtually intact from a father to all his sons. Because there are so few Y-linked genes, very few disorders are transferred from father to son on the Y chromosome. A rare example is that in the absence of certain Y-linked genes, an XY individual is male but does not produce normal sperm.

The human X chromosome contains approximately 1,100 genes, which are called **X-linked genes**. The fact that males and females inherit a different number of X chromosomes leads to a pattern of inheritance different from that produced by genes located on autosomes.

Inheritance of X-Linked Genes

While most Y-linked genes help determine sex, the X chromosomes have genes for many characters unrelated to sex. X-linked genes in humans follow the same pattern of inheritance that Morgan observed for the eye-color locus he studied in *Drosophila* (see Figure 15.4). Fathers pass X-linked

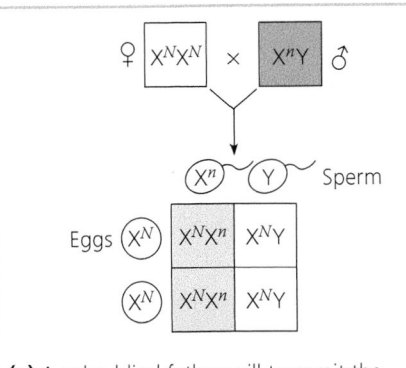

(a) A color-blind father will transmit the mutant allele to all daughters but to no sons. When the mother is a dominant homozygote, the daughters will have the normal phenotype but will be carriers of the mutation.

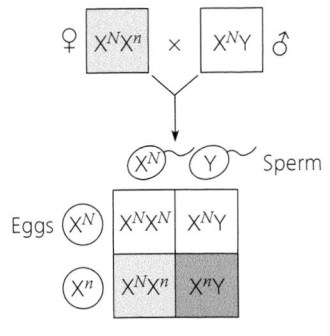

(b) If a carrier mates with a male who has normal color vision, there is a 50% chance that each daughter will be a carrier like her mother and a 50% chance that each son will have the disorder.

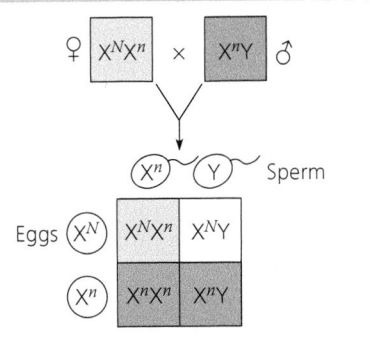

(c) If a carrier mates with a color-blind male, there is a 50% chance that each child born to them will have the disorder, regardless of sex. Daughters who have normal color vision will be carriers, whereas males who have normal color vision will be free of the recessive allele.

▲ **Figure 15.7 The transmission of X-linked recessive traits.** In this diagram, color blindness is used as an example. The superscript N represents the dominant allele for normal color vision carried on the X chromosome, and the superscript n represents the recessive allele, which has a mutation causing color blindness. White boxes indicate unaffected individuals, light orange boxes indicate carriers, and dark orange boxes indicate color-blind individuals.

? *If a color-blind woman married a man who had normal color vision, what would be the probable phenotypes of their children?*

alleles to all of their daughters but to none of their sons. In contrast, mothers can pass X-linked alleles to both sons and daughters, as shown in **Figure 15.7**.

If an X-linked trait is due to a recessive allele, a female will express the phenotype only if she is homozygous for that allele. Because males have only one locus, the terms *homozygous* and *heterozygous* lack meaning for describing their X-linked genes; the term *hemizygous* is used in such cases. Any male receiving the recessive allele from his mother will express the trait. For this reason, far more males than females have X-linked recessive disorders. However, even though the chance of a female inheriting a double dose of the mutant allele is much less than the probability of a male inheriting a single dose, there *are* females with X-linked disorders. For instance, color blindness is a mild disorder almost always inherited as an X-linked trait. A color-blind daughter may be born to a color-blind father whose mate is a carrier (see Figure 15.7c). Because the X-linked allele for color blindness is relatively rare, though, the probability that such a man and woman will mate is low.

A number of human X-linked disorders are much more serious than color blindness. An example is **Duchenne muscular dystrophy**, which affects about one out of every 3,500 males born in the United States. The disease is characterized by a progressive weakening of the muscles and loss of coordination. Affected individuals rarely live past their early 20s. Researchers have traced the disorder to the absence of a key muscle protein called dystrophin and have mapped the gene for this protein to a specific locus on the X chromosome.

Hemophilia is an X-linked recessive disorder defined by the absence of one or more of the proteins required for blood clotting. When a person with hemophilia is injured, bleeding is prolonged because a firm clot is slow to form. Small cuts in the skin are usually not a problem, but bleeding in the muscles or joints can be painful and can lead to serious damage. In the 1800s, hemophilia was widespread among the royal families of Europe. Queen Victoria of England is known to have passed the allele to several of her descendants. Subsequent intermarriage with royal family members of other nations, such as Spain and Russia, further spread this X-linked trait, and its incidence is well documented in royal pedigrees. Today, people with hemophilia are treated as needed with intravenous injections of the protein that is missing.

X Inactivation in Female Mammals

Female mammals, including humans, inherit two X chromosomes—twice the number inherited by males—so you may wonder whether females make twice as much as males of the proteins encoded by X-linked genes. In fact, most of one X chromosome in each cell in female mammals becomes inactivated during early embryonic development. As a result, the cells of females and males have the same effective dose (one copy) of most X-linked genes. The inactive X in each cell of a female condenses into a compact object called a **Barr body** (discovered by Canadian anatomist Murray Barr), which lies along the inside of the nuclear envelope. Most of the genes of the X chromosome that forms the Barr body are not expressed. In the ovaries, Barr-body chromosomes are reactivated in the cells that give rise to eggs, so every female gamete has an active X.

British geneticist Mary Lyon demonstrated that the selection of which X chromosome will form the Barr body occurs randomly and independently in each embryonic cell present at the time of X inactivation. As a consequence, females consist

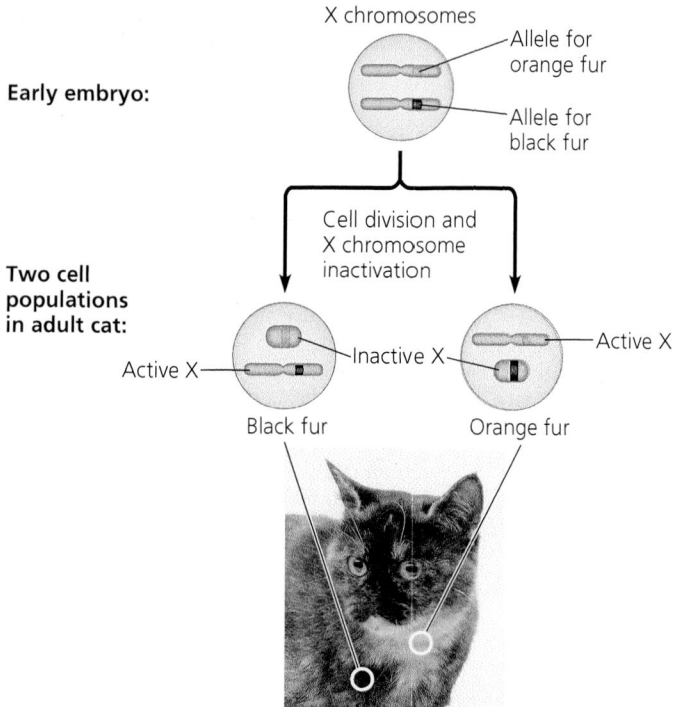

Early embryo:

X chromosomes

Allele for orange fur

Allele for black fur

Cell division and X chromosome inactivation

Two cell populations in adult cat:

Active X — Inactive X — Active X

Active X

Black fur   Orange fur

▲ **Figure 15.8 X inactivation and the tortoiseshell cat.** The tortoiseshell gene is on the X chromosome, and the tortoiseshell phenotype requires the presence of two different alleles, one for orange fur and one for black fur. Normally, only females can have both alleles, because only they have two X chromosomes. If a female cat is heterozygous for the tortoiseshell gene, she is tortoiseshell. Orange patches are formed by populations of cells in which the X chromosome with the orange allele is active; black patches have cells in which the X chromosome with the black allele is active. ("Calico" cats also have white areas, which are determined by yet another gene.)

of a *mosaic* of two types of cells: those with the active X derived from the father and those with the active X derived from the mother. After an X chromosome is inactivated in a particular cell, all mitotic descendants of that cell have the same inactive X. Thus, if a female is heterozygous for a sex-linked trait, about half her cells will express one allele, while the others will express the alternate allele. **Figure 15.8** shows how this mosaicism results in the mottled coloration of a tortoiseshell cat. In humans, mosaicism can be observed in a recessive X-linked mutation that prevents the development of sweat glands. A woman who is heterozygous for this trait has patches of normal skin and patches of skin lacking sweat glands.

Inactivation of an X chromosome involves modification of the DNA and the histone proteins bound to it, including attachment of methyl groups (—CH₃) to one of the nitrogenous bases of DNA nucleotides. (The regulatory role of DNA methylation is discussed further in Chapter 18.) A particular region of each X chromosome contains several genes involved in the inactivation process. The two regions, one on each X chromosome, associate briefly with each other in each cell at an early stage of embryonic development. Then one of the genes, called *XIST* (for <u>X</u>-<u>i</u>nactive <u>s</u>pecific

transcript) becomes active *only* on the chromosome that will become the Barr body. Multiple copies of the RNA product of this gene apparently attach to the X chromosome on which they are made, eventually almost covering it. Interaction of this RNA with the chromosome seems to initiate X inactivation, and the RNA products of other genes nearby on the X chromosome help to regulate the process.

CONCEPT CHECK 15.2

1. A white-eyed female *Drosophila* is mated with a red-eyed (wild-type) male, the reciprocal cross of the one shown in Figure 15.4. What phenotypes and genotypes do you predict for the offspring?
2. Neither Tim nor Rhoda has Duchenne muscular dystrophy, but their firstborn son does have it. What is the probability that a second child of this couple will have the disease? What is the probability if the second child is a boy? A girl?
3. **MAKE CONNECTIONS** Consider what you learned about dominant and recessive alleles in Concept 14.1 (p. 265). If a disorder were caused by a dominant X-linked allele, how would the inheritance pattern differ from what we see for recessive X-linked disorders?

For suggested answers, see Appendix A.

CONCEPT 15.3

Linked genes tend to be inherited together because they are located near each other on the same chromosome

The number of genes in a cell is far greater than the number of chromosomes; in fact, each chromosome has hundreds or thousands of genes. (The Y chromosome is an exception.) Genes located near each other on the same chromosome tend to be inherited together in genetic crosses; such genes are said to be genetically linked and are called **linked genes**. (Note the distinction between the terms *sex-linked gene*, referring to a single gene on a sex chromosome, and *linked genes*, referring to two or more genes on the same chromosome that tend to be inherited together.) When geneticists follow linked genes in breeding experiments, the results deviate from those expected from Mendel's law of independent assortment.

How Linkage Affects Inheritance

To see how linkage between genes affects the inheritance of two different characters, let's examine another of Morgan's *Drosophila* experiments. In this case, the characters are body color and wing size, each with two different phenotypes.

Wild-type flies have gray bodies and normal-sized wings. In addition to these flies, Morgan had managed to obtain, through breeding, doubly mutant flies with black bodies and wings much smaller than normal, called vestigial wings. The mutant alleles are recessive to the wild-type alleles, and neither gene is on a sex chromosome. In his investigation of these two genes, Morgan carried out the crosses shown in Figure 15.9. The first was a P generation cross to generate F_1 dihybrid flies, and the second was a testcross.

The resulting flies had a much higher proportion of the combinations of traits seen in the P generation flies (called parental phenotypes) than would be expected if the two genes assorted independently. Morgan thus concluded that body color and wing size are usually inherited together in

▼ Figure 15.9

INQUIRY

How does linkage between two genes affect inheritance of characters?

EXPERIMENT Morgan wanted to know whether the genes for body color and wing size were genetically linked, and if so, how this affected their inheritance. The alleles for body color are b^+ (gray) and b (black), and those for wing size are vg^+ (normal) and vg (vestigial).

Morgan mated true-breeding P (parental) generation flies—wild-type flies with black, vestigial-winged flies—to produce heterozygous F_1 dihybrids ($b^+ b\ vg^+ vg$), all of which are wild-type in appearance.

He then mated wild-type F_1 dihybrid females with black, vestigial-winged males. This testcross will reveal the genotype of the eggs made by the dihybrid female.

The male's sperm contributes only recessive alleles, so the phenotype of the offspring reflects the genotype of the female's eggs.

Note: Although only females (with pointed abdomens) are shown, half the offspring in each class would be males (with rounded abdomens).

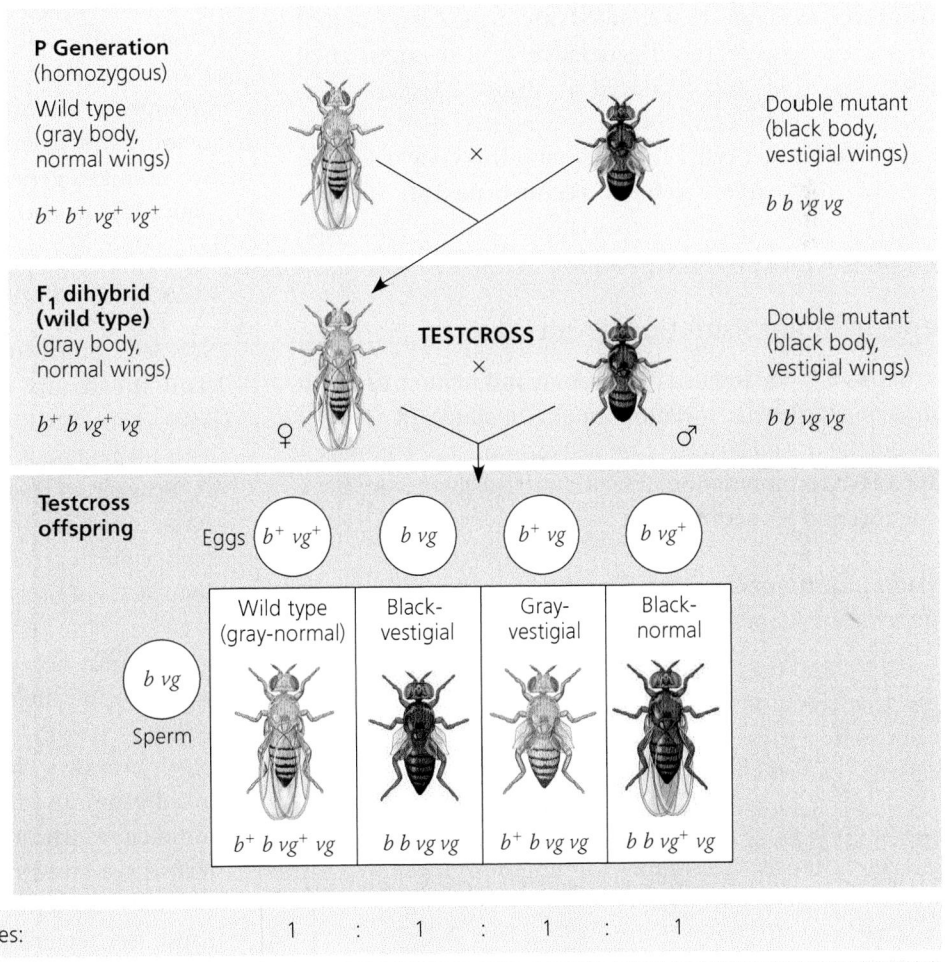

PREDICTED RATIOS

If genes are located on different chromosomes:	1	:	1	:	1	:	1
If genes are located on the same chromosome *and* parental alleles are always inherited together:	1	:	1	:	0	:	0

RESULTS

965	:	944	:	206	:	185

CONCLUSION Since most offspring had a parental (P generation) phenotype, Morgan concluded that the genes for body color and wing size are genetically linked on the same chromosome. However, the production of a relatively small number of offspring with nonparental phenotypes indicated that some mechanism occasionally breaks the linkage between specific alleles of genes on the same chromosome.

SOURCE: T. H. Morgan and C. J. Lynch, The linkage of two factors in *Drosophila* that are not sex-linked, *Biological Bulletin* 23:174–182 (1912).

WHAT IF? If the parental (P generation) flies had been true-breeding for gray body with vestigial wings and black body with normal wings, which phenotypic class(es) would be largest among the testcross offspring?

specific (parental) combinations because the genes for these characters are near each other on the same chromosome:

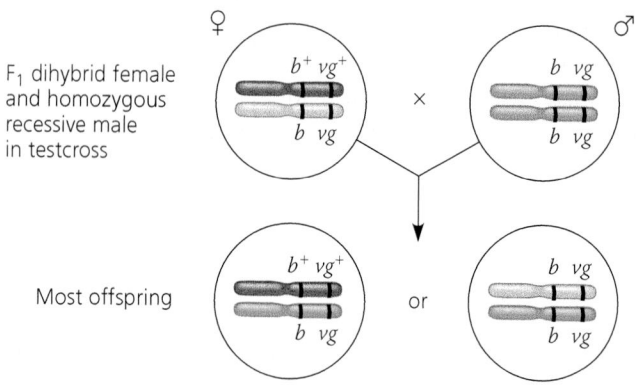

F₁ dihybrid female and homozygous recessive male in testcross

$b^+ vg^+$ / b vg × b vg / b vg

Most offspring $b^+ vg^+$ / b vg or b vg / b vg

However, as Figure 15.9 shows, both of the combinations of traits not seen in the P generation (called nonparental phenotypes) were also produced in Morgan's experiments, suggesting that the body-color and wing-size alleles are not always linked genetically. To understand this conclusion, we need to further explore **genetic recombination**, the production of offspring with combinations of traits that differ from those found in either parent.

Genetic Recombination and Linkage

In Chapter 13, you learned that meiosis and random fertilization generate genetic variation among offspring of sexually reproducing organisms. Here we will examine the chromosomal basis of recombination in relation to the genetic findings of Mendel and Morgan.

Recombination of Unlinked Genes: Independent Assortment of Chromosomes

Mendel learned from crosses in which he followed two characters that some offspring have combinations of traits that do not match those of either parent. For example, we can represent the cross between a pea plant with yellow-round seeds that is heterozygous for both seed color and seed shape (a dihybrid, *YyRr*) and a plant with green-wrinkled seeds (homozygous for both recessive alleles, *yyrr*) by the following Punnett square:

Gametes from yellow-round dihybrid parent (*YyRr*)

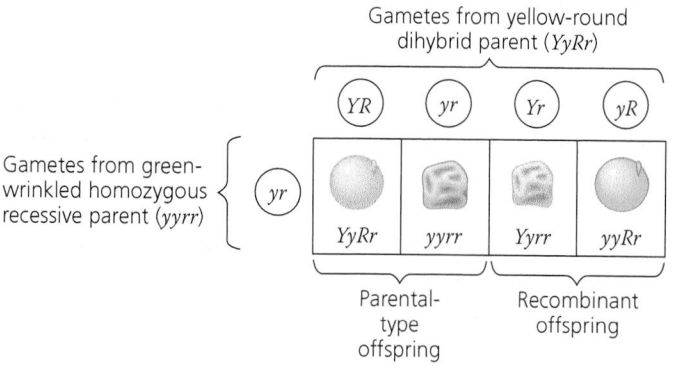

Gametes from green-wrinkled homozygous recessive parent (*yyrr*)

YR	yr	Yr	yR
YyRr	yyrr	Yyrr	yyRr

Parental-type offspring · Recombinant offspring

Notice in this Punnett square that one-half of the offspring are expected to inherit a phenotype that matches either of the parental (P generation) phenotypes. These offspring are called **parental types**. But two nonparental phenotypes are also found among the offspring. Because these offspring have new combinations of seed shape and color, they are called **recombinant types**, or **recombinants** for short. When 50% of all offspring are recombinants, as in this example, geneticists say that there is a 50% frequency of recombination. The predicted phenotypic ratios among the offspring are similar to what Mendel actually found in *YyRr* × *yyrr* crosses (a type of testcross because it reveals the genotype of the gametes made by the dihybrid *YyRr* plant).

A 50% frequency of recombination in such testcrosses is observed for any two genes that are located on different chromosomes and thus cannot be linked. The physical basis of recombination between unlinked genes is the random orientation of homologous chromosomes at metaphase I of meiosis, which leads to the independent assortment of the two unlinked genes (see Figure 13.10 and the question in the Figure 15.2 legend).

Recombination of Linked Genes: Crossing Over

Now let's return to Morgan's fly room to see how we can explain the results of the *Drosophila* testcross illustrated in Figure 15.9. Recall that most of the offspring from the testcross for body color and wing size had parental phenotypes. That suggested that the two genes were on the same chromosome, since the occurrence of parental types with a frequency greater than 50% indicates that the genes are linked. About 17% of offspring, however, were recombinants.

Faced with these results, Morgan proposed that some process must occasionally break the physical connection between specific alleles of genes on the same chromosome. Subsequent experiments demonstrated that this process, now called **crossing over**, accounts for the recombination of linked genes. In crossing over, which occurs while replicated homologous chromosomes are paired during prophase of meiosis I, a set of proteins orchestrates an exchange of corresponding segments of one maternal and one paternal chromatid (see Figure 13.11). In effect, end portions of two nonsister chromatids trade places each time a crossover occurs.

Figure 15.10 shows how crossing over in a dihybrid female fly resulted in recombinant eggs and ultimately recombinant offspring in Morgan's testcross. Most of the eggs had a chromosome with either the $b^+ vg^+$ or b vg parental genotype for body color and wing size, but some eggs had a recombinant chromosome ($b^+ vg$ or $b vg^+$). Fertilization of these various classes of eggs by homozygous recessive sperm (b vg) produced an offspring population in which 17% exhibited a nonparental, recombinant phenotype, reflecting combinations of alleles not seen before in either P generation parent.

Testcross parents

Gray body, normal wings (F₁ dihybrid)

$b^+ \quad vg^+$
$b \quad vg$

Black body, vestigial wings (double mutant)

$b \quad vg$
$b \quad vg$

♀

♂

Replication of chromosomes

$b^+ \quad vg^+$
$b^+ \quad vg^+$
$b \quad vg$
$b \quad vg$

Replication of chromosomes

$b \quad vg$
$b \quad vg$
$b \quad vg$
$b \quad vg$

Meiosis I: Crossing over between *b* and *vg* loci produces new allele combinations.

$b^+ \quad vg^+$
$b^+ \quad vg$
$b \quad vg^+$
$b \quad vg$

Meiosis I and II: No new allele combinations are produced.

Meiosis II: Separation of chromatids produces recombinant gametes with the new allele combinations.

Recombinant chromosomes

Eggs

b^+vg^+ | $b\ vg$ | $b^+\ vg$ | $b\ vg^+$

Testcross offspring

965 Wild type (gray-normal)	944 Black-vestigial	206 Gray-vestigial	185 Black-normal
$b^+ \quad vg^+$	$b \quad vg$	$b^+ \quad vg$	$b \quad vg^+$
$b \quad vg$	$b \quad vg$	$b \quad vg$	$b \quad vg$

$b \quad vg$

Sperm

Parental-type offspring — Recombinant offspring

$$\text{Recombination frequency} = \frac{391 \text{ recombinants}}{2{,}300 \text{ total offspring}} \times 100 = 17\%$$

▶ **Figure 15.10 Chromosomal basis for recombination of linked genes.** In these diagrams re-creating the testcross in Figure 15.9, we track chromosomes as well as genes. The maternal chromosomes are color-coded red and pink to distinguish one homolog from the other before any meiotic crossing over has taken place. Because crossing over between the *b* and *vg* loci occurs in some, but not all, egg-producing cells, more eggs with parental-type chromosomes than with recombinant ones are produced in the mating females. Fertilization of the eggs by sperm of genotype *b vg* gives rise to some recombinant offspring. The recombination frequency is the percentage of recombinant flies in the total pool of offspring.

DRAW IT *Suppose, as in the question at the bottom of Figure 15.9, the parental (P generation) flies were true-breeding for gray body with vestigial wings and black body with normal wings. Draw the chromosomes in each of the four possible kinds of eggs from an F₁ female, and label each chromosome as "parental" or "recombinant."*

New Combinations of Alleles: Variation for Natural Selection

EVOLUTION In Chapter 13, you learned how the physical behavior of chromosomes during meiosis contributes to the generation of variation in offspring. Each pair of homologous chromosomes lines up independently of other pairs during metaphase I, and crossing over prior to that, during prophase I, can mix and match parts of maternal and paternal homologs. Chapter 14 described Mendel's elegant experiments showing that the behavior of the abstract entities known as genes (or, more concretely, alleles of genes) also leads to variation in offspring. Now, putting these different ideas together, you can see that the recombinant chromosomes resulting from crossing over may bring alleles together in new combinations, and the

subsequent events of meiosis distribute to gametes the recombinant chromosomes in a multitude of combinations, such as the new variants seen in Figures 15.9 and 15.10. Random fertilization then increases even further the number of variant allele combinations that can be created.

This abundance of genetic variation provides the raw material on which natural selection works. If the traits conferred by particular combinations of alleles are better suited for a given environment, organisms possessing those genotypes will be expected to thrive and leave more offspring, ensuring the continuation of their genetic complement. In the next generation, of course, the alleles will be shuffled anew. Ultimately, the interplay between environment and genotype will determine which genetic combinations persist over time.

Mapping the Distance Between Genes Using Recombination Data: *Scientific Inquiry*

The discovery of linked genes and recombination due to crossing over led one of Morgan's students, Alfred H. Sturtevant, to a method for constructing a **genetic map**, an ordered list of the genetic loci along a particular chromosome.

Sturtevant hypothesized that the percentage of recombinant offspring, the *recombination frequency*, calculated from experiments like the one in Figures 15.9 and 15.10, depends on the distance between genes on a chromosome. He assumed that crossing over is a random event, with the chance of crossing over approximately equal at all points along a chromosome. Based on these assumptions, Sturtevant predicted that *the farther apart two genes are, the higher the probability that a crossover will occur between them and therefore the higher the recombination frequency.* His reasoning was simple: The greater the distance between two genes, the more points there are between them where crossing over can occur. Using recombination data from various fruit fly crosses, Sturtevant proceeded to assign relative positions to genes on the same chromosomes—that is, to *map* genes.

A genetic map based on recombination frequencies is called a **linkage map**. **Figure 15.11** shows Sturtevant's linkage map of three genes: the body-color (*b*) and wing-size (*vg*) genes depicted in Figure 15.10 and a third gene, called cinnabar (*cn*). Cinnabar is one of many *Drosophila* genes affecting eye color. Cinnabar eyes, a mutant phenotype, are a brighter red than the wild-type color. The recombination frequency between *cn* and *b* is 9%; that between *cn* and *vg*, 9.5%; and that between *b* and *vg*, 17%. In other words, crossovers between *cn* and *b* and between *cn* and *vg* are about half as frequent as crossovers between *b* and *vg*. Only a map that locates *cn* about midway between *b* and *vg* is consistent with these data, as you can prove to yourself by drawing alternative maps. Sturtevant expressed the distances between genes in **map units**, defining one map unit as equivalent to a 1% recombination frequency.

In practice, the interpretation of recombination data is more complicated than this example suggests. Some genes on a chromosome are so far from each other that a crossover between them is virtually certain. The observed frequency of recombination in crosses involving two such genes can have a maximum value of 50%, a result indistinguishable from that for genes on different chromosomes. In this case, the physical connection between genes on the same chromosome is not reflected in the results of genetic crosses. Despite being on the same chromosome and thus being *physically connected*, the genes are *genetically unlinked*; alleles of such genes assort independently, as if they were on different chromosomes. In fact, at least two of the genes for pea characters that Mendel studied are now known to be on the same chromosome, but the distance between them is so great that linkage is not observed in genetic crosses. Consequently, the two genes behaved as if they were on different chromosomes in Mendel's experiments.

RESEARCH METHOD

Constructing a Linkage Map

APPLICATION A linkage map shows the relative locations of genes along a chromosome.

TECHNIQUE A linkage map is based on the assumption that the probability of a crossover between two genetic loci is proportional to the distance separating the loci. The recombination frequencies used to construct a linkage map for a particular chromosome are obtained from experimental crosses, such as the cross depicted in Figures 15.9 and 15.10. The distances between genes are expressed as map units, with one map unit equivalent to a 1% recombination frequency. Genes are arranged on the chromosome in the order that best fits the data.

RESULTS In this example, the observed recombination frequencies between three *Drosophila* gene pairs (*b–cn* 9%, *cn–vg* 9.5%, and *b–vg* 17%) best fit a linear order in which *cn* is positioned about halfway between the other two genes:

The *b–vg* recombination frequency (17%) is slightly less than the sum of the *b–cn* and *cn–vg* frequencies (9 + 9.5 = 18.5%) because of the few times that one crossover occurs between *b* and *cn* and another crossover occurs between *cn* and *vg*. The second crossover would "cancel out" the first, reducing the observed *b–vg* recombination frequency while contributing to the frequency between each of the closer pairs of genes. The value of 18.5% (18.5 map units) is closer to the actual distance between the genes, so a geneticist would add the smaller distances in constructing a map.

Genes located far apart on a chromosome are mapped by adding the recombination frequencies from crosses involving closer pairs of genes lying between the two distant genes.

Using recombination data, Sturtevant and his colleagues were able to map numerous *Drosophila* genes in linear arrays. They found that the genes clustered into four groups of linked genes (*linkage groups*). Light microscopy had revealed four pairs of chromosomes in *Drosophila*, so the linkage map provided additional evidence that genes are located on chromosomes. Each chromosome has a linear array of specific genes, each gene with its own locus (**Figure 15.12**).

Because a linkage map is based strictly on recombination frequencies, it gives only an approximate picture of a chromosome. The frequency of crossing over is not actually uniform over the length of a chromosome, as Sturtevant assumed, and therefore map units do not correspond to actual physical distances (in nanometers, for instance). A linkage map does portray the order of genes along a chromosome, but it does not accurately portray the precise locations of those genes. Other methods enable geneticists to construct **cytogenetic maps** of chromosomes, which locate genes with respect to chromosomal

Mutant phenotypes

| Short aristae | Black body | Cinnabar eyes | Vestigial wings | Brown eyes |

| 0 | 48.5 | 57.5 | 67.0 | 104.5 |

| Long aristae (appendages on head) | Gray body | Red eyes | Normal wings | Red eyes |

Wild-type phenotypes

▲ **Figure 15.12 A partial genetic (linkage) map of a *Drosophila* chromosome.** This simplified map shows just a few of the genes that have been mapped on *Drosophila* chromosome II. The number at each gene locus indicates the number of map units between that locus and the locus for arista length (left). Notice that more than one gene can affect a given phenotypic characteristic, such as eye color. Also, note that in contrast to the homologous autosomes (II–IV), the X and Y sex chromosomes (I) have distinct shapes.

features, such as stained bands, that can be seen in the microscope. The ultimate maps, which we will discuss in Chapter 21, display the physical distances between gene loci in DNA nucleotides. Comparing a linkage map with such a physical map or with a cytogenetic map of the same chromosome, we find that the linear order of genes is identical in all the maps, but the spacing between genes is not.

CONCEPT CHECK 15.3

1. When two genes are located on the same chromosome, what is the physical basis for the production of recombinant offspring in a testcross between a dihybrid parent and a double-mutant (recessive) parent?
2. For each type of offspring of the testcross in Figure 15.9, explain the relationship between its phenotype and the alleles contributed by the female parent.
3. **WHAT IF?** Genes *A*, *B*, and *C* are located on the same chromosome. Testcrosses show that the recombination frequency between *A* and *B* is 28% and between *A* and *C* is 12%. Can you determine the linear order of these genes? Explain.

For suggested answers, see Appendix A.

Alterations of chromosome number or structure cause some genetic disorders

As you have learned so far in this chapter, the phenotype of an organism can be affected by small-scale changes involving individual genes. Random mutations are the source of all new alleles, which can lead to new phenotypic traits.

Large-scale chromosomal changes can also affect an organism's phenotype. Physical and chemical disturbances, as well as errors during meiosis, can damage chromosomes in major ways or alter their number in a cell. Large-scale chromosomal alterations in humans and other mammals often lead to spontaneous abortion (miscarriage) of a fetus, and individuals born with these types of genetic defects commonly exhibit various developmental disorders. Plants may tolerate such genetic defects better than animals do.

Abnormal Chromosome Number

Ideally, the meiotic spindle distributes chromosomes to daughter cells without error. But there is an occasional mishap, called a **nondisjunction**, in which the members of a pair of homologous chromosomes do not move apart properly during meiosis I or sister chromatids fail to separate during meiosis II **(Figure 15.13)**. In these cases, one gamete

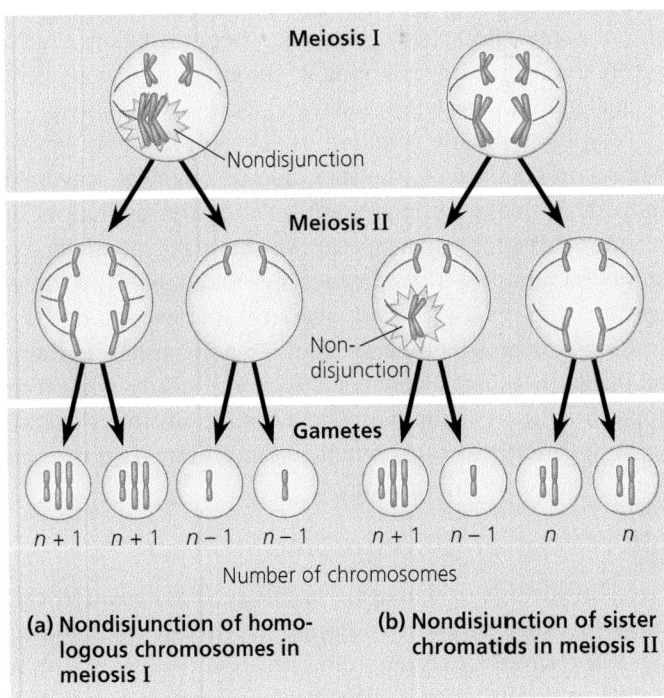

Meiosis I

Nondisjunction

Meiosis II

Nondisjunction

Gametes

| $n + 1$ | $n + 1$ | $n - 1$ | $n - 1$ | $n + 1$ | $n - 1$ | n | n |

Number of chromosomes

(a) Nondisjunction of homologous chromosomes in meiosis I

(b) Nondisjunction of sister chromatids in meiosis II

▲ **Figure 15.13 Meiotic nondisjunction.** Gametes with an abnormal chromosome number can arise by nondisjunction in either meiosis I or meiosis II. For simplicity, the figure does not show the spores formed by meiosis in plants. Ultimately, spores form gametes that have the defects shown. (See Figure 13.6.)

receives two of the same type of chromosome and another gamete receives no copy. The other chromosomes are usually distributed normally.

If either of the aberrant gametes unites with a normal one at fertilization, the zygote will also have an abnormal number of a particular chromosome, a condition known as **aneuploidy**. (Aneuploidy may involve more than one chromosome.) Fertilization involving a gamete that has no copy of a particular chromosome will lead to a missing chromosome in the zygote (so that the cell has $2n - 1$ chromosomes); the aneuploid zygote is said to be **monosomic** for that chromosome. If a chromosome is present in triplicate in the zygote (so that the cell has $2n + 1$ chromosomes), the aneuploid cell is **trisomic** for that chromosome. Mitosis will subsequently transmit the anomaly to all embryonic cells. If the organism survives, it usually has a set of traits caused by the abnormal dose of the genes associated with the extra or missing chromosome. Down syndrome is an example of trisomy in humans that will be discussed later. Nondisjunction can also occur during mitosis. If such an error takes place early in embryonic development, then the aneuploid condition is passed along by mitosis to a large number of cells and is likely to have a substantial effect on the organism.

Some organisms have more than two complete chromosome sets in all somatic cells. The general term for this chromosomal alteration is **polyploidy**; the specific terms *triploidy* (3n) and *tetraploidy* (4n) indicate three or four chromosomal sets, respectively. One way a triploid cell may arise is by the fertilization of an abnormal diploid egg produced by nondisjunction of all its chromosomes. Tetraploidy could result from the failure of a 2n zygote to divide after replicating its chromosomes. Subsequent normal mitotic divisions would then produce a 4n embryo.

Polyploidy is fairly common in the plant kingdom. As we will see in Chapter 24, the spontaneous origin of polyploid individuals plays an important role in the evolution of plants. Many of the plant species we eat are polyploid; for example, bananas are triploid, wheat hexaploid (6n), and strawberries octoploid (8n). Polyploid animal species are much less common, although some are found among fishes and amphibians. In general, polyploids are more nearly normal in appearance than aneuploids. One extra (or missing) chromosome apparently disrupts genetic balance more than does an entire extra set of chromosomes.

Alterations of Chromosome Structure

Errors in meiosis or damaging agents such as radiation can cause breakage of a chromosome, which can lead to four types of changes in chromosome structure (Figure 15.14). A **deletion** occurs when a chromosomal fragment is lost. The affected chromosome is then missing certain genes. (If the centromere is deleted, the entire chromosome will be lost.) The "deleted" fragment may become attached as an extra segment to a sister chromatid, producing a **duplication**.

▼ Figure 15.14 **Alterations of chromosome structure.** Red arrows indicate breakage points. Dark purple highlights the chromosomal parts affected by the rearrangements.

(a) Deletion

A **deletion** removes a chromosomal segment.

(b) Duplication

A **duplication** repeats a segment.

(c) Inversion

An **inversion** reverses a segment within a chromosome.

(d) Translocation

A **translocation** moves a segment from one chromosome to a nonhomologous chromosome. In a reciprocal translocation, the most common type, nonhomologous chromosomes exchange fragments.

Less often, a nonreciprocal translocation occurs: A chromosome transfers a fragment but receives none in return (not shown).

Alternatively, a detached fragment could attach to a nonsister chromatid of a homologous chromosome. In that case, though, the "duplicated" segments might not be identical because the homologs could carry different alleles of certain genes. A chromosomal fragment may also reattach to the original chromosome but in the reverse orientation, producing an **inversion**. A fourth possible result of chromosomal breakage is for the fragment to join a nonhomologous chromosome, a rearrangement called a **translocation**.

Deletions and duplications are especially likely to occur during meiosis. In crossing over, nonsister chromatids sometimes exchange unequal-sized segments of DNA, so that one partner gives up more genes than it receives. The products of such an unequal crossover are one chromosome with a deletion and one chromosome with a duplication.

A diploid embryo that is homozygous for a large deletion (or has a single X chromosome with a large deletion, in a male) is usually missing a number of essential genes, a condition that is ordinarily lethal. Duplications and translocations also tend to be harmful. In reciprocal translocations, in which segments are exchanged between nonhomologous chromosomes, and in inversions, the balance of genes is not abnormal—all genes are present in their normal doses. Nevertheless, translocations and inversions can alter phenotype because a gene's expression can be influenced by its location among neighboring genes; such events sometimes have devastating effects.

Human Disorders Due to Chromosomal Alterations

Alterations of chromosome number and structure are associated with a number of serious human disorders. As described earlier, nondisjunction in meiosis results in aneuploidy in gametes and any resulting zygotes. Although the frequency of aneuploid zygotes may be quite high in humans, most of these chromosomal alterations are so disastrous to development that the affected embryos are spontaneously aborted long before birth. However, some types of aneuploidy appear to upset the genetic balance less than others, with the result that individuals with certain aneuploid conditions can survive to birth and beyond. These individuals have a set of traits—a *syndrome*—characteristic of the type of aneuploidy. Genetic disorders caused by aneuploidy can be diagnosed before birth by fetal testing (see Figure 14.19).

Down Syndrome (Trisomy 21)

One aneuploid condition, **Down syndrome**, affects approximately one out of every 700 children born in the United States (Figure 15.15). Down syndrome is usually the result of an extra chromosome 21, so that each body cell has a total of 47 chromosomes. Because the cells are trisomic for chromosome 21, Down syndrome is often called *trisomy 21*. Down syndrome includes characteristic facial features, short stature, correctable heart defects, and developmental delays. Individuals with Down syndrome have an increased chance of developing leukemia and Alzheimer's disease but have a lower rate of high blood pressure, atherosclerosis (hardening of the arteries), stroke, and many types of solid tumors. Although people with Down syndrome, on average, have a life span shorter than normal, most, with proper medical treatment, live to middle age and beyond. Many live independently or at home with their families, are employed, and are valuable contributors to their communities. Almost all males and about half of females with Down syndrome are sexually underdeveloped and sterile.

The frequency of Down syndrome increases with the age of the mother. While the disorder occurs in just 0.04% of children born to women under age 30, the risk climbs to 0.92% for

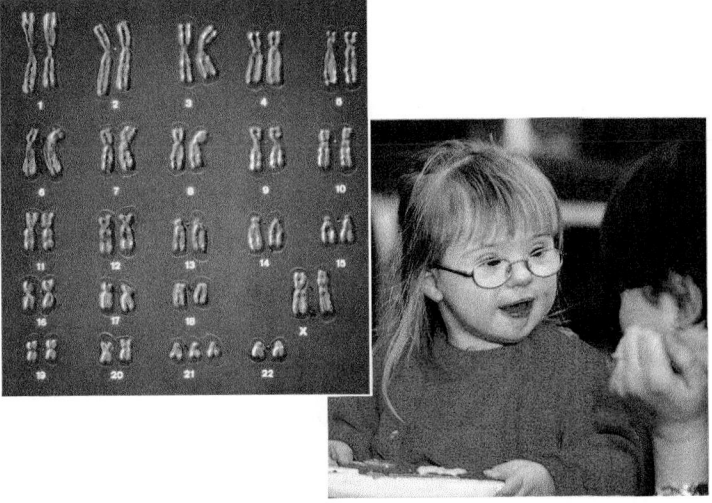

▲ **Figure 15.15 Down syndrome.** The karyotype shows trisomy 21, the most common cause of Down syndrome. The child exhibits the facial features characteristic of this disorder.

mothers at age 40 and is even higher for older mothers. The correlation of Down syndrome with maternal age has not yet been explained. Most cases result from nondisjunction during meiosis I, and some research points to an age-dependent abnormality in a meiosis checkpoint that normally delays anaphase until all the kinetochores are attached to the spindle (like the M phase checkpoint of the mitotic cell cycle; see Chapter 12). Trisomies of some other chromosomes also increase in incidence with maternal age, although infants with other autosomal trisomies rarely survive for long. Due to its low risk and its potential for providing useful information, prenatal screening for trisomies in the embryo is now offered to all pregnant women. In 2008, the Prenatally and Postnatally Diagnosed Conditions Awareness Act was signed into law in the United States. This law stipulates that medical practitioners give accurate, up-to-date information about any prenatal or postnatal diagnosis received by parents and that they connect parents with appropriate support services.

Aneuploidy of Sex Chromosomes

Nondisjunction of sex chromosomes produces a variety of aneuploid conditions. Most of these conditions appear to upset the genetic balance less than aneuploid conditions involving autosomes. This may be because the Y chromosome carries relatively few genes and because extra copies of the X chromosome become inactivated as Barr bodies in somatic cells.

An extra X chromosome in a male, producing XXY, occurs approximately once in every 500 to 1,000 live male births. People with this disorder, called *Klinefelter syndrome*, have male sex organs, but the testes are abnormally small and the man is sterile. Even though the extra X is inactivated, some breast enlargement and other female body characteristics are common. Affected individuals may have subnormal intelligence. About 1 of every 1,000 males is born with an extra Y chromosome (XYY). These males undergo normal sexual development and do not exhibit any well-defined syndrome, but they tend to be somewhat taller than average.

Females with trisomy X (XXX), which occurs once in approximately 1,000 live female births, are healthy and have no unusual physical features other than being slightly taller than average. Triple-X females are at risk for learning disabilities but are fertile. Monosomy X, called *Turner syndrome*, occurs about once in every 2,500 female births and is the only known viable monosomy in humans. Although these X0 individuals are phenotypically female, they are sterile because their sex organs do not mature. When provided with estrogen replacement therapy, girls with Turner syndrome do develop secondary sex characteristics. Most have normal intelligence.

Disorders Caused by Structurally Altered Chromosomes

Many deletions in human chromosomes, even in a heterozygous state, cause severe problems. One such syndrome, known as *cri du chat* ("cry of the cat"), results from a specific deletion in chromosome 5. A child born with this deletion is severely intellectually disabled, has a small head with unusual facial features, and has a cry that sounds like the mewing of a distressed cat. Such individuals usually die in infancy or early childhood.

Chromosomal translocations have been implicated in certain cancers, including *chronic myelogenous leukemia* (CML). This disease occurs when a reciprocal translocation happens during mitosis of cells that will become white blood cells. In these cells, the exchange of a large portion of chromosome 22 with a small fragment from a tip of chromosome 9 produces a much shortened, easily recognized chromosome 22, called the *Philadelphia chromosome* (Figure 15.16). Such an exchange causes cancer by activating a gene that leads to uncontrolled cell cycle progression. The mechanism of gene activation will be discussed in Chapter 18.

Normal chromosome 9

Normal chromosome 22

Reciprocal translocation

Translocated chromosome 9

Translocated chromosome 22
(Philadelphia chromosome)

▲ **Figure 15.16 Translocation associated with chronic myelogenous leukemia (CML).** The cancerous cells in nearly all CML patients contain an abnormally short chromosome 22, the so-called Philadelphia chromosome, and an abnormally long chromosome 9. These altered chromosomes result from the reciprocal translocation shown here, which presumably occurred in a single white blood cell precursor undergoing mitosis and was then passed along to all descendant cells.

CONCEPT **15.5**

Some inheritance patterns are exceptions to standard Mendelian inheritance

In the previous section, you learned about deviations from the usual patterns of chromosomal inheritance due to abnormal events in meiosis and mitosis. We conclude this chapter by describing two normally occurring exceptions to Mendelian genetics, one involving genes located in the nucleus and the other involving genes located outside the nucleus. In both cases, the sex of the parent contributing an allele is a factor in the pattern of inheritance.

Genomic Imprinting

Throughout our discussions of Mendelian genetics and the chromosomal basis of inheritance, we have assumed that a given allele will have the same effect whether it was inherited from the mother or the father. This is probably a safe assumption most of the time. For example, when Mendel crossed purple-flowered pea plants with white-flowered pea plants, he observed the same results regardless of whether the purple-flowered parent supplied the eggs or the sperm. In recent years, however, geneticists have identified two to three dozen traits in mammals that depend on which parent passed along the alleles for those traits. Such variation in phenotype depending on whether an allele is inherited from the male or female parent is called **genomic imprinting**. (Note that unlike sex-linked genes, most imprinted genes are on autosomes.)

Genomic imprinting occurs during gamete formation and results in the silencing of a particular allele of certain genes. Because these genes are imprinted differently in sperm and eggs, a zygote expresses only one allele of an imprinted gene, that inherited from either the female or the male parent. The imprints are then transmitted to all body cells during development. In each generation, the old imprints are "erased" in gamete-producing cells, and the chromosomes of the developing gametes are newly imprinted according to the sex of the individual forming the gametes. In a given species, the imprinted genes are always imprinted in the same way. For instance, a gene imprinted for maternal allele expression is always imprinted this way, generation after generation.

Consider, for example, the mouse gene for insulin-like growth factor 2 (*Igf2*), one of the first imprinted genes to be identified. Although this growth factor is required for normal prenatal growth, only the paternal allele is expressed (Figure 15.17a). Evidence that the *Igf2* gene is imprinted came initially from crosses between normal-sized (wild-type) mice and dwarf (mutant) mice homozygous for a recessive mutation in the *Igf2* gene. The phenotypes of heterozygous offspring (with one normal allele and one mutant) differed, depending on whether the mutant allele came from the mother or the father (Figure 15.17b).

What exactly is a genomic imprint? In many cases, it seems to consist of methyl (—CH₃) groups that are added to cytosine nucleotides of one of the alleles. Such methylation may silence the allele, an effect consistent with evidence that heavily methylated genes are usually inactive (see Chapter 18). However, for a few genes, methylation has been shown to *activate* expression of the allele. This is the case for the *Igf2* gene: Methylation of certain cytosines on the paternal chromosome leads to expression of the paternal *Igf2* allele. The apparent inconsistency as to whether methylation activates or silences alleles was resolved in part when researchers found that DNA methylation operates indirectly by recruiting enzymes that modify DNA-associated proteins (histones), leading to condensation of the local DNA. Depending on the original function of the condensed DNA in regulating allele expression, the result is either silencing or activation of a given allele.

Genomic imprinting is thought to affect only a small fraction of the genes in mammalian genomes, but most of the known imprinted genes are critical for embryonic development. In experiments with mice, for example, embryos engineered to inherit both copies of certain chromosomes from the same parent usually die before birth, whether that parent is male or female. A few years ago, however, scientists in Japan combined the genetic material from two eggs in a zygote while allowing expression of the *Igf2* gene from only one of the egg nuclei. The zygote developed into an apparently healthy mouse. Normal development seems to require that embryonic cells have exactly one active copy—not zero, not two—of certain genes. The association of aberrant imprinting

(a) Homozygote. A mouse homozygous for the wild-type *Igf2* allele is normal-sized. Only the paternal allele of this gene is expressed.

(b) Heterozygotes. Matings between wild-type mice and those homozygous for the recessive mutant *Igf2* allele produce heterozygous offspring. The dwarf (mutant) phenotype is seen only when the father contributed the mutant allele because the maternal allele is not expressed.

▲ Figure 15.17 **Genomic imprinting of the mouse *Igf2* gene.**

with abnormal development and certain cancers has stimulated numerous studies of how different genes are imprinted.

Inheritance of Organelle Genes

Although our focus in this chapter has been on the chromosomal basis of inheritance, we end with an important amendment: Not all of a eukaryotic cell's genes are located on nuclear chromosomes, or even in the nucleus; some genes are located in organelles in the cytoplasm. Because they are outside the nucleus, these genes are sometimes called *extranuclear genes* or *cytoplasmic genes*. Mitochondria, as well as chloroplasts and other plastids in plants, contain small circular DNA molecules that carry a number of genes. These organelles reproduce themselves and transmit their genes to daughter organelles. Organelle genes are not distributed to offspring according to the same rules that direct the distribution of nuclear chromosomes during meiosis, so they do not display Mendelian inheritance.

The first hint that extranuclear genes exist came from studies by the German scientist Karl Correns on the inheritance of yellow or white patches on the leaves of an otherwise green plant. In 1909, he observed that the coloration of the offspring was determined only by the maternal parent (the

◀ **Figure 15.18 Variegated leaves from English holly (*Ilex aquifolium*).** Variegated (striped or spotted) leaves result from mutations in pigment genes located in plastids, which generally are inherited from the maternal parent.

source of eggs) and not by the paternal parent (the source of sperm). Subsequent research showed that such coloration patterns, or variegation, are due to mutations in plastid genes that control pigmentation (**Figure 15.18**). In most plants, a zygote receives all its plastids from the cytoplasm of the egg and none from the sperm, which contributes little more than a haploid set of chromosomes. An egg may contain plastids with different alleles for a pigmentation gene. As the zygote develops, plastids containing wild-type or mutant pigmentation genes are distributed randomly to daughter cells. The pattern of leaf coloration exhibited by a plant depends on the ratio of wild-type to mutant plastids in its various tissues.

Similar maternal inheritance is also the rule for mitochondrial genes in most animals and plants, because almost all the mitochondria passed on to a zygote come from the cytoplasm of the egg. The products of most mitochondrial genes help make up the protein complexes of the electron transport chain and ATP synthase (see Chapter 9). Defects in one or more of these proteins, therefore, reduce the amount of ATP the cell can make and have been shown to cause a number of rare human disorders. Because the parts of the body most susceptible to energy deprivation are the nervous system and the muscles, most mitochondrial diseases primarily affect these systems. For example, *mitochondrial myopathy* causes weakness, intolerance of exercise, and muscle deterioration. Another mitochondrial disorder is *Leber's hereditary*

optic neuropathy, which can produce sudden blindness in people as young as their 20s or 30s. The four mutations found thus far to cause this disorder affect oxidative phosphorylation during cellular respiration, a crucial function for the cell.

In addition to the rare diseases clearly caused by defects in mitochondrial DNA, mitochondrial mutations inherited from a person's mother may contribute to at least some cases of diabetes and heart disease, as well as to other disorders that commonly debilitate the elderly, such as Alzheimer's disease. In the course of a lifetime, new mutations gradually accumulate in our mitochondrial DNA, and some researchers think that these mutations play a role in the normal aging process.

Wherever genes are located in the cell—in the nucleus or in cytoplasmic organelles—their inheritance depends on the precise replication of DNA, the genetic material. In the next chapter, you will learn how this molecular reproduction occurs.

CONCEPT CHECK 15.5

1. Gene dosage, the number of active copies of a gene, is important to proper development. Identify and describe two processes that establish the proper dosage of certain genes.
2. Reciprocal crosses between two primrose varieties, A and B, produced the following results: A female × B male → offspring with all green (nonvariegated) leaves; B female × A male → offspring with spotted (variegated) leaves. Explain these results.
3. **WHAT IF?** Mitochondrial genes are critical to the energy metabolism of cells, but mitochondrial disorders caused by mutations in these genes are generally not lethal. Why not?

For suggested answers, see Appendix A.

15 CHAPTER REVIEW

SUMMARY OF KEY CONCEPTS

CONCEPT 15.1

Mendelian inheritance has its physical basis in the behavior of chromosomes (pp. 286–289)

- The **chromosome theory of inheritance** states that genes are located on chromosomes and that the behavior of chromosomes during meiosis accounts for Mendel's laws of segregation and independent assortment.
- Morgan's discovery that transmission of the X chromosome in *Drosophila* correlates with inheritance of an eye-color trait was the first solid evidence indicating that a specific gene is associated with a specific chromosome.

? *What characteristic of the sex chromosomes allowed Morgan to correlate their behavior with that of the alleles of the eye-color gene?*

CONCEPT 15.2

Sex-linked genes exhibit unique patterns of inheritance (pp. 289–292)

- Sex is an inherited phenotypic character usually determined by which sex chromosomes are present. Humans and other mammals have an X-Y system in which sex is determined by whether a Y chromosome is present. Other systems are found in birds, fishes, and insects.
- The sex chromosomes carry **sex-linked genes** for some traits that are unrelated to sex characteristics. For instance, recessive alleles causing color blindness are **X-linked** (carried on the X chromosome). Fathers transmit this and other X-linked alleles to all daughters but to no sons. Any male who inherits such an allele from his mother will express the trait.
- In mammalian females, one of the two X chromosomes in each cell is randomly inactivated during early embryonic development,

becoming highly condensed into a **Barr body**. The descendant cells inherit the same inactivated X chromosome. If a female is heterozygous for a particular gene located on the X chromosome, she will be mosaic for that character, with about half her cells expressing the maternal allele and about half expressing the paternal allele.

? *Why are males affected much more often than females by X-linked disorders?*

CONCEPT 15.3

Linked genes tend to be inherited together because they are located near each other on the same chromosome (pp. 292–297)

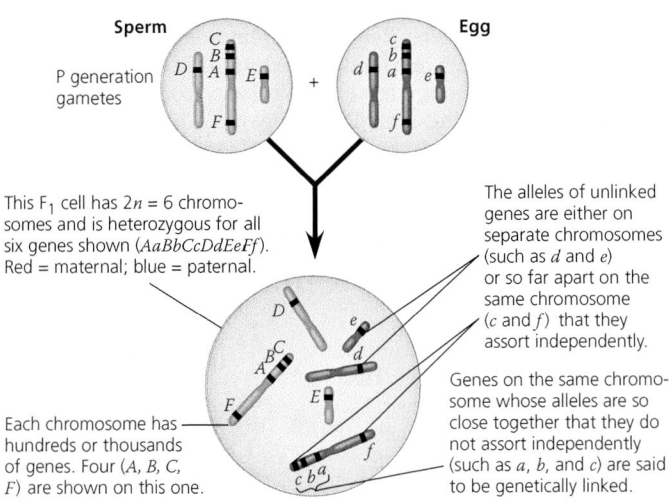

Sperm **Egg**

P generation gametes

This F₁ cell has $2n = 6$ chromosomes and is heterozygous for all six genes shown ($AaBbCcDdEeFf$). Red = maternal; blue = paternal.

Each chromosome has hundreds or thousands of genes. Four (A, B, C, F) are shown on this one.

The alleles of unlinked genes are either on separate chromosomes (such as d and e) or so far apart on the same chromosome (c and f) that they assort independently.

Genes on the same chromosome whose alleles are so close together that they do not assort independently (such as a, b, and c) are said to be genetically linked.

- Among offspring from an F₁ testcross, **parental types** have the same combination of traits as those in the P generation parents. **Recombinant types** (**recombinants**) exhibit new combinations of traits not seen in either P generation parent. Because of the independent assortment of chromosomes, unlinked genes exhibit a 50% frequency of recombination in the gametes. For genetically **linked genes**, **crossing over** between nonsister chromatids during meiosis I accounts for the observed recombinants, always less than 50% of the total.
- The order of genes on a chromosome and the relative distances between them can be deduced from recombination frequencies observed in genetic crosses. These data allow construction of a **linkage map** (a type of **genetic map**). The farther apart genes are, the more likely their allele combinations will be recombined during crossing over.

? *Why are specific alleles of two genes that are farther apart more likely to show recombination than those of two closer genes?*

CONCEPT 15.4

Alterations of chromosome number or structure cause some genetic disorders (pp. 297–300)

- **Aneuploidy**, an abnormal chromosome number, can result from **nondisjunction** during meiosis. When a normal gamete unites with one containing two copies or no copies of a particular chromosome, the resulting zygote and its descendant cells either have one extra copy of that chromosome (**trisomy**, $2n + 1$) or are missing a copy (**monosomy**, $2n - 1$). **Polyploidy** (more than two complete sets of chromosomes) can result from complete nondisjunction during gamete formation.
- Chromosome breakage can result in alterations of chromosome structure: **deletions**, **duplications**, **inversions**, and **translocations**. Translocations can be reciprocal or nonreciprocal.

- Changes in the number of chromosomes per cell or in the structure of individual chromosomes can affect the phenotype and, in some cases, lead to human disorders. Such alterations cause **Down syndrome** (usually due to trisomy of chromosome 21), certain cancers associated with chromosomal translocations, and various other human disorders.

? *Why are inversions and reciprocal translocations less likely to be lethal than are aneuploidy, duplications, deletions, and nonreciprocal translocations?*

CONCEPT 15.5

Some inheritance patterns are exceptions to standard Mendelian inheritance (pp. 300–302)

- In mammals, the phenotypic effects of a small number of particular genes depend on which allele is inherited from each parent, a phenomenon called **genomic imprinting**. Imprints are formed during gamete production, with the result that one allele (either maternal or paternal) is not expressed in offspring.
- The inheritance of traits controlled by the genes present in mitochondria and plastids depends solely on the maternal parent because the zygote's cytoplasm containing these organelles comes from the egg. Some diseases affecting the nervous and muscular systems are caused by defects in mitochondrial genes that prevent cells from making enough ATP.

? *Explain how genomic imprinting and inheritance of mitochondrial and chloroplast DNA are exceptions to standard Mendelian inheritance.*

> ### TEST YOUR UNDERSTANDING

LEVEL 1: KNOWLEDGE/COMPREHENSION

1. A man with hemophilia (a recessive, sex-linked condition) has a daughter of normal phenotype. She marries a man who is normal for the trait. What is the probability that a daughter of this mating will be a hemophiliac? That a son will be a hemophiliac? If the couple has four sons, what is the probability that all four will be born with hemophilia?

2. Pseudohypertrophic muscular dystrophy is an inherited disorder that causes gradual deterioration of the muscles. It is seen almost exclusively in boys born to apparently normal parents and usually results in death in the early teens. Is this disorder caused by a dominant or a recessive allele? Is its inheritance sex-linked or autosomal? How do you know? Explain why this disorder is almost never seen in girls.

3. A wild-type fruit fly (heterozygous for gray body color and normal wings) is mated with a black fly with vestigial wings. The offspring have the following phenotypic distribution: wild-type, 778; black-vestigial, 785; black-normal, 158; gray-vestigial, 162. What is the recombination frequency between these genes for body color and wing size?

4. What pattern of inheritance would lead a geneticist to suspect that an inherited disorder of cell metabolism is due to a defective mitochondrial gene?

5. A space probe discovers a planet inhabited by creatures that reproduce with the same hereditary patterns seen in humans. Three phenotypic characters are height (T = tall, t = dwarf), head appendages (A = antennae, a = no antennae), and nose morphology (S = upturned snout, s = downturned snout). Since the creatures are not "intelligent," Earth scientists are able to do some controlled breeding experiments using various heterozygotes in testcrosses. For tall heterozygotes with antennae, the offspring are

tall-antennae, 46; dwarf-antennae, 7; dwarf-no antennae, 42; tall-no antennae, 5. For heterozygotes with antennae and an up-turned snout, the offspring are antennae-upturned snout, 47; antennae-downturned snout, 2; no antennae-downturned snout, 48; no antennae-upturned snout, 3. Calculate the recombination frequencies for both experiments.

LEVEL 2: APPLICATION/ANALYSIS

6. Using the information from problem 5, scientists do a further testcross using a heterozygote for height and nose morphology. The offspring are: tall-upturned snout, 40; dwarf-upturned snout, 9; dwarf-downturned snout, 42; tall-downturned snout, 9. Calculate the recombination frequency from these data; then use your answer from problem 5 to determine the correct sequence of the three linked genes.

7. Red-green color blindness is caused by a sex-linked recessive allele. A color-blind man marries a woman with normal vision whose father was color-blind. What is the probability that they will have a color-blind daughter? What is the probability that their first son will be color-blind? (Note the different wording in the two questions.)

8. A wild-type fruit fly (heterozygous for gray body color and red eyes) is mated with a black fruit fly with purple eyes. The offspring are wild-type, 721; black-purple, 751; gray-purple, 49; black-red, 45. What is the recombination frequency between these genes for body color and eye color? Using information from problem 3, what fruit flies (genotypes and phenotypes) would you mate to determine the sequence of the body-color, wing-size, and eye-color genes on the chromosome?

9. **DRAW IT** A fruit fly that is true-breeding for gray body with vestigial wings ($b^+ \ b^+ \ vg \ vg$) is mated with one that is true-breeding for black body with normal wings ($b \ b \ vg^+ \ vg^+$).
   (a) Draw the chromosomes for the P generation flies, using red for the gray fly and pink for the black one. Show the position of each allele.
   (b) Draw the chromosomes and label the alleles of an F_1 fly.
   (c) Suppose an F_1 female is testcrossed. Draw the chromosomes of the resulting offspring in a Punnett square.
   (d) Knowing that the distance between these two genes is 17 map units, predict the phenotypic ratios of these offspring.

10. Women born with an extra X chromosome (XXX) are generally healthy and indistinguishable in appearance from normal XX women. What is a likely explanation for this finding? How could you test this explanation?

11. Determine the sequence of genes along a chromosome based on the following recombination frequencies: A–B, 8 map units; A–C, 28 map units; A–D, 25 map units; B–C, 20 map units; B–D, 33 map units.

12. Assume that genes A and B are on the same chromosome and are 50 map units apart. An animal heterozygous at both loci is crossed with one that is homozygous recessive at both loci. What percentage of the offspring will show recombinant phenotypes resulting from crossovers? Without knowing these genes are on the same chromosome, how would you interpret the results of this cross?

13. Two genes of a flower, one controlling blue (B) versus white (b) petals and the other controlling round (R) versus oval (r) stamens, are linked and are 10 map units apart. You cross a homozygous blue-oval plant with a homozygous white-round plant. The resulting F_1 progeny are crossed with homozygous white-oval plants, and 1,000 F_2 progeny are obtained. How many F_2 plants of each of the four phenotypes do you expect?

14. You design *Drosophila* crosses to provide recombination data for gene *a*, which is located on the chromosome shown in Figure 15.12. Gene *a* has recombination frequencies of 14% with the vestigial-wing locus and 26% with the brown-eye locus. Approximately where is *a* located along the chromosome?

LEVEL 3: SYNTHESIS/EVALUATION

15. Banana plants, which are triploid, are seedless and therefore sterile. Propose a possible explanation.

16. **EVOLUTION CONNECTION**
    You have seen that crossing over, or recombination, is thought to be evolutionarily advantageous because it continually shuffles genetic alleles into novel combinations, allowing evolutionary processes to occur. Until recently, it was thought that the genes on the Y chromosome might degenerate because they lack homologous genes on the X chromosome with which to recombine. However, when the Y chromosome was sequenced, eight large regions were found to be internally homologous to each other, and quite a few of the 78 genes represent duplicates. (Y chromosome researcher David Page has called it a "hall of mirrors.") What might be a benefit of these regions?

17. **SCIENTIFIC INQUIRY**
    Butterflies have an X-Y sex determination system that is different from that of flies or humans. Female butterflies may be either XY or XO, while butterflies with two or more X chromosomes are males. This photograph shows a tiger swallowtail *gynandromorph*, an individual that is half male (left side) and half female (right side). Given that the first division of the zygote divides the embryo into the future right and left halves of the butterfly, propose a hypothesis that explains how nondisjunction during the first mitosis might have produced this unusual-looking butterfly.

18. **WRITE ABOUT A THEME**
    The Genetic Basis of Life The continuity of life is based on heritable information in the form of DNA. In a short essay (100–150 words), relate the structure and behavior of chromosomes to inheritance in both asexually and sexually reproducing species.

For selected answers, see Appendix A.

Mastering BIOLOGY www.masteringbiology.com

1. MasteringBiology® Assignments
Make Connections Tutorial Chromosomal Inheritance (Chapter 15) and Independent Assortment of Alleles (Chapter 14)
Experimental Inquiry Tutorial What Is the Inheritance Pattern of Sex-Linked Traits?
Video Tutor Session Sex-Linked Pedigrees
Tutorials Sex Linkage • Linked Genes and Linkage Mapping • Chromosomal Mutations
Activities Sex-Linked Genes • Linked Genes and Crossing Over • Mistakes in Meiosis • Polyploid Plants
Questions Student Misconceptions • Reading Quiz • Multiple Choice • End-of-Chapter

2. eText
Read your book online, search, take notes, highlight text, and more.

3. The Study Area
Practice Tests • Cumulative Test • **BioFlix** 3-D Animations • MP3 Tutor Sessions • Videos • Activities • Investigations • Lab Media • Audio Glossary • Word Study Tools • Art

16

The Molecular Basis of Inheritance

▲ **Figure 16.1 How was the structure of DNA determined?**

KEY CONCEPTS

16.1 DNA is the genetic material
16.2 Many proteins work together in DNA replication and repair
16.3 A chromosome consists of a DNA molecule packed together with proteins

OVERVIEW

Life's Operating Instructions

In April 1953, James Watson and Francis Crick shook the scientific world with an elegant double-helical model for the structure of deoxyribonucleic acid, or DNA. **Figure 16.1** shows Watson (left) and Crick admiring their DNA model, which they built from tin and wire. Over the past 60 years or so, their model has evolved from a novel proposition to an icon of modern biology. Mendel's heritable factors and Morgan's genes on chromosomes are, in fact, composed of DNA. Chemically speaking, your genetic endowment is the DNA

you inherited from your parents. DNA, the substance of inheritance, is the most celebrated molecule of our time.

Of all nature's molecules, nucleic acids are unique in their ability to direct their own replication from monomers. Indeed, the resemblance of offspring to their parents has its basis in the precise replication of DNA and its transmission from one generation to the next. Hereditary information is encoded in the chemical language of DNA and reproduced in all the cells of your body. It is this DNA program that directs the development of your biochemical, anatomical, physiological, and, to some extent, behavioral traits. In this chapter, you will discover how biologists deduced that DNA is the genetic material and how Watson and Crick worked out its structure. You will also learn about **DNA replication**, the process by which a DNA molecule is copied, and how cells repair their DNA. Finally, you will explore how a molecule of DNA is packaged together with proteins in a chromosome.

CONCEPT 16.1

DNA is the genetic material

Today, even schoolchildren have heard of DNA, and scientists routinely manipulate DNA in the laboratory, often to change the heritable traits of cells in their experiments. Early in the 20th century, however, identifying the molecules of inheritance loomed as a major challenge to biologists.

The Search for the Genetic Material: *Scientific Inquiry*

Once T. H. Morgan's group showed that genes exist as parts of chromosomes (described in Chapter 15), the two chemical components of chromosomes—DNA and protein—became the candidates for the genetic material. Until the 1940s, the case for proteins seemed stronger, especially since biochemists had identified them as a class of macromolecules with great heterogeneity and specificity of function, essential requirements for the hereditary material. Moreover, little was known about nucleic acids, whose physical and chemical properties seemed far too uniform to account for the multitude of specific inherited traits exhibited by every organism. This view gradually changed as experiments with microorganisms yielded unexpected results. As with the work of Mendel and Morgan, a key factor in determining the identity of the genetic material was the choice of appropriate experimental organisms. The role of DNA in heredity was first worked out while studying bacteria and the viruses that infect them, which are far simpler than pea plants, fruit flies, or humans. In this section, we will trace the search for the genetic material in some detail as a case study in scientific inquiry.

Evidence That DNA Can Transform Bacteria

The discovery of the genetic role of DNA dates back to 1928. While attempting to develop a vaccine against pneumonia, a British medical officer named Frederick Griffith was studying *Streptococcus pneumoniae*, a bacterium that causes pneumonia in mammals. Griffith had two strains (varieties) of the bacterium, one pathogenic (disease-causing) and one nonpathogenic (harmless). He was surprised to find that when he killed the pathogenic bacteria with heat and then mixed the cell remains with living bacteria of the nonpathogenic strain, some of the living cells became pathogenic (Figure 16.2). Furthermore, this newly acquired trait of pathogenicity was inherited by all the descendants of the transformed bacteria. Clearly, some chemical component of the dead pathogenic cells caused this heritable change, although the identity of the substance was not known. Griffith called the phenomenon **transformation**, now defined as a change in genotype and phenotype due to the assimilation of external DNA by a cell. (This use of the word *transformation* should not be confused with the conversion of a normal animal cell to a cancerous one, discussed near the end of Concept 12.3)

Griffith's work set the stage for a 14-year effort by American bacteriologist Oswald Avery to identify the transforming substance. Avery focused on three main candidates: DNA, RNA (the other nucleic acid in cells), and protein. Avery broke open the heat-killed pathogenic bacteria and extracted the cellular contents. He treated each of three samples with an agent that inactivated one type of molecule, then tested the sample for its ability to transform live nonpathogenic bacteria. Only when DNA was allowed to remain active did transformation occur. In 1944, Avery and his colleagues Maclyn McCarty and Colin MacLeod announced that the transforming agent was DNA. Their discovery was greeted with interest but considerable skepticism, in part because of the lingering belief that proteins were better candidates for the genetic material. Moreover, many biologists were not convinced that the genes of bacteria would be similar in composition and function to those of more complex organisms. But the major reason for the continued doubt was that so little was known about DNA.

Evidence That Viral DNA Can Program Cells

Additional evidence for DNA as the genetic material came from studies of viruses that infect bacteria (Figure 16.3). These viruses are called **bacteriophages** (meaning "bacteria-eaters"), or **phages** for short. Viruses are much simpler than

▼ Figure 16.2 | INQUIRY

Can a genetic trait be transferred between different bacterial strains?

EXPERIMENT Frederick Griffith studied two strains of the bacterium *Streptococcus pneumoniae*. Bacteria of the S (smooth) strain can cause pneumonia in mice; they are pathogenic because they have an outer capsule that protects them from an animal's defense system. Bacteria of the R (rough) strain lack a capsule and are nonpathogenic. To test for the trait of pathogenicity, Griffith injected mice with the two strains:

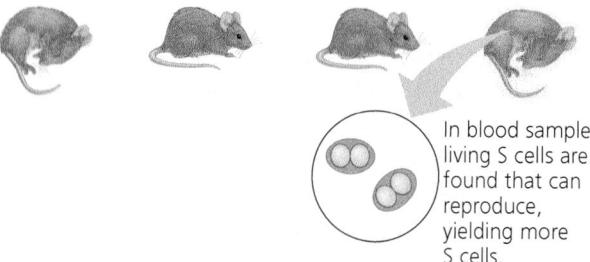

RESULTS

Mouse dies   Mouse healthy   Mouse healthy   Mouse dies

In blood sample, living S cells are found that can reproduce, yielding more S cells.

CONCLUSION Griffith concluded that the living R bacteria had been transformed into pathogenic S bacteria by an unknown, heritable substance from the dead S cells that allowed the R cells to make capsules.

SOURCE F. Griffith, The significance of pneumococcal types, *Journal of Hygiene* 27:113–159 (1928).

WHAT IF? How did this experiment rule out the possibility that the R cells could have simply used the capsules of the dead S cells to become pathogenic?

▲ Figure 16.3 **Viruses infecting a bacterial cell.** Phages called T2 attach to the host cell and inject their genetic material through the plasma membrane while the head and tail parts remain on the outer bacterial surface (colorized TEM).

cells. A **virus** is little more than DNA (or sometimes RNA) enclosed by a protective coat, which is often simply protein. To produce more viruses, a virus must infect a cell and take over the cell's metabolic machinery.

Phages have been widely used as tools by researchers in molecular genetics. In 1952, Alfred Hershey and Martha Chase performed experiments showing that DNA is the genetic material of a phage known as T2. This is one of many phages that infect *Escherichia coli* (*E. coli*), a bacterium that normally lives in the intestines of mammals and is a model organism for molecular biologists. At that time, biologists already knew that T2,

like many other phages, was composed almost entirely of DNA and protein. They also knew that the T2 phage could quickly turn an *E. coli* cell into a T2-producing factory that released many copies when the cell ruptured. Somehow, T2 could reprogram its host cell to produce viruses. But which viral component—protein or DNA—was responsible?

Hershey and Chase answered this question by devising an experiment showing that only one of the two components of T2 actually enters the *E. coli* cell during infection (**Figure 16.4**). In their experiment, they used a radioactive isotope of sulfur to tag protein in one batch of T2 and a radioactive isotope of

▼ Figure 16.4

INQUIRY

Is protein or DNA the genetic material of phage T2?

EXPERIMENT Alfred Hershey and Martha Chase used radioactive sulfur and phosphorus to trace the fates of protein and DNA, respectively, of T2 phages that infected bacterial cells. They wanted to see which of these molecules entered the cells and could reprogram them to make more phages.

RESULTS When proteins were labeled (batch 1), radioactivity remained outside the cells; but when DNA was labeled (batch 2), radioactivity was found inside the cells. Bacterial cells with radioactive phage DNA released new phages with some radioactive phosphorus.

CONCLUSION Phage DNA entered bacterial cells, but phage proteins did not. Hershey and Chase concluded that DNA, not protein, functions as the genetic material of phage T2.

SOURCE A. D. Hershey and M. Chase, Independent functions of viral protein and nucleic acid in growth of bacteriophage, *Journal of General Physiology* 36:39–56 (1952).

WHAT IF? How would the results have differed if proteins carried the genetic information?

phosphorus to tag DNA in a second batch. Because protein, but not DNA, contains sulfur, radioactive sulfur atoms were incorporated only into the protein of the phage. In a similar way, the atoms of radioactive phosphorus labeled only the DNA, not the protein, because nearly all the phage's phosphorus is in its DNA. In the experiment, separate samples of non-radioactive *E. coli* cells were allowed to be infected by the protein-labeled and DNA-labeled batches of T2. The researchers then tested the two samples shortly after the onset of infection to see which type of molecule—protein or DNA—had entered the bacterial cells and would therefore be capable of reprogramming them.

Hershey and Chase found that the phage DNA entered the host cells but the phage protein did not. Moreover, when these bacteria were returned to a culture medium, the infection ran its course, and the *E. coli* released phages that contained some radioactive phosphorus, further showing that the DNA inside the cell played an ongoing role during the infection process.

Hershey and Chase concluded that the DNA injected by the phage must be the molecule carrying the genetic information that makes the cells produce new viral DNA and proteins. The Hershey-Chase experiment was a landmark study because it provided powerful evidence that nucleic acids, rather than proteins, are the hereditary material, at least for viruses.

Additional Evidence That DNA Is the Genetic Material

Further evidence that DNA is the genetic material came from the laboratory of biochemist Erwin Chargaff. It was already known that DNA is a polymer of nucleotides, each consisting of three components: a nitrogenous (nitrogen-containing) base, a pentose sugar called deoxyribose, and a phosphate group (Figure 16.5). The base can be adenine (A), thymine (T), guanine (G), or cytosine (C). Chargaff analyzed the base composition of DNA from a number of different organisms. In 1950, he reported that the base composition of DNA varies from one species to another. For example, 30.3% of human DNA nucleotides have the base A, whereas DNA from the bacterium *E. coli* has only 26.0% A. This evidence of molecular diversity among species, which had been presumed absent from DNA, made DNA a more credible candidate for the genetic material.

Chargaff also noticed a peculiar regularity in the ratios of nucleotide bases. In the DNA of each species he studied, the number of adenines approximately equaled the number of thymines, and the number of guanines approximately equaled the number of cytosines. In human DNA, for example, the four bases are present in these percentages: A = 30.3% and T = 30.3%; G = 19.5% and C = 19.9%.

These two findings became known as *Chargaff's rules*: (1) the base composition varies between species, and (2) within a species, the number of A and T bases are equal and the number of G and C bases are equal. The basis for these rules remained unexplained until the discovery of the double helix.

▲ **Figure 16.5 The structure of a DNA strand.** Each DNA nucleotide monomer consists of a nitrogenous base (T, A, C, or G), the sugar deoxyribose (blue), and a phosphate group (yellow). The phosphate group of one nucleotide is attached to the sugar of the next, forming a "backbone" of alternating phosphates and sugars from which the bases project. The polynucleotide strand has directionality, from the 5' end (with the phosphate group) to the 3' end (with the —OH group of the sugar). 5' and 3' refer to the numbers assigned to the carbons in the sugar ring.

Building a Structural Model of DNA: *Scientific Inquiry*

Once most biologists were convinced that DNA was the genetic material, the challenge was to determine how the structure of DNA could account for its role in inheritance. By the early 1950s, the arrangement of covalent bonds in a nucleic acid polymer was well established (see Figure 16.5), and researchers focused on discovering the three-dimensional structure of DNA. Among the scientists working on the problem were Linus Pauling, at the California Institute of Technology, and Maurice Wilkins and Rosalind Franklin, at King's College in London. First to come up with the correct answer, however, were two scientists who were relatively unknown at the time—the American James Watson and the Englishman Francis Crick.

The brief but celebrated partnership that solved the puzzle of DNA structure began soon after Watson journeyed to Cambridge University, where Crick was studying protein structure with a technique called X-ray crystallography (see Figure 5.24). While visiting the laboratory of Maurice Wilkins, Watson saw an X-ray diffraction image of DNA produced by Wilkins's accomplished colleague Rosalind Franklin (Figure 16.6a). Images produced by X-ray crystallography are not actually pictures of molecules. The spots and smudges in Figure 16.6b were produced by X-rays that were diffracted (deflected) as they passed through aligned fibers of purified DNA. Watson was familiar with the type of X-ray diffraction pattern that helical molecules produce, and an examination of the photo that Wilkins showed him confirmed that DNA was helical in shape. It also augmented earlier data obtained by Franklin and others suggesting the width of the helix and the spacing of the nitrogenous bases along it. The pattern in this photo implied that the helix was made up of two strands, contrary to a three-stranded model that Linus Pauling had proposed a short time earlier. The presence of two strands accounts for the now-familiar term **double helix** (Figure 16.7).

Watson and Crick began building models of a double helix that would conform to the X-ray measurements and what was then known about the chemistry of DNA, including Chargaff's

(a) Rosalind Franklin

(b) Franklin's X-ray diffraction photograph of DNA

▲ **Figure 16.6 Rosalind Franklin and her X-ray diffraction photo of DNA.** Franklin, a very accomplished X-ray crystallographer, conducted critical experiments resulting in the photograph that allowed Watson and Crick to deduce the double-helical structure of DNA.

rule of base equivalences. Having also read an unpublished annual report summarizing Franklin's work, they knew she had concluded that the sugar-phosphate backbones were on the outside of the DNA molecule, contrary to their working model. Franklin's arrangement was appealing because it put the

(a) Key features of DNA structure. The "ribbons" in this diagram represent the sugar-phosphate backbones of the two DNA strands. The helix is "right-handed," curving up to the right. The two strands are held together by hydrogen bonds (dotted lines) between the nitrogenous bases, which are paired in the interior of the double helix.

(b) Partial chemical structure. For clarity, the two DNA strands are shown untwisted in this partial chemical structure. Strong covalent bonds link the units of each strand, while weaker hydrogen bonds hold one strand to the other. Notice that the strands are antiparallel, meaning that they are oriented in opposite directions.

(c) Space-filling model. The tight stacking of the base pairs is clear in this computer model. Van der Waals interactions between the stacked pairs play a major role in holding the molecule together (see Chapter 2).

▲ Figure 16.7 **The double helix.**

relatively hydrophobic nitrogenous bases in the molecule's interior, away from the surrounding aqueous solution, and the negatively charged phosphate groups wouldn't be forced together in the interior. Watson constructed a model with the nitrogenous bases facing the interior of the double helix. In this model, the two sugar-phosphate backbones are **antiparallel**—that is, their subunits run in opposite directions (see Figure 16.7). You can imagine the overall arrangement as a rope ladder with rigid rungs. The side ropes represent the sugar-phosphate backbones, and the rungs represent pairs of nitrogenous bases. Now imagine holding one end of the ladder and twisting the other end, forming a spiral. Franklin's X-ray data indicated that the helix makes one full turn every 3.4 nm along its length. With the bases stacked just 0.34 nm apart, there are ten layers of base pairs, or rungs of the ladder, in each full turn of the helix.

The nitrogenous bases of the double helix are paired in specific combinations: adenine (A) with thymine (T), and guanine (G) with cytosine (C). It was mainly by trial and error that Watson and Crick arrived at this key feature of DNA. At first, Watson imagined that the bases paired like with like—for example, A with A and C with C. But this model did not fit the X-ray data, which suggested that the double helix had a uniform diameter. Why is this requirement inconsistent with like-with-like pairing of bases? Adenine and guanine are purines, nitrogenous bases with two organic rings, while cytosine and thymine are nitrogenous bases called pyrimidines, which have a single ring. Thus, purines (A and G) are about twice as wide as pyrimidines (C and T). A purine-purine pair is too wide and a pyrimidine-pyrimidine pair too narrow to account for the 2-nm diameter of the double helix. Always pairing a purine with a pyrimidine, however, results in a uniform diameter:

Purine + purine: too wide

Pyrimidine + pyrimidine: too narrow

Purine + pyrimidine: width consistent with X-ray data

Watson and Crick reasoned that there must be additional specificity of pairing dictated by the structure of the bases. Each base has chemical side groups that can form hydrogen bonds with its appropriate partner: Adenine can form two hydrogen bonds with thymine and only thymine; guanine forms three hydrogen bonds with cytosine and only cytosine. In shorthand, A pairs with T, and G pairs with C (**Figure 16.8**).

The Watson-Crick model took into account Chargaff's ratios and ultimately explained them. Wherever one strand of a DNA molecule has an A, the partner strand has a T. And a G in one strand is always paired with a C in the complementary strand. Therefore, in the DNA of any organism, the amount of

Adenine (A)   Thymine (T)

Guanine (G)   Cytosine (C)

▲ **Figure 16.8 Base pairing in DNA.** The pairs of nitrogenous bases in a DNA double helix are held together by hydrogen bonds, shown here as black dotted lines.

adenine equals the amount of thymine, and the amount of guanine equals the amount of cytosine. Although the base-pairing rules dictate the combinations of nitrogenous bases that form the "rungs" of the double helix, they do not restrict the sequence of nucleotides *along* each DNA strand. The linear sequence of the four bases can be varied in countless ways, and each gene has a unique order, or base sequence.

In April 1953, Watson and Crick surprised the scientific world with a succinct, one-page paper in the journal *Nature*.* The paper reported their molecular model for DNA: the double helix, which has since become the symbol of molecular biology. Watson and Crick, along with Maurice Wilkins, were awarded the Nobel Prize in 1962 for this work. (Sadly, Rosalind Franklin died at the age of 38, in 1958, and was thus ineligible for the prize.) The beauty of the double helix model was that the structure of DNA suggested the basic mechanism of its replication.

CONCEPT CHECK 16.1

1. A fly has the following percentages of nucleotides in its DNA: 27.3% A, 27.6% T, 22.5% G, and 22.5% C. How do these numbers demonstrate Chargaff's rule about base ratios?
2. Given a polynucleotide sequence such as GAATTC, can you tell which is the 5' end? If not, what further information do you need to identify the ends? (See Figure 16.5.)
3. **WHAT IF?** Griffith did not expect transformation to occur in his experiment. What results was he expecting? Explain.

For suggested answers, see Appendix A.

*J. D. Watson and F. H. C. Crick, Molecular structure of nucleic acids: a structure for deoxyribose nucleic acids, *Nature* 171:737–738 (1953).

CONCEPT 16.2

Many proteins work together in DNA replication and repair

The relationship between structure and function is manifest in the double helix. The idea that there is specific pairing of nitrogenous bases in DNA was the flash of inspiration that led Watson and Crick to the double helix. At the same time, they saw the functional significance of the base-pairing rules. They ended their classic paper with this wry statement: "It has not escaped our notice that the specific pairing we have postulated immediately suggests a possible copying mechanism for the genetic material." In this section, you will learn about the basic principle of DNA replication, as well as some important details of the process.

The Basic Principle: Base Pairing to a Template Strand

In a second paper, Watson and Crick stated their hypothesis for how DNA replicates:

> Now our model for deoxyribonucleic acid is, in effect, a pair of templates, each of which is complementary to the other. We imagine that prior to duplication the hydrogen bonds are broken, and the two chains unwind and separate. Each chain then acts as a template for the formation onto itself of a new companion chain, so that eventually we shall have two pairs of chains, where we only had one before. Moreover, the sequence of the pairs of bases will have been duplicated exactly.*

*F. H. C. Crick and J. D. Watson, The complementary structure of deoxyribonucleic acid, *Proceedings of the Royal Society of London A* 223:80 (1954).

Figure 16.9 illustrates Watson and Crick's basic idea. To make it easier to follow, we show only a short section of double helix in untwisted form. Notice that if you cover one of the two DNA strands of Figure 16.9a, you can still determine its linear sequence of nucleotides by referring to the uncovered strand and applying the base-pairing rules. The two strands are complementary; each stores the information necessary to reconstruct the other. When a cell copies a DNA molecule, each strand serves as a template for ordering nucleotides into a new, complementary strand. Nucleotides line up along the template strand according to the base-pairing rules and are linked to form the new strands. Where there was one double-stranded DNA molecule at the beginning of the process, there are soon two, each an exact replica of the "parental" molecule. The copying mechanism is analogous to using a photographic negative to make a positive image, which can in turn be used to make another negative, and so on.

This model of DNA replication remained untested for several years following publication of the DNA structure. The requisite experiments were simple in concept but difficult to perform. Watson and Crick's model predicts that when a double helix replicates, each of the two daughter molecules will have one old strand, from the parental molecule, and one newly made strand. This **semiconservative model** can be distinguished from a conservative model of replication, in which the two parental strands somehow come back together after the process (that is, the parental molecule is conserved). In yet a third model, called the dispersive model, all four strands of DNA following replication have a mixture of old and new DNA. These three models are shown in

  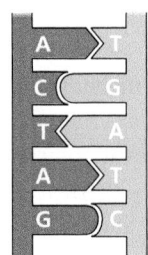

(a) The parental molecule has two complementary strands of DNA. Each base is paired by hydrogen bonding with its specific partner, A with T and G with C.

(b) The first step in replication is separation of the two DNA strands. Each parental strand can now serve as a template that determines the order of nucleotides along a new, complementary strand.

(c) The complementary nucleotides line up and are connected to form the sugar-phosphate backbones of the new strands. Each "daughter" DNA molecule consists of one parental strand (dark blue) and one new strand (light blue).

▲ Figure 16.9 **A model for DNA replication: the basic concept.** In this simplified illustration, a short segment of DNA has been untwisted into a structure that resembles a ladder. The side rails of the ladder are the sugar-phosphate backbones of the two DNA strands; the rungs are the pairs of nitrogenous bases. Simple shapes symbolize the four kinds of bases. Dark blue represents DNA strands present in the parental molecule; light blue represents newly synthesized DNA.

	Parent cell	First replication	Second replication

(a) Conservative model. The two parental strands reassociate after acting as templates for new strands, thus restoring the parental double helix.

(b) Semiconservative model. The two strands of the parental molecule separate, and each functions as a template for synthesis of a new, complementary strand.

(c) Dispersive model. Each strand of *both* daughter molecules contains a mixture of old and newly synthesized DNA.

▲ **Figure 16.10 Three alternative models of DNA replication.** Each short segment of double helix symbolizes the DNA within a cell. Beginning with a parent cell, we follow the DNA for two more generations of cells—two rounds of DNA replication. Newly made DNA is light blue.

Figure 16.10. Although mechanisms for conservative or dispersive DNA replication are not easy to devise, these models remained possibilities until they could be ruled out. After two years of preliminary work in the late 1950s, Matthew Meselson and Franklin Stahl devised a clever experiment that distinguished between the three models, described in detail in **Figure 16.11.** Their experiment supported the semiconservative model of DNA replication, as predicted by Watson and Crick, and is widely acknowledged among biologists to be a classic example of elegant experimental design.

The basic principle of DNA replication is conceptually simple. However, the actual process involves some complicated biochemical gymnastics, as we will now see.

DNA Replication: *A Closer Look*

The bacterium *E. coli* has a single chromosome of about 4.6 million nucleotide pairs. In a favorable environment, an *E. coli* cell

▼ **Figure 16.11**

INQUIRY

Does DNA replication follow the conservative, semiconservative, or dispersive model?

EXPERIMENT At the California Institute of Technology, Matthew Meselson and Franklin Stahl cultured *E. coli* for several generations in a medium containing nucleotide precursors labeled with a heavy isotope of nitrogen, ^{15}N. They then transferred the bacteria to a medium with only ^{14}N, a lighter isotope. A sample was taken after DNA replicated once; another sample was taken after DNA replicated again. They extracted DNA from the bacteria in the samples and then centrifuged each DNA sample to separate DNA of different densities.

1 Bacteria cultured in medium with ^{15}N (heavy isotope)

2 Bacteria transferred to medium with ^{14}N (lighter isotope)

RESULTS

3 DNA sample centrifuged after first replication

4 DNA sample centrifuged after second replication

Less dense

More dense

CONCLUSION Meselson and Stahl compared their results to those predicted by each of the three models in Figure 16.10, as shown below. The first replication in the ^{14}N medium produced a band of hybrid (^{15}N-^{14}N) DNA. This result eliminated the conservative model. The second replication produced both light and hybrid DNA, a result that refuted the dispersive model and supported the semiconservative model. They therefore concluded that DNA replication is semiconservative.

Predictions:	First replication	Second replication
Conservative model		
Semiconservative model		
Dispersive model		

SOURCE M. Meselson and F. W. Stahl, The replication of DNA in *Escherichia coli*, *Proceedings of the National Academy of Sciences USA* 44:671–682 (1958).

INQUIRY IN ACTION Read and analyze the original paper in *Inquiry in Action: Interpreting Scientific Papers.*

(MB) See the related Experimental Inquiry Tutorial in MasteringBiology.

WHAT IF? If Meselson and Stahl had first grown the cells in ^{14}N-containing medium and then moved them into ^{15}N-containing medium before taking samples, what would have been the result?

can copy all this DNA and divide to form two genetically identical daughter cells in less than an hour. Each of *your* cells has 46 DNA molecules in its nucleus, one long double-helical molecule per chromosome. In all, that represents about 6 billion nucleotide pairs, or over a thousand times more DNA than is found in a bacterial cell. If we were to print the one-letter symbols for these bases (A, G, C, and T) the size of the type you are now reading, the 6 billion nucleotide pairs of information in a diploid human cell would fill about 1,200 books as thick as this text. Yet it takes one of your cells just a few hours to copy all of this DNA. This replication of an enormous amount of genetic information is achieved with very few errors—only about one per 10 billion nucleotides. The copying of DNA is remarkable in its speed and accuracy.

More than a dozen enzymes and other proteins participate in DNA replication. Much more is known about how this "replication machine" works in bacteria (such as *E. coli*) than

in eukaryotes, and we will describe the basic steps of the process for *E. coli*, except where otherwise noted. What scientists have learned about eukaryotic DNA replication suggests, however, that most of the process is fundamentally similar for prokaryotes and eukaryotes.

Getting Started

The replication of a DNA molecule begins at particular sites called **origins of replication**, short stretches of DNA having a specific sequence of nucleotides. The *E. coli* chromosome, like many other bacterial chromosomes, is circular and has a single origin. Proteins that initiate DNA replication recognize this sequence and attach to the DNA, separating the two strands and opening up a replication "bubble." Replication of DNA then proceeds in both directions until the entire molecule is copied (**Figure 16.12a**). In contrast to a bacterial chromosome, a eukaryotic chromosome may have hundreds

▼ **Figure 16.12** **Origins of replication in *E. coli* and eukaryotes.** The red arrows indicate the movement of the replication forks and thus the overall directions of DNA replication within each bubble.

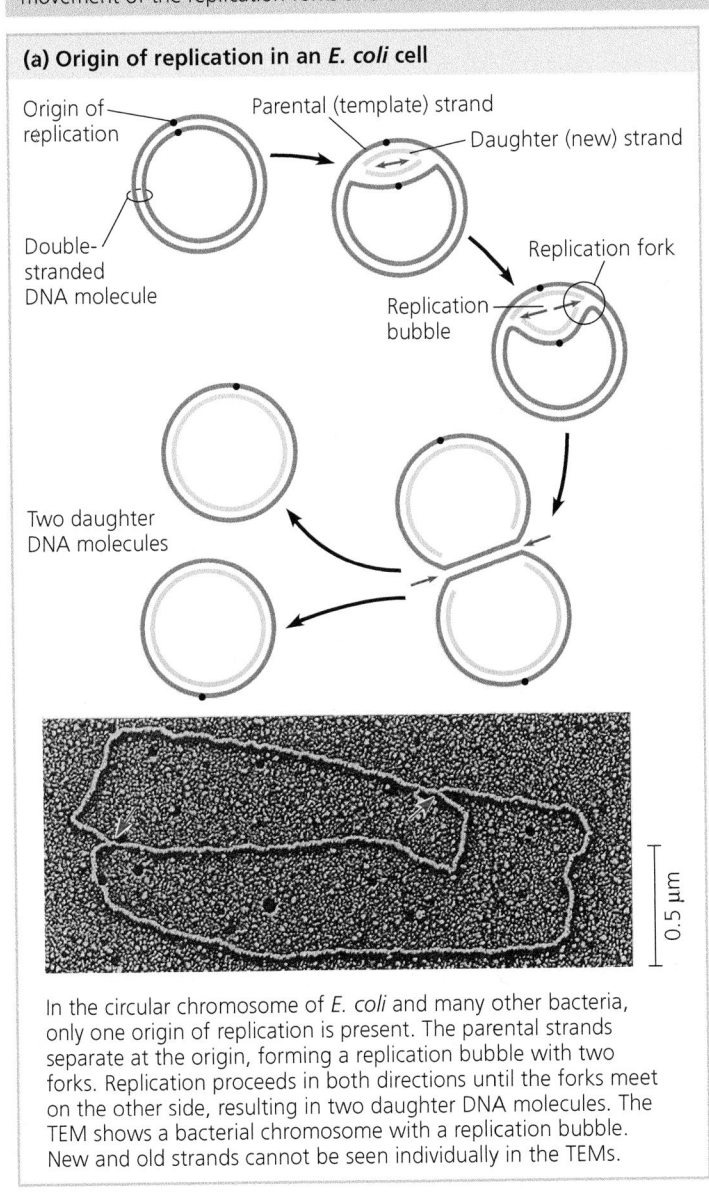

(a) Origin of replication in an *E. coli* cell

In the circular chromosome of *E. coli* and many other bacteria, only one origin of replication is present. The parental strands separate at the origin, forming a replication bubble with two forks. Replication proceeds in both directions until the forks meet on the other side, resulting in two daughter DNA molecules. The TEM shows a bacterial chromosome with a replication bubble. New and old strands cannot be seen individually in the TEMs.

(b) Origins of replication in a eukaryotic cell

In each linear chromosome of eukaryotes, DNA replication begins when replication bubbles form at many sites along the giant DNA molecule. The bubbles expand as replication proceeds in both directions. Eventually, the bubbles fuse and synthesis of the daughter strands is complete. The TEM shows three replication bubbles along the DNA of a cultured Chinese hamster cell.

DRAW IT *In the TEM in (b), add arrows for the third bubble.*

or even a few thousand replication origins. Multiple replication bubbles form and eventually fuse, thus speeding up the copying of the very long DNA molecules **(Figure 16.12b)**. As in bacteria, eukaryotic DNA replication proceeds in both directions from each origin.

At each end of a replication bubble is a **replication fork**, a Y-shaped region where the parental strands of DNA are being unwound. Several kinds of proteins participate in the unwinding **(Figure 16.13)**. **Helicases** are enzymes that untwist the double helix at the replication forks, separating the two parental strands and making them available as template strands. After the parental strands separate, **single-strand binding proteins** bind to the unpaired DNA strands, keeping them from re-pairing. The untwisting of the double helix causes tighter twisting and strain ahead of the replication fork. **Topoisomerase** helps relieve this strain by breaking, swiveling, and rejoining DNA strands.

The unwound sections of parental DNA strands are now available to serve as templates for the synthesis of new complementary DNA strands. However, the enzymes that synthesize DNA cannot *initiate* the synthesis of a polynucleotide; they can only add nucleotides to the end of an already existing chain that is base-paired with the template strand. The initial nucleotide chain that is produced during DNA synthesis is actually a short stretch of RNA, not DNA. This RNA chain is called a **primer** and is synthesized by the enzyme **primase** (see Figure 16.13). Primase starts a complementary RNA chain from a single RNA nucleotide, adding RNA nucleotides one at a time, using the parental DNA strand as a template. The completed primer, generally 5–10 nucleotides long, is thus base-paired to the template strand. The new DNA strand will start from the 3′ end of the RNA primer.

Synthesizing a New DNA Strand

Enzymes called **DNA polymerases** catalyze the synthesis of new DNA by adding nucleotides to a preexisting chain. In *E. coli*, there are several different DNA polymerases, but two appear to play the major roles in DNA replication: DNA polymerase III and DNA polymerase I. The situation in eukaryotes is more complicated, with at least 11 different DNA polymerases discovered so far; however, the general principles are the same.

Most DNA polymerases require a primer and a DNA template strand, along which complementary DNA nucleotides line up. In *E. coli*, DNA polymerase III (abbreviated DNA pol III) adds a DNA nucleotide to the RNA primer and then continues adding DNA nucleotides, complementary to the parental DNA template strand, to the growing end of the new DNA strand. The rate of elongation is about 500 nucleotides per second in bacteria and 50 per second in human cells.

Each nucleotide added to a growing DNA strand comes from a nucleoside triphosphate, which is a nucleoside (a sugar and a base) with three phosphate groups. You have already encountered such a molecule—ATP (adenosine triphosphate; see Figure 8.8). The only difference between the ATP of energy metabolism and dATP, the nucleoside triphosphate that supplies an adenine nucleotide to DNA, is the sugar component, which is deoxyribose in the building block of DNA but ribose in ATP. Like ATP, the nucleoside triphosphates used for DNA synthesis are chemically reactive, partly because their triphosphate tails have an unstable cluster of negative charge. As each monomer joins the growing end of a DNA strand, two phosphate groups are lost as a molecule of pyrophosphate ($\text{P}—\text{P}_i$). Subsequent hydrolysis of the pyrophosphate to two molecules of inorganic phosphate (P_i) is a coupled exergonic reaction that helps drive the polymerization reaction **(Figure 16.14)**.

Antiparallel Elongation

As we have noted previously, the two ends of a DNA strand are different, giving each strand directionality, like a one-way street (see Figure 16.5). In addition, the two strands of DNA in a double helix are antiparallel, meaning that they are oriented in opposite directions to each other, like a divided highway (see Figure 16.14). Clearly, the two new strands formed during DNA replication must also be antiparallel to their template strands.

Primase synthesizes RNA primers, using the parental DNA as a template.

Topoisomerase breaks, swivels, and rejoins the parental DNA ahead of the replication fork, relieving the strain caused by unwinding.

RNA primer

5′
3′

3′ 5′

5′

Helicase unwinds and separates the parental DNA strands.

Single-strand binding proteins stabilize the unwound parental strands.

▲ **Figure 16.13 Some of the proteins involved in the initiation of DNA replication.** The same proteins function at both replication forks in a replication bubble. For simplicity, only the left-hand fork is shown, and the DNA bases are drawn much larger in relation to the proteins than they are in reality.

New strand | Template strand
Sugar
Phosphate
Base
OH
3′
Nucleoside
triphosphate
Pyrophosphate

DNA polymerase

OH
3′

◀ **Figure 16.14 Incorporation of a nucleotide into a DNA strand.** DNA polymerase catalyzes the addition of a nucleoside triphosphate to the 3′ end of a growing DNA strand, with the release of two phosphates.

? *Use this diagram to explain what we mean when we say that each DNA strand has directionality.*

How does the antiparallel arrangement of the double helix affect replication? Because of their structure, DNA polymerases can add nucleotides only to the free 3′ end of a primer or growing DNA strand, never to the 5′ end (see Figure 16.14). Thus, a new DNA strand can elongate only in the 5′ → 3′ direction. With this in mind, let's examine one of the two replication forks in a bubble **(Figure 16.15)**. Along one template strand, DNA polymerase III can synthesize a complementary strand continuously by elongating the new DNA in the mandatory 5′ → 3′ direction. DNA pol III remains in the replication fork on that template strand and continuously adds nucleotides to the new complementary strand as the fork progresses. The DNA strand made by this mechanism is called the **leading strand**. Only one primer is required for DNA pol III to synthesize the leading strand (see Figure 16.15).

To elongate the other new strand of DNA in the mandatory 5′ → 3′ direction, DNA pol III must work along the other template strand in the direction *away from* the replication fork. The DNA strand elongating in this direction is called the **lagging strand**.* In contrast to the leading strand, which elongates continuously, the lagging strand is synthesized discontinuously, as a series of segments. These segments of the lagging strand are called **Okazaki fragments**, after the Japanese scientist who discovered them. The fragments are about 1,000–2,000 nucleotides long in *E. coli* and 100–200 nucleotides long in eukaryotes.

---

*Synthesis of the leading strand and synthesis of the lagging strand occur concurrently and at the same rate. The lagging strand is so named because its synthesis is delayed slightly relative to synthesis of the leading strand; each new fragment of the lagging strand cannot be started until enough template has been exposed at the replication fork.

Overview

Leading strand — Origin of replication — Lagging strand
Primer
Lagging strand — Overall directions of replication — Leading strand

❶ After RNA primer is made, DNA pol III starts to synthesize the leading strand.

Origin of replication

3′
5′
RNA primer
Sliding clamp
DNA pol III

Parental DNA

❷ The leading strand is elongated continuously in the 5′ → 3′ direction as the fork progresses.

▲ **Figure 16.15 Synthesis of the leading strand during DNA replication.** This diagram focuses on the left replication fork shown in the overview box. DNA polymerase III (DNA pol III), shaped like a cupped hand, is shown closely associated with a protein called the "sliding clamp" that encircles the newly synthesized double helix like a doughnut. The sliding clamp moves DNA pol III along the DNA template strand.

1 Primase joins RNA nucleotides into a primer.

Template strand

2 DNA pol III adds DNA nucleotides to the primer, forming Okazaki fragment 1.

RNA primer for fragment 1

3 After reaching the next RNA primer to the right, DNA pol III detaches.

Okazaki fragment 1

RNA primer for fragment 2

Okazaki fragment 2

4 Fragment 2 is primed. Then DNA pol III adds DNA nucleotides, detaching when it reaches the fragment 1 primer.

5 DNA pol I replaces the RNA with DNA, adding to the 3' end of fragment 2.

6 DNA ligase forms a bond between the newest DNA and the DNA of fragment 1.

7 The lagging strand in this region is now complete.

Overall direction of replication

▲ **Figure 16.16 Synthesis of the lagging strand.**

Figure 16.16 illustrates the steps in the synthesis of the lagging strand at one fork. Whereas only one primer is required on the leading strand, each Okazaki fragment on the lagging strand must be primed separately (steps **1** and **4**). After DNA pol III forms an Okazaki fragment (steps **2**–**4**), another DNA polymerase, DNA polymerase I (DNA pol I), replaces the RNA nucleotides of the adjacent primer with DNA nucleotides (step **5**). But DNA pol I cannot join the final nucleotide of this replacement DNA segment to the first DNA nucleotide of the adjacent Okazaki fragment. Another enzyme, **DNA ligase**, accomplishes this task, joining the sugar-phosphate backbones of all the Okazaki fragments into a continuous DNA strand (step **6**).

Figure 16.17 summarizes DNA replication. Please study it carefully before proceeding.

The DNA Replication Complex

It is traditional—and convenient—to represent DNA polymerase molecules as locomotives moving along a DNA "railroad track," but such a model is inaccurate in two important ways. First, the various proteins that participate in DNA replication actually form a single large complex, a "DNA replication machine." Many protein-protein interactions facilitate the efficiency of this complex. For example, by interacting with other proteins at the fork, primase apparently acts as a molecular brake, slowing progress of the replication fork and coordinating the placement of primers and the rates of replication on the leading and lagging strands. Second, the DNA replication complex may not move along the DNA; rather, the DNA may move through the complex during the replication process. In eukaryotic cells, multiple copies of the complex, perhaps grouped into "factories," may be anchored to the nuclear matrix, a framework of fibers extending through the interior of the nucleus. Recent studies support a model in which two DNA polymerase molecules, one on each template strand, "reel in" the parental DNA and extrude newly made daughter DNA molecules. Additional evidence suggests that the lagging strand is looped back through the complex (**Figure 16.18**).

Proofreading and Repairing DNA

We cannot attribute the accuracy of DNA replication solely to the specificity of base pairing. Although errors in the completed DNA molecule amount to only one in 10^{10} (10 billion) nucleotides, initial pairing errors between incoming nucleotides and those in the template strand are 100,000 times more common—an error rate of one in 10^5 nucleotides. During DNA replication, DNA polymerases proofread each nucleotide against its template as soon as it is added to the growing strand. Upon finding an incorrectly paired nucleotide, the polymerase removes the nucleotide and then resumes synthesis. (This action is similar to fixing a typing error by deleting the wrong letter and then entering the correct letter.)

③ The leading strand is synthesized continuously in the 5′ → 3′ direction by DNA pol III.

② Molecules of single-strand binding protein stabilize the unwound template strands.

① Helicase unwinds the parental double helix.

Overview

Origin of replication

Leading strand   Lagging strand

Lagging strand   Leading strand

Overall directions of replication

Leading strand

5′

3′

Parental DNA

DNA pol III

Primer   Primase

5′

3′

④ Primase begins synthesis of the RNA primer for the fifth Okazaki fragment.

⑤ DNA pol III is completing synthesis of the fourth fragment. When it reaches the RNA primer on the third fragment, it will detach and begin adding DNA nucleotides to the 3′ end of the fifth fragment primer in the replication fork.

DNA pol III

5′   4   3′   5′

Lagging strand

DNA pol I

DNA ligase

3   2   1   3′

5′

▲ **Figure 16.17 A summary of bacterial DNA replication.** The detailed diagram shows the left-hand replication fork of the replication bubble in the overview (upper right). Viewing each daughter strand in its entirety in the overview, you can see that half of it is made continuously as the leading strand, while the other half (on the other side of the origin) is synthesized in fragments as the lagging strand.

DRAW IT *Draw a similar diagram showing the right-hand fork of this bubble, numbering the Okazaki fragments appropriately.*

⑥ DNA pol I removes the primer from the 5′ end of the second fragment, replacing it with DNA nucleotides that it adds one by one to the 3′ end of the third fragment. The replacement of the last RNA nucleotide with DNA leaves the sugar-phosphate backbone with a free 3′ end.

⑦ DNA ligase joins the 3′ end of the second fragment to the 5′ end of the first fragment.

▲ **Figure 16.18 A current model of the DNA replication complex.** Two DNA polymerase III molecules work together in a complex, one on each template strand. The lagging strand template DNA loops through the complex.

 BioFlix Visit the Study Area at **www.masteringbiology.com** for the BioFlix® 3-D Animation on DNA Replication.

Mismatched nucleotides sometimes evade proofreading by a DNA polymerase. In **mismatch repair**, other enzymes remove and replace incorrectly paired nucleotides that have resulted from replication errors. Researchers spotlighted the importance of such repair enzymes when they found that a hereditary defect in one of them is associated with a form of colon cancer. Apparently, this defect allows cancer-causing errors to accumulate in the DNA faster than normal.

Incorrectly paired or altered nucleotides can also arise after replication. In fact, maintenance of the genetic information encoded in DNA requires frequent repair of various kinds of damage to existing DNA. DNA molecules are constantly subjected to potentially harmful chemical and physical agents, such as cigarette smoke and X-rays, as we'll discuss in Chapter 17. In addition, DNA bases often undergo spontaneous chemical changes under normal cellular conditions. However, these changes in DNA are usually corrected before they become permanent changes—*mutations*—perpetuated through successive replications. Each cell continuously monitors and repairs its genetic material. Because repair of damaged DNA is so important to the survival of an organism, it is no surprise that many different DNA repair enzymes have evolved. Almost 100 are known in *E. coli*, and about 130 have been identified so far in humans.

▲ **Figure 16.19 Nucleotide excision repair of DNA damage.**

① Teams of enzymes detect and repair damaged DNA, such as this thymine dimer (often caused by ultraviolet radiation), which distorts the DNA molecule.

② A nuclease enzyme cuts the damaged DNA strand at two points, and the damaged section is removed.

Nuclease

DNA polymerase

③ Repair synthesis by a DNA polymerase fills in the missing nucleotides.

DNA ligase

④ DNA ligase seals the free end of the new DNA to the old DNA, making the strand complete.

Most cellular systems for repairing incorrectly paired nucleotides, whether they are due to DNA damage or to replication errors, use a mechanism that takes advantage of the base-paired structure of DNA. In many cases, a segment of the strand containing the damage is cut out (excised) by a DNA-cutting enzyme—a **nuclease**—and the resulting gap is then filled in with nucleotides, using the undamaged strand as a template. The enzymes involved in filling the gap are a DNA polymerase and DNA ligase. One such DNA repair system is called **nucleotide excision repair** (Figure 16.19).

An important function of the DNA repair enzymes in our skin cells is to repair genetic damage caused by the ultraviolet rays of sunlight. One type of damage, shown in Figure 16.19, is the covalent linking of thymine bases that are adjacent on a DNA strand. Such *thymine dimers* cause the DNA to buckle and interfere with DNA replication. The importance of repairing this kind of damage is underscored by the disorder xeroderma pigmentosum, which in most cases is caused by an inherited defect in a nucleotide excision repair enzyme. Individuals with this disorder are hypersensitive to sunlight; mutations in their skin cells caused by ultraviolet light are left uncorrected, resulting in skin cancer.

Evolutionary Significance of Altered DNA Nucleotides

EVOLUTION Faithful replication of the genome and repair of DNA damage are important for the functioning of the organism and for passing on a complete, accurate genome to the next generation. The error rate after proofreading and repair is extremely low, but rare mistakes do slip through. Once a mismatched nucleotide pair is replicated, the sequence change is permanent in the daughter molecule that has the incorrect nucleotide as well as in any subsequent copies. As you know, a permanent change in the DNA sequence is called a mutation.

As you'll learn in Chapter 17, mutations can change the phenotype of an organism. And if they occur in germ cells (which give rise to gametes), mutations can be passed on from generation to generation. The vast majority of such changes are harmful, but a very small percentage can be beneficial. In either case, mutations are the source of the variation on which natural selection operates during evolution and are ultimately responsible for the appearance of new species. (You'll learn more about this process in Unit Four.) The balance between complete fidelity of DNA replication or repair and a low mutation rate has, over long periods of time, allowed the evolution of the rich diversity of species we see on Earth today.

Replicating the Ends of DNA Molecules

In spite of the impressive capabilities of DNA polymerases, there is a small portion of the cell's DNA that DNA polymerases can neither replicate nor repair. For linear DNA, such as the DNA of eukaryotic chromosomes, the fact that a DNA polymerase can add nucleotides only to the 3′ end of a preexisting polynucleotide leads to what might appear to be a problem. The usual replication machinery provides no way to complete the 5′ ends of daughter DNA strands. Even if an Okazaki fragment can be started with an RNA primer bound to the very end of the template strand, once that primer is removed, it cannot be replaced with DNA because there is no 3′ end available for nucleotide addition (Figure 16.20). As a result, repeated rounds of replication produce shorter and shorter DNA molecules with uneven ("staggered") ends.

Most prokaryotes have a circular chromosome, with no ends, so the shortening of DNA does not occur. But what protects the genes of linear eukaryotic chromosomes from being eroded away during successive rounds of DNA replication? It turns out that eukaryotic chromosomal DNA molecules have special nucleotide sequences called **telomeres** at their ends (Figure 16.21). Telomeres do not contain genes; instead, the DNA typically consists of multiple repetitions of one short nucleotide sequence. In each human telomere, for example, the six-nucleotide sequence TTAGGG is repeated between 100 and 1,000 times. Telomeric DNA acts as a kind of buffer zone that protects the organism's genes. In addition, specific proteins associated with telomeric DNA prevent the staggered ends of the daughter molecule from activating the cell's systems for monitoring DNA damage. (Staggered ends of a DNA molecule, which often result from double-strand breaks, can trigger signal transduction pathways leading to cell cycle arrest or cell death.)

Ends of parental DNA strands

5′

Leading strand
Lagging strand

3′

Last fragment   Next-to-last fragment

Lagging strand

RNA primer

5′
3′

Parental strand

Primer removed but cannot be replaced with DNA because no 3′ end available for DNA polymerase

Removal of primers and replacement with DNA where a 3′ end is available

5′
3′

Second round of replication

5′
New leading strand 3′

New lagging strand 5′
3′

Further rounds of replication

Shorter and shorter daughter molecules

▲ Figure 16.20 **Shortening of the ends of linear DNA molecules.** Here we follow the end of one strand of a DNA molecule through two rounds of replication. After the first round, the new lagging strand is shorter than its template. After a second round, both the leading and lagging strands have become shorter than the original parental DNA. Although not shown here, the other ends of these DNA molecules also become shorter.

1 μm

▲ Figure 16.21 **Telomeres.** Eukaryotes have repetitive, noncoding sequences called telomeres at the ends of their DNA. Telomeres are stained orange in these mouse chromosomes (LM).

Telomeres provide their protective function by postponing the erosion of genes located near the ends of DNA molecules. As shown in Figure 16.20, telomeres become shorter during every round of replication. As we would expect, telomeric DNA tends to be shorter in dividing somatic cells of older individuals and in cultured cells that have divided many times. It has been proposed that shortening of telomeres is somehow connected to the aging process of certain tissues and even to aging of the organism as a whole.

But what about cells whose genome must persist virtually unchanged from an organism to its offspring over many generations? If the chromosomes of germ cells became shorter in every cell cycle, essential genes would eventually be missing from the gametes they produce. However, this does not occur: An enzyme called **telomerase** catalyzes the lengthening of telomeres in eukaryotic germ cells, thus restoring their original length and compensating for the shortening that occurs during DNA replication. Telomerase is not active in most human somatic cells, but its activity in germ cells results in telomeres of maximum length in the zygote.

Normal shortening of telomeres may protect organisms from cancer by limiting the number of divisions that somatic cells can undergo. Cells from large tumors often have unusually short telomeres, as we would expect for cells that have undergone many cell divisions. Further shortening would presumably lead to self-destruction of the tumor cells. Intriguingly, researchers have found telomerase activity in cancerous somatic cells, suggesting that its ability to stabilize telomere length may allow these cancer cells to persist. Many cancer cells do seem capable of unlimited cell division, as do immortal strains of cultured cells (see Chapter 12). If telomerase is indeed an important factor in many cancers, it may provide a useful target for both cancer diagnosis and chemotherapy.

Thus far in this chapter, you have learned about the structure and replication of a DNA molecule. In the next section, we'll take a step back and examine how DNA is packaged into chromosomes, the structures that carry the genetic information.

CONCEPT CHECK 16.2

1. What role does complementary base pairing play in the replication of DNA?
2. Make a table listing the functions of seven proteins involved in DNA replication in *E. coli*.
3. **MAKE CONNECTIONS** What is the relationship between DNA replication and the S phase of the cell cycle? See Figure 12.6, page 231.
4. **WHAT IF?** If the DNA pol I in a given cell were nonfunctional, how would that affect the synthesis of a *leading* strand? In the overview box in Figure 16.17, point out where DNA pol I would normally function on the top leading strand.

For suggested answers, see Appendix A.

A chromosome consists of a DNA molecule packed together with proteins

The main component of the genome in most bacteria is one double-stranded, circular DNA molecule that is associated with a small amount of protein. Although we refer to this structure as the *bacterial chromosome*, it is very different from a eukaryotic chromosome, which consists of one linear DNA molecule associated with a large amount of protein. In *E. coli*, the chromosomal DNA consists of about 4.6 million nucleotide pairs, representing about 4,400 genes. This is 100 times more DNA than is found in a typical virus, but only about one-thousandth as much DNA as in a human somatic cell. Still, that is a lot of DNA to be packaged in such a small container.

Stretched out, the DNA of an *E. coli* cell would measure about a millimeter in length, 500 times longer than the cell.

▼ Figure 16.22

Exploring Chromatin Packing in a Eukaryotic Chromosome

This series of diagrams and transmission electron micrographs depicts a current model for the progressive levels of DNA coiling and folding. The illustration zooms out from a single molecule of DNA to a metaphase chromosome, which is large enough to be seen with a light microscope.

Nucleosome (10 nm in diameter)

DNA double helix (2 nm in diameter)

Histones

Histone tail

H1

DNA, the double helix

Shown here is a ribbon model of DNA, with each ribbon representing one of the sugar-phosphate backbones. As you will recall from Figure 16.7, the phosphate groups along the backbone contribute a negative charge along the outside of each strand. The TEM shows a molecule of naked DNA; the double helix alone is 2 nm across.

Histones

Proteins called **histones** are responsible for the first level of DNA packing in chromatin. Although each histone is small—containing only about 100 amino acids—the total mass of histone in chromatin approximately equals the mass of DNA. More than a fifth of a histone's amino acids are positively charged (lysine or arginine) and therefore bind tightly to the negatively charged DNA.

Four types of histones are most common in chromatin: H2A, H2B, H3, and H4. The histones are very similar among eukaryotes; for example, all but two of the amino acids in cow H4 are identical to those in pea H4. The apparent conservation of histone genes during evolution probably reflects the important role of histones in organizing DNA within cells.

The four main types of histones are critical to the next level of DNA packing. (A fifth type of histone, called H1, is involved in a further stage of packing.)

Nucleosomes, or "beads on a string" (10-nm fiber)

In electron micrographs, unfolded chromatin is 10 nm in diameter (the *10-nm fiber*). Such chromatin resembles beads on a string (see the TEM). Each "bead" is a **nucleosome**, the basic unit of DNA packing; the "string" between beads is called *linker DNA*.

A nucleosome consists of DNA wound twice around a protein core composed of two molecules each of the four main histone types. The amino end (N-terminus) of each histone (the *histone tail*) extends outward from the nucleosome.

In the cell cycle, the histones leave the DNA only briefly during DNA replication. Generally, they do the same during transcription, another process that requires access to the DNA by the cell's molecular machinery. Chapter 18 will discuss some recent findings about the role of histone tails and nucleosomes in the regulation of gene expression.

Within a bacterium, however, certain proteins cause the chromosome to coil and "supercoil," densely packing it so that it fills only part of the cell. Unlike the nucleus of a eukaryotic cell, this dense region of DNA in a bacterium, called the **nucleoid**, is not bounded by membrane (see Figure 6.5).

Eukaryotic chromosomes each contain a single linear DNA double helix that, in humans, averages about 1.5×10^8 nucleotide pairs. This is an enormous amount of DNA relative to a chromosome's condensed length. If completely stretched out, such a DNA molecule would be about 4 cm long, thousands of times the diameter of a cell nucleus—and that's not even considering the DNA of the other 45 human chromosomes!

In the cell, eukaryotic DNA is precisely combined with a large amount of protein. Together, this complex of DNA and protein, called **chromatin**, fits into the nucleus through an elaborate, multilevel system of packing. Our current view of the successive levels of DNA packing in a chromosome is outlined in **Figure 16.22**. Study this figure carefully before reading further.

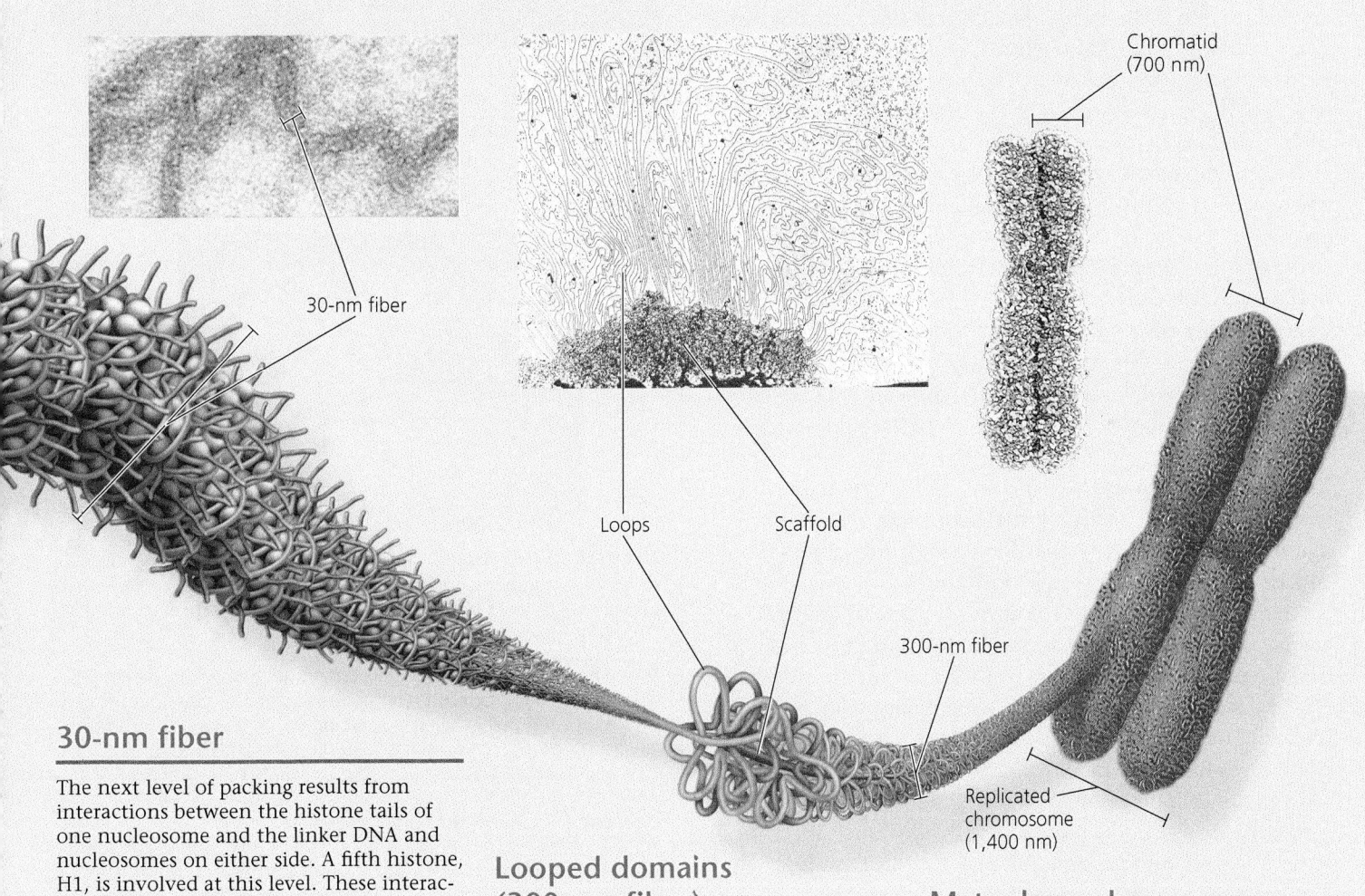

30-nm fiber

Chromatid (700 nm)

Loops

Scaffold

300-nm fiber

Replicated chromosome (1,400 nm)

30-nm fiber

The next level of packing results from interactions between the histone tails of one nucleosome and the linker DNA and nucleosomes on either side. A fifth histone, H1, is involved at this level. These interactions cause the extended 10-nm fiber to coil or fold, forming a chromatin fiber roughly 30 nm in thickness, the *30-nm fiber*. Although the 30-nm fiber is quite prevalent in the interphase nucleus, the packing arrangement of nucleosomes in this form of chromatin is still a matter of some debate.

Looped domains (300-nm fiber)

The 30-nm fiber, in turn, forms loops called *looped domains* attached to a chromosome scaffold made of proteins, thus making up a *300-nm fiber*. The scaffold is rich in one type of topoisomerase, and H1 molecules also appear to be present.

Metaphase chromosome

In a mitotic chromosome, the looped domains themselves coil and fold in a manner not yet fully understood, further compacting all the chromatin to produce the characteristic metaphase chromosome shown in the micrograph above. The width of one chromatid is 700 nm. Particular genes always end up located at the same places in metaphase chromosomes, indicating that the packing steps are highly specific and precise.

Chromatin undergoes striking changes in its degree of packing during the course of the cell cycle (see Figure 12.7). In interphase cells stained for light microscopy, the chromatin usually appears as a diffuse mass within the nucleus, suggesting that the chromatin is highly extended. As a cell prepares for mitosis, its chromatin coils and folds up (condenses), eventually forming a characteristic number of short, thick metaphase chromosomes that are distinguishable from each other with the light microscope.

Though interphase chromatin is generally much less condensed than the chromatin of mitotic chromosomes, it shows several of the same levels of higher-order packing. Some of the chromatin comprising a chromosome seems to be present as a 10-nm fiber, but much is compacted into a 30-nm fiber, which in some regions is further folded into looped domains. Early on, biologists assumed that interphase chromatin was a tangled mass in the nucleus, like a bowl of spaghetti, but this is far from the case. Although an interphase chromosome lacks an obvious scaffold, its looped domains appear to be attached to the nuclear lamina, on the inside of the nuclear envelope, and perhaps also to fibers of the nuclear matrix. These attachments may help organize regions of chromatin where genes are active. The chromatin of each chromosome occupies a specific restricted area within the interphase nucleus, and the chromatin fibers of different chromosomes do not become entangled (**Figure 16.23**).

Even during interphase, the centromeres and telomeres of chromosomes, as well as other chromosomal regions in some cells, exist in a highly condensed state similar to that seen in a metaphase chromosome. This type of interphase chromatin, visible as irregular clumps with a light microscope, is called **heterochromatin**, to distinguish it from the less compacted, more dispersed **euchromatin** ("true chromatin"). Because of its compaction, heterochromatic DNA is largely inaccessible to the machinery in the cell responsible for transcribing the genetic information coded in the DNA, a crucial early step in gene expression. In contrast, the looser packing of euchromatin makes its DNA accessible to this machinery, so the genes present in euchromatin can be transcribed. The chromosome is a dynamic structure that is condensed, loosened, modified, and remodeled as necessary for various cell processes, including mitosis, meiosis, and gene activity. Chemical modifications of histones affect the state of chromatin condensation and also have multiple effects on gene activity, as you will see in Chapter 18.

In this chapter, you have learned how DNA molecules are arranged in chromosomes and how DNA replication provides the copies of genes that parents pass to offspring. However, it is not enough that genes be copied and transmitted; the information they carry must be used by the cell. In other words, genes must also be "expressed." In the next chapter, we will examine how the cell expresses the genetic information encoded in DNA.

▼ Figure 16.23

IMPACT

Painting Chromosomes

Using techniques you'll learn about in Chapter 20, researchers have been able to treat human chromosomes with special molecular tags, such that each chromosome pair can be seen as a different color. Below on the left is a spread of chromosomes treated in this way; on the right they are organized into a karyotype.

WHY IT MATTERS The ability to visually distinguish among chromosomes has allowed researchers to see how the chromosomes are arranged in the interphase nucleus. As you can see in the interphase nucleus below, each chromosome appears to occupy a specific territory during interphase. In general, the two homologs of a pair are not located together.

FURTHER READING M. R. Speicher and N. P. Carter, The new cytogenetics: blurring the boundaries with molecular biology, *Nature Reviews Genetics* 6:782–792 (2005); J. L. Marx, New methods for expanding the chromosomal paint kit, *Science* 273:430 (1996).

MAKE CONNECTIONS If you arrested a human cell in metaphase I of meiosis and applied this technique, what would you observe? How would this differ from what you would see in metaphase of mitosis? Review Figure 13.8 (pp. 254–255) and Figure 12.7 (pp. 232–233).

CONCEPT CHECK 16.3

1. Describe the structure of a nucleosome, the basic unit of DNA packing in eukaryotic cells.
2. What two properties, one structural and one functional, distinguish heterochromatin from euchromatin?
3. **MAKE CONNECTIONS** Interphase chromosomes appear to be attached to the nuclear lamina and perhaps also the nuclear matrix. Describe these two structures. See page 102 and Figure 6.9 on page 103.

For suggested answers, see Appendix A.

CONCEPT 16.1

DNA is the genetic material (pp. 305–310)

- Experiments with bacteria and with **phages** provided the first strong evidence that the genetic material is DNA.
- Watson and Crick deduced that DNA is a **double helix** and built a structural model. Two **antiparallel** sugar-phosphate chains wind around the outside of the molecule; the nitrogenous bases project into the interior, where they hydrogen-bond in specific pairs, A with T, G with C.

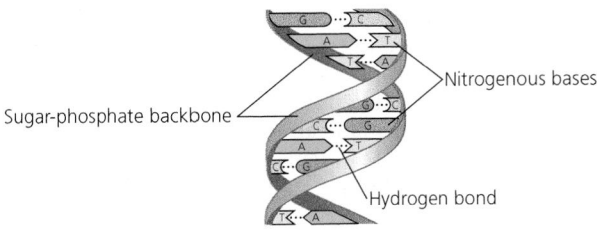

Sugar-phosphate backbone
Nitrogenous bases
Hydrogen bond

> ? *What does it mean when we say that the two DNA strands in the double helix are antiparallel? What would an end of the double helix look like if the strands were parallel?*

CONCEPT 16.2

Many proteins work together in DNA replication and repair (pp. 311–319)

- The Meselson-Stahl experiment showed that **DNA replication** is **semiconservative**: The parental molecule unwinds, and each strand then serves as a template for the synthesis of a new strand according to base-pairing rules.
- DNA replication at one **replication fork** is summarized here:

DNA pol III synthesizes leading strand continuously

Parental DNA

DNA pol III starts DNA synthesis at 3' end of primer, continues in 5' → 3' direction

Origin of replication

Helicase

Lagging strand synthesized in short Okazaki fragments, later joined by DNA ligase

Primase synthesizes a short RNA primer

DNA pol I replaces the RNA primer with DNA nucleotides

- DNA polymerases proofread new DNA, replacing incorrect nucleotides. In **mismatch repair**, enzymes correct errors that persist. **Nucleotide excision repair** is a general process by which **nucleases** cut out and replace damaged stretches of DNA.
- The ends of eukaryotic chromosomal DNA get shorter with each round of replication. The presence of **telomeres**, repetitive sequences at the ends of linear DNA molecules, postpones the erosion of genes. **Telomerase** catalyzes the lengthening of telomeres in germ cells.

> ? *Compare DNA replication on the leading and lagging strands, including both similarities and differences.*

CONCEPT 16.3

A chromosome consists of a DNA molecule packed together with proteins (pp. 320–322)

- The bacterial chromosome is usually a circular DNA molecule with some associated proteins, making up the **nucleoid** of the cell. Eukaryotic **chromatin** making up a chromosome is composed of DNA, **histones**, and other proteins. The histones bind to each other and to the DNA to form **nucleosomes**, the most basic units of DNA packing. Histone tails extend outward from each bead-like nucleosome core. Additional coiling and folding leads ultimately to the highly condensed chromatin of the metaphase chromosome. In interphase cells, most chromatin is less compacted (**euchromatin**), but some remains highly condensed (**heterochromatin**). Euchromatin, but not heterochromatin, is generally accessible for transcription of genes.

> ? *Describe the levels of chromatin packing you'd expect to see in an interphase nucleus.*

LEVEL 1: KNOWLEDGE/COMPREHENSION

1. In his work with pneumonia-causing bacteria and mice, Griffith found that
   a. the protein coat from pathogenic cells was able to transform nonpathogenic cells.
   b. heat-killed pathogenic cells caused pneumonia.
   c. some substance from pathogenic cells was transferred to nonpathogenic cells, making them pathogenic.
   d. the polysaccharide coat of bacteria caused pneumonia.
   e. bacteriophages injected DNA into bacteria.

2. What is the basis for the difference in how the leading and lagging strands of DNA molecules are synthesized?
   a. The origins of replication occur only at the 5' end.
   b. Helicases and single-strand binding proteins work at the 5' end.
   c. DNA polymerase can join new nucleotides only to the 3' end of a growing strand.
   d. DNA ligase works only in the 3' → 5' direction.
   e. Polymerase can work on only one strand at a time.

3. In analyzing the number of different bases in a DNA sample, which result would be consistent with the base-pairing rules?
   a. A = G
   b. A + G = C + T
   c. A + T = G + T
   d. A = C
   e. G = T

4. The elongation of the leading strand during DNA synthesis
   a. progresses away from the replication fork.
   b. occurs in the 3' → 5' direction.
   c. produces Okazaki fragments.
   d. depends on the action of DNA polymerase.
   e. does not require a template strand.

5. In a nucleosome, the DNA is wrapped around
   a. polymerase molecules.
   b. ribosomes.
   c. histones.
   d. a thymine dimer.
   e. satellite DNA.

LEVEL 2: APPLICATION/ANALYSIS

6. *E. coli* cells grown on ^{15}N medium are transferred to ^{14}N medium and allowed to grow for two more generations (two rounds of DNA replication). DNA extracted from these cells is centrifuged. What density distribution of DNA would you expect in this experiment?
   a. one high-density and one low-density band
   b. one intermediate-density band
   c. one high-density and one intermediate-density band
   d. one low-density and one intermediate-density band
   e. one low-density band

7. A biochemist isolates, purifies, and combines in a test tube a variety of molecules needed for DNA replication. When she adds some DNA to the mixture, replication occurs, but each DNA molecule consists of a normal strand paired with numerous segments of DNA a few hundred nucleotides long. What has she probably left out of the mixture?
   a. DNA polymerase
   b. DNA ligase
   c. nucleotides
   d. Okazaki fragments
   e. primase

8. The spontaneous loss of amino groups from adenine in DNA results in hypoxanthine, an uncommon base, opposite thymine. What combination of proteins could repair such damage?
   a. nuclease, DNA polymerase, DNA ligase
   b. telomerase, primase, DNA polymerase
   c. telomerase, helicase, single-strand binding protein
   d. DNA ligase, replication fork proteins, adenylyl cyclase
   e. nuclease, telomerase, primase

9. **MAKE CONNECTIONS** Although the proteins that cause the *E. coli* chromosome to coil are not histones, what property would you expect them to share with histones, given their ability to bind to DNA (see Figure 5.16, p. 79)?

LEVEL 3: SYNTHESIS/EVALUATION

10. The table below shows the base composition of DNA in several species. Explain how these data demonstrate Chargaff's rules.

Source	Adenine	Guanine	Cytosine	Thymine
E. coli	24.7%	26.0%	25.7%	23.6%
Wheat	28.1	21.8	22.7	27.4
Sea urchin	32.8	17.7	17.3	32.1
Salmon	29.7	20.8	20.4	29.1
Human	30.4	19.6	19.9	30.1
Ox	29.0	21.2	21.2	28.7

11. **EVOLUTION CONNECTION**
    Some bacteria may be able to respond to environmental stress by increasing the rate at which mutations occur during cell division. How might this be accomplished? Might there be an evolutionary advantage of this ability? Explain.

12. SCIENTIFIC INQUIRY

DRAW IT Model building can be an important part of the scientific process. The illustration shown above is a computer-generated model of a DNA replication complex. The parental and newly synthesized DNA strands are color-coded differently, as are each of the following three proteins: DNA pol III, the sliding clamp, and single-strand binding protein. Use what you've learned in this chapter to clarify this model by labeling each DNA strand and each protein and indicating the overall direction of DNA replication.

13. **WRITE ABOUT A THEME**
    The Genetic Basis of Life; Structure and Function The continuity of life is based on heritable information in the form of DNA, and structure and function are correlated at all levels of biological organization. In a short essay (100–150 words), describe how the structure of DNA is correlated with its role as the molecular basis of inheritance.

For selected answers, see Appendix A.

Mastering BIOLOGY® www.masteringbiology.com

1. MasteringBiology® Assignments
Experimental Inquiry Tutorial Does DNA Replication Follow the Conservative, Semiconservative, or Dispersive Model?
Video Tutor Session DNA Structure
BioFlix Tutorials DNA Replication: DNA Structure and Replication Machinery • Synthesis of the Leading and Lagging Strands
Tutorial DNA Replication
Activities The Hershey-Chase Experiment • DNA and RNA Structure • DNA Double Helix • DNA Replication: An Overview • DNA Replication: A Closer Look • DNA Replication: A Review • DNA Synthesis • DNA Packing
Questions Student Misconceptions • Reading Quiz • Multiple Choice • End-of-Chapter

2. eText
Read your book online, search, take notes, highlight text, and more.

3. The Study Area
Practice Tests • Cumulative Test • **BioFlix** 3-D Animations • MP3 Tutor Sessions • Videos • Activities • Investigations • Lab Media • Audio Glossary • Word Study Tools • Art

17

From Gene to Protein

▲ Figure 17.1 **How does a single faulty gene result in the dramatic appearance of an albino deer?**

KEY CONCEPTS

17.1 Genes specify proteins via transcription and translation

17.2 Transcription is the DNA-directed synthesis of RNA: *a closer look*

17.3 Eukaryotic cells modify RNA after transcription

17.4 Translation is the RNA-directed synthesis of a polypeptide: *a closer look*

17.5 Mutations of one or a few nucleotides can affect protein structure and function

17.6 While gene expression differs among the domains of life, the concept of a gene is universal

The Flow of Genetic Information

In 2006, a young albino deer seen frolicking with several brown deer in the mountains of eastern Germany elicited a public outcry (Figure 17.1). A local hunting organization announced that the albino deer suffered from a "genetic disorder" and should be shot. Some argued that the deer should merely be prevented from mating with other deer to safeguard the population's gene pool. Others favored relocating the albino deer to a nature reserve because they worried that it might be more noticeable to predators if left in the wild. A German rock star even held a benefit concert to raise funds for the relocation. What led to the striking phenotype of this deer, the cause of this lively debate?

You learned in Chapter 14 that inherited traits are determined by genes and that the trait of albinism is caused by a recessive allele of a pigmentation gene. The information content of genes is in the form of specific sequences of nucleotides along strands of DNA, the genetic material. But how does this information determine an organism's traits? Put another way, what does a gene actually say? And how is its message translated by cells into a specific trait, such as brown hair, type A blood, or, in the case of an albino deer, a total lack of pigment? The albino deer has a faulty version of a key protein, an enzyme required for pigment synthesis, and this protein is faulty because the gene that codes for it contains incorrect information.

This example illustrates the main point of this chapter: The DNA inherited by an organism leads to specific traits by dictating the synthesis of proteins and of RNA molecules involved in protein synthesis. In other words, proteins are the link between genotype and phenotype. **Gene expression** is the process by which DNA directs the synthesis of proteins (or, in some cases, just RNAs). The expression of genes that code for proteins includes two stages: transcription and translation. This chapter describes the flow of information from gene to protein in detail and explains how genetic mutations affect organisms through their proteins. Understanding the processes of gene expression, which are similar in all three domains of life, will allow us to revisit the concept of the gene in more detail at the end of the chapter.

CONCEPT 17.1

Genes specify proteins via transcription and translation

Before going into the details of how genes direct protein synthesis, let's step back and examine how the fundamental relationship between genes and proteins was discovered.

Evidence from the Study of Metabolic Defects

In 1902, British physician Archibald Garrod was the first to suggest that genes dictate phenotypes through enzymes that catalyze specific chemical reactions in the cell. Garrod postulated that the symptoms of an inherited disease reflect a person's inability to make a particular enzyme. He later referred to such diseases as "inborn errors of metabolism." Garrod gave as one example the hereditary condition called alkaptonuria. In this disorder, the urine is black because it contains the chemical alkapton, which darkens upon exposure to air. Garrod reasoned that most people have an enzyme that metabolizes alkapton, whereas people with alkaptonuria have inherited an inability to make that enzyme.

Garrod may have been the first to recognize that Mendel's principles of heredity apply to humans as well as peas. Garrod's realization was ahead of its time, but research several decades later supported his hypothesis that a gene dictates the production of a specific enzyme. Biochemists accumulated much evidence that cells synthesize and degrade most organic molecules via metabolic pathways, in which each chemical reaction in a sequence is catalyzed by a specific enzyme (see p. 142). Such metabolic pathways lead, for instance, to the synthesis of the pigments that give the brown deer in Figure 17.1 their fur color or fruit flies (*Drosophila*) their eye color (see Figure 15.3). In the 1930s, the American biochemist and geneticist George Beadle and his French colleague Boris Ephrussi speculated that in *Drosophila*, each of the various mutations affecting eye color blocks pigment synthesis at a specific step by preventing production of the enzyme that catalyzes that step. But neither the chemical reactions nor the enzymes that catalyze them were known at the time.

Nutritional Mutants in Neurospora: Scientific Inquiry

A breakthrough in demonstrating the relationship between genes and enzymes came a few years later at Stanford University, where Beadle and Edward Tatum began working with a bread mold, *Neurospora crassa*. They bombarded *Neurospora* with X-rays, shown in the 1920s to cause genetic changes, and then looked among the survivors for mutants that differed in their nutritional needs from the wild-type bread mold. Wild-type *Neurospora* has modest food requirements. It can grow in the laboratory on a simple solution of inorganic salts, glucose, and the vitamin biotin, incorporated into agar, a support medium. From this *minimal medium*, the mold cells use their metabolic pathways to produce all the other molecules they need. Beadle and Tatum identified mutants that could not survive on minimal medium, apparently because they were unable to synthesize certain essential molecules from the minimal ingredients. To ensure survival of these nutritional mutants, Beadle and Tatum allowed them to grow on a *complete growth medium*, which consisted of minimal medium supplemented with all 20 amino acids and a few other nutrients. The complete growth medium could support any mutant that couldn't synthesize one of the supplements.

To characterize the metabolic defect in each nutritional mutant, Beadle and Tatum took samples from the mutant growing on complete medium and distributed them to a number of different vials. Each vial contained minimal medium plus a single additional nutrient. The particular supplement that allowed growth indicated the metabolic defect. For example, if the only supplemented vial that supported growth of the mutant was the one fortified with the amino acid arginine, the researchers could conclude that the mutant was defective in the biochemical pathway that wild-type cells use to synthesize arginine.

In fact, such arginine-requiring mutants were obtained and studied by two colleagues of Beadle and Tatum, Adrian Srb and Norman Horowitz, who wanted to investigate the biochemical pathway for arginine synthesis in *Neurospora* (**Figure 17.2**). Srb and Horowitz pinned down each mutant's defect more specifically, using additional tests to distinguish among three classes of arginine-requiring mutants. Mutants in each class required a different set of compounds along the arginine-synthesizing pathway, which has three steps. These results, and those of many similar experiments done by Beadle and Tatum, suggested that each class was blocked at a different step in this pathway because mutants in that class lacked the enzyme that catalyzes the blocked step.

Because each mutant was defective in a single gene, Beadle and Tatum saw that, taken together, the collected results provided strong support for a working hypothesis they had proposed earlier. The *one gene–one enzyme hypothesis*, as they dubbed it, states that the function of a gene is to dictate the production of a specific enzyme. Further support for this hypothesis came from experiments that identified the specific enzymes lacking in the mutants. Beadle and Tatum shared a Nobel Prize in 1958 for "their discovery that genes act by regulating definite chemical events" (in the words of the Nobel committee).

The Products of Gene Expression: A Developing Story

As researchers learned more about proteins, they made revisions to the one gene–one enzyme hypothesis. First of all, not all proteins are enzymes. Keratin, the structural protein of animal hair, and the hormone insulin are two examples of nonenzyme proteins. Because proteins that are not enzymes are nevertheless gene products, molecular biologists began to think in terms of one gene–one protein. However, many proteins are constructed from two or more different polypeptide chains, and each polypeptide is specified by its own gene. For example, hemoglobin, the oxygen-transporting protein of vertebrate red blood cells, contains two kinds of polypeptides, and thus two genes code for this protein (see Figure 5.20). Beadle and Tatum's idea was therefore restated as the *one gene–one polypeptide hypothesis*. Even this description is not entirely accurate, though. First, many eukaryotic genes can each code for a set of closely related polypeptides via a process called alternative splicing, which you will learn about later in this chapter. Second, quite a few genes code for RNA molecules that have important functions in cells

INQUIRY

Do individual genes specify the enzymes that function in a biochemical pathway?

EXPERIMENT Working with the mold *Neurospora crassa*, Adrian Srb and Norman Horowitz, then at Stanford University, used Beadle and Tatum's experimental approach to isolate mutants that required arginine in their growth medium. The researchers showed that these mutants fell into three classes, each defective in a different gene. From other considerations, they suspected that the metabolic pathway of arginine biosynthesis involved a precursor nutrient and the intermediate molecules ornithine and citrulline. Their most famous experiment, shown here, tested both the one gene–one enzyme hypothesis and their postulated arginine-synthesizing pathway. In this experiment, they grew their three classes of mutants under the four different conditions shown in the Results section below. They included minimal medium (MM) as a control because they knew that wild-type cells could grow on MM but mutant cells could not. (See test tubes on the right.)

Growth: Wild-type cells growing and dividing — No growth: Mutant cells cannot grow and divide — Minimal medium

RESULTS The wild-type strain was capable of growth under all experimental conditions, requiring only the minimal medium. The three classes of mutants each had a specific set of growth requirements. For example, class II mutants could not grow when ornithine alone was added but could grow when either citrulline or arginine was added.

Classes of *Neurospora crassa*

Condition	Wild type	Class I mutants	Class II mutants	Class III mutants
Minimal medium (MM) (control)				
MM + ornithine				
MM + citrulline				
MM + arginine (control)				
Summary of results	Can grow with or without any supplements	Can grow on ornithine, citrulline, or arginine	Can grow only on citrulline or arginine	Require arginine to grow

CONCLUSION From the growth requirements of the mutants, Srb and Horowitz deduced that each class of mutant was unable to carry out one step in the pathway for synthesizing arginine, presumably because it lacked the necessary enzyme. Because each of their mutants was mutated in a single gene, they concluded that each mutated gene must normally dictate the production of one enzyme. Their results supported the one gene–one enzyme hypothesis proposed by Beadle and Tatum and also confirmed that the arginine pathway described in the mammalian liver also operates in *Neurospora*. (Notice in the Results that a mutant can grow only if supplied with a compound made *after* the defective step because this bypasses the defect.)

Gene (codes for enzyme)	Wild type	Class I mutants (mutation in gene *A*)	Class II mutants (mutation in gene *B*)	Class III mutants (mutation in gene *C*)
Gene *A* →	Precursor → Enzyme A	Precursor ✗ Enzyme A	Precursor → Enzyme A	Precursor → Enzyme A
Gene *B* →	Ornithine → Enzyme B	Ornithine → Enzyme B	Ornithine ✗ Enzyme B	Ornithine → Enzyme B
Gene *C* →	Citrulline → Enzyme C	Citrulline → Enzyme C	Citrulline → Enzyme C	Citrulline ✗ Enzyme C
	Arginine	Arginine	Arginine	Arginine

SOURCE A. M. Srb and N. H. Horowitz, The ornithine cycle in *Neurospora* and its genetic control, *Journal of Biological Chemistry* 154:129–139 (1944).

WHAT IF? Suppose the experiment had shown that class I mutants could grow only in MM supplemented by ornithine or arginine and that class II mutants could grow in MM supplemented by citrulline, ornithine, or arginine. What conclusions would the researchers have drawn from those results regarding the biochemical pathway and the defect in class I and class II mutants?

even though they are never translated into protein. For now, we will focus on genes that do code for polypeptides. (Note that it is common to refer to these gene products as proteins—a practice you will encounter in this book—rather than more precisely as polypeptides.)

Basic Principles of Transcription and Translation

Genes provide the instructions for making specific proteins. But a gene does not build a protein directly. The bridge between DNA and protein synthesis is the nucleic acid RNA. You learned in Chapter 5 that RNA is chemically similar to DNA except that it contains ribose instead of deoxyribose as its sugar and has the nitrogenous base uracil rather than thymine (see Figure 5.26). Thus, each nucleotide along a DNA strand has A, G, C, or T as its base, and each nucleotide along an RNA strand has A, G, C, or U as its base. An RNA molecule usually consists of a single strand.

It is customary to describe the flow of information from gene to protein in linguistic terms because both nucleic acids and proteins are polymers with specific sequences of monomers that convey information, much as specific sequences of letters communicate information in a language like English. In DNA or RNA, the monomers are the four types of nucleotides, which differ in their nitrogenous bases. Genes are typically hundreds or thousands of nucleotides long, each gene having a specific sequence of nucleotides. Each polypeptide of a protein also has monomers arranged in a particular linear order (the protein's primary structure), but its monomers are amino acids. Thus, nucleic acids and proteins contain information written in two different chemical languages. Getting from DNA to protein requires two major stages: transcription and translation.

Transcription is the synthesis of RNA using information in the DNA. The two nucleic acids are written in different forms of the same language, and the information is simply transcribed, or "rewritten," from DNA to RNA. Just as a DNA strand provides a template for making a new complementary strand during DNA replication, it also can serve as a template for assembling a complementary sequence of RNA nucleotides. For a protein-coding gene, the resulting RNA molecule is a faithful transcript of the gene's protein-building instructions. This type of RNA molecule is called **messenger RNA (mRNA)** because it carries a genetic message from the DNA to the protein-synthesizing machinery of the cell. (Transcription is the general term for the synthesis of *any* kind of RNA on a DNA template. Later, you will learn about some other types of RNA produced by transcription.)

Translation is the synthesis of a polypeptide using the information in the mRNA. During this stage, there is a change in language: The cell must translate the nucleotide sequence of an mRNA molecule into the amino acid sequence of a polypeptide. The sites of translation are **ribosomes**, complex particles that facilitate the orderly linking of amino acids into polypeptide chains.

Transcription and translation occur in all organisms, both those that lack a membrane-bounded nucleus (bacteria and archaea) and those that have one (eukaryotes). Because most studies of transcription and translation have used bacteria and eukaryotic cells, these are our main focus in this chapter. Our understanding of transcription and translation in archaea lags behind, but in the last section of the chapter we will discuss a few aspects of archaeal gene expression.

The basic mechanics of transcription and translation are similar for bacteria and eukaryotes, but there is an important difference in the flow of genetic information within the cells. Because bacteria do not have nuclei, their DNA is not separated by nuclear membranes from ribosomes and the other protein-synthesizing equipment (Figure 17.3a). As you will see later, this lack of compartmentalization allows translation of an mRNA to begin while its transcription is still in progress. In a eukaryotic cell, by contrast, the nuclear envelope separates transcription from translation in space and time (Figure 17.3b). Transcription occurs in the nucleus, and mRNA is then transported to the cytoplasm, where translation occurs. But before eukaryotic RNA transcripts from protein-coding genes can leave the nucleus, they are modified in various ways to produce the final, functional mRNA. The transcription of a protein-coding eukaryotic gene results in *pre-mRNA*, and further processing yields the finished mRNA. The initial RNA transcript from any gene, including those specifying RNA that is not translated into protein, is more generally called a **primary transcript**.

To summarize: Genes program protein synthesis via genetic messages in the form of messenger RNA. Put another way, cells are governed by a molecular chain of command with a directional flow of genetic information, shown here by arrows:

This concept was dubbed the *central dogma* by Francis Crick in 1956. How has the concept held up over time? In the 1970s, scientists were surprised to discover that some RNA molecules can act as templates for DNA synthesis, a process you'll read about in Chapter 19. However, these exceptions do not invalidate the idea that, in general, genetic information flows from DNA to RNA to protein. In the next section, we discuss how the instructions for assembling amino acids into a specific order are encoded in nucleic acids.

The Genetic Code

When biologists began to suspect that the instructions for protein synthesis were encoded in DNA, they recognized a problem: There are only four nucleotide bases to specify 20 amino acids. Thus, the genetic code cannot be a language like Chinese, where each written symbol corresponds to a word. How many nucleotides, then, correspond to an amino acid?

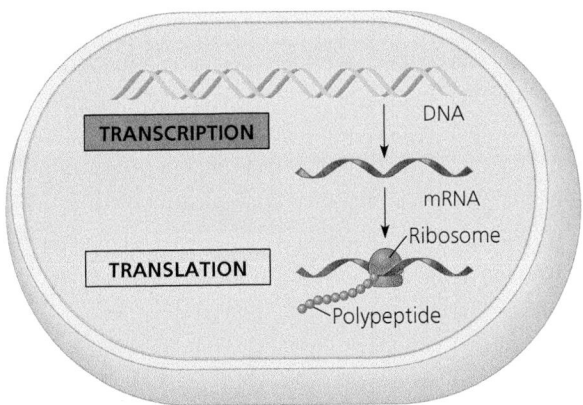

(a) Bacterial cell. In a bacterial cell, which lacks a nucleus, mRNA produced by transcription is immediately translated without additional processing.

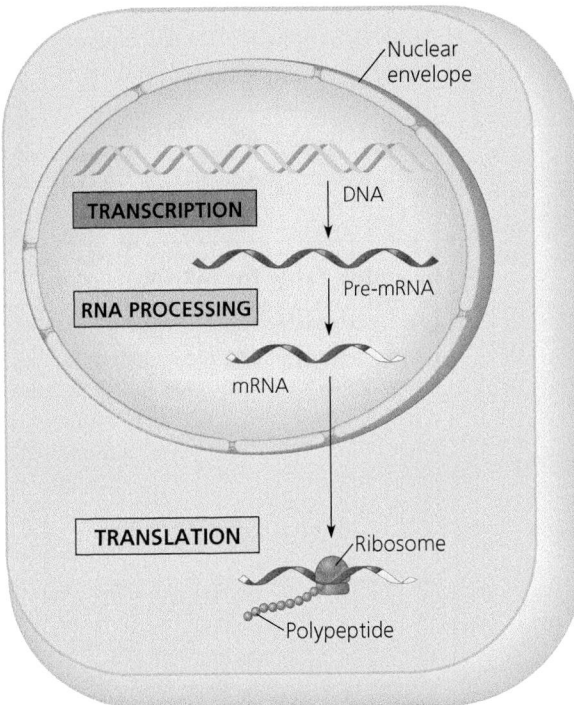

(b) Eukaryotic cell. The nucleus provides a separate compartment for transcription. The original RNA transcript, called pre-mRNA, is processed in various ways before leaving the nucleus as mRNA.

▲ **Figure 17.3 Overview: the roles of transcription and translation in the flow of genetic information.** In a cell, inherited information flows from DNA to RNA to protein. The two main stages of information flow are transcription and translation. A miniature version of part (a) or (b) accompanies several figures later in the chapter as an orientation diagram to help you see where a particular figure fits into the overall scheme.

Codons: Triplets of Nucleotides

If each kind of nucleotide base were translated into an amino acid, only 4 of the 20 amino acids could be specified. Would a language of two-letter code words suffice? The two-nucleotide sequence AG, for example, could specify one amino acid, and GT could specify another. Since there are four possible nucleotide bases in each position, this would give us 16 (that is, 4^2) possible arrangements—still not enough to code for all 20 amino acids.

Triplets of nucleotide bases are the smallest units of uniform length that can code for all the amino acids. If each arrangement of three consecutive nucleotide bases specifies an amino acid, there can be 64 (that is, 4^3) possible code words—more than enough to specify all the amino acids. Experiments have verified that the flow of information from gene to protein is based on a **triplet code**: The genetic instructions for a polypeptide chain are written in the DNA as a series of nonoverlapping, three-nucleotide words. The series of words in a gene is transcribed into a complementary series of nonoverlapping, three-nucleotide words in mRNA, which is then translated into a chain of amino acids **(Figure 17.4)**.

During transcription, the gene determines the sequence of nucleotide bases along the length of the RNA molecule that is being synthesized. For each gene, only one of the two DNA strands is transcribed. This strand is called the **template strand** because it provides the pattern, or template, for the sequence of nucleotides in an RNA transcript. For any given gene, the same strand is used as the template every time the gene is transcribed. For other genes on the same DNA molecule, however, the opposite strand may be the one that always functions as the template.

▲ **Figure 17.4 The triplet code.** For each gene, one DNA strand functions as a template for transcription of RNAs, such as mRNA. The base-pairing rules for DNA synthesis also guide transcription, except that uracil (U) takes the place of thymine (T) in RNA. During translation, the mRNA is read as a sequence of nucleotide triplets, called codons. Each codon specifies an amino acid to be added to the growing polypeptide chain. The mRNA is read in the 5′ → 3′ direction.

? *Compare the sequence of the mRNA to that of the nontemplate DNA strand, in both cases reading from 5′ → 3′.*

An mRNA molecule is complementary rather than identical to its DNA template because RNA nucleotides are assembled on the template according to base-pairing rules (see Figure 17.4). The pairs are similar to those that form during DNA replication, except that U, the RNA substitute for T, pairs with A and the mRNA nucleotides contain ribose instead of deoxyribose. Like a new strand of DNA, the RNA molecule is synthesized in an antiparallel direction to the template strand of DNA. (To review what is meant by "antiparallel" and the 5' and 3' ends of a nucleic acid chain, see Figure 16.7.) In the example in Figure 17.4, the nucleotide triplet ACC along the DNA (written as 3'-ACC-5') provides a template for 5'-UGG-3' in the mRNA molecule. The mRNA nucleotide triplets are called **codons**, and they are customarily written in the 5' → 3' direction. In our example, UGG is the codon for the amino acid tryptophan (abbreviated Trp). The term *codon* is also used for the DNA nucleotide triplets along the *nontemplate* strand. These codons are complementary to the template strand and thus identical in sequence to the mRNA, except that they have T instead of U. (For this reason, the nontemplate DNA strand is sometimes called the "coding strand.")

During translation, the sequence of codons along an mRNA molecule is decoded, or translated, into a sequence of amino acids making up a polypeptide chain. The codons are read by the translation machinery in the 5' → 3' direction along the mRNA. Each codon specifies which one of the 20 amino acids will be incorporated at the corresponding position along a polypeptide. Because codons are nucleotide triplets, the number of nucleotides making up a genetic message must be three times the number of amino acids in the protein product. For example, it takes 300 nucleotides along an mRNA strand to code for the amino acids in a polypeptide that is 100 amino acids long.

Cracking the Code

Molecular biologists cracked the genetic code of life in the early 1960s when a series of elegant experiments disclosed the amino acid translations of each of the RNA codons. The first codon was deciphered in 1961 by Marshall Nirenberg, of the National Institutes of Health, and his colleagues. Nirenberg synthesized an artificial mRNA by linking identical RNA nucleotides containing uracil as their base. No matter where this message started or stopped, it could contain only one codon in repetition: UUU. Nirenberg added this "poly-U" to a test-tube mixture containing amino acids, ribosomes, and the other components required for protein synthesis. His artificial system translated the poly-U into a polypeptide containing many units of the amino acid phenylalanine (Phe), strung together as a long polyphenylalanine chain. Thus, Nirenberg determined that the mRNA codon UUU specifies the amino acid phenylalanine. Soon, the amino acids specified by the codons AAA, GGG, and CCC were also determined.

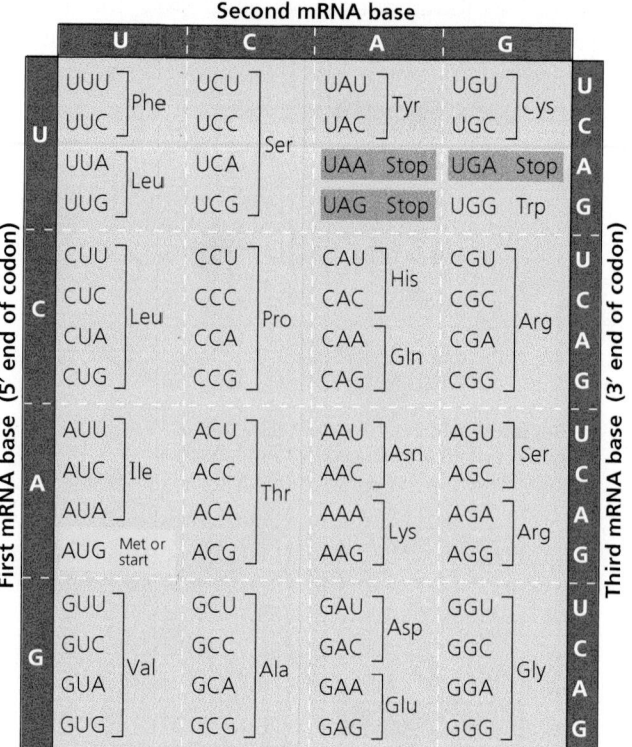

▲ **Figure 17.5 The codon table for mRNA.** The three nucleotide bases of an mRNA codon are designated here as the first, second, and third bases, reading in the 5' → 3' direction along the mRNA. (Practice using this table by finding the codons in Figure 17.4.) The codon AUG not only stands for the amino acid methionine (Met) but also functions as a "start" signal for ribosomes to begin translating the mRNA at that point. Three of the 64 codons function as "stop" signals, marking where ribosomes end translation. See Figure 5.16 for a list of the full names of all the amino acids.

Although more elaborate techniques were required to decode mixed triplets such as AUA and CGA, all 64 codons were deciphered by the mid-1960s. As **Figure 17.5** shows, 61 of the 64 triplets code for amino acids. The three codons that do not designate amino acids are "stop" signals, or termination codons, marking the end of translation. Notice that the codon AUG has a dual function: It codes for the amino acid methionine (Met) and also functions as a "start" signal, or initiation codon. Genetic messages usually begin with the mRNA codon AUG, which signals the protein-synthesizing machinery to begin translating the mRNA at that location. (Because AUG also stands for methionine, polypeptide chains begin with methionine when they are synthesized. However, an enzyme may subsequently remove this starter amino acid from the chain.)

Notice in Figure 17.5 that there is redundancy in the genetic code, but no ambiguity. For example, although codons GAA and GAG both specify glutamic acid (redundancy), neither of them ever specifies any other amino acid (no ambiguity). The redundancy in the code is not altogether random. In many cases, codons that are synonyms for a particular amino acid differ only in the third nucleotide base of the triplet. We will consider a possible benefit of this redundancy later in the chapter.

Our ability to extract the intended message from a written language depends on reading the symbols in the correct groupings—that is, in the correct **reading frame**. Consider this statement: "The red dog ate the bug." Group the letters incorrectly by starting at the wrong point, and the result will probably be gibberish: for example, "her edd oga tet heb ug." The reading frame is also important in the molecular language of cells. The short stretch of polypeptide shown in Figure 17.4, for instance, will be made correctly only if the mRNA nucleotides are read from left to right (5' → 3') in the groups of three shown in the figure: UGG UUU GGC UCA. Although a genetic message is written with no spaces between the codons, the cell's protein-synthesizing machinery reads the message as a series of nonoverlapping three-letter words. The message is *not* read as a series of overlapping words—UGGUUU, and so on—which would convey a very different message.

Evolution of the Genetic Code

EVOLUTION The genetic code is nearly universal, shared by organisms from the simplest bacteria to the most complex plants and animals. The RNA codon CCG, for instance, is translated as the amino acid proline in all organisms whose genetic code has been examined. In laboratory experiments, genes can be transcribed and translated after being transplanted from one species to another, sometimes with quite striking results, as shown in **Figure 17.6**! Bacteria can be pro-

grammed by the insertion of human genes to synthesize certain human proteins for medical use, such as insulin. Such applications have produced many exciting developments in the area of biotechnology (see Chapter 20).

Exceptions to the universality of the genetic code include translation systems in which a few codons differ from the standard ones. Slight variations in the genetic code exist in certain unicellular eukaryotes and in the organelle genes of some species. Despite these exceptions, the evolutionary significance of the code's *near* universality is clear. A language shared by all living things must have been operating very early in the history of life—early enough to be present in the common ancestor of all present-day organisms. A shared genetic vocabulary is a reminder of the kinship that bonds all life on Earth.

CONCEPT CHECK 17.1

1. **MAKE CONNECTIONS** In a research article about alkaptonuria published in 1902, Garrod suggested that humans inherit two "characters" (alleles) for a particular enzyme and that both parents must contribute a faulty version for the offspring to have the disorder. Today, would this disorder be called dominant or recessive? See Concept 14.4, pages 276–278.
2. What polypeptide product would you expect from a poly-G mRNA that is 30 nucleotides long?
3. **DRAW IT** The template strand of a gene contains the sequence 3'-TTCAGTCGT-5'. Draw the nontemplate sequence and the mRNA sequence, indicating 5' and 3' ends of each. Compare the two sequences.
4. **WHAT IF?** **DRAW IT** Imagine that the nontemplate sequence in question 3 was transcribed instead of the template sequence. Draw the mRNA sequence and translate it using Figure 17.5. (Be sure to pay attention to the 5' and 3' ends.) Predict how well the protein synthesized from the nontemplate strand would function, if at all.

For suggested answers, see Appendix A.

CONCEPT 17.2

Transcription is the DNA-directed synthesis of RNA: *a closer look*

Now that we have considered the linguistic logic and evolutionary significance of the genetic code, we are ready to re-examine transcription, the first stage of gene expression, in more detail.

Molecular Components of Transcription

Messenger RNA, the carrier of information from DNA to the cell's protein-synthesizing machinery, is transcribed from the template strand of a gene. An enzyme called an **RNA polymerase** pries the two strands of DNA apart and joins

 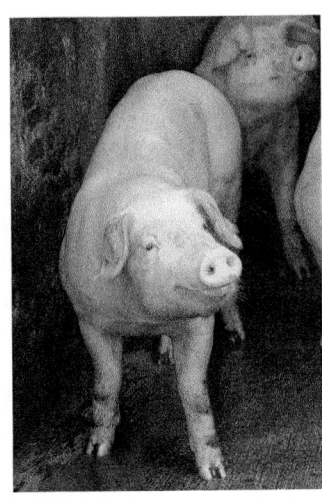

(a) Tobacco plant expressing a firefly gene. The yellow glow is produced by a chemical reaction catalyzed by the protein product of the firefly gene.

(b) Pig expressing a jellyfish gene. Researchers injected the gene for a fluorescent protein into fertilized pig eggs. One of the eggs developed into this fluorescent pig.

▲ **Figure 17.6 Expression of genes from different species.** Because diverse forms of life share a common genetic code, one species can be programmed to produce proteins characteristic of a second species by introducing DNA from the second species into the first.

together RNA nucleotides complementary to the DNA template strand, thus elongating the RNA polynucleotide (Figure 17.7). Like the DNA polymerases that function in DNA replication, RNA polymerases can assemble a polynucleotide only in its 5′ → 3′ direction. Unlike DNA polymerases, however, RNA polymerases are able to start a chain from scratch; they don't need a primer.

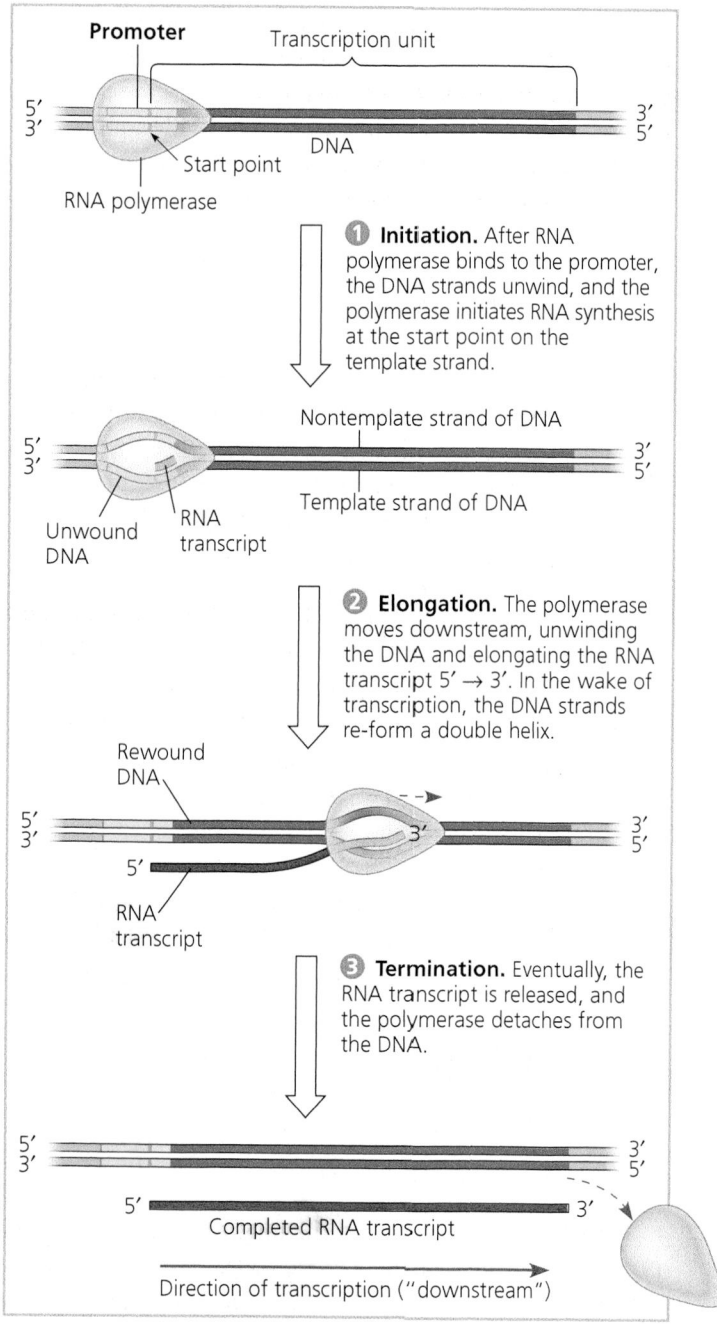

Promoter
Transcription unit

5′
3′

DNA

Start point

RNA polymerase

1 Initiation. After RNA polymerase binds to the promoter, the DNA strands unwind, and the polymerase initiates RNA synthesis at the start point on the template strand.

Nontemplate strand of DNA

5′
3′

3′
5′

Unwound DNA

RNA transcript

Template strand of DNA

2 Elongation. The polymerase moves downstream, unwinding the DNA and elongating the RNA transcript 5′ → 3′. In the wake of transcription, the DNA strands re-form a double helix.

Rewound DNA

5′
3′

3′
5′

3′

5′

RNA transcript

3 Termination. Eventually, the RNA transcript is released, and the polymerase detaches from the DNA.

5′
3′

3′
5′

5′

3′

Completed RNA transcript

Direction of transcription ("downstream")

▲ **Figure 17.7 The stages of transcription: initiation, elongation, and termination.** This general depiction of transcription applies to both bacteria and eukaryotes, but the details of termination differ, as described in the text. Also, in a bacterium, the RNA transcript is immediately usable as mRNA; in a eukaryote, the RNA transcript must first undergo processing.

MAKE CONNECTIONS *Compare the use of a template strand during transcription and replication. See Figure 16.17, page 317.*

Specific sequences of nucleotides along the DNA mark where transcription of a gene begins and ends. The DNA sequence where RNA polymerase attaches and initiates transcription is known as the **promoter**; in bacteria, the sequence that signals the end of transcription is called the **terminator**. (The termination mechanism is different in eukaryotes; we'll describe it later.) Molecular biologists refer to the direction of transcription as "downstream" and the other direction as "upstream." These terms are also used to describe the positions of nucleotide sequences within the DNA or RNA. Thus, the promoter sequence in DNA is said to be upstream from the terminator. The stretch of DNA that is transcribed into an RNA molecule is called a **transcription unit**.

Bacteria have a single type of RNA polymerase that synthesizes not only mRNA but also other types of RNA that function in protein synthesis, such as ribosomal RNA. In contrast, eukaryotes have at least three types of RNA polymerase in their nuclei. The one used for mRNA synthesis is called RNA polymerase II. The other RNA polymerases transcribe RNA molecules that are not translated into protein. In the discussion of transcription that follows, we start with the features of mRNA synthesis common to both bacteria and eukaryotes and then describe some key differences.

Synthesis of an RNA Transcript

The three stages of transcription, as shown in Figure 17.7 and described next, are initiation, elongation, and termination of the RNA chain. Study Figure 17.7 to familiarize yourself with the stages and the terms used to describe them.

RNA Polymerase Binding and Initiation of Transcription

The promoter of a gene includes within it the transcription **start point** (the nucleotide where RNA synthesis actually begins) and typically extends several dozen or more nucleotide pairs upstream from the start point. RNA polymerase binds in a precise location and orientation on the promoter, therefore determining where transcription starts and which of the two strands of the DNA helix is used as the template.

Certain sections of a promoter are especially important for binding RNA polymerase. In bacteria, the RNA polymerase itself specifically recognizes and binds to the promoter. In eukaryotes, a collection of proteins called **transcription factors** mediate the binding of RNA polymerase and the initiation of transcription. Only after transcription factors are attached to the promoter does RNA polymerase II bind to it. The whole complex of transcription factors and RNA polymerase II bound to the promoter is called a **transcription initiation complex**. Figure 17.8 shows the role of transcription factors and a crucial promoter DNA sequence called a **TATA box** in forming the initiation complex at a eukaryotic promoter.

The interaction between eukaryotic RNA polymerase II and transcription factors is an example of the importance of protein-protein interactions in controlling eukaryotic

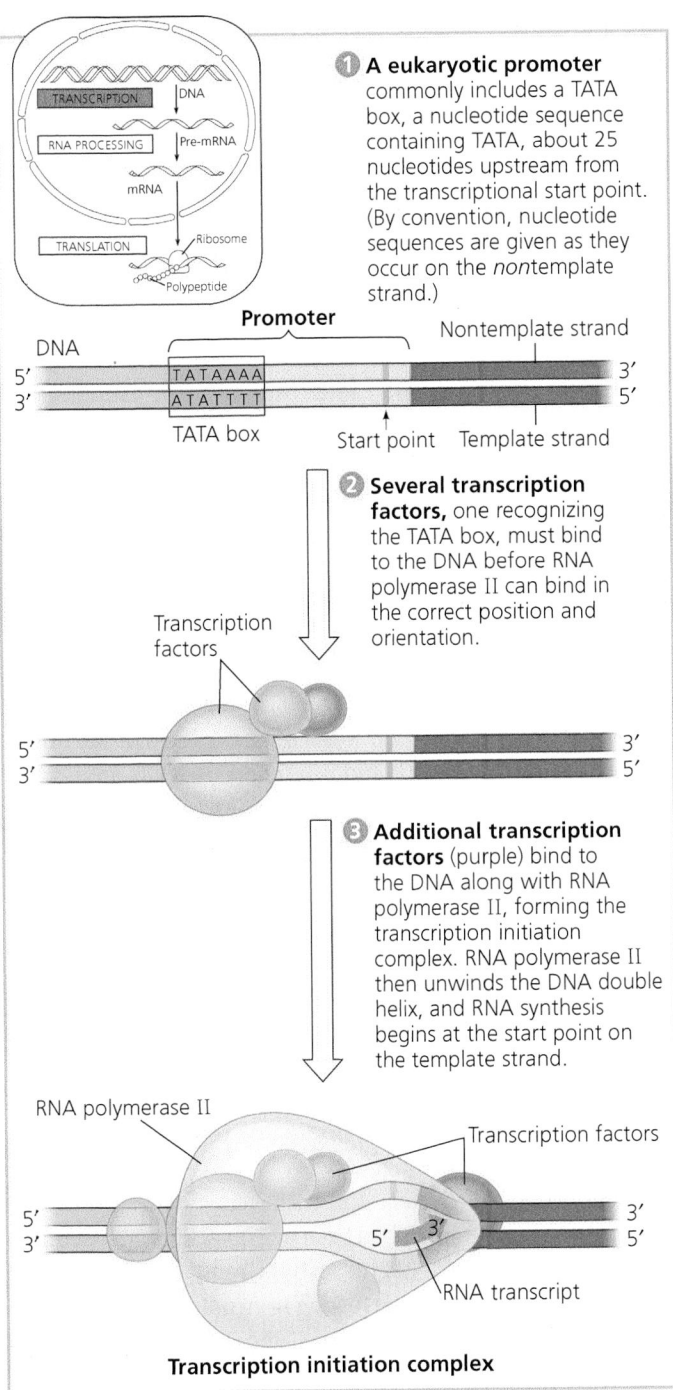

① A eukaryotic promoter commonly includes a TATA box, a nucleotide sequence containing TATA, about 25 nucleotides upstream from the transcriptional start point. (By convention, nucleotide sequences are given as they occur on the *non*template strand.)

② Several transcription factors, one recognizing the TATA box, must bind to the DNA before RNA polymerase II can bind in the correct position and orientation.

③ Additional transcription factors (purple) bind to the DNA along with RNA polymerase II, forming the transcription initiation complex. RNA polymerase II then unwinds the DNA double helix, and RNA synthesis begins at the start point on the template strand.

▲ **Figure 17.8 The initiation of transcription at a eukaryotic promoter.** In eukaryotic cells, proteins called transcription factors mediate the initiation of transcription by RNA polymerase II.

? *Explain how the interaction of RNA polymerase with the promoter would differ if the figure showed transcription initiation for bacteria.*

transcription. (And as you learned in Figure 16.22, the DNA of a eukaryotic chromosome is complexed with histones and other proteins in the form of chromatin. The roles of these proteins in making the DNA accessible to transcription factors will be discussed in Chapter 18). Once the appropriate transcription factors are firmly attached to the promoter DNA and the polymerase is bound in the correct orientation,

the enzyme unwinds the two DNA strands and starts transcribing the template strand.

Elongation of the RNA Strand

As RNA polymerase moves along the DNA, it continues to untwist the double helix, exposing about 10–20 DNA nucleotides at a time for pairing with RNA nucleotides **(Figure 17.9)**. The enzyme adds nucleotides to the 3′ end of the growing RNA molecule as it continues along the double helix. In the wake of this advancing wave of RNA synthesis, the new RNA molecule peels away from its DNA template, and the DNA double helix re-forms. Transcription progresses at a rate of about 40 nucleotides per second in eukaryotes.

A single gene can be transcribed simultaneously by several molecules of RNA polymerase following each other like trucks in a convoy. A growing strand of RNA trails off from each polymerase, with the length of each new strand reflecting how far along the template the enzyme has traveled from the start point (see the mRNA molecules in Figure 17.25). The congregation of many polymerase molecules simultaneously transcribing a single gene increases the amount of mRNA transcribed from it, which helps the cell make the encoded protein in large amounts.

Termination of Transcription

The mechanism of termination differs between bacteria and eukaryotes. In bacteria, transcription proceeds through a terminator sequence in the DNA. The transcribed terminator (an RNA sequence) functions as the termination signal,

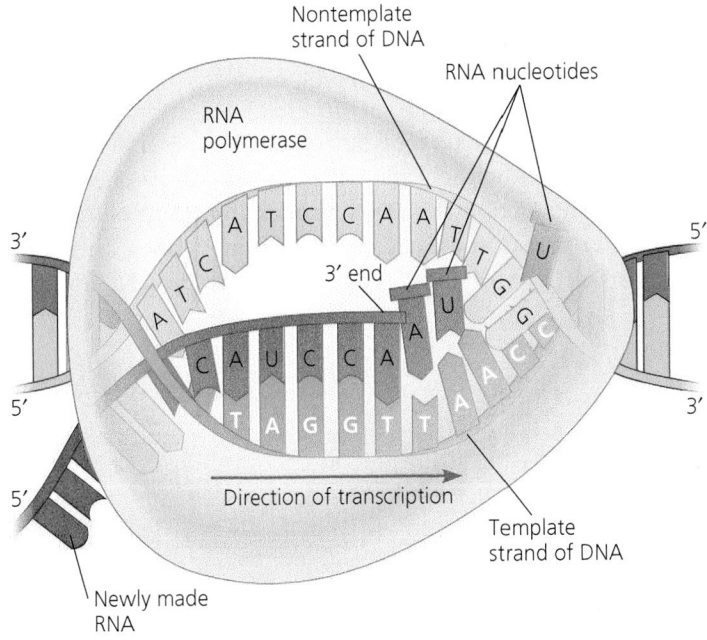

▲ **Figure 17.9 Transcription elongation.** RNA polymerase moves along the DNA template strand, joining complementary RNA nucleotides to the 3′ end of the growing RNA transcript. Behind the polymerase, the new RNA peels away from the template strand, which re-forms a double helix with the nontemplate strand.

causing the polymerase to detach from the DNA and release the transcript, which requires no further modification before translation. In eukaryotes, RNA polymerase II transcribes a sequence on the DNA called the polyadenylation signal sequence, which codes for a polyadenylation signal (AAUAAA) in the pre-mRNA. Then, at a point about 10–35 nucleotides downstream from the AAUAAA signal, proteins associated with the growing RNA transcript cut it free from the polymerase, releasing the pre-mRNA. The pre-mRNA then undergoes processing, the topic of the next section.

CONCEPT CHECK 17.2

1. **MAKE CONNECTIONS** Compare DNA polymerase and RNA polymerase in terms of how they function, the requirement for a template and primer, the direction of synthesis, and the type of nucleotides used. See Figure 16.17, page 317.
2. What is a promoter, and is it located at the upstream or downstream end of a transcription unit?
3. What enables RNA polymerase to start transcribing a gene at the right place on the DNA in a bacterial cell? In a eukaryotic cell?
4. **WHAT IF?** Suppose X-rays caused a sequence change in the TATA box of a particular gene's promoter. How would that affect transcription of the gene? (See Figure 17.8.)

For suggested answers, see Appendix A.

CONCEPT 17.3

Eukaryotic cells modify RNA after transcription

Enzymes in the eukaryotic nucleus modify pre-mRNA in specific ways before the genetic messages are dispatched to the cytoplasm. During this **RNA processing**, both ends of the primary transcript are altered. Also, in most cases, certain interior sections of the RNA molecule are cut out and the remaining parts spliced together. These modifications produce an mRNA molecule ready for translation.

Alteration of mRNA Ends

Each end of a pre-mRNA molecule is modified in a particular way (**Figure 17.10**). The 5′ end is synthesized first; it receives a **5′ cap**, a modified form of a guanine (G) nucleotide added onto the 5′ end after transcription of the first 20–40 nucleotides. The 3′ end of the pre-mRNA molecule is also modified before the mRNA exits the nucleus. Recall that the pre-mRNA is released soon after the polyadenylation signal, AAUAAA, is transcribed. At the 3′ end, an enzyme adds 50–250 more adenine (A) nucleotides, forming a **poly-A tail**. The 5′ cap and poly-A tail share several important functions. First, they seem to facilitate the export of the mature mRNA from the nucleus. Second, they help protect the mRNA from degradation by hydrolytic enzymes. And third, they help ribosomes attach to the 5′ end of the mRNA once the mRNA reaches the cytoplasm. Figure 17.10 shows a diagram of a eukaryotic mRNA molecule with cap and tail. The figure also shows the untranslated regions (UTRs) at the 5′ and 3′ ends of the mRNA (referred to as the 5′ UTR and 3′ UTR). The UTRs are parts of the mRNA that will not be translated into protein, but they have other functions, such as ribosome binding.

Split Genes and RNA Splicing

A remarkable stage of RNA processing in the eukaryotic nucleus is the removal of large portions of the RNA molecule that is initially synthesized—a cut-and-paste job called **RNA splicing**, similar to editing a video (**Figure 17.11**). The average length of a transcription unit along a human DNA molecule is about 27,000 nucleotide pairs, so the primary RNA transcript is also that long. However, it takes only 1,200 nucleotides in RNA to code for the average-sized protein of 400 amino acids. (Remember, each amino acid is encoded by a *triplet* of nucleotides.) This means that most eukaryotic genes and their RNA transcripts have long noncoding stretches of nucleotides, regions that are not translated. Even more surprising

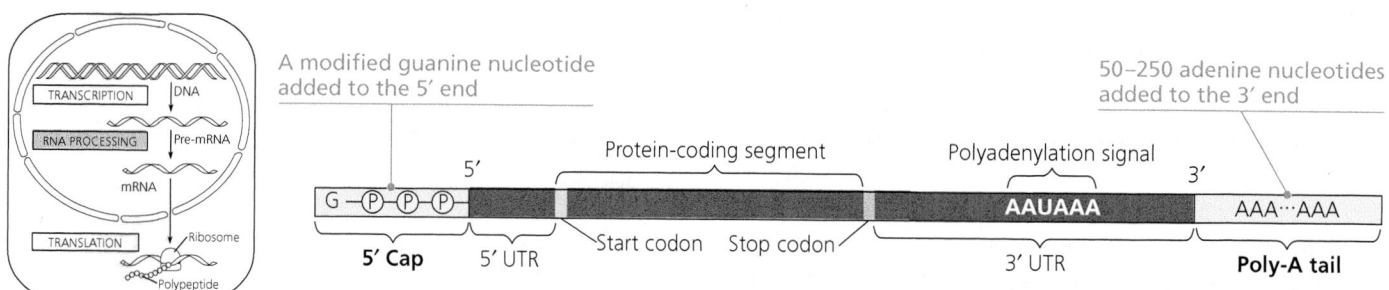

▲ **Figure 17.10 RNA processing: Addition of the 5′ cap and poly-A tail.** Enzymes modify the two ends of a eukaryotic pre-mRNA molecule. The modified ends may promote the export of mRNA from the nucleus, and they help protect the mRNA from degradation. When the mRNA reaches the cytoplasm, the modified ends, in conjunction with certain cytoplasmic proteins, facilitate ribosome attachment. The 5′ cap and poly-A tail are not translated into protein, nor are the regions called the 5′ untranslated region (5′ UTR) and 3′ untranslated region (3′ UTR).

Pre-mRNA
Codon numbers

5' Exon Intron Exon Intron Exon 3'

1–30 31–104 105–146

Introns cut out and exons spliced together

mRNA

5' Cap 1–146 Poly-A tail

5' UTR Coding segment 3' UTR

▲ **Figure 17.11 RNA processing: RNA splicing.** The RNA molecule shown here codes for β-globin, one of the polypeptides of hemoglobin. The numbers under the RNA refer to codons; β-globin is 146 amino acids long.

The β-globin gene and its pre-mRNA transcript have three exons, corresponding to sequences that will leave the nucleus as mRNA. (The 5' UTR and 3' UTR are parts of exons because they are included in the mRNA; however, they do not code for protein.) During RNA processing, the introns are cut out and the exons spliced together. In many genes, the introns are much larger than the exons.

is that most of these noncoding sequences are interspersed between coding segments of the gene and thus between coding segments of the pre-mRNA. In other words, the sequence of DNA nucleotides that codes for a eukaryotic polypeptide is usually not continuous; it is split into segments. The noncoding segments of nucleic acid that lie between coding regions are called *intervening sequences, or* **introns**. The other regions are called **exons**, because they are eventually *expressed*, usually by being translated into amino acid sequences. (Exceptions include the UTRs of the exons at the ends of the RNA, which make up part of the mRNA but are not translated into protein. Because of these exceptions, you may find it helpful to think of exons as sequences of RNA that *exit* the nucleus.) The terms *intron* and *exon* are used for both RNA sequences and the DNA sequences that encode them.

In making a primary transcript from a gene, RNA polymerase II transcribes both introns and exons from the DNA, but the mRNA molecule that enters the cytoplasm is an abridged version. The introns are cut out from the molecule and the exons joined together, forming an mRNA molecule with a continuous coding sequence. This is the process of RNA splicing.

How is pre-mRNA splicing carried out? Researchers have learned that the signal for RNA splicing is a short nucleotide sequence at each end of an intron. Joan Steitz, our interviewee for this unit (see pp. 246–247), discovered in 1979 that particles called *small nuclear ribonucleoproteins,* abbreviated *snRNPs* (pronounced "snurps"), recognize these splice sites. As the full name implies, snRNPs are located in the cell nucleus and are composed of RNA and protein molecules. The RNA in a snRNP particle is called a *small nuclear RNA (snRNA);* each snRNA molecule is about 150 nucleotides long. Several different snRNPs join with additional proteins to form an even larger assembly called a **spliceosome**, which is almost as big as a ribosome. The spliceosome interacts with certain sites along an intron, releasing the intron, which is rapidly degraded, and joining together the two exons that flanked the intron **(Figure 17.12)**. It turns out that snRNAs catalyze these processes, as well as participating in spliceosome assembly and splice site recognition.

▲ **Figure 17.12 The roles of snRNPs and spliceosomes in pre-mRNA splicing.** The diagram shows only a portion of the pre-mRNA transcript; additional introns and exons lie downstream from the ones pictured here. ❶ Small nuclear ribonucleoproteins (snRNPs) and other proteins form a molecular complex called a spliceosome on a pre-mRNA molecule containing exons and introns. ❷ Within the spliceosome, snRNA base-pairs with nucleotides at specific sites along the intron. ❸ The spliceosome cuts the pre-mRNA, releasing the intron for rapid degradation, and at the same time splices the exons together. The spliceosome then comes apart, releasing mRNA, which now contains only exons.

Ribozymes

The idea of a catalytic role for snRNA arose from the discovery of **ribozymes**, RNA molecules that function as enzymes. In some organisms, RNA splicing can occur without proteins or even additional RNA molecules: The intron RNA functions as a ribozyme and catalyzes its own excision! For example, in the ciliate protist *Tetrahymena*, self-splicing occurs in the production of ribosomal RNA (rRNA), a component of the organism's ribosomes. The pre-rRNA actually removes its own introns. The discovery of ribozymes rendered obsolete the idea that all biological catalysts are proteins.

Three properties of RNA enable some RNA molecules to function as enzymes. First, because RNA is single-stranded, a region of an RNA molecule may base-pair with a complementary region elsewhere in the same molecule, which gives the molecule a particular three-dimensional structure. A specific structure is essential to the catalytic function of ribozymes, just as it is for enzymatic proteins. Second, like certain amino acids in an enzymatic protein, some of the bases in RNA contain functional groups that may participate in catalysis. Third, the ability of RNA to hydrogen-bond with other nucleic acid molecules (either RNA or DNA) adds specificity to its catalytic activity. For example, complementary base pairing between the RNA of the spliceosome and the RNA of a primary RNA transcript precisely locates the region where the ribozyme catalyzes splicing. Later in this chapter, you will see how these properties of RNA also allow it to perform important noncatalytic roles in the cell, such as recognition of the three-nucleotide codons on mRNA.

The Functional and Evolutionary Importance of Introns

EVOLUTION Whether or not RNA splicing and the presence of introns have provided selective advantages during evolutionary history is a matter of some debate. In any case, it is informative to consider their possible adaptive benefits. Specific functions have not been identified for most introns, but at least some contain sequences that regulate gene expression, and many affect gene products.

One important consequence of the presence of introns in genes is that a single gene can encode more than one kind of polypeptide. Many genes are known to give rise to two or more different polypeptides, depending on which segments are treated as exons during RNA processing; this is called **alternative RNA splicing** (see Figure 18.13). For example, sex differences in fruit flies are largely due to differences in how males and females splice the RNA transcribed from certain genes. Results from the Human Genome Project (discussed in Chapter 21) suggest that alternative RNA splicing is one reason humans can get along with about the same number of genes as a nematode (roundworm). Because of alternative splicing, the number of different protein products an organism produces can be much greater than its number of genes.

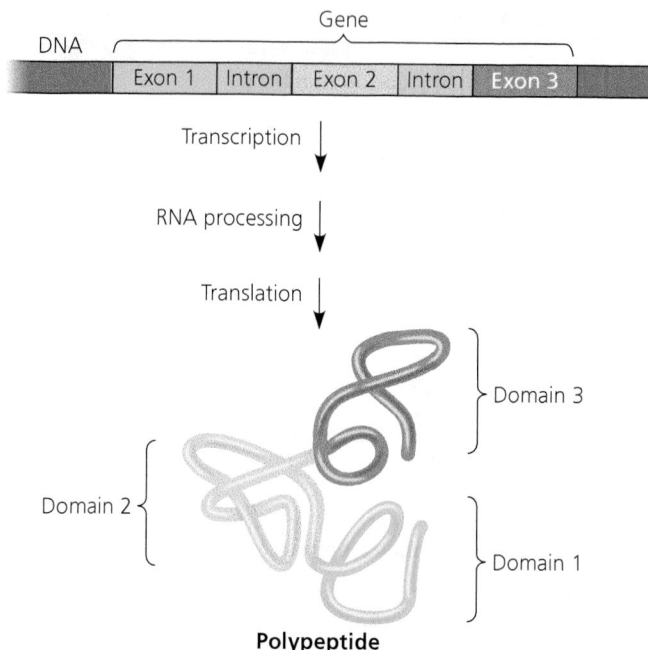

▲ Figure 17.13 **Correspondence between exons and protein domains.**

Proteins often have a modular architecture consisting of discrete structural and functional regions called **domains**. One domain of an enzyme, for example, might include the active site, while another might allow the enzyme to bind to a cellular membrane. In quite a few cases, different exons code for the different domains of a protein (Figure 17.13).

The presence of introns in a gene may facilitate the evolution of new and potentially beneficial proteins as a result of a process known as *exon shuffling*. Introns increase the probability of crossing over between the exons of alleles of a gene—simply by providing more terrain for crossovers without interrupting coding sequences. This might result in new combinations of exons and proteins with altered structure and function. We can also imagine the occasional mixing and matching of exons between completely different (nonallelic) genes. Exon shuffling of either sort could lead to new proteins with novel combinations of functions. While most of the shuffling would result in nonbeneficial changes, occasionally a beneficial variant might arise.

CONCEPT CHECK 17.3

1. How can human cells make 75,000–100,000 different proteins, given that there are about 20,000 human genes?
2. How is RNA splicing similar to editing a video? What would introns correspond to in this analogy?
3. **WHAT IF?** What would be the effect of treating cells with an agent that removed the cap from mRNAs?

For suggested answers, see Appendix A.

CONCEPT 17.4

Translation is the RNA-directed synthesis of a polypeptide: *a closer look*

We will now examine in greater detail how genetic information flows from mRNA to protein—the process of translation. As we did for transcription, we'll concentrate on the basic steps of translation that occur in both bacteria and eukaryotes, while pointing out key differences.

Molecular Components of Translation

In the process of translation, a cell "reads" a genetic message and builds a polypeptide accordingly. The message is a series of codons along an mRNA molecule, and the translator is called **transfer RNA (tRNA)**. The function of tRNA is to transfer amino acids from the cytoplasmic pool of amino acids to a growing polypeptide in a ribosome. A cell keeps its cytoplasm stocked with all 20 amino acids, either by synthesizing them from other compounds or by taking them up from the surrounding solution. The ribosome, a structure made of proteins and RNAs, adds each amino acid brought to it by tRNA to the growing end of a polypeptide chain **(Figure 17.14)**.

Translation is simple in principle but complex in its biochemistry and mechanics, especially in the eukaryotic cell. In dissecting translation, we'll concentrate on the slightly less complicated version of the process that occurs in bacteria. We'll begin by looking at the major players in this cellular process and then see how they act together in making a polypeptide.

The Structure and Function of Transfer RNA

The key to translating a genetic message into a specific amino acid sequence is the fact that molecules of tRNA are not all identical, and each type of tRNA molecule translates a particular mRNA codon into a particular amino acid. A tRNA molecule arrives at a ribosome bearing a specific amino acid at one end. At the other end of the tRNA is a nucleotide triplet called an **anticodon**, which base-pairs with a complementary codon on mRNA. For example, consider the mRNA codon GGC, which is translated as the amino acid glycine. The tRNA that base-pairs with this codon by hydrogen bonding has CCG as its anticodon and carries glycine at its other end (see the incoming tRNA approaching the ribosome in Figure 17.14). As an mRNA molecule is moved through a ribosome, glycine will be added to the polypeptide chain whenever the codon GGC is presented for translation. Codon by codon, the genetic message is translated as tRNAs deposit amino acids in the order prescribed, and the ribosome joins the amino acids into a chain. The tRNA molecule is a translator in the sense that it

▲ **Figure 17.14 Translation: the basic concept.** As a molecule of mRNA is moved through a ribosome, codons are translated into amino acids, one by one. The interpreters are tRNA molecules, each type with a specific anticodon at one end and a corresponding amino acid at the other end. A tRNA adds its amino acid cargo to a growing polypeptide chain when the anticodon hydrogen-bonds to a complementary codon on the mRNA. The figures that follow show some of the details of translation in a bacterial cell.

ANIMATION ***BioFlix*** Visit the Study Area at **www.masteringbiology.com** for the BioFlix® 3-D Animation on Protein Synthesis.

can read a nucleic acid word (the mRNA codon) and interpret it as a protein word (the amino acid).

Like mRNA and other types of cellular RNA, transfer RNA molecules are transcribed from DNA templates. In a eukaryotic cell, tRNA, like mRNA, is made in the nucleus and then travels from the nucleus to the cytoplasm, where translation occurs. In both bacterial and eukaryotic cells, each tRNA molecule is used repeatedly, picking up its designated amino acid in the cytosol, depositing this cargo onto a polypeptide chain at the ribosome, and then leaving the ribosome, ready to pick up another amino acid.

A tRNA molecule consists of a single RNA strand that is only about 80 nucleotides long (compared to hundreds of nucleotides for most mRNA molecules). Because of the presence of complementary stretches of nucleotide bases that can hydrogen-bond to each other, this single strand can fold back upon itself

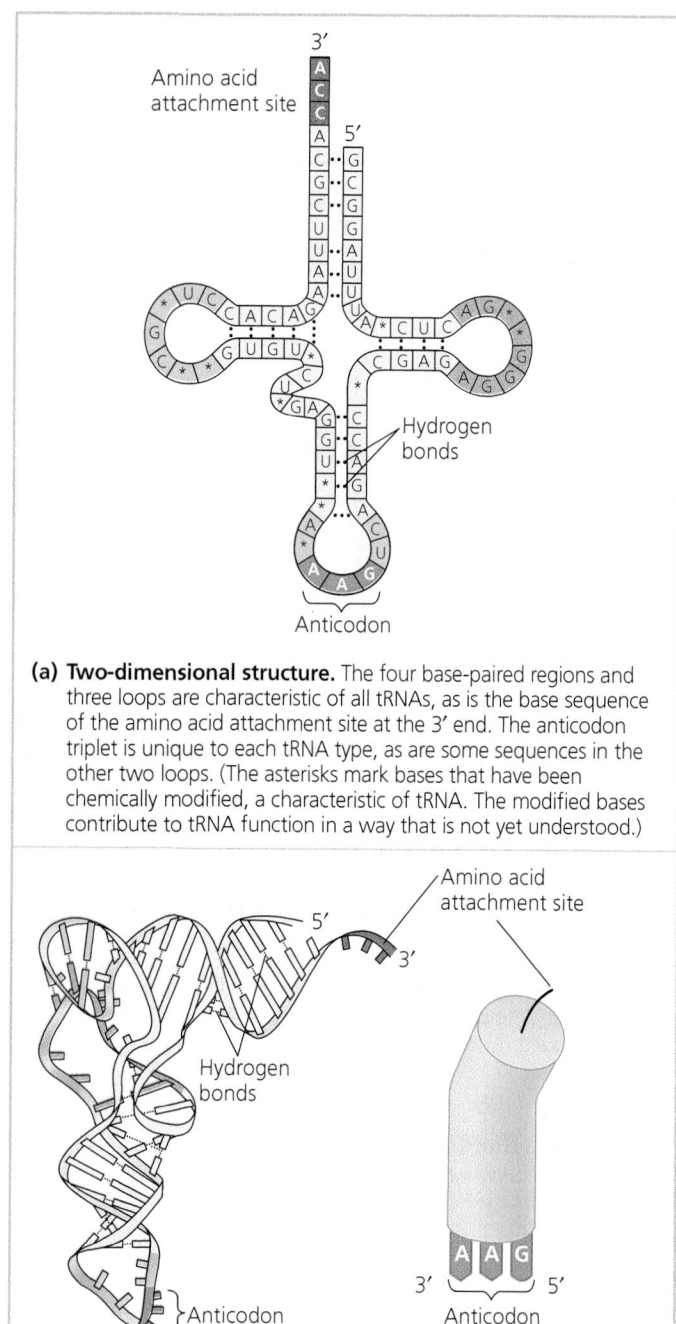

(a) Two-dimensional structure. The four base-paired regions and three loops are characteristic of all tRNAs, as is the base sequence of the amino acid attachment site at the 3' end. The anticodon triplet is unique to each tRNA type, as are some sequences in the other two loops. (The asterisks mark bases that have been chemically modified, a characteristic of tRNA. The modified bases contribute to tRNA function in a way that is not yet understood.)

(b) Three-dimensional structure

(c) Symbol used in this book

▲ **Figure 17.15 The structure of transfer RNA (tRNA).** Anticodons are conventionally written 3' → 5' to align properly with codons written 5' → 3' (see Figure 17.14). For base pairing, RNA strands must be antiparallel, like DNA. For example, anticodon 3'-AAG-5' pairs with mRNA codon 5'-UUC-3'.

and form a molecule with a three-dimensional structure. Flattened into one plane to clarify this base pairing, a tRNA molecule looks like a cloverleaf (**Figure 17.15a**). The tRNA actually twists and folds into a compact three-dimensional structure that is roughly L-shaped (**Figure 17.15b**). The loop extending from one end of the L includes the anticodon, the particular nucleotide triplet that base-pairs to a specific mRNA codon.

▲ **Figure 17.16 An aminoacyl-tRNA synthetase joining a specific amino acid to a tRNA.** Linkage of the tRNA and amino acid is an endergonic process that occurs at the expense of ATP. The ATP loses two phosphate groups, becoming AMP (adenosine monophosphate).

From the other end of the L-shaped tRNA molecule protrudes its 3' end, which is the attachment site for an amino acid. Thus, the structure of a tRNA molecule fits its function.

The accurate translation of a genetic message requires two instances of molecular recognition. First, a tRNA that binds to an mRNA codon specifying a particular amino acid must carry that amino acid, and no other, to the ribosome. The correct matching up of tRNA and amino acid is carried out by a family of related enzymes called **aminoacyl-tRNA synthetases** (**Figure 17.16**). The active site of each type of aminoacyl-tRNA synthetase fits only a specific combination of amino acid and tRNA. (Regions of both the amino acid attachment end and the anticodon end of the tRNA are instrumental in ensuring the specific fit.) There are 20 different synthetases, one for each amino acid; each synthetase is able to bind all the different tRNAs that code for its particular amino acid. The synthetase catalyzes the covalent attachment of the amino acid to its tRNA in a process driven by the hydrolysis of ATP. The resulting aminoacyl tRNA, also called a charged tRNA, is released from the enzyme and is then available to deliver its amino acid to a growing polypeptide chain on a ribosome.

The second instance of molecular recognition is the pairing of the tRNA anticodon with the appropriate mRNA codon. If one tRNA variety existed for each mRNA codon specifying an amino acid, there would be 61 tRNAs (see Figure 17.5). In fact, there are only about 45, signifying that some tRNAs must be able to bind to more than one codon. Such versatility is possible because the rules for base pairing between the third nucleotide base of a codon and the corresponding base of a tRNA anticodon are relaxed compared to those at other codon positions. For example, the nucleotide base U at the 5′ end of a tRNA anticodon can pair with either A or G in the third position (at the 3′ end) of an mRNA codon. The flexible base pairing at this codon position is called **wobble**. Wobble explains why the synonymous codons for a given amino acid most often differ in their third nucleotide base, but not in the other bases. For example, a tRNA with the anticodon 3′-UCU-5′ can base-pair with either the mRNA codon 5′-AGA-3′ or 5′-AGG-3′, both of which code for arginine (see Figure 17.5).

Ribosomes

Ribosomes facilitate the specific coupling of tRNA anticodons with mRNA codons during protein synthesis. A ribosome consists of a large subunit and a small subunit, each made up of proteins and one or more **ribosomal RNAs (rRNAs)** (Figure 17.17). In eukaryotes, the subunits are made in the nucleolus. Ribosomal RNA genes are transcribed, and the RNA is processed and assembled with proteins imported from the cytoplasm. The resulting ribosomal subunits are then exported via nuclear pores to the cytoplasm. In both bacteria and eukaryotes, large and small subunits join to form a functional ribosome only when they attach to an mRNA molecule. About one-third of the mass of a ribosome is made up of proteins; the rest consists of rRNAs, either three molecules (in bacteria) or four (in eukaryotes). Because most cells contain thousands of ribosomes, rRNA is the most abundant type of cellular RNA.

Although the ribosomes of bacteria and eukaryotes are very similar in structure and function, those of eukaryotes are slightly larger and differ somewhat from bacterial ribosomes in their molecular composition. The differences are medically significant. Certain antibiotic drugs can inactivate bacterial ribosomes without inhibiting the ability of eukaryotic ribosomes to make proteins. These drugs, including tetracycline and streptomycin, are used to combat bacterial infections.

(a) **Computer model of functioning ribosome.** This is a model of a bacterial ribosome, showing its overall shape. The eukaryotic ribosome is roughly similar. A ribosomal subunit is a complex of ribosomal RNA molecules and proteins.

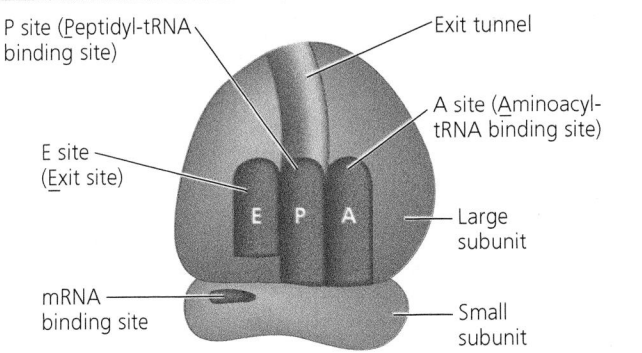

(b) **Schematic model showing binding sites.** A ribosome has an mRNA binding site and three tRNA binding sites, known as the A, P, and E sites. This schematic ribosome will appear in later diagrams.

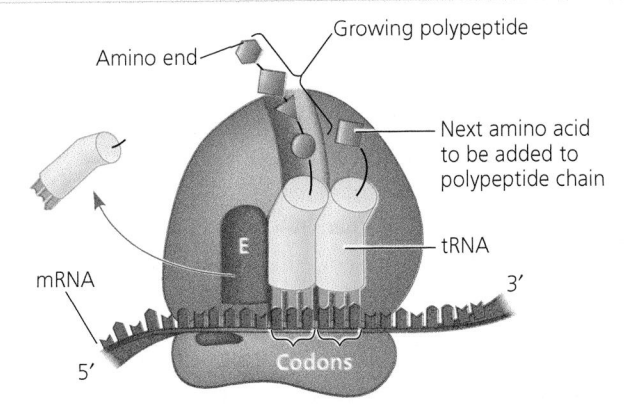

(c) **Schematic model with mRNA and tRNA.** A tRNA fits into a binding site when its anticodon base-pairs with an mRNA codon. The P site holds the tRNA attached to the growing polypeptide. The A site holds the tRNA carrying the next amino acid to be added to the polypeptide chain. Discharged tRNA leaves from the E site.

▲ Figure 17.17 **The anatomy of a functioning ribosome.**

The structure of a ribosome reflects its function of bringing mRNA together with tRNAs carrying amino acids. In addition to a binding site for mRNA, each ribosome has three binding sites for tRNA, as described in Figure 17.17. The **P site** (**p**eptidyl-tRNA binding site) holds the tRNA carrying the growing polypeptide chain, while the **A site** (**a**minoacyl-tRNA binding site) holds the tRNA carrying the next amino acid to be added to the chain. Discharged tRNAs leave the ribosome from the **E site** (**e**xit site). The ribosome holds the tRNA and mRNA in close proximity and positions the new amino acid for addition to the carboxyl end of the growing polypeptide. It then catalyzes the formation of the peptide bond. As the polypeptide becomes longer, it passes through an *exit tunnel* in the ribosome's large subunit. When the polypeptide is complete, it is released through the exit tunnel.

A lot of evidence strongly supports the hypothesis that rRNA, not protein, is primarily responsible for both the structure and the function of the ribosome. The proteins, which are largely on the exterior, support the shape changes of the rRNA molecules as they carry out catalysis during translation. Ribosomal RNA is the main constituent of the interface between the two subunits and of the A and P sites, and it is the catalyst of peptide bond formation. Thus, a ribosome can be regarded as one colossal ribozyme!

Building a Polypeptide

We can divide translation, the synthesis of a polypeptide chain, into three stages (analogous to those of transcription): initiation, elongation, and termination. All three stages require protein "factors" that aid in the translation process. For certain aspects of chain initiation and elongation, energy is also required. It is provided by the hydrolysis of guanosine triphosphate (GTP), a molecule closely related to ATP.

Ribosome Association and Initiation of Translation

The initiation stage of translation brings together mRNA, a tRNA bearing the first amino acid of the polypeptide, and the two subunits of a ribosome (Figure 17.18). First, a small ribosomal subunit binds to both mRNA and a specific initiator tRNA, which carries the amino acid methionine. In bacteria, the small subunit can bind these two in either order; it binds the mRNA at a specific RNA sequence, just upstream of the start codon, AUG. (Joan Steitz, our Unit Three interviewee, discovered the binding site on the mRNA and showed that complementary base pairing between this site and a ribosomal RNA was involved.) In

eukaryotes, the small subunit, with the initiator tRNA already bound, binds to the 5' cap of the mRNA and then moves, or *scans*, downstream along the mRNA until it reaches the start codon; the initiator tRNA then hydrogen-bonds to the AUG start codon. In either case, the start codon signals the start of translation; this is important because it establishes the codon reading frame for the mRNA.

The union of mRNA, initiator tRNA, and a small ribosomal subunit is followed by the attachment of a large ribosomal subunit, completing the *translation initiation complex*. Proteins called *initiation factors* are required to bring all these components together. The cell also expends energy obtained by hydrolysis of a GTP molecule to form the initiation complex. At the completion of the initiation process, the initiator tRNA sits in the P site of the ribosome, and the vacant A site is ready for the next aminoacyl tRNA. Note that a polypeptide is always synthesized in one direction, from the initial methionine at the amino end, also called the N-terminus, toward the final amino acid at the carboxyl end, also called the C-terminus (see Figure 5.17).

Elongation of the Polypeptide Chain

In the elongation stage of translation, amino acids are added one by one to the previous amino acid at the C-terminus of the growing chain. Each addition involves the participation of several proteins called *elongation factors* and occurs in a three-step cycle described in **Figure 17.19**. Energy expenditure occurs in the first and third steps. Codon recognition requires hydrolysis of one molecule of GTP, which increases the accuracy and efficiency of this step. One more GTP is hydrolyzed to provide energy for the translocation step.

1 A small ribosomal subunit binds to a molecule of mRNA. In a bacterial cell, the mRNA binding site on this subunit recognizes a specific nucleotide sequence on the mRNA just upstream of the start codon. An initiator tRNA, with the anticodon UAC, base-pairs with the start codon, AUG. This tRNA carries the amino acid methionine (Met).

2 The arrival of a large ribosomal subunit completes the initiation complex. Proteins called initiation factors (not shown) are required to bring all the translation components together. Hydrolysis of GTP provides the energy for the assembly. The initiator tRNA is in the P site; the A site is available to the tRNA bearing the next amino acid.

▲ Figure 17.18 **The initiation of translation.**

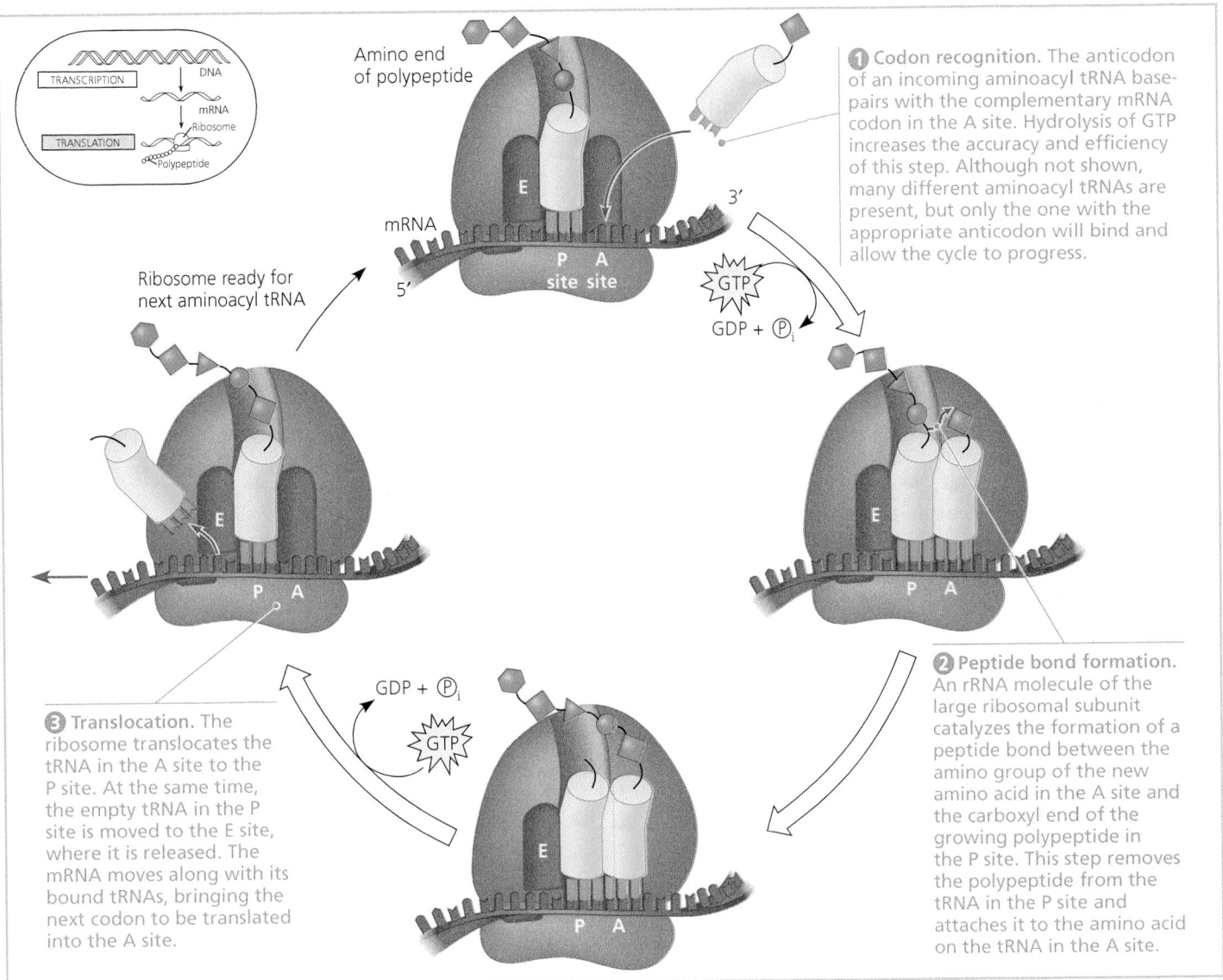

Amino end
of polypeptide

1 Codon recognition. The anticodon of an incoming aminoacyl tRNA base-pairs with the complementary mRNA codon in the A site. Hydrolysis of GTP increases the accuracy and efficiency of this step. Although not shown, many different aminoacyl tRNAs are present, but only the one with the appropriate anticodon will bind and allow the cycle to progress.

mRNA

Ribosome ready for
next aminoacyl tRNA

GTP

GDP + P$_i$

2 Peptide bond formation. An rRNA molecule of the large ribosomal subunit catalyzes the formation of a peptide bond between the amino group of the new amino acid in the A site and the carboxyl end of the growing polypeptide in the P site. This step removes the polypeptide from the tRNA in the P site and attaches it to the amino acid on the tRNA in the A site.

3 Translocation. The ribosome translocates the tRNA in the A site to the P site. At the same time, the empty tRNA in the P site is moved to the E site, where it is released. The mRNA moves along with its bound tRNAs, bringing the next codon to be translated into the A site.

GDP + P$_i$

GTP

▲ **Figure 17.19 The elongation cycle of translation.** The hydrolysis of GTP plays an important role in the elongation process. Not shown are the proteins called elongation factors.

The mRNA is moved through the ribosome in one direction only, 5′ end first; this is equivalent to the ribosome moving 5′ → 3′ on the mRNA. The important point is that the ribosome and the mRNA move relative to each other, unidirectionally, codon by codon. The elongation cycle takes less than a tenth of a second in bacteria and is repeated as each amino acid is added to the chain until the polypeptide is completed.

Termination of Translation

The final stage of translation is termination (Figure 17.20, on the next page). Elongation continues until a stop codon in the mRNA reaches the A site of the ribosome. The nucleotide base triplets UAG, UAA, and UGA do not code for amino acids but instead act as signals to stop translation. A *release factor*, a protein shaped like an aminoacyl tRNA, binds directly to the stop codon in the A site. The release factor causes the addition of a

water molecule instead of an amino acid to the polypeptide chain. (There are plenty of water molecules available in the aqueous cellular environment.) This reaction breaks (hydrolyzes) the bond between the completed polypeptide and the tRNA in the P site, releasing the polypeptide through the exit tunnel of the ribosome's large subunit. The remainder of the translation assembly then comes apart in a multistep process, aided by other protein factors. Breakdown of the translation assembly requires the hydrolysis of two more GTP molecules.

Polyribosomes

A single ribosome can make an average-sized polypeptide in less than a minute. Typically, however, multiple ribosomes translate an mRNA at the same time; that is, a single mRNA is used to make many copies of a polypeptide simultaneously. Once a ribosome is far enough past the start codon, a second ribosome can attach to the mRNA, eventually resulting in a number

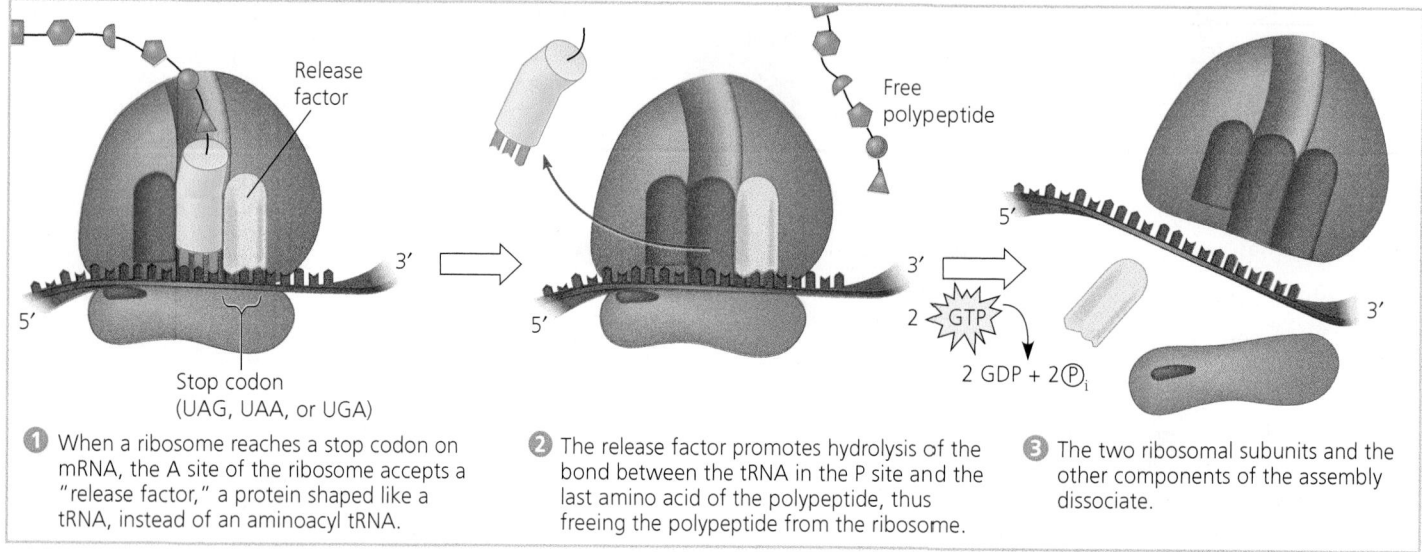

① When a ribosome reaches a stop codon on mRNA, the A site of the ribosome accepts a "release factor," a protein shaped like a tRNA, instead of an aminoacyl tRNA.

② The release factor promotes hydrolysis of the bond between the tRNA in the P site and the last amino acid of the polypeptide, thus freeing the polypeptide from the ribosome.

③ The two ribosomal subunits and the other components of the assembly dissociate.

▲ Figure 17.20 **The termination of translation.** Like elongation, termination requires GTP hydrolysis as well as additional protein factors, which are not shown here.

of ribosomes trailing along the mRNA. Such strings of ribosomes, called **polyribosomes** (or *polysomes*), can be seen with an electron microscope (**Figure 17.21**). Polyribosomes are found in both bacterial and eukaryotic cells. They enable a cell to make many copies of a polypeptide very quickly.

Completing and Targeting the Functional Protein

The process of translation is often not sufficient to make a functional protein. In this section, you will learn about modifications that polypeptide chains undergo after the translation process as well as some of the mechanisms used to target completed proteins to specific sites in the cell.

Protein Folding and Post-Translational Modifications

During its synthesis, a polypeptide chain begins to coil and fold spontaneously as a consequence of its amino acid sequence (primary structure), forming a protein with a specific shape: a three-dimensional molecule with secondary and tertiary structure (see Figure 5.20). Thus, a gene determines primary structure, and primary structure in turn determines shape. In many cases, a chaperone protein (chaperonin) helps the polypeptide fold correctly (see Figure 5.23).

Additional steps—*post-translational modifications*—may be required before the protein can begin doing its particular job in the cell. Certain amino acids may be chemically modified by the attachment of sugars, lipids, phosphate groups, or other additions. Enzymes may remove one or more amino acids from the leading (amino) end of the polypeptide chain. In some cases, a polypeptide chain may be enzymatically cleaved into two or more pieces. For example, the protein insulin is first synthesized as a single polypeptide chain but becomes active only after an enzyme cuts out a central part of the chain,

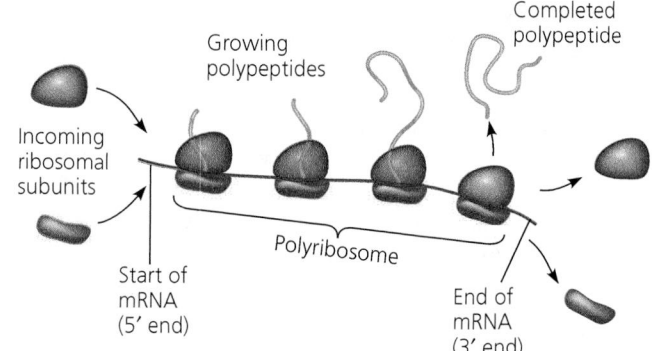

(a) An mRNA molecule is generally translated simultaneously by several ribosomes in clusters called polyribosomes.

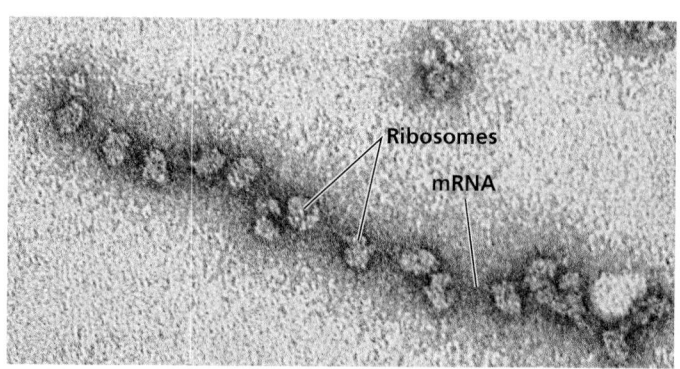

(b) This micrograph shows a large polyribosome in a bacterial cell. Growing polypeptides are not visible here (TEM).

▲ Figure 17.21 **Polyribosomes.**

leaving a protein made up of two polypeptide chains connected by disulfide bridges. In other cases, two or more polypeptides that are synthesized separately may come together, becoming the subunits of a protein that has quaternary structure. A familiar example is hemoglobin (see Figure 5.20).

Targeting Polypeptides to Specific Locations

In electron micrographs of eukaryotic cells active in protein synthesis, two populations of ribosomes (and polyribosomes) are evident: free and bound (see Figure 6.10). Free ribosomes are suspended in the cytosol and mostly synthesize proteins that stay in the cytosol and function there. In contrast, bound ribosomes are attached to the cytosolic side of the endoplasmic reticulum (ER) or to the nuclear envelope. Bound ribosomes make proteins of the endomembrane system (the nuclear envelope, ER, Golgi apparatus, lysosomes, vacuoles, and plasma membrane) as well as proteins secreted from the cell, such as insulin. It is important to note that the ribosomes themselves are identical and can switch their status from free to bound.

What determines whether a ribosome is free in the cytosol or bound to rough ER? Polypeptide synthesis always begins in the cytosol as a free ribosome starts to translate an mRNA molecule. There the process continues to completion—*unless* the growing polypeptide itself cues the ribosome to attach to the ER. The polypeptides of proteins destined for the endomembrane system or for secretion are marked by a **signal peptide**, which targets the protein to the ER **(Figure 17.22)**. The signal peptide, a sequence of about 20 amino acids at or near the

leading end (N-terminus) of the polypeptide, is recognized as it emerges from the ribosome by a protein-RNA complex called a **signal-recognition particle (SRP)**. This particle functions as an escort that brings the ribosome to a receptor protein built into the ER membrane. The receptor is part of a multiprotein translocation complex. Polypeptide synthesis continues there, and the growing polypeptide snakes across the membrane into the ER lumen via a protein pore. The signal peptide is usually removed by an enzyme. The rest of the completed polypeptide, if it is to be secreted from the cell, is released into solution within the ER lumen (as in Figure 17.22). Alternatively, if the polypeptide is to be a membrane protein, it remains partially embedded in the ER membrane.

Other kinds of signal peptides are used to target polypeptides to mitochondria, chloroplasts, the interior of the nucleus, and other organelles that are not part of the endomembrane system. The critical difference in these cases is that translation is completed in the cytosol before the polypeptide is imported into the organelle. The mechanisms of translocation also vary, but in all cases studied to date, the "postal zip codes" that address proteins for secretion or to cellular locations are signal peptides of some sort. Bacteria also employ signal peptides to target proteins to the plasma membrane for secretion.

1 Polypeptide synthesis begins on a free ribosome in the cytosol.

2 An SRP binds to the signal peptide, halting synthesis momentarily.

3 The SRP binds to a receptor protein in the ER membrane. This receptor is part of a protein complex (a translocation complex) that has a membrane pore and a signal-cleaving enzyme.

4 The SRP leaves, and polypeptide synthesis resumes, with simultaneous translocation across the membrane. (The signal peptide stays attached to the translocation complex.)

5 The signal-cleaving enzyme cuts off the signal peptide.

6 The rest of the completed polypeptide leaves the ribosome and folds into its final conformation.

Ribosome
mRNA
Signal peptide
Signal-recognition particle (SRP)
SRP receptor protein
CYTOSOL
Translocation complex
ER LUMEN
Signal peptide removed
ER membrane
Protein

▲ **Figure 17.22 The signal mechanism for targeting proteins to the ER.** A polypeptide destined for the endomembrane system or for secretion from the cell begins with a signal peptide, a series of amino acids that targets it for the ER. This figure shows the synthesis of a secretory protein and its simultaneous import into the ER. In the ER and then in the Golgi, the protein will be processed further. Finally, a transport vesicle will convey it to the plasma membrane for release from the cell (see Figure 7.12).

1. What two processes ensure that the correct amino acid is added to a growing polypeptide chain?
2. Discuss the ways in which rRNA structure likely contributes to ribosomal function.
3. Describe how a polypeptide to be secreted is transported to the endomembrane system.
4. **WHAT IF?** **DRAW IT** Draw a tRNA with the anticodon 3'-CGU-5'. What two different codons could it bind to? Draw each codon on an mRNA, labeling all 5' and 3' ends. Add the amino acid carried by this tRNA.

For suggested answers, see Appendix A.

CONCEPT **17.5**

Mutations of one or a few nucleotides can affect protein structure and function

Now that you have explored the process of gene expression, you are ready to understand the effects of changes to the genetic information of a cell (or virus). These changes, called **mutations**, are responsible for the huge diversity of genes found among organisms because mutations are the ultimate source of new genes. In Figure 15.14, we considered chromosomal rearrangements that affect long segments of DNA, which can be considered large-scale mutations. Here we examine small-scale mutations of one or a few nucleotide pairs, including **point mutations**, changes in a single nucleotide pair of a gene.

If a point mutation occurs in a gamete or in a cell that gives rise to gametes, it may be transmitted to offspring and to a succession of future generations. If the mutation has an adverse effect on the phenotype of an organism, the mutant condition is referred to as a genetic disorder or hereditary disease. For example, we can trace the genetic basis of sickle-cell disease to the mutation of a single nucleotide pair in the gene that encodes the β-globin polypeptide of hemoglobin. The change of a single nucleotide in the DNA's template strand leads to the production of an abnormal protein (**Figure 17.23**; also see Figure 5.21). In individuals who are homozygous for the mutant allele, the sickling of red blood cells caused by the altered hemoglobin produces the multiple symptoms associated with sickle-cell disease (see Chapter 14). Another disorder caused by a

point mutation is a heart condition, familial cardiomyopathy, that is responsible for some incidents of sudden death in young athletes. Point mutations in several genes have been identified, any of which can lead to this disorder.

Types of Small-Scale Mutations

Let's now consider how small-scale mutations affect proteins. Point mutations within a gene can be divided into two general categories: (1) single nucleotide-pair substitutions and (2) nucleotide-pair insertions or deletions. Insertions and deletions can involve one or more nucleotide pairs.

Substitutions

A **nucleotide-pair substitution** is the replacement of one nucleotide and its partner with another pair of nucleotides (**Figure 17.24a**). Some substitutions have no effect on the encoded protein, owing to the redundancy of the genetic code. For example, if 3'-CCG-5' on the template strand mutated to 3'-CCA-5', the mRNA codon that used to be GGC would become GGU, but a glycine would still be inserted at the proper location in the protein (see Figure 17.5). In other words, a change in a nucleotide pair may transform one codon into another that is translated into the same amino acid. Such a change is an example of a **silent mutation**, which has no observable effect on the phenotype. (Silent mutations can occur outside genes as well.) Substitutions that change one amino acid to another one are called **missense mutations**. Such a mutation may have little effect on the protein: The new amino acid may have properties similar to those of the amino acid it replaces, or it may be in a region of the protein where the exact sequence of amino acids is not essential to the protein's function.

▼ Figure 17.23 **The molecular basis of sickle-cell disease: a point mutation.** The allele that causes sickle-cell disease differs from the wild-type (normal) allele by a single DNA nucleotide pair.

▼ **Figure 17.24 Types of small-scale mutations that affect mRNA sequence.** All but one of the types shown here also affect the amino acid sequence of the encoded polypeptide.

However, the nucleotide-pair substitutions of greatest interest are those that cause a major change in a protein. The alteration of a single amino acid in a crucial area of a protein—such as in the part of hemoglobin shown in Figure 17.23 or in the active site of an enzyme as shown in Figure 8.18—will significantly alter protein activity. Occasionally, such a mutation leads to an improved protein or one with novel capabilities, but much more often such mutations are detrimental, leading to a useless or less active protein that impairs cellular function.

Substitution mutations are usually missense mutations; that is, the altered codon still codes for an amino acid and thus makes sense, although not necessarily the *right* sense. But a point mutation can also change a codon for an amino acid into a stop codon. This is called a **nonsense mutation**, and it causes translation to be terminated prematurely; the resulting polypeptide will be shorter than the polypeptide encoded by the normal gene. Nearly all nonsense mutations lead to nonfunctional proteins.

Insertions and Deletions

Insertions and **deletions** are additions or losses of nucleotide pairs in a gene **(Figure 17.24b)**. These mutations have a disastrous effect on the resulting protein more often than substitutions do. Insertion or deletion of nucleotides may alter the reading frame of the genetic message, the triplet grouping of nucleotides on the mRNA that is read during translation. Such a mutation, called a **frameshift mutation**, will occur whenever the number of nucleotides inserted or deleted is not a multiple of three. All the nucleotides that are downstream of the deletion or insertion will be improperly grouped into codons, and the result will be extensive missense, usually ending sooner or later in nonsense and premature termination. Unless the frameshift is very near the end of the gene, the protein is almost certain to be nonfunctional.

Mutagens

Mutations can arise in a number of ways. Errors during DNA replication or recombination can lead to nucleotide-pair substitutions, insertions, or deletions, as well as to mutations affecting longer stretches of DNA. If an incorrect nucleotide is added to a growing chain during replication, for example, the base on that nucleotide will then be mismatched with the nucleotide base on the other strand. In many cases, the error will be corrected by systems you learned about in Chapter 16. Otherwise, the incorrect base will be used as a template in the next round of replication, resulting in a mutation. Such mutations are called *spontaneous mutations*. It is difficult to calculate the rate at which such mutations occur. Rough estimates have been made of the rate of mutation during DNA replication for both *E. coli* and eukaryotes, and the numbers are similar: About one nucleotide in every 10^{10} is altered, and the change is passed on to the next generation of cells.

A number of physical and chemical agents, called **mutagens**, interact with DNA in ways that cause mutations. In the 1920s, Hermann Muller discovered that X-rays caused genetic changes in fruit flies, and he used X-rays to make *Drosophila* mutants for his genetic studies. But he also recognized an alarming implication of his discovery: X-rays and other forms of high-energy radiation pose hazards to the genetic material of people as well as laboratory organisms. Mutagenic radiation, a physical mutagen, includes ultraviolet (UV) light, which can cause disruptive thymine dimers in DNA (see Figure 16.19).

Chemical mutagens fall into several categories. Nucleotide analogs are chemicals that are similar to normal DNA nucleotides but that pair incorrectly during DNA replication. Some other chemical mutagens interfere with correct DNA replication by inserting themselves into the DNA and distorting the double helix. Still other mutagens cause chemical changes in bases that change their pairing properties.

Researchers have developed a variety of methods to test the mutagenic activity of chemicals. A major application of these tests is the preliminary screening of chemicals to identify those that may cause cancer. This approach makes sense because most carcinogens (cancer-causing chemicals) are mutagenic, and conversely, most mutagens are carcinogenic.

1. What happens when one nucleotide pair is lost from the middle of the coding sequence of a gene?
2. **MAKE CONNECTIONS** Individuals heterozygous for the sickle-cell allele are generally healthy but show phenotypic effects of the allele under some circumstances; see Concept 14.4, pages 277–278. Explain in terms of gene expression.
3. **WHAT IF?** **DRAW IT** The template strand of a gene includes this sequence: 3′-TACTTGTCCGATATC-5′. It is mutated to 3′-TACTTGTCCAATATC-5′. For both normal and mutant sequences, draw the double-stranded DNA, the resulting mRNA, and the amino acid sequence each encodes. What is the effect of the mutation on the amino acid sequence?

For suggested answers, see Appendix A.

CONCEPT 17.6

While gene expression differs among the domains of life, the concept of a gene is universal

Although bacteria and eukaryotes carry out transcription and translation in very similar ways, we have noted certain differences in cellular machinery and in details of the processes in these two domains. The division of organisms into three domains was established about 40 years ago, when archaea were recognized as distinct from bacteria. Like bacteria, archaea are prokaryotes. However, archaea share many aspects of the mechanisms of gene expression with eukaryotes, as well as a few with bacteria.

Comparing Gene Expression in Bacteria, Archaea, and Eukarya

Recent advances in molecular biology have enabled researchers to determine the complete nucleotide sequences of hundreds of genomes, including many genomes from each domain. This wealth of data allows us to compare gene and protein sequences across domains. Foremost among genes of interest are those that encode components of such fundamental biological processes as transcription and translation.

Bacterial and eukaryotic RNA polymerases differ significantly from each other, while the single archaeal RNA polymerase resembles the three eukaryotic ones. Archaea and eukaryotes use a complex set of transcription factors, unlike the smaller set of accessory proteins in bacteria. Transcription is terminated differently in bacteria and eukaryotes. The little that is known about archaeal transcription termination suggests that it is similar to the eukaryotic process.

As far as translation is concerned, archaeal ribosomes are the same size as bacterial ribosomes, but their sensitivities to chemical inhibitors more closely match those of eukaryotic ribosomes. We mentioned earlier that initiation of translation is slightly different in bacteria and eukaryotes. In this respect, the archaeal process is more like that of bacteria.

The most important differences between bacteria and eukaryotes with regard to gene expression arise from the bacterial cell's lack of compartmental organization. Like a one-room workshop, a bacterial cell ensures a streamlined operation. In the absence of a nucleus, it can simultaneously transcribe and translate the same gene (Figure 17.25), and the newly made protein can quickly diffuse to its site of function. Most researchers suspect that transcription and translation are coupled like this in archaeal cells as well, since archaea lack a nuclear envelope. In contrast, the eukaryotic cell's nuclear envelope segregates transcription from translation and provides a compartment for extensive RNA processing. This processing stage includes additional steps whose regulation can help coordinate the eukaryotic cell's elaborate activities (see Chapter 18).

Learning more about the proteins and RNAs involved in archaeal transcription and translation will tell us much about the evolution of these processes in all three domains. In spite of the differences in gene expression cataloged here, however, the idea of the gene itself is a unifying concept among all forms of life.

▲ **Figure 17.25 Coupled transcription and translation in bacteria.** In bacterial cells, the translation of mRNA can begin as soon as the leading (5′) end of the mRNA molecule peels away from the DNA template. The micrograph (TEM) shows a strand of *E. coli* DNA being transcribed by RNA polymerase molecules. Attached to each RNA polymerase molecule is a growing strand of mRNA, which is already being translated by ribosomes. The newly synthesized polypeptides are not visible in the micrograph but are shown in the diagram.

? *Which one of the mRNA molecules started transcription first? On that mRNA, which ribosome started translating first?*

What Is a Gene? *Revisiting the Question*

Our definition of a gene has evolved over the past few chapters, as it has through the history of genetics. We began with the Mendelian concept of a gene as a discrete unit of inheritance that affects a phenotypic character (Chapter 14). We saw that Morgan and his colleagues assigned such genes to specific loci on chromosomes (Chapter 15). We went on to view a gene as a region of specific nucleotide sequence along the length of the DNA molecule of a chromosome (Chapter 16). Finally, in this chapter, we have considered a functional definition of a gene as a DNA sequence that codes for a specific polypeptide chain. (Figure 17.26, on the next page, summarizes the path from gene to polypeptide in a eukaryotic cell.) All these definitions are useful, depending on the context in which genes are being studied.

Clearly, the statement that a gene codes for a polypeptide is too simple. Most eukaryotic genes contain noncoding segments (such as introns), so large portions of these genes have no corresponding segments in polypeptides. Molecular biologists also often include promoters and certain other regulatory regions of DNA within the boundaries of a gene. These DNA sequences are not transcribed, but they can be considered part of the functional gene because they must be present for transcription to occur. Our definition of a gene must also be broad enough to include the DNA that is transcribed into rRNA, tRNA, and other RNAs that are not translated. These genes have no polypeptide products but play crucial roles in the cell. Thus, we arrive at the following definition: *A gene is a region of DNA that can be expressed to produce a final functional product that is either a polypeptide or an RNA molecule.*

When considering phenotypes, however, it is often useful to start by focusing on genes that code for polypeptides. In this chapter, you have learned in molecular terms how a typical gene is expressed—by transcription into RNA and then translation into a polypeptide that forms a protein of specific structure and function. Proteins, in turn, bring about an organism's observable phenotype.

A given type of cell expresses only a subset of its genes. This is an essential feature in multicellular organisms: You'd be in trouble if the lens cells in your eyes started expressing the genes for hair proteins, which are normally expressed only in hair follicle cells! Gene expression is precisely regulated. We'll explore gene regulation in the next chapter, beginning with the simpler case of bacteria and continuing with eukaryotes.

CONCEPT CHECK 17.6

1. Would the coupling of processes shown in Figure 17.25 be found in a eukaryotic cell? Explain.
2. **WHAT IF?** In eukaryotic cells, mRNAs have been found to have a circular arrangement in which proteins hold the poly-A tail near the 5′ cap. How might this increase translation efficiency?

For suggested answers, see Appendix A.

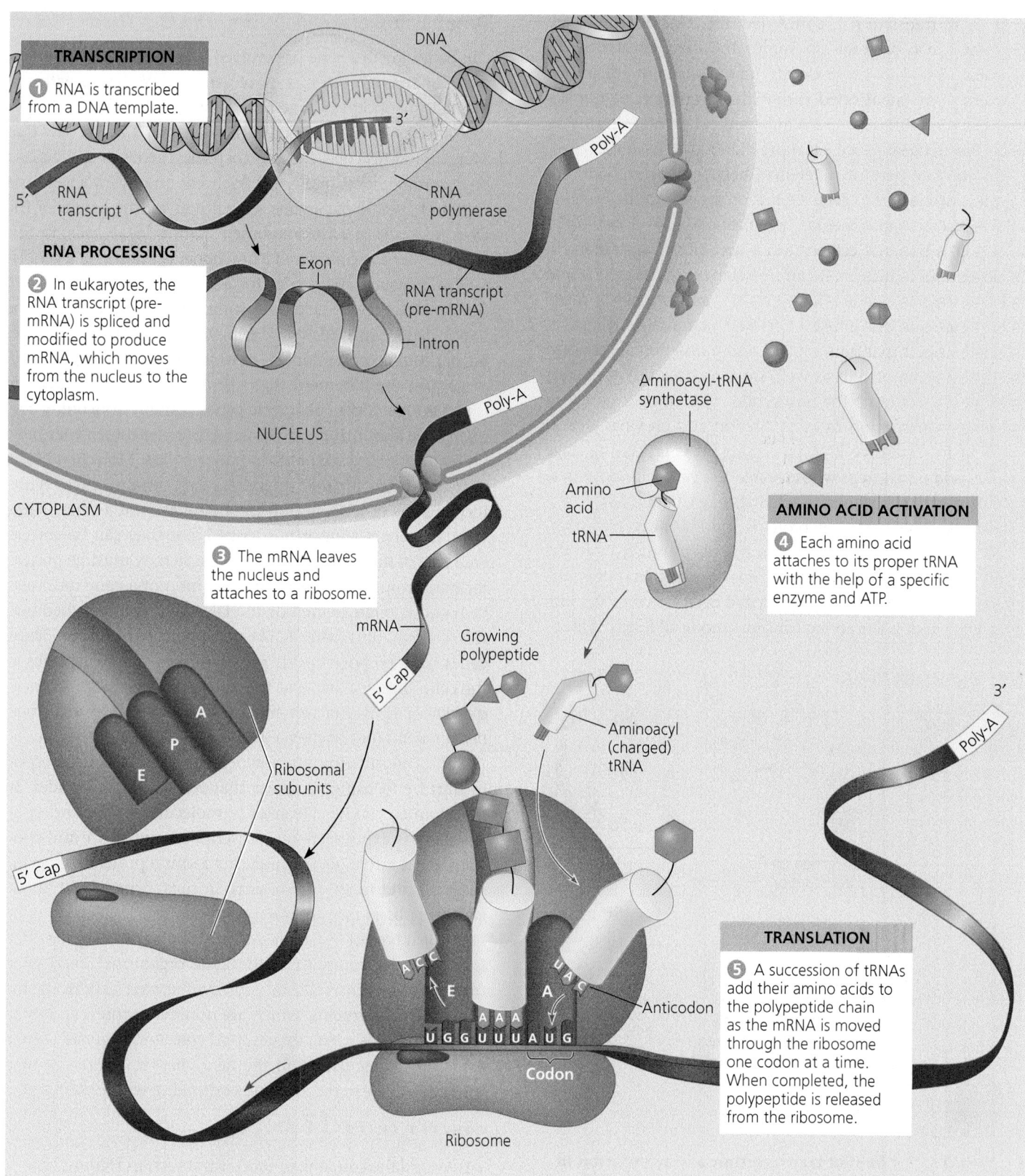

TRANSCRIPTION

1 RNA is transcribed from a DNA template.

DNA

RNA polymerase

RNA transcript

5′

RNA transcript (pre-mRNA)

Poly-A

RNA PROCESSING

2 In eukaryotes, the RNA transcript (pre-mRNA) is spliced and modified to produce mRNA, which moves from the nucleus to the cytoplasm.

Exon

Intron

3′

NUCLEUS

Poly-A

CYTOPLASM

AMINO ACID ACTIVATION

Aminoacyl-tRNA synthetase

Amino acid

tRNA

4 Each amino acid attaches to its proper tRNA with the help of a specific enzyme and ATP.

3 The mRNA leaves the nucleus and attaches to a ribosome.

mRNA

5′ Cap

Growing polypeptide

Aminoacyl (charged) tRNA

Ribosomal subunits

A
P
E

5′ Cap

TRANSLATION

5 A succession of tRNAs add their amino acids to the polypeptide chain as the mRNA is moved through the ribosome one codon at a time. When completed, the polypeptide is released from the ribosome.

Anticodon

ACC

E

A

UAC

AAA

UGGUUUAUG

Codon

Ribosome

3′

Poly-A

▲ **Figure 17.26 A summary of transcription and translation in a eukaryotic cell.** This diagram shows the path from one gene to one polypeptide. Keep in mind that each gene in the DNA can be transcribed repeatedly into many identical RNA molecules and that each mRNA can be translated repeatedly to yield many identical polypeptide molecules. (Also, remember that the final products of some genes are not polypeptides but RNA molecules, including tRNA and rRNA.) In general, the steps of transcription and translation are similar in bacterial, archaeal, and eukaryotic cells. The major difference is the occurrence of RNA processing in the eukaryotic nucleus. Other significant differences are found in the initiation stages of both transcription and translation and in the termination of transcription.

17 CHAPTER REVIEW

SUMMARY OF KEY CONCEPTS

CONCEPT 17.1

Genes specify proteins via transcription and translation (pp. 325–331)

- DNA controls metabolism by directing cells to make specific enzymes and other proteins, via the process of **gene expression**. Beadle and Tatum's studies of mutant strains of *Neurospora* led to the one gene–one polypeptide hypothesis. Genes code for polypeptide chains or specify RNA molecules.
- **Transcription** is the synthesis of RNA complementary to a **template strand** of DNA, providing a nucleotide-to-nucleotide transfer of information. **Translation** is the synthesis of a polypeptide whose amino acid sequence is specified by the nucleotide sequence in **mRNA**; this informational transfer thus involves a change of language, from that of nucleotides to that of amino acids.
- Genetic information is encoded as a sequence of nonoverlapping nucleotide triplets, or **codons**. A codon in messenger RNA (mRNA) either is translated into an amino acid (61 of the 64 codons) or serves as a stop signal (3 codons). Codons must be read in the correct **reading frame**.

? *Describe the process of gene expression, by which a gene affects the phenotype of an organism.*

CONCEPT 17.2

Transcription is the DNA-directed synthesis of RNA: *a closer look* (pp. 331–334)

- RNA synthesis is catalyzed by **RNA polymerase**, which links together RNA nucleotides complementary to a DNA template strand. This process follows the same base-pairing rules as DNA replication, except that in RNA, uracil substitutes for thymine.

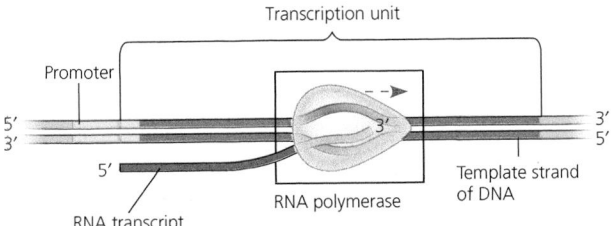

- The three stages of transcription are initiation, elongation, and termination. A **promoter**, often including a **TATA box** in eukaryotes, establishes where RNA synthesis is initiated. **Transcription factors** help eukaryotic RNA polymerase recognize promoter sequences, forming a **transcription initiation complex**. The mechanisms of termination are different in bacteria and eukaryotes.

? *What are the similarities and differences in the initiation of gene transcription in bacteria and eukaryotes?*

CONCEPT 17.3

Eukaryotic cells modify RNA after transcription (pp. 334–336)

- Before leaving the nucleus, eukaryotic mRNA molecules undergo **RNA processing**, which includes RNA splicing, the addition of a modified nucleotide **5′ cap** to the 5′ end, and the addition of a **poly-A tail** to the 3′ end.

- Most eukaryotic genes are split into segments: They have **introns** interspersed among the **exons** (the regions included in the mRNA). In **RNA splicing**, introns are removed and exons joined. RNA splicing is typically carried out by **spliceosomes**, but in some cases, RNA alone catalyzes its own splicing. The catalytic ability of some RNA molecules, called **ribozymes**, derives from the inherent properties of RNA. The presence of introns allows for **alternative RNA splicing**.

? *What function do the 5′ cap and the poly-A tail serve on a eukaryotic mRNA?*

CONCEPT 17.4

Translation is the RNA-directed synthesis of a polypeptide: *a closer look* (pp. 337–344)

- A cell translates an mRNA message into protein using **transfer RNAs (tRNAs)**. After being bound to a specific amino acid by an **aminoacyl-tRNA synthetase**, a tRNA lines up via its **anticodon** at the complementary codon on mRNA. A **ribosome**, made up of **ribosomal RNAs (rRNAs)** and proteins, facilitates this coupling with binding sites for mRNA and tRNA.

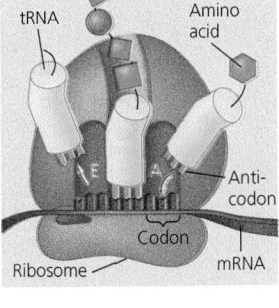

- Ribosomes coordinate the three stages of translation: initiation, elongation, and termination. The formation of peptide bonds between amino acids is catalyzed by rRNA as tRNAs move through the **A** and **P sites** and exit through the **E site**.
- A single mRNA molecule can be translated simultaneously by a number of ribosomes, forming a **polyribosome**.
- After translation, modifications to proteins can affect their three-dimensional shape. Free ribosomes in the cytosol initiate synthesis of all proteins, but proteins destined for the endomembrane system or for secretion are transported into the ER. Such proteins have a **signal peptide** to which a **signal-recognition particle (SRP)** binds, enabling the translating ribosome to bind to the ER.

? *What function do tRNAs serve in the process of translation?*

CONCEPT 17.5

Mutations of one or a few nucleotides can affect protein structure and function (pp. 344–346)

- Small-scale **mutations** include **point mutations**, changes in one DNA nucleotide pair, which may lead to production of nonfunctional proteins. **Nucleotide-pair substitutions** can cause **missense** or **nonsense mutations**. Nucleotide-pair **insertions** or **deletions** may produce **frameshift mutations**.
- Spontaneous mutations can occur during DNA replication, recombination, or repair. Chemical and physical **mutagens** cause DNA damage that can alter genes.

? *What will be the results of chemically modifying one nucleotide base of a gene? What role is played by DNA repair systems in the cell?*

While gene expression differs among the domains of life, the concept of a gene is universal (pp. 346–348)

- There are some differences in gene expression among bacteria, archaea, and eukaryotes. Because bacterial cells lack a nuclear envelope, translation can begin while transcription is still in progress. Archaeal cells show similarities to both eukaryotic and bacterial cells in their processes of gene expression. In a eukaryotic cell, the nuclear envelope separates transcription from translation, and extensive RNA processing occurs in the nucleus.
- A gene is a region of DNA whose final functional product is either a polypeptide or an RNA molecule.

? *How does the presence of a nuclear envelope affect gene expression in eukaryotes?*

TEST YOUR UNDERSTANDING

LEVEL 1: KNOWLEDGE/COMPREHENSION

1. In eukaryotic cells, transcription cannot begin until
   a. the two DNA strands have completely separated and exposed the promoter.
   b. several transcription factors have bound to the promoter.
   c. the 5′ caps are removed from the mRNA.
   d. the DNA introns are removed from the template.
   e. DNA nucleases have isolated the transcription unit.

2. Which of the following is *not* true of a codon?
   a. It consists of three nucleotides.
   b. It may code for the same amino acid as another codon.
   c. It never codes for more than one amino acid.
   d. It extends from one end of a tRNA molecule.
   e. It is the basic unit of the genetic code.

3. The anticodon of a particular tRNA molecule is
   a. complementary to the corresponding mRNA codon.
   b. complementary to the corresponding triplet in rRNA.
   c. the part of tRNA that bonds to a specific amino acid.
   d. changeable, depending on the amino acid that attaches to the tRNA.
   e. catalytic, making the tRNA a ribozyme.

4. Which of the following is *not* true of RNA processing?
   a. Exons are cut out before mRNA leaves the nucleus.
   b. Nucleotides may be added at both ends of the RNA.
   c. Ribozymes may function in RNA splicing.
   d. RNA splicing can be catalyzed by spliceosomes.
   e. A primary transcript is often much longer than the final RNA molecule that leaves the nucleus.

5. Which component is *not* directly involved in translation?
   a. mRNA   b. DNA   c. tRNA   d. ribosomes   e. GTP

LEVEL 2: APPLICATION/ANALYSIS

6. Using Figure 17.5, identify a 5′ → 3′ sequence of nucleotides in the DNA template strand for an mRNA coding for the polypeptide sequence Phe-Pro-Lys.
   a. 5′-UUUGGGAAA-3′   d. 5′-CTTCGGGAA-3′
   b. 5′-GAACCCCTT-3′   e. 5′-AAACCCUUU-3′
   c. 5′-AAAACCTTT-3′

7. Which of the following mutations would be *most* likely to have a harmful effect on an organism?
   a. a nucleotide-pair substitution
   b. a deletion of three nucleotides near the middle of a gene
   c. a single nucleotide deletion in the middle of an intron

d. a single nucleotide deletion near the end of the coding sequence
e. a single nucleotide insertion downstream of, and close to, the start of the coding sequence

8. **DRAW IT** Fill in the following table:

Type of RNA	Functions
Messenger RNA (mRNA)	
Transfer RNA (tRNA)	
	Plays catalytic (ribozyme) roles and structural roles in ribosomes
Primary transcript	
Small nuclear RNA (snRNA)	

LEVEL 3: SYNTHESIS/EVALUATION

9. **EVOLUTION CONNECTION** Most amino acids are coded for by a set of similar codons (see Figure 17.5). What evolutionary explanations can you give for this pattern? (*Hint*: There is one explanation relating to ancestry, and some less obvious ones of a "form-fits-function" type.)

10. **SCIENTIFIC INQUIRY**
    Knowing that the genetic code is almost universal, a scientist uses molecular biological methods to insert the human β-globin gene (shown in Figure 17.11) into bacterial cells, hoping the cells will express it and synthesize functional β-globin protein. Instead, the protein produced is nonfunctional and is found to contain many fewer amino acids than does β-globin made by a eukaryotic cell. Explain why.

11. **WRITE ABOUT A THEME**
    Evolution and The Genetic Basis of Life Evolution accounts for the unity and diversity of life, and the continuity of life is based on heritable information in the form of DNA. In a short essay (100–150 words), discuss how the fidelity with which DNA is inherited is related to the processes of evolution. (Review the discussion of proofreading and DNA repair in Concept 16.2, pp. 316–318.)

For selected answers, see Appendix A.

MasteringBIOLOGY   www.masteringbiology.com

1. MasteringBiology® Assignments
Make Connections Tutorial Point Mutations (Chapter 17) and Protein Structure (Chapter 5)
BioFlix Tutorials Protein Synthesis: Overview • Transcription and RNA Processing • Translation and Protein Targeting Pathways
Tutorials The Genetic Code • Following the Instructions in DNA • Types of RNA • Point Mutations
Activities Overview of Protein Synthesis • RNA Synthesis • Transcription • RNA Processing • Synthesizing Proteins • Translation • The Triplet Nature of the Genetic Code
Questions Student Misconceptions • Reading Quiz • Multiple Choice • End-of-Chapter

2. eText
Read your book online, search, take notes, highlight text, and more.

3. The Study Area
Practice Tests • Cumulative Test • **BioFlix** 3-D Animations • MP3 Tutor Sessions • Videos • Activities • Investigations • Lab Media • Audio Glossary • Word Study Tools • Art

18

Regulation of Gene Expression

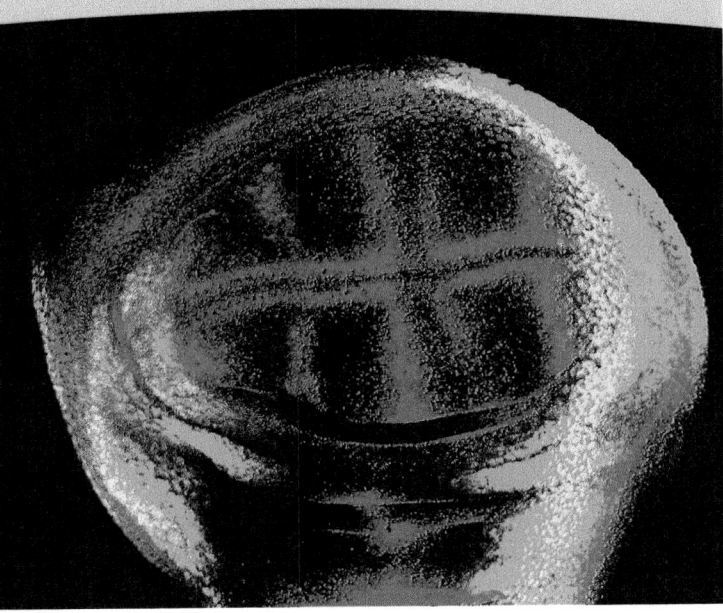

▲ **Figure 18.1 What regulates the precise pattern of gene expression in the developing wing of a fly embryo?**

KEY CONCEPTS

18.1 Bacteria often respond to environmental change by regulating transcription

18.2 Eukaryotic gene expression is regulated at many stages

18.3 Noncoding RNAs play multiple roles in controlling gene expression

18.4 A program of differential gene expression leads to the different cell types in a multicellular organism

18.5 Cancer results from genetic changes that affect cell cycle control

OVERVIEW

Conducting the Genetic Orchestra

It's almost concert time! Dissonance reigns as the orchestra members individually tune their instruments. Then, after a brief hush, the conductor's baton rises, pauses, and begins a series of elaborate movements, directing specific instruments to join in and others to raise or lower their volume at defined moments. Properly balanced and timed, discordant sounds are thus transformed into a beautiful symphony that enraptures the audience.

In a similar way, cells intricately and precisely regulate their gene expression. Both prokaryotes and eukaryotes must alter their patterns of gene expression in response to changes in environmental conditions. Multicellular eukaryotes must also develop and maintain multiple cell types. Each cell type contains the same genome but expresses a different subset of genes, a significant challenge in gene regulation.

An adult fruit fly, for example, develops from a single fertilized egg, passing through a wormlike stage called a larva. At every stage, gene expression is carefully regulated, ensuring that the right genes are expressed only at the correct time and place. In the larva, the adult wing forms in a disk-shaped pocket of several thousand cells, shown in **Figure 18.1**. The tissue in this image has been treated to reveal the mRNA for three genes—labeled red, blue, and green—using techniques covered in Chapter 20. (Red and green together appear yellow.) The intricate pattern of expression for each gene is the same from larva to larva at this stage, and it provides a graphic display of the precision of gene regulation. But what is the molecular basis for this pattern? Why is one particular gene expressed only in the few hundred cells that appear blue in this image and not in the other cells?

In this chapter, we first explore how bacteria regulate expression of their genes in response to different environmental conditions. We then examine how eukaryotes regulate gene expression to maintain different cell types. Gene expression in eukaryotes, as in bacteria, is often regulated at the stage of transcription, but control at other stages is also important. In recent years, researchers have been surprised to discover the many roles played by RNA molecules in regulating eukaryotic gene expression, a topic we cover next. We then consider what happens when a complex program of gene regulation works properly during embryonic development: A single cell—the fertilized egg—becomes a fully functioning organism made up of many different cell types. Finally, we investigate how cancer can result when gene regulation goes awry. Orchestrating proper gene expression by all cells is crucial to the functions of life.

CONCEPT 18.1

Bacteria often respond to environmental change by regulating transcription

Bacterial cells that can conserve resources and energy have a selective advantage over cells that are unable to do so. Thus, natural selection has favored bacteria that express only the genes whose products are needed by the cell.

Consider, for instance, an individual *E. coli* cell living in the erratic environment of a human colon, dependent for its nutrients on the whimsical eating habits of its host. If the environment is lacking in the amino acid tryptophan, which the bacterium needs to survive, the cell responds by activating a metabolic pathway that makes tryptophan from another compound. Later, if the human host eats a tryptophan-rich meal, the bacterial cell stops producing tryptophan, thus saving itself from squandering its resources to produce a substance that is available from the surrounding solution in prefabricated form. This is just one example of how bacteria tune their metabolism to changing environments.

Metabolic control occurs on two levels, as shown for the synthesis of tryptophan in **Figure 18.2**. First, cells can adjust the activity of enzymes already present. This is a fairly fast response, which relies on the sensitivity of many enzymes to chemical cues that increase or decrease their catalytic activity (see Chapter 8). The activity of the first enzyme in the tryptophan synthesis pathway is inhibited by the pathway's end product **(Figure 18.2a)**. Thus, if tryptophan accumulates in a cell, it shuts down the synthesis of more tryptophan by inhibiting enzyme activity. Such *feedback inhibition*, typical of

anabolic (biosynthetic) pathways, allows a cell to adapt to short-term fluctuations in the supply of a substance it needs.

Second, cells can adjust the production level of certain enzymes; that is, they can regulate the expression of the genes encoding the enzymes. If, in our example, the environment provides all the tryptophan the cell needs, the cell stops making the enzymes that catalyze the synthesis of tryptophan **(Figure 18.2b)**. In this case, the control of enzyme production occurs at the level of transcription, the synthesis of messenger RNA coding for these enzymes. More generally, many genes of the bacterial genome are switched on or off by changes in the metabolic status of the cell. One basic mechanism for this control of gene expression in bacteria, described as the *operon model*, was discovered in 1961 by François Jacob and Jacques Monod at the Pasteur Institute in Paris. Let's see what an operon is and how it works, using the control of tryptophan synthesis as our first example.

Operons: The Basic Concept

E. coli synthesizes the amino acid tryptophan from a precursor molecule in the multistep pathway shown in Figure 18.2. Each reaction in the pathway is catalyzed by a specific enzyme, and the five genes that code for the subunits of these enzymes are clustered together on the bacterial chromosome. A single promoter serves all five genes, which together constitute a transcription unit. (Recall from Chapter 17 that a promoter is a site where RNA polymerase can bind to DNA and begin transcription.) Thus, transcription gives rise to one long mRNA molecule that codes for the five polypeptides making up the enzymes in the tryptophan pathway. The cell can translate this one mRNA into five separate polypeptides because the mRNA is punctuated with start and stop codons that signal where the coding sequence for each polypeptide begins and ends.

A key advantage of grouping genes of related function into one transcription unit is that a single "on-off switch" can control the whole cluster of functionally related genes; in other words, these genes are *coordinately controlled*. When an *E. coli* cell must make tryptophan for itself because the nutrient medium lacks this amino acid, all the enzymes for the metabolic pathway are synthesized at one time. The switch is a segment of DNA called an **operator**. Both its location and name suit its function: Positioned within the promoter or, in some cases, between the promoter and the enzyme-coding genes, the operator controls the access of RNA polymerase to the genes. All together, the operator, the promoter, and the genes they control—the entire stretch of DNA required for enzyme production for the tryptophan pathway—constitute an **operon**. The *trp* operon (*trp* for tryptophan) is one of many operons in the *E. coli* genome **(Figure 18.3)**.

If the operator is the operon's switch for controlling transcription, how does this switch work? By itself, the *trp* operon is turned on; that is, RNA polymerase can bind to the promoter and transcribe the genes of the operon. The operon

▲ **Figure 18.2 Regulation of a metabolic pathway.** In the pathway for tryptophan synthesis, an abundance of tryptophan can both **(a)** inhibit the activity of the first enzyme in the pathway (feedback inhibition), a rapid response, and **(b)** repress expression of the genes encoding all subunits of the enzymes in the pathway, a longer-term response. Genes *trpE* and *trpD* encode the two subunits of enzyme 1, and genes *trpB* and *trpA* encode the two subunits of enzyme 3. (The genes were named before the order in which they functioned in the pathway was determined.) The ⊖ symbol stands for inhibition.

(a) Tryptophan absent, repressor inactive, operon on. RNA polymerase attaches to the DNA at the promoter and transcribes the operon's genes.

(b) Tryptophan present, repressor active, operon off. As tryptophan accumulates, it inhibits its own production by activating the repressor protein, which binds to the operator, blocking transcription.

▲ **Figure 18.3 The *trp* operon in *E. coli*: regulated synthesis of repressible enzymes.** Tryptophan is an amino acid produced by an anabolic pathway catalyzed by repressible enzymes. **(a)** The five genes encoding the polypeptide subunits of the enzymes in this pathway (see Figure 18.2) are grouped, along with a promoter, into the *trp* operon. The *trp* operator (the repressor binding site) is located within the *trp* promoter (the RNA polymerase binding site). **(b)** Accumulation of tryptophan, the end product of the pathway, represses transcription of the *trp* operon, thus blocking synthesis of all the enzymes in the pathway and shutting down tryptophan production.

? *Describe what happens to the* trp *operon as the cell uses up its store of tryptophan.*

can be switched off by a protein called the *trp* **repressor**. The repressor binds to the operator and blocks attachment of RNA polymerase to the promoter, preventing transcription of the genes. A repressor protein is specific for the operator of a particular operon. For example, the repressor that switches off the *trp* operon by binding to the *trp* operator has no effect on other operons in the *E. coli* genome.

The *trp* repressor is the protein product of a **regulatory gene** called *trpR*, which is located some distance from the *trp* operon and has its own promoter. Regulatory genes are expressed continuously, although at a low rate, and a few *trp* repressor molecules are always present in *E. coli* cells. Why, then, is the *trp* operon not switched off permanently? First, the binding of repressors to operators is reversible. An operator vacillates between two states: one without the repressor bound and one with the repressor bound. The relative duration of each state depends on the number of active repressor molecules around. Second, the *trp* repressor, like most regulatory proteins, is an allosteric protein, with two alternative

shapes, active and inactive (see Figure 8.20). The *trp* repressor is synthesized in an inactive form with little affinity for the *trp* operator. Only if tryptophan binds to the *trp* repressor at an allosteric site does the repressor protein change to the active form that can attach to the operator, turning the operon off.

Tryptophan functions in this system as a **corepressor**, a small molecule that cooperates with a repressor protein to switch an operon off. As tryptophan accumulates, more tryptophan molecules associate with *trp* repressor molecules, which can then bind to the *trp* operator and shut down production of the tryptophan pathway enzymes. If the cell's tryptophan level drops, transcription of the operon's genes resumes. The *trp* operon is one example of how gene expression can respond to changes in the cell's internal and external environment.

Repressible and Inducible Operons: Two Types of Negative Gene Regulation

The *trp* operon is said to be a *repressible operon* because its transcription is usually on but can be inhibited (repressed) when a specific small molecule (in this case, tryptophan) binds allosterically to a regulatory protein. In contrast, an *inducible operon* is usually off but can be stimulated (induced) when a specific small molecule interacts with a regulatory protein. The classic example of an inducible operon is the *lac* operon (*lac* for lactose), which was the subject of Jacob and Monod's pioneering research.

The disaccharide lactose (milk sugar) is available to *E. coli* in the human colon if the host drinks milk. Lactose metabolism begins with hydrolysis of the disaccharide into its component monosaccharides, glucose and galactose, a reaction catalyzed by the enzyme β-galactosidase. Only a few molecules of this enzyme are present in an *E. coli* cell growing in the absence of lactose. If lactose is added to the bacterium's environment, however, the number of β-galactosidase molecules in the cell increases a thousandfold within about 15 minutes.

The gene for β-galactosidase is part of the *lac* operon, which includes two other genes coding for enzymes that function in lactose utilization. The entire transcription unit is under the command of one main operator and promoter. The regulatory gene, *lacI*, located outside the operon, codes for an allosteric repressor protein that can switch off the *lac* operon by binding to the operator. So far, this sounds just like regulation of the *trp* operon, but there is one important difference. Recall that the *trp* repressor is inactive by itself and requires tryptophan as a corepressor in order to bind to the operator. The *lac* repressor, in contrast, is active by itself, binding to the operator and switching the *lac* operon off. In this case, a specific small molecule, called an **inducer**, *inactivates* the repressor.

For the *lac* operon, the inducer is allolactose, an isomer of lactose formed in small amounts from lactose that enters the cell. In the absence of lactose (and hence allolactose), the *lac* repressor is in its active configuration, and the genes of the *lac* operon are silenced **(Figure 18.4a)**. If lactose is added to the cell's surroundings, allolactose binds to the *lac* repressor and alters its conformation, nullifying the repressor's ability to attach to the operator. Without bound repressor, the *lac* operon is transcribed into mRNA for the lactose-utilizing enzymes **(Figure 18.4b)**.

In the context of gene regulation, the enzymes of the lactose pathway are referred to as *inducible enzymes* because their synthesis is induced by a chemical signal (allolactose, in this case). Analogously, the enzymes for tryptophan synthesis are said to be repressible. *Repressible enzymes* generally function in anabolic pathways, which synthesize essential end products from raw materials (precursors). By suspending production of an end product when it is already present in sufficient quantity, the cell can allocate its organic precursors and energy

(a) Lactose absent, repressor active, operon off. The *lac* repressor is innately active, and in the absence of lactose it switches off the operon by binding to the operator.

▼ **Figure 18.4 The *lac* operon in *E. coli*: regulated synthesis of inducible enzymes.** *E. coli* uses three enzymes to take up and metabolize lactose. The genes for these three enzymes are clustered in the *lac* operon. One gene, *lacZ*, codes for β-galactosidase, which hydrolyzes lactose to glucose and galactose. The second gene, *lacY*, codes for a permease, the membrane protein that transports lactose into the cell. The third gene, *lacA*, codes for an enzyme called transacetylase, whose function in lactose metabolism is still unclear. The gene for the *lac* repressor, *lacI*, happens to be adjacent to the *lac* operon, an unusual situation. The function of the teal region at the upstream end of the promoter (the left end in these diagrams) will be revealed in Figure 18.5.

(b) Lactose present, repressor inactive, operon on. Allolactose, an isomer of lactose, derepresses the operon by inactivating the repressor. In this way, the enzymes for lactose utilization are induced.

for other uses. In contrast, inducible enzymes usually function in catabolic pathways, which break down a nutrient to simpler molecules. By producing the appropriate enzymes only when the nutrient is available, the cell avoids wasting energy and precursors making proteins that are not needed.

Regulation of both the *trp* and *lac* operons involves the *negative* control of genes, because the operons are switched off by the active form of the repressor protein. It may be easier to see this for the *trp* operon, but it is also true for the *lac* operon. Allolactose induces enzyme synthesis not by acting directly on the genome, but by freeing the *lac* operon from the negative effect of the repressor. Gene regulation is said to be *positive* only when a regulatory protein interacts directly with the genome to switch transcription on. Let's look at an example of the positive control of genes, again involving the *lac* operon.

Positive Gene Regulation

When glucose and lactose are both present in its environment, *E. coli* preferentially uses glucose. The enzymes for glucose breakdown in glycolysis (see Figure 9.9) are continually present. Only when lactose is present *and* glucose is in short supply does *E. coli* use lactose as an energy source, and only then does it synthesize appreciable quantities of the enzymes for lactose breakdown.

How does the *E. coli* cell sense the glucose concentration and relay this information to the genome? Again, the mechanism depends on the interaction of an allosteric regulatory protein with a small organic molecule, in this case **cyclic AMP (cAMP)**, which accumulates when glucose is scarce (see Figure 11.11 for the structure of cAMP). The regulatory protein, called *catabolite activator protein (CAP)*, is an **activator**, a protein that binds to DNA and stimulates transcription of a gene. When cAMP binds to this regulatory protein, CAP assumes its active shape and can attach to a specific site at the upstream end of the *lac* promoter (**Figure 18.5a**). This attachment increases the affinity of RNA polymerase for the promoter, which is actually rather low even when no repressor is bound to the operator. By facilitating the binding of RNA polymerase to the promoter and thereby increasing the rate of transcription, the attachment of CAP to the promoter directly stimulates gene expression. Therefore, this mechanism qualifies as positive regulation.

If the amount of glucose in the cell increases, the cAMP concentration falls, and without cAMP, CAP detaches from the operon. Because CAP is inactive, RNA polymerase binds less efficiently to the promoter, and transcription of the *lac* operon proceeds at only a low level, even in the presence of lactose (**Figure 18.5b**). Thus, the *lac* operon is under dual control: negative control by the *lac* repressor and positive control by CAP. The state of the *lac* repressor (with or without bound allolactose) determines whether or not transcription of the *lac* operon's genes occurs at all; the state of CAP (with or without bound cAMP) controls the *rate* of transcription if

the operon is repressor-free. It is as though the operon has both an on-off switch and a volume control.

In addition to regulating the *lac* operon, CAP helps regulate other operons that encode enzymes used in catabolic pathways. All told, it may affect the expression of more than 100 genes in *E. coli*. When glucose is plentiful and CAP is inactive, the synthesis of enzymes that catabolize compounds other than glucose generally slows down. The ability to catabolize other compounds, such as lactose, enables a cell deprived of glucose to survive. The compounds present in the cell at the moment determine which operons are switched on—the result of simple interactions of activator and repressor proteins with the promoters of the genes in question.

(a) Lactose present, glucose scarce (cAMP level high): abundant *lac* mRNA synthesized. If glucose is scarce, the high level of cAMP activates CAP, and the *lac* operon produces large amounts of mRNA coding for the enzymes in the lactose pathway.

(b) Lactose present, glucose present (cAMP level low): little *lac* mRNA synthesized. When glucose is present, cAMP is scarce, and CAP is unable to stimulate transcription at a significant rate, even though no repressor is bound.

▲ **Figure 18.5 Positive control of the *lac* operon by catabolite activator protein (CAP).** RNA polymerase has high affinity for the *lac* promoter only when catabolite activator protein (CAP) is bound to a DNA site at the upstream end of the promoter. CAP attaches to its DNA site only when associated with cyclic AMP (cAMP), whose concentration in the cell rises when the glucose concentration falls. Thus, when glucose is present, even if lactose also is available, the cell preferentially catabolizes glucose and makes very little of the lactose-utilizing enzymes.

1. How does binding of the *trp* corepressor and the *lac* inducer to their respective repressor proteins alter repressor function and transcription in each case?
2. Describe the binding of RNA polymerase, repressors, and activators to the *lac* operon when both lactose and glucose are scarce. What is the effect of these scarcities on transcription of the *lac* operon?
3. **WHAT IF?** A certain mutation in *E. coli* changes the *lac* operator so that the active repressor cannot bind. How would this affect the cell's production of β-galactosidase?

For suggested answers, see Appendix A.

CONCEPT 18.2

Eukaryotic gene expression is regulated at many stages

All organisms, whether prokaryotes or eukaryotes, must regulate which genes are expressed at any given time. Both unicellular organisms and the cells of multicellular organisms must continually turn genes on and off in response to signals from their external and internal environments. Regulation of gene expression is also essential for cell specialization in multicellular organisms, which are made up of different types of cells, each with a distinct role. To perform its role, each cell type must maintain a specific program of gene expression in which certain genes are expressed and others are not.

Differential Gene Expression

A typical human cell might express about 20% of its protein-coding genes at any given time. Highly differentiated cells, such as muscle or nerve cells, express an even smaller fraction of their genes. Almost all the cells in an organism contain an identical genome. (Cells of the immune system are one exception, as you will see in Chapter 43.) However, the subset of genes expressed in the cells of each type is unique, allowing these cells to carry out their specific function. The differences between cell types, therefore, are due not to different genes being present, but to **differential gene expression**, the expression of different genes by cells with the same genome.

The function of any cell, whether a single-celled eukaryote or a particular cell type in a multicellular organism, depends on the appropriate set of genes being expressed. The transcription factors of a cell must locate the right genes at the right time, a task on a par with finding a needle in a haystack. When gene expression proceeds abnormally, serious imbalances and diseases, including cancer, can arise.

Figure 18.6 summarizes the entire process of gene expression in a eukaryotic cell, highlighting key stages in the expression of a protein-coding gene. Each stage depicted in

▲ **Figure 18.6 Stages in gene expression that can be regulated in eukaryotic cells.** In this diagram, the colored boxes indicate the processes most often regulated; each color indicates the type of molecule that is affected (blue = DNA, orange = RNA, purple = protein). The nuclear envelope separating transcription from translation in eukaryotic cells offers an opportunity for post-transcriptional control in the form of RNA processing that is absent in prokaryotes. In addition, eukaryotes have a greater variety of control mechanisms operating before transcription and after translation. The expression of any given gene, however, does not necessarily involve every stage shown; for example, not every polypeptide is cleaved.

Figure 18.6 is a potential control point at which gene expression can be turned on or off, accelerated, or slowed down.

Only 50 years ago, an understanding of the mechanisms that control gene expression in eukaryotes seemed almost hopelessly out of reach. Since then, new research methods, notably advances in DNA technology (see Chapter 20), have enabled molecular biologists to uncover many of the details of eukaryotic gene regulation. In all organisms, a common control point for gene expression is at transcription; regulation at this stage often occurs in response to signals coming from outside the cell, such as hormones or other signaling molecules. For this reason, the term *gene expression* is often equated with transcription for both bacteria and eukaryotes. While this is most often the case for bacteria, the greater complexity of eukaryotic cell structure and function provides opportunities for regulating gene expression at many additional stages (see Figure 18.6). In the remainder of this section, we'll examine some of the important control points of eukaryotic gene expression more closely.

Regulation of Chromatin Structure

Recall that the DNA of eukaryotic cells is packaged with proteins in an elaborate complex known as chromatin, the basic unit of which is the nucleosome (see Figure 16.22). The structural organization of chromatin not only packs a cell's DNA into a compact form that fits inside the nucleus, but also helps regulate gene expression in several ways. The location of a gene's promoter relative to nucleosomes and to the sites where the DNA attaches to the chromosome scaffold or nuclear lamina can affect whether the gene is transcribed. In addition, genes within heterochromatin, which is highly condensed, are usually not expressed. Lastly, certain chemical modifications to the histone proteins and to the DNA of chromatin can influence both chromatin structure and gene expression. Here we examine the effects of these modifications, which are catalyzed by specific enzymes.

Histone Modifications

There is abundant evidence that chemical modifications to histones, the proteins around which the DNA is wrapped in nucleosomes, play a direct role in the regulation of gene transcription. The N-terminus of each histone molecule in a nucleosome protrudes outward from the nucleosome (**Figure 18.7a**). These histone tails are accessible to various modifying enzymes that catalyze the addition or removal of specific chemical groups.

In **histone acetylation**, acetyl groups ($-COCH_3$) are attached to lysines in histone tails; deacetylation is the removal of acetyl groups. When the lysines are acetylated, their positive charges are neutralized and the histone tails no longer bind to neighboring nucleosomes (**Figure 18.7b**). Such binding promotes the folding of chromatin into a more compact structure; when this binding does not occur, chromatin has a looser structure. As a result, transcription proteins have easier

(a) **Histone tails protrude outward from a nucleosome.** The amino acids in the N-terminal tails are accessible for chemical modification.

(b) **Acetylation of histone tails promotes loose chromatin structure that permits transcription.** A region of chromatin in which nucleosomes are unacetylated forms a compact structure (left) in which the DNA is not transcribed. When nucleosomes are highly acetylated (right), the chromatin becomes less compact, and the DNA is accessible for transcription.

▲ Figure 18.7 **A simple model of histone tails and the effect of histone acetylation.** In addition to acetylation, histones can undergo several other types of modifications that also help determine the chromatin configuration in a region.

access to genes in an acetylated region. Researchers have shown that some enzymes that acetylate or deacetylate histones are closely associated with or even components of the transcription factors that bind to promoters (see Figure 17.8). These observations suggest that histone acetylation enzymes may promote the initiation of transcription not only by remodeling chromatin structure, but also by binding to and thus "recruiting" components of the transcription machinery.

Other chemical groups, such as methyl and phosphate groups, can be reversibly attached to amino acids in histone tails. Addition of methyl groups ($-CH_3$) to histone tails (histone methylation) can promote condensation of the chromatin, while addition of a phosphate group (phosphorylation) to an amino acid next to a methylated amino acid can have the opposite effect. The recent discovery that modifications to histone tails can affect chromatin structure and gene expression has led to the *histone code hypothesis*. This hypothesis proposes that specific combinations of modifications, as well as the order in which they have occurred, help determine the chromatin configuration, which in turn influences transcription.

DNA Methylation

While some enzymes methylate the tails of histone proteins, a different set of enzymes can methylate certain bases in the DNA itself, usually cytosine. Such **DNA methylation** occurs in most plants, animals, and fungi. Long stretches of inactive DNA, such as that of inactivated mammalian X chromosomes (see Figure 15.8), are generally more methylated than regions of actively transcribed DNA, although there are exceptions. On a smaller scale, individual genes are usually more heavily methylated in cells in which they are not expressed. Removal of the extra methyl groups can turn on some of these genes.

At least in some species, DNA methylation seems to be essential for the long-term inactivation of genes that occurs during normal cell differentiation in the embryo. For instance, experiments have shown that deficient DNA methylation (due to lack of a methylating enzyme) leads to abnormal embryonic development in organisms as different as mice and *Arabidopsis* (a mustard plant). Once methylated, genes usually stay that way through successive cell divisions in a given individual. At DNA sites where one strand is already methylated, enzymes methylate the correct daughter strand after each round of DNA replication. Methylation patterns are thus passed on, and cells forming specialized tissues keep a chemical record of what occurred during embryonic development. A methylation pattern maintained in this way also accounts for *genomic imprinting* in mammals, where methylation permanently regulates expression of either the maternal or paternal allele of particular genes at the start of development (see Figure 15.17).

Epigenetic Inheritance

The chromatin modifications that we have just discussed do not entail a change in the DNA sequence, yet they may be passed along to future generations of cells. Inheritance of traits transmitted by mechanisms not directly involving the nucleotide sequence is called **epigenetic inheritance**. Whereas mutations in the DNA are permanent changes, modifications to the chromatin can be reversed, by processes that are not yet fully understood. The molecular systems for chromatin modification may well interact with each other in a regulated way. In *Drosophila*, for example, experiments have suggested that a particular histone-modifying enzyme recruits a DNA methylation enzyme to one region and that the two enzymes collaborate to silence a particular set of genes. Working in the opposite order, proteins have also been found that first bind to methylated DNA and then recruit histone deacetylation enzymes. Thus, a dual mechanism, involving both DNA methylation and histone deacetylation, can repress transcription.

Researchers are amassing more and more evidence for the importance of epigenetic information in the regulation of gene expression. Epigenetic variations might help explain why one identical twin acquires a genetically based disease, such as schizophrenia, but the other does not, despite their identical genomes. Alterations in normal patterns of DNA methylation are seen in some cancers, where they are associated with inappropriate gene expression. Evidently, enzymes that modify chromatin structure are integral parts of the eukaryotic cell's machinery for regulating transcription.

Regulation of Transcription Initiation

Chromatin-modifying enzymes provide initial control of gene expression by making a region of DNA either more or less able to bind the transcription machinery. Once the chromatin of a gene is optimally modified for expression, the initiation of transcription is the next major step at which gene expression is regulated. As in bacteria, the regulation of transcription initiation in eukaryotes involves proteins that bind to DNA and either facilitate or inhibit binding of RNA polymerase. The process is more complicated in eukaryotes, however. Before looking at how eukaryotic cells control their transcription, let's review the structure of a typical eukaryotic gene and its transcript.

Organization of a Typical Eukaryotic Gene

A eukaryotic gene and the DNA elements (segments) that control it are typically organized as shown in **Figure 18.8**, which extends what you learned about eukaryotic genes in Chapter 17. Recall that a cluster of proteins called a *transcription initiation complex* assembles on the promoter sequence at the "upstream" end of the gene. One of these proteins, RNA polymerase II, then proceeds to transcribe the gene, synthesizing a primary RNA transcript (pre-mRNA). RNA processing includes enzymatic addition of a 5′ cap and a poly-A tail, as well as splicing out of introns, to yield a mature mRNA. Associated with most eukaryotic genes are multiple **control elements**, segments of noncoding DNA that serve as binding sites for the proteins called transcription factors, which in turn regulate transcription. Control elements and the transcription factors they bind are critical to the precise regulation of gene expression seen in different cell types.

The Roles of Transcription Factors

To initiate transcription, eukaryotic RNA polymerase requires the assistance of transcription factors. Some transcription factors, such as those illustrated in Figure 17.8, are essential for the transcription of *all* protein-coding genes; therefore, they are often called *general transcription factors*. Only a few general transcription factors independently bind a DNA sequence, such as the TATA box within the promoter; the others primarily bind proteins, including each other and RNA polymerase II. Protein-protein interactions are crucial to the initiation of eukaryotic transcription. Only when the complete initiation complex has assembled can the polymerase begin to move along the DNA template strand, producing a complementary strand of RNA.

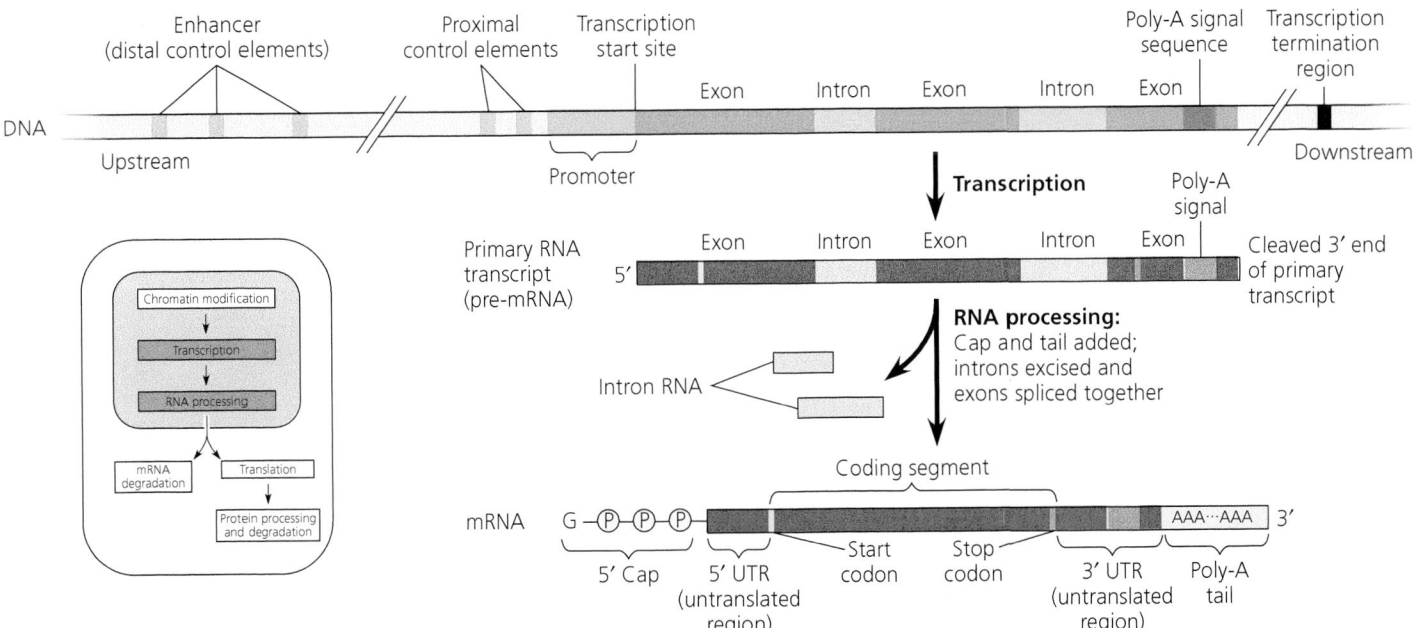

▲ Figure 18.8 A eukaryotic gene and its transcript. Each eukaryotic gene has a promoter, a DNA sequence where RNA polymerase binds and starts transcription, proceeding "downstream." A number of control elements (gold) are involved in regulating the initiation of transcription; these are DNA sequences located near (proximal to) or far from (distal to) the promoter. Distal control elements can be grouped together as enhancers, one of which is shown for this gene. A polyadenylation (poly-A) signal sequence in the last exon of the gene is transcribed into an RNA sequence that signals where the transcript is cleaved and the poly-A tail added. Transcription may continue for hundreds of nucleotides beyond the poly-A signal before terminating. RNA processing of the primary transcript into a functional mRNA involves three steps: addition of the 5′ cap, addition of the poly-A tail, and splicing. In the cell, the 5′ cap is added soon after transcription is initiated; splicing and poly-A tail addition may also occur while transcription is still under way (see Figure 17.10).

The interaction of general transcription factors and RNA polymerase II with a promoter usually leads to only a low rate of initiation and production of few RNA transcripts. In eukaryotes, high levels of transcription of particular genes at the appropriate time and place depend on the interaction of control elements with another set of proteins, which can be thought of as *specific transcription factors*.

Enhancers and Specific Transcription Factors As you can see in Figure 18.8, some control elements, named *proximal control elements*, are located close to the promoter. (Although some biologists consider proximal control elements part of the promoter, in this book we do not.) The more distant *distal control elements*, groupings of which are called **enhancers**, may be thousands of nucleotides upstream or downstream of a gene or even within an intron. A given gene may have multiple enhancers, each active at a different time or in a different cell type or location in the organism. Each enhancer, however, is generally associated with only that gene and no other.

In eukaryotes, the rate of gene expression can be strongly increased or decreased by the binding of specific transcription factors, either activators or repressors, to the control elements of enhancers. Hundreds of transcription activators have been discovered in eukaryotes; the structure of one example is shown in **Figure 18.9**. Researchers have identified two common structural elements in a large number of activator proteins: a DNA-binding domain—a part of the protein's three-dimensional structure that binds to DNA—and one or more activation domains. Activation domains bind other regulatory proteins or components of the transcription machinery, facilitating a series of protein-protein interactions that result in transcription of a given gene.

▲ Figure 18.9 The structure of MyoD, a specific transcription factor that acts as an activator. The MyoD protein is made up of two subunits (purple and salmon) with extensive regions of α helix. Each subunit has a DNA-binding domain and an activation domain (indicated by brackets for the purple subunit). The activation domain includes binding sites for the other subunit as well as other proteins. MyoD is involved in muscle development in vertebrate embryos and will be discussed further in Concept 18.4.

① **Activator proteins bind to distal control elements grouped as an enhancer in the DNA. This enhancer has three binding sites, each called a distal control element.**

Activators

DNA

Enhancer

Distal control element

Promoter

Gene

TATA box

② **A DNA-bending protein brings the bound activators closer to the promoter. General transcription factors, mediator proteins, and RNA polymerase II are nearby.**

DNA-bending protein

General transcription factors

Group of mediator proteins

RNA polymerase II

Chromatin modification

Transcription

RNA processing

mRNA degradation

Translation

Protein processing and degradation

③ **The activators bind to certain mediator proteins and general transcription factors, helping them form an active transcription initiation complex on the promoter.**

RNA polymerase II

Transcription initiation complex

RNA synthesis

▲ **Figure 18.10 A model for the action of enhancers and transcription activators.** Bending of the DNA by a protein enables enhancers to influence a promoter hundreds or even thousands of nucleotides away. Specific transcription factors called activators bind to the enhancer DNA sequences and then to a group of mediator proteins, which in turn bind to general transcription factors, assembling the transcription initiation complex. These protein-protein interactions facilitate the correct positioning of the complex on the promoter and the initiation of RNA synthesis. Only one enhancer (with three orange control elements) is shown here, but a gene may have several enhancers that act at different times or in different cell types.

Figure 18.10 shows a current model for how binding of activators to an enhancer located far from the promoter can influence transcription. Protein-mediated bending of the DNA is thought to bring the bound activators into contact with a group of *mediator proteins*, which in turn interact with proteins at the promoter. These multiple protein-protein interactions help assemble and position the initiation complex on the promoter. Support for this model includes a study showing that the proteins regulating a mouse globin gene contact both the gene's promoter and an enhancer located about 50,000 nucleotides upstream. Evidently, these two regions in the DNA must come together in a very specific fashion for this interaction to occur.

Specific transcription factors that function as repressors can inhibit gene expression in several different ways. Some repressors bind directly to control element DNA (in enhancers or elsewhere), blocking activator binding or, in some cases, turning off transcription even when activators are bound. Other repressors block the binding of activators to proteins that allow the activators to bind to DNA.

In addition to influencing transcription directly, some activators and repressors act indirectly by affecting chromatin structure. Studies using yeast and mammalian cells show that some activators recruit proteins that acetylate histones near the promoters of specific genes, thus promoting transcription (see Figure 18.7). Similarly, some repressors recruit proteins that deacetylate histones, leading to reduced transcription, a phenomenon referred to as *silencing*. Indeed, recruitment of chromatin-modifying proteins seems to be the most common mechanism of repression in eukaryotes.

Combinatorial Control of Gene Activation In eukaryotes, the precise control of transcription depends largely on the binding of activators to DNA control elements. Considering the great number of genes that must be regulated in a typical animal or plant cell, the number of completely different nucleotide sequences found in control elements is surprisingly small. A dozen or so short nucleotide sequences appear again and again in the control elements for different genes. On average, each enhancer is composed of about ten control elements, each of which can bind only one or two specific transcription factors. It is the particular *combination* of control elements in an enhancer associated with a gene, rather than the presence of a single unique control element, that is important in regulating transcription of the gene.

Even with only a dozen control element sequences available, a very large number of combinations are possible. A particular combination of control elements will be able to activate transcription only when the appropriate activator proteins are present, which may occur at a precise time during development or in a particular cell type. Figure 18.11 illustrates how the use of different combinations of just a few control elements can allow differential regulation of transcription in two cell types. This can occur because each cell type contains a different group of activator proteins. How these groups came to differ will be explored in Concept 18.4.

Coordinately Controlled Genes in Eukaryotes

How does the eukaryotic cell deal with genes of related function that need to be turned on or off at the same time? Earlier in this chapter, you learned that in bacteria, such coordinately controlled genes are often clustered into an operon, which is regulated by a single promoter and transcribed into a single mRNA molecule. Thus, the genes are expressed together, and the encoded proteins are produced concurrently. With a few minor exceptions, operons that work in this way have *not* been found in eukaryotic cells.

Co-expressed eukaryotic genes, such as genes coding for the enzymes of a metabolic pathway, are typically scattered over different chromosomes. In these cases, coordinate gene expression depends on the association of a specific combination of control elements with every gene of a dispersed group. The presence of these elements can be compared to the raised flags on a few mailboxes out of many, signaling to the mail carrier to check those boxes. Copies of the activators that recognize the control elements bind to them, promoting simultaneous transcription of the genes, no matter where they are in the genome.

(a) **Liver cell.** The albumin gene is expressed, and the crystallin gene is not.

(b) **Lens cell.** The crystallin gene is expressed, and the albumin gene is not.

▲ **Figure 18.11 Cell type–specific transcription.** Both liver cells and lens cells have the genes for making the proteins albumin and crystallin, but only liver cells make albumin (a blood protein) and only lens cells make crystallin (the main protein of the lens of the eye). The specific transcription factors made in a cell determine which genes are expressed. In this example, the genes for albumin and crystallin are shown at the top, each with an enhancer made up of three different control elements. Although the enhancers for the two genes share one control element (gray), each enhancer has a unique combination of elements. All the activators required for high-level expression of the albumin gene are present only in liver cells (a), whereas the activators needed for expression of the crystallin gene are present only in lens cells (b). For simplicity, we consider only the role of activators here, although the presence or absence of repressors may also influence transcription in certain cell types.

? *Describe the enhancer for the albumin gene in each cell. How would the nucleotide sequence of this enhancer in the liver cell compare with that in the lens cell?*

Coordinate control of dispersed genes in a eukaryotic cell often occurs in response to chemical signals from outside the cell. A steroid hormone, for example, enters a cell and binds to a specific intracellular receptor protein, forming a hormone-receptor complex that serves as a transcription activator (see Figure 11.9). Every gene whose transcription is stimulated by a particular steroid hormone, regardless of its chromosomal location, has a control element recognized by that hormone-receptor complex. This is how estrogen activates a group of genes that stimulate cell division in uterine cells, preparing the uterus for pregnancy.

Many signaling molecules, such as nonsteroid hormones and growth factors, bind to receptors on a cell's surface and never actually enter the cell. Such molecules can control gene expression indirectly by triggering signal transduction pathways that lead to activation of particular transcription activators or repressors (see Figure 11.15). Coordinate regulation in such pathways is the same as for steroid hormones: Genes with the same control elements are activated by the same chemical signals. Systems for coordinating gene regulation probably arose early in evolutionary history.

Nuclear Architecture and Gene Expression

You saw in Figure 16.23 that each chromosome in the interphase nucleus occupies a distinct territory. The chromosomes are not completely isolated, however. Recently, techniques have been developed that allow researchers to cross-link and identify regions of chromosomes that associate with each other during interphase. These studies reveal that loops of chromatin extend from individual chromosomal territories into specific sites in the nucleus (Figure 18.12). Different loops from the same chromosome and loops from other chromosomes may congregate in such sites, some of which are rich in RNA polymerases and other transcription-associated proteins. Like a recreation center that draws members from many different neighborhoods, these so-called *transcription factories* are thought to be areas specialized for a common function.

The old view that the nuclear contents are like a bowl of amorphous chromosomal spaghetti is giving way to a new model of a nucleus with a defined architecture and regulated movements of chromatin. Relocation of particular genes from their chromosomal territories to transcription factories may be part of the process of readying genes for transcription. This is an exciting area of current research that raises many fascinating questions for future study.

Mechanisms of Post-Transcriptional Regulation

Transcription alone does not constitute gene expression. The expression of a protein-coding gene is ultimately measured by the amount of functional protein a cell makes, and much happens between the synthesis of the RNA transcript and the activity of the protein in the cell. Researchers are discovering more and more regulatory mechanisms that operate at various stages after transcription (see Figure 18.6). These mechanisms allow a cell to fine-tune gene expression rapidly in response to environmental changes without altering its transcription patterns. Here we discuss how cells can regulate gene expression once a gene has been transcribed.

RNA Processing

RNA processing in the nucleus and the export of mature RNA to the cytoplasm provide several opportunities for regulating gene expression that are not available in prokaryotes. One example of regulation at the RNA-processing level is **alternative RNA splicing**, in which different mRNA molecules are produced from the same primary transcript, depending on which RNA segments are treated as exons and which as introns. Regulatory proteins specific to a cell type control intron-exon choices by binding to regulatory sequences within the primary transcript.

A simple example of alternative RNA splicing is shown in **Figure 18.13** for the troponin T gene, which encodes two different (though related) proteins. Other genes offer possibilities for far greater numbers of products. For instance, researchers have found a *Drosophila* gene with enough alternatively spliced exons to generate about 19,000 membrane proteins that have different extracellular domains. At least 17,500 (94%) of the alternative mRNAs are actually synthesized. Each developing nerve cell in the fly appears to synthesize a unique form of the protein, which acts as an identification badge on the cell surface.

It is clear that alternative RNA splicing can significantly expand the repertoire of a eukaryotic genome. In fact, alternative splicing was proposed as one explanation for the surprisingly low number of human genes counted when the human genome was sequenced about ten years ago. The number of human genes was found to be similar to that of a soil worm (nematode), a mustard plant, or a sea anemone. This discovery prompted questions about what, if not the number of genes, accounts for the more complex morphology (external form) of humans. It turns out that 75–100% of human genes that have multiple exons probably undergo alternative splicing. Thus, the extent of alternative splicing

Chromosomes in the interphase nucleus

Chromosome territory

10 μm

Chromatin loop

Transcription factory

▲ **Figure 18.12 Chromosomal interactions in the interphase nucleus.** Although each chromosome has its own territory (see Figure 16.23), loops of chromatin may extend into other sites in the nucleus. Some of these sites are transcription factories that are occupied by multiple chromatin loops from the same chromosome (blue loops) or other chromosomes (red and green loops).

Exons

DNA

Troponin T gene

Primary
RNA
transcript

RNA splicing

mRNA 1 2 3 5 or 1 2 4 5

◀ **Figure 18.13 Alternative RNA splicing of the troponin T gene.** The primary transcript of this gene can be spliced in more than one way, generating different mRNA molecules. Notice that one mRNA molecule has ended up with exon 3 (green) and the other with exon 4 (purple). These two mRNAs are translated into different but related muscle proteins.

greatly multiplies the number of possible human proteins, which may be better correlated with complexity of form.

mRNA Degradation

The life span of mRNA molecules in the cytoplasm is important in determining the pattern of protein synthesis in a cell. Bacterial mRNA molecules typically are degraded by enzymes within a few minutes of their synthesis. This short life span of mRNAs is one reason bacteria can change their patterns of protein synthesis so quickly in response to environmental changes. In contrast, mRNAs in multicellular eukaryotes typically survive for hours, days, or even weeks. For instance, the mRNAs for the hemoglobin polypeptides (α-globin and β-globin) in developing red blood cells are unusually stable, and these long-lived mRNAs are translated repeatedly in these cells.

Nucleotide sequences that affect how long an mRNA remains intact are often found in the untranslated region (UTR) at the 3′ end of the molecule (see Figure 18.8). In one experiment, researchers transferred such a sequence from the short-lived mRNA for a growth factor to the 3′ end of a normally stable globin mRNA. The globin mRNA was quickly degraded.

During the past few years, other mechanisms that degrade or block expression of mRNA molecules have come to light. These mechanisms involve an important group of newly discovered RNA molecules that regulate gene expression at several levels, and we will discuss them later in this chapter.

Initiation of Translation

Translation presents another opportunity for regulating gene expression; such regulation occurs most commonly at the initiation stage (see Figure 17.18). For some mRNAs, the initiation of translation can be blocked by regulatory proteins that bind to specific sequences or structures within the untranslated region at the 5′ or 3′ end (5′ or 3′ UTR), preventing the attachment of ribosomes. (Recall from Chapter 17 that both the 5′ cap and the poly-A tail of an mRNA molecule are important for ribosome binding.) A different mechanism for blocking translation is seen in a variety of mRNAs present in

the eggs of many organisms: Initially, these stored mRNAs lack poly-A tails of sufficient length to allow translation initiation. At the appropriate time during embryonic development, however, a cytoplasmic enzyme adds more adenine (A) nucleotides, prompting translation to begin.

Alternatively, translation of *all* the mRNAs in a cell may be regulated simultaneously. In a eukaryotic cell, such "global" control usually involves the activation or inactivation of one or more of the protein factors required to initiate translation. This mechanism plays a role in starting translation of mRNAs that are stored in eggs. Just after fertilization, translation is triggered by the sudden activation of translation initiation factors. The response is a burst of synthesis of the proteins encoded by the stored mRNAs. Some plants and algae store mRNAs during periods of darkness; light then triggers the reactivation of the translational apparatus.

Protein Processing and Degradation

The final opportunities for controlling gene expression occur after translation. Often, eukaryotic polypeptides must be processed to yield functional protein molecules. For instance, cleavage of the initial insulin polypeptide (pro-insulin) forms the active hormone. In addition, many proteins undergo chemical modifications that make them functional. Regulatory proteins are commonly activated or inactivated by the reversible addition of phosphate groups, and proteins destined for the surface of animal cells acquire sugars. Cell-surface proteins and many others must also be transported to target destinations in the cell in order to function. Regulation might occur at any of the steps involved in modifying or transporting a protein.

Finally, the length of time each protein functions in the cell is strictly regulated by means of selective degradation. Many proteins, such as the cyclins involved in regulating the cell cycle, must be relatively short-lived if the cell is to function appropriately (see Figure 12.17). To mark a particular protein for destruction, the cell commonly attaches molecules of a small protein called ubiquitin to the protein. Giant protein complexes called **proteasomes** then recognize the

① Multiple ubiquitin molecules are attached to a protein by enzymes in the cytosol.

② The ubiquitin-tagged protein is recognized by a proteasome, which unfolds the protein and sequesters it within a central cavity.

③ Enzymatic components of the proteasome cut the protein into small peptides, which can be further degraded by other enzymes in the cytosol.

Ubiquitin

Proteasome

Proteasome and ubiquitin to be recycled

Protein to be degraded

Ubiquitinated protein

Protein entering a proteasome

Protein fragments (peptides)

▲ **Figure 18.14 Degradation of a protein by a proteasome.** A proteasome, an enormous protein complex shaped like a trash can, chops up unneeded proteins in the cell. In most cases, the proteins attacked by a proteasome have been tagged with short chains of ubiquitin, a small protein. Steps 1 and 3 require ATP. Eukaryotic proteasomes are as massive as ribosomal subunits and are distributed throughout the cell. Their shape somewhat resembles that of chaperone proteins, which protect protein structure rather than destroy it (see Figure 5.23).

ubiquitin-tagged proteins and degrade them **(Figure 18.14)**. The importance of proteasomes is underscored by the finding that mutations making specific cell cycle proteins impervious to proteasome degradation can lead to cancer. The 2004 Nobel Prize in Chemistry was awarded to three scientists—two from Israel and one from the United States—who worked out the regulated process of protein degradation.

CONCEPT CHECK 18.2

1. In general, what is the effect of histone acetylation and DNA methylation on gene expression?
2. Compare the roles of general and specific transcription factors in regulating gene expression.
3. Suppose you compared the nucleotide sequences of the distal control elements in the enhancers of three genes that are expressed only in muscle tissue. What would you expect to find? Why?
4. Once mRNA encoding a particular protein reaches the cytoplasm, what are four mechanisms that can regulate the amount of the protein that is active in the cell?
5. **WHAT IF?** Examine Figure 18.11 and suggest a mechanism by which the yellow activator protein comes to be present in the liver cell but not in the lens cell.

For suggested answers, see Appendix A.

CONCEPT 18.3

Noncoding RNAs play multiple roles in controlling gene expression

Genome sequencing has revealed that protein-coding DNA accounts for only 1.5% of the human genome and a similarly small percentage of the genomes of many other multicellular eukaryotes. A very small fraction of the non-protein-coding DNA consists of genes for RNAs such as ribosomal RNA and transfer RNA. Until recently, most of the remaining DNA was assumed to be untranscribed. The idea was that since it didn't specify proteins or the few known types of RNA, such DNA didn't contain meaningful genetic information. However, a flood of recent data has contradicted this idea. For example, an in-depth study of a region comprising 1% of the human genome showed that more than 90% of that region was transcribed. Introns accounted for only a fraction of this transcribed, nontranslated RNA. These and other results suggest that a significant amount of the genome may be transcribed into non-protein-coding RNAs (also called *noncoding RNAs*, or *ncRNAs*), including a variety of small RNAs. While many questions about the functions of these RNAs remain unanswered, researchers are uncovering more evidence of their biological roles every day.

Biologists are excited about these recent discoveries, which hint at a large, diverse population of RNA molecules in the cell that play crucial roles in regulating gene expression—and have gone largely unnoticed until now. Clearly, we must revise our long-standing view that because mRNAs code for proteins, they are the most important RNAs functioning in the cell. This represents a major shift in the thinking of biologists, one that you are witnessing as students entering this field of study. It's as if our exclusive focus on a famous rock star has blinded us to the many backup musicians and songwriters working behind the scenes.

Regulation by both small and large ncRNAs is known to occur at several points in the pathway of gene expression, including mRNA translation and chromatin modification. We will focus mainly on two types of small ncRNAs that have been extensively studied in the past few years; the importance of these RNAs was acknowledged when they were the focus of the 2006 Nobel Prize in Physiology or Medicine.

Effects on mRNAs by MicroRNAs and Small Interfering RNAs

Since 1993, a number of research studies have uncovered small single-stranded RNA molecules, called **microRNAs (miRNAs)**, that are capable of binding to complementary sequences in mRNA molecules. The miRNAs are made from longer RNA precursors that fold back on themselves, forming one or more short double-stranded hairpin structures, each held together by hydrogen bonds (Figure 18.15). After each hairpin is cut away from the precursor, it is trimmed by an enzyme (fittingly called Dicer) into a short double-stranded fragment of about 22 nucleotide pairs. One of the two strands is degraded, while the other strand, which is the miRNA, forms a complex with one or more proteins; the miRNA allows the complex to bind to any mRNA molecule with 7–8 nucleotides of complementary sequence. The miRNA-protein complex then either degrades the target mRNA or blocks its translation. It has been estimated that expression of at least one-half of all human genes may be regulated by miRNAs, a remarkable figure given that the existence of miRNAs was unknown a mere two decades ago.

A growing understanding of the miRNA pathway provided an explanation for a perplexing observation: Researchers had found that injecting double-stranded RNA molecules into a cell somehow turned off expression of a gene with the same sequence as the RNA. They called this experimental phenomenon **RNA interference (RNAi)**. It was later shown to be due to **small interfering RNAs (siRNAs)**, which are similar in size and function to miRNAs. In fact, subsequent research showed that the same cellular machinery generates miRNAs and siRNAs and that both can associate with the same proteins, producing similar results. The distinction between miRNAs and siRNAs is based on the nature of the precursor molecule for each. While an miRNA is usually formed from a single hairpin in a precursor RNA (see Figure 18.15), multiple siRNAs are formed from a much longer, linear, double-stranded RNA molecule.

We mentioned that laboratory investigators had injected double-stranded RNAs into cells, and you may wonder whether such molecules are ever found naturally. As you will learn in Chapter 19, some viruses have double-stranded RNA genomes. Because the cellular RNAi pathway can lead to the destruction of RNAs with sequences complementary to those found in double-stranded RNAs, this pathway may have evolved as a natural defense against infection by such viruses. However, the fact that RNAi can also affect the expression of nonviral cellular genes may reflect a different evolutionary origin for the RNAi pathway. Moreover, many species, including mammals, apparently produce their own long, double-stranded RNA precursors to small RNAs such as siRNAs. Once produced, these RNAs can interfere with gene expression at stages other than translation, as we'll discuss next.

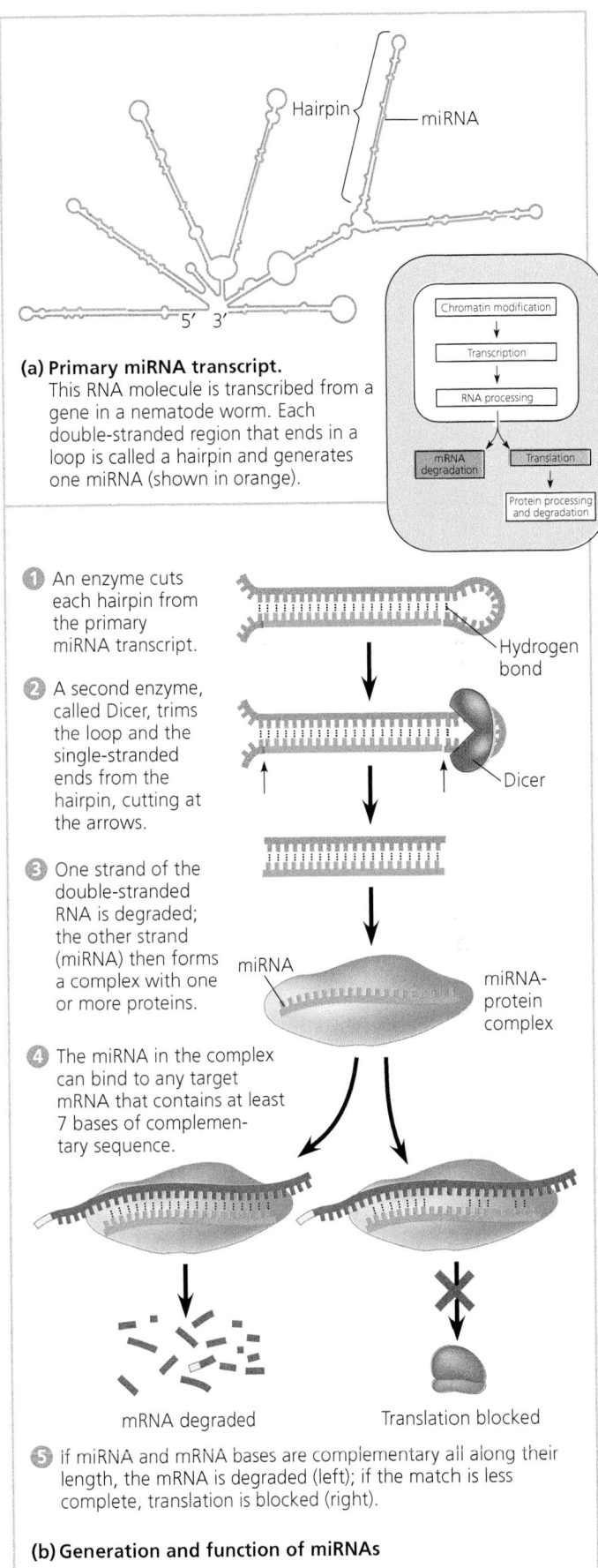

(a) Primary miRNA transcript.
This RNA molecule is transcribed from a gene in a nematode worm. Each double-stranded region that ends in a loop is called a hairpin and generates one miRNA (shown in orange).

1 An enzyme cuts each hairpin from the primary miRNA transcript.

2 A second enzyme, called Dicer, trims the loop and the single-stranded ends from the hairpin, cutting at the arrows.

3 One strand of the double-stranded RNA is degraded; the other strand (miRNA) then forms a complex with one or more proteins.

4 The miRNA in the complex can bind to any target mRNA that contains at least 7 bases of complementary sequence.

mRNA degraded   Translation blocked

5 If miRNA and mRNA bases are complementary all along their length, the mRNA is degraded (left); if the match is less complete, translation is blocked (right).

(b) Generation and function of miRNAs

▲ Figure 18.15 **Regulation of gene expression by miRNAs.**

Chromatin Remodeling and Effects on Transcription by ncRNAs

In addition to affecting mRNAs, small RNAs can cause remodeling of chromatin structure. In some yeasts, siRNAs produced by the yeast cells themselves are required for the formation of heterochromatin at the centromeres of chromosomes. According to one model, an RNA transcript produced from DNA in the centromeric region of the chromosome is copied into double-stranded RNA by a yeast enzyme and then processed into siRNAs. These siRNAs associate with a complex of proteins (different from the one shown in Figure 18.15) and act as a homing device, targeting the complex back to RNA transcripts being made from the centromeric sequences of DNA. Once there, proteins in the complex recruit enzymes that modify the chromatin, turning it into the highly condensed heterochromatin found at the centromere.

A newly discovered class of small ncRNAs called *piwi-associated RNAs* (*piRNAs*) also induce formation of heterochromatin, blocking expression of some parasitic DNA elements in the genome known as transposons. (Transposons are discussed in Chapter 21.) Usually 24–31 nucleotides in length, piRNAs are probably processed from single-stranded RNA precursors. They play an indispensable role in the germ cells of many animal species, where they appear to help re-establish appropriate methylation patterns in the genome during gamete formation.

The cases we have just described involve chromatin remodeling that blocks expression of large regions of the chromosome. Several recent experiments have shown that related RNA-based mechanisms may also block the transcription of specific genes. For instance, some plant miRNAs have sequences that bind to gene promoters and can repress transcription, and piRNAs can block expression of specific genes. And in a twist on the same theme, some cases have even been reported of *activation* of gene expression by miRNAs and piRNAs.

The Evolutionary Significance of Small ncRNAs

EVOLUTION Small ncRNAs can regulate gene expression at multiple steps and in many ways. In general, extra levels of gene regulation might allow evolution of a higher degree of complexity of form. Therefore, the versatility of miRNA regulation has led some biologists to hypothesize that an increase in the number of miRNAs specified by the genome of a given species has allowed morphological complexity to increase over evolutionary time. While this hypothesis is still being debated, it is logical to expand the discussion to include all small ncRNAs. Exciting new techniques for rapidly sequencing genomes are beginning to allow biologists to ask how many genes for ncRNAs are present in the genome of a given species. A survey of different species supports the notion that siRNAs evolved first, followed by miRNAs and later piRNAs, which are found only in animals. And while there

are hundreds of types of miRNAs, there appear to be many thousands of types of piRNAs, allowing the potential for very sophisticated gene regulation by piRNAs.

Given the extensive functions of ncRNAs, it is not surprising that many of the ncRNAs characterized thus far play important roles in embryonic development—the topic we turn to in the next section. Embryonic development is perhaps the ultimate example of precisely regulated gene expression.

CONCEPT CHECK 18.3

1. Compare and contrast miRNAs and siRNAs.
2. **WHAT IF?** If the mRNA being degraded in Figure 18.15 coded for a protein that promotes cell division in a multicellular organism, what would happen if a mutation disabled the gene encoding the miRNA that triggers this degradation?
3. **MAKE CONNECTIONS** In Concept 15.2 (pp. 291–292), you learned about inactivation of one of the X chromosomes in female mammals. Reread those pages, and suggest a model for how the *XIST* noncoding RNA functions to cause Barr body formation.

For suggested answers, see Appendix A.

CONCEPT 18.4

A program of differential gene expression leads to the different cell types in a multicellular organism

In the embryonic development of multicellular organisms, a fertilized egg (a zygote) gives rise to cells of many different types, each with a different structure and corresponding function. Typically, cells are organized into tissues, tissues into organs, organs into organ systems, and organ systems into the whole organism. Thus, any developmental program must produce cells of different types that form higher-level structures arranged in a particular way in three dimensions. The processes that occur during development in plants and animals are detailed in Chapters 35 and 47, respectively. In this chapter, we focus instead on the program of regulation of gene expression that orchestrates development, using a few animal species as examples.

A Genetic Program for Embryonic Development

The photos in **Figure 18.16** illustrate the dramatic difference between a zygote and the organism it becomes. This remarkable transformation results from three interrelated processes: cell division, cell differentiation, and morphogenesis. Through a succession of mitotic cell divisions, the zygote gives rise to a

(a) Fertilized eggs of a frog   (b) Newly hatched tadpole

▲ **Figure 18.16 From fertilized egg to animal: What a difference four days makes.** It takes just four days for cell division, differentiation, and morphogenesis to transform each of the fertilized frog eggs shown in (a) into a tadpole like the one in (b).

large number of cells. Cell division alone, however, would merely produce a great ball of identical cells, nothing like a tadpole. During embryonic development, cells not only increase in number, but also undergo cell **differentiation**, the process by which cells become specialized in structure and function. Moreover, the different kinds of cells are not randomly distributed but are organized into tissues and organs in a particular three-dimensional arrangement. The physical processes that give an organism its shape constitute **morphogenesis**, meaning "creation of form."

All three processes have their basis in cellular behavior. Even morphogenesis, the shaping of the organism, can be traced back to changes in the shape, motility, and other characteristics of the cells that make up various regions of the embryo. As you have seen, the activities of a cell depend on the genes it expresses and the proteins it produces. Almost all cells in an organism have the same genome; therefore, differential gene expression results from the genes being regulated differently in each cell type.

In Figure 18.11, you saw a simplified view of how differential gene expression occurs in two cell types, a liver cell and a lens cell. Each of these fully differentiated cells has a particular mix of specific activators that turn on the collection of genes whose products are required in the cell. The fact that both cells arose through a series of mitoses from a common fertilized egg inevitably leads to a question: How do different sets of activators come to be present in the two cells?

It turns out that materials placed into the egg by the mother set up a sequential program of gene regulation that is carried out as cells divide, and this program makes the cells become different from each other in a coordinated fashion. To understand how this works, we will consider two basic developmental processes: First, we'll explore how cells that arise from early embryonic mitoses develop the differences that start each cell along its own differentiation pathway. Second, we'll see how cellular differentiation leads to one particular cell type, using muscle development as an example.

Cytoplasmic Determinants and Inductive Signals

What generates the first differences among cells in an early embryo? And what controls the differentiation of all the various cell types as development proceeds? By this point in the chapter, you can probably deduce the answer: The specific genes expressed in any particular cell of a developing organism determine its path. Two sources of information, used to varying extents in different species, "tell" a cell which genes to express at any given time during embryonic development.

One important source of information early in development is the egg's cytoplasm, which contains both RNA and proteins encoded by the mother's DNA. The cytoplasm of an unfertilized egg is not homogeneous. Messenger RNA, proteins, other substances, and organelles are distributed unevenly in the unfertilized egg, and this unevenness has a profound impact on the development of the future embryo in many species. Maternal substances in the egg that influence the course of early development are called **cytoplasmic determinants** (Figure 18.17a, on the next page). After fertilization, early mitotic divisions distribute the zygote's cytoplasm into separate cells. The nuclei of these cells may thus be exposed to different cytoplasmic determinants, depending on which portions of the zygotic cytoplasm a cell received. The combination of cytoplasmic determinants in a cell helps determine its developmental fate by regulating expression of the cell's genes during the course of cell differentiation.

The other major source of developmental information, which becomes increasingly important as the number of embryonic cells increases, is the environment around a particular cell. Most influential are the signals impinging on an embryonic cell from other embryonic cells in the vicinity, including contact with cell-surface molecules on neighboring cells and the binding of growth factors secreted by neighboring cells. Such signals cause changes in the target cells, a process called **induction** (Figure 18.17b). The molecules conveying these signals within the target cell are cell-surface receptors and other proteins expressed by the embryo's own genes. In general, the signaling molecules send a cell down a specific developmental path by causing changes in its gene expression that eventually result in observable cellular changes. Thus, interactions between embryonic cells help induce differentiation of the many specialized cell types making up a new organism.

Sequential Regulation of Gene Expression During Cellular Differentiation

As the tissues and organs of an embryo develop and their cells differentiate, the cells become noticeably different in structure and function. These observable changes are actually the outcome of a cell's developmental history beginning at the first mitotic division of the zygote, as we have just seen. The

▼ **Figure 18.17 Sources of developmental information for the early embryo.**

(a) Cytoplasmic determinants in the egg

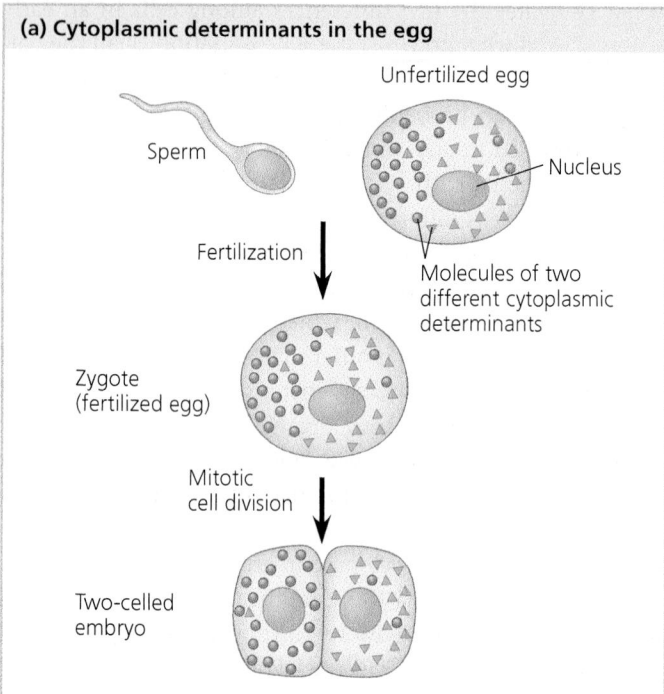

The unfertilized egg has molecules in its cytoplasm, encoded by the mother's genes, that influence development. Many of these cytoplasmic determinants, like the two shown here, are unevenly distributed in the egg. After fertilization and mitotic division, the cell nuclei of the embryo are exposed to different sets of cytoplasmic determinants and, as a result, express different genes.

(b) Induction by nearby cells

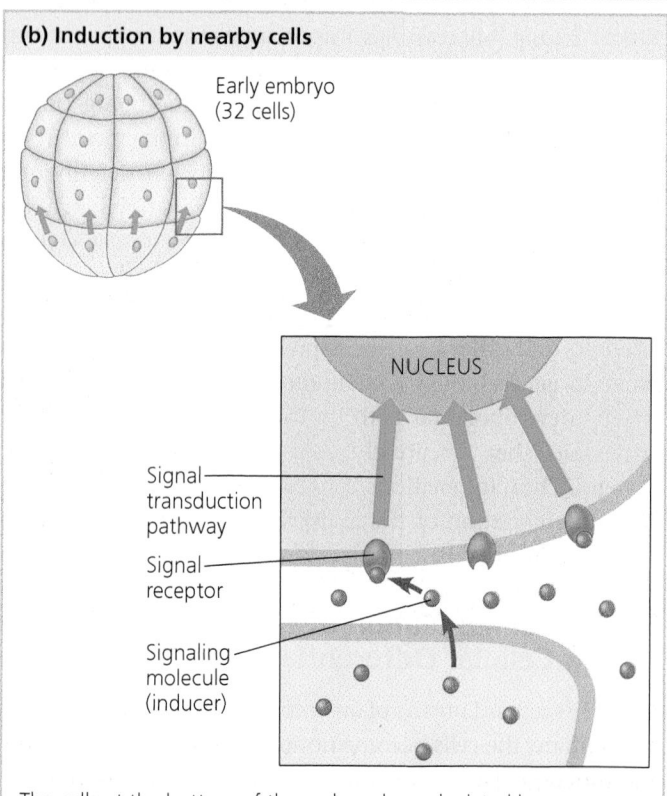

The cells at the bottom of the early embryo depicted here are releasing chemicals that signal nearby cells to change their gene expression.

earliest changes that set a cell on a path to specialization are subtle ones, showing up only at the molecular level. Before biologists knew much about the molecular changes occurring in embryos, they coined the term **determination** to refer to the events that lead to the observable differentiation of a cell. Once it has undergone determination, an embryonic cell is irreversibly committed to its final fate. If a committed cell is experimentally placed in another location in the embryo, it will still differentiate into the cell type that is its normal fate.

Today we understand determination in terms of molecular changes. The outcome of determination, observable cell differentiation, is marked by the expression of genes for *tissue-specific proteins*. These proteins are found only in a specific cell type and give the cell its characteristic structure and function. The first evidence of differentiation is the appearance of mRNAs for these proteins. Eventually, differentiation is observable with a microscope as changes in cellular structure. On the molecular level, different sets of genes are sequentially expressed in a regulated manner as new cells arise from division of their precursors. A number of the steps in gene expression may be regulated during differentiation, with transcription among the most important. In the fully differentiated cell, transcription remains the principal regulatory point for maintaining appropriate gene expression.

Differentiated cells are specialists at making tissue-specific proteins. For example, as a result of transcriptional regulation, liver cells specialize in making albumin, and lens cells specialize in making crystallin (see Figure 18.11). Skeletal muscle cells in vertebrates are another instructive example. Each of these cells is a long fiber containing many nuclei within a single plasma membrane. Skeletal muscle cells have high concentrations of muscle-specific versions of the contractile proteins myosin and actin, as well as membrane receptor proteins that detect signals from nerve cells.

Muscle cells develop from embryonic precursor cells that have the potential to develop into a number of cell types, including cartilage cells and fat cells, but particular conditions commit them to becoming muscle cells. Although the committed cells appear unchanged under the microscope, determination has occurred, and they are now *myoblasts*. Eventually, myoblasts start to churn out large amounts of muscle-specific proteins and fuse to form mature, elongated, multinucleate skeletal muscle cells **(Figure 18.18)**.

Researchers have worked out what happens at the molecular level during muscle cell determination by growing myoblasts in culture and analyzing them using molecular biological techniques you will learn about in Chapter 20. In a series of experiments, they isolated different genes, caused each to be expressed in a separate embryonic precursor cell, and then looked for differentiation into myoblasts and muscle cells. In this way, they identified several so-called "master regulatory genes" whose protein products commit the cells to becoming skeletal muscle. Thus, in the case of muscle cells,

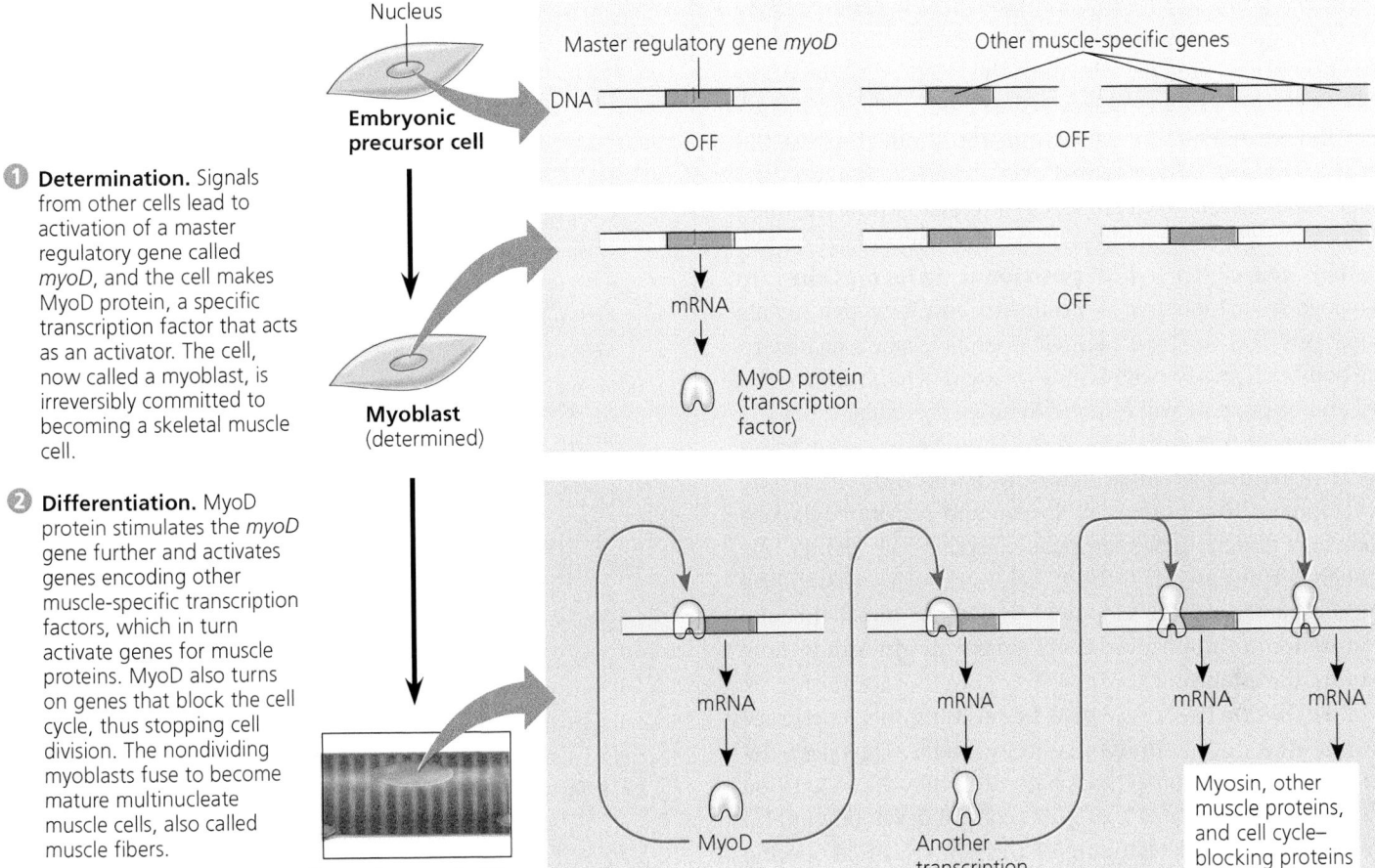

Determination. Signals from other cells lead to activation of a master regulatory gene called *myoD*, and the cell makes MyoD protein, a specific transcription factor that acts as an activator. The cell, now called a myoblast, is irreversibly committed to becoming a skeletal muscle cell.

Differentiation. MyoD protein stimulates the *myoD* gene further and activates genes encoding other muscle-specific transcription factors, which in turn activate genes for muscle proteins. MyoD also turns on genes that block the cell cycle, thus stopping cell division. The nondividing myoblasts fuse to become mature multinucleate muscle cells, also called muscle fibers.

Nucleus

Embryonic precursor cell

Master regulatory gene *myoD*　　Other muscle-specific genes

DNA

OFF　　　　OFF

Myoblast (determined)

mRNA

OFF

MyoD protein (transcription factor)

Part of a muscle fiber (fully differentiated cell)

mRNA　　mRNA　　mRNA　　mRNA

MyoD　　Another transcription factor　　Myosin, other muscle proteins, and cell cycle–blocking proteins

▲ **Figure 18.18 Determination and differentiation of muscle cells.** Skeletal muscle cells arise from embryonic cells as a result of changes in gene expression. (In this depiction, the process of gene activation is greatly simplified.)

WHAT IF? *What would happen if a mutation in the* myoD *gene resulted in a MyoD protein that could not activate the* myoD *gene?*

the molecular basis of determination is the expression of one or more of these master regulatory genes.

To understand more about how commitment occurs in muscle cell differentiation, let's focus on the master regulatory gene called *myoD* (see Figure 18.18). This gene encodes MyoD protein, a transcription factor that binds to specific control elements in the enhancers of various target genes and stimulates their expression (see Figure 18.9). Some target genes for MyoD encode still other muscle-specific transcription factors. MyoD also stimulates expression of the *myoD* gene itself, thus perpetuating its effect in maintaining the cell's differentiated state. Presumably, all the genes activated by MyoD have enhancer control elements recognized by MyoD and are thus coordinately controlled. Finally, the secondary transcription factors activate the genes for proteins such as myosin and actin that confer the unique properties of skeletal muscle cells.

The MyoD protein deserves its designation as a master regulatory gene. Researchers have shown that it is even capable of changing some kinds of fully differentiated nonmuscle cells, such as fat cells and liver cells, into muscle cells. Why

doesn't it work on *all* kinds of cells? One likely explanation is that activation of the muscle-specific genes is not solely dependent on MyoD but requires a particular *combination* of regulatory proteins, some of which are lacking in cells that do not respond to MyoD. The determination and differentiation of other kinds of tissues may play out in a similar fashion.

We have now seen how different programs of gene expression that are activated in the fertilized egg can result in differentiated cells and tissues. But for the tissues to function effectively in the organism as a whole, the organism's *body plan*—its overall three-dimensional arrangement—must be established and superimposed on the differentiation process. Next we'll investigate the molecular basis for the establishment of the body plan, using the well-studied *Drosophila* as an example.

Pattern Formation: Setting Up the Body Plan

Cytoplasmic determinants and inductive signals both contribute to the development of a spatial organization in which the tissues and organs of an organism are all in their characteristic places. This process is called **pattern formation**.

Pattern formation in animals begins in the early embryo, when the major axes of an animal are established. Before construction begins on a new building, the locations of the front, back, and sides are determined. In the same way, before the tissues and organs of a bilaterally symmetrical animal appear, the relative positions of the animal's head and tail, right and left sides, and back and front are set up, thus establishing the three major body axes. The molecular cues that control pattern formation, collectively called **positional information**, are provided by cytoplasmic determinants and inductive signals (see Figure 18.17). These cues tell a cell its location relative to the body axes and to neighboring cells and determine how the cell and its progeny will respond to future molecular signals.

During the first half of the 20th century, classical embryologists made detailed anatomical observations of embryonic development in a number of species and performed experiments in which they manipulated embryonic tissues. Although this research laid the groundwork for understanding the mechanisms of development, it did not reveal the specific molecules that guide development or determine how patterns are established.

Then, in the 1940s, scientists began using the genetic approach—the study of mutants—to investigate *Drosophila* development. That approach has had spectacular success. These studies have established that genes control development and have led to an understanding of the key roles that specific molecules play in defining position and directing differentiation. By combining anatomical, genetic, and biochemical approaches to the study of *Drosophila* development, researchers have discovered developmental principles common to many other species, including humans.

The Life Cycle of Drosophila

Fruit flies and other arthropods have a modular construction, an ordered series of segments. These segments make up the body's three major parts: the head, the thorax (the midbody, from which the wings and legs extend), and the abdomen (Figure 18.19a). Like other bilaterally symmetrical animals, *Drosophila* has an anterior-posterior (head-to-tail) axis, a dorsal-ventral (back-to-belly) axis, and a right-left axis. In *Drosophila*, cytoplasmic determinants that are localized in the unfertilized egg provide positional information for the placement of anterior-posterior and dorsal-ventral axes even before fertilization. We'll focus here on the molecules involved in establishing the anterior-posterior axis.

The *Drosophila* egg develops in the female's ovary, surrounded by ovarian cells called nurse cells and follicle cells (Figure 18.19b, top). These support cells supply the egg with nutrients, mRNAs, and other substances needed for development and make the egg shell. After fertilization and laying of the egg, embryonic development results in the formation of a segmented larva, which goes through three larval stages. Then, in a process much like that by which a caterpillar

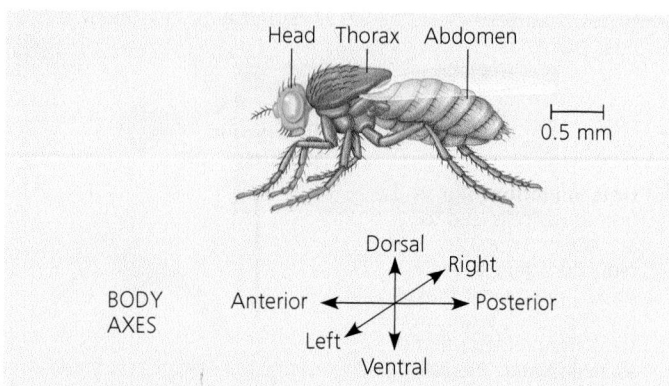

(a) Adult. The adult fly is segmented, and multiple segments make up each of the three main body parts—head, thorax, and abdomen. The body axes are shown by arrows.

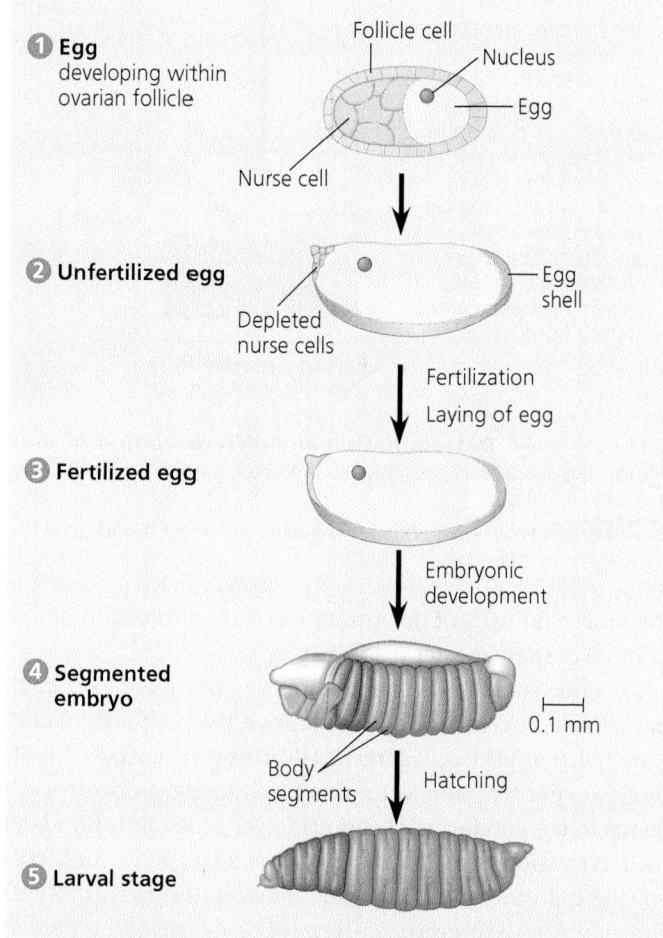

(b) Development from egg to larva. ① The egg (yellow) is surrounded by other cells that form a structure called the follicle within one of the mother's ovaries. ② The nurse cells shrink as they supply nutrients and mRNAs to the developing egg, which grows larger. Eventually, the mature egg fills the egg shell that is secreted by the follicle cells. ③ The egg is fertilized within the mother and then laid. ④ Embryonic development forms ⑤ a larva, which goes through three stages. The third stage forms a cocoon (not shown), within which the larva metamorphoses into the adult shown in (a).

▲ **Figure 18.19 Key developmental events in the life cycle of *Drosophila*.**

becomes a butterfly, the fly larva forms a cocoon in which it metamorphoses into the adult fly pictured in Figure 18.19a.

Genetic Analysis of Early Development: Scientific Inquiry

Edward B. Lewis was a visionary American biologist who, in the 1940s, first showed the value of the genetic approach to studying embryonic development in *Drosophila*. Lewis studied bizarre mutant flies with developmental defects that led to extra wings or legs in the wrong place (Figure 18.20). He located the mutations on the fly's genetic map, thus connecting the developmental abnormalities to specific genes. This research supplied the first concrete evidence that genes somehow direct the developmental processes studied by embryologists. The genes Lewis discovered, called **homeotic genes**, control pattern formation in the late embryo, larva, and adult.

Insight into pattern formation during early embryonic development did not come for another 30 years, when two researchers in Germany, Christiane Nüsslein-Volhard and Eric Wieschaus, set out to identify *all* the genes that affect segment formation in *Drosophila*. The project was daunting for three reasons. The first was the sheer number of *Drosophila* genes, now known to total about 13,700. The genes affecting segmentation might be just a few needles in a haystack or might be so numerous and varied that the scientists would be unable to make sense of them. Second, mutations affecting a

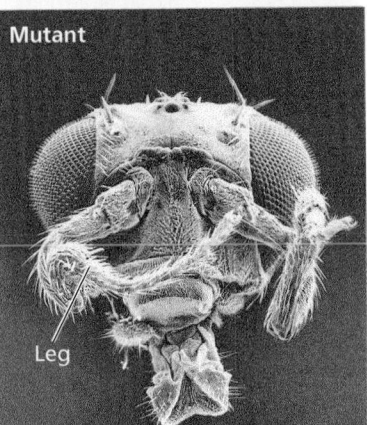

Wild type

Eye

Antenna

Mutant

Leg

◀ **Figure 18.20**
Abnormal pattern formation in Drosophila. Mutations in certain regulatory genes, called homeotic genes, cause a misplacement of structures in an animal. These scanning electron micrographs contrast the head of a wild-type fly, bearing a pair of small antennae, with that of a homeotic mutant (a fly with a mutation in a single gene), bearing a pair of legs in place of antennae.

process as fundamental as segmentation would surely be **embryonic lethals**, mutations with phenotypes causing death at the embryonic or larval stage. Because organisms with embryonic lethal mutations never reproduce, they cannot be bred for study. The researchers dealt with this problem by looking for recessive mutations, which can be propagated in heterozygous flies that act as genetic carriers. Third, cytoplasmic determinants in the egg were known to play a role in axis formation, so the researchers knew they would have to study the mother's genes as well as those of the embryo. It is the mother's genes that we will discuss further as we focus on how the anterior-posterior body axis is set up in the developing egg.

Nüsslein-Volhard and Wieschaus began their search for segmentation genes by exposing flies to a mutagenic chemical that affected the flies' gametes. They mated the mutagenized flies and then scanned their descendants for dead embryos or larvae with abnormal segmentation or other defects. For example, to find genes that might set up the anterior-posterior axis, they looked for embryos or larvae with abnormal ends, such as two heads or two tails, predicting that such abnormalities would arise from mutations in maternal genes required for correctly setting up the offspring's head or tail end.

Using this approach, Nüsslein-Volhard and Wieschaus eventually identified about 1,200 genes essential for pattern formation during embryonic development. Of these, about 120 were essential for normal segmentation. Over several years, the researchers were able to group these segmentation genes by general function, to map them, and to clone many of them for further study in the lab. The result was a detailed molecular understanding of the early steps in pattern formation in *Drosophila*.

When the results of Nüsslein-Volhard and Wieschaus were combined with Lewis's earlier work, a coherent picture of *Drosophila* development emerged. In recognition of their discoveries, the three researchers were awarded a Nobel Prize in 1995.

Let's consider further the genes that Nüsslein-Volhard, Wieschaus, and co-workers found for cytoplasmic determinants deposited in the egg by the mother. These genes set up the initial pattern of the embryo by regulating gene expression in broad regions of the early embryo.

Axis Establishment

As we mentioned earlier, cytoplasmic determinants in the egg are the substances that initially establish the axes of the *Drosophila* body. These substances are encoded by genes of the mother, fittingly called maternal effect genes. A **maternal effect gene** is a gene that, when mutant in the mother, results in a mutant phenotype in the offspring, regardless of the offspring's own genotype. In fruit fly development, the mRNA or protein products of maternal effect genes are placed in the egg while it is still in the mother's ovary. When the mother has a mutation in such a gene, she makes a defective gene product (or none at all), and her eggs are defective; when these eggs are fertilized, they fail to develop properly.

Because they control the orientation (polarity) of the egg and consequently of the fly, maternal effect genes are also called **egg-polarity genes**. One group of these genes sets up the anterior-posterior axis of the embryo, while a second group establishes the dorsal-ventral axis. Like mutations in segmentation genes, mutations in maternal effect genes are generally embryonic lethals.

Bicoid: A Morphogen Determining Head Structures To see how maternal effect genes determine the body axes of the offspring, we will focus on one such gene, called **bicoid**, a term meaning "two-tailed." An embryo whose mother has two mutant alleles of the *bicoid* gene lacks the front half of its body and has posterior structures at both ends **(Figure 18.21)**. This phenotype suggested to Nüsslein-Volhard and her colleagues that the product of the mother's *bicoid* gene is essential for setting up the anterior end of the fly and might be concentrated at the future anterior end of the embryo. This hypothesis is an example of the *morphogen gradient hypothesis* first proposed by embryologists a century ago; in this hypothesis, gradients of substances called **morphogens** establish an embryo's axes and other features of its form.

DNA technology and other modern biochemical methods enabled the researchers to test whether the *bicoid* product, a protein called Bicoid, is in fact a morphogen that determines the anterior end of the fly. The first question they asked was whether the mRNA and protein products of these genes are located in the egg in a position consistent with the hypothesis.

▲ **Figure 18.21 Effect of the *bicoid* gene on *Drosophila* development.** A wild-type fruit fly larva has a head, three thoracic (T) segments, eight abdominal (A) segments, and a tail. A larva whose mother has two mutant alleles of the *bicoid* gene has two tails and lacks all anterior structures (LMs).

They found that *bicoid* mRNA is highly concentrated at the extreme anterior end of the mature egg, as predicted by the hypothesis **(Figure 18.22)**. After the egg is fertilized, the mRNA is translated into protein. The Bicoid protein then diffuses from the anterior end toward the posterior, resulting in a gradient of protein within the early embryo, with the highest concentration at the anterior end. These results are consistent with the hypothesis that Bicoid protein specifies the fly's anterior end. To test the hypothesis more specifically, scientists injected pure *bicoid* mRNA into various regions of early embryos. The protein that resulted from its translation caused anterior structures to form at the injection sites.

▼ **Figure 18.22** **INQUIRY**

Is Bicoid a morphogen that determines the anterior end of a fruit fly?

EXPERIMENT Using a genetic approach to study *Drosophila* development, Christiane Nüsslein-Volhard and colleagues at the European Molecular Biology Laboratory in Heidelberg, Germany, analyzed expression of the *bicoid* gene. The researchers hypothesized that *bicoid* normally codes for a morphogen that specifies the head (anterior) end of the embryo. To test this hypothesis, they used molecular techniques to determine where the mRNA and protein encoded by this gene were found in the fertilized egg and early embryo of wild-type flies.

RESULTS Bicoid mRNA (dark blue) was confined to the anterior end of the unfertilized egg. Later in development, Bicoid protein (dark orange) was seen to be concentrated in cells at the anterior end of the embryo.

Bicoid mRNA in mature unfertilized egg

Bicoid protein in early embryo

Bicoid mRNA in mature unfertilized egg

Bicoid protein in early embryo

CONCLUSION The location of *bicoid* mRNA and the diffuse gradient of Bicoid protein seen later support the hypothesis that Bicoid protein is a morphogen specifying formation of head-specific structures.

SOURCE: C. Nüsslein-Volhard et al., Determination of anteroposterior polarity in *Drosophila*, *Science* 238:1675–1681 (1987); W. Driever and C. Nüsslein-Volhard, A gradient of *bicoid* protein in *Drosophila* embryos, *Cell* 54:83–93 (1988); T. Berleth et al., The role of localization of *bicoid* RNA in organizing the anterior pattern of the *Drosophila* embryo, *EMBO Journal* 7:1749–1756 (1988).

WHAT IF? If the hypothesis is correct, predict what would happen if you injected *bicoid* mRNA into the anterior end of an egg from a female with a mutation disabling the *bicoid* gene.

The *bicoid* research was groundbreaking for several reasons. First, it led to the identification of a specific protein required for some of the earliest steps in pattern formation. It thus helped us understand how different regions of the egg can give rise to cells that go down different developmental pathways. Second, it increased our understanding of the mother's critical role in the initial phases of embryonic development. Finally, the principle that a gradient of morphogens can determine polarity and position has proved to be a key developmental concept for a number of species, just as early embryologists had thought.

Maternal mRNAs are crucial during development of many species. In *Drosophila*, gradients of specific proteins encoded by maternal mRNAs determine the posterior and anterior ends and establish the dorsal-ventral axis. As the fly embryo grows, it reaches a point when the embryonic program of gene expression takes over, and the maternal mRNAs must be destroyed. (This process involves miRNAs in *Drosophila* and other species.) Later, positional information encoded by the embryo's genes, operating on an ever finer scale, establishes a specific number of correctly oriented segments and triggers the formation of each segment's characteristic structures. When the genes operating in this final step are abnormal, the pattern of the adult is abnormal, as you saw in Figure 18.20.

In this section, we have seen how a carefully orchestrated program of sequential gene regulation controls the transformation of a fertilized egg into a multicellular organism. The program is carefully balanced between turning on the genes for differentiation in the right place and turning off other genes. Even when an organism is fully developed, gene expression is regulated in a similarly fine-tuned manner. In the final section of the chapter, we'll consider how fine this tuning is by looking at how specific changes in expression of one or a few genes can lead to the development of cancer.

CONCEPT CHECK 18.4

1. As you learned in Chapter 12, mitosis gives rise to two daughter cells that are genetically identical to the parent cell. Yet you, the product of many mitotic divisions, are not composed of identical cells. Why?
2. **MAKE CONNECTIONS** Explain how the signaling molecules released by an embryonic cell can induce changes in a neighboring cell without entering the cell. (See Figures 11.15 and 11.16, pp. 219 and 220.)
3. Why are fruit fly maternal effect genes also called egg-polarity genes?
4. **WHAT IF?** In the blowup box in Figure 18.17b, the lower cell is synthesizing signaling molecules, whereas the upper cell is expressing receptors for these molecules. In terms of gene regulation, explain how these cells came to synthesize different molecules.

For suggested answers, see Appendix A.

Cancer results from genetic changes that affect cell cycle control

In Chapter 12, we considered cancer as a set of diseases in which cells escape from the control mechanisms that normally limit their growth. Now that we have discussed the molecular basis of gene expression and its regulation, we are ready to look at cancer more closely. The gene regulation systems that go wrong during cancer turn out to be the very same systems that play important roles in embryonic development, the immune response, and many other biological processes. Thus, research into the molecular basis of cancer has both benefited from and informed many other fields of biology.

Types of Genes Associated with Cancer

The genes that normally regulate cell growth and division during the cell cycle include genes for growth factors, their receptors, and the intracellular molecules of signaling pathways. (To review the cell cycle, see Chapter 12.) Mutations that alter any of these genes in somatic cells can lead to cancer. The agent of such change can be random spontaneous mutation. However, it is likely that many cancer-causing mutations result from environmental influences, such as chemical carcinogens, X-rays and other high-energy radiation, and some viruses.

Cancer research led to the discovery of cancer-causing genes called **oncogenes** (from the Greek *onco*, tumor) in certain types of viruses (see Chapter 19). Subsequently, close counterparts of viral oncogenes were found in the genomes of humans and other animals. The normal versions of the cellular genes, called **proto-oncogenes**, code for proteins that stimulate normal cell growth and division.

How might a proto-oncogene—a gene that has an essential function in normal cells—become an oncogene, a cancer-causing gene? In general, an oncogene arises from a genetic change that leads to an increase either in the amount of the proto-oncogene's protein product or in the intrinsic activity of each protein molecule. The genetic changes that convert proto-oncogenes to oncogenes fall into three main categories: movement of DNA within the genome, amplification of a proto-oncogene, and point mutations in a control element or in the proto-oncogene itself (**Figure 18.23**, on the next page).

Cancer cells are frequently found to contain chromosomes that have broken and rejoined incorrectly, translocating fragments from one chromosome to another (see Figure 15.14). Now that you have learned how gene expression is regulated, you can understand the possible consequences of such translocations. If a translocated proto-oncogene ends up near an especially active promoter (or other control element), its transcription may increase, making it an oncogene. The second main type of genetic change, amplification, increases the

▲ **Figure 18.23 Genetic changes that can turn proto-oncogenes into oncogenes.**

number of copies of the proto-oncogene in the cell through repeated gene duplication (discussed in Chapter 21). The third possibility is a point mutation either (1) in the promoter or an enhancer that controls a proto-oncogene, causing an increase in its expression, or (2) in the coding sequence, changing the gene's product to a protein that is more active or more resistant to degradation than the normal protein. All these mechanisms can lead to abnormal stimulation of the cell cycle and put the cell on the path to malignancy.

Tumor-Suppressor Genes

In addition to genes whose products normally promote cell division, cells contain genes whose normal products *inhibit* cell division. Such genes are called **tumor-suppressor genes** because the proteins they encode help prevent uncontrolled cell growth. Any mutation that decreases the normal activity of a tumor-suppressor protein may contribute to the onset of cancer, in effect stimulating growth through the absence of suppression.

The protein products of tumor-suppressor genes have various functions. Some tumor-suppressor proteins repair damaged DNA, a function that prevents the cell from accumulating cancer-causing mutations. Other tumor-suppressor proteins control the adhesion of cells to each other or to the extracellular matrix; proper cell anchorage is crucial in normal tissues—and is often absent in cancers. Still other tumor-suppressor proteins are components of cell-signaling pathways that inhibit the cell cycle.

Interference with Normal Cell-Signaling Pathways

The proteins encoded by many proto-oncogenes and tumor-suppressor genes are components of cell-signaling pathways. Let's take a closer look at how such proteins function in normal

cells and what goes wrong with their function in cancer cells. We will focus on the products of two key genes, the *ras* proto-oncogene and the *p53* tumor-suppressor gene. Mutations in *ras* occur in about 30% of human cancers, and mutations in *p53* in more than 50%.

The Ras protein, encoded by the **ras gene** (named for <u>ra</u>t <u>s</u>arcoma, a connective tissue cancer), is a G protein that relays a signal from a growth factor receptor on the plasma membrane to a cascade of protein kinases (see Figure 11.7). The cellular response at the end of the pathway is the synthesis of a protein that stimulates the cell cycle **(Figure 18.24a)**. Normally, such a pathway will not operate unless triggered by the appropriate growth factor. But certain mutations in the *ras* gene can lead to production of a hyperactive Ras protein that triggers the kinase cascade even in the absence of growth factor, resulting in increased cell division. In fact, hyperactive versions or excess amounts of any of the pathway's components can have the same outcome: excessive cell division.

Figure 18.24b shows a pathway in which a signal leads to the synthesis of a protein that suppresses the cell cycle. In this case, the signal is damage to the cell's DNA, perhaps as the result of exposure to ultraviolet light. Operation of this signaling pathway blocks the cell cycle until the damage has been repaired. Otherwise, the damage might contribute to tumor formation by causing mutations or chromosomal abnormalities. Thus, the genes for the components of the pathway act as tumor-suppressor genes. The **p53 gene**, named for the 53,000-dalton molecular weight of its protein product, is a tumor-suppressor gene. The protein it encodes is a specific transcription factor that promotes the synthesis of cell cycle–inhibiting proteins. That is why a mutation that knocks out the *p53* gene, like a mutation that leads to a hyperactive Ras protein, can lead to excessive cell growth and cancer **(Figure 18.24c)**.

(a) Cell cycle–stimulating pathway.
This pathway is triggered by ❶ a growth factor that binds to ❷ its receptor in the plasma membrane. The signal is relayed to ❸ a G protein called Ras. Like all G proteins, Ras is active when GTP is bound to it. Ras passes the signal to ❹ a series of protein kinases. The last kinase activates ❺ a transcription activator that turns on one or more genes for proteins that stimulate the cell cycle. If a mutation makes Ras or any other pathway component abnormally active, excessive cell division and cancer may result.

(b) Cell cycle–inhibiting pathway. In this pathway, ❶ DNA damage is an intracellular signal that is passed via ❷ protein kinases and leads to activation of ❸ p53. Activated p53 promotes transcription of the gene for a protein that inhibits the cell cycle. The resulting suppression of cell division ensures that the damaged DNA is not replicated. If the DNA damage is irreparable, the p53 signal leads to programmed cell death (apoptosis). Mutations causing deficiencies in any pathway component can contribute to the development of cancer.

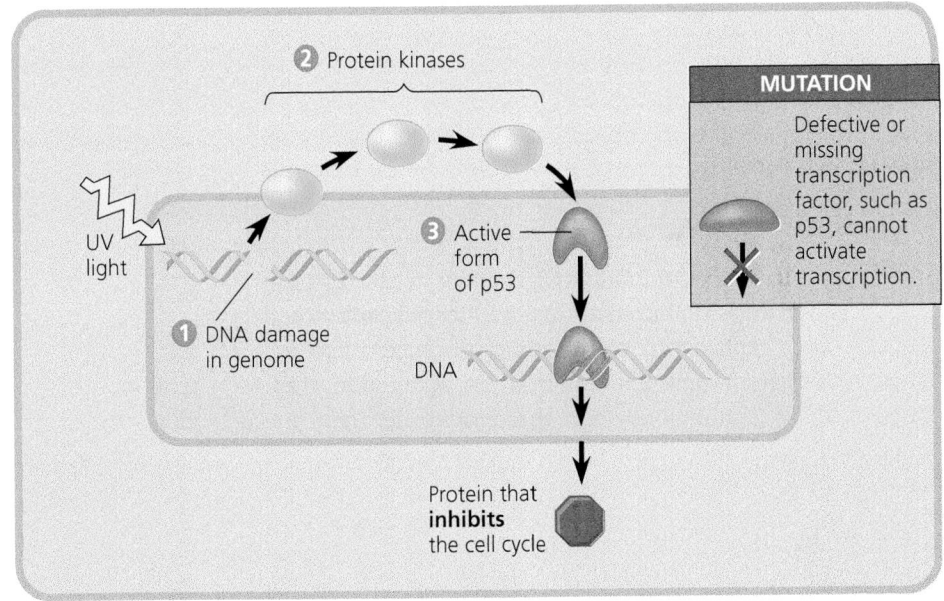

(c) Effects of mutations. Increased cell division, possibly leading to cancer, can result if the cell cycle is overstimulated, as in (a), or not inhibited when it normally would be, as in (b).

▲ **Figure 18.24 Signaling pathways that regulate cell division.** Both stimulatory and inhibitory pathways regulate the cell cycle, commonly by influencing transcription. Cancer can result from aberrations in such pathways, which may be caused by mutations, either spontaneous or environmentally triggered.

? *Looking at the pathway in (b), explain whether a cancer-causing mutation in a tumor-suppressor gene, such as p53, is more likely to be a recessive or a dominant mutation.*

The *p53* gene has been called the "guardian angel of the genome." Once the gene is activated—for example, by DNA damage—the p53 protein functions as an activator for several other genes. Often it activates a gene called *p21*, whose product halts the cell cycle by binding to cyclin-dependent kinases, allowing time for the cell to repair the DNA. Researchers recently showed that p53 also activates expression of a group of miRNAs, which in turn inhibit the cell cycle. In addition, the p53 protein can turn on genes directly involved in DNA repair. Finally, when DNA damage is irreparable, p53 activates "suicide" genes, whose protein products bring about programmed cell death (apoptosis; see Figure 11.21). Thus, p53 acts in several ways to prevent a cell from passing on mutations due to DNA damage. If mutations do accumulate and the cell survives through many divisions—as is more likely if the *p53* tumor-suppressor gene is defective or missing—cancer may ensue.

The many functions of p53 suggest a complex picture of regulation in normal cells, one that we do not yet fully understand. For the present, the diagram in Figure 18.24 is an accurate view of how mutations can contribute to cancer, but we still don't know exactly how a particular cell becomes a cancer cell. As we discover previously unknown aspects of gene regulation, it is informative to study their role in the onset of cancer. Such studies have shown, for instance, that DNA methylation and histone modification patterns differ in normal and cancer cells and that miRNAs probably participate in cancer development. While we've learned a lot about cancer by studying cell-signaling pathways, there is still a lot left to learn.

The Multistep Model of Cancer Development

More than one somatic mutation is generally needed to produce all the changes characteristic of a full-fledged cancer cell. This may help explain why the incidence of cancer increases greatly with age. If cancer results from an accumulation of mutations and if mutations occur throughout life, then the longer we live, the more likely we are to develop cancer.

The model of a multistep path to cancer is well supported by studies of one of the best-understood types of human cancer, colorectal cancer. About 135,000 new cases of colorectal cancer are diagnosed each year in the United States, and the disease causes 60,000 deaths each year. Like most cancers, colorectal cancer develops gradually (**Figure 18.25**). The first sign is often a polyp, a small, benign growth in the colon lining. The cells of the polyp look normal, although they divide unusually frequently. The tumor grows and may eventually become malignant, invading other tissues. The development of a malignant tumor is paralleled by a gradual accumulation of mutations that convert proto-oncogenes to oncogenes and knock out tumor-suppressor genes. A *ras* oncogene and a mutated *p53* tumor-suppressor gene are often involved.

About half a dozen changes must occur at the DNA level for a cell to become fully cancerous. These changes usually include the appearance of at least one active oncogene and the mutation or loss of several tumor-suppressor genes. Furthermore, since mutant tumor-suppressor alleles are usually recessive, in most cases mutations must knock out *both* alleles in a cell's genome to block tumor suppression. (Most oncogenes, on the other hand, behave as dominant alleles.) The order in which these changes must occur is still under investigation, as is the relative importance of different mutations.

Recently, technical advances in the sequencing of DNA and mRNA have allowed medical researchers to compare the genes expressed by different types of tumors and by the same type in different individuals. These comparisons have led to personalized cancer treatments based on the molecular characteristics of an individual's tumor (see Figure 12.21.)

Inherited Predisposition and Other Factors Contributing to Cancer

The fact that multiple genetic changes are required to produce a cancer cell helps explain the observation that cancers can run in families. An individual inheriting an oncogene or

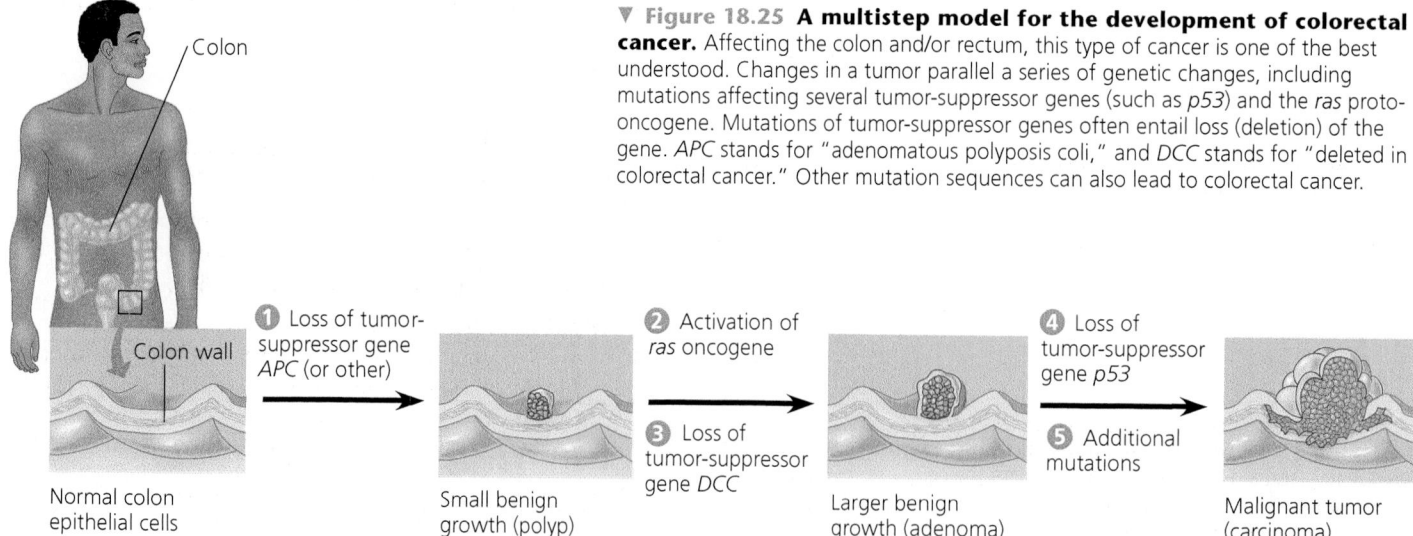

▼ **Figure 18.25 A multistep model for the development of colorectal cancer.** Affecting the colon and/or rectum, this type of cancer is one of the best understood. Changes in a tumor parallel a series of genetic changes, including mutations affecting several tumor-suppressor genes (such as *p53*) and the *ras* proto-oncogene. Mutations of tumor-suppressor genes often entail loss (deletion) of the gene. *APC* stands for "adenomatous polyposis coli," and *DCC* stands for "deleted in colorectal cancer." Other mutation sequences can also lead to colorectal cancer.

Colon

Colon wall

① Loss of tumor-suppressor gene *APC* (or other)

② Activation of *ras* oncogene

③ Loss of tumor-suppressor gene *DCC*

④ Loss of tumor-suppressor gene *p53*

⑤ Additional mutations

Normal colon epithelial cells

Small benign growth (polyp)

Larger benign growth (adenoma)

Malignant tumor (carcinoma)

a mutant allele of a tumor-suppressor gene is one step closer to accumulating the necessary mutations for cancer to develop than is an individual without any such mutations.

Geneticists are devoting much effort to identifying inherited cancer alleles so that predisposition to certain cancers can be detected early in life. About 15% of colorectal cancers, for example, involve inherited mutations. Many of these affect the tumor-suppressor gene called *adenomatous polyposis coli*, or *APC* (see Figure 18.25). This gene has multiple functions in the cell, including regulation of cell migration and adhesion. Even in patients with no family history of the disease, the *APC* gene is mutated in 60% of colorectal cancers. In these individuals, new mutations must occur in both *APC* alleles before the gene's function is lost. Since only 15% of colorectal cancers are associated with known inherited mutations, researchers continue in their efforts to identify "markers" that could predict the risk of developing this type of cancer.

There is evidence of a strong inherited predisposition in 5–10% of patients with breast cancer. This is the second most common type of cancer in the United States, striking over 180,000 women (and some men) annually and killing 40,000 each year. In 1990, after 16 years of research, geneticist Mary-Claire King convincingly demonstrated that mutations in one gene—*BRCA1*—were associated with increased susceptibility to breast cancer, a finding that flew in the face of medical opinion at the time. (*BRCA* stands for *br*east *ca*ncer.) Mutations in that gene or the related *BRCA2* gene are found in at least half of inherited breast cancers, and tests using DNA sequencing can detect these mutations (**Figure 18.26**). A woman who inherits one mutant *BRCA1* allele has a 60% probability of developing breast cancer before the age of 50, compared with only a 2% probability for an individual homozygous for the normal allele. Both *BRCA1* and *BRCA2* are considered tumor-suppressor genes because their wild-type alleles

protect against breast cancer and their mutant alleles are recessive. Apparently, the BRCA1 and BRCA2 proteins both function in the cell's DNA damage repair pathway. More is known about BRCA2, which, in association with another protein, helps repair breaks that occur in both strands of DNA; it is crucial for maintaining undamaged DNA in a cell's nucleus.

Because DNA breakage can contribute to cancer, it makes sense that the risk of cancer can be lowered by minimizing exposure to DNA-damaging agents, such as the ultraviolet radiation in sunlight and chemicals found in cigarette smoke. Novel methods for early diagnosis and treatment of specific cancers are being developed that rely on new techniques for analyzing, and perhaps interfering with, gene expression in tumors. Ultimately, such approaches may lower the death rate from cancer.

The study of genes associated with cancer, inherited or not, increases our basic understanding of how disruption of normal gene regulation can result in this disease. In addition to the mutations and other genetic alterations described in this section, a number of *tumor viruses* can cause cancer in various animals, including humans. In fact, one of the earliest breakthroughs in understanding cancer came in 1911, when Peyton Rous, an American pathologist, discovered a virus that causes cancer in chickens. The Epstein-Barr virus, which causes infectious mononucleosis, has been linked to several types of cancer in humans, notably Burkitt's lymphoma. Papillomaviruses are associated with cancer of the cervix, and a virus called HTLV-1 causes a type of adult leukemia. Worldwide, viruses seem to play a role in about 15% of the cases of human cancer.

Viruses may at first seem very different from mutations as a cause of cancer. However, we now know that viruses can interfere with gene regulation in several ways if they integrate their genetic material into the DNA of a cell. Viral integration may donate an oncogene to the cell, disrupt a tumor-suppressor gene, or convert a proto-oncogene to an oncogene. In addition, some viruses produce proteins that inactivate p53 and other tumor-suppressor proteins, making the cell more prone to becoming cancerous. Viruses are powerful biological agents, and you'll learn more about their function in Chapter 19.

▲ **Figure 18.26 Testing for mutations in *BRCA1* and *BRCA2*.** Genetic testing for mutations that increase the risk of breast cancer is available for individuals with a family history of breast cancer. New "high-throughput" sequencing techniques can sequence many DNA samples at once, as shown here.

CONCEPT CHECK 18.5

1. **MAKE CONNECTIONS** The p53 protein can activate genes involved in apoptosis, or programmed cell death. Review Concept 11.5 (pp. 223–225) and discuss how mutations in genes coding for proteins that function in apoptosis could contribute to cancer.

2. Under what circumstances is cancer considered to have a hereditary component?

3. **WHAT IF?** Explain how the types of mutations that lead to cancer are different for a proto-oncogene and a tumor-suppressor gene, in terms of the effect of the mutation on the activity of the gene product.

For suggested answers, see Appendix A.

SUMMARY OF KEY CONCEPTS

CONCEPT 18.1

Bacteria often respond to environmental change by regulating transcription (pp. 351–356)

- Cells control metabolism by regulating enzyme activity or the expression of genes coding for enzymes. In bacteria, genes are often clustered into **operons,** with one promoter serving several adjacent genes. An **operator** site on the DNA switches the operon on or off, resulting in coordinate regulation of the genes.

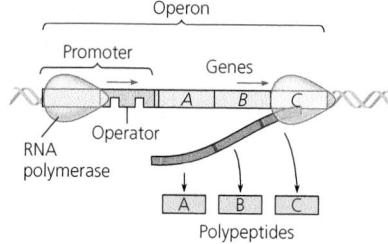

- Both repressible and inducible operons are examples of negative gene regulation. In either type of operon, binding of a specific **repressor** protein to the operator shuts off transcription. (The repressor is encoded by a separate **regulatory gene**.) In a repressible operon, the repressor is active when bound to a **corepressor,** usually the end product of an anabolic pathway.

In an inducible operon, binding of an **inducer** to an innately active repressor inactivates the repressor and turns on transcription. Inducible enzymes usually function in catabolic pathways.

- Some operons are also subject to positive gene regulation via a stimulatory **activator** protein, such as catabolite activator protein (CAP), which, when activated by **cyclic AMP,** binds to a site within the promoter and stimulates transcription.

> ? *Compare and contrast the roles of the corepressor and the inducer in negative regulation of an operon.*

CONCEPT 18.2

Eukaryotic gene expression is regulated at many stages (pp. 356–364)

> ? *Describe what must happen for a cell-type-specific gene to be transcribed in a cell of that type.*

CONCEPT 18.3

Noncoding RNAs play multiple roles in controlling gene expression (pp. 364–366)

> **?** Why are miRNAs called noncoding RNAs? Explain how they participate in gene regulation.

CONCEPT 18.4

A program of differential gene expression leads to the different cell types in a multicellular organism (pp. 366–373)

- Embryonic cells undergo **differentiation**, becoming specialized in structure and function. **Morphogenesis** encompasses the processes that give shape to the organism and its various parts. Cells differ in structure and function not because they contain different genes but because they express different portions of a common genome.
- **Cytoplasmic determinants** in the unfertilized egg regulate the expression of genes in the zygote that affect the developmental fate of embryonic cells. In the process called **induction**, signaling molecules from embryonic cells cause transcriptional changes in nearby target cells.
- Differentiation is heralded by the appearance of tissue-specific proteins, which enable differentiated cells to carry out their specialized roles.
- In animals, **pattern formation**, the development of a spatial organization of tissues and organs, begins in the early embryo. **Positional information**, the molecular cues that control pattern formation, tells a cell its location relative to the body's axes and to other cells. In *Drosophila*, gradients of **morphogens** encoded by **maternal effect genes** determine the body axes. For example, the gradient of **Bicoid** protein determines the anterior-posterior axis.

> **?** Describe the two main processes that cause embryonic cells to head down different pathways to their final fates.

CONCEPT 18.5

Cancer results from genetic changes that affect cell cycle control (pp. 373–377)

- The products of **proto-oncogenes** and **tumor-suppressor genes** control cell division. A DNA change that makes a proto-oncogene excessively active converts it to an **oncogene**, which may promote excessive cell division and cancer. A tumor-suppressor gene encodes a protein that inhibits abnormal cell division. A mutation in such a gene that reduces the activity of its protein product may also lead to excessive cell division and possibly to cancer.
- Many proto-oncogenes and tumor-suppressor genes encode components of growth-stimulating and growth-inhibiting signaling pathways, respectively, and mutations in these genes can interfere with normal cell-signaling pathways. A hyperactive version of a protein in a stimulatory pathway, such as **Ras** (a G protein), functions as an oncogene protein. A defective version of a protein in an inhibitory pathway, such as **p53** (a transcription activator), fails to function as a tumor suppressor.
- In the multistep model of cancer development, normal cells are converted to cancer cells by the accumulation of mutations affecting proto-oncogenes and tumor-suppressor genes. Technical advances in DNA and mRNA sequencing are enabling cancer treatments that are more individually based.
- Individuals who inherit a mutant oncogene or tumor-suppressor allele have a predisposition to develop a particular cancer. Certain viruses promote cancer by integration of viral DNA into a cell's genome.

> **?** Compare the usual functions of proteins encoded by proto-oncogenes with the functions of proteins encoded by tumor-suppressor genes.

LEVEL 1: KNOWLEDGE/COMPREHENSION

1. If a particular operon encodes enzymes for making an essential amino acid and is regulated like the *trp* operon, then
   a. the amino acid inactivates the repressor.
   b. the enzymes produced are called inducible enzymes.
   c. the repressor is active in the absence of the amino acid.
   d. the amino acid acts as a corepressor.
   e. the amino acid turns on transcription of the operon.

2. Muscle cells differ from nerve cells mainly because they
   a. express different genes.
   b. contain different genes.
   c. use different genetic codes.
   d. have unique ribosomes.
   e. have different chromosomes.

3. The functioning of enhancers is an example of
   a. transcriptional control of gene expression.
   b. a post-transcriptional mechanism to regulate mRNA.
   c. the stimulation of translation by initiation factors.
   d. post-translational control that activates certain proteins.
   e. a eukaryotic equivalent of prokaryotic promoter functioning.

4. Cell differentiation always involves
   a. the production of tissue-specific proteins, such as muscle actin.
   b. the movement of cells.
   c. the transcription of the *myoD* gene.
   d. the selective loss of certain genes from the genome.
   e. the cell's sensitivity to environmental cues, such as light or heat.

5. Which of the following is an example of post-transcriptional control of gene expression?
   a. the addition of methyl groups to cytosine bases of DNA
   b. the binding of transcription factors to a promoter
   c. the removal of introns and alternative splicing of exons
   d. gene amplification contributing to cancer
   e. the folding of DNA to form heterochromatin

LEVEL 2: APPLICATION/ANALYSIS

6. What would occur if the repressor of an inducible operon were mutated so it could not bind the operator?
   a. irreversible binding of the repressor to the promoter
   b. reduced transcription of the operon's genes
   c. buildup of a substrate for the pathway controlled by the operon
   d. continuous transcription of the operon's genes
   e. overproduction of catabolite activator protein (CAP)

7. Absence of *bicoid* mRNA from a *Drosophila* egg leads to the absence of anterior larval body parts and mirror-image duplication of posterior parts. This is evidence that the product of the *bicoid* gene
   a. is transcribed in the early embryo.
   b. normally leads to formation of tail structures.
   c. normally leads to formation of head structures.
   d. is a protein present in all head structures.
   e. leads to programmed cell death.

8. Which of the following statements about the DNA in one of your brain cells is true?
   a. Most of the DNA codes for protein.
   b. The majority of genes are likely to be transcribed.
   c. Each gene lies immediately adjacent to an enhancer.
   d. Many genes are grouped into operon-like clusters.
   e. It is the same as the DNA in one of your heart cells.

9. Within a cell, the amount of protein made using a given mRNA molecule depends partly on
   a. the degree of DNA methylation.
   b. the rate at which the mRNA is degraded.
   c. the presence of certain transcription factors.
   d. the number of introns present in the mRNA.
   e. the types of ribosomes present in the cytoplasm.

10. Proto-oncogenes can change into oncogenes that cause cancer. Which of the following best explains the presence of these potential time bombs in eukaryotic cells?
    a. Proto-oncogenes first arose from viral infections.
    b. Proto-oncogenes normally help regulate cell division.
    c. Proto-oncogenes are genetic "junk."
    d. Proto-oncogenes are mutant versions of normal genes.
    e. Cells produce proto-oncogenes as they age.

LEVEL 3: SYNTHESIS/EVALUATION

11. **DRAW IT** The diagram below shows five genes, including their enhancers, from the genome of a certain species. Imagine that orange, blue, green, black, red, and purple activator proteins exist that can bind to the appropriately color-coded control elements in the enhancers of these genes.

a. Draw an X above enhancer elements (of all the genes) that would have activators bound in a cell in which only gene 5 is transcribed. Which colored activators would be present?

b. Draw a dot above all enhancer elements that would have activators bound in a cell in which the green, blue, and orange activators are present. Which gene(s) would be transcribed?

c. Imagine that genes 1, 2, and 4 code for nerve-specific proteins, and genes 3 and 5 are skin specific. Which activators would have to be present in each cell type to ensure transcription of the appropriate genes?

12. **EVOLUTION CONNECTION**
DNA sequences can act as "tape measures of evolution" (see Chapter 5). Scientists analyzing the human genome sequence were surprised to find that some of the regions of the human genome that are most highly conserved (similar to comparable regions in other species) don't code for proteins. Propose a possible explanation for this observation.

13. **SCIENTIFIC INQUIRY**
Prostate cells usually require testosterone and other androgens to survive. But some prostate cancer cells thrive despite treatments that eliminate androgens. One hypothesis is that estrogen, often considered a female hormone, may be activating genes normally controlled by an androgen in these cancer cells. Describe one or more experiments to test this hypothesis. (See Figure 11.9, p. 214, to review the action of these steroid hormones.)

14. **SCIENCE, TECHNOLOGY, AND SOCIETY**
Trace amounts of dioxin were present in Agent Orange, a defoliant sprayed on vegetation during the Vietnam War. Animal tests suggest that dioxin can cause birth defects, cancer, liver and thymus damage, and immune system suppression, sometimes leading to death. But the animal tests are equivocal; a hamster is not affected by a dose that can kill a guinea pig. Dioxin acts somewhat like a steroid hormone, entering a cell and binding to a receptor protein that then attaches to the cell's DNA. How might this mechanism help explain the variety of dioxin's effects on different body systems and in different animals? How might you determine whether a type of illness is related to dioxin exposure? How might you determine whether a particular individual became ill as a result of exposure to dioxin? Which would be more difficult to demonstrate? Why?

15. **WRITE ABOUT A THEME**
Feedback Regulation In a short essay (100–150 words), discuss how the processes shown in Figure 18.24a and b are examples of feedback mechanisms regulating biological systems.

For selected answers, see Appendix A.

Mastering BIOLOGY®   www.masteringbiology.com

1. MasteringBiology® Assignments

Tutorials Regulation of Gene Expression in Bacteria • Regulation of Gene Expression in Eukaryotes • Pattern Formation
Activities The *lac* Operon • The *lac* Operon in *E. coli* • Transcription Initiation in Eukaryotes • Overview: Control of Gene Expression • Control of Transcription • Review: Control of Gene Expression • Early Pattern Formation in *Drosophila* • Role of *bicoid* Gene in *Drosophila* Development
Questions Student Misconceptions • Reading Quiz • Multiple Choice • End-of-Chapter

2. eText

Read your book online, search, take notes, highlight text, and more.

3. The Study Area

Practice Tests • Cumulative Test • *BioFlix* 3-D Animations • MP3 Tutor Sessions • Videos • Activities • Investigations • Lab Media • Audio Glossary • Word Study Tools • Art

19

Viruses

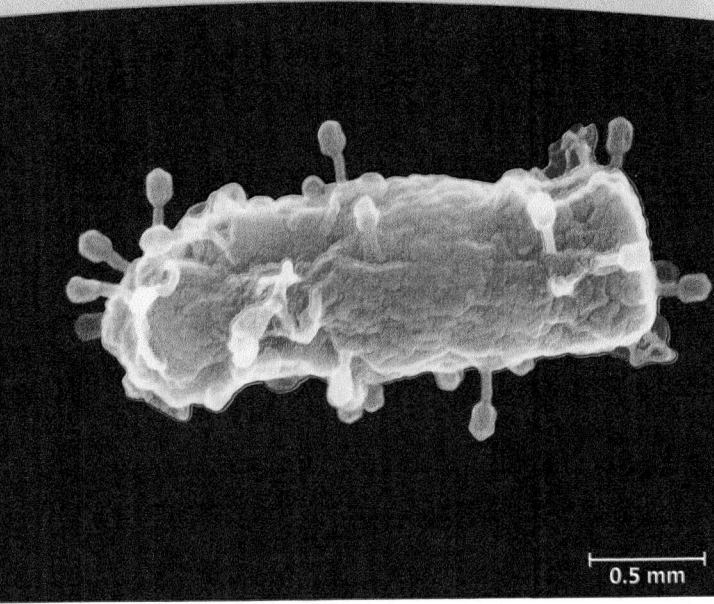

0.5 mm

▲ Figure 19.1 **Are the tiny viruses infecting this *E. coli* cell alive?**

KEY CONCEPTS

19.1 A virus consists of a nucleic acid surrounded by a protein coat

19.2 Viruses replicate only in host cells

19.3 Viruses, viroids, and prions are formidable pathogens in animals and plants

OVERVIEW

A Borrowed Life

The photo in **Figure 19.1** shows a remarkable event: the attack of a bacterial cell by numerous structures that resemble miniature lollipops. These structures, a type of virus called T4 bacteriophage, are seen infecting the bacterium *Escherichia coli* in this colorized SEM. By injecting its DNA into the cell, the virus sets in motion a genetic takeover of the bacterium, recruiting cellular machinery to mass-produce many new viruses.

Recall that bacteria and other prokaryotes are cells much smaller and more simply organized than the cells of eukaryotes, such as plants and animals. Viruses are smaller and simpler still. Lacking the structures and metabolic machinery found in a cell, a **virus** is an infectious particle consisting of little more than genes packaged in a protein coat.

Are viruses living or nonliving? Early on, they were considered biological chemicals; in fact, the Latin root for the word *virus* means "poison." Because viruses are capable of causing a wide variety of diseases and can be spread between organisms, researchers in the late 1800s saw a parallel with bacteria and proposed that viruses were the simplest of living forms. However, viruses cannot reproduce or carry out metabolic activities outside of a host cell. Most biologists studying viruses today would probably agree that they are not alive but exist in a shady area between life-forms and chemicals. The simple phrase used recently by two researchers describes them aptly enough: Viruses lead "a kind of borrowed life."

To a large extent, molecular biology was born in the laboratories of biologists studying viruses that infect bacteria. Experiments with viruses provided important evidence that genes are made of nucleic acids, and they were critical in working out the molecular mechanisms of the fundamental processes of DNA replication, transcription, and translation.

Beyond their value as experimental systems, viruses have unique genetic mechanisms that are interesting in their own right and that also help us understand how viruses cause disease. In addition, the study of viruses has led to the development of techniques that enable scientists to manipulate genes and transfer them from one organism to another. These techniques play an important role in basic research, biotechnology, and medical applications. For instance, viruses are used as agents of gene transfer in gene therapy (see Chapter 20).

In this chapter, we will explore the biology of viruses. We will begin with the structure of these simplest of all genetic systems and then describe the cycles by which they replicate. Next, we will discuss the role of viruses as disease-causing agents, or pathogens, and conclude by considering some even simpler infectious agents, viroids and prions.

CONCEPT **19.1**

A virus consists of a nucleic acid surrounded by a protein coat

Scientists were able to detect viruses indirectly long before they were actually able to see them. The story of how viruses were discovered begins near the end of the 19th century.

The Discovery of Viruses: *Scientific Inquiry*

Tobacco mosaic disease stunts the growth of tobacco plants and gives their leaves a mottled, or mosaic, coloration. In 1883, Adolf Mayer, a German scientist, discovered that he could transmit the disease from plant to plant by rubbing sap extracted from diseased leaves onto healthy plants. After an unsuccessful search for an infectious microbe in the sap, Mayer suggested that the disease was caused by unusually small bacteria that were invisible under a microscope. This hypothesis was tested a decade later by Dimitri Ivanowsky, a Russian biologist who passed sap from infected tobacco leaves through a filter designed to remove bacteria. After filtration, the sap still produced mosaic disease.

But Ivanowsky clung to the hypothesis that bacteria caused tobacco mosaic disease. Perhaps, he reasoned, the bacteria were small enough to pass through the filter or made a toxin that could do so. The second possibility was ruled out when the Dutch botanist Martinus Beijerinck carried out a classic series of experiments that showed that the infectious agent in the filtered sap could replicate (Figure 19.2).

In fact, the pathogen replicated only within the host it infected. In further experiments, Beijerinck showed that unlike bacteria used in the lab at that time, the mysterious agent of mosaic disease could not be cultivated on nutrient media in test tubes or petri dishes. Beijerinck imagined a replicating particle much smaller and simpler than a bacterium, and he is generally credited with being the first scientist to voice the concept of a virus. His suspicions were confirmed in 1935 when the American scientist Wendell Stanley crystallized the infectious particle, now known as tobacco mosaic virus (TMV). Subsequently, TMV and many other viruses were actually seen with the help of the electron microscope.

Structure of Viruses

The tiniest viruses are only 20 nm in diameter—smaller than a ribosome. Millions could easily fit on a pinhead. Even the largest known virus, which has a diameter of several hundred nanometers, is barely visible under the light microscope. Stanley's discovery that some viruses could be crystallized was exciting and puzzling news. Not even the simplest of cells can aggregate into regular crystals. But if viruses are not cells, then what are they? Examining the structure of a virus more closely reveals that it is an infectious particle consisting of nucleic acid enclosed in a protein coat and, for some viruses, surrounded by a membranous envelope.

Viral Genomes

We usually think of genes as being made of double-stranded DNA—the conventional double helix—but many viruses defy this convention. Their genomes may consist of double-stranded DNA, single-stranded DNA, double-stranded RNA, or single-stranded RNA, depending on the type of virus. A virus is called a DNA virus or an RNA virus, based on the kind of nucleic acid that makes up its genome. In either case, the genome is usually organized as a single linear or circular molecule of nucleic acid, although the genomes of

▼ Figure 19.2

INQUIRY

What causes tobacco mosaic disease?

EXPERIMENT In the late 1800s, Martinus Beijerinck, of the Technical School in Delft, the Netherlands, investigated the properties of the agent that causes tobacco mosaic disease (then called spot disease).

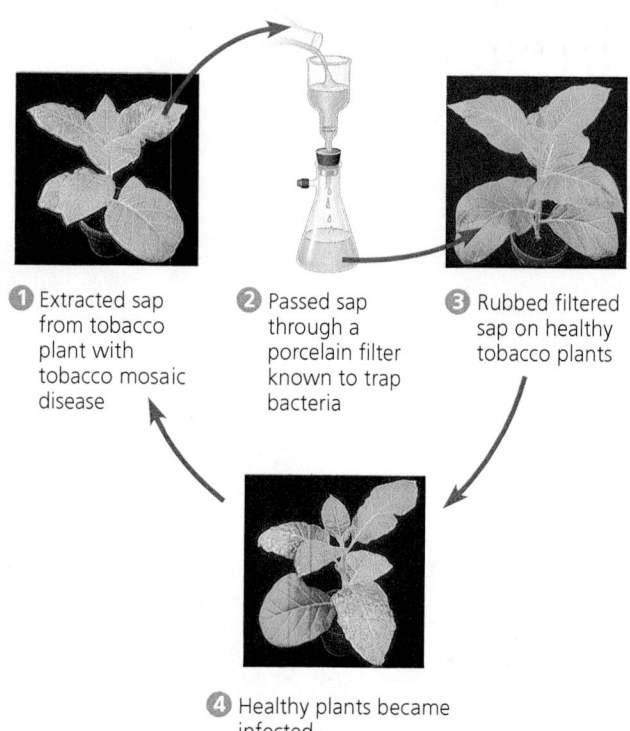

① Extracted sap from tobacco plant with tobacco mosaic disease

② Passed sap through a porcelain filter known to trap bacteria

③ Rubbed filtered sap on healthy tobacco plants

④ Healthy plants became infected

RESULTS When the filtered sap was rubbed on healthy plants, they became infected. Their sap, when extracted and filtered, could then act as the source of infection for another group of plants. Each successive group of plants developed the disease to the same extent as earlier groups.

CONCLUSION The infectious agent was apparently not a bacterium because it could pass through a bacterium-trapping filter. The pathogen must have been replicating in the plants because its ability to cause disease was undiluted after several transfers from plant to plant.

SOURCE M. J. Beijerinck, Concerning a *contagium vivum fluidum* as cause of the spot disease of tobacco leaves, *Verhandelingen der Koninkyke akademie Wettenschappen te Amsterdam* 65:3–21 (1898). Translation published in English as Phytopathological Classics Number 7 (1942), American Phytopathological Society Press, St. Paul, MN.

WHAT IF? If Beijerinck had observed that the infection of each group was weaker than that of the previous group and that ultimately the sap could no longer cause disease, what might he have concluded?

some viruses consist of multiple molecules of nucleic acid. The smallest viruses known have only four genes in their genome, while the largest have several hundred to a thousand. For comparison, bacterial genomes contain about 200 to a few thousand genes.

Capsids and Envelopes

The protein shell enclosing the viral genome is called a **capsid**. Depending on the type of virus, the capsid may be rod-shaped, polyhedral, or more complex in shape (like T4). Capsids are built from a large number of protein subunits called *capsomeres*, but the number of different *kinds* of proteins in a capsid is usually small. Tobacco mosaic virus has a rigid, rod-shaped capsid made from over a thousand molecules of a single type of protein arranged in a helix; rod-shaped viruses are commonly called *helical viruses* for this reason (Figure 19.3a). Adenoviruses, which infect the respiratory tracts of animals, have 252 identical protein molecules arranged in a polyhedral capsid with 20 triangular facets—an icosahedron; thus, these and other similarly shaped viruses are referred to as *icosahedral viruses* (Figure 19.3b).

Some viruses have accessory structures that help them infect their hosts. For instance, a membranous envelope surrounds the capsids of influenza viruses and many other viruses found in animals (Figure 19.3c). These **viral envelopes**, which are derived from the membranes of the host cell, contain host cell phospholipids and membrane proteins. They also contain proteins and glycoproteins of viral origin. (Glycoproteins are proteins with carbohydrates covalently attached.) Some viruses carry a few viral enzyme molecules within their capsids.

Many of the most complex capsids are found among the viruses that infect bacteria, called **bacteriophages**, or simply **phages**. The first phages studied included seven that infect *E. coli*. These seven phages were named type 1 (T1), type 2 (T2), and so forth, in the order of their discovery. The three T-even phages (T2, T4, and T6) turned out to be very similar in structure. Their capsids have elongated icosahedral heads

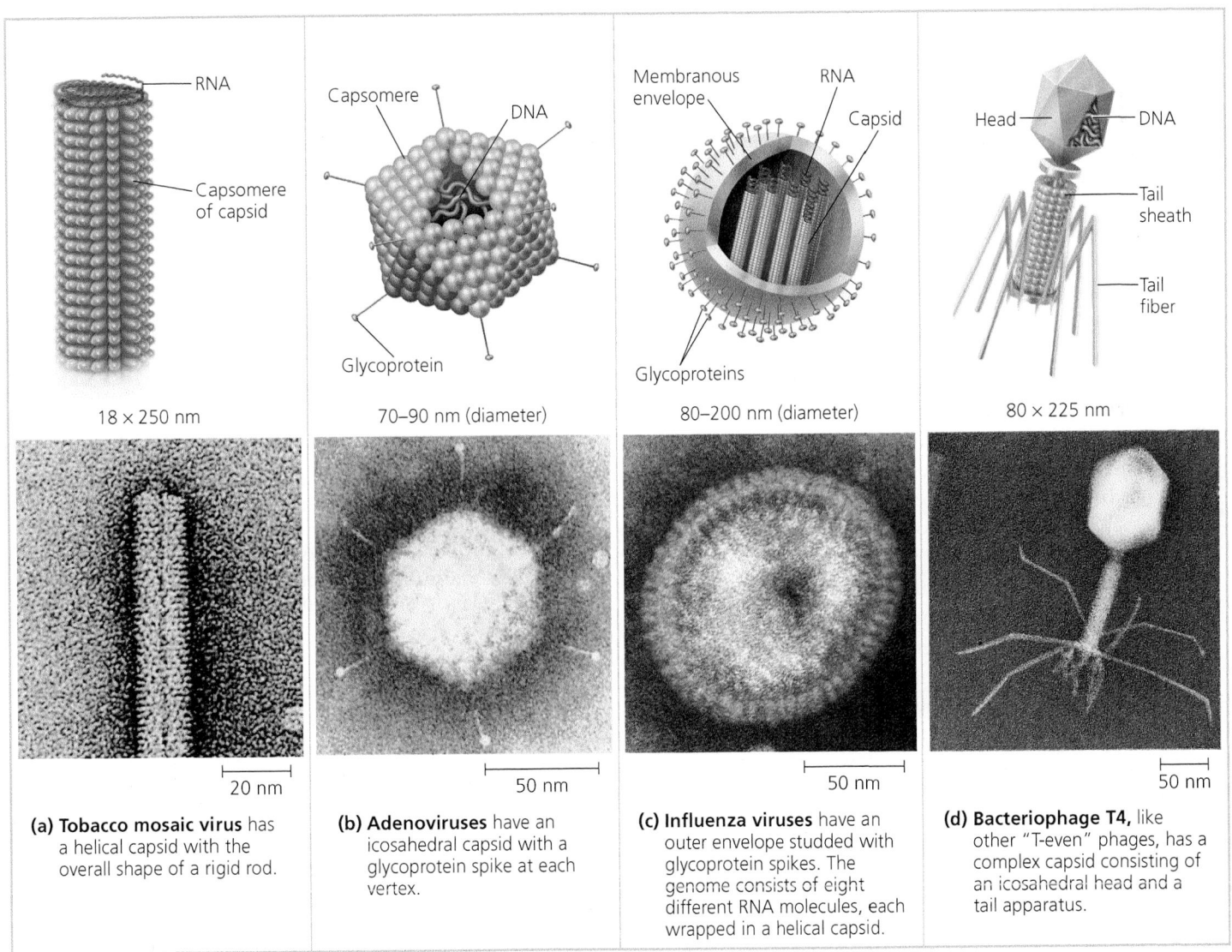

(a) **Tobacco mosaic virus** has a helical capsid with the overall shape of a rigid rod.

(b) **Adenoviruses** have an icosahedral capsid with a glycoprotein spike at each vertex.

(c) **Influenza viruses** have an outer envelope studded with glycoprotein spikes. The genome consists of eight different RNA molecules, each wrapped in a helical capsid.

(d) **Bacteriophage T4,** like other "T-even" phages, has a complex capsid consisting of an icosahedral head and a tail apparatus.

▲ Figure 19.3 **Viral structure.** Viruses are made up of nucleic acid (DNA or RNA) enclosed in a protein coat (the capsid) and sometimes further wrapped in a membranous envelope. The individual protein subunits making up the capsid are called capsomeres. Although diverse in size and shape, viruses have many common structural features. (All micrographs are colorized TEMs.)

enclosing their DNA. Attached to the head is a protein tail piece with fibers by which the phages attach to a bacterium (**Figure 19.3d**). In the next section, we'll examine how these few viral parts function together with cellular components to produce large numbers of viral progeny.

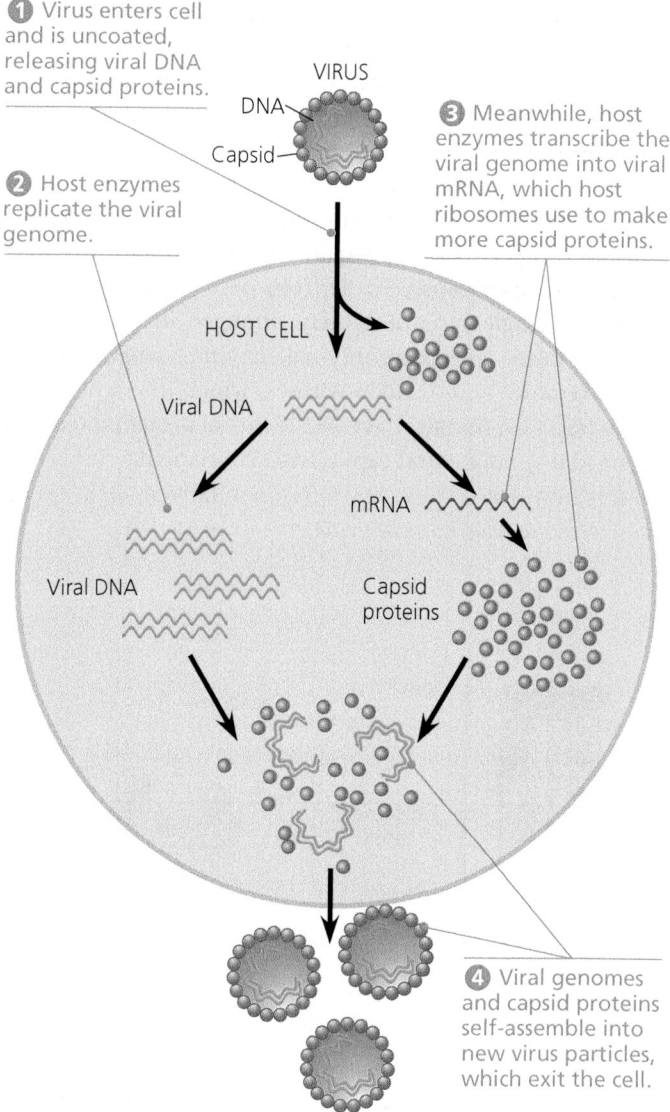

① Virus enters cell and is uncoated, releasing viral DNA and capsid proteins.

VIRUS

DNA

Capsid

② Host enzymes replicate the viral genome.

③ Meanwhile, host enzymes transcribe the viral genome into viral mRNA, which host ribosomes use to make more capsid proteins.

HOST CELL

Viral DNA

mRNA

Viral DNA

Capsid proteins

④ Viral genomes and capsid proteins self-assemble into new virus particles, which exit the cell.

▲ **Figure 19.4 A simplified viral replicative cycle.** A virus is an obligate intracellular parasite that uses the equipment and small molecules of its host cell to replicate. In this simplest of viral cycles, the parasite is a DNA virus with a capsid consisting of a single type of protein.

MAKE CONNECTIONS *Label each of the straight black arrows with one word representing the name of the process that is occurring. Review Figure 17.26 on page 348.*

CONCEPT CHECK 19.1

1. Compare the structures of tobacco mosaic virus (TMV) and influenza virus (see Figure 19.3).
2. **MAKE CONNECTIONS** In Figure 16.4 (p. 307), you learned how bacteriophages were used to provide evidence that DNA carries genetic information. Briefly describe the experiment carried out by Hershey and Chase, including in your description why the researchers chose to use phages.

For suggested answers, see Appendix A.

CONCEPT 19.2

Viruses replicate only in host cells

Viruses lack metabolic enzymes and equipment for making proteins, such as ribosomes. They are obligate intracellular parasites; in other words, they can replicate only within a host cell. It is fair to say that viruses in isolation are merely packaged sets of genes in transit from one host cell to another.

Each particular virus can infect cells of only a limited number of host species, called the **host range** of the virus. This host specificity results from the evolution of recognition systems by the virus. Viruses usually identify host cells by a "lock-and-key" fit between viral surface proteins and specific receptor molecules on the outside of cells. (According to one model, such receptor molecules originally carried out functions that benefited the host cell but were co-opted later by viruses as portals of entry.) Some viruses have broad host ranges. For example, West Nile virus and equine encephalitis virus are distinctly different viruses that can each infect mosquitoes, birds, horses, and humans. Other viruses have host ranges so narrow that they infect only a single species. Measles virus, for instance, can infect only humans. Furthermore, viral infection of multicellular eukaryotes is usually limited to particular tissues. Human cold viruses infect only the cells lining the upper respiratory tract, and the AIDS virus binds to receptors present only on certain types of white blood cells.

General Features of Viral Replicative Cycles

A viral infection begins when a virus binds to a host cell and the viral genome makes its way inside (**Figure 19.4**). The mechanism of genome entry depends on the type of virus and the type of host cell. For example, T-even phages use their elaborate tail apparatus to inject DNA into a bacterium (see Figure 19.3d). Other viruses are taken up by endocytosis or, in the case of

enveloped viruses, by fusion of the viral envelope with the plasma membrane. Once the viral genome is inside, the proteins it encodes can commandeer the host, reprogramming the cell to copy the viral nucleic acid and manufacture viral proteins. The host provides the nucleotides for making viral nucleic acids, as well as enzymes, ribosomes, tRNAs, amino acids, ATP, and other components needed for making the viral proteins. Many DNA viruses use the DNA polymerases of the host cell to synthesize new genomes along the templates provided by the viral DNA. In contrast, to replicate their genomes, RNA viruses use virally encoded RNA polymerases that can use RNA as a template. (Uninfected cells generally make no enzymes for carrying out this process.)

After the viral nucleic acid molecules and capsomeres are produced, they spontaneously self-assemble into new viruses. In fact, researchers can separate the RNA and capsomeres of TMV and then reassemble complete viruses simply by mixing the components together under the right conditions. The simplest type of viral replicative cycle ends with the exit of hundreds or thousands of viruses from the infected host cell, a process that often damages or destroys the cell. Such cellular damage and death, as well as the body's responses to this destruction, cause many of the symptoms associated with viral infections. The viral progeny that exit a cell have the potential to infect additional cells, spreading the viral infection.

There are many variations on the simplified viral replicative cycle we have just described. We will now take a look at some of these variations in bacterial viruses (phages) and animal viruses; later in the chapter, we will consider plant viruses.

Replicative Cycles of Phages

Phages are the best understood of all viruses, although some of them are also among the most complex. Research on phages led to the discovery that some double-stranded DNA viruses can replicate by two alternative mechanisms: the lytic cycle and the lysogenic cycle.

The Lytic Cycle

A phage replicative cycle that culminates in death of the host cell is known as a **lytic cycle**. The term refers to the last stage of infection, during which the bacterium lyses (breaks open) and releases the phages that were produced within the cell. Each of these phages can then infect a healthy cell, and a few successive lytic cycles can destroy an entire bacterial population in just a few hours. A phage that replicates only by a lytic cycle is a **virulent phage**. Figure 19.5 illustrates the major steps in the lytic cycle of T4, a typical virulent phage. Study this figure before proceeding.

After reading about the lytic cycle, you may wonder why phages haven't exterminated all bacteria. In fact, phage treatments have been used medically in some countries to help control bacterial infections in humans. Bacteria are not defenseless, however. First, natural selection favors bacterial mutants with receptors that are no longer recognized by a particular type of phage. Second, when phage DNA successfully enters a bacterium, the DNA often is identified as foreign and cut up by cellular enzymes called **restriction enzymes**, which are so named because their activity *restricts* the ability of the phage to infect the bacterium. The bacterial cell's own DNA is methylated in a way that prevents attack

▶ **Figure 19.5 The lytic cycle of phage T4, a virulent phage.** Phage T4 has almost 300 genes, which are transcribed and translated using the host cell's machinery. One of the first phage genes translated after the viral DNA enters the host cell codes for an enzyme that degrades the host cell's DNA (step 2); the phage DNA is protected from breakdown because it contains a modified form of cytosine that is not recognized by the enzyme. The entire lytic cycle, from the phage's first contact with the cell surface to cell lysis, takes only 20–30 minutes at 37°C.

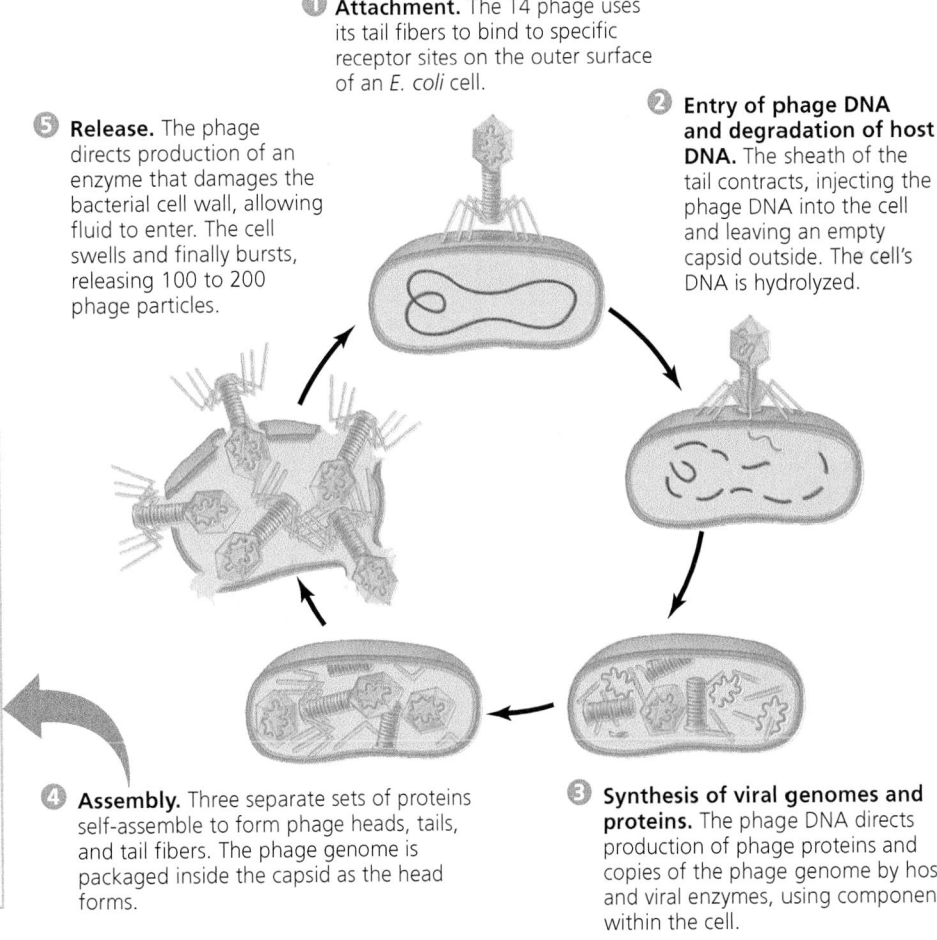

Phage assembly

Head   Tail   Tail fibers

① **Attachment.** The T4 phage uses its tail fibers to bind to specific receptor sites on the outer surface of an *E. coli* cell.

② **Entry of phage DNA and degradation of host DNA.** The sheath of the tail contracts, injecting the phage DNA into the cell and leaving an empty capsid outside. The cell's DNA is hydrolyzed.

③ **Synthesis of viral genomes and proteins.** The phage DNA directs production of phage proteins and copies of the phage genome by host and viral enzymes, using components within the cell.

④ **Assembly.** Three separate sets of proteins self-assemble to form phage heads, tails, and tail fibers. The phage genome is packaged inside the capsid as the head forms.

⑤ **Release.** The phage directs production of an enzyme that damages the bacterial cell wall, allowing fluid to enter. The cell swells and finally bursts, releasing 100 to 200 phage particles.

by its own restriction enzymes. But just as natural selection favors bacteria with mutant receptors or effective restriction enzymes, it also favors phage mutants that can bind the altered receptors or are resistant to particular restriction enzymes. Thus, the parasite-host relationship is in constant evolutionary flux.

There is yet a third important reason bacteria have been spared from extinction as a result of phage activity. Instead of lysing their host cells, many phages coexist with them in a state called lysogeny, which we'll now discuss.

The Lysogenic Cycle

In contrast to the lytic cycle, which kills the host cell, the **lysogenic cycle** allows replication of the phage genome without destroying the host. Phages capable of using both modes of replicating within a bacterium are called **temperate phages**. A temperate phage called lambda, written with the Greek letter λ, is widely used in biological research. Phage λ resembles T4, but its tail has only one short tail fiber.

Infection of an *E. coli* cell by phage λ begins when the phage binds to the surface of the cell and injects its linear DNA genome **(Figure 19.6)**. Within the host, the λ DNA molecule forms a circle. What happens next depends on the replicative

mode: lytic cycle or lysogenic cycle. During a lytic cycle, the viral genes immediately turn the host cell into a λ-producing factory, and the cell soon lyses and releases its viral products. During a lysogenic cycle, however, the λ DNA molecule is incorporated into a specific site on the *E. coli* chromosome by viral proteins that break both circular DNA molecules and join them to each other. When integrated into the bacterial chromosome in this way, the viral DNA is known as a **prophage**. One prophage gene codes for a protein that prevents transcription of most of the other prophage genes. Thus, the phage genome is mostly silent within the bacterium. Every time the *E. coli* cell prepares to divide, it replicates the phage DNA along with its own and passes the copies on to daughter cells. A single infected cell can quickly give rise to a large population of bacteria carrying the virus in prophage form. This mechanism enables viruses to propagate without killing the host cells on which they depend.

The term *lysogenic* implies that prophages are capable of generating active phages that lyse their host cells. This occurs when the λ genome is induced to exit the bacterial chromosome and initiate a lytic cycle. An environmental signal, such as a certain chemical or high-energy radiation, usually triggers the switchover from the lysogenic to the lytic mode.

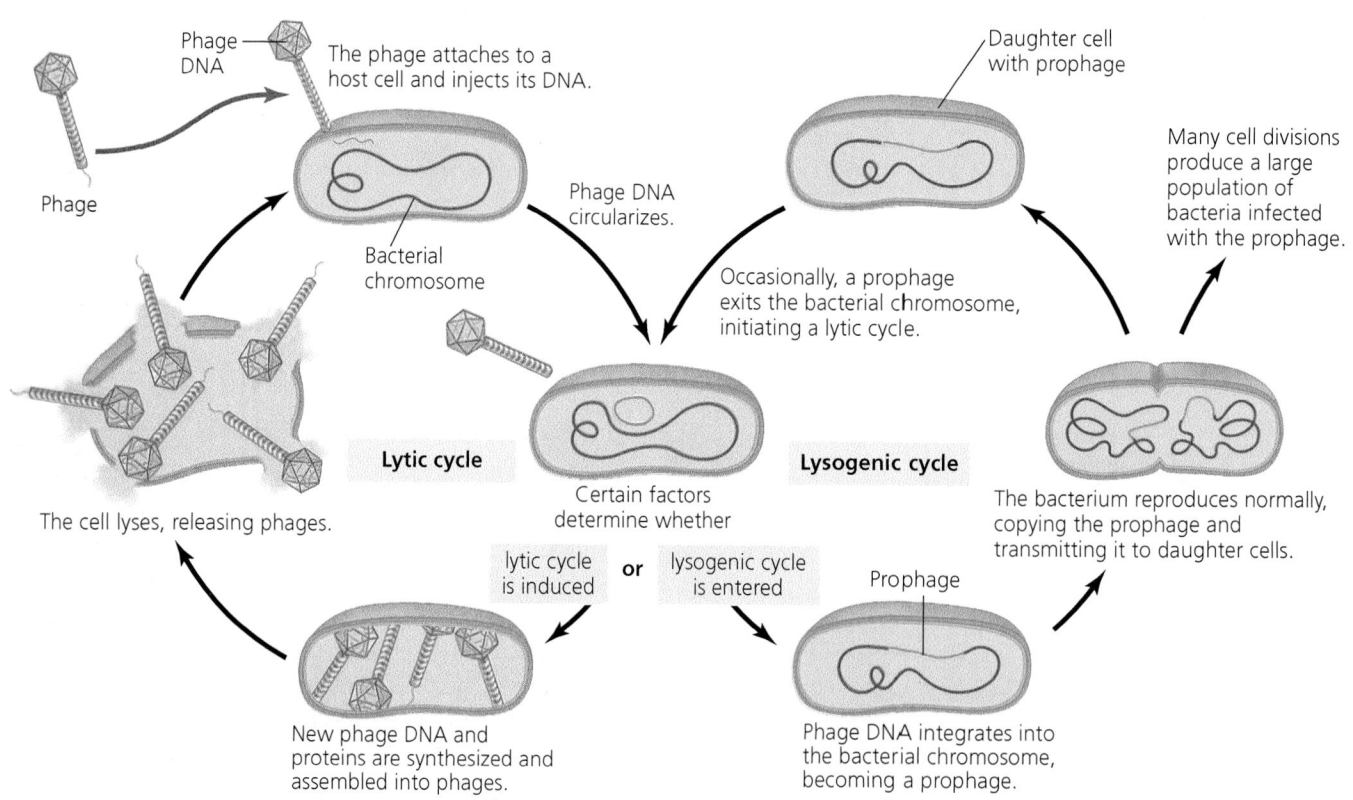

▲ **Figure 19.6 The lytic and lysogenic cycles of phage λ, a temperate phage.** After entering the bacterial cell and circularizing, the λ DNA can immediately initiate the production of a large number of progeny phages (lytic cycle) or integrate into the bacterial chromosome (lysogenic cycle). In most cases, phage λ follows the lytic pathway, which is similar to that detailed in Figure 19.5. However, once a lysogenic cycle begins, the prophage may be carried in the host cell's chromosome for many generations. Phage λ has one main tail fiber, which is short.

Table 19.1 Classes of Animal Viruses

Class/Family	Envelope	Examples That Cause Human Diseases
I. Double-Stranded DNA (dsDNA)		
Adenovirus (see Figure 19.3b)	No	Respiratory viruses; tumor-causing viruses
Papovavirus	No	Papillomavirus (warts, cervical cancer); polyomavirus (tumors)
Herpesvirus	Yes	Herpes simplex I and II (cold sores, genital sores); varicella zoster (shingles, chicken pox); Epstein-Barr virus (mononucleosis, Burkitt's lymphoma)
Poxvirus	Yes	Smallpox virus; cowpox virus
II. Single-Stranded DNA (ssDNA)		
Parvovirus	No	B19 parvovirus (mild rash)
III. Double-Stranded RNA (dsRNA)		
Reovirus	No	Rotavirus (diarrhea); Colorado tick fever virus
IV. Single-Stranded RNA (ssRNA); Serves as mRNA		
Picornavirus	No	Rhinovirus (common cold); poliovirus; hepatitis A virus; other enteric (intestinal) viruses
Coronavirus	Yes	Severe acute respiratory syndrome (SARS)
Flavivirus	Yes	Yellow fever virus; West Nile virus; hepatitis C virus
Togavirus	Yes	Rubella virus; equine encephalitis viruses
V. ssRNA; Template for mRNA Synthesis		
Filovirus	Yes	Ebola virus (hemorrhagic fever)
Orthomyxovirus (see Figures 19.3c and 19.9a)	Yes	Influenza virus
Paramyxovirus	Yes	Measles virus; mumps virus
Rhabdovirus	Yes	Rabies virus
VI. ssRNA; Template for DNA Synthesis		
Retrovirus (see Figure 19.8)	Yes	Human immunodeficiency virus (HIV/AIDS); RNA tumor viruses (leukemia)

In addition to the gene for the transcription-preventing protein, a few other prophage genes may be expressed during lysogeny. Expression of these genes may alter the host's phenotype, a phenomenon that can have important medical significance. For example, the three species of bacteria that cause the human diseases diphtheria, botulism, and scarlet fever would not be so harmful to humans without certain prophage genes that cause the host bacteria to make toxins. And the difference between the *E. coli* strain that resides in our intestines and the O157:H7 strain that has caused several deaths by food poisoning appears to be the presence of prophages in the O157:H7 strain.

Replicative Cycles of Animal Viruses

Everyone has suffered from viral infections, whether cold sores, influenza, or the common cold. Like all viruses, those that cause illness in humans and other animals can replicate only inside host cells. Many variations on the basic scheme of viral infection and replication are represented among the animal viruses. One key variable is the nature of the viral genome: Is it composed of DNA or RNA? Is it double-stranded or single-stranded? The nature of the genome is the basis for the common classification of viruses shown in Table 19.1. Single-stranded RNA viruses are further classified into three classes (IV–VI) according to how the RNA genome functions in a host cell.

Whereas few bacteriophages have an envelope or RNA genome, many animal viruses have both. In fact, nearly all animal viruses with RNA genomes have an envelope, as do some with DNA genomes (see Table 19.1). Rather than consider all the mechanisms of viral infection and replication, we will focus on the roles of viral envelopes and on the functioning of RNA as the genetic material of many animal viruses.

Viral Envelopes

An animal virus equipped with an envelope—that is, an outer membrane—uses it to enter the host cell. Protruding from the outer surface of this envelope are viral glycoproteins that bind to specific receptor molecules on the surface of a host cell. Figure 19.7, on the next page, outlines the events in the replicative cycle of an enveloped virus with an RNA genome. Ribosomes bound to the endoplasmic reticulum (ER) of the host cell make the protein parts of the envelope glycoproteins; cellular enzymes in the ER and Golgi apparatus then add the sugars. The resulting viral glycoproteins, embedded in host cell–derived membrane, are transported to the cell surface. In a process much like exocytosis, new viral capsids are wrapped in membrane as they bud from the cell. In other words, the viral envelope is derived from the host cell's plasma membrane, although some of the molecules of this membrane are specified by viral genes. The enveloped viruses are now free to infect other cells. This replicative cycle does not necessarily kill the host cell, in contrast to the lytic cycles of phages.

Some viruses have envelopes that are not derived from plasma membrane. Herpesviruses, for example, are temporarily cloaked in membrane derived from the nuclear envelope of the host; they then shed this membrane in the cytoplasm and

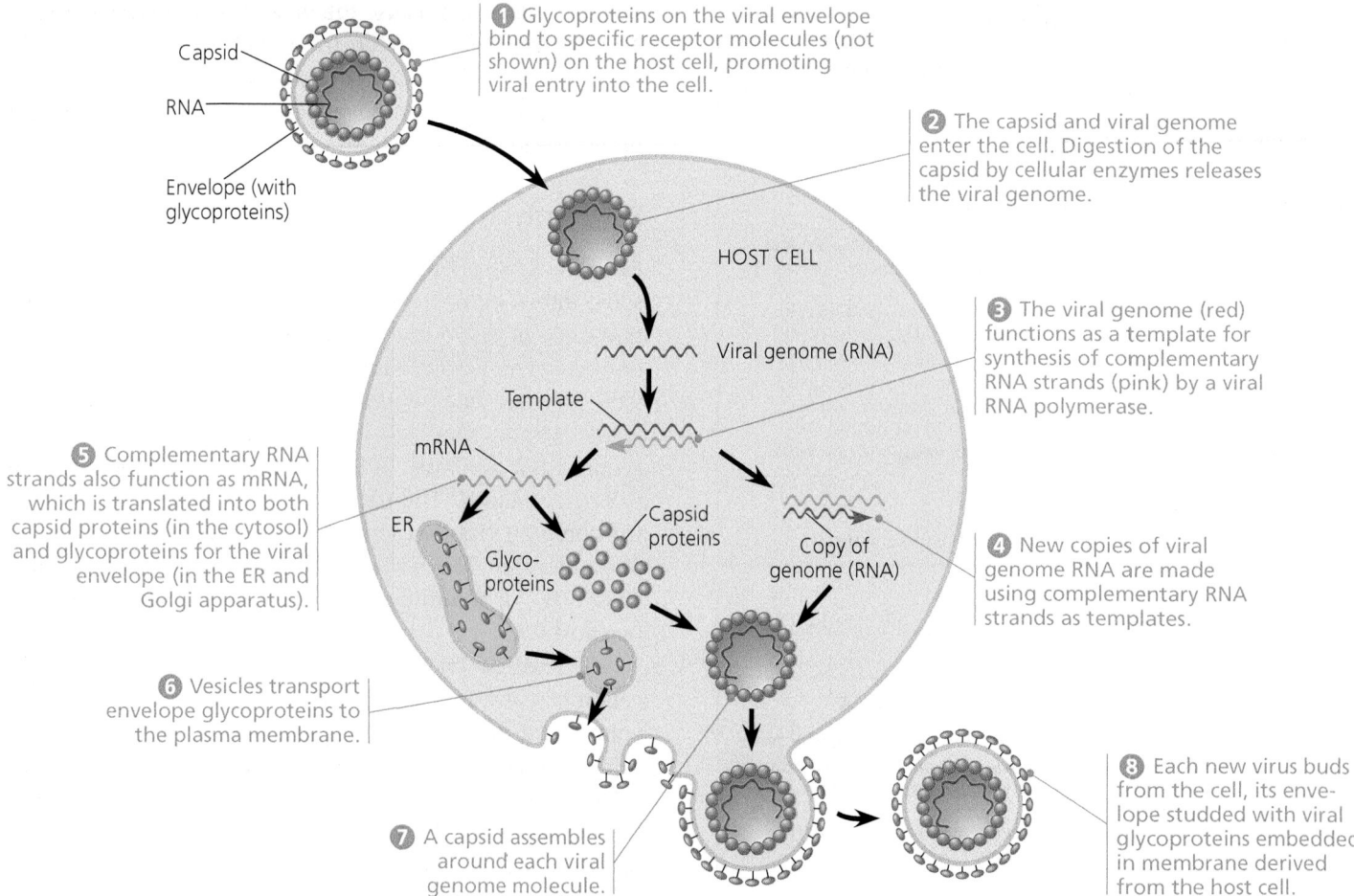

1 Glycoproteins on the viral envelope bind to specific receptor molecules (not shown) on the host cell, promoting viral entry into the cell.

2 The capsid and viral genome enter the cell. Digestion of the capsid by cellular enzymes releases the viral genome.

Capsid

RNA

Envelope (with glycoproteins)

HOST CELL

Viral genome (RNA)

Template

mRNA

3 The viral genome (red) functions as a template for synthesis of complementary RNA strands (pink) by a viral RNA polymerase.

5 Complementary RNA strands also function as mRNA, which is translated into both capsid proteins (in the cytosol) and glycoproteins for the viral envelope (in the ER and Golgi apparatus).

ER

Glyco-proteins

Capsid proteins

Copy of genome (RNA)

4 New copies of viral genome RNA are made using complementary RNA strands as templates.

6 Vesicles transport envelope glycoproteins to the plasma membrane.

7 A capsid assembles around each viral genome molecule.

8 Each new virus buds from the cell, its enve-lope studded with viral glycoproteins embedded in membrane derived from the host cell.

▲ **Figure 19.7 The replicative cycle of an enveloped RNA virus.** Shown here is a virus with a single-stranded RNA genome that functions as a template for synthesis of mRNA. Some enveloped viruses enter the host cell by fusion of the envelope with the cell's plasma membrane; others enter by endocytosis. For all enveloped RNA viruses, the formation of new envelopes for progeny viruses occurs by the mechanism depicted in this figure.

? *Name a virus that has infected you and has a replicative cycle matching this one. (Hint: See Table 19.1.)*

acquire a new envelope made from membrane of the Golgi apparatus. These viruses have a double-stranded DNA genome and replicate within the host cell nucleus, using a combination of viral and cellular enzymes to replicate and transcribe their DNA. In the case of herpesviruses, copies of the viral DNA can remain behind as mini-chromosomes in the nuclei of certain nerve cells. There they remain latent until some sort of physical or emotional stress triggers a new round of active virus production. The infection of other cells by these new viruses causes the blisters characteristic of herpes, such as cold sores or genital sores. Once someone acquires a herpesvirus infection, flare-ups may recur throughout the person's life.

RNA as Viral Genetic Material

Although some phages and most plant viruses are RNA viruses, the broadest variety of RNA genomes is found among the viruses that infect animals. Among the three types of single-stranded RNA genomes found in animal viruses, the genome of class IV viruses can directly serve as mRNA and thus can be translated into viral protein immediately after infection.

Figure 19.7 shows a virus of class V, in which the RNA genome serves as a *template* for mRNA synthesis. The RNA genome is transcribed into complementary RNA strands, which function both as mRNA and as templates for the synthesis of additional copies of genomic RNA. All viruses that require RNA → RNA synthesis to make mRNA use a viral enzyme capable of carrying out this process; there are no such enzymes in most cells. The viral enzyme is packaged with the genome inside the viral capsid.

The RNA animal viruses with the most complicated replicative cycles are the **retroviruses** (class VI). These viruses are equipped with an enzyme called **reverse transcriptase**, which transcribes an RNA template into DNA, providing an RNA → DNA information flow, the opposite of the usual direction. This unusual phenomenon is the source of the name retroviruses (*retro* means "backward"). Of particular medical importance is **HIV (human immunodeficiency virus)**, the retrovirus that causes **AIDS (acquired immunodeficiency syndrome)**. HIV and other retroviruses are enveloped viruses that contain two identical molecules of single-stranded RNA and two molecules of reverse transcriptase.

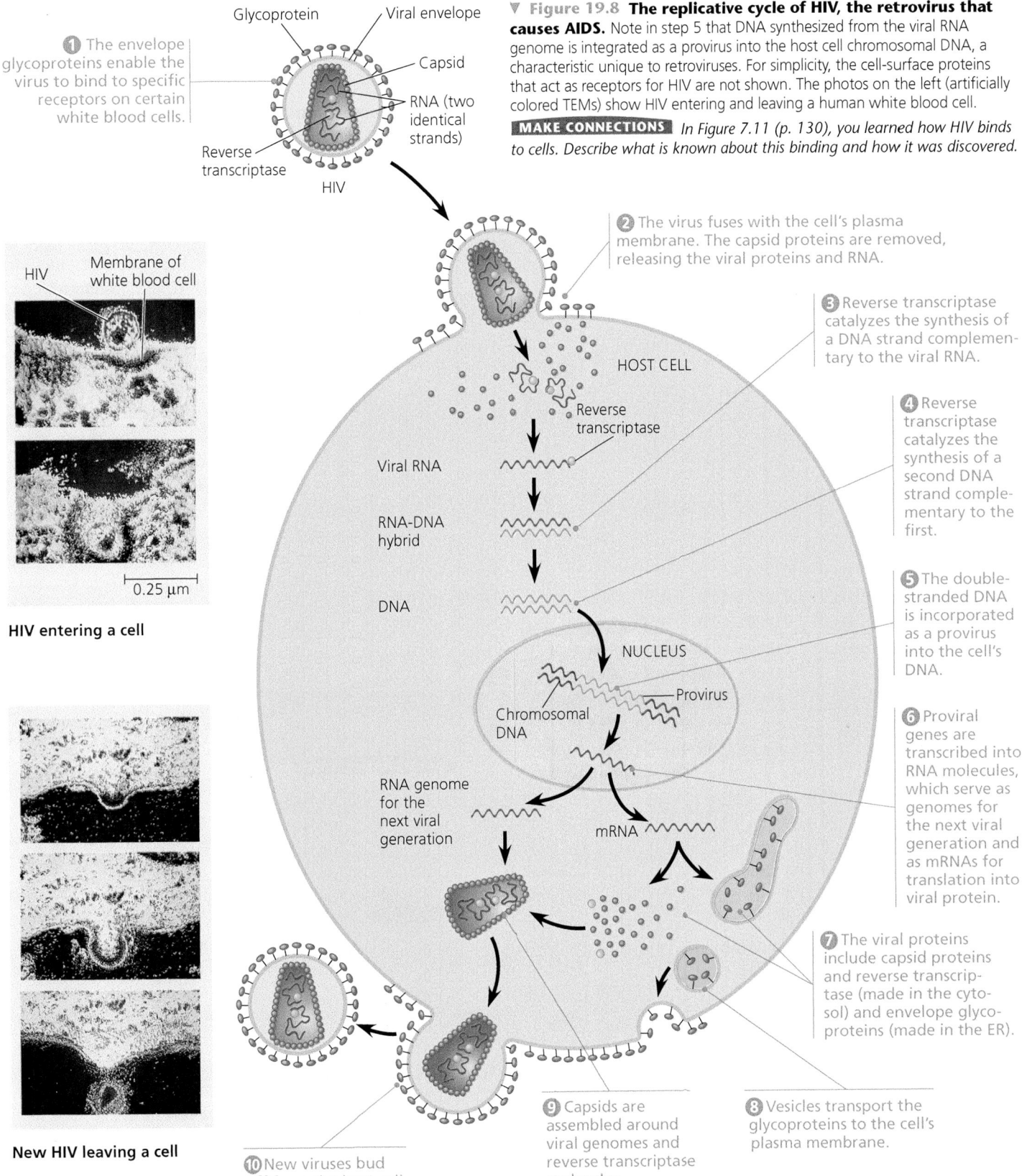

▼ **Figure 19.8** **The replicative cycle of HIV, the retrovirus that causes AIDS.** Note in step 5 that DNA synthesized from the viral RNA genome is integrated as a provirus into the host cell chromosomal DNA, a characteristic unique to retroviruses. For simplicity, the cell-surface proteins that act as receptors for HIV are not shown. The photos on the left (artificially colored TEMs) show HIV entering and leaving a human white blood cell.

MAKE CONNECTIONS *In Figure 7.11 (p. 130), you learned how HIV binds to cells. Describe what is known about this binding and how it was discovered.*

Glycoprotein — **Viral envelope**

1 The envelope glycoproteins enable the virus to bind to specific receptors on certain white blood cells.

Capsid

RNA (two identical strands)

Reverse transcriptase

HIV

HIV

Membrane of white blood cell

0.25 μm

HIV entering a cell

2 The virus fuses with the cell's plasma membrane. The capsid proteins are removed, releasing the viral proteins and RNA.

3 Reverse transcriptase catalyzes the synthesis of a DNA strand complementary to the viral RNA.

HOST CELL

Reverse transcriptase

Viral RNA

4 Reverse transcriptase catalyzes the synthesis of a second DNA strand complementary to the first.

RNA-DNA hybrid

DNA

5 The double-stranded DNA is incorporated as a provirus into the cell's DNA.

NUCLEUS

Provirus

Chromosomal DNA

6 Proviral genes are transcribed into RNA molecules, which serve as genomes for the next viral generation and as mRNAs for translation into viral protein.

RNA genome for the next viral generation

mRNA

7 The viral proteins include capsid proteins and reverse transcriptase (made in the cytosol) and envelope glycoproteins (made in the ER).

New HIV leaving a cell

10 New viruses bud off from the host cell.

9 Capsids are assembled around viral genomes and reverse transcriptase molecules.

8 Vesicles transport the glycoproteins to the cell's plasma membrane.

Figure 19.8 traces the HIV replicative cycle, which is typical of a retrovirus. After HIV enters a host cell, its reverse transcriptase molecules are released into the cytoplasm, where they catalyze synthesis of viral DNA. The newly made viral DNA then enters the cell's nucleus and integrates into the DNA of a chromosome. The integrated viral DNA, called a **provirus**, never leaves the host's genome, remaining a permanent resident of the cell. (Recall that a prophage, in contrast, leaves the host's genome at the start of a lytic cycle.) The host's RNA polymerase transcribes the proviral DNA into RNA molecules, which can function both as mRNA for the synthesis of viral proteins and as genomes for the new viruses that will be assembled and released from the cell. In Chapter 43, we describe how HIV causes the deterioration of the immune system that occurs in AIDS.

Evolution of Viruses

EVOLUTION We began this chapter by asking whether or not viruses are alive. Viruses do not really fit our definition of living organisms. An isolated virus is biologically inert, unable to replicate its genes or regenerate its own supply of ATP. Yet it has a genetic program written in the universal language of life. Do we think of viruses as nature's most complex associations of molecules or as the simplest forms of life? Either way, we must bend our usual definitions. Although viruses cannot replicate or carry out metabolic activities independently, their use of the genetic code makes it hard to deny their evolutionary connection to the living world.

How did viruses originate? Viruses have been found that infect every form of life—not just bacteria, animals, and plants, but also archaea, fungi, and algae and other protists. Because they depend on cells for their own propagation, it seems likely that viruses are not the descendants of precellular forms of life but evolved—possibly multiple times—*after* the first cells appeared. Most molecular biologists favor the hypothesis that viruses originated from naked bits of cellular nucleic acids that moved from one cell to another, perhaps via injured cell surfaces. The evolution of genes coding for capsid proteins may have facilitated the infection of uninjured cells. Candidates for the original sources of viral genomes include plasmids and transposons. *Plasmids* are small, circular DNA molecules found in bacteria and in the unicellular eukaryotes called yeasts. Plasmids exist apart from the cell's genome, can replicate independently of the genome, and are occasionally transferred between cells. *Transposons* are DNA segments that can move from one location to another within a cell's genome. Thus, plasmids, transposons, and viruses all share an important feature: They are *mobile genetic elements*. We will discuss plasmids in more detail in Chapters 20 and 27, and transposons in Chapter 21.

Consistent with this vision of pieces of DNA shuttling from cell to cell is the observation that a viral genome can have more in common with the genome of its host than with the genomes of viruses that infect other hosts. Indeed, some viral genes are essentially identical to genes of the host. On the other hand, recent sequencing of many viral genomes has shown that the genetic sequences of some viruses are quite similar to those of seemingly distantly related viruses; for example, some animal viruses share similar sequences with plant viruses. This genetic similarity may reflect the persistence of groups of viral genes that were favored by natural selection during the early evolution of viruses and the eukaryotic cells that served as their hosts.

The debate about the origin of viruses has been reinvigorated recently by reports of mimivirus, the largest virus yet discovered. Mimivirus is a double-stranded DNA virus with an icosahedral capsid that is 400 nm in diameter. (The beginning of its name is short for *mi*micking *micro*be because the virus is the size of a small bacterium.) Its genome contains 1.2 million bases (about 100 times as many as the influenza virus genome) and an estimated 1,000 genes. Perhaps the most surprising aspect of mimivirus, however, is that some of the genes appear to code for products previously thought to be hallmarks of cellular genomes. These products include proteins involved in translation, DNA repair, protein folding, and polysaccharide synthesis. The researchers who described mimivirus propose that it most likely evolved *before* the first cells and then developed an exploitative relationship with them. Other scientists disagree, maintaining that the virus evolved more recently than cells and has simply been efficient at scavenging genes from its hosts. The question of whether some viruses deserve their own early branch on the tree of life may not be answered for some time.

The ongoing evolutionary relationship between viruses and the genomes of their host cells is an association that makes viruses very useful experimental systems in molecular biology. Knowledge about viruses also allows many practical applications, since viruses have a tremendous impact on all organisms through their ability to cause disease.

CONCEPT CHECK 19.2

1. Compare the effect on the host cell of a lytic (virulent) phage and a lysogenic (temperate) phage.
2. **MAKE CONNECTIONS** The RNA virus in Figure 19.7 has a viral RNA polymerase that functions in step 3 of the virus's replicative cycle. Compare this RNA polymerase to the one in Figure 17.9 (p. 333) in terms of template and overall function.
3. Why is HIV called a retrovirus?
4. **WHAT IF?** If you were a researcher trying to combat HIV infection, what molecular processes could you attempt to block? (See Figure 19.8.)

For suggested answers, see Appendix A.

CONCEPT 19.3

Viruses, viroids, and prions are formidable pathogens in animals and plants

Diseases caused by viral infections afflict humans, agricultural crops, and livestock worldwide. Other smaller, less complex entities known as viroids and prions also cause disease in plants and animals, respectively.

Viral Diseases in Animals

A viral infection can produce symptoms by a number of different routes. Viruses may damage or kill cells by causing the release of hydrolytic enzymes from lysosomes. Some viruses cause infected cells to produce toxins that lead to disease symptoms, and some have molecular components that are toxic, such as envelope proteins. How much damage a virus causes depends partly on the ability of the infected tissue to regenerate by cell division. People usually recover completely from colds because the epithelium of the respiratory tract, which the viruses infect, can efficiently repair itself. In contrast, damage inflicted by poliovirus to mature nerve cells is permanent because these cells do not divide and usually cannot be replaced. Many of the temporary symptoms associated with viral infections, such as fever and aches, actually result from the body's own efforts at defending itself against infection rather than from cell death caused by the virus.

The immune system is a complex and critical part of the body's natural defenses (see Chapter 43). It is also the basis for the major medical tool for preventing viral infections—vaccines. A **vaccine** is a harmless variant or derivative of a pathogen that stimulates the immune system to mount defenses against the harmful pathogen. Smallpox, a viral disease that was at one time a devastating scourge in many parts of the world, was eradicated by a vaccination program carried out by the World Health Organization (WHO). The very narrow host range of the smallpox virus—it infects only humans—was a critical factor in the success of this program. Similar worldwide vaccination campaigns are currently under way to eradicate polio and measles. Effective vaccines are also available to protect against rubella, mumps, hepatitis B, and a number of other viral diseases.

Although vaccines can prevent certain viral illnesses, medical technology can do little, at present, to cure most viral infections once they occur. The antibiotics that help us recover from bacterial infections are powerless against viruses. Antibiotics kill bacteria by inhibiting enzymes specific to bacteria but have no effect on eukaryotic or virally encoded enzymes. However, the few enzymes that are encoded by viruses have provided targets for other drugs. Most antiviral drugs resemble nucleosides and as a result interfere with viral nucleic acid synthesis. One such drug is acyclovir, which impedes herpesvirus replication by inhibiting the viral polymerase that synthesizes viral DNA. Similarly, azidothymidine (AZT) curbs HIV replication by interfering with the synthesis of DNA by reverse transcriptase. In the past two decades, much effort has gone into developing drugs against HIV. Currently, multidrug treatments, sometimes called "cocktails," have been found to be most effective. Such treatments commonly include a combination of two nucleoside mimics and a protease inhibitor, which interferes with an enzyme required for assembly of the viruses.

Emerging Viruses

Viruses that suddenly become apparent are often referred to as *emerging viruses*. HIV, the AIDS virus, is a classic example: This virus appeared in San Francisco in the early 1980s, seemingly out of nowhere, although later studies uncovered a case in the Belgian Congo in 1959. The deadly Ebola virus, recognized initially in 1976 in central Africa, is one of several emerging viruses that cause *hemorrhagic fever*, an often fatal syndrome (set of symptoms) characterized by fever, vomiting, massive bleeding, and circulatory system collapse. A number of other dangerous emerging viruses cause encephalitis, inflammation of the brain. One example is the West Nile virus, which appeared in North America for the first time in 1999 and has spread to all 48 contiguous states in the United States.

In April 2009, a general outbreak, or **epidemic**, of a flu-like illness appeared in Mexico and the United States. The infectious agent was quickly identifed as an influenza virus related to viruses that cause the seasonal flu (**Figure 19.9a**). This particular virus was named H1N1 for reasons that will be

(a) 2009 pandemic H1N1 influenza A virus. Viruses (blue) are seen on an infected cell (green) in this colorized SEM.

(b) 2009 pandemic screening. At a South Korean airport, thermal scans were used to detect passengers with a fever who might have the H1N1 flu.

(c) 1918 flu pandemic. Many of those infected during the worst flu epidemic in the last 100 years were treated in large makeshift hospitals, such as this one.

▲ **Figure 19.9 Influenza in humans.**

explained shortly. The viral disease spread rapidly, prompting WHO to declare a global epidemic, or **pandemic**, in June 2009. By November, the disease had reached 207 countries, infecting over 600,000 people and killing almost 8,000. Public health agencies responded rapidly with guidelines for shutting down schools and other public places, and vaccine development and screening efforts were accelerated (**Figure 19.9b**).

How do such viruses burst on the human scene, giving rise to harmful diseases that were previously rare or even unknown? Three processes contribute to the emergence of viral diseases. The first, and perhaps most important, is the mutation of existing viruses. RNA viruses tend to have an unusually high rate of mutation because errors in replicating their RNA genomes are not corrected by proofreading. Some mutations change existing viruses into new genetic varieties (strains) that can cause disease, even in individuals who are immune to the ancestral virus. For instance, seasonal flu epidemics are caused by new strains of influenza virus genetically different enough from earlier strains that people have little immunity to them.

A second process that can lead to the emergence of viral diseases is the dissemination of a viral disease from a small, isolated human population. For instance, AIDS went unnamed and virtually unnoticed for decades before it began to spread around the world. In this case, technological and social factors, including affordable international travel, blood transfusions, sexual promiscuity, and the abuse of intravenous drugs, allowed a previously rare human disease to become a global scourge.

A third source of new viral diseases in humans is the spread of existing viruses from other animals. Scientists estimate that about three-quarters of new human diseases originate in this way. Animals that harbor and can transmit a particular virus but are generally unaffected by it are said to act as a natural reservoir for that virus. For example, the 2009 flu pandemic mentioned earlier was likely passed to humans from pigs; for this reason, it was originally called "swine flu."

In general, flu epidemics provide an instructive example of the effects of viruses moving between species. There are three types of influenza virus: types B and C, which infect only humans and have never caused an epidemic, and type A, which infects a wide range of animals, including birds, pigs, horses, and humans. Influenza A strains have caused four major flu epidemics among humans in the last 100 years. The worst was the first one, the "Spanish flu" pandemic of 1918–1919, which killed about 40 million people, including many World War I soldiers (**Figure 19.9c**).

Different strains of influenza A are given standardized names; for example, both the strain that caused the 1918 flu and the one that caused the 2009 pandemic flu are called H1N1. The name identifies which forms of two viral surface proteins are present: hemagglutinin (H) and neuraminidase

(N). There are 16 different types of hemagglutinin, a protein that helps the flu virus attach to host cells, and 9 types of neuraminidase, an enzyme that helps release new virus particles from infected cells. Waterbirds have been found that carry viruses with all possible combinations of H and N.

A likely scenario for the 1918 pandemic and others is that the virus mutated as it passed from one host species to another. When an animal like a pig or a bird is infected with more than one strain of flu virus, the different strains can undergo genetic recombination if the RNA molecules making up their genomes mix and match during viral assembly. Pigs are thought to have been the breeding ground for the 2009 flu virus, which contains sequences from bird, pig, and human flu viruses. Coupled with mutation, these reassortments can lead to the emergence of a viral strain that is capable of infecting human cells. Humans who have never been exposed to that particular strain before will lack immunity, and the recombinant virus has the potential to be highly pathogenic. If such a flu virus recombines with viruses that circulate widely among humans, it may acquire the ability to spread easily from person to person, dramatically increasing the potential for a major human outbreak.

Although the 2009 H1N1 flu was declared a pandemic, its toll in lives was significantly lower than that of the 1918 flu. Significantly, however, 79% of the confirmed H1N1 cases in 2009 occurred in people under 30 years of age, and the highest mortality rates occurred in people under 64, opposite to patterns seen for seasonal flu. Some scientists hypothesize that the 1918 flu virus was the ancestor of most subsequent H1N1 epidemic-causing viruses, including that responsible for the 2009 pandemic. Older people are likely to have been exposed to earlier H1N1 viruses and have probably built up immunity to them. This could explain why contracting the 2009 H1N1 virus was more deadly for younger people, who were less likely to have been exposed to H1N1 viruses and to have built up immune defenses.

Perhaps a greater long-term threat is the avian flu caused by an H5N1 virus carried by wild and domestic birds. The first documented transmission to humans was in 1997, when 18 people in Hong Kong were infected and 6 subsequently died. While the 2009 H1N1 flu virus spread easily from human to human, reports of human-to-human transmission of the H5N1 avian flu are quite rare. More alarming, however, is the overall mortality rate of the H5N1 virus, which is greater than 50%. Furthermore, the host range of H5N1 is expanding, which provides increasing opportunities for different strains of the virus to reassort their genetic material and for new strains to emerge. If the H5N1 avian flu virus evolves so that it can spread easily from person to person, it could represent a major global health threat akin to that of the 1918 pandemic.

As we have seen, emerging viruses are generally not new; rather, they are existing viruses that mutate, disseminate more widely in the current host species, or spread to new host species. Changes in host behavior or environmental changes can increase the viral traffic responsible for emerging diseases. For example, new roads built through remote areas can allow viruses to spread between previously isolated human populations. Also, the destruction of forests to expand cropland can bring humans into contact with other animals that may host viruses capable of infecting humans.

Viral Diseases in Plants

More than 2,000 types of viral diseases of plants are known, and together they account for an estimated annual loss of $15 billion worldwide due to their destruction of agricultural and horticultural crops. Common signs of viral infection include bleached or brown spots on leaves and fruits, stunted growth, and damaged flowers or roots, all tending to diminish the yield and quality of crops (Figure 19.10).

Plant viruses have the same basic structure and mode of replication as animal viruses. Most plant viruses discovered thus far, including tobacco mosaic virus (TMV), have an RNA genome. Many have a helical capsid, like TMV, while others have an icosahedral capsid (see Figure 19.3).

Viral diseases of plants spread by two major routes. In the first route, called *horizontal transmission*, a plant is infected from an external source of the virus. Because the invading virus must get past the plant's outer protective layer of cells (the epidermis), a plant becomes more susceptible to viral infections if it has been damaged by wind, injury, or herbivores. Herbivores, especially insects, pose a double threat because they can also act as carriers of viruses, transmitting disease from plant to plant. Moreover, farmers and gardeners may transmit plant viruses inadvertently on pruning shears and other tools. The other route of viral infection is *vertical transmission*, in which a plant inherits a viral infection from a parent. Vertical transmission can occur in asexual propagation (for example, through cuttings) or in sexual reproduction via infected seeds.

Once a virus enters a plant cell and begins replicating, viral genomes and associated proteins can spread throughout the plant by means of plasmodesmata, the cytoplasmic connections that penetrate the walls between adjacent plant cells (see Figure 36.20). The passage of viral macromolecules from cell to cell is facilitated by virally encoded proteins that cause enlargement of plasmodesmata. Scientists have not yet devised cures for most viral plant diseases. Consequently, research efforts are focused largely on reducing the transmission of such diseases and on breeding resistant varieties of crop plants.

Viroids and Prions: The Simplest Infectious Agents

As small and simple as viruses are, they dwarf another class of pathogens: **viroids**. These are circular RNA molecules, only a few hundred nucleotides long, that infect plants. Viroids do not encode proteins but can replicate in host plant cells, apparently using host cell enzymes. These small RNA molecules seem to cause errors in the regulatory systems that control plant growth; the typical signs of viroid diseases are abnormal development and stunted growth. One viroid disease, called cadang-cadang, has killed more than 10 million coconut palms in the Philippines.

An important lesson from viroids is that a single molecule can be an infectious agent that spreads a disease. But viroids are nucleic acids, whose ability to be replicated is well known. Even more surprising is the evidence for infectious *proteins*, called **prions**, which appear to cause a number of degenerative brain diseases in various animal species. These diseases include scrapie in sheep; mad cow disease, which has plagued the European beef industry in recent years; and Creutzfeldt-Jakob disease in humans, which has caused the death of some 150 people in Great Britain over the past decade. Prions are most likely transmitted in food, as may occur when people eat prion-laden beef from cattle with mad cow disease. Kuru, another human disease caused by prions, was identified in the early 1900s among the South Fore natives of New Guinea. A kuru epidemic peaked there in the 1960s, puzzling scientists, who at first thought the disease had a genetic basis. Eventually, however, anthropological investigations ferreted out how the disease was spread: ritual cannibalism, a widespread practice among South Fore natives at that time.

Two characteristics of prions are especially alarming. First, prions act very

▶ Figure 19.10 **Viral infection of plants.** Infection with particular viruses causes irregular brown patches on tomatoes (left), black blotching on squash (center), and streaking in tulips due to redistribution of pigment granules (right).

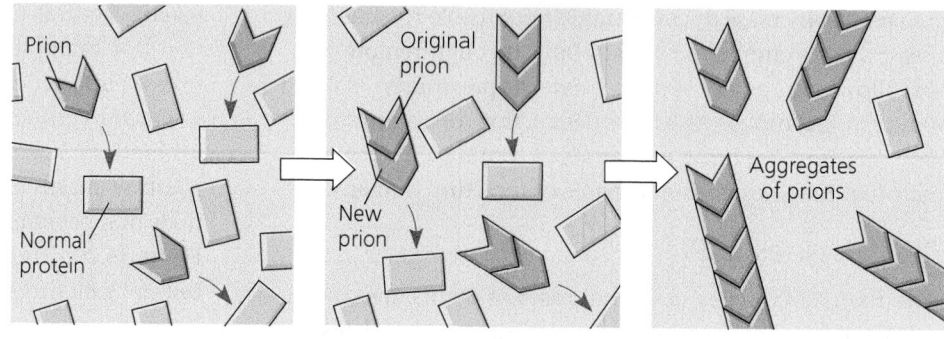

▶ **Figure 19.11 Model for how prions propagate.** Prions are misfolded versions of normal brain proteins. When a prion contacts a normally folded version of the same protein, it may induce the normal protein to assume the abnormal shape. The resulting chain reaction may continue until high levels of prion aggregation cause cellular malfunction and eventual degeneration of the brain.

slowly, with an incubation period of at least ten years before symptoms develop. The lengthy incubation period prevents sources of infection from being identified until long after the first cases appear, allowing many more infections to occur. Second, prions are virtually indestructible; they are not destroyed or deactivated by heating to normal cooking temperatures. To date, there is no known cure for prion diseases, and the only hope for developing effective treatments lies in understanding the process of infection.

How can a protein, which cannot replicate itself, be a transmissible pathogen? According to the leading model, a prion is a misfolded form of a protein normally present in brain cells. When the prion gets into a cell containing the normal form of the protein, the prion somehow converts normal protein molecules to the misfolded prion versions. Several prions then aggregate into a complex that can convert other normal proteins to prions, which join the chain **(Figure 19.11)**. Prion aggregation interferes with normal

cellular functions and causes disease symptoms. This model was greeted with much skepticism when it was first proposed by Stanley Prusiner in the early 1980s, but it is now widely accepted. Prusiner was awarded the Nobel Prize in 1997 for his work on prions.

CONCEPT CHECK 19.3

1. Describe two ways a preexisting virus can become an emerging virus.
2. Contrast horizontal and vertical transmission of viruses in plants.
3. **WHAT IF?** TMV has been isolated from virtually all commercial tobacco products. Why, then, is TMV infection not an additional hazard for smokers?

For suggested answers, see Appendix A.

19 CHAPTER REVIEW

SUMMARY OF KEY CONCEPTS

CONCEPT 19.1

A virus consists of a nucleic acid surrounded by a protein coat (pp. 381–384)

- Researchers discovered viruses in the late 1800s by studying a plant disease, tobacco mosaic disease.
- A **virus** is a small nucleic acid genome enclosed in a protein **capsid** and sometimes a membranous **viral envelope** containing viral proteins that help viruses enter cells. The genome may be single- or double-stranded DNA or RNA.

❓ *Are viruses generally considered living or nonliving? Explain.*

CONCEPT 19.2

Viruses replicate only in host cells (pp. 384–390)

- Viruses use enzymes, ribosomes, and small molecules of host cells to synthesize progeny viruses during replication. Each type of virus has a characteristic **host range**.

- **Phages** (viruses that infect bacteria) can replicate by two alternative mechanisms: the **lytic cycle** and the **lysogenic cycle**.

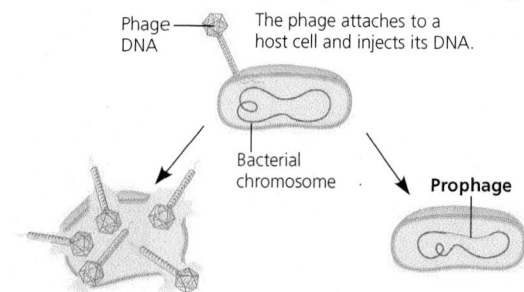

Lytic cycle	Lysogenic cycle
• **Virulent** or **temperate phage**	• **Temperate phage** only
• Destruction of host DNA	• Genome integrates into bacterial chromosome as **prophage**, which (1) is replicated and passed on to daughter cells and (2) can be induced to leave the chromosome and initiate a lytic cycle
• Production of new phages	
• Lysis of host cell causes release of progeny phages	

- Many animal viruses have an envelope. **Retroviruses** (such as **HIV**) use the enzyme **reverse transcriptase** to copy their RNA genome into DNA, which can be integrated into the host genome as a **provirus**.

- Since viruses can replicate only within cells, they probably evolved after the first cells appeared, perhaps as packaged fragments of cellular nucleic acid. The origin of viruses is still being debated.

> **?** *Describe enzymes that are not found in most cells but are necessary for the replication of viruses of certain types.*

CONCEPT 19.3

Viruses, viroids, and prions are formidable pathogens in animals and plants (pp. 390–394)

- Symptoms of viral diseases may be caused by direct viral harm to cells or by the body's immune response. **Vaccines** stimulate the immune system to defend the host against specific viruses.
- Outbreaks of "new" viral diseases in humans are usually caused by existing viruses that expand their host territory. The H1N1 2009 flu virus was a new combination of pig, human, and avian viral genes that caused a pandemic. The H5N1 avian flu virus has the potential to cause a high-mortality flu pandemic.
- Viruses enter plant cells through damaged cell walls (horizontal transmission) or are inherited from a parent (vertical transmission).
- **Viroids** are naked RNA molecules that infect plants and disrupt their growth. **Prions** are slow-acting, virtually indestructible infectious proteins that cause brain diseases in mammals.

> **?** *What aspect of an RNA virus makes it more likely than a DNA virus to become an emerging virus?*

TEST YOUR UNDERSTANDING

LEVEL 1: KNOWLEDGE/COMPREHENSION

1. Which of the following characteristics, structures, or processes is common to both bacteria and viruses?
   a. metabolism
   b. ribosomes
   c. genetic material composed of nucleic acid
   d. cell division
   e. independent existence

2. Emerging viruses arise by
   a. mutation of existing viruses.
   b. the spread of existing viruses to new host species.
   c. the spread of existing viruses more widely within their host species.
   d. all of the above
   e. none of the above

3. To cause a human pandemic, the H5N1 avian flu virus would have to
   a. spread to primates such as chimpanzees.
   b. develop into a virus with a different host range.
   c. become capable of human-to-human transmission.
   d. arise independently in chickens in North and South America.
   e. become much more pathogenic.

LEVEL 2: APPLICATION/ANALYSIS

4. A bacterium is infected with an experimentally constructed bacteriophage composed of the T2 phage protein coat and T4 phage DNA. The new phages produced would have
   a. T2 protein and T4 DNA.
   b. T2 protein and T2 DNA.
   c. a mixture of the DNA and proteins of both phages.
   d. T4 protein and T4 DNA.
   e. T4 protein and T2 DNA.

5. RNA viruses require their own supply of certain enzymes because
   a. host cells rapidly destroy the viruses.
   b. host cells lack enzymes that can replicate the viral genome.
   c. these enzymes translate viral mRNA into proteins.
   d. these enzymes penetrate host cell membranes.
   e. these enzymes cannot be made in host cells.

6. **DRAW IT** Redraw Figure 19.7 to show the replicative cycle of a virus with a single-stranded genome that can function as mRNA (a class IV virus).

LEVEL 3: SYNTHESIS/EVALUATION

7. **EVOLUTION CONNECTION**
   The success of some viruses lies in their ability to evolve rapidly within the host. Such a virus evades the host's defenses by mutating and producing many altered progeny viruses before the body can mount an attack. Thus, the viruses present late in infection differ from those that initially infected the body. Discuss this as an example of evolution in microcosm. Which viral lineages tend to predominate?

8. **SCIENTIFIC INQUIRY**
   When bacteria infect an animal, the number of bacteria in the body increases in an exponential fashion (graph A). After infection by a virulent animal virus with a lytic replicative cycle, there is no evidence of infection for a while. Then the number of viruses rises suddenly and subsequently increases in a series of steps (graph B). Explain the difference in the curves.

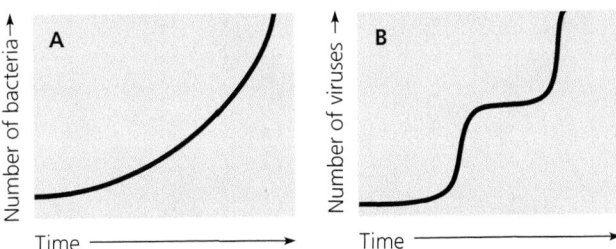

9. **WRITE ABOUT A THEME**
   Structure and Function While viruses are considered by most scientists to be nonliving, they do show some characteristics of life, including the correlation of structure and function. In a short essay (100–150 words), discuss how the structure of a virus correlates with its function.

For selected answers, see Appendix A.

Mastering BIOLOGY   www.masteringbiology.com

1. MasteringBiology® Assignments

Tutorial Viral Replication
Activities Simplified Viral Reproductive Cycle • Phage Lytic Cycle • Phage Lysogenic and Lytic Cycles • Retrovirus (HIV) Reproductive Cycle • The HIV Replicative Cycle • Discovery Channel Video: Emerging Diseases
Questions Student Misconceptions • Reading Quiz • Multiple Choice • End-of-Chapter

2. eText
Read your book online, search, take notes, highlight text, and more.

3. The Study Area
Practice Tests • Cumulative Test • ***BioFlix*** 3-D Animations • MP3 Tutor Sessions • Videos • Activities • Investigations • Lab Media • Audio Glossary • Word Study Tools • Art

20

Biotechnology

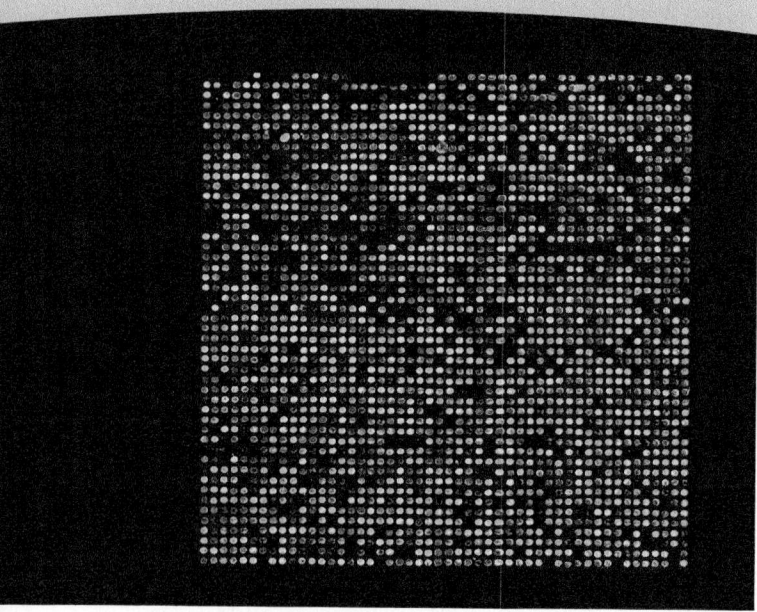

▲ **Figure 20.1 How can this array of spots be used to compare normal and cancerous tissues?**

KEY CONCEPTS

20.1 DNA cloning yields multiple copies of a gene or other DNA segment

20.2 DNA technology allows us to study the sequence, expression, and function of a gene

20.3 Cloning organisms may lead to production of stem cells for research and other applications

20.4 The practical applications of DNA technology affect our lives in many ways

OVERVIEW

The DNA Toolbox

In 2001, a major scientific milestone was announced: Researchers had completed a "first draft" sequence of all 3 billion base pairs of the human genome—only the fourth eukaryotic genome to be sequenced. This news electrified the scientific community. Few among them would have dared to dream that

a mere nine years later, genome sequencing would be under way for more than 7,000 species. By 2010, researchers had completed sequencing more than 1,000 bacterial, 80 archaeal, and 100 eukaryotic genomes, with many more in progress.

Ultimately, these achievements are attributable to advances in DNA technology—methods of working with and manipulating DNA—that had their roots in the 1970s. A key accomplishment was the invention of techniques for making **recombinant DNA**, DNA molecules formed when segments of DNA from two different sources—often different species—are combined *in vitro* (in a test tube). This advance gave rise to the development of powerful techniques for analyzing genes and gene expression. How scientists prepare recombinant DNA and use DNA technology to answer fundamental biological questions are one focus of this chapter. In the next chapter (Chapter 21), we'll see how these techniques have allowed the sequencing of whole genomes, and we'll consider what we've learned from these sequences about the evolution of species and of the genome itself.

Another focus of this chapter is how our lives are affected by **biotechnology**, the manipulation of organisms or their components to make useful products. Biotechnology includes such early practices as selective breeding of farm animals and using microorganisms to make wine and cheese. Today, biotechnology also encompasses **genetic engineering**, the direct manipulation of genes for practical purposes. Genetic engineering has launched a revolution in biotechnology, greatly expanding the scope of its potential applications. Tools from the DNA toolbox are now applied in ways that affect everything from agriculture to criminal law to medical research. For instance, on the DNA microarray in **Figure 20.1**, the colored spots represent the relative level of expression of 2,400 human genes in normal and cancerous tissue. Using microarray analysis, researchers can quickly compare gene expression in different samples, such as those tested here. The knowledge gained from such gene expression studies is making a significant contribution to the study of cancer and other diseases.

In this chapter, we'll first describe the main techniques for manipulating DNA and analyzing gene expression and function. Next, we'll explore advances in cloning organisms and producing stem cells, techniques that have both expanded our basic understanding of biology and enhanced our ability to apply this understanding to global problems. Finally, we'll survey the practical applications of biotechnology and consider some of the social and ethical issues that arise as biotechnology becomes more pervasive in our lives.

CONCEPT 20.1

DNA cloning yields multiple copies of a gene or other DNA segment

The molecular biologist studying a particular gene faces a challenge. Naturally occurring DNA molecules are very long, and a single molecule usually carries many genes. Moreover, in many eukaryotic genomes, genes occupy only a small proportion of the chromosomal DNA, the rest being noncoding nucleotide sequences. A single human gene, for example, might constitute only 1/100,000 of a chromosomal DNA molecule. As a further complication, the distinctions between a gene and the surrounding DNA are subtle, consisting only of differences in nucleotide sequence. To work directly with specific genes, scientists have developed methods for preparing well-defined segments of DNA in multiple identical copies, a process called *DNA cloning*.

DNA Cloning and Its Applications: *A Preview*

Most methods for cloning pieces of DNA in the laboratory share certain general features. One common approach uses bacteria, most often *Escherichia coli*. Recall from Figure 16.12 that the *E. coli* chromosome is a large circular molecule of DNA. In addition, *E. coli* and many other bacteria have **plasmids**, small circular DNA molecules that replicate separately from the bacterial chromosome. A plasmid has only a small number of genes; these genes may be useful when the bacterium is in a particular environment but may not be required for survival or reproduction under most conditions.

To clone pieces of DNA in the laboratory, researchers first obtain a plasmid (originally isolated from a bacterial cell and genetically engineered for efficient cloning) and insert DNA from another source ("foreign" DNA) into it **(Figure 20.2)**. The resulting plasmid is now a recombinant DNA molecule. The plasmid is then returned to a bacterial cell, producing a *recombinant bacterium*. This single cell reproduces through repeated cell divisions to form a clone of cells, a population of genetically identical cells. Because the dividing bacteria replicate the recombinant plasmid and pass it on to their descendants, the foreign DNA and any genes it carries are cloned at the same time. The production of multiple copies of a single gene is called **gene cloning**.

Gene cloning is useful for two basic purposes: to make many copies of, or *amplify*, a particular gene and to produce a protein product. Researchers can

isolate copies of a cloned gene from bacteria for use in basic research or to endow an organism with a new metabolic capability, such as pest resistance. For example, a resistance gene present in one crop species might be cloned and transferred into plants of another species. Alternatively, a protein with medical uses, such as human growth hormone, can be harvested in large quantities from cultures of bacteria carrying the cloned gene for the protein.

A single gene is usually a very small part of the total DNA in a cell. For example, a typical gene makes up only about one-millionth of the DNA in a human cell. The ability to

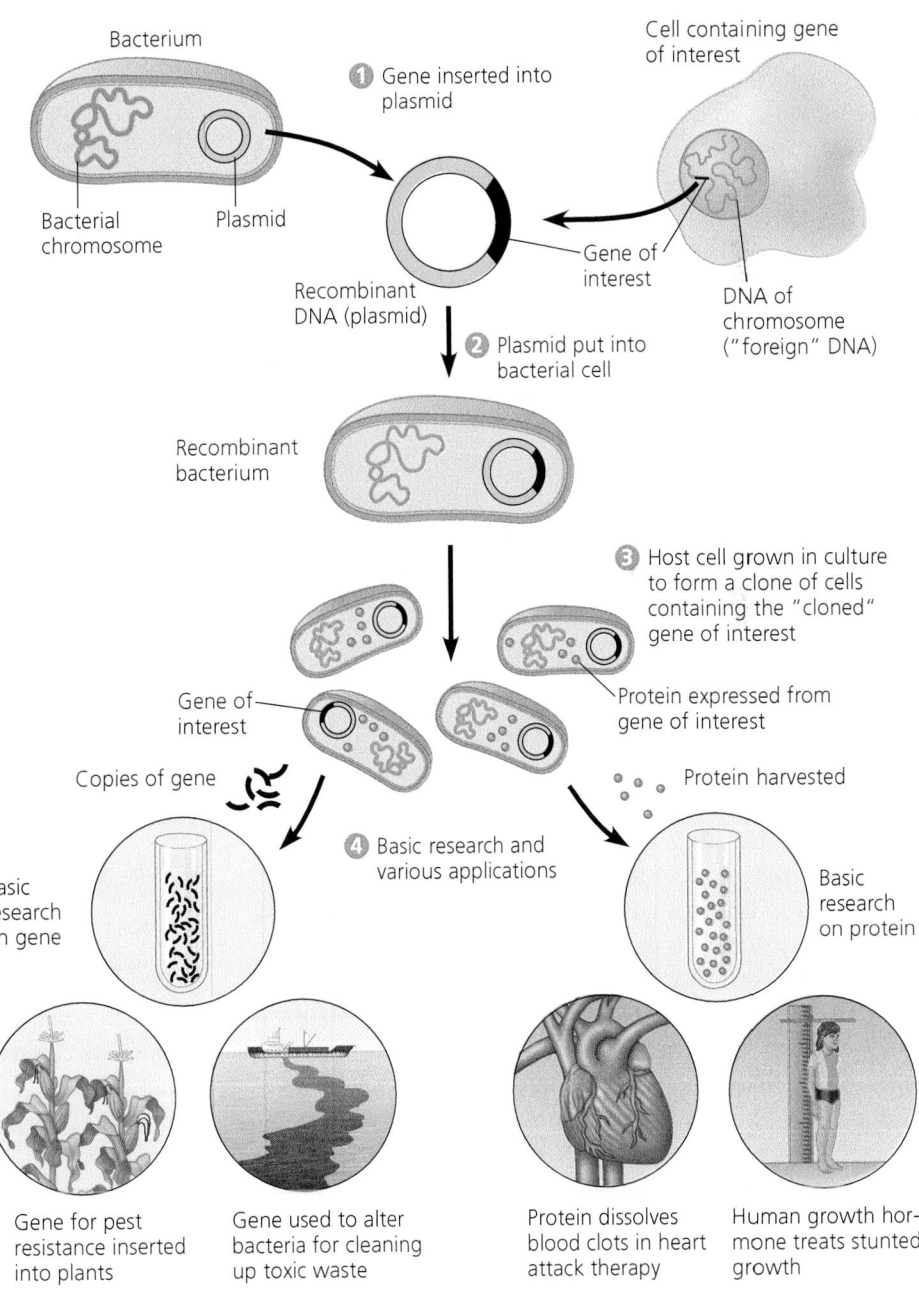

▲ **Figure 20.2 A preview of gene cloning and some uses of cloned genes.** In this simplified diagram of gene cloning, we start with a plasmid (originally isolated from a bacterial cell) and a gene of interest from another organism. Only one plasmid and one copy of the gene of interest are shown at the top of the figure, but the starting materials would include many of each.

amplify such rare DNA fragments is therefore crucial for any application involving a single gene.

Using Restriction Enzymes to Make Recombinant DNA

Gene cloning and genetic engineering rely on the use of enzymes that cut DNA molecules at a limited number of specific locations. These enzymes, called restriction endonucleases, or **restriction enzymes**, were discovered in the late 1960s by biologists doing basic research on bacteria. Restriction enzymes protect the bacterial cell by cutting up foreign DNA from other organisms or phages (see Chapter 19).

Hundreds of different restriction enzymes have been identified and isolated. Each restriction enzyme is very specific, recognizing a particular short DNA sequence, or **restriction site**, and cutting both DNA strands at precise points within this restriction site. The DNA of a bacterial cell is protected from the cell's own restriction enzymes by the addition of methyl groups (—CH₃) to adenines or cytosines within the sequences recognized by the enzymes.

The top of **Figure 20.3** illustrates a restriction site recognized by a particular restriction enzyme from *E. coli*. As shown in this example, most restriction sites are symmetrical. That is, the sequence of nucleotides is the same on both strands when read in the 5′ → 3′ direction. The most commonly used restriction enzymes recognize sequences containing four to eight nucleotides. Because any sequence this short usually occurs (by chance) many times in a long DNA molecule, a restriction enzyme will make many cuts in a DNA molecule, yielding a set of **restriction fragments**. All copies of a particular DNA molecule always yield the same set of restriction fragments when exposed to the same restriction enzyme. In other words, a restriction enzyme cuts a DNA molecule in a reproducible way. (Later you will learn how the different fragments can be separated and distinguished from each other.)

The most useful restriction enzymes cleave the sugar-phosphate backbones in the two DNA strands in a staggered manner, as indicated in Figure 20.3. The resulting double-stranded restriction fragments have at least one single-stranded end, called a **sticky end**. These short extensions can form hydrogen-bonded base pairs with complementary sticky ends on any other DNA molecules cut with the same enzyme. The associations formed in this way are only temporary but can be made permanent by the enzyme **DNA ligase**. As you saw in Figure 16.16, this enzyme catalyzes the formation of covalent bonds that close up the sugar-phosphate backbones of DNA strands; for example, it joins Okazaki fragments during replication. You can see at the bottom of Figure 20.3 that the ligase-catalyzed joining of DNA from two different sources produces a stable recombinant DNA molecule.

① Restriction enzyme cuts the sugar-phosphate backbones at each arrow.

② DNA fragment from another source is added. Base pairing of sticky ends produces various combinations.

Sticky end

Fragment from different DNA molecule cut by the same restriction enzyme

One possible combination

③ DNA ligase seals the strands.

Recombinant DNA molecule

▲ **Figure 20.3 Using a restriction enzyme and DNA ligase to make recombinant DNA.** The restriction enzyme in this example (called *Eco*RI) recognizes a specific six-base-pair sequence, the restriction site, and makes staggered cuts in the sugar-phosphate backbones within this sequence, producing fragments with sticky ends. Any fragments with complementary sticky ends can base-pair, including the two original fragments. If the fragments come from different DNA molecules, the ligated product is recombinant DNA.

DRAW IT *The restriction enzyme* Hind*III recognizes the sequence 5′-AAGCTT-3′, cutting between the two 'A's. Draw the double-stranded sequence before and after the enzyme cuts.*

Cloning a Eukaryotic Gene in a Bacterial Plasmid

Now that you've learned about restriction enzymes and DNA ligase, we can see how genes are cloned in plasmids. The original plasmid is called a **cloning vector**, defined as a DNA molecule that can carry foreign DNA into a host cell and replicate there. Bacterial plasmids are widely used as cloning vectors for several reasons: They can be readily obtained from commercial suppliers, manipulated to form recombinant plasmids by insertion of foreign DNA *in vitro*, and then introduced into bacterial cells. Moreover, recombinant bacterial plasmids (and the foreign DNA they carry) multiply rapidly owing to the high reproductive rate of their host cells.

Producing Clones of Cells Carrying Recombinant Plasmids

Let's say we are researchers interested in studying the β-globin gene in a particular species of hummingbird. We start by cloning all the hummingbird genes; later we'll isolate the β-globin gene from all the others, a task very much like finding a needle in a haystack. **Figure 20.4** details one method for cloning hummingbird genes using a bacterial plasmid as the cloning vector.

① First, we isolate hummingbird genomic DNA from hummingbird cells. We also obtain our chosen vector, a particular bacterial plasmid from *E. coli* cells. The plasmid has been engineered to carry two genes that will later prove useful: *amp*^{R}, which makes *E. coli* cells resistant to the antibiotic ampicillin, and *lacZ*, which encodes the enzyme β-galactosidase, which hydrolyzes lactose (see p. 354). This enzyme can also hydrolyze a similar synthetic molecule called X-gal to form a blue product. The plasmid contains only one copy of the restriction site recognized by the restriction enzyme used in the next step, and that site is within the *lacZ* gene.

② Both the plasmid and the hummingbird DNA are cut with the same restriction enzyme, and then ③ the fragments are mixed together, allowing base pairing between their complementary sticky ends. We then add DNA ligase, which covalently bonds the sugar-phosphate backbones of the fragments whose sticky ends have base-paired. Many of the resulting recombinant plasmids contain single hummingbird DNA fragments (three are shown in Figure 20.4), and at least one of them is expected to carry all or part of the β-globin gene. This step will also generate other products, such as plasmids containing multiple hummingbird DNA fragments, a combination of two plasmids, or a rejoined, nonrecombinant version of the original plasmid.

④ The DNA mixture is then added to bacteria that have a mutation in the *lacZ* gene on their own chromosome, making them unable to hydrolyze

▼ Figure 20.4

Cloning Genes in Bacterial Plasmids

APPLICATION Gene cloning is a process that produces many copies of a gene of interest. These copies can be used in sequencing the gene, in producing its encoded protein, or in basic research or other applications.

TECHNIQUE In this example, hummingbird genes are inserted into plasmids from *E. coli*. Only three plasmids and three hummingbird DNA fragments are shown, but millions of copies of the plasmid and a mixture of millions of different hummingbird DNA fragments would be present in the samples.

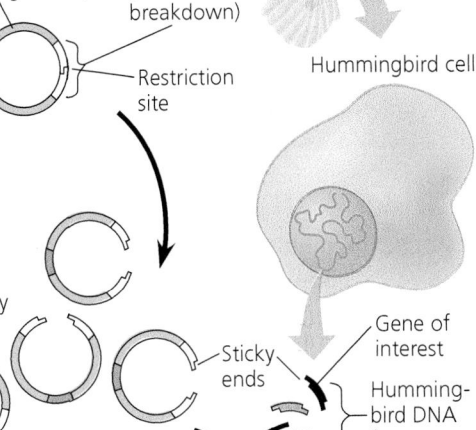

① Obtain engineered plasmid DNA and DNA from hummingbird cells. The hummingbird DNA contains the gene of interest.

② Cut both DNA samples with the same restriction enzyme, one that makes a single cut within the *lacZ* gene and many cuts within the hummingbird DNA.

③ Mix the cut plasmids and DNA fragments. Some join by base pairing; add DNA ligase to seal them together. The products include recombinant plasmids and many nonrecombinant plasmids.

④ Mix the DNA with bacterial cells that have a mutation in their own *lacZ* gene. Some cells take up a recombinant plasmid or other DNA molecule by transformation.

⑤ Plate the bacteria on nutrient-containing agar medium supplemented with ampicillin and X-gal, a molecule resembling lactose. Incubate until colonies grow.

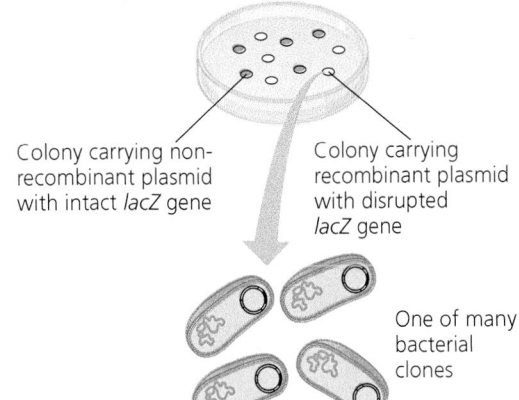

RESULTS Only a cell that took up a plasmid, which has the *amp*^{R} gene, will reproduce and form a colony. Colonies with nonrecombinant plasmids will be blue because they can hydrolyze X-gal, forming a blue product. Colonies with recombinant plasmids, in which *lacZ* is disrupted, will be white because they cannot hydrolyze X-gal.

WHAT IF? If the medium used in step 5 did not contain ampicillin, what other colonies would grow? What color would they be?

lactose or X-gal. Under suitable experimental conditions, the cells take up foreign DNA by transformation (see p. 306). Some cells acquire a recombinant plasmid carrying a gene, while others may take up a nonrecombinant plasmid, a fragment of noncoding hummingbird DNA, or nothing at all. The *amp^R* and *lacZ* genes on the plasmid can help us sort out these possibilities.

⑤ First, plating out all the bacteria on solid nutrient medium containing ampicillin allows us to distinguish the cells that have taken up plasmids, whether recombinant or not, from the other cells. Under these conditions, only cells with a plasmid will reproduce because only they have the *amp^R* gene conferring resistance to the ampicillin in the medium. Each reproducing bacterium forms a clone of cells. Once the clone contains between 10^5 and 10^8 cells, it is visible as a mass, or *colony*, on the agar. As cells reproduce, any foreign genes carried by recombinant plasmids are also copied (cloned).

Second, the presence of X-gal in the medium allows us to distinguish colonies with recombinant plasmids from those with nonrecombinant plasmids. Colonies containing nonrecombinant plasmids have the *lacZ* gene intact and will produce functional β-galactosidase. These colonies will be blue because the enzyme hydrolyzes the X-gal in the medium, forming a blue product. In contrast, no functional β-galactosidase is produced in colonies containing recombinant plasmids with foreign DNA inserted into the *lacZ* gene; these colonies will therefore be white.

The procedure to this point will have cloned many different hummingbird DNA fragments, not just the β-globin gene that interests us. In fact, taken together, the white colonies should represent all the DNA sequences from the hummingbird genome, including noncoding regions as well as genes. And because restriction enzymes do not recognize gene boundaries, some genes will be cut and divided up among two or more clones. Shortly, we will discuss the procedure we use to find the colony (cell clone) or colonies carrying the β-globin gene sequences among the many clones carrying other pieces of hummingbird DNA. To understand that procedure, we must first consider how the clones are stored.

Storing Cloned Genes in DNA Libraries

The cloning procedure in Figure 20.4, which starts with a mixture of fragments from the entire genome of an organism, is called a "shotgun" approach;

no single gene is targeted for cloning. Numerous different recombinant plasmids are produced in step 3, and a clone of cells carrying each type of plasmid ends up as a white colony in step 5. The complete set of plasmid-containing cell clones, each carrying copies of a particular segment from the initial genome, is referred to as a **genomic library** (Figure 20.5a). Each "plasmid clone" in the library is like a book containing specific information. Today, scientists often obtain such libraries (or even particular cloned genes) from another researcher, a commercial source, or a sequencing center.

Historically, certain bacteriophages have also been used as cloning vectors for making genomic libraries. Fragments of foreign DNA can be spliced into a trimmed-down version of a phage genome, as into a plasmid, by using a restriction enzyme and DNA ligase. The normal infection process allows production of many new phage particles, each carrying the foreign DNA insert. Today, phages are generally used for making genomic libraries only in special cases.

Another type of vector widely used in library construction is a **bacterial artificial chromosome (BAC)**. In spite of the name, these are simply large plasmids, trimmed down so they contain just the genes necessary to ensure replication. An advantage of using BACs as vectors is that while a standard plasmid can carry a DNA insert no larger than 10,000 base pairs (10 kb), a BAC can carry an insert of 100–300 kb

(a) Plasmid library. Shown are three of the thousands of "books" in a plasmid library. Each "book" is a clone of bacterial cells, which contain copies of a particular foreign genome fragment (pink, yellow, black segments) in their recombinant plasmids.

(b) BAC clone. Many BAC clones make up a BAC library.

(c) Storing genome libraries. Both plasmid and BAC genomic libraries are usually stored in a "multiwell" plastic plate; a 384-well plate is shown here. Each clone occupies one well. (The library of an entire genome would require many such plates.)

▲ **Figure 20.5 Genomic libraries.** A genomic library is a collection of many clones. Each clone carries copies of a particular DNA segment from a foreign genome, integrated into an appropriate DNA vector, such as a plasmid or a bacterial artificial chromosome (BAC). In a complete genomic library, the foreign DNA segments cover the entire genome of an organism. Note that the BACs are not drawn to scale; the genes carried are actually about 1,000 times larger than the vector itself.

(Figure 20.5b). The very large insert size minimizes the number of clones needed to make up the genomic library, but it also makes them more challenging to work with in the lab, so the insert may later be cut up into smaller pieces that are "subcloned" into plasmid vectors.

Clones are usually stored in multiwelled plastic plates, with one clone per well (Figure 20.5c). This orderly storage of clones, identified by their location in the plate, makes screening for the gene of interest very efficient, as you will see.

In a genomic library, the cloned β-globin gene would include not just exons containing the coding sequence, but also the promoter, untranslated regions, and any introns. Some biologists might be interested in the hummingbird β-globin protein itself—they might wonder, for instance, if this oxygen-carrying protein is different from its counterpart in other, less metabolically active species. Such researchers can make another kind of DNA library by starting with fully processed mRNA extracted from cells where the gene is expressed (Figure 20.6). The enzyme reverse transcriptase (obtained from retroviruses) is used *in vitro* to make a single-stranded DNA *reverse transcript* of each mRNA molecule. Recall that the 3' end of the mRNA has a stretch of

① Reverse transcriptase is added to a test tube containing mRNA isolated from a certain type of cell.

② Reverse transcriptase makes the first DNA strand using the mRNA as a template and a stretch of dT's as a DNA primer.

③ mRNA is degraded by another enzyme.

④ DNA polymerase synthesizes the second strand, using a primer in the reaction mixture. (Several options exist for primers.)

⑤ The result is cDNA, which carries the complete coding sequence of the gene but no introns.

▲ **Figure 20.6 Making complementary DNA (cDNA) from eukaryotic genes.** Complementary DNA is DNA made *in vitro* using mRNA as a template for the first strand. Because the mRNA contains only exons, the resulting double-stranded cDNA carries the complete coding sequence of the gene but no introns. Although only one mRNA is shown here, the final collection of cDNAs would reflect all the mRNAs that were present in the cell.

adenine (A) ribonucleotides called a poly-A tail. This feature allows use of a short strand of thymine deoxyribonucleotides (dT's) as a primer for the reverse transcriptase. Following enzymatic degradation of the mRNA, a second DNA strand, complementary to the first, is synthesized by DNA polymerase. The resulting double-stranded DNA is called **complementary DNA (cDNA)**. To create a library, the researchers must now modify the cDNA by adding restriction enzyme recognition sequences at each end. Then the cDNA is inserted into vector DNA in a manner similar to the insertion of genomic DNA fragments. The extracted mRNA is a mixture of all the mRNA molecules in the original cells, transcribed from many different genes. Therefore, the cDNAs that are cloned make up a **cDNA library** containing a collection of genes. However, a cDNA library represents only part of the genome—only the subset of genes that were transcribed in the cells from which the mRNA was isolated.

Genomic and cDNA libraries each have advantages, depending on what is being studied. If you want to clone a gene but don't know what cell type expresses it or cannot obtain enough cells of the appropriate type, a genomic library is almost certain to contain the gene. Also, if you are interested in the regulatory sequences or introns associated with a gene, a genomic library is necessary, since these sequences are absent from mRNAs used in making a cDNA library. On the other hand, to study a specific protein (like β-globin), a cDNA library made from cells expressing the gene (like red blood cells) is ideal. A cDNA library can also be used to study sets of genes expressed in particular cell types, such as brain or liver cells. Finally, by making cDNA from cells of the same type at different times in the life of an organism, researchers can trace changes in patterns of gene expression during development.

Screening a Library for Clones Carrying a Gene of Interest

Now, returning to the results in Figure 20.4, we're ready to screen all the colonies with recombinant plasmids (the white colonies) for a clone of cells containing the hummingbird β-globin gene. We can detect this gene's DNA by its ability to base-pair with a complementary sequence on another nucleic acid molecule, using **nucleic acid hybridization**. The complementary molecule, a short, single-stranded nucleic acid that can be either RNA or DNA, is called a **nucleic acid probe**. If we know at least part of the nucleotide sequence of the gene of interest (perhaps from knowing the amino acid sequence of the protein it encodes or, as in our case, the gene's nucleotide sequence in a closely related species), we can synthesize a probe complementary to it. For example, if part of the sequence on one strand of the desired gene were

5' ⬛⬛CTCATCACCGGC⬛⬛ 3'

then we would synthesize this probe:

3' GAGTAGTGGCCG 5'

Each probe molecule, which will hydrogen-bond specifically to a complementary sequence in the desired gene, is labeled with a radioactive isotope, a fluorescent tag, or another molecule so we can track it.

Recall that the clones in our hummingbird genomic library have been stored in a multiwell plate (see Figure 20.5c). If we transfer a few cells from each well to a defined location on a membrane made of nylon or nitrocellulose, we can screen a large number of clones simultaneously for the presence of DNA complementary to our DNA probe (Figure 20.7).

After we've identified the location of a clone carrying the β-globin gene, we can grow some cells from that colony in liquid culture in a large tank and then easily isolate many copies of the gene for our studies. We can also use the cloned gene as a probe to identify similar or identical genes in DNA from other sources, such as other species of birds.

Expressing Cloned Eukaryotic Genes

Once a particular gene has been cloned in host cells, its protein product can be produced in large amounts for research purposes or valuable practical applications, which we'll explore in Concept 20.4. Cloned genes can be expressed as protein in either bacterial or eukaryotic cells; each option has advantages and disadvantages.

Bacterial Expression Systems

Getting a cloned eukaryotic gene to function in bacterial host cells can be difficult because certain aspects of gene expression are different in eukaryotes and bacteria. To overcome differences in promoters and other DNA control sequences, scientists usually employ an **expression vector**, a cloning vector that contains a highly active bacterial promoter just upstream of a restriction site where the eukaryotic gene can be inserted in the correct reading frame. The bacterial host cell will recognize the promoter and proceed to express the foreign gene now linked to that promoter. Such expression vectors allow the synthesis of many eukaryotic proteins in bacterial cells.

▼ Figure 20.7   **RESEARCH METHOD**

Detecting a Specific DNA Sequence by Hybridization with a Nucleic Acid Probe

APPLICATION Hybridization with a complementary nucleic acid probe detects a specific DNA sequence within a mixture of DNA molecules. In this example, a collection of bacterial clones from a hummingbird genomic library is screened to identify clones that carry a recombinant plasmid bearing the gene of interest. The library is stored in many multiwell plates, with one clone per well (see Figure 20.5c).

TECHNIQUE Cells from each clone are applied to a special nylon membrane. Each membrane has room for thousands of clones (many more than are shown here), so only a few membranes are needed to hold samples of all the clones in the library. This set of membranes is an *arrayed library* that can be screened for a specific gene using a labeled probe. Here the label is a radioactive nucleotide, but other labels are also commonly linked covalently to the probe nucleotides. These include fluorescent tags or enzymes that can produce either a colored or luminescent product.

① Plate by plate, cells from each well, representing one clone, are transferred to a defined spot on a special nylon membrane. The nylon membrane is treated to break open the cells and denature their DNA; the resulting single-stranded DNA molecules stick to the membrane.

② The membrane is then incubated in a solution of radioactive probe molecules complementary to the gene of interest. Because the DNA immobilized on the membrane is single-stranded, the single-stranded probe can base-pair with any complementary DNA on the membrane. Excess DNA is then rinsed off. (One spot with radioactive probe–DNA hybrids is shown here in orange but would not be distinguishable yet.)

③ The membrane is laid under photographic film, allowing any radioactive areas to expose the film. Black spots on the film correspond to the locations on the membrane of DNA that has hybridized to the probe. Each spot can be traced back to the original well containing the bacterial clone that holds the gene of interest.

RESULTS For a radioactive probe, the location of the black spot on a piece of photographic film identifies the clone containing the gene of interest. (Probes labeled in other ways use other detection systems.) By using probes with different nucleotide sequences in different experiments, researchers can screen the collection of bacterial clones for different genes.

Another problem with expressing cloned eukaryotic genes in bacteria is the presence of noncoding regions (introns) in most eukaryotic genes. Introns can make a eukaryotic gene very long and unwieldy, and they prevent correct expression of the gene by bacterial cells, which do not have RNA-splicing machinery. This problem can be surmounted by using a cDNA form of the gene, which includes only the exons.

Eukaryotic Cloning and Expression Systems

Molecular biologists can avoid eukaryotic-bacterial incompatibility by using eukaryotic cells such as yeasts, rather than bacteria, as hosts for cloning and/or expressing eukaryotic genes of interest. Yeasts, single-celled fungi, offer two advantages: They are as easy to grow as bacteria, and they have plasmids, a rarity among eukaryotes. Scientists have even constructed recombinant plasmids that combine yeast and bacterial DNA and can replicate in either type of cell.

Another reason to use eukaryotic host cells for expressing a cloned eukaryotic gene is that many eukaryotic proteins will not function unless they are modified after translation, for example, by the addition of carbohydrate (glycosylation) or lipid groups. Bacterial cells cannot carry out these modifications, and if the gene product requiring such processing is from a mammal, even yeast cells may not be able to modify the protein correctly. Several cultured cell types have proved successful as host cells for this purpose, including some mammalian cell lines and an insect cell line that can be infected by a virus (called baculovirus) carrying recombinant DNA.

Besides using vectors, scientists have developed a variety of other methods for introducing recombinant DNA into eukaryotic cells. In **electroporation**, a brief electrical pulse applied to a solution containing cells creates temporary holes in their plasma membranes, through which DNA can enter. (This technique is now commonly used for bacteria as well.) Alternatively, scientists can inject DNA directly into single eukaryotic cells using microscopically thin needles. To get DNA into plant cells, the soil bacterium *Agrobacterium* can be used, as well as other methods you will learn about later. If the introduced DNA is incorporated into a cell's genome by genetic recombination, then it may be expressed by the cell.

Cross-Species Gene Expression and Evolutionary Ancestry

EVOLUTION The ability to express eukaryotic proteins in bacteria (even if the proteins aren't glycosylated properly) is quite remarkable when we consider how different eukaryotic and bacterial cells are. Examples abound of genes that are taken from one species and function perfectly well when transferred into another very different species. These observations underscore the shared evolutionary ancestry of species living today.

One example involves a gene called *Pax-6*, which has been found in animals as diverse as vertebrates and fruit flies. The vertebrate *Pax-6* gene product (the PAX-6 protein) triggers a complex program of gene expression resulting in formation of the vertebrate eye, which has a single lens. The fly *Pax-6* gene leads to formation of the compound fly eye, which is quite different from the vertebrate eye. When scientists cloned the mouse *Pax-6* gene and introduced it into a fly embryo, they were surprised to see that it led to formation of a compound fly eye (see Figure 50.16). Conversely, when the fly *Pax-6* gene was transferred into a vertebrate embryo—a frog, in this case—a frog eye formed. Although the genetic programs triggered in vertebrates and flies generate very different eyes, both versions of the *Pax-6* gene can substitute for each other, evidence of their evolution from a gene in a common ancestor.

Simpler examples are seen in Figure 17.6, where a firefly gene is expressed in a tobacco plant, and a jellyfish gene product is seen in a pig. The basic mechanisms of gene expression have ancient evolutionary roots, which is the basis of many recombinant DNA techniques described in this chapter.

Amplifying DNA *in Vitro*: The Polymerase Chain Reaction (PCR)

DNA cloning in cells remains the best method for preparing large quantities of a particular gene or other DNA sequence. However, when the source of DNA is scanty or impure, the **polymerase chain reaction**, or **PCR**, is quicker and more selective. In this technique, any specific target segment within one or many DNA molecules can be quickly amplified in a test tube. With automation, PCR can make billions of copies of a target segment of DNA in a few hours, significantly faster than the days it would take to obtain the same number of copies by screening a DNA library for a clone with the desired gene and letting it replicate within host cells. In fact, PCR is being used increasingly to make enough of a specific DNA fragment to insert it directly into a vector, entirely skipping the steps of making and screening a library. To continue our literary analogy, PCR is like photocopying a few pages rather than checking out a book from the library.

In the PCR procedure, a three-step cycle brings about a chain reaction that produces an exponentially growing population of identical DNA molecules. During each cycle, the reaction mixture is heated to denature (separate) the DNA strands and then cooled to allow annealing (hydrogen bonding) of short, single-stranded DNA primers complementary to sequences on opposite strands at each end of the target sequence; finally, a heat-stable DNA polymerase extends the primers in the $5' \rightarrow 3'$ direction. If a standard DNA polymerase were used, the protein would be denatured along with the DNA during the first heating step and would have to be replaced after each cycle. The key to automating PCR was the discovery of an unusual heat-stable DNA polymerase called Taq polymerase, named after the bacterial species from which it was first isolated. This bacterial species, *Thermus aquaticus*, lives in hot springs, so natural selection has resulted in a heat-stable DNA polymerase that can withstand the heat at the start of each cycle. **Figure 20.8** illustrates the steps in PCR.

Just as impressive as the speed of PCR is its specificity. Only minute amounts of DNA need be present in the starting material, and this DNA can be in a partially degraded state, as long as a few molecules contain the complete target sequence. The key to this high specificity is the primers, which hydrogen-bond *only* to sequences at opposite ends of the target segment. (For high specificity, the primers must be at least 15 or so nucleotides long.) By the end of the third cycle, one-fourth of the molecules are identical to the target segment, with both strands the appropriate length. With each successive cycle, the number of target segment molecules of the correct length doubles, so the number of molecules equals 2^n, where n is the number of cycles. After 30 more cycles, about a billion copies of the target sequence are present!

Despite its speed and specificity, PCR amplification cannot substitute for gene cloning in cells when large amounts of a gene are desired. Occasional errors during PCR replication impose limits on the number of good copies that can be made by this method. When PCR is used to provide the specific DNA fragment for cloning, the resulting clones are sequenced to select clones with error-free inserts. PCR errors also impose limits on the length of DNA fragments that can be copied.

Devised in 1985, PCR has had a major impact on biological research and biotechnology. PCR has been used to amplify DNA from a wide variety of sources: fragments of ancient DNA from a 40,000-year-old frozen woolly mammoth; DNA from fingerprints or from tiny amounts of blood, tissue, or semen found at crime scenes; DNA from single embryonic cells for rapid prenatal diagnosis of genetic disorders; and DNA of viral genes from cells infected with viruses that are difficult to detect, such as HIV. We'll return to applications of PCR later in the chapter.

▼ Figure 20.8

RESEARCH METHOD

The Polymerase Chain Reaction (PCR)

APPLICATION With PCR, any specific segment—the target sequence—within a DNA sample can be copied many times (amplified), completely *in vitro*.

TECHNIQUE PCR requires double-stranded DNA containing the target sequence, a heat-resistant DNA polymerase, all four nucleotides, and two 15- to 20-nucleotide DNA strands that serve as primers. One primer is complementary to one end of the target sequence on one strand; the second primer is complementary to the other end of the sequence on the other strand.

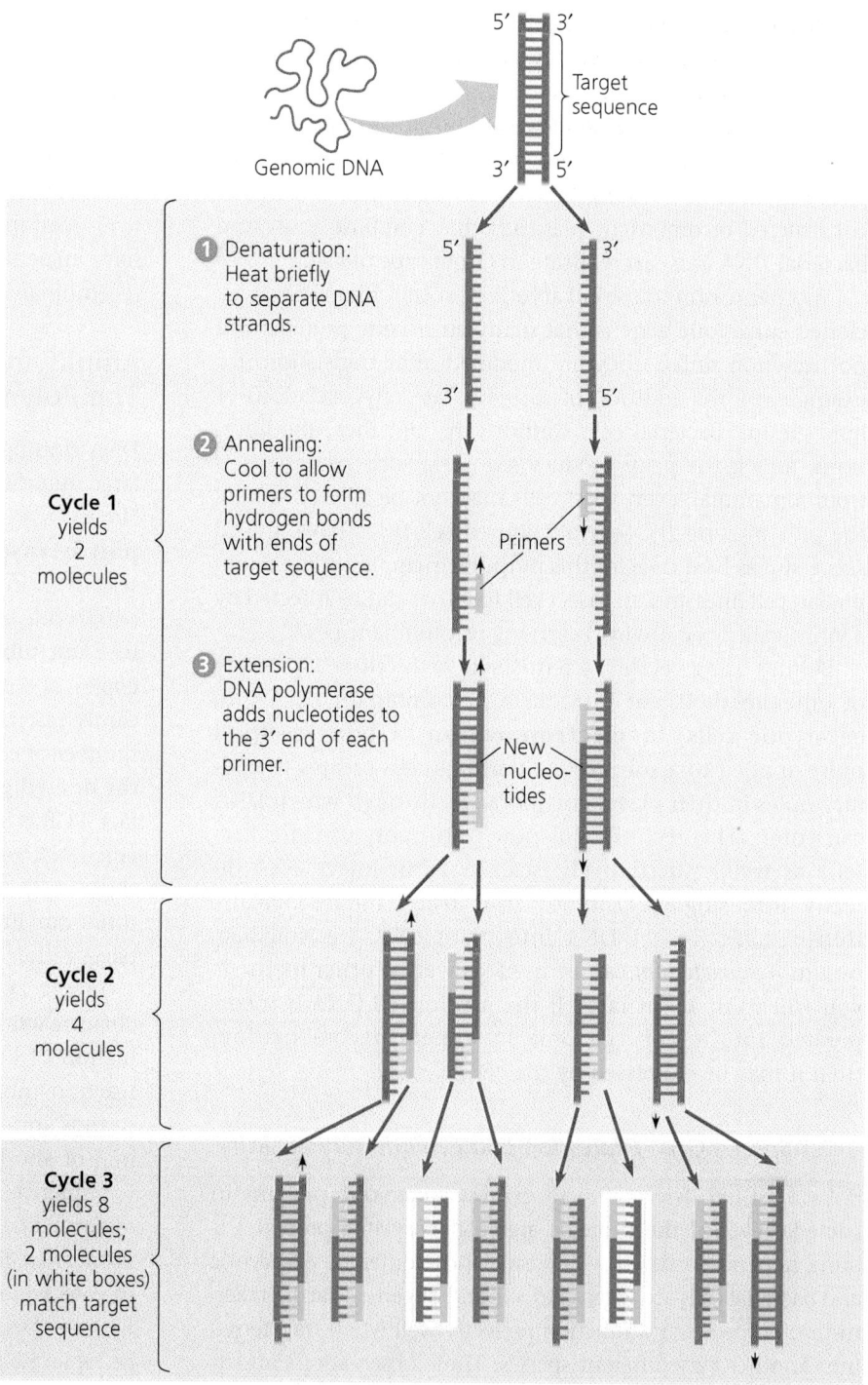

RESULTS After 3 cycles, two molecules match the target sequence exactly. After 30 more cycles, over 1 billion (10^9) molecules match the target sequence.

1. The restriction site for an enzyme called *Pvu*I is the following sequence:

   5′-C G A T C G-3′
   3′-G C T A G C-5′

   Staggered cuts are made between the T and C on each strand. What type of bonds are being cleaved?

2. **DRAW IT** One strand of a DNA molecule has the following sequence: 5′-CCTTGACGATCGTTACCG-3′. Draw the other strand. Will *Pvu*I cut this molecule? If so, draw the products.

3. What are some potential difficulties in using plasmid vectors and bacterial host cells to produce large quantities of proteins from cloned eukaryotic genes?

4. **MAKE CONNECTIONS** Compare Figure 20.8 with Figure 16.20 (p. 319). How does replication of DNA ends during PCR proceed without shortening the fragments each time?

For suggested answers, see Appendix A.

CONCEPT **20.2**

DNA technology allows us to study the sequence, expression, and function of a gene

Once DNA cloning has provided us with large quantities of specific DNA segments, we can tackle some interesting questions about a particular gene and its function. For example, does the sequence of the hummingbird β-globin gene suggest a protein structure that can carry oxygen more efficiently than its counterpart in less metabolically active species? Does a particular human gene differ from person to person, and are certain alleles of that gene associated with a hereditary disorder? Where in the body and when is a given gene expressed? And, ultimately, what role does a certain gene play in an organism?

Before we can begin to address such compelling questions, we must consider a few standard laboratory techniques that are used to analyze the DNA of genes.

Gel Electrophoresis and Southern Blotting

Many approaches for studying DNA molecules involve **gel electrophoresis**. This technique uses a gel made of a polymer, such as the polysaccharide *agarose*. The gel acts as a molecular sieve to separate nucleic acids or proteins on the basis of size, electrical charge, and other physical properties (**Figure 20.9**). Because nucleic acid molecules carry negative charges on their phosphate groups, they all travel toward the positive pole in an

▼ Figure 20.9 **RESEARCH METHOD**

Gel Electrophoresis

APPLICATION Gel electrophoresis is used for separating nucleic acids or proteins that differ in size, electrical charge, or other physical properties. DNA molecules are separated by gel electrophoresis in restriction fragment analysis of both cloned genes (see Figure 20.10) and genomic DNA (see Figure 20.11).

TECHNIQUE Gel electrophoresis separates macromolecules on the basis of their rate of movement through an agarose gel in an electric field: The distance a DNA molecule travels is inversely proportional to its length. A mixture of DNA molecules, usually fragments produced by restriction enzyme digestion (cutting) or PCR amplification, is separated into bands. Each band contains thousands of molecules of the same length.

1. Each sample, a mixture of DNA molecules, is placed in a separate well near one end of a thin slab of agarose gel. The gel is set into a small plastic support and immersed in an aqueous, buffered solution in a tray with electrodes at each end.

2. When the current is turned on, the negatively charged DNA molecules move toward the positive electrode, with shorter molecules moving faster than longer ones. Bands are shown here in blue, but in an actual gel, the bands would not be visible at this time.

RESULTS After the current is turned off, a DNA-binding dye (ethidium bromide) is added. This dye fluoresces pink in ultraviolet light, revealing the separated bands to which it binds. In the gel below, the pink bands correspond to DNA fragments of different lengths separated by electrophoresis. If all the samples were initially cut with the same restriction enzyme, then the different band patterns indicate that they came from different sources.

electric field. As they move, the thicket of agarose fibers impedes longer molecules more than it does shorter ones, separating them by length. Thus, gel electrophoresis separates a mixture of linear DNA molecules into bands, each band consisting of many thousands of DNA molecules of the same length.

One historically useful application of this technique has been *restriction fragment analysis*, which rapidly provides information about DNA sequences. With advances in sequencing technology, the approach taken in labs today is often simply to sequence the DNA sample in question. However, restriction fragment analysis is still done in some cases, and understanding how it is done will give you a better grasp of recombinant DNA technology. In this type of analysis, the DNA fragments produced by restriction enzyme digestion (cutting) of a DNA molecule are separated by gel electrophoresis. When the mixture of restriction fragments undergoes electrophoresis, it yields a band pattern characteristic of the starting molecule and the restriction enzyme used. In fact, the relatively small DNA molecules of viruses and plasmids can be identified simply by their restriction fragment patterns. Because DNA can be recovered undamaged from gels, the procedure also provides a way to prepare pure samples of individual fragments—assuming the bands can be clearly resolved. (Very large DNA molecules, such as those of eukaryotic chromosomes, yield so many fragments that they appear as a smear instead of distinct bands.)

Restriction fragment analysis can be used to compare two different DNA molecules—for example, two alleles of a gene—if the nucleotide difference affects a restriction site. A change in even one base pair of that sequence will prevent a restriction enzyme from cutting there. Variations in DNA sequence among a population are called *polymorphisms* (from the Greek for "many forms"), and this particular type of sequence change is called a **restriction fragment length polymorphism** (**RFLP**, pronounced "Rif-lip"). If one allele contains a RFLP, digestion with the enzyme that recognizes the site will produce a different mixture of fragments for each of the two alleles. Each mixture will give its own band pattern in gel electrophoresis.

For example, sickle-cell disease is caused by mutation of a single nucleotide located within a restriction sequence (a RFLP) in the human β-globin gene (see pp. 277–278 and Figure 17.23). Consequently, while other assays are preferred today, restriction fragment analysis was used for many years to distinguish the normal and sickle-cell alleles of the β-globin gene, as shown in **Figure 20.10**.

The starting materials in Figure 20.10 are samples of the cloned and purified β-globin alleles. But how could this test be done if we didn't have purified alleles to start with? If we wanted to determine whether a person is a heterozygous carrier of the mutant allele for sickle-cell disease, we would directly compare the genomic DNA from that person with DNA from both a person who has sickle-cell disease (and is homozygous for the mutant allele) and a person who is

(a) *Dde*I restriction sites in normal and sickle-cell alleles of the β-globin gene. Shown here are the cloned alleles, separated from the vector DNA but including some DNA next to the coding sequence. The normal allele contains two sites within the coding sequence recognized by the *Dde*I restriction enzyme. The sickle-cell allele lacks one of these sites.

(b) Electrophoresis of restriction fragments from normal and sickle-cell alleles. Samples of each purified allele were cut with the *Dde*I enzyme and then subjected to gel electrophoresis, resulting in three bands for the normal allele and two bands for the sickle-cell allele. (The tiny fragments on the ends of both initial DNA molecules are identical and are not seen here.)

▲ **Figure 20.10 Using restriction fragment analysis to distinguish the normal and sickle-cell alleles of the human β-globin gene. (a)** The sickle-cell mutation destroys one of the *Dde*I restriction sites within the gene. **(b)** As a result, digestion with the *Dde*I enzyme generates different sets of fragments from the normal and sickle-cell alleles.

WHAT IF? *Given bacterial clones with recombinant plasmids carrying each of these alleles, how would you isolate the pure DNA samples run on the gel in (b)? (Hint: Study Figures 20.4 and 20.9.)*

homozygous for the normal allele. As we mentioned already, electrophoresis of genomic DNA digested with a restriction enzyme and stained with a DNA-binding dye yields too many bands to distinguish them individually. However, a classic method called **Southern blotting** (developed by British biochemist Edwin Southern), which combines gel electrophoresis and nucleic acid hybridization, allows us to detect just those bands that include parts of the β-globin gene. The principle is the same as in nucleic acid hybridization for screening bacterial clones (see Figure 20.7). In Southern blotting, the probe is usually a radioactively or otherwise labeled single-stranded DNA molecule that is complementary to the gene of interest. **Figure 20.11** outlines the entire procedure and demonstrates how it can differentiate a heterozygote (in this case, for the sickle-cell allele) from an individual homozygous for the normal allele.

The identification of carriers of mutant alleles associated with genetic diseases is only one of the ways Southern blotting has been used. In fact, this technique was a laboratory workhorse for many years. Recently, however, it has been supplanted by more rapid methods, often involving PCR amplification of the specific parts of genomes that may differ.

DNA Sequencing

Once a gene is cloned, its complete nucleotide sequence can be determined. Today, sequencing is automated, carried out by sequencing machines (see Figure 1.12). The first automated procedure was based on a technique called the *dideoxyribonucleotide*

▼ Figure 20.11 | **RESEARCH METHOD**

Southern Blotting of DNA Fragments

APPLICATION Researchers can detect specific nucleotide sequences within a complex DNA sample with this method. In particular, Southern blotting can be used to compare the restriction fragments produced from different samples of genomic DNA.

TECHNIQUE In this example, we compare genomic DNA samples from three individuals: a homozygote for the normal β-globin allele (I), a homozygote for the mutant sickle-cell allele (II), and a heterozygote (III). As in Figure 20.7, we show a radioactively labeled probe, but other methods of probe labeling and detection are also used.

1 Preparation of restriction fragments. Each DNA sample is mixed with the same restriction enzyme, in this case *Dde*I. Digestion of each sample yields a mixture of thousands of restriction fragments.

2 Gel electrophoresis. The restriction fragments in each sample are separated by electrophoresis, forming a characteristic pattern of bands. (In reality, there would be many more bands than shown here, and they would be invisible unless stained.)

3 DNA transfer (blotting). With the gel arranged as shown above, capillary action pulls the alkaline solution upward through the gel, denaturing and transferring the DNA to a nitrocellulose membrane. This produces a blot with a pattern of DNA bands exactly like that of the gel.

4 Hybridization with labeled probe. The nitrocellulose blot is exposed to a solution containing a probe labeled in some way. In this example, the probe is radioactively labeled, single-stranded DNA complementary to the β-globin gene. Probe molecules attach by base-pairing to any restriction fragments containing a part of the β-globin gene. (The bands would not be visible yet.)

5 Probe detection. A sheet of photographic film is laid over the blot. The radioactivity in the bound probe exposes the film to form an image corresponding to those bands containing DNA that base-paired with the probe.

RESULTS The band patterns for the three samples are clearly different, so this method can be used to identify heterozygous carriers of the sickle-cell allele (III), as well as those with the disease, who have two mutant alleles (II), and unaffected individuals, who have two normal alleles (I). Band patterns for samples I and II resemble those seen for the purified normal and mutant alleles, respectively, seen in Figure 20.10b. The band pattern for the sample from the heterozygote (III) is a combination of the patterns for the two homozygotes (I and II).

RESEARCH METHOD

Dideoxy Chain Termination Method for Sequencing DNA

APPLICATION The sequence of nucleotides in any cloned DNA fragment of up to 800–1,000 base pairs in length can be determined rapidly with machines that carry out sequencing reactions and separate the labeled reaction products by length.

TECHNIQUE This method synthesizes a set of DNA strands complementary to the original DNA fragment. Each strand starts with the same primer and ends with a dideoxyribonucleotide (ddNTP), a modified nucleotide. Incorporation of a ddNTP terminates a growing DNA strand because it lacks a 3' —OH group, the site for attachment of the next nucleotide (see Figure 16.14). In the set of strands synthesized, each nucleotide position along the original sequence is represented by strands ending at that point with the complementary ddNTP. Because each type of ddNTP is tagged with a distinct fluorescent label, the identity of the ending nucleotides of the new strands, and ultimately the entire original sequence, can be determined.

1 The fragment of DNA to be sequenced is denatured into single strands and incubated in a test tube with the necessary ingredients for DNA synthesis: a primer designed to base-pair with the known 3' end of the template strand, DNA polymerase, the four deoxyribonucleotides, and the four dideoxyribonucleotides, each tagged with a specific fluorescent molecule.

2 Synthesis of each new strand starts at the 3' end of the primer and continues until a dideoxyribonucleotide is inserted, at random, instead of the normal equivalent deoxyribonucleotide. This prevents further elongation of the strand. Eventually, a set of labeled strands of various lengths is generated, with the color of the tag representing the last nucleotide in the sequence.

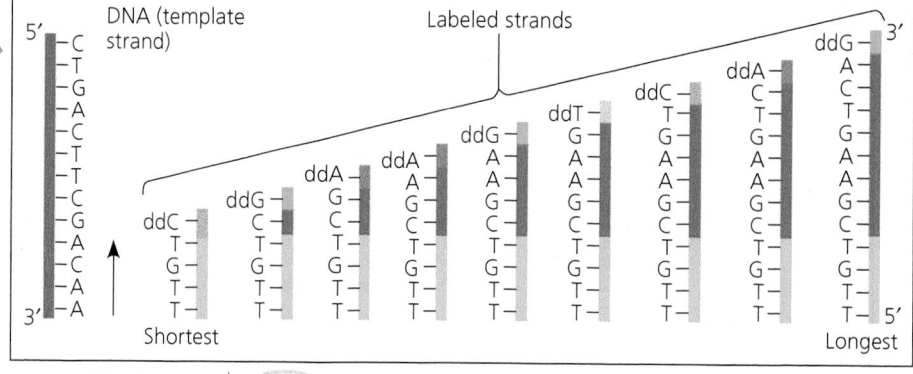

3 The labeled strands in the mixture are separated by passage through a polyacrylamide gel, with shorter strands moving through more quickly. For DNA sequencing, the gel is formed in a capillary tube rather than a slab like that shown in Figure 20.9. The small size of the tube allows a fluorescence detector to sense the color of each fluorescent tag as the strands come through. Strands differing in length by as little as one nucleotide can be distinguished from each other.

RESULTS The color of the fluorescent tag on each strand indicates the identity of the nucleotide at its end. The results can be printed out as a spectrogram, and the sequence, which is complementary to the template strand, can then be read from bottom (shortest strand) to top (longest strand). (Notice that the sequence here begins after the primer.)

(or *dideoxy*) *chain termination method*, for reasons you can see in Figure 20.12. This method was developed by British biochemist Frederick Sanger, who received the Nobel Prize in 1980 for this accomplishment. (One of only four people to win two Nobel Prizes, Sanger also won one in 1975 for determining the amino acid sequence of insulin.)

In the last ten years, "next-generation sequencing" techniques have been developed that do not rely on chain termination. Instead, a single template strand is immobilized, and reagents are added that allow so-called *sequencing by synthesis* of a complementary strand, one nucleotide at a time. A chemical trick enables electronic monitors to identify which of the four nucleotides is added, allowing determination of the sequence. Further technical changes have given rise to "third-generation sequencing," with each new technique being faster and less expensive than the previous. In Chapter 21, you'll learn more about how this rapid acceleration of sequencing technology has enhanced our study of genes and whole genomes.

Knowing the sequence of a gene allows researchers to compare it directly with genes in other species, where the function of the gene product may be known. If two genes from different species are quite similar in sequence, it is reasonable to suppose that their gene products perform similar functions. In this way, sequence comparisons provide clues to a gene's function, a topic we'll return to shortly. Another set of clues is provided by experimental approaches that analyze when and where a gene is expressed.

Analyzing Gene Expression

Having cloned a given gene, researchers can make labeled nucleic acid probes that will hybridize with mRNAs transcribed from the gene. The probes can provide information about when or where in the organism the gene is transcribed. Transcription levels are commonly used as a measure of gene expression.

Studying the Expression of Single Genes

Suppose we want to find out how the expression of the β-globin gene changes during the embryonic development of the hummingbird. There are at least two ways to do this.

The first is called **Northern blotting** (a play on words based on this method's close similarity to Southern blotting). In this method, we carry out gel electrophoresis on samples of mRNA from hummingbird embryos at different stages of development, transfer the samples to a nitrocellulose membrane, and then allow the mRNAs on the membrane to hybridize with a labeled probe recognizing β-globin mRNA. If we expose a film to the membrane, the resulting image will look similar to the Southern blot in Figure 20.11, with one band of a given size showing up in each sample. If the mRNA band is seen at a particular stage, we can hypothesize that the protein functions during events taking place at that stage. Like Southern blotting, Northern blotting has been a mainstay over the years, but it is being supplanted in many labs by other techniques.

A method that is quicker and more sensitive than Northern blotting (because it requires less mRNA) and therefore becoming more widely used is the **reverse transcriptase–polymerase chain reaction**, or **RT-PCR** (Figure 20.13). Analysis of hummingbird β-globin gene expression with RT-PCR begins similarly to Northern blotting, with the isolation of mRNAs from different developmental stages of hummingbird embryos. Reverse transcriptase is added next to make cDNA, which then serves as a template for PCR amplification using primers from the β-globin gene. When the products are run on a gel, copies of the amplified region will be observed as bands only in samples that originally contained the β-globin mRNA. In the case of hummingbird β-globin, for instance, we might expect to see a band appear at the stage when red blood cells begin forming, with all subsequent stages

▼ Figure 20.13   **RESEARCH METHOD**

RT-PCR Analysis of the Expression of Single Genes

APPLICATION RT-PCR uses the enzyme reverse transcriptase (RT) in combination with PCR and gel electrophoresis. RT-PCR can be used to compare gene expression between samples—for instance, in different embryonic stages, in different tissues, or in the same type of cell under different conditions.

TECHNIQUE In this example, samples containing mRNAs from six embryonic stages of hummingbird were processed as shown below. (The mRNA from only one stage is shown.)

1 **cDNA synthesis** is carried out by incubating the mRNAs with reverse transcriptase and other necessary components.

2 **PCR amplification** of the sample is performed using primers specific to the hummingbird β-globin gene.

3 **Gel electrophoresis** will reveal amplified DNA products only in samples that contained mRNA transcribed from the β-globin gene.

RESULTS The mRNA for this gene first is expressed at stage 2 and continues to be expressed through stage 6. The size of the amplified fragment (shown by its position on the gel) depends on the distance between the primers that were used.

▲ **Figure 20.14 Determining where genes are expressed by *in situ* hybridization analysis.** This *Drosophila* embryo was incubated in a solution containing probes for five different mRNAs, each probe labeled with a different fluorescently colored tag. The embryo was then viewed using fluorescence microscopy. Each color marks where a specific gene is expressed as mRNA.

showing the same band. RT-PCR can also be carried out with mRNAs collected from different tissues at one time to discover which tissue is producing a specific mRNA.

An alternative way to determine which tissues or cells are expressing certain genes is to track down the location of specific mRNAs using labeled probes in place, or *in situ*, in the intact organism. This technique, called ***in situ* hybridization**, is most often carried out with probes labeled by attachment of fluorescent dyes (see Chapter 6). Different probes can be labeled with different dyes, sometimes with strikingly beautiful results **(Figure 20.14)**.

Studying the Expression of Interacting Groups of Genes

A major goal of biologists is to learn how genes act together to produce and maintain a functioning organism. Now that the entire genomes of a number of organisms have been sequenced, it is possible to study the expression of large groups of genes—a systems approach. Researchers use genome sequences as probes to investigate which genes are transcribed in different situations, such as in different tissues or at different stages of development. They also look for groups of genes that are expressed in a coordinated manner, with the aim of identifying networks of gene expression across an entire genome.

The basic strategy in such global (genome-wide) expression studies is to isolate the mRNAs made in particular cells, use these molecules as templates for making the corresponding cDNAs by reverse transcription, and then employ nucleic acid hybridization to compare this set of cDNAs with a collection of DNA fragments representing all or part of the genome. The results identify the subset of genes in the genome that are being expressed at a given time or under certain conditions. DNA technology makes such studies possible; with automation, they are easily performed on a large scale. Scientists can now measure the expression of thousands of genes at one time.

Genome-wide expression studies are made possible by **DNA microarray assays**. A DNA microarray consists of tiny amounts of a large number of single-stranded DNA fragments representing different genes fixed to a glass slide in a tightly spaced array, or grid (see Figure 20.1). (The microarray is also called a *DNA chip* by analogy to a computer chip.) Ideally, these fragments represent all the genes of an organism. **Figure 20.15** outlines how the DNA fragments on a microarray are tested for hybridization with cDNA molecules that have been prepared from the mRNAs in particular cells of interest and labeled with fluorescent dyes.

Using this technique, researchers have performed DNA microarray assays on more than 90% of the genes of the nematode *Caenorhabditis elegans* during every stage of its life cycle. The results show that expression of nearly 60% of *C. elegans* genes changes dramatically during development and that many genes are expressed in a sex-specific pattern. This study supports the model held by most developmental biologists that embryonic development involves a complex and elaborate program of gene expression, rather than simply the expression of a small number of important genes. This example illustrates the ability of DNA microarrays to reveal general profiles of gene expression over the lifetime of an organism.

In addition to uncovering gene interactions and providing clues to gene function, DNA microarray assays may contribute to a better understanding of diseases and suggest new diagnostic techniques or therapies. For instance, comparing patterns of gene expression in breast cancer tumors and noncancerous breast tissue has already resulted in more informed and effective treatment protocols. Ultimately, information from DNA microarray assays should provide a grander view of how ensembles of genes interact to form an organism and maintain its vital systems.

Determining Gene Function

How do scientists determine the function of a gene identified by the techniques described thus far in the chapter? Perhaps the most common approach is to disable the gene and then observe the consequences in the cell or organism. In one application of this approach, called ***in vitro* mutagenesis**, specific mutations are introduced into a cloned gene, and then the mutated gene is returned to a cell in such a way that it disables ("knocks out") the normal cellular copies of the same gene. If the introduced mutations alter or destroy the function of the gene product, the phenotype of the mutant cell may help reveal the function of the missing normal protein. Using molecular and genetic techniques worked out in the 1980s, researchers can even generate mice with any given gene disabled, in order to study the role of that gene in development and in the adult. Mario Capecchi, Martin Evans, and Oliver Smithies received the Nobel Prize in 2007 for first accomplishing this feat.

RESEARCH METHOD

DNA Microarray Assay of Gene Expression Levels

APPLICATION With this method, researchers can test thousands of genes simultaneously to determine which ones are expressed in a particular tissue, under different environmental conditions, in various disease states, or at different developmental stages. They can also look for coordinated gene expression.

TECHNIQUE

❶ Isolate mRNA.

Tissue sample

mRNA molecules

❷ Make cDNA by reverse transcription, using fluorescently labeled nucleotides.

Labeled cDNA molecules (single strands)

❸ Apply the cDNA mixture to a microarray, a microscope slide on which copies of single-stranded DNA fragments from the organism's genes are fixed, with a different gene in each spot. The cDNA hybridizes with any complementary DNA on the microarray.

DNA fragments representing a specific gene

DNA microarray

❹ Rinse off excess cDNA; scan microarray for fluorescence. Each fluorescent spot (yellow) represents a gene expressed in the tissue sample.

DNA microarray with 2,400 human genes (actual size)

RESULTS The intensity of fluorescence at each spot is a measure of the expression in the tissue sample of the gene represented by that spot. Most often, as in the actual microarray above, two different samples are tested together by labeling the cDNAs prepared from each sample with labels of different colors, often green and red. The resulting color at a spot reveals the relative levels of expression of a particular gene in the two samples: Green indicates expression in one sample, red in the other, yellow in both, and black in neither. (See Figure 20.1 for a larger view.)

A newer method for silencing expression of selected genes exploits the phenomenon of **RNA interference (RNAi)**, described in Chapter 18. This experimental approach uses synthetic double-stranded RNA molecules matching the sequence of a particular gene to trigger breakdown of the gene's messenger RNA or to block its translation. In organisms such as the nematode and the fruit fly, RNAi has already proved valuable for analyzing the functions of genes on a large scale. In one study, RNAi was used to prevent expression of 86% of the genes in early nematode embryos, one gene at a time. Analysis of the phenotypes of the worms that developed from these embryos allowed the researchers to classify most of the genes into a small number of groups by function. This type of analysis, in which the functions of multiple genes are considered in a single study, is sure to become more common as research focuses on the importance of interactions between genes in the system as a whole. This is the basis of systems biology (see Chapter 21).

In humans, ethical considerations prohibit knocking out genes to determine their functions. An alternative approach is to analyze the genomes of large numbers of people with a certain phenotypic condition or disease, such as heart disease or diabetes, to try to find differences they all share compared with people without that condition. These large-scale analyses, called **genome-wide association studies**, do not require complete sequencing of all the genomes in the two groups. Instead, researchers test for *genetic markers*, DNA sequences that vary in the population. In a gene, such sequence variation is the basis of different alleles, as we saw earlier for sickle-cell disease. And just like coding sequences, noncoding DNA at a specific locus on a chromosome may exhibit small nucleotide differences (polymorphisms) among individuals.

Among the most useful of these genetic markers are single base-pair variations in the genomes of the human population. A single base-pair site where variation is found in at least 1% of the population is called a **single nucleotide polymorphism** (**SNP**, pronounced "snip"). A few million SNPs occur in the human genome, about once in 100–300 base pairs of both coding and noncoding DNA sequences. (Roughly 98.5% of our genome doesn't code for protein, as you will learn in Chapter 21.) It isn't necessary to sequence the DNA of multiple individuals to find SNPs; today they can be detected by very sensitive microarray analysis or by PCR.

Once a region is found that has a SNP shared by affected but not unaffected people, researchers focus on that region and sequence it. In the vast majority of cases, the SNP itself does not contribute to the disease, and most SNPs are in noncoding regions. Instead, if the SNP and a disease-causing allele are close enough, scientists can take advantage of the fact that crossing over between the marker and the gene is very unlikely during gamete formation. Therefore, the marker and gene will almost always be inherited together, even though the marker is not

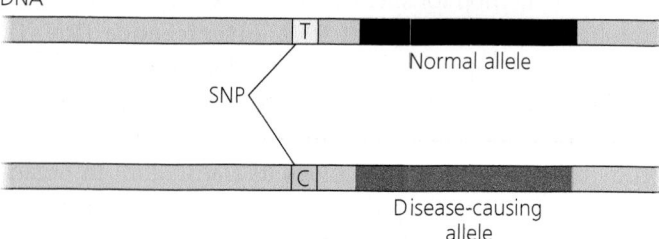

DNA

T

Normal allele

SNP

C

Disease-causing
allele

▲ **Figure 20.16 Single nucleotide polymorphisms (SNPs) as genetic markers for disease-causing alleles.** This diagram depicts homologous segments of DNA from two groups of individuals, those in one group having a particular disease or condition with a genetic basis. Unaffected people have a T at a particular SNP locus, while affected people have a C at that locus. A SNP that varies in this way is likely to be closely linked to one or more alleles of genes that contribute to the disease in question. (Here, only a single strand is shown for each DNA molecule.)

MAKE CONNECTIONS *What does it mean for a SNP to be "closely linked" to a disease-causing allele, and how does this allow the SNP to be used as a genetic marker? (See Concept 15.3, p. 296.)*

part of the gene **(Figure 20.16)**. SNPs have been found that correlate with diabetes, heart disease, and several types of cancer, and the search is on for genes that might be involved.

The techniques and experimental approaches you have learned about thus far have already taught us a great deal about genes and the functions of their products. This research is now being augmented by the development of powerful techniques for cloning whole multicellular organisms. An aim of this work is to obtain special types of cells, called stem cells, that give rise to all the different kinds of tissues. On a basic level, stem cells would allow scientists to use the DNA-based methods previously discussed to study the process of cell differentiation. On a more applied level, recombinant DNA techniques could be used to alter stem cells for the treatment of disease. Methods involving the cloning of organisms and production of stem cells are the subject of the next section.

CONCEPT CHECK 20.2

1. If you isolated DNA from human cells, treated it with a restriction enzyme, and analyzed the sample by gel electrophoresis, what would you see? Explain.
2. Describe the role of complementary base pairing during Southern blotting, DNA sequencing, Northern blotting, RT-PCR, and microarray analysis.
3. Distinguish between a SNP and a RFLP.
4. **WHAT IF?** Consider the microarray in Figure 20.1, a larger image of the one in Figure 20.15. If a sample from normal tissue is labeled with a green fluorescent dye, and a sample from cancerous tissue is labeled red, what can you conclude about a spot that is green? Red? Yellow? Black? Which genes would you be interested in examining further if you were studying cancer? Explain.

For suggested answers, see Appendix A.

Cloning organisms may lead to production of stem cells for research and other applications

In parallel with advances in DNA technology, scientists have been developing and refining methods for cloning whole multicellular organisms from single cells. In this context, cloning produces one or more organisms genetically identical to the "parent" that donated the single cell. This is often called *organismal cloning* to differentiate it from gene cloning and, more significantly, from cell cloning—the division of an asexually reproducing cell into a collection of genetically identical cells. (The common theme for all types of cloning is that the product is genetically identical to the parent. In fact, the word *clone* comes from the Greek *klon*, meaning "twig.") The current interest in organismal cloning arises primarily from its potential to generate stem cells, which can in turn generate many different tissues.

The cloning of plants and animals was first attempted over 50 years ago in experiments designed to answer basic biological questions. For example, researchers wondered if all the cells of an organism have the same genes (a concept called *genomic equivalence*) or if cells lose genes during the process of differentiation (see Chapter 18). One way to answer this question is to see whether a differentiated cell can generate a whole organism—in other words, whether cloning an organism is possible. Let's discuss these early experiments before we consider more recent progress in organismal cloning and procedures for producing stem cells.

Cloning Plants: Single-Cell Cultures

The successful cloning of whole plants from single differentiated cells was accomplished during the 1950s by F. C. Steward and his students at Cornell University, who worked with carrot plants **(Figure 20.17)**. They found that differentiated cells taken from the root (the carrot) and incubated in culture medium could grow into normal adult plants, each genetically identical to the parent plant. These results showed that differentiation does not necessarily involve irreversible changes in the DNA. In plants, at least, mature cells can "dedifferentiate" and then give rise to all the specialized cell types of the organism. Any cell with this potential is said to be **totipotent**.

Plant cloning is now used extensively in agriculture. For some plants, such as orchids, cloning is the only commercially practical means of reproducing plants. In other cases, cloning has been used to reproduce a plant with valuable characteristics, such as the ability to resist a plant pathogen. In fact, you yourself may be a plant cloner: If you have ever grown a new plant from a cutting, you have practiced cloning!

Cross section of carrot root

2-mg fragments

Fragments were cultured in nutrient medium; stirring caused single cells to shear off into the liquid.

Single cells free in suspension began to divide.

Embryonic plant developed from a cultured single cell.

Plantlet was cultured on agar medium. Later it was planted in soil.

Adult plant

▲ Figure 20.17 **The cloning of a whole carrot plant from a single carrot cell.**

Cloning Animals: Nuclear Transplantation

Differentiated cells from animals generally do not divide in culture, much less develop into the multiple cell types of a new organism. Therefore, early researchers had to use a different approach to the question of whether differentiated animal cells can be totipotent. Their approach was to remove the nucleus of an unfertilized or fertilized egg and replace it with the nucleus of a differentiated cell, a procedure called *nuclear transplantation*. If the nucleus from the differentiated donor cell retains its full genetic capability, then it should be able to direct development of the recipient cell into all the tissues and organs of an organism.

Such experiments were conducted on one species of frog (*Rana pipiens*) by Robert Briggs and Thomas King in the 1950s and on another (*Xenopus laevis*) by John Gurdon in the 1970s. These researchers transplanted a nucleus from an embryonic or tadpole cell into an enucleated (nucleus-lacking) egg of the same species. In Gurdon's experiments, the transplanted nucleus was often able to support normal development of the egg into a tadpole (Figure 20.18). However, he found that the potential of a transplanted nucleus to direct normal development was inversely related to the age of the donor: the older the donor nucleus, the lower the percentage of normally developing tadpoles.

From these results, Gurdon concluded that something in the nucleus *does* change as animal cells differentiate. In frogs and most other animals, nuclear potential tends to be restricted more and more as embryonic development and cell differentiation progress.

▼ Figure 20.18

INQUIRY

Can the nucleus from a differentiated animal cell direct development of an organism?

EXPERIMENT John Gurdon and colleagues at Oxford University, in England, destroyed the nuclei of frog (*Xenopus laevis*) eggs by exposing the eggs to ultraviolet light. They then transplanted nuclei from cells of frog embryos and tadpoles into the enucleated eggs.

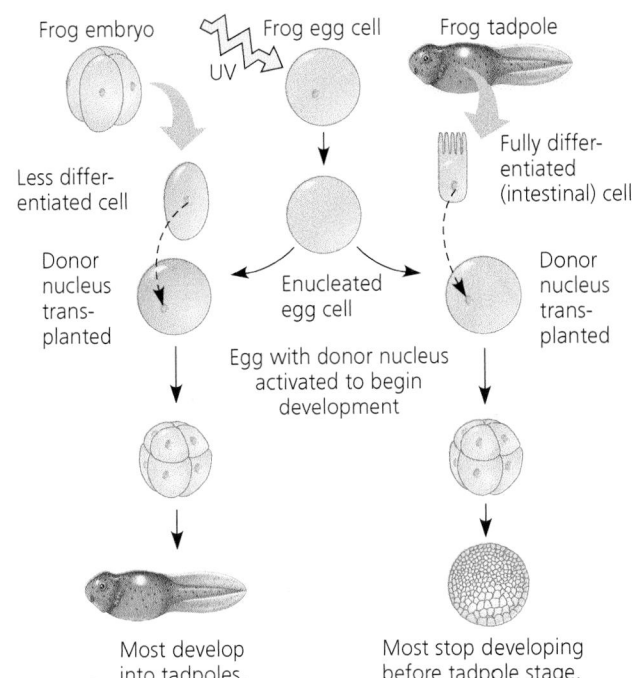

Frog embryo

Frog egg cell

UV

Frog tadpole

Less differentiated cell

Fully differentiated (intestinal) cell

Donor nucleus transplanted

Enucleated egg cell

Donor nucleus transplanted

Egg with donor nucleus activated to begin development

Most develop into tadpoles.

Most stop developing before tadpole stage.

RESULTS When the transplanted nuclei came from an early embryo, whose cells are relatively undifferentiated, most of the recipient eggs developed into tadpoles. But when the nuclei came from the fully differentiated intestinal cells of a tadpole, fewer than 2% of the eggs developed into normal tadpoles, and most of the embryos stopped developing at a much earlier stage.

CONCLUSION The nucleus from a differentiated frog cell can direct development of a tadpole. However, its ability to do so decreases as the donor cell becomes more differentiated, presumably because of changes in the nucleus.

SOURCE J. B. Gurdon et al., The developmental capacity of nuclei transplanted from keratinized cells of adult frogs, *Journal of Embryology and Experimental Morphology* 34:93–112 (1975).

WHAT IF? If each cell in a four-cell embryo was already so specialized that it was not totipotent, what results would you predict for the experiment on the left side of the figure?

Reproductive Cloning of Mammals

In addition to cloning frogs, researchers have long been able to clone mammals by transplanting nuclei or cells from a variety of early embryos. But it was not known whether a nucleus from a fully differentiated cell could be reprogrammed to succeed in acting as a donor nucleus. In 1997, however, researchers at the Roslin Institute in Scotland captured newspaper headlines when they announced the birth of Dolly, a

RESEARCH METHOD

Reproductive Cloning of a Mammal by Nuclear Transplantation

APPLICATION This method is used to produce cloned animals whose nuclear genes are identical to those of the animal supplying the nucleus.

TECHNIQUE Shown here is the procedure used to produce Dolly, the first reported case of a mammal cloned using the nucleus of a differentiated cell.

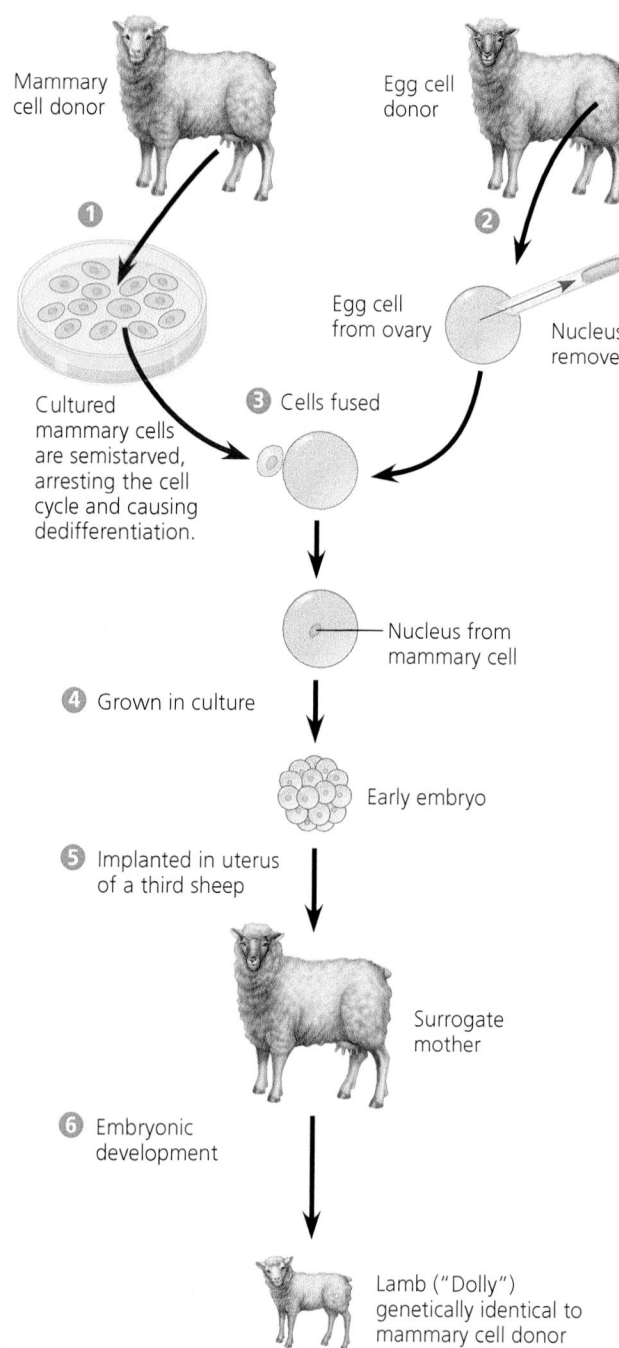

RESULTS The genetic makeup of the cloned animal is identical to that of the animal supplying the nucleus but differs from that of the egg donor and surrogate mother. (The latter two are "Scottish blackface" sheep, with dark faces.)

lamb cloned from an adult sheep by nuclear transplantation from a differentiated cell **(Figure 20.19)**. These researchers achieved the necessary dedifferentiation of donor nuclei by culturing mammary cells in nutrient-poor medium. They then fused these cells with enucleated sheep eggs. The resulting diploid cells divided to form early embryos, which were implanted into surrogate mothers. Out of several hundred implanted embryos, one successfully completed normal development, and Dolly was born.

Later analyses showed that Dolly's chromosomal DNA was indeed identical to that of the nucleus donor. (Her mitochondrial DNA came from the egg donor, as expected.) At the age of 6, Dolly suffered complications from a lung disease usually seen only in much older sheep and was euthanized. Dolly's premature death, as well as her arthritic condition, led to speculation that her cells were in some way not quite as healthy as those of a normal sheep, possibly reflecting incomplete reprogramming of the original transplanted nucleus.

Since 1997, researchers have cloned numerous other mammals, including mice, cats, cows, horses, pigs, dogs, and monkeys. In most cases, their goal has been the production of new individuals; this is known as *reproductive cloning*. We have already learned a lot from such experiments. For example, cloned animals of the same species do *not* always look or behave identically. In a herd of cows cloned from the same line of cultured cells, certain cows are dominant in behavior and others are more submissive. Another example of nonidentity in clones is the first cloned cat, named CC for Carbon Copy **(Figure 20.20)**. She has a calico coat, like her single female parent, but the color and pattern are different because of random X chromosome inactivation, which is a normal occurrence during embryonic development (see Figure 15.8). And identical human twins, which

▲ **Figure 20.20** **CC, the first cloned cat, and her single parent.** Rainbow (left) donated the nucleus in a cloning procedure that resulted in CC (right). However, the two cats are not identical: Rainbow is a classic calico cat with orange patches on her fur and has a "reserved personality," while CC has a gray and white coat and is more playful.

are naturally occurring "clones," are always slightly different. Clearly, environmental influences and random phenomena can play a significant role during development.

The successful cloning of so many mammals has heightened speculation about the cloning of humans. Scientists in several labs around the world have tackled the first steps of human cloning. In the most common approach, nuclei from differentiated human cells are transplanted into unfertilized enucleated eggs, and the eggs are stimulated to divide. In 2001, a research group at a biotechnology company in Massachusetts observed a few early cell divisions in such an experiment. A few years later, researchers at Seoul National University, in South Korea, reported cloning embryos to an early stage called the blastocyst stage, but the scientists were later found guilty of research misconduct and data fabrication. This episode sent shock waves through the scientific community. In 2007, the first primate (macaque) embryos were cloned by researchers at the Oregon National Primate Research Center; these clones reached the blastocyst stage. This achievement has moved the field one step closer to human cloning, the prospect of which raises unprecedented ethical issues.

Problems Associated with Animal Cloning

In most nuclear transplantation studies thus far, only a small percentage of cloned embryos develop normally to birth. And like Dolly, many cloned animals exhibit defects. Cloned mice, for instance, are prone to obesity, pneumonia, liver failure, and premature death. Scientists assert that even cloned animals that appear normal are likely to have subtle defects.

In recent years, we have begun to uncover some reasons for the low efficiency of cloning and the high incidence of abnormalities. In the nuclei of fully differentiated cells, a small subset of genes is turned on and expression of the rest is repressed. This regulation often is the result of epigenetic changes in chromatin, such as acetylation of histones or methylation of DNA (see Figure 18.7). During the nuclear transfer procedure, many of these changes must be reversed in the later-stage nucleus from a donor animal for genes to be expressed or repressed appropriately in early stages of development. Researchers have found that the DNA in cells from cloned embryos, like that of differentiated cells, often has more methyl groups than does the DNA in equivalent cells from normal embryos of the same species. This finding suggests that the reprogramming of donor nuclei requires chromatin restructuring, which occurs incompletely during cloning procedures. Because DNA methylation helps regulate gene expression, misplaced methyl groups in the DNA of donor nuclei may interfere with the pattern of gene expression necessary for normal embryonic development. In fact, the success of a cloning attempt may depend in large part on whether or not the chromatin in the donor nucleus can be artificially modified to resemble that of a newly fertilized egg.

Stem Cells of Animals

The major goal of cloning human embryos is not reproduction, but the production of stem cells for treating human diseases. A **stem cell** is a relatively unspecialized cell that can both reproduce itself indefinitely and, under appropriate conditions, differentiate into specialized cells of one or more types. Thus, stem cells are able both to replenish their own population and to generate cells that travel down specific differentiation pathways.

Many early animal embryos contain stem cells capable of giving rise to differentiated embryonic cells of any type. Stem cells can be isolated from early embryos at a stage called the blastula stage or its human equivalent, the blastocyst stage **(Figure 20.21)**. In culture, these *embryonic stem (ES) cells*

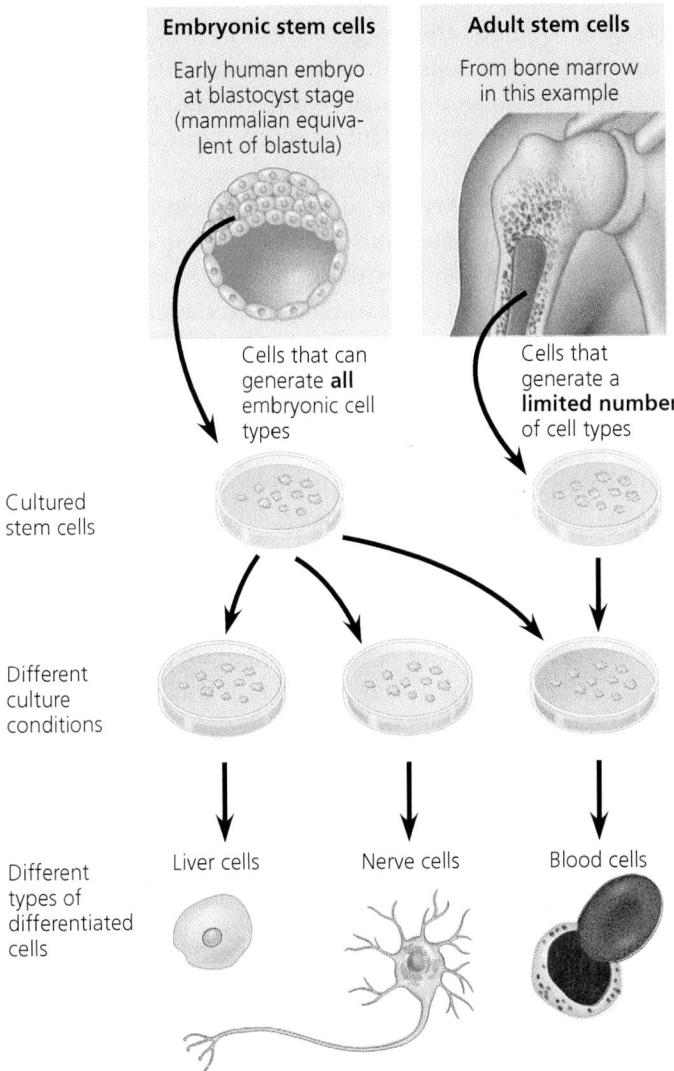

Embryonic stem cells

Early human embryo at blastocyst stage (mammalian equivalent of blastula)

Cells that can generate **all** embryonic cell types

Adult stem cells

From bone marrow in this example

Cells that generate a **limited number** of cell types

Cultured stem cells

Different culture conditions

Different types of differentiated cells

Liver cells

Nerve cells

Blood cells

▲ **Figure 20.21 Working with stem cells.** Animal stem cells, which can be isolated from early embryos or adult tissues and grown in culture, are self-perpetuating, relatively undifferentiated cells. Embryonic stem cells are easier to grow than adult stem cells and can theoretically give rise to *all* types of cells in an organism. The range of cell types that can arise from adult stem cells is not yet fully understood.

reproduce indefinitely; and depending on culture conditions, they can be made to differentiate into a wide variety of specialized cells, including even eggs and sperm.

The adult body also has stem cells, which serve to replace nonreproducing specialized cells as needed. In contrast to ES cells, *adult stem cells* are not able to give rise to all cell types in the organism, though they can generate multiple types. For example, one of the several types of stem cells in bone marrow can generate all the different kinds of blood cells (see Figure 20.21), and another can differentiate into bone, cartilage, fat, muscle, and the linings of blood vessels. To the surprise of many, the adult brain has been found to contain stem cells that continue to produce certain kinds of nerve cells there. And recently, researchers have reported finding stem cells in skin, hair, eyes, and dental pulp. Although adult animals have only tiny numbers of stem cells, scientists are learning to identify and isolate these cells from various tissues and, in some cases, to grow them in culture. With the right culture conditions (for instance, the addition of specific growth factors), cultured stem cells from adult animals have been made to differentiate into multiple types of specialized cells, although none are as versatile as ES cells.

Research with embryonic or adult stem cells is a source of valuable data about differentiation and has enormous potential for medical applications. The ultimate aim is to supply cells for the repair of damaged or diseased organs: for example, insulin-producing pancreatic cells for people with type 1 diabetes or certain kinds of brain cells for people with Parkinson's disease or Huntington's disease. Adult stem cells from bone marrow have long been used as a source of immune system cells in patients whose own immune systems are nonfunctional because of genetic disorders or radiation treatments for cancer.

The developmental potential of adult stem cells is limited to certain tissues. ES cells hold more promise than adult stem cells for most medical applications because ES cells are **pluripotent**, capable of differentiating into many different cell types. The only way to obtain ES cells thus far, however, has been to harvest them from human embryos, which raises ethical and political issues.

ES cells are currently obtained from embryos donated by patients undergoing infertility treatment or from long-term cell cultures originally established with cells isolated from donated embryos. If scientists were able to clone human embryos to the blastocyst stage, they might be able to use such clones as the source of ES cells in the future. Furthermore, with a donor nucleus from a person with a particular disease, they might be able to produce ES cells for treatment that match the patient and are thus not rejected by his or her immune system. When the main aim of cloning is to produce ES cells to treat disease, the process is called *therapeutic cloning*. Although most people believe that reproductive cloning of humans is unethical, opinions vary about the morality of therapeutic cloning.

Resolving the debate now seems less imperative because researchers have been able to turn back the clock in fully differentiated cells, reprogramming them to act like ES cells. The accomplishment of this feat, which posed formidable obstacles, was announced in 2007, first by labs using mouse skin cells and then by additional groups using cells from human skin and other organs or tissues. In all these cases, researchers transformed the differentiated cells into ES cells by using retroviruses to introduce extra cloned copies of four "stem cell" master regulatory genes. All the tests that were carried out at the time indicated that the transformed cells, known as *induced pluripotent stem (iPS) cells*, could do everything ES cells can do. More recently, however, several research groups have uncovered differences between iPS and ES cells in gene expression and other cellular functions, such as cell division. At least until these differences are fully understood, the study of ES cells will continue to make important contributions to the development of stem cell therapies. (In fact, ES cells will likely always be a focus of basic research as well.) In the meantime, work is proceeding using the iPS cells in hand.

There are two major potential uses for human iPS cells. First, cells from patients suffering from diseases can be reprogrammed to become iPS cells, which can act as model cells for studying the disease and potential treatments. Human iPS cell lines have already been developed from individuals with type 1 diabetes, Parkinson's disease, and at least a dozen other diseases. Second, in the field of regenerative medicine, a patient's own cells could be reprogrammed into iPS cells and then used to replace nonfunctional tissues (**Figure 20.22**). Developing techniques that direct iPS cells to become specific cell types for this purpose is an area of intense research, one that has already seen some success. The iPS cells created in this way could eventually provide tailor-made "replacement" cells for patients without using any human eggs or embryos, thus circumventing most ethical objections.

CONCEPT CHECK 20.3

1. Based on current knowledge, how would you explain the difference in the percentage of tadpoles that developed from the two kinds of donor nuclei in Figure 20.18?

2. If you were to clone a carrot using the technique shown in Figure 20.17, would all the progeny plants ("clones") look identical? Why or why not?

3. **WHAT IF?** If you were a doctor who wanted to use iPS cells to treat a patient with severe type 1 diabetes, what new technique would have to be developed?

4. **MAKE CONNECTIONS** Compare an individual carrot cell in Figure 20.17 with the fully differentiated muscle cell in Figure 18.18 (p. 369) in terms of their potential to develop into different cell types.

For suggested answers, see Appendix A.

IMPACT

The Impact of Induced Pluripotent Stem (iPS) Cells on Regenerative Medicine

While embryonic stem (ES) cells can generate every cell in an organism, the use of human embryos as their source is controversial. Several research groups have developed similar procedures for reprogramming fully differentiated cells to become induced pluripotent stem (iPS) cells, which act like ES cells. The technique is based on introducing transcription factors that are characteristic of stem cells into differentiated cells, such as skin cells.

WHY IT MATTERS Patients with diseases such as heart disease, diabetes, or Alzheimer's could have their own skin cells reprogrammed to become iPS cells. Once procedures have been developed for converting iPS cells into heart, pancreatic, or nervous system cells, the patients' own iPS cells might be used to treat their disease. This technique has already been used successfully to treat sickle-cell disease in a mouse that had been genetically engineered to have the disease. Shown below is how this therapy could work in humans, once researchers learn how iPS cells can be triggered to differentiate as desired (step 3).

① Remove skin cells from patient.

② Reprogram skin cells by introducing specific transcription factors so the cells become induced pluripotent stem (iPS) cells.

Patient with damaged heart tissue or other disease

③ Treat iPS cells with appropriate factors so that they differentiate into a specific cell type, such as heart cells.

④ Return cells to patient, where they can repair damaged tissue, such as heart tissue.

FURTHER READING G. Vogel and C. Holden, Field leaps forward with new stem cell advances, *Science* 318:1224–1225 (2007); K. Hochedlinger, Your inner healers, *Scientific American* 302:46–53 (2010).

WHAT IF? When organs are transplanted from a donor to a diseased recipient, the recipient's immune system may reject the transplant, a condition with serious and often fatal consequences. Would using converted iPS cells be expected to carry the same risk? Why or why not?

The practical applications of DNA technology affect our lives in many ways

DNA technology is in the news almost every day. Most often, the topic is a new and promising application in medicine, but this is just one of numerous fields benefiting from DNA technology and genetic engineering.

Medical Applications

One important use of DNA technology is the identification of human genes whose mutation plays a role in genetic diseases. These discoveries may lead to ways of diagnosing, treating, and even preventing such conditions. DNA technology is also contributing to our understanding of "nongenetic" diseases, from arthritis to AIDS, since a person's genes influence susceptibility to these diseases. Furthermore, diseases of all sorts involve changes in gene expression within the affected cells and often within the patient's immune system. By using DNA microarray assays or other techniques to compare gene expression in healthy and diseased tissues, as seen in Figure 20.1, researchers hope to find many of the genes that are turned on or off in particular diseases. These genes and their products are potential targets for prevention or therapy.

Diagnosis and Treatment of Diseases

A new chapter in the diagnosis of infectious diseases has been opened by DNA technology, in particular the use of PCR and labeled nucleic acid probes to track down pathogens. For example, because the sequence of the RNA genome of HIV is known, RT-PCR can be used to amplify, and thus detect, HIV RNA in blood or tissue samples (see Figure 20.13). RT-PCR is often the best way to detect an otherwise elusive infective agent.

Medical scientists can now diagnose hundreds of human genetic disorders by using PCR with primers that target the genes associated with these disorders. The amplified DNA product is then sequenced to reveal the presence or absence of the disease-causing mutation. Among the genes for human diseases that have been identified are those for sickle-cell disease, hemophilia, cystic fibrosis, Huntington's disease, and Duchenne muscular dystrophy. Individuals afflicted with such diseases can often be identified before the onset of symptoms, even before birth. PCR can also be used to identify symptomless carriers of potentially harmful recessive alleles, essentially replacing Southern blotting for this purpose.

As you learned earlier, genome-wide association studies have pinpointed SNPs (single nucleotide polymorphisms) that are linked to disease-causing alleles. Individuals can be tested by PCR and sequencing for a SNP that is correlated with the abnormal allele. The presence of particular SNPs is correlated with increased risk for conditions such as heart disease, Alzheimer's, and some types of cancer. Companies that offer individual genetic testing for risk factors like these are looking for the presence of previously identified, linked SNPs. It may be helpful for an individual to learn about their health risks, with the understanding that such genetic tests merely reflect correlations and do not make predictions.

The techniques described in this chapter have also prompted improvements in disease treatments. By analyzing the expression of many genes in breast cancer patients, researchers carrying out one genome-wide association study were able to identify 70 genes whose expression pattern could be correlated with the likelihood that the cancer would recur. Given that low-risk patients have a 96% survival rate over a ten-year period with no treatment, gene expression analysis allows doctors and patients access to valuable information when they are considering treatment options.

Many envision a future of "personalized medicine" where each person's genetic health profile can inform them about diseases or conditions for which they are especially at risk and help them make treatment choices. A genetic profile is currently taken to mean a set of genetic markers such as SNPs, but ultimately it could mean the complete DNA sequence of each individual—once sequencing becomes inexpensive enough.

Human Gene Therapy

Gene therapy—introducing genes into an afflicted individual for therapeutic purposes—holds great potential for treating the relatively small number of disorders traceable to a single defective gene. In theory, a normal allele of the defective gene could be inserted into the somatic cells of the tissue affected by the disorder.

For gene therapy of somatic cells to be permanent, the cells that receive the normal allele must be ones that multiply throughout the patient's life. Bone marrow cells, which include the stem cells that give rise to all the cells of the blood and immune system, are prime candidates. **Figure 20.23** outlines one possible procedure for gene therapy of an individual whose bone marrow cells do not produce a vital enzyme because of a single defective gene. One type of severe combined immunodeficiency (SCID) is caused by just this kind of defect. If the treatment is successful, the patient's bone marrow cells will begin producing the missing protein, and the patient may be cured.

The procedure shown in Figure 20.23 has been used in gene therapy trials for SCID. In a trial begun in France in 2000, ten young children with SCID were treated by the same procedure. Nine of these patients showed significant, definitive improvement after two years, the first indisputable success of gene therapy. However, three of the patients subsequently developed leukemia, a type of blood cell cancer, and one of them died. Two factors may have contributed to the development of leukemia: the insertion of the retroviral

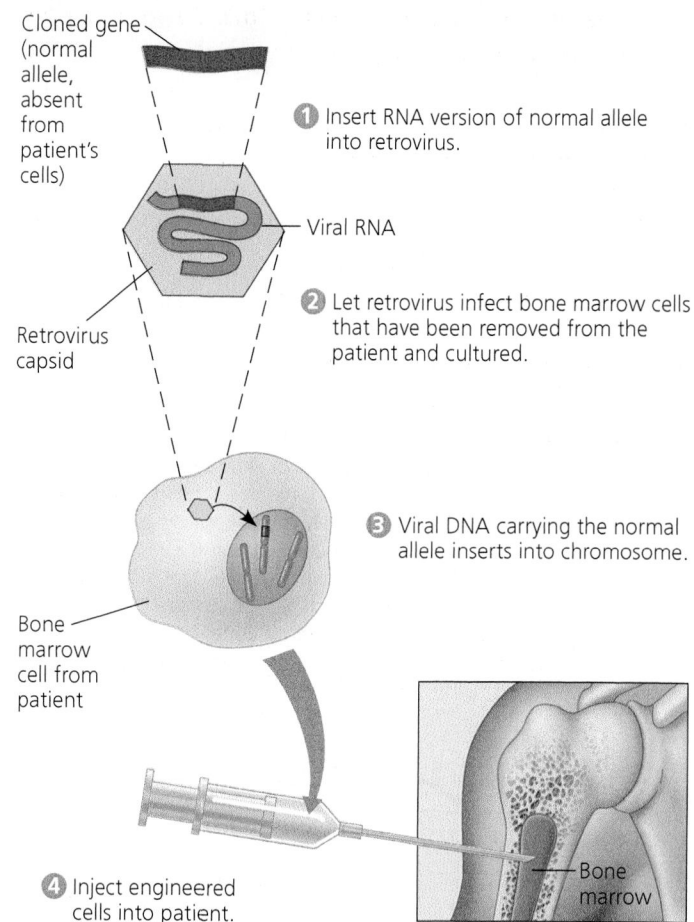

1. Insert RNA version of normal allele into retrovirus.

2. Let retrovirus infect bone marrow cells that have been removed from the patient and cultured.

3. Viral DNA carrying the normal allele inserts into chromosome.

4. Inject engineered cells into patient.

Cloned gene (normal allele, absent from patient's cells)

Viral RNA

Retrovirus capsid

Bone marrow cell from patient

Bone marrow

▲ **Figure 20.23 Gene therapy using a retroviral vector.** A retrovirus that has been rendered harmless is used as a vector in this procedure, which exploits the ability of a retrovirus to insert a DNA transcript of its RNA genome into the chromosomal DNA of its host cell (see Figure 19.8). If the foreign gene carried by the retroviral vector is expressed, the cell and its descendants will possess the gene product. Cells that reproduce throughout life, such as bone marrow cells, are ideal candidates for gene therapy.

vector near a gene involved in the proliferation of blood cells and an unknown function of the replacement gene itself. Two other genetic diseases have recently been treated somewhat successfully with gene therapy: one causing progressive blindness (see Figure 50.21) and the other leading to degeneration of the nervous system. The successful trials involve very few patients, but are still cause for cautious optimism.

Gene therapy raises many technical issues. For example, how can the activity of the transferred gene be controlled so that cells make appropriate amounts of the gene product at the right time and in the right place? How can we be sure that the insertion of the therapeutic gene does not harm some other necessary cell function? As more is learned about DNA control elements and gene interactions, researchers may be able to answer such questions.

In addition to technical challenges, gene therapy provokes ethical questions. Some critics believe that tampering with human genes in any way is immoral. Other observers see no fundamental difference between the transplantation of genes into somatic cells and the transplantation of organs. You might wonder whether scientists are considering engineering human germ-line cells in the hope of correcting a defect in future generations. At present, no one in the mainstream scientific community is pursuing this goal—it is considered much too risky. Such genetic engineering is routinely done in laboratory mice, though, and the technical problems relating to similar genetic engineering in humans will eventually be solved. Under what circumstances, if any, should we alter the genomes of human germ lines? Would this inevitably lead to the practice of eugenics, a deliberate effort to control the genetic makeup of human populations? While we may not have to resolve these questions right now, considering them is worthwhile because they will probably arise at some point in the future.

Pharmaceutical Products

The pharmaceutical industry derives significant benefit from advances in DNA technology and genetic research, applying them to the development of useful drugs to treat diseases. Pharmaceutical products are synthesized using methods of either organic chemistry or biotechnology, depending on the nature of the product.

Synthesis of Small Molecules for Use as Drugs Determining the sequence and structure of proteins crucial for tumor cell survival has led to the identification of small molecules that combat certain cancers by blocking the function of these proteins. One drug, imatinib (trade name Gleevec), is a small molecule that inhibits a specific receptor tyrosine kinase (see Figure 11.7). The overexpression of this receptor, resulting from a chromosomal translocation, is instrumental in causing chronic myelogenous leukemia (CML; see Figure 15.16). Patients in the early stages of CML who are treated with imatinib have exhibited nearly complete, sustained remission from the cancer. Drugs that work like this have also been used with success to treat a few types of lung and breast cancers. This approach is feasible only for cancers for which the molecular basis is fairly well understood.

Pharmaceutical products that are proteins can be synthesized on a large scale, using cells or whole organisms. Cell cultures are more widely used at present.

Protein Production in Cell Cultures You learned earlier in the chapter about DNA cloning and gene expression systems for producing large quantities of proteins that are present naturally in only minute amounts. The host cells used in such expression systems can even be engineered to secrete a protein as it is made, thereby simplifying the task of purifying it by traditional biochemical methods.

Among the first pharmaceutical products "manufactured" in this way were human insulin and human growth hormone (HGH). Some 2 million people with diabetes in the United

States depend on insulin treatment to control their disease. Human growth hormone has been a boon to children born with a form of dwarfism caused by inadequate amounts of HGH. Another important pharmaceutical product produced by genetic engineering is tissue plasminogen activator (TPA). If administered shortly after a heart attack, TPA helps dissolve blood clots and reduces the risk of subsequent heart attacks.

Protein Production by "Pharm" Animals In some cases, instead of using cell systems to produce large quantities of protein products, pharmaceutical scientists can use whole animals. They can introduce a gene from an animal of one genotype into the genome of another individual, often of a different species. This individual is then called a **transgenic** animal. To do this, they first remove eggs from a female of the recipient species and fertilize them *in vitro*. Meanwhile, they have cloned the desired gene from the donor organism. They then inject the cloned DNA directly into the nuclei of the fertilized eggs. Some of the cells integrate the foreign DNA, the *transgene*, into their genomes and are able to express the foreign gene. The engineered embryos are then surgically implanted in a surrogate mother. If an embryo develops successfully, the result is a transgenic animal that expresses its new, "foreign" gene.

Assuming that the introduced gene encodes a protein desired in large quantities, these transgenic animals can act as pharmaceutical "factories." For example, a transgene for a human blood protein such as antithrombin can be inserted into the genome of a goat in such a way that the transgene's product is secreted in the animal's milk **(Figure 20.24)**. The protein is then purified from the milk (which is easier than purification from a cell culture). Researchers have also engineered transgenic chickens that express large amounts of the transgene's product in eggs. Biotechnology companies consider the characteristics of candidate animals in deciding which to use for engineering. For

▲ **Figure 20.24 Goats as "pharm" animals.** This transgenic goat carries a gene for a human blood protein, antithrombin, which she secretes in her milk. Patients with a rare hereditary disorder in which this protein is lacking suffer from formation of blood clots in their blood vessels. Easily purified from the goat's milk, the protein has been approved in the United States and Europe for treating these patients.

example, goats reproduce faster than cows, and it is possible to harvest more protein from goat milk than from the milk of other rapidly reproducing mammals, such as rabbits.

Human proteins produced in transgenic farm animals for use in humans may differ in some ways from the naturally produced human proteins, possibly because of subtle differences in protein modification. Therefore, such proteins must be tested very carefully to ensure that they (or contaminants from the farm animals) will not cause allergic reactions or other adverse effects in patients who receive them.

Forensic Evidence and Genetic Profiles

In violent crimes, body fluids or small pieces of tissue may be left at the scene or on the clothes or other possessions of the victim or assailant. If enough blood, semen, or tissue is available, forensic laboratories can determine the blood type or tissue type by using antibodies to detect specific cell-surface proteins. However, such tests require fairly fresh samples in relatively large amounts. Also, because many people have the same blood or tissue type, this approach can only exclude a suspect; it cannot provide strong evidence of guilt.

DNA testing, on the other hand, can identify the guilty individual with a high degree of certainty, because the DNA sequence of every person is unique (except for identical twins). Genetic markers that vary in the population can be analyzed for a given person to determine that individual's unique set of genetic markers, or **genetic profile**. (This term is preferred over "DNA fingerprint" by forensic scientists, who want to emphasize the heritable aspect of these markers rather than the fact that they produce a pattern on a gel that, like a fingerprint, is visually recognizable.) The FBI started applying DNA technology to forensics in 1988, using RFLP analysis by Southern blotting to detect similarities and differences in DNA samples. This method required much smaller samples of blood or tissue than earlier methods—only about 1,000 cells.

Today, forensic scientists use an even more sensitive method that takes advantage of variations in length of genetic markers called **short tandem repeats (STRs)**. These are tandemly repeated units of two- to five-base sequences in specific regions of the genome. The number of repeats present in these regions is highly variable from person to person (polymorphic), and for one individual, the two alleles of an STR may even differ from each other. For example, one individual may have the sequence ACAT repeated 30 times at one genome locus and 15 times at the same locus on the other homolog, whereas another individual may have 18 repeats at this locus on each homolog. (These two genotypes can be expressed by the two repeat numbers: 30,15 and 18,18.) PCR is used to amplify particular STRs, using sets of primers that are labeled with different-colored fluorescent tags; the length of the region, and thus the number of repeats, can then be determined by electrophoresis. Because Southern blotting is not required, this method is quicker than RFLP analysis. And the PCR step allows use of the method even

when the DNA is in poor condition or available only in minute quantities. A tissue sample containing as few as 20 cells can be sufficient for PCR amplification.

In a murder case, for example, this method can be used to compare DNA samples from the suspect, the victim, and a small amount of blood found at the crime scene. The forensic scientist tests only a few selected portions of the DNA—usually 13 STR markers. However, even this small set of markers can provide a forensically useful genetic profile because the probability that two people (who are not identical twins) would have exactly the same set of STR markers is vanishingly small. The Innocence Project, a nonprofit organization dedicated to overturning wrongful convictions, uses STR analysis of archived samples from crime scenes to revisit old cases. As of 2010, more than 250 innocent people had been released from prison as a result of forensic and legal work by this group (Figure 20.25).

Genetic profiles can also be useful for other purposes. A comparison of the DNA of a mother, her child, and the purported father can conclusively settle a question of paternity. Sometimes paternity is of historical interest: Genetic profiles

(a) In 1984, Earl Washington was convicted and sentenced to death for the 1982 rape and murder of Rebecca Williams. His sentence was commuted to life in prison in 1993 due to new doubts about the evidence. In 2000, STR analysis by forensic scientists associated with The Innocence Project showed conclusively that he was innocent. This photo shows Washington just before his release in 2001, after 17 years in prison.

Source of sample	STR marker 1	STR marker 2	STR marker 3
Semen on victim	17,19	13,16	12,12
Earl Washington	16,18	14,15	11,12
Kenneth Tinsley	17,19	13,16	12,12

(b) In STR analysis, selected STR markers in a DNA sample are amplified by PCR, and the PCR products are separated by electrophoresis. The procedure reveals how many repeats are present for each STR locus in the sample. An individual has two alleles per STR locus, each with a certain number of repeats. This table shows the number of repeats for three STR markers in three samples: from semen found on the victim, from Washington, and from another man named Kenneth Tinsley, who was in prison because of an unrelated conviction. These and other STR data (not shown) exonerated Washington and led Tinsley to plead guilty to the murder.

▲ **Figure 20.25 STR analysis used to release an innocent man from prison.**

provided strong evidence that Thomas Jefferson or one of his close male relatives fathered at least one of the children of his slave Sally Hemings. Genetic profiles can also identify victims of mass casualties. The largest such effort occurred after the attack on the World Trade Center in 2001; more than 10,000 samples of victims' remains were compared with DNA samples from personal items, such as toothbrushes, provided by families. Ultimately, forensic scientists succeeded in identifying almost 3,000 victims using these methods.

Just how reliable is a genetic profile? The greater the number of markers examined in a DNA sample, the more likely it is that the profile is unique to one individual. In forensic cases using STR analysis with 13 markers, the probability of two people having identical DNA profiles is somewhere between one chance in 10 billion and one in several trillion. (For comparison, the world's population in 2009 was about 6.8 billion.) The exact probability depends on the frequency of those markers in the general population. Information on how common various markers are in different ethnic groups is critical because these marker frequencies may vary considerably among ethnic groups and between a particular ethnic group and the population as a whole. With the increasing availability of frequency data, forensic scientists can make extremely accurate statistical calculations. Thus, despite problems that can still arise from insufficient data, human error, or flawed evidence, genetic profiles are now accepted as compelling evidence by legal experts and scientists alike.

Environmental Cleanup

Increasingly, the remarkable ability of certain microorganisms to transform chemicals is being exploited for environmental cleanup. If the growth needs of such microbes make them unsuitable for direct use, scientists can now transfer the genes for their valuable metabolic capabilities into other microorganisms, which can then be used to treat environmental problems. For example, many bacteria can extract heavy metals, such as copper, lead, and nickel, from their environments and incorporate the metals into compounds such as copper sulfate or lead sulfate, which are readily recoverable. Genetically engineered microbes may become important in both mining minerals (especially as ore reserves are depleted) and cleaning up highly toxic mining wastes. Biotechnologists are also trying to engineer microbes that can degrade chlorinated hydrocarbons and other harmful compounds. These microbes could be used in wastewater treatment plants or by manufacturers before the compounds are ever released into the environment.

Agricultural Applications

Scientists are working to learn more about the genomes of agriculturally important plants and animals. For a number of years, they have been using DNA technology in an effort to improve agricultural productivity. The selective breeding of both livestock (animal husbandry) and crops has exploited naturally occurring mutations and genetic recombination for thousands of years.

As we described earlier, DNA technology enables scientists to produce transgenic animals, which speeds up the selective breeding process. The goals of creating a transgenic animal are often the same as the goals of traditional breeding—for instance, to make a sheep with better quality wool, a pig with leaner meat, or a cow that will mature in a shorter time. Scientists might, for example, identify and clone a gene that causes the development of larger muscles (muscles make up most of the meat we eat) in one breed of cattle and transfer it to other cattle or even to sheep. However, problems such as low fertility or increased susceptibility to disease are not uncommon among farm animals carrying genes from other species. Animal health and welfare are important issues to consider when developing transgenic animals.

Agricultural scientists have already endowed a number of crop plants with genes for desirable traits, such as delayed ripening and resistance to spoilage and disease. In one striking way, plants are easier to genetically engineer than most animals. For many plant species, a single tissue cell grown in culture can give rise to an adult plant (see Figure 20.17). Thus, genetic manipulations can be performed on an ordinary somatic cell and the cell then used to generate an organism with new traits.

The most commonly used vector for introducing new genes into plant cells is a plasmid, called the **Ti plasmid**, from the soil bacterium *Agrobacterium tumefaciens*. This plasmid integrates a segment of its DNA, known as T DNA, into the chromosomal DNA of its host plant cells. For vector purposes, researchers work with versions of the plasmid that do not cause disease (unlike the wild-type version) and that have been engineered to carry genes of interest within the borders of the T DNA. **Figure 20.26** (on the next page) outlines one method for using the Ti plasmid to produce transgenic plants.

Genetic engineering is rapidly replacing traditional plant-breeding programs, especially for useful traits, such as herbicide or pest resistance, determined by one or a few genes. Crops engineered with a bacterial gene making the plants resistant to herbicides can grow while weeds are destroyed, and genetically engineered crops that can resist destructive insects reduce the need for chemical insecticides. In India, the insertion of a salinity resistance gene from a coastal mangrove plant into the genomes of several rice varieties has resulted in rice plants that can grow in water three times as salty as seawater. The research foundation that carried out this feat of genetic engineering estimates that one-third of all irrigated land has high salinity owing to overirrigation and intensive use of chemical fertilizers, representing a serious threat to the food supply. Thus, salinity-resistant crop plants would be enormously valuable worldwide.

RESEARCH METHOD

Using the Ti Plasmid to Produce Transgenic Plants

APPLICATION Genes conferring useful traits, such as pest resistance, herbicide resistance, delayed ripening, and increased nutritional value, can be transferred from one plant variety or species to another using the Ti plasmid as a vector.

TECHNIQUE

Agrobacterium tumefaciens

❶ The Ti plasmid is isolated from the bacterium *Agrobacterium tumefaciens*. The segment of the plasmid that integrates into the genome of host cells is called T DNA.

Ti plasmid

Site where restriction enzyme cuts

T DNA

DNA with the gene of interest

❷ The foreign gene of interest is inserted into the middle of the T DNA using methods shown in Figure 20.4.

Recombinant Ti plasmid

❸ Recombinant plasmids can be introduced into cultured plant cells by electroporation. Or plasmids can be returned to *Agrobacterium*, which is then applied as a liquid suspension to the leaves of susceptible plants, infecting them. Once a plasmid is taken into a plant cell, its T DNA integrates into the cell's chromosomal DNA.

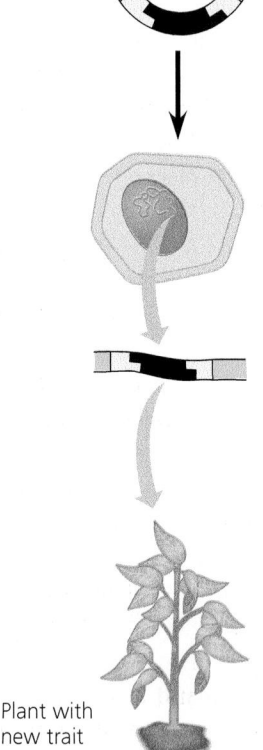

RESULTS Transformed cells carrying the transgene of interest can regenerate complete plants that exhibit the new trait conferred by the transgene.

Plant with new trait

Safety and Ethical Questions Raised by DNA Technology

Early concerns about potential dangers associated with recombinant DNA technology focused on the possibility that hazardous new pathogens might be created. What might happen, for instance, if cancer cell genes were transferred into bacteria or viruses? To guard against such rogue microbes, scientists developed a set of guidelines that were adopted as formal government regulations in the United States and some other countries. One safety measure is a set of strict laboratory procedures designed to protect researchers from infection by engineered microbes and to prevent the microbes from accidentally leaving the laboratory. In addition, strains of microorganisms to be used in recombinant DNA experiments are genetically crippled to ensure that they cannot survive outside the laboratory. Finally, certain obviously dangerous experiments have been banned.

Today, most public concern about possible hazards centers not on recombinant microbes but on **genetically modified (GM) organisms** used as food. A GM organism is one that has acquired by artificial means one or more genes from another species or even from another variety of the same species. Some salmon, for example, have been genetically modified by addition of a more active salmon growth hormone gene. However, the majority of the GM organisms that contribute to our food supply are not animals, but crop plants.

GM crops are widespread in the United States, Argentina, and Brazil; together these countries account for over 80% of the world's acreage devoted to such crops. In the United States, most corn, soybean, and canola crops are genetically modified, and GM products are not required to be labeled. However, the same foods are an ongoing subject of controversy in Europe, where the GM revolution has met with strong opposition. Many Europeans are concerned about the safety of GM foods and the possible environmental consequences of growing GM plants. Early in 2000, negotiators from 130 countries agreed on a Biosafety Protocol that requires exporters to identify GM organisms present in bulk food shipments and allows importing countries to decide whether the products pose environmental or health risks. (Although the United States declined to sign the agreement, it went into effect anyway because the majority of countries were in favor of it.) Since then, European countries have, on occasion, refused crops from the United States and other countries, leading to trade disputes. Although a small number of GM crops have been grown on European soil, these products have generally failed in local markets, and the future of GM crops in Europe is uncertain.

Advocates of a cautious approach toward GM crops fear that transgenic plants might pass their new genes to close relatives in nearby wild areas. We know that lawn and crop grasses, for example, commonly exchange genes with wild relatives via pollen transfer. If crop plants carrying genes for resistance to herbicides, diseases, or insect pests pollinated wild ones, the offspring might become "super weeds" that are very difficult to control. Another worry concerns possible risks to human health from GM foods. Some people fear that the protein products of transgenes might lead to allergic reactions. Although there is some evidence that this could happen, advocates claim that these proteins could be tested in advance to avoid producing ones that cause allergic reactions.

Today, governments and regulatory agencies throughout the world are grappling with how to facilitate the use of biotechnology in agriculture, industry, and medicine while ensuring that new products and procedures are safe. In the United States, such applications of biotechnology are evaluated for potential risks by various regulatory agencies, including the Food and Drug Administration, the Environmental Protection Agency, the National Institutes of Health, and the Department of Agriculture. Meanwhile, these same agencies and the public must consider the ethical implications of biotechnology.

Advances in biotechnology have allowed us to obtain complete genome sequences for humans and many other species, providing a vast treasure trove of information about genes. We can ask how certain genes differ from species to species, as well as how genes and, ultimately, entire genomes have evolved. (These are the subjects of Chapter 21.) At the same time, the increasing speed and falling cost of sequencing the genomes of

individuals are raising significant ethical questions. Who should have the right to examine someone else's genetic information? How should that information be used? Should a person's genome be a factor in determining eligibility for a job or insurance? Ethical considerations, as well as concerns about potential environmental and health hazards, will likely slow some applications of biotechnology. There is always a danger that too much regulation will stifle basic research and its potential benefits. However, the power of DNA technology and genetic engineering—our ability to profoundly and rapidly alter species that have been evolving for millennia—demands that we proceed with humility and caution.

CONCEPT CHECK 20.4

1. What is the advantage of using stem cells for gene therapy?
2. List at least three different properties that have been acquired by crop plants via genetic engineering.
3. **WHAT IF?** As a physician, you have a patient with symptoms that suggest a hepatitis A infection, but you have not been able to detect viral proteins in the blood. Knowing that hepatitis A is an RNA virus, what lab tests could you perform to support your diagnosis? Explain what the results would mean.

For suggested answers, see Appendix A.

20 CHAPTER REVIEW

SUMMARY OF KEY CONCEPTS

CONCEPT 20.1

DNA cloning yields multiple copies of a gene or other DNA segment (pp. 396–405)

- **Gene cloning** and other techniques, collectively termed DNA technology, can be used to manipulate and analyze DNA and to produce useful new products and organisms.
- In **genetic engineering**, bacterial **restriction enzymes** are used to cut DNA molecules within short, specific nucleotide sequences (**restriction sites**), yielding a set of double-stranded DNA fragments with single-stranded **sticky ends**.

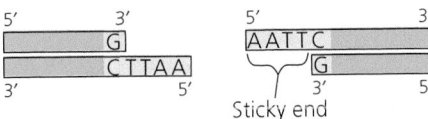
Sticky end

- The sticky ends on **restriction fragments** from one DNA source can base-pair with complementary sticky ends on fragments from other DNA molecules; sealing the base-paired fragments with **DNA ligase** produces **recombinant DNA** molecules.

- Cloning a eukaryotic gene in a bacterial plasmid:

Recombinant DNA plasmids

Cloning vectors include **plasmids** and **bacterial artificial chromosomes (BACs)**. Recombinant plasmids are returned to host cells, each of which divides to form a clone of cells. Collections of clones are stored as **genomic** or **complementary DNA (cDNA) libraries**. Libraries can be screened for a gene of interest using **nucleic acid hybridization** with a **nucleic acid probe**.
- Several technical difficulties hinder the expression of cloned eukaryotic genes in bacterial host cells. The use of cultured

eukaryotic cells (such as yeasts, insect cells, or cultured mammalian cells) as host cells, coupled with appropriate **expression vectors**, helps avoid these problems.
- The **polymerase chain reaction (PCR)** can produce many copies of (amplify) a specific target segment of DNA *in vitro*, using primers that bracket the desired sequence and a heat-resistant DNA polymerase.

> **?** *Describe how the process of gene cloning results in a cell clone containing a recombinant plasmid.*

CONCEPT 20.2

DNA technology allows us to study the sequence, expression, and function of a gene (pp. 405–412)

- DNA restriction fragments of different lengths can be separated by **gel electrophoresis**. Specific fragments can be identified by **Southern blotting**, using labeled probes that hybridize to the DNA immobilized on a "blot" of the gel. Historically, **restriction fragment length polymorphisms (RFLPs)** were used to screen for some disease-causing alleles, such as the sickle-cell allele.
- Relatively short DNA fragments can be sequenced by the dideoxy chain termination method, which can be performed in automated sequencing machines. The rapid development of faster and cheaper methods is ongoing.
- Expression of a gene can be investigated using hybridization with labeled probes to look for specific mRNAs, either on a gel (**Northern blotting**) or in a whole organism (*in situ* **hybridization**). Also, RNA can be transcribed into cDNA by reverse transcriptase and the cDNA amplified by PCR with specific primers (**RT-PCR**). **DNA microarrays** allow researchers to compare the expression of many genes at once in different tissues, at different times, or under different conditions.
- For a gene of unknown function, experimental inactivation of the gene and observation of the resulting phenotypic effects can provide clues to its function. In humans, **genome-wide association studies** use **single nucleotide polymorphisms (SNPs)** as genetic markers for alleles that are associated with particular conditions.

> **?** *Complementary base pairing is the basis of most procedures used to analyze gene expression. Explain.*

CONCEPT 20.3

Cloning organisms may lead to production of stem cells for research and other applications (pp. 412–417)

- Studies showing genomic equivalence (that an organism's cells have the same genome) provided the first examples of organismal cloning.
- Single differentiated cells from mature plants are often **totipotent**: capable of generating all the tissues of a complete new plant.
- Transplantation of the nucleus from a differentiated animal cell into an enucleated egg can sometimes give rise to a new animal.
- Certain embryonic stem (ES) or adult **stem cells** from animal embryos or adult tissues can reproduce and differentiate *in vitro* as well as *in vivo*, offering the potential for medical use. ES cells are **pluripotent** but difficult to acquire. Induced pluripotent stem (iPS) cells resemble ES cells in their capacity to differentiate; they can be generated by reprogramming differentiated cells. iPS cells hold promise for medical research and regenerative medicine.

> **?** *Describe how a researcher could carry out organismal cloning, production of ES cells, and generation of iPS cells, focusing on how the cells are reprogrammed and using mice as an example. (The procedures are basically the same in humans and mice.)*

CONCEPT 20.4

The practical applications of DNA technology affect our lives in many ways (pp. 417–423)

- DNA technology, including the analysis of genetic markers such as SNPs, is increasingly being used in the diagnosis of genetic and other diseases and offers potential for better treatment of genetic disorders (or even permanent cures through **gene therapy**), as well as more informed cancer therapies. Large-scale production of protein hormones and other proteins with therapeutic uses is possible with DNA technology. Some therapeutic proteins are being produced in **transgenic** "pharm" animals.
- Analysis of genetic markers such as **short tandem repeats (STRs)** in DNA isolated from tissue or body fluids found at crime scenes leads to a **genetic profile** that can provide definitive evidence that a suspect is innocent or strong evidence of guilt. Such analysis is also useful in parenthood disputes and in identifying the remains of crime victims.
- Genetically engineered microorganisms can be used to extract minerals from the environment or degrade various types of toxic waste materials.
- The aims of developing transgenic plants and animals are to improve agricultural productivity and food quality.
- The potential benefits of genetic engineering must be carefully weighed against the potential for harm to humans or the environment.

> **?** *What factors affect whether a given genetic disease would be a good candidate for successful gene therapy?*

TEST YOUR UNDERSTANDING

LEVEL 1: KNOWLEDGE/COMPREHENSION

1. Which of the following tools of recombinant DNA technology is *incorrectly* paired with its use?
   a. restriction enzyme—analysis of RFLPs
   b. DNA ligase—cutting DNA, creating sticky ends of restriction fragments
   c. DNA polymerase—polymerase chain reaction to amplify sections of DNA
   d. reverse transcriptase—production of cDNA from mRNA
   e. electrophoresis—separation of DNA fragments

2. Plants are more readily manipulated by genetic engineering than are animals because
   a. plant genes do not contain introns.
   b. more vectors are available for transferring recombinant DNA into plant cells.
   c. a somatic plant cell can often give rise to a complete plant.
   d. genes can be inserted into plant cells by microinjection.
   e. plant cells have larger nuclei.

3. A paleontologist has recovered a bit of tissue from the 400-year-old preserved skin of an extinct dodo (a bird). To compare a specific region of the DNA from the sample with DNA from living birds, which of the following would be most useful for increasing the amount of dodo DNA available for testing?
   a. RFLP analysis
   b. polymerase chain reaction (PCR)
   c. electroporation
   d. gel electrophoresis
   e. Southern blotting

4. DNA technology has many medical applications. Which of the following is *not* done routinely at present?
   a. production of hormones for treating diabetes and dwarfism
   b. production of microbes that can metabolize toxins
   c. introduction of genetically engineered genes into human gametes
   d. prenatal identification of genetic disease alleles
   e. genetic testing for carriers of harmful alleles

5. In recombinant DNA methods, the term *vector* can refer to
   a. the enzyme that cuts DNA into restriction fragments.
   b. the sticky end of a DNA fragment.
   c. a SNP marker.
   d. a plasmid used to transfer DNA into a living cell.
   e. a DNA probe used to identify a particular gene.

LEVEL 2: APPLICATION/ANALYSIS

6. Which of the following would *not* be true of cDNA produced using human brain tissue as the starting material?
   a. It could be amplified by the polymerase chain reaction.
   b. It could be used to create a complete genomic library.
   c. It was produced from mRNA using reverse transcriptase.
   d. It could be used as a probe to detect genes expressed in the brain.
   e. It lacks the introns of the human genes.

7. Expression of a cloned eukaryotic gene in a bacterial cell involves many challenges. The use of mRNA and reverse transcriptase is part of a strategy to solve the problem of
   a. post-transcriptional processing.
   b. electroporation.
   c. post-translational processing.
   d. nucleic acid hybridization.
   e. restriction fragment ligation.

8. Which of the following sequences in double-stranded DNA is most likely to be recognized as a cutting site for a restriction enzyme?
   a. AAGG   b. AGTC   c. GGCC   d. ACCA   e. AAAA
      TTCC   TCAG   CCGG   TGGT   TTTT

9. **DRAW IT** You are making a genomic library for the aardvark, using a bacterial plasmid as a vector. The green diagram below shows the plasmid, which contains the restriction site for the enzyme used in Figure 20.3. Above the plasmid is a segment of linear aardvark DNA. Diagram your cloning procedure, showing what would happen to these two molecules during each step. Use one color for the aardvark DNA and its bases and another color for those of the plasmid. Label each step and all 5′ and 3′ ends.

5′ TCCATGAATTCTAAAGCGCTTATGAATTCACGGC 3′
3′ AGGTACTTAAGATTTCGCGAATACTTAAGTGCCG 5′
Aardvark DNA

Plasmid

LEVEL 3: SYNTHESIS/EVALUATION

10. **WHAT IF?** Imagine you want to study one of the human crystallins, proteins present in the lens of the eye. To obtain a sufficient amount of the protein of interest, you decide to clone the gene that codes for it. Would you construct a genomic library or a cDNA library? What material would you use as a source of DNA or RNA?

11. **EVOLUTION CONNECTION**
    Ethical considerations aside, if DNA-based technologies became widely used, how might they change the way evolution proceeds, as compared with the natural evolutionary mechanisms of the past 4 billion years?

12. **SCIENTIFIC INQUIRY**
    You hope to study a gene that codes for a neurotransmitter protein produced in human brain cells. You know the amino acid sequence of the protein. Explain how you might (a) identify what genes are expressed in a specific type of brain cell, (b) identify (isolate) the neurotransmitter gene, (c) produce multiple copies of the gene for study, and (d) produce large quantities of the neurotransmitter for evaluation as a potential medication.

13. **SCIENCE, TECHNOLOGY, AND SOCIETY**
    Is there danger of discrimination based on testing for "harmful" genes? What policies can you suggest that would prevent such abuses?

14. **SCIENCE, TECHNOLOGY, AND SOCIETY**
    Government funding of embryonic stem cell research has been a contentious political issue. Why has this debate been so heated? Summarize the arguments for and against embryonic stem cell research, and explain your own position on the issue.

15. **WRITE ABOUT A THEME**
    The Genetic Basis of Life In a short essay (100–150 words), discuss how the genetic basis of life plays a central role in biotechnology.

For selected answers, see Appendix A.

Mastering**BIOLOGY**   www.masteringbiology.com

1. MasteringBiology® Assignments
Video Tutor Session DNA Profiling
Tutorial Restriction Enzymes, Recombinant DNA, and Gene Cloning
Activities Cloning a Gene in Bacteria • Producing Human Growth Hormone • Restriction Enzymes • The Polymerase Chain Reaction • Gel Electrophoresis of DNA • Analyzing DNA Fragments Using Gel Electrophoresis • Discovery Channel Video: Cloning • DNA Fingerprinting • Making Decisions About DNA Technology: Golden Rice • Discovery Channel Videos: DNA Forensics; Transgenics
Questions Student Misconceptions • Reading Quiz • Multiple Choice • End-of-Chapter

2. eText
Read your book online, search, take notes, highlight text, and more.

3. The Study Area
Practice Tests • Cumulative Test • *BioFlix* 3-D Animations • MP3 Tutor Sessions • Videos • Activities • Investigations • Lab Media • Audio Glossary • Word Study Tools • Art

21

Genomes and Their Evolution

▲ Figure 21.1 **What genomic information distinguishes a human from a chimpanzee?**

KEY CONCEPTS

21.1 New approaches have accelerated the pace of genome sequencing

21.2 Scientists use bioinformatics to analyze genomes and their functions

21.3 Genomes vary in size, number of genes, and gene density

21.4 Multicellular eukaryotes have much noncoding DNA and many multigene families

21.5 Duplication, rearrangement, and mutation of DNA contribute to genome evolution

21.6 Comparing genome sequences provides clues to evolution and development

Reading the Leaves from the Tree of Life

The chimpanzee (*Pan troglodytes*) is our closest living relative on the evolutionary tree of life. The boy in **Figure 21.1** and his chimpanzee companion are intently studying the same leaf, but only one of them is able to talk about it. What accounts for this difference between two primates that share so much of their evolutionary history? With the advent of recent techniques for rapidly sequencing complete genomes, we can now start to address the genetic basis of intriguing questions like this.

The chimpanzee genome was sequenced in 2005, two years after sequencing of the human genome was largely completed. Now that we can compare our genome with that of the chimpanzee base by base, we can tackle the more general issue of what differences in the genetic information account for the distinct characteristics of these two species of primates.

In addition to determining the sequences of the human and chimpanzee genomes, researchers have obtained complete genome sequences for *E. coli* and numerous other prokaryotes, as well as many eukaryotes, including *Zea mays* (corn), *Drosophila melanogaster* (fruit fly), *Mus musculus* (house mouse), and *Macaca mulatta* (rhesus macaque). In 2010, a draft sequence was announced for the genome of *Homo neanderthalensis*, an extinct species closely related to present-day humans. These whole and partial genomes are of great interest in their own right and are also providing important insights into evolution and other biological processes. Broadening the human-chimpanzee comparison to the genomes of other primates and more distantly related animals should reveal the sets of genes that control group-defining characteristics. Beyond that, comparisons with the genomes of bacteria, archaea, fungi, protists, and plants should enlighten us about the long evolutionary history of shared ancient genes and their products.

With the genomes of many species fully sequenced, scientists can study whole sets of genes and their interactions, an approach called **genomics**. The sequencing efforts that feed this approach have generated, and continue to generate, enormous volumes of data. The need to deal with this ever-increasing flood of information has spawned the field of **bioinformatics**, the application of computational methods to the storage and analysis of biological data.

We will begin this chapter by discussing two approaches to genome sequencing and some of the advances in bioinformatics and its applications. We will then summarize what has been learned from the genomes that have been sequenced thus far. Next, we will describe the composition of the human genome as a representative genome of a complex multicellular eukaryote. Finally, we will explore current ideas about how genomes evolve and about how the evolution of developmental mechanisms could have generated the great diversity of life on Earth today.

CONCEPT 21.1

New approaches have accelerated the pace of genome sequencing

Sequencing of the human genome, an ambitious undertaking, officially began as the **Human Genome Project** in 1990. Organized by an international, publicly funded consortium of scientists at universities and research institutes, the project involved 20 large sequencing centers in six countries plus a host of other labs working on small projects.

After sequencing of the human genome was largely completed in 2003, the sequence of each chromosome was carefully analyzed and described in a series of papers, the last of which covered chromosome 1 and was published in 2006. With this refinement, researchers termed the sequencing "virtually complete." To reach these milestones, the project proceeded through three stages that provided progressively more detailed views of the human genome: linkage mapping, physical mapping, and DNA sequencing.

Three-Stage Approach to Genome Sequencing

Even before the Human Genome Project began, earlier research had sketched a rough picture of the organization of the genomes of many organisms. For instance, the karyotyping of many species had revealed their chromosome numbers and banding patterns (see Figure 13.3). And some human genes had already been located on a particular region of a chromosome by fluorescence *in situ* hybridization (FISH), a method in which fluorescently labeled nucleic acid probes are allowed to hybridize to an immobilized array of whole chromosomes (see Figure 15.1). Cytogenetic maps based on this type of information provided the starting point for more detailed mapping of the human genome.

With these cytogenetic maps of the chromosomes in hand, the initial stage in sequencing the human genome was to construct a **linkage map** (a type of genetic map; see Figure 15.11) of several thousand genetic markers spaced throughout the chromosomes (**Figure 21.2**, stage ❶). The order of the markers and the relative distances between them on such a map are based on recombination frequencies. The markers can be genes or any other identifiable sequences in the DNA, such as RFLPs or short tandem repeats (STRs), both discussed in Chapter 20. By 1992, researchers had compiled a human linkage map with some 5,000 markers. Such a map enabled them to locate other markers, including genes, by testing for genetic linkage to the known markers. It was also valuable as a framework for organizing more detailed maps of particular regions. Remember from Chapter 15, however, that absolute distances between genes cannot be determined using this approach.

The next stage was the physical mapping of the human genome. In a **physical map**, the distances between markers

Cytogenetic map Chromosome banding pattern and location of specific genes by fluorescence *in situ* hybridization (FISH)

Chromosome bands

Genes located by FISH

❶ **Linkage mapping** Ordering of genetic markers such as RFLPs, STRs, and other polymorphisms (about 200 per chromosome)

Genetic markers

❷ **Physical mapping** Ordering of large overlapping fragments cloned in YAC and BAC vectors, followed by ordering of smaller fragments cloned in phage and plasmid vectors

Overlapping fragments

❸ **DNA sequencing** Determination of nucleotide sequence of each small fragment and assembly of the partial sequences into the complete genome sequence

···GACTTCATCGGTATCGAACT···

▲ **Figure 21.2 Three-stage approach to sequencing an entire genome.** Starting with a cytogenetic map of each chromosome, researchers with the Human Genome Project proceeded through three stages to reach the ultimate goal, the virtually complete nucleotide sequence of every chromosome.

are expressed by some physical measure, usually the number of base pairs along the DNA. For whole-genome mapping, a physical map is made by cutting the DNA of each chromosome into a number of restriction fragments and then determining the original order of the fragments in the chromosomal DNA. The key is to make fragments that overlap and then use probes or automated nucleotide sequencing of the ends to find the overlaps (see Figure 21.2, stage ❷). In this way, fragments can be assigned to a sequential order that corresponds to their order in a chromosome.

The DNA fragments used for physical mapping were prepared by DNA cloning. With such a large genome, researchers had to carry out several rounds of DNA cutting, cloning, and physical mapping. In this approach, the first cloning vector was often a yeast artificial chromosome (YAC), which can carry inserted fragments a million base pairs long, or a bacterial artificial chromosome (BAC), which typically carries inserts of 100,000–300,000 base pairs. After such long fragments were put in order, each fragment was cut into smaller pieces, which were cloned in plasmids or phages, ordered in turn, and finally sequenced.

The ultimate goal in mapping any genome is to determine the complete nucleotide sequence of each chromosome (see Figure 21.2, stage ❸). For the human genome, this was accomplished by sequencing machines, using the dideoxy chain termination method described in Figure 20.12. Even with automation, the sequencing of all 3 billion base pairs in a haploid set of human chromosomes presented a formidable challenge. In fact, a major thrust of the Human Genome Project was the development of technology for faster sequencing. Improvements over the years chipped away at each time-consuming step, enabling the rate of sequencing to accelerate impressively: Whereas a productive lab could typically sequence 1,000 base pairs a day in the 1980s, by the year 2000 each research center working on the Human Genome Project was sequencing 1,000 base pairs *per second*, 24 hours a day, seven days a week. Methods like this that can analyze biological materials very rapidly and produce enormous volumes of data are said to be "high-throughput." Sequencing machines are an example of high-throughput devices.

In practice, the three stages shown in Figure 21.2 overlapped in a way that our simplified version does not portray, but they accurately represent the overarching strategy employed in the Human Genome Project. During the project, however, an alternative strategy for genome sequencing emerged that was extremely efficient and became widely adopted.

Whole-Genome Shotgun Approach to Genome Sequencing

In 1992, emboldened by advances in sequencing and computer technology, molecular biologist J. Craig Venter devised an alternative approach to the sequencing of whole genomes. Called the *whole-genome shotgun approach*, it essentially skips the linkage mapping and physical mapping stages and starts directly with the sequencing of DNA fragments from randomly cut DNA. Powerful computer programs then assemble the resulting very large number of overlapping short sequences into a single continuous sequence **(Figure 21.3)**. In 1998, despite the skepticism of many scientists, Venter set up a company (Celera Genomics) and declared his intention to sequence the entire human genome. Five years later, and 13 years after the Human Genome Project began, Celera Genomics and the public consortium jointly announced that sequencing of the human genome was largely complete.

Representatives of the public consortium point out that Celera's accomplishment relied heavily on the consortium's maps and sequence data and that the infrastructure established by their approach was a tremendous aid to Celera's efforts. Venter, on the other hand, has argued for the efficiency and economy of Celera's methods, and indeed, the public consortium made some use of them as well. Evidently, both approaches made valuable contributions.

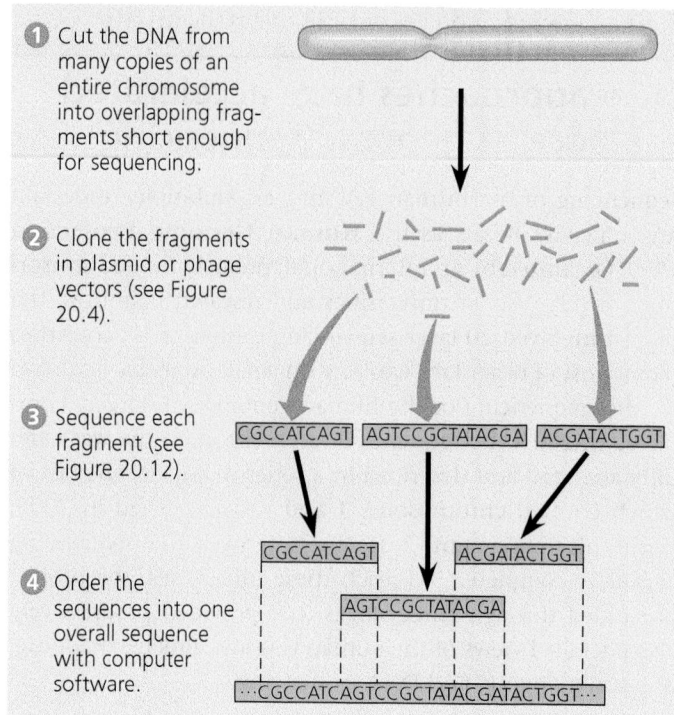

① Cut the DNA from many copies of an entire chromosome into overlapping fragments short enough for sequencing.

② Clone the fragments in plasmid or phage vectors (see Figure 20.4).

③ Sequence each fragment (see Figure 20.12).

CGCCATCAGT   AGTCCGCTATACGA   ACGATACTGGT

④ Order the sequences into one overall sequence with computer software.

CGCCATCAGT   ACGATACTGGT

AGTCCGCTATACGA

…CGCCATCAGTCCGCTATACGATACTGGT…

▲ **Figure 21.3 Whole-genome shotgun approach to sequencing.** In this approach, developed by Craig Venter and colleagues at the company he founded, Celera Genomics, random DNA fragments are sequenced and then ordered relative to each other. Compare this approach with the hierarchical, three-stage approach shown in Figure 21.2.

❓ *The fragments in stage 2 of this figure are depicted as scattered, whereas those in stage 2 of Figure 21.2 are drawn in a much more orderly fashion. How do these depictions reflect the two approaches?*

Today, the whole-genome shotgun approach is widely used. Also, the development of newer sequencing techniques, generally called *sequencing by synthesis* (see Chapter 20), has resulted in massive increases in speed and decreases in the cost of sequencing entire genomes. In these new techniques, many very small fragments (fewer than 100 base pairs) are sequenced at the same time, and computer software rapidly assembles the complete sequence. Because of the sensitivity of these techniques, the fragments can be sequenced directly; the cloning step (stage ② in Figure 21.3) is unnecessary. Whereas sequencing the first human genome took 13 years and cost $100 million, James Watson's genome was sequenced during four months in 2007 for about $1 million, and a group of researchers reported in 2010 that they had rapidly sequenced three human genomes for approximately $4,400 each!

These technological advances have also facilitated an approach called **metagenomics** (from the Greek *meta*, beyond), in which DNA from a group of species (a *metagenome*) is collected from an environmental sample and sequenced. Again, computer software accomplishes the task of sorting out the partial sequences and assembling them into specific genomes. So far, this approach has been applied to microbial communities found in environments as diverse as the Sargasso Sea and the human intestine. The ability to sequence the DNA of mixed populations eliminates the need to culture each species separately in the lab, a difficulty that has limited the study of many microbial species.

At first glance, genome sequences of humans and other organisms are simply dry lists of nucleotide bases—millions of A's, T's, C's, and G's in mind-numbing succession. Crucial to making sense of this massive amount of data have been new analytical approaches, which we discuss next.

CONCEPT 21.2

Scientists use bioinformatics to analyze genomes and their functions

Each of the 20 or so sequencing centers around the world working on the Human Genome Project churned out voluminous amounts of DNA sequence day after day. As the data began to accumulate, the need to coordinate efforts to keep track of all the sequences became clear. Thanks to the foresight of research scientists and government officials involved in the Human Genome Project, its goals included the establishment of banks of data, or databases, and the refining of analytical software. These databases and software programs would then be centralized and made readily accessible on the Internet. Accomplishing this aim has accelerated progress in DNA sequence analysis by making bioinformatics resources available to researchers worldwide and by speeding up the dissemination of information.

Centralized Resources for Analyzing Genome Sequences

Government-funded agencies carried out their mandate to establish databases and provide software with which scientists could analyze the sequence data. For example, in the United States, a joint endeavor between the National Library of Medicine and the National Institutes of Health (NIH) created the National Center for Biotechnology Information (NCBI), which maintains a website (www.ncbi.nlm.nih.gov) with extensive bioinformatics resources. On this site are links to databases, software, and a wealth of information about genomics and related topics. Similar websites have also been established by the European Molecular Biology Laboratory, the DNA Data Bank of Japan, and BGI (formerly known as the Beijing Genome Institute) in Shenzhen, China, three genome centers with which the NCBI collaborates. These large, comprehensive websites

are complemented by others maintained by individual or small groups of laboratories. Smaller websites often provide databases and software designed for a narrower purpose, such as studying genetic and genomic changes in one particular type of cancer.

The NCBI database of sequences is called GenBank. As of May 2010, it included the sequences of 119 million fragments of genomic DNA, totaling 114 billion base pairs! GenBank is constantly updated, and the amount of data it contains is estimated to double approximately every 18 months. Any sequence in the database can be retrieved and analyzed using software from the NCBI website or elsewhere.

One software program available on the NCBI website, called BLAST, allows the visitor to compare a DNA sequence with every sequence in GenBank, base by base, to look for similar regions. Another program allows comparison of predicted protein sequences. Yet a third can search any protein sequence for common stretches of amino acids (domains) for which a function is known or suspected, and it can show a three-dimensional model of the domain alongside other relevant information (Figure 21.4, on the next page). There is even a software program that can compare a collection of sequences, either nucleic acids or polypeptides, and diagram them in the form of an evolutionary tree based on the sequence relationships. (One such diagram is shown in Figure 21.16.)

Two research institutions, Rutgers University and the University of California, San Diego, also maintain a worldwide Protein Data Bank, a database of all three-dimensional protein structures that have been determined. (The database is accessible at www.wwpdb.org.) These structures can be rotated by the viewer to show all sides of the protein.

There is a vast array of resources available for researchers anywhere in the world to use. Let us now consider the types of questions scientists can address using these resources.

Identifying Protein-Coding Genes and Understanding Their Functions

Using available DNA sequences, geneticists can study genes directly, without having to infer genotype from phenotype as in classical genetics. But this approach, called *reverse genetics*, poses a new challenge: determining the phenotype from the genotype. Given a long DNA sequence from a database such as GenBank, the aim of scientists is to identify all protein-coding genes in the sequence and ultimately their functions. This process is called **gene annotation**.

In the past, gene annotation was carried out laboriously by individual scientists interested in particular genes, but the process has now been largely automated. The usual approach is to use software to scan the stored sequences for transcriptional and translational start and stop signals, for RNA-splicing sites, and for other telltale signs of protein-coding genes. The software also looks for certain short sequences that specify known mRNAs. Thousands of such sequences, called

In this window, a partial amino acid sequence from an unknown muskmelon protein ("Query") is aligned with sequences from other proteins that the computer program found to be similar. Each sequence represents a domain called WD40.

Four hallmarks of the WD40 domain are highlighted in yellow. (Sequence similarity is based on chemical aspects of the amino acids, so the amino acids in each hallmark region are not always identical.)

WD40 - Sequence Alignment Viewer

```
                        Query  ~~~ktGGIRL~RHfksVSAVEWHRk~~gDYLSTlvLreSRAVLIHQlsk
             Cow [transducin]  ~nvrvSRELA~GHtgyLSCCRFLDd~~nQIVTs~~Sg~DTTCALWDie~
     Mustard weed [transducin]  gtvpvSRMLT~GHrgyVSCCQYVPnedaHLITs~~Sg~DQTCILWDvtt
              Corn [GNB protein]  gnmpvSRILT~GHkgyVSSCQYVPdgetRLITS~~Sg~DQTCVLWDvt~
              Human [PAFA protein]  ~~~ecIRTMH~GHdhnVSSVAIMPg~dHIVSA~~Sr~DKTIKMWEvg~
     Nematode [unknown protein #1]  ~~~rcVKTLK~GHtnyVFCCCFNPs~~gTLIAS~~GsfDETIRIWCar~
     Nematode [unknown protein #2]  ~~~rmTKTLK~GHnnyVFCCNFNPq~~sSLVVS~~GsfDESVRIWDvk~
     Fission yeast [FWDR protein]  ~~~seCISILhGHtdsVLCLTFDS~~~~TLLVS~~GsaDCTVKLWHfs~
```

The Cn3D program displays a three-dimensional ribbon model of cow transducin (the protein highlighted in purple in the Sequence Alignment Viewer). This protein is the only one of those shown for which a structure has been determined. The sequence similarity of the other proteins to cow transducin suggests that their structures are likely to be similar.

This window displays information about the WD40 domain from the Conserved Domain Database.

CDD Descriptive Items

Name: WD40

WD40 domain, found in a number of eukaryotic proteins that cover a wide variety of functions including adaptor/regulatory modules in signal transduction, pre-mRNA processing and cytoskeleton assembly; typically contains a GH dipeptide 11-24 residues from its N-terminus and the WD dipeptide at its C-terminus and is 40 residues long, hence the name WD40;

WD40 - Cn3D 4.1

Cow transducin contains seven WD40 domains, one of which is highlighted here in gray.

The yellow segments correspond to the WD40 hallmarks highlighted in yellow in the window above.

▲ **Figure 21.4 Bioinformatics tools available on the Internet.** A website maintained by the National Center for Biotechnology Information allows scientists and the public to access DNA and protein sequences and other stored data. The site includes a link to a protein structure database (Conserved Domain Database, CDD) that can find and describe similar domains in related proteins, as well as software (Cn3D, "See in 3D") that displays three-dimensional models of domains for which the structure has been determined. Some results are shown from a search for regions of proteins similar to an amino acid sequence in a muskmelon protein.

expressed sequence tags, or *ESTs*, have been collected from cDNA sequences and are cataloged in computer databases. This type of analysis identifies sequences that may be previously unknown protein-coding genes.

The identities of about half of the human genes were known before the Human Genome Project began. But what about the others, the previously unknown genes revealed by analysis of DNA sequences? Clues about their identities and functions come from comparing sequences that might be genes with known genes from other organisms, using the software described previously. Due to redundancy in the genetic code, the DNA sequence itself may vary more than the protein sequence does. Thus, scientists interested in proteins often compare the predicted amino acid sequence of a protein to that of other proteins.

Sometimes a newly identified sequence will match, at least partially, the sequence of a gene or protein whose function is well known. For example, part of a new gene may match a known gene that encodes an important signaling pathway protein such as a protein kinase (see Chapter 11), suggesting that the new gene does, too. Alternatively, the new gene sequence may be similar to a previously encountered sequence whose function is still unknown. Another possibility is that the sequence is entirely unlike anything ever seen before. This was true for about a third of the genes of *E. coli* when its genome was sequenced. In the last case, protein function is usually deduced through a combination of biochemical and functional studies. The biochemical approach aims to determine the three-dimensional structure of the protein as well as other attributes, such as potential binding sites for other molecules. Functional studies usually involve blocking or disabling the gene to see how the phenotype is affected. RNAi, described in Chapter 20, is an example of an experimental technique used to block gene function.

Understanding Genes and Gene Expression at the Systems Level

The impressive computational power provided by the tools of bioinformatics allows the study of whole sets of genes and their interactions, as well as the comparison of genomes from different species. Genomics is a rich source of new insights into fundamental questions about genome organization, regulation of gene expression, growth and development, and evolution.

One informative approach has been taken by a research project called ENCODE (Encyclopedia of DNA Elements), which began in 2003. First, researchers focused intensively on 1% of the human genome and attempted to learn all they could about the functionally important elements in that sequence. They looked for protein-coding genes and genes for noncoding RNAs as well as sequences that regulate DNA replication, gene expression (such as enhancers and promoters), and chromatin modifications. The pilot project was completed in 2007, yielding a wealth of information. One big surprise, discussed in Concept 18.3, was that over 90% of the region was transcribed into RNA, even though less than 2% codes for proteins. The success of this approach has led to two follow-up studies, one extending the analysis to the entire human genome and the other analyzing in a similar fashion the genomes of two model organisms, the soil nematode *Caenorhabditis elegans* and the fruit fly *Drosophila melanogaster*. Because genetic and molecular biological experiments can be performed on these species, testing the activities of potentially functional DNA elements in their genomes will reveal much about how the human genome works.

The success in sequencing genomes and studying entire sets of genes has encouraged scientists to attempt similar systematic study of the full protein sets (*proteomes*) encoded by genomes, an approach called **proteomics**. Proteins, not the genes that encode them, actually carry out most of the activities of the cell. Therefore, we must study when and where proteins are produced in an organism, as well as how they interact in networks, if we are to understand the functioning of cells and organisms.

How Systems Are Studied: An Example

Genomics and proteomics are enabling molecular biologists to approach the study of life from an increasingly global perspective. Using the tools we have described, biologists have begun to compile catalogs of genes and proteins—listings of all the "parts" that contribute to the operation of cells, tissues, and organisms. With such catalogs in hand, researchers have shifted their attention from the individual parts to their functional integration in biological systems. As you may recall, in Chapter 1 we discussed this systems biology approach, which aims to model the dynamic behavior of whole biological systems.

One important use of the systems biology approach is to define gene circuits and protein interaction networks. To map the protein interaction network in the yeast *Saccharomyces cerevisiae*, for instance, researchers used sophisticated techniques to knock out (disable) pairs of genes, one pair at a time, creating doubly mutant cells. They then compared the fitness of each double mutant (based in part on the size of the cell colony it formed) to that predicted from the fitnesses of the two single mutants. The researchers reasoned that if the observed fitness matched the prediction, then the products of the two genes didn't interact with each other, but if the observed fitness was greater or less than predicted, then the gene products interacted in the cell. Computer software then mapped genes based on the similarity of their interactions; a network-like "functional map" of these genetic interactions is displayed in **Figure 21.5**. To process the vast number of protein-protein interactions generated by this experiment and integrate them

▲ **Figure 21.5 The systems biology approach to protein interactions.** This global protein interaction map shows the likely interactions (lines) among about 4,500 gene products (circles) in the yeast *Saccharomyces cerevisiae*. Circles of the same color represent gene products involved in one of the 13 cellular functions listed around the map. The blowup shows additional details of one map region where the gene products (blue circles) carry out amino acid biosynthesis, uptake, and related functions.

into the completed map required powerful computers, mathematical tools, and newly developed software. Thus, the systems biology approach has really been made possible by advances in computer technology and bioinformatics.

Application of Systems Biology to Medicine

The Cancer Genome Atlas is another example of systems biology in which a large group of interacting genes and gene products are analyzed together. This project, under the joint leadership of the National Cancer Institute and the NIH, aims to determine how changes in biological systems lead to cancer. A three-year pilot project beginning in 2007 set out to find all the common mutations in three types of cancer—lung cancer, ovarian cancer, and glioblastoma of the brain—by comparing gene sequences and patterns of gene expression in cancer cells with those in normal cells. Work on glioblastoma has confirmed the role of several suspected genes and identified a few unknown ones, suggesting possible new targets for therapies. The approach has proved so fruitful for these three types of cancer that it has been extended to ten other types, chosen because they are common and often lethal in humans.

Systems biology has tremendous potential in human medicine that is just starting to be explored. Silicon and glass "chips" have been developed that hold a microarray of most of the known human genes (**Figure 21.6**). Such chips are being used to analyze gene expression patterns in patients suffering from various cancers and other diseases, with the eventual aim of tailoring their treatment to their unique genetic makeup and the specifics of their cancers. This approach has had modest success in characterizing subsets of several cancers.

Ultimately, people may carry with their medical records a catalog of their DNA sequence, a sort of genetic bar code, with regions highlighted that predispose them to specific diseases. The use of such sequences for personalized medicine—disease prevention and treatment—has great potential.

Systems biology is a very efficient way to study emergent properties at the molecular level. Recall from Chapter 1 that according to the theme of emergent properties, novel properties arise at each successive level of biological complexity as a result of the arrangement of building blocks at the underlying

◀ **Figure 21.6 A human gene microarray chip.** Tiny spots of DNA arranged in a grid on this silicon wafer represent almost all of the genes in the human genome. Using this chip, researchers can analyze expression patterns for all these genes at the same time.

level. The more we can learn about the arrangement and interactions of the components of genetic systems, the deeper will be our understanding of whole organisms. The rest of this chapter will survey what we've learned from genomic studies thus far.

CONCEPT CHECK 21.2

1. What role does the Internet play in current genomics and proteomics research?
2. Explain the advantage of the systems biology approach to studying cancer versus the approach of studying a single gene at a time.
3. **MAKE CONNECTIONS** The ENCODE pilot project found that more than 90% of the genomic region being studied was transcribed into RNAs, far more than could be accounted for by protein-coding genes. Review Concept 18.3 (pp. 364–366) and suggest some roles that these RNAs might play.
4. **MAKE CONNECTIONS** In Concept 20.2 (p. 411), you learned about genome-wide association studies. Explain how these studies use the systems biology approach.

For suggested answers, see Appendix A.

CONCEPT 21.3
Genomes vary in size, number of genes, and gene density

By early 2010, the sequencing of about 1,200 genomes had been completed and that of over 5,500 genomes and over 200 metagenomes was in progress. In the completely sequenced group, about 1,000 are genomes of bacteria, and 80 are archaeal genomes. Among the 124 eukaryotic species in the group are vertebrates, invertebrates, protists, fungi, and plants. The accumulated genome sequences contain a wealth of information that we are now beginning to mine. What have we learned so far by comparing the genomes that have been sequenced? In this section, we will examine the characteristics of genome size, number of genes, and gene density. Because these characteristics are so broad, we will focus on general trends, for which there are often exceptions.

Genome Size

Comparing the three domains (Bacteria, Archaea, and Eukarya), we find a general difference in genome size between prokaryotes and eukaryotes (**Table 21.1**). While there are some exceptions, most bacterial genomes have between 1 and 6 million base pairs (Mb); the genome of *E. coli*, for instance, has 4.6 Mb. Genomes of archaea are, for the most part, within the size range of bacterial genomes. (Keep in mind, however, that many fewer archaeal genomes have

Table 21.1 Genome Sizes and Estimated Numbers of Genes*

Organism	Haploid Genome Size (Mb)	Number of Genes	Genes per Mb
Bacteria			
Haemophilus influenzae	1.8	1,700	940
Escherichia coli	4.6	4,400	950
Archaea			
Archaeoglobus fulgidus	2.2	2,500	1,130
Methanosarcina barkeri	4.8	3,600	750
Eukaryotes			
Saccharomyces cerevisiae (yeast, a fungus)	12	6,300	525
Caenorhabditis elegans (nematode)	100	20,100	200
Arabidopsis thaliana (mustard family plant)	120	27,000	225
Drosophila melanogaster (fruit fly)	165	13,700	83
Oryza sativa (rice)	430	42,000	98
Zea mays (corn)	2,300	32,000	14
Mus musculus (house mouse)	2,600	22,000	11
Ailuropoda melanoleuca (giant panda)	2,400	21,000	9
Homo sapiens (human)	3,000	<21,000	7
Fritillaria assyriaca (lily family plant)	124,000	ND	ND

*Some values given here are likely to be revised as genome analysis continues. Mb = million base pairs. ND = not determined.

been completely sequenced, so this picture may change.) Eukaryotic genomes tend to be larger: The genome of the single-celled yeast *Saccharomyces cerevisiae* (a fungus) has about 12 Mb, while most animals and plants, which are multicellular, have genomes of at least 100 Mb. There are 165 Mb in the fruit fly genome, while humans have 3,000 Mb, about 500 to 3,000 times as many as a typical bacterium.

Aside from this general difference between prokaryotes and eukaryotes, a comparison of genome sizes among eukaryotes fails to reveal any systematic relationship between genome size and the organism's phenotype. For instance, the genome of *Fritillaria assyriaca*, a flowering plant in the lily family, contains 124 billion base pairs (124,000 Mb), about 40 times the size of the human genome. Even more striking, there is a single-celled amoeba, *Polychaos dubia*, whose genome size has been estimated at 670,000 Mb. (This genome has not yet been sequenced.) On a finer scale, comparing two insect species, the cricket (*Anabrus simplex*) genome turns out to have 11 times as many base pairs as the *Drosophila melanogaster* genome. There

is a wide range of genome sizes within the groups of protists, insects, amphibians, and plants and less of a range within mammals and reptiles.

Number of Genes

The number of genes also varies between prokaryotes and eukaryotes: Bacteria and archaea, in general, have fewer genes than eukaryotes. Free-living bacteria and archaea have from 1,500 to 7,500 genes, while the number of genes in eukaryotes ranges from about 5,000 for unicellular fungi to at least 40,000 for some multicellular eukaryotes (see Table 21.1).

Within the eukaryotes, the number of genes in a species is often lower than expected from simply considering the size of its genome. Looking at Table 21.1, you can see that the genome of the nematode *C. elegans* is 100 Mb in size and contains roughly 20,000 genes. The *Drosophila* genome, in comparison, is much bigger (165 Mb) but has about two-thirds the number of genes—only 13,700 genes.

Considering an example closer to home, we noted that the human genome contains 3,000 Mb, well over ten times the size of either the *Drosophila* or *C. elegans* genome. At the outset of the Human Genome Project, biologists expected somewhere between 50,000 and 100,000 genes to be identified in the completed sequence, based on the number of known human proteins. As the project progressed, the estimate was revised downward several times, and in 2010, the most reliable count placed the number at fewer than 21,000. This relatively low number, similar to the number of genes in the nematode *C. elegans*, has surprised biologists, who had clearly expected many more human genes.

What genetic attributes allow humans (and other vertebrates) to get by with no more genes than nematodes? An important factor is that vertebrate genomes "get more bang for the buck" from their coding sequences because of extensive alternative splicing of RNA transcripts. Recall that this process generates more than one functional protein from a single gene (see Figure 18.13). A typical human gene contains about ten exons, and an estimated 93% or so of these multi-exon genes are spliced in at least two different ways. Some genes are expressed in hundreds of alternatively spliced forms, others in just two. It is not yet possible to catalog all of the different forms, but it is clear that the number of different proteins encoded in the human genome far exceeds the proposed number of genes.

Additional polypeptide diversity could result from post-translational modifications such as cleavage or the addition of carbohydrate groups in different cell types or at different developmental stages. Finally, the discovery of miRNAs and other small RNAs that play regulatory roles have added a new variable to the mix (see Concept 18.3). Some scientists think that this added level of regulation, when present, may contribute to greater organismal complexity for a given number of genes.

Gene Density and Noncoding DNA

In addition to genome size and number of genes, we can compare gene density in different species—in other words, how many genes there are in a given length of DNA. When we compare the genomes of bacteria, archaea, and eukaryotes, we see that eukaryotes generally have larger genomes but fewer genes in a given number of base pairs. Humans have hundreds or thousands of times as many base pairs in their genome as most bacteria, as we already noted, but only 5 to 15 times as many genes; thus, gene density is lower in humans (see Table 21.1). Even unicellular eukaryotes, such as yeasts, have fewer genes per million base pairs than bacteria and archaea. Among the genomes that have been sequenced completely thus far, humans and other mammals have the lowest gene density.

In all bacterial genomes studied so far, most of the DNA consists of genes for protein, tRNA, or rRNA; the small amount remaining consists mainly of nontranscribed regulatory sequences, such as promoters. The sequence of nucleotides along a bacterial protein-coding gene proceeds from start to finish without interruption by noncoding sequences (introns). In eukaryotic genomes, by contrast, most of the DNA neither encodes protein nor is transcribed into RNA molecules of known function, and the DNA includes more complex regulatory sequences. In fact, humans have 10,000 times as much noncoding DNA as bacteria. Some of this DNA in multicellular eukaryotes is present as introns within genes. Indeed, introns account for most of the difference in average length between human genes (27,000 base pairs) and bacterial genes (1,000 base pairs).

In addition to introns, multicellular eukaryotes have a vast amount of non-protein-coding DNA between genes. In the next section, we will describe the composition and arrangement of these great stretches of DNA in the human genome.

CONCEPT CHECK 21.3

1. According to the best current estimate, the human genome contains fewer than 21,000 genes. However, there is evidence that human cells produce many more than 21,000 different polypeptides. What processes might account for this discrepancy?

2. The number of sequenced genomes is constantly being updated. Go to www.genomesonline.org to find the current number of completed genomes for each domain as well as the number of genomes whose sequencing is in progress. (*Hint:* Click on "Enter GOLD," and then click on "Published Complete Genomes" for extra information.)

3. **WHAT IF?** What evolutionary processes might account for prokaryotes having smaller genomes than eukaryotes?

For suggested answers, see Appendix A.

CONCEPT 21.4

Multicellular eukaryotes have much noncoding DNA and many multigene families

We have spent most of this chapter, and indeed this unit, focusing on genes that code for proteins. Yet the coding regions of these genes and the genes for RNA products such as rRNA, tRNA, and miRNA make up only a small portion of the genomes of most multicellular eukaryotes. The bulk of many eukaryotic genomes consists of DNA sequences that neither code for proteins nor are transcribed to produce RNAs with known functions; this noncoding DNA was often described in the past as "junk DNA." However, much evidence is accumulating that this DNA plays important roles in the cell, an idea supported by its persistence in diverse genomes over many hundreds of generations. For example, comparison of the genomes of humans, rats, and mice has revealed the presence of almost 500 regions of noncoding DNA that are identical in sequence in all three species. This is a higher level of sequence conservation than is seen for protein-coding regions in these species, strongly suggesting that the noncoding regions have important functions. In this section, we examine how genes and noncoding DNA sequences are organized within genomes of multicellular eukaryotes, using the human genome as our main example. Genome organization tells us much about how genomes have evolved and continue to evolve, the next subject we'll consider.

Once the sequencing of the human genome was completed, it became clear that only a tiny part—1.5%—codes for proteins or is transcribed into rRNAs or tRNAs. **Figure 21.7** shows what is known about the makeup of the remaining 98.5%. Gene-related regulatory sequences and introns account, respectively, for 5% and about 20% of the human genome. The rest, located between functional genes, includes some unique noncoding DNA, such as gene fragments and **pseudogenes**, former genes that have accumulated mutations over a long time and no longer produce functional proteins. (The genes that produce small noncoding RNAs are a tiny percentage of the genome, distributed between the 20% introns and the 15% unique noncoding DNA.) Most intergenic DNA, however, is **repetitive DNA**, which consists of sequences that are present in multiple copies in the genome. Somewhat surprisingly, about 75% of this repetitive DNA (44% of the entire human genome) is made up of units called transposable elements and sequences related to them.

Transposable Elements and Related Sequences

Both prokaryotes and eukaryotes have stretches of DNA that can move from one location to another within the genome. These stretches are known as *transposable genetic elements*, or

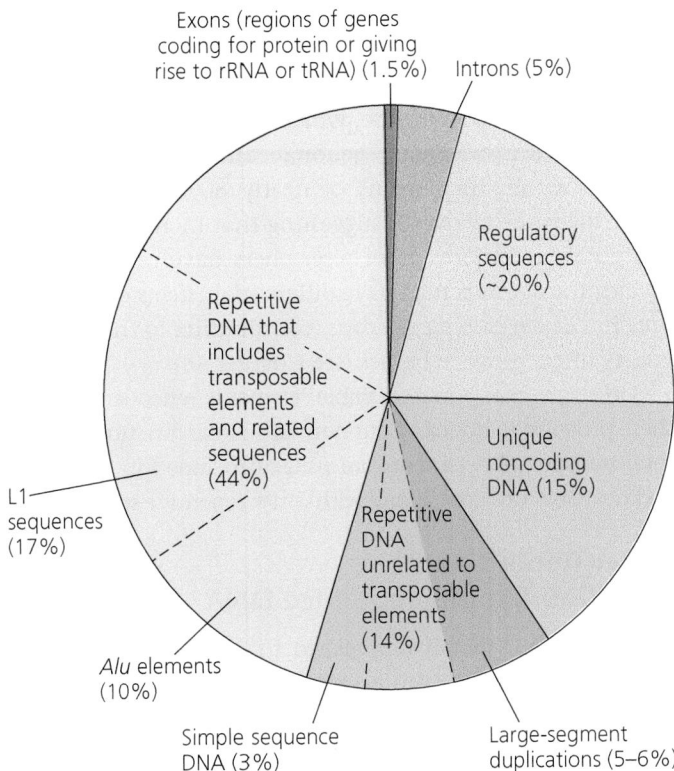

Exons (regions of genes coding for protein or giving rise to rRNA or tRNA) (1.5%)   Introns (5%)

Regulatory sequences (~20%)

Repetitive DNA that includes transposable elements and related sequences (44%)

Unique noncoding DNA (15%)

L1 sequences (17%)

Repetitive DNA unrelated to transposable elements (14%)

Alu elements (10%)

Simple sequence DNA (3%)

Large-segment duplications (5–6%)

▲ **Figure 21.7 Types of DNA sequences in the human genome.** The gene sequences that code for proteins or are transcribed into rRNA or tRNA molecules make up only about 1.5% of the human genome (dark purple in the pie chart), while introns and regulatory sequences associated with genes (light purple) make up about a quarter. The vast majority of the human genome does not code for proteins or give rise to known RNAs, and much of it is repetitive DNA (dark and light green and teal). Because repetitive DNA is the most difficult to sequence and analyze, classification of some portions is tentative, and the percentages given here may shift slightly as genome analysis proceeds. The genes that are transcribed into small noncoding RNAs such as miRNAs, which were recently discovered, are found among unique noncoding DNA sequences and within introns and thus would be included in two segments of this chart.

simply **transposable elements**. During the process called *transposition*, a transposable element moves from one site in a cell's DNA to a different target site by a type of recombination process. Transposable elements are sometimes called "jumping genes," but it should be kept in mind that they never completely detach from the cell's DNA. Instead, the original and new DNA sites are brought together by enzymes and other proteins that bend the DNA.

The first evidence for wandering DNA segments came from American geneticist Barbara McClintock's breeding experiments with Indian corn (maize) in the 1940s and 1950s **(Figure 21.8)**. As she tracked corn plants through multiple generations, McClintock identified changes in the color of corn kernels that made sense only if she postulated the existence of genetic elements capable of moving from other locations in the genome into the genes for kernel color, disrupting the genes so that the kernel color was changed. McClintock's discovery was met with great skepticism and virtually discounted at the time. Her

▲ **Figure 21.8 The effect of transposable elements on corn kernel color.** Barbara McClintock first proposed the idea of mobile genetic elements after observing variegations in corn kernel color (right).

careful work and insightful ideas were finally validated many years later when transposable elements were found in bacteria. In 1983, at the age of 81, McClintock received the Nobel Prize for her pioneering research.

Movement of Transposons and Retrotransposons

Eukaryotic transposable elements are of two types. The first type are **transposons**, which move within a genome by means of a DNA intermediate. Transposons can move by a "cut-and-paste" mechanism, which removes the element from the original site, or by a "copy-and-paste" mechanism, which leaves a copy behind **(Figure 21.9)**. Both mechanisms require an enzyme called *transposase*, which is generally encoded by the transposon.

Most transposable elements in eukaryotic genomes are of the second type, **retrotransposons**, which move by means of an RNA intermediate that is a transcript of the retrotransposon DNA. Retrotransposons always leave a copy at the original site during transposition, since they are initially transcribed

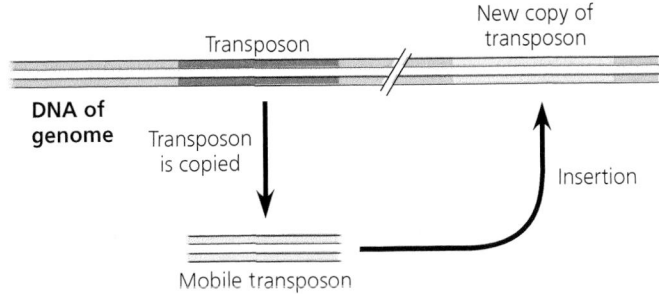

New copy of transposon

Transposon

DNA of genome

Transposon is copied

Insertion

Mobile transposon

▲ **Figure 21.9 Transposon movement.** Movement of transposons by either the cut-and-paste mechanism or the copy-and-paste mechanism (shown here) involves a double-stranded DNA intermediate that is inserted into the genome.

? *How would this figure differ if it showed the cut-and-paste mechanism?*

▲ Figure 21.10 Retrotransposon movement. Movement begins with formation of a single-stranded RNA intermediate. The remaining steps are essentially identical to part of the retrovirus replicative cycle (see Figure 19.8).

into an RNA intermediate (**Figure 21.10**). To insert at another site, the RNA intermediate is first converted back to DNA by reverse transcriptase, an enzyme encoded by the retrotransposon. (Reverse transcriptase is also encoded by retroviruses, as you learned in Chapter 19. In fact, retroviruses may have evolved from retrotransposons.) Another cellular enzyme catalyzes insertion of the reverse-transcribed DNA at a new site.

Sequences Related to Transposable Elements

Multiple copies of transposable elements and sequences related to them are scattered throughout eukaryotic genomes. A single unit is usually hundreds to thousands of base pairs long, and the dispersed "copies" are similar but usually not identical to each other. Some of these are transposable elements that can move; the enzymes required for this movement may be encoded by any transposable element, including the one that is moving. Others are related sequences that have lost the ability to move altogether. Transposable elements and related sequences make up 25–50% of most mammalian genomes (see Figure 21.7) and even higher percentages in amphibians and many plants. In fact, the very large size of some plant genomes is accounted for not by extra genes, but by extra transposable elements. For example, sequences like these make up 85% of the corn genome!

In humans and other primates, a large portion of transposable element–related DNA consists of a family of similar sequences called *Alu elements*. These sequences alone account for approximately 10% of the human genome. *Alu* elements are about 300 nucleotides long, much shorter than most functional transposable elements, and they do not code for any protein. However, many *Alu* elements are transcribed into RNA; its cellular function, if any, is currently unknown.

An even larger percentage (17%) of the human genome is made up of a type of retrotransposon called *LINE-1*, or *L1*. These sequences are much longer than *Alu* elements—about

6,500 base pairs—and have a low rate of transposition. What might account for this low rate? Recent research has uncovered the presence of sequences within L1 that block the progress of RNA polymerase, which is necessary for transposition. An accompanying genomic analysis found L1 sequences within the introns of nearly 80% of the human genes that were analyzed, suggesting that L1 may help regulate gene expression. Other researchers have proposed that L1 retrotransposons may have differential effects on gene expression in developing neurons, contributing to the great diversity of neuronal cell types (see Chapter 48).

Although many transposable elements encode proteins, these proteins do not carry out normal cellular functions. Therefore, transposable elements are usually included in the "noncoding" DNA category, along with other repetitive sequences.

Other Repetitive DNA, Including Simple Sequence DNA

Repetitive DNA that is not related to transposable elements probably arises due to mistakes during DNA replication or recombination. Such DNA accounts for about 14% of the human genome (see Figure 21.7). About a third of this (5–6% of the human genome) consists of duplications of long stretches of DNA, with each unit ranging from 10,000 to 300,000 base pairs. The large segments seem to have been copied from one chromosomal location to another site on the same or a different chromosome and probably include some functional genes.

In contrast to scattered copies of long sequences, **simple sequence DNA** contains many copies of tandemly repeated short sequences, as in the following example (showing one DNA strand only):

. . . GTTACGTTACGTTACGTTACGTTACGTTAC . . .

In this case, the repeated unit (GTTAC) consists of 5 nucleotides. Repeated units may contain as many as 500 nucleotides, but often contain fewer than 15 nucleotides, as in this example. When the unit contains 2–5 nucleotides, the series of repeats is called a **short tandem repeat**, or **STR**; we discussed the use of STR analysis in preparing genetic profiles in Chapter 20. The number of copies of the repeated unit can vary from site to site within a given genome. There could be as many as several hundred thousand repetitions of the GTTAC unit at one site, but only half that number at another. STR analysis is performed on sites selected because they have relatively few repeats. The repeat number can vary from person to person, and since humans are diploid, each person has two alleles per site, which can differ. This diversity produces the variation represented in the genetic profiles that result from STR analysis. Altogether, simple sequence DNA makes up 3% of the human genome.

Much of a genome's simple sequence DNA is located at chromosomal telomeres and centromeres, suggesting that this DNA plays a structural role for chromosomes. The DNA at centromeres is essential for the separation of chromatids in cell division (see Chapter 12). Centromeric DNA, along with simple sequence DNA located elsewhere, may also help organize the chromatin within the interphase nucleus. The simple sequence DNA located at telomeres, at the tips of chromosomes, prevents genes from being lost as the DNA shortens with each round of replication (see Chapter 16). Telomeric DNA also binds proteins that protect the ends of a chromosome from degradation and from joining to other chromosomes.

Genes and Multigene Families

We finish our discussion of the various types of DNA sequences in eukaryotic genomes with a closer look at genes. Recall that DNA sequences that code for proteins or give rise to tRNA or rRNA compose a mere 1.5% of the human genome (see Figure 21.7). If we include introns and regulatory sequences associated with genes, the total amount of DNA that is gene-related—coding and noncoding—constitutes about 25% of the human genome. Put another way, only about 6% (1.5% out of 25%) of the length of the average gene is represented in the final gene product.

Like the genes of bacteria, many eukaryotic genes are present as unique sequences, with only one copy per haploid set of chromosomes. But in the human genome and the genomes of many other animals and plants, solitary genes make up less than half of the total gene-related DNA. The rest occur in **multigene families**, collections of two or more identical or very similar genes.

In multigene families that consist of *identical* DNA sequences, those sequences are usually clustered tandemly and, with the notable exception of the genes for histone proteins, have RNAs as their final products. An example is the family of identical DNA sequences that are the genes for the three largest rRNA molecules **(Figure 21.11a)**. These rRNA molecules are transcribed from a single transcription unit that is repeated tandemly hundreds to thousands of times in one or several clusters in the genome of a multicellular eukaryote. The many copies of this rRNA transcription unit help cells to quickly make the millions of ribosomes needed for active protein synthesis. The primary transcript is cleaved to yield the three rRNA molecules, which combine with proteins and one other kind of rRNA (5S rRNA) to form ribosomal subunits.

The classic examples of multigene families of *nonidentical* genes are two related families of genes that encode globins, a group of proteins that include the α and β polypeptide subunits of hemoglobin. One family, located on chromosome 16 in humans, encodes various forms of α-globin; the other, on chromosome 11, encodes forms of β-globin **(Figure 21.11b)**. The different forms of each globin subunit are expressed at different times in development, allowing hemoglobin to function effectively in the changing environment of the developing animal. In humans, for example, the embryonic and fetal forms of hemoglobin have a higher affinity for oxygen

(a) Part of the ribosomal RNA gene family. The TEM at the top shows three of the hundreds of copies of rRNA transcription units in a salamander genome. Each "feather" corresponds to a single unit being transcribed by about 100 molecules of RNA polymerase (dark dots along the DNA), moving left to right (red arrow). The growing RNA transcripts extend from the DNA. In the diagram of a transcription unit below the TEM, the genes for three types of rRNA (blue) are adjacent to regions that are transcribed but later removed (yellow). A single transcript is processed to yield one of each of the three rRNAs (red), key components of the ribosome.

(b) The human α-globin and β-globin gene families. Adult hemoglobin is composed of two α-globin and two β-globin polypeptide subunits, as shown in the molecular model. The genes (dark blue) encoding α- and β-globins are found in two families, organized as shown here. The noncoding DNA separating the functional genes within each family includes pseudogenes (ψ; green), versions of the functional genes that no longer produce functional proteins. Genes and pseudogenes are named with Greek letters. Some genes are expressed only in the embryo or fetus.

▲ **Figure 21.11 Gene families.**

❓ *In (a), how could you determine the direction of transcription if it wasn't indicated by the red arrow?*

than the adult forms, ensuring the efficient transfer of oxygen from mother to fetus. Also found in the globin gene family clusters are several pseudogenes.

The arrangement of the genes in gene families has given biologists insight into the evolution of genomes. We will consider some of the processes that have shaped the genomes of different species over evolutionary time in the next section.

CONCEPT CHECK 21.4

1. Discuss the characteristics of mammalian genomes that make them larger than prokaryotic genomes.
2. Which of the three mechanisms described in Figures 21.9 and 21.10 result(s) in a copy remaining at the original site as well as appearing in a new location?
3. Contrast the organizations of the rRNA gene family and the globin gene families. For each, explain how the existence of a family of genes benefits the organism.
4. **MAKE CONNECTIONS** Assign each DNA segment at the top of Figure 18.8 (p. 359) to a sector in the pie chart in Figure 21.7.

For suggested answers, see Appendix A.

CONCEPT 21.5

Duplication, rearrangement, and mutation of DNA contribute to genome evolution

EVOLUTION The basis of change at the genomic level is mutation, which underlies much of genome evolution. It seems likely that the earliest forms of life had a minimal number of genes—those necessary for survival and reproduction. If this were indeed the case, one aspect of evolution must have been an increase in the size of the genome, with the extra genetic material providing the raw material for gene diversification. In this section, we will first describe how extra copies of all or part of a genome can arise and then consider subsequent processes that can lead to the evolution of proteins (or RNA products) with slightly different or entirely new functions.

Duplication of Entire Chromosome Sets

An accident in meiosis can result in one or more extra sets of chromosomes, a condition known as polyploidy. Although such accidents would most often be lethal, in rare cases they could facilitate the evolution of genes. In a polyploid organism, one set of genes can provide essential functions for the organism. The genes in the one or more extra sets can diverge by accumulating mutations; these variations may persist if the organism carrying them survives and reproduces. In this way, genes with novel functions can evolve. As long as one copy of an essential gene is expressed, the divergence of another copy can lead to its encoded protein acting in a novel way, thereby changing the organism's phenotype. The outcome of this accumulation of mutations may be the branching off of a new species, as happens often in flowering plants (see Chapter 24). Polyploid animals also exist, but they are much rarer; the tetraploid model organism *Xenopus laevis*, the African clawed frog, is an example.

Alterations of Chromosome Structure

Scientists have long known that sometime in the last 6 million years, when the ancestors of humans and chimpanzees diverged as species, the fusion of two ancestral chromosomes in the human line led to different haploid numbers for humans ($n = 23$) and chimpanzees ($n = 24$). The banding patterns in stained chromosomes suggested that the ancestral versions of current chimp chromosomes 12 and 13 fused end to end, forming chromosome 2 in an ancestor of the human lineage. With the recent explosion in genomic sequence information, we can now compare the chromosomal organizations of many different species on a much finer scale. This information allows us to make inferences about the evolutionary processes that shape chromosomes and may drive speciation. Sequencing and analysis of human chromosome 2 in 2005 provided very strong supporting evidence for the model we have just described **(Figure 21.12a)**.

In another study of broader scope, researchers compared the DNA sequence of each human chromosome with the whole-genome sequence of the mouse. **Figure 21.12b** shows the results of this comparison for human chromosome 16: Large blocks of genes on this chromosome are found on four mouse chromosomes, indicating that the genes in each block stayed together during the evolution of the mouse and human lineages.

Performing the same comparative analysis between chromosomes of humans and six other mammalian species allowed the researchers to reconstruct the evolutionary history of chromosomal rearrangements in these eight species. They found many duplications and inversions of large portions of chromosomes, the result of mistakes during meiotic recombination in which the DNA broke and was rejoined incorrectly. The rate of these events seems to have accelerated about 100 million years ago, around the time large dinosaurs became extinct and the number of mammalian species increased rapidly. The apparent coincidence is interesting because chromosomal rearrangements are thought to contribute to the generation of new species. Although two individuals with different arrangements could still mate and produce offspring, the offspring would have two nonequivalent sets of chromosomes, making meiosis inefficient or even impossible. Thus, chromosomal rearrangements would lead to two populations that could not successfully mate with each other, a step on the way to their becoming two separate species. (You'll learn more about this in Chapter 24.)

Human chromosome 2
Chimpanzee chromosomes

Telomere sequences

Centromere sequences

Telomere-like sequences

Centromere-like sequences

12

13

(a) Human and chimpanzee chromosomes. The positions of telomere-like and centromere-like sequences on human chromosome 2 (left) match those of telomeres on chimp chromosomes 12 and 13 and the centromere on chimp chromosome 13 (right). This suggests that chromosomes 12 and 13 in a human ancestor fused end to end to form human chromosome 2. The centromere from ancestral chromosome 12 remained functional on human chromosome 2, while the one from ancestral chromosome 13 did not. (Chimp chromosomes 12 and 13 have been renamed 2a and 2b, respectively.)

Human chromosome 16
Mouse chromosomes

7   8   16   17

(b) Human and mouse chromosomes. DNA sequences very similar to large blocks of human chromosome 16 (colored areas in this diagram) are found on mouse chromosomes 7, 8, 16, and 17. This suggests that the DNA sequence in each block has stayed together in the mouse and human lineages since the time they diverged from a common ancestor.

▲ **Figure 21.12 Related chromosome sequences among mammals.**

Somewhat unexpectedly, the same study also unearthed a pattern with medical relevance. Analysis of the chromosomal breakage points associated with the rearrangements showed that they were not randomly distributed; specific sites were used over and over again. A number of these recombination "hot spots" correspond to locations of chromosomal rearrangements within the human genome that are associated with congenital diseases. Researchers are, of course, looking at the other sites as well for their possible association with as yet unidentified diseases.

Duplication and Divergence of Gene-Sized Regions of DNA

Errors during meiosis can also lead to the duplication of chromosomal regions that are smaller than the ones we've just discussed, including segments the length of individual genes. Unequal crossing over during prophase I of meiosis, for instance, can result in one chromosome with a deletion and another with a duplication of a particular gene. As illustrated in **Figure 21.13**, transposable elements can provide homologous sites where nonsister chromatids can cross over, even when other chromatid regions are not correctly aligned.

Also, slippage can occur during DNA replication, such that the template shifts with respect to the new complementary strand, and a part of the template strand is either skipped by the replication machinery or used twice as a template. As a result, a segment of DNA is deleted or duplicated. It is easy to imagine how such errors could occur in regions of repeats. The variable number of repeated units of simple sequence DNA at a given site, used for STR analysis, is probably due to errors like these. Evidence that unequal crossing over and template slippage during DNA replication lead to duplication of genes is found in the existence of multigene families, such as the globin family.

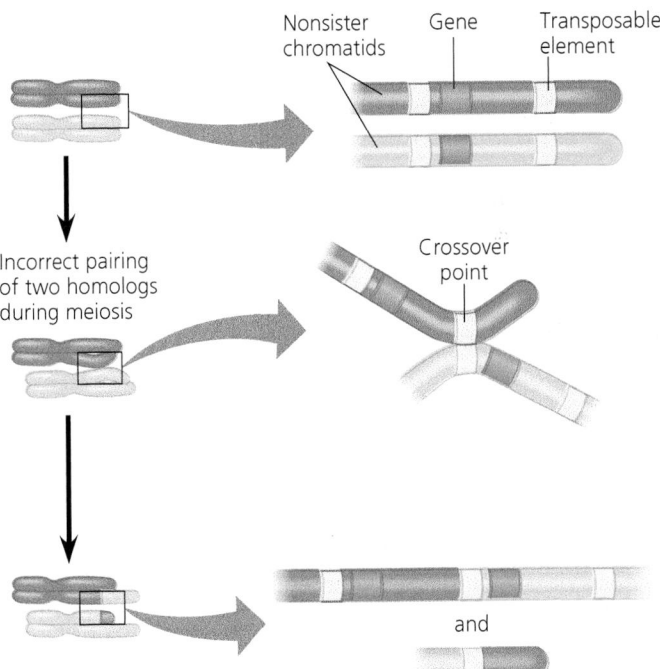

Nonsister chromatids   Gene   Transposable element

Incorrect pairing of two homologs during meiosis

Crossover point

and

▲ **Figure 21.13 Gene duplication due to unequal crossing over.** One mechanism by which a gene (or other DNA segment) can be duplicated is recombination during meiosis between copies of a transposable element flanking the gene. Such recombination between misaligned nonsister chromatids of homologous chromosomes produces one chromatid with two copies of the gene and one chromatid with no copy.

MAKE CONNECTIONS *Examine how crossing over occurs in Figure 13.11 (p. 259). In the middle panel above, draw a line through the portions that result in the upper chromatid in the bottom panel. Use a different color to do the same for the other chromatid.*

Evolution of Genes with Related Functions: The Human Globin Genes

Duplication events can lead to the evolution of genes with related functions, such as those of the α-globin and β-globin gene families (see Figure 21.11b). A comparison of gene sequences within a multigene family can suggest the order in which the genes arose. This approach to re-creating the evolutionary history of the globin genes indicates that they all evolved from one common ancestral globin gene that underwent duplication and divergence into the α-globin and β-globin ancestral genes about 450–500 million years ago (Figure 21.14). Each of these genes was later duplicated several times, and the copies then diverged from each other in sequence, yielding the current family members. In fact, the common ancestral globin gene also gave rise to the oxygen-binding muscle protein myoglobin and to the plant protein leghemoglobin. The latter two proteins function as monomers, and their genes are included in a "globin superfamily."

After the duplication events, the differences between the genes in the globin families undoubtedly arose from mutations that accumulated in the gene copies over many generations. The current model is that the necessary function provided by an α-globin protein, for example, was fulfilled by one gene, while other copies of the α-globin gene accumulated random mutations. Many mutations may have had an adverse effect on the organism and others may have had no effect, but a few mutations must have altered the function of the protein product in a way that was advantageous to the organism at a particular life stage without substantially changing the protein's oxygen-carrying function. Presumably, natural selection acted on these altered genes, maintaining them in the population.

The similarity in the amino acid sequences of the various α-globin and β-globin polypeptides supports this model of gene duplication and mutation (Table 21.2). The amino acid sequences of the β-globins, for instance, are much more similar to each other than to the α-globin sequences. The existence of several pseudogenes among the functional globin genes provides additional evidence for this model (see Figure 21.11b): Random mutations in these "genes" over evolutionary time have destroyed their function.

Evolution of Genes with Novel Functions

In the evolution of the globin gene families, gene duplication and subsequent divergence produced family members whose protein products performed similar functions (oxygen transport). Alternatively, one copy of a duplicated gene can undergo alterations that lead to a completely new function for the protein product. The genes for lysozyme and α-lactalbumin are good examples.

Lysozyme is an enzyme that helps protect animals against bacterial infection by hydrolyzing bacterial cell walls; α-lactalbumin is a nonenzymatic protein that plays a role in milk production in mammals. The two proteins are quite similar in their amino acid sequences and three-dimensional structures. Both genes are found in mammals, whereas only the lysozyme gene is present in birds. These findings suggest that at some time after the lineages leading to mammals and birds had separated, the lysozyme gene was duplicated in the

▲ **Figure 21.14 A model for the evolution of the human α-globin and β-globin gene families from a single ancestral globin gene.**

? *The green elements are pseudogenes. Explain how they could have arisen after gene duplication.*

Table 21.2 Percentage of Similarity in Amino Acid Sequence Between Human Globin Proteins

		α-Globins		β-Globins		
		α	ζ	β	γ	ε
α-Globins	α	—	58	42	39	37
	ζ	58	—	34	38	37
β-Globins	β	42	34	—	73	75
	γ	39	38	73	—	80
	ε	37	37	75	80	—

mammalian lineage but not in the avian lineage. Subsequently, one copy of the duplicated lysozyme gene evolved into a gene encoding α-lactalbumin, a protein with a completely different function.

Rearrangements of Parts of Genes: Exon Duplication and Exon Shuffling

Rearrangement of existing DNA sequences within genes has also contributed to genome evolution. The presence of introns in most genes of multicellular eukaryotes may have promoted the evolution of new and potentially useful proteins by facilitating the duplication or repositioning of exons in the genome. Recall from Chapter 17 that an exon often codes for a domain, a distinct structural or functional region of a protein.

We've already seen that unequal crossing over during meiosis can lead to duplication of a gene on one chromosome and its loss from the homologous chromosome (see Figure 21.13). By a similar process, a particular exon within a gene could be duplicated on one chromosome and deleted from the other. The gene with the duplicated exon would code for a protein containing a second copy of the encoded domain. This change in the protein's structure could augment its function by increasing its stability, enhancing its ability to bind a particular ligand, or altering some other property. Quite a few protein-coding genes have multiple copies of related exons, which presumably arose by duplication and then diverged. The gene encoding the extracellular matrix protein collagen is a good example. Collagen is a structural protein with a highly repetitive amino acid sequence, which is reflected in the repetitive pattern of exons in the collagen gene.

Alternatively, we can imagine the occasional mixing and matching of different exons either within a gene or between two different (nonallelic) genes owing to errors in meiotic recombination. This process, termed *exon shuffling*, could lead to new proteins with novel combinations of functions. As an example, let's consider the gene for tissue plasminogen activator (TPA). The TPA protein is an extracellular protein that helps control blood clotting. It has four domains of three types, each encoded by an exon; one exon is present in two copies. Because each type of exon is also found in other proteins, the gene for TPA is thought to have arisen by several instances of exon shuffling and duplication (Figure 21.15).

How Transposable Elements Contribute to Genome Evolution

The persistence of transposable elements as a large fraction of some eukaryotic genomes is consistent with the idea that they play an important role in shaping a genome over evolutionary time. These elements can contribute to the evolution of the genome in several ways. They can promote recombination, disrupt cellular genes or control elements, and carry entire genes or individual exons to new locations.

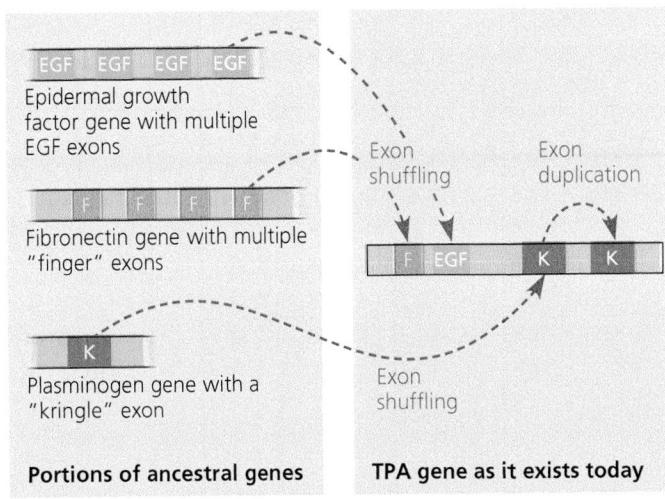

▲ Figure 21.15 Evolution of a new gene by exon shuffling. Exon shuffling could have moved exons, each encoding a particular domain, from ancestral forms of the genes for epidermal growth factor, fibronectin, and plasminogen (left) into the evolving gene for tissue plasminogen activator, TPA (right). Duplication of the "kringle" exon from the plasminogen gene after its movement could account for the two copies of this exon in the TPA gene.

? *How could the presence of transposable elements in introns have facilitated the exon shuffling shown here?*

Transposable elements of similar sequence scattered throughout the genome facilitate recombination between different chromosomes by providing homologous regions for crossing over. Most such recombination events are probably detrimental, causing chromosomal translocations and other changes in the genome that may be lethal to the organism. But over the course of evolutionary time, an occasional recombination event of this sort may be advantageous to the organism. (For the change to be heritable, of course, it must happen in a cell that will give rise to a gamete.)

The movement of a transposable element can have a variety of consequences. For instance, if a transposable element "jumps" into the middle of a protein-coding sequence, it will prevent the production of a normal transcript of the gene. If a transposable element inserts within a regulatory sequence, the transposition may lead to increased or decreased production of one or more proteins. Transposition caused both types of effects on the genes coding for pigment-synthesizing enzymes in McClintock's corn kernels. Again, while such changes are usually harmful, in the long run some may prove beneficial by providing a survival advantage.

During transposition, a transposable element may carry along a gene or group of genes to a new position in the genome. This mechanism probably accounts for the location of the α-globin and β-globin gene families on different human chromosomes, as well as the dispersion of the genes of certain other gene families. By a similar tag-along process, an exon from one gene may be inserted into another gene in a mechanism similar to that of exon shuffling during recombination. For example, an exon may be inserted by transposition into the intron of a protein-coding gene. If the inserted exon is retained in the RNA transcript during RNA splicing, the protein that is synthesized will have an additional domain, which may confer a new function on the protein.

All the processes discussed in this section most often produce either harmful effects, which may be lethal, or no effect at all. In a few cases, however, small beneficial heritable changes may occur. Over many generations, the resulting genetic diversity provides valuable raw material for natural selection. Diversification of genes and their products is an important factor in the evolution of new species. Thus, the accumulation of changes in the genome of each species provides a record of its evolutionary history. To read this record, we must be able to identify genomic changes. Comparing the genomes of different species allows us to do that and has increased our understanding of how genomes evolve. You will learn more about these topics in the final section.

CONCEPT CHECK 21.5

1. Describe three examples of errors in cellular processes that lead to DNA duplications.
2. Explain how multiple exons might have arisen in the ancestral EGF and fibronectin genes shown in Figure 21.15 (left).
3. What are three ways that transposable elements are thought to contribute to genome evolution?
4. **WHAT IF?** In 2005, Icelandic scientists reported finding a large chromosomal inversion present in 20% of northern Europeans, and they noted that Icelandic women with this inversion had significantly more children than women without it. What would you expect to happen to the frequency of this inversion in the Icelandic population in future generations?

For suggested answers, see Appendix A.

CONCEPT 21.6

Comparing genome sequences provides clues to evolution and development

EVOLUTION One researcher has likened the current state of biology to the Age of Exploration in the 15th century after major improvements in navigation and the building of faster ships. In the last 25 years, we have seen rapid advances in genome sequencing and data collection, new techniques for assessing gene activity across the whole genome, and refined approaches for understanding how genes and their products work together in complex systems. We are truly poised on the brink of a new world.

Comparisons of genome sequences from different species reveal much about the evolutionary history of life, from very ancient to more recent. Similarly, comparative studies of the genetic programs that direct embryonic development in different species are beginning to clarify the mechanisms that generated the great diversity of life-forms present today. In this final section of the chapter, we will discuss what has been learned from these two approaches.

Comparing Genomes

The more similar in sequence the genes and genomes of two species are, the more closely related those species are in their evolutionary history. Comparing genomes of closely related species sheds light on more recent evolutionary events, whereas comparing genomes of very distantly related species helps us understand ancient evolutionary history. In either case, learning about characteristics that are shared or divergent between groups enhances our picture of the evolution of life-forms and biological processes. As you learned in Chapter 1, the evolutionary relationships between species can be represented by a diagram in the form of a tree (often turned sideways), where each branch point marks the divergence of two lineages. **Figure 21.16** shows the evolutionary relationships of some groups and species we will be discussing. We will consider comparisons between distantly related species first.

▲ **Figure 21.16 Evolutionary relationships of the three domains of life.** This tree diagram shows the ancient divergence of bacteria, archaea, and eukaryotes. A portion of the eukaryote lineage is expanded in the inset to show the more recent divergence of three mammalian species discussed in this chapter.

Comparing Distantly Related Species

Determining which genes have remained similar—that is, are *highly conserved*—in distantly related species can help clarify evolutionary relationships among species that diverged from each other long ago. Indeed, comparisons of the complete genome sequences of bacteria, archaea, and eukaryotes indicate that these three groups diverged between 2 and 4 billion years ago and strongly support the theory that they are the fundamental domains of life (see Figure 21.16).

In addition to their value in evolutionary biology, comparative genomic studies confirm the relevance of research on model organisms to our understanding of biology in general and human biology in particular. Genes that evolved a very long time ago can still be surprisingly similar in disparate species. As a case in point, several genes in yeast are so similar to certain human disease genes that researchers have deduced the functions of the disease genes by studying their yeast counterparts. This striking similarity underscores the common origin of these two distantly related species.

Comparing Closely Related Species

The genomes of two closely related species are likely to be organized similarly because of their relatively recent divergence. As we mentioned earlier, this allows the fully sequenced genome of one species to be used as a scaffold for assembling the genomic sequences of a closely related species, accelerating mapping of the second genome. For instance, using the human genome sequence as a guide, researchers were able to quickly sequence the chimpanzee genome.

The recent divergence of two closely related species also underlies the small number of gene differences that are found when their genomes are compared. The particular genetic differences can therefore be more easily correlated with phenotypic differences between the two species. An exciting application of this type of analysis is seen as researchers compare the human genome with the genomes of the chimpanzee, mouse, rat, and other mammals. Identifying the genes shared by all of these species but not by nonmammals should give clues about what it takes to make a mammal, while finding the genes shared by chimpanzees and humans but not by rodents should tell us something about primates. And, of course, comparing the human genome with that of the chimpanzee should help us answer the tantalizing question we asked at the beginning of the chapter: What genomic information makes a human or a chimpanzee?

An analysis of the overall composition of the human and chimpanzee genomes, which are thought to have diverged only about 6 million years ago (see Figure 21.16), reveals some general differences. Considering single nucleotide substitutions, the two genomes differ by only 1.2%. When researchers looked at longer stretches of DNA, however, they were surprised to find a further 2.7% difference due to insertions or deletions of larger regions in the genome of one or the other species; many of the insertions were duplications or other repetitive DNA. In fact, a third of the human duplications are not present in the chimpanzee genome, and some of these duplications contain regions associated with human diseases. There are more *Alu* elements in the human genome than in the chimpanzee genome, and the latter contains many copies of a retroviral provirus not present in humans. All of these observations provide clues to the forces that might have swept the two genomes along different paths, but we don't have a complete picture yet. We also don't know how these differences might account for the distinct characteristics of each species.

To discover the basis for the phenotypic differences between the two species, biologists are studying specific genes and types of genes that differ between humans and chimpanzees and comparing them with their counterparts in other mammals. This approach has revealed a number of genes that are apparently changing (evolving) faster in the human than in either the chimpanzee or the mouse. Among them are genes involved in defense against malaria and tuberculosis and at least one gene that regulates brain size. When genes are classified by function, the genes that seem to be evolving the fastest are those that code for transcription factors. This discovery makes sense because transcription factors regulate gene expression and thus play a key role in orchestrating the overall genetic program.

One transcription factor whose gene shows evidence of rapid change in the human lineage is called FOXP2. Several lines of evidence suggest that the *FOXP2* gene functions in vocalization in vertebrates. For one thing, mutations in this gene can produce severe speech and language impairment in humans. Moreover, the *FOXP2* gene is expressed in the brains of zebra finches and canaries at the time when these songbirds are learning their songs. But perhaps the strongest evidence comes from a "knock-out" experiment in which researchers disrupted the *FOXP2* gene in mice and analyzed the resulting phenotype (**Figure 21.17**, on the next page). The homozygous mutant mice had malformed brains and failed to emit normal ultrasonic vocalizations, and mice with one faulty copy of the gene also showed significant problems with vocalization. These results support the idea that the *FOXP2* gene product turns on genes involved in vocalization.

Expanding on this analysis, another research group more recently replaced the *FOXP2* gene in mice with a "humanized" copy coding for the human versions of two amino acids that differ between human and chimp; these are the changes potentially responsible for a human's ability to speak. Although the mice were generally healthy, they had subtly different vocalizations and showed changes in brain cells in circuits associated with speech in human brains.

The *FOXP2* story is an excellent example of how different approaches can complement each other in uncovering biological phenomena of widespread importance. The

INQUIRY

What is the function of a gene (*FOXP2*) that is rapidly evolving in the human lineage?

EXPERIMENT Several lines of evidence support a role for the *FOXP2* gene in the development of speech and language in humans and of vocalization in other vertebrates. In 2005, Joseph Buxbaum and collaborators at the Mount Sinai School of Medicine and several other institutions tested the function of *FOXP2*. They used the mouse, a model organism in which genes can be easily knocked out, as a representative vertebrate that vocalizes: Mice produce ultrasonic squeaks (whistles) to communicate stress. The researchers used genetic engineering to produce mice in which one or both copies of *FOXP2* were disrupted.

Wild type: two normal copies of *FOXP2*	**Heterozygote: one copy of *FOXP2* disrupted**	**Homozygote: both copies of *FOXP2* disrupted**

They then compared the phenotypes of these mice. Two of the characters they examined are included here: brain anatomy and vocalization.

Experiment 1: Researchers cut thin sections of brain and stained them with reagents that allow visualization of brain anatomy in a UV fluorescence microscope.

Experiment 2: Researchers separated each newborn pup from its mother and recorded the number of ultrasonic whistles produced by the pup.

RESULTS

Experiment 1: Disruption of both copies of *FOXP2* led to brain abnormalities in which the cells were disorganized. Phenotypic effects on the brain of heterozygotes, with one disrupted copy, were less severe. (Each color reveals a different cell or tissue type.)

Experiment 2: Disruption of both copies of *FOXP2* led to an absence of ultrasonic vocalization in response to stress. The effect on vocalization in the heterozygote was also extreme.

Wild type

Heterozygote

Homozygote

Number of whistles (y-axis: 0, 100, 200, 300, 400)

Wild type — ~295; Hetero-zygote — ~70; Homo-zygote — (No whistles)

CONCLUSION *FOXP2* plays a significant role in the development of functional communication systems in mice. The results augment evidence from studies of birds and humans, supporting the hypothesis that *FOXP2* may act similarly in diverse organisms.

SOURCE W. Shu et al., Altered ultrasonic vocalization in mice with a disruption in the *Foxp2* gene, *Proceedings of the National Academy of Sciences* 102:9643–9648 (2005).

WHAT IF? Since the results support a role for mouse *FOXP2* in vocalization, you might wonder whether the human FOXP2 protein is a key regulator of speech. If you were given the amino acid sequences of wild-type and mutant human FOXP2 proteins and the wild-type chimpanzee FOXP2 protein, how would you investigate this question? What further clues could you obtain by comparing these sequences to that of the mouse FOXP2 protein?

FOXP2 experiments used mice as a model for humans because it would be unethical (as well as impractical) to carry out such experiments in humans. Mice and humans diverged about 65.5 million years ago (see Figure 21.16) and share about 85% of their genes. This genetic similarity can be exploited in studying human genetic disorders. If researchers know the organ or tissue that is affected by a particular genetic disorder, they can look for genes that are expressed in these locations in mice.

Further research efforts are under way to extend genomic studies to many more microbial species, additional primates, and neglected species from diverse branches of the tree of life.

These studies will advance our understanding of all aspects of biology, including health and ecology as well as evolution.

Comparing Genomes Within a Species

Another exciting consequence of our ability to analyze genomes is our growing understanding of the spectrum of genetic variation in humans. Because the history of the human species is so short—probably about 200,000 years—the amount of DNA variation among humans is small compared to that of many other species. Much of our diversity seems to be in the form of single nucleotide polymorphisms (SNPs, described in Chapter 20), usually detected by DNA sequencing. In the human genome, SNPs occur on average about once in 100–300 base pairs. Scientists have already identified the location of several million SNP sites in the human genome and continue to find more.

In the course of this search, they have also found other variations—including inversions, deletions, and duplications. The most surprising discovery has been the widespread occurrence of *copy-number variants* (CNVs), loci where some individuals have one or multiple copies of a particular gene or genetic region, rather than the standard two copies (one on each homolog). CNVs result from regions of the genome being duplicated or deleted inconsistently within the population. A 2010 study of 40 people found more than 8,000 CNVs involving 13% of the genes in the genome, and these CNVs probably represent just a small subset of the total. Since these variants encompass much longer stretches of DNA than the single nucleotides of SNPs, CNVs are more likely to have phenotypic consequences and to play a role in complex diseases and disorders. At the very least, the high incidence of copy-number variation casts doubt on the meaning of the phrase "a normal human genome."

Copy-number variants, SNPs, and variations in repetitive DNA such as short tandem repeats (STRs) will be useful genetic markers for studying human evolution. In 2010, the genomes of two Africans from different communities were sequenced: Archbishop Desmond Tutu, the South African civil rights advocate and a member of the Bantu tribe, the majority population in southern Africa; and !Gubi, a hunter-gatherer from the Khoisan community in Namibia, a minority African population that is probably the human group with the oldest known lineage. The comparison revealed many differences, as you might expect. The analysis was then broadened to compare the protein-coding regions of !Gubi's genome with those of three other Khoisan community members (self-identified Bushmen) living nearby. Remarkably, these four genomes differed more from each other than a European would from an Asian. These data highlight the extensive diversity among African genomes. Extending this approach will help us answer important questions about the differences between human populations and the migratory routes of human populations throughout history.

Comparing Developmental Processes

Biologists in the field of evolutionary developmental biology, or **evo-devo** as it is often called, compare developmental processes of different multicellular organisms. Their aim is to understand how these processes have evolved and how changes in them can modify existing organismal features or lead to new ones. With the advent of molecular techniques and the recent flood of genomic information, we are beginning to realize that the genomes of related species with strikingly different forms may have only minor differences in gene sequence or regulation. Discovering the molecular basis of these differences in turn helps us understand the origins of the myriad diverse forms that cohabit this planet, thus informing our study of evolution.

Widespread Conservation of Developmental Genes Among Animals

In Chapter 18, you learned about the homeotic genes in *Drosophila*, which specify the identity of body segments in the fruit fly (see Figure 18.20). Molecular analysis of the homeotic genes in *Drosophila* has shown that they all include a 180-nucleotide sequence called a **homeobox**, which specifies a 60-amino-acid *homeodomain* in the encoded proteins. An identical or very similar nucleotide sequence has been discovered in the homeotic genes of many invertebrates and vertebrates. The sequences are so similar between humans and fruit flies, in fact, that one researcher has whimsically referred to flies as "little people with wings." The resemblance even extends to the organization of these genes: The vertebrate genes homologous to the homeotic genes of fruit flies have kept the same chromosomal arrangement (**Figure 21.18**, on the next page). Homeobox-containing sequences have also been found in regulatory genes of much more distantly related eukaryotes, including plants and yeasts. From these similarities, we can deduce that the homeobox DNA sequence evolved very early in the history of life and was sufficiently valuable to organisms to have been conserved in animals and plants virtually unchanged for hundreds of millions of years.

Homeotic genes in animals were named *Hox* genes, short for *homeobox*-containing genes, because homeotic genes were the first genes found to have this sequence. Other homeobox-containing genes were later found that do not act as homeotic genes; that is, they do not directly control the identity of body parts. However, most of these genes, in animals at least, are associated with development, suggesting their ancient and fundamental importance in that process. In *Drosophila*, for example, homeoboxes are present not only in the homeotic genes but also in the egg-polarity gene *bicoid* (see Figures 18.21 and 18.22), in several of the segmentation genes, and in a master regulatory gene for eye development.

Researchers have discovered that the homeobox-encoded homeodomain is the part of a protein that binds to DNA

Figure 21.18 Conservation of homeotic genes in a fruit fly and a mouse. Homeotic genes that control the form of anterior and posterior structures of the body occur in the same linear sequence on chromosomes in *Drosophila* and mice. Each colored band on the chromosomes shown here represents a homeotic gene. In fruit flies, all homeotic genes are found on one chromosome. The mouse and other mammals have the same or similar sets of genes on four chromosomes. The color code indicates the parts of the embryos in which these genes are expressed and the adult body regions that result. All of these genes are essentially identical in flies and mice, except for those represented by black bands, which are less similar in the two animals.

when the protein functions as a transcriptional regulator. However, the shape of the homeodomain allows it to bind to any DNA segment; its own structure is not specific for a particular sequence. Instead, other, more variable domains in a homeodomain-containing protein determine which genes the protein regulates. Interaction of these variable domains with still other transcription factors helps a homeodomain-containing protein recognize specific enhancers in the DNA. Proteins with homeodomains probably regulate development by coordinating the transcription of batteries of developmental genes, switching them on or off. In embryos of

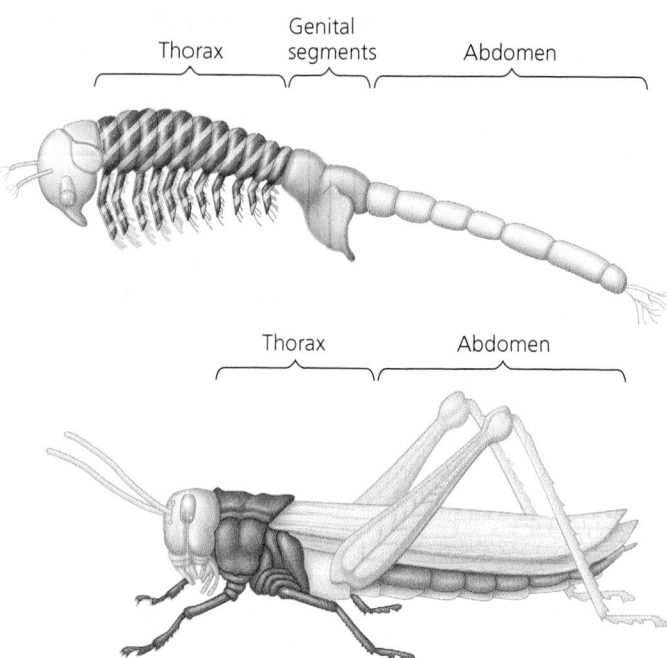

Figure 21.19 Effect of differences in *Hox* gene expression in crustaceans and insects. Changes in the expression patterns of *Hox* genes have occurred over evolutionary time. These changes account in part for the different body plans of the brine shrimp *Artemia*, a crustacean (top), and the grasshopper, an insect. Shown here are regions of the adult body color-coded for expression of four *Hox* genes that determine formation of particular body parts during embryonic development. Each color represents a specific *Hox* gene. Colored stripes on the thorax of *Artemia* indicate co-expression of three *Hox* genes.

Drosophila and other animal species, different combinations of homeobox genes are active in different parts of the embryo. This selective expression of regulatory genes, varying over time and space, is central to pattern formation.

Developmental biologists have found that in addition to homeotic genes, many other genes involved in development are highly conserved from species to species. These include numerous genes encoding components of signaling pathways. The extraordinary similarity among particular developmental genes in different animal species raises a question: How can the same genes be involved in the development of animals whose forms are so very different from each other?

Ongoing studies are suggesting answers to this question. In some cases, small changes in regulatory sequences of particular genes cause changes in gene expression patterns that can lead to major changes in body form. For example, the differing patterns of expression of the *Hox* genes along the body axis in insects and crustaceans can explain the variation in number of leg-bearing segments among these segmented animals (Figure 21.19). Also, recent research suggests that the same *Hox* gene product may have subtly dissimilar effects in different species, turning on new genes or turning on the same genes at higher or lower levels. In other cases, similar genes direct differing developmental processes in different organisms, resulting in diverse body shapes. Several *Hox* genes, for instance, are expressed in the embryonic and larval stages of the sea urchin, a nonsegmented animal that has a body plan quite different from those of insects and mice. Sea urchin adults make the pincushion-shaped shells you may have seen on the beach (see Figure 8.4). They are among the organisms long used in classical embryological studies (see Chapter 47).

Comparison of Animal and Plant Development

The last common ancestor of animals and plants was probably a single-celled eukaryote that lived hundreds of millions of years ago, so the processes of development must have evolved independently in the two multicellular lineages of organisms. Plants evolved with rigid cell walls, which rule out the morphogenetic movements of cells and tissues that are so important in animals. Instead, morphogenesis in plants relies primarily on differing planes of cell division and on selective cell enlargement. (You will learn about these processes in Chapter 35.) But despite the differences between animals and plants, there are similarities in the molecular mechanisms of development, which are legacies of their shared unicellular origin.

In both animals and plants, development relies on a cascade of transcriptional regulators turning on or turning off genes in a finely tuned series. For example, work on the small flowering plant *Arabidopsis thaliana* has shown that establishing the radial pattern of flower parts, like setting up the head-to-tail axis in *Drosophila*, involves a cascade of transcription factors (see Chapter 35). The genes that direct these processes, however, differ considerably in animals and plants. While quite a few of the master regulatory switches in *Drosophila* are homeobox-containing *Hox* genes, those in *Arabidopsis* belong to a completely different family of genes, called the *MADS-box* genes. And although homeobox-containing genes can be found in plants and *MADS-box* genes in animals, in neither case do they perform the same major roles in development that they do in the other group. Thus, molecular evidence supports the supposition that developmental programs evolved separately in animals and plants.

In this final chapter of the genetics unit, you have learned how studying genomic composition and comparing the genomes of different species can disclose much about how genomes evolve. Further, comparing developmental programs, we can see that the unity of life is reflected in the similarity of molecular and cellular mechanisms used to establish body pattern, although the genes directing development may differ among organisms. The similarities between genomes reflect the common ancestry of life on Earth. But the differences are also crucial, for they have created the huge diversity of organisms that have evolved. In the remainder of the book, we expand our perspective beyond the level of molecules, cells, and genes to explore this diversity on the organismal level.

CONCEPT CHECK 21.6

1. Would you expect the genome of the macaque (a monkey) to be more similar to the mouse genome or the human genome? Why?
2. The DNA sequences called homeoboxes, which help homeotic genes in animals direct development, are common to flies and mice. Given this similarity, explain why these animals are so different.
3. **WHAT IF?** There are three times as many *Alu* elements in the human genome as in the chimpanzee genome. How do you think these extra *Alu* elements arose in the human genome? Propose a role they might have played in the divergence of these two species.

For suggested answers, see Appendix A.

21 CHAPTER REVIEW

SUMMARY OF KEY CONCEPTS

CONCEPT 21.1

New approaches have accelerated the pace of genome sequencing (pp. 427–429)

- The **Human Genome Project** began in 1990, using a three-stage approach. In **linkage mapping**, the order of genes and other inherited markers in the genome and the relative distances between them can be determined from recombination frequencies. Next, **physical mapping** uses overlaps between DNA fragments to order the fragments and determine the distance in base pairs between markers. Finally, the ordered fragments are sequenced, providing the finished genome sequence.
- In the whole-genome shotgun approach, the whole genome is cut into many small, overlapping fragments that are sequenced; computer software then assembles the complete sequence. Correct assembly is made easier when mapping information is also available.

? *Why has the whole-genome shotgun approach been widely adopted for genome-sequencing projects?*

CONCEPT 21.2

Scientists use bioinformatics to analyze genomes and their functions (pp. 429–432)

- Websites on the Internet provide centralized access to genome sequence databases, analytical tools, and genome-related information.
- Computer analysis of genome sequences aids **gene annotation**, the identification of protein-coding sequences and determination of their function. Methods for determining gene function include comparing the sequences of newly discovered genes with those of known genes in other species and observing the phenotypic effects of experimentally inactivating genes of unknown function.
- In systems biology, scientists use the computer-based tools of **bioinformatics** to compare genomes and study sets of genes and proteins as whole systems (**genomics** and **proteomics**). Studies

include large-scale analyses of protein interactions, functional DNA elements, and genes contributing to medical conditions.

? *What was the most significant finding of the ENCODE pilot project? Why has the project been expanded to include other species?*

CONCEPT 21.3

Genomes vary in size, number of genes, and gene density (pp. 432–434)

	Bacteria	Archaea	Eukarya
Genome size	Most are 1–6 Mb		Most are 10–4,000 Mb, but a few are much larger
Number of genes	1,500–7,500		5,000–40,000
Gene density	Higher than in eukaryotes		Lower than in prokaryotes (Within eukaryotes, lower density is correlated with larger genomes.)
Introns	None in protein-coding genes	Present in some genes	Unicellular eukaryotes: present, but prevalent only in some species Multicellular eukaryotes: present in most genes
Other noncoding DNA	Very little		Can be large amounts; generally more repetitive noncoding DNA in multicellular eukaryotes

? *Compare genome size, gene number, and gene density (a) in the three domains and (b) among eukaryotes.*

CONCEPT 21.4

Multicellular eukaryotes have much noncoding DNA and many multigene families (pp. 434–438)

- Only 1.5% of the human genome codes for proteins or gives rise to rRNAs or tRNAs; the rest is noncoding DNA, including **pseudogenes** and **repetitive DNA** of unknown function.

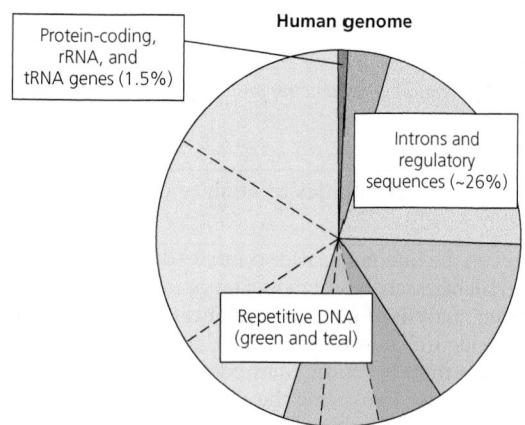

Human genome

Protein-coding, rRNA, and tRNA genes (1.5%)

Introns and regulatory sequences (~26%)

Repetitive DNA (green and teal)

- The most abundant type of repetitive DNA in multicellular eukaryotes consists of **transposable elements** and related sequences. In eukaryotes, there are two types of transposable elements: **transposons**, which move via a DNA intermediate,

and **retrotransposons**, which are more prevalent and move via an RNA intermediate.

- Other repetitive DNA includes short noncoding sequences that are tandemly repeated thousands of times (**simple sequence DNA**, which includes **STRs**); these sequences are especially prominent in centromeres and telomeres, where they probably play structural roles in the chromosome.

- Though many eukaryotic genes are present in one copy per haploid chromosome set, others (most, in some species) are members of a family of related genes, such as the human globin gene families:

α-Globin gene family	β-Globin gene family
Chromosome 16	Chromosome 11

ζ   ψ$_ζ$ ψ$_{α_2}$ ψ$_{α_1}$ α$_2$ α$_1$ ψ$_θ$ ε ^{G}γ ^{A}γ ψ$_β$ δ   β

? *Explain how the function of transposable elements might account for their prevalence in human noncoding DNA.*

CONCEPT 21.5

Duplication, rearrangement, and mutation of DNA contribute to genome evolution (pp. 438–442)

- Accidents in cell division can lead to extra copies of all or part of entire chromosome sets, which may then diverge if one set accumulates sequence changes.

- The chromosomal organization of genomes can be compared among species, providing information about evolutionary relationships. Within a given species, rearrangements of chromosomes are thought to contribute to the emergence of new species.

- The genes encoding the various globin proteins evolved from one common ancestral globin gene, which duplicated and diverged into α-globin and β-globin ancestral genes. Subsequent duplication and random mutation gave rise to the present globin genes, all of which code for oxygen-binding proteins. The copies of some duplicated genes have diverged so much that the functions of their encoded proteins (such as lysozyme and α-lactalbumin) are now substantially different.

- Rearrangement of exons within and between genes during evolution has led to genes containing multiple copies of similar exons and/or several different exons derived from other genes.

- Movement of transposable elements or recombination between copies of the same element occasionally generates new sequence combinations that are beneficial to the organism. Such mechanisms can alter the functions of genes or their patterns of expression and regulation.

? *How could chromosomal rearrangements lead to the emergence of new species?*

CONCEPT 21.6

Comparing genome sequences provides clues to evolution and development (pp. 442–447)

- Comparative studies of genomes from widely divergent and closely related species provide valuable information about ancient and more recent evolutionary history, respectively. Human and chimpanzee sequences show about 4% difference, mostly due to insertions, deletions, and duplications in one lineage. Along with nucleotide variations in specific genes (such as *FOXP2*, a gene affecting speech), these differences may account for the distinct characteristics of the two species. Analysis of single nucleotide polymorphisms (SNPs) and copy-number variants (CNVs) among individuals in a species can also yield information about the evolution of that species.

- Evolutionary developmental (**evo-devo**) biologists have shown that homeotic genes and some other genes associated with animal development contain a **homeobox** region whose sequence is highly conserved among diverse species. Related sequences are present in the genes of plants and yeasts. During embryonic development in both plants and animals, a cascade of transcription regulators turns genes on or off in a carefully regulated sequence. However, the genes that direct analogous developmental processes differ in plants and animals as a result of their remote ancestry.

? *What type of information can be obtained by comparing the genomes of closely related species? Of very distantly related species?*

TEST YOUR UNDERSTANDING

LEVEL 1: KNOWLEDGE/COMPREHENSION

1. Bioinformatics includes all of the following *except*
   a. using computer programs to align DNA sequences.
   b. analyzing protein interactions in a species.
   c. using molecular biology to combine DNA from two different sources in a test tube.
   d. developing computer-based tools for genome analysis.
   e. using mathematical tools to make sense of biological systems.

2. One of the characteristics of retrotransposons is that
   a. they code for an enzyme that synthesizes DNA using an RNA template.
   b. they are found only in animal cells.
   c. they generally move by a cut-and-paste mechanism.
   d. they contribute a significant portion of the genetic variability seen within a population of gametes.
   e. their amplification is dependent on a retrovirus.

3. Homeotic genes
   a. encode transcription factors that control the expression of genes responsible for specific anatomical structures.
   b. are found only in *Drosophila* and other arthropods.
   c. are the only genes that contain the homeobox domain.
   d. encode proteins that form anatomical structures in the fly.
   e. are responsible for patterning during plant development.

LEVEL 2: APPLICATION/ANALYSIS

4. Two eukaryotic proteins have one domain in common but are otherwise very different. Which of the following processes is most likely to have contributed to this similarity?
   a. gene duplication   d. histone modification
   b. RNA splicing   e. random point mutations
   c. exon shuffling

5. **DRAW IT** Below are the amino acid sequences (using the single-letter code; see Figure 5.16) of four short segments of the FOXP2 protein from six species: chimpanzee, orangutan, gorilla, rhesus macaque, mouse, and human. These segments contain all of the amino acid differences between the FOXP2 proteins of these species.

   1. ATETI...PKSSD...TSSTT...NARRD
   2. ATETI...PKSSE...TSSTT...NARRD
   3. ATETI...PKSSD...TSSTT...NARRD
   4. ATETI...PKSSD...TSSNT...SARRD
   5. ATETI...PKSSD...TSSTT...NARRD
   6. VTETI...PKSSD...TSSTT...NARRD

   Use a highlighter to color any amino acid that varies among the species. (Color that amino acid in all sequences.) Then answer the questions at the top of the next column.

(a) The chimpanzee, gorilla, and rhesus macaque (C, G, R) sequences are identical. Which lines correspond to those sequences?

(b) The human sequence differs from that of the C, G, R species at two amino acids. Which line corresponds to the human sequence? Underline the two differences.

(c) The orangutan sequence differs from the C, G, R sequence at one amino acid (having valine instead of alanine) and from the human sequence at three amino acids. Which line corresponds to the orangutan sequence?

(d) How many amino acid differences are there between the mouse and the C, G, R species? Circle the amino acid(s) that differ(s) in the mouse. How many amino acid differences are there between the mouse and the human? Draw a square around the amino acid(s) that differ(s) in the mouse.

(e) Primates and rodents diverged between 60 and 100 million years ago, and chimpanzees and humans diverged about 6 million years ago. Knowing that, what can you conclude by comparing the amino acid differences between the mouse and the C, G, R species with the differences between the human and the C, G, R species?

LEVEL 3: SYNTHESIS/EVALUATION

6. **EVOLUTION CONNECTION**

   Genes important in the embryonic development of animals, such as homeobox-containing genes, have been relatively well conserved during evolution; that is, they are more similar among different species than are many other genes. Why is this?

7. **SCIENTIFIC INQUIRY**

   The scientists mapping the SNPs in the human genome noticed that groups of SNPs tended to be inherited together, in blocks known as haplotypes, ranging in length from 5,000 to 200,000 base pairs. There are as few as four or five commonly occurring combinations of SNPs per haplotype. Propose an explanation for this observation, integrating what you've learned throughout this chapter and this unit.

8. **WRITE ABOUT A THEME**

   The Genetic Basis of Life The continuity of life is based on heritable information in the form of DNA. In a short essay (100–150 words), explain how mutations in protein-coding genes and regulatory DNA contribute to evolution.

For selected answers, see Appendix A.

Mastering BIOLOGY   www.masteringbiology.com

1. MasteringBiology® Assignments

Tutorial Shotgun Approach to Whole-Genome Sequencing • Using BLAST: Can You Identify a Pathogen from a Nucleotide Sequence?

Activity The Human Genome Project: Genes on Human Chromosome 17

Questions Student Misconceptions • Reading Quiz • Multiple Choice • End-of-Chapter

2. eText

Read your book online, search, take notes, highlight text, and more.

3. The Study Area

Practice Tests • Cumulative Test • *BioFlix* 3-D Animations • MP3 Tutor Sessions • Videos • Activities • Investigations • Lab Media • Audio Glossary • Word Study Tools • Art

Mechanisms of Evolution

An Interview with
Geerat J. Vermeij

Born in the Netherlands, Geerat Vermeij (pronounced "ver-may") lost his sight at the age of 3. Undeterred, he went on to earn degrees from Princeton and Yale and is now a Distinguished Professor at the University of California, Davis. A member of the Department of Geology, he nevertheless focuses on biology—the structure, evolution, and ecology of marine molluscs, both living and extinct. He is particularly well known for his work on the evolutionary "arms race" between long-extinct molluscs and their predators and more generally the roles of organismal interactions in evolution, although his many publications reflect much wider-ranging interests. (One of his books, *Nature: An Economic History*, relates the principles of evolution to the principles of economics; he has also written a memoir, *Privileged Hands: A Scientific Life*.) Dr. Vermeij has received numerous awards, including the MacArthur Award and the Daniel Giraud Elliot Medal from the National Academy of Sciences. His office at UC Davis features a large collection of marine shells and fossils and an extensive library. Jane Reece and Michael Cain spoke with him there.

How did you first become interested in biology?

As far back as I can recall, back to my earliest childhood, I've always liked natural history. When I was a child in the Netherlands, I liked pinecones and seeds and shells on the beach and leaves. I liked the whole ambience of being outside! Also, my parents were very good observers, and they spent a lot of time describing the world to me and letting me touch as much as I possibly could. When I moved to the U.S. at the age of 9, I found myself in a completely different environment. In New Jersey where we lived, there were wild forests full of huge vines, noisy crickets, cicadas, and strange birds, and I found this environment so different from the one I had left behind that I began to ask myself why this was.

When I was in the fourth grade, I had a wonderful teacher who brought shells from Florida to her classroom. And I explored these things and fell in love with them. And again, I wondered why these things were so different from anything I had collected in Holland.

They were beautiful, with lovely shapes and wonderful contrast between the outside surface and the inside. I was smitten. And from then on I knew I was going to do something scientific.

Much of your work focuses on marine molluscs. Please tell us about these animals.

Molluscs include snails, clams, squids, octopuses, and many lesser-known groups. There are something like 100,000 species living, and we know of fossils of tens of thousands of extinct ones, dating all the way back to at least 540 million years ago. Molluscs are a major animal group on the tree of life. Found on land and in fresh water and the sea, they do just about everything you can imagine—they range from top predators (such as squids) to suspension feeders, herbivores, detritus feeders, and parasites. Originally, all molluscs had some kind of mantle covering the major organs of the body. They probably started off as pretty simple creatures without shells, but shells soon evolved. Most living molluscs have shells, though some have lost their shell in the course of evolution.

How do you identify the shells you are studying?

Entirely by touch. You know, shells differ in size, shape, and texture, all of which are readily discernable by the fingers, and the same is true of fossils. Shells are ideally suited for a blind person like me.

In your research over the years, what are the main questions you have been trying to answer?

The questions have changed over the course of my career, but the overarching ones have been, What are the pathways of adaptation by which all the different lineages of organisms—not just molluscs, but all of life—have gotten here? How have the conditions to which organisms are exposed changed over time? How have organisms affected those conditions over time? I'm very interested in the history of life and how this history has been shaped.

What makes molluscs a good research focus for answering your questions?

Molluscs have several huge advantages. For me personally, of course, they are accessible. Most of them don't run away—squids and octopuses being exceptions. Their shells are extremely easy to observe with the hand, and importantly from a paleontologist's point of view, these hard mineralized objects have left a very good fossil record. That's a gigantic advantage. Not only can we trace molluscs all the way back through time, but because we know so much about how shells work, we can figure out how the extinct animals lived—even those that lived hundreds of millions of years ago.

What kinds of evolutionary insights can fossils provide that cannot be extracted from DNA evidence?

First of all, I should say that my collaborators and I do use DNA sequences ourselves to reconstruct the order of branching in evolutionary trees. But to estimate *when* these evolutionary lineages arose, we need to calibrate the tree with fossils of known age. Moreover, you can only get DNA from living things and a few rather recent fossils; so if you go back far enough, you find many lineages that no longer exist and for which, therefore, DNA evidence is simply unavailable. And yet these animals often have combinations of traits that we never see in living animals. Fossils give us a very good idea of what the ancestral organisms were like, which you couldn't get solely from DNA sequences of living organisms. So if you're trying to reconstruct early branches in the tree of life, fossils are very helpful.

How does your research relate to the mechanisms of evolution—to the principles as opposed to the pattern?

That's an important question. I do distinguish between describing what actually happened and the mechanisms that account for evolutionary events over time. A lot of our work is descriptive, figuring out what happened and what extinct animals were like. But we also try to determine the mechanisms that account for the phenomena. And given that I work on adaptive characteristics and on the fit between animals and plants and their environments, I am particularly interested in the mechanisms by which organisms become adapted to their environments. That's not simply natural selection; it's also the modification of environments by the animals and plants that reside there.

Tell us how you go about your work.

I have done a lot of fieldwork all over the world. In the field I observe molluscs in nature and occasionally do some experiments with them. I want to understand how the molluscs relate to their environments, including their predators. I am interested in how they live—for example, how quickly they move—and how their performance levels compare with the performance of the agents that are out there making the world tough for them.

Recently I've spent more time in museum collections. I also maintain a very large research collection, most of which I've collected myself over the years. All of these collections are critical for learning what the shapes of organisms are in different evolutionary groups. I also visit and learn from other scientists. And I do an enormous amount of reading, because I like to synthesize information and ideas, to put things together. I read hundreds of papers a year about a very wide variety of subjects, everything from biology to geology to economics and history, so that I can place the particular work that I do into a larger context. As a scientist, you can never read enough.

When you do this kind of work, whether in collections of specimens or in the field or library, you always come across wonderful surprises—perhaps a shell with a feature you've never seen or even a book you didn't know about. Every single day for me is like that.

You have written about the "arms race" of evolution. What do you mean by that, and how has it played out in the creatures you've studied?

All living things are exposed to competition for resources and also to predation, where one animal eats another animal or part of another animal. The animals I am working on mostly don't move very fast, and one of the typical results of predation is that armor in the form of shells evolves in the prey; the mollusc shell probably first evolved as armor. But as predators become more powerful thanks to competition among themselves, the performance criteria for an effective shell also escalate. Nowadays, in order to survive in tropical shallow water environments where there are lots of predators, a mollusc needs a very well-armored shell—one that has thick walls, bumps all over the place, a narrow opening, and many other features. In fact, if you look at shell architecture over geological time, keeping habitat as constant as you can, you find that some of these protective features (the narrow opening, for example) are found only in the more recent evolutionary lineages and don't appear at all in the first couple of hundred million years of mollusc history. Meanwhile, all sorts of ways of overcoming mollusc defenses have evolved in predators. They have developed stronger, more powerful jaws or claws. They have "learned" how to drill a hole through the

wall of a shell. They swallow or envelop larger prey. That tells us that there has been an arms race, an escalation of improvements in both shell architecture and methods of attack by predators.

In addition to arms races, what other kinds of ecological interactions have influenced evolutionary history?

Competition and predation are fundamental and inevitable, but the history of life from the very beginning is also a story of cooperation. The reason for that I think is simple: By cooperating, you can do things that neither party can do by itself. So, cooperation or some other kind of mutually beneficial relationship is a wonderful way to compete. Biology is absolutely filled with examples of social animals, mutually beneficial relationships between individuals of different species, and so forth. Cooperation is in some sense an emergent property of life as a whole. The interactions of organisms with one another give rise to properties that the individual components don't have. For example, a lichen, which is an alga and a fungus living together, has properties different from those of either participant.

How do the things you've been saying about the effects of ecological interactions on evolutionary history fit in with Darwin's main ideas?

Darwin was an incredibly smart guy. One of the many, many things that he got right was that natural selection is often brought about by the interactions of organisms with other organisms, as well as interactions of organisms with their physical environment. Natural selection isn't some nebulous agency out there that's choosing survivors over nonsurvivors.

Why is it important for people to understand evolution?

There are many reasons. An understanding of evolution is certainly of practical importance in medicine and agriculture. But an understanding of evolution also gives us a closer connection to the rest of life. Also, it's very important for people to understand that the theory of evolution, like all scientific theories, is a body of explanation and fact that explains natural phenomena and can predict them. A lot of the resistance to evolution comes down to the idea some people have that somehow evolution makes life meaningless or purposeless. To this I reply that meaning and purpose is an emergent property of evolution! It is our own responsibility to make life meaningful.

"When you do this kind of work . . . you always come across wonderful surprises. . . . Every single day for me is like that."

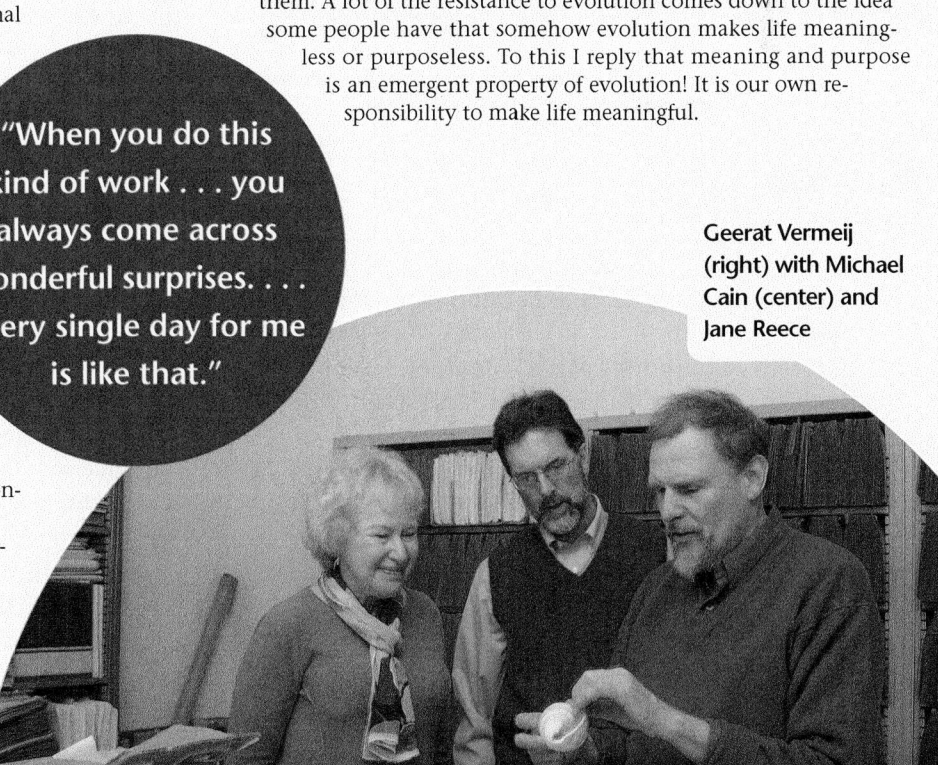

Geerat Vermeij (right) with Michael Cain (center) and Jane Reece

22

Descent with Modification: A Darwinian View of Life

▲ Figure 22.1 **How can this beetle survive in the desert, and what is it doing?**

KEY CONCEPTS

22.1 The Darwinian revolution challenged traditional views of a young Earth inhabited by unchanging species

22.2 Descent with modification by natural selection explains the adaptations of organisms and the unity and diversity of life

22.3 Evolution is supported by an overwhelming amount of scientific evidence

OVERVIEW

Endless Forms Most Beautiful

In the coastal Namib desert of southwestern Africa, a land where fog is common but virtually no rain falls, lives the beetle *Onymacris unguicularis*. To obtain the water it needs to survive, this insect relies on a peculiar "headstanding" behavior

(Figure 22.1). Tilting head-downward, the beetle faces into the winds that blow fog across the dunes. Droplets of moisture from the fog collect on the beetle's body and run down into its mouth.

Interesting in its own right, this headstander beetle is also a member of an astonishingly diverse group: the more than 350,000 species of beetles. In fact, nearly one of every five known species is a beetle. These beetles all share similar features, such as three pairs of legs, a hard outer surface, and two pairs of wings. But they also differ from one another. How did there come to be so many beetles, and what causes their similarities and differences?

The headstander beetle and its many close relatives illustrate three key observations about life:

- the striking ways in which organisms are suited for life in their environments*
- the many shared characteristics (unity) of life
- the rich diversity of life

A century and a half ago, Charles Darwin was inspired to develop a scientific explanation for these three broad observations. When he published his hypothesis in *The Origin of Species*, Darwin ushered in a scientific revolution—the era of evolutionary biology.

For now, we will define **evolution** as *descent with modification*, a phrase Darwin used in proposing that Earth's many species are descendants of ancestral species that were different from the present-day species. Evolution can also be defined more narrowly as a change in the genetic composition of a population from generation to generation, as discussed further in Chapter 23.

Whether it is defined broadly or narrowly, we can view evolution in two related but different ways: as a pattern and as a process. The *pattern* of evolutionary change is revealed by data from a range of scientific disciplines, including biology, geology, physics, and chemistry. These data are facts—they are observations about the natural world. The *process* of evolution consists of the mechanisms that produce the observed pattern of change. These mechanisms represent natural causes of the natural phenomena we observe. Indeed, the power of evolution as a unifying theory is its ability to explain and connect a vast array of observations about the living world.

As with all general theories in science, we continue to test our understanding of evolution by examining whether it can account for new observations and experimental results. In this and the following chapters, we'll examine how ongoing discoveries shape what we know about the pattern and process of evolution. To set the stage, we'll first retrace Darwin's quest to explain the adaptations, unity, and diversity of what he called life's "endless forms most beautiful."

---

*Here and throughout this book, the term *environment* refers to other organisms as well as to the physical aspects of an organism's surroundings.

1809
Lamarck publishes his hypothesis of evolution.

1798
Malthus publishes "Essay on the Principle of Population."

1795
Hutton proposes his principle of gradualism.

1812
Cuvier publishes his extensive studies of vertebrate fossils.

1830
Lyell publishes *Principles of Geology*.

1858
While studying species in the Malay Archipelago, Wallace sends Darwin his hypothesis of natural selection.

1790

1809
Charles Darwin is born.

1831–36
Darwin travels around the world on HMS *Beagle*.

1844
Darwin writes his essay on descent with modification.

1859
On the Origin of Species is published.

1870

Marine iguana in the Galápagos Islands

▲ **Figure 22.2** **The intellectual context of Darwin's ideas.**

The Darwinian revolution challenged traditional views of a young Earth inhabited by unchanging species

What impelled Darwin to challenge the prevailing views about Earth and its life? Darwin's revolutionary proposal developed over time, influenced by the work of others and by his travels (**Figure 22.2**). As we'll see, his ideas had deep historical roots.

Scala Naturae and Classification of Species

Long before Darwin was born, several Greek philosophers suggested that life might have changed gradually over time. But one philosopher who greatly influenced early Western science, Aristotle (384–322 BCE), viewed species as fixed (un-

changing). Through his observations of nature, Aristotle recognized certain "affinities" among organisms. He concluded that life-forms could be arranged on a ladder, or scale, of increasing complexity, later called the *scala naturae* ("scale of nature"). Each form of life, perfect and permanent, had its allotted rung on this ladder.

These ideas were generally consistent with the Old Testament account of creation, which holds that species were individually designed by God and therefore perfect. In the 1700s, many scientists interpreted the often remarkable match of organisms to their environment as evidence that the Creator had designed each species for a particular purpose.

One such scientist was Carolus Linnaeus (1707–1778), a Swedish physician and botanist who sought to classify life's diversity, in his words, "for the greater glory of God." Linnaeus developed the two-part, or *binomial*, format for naming species (such as *Homo sapiens* for humans) that is still used today. In contrast to the linear hierarchy of the *scala naturae*, Linnaeus adopted a nested classification system, grouping similar species into increasingly general categories. For example, similar species are grouped in the same genus, similar genera (plural of genus) are grouped in the same family, and so on (see Figure 1.14).

Linnaeus did not ascribe the resemblances among species to evolutionary kinship, but rather to the pattern of their creation. A century later, however, Darwin argued that classification should be based on evolutionary relationships. He also noted that scientists using the Linnaean system often grouped organisms in ways that reflected those relationships.

Ideas About Change over Time

Darwin drew from the work of scientists studying **fossils**, the remains or traces of organisms from the past. Many fossils are found in sedimentary rocks formed from the sand and mud that settle to the bottom of seas, lakes, swamps, and other aquatic habitats **(Figure 22.3)**. New layers of sediment cover older ones and compress them into superimposed layers of rock called **strata** (singular, *stratum*). The fossils in a particular stratum provide a glimpse of some of the organisms that populated Earth at the time that layer formed. Later, erosion may carve through upper (younger) strata, revealing deeper (older) strata that had been buried.

Paleontology, the study of fossils, was developed in large part by French scientist Georges Cuvier (1769–1832). In examining strata near Paris, Cuvier noted that the older the stratum, the more dissimilar its fossils were to current life-forms. He also observed that from one layer to the next, some new species appeared while others disappeared. He inferred that extinctions must have been a common occurrence in the history of life. Yet Cuvier staunchly opposed the idea of evolution. To explain his observations, he advocated **catastrophism**, the principle that events in the past occurred suddenly and were caused by mechanisms different from those operating in the present. Cuvier speculated that each boundary between strata represented a catastrophe, such as a flood, that had destroyed many of the species living at that time. He proposed that these periodic catastrophes were usually confined to local regions, which were later repopulated by different species immigrating from other areas.

In contrast, other scientists suggested that profound change could take place through the cumulative effect of slow but continuous processes. In 1795, Scottish geologist James Hutton (1726–1797) proposed that Earth's geologic features could be explained by gradual mechanisms still operating today. For example, he suggested that valleys were often formed by rivers wearing through rocks and that rocks containing marine fossils were formed when sediments that had eroded from the land were carried by rivers to the sea, where they buried dead marine organisms. The leading geologist of Darwin's time, Charles Lyell (1797–1875), incorporated Hutton's thinking into his principle of **uniformitarianism**, which stated that mechanisms of change are constant over time. Lyell proposed that the same geologic processes are operating today as in the past, and at the same rate.

Hutton and Lyell's ideas strongly influenced Darwin's thinking. Darwin agreed that if geologic change results from slow, continuous actions rather than from sudden events, then Earth must be much older than the widely accepted age of a few thousand years. It would, for example, take a very long time for a river to carve a canyon by erosion. He later reasoned that perhaps similarly slow and subtle processes could produce substantial biological change. Darwin was not the first to apply the idea of gradual change to biological evolution, however.

Lamarck's Hypothesis of Evolution

During the 18th century, several naturalists (including Darwin's grandfather, Erasmus Darwin) suggested that life evolves as environments change. But only one of Charles Darwin's predecessors proposed a mechanism for *how* life changes over time: French biologist Jean-Baptiste de Lamarck (1744–1829). Alas, Lamarck is primarily remembered today *not* for his visionary recognition that evolutionary change explains patterns in fossils and the match of organisms to their environments, but for the incorrect mechanism he proposed to explain how evolution occurs.

Lamarck published his hypothesis in 1809, the year Darwin was born. By comparing living species with fossil forms, Lamarck had found what appeared to be several lines of descent, each a chronological series of older to younger fossils leading to a living species. He explained his findings using two principles that were widely accepted at the time. The first was *use and disuse*, the idea that parts of the body that are used

① Rivers carry sediment into aquatic habitats such as seas and swamps. Over time, sedimentary rock layers (strata) form under water. Some strata contain fossils.

② As water levels change and the bottom surface is pushed upward, the strata and their fossils are exposed.

Younger stratum with more recent fossils

Older stratum with older fossils

▲ **Figure 22.3 Formation of sedimentary strata with fossils.**

▲ **Figure 22.4 Acquired traits cannot be inherited.** This bonsai tree was "trained" to grow as a dwarf by pruning and shaping. However, seeds from this tree would produce offspring of normal size.

extensively become larger and stronger, while those that are not used deteriorate. Among many examples, he cited a giraffe stretching its neck to reach leaves on high branches. The second principle, *inheritance of acquired characteristics*, stated that an organism could pass these modifications to its offspring. Lamarck reasoned that the long, muscular neck of the living giraffe had evolved over many generations as giraffes stretched their necks ever higher.

Lamarck also thought that evolution happens because organisms have an innate drive to become more complex. Darwin rejected this idea, but he, too, thought that variation was introduced into the evolutionary process in part through inheritance of acquired characteristics. Today, however, our understanding of genetics refutes this mechanism: Experiments show that traits acquired by use during an individual's life are not inherited in the way proposed by Lamarck (Figure 22.4).

Lamarck was vilified in his own time, especially by Cuvier, who denied that species ever evolve. In retrospect, however, Lamarck did recognize that the match of organisms to their environments can be explained by gradual evolutionary change, and he did propose a testable explanation for how this change occurs.

CONCEPT CHECK 22.1

1. How did Hutton's and Lyell's ideas influence Darwin's thinking about evolution?
2. **MAKE CONNECTIONS** In Concept 1.3 (pp. 19–20), you read that scientific hypotheses must be testable and falsifiable. Applying these criteria, are Cuvier's explanation of the fossil record and Lamarck's hypothesis of evolution scientific? Explain your answer in each case.

For suggested answers, see Appendix A.

Descent with modification by natural selection explains the adaptations of organisms and the unity and diversity of life

As the 19th century dawned, it was generally thought that species had remained unchanged since their creation. A few clouds of doubt about the permanence of species were beginning to gather, but no one could have forecast the thundering storm just beyond the horizon. How did Charles Darwin become the lightning rod for a revolutionary view of life?

Darwin's Research

Charles Darwin (1809–1882) was born in Shrewsbury, in western England. Even as a boy, he had a consuming interest in nature. When he was not reading nature books, he was fishing, hunting, and collecting insects. Darwin's father, a physician, could see no future for his son as a naturalist and sent him to medical school in Edinburgh. But Charles found medicine boring and surgery before the days of anesthesia horrifying. He quit medical school and enrolled at Cambridge University, intending to become a clergyman. (At that time in England, many scholars of science belonged to the clergy.)

At Cambridge, Darwin became the protégé of the Reverend John Henslow, a botany professor. Soon after Darwin graduated, Henslow recommended him to Captain Robert FitzRoy, who was preparing the survey ship HMS *Beagle* for a long voyage around the world. Darwin would pay his own way and serve as a conversation partner to the young captain. FitzRoy, who was himself an accomplished scientist, accepted Darwin because he was a skilled naturalist and because they were of the same social class and close in age.

The Voyage of the Beagle

Darwin embarked from England on the *Beagle* in December 1831. The primary mission of the voyage was to chart poorly known stretches of the South American coastline. While the ship's crew surveyed the coast, Darwin spent most of his time on shore, observing and collecting thousands of South American plants and animals. He noted the characteristics of plants and animals that made them well suited to such diverse environments as the humid jungles of Brazil, the expansive grasslands of Argentina, and the towering peaks of the Andes.

Darwin observed that the plants and animals in temperate regions of South America more closely resembled species living in the South American tropics than species living in temperate regions of Europe. Furthermore, the fossils he found, though clearly different from living species, were distinctly South American in their resemblance to the living organisms of that continent.

Darwin in 1840, after his return from the voyage

HMS *Beagle* in port

The Galápagos Islands

- Pinta
- Genovesa
- Marchena
- Santiago
- Daphne Islands
- Fernandina
- Pinzón
- Isabela
- Santa Cruz
- Santa Fe
- San Cristobal
- Florenza
- Española

PACIFIC OCEAN

Equator

0 20 40
Kilometers

NORTH AMERICA

ATLANTIC OCEAN

Great Britain

EUROPE

AFRICA

Equator

SOUTH AMERICA

Chile

Andes Mtns.

Brazil

Argentina

Cape Horn

PACIFIC OCEAN

Cape of Good Hope

Malay Archipelago

PACIFIC OCEAN

AUSTRALIA

Tasmania

New Zealand

▲ Figure 22.5 **The voyage of HMS *Beagle*.**

Darwin also spent much time thinking about geology. Despite bouts of seasickness, he read Lyell's *Principles of Geology* while aboard the *Beagle*. He experienced geologic change first-hand when a violent earthquake rocked the coast of Chile, and he observed afterward that rocks along the coast had been thrust upward by several feet. Finding fossils of ocean organisms high in the Andes, Darwin inferred that the rocks containing the fossils must have been raised there by many similar earthquakes. These observations reinforced what he had learned from Lyell: The physical evidence did not support the traditional view that Earth was only a few thousand years old.

Darwin's interest in the geographic distribution of species was further stimulated by the *Beagle*'s stop at the Galápagos, a group of volcanic islands located near the equator about 900 km west of South America (**Figure 22.5**). Darwin was fascinated by the unusual organisms there. The birds he collected included the finches mentioned in Chapter 1 and several kinds of mocking-birds. These mockingbirds, though similar to each other, seemed to be different species. Some were unique to individual islands, while others lived on two or more adjacent islands. Furthermore, although the animals on the Galápagos resembled species living on the South American mainland, most of the Galápagos species were not known from anywhere else in the world. Darwin hypothesized that the Galápagos had been colonized by organisms that had strayed from South America and then diversified, giving rise to new species on the various islands.

Darwin's Focus on Adaptation

During the voyage of the *Beagle*, Darwin observed many examples of **adaptations**, inherited characteristics of organisms that enhance their survival and reproduction in specific environments. Later, as he reassessed his observations, he began to perceive adaptation to the environment and the origin of new species as closely related processes. Could a new species arise from an ancestral form by the gradual accumulation of adaptations to a different environment? From studies made years after Darwin's voyage, biologists have concluded that this is indeed what happened to the diverse group of Galápagos finches (see Figure 1.22). The finches' various beaks and behaviors are adapted to the specific foods available on their home islands (**Figure 22.6**). Darwin realized that explaining such adaptations was essential to understanding evolution. As we'll explore further, his explanation of how adaptations arise centered on **natural selection**, a process in which individuals that have certain inherited traits tend to survive and reproduce at higher rates than other individuals *because of* those traits.

By the early 1840s, Darwin had worked out the major features of his hypothesis. He set these ideas on paper in 1844, when he wrote a long essay on descent with modification and its underlying mechanism, natural selection. Yet he was still reluctant to publish his ideas, apparently because he anticipated the uproar they would cause. During this time, Darwin continued to compile evidence in support of his hypothesis. By the mid-1850s, he had described his ideas to Lyell and a few others. Lyell, who was not yet convinced of evolution, nevertheless urged Darwin to publish on the subject before someone else came to the same conclusions and published first.

In June 1858, Lyell's prediction came true. Darwin received a manuscript from Alfred Russel Wallace (1823–1913), a British naturalist working in the South Pacific islands of the Malay

(a) Cactus-eater. The long, sharp beak of the cactus ground finch (*Geospiza scandens*) helps it tear and eat cactus flowers and pulp.

(b) Insect-eater. The green warbler finch (*Certhidea olivacea*) uses its narrow, pointed beak to grasp insects.

(c) Seed-eater. The large ground finch (*Geospiza magnirostris*) has a large beak adapted for cracking seeds that fall from plants to the ground.

▲ **Figure 22.6 Three examples of beak variation in Galápagos finches.** The Galápagos Islands are home to more than a dozen species of closely related finches, some found only on a single island. The most striking differences among them are their beaks, which are adapted for specific diets.

MAKE CONNECTIONS *Review Figure 1.22 (p. 17). To which of the other two species shown above is the cactus-eater more closely related (that is, with which does it share a more recent common ancestor)?*

Archipelago (see Figure 22.2). Wallace had developed a hypothesis of natural selection nearly identical to Darwin's. He asked Darwin to evaluate his paper and forward it to Lyell if it merited publication. Darwin complied, writing to Lyell: "Your words have come true with a vengeance. . . . I never saw a more striking coincidence . . . so all my originality, whatever it may amount to, will be smashed." On July 1, 1858, Lyell and a colleague presented Wallace's paper, along with extracts from Darwin's unpublished 1844 essay, to the Linnean Society of London. Darwin quickly finished his book, titled *On the Origin of Species by Means of Natural Selection* (commonly referred to as *The Origin of Species*), and published it the next year. Although Wallace had submitted his ideas for publication first, he admired Darwin and thought that Darwin had developed the idea of natural selection so extensively that he should be known as its main architect.

Within a decade, Darwin's book and its proponents had convinced most scientists that life's diversity is the product of evolution. Darwin succeeded where previous evolutionists had failed, mainly by presenting a plausible scientific mechanism with immaculate logic and an avalanche of evidence.

The Origin of Species

In his book, Darwin amassed evidence that descent with modification by natural selection explains the three broad observations about nature listed in the Overview: the unity of life, the diversity of life, and the match between organisms and their environments.

Descent with Modification

In the first edition of *The Origin of Species*, Darwin never used the word *evolution* (although the final word of the book is

"evolved"). Rather, he discussed *descent with modification*, a phrase that summarized his view of life. Organisms share many characteristics, leading Darwin to perceive unity in life. He attributed the unity of life to the descent of all organisms from an ancestor that lived in the remote past. He also thought that as the descendants of that ancestral organism lived in various habitats over millions of years, they accumulated diverse modifications, or adaptations, that fit them to specific ways of life. Darwin reasoned that over long periods of time, descent with modification eventually led to the rich diversity of life we see today.

Darwin viewed the history of life as a tree, with multiple branchings from a common trunk out to the tips of the youngest twigs **(Figure 22.7)**. The tips of the twigs represent the diversity of organisms living in the present. Each fork of the tree represents the most recent common ancestor of all the lines of evolution that subsequently branch from that point. As an example, consider the three living species of elephants: the Asian elephant (*Elephas maximus*) and African elephants

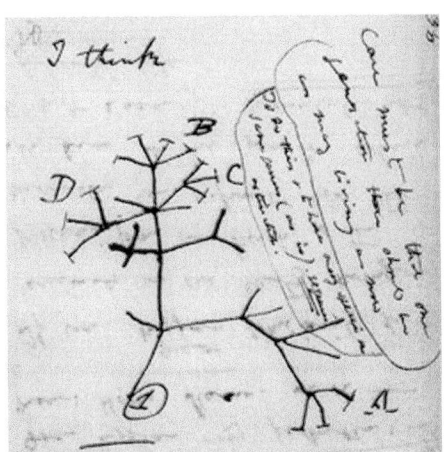

◀ **Figure 22.7 "I think. . ."** In this 1837 sketch, Darwin envisioned the branching pattern of evolution.

(*Loxodonta africana* and *L. cyclotis*). These closely related species are very similar because they shared the same line of descent until a relatively recent split from their common ancestor, as shown in the tree diagram in **Figure 22.8**. Note that seven lineages related to elephants have become extinct over the past 32 million years. As a result, there are no living species that fill the gap between the elephants and their nearest relatives today, the hyraxes and manatees. Such extinctions are not uncommon. In fact, many evolutionary branches, even some major ones, are dead ends: Scientists estimate that over 99% of all species that have ever lived are now extinct. As in Figure 22.8, fossils of extinct species can document the divergence of present-day groups by "filling in" gaps between them.

In his efforts at classification, Linnaeus had realized that some organisms resemble each other more closely than others, but he had not linked these resemblances to evolution. Nonetheless, because he had recognized that the great diversity of organisms could be organized into "groups subordinate to groups" (Darwin's phrase), Linnaeus's system meshed well with Darwin's hypothesis. To Darwin, the Linnaean hierarchy reflected the branching history of life, with organisms at the various levels related through descent from common ancestors.

Artificial Selection, Natural Selection, and Adaptation

Darwin proposed the mechanism of natural selection to explain the observable patterns of evolution. He crafted his argument carefully, to persuade even the most skeptical readers. First he discussed familiar examples of selective breeding of domesticated plants and animals. Humans have modified other species over many generations by selecting and breeding individuals that possess desired traits, a process called **artificial selection** (**Figure 22.9**). As a result of artificial selection, crops, livestock animals, and pets often bear little resemblance to their wild ancestors.

Darwin then argued that a similar process occurs in nature. He based his argument on two observations, from which he drew two inferences:

Observation #1: Members of a population often vary in their inherited traits (**Figure 22.10**).

Observation #2: All species can produce more offspring than their environment can support (**Figure 22.11**), and many of these offspring fail to survive and reproduce.

Inference #1: Individuals whose inherited traits give them a higher probability of surviving and reproducing in a given environment tend to leave more offspring than other individuals.

Inference #2: This unequal ability of individuals to survive and reproduce will lead to the accumulation of favorable traits in the population over generations.

Darwin saw an important connection between natural selection and the

▲ **Figure 22.8 Descent with modification.** This evolutionary tree of elephants and their relatives is based mainly on fossils—their anatomy, order of appearance in strata, and geographic distribution. Note that most branches of descent ended in extinction (denoted by the dagger symbol †). (Time line not to scale.)

? *Based on the tree shown here, approximately when did the most recent ancestor shared by Mammuthus (woolly mammoths), Asian elephants, and African elephants live?*

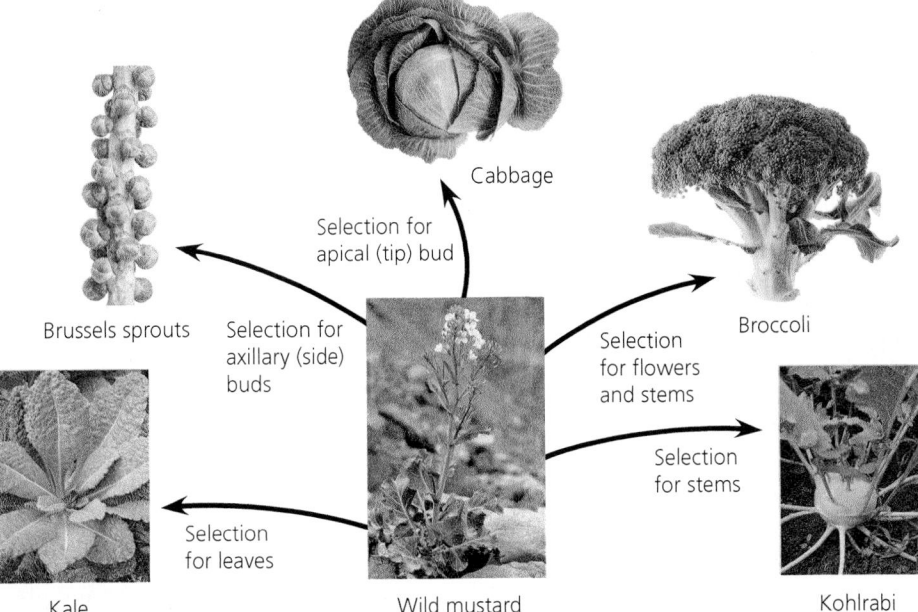

▶ Figure 22.9 **Artificial selection.** These different vegetables have all been selected from one species of wild mustard. By selecting variations in different parts of the plant, breeders have obtained these divergent results.

Cabbage

Selection for apical (tip) bud

Brussels sprouts

Selection for axillary (side) buds

Selection for flowers and stems

Broccoli

Selection for stems

Selection for leaves

Kale

Wild mustard

Kohlrabi

▲ Figure 22.10 **Variation in a population.** Individuals in this population of Asian ladybird beetles vary in color and spot pattern. Natural selection may act on these variations only if (1) they are heritable and (2) they affect the beetles' ability to survive and reproduce.

▶ Figure 22.11 **Overproduction of offspring.** A single puffball fungus can produce billions of offspring. If all of these offspring and their descendants survived to maturity, they would carpet the surrounding land surface.

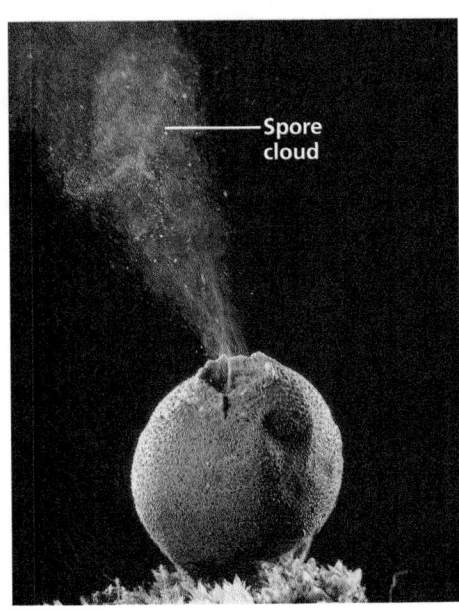

Spore cloud

capacity of organisms to "overreproduce." He began to make this connection after reading an essay by economist Thomas Malthus, who contended that much of human suffering—disease, famine, and war—was the inescapable consequence of the human population's potential to increase faster than food supplies and other resources. Darwin realized that the capacity to overreproduce was characteristic of all species. Of the many eggs laid, young born, and seeds spread, only a tiny fraction complete their development and leave offspring of their own. The rest are eaten, starved, diseased, unmated, or unable to tolerate physical conditions of the environment such as salinity or temperature.

An organism's heritable traits can influence not only its own performance, but also how well its offspring cope with environmental challenges. For example, an organism might have a trait that gives its offspring an advantage in escaping predators, obtaining food, or tolerating physical conditions. When such advantages increase the number of offspring that survive and reproduce, the traits that are favored will likely appear at a greater frequency in the next generation. Thus, over time, natural selection resulting from factors such as predators, lack of food, or adverse physical conditions can lead to an increase in the proportion of favorable traits in a population.

How rapidly do such changes occur? Darwin reasoned that if artificial selection can bring about dramatic change in a relatively short period of time, then natural selection should be capable of substantial modification of species over many hundreds of generations. Even if the advantages of some heritable traits over others are slight, the advantageous variations will gradually accumulate in the population, and less favorable variations will diminish. Over time, this process will increase the frequency of individuals with favorable adaptations and hence refine the match between organisms and their environment (see Figure 1.20).

Natural Selection: A Summary

Let's now recap the main ideas of natural selection:

- Natural selection is a process in which individuals that have certain heritable traits survive and reproduce at a higher rate than other individuals because of those traits.
- Over time, natural selection can increase the match between organisms and their environment (Figure 22.12).
- If an environment changes, or if individuals move to a new environment, natural selection may result in adaptation to these new conditions, sometimes giving rise to new species.

One subtle but important point is that although natural selection occurs through interactions between individual organisms and their environment, *individuals do not evolve*. Rather, it is the population that evolves over time.

A second key point is that natural selection can amplify or diminish only those heritable traits that differ among the individuals in a population. Thus, even if a trait is heritable, if all the individuals in a population are genetically identical for that trait, evolution by natural selection cannot occur.

Third, remember that environmental factors vary from place to place and over time. A trait that is favorable in one place or time may be useless—or even detrimental—in other places or times. Natural selection is always operating, but which traits are favored depends on the context in which a species lives and mates.

Next, we'll survey the wide range of observations that support a Darwinian view of evolution by natural selection.

CONCEPT CHECK 22.2

1. How does the concept of descent with modification explain both the unity and diversity of life?
2. **WHAT IF?** If you discovered a fossil of an extinct mammal that lived high in the Andes, would you predict that it would more closely resemble present-day mammals from South American jungles or present-day mammals that live high in African mountains? Explain.
3. **MAKE CONNECTIONS** Review Figures 14.4 and 14.6 (pp. 265 and 267) on the relationship between genotype and phenotype. In a particular pea population, suppose that flowers with the white phenotype are favored by natural selection. Predict what would happen over time to the frequency of the p allele in the population, and explain your reasoning.

For suggested answers, see Appendix A.

CONCEPT 22.3

Evolution is supported by an overwhelming amount of scientific evidence

In *The Origin of Species*, Darwin marshaled a broad range of evidence to support the concept of descent with modification. Still—as he readily acknowledged—there were instances in which key evidence was lacking. For example, Darwin referred to the origin of flowering plants as an "abominable mystery," and he lamented the lack of fossils showing how earlier groups of organisms gave rise to new groups.

In the last 150 years, new discoveries have filled many of the gaps that Darwin identified. The origin of flowering plants, for example, is much better understood (see Chapter 30), and many fossils have been discovered that signify the origin of new groups of organisms (see Chapter 25). In this section, we'll consider four types of data that document the pattern of evolution and illuminate the processes by which it occurs: direct observations of evolution, homology, the fossil record, and biogeography.

Direct Observations of Evolutionary Change

Biologists have documented evolutionary change in thousands of scientific studies. We'll examine many such studies throughout this unit, but let's look at two examples here.

(a) A flower mantid in Malaysia

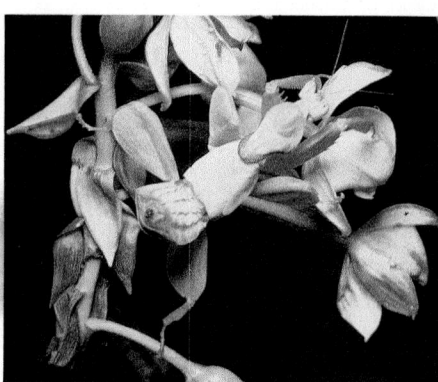

(b) A leaf mantid in Borneo

▲ **Figure 22.12 Camouflage as an example of evolutionary adaptation.** Related species of the insects called mantids have diverse shapes and colors that evolved in different environments.

? *Explain how these mantids demonstrate the three key observations about life introduced in this chapter's Overview: the match between organisms and their environments, unity, and diversity.*

Natural Selection in Response to Introduced Plant Species

Animals that eat plants, called herbivores, often have adaptations that help them feed efficiently on their primary food sources. What happens when herbivores begin to feed on a plant species with different characteristics than their usual food source?

An opportunity to study this question in nature is provided by soapberry bugs, which use their "beak," a hollow, needle-like mouthpart, to feed on seeds located within the fruits of various plants. In southern Florida, the soapberry bug *Jadera haematoloma* feeds on the seeds of a native plant, the balloon vine (*Cardiospermum corindum*). In central Florida, however, balloon vines have become rare. Instead, soapberry bugs in that region now feed on goldenrain tree (*Koelreuteria elegans*), a species recently introduced from Asia.

Soapberry bugs feed most effectively when their beak length closely matches the depth at which the seeds are found within the fruit. Goldenrain tree fruit consists of three flat lobes, and its seeds are much closer to the fruit surface than the seeds of the plump, round native balloon vine fruit. Researchers at the University of Utah predicted that in populations that feed on goldenrain tree, natural selection would result in beaks that are *shorter* than those in populations that feed on balloon vine **(Figure 22.13)**. Indeed, beak lengths are shorter in the populations that feed on goldenrain tree.

Researchers have also studied beak length evolution in soapberry bug populations that feed on plants introduced to Louisiana, Oklahoma, and Australia. In each of these locations, the fruit of the introduced plants is larger than the fruit of the native plant. Thus, in populations feeding on introduced species in these regions, the researchers predicted that natural selection would result in the evolution of *longer* beak length. Again, data collected in field studies upheld this prediction.

The adaptation observed in these soapberry bug populations had important consequences: In Australia, for example, the increase in beak length nearly doubled the success with which soapberry bugs could eat the seeds of the introduced species. Furthermore, since historical data show that the goldenrain tree reached central Florida just 35 years before the scientific studies were initiated, the results demonstrate that natural selection can cause rapid evolution in a wild population.

The Evolution of Drug-Resistant Bacteria

An example of ongoing natural selection that dramatically affects humans is the evolution of drug-resistant pathogens (disease-causing organisms and viruses). This is a particular problem with bacteria and viruses because resistant strains of these pathogens can proliferate very quickly.

Consider the evolution of drug resistance in the bacterium *Staphylococcus aureus*. About one in three people harbor this species on their skin or in their nasal passages with no negative effects. However, certain genetic varieties (strains) of this species, known as methicillin-resistant *S. aureus* (MRSA), are

---

▼ **Figure 22.13** | **INQUIRY**

Can a change in a population's food source result in evolution by natural selection?

FIELD STUDY Soapberry bugs (*Jadera haematoloma*) feed most effectively when the length of their "beak" closely matches the depth within the fruits of the seeds they eat. Scott Carroll and his colleagues measured beak lengths in soapberry bug populations in southern Florida feeding on the native balloon vine. They also measured beak lengths in populations in central Florida feeding on the introduced goldenrain tree, which has a flatter fruit shape than the balloon vine. The researchers then compared the measurements to those of museum specimens collected in the two areas before the goldenrain tree was introduced.

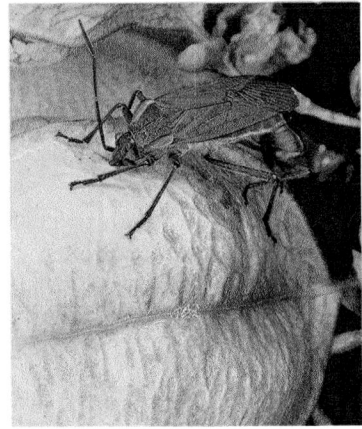

Soapberry bug with beak inserted in balloon vine fruit

RESULTS Beak lengths were shorter in populations feeding on the introduced species than in populations feeding on the native species, in which the seeds are buried more deeply. The average beak length in museum specimens from each population (indicated by red arrows) was similar to beak lengths in populations feeding on native species.

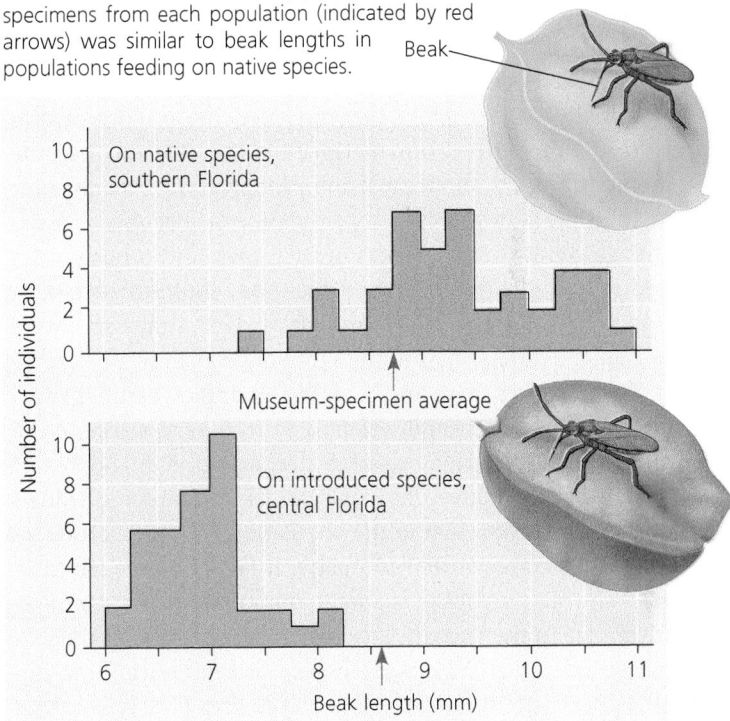

CONCLUSION Museum specimens and contemporary data suggest that a change in the size of the soapberry bug's food source can result in evolution by natural selection for matching beak size.

SOURCE S. P. Carroll and C. Boyd, Host race radiation in the soapberry bug: natural history with the history, *Evolution* 46: 1052–1069 (1992).

WHAT IF? When soapberry bug eggs from a population fed on balloon vine fruits were reared on goldenrain tree fruits (or vice versa), the beak lengths of the adult insects matched those in the population from which the eggs were obtained. Interpret these results.

formidable pathogens. The past decade has seen an alarming increase in virulent forms of MRSA such as clone USA300, a strain that can cause "flesh-eating disease" and potentially fatal infections (Figure 22.14). How did clone USA300 and other strains of MRSA become so dangerous?

The story begins in 1943, when penicillin became the first widely used antibiotic. Since then, penicillin and other antibiotics have saved millions of lives. However, by 1945, more than 20% of the *S. aureus* strains seen in hospitals were already resistant to penicillin. These bacteria had an enzyme, penicillinase, that could destroy penicillin. Researchers responded by developing antibiotics that were not destroyed by penicillinase, but some *S. aureus* populations developed resistance to each new drug within a few years.

In 1959, doctors began using the powerful antibiotic methicillin, but within two years, methicillin-resistant strains of *S. aureus* appeared. How did these resistant strains emerge? Methicillin works by deactivating a protein that bacteria use to synthesize their cell walls. However, *S. aureus* populations exhibited variations in how strongly their members were affected by the drug. In particular, some individuals were able to synthesize their cell walls using a different protein that was not affected by methicillin. These individuals survived the methicillin treatments and reproduced at higher rates than did other individuals. Over time, these resistant individuals became increasingly common, leading to the spread of MRSA.

Initially, MRSA could be controlled by antibiotics that worked differently from methicillin. But this has become increasingly difficult because some MRSA strains are resistant to multiple antibiotics—probably because bacteria can exchange genes with members of their own and other species (see Figure 27.13). Thus, the present-day multidrug-resistant strains may have emerged over time as MRSA strains that were resistant to different antibiotics exchanged genes.

The soapberry bug and *S. aureus* examples highlight two key points about natural selection. First, natural selection is a process of editing, not a creative mechanism. A drug does not *create* resistant pathogens; it *selects for* resistant individuals that are already present in the population. Second, natural selection depends on time and place. It favors those characteristics in a genetically variable population that provide advantage in the current, local environment. What is beneficial in one situation may be useless or even harmful in another. Beak lengths arise that match the size of the typical fruit eaten by a particular soapberry bug population. However, a beak length suitable for fruit of one size can be disadvantageous when the bug is feeding on fruit of another size.

Homology

A second type of evidence for evolution comes from analyzing similarities among different organisms. As we've discussed, evolution is a process of descent with modification: Characteristics present in an ancestral organism are altered (by natural

▼ Figure 22.14

IMPACT

The Rise of MRSA

Most methicillin-resistant *Staphylococcus aureus* (MRSA) infections are caused by recently appearing strains such as clone USA300. Resistant to multiple antibiotics and highly contagious, this strain and its close relatives can cause lethal infections of the skin, lungs, and blood. Researchers have identified key areas of the USA300 genome that code for its particularly virulent properties.

The circular chromosome of clone USA300 has been sequenced and contains 2,872,769 base pairs of DNA.

The highlighted regions contain genes that increase the strain's virulence (see the key).

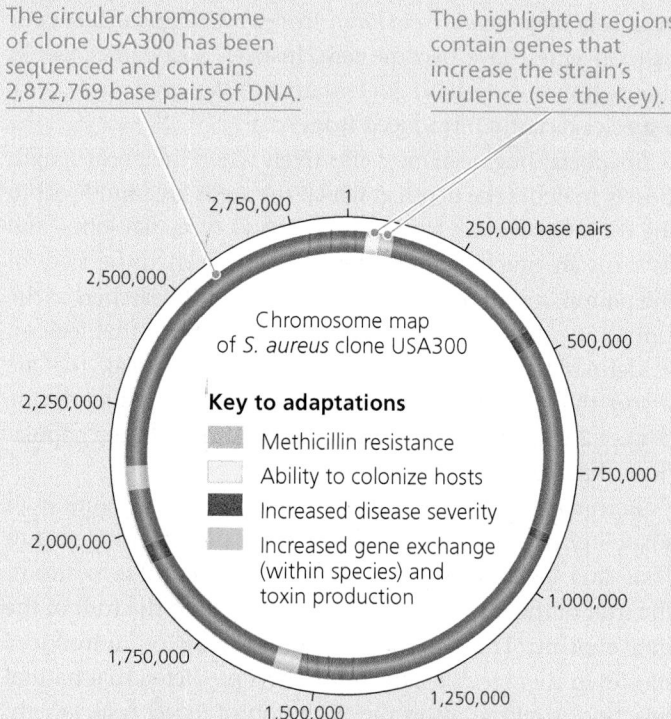

Chromosome map of *S. aureus* clone USA300

Key to adaptations

- Methicillin resistance
- Ability to colonize hosts
- Increased disease severity
- Increased gene exchange (within species) and toxin production

WHY IT MATTERS MRSA infections have proliferated dramatically in the past few decades, and the annual death toll in the United States is in the tens of thousands. There is grave concern about the continuing evolution of drug resistance and the resulting difficulty of treating MRSA infections. Ongoing studies of how MRSA strains colonize their hosts and cause disease may help scientists develop drugs to combat MRSA.

FURTHER READING General information about MRSA can be found on the Centers for Disease Control and Prevention (CDC) website (www.cdc.gov/mrsa) and in G. Taubes, The bacteria fight back, *Science* 321:356–361 (2008).

WHAT IF? Efforts are underway to develop drugs that target *S. aureus* specifically and to develop drugs that slow the growth of MRSA but do not kill it. Based on how natural selection works and on the fact that bacterial species can exchange genes, explain why each of these strategies might be effective.

selection) in its descendants over time as they face different environmental conditions. As a result, related species can have characteristics that have an underlying similarity yet function differently. Similarity resulting from common ancestry is known as **homology**. As this section will explain, an understanding of homology can be used to make testable predictions and explain observations that are otherwise puzzling.

Humerus

Radius
Ulna

Carpals
Metacarpals
Phalanges

Human   Cat   Whale   Bat

▲ Figure 22.15 **Mammalian forelimbs: homologous structures.** Even though they have become adapted for different functions, the forelimbs of all mammals are constructed from the same basic skeletal elements: one large bone (purple), attached to two smaller bones (orange and tan), attached to several small bones (gold), attached to several metacarpals (green), attached to approximately five digits, each of which is composed of phalanges (blue).

Anatomical and Molecular Homologies

The view of evolution as a remodeling process leads to the prediction that closely related species should share similar features—and they do. Of course, closely related species share the features used to determine their relationship, but they also share many other features. Some of these shared features make little sense except in the context of evolution. For example, the forelimbs of all mammals, including humans, cats, whales, and bats, show the same arrangement of bones from the shoulder to the tips of the digits, even though these appendages have very different functions: lifting, walking, swimming, and flying (Figure 22.15). Such striking anatomical resemblances would be highly unlikely if these structures had arisen anew in each species. Rather, the underlying skeletons of the arms, forelegs, flippers, and wings of different mammals are **homologous structures** that represent variations on a structural theme that was present in their common ancestor.

Comparing early stages of development in different animal species reveals additional anatomical homologies not visible in adult organisms. For example, at some point in their development, all vertebrate embryos have a tail located posterior to (behind) the anus, as well as structures called pharyngeal (throat) pouches (Figure 22.16). These homologous throat pouches ultimately develop into structures with very different functions, such as gills in fishes and parts of the ears and throat in humans and other mammals.

Some of the most intriguing homologies concern "leftover" structures of marginal, if any, importance to the organism. These **vestigial structures** are remnants of features that served a function in the organism's ancestors. For instance, the skeletons of some snakes retain vestiges of the pelvis and leg bones of walking ancestors. Another example is provided by eye remnants that are buried under scales in blind species of cave fishes. We would not expect to see these vestig-

ial structures if snakes and blind cave fishes had origins separate from other vertebrate animals.

Biologists also observe similarities among organisms at the molecular level. All forms of life use the same genetic language of DNA and RNA, and the genetic code is essentially universal. Thus, it is likely that all species descended from common ancestors that used this code. But molecular homologies go beyond a shared code. For example, organisms as dissimilar as humans and bacteria share genes inherited from a very distant common ancestor. Some of these homologous genes have acquired new functions, while others, such as those coding for the ribosomal subunits used in protein synthesis (see Figure 17.17), have retained their original functions. It is also common for organisms to have genes that have lost their function, even though the homologous genes in related species may be fully functional. Like vestigial structures, it appears that such inactive "pseudogenes" may be present simply because a common ancestor had them.

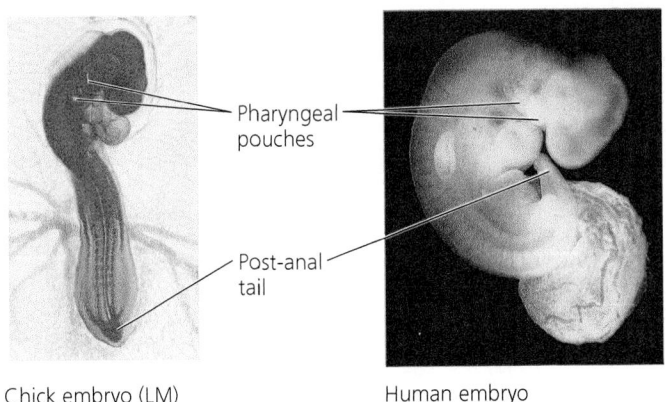

Pharyngeal pouches

Post-anal tail

Chick embryo (LM)   Human embryo

▲ **Figure 22.16 Anatomical similarities in vertebrate embryos.** At some stage in their embryonic development, all vertebrates have a tail located posterior to the anus (referred to as a post-anal tail), as well as pharyngeal (throat) pouches. Descent from a common ancestor can explain such similarities.

Homologies and "Tree Thinking"

Some homologous characteristics, such as the genetic code, are shared by all species because they date to the deep ancestral past. In contrast, homologous characteristics that evolved more recently are shared only within smaller groups of organisms. Consider the *tetrapods* (from the Greek *tetra*, four, and *pod*, foot), the vertebrate group that consists of amphibians, mammals, and reptiles (including birds—see Figure 22.17). All tetrapods have limbs with digits (see Figure 22.15), whereas other vertebrates do not. Thus, homologous characteristics form a nested pattern: All life shares the deepest layer, and each successive smaller group adds its own homologies to those it shares with larger groups. This nested pattern is exactly what we would expect to result from descent with modification from a common ancestor.

Biologists often represent the pattern of descent from common ancestors and the resulting homologies with an **evolutionary tree**, a diagram that reflects evolutionary relationships among groups of organisms. We will explore in detail how evolutionary trees are constructed in Chapter 26, but for now, let's consider how we can interpret and use such trees.

Figure 22.17 is an evolutionary tree of tetrapods and their closest living relatives, the lungfishes. In this diagram, each branch point represents the common ancestor of all species that descended from it. For example, lungfishes and all tetrapods descended from ancestor ❶, whereas mammals, lizards and snakes, crocodiles, and birds all descended from ancestor ❸. As expected, the three homologies shown on the tree—limbs with digits, the amnion (a protective embryonic membrane), and feathers—form a nested pattern. Limbs with digits were present in common ancestor ❷ and hence are found in all of the descendants of that ancestor (the tetrapods). The amnion was present only in ancestor ❸ and hence is shared only by some tetrapods (mammals and reptiles). Feathers were present only in common ancestor ❻ and hence are found only in birds.

To explore "tree thinking" further, note that in Figure 22.17, mammals are positioned closer to amphibians than to birds. As a result, you might conclude that mammals are more closely related to amphibians than they are to birds. However, mammals are actually more closely related to birds than to amphibians because mammals and birds share a more recent common ancestor (ancestor ❸) than do mammals and amphibians (ancestor ❷). Ancestor ❷ is also the most recent common ancestor of birds and amphibians, making mammals and birds equally related to amphibians. Finally, note that the tree in Figure 22.17 shows the relative timing of evolutionary events but not their actual dates. Thus, we can conclude that ancestor ❷ lived before ancestor ❸, but we do not know when that was.

Evolutionary trees are hypotheses that summarize our current understanding of patterns of descent. Our confidence in these relationships, as with any hypothesis, depends on the strength of the supporting data. In the case of Figure 22.17, the tree is supported by a variety of independent data sets, including both anatomical and DNA sequence data. As a result, biologists feel confident that it accurately reflects evolutionary history. As you will read in Chapter 26, scientists can use such well-supported evolutionary trees to make specific and sometimes surprising predictions about organisms.

A Different Cause of Resemblance: Convergent Evolution

Although organisms that are closely related share characteristics because of common descent, distantly related organisms can resemble one another for a different reason: **convergent evolution**, the independent evolution of similar features in different lineages. Consider marsupial mammals, many of which live in Australia. Marsupials are distinct from another group of mammals—the eutherians—few of which live in Australia. (Eutherians complete their embryonic development in the uterus, whereas marsupials

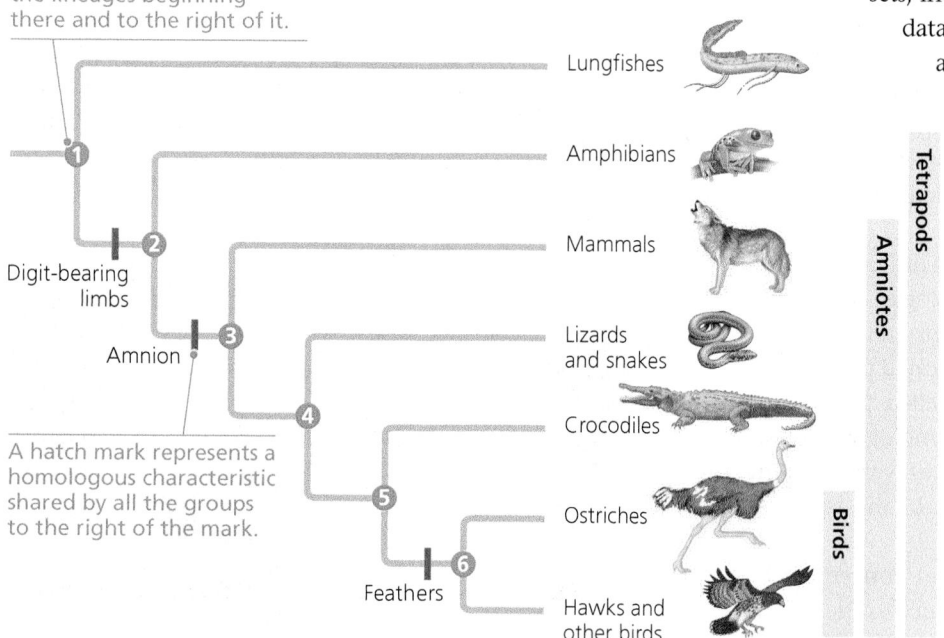

Each branch point represents the common ancestor of the lineages beginning there and to the right of it.

Digit-bearing limbs

Amnion

A hatch mark represents a homologous characteristic shared by all the groups to the right of the mark.

Feathers

Lungfishes
Amphibians
Mammals
Lizards and snakes
Crocodiles
Ostriches
Hawks and other birds

Tetrapods
Amniotes
Birds

▲ **Figure 22.17 Tree thinking: information provided in an evolutionary tree.** This evolutionary tree for tetrapods and their closest living relatives, the lungfishes, is based on anatomical and DNA sequence data. The purple bars indicate the origin of three important homologies, each of which evolved only once. Birds are nested within and evolved from reptiles; hence, the group of organisms called "reptiles" technically includes birds.

? *Are crocodiles more closely related to lizards or birds? Explain your answer.*

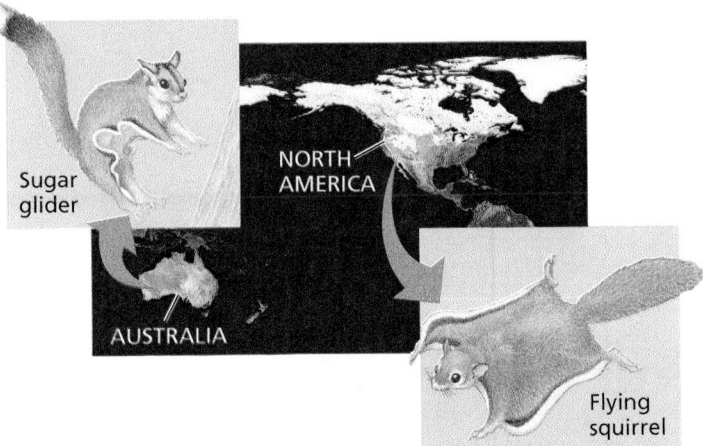

▲ **Figure 22.18 Convergent evolution.** The ability to glide through the air evolved independently in these two distantly related mammals.

are born as embryos and complete their development in an external pouch.) Some Australian marsupials have eutherian look-alikes with superficially similar adaptations. For instance, a forest-dwelling Australian marsupial called the sugar glider is superficially very similar to flying squirrels, gliding eutherians that live in North American forests (Figure 22.18). But the sugar glider has many other characteristics that make it a marsupial, much more closely related to kangaroos and other Australian marsupials than to flying squirrels or other eutherians. Once again, our understanding of evolution can explain these observations. Although they evolved independently from different ancestors, these two mammals have adapted to similar environments in similar ways. In such examples in which species share features because of convergent evolution, the resemblance is said to be **analogous**, not homologous. Analogous features share similar function, but not common ancestry, while homologous features share common ancestry, but not necessarily similar function.

The Fossil Record

A third type of evidence for evolution comes from fossils. As Chapter 25 discusses in more detail, the fossil record documents the pattern of evolution, showing that past organisms differed from present-day organisms and that many species have become extinct. Fossils also show the evolutionary changes that have occurred in various groups of organisms. To give one of hundreds of possible examples, researchers found that the pelvic bone in fossil stickleback fish became greatly reduced in size over time in a number of different lakes. The consistent nature of this change sug-

gests that the reduction in the size of the pelvic bone may have been driven by natural selection.

Fossils can also shed light on the origins of new groups of organisms. An example is the fossil record of cetaceans, the mammalian order that includes whales, dolphins, and porpoises. Some of these fossils provided an unexpected line of support for a hypothesis based on DNA data: that cetaceans are closely related to even-toed ungulates, a group that includes deer, pigs, camels, and cows (Figure 22.19). What else can fossils tell us about cetacean origins? The earliest cetaceans lived 50–60 million years ago. The fossil record indicates that prior to that time, most mammals were terrestrial. Although scientists had long realized that whales and other cetaceans originated from land mammals, few fossils had been found that revealed how cetacean limb structure had changed over time, leading eventually to the loss of hind limbs and the development of flippers and tail flukes. In the past few decades, however, a series of remarkable fossils have been discovered in Pakistan, Egypt, and North America. These fossils document steps in the transition from life on land to life in the sea, filling in some of the gaps between ancestral and living cetaceans (Figure 22.20, on the next page).

Collectively, the recent fossil discoveries document the formation of new species and the origin of a major new group of mammals, the cetaceans. These discoveries also show that cetaceans and their close living relatives (hippopotamuses, pigs, deer, and

▲ *Diacodexis*, an early even-toed ungulate

other even-toed ungulates) are much more different from each other than were *Pakicetus* and early even-toed ungulates, such as *Diacodexis*. Similar patterns are seen in fossils documenting the origins of other major new groups of organisms, including

Most mammals | **Cetaceans and even-toed ungulates**

(a) *Canis* (dog) (b) *Pakicetus* (c) *Sus* (pig) (d) *Odocoileus* (deer)

▲ **Figure 22.19 Ankle bones: one piece of the puzzle.** Comparing fossils and present-day examples of the astragalus (a type of ankle bone) provides one line of evidence that cetaceans are closely related to even-toed ungulates. **(a)** In most mammals, the astragalus is shaped like that of a dog, with a double hump on one end (indicated by the red arrows) but not at the opposite end (blue arrow). **(b)** Fossils show that the early cetacean *Pakicetus* had an astragalus with double humps at both ends, a unique shape that is otherwise found only in even-toed ungulates, as shown here for **(c)** a pig and **(d)** a deer.

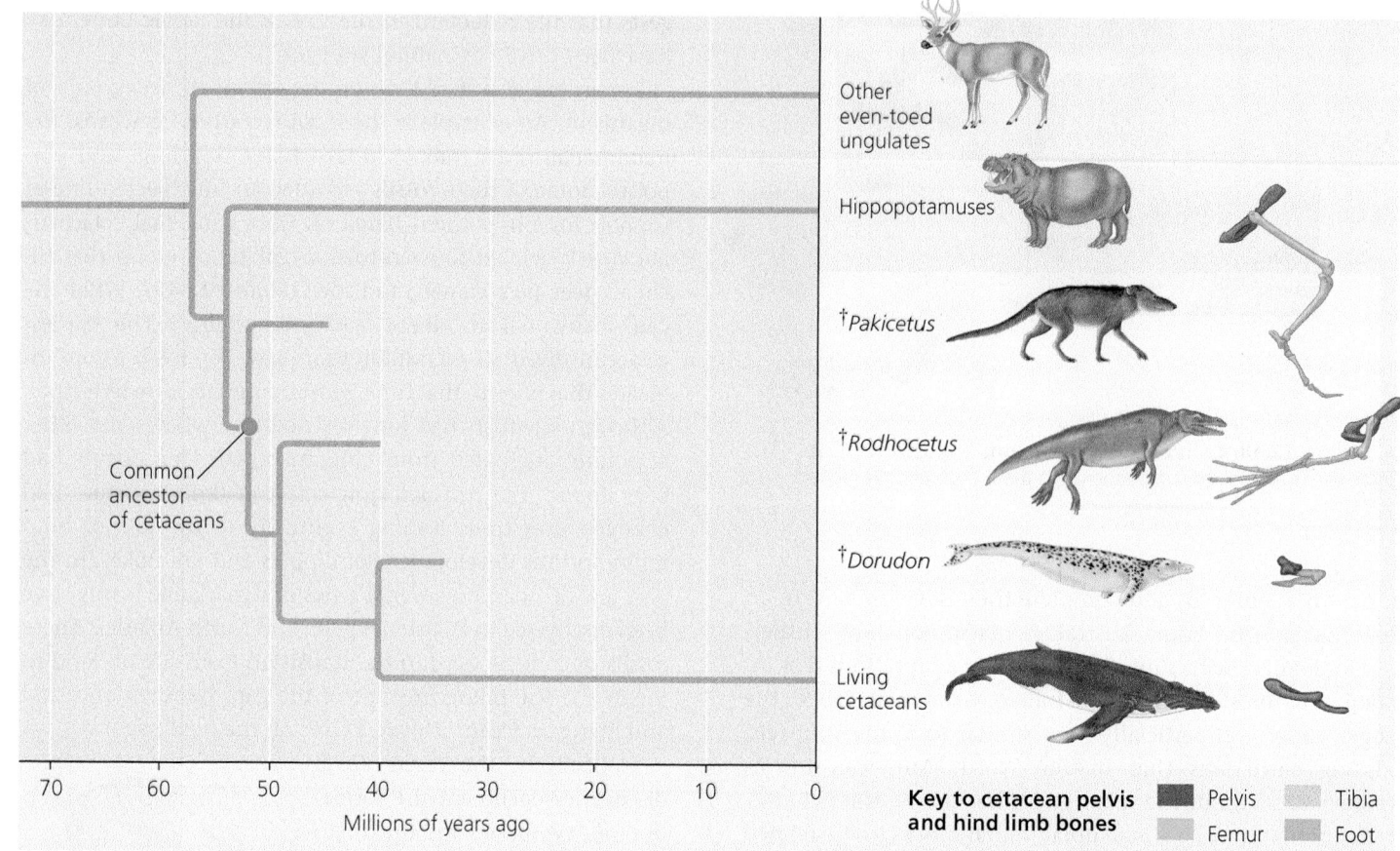

70   60   50   40   30   20   10   0
Millions of years ago

Key to cetacean pelvis and hind limb bones   ■ Pelvis   □ Tibia   □ Femur   ■ Foot

▲ **Figure 22.20 The transition to life in the sea.** Multiple lines of evidence support the hypothesis that cetaceans evolved from terrestrial mammals. Fossils document the reduction over time in the pelvis and hind limb bones of extinct cetacean ancestors, including *Pakicetus, Rodhocetus,* and *Dorudon.* DNA sequence data support the hypothesis that cetaceans are most closely related to hippopotamuses, even-toed ungulates.

? *Which happened first during the evolution of cetaceans: changes in hind limb structure or the origin of tail flukes?*

mammals (see Chapter 25), flowering plants (see Chapter 30), and tetrapods (see Chapter 34). In each of these cases, the fossil record shows that over time, descent with modification produced increasingly large differences among related groups of organisms, ultimately resulting in the diversity of life we see today.

Biogeography

A fourth type of evidence for evolution comes from **biogeography**, the geographic distribution of species. The geographic distribution of organisms is influenced by many factors, including *continental drift*, the slow movement of Earth's continents over time. About 250 million years ago, these movements united all of Earth's landmasses into a single large continent called **Pangaea** (see Figure 25.14). Roughly 200 million years ago, Pangaea began to break apart; by 20 million years ago, the continents we know today were within a few hundred kilometers of their present locations.

We can use our understanding of evolution and continental drift to predict where fossils of different groups of organisms might be found. For example, scientists have constructed evolutionary trees for horses based on anatomical data. These trees and the ages of fossils of horse ancestors suggest that present-day horse species originated 5 million years ago in North America. At that time, North and South America were close to their present locations, but they were not yet connected, making it difficult for horses to travel between them. Thus, we would predict that the oldest horse fossils should be found only on the continent on which horses originated—North America. This prediction and others like it for different groups of organisms have been upheld, providing more evidence for evolution.

We can also use our understanding of evolution to explain biogeographic data. For example, islands generally have many species of plants and animals that are **endemic**, which means they are found nowhere else in the world. Yet, as Darwin described in *The Origin of Species*, most island species are closely related to species from the nearest mainland or a neighboring island. He explained this observation by suggesting that islands are colonized by species from the nearest mainland. These colonists eventually give rise to new species as they adapt to their new environments. Such a process also explains why two islands with similar environments in distant parts of the world tend to be populated not by species that are closely related to each other, but rather by species related to those of the nearest mainland, where the environment is often quite different.

What Is Theoretical About Darwin's View of Life?

Some people dismiss Darwin's ideas as "just a theory." However, as we have seen, the *pattern* of evolution—the observation that life has evolved over time—has been documented directly and is supported by a great deal of evidence. In addition, Darwin's explanation of the *process* of evolution—that natural selection is the primary cause of the observed pattern of evolutionary change—makes sense of massive amounts of data. The effects of natural selection also can be observed and tested in nature.

What, then, is theoretical about evolution? Keep in mind that the scientific meaning of the term *theory* is very different from its meaning in everyday use. The colloquial use of the word *theory* comes close to what scientists mean by a hypothesis. In science, a theory is more comprehensive than a hypothesis. A theory, such as the theory of evolution by natural selection, accounts for many observations and explains and integrates a great variety of phenomena. Such a unifying theory does not become widely accepted unless its predictions stand up to thorough and continual testing by experiment and additional observation (see Chapter 1). As the next three chapters demonstrate, this has certainly been the case with the theory of evolution by natural selection.

The skepticism of scientists as they continue to test theories prevents these ideas from becoming dogma. For example, although Darwin thought that evolution was a very slow process, we now know that this isn't always true. New species can form in relatively short periods of time (a few thousand years or less; see Chapter 24). Furthermore, as we'll explore throughout this unit, evolutionary biologists now recognize that natural selection is not the only mechanism responsible for evolution. Indeed, the study of evolution today is livelier than ever as scientists find more ways to test predictions based on natural selection and other evolutionary mechanisms.

Although Darwin's theory attributes the diversity of life to natural processes, the diverse products of evolution nevertheless remain elegant and inspiring. As Darwin wrote in the final sentence of *The Origin of Species*, "There is grandeur in this view of life . . . [in which] endless forms most beautiful and most wonderful have been, and are being, evolved."

CONCEPT CHECK 22.3

1. Explain how the following statement is inaccurate: "Antibiotics have created drug resistance in MRSA."
2. How does evolution account for (a) the similar mammalian forelimbs with different functions shown in Figure 22.15 and (b) the similar lifestyle of the two distantly related mammals shown in Figure 22.18?
3. **WHAT IF?** The fossil record shows that dinosaurs originated 200–250 million years ago. Would you expect the geographic distribution of early dinosaur fossils to be broad (on many continents) or narrow (on one or a few continents only)? Explain.

For suggested answers, see Appendix A.

22 CHAPTER REVIEW

SUMMARY OF KEY CONCEPTS

CONCEPT 22.1

The Darwinian revolution challenged traditional views of a young Earth inhabited by unchanging species (pp. 453–455)

- Darwin proposed that life's diversity arose from ancestral species through natural selection, a departure from prevailing views.
- In contrast to **catastrophism** (the principle that events in the past occurred suddenly by mechanisms not operating today), Hutton and Lyell thought that geologic change results from mechanisms that operated in the past in the same manner as at the present time (**uniformitarianism**).
- Lamarck hypothesized that species evolve, but the underlying mechanisms he proposed are not supported by evidence.

? *Why was the age of Earth important for Darwin's ideas about evolution?*

CONCEPT 22.2

Descent with modification by natural selection explains the adaptations of organisms and the unity and diversity of life (pp. 455–460)

- Darwin's experiences during the voyage of the *Beagle* gave rise to his idea that new species originate from ancestral forms through the accumulation of **adaptations**. He refined his theory for many years and finally published it in 1859 after learning that Wallace had come to the same idea.
- In *The Origin of Species*, Darwin proposed that evolution occurs by **natural selection**.

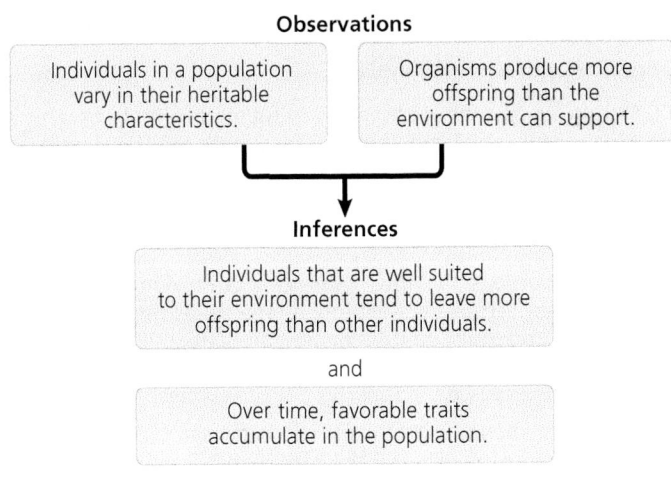

Observations

| Individuals in a population vary in their heritable characteristics. | Organisms produce more offspring than the environment can support. |

Inferences

Individuals that are well suited to their environment tend to leave more offspring than other individuals.

and

Over time, favorable traits accumulate in the population.

? *Describe how overreproduction and heritable variation relate to evolution by natural selection.*

Evolution is supported by an overwhelming amount of scientific evidence (pp. 460–467)

- Researchers have directly observed natural selection leading to adaptive evolution in many studies, including research on soapberry bug populations and on MRSA.
- Organisms share characteristics because of common descent (**homology**) or because natural selection affects independently evolving species in similar environments in similar ways (**convergent evolution**).
- Fossils show that past organisms differed from living organisms, that many species have become extinct, and that species have evolved over long periods of time; fossils also document the origin of major new groups of organisms.
- Evolutionary theory can explain biogeographic patterns.

? *Summarize the different lines of evidence supporting the hypothesis that cetaceans descended from land mammals and are closely related to even-toed ungulates.*

TEST YOUR UNDERSTANDING

Level 1: Knowledge/Comprehension

1. Which of the following is *not* an observation or inference on which natural selection is based?
   a. There is heritable variation among individuals.
   b. Poorly adapted individuals never produce offspring.
   c. Species produce more offspring than the environment can support.
   d. Individuals whose characteristics are best suited to the environment generally leave more offspring than those whose characteristics are less well suited.
   e. Only a fraction of an individual's offspring may survive.

2. Which of the following observations helped Darwin shape his concept of descent with modification?
   a. Species diversity declines farther from the equator.
   b. Fewer species live on islands than on the nearest continents.
   c. Birds can be found on islands located farther from the mainland than the birds' maximum nonstop flight distance.
   d. South American temperate plants are more similar to the tropical plants of South America than to the temperate plants of Europe.
   e. Earthquakes reshape life by causing mass extinctions.

Level 2: Application/Analysis

3. Within six months of effectively using methicillin to treat *S. aureus* infections in a community, all new infections were caused by MRSA. How can this result best be explained?
   a. *S. aureus* can resist vaccines.
   b. A patient must have become infected with MRSA from another community.
   c. In response to the drug, *S. aureus* began making drug-resistant versions of the protein targeted by the drug.
   d. Some drug-resistant bacteria were present at the start of treatment, and natural selection increased their frequency.
   e. The drug caused the *S. aureus* DNA to change.

4. The upper forelimbs of humans and bats have fairly similar skeletal structures, whereas the corresponding bones in whales have very different shapes and proportions. However, genetic data suggest that all three kinds of organisms diverged from a common ancestor at about the same time. Which of the following is the most likely explanation for these data?

   a. Humans and bats evolved by natural selection, and whales evolved by Lamarckian mechanisms.
   b. Forelimb evolution was adaptive in people and bats, but not in whales.
   c. Natural selection in an aquatic environment resulted in significant changes to whale forelimb anatomy.
   d. Genes mutate faster in whales than in humans or bats.
   e. Whales are not properly classified as mammals.

5. DNA sequences in many human genes are very similar to the sequences of corresponding genes in chimpanzees. The most likely explanation for this result is that
   a. humans and chimpanzees share a relatively recent common ancestor.
   b. humans evolved from chimpanzees.
   c. chimpanzees evolved from humans.
   d. convergent evolution led to the DNA similarities.
   e. humans and chimpanzees are not closely related.

Level 3: Synthesis/Evaluation

6. **EVOLUTION CONNECTION**
   Explain why anatomical and molecular features often fit a similar nested pattern. In addition, describe a process that can cause this not to be the case.

7. **SCIENTIFIC INQUIRY**
   DRAW IT Mosquitoes resistant to the pesticide DDT first appeared in India in 1959, but now are found throughout the world. (a) Graph the data in the table below. (b) Examining the graph, hypothesize why the percentage of mosquitoes resistant to DDT rose rapidly. (c) Suggest an explanation for the global spread of DDT resistance.

Month	0	8	12
Mosquitoes Resistant* to DDT	4%	45%	77%

   Source: C. F. Curtis et al., Selection for and against insecticide resistance and possible methods of inhibiting the evolution of resistance in mosquitoes, *Ecological Entomology* 3:273–287 (1978).
   *Mosquitoes were considered resistant if they were not killed within 1 hour of receiving a dose of 4% DDT.

8. **WRITE ABOUT A THEME**
   Environmental Interactions Write a short essay (about 100–150 words) evaluating whether changes to an organism's physical environment are likely to result in evolutionary change. Use an example to support your reasoning.

For selected answers, see Appendix A.

MasteringBIOLOGY® www.masteringbiology.com

1. MasteringBiology® Assignments:
   Tutorial Evidence for Evolution
   Activities Artificial Selection • Darwin and the Galápagos Islands • The Voyage of the *Beagle*: Darwin's Trip Around the World • Discovery Channel Video: Charles Darwin • Natural Selection for Antibiotic Resistance • Reconstructing Forelimbs
   Questions Student Misconceptions • Reading Quiz • Multiple Choice • End-of-Chapter

2. eText
   Read your book online, search, take notes, highlight text, and more.

3. The Study Area
   Practice Tests • Cumulative Test • *BioFlix* 3-D Animations • MP3 Tutor Sessions • Videos • Activities • Investigations • Lab Media • Audio Glossary • Word Study Tools • Art

The Evolution of Populations

▲ Figure 23.1 **Is this finch evolving?**

EVOLUTION

KEY CONCEPTS

23.1 Genetic variation makes evolution possible

23.2 The Hardy-Weinberg equation can be used to test whether a population is evolving

23.3 Natural selection, genetic drift, and gene flow can alter allele frequencies in a population

23.4 Natural selection is the only mechanism that consistently causes adaptive evolution

OVERVIEW

The Smallest Unit of Evolution

One common misconception about evolution is that individual organisms evolve. It is true that natural selection acts on individuals: Each organism's traits affect its survival and reproductive success compared with other individuals. But the evolutionary impact of natural selection is only apparent in the changes in a *population* of organisms over time.

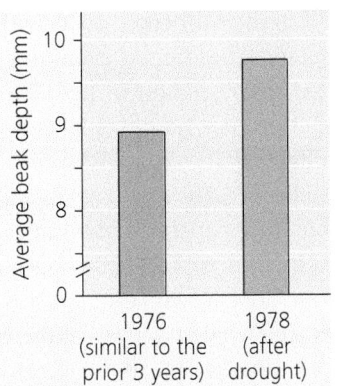

◀ Figure 23.2 **Evidence of selection by food source.** The data represent adult beak depth measurements of medium ground finches hatched in the generations before and after the 1977 drought. Beak sizes remained large until 1983, when changing conditions no longer favored large-beaked birds.

(MB) See the related Experimental Inquiry Tutorial in MasteringBiology.

Consider the medium ground finch (*Geospiza fortis*), a seed-eating bird that inhabits the Galápagos Islands (Figure 23.1). In 1977, the *G. fortis* population on the island of Daphne Major was decimated by a long period of drought: Of some 1,200 birds, only 180 survived. Researchers Peter and Rosemary Grant observed that during the drought, small, soft seeds were in short supply. The finches mostly fed on large, hard seeds that were more plentiful. Birds with larger, deeper beaks were better able to crack and eat these larger seeds, and they survived at a higher rate than finches with smaller beaks. Since beak depth is an inherited trait in these birds, the average beak depth in the next generation of *G. fortis* was greater than it had been in the pre-drought population (Figure 23.2). The finch population had evolved by natural selection. However, the *individual* finches did not evolve. Each bird had a beak of a particular size, which did not grow larger during the drought. Rather, the proportion of large beaks in the population increased from generation to generation: The population evolved, not its individual members.

Focusing on evolutionary change in populations, we can define evolution on its smallest scale, called **microevolution**, as change in allele frequencies in a population over generations. As we will see in this chapter, natural selection is not the only cause of microevolution. In fact, there are three main mechanisms that can cause allele frequency change: natural selection, genetic drift (chance events that alter allele frequencies), and gene flow (the transfer of alleles between populations). Each of these mechanisms has distinctive effects on the genetic composition of populations. However, only natural selection consistently improves the match between organisms and their environment (adaptation). Before we examine natural selection and adaptation more closely, let's revisit a prerequisite for these processes in a population: genetic variation.

CONCEPT 23.1

Genetic variation makes evolution possible

In *The Origin of Species*, Darwin provided abundant evidence that life on Earth has evolved over time, and he proposed natural selection as the primary mechanism for that change. He observed that individuals differed in their inherited traits and that selection acted on such differences, leading to evolutionary change. Thus, Darwin realized that variation in heritable traits was a prerequisite for evolution, but he did not know precisely how organisms pass heritable traits to their offspring.

Just a few years after Darwin published *The Origin of Species*, Gregor Mendel wrote a groundbreaking paper on inheritance in pea plants (see Chapter 14). In that paper, Mendel proposed a particulate model of inheritance in which organisms transmit discrete heritable units (now called genes) to their offspring. Although Darwin did not know about genes, Mendel's paper set the stage for understanding the genetic differences on which evolution is based. Here we'll examine such genetic differences and how they are produced.

Genetic Variation

You probably have no trouble recognizing your friends in a crowd. Each person is unique, exhibiting differences in their facial features, height, and voice. Indeed, individual variation occurs in all species. In addition to the differences that we can see or hear, individuals vary extensively at the molecular level. For example, you cannot identify a person's blood group (A, B, AB, or O) from his or her appearance, but this and many other molecular traits vary among individuals.

Individual variations often reflect **genetic variation**, differences among individuals in the composition of their genes or other DNA segments. As you read in earlier chapters, however, some phenotypic variation is not heritable (see **Figure 23.3** for a striking example in a caterpillar of the southwestern United States). Phenotype is the product of an inherited genotype and many environmental influences. In a human example, bodybuilders alter their phenotypes dramatically but do not pass their huge muscles on to the next generation. In general, only the genetically determined part of phenotypic variation can have evolutionary consequences. As

such, genetic variation provides the raw material for evolutionary change: Without genetic variation, evolution cannot occur.

Variation Within a Population

Characters that vary within a population may be discrete or quantitative. *Discrete characters*, such as the purple or white flower colors of Mendel's pea plants (see Figure 14.3), can be classified on an either-or basis (each plant has flowers that are either purple or white). Many discrete characters are determined by a single gene locus with different alleles that produce distinct phenotypes. However, most heritable variation involves *quantitative characters*, which vary along a continuum within a population. Heritable quantitative variation usually results from the influence of two or more genes on a single phenotypic character.

For both discrete and quantitative characters, biologists often need to describe how much genetic variation there is in a particular population. We can measure genetic variation at the whole-gene level (*gene variability*) and at the molecular level of DNA (*nucleotide variability*). Gene variability can be quantified as the **average heterozygosity**, the average percentage of loci that are heterozygous. (Recall that a heterozygous individual has two different alleles for a given locus, whereas a homozygous individual has two identical alleles for that locus.) As an example, on average the fruit fly *Drosophila melanogaster* is heterozygous for about 1,920 of its 13,700 loci (14%) and homozygous for all the rest. We can therefore say that a *D. melanogaster* population has an average heterozygosity of 14%. Analyses of this and many other species show that this level of genetic variation provides ample raw material for natural selection to operate, resulting in evolutionary change.

When determining gene variability, how do scientists identify heterozygous loci? One method is to survey the protein products of genes using gel electrophoresis (see Figure 20.9). However, this approach cannot detect silent mutations that

▲ **Figure 23.3 Nonheritable variation.** These caterpillars of the moth *Nemoria arizonaria* owe their different appearances to chemicals in their diets, not to differences in their genotypes. Caterpillars raised on a diet of oak flowers resembled the flowers **(a)**, whereas their siblings raised on oak leaves resembled oak twigs **(b)**.

alter the DNA sequence of a gene but not the amino acid sequence of the protein (see Figure 17.24). To include such silent mutations in their estimates of average heterozygosity, researchers must use other approaches, such as PCR-based methods and restriction fragment analyses (see Chapter 20).

To measure nucleotide variability, biologists compare the DNA sequences of two individuals in a population and then average the data from many such comparisons. The genome of *D. melanogaster* has about 180 million nucleotides, and the sequences of any two fruit flies differ on average by approximately 1.8 million (1%) of their nucleotides. Thus, the nucleotide variability of *D. melanogaster* populations is about 1%.

As in this example, gene variability tends to exceed nucleotide variability. Why is this true? Remember that a gene can consist of thousands of nucleotides. A difference at only one of these nucleotides can be sufficient to make two alleles of that gene different, increasing gene variability.

Variation Between Populations

In addition to variation observed within a population, species also exhibit **geographic variation**, differences in the genetic composition of separate populations. **Figure 23.4** illustrates geographic variation in populations of house mice (*Mus*

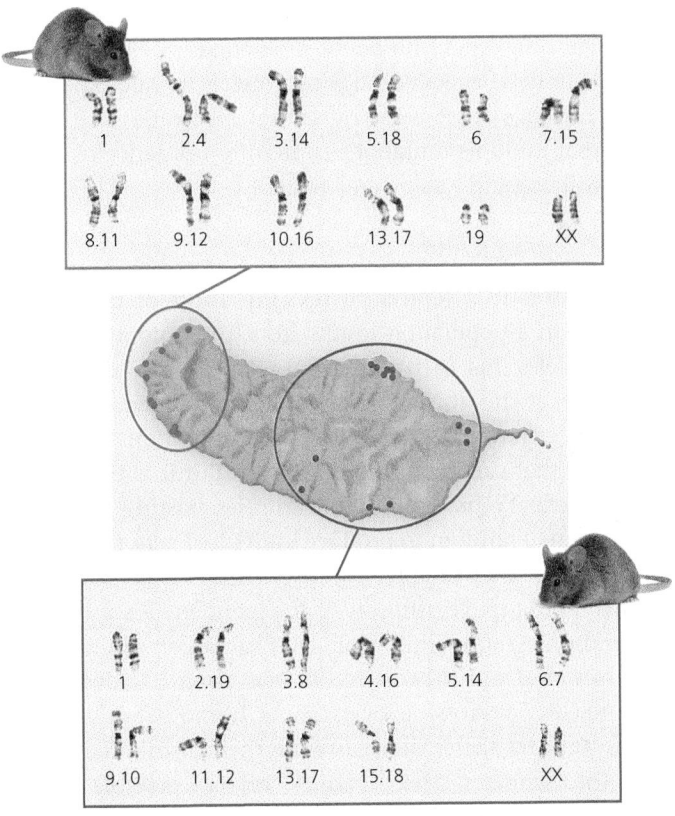

▲ **Figure 23.4 Geographic variation in isolated mouse populations on Madeira.** The number pairs represent fused chromosomes. For example, "2.4" indicates fusion of chromosome 2 and chromosome 4. Mice in the areas indicated by the blue dots have the set of fused chromosomes in the blue box; mice in the red-dot locales have the set of fused chromosomes in the red box.

▲ **Figure 23.5 A cline determined by temperature.** In mummichog fish, the frequency of the $Ldh\text{-}B^b$ allele for the enzyme lactate dehydrogenase-B (which functions in metabolism) decreases in fish sampled from Maine to Georgia. The $Ldh\text{-}B^b$ allele codes for a form of the enzyme that is a better catalyst in cold water than are other versions of the enzyme. Individuals with the $Ldh\text{-}B^b$ allele can swim faster in cold water than can individuals with other alleles.

musculus) separated by mountains on the Atlantic island of Madeira. Inadvertently introduced by Portuguese settlers in the 15th century, several populations of mice have evolved in isolation from one another. Researchers have observed differences in the karyotypes (chromosome sets) of these isolated populations. In certain populations, some of the chromosomes have become fused. However, the patterns of fused chromosomes differ from one population to another. Because these chromosome-level changes leave genes intact, their phenotypic effects on the mice seem to be neutral. Thus, the variation between these populations appears to have resulted from chance events (drift) rather than natural selection.

Other examples of geographic variation occur as a **cline**, a graded change in a character along a geographic axis. Some clines are produced by a gradation in an environmental variable, as illustrated by the impact of temperature on the frequency of a cold-adaptive allele in mummichog fish (*Fundulus heteroclitus*). Clines such as the one depicted in **Figure 23.5** probably result from natural selection—otherwise there would be no reason to expect a close association between the environmental variable and the frequency of the allele. But selection can only operate if multiple alleles exist for a given locus. Such variation in alleles can arise in several ways.

Sources of Genetic Variation

The genetic variation on which evolution depends originates when mutation, gene duplication, or other processes produce new alleles and new genes. Many new genetic variants can be produced in short periods of time in organisms that reproduce rapidly. Sexual reproduction can also result in genetic variation as existing genes are arranged in new ways.

Formation of New Alleles

As described in Chapters 17 and 21, new alleles can arise by *mutation*, a change in the nucleotide sequence of an organism's DNA. A mutation is like a shot in the dark—we cannot predict accurately which segments of DNA will be altered or in what way. In multicellular organisms, only mutations in cell lines that produce gametes can be passed to offspring. In plants and fungi, this is not as limiting as it may sound, since many different cell lines can produce gametes (see Figures 30.6 and 31.17). But in most animals, the majority of mutations occur in somatic cells and are lost when the individual dies.

A change of as little as one base in a gene, called a "point mutation," can have a significant impact on phenotype, as in sickle-cell disease (see Figure 17.23). Organisms reflect thousands of generations of past selection, and hence their phenotypes generally provide a close match to their environment. As a result, it's unlikely that a new mutation that alters a phenotype will improve it. In fact, most such mutations are at least slightly harmful. But much of the DNA in eukaryotic genomes does not code for protein products, and point mutations in these noncoding regions are often harmless. Also, because of the redundancy in the genetic code, even a point mutation in a gene that encodes a protein will have no effect on the protein's function if the amino acid composition is not changed. And even where there is a change in the amino acid, it may not affect the protein's shape and function. However, as will be discussed later in this chapter, a mutant allele may on rare occasions actually make its bearer better suited to the environment, enhancing reproductive success.

Altering Gene Number or Position

Chromosomal changes that delete, disrupt, or rearrange many loci at once are usually harmful. However, when such large-scale changes leave genes intact, their effects on organisms may be neutral (as in the case of the Madeira mice described in Figure 23.4). In rare cases, chromosomal rearrangements may even be beneficial. For example, the translocation of part of one chromosome to a different chromosome could link DNA segments in a way that results in a positive effect.

An important source of variation begins when genes are duplicated due to errors in meiosis (such as unequal crossing over), slippage during DNA replication, or the activities of transposable elements (see Chapters 15 and 21). Duplications of large chromosome segments, like other chromosomal aberrations, are often harmful, but the duplication of smaller pieces of DNA may not be. Gene duplications that do not have severe effects can persist over generations, allowing mutations to accumulate. The result is an expanded genome with new genes that may take on new functions.

Such beneficial increases in gene number appear to have played a major role in evolution. For example, the remote ancestors of mammals had a single gene for detecting odors that has since been duplicated many times. As a result, hu-

mans today have about 1,000 olfactory receptor genes, and mice have 1,300. This dramatic proliferation of olfactory genes probably helped early mammals, enabling them to detect faint odors and to distinguish among many different smells. More recently, about 60% of human olfactory receptor genes have been inactivated by mutations, whereas mice have lost only 20% of theirs. Since mutation rates in humans and mice are similar, this difference is likely due to strong selection against mice with mutations that inactivate their olfactory genes. A versatile sense of smell appears to be much more important to mice than to humans!

Rapid Reproduction

Mutation rates tend to be low in plants and animals, averaging about one mutation in every 100,000 genes per generation, and they are often even lower in prokaryotes. But prokaryotes typically have short generation spans, so mutations can quickly generate genetic variation in populations of these organisms. The same is true of viruses. For instance, HIV has a generation span of about two days. It also has an RNA genome, which has a much higher mutation rate than a typical DNA genome because of the lack of RNA repair mechanisms in host cells (see Chapter 19). For this reason, it is unlikely that a single-drug treatment would ever be effective against HIV; mutant forms of the virus that are resistant to a particular drug would no doubt proliferate in relatively short order. The most effective AIDS treatments to date have been drug "cocktails" that combine several medications. It is less likely that multiple mutations conferring resistance to *all* the drugs will occur in a short time period.

Sexual Reproduction

In organisms that reproduce sexually, most of the genetic variation in a population results from the unique combination of alleles that each individual receives from its parents. Of course, at the nucleotide level, all the differences among these alleles have originated from past mutations and other processes that can produce new alleles. But it is the mechanism of sexual reproduction that shuffles existing alleles and deals them at random to produce individual genotypes.

As described in Chapter 13, three mechanisms contribute to this shuffling: crossing over, independent assortment of chromosomes, and fertilization. During meiosis, homologous chromosomes, one inherited from each parent, trade some of their alleles by crossing over. These homologous chromosomes and the alleles they carry are then distributed at random into gametes. Then, because myriad possible mating combinations exist in a population, fertilization brings together gametes that are likely to have different genetic backgrounds. The combined effects of these three mechanisms ensure that sexual reproduction rearranges existing alleles into fresh combinations each generation, providing much of the genetic variation that makes evolution possible.

CONCEPT CHECK 23.1

1. (a) Explain why genetic variation within a population is a prerequisite for evolution. (b) What factors can produce genetic differences between populations?
2. Of all the mutations that occur in a population, why do only a small fraction become widespread?
3. **MAKE CONNECTIONS** If a population stopped reproducing sexually (but still reproduced asexually), how would its genetic variation be affected over time? Explain. (See Concept 13.4, pp. 257–259.)

For suggested answers, see Appendix A.

CONCEPT 23.2

The Hardy-Weinberg equation can be used to test whether a population is evolving

Although the individuals in a population must differ genetically for evolution to occur, the presence of genetic variation does not guarantee that a population will evolve. For that to happen, one of the factors that cause evolution must be at work. In this section, we'll explore one way to test whether evolution is occurring in a population. The first step in this process is to clarify what we mean by a population.

Gene Pools and Allele Frequencies

A **population** is a group of individuals of the same species that live in the same area and interbreed, producing fertile offspring. Different populations of a single species may be isolated geographically from one another, thus exchanging genetic material only rarely. Such isolation is common for species that live on widely separated islands or in different lakes. But not all populations are isolated, nor must populations have sharp boundaries **(Figure 23.6)**. Still, members of a population typically breed with one another and thus on average are more closely related to each other than to members of other populations.

We can characterize a population's genetic makeup by describing its **gene pool**, which consists of all copies of every type of allele at every locus in all members of the population. If only one allele exists for a particular locus in a population, that allele is said to be *fixed* in the gene pool, and all individuals are homozygous for that allele. But if there are two or more alleles for a particular locus in a population, individuals may be either homozygous or heterozygous.

Each allele has a frequency (proportion) in the population. For example, imagine a population of 500 wildflower plants with two alleles, C^R and C^W, for a locus that codes for flower pigment. These alleles show incomplete dominance (see Figure 14.10); thus, each genotype has a distinct phenotype.

Porcupine herd

Fortymile herd

▲ **Figure 23.6 One species, two populations.** These two caribou populations in the Yukon are not totally isolated; they sometimes share the same area. Still, members of either population are most likely to breed within their own population.

$C^R C^R$

$C^W C^W$

$C^R C^W$

Plants homozygous for the C^R allele ($C^R C^R$) produce red pigment and have red flowers; plants homozygous for the C^W allele ($C^W C^W$) produce no red pigment and have white flowers; and heterozygotes ($C^R C^W$) produce some red pigment and have pink flowers.

In our population, suppose there are 320 plants with red flowers, 160 with pink flowers, and 20 with white flowers. Because these are diploid organisms, there are a total of 1,000 copies of the gene for flower color in the population of 500 individuals. The C^R allele accounts for 800 of these copies ($320 \times 2 = 640$ for $C^R C^R$ plants, plus $160 \times 1 = 160$ for $C^R C^W$ plants).

When studying a locus with two alleles, the convention is to use p to represent the frequency of one allele and q to represent the frequency of the other allele. Thus, p, the frequency of the C^R allele in the gene pool of this population, is 800/1,000 = 0.8 = 80%. And because there are only two alleles for this gene, the frequency of the C^W allele, represented by q, must be 200/1,000 = 0.2 = 20%. For loci that have more than two alleles, the sum of all allele frequencies must still equal 1 (100%).

Next we'll see how allele and genotype frequencies can be used to test whether evolution is occurring in a population.

The Hardy-Weinberg Principle

One way to assess whether natural selection or other factors are causing evolution at a particular locus is to determine what the genetic makeup of a population would be if it were *not* evolving at that locus. We can then compare that scenario with data from a real population. If there are no differences, we can conclude that the real population is not evolving. If there are differences, this suggests that the real population may be evolving—and then we can try to figure out why.

Hardy-Weinberg Equilibrium

The gene pool of a population that is not evolving can be described by the **Hardy-Weinberg principle**, named for the British mathematician and German physician, respectively, who independently derived it in 1908. This principle states that the frequencies of alleles and genotypes in a population will remain constant from generation to generation, provided that only Mendelian segregation and recombination of alleles are at work. Such a gene pool is in *Hardy-Weinberg equilibrium*.

To use the Hardy-Weinberg principle, it is helpful to think about genetic crosses in a new way. Previously, we used Punnett squares to determine the genotypes of offspring in a genetic cross (see Figure 14.5). Here, instead of considering the possible allele combinations from one cross, consider the combination of alleles in *all* of the crosses in a population.

Imagine that all the alleles for a given locus from all the individuals in a population were placed in a large bin **(Figure 23.7)**.

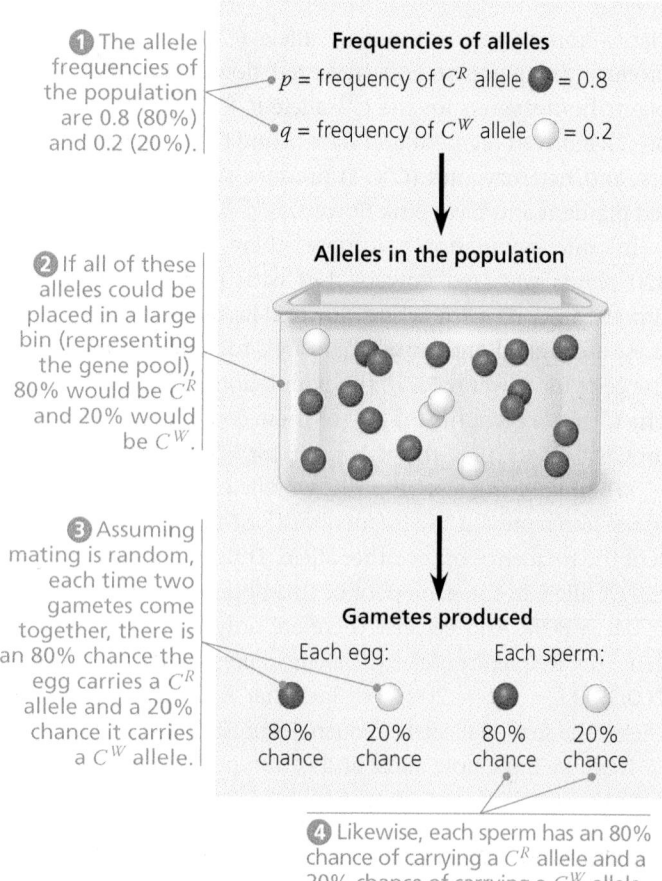

❶ The allele frequencies of the population are 0.8 (80%) and 0.2 (20%).

Frequencies of alleles

p = frequency of C^R allele ● = 0.8

q = frequency of C^W allele ○ = 0.2

❷ If all of these alleles could be placed in a large bin (representing the gene pool), 80% would be C^R and 20% would be C^W.

Alleles in the population

❸ Assuming mating is random, each time two gametes come together, there is an 80% chance the egg carries a C^R allele and a 20% chance it carries a C^W allele.

Gametes produced

Each egg:

| 80% chance | 20% chance |

Each sperm:

| 80% chance | 20% chance |

❹ Likewise, each sperm has an 80% chance of carrying a C^R allele and a 20% chance of carrying a C^W allele.

▲ **Figure 23.7 Selecting alleles at random from a gene pool.**

We can think of this bin as holding the population's gene pool for that locus. "Reproduction" occurs by selecting alleles at random from the bin; somewhat similar events occur in nature when fish release sperm and eggs into the water or when pollen (containing plant sperm) is blown about by the wind. By viewing reproduction as a process of randomly selecting and combining alleles from the bin (the gene pool), we are in effect assuming that mating occurs at random—that is, that all male-female matings are equally likely.

Let's apply the bin analogy to the hypothetical wildflower population discussed earlier. In that population of 500 flowers, the frequency of the allele for red flowers (C^R) is $p = 0.8$, and the frequency of the allele for white flowers (C^W) is $q = 0.2$. Thus, a bin holding all 1,000 copies of the flower-color gene in the population contains 800 C^R alleles and 200 C^W alleles. Assuming that gametes are formed by selecting alleles at random from the bin, the probability that an egg or sperm contains a C^R or C^W allele is equal to the frequency of these alleles in the bin. Thus, as shown in Figure 23.7, each egg has an 80% chance of containing a C^R allele and a 20% chance of containing a C^W allele; the same is true for each sperm.

Using the rule of multiplication (see Figure 14.9), we can now calculate the frequencies of the three possible genotypes, assuming random unions of sperm and eggs. The probability that two C^R alleles will come together is $p \times p = p^2 = 0.8 \times 0.8 = 0.64$. Thus, about 64% of the plants in the next generation will have the genotype $C^R C^R$. The frequency of $C^W C^W$ individuals is expected to be about $q \times q = q^2 = 0.2 \times 0.2 = 0.04$, or 4%. $C^R C^W$ heterozygotes can arise in two different ways. If the sperm provides the C^R allele and the egg provides the C^W allele, the resulting heterozygotes will be $p \times q = 0.8 \times 0.2 = 0.16$, or 16% of the total. If the sperm provides the C^W allele and the egg the C^R allele, the heterozygous offspring will make up $q \times p = 0.2 \times 0.8 = 0.16$, or 16%. The frequency of heterozygotes is thus the sum of these possibilities: $pq + qp = 2pq = 0.16 + 0.16 = 0.32$, or 32%.

As shown in **Figure 23.8** on the facing page, the genotype frequencies in the next generation must add up to 1 (100%). Thus, the equation for Hardy-Weinberg equilibrium states that at a locus with two alleles, the three genotypes will appear in the following proportions:

$$p^2 \quad + \quad 2pq \quad + \quad q^2 \quad = \quad 1$$

| Expected frequency of genotype $C^R C^R$ | Expected frequency of genotype $C^R C^W$ | Expected frequency of genotype $C^W C^W$ |

Note that for a locus with two alleles, only three genotypes are possible (in this case, $C^R C^R$, $C^R C^W$, and $C^W C^W$). As a result, the sum of the frequencies of the three genotypes must equal 1 (100%) in *any* population—regardless of whether the population is in Hardy-Weinberg equilibrium. A population is in Hardy-Weinberg equilibrium only if the genotype frequencies are such that the actual frequency of

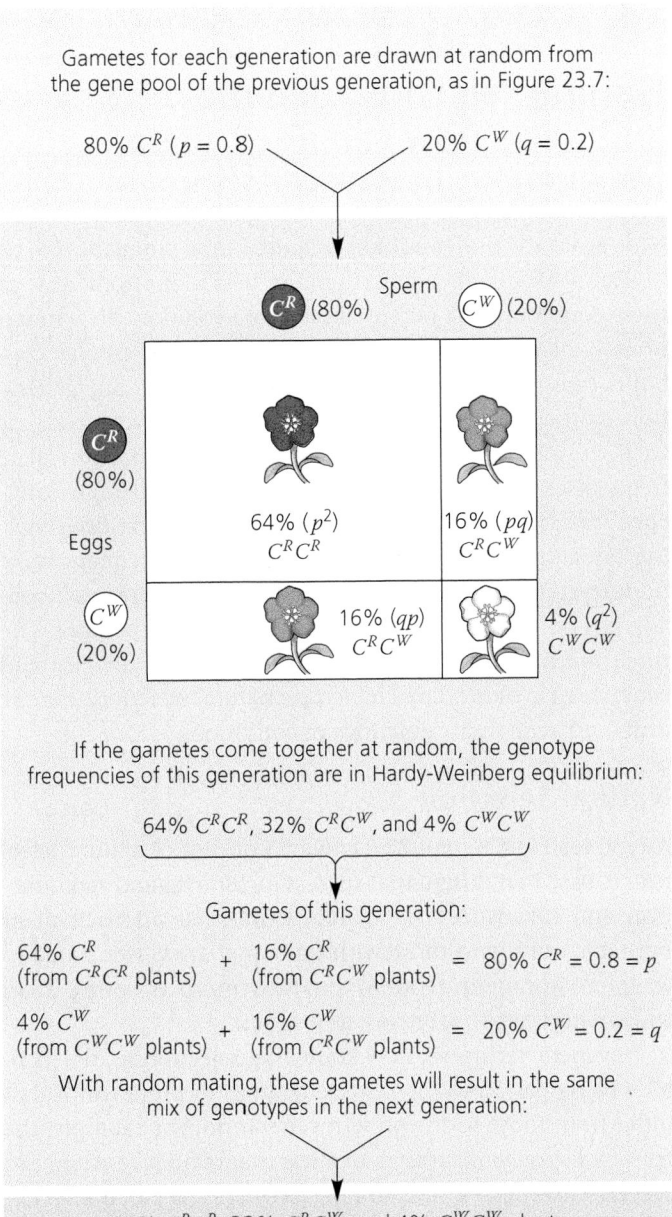

Gametes for each generation are drawn at random from the gene pool of the previous generation, as in Figure 23.7:

80% C^R ($p = 0.8$)   20% C^W ($q = 0.2$)

Sperm
C^R (80%) C^W (20%)

Eggs

C^R (80%)

64% (p^2) $C^R C^R$ 16% (pq) $C^R C^W$

C^W (20%)

16% (qp) $C^R C^W$ 4% (q^2) $C^W C^W$

If the gametes come together at random, the genotype frequencies of this generation are in Hardy-Weinberg equilibrium:

64% $C^R C^R$, 32% $C^R C^W$, and 4% $C^W C^W$

Gametes of this generation:

64% C^R (from $C^R C^R$ plants) + 16% C^R (from $C^R C^W$ plants) = 80% C^R = 0.8 = p

4% C^W (from $C^W C^W$ plants) + 16% C^W (from $C^R C^W$ plants) = 20% C^W = 0.2 = q

With random mating, these gametes will result in the same mix of genotypes in the next generation:

64% $C^R C^R$, 32% $C^R C^W$, and 4% $C^W C^W$ plants

▲ **Figure 23.8 The Hardy-Weinberg principle.** In our wildflower population, the gene pool remains constant from one generation to the next. Mendelian processes alone do not alter frequencies of alleles or genotypes.

? *If the frequency of the C^R allele is 60%, predict the frequencies of the $C^R C^R$, $C^R C^W$, and $C^W C^W$ genotypes.*

one homozygote is p^2, the actual frequency of the other homozygote is q^2, and the actual frequency of heterozygotes is $2pq$. Finally, as suggested by Figure 23.8, if a population such as our wildflowers is in Hardy-Weinberg equilibrium and its members continue to mate randomly generation after generation, allele and genotype frequencies will remain constant. The system operates somewhat like a deck of cards: No matter how many times the deck is reshuffled to deal out new hands, the deck itself remains the same. Aces do not grow more numerous than jacks. And the repeated shuffling of a

population's gene pool over the generations cannot, in itself, change the frequency of one allele relative to another.

Conditions for Hardy-Weinberg Equilibrium

The Hardy-Weinberg principle describes a hypothetical population that is not evolving. But in real populations, the allele and genotype frequencies often *do* change over time. Such changes can occur when at least one of the following five conditions of Hardy-Weinberg equilibrium is not met:

1. **No mutations.** The gene pool is modified if mutations alter alleles or if entire genes are deleted or duplicated.
2. **Random mating.** If individuals mate preferentially within a subset of the population, such as their close relatives (inbreeding), random mixing of gametes does not occur, and genotype frequencies change.
3. **No natural selection.** Differences in the survival and reproductive success of individuals carrying different genotypes can alter allele frequencies.
4. **Extremely large population size.** The smaller the population, the more likely it is that allele frequencies will fluctuate by chance from one generation to the next (a process called genetic drift).
5. **No gene flow.** By moving alleles into or out of populations, gene flow can alter allele frequencies.

Departure from these conditions usually results in evolutionary change, which, as we've already described, is common in natural populations. But it is also common for natural populations to be in Hardy-Weinberg equilibrium for specific genes. This apparent contradiction occurs because a population can be evolving at some loci, yet simultaneously be in Hardy-Weinberg equilibrium at other loci. In addition, some populations evolve so slowly that the changes in their allele and genotype frequencies are difficult to distinguish from those predicted for a nonevolving population.

Applying the Hardy-Weinberg Principle

The Hardy-Weinberg equation is often used as an initial test of whether evolution is occurring in a population (you'll encounter an example in Concept Check 23.2, question 3). The equation also has medical applications, such as estimating the percentage of a population carrying the allele for an inherited disease. For example, consider phenylketonuria (PKU), a metabolic disorder that results from homozygosity for a recessive allele and occurs in about one out of every 10,000 babies born in the United States. Left untreated, PKU results in mental disability and other problems. (Newborns are now tested for PKU, and symptoms can be largely avoided with a diet very low in phenylalanine. For this reason, products that contain phenylalanine, such as diet colas, carry warning labels.)

To apply the Hardy-Weinberg equation, we must assume that no new PKU mutations are being introduced into the population (condition 1), and that people neither choose their mates on the basis of whether or not they carry this gene nor generally mate with close relatives (condition 2). We must also ignore any effects of differential survival and reproductive success among PKU genotypes (condition 3) and assume that there are no effects of genetic drift (condition 4) or of gene flow from other populations into the United States (condition 5). These assumptions are reasonable: The mutation rate for the PKU gene is low, inbreeding is not common in the United States, selection occurs only against the rare homozygotes (and then only if dietary restrictions are not followed), the U.S. population is very large, and populations outside the country have PKU allele frequencies similar to those seen in the United States. If all these assumptions hold, then the frequency of individuals in the population born with PKU will correspond to q^2 in the Hardy-Weinberg equation (q^2 = frequency of homozygotes). Because the allele is recessive, we must estimate the number of heterozygotes rather than counting them directly as we did with the pink flowers. Since we know there is one PKU occurrence per 10,000 births (q^2 = 0.0001), the frequency of the recessive allele for PKU is

$$q = \sqrt{0.0001} = 0.01$$

and the frequency of the dominant allele is

$$p = 1 - q = 1 - 0.01 = 0.99$$

The frequency of carriers, heterozygous people who do not have PKU but may pass the PKU allele to offspring, is

$$2pq = 2 \times 0.99 \times 0.01 = 0.0198$$
(approximately 2% of the U.S. population)

Remember, the assumption of Hardy-Weinberg equilibrium yields an approximation; the real number of carriers may differ. Still, our calculations suggest that harmful recessive alleles at this and other loci can be concealed in a population because they are carried by healthy heterozygotes.

CONCEPT CHECK 23.2

1. Suppose a population of organisms with 20,000 gene loci is fixed at half of these loci and has two alleles at each of the other loci. How many different types of alleles are found in its entire gene pool? Explain.
2. If p is the frequency of allele A, use the Hardy-Weinberg equation to predict the frequency of individuals that have at least one A allele.
3. **WHAT IF?** A locus that affects susceptibility to a degenerative brain disease has two alleles, A and a. In a population, 16 people have genotype AA, 92 have genotype Aa, and 12 have genotype aa. Is this population evolving? Explain.

For suggested answers, see Appendix A.

CONCEPT **23.3**

Natural selection, genetic drift, and gene flow can alter allele frequencies in a population

Note again the five conditions required for a population to be in Hardy-Weinberg equilibrium. A deviation from any of these conditions is a potential cause of evolution. New mutations (violation of condition 1) can alter allele frequencies, but because mutations are rare, the change from one generation to the next is likely to be very small. Nevertheless, as we'll see, mutation ultimately can have a large effect on allele frequencies when it produces new alleles that strongly influence fitness in a positive or negative way. Nonrandom mating (violation of condition 2) can affect the frequencies of homozygous and heterozygous genotypes but by itself usually has no effect on allele frequencies in the gene pool. The three mechanisms that alter allele frequencies directly and cause most evolutionary change are natural selection, genetic drift, and gene flow (violations of conditions 3–5).

Natural Selection

As you read in Chapter 22, Darwin's concept of natural selection is based on differential success in survival and reproduction: Individuals in a population exhibit variations in their heritable traits, and those with traits that are better suited to their environment tend to produce more offspring than those with traits that are not as well suited.

In genetic terms, we now know that selection results in alleles being passed to the next generation in proportions that differ from those in the present generation. For example, the fruit fly *D. melanogaster* has an allele that confers resistance to several insecticides, including DDT. This allele has a frequency of 0% in laboratory strains of *D. melanogaster* established from flies collected in the wild in the early 1930s, prior to DDT use. However, in strains established from flies collected after 1960 (following 20 or more years of DDT use), the allele frequency is 37%. We can infer that this allele either arose by mutation between 1930 and 1960 or that it was present in 1930, but very rare. In any case, the rise in frequency of this allele most likely occurred because DDT is a powerful poison that is a strong selective force in exposed fly populations.

As the *D. melanogaster* example shows, an allele that confers insecticide resistance will increase in frequency in a population exposed to that insecticide. Such changes are not coincidental. By consistently favoring some alleles over others, natural selection can cause *adaptive evolution* (evolution that results in a better match between organisms and their environment). We'll explore this process in more detail a little later in this chapter.

Genetic Drift

If you flip a coin 1,000 times, a result of 700 heads and 300 tails might make you suspicious about that coin. But if you flip a coin only 10 times, an outcome of 7 heads and 3 tails would not be surprising. The smaller the number of coin flips, the more likely it is that chance alone will cause a deviation from the predicted result. (In this case, the prediction is an equal number of heads and tails.) Chance events can also cause allele frequencies to fluctuate unpredictably from one generation to the next, especially in small populations—a process called **genetic drift**.

Figure 23.9 models how genetic drift might affect a small population of our wildflowers. In this example, an allele is lost from the gene pool, but it is a matter of chance that the C^W allele is lost and not the C^R allele. Such unpredictable changes in allele frequencies can be caused by chance events associated with survival and reproduction. Perhaps a large animal such as a moose stepped on the three $C^W C^W$ individuals in generation 2, killing them and increasing the chance that only the C^R allele would be passed to the next generation. Allele frequencies can also be affected by chance events that occur during fertilization. For example, suppose two individuals of genotype $C^R C^W$ had a small number of offspring. By chance alone, every egg and sperm pair that generated offspring could happen to have carried the C^R allele and not the C^W allele.

Certain circumstances can result in genetic drift having a significant impact on a population. Two examples are the founder effect and the bottleneck effect.

The Founder Effect

When a few individuals become isolated from a larger population, this smaller group may establish a new population whose gene pool differs from the source population; this is called the **founder effect**. The founder effect might occur, for example, when a few members of a population are blown by a storm to a new island. Genetic drift, in which chance events alter allele frequencies, will occur in such a case if the storm indiscriminately transports some individuals (and their alleles), but not others, from the source population.

The founder effect probably accounts for the relatively high frequency of certain inherited disorders among isolated human populations. For example, in 1814, 15 British colonists founded a settlement on Tristan da Cunha, a group of small islands in the Atlantic Ocean midway between Africa and South America. Apparently, one of the colonists carried a recessive allele for retinitis pigmentosa, a progressive form of blindness that afflicts homozygous individuals. Of the founding colonists' 240 descendants on the island in the late 1960s, 4 had retinitis pigmentosa. The frequency of the allele that causes this disease is ten times

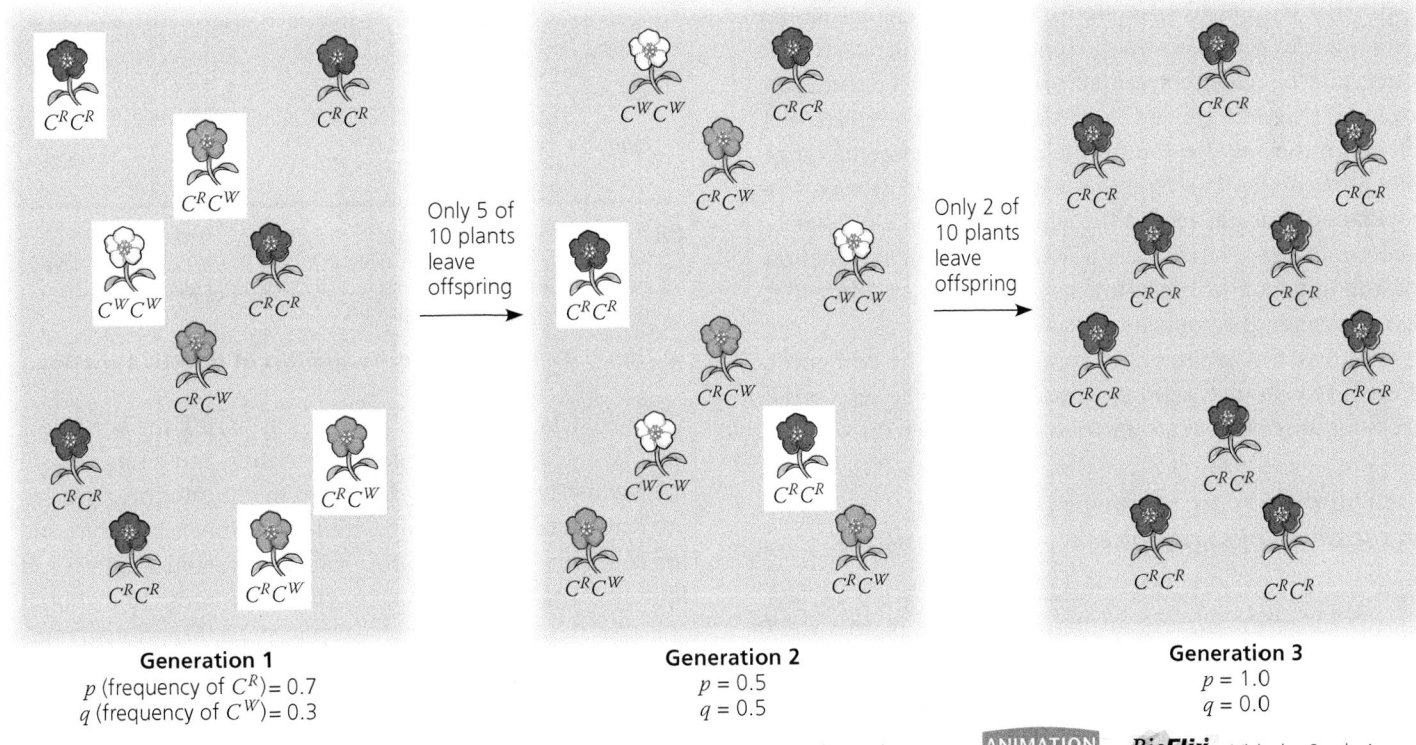

Generation 1
p (frequency of C^R) = 0.7
q (frequency of C^W) = 0.3

Generation 2
p = 0.5
q = 0.5

Generation 3
p = 1.0
q = 0.0

Only 5 of 10 plants leave offspring

Only 2 of 10 plants leave offspring

▲ **Figure 23.9 Genetic drift.** This small wildflower population has a stable size of ten plants. Suppose that by chance only five plants of generation 1 (those in white boxes) produce fertile offspring. (This could occur, for example, if only those plants happened to grow in a location that provided enough nutrients to support the production of offspring.) Again by chance, only two plants of generation 2 leave fertile offspring. As a result, by chance the frequency of the C^W allele first increases in generation 2, then falls to zero in generation 3.

ANIMATION **BioFlix** Visit the Study Area at **www.masteringbiology.com** for the BioFlix® 3-D Animation on Mechanisms of Evolution.

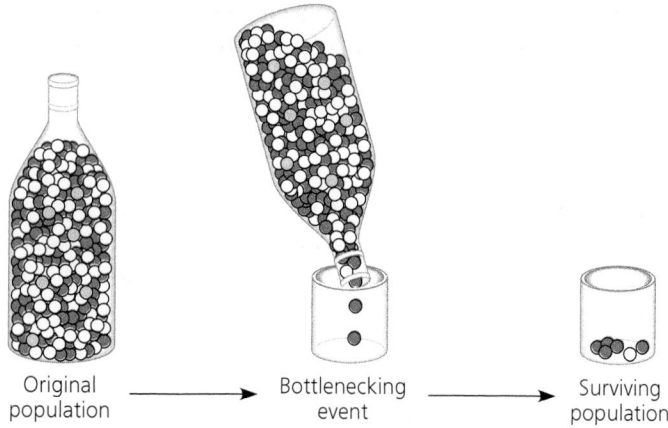

▲ Figure 23.10 **The bottleneck effect.** Shaking just a few marbles through the narrow neck of a bottle is analogous to a drastic reduction in the size of a population. By chance, blue marbles are overrepresented in the surviving population and gold marbles are absent.

higher on Tristan da Cunha than in the populations from which the founders came.

The Bottleneck Effect

A sudden change in the environment, such as a fire or flood, may drastically reduce the size of a population. A severe drop in population size can cause the **bottleneck effect**, so named because the population has passed through a "bottleneck" that reduces its size (**Figure 23.10**). By chance alone, certain alleles may be overrepresented among the survivors, others may be underrepresented, and some may be absent altogether. Ongoing genetic drift is likely to have substantial effects on the gene pool until the population becomes large enough that chance events have less impact. But even if a population that has passed through a bottleneck ultimately recovers in size, it may have low levels of genetic variation for a long period of time—a legacy of the genetic drift that occurred when the population was small.

One reason it is important to understand the bottleneck effect is that human actions sometimes create severe bottlenecks for other species, as the following example shows.

Case Study: *Impact of Genetic Drift on the Greater Prairie Chicken*

Millions of greater prairie chickens (*Tympanuchus cupido*) once lived on the prairies of Illinois. As these prairies were converted to farmland and other uses during the 19th and 20th centuries, the number of greater prairie chickens plummeted (**Figure 23.11a**). By 1993, only two Illinois populations remained, which together harbored fewer than 50 birds. The few surviving birds had low levels of genetic variation, and less than 50% of their eggs hatched, compared with much higher hatching rates of the larger populations in Kansas and Nebraska (**Figure 23.11b**).

(a) The Illinois population of greater prairie chickens dropped from millions of birds in the 1800s to fewer than 50 birds in 1993.

Location	Population size	Number of alleles per locus	Percentage of eggs hatched
Illinois			
1930–1960s	1,000–25,000	5.2	93
1993	<50	3.7	<50
Kansas, 1998 (no bottleneck)	750,000	5.8	99
Nebraska, 1998 (no bottleneck)	75,000–200,000	5.8	96

(b) As a consequence of the drastic reduction in the size of the Illinois population, genetic drift resulted in a drop in the number of alleles per locus (averaged across six loci studied) and a decrease in the percentage of eggs that hatched.

▲ Figure 23.11 **Genetic drift and loss of genetic variation.**

These data suggest that genetic drift during the bottleneck may have led to a loss of genetic variation and an increase in the frequency of harmful alleles. To investigate this hypothesis, Juan Bouzat, of Bowling Green State University, Ohio, and his colleagues extracted DNA from 15 museum specimens of Illinois greater prairie chickens. Of the 15 birds, 10 had been collected in the 1930s, when there were 25,000 greater prairie chickens in Illinois, and 5 had been collected in the 1960s, when there were 1,000 greater prairie chickens in Illinois. By studying the DNA of these specimens, the researchers were able to obtain a minimum, baseline estimate of how much genetic variation was present in the Illinois population *before* the population shrank to extremely low numbers. This baseline estimate is a key piece of information that is not usually available in cases of population bottlenecks.

The researchers surveyed six loci and found that the 1993 Illinois greater prairie chicken population had lost nine alleles that were present in the museum specimens. The 1993 population also had fewer alleles per locus than the pre-bottleneck Illinois or the current Kansas and Nebraska populations (see Figure 23.11b). Thus, as predicted, drift had reduced the genetic variation of the small 1993 population. Drift may also have increased the frequency of harmful alleles, leading to the low egg-hatching rate. To counteract these negative effects, 271 birds from neighboring states were added to the Illinois population over four years. This strategy succeeded: New alleles entered the population, and the egg-hatching rate improved to over 90%. Overall, studies on the Illinois greater prairie chicken illustrate the powerful effects of genetic drift in small populations and provide hope that in at least some populations, these effects can be reversed.

Effects of Genetic Drift: A Summary

The examples we've described highlight four key points:

1. **Genetic drift is significant in small populations.** Chance events can cause an allele to be disproportionately over- or underrepresented in the next generation. Although chance events occur in populations of all sizes, they tend to alter allele frequencies substantially only in small populations.

2. **Genetic drift can cause allele frequencies to change at random.** Because of genetic drift, an allele may increase in frequency one year, then decrease the next; the change from year to year is not predictable. Thus, unlike natural selection, which in a given environment consistently favors some alleles over others, genetic drift causes allele frequencies to change at random over time.

3. **Genetic drift can lead to a loss of genetic variation within populations.** By causing allele frequencies to fluctuate randomly over time, genetic drift can eliminate alleles from a population. Because evolution depends on genetic variation, such losses can influence how effectively a population can adapt to a change in the environment.

4. **Genetic drift can cause harmful alleles to become fixed.** Alleles that are neither harmful nor beneficial can be lost or become fixed entirely by chance through genetic drift. In very small populations, genetic drift can also cause alleles that are slightly harmful to become fixed. When this occurs, the population's survival can be threatened (as for the greater prairie chicken).

Gene Flow

Natural selection and genetic drift are not the only phenomena affecting allele frequencies. Allele frequencies can also change by **gene flow**, the transfer of alleles into or out of a population due to the movement of fertile individuals or their gametes. For example, suppose that near our original hypothetical wildflower population there is another population

consisting primarily of white-flowered individuals ($C^W C^W$). Insects carrying pollen from these plants may fly to and pollinate plants in our original population. The introduced C^W alleles would modify our original population's allele frequencies in the next generation. Because alleles are exchanged between populations, gene flow tends to reduce the genetic differences between populations. In fact, if it is extensive enough, gene flow can result in two populations combining into a single population with a common gene pool.

Alleles transferred by gene flow can also affect how well populations are adapted to local environmental conditions. Researchers studying the songbird *Parus major* (great tit) on the small Dutch island of Vlieland noted survival differences between two populations on the island. Females born in the eastern population survive twice as well as females born in the central population, regardless of where the females eventually settle and raise offspring (Figure 23.12). This finding suggests that females born in the eastern population are better adapted to life on the island than females born in the

▲ **Figure 23.12 Gene flow and local adaptation.** In *Parus major* populations on Vlieland, the yearly survival rate of females born in the eastern population is higher than that of females born in the central population. Gene flow from the mainland to the central population is 3.3 times higher than it is to the eastern population, and birds from the mainland are selected against in both populations. These data suggest that gene flow from the mainland has prevented the central population from adapting fully to its local conditions.

central population. But extensive field studies also showed that the two populations are connected by high levels of gene flow (mating), which should reduce genetic differences between them. So how can the eastern population be better adapted to life on Vlieland than the central population? The answer lies in the unequal amounts of gene flow from the mainland. In any given year, 43% of the first-time breeders in the central population are immigrants from the mainland, compared with only 13% in the eastern population. Birds with mainland genotypes survive and reproduce poorly on Vlieland, and in the eastern population, selection reduces the frequency of these genotypes. In the central population, however, gene flow from the mainland is so high that it overwhelms the effects of selection. As a result, females born in the central population have many immigrant genes, reducing the degree to which members of that population are adapted to life on the island. Researchers are currently investigating why gene flow is so much higher in the central population and why birds with mainland genotypes have low fitness on Vlieland.

Gene flow can also transfer alleles that improve the ability of populations to adapt to local conditions. For example, gene flow has resulted in the worldwide spread of several insecticide-resistance alleles in the mosquito *Culex pipiens*, a vector of West Nile virus and other diseases. Each of these alleles has a unique genetic signature that allowed researchers to document that it arose by mutation in one or a few geographic locations. In their population of origin, these alleles increased because they provided insecticide resistance. These alleles were then transferred to new populations, where again, their frequencies increased as a result of natural selection.

Finally, gene flow has become an increasingly important agent of evolutionary change in human populations. Humans today move much more freely about the world than in the past. As a result, mating is more common between members of populations that previously had very little contact, leading to an exchange of alleles and fewer genetic differences between those populations.

CONCEPT CHECK 23.3

1. In what sense is natural selection more "predictable" than genetic drift?
2. Distinguish genetic drift from gene flow in terms of (a) how they occur and (b) their implications for future genetic variation in a population.
3. **WHAT IF?** Suppose two plant populations exchange pollen and seeds. In one population, individuals of genotype *AA* are most common (9,000 *AA*, 900 *Aa*, 100 *aa*), while the opposite is true in the other population (100 *AA*, 900 *Aa*, 9,000 *aa*). If neither allele has a selective advantage, what will happen over time to the allele and genotype frequencies of these populations?

For suggested answers, see Appendix A.

CONCEPT **23.4**

Natural selection is the only mechanism that consistently causes adaptive evolution

Evolution by natural selection is a blend of chance and "sorting": chance in the creation of new genetic variations (as in mutation) and sorting as natural selection favors some alleles over others. Because of this favoring process, the outcome of natural selection is *not* random. Instead, natural selection consistently increases the frequencies of alleles that provide reproductive advantage and thus leads to adaptive evolution.

A Closer Look at Natural Selection

In examining how natural selection brings about adaptive evolution, we'll begin with the concept of relative fitness and the different ways that an organism's phenotype is subject to natural selection.

Relative Fitness

The phrases "struggle for existence" and "survival of the fittest" are commonly used to describe natural selection, but these expressions are misleading if taken to mean direct competitive contests among individuals. There *are* animal species in which individuals, usually the males, lock horns or otherwise do combat to determine mating privilege. But reproductive success is generally more subtle and depends on many factors besides outright battle. For example, a barnacle that is more efficient at collecting food than its neighbors may have greater stores of energy and hence be able to produce a larger number of eggs. A moth may have more offspring than other moths in the same population because its body colors more effectively conceal it from predators, improving its chance of surviving long enough to produce more offspring. These examples illustrate how in a given environment, certain traits can lead to greater **relative fitness**: the contribution an individual makes to the gene pool of the next generation *relative to* the contributions of other individuals.

Although we often refer to the relative fitness of a genotype, remember that the entity that is subjected to natural selection is the whole organism, not the underlying genotype. Thus, selection acts more directly on the phenotype than on the genotype; it acts on the genotype indirectly, via how the genotype affects the phenotype.

Directional, Disruptive, and Stabilizing Selection

Natural selection can alter the frequency distribution of heritable traits in three ways, depending on which phenotypes in a population are favored. These three modes of selection are called directional selection, disruptive selection, and stabilizing selection.

Directional selection occurs when conditions favor individuals exhibiting one extreme of a phenotypic range, thereby shifting a population's frequency curve for the phenotypic character in one direction or the other (Figure 23.13a). Directional selection is common when a population's environment changes or when members of a population migrate to a new (and different) habitat. For instance, an increase in the relative abundance of large seeds over small seeds led to an increase in beak depth in a population of Galápagos finches (see Figure 23.2).

Disruptive selection (Figure 23.13b) occurs when conditions favor individuals at both extremes of a phenotypic range over individuals with intermediate phenotypes. One example is a population of black-bellied seedcracker finches in Cameroon whose members display two distinctly different beak sizes. Small-billed birds feed mainly on soft seeds, whereas large-billed birds specialize in cracking hard seeds. It appears that birds with intermediate-sized bills are relatively inefficient at cracking both types of seeds and thus have lower relative fitness.

Stabilizing selection (Figure 23.13c) acts against both extreme phenotypes and favors intermediate variants. This mode of selection reduces variation and tends to maintain the status quo for a particular phenotypic character. For example, the birth weights of most human babies lie in the range of 3–4 kg (6.6–8.8 pounds); babies who are either much smaller or much larger suffer higher rates of mortality.

Regardless of the mode of selection, however, the basic mechanism remains the same. Selection favors individuals whose heritable phenotypic traits provide higher reproductive success than do the traits of other individuals.

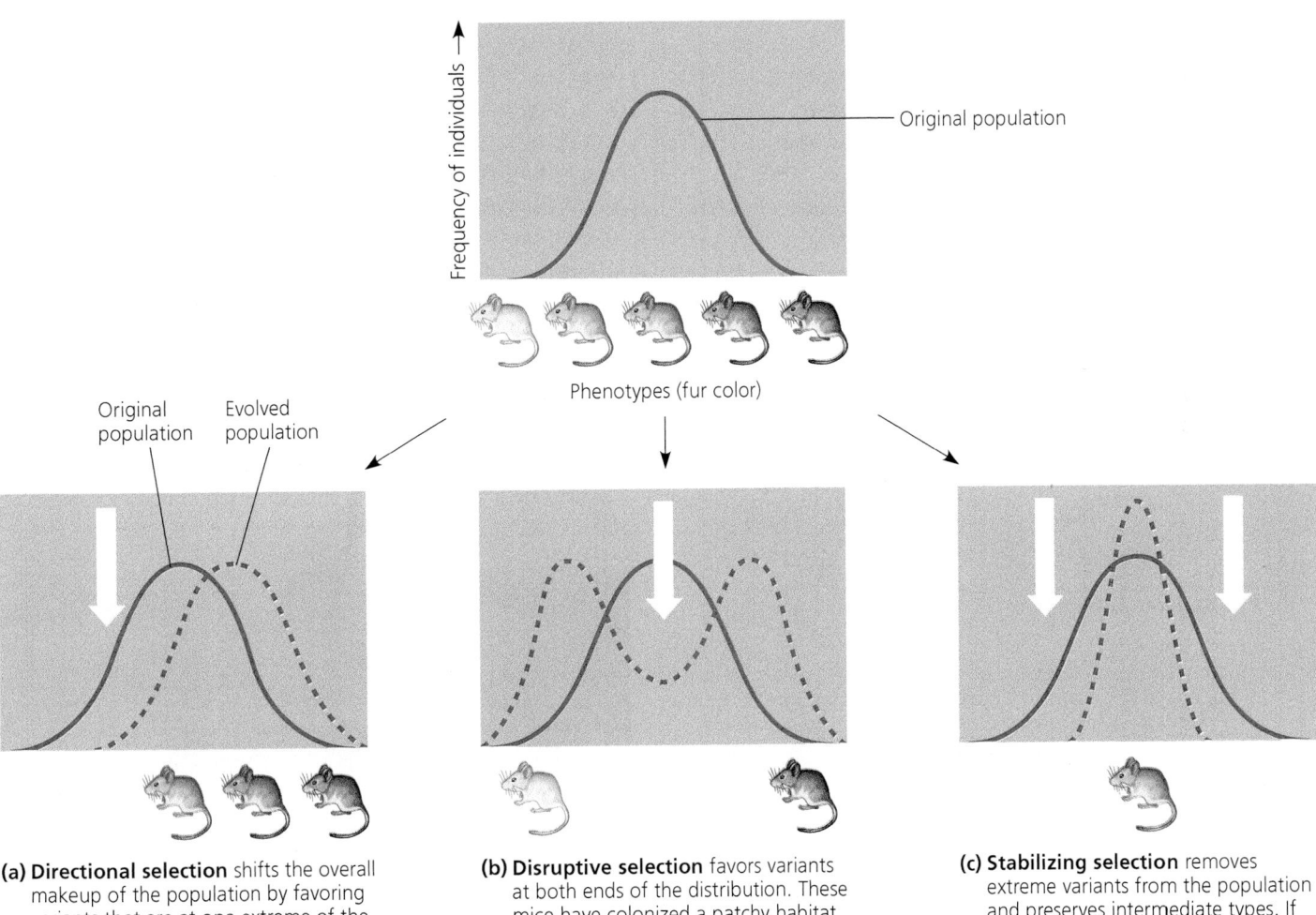

(a) Directional selection shifts the overall makeup of the population by favoring variants that are at one extreme of the distribution. In this case, lighter mice are selected against because they live among dark rocks, making it harder for them to hide from predators.

(b) Disruptive selection favors variants at both ends of the distribution. These mice have colonized a patchy habitat made up of light and dark rocks, with the result that mice of an intermediate color are selected against.

(c) Stabilizing selection removes extreme variants from the population and preserves intermediate types. If the environment consists of rocks of an intermediate color, both light and dark mice will be selected against.

▲ **Figure 23.13 Modes of selection.** These cases describe three ways in which a hypothetical deer mouse population with heritable variation in fur coloration from light to dark might evolve. The graphs show how the frequencies of individuals with different fur colors change over time. The large white arrows symbolize selective pressures against certain phenotypes.

MAKE CONNECTIONS *Review Figure 22.13 on p. 461. Which mode of selection has occurred in soapberry bug populations that feed on the introduced goldenrain tree? Explain.*

The Key Role of Natural Selection in Adaptive Evolution

The adaptations of organisms include many striking examples. Cuttlefish, for example, have the ability to change color rapidly, enabling them to blend into different backgrounds. Another example is the remarkable jaws of snakes (**Figure 23.14**), which allow them to swallow prey much larger than their own head (a feat analogous to a person swallowing a whole watermelon). Other adaptations, such as a version of an enzyme that shows improved function in cold environments (see Figure 23.5), may be less visually dramatic but just as important for survival and reproduction.

Such adaptations can arise gradually over time as natural selection increases the frequencies of alleles that enhance survival and reproduction. As the proportion of individuals that have favorable traits increases, the match between a species and its environment improves; that is, adaptive evolution occurs. However, as we saw in Chapter 22, the physical and biological components of an organism's environment may change over time. As a result, what constitutes a "good match" between an organism and its environment can be a moving target, making adaptive evolution a continuous, dynamic process.

And what about the two other important mechanisms of evolutionary change in populations, genetic drift and gene flow? Both can, in fact, increase the frequencies of alleles that improve the match between organisms and their environ-

ment, but neither does so consistently. Genetic drift can cause the frequency of a slightly beneficial allele to increase, but it also can cause the frequency of such an allele to decrease. Similarly, gene flow may introduce alleles that are advantageous or ones that are disadvantageous. Natural selection is the only evolutionary mechanism that consistently leads to adaptive evolution.

Sexual Selection

Charles Darwin was the first to explore the implications of **sexual selection**, a form of selection in which individuals with certain inherited characteristics are more likely than other individuals to obtain mates. Sexual selection can result in **sexual dimorphism**, a difference between the two sexes in secondary sexual characteristics (**Figure 23.15**). These distinctions include differences in size, color, ornamentation, and behavior.

How does sexual selection operate? There are several ways. In **intrasexual selection**, meaning selection within the same sex, individuals of one sex compete directly for mates of the opposite sex. In many species, intrasexual selection occurs among males. For example, a single male may patrol a group of females and prevent other males from mating with them. The patrolling male may defend his status by defeating smaller, weaker, or less fierce males in combat. More often, this male is the psychological victor in ritualized displays that discourage would-be competitors but do not risk injury that would reduce his own fitness (see Figure 51.17). Intrasexual selection has also been observed among females in a variety of species, including ring-tailed lemurs and broadnosed pipefish.

In **intersexual selection**, also called *mate choice*, individuals of one sex (usually the females) are choosy in selecting

The bones of the upper jaw that are shown in green are movable.

Ligament

The skull bones of most terrestrial vertebrates are relatively rigidly attached to one another, limiting jaw movement. In contrast, most snakes have movable bones in their upper jaw, allowing them to swallow food much larger than their head.

▲ **Figure 23.14 Movable jaw bones in snakes.**

▲ **Figure 23.15 Sexual dimorphism and sexual selection.** Peacocks (above left) and peahens (above right) show extreme sexual dimorphism. There is intrasexual selection between competing males, followed by intersexual selection when the females choose among the showiest males.

their mates from the other sex. In many cases, the female's choice depends on the showiness of the male's appearance or behavior (see Figure 23.15). What intrigued Darwin about mate choice is that male showiness may not seem adaptive in any other way and may in fact pose some risk. For example, bright plumage may make male birds more visible to predators. But if such characteristics help a male gain a mate, and if this benefit outweighs the risk from predation, then both the bright plumage and the female preference for it will be reinforced because they enhance overall reproductive success.

How do female preferences for certain male characteristics evolve in the first place? One hypothesis is that females prefer male traits that are correlated with "good genes." If the trait preferred by females is indicative of a male's overall genetic quality, both the male trait and female preference for it should increase in frequency. Figure 23.16 describes one experiment testing this hypothesis in gray tree frogs (*Hyla versicolor*).

Other researchers have shown that in several bird species, the traits preferred by females are related to overall male health. Here, too, female preference appears to be based on traits that reflect "good genes," in this case alleles indicative of a robust immune system.

The Preservation of Genetic Variation

Some of the genetic variation in populations represents **neutral variation**, differences in DNA sequence that do not confer a selective advantage or disadvantage. But variation is also found at loci affected by selection. What prevents natural selection from reducing genetic variation at those loci by culling all unfavorable alleles? The tendency for directional and stabilizing selection to reduce variation is countered by mechanisms that preserve or restore it.

Diploidy

In diploid eukaryotes, a considerable amount of genetic variation is hidden from selection in the form of recessive alleles. Recessive alleles that are less favorable than their dominant counterparts, or even harmful in the current environment, can persist by propagation in heterozygous individuals. This latent variation is exposed to natural selection only when both parents carry the same recessive allele and two copies end up in the same zygote. This happens only rarely if the frequency of the recessive allele is very low. Heterozygote protection maintains a huge pool of alleles that might not be favored under present conditions, but which could bring new benefits if the environment changes.

Balancing Selection

Selection itself may preserve variation at some loci. **Balancing selection** occurs when natural selection maintains two or

Do females select mates based on traits indicative of "good genes"?

EXPERIMENT Female gray tree frogs (*Hyla versicolor*) prefer to mate with males that give long mating calls. Allison Welch and colleagues, at the University of Missouri, tested whether the genetic makeup of long-calling (LC) males is superior to that of short-calling (SC) males. The researchers fertilized half the eggs of each female with sperm from an LC male and fertilized the remaining eggs with sperm from an SC male. The resulting half-sibling offspring were raised in a common environment, and several measures of their "performance" were tracked for two years.

RESULTS

Offspring Performance	1995	1996
Larval survival	LC better	NSD
Larval growth	NSD	LC better
Time to metamorphosis	LC better (shorter)	LC better (shorter)

NSD = no significant difference; LC better = offspring of LC males superior to offspring of SC males.

CONCLUSION Because offspring fathered by an LC male outperformed their half-siblings fathered by an SC male, the team concluded that the duration of a male's mating call is indicative of the male's overall genetic quality. This result supports the hypothesis that female mate choice can be based on a trait that indicates whether the male has "good genes."

SOURCE A. M. Welch et al., Call duration as an indicator of genetic quality in male gray tree frogs, *Science* 280:1928–1930 (1998).

INQUIRY IN ACTION Read and analyze the original paper in *Inquiry in Action: Interpreting Scientific Papers*.

WHAT IF? Why did the researchers split each female frog's eggs into two batches for fertilization by different males? Why didn't they mate each female with a single male frog?

more forms in a population. This type of selection includes heterozygote advantage and frequency-dependent selection.

Heterozygote Advantage If individuals who are heterozygous at a particular locus have greater fitness than do both kinds of homozygotes, they exhibit **heterozygote advantage**. In such a case, natural selection tends to maintain two or more alleles at that locus. Note that heterozygote advantage is defined in terms of *genotype*, not phenotype. Thus, whether heterozygote advantage represents stabilizing or directional selection depends on the relationship between the genotype and the phenotype. For example, if the phenotype of a heterozygote is intermediate to the phenotypes of both homozygotes, heterozygote advantage is a form of stabilizing selection.

An example of heterozygote advantage occurs at the locus in humans that codes for the β polypeptide subunit of hemoglobin, the oxygen-carrying protein of red blood cells. In homozygous individuals, a certain recessive allele at that locus causes sickle-cell disease. The red blood cells of people with sickle-cell disease become distorted in shape, or *sickled*, under low-oxygen conditions (see Figure 5.21), as occurs in the capillaries. These sickled cells can clump together and block the flow of blood in the capillaries, resulting in serious damage to organs such as the kidney, heart, and brain. Although some red blood cells become sickled in heterozygotes, not enough become sickled to cause sickle-cell disease.

Heterozygotes for the sickle-cell allele are protected against the most severe effects of malaria, a disease caused by a parasite that infects red blood cells (see Figure 28.10). This partial protection occurs because the body destroys sickled red blood cells rapidly, killing the parasites they harbor (but not affecting parasites inside normal red blood cells). Protection against malaria is important in tropical regions where the disease is a major killer. In such regions, selection favors heterozygotes over homozygous dominant individuals, who are more vulnerable to the effects of malaria, and also over homozygous recessive individuals, who develop sickle-cell disease. The frequency of the sickle-cell allele in Africa is generally highest in areas where the malaria parasite is most common (**Figure 23.17**). In some populations, it accounts for 20% of the hemoglobin alleles in the gene pool, a very high frequency for such a harmful allele.

Frequency-Dependent Selection In **frequency-dependent selection**, the fitness of a phenotype depends on how common it is in the population. Consider the scale-eating fish (*Perissodus microlepis*) of Lake Tanganyika, in Africa. These fish attack other fish from behind, darting in to remove a few scales from the flank of their prey. Of interest here is a peculiar feature of the scale-eating fish: Some are "left-mouthed" and some are "right-mouthed." Simple Mendelian inheritance determines these phenotypes, with the right-mouthed allele being domi-

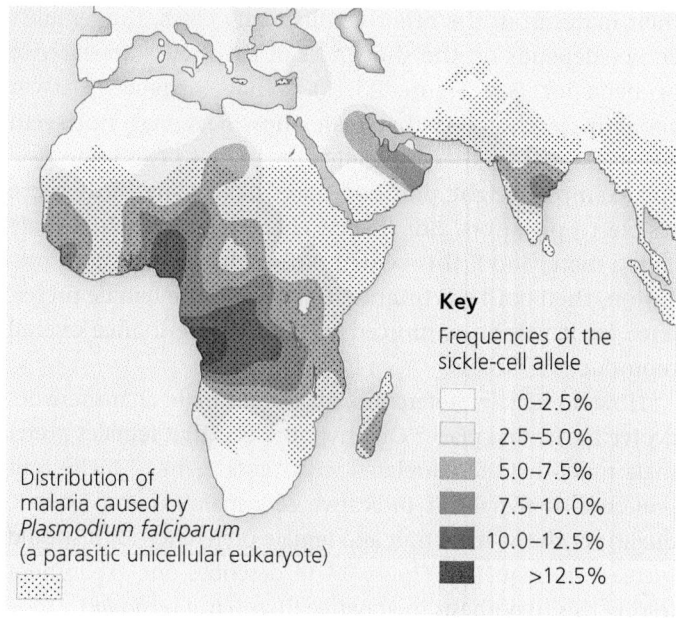

Key
Frequencies of the sickle-cell allele

	0–2.5%
	2.5–5.0%
	5.0–7.5%
	7.5–10.0%
	10.0–12.5%
	>12.5%

Distribution of malaria caused by *Plasmodium falciparum* (a parasitic unicellular eukaryote)

▲ **Figure 23.17 Mapping malaria and the sickle-cell allele.** The sickle-cell allele is most common in Africa, but it is not the only case of heterozygote advantage providing protection against malaria. Alleles at other loci (not shown on this map) are also favored by heterozygote advantage in populations near the Mediterranean Sea and in southeast Asia where malaria is widespread.

nant to the left-mouthed allele. Because their mouth twists to the left, left-mouthed fish always attack their prey's right flank (**Figure 23.18**). (To see why, twist your lower jaw and lips to the left and imagine trying to take a bite from the left side of a fish, approaching it from behind.) Similarly, right-mouthed fish always attack from the left. Prey species guard against attack from whatever phenotype of scale-eating fish is most common in the lake. Thus, from year to year, selection favors whichever mouth phenotype is least common. As a result, the frequency of left- and right-mouthed fish oscillates over time, and balancing selection (due to frequency dependence) keeps the frequency of each phenotype close to 50%.

Why Natural Selection Cannot Fashion Perfect Organisms

Though natural selection leads to adaptation, nature abounds with examples of organisms that are less than ideally "engineered" for their lifestyles. There are several reasons why.

1. **Selection can act only on existing variations.** Natural selection favors only the fittest phenotypes among those currently in the population, which may not be the ideal traits. New advantageous alleles do not arise on demand.
2. **Evolution is limited by historical constraints.** Each species has a legacy of descent with modification from ancestral forms. Evolution does not scrap the

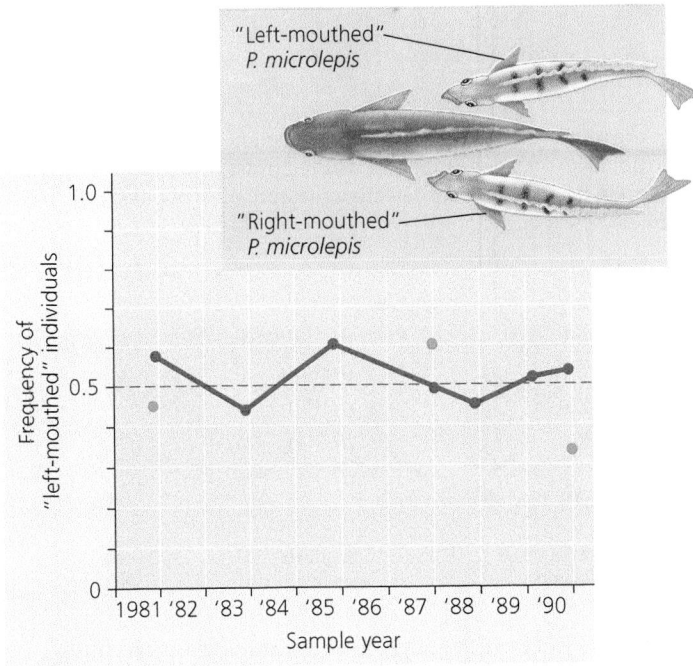

"Left-mouthed"
P. microlepis

"Right-mouthed"
P. microlepis

▲ **Figure 23.18 Frequency-dependent selection in scale-eating fish (*Perissodus microlepis*).** Michio Hori, of Kyoto University, Japan, noted that the frequency of left-mouthed individuals rises and falls in a regular manner. At each of three time periods when the phenotypes of breeding adults were assessed, adults that reproduced (represented by green dots) had the opposite phenotype of that which was most common in the population. Thus, it appeared that right-mouthed individuals were favored by selection when left-mouthed individuals were more common, and vice versa.

? *What did the researchers measure to determine which phenotype was favored by selection? Are any assumptions implied by this choice? Explain.*

ancestral anatomy and build each new complex structure from scratch; rather, evolution co-opts existing structures and adapts them to new situations. We could imagine that if a terrestrial animal were to adapt to an environment in which flight would be advantageous, it might be best just to grow an extra pair of limbs that would serve as wings. However, evolution does not work this way; instead, it operates on the traits an organism already has. Thus, in birds and bats, an existing pair of limbs took on new functions for flight as these organisms evolved from nonflying ancestors.

3. **Adaptations are often compromises.** Each organism must do many things. A seal spends part of its time on rocks; it could probably walk better if it had legs instead of flippers, but then it would not swim nearly as well. We humans owe much of our versatility and athleticism to our prehensile hands and flexible limbs, but these also make us prone to sprains, torn ligaments, and dislocations: Structural reinforcement has been compromised for agility. **Figure 23.19** depicts another example of evolutionary compromise.

▲ **Figure 23.19 Evolutionary compromise.** The loud call that enables a Túngara frog to attract mates also attracts more dangerous characters in the neighborhood—in this case, a bat about to seize a meal.

4. **Chance, natural selection, and the environment interact.** Chance events can affect the subsequent evolutionary history of populations. For instance, when a storm blows insects or birds hundreds of kilometers over an ocean to an island, the wind does not necessarily transport those individuals that are best suited to the new environment. Thus, not all alleles present in the founding population's gene pool are better suited to the new environment than the alleles that are "left behind." In addition, the environment at a particular location may change unpredictably from year to year, again limiting the extent to which adaptive evolution results in a close match between the organism and current environmental conditions.

With these four constraints, evolution does not tend to craft perfect organisms. Natural selection operates on a "better than" basis. We can, in fact, see evidence for evolution in the many imperfections of the organisms it produces.

CONCEPT CHECK 23.4

1. What is the relative fitness of a sterile mule? Explain.
2. Explain why natural selection is the only evolutionary mechanism that consistently leads to adaptive evolution.
3. **WHAT IF?** Consider a population in which heterozygotes at a certain locus have an extreme phenotype (such as being larger than homozygotes) that confers a selective advantage. Does such a situation represent directional, disruptive, or stabilizing selection? Explain your answer.
4. **WHAT IF?** Would individuals who are heterozygous for the sickle-cell allele be selected for or against in a region free from malaria? Explain.

For suggested answers, see Appendix A.

CONCEPT 23.1

Genetic variation makes evolution possible (pp. 469–473)

- **Genetic variation** refers to genetic differences among individuals within a population.
- The nucleotide differences that provide the basis of genetic variation arise by mutation and other processes that produce new alleles and new genes.
- New genetic variants are produced rapidly in organisms with short generation times. In sexually reproducing organisms, most of the genetic differences among individuals result from crossing over, the independent assortment of chromosomes, and fertilization.

? *Why do biologists estimate gene variability and nucleotide variability, and what do these estimates represent?*

CONCEPT 23.2

The Hardy-Weinberg equation can be used to test whether a population is evolving (pp. 473–476)

- A **population**, a localized group of organisms belonging to one species, is united by its **gene pool**, the aggregate of all the alleles in the population.
- The **Hardy-Weinberg principle** states that the allele and genotype frequencies of a population will remain constant if the population is large, mating is random, mutation is negligible, there is no gene flow, and there is no natural selection. For such a population, if p and q represent the frequencies of the only two possible alleles at a particular locus, then p^2 is the frequency of one kind of homozygote, q^2 is the frequency of the other kind of homozygote, and $2pq$ is the frequency of the heterozygous genotype.

? *Is it circular reasoning to calculate p and q from observed genotype frequencies and then use those values of p and q to test if the population is in Hardy-Weinberg equilibrium? Explain your answer. (Hint: Consider a specific case, such as a population with 195 individuals of genotype AA, 10 of genotype Aa, and 195 of genotype aa.)*

CONCEPT 23.3

Natural selection, genetic drift, and gene flow can alter allele frequencies in a population (pp. 476–480)

- In natural selection, individuals that have certain inherited traits tend to survive and reproduce at higher rates than other individuals *because of* those traits.
- In **genetic drift**, chance fluctuations in allele frequencies over generations tend to reduce genetic variation.
- **Gene flow**, the transfer of alleles between populations, tends to reduce genetic differences between populations over time.

? *Would two small, geographically isolated populations in very different environments be likely to evolve in similar ways? Explain.*

CONCEPT 23.4

Natural selection is the only mechanism that consistently causes adaptive evolution (pp. 480–485)

- One organism has greater **relative fitness** than a second organism if it leaves more fertile descendants than the second

organism. The modes of natural selection differ in how selection acts on phenotype (the white arrows in the summary diagram below represent selective pressure on a population).

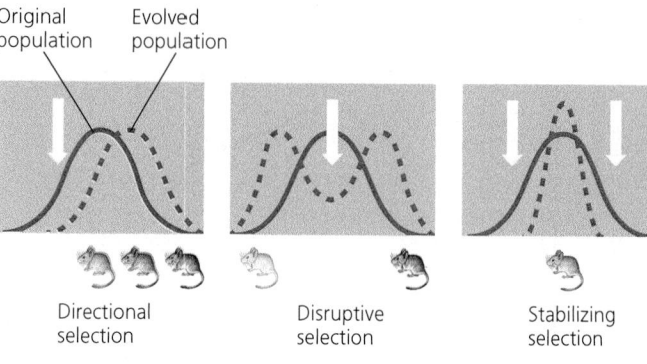

Original population / Evolved population

Directional selection   Disruptive selection   Stabilizing selection

- Unlike genetic drift and gene flow, natural selection consistently increases the frequencies of alleles that enhance survival and reproduction, thus improving the match between organisms and their environment.
- **Sexual selection** influences evolutionary change in secondary sex characteristics that can give individuals advantages in mating.
- Despite the winnowing effects of selection, populations have considerable genetic variation. Some of this variation represents **neutral variation**; additional variation can be maintained by diploidy and balancing selection.
- There are constraints to evolution: Natural selection can act only on available variation; structures result from modified ancestral anatomy; adaptations are often compromises; and chance, natural selection, and the environment interact.

? *How might secondary sex characteristics differ between males and females in a species in which females compete for mates?*

LEVEL 1: KNOWLEDGE/COMPREHENSION

1. Natural selection changes allele frequencies because some _____ survive and reproduce more successfully than others.
   a. alleles
   b. loci
   c. gene pools
   d. species
   e. individuals

2. No two people are genetically identical, except for identical twins. The main source of genetic variation among human individuals is
   a. new mutations that occurred in the preceding generation.
   b. genetic drift due to the small size of the population.
   c. the reshuffling of alleles in sexual reproduction.
   d. geographic variation within the population.
   e. environmental effects.

3. Sparrows with average-sized wings survive severe storms better than those with longer or shorter wings, illustrating
   a. the bottleneck effect.
   b. disruptive selection.
   c. frequency-dependent selection.
   d. neutral variation.
   e. stabilizing selection.

LEVEL 2: APPLICATION/ANALYSIS

4. If the nucleotide variability of a locus equals 0%, what is the gene variability and number of alleles at that locus?
   a. gene variability = 0%; number of alleles = 0
   b. gene variability = 0%; number of alleles = 1
   c. gene variability = 0%; number of alleles = 2
   d. gene variability > 0%; number of alleles = 2
   e. Without more information, gene variability and number of alleles cannot be determined.

5. There are 40 individuals in population 1, all with genotype *A1A1*, and there are 25 individuals in population 2, all with genotype *A2A2*. Assume that these populations are located far from each other and that their environmental conditions are very similar. Based on the information given here, the observed genetic variation is most likely an example of
   a. genetic drift.   d. discrete variation.
   b. gene flow.   e. directional selection.
   c. disruptive selection.

6. A fruit fly population has a gene with two alleles, *A1* and *A2*. Tests show that 70% of the gametes produced in the population contain the *A1* allele. If the population is in Hardy-Weinberg equilibrium, what proportion of the flies carry both *A1* and *A2*?
   a. 0.7   b. 0.49   c. 0.21   d. 0.42   e. 0.09

LEVEL 3: SYNTHESIS/EVALUATION

7. **EVOLUTION CONNECTION**
   How is the process of evolution revealed by the imperfections of living organisms?

8. **SCIENTIFIC INQUIRY**
   DRAW IT   Richard Koehn, of the State University of New York, Stony Brook, and Thomas Hilbish, of the University of South Carolina, studied genetic variation in the marine mussel *Mytilus edulis* around Long Island, New York. They measured the frequency of a particular allele (*lap94*) for an enzyme involved in regulating the mussel's internal saltwater balance. The researchers presented their data as a series of pie charts linked to sampling sites within Long Island Sound, where the salinity is highly variable, and along the coast of the open ocean, where salinity is constant:

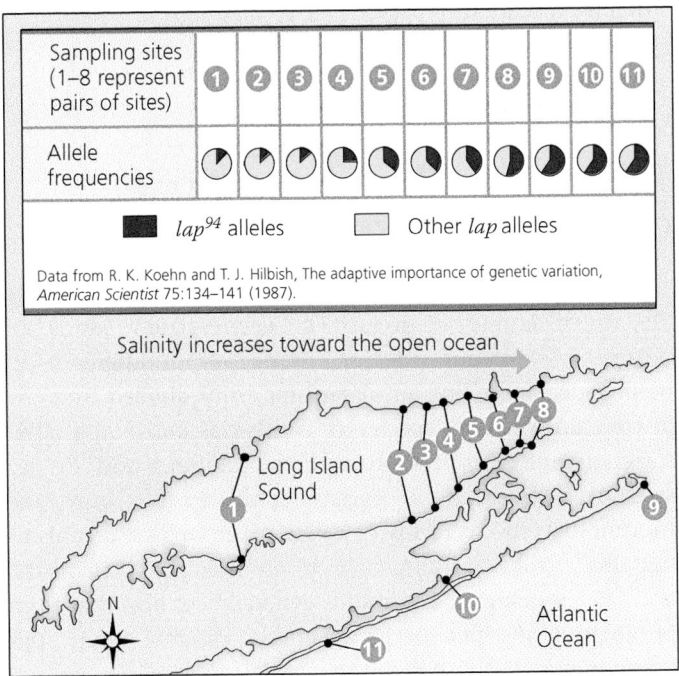

Data from R. K. Koehn and T. J. Hilbish, The adaptive importance of genetic variation, *American Scientist* 75:134–141 (1987).

(Question 8, continued)

Create a data table for the 11 sampling sites by estimating the frequency of *lap94* from the pie charts. (*Hint*: Think of each pie chart as a clock face to help you estimate the proportion of the shaded area.) Then graph the frequencies for sites 1–8 to show how the frequency of this allele changes with increasing salinity in Long Island Sound (from southwest to northeast). How do the data from sites 9–11 compare with the data from the sites within the Sound?

Construct a hypothesis that explains the patterns you observe in the data and that accounts for the following observations: (1) the *lap94* allele helps mussels maintain osmotic balance in water with a high salt concentration but is costly to use in less salty water; and (2) mussels produce larvae that can disperse long distances before they settle on rocks and grow into adults.

9. **WRITE ABOUT A THEME**

   Emergent Properties Heterozygotes at the sickle-cell locus produce both normal and abnormal (sickle-cell) hemoglobin (see Concept 14.4). When hemoglobin molecules are packed into a heterozygote's red blood cells, some cells receive relatively large quantities of abnormal hemoglobin, making these cells prone to sickling. In a short essay (approximately 100–150 words), explain how these molecular and cellular events lead to emergent properties at the individual and population levels of biological organization.

For selected answers, see Appendix A.

MasteringBIOLOGY   www.masteringbiology.com

1. MasteringBiology® Assignments
Make Connections Tutorial Hardy-Weinberg Principle (Chapter 23) and Inheritance of Alleles (Chapter 14)
Experimental Inquiry Tutorial Did Natural Selection of Ground Finches Occur When the Environment Changed?
BioFlix Tutorial Mechanisms of Evolution
Tutorial Hardy-Weinberg Principle
Activities Genetic Variation from Sexual Recombination • The Hardy-Weinberg Principle • Causes of Evolutionary Change • Three Modes of Natural Selection
Questions Student Misconceptions • Reading Quiz • Multiple Choice • End-of-Chapter

2. eText
Read your book online, search, take notes, highlight text, and more.

3. The Study Area
Practice Tests • Cumulative Test • **BioFlix** 3-D Animations • MP3 Tutor Sessions • Videos • Activities • Investigations • Lab Media • Audio Glossary • Word Study Tools • Art

24

The Origin of Species

▲ **Figure 24.1 How did this flightless bird come to live on the isolated Galápagos Islands?**

KEY CONCEPTS

24.1 The biological species concept emphasizes reproductive isolation

24.2 Speciation can take place with or without geographic separation

24.3 Hybrid zones reveal factors that cause reproductive isolation

24.4 Speciation can occur rapidly or slowly and can result from changes in few or many genes

OVERVIEW

That "Mystery of Mysteries"

Darwin came to the Galápagos Islands eager to explore landforms newly emerged from the sea. He noted that these volcanic islands, despite their geologic youth, were teeming with plants and animals found nowhere else in the world

(Figure 24.1). Later he realized that these species, like the islands, were relatively new. He wrote in his diary: "Both in space and time, we seem to be brought somewhat near to that great fact—that mystery of mysteries—the first appearance of new beings on this Earth."

The "mystery of mysteries" that captivated Darwin is **speciation**, the process by which one species splits into two or more species. Speciation fascinated Darwin (and many biologists since) because it is responsible for the tremendous diversity of life, repeatedly yielding new species that differ from existing ones. Speciation explains not only differences between species, but also similarities between them (the unity of life). When one species splits into two, the species that result share many characteristics because they are descended from this common ancestral species. For example, DNA similarities indicate that the flightless cormorant (*Phalacrocorax harrisi*) in Figure 24.1 is closely related to flying cormorants found in the Americas. This suggests that the flightless cormorant may have originated from an ancestral cormorant species that migrated from the mainland to the Galápagos.

Speciation also forms a conceptual bridge between **microevolution**, changes over time in allele frequencies in a population, and **macroevolution**, the broad pattern of evolution above the species level. An example of macroevolutionary change is the origin of new groups of organisms, such as mammals or flowering plants, through a series of speciation events. We examined microevolutionary mechanisms (mutation, natural selection, genetic drift, and gene flow) in Chapter 23, and we'll turn to macroevolution in Chapter 25. In this chapter, we will explore the "bridge"—the mechanisms by which new species originate from existing ones. First, however, we need to establish what we actually mean when we talk about "species."

CONCEPT **24.1**

The biological species concept emphasizes reproductive isolation

The word *species* is Latin for "kind" or "appearance." In daily life, we commonly distinguish between various "kinds" of organisms—dogs and cats, for instance—from differences in their appearance. But are organisms truly divided into the discrete units we call species, or is this classification an arbitrary attempt to impose order on the natural world? To answer this question, biologists compare not only the morphology (body form) of different groups of organisms but also less obvious differences in physiology, biochemistry, and DNA sequences. The results generally confirm that morphologically distinct species are indeed discrete groups, differing in many ways besides their body forms.

The Biological Species Concept

The primary definition of species used in this textbook is the **biological species concept**. According to this concept, a **species** is a group of populations whose members have the potential to interbreed in nature and produce viable, fertile offspring—but do not produce viable, fertile offspring with members of other such groups (Figure 24.2). Thus, the members of a biological species are united by being repro-ductively compatible, at least potentially. All human beings, for example, belong to the same species. A businesswoman in Manhattan may be unlikely to meet a dairy farmer in Mongolia, but if the two should happen to meet and mate, they could have viable babies that develop into fertile adults. In contrast, humans and chimpanzees remain distinct biological species even where they share territory, because many factors keep them from interbreeding and producing fertile offspring.

What holds the gene pool of a species together, causing its members to resemble each other more than they resemble other species? To answer this question, we need to return to the evolutionary mechanism called *gene flow*, the transfer of alleles between populations (see Chapter 23). Typically, gene flow occurs between the different populations of a species. This ongoing exchange of alleles tends to hold the populations together genetically. As we'll explore in the following sections, the absence of gene flow plays a key role in the formation of new species, as well as in keeping them apart once their potential to interbreed has been reduced.

(a) Similarity between different species. The eastern meadowlark (*Sturnella magna*, left) and the western meadowlark (*Sturnella neglecta*, right) have similar body shapes and colorations. Nevertheless, they are distinct biological species because their songs and other behaviors are different enough to prevent interbreeding should they meet in the wild.

Reproductive Isolation

Because biological species are defined in terms of reproductive compatibility, the formation of a new species hinges on **reproductive isolation**—the existence of biological factors (barriers) that impede members of two species from interbreeding and producing viable, fertile offspring. Such barriers block gene flow between the species and limit the formation of **hybrids**, offspring that result from an interspecific mating. Although a single barrier may not prevent all gene flow, a combination of several barriers can effectively isolate a species' gene pool.

Clearly, a fly cannot mate with a frog or a fern, but the reproductive barriers between more closely related species are not so obvious. These barriers can be classified according to whether they contribute to reproductive isolation before or after fertilization. **Prezygotic barriers** ("before the zygote") block fertilization from occurring. Such barriers typically act in one of three ways: by impeding members of different species from attempting to mate, by preventing an attempted mating from being completed successfully, or by hindering fertilization if mating is completed successfully. If a sperm cell from one species overcomes prezygotic barriers and fertilizes an ovum from another species, a variety of **postzygotic barriers** ("after the zygote") may contribute to reproductive isolation after the hybrid zygote is formed. For example, developmental errors may reduce survival among hybrid embryos. Or problems after birth may cause hybrids to be infertile or may decrease their chance of surviving long enough to reproduce. Figure 24.3, on the next two pages, describes prezygotic and postzygotic barriers in more detail.

(b) Diversity within a species. As diverse as we may be in appearance, all humans belong to a single biological species (*Homo sapiens*), defined by our capacity to interbreed successfully.

▲ **Figure 24.2 The biological species concept is based on the potential to interbreed rather than on physical similarity.**

Exploring Reproductive Barriers

Prezygotic barriers impede mating or hinder fertilization if mating does occur

| Habitat Isolation | Temporal Isolation | Behavioral Isolation | Mechanical Isolation |

Individuals of different species

MATING ATTEMPT

Habitat Isolation

Two species that occupy different habitats within the same area may encounter each other rarely, if at all, even though they are not isolated by obvious physical barriers, such as mountain ranges.

Example: Two species of garter snakes in the genus *Thamnophis* occur in the same geographic areas, but one lives mainly in water (a) while the other is primarily terrestrial (b).

Temporal Isolation

Species that breed during different times of the day, different seasons, or different years cannot mix their gametes.

Example: In North America, the geographic ranges of the western spotted skunk (*Spilogale gracilis*) (c) and the eastern spotted skunk (*Spilogale putorius*) (d) overlap, but *S. gracilis* mates in late summer and *S. putorius* mates in late winter.

Behavioral Isolation

Courtship rituals that attract mates and other behaviors unique to a species are effective reproductive barriers, even between closely related species. Such behavioral rituals enable *mate recognition*—a way to identify potential mates of the same species.

Example: Blue-footed boobies, inhabitants of the Galápagos, mate only after a courtship display unique to their species. Part of the "script" calls for the male to high-step (e), a behavior that calls the female's attention to his bright blue feet.

Mechanical Isolation

Mating is attempted, but morphological differences prevent its successful completion.

Example: The shells of two species of snails in the genus *Bradybaena* spiral in different directions: Moving inward to the center, one spirals in a counterclockwise direction (f, left), the other in a clockwise direction (f, right). As a result, the snails' genital openings (indicated by arrows) are not aligned, and mating cannot be completed.

Gametic Isolation

Reduced Hybrid Viability

Reduced Hybrid Fertility

Hybrid Breakdown

FERTILIZATION

VIABLE, FERTILE OFFSPRING

Sperm of one species may not be able to fertilize the eggs of another species. For instance, sperm may not be able to survive in the reproductive tract of females of the other species, or biochemical mechanisms may prevent the sperm from penetrating the membrane surrounding the other species' eggs.

Example: Gametic isolation separates certain closely related species of aquatic animals, such as sea urchins (g). Sea urchins release their sperm and eggs into the surrounding water, where they fuse and form zygotes. It is difficult for gametes of different species, such as the red and purple urchins shown here, to fuse because proteins on the surfaces of the eggs and sperm bind very poorly to each other.

The genes of different parent species may interact in ways that impair the hybrid's development or survival in its environment.

Example: Some salamander subspecies of the genus *Ensatina* live in the same regions and habitats, where they may occasionally hybridize. But most of the hybrids do not complete development, and those that do are frail (h).

Even if hybrids are vigorous, they may be sterile. If the chromosomes of the two parent species differ in number or structure, meiosis in the hybrids may fail to produce normal gametes. Since the infertile hybrids cannot produce offspring when they mate with either parent species, genes cannot flow freely between the species.

Example: The hybrid offspring of a male donkey (i) and a female horse (j) is a mule (k), which is robust but sterile. A "hinny" (not shown), the offspring of a female donkey and a male horse, is also sterile.

Some first-generation hybrids are viable and fertile, but when they mate with one another or with either parent species, offspring of the next generation are feeble or sterile.

Example: Strains of cultivated rice have accumulated different mutant recessive alleles at two loci in the course of their divergence from a common ancestor. Hybrids between them are vigorous and fertile (l, left and right), but plants in the next generation that carry too many of these recessive alleles are small and sterile (l, center). Although these rice strains are not yet considered different species, they have begun to be separated by postzygotic barriers.

Limitations of the Biological Species Concept

One strength of the biological species concept is that it directs our attention to a way by which speciation can occur: by the evolution of reproductive isolation. However, the number of species to which this concept can be usefully applied is limited. There is, for example, no way to evaluate the reproductive isolation of fossils. The biological species concept also does not apply to organisms that reproduce asexually all or most of the time, such as prokaryotes. (Many prokaryotes do transfer genes among themselves, as we will discuss in Chapter 27, but this is not part of their reproductive process.) Furthermore, in the biological species concept, species are designated by the *absence* of gene flow. But there are many pairs of species that are morphologically and ecologically distinct, and yet gene flow occurs between them. An example is the grizzly bear (*Ursus arctos*) and polar bear (*Ursus maritimus*), whose hybrid offspring have been dubbed "grolar bears" **(Figure 24.4)**. As we'll discuss, natural selection can cause such species to remain distinct even though some gene flow occurs between them. This observation has led some researchers to argue that the biological species concept overemphasizes gene flow and downplays the role of natural selection. Because of the limitations to the biological species concept, alternative species concepts are useful in certain situations.

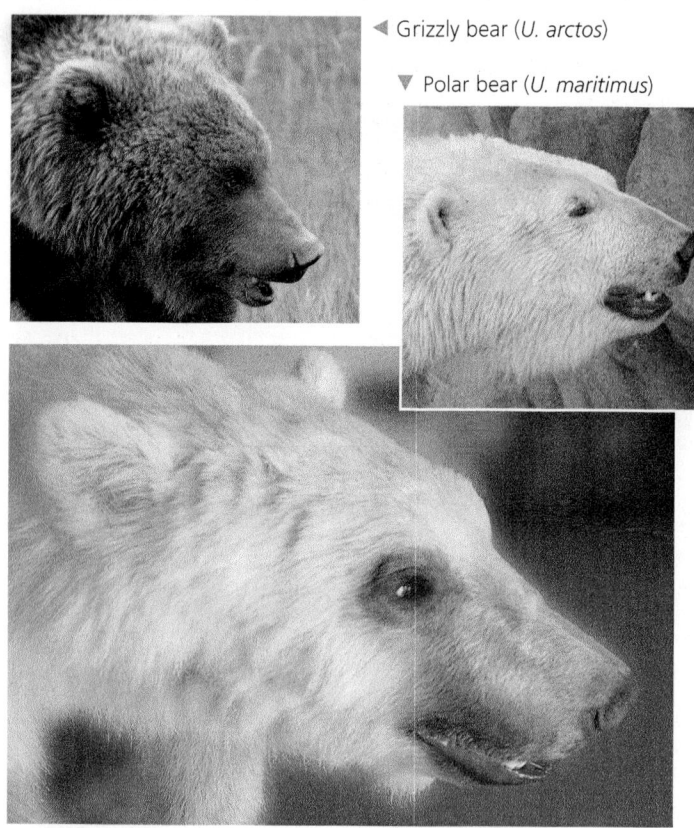

◄ Grizzly bear (*U. arctos*)

▼ Polar bear (*U. maritimus*)

▲ Hybrid "grolar bear"

▲ **Figure 24.4 Hybridization between two species of bears in the genus *Ursus*.**

Other Definitions of Species

While the biological species concept emphasizes the *separateness* of species from one another due to reproductive barriers, several other definitions emphasize the *unity within* a species. For example, the **morphological species concept** characterizes a species by body shape and other structural features. The morphological species concept can be applied to asexual and sexual organisms, and it can be useful even without information on the extent of gene flow. In practice, this is how scientists distinguish most species. One disadvantage, however, is that this definition relies on subjective criteria; researchers may disagree on which structural features distinguish a species.

The **ecological species concept** views a species in terms of its ecological niche, the sum of how members of the species interact with the nonliving and living parts of their environment (see Chapter 54). For example, two species of salamanders might be similar in appearance but differ in the foods they eat or in their ability to tolerate dry conditions. Unlike the biological species concept, the ecological species concept can accommodate asexual as well as sexual species. It also emphasizes the role of disruptive natural selection as organisms adapt to different environmental conditions.

The **phylogenetic species concept** defines a species as the smallest group of individuals that share a common ancestor, forming one branch on the tree of life. Biologists trace the phylogenetic history of a species by comparing its characteristics, such as morphology or molecular sequences, with those of other organisms. Such analyses can distinguish groups of individuals that are sufficiently different to be considered separate species. Of course, the difficulty with this species concept is determining the degree of difference required to indicate separate species.

In addition to those discussed here, more than 20 other species definitions have been proposed. The usefulness of each definition depends on the situation and the research questions being asked. For our purposes of studying how species originate, the biological species concept, with its focus on reproductive barriers, is particularly helpful.

CONCEPT CHECK 24.1

1. (a) Which species concept(s) could you apply to both asexual and sexual species? (b) Which would be most useful for identifying species in the field? Explain.
2. **WHAT IF?** Suppose you are studying two bird species that live in a forest and are not known to interbreed. One species feeds and mates in the treetops and the other on the ground. But in captivity, the birds can interbreed and produce viable, fertile offspring. What type of reproductive barrier most likely keeps these species separate in nature? Explain.

For suggested answers, see Appendix A.

CONCEPT 24.2

Speciation can take place with or without geographic separation

Now that we have a clearer sense of what constitutes a unique species, let's return to our discussion of the process by which such species arise from existing species. Speciation can occur in two main ways, depending on how gene flow is interrupted between populations of the existing species (Figure 24.5).

Allopatric ("Other Country") Speciation

In **allopatric speciation** (from the Greek *allos*, other, and *patra*, homeland), gene flow is interrupted when a population is divided into geographically isolated subpopulations. For example, the water level in a lake may subside, resulting in two or more smaller lakes that are now home to separated populations (see Figure 24.5a). Or a river may change course and divide a population of animals that cannot cross it. Allopatric speciation can also occur without geologic remodeling, such as when individuals colonize a remote area and their descendants become geographically isolated from the parent population. The flightless cormorant shown in Figure 24.1 most likely originated in this way from an ancestral flying species that reached the Galápagos Islands.

The Process of Allopatric Speciation

How formidable must a geographic barrier be to promote allopatric speciation? The answer depends on the ability of the organisms to move about. Birds, mountain lions, and coyotes can cross rivers and canyons—as can the windblown pollen of pine trees and the seeds of many flowering plants. In con-

▲ **Figure 24.6 Allopatric speciation of antelope squirrels on opposite rims of the Grand Canyon.** Harris's antelope squirrel (*Ammospermophilus harrisii*) inhabits the canyon's south rim (left). Just a few kilometers away on the north rim (right) lives the closely related white-tailed antelope squirrel (*Ammospermophilus leucurus*). Birds and other organisms that can disperse easily across the canyon have not diverged into different species on the two rims.

trast, small rodents may find a wide river or deep canyon a formidable barrier (Figure 24.6).

Once geographic separation has occurred, the separated gene pools may diverge. Different mutations arise, and natural selection and genetic drift may alter allele frequencies in different ways in the separated populations. Reproductive isolation may then arise as a by-product of selection or drift having caused the populations to diverge genetically. For example, on Andros Island, in the Bahamas, populations of the mosquitofish *Gambusia hubbsi* colonized a series of ponds that later became isolated from one another. Genetic analyses indicate that little or no gene flow currently occurs between the ponds. The environments of these ponds are very similar except that some contain many predatory fishes, while others do not. In the "high-predation" ponds, selection has favored the evolution of a mosquitofish body shape that enables rapid bursts of speed (Figure 24.7). In ponds lacking

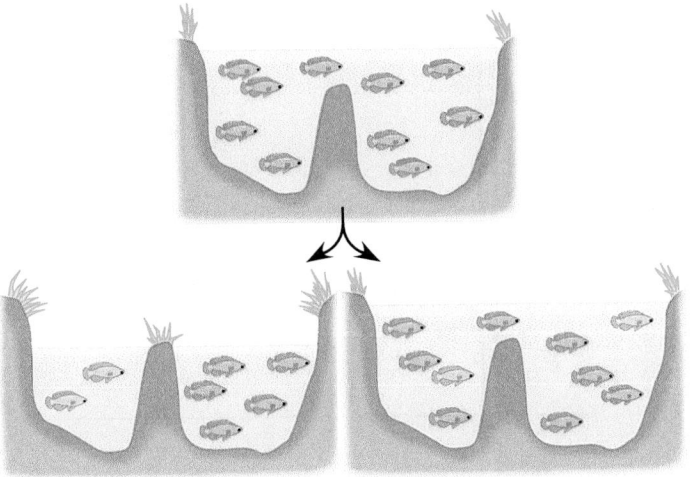

(a) Allopatric speciation. A population forms a new species while geographically isolated from its parent population.

(b) Sympatric speciation. A subset of a population forms a new species without geographic separation.

▲ Figure 24.5 **Two main modes of speciation.**

(a) Under high predation **(b) Under low predation**

In ponds with predatory fishes, the head region of the mosquitofish is streamlined and the tail region is powerful, enabling rapid bursts of speed.

In ponds without predatory fishes, mosquitofish have a different body shape that favors long, steady swimming.

▲ Figure 24.7 **Reproductive isolation as a by-product of selection.** After bringing together mosquitofish from different ponds, researchers concluded that selection for traits that enable mosquitofish in high-predation ponds to avoid predators has isolated them reproductively from mosquitofish in low-predation ponds.

predatory fishes, selection has favored a different body shape, one that improves the ability to swim for long periods of time. How have these different selective pressures affected the evolution of reproductive barriers? Researchers answered this question by bringing together mosquitofish from the two types of ponds. They found that female mosquitofish prefer to mate with males whose body shape is similar to their own. This preference establishes a barrier to reproduction between mosquitofish from ponds with predators and those from ponds without predators. Thus, as a by-product of selection for avoiding predators, reproductive barriers have started to form in these allopatric populations.

Evidence of Allopatric Speciation

Many studies provide evidence that speciation can occur in allopatric populations. Consider the 30 species of snapping shrimp in the genus *Alpheus* that live off the Isthmus of Panama, the land bridge that connects South and North America (**Figure 24.8**). Fifteen of these species live on the Atlantic side of the isthmus, while the other 15 live on the Pacific side. Before the isthmus formed, gene flow could occur between the Atlantic and Pacific populations of snapping shrimp. Did the species on different sides of the isthmus orig-

inate by allopatric speciation? Morphological and genetic data group these shrimp into 15 pairs of *sibling species*, pairs whose member species are each other's closest relative. In each of these 15 pairs, one of the sibling species lives on the Atlantic side of the isthmus, while the other lives on the Pacific side, strongly suggesting that the two species arose as a consequence of geographic separation. Furthermore, genetic analyses indicate that the *Alpheus* species originated from 9 to 3 million years ago, with the sibling species that live in the deepest water diverging first. These divergence times are consistent with geologic evidence that the isthmus formed gradually, starting 10 million years ago, and closing completely about 3 million years ago.

The importance of allopatric speciation is also suggested by the fact that regions that are isolated or highly subdivided by barriers typically have more species than do otherwise similar regions that lack such features. For example, many unique plants and animals are found on the geographically isolated Hawaiian Islands (we'll return to the origin of Hawaiian species in Chapter 25). Similarly, unusually high numbers of butterfly species are found in South American regions that are subdivided by many rivers.

Laboratory and field tests also provide evidence that reproductive isolation between two populations generally increases as the distance between them increases. In a study of dusky salamanders (*Desmognathus ochrophaeus*), biologists brought individuals from different populations into the laboratory and tested their ability to produce viable, fertile offspring (**Figure 24.9**). The researchers observed little reproductive isolation in salamanders from neighboring populations. In contrast, salamanders from widely separated populations often failed to reproduce, a result consistent with allopatric speciation. In other studies, researchers have tested whether intrinsic reproductive barriers develop when populations are isolated

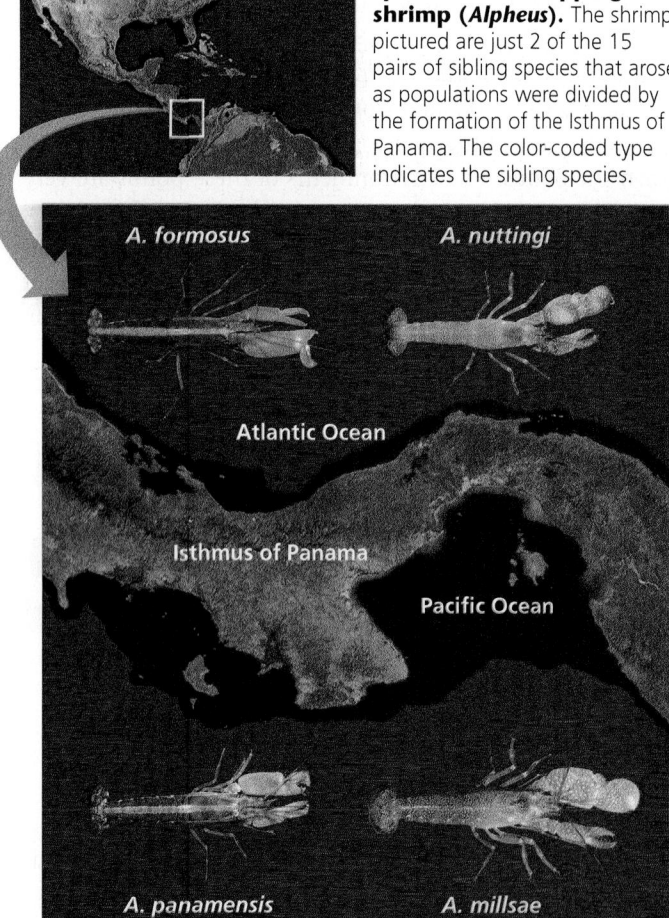

▼ **Figure 24.8 Allopatric speciation in snapping shrimp (*Alpheus*).** The shrimp pictured are just 2 of the 15 pairs of sibling species that arose as populations were divided by the formation of the Isthmus of Panama. The color-coded type indicates the sibling species.

▲ **Figure 24.9 Reproductive isolation increases with distance in populations of dusky salamanders.** The degree of reproductive isolation is represented here by an index ranging from 0 (no isolation) to 2 (complete isolation).

INQUIRY

Can divergence of allopatric populations lead to reproductive isolation?

EXPERIMENT Diane Dodd, then at Yale University, divided a laboratory population of the fruit fly *Drosophila pseudoobscura*, raising some flies on a starch medium and others on a maltose medium. After one year (about 40 generations), natural selection resulted in divergent evolution: Populations raised on starch digested starch more efficiently, while those raised on maltose digested maltose more efficiently. Dodd then put flies from the same or different populations in mating cages and measured mating frequencies. All flies used in the mating preference tests were reared for one generation on a standard cornmeal medium.

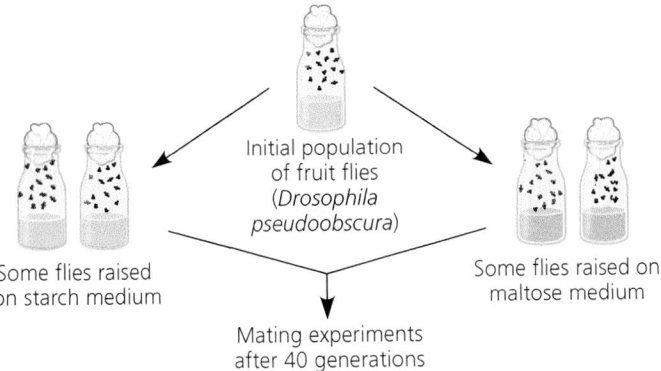

Initial population of fruit flies (*Drosophila pseudoobscura*)

Some flies raised on starch medium

Some flies raised on maltose medium

Mating experiments after 40 generations

RESULTS Mating patterns among populations of flies raised on different media are shown below. When flies from "starch populations" were mixed with flies from "maltose populations," the flies tended to mate with like partners. But in the control group (shown on the right), flies from different populations adapted to starch were about as likely to mate with each other as with flies from their own population; similar results were obtained for control groups adapted to maltose.

		Female	
		Starch	Maltose
Male	Starch	22	9
	Maltose	8	20

Number of matings in experimental group

		Female	
		Starch population 1	Starch population 2
Male	Starch population 1	18	15
	Starch population 2	12	15

Number of matings in control group

CONCLUSION In the experimental group, the strong preference of "starch flies" and "maltose flies" to mate with like-adapted flies indicates that a reproductive barrier was forming between these fly populations. Although this reproductive barrier was not absolute (some mating between starch flies and maltose flies did occur), after 40 generations it appeared to be under way. This barrier may have been caused by differences in courtship behavior that arose as an incidental by-product of differing selective pressures as these allopatric populations adapted to different sources of food.

SOURCE D. M. B. Dodd, Reproductive isolation as a consequence of adaptive divergence in *Drosophila pseudoobscura*, *Evolution* 43:1308–1311 (1989).

WHAT IF? Why were all flies used in the mating preference tests reared on a standard medium (rather than on a starch or maltose medium)?

experimentally and subjected to different environmental conditions. In such cases, too, the results provide strong support for allopatric speciation (Figure 24.10).

We need to emphasize here that although geographic isolation prevents interbreeding between allopatric populations, physical separation is not a biological barrier to reproduction. Biological reproductive barriers such as those described in Figure 24.3 are intrinsic to the organisms themselves. Hence, it is biological barriers that can prevent interbreeding when members of different populations come into contact with one another.

Sympatric ("Same Country") Speciation

In **sympatric speciation** (from the Greek *syn*, together), speciation occurs in populations that live in the same geographic area. How can reproductive barriers form between sympatric populations while their members remain in contact with each other? Although such contact (and the ongoing gene flow that results) makes sympatric speciation less common than allopatric speciation, sympatric speciation can occur if gene flow is reduced by such factors as polyploidy, habitat differentiation, and sexual selection. (Note that these factors can also promote allopatric speciation.)

Polyploidy

A species may originate from an accident during cell division that results in extra sets of chromosomes, a condition called **polyploidy**. Polyploid speciation occasionally occurs in animals; for example, the gray tree frog *Hyla versicolor* (see Figure 23.16) is thought to have originated in this way. However, polyploidy is far more common in plants. Botanists estimate that more than 80% of the plant species alive today are descended from ancestors that formed by polyploid speciation.

Two distinct forms of polyploidy have been observed in plant (and a few animal) populations. An **autopolyploid** (from the Greek *autos*, self) is an individual that has more than two chromosome sets that are all derived from a single species. In plants, for example, a failure of cell division could double a cell's chromosome number from the diploid number (2n) to a tetraploid number (4n).

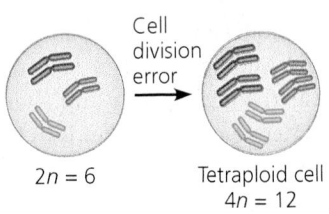

Cell division error

$2n = 6$

Tetraploid cell $4n = 12$

A tetraploid can produce fertile tetraploid offspring by self-pollinating or by mating with other tetraploids. In addition, the tetraploids are reproductively isolated from diploid plants of the original population, because the

$2n$

$2n$

Gametes produced by tetraploids

New species (4n)

triploid (3n) offspring of such unions have reduced fertility. Thus, in just one generation, autopolyploidy can generate reproductive isolation without any geographic separation.

A second form of polyploidy can occur when two different species interbreed and produce hybrid offspring. Most such hybrids are sterile because the set of chromosomes from one species cannot pair during meiosis with the set of chromosomes from the other species. However, an infertile hybrid may be able to propagate itself asexually (as many plants can do). In subsequent generations, various mechanisms can change a sterile hybrid into a fertile polyploid called an **allopolyploid** (Figure 24.11). The allopolyploids are fertile when mating with each other but cannot interbreed with either parent species; thus, they represent a new biological species.

Although polyploid speciation is relatively rare, even in plants, scientists have documented that at least five new plant species have originated in this way since 1850. One of these examples involves the origin of a new species of goatsbeard plant (genus *Tragopogon*) in the Pacific Northwest. *Tragopogon* first arrived in the region when humans introduced three European species in the early 1900s. These three species are now common weeds in abandoned parking lots and other urban sites. In 1950, a new *Tragopogon* species was discovered near the Idaho-Washington border, a region where all three European species also were found. Genetic analyses revealed that this new species, *Tragopogon miscellus*, is a tetraploid hybrid of two of the European species. Although the *T. miscellus* population grows mainly by reproduction of its own members, additional episodes of hybridization between the parent species continue to add new members to the *T. miscellus* population—just one of many examples in which scientists have observed speciation in progress.

Many important agricultural crops—such as oats, cotton, potatoes, tobacco, and wheat—are polyploids. The wheat used for bread, *Triticum aestivum*, is an allohexaploid (six sets of chromosomes, two sets from each of three different species). The first of the polyploidy events that eventually led to modern wheat probably occurred about 8,000 years ago in the Middle East as a spontaneous hybrid of an early cultivated wheat species and a wild grass. Today, plant geneticists generate new polyploids in the laboratory by using chemicals that induce meiotic and mitotic errors. By harnessing the evolutionary process, researchers can produce new hybrid species with desired qualities, such as a hybrid that combines the high yield of wheat with the hardiness of rye.

Habitat Differentiation

Sympatric speciation can also occur when genetic factors enable a subpopulation to exploit a habitat or resource not used by the parent population. Such is the case with the North American apple maggot fly (*Rhagoletis pomonella*), a

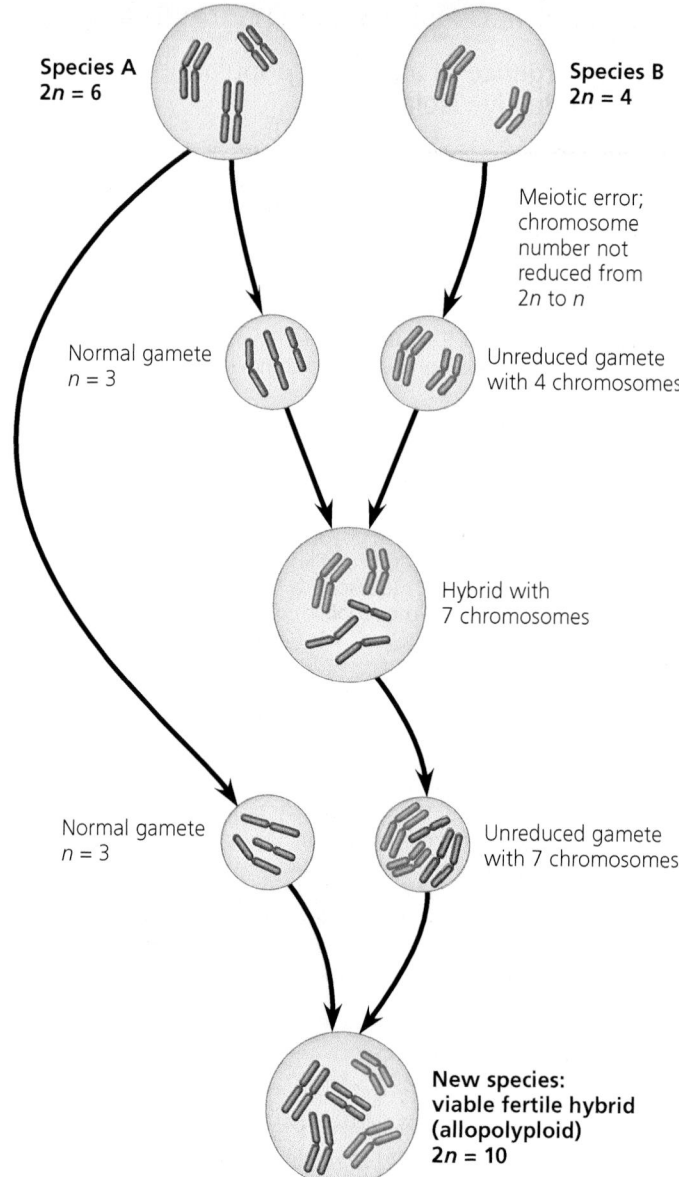

▲ Figure 24.11 **One mechanism for allopolyploid speciation in plants.** Most hybrids are sterile because their chromosomes are not homologous and cannot pair during meiosis. However, such a hybrid may be able to reproduce asexually. This diagram traces one mechanism that can produce fertile hybrids (allopolyploids) as new species. The new species has a diploid chromosome number equal to the sum of the diploid chromosome numbers of the two parent species.

pest of apples. The fly's original habitat was the native hawthorn tree, but about 200 years ago, some populations colonized apple trees that had been introduced by European settlers. As apples mature more quickly than hawthorn fruit, natural selection has favored apple-feeding flies with rapid development. These apple-feeding populations now show temporal isolation from the hawthorn-feeding *R. pomonella*, providing a prezygotic restriction to gene flow between the two populations. Researchers also have identified alleles that benefit the flies that use one host plant but harm the flies that use the other host plant. As a result, natural selection operating on these alleles provides a postzygotic barrier to reproduction, further limiting gene flow. Altogether, although the two populations are still classified as subspecies rather than separate species, sympatric speciation appears to be well under way.

Sexual Selection

There is evidence that sympatric speciation can also be driven by sexual selection. Clues to how this can occur have been found in cichlid fish from one of Earth's hot spots of animal speciation, East Africa's Lake Victoria. This lake was once home to as many as 600 species of cichlids. Genetic data indicate that these species originated within the last 100,000 years from a small number of colonizing species that arrived from rivers and lakes located elsewhere. How did so many species—more than double the number of freshwater fish species known in all of Europe—originate within a single lake?

One hypothesis is that subgroups of the original cichlid populations adapted to different food sources and that the resulting genetic divergence contributed to speciation in Lake Victoria. But sexual selection, in which (typically) females select males based on their appearance (see Chapter 23), may also have been a factor. Researchers have studied two closely related sympatric species of cichlids that differ mainly in the coloration of breeding males: Breeding *Pundamilia pundamilia* males have a blue-tinged back, whereas breeding *Pundamilia nyererei* males have a red-tinged back **(Figure 24.12)**. Their results suggest that mate choice based on male breeding coloration is the main reproductive barrier that normally keeps the gene pools of these two species separate.

Allopatric and Sympatric Speciation: A Review

Now let's recap the two main modes by which new species form. In allopatric speciation, a new species forms in geographic isolation from its parent population. Geographic isolation severely restricts gene flow. As a result, other reproductive barriers from the ancestral species may arise as a byproduct of genetic changes that occur within the isolated population. Many different processes can produce such genetic changes, including natural selection under different environmental conditions, genetic drift, and sexual selection. Once formed, intrinsic reproductive barriers that arise in allopatric populations can prevent interbreeding with the parent population even if the populations come back into contact.

Sympatric speciation, in contrast, requires the emergence of a reproductive barrier that isolates a subset of a population

INQUIRY

Does sexual selection in cichlids result in reproductive isolation?

EXPERIMENT Ole Seehausen and Jacques van Alphen, then at the University of Leiden, placed males and females of *Pundamilia pundamilia* and *P. nyererei* together in two aquarium tanks, one with natural light and one with a monochromatic orange lamp. Under normal light, the two species are noticeably different in male breeding coloration; under monochromatic orange light, the two species are very similar in color. The researchers then observed the mate choices of the females in each tank.

Normal light / Monochromatic orange light

P. pundamilia
P. nyererei

RESULTS Under normal light, females of each species strongly preferred males of their own species. But under orange light, females of each species responded indiscriminately to males of both species. The resulting hybrids were viable and fertile.

CONCLUSION Seehausen and van Alphen concluded that mate choice by females based on male breeding coloration is the main reproductive barrier that normally keeps the gene pools of these two species separate. Since the species can still interbreed when this prezygotic behavioral barrier is breached in the laboratory, the genetic divergence between the species is likely to be small. This suggests that speciation in nature has occurred relatively recently.

SOURCE O. Seehausen and J. J. M. van Alphen, The effect of male coloration on female mate choice in closely related Lake Victoria cichlids (*Haplochromis nyererei* complex), *Behavioral Ecology and Sociobiology* 42:1–8 (1998).

WHAT IF? If changing the light to orange had not affected the mating behavior of the cichlids, how might the researchers' conclusion have been different?

from the remainder of the population in the same area. Though rarer than allopatric speciation, sympatric speciation can occur when gene flow to and from the isolated subpopulation is blocked. This can occur as a result of polyploidy, a condition in which an organism has extra sets of chromosomes. Sympatric speciation also can occur when a subset of a population becomes reproductively isolated because of natural selection that results from a switch to a habitat or food source not used by the parent population. Finally, sympatric speciation can result from sexual selection.

Having reviewed the geographic context in which species originate, we'll next explore in more detail what can happen when new or partially formed species come into contact.

CONCEPT **24.3**

Hybrid zones reveal factors that cause reproductive isolation

What happens if species with incomplete reproductive barriers come into contact with one another? One possible outcome is the formation of a **hybrid zone**, a region in which members of different species meet and mate, producing at least some offspring of mixed ancestry. In this section, we'll explore hybrid zones and what they reveal about factors that cause the evolution of reproductive isolation.

Patterns Within Hybrid Zones

Some hybrid zones form as narrow bands, such as the one depicted in **Figure 24.13** for two species of toads in the genus *Bombina*, the yellow-bellied toad (*B. variegata*) and the fire-bellied toad (*B. bombina*). This hybrid zone, represented by the red line on the map, extends for 4,000 km but is less than 10 km wide in most places. The hybrid zone occurs where the

Fire-bellied toad, *Bombina bombina*: lives at lower altitudes

Yellow-bellied toad, *Bombina variegata*: lives at higher altitudes

▲ **Figure 24.13 A narrow hybrid zone for *Bombina* toads in Europe.** The graph shows the pattern of species-specific allele frequencies across the width of the zone near Krakow, Poland. Individuals with frequencies close to 1.0 are yellow-bellied toads, individuals with frequencies close to 0.0 are fire-bellied toads, and individuals with intermediate frequencies are considered hybrids.

? *Does the graph indicate that gene flow is spreading fire-bellied toad alleles into the range of the yellow-bellied toad? Explain.*

higher-altitude habitat of the yellow-bellied toad meets the lowland habitat of the fire-bellied toad. Across a given "slice" of the zone, the frequency of alleles specific to yellow-bellied toads typically decreases from close to 100% at the edge where only yellow-bellied toads are found, to 50% in the central portion of the zone, to 0% at the edge where only fire-bellied toads are found.

What causes such a pattern of allele frequencies across a hybrid zone? We can infer that there is an obstacle to gene flow—otherwise, alleles from one parent species would also be common in the gene pool of the other parent species. Are geographic barriers reducing gene flow? Not in this case, since the toads can move throughout the hybrid zone. A more important factor is that hybrid toads have increased rates of embryonic mortality and a variety of morphological abnormalities, including ribs that are fused to the spine and malformed tadpole mouthparts. Because the hybrids have poor survival and reproduction, they produce few viable offspring with members of the parent species. As a result, hybrid individuals rarely serve as a stepping-stone from which alleles are passed from one species to the other. Outside the hybrid zone, additional obstacles to gene flow may be provided by natural selection in the different environments in which the parent species live.

Other hybrid zones have more complicated spatial patterns. For example, many plant species only occur in locations that have a very particular set of environmental conditions. Favorable "patches" that have such conditions are often scattered irregularly across the landscape and are

isolated from one another. When two such plant species interbreed, the hybrid zone occurs in a group of disconnected patches, a more complex spatial pattern than the continuous band shown in Figure 24.13. But regardless of whether they have complex or simple spatial patterns, hybrid zones form when two species lacking complete barriers to reproduction come into contact. Once formed, how does a hybrid zone change over time?

Hybrid Zones over Time

Studying a hybrid zone is like observing a natural experiment on speciation. Will the hybrids become reproductively isolated from their parents and form a new species, as occurred by polyploidy in the goatsbeard plant of the Pacific Northwest? If not, there are three possible outcomes for the hybrid zone over time: reinforcement of barriers, fusion of species, or stability (Figure 24.14). Reproductive barriers between species may be reinforced over time (limiting the formation of hybrids) or weakened over time (causing the separating species to fuse into one species). Or hybrids may continue to be produced, creating a long-term and stable hybrid zone. Let's examine what studies in the field suggest about these three possibilities.

Reinforcement: Strengthening Reproductive Barriers

When hybrids are less fit than members of their parent species, as in the *Bombina* example, we might expect natural selection to strengthen prezygotic barriers to reproduction, thus reducing

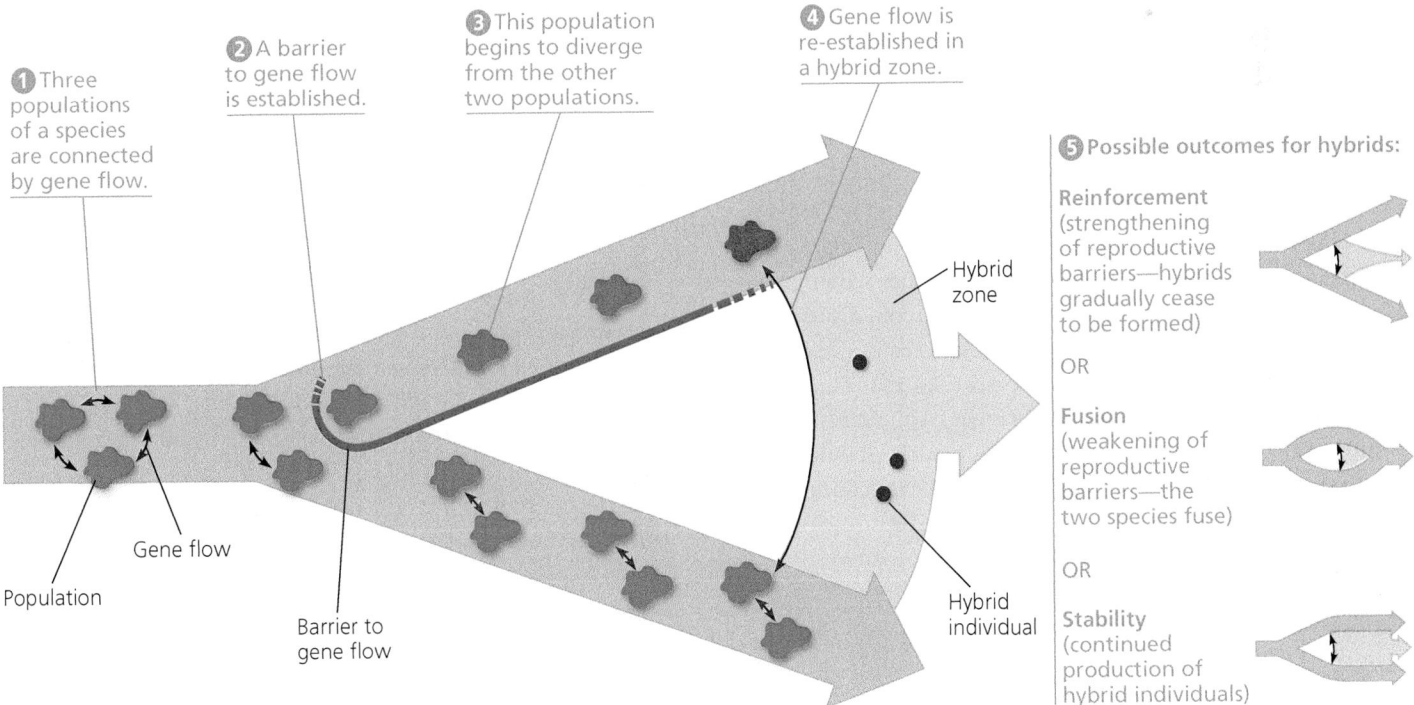

▲ **Figure 24.14 Formation of a hybrid zone and possible outcomes for hybrids over time.**
The thick colored arrows represent the passage of time.

WHAT IF? *Predict what might happen if gene flow were re-established at step 3 in this process.*

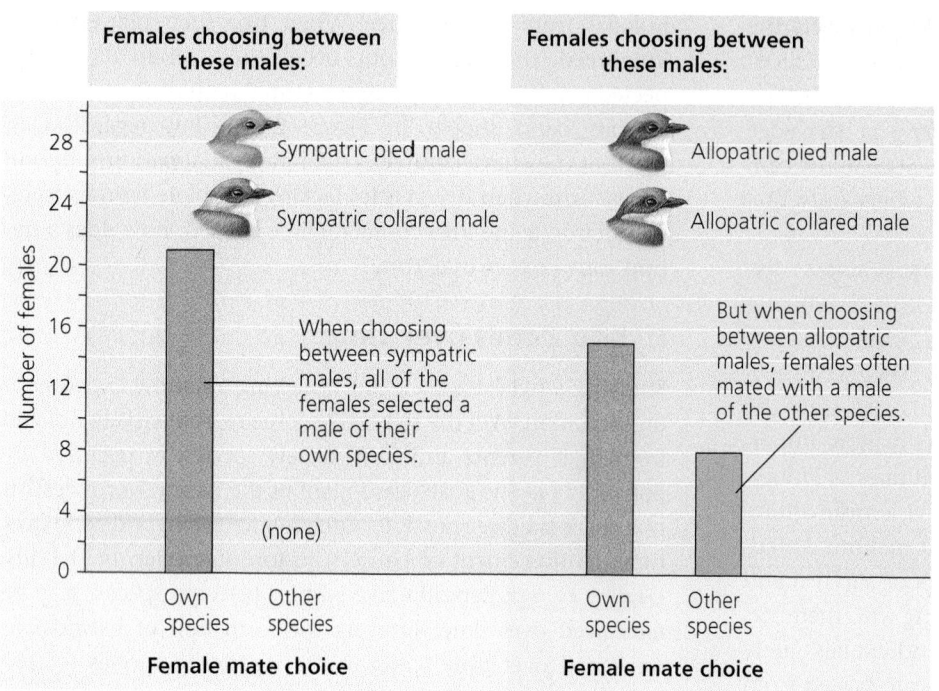

▲ **Figure 24.15 Reinforcement of barriers to reproduction in closely related species of European flycatchers.**

the formation of unfit hybrids. Because this process involves *reinforcing* reproductive barriers, it is called **reinforcement**. If reinforcement is occurring, a logical prediction is that barriers to reproduction between species should be stronger for sympatric populations than for allopatric populations.

As an example, let's consider the evidence for reinforcement in two closely related species of European flycatcher, the pied flycatcher and the collared flycatcher. In allopatric populations of these birds, males of the two species closely resemble one another. But in sympatric populations, the males of the two species look very different: Male pied flycatchers are a dull brown, whereas male collared flycatchers have enlarged patches of white. Female pied and collared flycatchers do not select males of the other species when given a choice between males from sympatric populations, but they frequently do make mistakes when selecting between males from allopatric populations **(Figure 24.15)**. Thus, barriers to reproduction appear to be stronger in birds from sympatric populations than in birds from allopatric populations, as you would predict if reinforcement is occurring. Similar results have been observed in a number of organisms, including fishes, insects, plants, and other birds. But interestingly, reinforcement does *not* appear to be at work in the case of the *Bombina* toads, as we'll discuss shortly.

Fusion: Weakening Reproductive Barriers

Next let's consider the case in which two species contact one another in a hybrid zone, but the barriers to reproduction are not strong. So much gene flow may occur that reproductive barriers weaken further and the gene pools of the two species become increasingly alike. In effect, the speciation process reverses, eventually causing the two hybridizing species to fuse into a single species.

Such a situation may be occurring among some of the Lake Victoria cichlids we discussed earlier. In the past 30 years, about 200 of the former 600 species of Lake Victoria cichlids have vanished. Some of these species were driven to extinction by an introduced predator, the Nile perch. But many species not eaten by Nile perch also have disappeared— perhaps in some cases by species fusion. Many pairs of ecologically similar cichlid species are reproductively isolated because the females of one species prefer to mate with males of one color, while females of the other species prefer to mate with males of a different color (see Figure 24.12). Researchers think that murky waters caused by pollution may have reduced the ability of females to use color to distinguish males of their own species from males of closely related species. If further evidence supports this hypothesis, it would seem that pollution in Lake Victoria has produced a cascade of related effects. First, by decreasing the ability of females to distinguish males of their own species, pollution has increased the frequency of mating between members of species that had been isolated reproductively from one another. Second, as a result of these matings, many hybrids have been produced, leading to fusion of the parent species' gene pools and a loss of species **(Figure 24.16)**.

Similar events may be affecting the polar bear (*Ursus maritimus*). Fossils and genetic analyses indicate that polar bears evolved from North American populations of grizzly bears (*U. arctos*) between 100,000 and 200,000 years ago. In recent decades, global warming has reduced the extent of the Arctic Ocean ice packs from which polar bears hunt for seals and other prey. As their ice-pack habitat disappears (placing them at risk of extinction), polar bears are more likely to be found on land, where they may encounter grizzly bears. Hybrid offspring of polar bears and grizzly bears in the wild have been documented (see Figure 24.4). As polar bear habitat continues to disappear, increasing numbers of such hybrids may cause the gene pools of these species to begin to fuse, thus contributing to the possible eventual extinction of the polar bear.

Pundamilia nyererei

Pundamilia pundamilia

Pundamilia "turbid water,"
hybrid offspring from a location
with turbid water

▲ **Figure 24.16 Fusion: The breakdown of reproductive barriers.** Increasingly cloudy water in Lake Victoria over the past 30 years may have weakened reproductive barriers between *P. nyererei* and *P. pundamilia*. In areas of cloudy water, the two species have hybridized extensively, causing their gene pools to fuse.

Stability: Continued Formation of Hybrid Individuals

Many hybrid zones are stable in the sense that hybrids continue to be produced. In some cases, this occurs because the hybrids survive or reproduce better than members of either parent species, at least in certain habitats or years. But stable hybrid zones have also been observed in cases where the hybrids are selected *against*—an unexpected result.

Recall that hybrids are at a strong disadvantage in the *Bombina* hybrid zone. As a result, the offspring of individuals that prefer to mate with members of their own species should survive or reproduce better than the unfit hybrid offspring of individuals that mate indiscriminately with members of the other species. This suggests that reinforcement should occur, strengthening reproductive barriers and thereby limiting the production of hybrid toads. But in more than 20 years of study, no evidence for reinforcement has been found, and hybrids continue to be produced.

What could explain this finding? One possibility relates to the narrowness of the *Bombina* hybrid zone (see Figure 24.13). Evidence suggests that members of both parent species migrate into the zone from the parent populations located outside the zone. Such movements lead to the continued production of hybrids, potentially overwhelming the selection for increased reproductive isolation inside the zone. If the hybrid zone were wider, this would be less likely to occur, since the center of the zone would receive little gene flow from distant parent populations located outside the hybrid zone.

In short, sometimes the outcomes in hybrid zones match our predictions (European flycatchers and cichlid fishes), and sometimes they don't (*Bombina*). But whether our predictions are upheld or not, events in hybrid zones can shed light on how barriers to reproduction between closely related species change over time. In the next section, we'll examine how interactions between hybridizing species can also provide a glimpse into the speed and genetic control of speciation.

CONCEPT CHECK 24.3

1. What are hybrid zones, and why can they be viewed as "natural laboratories" in which to study speciation?
2. **WHAT IF?** Consider two species that diverged while geographically separated but resumed contact before reproductive isolation was complete. Predict what would happen over time if the two species mated indiscriminately and (a) hybrid offspring survived and reproduced more poorly than offspring from intraspecific matings or (b) hybrid offspring survived and reproduced as well as offspring from intraspecific matings.

For suggested answers, see Appendix A.

CONCEPT 24.4

Speciation can occur rapidly or slowly and can result from changes in few or many genes

Darwin faced many unanswered questions when he began to ponder that "mystery of mysteries"—speciation. As you read in Chapter 22, he found answers to some of those questions when he realized that evolution by natural selection helped explain both the diversity of life and the adaptations of organisms. But biologists since Darwin have continued to ask fundamental questions about speciation. For example, how long does it take for new species to form? And how many genes change when one species splits into two? Answers to these questions are also beginning to emerge.

The Time Course of Speciation

We can gather information about how long it takes new species to form from broad patterns in the fossil record and from studies that use morphological data (including fossils) or molecular data to assess the time interval between speciation events in particular groups of organisms.

(a) In a punctuated pattern, new species change most as they branch from a parent species and then change little for the rest of their existence.

Time ⟶

(b) Other species diverge from one another much more gradually over time.

▲ Figure 24.17 **Two models for the tempo of speciation.**

Patterns in the Fossil Record

The fossil record includes many episodes in which new species appear suddenly in a geologic stratum, persist essentially unchanged through several strata, and then disappear. For example, there are dozens of species of marine invertebrates that make their debut in the fossil record with novel morphologies, but then change little for millions of years before becoming extinct. Paleontologists Niles Eldredge, of the American Museum of Natural History, and Stephen Jay Gould, of Harvard University, coined the term **punctuated equilibria** to describe these periods of apparent stasis punctuated by sudden change **(Figure 24.17a)**. Other species do not show a punctuated pattern; instead, they change more gradually over long periods of time **(Figure 24.17b)**.

What do punctuated and gradual patterns tell us about how long it takes new species to form? Suppose that a species survived for 5 million years, but most of the morphological changes that caused it to be designated a new species occurred during the first 50,000 years of its existence—just 1% of its total lifetime. Time periods this short (in geologic terms) often cannot be distinguished in fossil strata, in part because the rate of sediment accumulation is too slow to separate layers this close in time. Thus, based on its fossils, the species would seem to have appeared suddenly and then lingered with little or no change before becoming extinct. Even though such a species may have originated more slowly than its fossils suggest (in this case taking 50,000 years), a punctuated pattern indicates that speciation occurred relatively rapidly. For species whose fossils changed much more gradually, we also cannot tell exactly when a new biological species formed, since information about reproductive isolation does not fossilize. However, it is likely that speciation in such groups occurred relatively slowly, perhaps taking millions of years.

Speciation Rates

The punctuated pattern suggests that once the process of speciation begins, it can be completed relatively rapidly—a suggestion supported by a growing number of studies.

For example, research conducted at Indiana University suggests that rapid speciation produced the wild sunflower *Helianthus anomalus*. Genetic evidence indicates that this species originated by the hybridization of two other sunflower species, *H. annuus* and *H. petiolaris*. The hybrid species *H. anomalus* is ecologically distinct and reproductively isolated from both parent species **(Figure 24.18)**. Unlike the outcome of allopolyploid speciation, in which there is a change in chromosome number after hybridization, in these sunflowers the two parent species and the hybrid all have the same number of chromosomes ($2n = 34$). How, then, did speciation occur? To answer this question, the researchers performed an

▲ Figure 24.18 **A hybrid sunflower species and its dry sand dune habitat.** The wild sunflower *Helianthus anomalus* originated via the hybridization of two other sunflowers, *H. annuus* and *H. petiolaris*, which live in nearby but moister environments.

INQUIRY

How does hybridization lead to speciation in sunflowers?

EXPERIMENT At Indiana University, Loren Rieseberg and his colleagues crossed the two parent sunflower species, *H. annuus* and *H. petiolaris*, to produce experimental hybrids in the laboratory (for each gamete, only two of the $n = 17$ chromosomes are shown).

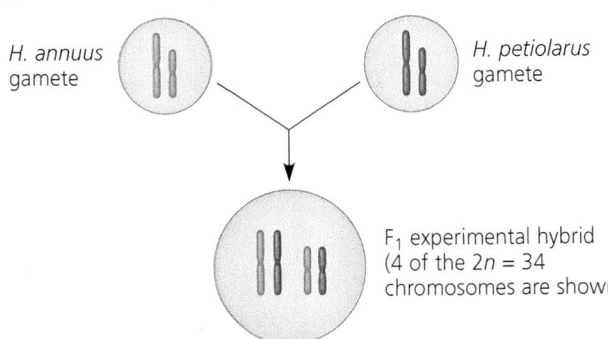

H. annuus gamete

H. petiolaris gamete

F_1 experimental hybrid (4 of the $2n = 34$ chromosomes are shown)

Note that in the first (F_1) generation, each chromosome of the experimental hybrids consisted entirely of DNA from one or the other parent species. The researchers then tested whether the F_1 and subsequent generations of experimental hybrids were fertile. They also used species-specific genetic markers to compare the chromosomes in the experimental hybrids with the chromosomes in the naturally occurring hybrid *H. anomalus*.

RESULTS Although only 5% of the F_1 experimental hybrids were fertile, after just four more generations the hybrid fertility rose to more than 90%. The chromosomes of individuals from this fifth hybrid generation differed from those in the F_1 generation but were similar to those in *H. anomalus* individuals from natural populations:

H. anomalus

Chromosome 1

Experimental hybrid

H. anomalus

Chromosome 2

Experimental hybrid

Comparison region containing *H. annuus*-specific marker

Comparison region containing *H. petiolarus*-specific marker

CONCLUSION Over time, the chromosomes in the population of experimental hybrids became similar to the chromosomes of *H. anomalus* individuals from natural populations. This suggests that the observed rise in the fertility of the experimental hybrids occurred as selection eliminated regions of DNA from the parent species that were not compatible with one another. Overall, it appeared that the initial steps of the speciation process occurred rapidly and could be mimicked in a laboratory experiment.

SOURCE L. H. Rieseberg et al., Role of gene interactions in hybrid speciation: evidence from ancient and experimental hybrids, *Science* 272:741–745 (1996).

WHAT IF? *The increased fertility of the experimental hybrids could have resulted from natural selection for thriving under laboratory conditions. Evaluate this alternative explanation for the results.*

experiment designed to mimic events in nature (Figure 24.19). Their results indicated that natural selection could produce extensive genetic changes in hybrid populations over short periods of time. These changes appear to have caused the hybrids to diverge reproductively from their parents and form a new species, *H. anomalus*.

The sunflower example, along with the apple maggot fly, Lake Victoria cichlid, and fruit fly examples discussed earlier, suggests that new species can arise rapidly *once divergence begins*. But what is the total length of time between speciation events? This interval consists of the time that elapses before populations of a newly formed species start to diverge from one another plus the time it takes for speciation to be complete once divergence begins. It turns out that the total time between speciation events varies considerably. For example, in a survey of data from 84 groups of plants and animals, the interval between speciation events ranged from 4,000 years (in cichlids of Lake Nabugabo, Uganda) to 40 million years (in some beetles). Overall, the time between speciation events averaged 6.5 million years and rarely took less than 500,000 years.

What can we learn from such data? First, the data suggest that on average, millions of years may pass before a newly formed species will itself give rise to another new species. As we'll see in Chapter 25, this result has implications for how long it takes life on Earth to recover from mass extinction events. Second, the extreme variability in the time it takes new species to form indicates that organisms do not have a "speciation clock" ticking inside them, causing them to produce new species at regular time intervals. Instead, speciation begins only after gene flow between populations is interrupted, perhaps by changing environmental conditions or by unpredictable events, such as a storm that transports a few individuals to an isolated area. Furthermore, once gene flow is interrupted, the populations must diverge genetically to such an extent that they become reproductively isolated—all before other events cause gene flow to resume, possibly reversing the speciation process (see Figure 24.16).

Studying the Genetics of Speciation

Studies of ongoing speciation (as in hybrid zones) can reveal traits that cause reproductive isolation. By identifying the genes that control those traits, scientists can explore a fundamental question of evolutionary biology: How many genes change when a new species forms?

In a few cases, the evolution of reproductive isolation is due to a change in a single gene. For example, in Japanese snails of the genus *Euhadra*, a change in a single gene can result in a mechanical barrier to reproduction. This gene controls the direction in which the shells spiral. When their shells spiral in different directions, the snails' genitalia are oriented in a manner that prevents mating (Figure 24.3f shows a similar example).

A major barrier to reproduction between two closely related species of monkey flower, *Mimulus cardinalis* and *M. lewisii*, also appears to be influenced by a relatively small number of genes. These two species are isolated by several prezygotic and postzygotic barriers. Of these, one prezygotic barrier, pollinator choice, accounts for most of the isolation: In a hybrid zone between *M. cardinalis* and *M. lewisii*, nearly 98% of pollinator visits were restricted to one species or the other.

The two monkey flower species are visited by different pollinators: Hummingbirds prefer the red-flowered *M. cardinalis*, and bumblebees prefer the pink-flowered *M. lewisii*. Douglas Schemske, of Michigan State University, and colleagues have shown that pollinator choice is affected by at least two loci in the monkey flowers, one of which, the "yellow upper," or *yup*, locus, influences flower color (Figure 24.20). By crossing the two parent species to produce F₁ hybrids and then performing repeated backcrosses of these F₁ hybrids to each parent species, Schemske and colleagues succeeded in transferring the *M. cardinalis* allele at this locus into *M. lewisii*, and vice versa. In a field experiment, *M. lewisii* plants with the *M. cardinalis yup* allele received 68-fold more visits from hummingbirds than did wild-type *M. lewisii*. Similarly, *M. cardinalis* plants with the *M. lewisii yup* allele received 74-fold more visits from bumblebees than did wild-type *M. cardinalis*. Thus, a mutation at a single locus can influence pollinator preference and hence contribute to reproductive isolation in monkey flowers.

In other organisms, the speciation process is influenced by larger numbers of genes and gene interactions. For example, hybrid sterility between two subspecies of the fruit fly *Drosophila pseudoobscura* results from gene interactions among at least four loci, and postzygotic isolation in the sunflower hybrid zone discussed earlier is influenced by at least 26 chromosome segments (and an unknown number of genes). Overall, studies suggest that few or many genes can influence the evolution of reproductive isolation and hence the emergence of a new species.

From Speciation to Macroevolution

As you've seen, speciation may begin with differences as seemingly small as the color on a cichlid's back. However, as speciation occurs again and again, such differences can accumulate and become more pronounced, eventually leading to the formation of new groups of organisms that differ greatly from their ancestors (as in the origin of whales from land-dwelling mammals; see Figure 22.20). Furthermore, as one group of organisms increases in size by producing many new species, another group of organisms may shrink, losing species to extinction. The cumulative effects of many such speciation and extinction events have helped shape the sweeping evolutionary changes that are documented in the fossil record. In the next chapter, we turn to such large-scale evolutionary changes as we begin our study of macroevolution.

(a) Typical *Mimulus lewisii*

(b) *M. lewisii* with an *M. cardinalis* flower-color allele

(c) Typical *Mimulus cardinalis*

(d) *M. cardinalis* with an *M. lewisii* flower-color allele

▲ Figure 24.20 **A locus that influences pollinator choice.** Pollinator preferences provide a strong barrier to reproduction between *Mimulus lewisii* and *M. cardinalis*. After transferring the *M. lewisii* allele for a flower-color locus into *M. cardinalis* and vice versa, researchers observed a shift in some pollinators' preferences.

WHAT IF? *If* M. cardinalis *individuals that had the* M. lewisii yup *allele were planted in an area that housed both monkey flower species, how might the production of hybrid offspring be affected?*

CONCEPT CHECK 24.4

1. Speciation can occur rapidly between diverging populations, yet the length of time between speciation events is often more than a million years. Explain this apparent contradiction.

2. Summarize evidence that the *yup* locus acts as a prezygotic barrier to reproduction in two species of monkey flowers. Do these results demonstrate that the *yup* locus alone controls barriers to reproduction between these species? Explain.

3. **MAKE CONNECTIONS** Compare Figure 13.11 (p. 259) with Figure 24.19 (p. 503). What cellular process could cause the hybrid chromosomes to contain DNA from both parent species? Explain.

For suggested answers, see Appendix A.

SUMMARY OF KEY CONCEPTS

CONCEPT 24.1

The biological species concept emphasizes reproductive isolation (pp. 488–492)

- A biological **species** is a group of populations whose individuals have the potential to interbreed and produce viable, fertile offspring with each other but not with members of other species. The **biological species concept** emphasizes reproductive isolation through prezygotic and postzygotic barriers that separate gene pools.
- Although helpful in thinking about how speciation occurs, the biological species concept has limitations. For instance, it cannot be applied to organisms known only as fossils or to organisms that reproduce only asexually. Thus, scientists use other species concepts, such as the **morphological species concept**, in certain circumstances.

> **?** *Explain the importance of gene flow to the biological species concept.*

CONCEPT 24.2

Speciation can take place with or without geographic separation (pp. 493–498)

- In **allopatric speciation**, gene flow is reduced when two populations of one species become geographically separated from each other. One or both populations may undergo evolutionary change during the period of separation, resulting in the establishment of prezygotic or postzygotic barriers to reproduction.
- In **sympatric speciation**, a new species originates while remaining in the same geographic area as the parent species. Plant species (and, more rarely, animal species) have evolved sympatrically through polyploidy. Sympatric speciation can also result from habitat shifts and sexual selection.

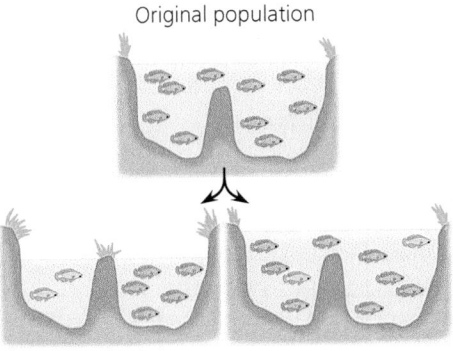

Original population

Allopatric speciation   Sympatric speciation

> **?** *Can factors that cause sympatric speciation also cause allopatric speciation? Explain.*

CONCEPT 24.3

Hybrid zones reveal factors that cause reproductive isolation (pp. 498–501)

- Many groups of organisms form **hybrid zones** in which members of different species meet and mate, producing at least some offspring of mixed ancestry.

- Many hybrid zones are *stable* in that hybrid offspring continue to be produced over time. In others, **reinforcement** strengthens prezygotic barriers to reproduction, thus decreasing the formation of unfit hybrids. In still other hybrid zones, barriers to reproduction may weaken over time, resulting in the *fusion* of the species' gene pools (reversing the speciation process).

> **?** *What factors can support the long-term stability of a hybrid zone if the parent species live in different environments?*

CONCEPT 24.4

Speciation can occur rapidly or slowly and can result from changes in few or many genes (pp. 501–504)

- New species can form rapidly once divergence begins—but it can take millions of years for that to happen. The time interval between speciation events varies considerably, from a few thousand years to tens of millions of years.
- New developments in genetics have enabled researchers to identify specific genes involved in some cases of speciation. Results show that speciation can be driven by few or many genes.

> **?** *Is speciation something that happened only in the distant past, or are new species continuing to arise today? Explain.*

TEST YOUR UNDERSTANDING

LEVEL 1: KNOWLEDGE/COMPREHENSION

1. The *largest* unit within which gene flow can readily occur is a
   - a. population.
   - b. species.
   - c. genus.
   - d. hybrid.
   - e. phylum.

2. Males of different species of the fruit fly *Drosophila* that live in the same parts of the Hawaiian Islands have different elaborate courtship rituals. These rituals involve fighting other males and making stylized movements that attract females. What type of reproductive isolation does this represent?
   - a. habitat isolation
   - b. temporal isolation
   - c. behavioral isolation
   - d. gametic isolation
   - e. postzygotic barriers

3. According to the punctuated equilibria model,
   - a. natural selection is unimportant as a mechanism of evolution.
   - b. given enough time, most existing species will branch gradually into new species.
   - c. most new species accumulate their unique features relatively rapidly as they come into existence, then change little for the rest of their duration as a species.
   - d. most evolution occurs in sympatric populations.
   - e. speciation is usually due to a single mutation.

LEVEL 2: APPLICATION/ANALYSIS

4. Bird guides once listed the myrtle warbler and Audubon's warbler as distinct species. Recently, these birds have been classified as eastern and western forms of a single species, the

yellow-rumped warbler. Which of the following pieces of evidence, if true, would be cause for this reclassification?

a. The two forms interbreed often in nature, and their offspring have good survival and reproduction.
b. The two forms live in similar habitats.
c. The two forms have many genes in common.
d. The two forms have similar food requirements.
e. The two forms are very similar in coloration.

5. Which of the following factors would *not* contribute to allopatric speciation?

a. A population becomes geographically isolated from the parent population.
b. The separated population is small, and genetic drift occurs.
c. The isolated population is exposed to different selection pressures than the ancestral population.
d. Different mutations begin to distinguish the gene pools of the separated populations.
e. Gene flow between the two populations is extensive.

6. Plant species A has a diploid number of 12. Plant species B has a diploid number of 16. A new species, C, arises as an allopolyploid from A and B. The diploid number for species C would probably be

a. 12. b. 14. c. 16. d. 28. e. 56.

LEVEL 3: SYNTHESIS/EVALUATION

7. Suppose that a group of male pied flycatchers migrated from a region where there were no collared flycatchers to a region where both species were present (see Figure 24.15). Assuming events like this are very rare, which of the following scenarios is *least* likely?

a. The frequency of hybrid offspring would increase.
b. Migrant pied males would produce fewer offspring than would resident pied males.
c. Pied females would rarely mate with collared males.
d. Migrant males would mate with collared females more often than with pied females.
e. The frequency of hybrid offspring would decrease.

8. **EVOLUTION CONNECTION**
What is the biological basis for assigning all human populations to a single species? Can you think of a scenario by which a second human species could originate in the future?

9. **SCIENCE, TECHNOLOGY, AND SOCIETY**
In the United States, the rare red wolf (*Canis lupus*) has been known to hybridize with coyotes (*Canis latrans*), which are much more numerous. Although red wolves and coyotes differ in terms of morphology, DNA, and behavior, genetic evidence suggests that living red wolf individuals are actually hybrids. Red wolves are designated as an endangered species and hence receive legal protection under the Endangered Species Act. Some people think that their endangered status should be withdrawn because the remaining red wolves are hybrids, not members of a "pure" species. Do you agree? Why or why not?

10. **SCIENTIFIC INQUIRY**
DRAW IT In this chapter, you read that bread wheat (*Triticum aestivum*) is an allohexaploid, containing two sets of chromosomes from each of three different parent species. Genetic analysis suggests that the three species pictured following this question each contributed chromosome sets to *T. aestivum*. (The capital letters here represent sets of chromosomes rather than individual genes.) Evidence also indicates that the first polyploidy event was a spontaneous hybridiza-

tion of the early cultivated wheat species *T. monococcum* and a wild *Triticum* grass species. Based on this information, draw a diagram of one possible chain of events that could have produced the allohexaploid *T. aestivum*.

Ancestral species:

AA
Triticum monococcum (2*n* = 14)

BB
Wild *Triticum* (2*n* = 14)

DD
Wild *T. tauschii* (2*n* = 14)

Product:

AA BB DD

T. aestivum (bread wheat) (2*n* = 42)

11. **WRITE ABOUT A THEME**
The Genetic Basis of Life In sexually reproducing species, each individual begins life with DNA inherited from both parent organisms. In a short essay (100–150 words), apply this idea to what occurs when organisms of two species that have homologous chromosomes mate and produce (F₁) hybrid offspring. What percentage of the DNA in the F₁ hybrids' chromosomes comes from each parent species? As the hybrids mate and produce F₂ and later-generation hybrid offspring, describe how recombination and natural selection may affect whether the DNA in hybrid chromosomes is derived from one parent species or the other.

For selected answers, see Appendix A.

25

The History of Life on Earth

▲ **Figure 25.1 What does fossil evidence say about where these dinosaurs lived?**

EVOLUTION

KEY CONCEPTS

25.1 Conditions on early Earth made the origin of life possible

25.2 The fossil record documents the history of life

25.3 Key events in life's history include the origins of single-celled and multicelled organisms and the colonization of land

25.4 The rise and fall of groups of organisms reflect differences in speciation and extinction rates

25.5 Major changes in body form can result from changes in the sequences and regulation of developmental genes

25.6 Evolution is not goal oriented

Lost Worlds

Visitors to Antarctica today encounter one of Earth's harshest, most barren environments. In this land of extreme cold where there is almost no liquid water, life is sparse and small—the largest fully terrestrial animal is a fly that is 5 mm long. But even as early Antarctic explorers struggled to survive, some of them made an astonishing discovery:

▲ *Cryolophosaurus* **skull**

fossil evidence that life once thrived where it now barely exists. Fossils reveal that 500 million years ago, the ocean waters surrounding Antarctica were warm and teeming with tropical invertebrates. Later, the continent was covered in forests for hundreds of millions of years. At various times, a wide range of animals stalked through these forests, including 3-m-tall predatory "terror birds" and giant dinosaurs such as the voracious *Cryolophosaurus* (**Figure 25.1**), a 7-m-long relative of *Tyrannosaurus rex*.

Fossils discovered in other parts of the world tell a similar, if not quite as surprising, story: Past organisms were very different from those presently living. The sweeping changes in life on Earth as revealed by fossils illustrate **macroevolution**, the broad pattern of evolution above the species level. Examples of macroevolutionary change include the emergence of terrestrial vertebrates through a series of speciation events, the impact of mass extinctions on the diversity of life, and the origin of key adaptations such as flight in birds.

Taken together, such changes provide a grand view of the evolutionary history of life on Earth. We'll examine that history in this chapter, beginning with hypotheses regarding the origin of life. The origin of life is the most speculative topic of the entire unit, for no fossil evidence of that seminal episode exists. We will then turn to evidence from the fossil record and what it tells us about major events in the history of life, paying particular attention to factors that have helped to shape the rise and fall of different groups of organisms over time.

CONCEPT **25.1**

Conditions on early Earth made the origin of life possible

Direct evidence of life on early Earth comes from fossils of microorganisms that are about 3.5 billion years old. But when and how did the first living cells appear? Observations and experiments in chemistry, geology, and physics have led scientists to propose one scenario that we'll examine here. They hypothesize that chemical and physical processes on early Earth, aided by the emerging force of natural selection, could have produced very simple cells through a sequence of four main stages:

1. The abiotic (nonliving) synthesis of small organic molecules, such as amino acids and nitrogenous bases
2. The joining of these small molecules into macromolecules, such as proteins and nucleic acids
3. The packaging of these molecules into **protocells**, droplets with membranes that maintained an internal chemistry different from that of their surroundings
4. The origin of self-replicating molecules that eventually made inheritance possible

Though speculative, this scenario leads to predictions that can be tested in the laboratory. In this section, we will examine some of the evidence for each stage.

Synthesis of Organic Compounds on Early Earth

There is scientific evidence that Earth and the other planets of the solar system formed about 4.6 billion years ago, condensing from a vast cloud of dust and rocks that surrounded the young sun. For the first few hundred million years, life probably could not have originated or survived on Earth because the planet was still being bombarded by huge chunks of rock and ice left over from the formation of the solar system. The collisions generated enough heat to vaporize the available water and prevent seas from forming. This early phase likely ended about 4.2–3.9 billion years ago.

As the bombardment of early Earth slowed, conditions on the planet were extremely different from those of today. The first atmosphere was probably thick with water vapor, along with various compounds released by volcanic eruptions, including nitrogen and its oxides, carbon dioxide, methane, ammonia, hydrogen, and hydrogen sulfide. As Earth cooled, the water vapor condensed into oceans, and much of the hydrogen escaped into space.

During the 1920s, Russian chemist A. I. Oparin and British scientist J. B. S. Haldane independently hypothesized that Earth's early atmosphere was a reducing (electron-adding) environment, in which organic compounds could have formed from simpler molecules. The energy for this organic synthesis could have come from lightning and intense UV radiation. Haldane suggested that the early oceans were a solution of organic molecules, a "primitive soup" from which life arose.

During 1953, Stanley Miller, working under the guidance of Harold Urey at the University of Chicago, tested the Oparin-Haldane hypothesis by creating laboratory conditions comparable to those that scientists at the time thought existed on early Earth (see Figure 4.2). His apparatus yielded a variety of amino acids found in organisms today, along with other organic compounds. Many laboratories have since repeated Miller's classic experiment using different recipes for the atmosphere, some of which also produced organic compounds.

However, it is unclear whether the atmosphere of early Earth contained enough methane and ammonia to be reducing. Some evidence suggests that the early atmosphere was made up primarily of nitrogen and carbon dioxide and was neither reducing nor oxidizing (electron-removing). Recent Miller-Urey-type experiments using such "neutral" atmospheres have also produced organic molecules. In addition, it is likely that small pockets of the early atmosphere—perhaps near the openings of volcanoes—were reducing. Perhaps the first organic compounds formed near volcanoes or deep-sea vents, where hot water and minerals gush into the ocean from Earth's interior. In a 2008 test of this volcanic-atmosphere hypothesis, researchers used modern equipment to reanalyze molecules that Miller had saved from one of his experiments. The study found that numerous amino acids had formed under conditions that simulated a volcanic eruption (Figure 25.2).

Miller-Urey-type experiments demonstrate that the abiotic synthesis of organic molecules is possible under various assumptions about the composition of the early atmosphere. A second source of organic molecules may have been meteorites. Among the meteorites that land on Earth are carbonaceous chondrites, rocks that are 1–2% carbon compounds by mass. Fragments of the Murchison meteorite, a 4.5-billion-year-old chondrite that fell to Australia in 1969, contain more than 80 amino acids, some in large amounts. These amino acids cannot be contaminants from Earth because they consist of an equal mix of D and L isomers (see Chapter 4). Organisms make and use only L isomers, with a few rare exceptions. Recent studies have shown that the Murchison meteorite also contained other key organic molecules, including lipids, simple sugars, and nitrogenous bases such as uracil.

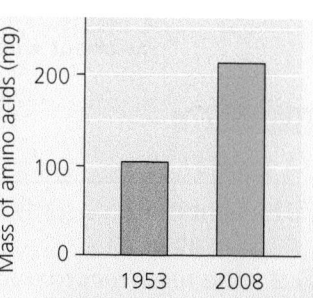

▲ **Figure 25.2 Amino acid synthesis in a simulated volcanic eruption.** In addition to his classic 1953 study, Miller also conducted an experiment simulating a volcanic eruption. In a 2008 reanalysis of those results, researchers found that far more amino acids were produced under simulated volcanic conditions than were produced in the conditions of the original 1953 experiment.

MAKE CONNECTIONS *After reviewing Concept 5.4 (pp. 78–80), explain how more than 20 amino acids could have been produced in the 2008 experiment.*

Abiotic Synthesis of Macromolecules

The presence of small organic molecules, such as amino acids and nitrogenous bases, is not sufficient for the emergence of life as we know it. Every cell has a vast assortment of macromolecules, including enzymes and other proteins and the nucleic acids that are essential for self-replication. Could such macromolecules have formed on early Earth? A 2009 study demonstrated that one key step, the abiotic synthesis of RNA monomers, can occur spontaneously from simple precursor molecules. In addition, by dripping solutions of amino acids or RNA nucleotides onto hot sand, clay, or rock, researchers have produced polymers of these molecules. The polymers formed spontaneously, without the help of enzymes or ribosomes. Unlike proteins, the amino acid polymers are a complex mix of linked and cross-linked amino acids. Nevertheless, it is possible that such polymers may have acted as weak catalysts for a variety of chemical reactions on early Earth.

Protocells

All organisms must be able to carry out reproduction and energy processing (metabolism). Life cannot persist without both of these functions. DNA molecules carry genetic information, including the instructions needed to replicate themselves accurately during reproduction. But the replication of DNA requires elaborate enzymatic machinery, along with a copious supply of nucleotide building blocks that are provided by the cell's metabolism (see Chapter 16). This suggests that self-replicating molecules and a metabolism-like source of the building blocks may have appeared together in early protocells. How did that happen?

The necessary conditions may have been met in *vesicles*, fluid-filled compartments bounded by a membrane-like structure. Recent experiments show that abiotically produced vesicles can exhibit certain properties of life, including simple reproduction and metabolism, as well as the maintenance of an internal chemical environment different from that of their surroundings.

For example, vesicles can form spontaneously when lipids or other organic molecules are added to water. When this occurs, the hydrophobic molecules in the mixture organize into a bilayer similar to the lipid bilayer of a plasma membrane. Adding substances such as *montmorillonite*, a soft mineral clay produced by the weathering of volcanic ash, greatly increases the rate of vesicle self-assembly (Figure 25.3a). This clay, which is thought to have been common on early Earth, provides surfaces on which organic molecules become concentrated, increasing the likelihood that the molecules will react with each other and form vesicles. Abiotically produced vesicles can "reproduce" on their own (Figure 25.3b), and they can increase in size ("grow") without dilution of their contents. Vesicles also can absorb montmorillonite particles, including those on which RNA and other organic molecules have become attached

(a) Self-assembly. The presence of montmorillonite clay greatly increases the rate of vesicle self-assembly.

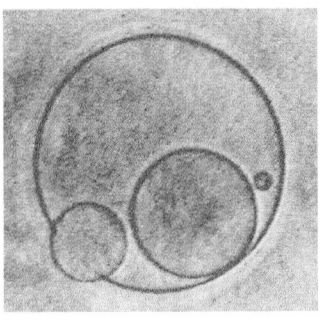

⊢—— 20 μm ——⊣

(b) Reproduction. Vesicles can divide on their own, as in this vesicle "giving birth" to smaller vesicles (LM).

(c) Absorption of RNA. This vesicle has incorporated montmorillonite clay particles coated with RNA (orange).

▲ **Figure 25.3 Features of abiotically produced vesicles.**

(Figure 25.3c). Finally, experiments have shown that some vesicles have a selectively permeable bilayer and can perform metabolic reactions using an external source of reagents—another important prerequisite for life.

Self-Replicating RNA and the Dawn of Natural Selection

The first genetic material was most likely RNA, not DNA. Thomas Cech, of the University of Colorado, and Sidney Altman, of Yale University, found that RNA, which plays a central role in protein synthesis, can also carry out a number of enzyme-like catalytic functions. Cech called these RNA catalysts **ribozymes**. Some ribozymes can make complementary copies of short pieces of RNA, provided that they are supplied with nucleotide building blocks.

Natural selection on the molecular level has produced ribozymes capable of self-replication in the laboratory. How does this occur? Unlike double-stranded DNA, which takes the form of a uniform helix, single-stranded RNA molecules assume a variety of specific three-dimensional shapes mandated by their nucleotide sequences. In a particular environment,

RNA molecules with certain base sequences are more stable and replicate faster and with fewer errors than other sequences. The RNA molecule whose sequence is best suited to the surrounding environment and has the greatest ability to replicate itself will leave the most descendant molecules. Occasionally, a copying error will result in a molecule that folds into a shape that is even more stable or more adept at self-replication than the ancestral sequence. Similar selection events may have occurred on early Earth. Thus, the molecular biology of today may have been preceded by an "RNA world," in which small RNA molecules that carried genetic information were able to replicate and to store information about the vesicles that carried them.

A vesicle with self-replicating, catalytic RNA would differ from its many neighbors that did not carry RNA or that carried RNA without such capabilities. If that vesicle could grow, split, and pass its RNA molecules to its daughters, the daughters would be protocells that had some of the properties of their parent. Although the first such protocells must have carried only limited amounts of genetic information, specifying only a few properties, their inherited characteristics could have been acted on by natural selection. The most successful of the early protocells would have increased in number because they could exploit their resources effectively and pass their abilities on to subsequent generations.

Once RNA sequences that carried genetic information appeared in protocells, many further changes would have been possible. For example, RNA could have provided the template on which DNA nucleotides were assembled. Double-stranded DNA is a more stable repository for genetic information than the more fragile single-stranded RNA. DNA also can be replicated more accurately. Accurate replication was advantageous as genomes grew larger through gene duplication and other processes and as more properties of the protocells became coded in genetic information. After DNA appeared, perhaps RNA molecules began to take on their present-day roles as regulators and intermediates in the translation of genes. The stage was now set for a blossoming of diverse life-forms—a change we see documented in the fossil record.

CONCEPT CHECK 25.1

1. What hypothesis did Miller test in his classic experiment?
2. How would the appearance of protocells have represented a key step in the origin of life?
3. **MAKE CONNECTIONS** In changing from an "RNA world" to today's "DNA world," genetic information must have flowed from RNA to DNA. After reviewing Figures 17.3 (p. 329) and 19.8 (p. 389), suggest how this could have occurred. Is such a flow a common occurrence today?

For suggested answers, see Appendix A.

CONCEPT 25.2

The fossil record documents the history of life

Starting with the earliest traces of life, the fossil record opens a window into the world of long ago and provides glimpses of the evolution of life over billions of years. In this section, we'll explore what the fossil record reveals about the major changes in the history of life—what those changes have been and how they may have occurred.

The Fossil Record

Recall from Chapter 22 that sedimentary rocks are the richest source of fossils. As a result, the fossil record is based primarily on the sequence in which fossils have accumulated in sedimentary rock layers, called *strata* (see Figure 22.3). Useful information is also provided by other types of fossils, such as insects preserved in amber (fossilized tree sap) and mammals frozen in ice.

The fossil record shows that there have been great changes in the kinds of organisms on Earth at different points in time (Figure 25.4). Many past organisms were unlike today's organisms, and many organisms that once were common are now extinct. As we'll see later, fossils also document how new groups of organisms arose from previously existing ones.

As substantial and significant as the fossil record is, keep in mind that it is an incomplete chronicle of evolutionary change. Many of Earth's organisms did not die in the right place at the right time to be preserved as fossils. Of those fossils that were formed, many were destroyed by later geologic processes, and only a fraction of the others have been discovered. As a result, the known fossil record is biased in favor of species that existed for a long time, were abundant and widespread in certain kinds of environments, and had hard shells, skeletons, or other parts that facilitated their fossilization. Even with its limitations, however, the fossil record is a remarkably detailed account of biological change over the vast scale of geologic time. Furthermore, as shown by the recently unearthed fossils of whale ancestors with hind limbs (see Figures 22.19 and 22.20), gaps in the fossil record continue to be filled by new discoveries.

Although some of these new discoveries are fortuitous, others illustrate the predictive nature of paleontology. For instance, researchers seeking to discover a close ancestor of early terrestrial vertebrates predicted that such a fossil would most likely be located in a river bed (which would have sedimentary rocks) containing rocks that were 375 million years old (an age based on previously known fossils). After digging for several years in one of the few such places on Earth, their predictions bore fruit with the discovery of *Tiktaalik*, an aquatic organism closely related to the first vertebrates to walk on land (see Figures 25.4 and 34.20).

▼ Figure 25.4 **Documenting the history of life.** These fossils illustrate representative organisms from different points in time. Although prokaryotes and unicellular eukaryotes are only shown at the base of the diagram, these organisms continue to thrive today. In fact, most organisms on Earth are unicellular.

Present

100 million years ago

▼ *Rhomaleosaurus victor*, a plesiosaur. These large marine reptiles were important predators from 200 million to 65.5 million years ago.

1 m

▼ *Dimetrodon*, the largest known carnivore of its day, was more closely related to mammals than to reptiles. The spectacular "sail" on its back probably functioned in temperature regulation.

0.5 m

175

200

▼ *Tiktaalik*, an extinct aquatic organism that is the closest known relative of the first vertebrates to walk on land

270

300

4.5 cm

▲ *Coccosteus cuspidatus*, a placoderm (fishlike vertebrate) that had a bony shield covering its head and front end

375

400

► *Hallucigenia*, a member of a morphologically diverse group of animals found in the Burgess Shale fossil bed in the Canadian Rockies

1 cm

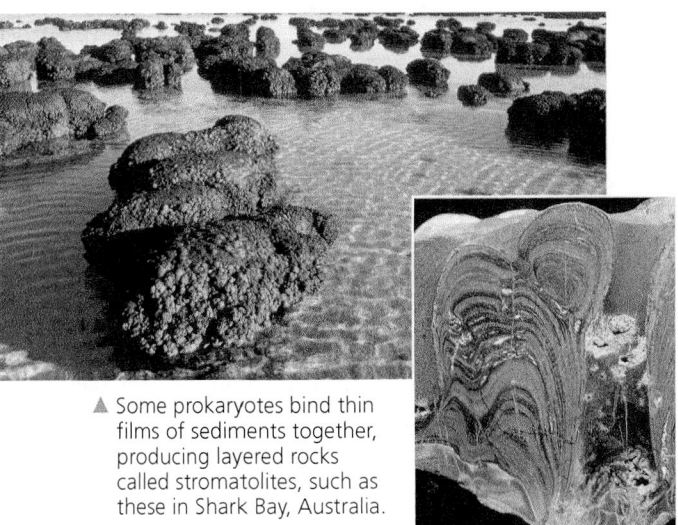

▲ Some prokaryotes bind thin films of sediments together, producing layered rocks called stromatolites, such as these in Shark Bay, Australia.

500

525

◄ *Dickinsonia costata*, a member of the Ediacaran biota, an extinct group of soft-bodied organisms

2.5 cm

565

▲ A section through a fossilized stromatolite

600

► A unicellular eukaryote, the alga *Tappania*, from northern Australia

1,500

3,500

How Rocks and Fossils Are Dated

Fossils are valuable data for reconstructing the history of life, but only if we can determine where they fit in that unfolding story. While the order of fossils in rock strata tells us the sequence in which the fossils were laid down—their relative ages—it does not tell us their actual (absolute) ages. Examining the relative positions of fossils in strata is like peeling off layers of wallpaper in an old house. You can determine the sequence in which the layers were applied, but not the year each layer was added.

How can we determine the absolute age of a fossil? (Note that "absolute" dating does not mean errorless dating, but only that an age is given in years rather than relative terms such as *before* and *after*.) One of the most common techniques is **radiometric dating**, which is based on the decay of radioactive isotopes (see Chapter 2). In this process, a radioactive "parent" isotope decays to a "daughter" isotope at a fixed rate. The rate of decay is expressed by the **half-life**, the time required for 50% of the parent isotope to decay (Figure 25.5). Each type of radioactive isotope has a characteristic half-life, which is not affected by temperature, pressure, or other environmental variables. For example, carbon-14 decays relatively quickly; it has a half-life of 5,730 years. Uranium-238 decays slowly; its half-life is 4.5 billion years.

Fossils contain isotopes of elements that accumulated in the organisms when they were alive. For example, a living organism contains the most common carbon isotope, carbon-12, as well as a radioactive isotope, carbon-14. When the organism dies, it stops accumulating carbon, and the amount of carbon-12 in its tissues does not change over time. However, the carbon-14 that it contains at the time of death slowly decays into another element, nitrogen-14. Thus, by measuring the ratio of carbon-14 to carbon-12 in a fossil, we can determine the fossil's age. This method works for fossils up to about 75,000 years old; fossils older than that contain too little carbon-14 to be detected with current techniques. Radioactive isotopes with longer half-lives are used to date older fossils.

Determining the age of these older fossils in sedimentary rocks is challenging. Organisms do not use radioisotopes with long half-lives, such as uranium-238, to build their bones or shells. Moreover, the sedimentary rocks themselves tend to consist of sediments of differing ages. Though we usually cannot date these old fossils directly, an indirect method can be used to infer the age of fossils that are sandwiched between two layers of volcanic rocks. As lava cools into volcanic rock, radioisotopes from the surrounding environment become trapped in the newly formed rock. Some of the trapped radioisotopes have long half-lives, allowing geologists to estimate the ages of ancient volcanic rocks. If two volcanic layers surrounding fossils are determined to be 525 million and 535 million years old, for example, then the fossils are roughly 530 million years old.

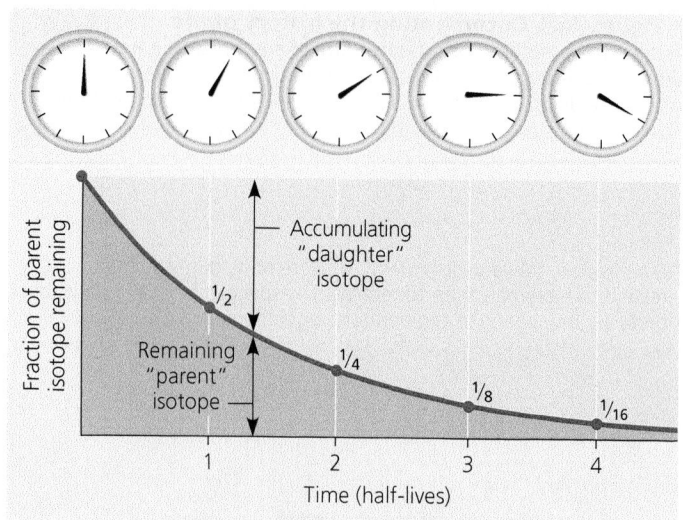

▲ **Figure 25.5 Radiometric dating.** In this diagram, each division of the clock face represents a half-life.

DRAW IT *Relabel the x-axis of this graph with time measurements in years to illustrate the radioactive decay of uranium-238 (half-life = 4.5 billion years).*

Now that we've seen how fossils can be dated, let's turn to an example of what we can learn from them.

The Origin of New Groups of Organisms

Some fossils provide a detailed look at the origin of new groups of organisms. Such fossils are central to our understanding of evolution; they illustrate how new features arise and how long it takes for such changes to occur. We'll examine one such case here: the origin of mammals.

Along with amphibians and reptiles, mammals belong to the group of animals called *tetrapods* (from the Greek *tetra*, four, and *pod*, foot), named for having four limbs. Mammals have a number of unique anatomical features that fossilize readily, allowing scientists to trace their origin. For example, the lower jaw is composed of one bone (the dentary) in mammals but several bones in other tetrapods. In addition, the lower and upper jaws hinge between a different set of bones in mammals than in other tetrapods. As we'll explore in Chapter 34, mammals also have a unique set of three bones that transmit sound in the middle ear (the hammer, anvil, and stirrup), whereas other tetrapods have only one such bone (the stirrup). Finally, the teeth of mammals are differentiated into incisors (for tearing), canines (for piercing), and the multi-pointed premolars and molars (for crushing and grinding). In contrast, the teeth of other tetrapods usually consist of a row of undifferentiated, single-pointed teeth.

As detailed in **Figure 25.6**, the fossil record shows that the unique features of mammalian jaws and teeth evolved gradually over time, in a series of steps. As you study Figure 25.6, bear in mind that it includes just a few examples of the fossil skulls that document the origin of mammals. If all the

Exploring The Origin of Mammals

Over the course of 120 million years, mammals originated gradually from a group of tetrapods called synapsids. Shown here are a few of the many fossil organisms whose morphological features represent intermediate steps between living mammals and their synapsid ancestors. The evolutionary context of the origin of mammals is shown in the tree diagram at right (the dagger symbol † indicates extinct lineages).

Key to skull bones

- ▨ Articular
- ▨ Dentary
- ▨ Quadrate
- ▨ Squamosal

Synapsid (300 mya)

Synapsids had multiple bones in the lower jaw and single-pointed teeth. The jaw hinge was formed by the articular and quadrate bones. Synapsids also had an opening called the *temporal fenestra* behind the eye socket. Powerful cheek muscles for closing the jaws probably passed through the temporal fenestra. Over time, this opening enlarged and moved in front of the hinge between the lower and upper jaws, thereby increasing the power and precision with which the jaws could be closed (much as moving a doorknob away from the hinge makes a door easier to close).

Therapsid (280 mya)

Later, a group of synapsids called therapsids appeared. Therapsids had large dentary bones, long faces, and the first examples of specialized teeth, large canines. These trends continued in a group of therapsids called cynodonts.

Early cynodont (260 mya)

In early cynodont therapsids, the dentary was the largest bone in the lower jaw, the temporal fenestra was large and positioned forward of the jaw hinge, and teeth with several cusps first appeared (not visible in the diagram). As in earlier synapsids, the jaw had an articular-quadrate hinge.

Later cynodont (220 mya)

Later cynodonts had teeth with complex cusp patterns and their lower and upper jaws hinged in two locations: They retained the original articular-quadrate hinge and formed a new, second hinge between the dentary and squamosal bones. (The temporal fenestra is not visible in this or the below cynodont skull at the angles shown.)

Very late cynodont (195 mya)

In some very late (non-mammalian) cynodonts and early mammals, the original articular-quadrate hinge was lost, leaving the dentary-squamosal hinge as the only hinge between the lower and upper jaws, as in living mammals. The articular and quadrate bones migrated into the ear region (not shown), where they functioned in transmitting sound. In the mammal lineage, these two bones later evolved into the familiar hammer (malleus) and anvil (incus) shown in Figure 34.31.

known fossils in the sequence were arranged by shape and placed side by side, their features would blend smoothly from one group to the next. Some of these fossils would reflect how the features of a group that dominates life today, the mammals, gradually arose in a previously existing group, the cynodonts. Others would reveal side branches on the tree of life—groups of organisms that thrived for millions of years but ultimately left no descendants that survive today.

CONCEPT CHECK 25.2

1. Your measurements indicate that a fossilized skull you unearthed has a carbon-14/carbon-12 ratio about 1/16 that of the skulls of present-day animals. What is the approximate age of the fossilized skull?
2. Describe an example from the fossil record that shows how life has changed over time.
3. **WHAT IF?** Suppose researchers discover a fossil of an organism that lived 300 million years ago but had mammalian teeth and a mammalian jaw hinge. What inferences might you draw from this fossil about the origin of mammals and the evolution of novel skeletal structures? Explain.

For suggested answers, see Appendix A.

CONCEPT 25.3

Key events in life's history include the origins of single-celled and multicelled organisms and the colonization of land

The study of fossils has helped geologists establish a **geologic record** of Earth's history, which is divided into three eons (**Table 25.1**, on the facing page). The first two eons—the Archaean and the Proterozoic—together lasted approximately 4 billion years. The Phanerozoic eon, roughly the last half billion years, encompasses most of the time that animals have existed on Earth. It is divided into three eras: the Paleozoic, Mesozoic, and Cenozoic. Each era represents a distinct age in the history of Earth and its life. For example, the Mesozoic era is sometimes called the "age of reptiles" because of its abundance of reptilian fossils, including those of dinosaurs. The boundaries between the eras correspond to major extinction events seen in the fossil record, when many forms of life disappeared and were replaced by forms that evolved from the survivors.

As we've seen, the fossil record provides a sweeping overview of the history of life over geologic time. Here we will focus on a few major events in that history, returning to study the details in Unit Five. **Figure 25.7** uses the analogy of a clock to place these events in the context of the geologic

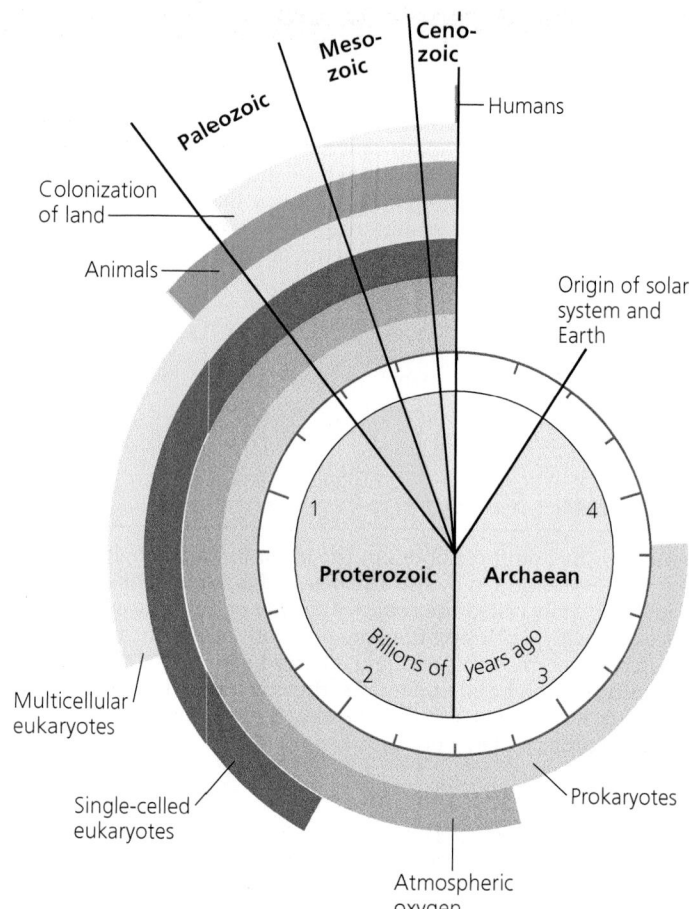

▲ **Figure 25.7 Clock analogy for some key events in Earth's history.** The clock ticks down from the origin of Earth 4.6 billion years ago to the present.

record. This clock will reappear at various points in this section as a quick visual reminder of when the events we are discussing took place.

The First Single-Celled Organisms

The earliest direct evidence of life, dating from 3.5 billion years ago, comes from fossilized stromatolites (see Figure 25.4). **Stromatolites** are layered rocks that form when certain prokaryotes bind thin films of sediment together. Present-day stromatolites are found in a few warm, shallow, salty bays. If microbial communities complex enough to form stromatolites existed 3.5 billion years ago, it is a reasonable hypothesis that single-celled organisms originated much earlier, perhaps as early as 3.9 billion years ago.

Early prokaryotes were Earth's sole inhabitants from at least 3.5 billion years ago to about 2.1 billion years ago. As we will see, these prokaryotes transformed life on our planet.

Table 25.1 The Geologic Record

Relative Duration of Eons	Era	Period	Epoch	Age (Millions of Years Ago)	Some Important Events in the History of Life
Phanerozoic	Cenozoic	Quaternary	Holocene	0.01	Historical time
			Pleistocene	2.6	Ice ages; origin of genus *Homo*
		Neogene	Pliocene	5.3	Appearance of bipedal human ancestors
			Miocene	23	Continued radiation of mammals and angiosperms; earliest direct human ancestors
		Paleogene	Oligocene	33.9	Origins of many primate groups
			Eocene	55.8	Angiosperm dominance increases; continued radiation of most present-day mammalian orders
			Paleocene	65.5	Major radiation of mammals, birds, and pollinating insects
Proterozoic	Mesozoic	Cretaceous		145.5	Flowering plants (angiosperms) appear and diversify; many groups of organisms, including most dinosaurs, become extinct at end of period
		Jurassic		199.6	Gymnosperms continue as dominant plants; dinosaurs abundant and diverse
		Triassic		251	Cone-bearing plants (gymnosperms) dominate landscape; dinosaurs evolve and radiate; origin of mammals
	Paleozoic	Permian		299	Radiation of reptiles; origin of most present-day groups of insects; extinction of many marine and terrestrial organisms at end of period
		Carboniferous		359	Extensive forests of vascular plants form; first seed plants appear; origin of reptiles; amphibians dominant
		Devonian		416	Diversification of bony fishes; first tetrapods and insects appear
		Silurian		444	Diversification of early vascular plants
		Ordovician		488	Marine algae abundant; colonization of land by diverse fungi, plants, and animals
		Cambrian		542	Sudden increase in diversity of many animal phyla (Cambrian explosion)
Archaean		Ediacaran		635	Diverse algae and soft-bodied invertebrate animals appear
				2,100	Oldest fossils of eukaryotic cells appear
				2,500	
				2,700	Concentration of atmospheric oxygen begins to increase
				3,500	Oldest fossils of cells (prokaryotes) appear
				3,800	Oldest known rocks on Earth's surface
				Approx. 4,600	Origin of Earth

Photosynthesis and the Oxygen Revolution

Atmospheric oxygen

Most atmospheric oxygen gas (O_2) is of biological origin, produced during the water-splitting step of photosynthesis. When oxygenic photosynthesis first evolved, the free O_2 it produced probably dissolved in the surrounding water until it reached a high enough concentration to react with dissolved iron. This would have caused the iron to precipitate as iron oxide, which accumulated as sediments. These sediments were compressed into banded iron formations, red layers of rock containing iron oxide that are a source of iron ore today. Once all of the dissolved iron had precipitated, additional O_2 dissolved in the water until the seas and lakes became saturated with O_2. After this occurred, the O_2 finally began to "gas out" of the water and enter the atmosphere. This change left its mark in the rusting of iron-rich terrestrial rocks, a process that began about 2.7 billion years ago. This chronology implies that bacteria similar to today's cyanobacteria (oxygen-releasing, photosynthetic bacteria) originated well before 2.7 billion years ago.

The amount of atmospheric O_2 increased gradually from about 2.7 to 2.3 billion years ago, but then shot up relatively rapidly to between 1% and 10% of its present level (Figure 25.8). This "oxygen revolution" had an enormous impact on life. In certain of its chemical forms, oxygen attacks chemical bonds and can inhibit enzymes and damage cells. As a result, the rising concentration of atmospheric O_2 probably doomed many prokaryotic groups. Some species survived in habitats that remained anaerobic, where we find their descendants living today (see Chapter 27). Among other survivors, diverse adaptations to the changing atmosphere

▲ **Figure 25.8 The rise of atmospheric oxygen.** Chemical analyses of ancient rocks have enabled this reconstruction of atmospheric oxygen levels during Earth's history.

evolved, including cellular respiration, which uses O_2 in the process of harvesting the energy stored in organic molecules.

As mentioned previously, the early, gradual rise in atmospheric O_2 levels was probably brought about by ancient cyanobacteria. A few hundred million years later, the rise in O_2 accelerated. What caused this acceleration? One hypothesis is that this rise followed the evolution of eukaryotic cells containing chloroplasts, as we will discuss next.

The First Eukaryotes

Single-celled eukaryotes

The oldest widely accepted fossils of eukaryotic organisms are about 2.1 billion years old. Recall that eukaryotic cells have more complex organization than prokaryotic cells: Eukaryotic cells have a nuclear envelope, mitochondria, endoplasmic reticulum, and other internal structures that prokaryotes lack. Also, unlike prokaryotic cells, eukaryotic cells have a cytoskeleton, a feature that enables eukaryotic cells to change their shape and thereby surround and engulf other cells.

How did these eukaryotic features evolve from prokaryotic cells? A range of evidence supports the **endosymbiont theory**, which posits that mitochondria and plastids (a general term for chloroplasts and related organelles) were formerly small prokaryotes that began living within larger cells. The term *endosymbiont* refers to a cell that lives within another cell, called the *host cell*. The prokaryotic ancestors of mitochondria and plastids probably gained entry to the host cell as undigested prey or internal parasites. Though such a process may seem unlikely, scientists have directly observed cases in which endosymbionts that began as prey or parasites came to have a mutually beneficial relationship with the host in as little as five years.

By whatever means the relationships began, we can hypothesize how the symbiosis could have become mutually beneficial. A host that is a heterotroph (an organism that eats other organisms or substances derived from them) could use nutrients released from photosynthetic endosymbionts. And in a world that was becoming increasingly aerobic, a host that was itself an anaerobe would have benefited from endosymbionts that turned the oxygen to advantage. Over time, the host and endosymbionts would have become a single organism, its parts inseparable. Although all eukaryotes have mitochondria or remnants of these organelles, they do not all have plastids. Thus, the hypothesis of **serial endosymbiosis** supposes that mitochondria evolved before plastids through a sequence of endosymbiotic events (Figure 25.9).

A great deal of evidence supports the endosymbiotic origin of mitochondria and plastids. The inner membranes of both organelles have enzymes and transport systems that are homologous to those found in the plasma membranes of

Cytoplasm

DNA

Plasma membrane

Ancestral prokaryote

Infolding of plasma membrane

Endoplasmic reticulum

Nucleus

Nuclear envelope

Engulfing of aerobic heterotrophic prokaryote

Cell with nucleus and endomembrane system

Mitochondrion

Mitochondrion

Engulfing of photosynthetic prokaryote by some cells

Ancestral heterotrophic eukaryote

Plastid

Ancestral photosynthetic eukaryote

▲ **Figure 25.9 A hypothesis for the origin of eukaryotes through serial endosymbiosis.** The proposed ancestors of mitochondria were aerobic, heterotrophic prokaryotes (meaning they used oxygen to metabolize organic molecules obtained from other organisms). The proposed ancestors of plastids were photosynthetic prokaryotes. In this figure, the arrows represent change over evolutionary time.

living prokaryotes. Mitochondria and plastids replicate by a splitting process that is similar to that of certain prokaryotes. In addition, each of these organelles contains a single, circular DNA molecule that, like the chromosomes of bacteria, is not associated with histones or large amounts of other proteins. As might be expected of organelles descended from free-living organisms, mitochondria and plastids also have the cellular machinery (including ribosomes) needed to transcribe and translate their DNA into proteins. Finally, in terms of size, RNA sequences, and sensitivity to certain antibiotics, the ribosomes of mitochondria and plastids are more similar to prokaryotic ribosomes than they are to the cytoplasmic ribosomes of eukaryotic cells.

The Origin of Multicellularity

An orchestra can play a greater variety of musical compositions than a violin soloist can; the increased complexity of the orchestra makes more variations possible. Likewise, the appearance of structurally complex eukaryotic cells sparked the evolution of greater morphological diversity than was possible for the simpler prokaryotic cells. After the first eukaryotes appeared, a great range of unicellular forms evolved, giving rise to the diversity of single-celled eukaryotes that continue to flourish today. Another wave of diversification also occurred: Some single-celled eukaryotes gave rise to multicellular forms, whose descendants include a variety of algae, plants, fungi, and animals.

The Earliest Multicellular Eukaryotes

Multicellular eukaryotes

Based on comparisons of DNA sequences, researchers have suggested that the common ancestor of multicellular eukaryotes lived 1.5 billion years ago. This result is in rough agreement with the fossil record; the oldest known fossils of multicellular eukaryotes are of relatively small algae that lived about 1.2 billion years ago. Larger and more diverse multicellular eukaryotes do not appear in the fossil record until about 575 million years ago (see Figure 25.4). These fossils, referred to as the Ediacaran biota, were of soft-bodied organisms—some over 1 m long—that lived from 575 to 535 million years ago.

Why were multicellular eukaryotes limited in size and diversity until the late Proterozoic? One hypothesis stems from geologic evidence indicating that a series of severe ice ages occurred from 750 to 580 million years ago. At various times during this period, glaciers covered all of the planet's landmasses, and the seas were largely iced over. The "snowball Earth" hypothesis suggests that most life would have been confined to areas near deep-sea vents and hot springs or to equatorial regions of the ocean that lacked ice cover. The fossil record of the first major diversification of multicellular eukaryotes (beginning about 575 million years ago) corresponds roughly to the time when snowball Earth thawed. As that diversification came to a close about 40 million years later, the stage was set for another, even more spectacular burst of evolutionary change.

The Cambrian Explosion

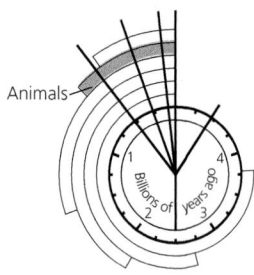

Many present-day animal phyla appear suddenly in fossils formed early in the Cambrian period (535–525 million years ago), a phenomenon referred to as the **Cambrian explosion**. Fossils of several animal groups—sponges, cnidarians (sea anemones and their relatives), and molluscs—appear in even older rocks dating from the late Proterozoic **(Figure 25.10)**.

Prior to the Cambrian explosion, all large animals were soft-bodied. The fossils of large pre-Cambrian animals reveal little evidence of predation. Instead, these animals appear to have been grazers (feeding on algae), suspension feeders, or scavengers, not hunters. The Cambrian explosion changed

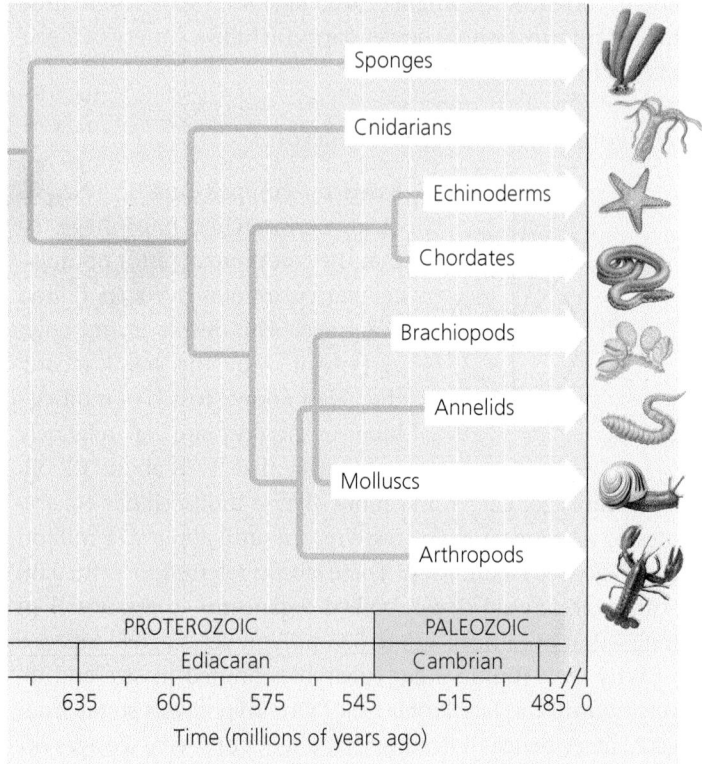

▲ **Figure 25.10 Appearance of selected animal groups.**
The white bars indicate earliest appearances of these animal groups in the fossil record.

DRAW IT *Circle the branch point that represents the most recent common ancestor of chordates and annelids. What is a minimum estimate of that ancestor's age?*

(a) Two-cell stage 150 μm **(b) Later stage** 200 μm

▲ **Figure 25.11 Proterozoic fossils that may be animal embryos (SEM).**

all of that. In a relatively short period of time (10 million years), predators over 1 m in length emerged that had claws and other features for capturing prey; simultaneously, new defensive adaptations, such as sharp spines and heavy body armor, appeared in their prey (see Figure 25.4).

Although the Cambrian explosion had an enormous impact on life on Earth, it is possible that many animal phyla originated long before that time. Some DNA analyses suggest that most animal phyla originated and began to diverge from one another as early as 700 million to 1 billion years ago. Even if these estimates are not correct, recent fossil discoveries in China suggest that animals similar to members of living animal phyla were present tens of millions of years before the Cambrian explosion. The discoveries include 575-million-year-old fossils of beautifully preserved specimens interpreted by most scientists either as animal embryos or as members of extinct groups closely related to animals **(Figure 25.11)**. Overall, it appears that the Cambrian explosion had a "long fuse"—at least 40 million years long, based on the Chinese fossils. The fuse may have been hundreds of millions of years long if some animal phyla originated as far back as some DNA-based estimates suggest.

The Colonization of Land

The colonization of land was another milestone in the history of life. There is fossil evidence that cyanobacteria and other photosynthetic prokaryotes coated damp terrestrial surfaces well over a billion years ago. However, larger forms of life, such as fungi, plants, and animals, did not begin to colonize land until about 500 million years ago. This gradual evolutionary venture out of aquatic environments was associated with adaptations that made it possible to reproduce on land and that helped prevent dehydration. For example, many land plants today have a vascular system for transporting materials internally and a waterproof coating of wax on their leaves that slows the loss of water to the air. Early signs of these adaptations were present 420 million years ago, at which time small plants (about 10 cm high) existed that had a vascular system but lacked true roots or leaves. By about 50 million years later, plants had diversified greatly and included reeds and treelike plants with true roots and leaves.

Plants colonized land in the company of fungi. Even today, the roots of most plants are associated with fungi that aid in the absorption of water and minerals from the soil (see Chapter 31). These root fungi, in turn, obtain their organic nutrients from the plants. Such mutually beneficial associations of plants and fungi are evident in some of the oldest fossilized roots, dating this relationship back to the early spread of life onto land.

Although many animal groups are now represented in terrestrial environments, the most widespread and diverse land animals are arthropods (particularly insects and spiders) and tetrapods. Arthropods were the first animals to colonize land, roughly 420 million years ago. The earliest tetrapods found in the fossil record lived about 365 million years ago and appear to have evolved from a group of lobe-finned fishes (see Chapter 34). Tetrapods include humans, although we are late arrivals on the scene. The human lineage diverged from other primates around 6–7 million years ago, and our species originated only about 195,000 years ago. If the clock of Earth's history were rescaled to represent an hour, humans appeared less than 0.2 second ago.

CONCEPT CHECK 25.3

1. The first appearance of free oxygen in the atmosphere likely triggered a massive wave of extinctions among the prokaryotes of the time. Why?
2. What evidence supports the hypothesis that mitochondria preceded plastids in the evolution of eukaryotic cells?
3. **WHAT IF?** What would a fossil record of life today look like?

For suggested answers, see Appendix A.

CONCEPT 25.4

The rise and fall of groups of organisms reflect differences in speciation and extinction rates

From its beginnings, life on Earth has seen the rise and fall of groups of organisms. Anaerobic prokaryotes originated, flourished, and then declined as the oxygen content of the atmosphere rose. Billions of years later, the first tetrapods emerged from the sea, giving rise to several major new groups of organisms. One of these, the amphibians, went on to dominate life on land for 100 million years, until other tetrapods (including dinosaurs and, later, mammals) replaced them as the dominant terrestrial vertebrates.

The rise and fall of these and other major groups of organisms have shaped the history of life. Narrowing our focus, we can also see that the rise or fall of any particular group is related to the speciation and extinction rates of its member species. Just as a population increases in size when there are more births than deaths, the rise of a group of organisms occurs when it produces more new species than are lost to extinction. The reverse occurs when a group is in decline. As we'll see, such changes in the fates of groups of organisms have been influenced by large-scale processes such as plate tectonics, mass extinctions, and adaptive radiations.

Plate Tectonics

If photographs of Earth were taken from space every 10,000 years and spliced together to make a movie, it would show something many of us find hard to imagine: The seemingly "rock solid" continents we live on move over time. Since the origin of multicellular eukaryotes roughly 1.5 billion years ago, there have been three occasions (1.1 billion, 600 million, and 250 million years ago) when most of the landmasses of Earth came together to form a supercontinent, then later broke apart. Each time they yielded a different configuration of continents. Looking into the future, some geologists have estimated that the continents will come together again and form a new supercontinent roughly 250 million years from now.

According to the theory of **plate tectonics**, the continents are part of great plates of Earth's crust that essentially float on the hot, underlying portion of the mantle (**Figure 25.12**). Movements in the mantle cause the plates to move over time in a process called *continental drift*. Geologists can measure the rate at which the plates are moving now, usually only a few centimeters per year. They can also infer the past locations of the continents using the magnetic signal recorded in rocks at the time of their formation. This method works because as a continent shifts its position over time, the direction of magnetic north recorded in its newly formed rocks also changes.

▶ **Figure 25.12 Cutaway view of Earth.** The thickness of the crust is exaggerated here.

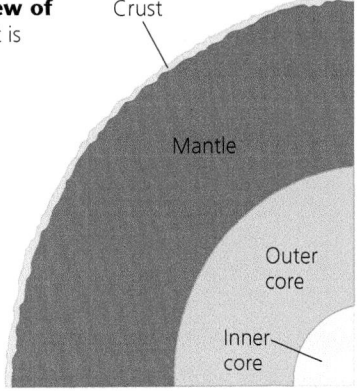

Crust

Mantle

Outer core

Inner core

Earth's major tectonic plates are shown in **Figure 25.13**. Many important geologic processes, including the formation of mountains and islands, occur at plate boundaries. In some cases, two plates are moving away from each other, as are the North American and Eurasian plates, which are currently drifting apart at a rate of about 2 cm per year. In other cases, two plates are sliding past each other, forming regions where earthquakes are common. California's infamous San Andreas Fault is part of a border where two plates slide past each other. In still other cases, two plates are colliding. Typically, oceanic plates (those found on the bottom of the ocean) are more dense than terrestrial plates. As a result, when an oceanic plate collides with a terrestrial plate, the oceanic plate usually sinks below the terrestrial plate. When two oceanic plates or two terrestrial plates collide with each other, violent upheavals occur and mountains form along the plate boundaries. One spectacular example of this occurred 45 million years ago, when the Indian plate crashed into the Eurasian plate, starting the formation of the Himalayan mountains.

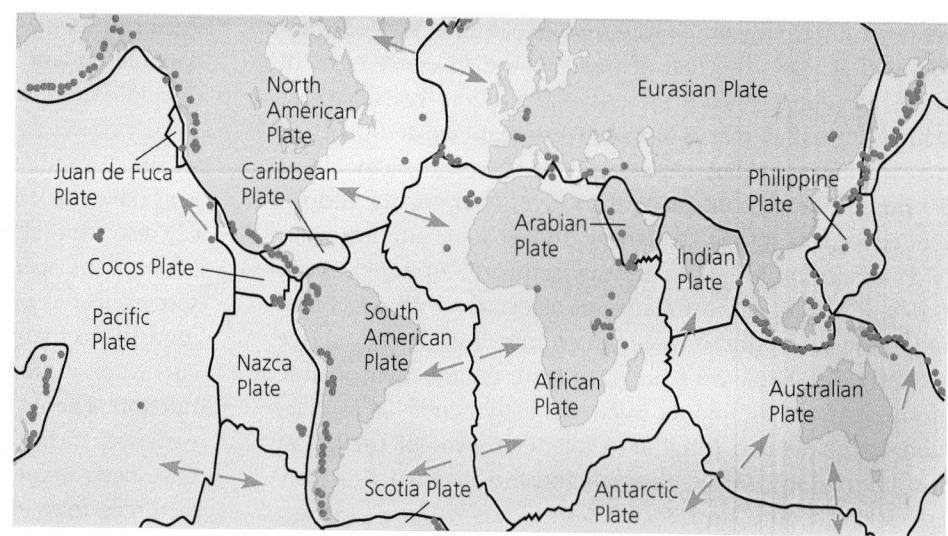

▲ Figure 25.13 **Earth's major tectonic plates.** The arrows indicate direction of movement. The reddish orange dots represent zones of violent tectonic activity.

Consequences of Continental Drift

Plate movements rearrange geography slowly, but their cumulative effects are dramatic. In addition to reshaping the physical features of our planet, continental drift also has a major impact on life on Earth.

One reason for its great impact on life is that continental drift alters the habitats in which organisms live. Consider the changes shown in **Figure 25.14**. About 250 million years ago, plate movements brought all the previously separated landmasses together into a supercontinent named **Pangaea**. Ocean basins became deeper, which lowered sea level and drained shallow coastal seas. At that time, as now, most marine species inhabited shallow waters, and the formation of Pangaea destroyed a considerable amount of that habitat. The interior of the vast continent was cold and dry, probably an even more severe environment than that of central Asia today. Overall, the formation of Pangaea had a tremendous impact on the physical environment and climate, which drove some species to extinction and provided new opportunities for groups of organisms that survived the crisis.

Another aspect of continental drift that affects organisms is the climate change that results when a continent shifts its location. The southern tip of Labrador, Canada, for example, once was located in the tropics but has moved 40° to the north over the last 200 million years. When faced with the changes in climate that such shifts in position entail, organisms adapt,

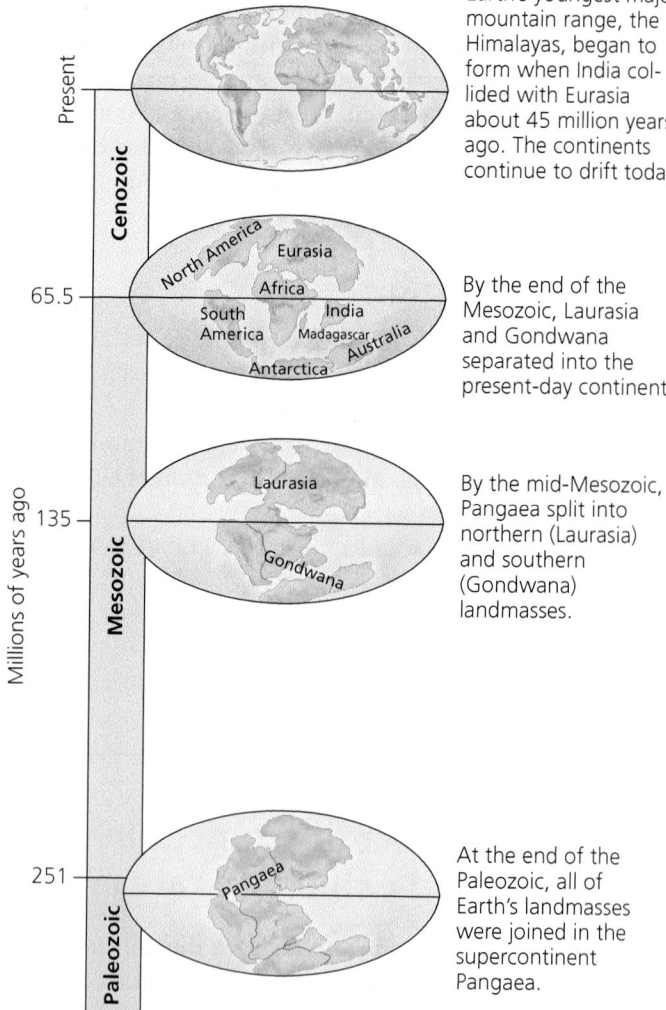

Earth's youngest major mountain range, the Himalayas, began to form when India collided with Eurasia about 45 million years ago. The continents continue to drift today.

By the end of the Mesozoic, Laurasia and Gondwana separated into the present-day continents.

By the mid-Mesozoic, Pangaea split into northern (Laurasia) and southern (Gondwana) landmasses.

At the end of the Paleozoic, all of Earth's landmasses were joined in the supercontinent Pangaea.

▲ Figure 25.14 **The history of continental drift during the Phanerozoic eon.**

move to a new location, or become extinct (this last outcome occurred for many organisms stranded on Antarctica).

Continental drift also promotes allopatric speciation on a grand scale. When supercontinents break apart, regions that once were connected become geographically isolated. As the continents drifted apart over the last 200 million years, each became a separate evolutionary arena, with lineages of plants and animals that diverged from those on other continents.

Finally, continental drift can help explain puzzles about the geographic distribution of extinct organisms, such as why fossils of the same species of Permian freshwater reptiles have been discovered in both Brazil and the West African nation of Ghana. These two parts of the world, now separated by 3,000 km of ocean, were joined together when these reptiles were living. Continental drift also explains much about the current distributions of organisms, such as why Australian fauna and flora contrast so sharply with those of the rest of the world. Marsupial mammals fill ecological roles in Australia analogous to those filled by eutherians (placental mammals) on other continents (see Figure 22.18). Fossil evidence suggests that marsupials originated in what is now Asia and reached Australia via South America and Antarctica while the continents were still joined. The subsequent breakup of the southern continents set Australia "afloat" like a giant raft of marsupials. In Australia, marsupials diversified, and the few eutherians that lived there became extinct; on other continents, most marsupials became extinct, and the eutherians diversified.

Mass Extinctions

The fossil record shows that the overwhelming majority of species that ever lived are now extinct. A species may become extinct for many reasons. Its habitat may have been destroyed, or its environment may have changed in a manner unfavorable to the species. For example, if ocean temperatures fall by even a few degrees, species that are otherwise well adapted may perish. Even if physical factors in the environment remain stable, biological factors may change—the origin of one species can spell doom for another.

Although extinction occurs on a regular basis, at certain times disruptive global environmental changes have caused the rate of extinction to increase dramatically. When this occurs, a **mass extinction** results, in which large numbers of species become extinct throughout Earth.

The "Big Five" Mass Extinction Events

Five mass extinctions are documented in the fossil record over the past 500 million years (**Figure 25.15**). These events are particularly well documented for the decimation of hard-bodied animals that lived in shallow seas, the organisms for which the fossil record is most complete. In each mass extinction, 50% or more of Earth's marine species became extinct.

Two mass extinctions—the Permian and the Cretaceous—have received the most attention. The Permian mass extinction, which defines the boundary between the Paleozoic and Mesozoic eras (251 million years ago), claimed about 96% of marine animal species and drastically altered life in the ocean.

◄ **Figure 25.15 Mass extinction and the diversity of life.** The five generally recognized mass extinction events, indicated by red arrows, represent peaks in the extinction rate of marine animal families (red line and left vertical axis). These mass extinctions interrupted the overall increase in the number of marine animal families over time (blue line and right vertical axis).

? *96% of marine animal species became extinct in the Permian mass extinction. Explain why the blue curve shows only a 50% drop at that time.*

Terrestrial life was also affected. For example, 8 out of 27 known orders of insects were wiped out. This mass extinction occurred in less than 500,000 years, possibly in just a few thousand years—an instant in the context of geologic time.

The Permian mass extinction occurred at the time of enormous volcanic eruptions in what is now Siberia. This period was the most extreme episode of volcanism to have occurred during the past half billion years. Geologic data indicate that an area of 1.6 million km^2 (roughly half the size of western Europe) was covered with a layer of lava hundreds to thousands of meters thick. Besides spewing enormous amounts of lava and ash, the eruptions may have produced enough carbon dioxide to warm the global climate by an estimated 6°C. Reduced temperature differences between the equator and the poles could have slowed the mixing of ocean water, which in turn could have led to a widespread drop in oxygen concentrations. The resulting low-oxygen condition, called *ocean anoxia*, would have suffocated oxygen-breathers and promoted the growth of anaerobic bacteria that emit a poisonous metabolic by-product, hydrogen sulfide (H_2S) gas. As this gas bubbled into the atmosphere, it could have caused further extinctions by directly killing land plants and animals and by initiating chemical reactions that destroy the ozone layer, a "shield" that ordinarily protects organisms from life-threatening levels of UV radiation.

The Cretaceous mass extinction occurred about 65.5 million years ago and marks the boundary between the Mesozoic and Cenozoic eras. This event extinguished more than half of all marine species and eliminated many families of terrestrial plants and animals, including all dinosaurs (except birds,

which are members of the same group; see Chapter 34). One clue to a possible cause of the Cretaceous mass extinction is a thin layer of clay enriched in iridium that separates sediments from the Mesozoic and Cenozoic eras. Iridium is an element that is very rare on Earth but common in many of the meteorites and other extraterrestrial objects that occasionally fall to Earth. Walter Alvarez and the late Luis Alvarez, of the University of California, Berkeley, and their colleagues proposed that this clay is fallout from a huge cloud of debris that billowed into the atmosphere when an asteroid or large comet collided with Earth. This cloud would have blocked sunlight and severely disturbed the global climate for several months.

Is there evidence of such an asteroid or comet? Research has focused on the Chicxulub crater, a 65-million-year-old scar beneath sediments off the Yucatán coast of Mexico (Figure 25.16). The crater is the right size to have been caused by an object with a diameter of 10 km. Critical evaluation of this and other hypotheses for mass extinctions continues.

Is a Sixth Mass Extinction Under Way?

As we will explore in Chapter 56, human actions, such as habitat destruction, are modifying the global environment to such an extent that many species are threatened with extinction. More than a thousand species have become extinct in the last 400 years. Scientists estimate that this rate is 100 to 1,000 times the typical background rate seen in the fossil record. Is a sixth mass extinction now in progress?

This question is difficult to answer, in part because it is hard to document the total number of extinctions occurring today. Tropical rain forests, for example, harbor many undiscovered

▲ **Figure 25.16 Trauma for Earth and its Cretaceous life.** Beneath the Caribbean Sea, the 65-million-year-old Chicxulub impact crater measures 180 km across. The horseshoe shape of the crater and the pattern of debris in sedimentary rocks indicate that an asteroid or comet struck at a low angle from the southeast. This artist's interpretation represents the impact and its immediate effect: a cloud of hot vapor and debris that could have killed many of the plants and animals in North America within hours.

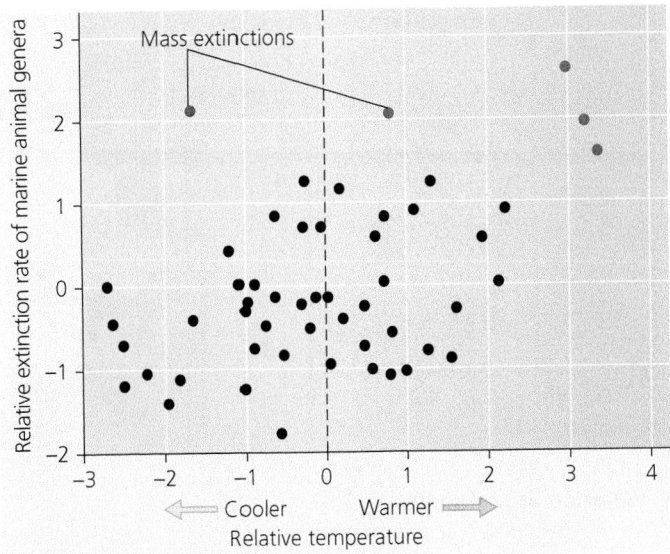

▲ **Figure 25.17 Fossil extinctions and temperature.** Extinction rates increased when global temperatures were high. Temperatures were estimated using ratios of oxygen isotopes and converted to an index in which 0 is the overall average temperature.

species. As a result, destroying tropical forest may drive species to extinction before we even learn of their existence. Such uncertainties make it hard to assess the full extent of the current extinction crisis. Even so, it is clear that losses to date have not reached those of the "big five" mass extinctions, in which large percentages of Earth's species became extinct. This does not in any way discount the seriousness of today's situation. Monitoring programs show that many species are declining at an alarming rate, and studies on polar bears, pine trees, and other species suggest that climate change may hasten some of these declines. Indeed, the fossil record indicates that over the last 500 million years, extinction rates have tended to increase when global temperatures were high **(Figure 25.17)**. Overall, present-day and fossil evidence both suggest that unless dramatic actions are taken, a sixth, human-caused mass extinction is likely to occur within the next few centuries or millennia.

Consequences of Mass Extinctions

Mass extinctions have significant and long-term effects. By eliminating large numbers of species, a mass extinction can reduce a thriving and complex ecological community to a pale shadow of its former self. And once an evolutionary lineage disappears, it cannot reappear. The course of evolution is changed forever. Consider what would have happened if the early primates living 66 million years ago had died out in the Cretaceous mass extinction. Humans would not exist, and life on Earth would differ greatly from what it is today.

The fossil record shows that it typically takes 5–10 million years for the diversity of life to recover to previous levels after a mass extinction. In some cases, it has taken much longer than that: It took about 100 million years for the number of marine families to recover after the Permian mass extinction (see Figure 25.15). These data have sobering implications. If current trends continue and a sixth mass extinction occurs, it will take millions of years for life on Earth to recover.

Mass extinctions can also alter ecological communities by changing the types of organisms found in them. For example, after the Permian and Cretaceous mass extinctions, the percentage of marine organisms that were predators increased substantially **(Figure 25.18)**. A rise in the number of predator species can increase both the pressures faced by prey and the competition among predators for food. In addition, mass extinctions can curtail lineages with highly advantageous features. For example, in the late Triassic a group of gastropods (snails and their relatives) arose that could drill through the shells of bivalves (such as clams) and feed on the animals inside. Although shell drilling provided access to a new and abundant source of food, this newly formed group was wiped out during the mass extinction at the end of the Triassic (about 200 million years ago). Another 120 million years passed before another group of gastropods (the oyster drills) exhibited the ability to drill through shells. As their predecessors might have done if they had not originated at an unfortunate time, oyster

◀ **Figure 25.18 Mass extinctions and ecology.** The Permian and Cretaceous mass extinctions (indicated by red arrows) altered the ecology of the oceans by increasing the percentage of marine genera that were predators.

drills have since diversified into many new species. Finally, by eliminating so many species, mass extinctions can pave the way for adaptive radiations, in which new groups of organisms proliferate.

Adaptive Radiations

The fossil record indicates that the diversity of life has increased over the past 250 million years (see blue line in Figure 25.15). This increase has been fueled by **adaptive radiations**, periods of evolutionary change in which groups of organisms form many new species whose adaptations allow them to fill different ecological roles, or niches, in their communities. Large-scale adaptive radiations occurred after each of the big five mass extinctions, when survivors became adapted to the many vacant ecological niches. Adaptive radiations have also occurred in groups of organisms that possessed major evolutionary innovations, such as seeds or armored body coverings, or that colonized regions in which they faced little competition from other species.

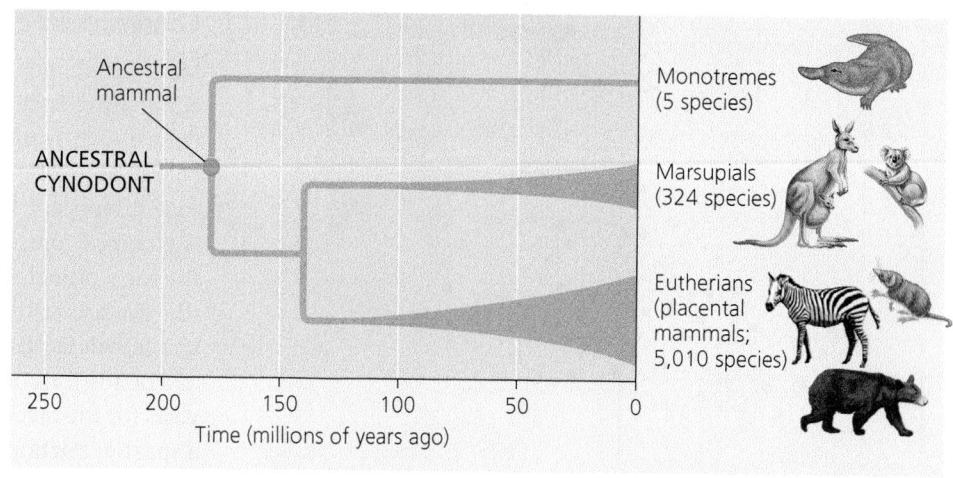

▲ Figure 25.19 **Adaptive radiation of mammals.**

Worldwide Adaptive Radiations

Fossil evidence indicates that mammals underwent a dramatic adaptive radiation after the extinction of terrestrial dinosaurs 65.5 million years ago (Figure 25.19). Although mammals originated about 180 million years ago, the mammal fossils older than 65.5 million years are mostly small and not morphologically diverse. Many species appear to have been nocturnal based on their large eye sockets, similar to those in living nocturnal mammals. A few early mammals were intermediate in size, such as *Repenomamus giganticus*, a 1-m-long predator that lived 130 million years ago—but none approached the size of many dinosaurs. Early mammals may have been restricted in size and diversity because they were eaten or outcompeted by the larger and more diverse dinosaurs. With the disappearance of the dinosaurs (except for birds), mammals expanded greatly in both diversity and size, filling the ecological roles once occupied by terrestrial dinosaurs.

The history of life has also been greatly altered by radiations in which groups of organisms increased in diversity as they came to play entirely new ecological roles in their communities. Examples include the rise of photosynthetic prokaryotes, the evolution of large predators in the Cambrian explosion, and the radiations following the colonization of land by plants, insects, and tetrapods. Each of these last three radiations was associated with major evolutionary innovations that facilitated life on land. The radiation of land plants, for example, was associated with key adaptations, such as stems that support plants against gravity and a waxy coat that protects leaves from water loss. Finally, organisms that arise in an adaptive radiation can serve as a new source of food for still other organisms. In fact, the diversification of land plants stimulated a series of adaptive radiations in insects that ate or pollinated plants, one reason that insects are the most diverse group of animals on Earth today.

Regional Adaptive Radiations

Striking adaptive radiations have also occurred over more limited geographic areas. Such radiations can be initiated when a few organisms make their way to a new, often distant location in which they face relatively little competition from other organisms. The Hawaiian archipelago is one of the world's great showcases of this type of adaptive radiation (Figure 25.20). Located about 3,500 km from the nearest continent, the volcanic islands are progressively older as one follows the chain toward the northwest; the youngest island, Hawaii, is less than a million years old and still has active volcanoes. Each island was born "naked" and was gradually populated by stray organisms that rode the ocean currents and winds either from far-distant land areas or from older islands of the archipelago itself. The physical diversity of each island, including immense variation in elevation and rainfall, provides many opportunities for evolutionary divergence by natural selection. Multiple invasions followed by speciation events have ignited an explosion of adaptive radiation in Hawaii. Most of the thousands of species that inhabit the islands are found nowhere else on Earth.

CONCEPT CHECK 25.4

1. Explain the consequences of continental drift for life on Earth.
2. What factors promote adaptive radiations?
3. **WHAT IF?** If a mass extinction were caused by a sudden catastrophic event, would dates of the last observation in the fossil record of species lost in the extinction differ for rare versus common species? Explain.

For suggested answers, see Appendix A.

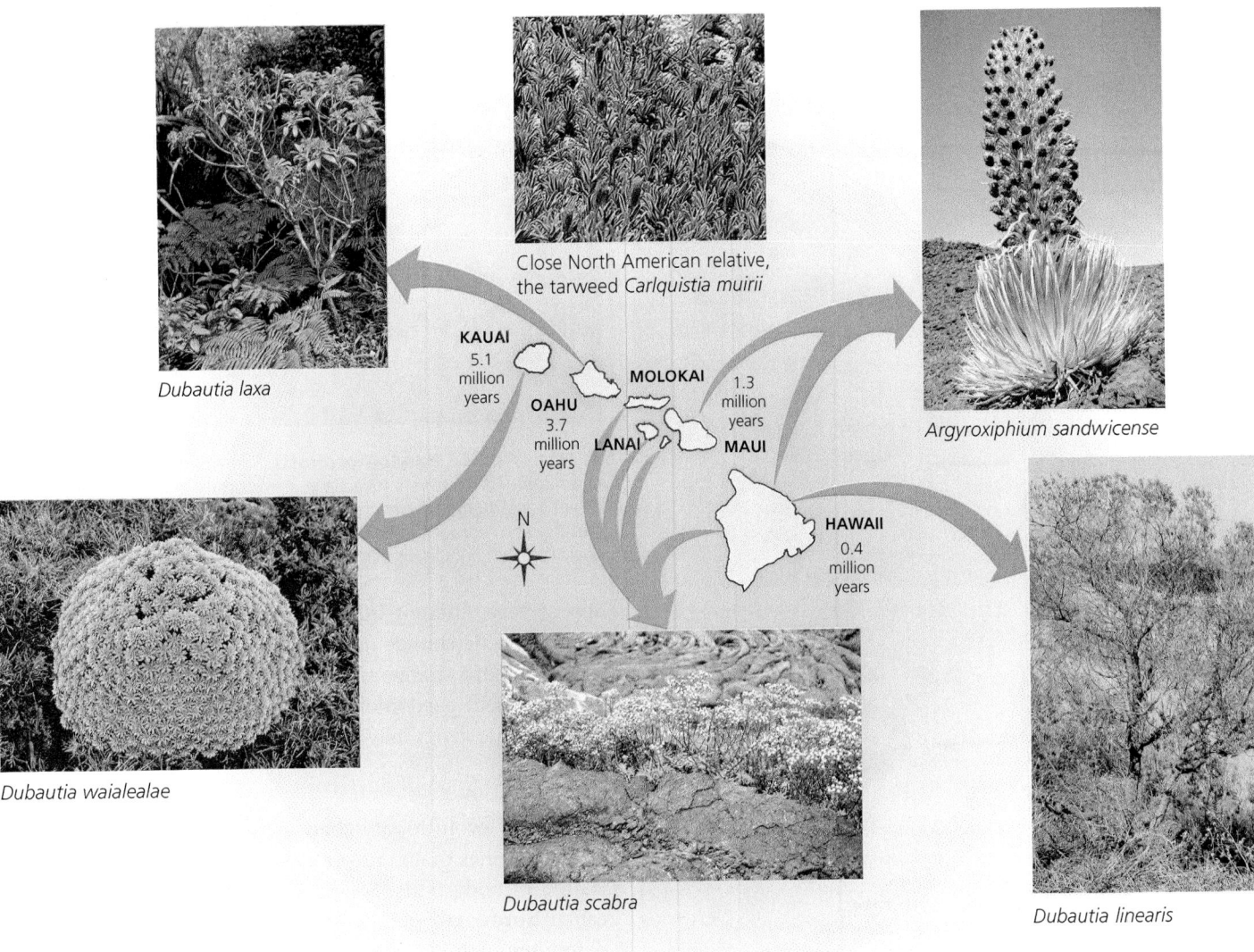

▲ Figure 25.20 Adaptive radiation on the Hawaiian Islands. Molecular analysis indicates that these remarkably varied Hawaiian plants, known collectively as the "silversword alliance," are all descended from an ancestral tarweed that arrived on the islands about 5 million years ago from North America. Members of the silversword alliance have since spread into different habitats and formed new species with strikingly different adaptations.

CONCEPT **25.5**

Major changes in body form can result from changes in the sequences and regulation of developmental genes

The fossil record tells us what the great changes in the history of life have been and when they occurred. Moreover, an understanding of plate tectonics, mass extinction, and adaptive radiation provides a picture of how those changes came about. But we can also seek to understand the intrinsic biological mechanisms that underlie changes seen in the fossil record. For this, we turn to genetic mechanisms of change, paying particular attention to genes that influence development.

Effects of Developmental Genes

As you read in Chapter 21, "evo-devo"—research at the interface between evolutionary biology and developmental biology—is illuminating how slight genetic divergences can produce major morphological differences between species. Genes that control development influence the rate, timing, and spatial pattern of change in an organism's form as it develops from a zygote into an adult.

Changes in Rate and Timing

Many striking evolutionary transformations are the result of **heterochrony** (from the Greek *hetero*, different, and *chronos*, time), an evolutionary change in the rate or timing of developmental events. For example, an organism's shape depends in part on the relative growth rates of different body parts

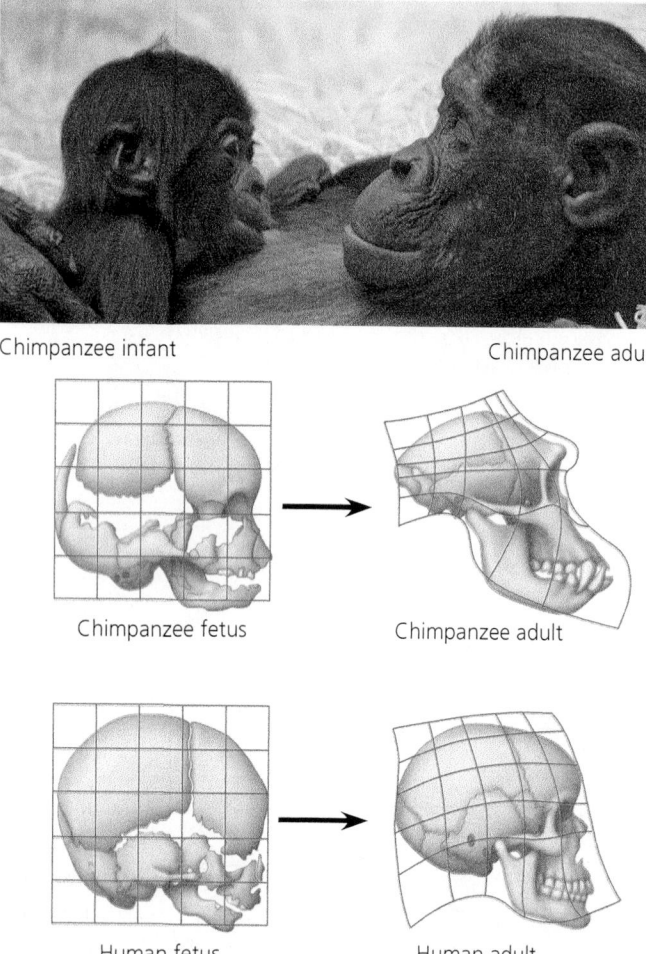

Chimpanzee infant   Chimpanzee adult

Chimpanzee fetus   Chimpanzee adult

Human fetus   Human adult

▲ Figure 25.21 **Relative skull growth rates.** In the human evolutionary lineage, mutations that slowed the growth of the jaw relative to other parts of the skull produced an adult whose head resembles that of a chimpanzee infant.

▲ Figure 25.22 **Paedomorphosis.** The adults of some species retain features that were juvenile in ancestors. This salamander is an axolotl, an aquatic species that grows to full size, becomes sexually mature, and reproduces while retaining certain larval (tadpole) characteristics, including gills.

during development. Changes to these rates can alter the adult form substantially, as seen in the contrasting shapes of human and chimpanzee skulls (**Figure 25.21**). Other examples of the dramatic evolutionary effects of heterochrony include how increased growth rates of finger bones yielded the skeletal structure of wings in bats (see Figure 22.15) and how slowed growth of leg and pelvic bones led to the reduction and eventual loss of hind limbs in whales (see Figure 22.20).

Heterochrony can also alter the timing of reproductive development relative to the development of nonreproductive organs. If reproductive organ development accelerates compared to other organs, the sexually mature stage of a species may retain body features that were juvenile structures in an ancestral species, a condition called **paedomorphosis** (from the Greek *paedos*, of a child, and *morphosis*, formation). For example, most salamander species have aquatic larvae that undergo metamorphosis in becoming adults. But some species grow to adult size and become sexually mature while retaining gills and other larval features (**Figure 25.22**). Such an evolutionary alteration of developmental timing can produce animals that

appear very different from their ancestors, even though the overall genetic change may be small. Indeed, recent evidence indicates that a change at a single locus was probably sufficient to bring about paedomorphosis in the axolotl salamander, although other genes may have contributed as well.

Changes in Spatial Pattern

Substantial evolutionary changes can also result from alterations in genes that control the placement and spatial organization of body parts. For example, master regulatory genes called **homeotic genes** (described in Chapters 18 and 21) determine such basic features as where a pair of wings and a pair of legs will develop on a bird or how a plant's flower parts are arranged.

The products of one class of homeotic genes, the *Hox* genes, provide positional information in an animal embryo. This information prompts cells to develop into structures appropriate for a particular location. Changes in *Hox* genes or in how they are expressed can have a profound impact on morphology. For example, among crustaceans, a change in the location where two *Hox* genes (*Ubx* and *Scr*) are expressed correlates with the conversion of a swimming appendage to a feeding appendage. Large effects are also seen in snakes, where changes in how two *Hox* genes (*HoxC6* and *HoxC8*) are expressed suppresses limb formation (**Figure 25.23**). Similarly, when comparing plant species, changes to the expression of homeotic genes known as *MADS-box* genes can produce flowers that differ dramatically in form (see Chapter 35).

The Evolution of Development

The 565-million-year-old fossils of Ediacaran animals in Figure 25.4 suggest that a set of genes sufficient to produce complex animals existed at least 30 million years *before* the Cambrian explosion. If such genes have existed for so long,

▲ **Figure 25.23** *Hox* **gene expression and limb development.** Regions of *HoxC6* gene expression (purple) correlate with limbless regions in the torsos of a snake embryo (left) and a chicken embryo (right).

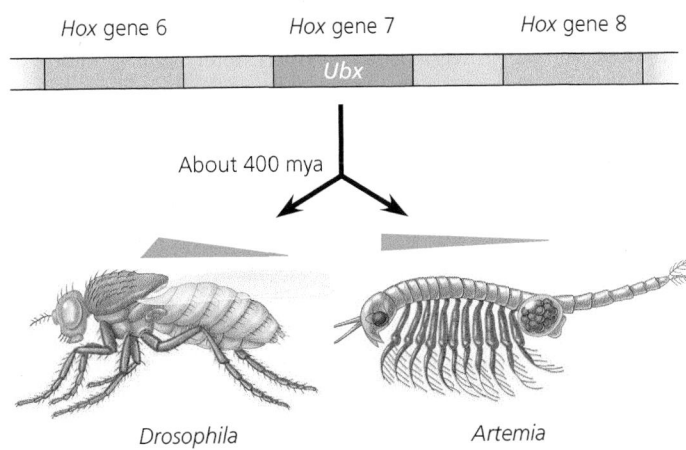

Hox gene 6   *Hox* gene 7   *Hox* gene 8

Ubx

About 400 mya

Drosophila   *Artemia*

▲ **Figure 25.24** **Origin of the insect body plan.** Expression of the *Hox* gene *Ubx* suppresses the formation of legs in fruit flies (*Drosophila*) but not in brine shrimp (*Artemia*), thus helping to build the insect body plan. Fruit fly and brine shrimp *Hox* genes have evolved independently for 400 million years. The green triangles indicate the relative amounts of *Ubx* expression in different body regions.

how can we explain the astonishing increases in diversity seen during and since the Cambrian explosion?

Adaptive evolution by natural selection provides one answer to this question. As we've seen throughout this unit, by sorting among differences in the sequences of protein-encoding genes, selection can improve adaptations rapidly. In addition, new genes (created by gene duplication events) can take on a wide range of new metabolic and structural functions. Thus, adaptive evolution of both new and existing genes may have played a key role in shaping the great diversity of life.

Examples in the previous section suggest that developmental genes may play a critical role. Next we'll examine how new morphological forms arise from changes in the nucleotide sequences or regulation of developmental genes.

Changes in Genes

New developmental genes arising after gene duplication events very likely facilitated the origin of novel morphological forms. But since other genetic changes also may have occurred at such times, it can be difficult to establish causal links between genetic and morphological changes that occurred in the past.

This difficulty was sidestepped in a recent study of developmental changes associated with the divergence of six-legged insects from crustacean-like ancestors that had more than six legs. In insects, such as *Drosophila*, the *Ubx* gene is expressed in the abdomen, while in crustaceans, such as *Artemia*, it is expressed in the main trunk of the body (**Figure 25.24**). When expressed, the *Ubx* gene suppresses leg formation in insects but not in crustaceans. To examine the workings of this gene, researchers cloned the *Ubx* gene from *Drosophila* and *Artemia*. Next, they genetically engineered fruit fly embryos to express either the *Drosophila Ubx* gene or the *Artemia Ubx* gene throughout their bodies. The *Drosophila* gene suppressed 100% of the limbs in the embryos, as expected, whereas *Artemia* gene suppressed only 15%.

The researchers then sought to uncover key steps involved in the evolutionary transition from a crustacean *Ubx* gene to an insect *Ubx* gene. Their approach was to identify mutations that would cause the *Artemia Ubx* gene to suppress leg formation, thus making the crustacean gene act more like an insect *Ubx* gene. To do this, they constructed a series of "hybrid" *Ubx* genes, each of which contained known segments of the *Drosophila Ubx* gene and known segments of the *Artemia Ubx* gene. By inserting these hybrid genes into fruit fly embryos (one hybrid gene per embryo) and observing their effects on leg development, the researchers were able to pinpoint the exact amino acid changes responsible for the suppression of additional limbs in insects. In so doing, this study provided evidence linking a particular change in the nucleotide sequence of a developmental gene to a major evolutionary change: the origin of the six-legged insect body plan.

Changes in Gene Regulation

Changes in the nucleotide sequence or regulation of developmental genes can result in morphological changes that harm the organism (see Chapter 18). Moreover, a change in the nucleotide sequence of a gene may affect its function wherever the gene is expressed. In contrast, changes in the regulation of gene expression can be limited to a single cell type (see Chapter 18). Thus, a change in the regulation of a developmental gene may have fewer harmful side effects than a change to the sequence of the gene. This line of reasoning has prompted researchers to suggest that changes in the form of organisms may often be caused by mutations that affect the regulation of developmental genes—not their sequences.

This idea is supported by studies in a variety of species, including threespine stickleback fish. These fish live in the open ocean and in shallow, coastal waters. In western Canada, they also live in lakes formed when the coastline receded during the past 12,000 years. Marine stickleback fish have a pair of spines on their ventral (lower) surface, which deter some predators. These spines are often reduced or absent in stickleback fish living in lakes that lack predatory fishes and that are also low in calcium. Spines may have been lost because they are not advantageous in the absence of predators, and the limited calcium is needed for purposes other than constructing spines.

At the genetic level, the developmental gene, *Pitx1*, was known to influence whether stickleback fish have ventral spines. Was the reduction of spines in some lake populations due to changes in the *Pitx1* gene or to changes in how the gene is expressed (Figure 25.25)? The researchers' results indicate that the regulation of gene expression has changed, not the DNA sequence of the gene. Furthermore, lake stickleback

▼ Figure 25.25

INQUIRY

What causes the loss of spines in lake stickleback fish?

EXPERIMENT Marine populations of the threespine stickleback fish (*Gasterosteus aculeatus*) have a set of protective spines on their lower (ventral) surface; however, these spines have been lost or reduced in some lake populations of this fish. Working at Stanford University, Michael Shapiro, David Kingsley, and colleagues performed genetic crosses and found that most of the reduction in spine size resulted from the effects of a single developmental gene, *Pitx1*. The researchers then tested two hypotheses about how *Pitx1* causes this morphological change.

Hypothesis A: A change in the DNA sequence of *Pitx1* had caused spine reduction in lake populations. To test this idea, the team used DNA sequencing to compare the coding sequence of the *Pitx1* gene between marine and lake stickleback populations.

Hypothesis B: A change in the regulation of the expression of *Pitx1* had caused spine reduction. To test this idea, the researchers monitored where in the developing embryo the *Pitx1* gene was expressed. They conducted whole-body *in situ* hybridization experiments (see Chapter 20) using *Pitx1* DNA as a probe to detect *Pitx1* mRNA in the fish.

Threespine stickleback (*Gasterosteus aculeatus*)

RESULTS

| Test of Hypothesis A: Are there differences in the coding sequence of the *Pitx1* gene in marine and lake stickleback fish? | Result: No → | The 283 amino acids of the *Pitx1* protein are identical in marine and lake stickleback populations. |

| Test of Hypothesis B: Are there any differences in the regulation of expression of *Pitx1*? | Result: Yes → | Red arrows (→) indicate regions of *Pitx1* gene expression in the photographs below. *Pitx1* is expressed in the ventral spine and mouth regions of developing marine stickleback fish but only in the mouth region of developing lake stickleback fish. |

Marine stickleback embryo   **Lake stickleback embryo**

Close-up of mouth

Close-up of ventral surface

CONCLUSION The loss or reduction of ventral spines in lake populations of threespine stickleback fish appears to have resulted primarily from a change in the regulation of *Pitx1* gene expression, not from a change in the gene's sequence.

SOURCE M. D. Shapiro et al., Genetic and developmental basis of evolutionary pelvic reduction in three-spine sticklebacks, *Nature* 428:717–723 (2004).

WHAT IF? Describe the set of results that would have led researchers to the conclusion that a change in the coding sequence of the *Pitx1* gene was more important than a change in regulation of gene expression.

fish do express the *Pitx1* gene in tissues not related to the production of spines (for example, the mouth), illustrating how morphological change can be caused by altering the expression of a developmental gene in some parts of the body but not others.

CONCEPT CHECK 25.5

1. How can heterochrony cause the evolution of different body forms?
2. Why is it likely that *Hox* genes have played a major role in the evolution of novel morphological forms?
3. **MAKE CONNECTIONS** Given that changes in morphology are often caused by changes in the regulation of gene expression, predict whether noncoding DNA is likely to be affected by natural selection. See Concept 18.3 (pp. 364–366) to review noncoding DNA and regulation of gene expression.

For suggested answers, see Appendix A.

CONCEPT 25.6

Evolution is not goal oriented

What does our study of macroevolution tell us about how evolution works? One lesson is that throughout the history of life, the origin of new species has been affected by both the bottom-up factors described in Chapter 24 (such as natural selection operating in populations) and the top-down factors described here (such as continental drift promoting bursts of speciation throughout the globe). Moreover, to paraphrase the Nobel Prize–winning geneticist François Jacob, evolution is like tinkering—a process in which new forms arise by the slight modification of existing forms. Even large changes, like the ones that produced the first mammals or the six-legged body plan of insects, can result from the modification of existing structures or existing developmental genes. Over time, such tinkering has led to three key features of the natural world described in Chapter 22: the striking ways in which organisms are suited for life in their environments; the many shared characteristics of life; and the rich diversity of life.

Evolutionary Novelties

François Jacob's view of evolution harkens back to Darwin's concept of descent with modification. As new species form, novel and complex structures can arise as gradual modifications of ancestral structures. In many cases, complex structures have evolved in increments from simpler versions that performed the same basic function. For example, consider the human eye, an intricate organ constructed from numerous parts that work together in forming an image and transmitting it to the brain. How could the human eye have evolved in gradual increments? Some argue that if the eye

needs all of its components to function, a partial eye could not have been of use to our ancestors.

The flaw in this argument, as Darwin himself noted, lies in the assumption that only complicated eyes are useful. In fact, many animals depend on eyes that are far less complex than our own (Figure 25.26). The simplest eyes that we know of are patches of light-sensitive photoreceptor cells. These simple eyes appear to have had a single evolutionary origin and are now found in a variety of animals, including small molluscs called limpets. Such eyes have no equipment for focusing images, but they do enable the animal to distinguish light from dark. Limpets cling more tightly to their rock when a shadow falls on them, a behavioral adaptation that reduces the risk of being eaten. Because limpets have had a long evolutionary history, we can conclude that their "simple" eyes are quite adequate to support their survival and reproduction.

▼ Figure 25.26 **A range of eye complexity among molluscs.**

(a) Patch of pigmented cells

Pigmented cells (photoreceptors)

Epithelium

Nerve fibers

The limpet *Patella* has a simple patch of photoreceptors.

(b) Eyecup

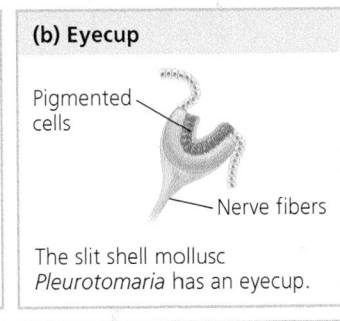

Pigmented cells

Nerve fibers

The slit shell mollusc *Pleurotomaria* has an eyecup.

(c) Pinhole camera-type eye

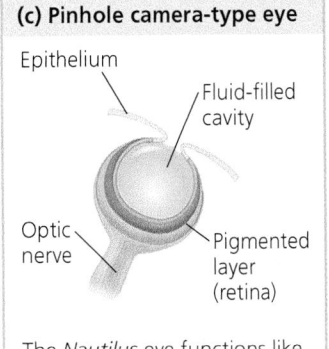

Epithelium

Fluid-filled cavity

Optic nerve

Pigmented layer (retina)

The *Nautilus* eye functions like a pinhole camera (an early type of camera lacking a lens).

(d) Eye with primitive lens

Cellular mass (lens)

Cornea

Optic nerve

The marine snail *Murex* has a primitive lens consisting of a mass of crystal-like cells. The cornea is a transparent region of tissue that protects the eye and helps focus light.

(e) Complex camera lens-type eye

Cornea

Lens

Retina

Optic nerve

The squid *Loligo* has a complex eye with features (cornea, lens, and retina) similar to those of vertebrate eyes. However, the squid eye evolved independently from vertebrate eyes.

In the animal kingdom, complex eyes have evolved independently from such basic structures many times. Some molluscs, such as squids and octopuses, have eyes as complex as those of humans and other vertebrates (see Figure 25.26). Although complex mollusc eyes evolved independently of vertebrate eyes, both evolved from a simple cluster of photoreceptor cells present in a common ancestor. In each case, the complex eye evolved through a series of incremental modifications that benefited the eyes' owners at every stage. Evidence of their independent evolution may also be found in their structure: Vertebrate eyes detect light at the back layer of the retina and conduct nerve impulses toward the front, while complex mollusc eyes do the reverse.

Throughout their evolutionary history, eyes retained their basic function of vision. But evolutionary novelties can also arise when structures that originally played one role gradually acquire a different one. For example, as cynodonts gave rise to early mammals, bones that formerly comprised the jaw hinge (the articular and quadrate; see Figure 25.6) were incorporated into the ear region of mammals, where they eventually took on a new function: the transmission of sound (see Chapter 34). Structures that evolve in one context but become co-opted for another function are sometimes called *exaptations* to distinguish them from the adaptive origin of the original structure. Note that the concept of exaptation does not imply that a structure somehow evolves in anticipation of future use. Natural selection cannot predict the future; it can only improve a structure in the context of its *current* utility. Novel features, such as the new jaw hinge and ear bones of early mammals, can arise gradually via a series of intermediate stages, each of which has some function in the organism's current context.

Evolutionary Trends

What else can we learn from patterns of macroevolution? Consider evolutionary "trends" observed in the fossil record. For instance, some evolutionary lineages exhibit a trend toward larger or smaller body size. An example is the evolution of the present-day horse (genus *Equus*), a descendant of the 55-million-year-old *Hyracotherium* (Figure 25.27). About the size of a large dog, *Hyracotherium* had four toes on its front feet, three toes on its hind feet, and teeth adapted for browsing on bushes and trees. In comparison, present-day horses are larger, have only one toe on each foot, and possess teeth modified for grazing on grasses.

Extracting a single evolutionary progression from the fossil record can be misleading, however; it is like describing a bush as growing toward a single point by tracing only the branches that lead to that twig. For example, by selecting certain species from the available fossils, it is possible to arrange a succession of animals intermediate between *Hyracotherium* and living horses that shows a trend toward large, single-toed species (follow the yellow highlighting in Figure 25.27). However, if we consider *all* fossil horses known today, this apparent trend vanishes. The genus *Equus* did not evolve in a straight line; it is the only surviving twig of an evolutionary tree that is so branched that it is more like a bush. *Equus* actually descended through a series of speciation episodes that included several adaptive radiations, not all of which led to large, one-toed, grazing horses. In fact, phylogenetic analyses suggest that all lineages that include grazers are closely related to *Parahippus*; the many other horse lineages, all of which are now extinct, remained multi-toed browsers for 35 million years.

Branching evolution *can* result in a real evolutionary trend even if some species counter the trend. One model of long-term trends proposed by Steven Stanley, of Johns Hopkins University, views species as analogous to individuals: Speciation is their birth, extinction is their death, and new species that diverge from them are their offspring. In this model, Stanley suggests that just as populations of individual organisms undergo natural selection, species undergo *species selection*. The species that endure the longest and generate the most new offspring species determine the direction of major evolutionary trends. The species selection model suggests that "differential speciation success" plays a role in macroevolution similar to the role of differential reproductive success in microevolution. Evolutionary trends can also result directly from natural selection. For example, when horse ancestors invaded the grasslands that spread during the mid-Cenozoic, there was strong selection for grazers that could escape predators by running faster. This trend would not have occurred without open grasslands.

Whatever its cause, an evolutionary trend does not imply that there is some intrinsic drive toward a particular phenotype. Evolution is the result of the interactions between organisms and their current environments; if environmental conditions change, an evolutionary trend may cease or even reverse itself. The cumulative effect of these ongoing interactions between organisms and their environments is enormous: It is through them that the staggering diversity of life—Darwin's "endless forms most beautiful"—has arisen.

CONCEPT CHECK 25.6

1. How can the Darwinian concept of descent with modification explain the evolution of such complex structures as the vertebrate eye?
2. **WHAT IF?** The myxoma virus kills up to 99.8% of infected European rabbits in populations with no previous exposure to the virus. The virus is transmitted between living rabbits by mosquitoes. Describe an evolutionary trend (in either the rabbit or virus) that might occur after a rabbit population first encounters the virus.

For suggested answers, see Appendix A.

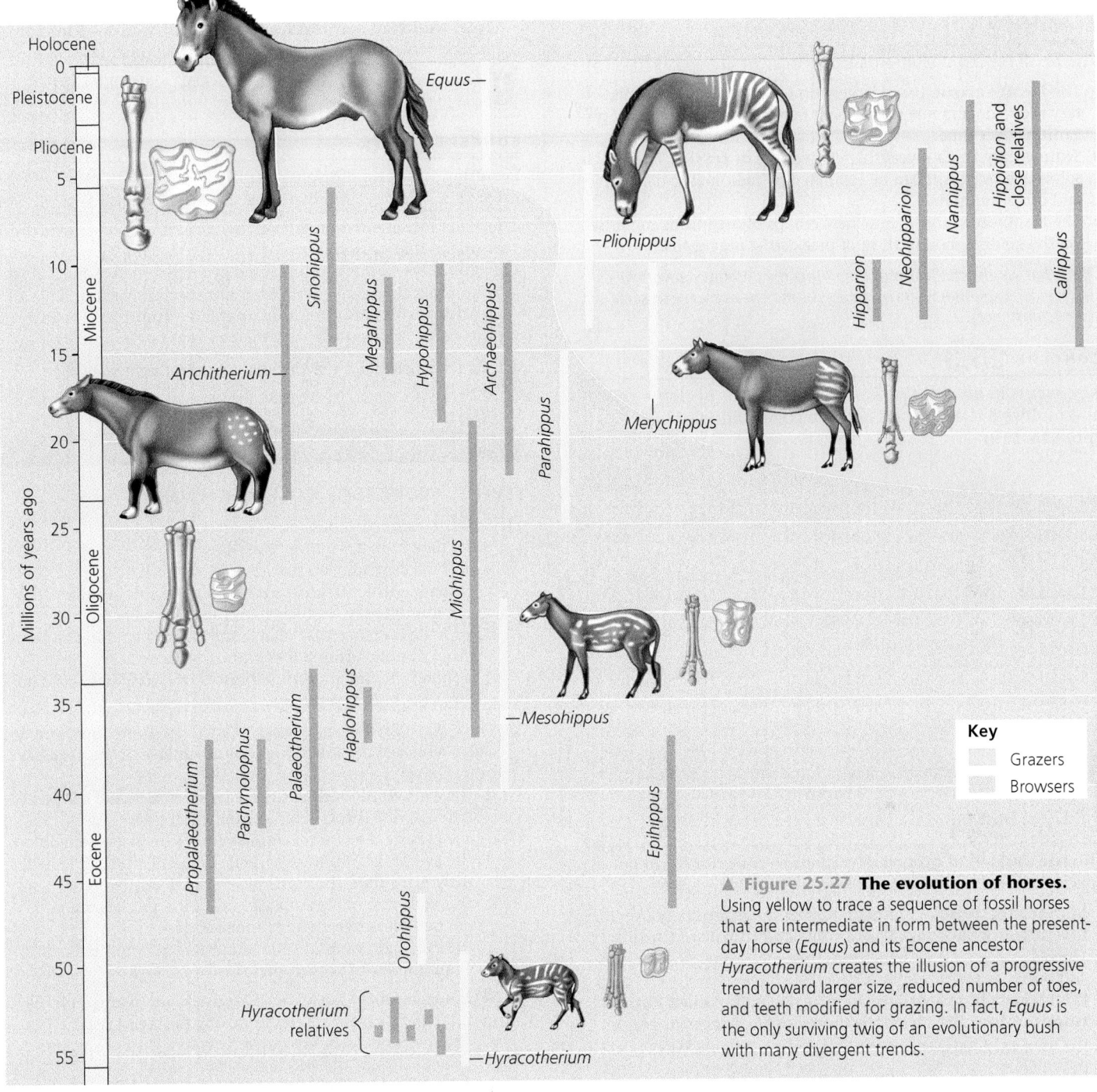

▲ Figure 25.27 The evolution of horses.
Using yellow to trace a sequence of fossil horses that are intermediate in form between the present-day horse (*Equus*) and its Eocene ancestor *Hyracotherium* creates the illusion of a progressive trend toward larger size, reduced number of toes, and teeth modified for grazing. In fact, *Equus* is the only surviving twig of an evolutionary bush with many divergent trends.

Key
Grazers
Browsers

25 CHAPTER REVIEW

SUMMARY OF KEY CONCEPTS

CONCEPT 25.1

Conditions on early Earth made the origin of life possible (pp. 507–510)

- Earth formed 4.6 billion years ago. Experiments simulating possible early atmospheres have produced organic molecules from inorganic precursors. Amino acids, lipids, sugars, and nitrogenous bases have also been found in meteorites.

- Amino acids and RNA nucleotides polymerize when dripped onto hot sand, clay, or rock. Organic compounds can spontaneously assemble into **protocells**, membrane-bounded droplets that have some properties of cells.

- The first genetic material may have been short pieces of RNA capable of guiding polypeptide synthesis and self-replication. Early protocells containing such RNA would have increased through natural selection.

> **?** *Describe the roles that montmorillonite clay and vesicles may have played in the origin of life.*

CONCEPT 25.2

The fossil record documents the history of life (pp. 510–514)

- The **fossil record**, based largely on fossils found in sedimentary rocks, documents the rise and fall of different groups of organisms over time.
- Sedimentary strata reveal the relative ages of **fossils**. The absolute ages of fossils can be estimated by radiometric dating and other methods.
- The fossil record shows how new groups of organisms can arise via the gradual modification of preexisting organisms.

> **?** *What are the challenges of estimating the absolute ages of old fossils? Explain how these challenges may be overcome in some circumstances.*

CONCEPT 25.3

Key events in life's history include the origins of single-celled and multicelled organisms and the colonization of land (pp. 514–519)

3.5 billion years ago (bya): First prokaryotes (single-celled)

2.1 bya: First eukaryotes (single-celled)

1.2 bya: First multicellular eukaryotes

500 mya: Colonization of land by fungi, plants, and animals

4,000 3,500 3,000 2,500 2,000 1,500 1,000 500
Millions of years ago (mya)

Present

535–525 mya: Cambrian explosion (great increase in diversity of animal forms)

> **?** *What is the "Cambrian explosion," and why is it significant?*

CONCEPT 25.4

The rise and fall of groups of organisms reflect differences in speciation and extinction rates (pp. 519–524)

- In **plate tectonics**, continental plates move gradually over time, altering the physical geography and climate of Earth. These changes lead to extinctions in some groups of organisms and bursts of speciation in others.
- Evolutionary history has been punctuated by five **mass extinctions** that radically altered the history of life. Some of these extinctions may have been caused by changes in continent positions, volcanic activity, or impacts from meteorites or comets.
- Large increases in the diversity of life have resulted from **adaptive radiations** that followed mass extinctions. Adaptive radiations have also occurred in groups of organisms that possessed major evolutionary innovations or that colonized new regions in which there was little competition from other organisms.

> **?** *Explain how the broad evolutionary changes seen in the fossil record are the cumulative result of speciation and extinction events.*

CONCEPT 25.5

Major changes in body form can result from changes in the sequences and regulation of developmental genes (pp. 525–529)

- Developmental genes affect morphological differences between species by influencing the rate, timing, and spatial patterns of change in an organism's form as it develops into an adult.

- The evolution of new forms can be caused by changes in the nucleotide sequences or regulation of developmental genes.

> **?** *How could changes in a single gene or DNA region ultimately lead to the origin of a new group of organisms?*

CONCEPT 25.6

Evolution is not goal oriented (pp. 529–531)

- Novel and complex biological structures can evolve through a series of incremental modifications, each of which benefits the organism that possesses it.
- Evolutionary trends can be caused by factors such as natural selection in a changing environment or species selection. Like all aspects of evolution, evolutionary trends result from interactions between organisms and their current environments.

> **?** *Explain the reasoning behind the statement "Evolution is not goal oriented."*

TEST YOUR UNDERSTANDING

LEVEL 1: KNOWLEDGE/COMPREHENSION

1. Fossilized stromatolites
   a. all date from 2.7 billion years ago.
   b. formed around deep-sea vents.
   c. resemble structures formed by bacterial communities that are found today in some warm, shallow, salty bays.
   d. provide evidence that plants moved onto land in the company of fungi around 500 million years ago.
   e. contain the first undisputed fossils of eukaryotes and date from 2.1 billion years ago.

2. The oxygen revolution changed Earth's environment dramatically. Which of the following took advantage of the presence of free oxygen in the oceans and atmosphere?
   a. the evolution of cellular respiration, which used oxygen to help harvest energy from organic molecules
   b. the persistence of some animal groups in anaerobic habitats
   c. the evolution of photosynthetic pigments that protected early algae from the corrosive effects of oxygen
   d. the evolution of chloroplasts after early protists incorporated photosynthetic cyanobacteria
   e. the evolution of multicellular eukaryotic colonies from communities of prokaryotes

3. Which factor most likely caused animals and plants in India to differ greatly from species in nearby southeast Asia?
   a. The species became separated by convergent evolution.
   b. The climates of the two regions are similar.
   c. India is in the process of separating from the rest of Asia.
   d. Life in India was wiped out by ancient volcanic eruptions.
   e. India was a separate continent until 45 million years ago.

4. Adaptive radiations can be a direct consequence of four of the following five factors. Select the exception.
   a. vacant ecological niches
   b. genetic drift
   c. colonization of an isolated region that contains suitable habitat and few competitor species
   d. evolutionary innovation
   e. an adaptive radiation in a group of organisms (such as plants) that another group uses as food

5. Which of the following steps has *not* yet been accomplished by scientists studying the origin of life?
   a. synthesis of small RNA polymers by ribozymes
   b. abiotic synthesis of polypeptides

c. formation of molecular aggregates with selectively permeable membranes

d. formation of protocells that use DNA to direct the polymerization of amino acids

e. abiotic synthesis of organic molecules

6. **DRAW IT** Use the unlabeled clock diagram below to test your memory of the sequence of key events in the history of life described in this chapter by labeling the colored bars. As a visual aid to help you study, add labels that represent other significant events, including the Cambrian explosion, origin of mammals, and Permian and Cretaceous mass extinctions.

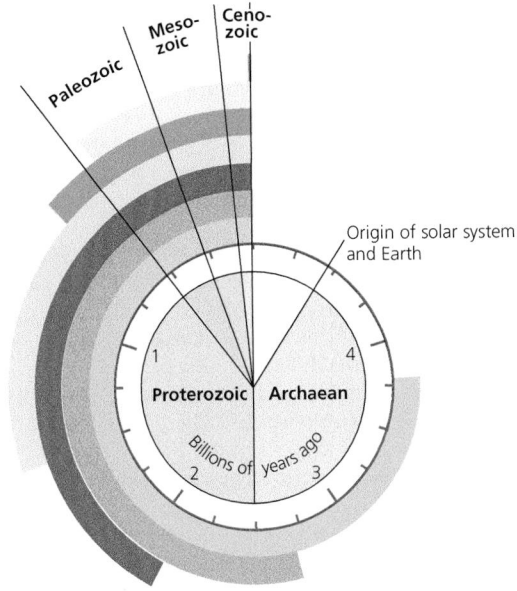

LEVEL 2: APPLICATION/ANALYSIS

7. A genetic change that caused a certain *Hox* gene to be expressed along the tip of a vertebrate limb bud instead of farther back helped make possible the evolution of the tetrapod limb. This type of change is illustrative of
   a. the influence of environment on development.
   b. paedomorphosis.
   c. a change in a developmental gene or in its regulation that altered the spatial organization of body parts.
   d. heterochrony.
   e. gene duplication.

8. A swim bladder is a gas-filled sac that helps fish maintain buoyancy. The evolution of the swim bladder from lungs of an ancestral fish is an example of
   a. an evolutionary trend.
   b. exaptation.
   c. changes in *Hox* gene expression.
   d. paedomorphosis.
   e. adaptive radiation.

LEVEL 3: SYNTHESIS/EVALUATION

9. **EVOLUTION CONNECTION**
   Describe how gene flow, genetic drift, and natural selection all can influence macroevolution.

10. **SCIENTIFIC INQUIRY**
   Herbivory (plant eating) has evolved repeatedly in insects, typically from meat-eating or detritus-feeding ancestors (detritus is dead organic matter). Moths and butterflies, for example, eat plants, whereas their "sister group" (the insect group

to which they are most closely related), the caddisflies, feed on animals, fungi, or detritus. As illustrated in the phylogenetic tree below, the combined moth/butterfly and caddisfly group shares a common ancestor with flies and fleas. Like caddisflies, flies and fleas are thought to have evolved from ancestors that did not eat plants.

There are 140,000 species of moths and butterflies and 7,000 species of caddisflies. State a hypothesis about the impact of herbivory on adaptive radiations in insects. How could this hypothesis be tested?

11. **SCIENCE, TECHNOLOGY, AND SOCIETY**
   Experts estimate that human activities cause the extinction of hundreds of species every year. In contrast, the natural rate of extinction is thought to average only a few species per year. If human actions continue to alter the global environment, especially by destroying tropical rain forests and changing Earth's climate, the likely result will be a wave of extinctions that could rival those at the end of the Cretaceous period. Considering that life has endured five mass extinctions, should we be concerned that we may cause a sixth mass extinction? How would such an extinction differ from previous extinctions? What might be some of the consequences?

12. **WRITE ABOUT A THEME**
   Structure and Function You have seen many examples of how form fits function at all levels of the biological hierarchy. However, we can imagine forms that would function better than some forms actually found in nature. For example, if the wings of a bird were not formed from its forelimbs, such a hypothetical bird could fly yet also hold objects with its forelimbs. In a short essay (100–150 words), use the concept of "evolution as tinkering" to explain why there are limits to the functionality of forms in nature.

For selected answers, see Appendix A.

Mastering**BIOLOGY**   www.masteringbiology.com

1. MasteringBiology® Assignments
Tutorial Fossil Record
Activities Discovery Channel Video: Early Life • The History of Life • A Scrolling Geologic Record • Discovery Channel Video: Mass Extinctions • Adaptive Radiation
Questions Student Misconceptions • Reading Quiz • Multiple Choice • End-of-Chapter

2. eText
Read your book online, search, take notes, highlight text, and more.

3. The Study Area
Practice Tests • Cumulative Test • *BioFlix* 3-D Animations • MP3 Tutor Sessions • Videos • Activities • Investigations • Lab Media • Audio Glossary • Word Study Tools • Art

An Interview with

W. Ford Doolittle

Brimming with curiosity about nature, W. Ford Doolittle is a passionate advocate for both science and scientists. Dr. Doolittle holds degrees in molecular biology from Harvard and Stanford Universities. Since 1971 he has worked at Dalhousie University in Halifax, Canada, where he is now a Professor Emeritus. The author of more than 270 scientific articles, Dr. Doolittle is well known for his work on the molecular biology of cyanobacteria and archaea, early steps in the evolution of eukaryotes, and the importance of horizontal gene transfer in prokaryotes. He has also nurtured dozens of young scientists, making Dalhousie a world-renowned center for the study of evolution. The recipient of numerous awards and honorary degrees, Dr. Doolittle is an elected member of the Royal Society of Canada and the U.S. National Academy of Sciences. He is also an avid photographer, and in 2011 he will receive a B.F.A. in photography from the Nova Scotia College of Art and Design. Surrounded by stacks of journal articles, photography projects, and the bustle of a busy laboratory, Michael Cain and Jane Reece spoke with Dr. Doolittle in his office at Dalhousie.

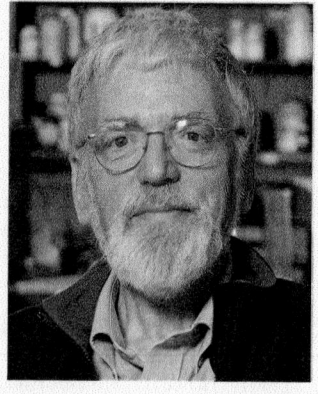

How did you get started in science?

I hadn't planned on studying science until, as a high school student, I got a job washing glassware in Sol Spiegelman's lab at the University of Illinois. [Spiegelman was a molecular biologist whose work on RNA played a key role in developing understanding of biology's "central dogma" (see Chapter 17).] In college, I continued working in Sol's lab during the summer. It was a very exciting place to be, kind of like a hospital emergency ward where everything was important, everything was urgent. Some people worked all day, some people worked all night, some people worked all day and night! The lab was abuzz with simple and elegant experiments in molecular biology. I got the feeling that science was important, which I have never lost. And I got the feeling that science was important for its own sake, which I also have never lost. Doing science seems to fill our human need to know, to understand what the universe is like.

Did you become interested in evolution while working in Sol's lab?

Well, that came a little later. When I arrived at Dalhousie in 1971, I began studying blue-green algae (now called cyanobacteria) because they were a pretty color and few people were working on them. So the field was wide open. Lynn Margulis had just published her book *Origin of Eukaryotic Cells*, which put forward a startling idea—the endosymbiont hypothesis—positing that mitochondria and chloroplasts were formerly aerobic bacteria and cyanobacteria, respectively, that began living within larger cells, ultimately leading to the origin of eukaryotes. Then a fortuitous thing happened: I hired Linda Bonen, who brought a new technique to our lab, called RNA cataloging, from which you could get RNA sequence information. It's not a full sequence, but it was enough to start comparing ribosomal RNA molecules (rRNAs). I realized that we could use this technique to test the endosymbiont hypothesis for the origin of chloroplasts. We compared the sequences of rRNAs from chloroplasts with those from cyanobacteria and found they were similar, just as Margulis had predicted! From there, I became more and more interested in evolution, which continues to fascinate me today.

What are the main questions you are asking in your research?

I've had a long-standing interest in the evolution of genes and genomes. Most of my current work is on prokaryotes, but I've also been interested in questions about eukaryotes, such as, Where did introns come from? How did eukaryotic genomes originate? In recent years, my students and I have been occupied with two main research areas. One is *metagenomics*, where we collect environmental samples, such as mud from the bottom of harbors, and then sequence the prokaryotic DNA contained in the samples. We use these DNA sequences to shed light on how microbes interact with each other and their environment. The other main area of my current research is *horizontal gene transfer*, the transfer of genetic information—usually whole genes but not necessarily—from one species to another.

How can genes move from one prokaryotic species to another?

This can happen in a variety of ways, and such transfers turn out to be surprisingly common. Mechanisms have evolved in some bacteria enabling them to take up DNA molecules directly from the environment—and these DNA molecules may have come from individuals of other species that have died and broken apart. When this happens, sometimes the DNA is incorporated into the bacterial chromosomes and hence becomes part of their own genetic heritage. Many prokaryotes can also form temporary bridges that connect two or more individuals to one another, enabling genes to move from one species to another. And as we mentioned earlier, sometimes entire genomes are transferred in endosymbiosis. These and other processes that result in horizontal gene transfer have occurred throughout the nearly 4 billion years of life on Earth—and they continue to occur today.

What impact has horizontal gene transfer had on the evolutionary history of life?

Horizontal gene transfer, or HGT for short, has been a major force in the history of life. For instance, the endosymbiotic origins of mitochondria and chloroplasts were profoundly important events in the origin of eukaryotic cells. We humans wouldn't be here if it weren't for mitochondria, and of course without chloroplasts there wouldn't be any plants. Furthermore, HGT has been a dominant force in prokaryotic evolution—probably *the* dominant force. Genes that control key metabolic processes, such as photosynthesis and nitrogen fixation, can be transferred readily between species, and this has had an enormous impact on the ecological and evolutionary success of prokaryotes. And while one can construct evolutionary trees that identify major groups of prokaryotes, such trees can obscure the fact that there has been a tremendous amount of HGT, affecting the majority of the genes.

Tell us more about evolutionary trees.

An evolutionary tree (or *phylogenetic tree*) is a branching diagram that represents the evolutionary history of a group of organisms. For example, we might use morphological and genetic data to figure out a phylogenetic tree of animals. Such a tree can provide a huge amount of information. For any particular group of animals, whether they be weevils, whales, or worms, our tree could identify the ancestors and closest relatives of the group. If we traced the history of animals all the way back, we could use the tree to help us answer questions such as, What did the earliest animals look like? What features did they pass on to all their descendants, including us? Phylogenetic trees also have great practical value. The same techniques we use to reconstruct evolutionary history have been used in forensics, where phylogenetic trees have helped solve criminal cases, and epidemiology, where trees have been used to estimate when and where diseases such as AIDS originated.

What have you learned during your career about the pattern and process of evolution?

We can document the *pattern* of evolution, the "what happened" part, with data from many scientific disciplines. For example, if we measure genetic change in a population, we are documenting an evolutionary pattern. The *process* of evolution is the "what caused it" part, which focuses on the mechanisms that produce the observed pattern. Sixty years ago, many scientists thought that natural selection was *the* mechanism that explained most evolutionary patterns. But we don't think that anymore; we now know that genetic drift and catastrophic events such as an asteroid striking Earth can explain many observed evolutionary patterns. I call this "process pluralism" to indicate that evolutionary patterns can result from many processes. Results from my research suggest that we should be considering "pattern pluralism" as well. Consider the tree of life, a phylogenetic tree that represents the history of all life as a series of branching events, in which a common ancestor gives rise to two descendant groups of organisms. This approach works well for organisms such as animals, but for prokaryotes the importance of HGT leads me to question whether the tree of life pattern is real. For prokaryotes, the pattern of evolution may be more like a tangled network of organisms exchanging DNA, not a simple branching tree.

Does this mean that Charles Darwin was wrong when he introduced the idea of a tree of life in *The Origin of Species*?

Darwin set out in his book to document the fact of evolution—the pattern of evolutionary change over time—and to show that natural selection could account for observed patterns of change. He did a great job on both accounts. We now recognize that well-understood genetic and ecological processes operating over nearly 4 billion years of evolution are adequate to explain diversity and adaptation in the living world. As for his ideas about the tree of life, Darwin was focused on plants and animals, two groups for which the tree of life idea works well. Remember, when Darwin formulated his ideas, many scientists still thought that bacteria formed spontaneously from rotten meat. It wasn't even clear that bacteria were organisms. So I would say that Darwin's idea about the tree of life is still true, but that certain restrictions apply. It is similar to the situation in physics: Newton's laws work well under certain conditions, but not as well under other conditions. The tree of life still works well for plants and animals, but less well for prokaryotes due to HGT. And after all, most of life is prokaryotic.

Have recent discoveries altered our understanding of the evolutionary history of life?

Certainly. For one thing, our view of genomes and genome evolution has changed greatly in recent years. Who would have thought that we humans only have about the same number of genes as a 1-mm-long worm? It's astonishing. Not that long ago, little was known about endosymbiosis or HGT or the astoundingly rapid rates at which bacterial populations can evolve. Overall, the importance of prokaryotes and protists (single-celled eukaryotes) has really become clear. I mentioned metagenomics earlier, an approach that has already revealed previously unsuspected levels of microbial diversity. I think metagenomics will play an increasingly important role in future discoveries. It might even help us understand the consequences of increased atmospheric carbon dioxide (CO_2) and global warming, among the most important problems we face today. Microorganisms absorb vast amounts of CO_2 from the atmosphere. How will ongoing global warming affect microorganisms? Will they absorb even more CO_2, thus reducing effects of global warming? Or will the opposite occur? We don't know, but we can use metagenomics to figure out how climate change is currently affecting microbial communities. Once we understand what is going on, perhaps that can help us fix it.

You've devoted much time and effort to mentoring others. Can you comment on that?

Working in Sol Spiegelman's lab when I was young was a big turning point in my life. And as I gained experience, I tried to provide similar opportunities for others. One way I've done that is to establish programs that provide opportunities for young scientists to work together and to learn from each other and from more experienced scientists. I've always thought that it really helps to get experience early in your career, so I welcome people seeking such experience. One of the best ways to find what you really love doing is to try different things and see what most excites you. I did not plan to be a scientist, but I started doing science and I loved it. I'm a big believer in hands-on experience as a way of learning.

"For prokaryotes, the pattern of evolution may be more like a tangled network of organisms exchanging DNA, not a simple branching tree."

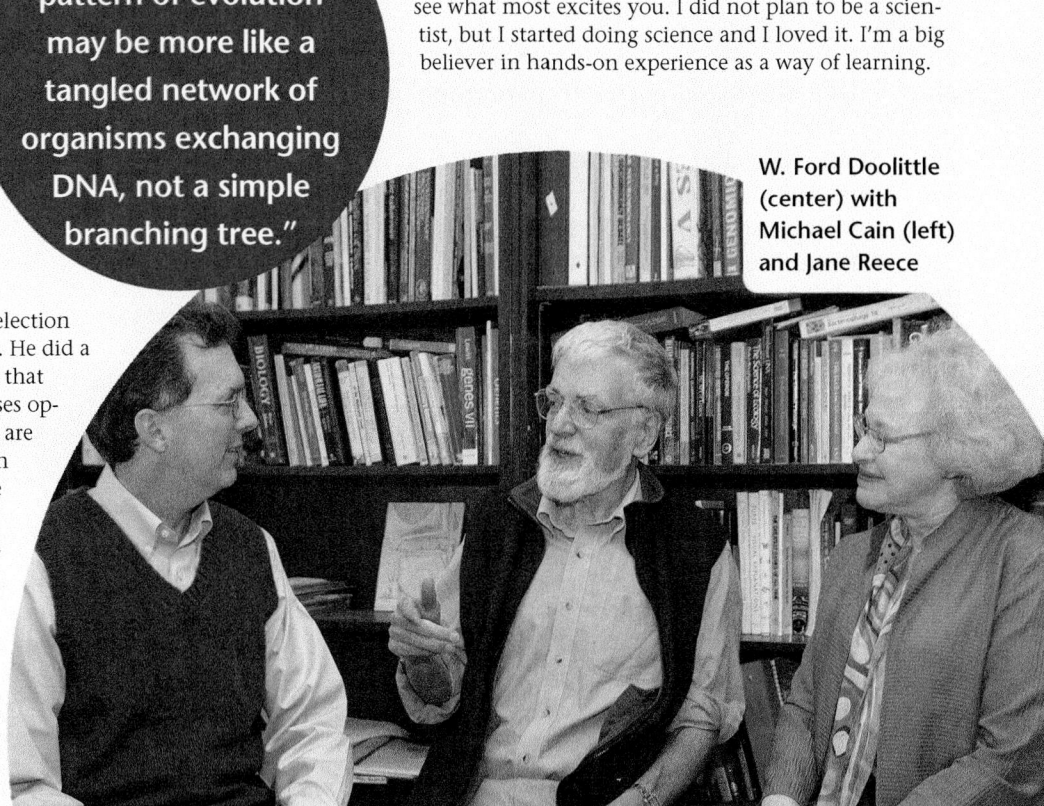

W. Ford Doolittle (center) with Michael Cain (left) and Jane Reece

26

Phylogeny and the Tree of Life

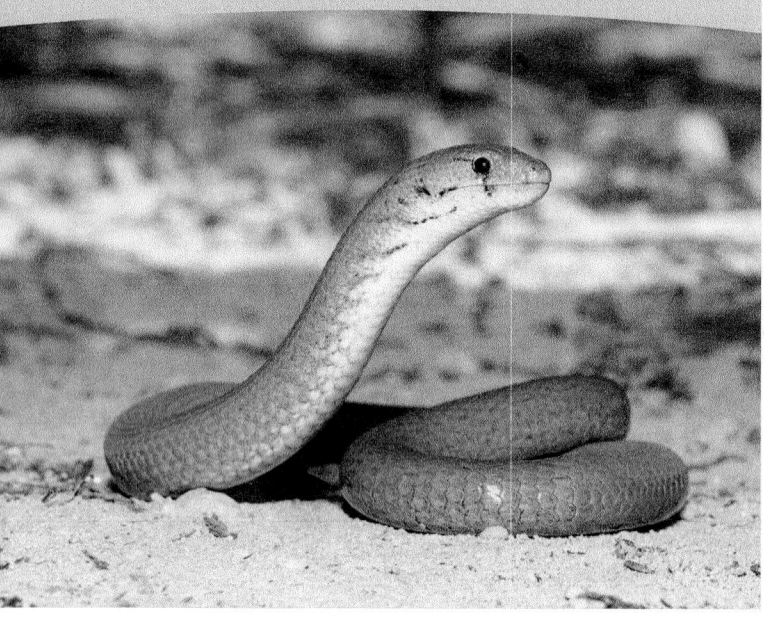

▲ Figure 26.1 **What is this organism?**

EVOLUTION

KEY CONCEPTS

26.1 Phylogenies show evolutionary relationships

26.2 Phylogenies are inferred from morphological and molecular data

26.3 Shared characters are used to construct phylogenetic trees

26.4 An organism's evolutionary history is documented in its genome

26.5 Molecular clocks help track evolutionary time

26.6 New information continues to revise our understanding of the tree of life

OVERVIEW

Investigating the Tree of Life

Look closely at the organism in Figure 26.1. Although it resembles a snake, this animal is actually an Australian legless lizard known as the common scaly-foot (*Pygopus lepidopodus*). Why isn't the scaly-foot considered a snake? More generally, how do biologists distinguish and categorize the millions of species on Earth?

An understanding of evolutionary relationships suggests one way to address these questions: We can decide in which "container" to place a species by comparing its traits with those of potential close relatives. For example, the scaly-foot does not have a fused eyelid, a highly mobile jaw, or a short tail posterior to the anus, three traits shared by all snakes. These and other characteristics suggest that despite a superficial resemblance, the scaly-foot is not a snake. Furthermore, a survey of the lizards reveals that the scaly-foot is not alone; the legless condition has evolved independently in several different groups of lizards. Most legless lizards are burrowers or live in grasslands, and like snakes, these species lost their legs over generations as they adapted to their environments.

Snakes and lizards are part of the continuum of life extending from the earliest organisms to the great variety of species alive today. In this unit, we will survey this diversity and describe hypotheses regarding how it evolved. As we do so, our emphasis will shift from the *process* of evolution (the evolutionary mechanisms described in Unit Four) to its *pattern* (observations of evolution's products over time).

To set the stage for surveying life's diversity, in this chapter we consider how biologists trace **phylogeny**, the evolutionary history of a species or group of species. A phylogeny of lizards and snakes, for example, indicates that both the scaly-foot and snakes evolved from lizards with legs—but that they evolved from different lineages of legged lizards. Thus, it appears that their legless conditions evolved independently.

To construct phylogenies, biologists utilize **systematics**, a discipline focused on classifying organisms and determining their evolutionary relationships. Systematists use data ranging from fossils to molecules and genes to infer evolutionary relationships (Figure 26.2). This information is enabling biologists to construct a tree of all life, which will continue to be refined as additional data are collected.

▲ Figure 26.2 **An unexpected family tree.** What are the evolutionary relationships between a human, a mushroom, and a tulip? A phylogeny based on DNA data reveals that—despite appearances—animals (including humans) and fungi (including mushrooms) are more closely related to each other than either is to plants.

CONCEPT 26.1

Phylogenies show evolutionary relationships

As we discussed in Chapter 22, organisms share many characteristics because of common ancestry. As a result, we can learn a great deal about a species if we know its evolutionary history. For example, an organism is likely to share many of its genes, metabolic pathways, and structural proteins with its close relatives. We'll consider practical applications of such information at the close of this section, but first we'll examine how organisms are named and classified, the scientific discipline of **taxonomy**. We'll also look at how we can interpret and use diagrams that represent evolutionary history.

Binomial Nomenclature

Common names for organisms—such as monkey, finch, and lilac—convey meaning in casual usage, but they can also cause confusion. Each of these names, for example, refers to more than one species. Moreover, some common names do not accurately reflect the kind of organism they signify. Consider these three "fishes": jellyfish (a cnidarian), crayfish (a small lobsterlike crustacean), and silverfish (an insect). And of course, a given organism has different names in different languages.

To avoid ambiguity when communicating about their research, biologists refer to organisms by Latin scientific names. The two-part format of the scientific name, commonly called a **binomial**, was instituted in the 18th century by Carolus Linnaeus (see Chapter 22). The first part of a binomial is the name of the **genus** (plural, *genera*) to which the species belongs. The second part, called the specific epithet, is unique for each species within the genus. An example of a binomial is *Panthera pardus*, the scientific name for the large cat commonly called the leopard. Notice that the first letter of the genus is capitalized and the entire binomial is italicized. (Newly created scientific names are also "latinized": You can name an insect you discover after a friend, but you must add a Latin ending.) Many of the more than 11,000 binomials assigned by Linnaeus are still used today, including the optimistic name he gave our own species—*Homo sapiens*, meaning "wise man."

Hierarchical Classification

In addition to naming species, Linnaeus also grouped them into a hierarchy of increasingly inclusive categories. The first grouping is built into the binomial: Species that appear to be closely related are grouped into the same genus. For example, the leopard (*Panthera pardus*) belongs to a genus that also includes the African lion (*Panthera leo*), the tiger (*Panthera tigris*), and the jaguar (*Panthera onca*). Beyond genera, taxonomists employ progressively more comprehensive categories of classification. The taxonomic system named after Linnaeus, the

Linnaean system, places related genera in the same **family**, families into **orders**, orders into **classes**, classes into **phyla** (singular, *phylum*), phyla into **kingdoms**, and, more recently, kingdoms into **domains** (Figure 26.3). The resulting biological classification of a particular organism is somewhat like a postal address identifying a person in a particular apartment, in a building with many apartments, on a street with many apartment buildings, in a city with many streets, and so on.

The named taxonomic unit at any level of the hierarchy is called a **taxon** (plural, *taxa*). In the leopard example, *Panthera* is a taxon at the genus level, and Mammalia is a taxon at the class level that includes all the many orders of mammals. Note that in the Linnaean system, taxa broader than the genus are not italicized, though they are capitalized.

Classifying species is a way to structure our human view of the world. We lump together various species of trees to which we give the common name of pines and distinguish them from other trees that we call firs. Taxonomists have decided

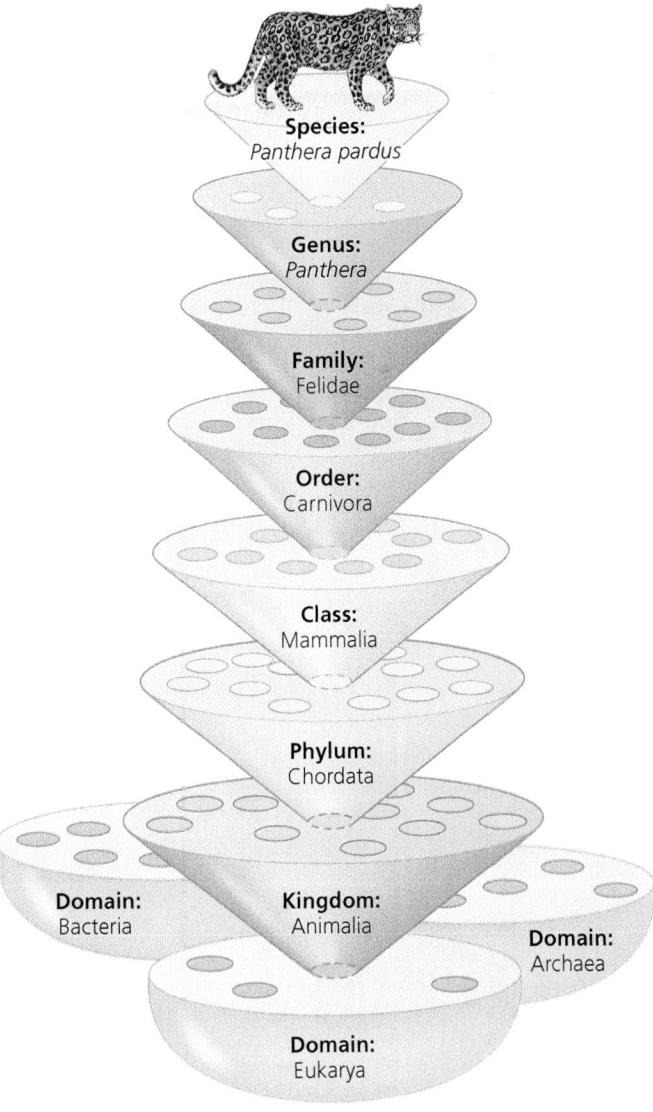

Species:
Panthera pardus

Genus:
Panthera

Family:
Felidae

Order:
Carnivora

Class:
Mammalia

Phylum:
Chordata

Domain:
Bacteria

Kingdom:
Animalia

Domain:
Archaea

Domain:
Eukarya

▲ **Figure 26.3 Linnaean classification.** At each level, or "rank," species are placed in groups within more inclusive groups.

that pines and firs are different enough to be placed in separate genera, yet similar enough to be grouped into the same family, Pinaceae. As with pines and firs, higher levels of classification are usually defined by particular characters chosen by taxonomists. However, characters that are useful for classifying one group of organisms may not be appropriate for other organisms. For this reason, the larger categories often are not comparable between lineages; that is, an order of snails does not exhibit the same degree of morphological or genetic diversity as an order of mammals. Furthermore, as we'll see, the placement of species into orders, classes, and so on, does not necessarily reflect evolutionary history.

Linking Classification and Phylogeny

The evolutionary history of a group of organisms can be represented in a branching diagram called a **phylogenetic tree**. As in **Figure 26.4**, the branching pattern often matches how taxonomists have classified groups of organisms nested within more inclusive groups. Sometimes, however, taxonomists have placed a species within a genus (or other group) to which it is *not* most closely related. One reason for misclassification might be that over the course of evolution, a species has lost a key feature shared by its close relatives. If DNA or other new evidence indicates that such a mistake has occurred, the organism may be reclassified to accurately reflect its evolutionary

history. Another issue is that while the Linnaean system may distinguish groups, such as mammals, reptiles, birds, and other classes of vertebrates, it tells us nothing about these groups' evolutionary relationships to one another.

In fact, such difficulties in aligning Linnaean classification with phylogeny have led some systematists to propose that classification be based entirely on evolutionary relationships. A system called **PhyloCode**, for example, only names groups that include a common ancestor and all of its descendants. While PhyloCode would change the way taxa are defined and recognized, the taxonomic names of most species would remain the same. But groups would no longer have "ranks" attached to them, such as family or class. Also, some commonly recognized groups would become part of other groups previously of the same rank. For example, because birds evolved from a group of reptiles, Aves (the Linnaean class to which birds are assigned) would be considered a subgroup of Reptilia (also a class in the Linnaean system). Although PhyloCode is controversial, many systematists are adopting the phylogenetic approach on which it is based.

Whether groups are named according to PhyloCode or according to Linnaean classification, a phylogenetic tree represents a hypothesis about evolutionary relationships. These relationships often are depicted as a series of dichotomies, or two-way **branch points**. Each branch point represents the divergence of two evolutionary lineages from a common ancestor. In **Figure 26.5**, for example, branch point ❸ represents the common ancestor of taxa A, B, and C. The position of branch point ❹ to the right of ❸ indicates that taxa B and C diverged after their shared lineage split from that of taxon A. (Tree branches can be rotated around a branch point without changing their evolutionary relationships.)

In Figure 26.5, taxa B and C are **sister taxa**, groups of organisms that share an immediate common ancestor (branch

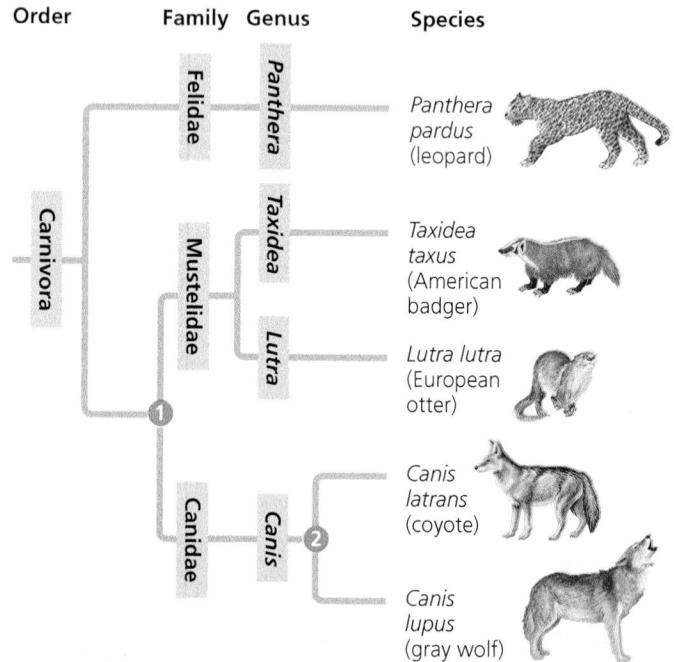

▲ **Figure 26.4 The connection between classification and phylogeny.** Hierarchical classification can reflect the branching patterns of phylogenetic trees. This tree traces possible evolutionary relationships between some of the taxa within order Carnivora, itself a branch of class Mammalia. The branch point ❶ represents the most recent common ancestor of all members of the weasel (Mustelidae) and dog (Canidae) families. The branch point ❷ represents the most recent common ancestor of coyotes and gray wolves.

Branch point: where lineages diverge

ANCESTRAL LINEAGE — ❶

Taxon A
Taxon B
Taxon C
Sister taxa
Taxon D
Taxon E
Taxon F
Taxon G
Basal taxon

This branch point represents the common ancestor of taxa A–G.

This branch point forms a polytomy: an unresolved pattern of divergence.

▲ **Figure 26.5 How to read a phylogenetic tree.**
DRAW IT *Redraw this tree, rotating the branches around branch points ❷ and ❹. Does your new version tell a different story about the evolutionary relationships between the taxa? Explain.*

point **❹**) and hence are each other's closest relatives. Note also that this tree, like most of the phylogenetic trees in this book, is **rooted**, which means that a branch point within the tree (often drawn farthest to the left) represents the most recent common ancestor of all taxa in the tree. The term **basal taxon** refers to a lineage that diverges early in the history of a group and hence, like taxon G in Figure 26.5, lies on a branch that originates near the common ancestor of the group. Finally, the lineage leading to taxa D–F includes a **polytomy**, a branch point from which more than two descendant groups emerge. A polytomy signifies that evolutionary relationships among the taxa are not yet clear.

What We Can and Cannot Learn from Phylogenetic Trees

Let's summarize three key points about phylogenetic trees. First, they are intended to show patterns of descent, not phenotypic similarity. Although closely related organisms often resemble one another due to their common ancestry, they may not if their lineages have evolved at different rates or faced very different environmental conditions. For example, even though crocodiles are more closely related to birds than to lizards (see Figure 22.17), they look more like lizards because morphology has changed dramatically in the bird lineage.

Second, the sequence of branching in a tree does not necessarily indicate the actual (absolute) ages of the particular species. For example, the tree in Figure 26.4 does not indicate that the wolf evolved more recently than the European otter; rather, the tree shows only that the most recent common ancestor of the wolf and otter (branch point **❶**) lived before the most recent common ancestor of the wolf and coyote (**❷**). To indicate when wolves and otters evolved, the tree would need to include additional divergences in each evolutionary lineage, as well as the dates when those splits occurred. Generally, unless given specific information about what the branch lengths in a phylogenetic tree mean—for example, that they are proportional to time—we should interpret the diagram solely in terms of patterns of descent. No assumptions should be made about when particular species evolved or how much change occurred in each lineage.

Third, we should not assume that a taxon on a phylogenetic tree evolved from the taxon next to it. Figure 26.4 does not indicate that wolves evolved from coyotes or vice versa. We can infer only that the lineage leading to wolves and the lineage leading to coyotes both evolved from the common ancestor **❷**. That ancestor, which is now extinct, was neither a wolf nor a coyote. However, its descendants include the two *extant* (living) species shown here, wolves and coyotes.

Applying Phylogenies

Understanding phylogeny can have practical applications. Consider maize (corn), which originated in the Americas and is now an important food crop worldwide. From a phylogeny of maize based on DNA data, researchers have been able to identify two species of wild grasses that may be maize's closest living relatives. These two close relatives may be useful as "reservoirs" of beneficial alleles that can be transferred to cultivated maize by cross-breeding or genetic engineering (see Chapter 20).

A different use of phylogenetic trees is described in **Figure 26.6**: investigating whether whale meat samples had

---

▼ **Figure 26.6** **INQUIRY**

What is the species identity of food being sold as whale meat?

EXPERIMENT C. S. Baker, then at the University of Auckland, New Zealand, and S. R. Palumbi, then at the University of Hawaii, purchased 13 samples of "whale meat" from Japanese fish markets. They sequenced a specific part of the mitochondrial DNA from each sample and compared their results with the comparable DNA sequence from known whale species. To infer the species identity of each sample, Baker and Palumbi constructed a *gene tree*, a phylogenetic tree that shows patterns of relatedness among DNA sequences rather than among taxa.

RESULTS The analysis yielded the following gene tree:

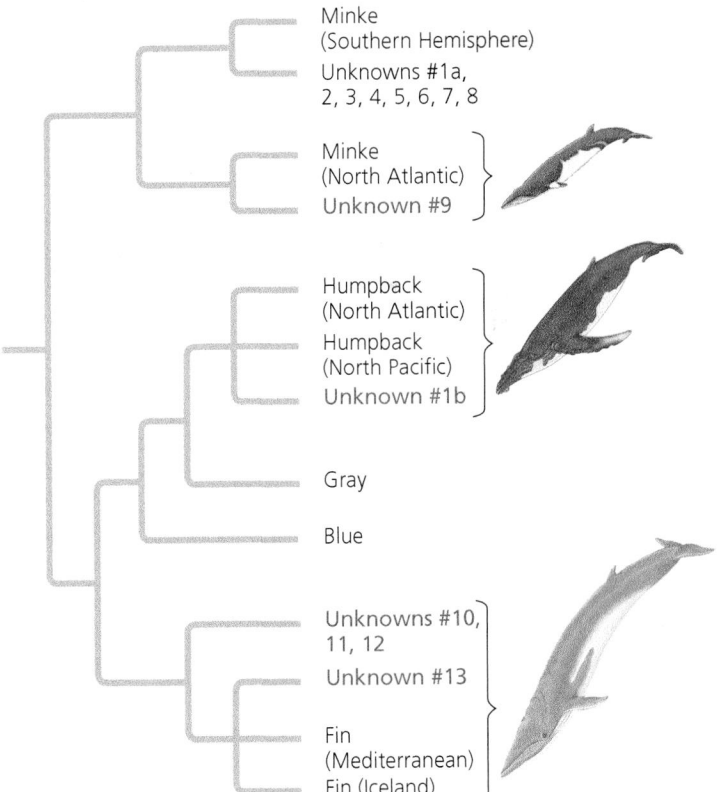

Minke (Southern Hemisphere)
Unknowns #1a, 2, 3, 4, 5, 6, 7, 8

Minke (North Atlantic)
Unknown #9

Humpback (North Atlantic)
Humpback (North Pacific)
Unknown #1b

Gray

Blue

Unknowns #10, 11, 12
Unknown #13

Fin (Mediterranean)
Fin (Iceland)

CONCLUSION This analysis indicated that DNA sequences of six of the unknown samples (in red) were most closely related to DNA sequences of whales that are not legal to harvest.

SOURCE C. S. Baker and S. R. Palumbi, Which whales are hunted? A molecular genetic approach to monitoring whaling, *Science* 265:1538–1539 (1994).

WHAT IF? What different results would have indicated that the whale meat had *not* been illegally harvested?

---

been illegally harvested from whale species protected under international law—rather than from species that can be harvested legally, such as Minke whales caught in the Southern Hemisphere. This phylogeny indicated that meat from humpback, fin, and Minke whales caught in the Northern Hemisphere was being sold illegally in some Japanese fish markets.

How do researchers construct trees like those we've considered here? In the next section, we'll begin to answer that question by examining the data used to determine phylogenies.

CONCEPT CHECK 26.1

1. Which levels of the classification in Figure 26.3 do humans share with leopards?
2. What does the phylogenetic tree in Figure 26.4 indicate about the evolutionary relationships of the leopard, badger, and wolf?
3. Which of the trees shown here depicts an evolutionary history different from the other two? Explain.

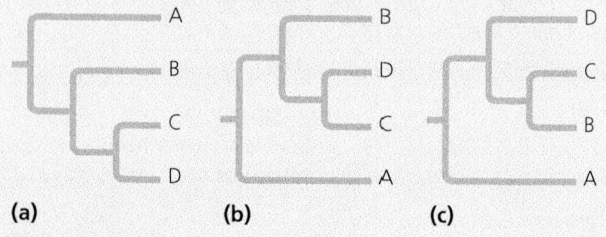

(a)   (b)   (c)

4. **WHAT IF?** Suppose new evidence indicates that taxon E in Figure 26.5 is the sister taxon of a group consisting of taxa D and F. Redraw the tree to accommodate this new finding.

For suggested answers, see Appendix A.

CONCEPT 26.2

Phylogenies are inferred from morphological and molecular data

To infer phylogeny, systematists must gather as much information as possible about the morphology, genes, and biochemistry of the relevant organisms. It is important to focus on features that result from common ancestry, because only such features reflect evolutionary relationships.

Morphological and Molecular Homologies

Recall that phenotypic and genetic similarities due to shared ancestry are called *homologies*. For example, the similarity in the number and arrangement of bones in the forelimbs of mammals is due to their descent from a common ancestor with the same bone structure; this is an example of a morphological homology (see Figure 22.15). In the same way, genes or other DNA sequences are homologous if they are descended from sequences carried by a common ancestor.

In general, organisms that share very similar morphologies or similar DNA sequences are likely to be more closely related than organisms with vastly different structures or sequences. In some cases, however, the morphological divergence between related species can be great and their genetic divergence small (or vice versa). Consider the Hawaiian silversword plants discussed in Chapter 25. These species vary dramatically in appearance throughout the islands. Some are tall, twiggy trees, and others are dense, ground-hugging shrubs (see Figure 25.20). But despite these striking phenotypic differences, the silverswords' genes are very similar. Based on these small molecular divergences, scientists estimate that the silversword group began to diverge 5 million years ago, which is also about the time when the oldest of the current islands formed. We'll discuss how scientists use molecular data to estimate such divergence times later in this chapter.

Sorting Homology from Analogy

A potential red herring in constructing a phylogeny is similarity due to convergent evolution—called **analogy**—rather than to shared ancestry (homology). As you read in Chapter 22, convergent evolution occurs when similar environmental pressures and natural selection produce similar (analogous) adaptations in organisms from different evolutionary lineages. For example, the two mole-like animals illustrated in **Figure 26.7** are very similar in their external appearance. However, their internal anatomy, physiology, and reproductive systems are very dissimilar. Australian "moles" are marsupials; their young complete their embryonic development in a pouch on the outside of the mother's body. North American moles, in contrast, are eutherians; their young complete

▲ Figure 26.7 **Convergent evolution of analogous burrowing characteristics.** An elongated body, enlarged front paws, small eyes, and a pad of thickened skin that protects a tapered nose all evolved independently in the marsupial Australian "mole" (top) and a eutherian North American mole (bottom).

their embryonic development in the uterus within the mother's body. Indeed, genetic comparisons and the fossil record provide evidence that the common ancestor of these moles lived 140 million years ago, about the time the marsupial and eutherian mammals diverged. This common ancestor and most of its descendants were not mole-like, but analogous characteristics evolved independently in these two mole lineages as they became adapted to similar lifestyles.

Distinguishing between homology and analogy is critical in reconstructing phylogenies. To see why, consider bats and birds, both of which have adaptations that enable flight. This superficial resemblance might imply that bats are more closely related to birds than they are to cats, which cannot fly. But a closer examination reveals that a bat's wing is far more similar to the forelimbs of cats and other mammals than to a bird's wing. Bats and birds descended from a common tetrapod ancestor that lived about 320 million years ago. This common ancestor could not fly. Thus, although the underlying skeletal systems of bats and birds are homologous, their *wings* are not. Flight is enabled in different ways—stretched membranes in the bat wing versus feathers in the bird wing. Fossil evidence also documents that bat wings and bird wings arose independently from the forelimbs of different tetrapod ancestors. Thus, with respect to flight, a bat's wing is *analogous*, not homologous, to a bird's wing. Analogous structures that arose independently are also called **homoplasies** (from the Greek, meaning "to mold in the same way").

Besides corroborative similarities and fossil evidence, another clue to distinguishing between homology and analogy is the complexity of the characters being compared. The more elements that are similar in two complex structures, the more likely it is that they evolved from a common ancestor. For instance, the skulls of an adult human and an adult chimpanzee both consist of many bones fused together. The compositions of the skulls match almost perfectly, bone for bone. It is highly improbable that such complex structures, matching in so many details, have separate origins. More likely, the genes involved in the development of both skulls were inherited from a common ancestor. The same argument applies to comparisons at the gene level. Genes are sequences of thousands of nucleotides, each of which represents an inherited character in the form of one of the four DNA bases: A (adenine), G (guanine), C (cytosine), or T (thymine). If genes in two organisms share many portions of their nucleotide sequences, it is likely that the genes are homologous.

Evaluating Molecular Homologies

Comparisons of DNA molecules often pose technical challenges for researchers. The first step after sequencing the molecules is to align comparable sequences from the species being studied. If the species are very closely related, the sequences probably differ at only one or a few sites. In contrast, comparable nucleic acid sequences in distantly related species usually have different bases at many sites and may have different lengths. This is because insertions and deletions accumulate over long periods of time.

Suppose, for example, that certain noncoding DNA sequences near a particular gene are very similar in two species, except that the first base of the sequence has been deleted in one of the species. The effect is that the remaining sequence shifts back one notch. A comparison of the two sequences that does not take this deletion into account would overlook what in fact is a very good match. To address such problems, researchers have developed computer programs that estimate the best way to align comparable DNA segments of differing lengths **(Figure 26.8)**.

Such molecular comparisons reveal that many base substitutions and other differences have accumulated in the comparable genes of an Australian mole and a North American mole. The many differences indicate that their lineages have diverged greatly since their common ancestor; thus, we say that the living species are not closely related. In contrast, the high degree of gene sequence similarity among the silverswords indicates that they are all very closely related, in spite of their considerable morphological differences.

Just as with morphological characters, it is necessary to distinguish homology from analogy in evaluating molecular similarities for evolutionary studies. Two sequences that resemble each other at many points along their length most likely are

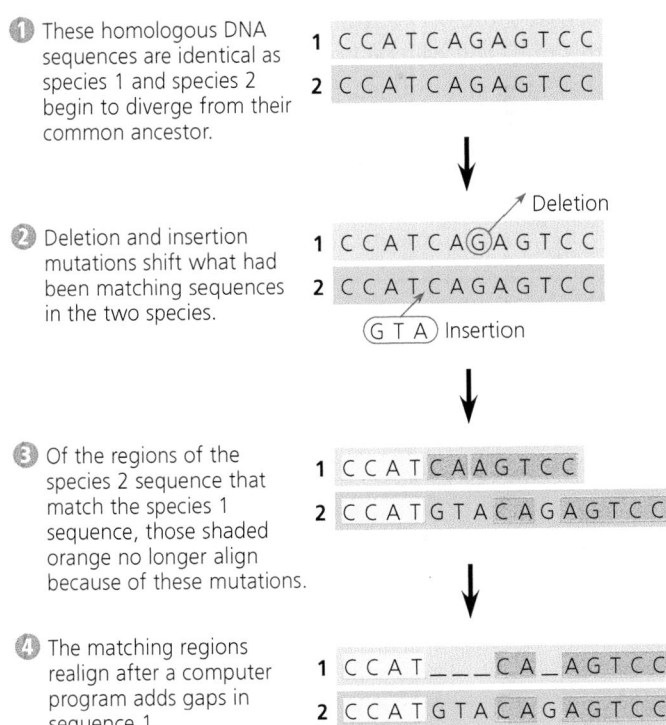

① These homologous DNA sequences are identical as species 1 and species 2 begin to diverge from their common ancestor.

1 C C A T C A G A G T C C
2 C C A T C A G A G T C C

② Deletion and insertion mutations shift what had been matching sequences in the two species.

Deletion

1 C C A T C A G A G T C C
2 C C A T C A G A G T C C

(G T A) Insertion

③ Of the regions of the species 2 sequence that match the species 1 sequence, those shaded orange no longer align because of these mutations.

1 C C A T C A A G T C C
2 C C A T G T A C A G A G T C C

④ The matching regions realign after a computer program adds gaps in sequence 1.

1 C C A T _ _ _ C A _ A G T C C
2 C C A T G T A C A G A G T C C

▲ **Figure 26.8 Aligning segments of DNA.** Systematists search for similar sequences along DNA segments from two species (only one DNA strand is shown for each species). In this example, 11 of the original 12 bases have not changed since the species diverged. Hence, those portions of the sequences still align once the length is adjusted.

```
A C G G A T A G T C C A C T A G G C A C T A
T C A C C G A C A G G T C T T T G A C T A G
```

▲ **Figure 26.9 A molecular homoplasy.** These two DNA sequences from organisms that are not closely related coincidentally share 25% of their bases. Statistical tools have been developed to determine whether DNA sequences that share more than 25% of their bases do so because they are homologous.

? *Why might you expect organisms that are not closely related to nevertheless share roughly 25% of their bases?*

homologous (see Figure 26.8). But in organisms that do not appear to be closely related, the bases that their otherwise very different sequences happen to share may simply be coincidental matches, called molecular homoplasies (Figure 26.9). Scientists have developed statistical tools that can help distinguish "distant" homologies from such coincidental matches in extremely divergent sequences.

To date, researchers have sequenced more than 110 billion bases of DNA from thousands of species. This enormous collection of data has fueled a boom in the study of phylogeny. The new data have supported earlier hypotheses regarding many evolutionary relationships, such as that between Australian and North American moles, and have clarified other relationships, such as those between the various silverswords. In the rest of this unit, you will see how our understanding of phylogeny has been transformed by **molecular systematics**, the discipline that uses data from DNA and other molecules to determine evolutionary relationships.

CONCEPT CHECK 26.2

1. Decide whether each of the following pairs of structures more likely represents analogy or homology, and explain your reasoning: (a) a porcupine's quills and a cactus's spines; (b) a cat's paw and a human's hand; (c) an owl's wing and a hornet's wing.
2. **WHAT IF?** Suppose that species 1 and species 2 have similar appearances but very divergent gene sequences and that species 2 and species 3 have very different appearances but similar gene sequences. Which pair of species is more likely to be closely related: 1 and 2, or 2 and 3? Explain.

For suggested answers, see Appendix A.

CONCEPT 26.3

Shared characters are used to construct phylogenetic trees

In reconstructing phylogenies, the first step is to distinguish homologous features from analogous ones (since only homology reflects evolutionary history). Next we must choose a method of inferring phylogeny from these homologous characters. A widely used set of methods is known as cladistics.

Cladistics

In the approach to systematics called **cladistics**, common ancestry is the primary criterion used to classify organisms. Using this methodology, biologists attempt to place species into groups called **clades**, each of which includes an ancestral species and all of its descendants (Figure 26.10a). Clades, like

▼ **Figure 26.10 Monophyletic, paraphyletic, and polyphyletic groups.**

(a) Monophyletic group (clade)

Group I, consisting of three species (A, B, C) and their common ancestor ❶, is a clade, also called a monophyletic group. A monophyletic group consists of an ancestral species and *all* of its descendants.

(b) Paraphyletic group

Group II is paraphyletic, meaning that it consists of an ancestral species ❷ and some of its descendants (species D, E, F) but not all of them (missing species G).

(c) Polyphyletic group

Group III is polyphyletic, meaning that some of its members have different ancestors. In this case, species A, B, and C share common ancestor ❶, but species D has a different ancestor: ❷.

taxonomic ranks, are nested within larger clades. In Figure 26.4, for example, the cat group (Felidae) represents a clade within a larger clade (Carnivora) that also includes the dog group (Canidae). However, a taxon is equivalent to a clade only if it is **monophyletic** (from the Greek, meaning "single tribe"), signifying that it consists of an ancestral species and all of its descendants (see Figure 26.10a). Contrast this with a **paraphyletic** ("beside the tribe") group, which consists of an ancestral species and some, but not all, of its descendants (Figure 26.10b), or a **polyphyletic** ("many tribes") group, which includes taxa with different ancestors (Figure 26.10c). Next we'll discuss how clades are identified using shared derived characters.

Shared Ancestral and Shared Derived Characters

As a result of descent with modification, organisms both share characteristics with their ancestors and differ from them. For example, all mammals have backbones, but a backbone does not distinguish mammals from other vertebrates because *all* vertebrates have backbones. The backbone predates the branching of mammals from other vertebrates. Thus for mammals, the backbone is a **shared ancestral character**, a character that originated in an ancestor of the taxon. In contrast, hair is a character shared by all mammals but *not* found in their ancestors. Thus, in mammals, hair is considered a **shared derived character**, an evolutionary novelty unique to a clade.

Note that it is a relative matter whether a particular character is considered ancestral or derived. A backbone can also qualify as a shared derived character, but only at a deeper branch point that distinguishes all vertebrates from other animals. Among mammals, a backbone is considered a shared ancestral character because it was present in the ancestor common to all mammals.

Inferring Phylogenies Using Derived Characters

Shared derived characters are unique to particular clades. Because all features of organisms arose at some point in the history of life, it should be possible to determine the clade in which each shared derived character first appeared and to use that information to infer evolutionary relationships.

To see how this analysis is done, consider the set of characters shown in **Figure 26.11a** for each of five vertebrates—a leopard, turtle, frog, bass, and lamprey (a jawless aquatic vertebrate). As a basis of comparison, we need to select an outgroup. An **outgroup** is a species or group of species from an evolutionary lineage that is known to have diverged before the lineage that includes the species we are studying (the **ingroup**). A suitable outgroup can be determined based on evidence from morphology, paleontology, embryonic development, and gene sequences. An appropriate outgroup for our example is the lancelet, a small animal that lives in mudflats and (like vertebrates) is a member of Chordata. Unlike the vertebrates, however, the lancelet does not have a backbone.

By comparing members of the ingroup with each other and with the outgroup, we can determine which characters were derived at the various branch points of vertebrate evolution. For example, *all* of the vertebrates in the ingroup have backbones: This character was present in the ancestral vertebrate, but not in the outgroup. Now note that hinged jaws are a character absent in lampreys but present in other members of the ingroup; this character helps us to identify an early branch point in the vertebrate clade. Proceeding in this way, we can translate the data in our table of characters into a phylogenetic tree that groups all the ingroup taxa into a hierarchy based on their shared derived characters (**Figure 26.11b**).

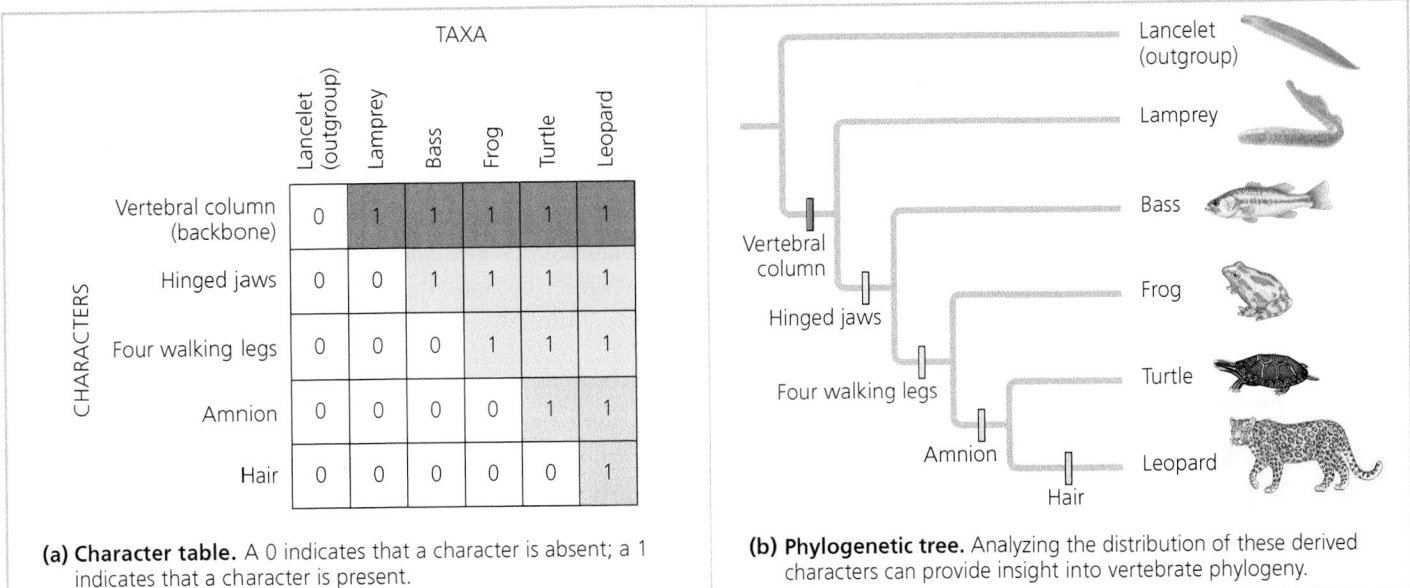

(a) **Character table.** A 0 indicates that a character is absent; a 1 indicates that a character is present.

(b) **Phylogenetic tree.** Analyzing the distribution of these derived characters can provide insight into vertebrate phylogeny.

▲ **Figure 26.11** **Constructing a phylogenetic tree.** The characters used here include the amnion, a membrane that encloses the embryo inside a fluid-filled sac (see Figure 34.25).

DRAW IT *In (b), circle the most inclusive clade for which a hinged jaw is a shared ancestral character.*

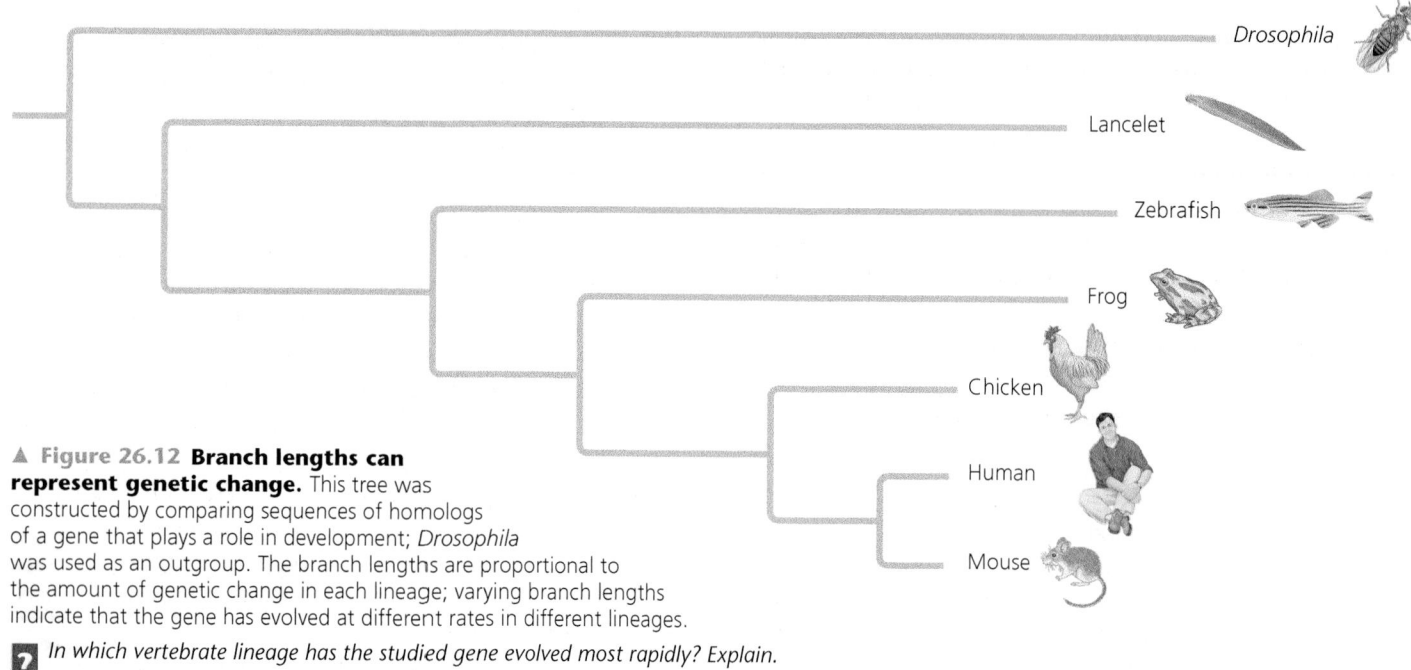

▲ **Figure 26.12 Branch lengths can represent genetic change.** This tree was constructed by comparing sequences of homologs of a gene that plays a role in development; *Drosophila* was used as an outgroup. The branch lengths are proportional to the amount of genetic change in each lineage; varying branch lengths indicate that the gene has evolved at different rates in different lineages.

? *In which vertebrate lineage has the studied gene evolved most rapidly? Explain.*

Phylogenetic Trees with Proportional Branch Lengths

In the phylogenetic trees we have presented so far, the lengths of the tree's branches do not indicate the degree of evolutionary change in each lineage. Furthermore, the chronology represented by the branching pattern of the tree is relative (earlier versus later) rather than absolute (how many millions of years ago). But in some tree diagrams, branch lengths are proportional to amount of evolutionary change or to the times at which particular events occurred.

In **Figure 26.12**, for example, the branch length of the phylogenetic tree reflects the number of changes that have taken place in a particular DNA sequence in that lineage. Note that the total length of the horizontal lines from the base of the tree to the mouse is less than that of the line leading to the outgroup species, the fruit fly *Drosophila*. This implies that in the time since the mouse and fly diverged from a common ancestor, more genetic changes have occurred in the *Drosophila* lineage than in the mouse lineage.

Even though the branches of a phylogenetic tree may have different lengths, among organisms alive today, all the different lineages that descend from a common ancestor have survived for the same number of years. To take an extreme example, humans and bacteria had a common ancestor that lived over 3 billion years ago. Fossils and genetic evidence indicate that this ancestor was a single-celled prokaryote. Even though bacteria have apparently changed little in their morphology since that common ancestor, there have nonetheless been 3 billion years of evolution in the bacterial lineage, just as there have been 3 billion years of evolution in the eukaryotic lineage that includes humans.

These equal spans of chronological time can be represented in a phylogenetic tree whose branch lengths are proportional to time (**Figure 26.13**). Such a tree draws on fossil data to place branch points in the context of geologic time. Additionally, it is possible to combine these two types of trees by labeling branch points with information about rates of genetic change or dates of divergence.

Maximum Parsimony and Maximum Likelihood

As the growing database of DNA sequences enables us to study more species, the difficulty of building the phylogenetic tree that best describes their evolutionary history also grows. What if you are analyzing data for 50 species? There are 3×10^{76} different ways to arrange 50 species into a tree! And which tree in this huge forest reflects the true phylogeny? Systematists can never be sure of finding the most accurate tree in such a large data set, but they can narrow the possibilities by applying the principles of maximum parsimony and maximum likelihood.

According to the principle of **maximum parsimony**, we should first investigate the simplest explanation that is consistent with the facts. (The parsimony principle is also called "Occam's razor" after William of Occam, a 14th-century English philosopher who advocated this minimalist problem-solving approach of "shaving away" unnecessary complications.) In the case of trees based on morphology, the most parsimonious tree requires the fewest evolutionary events, as measured by the origin of shared derived morphological characters. For phylogenies based on DNA, the most parsimonious tree requires the fewest base changes.

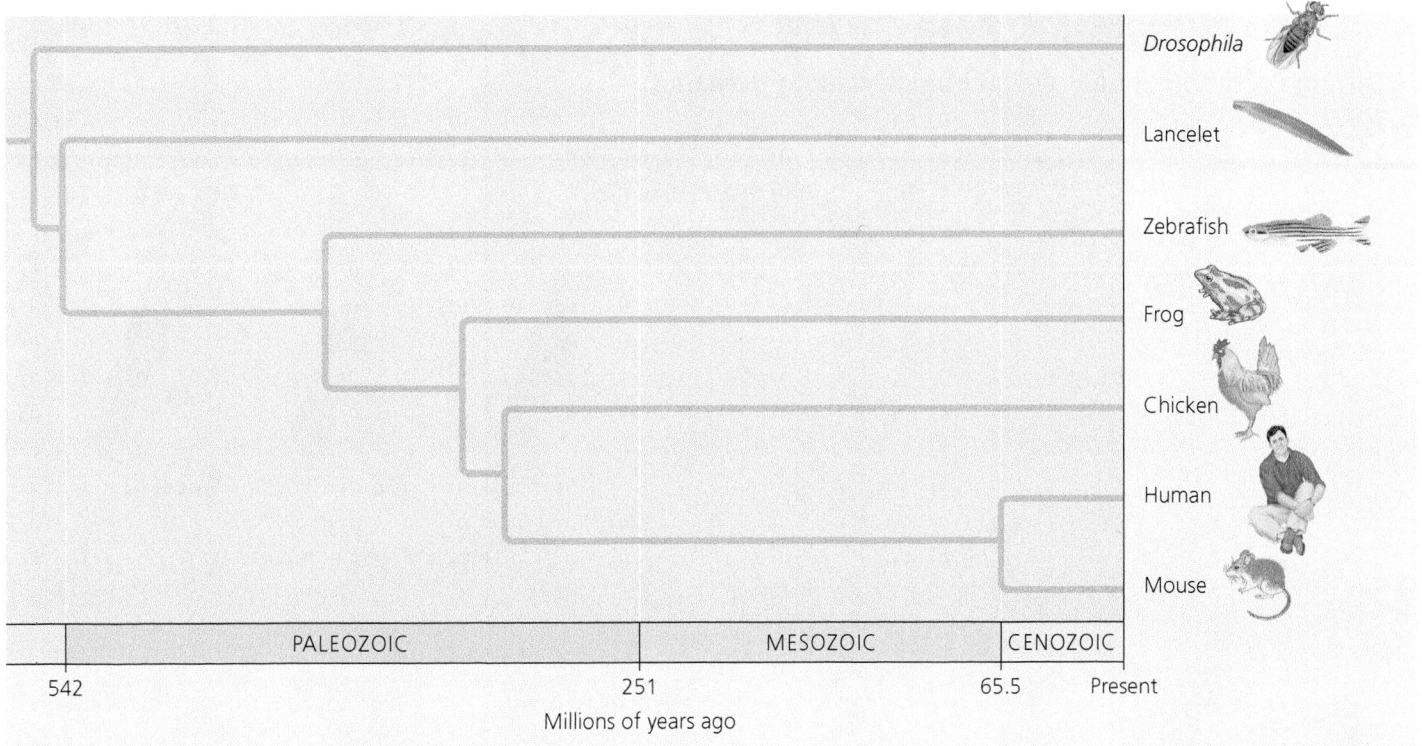

PALEOZOIC | MESOZOIC | CENOZOIC

542   251   65.5   Present

Millions of years ago

▲ **Figure 26.13 Branch lengths can indicate time.** This tree is based on the same molecular data as the tree in Figure 26.12, but here the branch points are mapped to dates based on fossil evidence. Thus, the branch lengths are proportional to time. Each lineage has the same total length from the base of the tree to the branch tip, indicating that all the lineages have diverged from the common ancestor for equal amounts of time.

The principle of **maximum likelihood** states that given certain probability rules about how DNA sequences change over time, a tree can be found that reflects the most likely sequence of evolutionary events. Maximum-likelihood methods are complex, but as a simple example, let us return to the phylogenetic relationships between a human, a mushroom, and a tulip. **Figure 26.14** shows two possible, equally parsimonious trees for this trio. Tree 1 is more likely if we assume that DNA changes have occurred at equal rates along all the branches of the tree from the common ancestor. Tree 2 requires assuming that the rate of evolution slowed greatly in the mushroom lineage and sped up greatly in the tulip lineage. Thus, assuming that equal rates are more common than unequal rates, tree 1 is more likely. We will soon see that many genes do evolve at approximately equal rates in different lineages. But note that if we find new evidence of unequal rates, tree 2 might be more likely! The likelihood of a tree depends on the assumptions on which it is based.

Scientists have developed many computer programs to search for trees that are parsimonious and likely. When a large amount of accurate data is available, the methods used in these programs usually yield similar trees. As an example of one

	Human	Mushroom	Tulip
Human	0	30%	40%
Mushroom		0	40%
Tulip			0

(a) Percentage differences between sequences

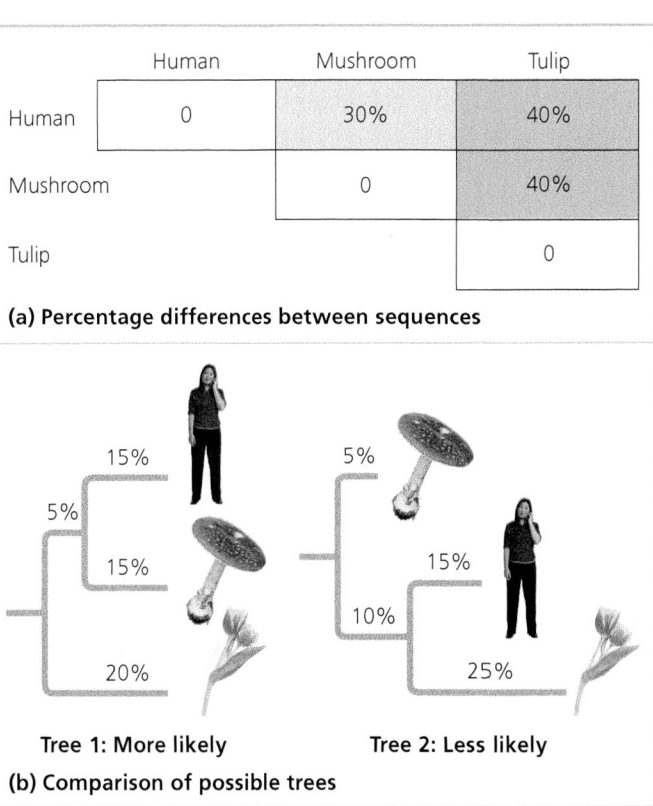

Tree 1: More likely   Tree 2: Less likely

(b) Comparison of possible trees

▲ **Figure 26.14 Trees with different likelihoods.** Based on percentage differences between genes in a human, a mushroom, and a tulip **(a)**, there are two phylogenetic trees with the same total branch length **(b)**. The sum of the percentages from a point of divergence in a tree equals the percentage differences in (a). For example, in tree 1, the human–tulip divergence is 15% + 5% + 20% = 40%. In tree 2, this divergence also equals 40% (15% + 25%). If the genes have evolved at the same rate in the different branches, tree 1 is more likely.

RESEARCH METHOD

Applying Parsimony to a Problem in Molecular Systematics

APPLICATION In considering possible phylogenies for a group of species, systematists compare molecular data for the species. An efficient way to begin is by identifying the most parsimonious hypothesis—the one that requires the fewest evolutionary events (molecular changes) to have occurred.

TECHNIQUE Follow the numbered steps as we apply the principle of parsimony to a hypothetical phylogenetic problem involving three closely related bird species.

Species I   Species II   Species III

1 First, draw the three possible phylogenies for the species. (Although only 3 trees are possible when ordering 3 species, the number of possible trees increases rapidly with the number of species: There are 15 trees for 4 species and 34,459,425 trees for 10 species.)

Three phylogenetic hypotheses:

2 Tabulate the molecular data for the species. In this simplified example, the data represent a DNA sequence consisting of just four nucleotide bases. Data from several outgroup species (not shown) were used to infer the ancestral DNA sequence.

	Site 1	2	3	4
Species I	C	T	A	T
Species II	C	T	T	C
Species III	A	G	A	C
Ancestral sequence	A	G	T	T

3 Now focus on site 1 in the DNA sequence. In the tree on the left, a single base-change event, represented by the purple hatchmark on the branch leading to species I and II (and labeled 1/C, indicating a change at site 1 to nucleotide C), is sufficient to account for the site 1 data. In the other two trees, two base-change events are necessary.

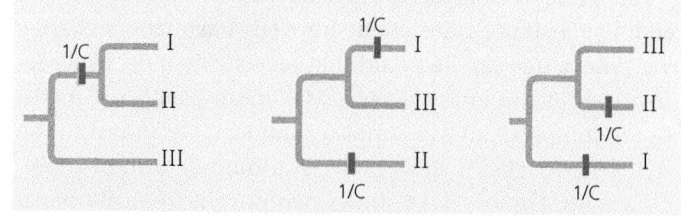

4 Continuing the comparison of bases at sites 2, 3, and 4 reveals that each of the three trees requires a total of five additional base-change events (purple hatchmarks).

RESULTS To identify the most parsimonious tree, we total all of the base-change events noted in steps 3 and 4. We conclude that the first tree is the most parsimonious of the three possible phylogenies. (In a real example, many more sites would be analyzed. Hence, the trees would often differ by more than one base-change event.)

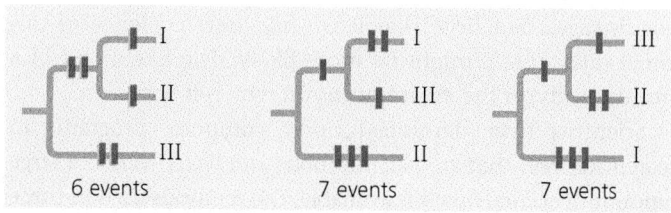

6 events   7 events   7 events

method, **Figure 26.15**, on the facing page, walks you through the process of identifying the most parsimonious molecular tree for a three-species problem. Computer programs use the principle of parsimony to estimate phylogenies in a similar way: They examine large numbers of possible trees and select the tree or trees that require fewest evolutionary changes.

Phylogenetic Trees as Hypotheses

This is a good place to reiterate that any phylogenetic tree represents a hypothesis about how the various organisms in the tree are related to one another. The best hypothesis is the one that best fits all the available data. A phylogenetic hypothesis may be modified when new evidence compels systematists to revise their trees. Indeed, while many older phylogenetic hypotheses have been supported by new morphological and molecular data, others have been changed or rejected.

Thinking of phylogenies as hypotheses also allows us to use them in a powerful way: We can make and test predictions based on the assumption that a phylogeny—our hypothesis—is correct. For example, in an approach known as *phylogenetic bracketing*, we can predict (by parsimony) that features shared by two groups of closely related organisms are present in their common ancestor and all of its descendants unless independent data indicate otherwise. (Note that "prediction" can refer to unknown past events as well as to evolutionary changes yet to occur.)

This approach has been used to make novel predictions about dinosaurs. For example, there is evidence that birds descended from the theropods, a group of bipedal saurischian dinosaurs. As seen in **Figure 26.16**, the closest living relatives of birds are crocodiles. Birds and crocodiles share numerous features: They have four-chambered hearts, they "sing" to defend territories and attract mates (although a crocodile's "song" is more like a bellow), and they build nests. Both birds and crocodiles also care for their eggs by *brooding*, a behavior in which a parent warms the eggs with its body. Birds brood by sitting on their eggs, whereas crocodiles cover their eggs with their neck. Reasoning that any feature shared by birds and crocodiles is likely to have been present in their common ancestor (denoted by the blue dot in Figure 26.16) and *all* of its descendants, biologists predicted that dinosaurs had four-chambered hearts, sang, built nests, and exhibited brooding.

Internal organs, such as the heart, rarely fossilize, and it is, of course, difficult to test whether dinosaurs sang to defend territories and attract mates. However, fossilized dinosaur eggs and nests have provided evidence supporting the prediction of brooding in dinosaurs. First, a fossil embryo of an *Oviraptor* dinosaur was found, still inside its egg. This egg was identical to those found in another fossil, one that showed an *Oviraptor* adult crouching over a group of eggs in a posture similar to that in brooding birds today (**Figure 26.17**). Researchers suggested that the *Oviraptor* dinosaur preserved in this second fossil died while incubating or protecting its eggs. The broader conclusion that emerged from this work—that

Front limb

Hind limb

Eggs

(a) Fossil remains of *Oviraptor* and eggs. The orientation of the bones, which surround and cover the eggs, suggests that the dinosaur died while incubating or protecting its eggs.

(b) Artist's reconstruction of the dinosaur's posture based on the fossil findings.

▲ **Figure 26.17 Fossil support for a phylogenetic prediction: Dinosaurs built nests and brooded their eggs.**

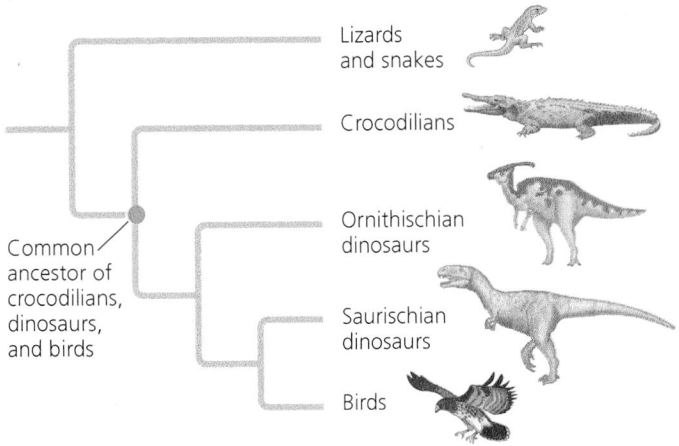

Lizards and snakes

Crocodilians

Ornithischian dinosaurs

Saurischian dinosaurs

Common ancestor of crocodilians, dinosaurs, and birds

Birds

▲ **Figure 26.16 A phylogenetic tree of birds and their close relatives.**

? *What is the most basal taxon represented in this tree?*

dinosaurs built nests and exhibited brooding—has since been strengthened by additional fossil discoveries that show that other species of dinosaurs built nests and sat on their eggs. Finally, by supporting predictions based on the phylogenetic hypothesis shown in Figure 26.16, fossil discoveries of nests and brooding in dinosaurs provide independent data that suggest that the hypothesis is correct.

CONCEPT CHECK 26.3

1. To distinguish a particular clade of mammals within the larger clade that corresponds to class Mammalia, would hair be a useful character? Why or why not?
2. The most parsimonious tree of evolutionary relationships can be inaccurate. How can this occur?
3. **WHAT IF?** Draw a phylogenetic tree that includes the relationships from both Figure 25.6 and Figure 26.16. Traditionally, all the taxa shown besides birds and mammals were classified as reptiles. Would a cladistic approach support that classification? Explain.

For suggested answers, see Appendix A.

CONCEPT 26.4

An organism's evolutionary history is documented in its genome

As you have seen in this chapter, molecular systematics—using comparisons of nucleic acids or other molecules to deduce relatedness—is a valuable approach for tracing evolutionary history. The molecular approach helps us understand phylogenetic relationships that cannot be determined by nonmolecular methods such as comparative anatomy. For example, molecular systematics helps us uncover evolutionary relationships between groups that have little common ground for morphological comparison, such as animals and fungi. And molecular methods allow us to reconstruct phylogenies among groups of present-day organisms for which the fossil record is poor or lacking entirely. Overall, molecular biology has helped to extend systematics to evolutionary relationships far above and below the species level, ranging from the major branches of the tree of life to its finest twigs.

Different genes evolve at different rates, even in the same evolutionary lineage. As a result, molecular trees can represent short or long periods of time, depending on which genes are used. For example, the DNA that codes for ribosomal RNA (rRNA) changes relatively slowly. Therefore, comparisons of DNA sequences in these genes are useful for investigating relationships between taxa that diverged hundreds of millions of years ago. Studies of rRNA sequences indicate, for instance, that fungi are more closely related to animals than to green plants (see Figure 26.2). In contrast, mitochondrial DNA (mtDNA) evolves relatively rapidly and can be used to ex-

plore recent evolutionary events. One research team has traced the relationships among Native American groups through their mtDNA sequences. The molecular findings corroborate other evidence that the Pima of Arizona, the Maya of Mexico, and the Yanomami of Venezuela are closely related, probably descending from the first of three waves of immigrants that crossed the Bering land bridge from Asia to the Americas about 15,000 years ago.

Gene Duplications and Gene Families

What does molecular systematics reveal about the evolutionary history of genome change? Consider gene duplication, which plays a particularly important role in evolution because it increases the number of genes in the genome, providing more opportunities for further evolutionary changes. Molecular techniques now allow us to trace the phylogenies of gene duplications and the influence of these duplications on genome evolution. These molecular phylogenies must account for repeated duplications that have resulted in *gene families*, groups of related genes within an organism's genome (see Figure 21.11). Accounting for such duplications leads us to distinguish two types of homologous genes: orthologous genes and paralogous genes. **Orthologous genes** (from the Greek *orthos*, exact) are those found in different species, and their divergence traces back to the speciation events that produced the species (Figure 26.18a). The cytochrome *c* genes (which code for an electron transport chain protein) in humans and dogs are orthologous. In **paralogous genes** (from the Greek *para*, in parallel), the homology results from gene duplication; hence, multiple copies of these genes have diverged from one another within a species (Figure 26.18b). In Chapter 23, you encountered the example of olfactory receptor genes, which have undergone many gene duplications in vertebrates. Humans and mice both have huge families of more than 1,000 of these paralogous genes.

Note that orthologous genes can only diverge after speciation has taken place, that is, after the genes are found in separate gene pools. For example, although the cytochrome *c* genes in humans and dogs serve the same function, the gene's sequence in humans has diverged from that in dogs in the time since these species last shared a common ancestor. Paralogous genes, on the other hand, can diverge within a species because they are present in more than one copy in the genome. The paralogous genes that make up the olfactory receptor gene family in humans have diverged from each other during our long evolutionary history. They now specify proteins that confer sensitivity to a wide variety of molecules, ranging from food odors to sex pheromones.

Genome Evolution

Now that we can compare the entire genomes of different organisms, including our own, two patterns have emerged. First, lineages that diverged long ago can share orthologous genes. For

▼ Figure 26.18 **Two types of homologous genes.** Colored bands mark regions of the genes where differences in base sequences have accumulated.

(a) Formation of orthologous genes: a product of speciation

Ancestral gene

Ancestral species

Speciation with divergence of gene

Orthologous genes

Species A   Species B

(b) Formation of paralogous genes: within a species

Ancestral gene

Species C

Gene duplication and divergence

Paralogous genes

Species C after many generations

example, though the human and mouse lineages diverged about 65 million years ago, 99% of the genes of humans and mice are orthologous. And 50% of human genes are orthologous with those of yeast, despite 1 billion years of divergent evolution. Such commonalities explain why disparate organisms nevertheless share many biochemical and developmental pathways.

Second, the number of genes a species has doesn't seem to increase through duplication at the same rate as perceived phenotypic complexity. Humans have only about four times as many genes as yeast, a single-celled eukaryote, even though—unlike yeast—we have a large, complex brain and a body with more than 200 different types of tissues. Evidence is emerging that many human genes are more versatile than those of yeast: A single human gene can encode multiple proteins that perform different tasks in various body tissues. Unraveling the mechanisms that cause this genomic versatility and phenotypic variation is an exciting challenge.

CONCEPT CHECK 26.4

1. Explain how comparing proteins of two species can yield data about the species' evolutionary relationship.
2. **WHAT IF?** Suppose gene A is orthologous in species 1 and species 2, and gene B is paralogous to gene A in species 1. Suggest a sequence of two evolutionary events that could result in the following: Gene A differs considerably between species, yet gene A and gene B show little divergence from each other.
3. **MAKE CONNECTIONS** Review Figure 18.13 (p. 363); then suggest how a particular gene could have different functions in different tissues within an organism.

For suggested answers, see Appendix A.

Molecular clocks help track evolutionary time

One goal of evolutionary biology is to understand the relationships among all organisms, including those for which there is no fossil record. However, if we attempt to determine the timing of molecular phylogenies that extend beyond the fossil record, we must rely on an assumption about how change occurs at the molecular level.

Molecular Clocks

We stated earlier that researchers have estimated that the common ancestor of Hawaiian silversword plants lived about 5 million years ago. How did they make this estimate? They relied on the concept of a **molecular clock**, a yardstick for measuring the absolute time of evolutionary change based on the observation that some genes and other regions of genomes appear to evolve at constant rates. The assumption underlying the molecular clock is that the number of nucleotide substitutions in orthologous genes is proportional to the time that has elapsed since the species branched from their common ancestor (divergence time). In the case of paralogous genes, the number of substitutions is proportional to the time since the ancestral gene was duplicated.

We can calibrate the molecular clock of a gene that has a reliable average rate of evolution by graphing the number of genetic differences—for example, nucleotide, codon, or amino acid differences—against the dates of evolutionary branch points that are known from the fossil record

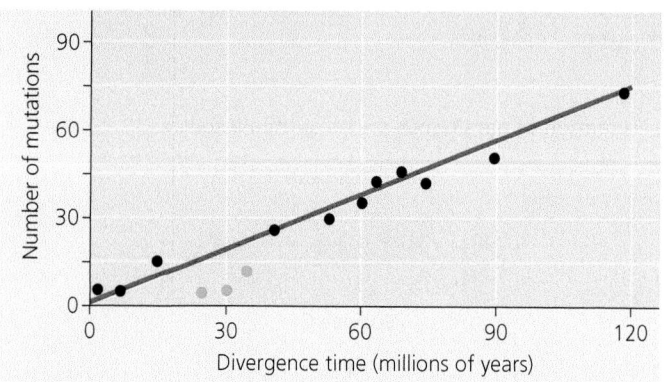

▲ **Figure 26.19 A molecular clock for mammals.** The number of accumulated mutations in seven proteins has increased over time in a consistent manner for most mammal species. The three green data points represent primate species, whose proteins appear to have evolved more slowly than those of other mammals. The divergence time for each data point was based on fossil evidence.

? *Use the graph to estimate the divergence time for a mammal with a total of 30 mutations in the seven proteins.*

(Figure 26.19). The average rates of genetic change inferred from such graphs can then be used to estimate the dates of events that cannot be discerned from the fossil record, such as the origin of the silverswords discussed earlier.

Of course, no gene marks time with complete precision. In fact, some portions of the genome appear to have evolved in irregular bursts that are not at all clocklike. And even those genes that seem to act as reliable molecular clocks are accurate only in the statistical sense of showing a fairly smooth *average* rate of change. Over time, there may still be deviations from that average rate. Furthermore, the same gene may evolve at different rates in different groups of organisms. And even among genes that are clocklike, the rate of the clock may vary greatly from one gene to another; some genes evolve a million times faster than others.

Neutral Theory

The observed regularity of change that enables us to use some genes as molecular clocks raises the possibility that many of the changes in these sequences result from mutations that have become fixed in a population by genetic drift (see Chapter 23) and that the changes are selectively neutral—neither beneficial nor detrimental. In the 1960s, Motoo Kimura, at the Japanese National Institute of Genetics, and Jack King and Thomas Jukes, at the University of California, Berkeley, independently published papers describing this **neutral theory**— that much evolutionary change in genes and proteins has no effect on fitness and therefore is not influenced by natural selection. Kimura pointed out that many new mutations are harmful and are removed quickly. But if most of the rest are neutral and have little or no effect on fitness, then the rate of molecular change should indeed be regular, like a clock. Differences in the clock rate for different genes are a function of how important a gene is. If the exact sequence of amino acids that a gene specifies is essential to survival, most of the mutational changes will be harmful and only a few will be neutral. As a result, such genes change only slowly. But if the exact sequence of amino acids is less critical, fewer of the new mutations will be harmful and more will be neutral. Such genes change more quickly.

Problems with Molecular Clocks

In fact, molecular clocks do not run as smoothly as neutral theory predicts. Many irregularities are likely to be the result of natural selection in which certain DNA changes are favored over others. Consequently, some scientists question the utility of molecular clocks for timing evolution. Their skepticism is part of a broader debate about the extent to which neutral genetic variation can account for some kinds of DNA diversity. Indeed, evidence suggests that almost half the amino acid differences in proteins of two *Drosophila* species, *D. simulans* and *D. yakuba*, are not neutral but have resulted from directional natural selection. But because the direction of natural selection may change repeatedly over long periods of time (and hence may average out), some genes experiencing selection can nevertheless serve as approximate markers of elapsed time.

Another question arises when researchers attempt to extend molecular clocks beyond the time span documented by the fossil record. Although some fossils are more than 3 billion years old, these are very rare. An abundant fossil record extends back only about 550 million years, but molecular clocks have been used to date evolutionary divergences that occurred a billion or more years ago. These estimates assume that the clocks have been constant for all that time. Such estimates are highly uncertain.

In some cases, problems may be avoided by calibrating molecular clocks with many genes rather than just one or a few genes (as is often done). By using many genes, fluctuations in evolutionary rate due to natural selection or other factors that vary over time may average out. For example, one group of researchers constructed molecular clocks of vertebrate evolution from published sequence data for 658 nuclear genes. Despite the broad period of time covered (nearly 600 million years) and the fact that natural selection probably affected some of these genes, their estimates of divergence times agreed closely with fossil-based estimates.

Applying a Molecular Clock: The Origin of HIV

Researchers have used a molecular clock to date the origin of HIV infection in humans. Phylogenetic analysis shows that HIV, the virus that causes AIDS, is descended from viruses that infect chimpanzees and other primates. (Most of these viruses do not cause AIDS-like diseases in their native hosts.) When did HIV jump to humans? There is no simple answer, because the virus has spread to humans more than once. The multiple origins of HIV are reflected in the variety of strains

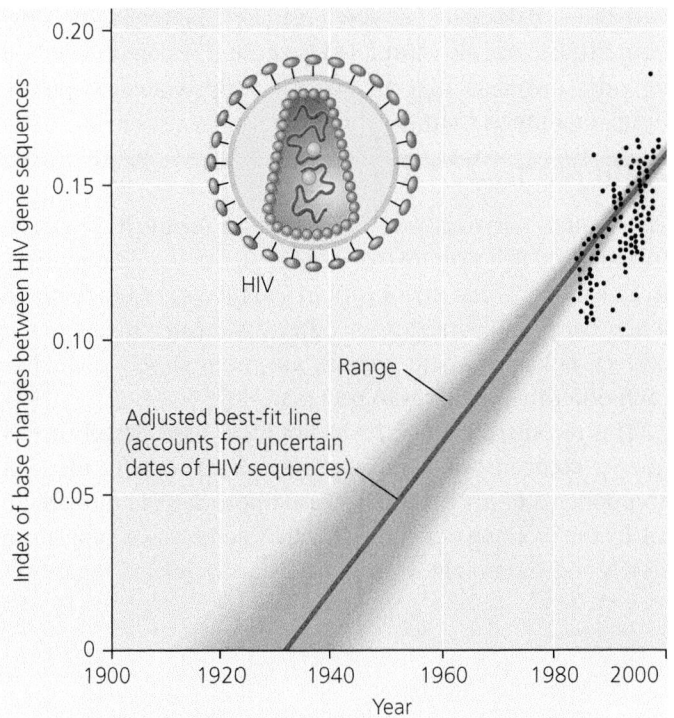

▲ **Figure 26.20 Dating the origin of HIV-1 M with a molecular clock.** The black data points are based on DNA sequences of an HIV gene in blood samples collected from patients. (The dates when these individual HIV gene sequences arose are not known with certainty because a person can harbor the virus for years before symptoms occur.) Projecting the gene's rate of change in the 1980s and 1990s backward in time suggests that the virus originated in the 1930s.

(genetic types) of the virus. HIV's genetic material is made of RNA, and like other RNA viruses, it evolves quickly.

The most widespread strain in humans is HIV-1 M. To pinpoint the earliest HIV-1 M infection, researchers compared samples of the virus from various times during the epidemic, including a sample from 1959. A comparison of gene sequences showed that the virus has evolved in a clocklike fashion (**Figure 26.20**). Extrapolating backward in time using the molecular clock indicates that the HIV-1 M strain first spread to humans during the 1930s.

CONCEPT CHECK 26.5

1. What is a molecular clock? What assumption underlies the use of a molecular clock?
2. **MAKE CONNECTIONS** Review Concept 17.5 (pp. 344–346). Then explain how numerous base changes could occur in an organism's DNA yet have no effect on its fitness.
3. **WHAT IF?** Suppose a molecular clock dates the divergence of two taxa at 80 million years ago, but new fossil evidence shows that the taxa diverged at least 120 million years ago. Explain how this could happen.

For suggested answers, see Appendix A.

New information continues to revise our understanding of the tree of life

The discovery that the scaly-foot in Figure 26.1 evolved from a different lineage of legless lizards than did snakes is one example of how systematics is used to reconstruct the evolutionary relationships of life's diverse forms. In recent decades, we have gained insight into even the very deepest branches of the tree of life through molecular systematics.

From Two Kingdoms to Three Domains

Early taxonomists classified all known species into two kingdoms: plants and animals. Even with the discovery of the diverse microbial world, the two-kingdom system persisted: Noting that bacteria had a rigid cell wall, taxonomists placed them in the plant kingdom. Eukaryotic unicellular organisms with chloroplasts were also considered plants. Fungi, too, were classified as plants, partly because most fungi, like most plants, are unable to move about (never mind the fact that fungi are not photosynthetic and have little in common structurally with plants!). In the two-kingdom system, unicellular eukaryotes that move and ingest food—protozoans—were classified as animals. Those such as *Euglena* that move and are photosynthetic were claimed by both botanists and zoologists and showed up in both kingdoms.

Taxonomic schemes with more than two kingdoms gained broad acceptance in the late 1960s, when many biologists recognized five kingdoms: Monera (prokaryotes), Protista (a diverse kingdom consisting mostly of unicellular organisms), Plantae, Fungi, and Animalia. This system highlighted the two fundamentally different types of cells, prokaryotic and eukaryotic, and set the prokaryotes apart from all eukaryotes by placing them in their own kingdom, Monera.

However, phylogenies based on genetic data soon began to reveal a problem with this system: Some prokaryotes differ as much from each other as they do from eukaryotes. Such difficulties have led biologists to adopt a three-domain system. The three domains—Bacteria, Archaea, and Eukarya—are a taxonomic level higher than the kingdom level. The validity of these domains is supported by many studies, including a recent study that analyzed nearly 100 completely sequenced genomes.

The domain Bacteria contains most of the currently known prokaryotes, including the bacteria closely related to chloroplasts and mitochondria. The second domain, Archaea, consists of a diverse group of prokaryotic organisms that inhabit a wide variety of environments. Some archaea can use hydrogen as an energy source, and others were the chief source of the natural gas deposits that are found throughout Earth's crust. As you will read in Chapter 27, bacteria differ from archaea in many structural, biochemical, and physiological characteristics. The third domain, Eukarya, consists of all the organisms that have cells containing true nuclei. This domain includes many groups of single-celled organisms (see Chapter 28) as well as multicellular plants (Chapters 29 and 30), fungi (Chapter 31), and animals (Chapters 32–34). **Figure 26.21** represents one possible phylogenetic tree for the three domains and the many lineages they encompass.

The three-domain system highlights the fact that much of the history of life has been about single-celled organisms. The two prokaryotic domains consist entirely of single-celled organisms, and even in Eukarya, only the branches shown in red (plants, fungi, and animals) are dominated by multicellular organisms. Of the five kingdoms previously recognized by taxonomists, most biologists continue to recognize Plantae, Fungi, and Animalia, but not Monera and Protista. The kingdom Monera is obsolete because it would have members in two different domains. As you'll read in Chapter 28, the kingdom Protista has also crumbled because it is polyphyletic—it includes members that are more closely related to plants, fungi, or animals than to other protists.

A Simple Tree of All Life

The evolutionary relationships shown in Figure 26.21 can be summarized in a simpler tree (see the figure legend question). In this tree, the first major split in the history of life occurred when bacteria diverged from other organisms. If this tree is correct, eukaryotes and archaea are more closely related to each other than either is to bacteria.

This reconstruction of the tree of life is based largely on sequence comparisons of rRNA genes, which code for the RNA components of ribosomes. Because ribosomes are fundamental to the workings of the cell, rRNA genes have evolved so slowly that homologies between distantly related organisms

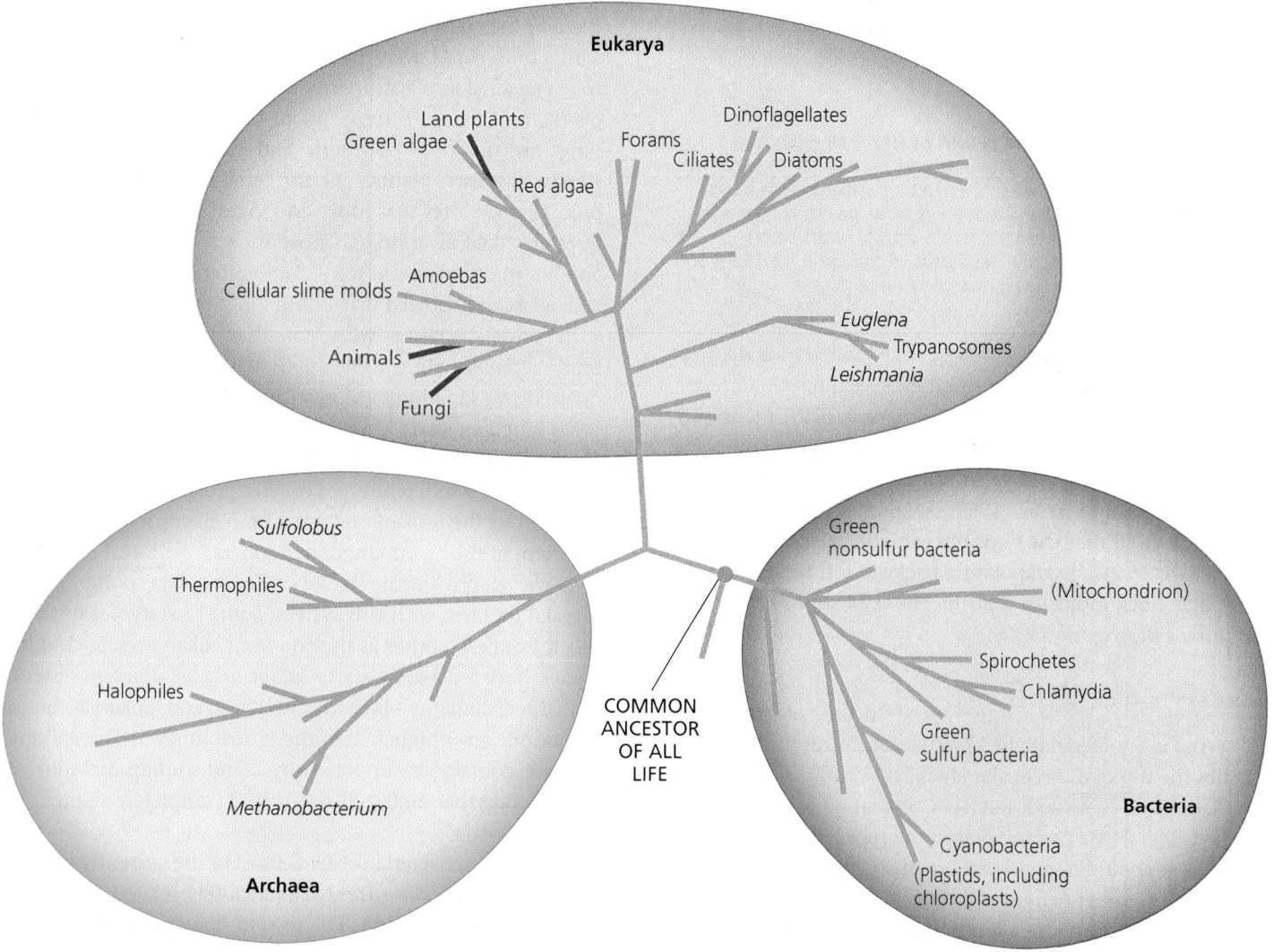

▲ **Figure 26.21 The three domains of life.** The phylogenetic tree shown here is based on rRNA gene sequences. Branch lengths are proportional to the amount of genetic change in each lineage. (To simplify the figure, only some branches are labeled.) In this diagram, the lineages within Eukarya that are dominated by multicellular organisms (plants, fungi, and animals) are shown in red. All other lineages consist solely or primarily of single-celled organisms.

DRAW IT *Redraw this tree as a horizontal tree that has just three branches, one for each domain. Which domain was the first to diverge? Which is the sister domain to Eukarya?*

can still be detected—making these genes very useful for determining evolutionary relationships between deep branches in the history of life. However, other genes reveal a different set of relationships. For example, researchers have found that many of the genes that influence metabolism in yeast (a unicellular eukaryote) are more similar to genes in the domain Bacteria than they are to genes in the domain Archaea—a finding that suggests that the eukaryotes may share a more recent common ancestor with bacteria than with archaea.

Comparisons of complete genomes from the three domains show that there have been substantial movements of genes between organisms in the different domains (Figure 26.22). These took place through **horizontal gene transfer**, a process in which genes are transferred from one genome to another through mechanisms such as exchange of transposable elements and plasmids, viral infection (see Chapter 19), and perhaps fusions of organisms. Recent research reinforces the view that horizontal gene transfer is important. For example, a 2008 analysis indicated that, on average, 80% of the genes in 181 prokaryotic genomes had moved between species at some point during the course of evolution. Because phylogenetic trees are based on the assumption that genes are passed vertically from one generation to the next, the occurrence of such horizontal transfer events helps to explain why trees built using different genes can give inconsistent results.

Is the Tree of Life Really a Ring?

Some biologists, including W. Ford Doolittle, interviewed on pages 534–535, have argued that horizontal gene transfer was

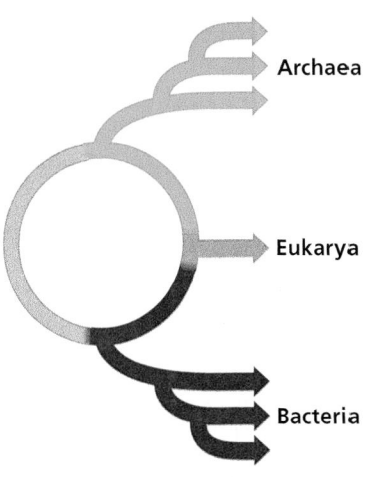

▲ **Figure 26.23 A ring of life.** In this hypothesis, the eukaryote lineage (orange) arose when an early archaean (teal) fused with an early bacterium (purple). Such an event is consistent with a "ring of life" but not with a tree of life. Three great domains (Archaea, Eukarya, and Bacteria) emerged from the ring and gave rise to the tremendous diversity of life we observe today.

so common that the early history of life should be represented as a tangled network of connected branches—not a simple, dichotomously branching tree like that in Figure 26.22. Others have suggested that relationships among early organisms are best represented by a ring, not a tree (Figure 26.23). In an analysis based on hundreds of genes, these researchers hypothesized that eukaryotes arose as a fusion between an early bacterium and an early archaean. If correct, eukaryotes are simultaneously most closely related to bacteria *and* archaea—an evolutionary relationship that cannot be depicted in a tree of life, but can be depicted in a *ring* of life.

Although scientists continue to debate whether early steps in the history of life are best represented as a tree, a ring, or a tangled web, in recent decades there have been many exciting discoveries about evolutionary events that occurred later in time. We'll explore such discoveries in the rest of this unit's chapters, beginning with Earth's earliest inhabitants, the prokaryotes.

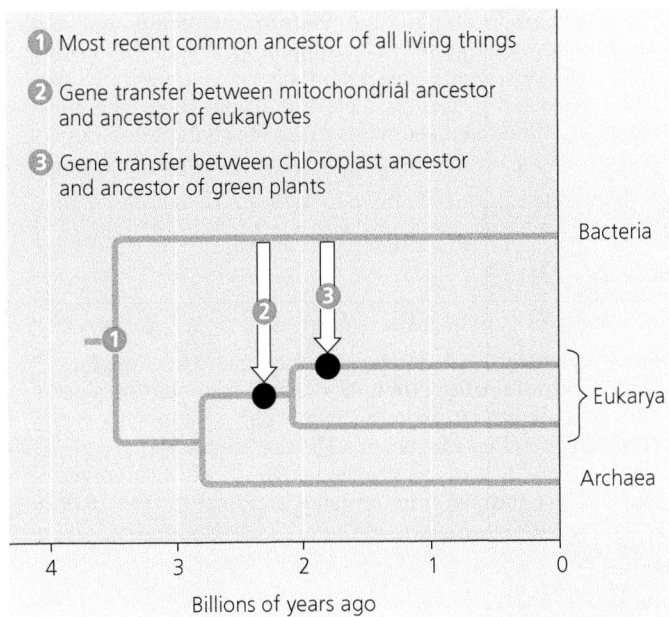

① Most recent common ancestor of all living things

② Gene transfer between mitochondrial ancestor and ancestor of eukaryotes

③ Gene transfer between chloroplast ancestor and ancestor of green plants

Bacteria

Eukarya

Archaea

4　3　2　1　0
Billions of years ago

▲ **Figure 26.22 The role of horizontal gene transfer in the history of life.** This tree shows two major episodes of horizontal gene transfer, the dates of which are uncertain. It is known that many more such events occurred. (Because the tree is horizontal, the arrows representing "horizontal" transfer are vertical here.)

CONCEPT CHECK 26.6

1. Why is the kingdom Monera no longer considered a valid taxon?
2. Explain why phylogenies based on different genes can yield different branching patterns for the tree of all life.
3. **WHAT IF?** Draw the three possible dichotomously branching trees showing evolutionary relationships for the domains Bacteria, Archaea, and Eukarya. Two of these trees have been supported by genetic data. Is it likely that the third tree might also receive such support? Explain your answer.

For suggested answers, see Appendix A.

26 CHAPTER REVIEW

SUMMARY OF KEY CONCEPTS

CONCEPT 26.1

Phylogenies show evolutionary relationships (pp. 537–540)

- Linnaeus's **binomial** classification system gives organisms two-part names: a **genus** plus a specific epithet.
- In the Linnaean system, species are grouped in increasingly broad taxa: Related genera are placed in the same family, families in orders, orders in classes, classes in phyla, phyla in kingdoms, and (more recently) kingdoms in domains.
- Systematists depict evolutionary relationships as branching **phylogenetic trees**. Many systematists propose that classification be based entirely on evolutionary relationships.

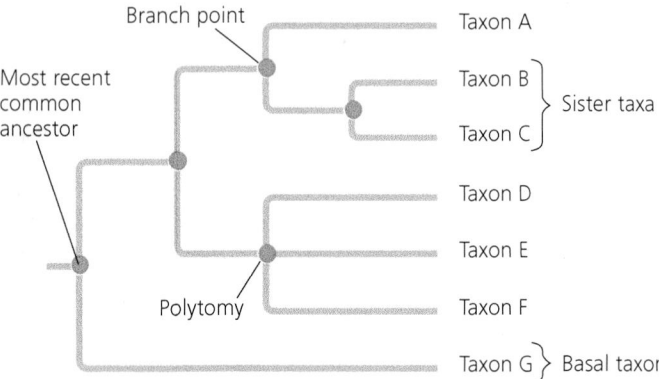

- Unless branch lengths are proportional to time or amount of genetic change, a phylogenetic tree indicates only patterns of descent.
- Much information can be learned about a species from its evolutionary history; hence, phylogenies are useful in a wide range of applications.

? *Humans and chimpanzees are sister species. Explain what that means.*

CONCEPT 26.2

Phylogenies are inferred from morphological and molecular data (pp. 540–542)

- Organisms with similar morphologies or DNA sequences are likely to be more closely related than organisms with very different structures and genetic sequences.
- To infer phylogeny, **homology** (similarity due to shared ancestry) must be distinguished from **analogy** (similarity due to convergent evolution).
- Computer programs are used to align comparable DNA sequences and to distinguish molecular homologies from coincidental matches between taxa that diverged long ago.

? *Why is it necessary to distinguish homology from analogy to infer phylogeny?*

CONCEPT 26.3

Shared characters are used to construct phylogenetic trees (pp. 542–548)

- A **clade** is a monophyletic grouping that includes an ancestral species and all of its descendants.

- Clades can be distinguished by their **shared derived characters**.

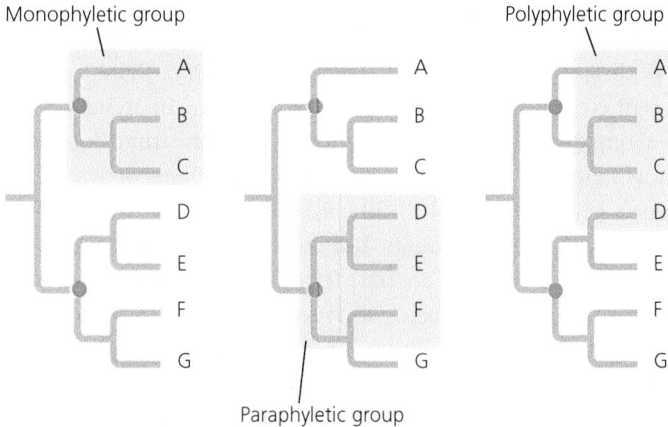

- Branch lengths can be drawn proportional to the amount of evolutionary change or time.
- Among phylogenies, the most parsimonious tree is the one that requires the fewest evolutionary changes. The most likely tree is the one based on the most likely pattern of changes.
- Well-supported phylogenetic hypotheses are consistent with a wide range of data.

? *Explain the logic of using shared derived characters to infer phylogeny.*

CONCEPT 26.4

An organism's evolutionary history is documented in its genome (pp. 548–549)

- **Orthologous genes** are homologous genes found in different species as a result of speciation. **Paralogous genes** are homologous genes within a species that result from gene duplication; such genes can diverge and potentially take on new functions.
- Distantly related species can have orthologous genes. The small variation in gene number in organisms of varying complexity suggests that genes are versatile and may have multiple functions.

? *When reconstructing phylogenies, is it better to compare orthologous or paralogous genes? Explain.*

CONCEPT 26.5

Molecular clocks help track evolutionary time (pp. 549–551)

- Some regions of DNA change at a rate consistent enough to serve as a **molecular clock**, in which the amount of genetic change is used to estimate the date of past evolutionary events. Other DNA regions change in a less predictable way.
- A molecular clock analysis suggests that the most common strain of HIV jumped from primates to humans in the 1930s.

? *Describe some assumptions and limitations of molecular clocks.*

CONCEPT 26.6

New information continues to revise our understanding of the tree of life (pp. 551–553)

- Past classification systems have given way to the current view of the tree of life, which consists of three great **domains**: Bacteria, Archaea, and Eukarya.

- Phylogenies based on rRNA genes suggest that eukaryotes are most closely related to archaea, while data from some other genes suggest a closer relationship to bacteria.
- Other genetic analyses suggest that eukaryotes arose as a fusion between a bacterium and an archaean, leading to a "ring of life" in which eukaryotes are equally closely related to bacteria and archaea.

? *Why was the five-kingdom system abandoned for a three-domain system?*

TESTING YOUR UNDERSTANDING

LEVEL 1: KNOWLEDGE/COMPREHENSION

1. In Figure 26.4, which similarly inclusive taxon descended from the same common ancestor as Canidae?
   a. Felidae
   b. Mustelidae
   c. Carnivora
   d. *Canis*
   e. *Lutra*

2. Three living species X, Y, and Z share a common ancestor T, as do extinct species U and V. A grouping that consists of species T, X, Y, and Z (but not U or V) makes up
   a. a valid taxon.
   b. a monophyletic clade.
   c. an ingroup, with species U as the outgroup.
   d. a paraphyletic group.
   e. a polyphyletic group.

3. In a comparison of birds and mammals, having four limbs is
   a. a shared ancestral character.
   b. a shared derived character.
   c. a character useful for distinguishing birds from mammals.
   d. an example of analogy rather than homology.
   e. a character useful for sorting bird species.

4. To apply parsimony to constructing a phylogenetic tree,
   a. choose the tree that assumes all evolutionary changes are equally probable.
   b. choose the tree in which the branch points are based on as many shared derived characters as possible.
   c. base phylogenetic trees only on the fossil record, as this provides the simplest explanation for evolution.
   d. choose the tree that represents the fewest evolutionary changes, in either DNA sequences or morphology.
   e. choose the tree with the fewest branch points.

LEVEL 2: APPLICATION/ANALYSIS

5. Based on this tree, which statement is *not* correct?

   a. The salamander lineage is a basal taxon.
   b. Salamanders are a sister group to the group containing lizards, goats, and humans.
   c. Salamanders are as closely related to goats as to humans.
   d. Lizards are more closely related to salamanders than to humans.
   e. The group highlighted by shading is paraphyletic.

6. If you were using cladistics to build a phylogenetic tree of cats, which of the following would be the best outgroup?
   a. lion   b. domestic cat   c. wolf   d. leopard   e. tiger

7. The relative lengths of the frog and mouse branches in the phylogeny in Figure 26.12 indicate that
   a. frogs evolved before mice.
   b. mice evolved before frogs.
   c. the genes of frogs and mice have only coincidental homoplasies.
   d. the homolog has evolved more slowly in mice.
   e. the homolog has evolved more rapidly in mice.

LEVEL 3: SYNTHESIS/EVALUATION

8. **EVOLUTION CONNECTION**
   Darwin suggested looking at a species' close relatives to learn what its ancestors may have been like. How does his suggestion anticipate recent methods, such as phylogenetic bracketing and the use of outgroups in cladistic analysis?

9. **SCIENTIFIC INQUIRY**
   DRAW IT (a) Draw a phylogenetic tree based on the first five characters in the table below. Place hatch marks on the tree to indicate the origin(s) of each of the six characters. (b) Assume that tuna and dolphins are sister species and redraw the phylogenetic tree accordingly. Place hatch marks on the tree to indicate the origin(s) of each of the six characters. (c) How many evolutionary changes are required in each tree? Which tree is most parsimonious?

Character	Lancelet (outgroup)	Lamprey	Tuna	Salamander	Turtle	Leopard	Dolphin
Backbone	0	1	1	1	1	1	1
Hinged jaw	0	0	1	1	1	1	1
Four limbs	0	0	0	1	1	1	1*
Amnion	0	0	0	0	1	1	1
Milk	0	0	0	0	0	1	1
Dorsal fin	0	0	1	0	0	0	1

*Although adult dolphins have only two obvious limbs (their flippers), as embryos they have two hind-limb buds, for a total of four limbs.

10. **WRITE ABOUT A THEME**
    The Cellular Basis of Life; The Genetic Basis of Life In a short essay (100–150 words), explain how these two themes—along with the process of descent with modification (see Chapter 22)—enable scientists to construct phylogenies that extend hundreds of millions of years back in time.

For selected answers, see Appendix A.

 www.masteringbiology.com

1. MasteringBiology® Assignments
   Video Tutor Sessions Phylogenetic Trees • Survey of Biodiversity
   Tutorial Constructing Phylogenetic Trees
   Activity Classification Schemes
   Questions Student Misconceptions • Reading Quiz • Multiple Choice • End-of-Chapter

2. eText
   Read your book online, search, take notes, highlight text, and more.

3. The Study Area
   Practice Tests • Cumulative Test • **BioFlix** 3-D Animations • MP3 Tutor Sessions • Videos • Activities • Investigations • Lab Media • Audio Glossary • Word Study Tools • Art

27

Bacteria and Archaea

▲ Figure 27.1 **Why is this lake's water pink?**

EVOLUTION

KEY CONCEPTS

27.1 Structural and functional adaptations contribute to prokaryotic success

27.2 Rapid reproduction, mutation, and genetic recombination promote genetic diversity in prokaryotes

27.3 Diverse nutritional and metabolic adaptations have evolved in prokaryotes

27.4 Molecular systematics is illuminating prokaryotic phylogeny

27.5 Prokaryotes play crucial roles in the biosphere

27.6 Prokaryotes have both beneficial and harmful impacts on humans

Masters of Adaptation

In the heat of summer, parts of Utah's Great Salt Lake turn pink (Figure 27.1), a sign of waters so salty that they would dehydrate your skin if you took a dip. The salt concentration can reach 32%, nearly ten times that of seawater. Yet despite these harsh conditions, the dramatic color of these waters is caused not by minerals or other nonliving sources, but by living things. What organisms can live in such an inhospitable environment, and how do they do it?

The pink color in the Great Salt Lake comes from trillions of prokaryotes in the domains Archaea and Bacteria, including archaea in the genus *Halobacterium*. These archaea have red membrane pigments, some of which capture the light energy that drives ATP synthesis. *Halobacterium* species are among the most salt-tolerant organisms on Earth; they thrive in salinities that dehydrate and kill other cells. *Halobacterium* compensates for water lost through osmosis by pumping potassium ions (K^+) into the cell until the ionic concentration inside the cell matches the concentration outside.

Like *Halobacterium*, many other prokaryotes can tolerate extreme conditions. Examples include *Deinococcus radiodurans*, which can survive 3 million rads of radiation (3,000 times the dose fatal to humans), and *Picrophilus oshimae*, which can grow at a pH of 0.03 (acidic enough to dissolve metal). Other prokaryotes live in environments that are too cold or too hot for most other organisms, and some have even been found living in rocks 3.2 km (2 miles) below Earth's surface.

Prokaryotic species are also very well adapted to more "normal" habitats—the lands and waters in which most other species are found. Their ability to adapt to a broad range of habitats helps explain why prokaryotes are the most abundant organisms on Earth: The number of prokaryotes in a handful of fertile soil is greater than the number of people who have ever lived. In this chapter, we'll examine the adaptations, diversity, and enormous ecological impact of these tiny organisms.

CONCEPT 27.1

Structural and functional adaptations contribute to prokaryotic success

As you read in Chapter 25, the first organisms to inhabit Earth were likely prokaryotes. Throughout their long evolutionary history, prokaryotic populations have been (and continue to be) subjected to natural selection in all kinds of environments, resulting in their enormous diversity today.

We'll begin by describing prokaryotes. Most prokaryotes are unicellular, although the cells of some species remain attached to each other after cell division. Prokaryotic cells typically have diameters of 0.5–5 μm, much smaller than the

10–100 μm diameter of many eukaryotic cells. (One notable exception, *Thiomargarita namibiensis*, can be 750 μm across—bigger than the dot on this i.) Prokaryotic cells have a variety of shapes (Figure 27.2). Finally, although they are unicellular and small, prokaryotes are well organized, achieving all of an organism's life functions within a single cell.

(a) Spherical   (b) Rod-shaped   (c) Spiral

▲ **Figure 27.2 The most common shapes of prokaryotes.** **(a)** Cocci (singular, *coccus*) are spherical prokaryotes. They occur singly, in pairs (diplococci), in chains of many cells (streptococci), and in clusters resembling bunches of grapes (staphylococci). **(b)** Bacilli (singular, *bacillus*) are rod-shaped prokaryotes. They are usually solitary, but in some forms the rods are arranged in chains (streptobacilli). **(c)** Spiral prokaryotes include spirilla, which range from comma-like shapes to loose coils, and spirochetes (shown here), which are corkscrew-shaped (colorized SEMs).

Cell-Surface Structures

A key feature of nearly all prokaryotic cells is the cell wall, which maintains cell shape, protects the cell, and prevents it from bursting in a hypotonic environment (see Chapter 7). In a hypertonic environment, most prokaryotes lose water and shrink away from their wall (plasmolyze), like other walled cells. Such water losses can inhibit cell reproduction. Thus, salt can be used to preserve foods because it causes prokaryotes to lose water, preventing them from rapidly multiplying.

The cell walls of prokaryotes differ in structure from those of eukaryotes. In eukaryotes that have cell walls, such as plants and fungi, the walls are usually made of cellulose or chitin (see Chapter 5). In contrast, most bacterial cell walls contain **peptidoglycan**, a polymer composed of modified sugars cross-linked by short polypeptides. This molecular fabric encloses the entire bacterium and anchors other molecules that extend from its surface. Archaeal cell walls contain a variety of polysaccharides and proteins but lack peptidoglycan.

Using a technique called the **Gram stain**, developed by the nineteenth-century Danish physician Hans Christian Gram, scientists can classify many bacterial species into two groups based on differences in cell wall composition. Samples are first stained with crystal violet dye and iodine, then rinsed in alcohol, and finally stained with a red dye such as safranin. The structure of a bacterium's cell wall determines the staining response (Figure 27.3). **Gram-positive** bacteria have simpler walls with a relatively large amount of peptidoglycan. **Gram-negative** bacteria have less peptidoglycan and are structurally more complex, with an outer membrane that contains lipopolysaccharides (carbohydrates bonded to lipids).

▼ **Figure 27.3 Gram staining.**

(a) Gram-positive bacteria

Gram-positive bacteria
Cell wall { Peptidoglycan layer
Plasma membrane
10 μm

Gram-positive bacteria have a thick cell wall made of peptidoglycan, which traps the crystal violet in the cytoplasm. The alcohol rinse does not remove the crystal violet, which masks the red safranin dye.

(b) Gram-negative bacteria

Gram-negative bacteria
Carbohydrate portion of lipopolysaccharide
Cell wall { Outer membrane
Peptidoglycan layer
Plasma membrane

Gram-negative bacteria have a thinner layer of peptidoglycan, and it is located in a layer between the plasma membrane and an outer membrane. The crystal violet is easily rinsed from the cytoplasm, and the cell appears pink or red from the dye.

▲ Figure 27.4 **Capsule.** The polysaccharide capsule around this *Streptococcus* bacterium enables the prokaryote to attach to cells in the respiratory tract—in this colorized TEM, a tonsil cell.

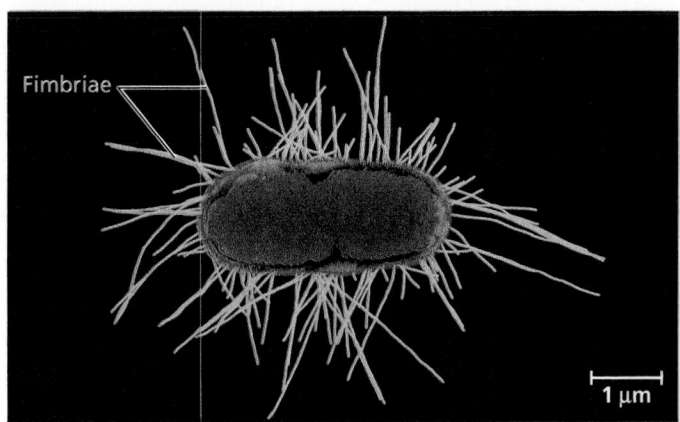

▲ Figure 27.5 **Fimbriae.** These numerous protein-containing appendages enable some prokaryotes to attach to surfaces or to other cells (colorized TEM).

Gram staining is a valuable tool in medicine for quickly determining if a patient's infection is due to gram-negative or to gram-positive bacteria. This information has treatment implications. The lipid portions of the lipopolysaccharides in the walls of many gram-negative bacteria are toxic, causing fever or shock. Furthermore, the outer membrane of a gram-negative bacterium helps protect it from the body's defenses. Gram-negative bacteria also tend to be more resistant than gram-positive species to antibiotics because the outer membrane impedes entry of the drugs. However, certain gram-positive species have virulent strains that are resistant to one or more antibiotics. (Figure 22.14 discusses one example: multidrug-resistant *Staphylococcus aureus*, which can cause lethal skin infections.)

The effectiveness of certain antibiotics, such as penicillin, derives from their inhibition of peptidoglycan cross-linking. The resulting cell wall may not be functional, particularly in gram-positive bacteria. Such drugs destroy many species of pathogenic bacteria without adversely affecting human cells, which do not have peptidoglycan.

The cell wall of many prokaryotes is surrounded by a sticky layer of polysaccharide or protein. This layer is called a **capsule** if it is dense and well-defined **(Figure 27.4)** or a *slime layer* if it is less well organized. Both kinds of sticky outer layers enable prokaryotes to adhere to their substrate or to other individuals in a colony. Some capsules and slime layers protect against dehydration, and some shield pathogenic prokaryotes from attacks by their host's immune system.

Some prokaryotes stick to their substrate or to one another by means of hairlike appendages called **fimbriae** (singular, *fimbria*) **(Figure 27.5)**. For example, the bacterium that causes gonorrhea, *Neisseria gonorrhoeae*, uses fimbriae to fasten itself to the mucous membranes of its host. Fimbriae are usually shorter and more numerous than **pili** (singular, *pilus*), appendages that pull two cells together prior to DNA transfer from one cell to the other (see Figure 27.12); pili are sometimes referred to as *sex pili*.

Motility

About half of all prokaryotes are capable of **taxis**, a directed movement toward or away from a stimulus (from the Greek *taxis*, to arrange). For example, prokaryotes that exhibit *chemotaxis* change their movement pattern in response to chemicals. They may move *toward* nutrients or oxygen (positive chemotaxis) or *away from* a toxic substance (negative chemotaxis). Some species can move at velocities exceeding 50 μm/sec—up to 50 times their body length per second. For perspective, consider that a person 1.7 m tall moving that fast would be running 306 km (190 miles) per hour!

Of the various structures that enable prokaryotes to move, the most common are flagella **(Figure 27.6)**. Flagella (singular, *flagellum*) may be scattered over the entire surface of the cell or concentrated at one or both ends. Prokaryotic flagella differ greatly from eukaryotic flagella: They are one-tenth the width and are not covered by an extension of the plasma membrane (see Figure 6.24). The flagella of prokaryotes are also very different in their molecular composition and their mechanism of propulsion. Among prokaryotes, bacterial and archaeal flagella are similar in size and rotation mechanism, but they are composed of different proteins. Overall, these structural and molecular comparisons suggest that the flagella of bacteria, archaea, and eukaryotes arose independently. Since the flagella of organisms in the three domains perform similar functions but probably are not related by common descent, it is likely that they are analogous, not homologous, structures.

Evolutionary Origins of Bacterial Flagella

The bacterial flagellum shown in Figure 27.6 has three main parts (the motor, hook, and filament) that are themselves composed of 42 different kinds of proteins. How could such a complex structure evolve? In fact, much evidence indicates that bacterial flagella originated as simpler structures that were modified in a stepwise fashion over time. As in the case of the

Two other proteins in the motor are homologous to proteins that function in ion transport. The proteins that comprise the rod, hook, and filament are all related to each other and are descended from an ancestral protein that formed a pilus-like tube. These findings suggest that the bacterial flagellum evolved as other proteins were added to an ancestral secretory system. This is an example of *exaptation*, the process in which existing structures take on new functions through descent with modification.

Internal Organization and DNA

The cells of prokaryotes are simpler than those of eukaryotes in both their internal structure and the physical arrangement of their DNA (see Figure 6.5). Prokaryotic cells lack the complex compartmentalization found in eukaryotic cells. However, some prokaryotic cells do have specialized membranes

▲ **Figure 27.6 A prokaryotic flagellum.** The motor of a prokaryotic flagellum consists of a system of rings embedded in the cell wall and plasma membrane (TEM). ATP-driven pumps in the motor transport protons out of the cell. The diffusion of protons back into the cell provides the force that turns a curved hook and thereby causes the attached filament to rotate and propel the cell. (This diagram shows flagellar structures characteristic of gram-negative bacteria.)

human eye (see Concept 25.6), biologists asked whether a less complex version of the flagellum could still benefit its owner. Analyses of hundreds of bacterial genomes indicate that only half of the flagellum's protein components appear to be necessary for it to function; the others are inessential or not encoded in the genomes of some species. Of the 21 proteins required by all species studied to date, 19 are modified versions of proteins that perform other tasks in bacteria. For example, a set of 10 proteins in the motor are homologous to 10 similar proteins in a secretory system found in bacteria. (A secretory system is a protein complex that enables a cell to secrete certain macromolecules.)

that perform metabolic functions (**Figure 27.7**). These membranes are usually infoldings of the plasma membrane.

The genome of a prokaryote is structurally different from a eukaryotic genome and in most cases has considerably less DNA. In the majority of prokaryotes, the genome consists of a circular chromosome with many fewer proteins than found in the linear chromosomes of eukaryotes (**Figure 27.8**). Also

(a) Aerobic prokaryote   **(b) Photosynthetic prokaryote**

▲ **Figure 27.7 Specialized membranes of prokaryotes.**
(a) Infoldings of the plasma membrane, reminiscent of the cristae of mitochondria, function in cellular respiration in some aerobic prokaryotes (TEM). **(b)** Photosynthetic prokaryotes called cyanobacteria have thylakoid membranes, much like those in chloroplasts (TEM).

▲ **Figure 27.8 A prokaryotic chromosome and plasmids.**
The thin, tangled loops surrounding this ruptured *E. coli* cell are parts of the cell's large, circular chromosome (colorized TEM). Three of the cell's plasmids, the much smaller rings of DNA, are also shown.

unlike eukaryotes, prokaryotes lack a membrane-bounded nucleus; their chromosome is located in the **nucleoid**, a region of cytoplasm that appears lighter than the surrounding cytoplasm in electron micrographs. In addition to its single chromosome, a typical prokaryotic cell may also have much smaller rings of independently replicating DNA molecules called **plasmids** (see Figure 27.8), most carrying only a few genes.

As explained in Chapters 16 and 17, DNA replication, transcription, and translation are fundamentally similar processes in prokaryotes and eukaryotes, although there are some differences. For example, prokaryotic ribosomes are slightly smaller than eukaryotic ribosomes and differ in their protein and RNA content. These differences allow certain antibiotics, such as erythromycin and tetracycline, to bind to ribosomes and block protein synthesis in prokaryotes but not in eukaryotes. As a result, people can use these antibiotics to kill or inhibit the growth of bacteria without harming themselves.

Reproduction and Adaptation

Prokaryotes are highly successful in part because of their potential to reproduce quickly in a favorable environment. By *binary fission* (see Figure 12.12), a single prokaryotic cell divides into 2 cells, which then divide into 4, 8, 16, and so on. Under optimal conditions, many prokaryotes can divide every 1–3 hours; some species can produce a new generation in only 20 minutes. If reproduction continued unchecked at this rate, a single prokaryotic cell could give rise to a colony outweighing Earth in only two days!

In reality, of course, prokaryotic reproduction is limited. The cells eventually exhaust their nutrient supply, poison themselves with metabolic wastes, face competition from other microorganisms, or are consumed by other organisms. For example, the well-studied bacterium *Escherichia coli* can divide every 20 minutes under ideal lab conditions, one reason it is used as a model organism in research. However, when growing in a human intestine, one of its natural environments, *E. coli* cells divide only once every 12–24 hours. But whether cell division occurs every 20 minutes or every few days, reproduction in prokaryotes draws attention to three key features of their biology: *They are small, they reproduce by binary fission, and they have short generation times.* As a result, prokaryotic populations can consist of many trillions of individuals—far more than populations of multicellular eukaryotes, such as plants and animals.

The ability of some prokaryotes to withstand harsh conditions also contributes to their success. Some, like *Halobacterium*, can survive in harsh environments because of particular biochemical adaptations; others, because of particular structural adaptations. Certain bacteria, for example, develop resistant cells called **endospores** when they lack an essential nutrient (Figure 27.9). The original cell produces a copy of its chromosome and surrounds it with a tough multilayered structure,

▲ **Figure 27.9 An endospore.** *Bacillus anthracis*, the bacterium that causes the disease anthrax, produces endospores (TEM). An endospore's protective, multilayered coat helps it survive in the soil for years.

forming the endospore. Water is removed from the endospore, and its metabolism halts. The original cell then lyses, releasing the endospore. Most endospores are so durable that they can survive in boiling water; killing them requires heating lab equipment to 121°C under high pressure. In less hostile environments, endospores can remain dormant but viable for centuries, able to rehydrate and resume metabolism when their environment improves.

Finally, in part because of their short generation times, prokaryotic populations can evolve substantially in short periods of time. For example, in a remarkable study that spanned 20,000 generations (roughly eight years) of evolution, researchers at Michigan State University documented adaptive evolution in bacterial populations (Figure 27.10). The ability of prokaryotes to adapt rapidly to new conditions highlights the point that although the structure of their cells is simpler than that of eukaryotic cells, prokaryotes are not "primitive" or "inferior" in an evolutionary sense. They are, in fact, highly evolved: For over 3.5 billion years, prokaryotic populations have responded successfully to many different types of environmental challenges. As we will see, one reason for this is that their populations harbor high levels of genetic diversity on which selection can act.

CONCEPT CHECK 27.1

1. Identify and explain at least two adaptations that enable prokaryotes to survive in environments too harsh for other organisms.

2. Contrast the cellular and DNA structures of prokaryotes and eukaryotes.

3. **MAKE CONNECTIONS** Suggest a hypothesis to explain why the thylakoid membranes of chloroplasts resemble those of cyanobacteria. Refer to Figure 6.18 (p. 111) and Figure 26.21 (p. 552).

For suggested answers, see Appendix A.

INQUIRY

Can prokaryotes evolve rapidly in response to environmental change?

EXPERIMENT Vaughn Cooper and Richard Lenski, of Michigan State University, tested the ability of *E. coli* populations to adapt to a new environment. They established 12 populations, each founded by a single cell from an *E. coli* strain, and followed these populations for 20,000 generations (3,000 days). To maintain a continual supply of resources, each day the researchers performed a *serial transfer*: They transferred 0.1 mL of each population to a new tube containing 9.9 mL of fresh growth medium. The growth medium used throughout the experiment provided a challenging environment that contained only low levels of glucose and other resources needed for growth.

Daily serial transfer

0.1 mL
(population sample)

Old tube
(discarded
after
transfer)

New tube
(9.9 mL
growth
medium)

Samples were periodically removed from the 12 populations and grown in competition with the common ancestral strain in the experimental (low-glucose) environment.

RESULTS The fitness of the experimental populations, as measured by the rate at which each population grew, increased rapidly for the first 5,000 generations (two years) and more slowly for the next 15,000 generations. The graph below shows the averages for the 12 populations.

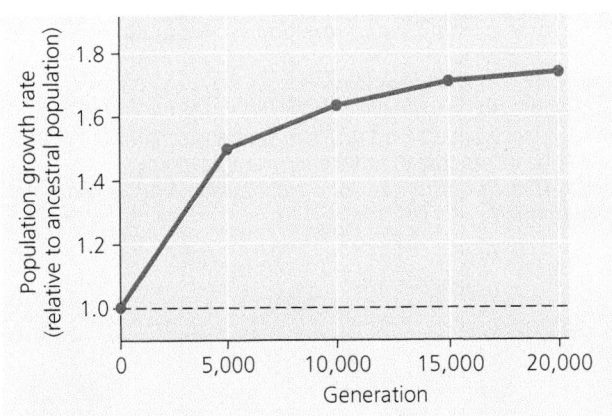

CONCLUSION Populations of *E. coli* continued to accumulate beneficial mutations for 20,000 generations, allowing rapid evolution of improved performance in their new environment.

SOURCE V. S. Cooper and R. E. Lenski, The population genetics of ecological specialization in evolving *Escherichia coli* populations, *Nature* 407:736–739 (2000).

WHAT IF? Suggest possible functions of the genes whose sequence or expression was altered as the experimental populations evolved in the low-glucose environment.

Rapid reproduction, mutation, and genetic recombination promote genetic diversity in prokaryotes

As we discussed in Unit Four, genetic variation is a prerequisite for natural selection to occur in a population. The diverse adaptations exhibited by prokaryotes suggest that their populations must have considerable genetic variation—and they do. For example, a ribosomal RNA gene can differ more between two strains of *E. coli* than it does between a human and a platypus. In this section, we'll examine three factors that give rise to high levels of genetic diversity in prokaryotes: rapid reproduction, mutation, and genetic recombination.

Rapid Reproduction and Mutation

In sexually reproducing species, the generation of a novel allele by a new mutation is rare for any particular gene. Instead, most of the genetic variation in sexual populations results from the way existing alleles are arranged in new combinations during meiosis and fertilization (see Chapter 13). Prokaryotes do not reproduce sexually, so at first glance their extensive genetic variation may seem puzzling. In fact, this variation can result from prokaryotes' rapid reproduction and mutation.

Consider a prokaryote reproducing by binary fission. After repeated rounds of division, most of the offspring cells are genetically identical to the original parent cell. However, if errors occur during DNA replication—such as insertions, deletions, or base-pair substitutions—some of the offspring cells may differ genetically. The probability of a spontaneous mutation occurring in a given *E. coli* gene averages only about one in 10 million (1×10^{-7}) per cell division. But among the 2×10^{10} new *E. coli* cells that arise each day in a person's intestine, there will be approximately $(2 \times 10^{10}) \times (1 \times 10^{-7}) = 2,000$ bacteria that have a mutation in that gene. The total number of mutations when all 4,300 *E. coli* genes are considered is about $4,300 \times 2,000 = 9$ million per day per human host.

The key point is that new mutations, though rare, can increase genetic diversity quickly in species with short generation times and large populations. This diversity, in turn, can lead to rapid evolution: Individuals that are genetically better equipped for their environment tend to survive and reproduce more prolifically than less fit individuals (see Figure 27.10).

Genetic Recombination

Although new mutations are a major source of variation in prokaryotic populations, additional diversity arises from *genetic recombination*, the combining of DNA from two sources. In eukaryotes, the sexual processes of meiosis and fertilization combine DNA from two individuals in a single zygote. But meiosis and fertilization do not occur in prokaryotes. Instead, three other mechanisms—transformation, transduction, and conjugation—can bring together prokaryotic DNA from different individuals (that is, cells). When the individuals are members of different species, this movement of genes from one organism to another is called *horizontal gene transfer*. Although scientists have found evidence that each of these mechanisms can transfer DNA within and between species in both domain Bacteria and domain Archaea, to date most of our knowledge comes from research on bacteria.

Transformation and Transduction

In **transformation**, the genotype and possibly phenotype of a prokaryotic cell are altered by the uptake of foreign DNA from its surroundings. For example, a harmless strain of *Streptococcus pneumoniae* can be transformed into pneumonia-causing cells if the cells are placed in a medium containing DNA from a pathogenic strain (see p. 306). This transformation occurs when a nonpathogenic cell takes up a piece of DNA carrying the allele for pathogenicity and replaces its own allele with the foreign allele, an exchange of homologous DNA segments. The cell is now a recombinant: Its chromosome contains DNA derived from two different cells.

For many years after transformation was discovered in laboratory cultures, most biologists thought the process to be too rare and haphazard to play an important role in natural bacterial populations. But researchers have since learned that many bacteria have cell-surface proteins that recognize DNA from closely related species and transport it into the cell. Once inside the cell, the foreign DNA can be incorporated into the genome by homologous DNA exchange.

In **transduction**, phages (from "bacteriophages," the viruses that infect bacteria) carry prokaryotic genes from one host cell to another. In most cases, transduction results from accidents that occur during the phage replicative cycle **(Figure 27.11)**. A virus that carries prokaryotic DNA may not be able to replicate because it lacks some or all of its own genetic material. However, the virus can attach to another prokaryotic cell (a recipient) and inject prokaryotic DNA acquired from the first cell (the donor). If some of this DNA is then incorporated into the recipient cell's chromosome by DNA recombination, a recombinant cell is formed.

Conjugation and Plasmids

In a process called **conjugation**, DNA is transferred between two prokaryotic cells (usually of the same species) that are temporarily joined. In bacteria, the DNA transfer is always one-way: One cell donates the DNA, and the other receives it. The best-understood mechanism is that used by *E. coli*, and we will focus on this organism for the rest of this section. In *E. coli*, a pilus of the donor cell attaches to the recipient **(Figure 27.12)**. The pilus then retracts, pulling the two cells together, much like a grappling hook. The next step is thought

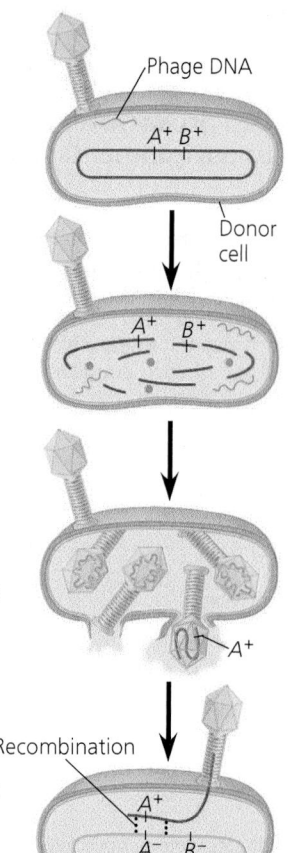

① A phage infects a bacterial cell that carries the A^+ and B^+ alleles on its chromosome (brown). This bacterium will be the "donor" cell.

② The phage DNA is replicated, and the cell makes many copies of the proteins encoded by its genes. Meanwhile, certain phage proteins halt the synthesis of proteins encoded by the host cell's DNA, and the host cell's DNA may be fragmented, as shown here.

③ As new phage particles assemble, a fragment of bacterial DNA carrying the A^+ allele happens to be packaged in a phage capsid.

④ The phage carrying the A^+ allele from the donor cell infects a recipient cell with alleles A^- and B^-. Recombination between donor DNA (brown) and recipient DNA (green) occurs at two places (dotted lines).

⑤ The genotype of the resulting recombinant cell (A^+B^-) differs from the genotypes of both the donor (A^+B^+) and the recipient (A^-B^-).

▲ **Figure 27.11 Transduction.** Phages may carry pieces of a bacterial chromosome from one cell (the donor) to another (the recipient). If recombination occurs after the transfer, genes from the donor may be incorporated into the recipient's genome.

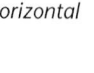 *Under what circumstances would transduction result in horizontal gene transfer?*

1 μm

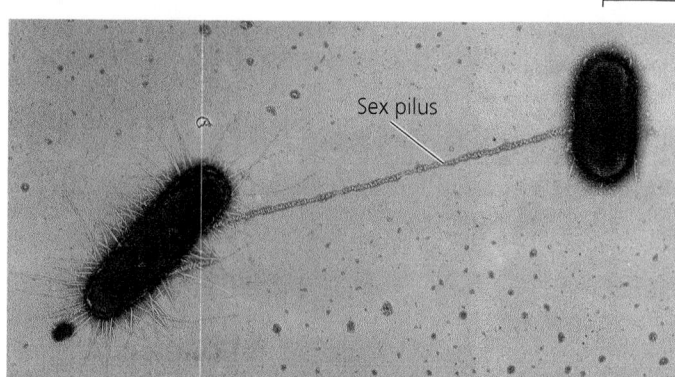

▲ **Figure 27.12 Bacterial conjugation.** The *E. coli* donor cell (left) extends a pilus that attaches to a recipient cell, a key first step in the transfer of DNA. The pilus is a flexible tube of protein subunits (TEM).

to be the formation of a temporary "mating bridge" between the two cells, through which the donor may transfer DNA to the recipient. This is an unsettled issue, however, and recent evidence indicates that DNA may pass directly through the pilus, which is hollow.

In either case, the ability to form pili and donate DNA during conjugation results from the presence of a particular piece of DNA called the **F factor** (F for *fertility*). The F factor of *E. coli* consists of about 25 genes, most required for the production of pili. The F factor can exist either as a plasmid or as a segment of DNA within the bacterial chromosome.

The F Factor as a Plasmid

The F factor in its plasmid form is called the **F plasmid**. Cells containing the F plasmid, designated F$^+$ cells, function as DNA donors during conjugation. Cells lacking the F factor, designated F$^-$, function as DNA re-

cipients during conjugation. The F$^+$ condition is transferable in the sense that an F$^+$ cell converts an F$^-$ cell to F$^+$ if a copy of the entire F$^+$ plasmid is transferred (**Figure 27.13a**).

The F Factor in the Chromosome

Chromosomal genes can be transferred during conjugation when the donor cell's F factor is integrated into the chromosome. A cell with the F factor built into its chromosome is called an *Hfr cell* (for *high frequency of recombination*). Like an F$^+$ cell, an Hfr cell functions as a donor during conjugation with an F$^-$ cell (**Figure 27.13b**). When chromosomal DNA from an Hfr cell enters an F$^-$ cell, homologous regions of the Hfr and F$^-$ chromosomes may align, allowing segments of their DNA to be exchanged. This results in the production of a recombinant bacterium that has genes derived from two different cells—a new genetic variant on which evolution can act.

① A cell carrying an F plasmid (an F$^+$ cell) forms a mating bridge with an F$^-$ cell. One strand of the plasmid's DNA breaks at the point marked by the arrowhead.

② Using the unbroken strand as a template, the cell synthesizes a new strand (light blue). Meanwhile, the broken strand peels off (red arrow), and one end enters the F$^-$ cell. There synthesis of its complementary strand begins.

③ DNA replication continues in both donor and recipient cells, as the transferred plasmid strand moves farther into the recipient cell.

④ Once DNA transfer and synthesis are completed, the plasmid in the recipient cell circularizes. Now both cells are F$^+$ cells.

(a) Conjugation and transfer of an F plasmid

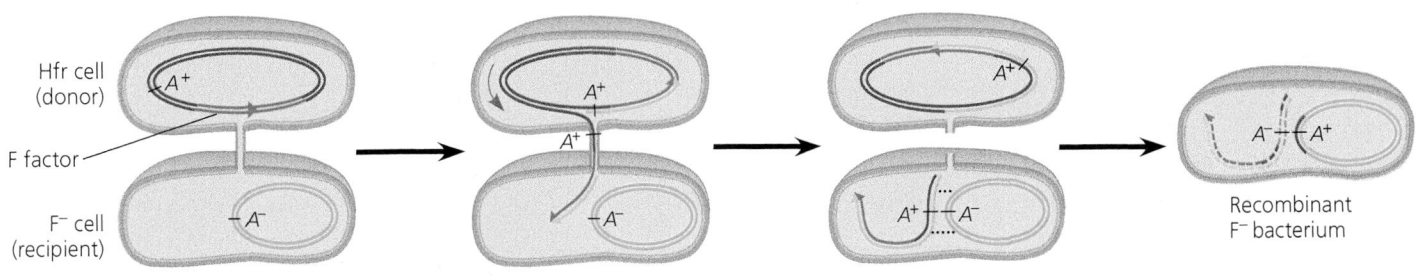

① In an Hfr cell, the F factor (dark blue) is integrated into the bacterial chromosome. Since an Hfr cell has all of the F-factor genes, it can form a mating bridge with an F$^-$ cell and transfer DNA.

② A single strand of the F factor breaks and begins to move through the bridge. DNA replication occurs in both donor and recipient cells, resulting in double-stranded DNA (daughter strands shown in lighter color).

③ The mating bridge usually breaks before the entire chromosome is transferred. DNA recombination (indicated by dotted lines) can result in the exchange of homologous genes between the transferred DNA (brown) and the recipient's chromosome (green).

④ Cellular enzymes degrade any linear DNA not incorporated into the chromosome. The recipient cell, with a new combination of genes but no F factor, is now a recombinant F$^-$ cell.

(b) Conjugation and transfer of part of an Hfr bacterial chromosome, resulting in recombination

▲ **Figure 27.13 Conjugation and recombination in *E. coli*.** The DNA replication that accompanies transfer of an F plasmid or part of an Hfr bacterial chromosome is called *rolling circle replication*. In effect, the intact circular parental DNA strand "rolls" as its other strand peels off and a new complementary strand is synthesized.

R Plasmids and Antibiotic Resistance During the 1950s in Japan, physicians started noticing that some hospital patients with bacterial dysentery, which produces severe diarrhea, did not respond to antibiotics that had generally been effective in the past. Apparently, resistance to these antibiotics had evolved in certain strains of *Shigella*, the bacterium that causes the disease.

Eventually, researchers began to identify the specific genes that confer antibiotic resistance in *Shigella* and other pathogenic bacteria. Sometimes, mutation in a chromosomal gene of the pathogen can confer resistance. For example, a mutation in one gene may make it less likely that the pathogen will transport a particular antibiotic into its cell. Mutation in a different gene may alter the intracellular target protein for an antibiotic molecule, reducing its inhibitory effect. In other cases, bacteria have "resistance genes," which code for enzymes that specifically destroy or otherwise hinder the effectiveness of certain antibiotics, such as tetracycline or ampicillin. Such resistance genes are carried by plasmids known as **R plasmids** (R for *resistance*).

Exposing a bacterial population to a specific antibiotic, whether in a laboratory culture or within a host organism, will kill antibiotic-sensitive bacteria but not those that happen to have R plasmids with genes that counter the antibiotic. Under these circumstances, we would predict that natural selection would cause the fraction of the bacterial population carrying genes for antibiotic resistance to increase, and that is exactly what happens. The medical consequences are also predictable: As you've read, resistant strains of pathogens are becoming more common, making the treatment of certain bacterial infections more difficult. The problem is compounded by the fact that many R plasmids, like F plasmids, have genes that encode pili and enable DNA transfer from one bacterial cell to another by conjugation. Making the problem still worse, some R plasmids carry as many as ten genes for resistance to that many antibiotics.

CONCEPT CHECK 27.2

1. What features of prokaryotes make it likely that considerable genetic variation will be added to their populations in each generation?
2. Distinguish between the three mechanisms of transferring DNA from one bacterial cell to another.
3. In a rapidly changing environment, which bacterial population would likely be more successful, one that includes individuals capable of conjugation or one that does not? Explain.
4. **WHAT IF?** If a nonpathogenic bacterium were to acquire resistance to antibiotics, could this strain pose a health risk to people? Explain. In general, how does DNA transfer among bacteria affect the spread of resistance genes?

For suggested answers, see Appendix A.

CONCEPT 27.3

Diverse nutritional and metabolic adaptations have evolved in prokaryotes

The extensive genetic variation found in prokaryotic populations is reflected in the diverse nutritional adaptations of prokaryotes. Like all organisms, prokaryotes can be categorized by how they obtain energy and the carbon used in building the organic molecules that make up cells. Every type of nutrition observed in eukaryotes is represented among prokaryotes, along with some nutritional modes unique to prokaryotes. In fact, prokaryotes have an astounding range of metabolic adaptations, much broader than that found in eukaryotes.

Organisms that obtain energy from light are called *phototrophs*, and those that obtain energy from chemicals are called *chemotrophs*. Organisms that need only CO_2 in some form as a carbon source are called *autotrophs*. In contrast, *heterotrophs* require at least one organic nutrient, such as glucose, to make other organic compounds. Combining possible energy sources and carbon sources results in four major modes of nutrition, summarized in **Table 27.1**.

The Role of Oxygen in Metabolism

Prokaryotic metabolism also varies with respect to oxygen (O_2). **Obligate aerobes** must use O_2 for cellular respiration (see Chapter 9) and cannot grow without it. **Obligate anaerobes**, on the other hand, are poisoned by O_2. Some obligate anaerobes live exclusively by fermentation; others extract chemical energy by **anaerobic respiration**, in which substances other than O_2, such as nitrate ions (NO_3^-) or sulfate ions (SO_4^{2-}), accept electrons at the "downhill" end of electron transport chains. **Facultative anaerobes** use O_2 if it is present but can also carry out fermentation or anaerobic respiration in an anaerobic environment.

Nitrogen Metabolism

Nitrogen is essential for the production of amino acids and nucleic acids in all organisms. Whereas eukaryotes can obtain nitrogen from only a limited group of nitrogen compounds, prokaryotes can metabolize nitrogen in a wide variety of forms. For example, some cyanobacteria and some methanogens (a group of archaea) convert atmospheric nitrogen (N_2) to ammonia (NH_3), a process called **nitrogen fixation**. The cells can then incorporate this "fixed" nitrogen into amino acids and other organic molecules. In terms of their nutrition, nitrogen-fixing cyanobacteria are some of the most self-sufficient organisms, since they need only light, CO_2, N_2, water, and some minerals to grow.

Nitrogen fixation by prokaryotes has a large impact on other organisms. For example, nitrogen-fixing prokaryotes can increase the nitrogen available to plants, which cannot use

Table 27.1 Major Nutritional Modes

Mode	Energy Source	Carbon Source	Types of Organisms
AUTOTROPH			
Photoautotroph	Light	CO_2, HCO_3^-, or related compound	Photosynthetic prokaryotes (for example, cyanobacteria); plants; certain protists (for example, algae)
Chemoautotroph	Inorganic chemicals (such as H_2S, NH_3, or Fe^{2+})	CO_2, HCO_3^-, or related compound	Unique to certain prokaryotes (for example, *Sulfolobus*)
HETEROTROPH			
Photoheterotroph	Light	Organic compounds	Unique to certain aquatic and salt-loving prokaryotes (for example, *Rhodobacter*, *Chloroflexus*)
Chemoheterotroph	Organic compounds	Organic compounds	Many prokaryotes (for example, *Clostridium*) and protists; fungi; animals; some plants

atmospheric nitrogen but can use the nitrogen compounds that the prokaryotes produce from ammonia. Chapter 55 discusses this and other essential roles that prokaryotes play in the nitrogen cycles of ecosystems.

Metabolic Cooperation

Cooperation between prokaryotic cells allows them to use environmental resources they could not use as individual cells. In some cases, this cooperation takes place between specialized cells of a filament. For instance, the cyanobacterium *Anabaena* has genes that encode proteins for photosynthesis and for nitrogen fixation, but a single cell cannot carry out both processes at the same time. The reason is that photosynthesis produces O_2, which inactivates the enzymes involved in nitrogen fixation. Instead of living as isolated cells, *Anabaena* forms filamentous chains **(Figure 27.14)**. Most cells in a filament carry out only photosynthesis, while a few specialized cells called **heterocysts** (sometimes called *heterocytes*) carry out only nitrogen fixation. Each heterocyst is surrounded by a thickened cell wall that restricts entry of O_2 produced by neighboring photosynthetic cells. Intercellular connections allow heterocysts to transport fixed nitrogen to neighboring cells and to receive carbohydrates.

Metabolic cooperation between different prokaryotic species often occurs in surface-coating colonies known as **biofilms**. Cells in a biofilm secrete signaling molecules that recruit nearby cells, causing the colonies to grow. The cells also produce polysaccharides and proteins that stick the cells to the substrate and to one another. Channels in the biofilm allow nutrients to reach cells in the interior and wastes to be expelled. Biofilms are common in nature, but they can cause problems by contaminating industrial products and medical equipment and contributing to tooth decay and more serious health problems. Altogether, damage caused by biofilms costs billions of dollars annually.

In another example of cooperation between prokaryotes, sulfate-consuming bacteria coexist with methane-consuming archaea in ball-shaped aggregates on the ocean floor. The bacteria appear to use the archaea's waste products, such as organic compounds and hydrogen. In turn, the bacteria produce sulfur compounds that the archaea use as oxidizing agents when they consume methane in the absence of oxygen. This partnership has global ramifications: Each year, these archaea consume an estimated 300 billion kilograms of methane, a major contributor to the greenhouse effect (see Chapter 55).

CONCEPT CHECK 27.3

1. Distinguish between the four major modes of nutrition, noting which are unique to prokaryotes.
2. A bacterium requires only the amino acid methionine as an organic nutrient and lives in lightless caves. What mode of nutrition does it employ? Explain.
3. **WHAT IF?** Describe what you might eat for a typical meal if humans, like cyanobacteria, could fix nitrogen.

For suggested answers, see Appendix A.

CONCEPT 27.4
Molecular systematics is illuminating prokaryotic phylogeny

Until the late 20th century, systematists based prokaryotic taxonomy on phenotypic criteria such as shape, motility, nutritional mode, and response to Gram staining. These criteria are still valuable in certain contexts, such as the rapid identification of pathogenic bacteria cultured from a patient's blood. But

▲ Figure 27.14 **Metabolic cooperation in a prokaryote.** In the filamentous cyanobacterium *Anabaena*, cells called heterocysts fix nitrogen, while the other cells carry out photosynthesis (LM). *Anabaena* is found in many freshwater lakes.

when it comes to prokaryotic phylogeny, comparing these characteristics does not reveal a clear evolutionary history. Applying molecular systematics to the investigation of prokaryotic phylogeny, however, has led to some dramatic conclusions.

Lessons from Molecular Systematics

As discussed in Chapter 26, microbiologists began comparing the sequences of prokaryotic genes in the 1970s. Using small-subunit ribosomal RNA as a marker for evolutionary relationships, Carl Woese and his colleagues concluded that many prokaryotes once classified as bacteria are actually more closely related to eukaryotes and belong in a domain of their own: Archaea. Microbiologists have since analyzed larger amounts of genetic data—including hundreds of entire genomes—and have concluded that a few traditional taxonomic groups, such as cyanobacteria, do appear to be monophyletic. However, other groups, such as gram-negative bacteria, are scattered throughout several lineages. **Figure 27.15** shows one phylogenetic hypothesis for some of the major taxa of prokaryotes based on molecular systematics.

One lesson from studying prokaryotic phylogeny is that the genetic diversity of prokaryotes is immense. When researchers began to sequence the genes of prokaryotes, they could investigate only the small fraction of species that could be cultured in the laboratory. In the 1980s, researchers began using the polymerase chain reaction (PCR; see Chapter 20) to analyze the genes of prokaryotes collected from the environment (such as from soil or water samples). Such "genetic prospecting" is now widely used; in fact, today entire prokaryotic genomes can be obtained from environmental samples using *metagenomics* (see Chapter 21). Each year these techniques add new branches to the tree of life. While only about 7,800 prokaryotic species have been assigned scientific names, a single handful of soil could contain 10,000 prokaryotic species by some estimates. Taking full stock of this diversity will require many years of research.

Another important lesson from molecular systematics is the apparent significance of horizontal gene transfer in the evolution of prokaryotes. Over hundreds of millions of years, prokaryotes have acquired genes from even distantly related species, and they continue to do so today. As a result, significant portions of the genomes of many prokaryotes are actually mosaics of genes imported from other species. As we saw in Chapter 26, such gene transfers can make it difficult to determine the root of the tree of life. Still, it is clear that for billions of years, the prokaryotes have evolved in two separate lineages, the archaea and the bacteria (see Figure 27.15).

Archaea

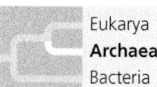

Archaea share certain traits with bacteria and other traits with eukaryotes **(Table 27.2)**. However, archaea also have many unique characteristics, as we would expect in a taxon that has followed a separate evolutionary path for so long.

▲ **Figure 27.15 A simplified phylogeny of prokaryotes.** This phylogenetic tree based on molecular data shows one of several debated hypotheses of the relationships between the major prokaryotic groups discussed in this chapter. Within Archaea, the placement of the korarchaeotes and nanoarchaeotes remains unclear.

Table 27.2 A Comparison of the Three Domains of Life

CHARACTERISTIC	DOMAIN		
	Bacteria	**Archaea**	**Eukarya**
Nuclear envelope	Absent	Absent	Present
Membrane-enclosed organelles	Absent	Absent	Present
Peptidoglycan in cell wall	Present	Absent	Absent
Membrane lipids	Unbranched hydrocarbons	Some branched hydrocarbons	Unbranched hydrocarbons
RNA polymerase	One kind	Several kinds	Several kinds
Initiator amino acid for protein synthesis	Formyl-methionine	Methionine	Methionine
Introns in genes	Very rare	Present in some genes	Present in many genes
Response to the antibiotics streptomycin and chloramphenicol	Growth inhibited	Growth not inhibited	Growth not inhibited
Histones associated with DNA	Absent	Present in some species	Present
Circular chromosome	Present	Present	Absent
Growth at temperatures > 100°C	No	Some species	No

The first prokaryotes assigned to domain Archaea live in environments so extreme that few other organisms can survive there. Such organisms are called **extremophiles**, meaning "lovers" of extreme conditions (from the Greek *philos*, lover), and include extreme halophiles and extreme thermophiles.

Extreme halophiles (from the Greek *halo*, salt) live in highly saline environments, such as the Great Salt Lake and the Dead Sea (see Figure 27.1). Some species merely tolerate salinity, while others require an environment that is several times saltier than seawater (which has a salinity of 3.5%). For example, the proteins and cell wall of *Halobacterium* have unusual features that improve function in extremely salty environments but render these organisms incapable of survival if the salinity drops below 9%.

Extreme thermophiles (from the Greek *thermos*, hot) thrive in very hot environments (Figure 27.16). For example, archaea in the genus *Sulfolobus* live in sulfur-rich volcanic springs as hot as 90°C. At temperatures this high, the cells of most organisms die because, for example, their DNA does not remain in a double helix and many of their proteins denature. *Sulfolobus* and other extreme thermophiles avoid this fate because their DNA and proteins have adaptations that make them stable at high temperatures. One extreme thermophile that lives near deep-sea hot springs called *hydrothermal vents* is informally known as "strain 121," since it can reproduce even at 121°C. Another extreme thermophile, *Pyrococcus furiosus*, is used in biotechnology as a source of DNA polymerase for the PCR technique (see Chapter 20).

Other archaea live in more moderate environments. Consider the **methanogens**, archaea that release methane as a by-product of their unique ways of obtaining energy. Many methanogens use CO_2 to oxidize H_2, a process that produces

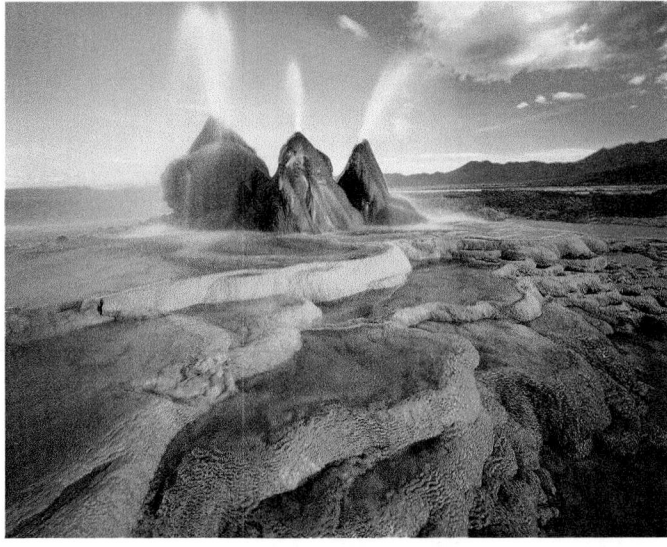

▲ **Figure 27.16 Extreme thermophiles.** Orange and yellow colonies of thermophilic prokaryotes grow in the hot water of a Nevada geyser.

MAKE CONNECTIONS *Review the discussion of enzymes in Concept 8.4 (pp. 155–156). How might the enzymes of thermophiles differ from those of other organisms?*

both energy and methane waste. Among the strictest of anaerobes, methanogens are poisoned by O_2. Although some methanogens live in extreme environments, such as under kilometers of ice in Greenland, others live in swamps and marshes where other microorganisms have consumed all the O_2. The "marsh gas" found in such environments is the methane released by these archaea. Other species of methanogens inhabit the anaerobic environment within the guts of cattle, termites, and other herbivores, playing an essential role in the nutrition of these animals. Methanogens also have an important application as decomposers in sewage treatment facilities.

Many extreme halophiles and all known methanogens are archaea in the clade Euryarchaeota (from the Greek *eurys*, broad, a reference to the habitat range of these prokaryotes). The euryarchaeotes also include some extreme thermophiles, though most thermophilic species belong to a second clade, Crenarchaeota (*cren* means "spring," such as a hydrothermal spring). Recently, genetic prospecting has revealed many species of euryarchaeotes and crenarchaeotes that are not extremophiles. These archaea exist in habitats ranging from farm soils to lake sediments to the surface waters of the open ocean.

New findings continue to update the picture of archaeal phylogeny. In 1996, researchers sampling a hot spring in Yellowstone National Park discovered archaea that do not appear to belong to either Euryarchaeota or Crenarchaeota. They placed these archaea in a new clade, Korarchaeota (from the Greek *koron*, young man). In 2002, researchers exploring hydrothermal vents off the coast of Iceland discovered archaeal cells only 0.4 µm in diameter attached to a much larger crenarchaeote. The genome of the smaller archaean is one of the smallest known of any organism, containing only 500,000 base pairs. Genetic analysis indicates that this prokaryote belongs to a fourth archaeal clade, Nanoarchaeota (from the Greek *nanos*, dwarf). Within a year after this clade was named, three other DNA sequences from nanoarchaeote species were isolated: one from Yellowstone's hot springs, one from hot springs in Siberia, and one from a hydrothermal vent in the Pacific. As prospecting continues, it seems likely that the tree in Figure 27.15 will undergo further changes.

Bacteria

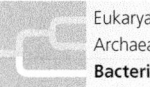

Eukarya
Archaea
Bacteria

Bacteria include the vast majority of prokaryotic species of which most people are aware, from the pathogenic species that cause strep throat and tuberculosis to the beneficial species used to make Swiss cheese and yogurt. Every major mode of nutrition and metabolism is represented among bacteria, and even a small taxonomic group of bacteria may contain species exhibiting many different nutritional modes. As we'll see, the diverse nutritional and metabolic capabilities of bacteria—and archaea—are behind the great impact of these tiny organisms on Earth and its life. Examine Figure 27.17, on the following two pages, for a closer look at several major groups of bacteria.

Exploring Major Groups of Bacteria

Proteobacteria

This large and diverse clade of gram-negative bacteria includes photo-autotrophs, chemoautotrophs, and heterotrophs. Some proteobacteria are anaerobic, while others are aerobic. Molecular systematists currently recognize five subgroups of proteobacteria; the phylogenetic tree at right shows their relationships based on molecular data.

Subgroup: Alpha Proteobacteria

Many of the species in this subgroup are closely associated with eukaryotic hosts. For example, *Rhizobium* species live in nodules within the roots of legumes (plants of the pea/bean family), where the bacteria convert atmospheric N_2 to compounds the host plant can use to make proteins. Species in the genus *Agrobacterium* produce tumors in plants; genetic engineers use these bacteria to carry foreign DNA into the genomes of crop plants (see Figure 20.26). As explained in Chapter 25, scientists hypothesize that mitochondria evolved from aerobic alpha proteobacteria through endosymbiosis.

Rhizobium (arrows) inside a root cell of a legume (TEM)

2.5 μm

Subgroup: Beta Proteobacteria

This nutritionally diverse subgroup includes *Nitrosomonas*, a genus of soil bacteria that play an important role in nitrogen recycling by oxidizing ammonium (NH_4^+), producing nitrite (NO_2^-) as a waste product.

Nitrosomonas (colorized TEM)

1 μm

Subgroup: Gamma Proteobacteria

This subgroup's autotrophic members include sulfur bacteria such as *Thiomargarita namibiensis* (see p. 557), which obtain energy by oxidizing H_2S, producing sulfur as a waste product (the small globules in the photograph at right). Some heterotrophic gamma proteobacteria are pathogens; for example, *Legionella* causes Legionnaires' disease, *Salmonella* is responsible for some cases of food poisoning, and *Vibrio cholerae* causes cholera. *Escherichia coli*, a common resident of the intestines of humans and other mammals, normally is not pathogenic.

Thiomargarita namibiensis containing sulfur wastes (LM)

200 μm

Subgroup: Delta Proteobacteria

This subgroup includes the slime-secreting myxobacteria. When the soil dries out or food is scarce, the cells congregate into a fruiting body that releases resistant "myxospores." These cells found new colonies in favorable environments. Another group of delta proteobacteria, the bdellovibrios, attack other bacteria, charging at up to 100 μm/sec (comparable to a human running 240 km/hr). The attack begins when a bdellovibrio attaches to specific molecules found on the outer covering of some bacterial species. The bdellovibrio then drills into its prey by using digestive enzymes and spinning at 100 revolutions per second.

Fruiting bodies of *Chondromyces crocatus*, a myxobacterium (SEM)

300 μm

Subgroup: Epsilon Proteobacteria

Most species in this subgroup are pathogenic to humans or other animals. Epsilon proteobacteria include *Campylobacter*, which causes blood poisoning and intestinal inflammation, and *Helicobacter pylori*, which causes stomach ulcers.

Helicobacter pylori (colorized TEM)

2 μm

Chlamydias

These parasites can survive only within animal cells, depending on their hosts for resources as basic as ATP. The gram-negative walls of chlamydias are unusual in that they lack peptidoglycan. One species, *Chlamydia trachomatis*, is the most common cause of blindness in the world and also causes nongonococcal urethritis, the most common sexually transmitted disease in the United States.

Chlamydia (arrows) inside an animal cell (colorized TEM)

2.5 µm

Spirochetes

These helical heterotrophs spiral through their environment by means of rotating, internal, flagellum-like filaments. Many spirochetes are free-living, but others are notorious pathogenic parasites: *Treponema pallidum* causes syphilis, and *Borrelia burgdorferi* causes Lyme disease (see Figure 27.20).

Leptospira, a spirochete (colorized TEM)

5 µm

Cyanobacteria

These photoautotrophs are the only prokaryotes with plantlike, oxygen-generating photosynthesis. (In fact, as we'll discuss in Chapter 28, chloroplasts likely evolved from an endosymbiotic cyanobacterium.) Both solitary and filamentous cyanobacteria are abundant components of freshwater and marine *phytoplankton*, the collection of photosynthetic organisms that drift near the water's surface. Some filaments have cells specialized for nitrogen fixation, the process that incorporates atmospheric N_2 into inorganic compounds that can be used in the synthesis of amino acids and other organic molecules (see Figure 27.14).

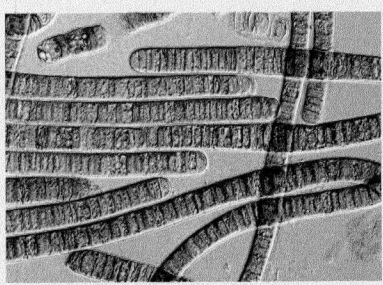

Oscillatoria, a filamentous cyanobacterium

40 µm

Gram-Positive Bacteria

Gram-positive bacteria rival the proteobacteria in diversity. Species in one subgroup, the actinomycetes (from the Greek *mykes*, fungus, for which these bacteria were once mistaken), form colonies containing branched chains of cells. Two species of actinomycetes cause tuberculosis and leprosy. However, most actinomycetes are free-living species that help decompose the organic matter in soil; their secretions are partly responsible for the "earthy" odor of rich soil. Soil-dwelling species in the genus *Streptomyces* (top) are cultured by pharmaceutical companies as a source of many antibiotics, including streptomycin.

Gram-positive bacteria include many solitary species, such as *Bacillus anthracis* (see Figure 27.9), which causes anthrax, and *Clostridium botulinum*, which causes botulism. The various species of *Staphylococcus* and *Streptococcus* are also gram-positive bacteria.

Mycoplasmas (bottom) are the only bacteria known to lack cell walls. They are also the tiniest known cells, with diameters as small as 0.1 µm, only about five times as large as a ribosome. Mycoplasmas have small genomes—*Mycoplasma genitalium* has only 517 genes, for example. Many mycoplasmas are free-living soil bacteria, but others are pathogens.

Streptomyces, the source of many antibiotics (SEM)

5 µm

Hundreds of mycoplasmas covering a human fibroblast cell (colorized SEM)

2 µm

CONCEPT 27.5

Prokaryotes play crucial roles in the biosphere

If humans were to disappear from the planet tomorrow, life on Earth would change for many species, but few would be driven to extinction. In contrast, prokaryotes are so important to the biosphere that if they were to disappear, the prospects of survival for many other species would be dim.

Chemical Recycling

The atoms that make up the organic molecules in all living things were at one time part of inorganic substances in the soil, air, and water. Sooner or later, those atoms will return there. Ecosystems depend on the continual recycling of chemical elements between the living and nonliving components of the environment, and prokaryotes play a major role in this process. For example, chemoheterotrophic prokaryotes function as **decomposers**, breaking down dead organisms as well as waste products and thereby unlocking supplies of carbon, nitrogen, and other elements. Without the actions of prokaryotes and other decomposers such as fungi, all life would cease. (See Chapter 55 for a detailed discussion of chemical cycles.)

Prokaryotes also convert some molecules to forms that can be taken up by other organisms. Cyanobacteria and other autotrophic prokaryotes use CO_2 to make organic compounds such as sugars, which are then passed up through food chains. Cyanobacteria also produce atmospheric O_2, and a variety of prokaryotes fix atmospheric nitrogen (N_2) into forms that other organisms can use to make the building blocks of proteins and nucleic acids. Under some conditions, prokaryotes can increase the availability of nutrients that plants require for growth, such as nitrogen, phosphorus, and potassium (Figure 27.18). Prokaryotes can also *decrease* the availability of key plant nutrients; this occurs when prokaryotes "immobilize" nutrients by using them to synthesize molecules that remain within their cells. Thus, prokaryotes can have complex effects on soil nutrient concentrations. In marine environments, a 2005 study found that an archaean from the clade Crenarchaeota can perform nitrification, a key step in the nitrogen

▲ Figure 27.18 Impact of bacteria on soil nutrient availability. Pine seedlings grown in sterile soils to which one of three strains of the bacterium *Burkholderia glathei* had been added absorbed more potassium (K) than did seedlings grown in soil without any bacteria. Other results (not shown) demonstrated that strain 3 increased the amount of K released from mineral crystals to the soil.

WHAT IF? *Estimate the average uptake of K for seedlings in soils with bacteria. What would you expect this average to be if bacteria had no effect on nutrient availability?*

cycle (see Figure 55.14). Crenarchaeotes dominate the oceans by numbers, comprising an estimated 10^{28} cells. The sheer abundance of these organisms suggests that they may have a large impact on the global nitrogen cycle; scientists are investigating this possibility.

Ecological Interactions

Prokaryotes play a central role in many ecological interactions. Consider **symbiosis** (from a Greek word meaning "living together"), an ecological relationship in which two species live in close contact with each other. Prokaryotes often form symbiotic associations with much larger organisms. In general, the larger organism in a symbiotic relationship is known as the **host**, and the smaller is known as the **symbiont**. There are many cases in which a prokaryote and its host participate in **mutualism**, an ecological interaction between two species in which both benefit (Figure 27.19). Other interactions take the form of **commensalism**, an ecological relationship in which one species benefits while the other is not harmed or helped in any significant way. For example, more than 150 bacterial species live on the surface of your body, covering portions of your skin with up to 10 million cells per square centimeter. Some of these species are commensalists: You provide them with food, such as the oils that exude from your pores, and a place to live, while they do not harm or benefit you. Finally, some prokaryotes engage in **parasitism**, an ecological relationship in which a **parasite** eats the cell contents, tissues, or body fluids of its host; as a group, parasites harm but usually do not kill their host, at least not immediately (unlike a predator). Parasites that cause disease are known as **pathogens**, many of which are prokaryotic.

▲ **Figure 27.19 Mutualism: bacterial "headlights."** The glowing oval below the eye of the flashlight fish (*Photoblepharon palpebratus*) is an organ harboring bioluminescent bacteria. The fish uses the light to attract prey and to signal potential mates. The bacteria receive nutrients from the fish.

(We'll discuss mutualism, commensalism, and parasitism in greater detail in Chapter 54.)

The very existence of an ecosystem can depend on prokaryotes. For example, consider the diverse ecological communities found at hydrothermal vents. These communities are densely populated by many different kinds of animals, including worms, clams, crabs, and fishes. But since sunlight does not penetrate to the deep ocean floor, the community does not include photosynthetic organisms. Instead, the energy that supports the community is derived from the metabolic activities of chemoautotrophic bacteria. These bacteria harvest chemical energy from compounds such as hydrogen sulfide (H_2S) that are released from the vent. An active hydrothermal vent may support hundreds of eukaryotic species, but when the vent stops releasing chemicals, the chemoautotrophic bacteria cannot survive. As a result, the entire vent community collapses.

CONCEPT CHECK 27.5

1. Explain how prokaryotes, though small, can be considered giants in their collective impact on Earth and its life.
2. **MAKE CONNECTIONS** After reviewing photosynthesis in Figure 10.6 (p. 188), summarize the main steps by which cyanobacteria produce O_2 and use CO_2 to make organic compounds.

For suggested answers, see Appendix A.

CONCEPT 27.6

Prokaryotes have both beneficial and harmful impacts on humans

Though the best-known prokaryotes tend to be the bacteria that cause illness in humans, these pathogens represent only a small fraction of prokaryotic species. Many other prokaryotes have positive interactions with humans, and some play essential roles in agriculture and industry.

Mutualistic Bacteria

As is true for many other eukaryotes, human well-being can depend on mutualistic prokaryotes. For example, our intestines are home to an estimated 500–1,000 species of bacteria; their cells outnumber all human cells in the body by a factor of ten. Different species live in different portions of the intestines, and they vary in their ability to process different foods. Many of these species are mutualists, digesting food that our own intestines cannot break down. In 2003, scientists published the first complete genome of one of these gut mutualists, *Bacteroides thetaiotaomicron*. The genome includes a large array of genes involved in synthesizing carbohydrates, vitamins, and other nutrients needed by humans. Signals from the bacterium activate human genes that build the network of intestinal blood vessels necessary to absorb nutrient molecules. Other signals induce human cells to produce antimicrobial compounds to which *B. thetaiotaomicron* is not susceptible. This action may reduce the population sizes of other, competing species, thus potentially benefiting both *B. thetaiotaomicron* and its human host.

Pathogenic Bacteria

All the pathogenic prokaryotes known to date are bacteria, and they deserve their negative reputation. Bacteria cause about half of all human diseases. Roughly 2 million people die each year of the lung disease tuberculosis, caused by *Mycobacterium tuberculosis*. And another 2 million people die each year from diarrheal diseases caused by various bacteria.

Some bacterial diseases are transmitted by other species, such as fleas or ticks. In the United States, the most widespread pest-carried disease is Lyme disease, which infects 15,000 to 20,000 people each year (**Figure 27.20**). Caused by a bacterium carried by ticks that live on deer and field mice,

▲ **Figure 27.20 Lyme disease.** Ticks in the genus *Ixodes* spread the disease by transmitting the spirochete *Borrelia burgdorferi* (colorized SEM). A rash may develop at the site of the tick's bite; the rash may be large and ring-shaped (as shown) or much less distinctive.

Lyme disease can result in debilitating arthritis, heart disease, nervous disorders, and death if untreated.

Pathogenic prokaryotes usually cause illness by producing poisons, which are classified as exotoxins or endotoxins. **Exotoxins** are proteins secreted by certain bacteria and other organisms. Cholera, a dangerous diarrheal disease, is caused by an exotoxin secreted by the proteobacterium *Vibrio cholerae*. The exotoxin stimulates intestinal cells to release chloride ions into the gut, and water follows by osmosis. In another example, the potentially fatal disease botulism is caused by botulinum toxin, an exotoxin secreted by the gram-positive bacterium *Clostridium botulinum* as it ferments various foods, including improperly canned meat, seafood, and vegetables. Like other exotoxins, the botulinum toxin can produce disease even if the bacteria that manufacture it are not present. In one such case, eight people contracted botulism after eating salted fish that did not contain any *C. botulinum* bacteria, but did contain the botulinum toxin. Even though the bacterium was no longer present, at some point in the fish preparation process, the bacterium had been able to grow and secrete the toxin.

Endotoxins are lipopolysaccharide components of the outer membrane of gram-negative bacteria. In contrast to exotoxins, endotoxins are released only when the bacteria die and their cell walls break down. Endotoxin-producing bacteria include species in the genus *Salmonella*, such as *Salmonella typhi*, which causes typhoid fever. You might have heard of food poisoning caused by other *Salmonella* species that are frequently found in poultry.

Since the 19th century, improved sanitation systems in the industrialized world have greatly reduced the threat of pathogenic bacteria. Antibiotics have saved a great many lives and reduced the incidence of disease. However, resistance to antibiotics is currently evolving in many bacterial strains. As you read earlier, the rapid reproduction of bacteria enables cells carrying resistance genes to quickly give rise to large populations as a result of natural selection, and these genes can also spread to other species by horizontal gene transfer.

Horizontal gene transfer can also spread genes associated with virulence, turning normally harmless bacteria into potent pathogens. *E. coli*, for instance, is ordinarily a harmless symbiont in the human intestines, but pathogenic strains that cause bloody diarrhea have emerged. One of the most dangerous strains, called O157:H7, is a global threat; in the United States alone, there are 75,000 cases of O157:H7 infection per year, often from contaminated beef or produce. In 2001, scientists sequenced the genome of O157:H7 and compared it with the genome of a harmless strain of *E. coli* called K-12. They discovered that 1,387 out of the 5,416 genes in O157:H7 have no counterpart in K-12. Many of these 1,387 genes are found in chromosomal regions that include phage DNA. This result suggests that at least some of the 1,387 genes were incorporated into the genome of O157:H7 through phage-mediated horizontal gene transfer (transduction). Some of the genes found only in O157:H7 are associated with virulence, including genes that code for adhesive fimbriae that enable O157:H7 to attach itself to the intestinal wall and extract nutrients.

Pathogenic bacteria also pose a potential threat as weapons of bioterrorism. For example, endospores of *Bacillus anthracis* sent through the mail in 2001 caused 18 people to develop inhalation anthrax, which was fatal in 5 of the cases. Such scenarios have stimulated more research on pathogenic prokaryotic species in the hope of developing new vaccines and antibiotics.

Prokaryotes in Research and Technology

On a positive note, we reap many benefits from the metabolic capabilities of both bacteria and archaea. For example, humans have long used bacteria to convert milk to cheese and yogurt. In recent years, our greater understanding of prokaryotes has led to an explosion of new applications in biotechnology; two examples are the use of *E. coli* in gene cloning (see Figure 20.2) and the use of *Agrobacterium tumefaciens* in producing transgenic plants such as Golden Rice (see Figure 20.26 and p. 816).

Bacteria may soon figure prominently in a major industry: plastics. Globally, each year about 350 billion pounds of plastic are produced from petroleum and used to make toys, storage containers, soft drink bottles, and many other items. These products degrade slowly, creating environmental problems. Bacteria can now be used to make natural plastics **(Figure 27.21a)**. For example, some bacteria synthesize a type of polymer known as PHA (polyhydroxyalkanoate), which they use to store chemical energy. The PHA they produce can be extracted, formed into pellets, and used to make durable, biodegradable plastics.

▲ **Figure 27.21 Some applications of prokaryotes. (a)** These bacteria synthesize and store PHA, which can be extracted and used to make biodegradable plastic products. **(b)** Spraying fertilizers on an oil-soaked area stimulates growth of native bacteria that metabolize the oil, speeding the natural breakdown process up to fivefold. **(c)** Current research seeks to develop bacteria that produce ethanol (E-85) fuel efficiently from renewable plant products.

Another way to harness prokaryotes is in **bioremediation**, the use of organisms to remove pollutants from soil, air, or water. For example, anaerobic bacteria and archaea decompose the organic matter in sewage, converting it to material that can be used as landfill or fertilizer after chemical sterilization. Other bioremediation applications include cleaning up oil spills (Figure 27.21b) and precipitating radioactive material (such as uranium) out of groundwater.

Through genetic engineering, humans can now modify bacteria to produce vitamins, antibiotics, hormones, and other products (see Chapter 20). Researchers are seeking to reduce fossil fuel use by engineering bacteria that can produce ethanol from various forms of biomass, including agricultural waste, switchgrass, municipal waste (such as paper products that are not recycled), and corn (Figure 27.21c).

The usefulness of prokaryotes largely derives from their diverse forms of nutrition and metabolism. All this metabolic versatility evolved prior to the appearance of the structural novelties that heralded the evolution of eukaryotic organisms, to which we devote the remainder of this unit.

CONCEPT CHECK 27.6

1. Identify at least two ways that prokaryotes have affected you positively today.
2. A pathogenic bacterium's toxin causes symptoms that increase the bacterium's chance of spreading from host to host. Does this information indicate whether the poison is an exotoxin or endotoxin? Explain.
3. **WHAT IF?** How might a sudden and dramatic change in your diet affect the diversity of prokaryotic species that live in your digestive tract?

For suggested answers, see Appendix A.

27 CHAPTER REVIEW

SUMMARY OF KEY CONCEPTS

CONCEPT 27.1

Structural and functional adaptations contribute to prokaryotic success (pp. 556–561)

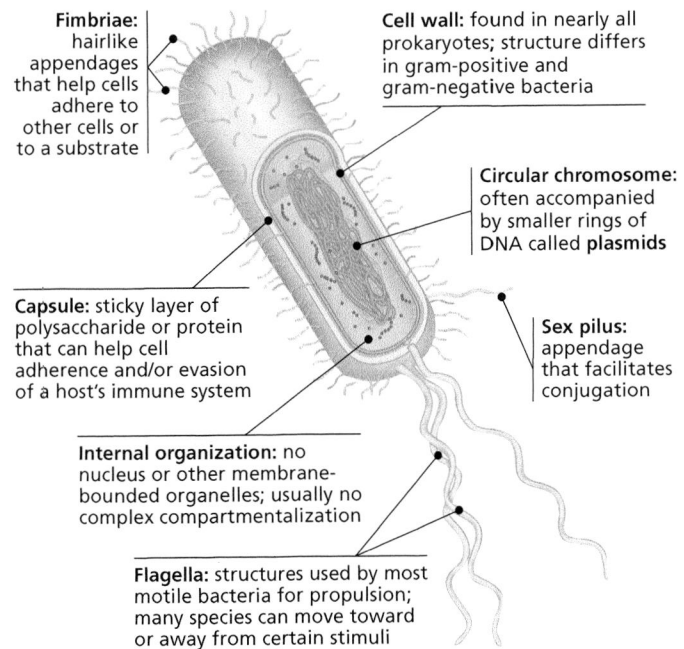

Fimbriae: hairlike appendages that help cells adhere to other cells or to a substrate

Cell wall: found in nearly all prokaryotes; structure differs in gram-positive and gram-negative bacteria

Circular chromosome: often accompanied by smaller rings of DNA called **plasmids**

Capsule: sticky layer of polysaccharide or protein that can help cell adherence and/or evasion of a host's immune system

Sex pilus: appendage that facilitates conjugation

Internal organization: no nucleus or other membrane-bounded organelles; usually no complex compartmentalization

Flagella: structures used by most motile bacteria for propulsion; many species can move toward or away from certain stimuli

- Prokaryotes can reproduce quickly by binary fission. Some form endospores, which can remain viable in harsh conditions for centuries. Prokaryotic populations can evolve in short periods of time in response to changing environmental conditions.

> *Describe features of prokaryotes that enable them to thrive in many different environments.*

CONCEPT 27.2

Rapid reproduction, mutation, and genetic recombination promote genetic diversity in prokaryotes (pp. 561–564)

- Because prokaryotes can often proliferate rapidly, mutations can quickly increase a population's genetic variation, making adaptive evolution possible.
- Genetic diversity in prokaryotes also can arise by recombination of the DNA from two different cells (via transformation, transduction, or conjugation). By transferring advantageous alleles, such as ones for antibiotic resistance, genetic recombination can promote adaptive evolution in prokaryotic populations.

> *Mutations are rare and prokaryotes reproduce asexually; yet their populations can have high genetic diversity. Explain how this can occur.*

CONCEPT 27.3

Diverse nutritional and metabolic adaptations have evolved in prokaryotes (pp. 564–565)

- Nutritional diversity is much greater in prokaryotes than in eukaryotes. As a group, prokaryotes perform all four modes of nutrition: **photoautotrophy, chemoautotrophy, photoheterotrophy,** and **chemoheterotrophy**.
- Among prokaryotes, **obligate aerobes** require O_2, **obligate anaerobes** are poisoned by O_2, and **facultative anaerobes** can survive with or without O_2.
- Unlike eukaryotes, prokaryotes can metabolize nitrogen in many different forms. Some can convert atmospheric nitrogen to ammonia, a process called **nitrogen fixation**.
- Prokaryotic cells and even species may cooperate metabolically. In *Anabaena*, photosynthetic cells and nitrogen-fixing cells exchange metabolic products. Metabolic cooperation also occurs in surface-coating **biofilms** that include different species.

> *Describe the range of prokaryotic metabolic adaptations.*

CONCEPT 27.4

Molecular systematics is illuminating prokaryotic phylogeny (pp. 565–570)

- Molecular systematics is leading to a phylogenetic classification of prokaryotes, allowing systematists to identify major new clades.
- Some archaea, such as extreme thermophiles and extreme halophiles, live in extreme environments. Other archaea live in moderate environments such as soils and lakes.
- Diverse nutritional types are scattered among the major groups of bacteria. The two largest groups are the proteobacteria and the gram-positive bacteria.

? *What impact have molecular data had on constructing prokaryotic phylogeny?*

CONCEPT 27.5

Prokaryotes play crucial roles in the biosphere (pp. 570–571)

- Decomposition by heterotrophic prokaryotes and the synthetic activities of autotrophic and nitrogen-fixing prokaryotes contribute to the recycling of elements in ecosystems.
- Many prokaryotes have a symbiotic relationship with a host; the relationships between prokaryotes and their hosts range from mutualism to commensalism to parasitism.

? *In what ways are prokaryotes key to the survival of many species?*

CONCEPT 27.6

Prokaryotes have both beneficial and harmful impacts on humans (pp. 571–573)

- Humans depend on mutualistic prokaryotes, including hundreds of species that live in our intestines and help digest food.
- Pathogenic bacteria typically cause disease by releasing **exotoxins** or **endotoxins** and are potential weapons of bioterrorism. Horizontal gene transfer can spread genes associated with virulence to harmless species or strains.
- Experiments with bacteria such as *E. coli* have led to important advances in DNA technology. Prokaryotes can be used in bioremediation, production of biodegradable plastics, and the synthesis of vitamins, antibiotics, and other products.

? *Describe beneficial and harmful impacts of prokaryotes on humans.*

TEST YOUR UNDERSTANDING

LEVEL 1: KNOWLEDGE/COMPREHENSION

1. Genetic variation in bacterial populations cannot result from
   a. transduction.
   b. transformation.
   c. conjugation.
   d. mutation.
   e. meiosis.

2. Photoautotrophs use
   a. light as an energy source and CO_2 as a carbon source.
   b. light as an energy source and methane as a carbon source.
   c. N_2 as an energy source and CO_2 as a carbon source.
   d. CO_2 as both an energy source and a carbon source.
   e. H_2S as an energy source and CO_2 as a carbon source.

3. Which of the following statements is *not* true?
   a. Archaea and bacteria have different membrane lipids.
   b. Both archaea and bacteria generally lack membrane-enclosed organelles.
   c. The cell walls of archaea lack peptidoglycan.
   d. Only bacteria have histones associated with DNA.
   e. Only some archaea use CO_2 to oxidize H_2, releasing methane.

4. Which of the following involves metabolic cooperation among prokaryotic cells?
   a. binary fission
   b. endospore formation
   c. endotoxin release
   d. biofilms
   e. photoautotrophy

5. Bacteria perform the following ecological roles. Which role typically does *not* involve symbiosis?
   a. skin commensalist
   b. decomposer
   c. aggregate with methane-consuming archaea
   d. gut mutualist
   e. pathogen

6. Plantlike photosynthesis that releases O_2 occurs in
   a. cyanobacteria.
   b. chlamydias.
   c. archaea.
   d. actinomycetes.
   e. chemoautotrophic bacteria.

LEVEL 2: APPLICATION/ANALYSIS

7. **EVOLUTION CONNECTION**

   In patients infected with nonresistant strains of the tuberculosis bacterium, antibiotics can relieve symptoms in a few weeks. However, it takes much longer to halt the infection, and patients may discontinue treatment while bacteria are still present. How might this result in the evolution of drug-resistant pathogens?

LEVEL 3: SYNTHESIS/EVALUATION

8. **SCIENTIFIC INQUIRY**

   DRAW IT The nitrogen-fixing bacterium *Rhizobium* infects the roots of some plant species, forming a mutualism in which the bacterium provides nitrogen, and the plant provides carbohydrates. Scientists measured the 12-week growth of one such plant species (*Acacia irrorata*) when infected by six different *Rhizobium* strains. (a) Graph the data. (b) Interpret your graph.

Rhizobium strain	1	2	3	4	5	6
Plant mass (g)	0.91	0.06	1.56	1.72	0.14	1.03

   Source: J. J. Burdon et al., Variation in the effectiveness of symbiotic associations between native rhizobia and temperate Australian *Acacia*: within species interactions, *Journal of Applied Ecology* 36:398–408 (1999).
   Note: Without *Rhizobium*, after 12 weeks, *Acacia* plants have a mass of about 0.1 g.

9. **WRITE ABOUT A THEME**

   Energy Transfer In a short essay (about 100–150 words), discuss how prokaryotes and other members of hydrothermal vent communities transfer and transform energy.

For selected answers, see Appendix A.

Mastering BIOLOGY   www.masteringbiology.com

1. MasteringBiology® Assignments

Make Connections Tutorial Bacterial Conjugation (Chapter 27) and Binary Fission (Chapter 12)
Tutorial Diversity in Bacteria
Activities Classification of Prokaryotes • The Tree of Life • Discovery Channel Videos: Bacteria; Antibiotics; Tasty Bacteria
Questions Student Misconceptions • Reading Quiz • Multiple Choice • End-of-Chapter

2. eText

Read your book online, search, take notes, highlight text, and more.

3. The Study Area

Practice Tests • Cumulative Test • *BioFlix* 3-D Animations • MP3 Tutor Sessions • Videos • Activities • Investigations • Lab Media • Audio Glossary • Word Study Tools • Art

28

Protists

▲ **Figure 28.1 Which of these organisms are prokaryotes and which are eukaryotes?**

EVOLUTION

KEY CONCEPTS

28.1 Most eukaryotes are single-celled organisms
28.2 Excavates include protists with modified mitochondria and protists with unique flagella
28.3 Chromalveolates may have originated by secondary endosymbiosis
28.4 Rhizarians are a diverse group of protists defined by DNA similarities
28.5 Red algae and green algae are the closest relatives of land plants
28.6 Unikonts include protists that are closely related to fungi and animals
28.7 Protists play key roles in ecological communities

Living Small

Knowing that most prokaryotes are extremely small organisms, you might assume that Figure 28.1 depicts six prokaryotes and one much larger eukaryote. But in fact, the only prokaryote is the organism immediately above the scale bar. The other six organisms are members of diverse, mostly unicellular groups of eukaryotes informally known as **protists**. Very small eukaryotes have intrigued scientists for more than 300 years, ever since the Dutch microscopist Antoni van Leeuwenhoek first laid eyes on them. As he discovered, viewing a drop of pond water under a light microscope can reveal a fascinating world of unicellular protists and prokaryotes. Some protists propel themselves with whipping flagella, while others creep along by means of blob-like appendages. Some are shaped like tiny trumpets; others resemble miniature jewelry. Recalling his observations, van Leeuwenhoek wrote, "No more pleasant sight has met my eye than this, of so many thousands of living creatures in one small drop of water."

Until recently, biologists thought that 300 years of observation had uncovered a representative sample of living protist species. But in the last decade, genetic prospecting has turned up a treasure trove of previously unknown protists within the world of microscopic life. Many of these newly discovered organisms are just 0.5–2 μm in diameter—as small as many prokaryotes.

The surprising discovery of many species of minuscule protists followed close on the heels of recent findings regarding protist phylogeny. All protists were once classified in a single kingdom, Protista, but advances in eukaryotic systematics have caused the kingdom to crumble. It has become clear that the kingdom Protista is in fact polyphyletic (see Figure 26.10): Some protists are more closely related to plants, fungi, or animals than they are to other protists. As a result, the kingdom Protista has been abandoned, and various lineages of protists are now recognized as kingdoms in their own right. Most biologists still use the term *protist*, but only as a convenient way to refer to eukaryotes that are not plants, animals, or fungi.

In this chapter, you will become acquainted with some of the most significant groups of protists. You will learn about their structural and biochemical adaptations as well as their enormous impact on ecosystems, agriculture, industry, and human health.

CONCEPT 28.1

Most eukaryotes are single-celled organisms

Protists, along with plants, animals, and fungi, are classified as eukaryotes; they are in domain Eukarya, one of the three domains of life. Unlike the cells of prokaryotes, eukaryotic cells have a nucleus and other membrane-bounded organelles, such as mitochondria and the Golgi apparatus. Such organelles provide specific locations in which particular cellular functions are accomplished, making the structure and organization of eukaryotic cells more complex than those of prokaryotic cells.

We'll survey the diversity of eukaryotes throughout the rest of this unit, beginning in this chapter with the protists. As you explore this material, bear in mind that

- the organisms in most eukaryotic lineages are protists, and
- most protists are unicellular.

Thus, life differs greatly from how most of us commonly think of it. The large, multicellular organisms that we know best (plants, animals, and fungi) are the tips of just a few branches on the great tree of life (see Figure 26.21).

Structural and Functional Diversity in Protists

Given the polyphyletic nature of the group once called Protista, it isn't surprising that few general characteristics of protists can be cited without exceptions. In fact, protists exhibit more structural and functional diversity than any other group of eukaryotes.

Most protists are unicellular, although there are some colonial and multicellular species. Single-celled protists are justifiably considered the simplest eukaryotes, but at the cellular level, many protists are very complex—the most elaborate of all cells. In multicellular organisms, essential biological functions are carried out by organs. Unicellular protists carry out the same essential functions, but they do so using subcellular organelles, not multicellular organs. The organelles that protists use are mostly those discussed in Chapter 6, including the nucleus, endoplasmic reticulum, Golgi apparatus, and lysosomes. Certain protists also rely on organelles not found in most other eukaryotic cells, such as contractile vacuoles that pump excess water from the protistan cell (see Figure 7.16).

Protists are more nutritionally diverse than other eukaryote groups. Some protists are photoautotrophs and contain chloroplasts. Some are heterotrophs, absorbing organic molecules or ingesting larger food particles. Still other protists, called **mixotrophs**, combine photosynthesis *and* heterotrophic nutrition. Photoautotrophy, heterotrophy, and mixotrophy have all arisen independently in many protist lineages.

Reproduction and life cycles also are highly varied among protists. Some protists are only known to reproduce asexually; others can also reproduce sexually or at least employ the sexual processes of meiosis and fertilization. All three basic types of sexual life cycles (see Figure 13.6) are represented among protists, along with some variations that do not quite fit any of these types. We will examine the life cycles of several protist groups later in this chapter.

Endosymbiosis in Eukaryotic Evolution

What gave rise to the enormous diversity of protists that exist today? There is abundant evidence that much of protist diversity has its origins in **endosymbiosis**, the process in which certain unicellular organisms engulf other cells, which become endosymbionts and ultimately organelles in the host cell. For example, as we discussed in Chapter 25, structural, biochemical, and DNA sequence data indicate that the first eukaryotes acquired mitochondria by engulfing an aerobic prokaryote (specifically, an alpha proteobacterium). The early origin of mitochondria is supported by the fact that all eukaryotes studied so far have either mitochondria or modified versions of them.

Much evidence also indicates that later in eukaryotic history, a lineage of heterotrophic eukaryotes acquired an additional endosymbiont—a photosynthetic cyanobacterium—that then evolved into plastids. As the hypothesis illustrated in Figure 28.2 shows, this plastid-bearing lineage gave rise to two lineages of photosynthetic protists, or **algae:** red algae and green algae. This hypothesis is supported by the observation that the DNA of plastid genes in red algae and green algae closely resembles the DNA of cyanobacteria. In addition, plastids in red algae and green algae are surrounded by two membranes. Transport proteins in these membranes are homologous to proteins in the inner and outer membranes of cyanobacterial endosymbionts, providing further support for the hypothesis.

On several occasions during eukaryotic evolution, red algae and green algae underwent **secondary endosymbiosis:** They were ingested in the food vacuoles of heterotrophic eukaryotes and became endosymbionts themselves. For example, protists known as chlorarachniophytes likely evolved when a heterotrophic eukaryote engulfed a green alga. Evidence for this process can be found within the engulfed cell, which contains a tiny vestigial nucleus, called a *nucleomorph*. Genes from the nucleomorph are still transcribed, and their DNA sequences indicate the engulfed cell was a green alga. Also consistent with the hypothesis that chlorarachniophytes evolved from a eukaryote that engulfed another eukaryote, their plastids are surrounded by *four* membranes. The two inner membranes originated as the inner and outer membranes of the ancient cyanobacterium. The third membrane is derived from the engulfed alga's plasma membrane, and the outermost membrane is derived from the heterotrophic eukaryote's food vacuole. In some other protists, plastids acquired by secondary endosymbiosis are surrounded by three membranes, indicating that one of the original four membranes was lost during the course of evolution.

Five Supergroups of Eukaryotes

Our understanding of the evolutionary history of protists has been in a state of flux in recent years. Not only has kingdom Protista been abandoned, but a variety of other hypotheses have been discarded as well. For example, in the early 1990s,

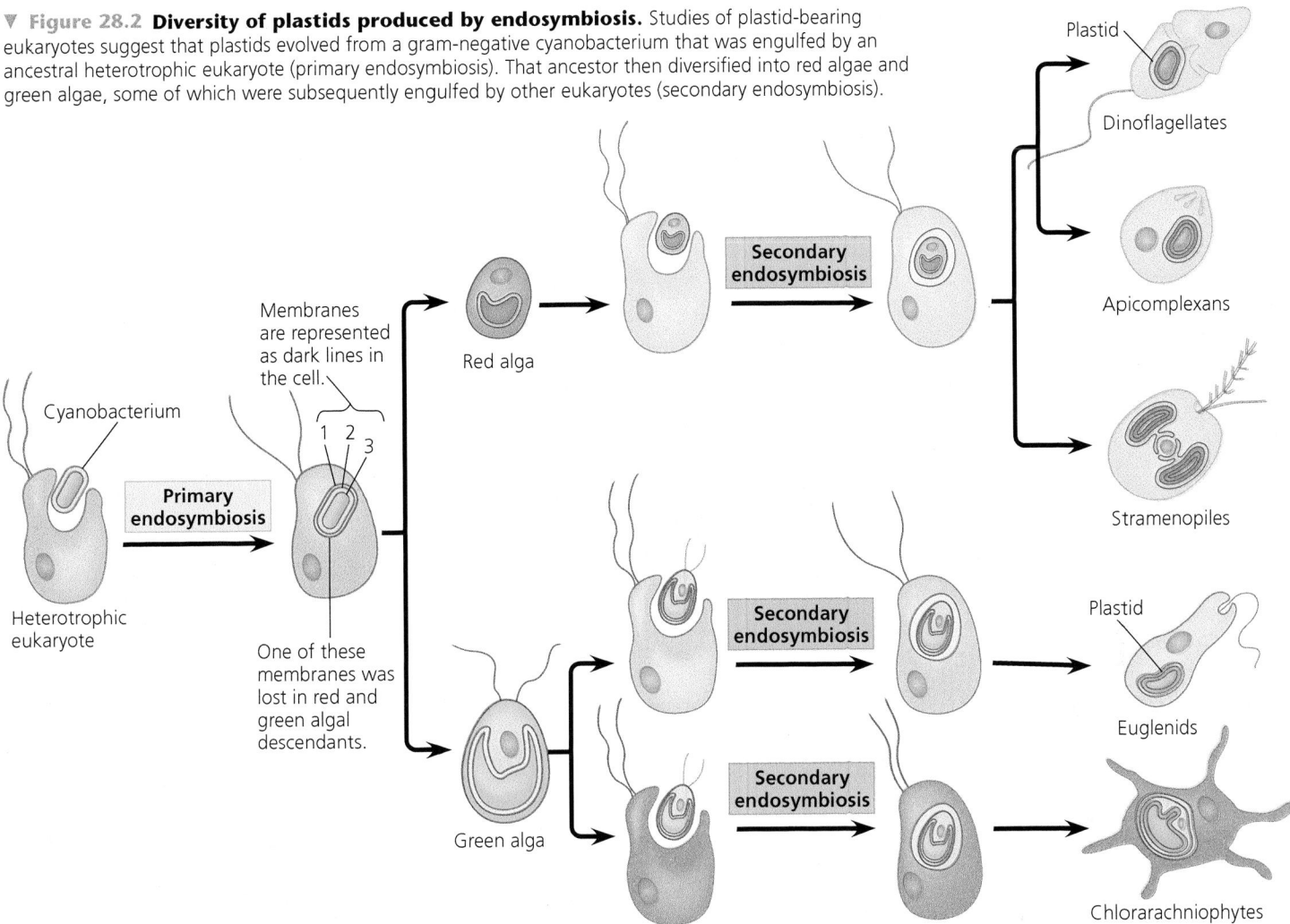

▼ **Figure 28.2** **Diversity of plastids produced by endosymbiosis.** Studies of plastid-bearing eukaryotes suggest that plastids evolved from a gram-negative cyanobacterium that was engulfed by an ancestral heterotrophic eukaryote (primary endosymbiosis). That ancestor then diversified into red algae and green algae, some of which were subsequently engulfed by other eukaryotes (secondary endosymbiosis).

Cyanobacterium

Heterotrophic eukaryote

Primary endosymbiosis

Membranes are represented as dark lines in the cell.

1 2 3

One of these membranes was lost in red and green algal descendants.

Red alga

Green alga

Secondary endosymbiosis

Secondary endosymbiosis

Secondary endosymbiosis

Plastid

Dinoflagellates

Apicomplexans

Stramenopiles

Plastid

Euglenids

Chlorarachniophytes

many biologists thought that the oldest lineage of living eukaryotes consisted of the *amitochondriate protists*, organisms without conventional mitochondria and with fewer membrane-bounded organelles than other protist groups. But recent structural and DNA data have undermined this hypothesis. Many of the so-called amitochondriate protists have been shown to have mitochondria—though reduced ones—and some of these organisms are now classified in entirely different groups. For example, microsporidians, once considered amitochondriate protists, are now classified as fungi.

The ongoing changes in our understanding of the phylogeny of protists pose challenges to students and instructors alike. Hypotheses about these relationships are a focus of scientific activity, changing rapidly as new data cause previous ideas to be modified or discarded. In this chapter, our discussion is organized around one current hypothesis: the five supergroups of eukaryotes shown in **Figure 28.3**, on the next two pages. Because the root of the eukaryotic tree is not known, all five supergroups are shown as diverging simultaneously from a common ancestor. We know that is not correct, but we do not know which organisms were the first to

diverge from the others. In addition, while some of the groups in Figure 28.3 are well supported by morphological and DNA data, others are more controversial. As you read this chapter, it may be helpful to focus less on the specific names of groups of organisms and more on why the organisms are important and how ongoing research is elucidating their evolutionary relationships.

CONCEPT CHECK 28.1

1. Cite at least four examples of structural and functional diversity among protists.
2. Summarize the role of endosymbiosis in eukaryotic evolution.
3. **WHAT IF?** After studying Figure 28.3, on the next two pages, draw a simplified version of the phylogenetic tree that shows only the five supergroups of eukaryotes. Now sketch how the tree would look if the unikonts were the first group of eukaryotes to diverge from other eukaryotes.

For suggested answers, see Appendix A.

Exploring Protistan Diversity

The tree below represents a phylogenetic hypothesis for the relationships among all the eukaryotes on Earth today. The eukaryotic groups at the branch tips are related in larger "supergroups," labeled vertically at the far right of the tree. The kingdoms Plantae (land plants), Fungi, and Animalia (animals) have survived from the five-kingdom system of classification. Groups that were formerly classified in the kingdom Protista are listed in beige boxes. Dotted lines indicate evolutionary relationships that are uncertain and proposed clades that are under active debate.

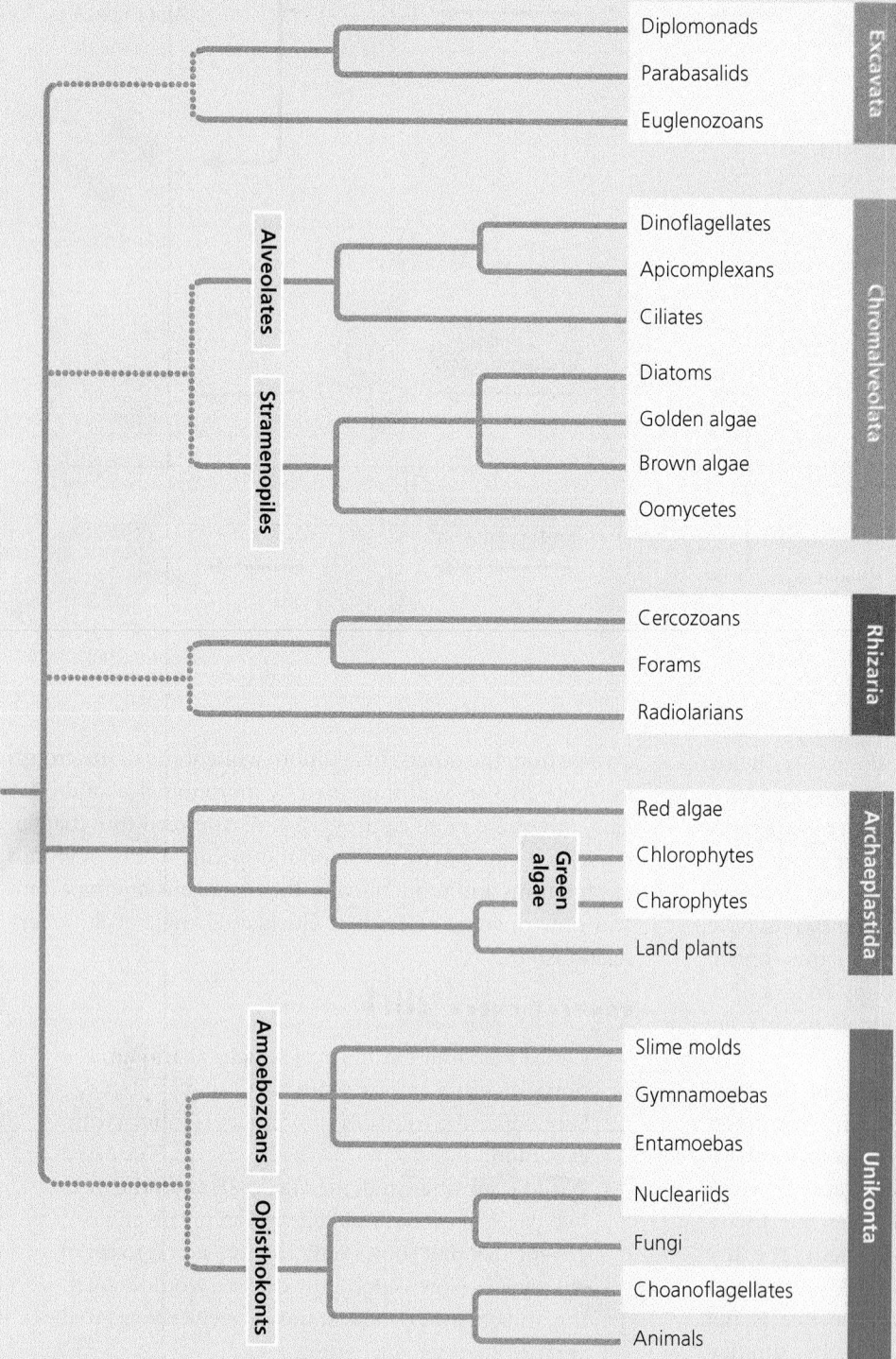

■ Excavata

Some members of this supergroup have an "excavated" groove on one side of the cell body. Two major clades (the parabasalids and diplomonads) have modified mitochondria; others (the euglenozoans) have flagella that differ in structure from those of other organisms. Excavates include parasites such as *Giardia*, as well as many predatory and photosynthetic species.

5 μm

Giardia intestinalis, **a diplomonad parasite.** This diplomonad (colorized SEM), which lacks the characteristic surface groove of the Excavata, can infect people when they drink water contaminated with feces containing *Giardia* cysts. Drinking such water—even from a seemingly pristine stream—can cause severe diarrhea. Boiling the water kills the parasite.

Chromalveolata

This group may have originated by an ancient secondary endosymbiosis event. Chromalveolates include some of the most important photosynthetic organisms on Earth, such as the diatoms shown here. The group also includes the brown algae that form underwater kelp "forests," as well as important pathogens, such as *Plasmodium*, which causes malaria, and *Phytophthora*, which caused the devastating potato famine in 19th-century Ireland.

50 μm

Diatom diversity. These beautiful single-celled protists are important photosynthetic organisms in aquatic communities (LM).

Rhizaria

This group contains many species of amoebas, most of which have pseudopodia that are threadlike in shape. Pseudopodia are extensions that can bulge from any portion of the cell; they are used in movement and in the capture of prey. Several recent molecular phylogenetic studies have suggested that Rhizaria should be nested within Chromalveolata; this hypothesis is currently being tested by other research groups.

100 μm

***Globigerina*, a foram in the supergroup Rhizaria.** Threadlike pseudopodia extend through pores in the shell, or *test* (LM). The inset SEM shows a foram test, which is hardened by calcium carbonate.

Archaeplastida

This group of eukaryotes includes red algae and green algae, along with land plants (kingdom Plantae, discussed in Chapters 29 and 30). Red algae and green algae include unicellular species, colonial species (such as the green alga *Volvox*), and multicellular species. Many of the large algae known informally as "seaweeds" are multicellular red or green algae. Protists in Archaeplastida include key photosynthetic species that form the base of the food web in some aquatic communities.

20 μm

50 μm

***Volvox*, a colonial freshwater green alga.** The colony is a hollow ball whose wall is composed of hundreds of biflagellated cells (see inset LM) embedded in a gelatinous matrix. The cells are usually connected by cytoplasmic strands; if isolated, these cells cannot reproduce. The large colonies seen here will eventually release the small "daughter" colonies within them (LM).

Unikonta

This group of eukaryotes includes amoebas that have lobe- or tube-shaped pseudopodia, as well as animals, fungi, and non-amoeba protists that are closely related to animals or fungi. According to one current hypothesis, the unikonts may have been the first group of eukaryotes to diverge from other eukaryotes (see Figure 28.23); however, this hypothesis has yet to be widely accepted.

A unikont amoeba. This amoeba (*Amoeba proteus*) is using its pseudopodia to move.

Excavates include protists with modified mitochondria and protists with unique flagella

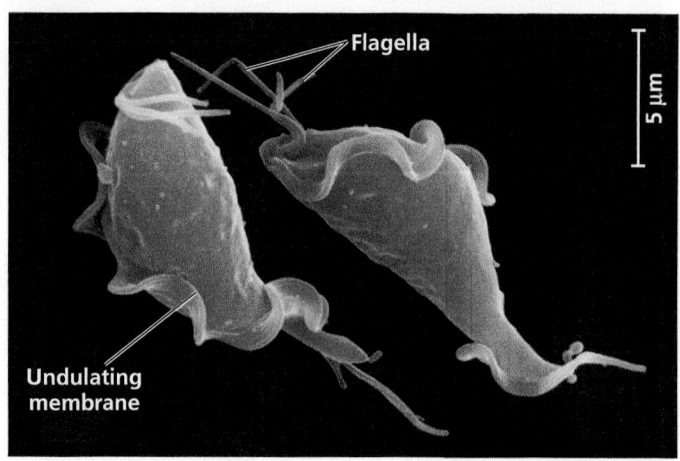

▲ Figure 28.4 **The parabasalid** *Trichomonas vaginalis* (colorized SEM).

Now that we have examined some of the broad patterns in eukaryotic evolution, we will look more closely at the five main groups of protists shown in Figure 28.3.

We begin this tour with **Excavata** (the excavates), a clade recently proposed based on morphological studies of the cytoskeleton. Some members of this diverse group also have an "excavated" feeding groove on one side of the cell body.

The excavates include the diplomonads, the parabasalids, and the euglenozoans. Molecular data indicate that each of these three groups is monophyletic, but the data have neither confirmed nor strongly refuted the monophyly of the excavate supergroup. Although many excavates share certain unique cytoskeletal features, we cannot yet tell whether that is because the excavates are monophyletic or because the common ancestor of eukaryotes had those features. Overall, support for the excavate clade is relatively weak, making it one of the more controversial of the five supergroups.

Diplomonads and Parabasalids

The protists in these two groups lack plastids and have modified mitochondria (until recently, they were thought to lack mitochondria altogether). Most diplomonads and parabasalids are found in anaerobic environments.

Diplomonads have modified mitochondria called *mitosomes*. These organelles lack functional electron transport chains and hence cannot use oxygen to help extract energy from carbohydrates and other organic molecules. Instead, diplomonads get the energy they need from anaerobic biochemical pathways.

Structurally, diplomonads have two equal-sized nuclei and multiple flagella. Recall that eukaryotic flagella are extensions of the cytoplasm, consisting of bundles of microtubules covered by the cell's plasma membrane (see Figure 6.24). They are quite different from prokaryotic flagella, which are filaments composed of the globular protein flagellin attached to the cell surface (see Figure 27.6).

Many diplomonads are parasites. An infamous example is *Giardia intestinalis* (also known as *Giardia lamblia*; see Figure 28.3), which inhabits the intestines of mammals.

Parabasalids also have reduced mitochondria; called *hydrogenosomes*, these organelles generate some energy anaerobically, releasing hydrogen gas as a by-product. The best-known parabasalid is *Trichomonas vaginalis*, a sexually transmitted parasite that infects some 5 million people each year. *T. vaginalis* travels along the mucus-coated lining of the human reproductive and urinary tracts by moving its flagella and by undulating part of its plasma membrane (Figure 28.4). In females, if the vagina's normal acidity is disturbed, *T. vaginalis* can outcompete beneficial microorganisms there and infect the vagina. (*Trichomonas* infections also can occur in the urethra of males, though often without symptoms.) *T. vaginalis* has a gene that allows it to feed on the vaginal lining, promoting infection. Studies suggest that the protist acquired this gene by horizontal gene transfer from bacterial parasites in the vagina.

Euglenozoans

Protists called **euglenozoans** belong to a diverse clade that includes predatory heterotrophs, photosynthetic autotrophs, and parasites. The main morphological feature that distinguishes protists in this clade is the presence of a rod with either a spiral or a crystalline structure inside each of their flagella (Figure 28.5). The two best-studied groups of euglenozoans are the kinetoplastids and the euglenids.

Kinetoplastids

Protists called **kinetoplastids** have a single, large mitochondrion that contains an organized mass of DNA called a *kinetoplast*. These protists include species that feed on prokaryotes in freshwater, marine, and moist terrestrial ecosystems, as well as species that parasitize animals, plants, and other protists. For example, kinetoplastids in the genus *Trypanosoma* infect humans and cause sleeping sickness, a neurological disease that is invariably fatal if not treated. The infection occurs via the bite of a vector (carrier) organism, the African tsetse fly (Figure 28.6). Trypanosomes also cause Chagas' disease, which

▲ **Figure 28.5 Euglenozoan flagellum.** Most euglenozoans have a crystalline rod inside one of their flagella (the TEM is a flagellum shown in cross section). The rod lies alongside the 9 + 2 ring of microtubules found in all eukaryotic flagella (compare with Figure 6.24).

▲ **Figure 28.6 *Trypanosoma*, the kinetoplastid that causes sleeping sickness.** The purple, ribbon-shaped cells among these red blood cells are the trypanosomes (colorized SEM).

is transmitted by bloodsucking insects and can lead to congestive heart failure.

Trypanosomes evade immune responses with an effective "bait-and-switch" defense. The surface of a trypanosome is coated with millions of copies of a single protein. However, before the host's immune system can recognize the protein and mount an attack, new generations of the parasite switch to another surface protein with a different molecular structure. Frequent changes in the surface protein prevent the host from developing immunity (see Figure 43.24). About a third of *Trypanosoma*'s genome is dedicated to producing these surface proteins.

Euglenids

A **euglenid** has a pocket at one end of the cell from which one or two flagella emerge **(Figure 28.7)**. Many species of the euglenid *Euglena* are mixotrophs: In sunlight they are autotrophic, but when sunlight is unavailable, they can become heterotrophic, absorbing organic nutrients from their environment. Many other euglenids engulf prey by phagocytosis.

CONCEPT CHECK 28.2

1. Why do some biologists describe the mitochondria of diplomonads and parabasalids as "highly reduced"?

2. **WHAT IF?** DNA sequence data for a diplomonad, a euglenid, a plant, and an unidentified protist suggest that the unidentified species is most closely related to the diplomonad. Further studies reveal that the unknown species has fully functional mitochondria. Based on these data, at what point on the phylogenetic tree in Figure 28.3 did the mystery protist's lineage probably diverge from other eukaryote lineages? Explain.

For suggested answers, see Appendix A.

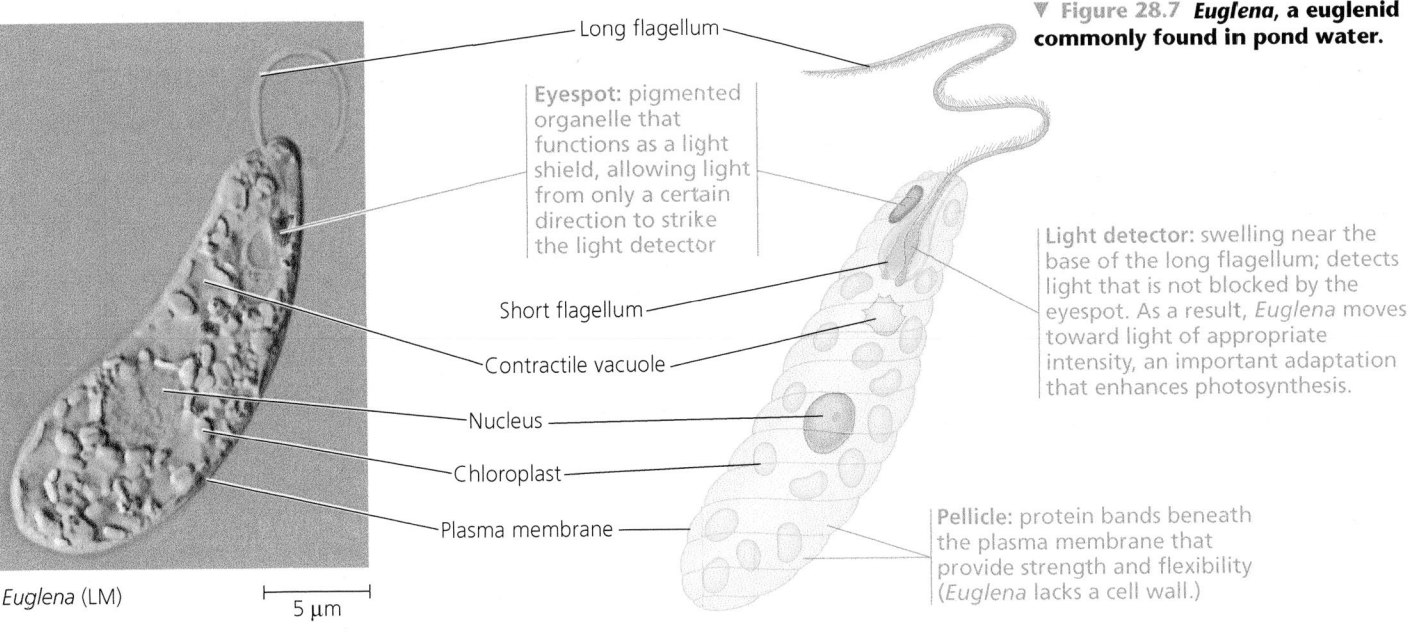

▼ **Figure 28.7 *Euglena*, a euglenid commonly found in pond water.**

Long flagellum

Eyespot: pigmented organelle that functions as a light shield, allowing light from only a certain direction to strike the light detector

Short flagellum

Contractile vacuole

Nucleus

Chloroplast

Plasma membrane

Light detector: swelling near the base of the long flagellum; detects light that is not blocked by the eyespot. As a result, *Euglena* moves toward light of appropriate intensity, an important adaptation that enhances photosynthesis.

Pellicle: protein bands beneath the plasma membrane that provide strength and flexibility (*Euglena* lacks a cell wall.)

Euglena (LM)

Chromalveolates may have originated by secondary endosymbiosis

The supergroup **Chromalveolata** (the chromalveolates), a large, extremely diverse clade of protists, has recently been proposed based on two lines of evidence. First, some (though not all) DNA sequence data suggest that the chromalveolates form a monophyletic group. Second, some data support the hypothesis that the chromalveolates originated more than a billion years ago, when a common ancestor of the group engulfed a single-celled, photosynthetic red alga. Because red algae are thought to have originated by primary endosymbiosis (see Figure 28.2), such an origin for the chromalveolates is referred to as secondary endosymbiosis.

How strong is the evidence that the chromalveolates originated by secondary endosymbiosis? Many species in the clade have plastids whose structure and DNA indicate that they are of red algal origin. Others have reduced plastids that seem to be derived from a red algal endosymbiont. Still other species lack plastids altogether, yet some of these species have plastid genes in their nuclear DNA. Such data have led researchers to suggest that the common ancestor of the chromalveolates had plastids of red algal origin, but that later, some evolutionary lineages within the group lost the plastids. Others question this idea, based on the absence of plastid genes in the genomes of several chromalveolates that lack plastids. Overall, the endosymbiotic origin of the chromalveolates is an interesting idea, but like any scientific hypothesis, new data may show it to be incorrect.

The chromalveolates are perhaps the most controversial of the five supergroups we describe in this chapter. Even so, for many scientists, this supergroup represents the best current hypothesis for the phylogeny of the two large protist clades to which we now turn: the alveolates and the stramenopiles.

Alveolates

The **alveolates** are a group of protists whose monophyly is well supported by molecular systematics. Structurally, species in this group have membrane-bounded sacs (alveoli) just under the plasma membrane (**Figure 28.8**). The function of the alveoli is unknown; researchers hypothesize that they may help stabilize the cell surface or regulate the cell's water and ion content.

The alveolates include three subgroups: a group of flagellates (the dinoflagellates), a group of parasites (the apicomplexans), and a group of protists that move using cilia (the ciliates).

Dinoflagellates

The **dinoflagellates** are characterized by cells that are reinforced by cellulose plates. Two flagella located in grooves in this "armor" make dinoflagellates (from the Greek *dinos*, whirling) spin as they move through the water (**Figure 28.9**). Dinoflagellates are abundant components of both marine and freshwater plankton, communities of mostly microscopic organisms that drift in currents near the water's surface. These dinoflagellates include some of the most important species of *phytoplankton* (photosynthetic plankton, which include photosynthetic bacteria as well as algae). However, many photosynthetic dinoflagellates are mixotrophic, and roughly half of all dinoflagellates are purely heterotrophic.

▲ **Figure 28.8 Alveoli.** These sacs under the plasma membrane are a characteristic that distinguishes alveolates from other eukaryotes (TEM).

▲ **Figure 28.9** *Pfiesteria shumwayae*, **a dinoflagellate.** Beating of the spiral flagellum, which lies in a groove that encircles the cell, makes this alveolate spin (colorized SEM).

Episodes of explosive population growth, or *blooms*, in dinoflagellates sometimes cause a phenomenon called "red tide." The blooms make coastal waters appear brownish red or pink because of the presence of carotenoids, the most common pigments in dinoflagellate plastids. Toxins produced by certain dinoflagellates (such as *Karenia brevis*, which inhabits the Gulf of Mexico) have caused massive kills of invertebrates and fishes. Humans who eat molluscs that have accumulated the toxins are affected as well, sometimes fatally.

Apicomplexans

Nearly all **apicomplexans** are parasites of animals, and some cause serious human diseases. The parasites spread through their host as tiny infectious cells called *sporozoites*. Apicomplexans are so named because one end (the *apex*) of the sporozoite cell contains a *complex* of organelles specialized for penetrating host cells and tissues. Although apicomplexans are not photosynthetic, recent data show that they retain a modified plastid (apicoplast), most likely of red algal origin.

Most apicomplexans have intricate life cycles with both sexual and asexual stages. Those life cycles often require two or more host species for completion. For example, *Plasmodium*, the parasite that causes malaria, lives in both mosquitoes and humans (Figure 28.10).

Historically, malaria has rivaled tuberculosis as the leading cause of human death by infectious disease. The incidence of malaria was greatly diminished in the 1960s by insecticides that reduced carrier populations of *Anopheles* mosquitoes and by drugs that killed *Plasmodium* in humans. But the emergence of resistant varieties of both *Anopheles* and *Plasmodium* has led

▼ **Figure 28.10 The two-host life cycle of *Plasmodium*, the apicomplexan that causes malaria.**

? *Are morphological differences between sporozoites, merozoites, and gametocytes caused by different genomes or by differences in gene expression? Explain.*

1 An infected *Anopheles* mosquito bites a person, injecting *Plasmodium* sporozoites in its saliva.

2 The sporozoites enter the person's liver cells. After several days, the sporozoites undergo multiple divisions and become merozoites, which use their apical complex to penetrate red blood cells (see TEM below).

8 An oocyst develops from the zygote in the wall of the mosquito's gut. The oocyst releases thousands of sporozoites, which migrate to the mosquito's salivary gland.

3 The merozoites divide asexually inside the red blood cells. At intervals of 48 or 72 hours (depending on the species), large numbers of merozoites break out of the blood cells, causing periodic chills and fever. Some of the merozoites infect other red blood cells.

7 Fertilization occurs in the mosquito's digestive tract, and a zygote forms.

4 Some merozoites form gametocytes.

6 Gametes form from gametocytes; each male gametocyte produces several slender male gametes.

5 Another *Anopheles* mosquito bites the infected person and picks up *Plasmodium* gametocytes along with blood.

Inside mosquito — Inside human

Sporozoites (*n*)

Merozoite — Apex — Red blood cell — 0.5 µm

Liver — Liver cell — Merozoite (*n*) — Red blood cells — Gametes — Gametocytes (*n*)

Oocyst — MEIOSIS — Zygote (2*n*) — FERTILIZATION

Key
- Haploid (*n*)
- Diploid (2*n*)

to a resurgence of malaria. About 250 million people in the tropics are currently infected, and 900,000 die each year.

The search for malarial vaccines has been hampered by the fact that *Plasmodium* lives mainly inside cells, hidden from the host's immune system. And, like trypanosomes, *Plasmodium* continually changes its surface proteins. The urgent need for treatments has inspired the sequencing of several *Plasmodium* genomes. Furthermore, researchers have now tracked the expression of most of the parasite's genes at nu-merous points in its life cycle. This research could help iden-tify vaccine targets. Drugs that target the apicoplast are also in development. This approach may be effective because the api-coplast, derived by secondary endosymbiosis from a prokary-ote, has metabolic pathways different from those in humans.

Ciliates

Ciliates are a large, varied group of protists named for their use of cilia to move and feed (**Figure 28.11a**). The cilia may

▼ **Figure 28.11** **Structure and function in the ciliate *Paramecium caudatum*.**

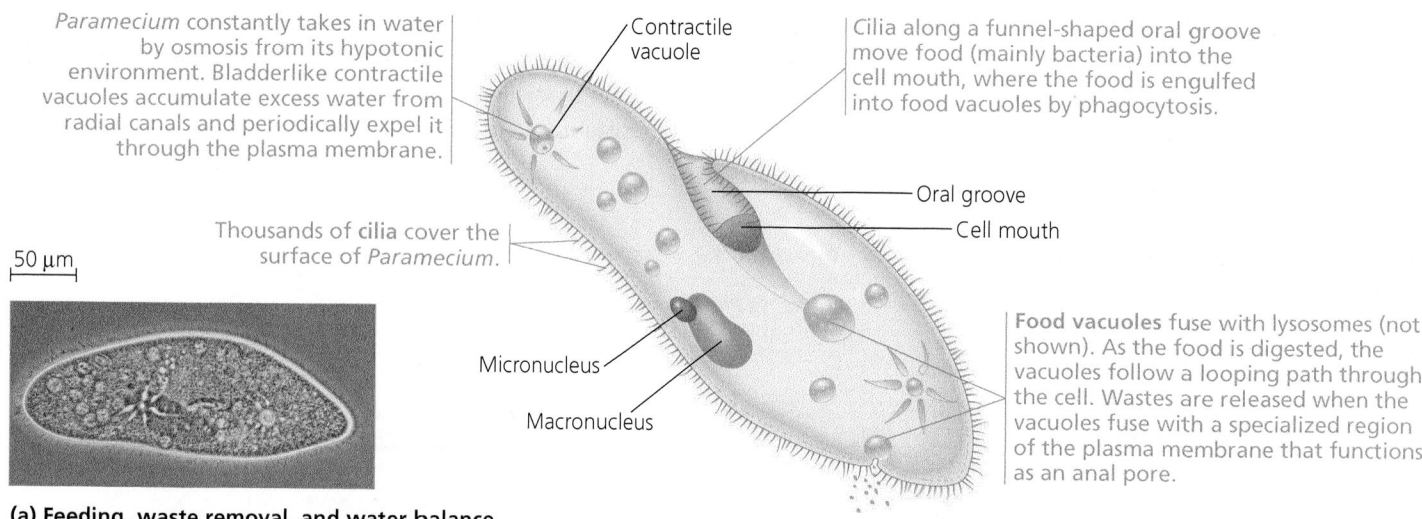

Paramecium constantly takes in water by osmosis from its hypotonic environment. Bladderlike contractile vacuoles accumulate excess water from radial canals and periodically expel it through the plasma membrane.

Contractile vacuole

Cilia along a funnel-shaped oral groove move food (mainly bacteria) into the cell mouth, where the food is engulfed into food vacuoles by phagocytosis.

Thousands of **cilia** cover the surface of *Paramecium*.

50 µm

Oral groove

Cell mouth

Micronucleus

Macronucleus

Food vacuoles fuse with lysosomes (not shown). As the food is digested, the vacuoles follow a looping path through the cell. Wastes are released when the vacuoles fuse with a specialized region of the plasma membrane that functions as an anal pore.

(a) Feeding, waste removal, and water balance.

❶ Two cells of compatible mating strains align side by side and partially fuse.

❷ Meiosis of micronuclei produces four haploid micronuclei in each cell.

❸ Three micronuclei in each cell disintegrate. The remaining micro-nucleus in each cell divides by mitosis.

MEIOSIS

❹ The cells swap one micronucleus.

Compatible mates

Diploid micronucleus

Haploid micronucleus

The original macronucleus disintegrates.

Diploid micronucleus

MICRONUCLEAR FUSION

❺ The cells separate.

❾ Two rounds of binary fission yield four daughter cells.

❽ Four micro-nuclei become macronuclei.

❼ Three rounds of mitosis produce eight micronuclei.

❻ The two micronuclei fuse.

Key

Conjugation

Asexual reproduction

(b) Conjugation and reproduction.

completely cover the cell surface or may be clustered in a few rows or tufts. In certain species, rows of tightly packed cilia function collectively in locomotion. Other ciliates scurry about on leg-like structures constructed from many cilia bonded together.

A distinctive feature of ciliates is the presence of two types of nuclei: tiny micronuclei and large macronuclei. A cell has one or more nuclei of each type. Genetic variation results from **conjugation**, a sexual process in which two individuals exchange haploid micronuclei but do not reproduce (Figure 28.11b). Ciliates generally reproduce asexually by binary fission, during which the existing macronucleus disintegrates and a new one is formed from the cell's micronuclei. Each macronucleus typically contains multiple copies of the ciliate's genome. Genes in the macronucleus control the everyday functions of the cell, such as feeding, waste removal, and maintaining water balance (see Figure 28.11a).

Stramenopiles

Another major subgroup of the chromalveolates is the **stramenopiles**, protists that include some of the most important photosynthetic organisms on the planet, as well as several clades of heterotrophs. Their name (from the Latin *stramen*, straw, and *pilos*, hair) refers to their characteristic flagellum, which has numerous fine, hairlike projections. In most stramenopiles, this "hairy" flagellum is paired with a shorter "smooth" (nonhairy) flagellum (Figure 28.12). Here we'll focus on four groups of stramenopiles: diatoms, golden algae, brown algae, and oomycetes.

Diatoms

Diatoms are unicellular algae that have a unique glass-like wall made of hydrated silica (silicon dioxide) embedded in an organic matrix. The wall consists of two parts that overlap like a shoe box and its lid. These walls provide effective protection from the crushing jaws of predators: Live diatoms can withstand pressures as great as 1.4 million kg/m², equal to the pressure under each leg of a table supporting an elephant! Much of the diatoms' strength comes from the delicate lacework of holes and grooves in their walls (Figure 28.13); if the walls were smooth, it would take 60% less force to crush them.

With an estimated 100,000 living species, diatoms are a highly diverse group of protists (see Figure 28.3). They are a major component of phytoplankton both in the ocean and in lakes: One bucket of water scooped from the surface of the sea may contain millions of these microscopic algae. The abundance of diatoms in the past is also evident in the fossil record, where massive accumulations of fossilized diatom walls are major constituents of sediments known as *diatomaceous earth*. These sediments are mined for their quality as a filtering medium and for many other uses.

▲ **Figure 28.12 Stramenopile flagella.** Most stramenopiles, such as *Synura petersenii*, have two flagella: one covered with fine, stiff hairs and a shorter one that is smooth.

▲ **Figure 28.13 The diatom *Triceratium morlandii*** (colorized SEM).

You might expect that since diatoms are so widespread and abundant, their photosynthetic activity would affect global carbon dioxide levels, and this is indeed the case. Diatoms have this effect in part because of the chain of events that follows their rapid population growth (a bloom) when ample nutrients are available. Typically, diatoms are eaten by a variety of protists and invertebrates, but during a bloom, many escape this fate. When these uneaten diatoms die, their bodies sink to the ocean floor. Diatoms that sink to the ocean floor are not very likely to be broken down by bacteria and other decomposers. Hence, the carbon in their bodies remains there, rather than being released as carbon dioxide as the decomposers respire. The overall effect of these events is that carbon dioxide absorbed by diatoms during photosynthesis is transported, or "pumped," to the ocean floor. With an eye toward reducing global warming by lowering atmospheric carbon dioxide levels, some scientists advocate promoting diatom blooms by fertilizing the ocean with essential nutrients such as iron. Other scientists question this strategy, noting that small-scale tests of this idea have yielded mixed results and that it is difficult to predict the effects of large-scale manipulations of ecological communities.

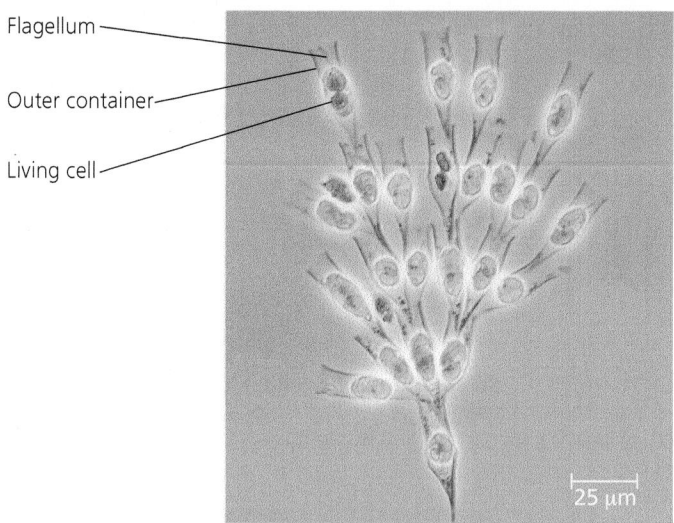

Flagellum
Outer container
Living cell

25 µm

▲ Figure 28.14 **Dinobryon, a colonial golden alga found in fresh water** (LM).

Golden Algae

The characteristic color of **golden algae** results from their yellow and brown carotenoids. The cells of golden algae are typically biflagellated, with both flagella attached near one end of the cell.

Many golden algae are components of freshwater and marine plankton. While all golden algae are photosynthetic, some species are mixotrophic. These mixotrophs can absorb dissolved organic compounds or ingest food particles, including living cells, by phagocytosis. Most species are unicellular, but some, such as those in the freshwater genus *Dinobryon*, are colonial (**Figure 28.14**). If environmental conditions deteriorate, many species form protective cysts that can survive for decades.

Brown Algae

The largest and most complex algae are **brown algae**. All are multicellular, and most are marine. Brown algae are especially common along temperate coasts, where the water is cool. They owe their characteristic brown or olive color to the carotenoids in their plastids.

Many of the species commonly called "seaweeds" are brown algae. (Some large, multicellular species of red and green algae are also referred to as seaweeds. We will examine them later in this chapter.) Brown algae include species that have the most complex multicellular anatomy of all algae; some even have specialized tissues and organs that resemble those in plants. But morphological and DNA evidence indicates that the similarities evolved independently in the algal and plant lineages and are thus analogous, not homologous.

The term **thallus** (plural, *thalli*; from the Greek *thallos*, sprout) refers to an algal body that is plantlike. Unlike the

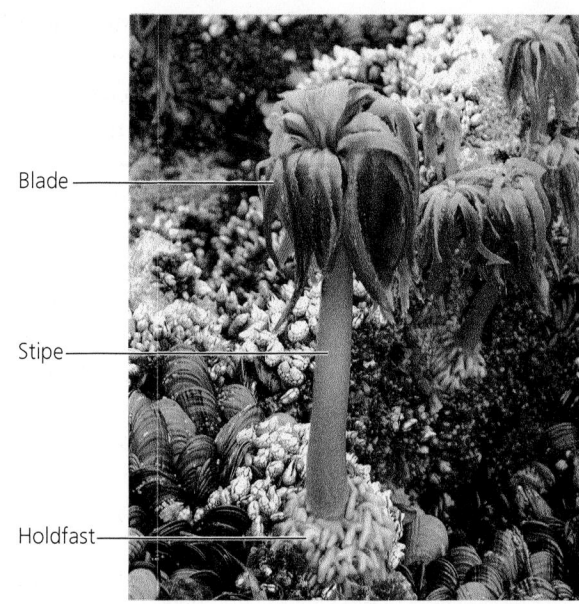

Blade
Stipe
Holdfast

▲ Figure 28.15 **Seaweeds: adapted to life at the ocean's margins.** The sea palm (*Postelsia*) lives on rocks along the coast of the northwestern United States and western Canada. The thallus of this brown alga is well adapted to maintaining a firm foothold despite the crashing surf.

body of a plant, however, a thallus lacks true roots, stems, and leaves. A typical thallus consists of a rootlike **holdfast**, which anchors the alga, and a stemlike **stipe**, which supports leaflike **blades** (**Figure 28.15**). The blades provide most of the alga's photosynthetic surface. Some brown algae are equipped with gas-filled, bubble-shaped floats, which help keep the blades up near the water surface. Beyond the intertidal zone in deeper waters live giant seaweeds known as kelps. The stipes of these brown algae may be as long as 60 m, more than half the length of a football field.

Brown algae that inhabit the intertidal zone must cope with water churned by waves and wind, along with low tides that expose the algae to the drying atmosphere and intense rays of the sun. Unique adaptations enable these seaweeds to survive. For example, their cell walls are composed of cellulose and gel-forming polysaccharides that help cushion the thalli from waves and reduce drying when the algae are exposed.

Brown algae are important commodities for humans. Some species are eaten, such as *Laminaria* (Japanese "kombu"), which is used in soups. In addition, the gel-forming substance in the cell walls of brown algae, called algin, is used to thicken many processed foods, including pudding and salad dressing.

Alternation of Generations

A variety of life cycles have evolved among the multicellular algae. The most complex life cycles include an **alternation of generations**, the alternation of multicellular haploid and diploid forms. Although haploid and diploid conditions alternate in *all* sexual life cycles—human gametes, for example, are haploid—the term *alternation of generations* applies only to life cycles in which both haploid and diploid stages are multicellular. As you will read in Chapter 29, alternation of generations also evolved in plants.

The complex life cycle of the brown alga *Laminaria* provides an example of alternation of generations (Figure 28.16). The diploid individual is called the *sporophyte* because it produces spores. The spores are haploid and move by means of flagella; they are called *zoospores*. The zoospores develop into haploid, multicellular male and female *gametophytes*, which produce gametes. The union of two gametes (fertilization, or syngamy)

results in a diploid zygote, which matures and gives rise to a new multicellular sporophyte.

In *Laminaria*, the two generations are **heteromorphic**, meaning that the sporophytes and gametophytes are structurally different. Other algal life cycles have an alternation of **isomorphic** generations, in which the sporophytes and gametophytes look similar to each other, although they differ in chromosome number.

Oomycetes (Water Molds and Their Relatives)

Oomycetes include the water molds, the white rusts, and the downy mildews. Based on their morphology, these organisms were previously classified as fungi (in fact, *oomycete* means

① The sporophytes are usually found in water just below the line of the lowest tides, attached to rocks by branching holdfasts.

② Cells on the surface of the blade develop into sporangia.

③ Sporangia produce zoospores by meiosis.

MEIOSIS

④ The zoospores are all structurally alike, but about half of them develop into male gametophytes and half into female gametophytes. The gametophytes are short, branched filaments that grow on subtidal rocks.

⑤ Male gametophytes release sperm, and female gametophytes produce eggs, which remain attached to the female gametophyte. Eggs secrete a chemical signal that attracts sperm of the same species, thereby increasing the probability of fertilization in the ocean.

⑥ Sperm fertilize the eggs.

⑦ The zygotes grow into new sporophytes while attached to the remains of the female gametophyte.

Sporangia

Sporophyte (2*n*)

Zoospore

Female

Gametophytes (*n*)

Male

Egg

Sperm

FERTILIZATION

Zygote (2*n*)

Developing sporophyte

Mature female gametophyte (*n*)

10 cm

Key

Haploid (*n*)

Diploid (2*n*)

▲ Figure 28.16 **The life cycle of the brown alga *Laminaria*: an example of alternation of generations.**

[?] *Are the sperm shown in ⑥ genetically identical to one another? Are they genetically identical to the egg in ⑥? Explain.*

"egg fungus"). For example, many oomycetes have multinucleate filaments (hyphae) that resemble fungal hyphae (Figure 28.17). However, there are key differences between oomycetes and fungi. Among the differences, oomycetes typically have cell walls made of cellulose, whereas the walls of fungi consist mainly of another polysaccharide, chitin. Data from molecular systematics have confirmed that oomycetes are not closely related to fungi. Their superficial similarity is a case of convergent evolution. In both oomycetes and fungi, the high surface-to-volume ratio of filamentous structures enhances the uptake of nutrients from the environment.

Although oomycetes descended from plastid-bearing ancestors, they no longer have plastids and do not perform photosynthesis. Instead, they typically acquire nutrients as decomposers or parasites. Most water molds are decomposers that grow as cottony masses on dead algae and animals, mainly in freshwater habitats (see Figure 28.17). White rusts and downy mildews generally live on land as plant parasites.

The ecological impact of oomycetes can be significant. For example, the oomycete *Phytophthora infestans* causes potato late blight, which turns the stalk and stem of potato plants to black slime. Late blight contributed to the devastating Irish famine of the 19th century, in which a million people died and at least that many were forced to leave Ireland. The disease remains a major problem today, causing crop losses of typically 15% in North America and as high as 70% in some parts of Russia where farmers cannot afford pesticides.

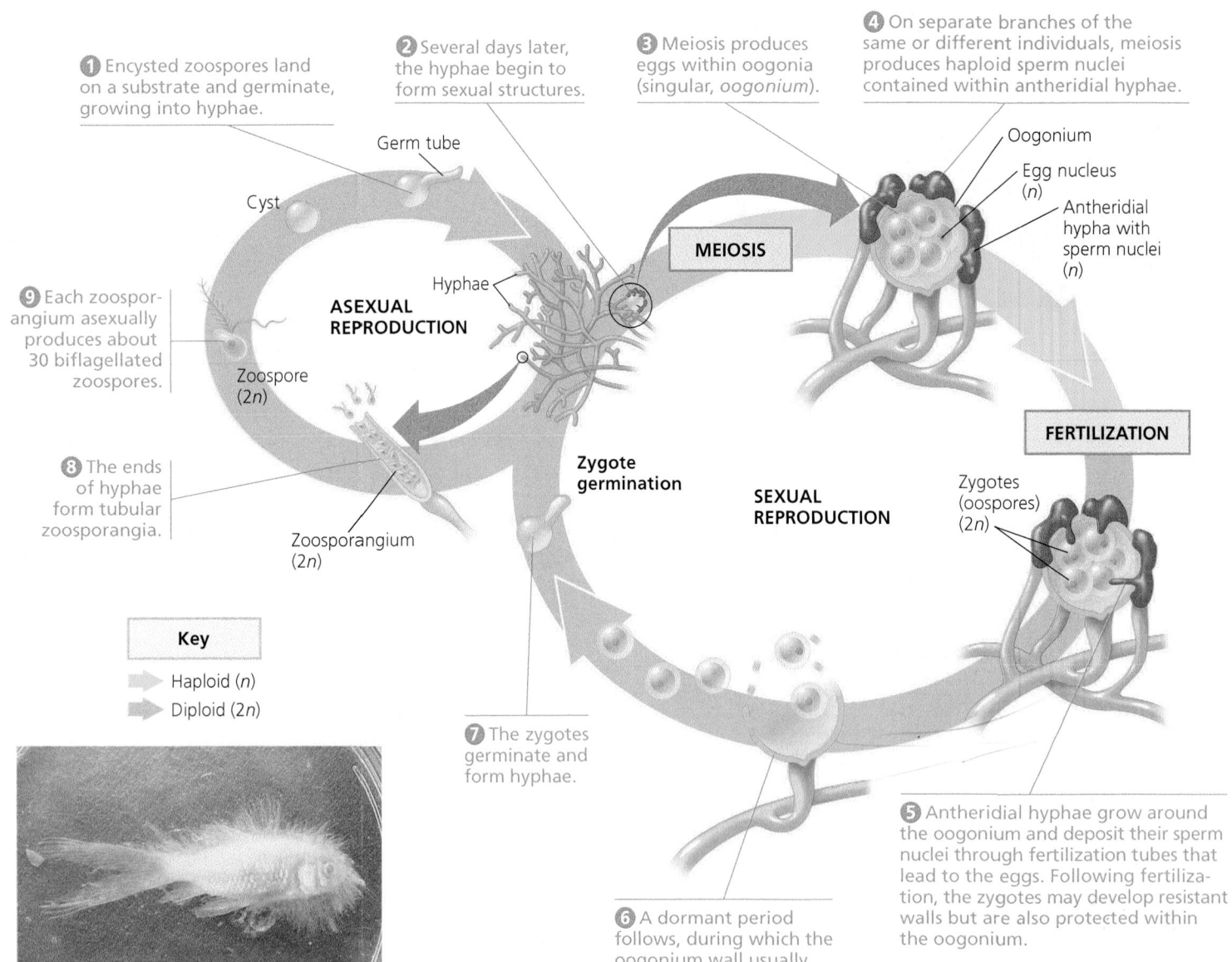

1 Encysted zoospores land on a substrate and germinate, growing into hyphae.

2 Several days later, the hyphae begin to form sexual structures.

3 Meiosis produces eggs within oogonia (singular, *oogonium*).

4 On separate branches of the same or different individuals, meiosis produces haploid sperm nuclei contained within antheridial hyphae.

Germ tube

Cyst

Oogonium

Egg nucleus (*n*)

Antheridial hypha with sperm nuclei (*n*)

MEIOSIS

Hyphae

9 Each zoosporangium asexually produces about 30 biflagellated zoospores.

ASEXUAL REPRODUCTION

Zoospore (2*n*)

8 The ends of hyphae form tubular zoosporangia.

Zoosporangium (2*n*)

Zygote germination

SEXUAL REPRODUCTION

FERTILIZATION

Zygotes (oospores) (2*n*)

Key

→ Haploid (*n*)
→ Diploid (2*n*)

7 The zygotes germinate and form hyphae.

6 A dormant period follows, during which the oogonium wall usually disintegrates.

5 Antheridial hyphae grow around the oogonium and deposit their sperm nuclei through fertilization tubes that lead to the eggs. Following fertilization, the zygotes may develop resistant walls but are also protected within the oogonium.

▲ Figure 28.17 **The life cycle of a water mold.** Water molds help decompose dead insects, fishes, and other animals in fresh water. (Note the hyphal mass growing on the goldfish in the photograph.)

To understand this pathogen better, molecular biologists have isolated DNA from a specimen of *P. infestans* preserved from the Irish potato blight of the 1840s. Genetic studies show that in recent decades, this oomycete has acquired genes that make it more aggressive and more resistant to pesticides. Scientists are looking within the genomes of both *Phytophthora* and potatoes to identify new weapons against the disease. Already, researchers have transferred genes from a blight-resistant strain of wild potato into domestic potatoes to produce a resistant crop strain.

CONCEPT CHECK 28.3

1. Summarize the evidence for and against the hypothesis that the species currently classified as chromalveolates are members of a single clade.
2. **WHAT IF?** Would you expect the plastid DNA of photosynthetic dinoflagellates, diatoms, and golden algae to be more similar to the nuclear DNA of plants (domain Eukarya) or to the chromosomal DNA of cyanobacteria (domain Bacteria)? Explain.
3. **MAKE CONNECTIONS** Which of the three life cycles in Figure 13.6 (p. 252) exhibits alternation of generations? How does it differ from the other two?

For suggested answers, see Appendix A.

CONCEPT 28.4

Rhizarians are a diverse group of protists defined by DNA similarities

Excavata
Chromalveolata

Radiolarians
Foraminiferans   Rhizaria
Cercozoans

Archaeplastida
Unikonta

The clade **Rhizaria** has recently been proposed based on results from molecular systematics. Although its members vary greatly in morphology, DNA evidence suggests that rhizarians are a monophyletic group. According to some recent phylogenetic studies, Rhizaria should be nested within Chromalveolata, as discussed in Figure 28.3.

Many species in Rhizaria are among the organisms referred to as amoebas. **Amoebas** were formerly defined as protists that move and feed by means of **pseudopodia**, extensions that may bulge from almost anywhere on the cell surface. An amoeba moves by extending a pseudopodium and anchoring the tip; more cytoplasm then streams into the pseudopodium. However, based on molecular systematics, it is now clear that amoebas do not constitute a monophyletic group but are dispersed across many distantly related eukaryotic

Pseudopodia

200 μm

▲ **Figure 28.18** **A radiolarian.** Numerous threadlike pseudopodia radiate from the central body of this radiolarian, which is found in the Red Sea (LM).

taxa. Most of those that belong to the clade Rhizaria are distinguished morphologically from other amoebas by having threadlike pseudopodia.

Rhizarians include three groups that we'll examine here: radiolarians, forams, and cercozoans.

Radiolarians

The protists called **radiolarians** have delicate, intricately symmetrical internal skeletons that are generally made of silica. The pseudopodia of these mostly marine protists radiate from the central body (Figure 28.18) and are reinforced by bundles of microtubules. The microtubules are covered by a thin layer of cytoplasm, which engulfs smaller microorganisms that become attached to the pseudopodia. Cytoplasmic streaming then carries the captured prey into the main part of the cell. After radiolarians die, their skeletons settle to the seafloor, where they have accumulated as an ooze that is hundreds of meters thick in some locations.

Forams

The protists called **foraminiferans** (from the Latin *foramen*, little hole, and *ferre*, to bear), or **forams**, are named for their porous shells, called **tests** (see Figure 28.3). Foram tests consist of a single piece of organic material hardened with calcium carbonate. The pseudopodia that extend through the pores function in swimming, test formation, and feeding. Many forams also derive nourishment from the photosynthesis of symbiotic algae that live within the tests.

Forams are found in both the ocean and fresh water. Most species live in sand or attach themselves to rocks or algae, but some are abundant in plankton. The largest forams, though single-celled, grow to a diameter of several centimeters.

Ninety percent of all identified species of forams are known from fossils. Along with the calcium-containing remains of other protists, the fossilized tests of forams are part of marine sediments, including sedimentary rocks that are now land formations. Foram fossils are excellent markers for correlating the ages of sedimentary rocks in different parts of the world.

Cercozoans

First identified in molecular phylogenies, the **cercozoans** form a large group that contains most of the amoeboid and flagellated protists that feed with threadlike pseudopodia. Cercozoan protists are common in marine, freshwater, and soil ecosystems.

Most cercozoans are heterotrophs. Many are parasites of plants, animals, or other protists; many others are predators. The predators include the most important consumers of bacteria in aquatic and soil ecosystems, along with species that eat other protists, fungi, and even small animals. One small group of cercozoans, the chlorarachniophytes (mentioned earlier in the discussion of secondary endosymbiosis), are mixotrophic: These organisms ingest smaller protists and bacteria as well as perform photosynthesis. At least one other cercozoan, *Paulinella chromatophora*, is an autotroph, deriving its energy from light and its carbon from carbon dioxide. This species has a distinctive sausage-shaped internal structure where photosynthesis is performed (**Figure 28.19**). Genetic and morphological analyses indicate that these structures were derived from a cyanobacterium, although not the same cyanobacterium from which all other plastids were derived. As such, *Paulinella* appears to represent an intriguing additional evolutionary example of a eukaryotic lineage that obtained its photosynthetic apparatus directly from a cyanobacterium.

Chromatophore

5 μm

▲ **Figure 28.19 A second case of primary endosymbiosis?** The cercozoan *Paulinella* conducts photosynthesis in a unique structure called a chromatophore (LM). Chromatophores are surrounded by a membrane with a peptidoglycan layer, suggesting that they are derived from a bacterium. DNA evidence indicates that chromatophores are derived from a different cyanobacterium than that from which other plastids are derived.

CONCEPT 28.5

Red algae and green algae are the closest relatives of land plants

As we described in Chapter 25, molecular systematics and studies of cell structure support the following scenario: More than a billion years ago, a heterotrophic protist acquired a cyanobacterial endosymbiont, and the photosynthetic descendants of this ancient protist evolved into red algae and green algae. At least 475 million years ago, the lineage that produced green algae gave rise to land plants. Together, red algae, green algae, and land plants make up the fourth eukaryotic supergroup, which is called **Archaeplastida**. Archaeplastida is a monophyletic group that descended from the ancient protist that engulfed a cyanobacterium. We will examine land plants in Chapters 29 and 30; here we will look at the diversity of their closest algal relatives, red algae and green algae.

Red Algae

Many of the 6,000 known species of **red algae** (rhodophytes, from the Greek *rhodos*, red) are reddish, owing to a photosynthetic accessory pigment called phycoerythrin, which masks the green of chlorophyll (**Figure 28.20**). However, species adapted to more shallow water have less phycoerythrin. As a result, red algal species may be greenish red in very shallow

► **Bonnemaisonia hamifera.** This red alga has a filamentous form.

8 mm

20 cm

◄ **Dulse (*Palmaria palmata*).** This edible species has a "leafy" form.

▼ **Nori.** The red alga *Porphyra* is the source of a traditional Japanese food.

The seaweed is grown on nets in shallow coastal waters.

The harvested seaweed is spread on bamboo screens to dry.

Paper-thin, glossy sheets of nori make a mineral-rich wrap for rice, seafood, and vegetables in sushi.

▲ **Figure 28.20 Red algae.**

water, bright red at moderate depths, and almost black in deep water. Some species lack pigmentation altogether and function heterotrophically as parasites on other red algae.

Red algae are the most abundant large algae in the warm coastal waters of tropical oceans. Their accessory pigments, including phycoerythrin, allow them to absorb blue and green light, which penetrate relatively far into the water. A

species of red alga has been discovered near the Bahamas at a depth of more than 260 m. There are also a small number of freshwater and terrestrial species.

Most red algae are multicellular. Although none are as big as the giant brown kelps, the largest multicellular red algae are included in the informal designation "seaweeds." You may have eaten one of these multicellular red algae, *Porphyra* (Japanese "nori"), as crispy sheets or as a wrap for sushi (see Figure 28.20). Red algae have especially diverse life cycles, and alternation of generations is common. But unlike other algae, they have no flagellated stages in their life cycle and depend on water currents to bring gametes together for fertilization.

Green Algae

The grass-green chloroplasts of **green algae** have a structure and pigment composition much like the chloroplasts of land plants. Molecular systematics and cellular morphology leave little doubt that green algae and land plants are closely related. In fact, some systematists now advocate including green algae in an expanded "plant" kingdom, Viridiplantae (from the Latin *viridis*, green). Phylogenetically, this change makes sense, since otherwise the green algae are a paraphyletic group.

Green algae are divided into two main groups, the charophytes and the chlorophytes. The charophytes are the algae most closely related to land plants, and so we will discuss them along with plants in Chapter 29.

The second group, the chlorophytes (from the Greek *chloros*, green), includes more than 7,000 species. Most live in fresh water, but there are also many marine and some terrestrial species. The simplest chlorophytes are unicellular organisms such as *Chlamydomonas*, which resemble gametes or zoospores of more complex chlorophytes. Various species of unicellular chlorophytes live in aquatic habitats as phytoplankton or inhabit damp soil. Some live symbiotically within other eukaryotes, contributing part of their photosynthetic output to the food supply of their hosts. Some chlorophytes have even adapted to one of the last habitats you might expect to find them: snow. These chlorophytes carry out photosynthesis despite subfreezing temperatures and intense visible and ultraviolet radiation. They are protected by the snow itself, which acts as a shield, and by radiation-blocking compounds in their cytoplasm. Other chlorophytes contain similar protective compounds in their cell wall or in a durable coat that surrounds the zygote.

Larger size and greater complexity evolved in chlorophytes by three different mechanisms:

1. The formation of colonies of individual cells, as seen in *Volvox* (see Figure 28.3) and in filamentous forms that contribute to the stringy masses known as pond scum

2. The formation of true multicellular bodies by cell division and differentiation, as in *Ulva* (Figure 28.21a)

3. The repeated division of nuclei with no cytoplasmic division, as in *Caulerpa* (Figure 28.21b)

Most chlorophytes have complex life cycles, with both sexual and asexual reproductive stages. Nearly all species of chlorophytes reproduce sexually by means of biflagellated gametes that have cup-shaped chloroplasts (Figure 28.22). Alternation of generations has evolved in some chlorophytes, including *Ulva*.

CONCEPT CHECK 28.5

1. Contrast red algae and brown algae.
2. Why is it accurate to say that *Ulva* is truly multicellular but *Caulerpa* is not?
3. **WHAT IF?** Suggest a possible reason why species in the green algal lineage may have been more likely to colonize land than species in the red algal lineage.

For suggested answers, see Appendix A.

(a) *Ulva,* **or sea lettuce.** This edible chlorophyte has a multicellular thallus differentiated into leaflike blades. Its rootlike holdfast anchors the alga.

(b) *Caulerpa,* **an intertidal chlorophyte.** The branched filaments lack cross-walls and thus are multinucleate. In effect, the thallus is one huge "supercell."

▲ **Figure 28.21 Multicellular chlorophytes.**

Flagella

Cell wall

Nucleus

Cross section of cup-shaped chloroplast

(TEM)

1 μm

❶ In *Chlamydomonas*, mature cells are haploid and contain a single cup-shaped chloroplast.

❷ In response to a nutrient shortage, drying of the enviroment, or other stress, cells develop into gametes.

❸ Gametes of different mating types (designated + and –) fuse (fertilization), forming a diploid zygote.

Gamete (*n*)

FERTILIZATION

❼ These daughter cells develop flagella and cell walls and then emerge as swimming zoospores from the parent cell. The zoospores develop into mature haploid cells.

Zoospore

Mature cell (*n*)

ASEXUAL REPRODUCTION

SEXUAL REPRODUCTION

Zygote (2*n*)

Key

Haploid (*n*)

Diploid (2*n*)

❻ When a mature cell reproduces asexually, it resorbs its flagella and then undergoes two rounds of mitosis, forming four cells (more in some species).

MEIOSIS

❹ The zygote secretes a durable coat that protects the cell from harsh conditions.

❺ After a dormant period, meiosis produces four haploid individuals (two of each mating type) that emerge and mature.

▲ **Figure 28.22 The life cycle of *Chlamydomonas*, a unicellular chlorophyte.**

DRAW IT *Circle the stage(s) in the diagram in which clones are formed, producing additional new daughter cells that are genetically identical to the parent cell(s).*

CONCEPT 28.6

Unikonts include protists that are closely related to fungi and animals

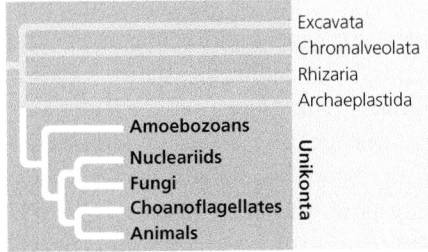

	Excavata
	Chromalveolata
	Rhizaria
	Archaeplastida
Amoebozoans	
Nucleariids	Unikonta
Fungi	
Choanoflagellates	
Animals	

Unikonta is a recently proposed, extremely diverse supergroup of eukaryotes that includes animals, fungi, and some protists. There are two major clades of unikonts, the amoebozoans and the opisthokonts (animals, fungi, and closely related protist groups). Each of these two major clades is strongly supported by molecular systematics. The close relationship between amoebozoans and opisthokonts is more controversial. Support for this close relationship is provided by comparisons of myosin proteins and by several studies based on hundreds of genes, but not by other studies based on single genes.

Another controversy involving the unikonts concerns the root of the eukaryotic tree. Recall that the root of a phylogenetic tree anchors the tree in time: Branch points close to the root are the oldest. At present, the root of the eukaryotic tree is uncertain; thus, we do not know which group of eukaryotes was the first to diverge from other eukaryotes. Some hypotheses, such as the amitochondriate hypothesis described earlier, have been abandoned, but researchers have yet to agree on an alternative. If the root of the eukaryotic tree were known, scientists could infer characteristics of the common ancestor of all eukaryotes. Such information could help resolve some of the current debates about the five supergroups of eukaryotes.

In trying to determine the root of the eukaryotic tree, researchers have based their phylogenies on different sets of genes, producing conflicting results. Researchers at Oxford University have described a different approach, results from which support a radical new hypothesis about the root of the eukaryotic tree (**Figure 28.23**). According to their hypothesis, the unikonts were the first eukaryotes to diverge from other eukaryotes. This hypothesis proposes that animals and fungi belong to an early-diverging group of eukaryotes, while protists that lack typical mitochondria (such as the diplomonads and parabasalids) diverged much later in the history of life. This idea remains controversial and will require more supporting evidence to be widely accepted.

Amoebozoans

As already mentioned, **amoebozoans** form a clade that is well supported by molecular data. This clade includes many species

---

▼ **Figure 28.23**   **INQUIRY**

What is the root of the eukaryotic tree?

EXPERIMENT Responding to the difficulty in determining the root of the eukaryotic phylogenetic tree, Alexandra Stechmann and Thomas Cavalier-Smith, of Oxford University, proposed a new approach. They studied two genes, one for the enzyme dihydrofolate reductase (DHFR), the other for the enzyme thymidylate synthase (TS). Their approach took advantage of a rare evolutionary event: In some organisms, the DHFR and TS genes have fused, leading to the production of a single protein with both enzyme activities. Stechmann and Cavalier-Smith amplified (using PCR; see Figure 20.8) and sequenced DHFR and TS genes in nine species (one choanoflagellate; two amoebozoans; one euglenozoan; two chromalveolates; and three rhizarians). They combined their data with previously published data for species of bacteria, animals, plants, and fungi.

RESULTS The bacteria studied all have separate DHFR and TS genes, suggesting that this is the ancestral condition (red dot on the tree below). Other taxa with separate genes are denoted by red type. Fused genes are a derived character, found in certain members (blue type) of the supergroups Excavata, Chromalveolata, Rhizaria, and Archaeplastida:

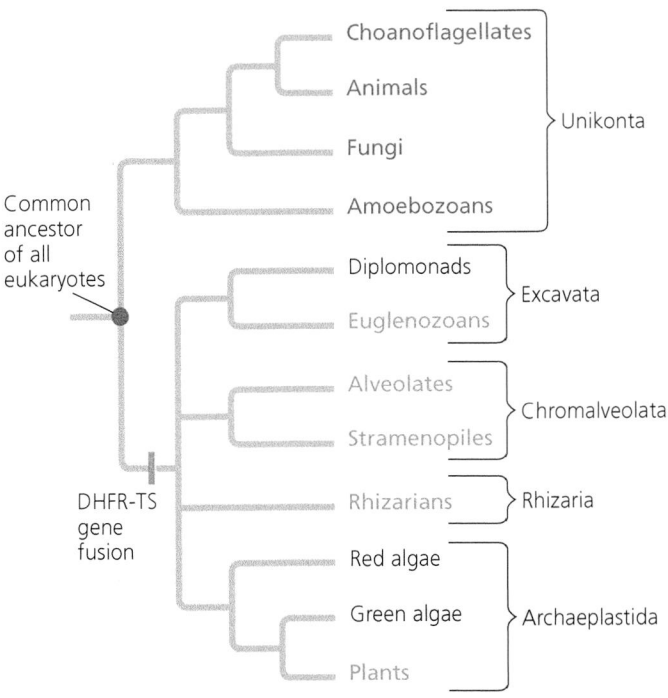

CONCLUSION These results support the hypothesis that the root of the tree is located between the unikonts and all other eukaryotes, suggesting that the unikonts were the first group of eukaryotes to diverge. Because support for this hypothesis is based on only one trait—the fusion of the DHFR and TS genes—more data are needed to evaluate its validity.

SOURCE A. Stechmann and T. Cavalier-Smith, Rooting the eukaryote tree by using a derived gene fusion, *Science* 297:89–91 (2002).

WHAT IF? Stechmann and Cavalier-Smith wrote that their conclusions are "valid only if the genes fused just once and were never secondarily split." Why is this assumption critical to their approach?

of amoebas that have lobe- or tube-shaped, rather than thread-like, pseudopodia. Amoebozoans include slime molds, gymnamoebas, and entamoebas.

Slime Molds

Slime molds, or mycetozoans (from the Latin, meaning "fungus animals"), were once thought to be fungi because, like fungi, they produce fruiting bodies that aid in spore dispersal. However, the resemblance between slime molds and fungi appears to be another example of evolutionary convergence. Molecular systematics places slime molds in Amoebozoa and suggests that they descended from unicellular ancestors. Slime molds have diverged into two main branches, plasmodial slime molds and cellular slime molds, distinguished in part by their unique life cycles.

Plasmodial Slime Molds Many **plasmodial slime molds** are brightly colored, often yellow or orange (Figure 28.24). At one stage in their life cycle, they form a mass called a **plasmodium**, which may grow to a diameter of many centimeters. (Don't confuse a slime mold's plasmodium with the genus *Plasmodium*, which includes the parasitic apicomplexan that causes malaria.) Despite its size, the plasmodium is not multicellular; it is a single mass of cytoplasm that is undivided by plasma membranes and that contains many nuclei. This "supercell" is the product of mitotic nuclear divisions that are not followed by cytokinesis.

Within the plasmodium, cytoplasm streams first one way, then the other, in pulsing flows that are beautiful to watch through a microscope. This cytoplasmic streaming apparently helps distribute nutrients and oxygen. The plasmodium extends pseudopodia through moist soil, leaf mulch, or rotting

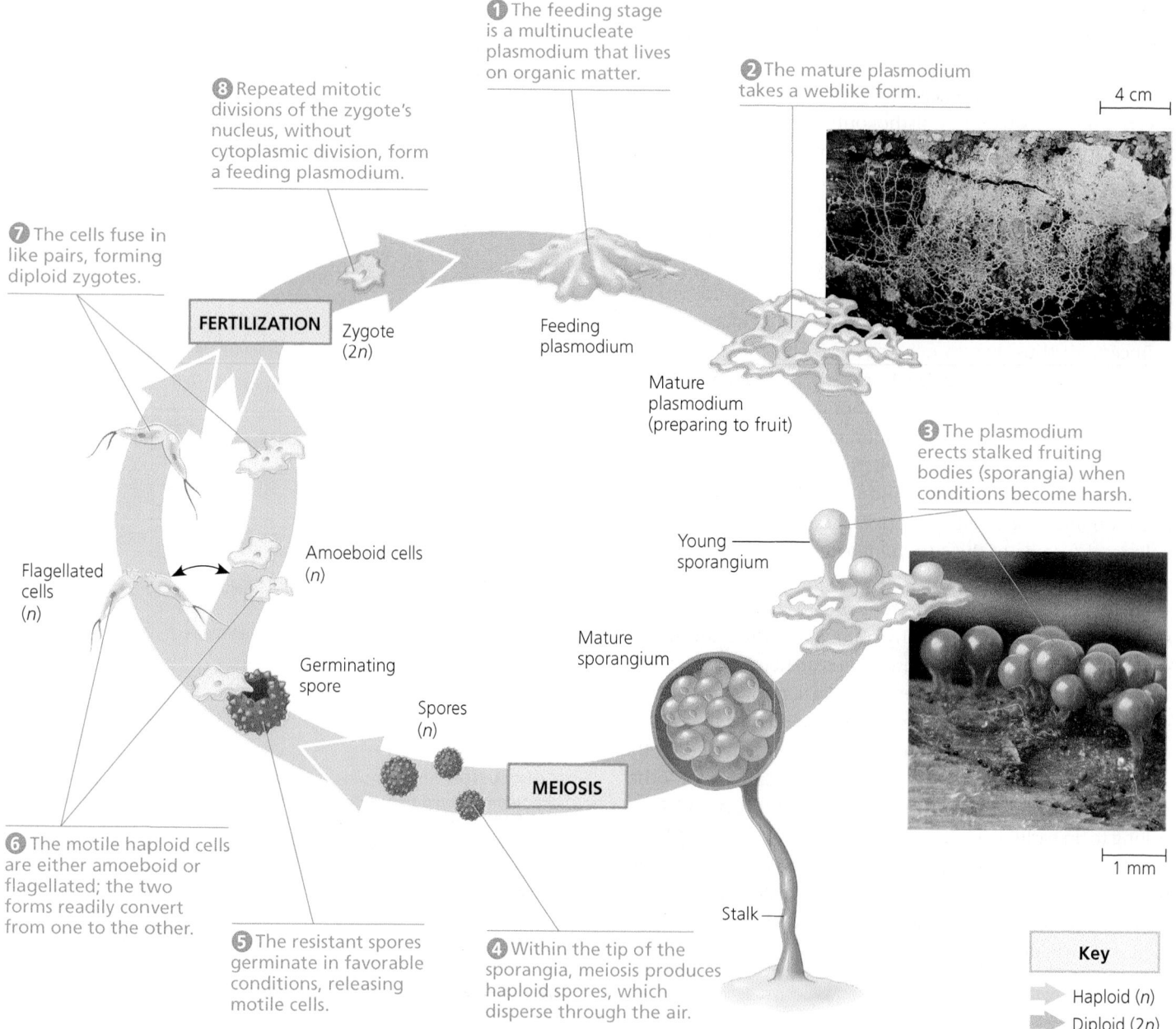

❶ The feeding stage is a multinucleate plasmodium that lives on organic matter.

❷ The mature plasmodium takes a weblike form.

4 cm

❽ Repeated mitotic divisions of the zygote's nucleus, without cytoplasmic division, form a feeding plasmodium.

❼ The cells fuse in like pairs, forming diploid zygotes.

FERTILIZATION

Zygote (2n)

Feeding plasmodium

Mature plasmodium (preparing to fruit)

❸ The plasmodium erects stalked fruiting bodies (sporangia) when conditions become harsh.

Amoeboid cells (n)

Flagellated cells (n)

Young sporangium

Mature sporangium

Germinating spore

Spores (n)

MEIOSIS

1 mm

❻ The motile haploid cells are either amoeboid or flagellated; the two forms readily convert from one to the other.

Stalk

❺ The resistant spores germinate in favorable conditions, releasing motile cells.

❹ Within the tip of the sporangia, meiosis produces haploid spores, which disperse through the air.

Key

Haploid (n)

Diploid (2n)

▲ Figure 28.24 **The life cycle of a plasmodial slime mold.**

logs, engulfing food particles by phagocytosis as it grows. If the habitat begins to dry up or there is no food left, the plasmodium stops growing and differentiates into fruiting bodies, which function in sexual reproduction.

Cellular Slime Molds The life cycle of the protists called **cellular slime molds** can prompt us to question what it means to be an individual organism. The feeding stage of these organisms consists of solitary cells that function individually, but when food is depleted, the cells form an aggregate that functions as a unit (Figure 28.25). Although this mass of cells superficially resembles a plasmodial slime mold, the cells remain separated by their individual plasma membranes. Cellular slime molds also differ from plasmodial slime molds in being haploid organisms (only the zygote is diploid) and in having fruiting bodies that function in asexual rather than sexual reproduction.

Dictyostelium discoideum, a cellular slime mold commonly found on forest floors, has become a model organism for studying the evolution of multicellularity. One line of research has focused on the slime mold's fruiting body stage. During this stage, the cells that form the stalk die as they dry out, while the spore cells at the top survive and have the potential to reproduce. Scientists have found that mutations in a single gene can turn individual *Dictyostelium* cells into "cheaters" that never become part of the stalk. Because these mutants gain a strong reproductive advantage over noncheaters, why don't all *Dictyostelium* cells cheat?

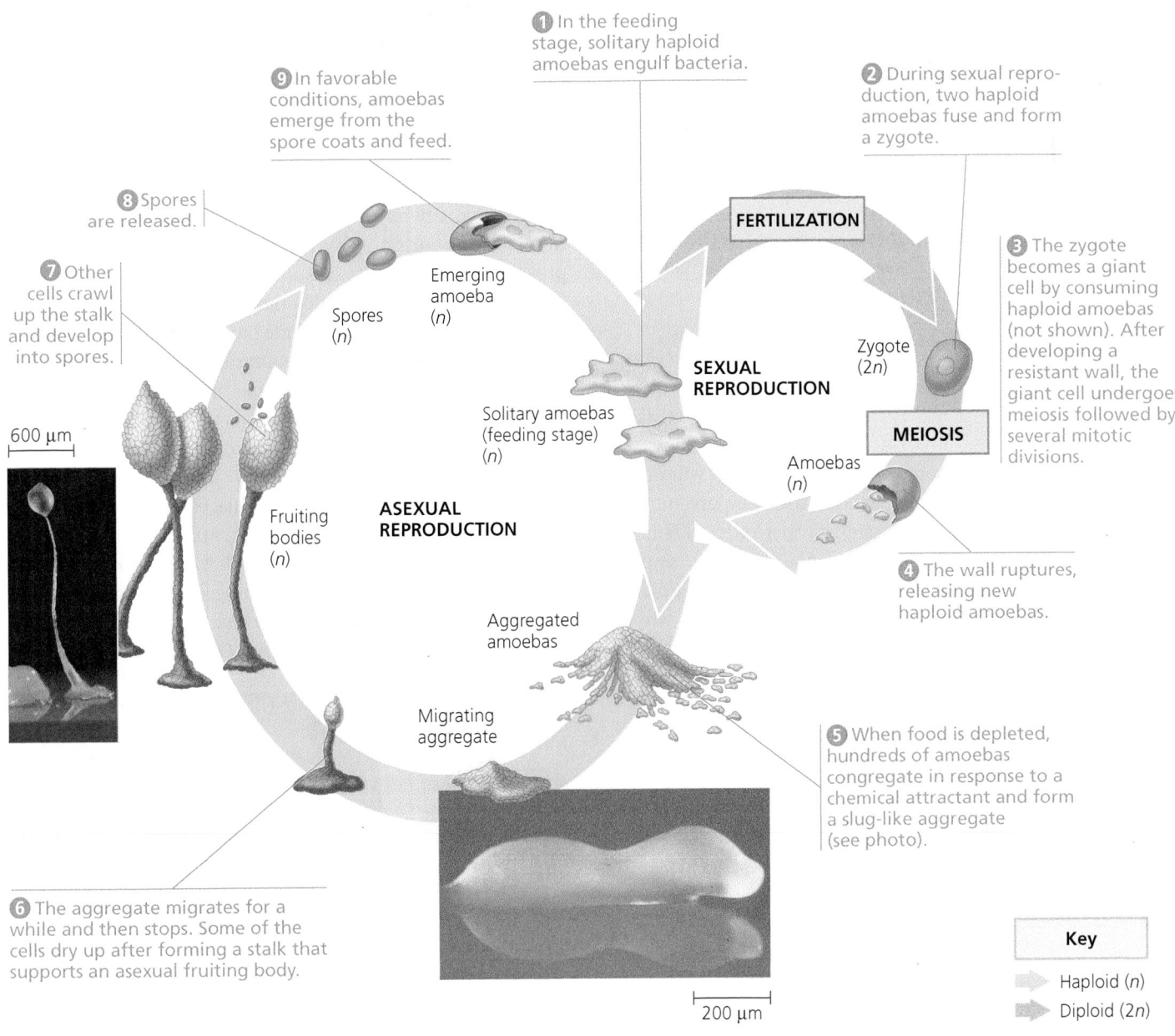

1 In the feeding stage, solitary haploid amoebas engulf bacteria.

9 In favorable conditions, amoebas emerge from the spore coats and feed.

2 During sexual reproduction, two haploid amoebas fuse and form a zygote.

FERTILIZATION

8 Spores are released.

3 The zygote becomes a giant cell by consuming haploid amoebas (not shown). After developing a resistant wall, the giant cell undergoes meiosis followed by several mitotic divisions.

7 Other cells crawl up the stalk and develop into spores.

Emerging amoeba (*n*)

Spores (*n*)

Zygote (*2n*)

SEXUAL REPRODUCTION

Solitary amoebas (feeding stage) (*n*)

MEIOSIS

600 μm

Amoebas (*n*)

ASEXUAL REPRODUCTION

Fruiting bodies (*n*)

4 The wall ruptures, releasing new haploid amoebas.

Aggregated amoebas

Migrating aggregate

5 When food is depleted, hundreds of amoebas congregate in response to a chemical attractant and form a slug-like aggregate (see photo).

6 The aggregate migrates for a while and then stops. Some of the cells dry up after forming a stalk that supports an asexual fruiting body.

200 μm

Key

Haploid (*n*)

Diploid (*2n*)

▲ **Figure 28.25 The life cycle of *Dictyostelium*, a cellular slime mold.**

Recent discoveries suggest an answer to this question. Cheating mutants lack a protein on their cell surface, and noncheating cells can recognize this difference. Noncheaters preferentially aggregate with other noncheaters, thus depriving cheaters of the opportunity to exploit them. Such a recognition system may have been important in the evolution of multicellular eukaryotes such as animals and plants.

Gymnamoebas

Gymnamoebas constitute a large and varied group of amoebozoans. These unicellular protists are ubiquitous in soil as well as freshwater and marine environments. Most are heterotrophs that actively seek and consume bacteria and other protists (see Figure 28.3). Some gymnamoebas also feed on detritus (nonliving organic matter).

Entamoebas

Whereas most amoebozoans are free-living, those that belong to the genus *Entamoeba* are parasites. They infect all classes of vertebrate animals as well as some invertebrates. Humans are host to at least six species of *Entamoeba*, but only one, *E. histolytica*, is known to be pathogenic. *E. histolytica* causes amebic dysentery and is spread via contaminated drinking water, food, or eating utensils. Responsible for up to 100,000 deaths worldwide every year, the disease is the third-leading cause of death due to eukaryotic parasites, after malaria (see Figure 28.10) and schistosomiasis (see Figure 33.11).

Opisthokonts

Opisthokonts are an extremely diverse group of eukaryotes that includes animals, fungi, and several groups of protists. We will discuss the evolutionary history of fungi and animals in Chapters 31–34. Of the opisthokont protists, we will discuss the nucleariids in Chapter 31 because they are more closely related to fungi than they are to other protists. Similarly, we will discuss choanoflagellates in Chapter 32, since they are more closely related to animals than they are to other protists. The nucleariids and choanoflagellates illustrate why scientists have abandoned the former kingdom Protista: A monophyletic group that included these single-celled eukaryotes would also have to include the multicellular animals and fungi that are closely related to them.

CONCEPT CHECK 28.6

1. Contrast the pseudopodia of amoebozoans and forams.
2. In what sense is "fungus animal" a fitting description of a slime mold? In what sense is it not fitting?
3. **WHAT IF?** If further evidence indicates that the root of the eukaryotic tree is as shown in Figure 28.23, would this evidence support, contradict, or have no bearing on the hypothesis that Excavata is monophyletic?

For suggested answers, see Appendix A.

CONCEPT 28.7

Protists play key roles in ecological communities

Most protists are aquatic, and they are found almost anywhere there is water, including moist terrestrial habitats such as damp soil and leaf litter. In oceans, ponds, and lakes, many protists are bottom-dwellers that attach to rocks and other substrates or creep through the sand and silt. Other protists are important constituents of plankton. We'll focus here on two key roles that protists play in the varied habitats in which they live: that of symbiont and that of producer.

Symbiotic Protists

Many protists form symbiotic associations with other species. For example, photosynthetic dinoflagellates are food-providing symbiotic partners of the coral polyps that build coral reefs. Coral reefs are highly diverse ecological communities. That diversity ultimately depends on corals—and on the mutualistic protist symbionts that nourish them. Corals support reef diversity by providing food to some species and habitat to many others.

Another example is the wood-digesting protists that inhabit the gut of many termite species **(Figure 28.26)**. Unaided, termites cannot digest wood, and they rely on protistan or prokaryotic symbionts to do so. Termites cause over $3.5 billion in damage annually to wooden homes in the United States.

Symbiotic protists also include parasites that have compromised the economies of entire countries. Consider the malaria-causing protist *Plasmodium*: Income levels in countries hard hit by malaria are 33% lower than in similar countries free of the disease. Protists can have devastating effects on other species too. Massive fish kills have been attributed to *Pfiesteria shumwayae* (see Figure 28.9), a dinoflagellate parasite that attaches to its victims and eats their skin. Among species that parasitize plants, the oomycete protist *Phytophthora ramorum* has emerged as a major new forest pathogen. This species causes sudden oak death (SOD), a disease that has killed millions of oaks and other trees in California and Oregon (see Chapter 54).

▶ **Figure 28.26 A symbiotic protist.** This organism is a hypermastigote, a member of a group of parabasalids that live in the gut of termites and certain cockroaches and enable the hosts to digest wood (SEM).

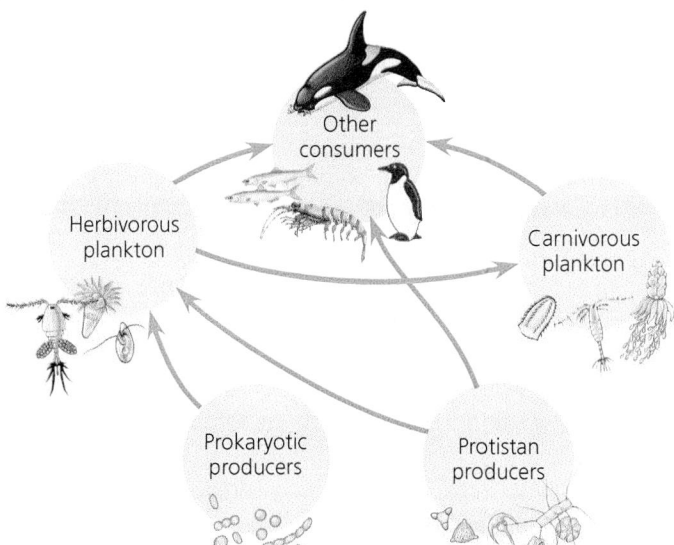

▲ **Figure 28.27 Protists: key producers in aquatic communities.** Arrows in this simplified food web lead from food sources to the organisms that eat them.

Photosynthetic Protists

Many protists are important **producers**, organisms that use energy from light (or inorganic chemicals) to convert carbon dioxide to organic compounds. Producers form the base of ecological food webs. In aquatic communities, the main producers are photosynthetic protists and prokaryotes. All other organisms in the community depend on them for food, either directly (by eating them) or indirectly (by eating an organism that ate a producer; **Figure 28.27**). Scientists estimate that roughly 30% of the world's photosynthesis is performed by diatoms, dinoflagellates, multicellular algae, and other aquatic protists. Photosynthetic prokaryotes contribute another 20%, and land plants are responsible for the remaining 50%.

Because producers form the foundation of food webs, factors that affect producers can dramatically affect their entire community. In aquatic environments, photosynthetic protists are often held in check by low concentrations of nitrogen, phosphorus, or iron. Various human actions can increase the concentrations of these elements in aquatic communities. For example, when fertilizer is applied to a field, some of the fertilizer may be washed by rainfall into a river that drains into a lake or ocean. When people add nutrients to aquatic communities in this or other ways, the abundance of photosynthetic protists can increase spectacularly. Such increases can alter the abundance of other species in the community, as we'll see in Chapter 55.

A pressing question is how global warming will affect protists and other producers. Satellite data indicate that the growth and biomass of photosynthetic protists and prokaryotes have declined in many regions as sea surface temperatures have increased (**Figure 28.28**). If sustained, these changes would likely have far-reaching effects on marine ecosystems, fishery yields, and the global carbon cycle (see Chapter 55). Global warming can also affect producers on land, but there the base of food webs is occupied not by protists but by land plants, which we will discuss in Chapters 29 and 30.

▼ **Figure 28.28**
IMPACT

Marine Protists in a Warmer World

Photosynthetic protists are important components of marine food webs, each day converting millions of tons of carbon in CO_2 to organic molecules on which other organisms depend. How has global warming affected these key marine producers? Satellite data indicate that the growth and biomass of marine producers are negatively correlated to sea surface temperature (SST) across much of the tropical and midlatitude oceans (between the heavy black lines on the map below). In regions where SSTs have risen and growth has declined, the available nutrient supply may have been reduced by the formation of a light, warm layer of water that acts as a barrier preventing the rise, or upwelling, of cold, nutrient-rich waters from below.

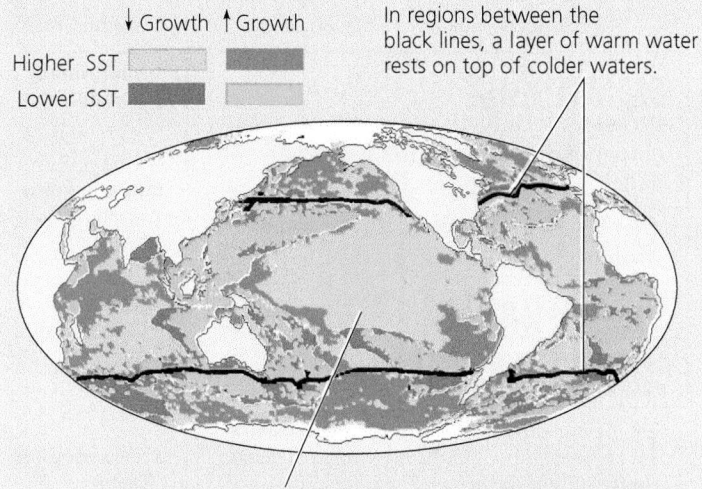

In regions between the black lines, a layer of warm water rests on top of colder waters.

In the yellow regions, high SSTs increase the temperature differences between warm and cold waters, which reduces upwelling. Marine producers rely on upwelled nutrients, so their growth decreases when upwelling decreases.

WHY IT MATTERS Major changes to marine ecosystems are expected if the growth and biomass of producers decrease as SSTs increase due to global warming. A decrease in diatom biomass, for example, would likely reduce both the amount of carbon pumped to the ocean floor and the catch of economically important fishes such as salmon and anchovies that feed on phytoplankton.

FURTHER READING M. J. Behrenfeld et al., Climate-driven trends in contemporary ocean productivity, *Nature* 444:752–755 (2006).

WHAT IF? If diatom populations continue to drop as the oceans warm, how might climate be affected in the future?

CONCEPT CHECK 28.7

1. Justify the claim that photosynthetic protists are among the biosphere's most important organisms.
2. Describe three symbioses that include protists.
3. **WHAT IF?** High water temperatures and pollution can cause corals to expel their dinoflagellate symbionts. Predict how such "coral bleaching" would affect corals and other species in the community.

For suggested answers, see Appendix A.

SUMMARY OF KEY CONCEPTS

CONCEPT 28.1

Most eukaryotes are single-celled organisms (pp. 575–579)

- Protists are more diverse than all other eukaryotes and are no longer classified in a single kingdom. Most are unicellular. Protists include photoautotrophs, heterotrophs, and mixotrophs. Protists are characterized by a wide diversity of life cycles.
- Mitochondria and plastids are thought to be descendants of bacteria that were engulfed by other cells and became endosymbionts. The plastid-bearing lineage eventually evolved into red algae and green algae. Other protist groups evolved from secondary endosymbiosis events in which red algae or green algae were themselves engulfed.

- In one hypothesis, eukaryotes are grouped into five super-groups, each a monophyletic clade: Excavata, Chromalveolata, Rhizaria, Archaeplastida, and Unikonta.

? *Describe similarities and differences between protists and other eukaryotes.*

Key Concept/Eukaryote Supergroup	Major Groups	Key Morphological Characteristics	Specific Examples
CONCEPT 28.2 Excavates include protists with modified mitochondria and protists with unique flagella (pp. 580–581) ? *What evidence indicates that the excavates form a clade?*	**Diplomonads and parabasalids**	Modified mitochondria	Giardia, Trichomonas
	Euglenozoans Kinetoplastids Euglenids	Spiral or crystalline rod inside flagella	Trypanosoma, Euglena
CONCEPT 28.3 Chromalveolates may have originated by secondary endosymbiosis (pp. 582–589) ? *If Chromalveolata originated by secondary endosymbiosis, what can be inferred about the plastids of its members? Explain.*	**Alveolates** Dinoflagellates Apicomplexans Ciliates	Membrane-bounded sacs (alveoli) beneath plasma membrane	Pfiesteria, Plasmodium, Paramecium
	Stramenopiles Diatoms Golden algae Brown algae Oomycetes	Hairy and smooth flagella	Phytophthora, Laminaria
CONCEPT 28.4 Rhizarians are a diverse group of protists defined by DNA similarities (pp. 589–590) ? *What are the main subgroups of rhizarians, and what unites these subgroups as a clade?*	**Radiolarians**	Amoebas with threadlike pseudopodia radiating from central body	Hexacontium
	Forams	Amoebas with threadlike pseudopodia and a porous shell	Globigerina
	Cercozoans	Amoebas and flagellated protists with threadlike pseudopodia	Paulinella
CONCEPT 28.5 Red algae and green algae are the closest relatives of land plants (pp. 590–592) (Archaeplastida) ? *On what basis do some systematists place land plants in the same supergroup (Archaeplastida) as red and green algae?*	**Red algae**	Phycoerythrin (accessory pigment)	Porphyra
	Green algae	Plant-type chloroplasts	Chlamydomonas, Ulva
	Land plants	(See Chapters 29 and 30.)	Mosses, ferns, conifers, flowering plants
CONCEPT 28.6 Unikonts include protists that are closely related to fungi and animals (pp. 593–596) ? *Describe a key feature for each of the main protist subgroups of Unikonta.*	**Amoebozoans** Slime molds Gymnamoebas Entamoebas	Amoebas with lobe-shaped pseudopodia	Amoeba, Entamoeba, Dictyostelium
	Opisthokonts	(Highly variable; see Chapters 31–34.)	Nucleariids, choanoflagellates, animals, fungi

Protists play key roles in ecological communities (pp. 596–597)

- Protists form a wide range of mutualistic and parasitic relationships that affect their symbiotic partners and many other members of the community.
- Photosynthetic protists are among the most important producers in aquatic communities. Because they are at the base of the food web, factors that affect photosynthetic protists affect many other species in the community.

? *Describe several protists that are ecologically important.*

TEST YOUR UNDERSTANDING

LEVEL 1: KNOWLEDGE/COMPREHENSION

1. Plastids that are surrounded by more than two membranes are evidence of
   a. evolution from mitochondria.
   b. fusion of plastids.
   c. origin of the plastids from archaea.
   d. secondary endosymbiosis.
   e. budding of the plastids from the nuclear envelope.

2. Biologists suspect that endosymbiosis gave rise to mitochondria before plastids partly because
   a. the products of photosynthesis could not be metabolized without mitochondrial enzymes.
   b. all eukaryotes have mitochondria (or their remnants), whereas many eukaryotes do not have plastids.
   c. mitochondrial DNA is less similar to prokaryotic DNA than is plastid DNA.
   d. without mitochondrial CO_2 production, photosynthesis could not occur.
   e. mitochondrial proteins are synthesized on cytosolic ribosomes, whereas plastids utilize their own ribosomes.

3. Which group is *incorrectly* paired with its description?
   a. rhizarians—morphologically diverse group defined by DNA similarities
   b. diatoms—important producers in aquatic communities
   c. red algae—acquired plastids by secondary endosymbiosis
   d. apicomplexans—parasites with intricate life cycles
   e. diplomonads—protists with modified mitochondria

4. Which protists are in the same eukaryotic supergroup as land plants?
   a. green algae
   b. dinoflagellates
   c. red algae
   d. brown algae
   e. both a and c

5. In life cycles with an alternation of generations, multicellular haploid forms alternate with
   a. unicellular haploid forms.
   b. unicellular diploid forms.
   c. multicellular haploid forms.
   d. multicellular diploid forms.
   e. multicellular polyploid forms.

LEVEL 2: APPLICATION/ANALYSIS

6. Based on the phylogenetic tree in Figure 28.3, which of the following statements is correct?
   a. The most recent common ancestor of Excavata is older than that of Chromalveolata.
   b. The most recent common ancestor of Chromalveolata is older than that of Rhizaria.
   c. The most recent common ancestor of red algae and land plants is older than that of nucleariids and fungi.
   d. The most basal (first to diverge) eukaryotic supergroup cannot be determined.
   e. Excavata is the most basal eukaryotic supergroup.

7. **EVOLUTION CONNECTION**
   DRAW IT Medical researchers seek to develop drugs that can kill or restrict the growth of human pathogens yet have few harmful effects on patients. These drugs often work by disrupting the metabolism of the pathogen or by targeting its structural features.

   Draw and label a phylogenetic tree that includes an ancestral prokaryote and the following groups of organisms: Excavata, Chromalveolata, Rhizaria, Archaeplastida, Unikonta, and, within Unikonta, amoebozoans, animals, choanoflagellates, fungi, and nucleariids. Based on this tree, hypothesize whether it would be most difficult to develop drugs to combat human pathogens that are prokaryotes, protists, animals, or fungi. (You do not need to consider the evolution of drug resistance by the pathogen.)

LEVEL 3: SYNTHESIS/EVALUATION

8. **SCIENTIFIC INQUIRY**
   Applying the "If . . . then" logic of science (see Chapter 1), what are a few of the predictions that arise from the hypothesis that plants evolved from green algae? Put another way, how could you test this hypothesis?

9. **WRITE ABOUT A THEME**
   Ecological Interactions Organisms interact with each other and the physical environment. In a short essay (100–150 words), explain how the response of diatom populations to a drop in nutrient availability can affect both other organisms and aspects of the physical environment (such as carbon dioxide concentrations).

For selected answers, see Appendix A.

 Mastering**BIOLOGY** www.masteringbiology.com

1. MasteringBiology® Assignments
Tutorial Life Cycles of Protists
Activities Tentative Phylogeny of Eukaryotes • Alternation of Generations in a Protist • Life Cycle of a Malaria Parasite
Questions Student Misconceptions • Reading Quiz • Multiple Choice • End-of-Chapter

2. eText
Read your book online, search, take notes, highlight text, and more.

3. The Study Area
Practice Tests • Cumulative Test • ***BioFlix*** 3-D Animations • MP3 Tutor Sessions • Videos • Activities • Investigations • Lab Media • Audio Glossary • Word Study Tools • Art

Plant Diversity I: How Plants Colonized Land

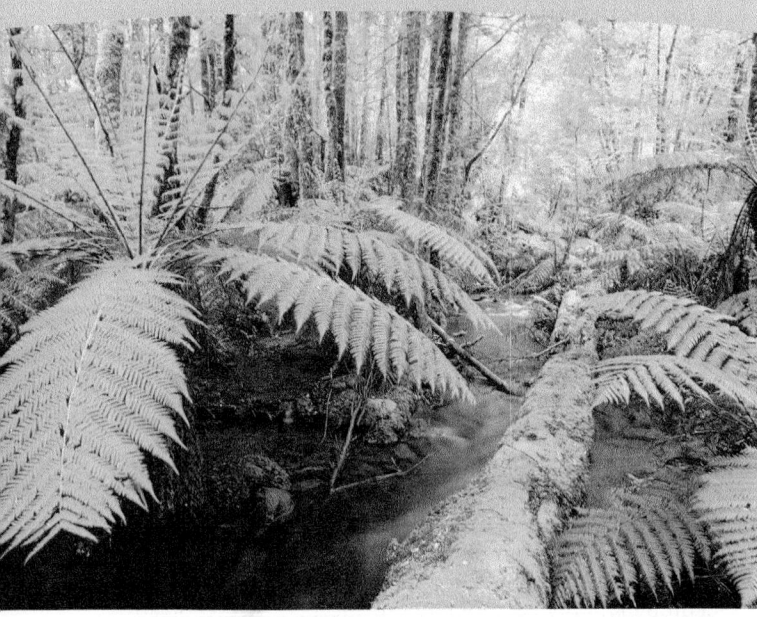

▲ Figure 29.1 **How did plants change the world?**

KEY CONCEPTS

29.1 Land plants evolved from green algae
29.2 Mosses and other nonvascular plants have life cycles dominated by gametophytes
29.3 Ferns and other seedless vascular plants were the first plants to grow tall

OVERVIEW

The Greening of Earth

Looking at a lush landscape, such as the forest scene in Figure 29.1, it is difficult to imagine the terrestrial environment without any plants or other organisms. Yet for more than 3 billion years of Earth's history, the land surface was largely lifeless. Geochemical evidence suggests that thin coatings of cyanobacteria existed on land about 1.2 billion years ago. But it was only within the last 500 million years that small plants as well as fungi and animals joined them

ashore. Finally, by about 385 million years ago, some plants appeared that could grow much taller, leading to the formation of the first forests (though with a very different set of species than those in Figure 29.1).

Since colonizing land, plants have diversified widely; today, there are more than 290,000 known plant species. Plants inhabit all but the harshest environments, such as some mountaintops, a few desert areas, and the polar regions. A few plant species, such as seagrasses, returned to aquatic habitats during their evolution, but most present-day plants live in terrestrial environments. In this chapter, we'll refer to all plants as *land* plants, even those that are now aquatic, to distinguish them from algae, which are photosynthetic protists.

The presence of land plants has enabled other life-forms—including animals—to survive on land. Plants supply oxygen and ultimately most of the food eaten by terrestrial animals. Also, plant roots create habitats for other organisms by stabilizing the soil in sand dunes and many other environments.

This chapter traces the first 100 million years of plant evolution, including the emergence of seedless plants such as mosses and ferns. Chapter 30 examines the later evolution of seed plants.

CONCEPT **29.1**

Land plants evolved from green algae

As you read in Chapter 28, researchers have identified green algae called charophytes as the closest relatives of land plants. What is the evidence for this relationship, and what does it suggest about the algal ancestors of land plants?

Morphological and Molecular Evidence

Many key traits of land plants also appear in some protists, primarily algae. For example, plants are multicellular, eukaryotic, photosynthetic autotrophs, as are brown, red, and certain green algae. Plants have cell walls made of cellulose, and so do green algae, dinoflagellates, and brown algae. And chloroplasts with chlorophylls *a* and *b* are present in green algae, euglenids, and a few dinoflagellates, as well as in plants.

However, the charophytes are the only algae that share the following four distinctive traits with land plants, strongly suggesting that they are the closest relatives of plants:

- **Rings of cellulose-synthesizing proteins.** The cells of both land plants and charophytes have distinctive circular rings of proteins in the plasma membrane (Figure 29.2). These protein rings synthesize the cellulose microfibrils of the cell wall. In contrast, noncharophyte algae have linear sets of proteins that synthesize cellulose.
- **Peroxisome enzymes.** The peroxisomes (see Figure 6.19) of both land plants and charophytes contain enzymes that help minimize the loss of organic products resulting from photorespiration (see Chapter 10).

▶ **Figure 29.2 Rings of cellulose-synthesizing proteins.** These circular sets of proteins embedded in the plasma membrane are found only in land plants and charophyte algae (SEM).

30 nm

- **Structure of flagellated sperm.** In species of land plants that have flagellated sperm, the structure of the sperm closely resembles that of charophyte sperm.
- **Formation of a phragmoplast.** Particular details of cell division occur only in land plants and certain charophytes, including the genera *Chara* and *Coleochaete*. For example, in land plants and certain charophytes, a group of microtubules known as the **phragmoplast** forms between the daughter nuclei of a dividing cell. A cell plate then develops in the middle of the phragmoplast, across the midline of the dividing cell (see Figure 12.10). The cell plate, in turn, gives rise to a new cross wall that separates the daughter cells.

Genetic evidence also supports the conclusion drawn from these four morphological and biochemical traits. Analyses of nuclear and chloroplast genes from a wide range of plants and algae indicate that charophytes—particularly *Chara* and *Coleochaete*—are the closest living relatives of land plants (Figure 29.3). Note that this does not mean that plants are descended from these living algae; however, present-day charophytes may tell us something about what the algal ancestors of plants were like.

Adaptations Enabling the Move to Land

Many species of charophyte algae inhabit shallow waters around the edges of ponds and lakes, where they are subject to occasional drying. In such environments, natural selection favors individual algae that can survive periods when they are not submerged in water. In charophytes, a layer of a durable polymer called **sporopollenin** prevents exposed zygotes from drying out. A similar chemical adaptation is found in the tough sporopollenin walls that encase the spores of plants.

The accumulation of such traits by at least one population of charophyte ancestors probably enabled their descendants—the first land plants—to live permanently above the waterline. These evolutionary novelties opened a new frontier: a terrestrial habitat that offered enormous benefits. The bright sunlight was unfiltered by water and plankton; the atmosphere offered more plentiful carbon dioxide than did water; the soil by the water's edge was rich in some mineral nutrients; and initially there were relatively few herbivores and pathogens. But these benefits were accompanied by challenges: a relative scarcity of water and a lack of structural support against gravity. (To appreciate why such support is important, picture how the soft body of a jellyfish sags when taken out of water.) Land

◀ *Chara* species, a pond organism

▼ *Coleochaete orbicularis*, a disk-shaped charophyte that also lives in ponds (LM)

5 mm

40 µm

▲ **Figure 29.3 Examples of charophytes, the closest algal relatives of land plants.**

plants diversified as adaptations evolved that enabled plants to thrive despite these challenges.

Today, what adaptations are unique to plants? The answer to this question depends on where you draw the boundary dividing land plants from algae (Figure 29.4). Many biologists equate the kingdom Plantae with embryophytes (plants with embryos). Others propose that the boundaries of the plant kingdom should be expanded to include some or all of the green algae (kingdoms Streptophyta and Viridiplantae). Since the debate is ongoing, this text retains the embryophyte definition of the plant kingdom and uses Plantae as the formal name for the taxon. In this context, let's now identify the derived traits that separate land plants from their closest algal relatives.

Derived Traits of Plants

Many of the adaptations that appear to have emerged after land plants diverged from their algal relatives facilitated survival and reproduction on dry land. Figure 29.5, on the next two pages, depicts four key traits that appear in land plants but not in the charophyte algae.

ANCESTRAL ALGA

Red algae

Chlorophytes

Charophytes

Embryophytes

Viridiplantae

Streptophyta

Plantae

▲ **Figure 29.4 Three possible "plant" kingdoms.**

Exploring Derived Traits of Land Plants

Charophyte algae lack the four key traits of land plants described in this figure: alternation of generations (with an associated trait of multicellular, dependent embryos), walled spores produced in sporangia, multicellular gametangia, and apical meristems. This suggests that these four traits were absent in the ancestor common to land plants and charophytes but instead evolved as derived traits of land plants. Note that some of these traits are not unique to plants, having evolved independently in other lineages. And not every land plant exhibits all four of these traits; certain lineages of plants have lost some traits over time.

Alternation of Generations and Multicellular, Dependent Embryos

The life cycles of all land plants alternate between two generations of multicellular organisms: gametophytes and sporophytes. As shown in the diagram (using a fern as an example), each generation gives rise to the other, a process that is called **alternation of generations**. This type of reproductive cycle evolved in various groups of algae but does not occur in the charophytes, the algae most closely related to land plants.

Take care not to confuse the alternation of generations in plants with the haploid and diploid stages in the life cycles of other sexually reproducing organisms (see Figure 13.6). In humans, for example, meiosis produces haploid gametes that unite, forming diploid zygotes that divide and become multicellular. The haploid stage is represented only by single-celled gametes. In contrast, alternation of generations is distinguished by the fact that the life cycle includes both multicellular haploid organisms and multicellular diploid organisms. The multicellular haploid **gametophyte** ("gamete-producing plant") is named for its production by mitosis of haploid gametes—eggs and sperm—that fuse during fertilization, forming diploid zygotes. Mitotic division of the zygote produces a multicellular diploid **sporophyte** ("spore-producing plant"). Meiosis in a mature sporophyte produces haploid **spores**,

Alternation of generations: five generalized steps

❶ The gametophyte produces haploid gametes by mitosis.

Gametophyte (n)

Mitosis

Gamete from another plant

Mitosis

❺ The spores develop into multicellular haploid gametophytes.

Spore

Gamete

❷ Two gametes unite (fertilization) and form a diploid zygote.

MEIOSIS

FERTILIZATION

❹ The sporophyte produces haploid spores by meiosis.

Zygote

❸ The zygote develops into a multicellular diploid sporophyte.

Sporophyte (2n)

Mitosis

Key

Haploid (n)

Diploid (2n)

reproductive cells that can develop into a new haploid organism without fusing with another cell. Mitotic division of the spore cell produces a new multicellular gametophyte, and the cycle begins again. In many seedless plants, such as the fern in the diagram, the gametophyte and sporophyte look like different types of plants, even though they are forms of the same species. In seed plants, the gametophytes are microscopic; the familiar plants we see are the sporophytes.

As part of a life cycle with alternation of generations, multicellular plant embryos develop from zygotes that are retained within the tissues of the female parent (a gametophyte). The parental tissues provide the developing embryo with nutrients, such as sugars and amino acids. The embryo has specialized **placental transfer cells**, sometimes present in the adjacent maternal tissue as well, which enhance the transfer of nutrients from parent to embryo through elaborate ingrowths of the wall surface (plasma membrane and cell wall). This interface is analogous to the nutrient-transferring embryo-mother interface of eutherian (placental) mammals. The multicellular, dependent embryo of land plants is such a significant derived trait that land plants are also known as **embryophytes**.

Embryo (LM) and placental transfer cell (TEM) of *Marchantia* (a liverwort)

Embryo

Maternal tissue

2 μm

10 μm

Wall ingrowths

Placental transfer cell (outlined in blue)

MAKE CONNECTIONS *Review sexual life cycles in Figure 13.6 on p. 252. Identify which life cycle has alternation of generations, and summarize how it differs from other life cycles.*

Walled Spores Produced in Sporangia

Plant spores are haploid reproductive cells that can grow into multicellular haploid gametophytes by mitosis. The polymer sporopollenin makes the walls of plant spores tough and resistant to harsh environments. This chemical adaptation enables spores to be dispersed through dry air without harm.

The sporophyte has multicellular organs called **sporangia** (singular, *sporangium*) that produce the spores. Within a sporangium, diploid cells called **sporocytes**, or spore mother cells, undergo meiosis and generate the haploid spores. The outer tissues of the sporangium protect the developing spores until they are released into the air. Multicellular sporangia that produce spores with sporopollenin-enriched walls are key terrestrial adaptations of land plants. Although charophytes also produce spores, these algae lack multicellular sporangia, and their flagellated, water-dispersed spores lack sporopollenin.

Sporophytes and sporangia of *Sphagnum* (a moss)

Multicellular Gametangia

Another feature distinguishing early land plants from their algal ancestors was the production of gametes within multicellular organs called **gametangia**. The female gametangia are called **archegonia** (singular, *archegonium*). Each archegonium is a pear-shaped organ that produces a single nonmotile egg retained within the bulbous part of the organ (the top for the species shown here). The male gametangia, called **antheridia** (singular, *antheridium*), produce sperm and release them into the environment. In many groups of present-day plants, the sperm have flagella and swim to the eggs through water droplets or a film of water. Each egg is fertilized within an archegonium, where the zygote develops into an embryo. As you will see in Chapter 30, the gametophytes of seed plants are so reduced in size that the archegonia and antheridia have been lost in many lineages.

Archegonia and antheridia of *Marchantia* (a liverwort)

Apical Meristems

In terrestrial habitats, a photosynthetic organism finds essential resources in two very different places. Light and CO_2 are mainly available above ground; water and mineral nutrients are found mainly in the soil. Though plants cannot move from place to place, their roots and shoots can elongate, increasing exposure to environmental resources. This growth in length is sustained throughout the plant's life by the activity of **apical meristems**, localized regions of cell division at the tips of roots and shoots. Cells produced by apical meristems differentiate into the outer epidermis, which protects the body, and various types of internal tissues. Shoot apical meristems also generate leaves in most plants. Thus, the complex bodies of plants have specialized below- and aboveground organs.

Apical meristems of plant roots and shoots. The LMs are longitudinal sections at the tips of a root and shoot.

In addition to the four traits shown in Figure 29.5, other derived traits that relate to terrestrial life have evolved in many plant species. For example, the epidermis in many species has a covering, the **cuticle**, which consists of wax and other polymers. Permanently exposed to the air, land plants run a far greater risk of desiccation (drying out) than their algal ancestors. The cuticle acts as waterproofing, helping prevent excessive water loss from the aboveground plant organs, while also providing some protection from microbial attack.

Early land plants lacked true roots and leaves. Without roots, how did these plants absorb nutrients from the soil? Fossils dating from 420 million years ago reveal an adaptation that may have aided early plants in nutrient uptake: They formed symbiotic associations with fungi similar in structure to beneficial associations observed today between plants and fungi. We'll describe these associations, called *mycorrhizae*, and their benefits to both plants and fungi in more detail in Chapter 31. For now, the main point is that mycorrhizal fungi form extensive networks of filaments through the soil, enabling them to absorb nutrients more effectively than a plant can on its own. The fungi transfer nutrients to their symbiotic plant partner, a benefit that may have helped plants without roots to colonize land.

Finally, many land plants produce molecules called *secondary compounds*, so named because they are products of secondary metabolic pathways—side branches off the primary metabolic pathways that produce the lipids, carbohydrates, amino acids, and other compounds common to all organisms. Secondary compounds include compounds called alkaloids, terpenes, tannins, and flavonoids. Various alkaloids, terpenes, and tannins have a bitter taste, strong odor, or toxic effect that helps defend a plant against herbivores and parasites. Flavonoids absorb harmful UV radiation, and some related compounds deter attack by pathogens. Humans also benefit from secondary compounds in plants, many of which are used in spices, medicines, and other products.

The Origin and Diversification of Plants

Paleobotanists seeking the evolutionary origin of plants have long debated what constitutes the oldest fossil evidence of land plants. In the 1970s, researchers found fossil spores dating to the Ordovician period, up to 475 million years old. Although the fossil spores resemble those of living plants, they also have some striking differences. For example, spores of present-day plants are typically dispersed as single grains, but the fossil spores are fused together in groups of two or four. This difference raises the possibility that the fossil spores were not produced by plants, but by some extinct algal relative. Furthermore, the oldest known fragments of plant body tissues are 50 million years younger than the puzzling spores.

In 2003, scientists from Britain and the Middle Eastern country of Oman shed some light on this mystery when they extracted spores from 475-million-year-old rocks from Oman

(a) Fossilized spores. Unlike the spores of most living plants, which are single grains, these spores found in Oman are in groups of four (left; one hidden) and two (right).

(b) Fossilized sporophyte tissue. The spores were embedded in tissue that appears to be from plants.

▲ Figure 29.6 **Ancient plant spores and tissue** (colorized SEMs).

(Figure 29.6a). Unlike previously discovered spores of this age, these were embedded in plant cuticle material that is similar to spore-bearing tissue in living plants **(Figure 29.6b)**. After uncovering other small fragments of tissue that clearly belonged to plants, the scientists concluded that the spores from Oman represent fossil plants rather than algae.

Whatever the precise age of the first land plants, those ancestral species gave rise to the vast diversity of living plants. **Table 29.1** summarizes the ten extant phyla in the taxonomic scheme used in this text. (Extant lineages are those that have surviving members, not only extinct ones.) As you read the rest of this section, look at Table 29.1 together with **Figure 29.7**, which reflects a view of plant phylogeny based on plant morphology, biochemistry, and genetics.

One way to distinguish groups of plants is whether or not they have an extensive system of **vascular tissue**, cells joined into tubes that transport water and nutrients throughout the plant body. Most present-day plants have a complex vascular tissue system and are therefore called **vascular plants**. Plants that do not have an extensive transport system—liverworts, mosses, and hornworts—are described as "nonvascular" plants, even though some mosses do have simple vascular tissue. Nonvascular plants are often informally called **bryophytes** (from the Greek *bryon*, moss, and *phyton*, plant).

Although the term *bryophyte* is commonly used to refer to all nonvascular plants, molecular studies and morphological analyses of sperm structure have concluded that bryophytes do not form a monophyletic group (a clade). Debate continues, however, over the relationships of liverworts, mosses, and hornworts to each other and to vascular plants. Regardless of the outcome of this debate, bryophytes share some derived traits with vascular plants, such as multicellular

Table 29.1 Ten Phyla of Extant Plants

	Common Name	Number of Known Species
Nonvascular Plants (Bryophytes)		
Phylum Hepatophyta	Liverworts	9,000
Phylum Bryophyta	Mosses	15,000
Phylum Anthocerophyta	Hornworts	100
Vascular Plants		
Seedless Vascular Plants		
Phylum Lycophyta	Lycophytes	1,200
Phylum Pterophyta	Pterophytes	12,000
Seed Plants		
Gymnosperms		
Phylum Ginkgophyta	Ginkgo	1
Phylum Cycadophyta	Cycads	130
Phylum Gnetophyta	Gnetophytes	75
Phylum Coniferophyta	Conifers	600
Angiosperms		
Phylum Anthophyta	Flowering plants	250,000

embryos and apical meristems, while lacking many innovations of vascular plants, such as roots and true leaves.

Vascular plants, which form a clade that comprises about 93% of all extant plant species, can be categorized further into smaller clades. Two of these clades are the **lycophytes** (club mosses and their relatives) and the **pterophytes** (ferns and their relatives). The plants in each of these clades lack seeds, which is why collectively the two clades are often informally called **seedless vascular plants**. However, notice in Figure 29.7 that seedless vascular plants are paraphyletic, not monophyletic. Groups such as the seedless vascular plants are sometimes referred to as a **grade**, a collection of organisms that share a key biological feature. Grades can be informative by grouping organisms according to features, such as lack of seeds. But members of a grade, unlike members of a clade, do not necessarily share the same ancestry. For example, even though pterophytes and lycophytes are all seedless plants, pterophytes share a more recent common ancestor with seed plants. As a result, we would expect pterophytes and seed plants to share key traits not found in lycophytes—and they do, as you'll read.

A third clade of vascular plants consists of seed plants, which represent the vast majority of living plant species. A **seed** is an embryo packaged with a supply of nutrients inside a protective coat. Seed plants can be divided into two groups, gymnosperms and angiosperms, based on the absence or

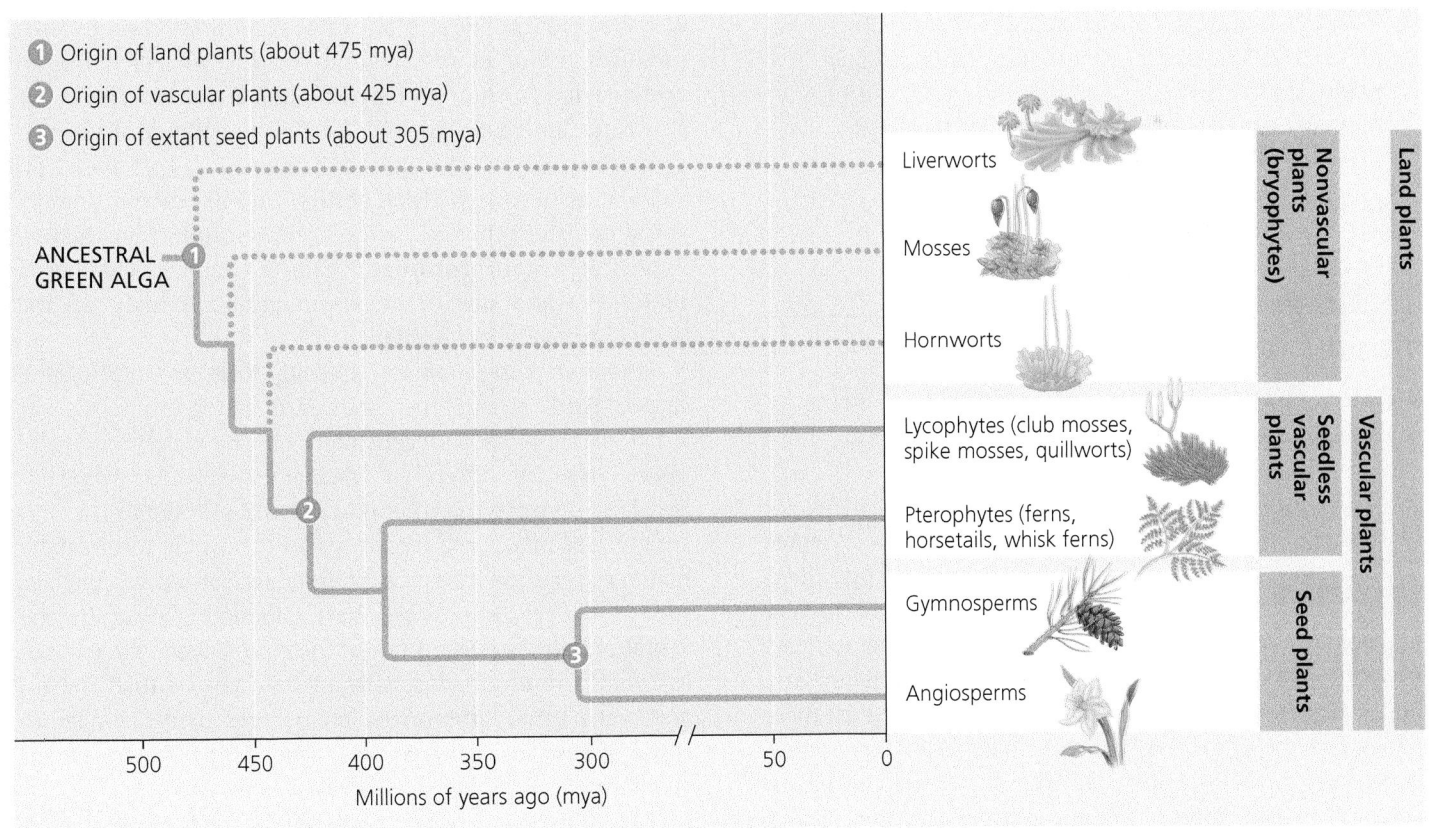

1. Origin of land plants (about 475 mya)
2. Origin of vascular plants (about 425 mya)
3. Origin of extant seed plants (about 305 mya)

▲ **Figure 29.7 Highlights of plant evolution.** The phylogeny shown here illustrates a leading hypothesis about the relationships between plant groups. The dotted lines indicate groups whose evolutionary relationships continue to be debated.

presence of enclosed chambers in which seeds mature. **Gymnosperms** (from the Greek *gymnos*, naked, and *sperm*, seed) are grouped together as "naked seed" plants because their seeds are not enclosed in chambers. Living gymnosperm species, the most familiar of which are the conifers, probably form a clade. **Angiosperms** (from the Greek *angion*, container) are a huge clade consisting of all flowering plants. Angiosperm seeds develop inside chambers called ovaries, which originate within flowers and mature into fruits. Nearly 90% of living plant species are angiosperms.

Note that the phylogeny depicted in Figure 29.7 focuses only on the relationships between extant plant lineages. Paleobotanists have also discovered fossils belonging to extinct plant lineages. As you'll read later in the chapter, many of these fossils reveal intermediate steps in the emergence of the distinctive plant groups found on Earth today.

CONCEPT CHECK 29.1

1. Why do researchers identify charophytes rather than another group as the closest relatives of land plants?
2. Identify three derived traits that distinguish plants from charophytes *and* facilitate life on land. Explain.
3. **WHAT IF?** What would the human life cycle be like if we had alternation of generations? Assume that the multicellular diploid stage is similar in form to an adult human.
4. **MAKE CONNECTIONS** Figure 29.7 identifies which lineages are land plants, nonvascular plants, vascular plants, seedless vascular plants, and seed plants. Which of these categories are monophyletic, and which are paraphyletic? Explain. See Figure 26.10 on p. 542.

For suggested answers, see Appendix A.

CONCEPT 29.2

Mosses and other nonvascular plants have life cycles dominated by gametophytes

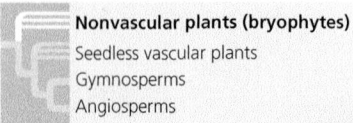

The nonvascular plants (bryophytes) are represented today by three phyla of small herbaceous (nonwoody) plants: **liverworts** (phylum Hepatophyta), **mosses** (phylum Bryophyta), and **hornworts** (phylum Anthocerophyta). Liverworts and hornworts are named for their shapes, plus the suffix *wort* (from the Anglo-Saxon for "herb"). Mosses are familiar to many people, although some plants commonly called "mosses" are not really mosses at all. These include Irish moss (a red seaweed), reindeer moss (a lichen), club mosses (seedless vascular plants), and Spanish mosses (lichens in some regions and flowering plants in others).

Note that the terms *Bryophyta* and *bryophyte* are not synonymous. Bryophyta is the formal taxonomic name for the phylum that consists solely of mosses. As mentioned earlier, the term *bryophyte* is used informally to refer to *all* nonvascular plants—liverworts, mosses, and hornworts.

Liverworts, mosses, and hornworts have acquired many unique adaptations over the long course of their evolution. Nevertheless, living bryophytes likely reflect some traits of the earliest plants. The oldest known fossils of plant fragments, for example, include tissues very similar to those inside liverworts. Researchers hope to discover more parts of these ancient plants to see if this resemblance is reflected more broadly.

Bryophyte Gametophytes

Unlike vascular plants, in all three bryophyte phyla the haploid gametophytes are the dominant stage of the life cycle: That is, they are usually larger and longer-living than the sporophytes, as shown in the moss life cycle in **Figure 29.8**. Sporophytes are typically present only part of the time.

When bryophyte spores are dispersed to a favorable habitat, such as moist soil or tree bark, they may germinate and grow into gametophytes. Germinating moss spores, for example, characteristically produce a mass of green, branched, one-cell-thick filaments known as a **protonema** (plural, *protonemata*; from the Greek *proto*, first, and *nema*, threads). A protonema has a large surface area that enhances absorption of water and minerals. In favorable conditions, a protonema produces one or more "buds." (Note that when referring to nonvascular plants, we typically use quotation marks for structures similar to the buds, stems, and leaves of vascular plants because the definitions of these terms are based on vascular plant organs.) Each of these bud-like growths has an apical meristem that generates a gamete-producing structure known as a **gametophore** ("gamete bearer"). Together, a protonema and one or more gametophores make up the body of a moss gametophyte.

Bryophyte gametophytes generally form ground-hugging carpets, partly because their body parts are too thin to support a tall plant. A second constraint on the height of many bryophytes is the absence of vascular tissue, which would enable long-distance transport of water and nutrients. (The thin structure of bryophyte organs makes it possible to distribute materials for short distances without specialized vascular tissue.) However, some mosses have conducting tissues in the center of their "stems." A few of these mosses can grow as tall as 2 m as a result. Phylogenetic analyses suggest that in these and some other bryophytes, conducting tissues similar to those of vascular plants arose independently by convergent evolution.

The gametophytes are anchored by delicate **rhizoids**, which are long, tubular single cells (in liverworts and hornworts) or filaments of cells (in mosses). Unlike roots, which are found in vascular plant sporophytes, rhizoids are not

▼ Figure 29.8 **The life cycle of a moss.**

? *In this diagram, does the sperm cell that fertilizes the egg cell differ genetically from the egg? Explain.*

1 Spores develop into threadlike protonemata.

2 The haploid protonemata produce "buds" that divide by mitosis and grow into gametophores.

3 Sperm must swim through a film of moisture to reach the egg.

Sperm

Antheridia

"Bud"

Male gametophyte (n)

Key

→ Haploid (n)
→ Diploid (2n)

Protonemata (n)

"Bud"

Gametophore

Spores

Female gametophyte (n)

Egg

Archegonia

Spore dispersal

Rhizoid

Peristome

7 Meiosis occurs and haploid spores develop in the capsule. When the capsule is mature, its lid pops off, and the spores are released.

FERTILIZATION
(within archegonium)

Sporangium

5 The sporophyte grows a long stalk (seta) that emerges from the archegonium.

MEIOSIS

Seta

Capsule (sporangium)

Foot

Mature sporophytes

Zygote (2n)

Embryo

4 The zygote develops into a sporophyte embryo.

Archegonium

Young sporophyte (2n)

6 Attached by its foot, the sporophyte remains nutritionally dependent on the gametophyte.

2 mm

Capsule with peristome (LM)

Female gametophytes

composed of tissues. Bryophyte rhizoids also lack specialized conducting cells and do not play a primary role in water and mineral absorption.

Gametophytes can form multiple gametangia, each of which produces gametes and is covered by protective tissue. Each archegonium produces one egg, whereas each antheridium produces many sperm. Some bryophyte gametophytes are bisexual, but in mosses the archegonia and antheridia are typically carried on separate female and male gametophytes. Flagellated sperm swim through a film of water toward eggs, entering the archegonia in response to chemical attractants.

Eggs are not released but instead remain within the bases of archegonia. After fertilization, embryos are retained within the archegonia. Layers of placental transfer cells help transport nutrients to the embryos as they develop into sporophytes.

Bryophyte sperm typically require a film of water to reach the eggs. Given this requirement, it is not surprising that many bryophyte species are found in moist habitats. The fact that sperm swim through water to reach the egg also means that in species with separate male and female gametophytes (most mosses), sexual reproduction is likely to be more successful when individuals are located close to one another.

Exploring Bryophyte Diversity

Liverworts (Phylum Hepatophyta)

This phylum's common and scientific names (from the Latin *hepaticus*, liver) refer to the liver-shaped gametophytes of its members, such as *Marchantia*, shown below. In medieval times, their shape was thought to be a sign that the plants could help treat liver diseases. Some liverworts, including *Marchantia*, are described as "thalloid" because of the flattened shape of their gametophytes. (Recall from Chapter 28 that the body of a multicellular alga is called a thallus.) *Marchantia* gametangia are elevated on gametophores that look like miniature trees. You would need a magnifying glass to see the sporophytes, which have a short seta (stalk) with an oval or round capsule. Other liverworts, such as *Plagiochila*, below, are called "leafy" because their stemlike gametophytes have many leaflike appendages. There are many more species of leafy liverworts than thalloid liverworts.

Thallus

Gametophore of female gametophyte

Sporophyte

Foot

Seta

Capsule (sporangium)

Marchantia polymorpha, a "thalloid" liverwort

Marchantia sporophyte (LM)

500 μm

Plagiochila deltoidea, a "leafy" liverwort

Hornworts (Phylum Anthocerophyta)

This phylum's common and scientific names (from the Greek *keras*, horn) refer to the long, tapered shape of the sporophyte. A typical sporophyte can grow to about 5 cm high. Unlike a liverwort or moss sporophyte, a hornwort sporophyte lacks a seta and consists only of a sporangium. The sporangium releases mature spores by splitting open, starting at the tip of the horn. The gametophytes, which are usually 1–2 cm in diameter, grow mostly horizontally and often have multiple sporophytes attached. Hornworts are frequently among the first species to colonize open areas with moist soils; a symbiotic relationship with nitrogen-fixing cyanobacteria contributes to their ability to do this (nitrogen is often in short supply in such areas).

An *Anthoceros* hornwort species

Sporophyte

Gametophyte

Mosses (Phylum Bryophyta)

Moss gametophytes, which range in height from less than 1 mm to up to 2 m, are less than 15 cm tall in most species. The familiar carpet of moss you observe consists mainly of gametophytes. The blades of their "leaves" are usually only one cell thick, but more complex "leaves" that have ridges coated with cuticle can be found on the common hairy-cap moss (*Polytrichum*, below) and its close relatives. Moss sporophytes are typically elongated and visible to the naked eye, with heights ranging up to about 20 cm. Though green and photosynthetic when young, they turn tan or brownish red when ready to release spores.

Polytrichum commune, hairy-cap moss

Capsule

Seta

Sporophyte (a sturdy plant that takes months to grow)

Gametophyte

Many bryophyte species can increase the number of individuals in a local area through various methods of asexual reproduction. For example, some mosses reproduce asexually by forming *brood bodies*, small plantlets (as shown at left) that detach from the parent plant and grow into new, genetically identical copies of their parent.

Bryophyte Sporophytes

Although bryophyte sporophytes are usually green and photosynthetic when young, they cannot live independently. They remain attached to their parental gametophytes, from which they absorb sugars, amino acids, minerals, and water.

Bryophytes have the smallest sporophytes of all extant plant groups, consistent with the hypothesis that larger sporophytes evolved only later, in the vascular plants. A typical bryophyte sporophyte consists of a foot, a seta, and a sporangium. Embedded in the archegonium, the **foot** absorbs nutrients from the gametophyte. The **seta** (plural, *setae*), or stalk, conducts these materials to the sporangium, also called a **capsule**, which uses them to produce spores by meiosis. One capsule can generate up to 50 million spores.

In most mosses, the seta becomes elongated, enhancing spore dispersal by elevating the capsule. Typically, the upper part of the capsule features a ring of interlocking, tooth-like structures known as the **peristome** (see Figure 29.8). These "teeth" open under dry conditions and close again when it is moist. This allows spores to be discharged gradually, via periodic gusts of wind that can carry them long distances.

Moss and hornwort sporophytes are often larger and more complex than those of liverworts. Both moss and hornwort sporophytes also have specialized pores called **stomata** (singular, *stoma*), which are also found in all vascular plants. These pores support photosynthesis by allowing the exchange of CO_2 and O_2 between the outside air and the sporophyte interior (see Figure 10.3). Stomata are also the main avenues by which water evaporates from the sporophyte. In hot, dry conditions, the stomata close, minimizing water loss.

The fact that stomata are present in mosses and hornworts but absent in liverworts suggests three possible hypotheses for their evolution. If liverworts are the deepest-branching lineage of land plants, as in Figure 29.7, then stomata may have evolved once in the ancestor of mosses, hornworts, and vascular plants. If hornworts are the deepest-branching lineage, stomata may have evolved once and then been lost in the liverwort lineage. Finally, if hornworts are the deepest-branching lineage and mosses are the closest relatives of vascular plants, it is also possible that hornworts acquired stomata independently of mosses and vascular plants. This question is important to understanding plant evolution because stomata play a crucial role in the success of vascular plants, as you will learn in Chapter 36.

Figure 29.9, on the facing page, shows some examples of gametophytes and sporophytes in the bryophyte phyla.

The Ecological and Economic Importance of Mosses

Wind dispersal of lightweight spores has distributed mosses throughout the world. These plants are particularly common and diverse in moist forests and wetlands. Some mosses colonize bare, sandy soil, where researchers have found they help retain nitrogen in the soil (**Figure 29.10**). In northern coniferous forests, species such as the feather moss *Pleurozium* harbor nitrogen-fixing cyanobacteria that increase the availability of nitrogen in the ecosystem. Other mosses inhabit such extreme environments as mountaintops, tundra, and deserts. Many mosses are able to live in very cold or dry habitats because they can survive the loss of most of their body water, then rehydrate when moisture is available. Few vascular plants can survive the same degree of desiccation.

▼ **Figure 29.10**

INQUIRY

Can bryophytes reduce the rate at which key nutrients are lost from soils?

EXPERIMENT Soils in terrestrial ecosystems are often low in nitrogen, a nutrient required for normal plant growth. Richard Bowden, of Allegheny College, measured annual inputs (gains) and outputs (losses) of nitrogen in a sandy-soil ecosystem dominated by the moss *Polytrichum*. Nitrogen inputs were measured from rainfall (dissolved ions, such as nitrate, NO_3^-), biological N_2 fixation, and wind deposition. Nitrogen losses were measured in leached water (dissolved ions, such as NO_3^-) and gaseous emissions (such as NO_2 emitted by bacteria). Bowden measured losses for soils with *Polytrichum* and for soils where the moss was removed two months before the experiment began.

RESULTS A total of 10.5 kg of nitrogen per hectare (kg/ha) entered the ecosystem each year. Little nitrogen was lost by gaseous emissions (0.10 kg/ha · yr). The results of comparing nitrogen losses by leaching are shown below.

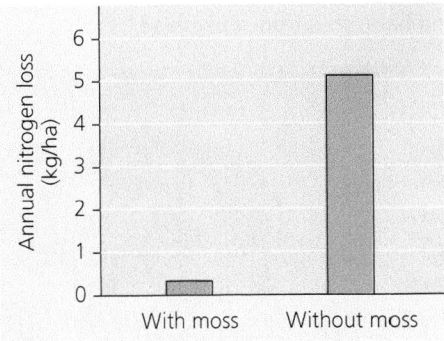

CONCLUSION The moss *Polytrichum* greatly reduced the loss of nitrogen by leaching in this ecosystem. Each year, the moss ecosystem retained over 95% of the 10.5 kg/ha of total nitrogen inputs (only 0.1 kg/ha and 0.3 kg/ha were lost to gaseous emissions and leaching, respectively).

SOURCE R. D. Bowden, Inputs, outputs, and accumulation of nitrogen in an early successional moss (*Polytrichum*) ecosystem, *Ecological Monographs* 61:207–223 (1991).

WHAT IF? How might the presence of *Polytrichum* affect plant species that typically colonize the sandy soils *after* the moss?

One wetland moss genus, *Sphagnum*, or "peat moss," is often a major component of deposits of partially decayed organic material known as **peat** (Figure 29.11a). Boggy regions with thick layers of peat are called peatlands. *Sphagnum* does not decay readily, in part because of phenolic compounds embedded in its cell walls. The low temperature, pH, and oxygen level of peatlands also inhibit decay of moss and other organisms in these boggy wetlands. As a result, some peatlands have preserved corpses for thousands of years (Figure 29.11b).

Peat has long been a fuel source in Europe and Asia, and it is still harvested for fuel today, notably in Ireland and Canada. Peat moss is also useful as a soil conditioner and for packing plant roots during shipment because it has large dead cells that can absorb roughly 20 times the moss's weight in water.

Peatlands cover 3% of Earth's land surface and contain roughly 30% of the world's soil carbon: Globally, an estimated 450 billion tons of organic carbon is stored as peat. These carbon reservoirs have helped to stabilize atmospheric CO_2

concentrations (see Chapter 55). Current overharvesting of *Sphagnum* may reduce peat's beneficial ecological effects and contribute to global warming by releasing stored CO_2. In addition, if global temperatures continue to rise, the water levels of some peatlands are expected to drop. Such a change would expose peat to air and cause it to decompose, thereby releasing additional stored CO_2 and contributing further to global warming. The historical and expected future effects of *Sphagnum* on the global climate underscore the importance of preserving and managing peatlands.

CONCEPT CHECK 29.2

1. How do bryophytes differ from other plants?
2. Give three examples of how structure fits function in bryophytes.
3. **WHAT IF?** For each hypothesis of stomatal evolution, label each gain and loss of stomata on an appropriately modified version of the tree in Figure 29.7.

For suggested answers, see Appendix A.

CONCEPT 29.3

Ferns and other seedless vascular plants were the first plants to grow tall

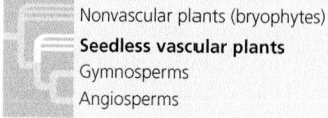

Nonvascular plants (bryophytes)
Seedless vascular plants
Gymnosperms
Angiosperms

During the first 100 million years of plant evolution, bryophytes or bryophyte-like plants were the prevalent vegetation. But it is vascular plants that dominate most landscapes today. Fossils and living seedless vascular plants can provide insights into plant evolution during the Devonian and Carboniferous periods, when vascular plants began to diversify but most groups of seed plants had not yet evolved. Fossils show that lycophytes, ferns, and other seedless vascular plants had well-developed vascular systems by the Devonian. As we'll see, this evolutionary innovation set the stage for vascular plants to grow taller than their bryophyte counterparts. As in nonvascular plants, however, the sperm of ferns and all other seedless vascular plants are flagellated and swim through a film of water to reach eggs. In part because of these swimming sperm, seedless vascular plants today are most common in damp environments.

Origins and Traits of Vascular Plants

Fossils of the forerunners of present-day vascular plants date back about 425 million years. Unlike the nonvascular plants, these species had branched sporophytes that were not dependent on gametophytes for nutrition (Figure 29.12). Although these ancestors of vascular plants were only about

(a) Peat being harvested from a peatland

(b) "Tollund Man," a bog mummy dating from 405–100 B.C.E.
The acidic, oxygen-poor conditions produced by *Sphagnum* can preserve human or other animal bodies for thousands of years.

▲ **Figure 29.11** *Sphagnum*, **or peat moss: a bryophyte with economic, ecological, and archaeological significance.**

► **Figure 29.12**
Sporophytes of *Aglaophyton major*, an ancient relative of present-day vascular plants. This reconstruction from 405-million-year-old fossils exhibits dichotomous (Y-shaped) branching with sporangia at the ends of the branches. Sporophyte branching characterizes living vascular plants but is lacking in living nonvascular plants (bryophytes).

Sporangia

15 cm tall, their branching made possible more complex bodies with multiple sporangia. As plant bodies became increasingly complex, competition for space and sunlight probably increased. As we'll see, that competition may have stimulated still more evolution in vascular plants.

The ancestors of vascular plants already had some derived traits of today's vascular plants, but they lacked roots and some other adaptations that evolved later. This section describes the main traits that characterize living vascular plants: life cycles with dominant sporophytes, transport in vascular tissues called xylem and phloem, and well-developed roots and leaves, including spore-bearing leaves called sporophylls.

Life Cycles with Dominant Sporophytes

Fossils suggest that the ancestors of vascular plants had gametophytes and sporophytes that were about equal in size. Among living vascular plants, however, the sporophyte (diploid) generation is the larger and more complex plant in the alternation of generations **(Figure 29.13)**. In ferns, for example, the familiar leafy plants are the sporophytes. You

▼ **Figure 29.13 The life cycle of a fern.**

WHAT IF? *If the ability to disperse sperm by wind evolved in a fern, how might its life cycle be affected?*

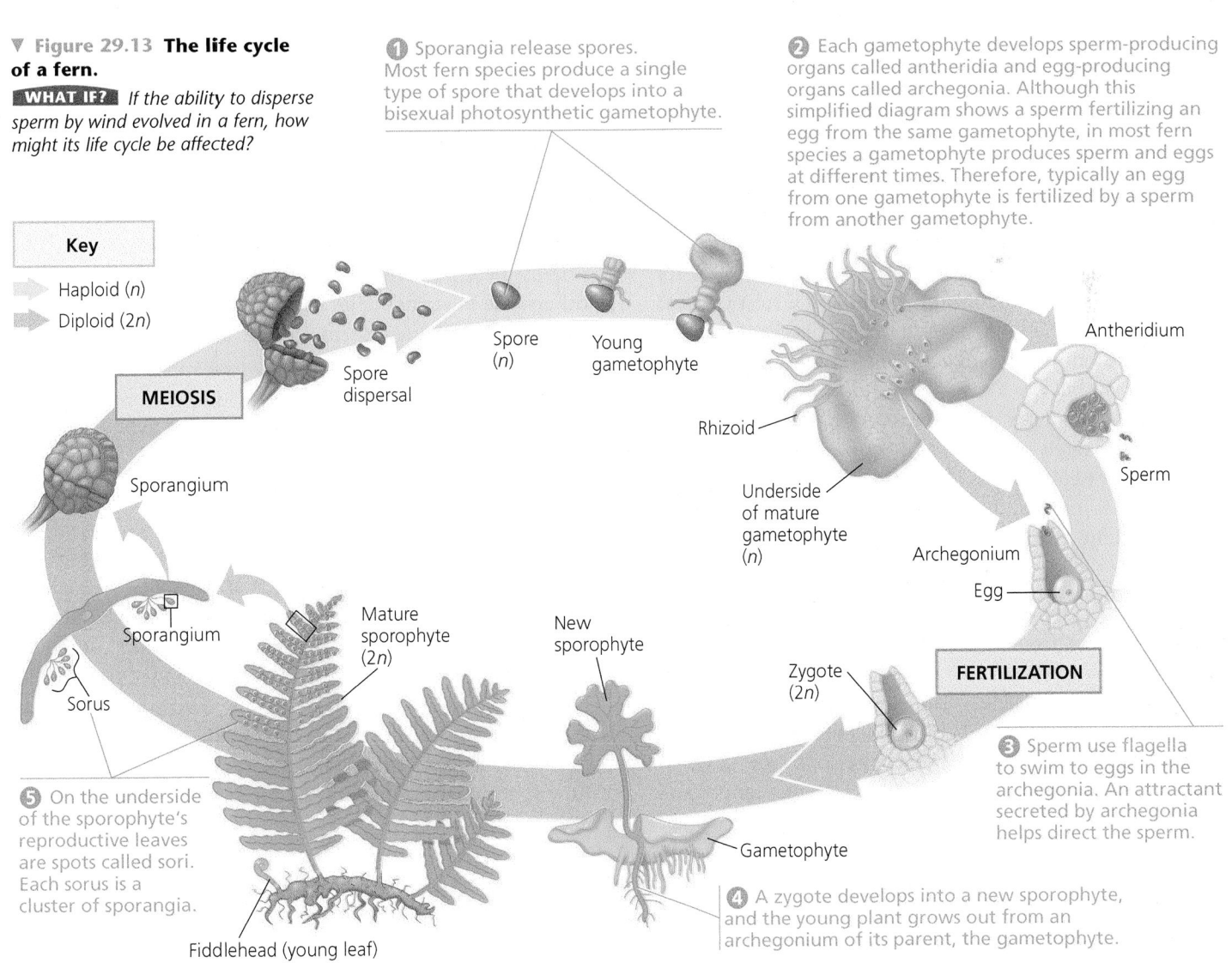

❶ Sporangia release spores. Most fern species produce a single type of spore that develops into a bisexual photosynthetic gametophyte.

❷ Each gametophyte develops sperm-producing organs called antheridia and egg-producing organs called archegonia. Although this simplified diagram shows a sperm fertilizing an egg from the same gametophyte, in most fern species a gametophyte produces sperm and eggs at different times. Therefore, typically an egg from one gametophyte is fertilized by a sperm from another gametophyte.

Key
→ Haploid (*n*)
→ Diploid (*2n*)

MEIOSIS

Spore dispersal

Spore (*n*)

Young gametophyte

Antheridium

Sperm

Rhizoid

Underside of mature gametophyte (*n*)

Archegonium

Egg

Sporangium

Sporangium

Mature sporophyte (*2n*)

New sporophyte

Zygote (*2n*)

FERTILIZATION

Sorus

❸ Sperm use flagella to swim to eggs in the archegonia. An attractant secreted by archegonia helps direct the sperm.

❺ On the underside of the sporophyte's reproductive leaves are spots called sori. Each sorus is a cluster of sporangia.

Gametophyte

❹ A zygote develops into a new sporophyte, and the young plant grows out from an archegonium of its parent, the gametophyte.

Fiddlehead (young leaf)

would have to get down on your hands and knees and search the ground carefully to find fern gametophytes, which are tiny structures that often grow on or just below the soil surface. Until you have a chance to do that, you can study the sporophyte-dominant life cycle of seedless vascular plants in Figure 29.13, which uses a fern as an example. Then, for review, compare this life cycle with Figure 29.8, which represents a gametophyte-dominated life cycle typical of mosses and other nonvascular plants. In Chapter 30, you will see that gametophytes became even more reduced during the evolution of seed plants.

Transport in Xylem and Phloem

Vascular plants have two types of vascular tissue: xylem and phloem. **Xylem** conducts most of the water and minerals. The xylem of most vascular plants includes **tracheids**, tube-shaped cells that carry water and minerals up from roots (see Figure 35.10). (Tracheids have been lost in some highly specialized species, such as *Wolffia*, a tiny aquatic angiosperm.) Because nonvascular plants lack tracheids, vascular plants are sometimes referred to as tracheophytes. The water-conducting cells in vascular plants are *lignified*; that is, their cell walls are strengthened by the polymer **lignin**. The tissue called **phloem** has cells arranged into tubes that distribute sugars, amino acids, and other organic products (see Figure 35.10).

Lignified vascular tissue permitted vascular plants to grow tall. Their stems became strong enough to provide support against gravity, and they could transport water and mineral nutrients high above the ground. Tall plants could also outcompete short plants for access to the sunlight needed for photosynthesis. In addition, the spores of tall plants could disperse farther than those of short plants, enabling tall species to colonize new environments rapidly. Overall, the ability to grow tall was a major evolutionary innovation that gave vascular plants a competitive edge over nonvascular plants, which rarely grow above 20 cm in height. Competition among vascular plants also increased, and taller growth forms were favored by natural selection—such as the trees that formed the first forests about 385 million years ago.

Evolution of Roots

Lignified vascular tissue also provides benefits below ground. Instead of the rhizoids seen in bryophytes, roots evolved in the sporophytes of almost all vascular plants. **Roots** are organs that absorb water and nutrients from the soil. Roots also anchor vascular plants, hence allowing the shoot system to grow taller.

Root tissues of living plants closely resemble stem tissues of early vascular plants preserved in fossils. This suggests that roots may have evolved from the lowest belowground portions of stems in ancient vascular plants. It is unclear whether roots evolved only once in the common ancestor of all vascular plants or independently in different lineages.

Although the roots of living members of these lineages of vascular plants share many similarities, fossil evidence hints at convergent evolution. The oldest lycophyte fossils, for example, already displayed simple roots 400 million years ago, when the ancestors of ferns and seed plants still had none. Studying genes that control root development in different vascular plant species may help resolve this question.

Evolution of Leaves

Leaves increase the surface area of the plant body and serve as the primary photosynthetic organ of vascular plants. In terms of size and complexity, leaves can be classified as either microphylls or megaphylls. All of the lycophytes (the oldest lineage of present-day vascular plants)—and only the lycophytes—have **microphylls**, small, usually spine-shaped leaves supported by a single strand of vascular tissue. Almost all other vascular plants have **megaphylls**, leaves with a highly branched vascular system; a few species have reduced leaves that appear to have evolved from megaphylls. So named because they are typically larger than microphylls, megaphylls support greater photosynthetic productivity than microphylls as a result of the greater surface area served by their network of veins. Microphylls first appear in the fossil record 410 million years ago, but megaphylls do not emerge until about 370 million years ago, toward the end of the Devonian period.

According to one model of leaf evolution, microphylls originated from sporangia located on the side of the stem (Figure 29.14a). Megaphylls, by contrast, may have evolved from a series of branches lying close together on a stem. As one of these branches came to grow above, or *overtop*, the others, the lower branches became flattened and developed webbing that joined them to one another. These joined branches thus became a leaf attached to the branch that overtopped them (Figure 29.14b). To better understand the origin of leaves, scientists are exploring the genetic control of leaf development.

Sporophylls and Spore Variations

One milestone in the evolution of plants was the emergence of **sporophylls**, modified leaves that bear sporangia. Sporophylls vary greatly in structure. For example, fern sporophylls produce clusters of sporangia known as **sori** (singular, *sorus*), usually on the undersides of the sporophylls (see Figure 29.13). In many lycophytes and in most gymnosperms, groups of sporophylls form cone-like structures called **strobili** (singular, *strobilus*; from the Greek *strobilos*, cone). In Chapter 30, you will see how sporophylls form gymnosperm strobili and parts of angiosperm flowers.

Most seedless vascular plant species are **homosporous**: They have one type of sporangium that produces one type of spore, which typically develops into a bisexual gametophyte, as in most ferns. In contrast, a **heterosporous** species has

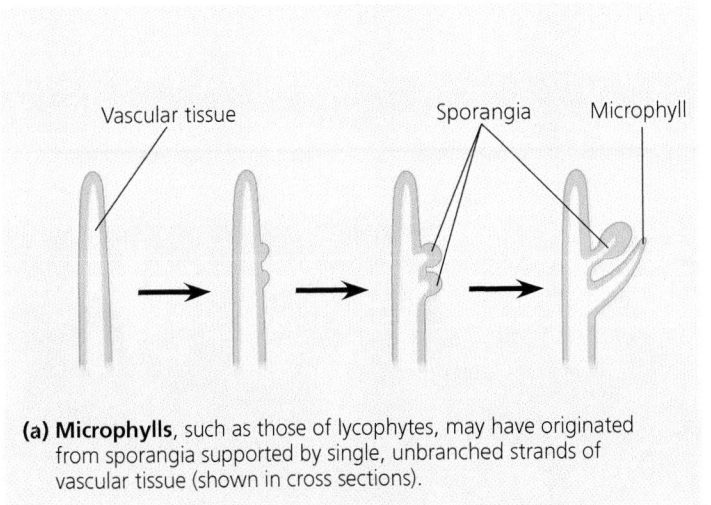

(a) **Microphylls**, such as those of lycophytes, may have originated from sporangia supported by single, unbranched strands of vascular tissue (shown in cross sections).

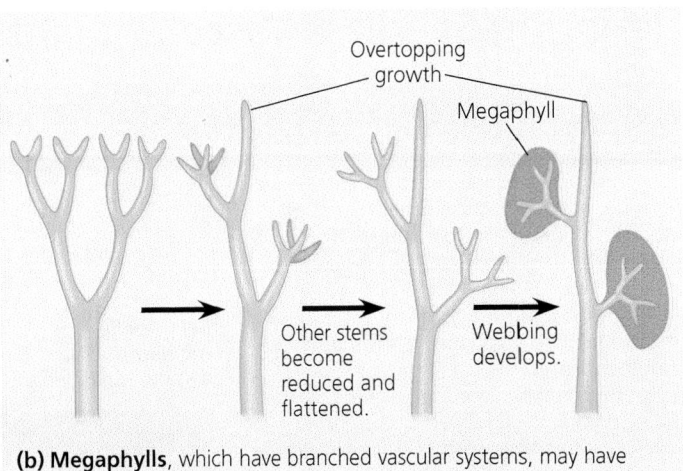

(b) **Megaphylls**, which have branched vascular systems, may have evolved by the fusion of branched stems.

▲ Figure 29.14 **Hypotheses for the evolution of leaves.**

two types of sporangia and produces two kinds of spores: Megasporangia on megasporophylls produce **megaspores**, which develop into female gametophytes; microsporangia on microsporophylls produce the comparatively smaller **microspores**, which develop into male gametophytes. All seed plants and a few seedless vascular plants are heterosporous. The following diagram compares the two conditions:

Classification of Seedless Vascular Plants

As we noted earlier, biologists recognize two clades of living seedless vascular plants: the lycophytes (phylum Lycophyta) and the pterophytes (phylum Pterophyta). The lycophytes include the club mosses, the spike mosses, and the quillworts. The pterophytes include the ferns, the horsetails, and the whisk ferns and their relatives. Because they differ greatly in appearance, the ferns, horsetails, and whisk ferns have long been considered separate phyla: phylum Pterophyta (ferns), phylum Sphenophyta (horsetails), and phylum Psilophyta (whisk ferns and a related genus). However, recent molecular comparisons provide convincing evidence that all three groups make up a clade. Accordingly, many systematists now classify them together as the phylum Pterophyta, as

we do in this chapter. Others refer to these groups as three separate phyla within a clade.

Figure 29.15, on the next page, describes the two main groups of seedless vascular plants.

Phylum Lycophyta: Club Mosses, Spike Mosses, and Quillworts

Present-day species of lycophytes, the most ancient group of vascular plants, are relicts of a far more impressive past. By the Carboniferous period (359–299 million years ago), the lycophyte evolutionary lineage included small herbaceous plants and giant trees with diameters of more than 2 m and heights of more than 40 m. The giant lycophyte trees thrived for millions of years in moist swamps, but they became extinct when Earth's climate became drier at the end of the Carboniferous period. The small lycophytes survived, represented today by about 1,200 species. Though some are commonly called club mosses and spike mosses, they are not true mosses (which, as discussed earlier, are nonvascular plants).

Phylum Pterophyta: Ferns, Horsetails, and Whisk Ferns and Relatives

Ferns radiated extensively from their Devonian origins and grew alongside lycophyte trees and horsetails in the great Carboniferous swamp forests. Today, ferns are by far the most widespread seedless vascular plants, numbering more than 12,000 species. Though most diverse in the tropics, many ferns thrive in temperate forests, and some species are even adapted to arid habitats.

As mentioned earlier, ferns and other pterophytes are more closely related to seed plants than to lycophytes. As a result, pterophytes and seed plants share traits that are not found in lycophytes, including overtopping growth (see Figure 29.14b), megaphyll leaves, and roots that can branch at various points along the length of an existing root. In lycophytes,

Exploring Seedless Vascular Plant Diversity

Lycophytes (Phylum Lycophyta)

Many lycophytes grow on tropical trees as *epiphytes*, plants that use other plants as a substrate but are not parasites. Other species grow on temperate forest floors. In some species, the tiny gametophytes live above ground and are photosynthetic. Others live below ground, nurtured by symbiotic fungi.

Sporophytes have upright stems with many small leaves, as well as ground-hugging stems that produce dichotomously branching roots. Spike mosses are usually relatively small and often grow horizontally. In many club mosses and spike mosses, sporophylls are clustered into club-shaped cones (strobili). Quillworts, named for their leaf shape, form a single genus whose members live in marshy areas or as submerged aquatic plants. Club mosses are all homosporous, whereas spike mosses and quillworts are all heterosporous. The spores of club mosses are released in clouds and are so rich in oil that magicians and photographers once ignited them to create smoke or flashes of light.

Selaginella moellendorffii, a spike moss

Isoetes gunnii, a quillwort

Strobili (clusters of sporophylls)

2.5 cm

1 cm

Diphasiastrum tristachyum, a club moss

Pterophytes (Phylum Pterophyta)

Athyrium filix-femina, lady fern

25 cm

Equisetum arvense, field horsetail

— Vegetative stem

— Strobilus on fertile stem

1.5 cm

Psilotum nudum, a whisk fern

4 cm

Ferns

Unlike the lycophytes, ferns have megaphylls (see Figure 29.14b). The sporophytes typically have horizontal stems that give rise to large leaves called fronds, often divided into leaflets. A frond grows as its coiled tip, the fiddlehead, unfurls.

Almost all species are homosporous. The gametophyte in some species shrivels and dies after the young sporophyte detaches itself. In most species, sporophytes have stalked sporangia with springlike devices that catapult spores several meters. Airborne spores can be carried far from their origin. Some species produce more than a trillion spores in a plant's lifetime.

Horsetails

The group's name refers to the brushy appearance of the stems, which have a gritty texture that made them historically useful as "scouring rushes" for pots and pans. Some species have separate fertile (cone-bearing) and vegetative stems. Horsetails are homosporous, with cones releasing spores that typically give rise to bisexual gametophytes.

Horsetails are also called arthrophytes ("jointed plants") because their stems have joints. Rings of small leaves or branches emerge from each joint, but the stem is the main photosynthetic organ. Large air canals carry oxygen to the roots, which often grow in waterlogged soil.

Whisk Ferns and Relatives

Like primitive vascular plant fossils, the sporophytes of whisk ferns (genus *Psilotum*) have dichotomously branching stems but no roots. Stems have scalelike outgrowths that lack vascular tissue and may have resulted from the evolutionary reduction of leaves. Each yellow knob on a stem consists of three fused sporangia. Species of the genus *Tmesipteris*, closely related to whisk ferns and found only in the South Pacific, also lack roots but have small, leaflike outgrowths in their stems, giving them a vine-like appearance. Both genera are homosporous, with spores giving rise to bisexual gametophytes that grow underground and are only about a centimeter long.

by contrast, roots branch only at the growing tip of the root, forming a Y-shaped structure.

The pterophytes called horsetails were very diverse during the Carboniferous period, some growing as tall as 15 m. Today, only 15 species survive as a single, widely distributed genus, *Equisetum*, found in marshy places and along streams.

Psilotum (whisk ferns) and a closely related genus, *Tmesipteris*, form a clade consisting mainly of tropical epiphytes. Plants in these two genera, the only vascular plants lacking true roots, are called "living fossils" because of their resemblance to fossils of ancient relatives of living vascular plants (see Figures 29.12 and 29.15). However, much evidence, including analyses of DNA sequences and sperm structure, indicates that the genera *Psilotum* and *Tmesipteris* are closely related to ferns. This hypothesis suggests that their ancestor's true roots were lost during evolution. Today, plants in these two genera absorb water and nutrients through numerous absorptive rhizoids.

Fern | Lycophyte trees | Horsetail | Tree trunk covered with small leaves | Lycophyte tree reproductive structures

▲ **Figure 29.16 Artist's conception of a Carboniferous forest based on fossil evidence.** In addition to plants, animals, including giant dragonflies like the one in the foreground, also thrived in the "coal forests" of the Carboniferous.

WHAT IF? *What would this forest look like if few lycophyte trees were reproducing (as would often have been the case)?*

The Significance of Seedless Vascular Plants

The ancestors of living lycophytes, horsetails, and ferns, along with their extinct seedless vascular relatives, grew to great heights during the Devonian and early Carboniferous, forming the first forests (Figure 29.16). How did their dramatic growth affect Earth and its other life? With the evolution of vascular tissue, roots, and leaves, these plants accelerated their rate of photosynthesis, dramatically increasing the removal of CO_2 from the atmosphere. Scientists estimate that CO_2 levels dropped by as much as a factor of five during the Carboniferous, causing global cooling that resulted in widespread glacier formation. Ancient CO_2 levels can be estimated in several ways. These include counting the number of stomata in fossil leaves (data from living species show that this number increases as CO_2 levels drop) and measuring carbon isotope levels in fossils of plankton. Different methods yield similar results, suggesting that reconstructions of past climates are accurate.

The seedless vascular plants that formed the first forests eventually became coal. In the stagnant waters of Carboniferous swamps, dead plants did not completely decay. This organic material turned to thick layers of peat, later covered by the sea. Marine sediments piled on top, and over millions of years, heat and pressure converted the peat to coal. In fact, Carboniferous coal deposits are the most extensive ever formed. Coal was crucial to the Industrial Revolution, and people worldwide still burn 6 billion tons a year. It is ironic

that coal, formed from plants that contributed to a global cooling, now contributes to global warming by returning carbon to the atmosphere (see Chapter 55).

Growing along with the seedless plants in Carboniferous swamps were primitive seed plants. Though seed plants were not dominant at that time, they rose to prominence after the swamps began to dry up at the end of the Carboniferous period. The next chapter traces the origin and diversification of seed plants, continuing our story of adaptation to life on land.

CONCEPT CHECK 29.3

1. List the key derived traits found in pterophytes and seed plants, but not in lycophytes.
2. How do the main similarities and differences between seedless vascular plants and nonvascular plants influence function in these plants?
3. **WHAT IF?** If (contrary to the evidence) lycophytes and pterophytes formed a clade, what could you conclude about how members of this clade gained (or lost) traits shared by pterophytes and seed plants?
4. **MAKE CONNECTIONS** In Figure 29.13, if fertilization occurred between gametes from one gametophyte, how would this affect the production of genetic variation from sexual reproduction? See page 258 of Concept 13.4.

For suggested answers, see Appendix A.

SUMMARY OF KEY CONCEPTS

CONCEPT 29.1

Land plants evolved from green algae (pp. 600–606)

- Morphological and biochemical traits, as well as similarities in nuclear and chloroplast genes, suggest that charophytes are the closest living relatives of land plants.
- A protective layer of **sporopollenin** and other traits allow charophytes to tolerate occasional drying along the edges of ponds and lakes. Such traits may have enabled the algal ancestors of plants to survive in terrestrial conditions, opening the way to the colonization of dry land.
- Derived traits that distinguish the clade of land plants from charophytes, their closest algal relatives, include the four shown here:

① Alternation of generations

② Apical meristems

③ Multicellular gametangia

④ Walled spores in sporangia

- Fossil evidence indicates that plants were on land at least 475 million years ago. Subsequently, plants diverged into several major groups, including nonvascular plants (bryophytes); seedless vascular plants, such as lycophytes and ferns; and the two groups of seed plants: gymnosperms and angiosperms.

> **?** Draw a phylogenetic tree illustrating our current understanding of land plant phylogeny; label the common ancestor of land plants and the origins of multicellular gametangia, vascular tissue, and seeds.

CONCEPT 29.2

Mosses and other nonvascular plants have life cycles dominated by gametophytes (pp. 606–610)

- Current evidence indicates that the three phyla of **bryophytes**—liverworts, mosses, and hornworts—do not form a clade.

- In bryophytes, the dominant and typically most visible generation consists of haploid **gametophytes**, such as those that make up a carpet of moss. **Rhizoids** anchor gametophytes to the substrate on which they grow. The flagellated sperm produced by **antheridia** require a film of water to travel to the eggs in the **archegonia**.
- The diploid stage of the bryophyte life cycle—the **sporophytes**—grow out of archegonia and are attached to the gametophytes and dependent on them for nourishment. Smaller and simpler than vascular plant sporophytes, they typically consist of a **foot**, **seta** (stalk), and **sporangium**.
- *Sphagnum*, or peat moss, is common in large regions known as peatlands and has many practical uses, including as a fuel.

> **?** Summarize the ecological importance of mosses.

CONCEPT 29.3

Ferns and other seedless vascular plants were the first plants to grow tall (pp. 610–615)

- Fossils of the forerunners of today's vascular plants date back about 425 million years and show that these small plants had independent, branching sporophytes. However, these ancestral species lacked other derived traits of living vascular plants, such as a life cycle with dominant sporophytes; lignified vascular tissue; well-developed roots and leaves; and sporophylls.
- Seedless vascular plants include the **lycophytes** (phylum Lycophyta: club mosses, spike mosses, and quillworts) and the **pterophytes** (phylum Pterophyta: ferns, horsetails, and whisk ferns and relatives). Ancient lycophytes included both small herbaceous plants and large trees. Present-day lycophytes are small herbaceous plants.
- Seedless vascular plants dominated the earliest forests. Their growth may have helped produce the major global cooling that characterized the end of the Carboniferous period. The decaying remnants of the first forests eventually became coal.

> **?** What trait(s) allowed vascular plants to grow tall, and why might increased height have been advantageous?

TEST YOUR UNDERSTANDING

LEVEL 1: KNOWLEDGE/COMPREHENSION

1. Which of the following is *not* evidence that charophytes are the closest algal relatives of plants?
   a. similar sperm structure
   b. the presence of chloroplasts
   c. similarities in cell wall formation during cell division
   d. genetic similarities in chloroplasts
   e. similarities in proteins that synthesize cellulose

2. Which of the following characteristics of plants is absent in their closest relatives, the charophyte algae?
   a. chlorophyll *b*
   b. cellulose in cell walls
   c. formation of a cell plate during cytokinesis
   d. sexual reproduction
   e. alternation of multicellular generations

3. In plants, which of the following are produced by meiosis?
   a. haploid sporophytes
   b. haploid gametes
   c. diploid gametes
   d. haploid spores
   e. diploid spores

4. Microphylls are found in which plant group?
   a. mosses
   b. liverworts
   c. lycophytes
   d. ferns
   e. hornworts

5. Which of the following is a land plant that has flagellated sperm and a sporophyte-dominated life cycle?
   a. fern
   b. moss
   c. liverwort
   d. charophyte
   e. hornwort

6. Identify each of the following structures as haploid or diploid.
   a. sporophyte
   b. spore
   c. gametophyte
   d. zygote
   e. sperm

LEVEL 2: APPLICATION/ANALYSIS

7. Suppose an efficient conducting system evolved in a moss that could transport water and other materials as high as a tall tree. Which of the following statements about "trees" of such a species would *not* be true?
   a. Fertilization would probably be more difficult.
   b. Spore dispersal distances would probably increase.
   c. Females could produce only one archegonium.
   d. Unless its body parts were strengthened, such a "tree" would probably flop over.
   e. Individuals would probably compete more effectively for access to light.

8. **EVOLUTION CONNECTION**

   DRAW IT Draw a phylogenetic tree that represents our current understanding of evolutionary relationships between a moss, a gymnosperm, a lycophyte, and a fern. Use a charophyte alga as the outgroup. (See Chapter 26 to review phylogenetic trees.) Label each branch point of the phylogeny with at least one derived character unique to the clade descended from the common ancestor represented by the branch point.

LEVEL 3: SYNTHESIS/EVALUATION

9. **SCIENTIFIC INQUIRY**

   DRAW IT The feather moss *Pleurozium schreberi* harbors species of symbiotic nitrogen-fixing bacteria. Scientists studying this moss in northern forests found that the percentage of the ground surface "covered" by the moss increased from about 5% in forests that had burned 35 to 41 years ago to about 70% in forests that had burned 170 or more years ago.

From mosses growing in these forests, they also obtained the following data on nitrogen fixation:

Age (years after fire)	N fixation rate (kg N per ha per yr)
35	0.001
41	0.005
78	0.08
101	0.3
124	0.9
170	2.0
220	1.3
244	2.1
270	1.6
300	3.0
355	2.3

Source: Data from O. Zackrisson et al., Nitrogen fixation increases with successional age in boreal forests, *Ecology* 85: 3327–3334 (2006).

   a. Use the data to draw a line graph, with age on the *x*-axis and the nitrogen fixation rate on the *y*-axis.
   b. Along with the nitrogen added by nitrogen fixation, about 1 kg of nitrogen per hectare per year is deposited into northern forests from the atmosphere as rain and small particles. Evaluate the extent to which *Pleurozium* affects nitrogen availability in northern forests of different ages.

10. **WRITE ABOUT A THEME**

   ENVIRONMENTAL INTERACTIONS Giant lycophyte trees had microphylls, whereas ferns and seed plants have megaphylls. Write a short essay (100–150 words) describing how a forest of lycophyte trees may have differed from a forest of large ferns or seed plants. In your answer, consider how the type of forest in which they grew may have affected interactions among small plants growing beneath the tall ones.

For selected answers, see Appendix A.

MasteringBIOLOGY®   www.masteringbiology.com

1. MasteringBiology® Assignments
Tutorial Nonvascular Plants
Activities Terrestrial Adaptations of Plants • Highlights of Plant Phylogeny • Moss Life Cycle • Fern Life Cycle
Questions Student Misconceptions • Reading Quiz • Multiple Choice • End-of-Chapter

2. eText
Read your book online, search, take notes, highlight text, and more.

3. The Study Area
Practice Tests • Cumulative Test • ***BioFlix*** 3-D Animations • MP3 Tutor Sessions • Videos • Activities • Investigations • Lab Media • Audio Glossary • Word Study Tools • Art

Plant Diversity II: The Evolution of Seed Plants

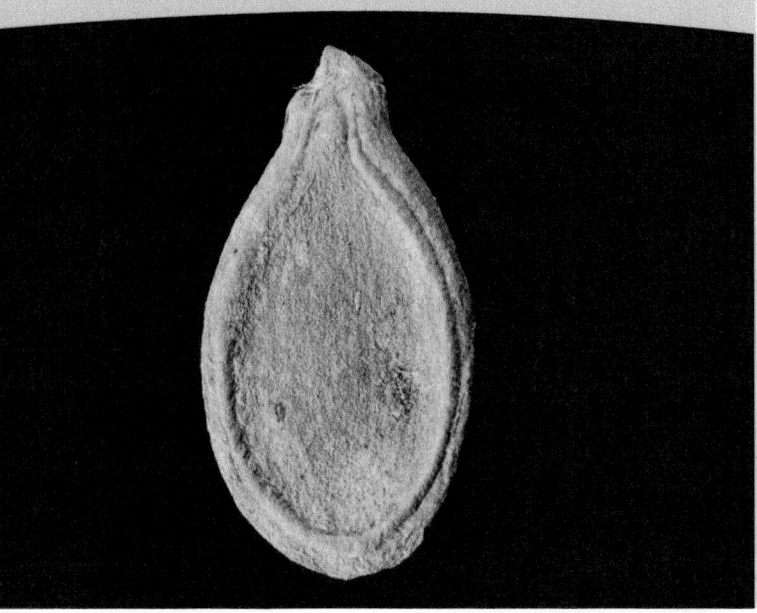

▲ **Figure 30.1 What human reproductive organ is functionally similar to this seed?**

KEY CONCEPTS

30.1 Seeds and pollen grains are key adaptations for life on land

30.2 Gymnosperms bear "naked" seeds, typically on cones

30.3 The reproductive adaptations of angiosperms include flowers and fruits

30.4 Human welfare depends greatly on seed plants

OVERVIEW

Transforming the World

Continuing the saga of how plants have transformed Earth, this chapter follows the emergence and diversification of seed plants. Fossils and comparative studies of living plants offer clues about the origin of seed plants some 360 million years ago. As this new group of plants became established, they

dramatically altered the course of plant evolution. We'll begin our exploration of how this occurred by looking at the innovation for which seed plants are named: seeds (**Figure 30.1**).

A **seed** consists of an embryo and its food supply, surrounded by a protective coat. When mature, seeds are dispersed from their parent by wind or other means. Because it nourishes and protects the embryo, yet can move away from the mother plant, a seed is analogous to a detachable and mobile version of a pregnant woman's uterus. As we'll see, seeds are a key adaptation that helped seed plants to become the dominant producers on land and to make up the vast majority of plant biodiversity today.

Seed plants have also had an enormous impact on human society. Starting about 12,000 years ago, humans began to cultivate wheat, figs, maize (commonly called corn in the United States), rice, and other wild seed plants. This practice emerged independently in various parts of the world, including the Near East, East Asia, Africa, and the Americas. One piece of evidence, the well-preserved squash seed in Figure 30.1, was found in a cave in Mexico and dates from between 8,000 and 10,000 years ago. This seed differs from wild squash seeds, suggesting that squash was being domesticated by that time. The domestication of seed plants, particularly angiosperms, produced the most important cultural change in human history, transforming most human societies from roving bands of hunter-gatherers to permanent settlements anchored by agriculture.

In this chapter, we will first examine the general characteristics of seed plants. Then we will look at the distinguishing features and evolution of gymnosperms and angiosperms.

CONCEPT 30.1

Seeds and pollen grains are key adaptations for life on land

We begin with an overview of terrestrial adaptations that seed plants added to those already present in nonvascular plants (bryophytes) and seedless vascular plants (see Chapter 29). In addition to seeds, the following are common to all seed plants: reduced gametophytes, heterospory, ovules, and pollen. As you'll read, these adaptations provided new ways for seed plants to cope with terrestrial conditions such as drought and exposure to the ultraviolet (UV) radiation in sunlight. Novel adaptations also freed seed plants from requiring water for fertilization, enabling reproduction to occur under a broader range of conditions than in seedless plants.

Advantages of Reduced Gametophytes

Mosses and other bryophytes have life cycles dominated by gametophytes, whereas ferns and other seedless vascular plants have sporophyte-dominated life cycles. The evolutionary trend of gametophyte reduction continued further in the vascular plant lineage that led to seed plants. While the gametophytes

PLANT GROUP		
	Mosses and other nonvascular plants	**Ferns and other seedless vascular plants**	**Seed plants (gymnosperms and angiosperms)**
Gametophyte	Dominant	Reduced, independent (photosynthetic and free-living)	Reduced (usually microscopic), dependent on surrounding sporophyte tissue for nutrition
Sporophyte	Reduced, dependent on gametophyte for nutrition	Dominant	Dominant
Example			

▲ **Figure 30.2 Gametophyte-sporophyte relationships in different plant groups.**
MAKE CONNECTIONS *In seed plants, how does retaining the gametophyte within the sporophyte likely affect embryo fitness? (See pp. 346, 472, and 480 in Chapters 17 and 23 to review mutagens, mutations, and fitness.)*

of seedless vascular plants are visible to the naked eye, the gametophytes of seed plants are mostly microscopic.

This miniaturization allowed for an important evolutionary innovation in seed plants: Their tiny gametophytes can develop from spores retained within the sporangia of the parental sporophyte. This arrangement protects the gametophytes from environmental stresses. The moist reproductive tissues of the sporophyte shield the gametophytes from UV radiation and protect them from drying out. This relationship also enables the dependent gametophytes to obtain nutrients from the sporophyte. In contrast, the free-living gametophytes of seedless plants must fend for themselves. **Figure 30.2** contrasts the gametophyte-sporophyte relationships in nonvascular plants, seedless vascular plants, and seed plants.

Heterospory: The Rule Among Seed Plants

You read in Chapter 29 that most seedless plants are *homosporous*—they produce one kind of spore, which usually gives rise to a bisexual gametophyte. Ferns and other close

relatives of seed plants are homosporous, suggesting that seed plants had homosporous ancestors. At some point, seed plants or their ancestors became *heterosporous*, producing two kinds of spores: Megasporangia produce *megaspores* that give rise to female gametophytes, and microsporangia produce *microspores* that give rise to male gametophytes. Each megasporangium has a single functional megaspore, whereas each microsporangium contains vast numbers of microspores.

As we noted previously, the miniaturization of seed plant gametophytes likely contributed to the great success of this clade. Next we will look at the development of the female gametophyte within an ovule and the development of the male gametophyte in a pollen grain. Then we will follow the transformation of a fertilized ovule into a seed.

Ovules and Production of Eggs

Although a few species of seedless plants are heterosporous, seed plants are unique in retaining the megasporangium within the parent sporophyte. A layer of sporophyte tissue

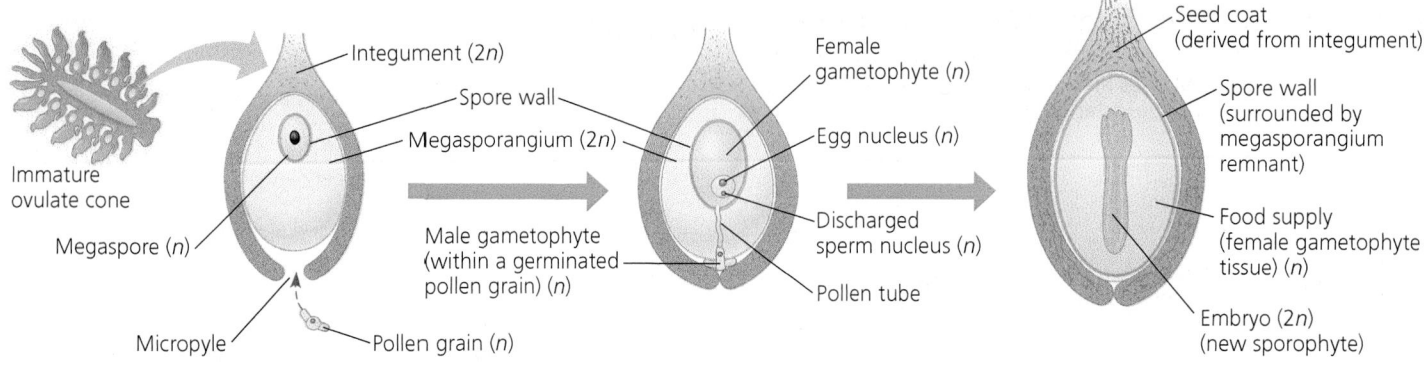

(a) Unfertilized ovule. In this longitudinal section through the ovule of a pine (a gymnosperm), a fleshy megasporangium is surrounded by a protective layer of tissue called an integument. The micropyle, the only opening through the integument, allows entry of a pollen grain.

(b) Fertilized ovule. A megaspore develops into a female gametophyte, which produces an egg. The pollen grain, which had entered through the micropyle, contains a male gametophyte. The male gametophyte develops a pollen tube that discharges sperm, thereby fertilizing the egg.

(c) Gymnosperm seed. Fertilization initiates the transformation of the ovule into a seed, which consists of a sporophyte embryo, a food supply, and a protective seed coat derived from the integument. The megasporangium dries out and collapses.

▲ Figure 30.3 **From ovule to seed in a gymnosperm.**

? *A gymnosperm seed contains cells from how many different plant generations? Identify the cells and whether each is haploid or diploid.*

called **integument** envelops and protects the megasporangium. Gymnosperm megasporangia are surrounded by one integument, whereas those in angiosperms usually have two integuments. The whole structure—megasporangium, megaspore, and their integument(s)—is called an **ovule** (**Figure 30.3a**). Inside each ovule (from the Latin *ovulum*, little egg), a female gametophyte develops from a megaspore and produces one or more eggs.

Pollen and Production of Sperm

A microspore develops into a **pollen grain** that consists of a male gametophyte enclosed within the pollen wall. (The outer layer of the pollen wall is composed of molecules secreted by sporophyte cells; hence, we refer to the male gametophyte as being *in* the pollen grain, not *equivalent to* the pollen grain.) The tough pollen wall, which contains the polymer sporopollenin, protects a pollen grain as it is transported from the parent plant by wind, for example, or by hitchhiking on the body of an animal. The transfer of pollen to the part of a seed plant that contains the ovules is called **pollination**. If a pollen grain germinates (begins growing), it gives rise to a pollen tube that discharges sperm into the female gametophyte within the ovule, as shown in **Figure 30.3b**.

Recall that in nonvascular plants and seedless vascular plants such as ferns, free-living gametophytes release flagellated sperm that swim through a film of water to reach eggs. The distance for this sperm transport rarely exceeds a few centimeters. By contrast, in seed plants a sperm-producing male gametophyte inside a pollen grain can be carried long distances by wind or by animals, eliminating the dependence on water for sperm transport. The sperm of seed plants also do not require motility because sperm are carried directly to the eggs by pollen tubes. Living gymnosperms provide evidence

of the evolutionary transition to nonmotile sperm. The sperm of some gymnosperm species (such as ginkgos and cycads, shown a little later in Figure 30.5) retain the ancient flagellated condition, but flagella have been lost in the sperm of most gymnosperms and all angiosperms.

The Evolutionary Advantage of Seeds

If a sperm fertilizes an egg of a seed plant, the zygote grows into a sporophyte embryo. As shown in **Figure 30.3c**, the whole ovule develops into a seed: the embryo, along with a food supply, packaged within a protective coat derived from the integument(s).

Until the advent of seeds, the spore was the only protective stage in any plant life cycle. Moss spores, for example, may survive even if the local environment becomes too cold, too hot, or too dry for the mosses themselves to live. Their tiny size enables the spores to be dispersed in a dormant state to a new area, where they can germinate and give rise to new moss gametophytes if and when conditions are favorable enough for them to break dormancy. Spores were the main way that mosses, ferns, and other seedless plants spread over Earth for the first 100 million years of plant life on land.

Although mosses and other seedless plants continue to be very successful today, seeds represent a major evolutionary innovation that contributed to the opening of new ways of life for seed plants. What advantages do seeds provide over spores? Spores are usually single-celled, whereas seeds are multicellular, consisting of an embryo protected by a layer of tissue, the seed coat. A seed can remain dormant for days, months, or even years after being released from the parent plant, whereas most spores have shorter lifetimes. Also, unlike spores, seeds have a supply of stored food. Under favorable conditions, the seed can emerge from dormancy and germinate, with its stored food providing critical support for growth as the sporophyte embryo emerges as a seedling. Most seeds land close to their parent sporophyte plant, but some are carried long distances (up to hundreds of kilometers) by wind or animals.

◀ **Figure 30.4 A progymnosperm.** *Archaeopteris,* which lived 380 million years ago, produced wood and was heterosporous, but it did not produce seeds. Growing up to 20 m tall, it had fernlike leaves.

CONCEPT CHECK 30.1

1. Contrast sperm delivery in seedless plants with sperm delivery in seed plants.
2. What features not present in seedless plants have contributed to the enormous success of seed plants on land?
3. **WHAT IF?** If a seed could not enter dormancy, how might that affect the embryo's transport or survival?

For suggested answers, see Appendix A.

CONCEPT 30.2

Gymnosperms bear "naked" seeds, typically on cones

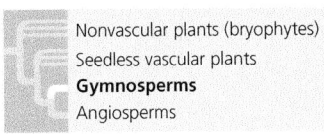

Nonvascular plants (bryophytes)
Seedless vascular plants
Gymnosperms
Angiosperms

As shown in this phylogeny, extant seed plants form two sister clades: gymnosperms and angiosperms. Recall from Chapter 29 that gymnosperms have "naked" seeds that are not enclosed in ovaries. Their seeds are exposed on modified leaves (sporophylls) that usually form cones (strobili). (Angiosperm seeds are enclosed in fruits, which are mature ovaries.) We turn now to the origin of gymnosperms and other early seed plants.

Gymnosperm Evolution

Fossils reveal that by the late Devonian period (about 380 million years ago), some plants had acquired adaptations characteristic of seed plants. For example, *Archaeopteris* was a heterosporous tree with a woody stem **(Figure 30.4)**. But it did not bear seeds. Such transitional species of seedless vascular plants are sometimes called **progymnosperms**.

The first seed plants to appear in the fossil record date from around 360 million years ago, 55 million years before the first gymnosperm fossils and more than 200 million years before the first angiosperm fossils. These early seed plants became extinct, as did several later lineages. It remains uncertain which of these extinct seed plant lineages ultimately gave rise to the gymnosperms.

The earliest fossils of gymnosperms are about 305 million years old. These early gymnosperms lived in Carboniferous ecosystems still dominated by lycophytes, horsetails, ferns, and other seedless vascular plants. As the Carboniferous period gave way to the Permian, markedly drier climatic conditions favored the spread of gymnosperms. The flora and fauna changed dramatically, as many groups of organisms

disappeared and others became prominent (see Chapter 25). Though most pronounced in the seas, the changeover also affected terrestrial life. For example, in the animal kingdom, amphibians decreased in diversity and were replaced by reptiles, which were especially well adapted to the arid conditions. Similarly, the lycophytes, horsetails, and ferns that dominated the Carboniferous swamps were largely replaced by gymnosperms, which were more suited to the drier climate. Gymnosperms have the key terrestrial adaptations found in all seed plants, such as seeds and pollen. In addition, some gymnosperms were particularly well suited to arid conditions because of the thick cuticles and relatively small surface areas of their needle-shaped leaves.

Geologists consider the end of the Permian period, about 251 million years ago, to be the boundary between the Paleozoic ("old life") and Mesozoic ("middle life") eras. Life changed profoundly as gymnosperms dominated terrestrial ecosystems throughout much of the Mesozoic, serving as the food supply for giant herbivorous dinosaurs. Toward the end of the Mesozoic, angiosperms began to replace gymnosperms in some ecosystems. The Mesozoic era ended 65 million years ago with mass extinctions of dinosaurs and many other animal groups, and further increases in the biodiversity and importance of angiosperms. Although angiosperms now dominate most terrestrial ecosystems, many gymnosperms remain an important part of Earth's flora. For example, vast regions in northern latitudes are covered by forests of cone-bearing gymnosperms called **conifers**, which include spruce, pine, fir, and redwood (see Figure 52.12, p. 1155).

Of the ten plant phyla in the taxonomic scheme adopted by this textbook (see Table 29.1), four are gymnosperms: Cycadophyta, Ginkgophyta, Gnetophyta, and Coniferophyta. The relationships of these four phyla to each other are uncertain. **Figure 30.5**, on the next two pages, surveys the diversity of extant gymnosperms.

Exploring Gymnosperm Diversity

Phylum Cycadophyta

Cycads are the next largest group of gymnosperms after the conifers. They have large cones and palmlike leaves (true palm species are angiosperms). Only about 130 species survive today, but cycads thrived during the Mesozoic era, known as the age of cycads as well as the age of dinosaurs.

Cycas revoluta

Phylum Ginkgophyta

Ginkgo biloba is the only surviving species of this phylum. Also known as the maidenhair tree, it has deciduous fanlike leaves that turn gold in autumn. It is a popular ornamental tree in cities because it tolerates air pollution well. Landscapers often plant only pollen-producing trees because the fleshy seeds smell rancid as they decay.

Phylum Gnetophyta

Plants in the phylum Gnetophyta, called gnetophytes, consist of three genera: *Gnetum*, *Ephedra*, and *Welwitschia*. Some species are tropical, whereas others live in deserts. Although very different in appearance, the genera are grouped together based on molecular data.

▶ **Welwitschia.** This genus consists of one species, *Welwitschia mirabilis*, a plant that lives only in the deserts of southwestern Africa. Its straplike leaves are among the largest leaves known.

Ovulate cones

◀ **Gnetum.** This genus includes about 35 species of tropical trees, shrubs, and vines, mainly native to Africa and Asia. Their leaves look similar to those of flowering plants, and their seeds look somewhat like fruits.

▶ **Ephedra.** This genus includes about 40 species that inhabit arid regions worldwide. These desert shrubs, commonly called "Mormon tea," produce the compound ephedrine, which is used medicinally as a decongestant.

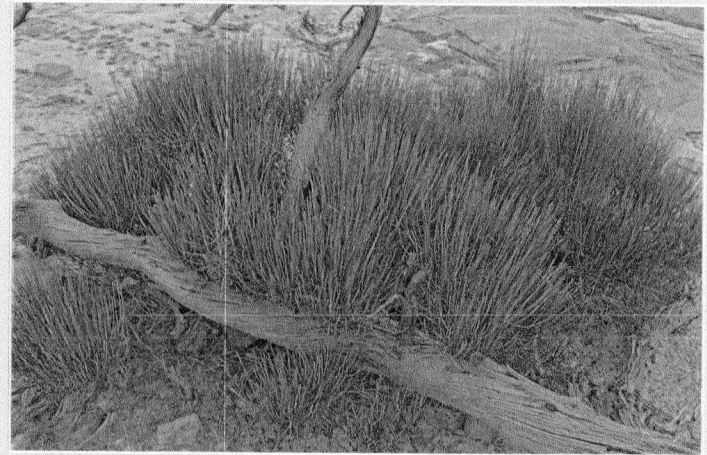

Phylum Coniferophyta

Phylum Coniferophyta is by far the largest of the gymnosperm phyla, consisting of about 600 species of conifers (from the Latin *conus*, cone, and *ferre*, to carry). Many are large trees, such as cypresses and redwoods. A few conifer species dominate vast forested regions of the Northern Hemisphere, where the growing season is relatively short because of latitude or altitude.

Most conifers are evergreens; they retain their leaves throughout the year. Even during winter, a limited amount of photosynthesis occurs on sunny days. When spring comes, conifers already have fully developed leaves that can take advantage of the sunnier, warmer days. Some conifers, such as the dawn redwood, tamarack, and larch, are deciduous trees that lose leaves each autumn.

▶ **Douglas fir.** This evergreen tree (*Pseudotsuga menziesii*) provides more timber than any other North American tree species. Some uses include house framing, plywood, pulpwood for paper, railroad ties, and boxes and crates.

▶ **Common juniper.** The "berries" of the common juniper (*Juniperus communis*) are actually ovule-producing cones consisting of fleshy sporophylls.

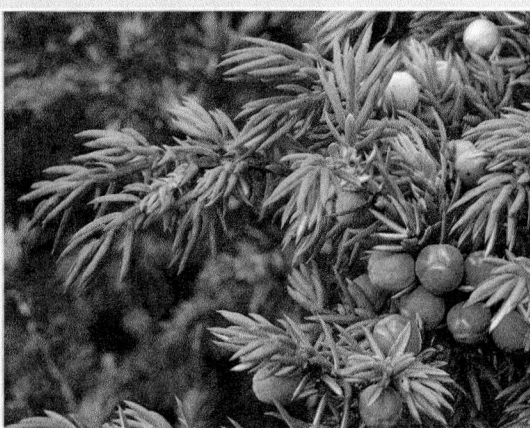

◀ **European larch.** The needle-like leaves of this deciduous conifer (*Larix decidua*) turn yellow before they are shed in autumn. Native to the mountains of central Europe, including Switzerland's Matterhorn, depicted here, this species is extremely cold-tolerant, able to survive winter temperatures that plunge to –50°C.

◀ **Wollemi pine.** Survivors of a conifer group once known only from fossils, living Wollemi pines (*Wollemia nobilis*) were discovered in 1994 in a national park only 150 km from Sydney, Australia. The species consists of just 40 known individuals in two small groves. The inset photo compares the leaves of this "living fossil" with actual fossils.

▶ **Sequoia.** This giant sequoia (*Sequoiadendron giganteum*) in California's Sequoia National Park weighs about 2,500 metric tons, equivalent to about 24 blue whales (the largest animals) or 40,000 people. The giant sequoia is one of the largest living organisms and also among the most ancient, with some individuals estimated to be between 1,800 and 2,700 years old. Their cousins, the coast redwoods (*Sequoia sempervirens*), grow to heights of more than 110 m (taller than the Statue of Liberty) and are found only in a narrow coastal strip of northern California and southern Oregon.

▶ **Bristlecone pine.** This species (*Pinus longaeva*), which is found in the White Mountains of California, includes some of the oldest living organisms, reaching ages of more than 4,600 years. One tree (not shown here) is called Methuselah because it may be the world's oldest living tree. To protect the tree, scientists keep its location a secret.

▼ **Figure 30.6 The life cycle of a pine.**

MAKE CONNECTIONS *What type of cell division occurs as a megaspore becomes a female gametophyte? (See Figure 13.9, p. 256.)*

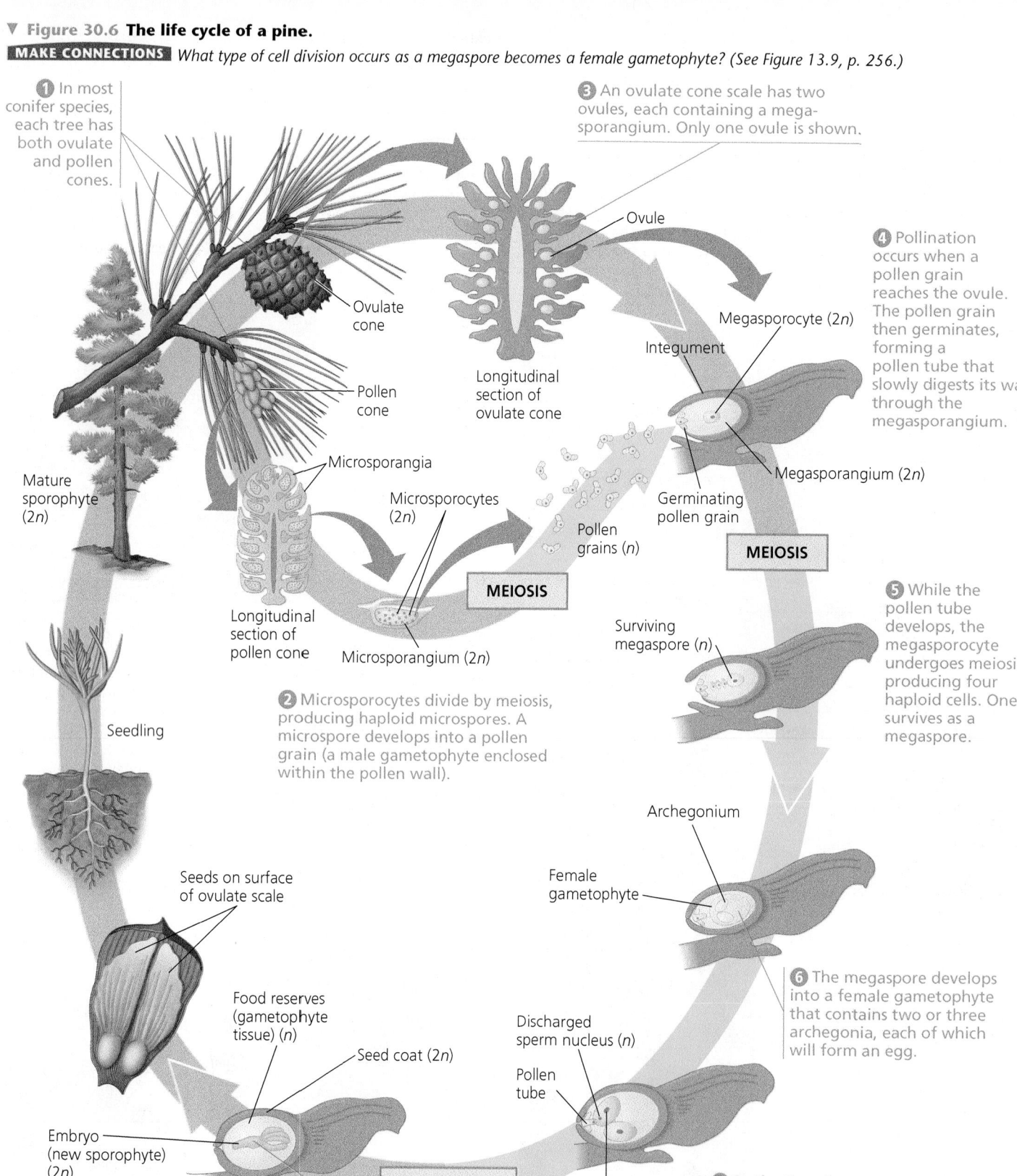

1 In most conifer species, each tree has both ovulate and pollen cones.

3 An ovulate cone scale has two ovules, each containing a mega-sporangium. Only one ovule is shown.

Ovule

Ovulate cone

Pollen cone

Longitudinal section of ovulate cone

4 Pollination occurs when a pollen grain reaches the ovule. The pollen grain then germinates, forming a pollen tube that slowly digests its way through the megasporangium.

Megasporocyte (2n)

Integument

Megasporangium (2n)

Germinating pollen grain

Microsporangia

Microsporocytes (2n)

Pollen grains (n)

MEIOSIS

Mature sporophyte (2n)

Longitudinal section of pollen cone

Microsporangium (2n)

2 Microsporocytes divide by meiosis, producing haploid microspores. A microspore develops into a pollen grain (a male gametophyte enclosed within the pollen wall).

MEIOSIS

5 While the pollen tube develops, the megasporocyte undergoes meiosis, producing four haploid cells. One survives as a megaspore.

Surviving megaspore (n)

Seedling

Archegonium

Female gametophyte

Seeds on surface of ovulate scale

6 The megaspore develops into a female gametophyte that contains two or three archegonia, each of which will form an egg.

Food reserves (gametophyte tissue) (n)

Discharged sperm nucleus (n)

Seed coat (2n)

Pollen tube

Embryo (new sporophyte) (2n)

FERTILIZATION

Egg nucleus (n)

7 By the time the eggs are mature, two sperm cells have developed in the pollen tube, which extends to the female gametophyte. Fertilization occurs when sperm and egg nuclei unite.

Key

→ Haploid (n)

→ Diploid (2n)

8 Fertilization usually occurs more than a year after pollination. All eggs may be fertilized, but usually only one zygote develops into an embryo. The ovule becomes a seed, consisting of an embryo, food supply, and seed coat.

The Life Cycle of a Pine: *A Closer Look*

As you read earlier, seed plant evolution has included three key reproductive adaptations: the increasing dominance of the sporophyte; the advent of the seed as a resistant, dispersible stage in the life cycle; and the appearance of pollen as an airborne agent that brings gametes together. **Figure 30.6**, on the facing page, shows how these adaptations come into play during the life cycle of a pine, a familiar conifer.

The pine tree is the sporophyte; its sporangia are located on scalelike structures packed densely in cones. Like all seed plants, conifers are heterosporous. In conifers, the two types of spores are produced by separate cones: small pollen cones and large ovulate cones. In most pine species, each tree has both types of cones. In pollen cones, microsporocytes (microspore mother cells) undergo meiosis, producing haploid microspores. Each microspore develops into a pollen grain containing a male gametophyte. In pines and other conifers, the yellow pollen is released in large amounts and carried by the wind, dusting everything in its path. Meanwhile, in ovulate cones, megasporocytes (megaspore mother cells) undergo meiosis and produce haploid megaspores inside the ovule. Surviving megaspores develop into multicellular female gametophytes, which are retained within the sporangia.

From the time young pollen and ovulate cones appear on the tree, it takes nearly three years for the male and female gametophytes to be produced and brought together and for mature seeds to form from the fertilized ovules. The scales of each ovulate cone then separate, and the seeds are dispersed by the wind. A seed that lands in a suitable environment then germinates, its embryo emerging as a pine seedling.

CONCEPT CHECK 30.2

1. Use examples from Figure 30.5 to describe how various gymnosperms are similar yet distinctive.
2. Explain how the pine life cycle in Figure 30.6 reflects the five adaptations common to all seed plants (see p. 618).
3. **MAKE CONNECTIONS** Does the hypothesis that gymnosperms and angiosperms are sister clades imply that they originated at the same time? (See pp. 538–539.)

For suggested answers, see Appendix A.

CONCEPT 30.3

The reproductive adaptations of angiosperms include flowers and fruits

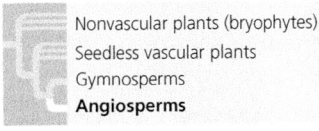

Nonvascular plants (bryophytes)
Seedless vascular plants
Gymnosperms
Angiosperms

Commonly known as flowering plants, angiosperms are seed plants that produce the reproductive structures called flowers and fruits. The name *angiosperm* (from the Greek *angion*, container) refers to seeds contained in fruits, the mature ovaries. Today, angiosperms are the most diverse and widespread of all plants, with more than 250,000 species (about 90% of all plant species).

Characteristics of Angiosperms

All angiosperms are classified in a single phylum, Anthophyta (from the Greek *anthos*, flower). Before considering the evolution of angiosperms, we will examine their key adaptations—flowers and fruits—and the roles of these structures in the angiosperm life cycle.

Flowers

The **flower** is an angiosperm structure specialized for sexual reproduction. In many angiosperm species, insects or other animals transfer pollen from one flower to the sex organs on another flower, which makes pollination more directed than the wind-dependent pollination of most gymnosperms. However, some angiosperms *are* wind-pollinated, particularly those species that occur in dense populations, such as grasses and tree species in temperate forests.

A flower is a specialized shoot that can have up to four rings of modified leaves (sporophylls) called floral organs: sepals, petals, stamens, and carpels (**Figure 30.7**). Starting at the base of the flower are the **sepals**, which are usually green and enclose the flower before it opens (think of a rosebud). Interior to the sepals are the **petals**, which are brightly colored in most flowers and aid in attracting pollinators. Flowers that are wind-pollinated, however, generally lack brightly colored parts. In all angiosperms, the sepals and petals are sterile floral organs, meaning that they do not produce sperm or eggs. Within the petals are two whorls of fertile floral organs that produce spores,

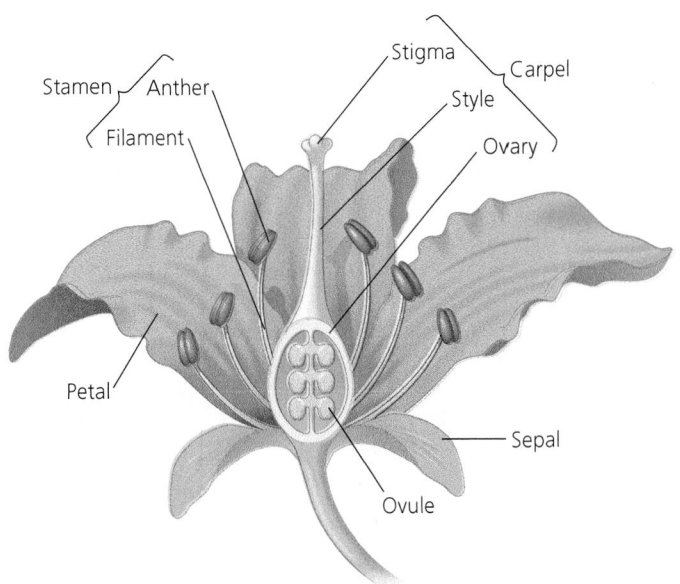

▲ **Figure 30.7** **The structure of an idealized flower.**

the stamens and carpels. **Stamens** produce microspores that develop into pollen grains containing male gametophytes. A stamen consists of a stalk called the **filament** and a terminal sac, the **anther**, where pollen is produced. **Carpels** make megaspores and their products, female gametophytes. Some flowers have a single carpel, whereas others have multiple carpels, which are either separate or fused together. At the tip of the carpel is a sticky **stigma** that receives pollen. A **style** leads from the stigma to the **ovary** at the base of the carpel; the ovary contains one or more ovules. If fertilized, an ovule develops into a seed.

Fruits

A **fruit** typically consists of a mature ovary but can also include other flower parts. As seeds develop from ovules after fertilization, the ovary wall thickens. A pea pod is an example of a fruit, with seeds (mature ovules, the peas) encased in the ripened ovary (the pod). (We'll examine the developmental origin of fruits in Figure 38.10.)

Fruits protect dormant seeds and aid in their dispersal. Mature fruits can be either fleshy or dry **(Figure 30.8)**.

▼ **Figure 30.8 Some variations in fruit structure.**

▼ Tomato, a fleshy fruit with soft outer and inner layers of pericarp (fruit wall)

▼ Ruby grapefruit, a fleshy fruit with a firm outer layer and soft inner layer of pericarp

▶ Nectarine, a fleshy fruit with a soft outer layer and hard inner layer (pit) of pericarp

▼ Hazelnut, a dry fruit that remains closed at maturity

◀ Milkweed, a dry fruit that splits open at maturity

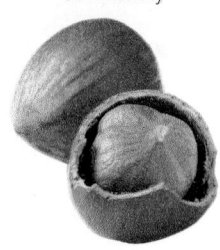

Tomatoes, plums, and grapes are examples of fleshy fruits, in which the wall (pericarp) of the ovary becomes soft during ripening. Dry fruits include beans, nuts, and grains. Some dry fruits split open at maturity to release seeds, whereas others remain closed. The dry, wind-dispersed fruits of grasses, harvested while on the plant, are major staple foods for humans. The cereal grains of maize, rice, wheat, and other grasses, though easily mistaken for seeds, are each actually a fruit with a dry outer covering (the former wall of the ovary) that adheres to the seed coat of the seed within.

As shown in **Figure 30.9**, various adaptations of fruits and seeds help to disperse seeds. The seeds of some flowering plants, such as dandelions and maples, are contained within fruits that function like parachutes or propellers, adaptations that enhance dispersal by wind. Some fruits, such as coconuts, are adapted to dispersal by water (see Figure 38.11). And many angiosperms rely on animals to carry seeds. Some of these plants have fruits modified as burrs that cling to animal fur (or the clothes of humans). Other angiosperms produce edible fruits, which are usually nutritious, sweet tasting, and vividly colored, advertising their ripeness. When an animal eats the fruit, it digests the fruit's fleshy part, but the tough seeds usually pass unharmed through the animal's digestive tract. Animals may deposit the seeds, along with a supply of natural fertilizer, many kilometers from where the fruit was eaten.

▼ **Figure 30.9 Fruit adaptations that enhance seed dispersal.**

▶ Wings enable maple fruits to be carried by the wind.

◀ Seeds within berries and other edible fruits are often dispersed in animal feces.

◀ The barbs of cockleburs facilitate seed dispersal by allowing the fruits to "hitchhike" on animals.

The Angiosperm Life Cycle

You can follow a typical angiosperm life cycle in **Figure 30.10**. The flower of the sporophyte produces microspores that form male gametophytes and megaspores that form female gametophytes. The male gametophytes are in the pollen grains, which develop within microsporangia in the anthers. Each male gametophyte has two haploid cells: a *generative cell* that divides, forming two sperm, and a *tube cell* that produces a pollen tube. Each ovule, which develops in the ovary, con-

tains a female gametophyte, also known as an **embryo sac**. The embryo sac consists of only a few cells, one of which is the egg. (We will discuss gametophyte development in more detail in Chapter 38.)

After its release from the anther, the pollen is carried to the sticky stigma at the tip of a carpel. Although some flowers self-pollinate, most have mechanisms that ensure **cross-pollination**, which in angiosperms is the transfer of pollen from an anther of a flower on one plant to the stigma of a flower on another plant of the same species. Cross-pollination enhances genetic

▼ **Figure 30.10** **The life cycle of an angiosperm.**

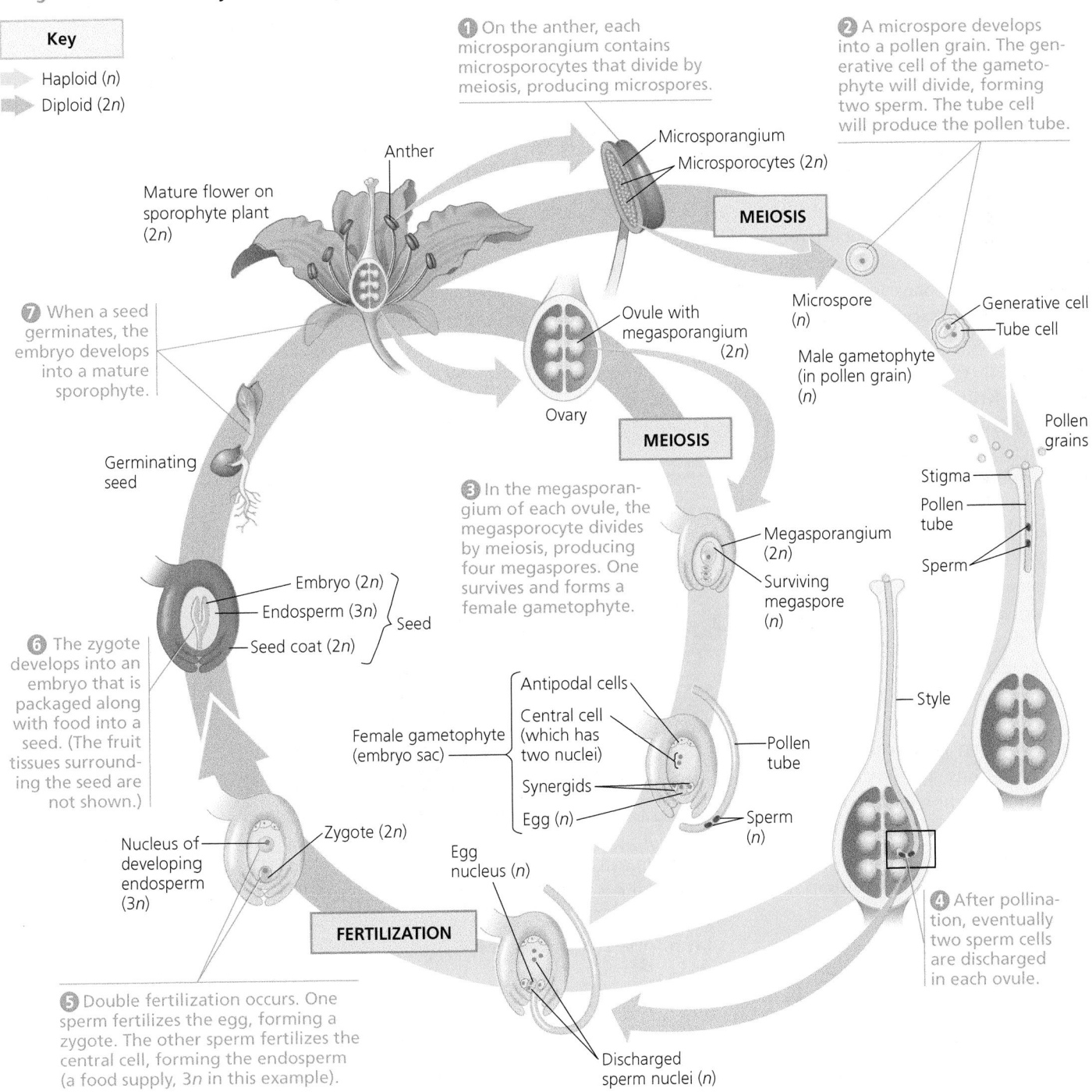

variability. In some species, stamens and carpels of a single flower may mature at different times, or they may be so arranged that self-pollination is unlikely.

The pollen grain absorbs water and germinates after it adheres to the stigma of a carpel. The tube cell produces a pollen tube that grows down within the style of the carpel. After reaching the ovary, the pollen tube penetrates through the **micropyle**, a pore in the integuments of the ovule, and discharges two sperm cells into the female gametophyte (embryo sac). One sperm fertilizes the egg, forming a diploid zygote. The other sperm fuses with the two nuclei in the large central cell of the female gametophyte, producing a triploid cell. This type of **double fertilization**, in which one fertilization event produces a zygote and the other produces a triploid cell, is unique to angiosperms.

After double fertilization, the ovule matures into a seed. The zygote develops into a sporophyte embryo with a rudimentary root and one or two seed leaves called **cotyledons**. The triploid central cell of the female gametophyte develops into **endosperm**, tissue rich in starch and other food reserves that nourish the developing embryo.

What is the function of double fertilization in angiosperms? One hypothesis is that double fertilization synchronizes the development of food storage in the seed with the development of the embryo. If a particular flower is not pollinated or sperm cells are not discharged into the embryo sac, fertilization does not occur, and neither endosperm nor embryo forms. So perhaps double fertilization is an adaptation that prevents flowering plants from squandering nutrients on infertile ovules.

Another type of double fertilization occurs in some gymnosperm species belonging to the phylum Gnetophyta. However, double fertilization in these species gives rise to two embryos rather than to an embryo and endosperm.

As you read earlier, the seed consists of the embryo, the endosperm, and a seed coat derived from the integuments. An ovary develops into a fruit as its ovules become seeds. After being dispersed, a seed may germinate if environmental conditions are favorable. The coat ruptures and the embryo emerges as a seedling, using food stored in the endosperm and cotyledons until it can produce its own food by photosynthesis.

Angiosperm Evolution

Clarifying the origin of angiosperms—what Charles Darwin once called an "abominable mystery"—poses fascinating challenges to evolutionary biologists.

Angiosperms originated at least 140 million years ago, and during the late Mesozoic, the major branches of the clade diverged from their common ancestor. By the mid-Cretaceous period (100 million years ago), angiosperms began to dominate many terrestrial ecosystems. Landscapes changed dramatically as conifers, cycads, and other gymnosperms gave way to flowering plants in many parts of the world.

The flowers and fruits of angiosperms distinguish them markedly from living gymnosperms, which makes the origins of angiosperms puzzling. To understand how the angiosperm body plan emerged, scientists are studying fossils, refining angiosperm phylogeny, and elucidating developmental patterns that underlie flowers and other angiosperm innovations. As we'll see, much progress has been made toward solving Darwin's mystery—but we still do not fully understand how angiosperms originated from earlier seed plants.

Fossil Angiosperms

In the late 1990s, scientists in China discovered several intriguing fossils of 125-million-year-old angiosperms. These fossils, now named *Archaefructus liaoningensis* and *Archaefructus sinensis* **(Figure 30.11)**, share some traits with living angiosperms but lack others. *Archaefructus sinensis*, for example, has anthers and also has seeds inside closed carpels but lacks petals and sepals. In 2002, scientists completed a phylogenetic comparison of *Archaefructus* with 173 living plant species. The researchers concluded that *Archaefructus* may belong to the earliest-diverging group of angiosperms known.

(a) *Archaefructus sinensis*, a 125-million-year-old fossil. This species may represent the sister group to all other angiosperms, or it may belong to the water lily group (see Figure 30.12). Researchers are testing these two hypotheses with phylogenetic analyses.

(b) Artist's reconstruction of *Archaefructus sinensis*

▲ Figure 30.11 **An early flowering plant.**

Based on *Archaefructus* fossils, can we infer traits of the common ancestor of *Archaefructus* and living angiosperms? The fossils indicate that *Archaefructus* had simple flowers and was herbaceous with bulbous structures that may have served as floats, suggesting it was aquatic. But investigating whether the angiosperm common ancestor had simple flowers and was herbaceous and aquatic also requires examining fossils of other seed plants thought to have been closely related to angiosperms. All of those plants were woody, indicating that the common ancestor was probably woody. Furthermore, paleobotanists have found angiosperm fossils from later-diverging lineages that became aquatic and have flowers resembling those of *Archaefructus*. This suggests that simple flowers and an aquatic growth form may have been derived traits of *Archaefructus* rather than traits of the common ancestor. Overall, while most researchers agree that the angiosperm common ancestor was woody, debate continues about many of its other features.

Angiosperm Phylogeny

To shed light on the body plan of early angiosperms, scientists have long sought to identify which seed plants, including fossil species, are most closely related to angiosperms. Molecular and morphological evidence suggests that living gymnosperms are a monophyletic group whose earliest lineages diverged from the ancestors of angiosperms about 305 million

years ago. Note that this does not necessarily imply that angiosperms originated 305 million years ago, but that the most recent common ancestor of gymnosperms and angiosperms lived at that time. Angiosperms may in fact be most closely related to extinct seed plants such as the Bennettitales, a group with flowerlike structures that may have been pollinated by insects (Figure 30.12a). Systematists hope to resolve this issue through phylogenetic studies that combine data from fossil and living species of a wide range of seed plants.

Making sense of the origin of angiosperms also depends on working out the order in which angiosperm clades diverged from one another. Here, dramatic progress has been made in recent years. Molecular and morphological evidence suggests that a small South Pacific shrub called *Amborella trichopoda* and water lilies are living representatives of two of the most ancient angiosperm lineages (Figure 30.12b).

Developmental Patterns in Angiosperms

Additional clues about the origin of flowering plants are emerging from studies of plant development. For example, a 2006 study demonstrated that in *Amborella*, eggs form from precursor cells that differ from the egg precursor cells of most other living angiosperms. Intriguingly, the way in which eggs form in *Amborella* has similarities to how eggs

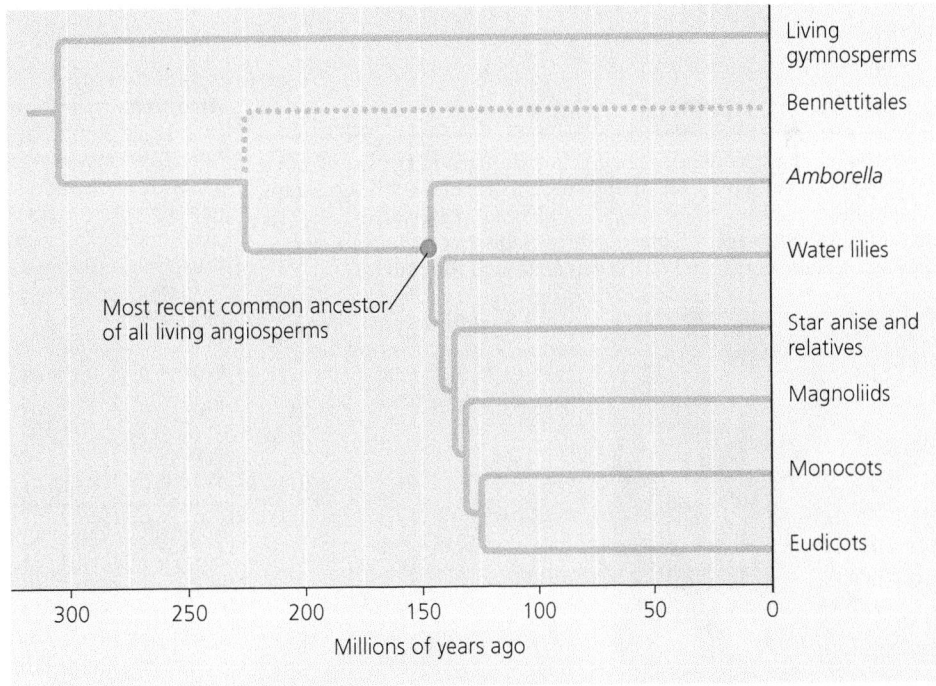

(a) **A possible ancestor of the angiosperms?** This reconstruction shows a cross section through the flowerlike structures found in the Bennettitales, an extinct group of seed plants hypothesized to be more closely related to angiosperms than to gymnosperms.

(b) **Angiosperm phylogeny.** This tree represents one current hypothesis of angiosperm evolutionary relationships, based on morphological and molecular evidence. Angiosperms originated at least 140 million years ago. The dotted line indicates the uncertain position of the Bennettitales, a possible sister group to the angiosperms.

▲ **Figure 30.12 Angiosperm evolutionary history.**

? *Would the branching order of the phylogeny in (b) necessarily have to be redrawn if a 150-million-year-old fossil monocot were discovered? Explain.*

form in gymnosperms—a possible link to the ancient common ancestor of gymnosperms and angiosperms. Other studies suggest that in a variety of early angiosperms (as well as in *Amborella*), the outer of the two protective integuments appears to be a modified leaf that originates separately from the inner integument. Because gymnosperms have only one integument, scientists are curious about exactly how the second integument originated in angiosperms. Researchers are also studying key developmental genes in gymnosperms and angiosperms, including genes that control flower development in angiosperms. Early results have uncovered developmental pathways shared by gymnosperms and angiosperms. These shared pathways may reveal clues about steps leading to the origin of flowering plants.

Angiosperm Diversity

From their humble beginnings in the Mesozoic, angiosperms have diversified into more than 250,000 living species. Until the late 1990s, most systematists divided flowering plants into two groups, based partly on the number of cotyledons, or seed leaves, in the embryo. Species with one cotyledon were called **monocots**, and those with two were called **dicots**. Other features, such as flower and leaf structure, were also used to define the two groups. For example, monocots typically have parallel leaf veins (think of a grass blade), whereas the veins of most dicots have a netlike pattern (think of an oak leaf). Some examples of monocots are orchids, palms, and grain crops such as maize, wheat, and rice. Some examples of dicots are roses, peas, sunflowers, and maples.

Recent DNA studies, however, indicate that the monocot-dicot distinction does not completely reflect evolutionary relationships. Current research supports the hypothesis that monocots form a clade but reveals that the species traditionally called dicots are polyphyletic. The vast majority of species once categorized as dicots form a large clade, now known as **eudicots** ("true" dicots). The rest of the former dicots are now grouped into several small lineages. Three of these lineages are informally called **basal angiosperms** because they appear to include the flowering plants belonging to the oldest lineages. A fourth lineage, called the **magnoliids**, evolved later. **Figure 30.13** provides an overview of angiosperm diversity.

▼ **Figure 30.13**

Exploring Angiosperm Diversity

Basal Angiosperms

Surviving basal angiosperms are currently thought to consist of three lineages comprising only about 100 species. The oldest lineage seems to be represented by a single species, *Amborella trichopoda* (right). The other surviving lineages diverged later: a clade that includes water lilies and a clade consisting of the star anise and its relatives.

Water lily (*Nymphaea "Rene Gerard"*). Water lilies are living members of a clade that may be predated only by the *Amborella* lineage.

Star anise (*Illicium*). This genus belongs to a third surviving lineage of basal angiosperms.

Amborella trichopoda. This small shrub, found only on the South Pacific island of New Caledonia, may be the sole survivor of a branch at the base of the angiosperm tree. *Amborella* lacks vessels, which are present in angiosperms in later-developing lineages. Consisting of xylem cells arranged in continuous tubes, vessels transport water more efficiently than tracheids. Their absence in *Amborella* indicates they may have evolved after the lineage that gave rise to *Amborella* diverged.

Magnoliids

Magnoliids consist of about 8,000 species, most notably magnolias, laurels, and black pepper plants. They include both woody and herbaceous species. Although they share some traits with basal angiosperms, such as a typically spiral rather than whorled arrangement of floral organs, magnoliids are more closely related to eudicots and monocots.

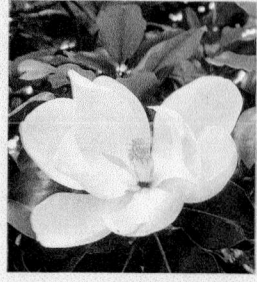

Southern magnolia (*Magnolia grandiflora*). This member of the magnolia family is a woody magnoliid. The variety of southern magnolia shown here, called "Goliath," has flowers that measure up to about a foot across.

Monocots

About one-quarter of angiosperm species are monocots—about 70,000 species. These examples represent some of the largest families.

Orchid (*Lemboglossum rossii*)

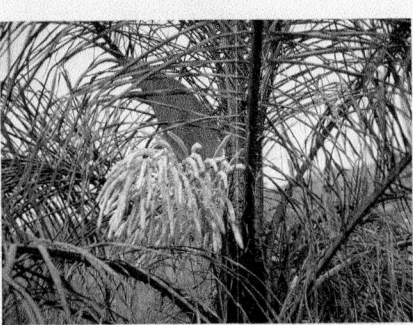

Pygmy date palm (*Phoenix roebelenii*)

Lily (*Lilium* "Enchantment")

Anther

Stigma

Ovary

Filament

Barley (*Hordeum vulgare*), a grass

Eudicots

More than two-thirds of angiosperm species are eudicots—roughly 170,000 species. Below is a sampling of eudicot floral diversity.

Monocot Characteristics		Eudicot Characteristics
	Embryos	
One cotyledon		Two cotyledons
	Leaf venation	
Veins usually parallel		Veins usually netlike
	Stems	
Vascular tissue scattered		Vascular tissue usually arranged in ring
	Roots	
Root system usually fibrous (no main root)		Taproot (main root) usually present
	Pollen	
Pollen grain with one opening		Pollen grain with three openings
	Flowers	
Floral organs usually in multiples of three		Floral organs usually in multiples of four or five

California poppy (*Eschscholzia californica*)

Pyrenean oak (*Quercus pyrenaica*)

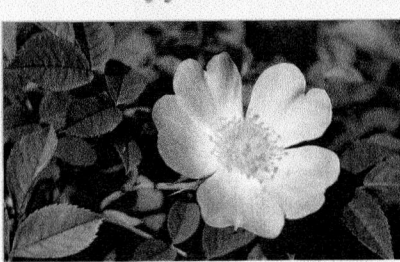

Dog rose (*Rosa canina*), a wild rose

Snow pea (*Pisum sativum*), a legume

Zucchini (*Cucurbita pepo*) flowers

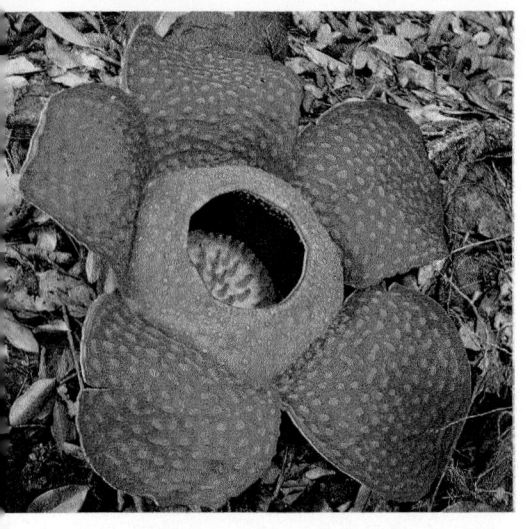

◀ Figure 30.14 **A plant pollinated by flies.** *Rafflesia arnoldii*, the "monster flower" of Indonesia, is the size of an automobile tire. It attracts fly pollinators with an odor like that of a decaying corpse.

Evolutionary Links Between Angiosperms and Animals

Ever since they colonized land, animals have influenced the evolution of terrestrial plants, and vice versa. For example, herbivores can reduce a plant's reproductive success by eating its roots, leaves, or seeds. As a result, if a novel and effective defense against herbivores originates in a group of plants, those plants may be favored by natural selection—as will any herbivores that can overcome this new defense. Plant-pollinator and other mutually beneficial interactions can have similar evolutionary effects, as seen in **Figure 30.14**.

In the examples we just discussed, interactions between plants and animals led to reciprocal evolution in the particular pairs of species involved. However, interactions between plants and animals also may have affected broader patterns in the history of life, such as rates at which new species form. Consider the evolutionary impact of how flower petals are arranged. Flower petals can be symmetrical in one direction only (*bilateral symmetry*, as in the pea blossom in Figure 30.13), or they can be symmetrical in all directions (*radial symmetry*, as in the dog rose in Figure 30.13). On a flower with bilateral symmetry, an insect pollinator may be able to obtain nectar only when it approaches the flower from a certain direction **(Figure 30.15)**. This constraint can make it more likely that

◀ Figure 30.15 **Pollinating a bilaterally symmetrical flower.** To harvest nectar (a sugary solution secreted by flower glands) from this bilaterally symmetrical Scottish broom flower, a honeybee must land as shown. This releases a tripping mechanism that arches the flower's stamens over the bee and dusts it with pollen. Later, some of this pollen will rub off onto the stigma of the next flower of this species that the bee visits.

as an insect moves from flower to flower, pollen is placed on a part of the insect's body that will come into contact with the stigma of a flower of the same species. Such specificity of pollen transfer tends to reduce gene flow between diverging populations and hence could lead to increased rates of plant speciation.

How can this hypothesis be tested? One approach is illustrated in this diagram:

A key step is to identify cases in which a clade with bilaterally symmetrical flowers shares an immediate common ancestor with a clade whose members have radially symmetrical flowers. One recent study identified 19 such pairs of closely related "bilateral" and "radial" clades. On average, the clade with bilaterally symmetrical flowers had nearly 2,400 more species than did its closely related clade with radially symmetrical flowers. This result suggests that flower shape can affect the rate at which new species form, with speciation occurring more rapidly in clades with bilateral symmetry. Overall, the effects of plant-pollinator interactions are thought to have contributed to the increasing dominance of flowering plants in the Cretaceous period, helping to make angiosperms of central importance in ecological communites.

CONCEPT CHECK 30.3

1. It has been said that an oak is an acorn's way of making more acorns. Write an explanation that includes these terms: sporophyte, gametophyte, ovule, seed, ovary, and fruit.
2. Compare and contrast a pine cone and a flower in terms of structure and function.
3. **WHAT IF?** Do speciation rates in closely related clades of flowering plants show that flower shape is *correlated with* the rate at which new species form, or that flower shape is *responsible for* this rate? Explain.

For suggested answers, see Appendix A.

CONCEPT 30.4

Human welfare depends greatly on seed plants

Throughout Unit Five, we are highlighting the ways in which humans depend on various organisms. In forests and on farms, seed plants are key sources of food, fuel, wood products, and medicine. Our reliance on them makes the preservation of plant diversity critical.

Products from Seed Plants

Most of our food comes from angiosperms. Just six crops—maize, rice, wheat, potatoes, cassava, and sweet potatoes—yield 80% of all the calories consumed by humans. We also depend on angiosperms to feed livestock: It takes 5–7 kg of grain to produce 1 kg of grain-fed beef.

Today's crops are the products of artificial selection—the result of plant domestication that began about 12,000 years ago. To appreciate the scale of this transformation, note how the number and size of seeds in domesticated plants are greater than those of their wild relatives, as in the case of maize and the grass teosinte (see Figure 38.16). Scientists can glean information about domestication by comparing the genes of crops with those of wild relatives. With maize, dramatic changes such as increased cob size and loss of the hard coating around teosinte kernels may have been initiated by as few as five mutations.

Flowering plants also provide other edible products. Two popular beverages come from tea leaves and coffee beans, and you can thank the tropical cacao tree for cocoa and chocolate. Spices are derived from various plant parts, such as flowers (cloves, saffron), fruits and seeds (vanilla, black pepper, mustard), leaves (basil, mint, sage), and even bark (cinnamon).

Many seed plants are sources of wood, which is absent in all living seedless plants. Wood consists of tough-walled xylem cells (see Figure 35.22). It is the primary source of fuel for much of the world, and wood pulp, typically derived from conifers such as fir and pine, is used to make paper. Wood also remains the most widely used construction material.

For centuries, humans have also depended on seed plants for medicines. Many cultures use herbal remedies, and scientists have extracted and identified the relevant secondary compounds (see p. 604) from many of these plants, and later synthesized them. Willow leaves and bark, for instance, have long been used in pain-relieving remedies, including prescriptions by the Greek physician Hippocrates. In the 1800s, scientists traced the willow's medicinal property to the chemical salicin. A synthesized derivative, acetylsalicylic acid, is what we call aspirin. Plants also remain a direct source of medicinal compounds. In the United States, about 25% of prescription drugs contain an active ingredient from plants, typically seed plants. Other ingredients were discovered in seed plants and then synthesized artificially. Table 30.1 lists some medicinal uses of secondary compounds found in seed plants.

Table 30.1 Examples of Plant-Derived Medicines

Compound	Source	Use
Atropine	Belladonna plant	Eye pupil dilator
Digitalin	Foxglove	Heart medication
Menthol	Eucalyptus tree	Throat soother
Quinine	Cinchona tree	Malaria preventive
Taxol	Pacific yew	Ovarian cancer drug
Tubocurarine	Curare tree	Muscle relaxant
Vinblastine	Periwinkle	Leukemia drug

Threats to Plant Diversity

Although plants may be a renewable resource, plant diversity is not. The exploding human population and its demand for space and resources are extinguishing plant species at a high rate. The problem is especially severe in the tropics, where more than two-thirds of the human population live and where population growth is fastest. About 55,000 km^2 (14 million acres) of tropical rain forest are cleared each year (Figure 30.16), a rate that would completely eliminate the remaining 11 million km^2

▼ Figure 30.16
IMPACT

Clear-Cutting of Tropical Forests

Over the past several hundred years, nearly half of Earth's tropical forests have been cut down and converted to farmland and other uses. Satellite images, such as those below, show that together these regions cover an area roughly the size of Canada. Living trees release large quantities of water to the atmosphere, cooling the local environment (much as evaporation of sweat cools your body) and putting moisture into the air that is recycled as rain. When trees are cut down, less moisture is released to the atmosphere, causing increased temperatures and decreased rainfall. Tree removal also reduces the absorption of atmospheric carbon dioxide (CO_2) that occurs during photosynthesis.

A satellite image from 2000 shows clear-cut areas in Brazil surrounded by dense tropical forest.

By 2009, much more of this same tropical forest had been cut down.

WHY IT MATTERS Higher temperatures and increased atmospheric CO_2 resulting from destruction of tropical forests contribute to global warming, making preservation of these forests a high priority. Moreover, changes in rainfall patterns are expected to reduce agricultural production in some of the poorest countries. Finally, tropical forests harbor 50% or more of all species on Earth. Hence, higher temperatures, reduced rainfall, and habitat loss caused by clear-cutting tropical forests may lead to extinction of many species.

FURTHER READING G. P. Asner, T. K. Rudel, T. M. Aide, R. Defries, and R. Emerson, A contemporary assessment of change in humid tropical forests, *Conservation Biology* 23:1386–1395 (2009).

WHAT IF? How would clear-cutting affect the temperature and moisture along the edges of a remaining forest fragment?

of tropical forests in 200 years. The most common cause of this destruction is slash-and-burn clearing of forests for agricultural use (see Chapter 56). As forests disappear, so do large numbers of plant species. Of course, once a species becomes extinct, it can never return.

The loss of plant species is often accompanied by the loss of insects and other rain forest animals. Researchers estimate that habitat destruction in rain forests and other ecosystems is pushing hundreds of species toward extinction each year. If current rates of loss in the tropics and elsewhere continue, scientists estimate that within the next few centuries, 50% or more of Earth's species will become extinct. Such losses would constitute a global mass extinction, rivaling the Permian and Cretaceous mass extinctions and forever changing the evolutionary history of land plants (and many other organisms).

Many people have ethical concerns about contributing to the extinction of living forms. In addition, there are practical reasons to be concerned about the loss of plant diversity. So far, we have explored the potential uses of only a tiny fraction of the more than 290,000 known plant species. For example,

almost all our food is based on the cultivation of only about two dozen species of seed plants. And fewer than 5,000 plant species have been studied as potential sources of medicines. The tropical rain forest may be a medicine chest of healing plants that could be extinct before we even know they exist. If we begin to view rain forests and other ecosystems as living treasures that can regenerate only slowly, we may learn to harvest their products at sustainable rates. What else can we do to preserve plant diversity? Few questions are as important, as we'll explore more fully in Unit Eight (Ecology).

CONCEPT CHECK 30.4

1. Explain why plant diversity can be considered a non-renewable resource.
2. **WHAT IF?** How could phylogenies be used to help researchers search more efficiently for novel medicines derived from seed plants?

For suggested answers, see Appendix A.

30 CHAPTER REVIEW

SUMMARY OF KEY CONCEPTS

CONCEPT 30.1

Seeds and pollen grains are key adaptations for life on land (pp. 618–621)

Five Derived Traits of Seed Plants

Reduced gametophytes	Microscopic male and female gametophytes (*n*) are nourished and protected by the sporophyte (2*n*)	Male gametophyte — Female gametophyte
Heterospory	Microspore (gives rise to a male gametophyte)	
	Megaspore (gives rise to a female gametophyte)	
Ovules	Ovule (gymnosperm) { Integument (2*n*) — Megaspore (*n*) — Megasporangium (2*n*)	
Pollen	Pollen grains make water unnecessary for fertilization	
Seeds	Seeds: survive better than unprotected spores, can be transported long distances { Seed coat — Food supply — Embryo	

? *Describe how the parts of an ovule (integument, megaspore, megasporangium) correspond to the parts of a seed.*

CONCEPT 30.2

Gymnosperms bear "naked" seeds, typically on cones (pp. 621–625)

- Gymnosperms appear early in the plant fossil record and dominated many Mesozoic terrestrial ecosystems. Living seed plants can be divided into two monophyletic groups: gymnosperms and angiosperms. Extant gymnosperms include cycads, *Ginkgo biloba*, gnetophytes, and conifers.
- Dominance of the sporophyte generation, the development of seeds from fertilized ovules, and the role of pollen in transferring sperm to ovules are key features of a typical gymnosperm life cycle.

? *Although there are fewer than 1,000 species of gymnosperms, the group is still very successful in terms of its evolutionary longevity, adaptations, and geographic distribution. Explain.*

CONCEPT 30.3

The reproductive adaptations of angiosperms include flowers and fruits (pp. 625–632)

- Flowers generally consist of four whorls of modified leaves: sepals, petals, stamens (which produce pollen), and carpels (which produce ovules). Ovaries ripen into fruits, which often carry seeds by wind, water, or animals to new locations.
- An adaptive radiation of angiosperms occurred during the Cretaceous period. Fossils, phylogenetic analyses, and developmental studies offer insights into the origin of flowers.
- Several groups of basal angiosperms have been identified. Other major clades of angiosperms include magnoliids, monocots, and eudicots.

- Pollination and other interactions between angiosperms and animals may have contributed to the success of flowering plants during the last 100 million years.

? *What makes the origin of angiosperms puzzling? Has Darwin's "abominable mystery" been solved? Explain.*

CONCEPT 30.4

Human welfare depends greatly on seed plants
(pp. 632–634)

- Humans depend on seed plants for products such as food, wood, and many medicines.
- Destruction of habitat threatens the extinction of many plant species and the animal species they support.

? *Explain why destroying the remaining tropical forests might harm humans and lead to a mass extinction.*

TEST YOUR UNDERSTANDING

LEVEL 1: KNOWLEDGE/COMPREHENSION

1. Where in an angiosperm would you find a megasporangium?
   a. in the style of a flower
   b. inside the tip of a pollen tube
   c. enclosed in the stigma of a flower
   d. within an ovule contained within an ovary of a flower
   e. packed into pollen sacs within the anthers found on a stamen

2. A fruit is most commonly
   a. a mature ovary.
   b. a thickened style.
   c. an enlarged ovule.
   d. a modified root.
   e. a mature female gametophyte.

3. With respect to angiosperms, which of the following is *incorrectly* paired with its chromosome count?
   a. egg—n
   b. megaspore—$2n$
   c. microspore—n
   d. zygote—$2n$
   e. sperm—n

4. Which of the following is *not* a characteristic that distinguishes gymnosperms and angiosperms from other plants?
   a. alternation of generations
   b. ovules
   c. integuments
   d. pollen
   e. dependent gametophytes

5. Gymnosperms and angiosperms have the following in common *except*
   a. seeds.
   b. pollen.
   c. vascular tissue.
   d. ovaries.
   e. ovules.

LEVEL 2: APPLICATION/ANALYSIS

6. **DRAW IT** Use the letters a–d to label where on the phylogenetic tree each of the following derived characters appear.
   a. flowers
   b. embryos
   c. seeds
   d. vascular tissue

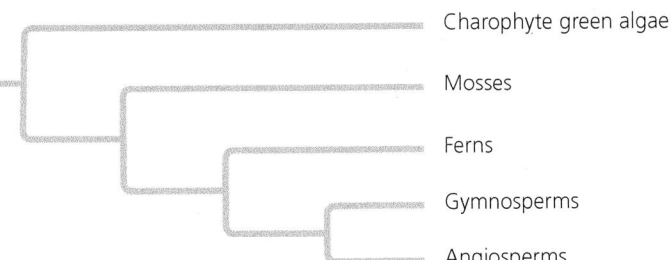

Charophyte green algae

Mosses

Ferns

Gymnosperms

Angiosperms

7. EVOLUTION CONNECTION

The history of life has been punctuated by several mass extinctions. For example, the impact of a meteorite may have wiped out most of the dinosaurs and many forms of marine life at the end of the Cretaceous period (see Chapter 25). Fossils indicate that plants were less severely affected by this and other mass extinctions. What adaptations may have enabled plants to withstand these disasters better than animals?

LEVEL 3: SYNTHESIS/EVALUATION

8. SCIENTIFIC INQUIRY

DRAW IT As will be described in detail in Chapter 38, the female gametophyte of angiosperms typically has seven cells, one of which, the central cell, contains two haploid nuclei. After double fertilization, the central cell develops into endosperm, which is triploid. Because magnoliids, monocots, and eudicots typically have female gametophytes with seven cells and triploid endosperm, scientists assumed that this was the ancestral state for angiosperms. Consider, however, the following recent discoveries:
- Our understanding of angiosperm phylogeny has changed to that shown in Figure 30.12b.
- *Amborella trichopoda* has eight-celled female gametophytes and triploid endosperm.
- Water lilies and star anise have four-celled female gametophytes and diploid endosperm.
   a. Draw a phylogeny of the angiosperms (see Figure 30.12b), incorporating the data given above about the number of cells in female gametophytes and the ploidy of the endosperm. Assume that all of the star anise relatives have four-celled female gametophytes and diploid endosperm.
   b. What does your labeled phylogeny suggest about the evolution of the female gametophyte and endosperm in angiosperms?

9. **WRITE ABOUT A THEME**

   The Cellular Basis of Life Cells are the basic units of structure and function in all organisms. A key feature in the life cycle of plants is the alternation of multicellular haploid and diploid generations. Imagine a lineage of flowering plants in which mitotic cell division did not occur between the events of meiosis and fertilization (see Figure 30.10). In a short essay (100–150 words), describe how this change in the timing of cell division would affect the structure and life cycle of plants in this lineage.

For selected answers, see Appendix A.

MasteringBIOLOGY® www.masteringbiology.com

1. MasteringBiology® Assignments
Tutorial Gymnosperms
Activities Pine Life Cycle • Angiosperm Life Cycle
Questions Student Misconceptions • Reading Quiz • Multiple Choice • End-of-Chapter

2. eText
Read your book online, search, take notes, highlight text, and more.

3. The Study Area
Practice Tests • Cumulative Test • *BioFlix* 3-D Animations • MP3 Tutor Sessions • Videos • Activities • Investigations • Lab Media • Audio Glossary • Word Study Tools • Art

31

Fungi

▲ Figure 31.1 **Can you spot the largest organism in this forest?**

KEY CONCEPTS

31.1 Fungi are heterotrophs that feed by absorption
31.2 Fungi produce spores through sexual or asexual life cycles
31.3 The ancestor of fungi was an aquatic, single-celled, flagellated protist
31.4 Fungi have radiated into a diverse set of lineages
31.5 Fungi play key roles in nutrient cycling, ecological interactions, and human welfare

OVERVIEW

Mighty Mushrooms

Hiking through the Malheur National Forest in eastern Oregon, you might notice a few clusters of honey mushrooms (*Armillaria ostoyae*) scattered here and there beneath the towering trees (**Figure 31.1**). The trees appear to dwarf the mushrooms, but as strange as it sounds, the reverse is actually true.

All these mushrooms are just the aboveground portion of a single enormous fungus. Its subterranean network of filaments spreads through 965 hectares of the forest—more than the area of 1,800 football fields. Based on its current growth rate, scientists estimate that this fungus, which weighs hundreds of tons, has been growing for more than 1,900 years.

The inconspicuous honey mushrooms on the forest floor are a fitting symbol of the neglected grandeur of the kingdom Fungi. Most of us are barely aware of these eukaryotes beyond the mushrooms we eat or the occasional brush with athlete's foot. Yet fungi are a huge and important component of the biosphere. While about 100,000 species have been described, it is estimated that there are actually as many as 1.5 million species of fungi. Some fungi are exclusively single-celled, though most have complex multicellular bodies, which in many cases include the structures we know as mushrooms. These diverse organisms are found in just about every imaginable terrestrial and aquatic habitat; airborne spores have even been found 160 km above ground.

Fungi are not only diverse and widespread; they are also essential for the well-being of most ecosystems. They break down organic material and recycle nutrients, allowing other organisms to assimilate essential chemical elements. Humans make use of fungi as a food source, for applications in agriculture and forestry, and in manufacturing products ranging from bread to antibiotics. But it is also true that some fungi cause disease in plants and animals.

In this chapter, we will investigate the structure and evolutionary history of fungi, survey the major groups of fungi, and discuss their ecological and commercial significance.

CONCEPT 31.1

Fungi are heterotrophs that feed by absorption

Despite their vast diversity, all fungi share some key traits, most importantly the way they derive nutrition. In addition, many fungi grow by forming multicellular filaments, a body structure that plays an important role in how they obtain food.

Nutrition and Ecology

Like animals, fungi are heterotrophs: They cannot make their own food as plants and algae can. But unlike animals, fungi do not ingest (eat) their food. Instead, a fungus absorbs nutrients from the environment outside of its body. Many fungi accomplish this task by secreting powerful hydrolytic enzymes into their surroundings. These enzymes break down complex molecules to smaller organic compounds that the fungi can absorb into their bodies and use. Other fungi use enzymes to penetrate the walls of cells, enabling the fungi to absorb nutrients from the cells. Collectively, the different enzymes found in various fungal species can digest compounds from a wide range of sources, living or dead.

This diversity of food sources corresponds to the varied roles of fungi in ecological communitities, with different species living as decomposers, parasites, or mutualists. Decomposer fungi break down and absorb nutrients from non-living organic material, such as fallen logs, animal corpses, and the wastes of living organisms. Parasitic fungi absorb nutrients from the cells of living hosts. Some parasitic fungi are pathogenic, including many species that cause diseases in plants. Mutualistic fungi also absorb nutrients from a host organism, but they reciprocate with actions that benefit the host. For example, mutualistic fungi that live inside certain termite species use their enzymes to break down wood, as do mutualistic protists in other termite species (see Figure 28.26).

The versatile enzymes that enable fungi to digest a wide range of food sources are not the only reason for their ecological success. Another important factor is how their body structure increases the efficiency of nutrient absorption.

Body Structure

The most common fungal body structures are multicellular filaments and single cells (**yeasts**). Many species can grow as both filaments and yeasts, but even more grow only as filaments; relatively few species grow only as yeasts. Yeasts often inhabit moist environments, including plant sap and animal tissues, where there is a ready supply of soluble nutrients, such as sugars and amino acids. We'll discuss yeasts again later in the chapter.

The morphology of multicellular fungi enhances their ability to grow into and absorb nutrients from their surroundings (**Figure 31.2**). The bodies of these fungi typically form a network of tiny filaments called **hyphae** (singular, *hypha*). Hyphae consist of tubular cell walls surrounding the plasma membrane and cytoplasm of the cells. Unlike plant cell walls, which contain cellulose, fungal cell walls are strengthened by **chitin**. This strong but flexible nitrogen-containing polysaccharide is also found in the external skeletons of insects and other arthropods.

Fungal hyphae form an interwoven mass called a **mycelium** (plural, *mycelia*) that infiltrates the material on which the fungus feeds. A mycelium's structure maximizes its surface-to-volume ratio, making feeding very efficient. Just 1 cm^3 of rich soil may contain as much as 1 km of hyphae with a total surface area of 300 cm^2 in contact with the soil. A fungal mycelium grows rapidly, as proteins and other materials synthesized by the fungus are channeled through cytoplasmic streaming to the tips of the extending hyphae. The fungus concentrates its energy and resources on adding hyphal length and thus overall absorptive surface area, rather than on increasing hyphal girth. Fungi are not motile in the typical sense—they cannot run, swim, or fly in search of food or mates. However, as they grow, fungi can move into new territory, swiftly extending the tips of their hyphae.

In most fungi, the hyphae are divided into cells by cross-walls, or **septa** (singular, *septum*) (**Figure 31.3a**). Septa generally have pores large enough to allow ribosomes, mitochondria, and even nuclei to flow from cell to cell. Some fungi lack septa (**Figure 31.3b**). Known as **coenocytic fungi**, these organisms consist of a continuous cytoplasmic mass having hundreds or thousands of nuclei. The coenocytic condition results from the repeated division of nuclei without cytokinesis. This description

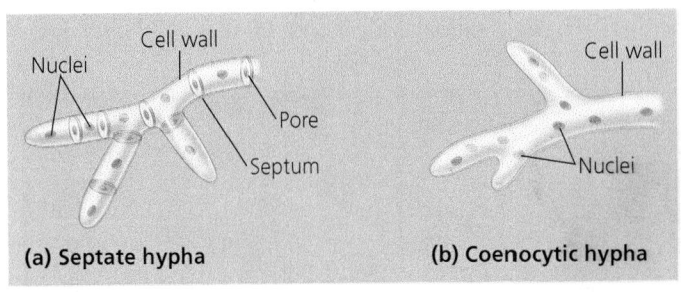

(a) Septate hypha   **(b) Coenocytic hypha**

▲ **Figure 31.3 Two forms of hyphae.**

Reproductive structure. Tiny haploid cells called spores are produced inside the mushroom.

Hyphae. The mushroom and its subterranean mycelium are a continuous network of hyphae.

Spore-producing structures

60 μm

Mycelium

▲ **Figure 31.2 Structure of a multicellular fungus.** The top photograph shows the sexual structures, in this case called mushrooms, of the penny bun fungus (*Boletus edulis*). The bottom photograph shows a mycelium growing on fallen conifer needles. The inset SEM shows hyphae.

? *Although the mushrooms in the top photograph appear to be different individuals, could their DNA be identical? Explain.*

may remind you of the plasmodial slime molds you read about in Chapter 28, which also consist of cytoplasmic masses containing many nuclei. This similarity is one reason that slime molds were once classified as fungi; molecular data have since shown that slime molds and fungi belong to distinct clades.

Specialized Hyphae in Mycorrhizal Fungi

Some fungi have specialized hyphae that allow them to feed on living animals (Figure 31.4a). Other fungal species have specialized hyphae called **haustoria**, which the fungi use to extract nutrients from, or exchange nutrients with, their plant hosts (Figure 31.4b). Mutually beneficial relationships between such fungi and plant roots are called **mycorrhizae** (the term means "fungus roots").

Mycorrhizal fungi (fungi that form mycorrhizae) can improve delivery of phosphate ions and other minerals to plants because the vast mycelial networks of the fungi are more efficient than the plants' roots at acquiring these minerals from the soil. In exchange, the plants supply the fungi with organic nutrients such as carbohydrates. There are two main types of mycorrhizal fungi. **Ectomycorrhizal fungi** (from the Greek *ektos*, out) form sheaths of hyphae over the surface of a root and typically grow into the extracellular spaces of the root cortex (see Figure 37.13a). **Arbuscular mycorrhizal fungi** (from the Latin *arbor*, tree) extend branching hyphae through the root cell wall and into tubes formed by invagination (pushing inward) of the root cell plasma membrane (see Figure 37.13b).

Mycorrhizae are enormously important in natural ecosystems and agriculture. Almost all vascular plants have mycorrhizae and rely on their fungal partners for essential nutrients. Many studies have demonstrated the significance of mycorrhizae by comparing the growth of plants with and without them (see Figure 37.14). Foresters commonly inoculate pine seedlings with mycorrhizal fungi to promote growth. In the absence of human intervention, mycorrhizal fungi colonize soils by dispersing haploid cells called **spores** that form new mycelia after germinating. Spore dispersal is a key component of how fungi reproduce and spread to new areas, as we discuss next.

(a) **Hyphae adapted for trapping and killing prey.** In *Arthrobotrys*, a soil fungus, portions of the hyphae are modified as hoops that can constrict around a nematode (roundworm) in less than a second. The fungus then penetrates its prey with hyphae and digests the prey's inner tissues (SEM).

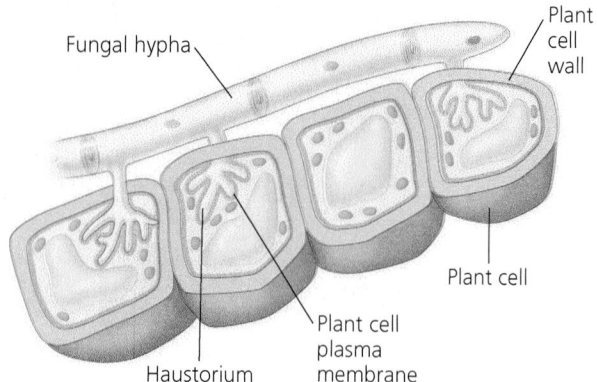

(b) **Haustoria.** Some mutualistic and parasitic fungi grow specialized hyphae called haustoria that can extract nutrients from living plant cells. Haustoria remain separated from a plant cell's cytoplasm by the plasma membrane of the plant cell (orange).

▲ **Figure 31.4 Specialized hyphae.**

CONCEPT CHECK 31.1

1. Compare and contrast the nutritional mode of a fungus with your own nutritional mode.
2. **WHAT IF?** Suppose a certain fungus is a mutualist that lives within an insect host, yet its ancestors were parasites that grew in and on the insect's body. What derived traits might you find in this mutualistic fungus?
3. **MAKE CONNECTIONS** Review Figure 10.4 (p. 186) and Figure 10.6 (p. 188). If a plant has mycorrhizae, where might carbon that enters the plant's stomata as CO_2 eventually be deposited: in the plant, in the mycorrhizal fungus, or in both? Explain.

For suggested answers, see Appendix A.

CONCEPT 31.2

Fungi produce spores through sexual or asexual life cycles

Most fungi propagate themselves by producing vast numbers of spores, either sexually or asexually. For example, puffballs, the reproductive structures of certain fungal species, may release trillions of spores in cloud-like bursts (see Figure 31.18). Spores can be carried long distances by wind or water. If they land in a moist place where there is food, they germinate, producing new mycelia. To appreciate how effective spores are at dispersing, leave a slice of melon exposed to the air. Even without a visible source of spores nearby, within a week or so, you will likely observe fuzzy mycelia growing from the microscopic spores that have fallen onto the melon.

Key

▷ Haploid (*n*)

▷ Heterokaryotic (unfused nuclei from different parents)

▷ Diploid (2*n*)

PLASMOGAMY (fusion of cytoplasm)

Heterokaryotic stage

Spore-producing structures

Spores

ASEXUAL REPRODUCTION

Mycelium

SEXUAL REPRODUCTION

KARYOGAMY (fusion of nuclei)

Zygote

GERMINATION

GERMINATION

MEIOSIS

Spores

▲ **Figure 31.5 Generalized life cycle of fungi.** Many—but not all—fungi reproduce both sexually and asexually. Some reproduce only sexually, others only asexually.

Figure 31.5 generalizes the many different life cycles that can produce fungal spores. In this section, we will survey general aspects of the sexual and asexual life cycles of fungi. Later, we'll examine more closely the life cycles of specific fungi.

Sexual Reproduction

The nuclei of fungal hyphae and the spores of most fungal species are haploid, although many fungi have transient diploid stages that form during sexual life cycles. In fungi, sexual reproduction often begins when hyphae from two mycelia release sexual signaling molecules called **pheromones**. If the mycelia are of different mating types, the pheromones from each partner bind to receptors on the other, and the hyphae extend toward the source of the pheromones. When the hyphae meet, they fuse. In species with such a "compatibility test," this process contributes to genetic variation by preventing hyphae from fusing with other hyphae from the same mycelium or another genetically identical mycelium.

The union of the cytoplasms of two parent mycelia is known as **plasmogamy**. In most fungi, the haploid nuclei contributed by each parent do not fuse right away. Instead, parts of the fused mycelium contain coexisting, genetically different nuclei. Such a mycelium is said to be a **heterokaryon** (meaning "different nuclei"). In some species, the different nuclei may even exchange chromosomes and genes in a process similar to crossing over (see Chapter 13). In other species, the haploid nuclei pair off two to a cell, one from each parent. Such a mycelium is **dikaryotic** (meaning "two nuclei"). As a dikaryotic mycelium grows, the two nuclei in each cell divide in tandem without fusing. Because these cells retain two separate haploid nuclei, they differ from diploid cells, which have pairs of homologous chromosomes within a single nucleus.

Hours, days, or (in some fungi) even centuries may pass between plasmogamy and the next stage in the sexual cycle, **karyogamy**. During karyogamy, the haploid nuclei contributed by the two parents fuse, producing diploid cells. Zygotes and other transient structures form during karyogamy, the only diploid stage in most fungi. Meiosis then restores the haploid condition, leading to the formation of spores that enable the fungus to disperse.

The sexual processes of karyogamy and meiosis generate extensive genetic variation, a prerequisite for natural selection. (See Chapters 13 and 23 to review how sex can increase genetic diversity in a population.) The heterokaryotic condition also offers some of the advantages of diploidy in that one haploid genome may compensate for harmful mutations in the other.

Asexual Reproduction

Many fungi can reproduce both sexually and asexually. Some 20,000 fungal species are only known to reproduce asexually. As with sexual reproduction, the processes of asexual reproduction vary widely among fungi.

Many fungi reproduce asexually by growing as filamentous fungi that produce (haploid) spores by mitosis; such species are known informally as **molds** if they form visible mycelia. Depending on your housekeeping habits, you may have observed molds in your kitchen, forming furry carpets on fruit, bread, and other foods (**Figure 31.6**). Molds typically grow rapidly and produce many spores asexually, enabling the fungi to colonize new sources of food. Many species that produce such spores can also reproduce sexually if they happen to contact a member of their species of a different mating type.

1.5 µm

▲ **Figure 31.6 *Penicillium*, a mold commonly encountered as a decomposer of food.** The bead-like clusters in the colorized SEM are conidia, structures involved in asexual reproduction.

Other fungi reproduce asexually by growing as single-celled yeasts. Instead of producing spores, asexual reproduction in yeasts occurs by ordinary cell division or by the pinching of small "bud cells" off a parent cell (Figure 31.7). As already mentioned, some fungi that grow as yeasts can also grow as filamentous mycelia, depending on the availability of nutrients.

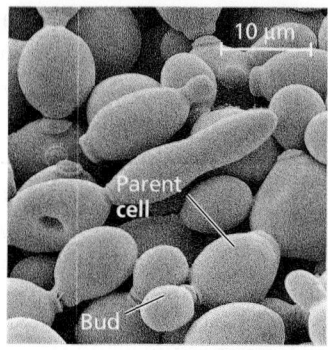

▲ Figure 31.7 **The yeast Saccharomyces cerevisiae in several stages of budding** (SEM).

Many yeasts and filamentous fungi have no known sexual stage in their life cycle. Since early mycologists (biologists who study fungi) classified fungi based mainly on their type of sexual structure, this posed a problem. Mycologists have traditionally lumped all fungi lacking sexual reproduction into a group called **deuteromycetes** (from the Greek *deutero*, second, and *mycete*, fungus). Whenever a sexual stage is discovered for a so-called deuteromycete, the species is reclassified in a particular phylum, depending on the type of sexual structures it forms. In addition to searching for sexual stages of such unassigned fungi, mycologists can now use genetic techniques to classify them.

CONCEPT CHECK 31.2

1. **MAKE CONNECTIONS** Compare Figure 31.5 with Figure 13.6 (p. 252). In terms of haploidy versus diploidy, how do the life cycles of fungi and humans differ?

2. **WHAT IF?** Suppose that you sample the DNA of two mushrooms on opposite sides of your yard and find that they are identical. Propose two hypotheses that could reasonably account for this result.

For suggested answers, see Appendix A.

CONCEPT 31.3

The ancestor of fungi was an aquatic, single-celled, flagellated protist

Data from both paleontology and molecular systematics offer insights into the early evolution of fungi. As a result, systematists now recognize that fungi and animals are more closely related to each other than either group is to plants or most other eukaryotes.

The Origin of Fungi

Phylogenetic systematics suggests that fungi evolved from a flagellated ancestor. While the majority of fungi lack flagella,

some of the earliest-diverging lineages of fungi (the chytrids, discussed later in this chapter) do have flagella. Moreover, most of the protists that share a close common ancestor with animals and fungi also have flagella. DNA sequence data indicate that these three groups of eukaryotes—the fungi, the animals, and their protistan relatives—form a clade (Figure 31.8). As discussed in Chapter 28, members of this clade are called **opisthokonts**, a name that refers to the posterior (*opistho-*) location of the flagellum in these organisms.

DNA sequence data also indicate that fungi are more closely related to several groups of single-celled protists than they are to animals, suggesting that the ancestor of fungi was unicellular. One such group of unicellular protists, the **nucleariids**, consists of amoebas that feed on algae and bacteria. DNA evidence further indicates that animals are more closely related to a *different* group of protists (the choanoflagellates) than they are to either fungi or nucleariids. Together, these results suggest that multicellularity must have evolved in animals and fungi independently, from different single-celled ancestors.

Based on molecular clock analysis (see Chapter 26), scientists have estimated that the ancestors of animals and fungi diverged into separate lineages about 1 billion years ago. However, the oldest undisputed fossils of fungi are only about 460 million years old (Figure 31.9). One possible explanation for this discrepancy is that the microscopic ancestors of today's terrestrial fungi fossilized poorly.

▲ Figure 31.8 **Fungi and their close relatives.** Molecular evidence indicates that the nucleariids, a group of single-celled protists, are the closest living relatives of fungi. The three parallel lines leading to the chytrids indicate that this group may be paraphyletic.

▶ Figure 31.9 **Fossil fungal hyphae and spores from the Ordovician period (about 460 million years ago)** (LM).

Host cell nucleus

Developing microsporidian

Spore

▲ **Figure 31.10 A eukaryotic cell infected by microsporidia.** A large vacuole inside this host eukaryotic cell contains spores and developing forms of the parasite *Encephalitozoon intestinalis* (TEM).

Are Microsporidia Fungi?

In addition to animals and protists such as the nucleariids, another group of organisms, the microsporidia, are closely related to fungi—and may in fact be fungi. Microsporidia are unicellular parasites of animals and protists (Figure 31.10). They are often used to control insect pests. While microsporidia do not normally cause illness in humans, they do pose a risk to people with AIDS and other immune-compromised conditions.

In many ways, microsporidia are unlike most other eukaryotes. They do not have conventional mitochondria, for example. As a result, microsporidia have been something of a taxonomic mystery, thought by some researchers to be a basal lineage of eukaryotes. In recent years, however, researchers have discovered that microsporidia actually have tiny organelles derived from mitochondria. In addition, most molecular comparisons indicate that microsporidia are fungi, suggesting that they are highly derived parasites. One such study, a 2006 analysis of DNA sequence data from six genes in nearly 200 fungal species, concluded that microsporidia are members of an early-diverging lineage of fungi. Additional genetic data from species belonging to early-diverging lineages of fungi are needed to fully resolve whether microsporidia are fungi or are a closely related but distinct group of organisms.

The Move to Land

Much of the fungal diversity we observe today may have originated during an adaptive radiation that began when multicellular plants and animals colonized land. For example, fossils of the earliest known vascular plants from the late Silurian period (420 million years ago) contain evidence of mycorrhizal relationships between plants and fungi. This evidence includes fossils of hyphae that have penetrated within plant cells and formed structures that closely resemble the haustoria of arbuscular mycorrhizae. Indeed, plants probably

existed in beneficial relationships with fungi from the earliest periods of colonization of land.

CONCEPT 31.4

Fungi have radiated into a diverse set of lineages

The phylogeny of fungi is currently the subject of much research. In the past decade, molecular analyses have helped clarify the evolutionary relationships between fungal groups, although there are still areas of uncertainty. Figure 31.11, on the next page, presents a simplified version of one current hypothesis. In this section, we will survey each of the major fungal groups identified in this phylogenetic tree.

Chytrids

Chytrids
Zygomycetes
Glomeromycetes
Ascomycetes
Basidiomycetes

The fungi classified in the phylum Chytridiomycota, called **chytrids**, are ubiquitous in lakes and soil. Some of the approximately 1,000 chytrid species are decomposers, while others are parasites of protists, other fungi, plants, or animals; as we'll see later in the chapter, one such chytrid parasite has likely contributed to the global decline of amphibian populations. Still other chytrids are important mutualists. For example, anaerobic chytrids that live in the digestive tracts of sheep and cattle help to break down plant matter, thereby contributing significantly to the animal's growth.

Molecular evidence supports the hypothesis that chytrids diverged early in fungal evolution. Like other fungi, chytrids have cell walls made of chitin, and they also share certain key enzymes and metabolic pathways with other fungal groups. Some chytrids form colonies with hyphae, while others exist as single spherical cells. But chytrids are unique among fungi in having flagellated spores, called **zoospores** (Figure 31.12).

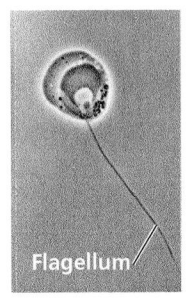

Flagellum

4 μm

▲ **Figure 31.12 Flagellated chytrid zoospore** (TEM).

Exploring Fungal Diversity

Most mycologists currently recognize five major groups of fungi, although the chytrids and zygomycetes are probably paraphyletic (as indicated by the parallel lines).

Chytrids (1,000 species)

In chytrids such as *Chytridium*, the globular fruiting body forms multicellular, branched hyphae (LM); other species are single-celled. Chytrids have flagellated spores and are thought to include some of the earliest fungal groups to diverge from other fungi.

Hyphae   25 μm

Zygomycetes (1,000 species)

The hyphae of some zygomycetes, including this mold in the genus *Mucor* (LM), grow rapidly into foods such as fruits and bread. As such, the fungi may act as decomposers (if the food is not alive) or parasites; other species live as neutral (commensal) symbionts. According to some recent analyses, the zygomycetes include the enigmatic group known as microsporidia; other studies have classified microsporidia as chytrids.

Fungal hypha   25 μm

Glomeromycetes (160 species)

The glomeromycetes (arbuscular mycorrhizal fungi) are of great ecological importance. Many plants form mycorrhizal associations with these fungi. This LM shows glomeromycete hyphae (stained dark blue) within a plant root.

Ascomycetes (65,000 species)

Also called sac fungi, members of this diverse group are common to many marine, freshwater, and terrestrial habitats. The cup-shaped ascocarp (fruiting body) of the ascomycete shown here (*Aleuria aurantia*) gives this species its common name: orange peel fungus.

Basidiomycetes (30,000 species)

Often important as decomposers and ectomycorrhizal fungi, basidiomycetes, or club fungi, are unusual in having a long-lived, dikaryotic mycelium. The fruiting bodies—commonly called mushrooms—of this fly agaric (*Amanita muscaria*) are a familiar sight in coniferous forests of the Northern Hemisphere.

Zygomycetes

Chytrids
Zygomycetes
Glomeromycetes
Ascomycetes
Basidiomycetes

There are approximately 1,000 known species of **zygomycetes**, fungi in the phylum Zygomycota. This diverse phylum includes species of fast-growing molds responsible for causing foods such as bread, peaches, strawberries, and sweet potatoes to rot during storage. Other zygomycetes live as parasites or as commensal (neutral) symbionts of animals.

The life cycle of *Rhizopus stolonifer* (black bread mold) is fairly typical of zygomycete species **(Figure 31.13)**. Its hyphae spread out over the food surface, penetrate it, and absorb nutrients. The hyphae are coenocytic, with septa found only where reproductive cells are formed. In the asexual phase, bulbous black sporangia develop at the tips of upright hyphae. Within each sporangium, hundreds of haploid spores develop and are dispersed through the air. Spores that happen to land on moist food germinate, growing into new mycelia.

If environmental conditions deteriorate—for instance, if the mold consumes all its food—*Rhizopus* may reproduce sexually. The parents in a sexual union are mycelia of different mating types, which possess different chemical markers but may appear identical. Plasmogamy produces a sturdy

1 Mycelia have various mating types (here designated (−), with red nuclei, and (+), with blue nuclei).

2 Neighboring mycelia of different mating types form hyphal extensions (gametangia), each of which encloses several haploid nuclei.

Key

Haploid (*n*)
Heterokaryotic (*n* + *n*)
Diploid (2*n*)

Mating type (−)

Mating type (+)

Gametangia with haploid nuclei

PLASMOGAMY

3 A zygosporangium forms, containing multiple haploid nuclei from the two parents.

Rhizopus growing on bread

Young zygosporangium (heterokaryotic)

100 µm

SEXUAL REPRODUCTION

8 The spores germinate and grow into new mycelia.

Zygosporangium

9 Mycelia can also reproduce asexually by forming sporangia that produce genetically identical haploid spores.

Dispersal and germination

KARYOGAMY

7 The sporangium disperses genetically diverse haploid spores.

Diploid nuclei

4 The zygosporangium develops a rough, thick-walled coating that can resist harsh conditions for months.

Sporangia

Sporangium

ASEXUAL REPRODUCTION

MEIOSIS

5 When conditions are favorable, karyogamy occurs, then meiosis.

50 µm

Dispersal and germination

Mycelium

6 The zygosporangium germinates into a sporangium on a short stalk.

▲ **Figure 31.13 The life cycle of the zygomycete *Rhizopus stolonifer* (black bread mold).**

▲ **Figure 31.14** *Pilobolus* **aiming its sporangia.** This zygomycete decomposes animal dung. Its spore-bearing hyphae bend toward light, where there are likely to be openings in the vegetation through which spores may reach fresh grass. The fungus then launches its sporangia in a jet of water that can travel up to 2.5 m. Grazing animals ingest the fungi with the grass and then scatter the spores in feces, thereby enabling the next generation of fungi to grow.

▲ **Figure 31.15** **Arbuscular mycorrhizae.** Most glomeromycetes form arbuscular mycorrhizae with plant roots, supplying minerals and other nutrients to the roots. This SEM depicts the branched hyphae—an arbuscule—of *Glomus mosseae* bulging into a root cell by pushing in the membrane (the root has been treated to remove the cytoplasm).

structure called a **zygosporangium**, in which karyogamy and then meiosis occur. Note that while a zygosporangium represents the zygote (2*n*) stage in the life cycle, it is not a zygote in the usual sense (that is, a cell with one diploid nucleus). Rather, a zygosporangium is a multinucleate structure, first heterokaryotic with many haploid nuclei from the two parents, then with many diploid nuclei after karyogamy.

Zygosporangia are resistant to freezing and drying and are metabolically inactive. When conditions improve, the nuclei of the zygosporangium undergo meiosis, the zygosporangium germinates into a sporangium, and the sporangium releases genetically diverse haploid spores that may colonize a new substrate. Some zygomycetes, such as *Pilobolus*, can actually "aim" and then shoot their sporangia toward bright light **(Figure 31.14)**.

Glomeromycetes

Chytrids
Zygomycetes
Glomeromycetes
Ascomycetes
Basidiomycetes

The **glomeromycetes**, fungi assigned to the phylum Glomeromycota, were formerly thought to be zygomycetes. But recent molecular studies, including a phylogenetic analysis of DNA sequence data from hundreds of fungal species, indicate that glomeromycetes form a separate clade (monophyletic group). Although only 160 species have been identified to date, the glomeromycetes are an ecologically significant group in that nearly all of them form arbuscular mycorrhizae **(Figure 31.15)**. The tips of the hyphae that push into plant root cells branch into tiny treelike arbuscules. About 90% of all plant species have such mutualistic partnerships with glomeromycetes.

Ascomycetes

Chytrids
Zygomycetes
Glomeromycetes
Ascomycetes
Basidiomycetes

Mycologists have described 65,000 species of **ascomycetes**, fungi in the phylum Ascomycota, from a wide variety of marine, freshwater, and terrestrial habitats. The defining feature of ascomycetes is the production of spores in saclike **asci** (singular, *ascus*) during sexual reproduction; thus, they are commonly called *sac fungi*. Unlike zygomycetes, during their sexual stage most ascomycetes develop fruiting bodies, called **ascocarps**, which range in size from microscopic to macroscopic **(Figure 31.16)**. The ascocarps contain the spore-forming asci.

▼ The edible ascocarp of *Morchella esculenta*, the tasty morel, is often found under trees in orchards.

▼ *Tuber melanosporum* is a truffle species that forms ectomycorrhizae with trees. The ascocarp grows underground and emits a strong odor. These ascocarps have been dug up and the middle one sliced open.

▲ **Figure 31.16** **Ascomycetes (sac fungi).**

? *Ascomycetes vary greatly in morphology (see also Figure 31.11). How could you confirm that a fungus is an ascomycete?*

Ascomycetes vary in size and complexity from unicellular yeasts to elaborate cup fungi and morels (see Figure 31.16). They include some of the most devastating plant pathogens, which we will discuss later. However, many ascomycetes are important decomposers, particularly of plant material. More than 25% of all ascomycete species live with green algae or cyanobacteria in beneficial symbiotic associations called lichens. Some ascomycetes form mycorrhizae with plants. Many others live between mesophyll cells in leaves; some of these species release toxic compounds that help protect the plant from insects.

Although the life cycles of various ascomycete groups differ in the details of their reproductive structures and processes,

we'll illustrate some common elements using the bread mold *Neurospora crassa* (Figure 31.17). Ascomycetes reproduce asexually by producing enormous numbers of asexual spores called **conidia** (singular, *conidium*). Conidia are not formed inside sporangia, as are the asexual spores of most zygomycetes. Rather, they are produced externally at the tips of specialized hyphae called conidiophores, often in clusters or long chains, from which they may be dispersed by the wind.

Conidia may also be involved in sexual reproduction, fusing with hyphae from a mycelium of a different mating type, as occurs in *Neurospora*. Fusion of two different mating types is followed by plasmogamy, resulting in the formation of dikaryotic cells, each with two haploid nuclei representing

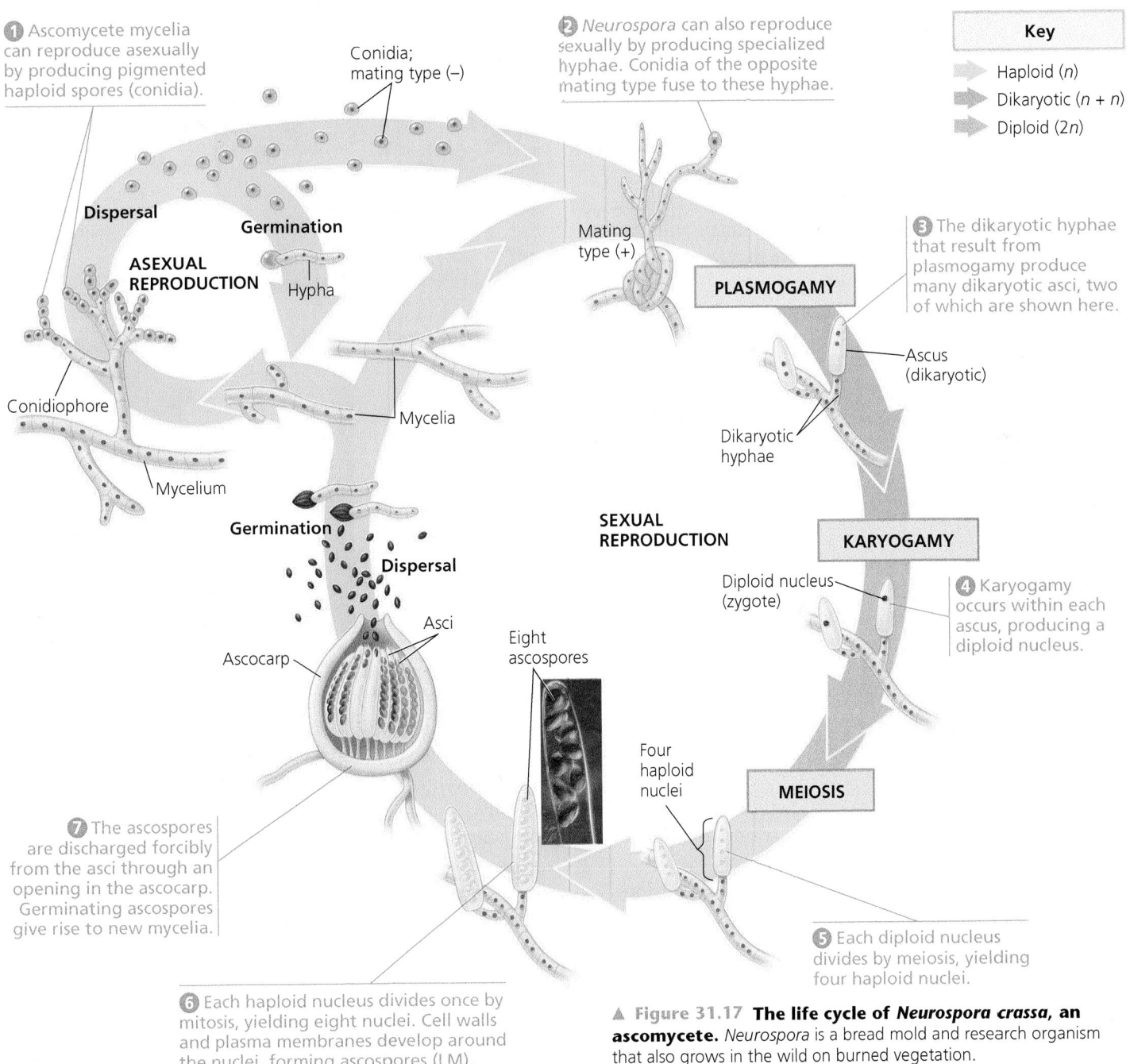

❶ Ascomycete mycelia can reproduce asexually by producing pigmented haploid spores (conidia).

Conidia; mating type (–)

Dispersal

Germination

ASEXUAL REPRODUCTION

Hypha

Conidiophore

Mycelium

Mycelia

Germination

Dispersal

Asci

Ascocarp

Eight ascospores

❷ *Neurospora* can also reproduce sexually by producing specialized hyphae. Conidia of the opposite mating type fuse to these hyphae.

Mating type (+)

Key
Haploid (*n*)
Dikaryotic (*n* + *n*)
Diploid (2*n*)

PLASMOGAMY

❸ The dikaryotic hyphae that result from plasmogamy produce many dikaryotic asci, two of which are shown here.

Ascus (dikaryotic)

Dikaryotic hyphae

SEXUAL REPRODUCTION

KARYOGAMY

Diploid nucleus (zygote)

❹ Karyogamy occurs within each ascus, producing a diploid nucleus.

Four haploid nuclei

MEIOSIS

❼ The ascospores are discharged forcibly from the asci through an opening in the ascocarp. Germinating ascospores give rise to new mycelia.

❺ Each diploid nucleus divides by meiosis, yielding four haploid nuclei.

❻ Each haploid nucleus divides once by mitosis, yielding eight nuclei. Cell walls and plasma membranes develop around the nuclei, forming ascospores (LM).

▲ Figure 31.17 **The life cycle of *Neurospora crassa*, an ascomycete.** *Neurospora* is a bread mold and research organism that also grows in the wild on burned vegetation.

the two parents. The cells at the tips of these dikaryotic hyphae develop into many asci. Within each ascus, karyogamy combines the two parental genomes, and then meiosis forms four genetically different nuclei. This is usually followed by a mitotic division, forming eight ascospores. The ascospores develop in and are eventually discharged from the ascocarp.

In contrast to the life cycle of zygomycetes, the extended dikaryotic stage of ascomycetes (and also basidiomycetes) provides increased opportunity for genetic recombination. In *Neurospora*, for example, many dikaryotic cells can develop into asci, recombining genomes during meiosis and resulting in a multitude of genetically different offspring from one mating event (see steps 2 and 3 in Figure 31.17).

Neurospora has a significant history in biological research. As we discussed in Chapter 17, biologists in the 1930s used *Neurospora* in research that led to the one gene–one enzyme hypothesis. Today, this ascomycete continues to serve as a model research organism. In 2003, its entire genome was published. With 10,000 genes, this tiny fungus has about three-fourths as many genes as the fruit fly *Drosophila* and about half as many as a human. The *Neurospora* genome is relatively compact, having few of the stretches of noncoding DNA that occupy so much space in the genomes of humans and many other eukaryotes. In fact, there is evidence that *Neurospora* has a genomic defense system that prevents noncoding DNA such as transposons from accumulating.

Basidiomycetes

Chytrids
Zygomycetes
Glomeromycetes
Ascomycetes
Basidiomycetes

Approximately 30,000 species, including mushrooms, puffballs, and shelf fungi, are called **basidiomycetes** and are classified in the phylum Basidiomycota **(Figure 31.18)**. This phylum also includes mutualists that form mycorrhizae and two groups of destructive plant parasites: rusts and smuts. The name of the phylum derives from the **basidium** (Latin for "little pedestal"), a cell in which karyogamy occurs, followed immediately by meiosis. The club-like shape of the basidium also gives rise to the common name *club fungus*.

Basidiomycetes are important decomposers of wood and other plant material. Of all the fungi, certain basidiomycetes are the best at decomposing the complex polymer lignin, an abundant component of wood. Many shelf fungi break down the wood of weak or damaged trees and continue to decompose the wood after the tree dies.

The life cycle of a basidiomycete usually includes a long-lived dikaryotic mycelium **(Figure 31.19)**. As in ascomycetes, this extended dikaryotic stage provides opportunities for many genetic recombination events, in effect multiplying the result of a single mating. Periodically, in response to environmental stimuli, the mycelium reproduces sexually by producing elaborate fruiting bodies called **basidiocarps**. The

▶ Shelf fungi, important decomposers of wood

◀ Puffballs emitting spores

▶ Maiden veil fungus (*Dictyphora*), a fungus with an odor like rotting meat

▲ **Figure 31.18 Basidiomycetes (club fungi).**

common white mushrooms in the supermarket are familiar examples of a basidiocarp.

By concentrating growth in the hyphae of mushrooms, a basidiomycete mycelium can erect its fruiting structures in just a few hours; a mushroom pops up as it absorbs water and as cytoplasm streams in from the dikaryotic mycelium. By this process, a ring of mushrooms, popularly called a "fairy ring," may appear literally overnight **(Figure 31.20)**. The mycelium below the fairy ring expands outward at a rate of about 30 cm per year, decomposing organic matter in the soil as it grows. Some giant fairy rings are produced by mycelia that are centuries old.

The numerous basidia in a basidiocarp are the sources of sexual spores called basidiospores. After a mushroom forms,

1 Two haploid mycelia of different mating types undergo plasmogamy.

2 A dikaryotic mycelium forms, growing faster than, and ultimately crowding out, the haploid parental mycelia.

PLASMOGAMY

Dikaryotic mycelium

3 Environmental cues such as rain or change in temperature induce the dikaryotic mycelium to form compact masses that develop into basidiocarps (mushrooms, in this case).

Mating type (−)

Mating type (+)

8 In a suitable environment, the basidiospores germinate and grow into short-lived haploid mycelia.

Haploid mycelia

SEXUAL REPRODUCTION

Gills lined with basidia

Basidiocarp (n + n)

7 When mature, the basidiospores are ejected and then dispersed by the wind.

Dispersal and germination

Basidiospores (n)

Basidium with four basidiospores

Basidium containing four haploid nuclei

Basidium

1 μm

Basidiospore

6 Each diploid nucleus yields four haploid nuclei, each of which develops into a basidiospore (SEM).

MEIOSIS

Diploid nuclei

Basidia (n + n)

4 The basidiocarp gills are lined with terminal dikaryotic cells called basidia.

KARYOGAMY

5 Karyogamy in each basidium produces a diploid nucleus, which then undergoes meiosis.

Key

Haploid (n)

Dikaryotic (n + n)

Diploid (2n)

▲ **Figure 31.19** **The life cycle of a mushroom-forming basidiomycete.**

its cap supports and protects a large surface area of dikaryotic basidia on gills. During karyogamy, the two nuclei in each basidium fuse, producing a diploid nucleus (see Figure 31.19). This nucleus then undergoes meiosis, yielding four haploid nuclei. The basidium then grows four appendages, and one haploid nucleus enters each appendage and develops into a basidiospore. Large numbers of basidiospores are produced: The gills of a common white mushroom have a surface area of about 200 cm² and may release a billion basidiospores, which drop from the bottom of the cap and are blown away.

▲ **Figure 31.20** **A fairy ring.** According to legend, these mushrooms spring up where fairies have danced in a ring on a moonlit night. (The text provides a biological explanation of how fairy rings form.)

1. What feature of chytrids supports the hypothesis that they represent an early-diverging fungal lineage?
2. Give examples of how form fits function in zygomycetes, glomeromycetes, ascomycetes, and basidiomycetes.
3. **WHAT IF?** Suppose that the mutation of an ascomycete changed its life cycle so that plasmogamy, karyogamy, and meiosis occurred in quick succession. How might this affect the ascospores and ascocarp?

For suggested answers, see Appendix A.

CONCEPT 31.5

Fungi play key roles in nutrient cycling, ecological interactions, and human welfare

In our survey of fungal classification, we've touched on some of the ways fungi influence other organisms. We will now look more closely at these impacts, focusing on how fungi act as decomposers, mutualists, and pathogens.

Fungi as Decomposers

Fungi are well adapted as decomposers of organic material, including the cellulose and lignin of plant cell walls. In fact, almost any carbon-containing substrate—even jet fuel and house paint—can be consumed by at least some fungi. As you might expect, researchers are developing ways to use a variety of fungal species in bioremediation projects. In addition, fungi and bacteria are primarily responsible for keeping ecosystems stocked with the inorganic nutrients essential for plant growth. Without these decomposers, carbon, nitrogen, and other elements would remain tied up in organic matter. Plants and the animals that eat them could not exist because elements taken from the soil would not be returned (see Chapter 55). Without decomposers, life as we know it would cease.

Fungi as Mutualists

Fungi may form mutualistic relationships with plants, algae, cyanobacteria, and animals. All of these relationships have profound ecological effects, often affecting the growth, survival, or reproduction of many species in a community.

Fungus-Plant Mutualisms

We've already considered the enormous importance of the mutualistic associations that most vascular plants form with mycorrhizal fungi. In addition, all plant species studied to date appear to harbor symbiotic **endophytes**, fungi that live inside leaves or other plant parts without causing harm. Most

▼ **Figure 31.21**

INQUIRY

Do endophytes benefit a woody plant?

EXPERIMENT Endophytes are symbiotic fungi found within the bodies of all plants examined to date. A. Elizabeth Arnold, at the University of Arizona, Tucson, and colleagues tested whether endophytes benefit the cacao tree (*Theobroma cacao*). This tree, whose name means "food of the gods" in Greek, is the source of the beans used to make chocolate, and it is cultivated throughout the tropics. Endophytes were added to the leaves of some cacao seedlings, but not others. (In cacao, endophytes colonize leaves after the seedling germinates.) The seedlings were then inoculated with a virulent pathogen, the protist *Phytophthora* (see Chapter 28).

RESULTS Fewer leaves were killed by the pathogen in seedlings with endophytes than in seedlings without endophytes. Among leaves that survived, pathogens damaged less of the leaf surface area in seedlings with endophytes than in seedlings without endophytes.

■ Endophyte not present; pathogen present (E−P+)
■ Both endophyte and pathogen present (E+P+)

CONCLUSION The presence of endophytes appears to benefit cacao trees by reducing the leaf mortality and damage caused by *Phytophthora*.

SOURCE A. E. Arnold et al., Fungal endophytes limit pathogen damage in a tropical tree, *Proceedings of the National Academy of Sciences* 100:15649–15654 (2003).

WHAT IF? Arnold and colleagues also performed control treatments. Suggest two controls they might have used, and explain how each would be helpful in interpreting the results described here.

endophytes identified to date are ascomycetes. Endophytes have been shown to benefit certain grasses and other nonwoody plants by making toxins that deter herbivores or by increasing host plant tolerance of heat, drought, or heavy metals. Seeking to discover how endophytes affect a woody plant, researchers tested whether leaf endophytes benefit seedlings of the cacao tree, *Theobroma cacao* (**Figure 31.21**). Their findings show that the endophytes of woody flowering plants can play an important role in defending against pathogens.

Fungus-Animal Mutualisms

As mentioned earlier, some fungi share their digestive services with animals, helping break down plant material in the guts of cattle and other grazing mammals. Many species of ants take advantage of the digestive power of fungi by raising them in "farms." Leaf-cutter ants, for example, scour tropical forests in search of leaves, which they cannot digest on their own but

▲ Figure 31.22 **Fungus-gardening insects.** These leaf-cutting ants depend on fungi to convert plant material to a form the insects can digest. The fungi, in turn, depend on the nutrients from the leaves the ants feed them.

carry back to their nests and feed to the fungi (Figure 31.22). As the fungi grow, their hyphae develop specialized swollen tips that are rich in proteins and carbohydrates. The ants feed primarily on these nutrient-rich tips. The fungi break down plant leaves into substances the insects can digest, and they also detoxify plant defensive compounds that would otherwise kill or harm the ants. In some tropical forests, the fungi have helped these insects become the major consumers of leaves.

The evolution of such farmer ants and that of their fungal "crops" have been tightly linked for over 50 million years. The fungi have become so dependent on their caretakers that in many cases they can no longer survive without the ants, and vice versa.

Lichens

A **lichen** is a symbiotic association between a photosynthetic microorganism and a fungus in which millions of photosynthetic cells are held in a mass of fungal hyphae. Lichens grow on the surfaces of rocks, rotting logs, trees, and roofs in various forms (Figure 31.23). The photosynthetic partners are unicellular or filamentous green algae or cyanobacteria. The fungal component is most often an ascomycete, but one glomeromycete and 75 basidiomycete lichens are known. The fungus usually gives a lichen its overall shape

and structure, and tissues formed by hyphae account for most of the lichen's mass. The algae or cyanobacteria generally occupy an inner layer below the lichen surface (Figure 31.24).

The merger of fungus and alga or cyanobacterium is so complete that lichens are given scientific names as though they were single organisms; to date, 17,000 lichen species have been described. As might be expected of such "dual organisms," asexual reproduction as a symbiotic unit is common. This can occur either by fragmentation of the parental lichen or by the formation of **soredia**, small clusters of hyphae with embedded algae (see Figure 31.24). The fungi of many lichens also reproduce sexually, and lichen algae can reproduce independently of the fungus by asexual cell division.

In most lichens, each partner provides something the other could not obtain on its own. The algae provide carbon compounds; the cyanobacteria also fix nitrogen (see Chapter 27) and provide organic nitrogen compounds. The fungi provide their photosynthetic partners with a suitable environment for growth. The physical arrangement of hyphae allows for gas

▼ Figure 31.23 **Variation in lichen growth forms.**

▼ Crustose (encrusting) lichens

▼ A foliose (leaflike) lichen

▶ A fruticose (shrublike) lichen

▼ Figure 31.24 **Anatomy of an ascomycete lichen** (colorized SEM).

Ascocarp of fungus

Fungal hyphae

Algal layer

Soredia

50 μm

Fungal hyphae

Algal cell

exchange, protects the photosynthetic partner, and retains water and minerals, most of which are absorbed either from airborne dust or from rain. The fungi also secrete acids, which aid in the uptake of minerals.

Lichens are important pioneers on cleared rock and soil surfaces, such as volcanic flows and burned forests. They break down the surface by physically penetrating and chemically attacking it, and they trap windblown soil. Nitrogen-fixing lichens also add organic nitrogen to some ecosystems. These processes make it possible for a succession of plants to grow (see Chapter 54). Lichens may also have aided the colonization of land by plants. Fossils of lichens or lichen-like organisms date to 550–600 million years ago, long before plants grew on land. Early lichens may have modified rocks and soil much as they do today, helping pave the way for plants.

As tough as lichens are, however, many do not stand up well to air pollution. Their passive mode of mineral uptake from rain and moist air makes them particularly sensitive to sulfur dioxide and other airborne poisons.

Fungi as Pathogens

About 30% of the 100,000 known species of fungi make a living as parasites or pathogens, mostly of plants (Figure 31.25). For example, *Cryphonectria parasitica*, the ascomycete fungus that causes chestnut blight, dramatically changed the landscape of the northeastern United States. Accidentally introduced on trees imported from Asia in the early 1900s, spores of the fungus enter cracks in the bark of American chestnut trees and produce hyphae, killing the tree. The once-common chestnuts now survive mainly as sprouts from the stumps of former trees. Another ascomycete, *Fusarium circinatum*, causes pine pitch canker, a disease that threatens pines throughout the world. Between 10% and 50% of the world's fruit harvest is lost annually due to fungi, and grain crops also suffer major losses each year.

Some fungi that attack food crops produce compounds that are toxic to humans. Certain species of the ascomycete *Aspergillus* contaminate grain and peanuts by secreting compounds called aflatoxins. Another example is the ascomycete *Claviceps purpurea*, which grows on rye plants, forming purple structures called ergots. If infected rye is milled into flour, toxins from the ergots can cause ergotism, characterized by gangrene, nervous spasms, burning sensations, hallucinations, and temporary insanity. An epidemic of ergotism around 944 CE killed more than 40,000 people in France. One compound that has been isolated from ergots is lysergic acid, the raw material from which the hallucinogen LSD is made.

Although animals are less susceptible to parasitic fungi than are plants, about 500 fungi are known to parasitize animals. One such parasite, the chytrid *Batrachochytrium dendrobatidis*, has been implicated in the recent decline or extinction of about 200 species of frogs and other amphibians (Figure 31.26). This chytrid can cause severe skin infections, leading to massive

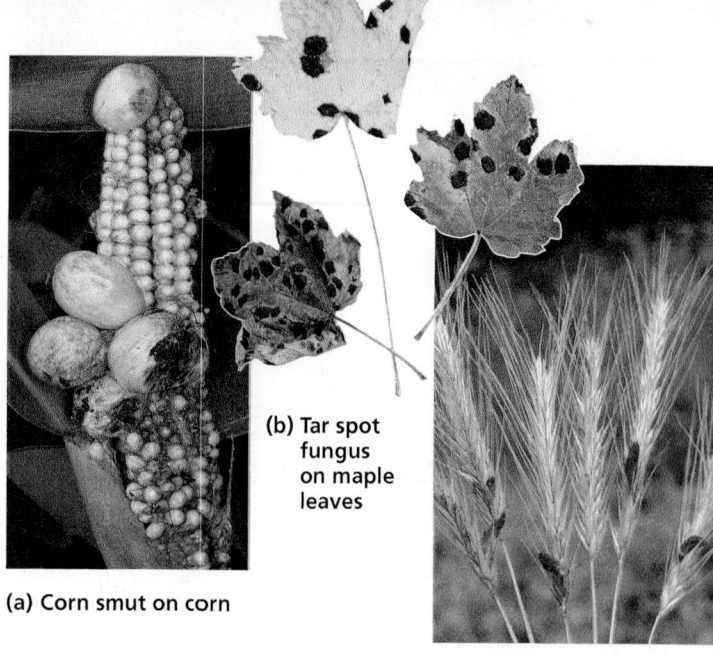

(a) Corn smut on corn

(b) Tar spot fungus on maple leaves

(c) Ergots on rye

▲ Figure 31.25 **Examples of fungal diseases of plants.**

die-offs. Field observations and studies of museum specimens indicate that *B. dendrobatidis* first appeared in frog populations shortly before their declines in Australia, Costa Rica, the United States, and other countries. In addition, in regions where it infects frogs, this chytrid has very low levels of genetic diversity. These findings are consistent with the hypothesis that *B. dendrobatidis* has emerged recently and spread rapidly across the globe, decimating many amphibian populations.

The general term for an infection caused by a fungal parasite is **mycosis**. In humans, skin mycoses include the disease ringworm, so named because it appears as circular red areas on the skin. The ascomycetes that cause ringworm can infect almost any skin surface. Most commonly, they grow on the feet, causing the intense itching and blisters known as athlete's foot. Though highly contagious, athlete's foot and other ringworm infections can be treated with fungicidal lotions and powders.

Systemic mycoses, by contrast, spread through the body and usually cause very serious illnesses. They are typically caused by inhaled spores. For example, coccidioidomycosis is a systemic mycosis that produces tuberculosis-like symptoms in the lungs. Each year, hundreds of cases in North America require treatment with antifungal drugs, without which the disease would be fatal.

Some mycoses are opportunistic, occurring only when a change in the body's microorganisms, chemical environment, or immune system allows fungi to grow unchecked. *Candida albicans*, for example, is one of the normal inhabitants of moist epithelia, such as the vaginal lining. Under certain circumstances, *Candida* can grow too rapidly and become pathogenic, leading to so-called "yeast infections." Many other opportunistic mycoses in humans have become more common in recent decades, due in part to AIDS, which compromises the immune system.

IMPACT

Amphibians Under Attack

Could a fungal parasite have caused the hundreds of amphibian population declines and extinctions during the last three decades? While habitat losses resulting from human activities have often been the culprit, the underlying causes have been unknown for nearly half the declining species. However, recent studies have implicated the global spread of a parasitic fungus, the chytrid *Batrachochytrium dendrobatidis*. For example, Vance Vredenburg, at San Francisco State University, and colleagues showed that the number of yellow-legged frogs (*Rana muscosa*) plummeted after the chytrid reached the Sixty Lake Basin area of California. Prior to the chytrid's 2004 arrival, on average there were 2,325 frogs in these lakes. By 2009, only 38 frogs remained. All the surviving frogs were in two lakes (yellow) where researchers had applied a fungicide to reduce the chytrid's impact.

▲ Yellow-legged frogs killed by *B. dendrobatidis* infection

Key

---- Boundary of chytrid spread

Lake status in 2009:

■ Frog population extinct

□ Treatment lake: frogs treated with fungicides and released

WHY IT MATTERS Worldwide, over one-third of amphibian species are suffering serious population declines. Information about the causes of these declines is essential if we are to protect these animals from extinction. Furthermore, because about 60% of human diseases originate from diseases in other animals, it is in our best interest to understand emerging diseases in amphibians.

FURTHER READING V. T. Vredenburg, et al., Large-scale amphibian die-offs driven by the dynamics of an emerging infectious disease, *Proceedings of the National Academy of Sciences* 107:9689-9694 (2010).

WHAT IF? Do the data depicted indicate that the chytrid *caused* or *is correlated to* the drop in frog numbers? Explain.

Practical Uses of Fungi

The dangers posed by fungi should not overshadow their immense benefits. We depend on their ecological services as decomposers and recyclers of organic matter. And without mycorrhizae, farming would be far less productive.

Mushrooms are not the only fungi of interest for human consumption. Fungi are used to ripen Roquefort and other blue cheeses. A species of *Aspergillus* produces citric acid used in colas. Morels and truffles, the edible fruiting bodies of various ascomycetes, are highly prized for their complex flavors (see Figure 31.16). These fungi can sell for hundreds to thousands of dollars a pound. Truffles release strong odors that attract mammals and insects, which in nature feed on them and disperse their spores. In some cases, the odors mimic the pheromones (sex attractants) of certain mammals. For example, the odors of several European truffles mimic the pheromones released by male pigs, which explains why *female* pigs are used to help find these delicacies.

Humans have used yeasts to produce alcoholic beverages and bread for thousands of years. Under anaerobic conditions, yeasts ferment sugars to alcohol and CO_2, which causes dough to rise. Only relatively recently have the yeasts involved been separated into pure cultures for more controlled use. The yeast *Saccharomyces cerevisiae* is the most important of all cultured fungi (see Figure 31.7). It is available as many strains of baker's yeast and brewer's yeast.

Many fungi have great medical value as well. For example, a compound extracted from ergots is used to reduce high blood pressure and to stop maternal bleeding after childbirth. Some fungi produce antibiotics that are effective in treating bacterial infections. In fact, the first antibiotic discovered was penicillin, made by the ascomycete mold *Penicillium* (**Figure 31.27**). Other examples of pharmaceuticals derived from fungi include cholesterol-lowering drugs and cyclosporine, a drug used to suppress the immune system after organ transplants.

Fungi also figure prominently in research. For example, the yeast *Saccharomyces cerevisiae* is used to study the molecular genetics of eukaryotes because its cells are easy to culture and manipulate. Scientists are gaining insight into the genes involved in Parkinson's disease and other human diseases by examining the functions of homologous genes in *S. cerevisiae*.

▲ **Figure 31.27 Fungal production of an antibiotic.** The mold *Penicillium* produces an antibiotic (penicillin) that inhibits the growth of *Staphylococcus* bacteria, resulting in the clear area between the mold and the bacteria.

Genetically modified fungi hold much promise. Although bacteria such as *Escherichia coli* can produce some useful proteins, they cannot synthesize glycoproteins because they lack enzymes that can attach carbohydrates to proteins. Fungi, on the other hand, do produce such enzymes. In 2003, scientists succeeded in engineering a strain of *S. cerevisiae* that produces human glycoproteins, including insulin-like growth factor. Such fungus-produced glycoproteins have the potential to treat people with medical conditions that prevent them from producing these compounds. Meanwhile, other researchers are sequencing the genome of the wood-digesting basidiomycete *Phanerochaete chrysosporium*, one of many "white rot" fungi. They hope to decipher the metabolic pathways by which white rot breaks down wood, with the goal of harnessing these pathways to produce paper pulp.

Having now completed our survey of the kingdom Fungi, we will turn in the remaining chapters of this unit to the closely related kingdom Animalia, to which we humans belong.

CONCEPT CHECK 31.5

1. What are some of the benefits that lichen algae can derive from their relationship with fungi?
2. What characteristics of pathogenic fungi result in their being efficiently transmitted?
3. **WHAT IF?** How might life on Earth differ from what we know today if no mutualistic relationships between fungi and other organisms had ever evolved?

For suggested answers, see Appendix A.

31 CHAPTER REVIEW

SUMMARY OF KEY CONCEPTS

CONCEPT 31.1

Fungi are heterotrophs that feed by absorption (pp. 636–638)

- All **fungi** (including decomposers and symbionts) are heterotrophs that acquire nutrients by absorption. Many fungi secrete enzymes that break down complex molecules to smaller molecules that can be absorbed.
- Most fungi grow as thin, multicellular filaments called **hyphae**; relatively few species grow only as single-celled **yeasts**. In their multicellular form, fungi consist of **mycelia**, networks of branched hyphae adapted for absorption. Mycorrhizal fungi have specialized hyphae that enable them to form a mutually beneficial relationship with plants.

? *How does the morphology of multicellular fungi affect the efficiency of nutrient absorption?*

CONCEPT 31.2

Fungi produce spores through sexual or asexual life cycles (pp. 638–640)

- The sexual cycle involves cytoplasmic fusion (**plasmogamy**) and nuclear fusion (**karyogamy**), with an intervening heterokaryotic stage in which cells have haploid nuclei from two parents. The diploid cells resulting from karyogamy are short-lived and undergo meiosis, producing haploid **spores**.
- Many fungi can reproduce asexually as filamentous fungi or yeasts. DNA sequence data now allow mycologists to classify all fungi, even those lacking a known sexual cycle.

DRAW IT *Draw a fungal life cycle, labeling asexual and sexual reproduction, meiosis, plasmogamy, karyogamy, and the points in the cycle when spores and the zygote are produced.*

CONCEPT 31.3

The ancestor of fungi was an aquatic, single-celled, flagellated protist (pp. 640–641)

- Molecular evidence supports the hypothesis that fungi and animals diverged from a common ancestor that was unicellular and had a flagellum.

- Unicellular parasites called microsporidia appear to be an early-diverging fungal lineage.
- Fungi were among the earliest colonizers of land, including species that were symbionts with early land plants.

? *Did multicellularity originate independently in fungi and animals? Explain.*

CONCEPT 31.4

Fungi have radiated into a diverse set of lineages (pp. 641–648)

Fungal Phylum	Distinguishing Features of Morphology and Life Cycles	
Chytridiomycota **(chytrids)**	Flagellated spores	
Zygomycota **(zygote fungi)**	Resistant zygosporangium as sexual stage	
Glomeromycota **(arbuscular mycorrhizal fungi)**	Arbuscular mycorrhizae formed with plants	
Ascomycota **(ascomycetes**, or **sac fungi)**	Sexual spores (ascospores) borne internally in sacs called asci; vast numbers of asexual spores (conidia) produced	
Basidiomycota **(basidiomycetes**, or **club fungi)**	Elaborate fruiting body (basidiocarp) containing many basidia that produce sexual spores (basidiospores)	

DRAW IT *Draw a phylogenetic tree showing relationships among the five major groups of fungi.*

CONCEPT 31.5

Fungi play key roles in nutrient cycling, ecological interactions, and human welfare (pp. 648–652)

- Fungi perform essential recycling of chemical elements between the living and nonliving world.
- Some **endophytes** help protect plants from herbivores and pathogens, while other fungi help certain animals digest plant tissue. **Lichens** are highly integrated symbiotic associations of fungi and algae or cyanobacteria.
- About 30% of all known fungal species are parasites, mostly of plants. Some fungi also cause disease in animals.
- Humans eat many fungi and use others to make cheeses, alcoholic beverages, and bread. Antibiotics produced by fungi treat bacterial infections. Genetic research on fungi is leading to applications in biotechnology.

? *Summarize how fungi are important as decomposers, mutualists, and pathogens.*

TEST YOUR UNDERSTANDING

LEVEL 1: KNOWLEDGE/COMPREHENSION

1. *All* fungi share which of the following characteristics?
   a. symbiotic
   b. heterotrophic
   c. flagellated
   d. pathogenic
   e. act as decomposers

2. Which feature seen in chytrids supports the hypothesis that they diverged earliest in fungal evolution?
   a. the absence of chitin within the cell wall
   b. coenocytic hyphae
   c. flagellated spores
   d. formation of resistant zygosporangia
   e. parasitic lifestyle

3. Which of the following cells or structures are associated with *asexual* reproduction in fungi?
   a. ascospores
   b. basidiospores
   c. zygosporangia
   d. conidiophores
   e. ascocarps

4. The photosynthetic symbiont of a lichen is often
   a. a moss.
   b. a green alga.
   c. a brown alga.
   d. an ascomycete.
   e. a small vascular plant.

5. Among the organisms listed here, which are thought to be the closest relatives of fungi?
   a. animals
   b. vascular plants
   c. mosses
   d. brown algae
   e. slime molds

LEVEL 2: APPLICATION/ANALYSIS

6. The adaptive advantage associated with the filamentous nature of fungal mycelia is primarily related to
   a. the ability to form haustoria and parasitize other organisms.
   b. avoiding sexual reproduction until the environment changes.
   c. the potential to inhabit almost all terrestrial habitats.
   d. the increased probability of contact between different mating types.
   e. an extensive surface area well suited for invasive growth and absorptive nutrition.

7. **SCIENTIFIC INQUIRY**
   DRAW IT The grass *Dichanthelium languinosum* lives in hot soils and houses fungi of the genus *Curvularia* as endophytes. Regina Redman, of Montana State University, and colleagues performed field experiments to test the impact of *Curvularia* on the heat tolerance of this grass. They grew plants without (E−) and with (E+) *Curvularia* endophytes in soils of different temperatures and measured plant mass and the number of new shoots the plants produced. Draw a bar graph of the results for plant mass versus temperature and interpret it.

Soil Temp.	Curvularia Presence	Plant Mass (g)	Number of New Shoots
30°C	E−	16.2	32
	E+	22.8	60
35°C	E−	21.7	43
	E+	28.4	60
40°C	E−	8.8	10
	E+	22.2	37
45°C	E−	0	0
	E+	15.1	24

Source: R. S. Redman et al., Thermotolerance generated by plant/fungal symbiosis, *Science* 298:1581 (2002).

LEVEL 3: SYNTHESIS/EVALUATION

8. **EVOLUTION CONNECTION**
   The fungus-alga symbiosis that makes up a lichen is thought to have evolved multiple times independently in different fungal groups. However, lichens fall into three well-defined growth forms (see Figure 31.23). What research could you perform to test the following hypotheses?

   Hypothesis 1: Crustose, foliose, and fruticose lichens each represent a monophyletic group.

   Hypothesis 2: Each lichen growth form represents convergent evolution by taxonomically diverse fungi.

9. **WRITE ABOUT A THEME**
   Emergent Properties As you read in this chapter, fungi have long formed symbiotic associations with plants and with algae. In a short essay (100–150 words), describe how these two types of associations may lead to emergent properties in biological communities.

For selected answers, see Appendix A.

MasteringBIOLOGY www.masteringbiology.com

1. MasteringBiology® Assignments
Tutorial Fungal Morphology and Nutrition
Activities Fungal Reproduction and Nutrition • Fungal Life Cycles • Life Cycle of a Mushroom • Discovery Channel Videos: Fungi; Leafcutter Ants
Questions Student Misconceptions • Reading Quiz • Multiple Choice • End-of-Chapter

2. eText
Read your book online, search, take notes, highlight text, and more.

3. The Study Area
Practice Tests • Cumulative Test • **BioFlix** 3-D Animations • MP3 Tutor Sessions • Videos • Activities • Investigations • Lab Media • Audio Glossary • Word Study Tools • Art

32

An Overview
of Animal Diversity

▲ Figure 32.1 **Which of these organisms are animals?**

EVOLUTION

KEY CONCEPTS

32.1 Animals are multicellular, heterotrophic eukaryotes with tissues that develop from embryonic layers

32.2 The history of animals spans more than half a billion years

32.3 Animals can be characterized by "body plans"

32.4 New views of animal phylogeny are emerging from molecular data

OVERVIEW

Welcome to Your Kingdom

Reading the last few chapters, you may have felt like a tourist among some unfamiliar organisms, such as slime molds, whisk ferns, and sac fungi. You probably are more at home with the topic introduced in this chapter—the animal

kingdom, which of course includes yourself. But animal diversity extends far beyond humans and the dogs, cats, birds, and other animals we humans regularly encounter. For example, the diverse organisms in **Figure 32.1** are all animals, including those that appear to resemble lacy branches, thick stems, and curly leaves. To date, biologists have identified 1.3 million extant (living) species of animals. Estimates of the actual number of animal species run far higher. This vast diversity encompasses a spectacular range of morphological variation, from corals to cockroaches to crocodiles.

In this chapter, we embark on a tour of the animal kingdom that will continue in the next two chapters. We will consider the characteristics that all animals share, as well as those that distinguish various taxonomic groups. This information is central to understanding animal phylogeny, a topic that is a lively arena of biological research and debate, as you will read.

CONCEPT 32.1

Animals are multicellular, heterotrophic eukaryotes with tissues that develop from embryonic layers

Listing features shared by all animals is challenging, as there are exceptions to nearly every criterion for distinguishing animals from other life-forms. When taken together, however, several characteristics of animals sufficiently describe the group for our discussion.

Nutritional Mode

Animals differ from both plants and fungi in their mode of nutrition. Plants are autotrophic eukaryotes capable of generating organic molecules through photosynthesis. Fungi are heterotrophs that grow on or near their food and that feed by absorption (often after they have released enzymes that digest the food outside their bodies). Unlike plants, animals cannot construct all of their own organic molecules and so, in most cases, they ingest them—either by eating other living organisms or by eating nonliving organic material. But unlike fungi, most animals do not feed by absorption; instead, animals ingest their food and then use enzymes to digest it within their bodies.

Cell Structure and Specialization

Animals are eukaryotes, and like plants and most fungi, animals are multicellular. In contrast to plants and fungi, however, animals lack the structural support of cell walls. Instead, a variety of proteins external to the cell membrane provide structural support to animal cells and connect them to one another (see Figure 6.30). The most abundant of these proteins is collagen, which is found only in animals.

Many animals have two types of specialized cells not found in other multicellular organisms: muscle cells and nerve cells. In most animals, these cells are organized into **tissues**, groups of cells that have a common structure, function, or both. Muscle tissue and nervous tissue are responsible for moving the body and conducting nerve impulses, respectively. The ability to move and conduct nerve impulses underlies many of the adaptations that differentiate animals from plants and fungi. For this reason, muscle and nerve cells are central to the animal lifestyle.

Reproduction and Development

Most animals reproduce sexually, and the diploid stage usually dominates the life cycle. In the haploid stage, sperm and egg cells are produced directly by meiotic division, unlike what occurs in plants and fungi (see Figure 13.6). In most animal species, a small, flagellated sperm fertilizes a larger, nonmotile egg, forming a diploid zygote. The zygote then undergoes **cleavage**, a succession of mitotic cell divisions without cell growth between the divisions. During the development of most animals, cleavage leads to the formation of a multicellular stage called a **blastula**, which in many animals takes the form of a hollow ball (Figure 32.2). Following the blastula stage is the process of **gastrulation**, during which the layers of embryonic tissues that will develop into adult body parts are produced. The resulting developmental stage is called a **gastrula**.

Although some animals, including humans, develop directly into adults, the life cycles of most animals include at least one larval stage. A **larva** is a sexually immature form of an animal that is morphologically distinct from the adult, usually eats different food, and may even have a different habitat than the adult, as in the case of the aquatic larva of a mosquito or dragonfly. Animal larvae eventually undergo **metamorphosis**, a developmental transformation that turns the animal into a juvenile that resembles an adult but is not yet sexually mature.

Although adult animals vary widely in morphology, the genes that control animal development are similar across a broad range of taxa. All animals have developmental genes that regulate the expression of other genes, and many of these regulatory genes contain sets of DNA sequences called *homeoboxes* (see Chapter 21). Most animals share a unique homeobox-containing family of genes, known as *Hox* genes. *Hox* genes play important roles in the development of animal embryos, controlling the expression of dozens or even hundreds of other genes that influence animal morphology (see Chapter 25).

Sponges, which are among the simplest extant animals, lack *Hox* genes. However, they have other homeobox genes that influence their shape, such as those that regulate the formation of water channels in the body wall, a key feature of sponge morphology (see Figure 33.4). In the ancestors of more complex animals, the *Hox* gene family arose via the duplication of

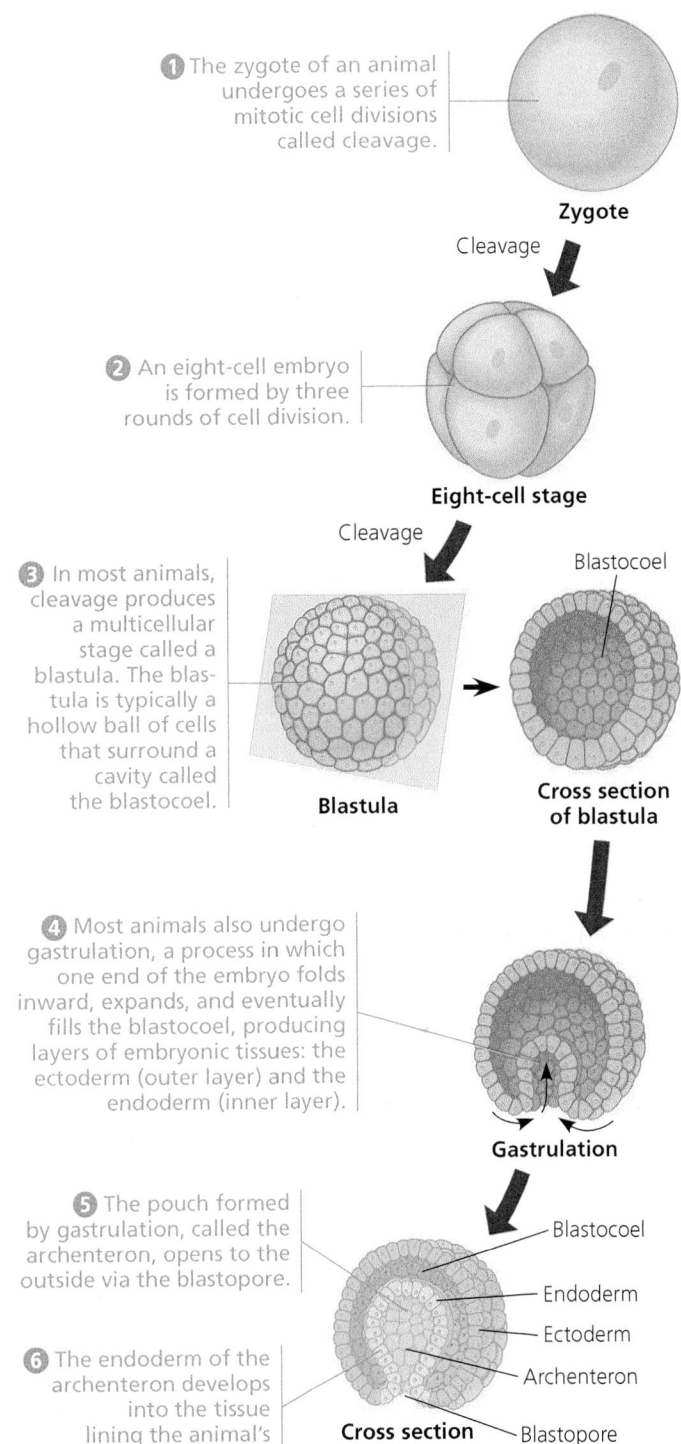

1 The zygote of an animal undergoes a series of mitotic cell divisions called cleavage.

Zygote

Cleavage

2 An eight-cell embryo is formed by three rounds of cell division.

Eight-cell stage

Cleavage

3 In most animals, cleavage produces a multicellular stage called a blastula. The blastula is typically a hollow ball of cells that surround a cavity called the blastocoel.

Blastocoel

Blastula

Cross section of blastula

4 Most animals also undergo gastrulation, a process in which one end of the embryo folds inward, expands, and eventually fills the blastocoel, producing layers of embryonic tissues: the ectoderm (outer layer) and the endoderm (inner layer).

Gastrulation

5 The pouch formed by gastrulation, called the archenteron, opens to the outside via the blastopore.

Blastocoel

Endoderm

Ectoderm

Archenteron

6 The endoderm of the archenteron develops into the tissue lining the animal's digestive tract.

Cross section of gastrula

Blastopore

▲ **Figure 32.2 Early embryonic development in animals.**

earlier homeobox genes. Over time, the *Hox* gene family underwent a series of duplications, yielding a versatile "toolkit" for regulating development. In vertebrates, insects, and most other animals, *Hox* genes regulate the formation of the anterior-posterior (front-to-back) axis, as well as other aspects of development. Similar sets of conserved genes govern the development of both flies and humans, despite their obvious differences and hundreds of millions of years of divergent evolution.

1. Summarize the main stages of animal development. What family of control genes plays a major role?
2. **WHAT IF?** What animal characteristics would be needed by an imaginary plant that could chase, capture, and digest its prey—yet could also extract nutrients from soil and conduct photosynthesis?
3. **MAKE CONNECTIONS** Humans have about the same number of protein-coding genes as do animals such as tunicates (see photograph) that have very simple body forms and few neurons. In contrast, humans have many more microRNA molecules (miRNAs) than these animals. Review Concept 18.3 (pp. 365–366); then suggest a possible reason for this observation.

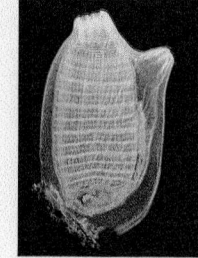

For suggested answers, see Appendix A.

CONCEPT 32.2

The history of animals spans more than half a billion years

The animal kingdom includes not only a great diversity of living species, but an even greater diversity of extinct ones. (Some paleontologists have estimated that over 99% of all animal species are extinct.) Various studies suggest that this great diversity originated during the last billion years. For example, some estimates based on molecular clocks suggest that the ancestors of animals diverged from the ancestors of fungi about a billion years ago. Other such studies have estimated that the common ancestor of living animals lived sometime between 800 and 675 million years ago.

To learn what this common ancestor may have been like, scientists have sought to identify protist groups that are closely related to animals. As shown in **Figure 32.3**, a combination of morphological and molecular evidence indicates that choanoflagellates are among the closest living relatives of animals. Based on such evidence, researchers hypothesize that the common ancestor of living animals may have been a suspension feeder similar to present-day choanoflagellates. We will next survey the fossil evidence for how animals evolved from their distant common ancestor over four geologic eras (see Table 25.1 to review the geologic time scale).

Neoproterozoic Era (1 Billion–542 Million Years Ago)

Despite the molecular data indicating an earlier origin of animals, the first generally accepted macroscopic fossils of animals date from 565 to 550 million years ago. These fossils are members of an early group of soft-bodied multicellular eukaryotes, known collectively as the **Ediacaran biota**. The name comes from the Ediacara Hills of Australia, where these animals were first discovered **(Figure 32.4)**. Similar fossils have since been found on other continents.

▼ Figure 32.3 **Three lines of evidence that choanoflagellates are closely related to animals.**

? *Are the data described in ❸ consistent with predictions that could be made from the evidence in ❶ and ❷? Explain.*

Choanoflagellates

OTHER EUKARYOTES

Animals

Sponges

Other animals

Individual choanoflagellate

❶ Morphologically, choanoflagellate cells and the collar cells (or *choanocytes*) of sponges are almost indistinguishable.

Collar cell (choanocyte)

❸ DNA sequence data indicate that choanoflagellates and animals are sister groups. In addition, genes for signaling and adhesion proteins previously known only from animals have been discovered in choanoflagellates.

❷ Similar collar cells have been identified in other animals, including cnidarians, flatworms, and echinoderms—but they have never been observed in non-choanoflagellate protists or in plants or fungi.

1.5 cm

0.4 cm

(a) *Mawsonites spriggi*   (b) *Spriggina floundersi*

▲ **Figure 32.4 Ediacaran fossils.** Fossils dating to 565–550 million years ago include animals **(a)** with simple, radial forms and **(b)** with many body segments.

Some are sponges, while others may be related to living cnidarians. Still others of these fossil organisms have proved difficult to classify, as they do not seem to be closely related to any living animal or algal groups.

In addition to these macroscopic fossils, Neoproterozoic rocks have also yielded what may be microscopic signs of early animals. As you read in Chapter 25, 575-million-year-old microfossils discovered in China appear to exhibit the basic structural organization of present-day animal embryos. However, debate continues about whether the fossil embryos are animals or are members of extinct groups that are closely related to animals (but are not actually animals). Though older fossils of animals may be discovered in the future, the fossil record as it is known today shows that the late Neoproterozoic era was a time of increasing animal diversity.

Paleozoic Era (542–251 Million Years Ago)

Another wave of animal diversification occurred 535–525 million years ago, during the Cambrian period of the Paleozoic era—a phenomenon referred to as the **Cambrian explosion** (see Chapter 25). In strata formed before the Cambrian explosion, only a few animal phyla have been observed. But in strata that are 535–525 million years old, paleontologists have found the oldest fossils of about half of all extant animal phyla, including the first arthropods, chordates, and echinoderms. Many of these distinctive fossils, which include the first animals with hard, mineralized skeletons, look very different from most living animals **(Figure 32.5)**. But for the most part, paleontologists have established that these Cambrian fossils are members of extant animal phyla, or at least are close relatives.

The increase in the diversity of animal phyla during the Cambrian was accompanied by a decline in the diversity of Ediacaran life-forms. What caused these trends? There are several current hypotheses. Some evidence suggests that during the Cambrian period, predators acquired novel adaptations,

▲ **Figure 32.5 A Cambrian seascape.** This artist's reconstruction depicts a diverse array of organisms found in fossils from the Burgess Shale site in British Columbia, Canada. The animals include *Pikaia* (eel-like chordate at top left), *Marella* (arthropod swimming at left), *Anomalocaris* (large animal with anterior grasping limbs and a circular mouth), and *Hallucigenia* (animals with toothpick-like spikes on the seafloor).

such as forms of locomotion that helped them catch prey, while prey species acquired new defenses, such as protective shells. As new predator-prey relationships emerged, natural selection may have led to the decline of some groups and the rise of others. Another hypothesis focuses on an increase in atmospheric oxygen that preceded the Cambrian explosion. More plentiful oxygen would have enabled animals with higher metabolic rates and larger body sizes to thrive, while potentially harming other species. A third hypothesis proposes that the origin of *Hox* genes and other genetic changes affecting the regulation of developmental genes facilitated the evolution of new body forms. These hypotheses are not mutually exclusive, however; predator-prey relationships, atmospheric changes, and changes in the regulation of development may each have played a role.

The Cambrian period was followed by the Ordovician, Silurian, and Devonian periods, when animal diversity continued to increase, although punctuated by episodes of mass extinction (see Figure 25.15). Vertebrates (fishes) emerged as the top predators of the marine food web. By 460 million years ago, groups that diversified during the Cambrian period were making an impact on land. Arthropods began to adapt to terrestrial habitats, as indicated by the appearance of millipedes and centipedes. Another clue is seen in fossilized fern galls—enlarged cavities that fern plants form in response to stimulation by resident insects, which then use the galls for protection. Fossils indicate that fern galls date back at least

302 million years, suggesting that insects and plants were influencing each other's evolution by that time.

Vertebrates made the transition to land around 365 million years ago and diversified into numerous terrestrial groups. Two of these survive today: the amphibians (such as frogs and salamanders) and the amniotes (reptiles, including birds, and mammals). We will explore these groups, known collectively as the tetrapods, in more detail in Chapter 34.

Mesozoic Era (251–65.5 Million Years Ago)

The animal phyla that had evolved during the Paleozoic now began to spread into new habitats. In the oceans, the first coral reefs formed, providing other marine animals with new habitats. Some reptiles returned to the water, leaving plesiosaurs (see Figure 25.4) and other large aquatic predators as their descendants. On land, descent with modification in some tetrapods led to the origin of wings and other flight equipment in pterosaurs and birds. Large and small dinosaurs emerged, both as predators and herbivores. At the same time, the first mammals—tiny nocturnal insect-eaters—appeared on the scene. In addition, as you read in Chapter 30, flowering plants (angiosperms) and insects both underwent dramatic diversifications during the late Mesozoic.

Cenozoic Era (65.5 Million Years Ago to the Present)

Mass extinctions of both terrestrial and marine animals ushered in a new era, the Cenozoic. Among the groups of species that disappeared were the large, nonflying dinosaurs and the marine reptiles. The fossil record of the early Cenozoic documents the rise of large mammalian herbivores and predators as mammals began to exploit the vacated ecological niches. The global climate gradually cooled throughout the Cenozoic, triggering significant shifts in many animal lineages. Among primates, for example, some species in Africa adapted to the open woodlands and savannas that replaced many of the former dense forests. The ancestors of our own species were among those grassland apes.

CONCEPT CHECK 32.2

1. Put the following milestones in animal evolution in chronological order from oldest to most recent: (a) origin of mammals, (b) earliest evidence of terrestrial arthropods, (c) Ediacaran fauna, (d) extinction of large, nonflying dinosaurs.
2. **WHAT IF?** Suppose the most recent common ancestor of fungi and animals lived 1 billion years ago. If the first fungi lived 990 million years ago, would animals also have been alive at that time? Explain.

For suggested answers, see Appendix A.

Animals can be characterized by "body plans"

Animal species vary tremendously in morphology, but their great diversity in form can be described by a relatively small number of major "body plans." A **body plan** is a particular set of morphological and developmental traits, integrated into a functional whole—the living animal. The term *plan* here does not imply that animal forms are the result of conscious planning or invention. But body plans do provide a succinct way to compare and contrast key animal features. They also are of interest in the study of *evo-devo*, the interface between evolution and development (see Chapters 21 and 25).

Like all features of organisms, animal body plans have evolved over time. Some of the evolutionary changes appear to have occurred early in the history of animal life. For example, recent research suggests that a key step in the molecular control of gastrulation has remained unchanged for more than 500 million years (Figure 32.6). This early evolutionary innovation was of fundamental importance: Gastrulation helps to explain why most animals are not a hollow ball of cells. As we'll discuss, however, other aspects of animal body plans have changed multiple times over the course of evolution. Thus, as we explore the major features of animal body plans, bear in mind that similar body forms may have evolved independently in different lineages. In addition, body features can be lost over the course of evolution, causing some closely related species to look very different from one another.

Symmetry

A basic feature of animal bodies is their type of symmetry—or absence of symmetry. (Many sponges, for example, lack symmetry altogether.) Some animals exhibit **radial symmetry**, the type of symmetry found in a flowerpot (Figure 32.7a). Sea anemones, for example, have a top side (where the mouth is located) and a bottom side. But they have no front and back ends and no left and right sides.

The two-sided symmetry seen in a shovel is an example of **bilateral symmetry** (Figure 32.7b). A bilateral animal has two axes of orientation: front to back and top to bottom. Such animals have a **dorsal** (top) side and a **ventral** (bottom) side, a left side and a right side, and an **anterior** (front) end and a **posterior** (back) end. Many animals with a bilaterally symmetrical body plan (such as arthropods and mammals) have sensory equipment concentrated at their anterior end, including a central nervous system ("brain") in the head—an evolutionary trend called **cephalization** (from the Greek *kephale*, head).

The symmetry of an animal generally fits its lifestyle. Many radial animals are sessile (living attached to a substrate) or planktonic (drifting or weakly swimming, such as jellies,

INQUIRY

Did β-catenin play an ancient role in the molecular control of gastrulation?

EXPERIMENT In most animals, gastrulation leads to the formation of three layers of embryonic cells. In some of these species, such as worms, sea urchins, and vertebrates, the protein β-catenin marks the site of gastrulation and activates the transcription of genes necessary for the process. Athula Wikramanayake and Mark Martindale, of the University of Hawaii, and colleagues tested whether β-catenin also helps to control gastrulation in the sea anemone *Nematostella vectensis*. This species is a member of the phylum Cnidaria, a group that predates the origin of animals whose embryos form three layers of cells.

RESULTS

① In early stages of development, β-catenin (here labeled with green fluorescent protein) is found throughout the *N. vectensis* embryo.

100 μm

② By the 32-cell stage, β-catenin is concentrated on the side of the embryo where gastrulation will occur.

Site of gastrulation

③ In the early gastrula stage, β-catenin activity (here stained a darker red) occurs in the inner layer of cells.

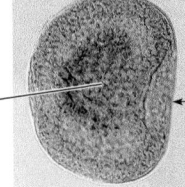

Site of gastrulation

④ In embryos in which β-catenin activity is blocked (by a protein that binds to β-catenin), gastrulation does not occur.

CONCLUSION In *N. vectensis*, β-catenin is required for gastrulation to occur and may help to determine the site of gastrulation. Since the fossil record indicates that cnidarians diverged more than 500 million years ago from species in which β-catenin is known to influence gastrulation, it seems likely that β-catenin played an ancient role in the molecular control of gastrulation.

SOURCE A. H. Wikramanayake et al., An ancient role for nuclear β-catenin in the evolution of axial polarity and germ layer segregation, *Nature* 426:446–450 (2003).

WHAT IF? β-catenin binds to DNA, thereby stimulating the transcription of genes necessary for gastrulation. Based on this information, suggest a different experiment that could be used to confirm the results in step 4. What would be the purpose of performing such an experiment?

(a) Radial symmetry. A radial animal, such as a sea anemone (phylum Cnidaria), does not have a left side and a right side. Any imaginary slice through the central axis divides the animal into mirror images.

(b) Bilateral symmetry. A bilateral animal, such as a lobster (phylum Arthropoda), has a left side and a right side. Only one imaginary cut divides the animal into mirror-image halves.

▲ **Figure 32.7 Body symmetry.** The flowerpot and shovel are included to help you remember the radial-bilateral distinction.

commonly called jellyfishes). Their symmetry equips them to meet the environment equally well from all sides. In contrast, bilateral animals typically move actively from place to place. Most bilateral animals have a central nervous system that enables them to coordinate the complex movements involved in crawling, burrowing, flying, or swimming. Fossil evidence indicates that these two fundamentally different kinds of symmetry have been present for at least 550 million years.

Tissues

Animal body plans also vary with regard to tissue organization. In animals, true tissues are collections of specialized cells isolated from other tissues by membranous layers. While sponges and a few other groups lack true tissues, in all other animals, the embryo becomes layered through the process of gastrulation (see Figure 32.2). As development progresses, these concentric layers, called *germ layers*, form the various tissues and organs of the body. **Ectoderm**, the germ layer covering the surface of the embryo, gives rise to the outer covering of the animal and, in some phyla, to the central nervous system. **Endoderm**, the innermost germ layer, lines the pouch that forms during gastrulation (the archenteron) and gives rise to the lining of the digestive tract (or cavity) and organs such as the liver and lungs of vertebrates.

Animals that have only these two germ layers are said to be **diploblastic**. Diploblasts include the animals called cnidarians (jellies and corals, for example) as well as the comb jellies (see Chapter 33). All bilaterally symmetrical animals have a third germ layer, called the **mesoderm**, which fills much of the space between the ectoderm and endoderm. Thus, animals with bilateral symmetry are also said to be **triploblastic** (having three germ layers). In triploblasts, the mesoderm forms the muscles and most other organs between the digestive tract and the outer covering of the animal. Triploblasts include a broad range of animals, from flatworms to arthropods to vertebrates. (Although some diploblasts actually do have a third germ layer, it is not nearly as well developed as the mesoderm of animals considered to be triploblastic.)

Body Cavities

Most triploblastic animals have a **body cavity**, a fluid- or air-filled space located between the digestive tract and the outer body wall. This body cavity is also called a **coelom** (from the Greek *koilos*, hollow). A so-called "true" coelom forms from tissue derived from mesoderm. The inner and outer layers of tissue that surround the cavity connect and form structures that suspend the internal organs. Animals with a true coelom are known as **coelomates** (Figure 32.8a).

Some triploblastic animals have a body cavity that is formed from mesoderm and endoderm (Figure 32.8b). Such a cavity is called a "pseudocoelom" (from the Greek *pseudo*, false), and the animals that have one are called **pseudocoelomates**. Despite its name, however, a pseudocoelom is not false; it is a fully functional body cavity. Finally, some triploblastic animals lack a body cavity altogether (Figure 32.8c). They are known collectively as **acoelomates** (from the Greek *a-*, without).

A body cavity has many functions. Its fluid cushions the suspended organs, helping to prevent internal injury. In soft-bodied coelomates, such as earthworms, the coelom contains noncompressible fluid that acts like a skeleton against which muscles can work. The cavity also enables the internal organs to grow and move independently of the outer body wall. If it were not for your coelom, for example, every beat of your heart or ripple of your intestine would warp your body's surface.

Terms such as *coelomates* and *pseudocoelomates* refer to organisms that have a similar body plan and hence belong to the same *grade* (a group whose members share key biological features). However, phylogenetic studies show that true coeloms and pseudocoeloms have been independently gained or lost multiple times in the course of animal evolution. As illustrated by this example, a grade is not necessarily equivalent to a *clade* (a group that includes an ancestral species and all of its descendants). Thus, while describing an organism as a coelomate or pseudocoelomate can be helpful in describing certain of its features, these terms must be interpreted with caution when seeking to understand evolutionary history.

Protostome and Deuterostome Development

Based on certain aspects of early development, many animals can be described as having one of two developmental modes: **protostome development** or **deuterostome**

▼ **Figure 32.8 Body cavities of triploblastic animals.** The various organ systems of a triploblastic animal develop from the three germ layers that form in the embryo. Blue represents tissue derived from ectoderm, red from mesoderm, and yellow from endoderm.

(a) Coelomate

Coelom

Body covering (from ectoderm)

Digestive tract (from endoderm)

Tissue layer lining coelom and suspending internal organs (from mesoderm)

Coelomate, such as earthworms, have a true coelom, a body cavity completely lined by tissue derived from mesoderm.

(b) Pseudocoelomate

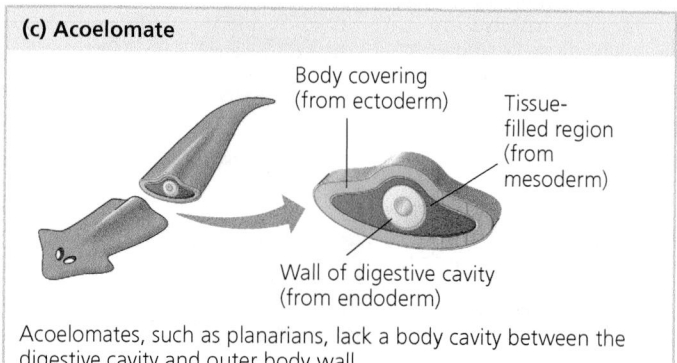

Body covering (from ectoderm)

Pseudocoelom

Muscle layer (from mesoderm)

Digestive tract (from endoderm)

Pseudocoelomates, such as roundworms, have a body cavity lined in part by tissue derived from mesoderm, but also by tissue derived from endoderm.

(c) Acoelomate

Body covering (from ectoderm)

Tissue-filled region (from mesoderm)

Wall of digestive cavity (from endoderm)

Acoelomates, such as planarians, lack a body cavity between the digestive cavity and outer body wall.

development. These modes can generally be distinguished by differences in cleavage, coelom formation, and fate of the blastopore.

Cleavage

Many animals with protostome development undergo **spiral cleavage**, in which the planes of cell division are diagonal to the vertical axis of the embryo; as seen in the eight-cell stage of the embryo, smaller cells are centered over the grooves between larger, underlying cells (Figure 32.9a, left). Furthermore, the so-called **determinate cleavage** of some animals with protostome development rigidly casts ("determines") the developmental fate of each embryonic cell very early. A cell

▶ **Figure 32.9** **A comparison of protostome and deuterostome development.** These are useful general distinctions, though there are many variations and exceptions to these patterns.

MAKE CONNECTIONS *Review Figure 20.21 (p. 415). As an early embryo, which would more likely have stem cells capable of giving rise to cells of any type: an animal with protostome development or with deuterostome development? Explain.*

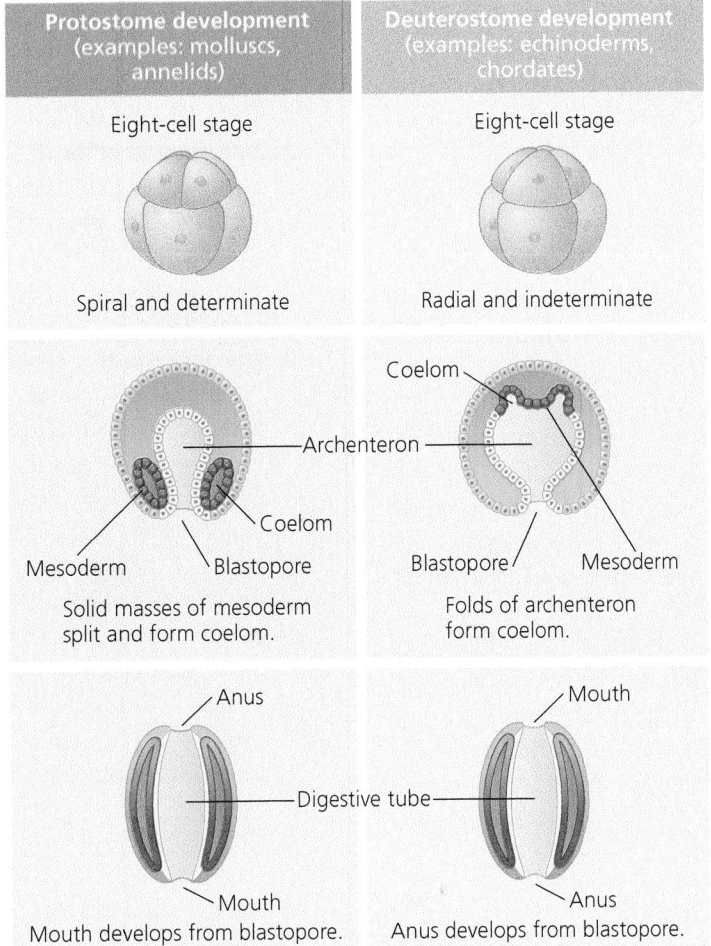

Protostome development (examples: molluscs, annelids)	Deuterostome development (examples: echinoderms, chordates)

(a) Cleavage. In general, protostome development begins with spiral, determinate cleavage. Deuterostome development is characterized by radial, indeterminate cleavage.

Eight-cell stage — Spiral and determinate

Eight-cell stage — Radial and indeterminate

(b) Coelom formation. Coelom formation begins in the gastrula stage. In protostome development, the coelom forms from splits in the mesoderm. In deuterostome development, the coelom forms from mesodermal outpocketings of the archenteron.

Archenteron — Coelom — Mesoderm — Blastopore — Solid masses of mesoderm split and form coelom.

Coelom — Blastopore — Mesoderm — Folds of archenteron form coelom.

(c) Fate of the blastopore. In protostome development, the mouth forms from the blastopore. In deuterostome development, the mouth forms from a secondary opening.

Anus — Digestive tube — Mouth — Mouth develops from blastopore.

Mouth — Digestive tube — Anus — Anus develops from blastopore.

Key
- Ectoderm
- Mesoderm
- Endoderm

isolated from a snail at the four-cell stage, for example, cannot develop into a whole animal. Instead, after repeated divisions, such a cell will form an inviable embryo that lacks many parts.

In contrast to the spiral cleavage pattern, deuterostome development is predominantly characterized by **radial cleavage**. The cleavage planes are either parallel or perpendicular to the vertical axis of the embryo; as seen at the eight-cell stage, the tiers of cells are aligned, one directly above the other (see Figure 32.9a, right). Most animals with deuterostome development also have **indeterminate cleavage**, meaning that each cell produced by early cleavage divisions retains the capacity to develop into a complete embryo. For example, if the cells of a sea urchin embryo are separated at the four-cell stage, each can form a complete larva. Similarly, it is the indeterminate cleavage of the human zygote that makes identical twins possible.

Coelom Formation

During gastrulation, an embryo's developing digestive tube initially forms as a blind pouch, the **archenteron**, which becomes the gut (Figure 32.9b). As the archenteron forms in protostome development, initially solid masses of mesoderm split and form the coelom. In contrast, in deuterostome development, the mesoderm buds from the wall of the archenteron, and its cavity becomes the coelom.

Fate of the Blastopore

Protostome and deuterostome development often differ in the fate of the **blastopore**, the indentation that during gastrulation leads to the formation of the archenteron (Figure 32.9c). After the archenteron develops, in most animals a second opening forms at the opposite end of the gastrula. In many species, the blastopore and this second opening become the two openings of the digestive tube: the mouth and the anus. In protostome development, the mouth generally develops from the first opening, the blastopore, and it is for this characteristic that the term *protostome* derives (from the Greek *protos*, first, and *stoma*, mouth). In deuterostome development (from the Greek *deuteros*, second), the mouth is derived from the secondary opening, and the blastopore usually forms the anus.

CONCEPT CHECK 32.3

1. Distinguish the terms *grade* and *clade*.
2. Compare three aspects of the early development of a snail (a mollusc) and a human (a chordate).
3. **WHAT IF?** Evaluate this claim: Ignoring the details of their specific anatomy, worms, humans, and most other triploblasts have a shape analogous to that of a doughnut.

For suggested answers, see Appendix A.

New views of animal phylogeny are emerging from molecular data

Zoologists currently recognize about three dozen animal phyla. But the boundaries of and relationships between these phyla continue to be debated. Although it might be frustrating that the phylogenies in textbooks cannot be memorized as set-in-stone truths, the uncertainty inherent in these diagrams is a healthy reminder that science is an ongoing, dynamic process of inquiry.

Researchers have long based their hypotheses about animal phylogeny on morphological data. Now biologists also reconstruct phylogenies using molecular data. Additional clues have come from studies of lesser-known animal phyla, along with fossil data that help clarify when key morphological traits arose in various groups.

Another important change has been the use of cladistics (see Chapter 26). Phylogenetic systematists seek to place organisms into clades, each of which includes an ancestral species and all of its descendants. Based on cladistic methods, a phylogenetic tree takes shape as a hierarchy of clades nested within larger clades—the finer and thicker branches of the tree, respectively. Clades are inferred from shared derived characters that are unique to members of the clade. For example, a clade might be inferred from key anatomical and embryological similarities that researchers conclude are homologous. Molecular data such as DNA sequences are another source of information for inferring common ancestry. But whether the data used are "traditional" morphological characters or "new" molecular sequences or a combination, the goal is the same: to reconstruct evolutionary history.

To get a sense of the debates in animal systematics, we'll compare a traditional view of animal phylogeny, based primarily on morphological data (Figure 32.10), with a more current view, based mainly on molecular data (Figure 32.11).

Points of Agreement

These two views agree on several significant aspects of animal phylogeny. Notice how the following points are reflected in Figures 32.10 and 32.11.

1. **All animals share a common ancestor.** Both trees indicate that animals are monophyletic, forming a clade called Metazoa. All extant and extinct animal lineages have descended from a common ancestor.

2. **Sponges are basal animals.** Among the extant taxa, sponges (phylum Porifera) branch from the base of both animal trees. Morphological and molecular analyses published in 2009 indicate that sponges are monophyletic, as shown here; some earlier studies had suggested that sponges are paraphyletic.

3. **Eumetazoa is a clade of animals with true tissues.** All animals except for sponges and a few others belong to a clade of **eumetazoans** ("true animals"). True tissues evolved in the common ancestor of living eumetazoans. Basal eumetazoans, which include the phyla Ctenophora (comb jellies) and Cnidaria, are diploblastic and generally have radial symmetry.

4. **Most animal phyla belong to the clade Bilateria.** Bilateral symmetry and the presence of three germ layers are shared derived characters that help define the clade Bilateria. This clade contains the majority of animal phyla, and its members are known as **bilaterians**. The Cambrian explosion was primarily a rapid diversification of bilaterians.

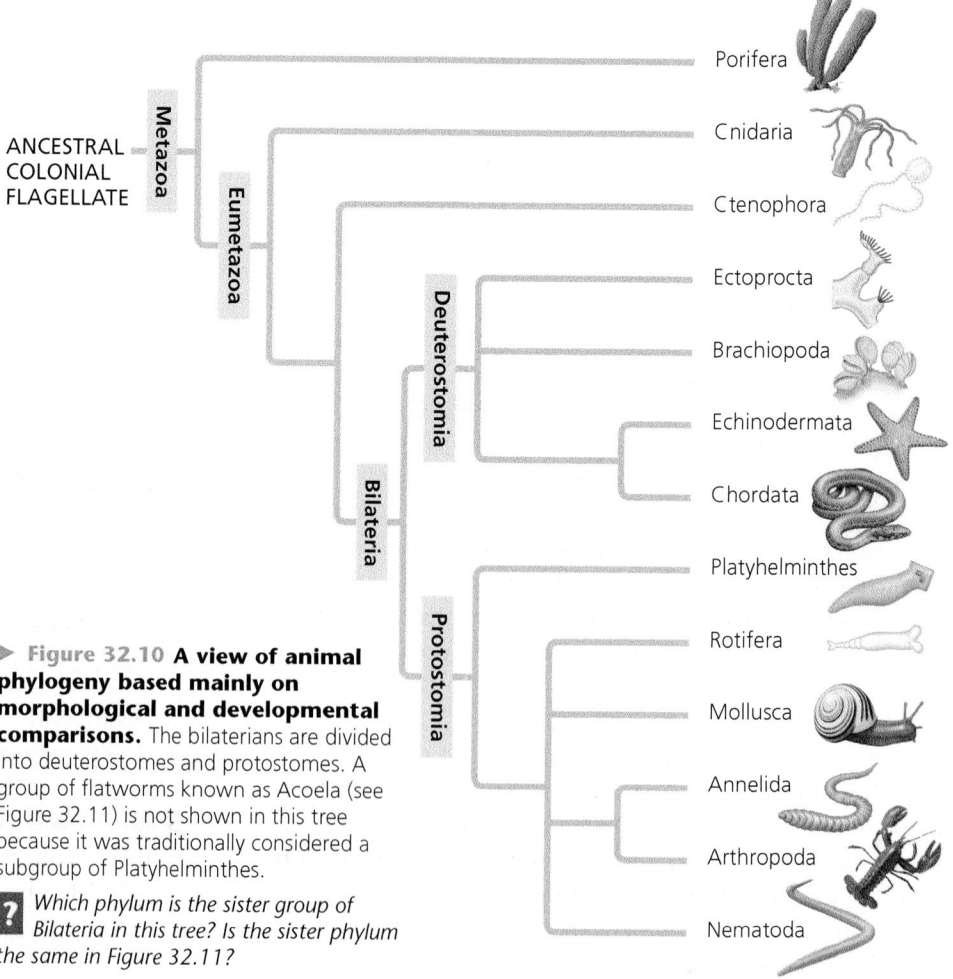

▶ **Figure 32.10 A view of animal phylogeny based mainly on morphological and developmental comparisons.** The bilaterians are divided into deuterostomes and protostomes. A group of flatworms known as Acoela (see Figure 32.11) is not shown in this tree because it was traditionally considered a subgroup of Platyhelminthes.

❓ *Which phylum is the sister group of Bilateria in this tree? Is the sister phylum the same in Figure 32.11?*

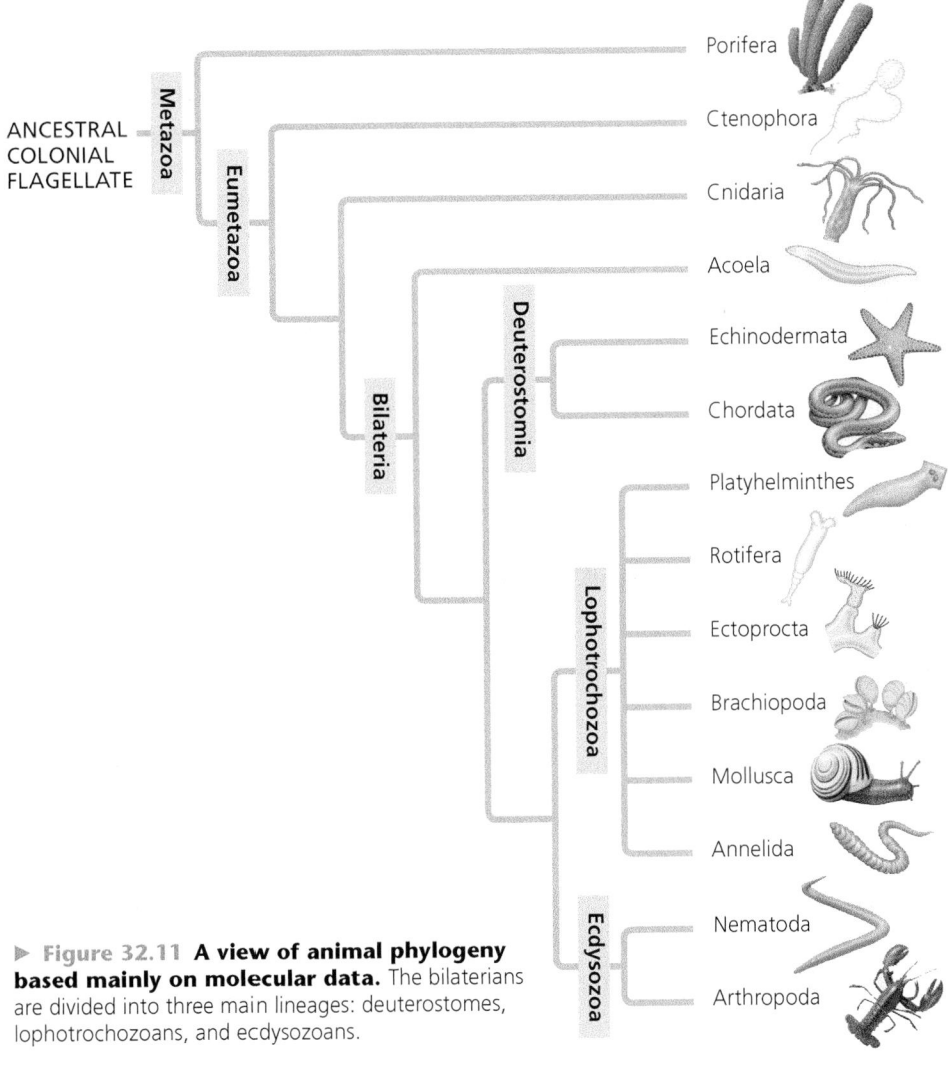

▶ Figure 32.11 A view of animal phylogeny based mainly on molecular data. The bilaterians are divided into three main lineages: deuterostomes, lophotrochozoans, and ecdysozoans.

Tree labels: ANCESTRAL COLONIAL FLAGELLATE, Metazoa, Eumetazoa, Bilateria, Deuterostomia, Lophotrochozoa, Ecdysozoa

Porifera, Ctenophora, Cnidaria, Acoela, Echinodermata, Chordata, Platyhelminthes, Rotifera, Ectoprocta, Brachiopoda, Mollusca, Annelida, Nematoda, Arthropoda

5. Chordates and some other phyla belong to the clade Deuterostomia. The term *deuterostome* refers not only to a mode of animal development, but also to the members of a clade that includes vertebrates and other chordates. (Note, however, that the traditional and molecular views of animal phylogeny disagree as to which other phyla are also deuterostomes.)

Progress in Resolving Bilaterian Relationships

While evolutionary relationships inferred from morphological data and molecular data are similar in many respects, there are some differences. For example, the morphology-based tree in Figure 32.10 divides the bilaterians into deuterostomes and protostomes. This view assumes that these two modes of development reflect a phylogenetic pattern. Within the protostomes, arthropods (such as insects and crustaceans) are grouped with annelids. Both groups have segmented bodies (think of the tail of a lobster, which is an arthropod, and an earthworm, which is an annelid).

A different view has emerged from molecular phylogenies based on ribosomal genes, *Hox* genes, and dozens of other protein-coding nuclear genes, as well as mitochondrial genes. Collectively, these studies indicate that there are three major clades of bilaterally symmetrical animals: the Deuterostomia, Lophotrochozoa, and Ecdysozoa (see Figure 32.11). In contrast to the traditional morphological view, the molecular phylogeny holds that the arthropods and annelids are not closely related to one another. Note also that Figure 32.11 includes a group of acoelomate flatworms (Acoela) not shown in Figure 32.10. Traditionally, acoelomate flatworms were classified with other flatworms in the phylum Platyhelminthes. However, recent research indicates that acoelomate flatworms are basal bilaterians, and not members of the phylum Platyhelminthes. Acoela's basal position suggests that the bilaterians may have descended from a common ancestor that resembled living acoelomate flatworms—that is, from an ancestor that had a simple nervous system, a saclike gut with a single opening (the "mouth"), and no excretory system.

As seen in Figure 32.11, the molecular phylogeny assigns the animal phyla that are not in Deuterostomia to two taxa rather than one: the **ecdysozoans** and the **lophotrochozoans**. The clade name Ecdysozoa refers to a characteristic shared by nematodes, arthropods, and some of the other ecdysozoan phyla that are not included in our survey. These animals secrete external skeletons (exoskeletons); the stiff covering of a cicada or cricket is an example. As the animal grows, it molts, squirming out of its old exoskeleton and secreting a larger one. The process of shedding the old exoskeleton is called *ecdysis* (Figure 32.12). Though named for this characteristic, the

◀ Figure 32.12 Ecdysis. This molting cicada is in the process of emerging from its old exoskeleton. The animal will now secrete a new, larger exoskeleton.

clade was proposed mainly on the basis of molecular data that support the common ancestry of its members. Furthermore, some taxa excluded from this clade by their molecular data, such as certain species of leeches, do in fact molt.

The name Lophotrochozoa refers to two different features observed in some animals belonging to this clade. Some lophotrochozoans, such as ectoprocts, develop a structure called a **lophophore** (from the Greek *lophos*, crest, and *pherein*, to carry), a crown of ciliated tentacles that function in feeding (Figure 32.13a). Individuals in other phyla, including molluscs and annelids, go through a distinctive developmental stage called the **trochophore larva** (Figure 32.13b)—hence the name lophotrochozoan.

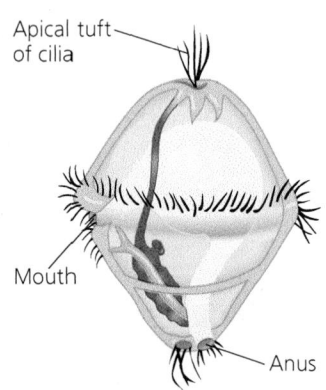

(a) Lophophore feeding structures of an ectoproct

(b) Structure of a trochophore larva

▲ Figure 32.13 **Morphological characteristics of lophotrochozoans.**

Future Directions in Animal Systematics

Like any area of scientific inquiry, animal systematics is a work in progress. At present, most systematists think that the tree shown in Figure 32.11 is more strongly supported than is the tree shown in Figure 32.10. Of course, as new information emerges, our understanding of the evolutionary relationships shown in these trees may change. Researchers continue to conduct large-scale analyses of multiple genes and morphological traits across a wide sample of animal phyla. A better understanding of the relationships between these phyla will give scientists a clearer picture of how the diversity of animal body plans arose. In Chapters 33 and 34, we will take a closer look at the diverse phyla of extant animals and their evolutionary history.

CONCEPT CHECK 32.4

1. Describe the evidence that cnidarians share a more recent common ancestor with other animals than with sponges.
2. How do the phylogenetic hypotheses presented in Figures 32.10 and 32.11 differ in structuring the major branches within the clade Bilateria?
3. **MAKE CONNECTIONS** Based on the phylogeny in Figure 32.11 and the information in Figure 25.10 (p. 518), evaluate this statement: "The Cambrian explosion actually consists of three explosions, not one."

For suggested answers, see Appendix A.

32 CHAPTER REVIEW

SUMMARY OF KEY CONCEPTS

CONCEPT 32.1

Animals are multicellular, heterotrophic eukaryotes with tissues that develop from embryonic layers (pp. 654–656)

- Animals are heterotrophs that ingest their food.
- Animals are multicellular eukaryotes. Their cells are supported and connected to one another by collagen and other structural proteins located outside the cell membrane. Nervous tissue and muscle tissue are key animal features.
- In most animals, **gastrulation** follows the formation of the **blastula** and leads to the formation of embryonic tissue layers. All animals have *Hox* genes that regulate the development of body form. Although *Hox* genes have been highly conserved over the course of evolution, they can produce a wide diversity of animal morphology.

? *Describe key ways that animals differ from plants and fungi.*

CONCEPT 32.2

The history of animals spans more than half a billion years (pp. 656–658)

? *What caused the Cambrian explosion? Describe current hypotheses.*

CONCEPT 32.3

Animals can be characterized by "body plans" (pp. 658–661)

- Animals may lack symmetry or may have radial or bilateral symmetry. Bilaterally symmetrical animals have dorsal and ventral sides, as well as anterior and posterior ends.

- Among eumetazoans (animals with true tissues), embryos may be **diploblastic** (having two germ layers) or **triploblastic** (having three germ layers).
- In triploblastic animals, a body cavity may be present or absent. A body cavity can be a **pseudocoelom** (derived from both mesoderm and endoderm) or a true **coelom** (derived only from mesoderm).
- **Protostome** and **deuterostome** development often differ in patterns of cleavage, coelom formation, and blastopore fate.

? *Describe how body plans provide useful information yet should be interpreted cautiously when scientists are trying to understand evolutionary relationships.*

CONCEPT 32.4

New views of animal phylogeny are emerging from molecular data (pp. 662–664)

This phylogenetic tree shows key steps in animal evolution:

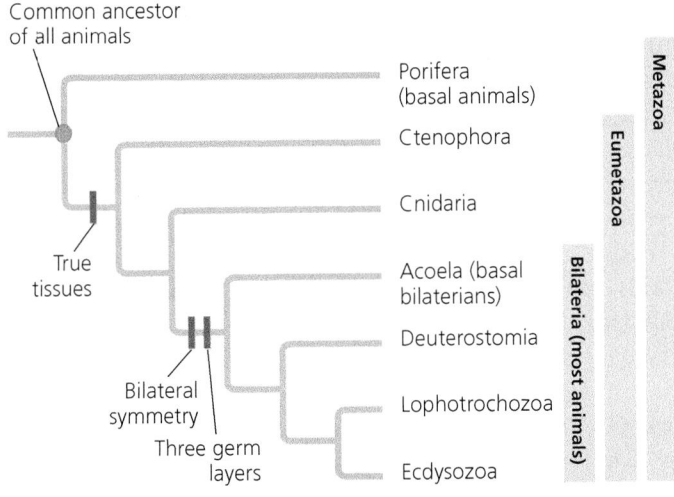

? *Describe the data and methods used today to reconstruct animal phylogeny.*

TEST YOUR UNDERSTANDING

LEVEL 1: KNOWLEDGE/COMPREHENSION

1. Among the characteristics unique to animals is
   a. gastrulation.
   b. multicellularity.
   c. sexual reproduction.
   d. flagellated sperm.
   e. heterotrophic nutrition.

2. The distinction between sponges and other animal phyla is based mainly on the absence versus the presence of
   a. a body cavity.
   b. a complete digestive tract.
   c. a circulatory system.
   d. true tissues.
   e. mesoderm.

3. Acoelomates are characterized by
   a. the absence of a brain.
   b. the absence of mesoderm.
   c. deuterostome development.
   d. a coelom that is not completely lined with mesoderm.
   e. a solid body without a cavity surrounding internal organs.

4. Which of the following was probably the *least* important factor in bringing about the Cambrian explosion?
   a. the emergence of predator-prey relationships among animals
   b. the accumulation of diverse adaptations, such as shells and different modes of locomotion
   c. the movement of animals onto land

   d. the origin of *Hox* genes and other genetic changes affecting the regulation of developmental genes
   e. the accumulation of sufficient atmospheric oxygen to support the more active metabolism of mobile animals

LEVEL 2: APPLICATION/ANALYSIS

5. Which of these is a point of conflict between the phylogenetic analyses presented in Figures 32.10 and 32.11?
   a. the monophyly of the animal kingdom
   b. the relationship of taxa of segmented animals to taxa of nonsegmented animals
   c. that sponges are basal animals
   d. that chordates are deuterostomes
   e. the monophyly of the bilaterians

LEVEL 3: SYNTHESIS/EVALUATION

6. **EVOLUTION CONNECTION**
   A professor begins a lecture on animal phylogeny by saying, "We are all worms." In this context, what did she mean?

7. **SCIENTIFIC INQUIRY**
   DRAW IT Redraw the bilaterian portion of Figure 32.11 for the nine phyla in the table below. Consider these blastopore fates: protostomy (mouth develops from the blastopore), deuterostomy (anus develops from the blastopore), or neither (the blastopore closes and the mouth develops elsewhere). Depending on the blastopore fate of its members, label each branch that leads to a phylum with P, D, N, or a combination of these letters. What is the ancestral blastopore fate? How many times has blastopore fate changed over the course of evolution? Explain.

Blastopore Fate	Phyla
Protostomy (P)	Platyhelminthes, Rotifera, Nematoda; most Mollusca, most Annelida; few Arthropoda
Deuterostomy (D)	Echinodermata, Chordata; most Arthropoda; few Mollusca, few Annelida
Neither (N)	Acoela

Source: A. Hejnol and M. Martindale, The mouth, the anus, and the blastopore—open questions about questionable openings. In *Animal Evolution: Genomes, Fossils and Trees*, eds. D. T. J. Littlewood and M. J. Telford, Oxford University Press, pp. 33–40 (2009).

8. **WRITE ABOUT A THEME**
   Feedback Regulation Animal life changed greatly during the Cambrian explosion, with some groups expanding in diversity and others declining. Write a short essay (100–150 words) interpreting these events as feedback regulation at the level of the biological community.

For selected answers, see Appendix A.

Mastering BIOLOGY www.masteringbiology.com

1. MasteringBiology® Assignments
Tutorial Animal Body Plans
Activities Protostome Diversity • Animal Phylogenetic Tree
Questions Student Misconceptions • Reading Quiz • Multiple Choice • End-of-Chapter

2. eText
Read your book online, search, take notes, highlight text, and more.

3. The Study Area
Practice Tests • Cumulative Test • *BioFlix* 3-D Animations • MP3 Tutor Sessions • Videos • Activities • Investigations • Lab Media • Audio Glossary • Word Study Tools • Art

33

An Introduction to Invertebrates

EVOLUTION

KEY CONCEPTS

33.1 Sponges are basal animals that lack true tissues

33.2 Cnidarians are an ancient phylum of eumetazoans

33.3 Lophotrochozoans, a clade identified by molecular data, have the widest range of animal body forms

33.4 Ecdysozoans are the most species-rich animal group

33.5 Echinoderms and chordates are deuterostomes

▲ Figure 33.1 **What function do the red whorls of this organism have?**

Life Without a Backbone

At first glance, you might mistake the organism shown in **Figure 33.1** for a type of seaweed. But this colorful inhabitant of coral reefs is actually an animal, not an alga. Specifically, it is a species of segmented worm known as a Christmas tree worm (*Spirobranchus giganteus*). The two tree-shaped whorls are tentacles, which the worm uses for gas exchange and for removing small food particles from the surrounding water. The tentacles emerge from a tube of calcium carbonate secreted by the worm that protects and supports its soft body. Light-sensitive structures on the tentacles can detect the shadow cast by a predator, triggering the worm to contract muscles that rapidly withdraw the tentacles into the tube.

Christmas tree worms are **invertebrates**—animals that lack a backbone. Invertebrates account for 95% of known animal species. They occupy almost every habitat on Earth, from the scalding water released by deep-sea hydrothermal vents to the rocky, frozen ground of Antarctica. Adaptation to these varied environments has produced an immense diversity of forms, ranging from a species consisting of a flat bilayer of cells to other species with features such as silk-spinning glands, pivoting spines, and tentacles covered with suction cups. Invertebrate species also show enormous variation in size, from microscopic organisms to organisms that can grow to 18 m long (1.5 times the length of a school bus).

In this chapter, we'll take a tour of the invertebrate world, using the phylogenetic tree in **Figure 33.2** as a guide. **Figure 33.3**, on the next three pages, surveys 23 invertebrate phyla. Serving as representatives of invertebrate diversity, many of those phyla are explored in more detail in the rest of this chapter.

▲ Figure 33.2 **Review of animal phylogeny.** Except for sponges (basal animals in phylum Porifera) and a few other groups, all animals have tissues and are in the clade Eumetazoa. Most animals are in the diverse clade Bilateria. The evolutionary tree shown here provides an overview of material covered in Chapter 32 but omits many groups; for a more complete view of animal relationships, see Figure 32.11.

Exploring Invertebrate Diversity

Kingdom Animalia encompasses 1.3 million known species, and estimates of total species range as high as 10–20 million species. Of the 23 phyla surveyed here, 12 are discussed more fully in this chapter, Chapter 32, or Chapter 34; cross-references are given at the end of their descriptions.

Porifera (5,500 species)

Animals in this phylum are informally called sponges. Sponges are sessile animals that lack true tissues. They live as suspension feeders, trapping particles that pass through the internal channels of their body (see Concept 33.1).

A sponge

Cnidaria (10,000 species)

Cnidarians include corals, jellies, and hydras. These animals have a diploblastic, radially symmetrical body plan that includes a gastrovascular cavity with a single opening that serves as both mouth and anus (see Concept 33.2).

A jelly

Acoela (400 species)

Acoel flatworms have a simple nervous system and a saclike gut, and thus were once placed in phylum Platyhelminthes. Molecular analyses, however, indicate that Acoela is a separate lineage that diverged before the three main bilaterian clades (see Concept 32.4).

Acoel flatworms (LM)

Placozoa (1 species)

The single known species in this phylum, *Trichoplax adhaerens*, doesn't even look like an animal. It consists of a simple bilayer of a few thousand cells. Placozoans are thought to be basal animals, but it is not yet known how they are related to other early-diverging animal groups such as Porifera and Cnidaria. *Trichoplax* can reproduce by dividing into two individuals or by budding off many multicellular individuals.

A placozoan (LM)

Ctenophora (100 species)

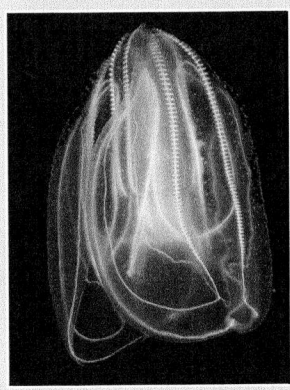

Ctenophores (comb jellies) are diploblastic and radially symmetrical like cnidarians, suggesting that both phyla diverged from other animals very early (see Figure 32.11). Comb jellies make up much of the ocean's plankton. They have many distinctive traits, including eight "combs" of cilia that propel the animals through the water. When a small animal contacts the tentacles of some comb jellies, specialized cells burst open, covering the prey with sticky threads.

A ctenophore, or comb jelly

Lophotrochozoa

Platyhelminthes (20,000 species)

Flatworms (including tapeworms, planarians, and flukes) have bilateral symmetry and a central nervous system that processes information from sensory structures. They have no body cavity or organs for circulation (see Concept 33.3).

A marine flatworm

Ectoprocta (4,500 species)

Ectoprocts (also known as bryozoans) live as sessile colonies and are covered by a tough exoskeleton (see Concept 33.3).

Ectoprocts

Rotifera (1,800 species)

Despite their microscopic size, rotifers have specialized organ systems, including an *alimentary canal* (a digestive tract with both a mouth and an anus). They feed on microorganisms suspended in water (see Concept 33.3).

A rotifer (LM)

Brachiopoda (335 species)

Brachiopods, or lamp shells, may be easily mistaken for clams or other molluscs. However, most brachiopods have a unique stalk that anchors them to their substrate, as well as a crown of cilia called a lophophore (see Concept 33.3).

A brachiopod

Continued on next page

Exploring Invertebrate Diversity

Lophotrochozoa (continued)

Acanthocephala (1,100 species)

Acanthocephalans are called spiny-headed worms because of the curved hooks on the proboscis at the anterior end of their body. All species are parasites. Some acanthocephalans manipulate the behavior of their intermediate hosts (generally arthropods) in ways that increase their chances of reaching their final hosts (generally vertebrates). For example, acanthocephalans that infect New Zealand mud crabs force their hosts to move to more visible areas on the beach, where the crabs are more likely to be eaten by birds, the worms' final hosts. Some phylogenetic analyses place the acanthocephalans within Rotifera.

An acanthocephalan (LM)

A ribbon worm

Nemertea (900 species)

Also called proboscis worms or ribbon worms, nemerteans swim through water or burrow in sand, extending a unique proboscis to capture prey. Like flatworms, they lack a true coelom. However, unlike flatworms, nemerteans have an alimentary canal and a closed circulatory system in which the blood is contained in vessels and hence is distinct from fluid in the body cavity.

Cycliophora (1 species)

A cycliophoran (colorized SEM)

The only known cyclio-phoran species, *Symbion pandora*, was discovered in 1995 on the mouthparts of a lobster. This tiny, vase-shaped creature has a unique body plan and a particularly bizarre life cycle. Males impregnate females that are still developing in their mothers' bodies. The fertilized females then escape, settle elsewhere on the lobster, and release their offspring. The offspring apparently leave that lobster and search for another one to which they attach.

Annelida (16,500 species)

Annelids, or segmented worms, are distinguished from other worms by their body segmentation. Earthworms are the most familiar annelids, but the phylum consists primarily of marine and freshwater species (see Concept 33.3).

A marine annelid

Mollusca (93,000 species)

Molluscs (including snails, clams, squids, and octopuses) have a soft body that in many species is protected by a hard shell (see Concept 33.3).

An octopus

Ecdysozoa

Loricifera (10 species)

Loriciferans (from the Latin *lorica*, corset, and *ferre*, to bear) are tiny animals that inhabit the deep-sea bottom. A loriciferan can telescope its head, neck, and thorax in and out of the lorica, a pocket formed by six plates surrounding the abdomen. Though the natural history of loriciferans is mostly a mystery, at least some species likely eat bacteria.

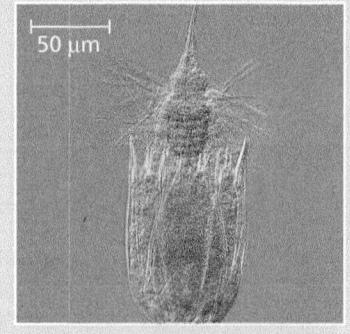

A loriciferan (LM)

Priapula (16 species)

A priapulan

Priapulans are worms with a large, rounded proboscis at the anterior end. (They are named after Priapos, the Greek god of fertility, who was symbolized by a giant penis.) Ranging from 0.5 mm to 20 cm in length, most species burrow through seafloor sediments. Fossil evidence suggests that priapulans were among the major predators during the Cambrian period.

Onychophora (110 species)

Onychophorans, also called velvet worms, originated during the Cambrian explosion (see Chapter 32). Originally, they thrived in the ocean, but at some point they succeeded in colonizing land. Today they live only in humid forests. Onychophorans have fleshy antennae and several dozen pairs of saclike legs.

An onychophoran

Tardigrada (800 species)

Tardigrades (from the Latin *tardus*, slow, and *gradus*, step) are sometimes called water bears for their rounded shape, stubby appendages, and lumbering, bearlike gait. Most tardigrades are less than 0.5 mm in length. Some live in oceans or fresh water, while others live on plants or animals. As many as 2 million tardigrades can be found on a square meter of moss. Harsh conditions may cause tardigrades to enter a state of dormancy; while dormant, they can survive temperatures as low as −272°C, close to absolute zero!

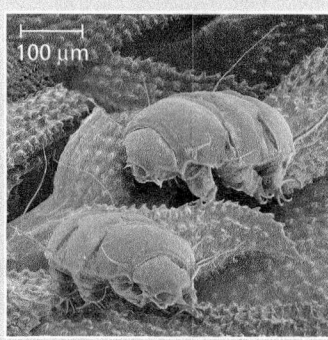

Tardigrades (colorized SEM)

Nematoda (25,000 species)

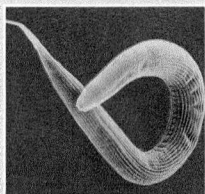

Also called roundworms, nematodes are enormously abundant and diverse in the soil and in aquatic habitats; many species parasitize plants and animals. Their most distinctive feature is a tough cuticle that coats the body (see Concept 33.4).

A roundworm (colored SEM)

Arthropoda (1,000,000 species)

The vast majority of known animal species, including insects, crustaceans, and arachnids, are arthropods. All arthropods have a segmented exoskeleton and jointed appendages (see Concept 33.4).

A scorpion (an arachnid)

Deuterostomia

Hemichordata (85 species)

Like echinoderms and chordates, hemichordates are members of the deuterostome clade (see Chapter 32). Hemichordates share some traits with chordates, such as gill slits and a dorsal nerve cord. The largest group of hemichordates is the enteropneusts, or acorn worms. Acorn worms are marine and generally live buried in mud or under rocks; they may grow to more than 2 m in length.

An acorn worm

Chordata (52,000 species)

More than 90% of all known chordate species have backbones (and thus are vertebrates). However, the phylum Chordata also includes three groups of invertebrates: lancelets, tunicates, and hagfishes. See Chapter 34 for a full discussion of this phylum.

A tunicate

Echinodermata (7,000 species)

Echinoderms, such as sand dollars, sea stars, and sea urchins, are marine animals in the deuterostome clade that are bilaterally symmetrical as larvae but not as adults. They move and feed by using a network of internal canals to pump water to different parts of their body (see Concept 33.5).

A sea urchin

Sponges are basal animals that lack true tissues

Porifera
Cnidaria
Lophotrochozoa
Ecdysozoa
Deuterostomia

Animals in the phylum Porifera are known informally as sponges. (Recent molecular studies indicate that sponges are monophyletic, and that is the phylogeny we follow here; this remains under debate, however, as some studies suggest that sponges are paraphyletic.) Among the simplest of animals, sponges are sedentary and were mistaken for plants by the ancient Greeks. They range in size from a few millimeters to a few meters, and most species are marine, though a few live in fresh water. Sponges are **suspension feeders**: They capture food particles suspended in the water that passes through their body, which in some species resembles a sac perforated with pores. Water is drawn through the pores into a central cavity, the **spongocoel**, and then flows out of the sponge through a larger opening called the **osculum** (Figure 33.4). More complex sponges have folded body walls, and many contain branched water canals and several oscula.

Sponges are basal animals; that is, they represent a lineage that originates near the root of the phylogenetic tree of animals. Unlike nearly all other animals, sponges lack true tissues, groups of similar cells that act as a functional unit and are isolated from other tissues by membranous layers. However, the sponge body does contain several different cell types. For example, lining the interior of the spongocoel are flagellated **choanocytes**, or collar cells (named for the finger-like projections that form a "collar" around the flagellum). These cells engulf bacteria and other food particles by phagocytosis. The similarity between choanocytes and the cells of choanoflagellates supports molecular evidence suggesting that animals evolved from a choanoflagellate-like ancestor (see Figure 32.3).

The body of a sponge consists of two layers of cells separated by a gelatinous region called the **mesohyl**. Because both cell layers are in contact with water, processes such as gas exchange and waste removal can occur by diffusion across the membranes of these cells. Other tasks are performed by cells called **amoebocytes**, named for their use of pseudopodia. These cells move through the mesohyl and have many functions. For example, they take up food from the surrounding water and from choanocytes, digest it, and carry nutrients to other cells. Amoebocytes also manufacture tough skeletal fibers within the mesohyl. In some sponges, these fibers are sharp spicules made from calcium carbonate or silica. Other sponges produce more flexible fibers composed of a protein called spongin; you may have seen these pliant skeletons

▼ Figure 33.4 **Anatomy of a sponge.**

Azure vase sponge (*Callyspongia plicifera*)

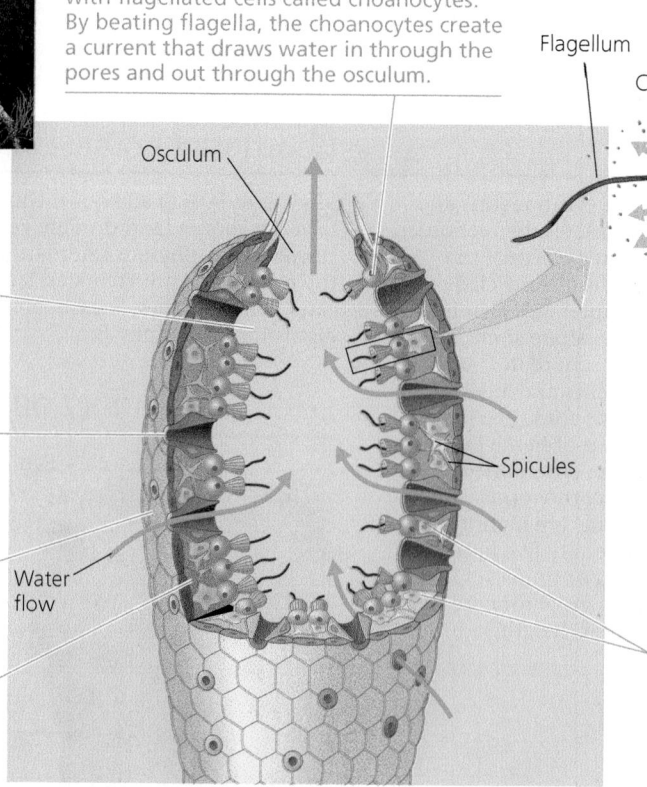

⑤ Choanocytes. The spongocoel is lined with flagellated cells called choanocytes. By beating flagella, the choanocytes create a current that draws water in through the pores and out through the osculum.

④ Spongocoel. Water passing through pores enters a cavity called the spongocoel.

③ Pores. Water enters the sponge through pores formed by doughnut-shaped cells that span the body wall.

② Epidermis. The outer layer consists of tightly packed epidermal cells.

① Mesohyl. The wall of this sponge consists of two layers of cells separated by a gelatinous matrix, the mesohyl ("middle matter").

Osculum

Water flow

Spicules

Flagellum

Collar

Food particles in mucus

Choanocyte

Phagocytosis of food particles

Amoebocyte

⑥ The movement of a choanocyte's flagellum also draws water through its collar of finger-like projections. Food particles are trapped in the mucus that coats the projections, engulfed by phagocytosis, and either digested or transferred to amoebocytes.

⑦ Amoebocytes. These cells can transport nutrients to other cells of the sponge body, produce materials for skeletal fibers (spicules), or become any type of sponge cell as needed.

being sold as brown bath sponges. Finally, and perhaps most importantly, amoebocytes are capable of becoming other types of sponge cells. This gives the sponge body remarkable flexibility, enabling it to adjust its shape in response to changes in its physical environment (such as the direction of water currents).

Most sponges are **hermaphrodites**, meaning that each individual functions as both male and female in sexual reproduction by producing sperm *and* eggs. Almost all sponges exhibit sequential hermaphroditism: They function first as one sex and then as the other.

Sponge gametes arise from choanocytes or amoebocytes. Eggs reside in the mesohyl, but sperm are carried out of the sponge by the water current. Cross-fertilization results from some of the sperm being drawn into neighboring individuals. Fertilization occurs in the mesohyl, where the zygotes develop into flagellated, swimming larvae that disperse from the parent sponge. After settling on a suitable substrate, a larva develops into a sessile adult.

Sponges produce a variety of antibiotics and other defensive compounds. Researchers are now isolating these compounds, which hold promise for fighting human diseases. For example, a compound called cribrostatin isolated from marine sponges can kill penicillin-resistant strains of the bacterium *Streptococcus*. Other sponge-derived compounds are being tested as possible anticancer agents.

CONCEPT CHECK 33.1

1. Describe how sponges feed.
2. **WHAT IF?** Some molecular evidence suggests that the sister group of animals is not the choanoflagellates, but rather a group of parasitic protists, Mesomycetozoa. Given that these parasites lack collar cells, can this hypothesis be correct? Explain.

For suggested answers, see Appendix A.

CONCEPT 33.2

Cnidarians are an ancient phylum of eumetazoans

All animals except sponges and a few other groups belong to the clade Eumetazoa, animals with true tissues (see Chapter 32). One of the oldest lineages in this clade is the phylum Cnidaria. Cnidarians have diversified into a wide range of sessile and motile forms, including hydras, corals, and jellies (commonly called "jellyfish"). Yet most cnidarians still exhibit the relatively simple, diploblastic, radial body plan that existed in early members of the group some 560 million years ago.

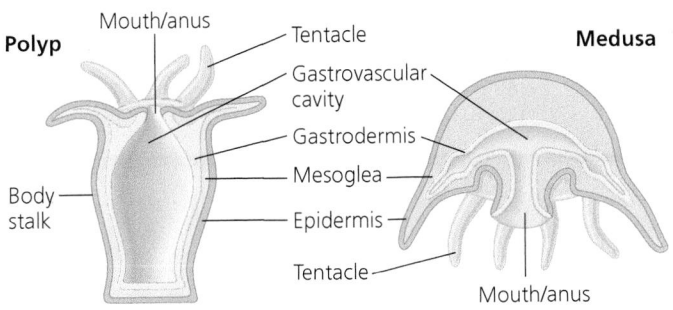

▲ **Figure 33.5 Polyp and medusa forms of cnidarians.** The body wall of a cnidarian has two layers of cells: an outer layer of epidermis (darker blue; derived from ectoderm) and an inner layer of gastrodermis (yellow; derived from endoderm). Digestion begins in the gastrovascular cavity and is completed inside food vacuoles in the gastrodermal cells. Flagella on the gastrodermal cells keep the contents of the gastrovascular cavity agitated and help distribute nutrients. Sandwiched between the epidermis and gastrodermis is a gelatinous layer, the mesoglea.

The basic body plan of a cnidarian is a sac with a central digestive compartment, the **gastrovascular cavity**. A single opening to this cavity functions as both mouth and anus. There are two variations on this body plan: the sessile polyp and the motile medusa (**Figure 33.5**). **Polyps** are cylindrical forms that adhere to the substrate by the aboral end of their body (the end opposite the mouth) and extend their tentacles, waiting for prey. Examples of the polyp form include hydras and sea anemones. A **medusa** (plural, *medusae*) resembles a flattened, mouth-down version of the polyp. It moves freely in the water by a combination of passive drifting and contractions of its bell-shaped body. Medusae include free-swimming jellies. The tentacles of a jelly dangle from the oral surface, which points downward. Some cnidarians exist only as polyps or only as medusae; others have both a polyp stage and a medusa stage in their life cycle.

Cnidarians are carnivores that often use tentacles arranged in a ring around their mouth to capture prey and push the food into their gastrovascular cavity, where digestion begins. Enzymes are secreted into the cavity, thus breaking down the prey into a nutrient-rich broth. Cells lining the cavity then absorb these nutrients and complete the digestive process; any undigested remains are expelled through the mouth/anus. The tentacles are armed with batteries of **cnidocytes**, cells unique to cnidarians that function in defense and prey capture (**Figure 33.6**). Cnidocytes contain *cnidae* (from the Greek *cnide*, nettle), capsule-like organelles that are capable of exploding outward and that give phylum Cnidaria its name. Specialized cnidae called **nematocysts** contain a stinging thread that can penetrate the body wall of the cnidarian's prey. Other kinds of cnidae have long threads that stick to or entangle small prey that bump into the cnidarian's tentacles.

Contractile tissues and nerves occur in their simplest forms in cnidarians. Cells of the epidermis (outer layer) and gastrodermis (inner layer) have bundles of microfilaments arranged into contractile fibers (see Chapter 6). The gastrovascular

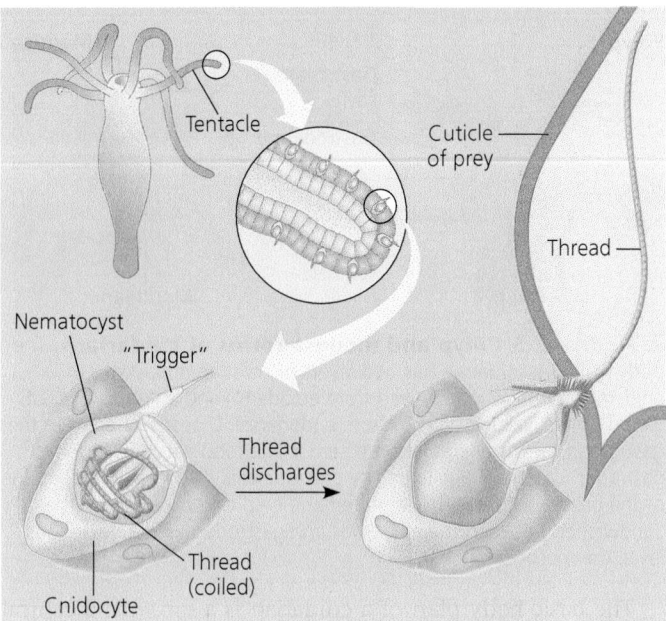

▲ Figure 33.6 **A cnidocyte of a hydra.** This type of cnidocyte contains a stinging capsule, the nematocyst, which contains a coiled thread. When a "trigger" is stimulated by touch or by certain chemicals, the thread shoots out, puncturing and injecting poison into prey.

cavity acts as a hydrostatic skeleton (see Concept 50.6) against which the contractile cells can work. When a cnidarian closes its mouth, the volume of the cavity is fixed, and contraction of selected cells causes the animal to change shape. Movements are coordinated by a nerve net. Cnidarians have no brain, and the noncentralized nerve net is associated with sensory structures that are distributed around the body. Thus, the animal can detect and respond to stimuli from all directions.

The phylum Cnidaria is divided into four major clades: Hydrozoa, Scyphozoa, Cubozoa, and Anthozoa (**Figure 33.7**).

Hydrozoans

Most hydrozoans alternate between the polyp and medusa forms, as seen in the life cycle of *Obelia* (**Figure 33.8**). The polyp stage, a colony of interconnected polyps in the case of *Obelia*, is more conspicuous than the medusa. Hydras, among the few cnidarians found in fresh water, are unusual hydrozoans in that they exist only in polyp form. When environmental conditions are favorable, a hydra reproduces asexually by budding, forming outgrowths that pinch off from the parent and live independently (see Figure 13.2). When conditions deteriorate, hydras can reproduce sexually, forming resistant zygotes that remain dormant until conditions improve.

Scyphozoans

The medusa is the predominant stage in the life cycle of most scyphozoans. The medusae of most species live among the plankton as jellies. Most coastal scyphozoans go through a stage as small polyps during their life cycle, whereas those that live in the open ocean generally lack the polyp stage altogether.

Cubozoans

As their name (which means "cube animals") suggests, cubozoans have a box-shaped medusa stage. Cubozoans can be distinguished from scyphozoans in other ways, such as having complex eyes embedded in the fringe of their medusae. They also are comparatively strong swimmers and as a result are less likely to be stranded on shore. Most cubozoans live in tropical oceans and are equipped with highly toxic cnidocytes. The sea wasp (*Chironex fleckeri*), a cubozoan that lives off the coast of northern Australia, is one of the deadliest organisms known: Its sting causes intense pain and can lead to respiratory failure, cardiac arrest, and death within minutes. The poison of sea wasps isn't universally fatal, however; sea turtles have defenses against it, allowing them to eat the cubozoan in great quantities.

(a) Hydrozoa. Some species, such as this one, live as colonial polyps.

(b) Scyphozoa. Many jellies are bioluminescent. Food captured by nematocyst-bearing tentacles is transferred to specialized oral arms (that lack nematocysts) for transport to the mouth.

(c) Cubozoa. A notorious example is the sea wasp (*Chironex fleckeri*). Its poison, which can subdue fish and other large prey, is more potent than cobra venom.

(d) Anthozoa. Sea anemones and other anthozoans exist only as polyps. Many anthozoans form symbiotic relationships with photosynthetic algae.

▲ Figure 33.7 **Cnidarians.**

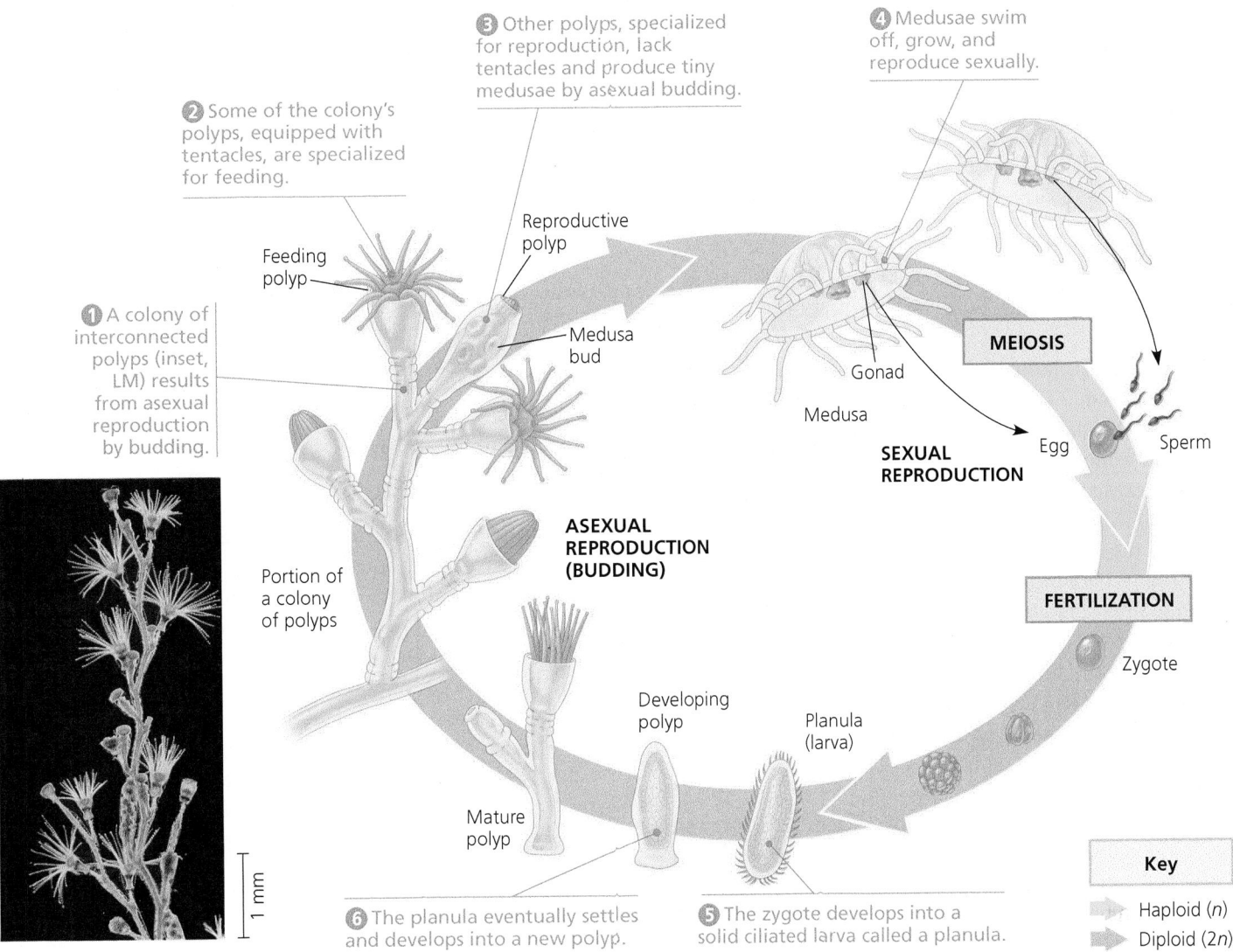

① A colony of interconnected polyps (inset, LM) results from asexual reproduction by budding.

② Some of the colony's polyps, equipped with tentacles, are specialized for feeding.

③ Other polyps, specialized for reproduction, lack tentacles and produce tiny medusae by asexual budding.

④ Medusae swim off, grow, and reproduce sexually.

Feeding polyp

Reproductive polyp

Medusa bud

Portion of a colony of polyps

MEIOSIS

Gonad

Medusa

SEXUAL REPRODUCTION

Egg

Sperm

ASEXUAL REPRODUCTION (BUDDING)

FERTILIZATION

Zygote

Developing polyp

Planula (larva)

Mature polyp

⑥ The planula eventually settles and develops into a new polyp.

⑤ The zygote develops into a solid ciliated larva called a planula.

Key
Haploid (*n*)
Diploid (2*n*)

1 mm

▲ **Figure 33.8 The life cycle of the hydrozoan *Obelia*.** The polyp is asexual, and the medusa is sexual, releasing eggs and sperm. These two stages alternate, one producing the other. Do not confuse this with the alternation of generations that occurs in plants and some algae: In *Obelia*, both the polyp and the medusa are diploid organisms. Typical of animals, only the single-celled gametes are haploid. By contrast, plants have a multicellular haploid generation and a multicellular diploid generation.

WHAT IF? *Suppose that* Obelia *medusae and gametes were haploid, but all other stages were diploid. What aspects of its actual life cycle would have to change for this to occur?*

Anthozoans

Sea anemones (see Figure 33.7d) and corals belong to the clade Anthozoa (meaning "flower animals"). These cnidarians occur only as polyps. Corals live as solitary or colonial forms, often forming symbioses with algae (see Chapter 28). Many species secrete a hard external skeleton of calcium carbonate. Each polyp generation builds on the skeletal remains of earlier generations, constructing "rocks" with shapes characteristic of their species. These skeletons are what we usually think of as coral.

Coral reefs are to tropical seas what rain forests are to tropical land areas: They provide habitat for many other species. Unfortunately, these reefs are being destroyed at an alarming rate. Pollution and overfishing are major threats, and global warming may also be contributing to their demise by raising seawater temperatures above the narrow range in which corals thrive.

CONCEPT CHECK 33.2

1. Compare and contrast the polyp and medusa forms of cnidarians.
2. Describe the structure and function of the stinging cells for which cnidarians are named.
3. **MAKE CONNECTIONS** As you read in Concept 25.3 (pp. 518–519), many new animal body plans emerged during and after the Cambrian explosion. In contrast, cnidarians today retain the same diploblastic, radial body plan found in cnidarians 560 million years ago. Are cnidarians therefore less successful or less "highly evolved" than other animal groups? Explain. (See also Concept 25.6, pp. 529–530.)

For suggested answers, see Appendix A.

Lophotrochozoans, a clade identified by molecular data, have the widest range of animal body forms

The vast majority of animal species belong to the clade Bilateria, whose members exhibit bilateral symmetry and triploblastic development (see Chapter 32). Most bilaterians also have a digestive tract with two openings (a mouth and an anus) and a coelom. While the sequence of bilaterian evolution is a subject of active investigation, the most recent common ancestor of living bilaterians probably existed in the late Proterozoic eon (about 575 million years ago). Many of the major groups of bilaterians first appeared in the fossil record during the Cambrian explosion.

As you read in Chapter 32, molecular evidence suggests that there are three major clades of bilaterally symmetrical animals: Lophotrochozoa, Ecdysozoa, and Deuterostomia. This section will focus on the first of these clades, the lophotrochozoans. Concepts 33.4 and 33.5 will explore the other two clades.

Although the clade Lophotrochozoa was identified by molecular data, its name comes from features found in some of its members. Some lophotrochozoans develop a structure called a *lophophore*, a crown of ciliated tentacles that functions in feeding, while others go through a distinctive stage called the *trochophore larva* (see Figure 32.13). Other members of the group have neither of these features. Few other unique morphological features are widely shared within the group—in fact, the lophotrochozoans are the most diverse bilaterian clade in terms of body plan. This diversity in form is reflected in the number of phyla classified in the group: Lophotrochozoa includes about 18 phyla, more than twice the number in any other clade of bilaterians.

We'll now introduce six diverse lophotrochozoan phyla: the flatworms, rotifers, ectoprocts, brachiopods, molluscs, and annelids.

Flatworms

Flatworms (phylum Platyhelminthes) live in marine, freshwater, and damp terrestrial habitats. In addition to free-living species, flatworms include many parasitic species, such as flukes and tapeworms. Flatworms are so named because they have thin bodies that are flattened dorsoventrally (between the dorsal and ventral surfaces); the word *platyhelminth* means "flat worm." (Note that *worm* is not a formal taxonomic name but rather refers to a grade of animals with long, thin bodies.) The smallest flatworms are nearly microscopic free-living species, while some tapeworms are more than 20 m long.

Although flatworms undergo triploblastic development, they are acoelomates (animals that lack a body cavity). Their flat shape places all their cells close to water in the surrounding environment or in their gut. Because of this proximity to water, gas exchange and the elimination of nitrogenous waste (ammonia) can occur by diffusion across the body surface. Flatworms have no organs specialized for gas exchange, and their relatively simple excretory apparatus functions mainly to maintain osmotic balance with their surroundings. This apparatus consists of **protonephridia**, networks of tubules with ciliated structures called *flame bulbs* that pull fluid through branched ducts opening to the outside (see Figure 44.11). Most flatworms have a gastrovascular cavity with only one opening. Though flatworms lack a circulatory system, the fine branches of the gastrovascular cavity distribute food directly to the animal's cells.

Early in their evolutionary history, flatworms separated into two lineages, Catenulida and Rhabditophora. Catenulida is a small clade of about 100 flatworm species, most of which live in freshwater habitats. Catenulids typically reproduce asexually by budding at their posterior end. The offspring often produce their own buds before detaching from the parent, thereby forming a chain of two to four genetically identical individuals—hence their informal name, "chain worms."

The other ancient flatworm lineage, Rhabditophora, is a diverse clade of about 20,000 freshwater and marine species, one example of which is shown in **Figure 33.9**. We'll explore this group in more detail, focusing on free-living and parasitic members of this clade.

Free-Living Species

Free-living rhabditophorans are important as predators and scavengers in a wide range of freshwater and marine habitats. The best-known members of this group are freshwater species in the genus *Dugesia*, commonly called **planarians**. Abundant in unpolluted ponds and streams, planarians prey on

▲ **Figure 33.9 A free-living marine flatworm.**

smaller animals or feed on dead animals. They move by using cilia on their ventral surface, gliding along a film of mucus they secrete. Some other rhabditophorans also use their muscles to swim through water with an undulating motion.

A planarian's head is equipped with a pair of light-sensitive eyespots and lateral flaps that function mainly to detect specific chemicals. The planarian nervous system is more complex and centralized than the nerve nets of cnidarians (Figure 33.10). Experiments have shown that planarians can learn to modify their responses to stimuli.

Some planarians can reproduce asexually through fission. The parent constricts roughly in the middle of its body, separating into a head end and a tail end; each end then regenerates the missing parts. Sexual reproduction also occurs. Planarians are hermaphrodites, and copulating mates typically cross-fertilize each other.

Parasitic Species

More than half of the known species of rhabditophorans live as parasites in or on other animals. Many have suckers that attach to the internal organs or outer surfaces of the host animal. In most species, a tough covering helps protect the parasites within their hosts. Reproductive organs occupy nearly the entire interior of these worms. We'll discuss two ecologically and economically important subgroups of parasitic rhabditophorans, the trematodes and the tapeworms.

Trematodes As a group, trematodes parasitize a wide range of hosts, and most species have complex life cycles with alternating sexual and asexual stages. Many trematodes require an intermediate host in which larvae develop before infecting the final host (usually a vertebrate), where the adult worms live. For example, trematodes that parasitize humans spend part of their lives in snail hosts (Figure 33.11). Around the world, some 200 million people are infected with trematodes called blood flukes (*Schistosoma*) and suffer from schistosomiasis, a disease whose symptoms include pain, anemia, and diarrhea.

Living within different hosts puts demands on trematodes that free-living animals don't face. A blood fluke, for instance, must evade the immune systems of both snails and humans. By mimicking the surface proteins of its hosts, the blood fluke creates a partial immunological camouflage for itself. It

▼ Figure 33.10 **Anatomy of a planarian.**

Pharynx. The mouth is at the tip of a muscular pharynx. Digestive juices are spilled onto prey, and the pharynx sucks small pieces of food into the gastrovascular cavity, where digestion continues.

Digestion is completed within the cells lining the gastrovascular cavity, which has many fine subbranches that provide an extensive surface area.

Undigested wastes are egested through the mouth.

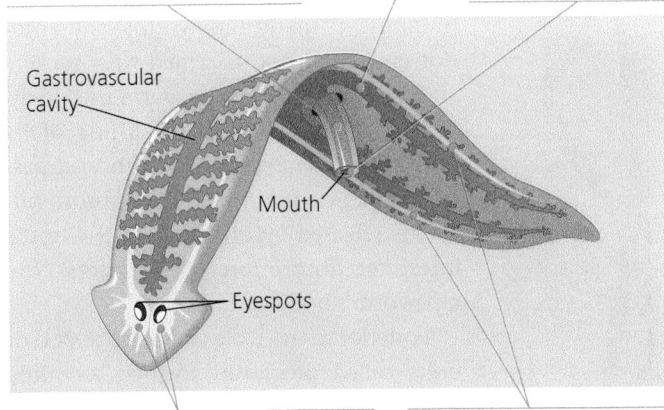

Gastrovascular cavity

Mouth

Eyespots

Ganglia. At the anterior end of the worm, near the main sources of sensory input, is a pair of ganglia, dense clusters of nerve cells.

Ventral nerve cords. From the ganglia, a pair of ventral nerve cords runs the length of the body.

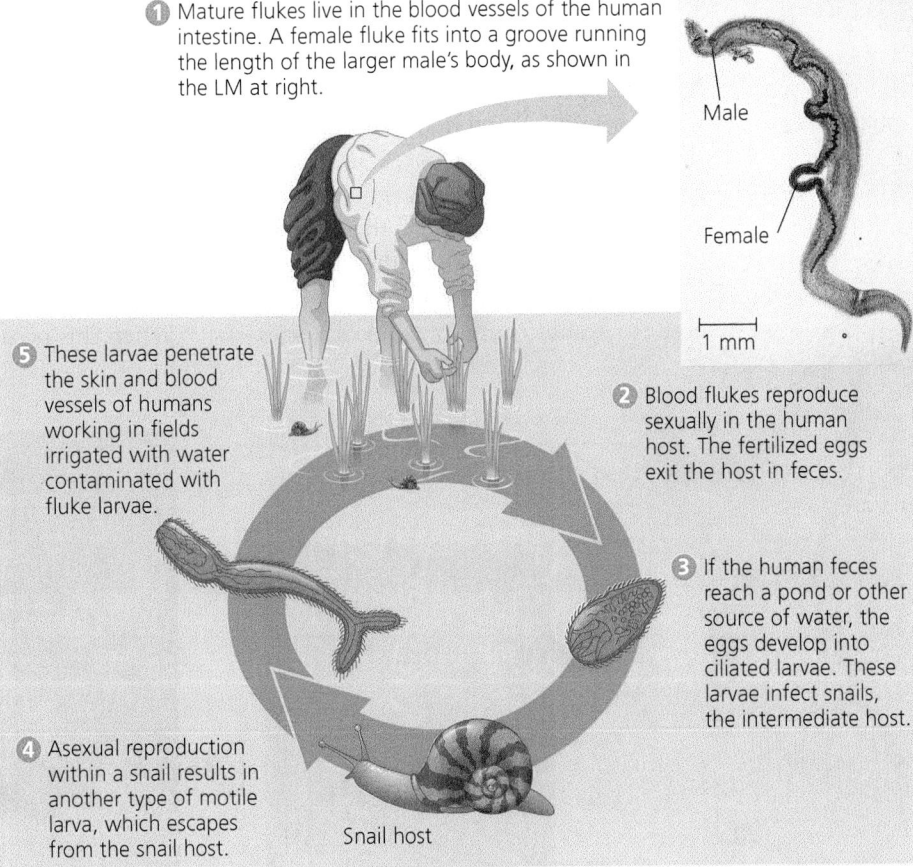

❶ Mature flukes live in the blood vessels of the human intestine. A female fluke fits into a groove running the length of the larger male's body, as shown in the LM at right.

Male

Female

1 mm

❺ These larvae penetrate the skin and blood vessels of humans working in fields irrigated with water contaminated with fluke larvae.

❷ Blood flukes reproduce sexually in the human host. The fertilized eggs exit the host in feces.

❸ If the human feces reach a pond or other source of water, the eggs develop into ciliated larvae. These larvae infect snails, the intermediate host.

❹ Asexual reproduction within a snail results in another type of motile larva, which escapes from the snail host.

Snail host

▲ Figure 33.11 **The life cycle of a blood fluke (*Schistosoma mansoni*), a trematode.**

WHAT IF? *Snails eat algae, whose growth is stimulated by nutrients found in fertilizer. How would the contamination of irrigation water with fertilizer likely affect the occurrence of schistosomiasis? Explain.*

also releases molecules that manipulate the hosts' immune systems into tolerating the parasite's existence. These defenses are so effective that individual blood flukes can survive in humans for more than 40 years.

Tapeworms The tapeworms are a second large and diverse group of parasitic rhabditophorans **(Figure 33.12)**. The adults live mostly inside vertebrates, including humans. In many tapeworms, the anterior end, or scolex, is armed with suckers and often hooks that the worm uses to attach itself to the intestinal lining of its host. Tapeworms lack a mouth and gastrovascular cavity; they simply absorb nutrients released by digestion in the host's intestine. Absorption occurs across the tapeworm's body surface.

Posterior to the scolex is a long ribbon of units called proglottids, which are little more than sacs of sex organs. After sexual reproduction, proglottids loaded with thousands of fertilized eggs are released from the posterior end of a tapeworm and leave the host's body in feces. In one type of life cycle, feces carrying the eggs contaminate the food or water of intermediate hosts, such as pigs or cattle, and the tapeworm eggs develop into larvae that encyst in muscles of these animals. A human acquires the larvae by eating undercooked meat containing the cysts, and the worms develop into mature adults within the human. Large tapeworms can block the intestines and rob enough nutrients from the human host to cause nutritional deficiencies.

Doctors have patients take the drug niclosamide by mouth to kill the adult worms.

Rotifers

Rotifers (phylum Rotifera) are tiny animals that inhabit freshwater, marine, and damp soil habitats. Ranging in size from about 50 μm to 2 mm, rotifers are smaller than many protists but nevertheless are multicellular and have specialized organ systems **(Figure 33.13)**. In contrast to cnidarians and flatworms, which have a gastrovascular cavity, rotifers have an **alimentary canal**, a digestive tube with two openings, a mouth and an anus. Internal organs lie within the pseudocoelom, a body cavity that is not completely lined by mesoderm (see Figure 32.8b). Fluid in the pseudocoelom serves as a hydrostatic skeleton. Movement of a rotifer's body distributes the fluid throughout the body, circulating nutrients.

The word *rotifer* is derived from the Latin meaning "wheel-bearer," a reference to the crown of cilia that draws a vortex of water into the mouth. Posterior to the mouth, a region of the digestive tract called the pharynx bears jaws called trophi that grind up food, mostly microorganisms suspended in the water. Digestion is then completed farther along the alimentary canal. Most other bilaterians also have an alimentary canal, which enables the stepwise digestion of a wide range of food particles.

Rotifers exhibit some unusual forms of reproduction. Some species consist only of females that produce more females from unfertilized eggs, a type of asexual reproduction called **parthenogenesis**. Some other invertebrates (for example, aphids and some bees) and even some vertebrates (for example, some lizards and some fishes) can also reproduce in this way. In addition to being able to produce females by parthenogeneis, some rotifers can also reproduce sexually under certain conditions, such as high levels of crowding. When this occurs, a female produces two types of eggs. Eggs

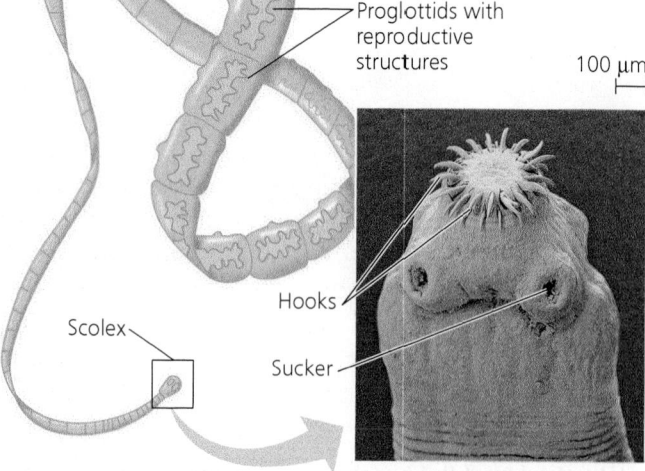

▲ **Figure 33.12 Anatomy of a tapeworm.** The inset shows a close-up of the scolex (colorized SEM).

Proglottids with reproductive structures

100 μm

Hooks

Scolex

Sucker

Jaws

Crown of cilia

Anus

Stomach

0.1 mm

▲ **Figure 33.13 A rotifer.** These pseudocoelomates, smaller than many protists, are generally more anatomically complex than flatworms (LM).

of one type develop into females, and eggs of the other type develop into males. In some cases, the males do not feed and survive only long enough to fertilize eggs. The fertilized eggs develop into resistant embryos capable of remaining dormant for years. Once the embryos break dormancy, they develop into a new female generation that reproduces by parthenogenesis until conditions once again favor sexual reproduction.

It is puzzling that many rotifer species survive without males. The vast majority of animals and plants reproduce sexually at least some of the time, and sexual reproduction has certain advantages over asexual reproduction (see Concept 46.1). For example, species that reproduce asexually tend to accumulate harmful mutations in their genomes faster than sexually reproducing species. As a result, asexual species should experience higher rates of extinction and lower rates of speciation.

Seeking to understand this unusual group, researchers have been studying a clade of asexual rotifers named Bdelloidea. Some 360 species of bdelloid rotifers are known, and all of them reproduce by parthenogenesis without any males. Paleontologists have discovered bdelloid rotifers preserved in 35-million-year-old amber, and the morphology of these fossils resembles only the female form, with no evidence of males. By comparing the DNA of bdelloids with that of their closest sexually reproducing rotifer relatives, scientists have concluded that bdelloids have likely been asexual for 100 million years. How these animals manage to flout the general rule against long-lasting asexuality remains a puzzle.

Lophophorates: Ectoprocts and Brachiopods

Bilaterians in the phyla Ectoprocta and Brachiopoda are among those known as lophophorates. These animals have a *lophophore*, a crown of ciliated tentacles around their mouth (see Figure 32.13a). As the cilia draw water toward the mouth, the tentacles trap suspended food particles. Other similarities, such as a U-shaped alimentary canal and the absence of a distinct head, reflect these organisms' sessile existence. In contrast to flatworms, which lack a body cavity, and rotifers, which have a pseudocoelom, lophophorates have a true coelom that is completely lined by mesoderm (see Figure 32.8a).

Ectoprocts (from the Greek *ecto*, outside, and *procta*, anus) are colonial animals that superficially resemble clumps of moss. (In fact, their common name, bryozoans, means "moss animals.") In most species, the colony is encased in a hard **exoskeleton** (external skeleton) studded with pores through which the lophophores extend **(Figure 33.14a)**. Most ectoproct species live in the sea, where they are among the most widespread and numerous sessile animals. Several species are important reef builders. Ectoprocts also live in lakes and rivers. Colonies of the freshwater ectoproct *Pectinatella magnifica* grow on submerged sticks or rocks and can grow into a gelatinous, ball-shaped mass more than 10 cm across.

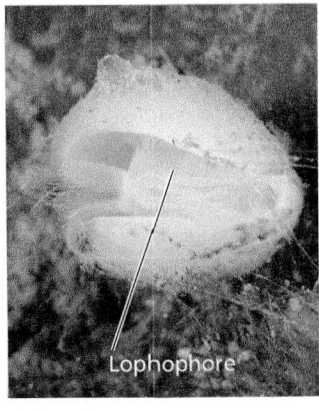

(a) Ectoprocts, such as this creeping bryozoan (*Plumatella repens*), are colonial lophophorates.

(b) Brachiopods, such as this lampshell (*Terebratulina retusa*), have a hinged shell. The two parts of the shell are dorsal and ventral.

▲ **Figure 33.14 Lophophorates.**

Brachiopods, or lamp shells, superficially resemble clams and other hinge-shelled molluscs, but the two halves of the brachiopod shell are dorsal and ventral rather than lateral, as in clams **(Figure 33.14b)**. All brachiopods are marine. Most live attached to the seafloor by a stalk, opening their shell slightly to allow water to flow through the lophophore. The living brachiopods are remnants of a much richer past that included 30,000 species in the Paleozoic and Mesozoic eras. Some living brachiopods, such as those in the genus *Lingula*, appear nearly identical to fossils of species that lived 400 million years ago.

Molluscs

Snails and slugs, oysters and clams, and octopuses and squids are all molluscs (phylum Mollusca). There are 93,000 known species, making them the second most diverse phylum of animals (after the arthropods, discussed later). Although the majority of molluscs are marine, roughly 8,000 species inhabit fresh water, and 28,000 species of snails and slugs live on land. All molluscs are soft-bodied (from the Latin *molluscus*, soft), and most secrete a hard protective shell made of calcium carbonate. Slugs, squids, and octopuses have a reduced internal shell or have lost their shell completely during their evolution.

Despite their apparent differences, all molluscs have a similar body plan **(Figure 33.15**, on the next page). Molluscs are coelomates, and their bodies have three main parts: a muscular **foot**, usually used for movement; a **visceral mass** containing most of the internal organs; and a **mantle**, a fold of tissue that drapes over the visceral mass and secretes a shell (if one is present). In many molluscs, the mantle extends beyond the visceral mass, producing a water-filled chamber, the **mantle cavity**, which houses the gills, anus, and excretory pores. Many molluscs feed by using a straplike organ called a **radula** to scrape up food.

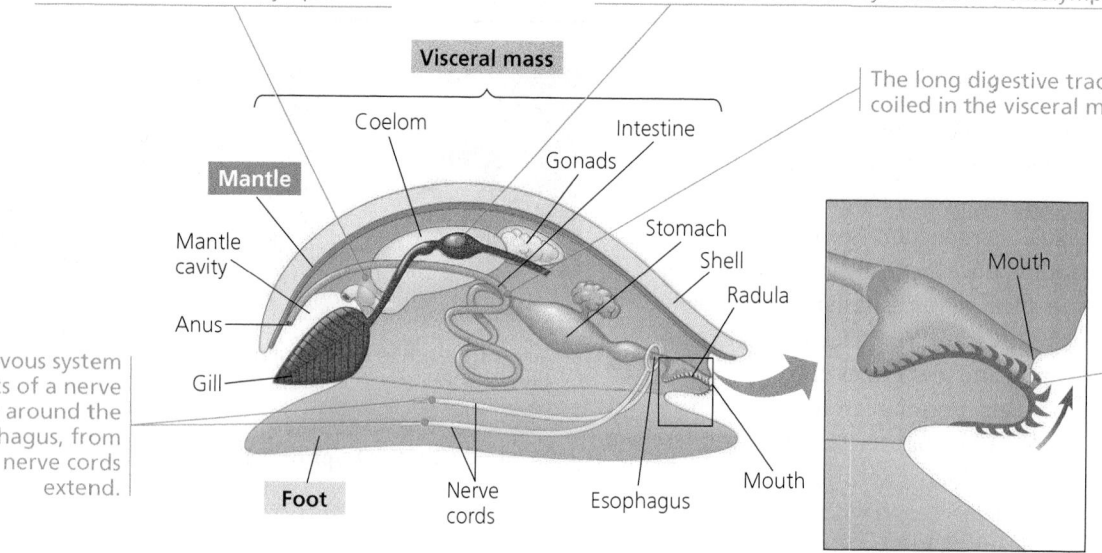

Nephridium. Excretory organs called nephridia remove metabolic wastes from the hemolymph.

Heart. Most molluscs have an open circulatory system. The dorsally located heart pumps circulatory fluid called hemolymph through arteries into sinuses (body spaces). The organs of the mollusc are thus continually bathed in hemolymph.

Visceral mass

Coelom

Intestine

Gonads

The long digestive tract is coiled in the visceral mass.

Mantle

Stomach

Shell

Mantle cavity

Radula

Anus

Mouth

The nervous system consists of a nerve ring around the esophagus, from which nerve cords extend.

Gill

Foot

Nerve cords

Esophagus

Mouth

Radula. The mouth region in many mollusc species contains a rasp-like feeding organ called a radula. This belt of backward-curved teeth repeatedly thrusts outward and then retracts into the mouth, scraping and scooping like a backhoe.

▲ Figure 33.15 **The basic body plan of a mollusc.**

Most molluscs have separate sexes, and their gonads (ovaries or testes) are located in the visceral mass. Many snails, however, are hermaphrodites. The life cycle of many marine molluscs includes a ciliated larval stage, the trochophore (see Figure 32.13b), which is also characteristic of marine annelids (segmented worms) and some other lophotrochozoans.

The basic body plan of molluscs has evolved in various ways in the phylum's seven or eight clades (experts disagree on the number). We'll examine four of those clades here: Polyplacophora (chitons), Gastropoda (snails and slugs), Bivalvia (clams, oysters, and other bivalves), and Cephalopoda (squids, octopuses, cuttlefishes, and chambered nautiluses). We will then focus on threats facing some groups of molluscs.

Chitons

Chitons have an oval-shaped body and a shell composed of eight dorsal plates (**Figure 33.16**). The chiton's body itself, however, is unsegmented. You can find these marine animals clinging to rocks along the shore during low tide. If you try to dislodge a chiton by hand, you will be surprised at how well its foot, acting as a suction cup, grips the rock. A chiton can also use its foot to creep slowly over the rock surface. Chitons use their radula to scrape algae off the rock surface.

Gastropods

About three-quarters of all living species of molluscs are gastropods (**Figure 33.17**). Most gastropods are marine, but there are also freshwater species. Still other gastropods have adapted to life on land, where snails and slugs thrive in habitats ranging from deserts to rain forests.

▲ Figure 33.16 **A chiton.** Note the eight-plate shell characteristic of molluscs in the clade Polyplacophora.

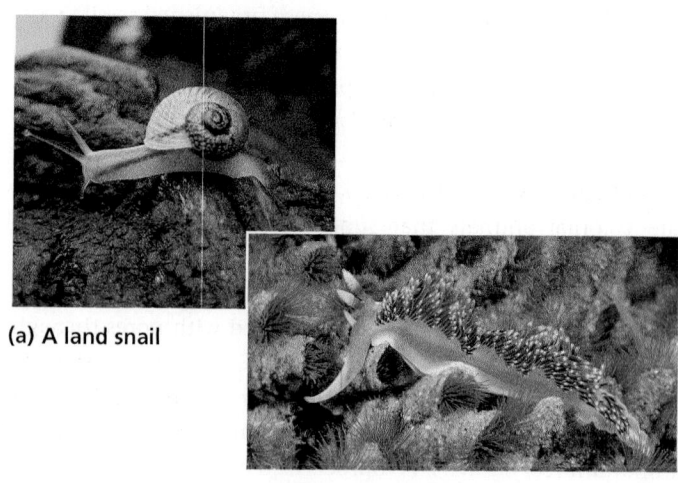

(a) A land snail

(b) A sea slug. Nudibranchs, or sea slugs, lost their shell during their evolution.

▲ Figure 33.17 **Gastropods.**

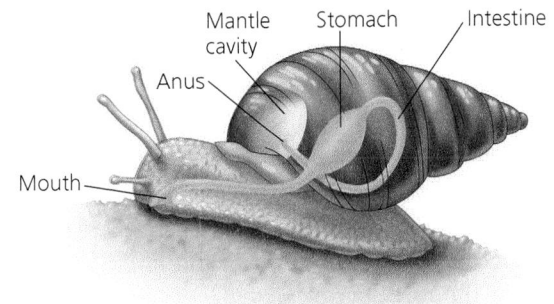

▲ **Figure 33.18 The results of torsion in a gastropod.** Because of torsion (twisting of the visceral mass) during embryonic development, the digestive tract is coiled and the anus is near the anterior end of the animal.

▲ **Figure 33.19 A bivalve.** This scallop has many eyes (dark blue spots) lining each half of its hinged shell.

Gastropods undergo a distinctive developmental process known as **torsion**. As a gastropod embryo develops, its visceral mass rotates up to 180°, causing the animal's anus and mantle cavity to wind up above its head (**Figure 33.18**). After torsion, some organs that were bilateral may be reduced in size, while others may be lost on one side of the body. Torsion should not be confused with the formation of a coiled shell, which is a separate developmental process.

Most gastropods have a single, spiraled shell into which the animal can retreat when threatened. The shell is often conical but is somewhat flattened in abalones and limpets. Many gastropods have a distinct head with eyes at the tips of tentacles. Gastropods move literally at a snail's pace by a rippling motion of their foot or by means of cilia, often leaving a trail of slime in their wake. Most gastropods use their radula to graze on algae or plants. Several groups, however, are predators, and their radula has become modified for boring holes in the shells of other molluscs or for tearing apart prey. In the cone snails, the teeth of the radula act as poison darts that are used to subdue prey (see the Unit 7 interview with Baldomero Olivera on pp. 850–851 to learn more about cone snails and their venom).

Terrestrial snails lack the gills typical of most aquatic gastropods. Instead, the lining of their mantle cavity functions as a lung, exchanging respiratory gases with the air.

Bivalves

The molluscs of the clade Bivalvia are all aquatic and include many species of clams, oysters, mussels, and scallops. Bivalves have a shell divided into two halves (**Figure 33.19**). The halves are hinged, and powerful adductor muscles draw them tightly together to protect the animal's soft body. Bivalves have no distinct head, and the radula has been lost. Some bivalves have eyes and sensory tentacles along the outer edge of their mantle.

The mantle cavity of a bivalve contains gills that are used for gas exchange as well as feeding in most species (**Figure 33.20**). Most bivalves are suspension feeders. They trap small food particles in mucus that coats their gills, and cilia then convey those particles to the mouth. Water enters the mantle cavity through an incurrent siphon, passes over the gills, and then exits the mantle cavity through an excurrent siphon.

Most bivalves lead sedentary lives, a characteristic suited to suspension feeding. Mussels secrete strong threads that tether them to rocks, docks, boats, and the shells of other animals. However, clams can pull themselves into the sand or mud, using their muscular foot for an anchor, and scallops can skitter along the seafloor by flapping their shells, rather like the mechanical false teeth sold in novelty shops.

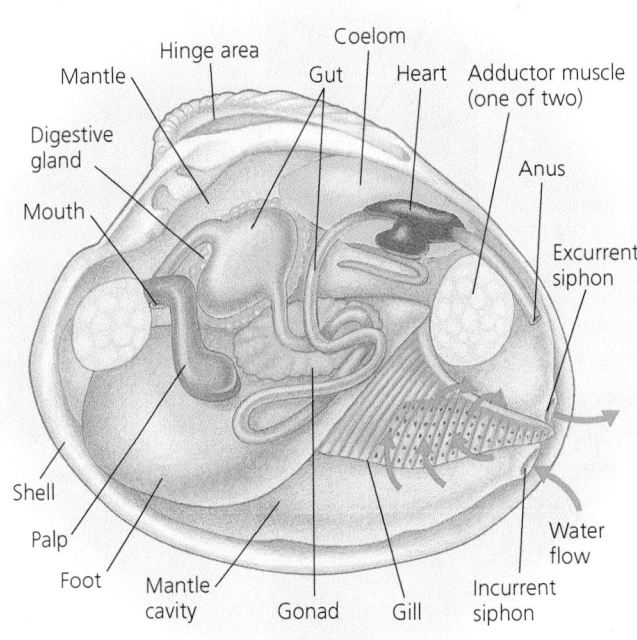

▲ **Figure 33.20 Anatomy of a clam.** Food particles suspended in water that enters through the incurrent siphon are collected by the gills and passed via cilia and the palps to the mouth.

Cephalopods

Cephalopods are active marine predators (Figure 33.21). They use their tentacles to grasp prey, which they then bite with beak-like jaws and immobilize with a poison present in their saliva. The foot of a cephalopod has become modified into a muscular excurrent siphon and part of the tentacles. Squids dart about by drawing water into their mantle cavity and then firing a jet of water through the excurrent siphon; they steer by pointing the siphon in different directions. Octopuses use a similar mechanism to escape predators.

The mantle covers the visceral mass of cephalopods, but the shell is generally reduced and internal (in most species) or missing altogether (in some cuttlefishes and some octopuses). One small group of cephalopods with external shells, the chambered nautiluses, survives today.

Cephalopods are the only molluscs with a *closed circulatory system*, in which the blood remains separate from fluid in the body cavity. They also have well-developed sense organs and a complex brain. The ability to learn and behave in a complex manner is probably more critical to fast-moving predators than to sedentary animals such as clams.

The ancestors of octopuses and squids were probably shelled molluscs that took up a predatory lifestyle; the shell was lost in later evolution. Shelled cephalopods called **ammonites**, some of them as large as truck tires, were the dominant invertebrate predators of the seas for hundreds of millions of years until their disappearance during the mass extinction at the end of the Cretaceous period, 65.5 million years ago (see Table 25.1).

Most species of squid are less than 75 cm long, but some are considerably larger. The giant squid *Architeuthis dux* was for a long time the largest squid known, with a mantle up to 2.25 m long and a total length of 18 m. In 2003, however, a specimen of the rare species *Mesonychoteuthis hamiltoni* was caught near Antarctica; its mantle was 2.5 m long. Some biologists think that this specimen was a juvenile and estimate that adults of its species could be twice as large! Unlike *A. dux*, which has large suckers and small teeth on its tentacles, *M. hamiltoni* has two rows of sharp hooks at the ends of its tentacles that can inflict deadly lacerations.

It is likely that *A. dux* and *M. hamiltoni* spend most of their time in the deep ocean, where they may feed on large fishes. Remains of both giant squid species have been found in the stomachs of sperm whales, which are probably their only natural predator. In 2005, scientists reported the first observations of *A. dux* in the wild, photographed while attacking baited hooks at a depth of 900 m. *M. hamiltoni* has yet to be observed in nature. Overall, these marine giants remain among the great mysteries of invertebrate life.

Protecting Freshwater and Terrestrial Molluscs

Species extinction rates have increased dramatically in the last 400 years, raising concern that a sixth, human-caused mass extinction may be under way (see Chapter 25). Among the many taxa under threat, molluscs have the dubious distinction of being the animal group with the largest number of documented extinctions (Figure 33.22).

Threats to molluscs are especially severe in two groups, freshwater bivalves and terrestrial gastropods. The pearl mussels, a group of freshwater bivalves that can make natural pearls (gems that form when a mussel or oyster secretes layers of a lustrous coating around a grain of sand or other small irritant), are among the world's most endangered animals. Roughly 10% of the 300 pearl mussel species that once lived in North America have become extinct in the last 100 years, and over two-thirds of those that remain are threatened by extinction. Terrestrial gastropods, such as the snail in Figure 33.22, fare no better. Hundreds of Pacific island land snails have disappeared since 1800. Overall, more than 50% of the Pacific island land snails are extinct or under imminent threat of extinction.

Threats faced by freshwater and terrestrial molluscs include habitat loss, pollution, and competition or predation by non-native species introduced by people. Is it too late to protect these molluscs? In some locations, reducing water pollution and changing how water is released from dams have led to dramatic rebounds in pearl mussel populations. Such results provide hope that with corrective measures, other endangered mollusc species can be revived.

▸ Squids are speedy carnivores with beak-like jaws and well-developed eyes.

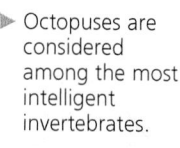

▸ Octopuses are considered among the most intelligent invertebrates.

◂ Chambered nautiluses are the only living cephalopods with an external shell.

▲ **Figure 33.21 Cephalopods.**

IMPACT

Molluscs: The Silent Extinction

Molluscs account for a largely unheralded but sobering 40% of all documented extinctions of animal species. These extinctions have resulted from habitat loss, pollution, introduced species, overharvesting, and other human actions. Many pearl mussel populations, for example, were driven to extinction by overharvesting for their shells, which were used to make buttons and other goods. Today, remaining populations of these and other freshwater bivalves face threats from pollution and introduced species. Terrestrial gastropods such as the species pictured above are highly vulnerable to the same threats and are among the world's most imperiled animal groups.

▲ An endangered Pacific island land snail, *Partula suturalis*

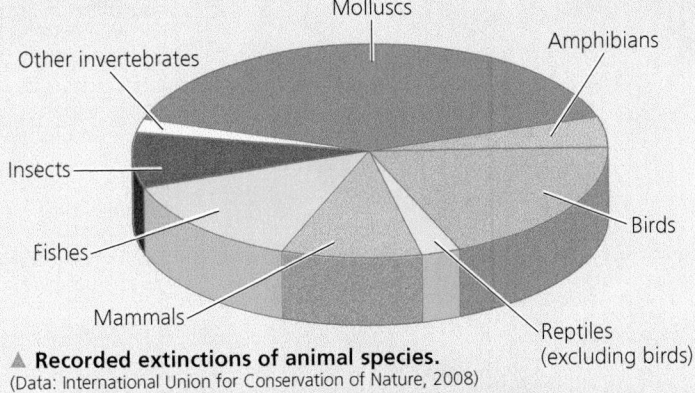

▲ **Recorded extinctions of animal species.**
(Data: International Union for Conservation of Nature, 2008)

▲ Workers on a mound of pearl mussels killed to make buttons (ca. 1919)

WHY IT MATTERS The extinctions of molluscs represent an irreversible loss of biological diversity and greatly threaten other organisms, too. Land snails, for example, play a key role in nutrient cycling, while the filtering activities of freshwater bivalves purify the waters of streams, rivers, and lakes.

FURTHER READING C. Lydeard et al., The global decline of nonmarine mollusks, *BioScience* 54:321–330 (2004).

MAKE CONNECTIONS Freshwater bivalves feed on and can reduce the abundance of photosynthetic protists and bacteria. As such, would the extinction of freshwater bivalves likely have weak or strong effects on aquatic communities (see Concept 28.7, p. 597)? Explain.

◀ **Figure 33.23 A polychaete.** *Hesiolyra bergi* lives on the seafloor around deep-sea hydrothermal vents.

Parapodia

Annelids

Annelida means "little rings," referring to the annelid body's resemblance to a series of fused rings. Annelids are segmented worms that live in the sea, in most freshwater habitats, and in damp soil. Annelids are coelomates, and they range in length from less than 1 mm to more than 3 m, the length of a giant Australian earthworm.

The phylum Annelida can be divided into two main groups: Polychaeta (the polychaetes) and Oligochaeta (the earthworms and their relatives, and the leeches). Some recent phylogenetic analyses have suggested that the oligochaetes are actually a subgroup of the polychaetes. However, since this idea continues to be debated, we discuss polychaetes and oligochaetes separately.

Polychaetes

Each segment of a polychaete (from the Greek *poly*, many, and *chaitē*, long hair) has a pair of paddle-like or ridge-like structures called parapodia ("beside feet") that function in locomotion **(Figure 33.23)**. Each parapodium has numerous chaetae, bristles made of chitin. In many polychaetes, the parapodia are richly supplied with blood vessels and also function as gills.

Polychaetes make up a large and diverse group, most of whose members are marine. A few species drift and swim among the plankton, many crawl on or burrow in the seafloor, and many others live in tubes. Some tube-dwellers, such as the fan worms, build their tubes by mixing mucus with bits of sand and broken shells. Others, such as Christmas tree worms (see Figure 33.1), construct tubes using only their own secretions.

Oligochaetes

Oligochaetes (*oligos*, few, and *chaitē*, long hair) are named for their relatively sparse chaetae (far fewer per segment than in polychaetes). Molecular data indicate that these segmented worms form a diverse clade that includes the earthworms and their aquatic relatives, along with the leeches.

Earthworms Earthworms eat their way through the soil, extracting nutrients as the soil passes through the alimentary canal.

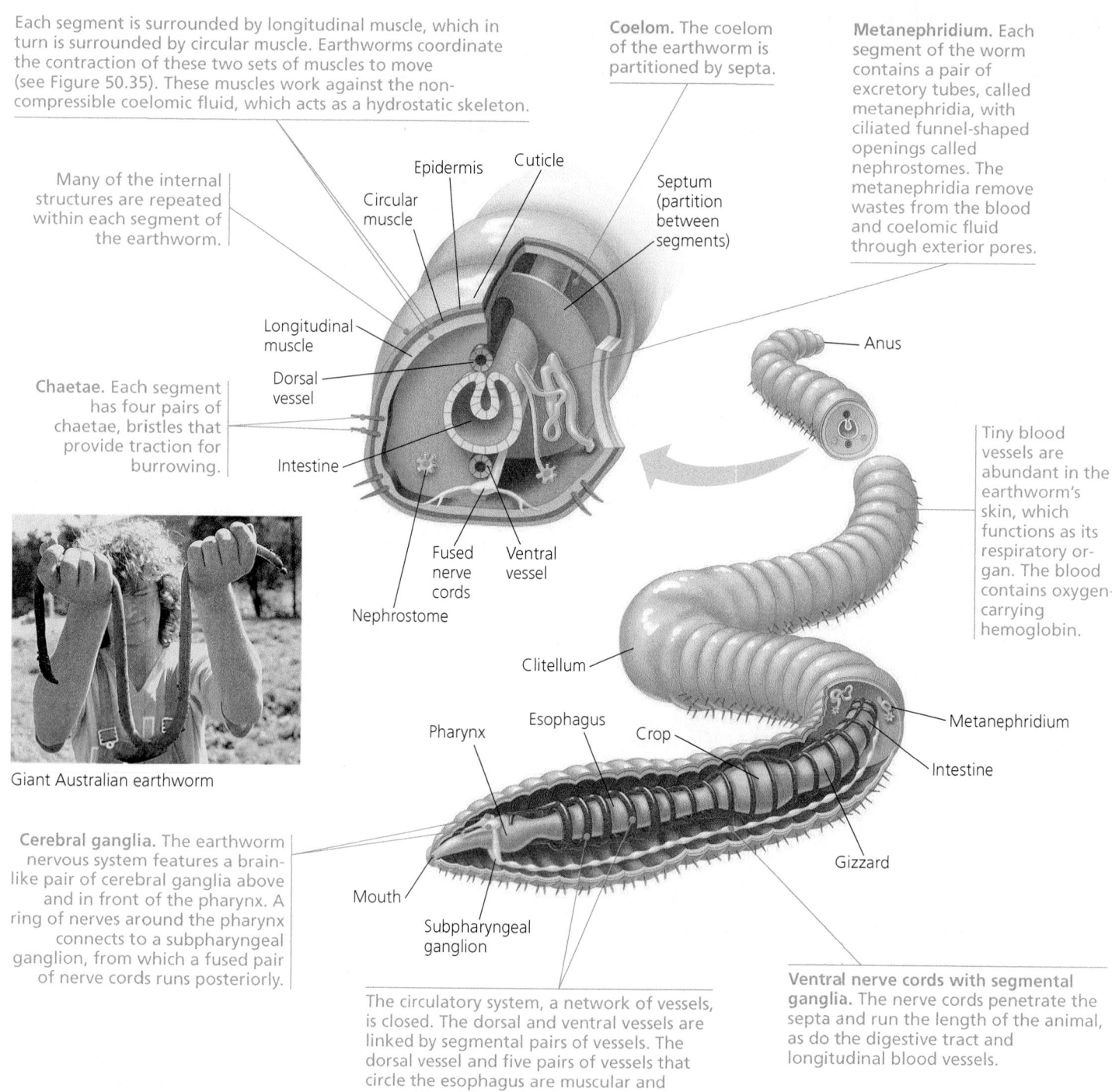

Each segment is surrounded by longitudinal muscle, which in turn is surrounded by circular muscle. Earthworms coordinate the contraction of these two sets of muscles to move (see Figure 50.35). These muscles work against the non-compressible coelomic fluid, which acts as a hydrostatic skeleton.

Many of the internal structures are repeated within each segment of the earthworm.

Chaetae. Each segment has four pairs of chaetae, bristles that provide traction for burrowing.

Giant Australian earthworm

Cerebral ganglia. The earthworm nervous system features a brain-like pair of cerebral ganglia above and in front of the pharynx. A ring of nerves around the pharynx connects to a subpharyngeal ganglion, from which a fused pair of nerve cords runs posteriorly.

Coelom. The coelom of the earthworm is partitioned by septa.

Metanephridium. Each segment of the worm contains a pair of excretory tubes, called metanephridia, with ciliated funnel-shaped openings called nephrostomes. The metanephridia remove wastes from the blood and coelomic fluid through exterior pores.

Epidermis
Cuticle
Circular muscle
Septum (partition between segments)

Longitudinal muscle
Dorsal vessel
Intestine

Anus

Tiny blood vessels are abundant in the earthworm's skin, which functions as its respiratory organ. The blood contains oxygen-carrying hemoglobin.

Fused nerve cords
Ventral vessel
Nephrostome

Clitellum

Metanephridium
Intestine

Pharynx
Esophagus
Crop

Mouth
Subpharyngeal ganglion

Gizzard

The circulatory system, a network of vessels, is closed. The dorsal and ventral vessels are linked by segmental pairs of vessels. The dorsal vessel and five pairs of vessels that circle the esophagus are muscular and pump blood through the circulatory system.

Ventral nerve cords with segmental ganglia. The nerve cords penetrate the septa and run the length of the animal, as do the digestive tract and longitudinal blood vessels.

▲ **Figure 33.24 Anatomy of an earthworm, an oligochaete.**

Undigested material, mixed with mucus secreted into the canal, is eliminated as fecal castings through the anus. Farmers value earthworms because the animals till and aerate the earth, and their castings improve the texture of the soil. (Charles Darwin estimated that a single acre of British farmland contains about 50,000 earthworms, producing 18 tons of castings per year.)

A guided tour of the anatomy of an earthworm, which is representative of annelids, is shown in **Figure 33.24**. Earthworms are hermaphrodites, but they do cross-fertilize. Two earthworms mate by aligning themselves in opposite directions in such a way that they exchange sperm, and then they separate. The received sperm are stored temporarily while an organ called the clitellum secretes a cocoon of mucus. The cocoon slides along the worm, picking up the eggs and then the stored sperm. The cocoon then slips off the worm's head and remains in the soil while the embryos develop. Some earthworms can also reproduce asexually by fragmentation followed by regeneration.

▶ **Figure 33.25 A leech.** A nurse applied this medicinal leech (*Hirudo medicinalis*) to a patient's sore thumb to drain blood from a hematoma (an abnormal accumulation of blood around an internal injury).

Leeches Most leeches inhabit fresh water, but there are also marine species and terrestrial leeches, which live in moist vegetation. Leeches range in length from 1 to 30 cm. Many are predators that feed on other invertebrates, but some are parasites that suck blood by attaching temporarily to other animals, including humans (**Figure 33.25**). Some parasitic species use bladelike jaws to slit the skin of their host, whereas others secrete enzymes that digest a hole through the skin. The host is usually oblivious to this attack because the leech secretes an anesthetic. After making the incision, the leech secretes another chemical, hirudin, which keeps the blood of the host from coagulating near the incision. The parasite then sucks as much blood as it can hold, often more than ten times its own weight. After this gorging, a leech can last for months without another meal.

Until the 20th century, leeches were frequently used for bloodletting. Today they are used to drain blood that accumulates in tissues following certain injuries or surgeries. Researchers have also investigated the potential use of purified hirudin to dissolve unwanted blood clots that form during surgery or as a result of heart disease. Several forms of hirudin have been developed using recombinant DNA techniques; two of these were recently approved for clinical use.

As a group, Lophotrochozoa encompasses a remarkable range of body plans, as illustrated by members of such phyla as Rotifera, Ectoprocta, Mollusca, and Annelida. Next we'll explore the diversity of Ecdysozoa, a dominant presence on Earth in terms of sheer number of species.

CONCEPT CHECK 33.3

1. Explain how tapeworms can survive without a coelom, a mouth, a digestive system, or an excretory system.
2. Annelid anatomy can be described as "a tube within a tube." Explain.
3. **MAKE CONNECTIONS** Explain how the molluscan foot in gastropods and the excurrent siphon in cephalopods represent an example of descent with modification (see Concept 22.2, pp. 457–460).

For suggested answers, see Appendix A.

CONCEPT 33.4

Ecdysozoans are the most species-rich animal group

Porifera
Cnidaria
Lophotrochozoa
Ecdysozoa
Deuterostomia

Although defined primarily by molecular evidence, the clade Ecdysozoa includes animals that shed a tough external coat (**cuticle**) as they grow; in fact, the group derives its name from this process, which is called *ecdysis*, or **molting**. Ecdysozoa consists of about eight animal phyla and contains more known species than all other animal, protist, fungus, and plant groups combined. Here we'll focus on the two largest ecdysozoan phyla, the nematodes and arthropods, which are among the most successful and abundant of all animal groups.

Nematodes

Among the most ubiquitous of animals, nematodes (phylum Nematoda), or roundworms, are found in most aquatic habitats, in the soil, in the moist tissues of plants, and in the body fluids and tissues of animals. In contrast to annelids, nematodes do not have segmented bodies. The cylindrical bodies of nematodes range from less than 1 mm to more than 1 m long, often tapering to a fine tip at the posterior end and to a blunter tip at the anterior end (**Figure 33.26**). A nematode's body is covered by a tough cuticle (a type of exoskeleton); as the worm grows, it periodically sheds its old cuticle and secretes a new, larger one. Nematodes have an alimentary canal, though they lack a circulatory system. Nutrients are transported throughout the body via fluid in the pseudocoelom. The body wall muscles are all longitudinal, and their contraction produces a thrashing motion.

Nematodes usually reproduce sexually, by internal fertilization. In most species, the sexes are separate and females are larger than males. A female may deposit 100,000 or more fertilized eggs (zygotes) per day. The zygotes of most species are resistant cells that can survive harsh conditions.

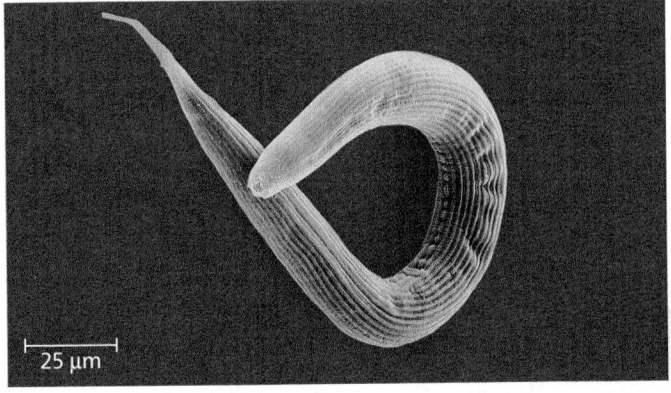

25 μm

▲ **Figure 33.26 A free-living nematode** (colorized SEM).

Multitudes of nematodes live in moist soil and in decomposing organic matter on the bottoms of lakes and oceans. While 25,000 species are known, perhaps 20 times that number actually exist. It has been said that if nothing of Earth or its organisms remained but nematodes, they would still preserve the outline of the planet and many of its features. These free-living worms play an important role in decomposition and nutrient cycling, but little is known about most species. One species of soil nematode, *Caenorhabditis elegans*, however, is very well studied and has become a model research organism in biology (see Chapter 47). Ongoing studies of *C. elegans* are revealing some of the mechanisms involved in aging in humans, among other findings.

Phylum Nematoda includes many species that parasitize plants, and some are major agricultural pests that attack the roots of crops. Other nematodes parasitize animals. Some of these species benefit humans by attacking insects such as cutworms that feed on the roots of crop plants. On the other hand, humans are hosts to at least 50 nematode species, including various pinworms and hookworms. One notorious nematode is *Trichinella spiralis*, the worm that causes trichinosis (**Figure 33.27**). Humans acquire this nematode by eating raw or undercooked pork or other meat (including wild game such as bear or walrus) that has juvenile worms encysted in the muscle tissue. Within the human intestines, the juveniles develop into sexually mature adults. Females burrow into the intestinal muscles and produce more juveniles, which bore through the body or travel in lymphatic vessels to other organs, including skeletal muscles, where they encyst.

Parasitic nematodes have an extraordinary molecular toolkit that enables them to redirect some of the cellular functions of their hosts and thus evade their immune systems. Some species inject their plant hosts with molecules that induce the development of root cells, which then supply nutrients to the parasites. *Trichinella*, which parasitizes animals, controls the expression of specific muscle cell genes that code for proteins that make the cell elastic enough to house the nematode. Additionally, the infected muscle cell releases signals that promote the growth of new blood vessels, which then supply the nematode with nutrients.

Arthropods

Zoologists estimate that there are about a billion billion (10^{18}) arthropods living on Earth. More than 1 million arthropod species have been described, most of which are insects. In fact, two out of every three known species are arthropods, and members of the phylum Arthropoda can be found in nearly all habitats of the biosphere. By the criteria of species diversity, distribution, and sheer numbers, arthropods must be regarded as the most successful of all animal phyla.

Arthropod Origins

Biologists hypothesize that the diversity and success of **arthropods** are related to their body plan—their segmented body, hard exoskeleton, and jointed appendages (*arthropod* means "jointed feet"). The earliest fossils with this body plan are from the Cambrian explosion (535–525 million years ago), indicating that the arthropods are at least that old.

Along with arthropods, the fossil record of the Cambrian explosion contains many species of *lobopods*, an extinct group from which arthropods may have evolved. Lobopods such as *Hallucigenia* (see Figure 25.4) had segmented bodies, but most of their body segments were identical to one another. Early arthropods, such as the trilobites, also showed little variation from segment to segment (**Figure 33.28**). As arthropods continued to evolve, the segments tended to fuse and become fewer, and the appendages became specialized for a variety of functions. These evolutionary changes resulted not only in great diversification but also in an efficient body plan that permits the division of labor among different body regions.

Encysted juveniles   Muscle tissue   ├── 50 μm ──┤

▲ Figure 33.27 **Juveniles of the parasitic nematode** *Trichinella spiralis* **encysted in human muscle tissue** (LM).

▶ **Figure 33.28 A trilobite fossil.** Trilobites were common denizens of the shallow seas throughout the Paleozoic era but disappeared with the great Permian extinctions about 250 million years ago. Paleontologists have described about 4,000 trilobite species.

▼ Figure 33.29

INQUIRY

Did the arthropod body plan result from new Hox genes?

EXPERIMENT How did the highly successful arthropod body plan arise? One hypothesis suggests that it resulted from the origin (by a gene duplication event) of two unusual *Hox* genes found in arthropods: *Ultrabithorax* (*Ubx*) and *abdominal-A* (*abd-A*). To test this hypothesis, Sean Carroll, of the University of Wisconsin, Madison, and colleagues turned to the onychophorans, a group of invertebrates closely related to arthropods. Unlike many living arthropods, onychophorans have a body plan in which most body segments are identical to one another. Thus, Carroll and colleagues reasoned that if the origin of the *Ubx* and *abd-A Hox* genes drove the evolution of body segment diversity in arthropods, these genes probably arose on the arthropod branch of the evolutionary tree:

According to this hypothesis, *Ubx* and *abd-A* would not have been present in the common ancestor of arthropods and onychophorans; hence, onychophorans should not have these genes. To find out whether this was the case, Carroll and colleagues examined the *Hox* genes of the onychophoran *Acanthokara kaputensis*.

RESULTS The onychophoran *A. kaputensis* has all arthropod *Hox* genes, including *Ubx* and *abd-A*.

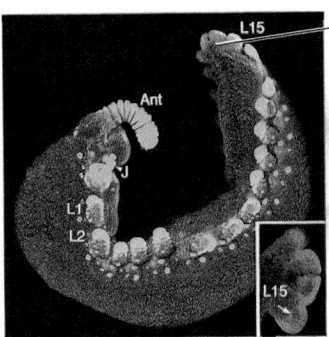

Red indicates the body regions of this onychophoran embryo in which *Ubx* or *abd-A* genes were expressed. (The inset shows this area enlarged.)

Ant = antenna
J = jaws
L1–L15 = body segments

CONCLUSION Since *A. kaputensis*, an onychophoran, has the arthropod *Hox* genes, the evolution of increased body segment diversity in arthropods must not have been related to the origin of new *Hox* genes.

SOURCE J. K. Grenier, S. Carroll, et al., Evolution of the entire arthropod *Hox* gene set predated the origin and radiation of the onychophoran/arthropod clade, *Current Biology* 7:547–553 (1997).

WHAT IF? If Carroll and colleagues had found that *A. kaputensis* did *not* have the *Ubx* and *abd-A Hox* genes, how would their conclusion have been affected? Explain.

What genetic changes led to the increasing complexity of the arthropod body plan? Arthropods today have two unusual *Hox* genes, both of which influence segmentation. To test whether these genes could have driven the evolution of increased body segment diversity in arthropods, researchers studied *Hox* genes in onychophorans (see Figure 33.3), close relatives of arthropods (Figure 33.29). Their results indicate that arthropod body plan diversity did *not* arise from the acquisition of new *Hox* genes. Instead, the evolution of body segment diversity in arthropods may have been driven by changes in the sequence or regulation of existing *Hox* genes. (See Chapter 25 for a discussion of how changes in form can result from changes in the sequence or regulation of developmental genes such as *Hox* genes.)

General Characteristics of Arthropods

Over the course of evolution, the appendages of some arthropods have become modified, specializing in functions such as walking, feeding, sensory reception, reproduction, and defense. Like the appendages from which they were derived, these modified structures are jointed and come in pairs. Figure 33.30 illustrates the diverse appendages and other arthropod characteristics of a lobster.

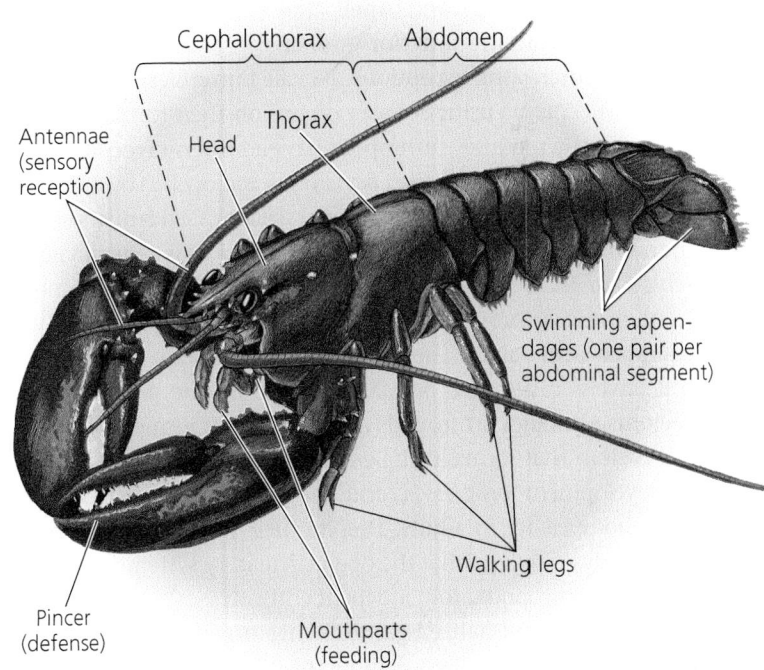

▲ **Figure 33.30 External anatomy of an arthropod.** Many of the distinctive features of arthropods are apparent in this dorsal view of a lobster, along with some uniquely crustacean characteristics. The body is segmented, but this characteristic is obvious only in the abdomen. The appendages (including antennae, pincers, mouthparts, walking legs, and swimming appendages) are jointed. The head bears a pair of compound (multilens) eyes, each situated on a movable stalk. The whole body, including appendages, is covered by an exoskeleton.

The body of an arthropod is completely covered by the cuticle, an exoskeleton constructed from layers of protein and the polysaccharide chitin. The cuticle can be thick and hard over some parts of the body and paper-thin and flexible over others, such as the joints. The rigid exoskeleton protects the animal and provides points of attachment for the muscles that move the appendages. But it also means that an arthropod cannot grow without occasionally shedding its exoskeleton and producing a larger one. This molting process is energetically expensive. A molting or recently molted arthropod is also vulnerable to predation and other dangers until its new, soft exoskeleton hardens.

When the arthropod exoskeleton first evolved in the sea, its main functions were probably protection and anchorage for muscles, but it later enabled certain arthropods to live on land. The exoskeleton's relative impermeability to water helped prevent desiccation, and its strength solved the problem of support when arthropods left the buoyancy of water. Arthropods began to diversify on land following the colonization of land by plants in the early Paleozoic. Evidence includes a 428-million-year-old fossil of a millipede found in 2004 by an amateur fossil hunter in Scotland. Fossilized tracks of other terrestrial arthropods date from about 450 million years ago.

Arthropods have well-developed sensory organs, including eyes, olfactory (smell) receptors, and antennae that function in both touch and smell. Most sensory organs are concentrated at the anterior end of the animal, although there are interesting exceptions. Female butterflies, for example, "taste" plants using sensory organs on their feet.

Like many molluscs, arthropods have an **open circulatory system**, in which fluid called *hemolymph* is propelled by a heart through short arteries and then into spaces called sinuses surrounding the tissues and organs. (The term *blood* is generally reserved for fluid in a closed circulatory system.) Hemolymph reenters the arthropod heart through pores that are usually equipped with valves. The hemolymph-filled body sinuses are collectively called the *hemocoel*, which is not part of the coelom. Although arthropods are coelomates, in most species the coelom that forms in the embryo becomes much reduced as development progresses, and the hemocoel becomes the main body cavity in adults. Despite their similarity, phylogenetic analyses suggest that the open circulatory systems of molluscs and arthropods arose independently.

A variety of specialized gas exchange organs have evolved in arthropods. These organs allow the diffusion of respiratory gases in spite of the exoskeleton. Most aquatic species have gills with thin, feathery extensions that place an extensive surface area in contact with the surrounding water. Terrestrial arthropods generally have internal surfaces specialized for gas exchange. Most insects, for instance, have tracheal systems, branched air ducts leading into the interior from pores in the cuticle.

▲ **Figure 33.31** **Horseshoe crabs (*Limulus polyphemus*).** Common on the Atlantic and Gulf coasts of the United States, these "living fossils" have changed little in hundreds of millions of years. They are surviving members of a rich diversity of chelicerates that once filled the seas.

Morphological and molecular evidence suggests that living arthropods consist of four major lineages that diverged early in the evolution of the phylum: **chelicerates** (sea spiders, horseshoe crabs, scorpions, ticks, mites, and spiders); **myriapods** (centipedes and millipedes); **hexapods** (insects and their wingless, six-legged relatives); and **crustaceans** (crabs, lobsters, shrimps, barnacles, and many others).

Chelicerates

Chelicerates (subphylum Chelicerata; from the Greek *cheilos*, lips, and *cheir*, arm) are named for clawlike feeding appendages called **chelicerae**, which serve as pincers or fangs. Chelicerates have an anterior cephalothorax and a posterior abdomen. They lack antennae, and most have simple eyes (eyes with a single lens).

The earliest chelicerates were **eurypterids**, or water scorpions. These marine and freshwater predators grew up to 3 m long; it is thought that some species could have walked on land, much as land crabs do today. Most of the marine chelicerates, including all of the eurypterids, are extinct. Among the marine chelicerates that survive today are the sea spiders (pycnogonids) and horseshoe crabs (**Figure 33.31**).

The bulk of modern chelicerates are **arachnids**, a group that includes scorpions, spiders, ticks, and mites (**Figure 33.32**). Ticks and many mites are among a large group of parasitic arthropods. Nearly all ticks are bloodsucking parasites that live on the body surfaces of reptiles or mammals. Parasitic mites live on or in a wide variety of vertebrates, invertebrates, and plants.

Arachnids have a cephalothorax that has six pairs of appendages: the chelicerae; a pair of appendages called *pedipalps* that function in sensing, feeding, or reproduction; and four pairs of walking legs (**Figure 33.33**). Spiders use their fang-like chelicerae, which are equipped with poison glands, to attack

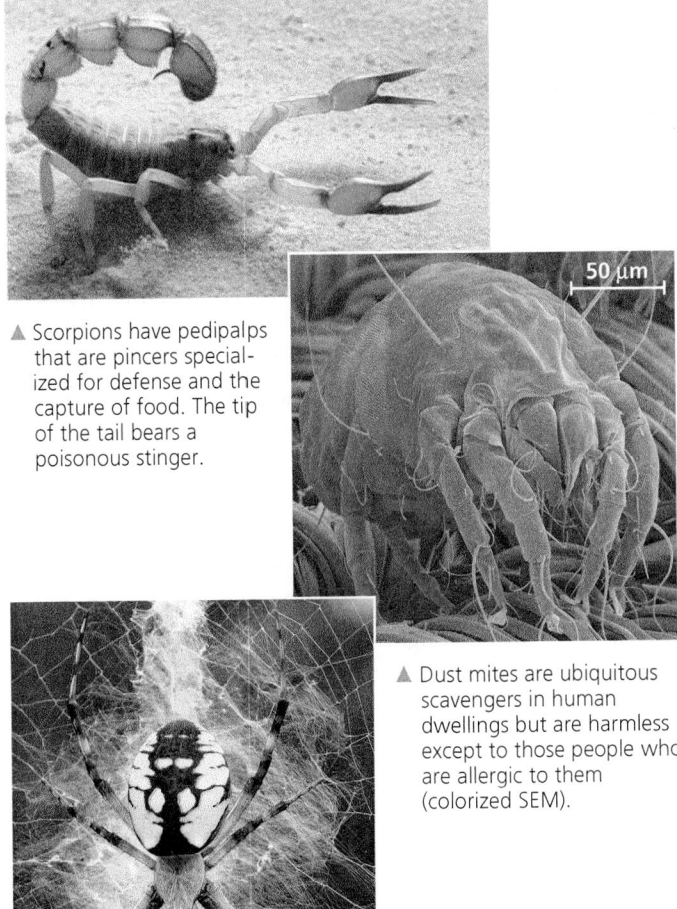

▲ Scorpions have pedipalps that are pincers specialized for defense and the capture of food. The tip of the tail bears a poisonous stinger.

50 μm

▲ Dust mites are ubiquitous scavengers in human dwellings but are harmless except to those people who are allergic to them (colorized SEM).

◀ Web-building spiders are generally most active during the daytime.

▲ **Figure 33.32 Arachnids.**

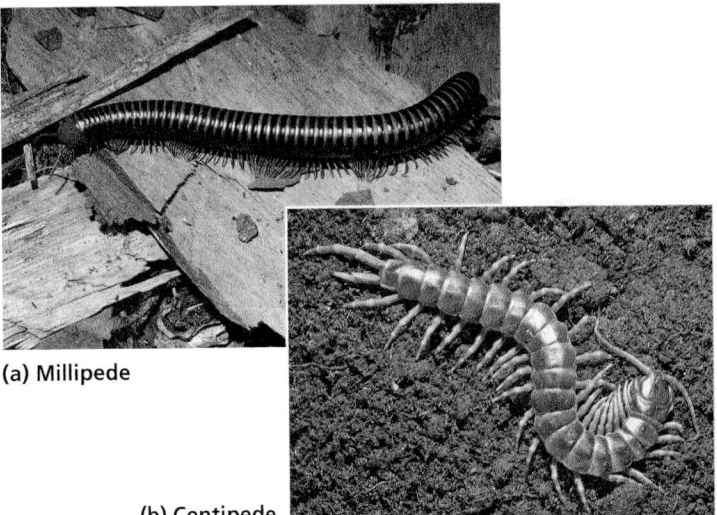

(a) Millipede

(b) Centipede

▲ Figure 33.34 **Myriapods.**

prey. As the chelicerae pierce the prey, the spider secretes digestive juices onto the prey's torn tissues. The food softens, and the spider sucks up the liquid meal.

In most spiders, gas exchange is carried out by **book lungs**, stacked platelike structures contained in an internal chamber (see Figure 33.33). The extensive surface area of these respiratory organs is a structural adaptation that enhances the exchange of O_2 and CO_2 between the hemolymph and air.

A unique adaptation of many spiders is the ability to catch insects by constructing webs of silk, a liquid protein produced by specialized abdominal glands. The silk is spun by organs called spinnerets into fibers that then solidify. Each spider engineers a web characteristic of its species and builds it perfectly on the first try, indicating that this complex behavior is inherited. Various spiders also use silk in other ways: as droplines for rapid escape, as a cover for eggs, and even as "gift wrap" for food that males offer females during courtship. Many small spiders also extrude silk into the air and let themselves be transported by wind, a behavior known as "ballooning."

Myriapods

Millipedes and centipedes belong to the subphylum Myriapoda (**Figure 33.34**). All living myriapods are terrestrial. The myriapod head has a pair of antennae and three pairs of appendages modified as mouthparts, including the jaw-like **mandibles**.

Millipedes have a large number of legs, though fewer than the thousand their name implies. Each trunk segment is formed from two fused segments and bears two pairs of legs (see Figure 33.34a). Millipedes eat decaying leaves and other plant matter. They may have been among the earliest animals on land, living on mosses and early vascular plants.

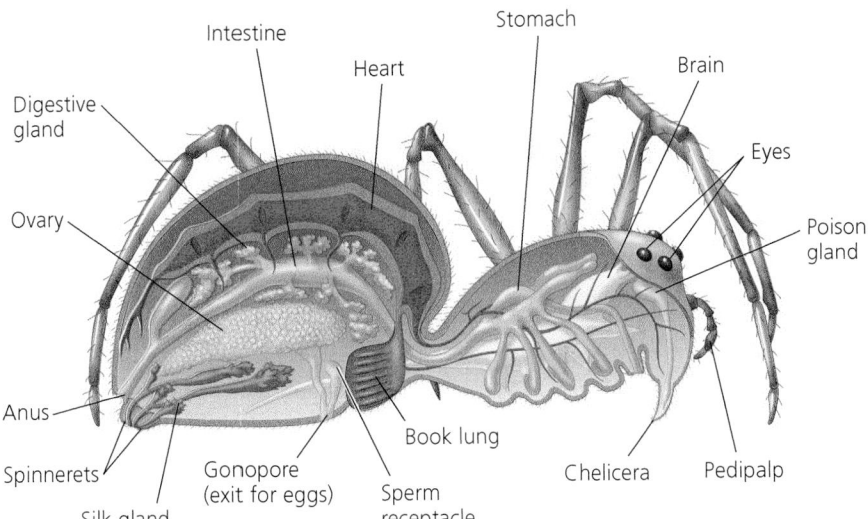

Intestine
Stomach
Heart
Brain
Digestive gland
Eyes
Ovary
Poison gland
Anus
Book lung
Spinnerets
Gonopore (exit for eggs)
Chelicera
Pedipalp
Silk gland
Sperm receptacle

▲ **Figure 33.33 Anatomy of a spider.**

Unlike millipedes, centipedes are carnivores. Each segment of a centipede's trunk region has one pair of legs (see Figure 33.34b). Centipedes have poison claws on their foremost trunk segment that paralyze prey and aid in defense.

Insects

Insects and their relatives (subphylum Hexapoda) are more species-rich than all other forms of life combined. They live in almost every terrestrial habitat and in fresh water, and flying insects fill the air. Insects are rare, though not absent, in marine habitats, where crustaceans are the dominant arthropods. The internal anatomy of an insect includes several complex organ systems, which are highlighted in **Figure 33.35**.

The oldest insect fossils date from the Devonian period, which began about 416 million years ago. However, when insect flight evolved during the Carboniferous and Permian periods, it spurred an explosion in insect diversity. A fossil record of diverse insect mouthparts indicates that specialized feeding on gymnosperms and other Carboniferous plants also contributed to early adaptive radiations of insects. Later, a major increase in insect diversity appears to have been stimulated by the evolutionary expansion of flowering plants

during the mid-Cretaceous period (about 90 million years ago). Although insect and plant diversity decreased during the Cretaceous mass extinction, both groups rebounded over the next 65 million years. Studies indicate that increases in the diversity of particular insect groups often were associated with radiations of the flowering plants on which they fed.

Flight is obviously one key to the great success of insects. An animal that can fly can escape many predators, find food and mates, and disperse to new habitats much faster than an animal that must crawl about on the ground. Many insects have one or two pairs of wings that emerge from the dorsal side of the thorax **(Figure 33.36)**. Because the wings are extensions of the cuticle and not true appendages, insects can fly without sacrificing any walking legs. By contrast, the flying vertebrates—birds and bats—have one of their two pairs of walking legs modified into wings, making some of these species clumsy on the ground.

Insect wings may have first evolved as extensions of the cuticle that helped the insect body absorb heat, only later becoming organs for flight. Other hypotheses suggest that wings allowed terrestrial insects to glide from vegetation to the ground or that they served as gills in aquatic insects. Still another hypothesis is that insect wings functioned for swimming before they functioned for flight.

The insect body has three regions: head, thorax, and abdomen. The segmentation of the thorax and abdomen is obvious, but the segments that form the head are fused.

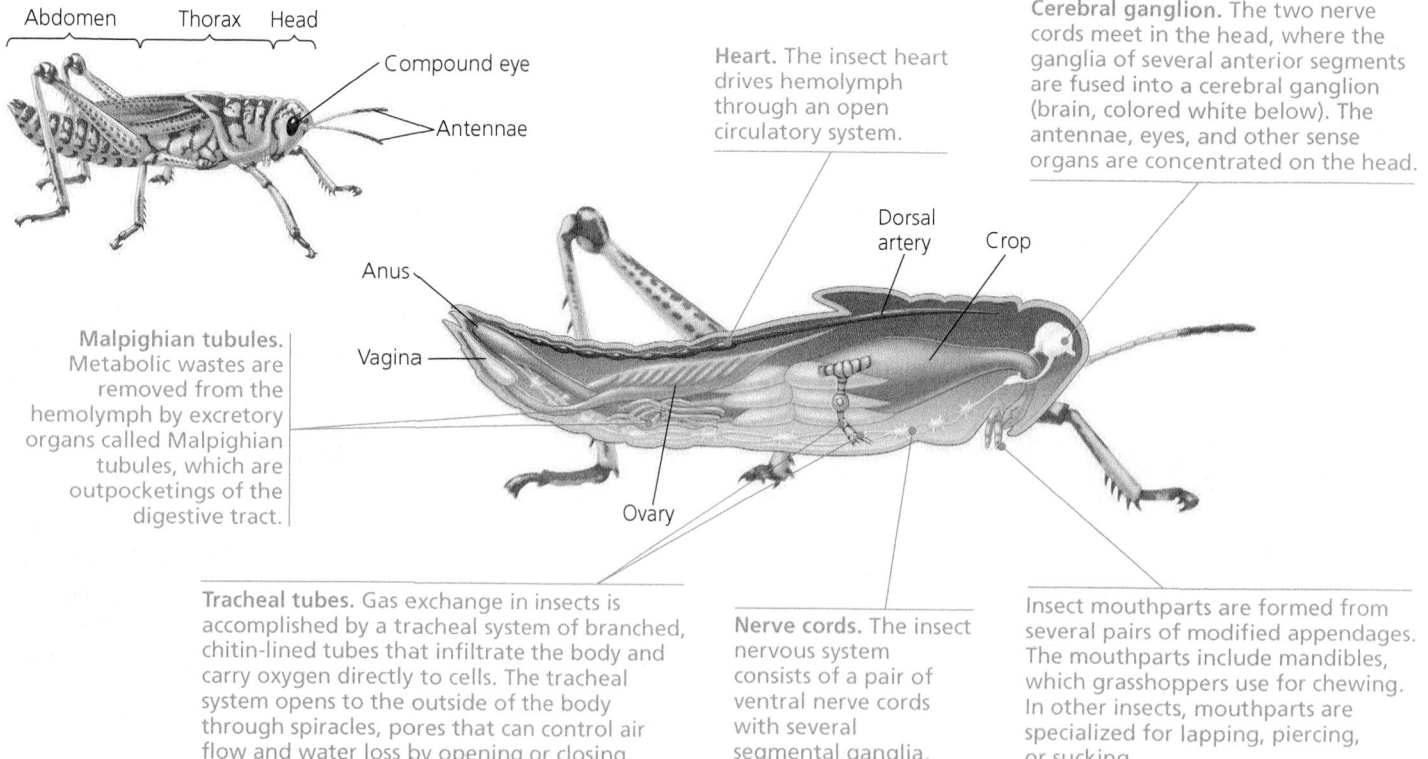

Cerebral ganglion. The two nerve cords meet in the head, where the ganglia of several anterior segments are fused into a cerebral ganglion (brain, colored white below). The antennae, eyes, and other sense organs are concentrated on the head.

Heart. The insect heart drives hemolymph through an open circulatory system.

Malpighian tubules. Metabolic wastes are removed from the hemolymph by excretory organs called Malpighian tubules, which are outpocketings of the digestive tract.

Tracheal tubes. Gas exchange in insects is accomplished by a tracheal system of branched, chitin-lined tubes that infiltrate the body and carry oxygen directly to cells. The tracheal system opens to the outside of the body through spiracles, pores that can control air flow and water loss by opening or closing.

Nerve cords. The insect nervous system consists of a pair of ventral nerve cords with several segmental ganglia.

Insect mouthparts are formed from several pairs of modified appendages. The mouthparts include mandibles, which grasshoppers use for chewing. In other insects, mouthparts are specialized for lapping, piercing, or sucking.

▲ **Figure 33.35 Anatomy of a grasshopper, an insect.**

Morphological and molecular data indicate that wings evolved only once in insects. Dragonflies, which have two similar pairs of wings, were among the first insects to fly. Several insect orders that evolved later than dragonflies have modified flight equipment. The wings of bees and wasps, for instance, are hooked together and move as a single pair. Butterfly wings operate in a similar fashion because the anterior pair overlaps the posterior wings. In beetles, the posterior wings function in flight, while the anterior ones are modified as covers that protect the flight wings when the beetle is walking on the ground or burrowing.

Many insects undergo metamorphosis during their development. In the **incomplete metamorphosis** of grasshoppers and some other insect groups, the young (called nymphs) resemble adults but are smaller, have different body proportions, and lack wings. The nymph undergoes a series of molts, each time looking more like an adult. With the final molt, the insect reaches full size, acquires wings, and becomes sexually mature. Insects with **complete metamorphosis** have larval stages specialized for eating and growing that are known by such names as caterpillar, maggot, or grub. The larval stage looks entirely different from the adult stage, which is specialized for dispersal and reproduction. Metamorphosis from the larval stage to the adult occurs during a pupal stage (Figure 33.37).

Reproduction in insects is usually sexual, with separate male and female individuals. Adults come together and recognize each other as members of the same species by advertising with bright colors (as in butterflies), sounds (as in crickets), or odors (as in moths). Fertilization is generally internal. In most species, sperm are deposited directly into the female's vagina at the time of copulation, though in some species the male deposits a sperm packet outside the female, and the female picks it up. An internal structure in the female called the spermatheca stores the sperm, usually enough to fertilize more than one batch of eggs. Many insects mate only once in a lifetime. After mating, a female often lays her eggs on an appropriate food source where the next generation can begin eating as soon as it hatches.

Insects are classified in more than 30 orders, 8 of which are introduced in Figure 33.38.

(a) Larva (caterpillar)

(b) Pupa

(c) Later-stage pupa

(d) Emerging adult

(e) Adult

▲ Figure 33.37 **Complete metamorphosis of a butterfly.** (a) The larva (caterpillar) spends its time eating and growing, molting as it grows. (b) After several molts, the larva develops into a pupa. (c) Within the pupa, the larval tissues are broken down, and the adult is built by the division and differentiation of cells that were quiescent in the larva. (d) Eventually, the adult begins to emerge from the pupal cuticle. (e) Hemolymph is pumped into veins of the wings and then withdrawn, leaving the hardened veins as struts supporting the wings. The insect will fly off and reproduce, deriving much of its nourishment from the food reserves stored by the feeding larva.

Exploring Insect Diversity

Although there are more than 30 orders of insects, we'll focus on just 8 here. Two early-diverging groups of wingless insects are the bristletails (Archaeognatha) and silverfish (Thysanura). Evolutionary relationships among the other groups discussed here are under debate and so are not depicted on the tree.

Archaeognatha (bristletails; 350 species)

These wingless insects are found under bark and in other moist, dark habitats such as leaf litter, compost piles, and rock crevices. They feed on algae, plant debris, and lichens.

Thysanura (silverfish; 450 species)

These small, wingless insects have a flattened body and reduced eyes. They live in leaf litter or under bark. They can also infest buildings, where they can become pests.

Winged insects (many orders; six are shown below)

Complete metamorphosis

Coleoptera (beetles; 350,000 species)

Beetles, such as this male snout weevil (*Rhiastus lasternus*), constitute the most species-rich order of insects. They have two pairs of wings, one of which is thick and stiff, the other membranous. They have an armored exoskeleton and mouthparts adapted for biting and chewing.

Diptera (151,000 species)

Dipterans have one pair of wings; the second pair has become modified into balancing organs called halteres. Their mouthparts are adapted for sucking, piercing, or lapping. Flies and mosquitoes are among the best-known dipterans, which live as scavengers, predators, and parasites. Like many other insects, flies such as this red tachinid (*Adejeania vexatrix*) have well-developed compound eyes that provide a wide-angle view and excel at detecting fast movements.

Hymenoptera (125,000 species)

Most hymenopterans, which include ants, bees, and wasps, are highly social insects. They have two pairs of membranous wings, a mobile head, and chewing or sucking mouthparts. The females of many species have a posterior stinging organ. Many species, such as this European paper wasp (*Polistes dominulus*), build elaborate nests.

Proboscis

Lepidoptera (120,000 species)

Butterflies and moths have two pairs of wings covered with tiny scales. To feed, they uncoil a long proboscis, visible in this photograph of a hummingbird hawkmoth (*Macroglossum stellatarum*). This moth's name refers to its ability to hover in the air while feeding from a flower. Most lepidopterans feed on nectar, but some species feed on other substances, including animal blood or tears.

Incomplete metamorphosis

Hemiptera (85,000 species)

Hemipterans include so-called "true bugs," such as stink bugs, bed bugs, and assassin bugs. (Insects in other orders are sometimes erroneously called bugs.) Hemipterans have two pairs of wings, one pair partly leathery, the other pair membranous. They have piercing or sucking mouthparts and undergo incomplete metamorphosis, as shown in this image of an adult stink bug guarding its offspring (nymphs).

Orthoptera (13,000 species)

Grasshoppers, crickets, and their relatives are mostly herbivorous. They have large hind legs adapted for jumping, two pairs of wings (one leathery, one membranous), and biting or chewing mouthparts. This aptly named spear-bearer katydid (*Cophiphora* sp.) has a face and legs well adapted to making a threatening display. Male orthopterans commonly make courtship sounds by rubbing together body parts, such as ridges on their hind legs.

Animals as numerous, diverse, and widespread as insects are bound to affect the lives of most other terrestrial organisms, including humans. Insects consume enormous quantities of plant matter; play key roles as predators, parasites, and decomposers; and are an essential source of food for larger animals such as lizards, rodents, and birds. Humans depend on bees, flies, and many other insects to pollinate crops and orchards. In addition, people in many parts of the world eat insects as an important source of protein. On the other hand, insects are carriers for many diseases, including African sleeping sickness (spread by tsetse flies that carry the protist *Trypanosoma*; see Figure 28.6) and malaria (spread by mosquitoes that carry the protist *Plasmodium*; see Figure 28.10).

Insects also compete with humans for food. In parts of Africa, for instance, insects claim about 75% of the crops. In the United States, billions of dollars are spent each year on pesticides, spraying crops with massive doses of some of the deadliest poisons ever invented. Try as they may, not even humans have challenged the preeminence of insects and their arthropod kin. As Cornell University entomologist Thomas Eisner puts it: "Bugs are not going to inherit the Earth. They own it now. So we might as well make peace with the landlord."

Crustaceans

While arachnids and insects thrive on land, crustaceans, for the most part, have remained in marine and freshwater environments. Crustaceans (subphylum Crustacea) typically have highly specialized appendages. Lobsters and crayfishes, for instance, have a toolkit of 19 pairs of appendages (see Figure 33.30). The anterior-most appendages are antennae; crustaceans are the only arthropods with two pairs. Three or more pairs of appendages are modified as mouthparts, including the hard mandibles. Walking legs are present on the thorax, and, unlike insects, crustaceans also have appendages on their abdomen. A lost appendage can be regenerated at the next molt.

Small crustaceans exchange gases across thin areas of the cuticle; larger species have gills. Nitrogenous wastes also diffuse through thin areas of the cuticle, but a pair of glands regulates the salt balance of the hemolymph.

Sexes are separate in most crustaceans. In the case of lobsters and crayfishes, the male uses a specialized pair of abdominal appendages to transfer sperm to the reproductive pore of the female during copulation. Most aquatic crustaceans go through one or more swimming larval stages.

One of the largest groups of crustaceans (numbering over 11,000 species) is the **isopods**, which include terrestrial, freshwater, and marine species. Some isopod species are abundant in habitats at the bottom of the deep ocean. Among the terrestrial isopods are the pill bugs, or wood lice, common on the undersides of moist logs and leaves.

Lobsters, crayfishes, crabs, and shrimps are all relatively large crustaceans called **decapods** (Figure 33.39a). The cuticle of

(a) Ghost crabs live on sandy ocean beaches worldwide. Primarily nocturnal, they take shelter in burrows during the day.

(b) Planktonic crustaceans known as krill are consumed in vast quantities by some whales.

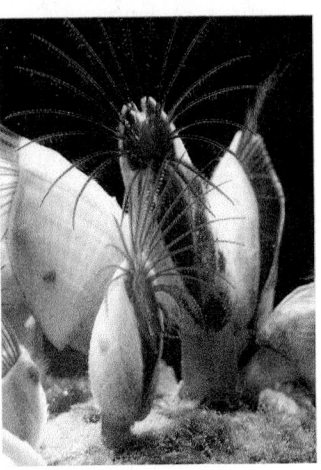

(c) The jointed appendages projecting from the shells of these barnacles capture organisms and organic particles suspended in the water.

▲ Figure 33.39 **Crustaceans.**

decapods is hardened by calcium carbonate; the portion that covers the dorsal side of the cephalothorax forms a shield called the carapace. Most decapod species are marine. Crayfishes, however, live in fresh water, and some tropical crabs live on land.

Many small crustaceans are important members of marine and freshwater plankton communities. Planktonic crustaceans include many species of **copepods**, which are among the most numerous of all animals. Some copepods are grazers that feed upon algae, while others are predators that eat small animals (including smaller copepods!). Copepods are rivaled in abundance by the shrimplike krill, which grow to about 5 cm long (Figure 33.39b). A major food source for baleen whales (including blue whales, humpbacks, and right whales), krill are now being harvested in great numbers by humans for food and agricultural fertilizer. The larvae of many larger-bodied crustaceans are also planktonic.

With the exception of a few parasitic species, barnacles are a group of sessile crustaceans whose cuticle is hardened into a shell containing calcium carbonate (Figure 33.39c). Most barnacles anchor themselves to rocks, boat hulls, pilings, and other submerged surfaces. Their natural adhesive is as strong as synthetic glues. These barnacles feed by extending appendages from their shell to strain food from the water. Barnacles were not recognized as crustaceans until the 1800s, when naturalists discovered that barnacle larvae resemble the larvae of other crustaceans. The remarkable mix of unique traits and crustacean homologies found in barnacles was a major inspiration to Charles Darwin as he developed his theory of evolution.

CONCEPT CHECK 33.4

1. How do nematode and annelid body plans differ?
2. Describe two adaptations that have enabled insects to thrive on land.
3. In contrast to mammalian jaws, which move up and down, the mouthparts of arthropods move side to side. Explain this feature of arthropods in terms of the origin of their mouthparts.
4. **MAKE CONNECTIONS** Traditionally, annelids and arthropods were viewed as closely related because both have body segmentation. Yet DNA sequence data indicate that annelids belong to one clade (Lophotrochozoa) and arthropods to another (Ecdysozoa). Could traditional and molecular hypotheses be tested by studying the expression of *Hox* genes that control body segmentation (see Concept 21.6, pp. 442–447)? Explain.

For suggested answers, see Appendix A.

CONCEPT 33.5

Echinoderms and chordates are deuterostomes

Porifera
Cnidaria
Lophotrochozoa
Ecdysozoa
Deuterostomia

Sea stars, sea urchins, and other echinoderms (phylum Echinodermata) may seem to have little in common with vertebrates (animals that have a backbone) and other members of phylum Chordata. Nevertheless, DNA evidence indicates that echinoderms and chordates are closely related, with both phyla belonging to the Deuterostomia clade of bilaterian animals. Echinoderms and chordates also share features characteristic of a deuterostome mode of development, such as radial cleavage and formation of the anus from the blastopore (see Figure 32.9). As discussed in Chapter 32, however, some animal phyla with members that have deuterostome developmental features, including ectoprocts and brachiopods, are not in the deuterostome clade. Hence, despite its name, the clade Deuterostomia is defined primarily by DNA similarities—not developmental similarities.

Echinoderms

Sea stars (commonly called starfish) and most other **echinoderms** (from the Greek *echin*, spiny, and *derma*, skin) are slow-moving or sessile marine animals. A thin epidermis covers an endoskeleton of hard calcareous plates. Most echinoderms are prickly from skeletal bumps and spines. Unique to echinoderms is the **water vascular system**, a network of hydraulic canals branching into extensions called **tube feet** that function in locomotion and feeding (Figure 33.40). Sexual reproduction of echinoderms usually involves separate male and female individuals that release their gametes into the water.

The internal and external parts of most adult echinoderms radiate from the center, often as five spokes. However, echinoderm larvae have bilateral symmetry. Furthermore, the symmetry of adult echinoderms is not truly radial. For example, the opening (madreporite) of a sea star's water vascular system is not central but shifted to one side.

Living echinoderms are divided into five clades.

Asteroidea: Sea Stars and Sea Daisies

Sea stars have arms radiating from a central disk; the undersurfaces of the arms bear tube feet. By a combination of muscular and chemical actions, the tube feet can attach to or detach from a substrate. The sea star adheres firmly to rocks or creeps along slowly as its tube feet extend, grip, release, extend, and grip again. Although the base of the tube foot has a flattened disk that resembles a suction cup, the gripping action results from adhesive chemicals, not suction (see Figure 33.40).

Sea stars also use their tube feet to grasp prey, such as clams and oysters. The arms of the sea star embrace the closed bivalve, clinging tightly with their tube feet. The sea star then turns part of its stomach inside out, everting it through its mouth and into the narrow opening between the halves of the bivalve's shell. Next, the digestive system of the sea star secretes juices that begin digesting the mollusc within its own shell. The stomach is then brought back inside the seastar's body, where digestion of the mollusc's (now liquefied) body is completed. The ability to begin the digestive process outside of its body allows a sea star to consume bivalves and other prey species that are much larger than its mouth.

Sea stars and some other echinoderms have considerable powers of regeneration. Sea stars can regrow lost arms, and members of one genus can even regrow an entire body from a single arm if part of the central disk remains attached.

The clade Asteroidea, to which sea stars belong, also includes a small group of armless species, the *sea daisies*. Discovered in 1986, only three species of sea daisies are known, all of which live on submerged wood. A sea daisy's body is typically disk-shaped; it has a five-sided organization and measures less than a centimeter in diameter (Figure 33.41). The edge of the body is ringed with small spines. Sea daisies absorb nutrients through a membrane that surrounds their body.

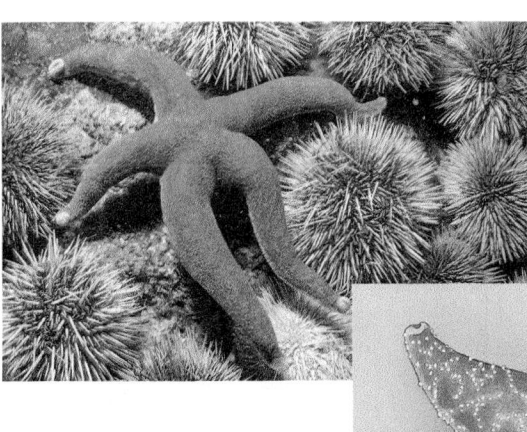

A short digestive tract runs from the mouth on the bottom of the central disk to the anus on top of the disk.

The surface of a sea star is covered by spines that help defend against predators, as well as by small gills that provide gas exchange.

Anus

Stomach

Spine

Gills

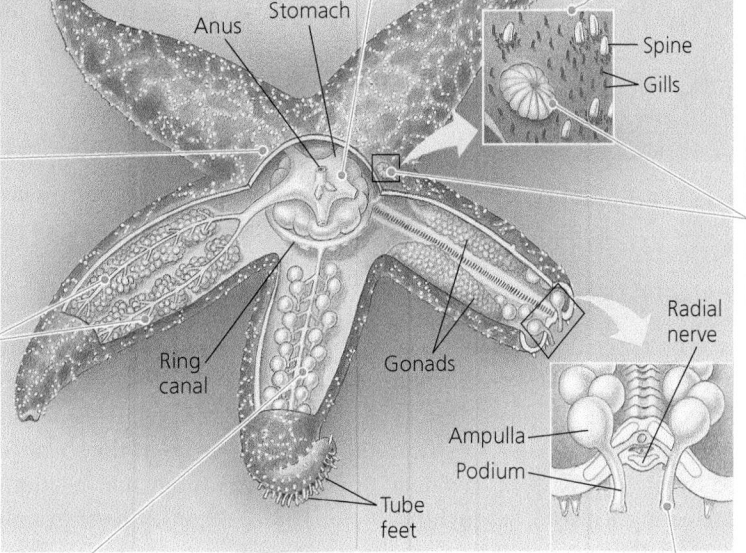

Central disk. The central disk has a nerve ring and nerve cords radiating from the ring into the arms.

Digestive glands secrete digestive juices and aid in the absorption and storage of nutrients.

Ring canal

Gonads

Madreporite. Water can flow in or out of the water vascular system into the surrounding water through the madreporite.

Radial nerve

Ampulla

Podium

Tube feet

Radial canal. The water vascular system consists of a ring canal in the central disk and five radial canals, each running in a groove down the entire length of an arm. Branching from each radial canal are hundreds of hollow, muscular tube feet filled with fluid.

Each tube foot consists of a bulb-like ampulla and a podium (foot portion). When the ampulla squeezes, water is forced into the podium, which expands and contacts the substrate. Adhesive chemicals are then secreted from the base of the podium, attaching it to the substrate. To detach the tube foot, de-adhesive chemicals are secreted and muscles in the podium contract, forcing water back into the ampulla and shortening the podium. As it moves, a sea star leaves an observable "footprint" of adhesive material on the substrate.

▲ **Figure 33.40 Anatomy of a sea star, an echinoderm.**

▶ **Figure 33.41 A sea daisy (clade Asteroidea).**

▲ **Figure 33.42 A brittle star (clade Ophiuroidea).**

Ophiuroidea: Brittle Stars

Brittle stars have a distinct central disk and long, flexible arms (Figure 33.42). They move primarily by lashing their arms in serpentine movements. The base of a brittle star tube foot lacks the flattened disk found in sea stars but does secrete adhesive chemicals. Hence, like sea stars and other echinoderms, brittle stars can use their tube feet to grip substrates. Some species are suspension feeders; others are predators or scavengers.

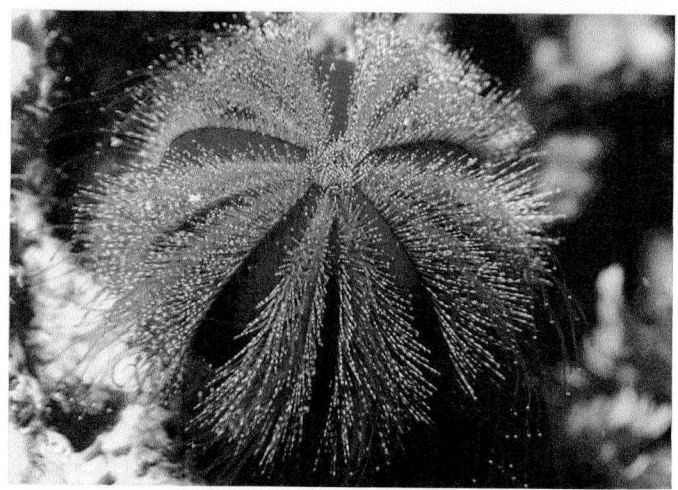

▲ Figure 33.43 **A sea urchin (clade Echinoidea).**

▲ Figure 33.45 **A sea cucumber (clade Holothuroidea).**

Echinoidea: Sea Urchins and Sand Dollars

Sea urchins and sand dollars have no arms, but they do have five rows of tube feet that function in slow movement. Sea urchins also have muscles that pivot their long spines, which aid in locomotion as well as protection (**Figure 33.43**). The mouth of a sea urchin is ringed by highly complex, jaw-like structures that are well adapted to eating seaweed. Sea urchins are roughly spherical, whereas sand dollars are flat disks.

Crinoidea: Sea Lilies and Feather Stars

Sea lilies live attached to the substrate by a stalk; feather stars crawl about by using their long, flexible arms. Both use their arms in suspension feeding. The arms encircle the mouth, which is directed upward, away from the substrate (**Figure 33.44**). Crinoidea is an ancient group whose morphology has changed little over the course of evolution; fossilized sea lilies some 500 million years old are extremely similar to present-day members of the clade.

Holothuroidea: Sea Cucumbers

On casual inspection, sea cucumbers do not look much like other echinoderms. They lack spines, and their endoskeleton is much reduced. They are also elongated in their oral-aboral axis, giving them the shape for which they are named and further disguising their relationship to sea stars and sea urchins (**Figure 33.45**). Closer examination, however, reveals that sea cucumbers have five rows of tube feet. Some of the tube feet around the mouth are developed as feeding tentacles.

Chordates

Phylum Chordata consists of two subphyla of invertebrates, as well as the hagfishes and the vertebrates. Chordates are bilaterally symmetrical coelomates with segmented bodies. The close relationship between echinoderms and chordates does not mean that one phylum evolved from the other. In fact, echinoderms and chordates have evolved independently of one another for over 500 million years. We will trace the phylogeny of chordates in Chapter 34, focusing on the history of vertebrates.

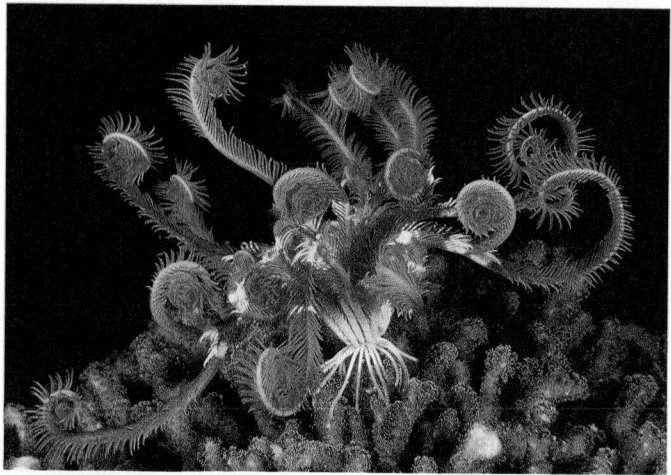

▲ Figure 33.44 **A feather star (clade Crinoidea).**

CONCEPT CHECK 33.5

1. How do sea star tube feet attach to substrates?
2. **WHAT IF?** The insect *Drosophila melanogaster* and the nematode *Caenorhabditis elegans* are prominent model organisms. Are these species the most appropriate invertebrates for making inferences about humans and other vertebrates? Explain.
3. **MAKE CONNECTIONS** Describe how the features and diversity of echinoderms illustrate the unity of life, the diversity of life, and the match between organisms and their environments (see Concept 22.2, pp. 455–460).

For suggested answers, see Appendix A.

SUMMARY OF KEY CONCEPTS

The table below summarizes the groups of animals surveyed in this chapter.

Selected Animal Phyla

Key Concept			Phylum	Description
Concept 33.1 Sponges are basal animals that lack true tissues (pp. 670–671) **?** *Lacking tissues and organs, how do sponges accomplish tasks such as gas exchange, nutrient transport, and waste removal?*			Porifera (sponges)	Lack true tissues; have choanocytes (collar cells—flagellated cells that ingest bacteria and tiny food particles)
Concept 33.2 Cnidarians are an ancient phylum of eumetazoans (pp. 671–673) **?** *Describe the cnidarian body plan and its two major variations.*			Cnidaria (hydras, jellies, sea anemones, corals)	Unique stinging structures (nematocysts) housed in specialized cells (cnidocytes); diploblastic; radially symmetrical; gastrovascular cavity (digestive compartment with a single opening)
Concept 33.3 Lophotrochozoans, a clade identified by molecular data, have the widest range of animal body forms (pp. 674–683) **?** *Is the lophotrochozoan clade united by unique morphological features shared by all of its members? Explain.*			Platyhelminthes (flatworms)	Dorsoventrally flattened, unsegmented acoelomates; gastrovascular cavity or no digestive tract
			Rotifera (rotifers)	Pseudocoelomates with alimentary canal (digestive tube with mouth and anus); jaws (trophi) in pharynx; head with ciliated crown
			Lophophorates: Ectoprocta, Brachiopoda	Coelomates with lophophores (feeding structures bearing ciliated tentacles)
			Mollusca (clams, snails, squids)	Coelomates with three main body parts (muscular foot, visceral mass, mantle); coelom reduced; most have hard shell made of calcium carbonate
			Annelida (segmented worms)	Coelomates with segmented body wall and internal organs (except digestive tract, which is unsegmented)
Concept 33.4 Ecdysozoans are the most species-rich animal group (pp. 683–692) **?** *Describe ecological roles of nematodes and arthropods.*			Nematoda (roundworms)	Cylindrical, unsegmented pseudocoelomates with tapered ends; no circulatory system; undergo ecdysis
			Arthropoda (crustaceans, insects, spiders)	Coelomates with segmented body, jointed appendages, and exoskeleton made of protein and chitin
Concept 33.5 Echinoderms and chordates are deuterostomes (pp. 692–694) **?** *You've read that echinoderms and chordates are closely related and have evolved independently for over 500 million years. Explain how both of these statements can be correct.*			Echinodermata (sea stars, sea urchins)	Coelomates with bilaterally symmetrical larvae and five-part body organization as adults; unique water vascular system; endoskeleton
			Chordata (lancelets, tunicates, vertebrates)	Coelomates with notochord; dorsal, hollow nerve cord; pharyngeal slits; post-anal tail (see Chapter 34)

Bracketing categories (outer to inner): Metazoa; Eumetazoa; Bilateria; Lophotrochozoa; Ecdysozoa; Deuterostomia

LEVEL 1: KNOWLEDGE/COMPREHENSION

1. A land snail, a clam, and an octopus all share
   a. a mantle.
   b. a radula.
   c. gills.
   d. embryonic torsion.
   e. distinct cephalization.

2. Which phylum is characterized by animals that have a segmented body?
   a. Cnidaria
   b. Platyhelminthes
   c. Porifera
   d. Arthropoda
   e. Mollusca

3. The water vascular system of echinoderms
   a. functions as a circulatory system that distributes nutrients to body cells.
   b. functions in locomotion and feeding.
   c. is bilateral in organization, even though the adult animal is not bilaterally symmetrical.
   d. moves water through the animal's body during suspension feeding.
   e. is analogous to the gastrovascular cavity of flatworms.

4. Which of the following combinations of phylum and description is *incorrect*?
   a. Echinodermata—bilateral symmetry as a larva, coelom present
   b. Nematoda—roundworms, pseudocoelomate
   c. Cnidaria—radial symmetry, polyp and medusa body forms
   d. Platyhelminthes—flatworms, gastrovascular cavity, acoelomate
   e. Porifera—gastrovascular cavity, coelom present

LEVEL 2: APPLICATION/ANALYSIS

5. In Figure 33.2, which two main clades branch from the most recent common ancestor of the eumetazoans?
   a. Porifera and Cnidaria
   b. Lophotrochozoa and Ecdysozoa
   c. Cnidaria and Bilateria
   d. Rotifera and Deuterostomia
   e. Deuterostomia and Bilateria

6. **MAKE CONNECTIONS** In Figure 33.8, assume that the two medusae shown at step 4 were produced by one polyp colony. Review Concept 12.1 (pp. 229–230) and Concept 13.4 (pp. 257–260), and then use your understanding of mitosis and meiosis to evaluate whether the following sentence is true or false. If false, select the answer that provides the correct reason.

   Although the two medusae are genetically identical, a sperm produced by one will differ genetically from an egg produced by the other.

   a. F (the medusae are genetically identical, but so are the gametes)
   b. F (neither the medusae or the gametes are genetically identical)
   c. F (the medusae are not identical but the gametes are)
   d. T

LEVEL 3: SYNTHESIS/EVALUATION

7. **EVOLUTION CONNECTION**
   DRAW IT Draw a phylogenetic tree of Bilateria that includes the ten phyla of bilaterians discussed in detail in this chapter. Label each branch that leads to a phylum with a C, P, or A, depending on whether members of the phylum are coelomates (C), pseudocoelomates (P), or acoelomates (A). Use your labeled tree to answer the following questions:
   a. For each of the three major clades of bilaterians, what (if anything) can be inferred about whether the common ancestor of the clade had a true coelom?
   b. To what extent has the presence of a true coelom in animals changed over the course of evolution?

8. **SCIENTIFIC INQUIRY**
   Bats emit ultrasonic sounds and then use the returning echoes of those sounds to locate and capture flying insects, such as moths, in the dark. In response to bat attacks, some tiger moths make ultrasonic clicks of their own. Researchers hypothesize that tiger moth clicks likely either (1) jam the bat's sonar or (2) warn the bat about the moth's toxic chemical defenses. The graph below shows two patterns observed in studies of moth capture rates over time.

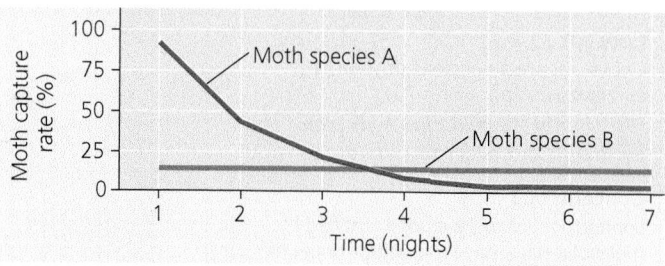

   Bats in these experiments were "naive," meaning that prior to the study the bats had not previously hunted tiger moths. Do the results support hypothesis (1), hypothesis (2), or both? Why did the researchers use naive bats? Explain.

9. **WRITE ABOUT A THEME**
   Structure and Function Write a short essay (100–150 words) that explains how the structure of the digestive tract in different invertebrate groups affects the size of the organisms that they can eat.

For selected answers, see Appendix A.

Mastering BIOLOGY www.masteringbiology.com

1. MasteringBiology® Assignments
   Tutorial Ecdysozoans
   Activities Characteristics of Invertebrates • Discovery Channel Video: Invertebrates
   Questions Student Misconceptions • Multiple Choice • Reading Quiz • End-of-Chapter

2. eText
   Read your book online, search, take notes, highlight text, and more.

3. The Study Area
   Practice Tests • Cumulative Test • *BioFlix* 3-D Animations • MP3 Tutor Sessions • Videos • Activities • Investigations • Lab Media • Audio Glossary • Word Study Tools • Art

34

The Origin and Evolution of Vertebrates

▲ **Figure 34.1 What is the relationship of this ancient organism to humans?**

KEY CONCEPTS

34.1 Chordates have a notochord and a dorsal, hollow nerve cord

34.2 Craniates are chordates that have a head

34.3 Vertebrates are craniates that have a backbone

34.4 Gnathostomes are vertebrates that have jaws

34.5 Tetrapods are gnathostomes that have limbs

34.6 Amniotes are tetrapods that have a terrestrially adapted egg

34.7 Mammals are amniotes that have hair and produce milk

34.8 Humans are mammals that have a large brain and bipedal locomotion

Half a Billion Years of Backbones

Early in the Cambrian period, some 530 million years ago, an immense variety of invertebrate animals inhabited Earth's oceans. Predators used sharp claws and mandibles to skewer their prey. Many animals had protective spikes or armor as well as modified mouthparts that enabled their bearers to filter food from the water. Worms slithered in the bottom muck, feeding on organic matter. Amidst this bustle, it would have been easy to overlook certain slender, 3-cm-long creatures gliding through the water: *Myllokunmingia fengjiaoa* (**Figure 34.1**). Although lacking armor and appendages, this ancient species was closely related to one of the most successful groups of animals ever to swim, walk, slither, or fly: the **vertebrates**, which derive their name from vertebrae, the series of bones that make up the vertebral column, or backbone.

For more than 150 million years, vertebrates were restricted to the oceans, but about 365 million years ago, the evolution of limbs in one lineage of vertebrates set the stage for these vertebrates to colonize land. There they diversified into amphibians, reptiles (including birds), and mammals.

There are approximately 52,000 species of vertebrates, a relatively small number compared to, say, the 1 million insect species on Earth. But what vertebrates lack in species diversity they make up for in *disparity*, varying enormously in characteristics such as body mass. Vertebrates include the heaviest animals ever to walk on land, plant-eating dinosaurs as massive as 40,000 kg (more than 13 pickup trucks). They also include the biggest animal ever to exist on Earth, the blue whale, which can exceed a mass of 100,000 kg. On the other end of the spectrum, a fish discovered in 2004 is just 8.4 mm long and has a mass roughly 100 billion times smaller than that of a blue whale.

In this chapter, you will learn about current hypotheses regarding the origins of vertebrates from invertebrate ancestors. We will track the evolution of the vertebrate body plan, from a notochord to a head to a mineralized skeleton. We'll also explore the major groups of vertebrates (both living and extinct), as well as the evolutionary history of our own species.

CONCEPT 34.1

Chordates have a notochord and a dorsal, hollow nerve cord

Vertebrates are members of the phylum Chordata, the chordates. **Chordates** are bilaterian (bilaterally symmetrical) animals, and within Bilateria, they belong to the clade of animals known as Deuterostomia (see Chapter 32). The best-known deuterostomes, aside from vertebrates, are the echinoderms, the group that includes sea stars and sea urchins.

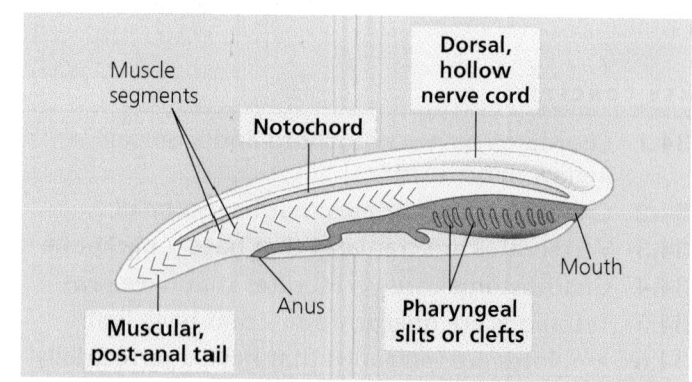

▲ **Figure 34.2 Phylogeny of living chordates.**
This phylogenetic hypothesis shows the major clades of
chordates in relation to the other main deuterostome
clade, Echinodermata (see Chapter 33). For selected
clades, some of the derived characters are listed; for
example, all chordates, and only chordates, have a
notochord.

However, as shown in **Figure 34.2**, the cephalochordates and
the urochordates are two groups of invertebrate deuterostomes that are more closely related to vertebrates than to
other invertebrates. Along with the hagfishes and the vertebrates, they make up the chordates.

Derived Characters of Chordates

All chordates share a set of derived characters, though many
species possess some of these traits only during embryonic
development. **Figure 34.3** illustrates four key characters of
chordates: a notochord; a dorsal, hollow nerve cord; pharyngeal slits or clefts; and a muscular, post-anal tail.

Notochord

Chordates are named for a skeletal structure, the notochord,
present in all chordate embryos as well as in some adult chordates. The **notochord** is a longitudinal, flexible rod located
between the digestive tube and the nerve cord. It is composed
of large, fluid-filled cells encased in fairly stiff, fibrous tissue.
The notochord provides skeletal support throughout most of

▲ **Figure 34.3 Chordate characteristics.** All chordates possess
the four highlighted structural trademarks at some point during their
development.

the length of a chordate, and in larvae or adults that retain it, it
also provides a firm but flexible structure against which muscles can work during swimming. In most vertebrates, a more
complex, jointed skeleton develops around the ancestral notochord, and the adult retains only remnants of the embryonic

notochord. In humans, the notochord is reduced and forms part of the gelatinous disks sandwiched between the vertebrae.

Dorsal, Hollow Nerve Cord

The nerve cord of a chordate embryo develops from a plate of ectoderm that rolls into a tube located dorsal to the notochord. The resulting dorsal, hollow nerve cord is unique to chordates. Other animal phyla have solid nerve cords, and in most cases they are ventrally located. The nerve cord of a chordate embryo develops into the central nervous system: the brain and spinal cord.

Pharyngeal Slits or Clefts

The digestive tube of chordates extends from the mouth to the anus. The region just posterior to the mouth is the pharynx. In all chordate embryos, a series of pouches separated by grooves forms along the sides of the pharynx. In most chordates, these grooves (known as **pharyngeal clefts**) develop into slits that open to the outside of the body. These **pharyngeal slits** allow water entering the mouth to exit the body without passing through the entire digestive tract. Pharyngeal slits function as suspension-feeding devices in many invertebrate chordates. In vertebrates (with the exception of vertebrates with limbs, the tetrapods), these slits and the structures that support them have been modified for gas exchange and are known as gill slits. In tetrapods, the pharyngeal clefts do not develop into slits. Instead, they play an important role in the development of parts of the ear and other structures in the head and neck.

Muscular, Post-Anal Tail

Chordates have a tail that extends posterior to the anus, although in many species it is greatly reduced during embryonic development. In contrast, most nonchordates have a digestive tract that extends nearly the whole length of the body. The chordate tail contains skeletal elements and muscles, and it helps propel many aquatic species in the water.

Lancelets

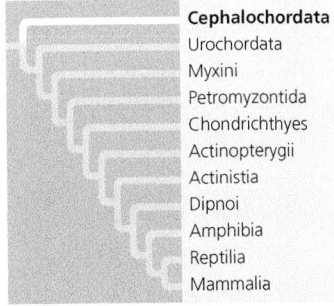

Cephalochordata
Urochordata
Myxini
Petromyzontida
Chondrichthyes
Actinopterygii
Actinistia
Dipnoi
Amphibia
Reptilia
Mammalia

The most basal (earliest-diverging) group of living chordates are animals called **lancelets** (Cephalochordata), which get their name from their bladelike shape **(Figure 34.4)**. As larvae, lancelets develop a notochord, a dorsal, hollow nerve cord, numerous pharyngeal slits, and a post-anal tail. The larvae feed on plankton in the water column, alternating between upward swimming and passive sinking. As the larvae sink, they trap plankton and other suspended particles in their pharynx.

Adult lancelets can reach 6 cm in length. They retain key chordate traits, closely resembling the idealized chordate shown in Figure 34.3. Following metamorphosis, an adult lancelet swims down to the seafloor and wriggles backward into the sand, leaving only its anterior end exposed. Cilia draw seawater into the lancelet's mouth. A net of mucus secreted across the pharyngeal slits removes tiny food particles as the water passes through the slits, and the trapped food enters the intestine. The pharynx and pharyngeal slits play a minor role in gas exchange, which occurs mainly across the external body surface.

A lancelet frequently leaves its burrow to swim to a new location. Though feeble swimmers, these invertebrate chordates display, in a simple form, the swimming mechanism of fishes.

◄ **Figure 34.4 The lancelet *Branchiostoma*, a cephalochordate.** This small invertebrate displays all four main chordate characters. Water enters the mouth and passes through the pharyngeal slits into the atrium, a chamber that vents to the outside via the atriopore; large particles are blocked from entering the mouth by tentacle-like cirri. The serially arranged segmental muscles produce the lancelet's wavelike swimming movements.

Coordinated contraction of muscles arranged like rows of chevrons (<<<<) along the sides of the notochord flexes the notochord, producing side-to-side undulations that thrust the body forward. This serial arrangement of muscles is evidence of the lancelet's segmentation. The muscle segments develop from blocks of mesoderm called *somites*, which are found along each side of the notochord in all chordate embryos.

Globally, lancelets are rare, but in a few regions (including Tampa Bay, along the Florida coast), they occasionally reach densities in excess of 5,000 individuals per square meter.

Tunicates

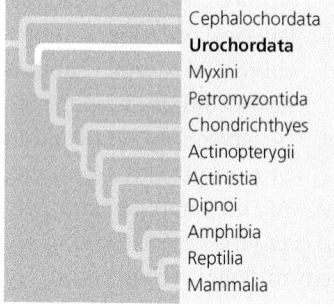

Cephalochordata
Urochordata
Myxini
Petromyzontida
Chondrichthyes
Actinopterygii
Actinistia
Dipnoi
Amphibia
Reptilia
Mammalia

Contrary to what was formerly thought, recent molecular studies suggest that the **tunicates** (Urochordata) are more closely related to other chordates than are lancelets. The chordate characters of tunicates are most apparent during their larval stage, which may be as brief as a few minutes (Figure 34.5a). In many species, the larva uses its tail muscles and notochord to swim through water in search of a suitable substrate on which it can settle, guided by cues it receives from light- and gravity-sensitive cells.

Once a tunicate has settled on a substrate, it undergoes a radical metamorphosis in which many of its chordate characters disappear. Its tail and notochord are resorbed; its nervous system degenerates; and its remaining organs rotate 90°. As an adult, a tunicate draws in water through an incurrent siphon;

the water then passes through the pharyngeal slits into a chamber called the atrium and exits through an excurrent siphon (Figure 34.5b and c). Food particles are filtered from the water by a mucous net and transported by cilia to the esophagus. The anus empties into the excurrent siphon. Some tunicate species shoot a jet of water through their excurrent siphon when attacked, earning them the informal name of "sea squirts."

The loss of chordate characters in the adult stage of tunicates appears to have occurred after the tunicate lineage branched off from other chordates. Even the tunicate larva appears to be highly derived. For example, tunicates have 9 *Hox* genes, whereas all other chordates studied to date—including the early-diverging lancelets—share a set of 13 *Hox* genes. The apparent loss of 4 *Hox* genes indicates that the chordate body plan of a tunicate larva is built using a different set of genetic controls than other chordates.

Early Chordate Evolution

Although lancelets and tunicates are relatively obscure animals, they occupy key positions in the history of life and can provide clues about the evolutionary origin of vertebrates. As you have read, for example, lancelets display key chordate characters as adults, and their lineage branches from the base of the chordate phylogenetic tree. These findings suggest that the ancestral chordate may have looked something like a lancelet—that is, it had an anterior end with a mouth; a notochord; a dorsal, hollow nerved cord; pharyngeal slits; and a post-anal tail.

Research on lancelets has also revealed important clues about the evolution of the chordate brain. Rather than a full-fledged brain, lancelets have only a slightly swollen tip on the anterior end of their dorsal nerve cord. But the same *Hox* genes that organize major regions of the forebrain, midbrain,

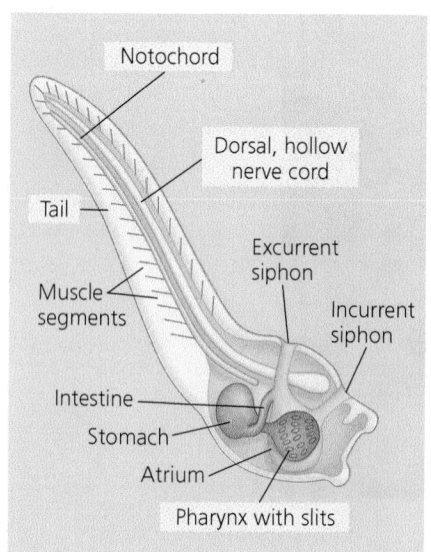

(a) A tunicate larva is a free-swimming but nonfeeding "tadpole" in which all four main characters of chordates are evident.

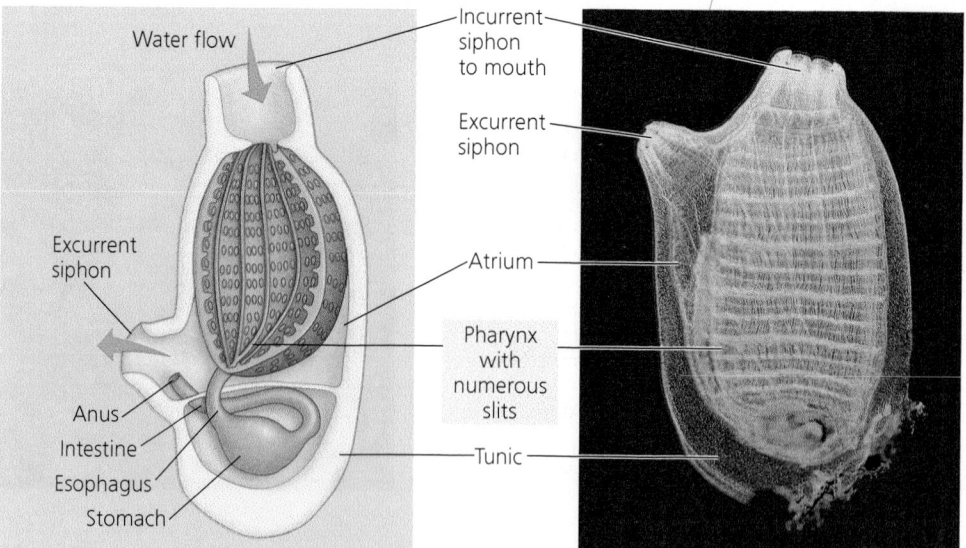

(b) In the adult, prominent pharyngeal slits function in suspension feeding, but other chordate characters are not obvious.

(c) An adult tunicate, or sea squirt, is a sessile animal (photo is approximately life-sized).

▲ Figure 34.5 **A tunicate, a urochordate.**

BF1
Otx
Hox3

Nerve cord of lancelet embryo

BF1
Otx
Hox3

Brain of vertebrate embryo
(shown straightened)

Forebrain Midbrain Hindbrain

▲ Figure 34.6 **Expression of developmental genes in lancelets and vertebrates.** *Hox* genes (including *BF1*, *Otx*, and *Hox3*) control the development of major regions of the vertebrate brain. These genes are expressed in the same anterior-to-posterior order in lancelets and vertebrates. Each colored bar is positioned above the portion of the brain whose development that gene controls.

MAKE CONNECTIONS *What do these results and those in Figure 21.18 indicate about* Hox *genes and their evolution?*

and hindbrain of vertebrates express themselves in a corresponding pattern in this small cluster of cells in the lancelet's nerve cord (Figure 34.6). This suggests that the vertebrate brain is an elaboration of an ancestral structure similar to the lancelet's simple nerve cord tip.

As for tunicates, their genome has been completely sequenced and can be used to identify genes likely to have been present in early chordates. Researchers taking this approach have suggested that ancestral chordates had genes associated with vertebrate organs such as the heart and thyroid gland. These genes are found in tunicates and vertebrates but are absent from nonchordate invertebrates. In contrast, tunicates lack many genes that in vertebrates are associated with the long-range transmission of nerve impulses. This result suggests that such genes arose in an early vertebrate and are unique to the vertebrate evolutionary lineage.

CONCEPT CHECK 34.1

1. Identify four derived characters that all chordates have at some point during their life.
2. You are a chordate, yet you lack most of the main derived characters of chordates. Explain.
3. **WHAT IF?** Suppose lancelets lacked a gene found in tunicates and vertebrates. Would this imply that the chordates' most recent common ancestor also lacked this gene? Explain.

For suggested answers, see Appendix A.

CONCEPT 34.2

Craniates are chordates that have a head

After the evolution of the basic chordate body plan, that seen in lancelets and tunicate larvae, the next major transition in chordate evolution was the appearance of a head. Chordates with a head are known as **craniates** (from the word *cranium*, skull). The origin of a head—consisting of a brain at the anterior end of the dorsal nerve cord, eyes and other sensory organs, and a skull—enabled chordates to coordinate more complex movement and feeding behaviors. (Note that heads evolved independently in other animal lineages as well; see Chapter 33.)

Derived Characters of Craniates

Living craniates share a set of derived characters that distinguish them from other chordates. As a result of gene duplication, craniates possess two or more sets of *Hox* genes (lancelets and tunicates have only one). Other important families of genes that produce signaling molecules and transcription factors are also duplicated in craniates. Divergence of sequences in the duplicate genes led to additional genetic complexity. This may have made it possible for craniates to develop more complex morphologies than those of lancelets and tunicates.

One feature unique to craniates is the **neural crest**, a collection of cells that appears near the dorsal margins of the closing neural tube in an embryo (Figure 34.7). Neural crest cells disperse throughout the body, where they give rise to a variety of structures, including teeth, some of the bones and cartilage of the skull, the inner layer of skin (dermis) of the facial region, several types of neurons, and the sensory capsules in which eyes and other sense organs develop.

In aquatic craniates, the pharyngeal clefts evolved into gill slits. Unlike the pharyngeal slits of lancelets, which are used primarily for suspension feeding, gill slits are associated with muscles and nerves that allow water to be pumped through

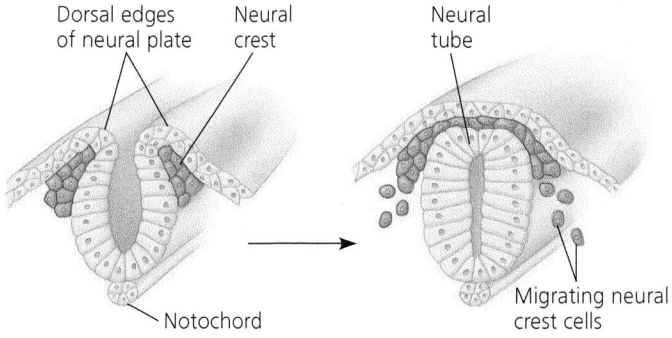

Dorsal edges of neural plate   Neural crest

Neural tube

Notochord

Migrating neural crest cells

(a) The neural crest consists of bilateral bands of cells near the margins of the embryonic folds that form the neural tube.

(b) Neural crest cells migrate to distant sites in the embryo.

(c) The migrating neural crest cells give rise to some of the anatomical structures unique to vertebrates, including some of the bones and cartilage of the skull. (A fetal human skull is depicted here.)

▲ Figure 34.7 **The neural crest, embryonic source of many unique craniate characters.**

the slits. This pumping can assist in sucking in food, and it facilitates gas exchange. (In terrestrial craniates, the pharyngeal clefts develop into other structures, as we'll explain later.)

Craniates, which are more active than lancelets and tunicates, also have a higher metabolic rate and a much more extensive muscular system. Muscles lining their digestive tract aid digestion by moving food through the tract. Craniates also have a heart with at least two chambers, red blood cells with hemoglobin, and kidneys that remove waste products from the blood.

The Origin of Craniates

In the late 1990s, paleontologists working in China discovered a vast supply of fossils of early chordates that appear to straddle the transition to craniates. The fossils were formed during the Cambrian explosion 530 million years ago, when many groups of animals were diversifying (see Chapter 32).

The most primitive of the fossils are the 3-cm-long *Haikouella* (**Figure 34.8**). In many ways, *Haikouella* resembled a lancelet. Its mouth structure indicates that, like lancelets, it probably was a suspension feeder. However, *Haikouella* also had some of the characters of craniates. For example, it had a well-formed brain, small eyes, and muscle segments along the body, as do the vertebrate fishes. It also had respiratory gills in its pharynx, which all the more basal chordates lack. However, *Haikouella* did not have a skull or ear organs, suggesting that these characters emerged with further innovations to the

chordate nervous system. (The earliest "ears" were organs for maintaining balance, a function still performed by the ears of humans and other living vertebrates.)

In other Cambrian rocks, paleontologists have found fossils of more advanced chordates, such as *Myllokunmingia* (see Figure 34.1). About the same size as *Haikouella*, *Myllokunmingia* had ear capsules and eye capsules, parts of the skull that surround these organs. Based on these and other characters, paleontologists have identified *Myllokunmingia* as a true craniate.

Hagfishes

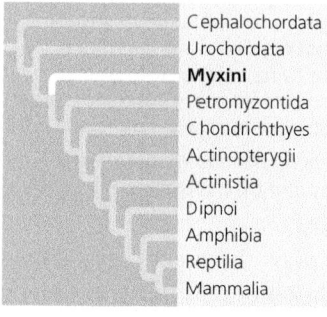

The most basal group of craniates is Myxini, the hagfishes (**Figure 34.9**). Hagfishes have a skull made of cartilage, but they lack jaws and vertebrae. They swim in a snakelike fashion by using their segmental muscles to exert force against their notochord, which they retain in adulthood as a strong, flexible rod of cartilage. Hagfishes have a small brain, eyes, ears, and a nasal opening that connects with the pharynx. Their mouths contain toothlike formations made of the protein keratin.

All of the 30 living species of hagfishes are marine. Measuring up to 60 cm in length, most are bottom-dwelling scavengers that feed on worms and sick or dead fish. Rows of slime glands on a hagfish's flanks secrete a substance that absorbs water, forming a slime that may repulse other scavengers when a hagfish is feeding (see Figure 34.9). When attacked by a predator, a hagfish can produce several liters of slime in less than a minute. The slime coats the gills of the attacking fish, sending it into retreat or even suffocating it. Several teams of biologists and engineers are investigating the properties of hagfish slime in hopes of producing an artificial slime that could act as a space-filling gel. Such a gel might be used, for instance, to curtail bleeding during surgery.

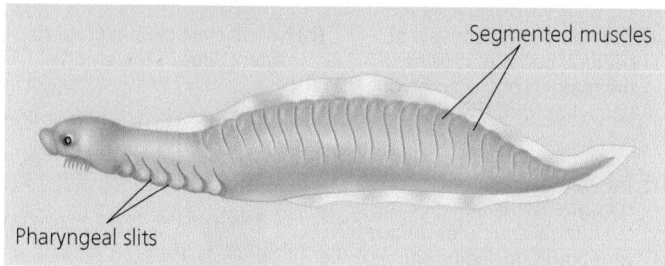

▲ **Figure 34.8 Fossil of an early chordate.** Discovered in 1999 in southern China, *Haikouella* had eyes and a brain but lacked a skull, a derived trait of craniates. The colors in the illustration are fanciful.

▲ **Figure 34.9 A hagfish.**

CONCEPT CHECK 34.2

1. What characteristics do hagfishes have that lancelets and tunicates lack?
2. Which extinct chordate is more closely related to humans, *Myllokunmingia* or *Haikouella*? Explain.
3. **WHAT IF?** In several different animal lineages, organisms with a head first appeared roughly 530 million years ago. Does this finding constitute proof that having a head is favored by natural selection? Explain.

For suggested answers, see Appendix A.

CONCEPT 34.3

Vertebrates are craniates that have a backbone

During the Cambrian period, a lineage of craniates gave rise to vertebrates. With a more complex nervous system and a more elaborate skeleton than those of their ancestors, vertebrates became more efficient at two essential tasks: capturing food and avoiding being eaten.

Derived Characters of Vertebrates

After vertebrates branched off from other craniates, they underwent another gene duplication, this one involving a group of transcription factor genes called the *Dlx* family. The resulting additional genetic complexity may be associated with innovations in the vertebrate nervous system and skeleton, including a more extensive skull and a backbone composed of vertebrae. In some vertebrates, the vertebrae are little more than small prongs of cartilage arrayed dorsally along the notochord. In the majority of vertebrates, however, the vertebrae enclose the spinal cord and have taken over the mechanical roles of the notochord. Aquatic vertebrates also acquired dorsal, ventral, and anal fins stiffened by bony structures called fin rays, which provide thrust and steering control when swimming after prey or away from predators. Faster swimming was supported by other adaptations, including a more efficient gas exchange system in the gills.

Lampreys

Cephalochordata
Urochordata
Myxini
Petromyzontida
Chondrichthyes
Actinopterygii
Actinistia
Dipnoi
Amphibia
Reptilia
Mammalia

Lampreys (Petromyzontida) are the most basal lineage of living vertebrates. Like hagfishes, lampreys may offer clues to early chordate evolution, but they have also acquired unique characters.

There are about 35 species of lampreys inhabiting

▲ **Figure 34.10 A sea lamprey.** Most lampreys use their mouth (inset) and tongue to bore a hole in the side of a fish. The lamprey then ingests the blood and other tissues of its host.

various marine and freshwater environments (**Figure 34.10**). Most are parasites that feed by clamping their round, jawless mouth onto the flank of a live fish. They then use their rasping tongue to penetrate the skin of the fish and ingest the fish's blood.

As larvae, lampreys live in freshwater streams. The larva is a suspension feeder that resembles a lancelet and spends much of its time partially buried in sediment. Some species of lampreys feed only as larvae; following several years in streams, they mature sexually, reproduce, and die within a few days. Most lampreys, however, migrate to the sea or lakes as they mature into adults. Sea lampreys (*Petromyzon marinus*) have invaded the Great Lakes over the past 170 years and have devastated a number of fisheries there.

The skeleton of lampreys is made of cartilage. Unlike the cartilage found in most vertebrates, lamprey cartilage contains no collagen. Instead, it is a stiff matrix of other proteins. The notochord of lampreys persists as the main axial skeleton in the adult, as it does in hagfishes. However, lampreys also have a flexible sheath around their rodlike notochord. Along the length of this sheath, pairs of cartilaginous projections related to vertebrae extend dorsally, partially enclosing the nerve cord.

Fossils of Early Vertebrates

After the ancestors of lampreys branched off from other vertebrates during the Cambrian period, many other lineages of vertebrates emerged. Like lampreys, the early members of these lineages lacked jaws, but the resemblance stopped there.

Conodonts were slender, soft-bodied vertebrates with prominent eyes controlled by numerous muscles. Most conodonts were 3–10 cm in length, although some may have been as long as 30 cm. They probably hunted with the help of their large eyes, impaling prey on a set of barbed hooks at the anterior end of their mouth. These hooks were made of dental tissues that were *mineralized*—composed of minerals such as calcium that provide rigidity (**Figure 34.11**). The food was then passed back to the pharynx, where a different set of dental elements sliced and crushed the food.

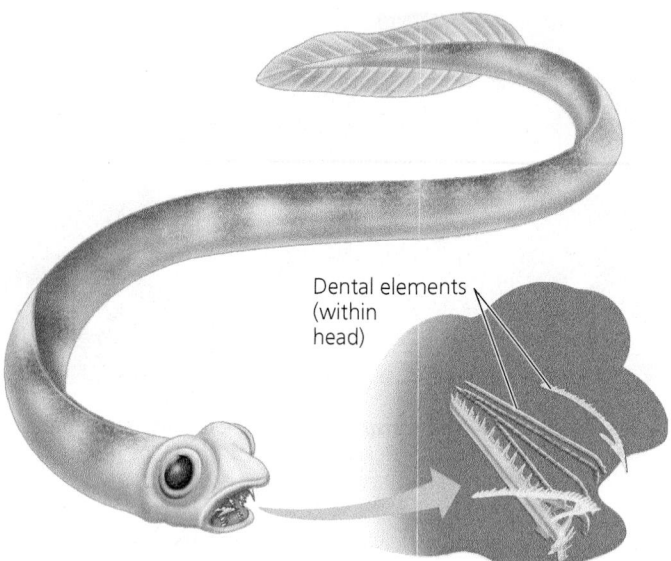

▲ **Figure 34.11 A conodont.** Conodonts were early vertebrates that lived from the late Cambrian until the late Triassic. Unlike lampreys, conodonts had mineralized mouthparts, which they used for either predation or scavenging.

Dental elements (within head)

Conodonts were extremely abundant for over 300 million years. Their fossilized dental elements are so plentiful that they have been used for decades by petroleum geologists as guides to the age of rock layers in which they search for oil. (These elements also gave conodonts their name, which means "cone teeth.")

Vertebrates with additional innovations emerged during the Ordovician, Silurian, and Devonian periods. These vertebrates had paired fins and, as in lampreys, an inner ear with two semicircular canals that provided a sense of balance. Although they, too, lacked jaws, they had a muscular pharynx, which they may have used to suck in bottom-dwelling organisms or detritus. They were also armored with mineralized bone, which covered varying amounts of their body **(Figure 34.12)**. The armor, which in some species included spines, may have offered protection from predators. There were many species of these

Pteraspis

Pharyngolepis

▲ **Figure 34.12 Jawless armored vertebrates.** *Pteraspis* and *Pharyngolepis* were two of many genera of jawless vertebrates that emerged during the Ordovician, Silurian, and Devonian periods.

jawless, armored swimming vertebrates, but they all became extinct by the end of the Devonian period.

Origins of Bone and Teeth

The human skeleton is heavily mineralized bone, whereas cartilage plays a fairly minor role. But a bony skeleton was a relatively late development in the history of vertebrates. As we've seen, the vertebrate skeleton evolved initially as a structure made of unmineralized cartilage.

What initiated the process of mineralization in vertebrates? One hypothesis is that mineralization was associated with a transition in feeding mechanisms. Early chordates probably were suspension feeders, like lancelets, but over time they became larger and were able to ingest larger particles, including some small animals. The earliest known mineralized structures in vertebrates—conodont dental elements—were an adaptation that may have allowed these animals to become scavengers and predators. In addition, when the bony armor of later jawless vertebrates was examined under the microscope, scientists found that it was composed of small tooth-like structures. These findings suggest that mineralization of the vertebrate body may have begun in the mouth and later was incorporated into protective armor. Only in more derived vertebrates did the endoskeleton begin to mineralize, starting with the skull. As you'll read in the next section, more recent lineages of vertebrates underwent even further mineralization.

CONCEPT CHECK 34.3

1. How are differences in the anatomy of lampreys and conodonts reflected in each animal's feeding method?
2. **WHAT IF?** Suggest key roles that mineralized bone might have played in early vertebrates.

For suggested answers, see Appendix A.

CONCEPT 34.4

Gnathostomes are vertebrates that have jaws

Hagfishes and lampreys are survivors from the early Paleozoic era, when jawless craniates were common. Since then, jawless vertebrates have been far outnumbered by jawed vertebrates, known as **gnathostomes**. Living gnathostomes are a diverse group that includes sharks and their relatives, ray-finned fishes, lobe-finned fishes, amphibians, reptiles (including birds), and mammals.

Derived Characters of Gnathostomes

Gnathostomes ("jaw mouth") are named for their jaws, hinged structures that, especially with the help of teeth, enable gnathostomes to grip food items firmly and slice them.

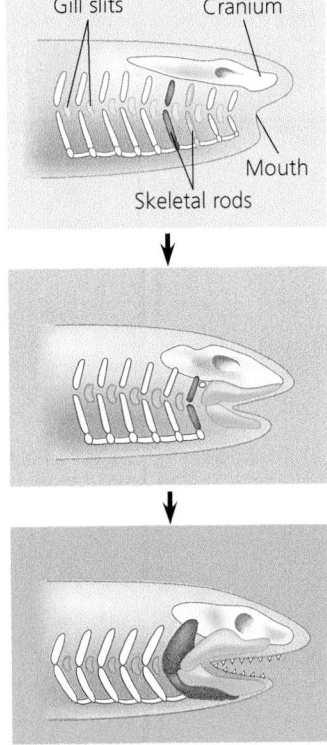

▶ **Figure 34.13 Hypothesis for the evolution of vertebrate jaws.** The skeleton of the jaws and their supports may have evolved from two pairs of skeletal rods (red and green) located between gill slits near the mouth. According to this hypothesis, pairs of rods anterior to those that formed the jaws were either lost or incorporated into the cranium or jaws.

Gill slits
Cranium
Mouth
Skeletal rods

0.5 m

▲ **Figure 34.14 Fossil of an early gnathostome.** The placoderm *Dunkleosteus* grew up to 10 m in length. A 2006 analysis of its jaw structure concluded that *Dunkleosteus* could exert a force of 560 kg/cm² (8,000 pounds per square inch) at the tip of its jaws.

According to one hypothesis, gnathostome jaws evolved by modification of the skeletal rods that had previously supported the anterior pharyngeal (gill) slits (Figure 34.13). The remaining gill slits, no longer required for suspension feeding, remained as the major sites of respiratory gas exchange with the external environment.

Gnathostomes share other derived characters besides jaws. The common ancestors of all gnathostomes underwent an additional duplication of *Hox* genes, such that the single set present in early chordates became four. In fact, the entire genome appears to have duplicated, and together these genetic changes likely enabled the origin of jaws and other novel features in gnathostomes. The gnathostome forebrain is enlarged compared to that of other craniates, mainly in association with enhanced senses of smell and vision. Another characteristic of aquatic gnathostomes is the **lateral line system**, organs that form a row along each side of the body and are sensitive to vibrations in the surrounding water. Precursors of these organs were present in the head shields of some jawless vertebrates.

Fossil Gnathostomes

Gnathostomes appeared in the fossil record in the late Ordovician period, about 450 million years ago, and steadily became more diverse. Their success probably resulted from a combination of anatomical features: Their paired fins and tail (which were also found in jawless vertebrates) allowed them to swim efficiently after prey, and their jaws enabled them to grab prey or simply bite off chunks of flesh.

The earliest gnathostomes in the fossil record include extinct lineages of armored vertebrates known as **placoderms**,

which means "plate-skinned." Most placoderms were less than a meter long, though some giants measured more than 10 m (Figure 34.14). Other groups of jawed vertebrates, collectively called **acanthodians**, emerged at roughly the same time and radiated during the Silurian and Devonian periods (444–359 million years ago). Placoderms had disappeared by 359 million years ago, and acanthodians became extinct about 70 million years later.

In the past several years, new fossil discoveries have revealed that 450–420 million years ago was a period of tumultuous evolutionary change. Gnathostomes that lived during this period had highly variable forms, and by 420 million years ago, they had diverged into the three lineages of jawed vertebrates that survive today: chondrichthyans, ray-finned fishes, and lobe-fins.

Chondrichthyans (Sharks, Rays, and Their Relatives)

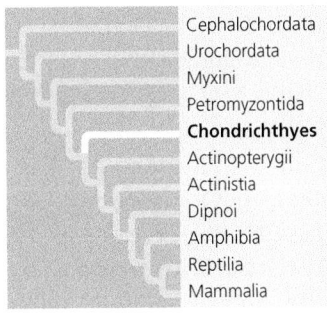

Cephalochordata
Urochordata
Myxini
Petromyzontida
Chondrichthyes
Actinopterygii
Actinistia
Dipnoi
Amphibia
Reptilia
Mammalia

Sharks, rays, and their relatives include some of the biggest and most successful vertebrate predators in the oceans. They belong to the clade Chondrichthyes, which means "cartilage fish." As their name indicates, the **chondrichthyans** have a skeleton composed predominantly of cartilage, though often impregnated with calcium.

When the name Chondrichthyes was first coined in the 1800s, scientists thought that chondrichthyans represented an early stage in the evolution of the vertebrate skeleton and that mineralization had evolved only in more derived lineages (such as "bony fishes"). However, as conodonts and armored jawless vertebrates demonstrate, the mineralization of the vertebrate skeleton had already begun before the chondrichthyan lineage branched off from other vertebrates. Moreover, bone-like tissues have been found in early chondrichthyans, such as the fin skeleton of a shark that lived in the Carboniferous period. Traces of bone can also be found in living chondrichthyans—in their scales, at the base of their teeth, and, in some sharks, in a thin layer on the surface of their vertebrae. Such findings strongly suggest that the restricted distribution of bone in the chondrichthyan body is a derived condition, emerging after chondrichthyans diverged from other gnathostomes.

There are about 1,000 species of living chondrichthyans. The largest and most diverse group consists of the sharks, rays, and skates (Figure 34.15a and b). A second group is composed of a few dozen species of ratfishes, or chimaeras (Figure 34.15c).

Most sharks have a streamlined body and are swift swimmers, but they do not maneuver very well. Powerful movements of the trunk and the tail fin propel them forward. The dorsal fins function mainly as stabilizers, and the paired pectoral (fore) and pelvic (hind) fins are important for maneuvering. Although a shark gains buoyancy by storing a large amount of oil in its huge liver, the animal is still more dense than water, and if it stops swimming it sinks. Continual swimming also ensures that water flows into the shark's mouth and out through the gills, where gas exchange occurs. However, some sharks and many skates and rays spend a good deal of time resting on the seafloor. When resting, they use muscles of their jaws and pharynx to pump water over the gills.

The largest sharks and rays are suspension feeders that consume plankton. Most sharks, however, are carnivores that swallow their prey whole or use their powerful jaws and sharp teeth to tear flesh from animals too large to swallow in one piece. Sharks have several rows of teeth that gradually move to the front of the mouth as old teeth are lost. The digestive tract of many sharks is proportionately shorter than that of many other vertebrates. Within the shark intestine is a *spiral valve*, a corkscrew-shaped ridge that increases surface area and prolongs the passage of food through the digestive tract.

Acute senses are adaptations that go along with the active, carnivorous lifestyle of sharks. Sharks have sharp vision but cannot distinguish colors. The nostrils of sharks, like those of most aquatic vertebrates, open into dead-end cups. They function only for olfaction (smelling), not for breathing. Like some other vertebrates, sharks have a pair of regions in the skin of their head that can detect electric fields generated by the muscle contractions of nearby animals. Like all (non-mammalian) aquatic vertebrates, sharks have no eardrums, structures that terrestrial vertebrates use to transmit sound waves in air to the auditory organs. Sound reaches a shark through water, and the animal's entire body transmits the sound to the hearing organs of the inner ear.

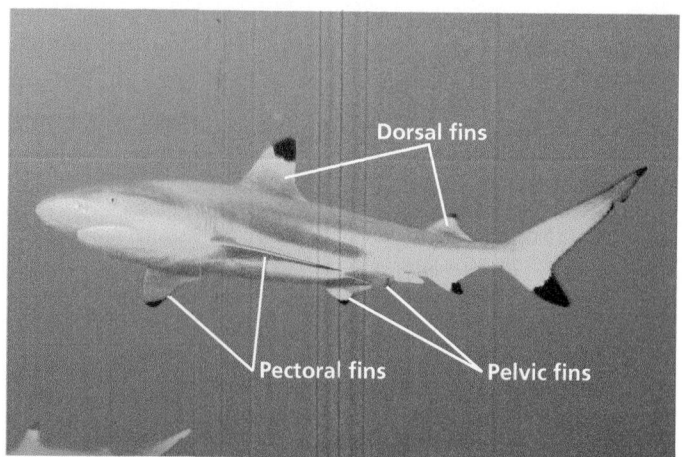

(a) **Blacktip reef shark (*Carcharhinus melanopterus*).** Sharks are fast swimmers with acute senses. Like all gnathosomes, they have paired pectoral and pelvic fins.

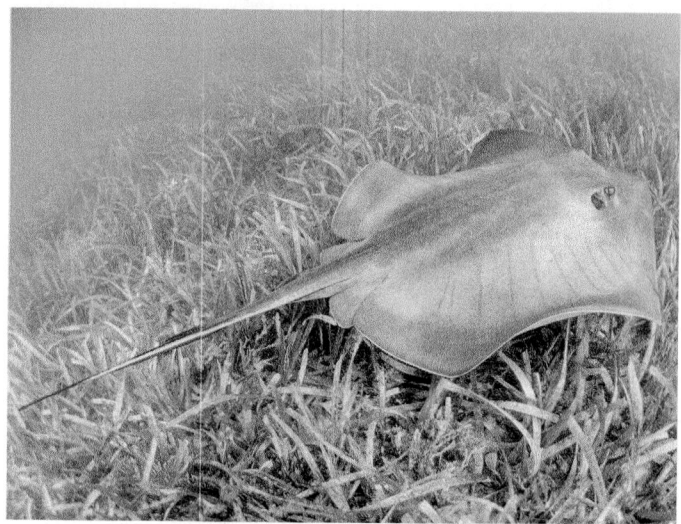

(b) **Southern stingray (*Dasyatis americana*).** Most rays are bottom-dwellers that feed on molluscs and crustaceans. Some rays cruise in open water and scoop food into their gaping mouth.

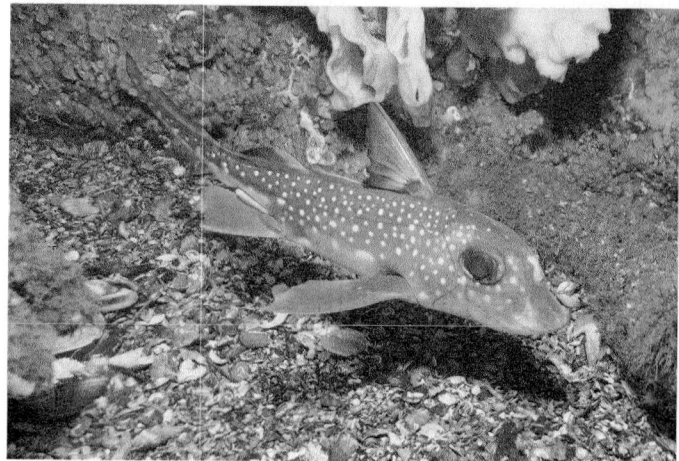

(c) **Spotted ratfish (*Hydrolagus colliei*).** Ratfishes, or chimaeras, typically live at depths greater than 80 m and feed on shrimp, molluscs, and sea urchins. Some species have a venomous spine at the front of their first dorsal fin.

▲ Figure 34.15 **Chondrichthyans.**

Shark eggs are fertilized internally. The male has a pair of claspers on its pelvic fins that transfer sperm into the reproductive tract of the female. Some species of sharks are **oviparous**; they lay eggs that hatch outside the mother's body. These sharks release their eggs after encasing them in protective coats. Other species are **ovoviviparous**; they retain the fertilized eggs in the oviduct. Nourished by the egg yolk, the embryos develop into young that are born after hatching within the uterus. A few species are **viviparous**; the young develop within the uterus and obtain nourishment prior to birth by receiving nutrients from the mother's blood through a yolk sac placenta, by absorbing a nutritious fluid produced by the uterus, or by eating other eggs. The reproductive tract of the shark empties along with the excretory system and digestive tract into the **cloaca**, a common chamber that has a single opening to the outside.

Although rays are closely related to sharks, they have adopted a very different lifestyle. Most rays are bottom-dwellers that feed by using their jaws to crush molluscs and crustaceans. They have a flattened shape and use their greatly enlarged pectoral fins like water wings to propel themselves through the water. The tail of many rays is whiplike and, in some species, bears venomous barbs that function in defense.

Chondrichthyans have thrived for over 400 million years. Today, however, they are severely threatened with overfishing. A recent report indicated that shark stocks in the northwest Atlantic had declined 75% over a 15-year period.

Ray-Finned Fishes and Lobe-Fins

Cephalochordata
Urochordata
Myxini
Petromyzontida
Chondrichthyes
Actinopterygii
Actinistia
Dipnoi
Amphibia
Reptilia
Mammalia

The vast majority of vertebrates belong to the clade of gnathostomes called Osteichthyes. Unlike chondrichthyans, nearly all living **osteichthyans** have an ossified (bony) endoskeleton with a hard matrix of calcium phosphate. Like many other taxonomic names, the name Osteichthyes ("bony fish") was coined long before the advent of phylogenetic systematics. When it was originally defined, the group excluded tetrapods, but we now know that such a taxon would be paraphyletic (see Figure 34.2). Therefore, systematists today include tetrapods along with bony fishes in the clade Osteichthyes. Clearly, the name of the group does not accurately describe all of its members.

In this section, we'll discuss the aquatic osteichthyans known informally as fishes. Most fishes breathe by drawing water over four or five pairs of gills located in chambers covered by a protective bony flap called the **operculum** (Figure 34.16). Water is drawn into the mouth, through the pharynx, and out between the gills by movement of the operculum and contraction of muscles surrounding the gill chambers.

Most fishes can control their buoyancy with an air sac known as a **swim bladder**. Movement of gases from the blood to the swim bladder increases buoyancy, making the animal rise; transfer of gas back to the blood causes the animal to sink. Charles Darwin proposed that the lungs of tetrapods evolved from swim bladders, but strange as it may sound, the opposite seems to be true. Osteichthyans in many early-branching lineages have lungs, which they use to breathe air as a supplement to gas exchange in their gills. The weight of evidence indicates that lungs arose in early osteichthyans; later, swim bladders evolved from lungs in some lineages.

In nearly all fishes, the skin is covered by flattened, bony scales that differ in structure from the tooth-like scales of sharks. Glands in the skin secrete a slimy mucus over the skin, an adaptation that reduces drag during swimming. Like the ancient aquatic gnathostomes mentioned earlier, fishes have a lateral line system, which is evident as a row of tiny pits in the skin on either side of the body.

The details of fish reproduction vary extensively. Most species are oviparous, reproducing by external fertilization after the female sheds large numbers of small eggs. However, internal fertilization and birthing characterize other species.

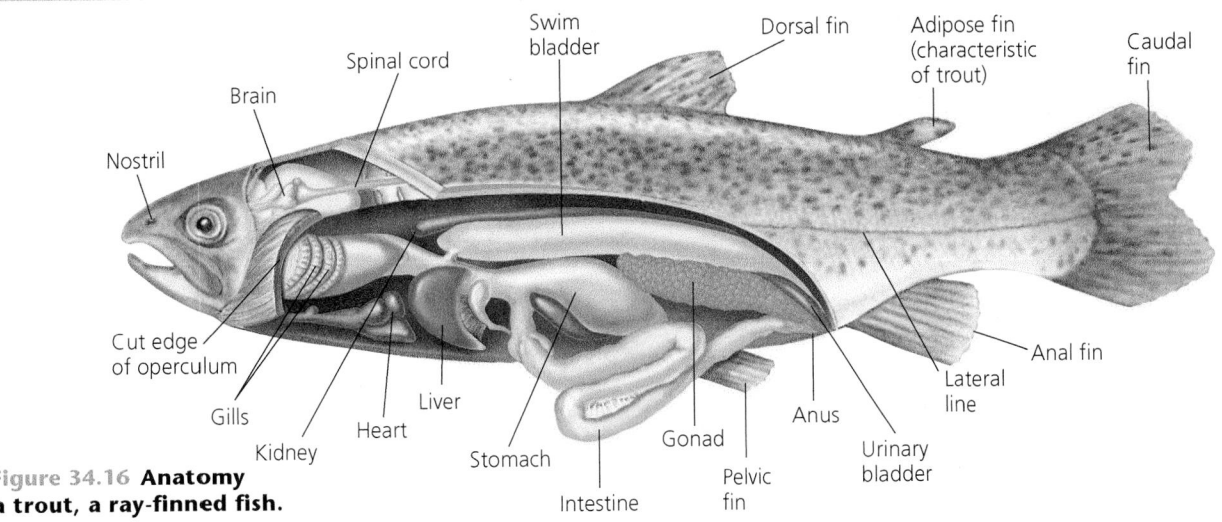

▲ **Figure 34.16 Anatomy of a trout, a ray-finned fish.**

Ray-Finned Fishes

Nearly all the aquatic osteichthyans familiar to us are among the over 27,000 species of **ray-finned fishes** (Actinopterygii) **(Figure 34.17)**. Named for the bony rays that support their fins, the ray-finned fishes originated during the Silurian period (444–416 million years ago). The group has diversified greatly since that time, as suggested by modifications in body form and fin structure that affect maneuvering, defense, and other functions (see Figure 34.17).

▲ Yellowfin tuna (*Thunnus albacares*) is a fast-swimming, schooling fish that is commercially important worldwide.

▶ Native to coral reefs of the Pacific Ocean, the brightly colored red lionfish (*Pterois volitans*) can inject venom through its spines, causing a severe and painful reaction in humans.

▲ The sea horse has a highly modified body form, as exemplified by *Hippocampus ramulosus*, shown above. Sea horses are unusual among animals in that the male carries the young during their embryonic development.

▲ The fine-spotted moray eel (*Gymnothorax dovii*) is a predator that ambushes prey from crevices in its coral reef habitat.

▲ **Figure 34.17 Ray-finned fishes (Actinopterygii).**

Ray-finned fishes serve as a major source of protein for humans, who have harvested them for thousands of years. However, industrial-scale fishing operations appear to have driven some of the world's biggest fisheries to collapse. For example, after decades of abundant harvests, in the 1990s the catch of cod (*Gadus morhua*) in the northwest Atlantic plummeted to just 5% of its historic maximum, bringing codfishing there to a near halt. Despite ongoing restrictions on the fishery, cod populations have yet to recover to sustainable levels. Ray-finned fishes also face other pressures from humans, such as the diversion of rivers by dams. Changing water flow patterns can hamper the fishes' ability to obtain food and interferes with migratory pathways and spawning grounds.

Lobe-Fins

Like the ray-finned fishes, the other major lineage of osteichthyans, the **lobe-fins** (Sarcopterygii), also originated during the Silurian period **(Figure 34.18)**. The key derived character of lobe-fins is the presence of rod-shaped bones surrounded by a thick layer of muscle in their pectoral and pelvic fins. During the Devonian (416–359 million years ago), many lobe-fins lived in brackish waters, such as in coastal wetlands. There they may have used their lobed fins to swim and "walk" underwater across the substrate (as do some living lobe-fins). Some Devonian lobe-fins were gigantic predators. It is not uncommon to find spike-shaped fossils of Devonian lobe-fin teeth as big as your thumb.

By the end of the Devonian period, lobe-fin diversity was dwindling, and today only three lineages survive. One lineage,

5 cm

Lower jaw   Scaly covering   Dorsal spine

▲ **Figure 34.18 A reconstruction of an ancient lobe-fin.** Discovered in 2009, *Guiyu oneiros* is the earliest known lobe-fin, dating to 420 million years ago. The fossil of this species was nearly complete, allowing for an accurate reconstruction.

▲ **Figure 34.19 A coelacanth (*Latimeria*).** These lobe-fins were found living off the coasts of southern Africa and Indonesia.

the coelacanths (Actinistia), was thought to have become extinct 75 million years ago. However, in 1938, fishermen caught a living coelacanth off the east coast of South Africa (Figure 34.19). Until the 1990s, all subsequent discoveries were near the Comoros Islands in the western Indian Ocean. Since 1999, coelacanths have also been found at various places along the eastern coast of Africa and in the eastern Indian Ocean, near Indonesia. The Indonesian population may represent a second species.

The second lineage of living lobe-fins, the lungfishes (Dipnoi), is represented today by six species in three genera, all of which are found in the Southern Hemisphere. Lungfishes arose in the ocean but today are found only in fresh water, generally in stagnant ponds and swamps. They surface to gulp air into lungs connected to their pharynx. Lungfishes also have gills, which are the main organs for gas exchange in Australian lungfishes. When ponds shrink during the dry season, some lungfishes can burrow into the mud and estivate (wait in a state of torpor; see Chapter 40).

The third lineage of lobe-fins that survives today is far more diverse than the coelacanths or the lungfishes. During the mid-Devonian, these organisms adapted to life on land and gave rise to vertebrates with limbs and feet, called tetrapods—a lineage that includes humans. The tetrapod clade is the topic of the next section.

CONCEPT CHECK 34.4

1. What derived characters do sharks and tuna share? What are some characteristics that distinguish tuna from sharks?
2. Describe key adaptations of aquatic gnathostomes.
3. **WHAT IF?** Imagine that we could replay the history of life. Is it possible that a group of vertebrates that colonized land could have arisen from aquatic gnathostomes other than the lobe-fins? Explain.

For suggested answers, see Appendix A.

CONCEPT 34.5

Tetrapods are gnathostomes that have limbs

One of the most significant events in vertebrate history took place about 365 million years ago, when the fins of some lobe-fins evolved into the limbs and feet of tetrapods. Until then, all vertebrates had shared the same basic fishlike anatomy. After tetrapods moved onto land, they took on many new forms, from leaping frogs to flying eagles to bipedal humans.

Derived Characters of Tetrapods

The most significant character of **tetrapods** gives the group its name, which means "four feet" in Greek. In place of pectoral and pelvic fins, tetrapods have limbs with digits. Limbs support a tetrapod's weight on land, while feet with digits efficiently transmit muscle-generated forces to the ground when it walks.

Life on land brought numerous other changes to the tetrapod body plan. In tetrapods, the head is separated from the body by a neck that originally had one vertebra on which the skull could move up and down. Later, with the origin of a second vertebra in the neck, the head could also swing from side to side. The bones of the pelvic girdle, to which the hind legs are attached, are fused to the backbone, permitting forces generated by the hind legs against the ground to be transferred to the rest of the body. Except for some fully aquatic species (such as the axolotl discussed below), the adults of living tetrapods do not have gills; during embryonic development, the pharyngeal clefts instead give rise to parts of the ears, certain glands, and other structures.

As you will see, some of these characters were dramatically altered or lost in various lineages of tetrapods. In birds, for example, the pectoral limbs became wings, and in whales, the entire body converged toward a fishlike shape.

The Origin of Tetrapods

As you have read, the Devonian coastal wetlands were home to a wide range of lobe-fins. Those that entered particularly shallow, oxygen-poor water could use their lungs to breathe air. Some species probably used their stout fins to help them move across logs or the muddy bottom. Thus, the tetrapod body plan did not evolve "out of nowhere" but was simply a modification of a preexisting body plan.

The recent discovery of a fossil called *Tiktaalik* has provided new details on how this process occurred. Like a fish, this species had fins, gills, and lungs, and its body was covered in scales. But unlike a fish, *Tiktaalik* had a full set of ribs

IMPACT

Discovery of a "Fishapod": *Tiktaalik*

Paleontologists were on the hunt for fossils that could shed light on the evolutionary origin of tetrapods. Based on the ages of previously discovered fossils, researchers were looking for a dig site with rocks about 365–385 million years old. Ellesmere Island, in the Canadian Arctic, was one of the few such sites likely to contain fossils, because it was once a river. The search at this site was rewarded by the discovery of fossils of a 375-million-year-old lobe-fin, named *Tiktaalik*. As shown in the chart and photographs below, *Tiktaalik* exhibits both fish and tetrapod characters. (Figure 34.21, on the facing page, includes an artist's conception of what *Tiktaalik* might have looked like.)

WHY IT MATTERS As the most tetrapod-like fish known, *Tiktaalik* documents key steps in the vertebrate transition from water to land. Since *Tiktaalik* predates the oldest known tetrapod by 10 million years, its features suggest that key "tetrapod" traits, such as a wrist, ribs, and a neck, were in fact ancestral to the tetrapod lineage. The discovery also shows the predictive capacity of paleontology in identifying likely locations of fossils of interest.

FURTHER READING E. B. Daeschler, N. H. Shubin, and F. A. Jenkins, A Devonian tetrapod-like fish and the evolution of the tetrapod body plan, *Nature* 440:757–763 (2006).

MAKE CONNECTIONS Describe how *Tiktaalik*'s features illustrate Darwin's concept of descent with modification (see Concept 22.2, pp. 457–460).

Fish Characters	Tetrapod Characters
Scales	Neck
Fins	Ribs
Gills and lungs	Fin skeleton
	Flat skull
	Eyes on top of skull

that would have helped it breathe air and support its body (**Figure 34.20**). Also unlike a fish, *Tiktaalik* had a neck and shoulders, allowing it to move its head about. Finally, the bones of *Tiktaalik*'s front fin have the same basic pattern found in all limbed animals: one bone (the humerus), followed by two bones (the radius and ulna), followed by a group of small bones that comprise the wrist. Although it is unlikely that *Tiktaalik* could walk on land, its front fin skeleton suggests that it could prop itself up in water on its fins.

Tiktaalik and other extraordinary fossil discoveries have allowed paleontologists to reconstruct how fins became progressively more limb-like over time, culminating in the appearance of the first tetrapods 365 million years ago (**Figure 34.21**). Over the next 60 million years, a great diversity of tetrapods arose. Judging from the morphology and locations of their fossils, most of these early tetrapods probably remained tied to water, a characteristic they share with some members of a group of living tetrapods called amphibians.

Amphibians

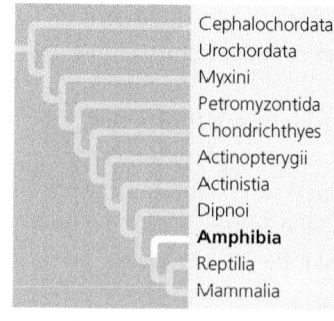

Cephalochordata
Urochordata
Myxini
Petromyzontida
Chondrichthyes
Actinopterygii
Actinistia
Dipnoi
Amphibia
Reptilia
Mammalia

The **amphibians** (class Amphibia) are represented today by about 6,150 species of salamanders (order Urodela, "tailed ones"), frogs (order Anura, "tail-less ones"), and caecilians (order Apoda, "legless ones").

About 550 species of urodeles are known. Some are entirely aquatic, but others live on land as adults or

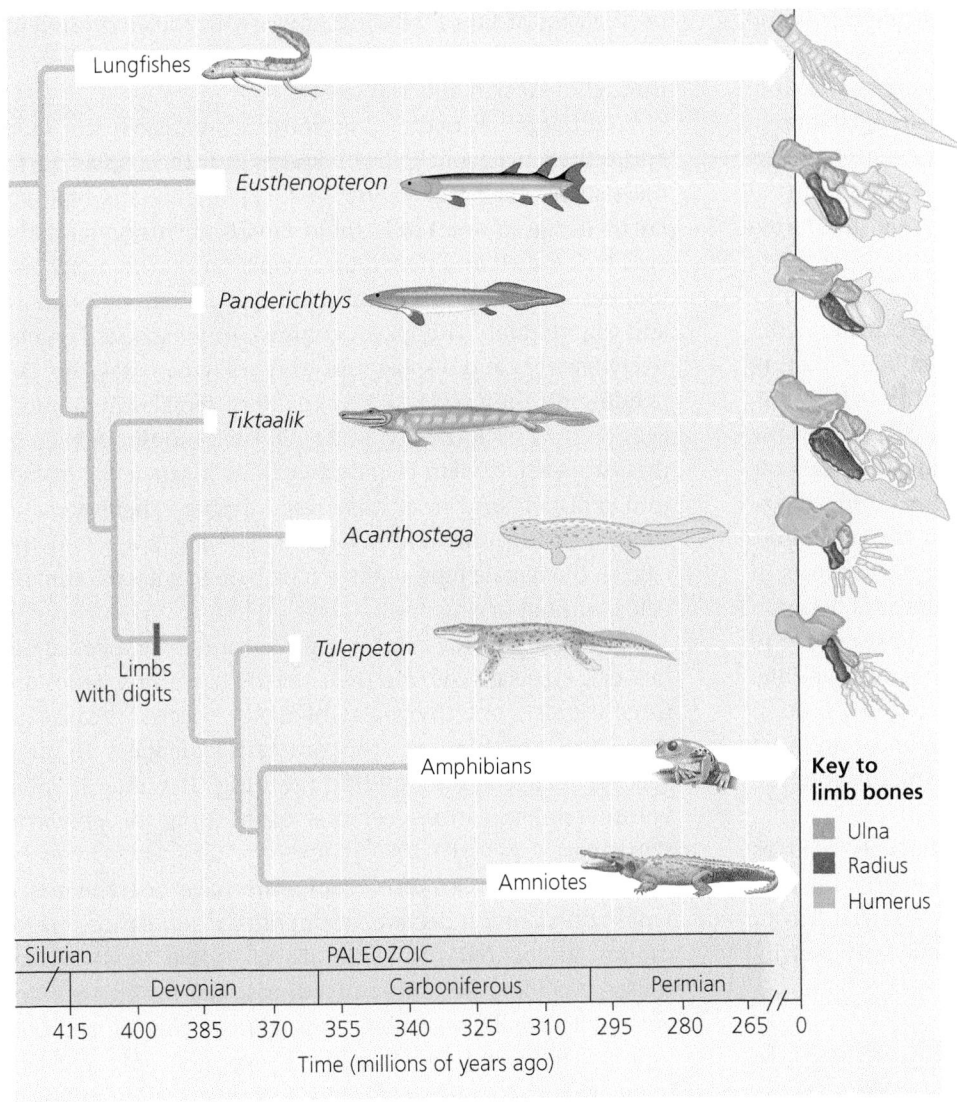

Lungfishes

Eusthenopteron

Panderichthys

Tiktaalik

Acanthostega

Limbs
with digits

Tulerpeton

Amphibians

Amniotes

WHAT IF? *If the most recent common ancestor of* Tulerpeton *and living tetrapods originated 380 million years ago, what range of dates would include the origin of amphibians?*

Key to limb bones

■ Ulna
■ Radius
■ Humerus

Silurian	PALEOZOIC		
	Devonian	Carboniferous	Permian

415   400   385   370   355   340   325   310   295   280   265   0
Time (millions of years ago)

---

throughout life. Most salamanders that live on land walk with a side-to-side bending of the body, a trait also found in early terrestrial tetrapods **(Figure 34.22a)**. Paedomorphosis is common among aquatic salamanders; the axolotl, for instance, retains larval features even when it is sexually mature (see Figure 25.22).

Anurans, numbering about 5,420 species, are more specialized than urodeles for moving on land **(Figure 34.22b)**. Adult frogs use their powerful hind legs to hop along the terrain. Although often distinctive in appearance, the animals known as "toads" are simply frogs that have leathery skin or other adaptations for life on land. A frog nabs insects and other prey by flicking out its long, sticky tongue, which is attached to the front of the mouth. Frogs display a great variety of adaptations that help them avoid being eaten by larger predators. Their skin glands secrete distasteful or even poisonous mucus. Many poisonous species have bright coloration, which predators apparently associate with danger (see Figure 54.5b). Other frogs have color patterns that camouflage them (see Figure 54.5a).

(a) Order Urodela. Urodeles (salamanders) retain their tail as adults.

(b) Order Anura. Anurans, such as this poison dart frog, lack a tail as adults.

▶ **Figure 34.22 Amphibians.**

(c) Order Apoda. Apodans, or caecilians, are legless, mainly burrowing amphibians.

Apodans, the caecilians (about 170 species), are legless and nearly blind, and superficially they resemble earthworms (Figure 34.22c). Their absence of legs is a secondary adaptation, as they evolved from a legged ancestor. Caecilians inhabit tropical areas, where most species burrow in moist forest soil. A few South American species live in freshwater ponds and streams.

Amphibian (derived from *amphibious*, meaning "both ways of life") refers to the life stages of many frog species that live first in water and then on land (Figure 34.23). The larval stage of a frog, called a tadpole, is usually an aquatic herbivore with gills, a lateral line system resembling that of aquatic vertebrates, and a long, finned tail. The tadpole initially lacks legs; it swims by undulating its tail. During the metamorphosis that leads to the "second life," the tadpole develops legs, lungs, a pair of external eardrums, and a digestive system adapted to a carnivorous diet. At the same time, the gills disappear; the lateral line system also disappears in most species. The young frog crawls onto shore and becomes a terrestrial hunter. In spite of their name, however, many amphibians do not live a dual—aquatic and terrestrial—life. There are some strictly aquatic or strictly terrestrial frogs, salamanders, and caecilians. Moreover, salamander and caecilian larvae look much like the adults, and typically both the larvae and the adults are carnivorous.

Most amphibians are found in damp habitats such as swamps and rain forests. Even those adapted to drier habitats spend much of their time in burrows or under moist leaves, where humidity is high. Amphibians generally rely heavily on their moist skin for gas exchange with the environment. Some terrestrial species lack lungs and breathe exclusively through their skin and oral cavity.

Fertilization is external in most amphibians; the male grasps the female and spills his sperm over the eggs as the female sheds them (see Figure 34.23c). Amphibians typically lay their eggs in water or in moist environments on land; the eggs lack a shell and dehydrate quickly in dry air. Some amphibian species lay vast numbers of eggs in temporary pools, and egg mortality is high. In contrast, other species lay relatively few eggs and display various types of parental care. Depending on the species, either males or females may house eggs on their back (Figure 34.24), in their mouth, or even in their stomach. Certain tropical tree frogs stir their egg masses into moist, foamy nests that resist drying. There are also some ovoviviparous and viviparous species that retain the eggs in the female reproductive tract, where embryos can develop without drying out.

Many amphibians exhibit complex and diverse social behaviors, especially during their breeding seasons. Frogs are usually quiet, but the males of many species vocalize to defend their breeding territory or to attract females. In some species, migrations to specific breeding sites may involve vocal communication, celestial navigation, or chemical signaling.

Over the past 30 years, zoologists have documented a rapid and alarming decline in amphibian populations in locations throughout the world. There appear to be several causes, including the spread of a disease-causing chytrid fungus (see Figure 31.26), habitat loss, climate change, and pollution. These and other factors have not only reduced populations, but led to extinctions. A recent study indicates that at least 9 amphibian species have become extinct since 1980; more than 100 other species have not been seen since that time and are considered possibly extinct.

(a) The tadpole is an aquatic herbivore with a fishlike tail and internal gills.

(b) During metamorphosis, the gills and tail are resorbed, and walking legs develop. The adult frog will live on land.

(c) The adults return to water to mate. The male grasps the female, stimulating her to release eggs. The eggs are laid and fertilized in water. They have a jelly coat but lack a shell and would desiccate in air.

▲ Figure 34.23 **The "dual life" of a frog (*Rana temporaria*).**

▲ Figure 34.24 **A mobile nursery.** A female pygmy marsupial frog, *Flectonotus pygmaeus*, incubates her eggs in a pouch of skin on her back, helping to protect the eggs from predators. When the eggs hatch, the female deposits the tadpoles in water where they begin life on their own.

1. Describe the origin of tetrapods and identify some of their key derived traits.
2. Some amphibians never leave the water, whereas others can survive in relatively dry terrestrial environments. Contrast the adaptations that facilitate these two lifestyles.
3. **WHAT IF?** Scientists think that amphibian populations may provide an early warning system of environmental problems. What features of amphibians might make them particularly sensitive to environmental problems?

For suggested answers, see Appendix A.

Amniotes are tetrapods that have a terrestrially adapted egg

The **amniotes** are a group of tetrapods whose extant members are the reptiles (including birds) and mammals (Figure 34.25). During their evolution, amniotes acquired a number of new adaptations to life on land.

Derived Characters of Amniotes

Amniotes are named for the major derived character of the clade, the **amniotic egg**, which contains four specialized membranes: the amnion, the chorion, the yolk sac, and the

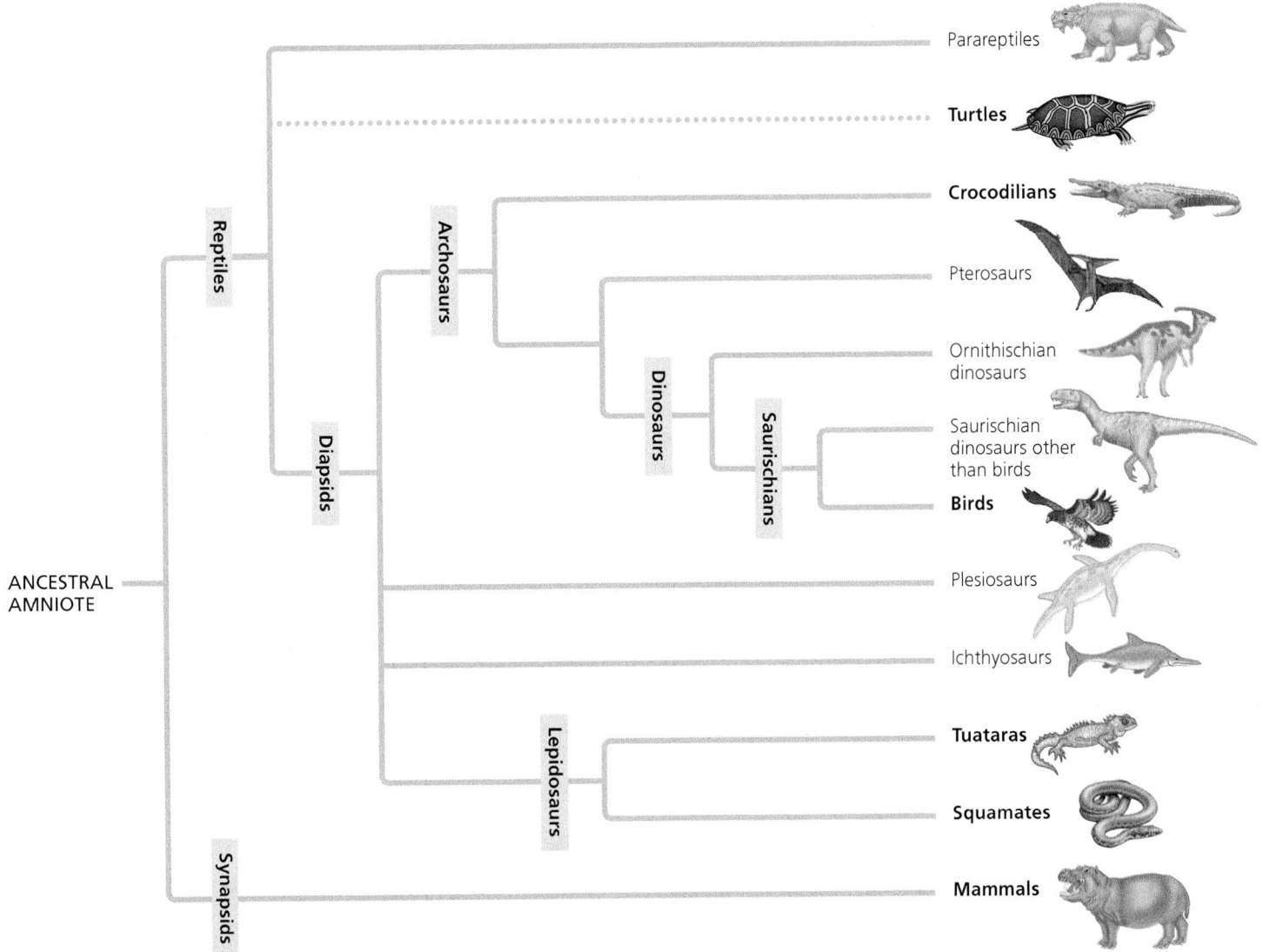

Pararreptiles

Turtles

Crocodilians

Pterosaurs

Ornithischian dinosaurs

Saurischian dinosaurs other than birds

Birds

Plesiosaurs

Ichthyosaurs

Tuataras

Squamates

Mammals

ANCESTRAL AMNIOTE

Reptiles · Archosaurs · Diapsids · Dinosaurs · Saurischians · Lepidosaurs · Synapsids

▲ **Figure 34.25 A phylogeny of amniotes.** Extant groups are named at the tips of the branches in boldface type. The dotted line of the turtle branch indicates the uncertain relationship of turtles to other reptiles. Turtles may be a sister group to parareptiles (as indicated by some morphological data), or they may be diapsids more closely related to lepidosaurs (as indicated by other morphological analyses) or to archosaurs (as indicated by many molecular studies).

? *Based on this phylogeny, DNA sequences in birds are likely most similar to DNA sequences in which other extant group of amniotes? Explain.*

► Figure 34.26 **The amniotic egg.**
The embryos of reptiles and mammals form four extraembryonic membranes: the amnion, chorion, yolk sac, and allantois. This diagram shows these membranes in the shelled egg of a reptile.

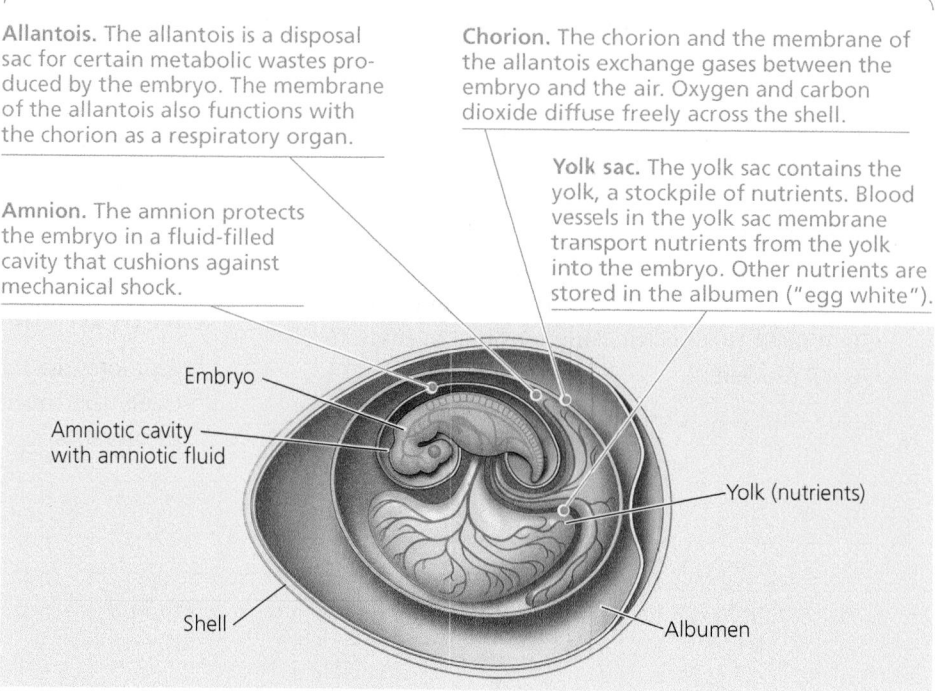

Allantois. The allantois is a disposal sac for certain metabolic wastes produced by the embryo. The membrane of the allantois also functions with the chorion as a respiratory organ.

Chorion. The chorion and the membrane of the allantois exchange gases between the embryo and the air. Oxygen and carbon dioxide diffuse freely across the shell.

Amnion. The amnion protects the embryo in a fluid-filled cavity that cushions against mechanical shock.

Yolk sac. The yolk sac contains the yolk, a stockpile of nutrients. Blood vessels in the yolk sac membrane transport nutrients from the yolk into the embryo. Other nutrients are stored in the albumen ("egg white").

Embryo

Amniotic cavity with amniotic fluid

Yolk (nutrients)

Shell

Albumen

allantois (**Figure 34.26**). Called *extraembryonic membranes* because they are not part of the body of the embryo itself, these membranes develop from tissue layers that grow out from the embryo. The amniotic egg is named for the amnion, which encloses a compartment of fluid that bathes the embryo and acts as a hydraulic shock absorber. The other membranes in the egg function in gas exchange, the transfer of stored nutrients to the embryo, and waste storage. The amniotic egg was a key evolutionary innovation for terrestrial life: It allowed the embryo to develop on land in its own private "pond," hence reducing the dependence of tetrapods on an aqueous environment for reproduction.

In contrast to the shell-less eggs of amphibians, the amniotic eggs of most reptiles and some mammals have a shell. The shells of bird eggs are calcareous (made of calcium carbonate) and inflexible, while the eggshells of many other reptiles are leathery and flexible. Either kind of shell significantly slows dehydration of the egg in air, an adaptation that helped amniotes to occupy a wider range of terrestrial habitats than amphibians, their closest living relatives. (Seeds played a similar role in the evolution of land plants, as we discussed in Chapter 30.) Most mammals have dispensed with the eggshell over the course of their evolution, and the embryo avoids desiccation by developing within the amnion inside the mother's body.

Amniotes have acquired other key adaptations to life on land. For example, amniotes use their rib cage to ventilate their lungs. This method is more efficient than throat-based ventilation, which amphibians use as a supplement to breathing through their skin. The increased efficiency of rib cage ventilation may

have allowed amniotes to abandon breathing through their skin and develop less permeable skin, thereby conserving water.

Early Amniotes

The most recent common ancestor of living amphibians and amniotes likely lived about 350 million years ago. No fossils of amniotic eggs have been found from that time, which is not surprising given how delicate they are. Thus, it is not yet possible to say when the amniotic egg evolved, although it must have existed in the last common ancestor of living amniotes, which all have amniotic eggs.

Based on where their fossils have been found, the earliest amniotes lived in warm, moist environments, as did the first tetrapods. Over time, however, early amniotes expanded into a wide range of new environments, including dry and high-latitude regions. The earliest amniotes were small and had sharp teeth, a sign that they were predators (**Figure 34.27**). Later groups also included herbivores, as evidenced by their grinding teeth and other features.

▲ Figure 34.27 **Artist's reconstruction of *Hylonomus*, an early amniote.** About 25 cm long, this species lived 310 million years ago and probably ate insects and other small invertebrates.

Reptiles

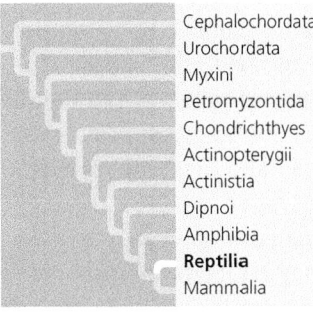

Cephalochordata
Urochordata
Myxini
Petromyzontida
Chondrichthyes
Actinopterygii
Actinistia
Dipnoi
Amphibia
Reptilia
Mammalia

The **reptile** clade includes tuataras, lizards, snakes, turtles, crocodilians, and birds, along with a number of extinct groups, such as plesiosaurs and ichthyosaurs (see Figure 34.25).

Fossil evidence indicates that the earliest reptiles lived about 310 million years ago and resembled lizards. Reptiles have diverged greatly since that time, but as a group they share several derived characters that distinguish them from other tetrapods. For example, unlike amphibians, reptiles have scales that contain the protein keratin (as does a human nail). Scales help protect the animal's skin from desiccation and abrasion. In addition, most reptiles lay their shelled eggs on land (Figure 34.28). Fertilization must occur internally, before the eggshell is secreted. Many species of snakes and lizards are viviparous; in such species, the extraembryonic membranes form a kind of placenta that enables the embryo to obtain nutrients from its mother.

Reptiles such as lizards and snakes are sometimes described as "cold-blooded" because they do not use their metabolism extensively to control their body temperature. However, they do regulate their body temperature by using behavioral adaptations. For example, many lizards bask in the sun when the air is cool and seek shade when the air is too warm. A more accurate description of these reptiles is to say that they are **ectothermic**, which means that they absorb external heat as their main source of body heat. (This topic is discussed in more detail in Chapter 40.) By warming themselves directly with solar energy rather than through the metabolic breakdown of food, an ectothermic reptile can survive on less than 10% of the food energy required by a mammal of the same size. But the reptile clade is not entirely ectothermic; birds are **endothermic**, capable of maintaining body temperature through metabolic activity.

The Origin and Evolutionary Radiation of Reptiles

The oldest reptilian fossils, found in rocks from Nova Scotia, date from the late Carboniferous period. As reptiles diverged from their lizard-like ancestors, one of the first major groups to emerge were the **parareptiles**, which were mostly large, stocky, quadrupedal herbivores. Some parareptiles had plates on their skin that may have provided them with defense against predators. Parareptiles died out by about 200 million years ago, at the end of the Triassic period.

As parareptiles were dwindling, another ancient clade of reptiles, the **diapsids**, was diversifying. One of the most obvious derived characters of diapsids is a pair of holes on each side of the skull, behind the eye socket; muscles pass through these holes and attach to the jaw, controlling jaw movement. The diapsids are composed of two main lineages. One lineage gave rise to the **lepidosaurs**, which include tuataras, lizards, and snakes. This lineage also produced a number of marine reptiles, including the giant mososaurs. Some of these marine species rivaled today's whales in length; all of them are extinct. (We'll say more about living lepidosaurs shortly.)

The other diapsid lineage, the **archosaurs**, produced the crocodilians (which we'll discuss later), pterosaurs, and dinosaurs. **Pterosaurs**, which originated in the late Triassic, were the first tetrapods to exhibit flapping flight. The pterosaur wing was completely different from the wings of birds and bats. It consisted of a collagen-strengthened membrane that stretched between the trunk or hind leg and a very long digit on the foreleg. Well-preserved fossils show evidence of muscles, blood vessels, and nerves in the wing membranes, suggesting that pterosaurs could dynamically adjust their membranes to assist their flight.

The smallest pterosaurs were no bigger than a sparrow, and the largest had a wingspan of nearly 11 m. They appear to have converged on many of the ecological roles later played by birds; some were insect-eaters, others grabbed fish out of the ocean, and still others filtered small animals through thousands of fine needlelike teeth. But by the end of the Cretaceous period 65 million years ago, pterosaurs had become extinct.

On land, the **dinosaurs** diversified into a vast range of shapes and sizes, from bipeds the size of a pigeon to 45-m-long quadrupeds with necks long enough to let them browse the tops of trees. One lineage of dinosaurs, the ornithischians, were herbivores; they included many species with elaborate defenses against predators, such as tail clubs and horned crests. The other main lineage of dinosaurs, the saurischians, included the

▲ **Figure 34.28 Hatching reptiles.** These bushmaster snakes (*Lachesis muta*) are breaking out of their parchment-like shells, a common type of shell among living reptiles other than birds.

long-necked giants and a group called the **theropods**, which were bipedal carnivores. Theropods included the famous *Tyrannosaurus rex* as well as the ancestors of birds.

There is continuing debate about the metabolism of dinosaurs. Some researchers have pointed out that the Mesozoic climate over much of the dinosaurs' range was relatively warm and unvarying, and they have suggested that the low surface-to-volume ratios of large dinosaurs combined with behavioral adaptations such as basking may have been sufficient for an ectotherm to maintain a suitable body temperature. However, some anatomical evidence supports the hypothesis that at least some dinosaurs were endotherms. Furthermore, paleontologists have found fossils of dinosaurs in both Antarctica and the Arctic; although the climate in these areas was milder when dinosaurs existed than it is today, it was cool enough that small dinosaurs may have had difficulty maintaining a high body temperature through ectothermy. The dinosaur that gave rise to birds was *certainly* endothermic, as are all birds.

Traditionally, dinosaurs were considered slow, sluggish creatures. Since the early 1970s, however, fossil discoveries and research have led to the conclusion that many dinosaurs were agile and fast moving. Dinosaurs had a limb structure that enabled them to walk and run more efficiently than could earlier tetrapods, which had a sprawling gait. Fossilized footprints and other evidence suggest that some species were social—they lived and traveled in groups, much as many mammals do today. Paleontologists have also discovered evidence that some dinosaurs built nests and brooded their eggs, as birds do today (see Figure 26.17).

All dinosaurs except birds became extinct by the end of the Cretaceous period. Their extinction may have been caused at least in part by the asteroid or comet impact you read about in Chapter 25. Some analyses of the fossil record are consistent with this idea in that they show a sudden decline in dinosaur diversity at the end of the Cretaceous. However, other analyses indicate that the number of dinosaur species had begun to decline several million years before the Cretaceous ended. Further fossil discoveries and new analyses will be needed to resolve this debate.

Lepidosaurs

One surviving lineage of lepidosaurs is represented by two species of lizard-like reptiles called tuataras (**Figure 34.29a**). Fossil evidence indicates that tuatara ancestors lived at least 220 million years ago. These organisms thrived on many

▼ **Figure 34.29 Extant reptiles (other than birds).**

(a) Tuatara (*Sphenodon punctatus*)

(b) Australian thorny devil lizard (*Moloch horridus*)

(c) Wagler's pit viper (*Tropidolaemus wagleri*)

(d) Eastern box turtle (*Terrapene carolina carolina*)

(e) American alligator (*Alligator mississippiensis*)

continents well into the Cretaceous period, reaching up to a meter in length. Today, however, tuataras are found only on 30 islands off the coast of New Zealand. When humans arrived in New Zealand 750 years ago, the rats that accompanied them devoured tuatara eggs, eventually eliminating the reptiles on the main islands. The tuataras that remain on the outlying islands are about 50 cm long and feed on insects, small lizards, and bird eggs and chicks. They can live to be over 100 years old. Their future survival depends on whether their remaining habitats are kept rat-free.

The other major living lineage of lepidosaurs consists of the lizards and snakes, or squamates, which number about 7,900 species. Lizards are the most numerous and diverse reptiles (apart from birds) alive today (Figure 34.29b). Many lizards are small; the Jaragua lizard, discovered in the Dominican Republic in 2001, is only 16 mm long—small enough to fit comfortably on a dime. In contrast, the Komodo dragon of Indonesia is a lizard that can reach a length of 3 m. It hunts deer and other large prey, delivering venom with its bite.

Snakes are legless lepidosaurs (Figure 34.29c). As described in Chapter 26, snakes descended from lizards with legs. Today, some species of snakes retain vestigial pelvic and limb bones, providing evidence of their ancestry. Despite their lack of legs, snakes are quite proficient at moving on land, most often by producing waves of lateral bending that pass from head to tail. Force exerted by the bends against solid objects pushes the snake forward. Snakes can also move by gripping the ground with their belly scales at several points along the body while the scales at intervening points are lifted slightly off the ground and pulled forward.

Snakes are carnivorous, and a number of adaptations aid them in hunting and eating prey. They have acute chemical sensors, and though they lack eardrums, they are sensitive to ground vibrations, which helps them detect the movements of prey. Heat-detecting organs between the eyes and nostrils of pit vipers, including rattlesnakes, are sensitive to minute temperature changes, enabling these night hunters to locate warm animals. Venomous snakes inject their toxin through a pair of sharp teeth that may be hollow or grooved. The flicking tongue is not venomous but helps fan odors toward olfactory (smell) organs on the roof of the mouth. Loosely articulated jawbones and elastic skin enable most snakes to swallow prey larger than the diameter of the snake's head (see Figure 23.14).

Turtles

Turtles are one of the most distinctive group of reptiles alive today. All turtles have a boxlike shell made of upper and lower shields that are fused to the vertebrae, clavicles (collarbones), and ribs (Figure 34.29d). Most of the 307 known species of turtles have a hard shell, providing excellent defense against predators. A 2008 study reported the discovery of the oldest known fossil of the turtle lineage, dating to 220 million years ago. This fossil has a complete lower shell but an incomplete upper shell, suggesting that turtles may have acquired full shells in stages. The marine sediments in which this fossil was found also suggest that turtles may have originated in shallow coastal waters. However, as other scientists have argued, it is also possible that turtles originated on land and that the incomplete upper shell of this fossil may have been a specialized adaptation for an aquatic lifestyle. Scientists continue to hunt for fossils that could shed light on the origin of the turtle shell.

The earliest turtles could not retract their head into their shell, but mechanisms for doing so evolved independently in two separate branches of turtles. The side-necked turtles fold their neck horizontally, while the vertical-necked turtles fold their neck vertically.

Some turtles have adapted to deserts, and others live almost entirely in ponds and rivers. Still others have returned to the sea. Sea turtles have a reduced shell and enlarged forelimbs that function as flippers. They include the largest living turtles, the deep-diving leatherbacks, which can exceed a mass of 1,500 kg and feed on jellies. Leatherbacks and other sea turtles are endangered by being caught in fishing nets, as well as by development of the beaches where the turtles lay their eggs.

Alligators and Crocodiles

Alligators and crocodiles (collectively called crocodilians) belong to a lineage that reaches back to the late Triassic (Figure 34.29e). The earliest members of this lineage were small terrestrial quadrupeds with long, slender legs. Later species became larger and adapted to aquatic habitats, breathing air through their upturned nostrils. Some Mesozoic crocodilians grew as long as 12 m and may have attacked dinosaurs and other prey at the water's edge.

The 23 known species of living crocodilians are confined to warm regions of the globe. Alligators in the southeastern United States have made a comeback after spending years on the endangered species list.

Birds

There are about 10,000 species of birds in the world. Like crocodilians, birds are archosaurs, but almost every feature of their anatomy has been modified in their adaptation to flight.

Derived Characters of Birds Many of the characters of birds are adaptations that facilitate flight, including weight-saving modifications that make flying more efficient. For example, birds lack a urinary bladder, and the females of most species have only one ovary. The gonads of both females and males are usually small, except during the breeding season, when they increase in size. Living birds are also toothless, an adaptation that trims the weight of the head.

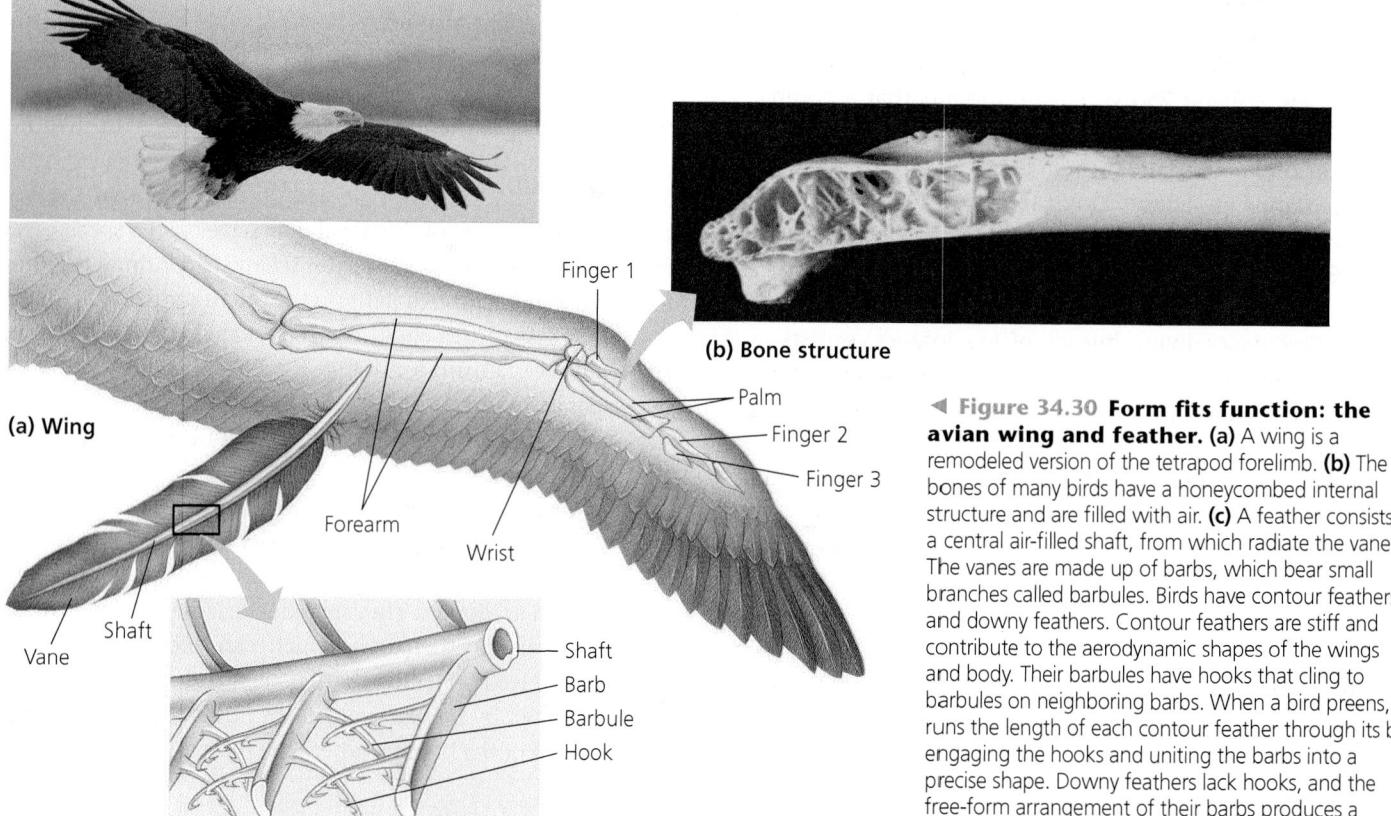

(a) Wing

Finger 1

(b) Bone structure

Palm
Finger 2
Finger 3

Forearm
Wrist

Shaft
Vane

Shaft
Barb
Barbule
Hook

(c) Feather structure

◀ **Figure 34.30 Form fits function: the avian wing and feather. (a)** A wing is a remodeled version of the tetrapod forelimb. **(b)** The bones of many birds have a honeycombed internal structure and are filled with air. **(c)** A feather consists of a central air-filled shaft, from which radiate the vanes. The vanes are made up of barbs, which bear small branches called barbules. Birds have contour feathers and downy feathers. Contour feathers are stiff and contribute to the aerodynamic shapes of the wings and body. Their barbules have hooks that cling to barbules on neighboring barbs. When a bird preens, it runs the length of each contour feather through its bill, engaging the hooks and uniting the barbs into a precise shape. Downy feathers lack hooks, and the free-form arrangement of their barbs produces a fluffiness that provides insulation by trapping air.

A bird's most obvious adaptations for flight are its wings and feathers **(Figure 34.30)**. Feathers are made of the protein β-keratin, which is also found in the scales of other reptiles. The shape and arrangement of the feathers form the wings into airfoils, and they illustrate some of the same principles of aerodynamics as the wings of an airplane. Power for flapping the wings comes from contractions of large pectoral (breast) muscles anchored to a keel on the sternum (breastbone). Some birds, such as eagles and hawks, have wings adapted for soaring on air currents and flap their wings only occasionally; other birds, including hummingbirds, must flap continuously to stay aloft (see Figure 34.34). Among the fastest birds are the appropriately named swifts, which can fly up to 170 km/hr.

Flight provides numerous benefits. It enhances hunting and scavenging; many birds consume flying insects, an abundant, highly nutritious food resource. Flight also provides ready escape from earthbound predators and enables some birds to migrate great distances to exploit different food resources and seasonal breeding areas.

Flying requires a great expenditure of energy from an active metabolism. Birds are endothermic; they use their own metabolic heat to maintain a high, constant body temperature. Feathers and in some species a layer of fat provide insulation that enables birds to retain body heat. The lungs have

tiny tubes leading to and from elastic air sacs that improve airflow and oxygen uptake. This efficient respiratory system and a circulatory system with a four-chambered heart keep tissues well supplied with oxygen and nutrients, supporting a high rate of metabolism.

Flight also requires both acute vision and fine muscle control. Birds have color vision and excellent eyesight. The visual and motor areas of the brain are well developed, and the brain is proportionately larger than those of amphibians and nonbird reptiles.

Birds generally display very complex behaviors, particularly during breeding season, when they engage in elaborate courtship rituals. Because eggs have shells by the time they are laid, fertilization must be internal. Copulation usually involves contact between the mates' vents, the openings to their cloacas. After eggs are laid, the avian embryo must be kept warm through brooding by the mother, the father, or both, depending on the species.

The Origin of Birds Cladistic analyses of birds and reptilian fossils indicate that birds belong to the group of bipedal saurischian dinosaurs called theropods. Since the late 1990s, Chinese paleontologists have unearthed a spectacular trove of feathered theropod fossils that are shedding light on the origin of birds. Several species of dinosaurs closely related to birds had feathers with vanes, and a wider range of species had filamentous feathers. Such findings imply that feathers evolved long before powered flight. Among the possible functions of these early feathers were insulation, camouflage, and courtship display.

How did flight evolve in the theropods? In one scenario, feathers may have enabled small, running dinosaurs chasing prey or escaping predators to gain extra lift as they jumped into the air. Or small dinosaurs could have gained traction as they ran up hills by flapping their feathered forelimbs—a behavior seen in some birds today. In a third scenario, some dinosaurs could have climbed trees and glided, aided by feathers. Whether birds took to the air from the ground up or the trees down, an essential question being studied by scientists ranging from paleontologists to engineers is how their efficient flight stroke evolved.

By 150 million years ago, feathered theropods had evolved into birds. *Archaeopteryx*, which was discovered in a German limestone quarry in 1861, remains the earliest known bird **(Figure 34.31)**. It had feathered wings but retained ancestral characters such as teeth, clawed digits in its wings, and a long tail. *Archaeopteryx* flew well at high speeds, but unlike a present-day bird, it could not take off from a standing position. Fossils of later birds from the Cretaceous show a gradual loss of certain ancestral dinosaur features, such as teeth and clawed forelimbs, as well as the acquisition of innovations found in extant birds, including a short tail covered by a fan of feathers.

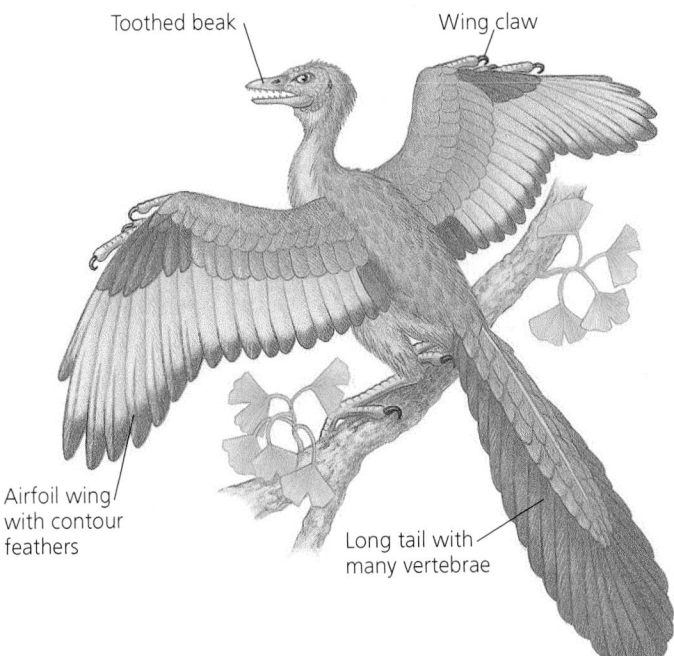

Toothed beak
Wing claw
Airfoil wing with contour feathers
Long tail with many vertebrae

▲ **Figure 34.31 Artist's reconstruction of *Archaeopteryx*, the earliest known bird.** Fossil evidence indicates that *Archaeopteryx* was capable of powered flight but retained many characters of nonbird dinosaurs.

▲ **Figure 34.32 An emu (*Dromaius novaehollandiae*), a flightless bird native to Australia.**

Living Birds Clear evidence of Neornithes, the clade that includes the 28 orders of living birds, can be found before the Cretaceous-Paleogene boundary 65.5 million years ago. Several groups of living and extinct birds include one or more flightless species. The **ratites** (order Struthioniformes), which consist of the ostrich, rhea, kiwi, cassowary, and emu, are all flightless **(Figure 34.32)**. In ratites, the sternal keel is absent, and the pectoral muscles are small relative to those of birds that can fly.

Penguins make up the flightless order Sphenisciformes, but, like flying birds, they have powerful pectoral muscles. They use these muscles to "fly" in the water: As they swim, they flap their flipper-like wings in a manner that resembles the flight stroke of a more typical bird **(Figure 34.33)**. Certain species of rails, ducks, and pigeons are also flightless.

Although the demands of flight have rendered the general body forms of many flying birds similar to one another, experienced bird-watchers can distinguish species by their profile, colors, flying style, behavior, and beak shape. The skeleton of a hummingbird wing is unique, making them the only birds

▲ **Figure 34.33 A king penguin (*Aptenodytes patagonicus*) "flying" underwater.** With their streamlined shape and powerful pectoral muscles, penguins are fast and agile swimmers.

◀ **Figure 34.34 Hummingbird feeding while hovering.** A hummingbird can rotate its wings in all directions, enabling it to hover and fly backwards.

CONCEPT CHECK 34.6

1. Describe three key amniote adaptations for life on land.
2. Are snakes tetrapods? Explain.
3. Identify four avian adaptations for flight.
4. **WHAT IF?** Suppose turtles are more closely related to lepidosaurs than to other reptiles. Redraw Figure 34.25 to show this relationship, and mark the node that represents the most recent common ancestor shared by all living reptiles. Defining the reptile clade as consisting of all descendants of that ancestor, list the reptiles.

For suggested answers, see Appendix A.

that can hover and fly backwards (**Figure 34.34**). Adult birds lack teeth, but during the course of avian evolution their beaks have taken on a variety of shapes suited to different diets. Some birds, such as parrots, have crushing beaks with which they can crack open hard nuts and seeds. Other birds, such as flamingoes, are filter feeders. Their beaks have remarkable 'strainers' that enable them to capture food particles from the water (**Figure 34.35**). Foot structure, too, shows considerable variation. Various birds use their feet for perching on branches (**Figure 34.36**), grasping food, defense, swimming or walking, and even courtship (see Figure 24.3e).

◀ **Figure 34.35 Specialized beaks.** This greater flamingo (*Phoenicopterus ruber*) dips its beak into the water and strains out the food.

▲ **Figure 34.36 Feet adapted to perching.** This great tit (*Parus major*) is a member of the Passeriformes, the perching birds. The toes of these birds can lock around a branch or wire, enabling the bird to rest for long periods.

CONCEPT 34.7

Mammals are amniotes that have hair and produce milk

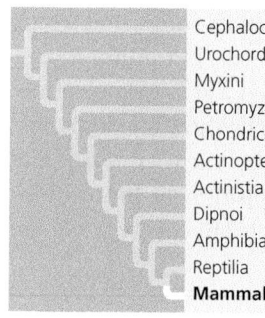

Cephalochordata
Urochordata
Myxini
Petromyzontida
Chondrichthyes
Actinopterygii
Actinistia
Dipnoi
Amphibia
Reptilia
Mammalia

The reptiles we have been discussing represent one of the two living lineages of amniotes. The other amniote lineage is our own, the **mammals** (class Mammalia). Today, there are more than 5,300 known species of mammals on Earth.

Derived Characters of Mammals

The distinctive character from which mammals derive their name is their mammary glands, which produce milk for offspring. All mammalian mothers nourish their young with milk, a balanced diet rich in fats, sugars, proteins, minerals, and vitamins. Hair, another mammalian characteristic, and a fat layer under the skin help the body retain heat. Like birds, mammals are endothermic, and most have a high metabolic rate. Efficient respiratory and circulatory systems (including a four-chambered heart) support a mammal's metabolism. A sheet of muscle called the diaphragm helps ventilate the lungs.

Like birds, mammals generally have a larger brain than other vertebrates of equivalent size, and many species are capable learners. And as in birds, the relatively long duration of parental care extends the time for offspring to learn important survival skills by observing their parents.

Differentiated teeth are another important mammalian trait. Whereas the teeth of reptiles are generally uniform in size and shape, the jaws of mammals bear a variety of teeth with sizes and shapes adapted for chewing many kinds of foods. Humans, like most mammals, have teeth modified for shearing (incisors and canine teeth) and for crushing and grinding (premolars and molars; see Figure 41.16).

Early Evolution of Mammals

Mammals belong to a group of amniotes known as **synapsids**. Early nonmammalian synapsids lacked hair, had a sprawling gait, and laid eggs. A distinctive characteristic of synapsids is the single temporal fenestra, a hole behind the eye socket on each side of the skull. Humans retain this feature; your jaw muscles pass through the temporal fenestra and anchor on your temple. Fossil evidence shows that the jaw was remodeled as mammalian features arose gradually in successive lineages of earlier synapsids (see Figure 25.6); in all, these changes took more than 100 million years. In addition, two of the bones that formerly made up the jaw joint were incorporated into the mammalian middle ear (Figure 34.37). This evolutionary change is reflected in changes that occur during development. For example, as a mammalian embryo grows, the posterior region of its jaw—which in a reptile forms the articular bone—can be observed to detach from the jaw and migrate to the ear, where it forms the malleus.

Synapsids evolved into large herbivores and carnivores during the Permian period, and for a time they were the dominant tetrapods. However, the Permian-Triassic extinctions took a heavy toll on them, and their diversity fell during the Triassic (251–200 million years ago). Increasingly mammal-like synapsids emerged by the end of the Triassic. While not true mammals, these synapsids had acquired a number of the derived characters that distinguish mammals from other amniotes. They were small and probably hairy, and they likely fed on insects at night. Their bones show that they grew faster than other synapsids, suggesting that they probably had a relatively high metabolic rate; however, they still laid eggs.

During the Jurassic (200–145 million years ago), the first true mammals arose and diversified into many short-lived lineages. A diverse set of mammal species coexisted with dinosaurs in Jurassic and Cretaceous periods, but these species were not abundant or dominant members of their community, and most measured less than 1 m. One possible explanation for their small size is that dinosaurs already occupied ecological niches of large-bodied animals.

By the early Cretaceous, the three major lineages of mammals had emerged: those leading to monotremes (egg-laying mammals), marsupials (mammals with a pouch), and eutherians (placental mammals). After the extinction of large dinosaurs, pterosaurs, and marine reptiles during the late Cretaceous period, mammals underwent an adaptive radiation, giving rise to large predators and herbivores as well as flying and aquatic species.

Monotremes

Monotremes are found only in Australia and New Guinea and are represented by one species of platypus and four species of echidnas (spiny anteaters). Monotremes lay eggs, a character that is ancestral for amniotes and retained in most

Key	
	Articular
	Quadrate
	Dentary
	Squamosal

◀ Figure 34.37 **The evolution of the mammalian ear bones.** *Biarmosuchus* was a synapsid, a lineage that eventually gave rise to the mammals. Bones that transmit sound in the ear of mammals arose from the modification of bones in the jaw of nonmammalian synapsids.

MAKE CONNECTIONS *Review the definition of exaptation in Concept 25.6 (p. 530). Summarize the process by which exaptation occurs and explain how the incorporation of the articular and quadrate bones into the mammalian inner ear is an example.*

Biarmosuchus, a synapsid

Temporal fenestra

Jaw joint

(a) In *Biarmosuchus,* the articular and quadrate bones formed the jaw joint.

Middle ear

Eardrum   Stapes   Inner ear

Sound

Present-day reptile

Eardrum   Middle ear

Inner ear

Stapes

Incus (quadrate)

Malleus (articular)

Sound

Present-day mammal

(b) During the evolutionary remodeling of the mammalian skull, a new jaw joint formed between the dentary and squamosal bones (see Figure 25.6). No longer used in the jaw, the quadrate and articular bones became incorporated into the middle ear as two of the three bones that transmit sound from the eardrum to the inner ear.

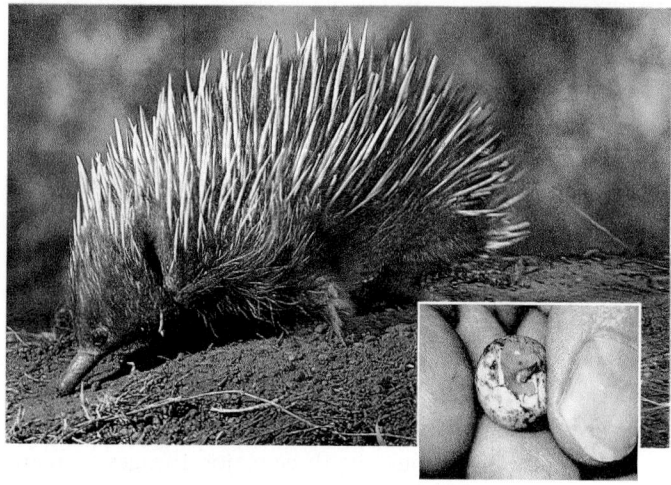

▲ Figure 34.38 **Short-beaked echidna (*Tachyglossus aculeatus*), an Australian monotreme.** Monotremes have hair and produce milk, but they lack nipples. Monotremes are the only mammals that lay eggs (inset).

(a) A young brushtail possum. The offspring of marsupials are born very early in their development. They finish their growth while nursing from a nipple (in their mother's pouch in most species).

(b) Long-nosed bandicoot. Most bandicoots are diggers and burrowers that eat mainly insects but also some small vertebrates and plant material. Their rear-opening pouch helps protect the young from dirt as the mother digs. Other marsupials, such as kangaroos, have a pouch that opens to the front.

▲ Figure 34.39 **Australian marsupials.**

reptiles (Figure 34.38). Like all mammals, monotremes have hair and produce milk, but they lack nipples. Milk is secreted by glands on the belly of the mother. After hatching, the baby sucks the milk from the mother's fur.

Marsupials

Opossums, kangaroos, and koalas are examples of **marsupials**. Both marsupials and eutherians share derived characters not found among monotremes. They have higher metabolic rates and nipples that provide milk, and they give birth to live young. The embryo develops inside the uterus of the female's reproductive tract. The lining of the uterus and the extraembryonic membranes that arise from the embryo form a **placenta**, a structure in which nutrients diffuse into the embryo from the mother's blood.

A marsupial is born very early in its development and completes its embryonic development while nursing. In most species, the nursing young are held within a maternal pouch called a *marsupium* (Figure 34.39a). A red kangaroo, for instance, is about the size of a honeybee at its birth, just 33 days after fertilization. Its back legs are merely buds, but its front legs are strong enough for it to crawl from the exit of its mother's reproductive tract to a pouch that opens to the front of her body, a journey that lasts a few minutes. In other species, the marsupium opens to the rear of the mother's body; in bandicoots, this protects the young as their mother burrows in the dirt (Figure 34.39b).

Marsupials existed worldwide during the Mesozoic era, but today they are found only in the Australian region and in North and South America. The biogeography of marsupials is an example of the interplay between biological and geologic evolution (see Concept 25.4). After the breakup of the supercontinent Pangaea, South America and Australia became island

continents, and their marsupials diversified in isolation from the eutherians that began an adaptive radiation on the northern continents. Australia has not been in contact with another continent since early in the Cenozoic era, about 65 million years ago. In Australia, convergent evolution has resulted in a diversity of marsupials that resemble eutherians in similar ecological roles in other parts of the world (Figure 34.40). In contrast, although South America had a diverse marsupial fauna throughout the Paleogene, it has experienced several migrations of eutherians. One of the most important migrations occurred about 3 million years ago, when North and South America joined at the Panamanian isthmus and extensive two-way traffic of animals took place over the land bridge. Today, only three families of marsupials live outside the Australian region, and the only marsupials found in the wild in North America are a few species of opossum.

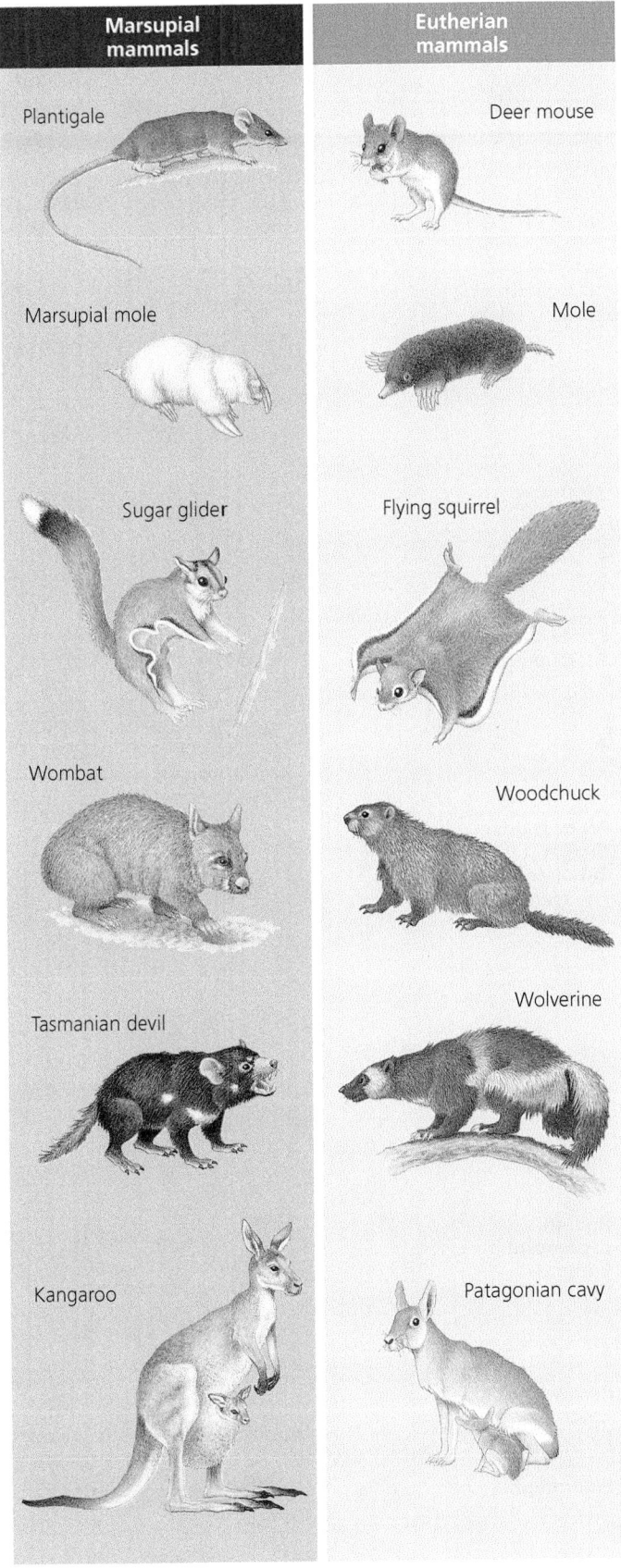

Marsupial mammals	Eutherian mammals
Plantigale	Deer mouse
Marsupial mole	Mole
Sugar glider	Flying squirrel
Wombat	Woodchuck
Tasmanian devil	Wolverine
Kangaroo	Patagonian cavy

▲ Figure 34.40 **Convergent evolution of marsupials and eutherians (placental mammals).** (Drawings are not to scale.)

Eutherians (Placental Mammals)

Eutherians are commonly called placental mammals because their placentas are more complex than those of marsupials. Eutherians have a longer pregnancy than marsupials. Young eutherians complete their embryonic development within the uterus, joined to their mother by the placenta. The eutherian placenta provides an intimate and long-lasting association between the mother and her developing young.

The major groups of living eutherians are thought to have diverged from one another in a burst of evolutionary change. The timing of this burst is uncertain: It is dated to 100 million years ago by molecular data and 60 million years ago by morphological data. **Figure 34.41**, on the next two pages, explores the major eutherian orders and their possible phylogenetic relationships with each other as well as with the monotremes and marsupials.

Primates

The mammalian order Primates includes the lemurs, tarsiers, monkeys, and apes. Humans are members of the ape group.

Derived Characters of Primates Most primates have hands and feet adapted for grasping, and their digits have flat nails instead of the narrow claws of other mammals. There are other characteristic features of the hands and feet, too, such as skin ridges on the fingers (which account for human fingerprints). Relative to other mammals, primates have a large brain and short jaws, giving them a flat face. Their forward-looking eyes are close together on the front of the face. Primates also exhibit relatively well-developed parental care and complex social behavior.

The earliest known primates were tree-dwellers, and many of the characteristics of primates are adaptations to the demands of living in the trees. Grasping hands and feet allow primates to hang onto tree branches. All living primates, except humans, have a big toe that is widely separated from the other toes, enabling them to grasp branches with their feet. All primates also have a thumb that is relatively movable and separate from the fingers, but monkeys and apes have a fully **opposable thumb**; that is, they can touch the ventral surface (fingerprint side) of the tip of all four fingers with the ventral surface of the thumb of the same hand. In monkeys and apes other than humans, the opposable thumb functions in a grasping "power grip." In humans, a distinctive bone structure at the base of the thumb allows it to be used for more precise manipulation. The unique dexterity of humans represents descent with modification from our tree-dwelling ancestors. Arboreal maneuvering also requires excellent eye-hand coordination. The overlapping visual fields of the two forward-facing eyes enhance depth perception, an obvious advantage when brachiating (traveling by swinging from branch to branch in trees).

Exploring Mammalian Diversity

Phylogenetic Relationships of Mammals

Evidence from numerous fossils and molecular analyses indicates that monotremes diverged from other mammals about 180 million years ago and that marsupials diverged from eutherians (placental mammals) about 140 million years ago. Molecular systematics has helped to clarify the evolutionary relationships between the eutherian orders, though there is still no broad consensus on a phylogenetic tree. One current hypothesis, represented by the tree shown below, clusters the eutherian orders into four main clades.

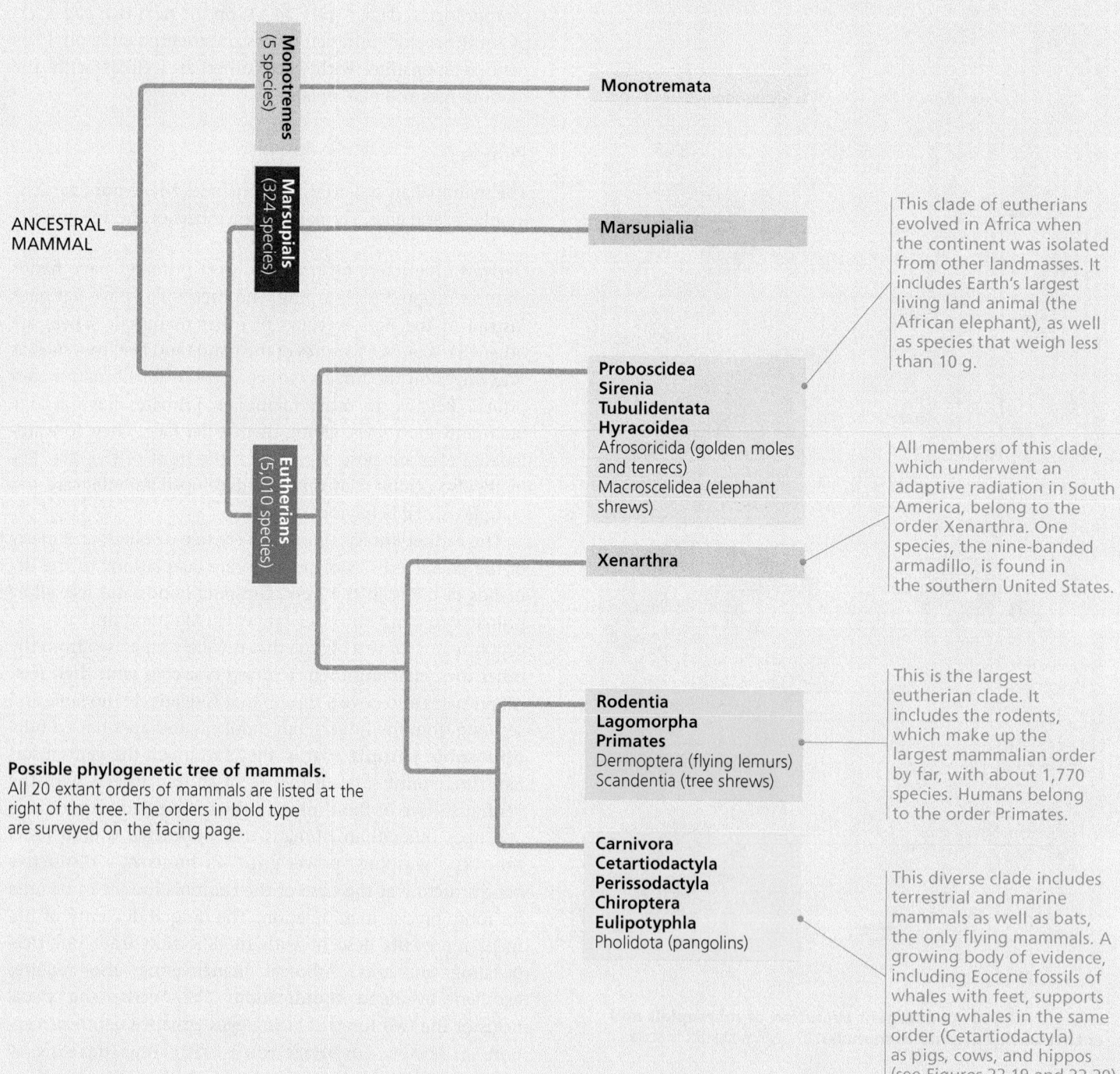

This clade of eutherians evolved in Africa when the continent was isolated from other landmasses. It includes Earth's largest living land animal (the African elephant), as well as species that weigh less than 10 g.

All members of this clade, which underwent an adaptive radiation in South America, belong to the order Xenarthra. One species, the nine-banded armadillo, is found in the southern United States.

This is the largest eutherian clade. It includes the rodents, which make up the largest mammalian order by far, with about 1,770 species. Humans belong to the order Primates.

This diverse clade includes terrestrial and marine mammals as well as bats, the only flying mammals. A growing body of evidence, including Eocene fossils of whales with feet, supports putting whales in the same order (Cetartiodactyla) as pigs, cows, and hippos (see Figures 22.19 and 22.20).

Possible phylogenetic tree of mammals.
All 20 extant orders of mammals are listed at the right of the tree. The orders in bold type are surveyed on the facing page.

Orders and Examples	Main Characteristics	Orders and Examples	Main Characteristics
Monotremata Platypuses, echidnas Echidna	Lay eggs; no nipples; young suck milk from fur of mother	**Marsupialia** Kangaroos, opossums, koalas Koala	Completes embryonic development in pouch on mother's body
Proboscidea Elephants African elephant	Long, muscular trunk; thick, loose skin; upper incisors elongated as tusks	**Tubulidentata** Aardvarks Aardvark	Teeth consisting of many thin tubes cemented together; eats ants and termites
Sirenia Manatees, dugongs Manatee	Aquatic; finlike fore-limbs and no hind limbs; herbivorous	**Hyracoidea** Hyraxes Rock hyrax	Short legs; stumpy tail; herbivorous; complex, multi-chambered stomach
Xenarthra Sloths, anteaters, armadillos Tamandua	Reduced teeth or no teeth; herbivorous (sloths) or carnivorous (anteaters, armadillos)	**Rodentia** Squirrels, beavers, rats, porcupines, mice Red squirrel	Chisel-like, continuously growing incisors worn down by gnawing; herbivorous
Lagomorpha Rabbits, hares, picas Jackrabbit	Chisel-like incisors; hind legs longer than forelegs and adapted for running and jumping; herbivorous	**Primates** Lemurs, monkeys, chimpanzees, gorillas, humans Golden lion tamarin	Opposable thumbs; forward-facing eyes; well-developed cerebral cortex; omnivorous
Carnivora Dogs, wolves, bears, cats, weasels, otters, seals, walruses Coyote	Sharp, pointed canine teeth and molars for shearing; carnivorous	**Perissodactyla** Horses, zebras, tapirs, rhinoceroses Indian rhinoceros	Hooves with an odd number of toes on each foot; herbivorous
Cetartiodactyla Artiodactyls Sheep, pigs, cattle, deer, giraffes Bighorn sheep	Hooves with an even number of toes on each foot; herbivorous	**Chiroptera** Bats Frog-eating bat	Adapted for flight; broad skinfold that extends from elongated fingers to body and legs; carnivorous or herbivorous
Cetaceans Whales, dolphins, porpoises Pacific white-sided porpoise	Aquatic; streamlined body; paddle-like fore-limbs and no hind limbs; thick layer of insulating blubber; carnivorous	**Eulipotyphla** "Core insectivores": some moles, some shrews Star-nosed mole	Eat mainly insects and other small invertebrates

Living Primates There are three main groups of living primates: (1) the lemurs of Madagascar (**Figure 34.42**) and the lorises and bush babies of tropical Africa and southern Asia; (2) the tarsiers, which live in Southeast Asia; and (3) the **anthropoids**, which include monkeys and apes and are found worldwide. The first group—lemurs, lorises, and bush babies—probably resemble early arboreal primates. The oldest known anthropoid fossils, discovered in China in mid-Eocene strata dating to 45 million years ago, indicate that tarsiers are more closely related to anthropoids than to the lemur group (**Figure 34.43**).

You can see in Figure 34.38 that monkeys do not form a clade but rather consist of two groups, the New and Old World monkeys. Both of these groups are thought to have originated in Africa or Asia. The fossil record indicates that New World monkeys first colonized South America roughly 25 million years ago. By that time, South America and Africa had drifted apart, and monkeys may have reached South America from Africa by rafting on logs or other debris. What is certain is that New World monkeys and Old World monkeys underwent separate adaptive radiations during their many millions of years of separation (**Figure 34.44**). All species of New World monkeys are arboreal, whereas Old World monkeys include ground-dwelling as well as arboreal species. Most monkeys in both groups are diurnal (active during the day) and usually live in bands held together by social behavior.

The other group of anthropoids consists of primates informally called apes (**Figure 34.45**). The ape group includes the genera *Hylobates* (gibbons), *Pongo* (orangutans), *Gorilla* (gorillas), *Pan* (chimpanzees and bonobos), and *Homo* (humans).

▶ **Figure 34.42**
Coquerel's sifakas (*Propithecus verreauxi coquereli*), a type of lemur.

ANCESTRAL PRIMATE

Lemurs, lorises, and bush babies

Tarsiers

New World monkeys

Old World monkeys

Gibbons

Orangutans

Gorillas

Chimpanzees and bonobos

Humans

Anthropoids

▲ **Figure 34.43 A phylogenetic tree of primates.** The fossil record indicates that anthropoids began diverging from other primates about 50 million years ago. New World monkeys, Old World monkeys, and apes (the clade that includes gibbons, orangutans, gorillas, chimpanzees, and humans) have been evolving as separate lineages for over 20 million years. The lineages leading to humans branched off from other apes sometime between 6 and 7 million years ago.

? *Is the phylogeny shown here consistent with the idea that humans evolved from chimpanzees? Explain.*

60   50   40   30   20   10   0

Time (millions of years ago)

▼ **Figure 34.44** **New World monkeys and Old World monkeys.**

(a) New World monkeys, such as spider monkeys (shown here), squirrel monkeys, and capuchins, have a prehensile tail and nostrils that open to the sides.

(b) Old World monkeys lack a prehensile tail, and their nostrils open downward. This group includes macaques (shown here), mandrils, baboons, and rhesus monkeys.

The apes diverged from Old World monkeys about 20–25 million years ago. Today, nonhuman apes are found exclusively in tropical regions of the Old World. With the exception of gibbons, living apes are larger than either New or Old World monkeys. All living apes have relatively long arms, short legs, and no tail. Although all nonhuman apes spend time in trees, only gibbons and orangutans are primarily arboreal. Social organization varies among the apes; gorillas and chimpanzees are highly social. Finally, compared to other primates, apes have a larger brain in proportion to their body size, and their behavior is more flexible. These two characteristics are especially prominent in the next group we'll consider, the hominins.

(a) Gibbons, such as this Muller's gibbon, are found only in southeastern Asia. Their very long arms and fingers are adaptations for brachiating (swinging by the arms from branch to branch).

(b) Orangutans are shy apes that live in the rain forests of Sumatra and Borneo. They spend most of their time in trees; note the foot adapted for grasping and the opposable thumb.

(c) Gorillas are the largest apes; some males are almost 2 m tall and weigh about 200 kg. Found only in Africa, these herbivores usually live in groups of up to about 20 individuals.

(d) Chimpanzees live in tropical Africa. They feed and sleep in trees but also spend a great deal of time on the ground. Chimpanzees are intelligent, communicative, and social.

▲ **Figure 34.45** **Nonhuman apes.**

(e) Bonobos are in the same genus (*Pan*) as chimpanzees but are smaller. They survive today only in the African nation of Congo.

1. Contrast monotremes, marsupials, and eutherians in terms of how they bear young.
2. Identify at least five derived traits of primates.
3. **MAKE CONNECTIONS** Develop a hypothesis to explain why the diversity of mammals increased in the Cenozoic. Your explanation should consider mammalian adaptations as well as factors such as mass extinctions and continental drift (review these factors in Concept 25.4, pp. 519–524).

For suggested answers, see Appendix A.

CONCEPT 34.8

Humans are mammals that have a large brain and bipedal locomotion

In our tour of Earth's biodiversity, we come at last to our own species, *Homo sapiens*, which is about 200,000 years old. When you consider that life has existed on Earth for at least 3.5 billion years, we are clearly evolutionary newcomers.

Derived Characters of Humans

Many characters distinguish humans from other apes. Most obviously, humans stand upright and are bipedal (walk on two legs). Humans have a much larger brain and are capable of language, symbolic thought, artistic expression, and the manufacture and use of complex tools. Humans also have reduced jawbones and jaw muscles, along with a shorter digestive tract.

At the molecular level, the list of derived characters of humans is growing as scientists compare the genomes of humans and chimpanzees. Although the two genomes are 99% identical, a difference of 1% can translate into a large number of changes in a genome that contains 3 billion base pairs. Furthermore, changes in a small number of genes can have large effects. This point was highlighted by recent results showing that humans and chimpanzees differ in the expression of 19 regulatory genes. These genes turn other genes on and off and hence may account for many differences between humans and chimpanzees.

Bear in mind that such genomic differences—and whatever derived phenotypic traits they code for—separate humans from other *living* apes. But many of these new characters first emerged in our ancestors, long before our own species appeared. We will consider some of these ancestors to see how these characters originated.

The Earliest Hominins

The study of human origins is known as **paleoanthropology**. Paleoanthropologists have unearthed fossils of approximately 20 extinct species that are more closely related to humans than to chimpanzees. These species are known as **hominins** (Figure 34.46, on the facing page). (Although a majority of anthropologists now use the term *hominin*, its older synonym, *hominid*, continues to be used by some). Since 1994, fossils of four hominin species dating to more than 4 million years ago have been discovered. The oldest of these hominins, *Sahelanthropus tchadensis*, lived about 6.5 million years ago.

Sahelanthropus and other early hominins shared some of the derived characters of humans. For example, they had reduced canine teeth, and some fossils suggest that they had relatively flat faces. They also show signs of having been more upright and bipedal than other apes. One clue to their upright stance can be found in the foramen magnum, the hole at the base of the skull through which the spinal cord exits. In chimpanzees, the foramen magnum is relatively far back on the skull, while in early hominins (and in humans), it is located underneath the skull. This position allows us to hold our head directly over our body, as apparently early hominins did as well. The pelvis, leg bones, and feet of the 4.4-million-year-old *Ardipithecus ramidus* also suggest that early hominins were increasingly bipedal (Figure 34.47). (We will return to the subject of bipedalism later.)

Note that the characters that distinguish humans from other living apes did not all evolve in tight unison. While early hominins were showing signs of bipedalism, their brains remained small—about 300–450 cm^3 in volume, compared with an average of 1,300 cm^3 for *Homo sapiens*. The earliest hominins were also small overall. *A. ramidus*, for example, is

◀ Figure 34.47 **The skeleton of "Ardi," a 4.4-million-year-old hominin, *Ardipithecus ramidus*.**

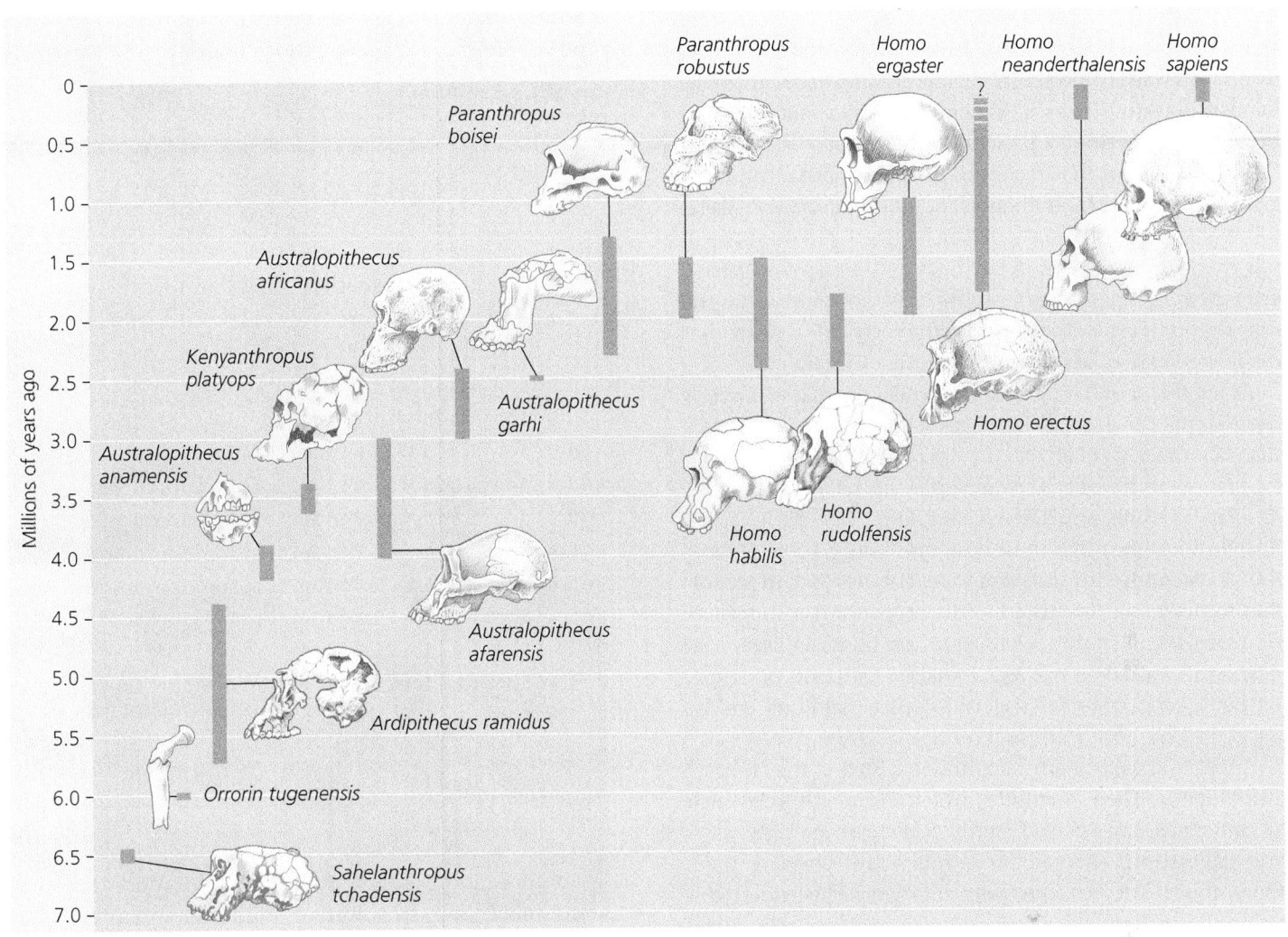

▲ **Figure 34.46 A timeline for some selected hominin species.** Most of these fossils come from sites in eastern and southern Africa. Note that at most times in hominin history, two or more hominin species were contemporaries. Some of the species are controversial, reflecting phylogenetic debates about the interpretation of skeletal details and biogeography.

estimated to have weighed only 50 kg, with relatively large teeth and a jaw that projected beyond the upper part of the face. Humans, in contrast, have a relatively flat face; compare your own face with that of the chimpanzees in Figure 34.45d.

It's important to avoid two common misconceptions when considering early hominins. One is to think of them either as chimpanzees or as having evolved from chimpanzees. Chimpanzees represent the tip of a separate branch of evolution, and they acquired derived characters of their own after they diverged from their common ancestor with humans.

Another misconception is to think of human evolution as a ladder leading directly from an ancestral ape to *Homo sapiens*. This error is often illustrated as a parade of fossil species that become progressively more like ourselves as they march across the page. If human evolution is a parade, it is a very disorderly one, with many groups breaking away to wander other evolutionary paths. At times, several hominin species coexisted. These species often differed in skull shape, body size, and diet

(as inferred from their teeth). Ultimately, all but one lineage—the one that gave rise to *Homo sapiens*—ended in extinction. But when the characteristics of all hominins that lived over the past 6 million years are considered, *H. sapiens* appears not as the end result of a straight evolutionary path, but rather as the only surviving member of a highly branched evolutionary tree.

Australopiths

The fossil record indicates that hominin diversity increased dramatically between 4 and 2 million years ago. Many of the hominins from this period are collectively called australopiths. Their phylogeny remains unresolved on many points, but as a group, they are almost certainly paraphyletic. The earliest member of the group, *Australopithecus anamensis*, lived 4.2–3.9 million years ago, close in time to older hominins such as *Ardipithecus ramidus*.

Australopiths got their name from the 1924 discovery in South Africa of *Australopithecus africanus* ("southern ape of

Africa"), which lived between 3 and 2.4 million years ago. With the discovery of more fossils, it became clear that *A. africanus* walked fully erect (was bipedal) and had human-like hands and teeth. However, its brain was only about one-third the size of the brain of a present-day human.

In 1974, in the Afar region of Ethiopia, paleoanthropologists discovered a 3.2-million-year-old *Australopithecus* skeleton that was 40% complete. "Lucy," as the fossil was named, was short—only about 1 m tall. Lucy and similar fossils have been given the species name *Australopithecus afarensis* (for the Afar region). Fossils discovered in the early 1990s show that *A. afarensis* existed as a species for at least 1 million years.

At the risk of oversimplifying, we could say that *A. afarensis* had fewer of the derived characters of humans above the neck than below. Lucy's brain was the size of a softball, a size similar to that expected for a chimpanzee of Lucy's body size. *A. afarensis* skulls also have a long lower jaw. Skeletons of *A. afarensis* suggest that these hominins were capable of arboreal locomotion, with arms that were relatively long in proportion to body size (compared to the proportions in humans). However, fragments of pelvic and skull bones indicate that *A. afarensis* walked on two legs. Fossilized footprints in Laetoli, Tanzania, corroborate the skeletal evidence that hominins living at the time of *A. afarensis* were bipedal (Figure 34.48).

Another lineage of australopiths consisted of the "robust" australopiths. These hominins, which included species such as *Paranthropus boisei*, had sturdy skulls with powerful jaws and large teeth, adapted for grinding and chewing hard, tough foods. They contrast with the "gracile" (slender) australopiths, including *A. afarensis* and *A. africanus*, which had lighter feeding equipment adapted for softer foods.

Combining evidence from the earliest hominins with the much richer fossil record of later australopiths makes it possible to formulate hypotheses about significant trends in hominin evolution. Let's consider two of these trends: the emergence of bipedalism and tool use.

Bipedalism

Our anthropoid ancestors of 35–30 million years ago were still tree-dwellers. But by about 10 million years ago, the Himalayan mountain range had formed, thrust up in the aftermath of the Indian plate's collision with the Eurasian plate (see Figure 25.13). The climate became drier, and the forests of what are now Africa and Asia contracted. The result was an increased area of savanna (grassland) habitat, with fewer trees. For decades, paleoanthropologists have seen a strong connection between the rise of savannas and the rise of bipedal hominins. According to one hypothesis, tree-dwelling hominins could no longer move through the canopy, so natural selection favored adaptations that made moving over open ground more efficient. Underlying this idea is the fact that while nonhuman apes are superbly adapted for climbing trees, they are less well suited for

▶ **Figure 34.48**
Evidence that hominins walked upright 3.5 million years ago.

(a) The Laetoli footprints, more than 3.5 million years old, confirm that upright posture evolved quite early in hominin history.

(b) An artist's reconstruction of *A. afarensis*, a hominin alive at the time of the Laetoli footprints.

ground travel. For example, as a chimpanzee walks, it uses four times the amount of energy used by a human.

Although elements of this hypothesis survive, the picture now appears somewhat more complex. Although all recently discovered fossils of early hominins show indications of bipedalism, none of these hominins lived in savannas. Instead, they lived in mixed habitats ranging from forests to open woodlands. Furthermore, whatever the selective pressure that led to bipedalism, hominins did not become more bipedal in a simple, linear fashion. *Ardipithecus* had skeletal elements indicating that it could switch to upright walking but also was well suited for climbing trees. Australopiths seem to have had various locomotor styles, and some species spent more time on the ground than others. Only about 1.9 million years ago did hominins begin to walk long distances on two legs. These hominins lived in more arid environments, where bipedal walking requires less energy than walking on all fours.

Tool Use

As you read earlier, the manufacture and use of complex tools is a derived behavioral character of humans. Determining the origin of tool use in hominin evolution is one of paleoanthropology's great challenges. Other apes are capable of surprisingly sophisticated tool use. Orangutans, for example, can fashion sticks into probes for retrieving insects from their nests. Chimpanzees are even more adept, using rocks to smash open food and putting leaves on their feet to walk over thorns. It's likely that early hominins were capable of this sort of simple tool use, but finding fossils of modified sticks or leaves that were used as shoes is practically impossible.

The oldest generally accepted evidence of tool use by hominins is 2.5-million-year-old cut marks on animal bones found in Ethiopia. These marks suggest that hominins cut flesh from the bones of animals using stone tools. Interestingly, the hominins whose fossils were found near the site where the bones were discovered had a relatively small brain. If these hominins, which have been named *Australopithecus garhi*, were in fact the creators of the stone tools used on the bones, that would suggest that stone tool use originated before the evolution of large brains in hominins.

Early *Homo*

The earliest fossils that paleoanthropologists place in our genus, *Homo*, include those of the species *Homo habilis*. These fossils, ranging in age from about 2.4 to 1.6 million years, show clear signs of certain derived hominin characters above the neck. Compared to the australopiths, *H. habilis* had a shorter jaw and a larger brain volume, about 600–750 cm³. Sharp stone tools have also been found with some fossils of *H. habilis* (the name means "handy man").

Fossils from 1.9 to 1.5 million years ago mark a new stage in hominin evolution. A number of paleoanthropologists recognize these fossils as those of a distinct species, *Homo ergaster*. *Homo ergaster* had a substantially larger brain than *H. habilis* (over 900 cm³), as well as long, slender legs with hip joints well adapted for long-distance walking (**Figure 34.49**). The fingers were relatively short and straight, suggesting that *H. ergaster* did not climb trees like earlier hominins. *Homo ergaster* fossils have been discovered in far more arid environments than earlier hominins and have been associated with more sophisticated stone tools. Its smaller teeth also suggest that *H. ergaster* either ate different foods than australopiths (more meat and less plant material) or prepared some of its food before chewing, perhaps by cooking or mashing the food.

Homo ergaster marks an important shift in the relative sizes of the sexes. In primates, a size difference between males and females is a major component of sexual dimorphism (see Chapter 23). On average, male gorillas and orangutans weigh about twice as much as females of their species. In chimpanzees and bonobos, males are only about 1.35 times as heavy as females, on average. In *Australopithecus afarensis*, males were 1.5 times as heavy as females. But in early *Homo*, sexual dimorphism was significantly reduced, and this trend continues through our own species: Human males average about 1.2 times the weight of females.

▶ **Figure 34.49 Fossil of Homo ergaster.** This 1.7-million-year-old fossil from Kenya belongs to a young *Homo ergaster* male. This individual was tall, slender, and fully bipedal, and he had a relatively large brain.

The reduced sexual dimorphism may offer some clues to the social systems of extinct hominins. In extant primates, extreme sexual dimorphism is associated with intense male-male competition for multiple females. In species that undergo more pair-bonding (including our own), sexual dimorphism is less dramatic. In *H. ergaster*, therefore, males and females may have engaged in more pair-bonding than earlier hominins did. This shift may have been associated with long-term care of the young by both parents. Human babies depend on their parents for food and protection much longer than do the young of other apes.

Fossils now generally recognized as *H. ergaster* were originally considered early members of another species, *Homo erectus*, and some paleoanthropologists still hold this position. *Homo erectus* originated in Africa and was the first hominin to migrate out of Africa. The oldest fossils of hominins outside Africa, dating back 1.8 million years, were discovered in 2000 in the former Soviet Republic of Georgia. *Homo erectus* eventually migrated as far as the Indonesian archipelago. Fossil evidence indicates that *H. erectus* became extinct sometime after 200,000 years ago; one group may have persisted on Java until roughly 50,000 years ago.

Neanderthals

In 1856, miners discovered some mysterious human fossils in a cave in the Neander Valley in Germany. The 40,000-year-old fossils belonged to a thick-boned hominin with a prominent brow. The hominin was named *Homo neanderthalensis* and is commonly called a Neanderthal. Neanderthals were living in Europe by 350,000 years ago and later spread to the Near East, central Asia, and southern Siberia. They had a brain as large as that of present-day humans, buried their dead, and made hunting tools from stone and wood. But despite their adaptations and culture, Neanderthals apparently became extinct about 28,000 years ago.

At one time, many paleoanthropologists considered Neanderthals to be a stage in the evolution of *Homo erectus* into *Homo sapiens*. Now most have abandoned this view, partly due to the analysis of mitochondrial DNA (**Figure 34.50**). These and other genetic results suggest that Neanderthals may have contributed little to the gene pool of *H. sapiens*. However, a 2010 analysis of the DNA sequence of the Neanderthal genome appears to be consistent with limited gene flow between the two species. In addition, some researchers have argued that evidence of gene flow can be found in fossils that show a mixture of *H. sapiens* and Neanderthal characteristics. Further genetic analyses and fossil discoveries will be needed to resolve the ongoing debate over the extent of genetic exchange between the two species.

Homo sapiens

Evidence from fossils, archaeology, and DNA studies has led to a compelling hypothesis about how our own species, *Homo sapiens*, emerged and spread around the world.

Fossil evidence indicates that the ancestors of humans originated in Africa. Older species (perhaps *H. ergaster* or *H. erectus*) gave rise to later species, ultimately including *H. sapiens*. Furthermore, the oldest known fossils of our own species have been found at two different sites in Ethiopia and include specimens that are 195,000 and 160,000 years old (**Figure 34.51**). These early humans had less pronounced browridges than found in *H. erectus* and Neanderthals, and they were more slender than other recent hominins.

The Ethiopian fossils support inferences about the origin of humans from molecular evidence. As shown in Figure 34.50, DNA analyses indicate that all living humans are more closely related to one another than to Neanderthals. Other studies on human DNA show that Europeans and Asians share a relatively recent common ancestor and that many African lineages branched off more basal positions on the human family tree. These findings strongly suggest that all living humans have ancestors that originated as *H. sapiens* in Africa, which is further supported by analysis of mitochondrial DNA and Y chromosomes from members of various human populations.

The oldest fossils of *H. sapiens* outside Africa are from the Middle East and date back about 115,000 years.

▲ **Figure 34.51 A 160,000-year-old fossil of Homo sapiens.** This skull, discovered in Ethiopia in 2003, differs little from the skulls of living humans.

INQUIRY

Did Neanderthals give rise to European humans?

EXPERIMENT People have long been fascinated by Neanderthals and their relationship to *Homo sapiens*. Several fossils discovered in Europe have been interpreted by some researchers as showing a mixture of Neanderthal and human features, leading to the suggestion that European humans bred extensively with or descended from Neanderthals. Igor Ovchinnikov and William Goodwin, then at the University of Glasgow, and their team used genetic methods to assess the relationship between Neanderthals and *H. sapiens*. The team extracted mitochondrial DNA (mtDNA) from a Neanderthal fossil (Neanderthal 1) and compared its sequence to an mtDNA sequence that other researchers had obtained three years earlier from a different Neanderthal fossil (Neanderthal 2). Mitochondrial DNA sequences were also obtained for a number of living humans from Europe, Africa, and Asia. The researchers then used Neanderthal and *H. sapiens* mtDNA sequences to construct a phylogenetic tree for Neanderthals and humans; data from chimpanzees were used to root the tree. This approach permitted the researchers to test the following hypothesis:

Hypothesis: Neanderthals gave rise to European humans.

Expected phylogeny:

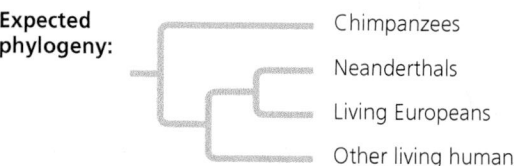

Chimpanzees

Neanderthals

Living Europeans

Other living humans

RESULTS The two Neanderthal mtDNA sequences differed at 3.5% of the bases, whereas on average, the Neanderthal and *H. sapiens* mtDNA differed at 24% of the bases. The phylogenetic analysis yielded the following tree:

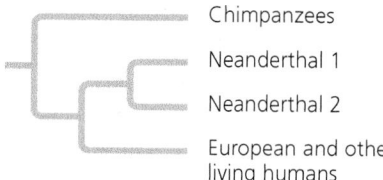

Chimpanzees

Neanderthal 1

Neanderthal 2

European and other living humans

CONCLUSION The Neanderthals form one clade, and living humans form another, separate clade. Thus, it is not likely that Neanderthals gave rise to European humans.

SOURCE I. V. Ovchinnikov et al., Molecular analysis of Neanderthal DNA from the northern Caucasus, *Nature* 404:490–493 (2000).

WHAT IF? The human and chimpanzee lineages diverged about 6 million years ago. Can the phylogeny shown in RESULTS be used to infer when Neanderthal and human lineages diverged? Explain.

Studies of the human Y chromosome suggest that humans spread beyond Africa in one or more waves, first into Asia and then to Europe and Australia. The date of the first arrival of humans in the New World is uncertain, although the oldest generally accepted evidence puts that date at about 15,000 years ago.

New findings continually update our understanding of the evolution of *H. sapiens*. For example, in 2004, researchers reported an astonishing find: skeletal remains of adult hominins dating from just 18,000 years ago and representing a previously unknown species, which they named *Homo floresiensis*. Discovered in a limestone cave on the Indonesian island of Flores, the individuals were much shorter and had a much smaller brain volume than *H. sapiens*—more similar, in fact, to an australopith. The researchers who discovered these fossils argue that the skeletons also display many derived traits, including skull thickness and proportions and teeth shape, suggesting that the species is descended from the larger *H. erectus*. Not convinced, some researchers have argued that the fossils represent small *H. sapiens* individuals with deformed, miniature brains, a condition called microcephaly.

However, a 2007 study found that the wrist bones of the Flores fossils are similar in shape to those of nonhuman apes and early hominins, but different from those of Neanderthals and *H. sapiens*. These researchers concluded that the Flores fossils represent a species whose lineage branched off before the origin of the clade that includes Neanderthals and humans. A later study comparing the foot bones of the Flores fossils with those of other hominins also indicated that *H. floresiensis* arose before *H. sapiens*; in fact, these researchers suggested that *H. floresiensis* may have descended from an as-yet-unidentified hominin that lived even earlier than *H. erectus*.

If further evidence continues to support the designation of *H. floresiensis* as a new hominin, one intriguing explanation for this species' apparent "shrinkage" is that isolation on the island may have resulted in selection for greatly reduced size. Such dramatic size reduction is well studied in other dwarf mammalian species that are endemic to islands, including primitive pygmy elephants found near the Flores fossils. One such study found that on islands, the brains of dwarf fossil hippos were proportionally even smaller than their bodies. One possible explanation for this finding is that smaller brains resulted from selection for reduced energy consumption (the mammalian brain uses large amounts of energy). Applying their results to the Flores fossils, the researchers concluded that the brain size of *H. floresiensis* closely matches that predicted for a dwarf hominin of its body size. Compelling questions that may yet be answered from the cache of anthropological and archaeological finds on Flores include how *H. floresiensis* originated and whether it encountered *H. sapiens*, which also was living in Indonesia 18,000 years ago.

The rapid expansion of our species may have been spurred by changes in human cognition as *H. sapiens* evolved in Africa. Evidence of sophisticated thought in *H. sapiens* includes a 2002 discovery in South Africa of 77,000-year-old art—geometric markings made on pieces of ochre (Figure 34.52). And in 2004, archaeologists working in southern and eastern Africa found 75,000-year-old ostrich eggs and snail shells with holes neatly drilled through them. By 36,000 years ago, humans were producing spectacular cave paintings (see Figure 56.33a). While these developments can help us understand the spread of *H. sapiens*, it is not clear whether they played a role in the extinction of other hominins. Neanderthals, for example, also

▲ **Figure 34.52 Art, a human hallmark.** The engravings on this 77,000-year-old piece of ochre, discovered in South Africa's Blombos Cave, are among the earliest signs of symbolic thought in humans.

made complex tools and showed a capacity for symbolic thought. As a result, the earlier suggestion that Neanderthals were driven to extinction by competition with *H. sapiens* is now being questioned by some scientists.

Our discussion of humans brings this unit on biological diversity to an end. But this organization isn't meant to imply that life consists of a ladder leading from lowly microorganisms to lofty humanity. Biological diversity is the product of branching phylogeny, not ladderlike "progress," however we choose to measure it. The fact that there are more species of ray-finned fishes alive today than all other vertebrates combined is a clear indication that our finned relatives are not outmoded underachievers that failed to leave the water. The tetrapods—amphibians, reptiles, and mammals—are derived from one lineage of lobe-finned vertebrates. As tetrapods diversified on land, fishes continued their branching evolution in the greatest portion of the biosphere's volume. Similarly, the ubiquity of diverse prokaryotes throughout the biosphere today is a reminder of the enduring ability of these relatively simple organisms to keep up with the times through adaptive evolution. Biology exalts life's diversity, past and present.

CONCEPT CHECK 34.8

1. Identify some characters that distinguish hominins from other apes.
2. Provide an example in which different features of organisms in the hominin evolutionary lineage evolved at different rates.
3. **WHAT IF?** Some genetic studies suggest that the most recent common ancestor of *Homo sapiens* that lived outside of Africa spread from Africa about 50,000 years ago. Compare this date with the dates of fossils given in the text. Can both the genetic results and the dates ascribed to the fossils be correct? Explain.

For suggested answers, see Appendix A.

SUMMARY OF KEY CONCEPTS

Key Concept	Clade	Description
Concept 34.1 Chordates have a notochord and a dorsal, hollow nerve cord (pp. 697–701) **?** *Describe likely features of the chordate common ancestor and explain your reasoning.*	Cephalochordata (lancelets)	Basal chordates; marine suspension feeders that exhibit four key derived characters of chordates
	Urochordata (tunicates)	Marine suspension feeders; larvae display the derived traits of chordates
Concept 34.2 Craniates are chordates that have a head (pp. 701–703) **?** *Compare the typical lifestyle of craniates with that of lancelets and tunicates.*	Myxini (hagfishes and relatives)	Jawless marine organisms; have head that includes a skull and brain, eyes, and other sensory organs
Concept 34.3 Vertebrates are craniates that have a backbone (pp. 703–704) **?** *Identify the shared features of early fossil vertebrates.*	Petromyzontida (lampreys)	Jawless vertebrates; typically feed by attaching to a live fish and ingesting its blood
Concept 34.4 Gnathostomes are vertebrates that have jaws (pp. 704–709) **?** *How would the appearance of organisms with jaws have altered ecological interactions? Provide supporting evidence.*	Chondrichthyes (sharks, rays, skates, ratfishes)	Aquatic gnathostomes; have cartilaginous skeleton, a derived trait formed by the reduction of an ancestral mineralized skeleton
	Actinopterygii (ray-finned fishes)	Aquatic gnathostomes; have bony skeleton and maneuverable fins supported by rays
	Actinistia (coelacanths)	Ancient lineage of aquatic lobe-fins still surviving in Indian Ocean
	Dipnoi (lungfishes)	Freshwater lobe-fins with both lungs and gills; sister group of tetrapods
Concept 34.5 Tetrapods are gnathostomes that have limbs (pp. 709–713) **?** *Which features of amphibians restrict most species to living in aquatic or moist terrestrial habitats?*	Amphibia (salamanders, frogs, caecilians)	Have four limbs descended from modified fins; most have moist skin that functions in gas exchange; many live both in water (as larvae) and on land (as adults)
Concept 34.6 Amniotes are tetrapods that have a terrestrially adapted egg (pp. 713–720) **?** *Explain why birds are considered reptiles.*	Reptilia (tuataras, lizards and snakes, turtles, crocodilians, birds)	One of two groups of living amniotes; have amniotic eggs and rib cage ventilation, key adaptations for life on land
Concept 34.7 Mammals are amniotes that have hair and produce milk (pp. 720–728) **?** *Describe the origin and early evolution of mammals.*	Mammalia (monotremes, marsupials, eutherians)	Evolved from synapsid ancestors; include egg-laying monotremes (echidnas, platypus); pouched marsupials (such as kangaroos, opossums); and eutherians (placental mammals, such as rodents, primates)

Phylogenetic bracket labels (read vertically):
- **Chordates:** notochord; dorsal, hollow nerve cord; pharyngeal slits; post-anal tail
- **Craniates:** two sets of *Hox* genes, neural crest
- **Vertebrates:** *Dlx* genes duplication, backbone of vertebrae
- **Gnathostomes:** hinged jaws, four sets of *Hox* genes
- **Osteichthyans:** bony skeleton
- **Lobe-fins:** muscular fins or limbs
- **Tetrapods:** four limbs, neck, fused pelvic girdle
- **Amniotes:** amniotic egg, rib cage ventilation

CONCEPT 34.8

Humans are mammals that have a large brain and bipedal locomotion (pp. 728–733)

- Derived characters of humans include that we are bipedal and have a larger brain and reduced jaw compared with other apes.
- Hominins—humans and species that are more closely related to humans than to chimpanzees—originated in Africa at least 6 million years ago. Early hominins had a small brain but probably walked upright.
- The oldest evidence of tool use is 2.5 million years old.
- *Homo ergaster* was the first fully bipedal, large-brained hominin. *Homo erectus* was the first hominin to leave Africa.
- Neanderthals lived in Europe and the Near East from about 350,000 to 28,000 years ago.
- *Homo sapiens* originated in Africa about 195,000 years ago and began to spread to other continents about 115,000 years ago.

? *Explain why it is misleading to portray human evolution as a "ladder" leading to* Homo sapiens.

TEST YOUR UNDERSTANDING

LEVEL 1: KNOWLEDGE/COMPREHENSION

1. Vertebrates and tunicates share
   a. jaws adapted for feeding.
   b. a high degree of cephalization.
   c. the formation of structures from the neural crest.
   d. an endoskeleton that includes a skull.
   e. a notochord and a dorsal, hollow nerve cord.

2. Some animals that lived 530 million years ago resembled lancelets but had a brain and a skull. These animals may represent
   a. the first chordates.
   b. a "missing link" between urochordates and cephalochordates.
   c. early craniates.
   d. marsupials.
   e. nontetrapod gnathostomes.

3. Which of the following could be considered the most recent common ancestor of living tetrapods?
   a. a sturdy-finned, shallow-water lobe-fin whose appendages had skeletal supports similar to those of terrestrial vertebrates
   b. an armored, jawed placoderm with two pairs of appendages
   c. an early ray-finned fish that developed bony skeletal supports in its paired fins
   d. a salamander that had legs supported by a bony skeleton but moved with the side-to-side bending typical of fishes
   e. an early terrestrial caecilian whose legless condition had evolved secondarily

4. Unlike eutherians, *both* monotremes and marsupials
   a. lack nipples.
   b. have some embryonic development outside the uterus.
   c. lay eggs.
   d. are found in Australia and Africa.
   e. include only insectivores and herbivores.

5. Which clade does *not* include humans?
   a. synapsids
   b. lobe-fins
   c. diapsids
   d. craniates
   e. osteichthyans

6. As hominins diverged from other primates, which of the following appeared first?
   a. reduced jawbones
   b. language
   c. bipedal locomotion
   d. the making of stone tools
   e. an enlarged brain

LEVEL 2: APPLICATION/ANALYSIS

7. **EVOLUTION CONNECTION**
   Living members of a vertebrate lineage can be very different from early members of the lineage, and evolutionary reversals (character losses) are common. Give examples that illustrate these observations, and explain their evolutionary causes.

LEVEL 3: SYNTHESIS/EVALUATION

8. **SCIENTIFIC INQUIRY**
   DRAW IT As a consequence of size alone, organisms that are large tend to have larger brains than organisms that are small. However, some organisms have brains that are considerably larger than expected for an animal of their size. There are high energetic costs associated with the development and maintenance of brains that are large relative to body size.
   (a) The fossil record documents trends in which brains that are large relative to body size evolved in certain lineages, including hominins. In such lineages, what can you infer about the relative magnitude of the costs and benefits of large brains?
   (b) Hypothesize how natural selection might favor the evolution of large brains despite their high maintenance costs.
   (c) Data for 14 bird species are listed below. Graph the data, placing deviation from expected brain size on the *x*-axis and mortality rate on the *y*-axis. What can you conclude about the relationship between brain size and mortality?

Deviation from Expected Brain Size*	−2.4	−2.1	2.0	−1.8	−1.0	0.0	0.3	0.7	1.2	1.3	2.0	2.3	3.0	3.2
Mortality Rate	0.9	0.7	0.5	0.9	0.4	0.7	0.8	0.4	0.8	0.3	0.6	0.6	0.3	0.6

D. Sol et al., Big-brained birds survive better in nature, *Proceedings of the Royal Society B* 274:763–769 (2007).

*Values <0 indicate brain sizes smaller than expected; values >0 indicate sizes larger than expected.

9. **WRITE ABOUT A THEME**
   Emergent Properties Early tetrapods had a sprawling gait (like that of a lizard): As the right front foot moved forward, the body twisted to the left and the left rib cage and lung were compressed; the reverse occurred with the next step. Normal breathing, in which both lungs expand equally with each breath, was hindered during walking and prevented during running. In a short essay (100–150 words), explain how the origin of organisms such as dinosaurs, whose gait allowed them to move without compressing their lungs, could have led to emergent properties in biological communities.

For selected answers, see Appendix A.

Mastering BIOLOGY www.masteringbiology.com

1. MasteringBiology® Assignments
Tutorial Chordates
Activities Deuterostome Diversity • Characteristics of Chordates • Primate Diversity • Human Evolution
Questions Student Misconceptions • Reading Quiz • Multiple Choice • End-of-Chapter

2. eText
Read your book online, search, take notes, highlight text, and more.

3. The Study Area
Practice Tests • Cumulative Test • **BioFlix** 3-D Animations • MP3 Tutor Sessions • Videos • Activities • Investigations • Lab Media • Audio Glossary • Word Study Tools • Art

6 UNIT

Plant Form and Function

An Interview with
Luis Herrera-Estrella

Luis Herrera-Estrella is a leading advocate for the use of genetic engineering to improve the lives of poor farmers in Mexico and other developing countries. He graduated with a B.Sc. in Biochemical Engineering from the National Polytechnic Institute (NPI) in Mexico City in 1978. In 1980 he received his M.Sc. from the Center for Research and Advanced Studies at NPI (where he heads a laboratory today) and in 1984 his Ph.D. from Ghent University, in Belgium. While still a graduate student, he published the first report of the successful transfer and expression of a bacterial gene in plant cells. He also pioneered the development of selectable markers and the use of reporter genes for plant systems, which have since become two of the most important tools in developing gene transfer systems for crops. More recently, his work has focused on improving plant tolerance to acidic and phosphate-deficient soils. Among other honors, Dr. Herrera is a Scholar of the Howard Hughes Biomedical Institute, a member of the Mexican Academy of Sciences, a foreign associate member of the U.S. National Academy of Sciences, and a past president of the International Society for Plant Molecular Biology.

What sparked your interest in science?
My childhood interest in science came from reading books and watching TV programs about science and technology. As a child, I wanted to be an inventor. However, because I came from a lower middle-class family in Mexico and had no contact with scientists or academics, I didn't really know what science or research was. When I finished high school, I wanted to become a nuclear physicist, but I was told that nuclear physics didn't have a future in Mexico. So I studied biochemical engineering. I had an inspirational teacher, a microbiologist who taught me about molecular biology. I was fascinated and decided to pursue a Ph.D.

How did you become interested in plant molecular biology?
I thought about how I could use molecular biology. Agriculture is important in Mexico, so I decided to study plant molecular biology

even though I had absolutely no background in plant biology! When I reached this decision, Francisco Bolívar, one of the scientists who had developed a type of plasmid widely used in genetic engineering, had just returned to Mexico. So I asked him if I could work with him before entering a Ph.D. program. Very kindly, he accepted me. When I was in his lab, a visiting scientist from Belgium, Marc van Montagu, gave a seminar about *Agrobacterium* and the potential use of this bacterium for genetically modifying plants. I immediately thought, "That's my future!"

Agrobacterium tumefaciens is a bacterial pathogen that causes crown gall disease. How does one make the creative leap to change a disease into a useful tool?
Agrobacterium causes disease by transferring genes into the host plant's chromosomes and modifying the cell's metabolism for its own benefit. When I went to Belgium, the plant molecular biologist Patricia Zambryski was already studying the mechanism by which tumor-inducing (Ti) plasmids of *Agrobacterium* integrate into plant chromosomes. She had been able to produce "disarmed Ti plasmids"—modified plasmids that failed to produce tumors or alter the host's metabolism but were still effective in DNA transfer. But we didn't have a way to quickly identify which cells were modified because the transformed cells had no selective advantage. I started working on a way to get plant cells to express foreign genes. Scientists had just identified the sequences of two genes in the DNA transferred by *Agrobacterium* to its host. So I figured that the promoter sequence and terminator sequences of these genes could be used to express any gene we chose. We took a gene that confers resistance to the protein synthesis inhibitor kanamycin (because we could select for that gene) and integrated it into a disarmed Ti plasmid. We then transformed plant cells with these plasmids and obtained transgenic plant cells that were resistant to kanamycin! The next question was whether genetic transformation had affected the ability of the cells to regenerate from tiny clumps of cells into whole plants. It was exciting to see that when we put these cells in tissue culture medium, little plants emerged, and they were still kanamycin resistant. Finally, we determined that the transgenes were passed on according to Mendel's laws, just like any other gene!

How is your more recent research contributing to agriculture?
One of the major problems faced by farmers in the tropics is acidic soil. The problem stems from the fact that aluminum, which is high in tropical soils, becomes soluble under acidic conditions, and the ions are quite toxic to plants. We have been able to genetically alter plants to secrete more organic acids from their roots. The organic anions bind the aluminum cations and eliminate the toxicity.

We are also interested in how plants alter their architecture in response to deficiencies in phosphorus, an essential plant nutrient. Phosphorus availability is one of the most limiting factors for plant productivity in many natural and agricultural ecosystems. We have found that in low-phosphorus conditions, root systems become more branched, and root hairs become denser and longer. What controls these changes? You don't see this in animals. We don't develop extra arms or extra legs in response to environmental changes.

What are the steps for transferring the results of basic research to products in the field, and why do some people oppose genetically engineered crops?
To go from a discovery in the lab to the commercial release of a transgenic plant is a long process that requires extensive testing in the lab, in the greenhouse, and eventually in the field. You have to demonstrate that the transgenic crop performs consistently under different environments and that it has no negative effects on yield

or quality. And then you have to go through the process of approval for human consumption and show that the protein that you introduce is not toxic or allergenic. Unfortunately, it can cost $10–50 million to go through this regulatory process. Nowadays, the only organizations that can afford to commercialize transgenic plants are large, multinational companies.

Because multinational companies have monopolized the commercialization of transgenic plants, there has been a strong reaction from people who oppose the control of food production by such companies. Other issues are raised—for example, that GMOs (genetically modified organisms) could harm the environment or human health. But in fact most of the products commercially released to date have been shown to be totally innocuous for human and animal health and have no different impact on the environment than traditional crops. The opposition to GMOs initially started in Europe, where most people have enough money to buy food and don't need transgenic crops. It's not the same case in other countries where any technology that helps to produce more and better food is strongly needed. I do not think that recombinant technology is a miracle that is going to solve the problem of hunger in the world, but it's going to be a very important tool for making agriculture more productive.

Tell us about the debate surrounding GMOs in Mexico.

When I returned to Mexico in 1986, some field trials of transgenic plants were under way. There wasn't much controversy because few people knew what a transgenic plant was. Government officials had heard about the potential applications of genetic engineering, and they were happy that Mexico was involved in this new technology. But then people who oppose multinational companies and some ecologists started to protest, and the government officials became concerned. The government decided that if the scientists couldn't agree, then it would be better to err on the side of caution, and an official moratorium was imposed against planting transgenic crops in Mexico. The farmers, however, wanted the technology, and they began smuggling the seeds of genetically modified plants, especially maize, into Mexico and planting them illegally. This is a bad situation because you don't know what, where, or how much they are planting. We argued that the only way of assessing whether GMOs are actually going to have a negative effect on the environment and alter the genomes of indigenous varieties of maize is to do small, controlled experiments employing every conceivable biological safety measure. Eventually, the government agreed and lifted the moratorium.

Maize cross-fertilizes very easily and over long distances, so it's impossible to avoid the transfer of genes from transgenic maize into Mexico's indigenous varieties of maize. Is this a problem? Personally, I don't think so. Plants, particularly maize, are full of transposable elements that jump from one place in the genome to another. So, the maize genome is already a "mess." Introducing one more gene is not going to be any different from a transposon moving an enhancer or a complete gene from one place in the genome to another. Of course we have to analyze each transgenic line to make sure that the gene is not going to cause any problem for the environment or for the health of humans or other animals.

> "... our attempts to modify maize are quite modest compared with what the ancient Native American farmers accomplished."

How can genetic engineering improve the welfare of poor farmers in developing countries?

Those who would benefit the most from genetic engineering are the poorest farmers. For example, the average production of maize in Mexico is about 2.5 tons per acre. But in central Mexico, where I live, the production of maize is around 8–10 tons per acre. That means that in many places, people are producing only 1 ton per acre. If, by using recombinant DNA technology, we can increase the yields of these poor farmers to 3 tons per acre, these people will triple their incomes. Of course, the big seed companies tailor their products for large farms, but they are willing to donate their expertise toward programs aimed at developing the types of crop varieties needed by subsistence farmers. People who oppose the use of the transgenic crops simply because they are controlled by large companies are making it more difficult for scientists in the developing world to create the varieties that are needed by the poor farmers in their countries.

By altering plants you are continuing a great and ancient Mexican tradition: plant domestication. How did farmers create maize over 10,000 years ago?

Well, first I must say that our attempts to modify maize are quite modest compared with what the ancient Native American farmers accomplished. Maize is derived from a wild grass called teosinte. The two plants look fairly similar. It's very hard, for example, to distinguish between the leaves of teosinte and maize. The really fantastic difference is in the reproductive organs. When a teosinte seed matures, it goes "pop!" and lands on the ground. Picking up these small seeds is laborious, so the ancient farmers selected plants that had cobs that held onto their seeds. Also, because teosinte seeds have a very hard coat, making them difficult to cook, the farmers selected for a thinner seed coat. And teosinte has only a single row of seeds, so these early farmers selected for two rows of seeds, and then four and eight, and so on. What we are doing now with genetic engineering is absolutely nothing compared with the domestication of maize.

You have published research on plants, fungi, and bacteria. What has led you to cast such a wide intellectual net?

Curiosity about life and nature and the world around me. I don't share the ambition of people who embrace a single question, topic, or model system at the beginning of their career and then die studying the same thing. I'm always eager to explore new processes and new phenomena, even if I have to switch to a completely different field. Currently, I'm sequencing the genome of plant species native to Mexico—but truthfully, I don't know what I'm going to be doing in four years.

Luis Herrera-Estrella (right) with Peter Minorsky (left) and Jane Reece

35

Plant Structure, Growth, and Development

▲ Figure 35.1 **Computer art?**

KEY CONCEPTS

35.1 Plants have a hierarchical organization consisting of organs, tissues, and cells
35.2 Meristems generate cells for primary and secondary growth
35.3 Primary growth lengthens roots and shoots
35.4 Secondary growth increases the diameter of stems and roots in woody plants
35.5 Growth, morphogenesis, and cell differentiation produce the plant body

OVERVIEW

Are Plants Computers?

The object in **Figure 35.1** is not the creation of a computer genius with a flair for the artistic. It is a head of romanesco, an edible relative of broccoli. Romanesco's mesmerizing beauty is attributable to the fact that each of its smaller buds

resembles in miniature the entire vegetable. (Mathematicians refer to such repetitive patterns as *fractals*.) Romanesco looks as if it were generated by a computer because its growth pattern follows a repetitive sequence of instructions. As in most plants, the growing shoot tips lay down a pattern of leaf . . . bud . . . stem, over and over again. These repetitive developmental patterns are genetically determined and subject to natural selection. For example, a mutation that shortens the stem segments between leaves will generate a bushier plant. If this altered architecture enhances the plant's ability to access resources such as light and, by doing so, to leave more offspring, then this trait will occur more frequently in later generations—evolution will have occurred.

Romanesco is unusual in adhering so rigidly to its basic body organization. Most plants show much greater diversity in their individual forms because the growth of most plants, much more than in animals, is affected by local environmental conditions. All lions, for example, have four legs and are of roughly the same size, but oak trees vary in the number and arrangement of their branches. This is because lions and other animals respond to challenges and opportunities in their local environment by movement, whereas plants respond by altering their growth. Illumination of a plant from the side, for example, creates asymmetries in its basic body plan. Branches grow more quickly from the illuminated side of a shoot than from the shaded side, an architectural change of obvious benefit for photosynthesis. Recognizing the highly adaptive development of plants is critical for understanding how plants interact with their environment.

Chapters 29 and 30 described the evolution of plants from green algae to angiosperms (flowering plants). In Unit Six, we focus primarily on angiosperms because they serve as the primary producers in many ecosystems and are of great agricultural importance. We begin by discussing the structure of flowering plants and how these plants develop.

CONCEPT 35.1

Plants have a hierarchical organization consisting of organs, tissues, and cells

Plants, like most animals, have organs composed of different tissues, which in turn are composed of different cell types. A **tissue** is a group of cells, consisting of one or more cell types, that together perform a specialized function. An **organ** consists of several types of tissues that together carry out particular functions. In looking at the hierarchy of plant organs, tissues, and cells, we begin with organs because they are the most familiar and easily observed plant structures. As you learn about the hierarchy of plant structure, keep in mind how natural selection has produced plant forms that fit plant function at all levels of organization.

The Three Basic Plant Organs: Roots, Stems, and Leaves

The basic morphology of vascular plants reflects their evolutionary history as terrestrial organisms that inhabit and draw resources from two very different environments—below the ground and above the ground. They must absorb water and minerals from below the ground surface and CO_2 and light from above the ground surface. The ability to acquire these resources efficiently is traceable to the evolution of three basic organs—roots, stems, and leaves. These organs form a **root system** and a **shoot system**, the latter consisting of stems and leaves **(Figure 35.2)**. With few exceptions, vascular plants rely completely on both systems for survival. Roots typically are not photosynthetic; they starve unless *photosynthates*, the sugars and other carbohydrates produced during photosynthesis, are imported from the shoot system. Conversely, the shoot system depends on the water and minerals that roots absorb from the soil.

Vegetative growth—production of nonreproductive leaves, stems, and roots—is only one stage in a plant's life. Most plants also undergo growth relating to sexual reproduction. In angiosperms, reproductive shoots bear flowers, which consist of leaves that are highly modified for sexual reproduction.

Later in this chapter, we'll discuss the transition from vegetative shoot formation to reproductive shoot formation.

In describing plant organs, we'll draw examples mainly from the two major groups of angiosperms: monocots and eudicots (see Figure 30.13).

Roots

A **root** is an organ that anchors a vascular plant in the soil, absorbs minerals and water, and often stores carbohydrates. Most eudicots and gymnosperms have a *taproot system*, consisting of one main vertical root, the **taproot**, which develops from an embryonic root. The taproot gives rise to **lateral roots**, also called branch roots (see Figure 35.2). Taproot systems generally penetrate deeply and are therefore well adapted to deep soils, where the groundwater is not close to the surface.

In most monocots, such as grasses, the embryonic root dies early on and does not form a taproot. Instead, many small roots emerge from the stem. Such roots are said to be *adventitious* (from the Latin *adventicus*, extraneous), a term describing a plant organ that grows in an unusual location, such as roots arising from stems or leaves. Each small root forms its own lateral roots. The result is a *fibrous root system*—a mat of generally thin roots spreading out below the soil surface (see Figure 30.13). Fibrous root systems usually do not penetrate deeply and are therefore best adapted to shallow soils or regions where rainfall is light and does not moisten the soil much below the surface layer. Most grasses have shallow roots, concentrated in the upper few centimeters of the soil. Because these shallow roots hold the topsoil in place, grass makes excellent ground cover for preventing erosion.

Although the entire root system helps anchor a plant, in most plants the absorption of water and minerals occurs primarily near the tips of roots, where vast numbers of **root hairs** emerge and increase the surface area of the root enormously **(Figure 35.3)**. A root hair is a thin, tubular extension of a root epidermal cell. It should not be confused with a lateral root, which is an organ. Despite their great surface

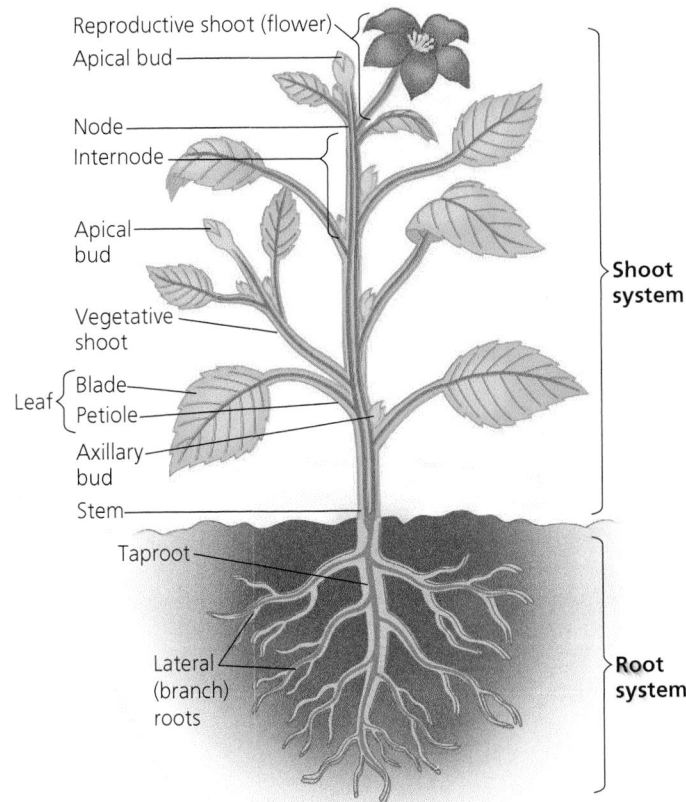

Reproductive shoot (flower)
Apical bud
Node
Internode
Apical bud
Vegetative shoot
Leaf { Blade / Petiole
Axillary bud
Stem
Shoot system

Taproot
Lateral (branch) roots
Root system

▲ **Figure 35.2 An overview of a flowering plant.** The plant body is divided into a root system and a shoot system, connected by vascular tissue (purple strands in this diagram) that is continuous throughout the plant. The plant shown is an idealized eudicot.

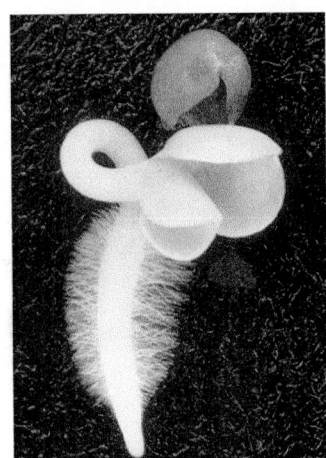

◀ **Figure 35.3 Root hairs of a radish seedling.** Root hairs grow by the thousands just behind the tip of each root. By increasing the root's surface area, they greatly enhance the absorption of water and minerals from the soil.

area, root hairs, unlike lateral roots, contribute little to plant anchorage. Their main function is absorption.

Many plants have root adaptations with specialized functions (Figure 35.4). Some of these arise from the roots, and others are adventitious, developing from stems or, in rare cases, leaves. Some modified roots add support and anchorage. Others store water and nutrients or absorb oxygen from the air.

Stems

A **stem** is an organ that raises or separates leaves, exposing them to sunlight. Stems also raise reproductive structures, facilitating dispersal of pollen and fruit. Each stem consists of an alternating system of **nodes**, the points at which leaves are attached, and **internodes**, the stem segments between nodes (see Figure 35.2). In the upper angle (axil) formed by each leaf and the stem is an **axillary bud**, a structure that can form a lateral shoot, commonly called a branch. Young axillary buds typically grow very slowly: Most of the growth of a young shoot is concentrated near the shoot tip, which consists of an **apical bud**, or terminal bud, that is composed of developing leaves and a compact series of nodes and internodes.

The proximity of the axillary buds to the apical bud is partly responsible for their dormancy. The inhibition of axillary buds by an apical bud is called **apical dominance**. If an animal eats the end of the shoot or if shading results in

▼ **Figure 35.4 Evolutionary adaptations of roots.**

▲ **Prop roots.** The aerial roots of hala trees are examples of prop roots, so named because they support the tall, top-heavy trees. Hala trees grow along coastal areas in the South Pacific where the sandy soils are shallow and unstable.

◀ **Storage roots.** Many plants, such as the common beet, store food and water in their roots.

◀ **"Strangling" aerial roots.** The seeds of this strangler fig germinate in the branches of tall trees of other species and send numerous aerial roots to the ground. These snakelike roots gradually wrap around the host tree and objects such as this Cambodian temple ruin. Eventually, the host tree dies of shading by the fig leaves.

▼ **Buttress roots.** Because of moist conditions in the tropics, root systems of many of the tallest trees are surprisingly shallow. Aerial roots that look like buttresses, such as seen in this ceiba tree in Central America, give architectural support to the trunks of such trees.

▲ **Pneumatophores.** Also known as air roots, pneumatophores are produced by trees such as mangroves that inhabit tidal swamps. By projecting above the water's surface, they enable the root system to obtain oxygen, which is lacking in the thick, waterlogged mud.

the light being more intense to the side of the shoot, axillary buds break dormancy; that is, they start growing. A growing axillary bud gives rise to a lateral shoot, complete with its own apical bud, leaves, and axillary buds. Removing the apical bud stimulates the growth of axillary buds, resulting in more lateral shoots. That is why pruning trees and shrubs and pinching back houseplants will make them bushier. The hormonal changes underlying apical dominance are discussed in Chapter 39.

Some plants have stems with additional functions, such as food storage and asexual reproduction. These modified stems, which include rhizomes, bulbs, stolons, and tubers, are often mistaken for roots (Figure 35.5).

▼ Figure 35.5 **Evolutionary adaptations of stems.**

◀ **Rhizomes.** The base of this iris plant is an example of a rhizome, a horizontal shoot that grows just below the surface. Vertical shoots emerge from axillary buds on the rhizome.

▶ **Bulbs.** Bulbs are vertical underground shoots consisting mostly of the enlarged bases of leaves that store food. You can see the many layers of modified leaves attached to the short stem by slicing an onion bulb lengthwise.

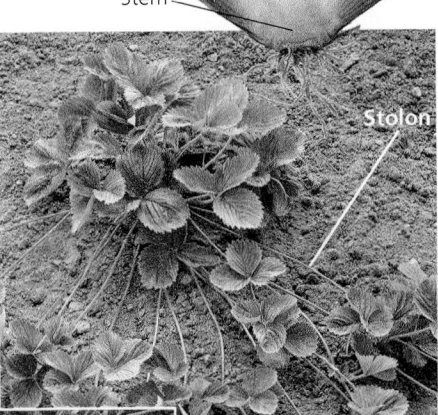

▶ **Stolons.** Shown here on a strawberry plant, stolons are horizontal shoots that grow along the surface. These "runners" enable a plant to reproduce asexually, as plantlets form at nodes along each runner.

◀ **Tubers.** Tubers, such as these potatoes, are enlarged ends of rhizomes or stolons specialized for storing food. The "eyes" of a potato are clusters of axillary buds that mark the nodes.

Leaves

In most vascular plants, the **leaf** is the main photosynthetic organ, although green stems also perform photosynthesis. Leaves vary extensively in form but generally consist of a flattened **blade** and a stalk, the **petiole**, which joins the leaf to the stem at a node (see Figure 35.2). Grasses and many other monocots lack petioles; instead, the base of the leaf forms a sheath that envelops the stem.

Monocots and eudicots differ in the arrangement of **veins**, the vascular tissue of leaves. Most monocots have parallel major veins that run the length of the blade. Eudicots generally have a branched network of major veins (see Figure 30.13).

In identifying angiosperms according to structure, taxonomists rely mainly on floral morphology, but they also use variations in leaf morphology, such as leaf shape, the branching pattern of veins, and the spatial arrangement of leaves. Figure 35.6 illustrates a difference in leaf shape: simple versus compound. Many leaves, such as those of poison ivy, are

▼ Figure 35.6 **Simple versus compound leaves.**

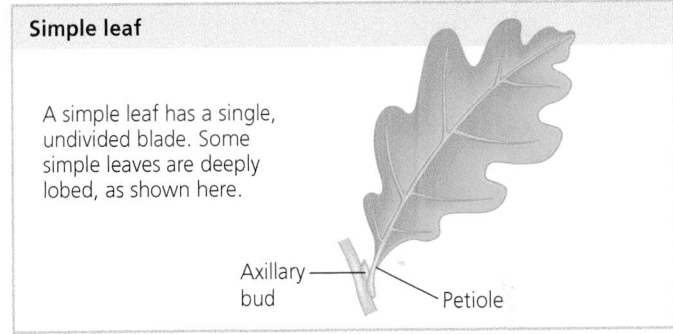

Simple leaf

A simple leaf has a single, undivided blade. Some simple leaves are deeply lobed, as shown here.

Axillary bud

Petiole

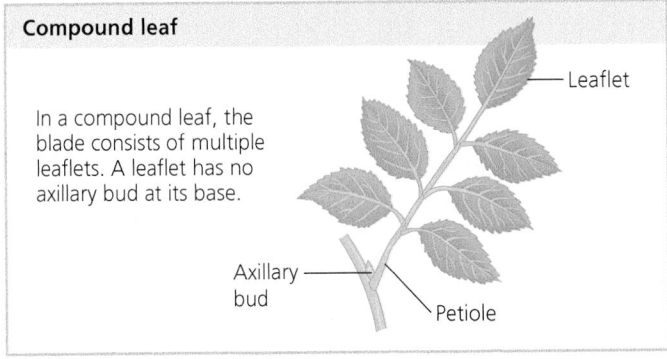

Compound leaf

In a compound leaf, the blade consists of multiple leaflets. A leaflet has no axillary bud at its base.

Leaflet

Axillary bud

Petiole

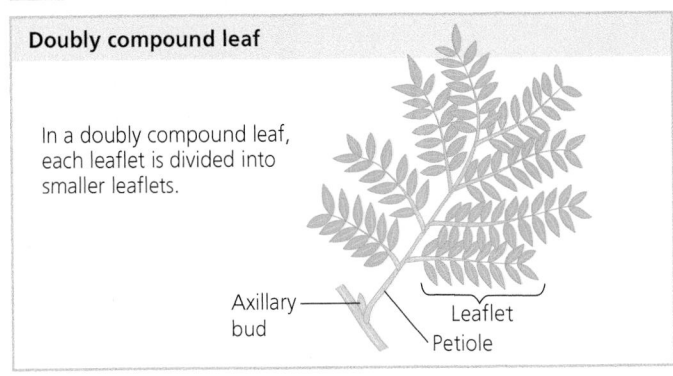

Doubly compound leaf

In a doubly compound leaf, each leaflet is divided into smaller leaflets.

Axillary bud

Leaflet

Petiole

compound or doubly compound. This structural adaptation may enable leaves to withstand strong wind with less tearing. It may also confine some pathogens (disease-causing organisms and viruses) that invade the leaf to a single leaflet, rather than allowing them to spread to the entire leaf.

Almost all leaves are specialized for photosynthesis. However, some species have leaves with adaptations that enable them to perform additional functions, such as support, protection, storage, or reproduction **(Figure 35.7)**.

▼ **Figure 35.7 Evolutionary adaptations of leaves.**

▶ **Tendrils.** The tendrils by which this pea plant clings to a support are modified leaves. After it has "lassoed" a support, a tendril forms a coil that brings the plant closer to the support. Tendrils are typically modified leaves, but some tendrils are modified stems, as in grapevines.

◀ **Spines.** The spines of cacti, such as this prickly pear, are actually leaves; photosynthesis is carried out by the fleshy green stems.

◀ **Storage leaves.** Most succulents, such as this ice plant, have leaves adapted for storing water.

◀ **Reproductive leaves.** The leaves of some succulents, such as *Kalanchoë daigremontiana*, produce adventitious plantlets, which fall off the leaf and take root in the soil.

▶ **Bracts.** Often mistaken for petals, the red parts of the poinsettia are actually modified leaves called bracts that surround a group of flowers. Such brightly colored leaves attract pollinators.

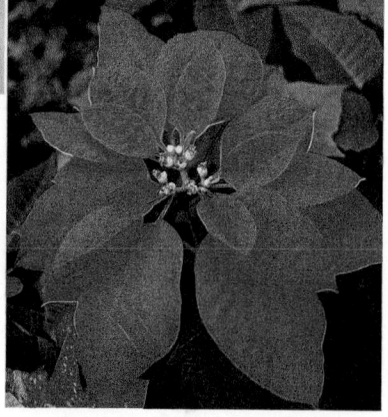

Dermal, Vascular, and Ground Tissues

Each plant organ—root, stem, or leaf—has dermal, vascular, and ground tissues. Each of these three categories forms a **tissue system**, a functional unit connecting all of the plant's organs. Although each tissue system is continuous throughout the plant, specific characteristics of the tissues and their spatial relationships to one another vary in different organs **(Figure 35.8)**.

The **dermal tissue system** is the plant's outer protective covering. Like our skin, it forms the first line of defense against physical damage and pathogens. In nonwoody plants, it is usually a single tissue called the **epidermis**, a layer of tightly packed cells. In leaves and most stems, the **cuticle**, a waxy coating on the epidermal surface, helps prevent water loss. In woody plants, protective tissues called **periderm** replace the epidermis in older regions of stems and roots. In addition to protecting the plant from water loss and disease, the epidermis has specialized characteristics in each organ. For example, a root hair is an extension of an epidermal cell near the tip of a root. *Trichomes* are hairlike outgrowths of the shoot epidermis. In some desert species, they reduce water loss and reflect excess light, but their most common function

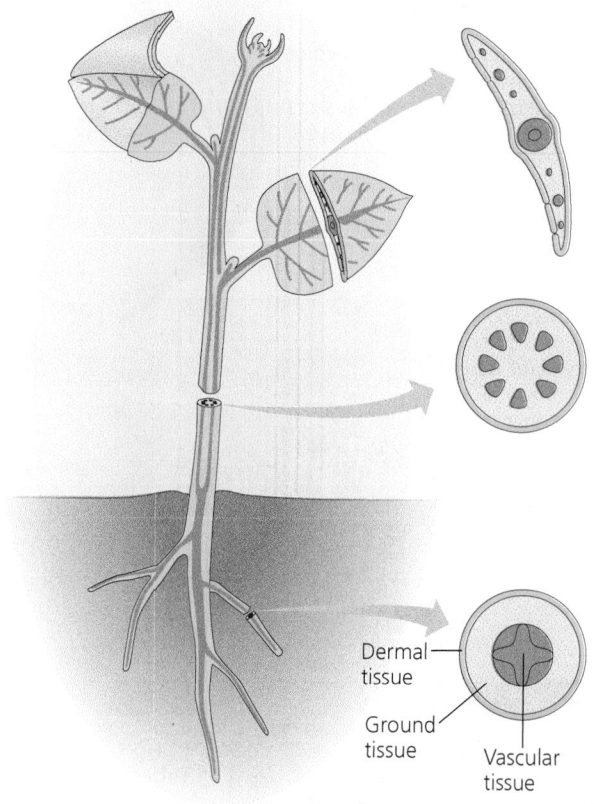

▲ **Figure 35.8 The three tissue systems.** The dermal tissue system (blue) provides a protective cover for the entire body of a plant. The vascular tissue system (purple), which transports materials between the root and shoot systems, is also continuous throughout the plant, but is arranged differently in each organ. The ground tissue system (yellow), which is responsible for most of the plant's metabolic functions, is located between the dermal tissue and the vascular tissue in each organ.

is to provide defense against insects by forming a barrier or by secreting sticky fluids or toxic compounds. For instance, the trichomes on aromatic leaves such as mint secrete oils that protect the plants from herbivores and disease. **Figure 35.9** describes an investigation of the relationship between trichome density on soybean pods and damage by beetles.

▼ Figure 35.9

INQUIRY

Do soybean pod trichomes deter herbivores?

EXPERIMENT Bean leaf beetles (*Cerotoma trifurcata*) feed on developing legume pods, causing pod scarring and decreased seed quality. W. F. Lam and L. P. Pedigo, of Purdue University, investigated whether the stiff trichomes on soybean pods (*Glycine max*) physically deter these beetles. The researchers placed hungry beetles in muslin bags and sealed the bags around the pods of adjacent plants expressing different pod hairiness. The amount of damage to the pods was assessed after 24 hours.

Very hairy pod
(10 trichomes/
mm²)

Slightly hairy pod
(2 trichomes/
mm²)

Bald pod
(no trichomes)

RESULTS Beetle damage to very hairy soybean pods was much lower than damage to the other pod types.

Very hairy pod:
10% damage

Slightly hairy pod:
25% damage

Bald pod:
40% damage

CONCLUSION Soybean pod trichomes protect against beetle damage.

SOURCE W. F. Lam and L. P. Pedigo, Effect of trichome density on soybean pod feeding by adult bean leaf beetles (Coleoptera: Chrysomelidae), *Journal of Economic Entomology* 94:1459–1463 (2001).

WHAT IF? The pod trichomes of most soybean varieties are white, but some varieties have tan-colored trichomes. Suppose that the effects of trichome density on beetle feeding were observed only in tan-haired varieties. What might this finding suggest about how these trichomes deter beetles?

The **vascular tissue system** carries out long-distance transport of materials between the root and shoot systems. The two types of vascular tissues are xylem and phloem. **Xylem** conducts water and dissolved minerals upward from roots into the shoots. **Phloem** transports sugars, the products of photosynthesis, from where they are made (usually the leaves) to where they are needed—usually roots and sites of growth, such as developing leaves and fruits. The vascular tissue of a root or stem is collectively called the **stele** (the Greek word for "pillar"). The arrangement of the stele varies, depending on the species and organ. In angiosperms, for example, the root stele is a solid central *vascular cylinder* of xylem and phloem, whereas the stele of stems and leaves consists of *vascular bundles*, separate strands containing xylem and phloem (see Figure 35.8). Both xylem and phloem are composed of a variety of cell types, including cells that are highly specialized for transport or support.

Tissues that are neither dermal nor vascular are part of the **ground tissue system**. Ground tissue that is internal to the vascular tissue is known as **pith**, and ground tissue that is external to the vascular tissue is called **cortex**. The ground tissue system is not just filler. It includes various cells specialized for functions such as storage, photosynthesis, and support.

Common Types of Plant Cells

Like any multicellular organism, a plant is characterized by cell differentiation, the specialization of cells in structure and function. Cell differentiation may involve changes both in the cytoplasm and its organelles and in the cell wall. **Figure 35.10**, on the next two pages, focuses on the major types of plant cells: parenchyma cells, collenchyma cells, sclerenchyma cells, the water-conducting cells of the xylem, and the sugar-conducting cells of the phloem. Notice the structural adaptations in the different cells that make their specific functions possible. You may also wish to review Figures 6.9 and 6.28, which show basic plant cell structure.

CONCEPT CHECK 35.1

1. How does the vascular tissue system enable leaves and roots to function together in supporting growth and development of the whole plant?
2. What plant structure is each of the following? (a) brussels sprouts; (b) celery; (c) onions; (d) carrots
3. **WHAT IF?** If humans were photoautotrophs, making food by capturing light energy for photosynthesis, how might our anatomy be different?
4. **MAKE CONNECTIONS** Explain how central vacuoles and cellulose cell walls contribute to plant growth (see Chapter 6, pp. 108 and 118–119).

For suggested answers, see Appendix A.

▼ Figure 35.10

Exploring Examples of Differentiated Plant Cells

Parenchyma Cells

Mature **parenchyma cells** have primary walls that are relatively thin and flexible, and most lack secondary walls. (See Figure 6.28 to review primary and secondary cell walls.) When mature, parenchyma cells generally have a large central vacuole. Parenchyma cells perform most of the metabolic functions of the plant, synthesizing and storing various organic products. For example, photosynthesis occurs within the chloroplasts of parenchyma cells in the leaf. Some parenchyma cells in stems and roots have colorless plastids that store starch. The fleshy tissue of many fruits is composed mainly of parenchyma cells. Most parenchyma cells retain the ability to divide and differentiate into other types of plant cells under particular conditions—during wound repair, for example. It is even possible to grow an entire plant from a single parenchyma cell.

Parenchyma cells in *Elodea* leaf, with chloroplasts (LM)   60 μm

Collenchyma Cells

Grouped in strands, **collenchyma cells** (seen here in cross section) help support young parts of the plant shoot. Collenchyma cells are generally elongated cells that have thicker primary walls than parenchyma cells, though the walls are unevenly thickened. Young stems and petioles often have strands of collenchyma cells just below their epidermis (for example, the "strings" of a celery stalk, which is a petiole). Collenchyma cells provide flexible support without restraining growth. At maturity, these cells are living and flexible, elongating with the stems and leaves they support—unlike sclerenchyma cells, which we discuss next.

Collenchyma cells (in *Helianthus* stem) (LM)   5 μm

Sclerenchyma Cells

5 μm

Sclereid cells in pear (LM)

25 μm

Cell wall

Fiber cells (cross section from ash tree) (LM)

Sclerenchyma cells also function as supporting elements in the plant, but are much more rigid than collenchyma cells. The secondary walls of sclerenchyma cells are thick and contain large amounts of lignin. This relatively indigestible strengthening polymer accounts for more than a quarter of the dry mass of wood. Lignin is present in all vascular plants, but not in bryophytes. Mature sclerenchyma cells cannot elongate, and they occur in regions of the plant that have stopped growing in length. Sclerenchyma cells are so specialized for support that many are dead at functional maturity, but they produce secondary walls before the protoplast (the living part of the cell) dies. The rigid walls remain as a "skeleton" that supports the plant, in some cases for hundreds of years.

Two types of sclerenchyma cells, known as **sclereids** and **fibers**, are specialized entirely for support and strengthening. Sclereids, which are boxier than fibers and irregular in shape, have very thick, lignified secondary walls. Sclereids impart the hardness to nutshells and seed coats and the gritty texture to pear fruits. Fibers, which are usually grouped in strands, are long, slender, and tapered. Some are used commercially, such as hemp fibers for making rope and flax fibers for weaving into linen.

Water-Conducting Cells of the Xylem

The two types of water-conducting cells, **tracheids** and **vessel elements**, are tubular, elongated cells that are dead at functional maturity. Tracheids are in the xylem of nearly all vascular plants. In addition to tracheids, most angiosperms, as well as a few gymnosperms and a few seedless vascular plants, have vessel elements. When the living cellular contents of a tracheid or vessel element disintegrate, the cell's thickened walls remain behind, forming a nonliving conduit through which water can flow. The secondary walls of tracheids and vessel elements are often interrupted by pits, thinner regions where only primary walls are present (see Figure 6.28 to review primary and secondary walls). Water can migrate laterally between neighboring cells through pits.

Tracheids are long, thin cells with tapered ends. Water moves from cell to cell mainly through the pits, where it does not have to cross thick secondary walls.

Vessel elements are generally wider, shorter, thinner walled, and less tapered than the tracheids. They are aligned end to end, forming long micropipes known as **vessels**. The end walls of vessel elements have perforation plates that enable water to flow freely through the vessels.

The secondary walls of tracheids and vessel elements are hardened with lignin. This hardening prevents collapse under the tensions of water transport and also provides support.

Tracheids and vessels
(colorized SEM)

Vessel elements, with perforated end walls

Tracheids

Sugar-Conducting Cells of the Phloem

Unlike the water-conducting cells of the xylem, the sugar-conducting cells of the phloem are alive at functional maturity. In seedless vascular plants and gymnosperms, sugars and other organic nutrients are transported through long, narrow cells called sieve cells. In the phloem of angiosperms, these nutrients are transported through sieve tubes, which consist of chains of cells called **sieve-tube elements**, or sieve-tube members.

Though alive, sieve-tube elements lack a nucleus, ribosomes, a distinct vacuole, and cytoskeletal elements. This reduction in cell contents enables nutrients to pass more easily through the cell. The end walls between sieve-tube elements, called **sieve plates**, have pores that facilitate the flow of fluid from cell to cell along the sieve tube. Alongside each sieve-tube element is a nonconducting cell called a **companion cell**, which is connected to the sieve-tube element by numerous channels called plasmodesmata (see Figure 6.28). The nucleus and ribosomes of the companion cell serve not only that cell itself but also the adjacent sieve-tube element. In some plants, the companion cells in leaves also help load sugars into the sieve-tube elements, which then transport the sugars to other parts of the plant.

Sieve-tube element (left) and companion cell: cross section (TEM)

Sieve-tube elements: longitudinal view

Sieve-tube elements: longitudinal view (LM)

Sieve plate with pores (LM)

BioFlix Visit the Study Area at **www.masteringbiology.com** for the BioFlix® 3-D Animation called Tour of a Plant Cell.

CONCEPT 35.2

Meristems generate cells for primary and secondary growth

How do plant cells and tissues develop into mature organs? A major difference between plants and most animals is that plant growth is not limited to an embryonic or juvenile period. Instead, growth occurs throughout the plant's life, a process known as **indeterminate growth**. At any given time, a typical plant has embryonic, developing, and mature organs. Except for dormant periods, most plants grow continuously. In contrast, most animals and some plant organs—such as leaves, thorns, and flowers—undergo **determinate growth**; that is, they stop growing after reaching a certain size.

Plants are capable of indeterminate growth because they have perpetually undifferentiated tissues called **meristems** that divide when conditions permit, leading to new cells that can elongate. There are two main types of meristems: apical meristems and lateral meristems **(Figure 35.11)**. **Apical meristems**, located at the tips of roots and shoots and in axillary buds of shoots, provide additional cells that enable growth in length, a process known as **primary growth**. Primary growth allows roots to extend throughout the soil and shoots to increase their exposure to light. In herbaceous (nonwoody) plants, primary growth produces all, or almost all, of the plant body. Woody plants, however, also grow in circumference in the parts of stems and roots that no longer grow in length. This growth in thickness, known as **secondary growth**, is caused by **lateral meristems** called the vascular cambium and cork cambium. These cylinders of dividing cells extend along the length of roots and stems. The **vascular cambium** adds layers of vascular tissue called secondary xylem (wood) and secondary phloem. The **cork cambium** replaces the epidermis with the thicker, tougher periderm.

The cells within meristems divide relatively frequently, generating additional cells. Some new cells remain in the meristem and produce more cells, while others differentiate and are incorporated into tissues and organs of the growing plant. Cells that remain as sources of new cells have traditionally been called *initials* but are increasingly being called *stem cells* to correspond to animal stem cells that also perpetually divide and remain undifferentiated. The new cells displaced from the meristem, called *derivatives*, divide until the cells they produce become specialized in mature tissues.

The relationship between primary and secondary growth is clearly seen in the winter twig of a deciduous tree. At the shoot tip is the dormant apical bud, enclosed by scales that protect its apical meristem **(Figure 35.12)**. In spring, the bud sheds its scales and begins a new spurt of primary growth, producing a series of nodes and internodes. Along each growth segment, nodes are marked by scars that were left when leaves fell. Above each leaf scar is an axillary bud or a branch formed by an axillary bud. Farther down the twig are bud scars from the whorls of scales that enclosed the apical bud during the previous winter. During each growing season, primary growth extends the shoots, and secondary growth thickens the parts that formed in previous years.

Although plants grow throughout their lives, they do die, of course. Based on the length of their life cycle, flowering

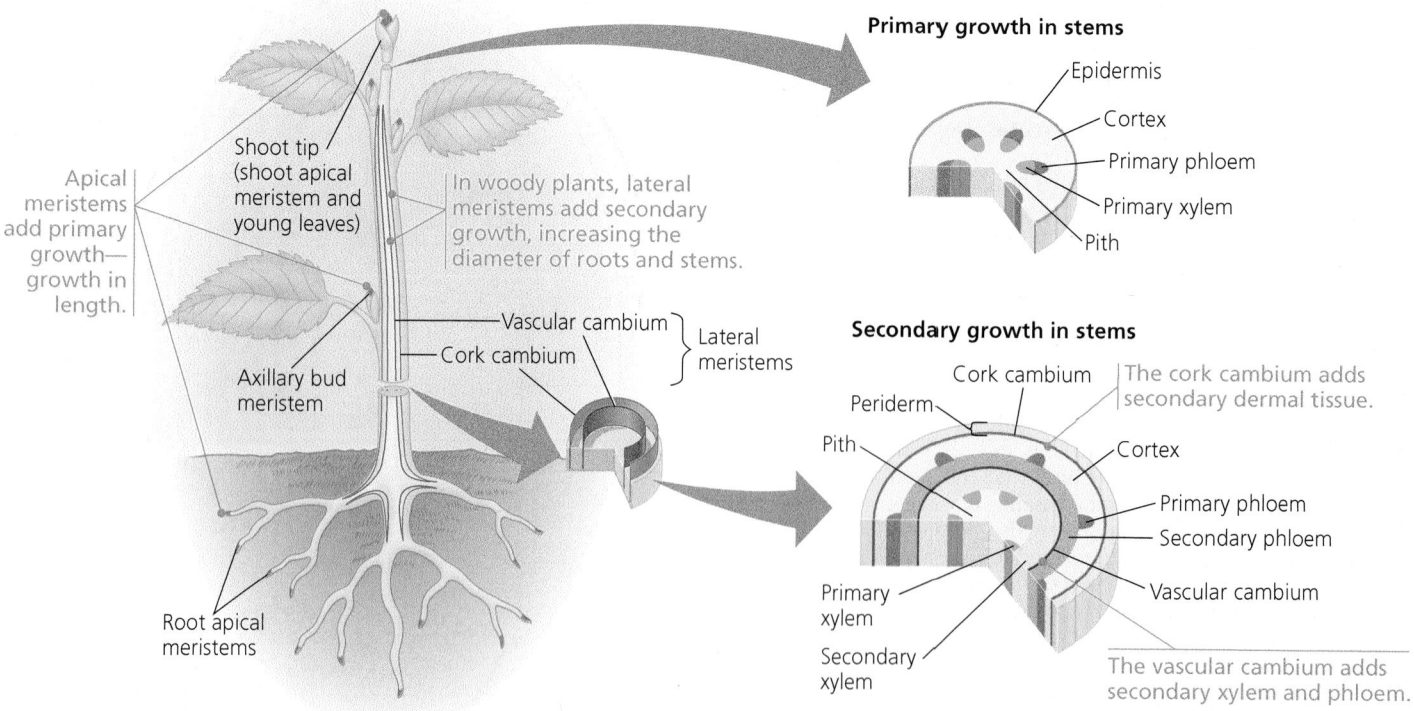

▲ **Figure 35.11 An overview of primary and secondary growth.**

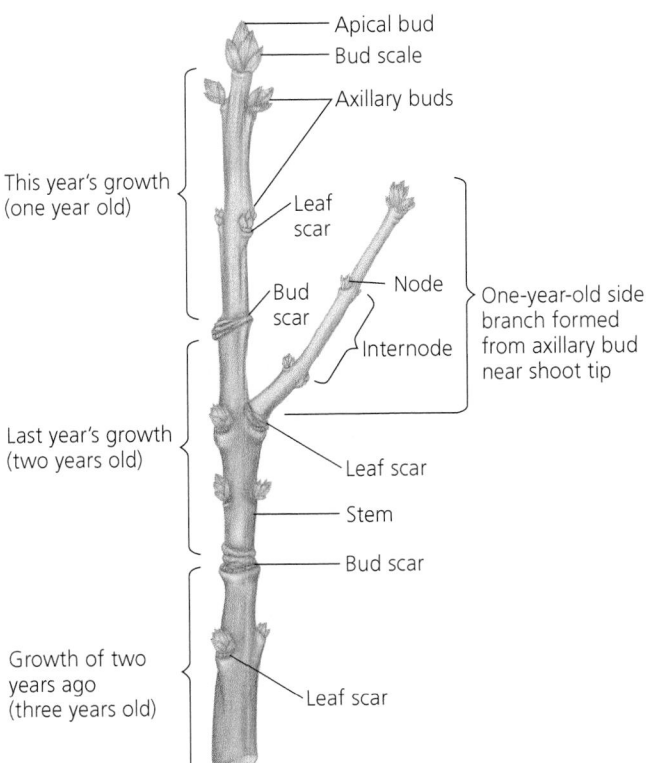

Apical bud
Bud scale
Axillary buds

This year's growth
(one year old)

Leaf
scar

Bud
scar
Node
Internode

One-year-old side
branch formed
from axillary bud
near shoot tip

Last year's growth
(two years old)

Leaf scar

Stem

Bud scar

Growth of two
years ago
(three years old)

Leaf scar

▲ Figure 35.12 **Three years' growth in a winter twig.**

plants can be categorized as annuals, biennials, or perennials. *Annuals* complete their life cycle—from germination to flowering to seed production to death—in a single year or less. Many wildflowers are annuals, as are most staple food crops, including legumes and cereal grains such as wheat and rice. *Biennials*, such as turnips, generally require two growing seasons to complete their life cycle, flowering and fruiting only in their second year. *Perennials* live many years and include trees, shrubs, and some grasses. Some buffalo grass of the North American plains is thought to have been growing for 10,000 years from seeds that sprouted at the close of the last ice age.

CONCEPT CHECK 35.2

1. Distinguish between primary and secondary growth.
2. Cells in lower layers of your skin divide and replace dead cells sloughed from the surface. Are such regions of cell division comparable to a plant meristem? Explain your answer.
3. Roots and stems grow indeterminately, but leaves do not. How might this benefit the plant?
4. **WHAT IF?** Suppose a gardener uproots some carrots after one season and sees they are too small. Carrots are biennials, and so the gardener leaves the remaining plants in the ground, thinking their roots will grow larger during their second year. Is this a good idea? Explain.

For suggested answers, see Appendix A.

Primary growth lengthens roots and shoots

As you have learned, primary growth arises directly from cells produced by apical meristems. In herbaceous plants, the entire plant consists of primary growth, whereas in woody plants, only the nonwoody, more recently formed parts of the plant are primary growth. Although the elongation of both roots and shoots arises from cells derived from apical meristems, the primary growth of roots and primary growth of shoots differ in many ways.

Primary Growth of Roots

The tip of a root is covered by a thimble-like **root cap**, which protects the delicate apical meristem as the root pushes through the abrasive soil during primary growth. The root cap also secretes a polysaccharide slime that lubricates the soil around the tip of the root. Growth occurs just behind the tip in three overlapping zones of cells at successive stages of primary growth. These are the zones of cell division, elongation, and differentiation (Figure 35.13).

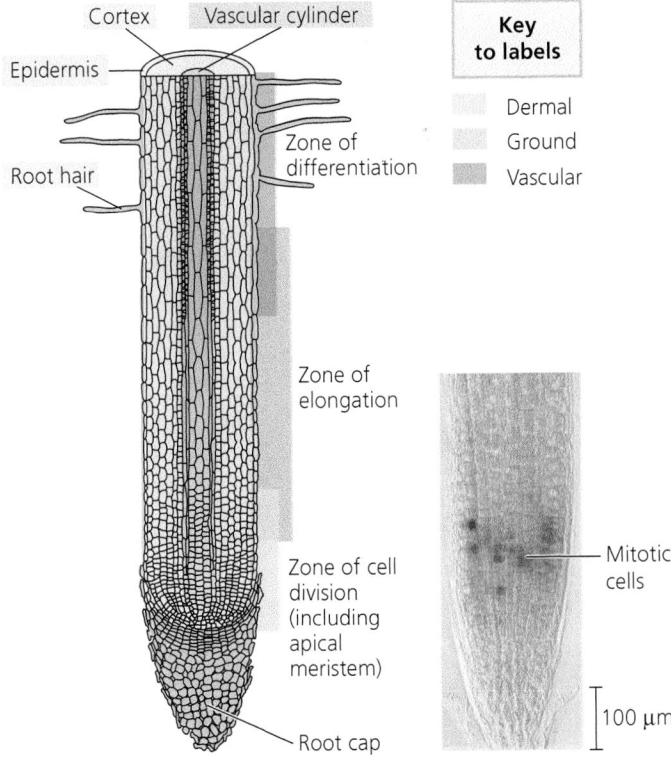

Cortex   Vascular cylinder

Epidermis

Root hair

Zone of
differentiation

Key to labels

Dermal
Ground
Vascular

Zone of
elongation

Zone of cell
division
(including
apical
meristem)

Mitotic
cells

100 μm

Root cap

▲ Figure 35.13 **Primary growth of a root.** The diagram depicts the anatomical features of the tip of a typical eudicot root. The apical meristem produces all the cells of the root and the root cap. Most lengthening of the root occurs in the zone of elongation. In the micrograph, cells undergoing mitosis in the apical meristem are revealed by staining for cyclin, a protein that plays an important role in cell division (LM).

The *zone of cell division* includes the root apical meristem and its derivatives. New root cells are produced in this region, including cells of the root cap. Typically, a few millimeters behind the tip of the root is the *zone of elongation*, where most of the growth occurs as root cells elongate—sometimes to more than ten times their original length. Cell elongation in this zone pushes the tip farther into the soil. Meanwhile, the root apical meristem keeps adding cells to the younger end of the zone of elongation. Even before the root cells finish lengthening, many begin specializing in structure and function. In the *zone of differentiation*, or zone of maturation, cells complete their differentiation and become distinct cell types.

The primary growth of a root produces its epidermis, ground tissue, and vascular tissue. **Figure 35.14** shows in cross section the three primary tissue systems in the young roots of a eudicot (*Ranunculus*, buttercup) and a monocot (*Zea*, maize). Water and minerals absorbed from the soil must enter through the root's epidermis. Root hairs, which account for much of this absorption, enhance this process by greatly increasing the surface area of the epidermis.

In angiosperm roots, the stele is a vascular cylinder, consisting of a solid core of xylem and phloem **(Figure 35.14a)**. In most eudicot roots, the xylem has a starlike appearance in cross section and the phloem occupies the indentations between the arms of the xylem "star." In many monocot roots, the vascular tissue consists of a central core of parenchyma cells surrounded by a ring of xylem and a ring of phloem **(Figure 35.14b)**.

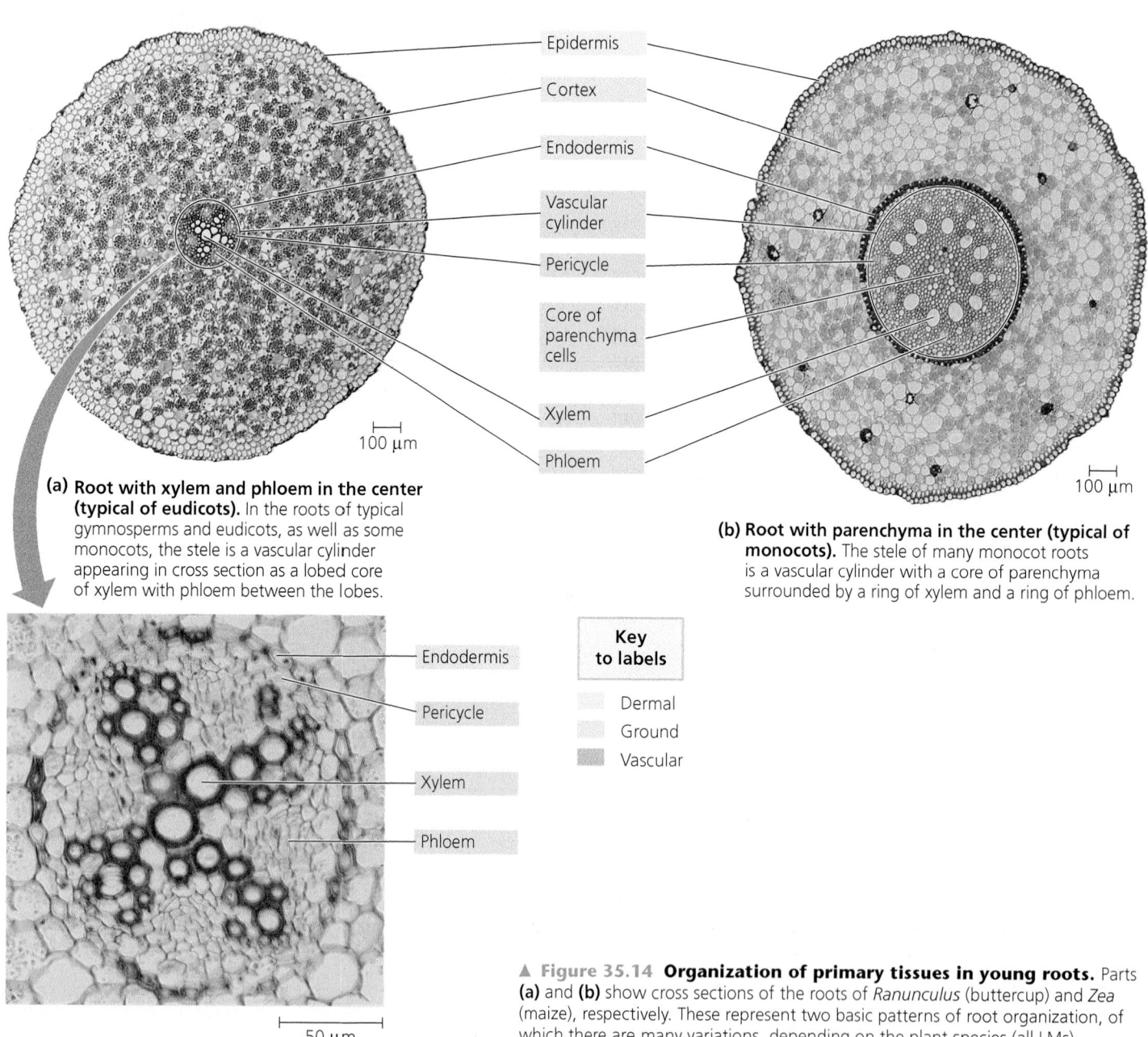

(a) **Root with xylem and phloem in the center (typical of eudicots).** In the roots of typical gymnosperms and eudicots, as well as some monocots, the stele is a vascular cylinder appearing in cross section as a lobed core of xylem with phloem between the lobes.

(b) **Root with parenchyma in the center (typical of monocots).** The stele of many monocot roots is a vascular cylinder with a core of parenchyma surrounded by a ring of xylem and a ring of phloem.

Epidermis
Cortex
Endodermis
Vascular cylinder
Pericycle
Core of parenchyma cells
Xylem
Phloem

100 µm

100 µm

Endodermis
Pericycle
Xylem
Phloem

50 µm

Key to labels

Dermal
Ground
Vascular

▲ **Figure 35.14 Organization of primary tissues in young roots.** Parts **(a)** and **(b)** show cross sections of the roots of *Ranunculus* (buttercup) and *Zea* (maize), respectively. These represent two basic patterns of root organization, of which there are many variations, depending on the plant species (all LMs).

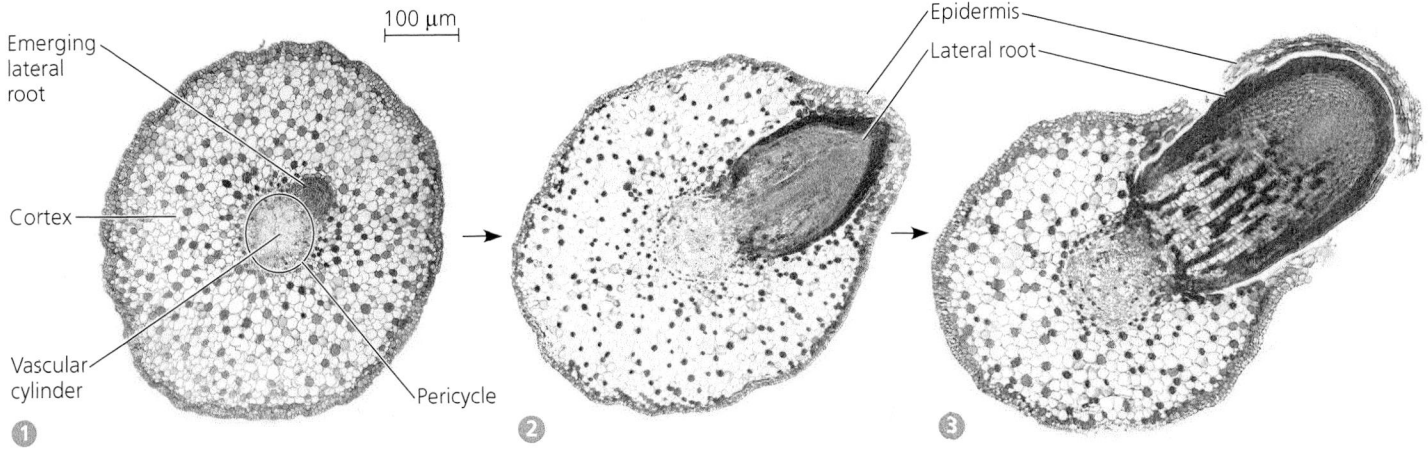

▲ Figure 35.15 **The formation of a lateral root.** A lateral root originates in the pericycle, the outermost layer of the vascular cylinder of a root, and grows out through the cortex and epidermis. In this series of light micrographs, the view of the original root is a cross section, while the view of the lateral root is a longitudinal section.

The ground tissue of roots, consisting mostly of parenchyma cells, fills the cortex, the region between the vascular cylinder and epidermis. Cells within the ground tissue store carbohydrates and absorb water and minerals from the soil. The innermost layer of the cortex is called the **endodermis**, a cylinder one cell thick that forms the boundary with the vascular cylinder. As you will see in Chapter 36, the endodermis is a selective barrier that regulates passage of substances from the soil into the vascular cylinder.

Lateral roots arise from the **pericycle**, the outermost cell layer in the vascular cylinder, which is adjacent to and just inside the endodermis (see Figure 35.14). A lateral root pushes through the cortex and epidermis until it emerges from the established root **(Figure 35.15)**.

Primary Growth of Shoots

A shoot apical meristem is a dome-shaped mass of dividing cells at the shoot tip **(Figure 35.16)**. Leaves develop from **leaf primordia** (singular, *primordium*), finger-like projections along the sides of the apical meristem. Within a bud, young leaves are spaced close together because the internodes are very short. Shoot elongation is due to the lengthening of internode cells below the shoot tip.

Branching, which is also part of primary growth, arises from the activation of axillary buds. Within each axillary bud is a shoot apical meristem. Its dormancy depends mainly on its proximity to an active apical bud. Generally, the closer an axillary bud is to an active apical bud, the more inhibited it is.

In some monocots, particularly grasses, meristematic activity occurs at the bases of stems and leaves. These areas, called *intercalary meristems*, allow damaged leaves to rapidly regrow, which accounts for the ability of lawns to grow following mowing. The ability of grasses to regrow leaves by intercalary meristems enables the plant to recover more effectively from damage incurred from grazing herbivores.

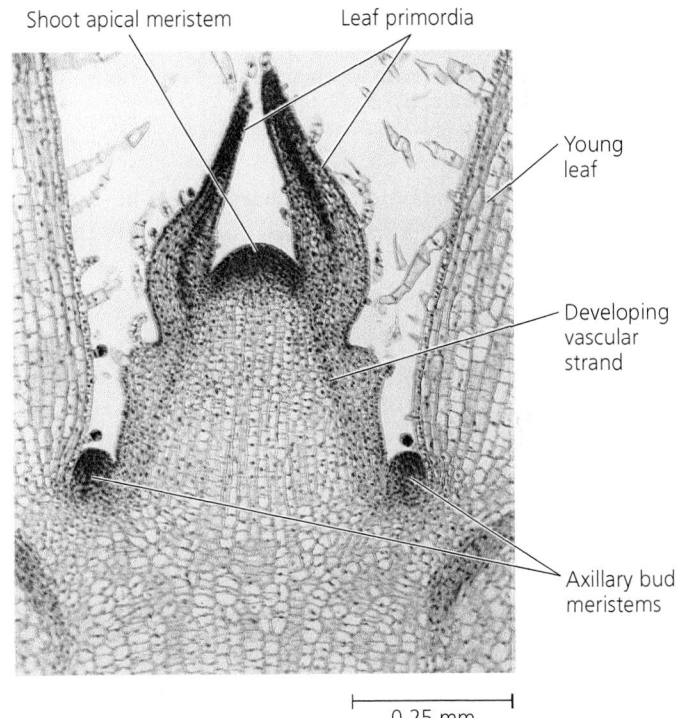

▲ Figure 35.16 **The shoot tip.** Leaf primordia arise from the flanks of the dome of the apical meristem. This is a longitudinal section of the shoot tip of *Coleus* (LM).

Tissue Organization of Stems

The epidermis covers stems as part of the continuous dermal tissue system. Vascular tissue runs the length of a stem in vascular bundles. Unlike lateral roots, which arise from vascular tissue deep within a root and disrupt the vascular cylinder, cortex, and epidermis as they emerge (see Figure 35.15), lateral shoots develop from axillary bud meristems on the stem's surface and disrupt no other tissues (see Figure 35.16). The vascular bundles of the stem converge with the root's vascular cylinder in a zone of transition located near the soil surface.

Phloem   Xylem

Sclerenchyma
(fiber cells)

Ground tissue
connecting
pith to cortex

Ground
tissue

Pith

Epidermis

Key
to labels

Epidermis

Cortex

Vascular
bundle

Vascular
bundles

Dermal

Ground

Vascular

1 mm

1 mm

(a) Cross section of stem with vascular bundles forming a ring (typical of eudicots). Ground tissue toward the inside is called pith, and ground tissue toward the outside is called cortex (LM).

(b) Cross section of stem with scattered vascular bundles (typical of monocots). In such an arrangement, ground tissue is not partitioned into pith and cortex (LM).

▲ **Figure 35.17 Organization of primary tissues in young stems.**

? *Why aren't the terms* pith *and* cortex *used to describe the ground tissue of monocot stems?*

In most eudicot species, the vascular tissue consists of vascular bundles arranged in a ring (**Figure 35.17a**). The xylem in each vascular bundle is adjacent to the pith, and the phloem in each bundle is adjacent to the cortex. In most monocot stems, the vascular bundles are scattered throughout the ground tissue rather than forming a ring (**Figure 35.17b**). In the stems of both monocots and eudicots, the ground tissue consists mostly of parenchyma cells. However, collenchyma cells just beneath the epidermis strengthen many stems. Sclerenchyma cells, especially fiber cells, also provide support in those parts of the stems that are no longer elongating.

Tissue Organization of Leaves

Figure 35.18 provides an overview of leaf structure. The epidermis is interrupted by pores called **stomata** (singular, *stoma*), which allow exchange of CO_2 and O_2 between the surrounding air and the photosynthetic cells inside the leaf. In addition to regulating CO_2 uptake for photosynthesis, stomata are major avenues for the evaporative loss of water. The term *stoma* can refer to the stomatal pore or to the entire stomatal complex consisting of a pore flanked by two **guard cells**, which regulate the opening and closing of the pore. We'll discuss stomata in detail in Chapter 36.

The ground tissue of a leaf, a region called the **mesophyll** (from the Greek *mesos*, middle, and *phyll*, leaf), is sandwiched

between the upper and lower epidermal layers. Mesophyll consists mainly of parenchyma cells specialized for photosynthesis. The mesophylls of many eudicots have two distinct layers: palisade mesophyll and spongy mesophyll. *Palisade mesophyll* consists of one or more layers of elongated parenchyma cells on the upper part of the leaf. *Spongy mesophyll* is below the palisade mesophyll. These parenchyma cells are more loosely arranged, with a labyrinth of air spaces through which CO_2 and oxygen circulate around the cells and up to the palisade region. The air spaces are particularly large in the vicinity of stomata, where CO_2 is taken up from the outside air and O_2 is discharged.

The vascular tissue of each leaf is continuous with the vascular tissue of the stem. Veins subdivide repeatedly and branch throughout the mesophyll. This network brings xylem and phloem into close contact with the photosynthetic tissue, which obtains water and minerals from the xylem and loads its sugars and other organic products into the phloem for transport to other parts of the plant. The vascular structure also functions as a framework that reinforces the shape of the leaf. Each vein is enclosed by a protective *bundle sheath*, consisting of one or more layers of cells, usually parenchyma cells. Bundle sheath cells are particularly prominent in leaves of plant species that undergo C_4 photosynthesis (see Chapter 10).

Key to labels

Dermal
Ground
Vascular

Cuticle

Sclerenchyma fibers

Stoma

Bundle-sheath cell

Xylem
Phloem

Guard cells

(a) Cutaway drawing of leaf tissues

Guard cells
Stomatal pore
Epidermal cell

(b) Surface view of a spiderwort (*Tradescantia*) leaf (LM)

Upper epidermis
Palisade mesophyll
Spongy mesophyll
Lower epidermis
Cuticle
Vein

50 μm

Vein   Air spaces   Guard cells

100 μm

(c) Cross section of a lilac (*Syringa*) leaf (LM)

CONCEPT CHECK **35.3**

1. Contrast primary growth in roots and shoots.
2. **WHAT IF?** If a plant species has vertically oriented leaves, would you expect its mesophyll to be divided into spongy and palisade layers? Explain.
3. **MAKE CONNECTIONS** How are root hairs and microvilli analogous structures? (See Figure 6.8 on p. 100 and the discussion of analogy on p. 540 of Concept 26.2.)

For suggested answers, see Appendix A.

CONCEPT **35.4**

Secondary growth increases the diameter of stems and roots in woody plants

As you have seen, primary growth arises from apical meristems and involves the production and elongation of roots, stems, and leaves. In contrast, secondary growth, the growth in thickness produced by lateral meristems, occurs in stems and roots of woody plants, but rarely in leaves. Secondary growth consists of the tissues produced by the vascular cambium and cork cambium. The vascular cambium adds secondary xylem (wood) and secondary phloem, thereby increasing vascular flow and support for the shoots. The cork cambium produces a tough, thick covering consisting mainly of wax-impregnated cells that protect the stem from water loss and from invasion by insects, bacteria, and fungi. All gymnosperm species and many eudicot species undergo secondary growth, but it is rare in monocots.

In woody plants, primary growth and secondary growth occur simultaneously. As primary growth adds leaves and lengthens stems and roots in the younger regions of a plant, secondary growth thickens stems and roots in older regions where primary growth has stopped. The process is similar in shoots and roots. **Figure 35.19**, on the next page, provides an overview of growth in a woody stem.

The Vascular Cambium and Secondary Vascular Tissue

The vascular cambium is a cylinder of meristematic cells, often only one cell thick. It increases in circumference and also adds layers of secondary xylem to its interior and secondary phloem to its exterior. Each layer has a larger diameter than the previous layer (see Figure 35.19). In this way, the vascular cambium thickens roots and stems.

In a typical woody stem, the vascular cambium consists of a continuous cylinder of undifferentiated parenchyma cells, located outside the pith and primary xylem and to the inside of the cortex and primary phloem. In a typical woody root, the vascular cambium forms to the exterior of the primary xylem and interior to the primary phloem and pericycle.

(a) Primary and secondary growth in a two-year-old woody stem

Epidermis
Cortex
Primary phloem
Vascular cambium
Primary xylem
Pith

Periderm (mainly cork cambia and cork)

Primary phloem
Secondary phloem
Vascular cambium
Secondary xylem
Primary xylem
Pith

① Pith
Primary xylem
Vascular cambium
Primary phloem
Epidermis
Cortex

② Growth

③ Vascular ray
Primary xylem
Secondary xylem
Vascular cambium
Secondary phloem
Primary phloem
First cork cambium
④
Cork

Growth ⑥

Secondary xylem (two years of production) ⑤
Vascular cambium
Secondary phloem
⑦ Most recent cork cambium
Cork
⑨ Bark
⑧ Layers of periderm

① Primary growth from the activity of the apical meristem is nearing completion. The vascular cambium has just formed.

② Although primary growth continues in the apical bud, only secondary growth occurs in this region. The stem thickens as the vascular cambium forms secondary xylem to the inside and secondary phloem to the outside.

③ Some initials of the vascular cambium give rise to vascular rays (see next page).

④ As the vascular cambium's diameter increases, the secondary phloem and other tissues external to the cambium can't keep pace because their cells no longer divide. As a result, these tissues, including the epidermis, will eventually rupture. A second lateral meristem, the cork cambium, develops from parenchyma cells in the cortex. The cork cambium produces cork cells, which replace the epidermis.

⑤ In year 2 of secondary growth, the vascular cambium produces more secondary xylem and phloem, and the cork cambium produces more cork.

⑥ As the stem's diameter increases, the outermost tissues exterior to the cork cambium rupture and are sloughed off.

⑦ In many cases, the cork cambium re-forms deeper in the cortex. When none of the cortex is left, the cambium develops from phloem parenchyma cells.

⑧ Each cork cambium and the tissues it produces form a layer of periderm.

⑨ Bark consists of all tissues exterior to the vascular cambium.

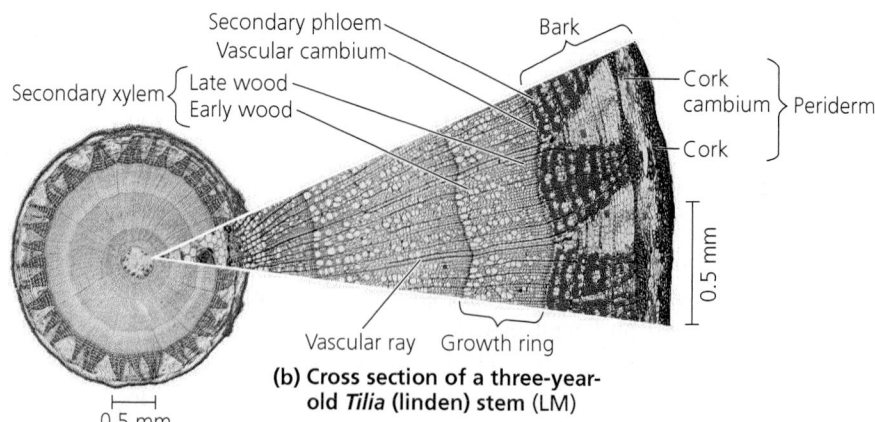

Secondary phloem
Vascular cambium
Secondary xylem { Late wood, Early wood }
Bark
Cork cambium } Periderm
Cork
0.5 mm
Vascular ray   Growth ring

(b) Cross section of a three-year-old _Tilia_ (linden) stem (LM)

0.5 mm

▲ Figure 35.19 **Primary and secondary growth of a woody stem.** The progress of secondary growth can be tracked by examining the sections through sequentially older parts of the stem.

? _How does the vascular cambium cause some tissues to rupture?_

Viewed in cross section, the vascular cambium appears as a ring of initials (stem cells). As these meristematic cells divide, they increase the circumference of the vascular cambium and also add secondary xylem to the inside of the cambium and secondary phloem to the outside (Figure 35.20). Some initials are elongated and are oriented with their long axis parallel to the axis of the stem or root. They produce cells such as the tracheids, vessel elements, and fibers of the xylem, as well as the sieve-tube elements, companion cells, axially oriented parenchyma, and fibers of the phloem. The other initials are shorter and are oriented perpendicular to the axis of the stem or root. They produce *vascular rays*—radial files of mostly parenchyma cells that connect the secondary xylem and phloem (see Figure 35.19b). The cells of a vascular ray move water and nutrients between the secondary xylem and phloem, store carbohydrates, and aid in wound repair.

As secondary growth continues over many years, layers of secondary xylem (wood) accumulate, consisting mainly of tracheids, vessel elements, and fibers (see Figure 35.10). Gymnosperms have only tracheids, whereas most angiosperms have tracheids and vessel elements. The walls of secondary xylem cells are heavily lignified and account for the hardness and strength of wood. In temperate regions, wood that develops early in the spring, known as early (or spring) wood, usually consists of secondary xylem cells with relatively large diameters and thin cell walls (see Figure 35.19b). This structure maximizes delivery of water to new leaves. Wood produced during the rest of the growing season is called late (or summer) wood. It is composed of thick-walled cells that do not transport as much water but provide more support.

In temperate regions, the vascular cambium becomes inactive during winter, and after growth resumes in spring, there is a marked contrast between the large cells of the new early wood and the smaller cells of the late wood of the previous growing season. A year's growth appears as a distinct ring in the cross sections of most tree trunks and roots. Therefore, researchers can estimate a tree's age by counting its annual rings. *Dendrochronology* (from the Greek *dendron*, trees) is the science of analyzing tree ring growth patterns. Rings can vary in thicknesses, depending on seasonal growth. Trees grow well in wet and warm years but may grow hardly at all in cold or dry years. Because a thick ring indicates a warm year and a thin ring indicates a cold or dry one, scientists can use ring patterns to study climate changes (Figure 35.21).

▼ Figure 35.21   **RESEARCH METHOD**

Using Dendrochronology to Study Climate

APPLICATION Dendrochronology, the science of analyzing tree rings, is useful in studying climate change. Most scientists attribute recent global warming to the burning of fossil fuels and release of CO_2 and other greenhouse gases, whereas a minority think it is a natural variation. Studying climate patterns requires comparing past and present temperatures, but instrumental climate records span only the last two centuries and apply only to some regions. By examining growth rings of Mongolian conifers dating back to the mid-1500s, G. C. Jacoby and Rosanne D'Arrigo, of the Lamont-Doherty Earth Observatory, and colleagues sought to learn whether Mongolia experienced similar warm periods in the past.

TECHNIQUE Researchers can analyze patterns of rings in living and dead trees. They can even study wood used for building long ago by matching samples with those from naturally situated specimens of overlapping age. Core samples, each about the diameter of a pencil, are taken from the bark to the center of the trunk. Each sample is dried and sanded to reveal the rings. By comparing, aligning, and averaging many samples from the Mongolian conifers, the researchers compiled a chronology. In this way, the trees served as a chronicle of environmental change.

RESULTS

This graph summarizes a composite record of ring-width indexes for the Mongolian conifers from 1550 to 1993. Higher indexes indicate wider rings and higher temperatures. The highest growth period was from 1974 to 1993, and 17 of the 20 highest-growth years occurred since 1946, suggesting unusual warming during the 1900s.

SOURCE G. C. Jacoby et al., Mongolian Tree Rings and 20th-Century Warming, *Science* 273:771–773 (1996).

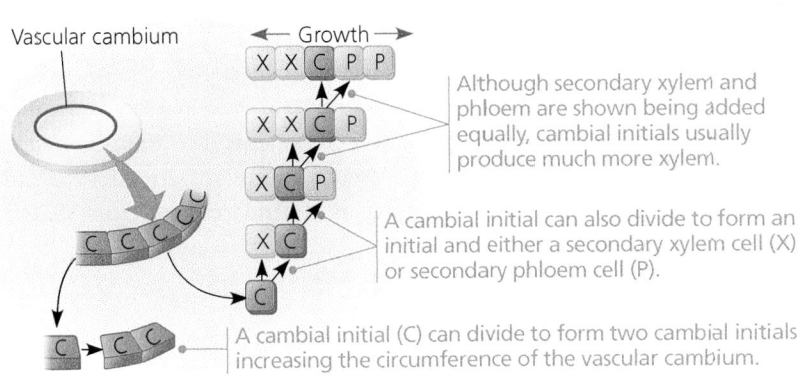

Although secondary xylem and phloem are shown being added equally, cambial initials usually produce much more xylem.

A cambial initial can also divide to form an initial and either a secondary xylem cell (X) or secondary phloem cell (P).

A cambial initial (C) can divide to form two cambial initials, increasing the circumference of the vascular cambium.

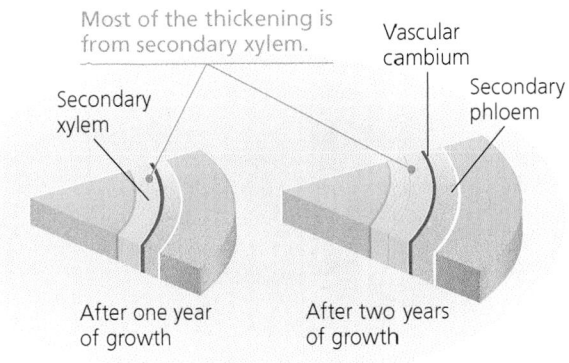

Most of the thickening is from secondary xylem.

After one year of growth

After two years of growth

▲ Figure 35.20 **Secondary growth produced by the vascular cambium.**

As a tree or woody shrub ages, the older layers of secondary xylem no longer transport water and minerals (a solution called xylem sap). These layers are called *heartwood* because they are closer to the center of a stem or root (Figure 35.22). The newest, outer layers of secondary xylem still transport xylem sap and are therefore known as *sapwood*. That is why a large tree can survive even if the center of its trunk is hollow (Figure 35.23). Because each new layer of secondary xylem has a larger circumference, secondary growth enables the xylem to transport more sap each year, supplying an increasing number of leaves. The heartwood is generally darker than sapwood because of resins and other compounds that permeate the cell cavities and help protect the core of the tree from fungi and wood-boring insects.

Only the youngest secondary phloem, closest to the vascular cambium, functions in sugar transport. As a stem or root increases in circumference, the older secondary phloem is sloughed off, which is one reason secondary phloem does not accumulate as extensively as secondary xylem.

The Cork Cambium and the Production of Periderm

During the early stages of secondary growth, the epidermis is pushed outward, causing it to split, dry, and fall off the stem or root. It is replaced by two tissues produced by the first cork cambium, a cylinder of dividing cells that arises in the outer cortex of stems (see Figure 35.19a) and in the outer layer of the pericycle in roots. One tissue, called *phelloderm*, is a thin layer of parenchyma cells that forms to the interior of the cork cambium. The other tissue consists of cork cells that accumulate to the exterior of the cork cambium. As cork cells mature, they deposit a waxy, hydrophobic material called *suberin* in their walls and then die. The cork tissue then functions as a barrier that helps protect the stem or root from water loss, physical damage, and pathogens. Each cork cambium and the tissues it produces comprise a layer of periderm.

Because cork cells have suberin and are usually compacted together, most of the periderm is impermeable to water and gases, unlike the epidermis. In most plants, therefore, water and minerals are absorbed primarily in the youngest parts of roots. The older parts of roots anchor the plant and transport water and solutes between the soil and shoots. Dotting the periderm are small, raised areas called **lenticels**, in which there is more space between cork cells, enabling living cells within a woody stem or root to exchange gases with the outside air. Lenticels often appear as horizontal slits, as shown on the stem in Figure 35.19a.

The thickening of a stem or root often splits the first cork cambium, which loses its meristematic activity and differentiates into cork cells. A new cork cambium forms to the inside, resulting in another layer of periderm. As this process continues, older layers of periderm are sloughed off, as you can see in the cracked, peeling bark of many tree trunks.

There is a popular misconception that bark consists only of the protective outer covering of a woody stem or root. Actually, **bark** includes all tissues external to the vascular cambium. Moving outward, its main components are the secondary phloem (produced by the vascular cambium), the most recent periderm, and all the older layers of periderm (see Figure 35.22).

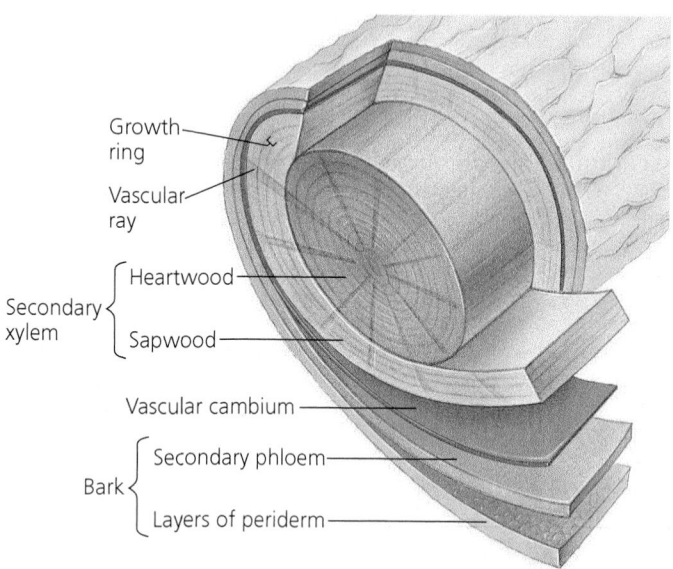

▲ **Figure 35.22 Anatomy of a tree trunk.**

Growth ring
Vascular ray
Heartwood
Secondary xylem { Sapwood
Vascular cambium
Secondary phloem
Bark { Layers of periderm

◀ **Figure 35.23 Is this tree living or dead?** The Wawona Sequoia tunnel in Yosemite National Park in California was cut in 1881 as a tourist attraction. This giant sequoia (*Sequoiadendron giganteum*) lived for another 88 years before falling during a severe winter. It was 71.3 m tall and estimated to be 2,100 years old. Though conservation policies today would forbid the mutilation of such an important specimen, the Wawona Sequoia did teach a valuable botanical lesson: Trees can survive the excision of large portions of their heartwood.

Evolution of Secondary Growth

EVOLUTION Although the genome of one tree species, the poplar (*Populus trichocarpa*), has been sequenced, studying the molecular biology of secondary growth is difficult because woody plants take years to develop and require large areas to grow. Surprisingly, some insights into the evolution of secondary growth have been achieved by studying the herbaceous plant *Arabidopsis thaliana*. Researchers have found that they can stimulate some secondary growth in *Arabidopsis* stems by adding weights to the plant. These findings suggest that weight carried by the stem activates a developmental program leading to wood formation. Moreover, several developmental genes that regulate shoot apical meristems in *Arabidopsis* have been found to regulate vascular cambium activity in *Populus*. This suggests that the processes of primary and secondary growth are evolutionarily more closely related than previously thought.

CONCEPT CHECK 35.4

1. A sign is hammered into a tree 2 m from the tree's base. If the tree is 10 m tall and elongates 1 m each year, how high will the sign be after 10 years?
2. Stomata and lenticels are both involved in exchange of CO_2 and O_2. Why do stomata need to be able to close, but lenticels do not?
3. Would you expect a tropical tree to have distinct growth rings? Why or why not?
4. **WHAT IF?** If a complete ring of bark is removed around a tree trunk (a process called girdling), the tree usually dies. Explain why.

For suggested answers, see Appendix A.

CONCEPT 35.5

Growth, morphogenesis, and cell differentiation produce the plant body

As you'll recall, the specific series of changes by which cells form tissues, organs, and organisms is called **development**. Development unfolds according to the genetic information that an organism inherits from its parents but is also influenced by the external environment. A single genotype can produce different phenotypes in different environments. For example, the aquatic plant called the fanwort (*Cabomba caroliniana*) forms two very different types of leaves, depending on whether or not the shoot apical meristem is submerged (**Figure 35.24**). This ability to alter form in response to local environmental conditions is called *developmental plasticity*. Dramatic examples of plasticity, as in *Cabomba,* are much more common in plants than in animals and may help compensate for plants' inability to escape adverse conditions by moving.

Let's briefly review the three overlapping processes in development: growth, morphogenesis, and cell differentiation. **Growth** is an irreversible increase in size. **Morphogenesis** (from the Greek *morphê*, shape, and *genesis*, creation) is the

▲ **Figure 35.24 Developmental plasticity in the aquatic plant *Cabomba caroliniana*.** The underwater leaves of *Cabomba* are feathery, an adaptation that protects them from damage by lessening their resistance to moving water. In contrast, the surface leaves are pads that aid in flotation. Both leaf types have genetically identical cells, but their different environments result in the turning on or off of different genes during leaf development.

process that gives a tissue, organ, or organism its shape and determines the positions of cell types. Cell **differentiation** is the process by which cells with the same genes become different from one another. We'll examine these three processes in turn, but first we'll discuss how applying techniques of modern molecular biology to model organisms, particularly *Arabidopsis thaliana*, has revolutionized the study of plant development.

Model Organisms: Revolutionizing the Study of Plants

As in other branches of biology, molecular biological techniques and a focus on model organisms such as *Arabidopsis thaliana* have catalyzed a research explosion in the last two decades. *Arabidopsis*, a tiny weed in the mustard family, has no inherent agricultural value but is a favored model organism of plant geneticists and molecular biologists for many reasons. It is so small that thousands of plants can be cultivated in a few square meters of lab space. It also has a short generation time, taking about six weeks for a seed to grow into a mature plant that produces more seeds. This rapid maturation enables biologists to conduct genetic cross experiments in a relatively short time frame. One plant can produce over 5,000 seeds, another property that makes *Arabidopsis* useful for genetic analysis.

Beyond these basic traits, the plant's genome makes it particularly well suited for analysis by molecular genetic methods. The *Arabidopsis* genome, which includes about 27,400 protein-encoding genes, is among the smallest known in plants. Furthermore, the plant has only five pairs

Table 35.1 *Arabidopsis thaliana* Gene Functions		
Gene Function	Number of Genes	Percent of Total*
Unknown function	9,967	36%
Protein metabolism	3,204	12%
Transport	2,253	8%
Transcription	2,039	7%
Response to stress	1,811	7%
Development	1,627	6%
Environmental sensing	1,627	6%
Cell division and organization	1,201	4%
Signal transduction	1,097	4%
Nucleic acid metabolism	333	1%
Energy pathways	304	1%
Other cellular processes	8,959	33%
Other metabolic processes	8,476	31%
Other biological processes	1,592	6%

Source: The *Arabidopsis* Information Resource, 2010
*The percentages total more than 100% because some genes are listed in more than one category.

of chromosomes, making it easier for geneticists to locate specific genes. Because *Arabidopsis* has such a small genome, it was the first plant to have its entire genome sequenced—a six-year, multinational effort (Table 35.1).

Another property that makes *Arabidopsis* attractive to molecular biologists is that the plant's cells are easy to transform with foreign DNA. The transformation of *Arabidopsis* cells is useful for studying how genes function and interact with other genes. Biologists usually transform plant cells by infecting them with genetically altered varieties of the bacterium *Agrobacterium tumefaciens* (see Figure 20.26). *Arabidopsis* researchers also use a variation of this technique to create a plant with a particular mutation. Studying the effect of a mutation in a gene often yields important information about the gene's normal function. Because *Agrobacterium* inserts its transforming DNA randomly into the genome, the DNA may be inserted in the middle of a gene. Such an insertion usually destroys the function of the disrupted gene, resulting in a "knock-out mutant."

Large-scale projects using this technique are under way to determine the function of every gene in *Arabidopsis*. By identifying each gene's function and tracking every biochemical pathway, researchers aim to determine the blueprints for plant development, a major goal of systems biology. It may one day be possible to create a computer-generated "virtual plant" that enables researchers to visualize which genes are activated in different parts of the plant as the plant develops.

Basic research involving model organisms such as *Arabidopisis* has accelerated the pace of discovery in the plant

sciences, including the identification of the complex genetic pathways underlying plant structure. As you read more about this, you'll be able to appreciate not just the power of studying model organisms but also the rich history of plant investigation that underpins all modern plant research.

Growth: Cell Division and Cell Expansion

Cell division enhances the potential for growth by increasing the number of cells, but plant growth itself is brought about by cell enlargement. The process of plant cell division is described more fully in Chapter 12 (see Figure 12.10), and Chapter 39 discusses the process of cell elongation (see Figure 39.8). Here we are more concerned with how these processes contribute to plant form.

The Plane and Symmetry of Cell Division

The new cell walls that bisect plant cells during cytokinesis develop from the cell plate (see Figure 12.10). The precise plane of cell division, determined during late interphase, usually corresponds to the shortest path that will halve the volume of the parent cell. The first sign of this spatial orientation is rearrangement of the cytoskeleton. Microtubules in the cytoplasm become concentrated into a ring called the *preprophase band* (Figure 35.25). The band disappears before metaphase but predicts the future plane of cell division.

It has long been thought that the plane of cell division provides the foundation for the forms of plant organs, but studies of an internally disorganized maize mutant called *tangled-1* have led researchers to question that view. In wild-type maize plants, leaf cells divide either transversely (crosswise) or longitudinally relative to the axis of the parent cell. Transverse divisions are associated with leaf elongation, and longitudinal divisions are associated with leaf broadening. In *tangled-1* leaves, transverse divisions are normal, but most longitudinal divisions are oriented abnormally, leading to cells that are crooked or curved (Figure 35.26). However, these abnormal cell divisions do not affect leaf shape. Mutant leaves grow more slowly than wild-type leaves, but their overall shapes remain normal, indicating that leaf shape does not depend solely on precise spatial control of cell division. In addition,

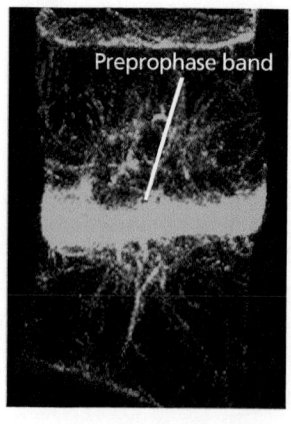

Preprophase band

7 μm

◀ Figure 35.25 **The preprophase band and the plane of cell division.** The location of the preprophase band predicts the plane of cell division. In this light micrograph, the preprophase band has been stained with green fluorescent protein bound to a microtubule-associated protein.

Leaf epidermal cells of wild-type maize

Leaf epidermal cells of *tangled-1* maize mutant

▲ Figure 35.26 **Cell division patterns in wild-type versus mutant maize plants.** Compared with the epidermal cells of wild-type maize plants (left), the epidermal cells of the *tangled-1* mutant of maize (right) are highly disordered. Nevertheless, *tangled-1* maize plants produce normal-looking leaves.

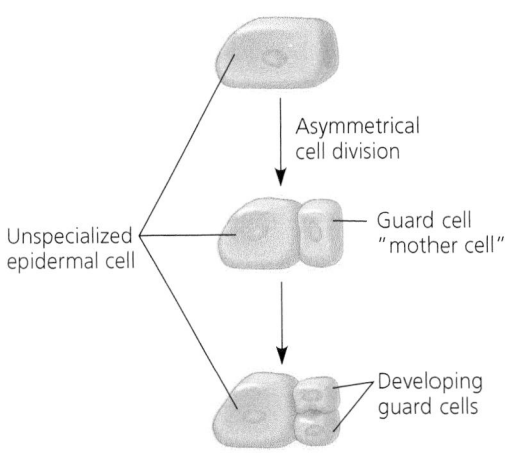

▲ Figure 35.27 **Asymmetrical cell division and stomatal development.** An asymmetrical cell division precedes the development of epidermal guard cells, the cells that border stomata (see Figure 35.18).

recent evidence suggests that the shape of the shoot apex in *Arabidopsis* depends not on the plane of cell division but on microtubule-dependent mechanical stresses stemming from the "crowding" associated with cell proliferation and growth.

Although the *plane* of cell division does not determine the shape of plant organs, the *symmetry* of cell division—the distribution of cytoplasm between daughter cells—is important in determining cell fate. Not all plant cells divide into two equal halves during mitosis. Although chromosomes are allocated to daughter cells equally during mitosis, the cytoplasm may sometimes divide asymmetrically. *Asymmetrical cell division*, in which one daughter cell receives more cytoplasm than the other during mitosis, usually signals a key event in development. For example, the formation of guard cells typically involves both an asymmetrical cell division and a change in the plane of cell division. An epidermal cell divides asymmetrically, forming a large cell that remains an unspecialized epidermal cell and a small cell that becomes the guard cell "mother cell." Guard cells form when this small mother cell divides in a plane perpendicular to the first cell division (**Figure 35.27**). Thus, asymmetrical cell division generates cells with different fates—that is, cells that mature into different types.

Asymmetrical cell divisions also play a role in the establishment of **polarity**, the condition of having structural or chemical differences at opposite ends of an organism. Plants typically have an axis, with a root end and a shoot end. Such polarity is most obvious in morphological differences, but it is also apparent in physiological properties, including the movement of the hormone auxin in a single direction and the emergence of adventitious roots and shoots from "cuttings." Adventitious roots form within the root end of a stem cutting, and adventitious shoots arise from the shoot end of a root cutting.

The first division of a plant zygote is normally asymmetrical, initiating polarization of the plant body into shoot

and root. This polarity is difficult to reverse experimentally, indicating that the proper establishment of axial polarity is a critical step in a plant's morphogenesis. In the *gnom* (from the German for a dwarf and misshapen creature) mutant of *Arabidopsis*, the establishment of polarity is defective. The first cell division of the zygote is abnormal because it is symmetrical, and the resulting ball-shaped plant has neither roots nor leaves (**Figure 35.28**).

Orientation of Cell Expansion

Before discussing how cell expansion contributes to plant form, it is useful to consider the difference in cell expansion between plants and animals. Animal cells grow mainly by synthesizing protein-rich cytoplasm, a metabolically expensive process. Growing plant cells also produce additional protein-rich material in their cytoplasm, but water uptake typically accounts for about 90% of expansion. Most of this

◀ Figure 35.28 **Establishment of axial polarity.** The normal *Arabidopsis* seedling (left) has a shoot end and a root end. In the *gnom* mutant (right), the first division of the zygote was not asymmetrical; as a result, the plant is ball-shaped and lacks leaves and roots. The defect in *gnom* mutants has been traced to an inability to transport the hormone auxin in a polar manner.

water is packaged in the large central vacuole. Vacuolar sap is very dilute and nearly devoid of the energetically expensive macromolecules that are found in great abundance in the rest of the cytoplasm. Large vacuoles are therefore a "cheap" way of filling space, enabling a plant to grow rapidly and economically. Bamboo shoots, for instance, can elongate more than 2 m per week. Rapid and efficient extensibility of shoots and roots was an important evolutionary adaptation that increased their exposure to light and soil.

Plant cells rarely expand equally in all directions. Their greatest expansion is usually oriented along the plant's main axis. For example, cells near the tip of the root may elongate up to 20 times their original length, with relatively little increase in width. The orientation of cellulose microfibrils in the innermost layers of the cell wall causes this differential growth. The microfibrils do not stretch, so the cell expands mainly perpendicular to the main orientation of the microfibrils, as shown in **Figure 35.29**. As with the plane of cell division, microtubules play a key role in regulating the plane of cell expansion. It is the orientation of microtubules in the cell's outermost cytoplasm that determines the orientation of cellulose microfibrils, the basic structural units of the cell wall.

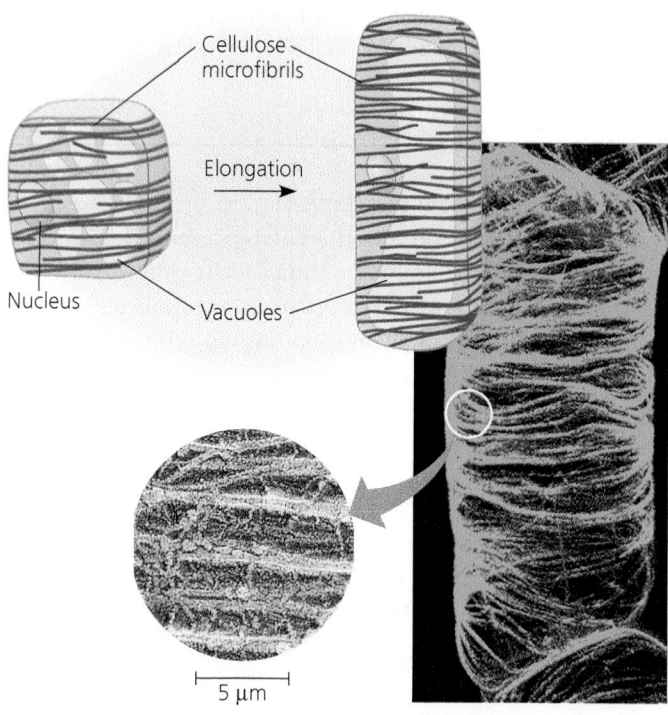

▲ **Figure 35.29 The orientation of plant cell expansion.** Growing plant cells expand mainly through water uptake. In a growing cell, enzymes weaken cross-links in the cell wall, allowing it to expand as water diffuses into the vacuole by osmosis; at the same time, more microfibrils are made. The orientation of cell growth is mainly in the plane perpendicular to the orientation of cellulose microfibrils in the wall. The orientation of microtubules in the cell's outermost cytoplasm determines the orientation of the cellulose microfibrils (fluorescent LM). The microfibrils are embedded in a matrix of other (noncellulose) polysaccharides, some of which form the cross-links visible in the TEM.

Morphogenesis and Pattern Formation

A plant's body is more than a collection of dividing and expanding cells. During morphogenesis, cells acquire different identities in an ordered spatial arrangement. For example, dermal tissue forms on the exterior, and vascular tissue in the interior—never the other way around. The development of specific structures in specific locations is called **pattern formation**.

Two types of hypotheses have been put forward to explain how the fate of plant cells is determined during pattern formation. Hypotheses based on *lineage-based mechanisms* propose that cell fate is determined early in development and that cells pass on this destiny to their progeny. According to this view, the basic pattern of cell differentiation is mapped out according to the directions in which meristematic cells divide and expand. On the other hand, hypotheses based on *position-based mechanisms* propose that the cell's final position in an emerging organ determines what kind of cell it will become. In support of this view, experimental manipulations of cell positions by surgically destroying certain cells with lasers have demonstrated that a plant cell's fate is established late in development and largely depends on signaling from neighboring cells.

In contrast, cell fate in animals is largely determined by lineage-dependent mechanisms involving transcription factors. The homeotic (*Hox*) genes that encode such transcription factors are critical for the proper number and placement of embryonic structures, such as legs and antennae, in the fruit fly *Drosophila* (see Figure 18.19). Interestingly, maize has a homolog of *Hox* genes called *KNOTTED-1*, but unlike its counterparts in the animal world, *KNOTTED-1* does not affect the proper number or placement of plant organs. As you will see, an unrelated class of transcription factors called *MADS-box* proteins plays that role in plants. *KNOTTED-1* is, however, important in the development of leaf morphology, including the production of compound leaves. If the *KNOTTED-1* gene is expressed in greater quantity than normal in the genome of tomato plants, the normally compound leaves become "super-compound" **(Figure 35.30)**.

▲ **Figure 35.30 Overexpression of a *Hox*-like gene in leaf formation.** *KNOTTED-1* is a gene involved in leaf and leaflet formation. An increase in its expression in tomato plants results in leaves that are "super-compound" (right) compared with normal leaves (left).

Gene Expression and Control of Cell Differentiation

Cells of a developing organism can synthesize different proteins and diverge in structure and function even though they share a common genome. If a mature cell removed from a root or leaf can dedifferentiate in tissue culture and give rise to the diverse cell types of a plant, then it must possess all the genes necessary to make any kind of plant cell (see Figure 20.17). Therefore, cell differentiation depends, to a large degree, on the control of gene expression—the regulation of transcription and translation, resulting in the production of specific proteins.

Although cell differentiation depends on the control of gene expression, the fate of a plant cell is determined by its final position in the developing organ, not by cell lineage. If an undifferentiated cell is displaced, it will differentiate into a cell type appropriate to its new position. One aspect of plant cell interaction is the communication of positional information from one cell to another.

Evidence suggests that the activation or inactivation of specific genes involved in cell differentiation depends largely on cell-to-cell communication. For example, two cell types arise in the root epidermis of *Arabidopsis*: root hair cells and hairless epidermal cells. Cell fate is associated with the position of the epidermal cells. The immature epidermal cells that are in contact with two underlying cells of the root cortex differentiate into root hair cells, whereas the immature epidermal cells in contact with only one cortical cell differentiate into mature hairless cells. Differential expression of a homeotic gene called *GLABRA-2* (from the Latin *glaber*, bald) is required for appropriate root hair distribution (**Figure 35.31**). Researchers have demonstrated this by coupling the *GLABRA-2* gene to a "reporter gene" that causes every cell expressing *GLABRA-2* in the root to turn pale blue following a certain treatment. The *GLABRA-2* gene is normally expressed only in epidermal cells that will not develop root hairs.

Shifts in Development: Phase Changes

Multicellular organisms generally pass through developmental stages. In humans, these are infancy, childhood, adolescence, and adulthood, with puberty as the dividing line between the nonreproductive and reproductive stages. Plants also pass through stages, developing from a juvenile stage to an adult vegetative stage to an adult reproductive stage. In animals, the developmental changes take place throughout the entire organism, such as when a larva develops into an adult animal. In contrast, plant developmental stages, called *phases*, occur within a single region, the shoot apical meristem. The morphological changes that arise from these transitions in shoot apical meristem activity are called **phase changes**. During the transition from a juvenile phase to an adult phase, the most obvious morphological changes typically occur in leaf size and shape (**Figure 35.32**). Juvenile nodes and internodes

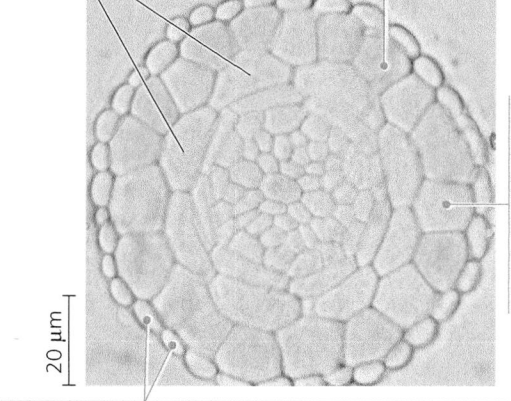

Cortical cells

When an epidermal cell borders a single cortical cell, the homeotic gene *GLABRA-2* is expressed, and the cell remains hairless. (The blue color indicates cells in which *GLABRA-2* is expressed.)

Here an epidermal cell borders two cortical cells. *GLABRA-2* is not expressed, and the cell will develop a root hair.

20 μm

The root cap cells external to the epidermal layer will be sloughed off before root hairs emerge.

▲ **Figure 35.31 Control of root hair differentiation by a homeotic gene** (LM).

WHAT IF? *What would the roots look like if GLABRA-2 were rendered dysfunctional by a mutation?*

Leaves produced by adult phase of apical meristem

Leaves produced by juvenile phase of apical meristem

▲ **Figure 35.32 Phase change in the shoot system of *Acacia koa*.** This native of Hawaii has compound juvenile leaves, consisting of many small leaflets, and simple mature leaves. This dual foliage reflects a phase change in the development of the apical meristem of each shoot. Once a node forms, the developmental phase—juvenile or adult—is fixed; that is, compound leaves do not mature into simple leaves.

retain their juvenile status even after the shoot continues to elongate and the shoot apical meristem has changed to the adult phase. Therefore, any *new* leaves that develop on branches that emerge from axillary buds at juvenile nodes will also be juvenile, even though the apical meristem of the stem's main axis may have been producing mature nodes for years.

If environmental conditions permit, an adult plant is induced to flower. Biologists have made great progress in explaining the genetic control of floral development—the topic of the next section.

Genetic Control of Flowering

Flower formation involves a phase change from vegetative growth to reproductive growth. This transition is triggered by a combination of environmental cues, such as day length, and internal signals, such as hormones. (You will learn more about the roles of these signals in flowering in Chapter 39.) Unlike vegetative growth, which is indeterminate, floral growth is determinate: The production of a flower by a shoot apical meristem stops the primary growth of that shoot. The transition from vegetative growth to flowering is associated with the switching on of floral **meristem identity genes**. The protein products of these genes are transcription factors that regulate the genes required for the conversion of the indeterminate vegetative meristems to determinate floral meristems.

When a shoot apical meristem is induced to flower, the order of each primordium's emergence determines its development into a specific type of floral organ—a sepal, petal, stamen, or carpel (see Figure 30.7 to review basic flower structure). These floral organs form four whorls that can be described roughly as concentric "circles" when viewed from above. Sepals form the first (outermost) whorl; petals form the second; stamens form the third; and carpels form the fourth (innermost) whorl. Plant biologists have identified several **organ identity genes** belonging to the *MADS-box* family that encode transcription factors that regulate the development of this characteristic floral pattern. Positional information determines which organ identity genes are expressed in a particular floral organ primordium. The result is the development of an emerging floral primordium into a specific floral organ. A mutation in a plant organ identity gene can cause abnormal floral development, such as petals growing in place of stamens **(Figure 35.33)**. Some homeotic mutants with increased petal numbers produce showier flowers that are prized by gardeners.

By studying mutants with abnormal flowers, researchers have identified and cloned three classes of floral organ identity genes, and their studies are beginning to reveal how these genes function. **Figure 35.34a** shows a simplified version of the **ABC hypothesis** of flower formation, which proposes that three classes of genes direct the formation of the four types of floral organs. According to the ABC hypothesis, each class of organ identity genes is switched on in two specific whorls of the floral meristem. Normally, *A* genes are switched on in the two outer whorls (sepals and petals); *B* genes are switched on in the two middle whorls (petals and stamens); and *C* genes are switched on in the two inner whorls (stamens and carpels). Sepals arise from those parts of the floral meristems in which only *A* genes are active; petals arise where *A* and *B* genes are active; stamens where *B* and *C* genes are active; and carpels where only *C* genes are active. The ABC hypothesis can account for the phenotypes of mutants lacking *A*, *B*, or *C* gene activity, with one addition: Where gene *A* activity is present, it inhibits *C*, and vice versa. If either *A* or *C* is missing, the other takes its place. **Figure 35.34b** shows the floral patterns of mutants lacking each of the three classes of organ identity genes and depicts how the hypothesis accounts for the floral phenotypes. By constructing such hypotheses and designing experiments to test them, researchers are tracing the genetic basis of plant development.

(a) **Normal *Arabidopsis* flower.** *Arabidopsis* normally has four whorls of flower parts: sepals (Se), petals (Pe), stamens (St), and carpels (Ca).

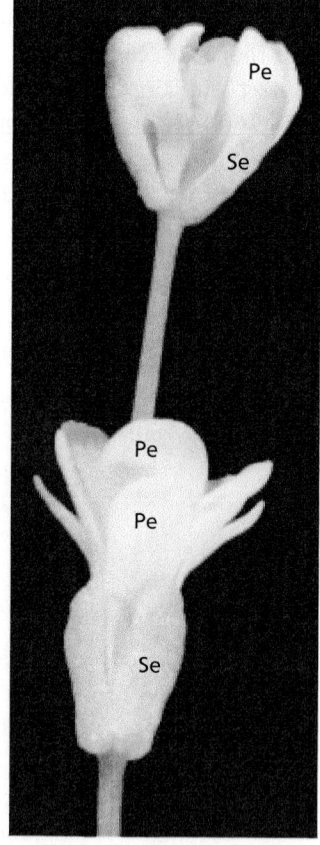

(b) **Abnormal *Arabidopsis* flower.** Researchers have identified several mutations of organ identity genes that cause abnormal flowers to develop. This flower has an extra set of petals in place of stamens and an internal flower where normal plants have carpels.

▲ **Figure 35.33 Organ identity genes and pattern formation in flower development.**

MAKE CONNECTIONS *Review Concept 18.4 on pages 366–373, and provide another example of a homeotic gene mutation that leads to organs being produced in the wrong place.*

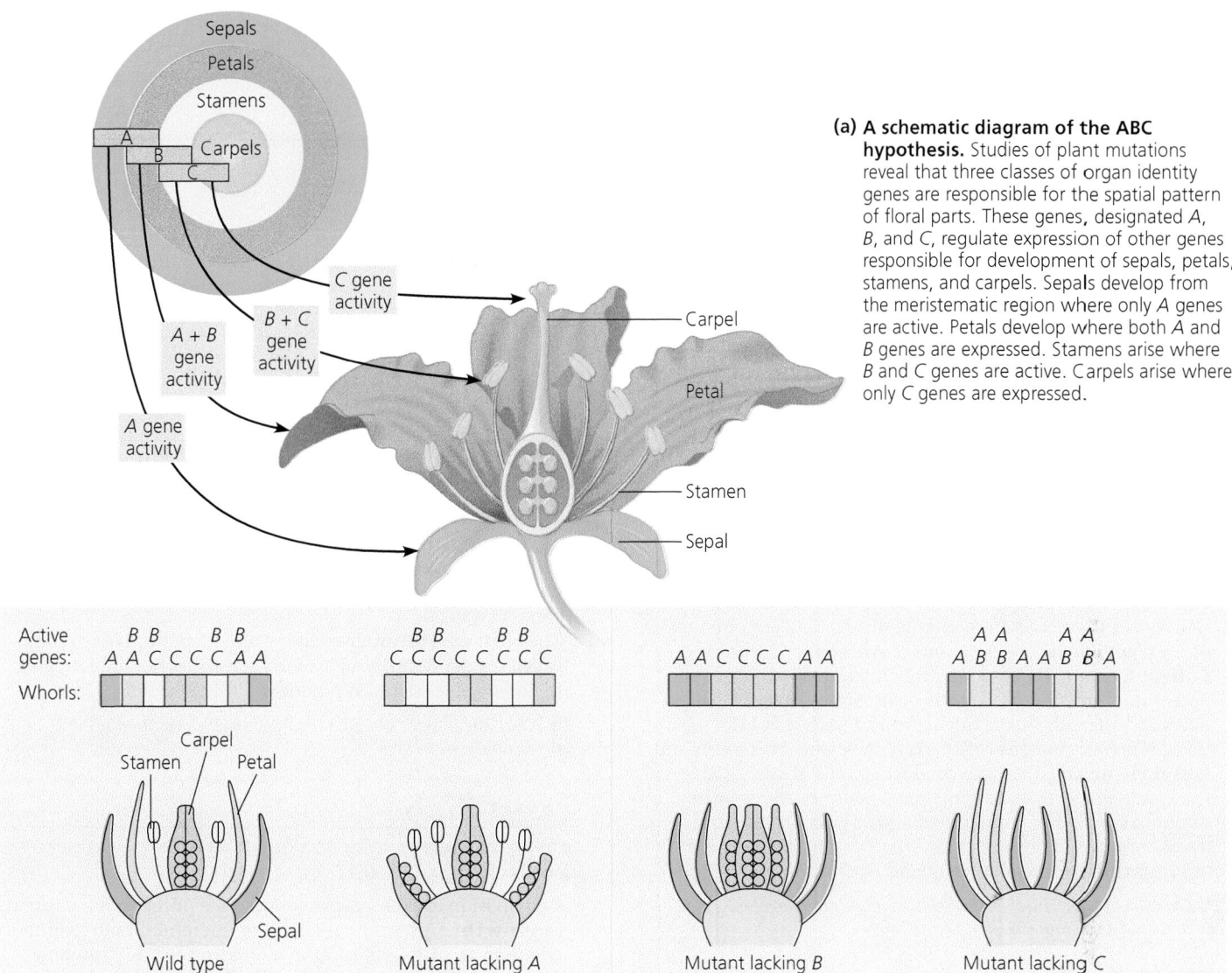

(a) **A schematic diagram of the ABC hypothesis.** Studies of plant mutations reveal that three classes of organ identity genes are responsible for the spatial pattern of floral parts. These genes, designated *A*, *B*, and *C*, regulate expression of other genes responsible for development of sepals, petals, stamens, and carpels. Sepals develop from the meristematic region where only *A* genes are active. Petals develop where both *A* and *B* genes are expressed. Stamens arise where *B* and *C* genes are active. Carpels arise where only *C* genes are expressed.

(b) **Side view of flowers with organ identity mutations.** The phenotype of mutants lacking a functional *A*, *B*, or *C* organ identity gene can be explained by combining the model in part (a) with the rule that if *A* or *C* activity is missing, the other activity occurs through all four whorls.

▲ **Figure 35.34 The ABC hypothesis for the functioning of organ identity genes in flower development.**

WHAT IF? *What would a flower look like if the* A *genes and* B *genes were inactivated?*

In dissecting the plant to examine its parts, as we have done in this chapter, we must remember that the whole plant functions as an integrated organism. In the following chapters, you'll learn more about how materials are transported within vascular plants (Chapter 36), how plants obtain nutrients (Chapter 37), how plants reproduce (Chapter 38, focusing on flowering plants), and how plant functions are coordinated (Chapter 39). As you read further, your understanding of plants will be enhanced by bearing in mind that the plant structures largely reflect evolutionary adaptations to the challenges of a photoautotrophic existence on land.

CONCEPT CHECK 35.5

1. How can two cells in a plant have vastly different structures even though they have the same genome?
2. What are three differences between animal development and plant development?
3. **WHAT IF?** In some species, sepals look like petals, and both are collectively called "tepals." Suggest an extension to the ABC hypothesis that could hypothetically account for the origin of tepals.

For suggested answers, see Appendix A.

35 CHAPTER REVIEW

SUMMARY OF KEY CONCEPTS

CONCEPT 35.1

Plants have a hierarchical organization consisting of organs, tissues, and cells (pp. 738–745)

- Vascular plants have shoots consisting of **stems**, **leaves**, and, in angiosperms, flowers. **Roots** anchor the plant, absorb and conduct water and minerals, and store food. Leaves are attached to stem **nodes** and are the main **organs** of photosynthesis. **Axillary buds**, in axils of leaves and stems, give rise to branches. Plant organs may be adapted for specialized functions.
- Vascular plants have three **tissue systems**—dermal, vascular, and ground—which are continuous throughout the plant. **Dermal tissue** protects against pathogens, herbivores, and drought and aids in the absorption of water, minerals, and carbon dioxide. **Vascular tissues** (**xylem** and **phloem**) facilitate the long-distance transport of substances. **Ground tissues** function in storage, metabolism, and regeneration.
- **Parenchyma cells** are relatively unspecialized and thin-walled cells that retain the ability to divide; they perform most of the plant's metabolic functions of synthesis and storage. **Collenchyma cells** have unevenly thickened walls; they support young, growing parts of the plant. **Sclerenchyma cells**—fibers and sclereids—have thick, lignified walls that help support mature, nongrowing parts of the plant. **Tracheids** and **vessel elements**, the water-conducting cells of xylem, have thick walls and are dead at functional maturity. **Sieve-tube elements** are living but highly modified cells that are largely devoid of internal organelles; they function in the transport of sugars through the phloem of angiosperms.

> **?** *Describe at least three specializations in plant organs and plant cells that are adaptations to life on land.*

CONCEPT 35.2

Meristems generate cells for primary and secondary growth (pp. 746–747)

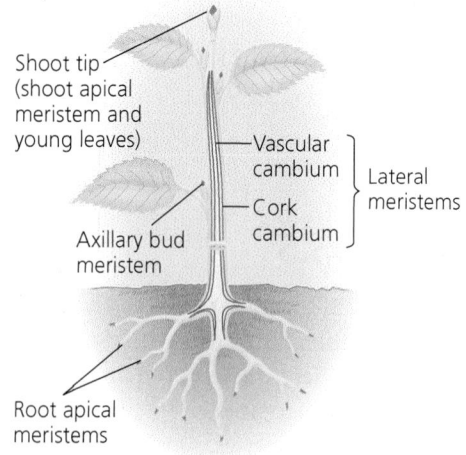

Shoot tip (shoot apical meristem and young leaves)

Axillary bud meristem

Vascular cambium — Cork cambium } Lateral meristems

Root apical meristems

> **?** *Which plant organs originate from the activity of meristems?*

CONCEPT 35.3

Primary growth lengthens roots and shoots (pp. 747–751)

- The root **apical meristem** is located near the tip of the root, where it generates cells for the growing root axis and the **root cap**.
- The apical meristem of a shoot is located in the **apical bud**, where it gives rise to alternating **internodes** and leaf-bearing nodes.

> **?** *How does branching differ in roots versus stems?*

CONCEPT 35.4

Secondary growth increases the diameter of stems and roots in woody plants (pp. 751–755)

- The **vascular cambium** is a meristematic cylinder that produces secondary xylem and secondary phloem during **secondary growth**. Older layers of secondary xylem (heartwood) become inactive, whereas younger layers (sapwood) still conduct water.
- The **cork cambium** gives rise to a thick protective covering called the periderm, which consists of the cork cambium plus the layers of cork cells it produces.

> **?** *What advantages did plants gain from the evolution of secondary growth?*

CONCEPT 35.5

Growth, morphogenesis, and cell differentiation produce the plant body (pp. 755–761)

- Cell division and cell expansion are the primary determinants of **growth**. A preprophase band of microtubules determines where a cell plate will form in a dividing cell. Microtubule orientation also affects the direction of cell elongation by controlling the orientation of cellulose microfibrils in the cell wall.
- **Morphogenesis**, the development of body shape and organization, depends on cells responding to positional information from its neighbors.
- **Cell differentiation**, arising from differential gene activation, enables cells within the plant to assume different functions despite having identical genomes. The way in which a plant cell differentiates is determined largely by the cell's position in the developing plant.
- Internal or environmental cues may cause a plant to switch from one developmental stage to another—for example, from developing juvenile leaves to developing mature leaves. Such morphological changes are called **phase changes**.
- Research on **organ identity genes** in developing flowers provides a model system for studying **pattern formation**. The **ABC hypothesis** identifies how three classes of organ identity genes control formation of sepals, petals, stamens, and carpels.

> **?** *By what mechanism do plant cells tend to elongate along one axis instead of expanding like a balloon in all directions?*

LEVEL 1: KNOWLEDGE/COMPREHENSION

1. Most of the growth of a plant body is the result of
   a. cell differentiation.
   b. morphogenesis.
   c. cell division.
   d. cell elongation.
   e. reproduction.

2. The innermost layer of the root cortex is the
   a. core.
   b. pericycle.
   c. endodermis.
   d. pith.
   e. vascular cambium.

3. Heartwood and sapwood consist of
   a. bark.
   b. periderm.
   c. secondary xylem.
   d. secondary phloem.
   e. cork.

4. The phase change of an apical meristem from the juvenile to the mature vegetative phase is often revealed by
   a. a change in the morphology of the leaves produced.
   b. the initiation of secondary growth.
   c. the formation of lateral roots.
   d. a change in the orientation of preprophase bands and cytoplasmic microtubules in lateral meristems.
   e. the activation of floral meristem identity genes.

LEVEL 2: APPLICATION/ANALYSIS

5. Based on the ABC hypothesis, what would be the structure of a flower from the outermost whorl that had normal expression of genes *A* and *C* and expression of gene *B* in all four whorls?
   a. carpel-petal-petal-carpel
   b. petal-petal-stamen-stamen
   c. sepal-carpel-carpel-sepal
   d. sepal-sepal-carpel-carpel
   e. carpel-carpel-carpel-carpel

6. Which of the following arise, directly or indirectly, from meristematic activity?
   a. secondary xylem
   b. leaves
   c. dermal tissue
   d. tubers
   e. all of the above

7. Which of the following would not be seen in a cross-section through the woody part of a root?
   a. sclerenchyma cells
   b. parenchyma cells
   c. sieve-tube elements
   d. root hairs
   e. vessel elements

8. **DRAW IT** On this cross section from a woody eudicot, label a growth ring, late wood, early wood, and a vessel element. Then draw an arrow in the pith-to-cork direction.

LEVEL 3: SYNTHESIS/EVALUATION

9. **EVOLUTION CONNECTION**
   Evolutionary biologists have coined the term *exaptation* to describe a common occurrence in the evolution of life: A limb or organ evolves in a particular context but over time takes on a new function (see Chapter 25). What are some examples of exaptations in plant organs?

10. **SCIENTIFIC INQUIRY**
    Grasslands typically do not flourish when large herbivores are removed. In fact, they are soon replaced by broad-leaved herbaceous eudicots, shrubs, and trees. Based on your knowledge of the structure and growth habits of monocots versus eudicots, suggest a reason why.

11. **SCIENCE, TECHNOLOGY, AND SOCIETY**
    Hunger and malnutrition are urgent problems for many poor countries, and yet plant biologists in wealthy nations have focused most of their research efforts on *Arabidopsis thaliana*. Some people have argued that if plant biologists are truly concerned about fighting world hunger, they should focus their studies on crops such as cassava and plantain because they are staples for many of the world's poor. If you were an *Arabidopsis* researcher, how might you respond to these arguments?

12. **WRITE ABOUT A THEME**
    Structure and Function In a short essay (100–150 words), explain how the evolution of lignin affected vascular plant structure and function.

For selected answers, see Appendix A.

MasteringBIOLOGY®   www.masteringbiology.com

1. MasteringBiology® Assignments:
Tutorials Primary and Secondary Growth in Plants • Developmental Biology of Plants • The ABC Model of Flowering
Activities Root, Stem, and Leaf Sections • Plant Growth • Primary and Secondary Growth
Questions Student Misconceptions • Reading Quiz • Multiple Choice • End-of-Chapter

2. eText
Read your book online, search, take notes, highlight text, and more.

3. The Study Area
Practice Tests • Cumulative Test • *BioFlix* 3-D Animations • MP3 Tutor Sessions • Videos • Activities • Investigations • Lab Media • Audio Glossary • Word Study Tools • Art

36

Resource Acquisition and Transport in Vascular Plants

▲ Figure 36.1 **Plants or pebbles?**

KEY CONCEPTS

36.1 Adaptations for acquiring resources were key steps in the evolution of vascular plants

36.2 Different mechanisms transport substances over short or long distances

36.3 Transpiration drives the transport of water and minerals from roots to shoots via the xylem

36.4 The rate of transpiration is regulated by stomata

36.5 Sugars are transported from sources to sinks via the phloem

36.6 The symplast is highly dynamic

OVERVIEW

Underground Plants

The Kalahari Desert of southern Africa receives only about 20 cm of precipitation a year, almost entirely during the summer, when daytime temperatures reach a scorching 35–45°C (95–113°F). Many animals escape the desert heat by seeking shelter underground. A peculiar genus of perennial plants called stone plants (*Lithops*) has a similar, mostly subterranean lifestyle (**Figure 36.1**). Except for the tips of two succulent leaves that are exposed to the surface, a stone plant lives entirely below ground. Each leaf tip has a region of clear, lens-like cells that allow light to penetrate to the photosynthetic tissues underground. These adaptations enable stone plants to conserve moisture, hide from grazing tortoises, and avoid the potentially harmful temperatures and high light intensities of the desert.

The remarkable growth habit of *Lithops* reminds us that the success of plants depends largely on their ability to gather and conserve resources from their environment. Through natural selection, many plant species have become highly proficient in acquiring or conserving resources that are especially limited in their environment, but there are often trade-offs in such specializations. For example, the mostly subterranean lifestyle of stone plants reduces water loss from evaporation but inhibits photosynthesis. As a result, stone plants grow very slowly.

The first concept in this chapter examines structural features of shoot and root systems that increase their efficiency in acquiring resources. Resource acquisition, however, is not the end of the story but the beginning. Resources must be transported within the plant to where they are needed. Therefore, the rest of the chapter focuses on how water, minerals, and the products of photosynthesis (sugars) are transported in vascular plants.

CONCEPT 36.1

Adaptations for acquiring resources were key steps in the evolution of vascular plants

EVOLUTION Land plants typically inhabit two worlds—above ground, where their shoot systems acquire sunlight and CO_2, and below ground, where their root systems acquire water and minerals. Without adaptations that allow acquisition of these resources, plants could not have colonized land.

The algal ancestors of land plants absorbed water, minerals, and CO_2 directly from the water in which they lived. Transport in these algae was relatively simple because every cell was close to the source of these substances. The earliest land plants were nonvascular plants that grew photosynthetic shoots above the shallow fresh water in which they lived. These leafless shoots typically had waxy cuticles and few stomata, which allowed them to avoid excessive water loss while still permitting some exchange of CO_2 and O_2 for photosynthesis. The anchoring and absorbing functions of early land plants were assumed by the base of the stem or by threadlike rhizoids (see Figure 29.8).

As land plants evolved and increased in number, competition for light, water, and nutrients intensified. Taller plants with broad, flat appendages had an advantage in absorbing light. This increase in surface area, however, resulted in more evaporation and therefore a greater need for water. Larger shoots also required more anchorage. These needs favored the production of multicellular, branching roots. Meanwhile, as greater shoot heights further separated the top of the photosynthetic shoot from the nonphotosynthetic parts below ground, natural selection favored plants capable of efficient long-distance transport of water, minerals, and products of photosynthesis.

The evolution of vascular tissue consisting of xylem and phloem made possible the development of extensive root and shoot systems that carry out long-distance transport (see Figure 35.10). The xylem transports water and minerals from roots to shoots. The phloem transports products of photosynthesis from where they are made or stored to where they are needed. **Figure 36.2** provides an overview of resource acquisition and transport in a vascular plant.

Because plant success depends on photosynthesis, evolution has resulted in many structural adaptations for efficiently acquiring light from the sun, CO_2 from the air, and water from the ground. Perhaps just as importantly, land plants must minimize the evaporative loss of water, particularly in environments where water is scarce. The adaptations of each species represent compromises between enhancing photosynthesis and minimizing water loss in the species' particular habitat. Later in the chapter, we discuss how plants enhance CO_2 uptake and minimize water loss by regulating stomatal pores. Here, we examine how the basic architecture of shoots and roots helps plants acquire resources.

Shoot Architecture and Light Capture

In shoot systems, stems serve as supporting structures for leaves and as conduits for the transport of water and nutrients. Variations in shoot systems arise largely from the form and arrangement of leaves, the outgrowth of axillary buds, and the relative growth in stem length and thickness.

Leaf size and structure account for much of the outward diversity in plant form. Leaves range in length from the minuscule 1.3-mm leaves of the pygmy weed (*Crassula erecta*), a native of dry, sandy regions in the western United States, to the 20-m leaves of the palm *Raphia regalis*, a native of African rain forests. These species represent extreme examples of a general correlation observed between water availability and leaf size. The largest leaves are typically found in species from tropical rain forests, whereas the smallest are usually found in species from dry or very cold environments, where liquid water is scarce and evaporative loss from leaves is potentially more problematic.

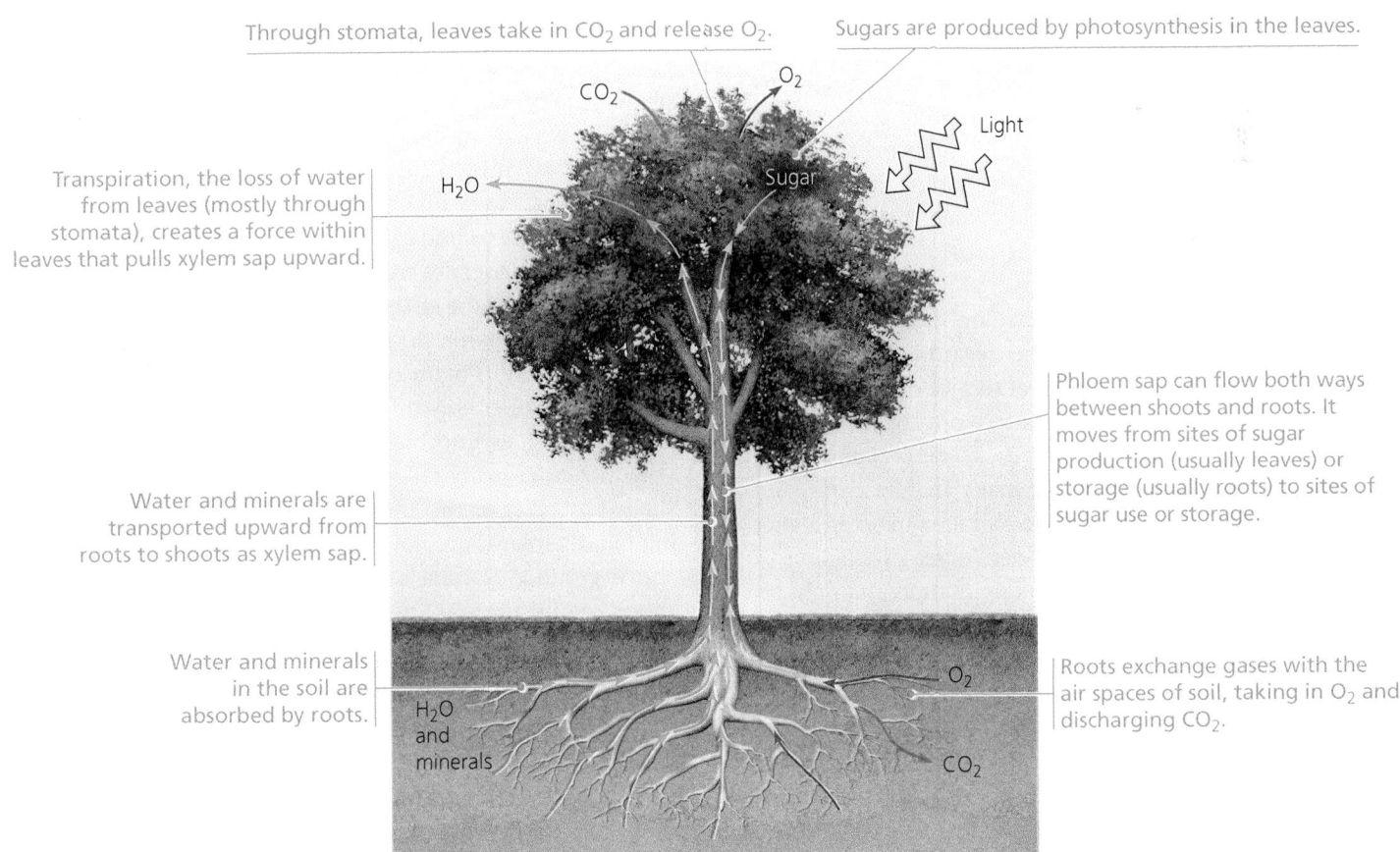

Through stomata, leaves take in CO_2 and release O_2.

Sugars are produced by photosynthesis in the leaves.

Transpiration, the loss of water from leaves (mostly through stomata), creates a force within leaves that pulls xylem sap upward.

Phloem sap can flow both ways between shoots and roots. It moves from sites of sugar production (usually leaves) or storage (usually roots) to sites of sugar use or storage.

Water and minerals are transported upward from roots to shoots as xylem sap.

Water and minerals in the soil are absorbed by roots.

Roots exchange gases with the air spaces of soil, taking in O_2 and discharging CO_2.

▲ Figure 36.2 **An overview of resource acquisition and transport in a vascular plant.**

▲ **Figure 36.3 Emerging phyllotaxy of Norway spruce.** This SEM, taken from above a shoot tip, shows the pattern of emergence of leaves. The leaves are numbered, with 1 being the youngest. (Some numbered leaves are not visible in the close-up.)

? *With your finger, trace the progression of leaf emergence, starting with leaf number 29. What is the pattern?*

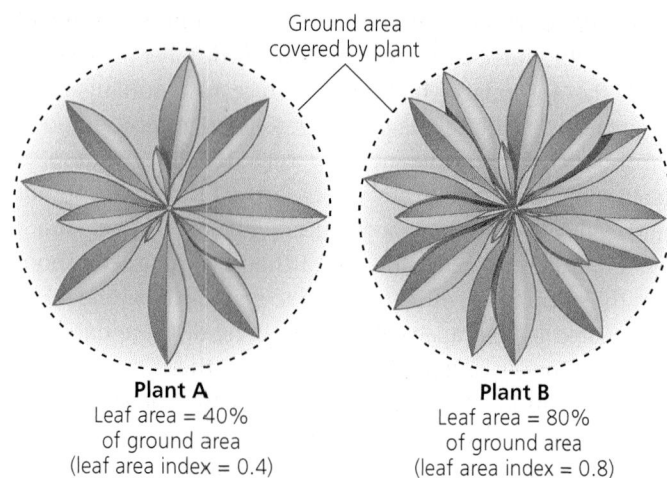

▲ **Figure 36.4 Leaf area index.** The leaf area index of a single plant is the ratio of the total area of the top surfaces of the leaves to the area of ground covered by the plant, as shown in this illustration of two plants viewed from the top. With many layers of leaves, a leaf area index value can easily exceed 1.

? *Would a higher leaf area index always increase the amount of photosynthesis? Explain.*

The arrangement of leaves on a stem, known as **phyllotaxy**, is an architectural feature of immense importance in light capture. Phyllotaxy is determined by the shoot apical meristem (see Figure 35.16) and is specific to each species (Figure 36.3). A species may have one leaf per node (alternate, or spiral, phyllotaxy), two leaves per node (opposite phyllotaxy), or more (whorled phyllotaxy). Most angiosperms have alternate phyllotaxy, with leaves arranged in an ascending spiral around the stem, each successive leaf emerging 137.5° from the site of the previous one. Why 137.5°? Mathematical analyses suggest that this angle minimizes shading of the lower leaves by those above. In environments where intense sunlight can harm leaves, the greater shading provided by oppositely arranged leaves may be advantageous.

Plant features that reduce self-shading increase light capture. A useful measurement in this regard is the *leaf area index*, the ratio of the total upper leaf surface of a single plant or an entire crop divided by the surface area of the land on which the plant or crop grows (Figure 36.4). Leaf area index values of up to 7 are common for many mature crops, and there is little agricultural benefit to leaf area indexes higher than this value. Adding more leaves increases shading of lower leaves to the point that they respire more than photosynthesize. When this happens, the nonproductive leaves or branches undergo programmed cell death and are eventually shed, a process called *self-pruning*.

Another factor affecting light capture is leaf orientation. Some plants have horizontally oriented leaves; others, such as grasses, have leaves that are vertically oriented. In low-light conditions, horizontal leaves capture sunlight much more effectively than vertical leaves. In grasslands or other sunny regions, however, horizontal orientation may expose upper leaves

to overly intense light, injuring leaves and reducing photosynthesis. But if a plant's leaves are nearly vertical, light rays are essentially parallel to the leaf surfaces, so no leaf receives too much light, and light penetrates more deeply to the lower leaves.

The height of shoots and their branching patterns are two other architectural features affecting light capture. Plants that grow tall avoid shading from neighboring plants. Most tall plants require thick stems, which enable greater vascular flow to the leaves and mechanical support for them. Vines are an exception, relying on other structures (usually other plants) to raise their leaves higher. In woody plants, stems become thicker through secondary growth (see Figure 35.11).

Branching generally enables plants to harvest sunlight for photosynthesis more effectively. However, some species, such as the coconut palm, do not branch at all. Why is there so much variation in branching patterns? Plants have only a finite amount of energy to devote to shoot growth. If most of that energy goes into branching, there is less energy to devote toward growing tall, and there is increased risk of being shaded by taller plants. If most of the energy goes into growing tall, the plants are not optimally exploiting the resources above ground. Natural selection has produced varieties of shoot architectures among species, optimizing light absorption in the ecological niche each species occupies.

Root Architecture and Acquisition of Water and Minerals

Just as carbon dioxide and sunlight are resources exploited by the shoot system, soil contains resources mined by the root system. The evolution of root branching enabled land plants to more effectively acquire water and nutrients from the soil while also providing strong anchorage. The tallest plant species, including gymnosperms and eudicots, are typically anchored by strong taproot systems with numerous branches (see Figure 35.2). Although there are exceptions, such as palms, most monocots do not reach treelike heights because their fibrous root systems do not anchor a tall plant as strongly as a taproot system (see Figure 30.13).

Plants can rapidly adjust the architecture and physiology of their roots to exploit patches of available nutrients in the soil. The roots of many plants, for example, respond to pockets of low nitrate availability in soils by extending straight through the pockets instead of branching within them. Conversely, when encountering a pocket rich in nitrate, a root will often branch extensively there. Root cells also respond to high soil nitrate levels by synthesizing more proteins involved in nitrate transport and assimilation. Thus, not only does the plant devote more of its mass to exploiting a nitrate-rich patch; the cells also absorb nitrate more efficiently.

Researchers have uncovered a fascinating physiological mechanism that reduces competition within the root system of a plant. Cuttings from the stolons of buffalo grass (*Buchloe dactyloides*) develop fewer and shorter roots in the presence of cuttings from the same plant than they do in the presence of cuttings from another buffalo grass plant. Although the mechanism underlying this ability to distinguish self from nonself is unknown, avoiding competition between roots of the same plant for the same limited pool of resources certainly seems beneficial.

The evolution of mutualistic associations between roots and fungi called **mycorrhizae** (Figure 36.5) was a critical step in the successful colonization of land by vascular plants, especially given the poorly developed soils available at that time. About 80% of extant land plant species form mycorrhizal associations. Mycorrhizal hyphae endow the fungus and plant roots with an enormous surface area for absorbing water and minerals, particularly phosphate. The role of mycorrhizae in plant nutrition will be examined more fully in Chapter 37.

Once acquired, resources must be transported to other parts of the plant that need them. In the next section, we examine the processes and pathways that enable resources such as water, minerals, and sugars to be transported throughout the plant.

CONCEPT CHECK 36.1

1. Why is long-distance transport important for vascular plants?
2. What architectural features influence self-shading?
3. Some plants can detect increased levels of light reflected from leaves of encroaching neighbors. This detection elicits stem elongation, production of erect leaves, and reduced lateral branching. How do these responses help the plant compete?
4. **WHAT IF?** If you prune a plant's shoot tips, what will be the short-term effect on the plant's branching and leaf area index?
5. **MAKE CONNECTIONS** Explain how fungal hyphae provide more surface area for nutrient absorption. See pp. 637–638 of Concept 31.1.

For suggested answers, see Appendix A.

CONCEPT 36.2

Different mechanisms transport substances over short or long distances

Given the diversity of substances that move through plants and the great range of distances and barriers over which such substances must be transported, it is not surprising that plants employ a variety of transport processes. Before examining these processes, however, we will look at the two major pathways of transport: the apoplast and the symplast.

The Apoplast and Symplast: Transport Continuums

Plant tissues may be viewed as having two major compartments—the apoplast and the symplast. The **apoplast** consists of everything external to the plasma membranes of living cells and includes cell walls, extracellular spaces, and the interior of dead cells such as vessel elements and tracheids (see Figure 35.10). The **symplast** consists of the entire mass of cytosol of all the living cells in a plant, as well as the plasmodesmata, the cytoplasmic channels that interconnect them.

▲ **Figure 36.5 A mycorrhiza, a mutualistic association of fungus and roots.** The fine fungal hyphae provide an extensive surface area for the absorption of water and minerals.

Roots

Fungus

► Figure 36.6 **Cell compartments and routes for short-distance transport.** Some substances may use more than one transport route.

The apoplast is the continuum of cell walls and extracellular spaces.

The symplast is the continuum of cytosol connected by plasmodesmata.

Cell wall

Cytosol

Apoplastic route

Symplastic route

Transmembrane route

Plasmodesma

Plasma membrane

Key

Apoplast

Symplast

The compartmental structure of plants provides three routes for transport within a plant tissue or organ: the apoplastic, symplastic, and transmembrane routes (**Figure 36.6**). In the *apoplastic route*, water and solutes (dissolved chemicals) move along the continuum of cell walls and extracellular spaces. In the *symplastic route*, water and solutes move along the continuum of cytosol. This route requires substances to cross a plasma membrane once, when they first enter the plant. After entering one cell, substances can move from cell to cell via plasmodesmata. In the *transmembrane route*, water and solutes move out of one cell, across the cell wall, and into the neighboring cell, which may pass them to the next cell in the same way. The transmembrane route requires repeated crossings of plasma membranes as substances exit one cell and enter the next. These three routes are not mutually exclusive, and some substances may use more than one route to varying degrees.

Short-Distance Transport of Solutes Across Plasma Membranes

In plants, as in any organism, the selective permeability of the plasma membrane controls the short-distance movement of substances into and out of cells (see Chapter 7). Both active and passive transport mechanisms occur in plants, and plant cell membranes are equipped with the same general types of pumps and transport proteins (channel proteins, carrier proteins, and cotransporters) that function in other cells. In this section, we focus on some ways that plants differ from animals in solute transport across plasma membranes.

Hydrogen ions (H^+), rather than sodium ions (Na^+), play the primary role in basic transport processes in plant cells. For example, in plant cells the membrane potential (the voltage across the membrane) is established mainly through the pumping of H^+ by proton pumps (**Figure 36.7a**), rather than the pumping of Na^+ by sodium-potassium pumps. Also, H^+ is most often cotransported in plants, whereas Na^+ is typically cotransported in animals. During cotransport,

plant cells use the energy in the H^+ gradient and membrane potential to drive the active transport of many different solutes. For instance, cotransport with H^+ is responsible for absorption of neutral solutes, such as the sugar sucrose, by phloem cells and other plant cells. An H^+/sucrose cotransporter couples movement of sucrose against its concentration gradient with movement of H^+ down its electrochemical gradient (**Figure 36.7b**). Cotransport with H^+ also facilitates movement of ions, as in the uptake of nitrate (NO_3^-) by root cells (**Figure 36.7c**).

The membranes of plant cells also have ion channels that allow only certain ions to pass (**Figure 36.7d**). As in animal cells, most channels are gated, opening or closing in response to stimuli such as chemicals, pressure, or voltage. Later in this chapter, we discuss how K^+ ion channels in guard cells function in opening and closing stomata. Ion channels are also involved in producing electrical signals analogous to the action potentials of animals (see Chapter 48). However, these signals are 1,000 times slower and employ Ca^{2+}-activated anion channels rather than the Na^+ ion channels used by animal cells.

Short-Distance Transport of Water Across Plasma Membranes

The absorption or loss of water by a cell occurs by **osmosis**, the diffusion of free water—water that is not bound to solutes or surfaces—across a membrane (see Figure 7.14). The physical property that predicts the direction in which water will flow is called **water potential**, a quantity that includes the effects of solute concentration and physical pressure. Free water moves from regions of higher water potential to regions of lower water potential if there is no barrier to its flow. For example, if a plant cell is immersed in a solution that has a higher water potential than the cell, water will move into the cell. As it moves, water can perform work, such as cell expansion. The word *potential* in the term *water potential* refers to water's potential energy—

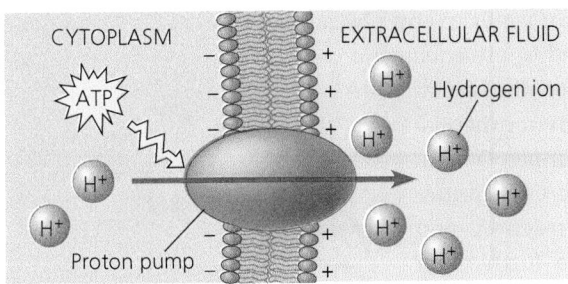

CYTOPLASM — EXTRACELLULAR FLUID

ATP

Hydrogen ion
H^+

Proton pump

(a) H^+ and membrane potential. The plasma membranes of plant cells use ATP-dependent proton pumps to pump H^+ out of the cell. These pumps contribute to the membrane potential and the establishment of a pH gradient across the membrane. These two forms of potential energy can drive the transport of solutes.

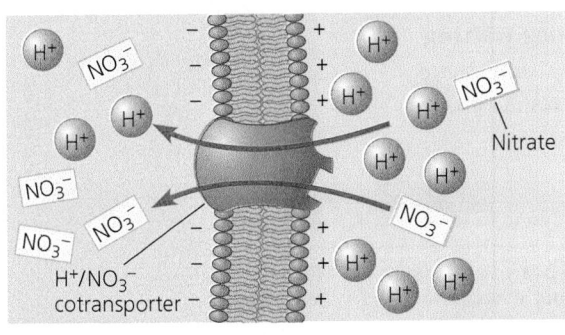

H^+/sucrose cotransporter

Sucrose (neutral solute)

(b) H^+ and cotransport of neutral solutes. Neutral solutes such as sugars can be loaded into plant cells by cotransport with H^+ ions. H^+/sucrose cotransporters, for example, play a key role in loading sugar into the phloem prior to its transport throughout the plant.

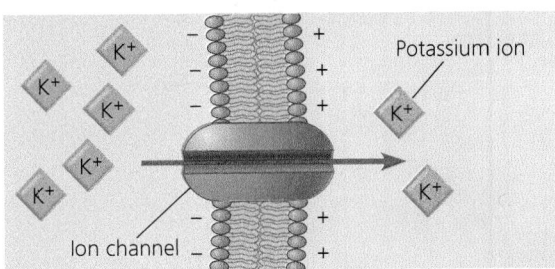

H^+/NO_3^- cotransporter

Nitrate

(c) H^+ and cotransport of ions. Cotransport mechanisms involving H^+ also participate in regulating ion fluxes into and out of cells. For example, H^+/NO_3^- cotransporters in the plasma membranes of root cells are important for the uptake of NO_3^- by plant roots.

Potassium ion

Ion channel

(d) Ion channels. Plant ion channels open and close in response to voltage, stretching of the membrane, and chemical factors. When open, ion channels allow specific ions to diffuse across membranes. For example, a K^+ ion channel is involved in the release of K^+ from guard cells when stomata close.

▲ **Figure 36.7 Solute transport across plant cell plasma membranes.**

? *Assume that a plant cell has all four of the plasma membrane transport proteins shown above. Assume also that you have specific inhibitors for each of the four transport proteins. Then predict what effect the individual application of each inhibitor would have on the cell's membrane potential.*

living plant cell due to the osmotic uptake of water is approximately 0.5 MPa, about twice the air pressure inside an inflated car tire.

How Solutes and Pressure Affect Water Potential

Both solute concentration and physical pressure can affect water potential, as expressed in the *water potential equation*:

$$\psi = \psi_S + \psi_P$$

where ψ is the water potential, ψ_S is the solute potential (osmotic potential), and ψ_P is the pressure potential. The **solute potential** (ψ_S) of a solution is directly proportional to its molarity. Solute potential is also called *osmotic potential* because solutes affect the direction of osmosis. The solutes in plants are typically mineral ions and sugars. By definition, the ψ_S of pure water is 0. When solutes are added, they bind water molecules. As a result, there are fewer free water molecules, reducing the capacity of the water to move and do work. In this way, an increase in solutes has a negative effect on water potential, which is why the ψ_S of a solution is always expressed as a negative number. For example, a 0.1 *M* solution of a sugar has a ψ_S of -0.23 MPa. As the solute concentration increases, ψ_S becomes more negative.

Pressure potential (ψ_P) is the physical pressure on a solution. Unlike ψ_S, ψ_P can be positive or negative relative to atmospheric pressure. For example, the water in the hollow nonliving xylem cells (tracheids and vessel elements) of a plant is often under a negative pressure potential (tension) of less than -2 MPa. Conversely, much like the air in a tire's inner tube, the water in living cells is usually under positive pressure due to the osmotic uptake of water. Specifically, the cell contents press the plasma membrane against the cell wall, and the cell wall then presses against the **protoplast** (the living part of the cell, which also includes the plasma membrane), producing what is called **turgor pressure**. This internal pressure is critical for plant function because it helps maintain the stiffness of plant tissues and also serves as the driving force for cell elongation.

water's capacity to perform work when it moves from a region of higher water potential to a region of lower water potential.

Water potential is abbreviated by the Greek letter ψ (psi, pronounced "sigh"). Plant biologists measure ψ in a unit of pressure called a **megapascal** (abbreviated MPa). By definition, the ψ of pure water in a container open to the atmosphere under standard conditions (at sea level and at room temperature) is 0 MPa. One MPa is equal to about 10 times atmospheric pressure at sea level. The internal pressure of a

A U-shaped tube can be used to demonstrate the effects of solutes and pressure on water movement across a selectively permeable membrane (Figure 36.8). As you consider this model, keep in mind the key point: *Water moves from regions of higher water potential to regions of lower water potential.*

Water Movement Across Plant Cell Membranes

Now let's consider how water potential affects absorption and loss of water by a living plant cell. First, imagine a cell that is **flaccid** (limp) as a result of losing water. The cell has a ψ_P of 0 MPa. Suppose this flaccid cell is bathed in a solution of higher solute concentration (more negative solute potential) than the cell itself (Figure 36.9a). Since the external solution has the lower (more negative) water potential, water diffuses out of the cell. The cell's protoplast undergoes **plasmolysis**—that is, it shrinks and pulls away from the cell wall. If we place the same flaccid cell in pure water ($\psi = 0$ MPa) (Figure 36.9b), the cell, because it contains solutes, has a lower water potential than the water, and water enters the cell by osmosis. The contents of the cell begin to swell and press the plasma membrane against the cell wall. The partially elastic wall, exerting turgor pressure, confines the pressurized protoplast. When this pressure is enough to offset the

tendency for water to enter because of the solutes in the cell, then ψ_P and ψ_S are equal, and $\psi = 0$. This matches the water potential of the extracellular environment—in this example, 0 MPa. A dynamic equilibrium has been reached, and there is no further net movement of water.

Turgid

In contrast to a flaccid cell, a walled cell with a greater solute concentration than its surroundings is **turgid**, or very firm. When turgid cells in a nonwoody tissue push against each other, the tissue is stiffened. The effects of turgor loss are seen during **wilting**, when leaves and stems droop as a result of cells losing water.

Wilted

▼ **Figure 36.8 Effects of solutes and pressure on water potential (ψ) and water movement.**

| Solutes have a negative effect on ψ by binding water molecules. | Positive pressure has a positive effect on ψ by pushing water. | Solutes and positive pressure have opposing effects on water movement. | Negative pressure (tension) has a negative effect on ψ by pulling water. |

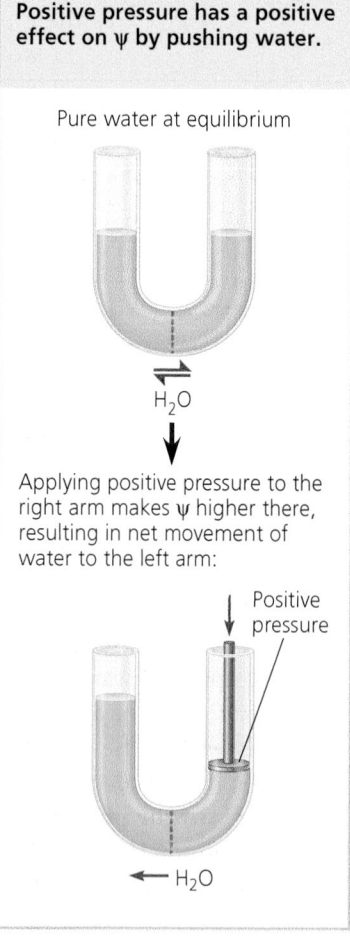

Adding solutes to the right arm makes ψ lower there, resulting in net movement of water to the right arm:

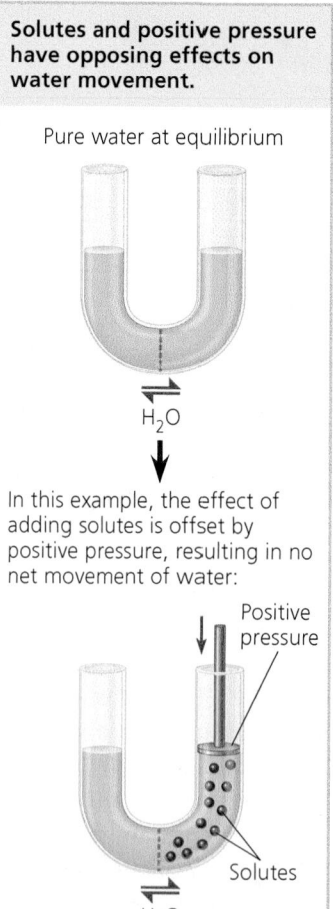

Applying positive pressure to the right arm makes ψ higher there, resulting in net movement of water to the left arm:

In this example, the effect of adding solutes is offset by positive pressure, resulting in no net movement of water:

Applying negative pressure to the right arm makes ψ lower there, resulting in net movement of water to the right arm:

Initial flaccid cell:
$\psi_P = 0$
$\psi_S = -0.7$
$\psi = -0.7$ MPa

0.4 *M* sucrose solution:
$\psi_P = 0$
$\psi_S = -0.9$
$\psi = -0.9$ MPa

Pure water:
$\psi_P = 0$
$\psi_S = 0$
$\psi = 0$ MPa

Plasmolyzed cell
at osmotic equilibrium
with its surroundings
$\psi_P = 0$
$\psi_S = -0.9$
$\psi = -0.9$ MPa

Turgid cell
at osmotic equilibrium
with its surroundings
$\psi_P = 0.7$
$\psi_S = -0.7$
$\psi = 0$ MPa

(a) Initial conditions: cellular ψ > environmental ψ. The cell loses water and plasmolyzes. After plasmolysis is complete, the water potentials of the cell and its surroundings are the same.

(b) Initial conditions: cellular ψ < environmental ψ. There is a net uptake of water by osmosis, causing the cell to become turgid. When this tendency for water to enter is offset by the back pressure of the elastic wall, water potentials are equal for the cell and its surroundings. (The volume change of the cell is exaggerated in this diagram.)

▲ Figure 36.9 **Water relations in plant cells.** In these experiments, flaccid cells (cells in which the protoplast contacts the cell wall but lacks turgor pressure) are placed in two environments. Blue arrows indicate initial net water movement.

Aquaporins: Facilitating Diffusion of Water

A difference in water potential determines the *direction* of water movement across membranes, but how do water molecules actually cross the membranes? Water molecules are small enough to diffuse across the phospholipid bilayer, even though the bilayer's interior is hydrophobic. However, their movement across biological membranes is too rapid to be explained by unaided diffusion. The transport of water molecules across membranes is facilitated by transport proteins called **aquaporins** (see Chapter 7). These selective channels affect the *rate* at which water moves osmotically across the membrane. Aquaporin channel proteins are highly dynamic: Their permeability is decreased by increases in cytosolic Ca^{2+} or decreases in cytosolic pH.

Long-Distance Transport: The Role of Bulk Flow

Diffusion is an effective transport mechanism over the spatial scales typically found at the cellular level. However, diffusion is much too slow to function in long-distance transport within a plant. Although diffusion from one end of a cell to the other takes just seconds, diffusion from the roots to the top of a giant redwood would take several centuries. Instead, long-distance transport occurs through **bulk flow**, the movement of liquid in response to a pressure gradient. The bulk flow of material always occurs from higher to lower pressure. Unlike osmosis, bulk flow is independent of solute concentration.

Long-distance bulk flow occurs within the tracheids and vessel elements of the xylem and within the sieve-tube elements of the phloem. The structures of these conducting cells facilitate bulk flow. As you saw in Figure 35.10, mature tracheids and vessel elements are dead cells and therefore have no cytoplasm, and the cytoplasm of sieve-tube elements is almost devoid of internal organelles. If you have ever dealt with a partially clogged drain, you know that the volume of flow depends on the pipe's diameter. Clogs reduce the effective diameter of the drainpipe. Such experiences help us understand how the structures of plant cells specialized for bulk flow fit their function. Like the unplugging of a kitchen drain, the absence or reduction of cytoplasm in a plant's "plumbing" allows for efficient bulk flow through the xylem and phloem. Bulk flow is also enhanced by the perforation plates at the ends of vessel elements and the porous sieve plates connecting sieve-tube elements.

Diffusion, active transport, and bulk flow act in concert to transport resources throughout the whole plant. For example, bulk flow due to a pressure difference is the mechanism of long-distance transport of sugars in the phloem, but active transport of sugar at the cellular level maintains this pressure difference. In the next three sections, we examine in more detail the transport of water and minerals from roots to shoots, the control of evaporation, and the transport of sugars.

CONCEPT CHECK 36.2

1. If a plant cell immersed in distilled water has a ψ_S of -0.7 MPa and a ψ of 0 MPa, what is the cell's ψ_P? If you put it in an open beaker of solution that has a ψ of -0.4 MPa, what would be its ψ_P at equilibrium?
2. How would a reduction in the number of aquaporin channels affect a plant cell's ability to adjust to new osmotic conditions?
3. How would the long-distance transport of water be affected if tracheids and vessel elements were alive at maturity? Explain.
4. **WHAT IF?** What would happen if you put plant protoplasts in pure water? Explain.

For suggested answers, see Appendix A.

Transpiration drives the transport of water and minerals from roots to shoots via the xylem

Picture yourself struggling to carry a 19-L (5-gallon) container of water weighing 19 kg (42 pounds) up several flights of stairs. Imagine doing this 40 times a day. Then consider the fact that an averaged-sized tree, despite having neither heart nor muscle, transports a similar volume of water effortlessly on a daily basis. How do trees accomplish this feat? To answer this question, we'll follow each step in the journey of water and minerals from the tips of roots to leaves.

Absorption of Water and Minerals by Root Cells

Although all living plant cells absorb nutrients across their plasma membranes, the cells near the tips of roots are particularly important because most of the absorption of water and minerals occurs there. In this region, the epidermal cells are permeable to water, and many are differentiated into root hairs, modified cells that account for much of the absorption of water by roots (see Figure 35.3). The root hairs absorb the soil solution, which consists of water molecules and dissolved mineral ions that are not bound tightly to soil particles. The soil solution is drawn into the hydrophilic walls of epidermal cells and passes freely along the cell walls and the extracellular spaces into the root cortex. This flow enhances the exposure of the cells of the cortex to the soil solution, providing a much greater membrane surface area for absorption than the surface area of the epidermis alone. Although the soil solution usually has a low mineral concentration, active transport enables roots to accumulate essential minerals, such as K^+, to concentrations hundreds of times greater than in the soil.

Transport of Water and Minerals into the Xylem

Water and minerals that pass from the soil into the root cortex cannot be transported to the rest of the plant until they enter the xylem of the vascular cylinder, or stele. The **endodermis**, the innermost layer of cells in the root cortex, functions as a last checkpoint for the selective passage of minerals from the cortex into the vascular cylinder (Figure 36.10). Minerals already in the symplast when they reach the endodermis continue through the plasmodesmata of endodermal cells and pass into the vascular cylinder. These minerals were already screened by the plasma membrane they had to cross to enter the symplast in the epidermis or cortex. Those minerals that reach the endodermis via the apoplast encounter a dead end that blocks their passage into the vascular cylinder. This barrier, located in the transverse and radial walls of each endodermal cell, is the **Casparian strip**, a belt made of suberin, a waxy material impervious to water and dissolved minerals (see Figure 36.10). Thus, water and minerals cannot cross the endodermis and enter the vascular cylinder via the apoplast. The Casparian strip forces water and minerals that are passively moving through the apoplast to cross the plasma membrane of an endodermal cell before they can enter the vascular cylinder.

The endodermis, with its Casparian strip, ensures that no minerals can reach the vascular tissue of the root without crossing a selectively permeable plasma membrane. The endodermis also prevents solutes that have accumulated in the xylem from leaking back into the soil solution. The structure of the endodermis and its strategic location fit its function as an apoplastic barrier between the cortex and the vascular cylinder. The endodermis transports needed minerals from the soil into the xylem and keeps many unneeded or toxic substances out.

The last segment in the soil-to-xylem pathway is the passage of water and minerals into the tracheids and vessel elements of the xylem. These water-conducting cells lack protoplasts when mature and are therefore parts of the apoplast. Endodermal cells, as well as living cells within the vascular cylinder, discharge minerals from their protoplasts into their own cell walls. Both diffusion and active transport are involved in this transfer of solutes from symplast to apoplast, and the water and minerals are now free to enter the tracheids and vessel elements, where they are transported to the shoot system by bulk flow.

Bulk Flow Transport via the Xylem

Water and minerals from the soil enter the plant through the epidermis of roots, cross the root cortex, and pass into the vascular cylinder. From there the **xylem sap**, the water and dissolved minerals in the xylem, gets transported long distances by bulk flow to the veins that branch throughout each leaf. As noted earlier, bulk flow is much faster than diffusion or active transport. Peak velocities in the transport of xylem sap can range from 15 to 45 m/hr for trees with wide vessel elements. Stems and leaves depend on this efficient delivery system for their supply of water and minerals.

The process of transporting xylem sap involves the loss of an astonishing amount of water by **transpiration**, the loss of water vapor from leaves and other aerial parts of the plant. A single maize plant, for example, transpires 60 L of water (the equivalent of 170 12-ounce bottles) during a growing season. A maize crop growing at a typical density of 60,000 plants per hectare transpires almost 4 million L of water per hectare every growing season (about 400,000 gallons of water per acre per growing season). Unless the transpired water is replaced by water transported up from the roots, the leaves will wilt, and the plants will eventually die.

Xylem sap rises to heights of more than 120 m in the tallest trees. Is the sap mainly *pushed* upward from the roots, or is it mainly *pulled* upward? Let's evaluate the relative contributions of these two mechanisms.

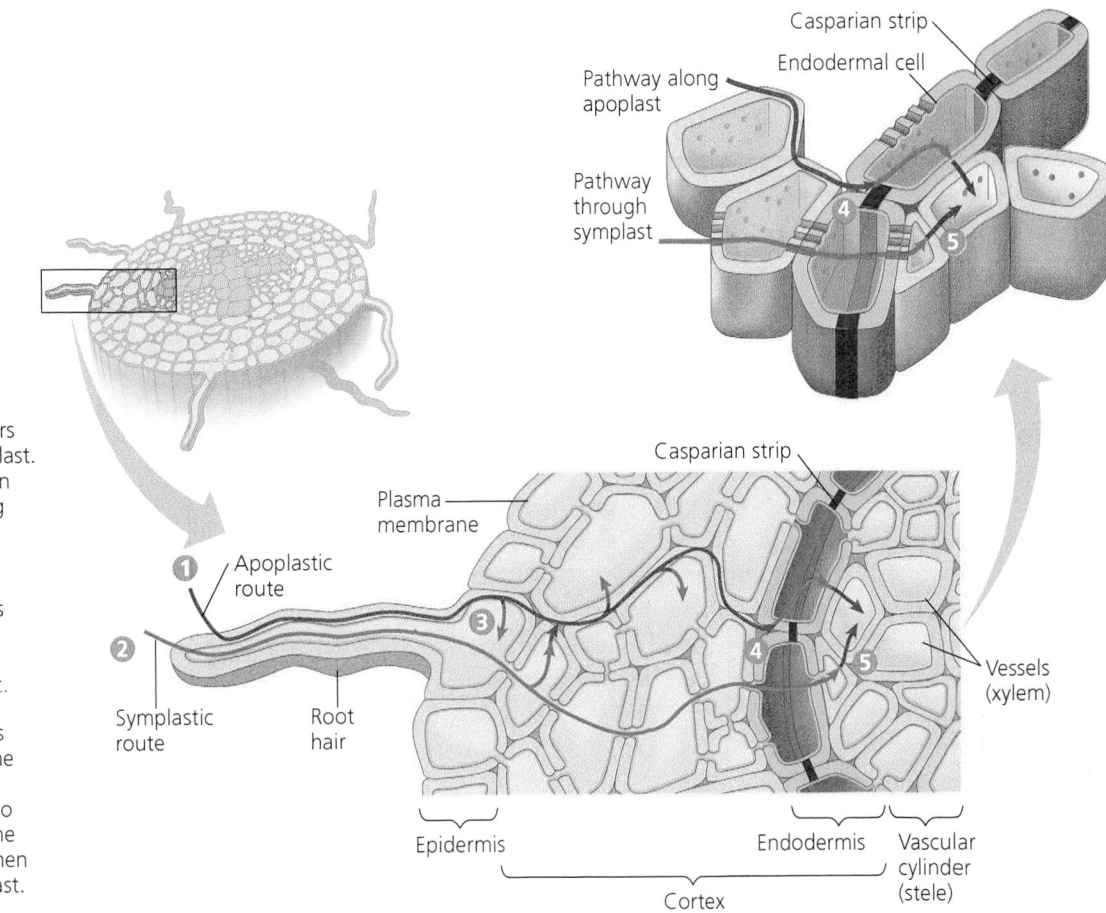

1 Apoplastic route. Uptake of soil solution by the hydrophilic walls of root hairs provides access to the apoplast. Water and minerals can then diffuse into the cortex along this matrix of walls and extracellular spaces.

2 Symplastic route. Minerals and water that cross the plasma membranes of root hairs can enter the symplast.

3 Transmembrane route. As soil solution moves along the apoplast, some water and minerals are transported into the protoplasts of cells of the epidermis and cortex and then move inward via the symplast.

4 The endodermis: controlled entry to the vascular cylinder (stele). Within the transverse and radial walls of each endodermal cell is the Casparian strip, a belt of waxy material (purple band) that blocks the passage of water and dissolved minerals. Only minerals already in the symplast or entering that pathway by crossing the plasma membrane of an endodermal cell can detour around the Casparian strip and pass into the vascular cylinder (stele).

5 Transport in the xylem. Endodermal cells and also living cells within the vascular cylinder discharge water and minerals into their walls (apoplast). The xylem vessels then transport the water and minerals by bulk flow upward into the shoot system.

▲ **Figure 36.10 Transport of water and minerals from root hairs to the xylem.**

? *How does the Casparian strip force water and minerals to pass through the plasma membranes of endodermal cells?*

Pushing Xylem Sap: Root Pressure

At night, when there is almost no transpiration, root cells continue actively pumping mineral ions into the xylem of the vascular cylinder. Meanwhile, the Casparian strip of the endodermis prevents the ions from leaking back out into the cortex and soil. The resulting accumulation of minerals lowers the water potential within the vascular cylinder. Water flows in from the root cortex, generating **root pressure**, a push of xylem sap. The root pressure sometimes causes more water to enter the leaves than is transpired, resulting in **guttation**, the exudation of water droplets that can be seen in the morning on the tips or edges of some plant leaves (Figure 36.11). Guttation fluid should not be confused with dew, which is condensed atmospheric moisture.

In most plants, root pressure is a minor mechanism driving the ascent of xylem sap, at most pushing water only a few

▲ **Figure 36.11 Guttation.** Root pressure is forcing excess water from this strawberry leaf.

meters. The positive pressures produced are simply too weak to overcome the gravitational force of the water column in the xylem, particularly in tall plants. Many plants do not generate any root pressure or do so only during part of the growing season. Even in plants that display guttation, root pressure cannot keep pace with transpiration after sunrise. For the most part, xylem sap is not pushed from below by root pressure but is pulled up.

Pulling Xylem Sap: The Cohesion-Tension Hypothesis

As we have seen, root pressure, which depends on the active transport of solutes by plants, is only a minor force in the ascent of xylem sap. Far from depending on the metabolic activity of cells, most of the xylem sap that rises through a tree does not even require living cells to do so. As demonstrated by Eduard Strasburger in 1891, leafy stems with their lower end immersed in toxic solutions of copper sulfate or acid will readily draw these poisons up if the stem is cut below the surface of the liquid. As the toxic solutions ascend, they kill all living cells in their path, eventually arriving in the transpiring leaves and killing the leaf cells as well. Nevertheless, as Strasburger noted, the uptake of the toxic solutions and the loss of water from the dead leaves can continue for weeks.

In 1894, a few years after Strasburger's findings, two Irish scientists, John Joly and Henry Dixon, put forward a hypothesis that remains the leading explanation of the ascent of xylem sap. According to their **cohesion-tension hypothesis**, transpiration provides the pull for the ascent of xylem sap, and

the cohesion of water molecules transmits this pull along the entire length of the xylem from shoots to roots. Hence, xylem sap is normally under negative pressure, or tension. Since transpiration is a "pulling" process, our exploration of the rise of xylem sap by the cohesion-tension mechanism begins not with the roots but with the leaves, where the driving force for transpirational pull begins.

Transpirational Pull Stomata on a leaf's surface lead to a maze of internal air spaces that expose the mesophyll cells to the CO_2 they need for photosynthesis. The air in these spaces is saturated with water vapor because it is in contact with the moist walls of the cells. On most days, the air outside the leaf is drier; that is, it has lower water potential than the air inside the leaf. Therefore, water vapor in the air spaces of a leaf diffuses down its water potential gradient and exits the leaf via the stomata. It is this loss of water vapor by diffusion and evaporation that we call transpiration.

But how does loss of water vapor from the leaf translate into a pulling force for upward movement of water through a plant? The negative pressure potential that causes water to move up through the xylem develops at the surface of mesophyll cell walls in the leaf (Figure 36.12). The cell wall acts like a very thin capillary network. Water adheres to the cellulose microfibrils and other hydrophilic components of the cell wall. As water evaporates from the water film that covers the cell walls of mesophyll cells, the air-water interface retreats farther into the cell wall. Because of the high surface tension of water, the curvature of the interface induces a tension, or negative pressure potential, in the water. As more

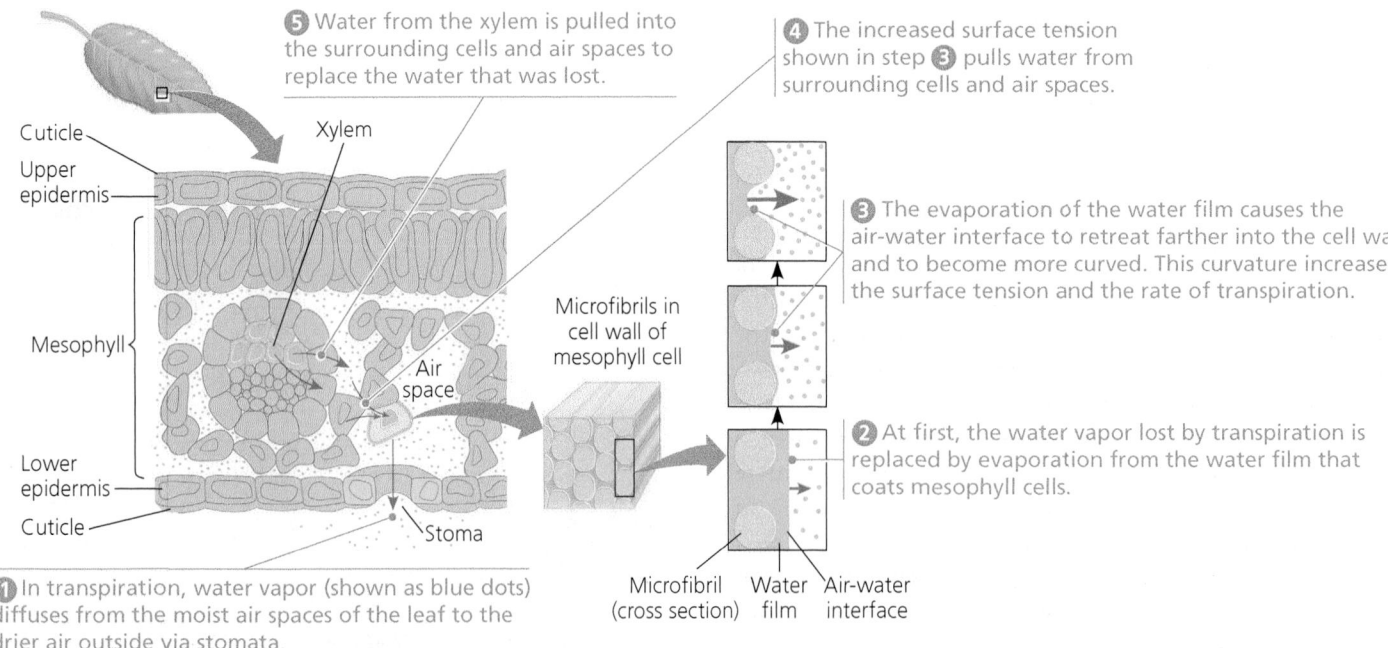

⑤ Water from the xylem is pulled into the surrounding cells and air spaces to replace the water that was lost.

④ The increased surface tension shown in step ③ pulls water from surrounding cells and air spaces.

③ The evaporation of the water film causes the air-water interface to retreat farther into the cell wall and to become more curved. This curvature increases the surface tension and the rate of transpiration.

② At first, the water vapor lost by transpiration is replaced by evaporation from the water film that coats mesophyll cells.

① In transpiration, water vapor (shown as blue dots) diffuses from the moist air spaces of the leaf to the drier air outside via stomata.

Cuticle
Upper epidermis
Xylem
Mesophyll
Air space
Lower epidermis
Cuticle
Stoma

Microfibrils in cell wall of mesophyll cell

Microfibril (cross section)   Water film   Air-water interface

▲ **Figure 36.12 Generation of transpirational pull.** Negative pressure (tension) at the air-water interface in the leaf is the basis of transpirational pull, which draws water out of the xylem.

water evaporates from the cell wall, the curvature of the air-water interface increases and the pressure of the water becomes more negative. Water molecules from the more hydrated parts of the leaf are then pulled toward this area, reducing the tension. These pulling forces are transferred to the xylem because each water molecule is cohesively bound to the next by hydrogen bonds. Thus, transpirational pull depends on several of the properties of water discussed in Chapter 3: adhesion, cohesion, and surface tension.

The role of negative pressure potential in transpiration is consistent with the water potential equation because negative pressure potential (tension) *lowers* water potential (see Figure 36.8). Because water moves from areas of higher water potential to areas of lower water potential, the more negative pressure potential at the air-water interface causes water in xylem cells to be "pulled" into mesophyll cells, which lose water to the air spaces, the water diffusing out through stomata. In this way, the negative water potential of leaves provides the "pull" in transpirational pull. The transpirational pull on xylem sap is transmitted all the way from the leaves to the root tips and even into the soil solution (**Figure 36.13**).

Adhesion and Cohesion in the Ascent of Xylem Sap Adhesion and cohesion facilitate the transport of water by bulk flow. Adhesion is the attractive force between water molecules and other polar substances. Because both water and cellulose are polar molecules, there is a strong attraction between water molecules and the cellulose molecules in the xylem cell walls. Cohesion is the attractive force between molecules of the same substance. Water has an unusually high cohesive force due to the hydrogen bonds each water molecule can potentially make with other water molecules. It is estimated that water's cohesive force within the xylem gives it a tensile strength equivalent to that of a steel wire of similar diameter. The cohesion of water makes it possible to pull a column of xylem sap from above without the water molecules separating. Water molecules exiting the xylem in the leaf tug on adjacent water molecules, and this pull is relayed, molecule by molecule, down the entire column of water

in the xylem. Meanwhile, the strong adhesion of water molecules (again by hydrogen bonds) to the hydrophilic walls of xylem cells helps offset the downward force of gravity.

The upward pull on the sap creates tension within the vessel elements and tracheids, which are like elastic pipes. Positive pressure causes an elastic pipe to swell, whereas tension pulls the walls of the pipe inward. On a warm day, a decrease in the diameter of a tree trunk can even be measured. As transpirational pull puts the vessel elements and tracheids under tension, their thick secondary walls prevent them from collapsing, much as wire rings maintain the shape of a vacuum-cleaner hose. The tension produced by transpirational pull

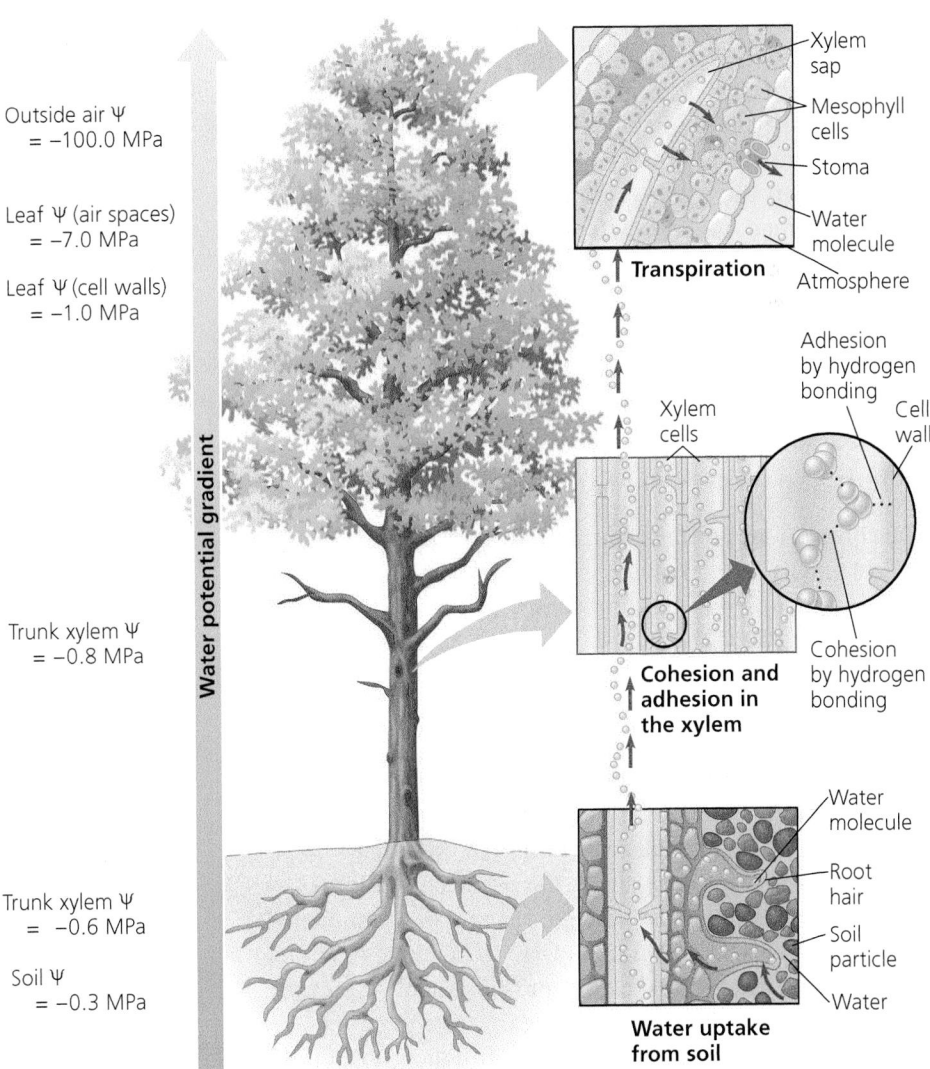

▲ **Figure 36.13 Ascent of xylem sap.** Hydrogen bonding forms an unbroken chain of water molecules extending from leaves to the soil. The force driving the ascent of xylem sap is a gradient of water potential (ψ). For bulk flow over long distance, the ψ gradient is due mainly to a gradient of the pressure potential (ψ_P). Transpiration results in the ψ_P at the leaf end of the xylem being lower than the ψ_P at the root end. The ψ values shown at the left are a "snapshot." They may vary during daylight, but the direction of the ψ gradient remains the same.

 BioFlix Visit the Study Area at **www.masteringbiology.com** for the BioFlix® 3-D Animation on Water Transport in Plants.

lowers water potential in the root xylem to such an extent that water flows passively from the soil, across the root cortex, and into the vascular cylinder.

Transpirational pull can extend down to the roots only through an unbroken chain of water molecules. Cavitation, the formation of a water vapor pocket, breaks the chain. It is more common in wide vessel elements than in tracheids and can occur during drought stress or when xylem sap freezes in winter. The air bubbles resulting from cavitation expand and block water channels of the xylem. The rapid expansion of air bubbles produces clicking noises that can be heard by placing sensitive microphones at the surface of the stem.

The interruption of xylem sap transport by cavitation is not always permanent. The chain of water molecules can detour around the air bubbles through pits between adjacent tracheids or vessel elements (see Figure 35.10). Moreover, root pressure enables small plants to refill blocked vessel elements. Recent evidence suggests that cavitation may even be repaired when the xylem sap is under negative pressure, although the mechanism by which this occurs is uncertain. In addition, secondary growth adds a layer of new xylem each year. Only the youngest, outermost secondary xylem layers transport water. Although the older secondary xylem no longer transports water, it does provide support for the tree (see Figure 35.22).

Xylem Sap Ascent by Bulk Flow: *A Review*

The cohesion-tension mechanism that transports xylem sap against gravity is an excellent example of how physical principles apply to biological processes. In the long-distance transport of water from roots to leaves by bulk flow, the movement of fluid is driven by a water potential difference at opposite ends of xylem tissue. The water potential difference is created at the leaf end of the xylem by the evaporation of water from leaf cells. Evaporation lowers the water potential at the air-water interface, thereby generating the negative pressure (tension) that pulls water through the xylem.

Bulk flow in the xylem differs from diffusion in some key ways. First, it is driven by differences in pressure potential (ψ_P); solute potential (ψ_S) is not a factor. Therefore, the water potential gradient within the xylem is essentially a pressure gradient. Also, the flow does not occur across plasma membranes of living cells, but instead within hollow, dead cells. Furthermore, it moves the entire solution together—not just water or solutes—and at much greater speed than diffusion.

The plant expends no energy to lift xylem sap by bulk flow. Instead, the absorption of sunlight drives most of transpiration by causing water to evaporate from the moist walls of mesophyll cells and by lowering the water potential in the air spaces within a leaf. Thus, the ascent of xylem sap, like the process of photosynthesis, is ultimately solar powered.

CONCEPT 36.4

The rate of transpiration is regulated by stomata

Leaves generally have large surface areas and high surface-to-volume ratios. The large surface area enhances light absorption for photosynthesis. The high surface-to-volume ratio aids in CO_2 absorption during photosynthesis as well as in the release of O_2, a by-product of photosynthesis. Upon diffusing through the stomata, CO_2 enters a honeycomb of air spaces formed by the spongy mesophyll cells (see Figure 35.18). Because of the irregular shapes of these cells, the leaf's internal surface area may be 10 to 30 times greater than the external surface area.

Although large surface areas and high surface-to-volume ratios increase the rate of photosynthesis, they also increase water loss by way of the stomata. Thus, a plant's tremendous requirement for water is largely a consequence of the shoot system's need for ample exchange of CO_2 and O_2 for photosynthesis. By opening and closing the stomata, guard cells help balance the plant's requirement to conserve water with its requirement for photosynthesis (Figure 36.14).

Stomata: Major Pathways for Water Loss

About 95% of the water a plant loses escapes through stomata, although these pores account for only 1–2% of the external leaf surface. The waxy cuticle limits water loss through the remaining surface of the leaf. Each stoma is flanked by a pair of guard cells. Guard cells control the diameter of the stoma by changing shape, thereby widening or narrowing the gap between the guard cell pair. Under the same environmental conditions, the amount of water lost by a leaf

▲ Figure 36.14 **An open stoma (left) and closed stoma** (LMs).

depends largely on the number of stomata and the average size of their pores.

The stomatal density of a leaf, which may be as high as 20,000 per square centimeter, is under both genetic and environmental control. For example, as a result of evolution by natural selection, desert plants are genetically programmed to have lower stomatal densities than do marsh plants. Stomatal density, however, is a developmentally plastic feature of many plants. High light exposures and low CO_2 levels during leaf development lead to increased density in many species. By measuring the stomatal density of leaf fossils, scientists have gained insight into the levels of atmospheric CO_2 in past climates. A recent British survey found that stomatal density of many woodland species has decreased since 1927, when a similar survey was made. This observation is consistent with other findings that atmospheric CO_2 levels increased dramatically during the late 20th century.

Mechanisms of Stomatal Opening and Closing

When guard cells take in water from neighboring cells by osmosis, they become more turgid. In most angiosperm species, the cell walls of guard cells are uneven in thickness, and the cellulose microfibrils are oriented in a direction that causes the guard cells to bow outward when turgid (**Figure 36.15a**). This bowing outward increases the size of the pore between the guard cells. When the cells lose water and become flaccid, they become less bowed, and the pore closes.

The changes in turgor pressure in guard cells result primarily from the reversible absorption and loss of K^+. Stomata open when guard cells actively accumulate K^+ from neighboring epidermal cells (**Figure 36.15b**). The flow of K^+ across the plasma membrane of the guard cell is coupled to the generation of a membrane potential by proton pumps (see Figure 36.7a). Stomatal opening correlates with active transport of H^+ out of the guard cell. The resulting voltage (membrane potential) drives K^+ into the cell through specific membrane channels.

Guard cells turgid/Stoma open   Guard cells flaccid/Stoma closed

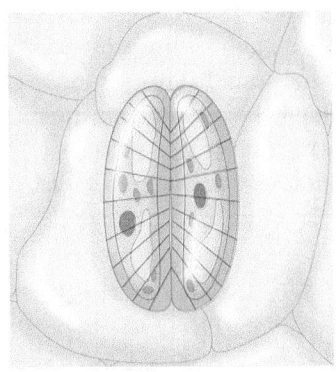

(a) Changes in guard cell shape and stomatal opening and closing (surface view). Guard cells of a typical angiosperm are illustrated in their turgid (stoma open) and flaccid (stoma closed) states. The radial orientation of cellulose microfibrils in the cell walls causes the guard cells to increase more in length than width when turgor increases. Since the two guard cells are tightly joined at their tips, they bow outward when turgid, causing the stomatal pore to open.

(b) Role of potassium in stomatal opening and closing. The transport of K^+ (potassium ions, symbolized here as red dots) across the plasma membrane and vacuolar membrane causes the turgor changes of guard cells. The uptake of anions, such as malate and chloride ions (not shown), also contributes to guard cell swelling.

▲ Figure 36.15 **Mechanisms of stomatal opening and closing.**

The absorption of K^+ causes the water potential to become more negative within the guard cells, and the cells become more turgid as water enters by osmosis. Because most of the K^+ and water are stored in the vacuole, the vacuolar membrane also plays a role in regulating guard cell dynamics. Stomatal closing results from a loss of K^+ from guard cells to neighboring cells, which leads to an osmotic loss of water. Aquaporins also help regulate the osmotic swelling and shrinking of guard cells.

Stimuli for Stomatal Opening and Closing

In general, stomata are open during the day and mostly closed at night, preventing the plant from losing water under conditions when photosynthesis cannot occur. At least three cues contribute to stomatal opening at dawn: light, CO_2 depletion, and an internal "clock" in guard cells.

The light stimulates guard cells to accumulate K^+ and become turgid. This response is triggered by illumination of blue-light receptors in the plasma membrane of guard cells. Activation of these receptors stimulates the activity of proton pumps in the plasma membrane of the guard cells, in turn promoting absorption of K^+.

The stomata also open in response to depletion of CO_2 within the leaf's air spaces as a result of photosynthesis. As CO_2 concentrations decrease during the day, the stomata progressively open if sufficient water is supplied to the leaf.

A third cue, the internal "clock" in the guard cells, ensures that stomata continue their daily rhythm of opening and closing. This rhythm occurs even if a plant is kept in a dark location. All eukaryotic organisms have internal clocks that regulate cyclic processes. Cycles with intervals of approximately 24 hours are called **circadian rhythms**, which you'll learn more about in Chapter 39.

Environmental stresses, such as drought, high temperature, and wind, can cause stomata to close during the daytime. When the plant has a water deficiency, guard cells may lose turgor and close stomata. In addition, a hormone called **abscisic acid (ABA)**, produced in roots and leaves in response to water deficiency, signals guard cells to close stomata. This response reduces wilting but also restricts CO_2 absorption, thereby slowing photosynthesis. Since turgor is necessary for cell elongation, growth ceases throughout the plant. These are some reasons why droughts reduce crop yields.

Guard cells control the photosynthesis-transpiration compromise on a moment-to-moment basis by integrating a variety of internal and external stimuli. Even the passage of a cloud or a transient shaft of sunlight through a forest can affect the rate of transpiration.

Effects of Transpiration on Wilting and Leaf Temperature

As long as most stomata remain open, transpiration is greatest on a day that is sunny, warm, dry, and windy because these environmental factors increase evaporation. If transpiration cannot pull sufficient water to the leaves, the shoot becomes slightly wilted as cells lose turgor pressure. Although plants respond to such mild drought stress by rapidly closing stomata, some evaporative water loss still occurs through the cuticle. Under prolonged drought conditions, leaves can become severely wilted and irreversibly injured.

Transpiration also results in evaporative cooling, which can lower a leaf's temperature by as much as 10°C compared with the surrounding air. This cooling prevents the leaf from reaching temperatures that could denature enzymes involved in photosynthesis and other metabolic processes.

Adaptations That Reduce Evaporative Water Loss

Plants adapted to arid environments, such as the stone plants of the Kalahari Desert (see Figure 36.1), are called **xerophytes** (from the Greek *xero*, dry). **Figure 36.16** shows other examples. Dry soils are relatively unproductive because plants need a sufficient quantity of liquid water to carry out photosynthesis. However, the reason why water availability is so tied to plant productivity is not related to photosynthesis's direct need for water as a substrate but rather because freely available water allows plants to keep stomata open and take up more CO_2.

Many species of desert plants avoid drying out by completing their short life cycles during the brief rainy seasons. Rain comes infrequently in deserts, but when it arrives, the vegetation is transformed as dormant seeds of annual species quickly germinate and bloom, completing their life cycle before dry conditions return. Longer-lived species have unusual physiological or morphological adaptations that enable them to withstand the harsh desert conditions. Many xerophytes, such as cacti, have highly reduced leaves that resist excessive water loss; they carry out photosynthesis mainly in their stems. The stems of many xerophytes are fleshy because they store water for use during long dry periods. Some desert plants, such as mesquite, have roots more than 20 m long, allowing them to acquire moisture at or near the water table.

Another adaptation to arid habitats is crassulacean acid metabolism (CAM), a specialized form of photosynthesis found in succulents of the family Crassulaceae and several other families (see Figure 10.21). Because the leaves of CAM plants take in CO_2 at night, the stomata can remain closed during the day, when evaporative stresses are greater. Stomata are the most important mediators of the conflicting demands of CO_2 acquisition and water retention.

CONCEPT CHECK 36.4

1. What are the stimuli that control the opening and closing of stomata?
2. The pathogenic fungus *Fusicoccum amygdali* secretes a toxin called fusicoccin that activates the plasma membrane proton pumps of plant cells and leads to uncontrolled water loss. Suggest a mechanism by which the activation of proton pumps could lead to severe wilting.
3. **WHAT IF?** If you buy cut flowers, why might the florist recommend cutting the stems underwater and then transferring the flowers to a vase while the cut ends are still wet?
4. **MAKE CONNECTIONS** Explain why the evaporation of water from leaves lowers their temperature. See p. 49 of Concept 3.2.

For suggested answers, see Appendix A.

▼ Figure 36.16 Some xerophytic adaptations.

▶ Ocotillo (*Fouquieria splendens*) is common in the southwestern region of the United States and northern Mexico. It is leafless during most of the year, thereby avoiding excessive water loss (right). Immediately after a heavy rainfall, it produces small leaves (below and inset). As the soil dries, the leaves quickly shrivel and die.

▼ Oleander (*Nerium oleander*), shown in the inset, is commonly found in arid climates. Its leaves have a thick cuticle and multiple-layered epidermal tissue that reduce water loss. Stomata are recessed in cavities called "crypts," an adaptation that reduces the rate of transpiration by protecting the stomata from hot, dry wind. Trichomes help minimize transpiration by breaking up the flow of air, allowing the chamber of the crypt to have a higher humidity than the surrounding atmosphere (LM).

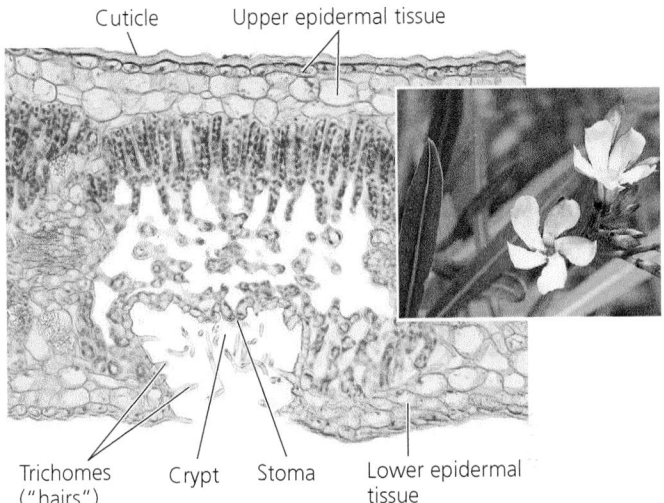

Cuticle   Upper epidermal tissue

100 μm

Trichomes   Crypt   Stoma   Lower epidermal
("hairs")   tissue

▶ This is a close-up view of stems of old man cactus (*Cephalocereus senilis*), a Mexican desert plant. The long, white, hairlike bristles help reflect the sun.

CONCEPT 36.5

Sugars are transported from sources to sinks via the phloem

You have read how water and minerals are absorbed by root cells, transported through the endodermis, released into the vessel elements and tracheids of the xylem, and carried to the tops of plants by the bulk flow driven by transpiration. However, transpiration cannot meet all the long-distance transport needs of the plant. The flow of water and minerals from soil to roots to leaves is largely in a direction opposite to the direction necessary for transporting sugars from mature leaves to lower parts of the plant, such as root tips that require large amounts of sugars for energy and growth. The transport of the products of photosynthesis, known as **translocation**, is carried out by another tissue, the phloem.

Movement from Sugar Sources to Sugar Sinks

In angiosperms, the specialized cells that are conduits for translocation are the sieve-tube elements. Arranged end to end, they form long sieve tubes (see Figure 35.10). Between these cells are sieve plates, structures that allow the flow of sap along the sieve tube.

Phloem sap, the aqueous solution that flows through sieve tubes, differs markedly from the xylem sap that is transported by tracheids and vessel elements. By far the most prevalent solute in phloem sap is sugar, typically sucrose in most species. The sucrose concentration may be as high as 30% by weight, giving the sap a syrupy thickness. Phloem sap may also contain amino acids, hormones, and minerals.

In contrast to the unidirectional transport of xylem sap from roots to leaves, phloem sap moves from sites of sugar production to sites of sugar use or storage (see Figure 36.2). A

sugar source is a plant organ that is a net producer of sugar, by photosynthesis or by breakdown of starch. A **sugar sink** is an organ that is a net consumer or depository of sugar. Growing roots, buds, stems, and fruits are sugar sinks. Although expanding leaves are sugar sinks, mature leaves, if well illuminated, are sugar sources. A storage organ, such as a tuber or a bulb, may be a source or a sink, depending on the season. When stockpiling carbohydrates in the summer, it is a sugar sink. After breaking dormancy in the spring, it is a sugar source because its starch is broken down to sugar, which is carried to the growing shoot tips.

Sinks usually receive sugar from the nearest sugar sources. The upper leaves on a branch, for example, may export sugar to the growing shoot tip, whereas the lower leaves may export sugar to the roots. A growing fruit may monopolize the sugar sources that surround it. For each sieve tube, the direction of transport depends on the locations of the sugar source and sugar sink that are connected by that tube. Therefore, neighboring sieve tubes may carry sap in opposite directions if they originate and end in different locations.

Sugar must be transported, or loaded, into sieve-tube elements before being exported to sugar sinks. In some species, it moves from mesophyll cells to sieve-tube elements via the symplast, passing through plasmodesmata. In other species, it moves by symplastic and apoplastic pathways. In maize leaves, for example, sucrose diffuses through the symplast from photosynthetic mesophyll cells into small veins. Much of it then moves into the apoplast and is accumulated by nearby sieve-tube elements, either directly or through companion cells (Figure 36.17a). In some plants, the walls of the companion cells feature many ingrowths, enhancing solute transfer between apoplast and symplast.

In many plants, sugar movement into the phloem requires active transport because sucrose is more concentrated in sieve-tube elements and companion cells than in mesophyll. Proton pumping and H^+/sucrose cotransport enable sucrose to move from mesophyll cells to sieve-tube elements or companion cells (Figure 36.17b).

Sucrose is unloaded at the sink end of a sieve tube. The process varies by species and organ. However, the concentration of free sugar in the sink is always lower than in the sieve tube because the unloaded sugar is consumed during growth and metabolism of the cells of the sink or converted to insoluble polymers such as starch. As a result of this sugar concentration gradient, sugar molecules diffuse from the phloem into the sink tissues, and water follows by osmosis.

Bulk Flow by Positive Pressure: The Mechanism of Translocation in Angiosperms

Phloem sap flows from source to sink at rates as great as 1 m/hr, much faster than diffusion or cytoplasmic streaming. Researchers have concluded that phloem sap moves through the sieve tubes of angiosperms by bulk flow driven by positive pressure, known as *pressure flow* (Figure 36.18). The building of pressure at the source and reduction of that pressure at the sink cause sap to flow from source to sink.

The pressure-flow hypothesis explains why phloem sap flows from source to sink, and experiments build a strong case for pressure flow as the mechanism of translocation in angiosperms (Figure 36.19). However, studies using electron microscopes suggest that in nonflowering vascular plants, the pores between phloem cells may be too small or obstructed to permit pressure flow.

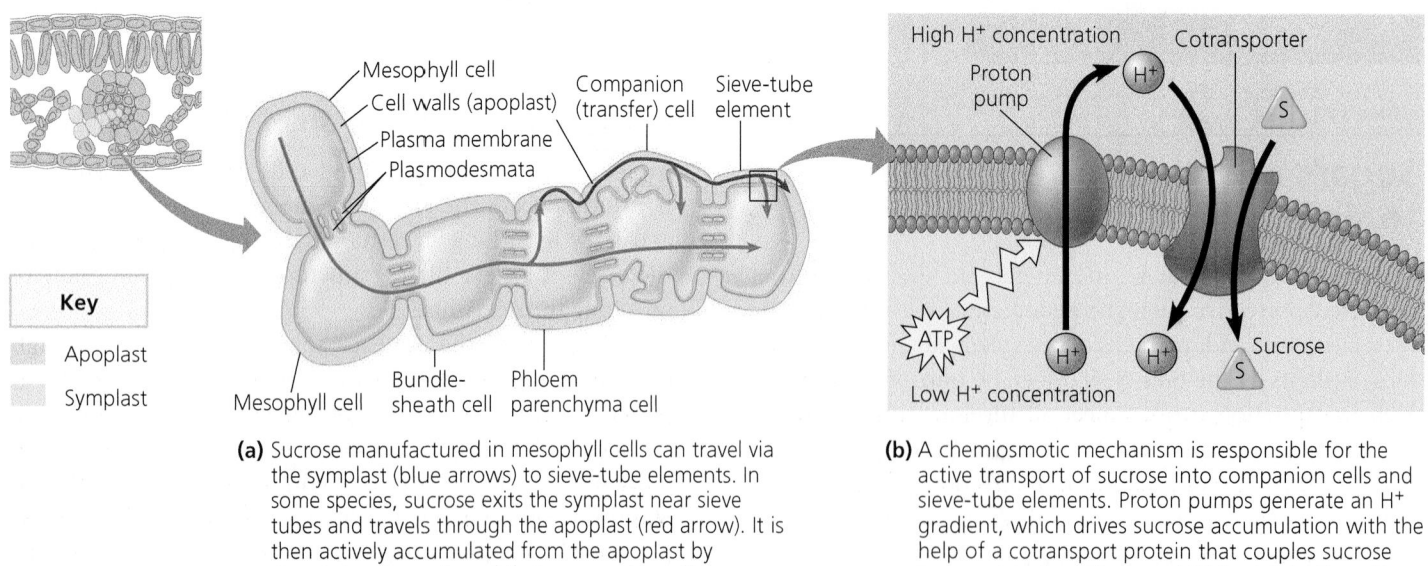

Key

Apoplast

Symplast

(a) Sucrose manufactured in mesophyll cells can travel via the symplast (blue arrows) to sieve-tube elements. In some species, sucrose exits the symplast near sieve tubes and travels through the apoplast (red arrow). It is then actively accumulated from the apoplast by sieve-tube elements and their companion cells.

(b) A chemiosmotic mechanism is responsible for the active transport of sucrose into companion cells and sieve-tube elements. Proton pumps generate an H^+ gradient, which drives sucrose accumulation with the help of a cotransport protein that couples sucrose transport to the diffusion of H^+ back into the cell.

▲ Figure 36.17 **Loading of sucrose into phloem.**

Vessel (xylem)   **Sieve tube (phloem)**   **Source cell (leaf)**

Bulk flow by negative pressure

Bulk flow by positive pressure

H₂O

Sucrose

H₂O

Sink cell (storage root)

Sucrose

H₂O

① Loading of sugar (green dots) into the sieve tube at the source reduces water potential inside the sieve-tube elements. This causes the tube to take up water by osmosis.

② This uptake of water generates a positive pressure that forces the sap to flow along the tube.

③ The pressure is relieved by the unloading of sugar and the consequent loss of water at the sink.

④ In leaf-to-root translocation, xylem recycles water from sink to source.

▲ **Figure 36.18 Bulk flow by positive pressure (pressure flow) in a sieve tube.**

Sinks vary in energy demands and capacity to unload sugars. Sometimes there are more sinks than can be supported by sources. In such cases, a plant might abort some flowers, seeds, or fruits—a phenomenon called *self-thinning*. Removing sinks can also be a horticulturally useful practice. For example, since large apples command a much better price than small ones, growers sometimes remove flowers or young fruits so that their trees produce fewer but larger apples.

CONCEPT CHECK 36.5

1. Compare and contrast the forces that move phloem sap and xylem sap over long distance.
2. Identify plant organs that are sugar sources, organs that are sugar sinks, and organs that might be either. Explain.
3. Why can xylem transport water and minerals using dead cells, whereas phloem requires living cells?
4. **WHAT IF?** Apple growers in Japan sometimes make a nonlethal spiral slash around the bark of trees that are destined for removal after the growing season. This practice makes the apples sweeter. Why?

For suggested answers, see Appendix A.

Does phloem sap contain more sugar near sources than sinks?

EXPERIMENT The pressure-flow hypothesis predicts that phloem sap near sources should have a higher sugar content than phloem sap near sinks. To test this aspect of the hypothesis, researchers used aphids that feed on phloem sap. An aphid probes with a hypodermic-like mouthpart called a stylet that penetrates a sieve-tube element. As sieve-tube pressure forced out phloem sap into the stylets, the researchers separated the aphids from the stylets, which then acted as taps exuding sap for hours. Researchers measured the sugar concentration of sap from stylets at different points between a source and sink.

25 μm

Sieve-tube element

Sap droplet

Stylet

Sap droplet

Aphid feeding   Stylet in sieve-tube element   Separated stylet exuding sap

RESULTS The closer the stylet was to a sugar source, the higher its sugar concentration.

CONCLUSION The results of such experiments support the pressure-flow hypothesis, which predicts that sugar concentrations should be higher in sieve tubes closer to sugar sources.

SOURCE S. Rogers and A. J. Peel, Some evidence for the existence of turgor pressure in the sieve tubes of willow (*Salix*), *Planta* 126:259–267 (1975).

WHAT IF? Spittlebugs are xylem sap feeders that use strong muscles to pump xylem sap through their guts. Could you isolate xylem sap from the excised stylets of spittlebugs?

CONCEPT 36.6

The symplast is highly dynamic

Although we have been discussing transport in mostly physical terms, almost like the flow of solutions through pipes, plant transport is a finely tuned process. That is, the transport needs of a plant cell typically change during its development. A leaf, for example, may begin as a sugar sink but spend most of its life as a sugar source. Also, environmental changes may trigger marked responses in plant transport processes. Water stress may activate signal transduction pathways that greatly alter the membrane transport proteins governing the overall transport of water and minerals. Because the symplast is living tissue, it is largely responsible for the dynamic changes in plant transport processes.

Changes in Plasmodesmata

Plasmodesmata are highly dynamic components of the symplast. Mostly on the basis of static images from electron microscopy, biologists formerly thought of plasmodesmata as unchanging pore-like structures. Recently, however, new techniques have revealed that plasmodesmata are highly dynamic structures that can change in permeability and number. They can open or close rapidly in response to changes in turgor pressure, cytosolic Ca^{2+} levels, or cytosolic pH. Although some form during cytokinesis, they can also form much later. Moreover, loss of function is common during differentiation. For example, as a leaf matures from a sink to a source, its plasmodesmata either close or are eliminated, causing phloem unloading to cease.

Early studies by plant physiologists and pathologists came to differing conclusions regarding pore sizes of plasmodesmata. Physiologists injected fluorescent probes of different molecular sizes into cells and recorded whether the molecules passed into adjacent cells. Based on these observations, they concluded that the pore sizes were approximately 2.5 nm—too small for macromolecules such as proteins to pass. In contrast, pathologists provided electron micrographs showing evidence of the passage of virus particles with diameters of 10 nm or greater (Figure 36.20). One hypothesis to explain these discordant findings was that viruses dilate plasmodesmata.

Subsequently, it was learned that plant viruses produce *viral movement proteins* that cause plasmodesmata to dilate, enabling viral RNA to pass between cells. More recent evidence shows that plant cells themselves regulate plasmodesmata as part of a communication network. Viruses subvert this network by mimicking the cell's regulators of plasmodesmata.

A high degree of cytosolic interconnectedness exists only within certain groups of cells and tissues, known as *symplastic domains*. Informational molecules, such as proteins and RNAs, coordinate development between cells within each symplastic domain. If symplastic communication is disrupted, development can be grossly affected.

Plasmodesma — Virus particles — Cell wall — 100 nm

▲ **Figure 36.20 Virus particles moving cell to cell through a plasmodesma connecting turnip leaf cells** (TEM).

Phloem: An Information Superhighway

In addition to transporting sugars, the phloem is a "superhighway" for the transport of macromolecules and viruses. This transport is systemic (throughout the body), affecting many or all of the plant's systems or organs. Macromolecules translocated through the phloem include proteins and various types of RNA that enter the sieve tubes through plasmodesmata. Although they are often likened to the gap junctions between animal cells, plasmodesmata are unique in their ability to traffic proteins and RNA.

Systemic communication through the phloem helps integrate the functions of the whole plant. One classic example is the delivery of a flower-inducing signal from leaves to vegetative meristems. Another is a defensive response to localized infection, in which signals traveling through the phloem activate defense genes in noninfected tissues.

Electrical Signaling in the Phloem

Rapid, long-distance electrical signaling through the phloem is another dynamic feature of the symplast. Electrical signaling has been studied extensively in plants that have rapid leaf movements, such as the sensitive plant (*Mimosa pudica*) and Venus flytrap (*Dionaea muscipula*). However, its role in other species is less clear. Some studies have revealed that a stimulus in one part of a plant can trigger an electrical signal in the phloem that affects another part, where it may elicit a change in gene transcription, respiration, photosynthesis, phloem unloading, or hormonal levels. Thus, the phloem can serve a nerve-like function, allowing for swift electrical communication between widely separated organs.

The coordinated transport of materials and information is central to plant survival. Plants acquire only so many resources in the course of their lifetimes. Ultimately, the successful acquisition of resources and their optimal distribution are the most critical determinants of whether the plant will compete successfully.

CONCEPT CHECK 36.6

1. How do plasmodesmata differ from gap junctions?
2. Nerve-like signals in animals are thousands of times faster than their plant counterparts. Suggest a behavioral reason for the difference.
3. **WHAT IF?** Suppose plants were genetically modified to be unresponsive to viral movement proteins. Would this be a good way to prevent the spread of infection? Explain.

For suggested answers, see Appendix A.

36 CHAPTER REVIEW

SUMMARY OF KEY CONCEPTS

CONCEPT 36.1

Adaptations for acquiring resources were key steps in the evolution of vascular plants (pp. 764–767)

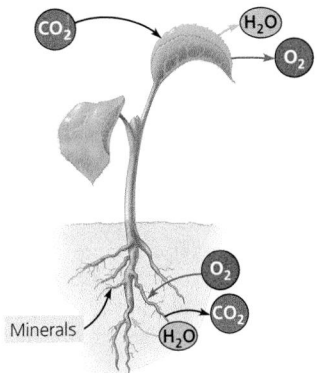

- Leaves typically function in gathering sunlight and CO_2. Stems serve as supporting structures for leaves and as conduits for the long-distance transport of water and nutrients. Roots mine the soil for water and minerals and anchor the whole plant. **Mycorrhizae** are mutualistic associations formed between roots and certain soil fungi that aid in the absorption of minerals and water.
- Natural selection has produced plant architectures that optimize resource acquisition in the ecological niche in which the plant species naturally exists.

> ? How did the evolution of xylem and phloem contribute to the successful colonization of land by vascular plants?

CONCEPT 36.2

Different mechanisms transport substances over short or long distances (pp. 767–771)

- The selective permeability of the plasma membrane controls the movement of substances into and out of cells. Both active and passive transport mechanisms occur in plants.
- Plant tissues have two major compartments: the **apoplast** (everything outside the cells' plasma membranes) and the **symplast** (the cytosol and connecting plasmodesmata).
- The direction of water movement depends on the **water potential**, a quantity incorporating solute concentration and physical pressure. The osmotic uptake of water by plant cells and the resulting internal pressure that builds up make plant cells **turgid**.
- Long-distance transport occurs through **bulk flow**, the movement of liquid in response to a pressure gradient. Bulk flow occurs within the tracheids and vessel elements of the xylem and within the sieve-tube elements of the phloem.

> ? Is xylem sap usually pulled or pushed up the plant?

CONCEPT 36.3

Transpiration drives the transport of water and minerals from roots to shoots via the xylem (pp. 772–776)

- Water and minerals from the soil enter the plant through the epidermis of roots, cross the root cortex, and then pass into the vascular cylinder by way of the selectively permeable cells of the **endodermis**. From the vascular cylinder, the **xylem sap** is transported long distances by bulk flow to the veins that branch throughout each leaf.
- The **cohesion-tension hypothesis** proposes that the movement of xylem sap is driven by a water potential difference created at the leaf end of the xylem by the evaporation of water from leaf cells. Evaporation lowers the water potential at the air-water interface, thereby generating the negative pressure that pulls water through the xylem.

> ? Why is the ability of water molecules to form hydrogen bonds important for the movement of xylem sap?

CONCEPT 36.4

The rate of transpiration is regulated by stomata (pp. 776–778)

- **Transpiration** is the loss of water vapor from plants. **Wilting** occurs when the water lost by transpiration is not replaced by absorption from roots.
- Stomata are the major pathway for water loss from plants. Guard cells widen or narrow the stomatal pores. When guard cells take up K^+, the pore widens. The opening and closing of stomata is controlled by light, CO_2, the drought hormone **abscisic acid**, and a **circadian rhythm**.
- Reduced leaves and CAM photosynthesis are examples of adaptations to arid environments.

> ? Why are stomata necessary?

CONCEPT 36.5

Sugars are transported from sources to sinks via the phloem (pp. 779–781)

- Mature leaves are the main **sugar sources**, although storage organs can be seasonal sources. Growing organs such as roots, stems, and fruits are the main **sugar sinks**.
- Phloem loading depends on the active transport of sucrose. Sucrose is cotransported with H^+, which diffuses down a gradient generated by proton pumps. Loading of sugar at the source and unloading at the sink maintain a pressure difference that keeps sap flowing through a sieve tube.

> ? Why is phloem transport considered an active process?

CONCEPT 36.6

The symplast is highly dynamic (pp. 781–782)

- **Plasmodesmata** can change in permeability and number. When dilated, they provide a passageway for the symplastic transport of proteins, RNAs, and other macromolecules over long distances. The phloem also conducts nerve-like electrical signals that help integrate whole-plant function.

> ? By what mechanisms is symplastic communication regulated?

LEVEL 1: KNOWLEDGE/COMPREHENSION

1. The symplast transports all of the following *except*
   a. sugars.
   b. mRNA.
   c. DNA.
   d. proteins.
   e. viruses.

2. Which of the following is an adaptation that enhances the uptake of water and minerals by roots?
   a. mycorrhizae
   b. cavitation
   c. active uptake by vessel elements
   d. rhythmic contractions by cortical cells
   e. pumping through plasmodesmata

3. Which structure or compartment is part of the symplast?
   a. the interior of a vessel element
   b. the interior of a sieve tube
   c. the cell wall of a mesophyll cell
   d. an extracellular air space
   e. the cell wall of a root hair

4. Movement of phloem sap from a source to a sink
   a. occurs through the apoplast of sieve-tube elements.
   b. depends ultimately on the activity of proton pumps.
   c. depends on tension, or negative pressure potential.
   d. depends on pumping water into sieve tubes at the source.
   e. results mainly from diffusion.

LEVEL 2: APPLICATION/ANALYSIS

5. Photosynthesis ceases when leaves wilt, mainly because
   a. the chlorophyll in wilting leaves is degraded.
   b. flaccid mesophyll cells are incapable of photosynthesis.
   c. stomata close, preventing CO_2 from entering the leaf.
   d. photolysis, the water-splitting step of photosynthesis, cannot occur when there is a water deficiency.
   e. accumulation of CO_2 in the leaf inhibits enzymes.

6. What would enhance water uptake by a plant cell?
   a. decreasing the ψ of the surrounding solution
   b. increasing the pressure exerted by the cell wall
   c. the loss of solutes from the cell
   d. increasing the ψ of the cytoplasm
   e. positive pressure on the surrounding solution

7. A plant cell with a ψ_S of –0.65 MPa maintains a constant volume when bathed in a solution that has a ψ_S of –0.30 MPa and is in an open container. The cell has a
   a. ψ_P of +0.65 MPa.
   b. ψ of –0.65 MPa.
   c. ψ_P of +0.35 MPa.
   d. ψ_P of +0.30 MPa.
   e. ψ of 0 MPa.

8. Compared with a cell with few aquaporin proteins in its membrane, a cell containing many aquaporin proteins will
   a. have a faster rate of osmosis.
   b. have a lower water potential.
   c. have a higher water potential.
   d. have a faster rate of active transport.
   e. accumulate water by active transport.

9. Which of the following would tend to increase transpiration?
   a. a rainstorm
   b. sunken stomata
   c. a thicker cuticle
   d. higher stomatal density
   e. spiny leaves

10. **DRAW IT** Trace the uptake of water and minerals from root hairs to the endodermis in a root, following a symplastic route and an apoplastic route. Label the routes on the diagram below.

LEVEL 3: SYNTHESIS/EVALUATION

11. **EVOLUTION CONNECTION**
    Large brown algae called kelps can grow as tall as 25 m. Kelps consist of a holdfast anchored to the ocean floor, blades that float at the surface and collect light, and a long stalk connecting the blades to the holdfast (see Figure 28.15). Specialized cells in the stalk, although nonvascular, can transport sugar. Suggest a reason why these structures analogous to sieve-tube elements might have evolved in kelps.

12. **SCIENTIFIC INQUIRY**
    Cotton plants wilt within a few hours of flooding their roots. The flooding leads to low-oxygen conditions, increases in cytosolic Ca^{2+}, and decreases in cytosolic pH. Suggest a hypothesis to explain how flooding leads to wilting.

13. **WRITE ABOUT A THEME**
    Structure and Function Natural selection has led to changes in the architecture of plants that enable them to photosynthesize more efficiently in the ecological niches they occupy. In a short essay (100–150 words), explain how shoot architecture enhances photosynthesis.

For selected answers, see Appendix A.

Mastering BIOLOGY   www.masteringbiology.com

1. MasteringBiology® Assignments:
   Make Connections Tutorial Ascent of Xylem Sap (Chapter 36) and Hydrogen Bonding (Chapter 3)
   BioFlix Tutorials Water Transport in Plants: The Transpiration-Cohesion-Tension Mechanism • Water Transport in Plants: Transpiration
   Activities Transport of Xylem Sap • Translocation of Phloem Sap • Solute Transport in Plants
   Questions Student Misconceptions • Reading Quiz • Multiple Choice • End-of-Chapter

2. eText
   Read your book online, search, take notes, highlight text, and more.

3. The Study Area
   Practice Tests • Cumulative Test • **BioFlix** 3-D Animations • MP3 Tutor Sessions • Videos • Activities • Investigations • Lab Media • Audio Glossary • Word Study Tools • Art

Soil and Plant Nutrition

▲ Figure 37.1 **A rat trap?**

KEY CONCEPTS

37.1 Soil contains a living, complex ecosystem
37.2 Plants require essential elements to complete their life cycle
37.3 Plant nutrition often involves relationships with other organisms

OVERVIEW

A Horrifying Discovery

In 1858, two British explorers made a grisly discovery during their ascent of Mount Kinabalu, in northern Borneo: a dead rat. What was unusual about this rat was that it was the partially digested meal of *Nepenthes rajah*, a member of a group of carnivorous plants called "pitcher plants" because their highly modified leaves resemble pitchers (Figure 37.1).

Each pitcher contains a slightly viscous fluid of the plant's own production, which is used to drown prey. Along the upper lip of the trap is a slick waxy coating that makes the escape of its prey virtually impossible. Above the lip is a lid that in many species keeps rain from diluting the viscous fluid within the pitcher. The lower part of the trap contains glands that absorb nutrients from the captured prey. Although carnivory by pitcher plants is well documented, what sets *N. rajah* apart from other *Nepenthes* species is the size of its pitcher and the size of its prey: The pitcher of *N. rajah* holds several liters of solution, and it is one of only a few *Nepenthes* species documented as having caught mammals in the wild.

To understand the reason for this marvelous adaptation, it is necessary to consider the unproductive serpentine soil found on the slopes of Mount Kinabalu. Serpentine soils are notoriously poor soils derived from Earth's molten magma: They typically have a high metal content but contain low amounts of nutrient elements such as calcium, potassium, and phosphorus. The unusual carnivorous habit of *N. rajah* is an adaptation that allows the plant to supplement its meager mineral rations from the soil with minerals released from its digested prey.

Plant nutrition is the study of the chemical elements that are necessary for plant growth. As discussed in Chapter 36, plants obtain nutrients from both the atmosphere and the soil. Using sunlight as an energy source, plants produce organic nutrients by reducing carbon dioxide to sugars through the process of photosynthesis. Land plants also take up water and various mineral nutrients from the soil through their root systems. In this chapter, we discuss the basic physical properties of soils and the factors that govern soil quality. We then explore why certain inorganic nutrients are essential for plant function. Finally, we examine some nutritional adaptations that have evolved in plants, often in relationships with other organisms.

CONCEPT 37.1

Soil contains a living, complex ecosystem

The upper layers of the soil, from which plants absorb nearly all of the water and minerals they require, contain a wide range of living organisms that interact with each other and with the physical environment. This complex ecosystem may take centuries to form but can be destroyed by human mismanagement in just a few years. To understand why soil must be conserved and why particular plants grow where they do, it is necessary to first consider the basic physical properties of soil: its texture and composition.

Soil Texture

The texture of soil depends on the sizes of its particles. Soil particles can range from coarse sand (0.02–2 mm in diameter) to silt (0.002–0.02 mm) to microscopic clay particles (less than 0.002 mm). These different-sized particles arise ultimately from the weathering of rock. Water freezing in the crevices of rocks causes mechanical fracturing, and weak acids in the soil break rocks down chemically. When organisms penetrate the rock, they accelerate breakdown by chemical and mechanical means. Plant roots, for example, secrete acids that dissolve the rock, and their growth in fissures leads to mechanical fracturing. The mineral particles released by weathering become mixed with living organisms and **humus**, the remains of dead organisms and other organic matter, forming **topsoil**. The topsoil and other distinct soil layers are called **soil horizons** (Figure 37.2). The topsoil, or A horizon, can range in depth from millimeters to meters. We focus mostly on the properties of topsoil because it is generally the most important soil layer for the growth of plants.

In the topsoil, plants are nourished by the soil solution, the water and dissolved minerals in the pores between soil particles. The pores also contain air pockets. After a heavy rainfall, water drains away from the larger spaces in the soil, but smaller spaces retain water because water molecules are attracted to the negatively charged surfaces of clay and other soil particles.

The topsoils that are the most fertile—supporting the most abundant growth—are **loams**, which are composed of roughly equal amounts of sand, silt, and clay. Loamy soils have enough small silt and clay particles to provide ample surface area for the adhesion and retention of minerals and water. Meanwhile,

the large spaces between sand particles enable efficient diffusion of oxygen to the roots. Sandy soils generally don't retain enough water to support vigorous plant growth, and clayey soils tend to retain too much water. When soil does not drain adequately, the air is replaced by water, and the roots suffocate from lack of oxygen. Typically, the most fertile topsoils have pores that are about half water and half air, providing a good balance between aeration, drainage, and water storage capacity. The physical properties of soils can be adjusted by adding soil amendments, such as peat moss, compost, manure, or sand.

Topsoil Composition

A soil's composition encompasses its inorganic (mineral) and organic chemical components. The organic components include the many life-forms that inhabit the soil.

Inorganic Components

The surface charges of soil particles determine their ability to bind many nutrients. Most soil particles are negatively charged. Positively charged ions (cations)—such as potassium (K^+), calcium (Ca^{2+}), and magnesium (Mg^{2+})—adhere to these particles and are therefore not easily lost by *leaching*, the percolation of water through the soil. Roots, however, do not absorb mineral cations directly from soil particles; they absorb them from the soil solution. Mineral cations enter the soil solution by **cation exchange**, a process in which cations are displaced from soil particles by other cations, particularly H^+ (Figure 37.3). Therefore, a soil's capacity to exchange cations is determined by the number of cation adhesion sites

The A horizon is the topsoil, a mixture of broken-down rock of various textures, living organisms, and decaying organic matter.

The B horizon contains much less organic matter than the A horizon and is less weathered.

The C horizon is composed mainly of partially broken-down rock. Some of the rock served as "parent" material for minerals that later helped form the upper horizons.

▲ **Figure 37.2 Soil horizons.**

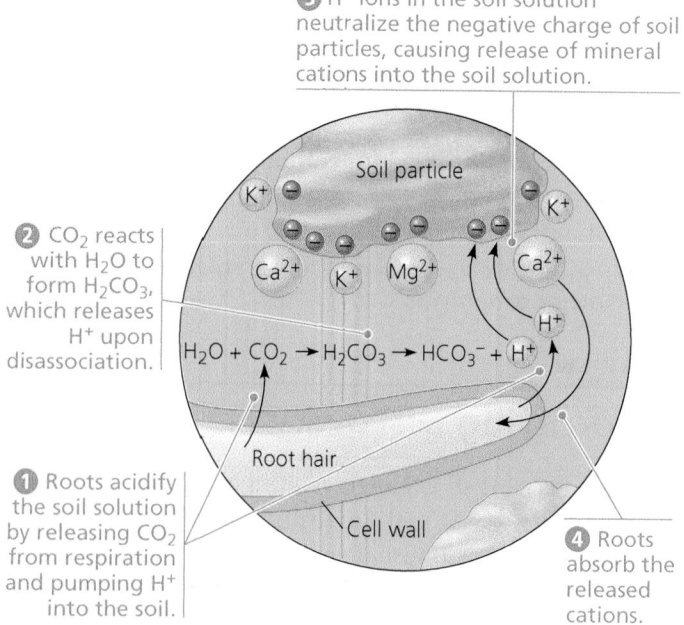

❸ H^+ ions in the soil solution neutralize the negative charge of soil particles, causing release of mineral cations into the soil solution.

❷ CO_2 reacts with H_2O to form H_2CO_3, which releases H^+ upon disassociation.

❶ Roots acidify the soil solution by releasing CO_2 from respiration and pumping H^+ into the soil.

❹ Roots absorb the released cations.

Soil particle

$H_2O + CO_2 \rightarrow H_2CO_3 \rightarrow HCO_3^- + H^+$

Root hair

Cell wall

▲ **Figure 37.3 Cation exchange in soil.**

❓ *Which are more likely to be leached from the soil by heavy rains—cations or anions? Explain.*

and by the soil's pH. Soils with higher capacities generally have a larger reserve of mineral nutrients.

Negatively charged ions (anions)—such as the plant nutrients nitrate (NO_3^-), phosphate ($H_2PO_4^-$), and sulfate (SO_4^{2-})—do not bind to the negatively charged soil particles and are therefore easily released. During heavy rain or irrigation, they are leached into the groundwater, making them unavailable for uptake by roots.

Organic Components

The major organic component of topsoil is humus, which consists of organic material produced by the decomposition of dead organisms, feces, fallen leaves, and other organic matter by bacteria and fungi. Humus prevents clay particles from packing together and forms a crumbly soil that retains water but is still porous enough to aerate roots adequately. Humus also increases the soil's capacity to exchange cations and serves as a reservoir of mineral nutrients that return gradually to the soil as microorganisms decompose the organic matter.

Topsoil is home to an astonishing number and variety of organisms. A teaspoon of topsoil has about 5 billion bacteria, which cohabit with fungi, algae and other protists, insects, earthworms, nematodes, and plant roots. The activities of all these organisms affect the soil's physical and chemical properties. Earthworms, for example, consume organic matter and derive their nutrition from the bacteria and fungi growing on this material. They excrete wastes and move large amounts of material to the soil surface. In addition, they move organic matter into deeper layers of the soil. In effect, earthworms mix and clump the soil particles, allowing for better gaseous diffusion and retention of water. Plant roots also affect soil texture and composition. For example, by binding the soil, they reduce erosion, and by excreting acids, they lower soil pH.

Soil Conservation and Sustainable Agriculture

Ancient farmers recognized that yields on a particular plot of land decreased over the years. Moving to uncultivated areas, they observed the same pattern of reduced yields over time. Eventually, they realized that fertilization could make soil a renewable resource that enabled crops to be cultivated season after season at a fixed location. This sedentary agriculture facilitated a new way of life. Humans began to build permanent dwellings—the first villages. They also stored food for use between harvests, and food surpluses enabled some members of these early communities to specialize in nonfarming occupations. In short, soil management, by fertilization and other practices, helped prepare the way for modern societies.

Unfortunately, soil mismanagement has been a recurrent problem throughout human history, as exemplified by the American Dust Bowl, an ecological and human disaster that ravaged the southwestern Great Plains of the United States in the 1930s. This region suffered through devastating dust

▲ **Figure 37.4 A massive dust storm in the American Dust Bowl during the 1930s.**

storms that resulted from a prolonged drought and decades of inappropriate farming techniques. Before the arrival of farmers, the Great Plains had been covered by hardy grasses that held the soil in place in spite of recurring droughts and torrential rains. But in the late 1800s and early 1900s, many homesteaders settled in the region, planting wheat and raising cattle. These land uses left the soil exposed to erosion by winds. A few years of drought made the problem worse. During the 1930s, huge quantities of fertile soil were blown away in "black blizzards," rendering millions of hectares of farmland useless (Figure 37.4). In one of the worst dust storms, clouds of dust blew eastward to Chicago, where soil fell like snow, and even reached the Atlantic coast. Hundreds of thousands of people in the Dust Bowl region were forced to abandon their homes and land, a plight immortalized in John Steinbeck's novel *The Grapes of Wrath*.

Soil mismanagement continues to be a major problem to this day. More than 30% of the world's farmland has reduced productivity stemming from poor soil conditions, such as chemical contamination, mineral deficiencies, acidity, salinity, and poor drainage. As the world's population continues to grow, the demand for food increases. Because soil quality is a major determinant of crop yield, the need to manage soil resources prudently has never been greater.

We'll now discuss how farmers irrigate and modify soil in order to maintain good crop yields. The goal is **sustainable agriculture**, a commitment embracing a variety of farming methods that are conservation minded, environmentally safe, and profitable. We will also examine problems and solutions relating to soil degradation.

Irrigation

Because water is often the limiting factor in plant growth, perhaps no technology has increased crop yield as much as irrigation. However, irrigation is a huge drain on freshwater resources. Globally, about 75% of all freshwater use is devoted to agriculture. Many rivers in arid regions have been reduced

▲ **Figure 37.5 Sudden land subsidence.** Overuse of groundwater for irrigation triggered formation of this sinkhole in Florida.

to trickles by the diversion of water for irrigation. The primary source of irrigation water, however, is not surface waters, such as rivers and lakes, but underground water reserves called *aquifers*. In some parts of the world, the rate of water removal is exceeding the natural refilling of the aquifers. The result is *land subsidence*, a gradual settling or sudden sinking of Earth's surface (**Figure 37.5**). Land subsidence alters drainage patterns, causes damage to human-made structures, contributes to loss of underground springs, and increases the risk of flooding.

Irrigation, particularly from groundwater, can also lead to soil *salinization*—the addition of salts to the soil that make it too salty for cultivating plants. Salts dissolved in irrigation water accumulate in the soil as the water evaporates, making the water potential of the soil solution more negative. The water potential gradient from soil to roots is reduced, diminishing water uptake (see Chapter 36).

Many forms of irrigation, such as the flooding of fields, are wasteful because much of the water evaporates. To use water efficiently, farmers must understand the water-holding capacity of their soil, the water needs of their crops, and the appropriate irrigation technology. One popular technology is *drip irrigation*, the slow release of water to soil and plants from perforated plastic tubing placed directly at the root zone. Because drip irrigation requires less water and reduces salinization, it is used in many arid agricultural regions.

Fertilization

In natural ecosystems, mineral nutrients are usually recycled by the excretion of animal wastes and the decomposition of humus. Agriculture, however, is unnatural. The lettuce you eat, for example, contains minerals extracted from a farmer's field. As you excrete wastes, these minerals are deposited far from their original source. Over many harvests, the farmer's field will eventually become depleted of nutrients. Nutrient depletion is a major cause of global soil degradation. Farmers must reverse nutrient depletion by **fertilization**, the addition of mineral nutrients to the soil.

Today, most farmers in industrialized nations use fertilizers containing minerals that are either mined or prepared by energy-intensive processes. These fertilizers are usually enriched in nitrogen (N), phosphorus (P), and potassium (K)—the nutrients most commonly deficient in depleted soils. You may have seen fertilizers labeled with a three-number code, called the N-P-K ratio. A fertilizer marked "15-10-5," for instance, is 15% N (as ammonium or nitrate), 10% P (as phosphate), and 5% K (as the mineral potash).

Manure, fishmeal, and compost are called "organic" fertilizers because they are of biological origin and contain decomposing organic material. Before plants can use organic material, however, it must be decomposed into the inorganic nutrients that roots can absorb. Whether from organic fertilizer or a chemical factory, the minerals a plant extracts are in the same form. However, organic fertilizers release them gradually, whereas minerals in commercial fertilizers are immediately available but may not be retained by the soil for long. Minerals not absorbed by roots are often leached from the soil by rainwater or irrigation. To make matters worse, mineral runoff into lakes may lead to explosions in algal populations that can deplete oxygen levels and decimate fish populations.

Adjusting Soil pH

Soil pH is an important factor that influences mineral availability by its effect on cation exchange and the chemical form of minerals. Depending on the soil pH, a particular mineral may be bound too tightly to clay particles or may be in a chemical form that the plant cannot absorb. Most plants prefer slightly acidic soil because the high H^+ concentrations can displace positively charged minerals from soil particles, making them more available for absorption. Adjusting soil pH for optimal crop growth is tricky because a change in H^+ concentration may make one mineral more available but another less available. At pH 8, for instance, plants can absorb calcium, but iron is almost unavailable. The soil pH should be matched to a crop's mineral needs. If the soil is too alkaline, adding sulfate will lower the pH. Soil that is too acidic can be adjusted by adding lime (calcium carbonate or calcium hydroxide).

When the soil pH dips to 5 or lower, toxic aluminum ions (Al^{3+}) become more soluble and are absorbed by roots, stunting root growth and preventing the uptake of calcium, a needed plant nutrient. Some plants can cope with high Al^{3+} levels by secreting organic anions that bind Al^{3+} and render it harmless. However, low soil pH and Al^{3+} toxicity continue to pose serious problems, especially in tropical regions, where the pressure of producing food for a growing population is often most acute.

Controlling Erosion

As happened most dramatically in the Dust Bowl, water and wind erosion can remove considerable amounts of topsoil.

▲ Figure 37.6 **Contour tillage.** These crops are planted in rows that go around, rather than up and down, the hills. Contour tillage helps slow water runoff and topsoil erosion after heavy rains.

Erosion is a major cause of soil degradation because soil nutrients are carried away by wind and streams. To limit erosion, farmers plant rows of trees as windbreaks, terrace hillside crops, and cultivate crops in a contour pattern (Figure 37.6). Crops such as alfalfa and wheat provide good ground cover and protect the soil better than maize and other crops that are usually planted in more widely spaced rows.

Erosion can also be reduced by a plowing technique called **no-till agriculture**. In traditional plowing, the entire field is tilled, or turned over. This practice helps control weeds but disrupts the meshwork of roots that holds the soil in place, leading to increased surface runoff and erosion. In no-till agriculture, a special plow creates narrow furrows for seeds and fertilizer. In this way, the field can be seeded with minimal disturbance to the soil, while also requiring less fertilizer.

Phytoremediation

Some land areas are unfit for cultivation because toxic heavy metals or organic pollutants have contaminated the soil or groundwater. Traditionally, soil remediation, the detoxification of contaminated soils, has focused on nonbiological technologies, such as removing and storing contaminated soil in landfills, but these techniques are very costly and often disrupt the landscape. **Phytoremediation** is a nondestructive biotechnology that harnesses the ability of some plants to extract soil pollutants and concentrate them in portions of the plant that can be easily removed for safe disposal. For example, alpine pennycress (*Thlaspi caerulescens*) can accumulate zinc in its shoots at concentrations 300 times higher than most plants can tolerate. The shoots can then be harvested and the contaminating zinc removed. Such plants show promise for cleaning up areas contaminated by smelters, mining operations, or nuclear testing. Phytoremediation is a type of bioremediation, which also includes the use of prokaryotes and protists to detoxify polluted sites (see Chapters 27 and 55).

We have discussed the importance of soil conservation for sustainable agriculture. Mineral nutrients contribute greatly to soil fertility, but which minerals are most important, and why do plants need them? These are the topics of the next section.

CONCEPT CHECK 37.1

1. Explain how the phrase "too much of a good thing" can apply to watering and fertilizing plants.
2. Some lawn mowers collect clippings for easy disposal. What is a drawback of this practice with respect to plant nutrition?
3. **WHAT IF?** How would adding clay to loamy soil affect the soil's capacity to exchange cations and retain water? Explain.
4. **MAKE CONNECTIONS** Note three ways in which the properties of water contribute to soil formation. See pages 47–51 of Concept 3.2.

For suggested answers, see Appendix A.

CONCEPT 37.2

Plants require essential elements to complete their life cycle

Watch a large plant grow from a tiny seed, and you cannot help wondering where all the mass comes from. Aristotle hypothesized that plants "ate" soil because they were seen to arise from the ground. In the 1640s, Jan Baptista van Helmont tested the hypothesis that plants grow by consuming soil. He planted a small willow in a pot that contained 90.9 kg of soil. After five years, the plant weighed 76.8 kg, but only 0.06 kg of soil had disappeared from the pot. He concluded that the willow had grown mainly from the water added. A century later, the English physiologist Stephen Hales, armed with knowledge from advances in physics and chemistry that air is a substance with mass, postulated that plants are nourished mostly by air.

There is some truth to all three hypotheses because soil, water, and air all contribute to plant growth. The water content of a plant can be measured by comparing the plant's mass before and after drying. Typically, 80–90% of a plant's fresh mass is water. We can also analyze the chemical composition of the dry residue. Inorganic substances generally account for about 4% of the dry mass. Thus, inorganic nutrients from the soil, although essential for plant survival, contribute very little to the plant's mass. Some 96% of the dry mass consists of organic compounds produced by photosynthesis. The carbon and most of the oxygen atoms in these compounds come from CO_2 assimilated from the air, while water supplies most of the hydrogen atoms and some oxygen atoms (see Figure 10.5). Most of the organic material of plants is carbohydrate, including the cellulose of cell walls. Thus, the components of carbohydrates—carbon, oxygen, and hydrogen—are the most abundant elements in a dried plant. Because many macromolecules contain nitrogen, sulfur, or phosphorus, these elements are also relatively abundant in plants.

Macronutrients and Micronutrients

The inorganic substances in plants contain more than 50 chemical elements. In studying the chemical composition of plants, we must distinguish elements that are essential from those that are merely present in the plant. A chemical element is considered an **essential element** only if it is required for a plant to complete its life cycle and produce another generation.

To determine which chemical elements are essential, researchers use **hydroponic culture**, in which plants are grown in mineral solutions instead of soil (Figure 37.7). Such studies have helped identify 17 essential elements needed by all plants (Table 37.1). Hydroponic culture is also used on a small scale to grow some greenhouse crops.

Nine of the essential elements are called **macronutrients** because plants require them in relatively large amounts. Six of these are the major components of organic compounds forming a plant's structure: carbon, oxygen, hydrogen, nitrogen, phosphorus, and sulfur. The other three macronutrients are potassium, calcium, and magnesium. Of all the mineral nutrients, nitrogen contributes the most to plant growth and crop yields. Plants require nitrogen as a component of proteins, nucleic acids, chlorophyll, and other important organic molecules.

The remaining eight essential elements are known as **micronutrients** because plants need them in only tiny quantities. They are chlorine, iron, manganese, boron, zinc, copper, nickel, and molybdenum. In some cases, sodium may be a ninth essential micronutrient: Plants that use the C_4 and CAM pathways of photosynthesis (see Chapter 10) require sodium ions to regenerate phosphophenolpyruvate, which is the CO_2 acceptor in these two types of carbon fixation.

Micronutrients function in plants mainly as cofactors, nonprotein helpers in enzymatic reactions (see Chapter 8). Iron, for example, is a metallic component of cytochromes, the proteins in the electron transport chains of chloroplasts and mitochondria. It is because micronutrients generally play catalytic roles that plants need only tiny quantities. The requirement for molybdenum, for instance, is so modest that there is only one atom of this rare element for every 60 million atoms of hydrogen in dried plant material. Yet a deficiency of molybdenum or any other micronutrient can weaken or kill a plant.

Symptoms of Mineral Deficiency

The symptoms of a deficiency depend partly on the mineral's function as a nutrient. For example, a deficiency of magnesium, a component of chlorophyll, causes *chlorosis*, yellowing of the leaves. In some cases, the relationship between a mineral deficiency and its symptoms is less direct. For instance, iron deficiency can cause chlorosis even though chlorophyll contains no iron, because iron ions are required as a cofactor in one of the enzymatic steps of chlorophyll synthesis.

Mineral deficiency symptoms depend not only on the role of the nutrient but also on its mobility within the plant. If a

▼ Figure 37.7 **RESEARCH METHOD**

Hydroponic Culture

APPLICATION In hydroponic culture, plants are grown in mineral solutions without soil. One use of hydroponic culture is to identify essential elements in plants.

TECHNIQUE Plant roots are bathed in aerated solutions of known mineral composition. Aerating the water provides the roots with oxygen for cellular respiration. (Note: The flasks would normally be opaque to prevent algal growth.) A mineral, such as potassium, can be omitted to test whether it is essential.

Control: Solution containing all minerals

Experimental: Solution without potassium

RESULTS If the omitted mineral is essential, mineral deficiency symptoms occur, such as stunted growth and discolored leaves. By definition, the plant would not be able to complete its life cycle. Deficiencies of different elements may have different symptoms, which can aid in diagnosing mineral deficiencies in soil.

nutrient moves about freely, symptoms appear first in older organs because young, growing tissues are a greater sink for nutrients that are in short supply. For example, magnesium is relatively mobile and is shunted preferentially to young leaves. Therefore, a plant deficient in magnesium first shows signs of chlorosis in its older leaves. The mechanism for preferential routing is the source-to-sink translocation in phloem, as minerals move along with sugars to the growing tissues (see Figure 36.18). In contrast, a deficiency of a mineral that is relatively immobile affects young parts of the plant first. Older tissues may have adequate amounts that they retain during periods of short supply. For example, iron does not move freely within a plant, and an iron deficiency causes yellowing of young leaves before any effect on older leaves is visible. The mineral requirements of a plant may also change with the time of the year and the age of the plant. Young seedlings, for example, rarely show mineral deficiency symptoms because their mineral requirements are met largely by minerals released from stored reserves in the seed itself.

Table 37.1 **Essential Elements in Plants**

Element	Form Primarily Absorbed by Plants	% Mass in Dry Tissue	Major Functions
Macronutrients			
Carbon	CO_2	45%	Major component of plant's organic compounds
Oxygen	CO_2	45%	Major component of plant's organic compounds
Hydrogen	H_2O	6%	Major component of plant's organic compounds
Nitrogen	NO_3^-, NH_4^+	1.5%	Component of nucleic acids, proteins, hormones, chlorophyll, coenzymes
Potassium	K^+	1.0%	Cofactor that functions in protein synthesis; major solute functioning in water balance; operation of stomata
Calcium	Ca^{2+}	0.5%	Important in formation and stability of cell walls and in maintenance of membrane structure and permeability; activates some enzymes; regulates many responses of cells to stimuli
Magnesium	Mg^{2+}	0.2%	Component of chlorophyll; cofactor and activator of many enzymes
Phosphorus	$H_2PO_4^-$, HPO_4^{2-}	0.2%	Component of nucleic acids, phospholipids, ATP, several coenzymes
Sulfur	SO_4^{2-}	0.1%	Component of proteins, coenzymes
Micronutrients			
Chlorine	Cl^-	0.01%	Required for water-splitting step of photosynthesis; functions in water balance
Iron	Fe^{3+}, Fe^{2+}	0.01%	Component of cytochromes; cofactor of some enzymes; needed for photosynthesis
Manganese	Mn^{2+}	0.005%	Active in formation of amino acids; activates some enzymes; required for water-splitting step of photosynthesis
Boron	$H_2BO_3^-$	0.002%	Cofactor in chlorophyll synthesis; may be involved in carbohydrate transport and nucleic acid synthesis; role in cell wall function
Zinc	Zn^{2+}	0.002%	Active in formation of chlorophyll; cofactor of some enzymes; needed for DNA transcription
Copper	Cu^+, Cu^{2+}	0.001%	Component of many redox and lignin-biosynthetic enzymes
Nickel	Ni^{2+}	0.001%	Cofactor for an enzyme functioning in nitrogen metabolism
Molybdenum	MoO_4^{2-}	0.0001%	Essential for mutualistic relationship with nitrogen-fixing bacteria; cofactor in nitrate reduction

MAKE CONNECTIONS *Three of the mineral requirements for humans in Table 41.2, on page 878, come from plants but are not essential for plant survival. What are those minerals, and how can plants be a source when they don't need them to complete their life cycle?*

Deficiencies of phosphorus, potassium, and especially nitrogen are most common. Micronutrient shortages are less common and tend to occur in certain geographic regions because of differences in soil composition. The symptoms of a mineral deficiency may vary between species but are often distinctive enough for a plant physiologist or farmer to diagnose the cause (Figure 37.8). One way to confirm a diagnosis is to analyze the mineral content of the plant or soil. The amount of a micronutrient needed to correct a deficiency is usually quite small. For example, a zinc deficiency in fruit trees can usually be cured by hammering a few zinc nails into each tree trunk. Moderation is important because overdoses of many nutrients can be detrimental or toxic to plants. Too much nitrogen, for example, can lead to excessive vine growth in tomato plants at the expense of good fruit production.

Healthy

Phosphate-deficient

Potassium-deficient

Nitrogen-deficient

▶ Figure 37.8 **The most common mineral deficiencies, as seen in maize leaves.** Mineral deficiency symptoms may vary in different species. In maize, phosphate-deficient plants have reddish purple margins, particularly in young leaves. Potassium-deficient maize plants exhibit "firing," or drying, along tips and margins of older leaves. Nitrogen deficiency is evident in a yellowing that starts at the tip and moves along the center (midrib) of older leaves.

Improving Plant Nutrition by Genetic Modification: Some Examples

In exploring plant nutrition so far, we have discussed how farmers use irrigation, fertilization, and other means to tailor the soil conditions to fit the needs of a crop. An opposite approach involves tailoring the plant by genetic engineering to better fit the soil conditions. Here we highlight a few examples of how genetic engineering is improving plant nutrition and fertilizer usage.

Resistance to Aluminum Toxicity

As previously discussed, aluminum in acidic soils damages roots and greatly reduces crop yields. The major mechanism of aluminum resistance is the secretion of organic acids (such as malic acid and citric acid) by roots. These acids bind to free aluminum ions and lower the levels of toxic aluminum in the soil. Luis Herrera-Estrella and colleagues (see the Unit Six interview on pages 736–737), at the National Polytechnic Institute in Mexico, altered tobacco and papaya plants by introducing a citrate synthase gene from a bacterium into the plants' genomes. The resulting overproduction of citric acid increased aluminum resistance in these two crops.

Flood Tolerance

Waterlogged soil not only deprives roots of oxygen but also can injure plants as ethanol and other toxic products of alcoholic fermentation by the plant accumulate. In Asian countries, flooding during the monsoon season often destroys rice crops. Although most varieties of rice die after being submerged for a week, some types can survive weeks of flooding. A gene called *Submergence 1A-1* (*Sub1A-1*) is the main source of submergence tolerance in flood-resistant rice. The Sub1A-1 protein regulates the expression of genes that are normally activated under anaerobic conditions, such as those that code for alcohol dehydrogenase, an enzyme that breaks down ethanol. The heightened expression of *Sub1A-1* in flooding-intolerant varieties of rice increases the alcohol dehydrogenase levels of the plants and confers tolerance to submergence. Increasing the expression of *Sub1A-1* by genetic engineering may enhance flood tolerance in other crop species.

Smart Plants

Agricultural researchers are developing ways to maintain crop yields while reducing fertilizer use. One approach is to genetically engineer "smart" plants that signal when a nutrient deficiency is imminent—but *before* damage has occurred. One type of smart plant takes advantage of a promoter (a DNA sequence indicating where the transcription of a gene starts) that more readily binds RNA polymerase (the transcription enzyme) when the phosphorus content of the plant's tissues begins to decline. This promoter is linked to a "reporter" gene that leads to production of a light blue

  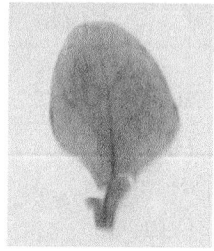

No phosphorus deficiency   Beginning phosphorus deficiency   Well-developed phosphorus deficiency

▲ **Figure 37.9 Deficiency warnings from "smart" plants.** Some plants have been genetically modified to signal an impending nutrient deficiency before irreparable damage occurs. For example, after laboratory treatments, the research plant *Arabidopsis* develops a blue color in response to an imminent phosphate deficiency.

pigment in the leaf cells (**Figure 37.9**). When leaves of these smart plants develop a blue tinge, the farmer knows it is time to add phosphate-containing fertilizer.

So far, you have learned that soil, to support vigorous plant growth, must have an adequate supply of mineral nutrients, sufficient aeration, good water-holding capacity, low salinity, and a pH near neutrality. It must also be free of toxic concentrations of minerals and other chemicals. These physical and chemical features of soil, however, are just part of the story: We must also consider the living components of soil.

CONCEPT CHECK 37.2

1. Explain how Table 37.1 supports Stephen Hales's hypothesis.
2. Are some essential elements more important than others? Explain.
3. **WHAT IF?** If an element increases the growth rate of a plant, can it be defined as an essential element?
4. **MAKE CONNECTIONS** Based on Figure 9.18, on page 179, explain why ethanol accumulates in plant roots subjected to waterlogging.

For suggested answers, see Appendix A.

CONCEPT 37.3

Plant nutrition often involves relationships with other organisms

To this point, we have portrayed plants as exploiters of soil resources. But plants and soil have a two-way relationship. Dead plants provide much of the energy needed by soil-dwelling microorganisms, while secretions from living roots support a wide variety of microbes in the near-root environment. Here we'll focus on some *mutualistic*—mutually beneficial—relationships between plants and soil bacteria or fungi. Then we'll look at some unusual plants that form nonmutualistic relationships with other plants or, in a few cases, with animals.

Soil Bacteria and Plant Nutrition

Some soil bacteria engage in mutually beneficial chemical exchanges with plant roots. Others enhance the decomposition of organic materials and increase nutrient availability. Some even live inside roots and convert nitrogen from the air.

Rhizobacteria

Rhizobacteria are soil bacteria with especially large populations in the **rhizosphere**, the soil layer that surrounds the plant's roots. Different soils vary greatly in the types and number of rhizobacteria they harbor. Microbial activity within a plant's rhizosphere is 10 to 100 times higher than in nearby soil because the roots secrete nutrients such as sugars, amino acids, and organic acids. Up to 20% of a plant's photosynthetic production fuels the organisms in this miniature ecosystem. As a result of diverse plant-microbe interactions, the composition of this microbial population often differs greatly from the surrounding soil and the rhizospheres of other plant species. Each rhizosphere contains a unique and complex cocktail of root secretions and microbial products.

Rhizobacteria known as *plant-growth-promoting rhizobacteria* enhance plant growth by a variety of mechanisms. Some produce chemicals that stimulate plant growth. Others produce antibiotics that protect roots from disease. Still others absorb toxic metals or make nutrients more available to roots. Inoculation of seeds with plant-growth-promoting rhizobacteria can increase crop yield and reduce the need for fertilizers and pesticides. How do the bacteria benefit by interacting with plants? Root secretions supply most of the energy in the rhizosphere, so bacterial adaptations that help a plant thrive and secrete nutrients also help the bacteria.

Bacteria in the Nitrogen Cycle

Plants have mutualistic relationships with several groups of bacteria that help make nitrogen more available. From a global perspective, no mineral nutrient is more limiting to plant growth than nitrogen, which is required in large amounts for synthesizing proteins and nucleic acids. The **nitrogen cycle**, discussed in Chapter 55, describes transformations of nitrogen and nitrogenous compounds in nature. Here we focus on processes leading directly to nitrogen assimilation by plants.

Unlike other soil minerals, ammonium ions (NH_4^+) and nitrate ions (NO_3^-)—the forms of nitrogen that plants can use—are not derived from the weathering of rocks. Although lightning produces small amounts of NO_3^- that get carried to the soil in rain, most soil nitrogen comes from the activity of bacteria **(Figure 37.10)**. *Ammonifying bacteria*, which are usually decomposers living in humus-rich soil, release ammonia (NH_3) by breaking down proteins and other organic compounds in humus. *Nitrogen-fixing bacteria* convert gaseous nitrogen (N_2) to NH_3 in a process we'll discuss shortly. In either case, the NH_3 produced picks up another H^+ in the soil solution to form NH_4^+. However, plants acquire nitrogen mainly in the form of NO_3^-. Soil NO_3^- is largely formed by a two-step process called *nitrification*, which consists of the oxidation of NH_3 to nitrite (NO_2^-), followed by oxidation of nitrite to nitrate (NO_3^-). Different types of *nitrifying bacteria* mediate each step. After the roots absorb NO_3^-, a plant enzyme reduces it back to NH_4^+, which other enzymes incorporate into amino acids and other organic compounds. Most plant species export nitrogen from roots to shoots via the xylem as NO_3^- or organic compounds synthesized in the roots. Some soil nitrogen is lost, particularly in anaerobic soils, when denitrifying bacteria convert NO_3^- to N_2, which diffuses into the atmosphere.

▲ **Figure 37.10 The roles of soil bacteria in the nitrogen nutrition of plants.** Ammonium is made available to plants by two types of soil bacteria: those that fix atmospheric N_2 (nitrogen-fixing bacteria) and those that decompose organic material (ammonifying bacteria). Although plants absorb some ammonium from the soil, they absorb mainly nitrate, which is produced from ammonium by nitrifying bacteria. Plants reduce nitrate back to ammonium before incorporating the nitrogen into organic compounds.

Nitrogen-Fixing Bacteria: A Closer Look

Although Earth's atmosphere is 79% nitrogen, plants cannot use free gaseous nitrogen (N_2) because there is a triple bond between the two nitrogen atoms, making the molecule almost inert. For atmospheric N_2 to be of use to plants, it must be reduced to NH_3 by a process called **nitrogen fixation**. All N_2-fixing organisms are bacteria, and some that carry out this process are free-living (see Figure 37.10). One of the more important bacteria involved in N_2 fixation is the genus *Rhizobium*, which forms intimate associations with the roots of legumes (such as peas, soybeans, alfalfa, and peanuts) and markedly alters their root structure. Although *Rhizobium* can be free-living in the soil, it cannot fix N_2 in its free state, nor can legume roots fix N_2 without the bacteria.

The conversion of N_2 to NH_3 is a complicated, multistep process, but the reactants and products in nitrogen fixation can be summarized as follows:

$$N_2 + 8\,e^- + 8\,H^+ + 16\,ATP \rightarrow 2\,NH_3 + H_2 + 16\,ADP + 16\,\textcircled{P}_i$$

The enzyme complex *nitrogenase* catalyzes the entire reaction sequence, which reduces N_2 to NH_3 by adding electrons and H^+. Because the process of nitrogen fixation requires eight ATP molecules for each NH_3 synthesized, nitrogen-fixing bacteria require a rich supply of carbohydrates from decaying material, root secretions, or (in the case of *Rhizobium*) the vascular tissue of roots.

The specialized mutualism between *Rhizobium* bacteria and legume roots involves dramatic changes in root structure. Along a legume's roots are swellings called **nodules**, composed of plant cells that have been "infected" by *Rhizobium* ("root living") bacteria (**Figure 37.11a**). Inside each nodule, *Rhizobium* bacteria assume a form called **bacteroids**, which are contained within vesicles formed in the root cells (**Figure 37.11b**). Legume-*Rhizobium* relationships generate more usable nitrogen for plants than all industrial fertilizers used today, and the mutualism provides the right amount of nitrogen at the right time at virtually no cost to the farmer. In addition to supplying the legume with nitrogen, this nitrogen fixation significantly reduces spending on fertilizers for subsequent crops.

The location of the bacteroids inside living, nonphotosynthetic cells is conducive to nitrogen fixation, which requires an anaerobic environment. Lignified external layers of root nodules also limit gas exchange. Some root nodules appear reddish because of a molecule called leghemoglobin (*leg-* for "legume"), an iron-containing protein that binds reversibly to oxygen (similar to the hemoglobin in human red blood cells). This protein is an oxygen "buffer," reducing the concentration of free oxygen and thereby providing an anaerobic environment for nitrogen fixation while regulating the oxygen supply for the intense cellular respiration required to produce ATP for nitrogen fixation.

Each legume species is associated with a particular strain of *Rhizobium*. **Figure 37.12** describes how a root nodule develops after bacteria enter through an "infection thread." The symbiotic relationship between a legume and nitrogen-fixing bacteria is mutualistic in that the bacteria supply the host plant with fixed nitrogen while the plant provides the bacteria with carbohydrates and other organic compounds. The root nodules use most of the ammonium produced to make

(a) Soybean root. The bumps on this soybean root are nodules containing *Rhizobium* bacteria. The bacteria fix nitrogen and obtain photosynthetic products supplied by the plant.

Nodules

Roots

(b) Bacteroids in a soybean root nodule. In this TEM, a cell from a soybean root nodule is filled with bacteroids in vesicles. The cells on the left are uninfected.

Bacteroids within vesicle

5 µm

◀ **Figure 37.11 Root nodules on a legume.** The coordinated activities of the legume and the *Rhizobium* bacteria depend on chemical signals between the mutualistic partners.

? *How is the relationship between legume plants and* Rhizobium *bacteria mutualistic?*

① Roots emit chemical signals that attract *Rhizobium* bacteria. The bacteria then emit signals that stimulate root hairs to elongate and to form an infection thread by an invagination of the plasma membrane.

Infection thread

Rhizobium bacteria

Dividing cells in root cortex

Bacteroid

Infected root hair

Nodule vascular tissue

② The infection thread containing the bacteria penetrates the root cortex. Cells of the cortex and pericycle begin dividing, and vesicles containing the bacteria bud into cortical cells from the branching infection thread. Bacteria within the vesicles develop into nitrogen-fixing bacteroids.

Dividing cells in pericycle

Bacteroid

Root hair sloughed off

Bacteroids

Developing root nodule

③ Growth continues in the affected regions of the cortex and pericycle, and these two masses of dividing cells fuse, forming the nodule.

Sclerenchyma cells

⑤ The mature nodule grows to be many times the diameter of the root. A layer of lignin-rich sclerenchyma cells forms, reducing absorption of oxygen and thereby helping maintain the anaerobic environment needed for nitrogen fixation.

Nodule vascular tissue

Bacteroid

④ The nodule develops vascular tissue (individual cells not shown) that supplies nutrients to the nodule and carries nitrogenous compounds into the vascular cylinder for distribution throughout the plant.

▲ Figure 37.12 **Development of a soybean root nodule.**

? *What plant tissue systems are modified by root nodule formation?*

amino acids, which are then transported up to the shoot through the xylem.

How does a legume species recognize a certain strain of *Rhizobium* among the many bacterial strains in the soil? And how does an encounter with that specific *Rhizobium* strain lead to development of a nodule? These two questions have led researchers to uncover a chemical dialogue between the bacteria and the root. Each partner responds to chemical signals from the other by expressing certain genes whose products contribute to nodule formation. By understanding the molecular biology underlying the formation of root nodules, researchers hope to learn how to induce *Rhizobium* uptake and nodule formation in crop plants that do not normally form such nitrogen-fixing mutualistic relationships.

Nitrogen Fixation and Agriculture

The agricultural benefits of mutualistic nitrogen fixation underlie most types of **crop rotation**. In this practice, a nonlegume such as maize is planted one year, and the following year alfalfa or some other legume is planted to restore the concentration of fixed nitrogen in the soil. To ensure that the legume encounters

its specific *Rhizobium* strain, the seeds are exposed to bacteria before sowing. Instead of being harvested, the legume crop is often plowed under so that it will decompose as "green manure," reducing the need for manufactured fertilizers.

Many plant families besides legumes include species that benefit from mutualistic nitrogen fixation. For example, alder trees and certain tropical grasses host nitrogen-fixing actinomycete bacteria (see the gram-positive bacteria in Figure 27.17). Rice, a crop of great commercial importance, benefits indirectly from mutualistic nitrogen fixation. Rice farmers culture a free-floating aquatic fern, *Azolla*, which has mutualistic cyanobacteria that fix nitrogen. The growing rice eventually shades and kills the *Azolla*, and decomposition of this nitrogen-rich organic material increases the paddy's fertility.

Fungi and Plant Nutrition

Certain species of soil fungi also form mutualistic relationships with roots and play a major role in plant nutrition. **Mycorrhizae** ("fungus roots") are mutualistic associations of roots and fungi (see Figures 31.15 and 36.5). The host plant provides the fungus with a steady supply of sugar. Meanwhile, the fungus increases the surface area for water uptake and also supplies the plant with phosphate and other minerals absorbed from the soil. The fungi of mycorrhizae also secrete growth factors that stimulate roots to grow and branch, as well as antibiotics that help protect the plant from pathogens in the soil.

Mycorrhizae and Plant Evolution

EVOLUTION Mycorrhizae are not oddities; they are formed by most plant species. In fact, this plant-fungus mutualism might have been one of the evolutionary adaptations that helped plants initially colonize land (see Chapter 29). New fossil evidence has pushed the date for the appearance of mycorrhizae back to 460 million years ago, predating vascular plants. In early terrestrial ecosystems, the soil was probably poor in nutrients. The fungi of mycorrhizae, which are more efficient at absorbing minerals than the roots themselves, would have helped nourish the pioneering plants.

The Two Main Types of Mycorrhizae

The major mutualistic symbioses of fungi and plants are classified as either ectomycorrhizae or arbuscular mycorrhizae (sometimes called endomycorrhizae). In **ectomycorrhizae**, the mycelium (mass of branching hyphae; see Chapter 31) forms a dense sheath, or mantle, over the surface of the root **(Figure 37.13a)**. Fungal hyphae extend from the mantle into

the soil, greatly increasing the surface area for water and mineral absorption. Hyphae also grow into the root cortex. These hyphae do not penetrate the root cells but form a network in the apoplast, or extracellular space, that facilitates nutrient exchange between the fungus and the plant. Compared with "uninfected" roots, ectomycorrhizae are generally thicker, shorter, and more branched. They typically do not form root hairs, which would be superfluous given the extensive surface area of the fungal mycelium. About 10% of plant families have species that form ectomycorrhizae, and the vast majority of these species are woody, including members of the pine, spruce, oak, walnut, birch, willow, and eucalyptus families.

In contrast, **arbuscular mycorrhizae** do not have a dense mantle ensheathing the root **(Figure 37.13b)**. Mycorrhizal associations start when microscopic soil hyphae respond to the presence of a root by growing toward it, establishing contact, and growing along its surface. Hyphae penetrate between epidermal cells and then enter the root cortex. These hyphae digest small patches of the cortical cell walls, but they do not actually pierce the plasma membrane and enter the cytoplasm. Instead, a hypha grows into a tube formed by invagination of the root cell's membrane. The process is analogous to poking a finger gently into a balloon without popping it; your finger is like the fungal hypha, and the balloon skin is like the root cell's membrane. After the fungal hyphae have penetrated in this way, some branch densely, forming structures called

(a) Ectomycorrhizae. The mantle of the fungal mycelium ensheathes the root. Fungal hyphae extend from the mantle into the soil, absorbing water and minerals, especially phosphate. Hyphae also extend into the extracellular spaces of the root cortex, providing extensive surface area for nutrient exchange between the fungus and its host plant.

(Colorized SEM)
Mantle (fungal sheath)
⊢ 1.5 mm ⊣

Epidermis — Cortex — Mantle (fungal sheath)
Epidermal cell
Endodermis
Fungal hyphae between cortical cells
(LM) ⊢ 50 μm ⊣

(b) Arbuscular mycorrhizae (endomycorrhizae). No mantle forms around the root, but microscopic fungal hyphae extend into the root. Within the root cortex, the fungus makes extensive contact with the plant through branching of hyphae that form arbuscules, providing an enormous surface area for nutrient swapping. The hyphae penetrate the cell walls, but not the plasma membranes, of cells within the cortex.

Fungal hyphae
Root hair
Epidermis — Cortex
Cortical cell
Endodermis
Fungal vesicle
Casparian strip
Arbuscules
Plasma membrane
(LM)
10 μm

▲ Figure 37.13 **Mycorrhizae.**

arbuscules ("little trees"), which are important sites of nutrient transfer between the fungus and the plant. Within the hyphae themselves, oval vesicles may form, possibly serving as food storage sites for the fungus. To the unaided eye, arbuscular mycorrhizae look like "normal" roots with root hairs, but a microscope reveals the enormous extent of the mutualistic relationship. Arbuscular mycorrhizae are much more common than ectomycorrhizae and are found in over 85% of plant species, including crop plants such as grains and legumes.

Agricultural and Ecological Importance of Mycorrhizae

Roots can form mycorrhizal symbioses only if exposed to the appropriate species of fungus. In most ecosystems, these fungi are present in the soil, and seedlings develop mycorrhizae. But if seeds are collected in one environment and planted in foreign soil, the plants may show signs of malnutrition (particularly phosphorus deficiency), resulting from the absence of fungal partners. Treating seeds with spores of mycorrhizal fungi can sometimes help seedlings to form mycorrhizae and improve crop yield.

Mycorrhizal associations are also important in understanding ecological relationships. Invasive exotic plants sometimes colonize areas by disrupting interactions between native organisms. For example, garlic mustard (*Alliaria petiolata*), introduced into New England from Europe during the 1800s, has invaded woodlands throughout the eastern and middle United States, suppressing tree seedlings and other native plants. Researchers at Harvard University have produced compelling evidence that its invasive properties may be related to an ability to slow the growth of other plant species by preventing the growth of arbuscular mycorrhizal fungi (Figure 37.14).

Epiphytes, Parasitic Plants, and Carnivorous Plants

Almost all plant species have mutualistic symbiotic relationships with soil fungi or bacteria or both. Though rarer, there are also plant species with nutritional adaptations that use other organisms in nonmutualistic ways. Figure 37.15, on the next page, provides an overview of three unusual adaptations: epiphytes, parasitic plants, and carnivorous plants.

CONCEPT CHECK 37.3

1. Why is the study of the rhizosphere critical to understanding plant nutrition?
2. How do soil bacteria and mycorrhizae contribute to plant nutrition?
3. **WHAT IF?** A peanut farmer finds that the older leaves of his plant are turning yellow following a long period of wet weather. Suggest a reason why.

For suggested answers, see Appendix A.

▼ **Figure 37.14**　**INQUIRY**

Does the invasive weed garlic mustard disrupt mutualistic associations between native tree seedlings and arbuscular mycorrhizal fungi?

EXPERIMENT Kristina Stinson, of Harvard University, and colleagues investigated the effect of invasive garlic mustard on the growth of native tree seedlings and associated mycorrhizal fungi. In one experiment, they grew seedlings of three North American trees—sugar maple, red maple, and white ash—in four different soils. Two of the soil samples were collected from a location where garlic mustard was growing, and one of these samples was sterilized. The other two soil samples were collected from a location devoid of garlic mustard, and one was then sterilized. After four months of growth, the researchers harvested the shoots and roots and determined the dried biomass. The roots were also analyzed for percent colonization by arbuscular mycorrhizal fungi.

RESULTS Native tree seedlings grew more slowly and were less able to form mycorrhizal associations when grown either in sterilized soil or in unsterilized soil collected from a location that had been invaded by garlic mustard.

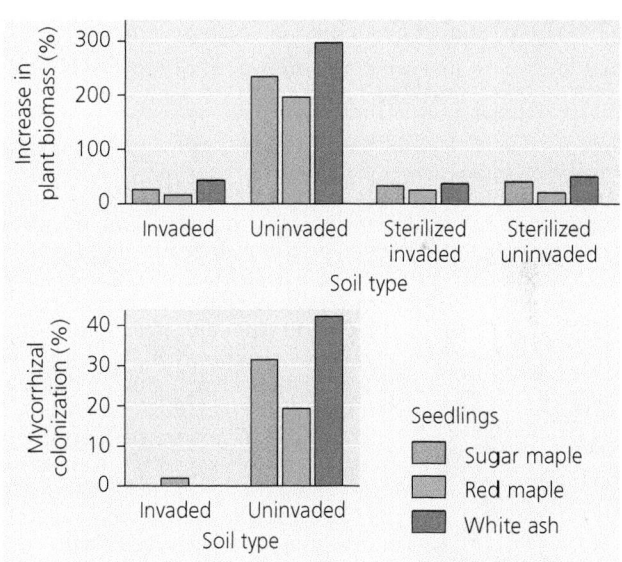

CONCLUSION The data support the hypothesis that garlic mustard suppresses growth of native trees by affecting the soil in a way that disrupts mutualistic associations between the trees and arbuscular mycorrhizal fungi.

SOURCE K. A. Stinson et al., Invasive plant suppresses the growth of native tree seedlings by disrupting belowground mutualisms, *PLoS Biol* (*Public Library of Science: Biology*) 4(5): e140 (2006).

INQUIRY IN ACTION Read and analyze the original paper in *Inquiry in Action: Interpreting Scientific Papers*.

WHAT IF? What effect would applying inorganic phosphate to soil invaded by garlic mustard have on the plant's ability to outcompete native species?

Exploring Unusual Nutritional Adaptations in Plants

Epiphytes

An **epiphyte** (from the Greek *epi*, upon, and *phyton*, plant) is a plant that grows on another plant. Epiphytes produce and gather their own nutrients; they do not tap into their hosts for sustenance. Usually anchored to the branches or trunks of living trees, epiphytes absorb water and minerals from rain, mostly through leaves rather than roots. Some examples are staghorn ferns, bromeliads, and many orchids, including the vanilla plant.

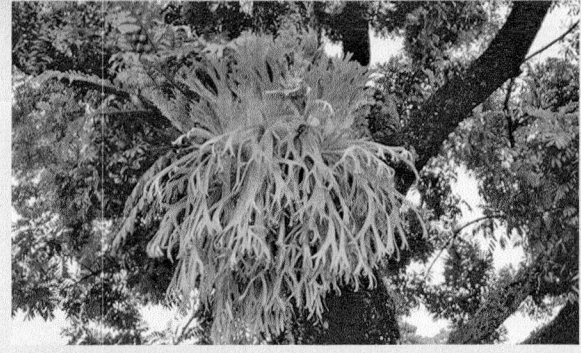

▶ **Staghorn fern**, an epiphyte

Parasitic Plants

Unlike epiphytes, parasitic plants absorb water, minerals, and sometimes products of photosynthesis from their living hosts. Many species have roots that function as haustoria, nutrient-absorbing projections that tap into the host plant. Some parasitic species, such as orange-colored, spaghetti-like dodder (genus *Cuscuta*), lack chlorophyll entirely, whereas others, such as mistletoe (genus *Phoradendron*), are photosynthetic. Still others, such as Indian pipe (*Monotropa uniflora*), absorb nutrients from the hyphae of mycorrhizae associated with other plants.

◀ **Mistletoe**, a photosynthetic parasite

▲ **Dodder**, a nonphoto-synthetic parasite (orange)

▲ **Indian pipe**, a nonphoto-synthetic parasite of mycorrhizae

Carnivorous Plants

Carnivorous plants are photosynthetic but supplement their mineral diet by capturing insects and other small animals. They live in acid bogs and other habitats where soils are poor in nitrogen and other minerals. Pitcher plants such as *Nepenthes* and *Sarracenia* have water-filled funnels into which prey slip and drown, eventually to be digested by enzymes (see also Figure 37.1). Sundews (genus *Drosera*) exude a sticky fluid from tentacle-like glands on highly modified leaves. Stalked glands secrete sweet mucilage that attracts and ensnares insects, and they also release digestive enzymes. Other glands then absorb the nutrient "soup." The highly modified leaves of Venus flytrap (*Dionaea muscipula*) close quickly but partially when a prey hits two trigger hairs in rapid enough succession. Smaller insects can escape, but larger ones are trapped by the teeth lining the margins of the lobes. Excitation by the prey causes the trap to narrow more and digestive enzymes to be released.

▲ **Sundews**

◀ **Pitcher plants**

◀ **Venus flytrap**

37 CHAPTER REVIEW

SUMMARY OF KEY CONCEPTS

CONCEPT 37.1

Soil contains a living, complex ecosystem (pp. 785–789)

- Soil particles of various sizes derived from the breakdown of rock are found in soil. Soil particle size affects the availability of water, oxygen, and minerals in the soil.
- A soil's composition refers to its inorganic and organic components. **Topsoil** is a complex ecosystem teeming with bacteria, fungi, protists, animals, and the roots of plants.
- Some agricultural practices can deplete the mineral content of soil, tax water reserves, and promote erosion. The goal of soil conservation is to minimize this damage.

? *How is soil a complex ecosystem?*

CONCEPT 37.2

Plants require essential elements to complete their life cycle (pp. 789–792)

- **Macronutrients**, elements required in relatively large amounts, include carbon, oxygen, hydrogen, nitrogen, and other major ingredients of organic compounds. **Micronutrients**, elements required in very small amounts, typically have catalytic functions as cofactors of enzymes.
- Deficiency of a mobile nutrient usually affects older organs more than younger ones; the reverse is true for nutrients that are less mobile within a plant. Macronutrient deficiencies are most common, particularly deficiencies of nitrogen, phosphorus, and potassium.
- Rather than tailoring the soil to match the plant, genetic engineers are tailoring the plant to match the soil.

? *Do plants need soil to grow? Explain.*

CONCEPT 37.3

Plant nutrition often involves relationships with other organisms (pp. 792–798)

- **Rhizobacteria** derive their energy from the rhizosphere, a microbe-enriched ecosystem intimately associated with roots. Plant secretions support the energy needs of the rhizosphere. Some rhizobacteria produce antibiotics, whereas others make nutrients more available for plants. Most are free-living, but some live inside plants. Plants satisfy most of their huge needs for nitrogen from the bacterial decomposition of **humus** and the fixation of gaseous nitrogen.

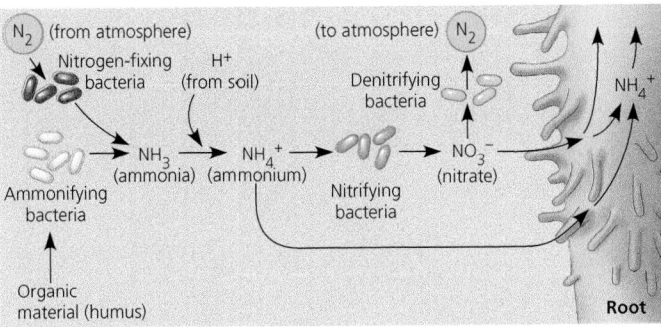

Nitrogen-fixing bacteria convert atmospheric N_2 to nitrogenous minerals that plants can absorb as a nitrogen source for organic synthesis. The most efficient mutualism between plants and nitrogen-fixing bacteria occurs in the nodules formed by *Rhizobium* bacteria growing in the roots of legumes. These bacteria obtain sugar from the plant and supply the plant with fixed nitrogen. In agriculture, legume crops are rotated with other crops to restore nitrogen to the soil.

- **Mycorrhizae** are mutualistic associations of fungi and roots. The fungal hyphae of mycorrhizae absorb water and minerals, which they supply to their plant hosts.
- **Epiphytes** grow on the surfaces of other plants but acquire water and minerals from rain. Parasitic plants absorb nutrients from host plants. Carnivorous plants supplement their mineral nutrition by digesting animals.

? *Do all plants gain their energy directly from photosynthesis? Explain.*

TEST YOUR UNDERSTANDING

LEVEL 1: KNOWLEDGE/COMPREHENSION

1. Most of the mass of organic material of a plant comes from
   a. water.
   b. carbon dioxide.
   c. soil minerals.
   d. atmospheric oxygen.
   e. nitrogen.

2. Micronutrients are needed in very small amounts because
   a. most of them are mobile in the plant.
   b. most serve mainly as cofactors of enzymes.
   c. most are supplied in large enough quantities in seeds.
   d. they play only a minor role in the growth and health of the plant.
   e. only the most actively growing regions of the plants require micronutrients.

3. Mycorrhizae enhance plant nutrition mainly by
   a. absorbing water and minerals through the fungal hyphae.
   b. providing sugar to root cells, which have no chloroplasts.
   c. converting atmospheric nitrogen to ammonia.
   d. enabling the roots to parasitize neighboring plants.
   e. stimulating the development of root hairs.

4. Epiphytes are
   a. fungi that attack plants.
   b. fungi that form mutualistic associations with roots.
   c. nonphotosynthetic parasitic plants.
   d. plants that capture insects.
   e. plants that grow on other plants.

5. Some of the problems associated with intensive irrigation include all but
   a. mineral runoff.
   b. overfertilization.
   c. land subsidence.
   d. aquifer depletion.
   e. soil salinization.

LEVEL 2: APPLICATION/ANALYSIS

6. A mineral deficiency is likely to affect older leaves more than younger leaves if
   a. the mineral is a micronutrient.
   b. the mineral is very mobile within the plant.
   c. the mineral is required for chlorophyll synthesis.
   d. the mineral is a macronutrient.
   e. the older leaves are in direct sunlight.

7. We would expect the greatest difference in plant health between two groups of plants of the same species, one group with mycorrhizae and one group without mycorrhizae, in an environment
   a. where nitrogen-fixing bacteria are abundant.
   b. that has soil with poor drainage.
   c. that has hot summers and cold winters.
   d. in which the soil is relatively deficient in mineral nutrients.
   e. that is near a body of water, such as a pond or river.

8. Two groups of tomatoes were grown under laboratory conditions, one with humus added to the soil and one a control without humus. The leaves of the plants grown without humus were yellowish (less green) compared with those of the plants grown in humus-enriched soil. The best explanation for this difference is that
   a. the healthy plants used the food in the decomposing leaves of the humus for energy to make chlorophyll.
   b. the humus made the soil more loosely packed, so water penetrated more easily to the roots.
   c. the humus contained minerals such as magnesium and iron, needed for the synthesis of chlorophyll.
   d. the heat released by the decomposing leaves of the humus caused more rapid growth and chlorophyll synthesis.
   e. the healthy plants absorbed chlorophyll from the humus.

9. The specific relationship between a legume and its mutualistic *Rhizobium* strain probably depends on
   a. each legume having a chemical dialogue with a fungus.
   b. each *Rhizobium* strain having a form of nitrogenase that works only in the appropriate legume host.
   c. each legume being found where the soil has only the *Rhizobium* specific to that legume.
   d. specific recognition between the chemical signals and signal receptors of the *Rhizobium* strain and legume species.
   e. destruction of all incompatible *Rhizobium* strains by enzymes secreted from the legume's roots.

10. **DRAW IT** Draw a simple sketch of cation exchange, showing a root hair, a soil particle with anions, and a hydrogen ion displacing a mineral cation.

LEVEL 3: SYNTHESIS/EVALUATION

11. **EVOLUTION CONNECTION**
    Imagine taking the plant out of the picture in Figure 37.10. Write a paragraph explaining how soil bacteria could sustain the recycling of nitrogen *before* land plants evolved.

12. **SCIENTIFIC INQUIRY**
    Acid precipitation has an abnormally high concentration of hydrogen ions (H^+). One effect of acid precipitation is to deplete the soil of nutrients such as calcium (Ca^{2+}), potassium (K^+), and magnesium (Mg^{2+}). Suggest a hypothesis to explain how acid precipitation washes these nutrients from the soil. How might you test your hypothesis?

13. **SCIENCE, TECHNOLOGY, AND SOCIETY**
    In many countries, irrigation is depleting aquifers to such an extent that land is subsiding, harvests are decreasing, and it is becoming necessary to drill wells deeper. In many cases, the withdrawal of groundwater has now greatly surpassed the aquifers' rates of natural recharge. Discuss the possible consequences of this trend. What can society and science do to help alleviate this growing problem?

14. **WRITE ABOUT A THEME**
    Environmental Interactions The soil in which plants grow teems with organisms from every taxonomic kingdom. In a short essay (100–150 words), discuss examples of how the mutualistic interactions of plants with bacteria, fungi, and animals improve plant nutrition.

For selected answers, see Appendix A.

Mastering**BIOLOGY**®   www.masteringbiology.com

1. MasteringBiology® Assignments
Tutorial Nitrogen Nutrition in Plants
Activities How Plants Obtain Minerals from Soil • Graph It!: Global Soil Degradation • Soil Formation and Nutrient Uptake
Questions Student Misconceptions • Reading Quiz • Multiple Choice • End-of-Chapter

2. eText
Read your book online, search, take notes, highlight text, and more.

3. The Study Area
Practice Tests • Cumulative Test • *BioFlix* 3-D Animations • MP3 Tutor Sessions • Videos • Activities • Investigations • Lab Media • Audio Glossary • Word Study Tools • Art

38

Angiosperm Reproduction and Biotechnology

▲ **Figure 38.1 Why is this wasp trying to mate with this flower?**

KEY CONCEPTS

38.1 Flowers, double fertilization, and fruits are unique features of the angiosperm life cycle

38.2 Flowering plants reproduce sexually, asexually, or both

38.3 Humans modify crops by breeding and genetic engineering

OVERVIEW

Flowers of Deceit

Male wasps of the species *Campsoscolia ciliata* often attempt to copulate with the flowers of the Mediterranean orchid *Ophrys speculum* **(Figure 38.1)**. During this encounter, a sac of pollen becomes glued to the insect's body. Eventually frustrated, the wasp flies off and deposits the pollen onto another *Ophrys* flower that has become the object of his misplaced ardor. *Ophrys* flowers offer no reward such as nectar to the male wasps, only sexual frustration. So what makes the male wasps so enamored of this orchid? The traditional answer has been that the shape of the orchid's largest petal and the frill of orange bristles around it vaguely resemble the female wasp. These visual cues, however, are only part of the deception: *Ophrys* orchids also emit chemicals with a scent similar to that produced by sexually receptive female wasps.

This orchid and its wasp pollinators are one example of the amazing ways in which angiosperms (flowering plants) reproduce sexually with spatially distant members of their own species. Sex, however, is not their only means of reproduction. Many species also reproduce asexually, creating offspring that are genetically identical to the parent.

An unusual aspect of the orchid and wasp example is that the insect does not profit from interacting with the flower. In fact, by wasting time and energy, the wasp is probably rendered less fit. More typically, a plant lures an animal pollinator to its flowers not with offers of sex but with rewards of energy-rich nectar or pollen. Thus, both plant and pollinator benefit; that is, the relationship is mutually beneficial. Participating in such beneficial relationships with other organisms is very common in the plant kingdom. In fact, in recent evolutionary times, some flowering plants have formed relationships with an animal that not only disperses their seeds but also provides the plants with water and mineral nutrients and vigorously protects them from encroaching competitors, pathogens, and predators. In return for these favors, the animal typically gets to eat a fraction of the plants' seeds and fruits. The plants involved in these reciprocally beneficial interactions are called crops; the animals are humans.

Since the origins of crop domestication over 10,000 years ago, plant breeders have genetically manipulated the traits of a few hundred wild angiosperm species by artificial selection, transforming them into the crops we grow today. Genetic engineering has dramatically increased the variety of ways and the speed with which we can now modify plants.

In Chapters 29 and 30, we approached plant reproduction from an evolutionary perspective, tracing the descent of land plants from algal ancestors. Here, we'll explore the reproductive biology of flowering plants in greater detail because they are the most important group of plants in most terrestrial ecosystems and in agriculture. After discussing the sexual and asexual reproduction of angiosperms, we'll examine the role of humans in genetically altering crop species, as well as the controversies surrounding modern plant biotechnology.

CONCEPT 38.1

Flowers, double fertilization, and fruits are unique features of the angiosperm life cycle

The life cycles of plants are characterized by an alternation of generations, in which multicellular haploid (*n*) and diploid (*2n*)

generations take turns producing each other (see Figures 29.5 and 30.10). The diploid plant, the sporophyte, produces haploid spores by meiosis. These spores divide by mitosis, giving rise to the multicellular gametophytes, the male and female haploid plants that produce gametes (sperm and eggs). **Fertilization**, the fusion of gametes, results in diploid zygotes, which divide by mitosis and form new sporophytes. In angiosperms, the sporophyte is the dominant generation: It is larger, more conspicuous, and longer-lived than the gametophyte. Over the course of seed plant evolution, gametophytes became reduced in size and wholly dependent on the sporophyte for nutrients. Angiosperm gametophytes are the most reduced of all plants, consisting of only a few cells. **Figure 38.2** reviews the angiosperm life cycle, which is shown in more detail in Figure 30.10. The key derived traits of the angiosperm life cycle can be remembered as the "three Fs"—*f*lowers, double *f*ertilization, and *f*ruits. Since angiosperms, along with gymnosperms, are seed plants, a knowledge of seed structure and function is also critical to understanding the angiosperm life cycle.

Flower Structure and Function

Flowers, the reproductive shoots of angiosperm sporophytes, are typically composed of four whorls of modified leaves called floral organs. Unlike vegetative shoots, flowers are determinate shoots; they cease growing after the flower and fruit are formed.

Floral organs—**sepals**, **petals**, **stamens**, and **carpels**—are attached to a part of the stem called the **receptacle**. Stamens and carpels are reproductive organs, whereas sepals and petals are sterile. Sepals, which enclose and protect unopened floral buds, are usually more leafy in appearance than the other floral organs. Petals are typically more brightly colored than sepals and advertise the flower to insects and other pollinators.

A stamen consists of a stalk called the *filament* and a terminal structure called the **anther**; within the anther are chambers called microsporangia (pollen sacs) that produce pollen. A carpel has an **ovary** at its base and a long, slender neck called the **style**. At the top of the style is a generally sticky structure called the **stigma** that captures pollen. Within the ovary are one or more **ovules**; the number of ovules depends on the species. The flower shown in Figure 38.2 has a single carpel, but many species have multiple carpels. In most species, two or more carpels are fused into a single structure; the result is an ovary with two or more chambers, each containing one or more ovules. The term **pistil** is sometimes used to refer to a single carpel or two or more fused carpels.

Complete flowers have all four basic floral organs (see Figure 38.2a). Some species have **incomplete flowers**, lacking sepals, petals, stamens, or carpels. For example, most grass flowers lack petals. Some incomplete flowers are sterile, lacking functional stamens and carpels; others are *unisexual*, lacking either stamens or carpels. Flowers also vary in size, shape, color, odor, organ arrangement, and time of opening. Some are borne singly, while others are arranged in showy clusters called **inflorescences**. For example, a sunflower's central disk consists of hundreds of tiny incomplete flowers, and what look like petals are actually sterile flowers (see Figure 1.3). Much of floral diversity represents adaptation to specific pollinators.

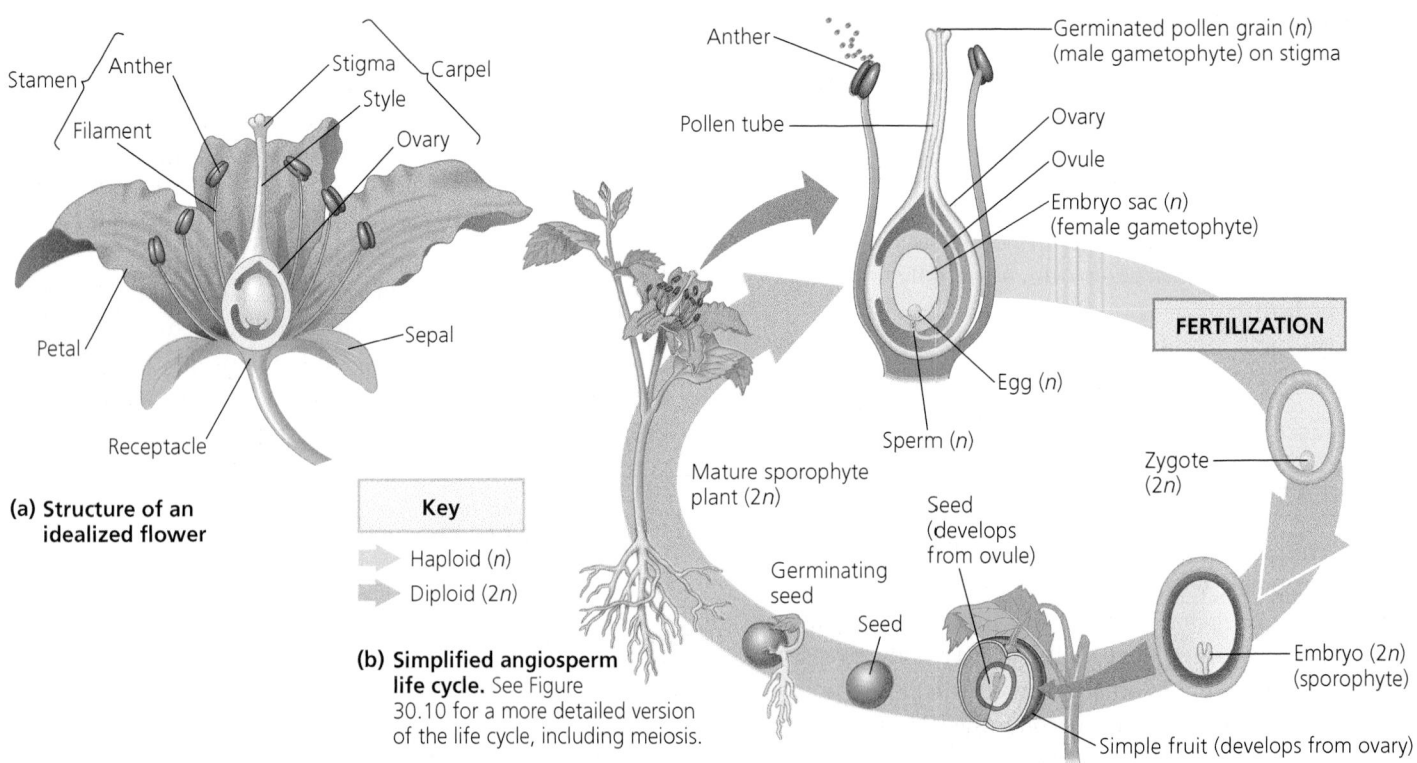

(a) Structure of an idealized flower

Key
Haploid (*n*)
Diploid (*2n*)

(b) Simplified angiosperm life cycle. See Figure 30.10 for a more detailed version of the life cycle, including meiosis.

▲ **Figure 38.2 An overview of angiosperm reproduction.**

Development of Male Gametophytes in Pollen Grains

Each anther contains four microsporangia, also known as pollen sacs. Within the microsporangia are many diploid cells called *microsporocytes,* or microspore mother cells **(Figure 38.3a)**. Each microsporocyte undergoes meiosis, forming four haploid **microspores**, each of which eventually gives rise to a haploid male gametophyte. Each microspore then undergoes mitosis, producing a male gametophyte consisting of only two cells: the *generative cell* and the *tube cell*. Together, these two cells and the spore wall constitute a **pollen grain**. The spore wall, which consists of material produced by both the microspore and the anther, usually exhibits an elaborate pattern unique to the species. During maturation of the male gametophyte, the generative cell passes into the tube cell, and the spore wall is completed. The tube cell now has a completely free-standing cell inside it. After the microsporangium breaks open and releases the pollen, a pollen grain may be transferred to a receptive surface of a stigma. There, the tube cell produces the **pollen tube**, a long cellular protuberance that delivers sperm to the female gametophyte. Pollen tubes can grow very quickly, at rates of 1 cm/hr or more. As a pollen tube elongates through the style, the generative cell usually divides and produces two sperm cells, which remain inside the tube cell (see Figure 30.10). The pollen tube grows through the style and into the ovary, where it releases the sperm cells in the vicinity of the female gametophyte.

Development of Female Gametophytes (Embryo Sacs)

Among angiosperm species, there are over 15 variations in the development of the female gametophyte, also known as an **embryo sac**. We'll focus on just one common variation. The entire process occurs in a tissue within each ovule called the megasporangium. Two *integuments* (layers of protective sporophytic tissue that will develop into the seed coat) surround each megasporangium except at a gap called the *micropyle*. Female gametophyte development begins when one cell in the megasporangium of each ovule, the *megasporocyte* (or megaspore mother cell), enlarges and undergoes meiosis, producing four haploid **megaspores** **(Figure 38.3b)**. Only one megaspore survives; the others degenerate.

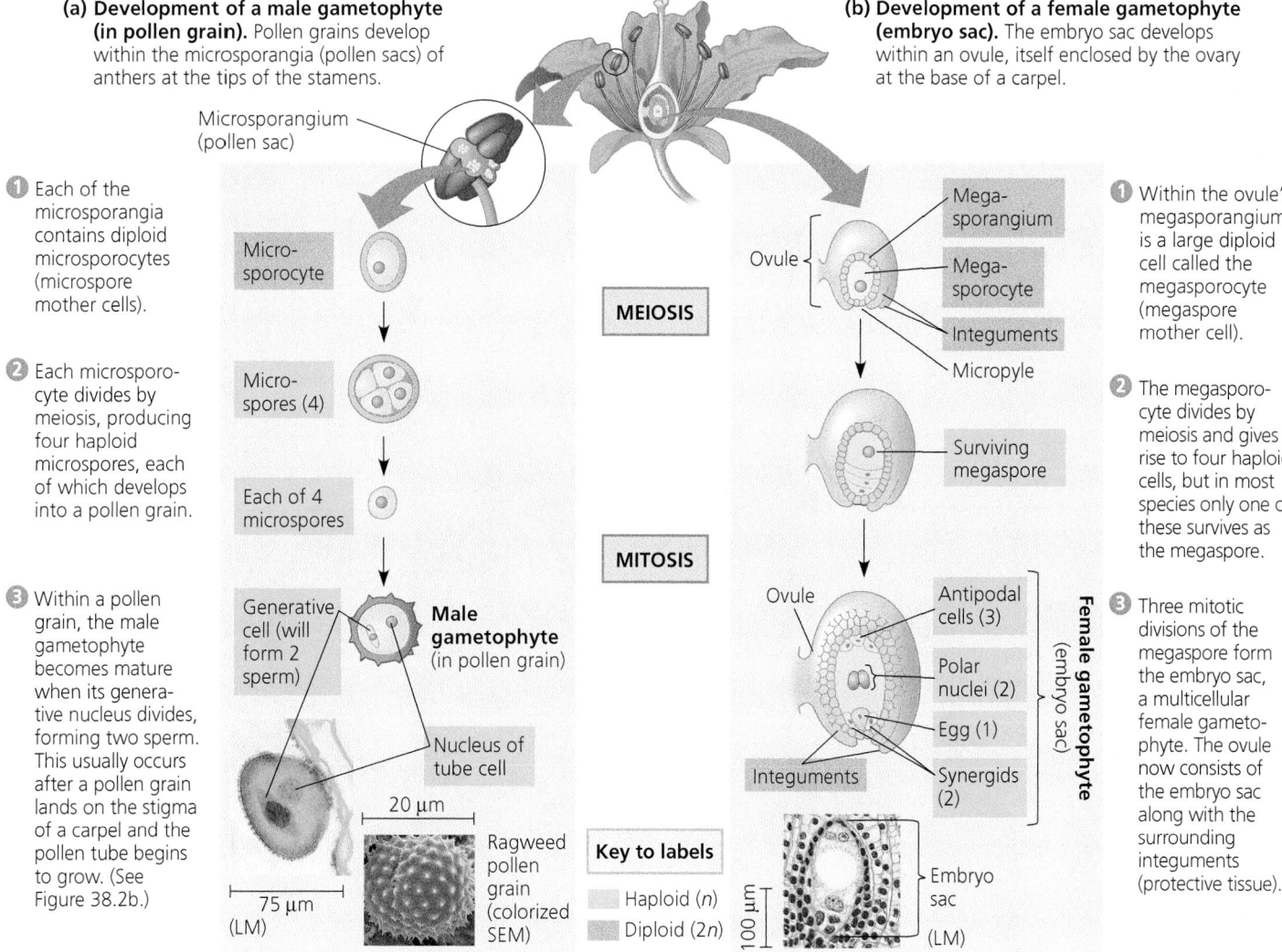

(a) Development of a male gametophyte (in pollen grain). Pollen grains develop within the microsporangia (pollen sacs) of anthers at the tips of the stamens.

Microsporangium (pollen sac)

1 Each of the microsporangia contains diploid microsporocytes (microspore mother cells).

2 Each microsporocyte divides by meiosis, producing four haploid microspores, each of which develops into a pollen grain.

3 Within a pollen grain, the male gametophyte becomes mature when its generative nucleus divides, forming two sperm. This usually occurs after a pollen grain lands on the stigma of a carpel and the pollen tube begins to grow. (See Figure 38.2b.)

Microsporocyte

Microspores (4)

Each of 4 microspores

Generative cell (will form 2 sperm)

Male gametophyte (in pollen grain)

Nucleus of tube cell

MEIOSIS

MITOSIS

20 μm

75 μm (LM)

Ragweed pollen grain (colorized SEM)

Key to labels

Haploid (*n*)
Diploid (2*n*)

(b) Development of a female gametophyte (embryo sac). The embryo sac develops within an ovule, itself enclosed by the ovary at the base of a carpel.

Ovule

Mega-sporangium

Mega-sporocyte

Integuments

Micropyle

Surviving megaspore

Ovule

Antipodal cells (3)

Polar nuclei (2)

Egg (1)

Synergids (2)

Integuments

Embryo sac

Female gametophyte (embryo sac)

100 μm

(LM)

1 Within the ovule's megasporangium is a large diploid cell called the megasporocyte (megaspore mother cell).

2 The megasporocyte divides by meiosis and gives rise to four haploid cells, but in most species only one of these survives as the megaspore.

3 Three mitotic divisions of the megaspore form the embryo sac, a multicellular female gametophyte. The ovule now consists of the embryo sac along with the surrounding integuments (protective tissue).

▲ **Figure 38.3** **The development of male and female gametophytes in angiosperms.**

The nucleus of the surviving megaspore divides by mitosis three times without cytokinesis, resulting in one large cell with eight haploid nuclei. The multinucleate mass is partitioned by membranes into a multicellular female gametophyte—the embryo sac. The cell fates of the nuclei are determined by a gradient of the hormone auxin originating near the micropyle. At the micropylar end, two cells called synergids flank the egg and help attract and guide the pollen tube to the embryo sac. At the opposite end of the embryo sac are three antipodal cells of unknown function. The other two nuclei, called polar nuclei, are not partitioned into separate cells but share the cytoplasm of the large central cell of the embryo sac. The ovule, which will become a seed, now consists of the embryo sac and two surrounding integuments.

▼ Figure 38.4

Exploring Flower Pollination

Most angiosperm species rely on a living (biotic) or nonliving (abiotic) pollinating agent that can move pollen from the anther of a flower on one plant to the stigma of a flower on another plant. Approximately 80% of all angiosperm pollination is biotic, employing animal go-betweens. Among abiotically pollinated species, 98% rely on wind and 2% on water. (Some angiosperm species can self-pollinate, but such species are limited to inbreeding in nature.)

Abiotic Pollination by Wind

About 20% of all angiosperm species are wind-pollinated. Since their reproductive success does not depend on attracting pollinators, there has been no selective pressure favoring colorful or scented flowers. Accordingly, the flowers of wind-pollinated species are often small, green, and inconspicuous, and they produce neither nectar nor scent. Most temperate trees and grasses are wind-pollinated. The flowers of hazel (*Corylus avellana*, shown here) and many other temperate, wind-pollinated trees appear in the early spring, when leaves are not present to interfere with pollen movement. The relative inefficiency of wind pollination is compensated for by production of copious amounts of pollen grains. Wind tunnel studies reveal that wind pollination is often more efficient than it appears because floral structures can create eddy currents that aid in pollen capture.

▲ Hazel staminate flowers (stamens only)

▶ Hazel carpellate flower (carpels only)

Pollination by Bees

About 65% of all flowering plants require insects for pollination; the percentage is even greater for major crops. Bees are the most important insect pollinators, and there is great concern in Europe and North America that honeybee populations have shrunk. Pollinating bees depend on nectar and pollen for food. Typically, bee-pollinated flowers have a delicate, sweet fragrance. Bees are attracted to bright colors, primarily yellow and blue. Red appears dull to them, but they can see ultraviolet radiation. Many bee-pollinated flowers, such as the common dandelion (*Taraxacum vulgare*), have ultraviolet markings called "nectar guides" that help insects locate the nectaries (nectar-producing glands) but are only visible to human eyes under ultraviolet light.

▲ Common dandelion under normal light

▲ Common dandelion under ultraviolet light

Pollination

In angiosperms, **pollination** is the transfer of pollen from an anther to a stigma. It is accomplished by wind, water, or animals (Figure 38.4). In wind-pollinated species, including grasses and many trees, the release of enormous quantities of smaller-sized pollen compensates for the randomness of dispersal by the wind. At certain times of the year, the air is loaded with pollen grains, as anyone who is plagued with pollen allergies can attest. Some species of aquatic plants rely on water to disperse pollen. Most angiosperm species, however, depend on insects, birds, or other animal pollinators to transfer pollen directly from one flower to another. If pollination is successful, a pollen grain produces a pollen tube, which then grows down into the ovary via the style.

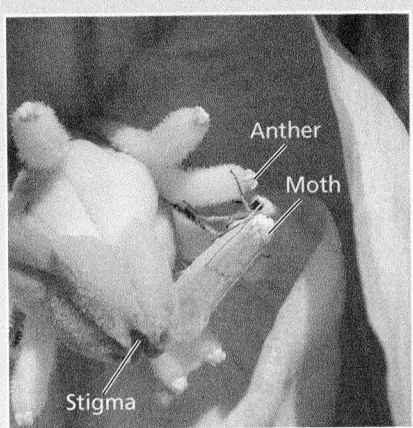

▲ Moth on yucca flower

▲ Blowfly on carrion flower

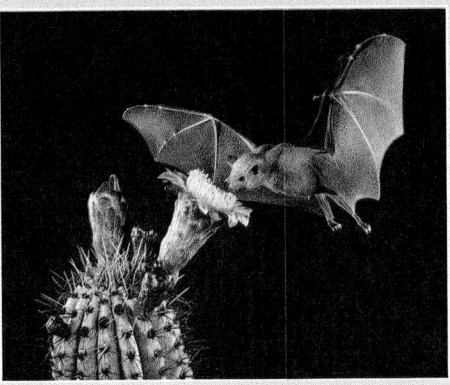

▲ Long-nosed bat feeding on cactus flower at night

Pollination by Moths and Butterflies

Moths and butterflies detect odors, and the flowers they pollinate are often sweetly fragrant. Butterflies perceive many bright colors, but moth-pollinated flowers are usually white or yellow, which stand out at night when moths are active. A yucca plant (shown here) is typically pollinated by a single species of moth with appendages that pack pollen onto the stigma. The moth then deposits eggs directly into the ovary. The larvae eat some developing seeds, but this cost is outweighed by the benefit of an efficient and reliable pollinator. If a moth deposits too many eggs, the flower aborts and drops off, selecting against individuals that overexploit the plant.

? *What are the benefits and dangers to a plant of having a highly specific animal pollinator?*

Pollination by Flies

Many fly-pollinated flowers are reddish and fleshy, with an odor like rotten meat. Blowflies visiting carrion flowers (*Stapelia* species) mistake the flower for a rotting corpse and lay their eggs on it. In the process, the blowflies become dusted with pollen that they carry to other flowers. When the eggs hatch, the larvae find no carrion to eat and therefore die.

Pollination by Birds

Bird-pollinated flowers, such as columbine flowers, are usually large and bright red or yellow, but they have little odor. Since birds often do not have a well-developed sense of smell, there has been no selective pressure favoring scent production. However, the flowers produce the sugary solution called nectar that helps meet the high energy demands of the pollinating birds. The primary function of nectar, which is produced by nectaries at the base of many flowers, is to "reward" the pollinator. The petals of such flowers are often fused, forming a bent floral tube that fits the curved beak of the bird.

Pollination by Bats

Bat-pollinated flowers, like moth-pollinated flowers, are light-colored and aromatic, attracting their nocturnal pollinators. The lesser long-nosed bat (*Leptonycteris curasoae yerbabuenae*) feeds on the nectar and pollen of agave and cactus flowers in the southwestern United States and Mexico. In feeding, the bats transfer pollen from plant to plant. Long-nosed bats are an endangered species.

▶ Hummingbird drinking nectar of columbine flower

805

Coevolution of Flower and Pollinator

EVOLUTION The joint evolution of two interacting species, each in response to selection imposed by the other, is called **coevolution**. Many species of flowering plants have coevolved with specific pollinators. Natural selection favors individual plants or insects having slight deviations of structure that enhance the flower-pollinator mutualism. For example, some species have flower petals fused together, forming long, tube-like structures bearing nectaries tucked deep inside. Charles Darwin suggested that a race between flower and insect might lead to correspondences between the length of a floral tube and the length of an insect's proboscis, a straw-like mouthpart. Imagine an insect with a tongue long enough to drink the nectar of flowers without picking up pollen on its body. The resulting failure of these plants to fertilize others would render them less evolutionarily fit. Natural selection would then favor flowers with longer tubes. At the same time, an insect with a tongue that was too short for the tube wouldn't be able to use the nectar as a food source and therefore would be at a selective disadvantage compared with long-tongued rivals. As a result, the shapes and sizes of flowers often show a close correspondence to the pollen-adhering parts of their animal pollinators. In fact, based on the length of a long, tubular flower that grows in Madagascar, Darwin predicted the existence of a pollinating moth with a 28-cm-long proboscis. Such a moth was discovered two decades after Darwin's death (Figure 38.5).

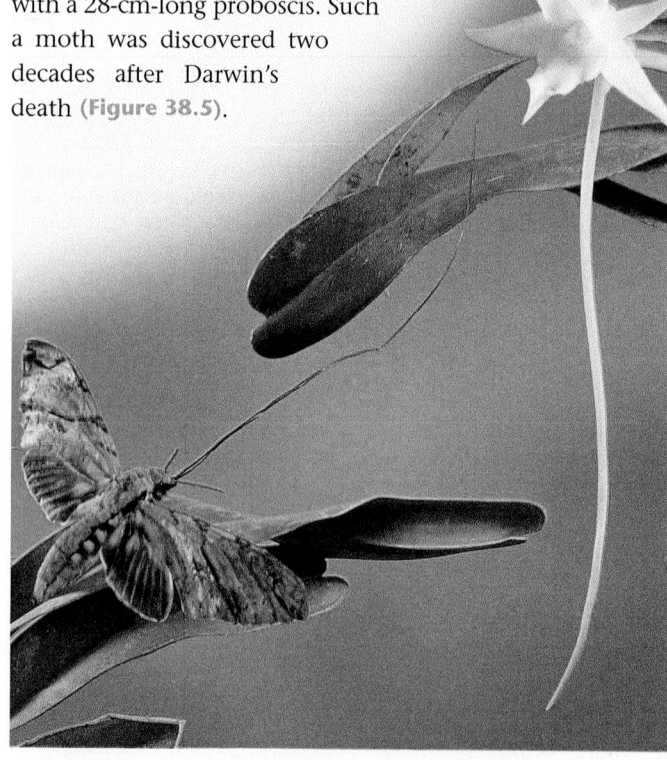

▲ **Figure 38.5 Coevolution of a flower and an insect pollinator.** The long floral tube of the Madagascar orchid *Angraecum sesquipedale* has coevolved with the 28-cm-long proboscis of its pollinator, the hawkmoth *Xanthopan morganii praedicta*. The moth is named in honor of Darwin's prediction of its existence.

Double Fertilization

At the time of pollination, the pollen grain typically consists of only the tube cell and the generative cell. After a pollen grain lands on a suitable stigma, it absorbs water and germinates by producing a pollen tube, which grows between the cells of the style toward the ovary (Figure 38.6). The nucleus of the generative cell divides by mitosis and forms two sperm. In response to chemical attractants produced by the synergids, the tip of the pollen tube grows toward the micropyle. Its arrival initiates the death of one of the two synergids, thereby providing a passageway into the embryo sac for the two sperm that are discharged from the pollen tube.

Upon reaching the female gametophyte, one sperm fertilizes the egg, forming the zygote. The other sperm combines with the two polar nuclei, forming a triploid (3*n*) nucleus in the

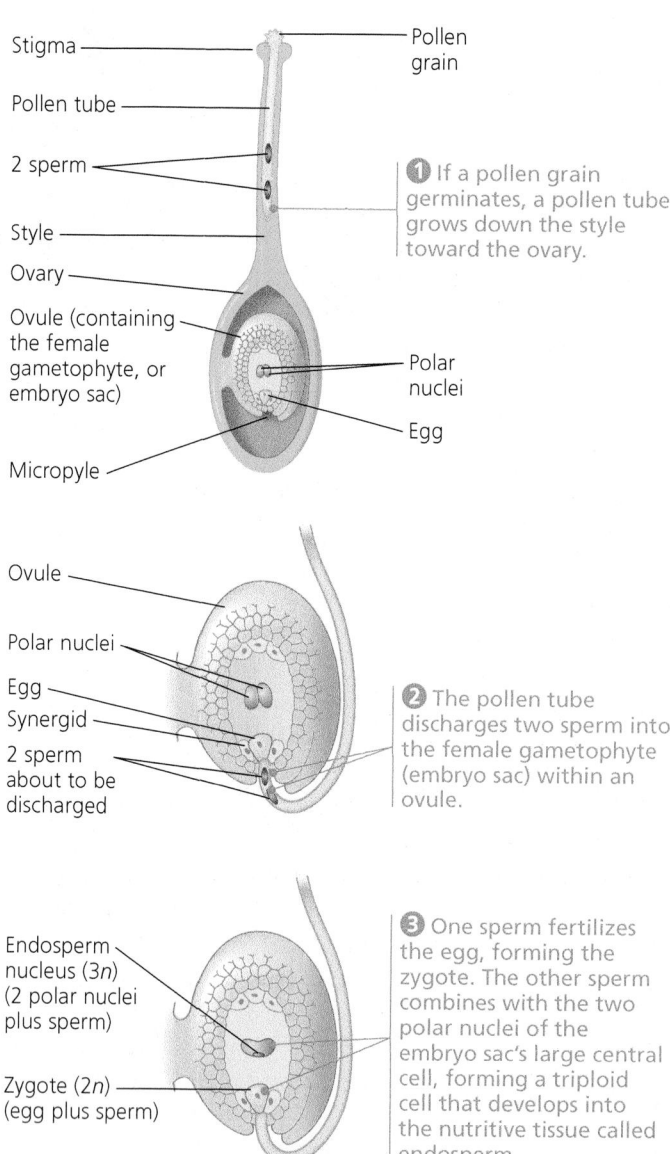

Stigma
Pollen grain
Pollen tube
2 sperm
Style
Ovary
Ovule (containing the female gametophyte, or embryo sac)
Micropyle
Polar nuclei
Egg

1 If a pollen grain germinates, a pollen tube grows down the style toward the ovary.

Ovule
Polar nuclei
Egg
Synergid
2 sperm about to be discharged

2 The pollen tube discharges two sperm into the female gametophyte (embryo sac) within an ovule.

Endosperm nucleus (3*n*) (2 polar nuclei plus sperm)
Zygote (2*n*) (egg plus sperm)

3 One sperm fertilizes the egg, forming the zygote. The other sperm combines with the two polar nuclei of the embryo sac's large central cell, forming a triploid cell that develops into the nutritive tissue called endosperm.

▲ **Figure 38.6 Growth of the pollen tube and double fertilization.**

center of the large central cell of the female gametophyte. This large cell will give rise to the **endosperm**, a food-storing tissue of the seed. The union of two sperm cells with different nuclei of the female gametophyte is called **double fertilization**. Double fertilization ensures that endosperm develops only in ovules where the egg has been fertilized, thereby preventing angiosperms from squandering nutrients on infertile ovules.

The tissues surrounding the female gametophyte have prevented researchers from directly observing fertilization in plants grown under normal conditions. Scientists have, however, isolated sperm from germinated pollen grains and eggs from female gametophytes and observed the merging of plant gametes *in vitro* (in an artificial environment). The first cellular event that takes place after gamete fusion is an increase in the levels of cytoplasmic calcium ions (Ca^{2+}) in the egg, as also occurs during animal gamete fusion (see Chapter 47). Another similarity to animals is the establishment of a block to *polyspermy*, the fertilization of an egg by multiple sperm. Thus, sperm cannot fuse with zygotes even *in vitro*. In maize (*Zea mays*), for example, this barrier to polyspermy is established as early as 45 seconds after the initial fusion of sperm with egg.

Seed Development, Form, and Function

After double fertilization, each ovule develops into a seed, and the ovary develops into a fruit enclosing the seed(s). As the embryo develops from the zygote, the seed stockpiles proteins, oils, and starch to varying degrees, depending on the species. This is why seeds are such a major nutrient drain. Initially, carbohydrates and other nutrients are stored in the seed's endosperm, but later, depending on the species, the swelling cotyledons (seed leaves) of the embryo may take over this function.

Endosperm Development

Endosperm usually develops before the embryo does. After double fertilization, the triploid nucleus of the ovule's central cell divides, forming a multinucleate "supercell" that has a milky consistency. This liquid mass, the endosperm, becomes multicellular when cytokinesis partitions the cytoplasm by forming membranes between the nuclei. Eventually, these "naked" cells produce cell walls, and the endosperm becomes solid. Coconut "milk" and "meat" are examples of liquid and solid endosperm, respectively. The white fluffy part of popcorn is also endosperm.

In grains and most other species of monocots, as well as many eudicots, the endosperm stores nutrients that can be used by the seedling after germination. In other eudicot seeds, the food reserves of the endosperm are completely exported to the cotyledons before the seed completes its development; consequently, the mature seed lacks endosperm.

Embryo Development

The first mitotic division of the zygote splits the fertilized egg into a basal cell and a terminal cell **(Figure 38.7)**. The

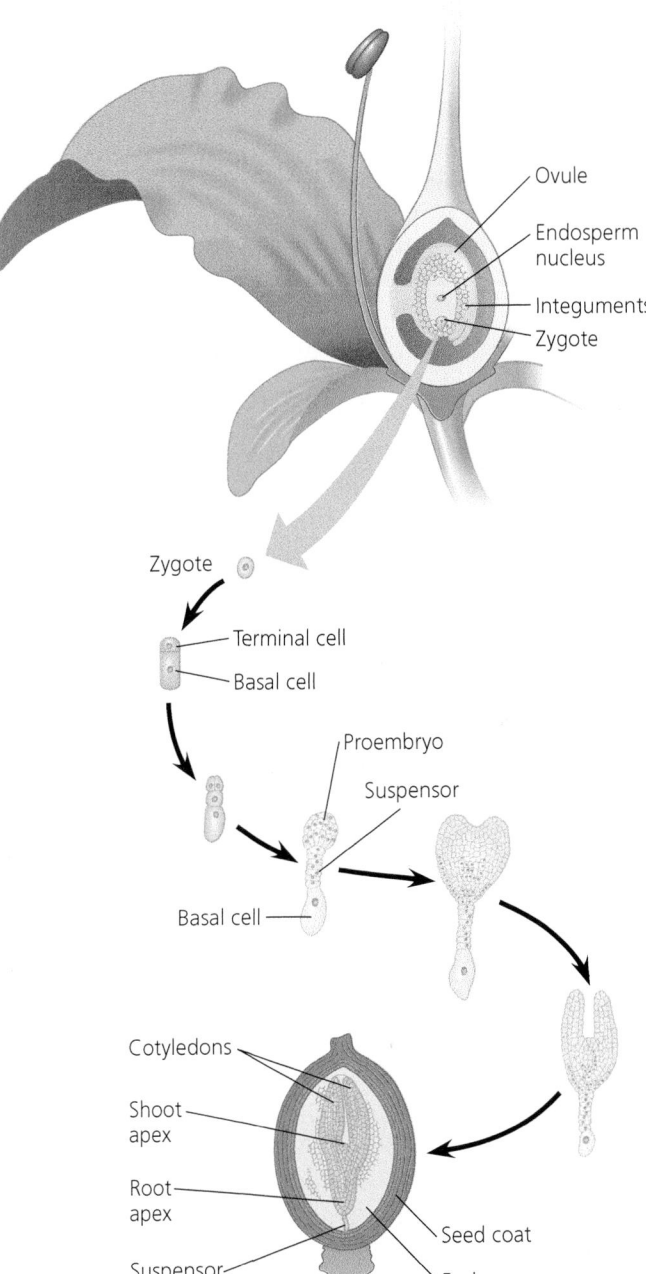

▲ **Figure 38.7 The development of a eudicot plant embryo.** By the time the ovule becomes a mature seed and the integuments harden and thicken into the seed coat, the zygote has given rise to an embryonic plant with rudimentary organs.

terminal cell eventually gives rise to most of the embryo. The basal cell continues to divide, producing a thread of cells called the *suspensor*, which anchors the embryo to the parent plant. The suspensor helps in transferring nutrients to the embryo from the parent plant and, in some species of plants, from the endosperm. As the suspensor elongates, it pushes the embryo deeper into the nutritive and protective tissues. Meanwhile, the terminal cell divides several times and forms a spherical proembryo (early embryo) attached to the suspensor. The cotyledons begin to form as bumps on the proembryo. A eudicot, with its two cotyledons, is heart-shaped at this stage. Only one cotyledon develops in monocots.

Soon after the rudimentary cotyledons appear, the embryo elongates. Cradled between the two cotyledons is the embryonic shoot apex. At the opposite end of the embryo's axis, where the suspensor attaches, an embryonic root apex forms. After the seed germinates—indeed, for the rest of the plant's life—the apical meristems at the apices of shoots and roots sustain primary growth (see Figure 35.11).

Structure of the Mature Seed

During the last stages of its maturation, the seed dehydrates until its water content is only about 5–15% of its weight. The embryo, which is surrounded by a food supply (cotyledons, endosperm, or both), enters **dormancy**; that is, it stops growing and its metabolism nearly ceases. The embryo and its food supply are enclosed by a hard, protective **seed coat** formed from the integuments of the ovule. In some species, dormancy is imposed by the presence of an intact seed coat rather than by the embryo itself.

You can take a closer look at one type of eudicot seed by splitting open the seed of a common garden bean. The embryo consists of an elongate structure, the embryonic axis, attached to fleshy cotyledons (**Figure 38.8a**). Below where the cotyledons are attached, the embryonic axis is called the **hypocotyl** (from the Greek *hypo*, under). The hypocotyl terminates in the **radicle**, or embryonic root. The portion of the embryonic axis above where the cotyledons are attached and below the first pair of miniature leaves is the **epicotyl** (from the Greek *epi*, on, over). The epicotyl, young leaves, and shoot apical meristem are collectively called the *plumule*.

The cotyledons of the common garden bean are packed with starch before the seed germinates because they absorbed carbohydrates from the endosperm when the seed was developing. However, the seeds of some eudicot species, such as castor beans (*Ricinus communis*), retain their food supply in the endosperm and have very thin cotyledons (**Figure 38.8b**). The cotyledons absorb nutrients from the endosperm and transfer them to the rest of the embryo when the seed germinates.

The embryos of monocots possess only a single cotyledon (**Figure 38.8c**). Grasses, including maize and wheat, have a specialized cotyledon called a *scutellum* (from the Latin *scutella*, small shield, a reference to its shape). The scutellum, which has a large surface area, is pressed against the endosperm, from which it absorbs nutrients during germination. The embryo of a grass seed is enclosed within two protective sheathes: a **coleoptile**, which covers the young shoot, and a **coleorhiza**, which covers the young root. Both structures aid in soil penetration after germination.

Seed weights range from less than 1 µg for some orchids to 20 kg for coco-de-mer palms. Orchid seeds have almost no

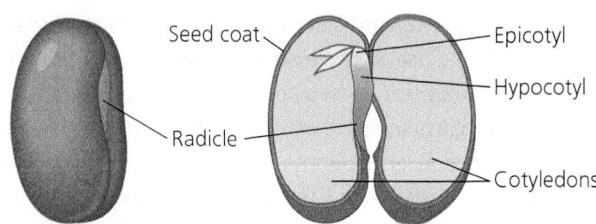

(a) Common garden bean, a eudicot with thick cotyledons. The fleshy cotyledons store food absorbed from the endosperm before the seed germinates.

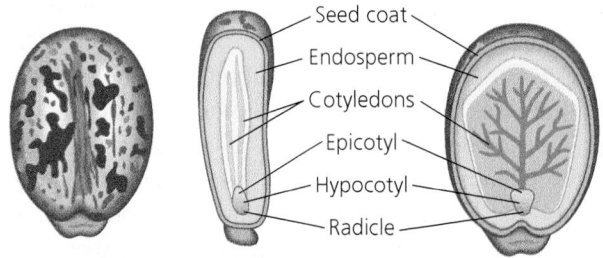

(b) Castor bean, a eudicot with thin cotyledons. The narrow, membranous cotyledons (shown in edge and flat views) absorb food from the endosperm when the seed germinates.

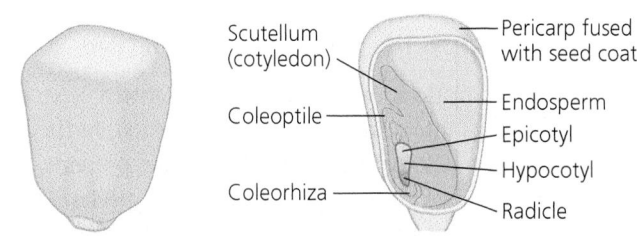

(c) Maize, a monocot. Like all monocots, maize has only one cotyledon. Maize and other grasses have a large cotyledon called a scutellum. The rudimentary shoot is sheathed in a structure called the coleoptile, and the coleorhiza covers the young root.

▲ **Figure 38.8 Seed structure.**

MAKE CONNECTIONS *In addition to cotyledon number, what are some others ways that the structures of monocots and eudicots differ? (See Figure 30.13 on p. 631.)*

food reserves and must bond symbiotically with mycorrhizae prior to germination. Large, endosperm-rich palm seeds are an adaptation for seedling establishment on nutrient-poor beaches.

Seed Dormancy: An Adaptation for Tough Times

Environmental conditions required to break seed dormancy vary among species. Seeds of some species germinate as soon as they are in a suitable environment. Others remain dormant, even if sown in a favorable place, until a specific environmental cue causes them to break dormancy.

The requirement for specific cues to break seed dormancy increases the chances that germination will occur at a time and place most advantageous to the seedling. Seeds of many desert plants, for instance, germinate only after a substantial rainfall. If they were to germinate after a mild drizzle, the soil might soon become too dry to support the seedlings. Where natural fires are common, many seeds require intense heat or smoke to break dormancy; seedlings are therefore most abundant after fire has cleared away competing vegetation. Where winters are harsh, seeds may require extended exposure to cold. Seeds sown during summer or fall will then not germinate until the following spring, ensuring a long growth season before the next winter. Certain small seeds, such as those of some lettuce varieties, require light for germination and will break dormancy only if buried shallow enough for the seedlings to poke through the soil surface. Some seeds have coats that must be weakened by chemical attack as they pass through an animal's digestive tract and thus are usually carried a considerable distance before germinating from dropped feces.

The length of time a dormant seed remains viable and capable of germinating varies from a few days to decades or even longer, depending on the plant species and environmental conditions. The oldest carbon-14–dated seed that has grown into a viable plant was a 2,000-year-old date palm seed recovered from excavations of Herod's palace in Israel. Most seeds are durable enough to last a year or two until conditions are favorable for germinating. Thus, the soil has a bank of ungerminated seeds that may have accumulated for several years. This is one reason vegetation reappears so rapidly after an environmental disruption such as fire.

Seed Germination and Seedling Development

Germination depends on **imbibition**, the uptake of water due to the low water potential of the dry seed. Imbibing water causes the seed to expand and rupture its coat and also triggers metabolic changes in the embryo that enable it to resume growth. Following hydration, enzymes begin digesting the storage materials of the endosperm or cotyledons, and the nutrients are transferred to the growing regions of the embryo.

The first organ to emerge from the germinating seed is the radicle, the embryonic root. Next, the shoot tip must break through the soil surface. In garden beans and many other eudicots, a hook forms in the hypocotyl, and growth pushes the hook above ground (**Figure 38.9a**). In response to light, the hypocotyl straightens, the cotyledons separate, and the delicate epicotyl, now exposed, spreads its first true leaves (as distinct from the cotyledons, or seed leaves). These leaves expand, become green, and begin making food by photosynthesis. The cotyledons shrivel and fall away from the seedling, their food reserves having been exhausted by the germinating embryo.

Some monocots, such as maize and other grasses, use a different method for breaking ground when they germinate (**Figure 38.9b**). The coleoptile, the sheath enclosing and protecting the embryonic shoot, pushes upward through the soil and into the air. The shoot tip then grows straight up through the tunnel provided by the tubular coleoptile and eventually breaks out through the coleoptile's tip.

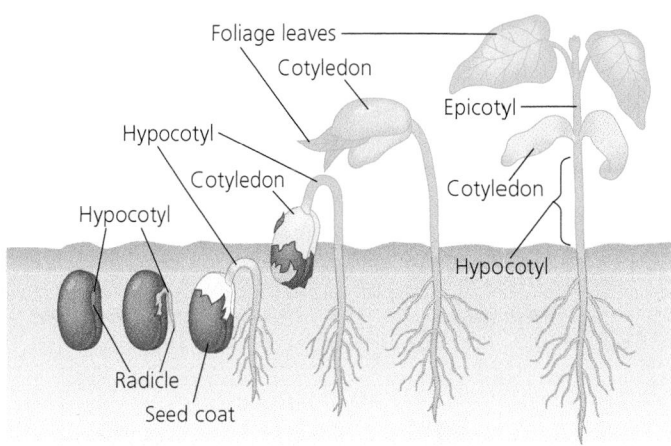

(a) Common garden bean. In common garden beans, straightening of a hook in the hypocotyl pulls the cotyledons from the soil.

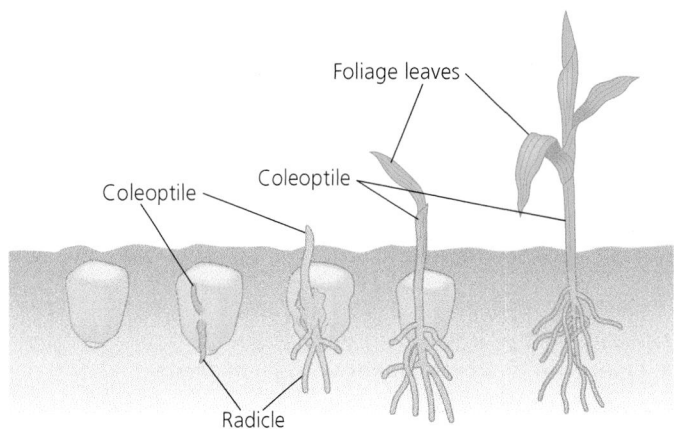

(b) Maize. In maize and other grasses, the shoot grows straight up through the tube of the coleoptile.

▲ **Figure 38.9 Two common types of seed germination.**

? *How do bean and maize seedlings protect their shoot systems as they push through the soil?*

Fruit Form and Function

While the seeds are developing from ovules, the ovary of the flower is developing into a **fruit**, which protects the enclosed seeds and, when mature, aids in their dispersal by wind or animals. Fertilization triggers hormonal changes that cause the ovary to begin its transformation into a fruit. If a flower has not been pollinated, fruit typically does not develop, and the entire flower usually withers and falls away.

During fruit development, the ovary wall becomes the pericarp, the thickened wall of the fruit. As the ovary grows, the other parts of the flower usually wither and are shed. For example, the pointed tip of a pea pod is the withered remains of the pea flower's stigma.

Fruits are classified into several types, depending on their developmental origin. Most fruits are derived from a single

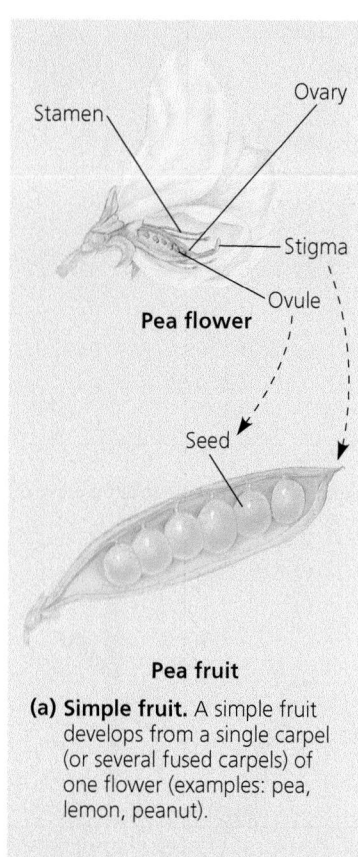

Stamen — Ovary

Stamen

Stigma

Ovule

Pea flower

Seed

Pea fruit

(a) Simple fruit. A simple fruit develops from a single carpel (or several fused carpels) of one flower (examples: pea, lemon, peanut).

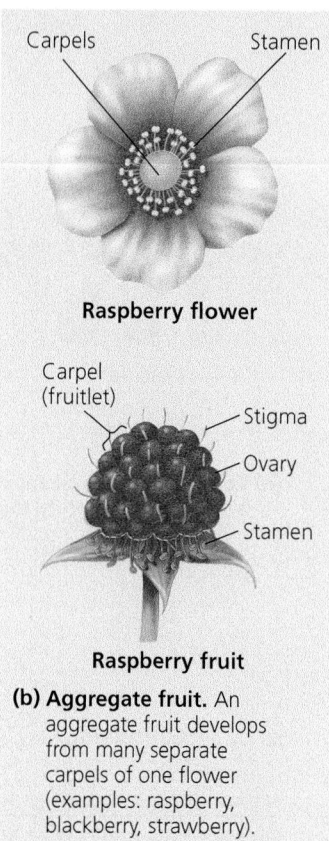

Carpels — Stamen

Raspberry flower

Carpel (fruitlet) — Stigma

Ovary

Stamen

Raspberry fruit

(b) Aggregate fruit. An aggregate fruit develops from many separate carpels of one flower (examples: raspberry, blackberry, strawberry).

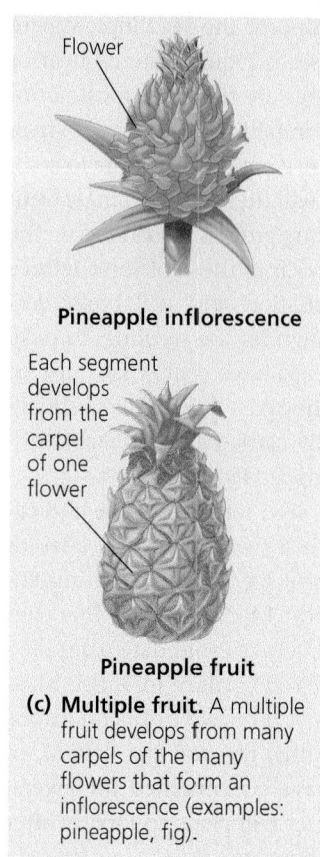

Flower

Pineapple inflorescence

Each segment develops from the carpel of one flower

Pineapple fruit

(c) Multiple fruit. A multiple fruit develops from many carpels of the many flowers that form an inflorescence (examples: pineapple, fig).

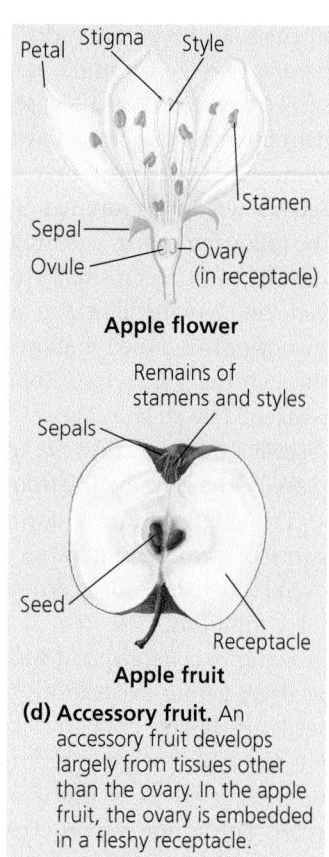

Petal — Stigma — Style

Stamen

Sepal

Ovule — Ovary (in receptacle)

Apple flower

Remains of stamens and styles

Sepals

Seed

Receptacle

Apple fruit

(d) Accessory fruit. An accessory fruit develops largely from tissues other than the ovary. In the apple fruit, the ovary is embedded in a fleshy receptacle.

▲ Figure 38.10 **Developmental origin of fruits.**

carpel or several fused carpels and are called **simple fruits** (Figure 38.10a). Some simple fruits are dry, such as a pea pod or a nut, whereas others are fleshy, such as a nectarine (see Figure 30.8). An **aggregate fruit** results from a single flower that has more than one separate carpel, each forming a small fruit (Figure 38.10b). These "fruitlets" are clustered together on a single receptacle, as in a raspberry. A **multiple fruit** develops from an inflorescence, a group of flowers tightly clustered together. When the walls of the many ovaries start to thicken, they fuse together and become incorporated into one fruit, as in a pineapple (Figure 38.10c).

In some angiosperms, other floral parts contribute to what we commonly call the fruit. Such fruits are called **accessory fruits**. In apple flowers, the ovary is embedded in the receptacle, and the fleshy part of this simple fruit is derived mainly from the enlarged receptacle; only the apple core develops from the ovary (Figure 38.10d). Another example is the strawberry, an aggregate fruit consisting of an enlarged receptacle studded with tiny, partially embedded fruits, each bearing a single seed.

A fruit usually ripens about the same time that its seeds complete their development. Whereas the ripening of a dry fruit, such as a soybean pod, involves the aging and drying out of fruit tissues, the process in a fleshy fruit is more elaborate. Complex interactions of hormones result in an edible

fruit that entices animals that help disperse the seeds. The fruit's "pulp" becomes softer as a result of enzymes digesting components of the cell walls. The color usually changes from green to another color, such as red, orange, or yellow. The fruit becomes sweeter as organic acids or starch molecules are converted to sugar, which may reach a concentration of as much as 20% in a ripe fruit. Figure 38.11 examines some mechanisms of fruit dispersal in more detail.

In this section, you have learned about the unique features of sexual reproduction in angiosperms—flowers, fruits, and double fertilization. Next, we'll examine asexual reproduction.

CONCEPT CHECK 38.1

1. Distinguish between pollination and fertilization.
2. What is the benefit of seed dormancy?
3. **WHAT IF?** If flowers had shorter styles, pollen tubes would more easily reach the embryo sac. Suggest an explanation for why very long styles have evolved in most flowering plants.
4. **MAKE CONNECTIONS** Does the life cycle of animals have any structures analogous to plant gametophytes? Explain your answer. (See Figure 13.6 on p. 252.)

For suggested answers, see Appendix A.

Exploring Fruit and Seed Dispersal

A plant's life depends on finding fertile ground. But a seed that falls and sprouts beneath the parent plant will stand little chance of competing successfully for nutrients. To prosper, seeds must be widely dispersed. Plants use biotic dispersal agents as well as abiotic agents such as water and wind.

Dispersal by Water

▶ Some buoyant seeds and fruits can survive months or years at sea. In coconut, the seed embryo and fleshy white "meat" (endosperm) are within a hard layer (endocarp) surrounded by a thick and buoyant fibrous husk.

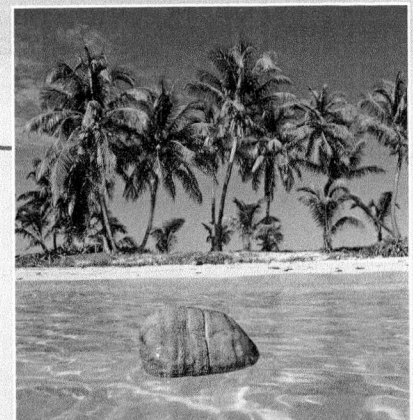

Dispersal by Wind

▶ The winged seed of the tropical Asian climbing gourd *Alsomitra macrocarpa* glides through the air of the rain forest in wide circles when released.

▼ The winged fruit of a maple spins like a helicopter blade, slowing descent and increasing the chance of being carried farther by horizontal winds.

Dandelion fruit

▶ Tumbleweeds break off at the ground and tumble across the terrain, scattering their seeds.

▲ Some seeds and fruits are attached to umbrella-like "parachutes" that are made of intricately branched hairs and often produced in puffy clusters. These dandelion "seeds" (actually one-seeded fruits) are carried aloft by the slightest gust of wind.

Dispersal by Animals

◀ The sharp, tack-like spines on the fruits of puncture vine (*Tribulus terrestris*) can pierce bicycle tires and injure animals, including humans. When these painful "tacks" are removed and discarded, the seeds are dispersed.

◀ Some animals, such as squirrels, hoard seeds or fruits in underground caches. If the animal dies or forgets the cache's location, the buried seeds are well positioned to germinate.

▶ Seeds in edible fruits are often dispersed in feces, such as the black bear feces shown here. Such dispersal may carry seeds far from the parent plant.

▶ Ants are chemically attracted to seeds with "food bodies" rich in fatty acids, amino acids, and sugars. The ants carry the seed to their underground nest, where the food body (the lighter-colored portion shown here) is removed and fed to larvae. Due to the seed's size, unwieldy shape, or hard coating, the remainder is usually left intact in the nest, where it germinates.

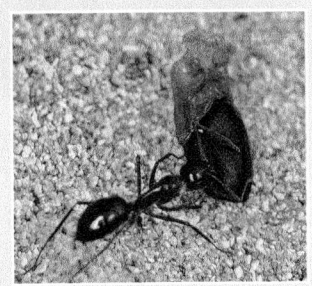

CONCEPT 38.2

Flowering plants reproduce sexually, asexually, or both

Imagine chopping off your finger and watching it develop into an exact copy of you. If this could actually occur, it would be an example of **asexual reproduction**, in which offspring are derived from a single parent without fusion of egg and sperm. The result would be a clone, an asexually produced, genetically identical organism. Asexual reproduction is common in angiosperms, as well as in other plants, and for some plant species it is the predominant mode of reproduction.

Mechanisms of Asexual Reproduction

Asexual reproduction in plants is typically an extension of the capacity for indeterminate growth. As described in Concept 35.2, plant growth can be sustained or renewed indefinitely by meristems, regions of undifferentiated, dividing cells. In addition, parenchyma cells throughout the plant can divide and differentiate into more specialized types of cells, enabling plants to regenerate lost parts. Detached vegetative fragments of some plants can develop into whole offspring; for example, pieces of a potato with an "eye" (vegetative bud) can each regenerate a whole plant. Such **fragmentation**, the separation of a parent plant into parts that develop into whole plants, is one of the most common modes of asexual reproduction. The adventitious plantlets on *Kalanchoë* leaves exemplify an unusual type of fragmentation (see Figure 35.7). In other cases, the root system of a single parent, such as an aspen tree, can give rise to many adventitious shoots that become separate shoot systems **(Figure 38.12)**. One aspen clone in Utah has been estimated to be composed of 47,000 stems of genetically identical trees. Although it is likely that some of the root system connections have been severed, making some of the trees isolated from the rest of the clone, each tree still shares a common genome.

An entirely different mechanism of asexual reproduction has evolved in dandelions and some other plants. These plants can sometimes produce seeds without pollination or fertilization. This asexual production of seeds is called **apomixis** (from the Greek words meaning "away from the act of mixing") because there is no joining or, indeed, production of sperm and egg. Instead, a diploid cell in the ovule gives rise to the embryo, and the ovules mature into seeds, which in the dandelion are dispersed by windblown fruits. Thus, these plants clone themselves by an asexual process but have the advantage of seed dispersal, usually associated with sexual reproduction. Introducing apomixis into hybrid crops is of great interest to plant breeders because apomixis would allow hybrid plants to pass on their desirable genomes intact to their offspring.

Advantages and Disadvantages of Asexual Versus Sexual Reproduction

An advantage of asexual reproduction is that there is no need for a pollinator. This may be beneficial in situations where plants of the same species are sparsely distributed and unlikely to be visited by the same pollinator. Asexual reproduction also allows the plant to pass on all of its genetic legacy intact to its progeny. In contrast, when reproducing sexually, a plant passes on only half of its alleles. If a plant is superbly suited to its environment, asexual reproduction can be advantageous. A vigorous plant can potentially clone many copies of itself, and if the environmental circumstances remain stable, these offspring will also be genetically well adapted to the same environmental conditions under which the parent flourished.

Generally, the progeny produced by asexual reproduction are stronger than seedlings produced by sexual reproduction. The offspring usually arise from mature vegetative fragments from the parent plant, which is why asexual reproduction in plants is also known as **vegetative reproduction**. In contrast, seed germination is a precarious stage in a plant's life. The tough seed gives rise to a fragile seedling that may face exposure to predators, parasites, wind, and other hazards. In the wild, only a small fraction of seedlings survive to become parents themselves. Production of enormous numbers of seeds compensates for the odds against individual survival and gives natural selection ample genetic variations to screen. However, this is an expensive means of reproduction in terms of the resources consumed in flowering and fruiting.

Because sexual reproduction generates variation in offspring and populations, it can be advantageous in unstable environments where evolving pathogens and other fluctuating conditions affect survival and reproductive success. In contrast, the genotypic uniformity of asexually produced plants puts them at great risk of local extinction if there is a

▲ **Figure 38.12 Asexual reproduction in aspen trees.** Some aspen groves, such as those shown here, consist of thousands of trees descended by asexual reproduction. Each grove of trees derives from the root system of one parent. Thus, the grove is a clone. Notice that genetic differences between groves descended from different parents result in different timing for the development of fall color.

catastrophic environmental change, such as a new strain of disease. Moreover, seeds (which are almost always produced sexually) facilitate the dispersal of offspring to more distant locations. Finally, seed dormancy allows growth to be suspended until environmental conditions become more favorable.

Although sexual reproduction involving two genetically different plants has the benefit of producing the most genetically diverse offspring, some plants, such as garden peas, usually self-fertilize. This process, called "selfing," can be a desirable attribute in some crop plants because it ensures that every ovule will develop into a seed. In many angiosperm species, however, mechanisms have evolved that make it difficult or impossible for a flower to fertilize itself, as we'll discuss next.

Mechanisms That Prevent Self-Fertilization

The various mechanisms that prevent self-fertilization contribute to genetic variety by ensuring that the sperm and egg come from different parents. In the case of **dioecious** species, plants cannot self-fertilize because different individuals have either staminate flowers (lacking carpels) or carpellate flowers (lacking stamens) (Figure 38.13a). Other plants have flowers with functional stamens and carpels that mature at different times or are structurally arranged in such a way that it is unlikely that an animal pollinator could transfer pollen from an anther to a stigma of the same flower (Figure 38.13b). However, the most common anti-selfing mechanism in flowering plants is **self-incompatibility**, the ability of a plant to reject its own pollen and sometimes the pollen of closely related individuals. If a pollen grain lands on a stigma of a flower on the same plant, a biochemical block prevents the pollen from completing its development and fertilizing an egg.

Researchers are unraveling the molecular mechanisms involved in self-incompatibility. This plant response is analogous to the immune response of animals in that both are based on the ability to distinguish the cells of "self" from those of "nonself." The key difference is that the animal immune system rejects nonself, as when the system mounts a defense against a pathogen or rejects a transplanted organ (see Chapter 43). Self-incompatibility in plants, in contrast, is a rejection of self.

Recognition of "self" pollen is based on genes for self-incompatibility, called *S*-genes. In the gene pool of a plant population, there can be dozens of alleles of an *S*-gene. If a pollen grain has an allele that matches an allele of the stigma on which it lands, the pollen tube fails to grow. Depending on the species, self-recognition blocks pollen tube growth by one of two molecular mechanisms: gametophytic self-incompatibility or sporophytic self-incompatibility.

In gametophytic self-incompatibility, the *S*-allele in the pollen genome governs the blocking of fertilization. For example, an S_1 pollen grain from an S_1S_2 parental sporophyte cannot fertilize eggs of an S_1S_2 flower but can fertilize an S_2S_3 flower. An S_2 pollen grain cannot fertilize either flower. Self-recognition of this kind involves the enzymatic destruction of RNA within a pollen tube. RNA-hydrolyzing enzymes are produced by the style and enter the pollen tube. If the pollen tube is a "self" type, these enzymes destroy its RNA.

In sporophytic self-incompatibility, fertilization is blocked by *S*-allele gene products in tissues of the parental sporophyte that adhere to the pollen grain wall. For example, neither an S_1 nor S_2 pollen grain from an S_1S_2 parental sporophyte can fertilize eggs of an S_1S_2 flower or S_2S_3 flower, due to the S_1S_2 parental tissue attached to the pollen wall. Sporophytic incompatibility involves a signal transduction pathway in epidermal cells of the stigma that prevents germination of the pollen grain.

Some crops, such as peas, maize, and tomatoes, routinely self-fertilize with satisfactory results. However, plant breeders frequently hybridize different varieties of a crop plant to combine the best traits of the varieties and counter the loss of vigor that can often result from excessive inbreeding. To obtain hybrid seeds, plant breeders today must prevent self-fertilization either by laboriously removing the anthers from the parent plants that provide the seeds (as Mendel did) or by developing male-sterile plants. The latter option is increasingly common. Eventually, it may also be possible to impose self-incompatibility genetically on crop species that are normally self-compatible. Basic research on mechanisms of self-incompatibility may thus have agricultural applications.

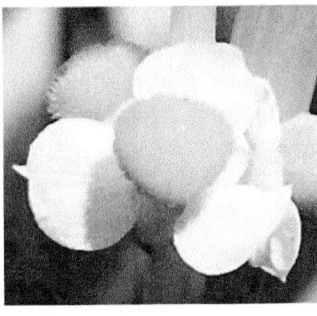

(a) Some species, such as *Sagittaria latifolia* (common arrowhead), are dioecious, having plants that produce only staminate flowers (left) or carpellate flowers (right).

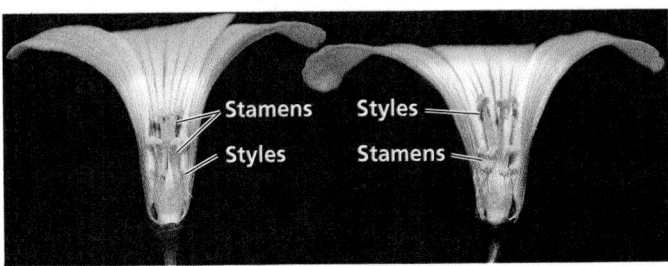

Thrum flower   Pin flower

(b) Some species, such as *Oxalis alpina* (alpine woodsorrel), produce two types of flowers on different individuals: "thrums," which have short styles and long stamens, and "pins," which have long styles and short stamens. An insect foraging for nectar would collect pollen on different parts of its body; thrum pollen would be deposited on pin stigmas, and vice versa.

▲ **Figure 38.13 Some floral adaptations that prevent self-fertilization.**

Vegetative Propagation and Agriculture

With the objective of improving crops and ornamental plants, humans have devised various methods for asexual propagation of angiosperms. Most of these methods are based on the ability of plants to form adventitious roots or shoots.

Clones from Cuttings

Most houseplants, woody ornamentals, and orchard trees are asexually reproduced from plant fragments called cuttings. In some cases, shoot cuttings are used. At the cut end of the shoot, a mass of dividing, undifferentiated cells called a **callus** forms, and adventitious roots then develop from the callus. If the shoot fragment includes a node, then adventitious roots form without a callus stage. Some plants, including African violets, can be propagated from single leaves rather than stems. For other plants, cuttings are taken from specialized storage stems, such as potato tubers. The Bartlett pear and the Red Delicious apple are examples of varieties that have been propagated asexually for over 150 years.

Grafting

In a modification of vegetative reproduction from cuttings, a twig or bud from one plant can be grafted onto a plant of a closely related species or a different variety of the same species. Grafting makes it possible to combine the best qualities of different species or varieties into a single plant. The plant that provides the root system is called the **stock**; the twig grafted onto the stock is referred to as the **scion**. For example, scions from French varieties of vines that produce superior wine grapes are grafted onto rootstocks of American varieties that produce inferior grapes but are more resistant to certain soil pathogens. The genes of the scion determine the quality of the fruit.

Test-Tube Cloning and Related Techniques

Plant biologists have adopted *in vitro* methods to clone novel plant varieties. They can grow whole plants by culturing small pieces of tissue from the parent plant on an artificial medium containing nutrients and hormones. The cells or tissues can come from any part of a plant, but growth may vary depending on the plant part, species, and artificial medium. In some media, the cultured cells divide and form a callus of undifferentiated cells **(Figure 38.14a)**. When the concentrations of hormones and nutrients are manipulated appropriately, a callus can sprout shoots and roots with fully differentiated cells **(Figure 38.14b,c)**. The plantlets can then be transferred to soil, where they continue their growth. A single plant can be cloned into thousands of copies by dividing calluses as they grow. This method is now used for propagating orchids as well as a wide variety of trees and shrubs.

▲ **Figure 38.14 Cloning a garlic plant. (a)** A root from a garlic clove gave rise to this callus culture, a mass of undifferentiated cells. **(b and c)** The differentiation of a callus into a plantlet depends on the nutrient levels and hormone concentrations in the artificial medium, as can be seen in these cultures grown for different lengths of time.

Plant tissue culture also facilitates genetic engineering. Most techniques for the introduction of foreign genes into plants require small pieces of plant tissue or single plant cells as the starting material. The term **transgenic** is used to describe genetically modified (GM) organisms that have been engineered to express a gene from another species. Test-tube culture makes it possible to regenerate GM plants from a single plant cell into which the foreign DNA has been incorporated. The techniques of genetic engineering are discussed in more detail in Chapter 20.

Some researchers couple a technique known as **protoplast fusion** with tissue culture methods to invent new plant varieties that can be cloned. Protoplasts are plant cells with their cell walls removed by treatment with enzymes (cellulases and pectinases) isolated from fungi **(Figure 38.15)**. In some cases, it is possible to fuse two protoplasts from different plant species that would otherwise be reproductively incompatible and then culture the hybrid protoplasts. Each protoplast can regenerate a wall and eventually form a hybrid plantlet. The hybrid produced by the protoplast fusion

◀ **Figure 38.15 Protoplasts.** These plant cells without walls are prepared by treating cells or tissues with wall-degrading enzymes isolated from certain fungi. Researchers can fuse protoplasts from different species to make hybrid cells and can then culture the cells to produce a new plant (LM).

50 μm

of two *Datura* species, for example, produces fertile seeds and is considered a new species. This hybrid can grow larger than the two parent species and is about 25% richer in medicinal alkaloids.

The *in vitro* culturing of plant cells and tissues is fundamental to most types of plant biotechnology. The other basic process is the production of transgenic plants through various methods of genetic engineering. In the next section, we take a closer look at plant biotechnology.

CONCEPT CHECK 38.2

1. The seedless banana, the world's most popular fruit, is losing the battle against two fungal epidemics. Why do such epidemics generally pose a greater risk to asexually propagated crops?
2. Self-fertilization, or selfing, seems to have obvious disadvantages as a reproductive "strategy" in nature, and it has even been called an "evolutionary dead end." So it is surprising that about 20% of angiosperm species primarily rely on selfing. Suggest a reason why selfing might be advantageous and yet still be an evolutionary dead end.
3. **WHAT IF?** Potatoes (*Solanum tuberosum*) and tomatoes (*Solanum lycopersicum*) are fairly closely related species. If you managed to cross the two, would it be possible to have a hybrid that makes potato-like tubers and tomato-like fruits on the same plant?

For suggested answers, see Appendix A.

CONCEPT 38.3

Humans modify crops by breeding and genetic engineering

Humans have intervened in the reproduction and genetic makeup of plants since the dawn of agriculture. As explained by Luis Herrera-Estrella in the Unit Six interview (see pp. 736–737), maize owes its existence to humans. Left on its own in nature, maize would soon become extinct for the simple reason that it cannot spread its seeds. Maize kernels are not only permanently attached to the central axis (the "cob") but also permanently protected by tough, overlapping leaf sheaths (the "husk") **(Figure 38.16)**. These attributes arose by artificial selection by humans. (See Chapter 22 to review the basic concept of artificial selection.) Despite having no understanding of the scientific principles underlying plant breeding, Neolithic (late Stone Age) humans domesticated most of our crop species over a relatively short period about 10,000 years ago. But genetic modification began long before humans started altering crops by artificial selection. For example,

▲ Figure 38.16 **Maize: a product of artificial selection.** Modern maize (bottom) was derived from teosinte (top). Teosinte kernels are tiny, and each row has a husk that must be removed to get at the kernel. The seeds are loose at maturity, allowing dispersal, which probably made harvesting difficult for early farmers. Neolithic farmers selected seeds from plants with larger cob and kernel size as well as the permanent attachment of seeds to the cob and the encasing of the entire cob by a tough husk.

the wheat species we rely on for much of our food evolved by the natural hybridization between different species of grasses. Such hybridization is common in plants and has long been exploited by breeders to introduce genetic variation for artificial selection and crop improvement.

Plant Breeding

The art of recognizing valuable traits is important in plant breeding. Breeders scrutinize their fields carefully and travel to other countries searching for domesticated varieties or wild relatives with desirable traits. Such traits occasionally arise spontaneously through mutation, but the natural rate of mutation is too slow and unreliable to produce all the mutations that breeders would like to study. Breeders sometimes hasten mutations by treating large batches of seeds or seedlings with radiation or chemicals.

When a desirable trait is identified in a wild species, the wild species is crossed with a domesticated variety. Generally, those progeny that have inherited the desirable trait from the wild parent have also inherited many traits that are not desirable for agriculture, such as small fruits or low yields. The progeny that express the desired trait are again crossed with members of the domesticated species and their progeny examined for the desired trait. This process is continued until the progeny with the desired wild trait resemble the original domesticated parent in their other agricultural attributes.

While most breeders cross-pollinate plants of a single species, some breeding methods rely on hybridization between two distant species of the same genus. Such crosses often result in the abortion of the hybrid seed during development. Very often the embryo begins to develop, but the endosperm does not. Hybrid embryos are sometimes rescued by surgically removing them from the ovule and culturing them *in vitro*.

Less commonly, hybridization is carried out on members of two different genera. A cross between wheat (*Triticum aestivum*) and rye (*Secale cereale*), for example, produced a novel grain called triticale, which contains a copy of all the chromosomes from both species. When triticale was first produced in the 1870s, it was considered little more than a botanical oddity. In the mid-1900s, however, plant breeders realized that triticale could potentially be developed into a crop with the yield and quality of bread wheat and with rye's tolerance of cold stress, moisture stress, and acidic soils. The early triticales were plagued with problems. These tall, late-maturing plants tended to fall over, were partially sterile, and were low yielding. They typically produced shriveled seeds that germinated poorly and were of poor quality for milling and baking. But through continued artificial selection, these problems were overcome, and triticale is now grown worldwide on more than 1 million hectares of marginal (poor-quality) farmland (1 ha = 2.47 acres). If we are to feed the rapidly growing world population in the 21st century, such marginal lands will have to become increasingly productive.

Plant Biotechnology and Genetic Engineering

Plant biotechnology has two meanings. In the general sense, it refers to innovations in the use of plants (or substances obtained from plants) to make products of use to humans—an endeavor that began in prehistory. In a more specific sense, biotechnology refers to the use of GM organisms in agriculture and industry. Indeed, in the last two decades, genetic engineering has become such a powerful force that the terms *genetic engineering* and *biotechnology* have become synonymous in the media.

Unlike traditional plant breeders, modern plant biotechnologists, using techniques of genetic engineering, are not limited to the transfer of genes between closely related species or genera. For example, traditional breeding techniques could not be used to insert a desired gene from daffodil into rice because the many intermediate species between rice and daffodil and their common ancestor are extinct. In theory, if breeders had the intermediate species, over the course of several centuries they could probably introduce a daffodil gene into rice by traditional hybridization and breeding methods. With genetic engineering, however, such gene transfers can be done more quickly, more specifically, and without the need for intermediate species.

In the remainder of this chapter, we expand on discussions in Chapter 20 by examining the prospects and controversies surrounding the use of GM crops. The advocates of plant biotechnology believe that the genetic engineering of crop plants is the key to overcoming some of the most pressing problems of the 21st century, including world hunger and fossil fuel dependency.

Reducing World Hunger and Malnutrition

Currently, 800 million people suffer from nutritional deficiencies, with 40,000 dying each day of malnutrition, half of them children. There is much disagreement about the causes of such hunger. Some argue that food shortages arise from inequities in distribution and that the dire poor simply cannot afford food. Others regard food shortages as evidence that the world is overpopulated—that the human species has exceeded the carrying capacity of the planet (see Chapter 53). Whatever the social and demographic causes of malnutrition, increasing food production is a humane objective. Because land and water are the most limiting resources, the best option is to increase yields on already existing farmland. Indeed, there is very little "extra" land that can be farmed, especially if the few remaining pockets of wilderness are to be preserved. Based on conservative estimates of population growth, farmers will have to produce 40% more grain per hectare to feed the human population in 2030. Plant biotechnology can help make these crop yields possible.

The commercial use of transgenic crops has been one of the most dramatic examples of rapid technology adoption in the history of agriculture. These crops include varieties and hybrids of cotton, maize, and potatoes that contain genes from the bacterium *Bacillus thuringiensis*. These "transgenes" encode a protein (*Bt* toxin) that is toxic to insect pests. The use of such plant varieties greatly reduces the need for chemical insecticides. The *Bt* toxin used in crops is produced in the plant as a harmless protoxin that only becomes toxic if activated by alkaline conditions, such as occur in the guts of insects. Because vertebrates have highly acidic stomachs, protoxin consumed by humans or farm animals is destroyed without becoming active.

Considerable progress has also been made in developing transgenic crops that tolerate certain herbicides. The cultivation of these plants may reduce production costs by enabling farmers to "weed" crops with herbicides that do not damage the transgenic crop plants, instead of using heavy tillage, which can cause soil erosion. Researchers are also engineering plants with enhanced resistance to disease. In one case, a transgenic papaya resistant to a ring spot virus was introduced into Hawaii, thereby saving its papaya industry.

The nutritional quality of plants is also being improved. For example, some 250,000 to 500,000 children go blind each year because of vitamin A deficiencies. More than half of these children die within a year of becoming blind. In response to this crisis, genetic engineers have created "Golden Rice," a transgenic variety supplemented with two daffodil genes that enable it to produce grain containing beta-carotene, a precursor of vitamin A. Another target for improvement by genetic

Fighting World Hunger with Transgenic Cassava

Plant biologists are racing to mold cassava (*Manihot esculenta*) into the perfect food. This starchy root crop is plentiful and easy to grow and is the primary food for 800 million of the world's poor. But it has several drawbacks. Composed almost entirely of carbohydrates, it provides plenty of calories but not a complete and balanced diet. Moreover, it must be processed to remove chemicals that release cyanide, and workers can be sickened by chronic exposure to this toxin. However, transgenic cassava plants have been developed with greatly enriched levels of protein, iron, and beta-carotene (a vitamin A precursor), and cyanide-producing chemicals have been almost eliminated from the roots. Researchers have also created cassava plants with root masses twice the normal size.

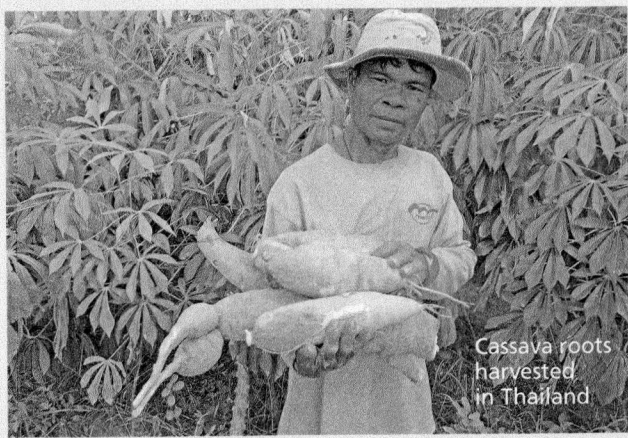

Cassava roots harvested in Thailand

WHY IT MATTERS Feeding the world's hungry will continue to be a daunting challenge in the 21st century because their population continues to climb. Untold human misery can be avoided if plant biologists can produce a cassava variety so nutritious that a 500-gram serving a day will provide a full and healthy diet.

FURTHER READING N. Nassar and R. Ortiz, Breeding cassava to feed the poor, *Scientific American* 302:78–84 (2010).

MAKE CONNECTIONS Genetic transformation using *Agrobacterium tumefaciens*, which causes crown gall disease, is the preferred method for transporting new genes into cassava cells. Review Concept 20.4, page 421, and explain why the use of this pathogen in genetic engineering does not produce crown gall disease in transgenic plants.

engineering is cassava, a staple for 800 million of the poorest people on our planet (Figure 38.17).

Reducing Fossil Fuel Dependency

Global sources of inexpensive fossil fuels, particularly oil, are rapidly being depleted. Moreover, most climatologists attribute global warming mainly to the rampant burning of fossil fuels, such as coal and oil, and the resulting release of the greenhouse gas CO_2. How can the world meet its energy demands in the 21st century in an economical and nonpolluting way? In certain localities, wind or solar power may become economically viable, but such alternative energy sources are unlikely to fill the global energy demands completely. Many scientists predict that biomass from extremely fast-growing plants, such as switchgrass (*Panicum virgatum*) and poplar (*Populus trichocarpa*), could produce a sizable fraction of the world's energy needs in the not-too-distant future.

Under optimal conditions, poplars can grow 3–4 m each year, and switchgrass grows well under a wide variety of conditions found in regions where most types of agriculture are not economically viable. Scientists do not envisage the plant biomass being burned directly. Instead, the polymers in cell walls, such as cellulose and hemicellulose, which constitute the most abundant organic compounds on Earth, would be broken down into sugars by enzymatic reactions. These sugars, in turn, would be fermented into alcohol and distilled to yield **biofuels**.

The use of biofuels from plant biomass would reduce the net emission of CO_2. Whereas burning fossil fuels increases atmospheric CO_2 concentrations, biofuel crops reabsorb by photosynthesis the CO_2 emitted when biofuels are burned, creating a cycle that is carbon neutral. Plant breeders are trying to genetically engineer faster-growing poplar trees that produce more readily convertible biomass.

Biofuel technology does have its critics. For example, ecologist David Pimentel, of Cornell University, and geoengineer Tad Patzek, of the University of California, Berkeley, have estimated that more energy may be required to produce biofuels than would be produced from combustion of these products. Biofuel advocates, in turn, have questioned the accuracy of the data underlying these estimates.

The Debate over Plant Biotechnology

Much of the debate about GM organisms (GMOs) in agriculture is political, social, economic, or ethical and therefore outside the scope of this book. But we *should* consider the biological concerns about GM crops. Some biologists, particularly ecologists, are concerned about the unknown risks associated with the release of GMOs into the environment. The debate centers on the extent to which GMOs could harm the environment or human health. Those who want to proceed more slowly with agricultural biotechnology (or end it) are concerned about the unstoppable nature of the "experiment." If a drug trial produces unanticipated harmful results, the trial is stopped. But we may not be able to stop the "trial" of introducing novel organisms into the biosphere.

Chapter 20 introduced the key concerns regarding biotechnology in general. Here we take a closer look at some issues as they relate to plant biotechnology. Laboratory and field studies continue to examine the possible consequences of using GM crops, including the effects on human health and nontarget organisms and the potential for transgene escape.

Issues of Human Health

Many GMO opponents worry that genetic engineering may inadvertently transfer allergens, molecules to which some people are allergic, from a species that produces an allergen to a plant used for food. However, biotechnologists are already engaged in removing genes that encode allergenic proteins from soybeans and other crops. So far, there is no credible evidence that GM plants specifically designed for human consumption have adverse effects on human health. In fact, some GM foods are potentially healthier than non-GM foods. For example, *Bt* maize (the transgenic variety with the *Bt* toxin) contains 90% less of a cancer-causing and birth defect–causing fungal toxin than non-*Bt* maize. Called fumonisin, this toxin is highly resistant to degradation and has been found in alarmingly high concentrations in some batches of processed maize products, ranging from cornflakes to beer. Fumonisin is produced by a fungus (*Fusarium*) that infects insect-damaged maize. Because *Bt* maize generally suffers less insect damage than non-GM maize, it contains much less fumonisin.

Nevertheless, because of health concerns, GMO opponents lobby for the clear labeling of all foods containing products of GMOs. Some also argue for strict regulations against the mixing of GM foods with non-GM foods during food transport, storage, and processing. Biotechnology advocates, however, note that similar demands were not made when "transgenic" crops produced by traditional plant-breeding techniques were put on the market. There are, for example, some commercially grown varieties of wheat derived by traditional plant-breeding techniques that contain entire chromosomes (and thousands of genes) from rye.

Possible Effects on Nontarget Organisms

Many ecologists are concerned that the growing of GM crops might have unforeseen effects on nontarget organisms. One laboratory study indicated that the larvae (caterpillars) of monarch butterflies responded adversely and even died after eating milkweed leaves (their preferred food) heavily dusted with pollen from transgenic *Bt* maize. This study has since been discredited, affording a good example of the self-correcting nature of science. As it turns out, when the original researchers shook the male maize inflorescences onto the milkweed leaves in the laboratory, the filaments of stamens, opened microsporangia, and other floral parts also rained onto the leaves. Subsequent research found that it was these other floral parts, *not* the pollen, that contained *Bt* toxin in high concentrations. Unlike pollen, these floral parts would not be carried by the wind to neighboring milkweed plants when shed under natural field conditions. Only one *Bt* maize line, accounting for less than 2% of commercial *Bt* maize production (and now discontinued), produced pollen with high *Bt* toxin concentrations.

In considering the negative effects of *Bt* pollen on monarch butterflies, one must also weigh the effects of an alternative to the cultivation of *Bt* maize—the spraying of non-*Bt* maize with chemical pesticides. Recent studies have shown that such spraying is much more harmful to nearby monarch populations than is *Bt* maize production. Although the effects of *Bt* maize pollen on monarch butterfly larvae appear to be minor, the controversy has emphasized the need for accurate field testing of all GM crops and the importance of targeting gene expression to specific tissues to improve safety.

Addressing the Problem of Transgene Escape

Perhaps the most serious concern raised about GM crops is the possibility of the introduced genes escaping from a transgenic crop into related weeds through crop-to-weed hybridization. The fear is that the spontaneous hybridization between a crop engineered for herbicide resistance and a wild relative might give rise to a "superweed" that would have a selective advantage over other weeds in the wild and would be much more difficult to control in the field. Some crops *do* hybridize with weedy relatives, and crop-to-weed transgene escape is a possibility. Its likelihood depends on the ability of the crop and weed to hybridize and on how the transgenes affect the overall fitness of the hybrids. A desirable crop trait—a dwarf phenotype, for example—might be disadvantageous to a weed growing in the wild. In other instances, there are no weedy relatives nearby with which to hybridize; soybean, for example, has no wild relatives in the United States. However, canola, sorghum, and many other crops do hybridize readily with weeds.

Many different strategies are being pursued with the goal of preventing transgene escape. For example, if male sterility could be engineered into plants, these plants would still produce seeds and fruit if pollinated by nearby nontransgenic plants, but they would produce no viable pollen. A second approach involves genetically engineering apomixis into transgenic crops. When a seed is produced by apomixis, the embryo and endosperm develop without fertilization. The transfer of this trait to transgenic crops would therefore minimize the possibility of transgene escape via pollen because plants could be male-sterile without compromising seed or fruit production. A third approach is to engineer the transgene into the chloroplast DNA of the crop. Chloroplast DNA in many plant species is inherited strictly from the egg, so transgenes in the chloroplast cannot be transferred by pollen (see Chapter 15 to review maternal inheritance). A fourth approach for preventing transgene escape is to genetically engineer flowers that develop normally but fail to open. Consequently, self-pollination would occur, but pollen would be unlikely to escape from the flower. This solution would require modifications to flower design. Several floral genes have been identified that could be manipulated to this end.

The continuing debate about GMOs in agriculture exemplifies one of this textbook's recurring ideas: the relationship of science and technology to society. Technological advances almost always involve some risk of unintended outcomes. In plant biotechnology, zero risk is probably unattainable. Therefore, scientists and the public must assess on a case-by-case basis the possible benefits of transgenic products versus the risks that society is willing to take. The best scenario is for these discussions and decisions to be based on sound scientific information and rigorous testing rather than on reflexive fear or blind optimism.

CONCEPT CHECK 38.3

1. Compare traditional plant-breeding methods with genetic engineering.
2. Explain some benefits and risks of GM crops.
3. Why does *Bt* maize have less fumonisin than non-GM maize?
4. **WHAT IF?** In a few species, chloroplast genes are inherited only from sperm. How might this influence efforts to prevent transgene escape?

For suggested answers, see Appendix A.

38 CHAPTER REVIEW

SUMMARY OF KEY CONCEPTS

CONCEPT 38.1

Flowers, double fertilization, and fruits are unique features of the angiosperm life cycle (pp. 801–811)

- Angiosperm reproduction involves an alternation of generations between a multicellular diploid sporophyte generation and a multicellular haploid gametophyte generation. Flowers, produced by the sporophyte, function in sexual reproduction.
- The four floral organs are sepals, petals, stamens, and carpels. **Sepals** protect the floral bud. **Petals** help attract pollinators. **Stamens** bear anthers in which haploid **microspores** develop into **pollen grains** containing a male gametophyte. **Carpels** contain ovules (immature seeds) in their swollen bases. Within the ovules, **embryos sacs** (female gametophytes) develop from megaspores.
- **Pollination**, which precedes fertilization, is the placing of pollen on the stigma of a carpel. After pollination, the pollen tube discharges two sperm into the female gametophyte. Two sperm are needed for **double fertilization**, a process in which one sperm fertilizes the egg, forming a zygote and eventually an embryo, while the other sperm combines with the polar nuclei, giving rise to food-storing endosperm.

Endosperm nucleus (3*n*) (2 polar nuclei plus sperm)

Zygote (2*n*) (egg plus sperm)

- The **seed coat** encloses the embryo along with a food supply stocked in either the **endosperm** or the **cotyledons**. Seed **dormancy** ensures that seeds germinate only when conditions for seedling survival are optimal. The breaking of dormancy often requires environmental cues, such as temperature or lighting changes.
- The **fruit** protects the enclosed seeds and aids in wind dispersal or in the attraction of seed-dispersing animals.

? *What changes occur to the four types of floral parts as a flower changes into a fruit?*

CONCEPT 38.2

Flowering plants reproduce sexually, asexually, or both (pp. 812–815)

- **Asexual reproduction** enables successful plants to proliferate quickly. Sexual reproduction generates most of the genetic variation that makes evolutionary adaptation possible.
- Plants have evolved many mechanisms to avoid self-fertilization, including dioecy (male and female flowers on different individuals), nonsynchronous production of male and female parts within a single flower, and **self-incompatibility** reactions in which pollen grains that bear an allele identical to one in the female are rejected.
- Plants can be cloned from single cells, which can be genetically manipulated before being allowed to develop into a plant.

? *What are the advantages and disadvantages of asexual reproduction?*

CONCEPT 38.3

Humans modify crops by breeding and genetic engineering (pp. 815–819)

- Hybridization of different varieties and even species of plants is common in nature and has been used by breeders, ancient and modern, to introduce new genes into crops. After two plants are successfully hybridized, plant breeders select those progeny that have the desired traits.
- In genetic engineering, genes from unrelated organisms are incorporated into plants. Genetically modified (GM) plants have the potential of increasing the quality and quantity of food worldwide and may also become increasingly important as biofuels.
- Two important GM crops are Golden Rice, which provides more vitamin A, and *Bt* maize, which is insect resistant.
- There are concerns about the unknown risks of releasing GM organisms into the environment, but the potential benefits of transgenic crops need to be considered.

? *Give three examples of how genetic engineering has improved food quality or agricultual productivity.*

LEVEL 1: KNOWLEDGE/COMPREHENSION

1. A seed develops from
   a. an ovum.
   b. a pollen grain.
   c. an ovule.
   d. an ovary.
   e. an embryo.

2. A fruit is
   a. a mature ovary.
   b. a mature ovule.
   c. a seed plus its integuments.
   d. a fused carpel.
   e. an enlarged embryo sac.

3. Double fertilization means that
   a. flowers must be pollinated twice to yield fruits and seeds.
   b. every egg must receive two sperm to produce an embryo.
   c. one sperm is needed to fertilize the egg, and a second sperm is needed to fertilize the polar nuclei.
   d. the egg of the embryo sac is diploid.
   e. every sperm has two nuclei.

4. "Golden Rice"
   a. is resistant to various herbicides, making it practical to weed rice fields with those herbicides.
   b. is resistant to a virus that commonly attacks rice fields.
   c. includes bacterial genes that produce a toxin that reduces damage from insect pests.
   d. produces larger, golden grains that increase crop yields.
   e. contains daffodil genes that increase vitamin A content.

5. Which statement concerning grafting is correct?
   a. Stocks and scions refer to twigs of different species.
   b. Stocks come from vines, but scions come from trees.
   c. Stocks provide root systems for grafting.
   d. Grafting creates new species.
   e. Stocks and scions must come from unrelated species.

LEVEL 2: APPLICATION/ANALYSIS

6. Some dioecious species have the XY genotype for male and XX for female. After double fertilization, what would be the genotypes of the embryos and endosperm nuclei?
   a. embryo X/endosperm XX or embryo Y/endosperm XY
   b. embryo XX/endosperm XX or embryo XY/endosperm XY
   c. embryo XX/endosperm XXX or embryo XY/endosperm XYY
   d. embryo XX/endosperm XXX or embryo XY/endosperm XXY
   e. embryo XY/endosperm XXX or embryo XX/endosperm XXY

7. A small flower with green petals is most likely
   a. bee-pollinated.
   b. bird-pollinated.
   c. bat-pollinated.
   d. wind-pollinated.
   e. moth-pollinated.

8. The pollen produced by wind-pollinated plants is often smaller than the pollen produced by animal-pollinated plants. A reason for this might be that
   a. wind-pollinated plants, in general, are smaller than animal pollinated plants.
   b. wind-pollinated plants release pollen in the spring, before the plant has stored enough energy to make large pollen grains.
   c. small pollen grains can be carried farther by the wind.
   d. animal pollinators are more facile at picking up large pollen grains.
   e. wind-pollinated flowers don't need large pollen grains because they don't have to attract animal pollinators.

9. The black dots that cover strawberries are actually individual fruits. The fleshy and tasty portion of a strawberry derives from the receptacle of a flower with many separate carpels. Therefore, a strawberry is
   a. both a multiple fruit and an aggregate fruit.
   b. both a multiple fruit and an accessory fruit.
   c. both a simple fruit and an aggregate fruit.
   d. both an aggregrate fruit and an accessory fruit.
   e. a simple fruit with many seeds.

10. **DRAW IT** Draw and label the parts of a flower.

LEVEL 3: SYNTHESIS/EVALUATION

11. **EVOLUTION CONNECTION**
    With respect to sexual reproduction, some plant species are fully self-fertile, others are fully self-incompatible, and some exhibit a "mixed strategy" with partial self-incompatibility. These reproductive strategies differ in their implications for evolutionary potential. How, for example, might a self-incompatible species fare as a small founder population or remnant population in a severe population bottleneck (see Chapter 23), as compared with a self-fertile species?

12. **SCIENTIFIC INQUIRY**
    Critics of GM foods have argued that foreign genes may disturb normal cellular functioning, causing unexpected and potentially harmful substances to appear inside cells. Toxic intermediary substances that normally occur in very small amounts may arise in larger amounts, or new substances may appear. The disruption may also lead to loss of substances that help maintain normal metabolism. If you were your nation's chief scientific advisor, how would you respond to these criticisms?

13. **SCIENCE, TECHNOLOGY, AND SOCIETY**
    Humans have engaged in genetic manipulation for millennia, producing plant and animal varieties through selective breeding and hybridization processes that significantly modify the genomes of organisms. Why do you think modern genetic engineering, which often entails introducing or modifying only one or a few genes, has met with so much public opposition? Should some forms of genetic engineering be of greater concern than others? Explain.

14. **WRITE ABOUT A THEME**
    Emergent Properties In a short essay (100–150 words), discuss how the ability of a flower to reproduce with other flowers of the same species is an emergent property that arises from its floral parts and their organization.

For selected answers, see Appendix A.

www.masteringbiology.com

1. MasteringBiology® Assignments
Tutorial Angiosperm Life Cycle
Activities Discovery Channel Video: Plant Pollination • Reproduction in Flowering Plants • Seed and Fruit Development • Fruit Structure and Development • Discovery Channel Video: Colored Cotton
Questions Student Misconceptions • Reading Quiz • Multiple Choice • End-of-Chapter

2. eText
Read your book online, search, take notes, highlight text, and more.

3. The Study Area
Practice Tests • Cumulative Test • *BioFlix* 3-D Animations • MP3 Tutor Sessions • Videos • Activities • Investigations • Lab Media • Audio Glossary • Word Study Tools • Art

Plant Responses to Internal and External Signals

▲ Figure 39.1 **Can flowers tell you the time of day?**

KEY CONCEPTS

39.1 Signal transduction pathways link signal reception to response

39.2 Plant hormones help coordinate growth, development, and responses to stimuli

39.3 Responses to light are critical for plant success

39.4 Plants respond to a wide variety of stimuli other than light

39.5 Plants respond to attacks by herbivores and pathogens

OVERVIEW

Stimuli and a Stationary Life

Carolus Linnaeus, the father of taxonomy, was a keen naturalist. He noted that each plant species opened and closed its flowers at a characteristic time of the day. Therefore, one could estimate the time of day by observing which species had open or closed flowers. If the times of opening and closing were arranged in sequence, they could serve as a kind of floral clock, or *horologium florae*, as Linnaeus called it. Figure 39.1 shows a modern representation as a 12-hour clock face. Why does the timing vary? The time at which flowers open presumably reflects the time when their insect pollinators are most active, just one example of the numerous environmental factors that a plant must sense to compete successfully.

This chapter focuses on the mechanisms by which flowering plants sense and respond to external and internal cues. At the organismal level, plants and animals respond to environmental stimuli by different means. Animals, being mobile, respond mainly by moving toward positive stimuli and away from negative stimuli. In contrast, plants are stationary and generally respond to environmental cues by adjusting their individual patterns of growth and development. For this reason, plants of the same species vary in body form much more than do animals of the same species. But just because plants do not move in the same manner as animals does not mean that plants lack sensitivity. Before a plant can initiate alterations to growth patterns in response to environmental signals, it must first detect the change in its environment. As we will see, the molecular processes underlying plant responses are as complex as those used by animal cells and are often homologous to them.

CONCEPT **39.1**

Signal transduction pathways link signal reception to response

Plants receive specific signals and respond to them in ways that enhance survival and reproductive success. Consider, for example, a forgotten potato in the back corner of a kitchen cupboard. This modified underground stem, or tuber, has sprouted shoots from its "eyes" (axillary buds). These shoots, however, scarcely resemble those of a typical plant. Instead of sturdy stems and broad green leaves, this plant has ghostly pale stems and unexpanded leaves, as well as short, stubby roots (Figure 39.2a). These morphological adaptations for growing in darkness, collectively referred to as **etiolation**, make sense if we consider that a young potato plant in nature usually encounters continuous darkness when sprouting underground. Under these circumstances, expanded leaves would be a hindrance to soil penetration and would be damaged as the shoots pushed through the soil. Because the leaves are unexpanded and underground, there is little evaporative loss of water and little requirement for an extensive root system to replace the water lost by transpiration. Moreover, the energy expended in producing

(a) Before exposure to light. A dark-grown potato has tall, spindly stems and nonexpanded leaves—morphological adaptations that enable the shoots to penetrate the soil. The roots are short, but there is little need for water absorption because little water is lost by the shoots.

(b) After a week's exposure to natural daylight. The potato plant begins to resemble a typical plant with broad green leaves, short sturdy stems, and long roots. This transformation begins with the reception of light by a specific pigment, phytochrome.

▲ **Figure 39.2 Light-induced de-etiolation (greening) of dark-grown potatoes.**

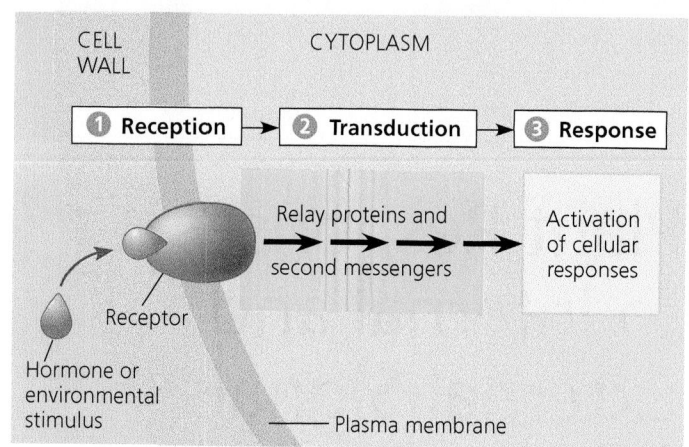

▲ **Figure 39.3 Review of a general model for signal transduction pathways.** As discussed in Chapter 11, a hormone or other kind of stimulus interacting with a specific receptor protein can trigger the sequential activation of relay proteins and also the production of second messengers that participate in the pathway. The signal is passed along, ultimately bringing about cellular responses. In this diagram, the receptor is on the surface of the target cell; in other cases, the stimulus interacts with receptors inside the cell.

green chlorophyll would be wasted because there is no light for photosynthesis. Instead, a potato plant growing in the dark allocates as much energy as possible to elongating its stems. This adaptation enables the shoots to break ground before the nutrient reserves in the tuber are exhausted. The etiolation response is one example of how a plant's morphology and physiology are tuned to its surroundings by complex interactions between environmental and internal signals.

When a shoot reaches light, the plant undergoes profound changes, collectively called **de-etiolation** (informally known as greening). Stem elongation slows; leaves expand; roots elongate; and the shoot produces chlorophyll. In short, it begins to resemble a typical plant (**Figure 39.2b**). In this section, we will use this de-etiolation response as an example of how a plant cell's reception of a signal—in this case, light—is transduced into a response (greening). Along the way, we will explore how studies of mutants provide insights into the molecular details of the stages of cell signal processing: reception, transduction, and response (**Figure 39.3**).

Reception

Signals are first detected by receptors, proteins that undergo changes in shape in response to a specific stimulus. The receptor involved in de-etiolation is a type of *phytochrome*, a member of a class of photoreceptors that we'll discuss more fully later in the chapter. Unlike most receptors, which are built into the plasma membrane, the type of phytochrome that functions in de-etiolation is located in the cytoplasm. Researchers demonstrated the requirement for phytochrome in

de-etiolation through studies of the tomato, a close relative of the potato. The *aurea* mutant of tomato, which has reduced levels of phytochrome, greens less than wild-type tomatoes when exposed to light. (*Aurea* is Latin for "gold." In the absence of chlorophyll, the yellow and orange accessory pigments called carotenoids are more obvious.) Researchers produced a normal de-etiolation response in individual *aurea* leaf cells by injecting phytochrome from other plants and then exposing the cells to light. Such experiments indicated that phytochrome functions in light detection during de-etiolation.

Transduction

Receptors can be sensitive to very weak environmental or chemical signals. Some de-etiolation responses are triggered by extremely low levels of light, in certain cases as little as the equivalent of a few seconds of moonlight. The transduction of these extremely weak signals involves **second messengers**— small molecules and ions in the cell that amplify the signal and transfer it from the receptor to other proteins that carry out the response (**Figure 39.4**). In Chapter 11, we discussed several kinds of second messengers (see Figures 11.12 and 11.14). Here, we examine the particular roles of two types of second messengers in de-etiolation: calcium ions (Ca^{2+}) and cyclic GMP (cGMP).

Changes in cytosolic Ca^{2+} levels play an important role in phytochrome signal transduction. The concentration of cytosolic Ca^{2+} is generally very low (about 10^{-7} M), but phytochrome activation leads to the opening of Ca^{2+} channels and a transient 100-fold increase in cytosolic

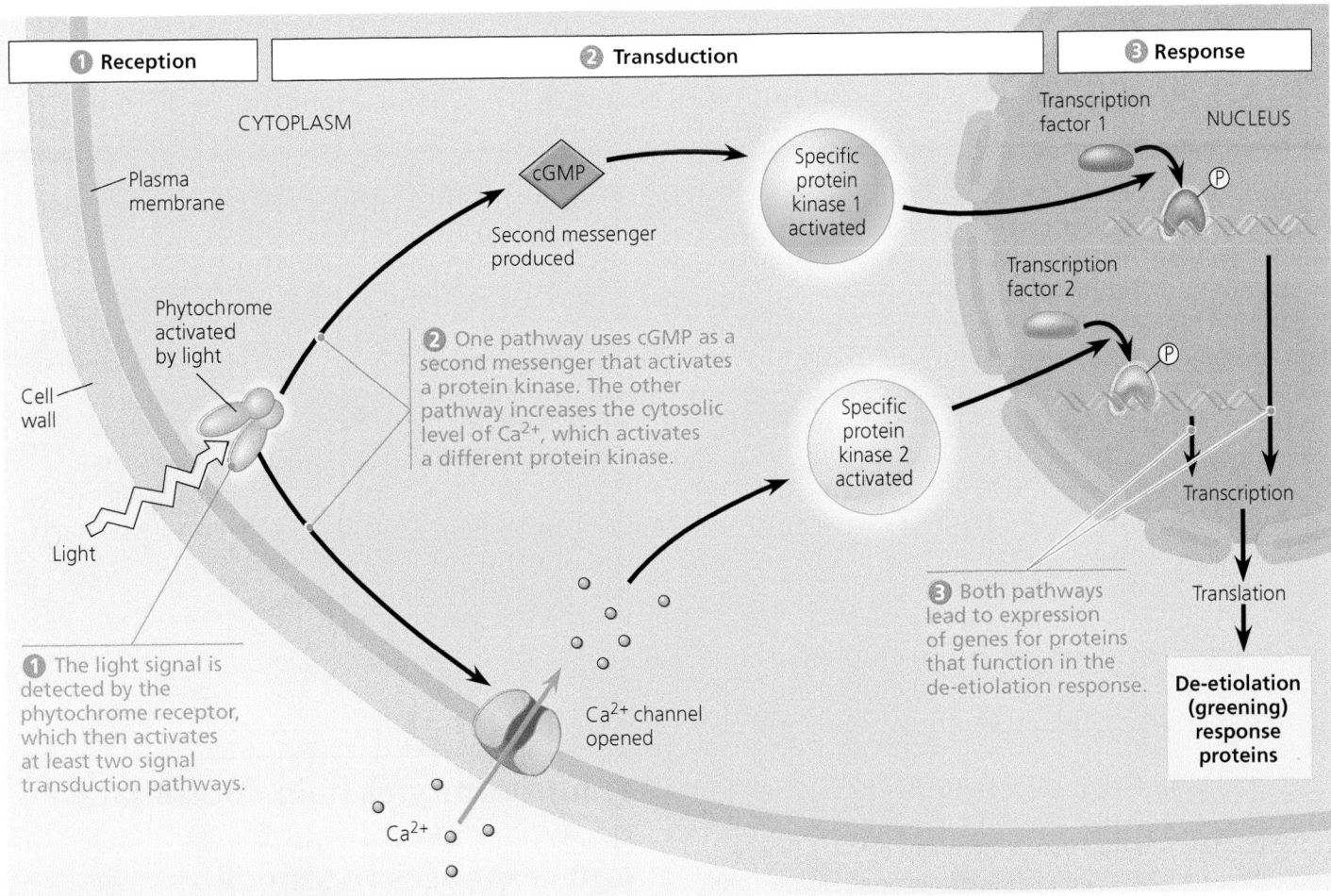

CYTOPLASM

Plasma membrane

cGMP

Second messenger produced

Specific protein kinase 1 activated

Transcription factor 1

NUCLEUS

Transcription factor 2

Phytochrome activated by light

② One pathway uses cGMP as a second messenger that activates a protein kinase. The other pathway increases the cytosolic level of Ca^{2+}, which activates a different protein kinase.

Cell wall

Specific protein kinase 2 activated

Light

① The light signal is detected by the phytochrome receptor, which then activates at least two signal transduction pathways.

③ Both pathways lead to expression of genes for proteins that function in the de-etiolation response.

Transcription

Translation

Ca^{2+} channel opened

De-etiolation (greening) response proteins

Ca^{2+}

▲ Figure 39.4 **An example of signal transduction in plants: the role of phytochrome in the de-etiolation (greening) response.**

MAKE CONNECTIONS *Which panel in Figure 11.18 (p. 222) best exemplifies the phytochrome-dependent signal transduction pathway during de-etiolation? Explain.*

Ca^{2+} levels. In response to light, phytochrome undergoes a change in shape that leads to the activation of guanylyl cyclase, an enzyme that produces the second messenger cyclic GMP. Both Ca^{2+} and cGMP must be produced for a complete de-etiolation response. The injection of cGMP into *aurea* tomato leaf cells, for example, induces only a partial de-etiolation response.

Response

Ultimately, second messengers regulate one or more cellular activities. In most cases, these responses involve the increased activity of particular enzymes. There are two main mechanisms by which a signaling pathway can enhance an enzymatic step in a biochemical pathway: post-translational modification and transcriptional regulation. Post-translational modification activates preexisting enzymes. Transcriptional regulation increases or decreases the synthesis of mRNA encoding a specific enzyme.

Post-Translational Modification of Preexisting Proteins

In most signal transduction pathways, preexisting proteins are modified by the phosphorylation of specific amino acids, which alters the protein's hydrophobicity and activity. Many second messengers, including cGMP and Ca^{2+}, activate protein kinases directly. Often, one protein kinase will phosphorylate another protein kinase, which then phosphorylates another, and so on (see Figure 11.10). Such kinase cascades may link initial stimuli to responses at the level of gene expression, usually via the phosphorylation of transcription factors. As we'll discuss on the next page, many signal transduction pathways ultimately regulate the synthesis of new proteins by turning specific genes on or off.

Signal transduction pathways must also have a means for turning off when the initial signal is no longer present, such as when a sprouting potato is put back into the cupboard. Protein phosphatases, which are enzymes that dephosphorylate specific proteins, are important in these "switch-off" processes. At any particular moment, a cell's functioning depends on the balance of activity of many types of protein kinases and protein phosphatases.

Transcriptional Regulation

As discussed in Chapter 18, the proteins we call *specific transcription factors* bind to specific regions of DNA and control the transcription of specific genes (see Figure 18.9). In the case of phytochrome-induced de-etiolation, several such transcription factors are activated by phosphorylation in response to the appropriate light conditions. The activation of some of these transcription factors depends on their phosphorylation by protein kinases activated by cGMP or Ca^{2+}.

The mechanism by which a signal promotes developmental changes may depend on transcription factors that are activators (which *increase* transcription of specific genes) or repressors (which *decrease* transcription) or both. For example, some *Arabidopsis* mutants, except for their pale color, have a light-grown morphology when grown in the dark; they have expanded leaves and short, sturdy stems but are not green because the final step in chlorophyll production requires light directly. These mutants have defects in a repressor that normally inhibits the expression of other genes that are activated by light. When the repressor is eliminated by mutation, the pathway that is normally blocked proceeds. Thus, these mutants appear to have been grown in the light, except for their pale color.

De-Etiolation ("Greening") Proteins

What types of proteins are either activated by phosphorylation or newly transcribed during the de-etiolation process? Many are enzymes that function in photosynthesis directly; others are enzymes involved in supplying the chemical precursors necessary for chlorophyll production; still others affect the levels of plant hormones that regulate growth. For example, the levels of auxin and brassinosteroids, hormones that enhance stem elongation, decrease following the activation of phytochrome. That decrease explains the slowing of stem elongation that accompanies de-etiolation.

We have discussed the signal transduction involved in the de-etiolation response of a potato plant in some detail to give you a sense of the complexity of biochemical changes that underlie this one process. Every plant hormone and every environmental stimulus triggers one or more signal transduction pathways of comparable complexity. As in the studies on the *aurea* mutant tomato, the isolation of mutants (a genetic approach) and techniques of molecular biology are helping researchers identify these various pathways. But this recent research builds on a long history of careful physiological and biochemical investigations

into how plants work. As you will read in the next section, classic experiments provided the first clues that transported signaling molecules called hormones are internal regulators of plant growth.

CONCEPT CHECK 39.1

1. What are the morphological differences between dark- and light-grown plants? Explain how etiolation helps a seedling compete successfully.
2. Cycloheximide is a drug that inhibits protein synthesis. Predict what effect cycloheximide would have on de-etiolation.
3. **WHAT IF?** The sexual dysfunction drug Viagra inhibits an enzyme that breaks down cyclic GMP. If tomato leaf cells have a similar enzyme, would applying Viagra to these cells cause a normal de-etiolation of *aurea* mutant tomato leaves?

For suggested answers, see Appendix A.

CONCEPT 39.2

Plant hormones help coordinate growth, development, and responses to stimuli

A **hormone**, in the original meaning of the term, is a signaling molecule that is produced in tiny amounts by one part of an organism's body and transported to other parts, where it binds to a specific receptor and triggers responses in target cells and tissues. In animals, hormones are usually transported through the circulatory system, a criterion often included in definitions of the term.

The hormone concept originated from studies of animals and was adopted by plant physiologists in the early 1900s. Many modern plant biologists, however, argue that it is too limiting to describe plant physiological processes using the narrow definitions established by animal physiologists. For example, plants don't have circulating blood to transport hormone-like signaling molecules. Moreover, some signaling molecules that are considered plant hormones act only locally. Finally, there are some signaling molecules in plants, such as sucrose, that typically occur in plants at concentrations that are hundreds of thousands times greater than a typical hormone. Nevertheless, they are transported through plants and activate signal transduction pathways that greatly alter the functioning of plants in a manner similar to a hormone. Thus, many plant biologists prefer the broader term *plant growth regulator* to describe organic compounds, either natural or synthetic, that modify or control one or more specific physiological processes within a plant.

At this point in time, the terms *plant hormone* and *plant growth regulator* are used about equally, but for historical continuity we will use the term *plant hormone* and adhere to the criterion that plant hormones are active at very low concentrations.

Virtually every aspect of plant growth and development is under hormonal control to some degree. A single hormone can regulate an amazingly diverse array of cellular and developmental processes. Conversely, multiple hormones can influence a single process.

The Discovery of Plant Hormones

The idea that chemical messengers exist in plants emerged from a series of classic experiments on how stems respond to light. As you know, the shoot of a houseplant on a windowsill grows toward light. Any growth response that results in plant organs curving toward or away from stimuli is called a **tropism** (from the Greek *tropos*, turn). The growth of a shoot toward light or away from it is called **phototropism**; the former is positive phototropism, and the latter is negative phototropism.

In natural ecosystems where plants may be crowded, phototropism directs shoot growth toward the sunlight that powers photosynthesis. This response results from a differential growth of cells on opposite sides of the shoot; the cells on the darker side elongate faster than the cells on the brighter side.

Charles Darwin and his son Francis conducted some of the earliest experiments on phototropism in the late 1800s (Figure 39.5). They observed that a grass seedling ensheathed in its coleoptile (see Figure 38.9b) could bend toward light only if the tip of the coleoptile was present. If the tip was removed, the coleoptile did not curve. The seedling also failed to grow toward light if the tip was covered with an opaque cap; but neither a transparent cap over the tip nor an opaque shield placed below the coleoptile tip prevented the phototropic response. It was the tip of the coleoptile, the Darwins concluded, that was responsible for sensing light. However, they noted that the differential growth response that led to curvature of the coleoptile occurred some distance below the tip. The Darwins postulated that some signal was transmitted downward from the tip to the elongating region of the coleoptile. A few decades later, the Danish scientist Peter Boysen-Jensen demonstrated that the signal was a mobile chemical substance. He separated the tip from the remainder of the coleoptile by a cube of gelatin, which prevented cellular contact but allowed chemicals to pass through. These seedlings responded normally, bending toward light. However, if the tip was experimentally separated from the lower coleoptile by an impermeable barrier, such as the mineral mica, no phototropic response occurred.

▼ Figure 39.5

What part of a grass coleoptile senses light, and how is the signal transmitted?

EXPERIMENT In 1880, Charles and Francis Darwin removed and covered parts of grass coleoptiles to determine what part senses light. In 1913, Peter Boysen-Jensen separated coleoptiles with different materials to determine how the signal for phototropism is transmitted.

RESULTS

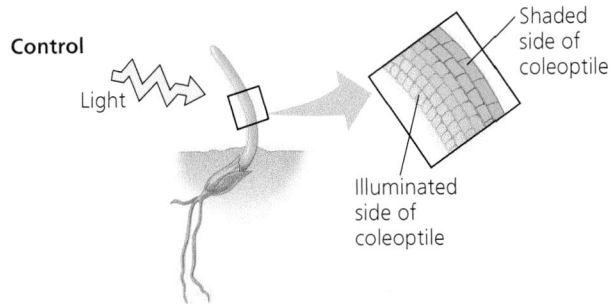

Darwin and Darwin: Phototropism occurs only when the tip is illuminated.

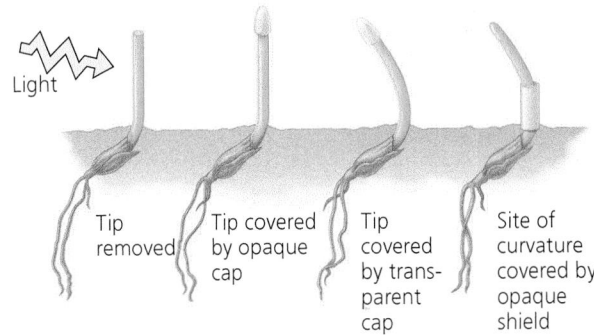

Boysen-Jensen: Phototropism occurs when the tip is separated by a permeable barrier but not an impermeable barrier.

CONCLUSION The Darwins' experiment suggested that only the tip of the coleoptile senses light. The phototropic bending, however, occurred at a distance from the site of light perception (the tip). Boysen-Jensen's results suggested that the signal for the bending is a light-activated mobile chemical.

SOURCE C. R. Darwin, *The power of movement in plants*, John Murray, London (1880). P. Boysen-Jensen, Concerning the performance of phototropic stimuli on the *Avena* coleoptile, *Berichte der Deutschen Botanischen Gesellschaft* (*Reports of the German Botanical Society*) 31:559–566 (1913).

WHAT IF? How could you experimentally determine which colors of light cause the most phototropic bending?

INQUIRY

Does asymmetrical distribution of a growth-promoting chemical cause a coleoptile to grow toward the light?

EXPERIMENT In 1926, Frits Went's experiment identified how a growth-promoting chemical causes a coleoptile to grow toward light. He placed coleoptiles in the dark and removed their tips, putting some tips on agar cubes that he predicted would absorb the growth-promoting chemical. On a control coleoptile, he placed a cube that lacked the chemical. On others, he placed cubes containing the chemical, either centered on top of the coleoptile to distribute the chemical evenly or offset to increase the concentration on one side.

RESULTS The coleoptile grew straight if the growth-promoting chemical was distributed evenly. If the chemical was distributed unevenly, the coleoptile curved away from the side with the cube, as if growing toward light, even though it was grown in the dark.

Excised tip placed on agar cube

Growth-promoting chemical diffuses into agar cube

Control (agar cube lacking chemical) has no effect

Agar cube with chemical stimulates growth

Control

Offset cubes cause curvature

CONCLUSION Went concluded that a coleoptile curves toward light because its dark side has a higher concentration of the growth-promoting chemical, which he named auxin.

SOURCE F. Went, A growth substance and growth, *Recueils des Travaux Botaniques Néerlandais* (*Collections of Dutch Botanical Works*) 25:1–116 (1928).

(MB) See the related Experimental Inquiry Tutorial in MasteringBiology.

WHAT IF? Triiodobenzoic acid (TIBA) inhibits auxin transport. If a tiny agar bead containing TIBA were placed off center on the tip of an intact coleoptile, which way would the coleoptile bend: toward the side with the bead or away from it? Explain.

In 1926, Frits Went, a Dutch graduate student, extracted the chemical messenger for phototropism by modifying the experiments of Boysen-Jensen (Figure 39.6). Went removed the coleoptile tip and placed it on a cube of agar, a gelatinous material. The chemical messenger from the tip, Went reasoned, should diffuse into the agar, and the agar block should then be able to substitute for the coleoptile tip. Went placed the agar blocks on decapitated coleoptiles that were kept in the dark. A block that was centered on top of the coleoptile caused the stem to grow straight upward. However, when the block was placed off center, the coleoptile began to bend away from the side with the agar block, as though growing toward light. Went concluded that the agar block contained a chemical produced in the coleoptile tip, that this chemical stimulated growth as it passed down the coleoptile, and that a coleoptile curved toward light because of a higher concentration of the growth-promoting chemical on the darker side of the coleoptile. For this chemical messenger, or hormone, Went chose the name auxin (from the Greek *auxein*, to increase). The major type of auxin was later purified, and its chemical structure was determined to be indoleacetic acid (IAA).

The classic hypothesis for what causes grass coleoptiles to grow toward light, based on the work of the Darwins, Boysen-Jensen, and Went, is that an asymmetrical distribution of auxin moving down from the coleoptile tip causes cells on the darker side to elongate faster than cells on the brighter side. But studies of phototropism in organs other than grass coleoptiles provide less support for this idea. There is no evidence that illumination from one side causes asymmetrical distribution of auxin in stems of sunflowers or other eudicots. There *is*, however, asymmetrical distribution of certain substances that may act as growth *inhibitors*, and these substances are more concentrated on the lighted side of a stem.

A Survey of Plant Hormones

The discovery of auxin stimulated the search for other plant hormones. Table 39.1 previews some major classes of plant hormones: auxin, cytokinins, gibberellins, brassinosteroids, abscisic acid, strigolactones, and ethylene. Many molecules in plants that function in defense against pathogens are probably plant hormones as well. (We'll discuss these molecules later in the chapter.)

Plant hormones are produced in very low concentrations, but a tiny amount of hormone can have a profound effect on the growth and development of a plant organ. Signal transduction pathways amplify the hormonal signal and connect it to a cell's specific responses. In general, hormones control plant growth and development by affecting the division, elongation, and differentiation of cells. Some hormones also mediate shorter-term physiological responses of plants to environmental stimuli. Each hormone has multiple effects,

Table 39.1 Overview of Plant Hormones

Hormone	Where Produced or Found in Plant	Major Functions
Auxin (IAA)	Shoot apical meristems and young leaves are the primary sites of auxin synthesis. Root apical meristems also produce auxin, although the root depends on the shoot for much of its auxin. Developing seeds and fruits contain high levels of auxin, but it is unclear whether it is newly synthesized or transported from maternal tissues.	Stimulates stem elongation (low concentration only); promotes the formation of lateral and adventitious roots; regulates development of fruit; enhances apical dominance; functions in phototropism and gravitropism; promotes vascular differentiation; retards leaf abscission.
Cytokinins	These are synthesized primarily in roots and transported to other organs, although there are many minor sites of production as well.	Regulate cell division in shoots and roots; modify apical dominance and promote lateral bud growth; promote movement of nutrients into sink tissues; stimulate seed germination; delay leaf senescence.
Gibberellins	Meristems of apical buds and roots, young leaves, and developing seeds are the primary sites of production.	Stimulate stem elongation, pollen development, pollen tube growth, fruit growth, and seed development and germination; regulate sex determination and the transition from juvenile to adult phases.
Brassinosteroids	These compounds are present in all plant tissues, although different intermediates predominate in different organs. Internally produced brassinosteroids act near the site of synthesis.	Promote cell expansion and cell division in shoots; promote root growth at low concentrations; inhibit root growth at high concentrations; promote xylem differentiation and inhibit phloem differentiation; promote seed germination and pollen tube elongation.
Abscisic acid (ABA)	Almost all plant cells have the ability to synthesize abscisic acid, and its presence has been detected in every major organ and living tissue; may be transported in the phloem or xylem.	Inhibits growth; promotes stomatal closure during drought stress; promotes seed dormancy and inhibits early germination; promotes leaf senescence; promotes desiccation tolerance.
Strigolactones	These carotenoid-derived hormones and extracellular signals are produced in roots in response to low phosphate conditions or high auxin flow from the shoot.	Promote seed germination, control of apical dominance, and the attraction of mycorrhizal fungi to the root.
Ethylene	This gaseous hormone can be produced by most parts of the plant. It is produced in high concentrations during senescence, leaf abscission, and the ripening of some types of fruits. Synthesis is also stimulated by wounding and stress.	Promotes ripening of many types of fruit, leaf abscission, and the triple response in seedlings (inhibition of stem elongation, promotion of lateral expansion, and horizontal growth); enhances the rate of senescence; promotes root and root hair formation; promotes flowering in the pineapple family.

depending on its site of action, its concentration, and the developmental stage of the plant.

Response to a hormone usually depends not so much on the amount of that hormone as on its relative concentration compared with other hormones. It is often the interactions between different hormones, rather than hormones acting in isolation, that control growth and development. These interactions will become apparent in the following survey of hormone function.

Auxin

The term **auxin** is used for any chemical substance that promotes elongation of coleoptiles, although auxins have multiple functions in flowering plants. The major natural auxin in plants is indoleacetic acid (IAA), although several other compounds, including some synthetic ones, have auxin activity.

(Unless mentioned otherwise, we will use the term *auxin* synonymously with IAA.) Although IAA was the first plant hormone to be discovered, much remains to be learned about auxin signal transduction and the regulation of auxin biosynthesis.

Auxin is produced predominantly in shoot tips and is transported from cell to cell down the stem at a rate of about 1 cm/hr. It moves only from tip to base, not in the reverse direction. This unidirectional transport of auxin is called *polar transport*.

Polar transport has nothing to do with gravity; experiments have shown that auxin travels upward when a stem or coleoptile segment is placed upside down. Rather, the polarity of auxin movement is attributable to the polar distribution of auxin transport protein in the cells. Concentrated at the basal end of a cell, the auxin transporters move the

▼ Figure 39.7

INQUIRY

What causes polar movement of auxin from shoot tip to base?

EXPERIMENT To investigate how auxin is transported unidirectionally, Leo Gälweiler and colleagues designed an experiment to identify the location of the auxin transport protein. They used a greenish yellow fluorescent molecule to label antibodies that bind to the auxin transport protein. Then they applied the antibodies to longitudinally sectioned *Arabidopsis* stems.

RESULTS The light micrograph on the left shows that auxin transport proteins are not found in all stem tissues, but only in the xylem parenchyma. In the light micrograph on the right, a higher magnification reveals that these proteins are primarily localized at the basal ends of the cells.

CONCLUSION The results support the hypothesis that concentration of the auxin transport protein at the basal ends of cells mediates the polar transport of auxin.

SOURCE L. Gälweiler et al., Regulation of polar auxin transport by AtPIN1 in *Arabidopsis* vascular tissue, *Science* 282:2226–2230 (1998).

WHAT IF? If auxin transport proteins were equally distributed at both ends of the cells, would polar auxin transport still be possible? Explain.

hormone out of the cell. The auxin can then enter the apical end of the neighboring cell **(Figure 39.7)**. Auxin has a variety of effects, including stimulating cell elongation and regulating plant architecture.

The Role of Auxin in Cell Elongation One of auxin's chief functions is to stimulate elongation of cells within young developing shoots. As auxin from the shoot apex moves down to the region of cell elongation (see Figure 35.16), the hormone stimulates cell growth, probably by binding to a receptor in the plasma membrane. Auxin stimulates growth only over a certain concentration range, from about 10^{-8} to 10^{-4} M. At higher concentrations, auxin may inhibit cell elongation, probably by inducing production of ethylene, a hormone that

generally hinders growth. We will return to this hormonal interaction when we discuss ethylene.

According to a model called the *acid growth hypothesis*, proton pumps play a major role in the growth response of cells to auxin. In a shoot's region of elongation, auxin stimulates the plasma membrane's proton (H^+) pumps. This pumping of H^+ increases the voltage across the membrane (membrane potential) and lowers the pH in the cell wall within minutes **(Figure 39.8)**. Acidification of the wall activates enzymes called **expansins** that break the cross-links (hydrogen bonds) between cellulose microfibrils and other cell wall constituents, loosening the wall's fabric. (Expansins can even weaken the integrity of filter paper made of pure cellulose.) Increasing the membrane potential enhances ion uptake into the cell, which causes osmotic uptake of water and increased turgor. Increased turgor and increased cell wall plasticity enable the cell to elongate.

Auxin also rapidly alters gene expression, causing cells in the region of elongation to produce new proteins within minutes. Some of these proteins are short-lived transcription factors that repress or activate the expression of other genes. For sustained growth after this initial spurt, cells must make more cytoplasm and wall material. Auxin also stimulates this sustained growth response.

Auxin's Role in Plant Development The polar transport of auxin is a central element controlling the spatial organization, or *pattern formation*, of the developing plant. As we will see, auxin plays a role in almost all aspects of plant pattern formation.

Auxin is synthesized in shoot tips, and it carries integrated information about the development, size, and environment of individual branches. This flow of information controls branching patterns. A reduced flow of auxin from a branch, for example, indicates that the branch is not being sufficiently productive: New branches are needed elsewhere. Thus, lateral buds below the branch are released from dormancy and begin to grow.

Auxin transport also plays a key role in establishing *phyllotaxy* (see Figure 36.3), the arrangement of leaves on the stem. A leading model proposes that polar auxin transport in the shoot apex generates local peaks in auxin concentration that determine the site of leaf primordium formation and thereby the different phyllotaxies found in nature.

The polar transport of auxin from the leaf margin also directs the patterns of leaf veins. Inhibitors of polar auxin transport result in leaves that lack vascular continuity through the petiole and have broad, loosely organized main veins, an increased number of secondary veins, and a dense band of irregularly shaped vascular cells adjacent to the leaf margin.

The activity of the vascular cambium, the meristem that produces woody tissues, is also under the control of auxin transport. When a plant becomes dormant at the end of a

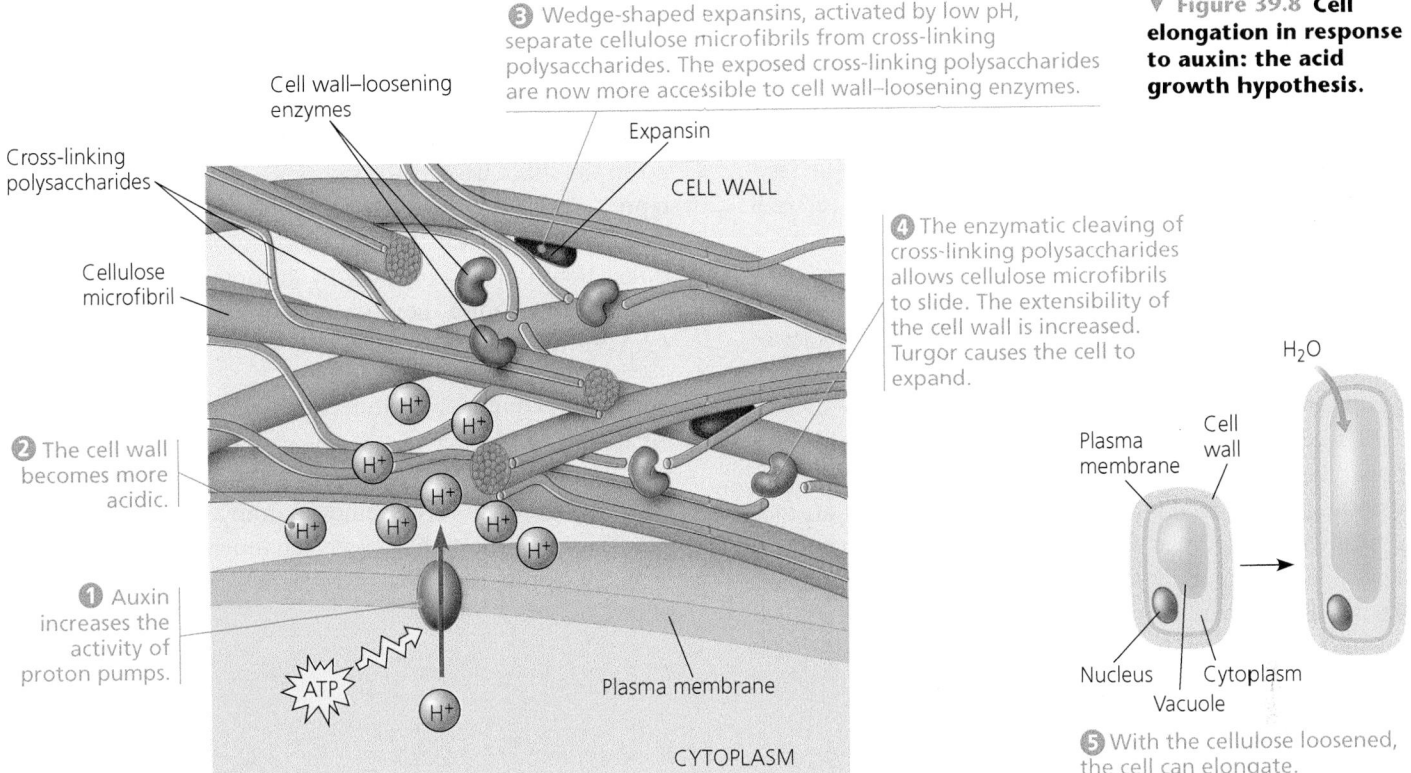

3 Wedge-shaped expansins, activated by low pH, separate cellulose microfibrils from cross-linking polysaccharides. The exposed cross-linking polysaccharides are now more accessible to cell wall–loosening enzymes.

▼ Figure 39.8 **Cell elongation in response to auxin: the acid growth hypothesis.**

Cell wall–loosening enzymes

Cross-linking polysaccharides

Cellulose microfibril

Expansin

CELL WALL

4 The enzymatic cleaving of cross-linking polysaccharides allows cellulose microfibrils to slide. The extensibility of the cell wall is increased. Turgor causes the cell to expand.

2 The cell wall becomes more acidic.

1 Auxin increases the activity of proton pumps.

ATP

H⁺

Plasma membrane

CYTOPLASM

H₂O

Plasma membrane

Cell wall

Nucleus

Cytoplasm

Vacuole

5 With the cellulose loosened, the cell can elongate.

growing season, there is a reduction in auxin transport capacity and the expression of genes encoding auxin transporters.

Auxin's effects on plant development are not limited to the familiar sporophyte plant that we see. Recent evidence suggests that the organization of the microscopic angiosperm female gametophytes is regulated by an auxin gradient.

Practical Uses for Auxins Auxins, both natural and synthetic, have many commercial applications. For example, the natural auxin indolebutyric acid (IBA) is used in the vegetative propagation of plants by cuttings. (The formation of lateral roots in intact plants is one case where IBA seems to be a more important auxin than IAA.) Treating a detached leaf or stem with powder containing IBA often causes adventitious roots to form near the cut surface.

Certain synthetic auxins, including 2,4-dichlorophenoxyacetic acid (2,4-D), are widely used as herbicides. Monocots, such as maize and turfgrass, can rapidly inactivate such synthetic auxins. However, eudicots cannot and therefore die from hormonal overdose. Spraying cereal fields or turf with 2,4-D eliminates eudicot (broadleaf) weeds.

Developing seeds produce auxin, which promotes fruit growth. In tomato plants grown in greenhouses, often fewer seeds are produced, resulting in poorly developed tomato fruits. However, spraying synthetic auxins on greenhouse-grown tomato vines induces normal fruit development, making the greenhouse-cultivated tomatoes commercially viable.

Cytokinins

Trial-and-error attempts to find chemical additives that would enhance the growth and development of plant cells in tissue culture led to the discovery of **cytokinins**. In the 1940s, researchers stimulated the growth of plant embryos in culture by adding coconut milk, the liquid endosperm of a coconut's giant seed. Subsequent researchers found that they could induce cultured tobacco cells to divide by adding degraded DNA samples. The active ingredients of both experimental additives turned out to be modified forms of adenine, a component of nucleic acids. These growth regulators were named cytokinins because they stimulate cytokinesis, or cell division. The most common natural cytokinin is zeatin, so named because it was discovered first in maize (*Zea mays*). Although much remains to be learned about cytokinin synthesis and signal transduction, the effects of cytokinins on cell division and differentiation, apical dominance, and aging are well documented.

Control of Cell Division and Differentiation Cytokinins are produced in actively growing tissues, particularly in roots, embryos, and fruits. Cytokinins produced in roots reach their target tissues by moving up the plant in the xylem sap. Acting in concert with auxin, cytokinins stimulate cell division and influence the pathway of differentiation. The effects of cytokinins on cells growing in tissue culture provide clues about how this class of hormones may function in an intact plant. When a piece of parenchyma tissue from a stem is cultured in the absence of cytokinins, the cells grow very large but do not divide. But if cytokinins are added along with auxin, the cells divide. Cytokinins alone have no effect. The ratio of cytokinins to auxin controls cell differentiation. When the concentrations of these two hormones are at certain levels, the mass of cells continues to grow, but it remains a cluster of undifferentiated cells called a callus (see Figure 38.14). If cytokinin levels increase, shoot buds develop from the callus. If auxin levels increase, roots form.

Control of Apical Dominance Cytokinins, auxin, and newly discovered plant hormones called strigolactones interact in the control of apical dominance, the ability of the apical bud to suppress the development of axillary buds (**Figure 39.9a**). Until recently, the leading hypothesis to explain the hormonal regulation of apical dominance—the direct inhibition hypothesis—proposed that auxin and cytokinins act antagonistically in regulating axillary bud growth. According to this view, auxin transported down the shoot from the apical bud directly inhibits axillary buds from growing, causing a shoot to lengthen at the expense of lateral branching. Meanwhile, cytokinins entering the shoot system from roots counter the action of auxin by signaling axillary buds to begin growing. Thus, the ratio of auxin and cytokinins was viewed as the critical factor in controlling axillary bud inhibition.

Many observations are consistent with the direct inhibition hypothesis. If the apical bud, the primary source of auxin, is removed, the inhibition of axillary buds is removed and the plant becomes bushier (**Figure 39.9b**). Applying auxin to the cut surface of the decapitated shoot resuppresses the growth of the lateral buds (**Figure 39.9c**). Mutants that overproduce cytokinins or plants treated with cytokinins also tend to be bushier than normal. It now appears, however, that auxin's effects are partially indirect. The polar flow of auxin down the shoot triggers the synthesis of strigolactones, which repress bud growth. Moreover, another signal, perhaps an electrical one, appears to cause buds to begin growing much earlier than can be explained by disrupted auxin flow. Thus, the control of apical dominance is much more complicated than previously thought.

Anti-Aging Effects Cytokinins slow the aging of certain plant organs by inhibiting protein breakdown, stimulating RNA and protein synthesis, and mobilizing nutrients from surrounding tissues. If leaves removed from a plant are dipped in a cytokinin solution, they stay green much longer than otherwise. Cytokinins also slow the progress of **apoptosis**, a type of programmed cell death.

Gibberellins

In the early 1900s, farmers in Asia noticed that some rice seedlings in their paddies grew so tall and spindly that they toppled over before they could mature. In 1926, it was discovered that a fungus of the genus *Gibberella* causes this "foolish seedling disease." By the 1930s, it was determined that the fungus causes hyperelongation of rice stems by secreting a chemical, which was given the name **gibberellin**. In the 1950s, researchers discovered that plants also produce gibberellins (GAs). Since that time, scientists have identified more than 100 different gibberellins that occur naturally in plants, although a much smaller number occur in each plant species. "Foolish rice" seedlings, it seems, suffer from too much gibberellin. Gibberellins have a variety of effects, such as stem elongation, fruit growth, and seed germination.

Stem Elongation The major sites of gibberellin production are young roots and leaves. Gibberellins are best known for stimulating stem and leaf growth by enhancing cell elongation *and* cell division. One hypothesis proposes that they activate enzymes that loosen cell walls, facilitating entry of expansin proteins. Thus, gibberellins act in concert with auxin to promote stem elongation.

The effects of gibberellins in enhancing stem elongation are evident when certain dwarf (mutant) varieties of plants are treated with gibberellins. For instance,

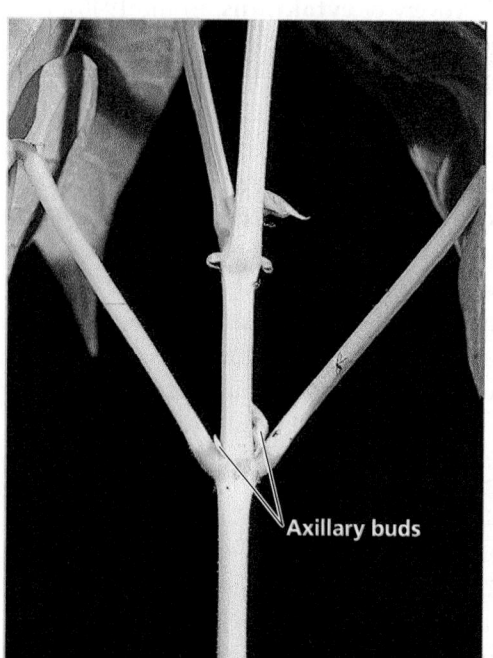

(a) Apical bud intact (not shown in photo)

Axillary buds

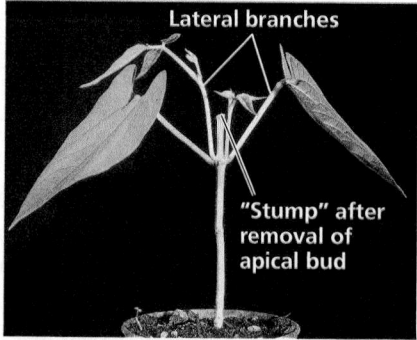

Lateral branches

"Stump" after removal of apical bud

(b) Apical bud removed

(c) Auxin added to decapitated stem

▲ **Figure 39.9 Apical dominance. (a)** The inhibition of growth of axillary buds, possibly influenced by auxin from the apical bud, favors elongation of the shoot's main axis. **(b)** Removal of the apical bud from the same plant enables lateral branches to grow. **(c)** Applying a gelatin capsule containing auxin to the stump prevents the lateral branches from growing.

(b) The Thompson seedless grape bunch on the left is from an untreated control vine. The bunch on the right is growing from a vine that was sprayed with gibberellin during fruit development.

(a) Some plants develop in a rosette form, low to the ground with very short internodes, as in the *Arabidopsis* plant shown at the left. As the plant switches to reproductive growth, a surge of gibberellins induces bolting: Internodes elongate rapidly, elevating floral buds that develop at stem tips (right).

◄ **Figure 39.10 Effects of gibberellins on stem elongation and fruit growth.**

some dwarf pea plants (including the variety Mendel studied; see Chapter 14) grow tall if treated with gibberellins. But there is often no response if the gibberellins are applied to wild-type plants. Apparently, these plants already produce an optimal dose of the hormone. The most dramatic example of gibberellin-induced stem elongation is *bolting*, rapid growth of the floral stalk **(Figure 39.10a)**.

Fruit Growth In many plants, both auxin and gibberellins must be present for fruit to develop. The most important commercial application of gibberellins is in the spraying of Thompson seedless grapes **(Figure 39.10b)**. The hormone makes the individual grapes grow larger, a trait valued by the consumer. The gibberellin sprays also make the internodes of the grape bunch elongate, allowing more space for the individual grapes. By enhancing air circulation between the grapes, this increase in space also makes it harder for yeasts and other microorganisms to infect the fruit.

Germination The embryo of a seed is a rich source of gibberellins. After water is imbibed, the release of gibberellins from the embryo signals the seed to break dormancy and germinate. Some seeds that normally require particular environmental conditions to germinate, such as exposure to light or low temperatures, break dormancy if they are treated with

gibberellins. Gibberellins support the growth of cereal seedlings by stimulating the synthesis of digestive enzymes such as α-amylase that mobilize stored nutrients **(Figure 39.11)**.

Brassinosteroids

Brassinosteroids are steroids similar to cholesterol and the sex hormones of animals. They induce cell elongation and division in stem segments and seedlings at concentrations as low as 10^{-12} *M*. They also slow leaf abscission (leaf drop) and promote xylem differentiation. These effects are so qualitatively similar to those of auxin that it took years for plant physiologists to determine that brassinosteroids were not types of auxins.

The identification of brassinosteroids as plant hormones arose from studies of an *Arabidopsis* mutant that exhibited morphological features similar to those of light-grown plants even when grown in the dark. The researchers discovered that the mutation affects a gene that normally codes for an enzyme similar to one involved in steroid synthesis in mammals. They also found that this brassinosteroid-deficient mutant could be restored to the wild-type phenotype by applying brassinosteroids.

Abscisic Acid

In the 1960s, one research group studying the chemical changes that precede bud dormancy and leaf abscission in deciduous trees and another team investigating chemical changes preceding abscission of cotton fruits isolated the same compound, **abscisic acid (ABA)**. Ironically, ABA is no longer thought to play a primary role in bud dormancy or leaf abscission, but it is very

1 After a seed imbibes water, the embryo releases gibberellin (GA), which sends a signal to the aleurone, the thin outer layer of the endosperm.

2 The aleurone responds to GA by synthesizing and secreting digestive enzymes that hydrolyze nutrients stored in the endosperm. One example is α-amylase, which hydrolyzes starch.

3 Sugars and other nutrients absorbed from the endosperm by the scutellum (cotyledon) are consumed during growth of the embryo into a seedling.

▲ **Figure 39.11 Mobilization of nutrients by gibberellins during the germination of grain seeds such as barley.**

important in other functions. Unlike the growth-stimulating hormones we have discussed so far—auxin, cytokinins, gibberellins, and brassinosteroids—ABA *slows* growth. ABA often antagonizes the actions of growth hormones, and the ratio of ABA to one or more growth hormones determines the final physiological outcome. We will consider here two of ABA's many effects: seed dormancy and drought tolerance.

Seed Dormancy Seed dormancy increases the likelihood that seeds will germinate only when there are sufficient amounts of light, temperature, and moisture for the seedlings to survive (see Chapter 38). What prevents seeds dispersed in autumn from germinating immediately, only to die in the winter? What mechanisms ensure that such seeds do not germinate until spring? For that matter, what prevents seeds from germinating in the dark, moist interior of the fruit? The answer to these questions is ABA. The levels of ABA may increase 100-fold during seed maturation. The high levels of ABA in maturing seeds inhibit germination and induce the production of proteins that help the seeds withstand the extreme dehydration that accompanies maturation.

Many types of dormant seeds germinate when ABA is removed or inactivated. The seeds of some desert plants break dormancy only when heavy rains wash ABA out of them. Other seeds require light or prolonged exposure to cold to inactivate ABA. Often, the ratio of ABA to gibberellins determines whether seeds remain dormant or germinate, and adding ABA to seeds that are primed to germinate makes them dormant again. Inactivated ABA or low levels of ABA can lead to precocious (early) germination **(Figure 39.12)**. For example, a maize mutant with grains that germinate while still on the cob lacks a functional transcription factor required for ABA to induce expression of certain genes. Precocious germination of red mangrove seeds, due to low ABA levels, is actually an adaptation that helps the young seedlings to plant themselves like darts in the soft mud below the parent tree.

Drought Tolerance ABA plays a major role in drought signaling. When a plant begins to wilt, ABA accumulates in the leaves and causes stomata to close rapidly, reducing transpiration and preventing further water loss. By affecting second messengers such as calcium, ABA causes potassium channels in the plasma membrane of guard cells to open, leading to a massive loss of potassium ions from the cells. The accompanying osmotic loss of water reduces guard cell turgor and leads to closing of the stomatal pores (see Figure 36.15). In some cases, water shortage stresses the root system before the shoot system, and ABA transported from roots to leaves may function as an "early warning system." Many mutants that are especially prone to wilting are deficient in ABA production.

Strigolactones

The hormones called **strigolactones** are upwardly mobile signals that stimulate seed germination, help establish

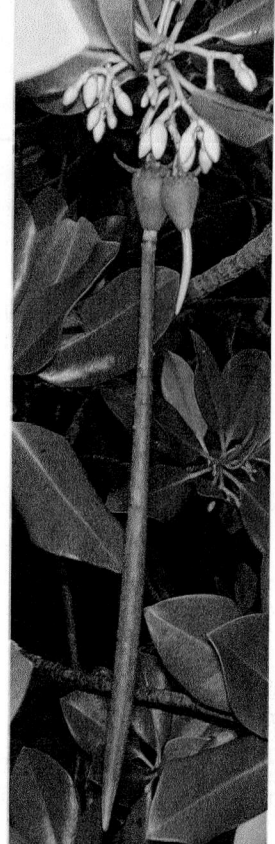

◄ Red mangrove (*Rhizophora mangle*) seeds produce only low levels of ABA, and their seeds germinate while still on the tree. In this case, early germination is a useful adaptation. When released, the radicle of the dart-like seedling deeply penetrates the soft mudflats in which the mangroves grow.

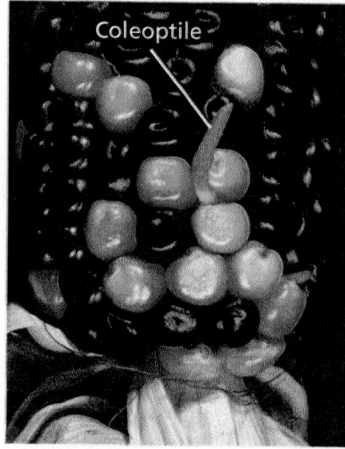

Coleoptile

▲ Precocious germination in this maize mutant is caused by lack of a functional transcription factor required for ABA action.

▲ **Figure 39.12 Precocious germination of wild-type mangrove and mutant maize seeds.**

mycorrhizal associations, and (as noted earlier) help control apical dominance. Their recent discovery relates back to studies of their namesake, *Striga*, a colorfully named genus of rootless parasitic plants that penetrate the roots of other plants, diverting essential nutrients from them and stunting their growth. (In Romanian legend, Striga is a vampire-like creature that lives for thousands of years, only needing to feed every 25 years or so.) Also known as witchweed, *Striga* may be the greatest obstacle to food production in Africa, infesting about two-thirds of the area devoted to cereal crops. Each *Striga* plant produces tens of thousands of tiny seeds that can remain dormant in the soil for many years until a suitable host begins to grow. Thus, *Striga* cannot be eradicated by growing non-grain crops for several years. Strigolactones, exuded by the host roots, were first identified as the chemical signals that stimulate the germination of *Striga* seeds.

Ethylene

During the 1800s, when coal gas was used as fuel for streetlights, leakage from gas pipes caused nearby trees to drop leaves prematurely. In 1901, the gas **ethylene** was demonstrated to be the active factor in coal gas. But the idea that it is a plant hormone was not widely accepted until the advent of a technique called gas chromatography simplified its identification.

Plants produce ethylene in response to stresses such as drought, flooding, mechanical pressure, injury, and infection. Ethylene is also produced during fruit ripening and programmed cell death and in response to high concentrations of externally applied auxin. Indeed, many effects previously ascribed to auxin, such as inhibition of root elongation, may be due to auxin-induced ethylene production. We will focus here on four of ethylene's many effects: response to mechanical stress, senescence, leaf abscission, and fruit ripening.

The Triple Response to Mechanical Stress Imagine a pea seedling pushing upward through the soil, only to come up against a stone. As it pushes against the obstacle, the stress in its delicate tip induces the seedling to produce ethylene. The hormone then instigates a growth maneuver known as the **triple response** that enables the shoot to avoid the obstacle. The three parts of this response are a slowing of stem elongation, a thickening of the stem (which makes it stronger), and a curvature that causes the stem to start growing horizontally. As the effects of the initial ethylene pulse lessen, the stem resumes vertical growth. If it again contacts a barrier, another burst of ethylene is released, and horizontal growth resumes. However, if the upward touch detects no solid object, then ethylene production decreases, and the stem, now clear of the obstacle, resumes its normal upward growth. It is ethylene that induces the stem to grow horizontally rather than the physical obstruction itself; when ethylene is applied to normal seedlings growing free of physical impediments, they still undergo the triple response (**Figure 39.13**).

Studies of *Arabidopsis* mutants with abnormal triple responses are an example of how biologists identify a signal transduction pathway. Scientists isolated ethylene-insensitive (*ein*) mutants, which fail to undergo the triple response after exposure to ethylene (**Figure 39.14a**). Some types of *ein* mutants are insensitive to ethylene because they lack a functional ethylene receptor. Mutants of a different sort undergo the triple response even out of soil, in the air, where there are no physical obstacles. Some of these mutants have a regulatory defect that causes them to produce ethylene at rates 20 times normal. The phenotype of such ethylene-overproducing (*eto*) mutants can be restored to wild-type by treating the seedlings with inhibitors of ethylene synthesis. Other mutants, called constitutive triple-response (*ctr*) mutants, undergo the triple response in air but do not respond to inhibitors of ethylene synthesis (**Figure 39.14b**). (Constitutive genes are genes that are continually expressed in all cells of an organism.) In *ctr* mutants, ethylene signal transduction is permanently turned on, even though ethylene is not present.

The affected gene in *ctr* mutants codes for a protein kinase. The fact that this mutation *activates* the ethylene response suggests that the normal kinase product of the wild-type allele is a *negative* regulator of ethylene signal transduction. Thus, binding of the hormone ethylene to the ethylene receptor normally leads to inactivation of the kinase; and the inactivation of this negative regulator allows synthesis of the proteins required for the triple response.

Senescence Consider the shedding of a leaf in autumn or the death of an annual after flowering. Or think about the final

▲ **Figure 39.13 The ethylene-induced triple response.** In response to ethylene, a gaseous plant hormone, germinating pea seedlings grown in the dark undergo the triple response—slowing of stem elongation, stem thickening, and horizontal stem growth. The response is greater with increased ethylene concentration.

Ethylene concentration (parts per million)

0.00 0.10 0.20 0.40 0.80

ein mutant

ctr mutant

(a) ***ein* mutant.** An ethylene-insensitive (*ein*) mutant fails to undergo the triple response in the presence of ethylene.

(b) ***ctr* mutant.** A constitutive triple-response (*ctr*) mutant undergoes the triple response even in the absence of ethylene.

▲ **Figure 39.14 Ethylene triple-response *Arabidopsis* mutants.**

step in differentiation of a vessel element, when its living contents are destroyed, leaving a hollow tube behind. Such events involve **senescence**—the programmed death of certain cells or organs or the entire plant. Cells, organs, and plants genetically programmed to die on a schedule do not simply shut down cellular machinery and await death. Instead, at the molecular level, the onset of the programmed cell death called apoptosis is a very busy time in a cell's life, requiring new gene expression (see pp. 223–225). During apoptosis, newly formed enzymes break down many chemical components, including chlorophyll, DNA, RNA, proteins, and membrane lipids. The plant salvages many of the breakdown products. A burst of ethylene is almost always associated with the apoptosis of cells during senescence.

Leaf Abscission The loss of leaves from deciduous trees helps prevent desiccation during seasonal periods of climatic stress that severely limit the availability of water to the roots. Before dying leaves abscise, many essential elements are salvaged from them and stored in stem parenchyma cells. These nutrients are recycled back to developing leaves the following spring. Autumn leaf color is due to newly made red pigments as well as yellow and orange carotenoids (see Chapter 10) that were already present in the leaf and are rendered visible by the breakdown of the dark green chlorophyll in autumn.

When an autumn leaf falls, the breaking point is an abscission layer that develops near the base of the petiole (**Figure 39.15**). The small parenchyma cells of this layer have very thin walls, and there are no fiber cells around the vascular tissue. The abscission layer is further weakened when enzymes hydrolyze polysaccharides in the cell walls. Finally, the weight of the leaf, with the help of the wind, causes a separation within the abscission layer. Even before the leaf falls, a

layer of cork forms a protective scar on the twig side of the abscission layer, preventing pathogens from invading the plant.

A change in the ratio of ethylene to auxin controls abscission. An aging leaf produces less and less auxin, rendering the cells of the abscission layer more sensitive to ethylene. As the influence of ethylene on the abscission layer prevails, the cells produce enzymes that digest the cellulose and other components of cell walls.

Fruit Ripening Immature fleshy fruits are generally tart, hard, and green—features that help protect the developing seeds from herbivores. After ripening, the mature fruits help *attract* animals that disperse the seeds (see Figures 30.8 and 30.9). In many cases, a burst of ethylene production in the fruit triggers the ripening process. The enzymatic breakdown of cell wall components softens the fruit, and the conversion of starches and acids to sugars makes the fruit sweet. The production of new scents and colors helps advertise ripeness to animals, which eat the fruits and disperse the seeds.

A chain reaction occurs during ripening: Ethylene triggers ripening, and ripening triggers more ethylene production. The result is a huge burst in ethylene production. Because ethylene is a gas, the signal to ripen spreads from fruit to fruit. If you pick or buy green fruit, you may be able to speed ripening by storing the fruit in a paper bag, allowing ethylene to accumulate. On a commercial scale, many kinds of fruits are ripened in huge storage containers in which ethylene levels are enhanced. In other cases, fruit producers take measures to slow ripening caused by natural ethylene. Apples, for instance, are stored in bins flushed with carbon dioxide. Circulating the air prevents ethylene from accumulating, and carbon dioxide inhibits synthesis of new ethylene. Stored in this way, apples picked in autumn can still be shipped to grocery stores the following summer.

Given the importance of ethylene in the postharvest physiology of fruits, the genetic engineering of ethylene signal transduction pathways has potential commercial applications. For example, by engineering a way to block the transcription of one of the genes required for ethylene synthesis, molecular biologists have created tomato fruits that ripen on demand. These fruits are picked while green and will not ripen unless ethylene gas is added. As such methods are refined, they will reduce spoilage of fruits and vegetables, a problem that ruins almost half the produce harvested in the United States.

Systems Biology and Hormone Interactions

As we have discussed, plant responses often involve the interactions of many hormones and their signal transduction pathways. The study of hormone interactions can be a complex problem. For example, as you saw in the description of apical dominance, the growth of lateral buds is controlled by cross-talk between the signal transduction pathways triggered by cytokinins, auxin, and strigolactones. Imagine yourself as a

0.5 mm

Protective layer — Abscission layer
Stem — Petiole

▲ **Figure 39.15 Abscission of a maple leaf.** Abscission is controlled by a change in the ratio of ethylene to auxin. The abscission layer is seen in this longitudinal section as a vertical band at the base of the petiole. After the leaf falls, a protective layer of cork becomes the leaf scar that helps prevent pathogens from invading the plant (LM).

molecular biologist assigned the task of genetically engineering a bushier plant phenotype. Would the best molecular target for genetic manipulation be an enzyme that inactivates IAA? An enzyme that produces more cytokinin? A strigolactone receptor? It is difficult to predict. And this is by no means an unusual problem. Virtually every plant response discussed in this chapter is of comparable complexity. Because of the pervasive nature of complex interactions in plant physiology, many plant biologists are promoting a new, systems-based approach to plant biology.

In Chapter 1, we provided a general description of systems biology, which attempts to discover and understand biological properties that emerge from the interactions of many system elements (for example, mRNAs, proteins, hormones, and metabolites). Using genomic techniques, biologists can now identify all the genes in a plant. The genomes of many plant species have now been sequenced, including *Arabidopsis*, rice, grape, maize, and poplar trees. Moreover, using microarray and proteomic techniques (see Chapters 20 and 21), scientists can determine which genes are activated or inactivated during development or in response to an environmental change. However, simply identifying all the genes and proteins (system elements) in an organism is comparable to listing all the parts of an airplane. Although such a list provides a catalog of components, it is not sufficient for understanding the complexity underlying the integrated system. What plant biologists really need to know is how all these system elements interact.

A systems-based approach may greatly alter how plants are studied. One vision is laboratories equipped with high-throughput robotic scanners that record which genes in a plant's genome are activated in which cells and under what conditions. New hypotheses and avenues of research will emerge from analysis of these comprehensive data sets. Ultimately, one goal of systems biology is to model an entire living plant. Armed with such detailed knowledge, a biologist attempting to genetically engineer a bushier plant could proceed much more efficiently. The ability to model a living plant could make it possible to predict the result of a genetic manipulation before setting foot in the laboratory.

CONCEPT CHECK 39.2

1. Suggest a reason why cut flowers such as carnations are often treated with cytokinins prior to shipping.
2. Fusicoccin is a fungal toxin that stimulates the plasma membrane H$^+$ pumps of plant cells. How may it affect the growth of isolated stem sections?
3. **WHAT IF?** If a plant has the double mutation *ctr* and *ein*, what is its triple-response phenotype? Explain your answer.
4. **MAKE CONNECTIONS** What type of feedback process is exemplified by the production of ethylene during fruit ripening? Explain. (See Figure 1.13, on p. 11.)

For suggested answers, see Appendix A.

CONCEPT 39.3

Responses to light are critical for plant success

Light is an especially important environmental factor in the lives of plants. In addition to being required for photosynthesis, light triggers many key events in plant growth and development. The effects of light on plant morphology are called **photomorphogenesis**. Light reception also allows plants to measure the passage of days and seasons.

Plants detect not only the presence of light but also its direction, intensity, and wavelength (color). As you saw in Figure 10.10b for photosynthesis, a graph called an **action spectrum** depicts the relative effectiveness of different wavelengths of radiation in driving a particular process. Action spectra are useful in studying *any* process that depends on light, including phototropism (**Figure 39.16**). By comparing action spectra of various plant responses, researchers determine which responses are mediated by the same photoreceptor (pigment).

(a) This action spectrum illustrates that only light wavelengths below 500 nm (blue and violet light) induce curvature.

(b) These photographs of coleoptiles were taken before and after 90-minute exposures to light sources of the colors indicated.

▲ **Figure 39.16 Action spectrum for blue-light-stimulated phototropism in maize coleoptiles.** Phototropic bending toward light is controlled by phototropin, a photoreceptor sensitive to blue and violet light, particularly blue light.

They also compare action spectra with absorption spectra of pigments; a close correspondence for a given pigment suggests that the pigment is the photoreceptor mediating the response. Action spectra reveal that red and blue light are the most important colors in regulating a plant's photomorphogenesis. These observations led researchers to two major classes of light receptors: **blue-light photoreceptors** and **phytochromes**, photoreceptors that absorb mostly red light.

Blue-Light Photoreceptors

Blue light initiates a variety of responses in plants, including phototropism, the light-induced opening of stomata (see Figure 36.14), and the light-induced slowing of hypocotyl elongation that occurs when a seedling breaks ground. The biochemical identity of the blue-light photoreceptor was so elusive that in the 1970s, plant physiologists began to call this receptor "cryptochrome" (from the Greek *kryptos*, hidden, and *chrom*, pigment). In the 1990s, molecular biologists analyzing *Arabidopsis* mutants found that plants use as many as three different types of pigments to detect blue light. *Cryptochromes*, molecular relatives of DNA repair enzymes, are involved in the blue-light-induced inhibition of stem elongation that occurs, for example, when a seedling first emerges from the soil. *Phototropin* is a protein kinase involved in mediating phototropic curvatures, such as those studied in grass seedlings by the Darwins, and in chloroplast movements in response to light. There is currently much debate about whether phototropin or a carotenoid-based photoreceptor called *zeaxanthin* is the major blue-light photoreceptor involved in blue-light-mediated stomatal opening.

Phytochromes as Photoreceptors

When introducing signal transduction in plants earlier in the chapter, we discussed the role of the plant pigments called phytochromes in the de-etiolation process. Phytochromes regulate many plant responses to light. Let's look at two more examples: seed germination and shade avoidance.

Phytochromes and Seed Germination

Studies of seed germination led to the discovery of phytochromes. Because of limited nutrient reserves, many types of seeds, especially small ones, germinate only when the light environment and other conditions are near optimal. Such seeds often remain dormant for years until light conditions change. For example, the death of a shading tree or the plowing of a field may create a favorable light environment.

In the 1930s, scientists at the U.S. Department of Agriculture determined the action spectrum for light-induced germination of lettuce seeds. They exposed water-swollen seeds to a few minutes of monochromatic (single-colored) light of various wavelengths and then stored the seeds in the dark. After two days, the researchers counted the

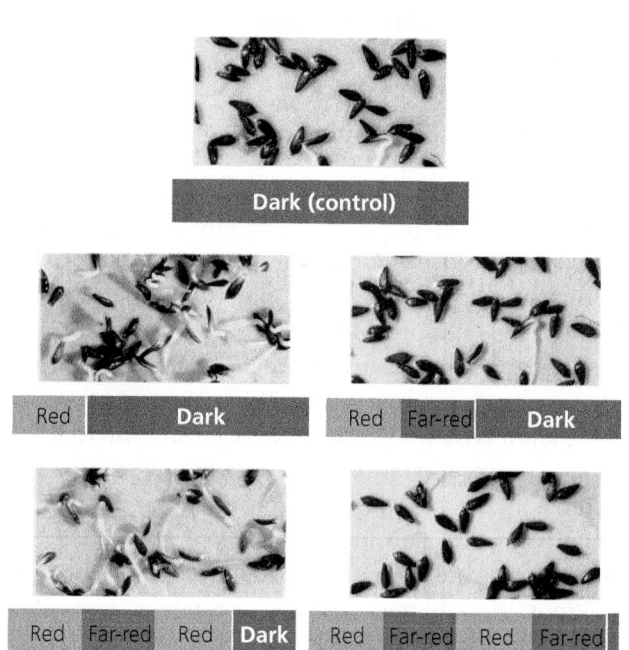

▼ **Figure 39.17**   **INQUIRY**

How does the order of red and far-red illumination affect seed germination?

EXPERIMENT Scientists at the U.S. Department of Agriculture briefly exposed batches of lettuce seeds to red light or far-red light to test the effects on germination. After the light exposure, the seeds were placed in the dark, and the results were compared with control seeds that were not exposed to light.

RESULTS The bar below each photo indicates the sequence of red light exposure, far-red light exposure, and darkness. The germination rate increased greatly in groups of seeds that were last exposed to red light (left). Germination was inhibited in groups of seeds that were last exposed to far-red light (right).

CONCLUSION Red light stimulates germination, and far-red light inhibits germination. The final light exposure is the determining factor. The effects of red and far-red light are reversible.

SOURCE H. Borthwick et al., A reversible photoreaction controlling seed germination, *Proceedings of the National Academy of Sciences, USA* 38:662–666 (1952).

WHAT IF? Phytochrome responds faster to red light than to far-red. If the seeds had been placed in white light instead of the dark after their red and far-red light treatments, would the results have been different?

number of seeds that had germinated under each light regimen. They found that red light of wavelength 660 nm increased the germination percentage of lettuce seeds maximally, whereas far-red light—that is, light of wavelengths near the upper edge of human visibility (730 nm)—*inhibited* germination compared with dark controls (**Figure 39.17**). What happens when the lettuce seeds are subjected to a flash of red light followed by a flash of far-red light or, conversely, to far-red light followed by red

Two identical subunits. Each subunit has two domains.

Chromophore

Photoreceptor activity. In each subunit, one domain, which functions as the photoreceptor, is covalently bonded to a nonprotein pigment, or chromophore.

Kinase activity. The other domain has protein kinase activity. The photoreceptor domains interact with the kinase domains, linking light reception to cellular responses triggered by the kinase.

▲ Figure 39.18 **Structure of a phytochrome.**

light? The *last* flash of light determines the seeds' response: The effects of red and far-red light are reversible.

The photoreceptors responsible for the opposing effects of red and far-red light are phytochromes. A phytochrome has two identical subunits, each consisting of a polypeptide component covalently bonded to a nonpolypeptide *chromophore*, the light-absorbing part of the subunit (**Figure 39.18**). So far, researchers have identified five phytochromes in *Arabidopsis*, each with a slightly different polypeptide component.

The chromophore of a phytochrome is photoreversible, reverting back and forth between two isomeric forms, depending on the color of light provided (see Figure 4.7 to review isomers). In its P_r isomer form, a phytochrome absorbs red (r) light maximally, whereas in its P_{fr} isomer form, it absorbs far-red (fr) light:

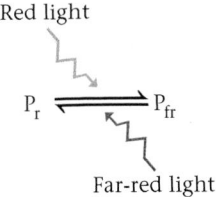

Red light

$$P_r \rightleftarrows P_{fr}$$

Far-red light

▶ Figure 39.19 **Phytochrome: a molecular switching mechanism.** Absorption of red light causes the P_r to change to the P_{fr}. Far-red light reverses this conversion. In most cases, it is the P_{fr} form of the pigment that switches on physiological and developmental responses in the plant.

This $P_r \longleftrightarrow P_{fr}$ interconversion is a switching mechanism that controls various light-induced events in the life of the plant (**Figure 39.19**). P_{fr} is the form of phytochrome that triggers many of a plant's developmental responses to light. For example, P_r in lettuce seeds exposed to red light is converted to P_{fr}, stimulating the cellular responses that lead to germination. When red-illuminated seeds are then exposed to far-red light, the P_{fr} is converted back to P_r, inhibiting the germination response.

How does phytochrome switching explain light-induced germination in nature? Plants synthesize phytochrome as P_r, and if seeds are kept in the dark, the pigment remains almost entirely in the P_r form (see Figure 39.19). Sunlight contains both red light and far-red light, but the conversion to P_{fr} is faster than the conversion to P_r. Therefore, the ratio of P_{fr} to P_r increases in the sunlight. When seeds are exposed to adequate sunlight, the production and accumulation of P_{fr} will trigger their germination.

Phytochromes and Shade Avoidance

The phytochrome system also provides the plant with information about the *quality* of light. Because sunlight includes both red and far-red radiation, during the day the $P_r \longleftrightarrow P_{fr}$ interconversion reaches a dynamic equilibrium, with the ratio of the two phytochrome forms indicating the relative amounts of red and far-red light. This sensing mechanism enables plants to adapt to changes in light conditions. Consider, for example, the "shade avoidance" response of a tree that requires relatively high light intensity. If other trees in a forest shade this tree, the phytochrome ratio shifts in favor of P_r because the forest canopy screens out more red light than far-red light. This is because the chlorophyll pigments in the leaves of the canopy absorb red light and allow far-red light to pass. The shift in the ratio of red to far-red light induces the tree to allocate more of its resources to growing taller. In contrast, direct sunlight increases the proportion of P_{fr}, which stimulates branching and inhibits vertical growth.

In addition to helping plants detect light, phytochrome helps a plant keep track of the passage of days and seasons. To understand phytochrome's role in these timekeeping processes, we must first examine the nature of the plant's internal clock.

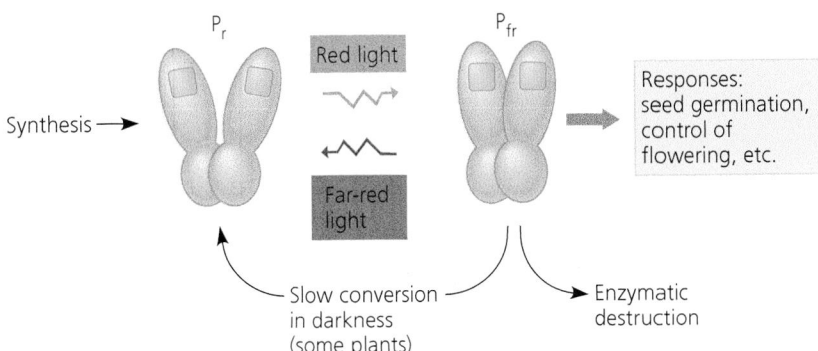

P_r P_{fr}

Red light

Far-red light

Synthesis →

Responses: seed germination, control of flowering, etc.

Slow conversion in darkness (some plants)

Enzymatic destruction

Biological Clocks and Circadian Rhythms

Many plant processes, such as transpiration and the synthesis of certain enzymes, undergo a daily oscillation. Some of these cyclic variations are responses to the changes in light levels, temperature, and relative humidity that accompany the 24-hour cycle of day and night. We can control these external factors by growing plants in growth chambers under rigidly maintained conditions of light, temperature, and humidity. But even under artificially constant conditions, many physiological processes in plants, such as the opening and closing of stomata and the production of photosynthetic enzymes, continue to oscillate with a frequency of about 24 hours. For example, many legumes lower their leaves in the evening and raise them in the morning (**Figure 39.20**). A bean plant continues these "sleep movements" even if kept in constant light or constant darkness; the leaves are not simply responding to sunrise and sunset. Such cycles, with a frequency of about 24 hours and not directly controlled by any known environmental variable, are called **circadian rhythms** (from the Latin *circa*, approximately, and *dies*, day).

Recent research supports the idea that the molecular "gears" of the circadian clock really are internal and not a daily response to some subtle but pervasive environmental cycle, such as geomagnetism or cosmic radiation. Organisms, including plants and humans, continue their rhythms even when placed in deep mine shafts or when orbited in satellites, conditions that alter these subtle geophysical periodicities. However, daily signals from the environment can entrain (set) the circadian clock to a period of precisely 24 hours.

If an organism is kept in a constant environment, its circadian rhythms deviate from a 24-hour period (a period is the duration of one cycle). These free-running periods, as they are called, vary from about 21 to 27 hours, depending on the particular rhythmic response. The sleep movements of bean plants, for instance, have a period of 26 hours when the plants are kept in the free-running condition of constant darkness. Deviation of the free-running period from exactly

24 hours does not mean that biological clocks drift erratically. Free-running clocks are still keeping perfect time, but they are not synchronized with the outside world. To understand the mechanisms underlying circadian rhythms, we must distinguish between the clock and the rhythmic processes it controls. For example, the leaves of the bean plant in Figure 39.20 are the clock's "hands" but are not the essence of the clock itself. If bean leaves are restrained for several hours and then released, they will reestablish the position appropriate for the time of day. We can interfere with a biological rhythm, but the underlying clockwork continues to tick.

At the heart of the molecular mechanisms underlying circadian rhythms are oscillations in the transcription of certain genes. The monitoring of *Arabidopsis* over a 24-hour cycle revealed that approximately 5% of its mRNAs undergo a circadian rhythm in synthesis. Some of these mRNAs are more abundant at dawn, others at dusk, and some in the middle of the day. Mathematical models propose that the 24-hour period arises from negative-feedback loops involving the transcription of a few central "clock genes." Some clock genes may encode transcription factors that inhibit, after a time delay, the transcription of the gene that encodes the transcription factor itself. Such negative-feedback loops, together with a time delay, are enough to produce oscillations.

Researchers have recently used a novel technique to identify clock mutants of *Arabidopsis*. One prominent circadian rhythm in plants is the daily production of certain photosynthesis-related proteins. Molecular biologists traced the source of this rhythm to the promoter that initiates the transcription of the genes for these photosynthesis proteins. To identify clock mutants, scientists spliced the gene for an enzyme responsible for the bioluminescence of fireflies, called luciferase, to the promoter. When the biological clock turned on the promoter in the *Arabidopsis* genome, it also turned on the production of luciferase. The plants began to glow with a circadian periodicity. Clock mutants were then isolated by selecting specimens that glowed for a longer or shorter time than normal. The genes altered in some of these mutants affect proteins that normally bind photoreceptors. Perhaps these particular mutations disrupt a light-dependent mechanism that sets the biological clock.

The Effect of Light on the Biological Clock

As we have discussed, the free-running period of the circadian rhythm of bean leaf movements is 26 hours. Consider a bean plant placed at dawn in a dark cabinet for 72 hours: Its leaves would not rise again until 2 hours after natural dawn on the second day, 4 hours after natural dawn on the third day, and so on. Shut off from environmental cues, the plant becomes desynchronized. Desynchronization happens to humans when we fly across several time zones; when we reach our destination, the clocks on the wall are not synchronized with our internal clocks. Most organisms are probably prone to jet lag.

Noon   Midnight

▲ **Figure 39.20 Sleep movements of a bean plant (*Phaseolus vulgaris*).** The movements are caused by reversible changes in the turgor pressure of cells on opposing sides of the pulvini, motor organs of the leaf.

The factor that entrains the biological clock to precisely 24 hours every day is light. Both phytochromes and blue-light photoreceptors can entrain circadian rhythms in plants, but our understanding of how phytochromes do this is more complete. The mechanism involves turning cellular responses on and off by means of the $P_r \longleftrightarrow P_{fr}$ switch.

Consider again the photoreversible system in Figure 39.19. In darkness, the phytochrome ratio shifts gradually in favor of the P_r form, partly as a result of turnover in the overall phytochrome pool. The pigment is synthesized in the P_r form, and enzymes destroy more P_{fr} than P_r. In some plant species, P_{fr} present at sundown slowly converts to P_r. In darkness, there is no means for the P_r to be reconverted to P_{fr}, but upon illumination, the P_{fr} level suddenly increases again as P_r is rapidly converted. This increase in P_{fr} each day at dawn resets the biological clock: Bean leaves reach their most extreme night position 16 hours after dawn.

In nature, interactions between phytochrome and the biological clock enable plants to measure the passage of night and day. The relative lengths of night and day, however, change over the course of the year (except at the equator). Plants use this change to adjust activities in synchrony with the seasons.

Photoperiodism and Responses to Seasons

Imagine the consequences if a plant produced flowers when pollinators were not present or if a deciduous tree produced leaves in the middle of winter. Seasonal events are of critical importance in the life cycles of most plants. Seed germination, flowering, and the onset and breaking of bud dormancy are all stages that usually occur at specific times of the year. The environmental stimulus that plants use most often to detect the time of year is the photoperiod, the relative lengths of night and day. A physiological response to photoperiod, such as flowering, is called **photoperiodism.**

Photoperiodism and Control of Flowering

An early clue to how plants detect seasons came from a mutant variety of tobacco, Maryland Mammoth, which grew tall but failed to flower during summer. It finally bloomed in a greenhouse in December. After trying to induce earlier flowering by varying temperature, moisture, and mineral nutrition, researchers learned that the shortening days of winter stimulated this variety to flower. If the plants were kept in light-tight boxes so that lamps could manipulate "day" and "night," flowering occurred only if the day length was 14 hours or shorter. It did not flower during summer because at Maryland's latitude, the summer days were too long.

The researchers called Maryland Mammoth a **short-day plant** because it apparently required a light period *shorter* than a critical length to flower. Chrysanthemums, poinsettias, and some soybean varieties are also short-day plants, which generally flower in late summer, fall, or winter. Another group of plants flower only when the light period is *longer* than a certain number of hours. These **long-day plants** generally flower in late spring or early summer. Spinach, for example, flowers when days are 14 hours or longer. Radishes, lettuce, irises, and many cereal varieties are also long-day plants. **Day-neutral plants**, such as tomatoes, rice, and dandelions, are unaffected by photoperiod and flower when they reach a certain stage of maturity, regardless of day length.

Critical Night Length In the 1940s, researchers learned that flowering and other responses to photoperiod are actually controlled by night length, not day length. Many of these scientists worked with cocklebur (*Xanthium strumarium*), a short-day plant that flowers only when days are 16 hours or shorter (and nights are at least 8 hours long). These researchers found that if the light portion of the photoperiod is broken by a brief exposure to darkness, flowering proceeds. However, if the dark part of the photoperiod is interrupted by even a few minutes of dim light, cocklebur will not flower, and this turned out to be true for other short-day plants as well **(Figure 39.21a)**. Cocklebur is unresponsive to day length, but it requires at least 8 hours of continuous darkness to flower. Short-day plants are really long-night plants, but the older term is embedded firmly in the lexicon of plant physiology. Similarly, long-day plants are actually short-night plants. A long-day plant grown on photoperiods of long nights that would not normally induce flowering will flower if the period of continuous darkness is interrupted by a few minutes of light **(Figure 39.21b)**. Notice that we distinguish long-day from short-day plants *not* by an absolute night length but by whether the critical night length sets a maximum

(a) **Short-day (long-night) plant.** Flowers when night exceeds a critical dark period. A flash of light interrupting the dark period prevents flowering.

(b) **Long-day (short-night) plant.** Flowers only if the night is shorter than a critical dark period. A brief flash of light artificially interrupts a long dark period, thereby inducing flowering.

▲ **Figure 39.21 Photoperiodic control of flowering.**

(long-day plants) or minimum (short-day plants) number of hours of darkness required for flowering. In both cases, the actual number of hours in the critical night length is specific to each species of plant.

Red light is the most effective color in interrupting the nighttime portion of the photoperiod. Action spectra and photoreversibility experiments show that phytochrome is the pigment that detects the red light (Figure 39.22). For example, if a flash of red (R) light during the dark period is followed by a flash of far-red (FR) light, then the plant detects no interruption of night length. As in the case of phytochrome-mediated seed germination, red/far-red photoreversibility occurs.

Plants detect night length very precisely; some short-day plants will not flower if night is even 1 minute shorter than the critical length. Some plant species always flower on the same day each year. It appears that plants use their biological clock, entrained by night length with the help of phytochrome, to tell the season of the year. The floriculture (flower-growing) industry applies this knowledge to produce flowers out of season. Chrysanthemums, for instance, are short-day plants that normally bloom in fall, but their blooming can be stalled until Mother's Day in May by punctuating each long night with a flash of light, thus turning one long night into two short nights.

Some plants bloom after a single exposure to the photoperiod required for flowering. Other species need several successive days of the appropriate photoperiod. Still others respond to a photoperiod only if they have been previously exposed to some other environmental stimulus, such as a period of cold. Winter wheat, for example, will not flower unless it has been exposed to several weeks of temperatures below 10°C. The use of pretreatment with cold to induce flowering is called **vernalization** (from the Latin for "spring"). Several weeks after winter wheat is vernalized, a photoperiod with long days (short nights) induces flowering.

A Flowering Hormone?

Although flowers form from apical or axillary bud meristems, it is leaves that detect changes in photoperiod and produce signaling molecules that cue buds to develop as flowers. In many short-day and long-day plants, exposing just one leaf to the appropriate photoperiod is enough to induce flowering. Indeed, as long as one leaf is left on the plant, photoperiod is detected and floral buds are induced. If all leaves are removed, the plant is insensitive to photoperiod.

Classic experiments revealed that the floral stimulus could move across a graft from an induced plant to a noninduced plant and trigger flowering in the latter. Moreover, the flowering stimulus appears to be the same for short-day and long-day plants, despite the different photoperiodic conditions required for leaves to send this signal (Figure 39.23). The hypothetical signaling molecule for flowering, called **florigen**, remained unidentified for over 70 years as scientists focused on small hormone-like molecules. However, as discussed in Chapter 36, large macromolecules, such as mRNA and proteins, can move

▲ **Figure 39.22 Reversible effects of red and far-red light on photoperiodic response.** A flash of red (R) light shortens the dark period. A subsequent flash of far-red (FR) light cancels the red flash's effect.

? *How would a single flash of full-spectrum light affect each plant?*

▲ **Figure 39.23 Experimental evidence for a flowering hormone.** If grown individually under short-day conditions, a short-day plant will flower and a long-day plant will not. However, both will flower if grafted together and exposed to short days. This result indicates that a flower-inducing substance (florigen) is transmitted across grafts and induces flowering in both short-day and long-day plants.

WHAT IF? *If flowering were inhibited in both parts of the grafted plants, what would you conclude?*

by the symplastic route via plasmodesmata (see Figure 36.6) and regulate plant development. It now appears that florigen is a macromolecule. A gene called *FLOWERING LOCUS T* (*FT*) is activated in leaf cells during conditions favoring flowering, and the FT protein travels through the symplasm to the shoot apical meristem and initiates flowering.

Whatever combination of environmental cues (such as photoperiod or vernalization) and internal signaling molecules (such as the FT protein) is necessary for flowering, the outcome is the transition of a bud's meristem from a vegetative to a flowering state. This transition requires changes in the expression of genes that regulate pattern formation. Meristem identity genes that induce the bud to form a flower instead of a vegetative shoot must be switched on. Then the organ identity genes that specify the spatial organization of the floral organs—sepals, petals, stamens, and carpels—are activated in the correct regions of the meristem (see Figure 35.34).

CONCEPT CHECK 39.3

1. If an enzyme in field-grown soybean leaves is most active at noon and least active at midnight, is its activity under circadian regulation?
2. A guard absentmindedly turns on the lights in a greenhouse one night, but the plants still flower on schedule. Suggest two reasons why they were not affected by the interruption of darkness.
3. Some vine seedlings grow toward darkness until reaching an upright structure. This adaptation helps them "find" a shaded object to climb. How might you test whether this negative phototropism is mediated by blue-light photoreceptors or by phytochrome?
4. **WHAT IF?** If a plant flowers in a controlled chamber with a daily cycle of 10 hours of light and 14 hours of darkness, is it a short-day plant? Explain.
5. **MAKE CONNECTIONS** Plants detect the quality of their light environment by using blue-light photoreceptors and red-light-absorbing phytochromes. After reviewing Figure 10.10 (p. 191), suggest a reason why plants are so sensitive to these colors of light.

For suggested answers, see Appendix A.

CONCEPT 39.4

Plants respond to a wide variety of stimuli other than light

EVOLUTION Plants can neither migrate to a watering hole when water is scarce nor seek shelter from wind. A seed landing upside down in the soil cannot maneuver itself into an upright position. Plants are immobile, but mechanisms have evolved by natural selection that enable them to adjust to a wide range of environmental circumstances by developmental or physiological means. Light is so important in the life of a plant that we devoted the entire previous section to a plant's reception of and response to this one environmental factor. In this section, we examine responses to some of the other environmental stimuli that a plant commonly encounters.

Gravity

Because plants are solar-powered organisms, it is not surprising that mechanisms for growing toward sunlight have evolved. But what environmental cue does the shoot of a young seedling use to grow upward when it is completely underground and there is no light for it to detect? Similarly, what environmental factor prompts the young root to grow downward? The answer to both questions is gravity.

Place a plant on its side, and it adjusts its growth so that the shoot bends upward and the root curves downward. In their responses to gravity, or **gravitropism**, roots display positive gravitropism (Figure 39.24a) and shoots exhibit negative gravitropism. Gravitropism occurs as soon as a seed germinates, ensuring that the root grows into the soil and the shoot grows toward sunlight, regardless of how the seed is oriented when it lands.

Plants may detect gravity by the settling of **statoliths**, dense cytoplasmic components that settle under the influence of gravity to the lower portions of the cell. The statoliths of vascular plants are specialized plastids containing dense starch grains (Figure 39.24b). In roots, statoliths are located in certain cells of the root cap. According to one

Statoliths
20 μm

(a) Over the course of hours, a horizontally oriented primary root of maize bends gravitropically until its growing tip becomes vertically oriented (LMs).

(b) Within minutes after the root is placed horizontally, plastids called statoliths begin settling to the lowest sides of root cap cells. This settling may be the gravity-sensing mechanism that leads to redistribution of auxin and differing rates of elongation by cells on opposite sides of the root (LMs).

▲ **Figure 39.24 Positive gravitropism in roots: the statolith hypothesis.**

hypothesis, the aggregation of statoliths at the low points of these cells triggers a redistribution of calcium, which causes lateral transport of auxin within the root. The calcium and auxin accumulate on the lower side of the root's zone of elongation. At high concentration, auxin inhibits cell elongation, an effect that slows growth on the root's lower side. The more rapid elongation of cells on the upper side causes the root to curve as it grows. This tropism continues until the root grows straight down.

Based on new experiments, plant physiologists are refining the "falling statolith" hypothesis of root gravitropism. For example, they have found mutants of *Arabidopsis* and tobacco that lack statoliths but are still capable of gravitropism, though the response is slower than in wild-type plants. It could be that the entire cell helps the root sense gravity by mechanically pulling on proteins that tether the protoplast to the cell wall, stretching the proteins on the "up" side and compressing the proteins on the "down" side of the root cells. Dense organelles, in addition to starch granules, may also contribute by distorting the cytoskeleton as they are pulled by gravity. Statoliths, because of their density, may enhance gravitational sensing by a mechanism that simply works more slowly in their absence.

Mechanical Stimuli

A tree growing on a windy mountain ridge usually has a shorter, stockier trunk than a tree of the same species growing in a more sheltered location. The advantage of this stunted morphology is that it enables the plant to hold its ground against strong gusts of wind. The term **thigmomorphogenesis** (from the Greek *thigma*, touch) refers to the changes in form that result from mechanical perturbation. Plants are very sensitive to mechanical stress: Even the act of measuring the length of a leaf with a ruler alters its subsequent growth. Rubbing the stems of a young plant a couple of times daily results in plants that are shorter than controls **(Figure 39.25)**.

Some plant species have become, over the course of their evolution, "touch specialists." Acute responsiveness to mechanical stimuli is an integral part of these plants' "life strategies." Most vines and other climbing plants have tendrils that coil rapidly around supports (see Figure 35.7). These grasping organs usually grow straight until they touch something; the contact stimulates a coiling response caused by differential growth of cells on opposite sides of the tendril. This directional growth in response to touch is called **thigmotropism**, and it allows the vine to take advantage of whatever mechanical supports it comes across as it climbs upward toward a forest canopy.

Other examples of touch specialists are plants that undergo rapid leaf movements in response to mechanical stimulation. For example, when the compound leaf of the sensitive plant *Mimosa pudica* is touched, it collapses and its leaflets fold

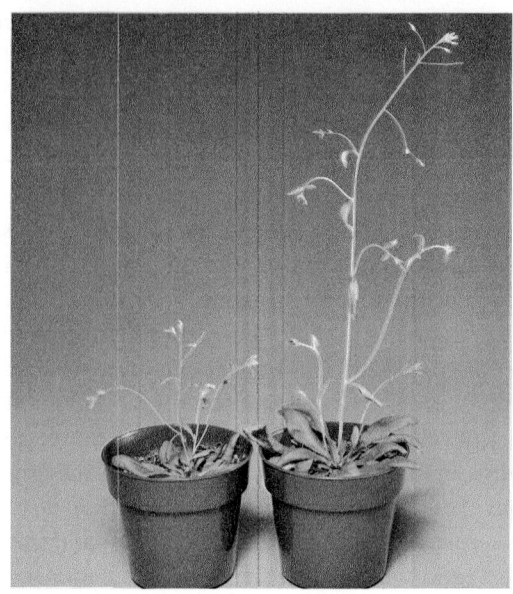

▲ **Figure 39.25 Altering gene expression by touch in** *Arabidopsis.* The shorter plant on the left was rubbed twice a day. The untouched plant (right) grew much taller.

together **(Figure 39.26)**. This response, which takes only a second or two, results from a rapid loss of turgor in cells within pulvini, specialized motor organs located at the joints of the leaf. The motor cells suddenly become flaccid after stimulation because they lose potassium ions, causing water to leave the cells by osmosis. It takes about 10 minutes for the cells to regain their turgor and restore the "unstimulated" form of the leaf. The function of the sensitive plant's behavior invites speculation. Perhaps by folding its leaves and reducing its surface area when jostled by strong winds, the plant conserves water. Or perhaps because the collapse of the leaves exposes thorns on the stem, the rapid response of the sensitive plant discourages herbivores.

A remarkable feature of rapid leaf movements is the mode of transmission of the stimulus through the plant. If one leaflet on a sensitive plant is touched, first that leaflet responds, then the adjacent leaflet responds, and so on, until all the leaflet pairs have folded together. From the point of stimulation, the signal that produces this response travels at a speed of about 1 cm/sec. An electrical impulse traveling at the same rate can be detected when electrodes are attached to the leaf. These impulses, called **action potentials**, resemble nerve impulses in animals, though the action potentials of plants are thousands of times slower. Action potentials have been discovered in many species of algae and plants and may be used as a form of internal communication. For example, in the Venus flytrap (*Dionaea muscipula*), action potentials are transmitted from sensory hairs in the trap to the cells that respond by closing the trap (see Figure 37.15). In the case of *Mimosa pudica*, more violent stimuli, such as touching a leaf

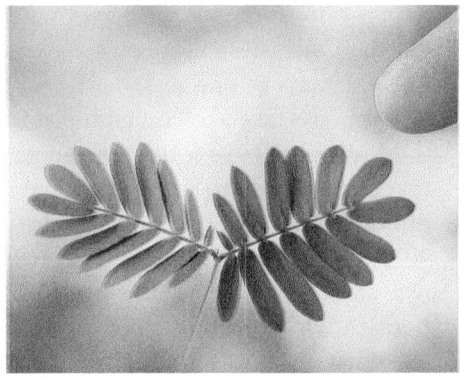

(a) Unstimulated state (leaflets spread apart)

(b) Stimulated state (leaflets folded)

Leaflets after stimulation

Pulvinus (motor organ)

Side of pulvinus with flaccid cells

Side of pulvinus with turgid cells

Vein

0.5 μm

(c) Cross section of a leaflet pair in the stimulated state (LM). The pulvinus (motor organ) becomes curved when motor cells on one side of the pulvinus lose water and become flaccid while cells on the opposite side retain their turgor.

▲ **Figure 39.26 Rapid turgor movements by the sensitive plant (*Mimosa pudica*).**

with a hot needle, causes *all* the leaves and leaflets on a plant to droop, but this whole-plant response involves the spread of signaling molecules released from the injured area to other parts of the shoot.

Environmental Stresses

Certain factors in the environment may change severely enough to have a potentially adverse effect on a plant's survival, growth, and reproduction. Environmental stresses, such as flooding, drought, or extreme temperatures, can have a devastating impact on crop yields in agriculture. In natural ecosystems, plants that cannot tolerate an environmental stress will either succumb or be outcompeted by other plants, and they will become locally extinct. Thus, environmental stresses are an important factor in determining the geographic ranges of plants. Here we will consider some of the more common **abiotic** (nonliving) stresses that plants encounter. In the last section of this chapter, we will examine the defensive responses of plants to common **biotic** (living) stresses, such as herbivores and pathogens.

Drought

On a sunny, dry day, a plant may wilt because its water loss by transpiration exceeds the ability of the root system to absorb water from the soil. Prolonged drought can stress crops and the plants of natural ecosystems for weeks or months. Severe water deficit, of course, will kill a plant, as you may know from experience with neglected houseplants. But plants have control systems that enable them to cope with less extreme water deficits.

Many of a plant's responses to water deficit help the plant conserve water by reducing the rate of transpiration. Water deficit in a leaf causes guard cells to lose turgor, a simple control mechanism that slows transpiration by closing stomata (see Figure 36.15). Water deficit also stimulates increased synthesis and release of abscisic acid in the leaf; this hormone helps keep stomata closed by acting on guard cell membranes. Leaves respond to water deficit in several other ways. For example, when the leaves of grasses wilt, they roll into a tubelike shape that reduces transpiration by exposing less leaf surface to dry air and wind. Other plants, such as ocotillo (see Figure 36.16), shed their leaves in response to seasonal drought. Although these leaf responses conserve water, they also reduce photosynthesis, which is one reason why a drought diminishes crop yield.

Root growth also responds to water deficit. During a drought, the soil usually dries from the surface down. This inhibits the growth of shallow roots, partly because cells cannot maintain the turgor required for elongation. Deeper roots surrounded by soil that is still moist continue to grow. Thus, the root system proliferates in a way that maximizes exposure to soil water.

Flooding

Too much water is also a problem for a plant. An overwatered houseplant may suffocate because the soil lacks the air spaces that provide oxygen for cellular respiration in the roots. Some plants are structurally adapted to very wet habitats. For example, the submerged roots of mangroves, which inhabit coastal marshes, are continuous with aerial roots exposed to oxygen (see Figure 35.4). But how do less specialized plants cope with oxygen deprivation in waterlogged soils? Oxygen deprivation stimulates the production of ethylene, which causes some

Vascular cylinder

Air tubes

Epidermis

100 μm   100 μm

(a) Control root (aerated)   **(b) Experimental root (nonaerated)**

▲ Figure 39.27 **A developmental response of maize roots to flooding and oxygen deprivation. (a)** A cross section of a control root grown in an aerated hydroponic medium. **(b)** A root grown in a nonaerated hydroponic medium. Ethylene-stimulated apoptosis (programmed cell death) creates the air tubes (SEMs).

cells in the root cortex to undergo apoptosis. The destruction of these cells creates air tubes that function as "snorkels," providing oxygen to the submerged roots (**Figure 39.27**).

Salt Stress

An excess of sodium chloride or other salts in the soil threatens plants for two reasons. First, by lowering the water potential of the soil solution, salt can cause a water deficit in plants even though the soil has plenty of water. As the water potential of the soil solution becomes more negative, the water potential gradient from soil to roots is lowered, thereby reducing water uptake (see Chapter 36). Another problem with saline soil is that sodium and certain other ions are toxic to plants when their concentrations are so high that they overwhelm the selective permeability capabilities of the root cell membranes. Many plants can respond to moderate soil salinity by producing solutes that are well tolerated at high concentrations: These mostly organic compounds keep the water potential of cells more negative than that of the soil solution without admitting toxic quantities of salt. However, most plants cannot survive salt stress for long. The exceptions are halophytes, salt-tolerant plants with adaptations such as salt glands that pump salts out across the leaf epidermis.

Heat Stress

As is true for other organisms, excessive heat harms and even kills a plant by denaturing its enzymes and disrupting its metabolism. One result of transpiration is evaporative cooling. On a warm day, for example, the temperature of a leaf may be 3–10°C below the ambient air temperature. Hot, dry weather also tends to dehydrate many plants; the closing of stomata in

response to this stress conserves water but then sacrifices evaporative cooling. This dilemma is one reason why very hot, dry days take a toll on most plants.

Most plants have a backup response that enables them to survive heat stress. Above a certain temperature—about 40°C for most plants in temperate regions—plant cells begin synthesizing **heat-shock proteins**, which help protect other proteins from heat stress. This response also occurs in heat-stressed animals and microorganisms. Some heat-shock proteins are chaperone proteins (chaperonins), which function in unstressed cells as temporary scaffolds that help other proteins fold into their functional shapes (see Chapter 5). In their roles as heat-shock proteins, perhaps these molecules bind to other proteins and help prevent their denaturation.

Cold Stress

One problem plants face when the temperature of the environment falls is a change in the fluidity of cell membranes. Recall from Chapter 7 that a biological membrane is a fluid mosaic, with proteins and lipids moving laterally in the plane of the membrane. When a membrane cools below a critical point, it loses its fluidity as the lipids become locked into crystalline structures. This alters solute transport across the membrane and also adversely affects the functions of membrane proteins. Plants respond to cold stress by altering the lipid composition of their membranes. For example, membrane lipids increase in their proportion of unsaturated fatty acids, which have shapes that help keep membranes fluid at lower temperatures by impeding crystal formation (see Figure 7.8a). Such membrane modification requires from several hours to days, which is one reason why unseasonably cold temperatures are generally more stressful to plants than the more gradual seasonal drop in air temperature.

Freezing is another type of cold stress. At subfreezing temperatures, ice forms in the cell walls and intercellular spaces of most plants. The cytosol generally does not freeze at the cooling rates encountered in nature because it contains more solutes than the very dilute solution found in the cell wall, and solutes lower the freezing point of a solution. The reduction in liquid water in the cell wall caused by ice formation lowers the extracellular water potential, causing water to leave the cytoplasm. The resulting increase in the concentration of ions in the cytoplasm is harmful and can lead to cell death. Whether the cell survives depends largely on how well it resists dehydration. In regions with cold winters, native plants are adapted to cope with freezing stress. For example, before the onset of winter, the cells of many frost-tolerant species increase cytoplasmic levels of specific solutes, such as sugars, that are well tolerated at high concentrations and that help reduce the loss of water from the cell during extracellular freezing. The unsaturation of membrane lipids also increases, thereby maintaining proper levels of membrane fluidity.

Many organisms, including certain vertebrates, fungi, bacteria, and many species of plants, have special proteins that hinder ice crystals from growing, helping the organism escape freezing damage. First described in Arctic fish in the 1950s, these *antifreeze proteins* permit survival at temperatures below 0°C. Antifreeze proteins bind to small ice crystals and inhibit their growth or, in the case of plants, prevent the crystallization of ice. The five major classes of antifreeze proteins differ markedly in their amino acid sequences but have a similar three-dimensional structure, suggesting convergent evolution. Surprisingly, antifreeze proteins from winter rye are homologous to antifungal proteins called PR proteins that you'll learn about later in the chapter, but they are produced in response to cold temperatures and shorter days, not fungal pathogens. Progress is being made in increasing the freezing tolerance of crop plants by genetically engineering antifreeze protein genes into their genomes.

CONCEPT CHECK 39.4

1. Thermal images are photographs of the heat emitted by an object. Researchers have used thermal imaging of plants to isolate mutants that overproduce abscisic acid. Suggest a reason why these mutants are warmer than wild-type plants under conditions that are normally nonstressful.
2. A greenhouse worker finds that potted chrysanthemums nearest to the aisles are often shorter than those in the middle of the bench. Explain this "edge effect," a common problem in horticulture.
3. **WHAT IF?** If you removed the root cap from a root, would the root still respond to gravity? Explain.

For suggested answers, see Appendix A.

CONCEPT 39.5

Plants respond to attacks by herbivores and pathogens

EVOLUTION Through natural selection, plants have evolved many types of interactions with other species in their communities. Some interspecific interactions are mutually beneficial, such as the associations of plants with mycorrhizal fungi (see Figure 37.13) or with pollinators (see Figure 38.4). Most of a plant's interactions with other organisms, however, do not benefit the plant. As primary producers, plants are at the base of most food webs and are subject to attack by a wide range of plant-eating (herbivorous) animals. A plant is also subject to infection by diverse viruses, bacteria, and fungi that can damage tissues or even kill the plant. Plants counter these threats with defense systems that deter herbivory and prevent infection or combat pathogens that infect the plant.

Defenses Against Herbivores

Herbivory—animals eating plants—is a stress that plants face in any ecosystem. Plants prevent excessive herbivory by using both physical defenses, such as thorns and trichomes, and chemical defenses, such as the production of distasteful or toxic compounds. For example, some plants produce an unusual amino acid called *canavanine*, named for one of its sources, the jackbean (*Canavalia ensiformis*). Canavanine resembles arginine, one of the 20 amino acids that organisms incorporate into their proteins. If an insect eats a plant containing canavanine, the molecule is incorporated into the insect's proteins in place of arginine. Because canavanine is different enough from arginine to adversely affect the shape and hence the function of the proteins, the insect dies.

Some plants even "recruit" predatory animals that help defend the plant against specific herbivores. Consider the insects called parasitoid wasps, which inject their eggs into caterpillars feeding on plants. The eggs hatch within the caterpillars, and the larvae eat through their organic containers from the inside out. The plant, which benefits from the destruction of the herbivorous caterpillars, has an active role in this drama. A leaf damaged by caterpillars releases volatile compounds that attract parasitoid wasps. The stimulus for this response is a combination of physical damage to the leaf caused by the munching caterpillar and a specific compound in the caterpillar's saliva (**Figure 39.28**).

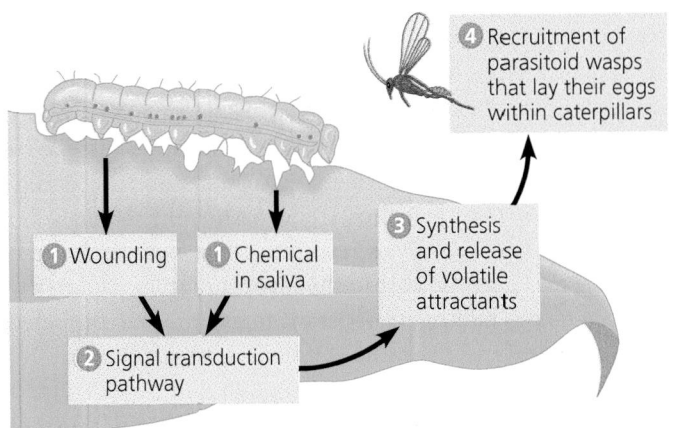

▲ **Figure 39.28 A maize leaf "recruiting" a parasitoid wasp as a defensive response to an armyworm caterpillar, an herbivore.**

The volatile molecules a plant releases in response to herbivore damage can also function as an early warning system for nearby plants of the same species. For example, lima bean plants infested with spider mites release a cocktail of volatile chemicals, including methyljasmonic acid, that signal "news" of the attack to neighboring, noninfested lima bean plants. In response to these volatile compounds, the neighbors instigate biochemical changes that make themselves less susceptible, including the release of volatile chemicals that attract another predatory mite species that feeds on spider mites. Researchers have even transgenically engineered *Arabidopsis* plants to produce two volatile chemicals that normally are not made by *Arabidopsis* but which have been found to attract carnivorous predatory mites in other plants. The predatory mites become attracted to the genetically modified *Arabidopsis*, a finding that could have implications for the genetic engineering of insect resistance in crop plants.

Defenses Against Pathogens

A plant's first line of defense against infection is the physical barrier presented by the epidermis and periderm of the plant body (see Figure 35.19). This first defense system, however, is not impenetrable. The mechanical wounding of leaves by herbivores, for example, opens up portals for invasion by pathogens. Even when plant tissues are intact, viruses, bacteria, and the spores and hyphae of fungi can still enter the plant through natural openings in the epidermis, such as stomata.

When a pathogen invades a plant, the plant mounts a second line of defense, a chemical attack that destroys the pathogen and prevents its spread from the site of infection. This second defense system is enhanced by the plant's ability to recognize certain pathogens. Successful pathogens cause disease because they evade recognition or suppress the host's defense mechanisms.

Host-Pathogen Coevolution

Pathogens against which a plant has little specific defense are **virulent** pathogens. Strains of pathogens that mildly harm but do not kill the host plant are said to be **avirulent** pathogens. Virulent pathogens are the exceptions. If they were not, hosts and pathogens would soon perish together. Complete resistance to a pathogen often comes at an energetic cost to the plant, however, and in the absence of the pathogen, resistant plants are outcompeted by those with less resistance. Of course, plants with no resistance will succumb to a pathogen outbreak. Thus, a "compromise" has evolved between plants and most of their pathogens: The pathogen gains enough access to its host to enable it to perpetuate itself without severely damaging or killing the plant.

Gene-for-gene recognition is a form of plant disease resistance in which pathogen-derived molecules called *effectors* are recognized by one of the hundreds of resistance (*R*) genes in a plant's genome. Protein effectors, encoded by the pathogen's avirulence (*Avr*) genes, can facilitate infection in plants that lack the appropriate R protein by redirecting the host's metabolism to the pathogen's advantage. In those plants that do have the appropriate R protein, however, such effector proteins can directly trigger a suite of strong defense responses. The recognition of effectors by R proteins triggers signal transduction pathways leading to the activation of an arsenal of defense responses, including a local defense called the hypersensitive response and a general defense called systemic acquired resistance. Local and systemic responses to pathogens require extensive genetic reprogramming and commitment of cellular resources. Therefore, a plant activates these defenses only after detecting an invading pathogen.

The Hypersensitive Response

The **hypersensitive response** is a defense response that causes cell and tissue death near the infection site, thereby restricting the spread of a pathogen. After the cells at the infection site mount a chemical defense and seal off the area, they destroy themselves. As indicated in **Figure 39.29**, the hypersensitive response is initiated when pathogen effectors bind to R proteins and stimulate the production of phytoalexins, which are compounds having fungicidal and bactericidal properties. The hypersensitive response also induces production of *PR proteins* (pathogenesis-related proteins), many of which are enzymes that hydrolyze components in the cell walls of pathogens. Infection also stimulates the formation of lignin and the cross-linking of molecules within the plant cell wall, responses that hinder the spread of the pathogen to other parts of the plant. We can see the result of a hypersensitive response as lesions on a leaf, as shown at the upper right in the figure. As "sick" as such a leaf appears, it will still survive, and its defensive response will help protect the rest of the plant.

Systemic Acquired Resistance

The hypersensitive response is localized and specific. However, as noted previously, pathogen invasions can also produce signaling molecules that "sound the alarm" of infection to the whole plant. The resulting **systemic acquired resistance** arises from the plant-wide expression of defense genes. It is nonspecific, providing protection against a diversity of pathogens that lasts for days. The search for a signaling molecule that moves from the infection site to elicit systemic acquired resistance led to the identification of *methylsalicylic acid* as the most likely candidate. Methylsalicylic acid is produced around the infection site and carried by the phloem throughout the plant, where it is converted to

④ Before they die, infected cells release the signaling molecule methylsalicylic acid.

③ In a hypersensitive response, plant cells produce anti-microbial molecules, seal off infected areas by modifying their walls, and then destroy themselves. This localized response produces lesions and protects other parts of an infected leaf.

② The identification in step ① triggers a signal transduction pathway.

① Specific resistance is based on the binding of pathogen effector molecules to specific plant resistance (R) proteins.

④ Signal

③ Hypersensitive response

② Signal transduction pathway

R protein

Avirulent pathogen

Avr effector protein

R-Avr recognition and hypersensitive response

⑤

Signal transduction pathway ⑥

⑦ Acquired resistance

Systemic acquired resistance

Infected tobacco leaf with lesions

⑤ The signaling molecule is distributed to the rest of the plant.

⑥ In cells remote from the infection site, methylsalicylic acid is converted to salicylic acid, which initiates a signal transduction pathway.

⑦ Systemic acquired resistance is activated: the production of molecules that help protect the cell against a diversity of pathogens for several days.

▲ Figure 39.29 **Defense responses against an avirulent pathogen.** Plants can often prevent the systemic spread of infection by instigating a hypersensitive response. This response helps isolate the pathogen by producing lesions that form "rings of death" around the sites of infection.

salicylic acid in areas remote from the sites of infection. Salicylic acid activates a signal transduction pathway that induces the production of PR proteins and resistance to pathogen attack (see Figure 39.29).

Plant disease epidemics, such as the potato blight (see pp. 588–589) that caused the Irish potato famine of the 1840s, can lead to incalculable human misery. Other diseases, such as chestnut blight (see p. 650) and sudden oak death (see p. 1214), can dramatically alter community structures. Plant epidemics are often the result of infected plants or timber being inadvertently transported around the world. As global commerce increases, such epidemics will become increasingly more common. To prepare for such outbreaks, plant biologists are stockpiling the seeds of wild relatives of crop plants in special storage facilities. Scientists hope that undomesticated relatives may have genes that will be able to curb the next plant epidemic. These scientists, along with thousands of other plant biologists, are extending an age-old tradition of curiosity about the green organisms that feed our species and the biosphere.

CONCEPT CHECK 39.5

1. What are some drawbacks of spraying fields with general-purpose insecticides?
2. Chewing insects mechanically damage plants and lessen the surface area of leaves for photosynthesis. In addition, these insects make plants more vulnerable to pathogen attack. Suggest a reason why.
3. Many fungal pathogens get their food by causing plant cells to become leaky, thereby releasing nutrients into the intercellular spaces. Would it benefit the fungus to kill the host plant in a way that results in all the nutrients leaking out?
4. **WHAT IF?** Suppose a scientist finds that a population of plants growing in a breezy location is more prone to herbivory by insects than a population of the same species growing in a sheltered area. Suggest a hypothesis to account for this observation.

For suggested answers, see Appendix A.

SUMMARY OF KEY CONCEPTS

CONCEPT 39.1

Signal transduction pathways link signal reception to response (pp. 821–824)

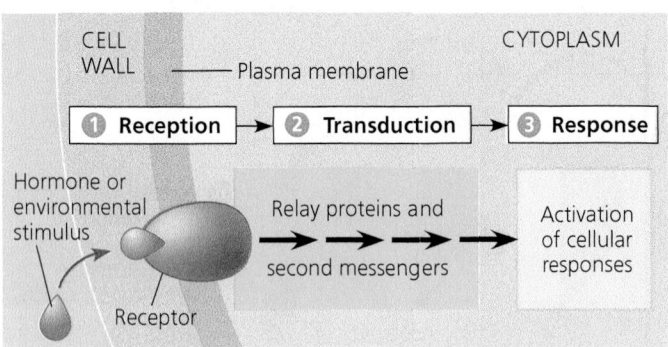

> **?** *What are two common ways by which signal transduction pathways enhance the activity of specific enzymes?*

CONCEPT 39.2

Plant hormones help coordinate growth, development, and responses to stimuli (pp. 824–835)

- Hormones control plant growth and development by affecting the division, elongation, and differentiation of cells. Some hormones also mediate the responses of plants to environmental stimuli.

Plant Hormone	Major Responses
Auxin	Stimulates cell elongation; regulates branching and organ bending.
Cytokinins	Stimulate plant cell division; promote later bud growth; slow organ death.
Gibberellins	Promote stem elongation; help seeds break dormancy and use stored reserves.
Brassinosteroids	Chemically similar to the sex hormones of animals; induce cell elongation and division.
Abscisic acid	Promotes stomatal closure in response to drought; promotes seed dormancy.
Strigolactones	Regulate apical dominance, seed germination, and mycorrhizal associations.
Ethylene	Mediates fruit ripening.

> **?** *Is there any truth to the old adage, "One bad apple spoils the whole bunch?" Explain.*

CONCEPT 39.3

Responses to light are critical for plant success (pp. 835–841)

- **Blue-light photoreceptors** control hypocotyl elongation, stomatal opening, and phototropism.

- **Phytochromes** act like molecular "on-off" switches. Red light turns phytochrome "on," and far-red light turns it "off." Phytochrome regulates shade avoidance and the germination of many seed types.

Photoreversible states of phytochrome:

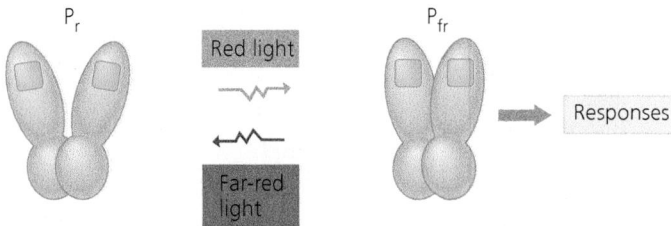

- Phytochrome conversion also provides information about the relative lengths of day and night (photoperiod) and hence the time of year. Photoperiodism regulates the time of flowering in many species. **Short-day plants** require a night longer than a critical length to flower. **Long-day plants** need a night length shorter than a critical period to flower.
- Many daily rhythms in plant behavior are controlled by an internal circadian clock. Free-running circadian cycles are approximately 24 hours long but are entrained to exactly 24 hours by dawn and dusk effects on phytochrome form.

> **?** *Why did plant physiologists propose the existence of a mobile molecule (florigen) that triggers flowering?*

CONCEPT 39.4

Plants respond to a wide variety of stimuli other than light (pp. 841–845)

- **Gravitropism** is the bending of an organ in response to gravity. Roots show positive gravitropism, and stems show negative gravitropism. **Statoliths**, starch-filled plastids, enable plant roots to detect gravity.
- Plants are highly sensitive to touch. **Thigmotropism** is a growth response to touch. Rapid leaf movements involve transmission of electrical impulses called action potentials.
- Plants are sensitive to environmental stresses, including drought, flooding, high salinity, and extremes of temperature.

Environmental Stress	Major Response
Drought	ABA production, reducing water loss by closing stomata
Flooding	Formation of air tubes that help roots survive oxygen deprivation
Salt	Avoiding osmotic water loss by producing solutes tolerated at high concentrations
Heat	Synthesis of heat-shock proteins, which reduce protein denaturation at high temperatures
Cold	Adjusting membrane fluidity; avoiding osmotic water loss; producing antifreeze proteins

> **?** *Plants that have acclimated to drought stress are often more resistant to freezing stress as well. Suggest a reason why.*

Plants respond to attacks by herbivores and pathogens
(pp. 845–847)

- In addition to physical defenses such as thorns and trichomes, plants produce distasteful or toxic chemicals, as well as attractants that recruit animals that destroy herbivores.
- The **hypersensitive response** seals off an infection and destroys both pathogen and host cells in the region. **Systemic acquired resistance** is a generalized defense response in organs distant from the infection site.

? *How do chewing insects make plants more susceptible to pathogens?*

TEST YOUR UNDERSTANDING

LEVEL 1: KNOWLEDGE/COMPREHENSION

1. The hormone that helps plants respond to drought is
   a. auxin.
   b. gibberellin.
   c. cytokinin.
   d. ethylene.
   e. abscisic acid.

2. Auxin enhances cell elongation in all of these ways *except*
   a. increased uptake of solutes.
   b. gene activation.
   c. acid-induced denaturation of cell wall proteins.
   d. increased activity of plasma membrane proton pumps.
   e. cell wall loosening.

3. Charles and Francis Darwin discovered that
   a. auxin is responsible for phototropic curvature.
   b. auxin can pass through agar.
   c. light destroys auxin.
   d. light is perceived by the tips of coleoptiles.
   e. red light is most effective in shoot phototropism.

4. How may a plant respond to *severe* heat stress?
   a. by reorienting leaves to increase evaporative cooling
   b. by creating air tubes for ventilation
   c. by initiating a systemic acquired resistance response
   d. by increasing the proportion of unsaturated fatty acids in cell membranes, reducing their fluidity
   e. by producing heat-shock proteins, which may protect the plant's proteins from denaturing

LEVEL 2: APPLICATION/ANALYSIS

5. The signaling molecule for flowering might be released earlier than usual in a long-day plant exposed to flashes of
   a. far-red light during the night.
   b. red light during the night.
   c. red light followed by far-red light during the night.
   d. far-red light during the day.
   e. red light during the day.

6. If a long-day plant has a critical night length of 9 hours, which 24-hour cycle would prevent flowering?
   a. 16 hours light/8 hours dark
   b. 14 hours light/10 hours dark
   c. 15.5 hours light/8.5 hours dark
   d. 4 hours light/8 hours dark/4 hours light/8 hours dark
   e. 8 hours light/8 hours dark/light flash/8 hours dark

7. A plant mutant that shows normal gravitropic bending but does not store starch in its plastids would require a reevaluation of the role of _____ in gravitropism.
   a. auxin
   b. calcium
   c. statoliths
   d. light
   e. differential growth

8. Which type of mutant would be most likely to produce a bushier phenotype?
   a. auxin overproducer
   b. strigolactone overproducer
   c. cytokinin underproducer
   d. gibberellin overproducer
   e. strigolactone underproducer

9. **DRAW IT** Indicate the response to each condition by drawing a straight seedling or one with the triple response.

	Control	Ethylene added	Ethylene synthesis inhibitor
Wild-type			
Ethylene insensitive (*ein*)			
Ethylene overproducing (*eto*)			
Constitutive triple response (*ctr*)			

LEVEL 3: SYNTHESIS/EVALUATION

10. **EVOLUTION CONNECTION**
    As a general rule, light-sensitive germination is more pronounced in small seeds compared with large seeds. Suggest a reason why.

11. **SCIENTIFIC INQUIRY**
    A plant biologist observed a peculiar pattern when a tropical shrub was attacked by caterpillars. After a caterpillar ate a leaf, it would skip over nearby leaves and attack a leaf some distance away. Simply removing a leaf did not deter caterpillars from eating nearby leaves. The biologist suspected that an insect-damaged leaf sent out a chemical that signaled nearby leaves. How could the researcher test this hypothesis?

12. **SCIENCE, TECHNOLOGY, AND SOCIETY**
    Describe how our knowledge about the control systems of plants is being applied to agriculture or horticulture.

13. **WRITE ABOUT A THEME**
    Environmental Interactions In a short essay (100–150 words), summarize phytochrome's role in altering shoot growth for the enhancement of light capture.

For selected answers, see Appendix A.

Mastering BIOLOGY   www.masteringbiology.com

1. MasteringBiology® Assignments
Experimental Inquiry Tutorial What Effect Does Auxin Have on Coleoptile Growth?
Tutorial Plant Responses to Light
Activities Leaf Abscission • Flowering Lab • Plant Hormones • Plant Defenses
Questions Student Misconceptions • Reading Quiz • Multiple Choice • End-of-Chapter

2. eText
Read your book online, search, take notes, highlight text, and more.

3. The Study Area
Practice Tests • Cumulative Test • *BioFlix* 3-D Animations • MP3 Tutor Sessions • Videos • Activities • Investigations • Lab Media • Audio Glossary • Word Study Tools • Art

UNIT 7

Animal Form and Function

An Interview with
Baldomero M. Olivera

Growing up in the Philippines, Baldomero (Toto) Olivera collected the shells of venomous cone snails as a hobby. Today, he is a leading expert on the use of cone snail toxins for exploring and modifying the activity of the mammalian nervous system. After graduating summa cum laude from the University of the Philippines, he earned a Ph.D. in Chemistry from the California Institute of Technology (Caltech). In 1970, Dr. Olivera joined the faculty at the University of Utah, where he is now a Distinguished Professor of Biology. In 2009, he became the first Filipino to be elected to the U.S. National Academy of Sciences.

How did you get started in science?
In high school I had a great teacher in both biology and chemistry. After I finished college, she encouraged me to go on to graduate school. She put an article in front of me about Caltech and told me to apply there. Fortunately, they accepted me.

When I got to Caltech, I assumed that since I'd taken five courses at a time as an undergraduate, I'd be expected to take even more in graduate school, so in my first semester I was taking seven courses. One was the only statistical mechanics course at Caltech, so not only chemists like me, but also physicists took it. The first day, the professor, Norman Davidson, reviewed all of classical mechanics, which I had never had. The second day he reviewed all of quantum mechanics. After the fourth lecture I went to him and said, "You know, Professor, I haven't understood a word you've said." He said, "Don't worry about it. Just hang in there." I did, and I ended up doing my Ph.D. research in his lab, studying DNA.

After graduate school I went to Stanford and continued to work on DNA as a postdoctoral fellow. I then took a faculty job in the Philippines, but soon found out that I probably would have no large lab equipment for at least a year. I decided to look for a project that we could start immediately with no equipment and, if at all possible, that would have some local advantages. Since I'd collected shells as a hobby, I knew that some of the local snails, called cone snails, had a venomous sting that could kill people. So we set out to purify the substances in the venom that were lethal to mammals.

Why do cone snails produce venom?
Not much was known about this until 1956, when a Yale graduate student, Alan Kohn, discovered that a cone snail he had in an aquarium hunted fish. (Kohn went on to become a leading expert on the ecology and taxonomy of cone snails.) We now know that about 100 of the 500–700 species of cone snails hunt fish. A similar number hunt other molluscs, and the rest hunt marine worms.

When a cone snail hunts, it first sniffs the fish by means of chemoreceptors, specialized cells that function in sensing smell or taste. Chemoreception by a cone snail in the marine environment is amazing. For example, fish-hunting cone snails in a large aquarium react the moment you drop in a fish. They move their siphon, which is sensory, back and forth so they can locate the fish. When the siphon touches fish skin, a disposable, harpoon-like tooth shoots out of the snail's proboscis and pierces the scales of the fish. The venom flows through the tooth into the fish. So the tooth, which is barbed, is both a harpoon and a hypodermic needle. The venom very rapidly immobilizes the harpooned fish, which the cone snail can then consume.

Some other animals hunt cone snails, which explains their cone-like shape. Among the major predators are crabs. If you're a crab, you grab the snail's shell and try to break it. But if the snail is cone-shaped, the crab claw slips, making it hard to break the shell. So the cone shape is a defensive adaptation. However, a cone-shaped snail shell that narrows to a point has an opening too small to allow a large prey animal to be pulled into the shell. So fish-hunting cone snails tend to be more cylindrical.

What did you hope to learn by studying cone snail venom?
We knew that venoms could be useful because the toxins of the pufferfish—*fugu* in Japanese—and the krait, a cobra-like snake, had been used to study ion channels in the nervous system. Ion channels are found on the surface of neurons, and they let ions in and out of the cell. This movement of ions mediates the electrical signaling within neurons and controls the transfer of a signal from one neuron to another. Venoms that interfere with that ion movement wipe out the prey animal's nervous system—that's why they're deadly.

The toxins in venoms are quite specific. The toxin of the pufferfish targets a sodium ion channel. The toxin of the krait targets a different type of ion channel, called a nicotinic receptor. By using these toxins in the lab to interfere with the function of particular kinds of ion channels, you can learn a great deal about how the nervous system normally functions.

How did you study the cone snail toxins?
In the Philippines, people eat marine snails, and the shells are by-products. Since I'd collected shells, I knew the people who sold them commercially and asked them to get me some live snails.

When you work with cone snails, you of course don't want to be stung. We put the snails on ice and they became very lethargic. We then dissected out the venom duct and pressed out the venom. The next step was to measure the activity of the venom. The medical literature said people stung by cone snails died because their diaphragms became paralyzed. So we assayed (tested) for paralysis. We would inject mice with various fractions of the venom and then immediately put them on a wire screen, upside down. Mice can actually stay attached this way indefinitely, but when paralysis sets in, they fall off. All we did was measure the time until they fell. It turns out that the falling time changes with the amount of toxin in a very reproducible way.

Using this falling-time assay, we purified an active peptide from two different fractions of the venom of the species *Conus geographus*. One of these peptides has only 13 amino acids; the other has 22. We found out that the peptide with 13 amino acids bound to exactly the same site on an ion channel as the krait toxin, which has about 80 amino acids. It was remarkable that a toxin had evolved in snails that was so much smaller but had the same activity.

How did the big breakthrough in your cone snail studies come about?

When I started as a full-time faculty member here at Utah, all our funding was still for experiments with DNA, and my graduate students all studied DNA. So we started recruiting undergraduates to work on the cone snail project—and that led to a very lucky break. One of the undergraduates, Craig Clark, said, "You guys are injecting into the body cavity of the mice. I think we should inject directly into the central nervous system." That was purely his idea. I thought it would probably just kill the mice.

At the time, we were beginning to use new techniques to separate the venom into many fractions, each containing different peptides. Using our falling-time assay, most fractions were inactive. But when Craig started injecting fractions into the central nervous system, the results were truly astonishing. Almost every fraction changed the mice's behavior in some way, and many of the effects were really bizarre. Some fractions made mice run around in circles. Others made mice scratch themselves. Still others made mice get up on their hind legs and move their front legs as if they were boxing. There was even a fraction that put juvenile, but not adult, mice into a sleeplike state. Craig purified the peptide with that activity, which he called the "sleeper peptide." I think the reason why university research is typically the most creative is that students sometimes do what they want, not what their professors tell them to do!

From then on, we let undergraduates pick which active fraction they wanted to study. Their job was to purify the peptide, which we would then synthesize and work on further.

Why and how did so much toxin diversity evolve in cone snails?

My suspicion is that if your survival depends on influencing the behavior of another animal and your strategy is purely chemical, it takes a very complex strategy for that to be successful in evolution. The adaptations that evolved in cone snails are in essence what we're just discovering in modern medical practice. To treat cancer or AIDS effectively, you can't use just one chemical; you use combination drug therapy. I think the evolution of venoms in cone snails followed the same principle.

For the cone snail toxins there are a few gene superfamilies, and they are subject to very accelerated evolution. There are parallels to the vertebrate adaptive immune system in that there are conserved and highly variable regions in the genes. The conserved regions are mostly all cut out. So, if you like, a cone snail peptide is equivalent to the highly variable part that makes an antibody very specific.

How did your studies with snails lead to a discovery that was medically important?

After Craig discovered that you could study the effects of toxins by injecting them into the central nervous system of mice, he recruited a high school student, Michael McIntosh, to the lab. Mike decided to work with a different snail, called *Conus magus*, or the magician's cone. One of the most striking discoveries he made was a peptide that gave mice a characteristic tremor, or shake.

When Mike purified the "shaker peptide," we learned that it blocks a certain type of calcium channel. In fish these calcium channels control the release of the neurotransmitter that carries signals from nerve to muscle. When shaker peptide blocks these channels, the neurotransmitter is not released, and the fish becomes paralyzed. In mammals, this type of calcium channel is found only in the pain circuitry. When you experience severe pain, pain fibers send signals to a nerve cell in your spinal cord that takes the pain signal up to your brain. The pain fibers in mammals release signals to the nerves using the same type of calcium channel that in fish carries signals to muscles to direct movement. This difference in receptor location and function is why the shaker peptide paralyzes and kills fish, but not mammals.

The shaker peptide is now an approved drug. If a patient has very severe pain and the shaker peptide is injected where the pain fiber connects to the nerve, the perception of pain stops because the pain fiber no longer releases the chemical signal to the nerve. Doctors are using the shaker peptide in this way for people who are suffering from severe pain and no longer get pain relief from morphine due to tolerance built up over time. A surgically implanted pump introduces the shaker peptide to the spinal cord at the site where the pain fiber makes its connection.

What other discoveries do you hope to see come out of studying cone snails?

There are 500–700 species of cone snails, but the total biodiversity of molluscs with venom is probably 12,000 species. The biggest group is the turrids. You don't find many of them in shallow water, but at 400 meters, where there are no cone snails, you find hundreds of species of turrids. Many of them are just a few millimeters in length, and nobody knows anything about their biology. Fortunately, hobbyists are extremely interested in their tiny shells, so fishermen in the Philippines gather them. They tie all their broken fine-mesh fishing nets into bundles, which they sink in water for 3 to 6 months. When they lift these bundles, each will contain several thousand marine animals, almost all of them alive. For gastropods alone, a net will hold something like 250 different species, of which 40 are venomous. Each venom has 200 compounds. So this is a vast new world.

What advice would you give students interested in biology or medicine?

One piece of advice is to get as good a basic science background as you possibly can. I started out with very basic chemistry and very basic biology, and then of course the science grew as my research career grew. Having strong basic science training allows you to feel confident that even if you don't understand a problem at first (like quantum mechanics), you can still tackle it. A second thing is that you ought to know what it is in science that really turns you on. Third, keep in mind that it is always fun to learn something new.

"The adaptations that evolved in cone snails are in essence what we're just discovering in modern medical practice."

Baldomero Olivera (center) with Jane Reece and Steve Wasserman (right)

40

Basic Principles of Animal Form and Function

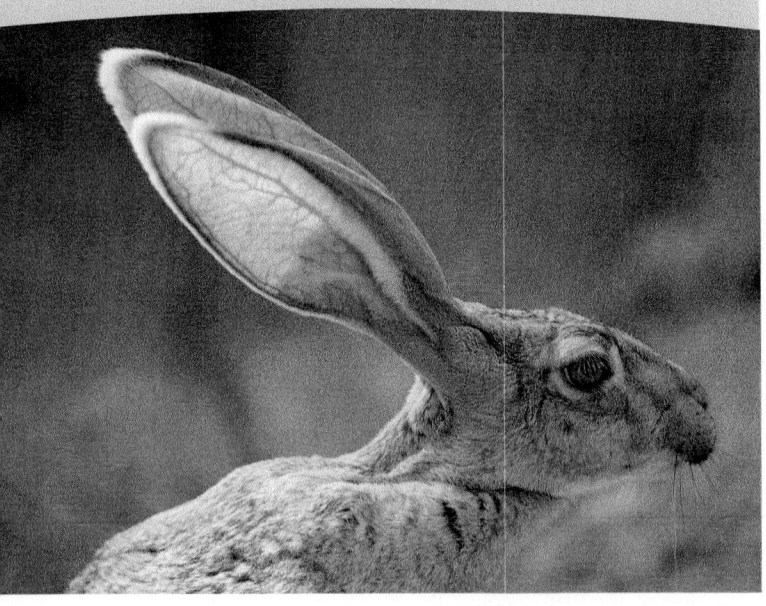

▲ **Figure 40.1 How does a jackrabbit keep from overheating?**

KEY CONCEPTS

40.1 Animal form and function are correlated at all levels of organization

40.2 Feedback control maintains the internal environment in many animals

40.3 Homeostatic processes for thermoregulation involve form, function, and behavior

40.4 Energy requirements are related to animal size, activity, and environment

OVERVIEW

Diverse Forms, Common Challenges

The ears of the jackrabbit (*Lepus alleni*) in **Figure 40.1** are thin and remarkably large. They provide this hare with an acute sense of hearing, a primary defense against predators. The ears also help the jackrabbit shed excess heat. Blood flowing through each ear's network of vessels transfers heat to the surrounding air. However, when the air is warmer than the jackrabbit, blood passing through the ears could absorb heat, raising body temperature to a dangerous level. How, then, does a big-eared jackrabbit survive in the midday desert heat? To answer this question, we need to look more closely at the biological form, or **anatomy**, of the animal.

Over the course of its life, a jackrabbit faces the same fundamental challenges as any other animal, whether hydra, hawk, or human. All animals must obtain oxygen and nutrients, fight off infection, and produce offspring. Given that they share these and other basic requirements, why do species vary so enormously in makeup, complexity, organization, and appearance? The answer is adaptation: Natural selection favors those variations in a population that increase relative fitness (see Chapter 23). The solutions to the challenges of survival vary among environments and species, but they frequently result in a close match of form to function.

Because form and function are correlated, examining anatomy often provides clues to **physiology**—biological function. In the case of the jackrabbit, researchers noted that its large, pink-tinged ears turn pale when the air temperature exceeds 40°C (104°F), the normal temperature of the jackrabbit's body. The color change reflects a temporary narrowing of blood vessels in response to a hot environment. With their blood supply reduced, the ears can absorb heat without overheating the rest of the body. When the air cools, blood flow increases, and the large ears again help release excess heat.

In this chapter, we will begin our study of animal form and function by examining the levels of organization in the animal body and the systems for coordinating the activities of distinct body parts. Next, we will use the example of body temperature regulation to illustrate how animals control their internal environment. Finally, we will explore how anatomy and physiology relate to an animal's interactions with the environment and its management of energy use.

CONCEPT 40.1

Animal form and function are correlated at all levels of organization

An animal's size and shape are fundamental aspects of form that significantly affect the way the animal interacts with its environment. Although we may refer to size and shape as elements of a "body plan" or "design," this does not imply a process of conscious invention. The body plan of an animal is the result of a pattern of development programmed by the genome, itself the product of millions of years of evolution.

Evolution of Animal Size and Shape

EVOLUTION Many different body plans have arisen during the course of evolution, but these variations fall within certain bounds. Physical laws that govern strength, diffusion, movement, and heat exchange limit the range of animal forms.

As an example of how physical laws constrain evolution, let's consider how some properties of water limit the possible shapes for animals that are fast swimmers. Water is about a thousand times denser than air and also far more viscous. Therefore, any bump on an animal's body surface that causes drag impedes a swimmer more than it would a runner or flyer. Tuna and other fast ray-finned fishes can swim at speeds up to 80 km/hr (50 miles/hour). Sharks, penguins, dolphins, and seals are also fast swimmers. As is apparent in the examples in **Figure 40.2**, such animals share a streamlined body contour: a shape that is fusiform, meaning tapered on both ends. The similar shape found in these speedy vertebrates is an example of convergent evolution (see Chapter 22). Natural selection often results in similar adaptations when diverse organisms face the same environmental challenge, such as overcoming drag during swimming.

Physical laws also influence animal body plans with regard to maximum size. As body dimensions increase, thicker skeletons are required to maintain adequate support. This limitation affects internal skeletons, such as those of vertebrates, as well as external skeletons, such as those of insects and other arthropods. In addition, as bodies increase in size, the muscles required for locomotion must represent an ever-larger fraction of the total body mass. At some point, mobility becomes limited. By considering the fraction of body mass in leg muscles and the effective force such muscles generate, scientists can estimate maximum running speed for a wide range of body plans. Such calculations indicate that the dinosaur *Tyrannosaurus rex*, which stood more than 6 m tall, probably could reach speeds of 30 km/hr (19 miles/hour), about as fast as the fastest humans can run.

Exchange with the Environment

Animals must exchange materials with their environment, and this requirement imposes limitations on their body plans (as it does for all multicellular organisms). Exchange occurs as substances dissolved in an aqueous solution move across the plasma membrane of each cell. The rates of exchange for nutrients, waste products, and gases are proportional to membrane surface area, whereas the amount of material that must be exchanged to sustain life is proportional to cell volume.

The opportunity for exchange depends on the number of cells in an organism's body. A single-celled organism, such as the amoeba in **Figure 40.3a**, has a sufficient membrane surface area in contact with its environment to carry out all necessary exchange. In contrast, an animal is composed of many cells, each with its own plasma membrane across which exchange must occur. A multicellular organization therefore works only if every cell has access to a suitable aqueous environment, either inside or outside the animal's body.

Many animals with a simple internal organization have body plans that enable direct exchange between almost all their cells and the external environment. For example, a pond-dwelling hydra, which has a saclike body plan, has a body wall only two cell layers thick (**Figure 40.3b**). Because its

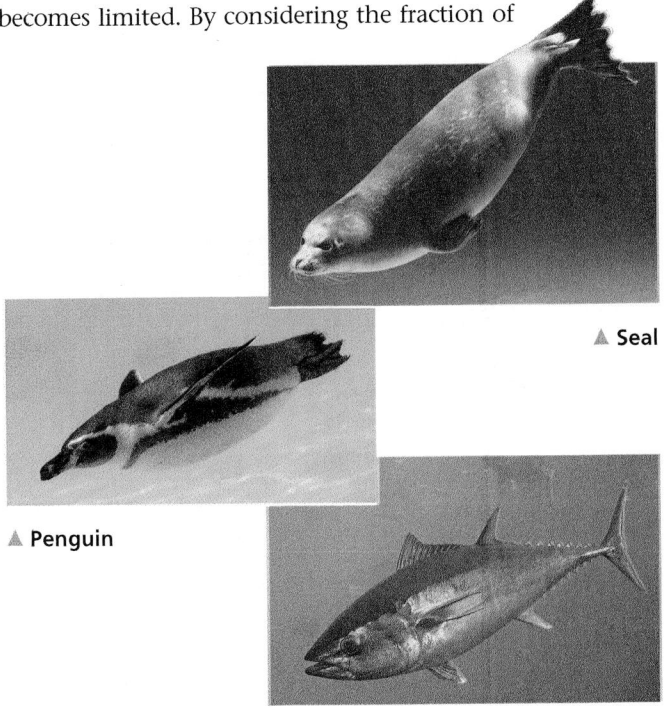

▲ **Figure 40.2 Convergent evolution in fast swimmers.**

(Labels: ▲ Seal, ▲ Penguin, ▲ Tuna)

(a) Single cell — 0.1 mm

(b) Two layers of cells — Mouth, Gastrovascular cavity, Exchange — 1 mm

▲ **Figure 40.3 Contact with the environment. (a)** In a single-celled organism, such as an amoeba, the entire surface area contacts the environment. **(b)** Although all animals are multicellular, some have a simple organization in which all or nearly all cells contact the environment. For example, a hydra's body consists of two layers of cells. As fluid moves in and out of the hydra's mouth, every body cell can exchange material directly with the aqueous environment.

gastrovascular cavity opens to the external environment, both the outer and inner layers of cells are constantly bathed by pond water. Another common body plan that maximizes exposure to the surrounding medium is a flat shape. Consider, for instance, a parasitic tapeworm, which can reach several meters in length (see Figure 33.12). A thin, flat shape places most cells of the worm in direct contact with its particular environment—the nutrient-rich intestinal fluid of a vertebrate host.

The bodies of most animals are composed of compact masses of cells, with an internal organization much more complex than that of a hydra or a tapeworm. For such a body plan, increasing the number of cells decreases the ratio of outer surface area to total volume. As an extreme comparison, the ratio of outer surface to volume for a whale is hundreds of thousands of times smaller than that for a water flea (*Daphnia*). Nevertheless, every cell in the whale must be bathed in fluid and have access to oxygen, nutrients, and other resources. How is this accomplished?

In whales and most other animals, the evolutionary adaptations that enable sufficient exchange with the environment are specialized surfaces that are extensively branched or folded (Figure 40.4). In almost all cases, these exchange surfaces lie within the body, an arrangement that protects their delicate tissues from abrasion or dehydration and allows for streamlined body contours. In humans, the internal exchange surfaces of the digestive, respiratory, and circulatory systems each have an area more than 25 times that of the skin.

Internal body fluids link exchange surfaces to body cells. The spaces between cells are filled with fluid, in many animals called **interstitial fluid** (from the Latin for "stand between"). Complex body plans also include a circulatory fluid, such as blood. Exchange between the interstitial fluid and the circulatory fluid enables cells throughout the body to obtain nutrients and get rid of wastes (see Figure 40.4).

Despite the greater challenges of exchange with the environment, complex body plans have distinct benefits over simple

The lining of the small intestine has finger-like projections that expand the surface area for nutrient absorption (SEM).

A microscopic view of the lung reveals that it is much more sponge-like than balloon-like. This construction provides an expansive wet surface for gas exchange with the environment (SEM).

Within the kidney, blood is filtered across the surface of long, narrow blood vessels packed into ball-shaped structures (SEM).

▲ **Figure 40.4 Internal exchange surfaces of complex animals.** This diagram provides an overview of chemical exchange between an animal body and the environment. Most animals have surfaces that are specialized for exchanging chemicals with the surroundings. These exchange surfaces are usually internal but are connected to the environment via openings on the body surface (the mouth, for example). The exchange surfaces are finely branched or folded, giving them a very large area. The digestive, respiratory, and excretory systems all have such exchange surfaces. The circulatory system carries chemicals transported across these surfaces throughout the body.

? *In what sense are exchange surfaces such as the lining of the digestive system both internal and external?*

ones. For example, an external skeleton can protect against predators, and sensory organs can provide detailed information on the animal's surroundings. Internal digestive organs can break down food gradually, controlling the release of stored energy. In addition, specialized filtration systems can adjust the composition of the internal fluid that bathes the animal's body cells. In this way, an animal can maintain a relatively stable internal environment while living in a changeable external environment. A complex body plan is especially advantageous for animals living on land, where the external environment may be highly variable.

Hierarchical Organization of Body Plans

Cells form a functional animal body through their emergent properties. Recall from Chapter 1 that emergent properties arise by way of successive levels of structural and functional organization. Cells are organized into **tissues**, groups of cells with a similar appearance and a common function. Different types of tissues are further organized into functional units called **organs**. (The simplest animals, such as sponges, lack organs or even true tissues.) Groups of organs that work together provide an additional level of organization and coordination and make up an **organ system** (Table 40.1). Thus, for example, the skin is an organ of the integumentary system, which protects against infection and helps regulate body temperature.

Many organs contain tissues with distinct physiological roles. In some cases, the roles are different enough that we consider the organ to belong to more than one organ sys-

tem. The pancreas, for instance, produces enzymes critical to the function of the digestive system and also regulates the level of sugar in the blood as a vital part of the endocrine system.

Just as viewing the body's organization from the "bottom up" (from cells to organ systems) reveals emergent properties, a "top-down" view of the hierarchy reveals the multilayered basis of specialization. Consider the human digestive system: the mouth, pharynx, esophagus, stomach, small and large intestines, accessory organs, and anus. Each organ has specific roles in digestion. One function of the stomach, for example, is to initiate the breakdown of proteins. This process requires a churning motion powered by stomach muscles, as well as digestive juices secreted by the stomach lining. Producing digestive juices, in turn, requires highly specialized cell types: One cell type secretes a protein-digesting enzyme, a second generates concentrated hydrochloric acid, and a third produces mucus, which protects the stomach lining.

The specialized and complex organ systems of animals are built from a limited set of cell and tissue types. For example, lungs and blood vessels have distinct functions but are lined by tissues that are of the same basic type and that therefore share many properties.

There are four main types of animal tissues: epithelial, connective, muscle, and nervous. Figure 40.5, on the next three pages, explores the structure and function of each type. In later chapters, we'll discuss how the tissues described here contribute to the functions of each organ system.

Organ System	Main Components	Main Functions
Digestive	Mouth, pharynx, esophagus, stomach, intestines, liver, pancreas, anus	Food processing (ingestion, digestion, absorption, elimination)
Circulatory	Heart, blood vessels, blood	Internal distribution of materials
Respiratory	Lungs, trachea, other breathing tubes	Gas exchange (uptake of oxygen; disposal of carbon dioxide)
Immune and lymphatic	Bone marrow, lymph nodes, thymus, spleen, lymph vessels, white blood cells	Body defense (fighting infections and cancer)
Excretory	Kidneys, ureters, urinary bladder, urethra	Disposal of metabolic wastes; regulation of osmotic balance of blood
Endocrine	Pituitary, thyroid, pancreas, adrenal, and other hormone-secreting glands	Coordination of body activities (such as digestion and metabolism)
Reproductive	Ovaries or testes and associated organs	Reproduction
Nervous	Brain, spinal cord, nerves, sensory organs	Coordination of body activities; detection of stimuli and formulation of responses to them
Integumentary	Skin and its derivatives (such as hair, claws, skin glands)	Protection against mechanical injury, infection, dehydration; thermoregulation
Skeletal	Skeleton (bones, tendons, ligaments, cartilage)	Body support, protection of internal organs, movement
Muscular	Skeletal muscles	Locomotion and other movement

Table 40.1 Organ Systems in Mammals

Exploring Structure and Function in Animal Tissues

Epithelial Tissue

Occurring as sheets of cells, **epithelial tissues**, or **epithelia** (singular, *epithelium*), cover the outside of the body and line organs and cavities within the body. Because epithelial cells are closely packed, often with tight junctions (see Figure 6.32), they function as a barrier against mechanical injury, pathogens, and fluid loss. Epithelia also form active interfaces with the environment. For example, the epithelium that lines the nasal passages is crucial for olfaction, the sense of smell. Note how different cell shapes and arrangements correlate with distinct functions.

Stratified squamous epithelium

A stratified squamous epithelium is multilayered and regenerates rapidly. New cells formed by division near the basal lamina (see micrograph below) push outward, replacing cells that are sloughed off. This epithelium is commonly found on surfaces subject to abrasion, such as the outer skin and the linings of the mouth, anus, and vagina.

Cuboidal epithelium

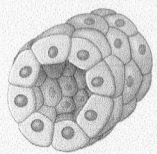

Cuboidal epithelium, with dice-shaped cells specialized for secretion, makes up the epithelium of kidney tubules and many glands, including the thyroid gland and salivary glands.

Simple columnar epithelium

The large, brick-shaped cells of simple columnar epithelia are often found where secretion or active absorption is important. For example, a simple columnar epithelium lines the intestines, secreting digestive juices and absorbing nutrients.

Simple squamous epithelium

The single layer of platelike cells that form a simple squamous epithelium functions in the exchange of material by diffusion. This type of epithelium, which is thin and leaky, lines blood vessels and the air sacs of the lungs, where diffusion of nutrients and gases is critical.

Pseudostratified columnar epithelium

A pseudostratified epithelium consists of a single layer of cells varying in height. In many vertebrates, a pseudostratified epithelium of ciliated cells forms a mucous membrane that lines portions of the respiratory tract. The beating cilia sweep the film of mucus along the surface.

Apical surface

Basal surface

Basal lamina

40 μm

Polarity of epithelia

All epithelia are polarized, meaning that they have two different sides. The *apical* surface faces the lumen (cavity) or outside of the organ and is therefore exposed to fluid or air. Specialized projections often cover this surface. For example, the apical surface of the epithelium lining the small intestine is covered with microvilli, projections that increase the surface area available for absorbing nutrients. The opposite side of each epithelium is the *basal* surface. The basal surface is attached to a *basal lamina*, a dense mat of extracellular matrix that separates the epithelium from the underlying tissue.

(All photos in figure are LMs.)

Connective tissue, consisting of a sparse population of cells scattered through an extracellular matrix, holds many tissues and organs together and in place. The matrix generally consists of a web of fibers embedded in a liquid, jellylike, or solid foundation. Within the matrix are numerous cells called **fibroblasts**, which secrete fiber proteins, and **macrophages**, which engulf foreign particles and any cell debris by phagocytosis (see Chapter 6).

Connective tissue fibers are of three kinds: *Collagenous fibers* provide strength and flexibility,

reticular fibers join connective tissue to adjacent tissues, and *elastic fibers* make tissues elastic. If you pinch a fold of tissue on the back of your hand, the collagenous and reticular fibers prevent the skin from being pulled far from the bone, whereas the elastic fibers restore the skin to its original shape when you release your grip. Different mixtures of fibers and foundation form the major types of connective tissue shown below.

Loose connective tissue

The most widespread connective tissue in the vertebrate body is *loose connective tissue,* which binds epithelia to underlying tissues and holds organs in place. Loose connective tissue gets its name from the loose weave of its fibers, which include all three types. It is found in the skin and throughout the body.

Collagenous fiber

120 μm

Elastic fiber

Fibrous connective tissue

Fibrous connective tissue is dense with collagenous fibers. It is found in **tendons**, which attach muscles to bones, and in **ligaments**, which connect bones at joints.

30 μm

Nuclei

Bone

The skeleton of most vertebrates is made of **bone**, a mineralized connective tissue. Bone-forming cells called *osteoblasts* deposit a matrix of collagen. Calcium, magnesium, and phosphate ions combine into a hard mineral within the matrix. The microscopic structure of hard mammalian bone consists of repeating units called *osteons*. Each osteon has concentric layers of the mineralized matrix, which are deposited around a central canal containing blood vessels and nerves.

Central canal

700 μm

Osteon

Blood

Blood has a liquid extracellular matrix called plasma, which consists of water, salts, and dissolved proteins. Suspended in plasma are erythrocytes (red blood cells), leukocytes (white blood cells), and cell fragments called platelets. Red cells carry oxygen, white cells function in defense, and platelets aid in blood clotting.

Plasma

White blood cells

55 μm

Red blood cells

Adipose tissue

Adipose tissue is a specialized loose connective tissue that stores fat in adipose cells distributed throughout its matrix. Adipose tissue pads and insulates the body and stores fuel as fat molecules (see Figure 4.6). Each adipose cell contains a large fat droplet that swells when fat is stored and shrinks when the body uses that fat as fuel.

Fat droplets

150 μm

Cartilage

Cartilage contains collagenous fibers embedded in a rubbery protein-carbohydrate complex called chondroitin sulfate. Cells called *chondrocytes* secrete the collagen and chondroitin sulfate, which together make cartilage a strong yet flexible support material. The skeletons of many vertebrate embryos contain cartilage that is replaced by bone as the embryo matures. Cartilage remains in some locations, such as the disks that act as cushions between vertebrae.

Chondrocytes

100 μm

Chondroitin sulfate

Exploring Structure and Function in Animal Tissues

Muscle Tissue

The tissue responsible for nearly all types of body movement is **muscle tissue**. All muscle cells consist of filaments containing the proteins actin and myosin, which together enable muscles to contract. There are three types of muscle tissue in the vertebrate body: skeletal, smooth, and cardiac.

Skeletal muscle

Attached to bones by tendons, **skeletal muscle**, or *striated muscle*, is responsible for voluntary movements. Skeletal muscle consists of bundles of long cells called muscle fibers. During development, skeletal muscle fibers form by the fusion of many cells, resulting in multiple nuclei in each muscle cell or fiber. The arrangement of contractile units, or sarcomeres, along the fibers gives the cells a striped (striated) appearance. In adult mammals, building muscle increases the size but not the number of muscle fibers.

Smooth muscle

Smooth muscle, which lacks striations, is found in the walls of the digestive tract, urinary bladder, arteries, and other internal organs. The cells are spindle-shaped. Smooth muscles are responsible for involuntary body activities, such as churning of the stomach and constriction of arteries.

Cardiac muscle

Cardiac muscle forms the contractile wall of the heart. It is striated like skeletal muscle and has similar contractile properties. Unlike skeletal muscle, however, cardiac muscle has fibers that interconnect via intercalated disks, which relay signals from cell to cell and help synchronize heart contraction.

Nuclei

Muscle fiber

Sarcomere

100 μm

Nucleus   Muscle fibers   25 μm

Nucleus   Intercalated disk   50 μm

Nervous Tissue

Nervous tissue functions in the receipt, processing, and transmission of information. Nervous tissue contains **neurons**, or nerve cells, which transmit nerve impulses, as well as support cells called **glial cells**, or simply **glia**. In many animals, a concentration of nervous tissue forms a brain, an information-processing center.

Neurons

Neurons are the basic units of the nervous system. A neuron receives nerve impulses from other neurons via its cell body and multiple extensions called dendrites. Neurons transmit impulses to neurons, muscles, or other cells via extensions called axons, which are often bundled together into nerves.

Neuron:

Dendrites

Cell body

Axon

40 μm

(Fluorescent LM)

Glia

The various types of glia help nourish, insulate, and replenish neurons, and in some cases, modulate neuron function.

Glia

15 μm

Axons of neurons

Blood vessel

(Confocal LM)

Coordination and Control

An animal's tissues, organs, and organ systems must act in concert with one another. For example, during long dives, the harbor seal in Figure 40.2 slows its heart rate, collapses its lungs, and lowers its body temperature while propelling itself forward with its hind flippers. Coordinating activity across an animal's body in this way requires communication between different locations in the body. What signals are used? How do the signals move within the body? There are two sets of answers to these questions, reflecting the two major systems for controlling and coordinating responses to stimuli (Figure 40.6).

In the endocrine system, signaling molecules released into the bloodstream by endocrine cells reach all locations in the body. In the nervous system, neurons transmit signals, called

nerve impulses, between specific locations in the body. In each system, the type of pathway used is the same regardless of whether the signal reaches across the length of the body or ends up just a few cell diameters away.

The signaling molecules broadcast throughout the body by the endocrine system are called **hormones**. Different hormones cause distinct effects, and only cells that have receptors for a particular hormone respond (Figure 40.6a). Depending on which cells have receptors for that hormone, the hormone may have an effect in just a single location or in sites throughout the body. For example, only cells of the thyroid gland have the receptor for thyroid-stimulating hormone (TSH). Upon binding TSH, thyroid cells release thyroid hormone, which acts directly on cells in nearly every tissue to increase oxygen consumption and heat production.

Hormones are relatively slow acting. It takes many seconds for TSH and other hormones to be released into the bloodstream and carried throughout the body. The effects of hormones are often long-lasting, however, because hormones remain in the bloodstream for seconds, minutes, or even hours.

In the nervous system, signals are not broadcast throughout the entire body. Instead, each nerve impulse travels to specific target cells along dedicated communication lines consisting mainly of axons (Figure 40.6b). Four types of cells can receive nerve impulses: other neurons, muscle cells, endocrine cells, and exocrine cells. Unlike the endocrine system, the nervous system conveys information by the *pathway* the signal takes. For example, a person can distinguish different musical notes because each note's frequency activates different neurons connecting the ear to the brain.

Communication in the nervous system usually involves more than one type of signal. Nerve impulses travel along axons, sometimes over long distances, as changes in voltage. But in many cases, passing information from one neuron to another involves very short-range chemical signals. Overall, transmission is extremely fast; nerve impulses take only a fraction of a second to reach the target and last only a fraction of a second.

Because the two major communication systems of the body differ in signal type, transmission, speed, and duration, they are adapted to different functions. The endocrine system is well suited for coordinating gradual changes that affect the entire body, such as growth and development, reproduction, metabolic processes, and digestion. The nervous system is well suited for directing immediate and rapid responses to the environment, especially in controlling fast locomotion and behavior.

Although the functions of the endocrine and nervous systems are distinct, the two systems often work in close coordination. Both contribute to maintaining a stable internal environment, our next topic of discussion.

▼ Figure 40.6 **Signaling in the endocrine and nervous systems**

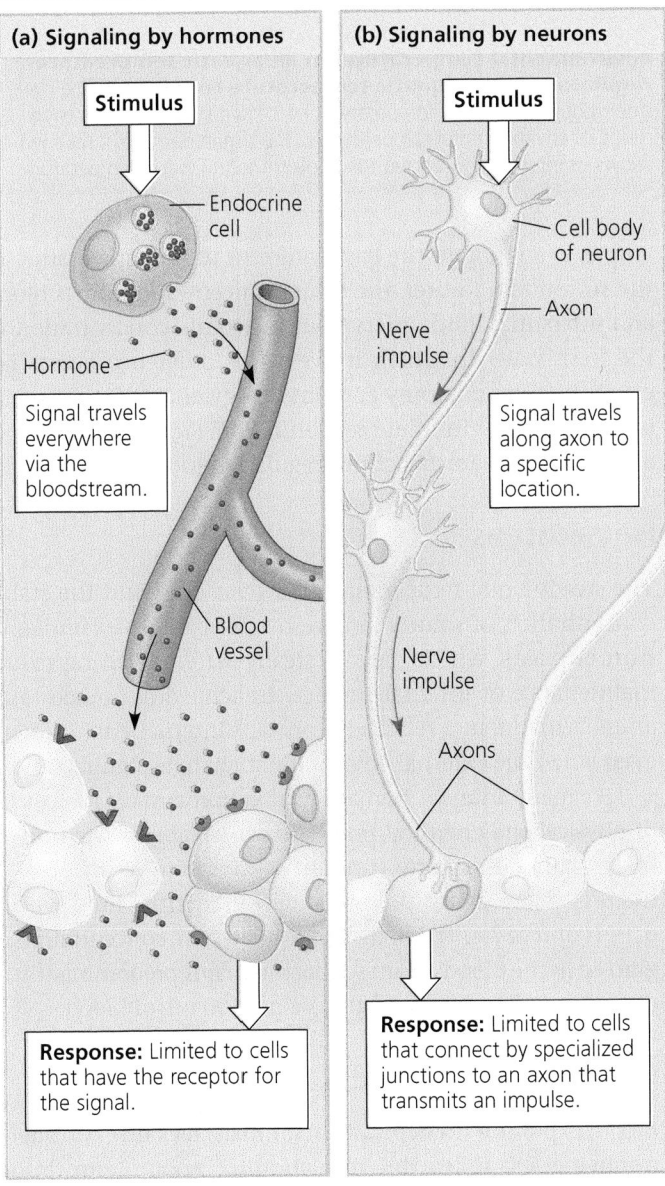

(a) Signaling by hormones

Stimulus

Endocrine cell

Hormone

Signal travels everywhere via the bloodstream.

Blood vessel

Response: Limited to cells that have the receptor for the signal.

(b) Signaling by neurons

Stimulus

Cell body of neuron

Axon

Nerve impulse

Signal travels along axon to a specific location.

Nerve impulse

Axons

Response: Limited to cells that connect by specialized junctions to an axon that transmits an impulse.

1. What properties are shared by all types of epithelia?
2. In cool weather, jackrabbits sometimes flatten their ears against their body. What advantage and disadvantage do you think this body posture offers for survival?
3. **WHAT IF?** Suppose you are standing at the edge of a cliff and suddenly slip—you barely manage to keep your balance and avoid falling. As your heart races, you feel a burst of energy, due in part to a surge of blood into dilated (widened) vessels in your muscles and an upward spike in the level of glucose in your blood. Why might you expect that this "fight-or-flight" response requires both the nervous and endocrine systems?

For suggested answers, see Appendix A.

CONCEPT 40.2

Feedback control maintains the internal environment in many animals

Imagine that your body temperature soared every time you took a hot shower or drank a freshly brewed cup of coffee. Managing the state of the internal environment is a major challenge for the animal body. Faced with environmental fluctuations, animals manage their internal environment by either regulating or conforming.

Regulating and Conforming

An animal is said to be a **regulator** for a particular environmental variable if it uses internal mechanisms to control internal change in the face of external fluctuation. The river otter in **Figure 40.7** is a regulator for temperature, keeping its body at a temperature that is largely independent of that of the water in which it swims.

An animal is said to be a **conformer** for a particular environmental variable if it allows its internal condition to change in accordance with external changes in the variable. The largemouth bass in Figure 40.7 conforms to the temperature of the lake it inhabits. As the water warms or cools, so does the body of the bass. Some animals conform to more constant environments. For example, many marine invertebrates, such as spider crabs of the genus *Libinia*, let their internal solute concentration conform to the relatively stable solute concentration (salinity) of their ocean environment.

Regulating and conforming represent extremes on a continuum. An animal may regulate some internal conditions while allowing others to conform to the environment. For ex-

▲ **Figure 40.7 The relationship between body and environmental temperatures in an aquatic temperature regulator and an aquatic temperature conformer.** The river otter regulates its body temperature, keeping it stable across a wide range of environmental temperatures. The largemouth bass, meanwhile, allows its internal environment to conform to the water temperature.

ample, even though the bass conforms to the temperature of the surrounding water, the solute concentration in its blood and interstitial fluid differs from the solute concentration of the fresh water in which it lives. This difference occurs because the fish's anatomy and physiology enable it to regulate internal changes in solute concentration. (You will learn more about the mechanisms of this regulation in Chapter 44.)

Homeostasis

The steady body temperature of a river otter and the stable concentration of solutes in a freshwater bass are examples of **homeostasis**, which means "steady state," referring to the maintenance of internal balance. In achieving homeostasis, animals maintain a relatively constant internal environment even when the external environment changes significantly.

Like many animals, humans exhibit homeostasis for a range of physical and chemical properties. For example, the human body maintains a fairly constant temperature of about 37°C (98.6°F) and a pH of the blood and interstitial fluid within 0.1 pH unit of 7.4. The body also regulates the concentration of glucose in the bloodstream so that it remains predominantly in the range of 70–110 mg of glucose per 100 mL of blood.

Mechanisms of Homeostasis

Before exploring homeostasis in animals, let's first consider a nonliving example: the regulation of room temperature

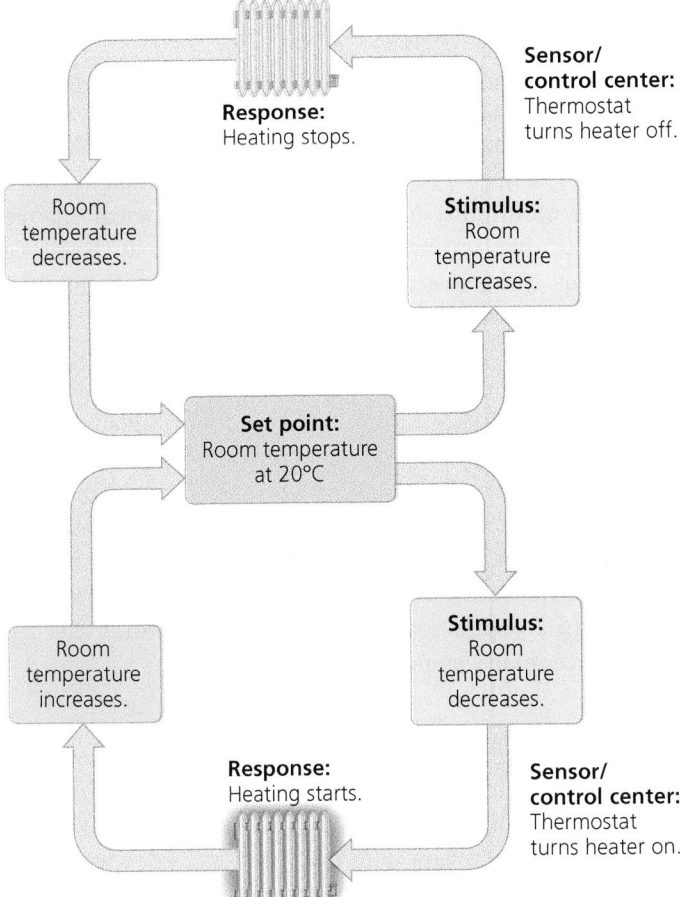

Response:
Heating stops.

Sensor/control center:
Thermostat turns heater off.

Room temperature decreases.

Stimulus:
Room temperature increases.

Set point:
Room temperature at 20°C

Room temperature increases.

Stimulus:
Room temperature decreases.

Response:
Heating starts.

Sensor/control center:
Thermostat turns heater on.

▲ **Figure 40.8 A nonliving example of temperature regulation: control of room temperature.** Regulating room temperature depends on a control center (a thermostat) that detects temperature change and activates mechanisms that reverse that change.

WHAT IF? *How would adding an air conditioner to the system contribute to homeostasis?*

(Figure 40.8). Let's assume you want to keep a room at 20°C (68°F), a comfortable temperature for normal activity. You adjust a control device—the thermostat—to 20°C and allow a thermometer in the thermostat to monitor temperature. If the room temperature falls below 20°C, the thermostat responds by turning on a radiator, furnace, or other heater. Heat is produced until the room reaches 20°C, at which point the thermostat switches off the heater. Whenever the temperature in the room again drifts below 20°C, the thermostat activates another heating cycle.

Like a home heating system, an animal achieves homeostasis by maintaining a variable, such as body temperature or solute concentration, at or near a particular value, or **set point**. Fluctuations in the variable above or below the set point serve as the **stimulus** detected by a receptor, or **sensor**. Upon receiving a signal from the sensor, a *control center* generates output that triggers a **response**, a physiological activity that helps return the variable to the set point. In the home heating example, a drop in temperature

below the set point acts as a stimulus, the thermostat serves as the sensor and control center, and the heater produces the response.

Feedback Control in Homeostasis

Like the regulatory circuit shown in Figure 40.8, homeostasis in animals relies largely on **negative feedback**, a control mechanism that reduces, or "damps," the stimulus. For example, when you exercise vigorously, you produce heat, which increases body temperature. Your nervous system detects this increase and triggers sweating. As you sweat, the evaporation of moisture from your skin cools your body, helping return your body temperature to its set point.

Homeostasis is a dynamic equilibrium, the interplay between external factors that tend to change the internal environment and internal control mechanisms that oppose such changes. Note that physiological responses to stimuli are not instantaneous, just as switching on a furnace does not immediately warm a room. As a result, homeostasis moderates but doesn't eliminate changes in the internal environment. Additional fluctuation occurs if a variable has a *normal range*—an upper and lower limit—rather than a single set point. This is equivalent to a heating system that begins producing heat when the room temperature drops to 19°C (66°F) and stops heating when the temperature reaches 21°C (70°F). Regardless of whether there is a set point or a normal range, homeostasis is enhanced by adaptations that reduce fluctuations, such as insulation in the case of temperature and physiological buffers in the case of pH.

Unlike negative feedback, **positive feedback** is a control mechanism that amplifies rather than reduces the stimulus (see Figure 1.13). Positive-feedback loops in animals do not play a major role in homeostasis, but instead help drive processes to completion. During childbirth, for instance, the pressure of the baby's head against receptors near the opening of the mother's uterus stimulates the uterus to contract. These contractions result in greater pressure against the opening of the uterus, heightening the contractions and thereby causing even greater pressure, until the baby is born.

Alterations in Homeostasis

The set points and normal ranges for homeostasis can change under various circumstances. In fact, *regulated changes* in the internal environment are essential to normal body functions. Some regulated changes are associated with a particular stage in life, such as the radical shift in hormone balance that occurs during puberty. Other regulated changes are cyclic, such as the variation in hormone levels responsible for a woman's menstrual cycle (see Figure 46.14).

In all animals (and plants, too), certain cyclic alterations in metabolism reflect a **circadian rhythm**, a set of physiological changes that occur roughly every 24 hours. For example, your body temperature typically undergoes a cyclic rise and fall of more than 0.6°C (1°F) in every 24-hour period. Remarkably, a biological clock maintains this rhythm even when variations in human activity, room temperature, and light levels are minimized (Figure 40.9a). A circadian rhythm is thus intrinsic to the body, although the biological clock is normally coordinated with the cycle of light and darkness in the environment (Figure 40.9b). For example, the hormone melatonin is secreted at night, and more is released during the longer nights of winter. External stimuli can reset the biological clock, but the effect is not immediate. That is why flying across several time zones results in jet lag, a mismatch between the circadian rhythm and local environment that persists until the clock fully resets.

One way in which the normal range of homeostasis may change is through **acclimatization**, the gradual process by which an animal adjusts to changes in its external environment. For example, when an elk or other mammal moves up into the mountains from sea level, physiological changes that occur over several days facilitate activity at the higher elevations. The lower oxygen concentration in the air stimulates the animal to breathe more rapidly and deeply. It therefore loses more CO_2 through exhalation, raising blood pH above its set point. As the animal acclimatizes, changes in kidney function result in excretion of more alkaline urine, returning blood pH to its normal range. Other changes during acclimatization to a higher altitude include increased production of red blood cells, which carry oxygen. Note that acclimatization, a temporary change during an animal's lifetime, should not be confused with adaptation, a process of change in a population brought about by natural selection acting over many generations.

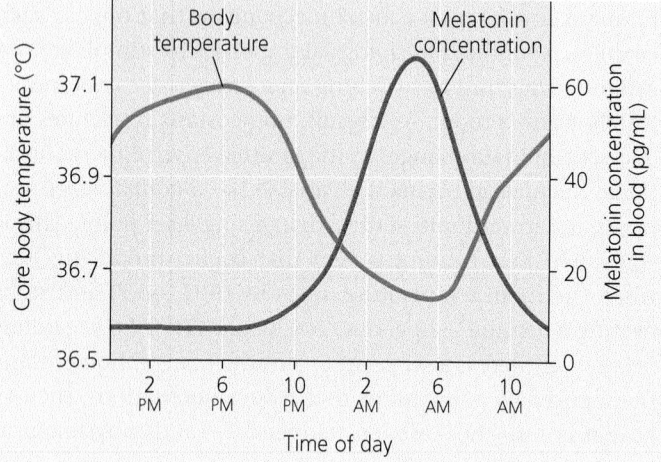

(a) **Variation in core body temperature and melatonin concentration in blood.** Researchers measured these two variables in resting but awake volunteers in an isolation chamber with constant temperature and low light. (Melatonin is a hormone that appears to be involved in sleep/wake cycles; see Chapter 45.)

(b) **The human circadian clock.** Metabolic activities undergo daily cycles in response to the circadian clock. As illustrated for a typical individual who rises early in the morning, eats lunch around noon, and sleeps at night, this variation in metabolism is apparent both day and night.

▲ **Figure 40.9 Human circadian rhythm.**

CONCEPT CHECK 40.2

1. **MAKE CONNECTIONS** Figure 8.21 (p. 160) illustrates feedback inhibition in an enzyme-catalyzed biosynthetic process. How does this type of negative feedback differ from that in thermoregulation?
2. If you were deciding where to put the thermostat in a house, what factors would govern your decision? How do these factors relate to the fact that many homeostatic control sensors in humans are located in the brain?
3. **MAKE CONNECTIONS** Like animals, cyanobacteria have a circadian rhythm. By analyzing the genes that maintain biological clocks, scientists were able to conclude that the 24-hour rhythms of humans and cyanobacteria reflect convergent evolution (see Concept 26.2, pp. 540–541). What evidence would have supported this conclusion? Explain.

For suggested answers, see Appendix A.

CONCEPT **40.3**

Homeostatic processes for thermoregulation involve form, function, and behavior

In this section, we will examine the regulation of body temperature as an example of how form and function work together in regulating an animal's internal environment. Later chapters in this unit will discuss other physiological systems involved in maintaining homeostasis.

Thermoregulation is the process by which animals maintain an internal temperature within a tolerable range. Thermoregulation is critical to survival because most biochemical and physiological processes are very sensitive to changes in body temperature. For every 10°C (18°F) decrease in temperature, the rates of most enzyme-mediated reactions decrease two- to threefold. Increases in temperature speed up reactions but cause some proteins to become less active. For instance, the oxygen carrier molecule hemoglobin becomes less effective at binding oxygen as temperature increases. Membranes can also change fluidity, becoming increasingly fluid or rigid as temperatures rise or fall, respectively.

Each animal species has an optimal temperature range. Thermoregulation helps maintain body temperature within that optimal range, enabling cells to function effectively even as the external temperature fluctuates.

Endothermy and Ectothermy

Internal metabolism and the external environment are the sources of heat for thermoregulation. Birds and mammals are mainly **endothermic**, meaning that they are warmed mostly by heat generated by metabolism. A few nonavian reptiles, some fishes, and many insect species are also mainly endothermic. In contrast, amphibians, lizards, snakes, turtles, many fishes, and most invertebrates are mainly **ectothermic**, meaning that they gain most of their heat from external sources.

Animals that are mainly endothermic are referred to as endotherms; those that are mainly ectothermic are known as ectotherms. Keep in mind, though, that endothermy and ectothermy are not mutually exclusive modes of thermoregulation. For example, a bird is mainly endothermic, but it may warm itself in the sun on a cold morning, much as an ectothermic lizard does.

Endotherms can maintain a stable body temperature even in the face of large fluctuations in the environmental temperature. For example, few ectotherms are active in the below-freezing weather that prevails during winter over much of Earth's surface, but many endotherms function very well in these conditions (Figure 40.10a). In a cold environment, an endotherm generates enough heat to keep its body substantially warmer than its surroundings. In a hot environment, endothermic vertebrates have mechanisms for cooling their bodies, enabling them to withstand heat loads that are intolerable for most ectotherms.

Because their heat source is largely environmental, ectotherms generally need to consume much less food than endotherms of equivalent size—an advantage if food supplies are limited. Ectotherms also usually tolerate larger fluctuations in their internal temperature. Although ectotherms do not generate enough heat for thermoregulation, many adjust body temperature by behavioral means, such as seeking out shade

(a) A walrus, an endotherm

(b) A lizard, an ectotherm

▲ Figure 40.10 **Endothermy and ectothermy.**

or basking in the sun (Figure 40.10b). Overall, ectothermy is an effective and successful strategy in most environments, as shown by the abundance and diversity of ectothermic animals.

Variation in Body Temperature

Animals can have either a variable or a constant body temperature. An animal whose body temperature varies with its environment is called a *poikilotherm* (from the Greek *poikilos*, varied). In contrast, a *homeotherm* has a relatively constant body temperature. For example, the largemouth bass is a poikilotherm, and the river otter is a homeotherm (see Figure 40.7).

From the descriptions of ectotherms and endotherms, it might seem that all ectotherms are poikilothermic and all endotherms are homeothermic. In fact, there is no fixed relationship between the source of heat and the stability of body temperature. For example, many ectothermic marine fishes and invertebrates inhabit waters with such stable temperatures that their body temperature varies less than that of endotherms such as humans and other mammals. Conversely, the body temperature of a few endotherms varies considerably. For example, bats and hummingbirds may periodically enter an inactive state in which they maintain a lower body temperature.

It is a common misconception that ectotherms are "cold-blooded" and endotherms are "warm-blooded." Ectotherms do not necessarily have low body temperatures. In fact, when sitting in the sun, many ectothermic lizards have higher body temperatures than mammals. Thus, the terms *cold-blooded* and *warm-blooded* are misleading and are avoided in scientific communication.

Balancing Heat Loss and Gain

Thermoregulation depends on an animal's ability to control the exchange of heat with its environment. Any organism, like any object, exchanges heat by four physical processes: radiation, evaporation, convection, and conduction. **Figure 40.11** distinguishes these processes, which account for the flow of heat both within an organism and between an organism and its external environment. Note that heat is always transferred from an object of higher temperature to one of lower temperature.

The essence of thermoregulation is maintaining rates of heat gain that equal rates of heat loss. Animals do this through mechanisms that either reduce heat exchange overall or favor heat exchange in a particular direction. In mammals, several of these mechanisms involve the **integumentary system**,

Radiation is the emission of electromagnetic waves by all objects warmer than absolute zero. Here, a lizard absorbs heat radiating from the distant sun and radiates a smaller amount of energy to the surrounding air.

Evaporation is the removal of heat from the surface of a liquid that is losing some of its molecules as gas. Evaporation of water from a lizard's moist surfaces that are exposed to the environment has a strong cooling effect.

Convection is the transfer of heat by the movement of air or liquid past a surface, as when a breeze contributes to heat loss from a lizard's dry skin or when blood moves heat from the body core to the extremities.

Conduction is the direct transfer of thermal motion (heat) between molecules of objects in contact with each other, as when a lizard sits on a hot rock.

▲ **Figure 40.11 Heat exchange between an organism and its environment.**

the outer covering of the body, consisting of the skin, hair, and nails (claws or hooves in some species).

Insulation

A major thermoregulatory adaptation in mammals and birds is insulation, which reduces the flow of heat between an animal and its environment. Sources of insulation include hair, feathers, and layers of fat formed by adipose tissue.

Many animals that rely on insulation to reduce overall heat exchange also adjust their insulating layers to help thermoregulate. Most land mammals and birds, for example, react to cold by raising their fur or feathers. This action traps a thicker layer of air, thereby increasing the insulating power of the fur or feather layer. To repel water that would reduce the insulating capacity of feathers or fur, some animals secrete oily substances, such as the oils that birds apply to their feathers during preening. Lacking feathers or fur, humans must rely primarily on fat for insulation. "Goose bumps" are a vestige of hair raising inherited from our furry ancestors.

Insulation is particularly important for marine mammals, such as whales and walruses. These animals swim in water colder than their body core, and many species spend at least part of the year in nearly freezing polar seas. The problem of thermoregulation is made worse by the fact that the transfer of heat to water occurs 50 to 100 times more rapidly than heat transfer to air. Just under their skin, marine mammals have a very thick layer of insulating fat called blubber. The insulation that blubber provides is so effective that marine mammals can maintain body core temperatures of about 36–38°C (97–100°F) without requiring much more energy from food than land mammals of similar size.

Circulatory Adaptations

Circulatory systems provide a major route for heat flow between the interior and exterior of the body. Adaptations that regulate the extent of blood flow near the body surface or that trap heat within the body core play a significant role in thermoregulation.

In response to changes in the temperature of their surroundings, many animals alter the amount of blood (and hence heat) flowing between their body core and their skin. Nerve signals that relax the muscles of the vessel walls result in *vasodilation*, a widening of superficial blood vessels (those near the body surface). As a consequence of the increase in vessel diameter, blood flow in the skin increases. In endotherms, vasodilation usually warms the skin and increases the transfer of body heat to the environment by radiation, conduction, and convection (see Figure 40.11). The reverse process, *vasoconstriction*, reduces blood flow and heat transfer by decreasing the diameter of superficial vessels. It is vasoconstriction in blood vessels of the ear that allows the jackrabbit shown in Figure 40.1 to avoid overheating on hot desert days.

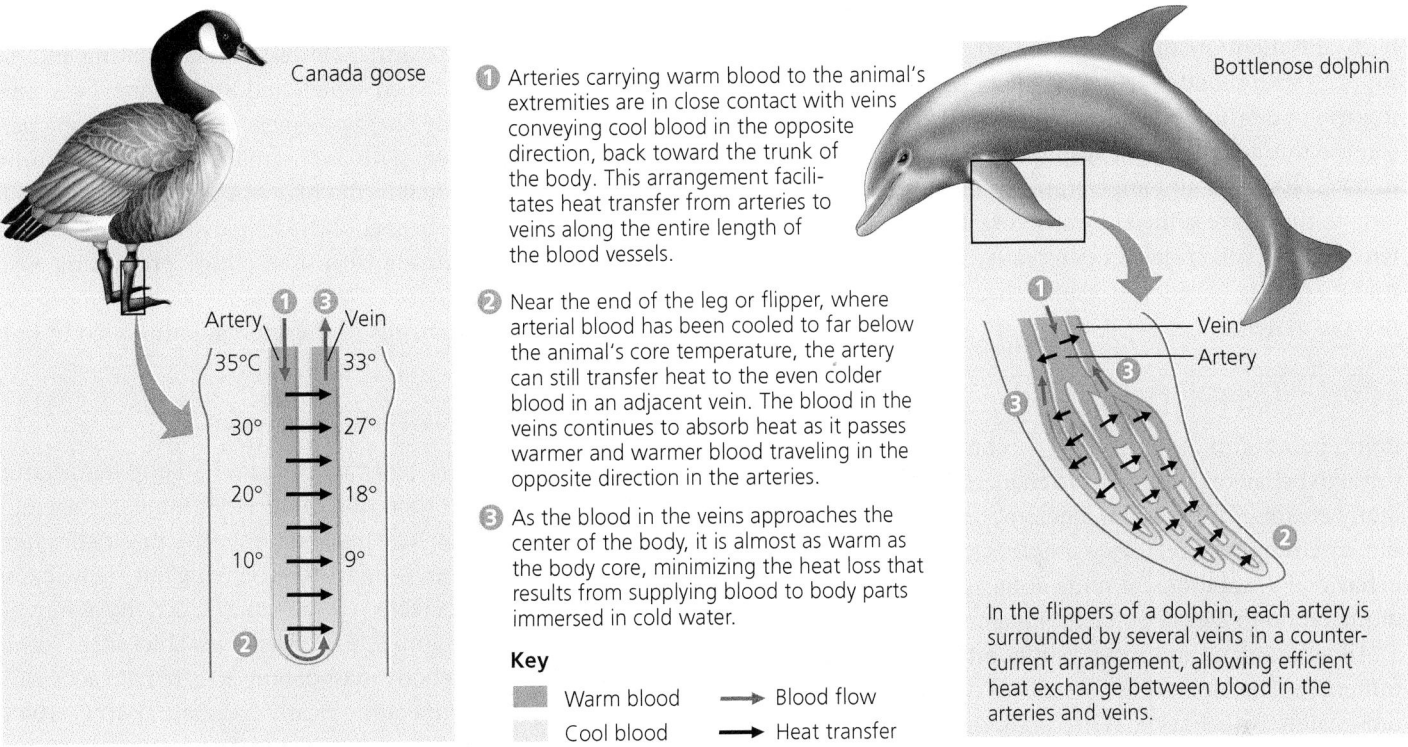

Canada goose

1 Arteries carrying warm blood to the animal's extremities are in close contact with veins conveying cool blood in the opposite direction, back toward the trunk of the body. This arrangement facilitates heat transfer from arteries to veins along the entire length of the blood vessels.

2 Near the end of the leg or flipper, where arterial blood has been cooled to far below the animal's core temperature, the artery can still transfer heat to the even colder blood in an adjacent vein. The blood in the veins continues to absorb heat as it passes warmer and warmer blood traveling in the opposite direction in the arteries.

3 As the blood in the veins approaches the center of the body, it is almost as warm as the body core, minimizing the heat loss that results from supplying blood to body parts immersed in cold water.

Key

Warm blood   → Blood flow
Cool blood   → Heat transfer

Bottlenose dolphin

In the flippers of a dolphin, each artery is surrounded by several veins in a countercurrent arrangement, allowing efficient heat exchange between blood in the arteries and veins.

▲ **Figure 40.12 Countercurrent heat exchangers.** A countercurrent exchange system traps heat in the body core, thus reducing heat loss from the extremities, particularly when they are immersed in cold water or in contact with ice or snow. In essence, heat in the arterial blood emerging from the body core is transferred directly to the returning venous blood instead of being lost to the environment.

Like endotherms, some ectotherms control heat exchange by regulating blood flow. For example, when the marine iguana of the Galápagos Islands swims in the cold ocean, its superficial blood vessels undergo vasoconstriction. This process routes more blood to the central core of the iguana's body, conserving body heat.

In many birds and mammals, reducing heat loss from the body relies on **countercurrent exchange**, the transfer of heat (or solutes) between fluids that are flowing in opposite directions. In a countercurrent heat exchanger, arteries and veins are located adjacent to each other **(Figure 40.12)**. As warm blood moves from the body core in the arteries, it transfers heat to the colder blood returning from the extremities in the veins. Because blood flows through the arteries and veins in opposite directions, heat is transferred along the entire length of the exchanger, maximizing the rate of heat exchange.

Certain sharks, fishes, and insects also use countercurrent heat exchange. Although most sharks and fishes are temperature conformers, countercurrent heat exchangers are found in some large, powerful swimmers, including great white sharks, bluefin tuna, and swordfish. By keeping the main swimming muscles several degrees warmer than tissues near the animal's surface, this adaptation enables the vigorous, sustained activity that is characteristic of these animals. Similarly, many endothermic insects (bumblebees, honeybees, and some moths) have a countercurrent exchanger that helps maintain a high temperature in their thorax, where flight muscles are located.

In controlling heat gain and loss, some species regulate the extent of blood flow to the countercurrent exchanger. By allowing blood to pass through the heat exchanger or diverting it to other blood vessels, these animals alter the rate of heat loss as their physiological state or environment changes. For example, insects flying in hot weather run the risk of overheating because of the large amount of heat produced by working flight muscles. In some species, the countercurrent mechanism can be "shut down," allowing muscle-produced heat to be lost from the thorax to the abdomen and then to the environment.

Cooling by Evaporative Heat Loss

Many mammals and birds live in places where thermoregulation requires cooling as well as warming. If the environmental temperature is above their body temperature, animals gain heat from the environment as well as from metabolism, and evaporation is the only way to keep body temperature from rising. Terrestrial animals lose water by evaporation from their skin and respiratory surfaces. Water absorbs considerable heat when it evaporates (see Chapter 3); this heat is carried away from the body surface with the water vapor.

Some animals have adaptations that can greatly augment the cooling effect of evaporation. Panting is important in birds and many mammals. Some birds have a pouch richly supplied with blood vessels in the floor of the mouth; fluttering the pouch increases evaporation. Pigeons, for example, can use this adaptation to keep their body temperature close to 40°C (104°F) in air temperatures as high as 60°C (140°F), as long as they have sufficient water. Sweating or bathing moistens the skin and enhances evaporative cooling. Many terrestrial mammals have sweat glands that are controlled by the nervous system.

Behavioral Responses

Both endotherms and ectotherms control body temperature through behavioral responses to changes in the environment. Many ectotherms maintain a nearly constant body temperature by engaging in relatively simple behaviors. More extreme behavioral adaptations in some animals include hibernation or migration to a more suitable climate.

All amphibians and most reptiles other than birds are ectothermic. Therefore, these organisms control body temperature mainly by behavior. When cold, they seek warm places, orienting themselves toward heat sources and expanding the portion of their body surface exposed to the heat source (see Figure 40.10b). When hot, they move to cool areas or turn in another direction.

Many terrestrial invertebrates can adjust internal temperature by the same behavioral mechanisms used by vertebrate ectotherms. The desert locust (*Schistocerca gregaria*), for example, must reach a certain temperature to become active, and on cold days it orients itself in a direction that maximizes the absorption of sunlight. Other terrestrial invertebrates have certain postures that enable them to maximize or minimize their absorption of heat from the sun (Figure 40.13).

Honeybees use a thermoregulatory mechanism that depends on social behavior. In cold weather, they increase heat production and huddle together, thereby retaining heat. Individuals move between the cooler outer edges of

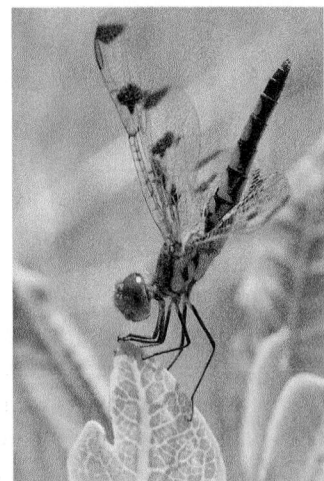

▶ Figure 40.13
Thermoregulatory behavior in a dragonfly. This dragonfly's "obelisk" posture is an adaptation that minimizes the amount of body surface exposed to the sun. This posture helps reduce heat gain by radiation.

the cluster and the warmer center, thus circulating and distributing the heat. Even when huddling, honeybees must expend considerable energy to keep warm during long periods of cold weather. (This is the main function of storing large quantities of fuel in the hive in the form of honey.) In hot weather, honeybees cool the hive by transporting water to the hive and fanning with their wings, promoting evaporation and convection. Thus, a colony of honeybees uses many of the mechanisms of thermoregulation seen in individual organisms.

Adjusting Metabolic Heat Production

Because endotherms generally maintain a body temperature considerably higher than that of the environment, they must counteract continual heat loss. Endotherms can vary heat production—*thermogenesis*—to match changing rates of heat loss. Thermogenesis is increased by such muscle activity as moving or shivering. For example, shivering helps chickadees (genus *Poecile*), birds with a body mass of only 20 g, remain active and hold their body temperature nearly constant at 40°C (104°F) in environmental temperatures as low as −40°C (−40°F), as long as they have adequate food.

In some mammals, certain hormones can cause mitochondria to increase their metabolic activity and produce heat instead of ATP. This process, called *nonshivering thermogenesis*, takes place throughout the body; some mammals also have a tissue called *brown fat* in their neck and between their shoulders that is specialized for rapid heat production. (In human infants, brown fat represents about 5% of total body weight. In 2009, brown fat was found for the first time in human adults, with greater amounts being detected when outdoor temperatures were lower.) Through shivering and nonshivering thermogenesis, mammals and birds in cold environments can increase their metabolic heat production by as much as five to ten times the levels that occur in warm conditions.

A few large reptiles become endothermic in particular circumstances. In the early 1960s, Herndon Dowling documented this phenomenon for a female Burmese python (*Python molurus bivittatus*). Placing temperature-recording devices along the snake's coils, Dowling found that the snake maintained a body temperature roughly 6°C (11°F) above that of the surrounding air during the month when she was incubating eggs. Where did the heat come from? Further studies by Dowling and colleagues showed that pythons, like mammals and birds, can raise their body temperature through shivering (Figure 40.14). These and other findings have led to new insights into thermoregulation in reptiles and have contributed to the idea, still under debate, that certain groups of Mesozoic dinosaurs were endothermic (see Chapter 34).

As mentioned earlier, many species of flying insects, such as bees and moths, are endothermic—the smallest of all endotherms. The capacity of such endothermic insects to elevate

INQUIRY

How does a Burmese python generate heat while incubating eggs?

EXPERIMENT Herndon Dowling, graduate student Allen Vinegar, and the student's research supervisor, Victor Hutchison, at the Bronx Zoo in New York, observed that when a female Burmese python incubated eggs by wrapping her body around them, she raised her body temperature and frequently contracted the muscles in her coils. To learn if the contractions were elevating her body temperature, they placed the python and her eggs in a chamber. As they varied the chamber's temperature, they monitored the python's muscle contractions as well as her oxygen uptake, a measure of her rate of cellular respiration.

RESULTS The python's oxygen consumption increased when the temperature in the chamber decreased. Her oxygen consumption also increased with the rate of muscle contraction.

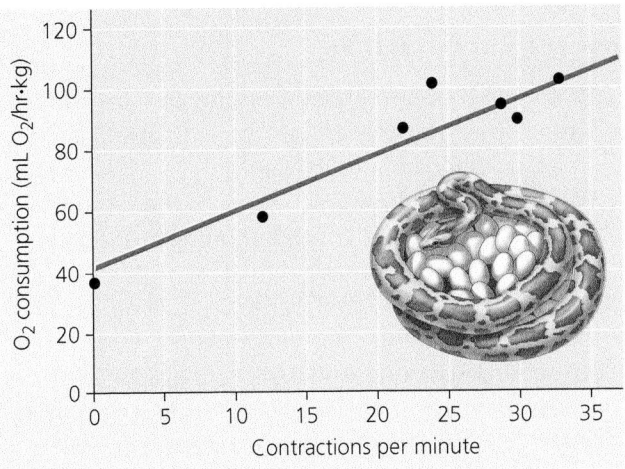

CONCLUSION Because oxygen consumption generates heat through cellular respiration and increases linearly with the rate of muscle contraction, the researchers concluded that the muscle contractions, a form of shivering, were the source of the Burmese python's elevated body temperature.

SOURCE V. H. Hutchison, H. G. Dowling, and A. Vinegar, Thermoregulation in a brooding female Indian python, *Python molurus bivittatus*, *Science* 151:694–696 (1966).

WHAT IF? Suppose you varied air temperature and measured oxygen consumption for a female Burmese python without a clutch of eggs. Since she would not show shivering behavior, how would you expect the snake's oxygen consumption to vary with environmental temperature?

body temperature depends on powerful flight muscles, which generate large amounts of heat when contracting. Many endothermic insects warm up by shivering before taking off. As they contract their flight muscles in synchrony, only slight wing movements occur, but considerable heat is produced. Chemical reactions, and hence cellular respiration, speed up in the warmed-up flight "motors," enabling these insects to fly even when the air is cold **(Figure 40.15)**.

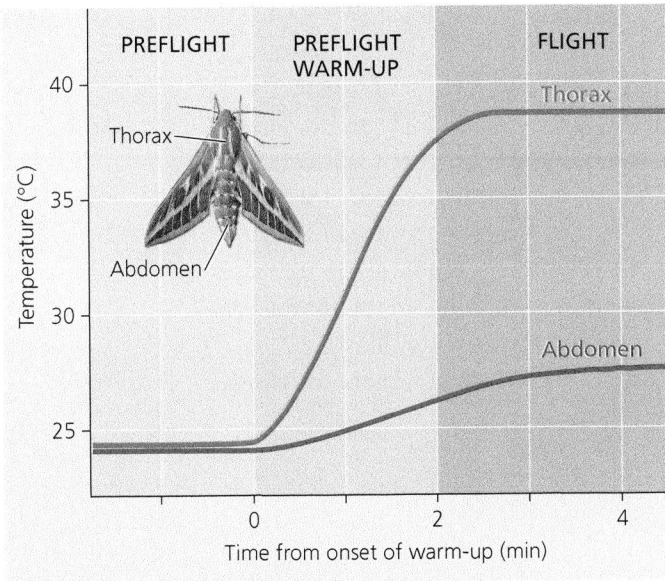

▲ Figure 40.15 **Preflight warm-up in the hawkmoth.** The hawkmoth (*Manduca sexta*) is one of many insect species that use a shivering-like mechanism for preflight warm-up of thoracic flight muscles. Warming up helps these muscles produce enough power to let the animal take off. Once the moth is airborne, flight muscle activity maintains a high thoracic temperature.

Acclimatization in Thermoregulation

Acclimatization contributes to thermoregulation in many animal species. In birds and mammals, acclimatization to seasonal temperature changes often includes adjusting insulation—growing a thicker coat of fur in the winter and shedding it in the summer, for example. These changes help endotherms keep a constant body temperature year-round.

Acclimatization in ectotherms often includes adjustments at the cellular level. Cells may produce variants of enzymes that have the same function but different optimal temperatures. Also, the proportions of saturated and unsaturated lipids in membranes may change; unsaturated lipids help keep membranes fluid at lower temperatures (see Figure 7.5). Some ectotherms that experience subzero body temperatures protect themselves by producing "antifreeze" compounds that prevent ice formation in their cells. In the Arctic Ocean and Southern (Antarctic) Ocean, these compounds enable certain fishes to survive in water as cold as −2°C (28°F), below the freezing point of unprotected body fluids (about −1°C, or 30°F).

Physiological Thermostats and Fever

The regulation of body temperature in humans and other mammals is brought about by a complex system based on feedback mechanisms. The sensors for thermoregulation are concentrated in a brain region called the **hypothalamus**. A group of nerve cells in the hypothalamus functions as a thermostat, responding to body temperatures outside a normal range by activating mechanisms that promote heat loss

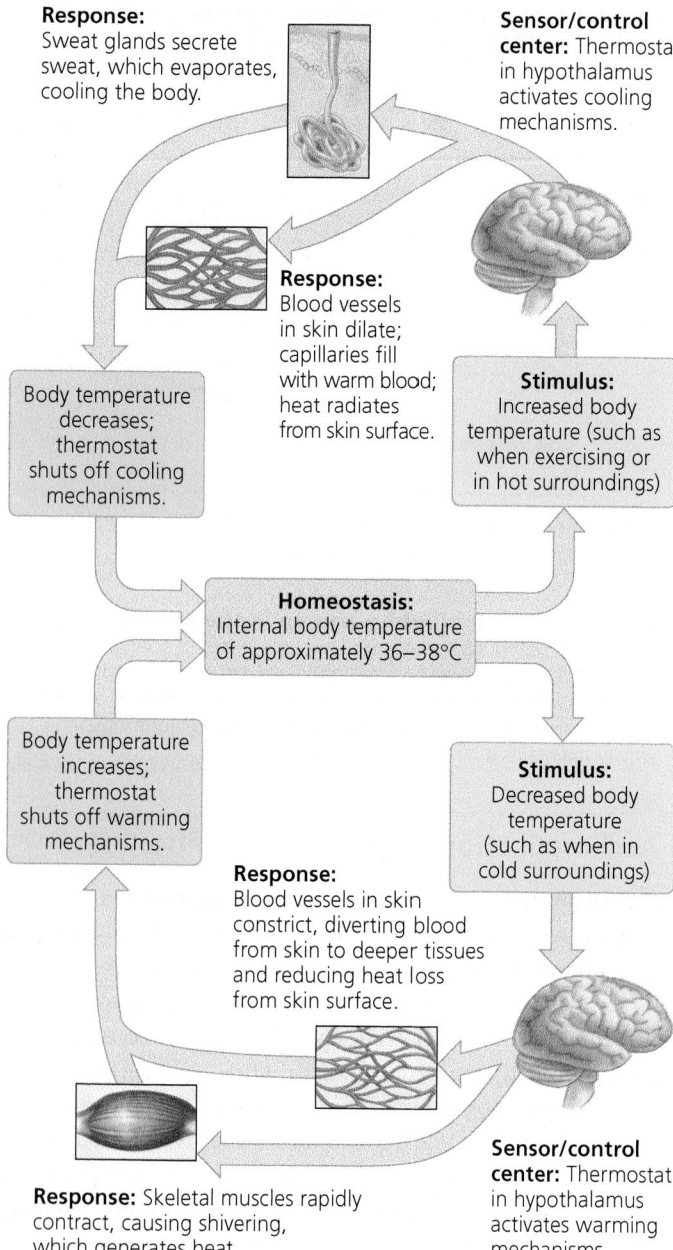

Response:
Sweat glands secrete sweat, which evaporates, cooling the body.

Sensor/control center: Thermostat in hypothalamus activates cooling mechanisms.

Response:
Blood vessels in skin dilate; capillaries fill with warm blood; heat radiates from skin surface.

Body temperature decreases; thermostat shuts off cooling mechanisms.

Stimulus:
Increased body temperature (such as when exercising or in hot surroundings)

Homeostasis:
Internal body temperature of approximately 36–38°C

Body temperature increases; thermostat shuts off warming mechanisms.

Stimulus:
Decreased body temperature (such as when in cold surroundings)

Response:
Blood vessels in skin constrict, diverting blood from skin to deeper tissues and reducing heat loss from skin surface.

Sensor/control center: Thermostat in hypothalamus activates warming mechanisms.

Response: Skeletal muscles rapidly contract, causing shivering, which generates heat.

▲ **Figure 40.16 The thermostatic function of the hypothalamus in human thermoregulation.**

or gain (**Figure 40.16**). Warm receptors signal the hypothalamic thermostat when temperatures increase; cold receptors signal when temperatures decrease. (Because the same blood vessel supplies the hypothalamus and ears, an ear thermometer records the temperature detected by the hypothalamic thermostat.) At body temperatures below the normal range, the thermostat inhibits heat loss mechanisms and activates heat-saving ones, such as vasoconstriction and the raising of fur, while stimulating heat-generating mechanisms (shivering and nonshivering thermogenesis). In response to elevated body temperature, the thermostat shuts down heat retention mechanisms and promotes cooling the body by vasodilation, sweating, or panting.

In the course of certain bacterial and viral infections, mammals and birds develop fever, an elevated body temperature. A variety of experiments have shown that fever reflects an increase in the set point for the biological thermostat. For example, artificially raising the temperature of the hypothalamus in an infected animal reduces fever in the rest of the body!

Although only endotherms develop fever, lizards exhibit a related response. When infected with certain bacteria, the desert iguana (*Dipsosaurus dorsalis*) seeks a warmer environment and then maintains a body temperature that is elevated by 2–4°C (4–7°F). Similar observations in fishes, amphibians, and even cockroaches indicate that this response to certain infections is a common feature of many animal species.

Having explored thermoregulation in depth, we'll now consider some other energy-consuming processes and the different ways that animals allocate, use, and conserve energy.

CONCEPT CHECK 40.3

1. What mode of heat exchange is involved in "wind chill," when moving air feels colder than still air at the same temperature? Explain.
2. Flowers differ in how much sunlight they absorb. Why might this matter to a hummingbird seeking nectar on a cool morning?
3. **WHAT IF?** Suppose at the end of a hard run on a hot day you find that there are no drinks left in the cooler. If, out of desperation, you dunk your head into the cooler, how might the ice-cold water affect the rate at which your body temperature returns to normal?

For suggested answers, see Appendix A.

CONCEPT **40.4**

Energy requirements are related to animal size, activity, and environment

One of the unifying themes of biology introduced in Chapter 1 is that life requires energy transfer and transformation. Like other organisms, animals use chemical energy for growth, repair, activity, and reproduction. The overall flow and transformation of energy in an animal—its **bioenergetics**—determines nutritional needs and is related to the animal's size, activity, and environment.

Energy Allocation and Use

As we have discussed in other chapters, organisms can be classified by how they obtain chemical energy. Most autotrophs, such as plants, use light energy to build energy-rich organic molecules and then use those organic molecules for fuel. Most heterotrophs, such as animals, must obtain their chemical

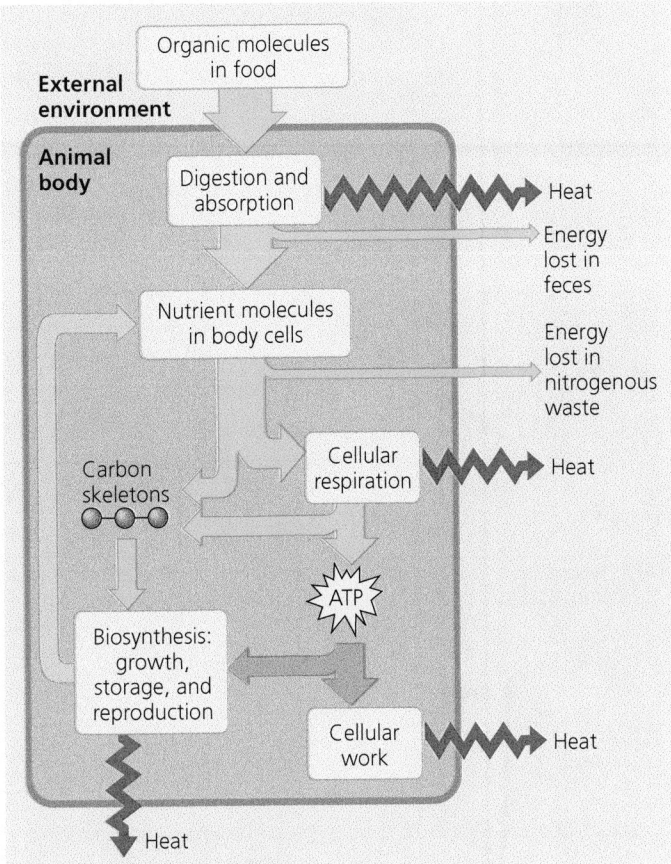

▲ **Figure 40.17 Bioenergetics of an animal: an overview.**

MAKE CONNECTIONS *Review the idea of energy coupling in Concept 8.3 (pp. 149–151). Then use that idea to explain why heat is produced in the absorption of nutrients, in cellular respiration, and in the synthesis of biopolymers.*

▲ **Figure 40.18 Measuring the rate of oxygen consumption by a swimming shark.** A researcher monitors the drop in oxygen level in the recirculating water of a juvenile hammerhead's tank.

energy from food, which contains organic molecules synthesized by other organisms.

Animals use chemical energy harvested from the food they eat to fuel metabolism and activity (**Figure 40.17**). Food is digested by enzymatic hydrolysis (see Figure 5.2b), and nutrients are absorbed by body cells. Most nutrient molecules are used to generate ATP. ATP produced by cellular respiration and fermentation powers cellular work, enabling cells, organs, and organ systems to perform the functions that keep an animal alive. Energy in the form of ATP is also used in biosynthesis, which is needed for body growth and repair, synthesis of storage material such as fat, and production of gametes. The production and use of ATP generates heat, which the animal eventually gives off to its surroundings.

Quantifying Energy Use

How much of the total energy an animal obtains from food does it need just to stay alive? How much energy must be expended to walk, run, swim, or fly from one place to another? What fraction of the energy intake is used for reproduction? Physiologists answer such questions by measuring the rate at

which an animal uses chemical energy and how this rate changes in different circumstances.

The amount of energy an animal uses in a unit of time is called its **metabolic rate**—the sum of all the energy used in biochemical reactions over a given time interval. Energy is measured in joules (J) or in calories (cal) and kilocalories (kcal). (A kilocalorie equals 1,000 calories, or 4,184 joules. The unit Calorie, with a capital C, as used by many nutritionists, is actually a kilocalorie.)

Metabolic rate can be determined in several ways. Because nearly all of the chemical energy used in cellular respiration eventually appears as heat, metabolic rate can be measured by monitoring an animal's rate of heat loss. For this approach, researchers use a calorimeter, which is a closed, insulated chamber equipped with a device that records an animal's heat loss. Metabolic rate can also be determined from the amount of oxygen consumed or carbon dioxide produced by an animal's cellular respiration (**Figure 40.18**). To calculate metabolic rate over longer periods, researchers record the rate of food consumption, the energy content of the food (about 4.5–5 kcal per gram of protein or carbohydrate and about 9 kcal per gram of fat), and the chemical energy lost in waste products (feces and nitrogenous waste).

Minimum Metabolic Rate and Thermoregulation

Animals must maintain a minimum metabolic rate for basic functions such as cell maintenance, breathing, and heartbeat. Researchers measure this minimum metabolic rate differently for endotherms and ectotherms. The minimum metabolic rate of a nongrowing endotherm that is at rest, has an empty stomach, and is not experiencing stress is called the **basal metabolic rate (BMR)**. BMR is measured under a "comfortable" temperature range—a range that requires no generation or shedding of heat above the minimum. The minimum metabolic rate of ectotherms is determined at a specific temperature because changes in the environmental temperature alter body temperature and therefore metabolic rate. The metabolic rate of a fasting, nonstressed ectotherm at rest at a particular temperature is called its **standard metabolic rate (SMR)**.

Comparisons of minimum metabolic rates reveal that endothermy and ectothermy have different energy costs. The BMR for humans averages 1,600–1,800 kcal per day for adult males and 1,300–1,500 kcal per day for adult females. These BMRs are about equivalent to the rate of energy use by a 75-watt light bulb. In contrast, the SMR of an American alligator is only about 60 kcal per day at 20°C (68°F). Since this represents less than ¹⁄₂₀ the energy used by a comparably sized adult human, the lower energetic requirement of ectothermy is readily apparent.

Influences on Metabolic Rate

Metabolic rate is affected by many factors besides whether the animal is an endotherm or an ectotherm. Some key factors are age, sex, size, activity, temperature, and nutrition. Here we'll examine the effects of size and activity.

Size and Metabolic Rate

Larger animals have more body mass and therefore require more chemical energy. Remarkably, the relationship between overall metabolic rate and body mass is constant across a wide range of sizes and forms, as illustrated for various mammals in **Figure 40.19a**. In fact, for even more varied organisms ranging in size from bacteria to blue whales, metabolic rate remains roughly proportional to body mass to the three-quarter power ($m^{3/4}$). Scientists are still researching the basis of this relationship, which applies to ectotherms as well as endotherms.

The relationship of metabolic rate to size profoundly affects energy consumption by body cells and tissues. As shown in **Figure 40.19b**, the energy it takes to maintain each gram of body mass is inversely related to body size. Each gram of a mouse, for instance, requires about 20 times as many calories as a gram of an elephant, even though the whole elephant uses far more calories than the whole mouse. The smaller animal's higher metabolic rate per gram demands a higher rate of oxygen delivery. Correlated with its higher metabolic rate per gram, the smaller animal has a higher breathing rate, blood volume (relative to its size), and heart rate. Also, it must eat much more food per unit of body mass.

Bioenergetic considerations associated with body size provide a clear example of how trade-offs shape the evolution of body plans. As body size becomes smaller, each gram of tissue increases in energy cost. As body size increases, energy costs per gram of tissue decrease, but an ever-larger fraction of body tissue is required for exchange, support, and locomotion.

Activity and Metabolic Rate

For both ectotherms and endotherms, activity greatly affects metabolic rate. Even a person reading quietly at a desk or an

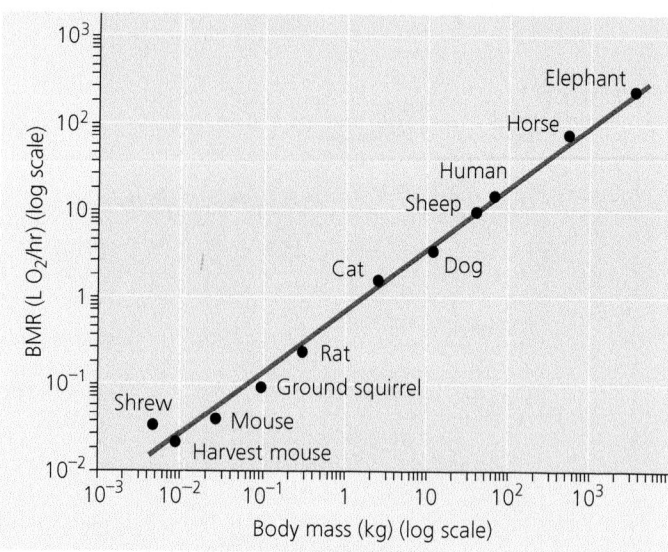

(a) Relationship of basal metabolic rate (BMR) to body size for various mammals. From shrew to elephant, size increases 1 millionfold.

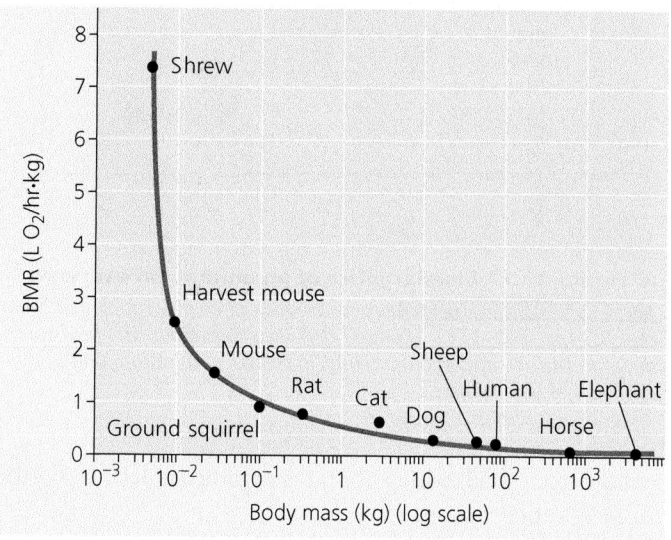

(b) Relationship of BMR per kilogram of body mass to body size for the same mammals as in (a).

▲ **Figure 40.19 The relationship of metabolic rate to body size.**

insect twitching its wings consumes energy beyond the BMR or SMR. Maximum metabolic rates (the highest rates of ATP use) occur during peak activity, such as lifting heavy weights, sprinting, or high-speed swimming. In general, the maximum metabolic rate an animal can sustain is inversely related to the duration of activity.

For most terrestrial animals, the average daily rate of energy consumption is 2 to 4 times BMR (for endotherms) or SMR (for ectotherms). Humans in most developed countries have an unusually low average daily metabolic rate of about 1.5 times BMR—an indication of their relatively sedentary lifestyles.

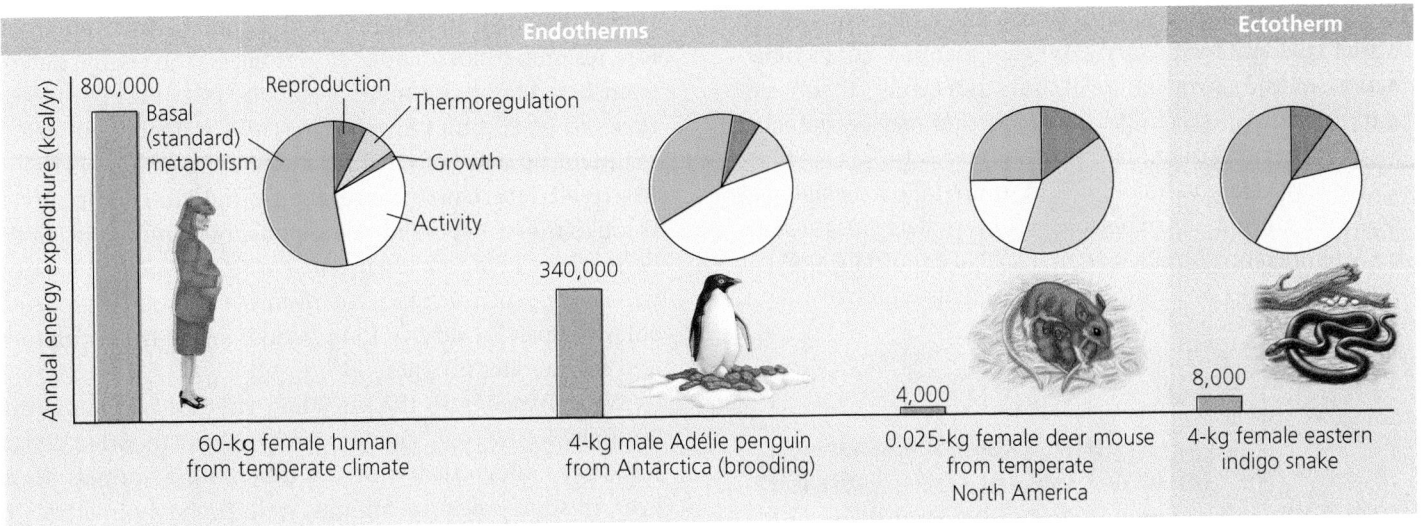

▲ **Figure 40.20 Energy budgets for four animals.** The slices of the pie charts indicate annual energy expenditures for various functions.

Energy Budgets

As we have seen, the ways in which animals use the chemical energy of food depend on environment, behavior, size, and thermoregulation. To understand how these influences affect bioenergetics in animal bodies, let's consider typical annual energy "budgets" of four terrestrial vertebrates varying in size and thermoregulatory strategy: a 60-kg female human, a 4-kg male Adélie penguin, a 25-g (0.025-kg) female deer mouse, and a 4-kg female eastern indigo snake (Figure 40.20). Reproduction is included in these energy budgets because it can greatly influence energy allocation and is critical to species survival.

The female human, an endothermic mammal, spends the largest fraction of her annual energy budget for BMR and comparatively less for activity and thermoregulation. The small amount of growth, about 1%, is equivalent to adding about 1 kg of body fat or 5–6 kg of other tissues. (Growth is not shown in the budgets for the penguin and deer mouse because these animals don't typically gain weight year to year after they are adults.) The cost of nine months of pregnancy and several months of breast-feeding is only 5–8% of the mother's energy requirements for a year.

A male penguin spends the largest fraction of his energy for activity because he must swim to catch food. Being well insulated and fairly large, he has relatively low costs of thermoregulation in spite of living in the cold Antarctic. His reproductive costs, about 6% of annual energy expenditures, come mainly from incubating eggs (brooding) and bringing food to his chicks.

Despite living in a temperate climate, the female deer mouse spends a large fraction of her energy budget for temperature regulation. Because of the high surface-to-volume ratio that goes with small size, deer mice lose body heat rapidly

and must constantly generate metabolic heat to maintain body temperature.

In contrast with these endothermic animals, the ectothermic snake has no thermoregulation costs. Like most snakes, she grows continuously throughout her life. In the example in Figure 40.20, the snake adds about 750 g of new body tissue in a year. She also produces about 650 g of eggs. The snake's economical ectothermic strategy is revealed by her very low energy expenditure, only $\frac{1}{40}$ the energy expended by the similarly sized endothermic penguin.

For all the animals in Figure 40.20, locomotion and other activities are a major part of the energy budget. Some animals can conserve energy by temporarily decreasing their activity to a very low level, a process we will consider next.

Torpor and Energy Conservation

Despite their many adaptations for homeostasis, animals may encounter conditions that severely challenge their abilities to balance their heat, energy, and materials budgets. For example, at certain times of the day or year, their surroundings may be extremely hot or cold, or food may be unavailable. **Torpor**, a physiological state of decreased activity and metabolism, is an adaptation that enables animals to save energy while avoiding difficult and dangerous conditions.

Many small mammals and birds exhibit a daily torpor that seems to be adapted to feeding patterns. For instance, some bats feed at night and go into torpor in daylight. Chickadees and hummingbirds feed during the day and often go into torpor on cold nights; the body temperature of chickadees drops as much as 10°C (18°F) at night, and the temperature of hummingbirds can fall 25°C (45°F) or more. All endotherms that exhibit daily torpor are relatively small; when active, they have high metabolic rates and thus very high rates of energy consumption.

Hibernation is long-term torpor that is an adaptation to winter cold and food scarcity. When a mammal enters hibernation, its body temperature declines as its body's thermostat is turned down. The temperature reduction may be dramatic: Some hibernating mammals cool to as low as 1–2°C (34–36°F), and at least one, the Arctic ground squirrel (*Spermophilus parryii*), can enter a supercooled (unfrozen) state in which its body temperature dips below 0°C (32°F). Periodically, perhaps every two weeks or so, hibernating animals undergo arousal, raising their body temperature and becoming active briefly before resuming hibernation. Nevertheless, the energy savings from hibernation are huge: Metabolic rates during hibernation can be 20 times lower than if the animal attempted to maintain normal body temperatures of 36–38°C (97–100°F). As a result, hibernators such as the ground squirrel can survive through the winter on limited supplies of energy stored in the body tissues or as food cached in a burrow. Similarly, the slow metabolism and inactivity of *estivation*, or summer torpor, enables animals to survive long periods of high temperatures and scarce water supplies.

What happens to the circadian rhythm in hibernating animals? In the past, some researchers have reported detecting daily biological rhythms in hibernating animals. However, in some cases the animals were probably in a state of torpor, from which they could readily arouse, rather than "deep" hibernation. Recently, a group of researchers in France addressed this question in a different way, examining the machinery of the biological clock rather than the rhythms it controls (**Figure 40.21**). Working with the European hamster, they found that molecular components of the clock stopped oscillating during hibernation. These findings support the hypothesis that the circadian clock ceases operation during hibernation, at least in this species.

From discussing body shape to considering energy conservation, this chapter has focused on the whole animal. We surveyed common tissue types that make up organs and organ systems. We also investigated how body plans provide for exchange of materials with the environment, how some animals maintain a constant internal environment, and how size and activity affect metabolic rate. For much of the rest of this unit, we'll explore how specialized organs and organ systems enable animals to meet the basic challenges of life.

▼ Figure 40.21

INQUIRY

What happens to the circadian clock during hibernation?

EXPERIMENT To determine whether the 24-hour biological clock continues to run during hibernation, Paul Pévet and colleagues at the University of Louis Pasteur in Strasbourg, France, studied molecular components of the circadian clock in the European hamster (*Cricetus cricetus*). The researchers measured RNA levels for two clock genes—*Per2* and *Bmal1*—during normal activity (euthermia) and during hibernation in constant darkness. The RNA samples were obtained from the suprachiasmatic nuclei (SCN), a pair of structures in the mammalian brain that control circadian rhythms.

RESULTS

CONCLUSION Hibernation disrupted circadian variation in the hamster's clock gene RNA levels. Further experiments demonstrated that this disruption was not simply due to the dark environment during hibernation, since for nonhibernating animals RNA levels during a darkened daytime were the same as in daylight. The researchers concluded that the biological clock stops running in hibernating European hamsters and, perhaps, in other hibernators as well.

SOURCE F. G. Revel et al., The circadian clock stops ticking during deep hibernation in the European hamster, *Proceedings of the National Academy of Sciences USA* 104:13816–13820 (2007).

WHAT IF? Suppose you discovered a new hamster gene and found that the levels of RNA for this gene were constant during hibernation. What could you conclude about the day and night RNA levels for this gene during euthermia?

CONCEPT CHECK 40.4

1. If a mouse and a small lizard of the same mass (both at rest) were placed in experimental chambers under identical environmental conditions, which animal would consume oxygen at a higher rate? Explain.
2. Which animal must eat a larger proportion of its weight in food each day: a house cat or an African lion caged in a zoo? Explain.
3. **WHAT IF?** If you monitored energy allocation in the penguin in Figure 40.20 for just a few months instead of an entire year, you might find the "growth" category to be a significant part of the pie chart. Given that adult penguins don't grow from year to year, how would you explain this finding?

For suggested answers, see Appendix A.

40 CHAPTER REVIEW

SUMMARY OF KEY CONCEPTS

CONCEPT 40.1

Animal form and function are correlated at all levels of organization (pp. 852–860)

- Physical laws constrain the evolution of an animal's size and shape. These constraints contribute to convergent evolution, the similar but independent adaptations of different species to a common environmental challenge.
- Each animal cell must have access to an aqueous environment. Simple two-layered sacs and flat shapes maximize exposure to the surrounding medium. More complex body plans have highly folded internal surfaces specialized for exchanging materials.
- In the hierarchical organization of animal bodies, groups of cells with a common structure and function make up **tissues**. Different tissues make up **organs**, which together make up **organ systems**. Animal tissues fall into four main groups, each with distinct functions. **Epithelial tissue** forms active interfaces with the environment on external and internal surfaces of the body. **Connective tissue** binds and supports other tissues. **Muscle tissue** contracts, moving the parts of the body. **Nervous tissue** transmits nerve impulses throughout the body.
- The endocrine and nervous systems are the two means of communication between different locations in the body. The endocrine system broadcasts signaling molecules called **hormones** everywhere via the bloodstream, but only certain cells are responsive to each hormone. The nervous system uses dedicated cellular circuits involving electrical and chemical signals to send information to specific locations.

> **?** *For a large animal, what challenges would a spherical shape pose for carrying out exchange with the environment?*

CONCEPT 40.2

Feedback control maintains the internal environment in many animals (pp. 860–862)

- Faced with environmental fluctuations, animals *regulate* (control) certain internal variables while allowing other internal variables to *conform* to (correspond to) external changes. **Homeostasis** is the maintenance of a steady state despite internal and external changes.
- Homeostatic mechanisms are usually based on **negative feedback**, in which the **response** reduces the **stimulus**.

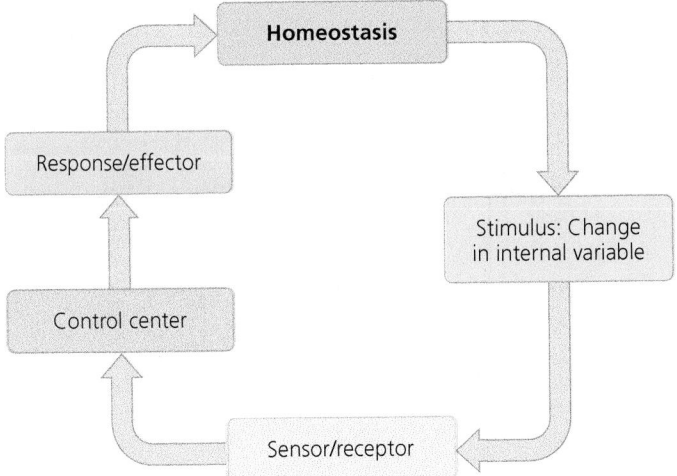

In contrast, **positive feedback** involves amplification of a stimulus by the response and often brings about a change in state, such as the transition from pregnancy to childbirth.

- Regulated change in the internal environment is essential to normal function. **Circadian rhythms** are daily fluctuations in metabolism and behavior tuned to the cycles of light and dark in the environment. Other environmental changes may trigger **acclimatization**, a temporary shift in the steady state.

> **?** *Is it accurate to define homeostasis as a constant internal environment? Explain.*

CONCEPT 40.3

Homeostatic processes for thermoregulation involve form, function, and behavior (pp. 862–868)

- An animal maintains its internal temperature within a tolerable range by **thermoregulation**. **Endotherms** are warmed mostly by heat generated by metabolism. **Ectotherms** get most of their heat from external sources. Endothermy requires a greater expenditure of energy. Body temperature may vary with environmental temperature, as in *poikilotherms*, or be relatively constant, as in *homeotherms*.
- In thermoregulation, physiological and behavioral adjustments balance heat gain and loss, which occur through **radiation**, **evaporation**, **convection**, and **conduction**. Insulation and **countercurrent exchange** reduce heat loss, whereas panting, sweating, and bathing increase evaporation, cooling the body. Both ectotherms and endotherms adjust their rate of heat exchange with their surroundings by vasodilation or vasoconstriction and by behavioral responses.
- Many mammals and birds adjust their amount of body insulation in response to changes in environmental temperature. Ectotherms undergo a variety of changes at the cellular level to acclimatize to shifts in temperature.
- The **hypothalamus** acts as the thermostat in mammalian regulation of body temperature. Fever reflects a resetting of this thermostat to a higher set point in response to infection.

> **?** *Given that humans thermoregulate, explain why your skin is cooler than your body core.*

CONCEPT 40.4

Energy requirements are related to animal size, activity, and environment (pp. 868–872)

- Animals obtain chemical energy from food, storing it for short-term use in ATP. The total amount of energy used in a unit of time defines an animal's **metabolic rate**. Metabolic rates are generally higher for endotherms than for ectotherms.
- Under similar conditions and for animals of the same size, the **basal metabolic rate** of endotherms is substantially higher than the **standard metabolic rate** of ectotherms. Minimum metabolic rate per gram is inversely related to body size among similar animals. Animals allocate energy for basal (or standard) metabolism, activity, homeostasis, growth, and reproduction.
- **Torpor**, a state of decreased activity and metabolism, conserves energy during environmental extremes. Animals may enter torpor during sleep periods (daily torpor), in winter (**hibernation**), or in summer (estivation).

> **?** *Most hibernators are small. After reviewing Figure 40.19, suggest an explanation for this observation.*

LEVEL 1: KNOWLEDGE/COMPREHENSION

1. The body tissue that consists largely of material located outside of cells is
   a. epithelial tissue.
   b. connective tissue.
   c. skeletal muscle.
   d. smooth muscle.
   e. nervous tissue.

2. Which of the following would increase the rate of heat exchange between an animal and its environment?
   a. feathers or fur
   b. vasoconstriction
   c. wind blowing across the body surface
   d. countercurrent heat exchanger
   e. blubber or fat layer

3. Consider the energy budgets for a human, an elephant, a penguin, a mouse, and a snake. The _____ would have the highest total annual energy expenditure, and the _____ would have the highest energy expenditure per unit mass.
   a. elephant; mouse
   b. elephant; human
   c. human; penguin
   d. mouse; snake
   e. penguin; mouse

LEVEL 2: APPLICATION/ANALYSIS

4. Compared with a smaller cell, a larger cell of the same shape has
   a. less surface area.
   b. less surface area per unit of volume.
   c. the same surface-to-volume ratio.
   d. a smaller average distance between its mitochondria and the external source of oxygen.
   e. a smaller cytoplasm-to-nucleus ratio.

5. An animal's inputs of energy and materials would exceed its outputs
   a. if the animal is an endotherm, which must always take in more energy because of its high metabolic rate.
   b. if it is actively foraging for food.
   c. if it is hibernating.
   d. if it is growing and increasing its mass.
   e. never; homeostasis makes these energy and material budgets always balance.

6. You are studying a large tropical reptile that has a high and relatively stable body temperature. How would you determine whether this animal is an endotherm or an ectotherm?
   a. You know from its high and stable body temperature that it must be an endotherm.
   b. You know that it is an ectotherm because it is not a bird or mammal.
   c. You subject this reptile to various temperatures in the lab and find that its body temperature and metabolic rate change with the ambient temperature. You conclude that it is an ectotherm.
   d. You note that its environment has a high and stable temperature. Because its body temperature matches the environmental temperature, you conclude that it is an ectotherm.
   e. You measure the metabolic rate of the reptile, and because it is higher than that of a related species that lives in temperate forests, you conclude that this reptile is an endotherm and its relative is an ectotherm.

7. Which of the following animals uses the largest percentage of its energy budget for homeostatic regulation?
   a. a hydra
   b. a marine jelly (an invertebrate)
   c. a snake in a temperate forest
   d. a desert insect
   e. a desert bird

8. **DRAW IT** Draw a model of the control circuit(s) required for driving an automobile at a fairly constant speed over a hilly road. Indicate each feature that represents a sensor, stimulus, or response.

LEVEL 3: SYNTHESIS/EVALUATION

9. **EVOLUTION CONNECTION**
   In 1847, the German biologist Christian Bergmann noted that mammals and birds living at higher latitudes (farther from the equator) are on average larger and bulkier than related species found at lower latitudes. Suggest an evolutionary hypothesis to explain this observation.

10. **SCIENTIFIC INQUIRY**
    Eastern tent caterpillars (*Malacosoma americanum*) live in large groups in silk nests, or tents, which they build in trees. They are among the first insects to be active in early spring, when daily temperature fluctuates from freezing to very hot. Over the course of a day, they display striking differences in behavior: Early in the morning, they rest in a tightly packed group on the tent's east-facing surface. In midafternoon, they are on its undersurface, each caterpillar hanging by a few of its legs. Propose a hypothesis to explain this behavior. How could you test it?

11. **SCIENCE, TECHNOLOGY, AND SOCIETY**
    Medical researchers are investigating artificial substitutes for various human tissues. Why might artificial blood or skin be useful? What characteristics would these substitutes need in order to function well in the body? Why do real tissues work better? Why not use the real tissues if they work better? What other artificial tissues might be useful? What problems do you anticipate in developing and applying them?

12. **WRITE ABOUT A THEME**
    Feedback Regulation In a short essay (about 100–150 words) focusing on feedback control in thermoregulation, explain why shivering is likely during the onset of a fever.

For selected answers, see Appendix A.

MasteringBIOLOGY   www.masteringbiology.com

1. MasteringBiology® Assignments
Tutorial Thermoregulation
Activities Overview of Animal Tissues • Epithelial Tissue • Connective Tissue • Muscle Tissue • Nervous Tissue • Homeostasis • Regulation: Negative and Positive Feedback • Discovery Channel Video: An Introduction to the Human Body
Questions Student Misconceptions • Reading Quiz • Multiple Choice • End-of-Chapter

2. eText
Read your book online, search, take notes, highlight text, and more.

3. The Study Area
Practice Tests • Cumulative Test • *BioFlix* 3-D Animations • MP3 Tutor Sessions • Videos • Activities • Investigations • Lab Media • Audio Glossary • Word Study Tools • Art

41

Animal Nutrition

▲ Figure 41.1 **How does a lean fish help a bear make fat?**

KEY CONCEPTS

41.1 An animal's diet must supply chemical energy, organic molecules, and essential nutrients

41.2 The main stages of food processing are ingestion, digestion, absorption, and elimination

41.3 Organs specialized for sequential stages of food processing form the mammalian digestive system

41.4 Evolutionary adaptations of vertebrate digestive systems correlate with diet

41.5 Feedback circuits regulate digestion, energy storage, and appetite

The Need to Feed

Dinnertime has arrived for the Kodiak bear in **Figure 41.1** (and for the salmon, though in quite a different sense). The skin, muscles, and other parts of the fish will be chewed into pieces, broken down by acid and enzymes in the bear's digestive system, and finally absorbed as small molecules into the body of the bear. Such a process is what is meant by animal **nutrition**: food being taken in, taken apart, and taken up.

Although a diet of fish plucked from a waterfall is not common, all animals eat other organisms—dead or alive, piecemeal or whole. Unlike plants, animals must consume food for both energy and the organic molecules used to assemble new molecules, cells, and tissues. Despite this shared need, animals have diverse diets. **Herbivores**, such as cattle, sea slugs, and termites, dine mainly on plants or algae. **Carnivores**, such as sharks, hawks, and spiders, mostly eat other animals. Bears and other **omnivores** (from the Latin *omni*, all) don't in fact eat everything, but they do regularly consume animals as well as plants or algae. We humans are typically omnivores, as are cockroaches and crows.

The terms *herbivore*, *carnivore*, and *omnivore* represent the kinds of food an animal usually eats. Keep in mind, however, that most animals are opportunistic feeders, eating foods outside their standard diet when their usual foods aren't available. For example, deer are herbivores, but in addition to feeding on grass and other plants, they occasionally eat insects, worms, or bird eggs. Note as well that microorganisms are an unavoidable "supplement" in every animal's diet.

Animals must eat. But to survive and reproduce, they must also balance their consumption, storage, and use of food. Bears, for example, store energy, largely in the form of body fat, in preparation for winter sleep. Eating too little food, too much food, or the wrong mixture of foods can endanger an animal's health. In this chapter, we will survey the nutritional requirements of animals, explore some of the diverse evolutionary adaptations for obtaining and processing food, and investigate the regulation of energy intake and expenditure.

CONCEPT 41.1

An animal's diet must supply chemical energy, organic molecules, and essential nutrients

Overall, an adequate diet must satisfy three nutritional needs: chemical energy for cellular processes, organic building blocks for macromolecules, and essential nutrients.

The activities of cells, tissues, organs, and whole animals depend on sources of chemical energy in the diet. This energy is used to produce ATP, which powers processes ranging from DNA replication and cell division to vision and flight. To meet the continuous requirement for ATP, animals ingest and digest nutrients, including carbohydrates, proteins, and lipids, for use in cellular respiration and energy storage.

In addition to providing fuel for ATP production, an animal's diet must supply the raw materials needed for biosynthesis. To build the complex molecules it needs to grow, maintain itself, and reproduce, an animal must obtain two types of organic precursors from its food. Animals need a source of organic carbon (such as sugar) and a source of organic nitrogen (such as protein). Starting with these materials, animals can construct a great variety of organic molecules.

The materials that an animal's cells require but cannot synthesize are called **essential nutrients**. Obtained from dietary sources, these nutrients include certain minerals and preassembled organic molecules. Some nutrients are essential for all animals, whereas others are needed only by certain species. For instance, ascorbic acid (vitamin C) is an essential nutrient for humans and other primates, guinea pigs, and some birds and snakes, but not for most other animals.

Essential Nutrients

There are four classes of essential nutrients: essential amino acids, essential fatty acids, vitamins, and minerals.

Essential Amino Acids

Animals require 20 amino acids to make proteins (see Figure 5.16). The majority of animal species have the enzymes to synthesize about half of these amino acids, as long as their diet includes sulfur and organic nitrogen. The remaining amino acids must be obtained from food in prefabricated form and are therefore called **essential amino acids**. Most animals, including adult humans, require eight amino acids in their diet (infants also need a ninth, histidine).

The proteins in animal products such as meat, eggs, and cheese are "complete," which means that they provide all the essential amino acids in their proper proportions. In contrast, most plant proteins are "incomplete," being deficient in one or more essential amino acids. Corn (maize), for example, is deficient in tryptophan and lysine, whereas beans are lacking in methionine. However, vegetarians can easily obtain all of the essential amino acids by eating a varied diet of plant proteins.

Some animals have adaptations that help them through periods when their bodies demand extraordinary amounts of protein. In penguins, for example, muscle protein provides a source of amino acids for making new proteins when feathers are replaced after molting (**Figure 41.2**).

Essential Fatty Acids

Animals produce the enzymes to synthesize most, but not all, of the fatty acids they need. The **essential fatty acids**, the ones they cannot make, are certain fatty acids that contain

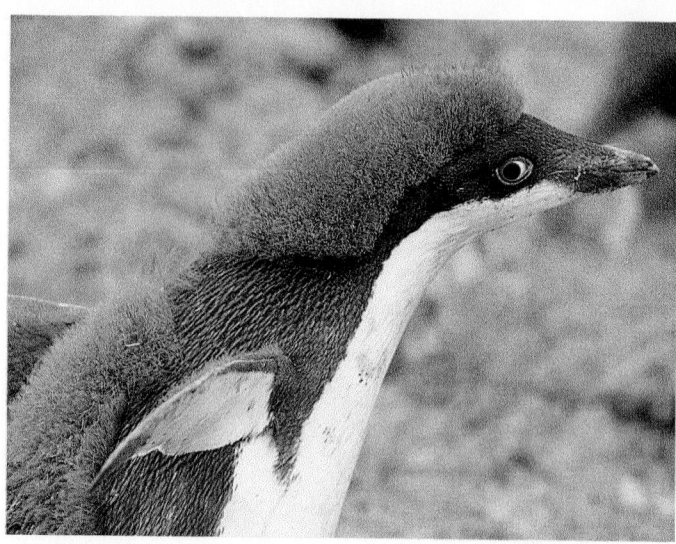

▲ **Figure 41.2 Storing protein for growth.** Penguins, such as this Adélie from Antarctica, must make an abundance of new proteins when they molt and grow new feathers. Because of the temporary loss of their insulating coat of feathers, penguins cannot swim—or feed—when molting. How, then, do they obtain amino acids for production of feather protein? Before molting, a penguin greatly increases its muscle mass. The penguin then breaks down the extra muscle protein, which supplies the amino acids for growing new feathers.

MAKE CONNECTIONS *Taking into account the examples in Figure 5.15, what generalization can you make about the circumstances under which animals commonly use proteins for amino acid storage?*

one or more double bonds and are thus unsaturated (see Figure 5.11). For example, humans require linoleic acid to make some membrane phospholipids. Because seeds, grains, and vegetables in the diets of humans and other animals generally furnish ample quantities of essential fatty acids, deficiencies in this class of nutrients are rare.

Vitamins

As Nobel Prize winner Albert Szent-Györgyi pointed out, "A vitamin is a substance that makes you ill if you *don't* eat it." **Vitamins** are organic molecules that have diverse functions and are required in the diet in very small amounts. Vitamin B_2, for example, is converted in the body to FAD, a coenzyme used in many metabolic processes, including cellular respiration (see Figure 9.12). For humans, 13 vitamins have been identified. Depending on the vitamin, the required amount ranges from about 0.01 to 100 mg per day.

Vitamins are classified as water-soluble or fat-soluble (**Table 41.1**). The water-soluble vitamins include the B vitamins, which are compounds that generally function as coenzymes, and vitamin C, which is required for the production of connective tissue. Among the fat-soluble vitamins are vitamin A, which is incorporated into visual pigments of the eye, and vitamin K, which functions in blood clotting. Another is vitamin D, which aids in calcium absorption and bone formation.

Table 41.1 Vitamin Requirements of Humans

Vitamin	Major Dietary Sources	Major Functions in the Body	Symptoms of Deficiency
Water-Soluble Vitamins			
B_1 (thiamine)	Pork, legumes, peanuts, whole grains	Coenzyme used in removing CO_2 from organic compounds	Beriberi (tingling, poor coordination, reduced heart function)
B_2 (riboflavin)	Dairy products, meats, enriched grains, vegetables	Component of coenzymes FAD and FMN	Skin lesions, such as cracks at corners of mouth
B_3 (niacin)	Nuts, meats, grains	Component of coenzymes NAD^+ and $NADP^+$	Skin and gastrointestinal lesions, delusions, confusion
B_5 (pantothenic acid)	Meats, dairy products, whole grains, fruits, vegetables	Component of coenzyme A	Fatigue, numbness, tingling of hands and feet
B_6 (pyridoxine)	Meats, vegetables, whole grains	Coenzyme used in amino acid metabolism	Irritability, convulsions, muscular twitching, anemia
B_7 (biotin)	Legumes, other vegetables, meats	Coenzyme in synthesis of fat, glycogen, and amino acids	Scaly skin inflammation, neuromuscular disorders
B_9 (folic acid)	Green vegetables, oranges, nuts, legumes, whole grains	Coenzyme in nucleic acid and amino acid metabolism	Anemia, birth defects
B_{12} (cobalamin)	Meats, eggs, dairy products	Production of nucleic acids and red blood cells	Anemia, numbness, loss of balance
C (ascorbic acid)	Citrus fruits, broccoli, tomatoes	Used in collagen synthesis; antioxidant	Scurvy (degeneration of skin and teeth), delayed wound healing
Fat-Soluble Vitamins			
A (retinol)	Dark green and orange vegetables and fruits, dairy products	Component of visual pigments; maintenance of epithelial tissues	Blindness, skin disorders, impaired immunity
D	Dairy products, egg yolk	Aids in absorption and use of calcium and phosphorus	Rickets (bone deformities) in children, bone softening in adults
E (tocopherol)	Vegetable oils, nuts, seeds	Antioxidant; helps prevent damage to cell membranes	Nervous system degeneration
K (phylloquinone)	Green vegetables, tea; also made by colon bacteria	Important in blood clotting	Defective blood clotting

Our dietary requirement for vitamin D is variable because we synthesize this vitamin from other molecules when the skin is exposed to sunlight.

For people with poorly balanced diets, taking vitamin supplements that provide recommended daily levels is certainly reasonable. It is much less clear whether massive doses of vitamins confer any health benefits or are, in fact, safe. Moderate overdoses of water-soluble vitamins are probably harmless because excesses of these vitamins are excreted in urine. However, excesses of fat-soluble vitamins are deposited in body fat, so overconsumption may result in accumulating toxic levels of these compounds.

Minerals

Dietary **minerals** are inorganic nutrients, such as iron and sulfur, that are usually required in small amounts—from less than 1 mg to about 2,500 mg per day. As shown in Table 41.2 on the next page, minerals have diverse functions in animal physiology. Some are cofactors built into the structure of enzymes; magnesium, for example, is present in enzymes that split ATP. In contrast, sodium, potassium, and chloride are important in the functioning of nerves and in maintaining osmotic balance between cells and the surrounding body fluid. Vertebrates use one mineral—iodine—specifically to make thyroid hormones, which regulate metabolic rate. Vertebrates also require relatively large quantities of calcium and phosphorus for building and maintaining bone.

Ingesting large amounts of some minerals can upset homeostatic balance and impair health. For example, excess salt (sodium chloride) intake can contribute to high blood pressure. This is a particular problem in the United States, where the typical person consumes enough salt to provide about 20 times the required amount of sodium. Packaged (prepared) foods often contain large amounts of sodium chloride, even if they do not taste very salty. Excessive consumption of iron can also endanger health: Liver damage due to iron overload affects as much as 10% of the human population in some regions of Africa where the water supply is especially iron-rich.

Table 41.2 **Mineral Requirements of Humans**[*]

	Mineral	Major Dietary Sources	Major Functions in the Body	Symptoms of Deficiency
Greater than 200 mg per day required	Calcium (Ca)	Dairy products, dark green vegetables, legumes	Bone and tooth formation, blood clotting, nerve and muscle function	Impaired growth, loss of bone mass
	Phosphorus (P)	Dairy products, meats, grains	Bone and tooth formation, acid-base balance, nucleotide synthesis	Weakness, loss of minerals from bone, calcium loss
	Sulfur (S)	Proteins from many sources	Component of certain amino acids	Impaired growth, fatigue, swelling
	Potassium (K)	Meats, dairy products, many fruits and vegetables, grains	Acid-base balance, water balance, nerve function	Muscular weakness, paralysis, nausea, heart failure
	Chlorine (Cl)	Table salt	Acid-base balance, formation of gastric juice, nerve function, osmotic balance	Muscle cramps, reduced appetite
	Sodium (Na)	Table salt	Acid-base balance, water balance, nerve function	Muscle cramps, reduced appetite
	Magnesium (Mg)	Whole grains, green leafy vegetables	Enzyme cofactor; ATP bioenergetics	Nervous system disturbances
	Iron (Fe)	Meats, eggs, legumes, whole grains, green leafy vegetables	Component of hemoglobin and of electron carriers; enzyme cofactor	Iron-deficiency anemia, weakness, impaired immunity
	Fluorine (F)	Drinking water, tea, seafood	Maintenance of tooth structure	Higher frequency of tooth decay
	Iodine (I)	Seafood, iodized salt	Component of thyroid hormones	Goiter (enlarged thyroid gland)

[*]Additional minerals required in trace amounts are chromium (Cr), cobalt (Co), copper (Cu), manganese (Mn), molybdenum (Mo), selenium (Se), and zinc (Zn). All of these minerals, as well as those in the table, are harmful when consumed in excess.

Dietary Deficiencies

A diet that lacks one or more essential nutrients or consistently supplies less chemical energy than the body requires results in *malnutrition*, a failure to obtain adequate nutrition. Malnutrition resulting from either type of dietary deficiency can have negative impacts on health and survival.

Deficiencies in Essential Nutrients

Insufficient intake of essential nutrients can cause deformities, disease, and even death. For example, cattle, deer, and other herbivores may develop dangerously fragile bones if they graze on plants growing in soil that lacks phosphorus. Some grazing animals obtain otherwise missing nutrients by consuming concentrated sources of salt or other minerals (Figure 41.3). Among carnivores, spiders have been found to adjust for dietary deficiencies by switching to prey that restores nutritional balance.

Like other animals, humans sometimes suffer from diets lacking in essential nutrients. A diet that provides insufficient amounts of one or more essential amino acids causes protein deficiency, the most common type of malnutrition among humans. For example, protein deficiency may arise if a child's diet shifts from consisting of breast milk to consisting solely of foods that provide almost all of their calories in the form of starch and other carbohydrates. Such children, if they survive infancy, often have impaired physical and mental development.

▲ Figure 41.3 **Obtaining essential nutrients.** A juvenile chamois (*Rupicapra rupicapra*), an herbivore, licks exposed salts and minerals in its rocky alpine habitat. This behavior is common among herbivores living where soils and plants provide insufficient amounts of essential nutrients, such as sodium, calcium, phosphorus, and iron.

Among populations subsisting on simple rice diets, individuals are often afflicted with vitamin A deficiency, which can cause blindness or death. To overcome this problem, scientists have engineered a strain of rice to synthesize beta-carotene, the orange-colored pigment that is abundant in carrots. Once absorbed into the body, beta-carotene is converted to vitamin A.

The potential benefit of this "Golden Rice" (see Chapter 38) is enormous because 1–2 million young children worldwide die every year from vitamin A deficiency.

Undernutrition

A diet that fails to provide adequate sources of chemical energy results in *undernutrition*. When an animal is undernourished, a series of events unfold: The body uses up stored carbohydrates and fat and then begins breaking down its own proteins for fuel; muscles begin to decrease in size; and the brain may become protein-deficient. If energy intake remains less than energy expenditures, the animal will eventually die. Even if a seriously undernourished animal survives, some of the damage may be irreversible.

Human undernutrition is most common when drought, war, or another crisis severely disrupts the food supply. In sub-Saharan Africa, where the AIDS epidemic has crippled both rural and urban communities, approximately 200 million children and adults cannot obtain enough food.

Sometimes undernutrition occurs within well-fed human populations as a result of eating disorders. For example, anorexia nervosa leads individuals, usually female, to starve themselves compulsively.

Assessing Nutritional Needs

Determining the ideal diet for the human population is an important but difficult problem for scientists. As objects of study, people present many challenges. Unlike laboratory animals, humans are genetically diverse. They also live in settings far more varied than the stable and uniform environment that scientists use to facilitate comparisons in laboratory experiments. Ethical concerns present an additional barrier. For example, it is not acceptable to investigate the nutritional needs of children in a way that might harm a child's growth or development.

The methods used to study human nutrition have changed dramatically over time. To avoid harming others, several of the researchers who discovered vitamins a century ago used themselves as subject animals. Today, researchers typically rely on the study of genetic defects that disrupt food uptake, storage, or use. For example, a genetic disorder called hemochromatosis causes iron buildup in the absence of any abnormal iron consumption or exposure. Fortunately, this common disorder is remarkably easy to treat: Drawing blood regularly removes enough iron from the body to restore homeostasis. By studying the defective genes that can cause the disease, scientists have learned a great deal about the regulation of iron absorption.

Many insights into human nutrition have come from *epidemiology*, the study of human health and disease at the population level. In the 1970s, for instance, researchers

▼ **Figure 41.4** **INQUIRY**

Can diet influence the frequency of birth defects?

EXPERIMENT Richard Smithells, of the University of Leeds, in England, examined the effect of vitamin supplementation on the risk of neural tube defects. Women who had had one or more babies with such a defect were put into two study groups. The experimental group consisted of those who were planning a pregnancy and began taking a multivitamin at least four weeks before attempting conception. The control group, who were not given vitamins, included women who declined them and women who were already pregnant. The numbers of neural tube defects resulting from the pregnancies were recorded for each group.

RESULTS

Group	Number of infants/fetuses studied	Infants/fetuses with a neural tube defect
Vitamin supplements (experimental group)	141	1 (0.7%)
No vitamin supplements (control group)	204	12 (5.9%)

CONCLUSION This study provided evidence that vitamin supplementation protects against neural tube defects, at least after the first pregnancy. Follow-up trials demonstrated that folic acid alone provided an equivalent protective effect.

SOURCE R. W. Smithells et al., Possible prevention of neural-tube defects by periconceptional vitamin supplementation, *Lancet* 315: 339–340 (1980).

INQUIRY IN ACTION Read and analyze the original paper in *Inquiry in Action: Interpreting Scientific Papers*.

WHAT IF? Subsequent studies were designed to learn if folic acid supplements prevent neural tube defects during first-time pregnancies. To determine the required number of subjects, what type of additional information did the researchers need?

discovered that children born to women of low socioeconomic status were more likely to have neural tube defects, which occur when tissue fails to enclose the developing brain and spinal cord (see Chapter 47). The English scientist Richard Smithells thought that malnutrition among these women might be responsible. As described in **Figure 41.4**, he found that vitamin supplementation greatly reduced the risk of neural tube defects. In other studies, he obtained evidence that folic acid (vitamin B_9) was the specific vitamin responsible, a finding confirmed by other researchers. Based on this evidence, the United States in 1998 began to require that folic acid be added to enriched grain products used to make bread, cereals, and other foods. Follow-up studies have documented the effectiveness of this program in reducing the frequency of neural tube defects. Thus, at a time when microsurgery and sophisticated diagnostic imaging dominate the headlines, a simple dietary change such as folic acid supplementation or consumption of Golden Rice may be among the greatest contributors to human health.

CONCEPT 41.2

The main stages of food processing are ingestion, digestion, absorption, and elimination

In this section, we turn from nutritional requirements to the mechanisms by which animals process food. Food processing can be divided into four distinct stages: ingestion, digestion, absorption, and elimination (**Figure 41.5**). The first stage, **ingestion**, is the act of eating or feeding. **Figure 41.6** surveys and classifies the principal feeding mechanisms that have evolved in animals. Given the variation in food sources among animal species, it is not surprising that strategies for extracting resources from food also differ widely. We will focus, however, on the shared processes, pausing periodically to consider some adaptations to particular diets or environments.

In **digestion**, the second stage of food processing, food is broken down into molecules small enough for the body to absorb. Mechanical digestion, such as chewing, typically precedes chemical digestion. Mechanical digestion breaks food into smaller pieces, increasing the surface area available for

1 Ingestion   2 Digestion   3 Absorption   4 Elimination

▲ **Figure 41.5 The four stages of food processing.**

chemical processes. Chemical digestion is necessary because animals cannot directly use the proteins, carbohydrates, nucleic acids, fats, and phospholipids in food. One problem is that these molecules are too large to pass through membranes and enter the cells of the animal. In addition, the large molecules in food are not all identical to those the animal needs for its particular tissues and functions. When large molecules in food are broken down into their components, however, the animal can use these smaller molecules to assemble the large molecules it needs. For example, although fruit flies and humans have very different diets, both convert proteins in their food to the same 20 amino acids from which they assemble all of the proteins specific for their species.

Recall from Chapter 5 that a cell makes a macromolecule or fat by linking together smaller components; it does so by removing a molecule of water for each new covalent bond formed. Chemical digestion by enzymes reverses this process by breaking bonds with the addition of water (see Figure 5.2). This splitting process is called *enzymatic hydrolysis*. A variety of enzymes catalyze the digestion of large molecules in food. Polysaccharides and disaccharides are split into simple sugars; proteins are broken down into amino acids; and nucleic acids are cleaved into nucleotides and their components. Enzymatic hydrolysis also releases fatty acids and other components from fats and phospholipids.

The last two stages of food processing occur after the food is digested. In the third stage, **absorption**, the animal's cells take up (absorb) small molecules such as amino acids and simple sugars. **Elimination** completes the process as undigested material passes out of the digestive system.

Digestive Compartments

In our overview of food processing, we have seen that digestive enzymes hydrolyze the same biological materials (such as proteins, fats, and carbohydrates) that make up the bodies of the animals themselves. How, then, are animals able to digest food without digesting their own cells and tissues? The evolutionary adaptation found across a wide range of animal species is the processing of food within specialized compartments. Such compartments can be intracellular, in the form of food vacuoles, or extracellular, as in digestive organs and systems.

Intracellular Digestion

Food vacuoles—cellular organelles in which hydrolytic enzymes break down food—are the simplest digestive compartments. The hydrolysis of food inside vacuoles, called *intracellular digestion*, begins after a cell engulfs solid food by phagocytosis or liquid food by pinocytosis (see Figure 7.22). Newly formed food vacuoles fuse with lysosomes, organelles containing hydrolytic enzymes. This fusion of organelles brings food in contact with the enzymes, allowing digestion to occur safely within a compartment

Exploring Four Main Feeding Mechanisms of Animals

Suspension Feeders and Filter Feeders

Baleen

Many aquatic animals are **suspension feeders**, which eat small organisms or food particles suspended in the water. For example, clams and oysters feed on tiny morsels of food in the water that passes over their gills; cilia sweep the food particles to the animal's mouth in a film of mucus. **Filter feeders** such as the humpback whale shown above move water through a filtering structure to obtain food. Attached to the whale's upper jaw are comblike plates called baleen, which strain small invertebrates and fish from enormous volumes of water.

Substrate Feeders

Substrate feeders are animals that live in or on their food source. This leaf miner caterpillar, the larva of a moth, is eating through the soft tissue of an oak leaf, leaving a dark trail of feces in its wake. Some other substrate feeders include maggots (fly larvae), which burrow into animal carcasses.

Caterpillar   Feces

Fluid Feeders

Fluid feeders suck nutrient-rich fluid from a living host. This mosquito has pierced the skin of its human host with hollow, needlelike mouthparts and is consuming a blood meal (colorized SEM). Similarly, aphids are fluid feeders that tap the phloem sap of plants. In contrast to such parasites, some fluid feeders actually benefit their hosts. For example, hummingbirds and bees move pollen between flowers as they fluid-feed on nectar.

Bulk Feeders

Most animals, including humans, are **bulk feeders**, which eat relatively large pieces of food. Their adaptations include tentacles, pincers, claws, poisonous fangs, jaws, and teeth that kill their prey or tear off pieces of meat or vegetation. In this amazing scene, a rock python is beginning to ingest a gazelle it has captured and killed. Snakes cannot chew their food into pieces and must swallow it whole—even if the prey is much bigger than the diameter of the snake. They can do so because the lower jaw is loosely hinged to the skull by an elastic ligament that permits the mouth and throat to open very wide. After swallowing its prey, which may take more than an hour, the python will spend two weeks or more digesting its meal.

enclosed by a protective membrane. A few animals, such as sponges, digest their food entirely by this intracellular mechanism (see Figure 33.4).

Extracellular Digestion

In most animal species, at least some hydrolysis occurs by *extracellular digestion*, the breakdown of food in compartments that are continuous with the outside of the animal's body. Having one or more extracellular compartments for digestion enables an animal to devour much larger pieces of food than can be ingested by phagocytosis.

Many animals with relatively simple body plans have a digestive compartment with a single opening **(Figure 41.7)**. This pouch, called a **gastrovascular cavity**, functions in digestion as well as in the distribution of nutrients throughout the body (hence the *vascular* part of the term). The carnivorous cnidarians called hydras provide a good example of how a gastrovascular cavity works. A hydra uses its tentacles to stuff captured prey through its mouth into its gastrovascular cavity. Specialized gland cells of the hydra's gastrodermis, the tissue layer that lines the cavity, then secrete digestive enzymes that break the soft tissues of the prey into tiny pieces. Other cells of the gastrodermis engulf these food particles, and most of the hydrolysis of macromolecules occurs intracellularly, as in sponges. After a hydra has digested its meal, undigested materials that remain in the gastrovascular cavity, such as exoskeletons of small crustaceans, are eliminated through the same opening by which food entered. Many flatworms also have a gastrovascular cavity with a single opening (see Figure 33.10).

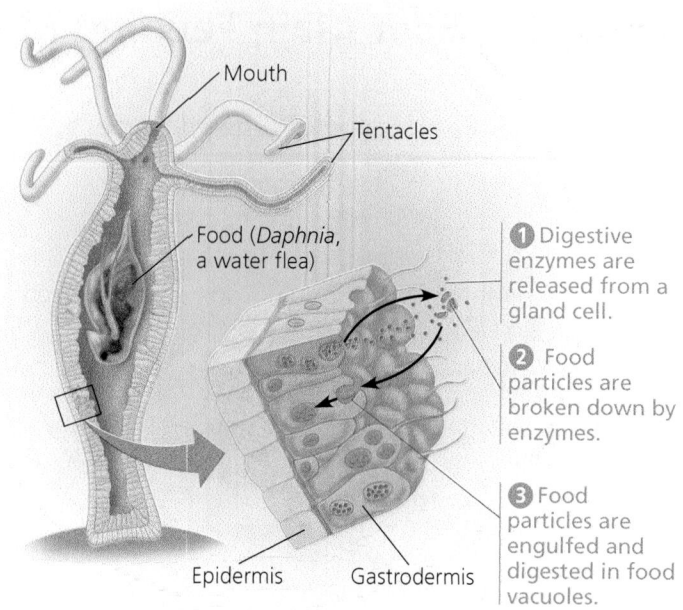

1 Digestive enzymes are released from a gland cell.

2 Food particles are broken down by enzymes.

3 Food particles are engulfed and digested in food vacuoles.

▲ **Figure 41.7 Digestion in a hydra.** Digestion begins in the gastrovascular cavity and is completed intracellularly after small food particles are engulfed by specialized cells of the gastrodermis.

In contrast with cnidarians and flatworms, most animals have a digestive tube extending between two openings, a mouth and an anus **(Figure 41.8)**. Such a tube is called a *complete digestive tract* or, more commonly, an **alimentary canal**. Because food moves along the alimentary canal in a single direction, the tube can be organized into specialized compartments that carry out digestion and nutrient absorption in a stepwise fashion. An animal with an alimentary canal can ingest food while earlier meals are still being digested, a feat that

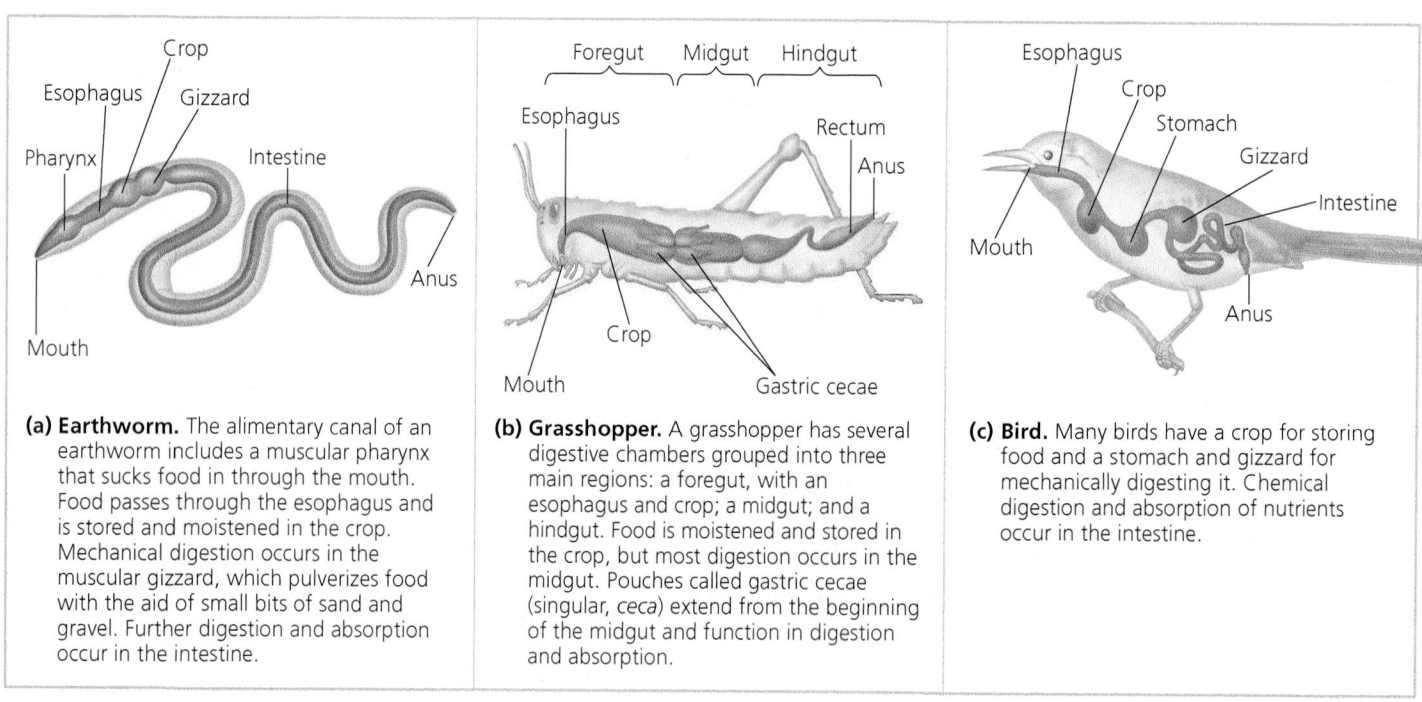

(a) Earthworm. The alimentary canal of an earthworm includes a muscular pharynx that sucks food in through the mouth. Food passes through the esophagus and is stored and moistened in the crop. Mechanical digestion occurs in the muscular gizzard, which pulverizes food with the aid of small bits of sand and gravel. Further digestion and absorption occur in the intestine.

(b) Grasshopper. A grasshopper has several digestive chambers grouped into three main regions: a foregut, with an esophagus and crop; a midgut; and a hindgut. Food is moistened and stored in the crop, but most digestion occurs in the midgut. Pouches called gastric cecae (singular, *ceca*) extend from the beginning of the midgut and function in digestion and absorption.

(c) Bird. Many birds have a crop for storing food and a stomach and gizzard for mechanically digesting it. Chemical digestion and absorption of nutrients occur in the intestine.

▲ **Figure 41.8 Variation in alimentary canals.**

is likely to be difficult or inefficient for animals with gastrovascular cavities. In the next section, we'll explore the spatial and functional organization of an alimentary canal.

CONCEPT CHECK 41.2

1. Distinguish the overall structure of a gastrovascular cavity from that of an alimentary canal.
2. In what sense are nutrients from a recently ingested meal not really "inside" your body prior to the absorption stage of food processing?
3. **WHAT IF?** Thinking in broad terms, what similarities can you identify between digestion in an animal body and the breakdown of gasoline in an automobile? (You don't have to know about auto mechanics.)

For suggested answers, see Appendix A.

CONCEPT 41.3

Organs specialized for sequential stages of food processing form the mammalian digestive system

Because most animals, including mammals, have an alimentary canal, we can use the mammalian digestive system as a representative example of the general principles of food pro-cessing. In mammals, the digestive system consists of the alimentary canal and various accessory glands that secrete digestive juices through ducts into the canal (Figure 41.9). The accessory glands of the mammalian digestive system are three pairs of salivary glands, the pancreas, the liver, and the gallbladder.

Food is pushed along the alimentary canal by **peristalsis**, alternating waves of contraction and relaxation in the smooth muscles lining the canal. At some of the junctions between specialized compartments, the muscular layer forms ringlike valves called **sphincters**. Acting like drawstrings to close off the alimentary canal, sphincters regulate the passage of material between compartments.

Using the human digestive system as a model, let's now follow a meal through the alimentary canal. As we do so, we'll examine in more detail what happens to the food in each digestive compartment along the way.

The Oral Cavity, Pharynx, and Esophagus

Ingestion and the initial steps of digestion occur in the mouth, or **oral cavity**. Mechanical digestion begins as teeth of various shapes cut, mash, and grind food, making the food easier to swallow and increasing its surface area. Meanwhile, the presence of food stimulates a nervous reflex that causes the **salivary glands** to deliver saliva through ducts to the oral cavity. Saliva may also be released before food enters the mouth, triggered by a learned association between eating and the time of day, a cooking odor, or another stimulus.

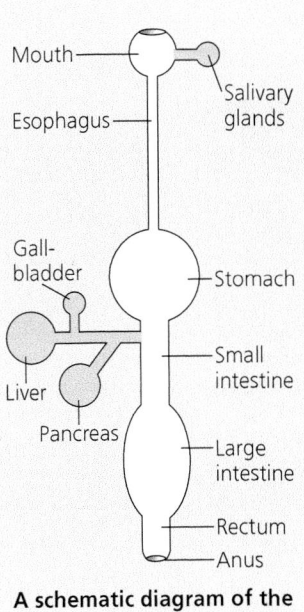

◀ **Figure 41.9 The human digestive system.** After food is chewed and swallowed, it takes 5–10 seconds for it to pass down the esophagus and into the stomach, where it spends 2–6 hours being partially digested. Final digestion and nutrient absorption occur in the small intestine over a period of 5–6 hours. In 12–24 hours, any undigested material passes through the large intestine, and feces are expelled through the anus.

A schematic diagram of the human digestive system (accessory glands in purple)

Saliva initiates chemical digestion while also protecting the oral cavity. The enzyme **amylase**, found in saliva, hydrolyzes starch (a glucose polymer from plants) and glycogen (a glucose polymer from animals) into smaller polysaccharides and the disaccharide maltose. Much of the protective effect of saliva is provided by **mucus**, which is a viscous mixture of water, salts, cells, and slippery glycoproteins (carbohydrate-protein complexes) called mucins. Mucus in saliva protects the lining of the mouth from abrasion and lubricates food for easier swallowing. Additional components of saliva include buffers, which help prevent tooth decay by neutralizing acid, and antimicrobial agents (such as lysozyme; see Figure 5.18), which protect against bacteria that enter the mouth with food.

Much as a doorman screens and assists people entering a building, the tongue aids digestive processes by evaluating ingested material and then enabling its further passage. When food arrives at the oral cavity, the tongue plays a critical role in distinguishing which foods should be processed further. (See Chapter 50 for a discussion of the sense of taste.) After food is deemed acceptable and chewing commences, tongue movements manipulate the food, helping shape it into a ball called a **bolus**. During swallowing, the tongue provides further help, pushing the bolus to the back of the oral cavity and into the pharynx.

The **pharynx**, or throat region, opens to two passageways: the esophagus and the trachea (windpipe). The **esophagus** connects to the stomach, whereas the trachea leads to the lungs. Swallowing must therefore be carefully choreographed to keep food from entering and blocking the airway. When you swallow, a flap of cartilage called the *epiglottis* covers the *glottis*—the vocal cords and the opening between them. Guided by the movements of the *larynx*, the upper part of the respiratory tract, this swallowing reflex directs each bolus into the entrance of the esophagus (**Figure 41.10**, ❶–❹). If the swallowing reflex fails, food or liquids can reach the trachea and cause choking, a blockage of the trachea. The resulting lack of airflow into the lungs can be fatal if the material is not dislodged by vigorous coughing, a series of back slaps, or a forced upward thrust of the diaphragm (the Heimlich maneuver).

The esophagus contains both striated and smooth muscle (see Figure 40.5). The striated muscle is situated at the top of the esophagus and is active during swallowing. Throughout the rest of the esophagus, smooth muscle functions in peristalsis. The rhythmic cycles of contraction move each bolus to the stomach (see Figure 41.10, ❻). As with other parts of the digestive system, the form of the esophagus fits its function and varies among species. For example, fishes have no lungs to bypass and therefore have a very short esophagus. And it will come as no surprise that giraffes have a very long esophagus.

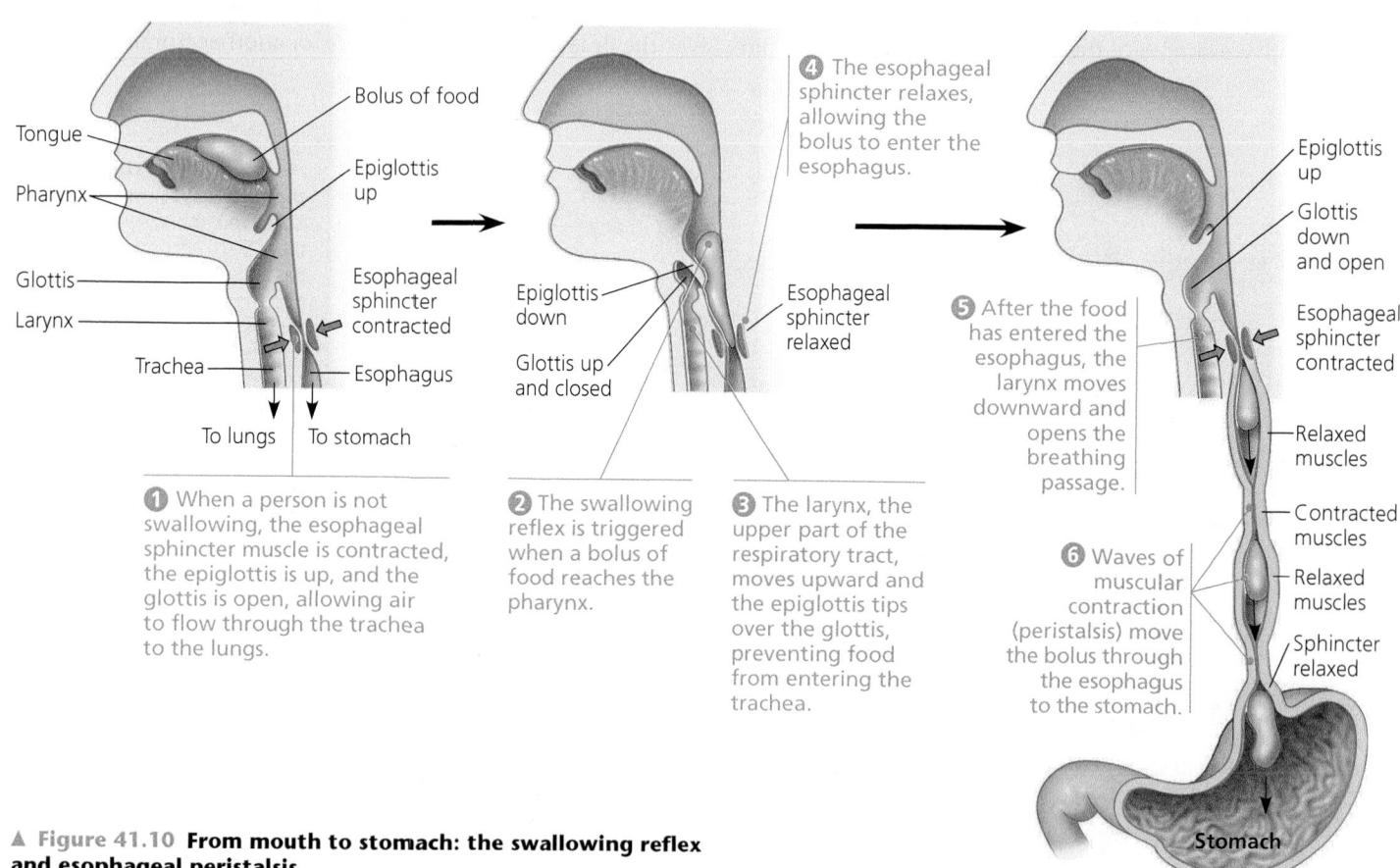

▲ **Figure 41.10 From mouth to stomach: the swallowing reflex and esophageal peristalsis.**

❶ When a person is not swallowing, the esophageal sphincter muscle is contracted, the epiglottis is up, and the glottis is open, allowing air to flow through the trachea to the lungs.

❷ The swallowing reflex is triggered when a bolus of food reaches the pharynx.

❸ The larynx, the upper part of the respiratory tract, moves upward and the epiglottis tips over the glottis, preventing food from entering the trachea.

❹ The esophageal sphincter relaxes, allowing the bolus to enter the esophagus.

❺ After the food has entered the esophagus, the larynx moves downward and opens the breathing passage.

❻ Waves of muscular contraction (peristalsis) move the bolus through the esophagus to the stomach.

Digestion in the Stomach

The **stomach**, which is located just below the diaphragm, stores food and begins digestion of proteins. With accordion-like folds and a very elastic wall, this organ can stretch to accommodate about 2 L of food and fluid. The stomach secretes a digestive fluid called **gastric juice** and mixes this secretion with the food through a churning action. This mixture of ingested food and digestive juice is called **chyme**.

Chemical Digestion in the Stomach

Two components of gastric juice carry out chemical digestion. One is hydrochloric acid (HCl), which disrupts the extracellular matrix that binds cells together in meat and plant material. The concentration of HCl is so high that the pH of gastric juice is about 2, acidic enough to dissolve iron nails (and to kill most bacteria). This low pH denatures (unfolds) proteins in food, increasing exposure of their peptide bonds. The exposed bonds are attacked by the second component of gastric juice—a **protease**, or protein-digesting enzyme, called **pepsin**. Unlike most enzymes, pepsin works best in a strongly acidic environment. By breaking peptide bonds, it cleaves proteins into smaller polypeptides. Further digestion to individual amino acids occurs in the small intestine.

Why doesn't gastric juice destroy the stomach cells that make it? The answer is that the ingredients of gastric juice are kept inactive until they are released into the lumen (cavity) of the stomach. The components of gastric juice are produced by cells in the gastric glands of the stomach (Figure 41.11). *Parietal cells* secrete hydrogen and chloride ions, which form HCl. Using an ATP-driven pump, the parietal cells expel hydrogen ions into the lumen. There, the hydrogen ions combine with chloride ions that diffuse into the lumen through specific membrane channels of the parietal cells. Meanwhile, *chief cells* release pepsin into the lumen in an inactive form called **pepsinogen**. HCl converts pepsinogen to active pepsin by clipping off a small portion of the molecule and exposing its active site. Through these processes, both HCl and pepsin form in the lumen of the stomach, not within the cells of the gastric glands.

After hydrochloric acid converts a small amount of pepsinogen to pepsin, pepsin itself helps activate the remaining pepsinogen. Pepsin, like HCl, can clip pepsinogen to expose the enzyme's active site. This generates more pepsin,

▶ Figure 41.11 **The stomach and its secretions.** The micrograph (colorized SEM) shows a gastric pit on the interior surface of the stomach, through which digestive juices are secreted.

Interior surface of stomach. The interior surface of the stomach wall is highly folded and dotted with pits leading into tubular gastric glands.

Gastric gland. The gastric glands have three types of cells that secrete different components of the gastric juice: mucous cells, chief cells, and parietal cells.

Mucous cells secrete mucus, which lubricates and protects the cells lining the stomach.

Chief cells secrete pepsinogen, an inactive form of the digestive enzyme pepsin.

Parietal cells secrete hydrochloric acid (HCl).

Esophagus

Sphincter

Stomach

Sphincter

Small intestine

Folds of epithelial tissue

Epithelium

10 μm

Pepsinogen → Pepsin (active enzyme)

HCl

Chief cell

H⁺

Cl⁻

Parietal cell

The production of gastric juice

① Pepsinogen and HCl are secreted into the lumen of the stomach.

② HCl converts pepsinogen to pepsin.

③ Pepsin then activates more pepsinogen, starting a chain reaction. Pepsin begins the chemical digestion of proteins.

which activates more pepsinogen, forming more active enzyme. This series of events is an example of positive feedback, which amplifies the effect of an initially small input.

When HCl and pepsin form within the stomach lumen, why aren't the cells that line the stomach damaged? Actually, these cells are vulnerable to gastric juice as well as to acid-tolerant pathogens in food or water. However, the stomach lining protects against self-digestion by secreting mucus. In addition, cell division adds a new epithelial layer every three days, replacing cells eroded by digestive juices. Despite these defenses, damaged areas of the stomach lining called gastric ulcers may appear. For decades, scientists thought they were caused by psychological stress and resulting excess acid secretion. In 1982, however, Australian researchers Barry Marshall and Robin Warren reported that infection by the acid-tolerant bacterium *Helicobacter pylori* causes ulcers. They also demonstrated that an antibiotic treatment could cure most gastric ulcers. For these findings, they were awarded the Nobel Prize in 2005.

Stomach Dynamics

Chemical digestion by gastric juice is facilitated by the churning action of the stomach. This coordinated series of muscle contractions and relaxations mixes the stomach contents about every 20 seconds. As a result of mixing and enzyme action, what begins as a recently swallowed meal becomes the acidic, nutrient-rich broth known as chyme. Most of the time, the stomach is closed off at both ends (see Figure 41.9). The sphincter between the esophagus and the stomach normally opens only when a bolus arrives. Occasionally, however, a person experiences acid reflux, a backflow of chyme from the stomach into the lower end of the esophagus. The resulting irritation of the esophagus is commonly called "heartburn."

The contents of the stomach typically pass into the small intestine within 2–6 hours after a meal. The sphincter located where the stomach opens to the small intestine helps regulate passage into the small intestine, allowing only one squirt of chyme at a time.

▼ **Figure 41.12 Chemical digestion in the human digestive system.**

? *Pepsin is resistant to the denaturing effect of the low pH environment of the stomach. Thinking about the different digestive processes that occur in the small intestine, what adaptation do you think the digestive enzymes in that compartment share?*

Digestion in the Small Intestine

Although chemical digestion of some nutrients begins in the oral cavity or stomach, most enzymatic hydrolysis of the macromolecules from food occurs in the **small intestine** (Figure 41.12, on p. 886). Over 6 m (20 feet) long in humans, the small intestine is the alimentary canal's longest compartment. Its name refers to its small diameter, compared with that of the large intestine. The first 25 cm (10 inches) or so of the small intestine forms the **duodenum**. It is here that chyme from the stomach mixes with digestive juices from the pancreas, liver, and gallbladder, as well as from gland cells of the intestinal wall itself. As you will see in Concept 41.5, hormones released by the stomach and duodenum control the digestive secretions into the alimentary canal.

Pancreatic Secretions

The **pancreas** aids chemical digestion by producing an alkaline solution rich in bicarbonate as well as several enzymes. The bicarbonate neutralizes the acidity of chyme and acts as a buffer. Among the pancreatic enzymes are trypsin and chymotrypsin, proteases secreted into the duodenum in inactive forms (see Figure 41.12). In a chain reaction similar to activation of pepsin, they are activated when safely located in the lumen within the duodenum.

Bile Production by the Liver

Digestion of fats and other lipids begins in the small intestine and relies on the production of **bile**, a mixture of substances that is made in the **liver**. Bile contains bile salts, which act as emulsifiers (detergents) that aid in digestion and absorption of lipids. Bile is stored and concentrated in the **gallbladder**.

Bile production is integral to one of the other vital functions of the liver: the destruction of red blood cells that are no longer fully functional. In producing bile, the liver incorporates some pigments that are by-products of red blood cell disassembly. These bile pigments are then eliminated from the body with the feces. In some liver or blood disorders, bile pigments accumulate in the skin, resulting in a characteristic yellowing called jaundice.

Secretions of the Small Intestine

The epithelial lining of the duodenum is the source of several digestive enzymes (see Figure 41.12). Some are secreted into the lumen of the duodenum, whereas others are bound to the surface of epithelial cells.

While enzymatic hydrolysis proceeds, peristalsis moves the mixture of chyme and digestive juices along the small intestine. Most digestion is completed in the duodenum. The remaining regions of the small intestine, called the *jejunum* and *ileum*, function mainly in the absorption of nutrients and water.

Absorption in the Small Intestine

To reach body tissues, nutrients in the lumen must first cross the lining of the alimentary canal. Most of this absorption occurs across the highly folded surface of the small intestine, as illustrated in **Figure 41.13**. Large folds in the lining encircle

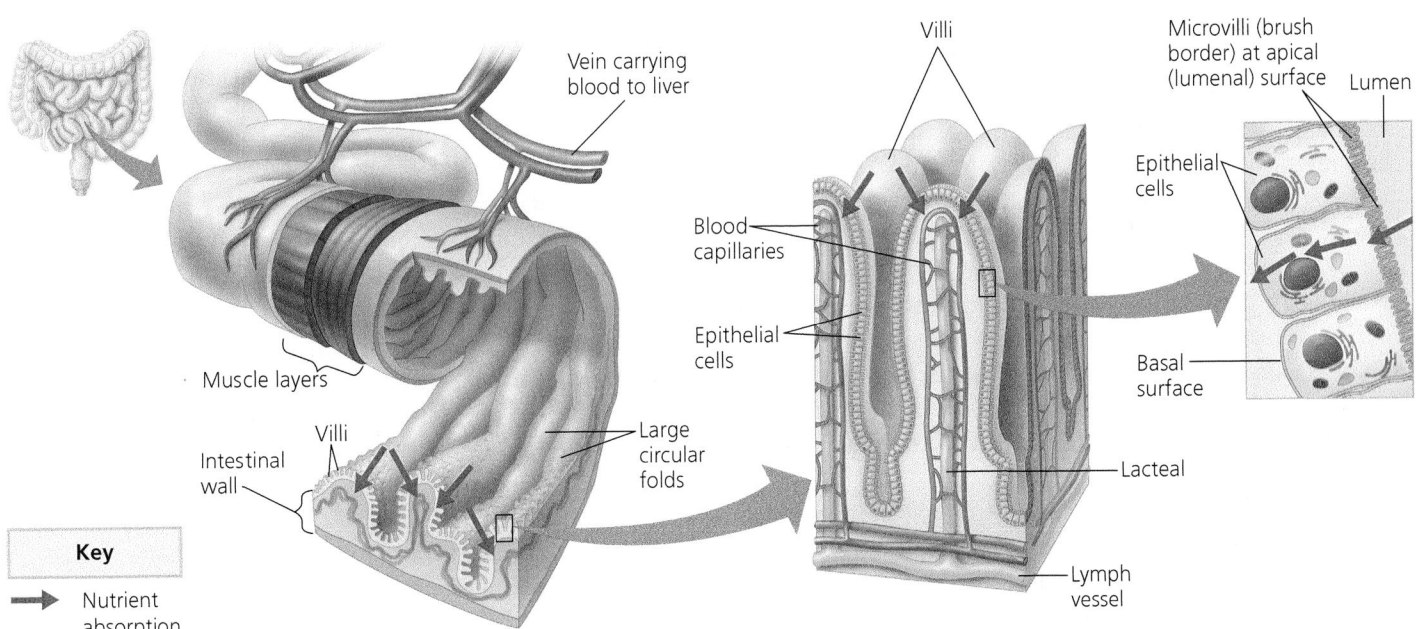

Key

→ Nutrient absorption

▲ **Figure 41.13 Nutrient absorption in the small intestine.**

? *Tapeworms sometimes infect humans, anchoring themselves to the wall of the small intestine. Based on how digestion is compartmentalized along the mammalian alimentary canal, what digestive functions would you expect these parasites to have?*

ANIMATION ***BioFlix*** Visit the Study Area at **www.masteringbiology.com** for the BioFlix® 3-D Animation on Membrane Transport.

the intestine and are studded with finger-like projections called **villi**. In turn, each epithelial cell of a villus has on its apical surface many microscopic projections, or **microvilli**, that are exposed to the intestinal lumen. The many side-by-side microvilli give cells of the intestinal epithelium a brush-like appearance—reflected in the name *brush border*. Together, the folds, villi, and microvilli of the small intestine have a surface area of 300 m², roughly the size of a tennis court. This enormous surface area is an evolutionary adaptation that greatly increases the rate of nutrient absorption.

Depending on the nutrient, transport across the epithelial cells can be passive or active (see Chapter 7). The sugar fructose, for example, moves by facilitated diffusion down its concentration gradient from the lumen of the small intestine into the epithelial cells. From there, fructose exits the basal surface and is absorbed into microscopic blood vessels, or capillaries, at the core of each villus. Other nutrients, including amino acids, small peptides, vitamins, and most glucose molecules, are pumped against concentration gradients by the epithelial cells of the villus. This active transport allows much more absorption of nutrients than would be possible with passive diffusion alone.

The capillaries and veins that carry nutrient-rich blood away from the villi all converge into the **hepatic portal vein**, a blood vessel that leads directly to the liver. From the liver, blood travels to the heart and then to other tissues and organs. This arrangement serves two major functions. First, it allows the liver to regulate the distribution of nutrients to the rest of the body. Because the liver can interconvert many organic molecules, blood that leaves the liver may have a very different nutrient balance than the blood that entered via the hepatic portal vein. Second, the arrangement allows the liver to remove toxic substances before the blood circulates broadly. The liver is the primary site for the detoxification of many organic molecules, including drugs, that are foreign to the body.

Although many nutrients leave the intestine through the bloodstream, some products of fat (triglyceride) digestion take a different path. As shown in **Figure 41.14**, hydrolysis of fats by lipase in the small intestine generates fatty acids and monoglycerides (glycerol joined to a single fatty acid). These products are absorbed by epithelial cells and recombined into triglycerides. They are then coated with phospholipids, cholesterol, and proteins, forming water-soluble globules called **chylomicrons**.

In exiting the intestine, chylomicrons are first transported from an epithelial cell into a **lacteal**, a vessel at the core of each villus (see Figures 41.13 and 41.14). Lacteals are part of the vertebrate lymphatic system, which is a network of vessels that are filled with a clear fluid called lymph. Starting at the lacteals, lymph containing the chylomicrons passes into the larger vessels of the lymphatic system and eventually into large veins that return the blood to the heart.

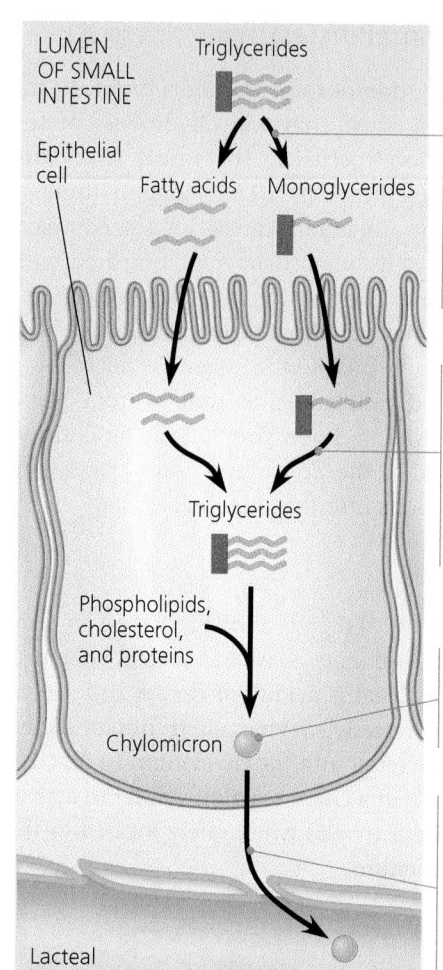

① In the lumen, triglycerides (fat molecules) exposed on the surface of fat droplets (not shown) are subject to enzymatic hydrolysis. The enzyme lipase breaks the triglycerides down to fatty acids and monoglycerides.

② After diffusing into epithelial cells, monoglycerides and fatty acids are re-formed into triglycerides. (Some glycerol and fatty acids pass directly into capillaries.)

③ Triglycerides are incorporated into water-soluble globules called chylomicrons.

④ Chylomicrons leave epithelial cells by exocytosis and enter lacteals, where they are carried away by the lymph and later pass into large veins.

▲ **Figure 41.14 Absorption of fats.** Because fats are insoluble in water, adaptations are needed to digest and absorb them. Bile salts (not shown) break up large fat droplets and maintain a small droplet size in the intestinal lumen, exposing more of the fat at the surface for enzymatic hydrolysis. The fatty acids and monoglycerides released by hydrolysis can diffuse into epithelial cells, where fats are reassembled and incorporated into water-soluble chylomicrons that enter the lymphatic system.

Absorption in the Large Intestine

The alimentary canal ends with the **large intestine**, which includes the colon, cecum, and rectum. The small intestine connects to the large intestine at a T-shaped junction **(Figure 41.15)**. One arm of the T is the 1.5-m-long **colon**, which leads to the rectum and anus. The other arm is a pouch called the **cecum**. The cecum is important for fermenting ingested material, especially in animals that eat large amounts of plant material. Compared with many other mammals,

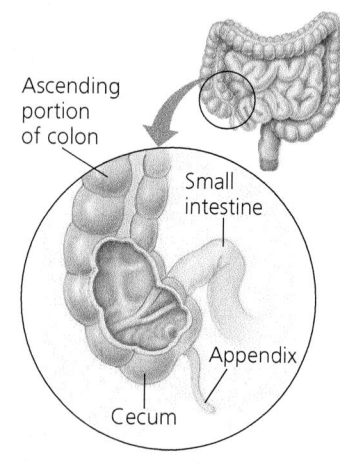

▲ **Figure 41.15 Junction of the small and large intestines.**

humans have a small cecum. The **appendix**, a finger-like extension of the human cecum, has a minor and dispensable role in immunity.

A major function of the colon is to recover water that has entered the alimentary canal as the solvent of digestive juices. About 7 L of fluid is secreted into the lumen of the alimentary canal each day, and about 90% of that is reabsorbed in the small intestine and colon. There is no mechanism for active transport of water. Instead, water is reabsorbed by osmosis when Na^+ and other ions are pumped out of the lumen of the colon.

The **feces**, the wastes of the digestive system, become increasingly solid as they are moved along the colon by peristalsis. It takes approximately 12–24 hours for material to travel the length of the colon. If the lining of the colon is irritated—by a viral or bacterial infection, for instance—less water than normal may be reabsorbed, resulting in diarrhea. The opposite problem, constipation, occurs when the feces move along the colon too slowly. An excess of water is reabsorbed, and therefore the feces become compacted.

A rich community of mostly harmless bacteria lives on unabsorbed organic material in the human colon, contributing approximately one-third of the dry weight of feces. One inhabitant, *Escherichia coli*, is so common in the human digestive system that its presence in lakes and streams is a useful indicator of contamination by untreated sewage. As by-products of their metabolism, many colon bacteria generate gases, including methane and hydrogen sulfide, which has an offensive odor. These gases and ingested air are expelled through the anus. Some bacteria produce vitamins, such as vitamin K, biotin, and folic acid, that supplement our dietary intake when absorbed into the blood.

Besides bacteria, feces contain undigested material, including cellulose fiber. Although it has no caloric value to humans, fiber helps move food along the alimentary canal.

The terminal portion of the large intestine is the **rectum**, where feces are stored until they can be eliminated. Between the rectum and the anus are two sphincters, the inner one being involuntary and the outer one being voluntary. Periodically, strong contractions of the colon create an urge to defecate. Because filling of the stomach triggers a reflex that increases the rate of contractions in the colon, the urge to defecate often follows a meal.

We have followed a meal from one opening (the mouth) of the alimentary canal to the other (the anus). Next we'll see how some digestive adaptations may have evolved.

CONCEPT CHECK 41.3

1. How does swallowed food reach the stomach of a weightless astronaut in orbit?
2. Explain why a proton pump inhibitor, such as the drug Prilosec, relieves the symptoms of acid reflux.
3. **WHAT IF?** If you mixed gastric juice with crushed food in a test tube, what would happen?

For suggested answers, see Appendix A.

CONCEPT 41.4

Evolutionary adaptations of vertebrate digestive systems correlate with diet

EVOLUTION The digestive systems of mammals and other vertebrates are variations on a common plan, but there are many intriguing adaptations, often associated with the animal's diet. To highlight how form fits function, we'll examine a few of them.

Dental Adaptations

Dentition, an animal's assortment of teeth, is one example of structural variation reflecting diet (Figure 41.16). The evolutionary adaptation of teeth for processing different kinds of

▼ Figure 41.16 **Dentition and diet.**

Carnivore

Carnivores, such as members of the dog and cat families, generally have large, pointed incisors and canines that can be used to kill prey and rip or cut away pieces of flesh. The jagged premolars and molars crush and shred food.

Herbivore

Herbivores, such as horses and deer, usually have premolars and molars with broad, ridged surfaces that grind tough plant material. The incisors and canines are generally modified for biting off pieces of vegetation. In some herbivores, canines are absent.

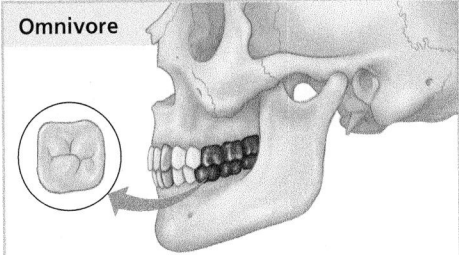

Omnivore

As omnivores, humans are adapted to eating both plants and meat. Adults have 32 teeth. From front to back along either side of the mouth are four bladelike incisors for biting, a pair of pointed canines for tearing, four premolars for grinding, and six molars for crushing (see inset, top view).

Key Incisors Canines Premolars Molars

food is one of the major reasons mammals have been so successful. Nonmammalian vertebrates generally have less specialized dentition, but there are interesting exceptions. For example, poisonous snakes, such as rattlesnakes, have fangs, modified teeth that inject venom into prey. Some fangs are hollow, like syringes, whereas others drip the poison along grooves on the surfaces of the teeth.

Stomach and Intestinal Adaptations

Large, expandable stomachs are common in carnivorous vertebrates, which may go for a long time between meals and must eat as much as they can when they do catch prey. A 200-kg African lion can consume 40 kg of meat in one meal!

The length of the vertebrate digestive system is also correlated with diet. In general, herbivores and omnivores have longer alimentary canals relative to their body size than do carnivores. Vegetation is more difficult to digest than meat because it contains cell walls. A longer digestive tract furnishes more time for digestion and more surface area for the absorption of nutrients. As an example, consider the koala and coyote in **Figure 41.17**. Although these two mammals are about the same size, the koala's intestines are much longer, enhancing the processing of fibrous, protein-poor eucalyptus leaves from which the koala obtains virtually all its food and water.

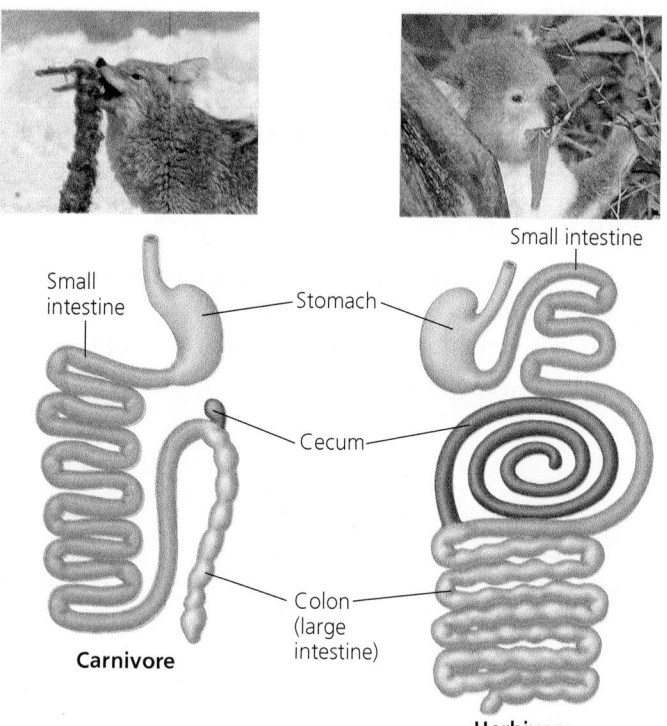

▲ **Figure 41.17 The alimentary canals of a carnivore (coyote) and herbivore (koala).** The koala's alimentary canal is specialized for digesting eucalyptus leaves. Extensive chewing chops the leaves into tiny pieces, increasing exposure to digestive juices. In the long cecum and the upper portion of the colon, symbiotic bacteria convert the shredded leaves to a more nutritious diet.

Mutualistic Adaptations

Some digestive adaptations involve mutualistic symbiosis, a mutually beneficial interaction between two species (see Chapter 54). For example, microorganisms help herbivores digest plants. Much of the chemical energy in herbivore diets comes from the cellulose of plant cell walls, but animals do not produce enzymes that hydrolyze cellulose. Instead, many vertebrates (as well as termites, whose wood diets consist largely of cellulose) house large populations of mutualistic bacteria and protists in fermentation chambers in their alimentary canals. These microorganisms have enzymes that can digest cellulose to simple sugars and other compounds that the animal can absorb. In many cases, the microorganisms also use the sugars from digested cellulose in the production of a variety of nutrients essential to the animal, such as vitamins and amino acids.

The location of mutualistic microbes in alimentary canals varies, depending on the type of herbivore. For example:

- The hoatzin, an herbivorous bird that lives in the South American rain forests, has a large, muscular crop (an esophageal pouch; see Figure 41.8) that houses mutualistic microorganisms. Hard ridges in the wall of the crop grind plant leaves into small fragments, and the microorganisms break down cellulose.
- Horses and many other herbivorous mammals house mutualistic microorganisms in a large cecum. The koala also has an enlarged cecum, where mutualistic bacteria ferment finely shredded eucalyptus leaves.
- In rabbits and some rodents, mutualistic bacteria live in the large intestine as well as in the cecum. Since most nutrients are absorbed in the small intestine, nourishing byproducts of fermentation by bacteria in the large intestine are initially lost with the feces. Rabbits and rodents recover these nutrients by *coprophagy* (from the Greek, meaning "dung eating"), feeding on some of their feces and then passing the food through the alimentary canal a second time. The familiar rabbit "pellets," which are not reingested, are the feces eliminated after food has passed through the digestive tract twice.
- The most elaborate adaptations for an herbivorous diet have evolved in the animals called **ruminants**, which include deer, sheep, and cattle (**Figure 41.18**).

Although we have focused our discussion on vertebrates, adaptations related to digestion are also widespread among other animals. Some of the most remarkable examples are the giant tubeworms (over 3 m long) that live at pressures as high as 260 atmospheres around deep-sea hydrothermal vents (see Figure 52.16). These worms have no mouth or digestive system. Instead, they rely entirely on mutualistic bacteria to generate energy and nutrients from the carbon dioxide, oxygen,

① Rumen. When the cow first chews and swallows a mouthful of grass, boluses (green arrows) enter the rumen.

② Reticulum. Some boluses also enter the reticulum. In both the rumen and the reticulum, mutualistic prokaryotes and protists (mainly ciliates) go to work on the cellulose-rich meal. As by-products of their metabolism, the microorganisms secrete fatty acids. The cow periodically regurgitates and rechews the cud (red arrows), which further breaks down the fibers, making them more accessible to further microbial action.

◄ **Figure 41.18 Ruminant digestion.** The stomach of a ruminant has four chambers. Because of the microbial action in the chambers, the diet from which a ruminant actually absorbs its nutrients is much richer than the grass the animal originally eats. In fact, a ruminant eating grass or hay obtains many of its nutrients by digesting the mutualistic microorganisms, which reproduce rapidly enough in the rumen to maintain a stable population.

Esophagus

Intestine

④ Abomasum. The cud, containing great numbers of microorganisms, finally passes to the abomasum for digestion by the cow's own enzymes (black arrows).

③ Omasum. The cow then reswallows the cud (blue arrows), which moves to the omasum, where water is removed.

hydrogen sulfide, and nitrate available at the vents. Thus, for invertebrates and vertebrates alike, mutualistic symbiosis has evolved as a general strategy for expanding the sources of nutrition available to animals.

Having examined how animals optimize their extraction of nutrients from food, we will next turn to the challenge of balancing the use of these nutrients.

CONCEPT CHECK 41.4

1. What are two advantages of a longer alimentary canal for processing plant material that is difficult to digest?
2. What features of a mammal's digestive system make it an attractive habitat for mutualistic microorganisms?
3. **WHAT IF?** "Lactose-intolerant" people have a shortage of lactase, the enzyme that breaks down lactose in milk. As a result, they sometimes develop cramps, bloating, or diarrhea after consuming dairy products. Suppose such a person ate yogurt containing bacteria that produce lactase. Why would eating yogurt likely provide at best only temporary relief of the symptoms?

For suggested answers, see Appendix A.

CONCEPT 41.5

Feedback circuits regulate digestion, energy storage, and appetite

Having examined the processes that enable an animal to obtain nutrients, we will finish our discussion of nutrition by considering how these processes are matched to circumstance and need.

Regulation of Digestion

Many animals go for long intervals between meals and do not need their digestive systems to be active continuously. Instead, each step in processing is activated as food reaches a new compartment in the alimentary canal. The arrival of food triggers the secretion of substances that promote the next stage of chemical digestion, as well as muscular contractions that propel food farther along the canal. For example, you learned earlier that nervous reflexes stimulate the release of saliva when food enters the oral cavity and orchestrate swallowing when a bolus of food reaches the pharynx. Similarly, the arrival of food in the stomach triggers churning and the release of gastric juices. A branch of the nervous system

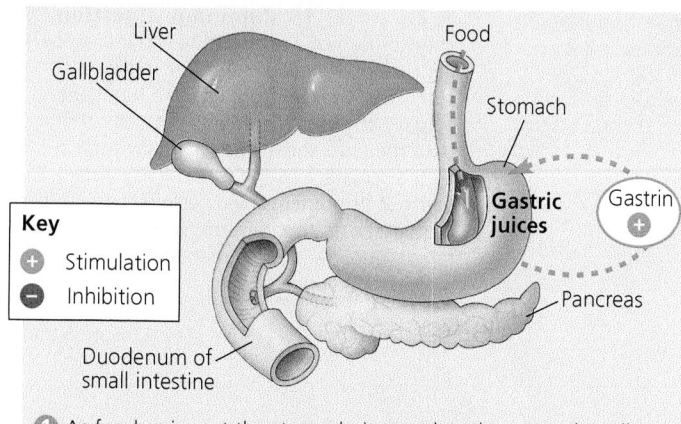

① As food arrives at the stomach, it stretches the stomach walls, triggering release of the hormone **gastrin**. Gastrin circulates via the bloodstream back to the stomach, where it stimulates production of gastric juices.

Key
- ➕ Stimulation
- ➖ Inhibition

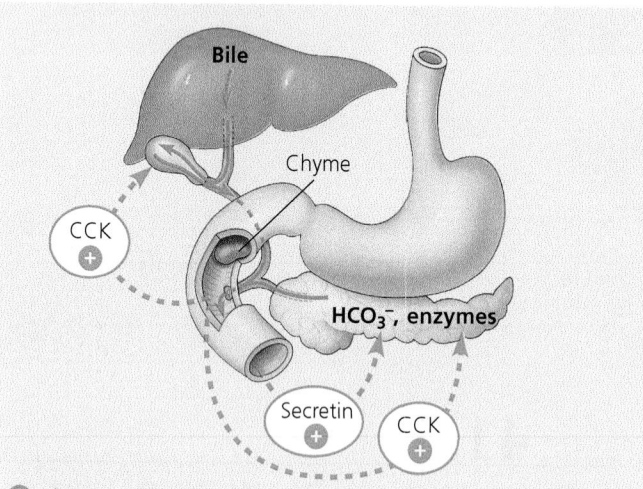

② Chyme—an acidic mixture of partially digested food—eventually passes from the stomach to the duodenum. The duodenum responds to amino acids or fatty acids in the chyme by releasing the digestive hormones cholecystokinin and secretin. **Cholecystokinin (CCK)** stimulates the release of digestive enzymes from the pancreas and of bile from the gallbladder. **Secretin** stimulates the pancreas to release bicarbonate (HCO_3^-), which neutralizes chyme.

③ If the chyme is rich in fats, the high levels of secretin and CCK released act on the stomach to inhibit peristalsis and secretion of gastric juices, thereby slowing digestion.

▲ **Figure 41.19 Hormonal control of digestion.**

called the *enteric division*, which is dedicated to the digestive organs, regulates these events as well as peristalsis in the small and large intestines.

The endocrine system also plays a critical role in controlling digestion. As described in **Figure 41.19**, a series of hormones released by the stomach and duodenum help ensure that digestive secretions are present only when needed. Like all hormones, they are transported through the bloodstream. This is true even for the hormone gastrin, whose target (the stomach) is the same organ that secretes it.

Regulation of Energy Storage

As discussed in Chapter 40, when an animal takes in more energy-rich molecules than it needs for metabolism and activity, it stores the excess energy. In concluding our overview of nutrition, we'll examine some ways in which animals manage their energy allocation.

In humans, the first sites used for energy storage are liver and muscle cells. In these cells, excess energy from the diet is stored in glycogen, a polymer made up of many glucose units (see Figure 5.6b). Once glycogen depots are full, any additional excess energy is usually stored in fat in adipose cells.

When fewer calories are taken in than are expended— perhaps because of sustained heavy exercise or lack of food— the human body generally expends liver glycogen first and then draws on muscle glycogen and fat. Fats are especially rich in energy; oxidizing a gram of fat liberates about twice the energy liberated from a gram of carbohydrate or protein. For this reason, adipose tissue provides the most space-efficient way for the body to store large amounts of energy. Most healthy people have enough stored fat to sustain them through several weeks without food.

Glucose Homeostasis

The synthesis and breakdown of glycogen is central not only to energy storage, but also to maintaining metabolic balance through glucose homeostasis. Tissues throughout the body rely on the generation of ATP by oxidation of glucose to fuel cellular processes (see Chapter 9). The pancreatic hormones insulin and glucagon maintain glucose homeostasis by tightly regulating the synthesis and breakdown of glycogen.

The liver is a key site for glucose homeostasis (**Figure 41.20**). When insulin levels rise after a carbohydrate-rich meal, glucose entering the liver in the hepatic portal vein is used to synthesize glycogen. Between meals, when blood in the hepatic portal vein has a much lower glucose concentration, glucagon stimulates the liver to break down glycogen, releasing glucose into the blood. Through the combined action of insulin and glucagon, blood exiting the liver has a glucose concentration of 70–110 mg per 100 mL at nearly all times.

We will return to the mechanism of glucose homeostasis (and explore the consequences when it fails) in our discussion of the endocrine system in Chapter 45.

Figure 41.20 and surrounding labels

Insulin enhances the transport of glucose into body cells and stimulates liver and muscle cells to store glucose as glycogen. As a result, the blood glucose level drops.

The pancreas secretes the hormone insulin into the blood.

Stimulus: Blood glucose level rises after eating.

Homeostasis: 70–110 mg glucose/100 mL blood

Stimulus: Blood glucose level drops below set point.

Glucagon promotes the breakdown of glycogen in the liver and the release of glucose into the blood, increasing the blood glucose level.

The pancreas secretes the hormone glucagon into the blood.

◀ **Figure 41.20 Homeostatic regulation of cellular fuel.** After a meal is digested, glucose and other monomers are absorbed into the blood from the digestive tract. The human body regulates the use and storage of glucose, a major cellular fuel.

MAKE CONNECTIONS *What form of feedback control does each of these regulatory circuits reflect (see Concept 40.2, p. 861)?*

ANIMATION **BioFlix** Visit the Study Area at **www.masteringbiology.com** for the BioFlix® 3-D Animation on Homeostasis: Regulating Blood Sugar.

Regulation of Appetite and Consumption

Overnourishment, the consumption of more calories than the body needs for normal metabolism, causes obesity, the excessive accumulation of fat. Obesity, in turn, contributes to a number of health problems, including the most common type of diabetes (type 2), cancer of the colon and breast, and cardiovascular disease that can lead to heart attacks and strokes. It is estimated that obesity is a factor in about 300,000 deaths per year in the United States alone.

Researchers have discovered several homeostatic mechanisms that help regulate body weight. Operating as feedback circuits, these mechanisms control the storage and metabolism of fat. Several hormones regulate long-term and short-term appetite by affecting a "satiety center" in the brain **(Figure 41.21)**. In addition, a network of neurons relays and integrates information from the digestive system to regulate hormone release. To a large extent, this neuronal network functions independent of inputs from the central nervous system.

Mutations that cause mice to be chronically obese have played a key role in advancing our understanding of the satiety pathway. Mice with mutations in the *ob* or *db* gene eat voraciously and become much heavier than normal. Doug Coleman investigated how *ob* and *db* mutations disrupt normal

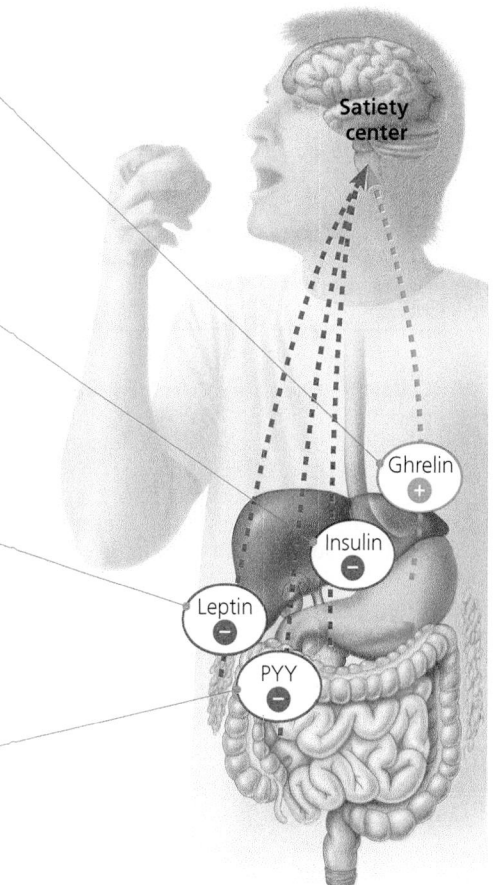

Secreted by the stomach wall, **ghrelin** is one of the signals that triggers feelings of hunger as mealtimes approach. In dieters who lose weight, ghrelin levels increase, which may be one reason it's so hard to stay on a diet.

A rise in blood sugar level after a meal stimulates the pancreas to secrete **insulin** (see Figure 41.20). In addition to its other functions, insulin suppresses appetite by acting on the brain.

Produced by adipose (fat) tissue, **leptin** suppresses appetite. When the amount of body fat decreases, leptin levels fall, and appetite increases.

The hormone **PYY**, secreted by the small intestine after meals, acts as an appetite suppressant that counters the appetite stimulant ghrelin.

▲ **Figure 41.21 A few of the appetite-regulating hormones.** Secreted by various organs and tissues, the hormones reach the brain via the bloodstream. These signals act on a region of the brain that in turn controls the "satiety center," which generates the nervous impulses that make us feel either hungry or satiated ("full"). The hormone ghrelin is an appetite stimulant; the other three hormones shown here are appetite suppressants.

INQUIRY

What are the roles of the *ob* and *db* genes in appetite regulation?

EXPERIMENT Margaret Dickie, Katherine Hummel, and Doug Coleman, of the Jackson Laboratory in Bar Harbor, Maine, discovered that mice mutant for the *ob* gene (*ob ob*) or for the *db* gene (*db db*) eat voraciously and grow much more massive than mice with the wild-type (nonmutant) forms of both genes (designated *ob*⁺ and *db*⁺).

Obese mouse with mutant *ob* gene (left) next to wild-type mouse.

To explore further the roles of the two genes, Coleman measured the body masses of young mice with various genotypes and then surgically linked the circulatory system of each subject to that of another mouse. This procedure ensured that any factor circulating in the bloodstream of either mouse would be transferred to the other. After eight weeks, he again measured the mass of each subject.

RESULTS

Genotype pairing (red type indicates mutant genes)		Average change in body mass (g) of subject
Subject	Paired with	
ob⁺*ob*⁺, *db*⁺*db*⁺	*ob*⁺*ob*⁺, *db*⁺*db*⁺	8.3
ob ob, *db*⁺*db*⁺	*ob ob*, *db*⁺*db*⁺	38.7
ob ob, *db*⁺*db*⁺	*ob*⁺*ob*⁺, *db*⁺*db*⁺	8.2
ob ob, *db*⁺*db*⁺	*ob*⁺*ob*⁺, *db db*	−14.9*

*Due to pronounced weight loss and weakening, subjects in this pairing were reweighed after less than eight weeks.

CONCLUSION Because an *ob* mouse gains less weight when surgically joined with an *ob*⁺ mouse than when joined with an *ob* mouse, Coleman concluded that the *ob* mouse fails to make a satiety factor but can respond to the factor when it is present. To explain the weight loss in an *ob* mouse that receives circulating factors from a *db* mouse, he reasoned that the *db* mutation blocks the response to the satiety factor but not its production, leading to an overproduction of the factor by the *db* mouse.

Subsequent molecular studies demonstrated the validity of both parts of Coleman's conclusion. The *ob* gene product is leptin, the satiety factor, whereas the *db* gene product is the leptin receptor. Thus, mice with the *ob* mutation cannot produce leptin, and mice with the *db* mutation produce leptin but cannot respond to it.

SOURCE D. L. Coleman, Effects of parabiosis of obese mice with diabetes and normal mice. *Diabetologia* 9:294–298 (1973).

MB See the related Experimental Inquiry Tutorial in MasteringBiology.

WHAT IF? Suppose you collected blood from a wild-type mouse and a *db* mouse over the course of a day. What changes would you expect in the concentration of leptin, the satiety factor, in each mouse? Explain your reasoning.

control of appetite (Figure 41.22). Based on his experiments, Coleman deduced that the *ob* gene is required to produce the satiety factor, and the *db* gene is required to respond to the factor.

Cloning of the *ob* gene led to the demonstration that it codes for the hormone now known as **leptin** (from the Greek *lepto*, thin). The *db* gene encodes the leptin receptor. Leptin and the leptin receptor are key components of the circuitry that regulates appetite over the long term. Because leptin is a product of adipose cells, levels rise when the amount of body fat increases, cuing the brain to suppress appetite (see Figure 41.20). Conversely, loss of fat decreases leptin levels, signaling the brain to increase appetite. In this way, the feedback signals provided by leptin maintain body fat levels within a set range.

Our understanding of leptin may lead to treatments for obesity, but uncertainties remain. For one thing, leptin has complex functions, including a role in how the nervous system develops. Also, most obese people have an abnormally high leptin level, which somehow fails to elicit a response from the brain's satiety center. Clearly, there is much to learn in this important area of human physiology.

Obesity and Evolution

EVOLUTION The relationship between fat storage and evolutionary adaptation in animals is sometimes complex. Consider the plump offspring of the seabirds called petrels (Figure 41.23). Their parents must fly long distances to find food. Most of the food that they bring to their chicks is very rich in lipids. The fact that fat has about twice as many calories per gram as other fuels minimizes the number of foraging trips. However, growing petrels need lots of protein for building new tissues, and there is relatively little in their oily

▲ **Figure 41.23 A plump petrel.** Too heavy to fly, the petrel chick (right) will have to lose weight before it takes wing. In the meantime, its stored fat provides energy during times when its parents fail to bring enough food.

diet. To get all the protein they need, young petrels must consume many more calories than they burn in metabolism, and consequently they become obese. Their fat depots nevertheless help them survive periods when their parents cannot find enough food. When food is plentiful, chicks at the end of the growth period weigh much more than their parents. The youngsters must then fast for several days to lose enough weight to be capable of flight.

Though fat hoarding in humans can be a health liability, it may have been an advantage in our evolutionary past. Our ancestors on the African savanna were hunter-gatherers who probably survived mainly on seeds and other plant products, a diet only occasionally supplemented by hunting game or scavenging meat from animals killed by other predators. In such a feast-or-famine existence, natural selection may have favored those individuals with a physiology that induced them to gorge on rich, fatty foods on those rare occasions when such treats were abundantly available. Individuals with genes promoting the storage of high-energy molecules during feasts may have been more likely to survive famines. Thus, our present-day taste for fats may be partly an evolutionary vestige of less nutritious times.

In the next chapter, we'll see that obtaining food, digesting it, and absorbing nutrients are parts of a larger story. Provisioning the body also involves distributing nutrients (circulation), and using nutrients for metabolism requires exchanging respiratory gases with the environment.

CONCEPT CHECK 41.5

1. Explain how people can become obese even if their intake of dietary fat is relatively low compared with carbohydrate intake.
2. After reviewing Figure 41.21, explain how PYY and leptin complement each other in regulating body weight.
3. **WHAT IF?** Suppose you were studying two groups of obese people with genetic abnormalities in the leptin pathway. In one group, the leptin levels are abnormally high; in the other group, they are abnormally low. How would each group's leptin levels change if both groups were placed on a low-calorie diet for an extended period? Explain.

For suggested answers, see Appendix A.

41 CHAPTER REVIEW

SUMMARY OF KEY CONCEPTS

- Animals have diverse diets. **Herbivores** mainly eat plants; **carnivores** mainly eat other animals; and **omnivores** eat both. Animals must balance consumption, storage, and use of food.

CONCEPT 41.1

An animal's diet must supply chemical energy, organic molecules, and essential nutrients (pp. 875–880)

- Food provides animals with energy for ATP production, carbon skeletons for biosynthesis, and **essential nutrients**—nutrients that must be supplied in preassembled form. Essential nutrients include certain amino acids and fatty acids that animals cannot synthesize; **vitamins**, which are organic molecules; and **minerals**, which are inorganic substances.
- Animals can suffer from two types of malnutrition: an inadequate intake of essential nutrients and a deficiency in sources of chemical energy. Studies of genetic defects and of disease at the population level help researchers determine human dietary requirements.

? *Propose a reason why the diet of many mammals doesn't need to include vitamin C, a substance that is important for collagen synthesis.*

CONCEPT 41.2

The main stages of food processing are ingestion, digestion, absorption, and elimination (pp. 880–883)

- Food processing in animals involves **ingestion** (eating), **digestion** (enzymatic breakdown of large molecules), **absorption** (uptake of nutrients by cells), and **elimination** (passage of undigested materials out of the body in feces).

- Animals differ in the ways they obtain and ingest food. Most animals are **bulk feeders**, eating large pieces of food.
- Compartmentalization is necessary to avoid self-digestion. In intracellular digestion, food particles are engulfed by endocytosis and digested within food vacuoles that have fused with lysosomes. In extracellular digestion, which is used by most animals, enzymatic hydrolysis occurs outside cells in a **gastrovascular cavity** or **alimentary canal**.

? *Propose an artificial diet that would eliminate the need for one of the first three steps in food processing.*

CONCEPT 41.3

Organs specialized for sequential stages of food processing form the mammalian digestive system (pp. 883–889)

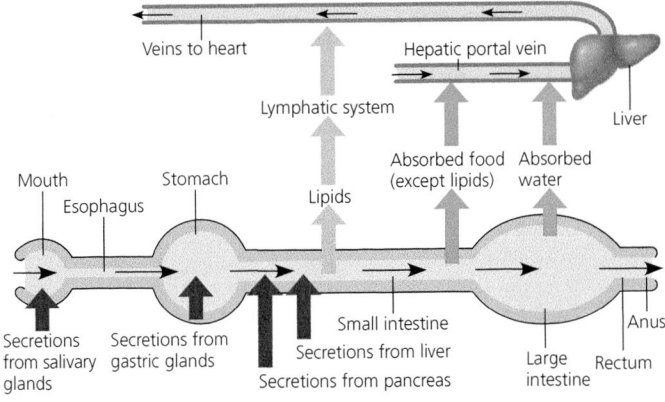

? *What structural feature of the small intestine makes it better suited for absorption of nutrients than the stomach?*

CONCEPT 41.4

Evolutionary adaptations of vertebrate digestive systems correlate with diet (pp. 889–891)

- Vertebrate digestive systems display many evolutionary adaptations associated with diet. For example, dentition, which is the assortment of teeth, generally correlates with diet. In addition, herbivores usually have longer alimentary canals than carnivores, reflecting the longer time needed to digest vegetation. Many herbivores, including cows, also have fermentation chambers where microorganisms digest cellulose, a form of mutualism.

? *How does our anatomy indicate that our ancestors were not vegetarians?*

CONCEPT 41.5

Feedback circuits regulate digestion, energy storage, and appetite (pp. 891–895)

- Nutrition is regulated at multiple levels. Food in the alimentary canal triggers nervous and hormonal responses that control the secretion of digestive juices and that promote the movement of ingested material through the canal. The availability of glucose for energy production is regulated by the hormones insulin and glucagon, which control the synthesis and breakdown of glycogen.
- Vertebrates store excess calories in glycogen (in liver and muscle cells) and in fat (in adipose cells). These energy stores can be tapped when an animal expends more calories than it consumes. If, however, an animal consumes more calories than it needs for normal metabolism, the resulting overnourishment can lead to the serious health problem of obesity.
- Several hormones, including leptin and insulin, regulate appetite by affecting the brain's satiety center. The problem of maintaining a healthy weight may stem partly from our evolutionary past, when fat hoarding may have been important for survival.

? *Explain why your stomach might make growling noises when you skip a meal.*

TEST YOUR UNDERSTANDING

LEVEL 1: KNOWLEDGE/COMPREHENSION

1. Which of the following animals is *incorrectly* paired with its feeding mechanism?
   a. lion—substrate feeder
   b. baleen whale—suspension feeder
   c. aphid—fluid feeder
   d. clam—suspension feeder
   e. snake—bulk feeder

2. The mammalian trachea and esophagus both connect to the
   a. large intestine.   d. rectum.
   b. stomach.   e. epiglottis.
   c. pharynx.

3. Which of the following organs is *incorrectly* paired with its function?
   a. stomach—protein digestion
   b. oral cavity—starch digestion
   c. large intestine—bile production
   d. small intestine—nutrient absorption
   e. pancreas—enzyme production

4. Which of the following is *not* a major activity of the stomach?
   a. mechanical digestion   d. nutrient absorption
   b. HCl secretion   e. enzyme secretion
   c. mucus secretion

LEVEL 2: APPLICATION/ANALYSIS

5. After surgical removal of an infected gallbladder, a person must be especially careful to restrict dietary intake of
   a. starch.   b. protein.   c. sugar.   d. fat.   e. water.

6. If you were to jog 1 km a few hours after lunch, which stored fuel would you probably tap?
   a. muscle proteins
   b. muscle and liver glycogen
   c. fat stored in the liver
   d. fat stored in adipose tissue
   e. blood proteins

LEVEL 3: SYNTHESIS/EVALUATION

7. **DRAW IT** Make a flowchart of the events that occur after partially digested food leaves the stomach. Use the following terms: bicarbonate secretion, circulation, decrease in acidity, secretin secretion, increase in acidity, signal detection. Next to each term, indicate the compartment(s) involved. You may use a term more than once.

8. **EVOLUTION CONNECTION**
   The human esophagus and trachea share a passage leading from the mouth and nasal passages, which can cause problems. After reviewing vertebrate evolution in Chapter 34, explain the evolutionary basis for this "imperfect" anatomy.

9. **SCIENTIFIC INQUIRY**
   In human populations of northern European origin, the disorder called hemochromatosis causes excess iron uptake from food and affects one in 200 adults. Men are ten times as likely as women to suffer from iron overload. Devise a hypothesis for the difference in the disease between the two sexes.

10. **WRITE ABOUT A THEME**
    Emergent Properties Hair is largely made up of the protein keratin. In a short essay (100–150 words), explain why a shampoo containing protein is not effective in replacing the protein in damaged hair.

For selected answers, see Appendix A.

Mastering BIOLOGY www.masteringbiology.com

1. MasteringBiology® Assignments
Make Connections Tutorial Fat Absorption (Chapter 41) and Fat Structure (Chapter 5)
Experimental Inquiry Tutorial What Role Do Genes Play in Appetite Regulation?
BioFlix Tutorials Membrane Transport • Homeostasis: Regulating Blood Sugar
Tutorial Vitamins
Activities Digestive System Function • Hormonal Control of Digestion • The Digestion and Absorption of Food • Discovery Channel Video: Nutrition
Questions Student Misconceptions • Reading Quiz • Multiple Choice • End-of-Chapter

2. eText
Read your book online, search, take notes, highlight text, and more.

3. The Study Area
Practice Tests • Cumulative Test • **BioFlix** 3-D Animations • MP3 Tutor Sessions • Videos • Activities • Investigations • Lab Media • Audio Glossary • Word Study Tools • Art

42

Circulation and Gas Exchange

▲ Figure 42.1 **How does a feathery fringe help this animal survive?**

KEY CONCEPTS

42.1 Circulatory systems link exchange surfaces with cells throughout the body

42.2 Coordinated cycles of heart contraction drive double circulation in mammals

42.3 Patterns of blood pressure and flow reflect the structure and arrangement of blood vessels

42.4 Blood components function in exchange, transport, and defense

42.5 Gas exchange occurs across specialized respiratory surfaces

42.6 Breathing ventilates the lungs

42.7 Adaptations for gas exchange include pigments that bind and transport gases

Trading Places

The animal in **Figure 42.1** may look like a creature from a science fiction film, but it's actually an axolotl, a salamander native to shallow ponds in central Mexico. The feathery red appendages jutting out from the head of this albino adult are gills. Although external gills are uncommon in adult animals, they help satisfy the need shared by all animals to exchange substances with their environment.

Exchange between an axolotl or any other animal and its surroundings ultimately occurs at the cellular level. The resources that animal cells require, such as nutrients and oxygen (O_2), enter the cytoplasm by crossing the plasma membrane. Metabolic by-products, such as carbon dioxide (CO_2), exit the cell by crossing the same membrane. In unicellular organisms, exchange occurs directly with the external environment. For most multicellular organisms, however, direct transfer of materials between every cell and the environment is not possible. Instead, these organisms rely on specialized systems that carry out exchange with the environment and that transport materials between sites of exchange and the rest of the body.

The reddish color and branching structure of the axolotl's gills reflect the intimate association between exchange and transport. Tiny blood vessels lie close to the surface of each filament in the gills. Across this surface, there is a net diffusion of O_2 from the surrounding water into the blood and of CO_2 from the blood into the water. The short distances involved allow diffusion to be rapid. Pumping of the axolotl's heart propels the oxygen-rich blood from the gill filaments to all other tissues of the body. There, more short-range exchange occurs, involving nutrients and O_2 as well as CO_2 and other wastes.

Because internal transport and gas exchange are functionally related in most animals, not just axolotls, we will examine both circulatory and respiratory systems in this chapter. We will explore the remarkable variation in form and organization of these systems by considering examples from a number of species. We will also highlight the roles of circulatory and respiratory systems in maintaining homeostasis under a range of physiological and environmental conditions.

CONCEPT 42.1

Circulatory systems link exchange surfaces with cells throughout the body

The molecular trade that an animal carries out with its environment—gaining O_2 and nutrients while shedding CO_2 and other waste products—must ultimately involve every cell in the body. As you learned in Chapter 7, small, nonpolar molecules such as O_2 and CO_2 can move between cells and their immediate surroundings by diffusion. But diffusion is very slow for distances of more than a few millimeters. That's because the time it takes for a substance to diffuse from one place to another is proportional to the *square* of the distance. For example, if it takes 1 second for a given quantity of glucose to diffuse 100 µm, it will take 100 seconds for the same quantity to diffuse 1 mm and almost 3 hours to diffuse 1 cm! This relationship between diffusion time and distance places a substantial constraint on the body plan of any animal.

Given that diffusion is rapid only over very small distances, how does each cell of an animal participate in exchange? Natural selection has resulted in two general solutions to this problem. The first solution is a body size and shape that keep many or all cells in direct contact with the environment. Each cell can thus exchange materials directly with the surrounding medium. This type of body plan is found only in certain invertebrates, including cnidarians and flatworms. The second solution, found in all other animals, is a circulatory system that moves fluid between each cell's immediate surroundings and the tissues where exchange with the environment occurs.

Gastrovascular Cavities

Let's begin by looking at animals that lack a distinct circulatory system. In hydras, jellies, and other cnidarians, a central gastrovascular cavity functions in the distribution of substances throughout the body and in digestion (see Figure 41.7). An opening at one end connects the cavity to the surrounding water. In a hydra, thin branches of the gastrovascular cavity extend into the animal's tentacles. In jellies and some other cnidarians, the gastrovascular cavity has a much more elaborate branching pattern (**Figure 42.2a**).

In animals with a gastrovascular cavity, fluid bathes both the inner and outer tissue layers, facilitating exchange of gases and cellular waste. Only the cells lining the cavity have direct access to nutrients released by digestion. However, because the body wall is a mere two cells thick, nutrients need diffuse only a short distance to reach the cells of the outer tissue layer.

Planarians and most other flatworms also survive without a circulatory system. Their combination of a gastrovascular cavity and a flat body is well suited for exchange with the environment (**Figure 42.2b**). A flat body

optimizes diffusional exchange by increasing surface area and minimizing diffusion distances.

Evolutionary Variation in Circulatory Systems

EVOLUTION For animals with many cell layers, diffusion distances are too great for adequate exchange of nutrients and wastes by a gastrovascular cavity. In these organisms, a circulatory system minimizes the distances that substances must diffuse to enter or leave a cell.

General Properties of Circulatory Systems

A circulatory system has three basic components: a circulatory fluid, a set of interconnecting vessels, and a muscular pump, the **heart**. The heart powers circulation by using metabolic energy to elevate the hydrostatic pressure of the circulatory fluid, which then flows through the vessels and back to the heart.

By transporting fluid throughout the body, the circulatory system functionally connects the aqueous environment of the body cells to the organs that exchange gases, absorb nutrients, and dispose of wastes. In mammals, for example, O_2 from inhaled air diffuses across only two layers of cells in the lungs before reaching the blood. The circulatory system, powered by the heart, then carries the oxygen-rich blood to all parts of the body. As the blood streams throughout the body tissues in tiny blood vessels, O_2 in the blood diffuses only a short distance before entering the fluid that directly bathes the cells.

Several basic types of circulatory systems have arisen during evolution, each representing adaptations to constraints imposed by anatomy and environment. Circulatory systems are either open or closed, vary with regard to the number of circuits in the body, and rely on pumps that differ in structure and organization. We'll examine each of these variations and their physiological consequences in turn.

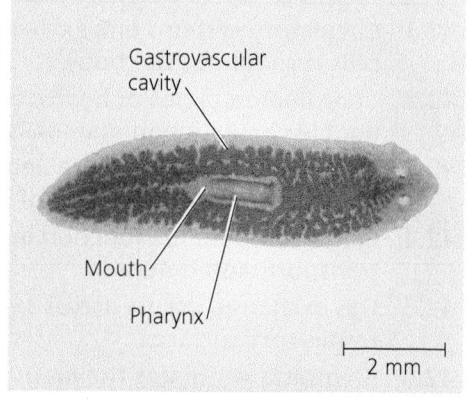

▶ Figure 42.2 **Internal transport in gastrovascular cavities.**

WHAT IF? *Suppose a gastrovascular cavity were open at two ends, with fluid entering one end and leaving the other. How would this affect the gastrovascular cavity's functions in gas exchange and digestion?*

(a) The moon jelly *Aurelia*, a cnidarian. The jelly is viewed here from its underside (oral surface). The mouth leads to an elaborate gastrovascular cavity that consists of radial canals leading to and from a circular canal. Ciliated cells lining the canals circulate fluid within the cavity.

(b) The planarian *Dugesia*, a flatworm. The mouth and pharynx on the ventral side lead to the highly branched gastrovascular cavity, stained dark red in this specimen (LM).

Open and Closed Circulatory Systems

Arthropods and most molluscs have an **open circulatory system**, in which the circulatory fluid bathes the organs directly (Figure 42.3a). In these animals, the circulatory fluid, called **hemolymph**, is also the *interstitial fluid* that bathes body cells. Contraction of one or more hearts pumps the hemolymph through the circulatory vessels into interconnected sinuses, spaces surrounding the organs. Within the sinuses, chemical exchange occurs between the hemolymph and body cells. Relaxation of the heart draws hemolymph

back in through pores, which are equipped with valves that close when the heart contracts. Body movements help circulate the hemolymph by periodically squeezing the sinuses. The open circulatory system of larger crustaceans, such as lobsters and crabs, includes a more extensive system of vessels as well as an accessory pump.

In a **closed circulatory system**, a circulatory fluid called **blood** is confined to vessels and is distinct from the interstitial fluid (Figure 42.3b). One or more hearts pump blood into large vessels that branch into smaller ones that infiltrate the organs. Chemical exchange occurs between the blood and the interstitial fluid, as well as between the interstitial fluid and body cells. Annelids (including earthworms), cephalopods (including squids and octopuses), and all vertebrates have closed circulatory systems.

The fact that both open and closed circulatory systems are widespread among animals suggests that there are advantages to each system. The lower hydrostatic pressures associated with open circulatory systems make them less costly than closed systems in terms of energy expenditure. In some invertebrates, open circulatory systems serve additional functions. For example, spiders use the hydrostatic pressure generated by their open circulatory system to extend their legs.

The benefits of closed circulatory systems include relatively high blood pressures, which enable the effective delivery of O_2 and nutrients to the cells of larger and more active animals. Among the molluscs, for instance, closed circulatory systems are found in the largest and most active species, the squids and octopuses. Closed systems are also particularly well suited to regulating the distribution of blood to different organs, as you'll learn later in this chapter. In examining closed circulatory systems in more detail, we will focus on the vertebrates.

Organization of Vertebrate Circulatory Systems

The closed circulatory system of humans and other vertebrates is often called the **cardiovascular system**. Blood circulates to and from the heart through an amazingly extensive network of vessels: The total length of blood vessels in an average human adult is twice Earth's circumference at the equator!

Arteries, veins, and capillaries are the three main types of blood vessels. Within each type, blood flows in only one direction. **Arteries** carry blood away from the heart to organs throughout the body. Within organs, arteries branch into **arterioles**, small vessels that convey blood to the capillaries. **Capillaries** are microscopic vessels with very thin, porous walls. Networks of these vessels, called **capillary beds**, infiltrate every tissue, passing within a few cell diameters of every cell in the body. Across the thin walls of capillaries, chemicals, including dissolved gases, are exchanged by diffusion between the blood and the interstitial fluid around the tissue cells. At their "downstream" end, capillaries converge into **venules**, and venules converge into **veins**, the vessels that carry blood back to the heart.

▼ Figure 42.3 **Open and closed circulatory systems.**

(a) An open circulatory system

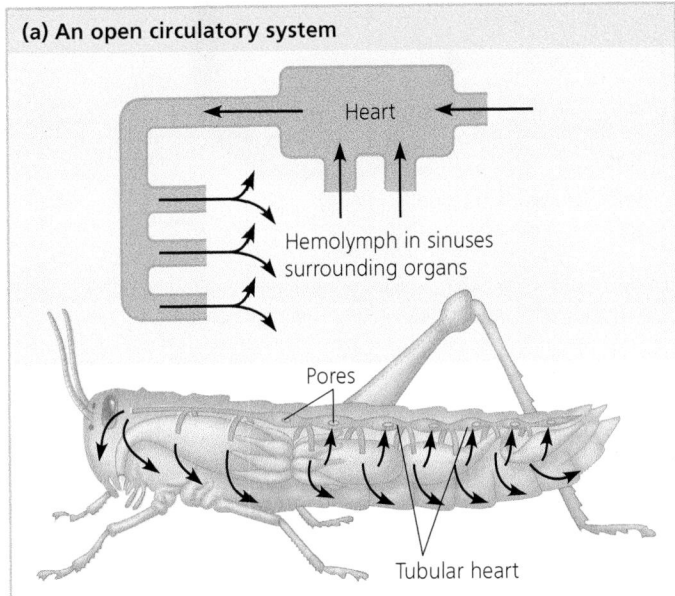

Heart

Hemolymph in sinuses surrounding organs

Pores

Tubular heart

In an open circulatory system, such as that of a grasshopper, hemolymph surrounding body tissues also acts as the circulatory fluid.

(b) A closed circulatory system

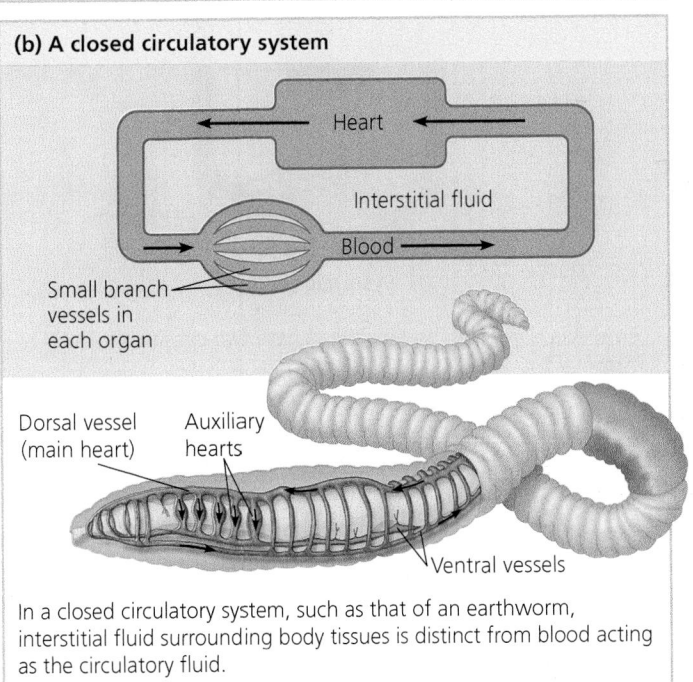

Heart

Interstitial fluid

Blood

Small branch vessels in each organ

Dorsal vessel (main heart)

Auxiliary hearts

Ventral vessels

In a closed circulatory system, such as that of an earthworm, interstitial fluid surrounding body tissues is distinct from blood acting as the circulatory fluid.

Arteries and veins are distinguished by the *direction* in which they carry blood, not by the O_2 content or other characteristics of the blood they contain. Arteries carry blood from the heart *toward* capillaries, and veins return blood to the heart *from* capillaries. The only exceptions are the portal veins, which carry blood between pairs of capillary beds. The hepatic portal vein, for example, carries blood from capillary beds in the digestive system to capillary beds in the liver (see Chapter 41). From the liver, blood passes into the hepatic veins, which conduct blood toward the heart.

The hearts of all vertebrates contain two or more muscular chambers. The chambers that receive blood entering the heart are called **atria** (singular, *atrium*). The chambers responsible for pumping blood out of the heart are called **ventricles**. The number of chambers and the extent to which they are separated from one another differ substantially among groups of vertebrates, as we will discuss next. These important differences reflect the close fit of form to function that arises from natural selection.

Single Circulation

In bony fishes, rays, and sharks, the heart consists of two chambers: an atrium and a ventricle. The blood passes through the heart once in each complete circuit, an arrangement called **single circulation** (Figure 42.4a). Blood entering the heart collects in the atrium before transfer to the ventricle. Contraction of the ventricle pumps blood to the gills, where there is a net diffusion of O_2 into the blood and of CO_2 out of the blood. As blood leaves the gills, the capillaries converge into a vessel that carries oxygen-rich blood to capillary beds throughout the body. Blood then returns to the heart.

In single circulation, blood that leaves the heart passes through two capillary beds before returning to the heart. When blood flows through a capillary bed, blood pressure drops substantially, for reasons we will explain shortly. The drop in blood pressure in the gills limits the rate of blood flow in the rest of the animal's body. As the animal swims, however, the contraction and relaxation of its muscles help accelerate the relatively sluggish pace of circulation.

Double Circulation

The circulatory systems of amphibians, reptiles, and mammals have two circuits, an arrangement called **double circulation** (Figure 42.4b). The pumps for the two circuits are combined into a single organ, the heart. Having both pumps within a single heart simplifies coordination of the pumping cycles.

One pump, the right side of the heart, delivers oxygen-poor blood to the capillary beds of the gas exchange tissues, where there is a net movement of O_2 into the blood and of CO_2 out of the blood. This part of the circulation is called a **pulmonary circuit** if the capillary beds involved are all in the lungs, as in reptiles and mammals. It is called a **pulmocutaneous circuit** if it includes capillaries in both the lungs and the skin, as in many amphibians.

(a) Single circulation

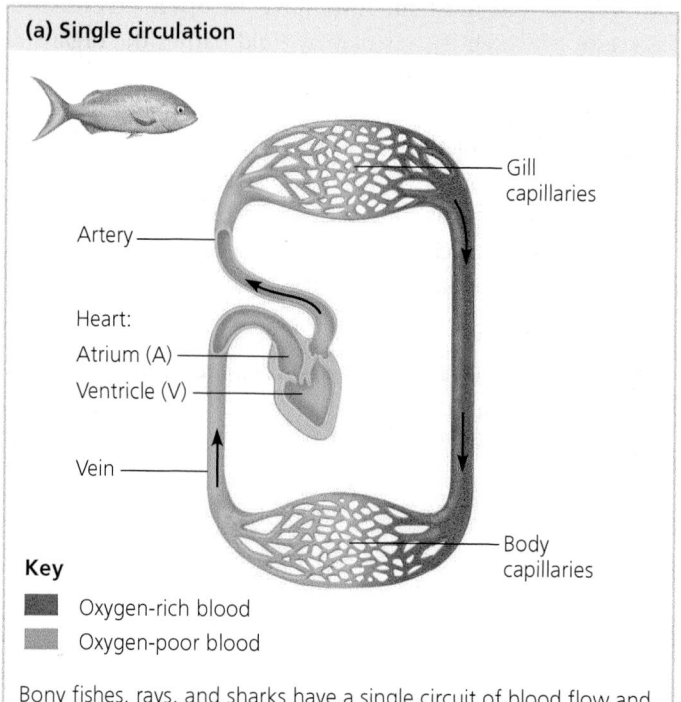

Key

■ Oxygen-rich blood
■ Oxygen-poor blood

Bony fishes, rays, and sharks have a single circuit of blood flow and a single circulatory pump—a heart with two chambers.

(b) Double circulation

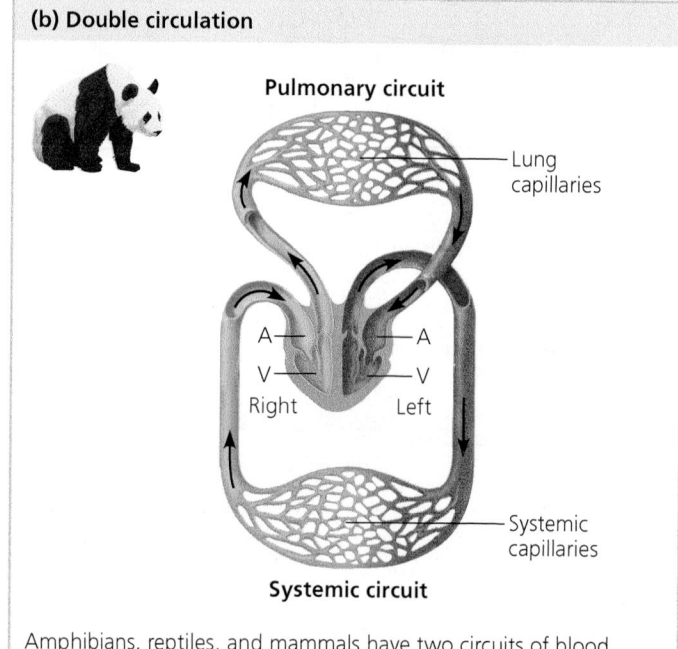

Amphibians, reptiles, and mammals have two circuits of blood flow and two pumps fused into a multi-chambered heart. Note that circulatory systems are depicted as if the animal is facing you: The right side of the heart is shown on the left, and vice versa.

After the oxygen-enriched blood leaves the gas exchange tissues, it enters the other pump, the left side of the heart. Contraction of the heart propels this blood to capillary beds in organs and tissues throughout the body. Following the exchange of O_2 and CO_2, as well as nutrients and waste products, the now oxygen-poor blood returns to the heart, completing the **systemic circuit**.

Double circulation provides a vigorous flow of blood to the brain, muscles, and other organs because the heart repressurizes the blood destined for these tissues after it passes through the capillary beds of the lungs or skin. Indeed, blood pressure is often much higher in the systemic circuit than in the gas exchange circuit. This contrasts sharply with single circulation, in which blood flows under reduced pressure directly from the gas exchange organs to other organs.

To explore the adaptations of double circulation that meet the particular needs of different vertebrates, we conclude our overview of circulatory systems with Figure 42.5. In the next section, we will restrict our focus to circulation in mammals and to the anatomy and physiology of the key circulatory organ—the heart.

▼ Figure 42.5

Exploring Double Circulation in Vertebrates

    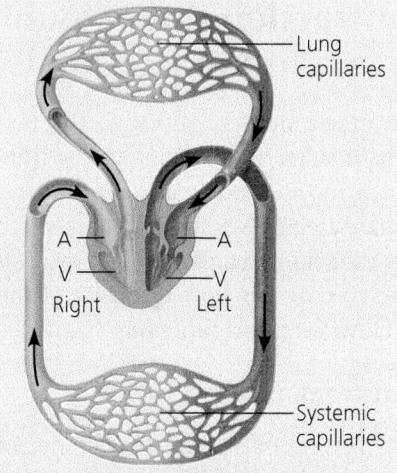

Amphibians

Pulmocutaneous circuit

Systemic circuit

Reptiles (Except Birds)

Pulmonary circuit

Systemic circuit

Mammals and Birds

Pulmonary circuit

Systemic circuit

Frogs and other amphibians have a heart with three chambers: two atria and one ventricle. A ridge within the ventricle diverts most (about 90%) of the oxygen-poor blood from the right atrium into the pulmocutaneous circuit and most of the oxygen-rich blood from the left atrium into the systemic circuit. When underwater, a frog adjusts its circulation, for the most part shutting off blood flow to its temporarily ineffective lungs. Blood flow continues to the skin, which acts as the sole site of gas exchange while the frog is submerged.

In the three-chambered heart of turtles, snakes, and lizards, an incomplete septum partially divides the single ventricle into separate right and left chambers. Two major arteries, called aortas, lead to the systemic circulation. The detailed anatomy of the heart varies among these three groups of reptiles, with some adaptations allowing control of the relative amount of blood flowing to the lungs and the body.

In alligators, caimans, and other crocodilians, the ventricles are divided by a complete septum (not shown), but the pulmonary and systemic circuits connect where the arteries exit the heart. This connection enables arterial valves to shunt blood flow away from the lungs temporarily, such as when the animal is underwater.

In mammals and birds, there are two atria and two completely divided ventricles. The left side of the heart receives and pumps only oxygen-rich blood, while the right side receives and pumps only oxygen-poor blood. (In birds, the major vessels near the heart are slightly different than shown.) As endotherms, mammals and birds use about ten times as much energy as equal-sized ectotherms. Their circulatory systems therefore need to deliver about ten times as much fuel and O_2 to their tissues (and remove ten times as much CO_2 and other wastes). This large traffic of substances is made possible by separate and independently powered systemic and pulmonary circuits and by large hearts that pump the necessary volume of blood. A powerful four-chambered heart arose independently in the distinct ancestors of mammals and birds and thus reflects convergent evolution (see Chapter 34).

Key

Oxygen-rich blood
Oxygen-poor blood

1. How is the flow of hemolymph through an open circulatory system similar to the flow of water through an outdoor fountain?

2. Three-chambered hearts with incomplete septa were once viewed as being less adapted to circulatory function than mammalian hearts. What advantage of such hearts did this viewpoint overlook?

3. **WHAT IF?** The heart of a normally developing human fetus has a hole between the left and right atria. In some cases, this hole does not close completely before birth. If the hole weren't surgically corrected, how would it affect the O_2 content of the blood entering the systemic circuit?

For suggested answers, see Appendix A.

CONCEPT **42.2**

Coordinated cycles of heart contraction drive double circulation in mammals

The timely delivery of O_2 to the body's organs is critical: Some brain cells, for example, die if their O_2 supply is interrupted for as little as a few minutes. How does the mammalian cardiovascular system meet the body's continuous but variable demand for O_2? To answer this question, we need to consider how the parts of the system are arranged and how each part functions.

Mammalian Circulation

Let's first examine the overall organization of the mammalian cardiovascular system, beginning with the pulmonary circuit. (The circled numbers refer to corresponding locations in **Figure 42.6**.) ❶ Contraction of the right ventricle pumps blood to the lungs via ❷ the pulmonary arteries. As the blood flows through ❸ capillary beds in the left and right lungs, it loads O_2 and unloads CO_2. Oxygen-rich blood returns from the lungs via the pulmonary veins to ❹ the left atrium of the heart. Next, the oxygen-rich blood flows into ❺ the heart's left ventricle, which pumps the oxygen-rich blood out to body tissues through the systemic circuit. Blood leaves the left ventricle via ❻ the aorta, which conveys blood to arteries leading throughout the body. The first branches leading from the aorta are the coronary arteries (not shown), which supply blood to the heart muscle itself. Then branches lead to ❼ capillary beds in the head and arms (forelimbs). The aorta then descends into the abdomen, supplying oxygen-rich blood to arteries leading to ❽ capillary beds in the abdominal organs and legs (hind limbs). Within the capillaries, there is a net diffusion of O_2 from the blood to the tissues

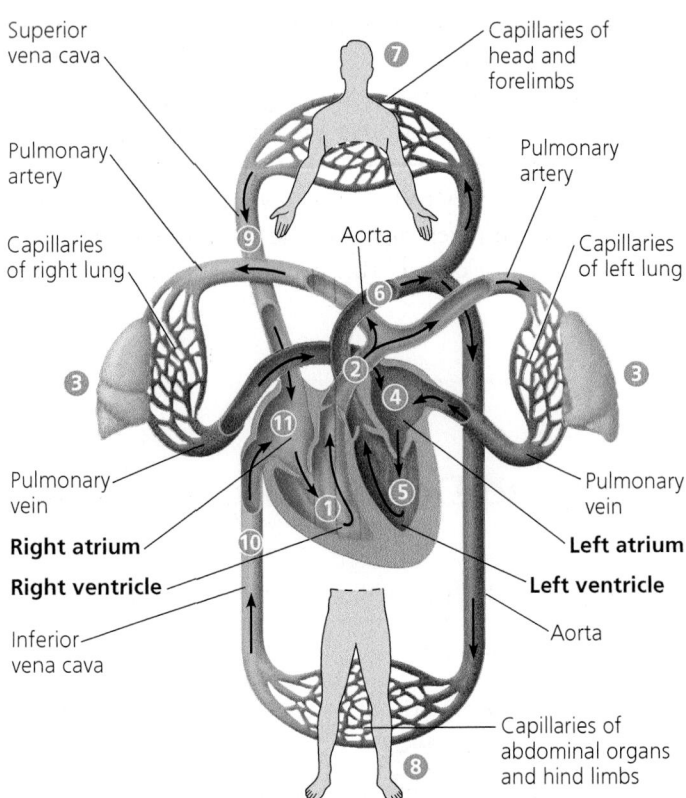

▲ **Figure 42.6 The mammalian cardiovascular system: an overview.** Note that the dual circuits operate simultaneously, not in the serial fashion that the numbering in the diagram suggests. The two ventricles pump almost in unison; while some blood is traveling in the pulmonary circuit, the rest of the blood is flowing in the systemic circuit.

and of CO_2 (produced by cellular respiration) into the blood. Capillaries rejoin, forming venules, which convey blood to veins. Oxygen-poor blood from the head, neck, and forelimbs is channeled into a large vein, ❾ the superior vena cava. Another large vein, ❿ the inferior vena cava, drains blood from the trunk and hind limbs. The two venae cavae empty their blood into ⓫ the right atrium, from which the oxygen-poor blood flows into the right ventricle.

The Mammalian Heart: *A Closer Look*

Using the human heart as an example, let's now take a closer look at how the mammalian heart works (**Figure 42.7**). Located behind the sternum (breastbone), the human heart is about the size of a clenched fist and consists mostly of cardiac muscle (see Figure 40.5). The two atria have relatively thin walls and serve as collection chambers for blood returning to the heart from the lungs or other body tissues. Much of the blood that enters the atria flows into the ventricles while all heart chambers are relaxed. The remainder is transferred by contraction of the atria before the ventricles begin to contract. The ventricles have thicker walls and contract much more forcefully than the atria—especially the left ventricle, which pumps blood to all body organs through the systemic circuit. Although the left ventricle contracts with

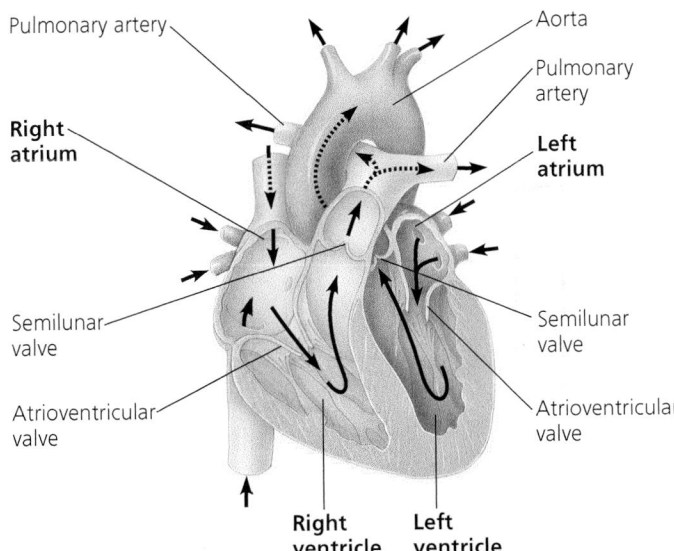

Pulmonary artery

Aorta

Pulmonary artery

Right atrium

Left atrium

Semilunar valve

Semilunar valve

Atrioventricular valve

Atrioventricular valve

Right ventricle

Left ventricle

▲ **Figure 42.7 The mammalian heart: a closer look.** Notice the locations of the valves, which prevent backflow of blood within the heart. Also notice how the atria and left and right ventricles differ in the thickness of their muscular walls.

❶ **Atrial and ventricular diastole.** During a relaxation phase, blood returning from the large veins flows into the atria and then into the ventricles through the AV valves.

❷ **Atrial systole and ventricular diastole.** A brief period of atrial contraction then forces all blood remaining in the atria into the ventricles.

0.1 sec

0.3 sec

0.4 sec

❸ **Ventricular systole and atrial diastole.** During the remainder of the cycle, ventricular contraction pumps blood into the large arteries through the semilunar valves.

▲ **Figure 42.8 The cardiac cycle.** For an adult human at rest with a heart rate of about 72 beats per minute, one complete cardiac cycle takes about 0.8 second. Note that during all but 0.1 second of the cardiac cycle, the atria are relaxed and are filling with blood returning via the veins.

greater force than the right ventricle, it pumps the same volume of blood as the right ventricle during each contraction.

The heart contracts and relaxes in a rhythmic cycle. When it contracts, it pumps blood; when it relaxes, its chambers fill with blood. One complete sequence of pumping and filling is referred to as the **cardiac cycle**. The contraction phase of the cycle is called **systole**, and the relaxation phase is called **diastole** (Figure 42.8).

The volume of blood each ventricle pumps per minute is the **cardiac output**. Two factors determine cardiac output: the rate of contraction, or **heart rate** (number of beats per minute), and the **stroke volume**, the amount of blood pumped by a ventricle in a single contraction. The average stroke volume in humans is about 70 mL. Multiplying this stroke volume by a resting heart rate of 72 beats per minute yields a cardiac output of 5 L/min—about equal to the total volume of blood in the human body. During heavy exercise, cardiac output increases as much as fivefold.

Four valves in the heart prevent backflow and keep blood moving in the correct direction (see Figures 42.7 and 42.8). Made of flaps of connective tissue, the valves open when pushed from one side and close when pushed from the other. An **atrioventricular (AV) valve** lies between each atrium and ventricle. The AV valves are anchored by strong fibers that prevent them from turning inside out. Pressure generated by the powerful contraction of the ventricles closes the AV valves, keeping blood from flowing back into the atria. **Semilunar valves** are located at the two exits of the heart: where the aorta leaves the left ventricle and where the pulmonary artery leaves the right ventricle. These valves are pushed open by the pressure generated during contraction of

the ventricles. When the ventricles relax, blood pressure built up in the aorta closes the semilunar valves and prevents significant backflow.

You can follow the closing of the two sets of heart valves either with a stethoscope or by pressing your ear tightly against the chest of a friend (or a friendly dog). The sound pattern is "lub-dup, lub-dup, lub-dup." The first heart sound ("lub") is created by the recoil of blood against the closed AV valves. The second sound ("dup") is produced by the recoil of blood against the closed semilunar valves.

If blood squirts backward through a defective valve, it may produce an abnormal sound called a **heart murmur**. Some people are born with heart murmurs; in others, the valves may be damaged by infection (from rheumatic fever, for instance). When a valve defect is severe enough to endanger health, surgeons may implant a mechanical replacement valve. However, not all heart murmurs are caused by a defect, and most valve defects do not reduce the efficiency of blood flow enough to warrant surgery.

▶ **Figure 42.9 The control of heart rhythm.** The sequence of electrical events in the heart is shown at the top; red highlights specialized muscle cells involved in the electrical control of the rhythm. The corresponding components of an electrocardiogram (ECG) are highlighted at the bottom in yellow. In step 4, the portion of the ECG to the right of the "spike" represents electrical activity that reprimes the ventricles for the next round of contraction.

WHAT IF? *If a doctor gave you a copy of your ECG recording, how could you determine what your heart rate had been during the test?*

1 Signals (yellow) from SA node spread through atria.

SA node (pacemaker)

2 Signals are delayed at AV node.

AV node

3 Bundle branches pass signals to heart apex.

Bundle branches   Heart apex

4 Signals spread throughout ventricles.

Purkinje fibers

ECG

Maintaining the Heart's Rhythmic Beat

In vertebrates, the heartbeat originates in the heart itself. Some cardiac muscle cells are autorhythmic, meaning they contract and relax repeatedly without any signal from the nervous system. You can even see these rhythmic contractions in tissue that has been removed from the heart and placed in a dish in the laboratory! Because each of these cells has its own intrinsic contraction rhythm, how are their contractions coordinated in the intact heart? The answer lies in a group of autorhythmic cells located in the wall of the right atrium, near where the superior vena cava enters the heart. This cluster of cells is called the **sinoatrial (SA) node**, or *pacemaker*, and it sets the rate and timing at which all cardiac muscle cells contract. (In contrast to vertebrates, some arthropods have pacemakers located in the nervous system, outside the heart.)

The SA node generates electrical impulses much like those produced by nerve cells. Because cardiac muscle cells are electrically coupled through gap junctions (see Figure 6.32), impulses from the SA node spread rapidly within heart tissue. In addition, these impulses generate currents that are conducted to the skin via body fluids. In an **electrocardiogram** (**ECG** or, often, **EKG**, from the German spelling), these currents are recorded by electrodes placed on the skin. The resulting graph of current against time has a characteristic shape that represents the stages in the cardiac cycle (**Figure 42.9**).

Impulses from the SA node first spread rapidly through the walls of the atria, causing both atria to contract in unison. During atrial contraction, the impulses originating at the SA node reach other autorhythmic cells located in the wall between the left and right atria. These cells form a relay point called the **atrioventricular (AV) node**. Here the impulses are delayed for about 0.1 second before spreading to the heart apex. This delay allows the atria to empty completely before the ventricles contract. Then the signals from the AV node are conducted to the heart apex and throughout the ventricular walls by specialized muscle fibers called bundle branches and Purkinje fibers.

Physiological cues alter heart tempo by regulating the SA node. Two portions of the nervous system, the sympathetic and parasympathetic divisions, are largely responsible for this regulation. They function like the spurs and reins used in riding a horse: The sympathetic division speeds up the pacemaker, and the parasympathetic division slows it down. For example, when you stand up and start walking, the sympathetic division increases your heart rate, an adaptation that enables your circulatory system to provide the additional O_2 needed by the muscles that are powering your activity. If you then sit down and relax, the parasympathetic division decreases your heart rate, an adaptation that conserves energy. Hormones secreted into the blood also influence the pacemaker. For instance, epinephrine, the "fight-or-flight" hormone secreted by the adrenal glands, causes the heart rate to increase. A third type of input that affects the pacemaker is body temperature. An increase of only 1°C raises the heart rate by about 10 beats per minute. This is the reason your heart beats faster when you have a fever.

Having examined the operation of the circulatory pump, we turn in the next section to the forces and structures that influence blood flow in the vessels of each circuit.

CONCEPT CHECK 42.2

1. Explain why blood in the pulmonary veins has a higher O_2 concentration than blood in the venae cavae, which are also veins.
2. Why is it important that the AV node delay the electrical impulse moving from the SA node and the atria to the ventricles?
3. **WHAT IF?** After exercising regularly for several months, you find that your resting heart rate has decreased. What other change in the function of your heart at rest would you expect to find? Explain.

For suggested answers, see Appendix A.

Patterns of blood pressure and flow reflect the structure and arrangement of blood vessels

The vertebrate circulatory system enables blood to deliver oxygen and nutrients and remove wastes throughout the body. In doing so, the circulatory system relies on a branching network of vessels much like the plumbing system that delivers fresh water to a city and removes its wastes. In fact, the same physical principles that govern the operation of plumbing systems apply to the functioning of blood vessels.

Blood Vessel Structure and Function

Blood vessels contain a central lumen (cavity) lined with an **endothelium**, a single layer of flattened epithelial cells. The smooth surface of the endothelium minimizes resistance to the flow of blood. Surrounding the endothelium are layers of tissue that differ in capillaries, arteries, and veins, reflecting the specialized functions of these vessels.

Capillaries are the smallest blood vessels, having a diameter only slightly greater than that of a red blood cell (Figure 42.10). Capillaries also have very thin walls, which consist of just the endothelium and its basal lamina. This structural organization facilitates the exchange of substances between the blood in capillaries and the interstitial fluid.

The walls of arteries and veins have a more complex organization than those of capillaries. Both arteries and veins have two layers of tissue surrounding the endothelium: an outer layer of connective tissue containing elastic fibers, which allow the vessel to stretch and recoil, and a middle layer containing smooth muscle and more elastic fibers. However, the walls of arteries and veins also differ, reflecting distinct adaptations of these vessels to their particular functions in circulation.

The walls of arteries are thick and strong, accommodating blood pumped at high pressure by the heart. Arterial walls also have an elastic recoil that helps maintain blood pressure and flow to capillaries when the heart relaxes between contractions. Signals from the nervous system and hormones circulating in the blood act on the smooth muscle in arteries and arterioles, dilating or constricting these vessels and thus controlling blood flow to different parts of the body.

Because veins convey blood back to the heart at a lower pressure, they do not require thick walls. For a given blood vessel diameter, a vein has a wall only about a third as thick as that of an artery. Valves inside the veins maintain a unidirectional flow of blood despite the low blood pressure.

We consider next how blood vessel diameter, vessel number, and pressure influence the speed at which blood flows in different locations within the body.

Blood Flow Velocity

To understand how blood vessel diameter influences blood flow, consider how water flows through a thick hose connected to a faucet. When the faucet is turned on, water flows at the same velocity at each point along the hose. However, if a narrow nozzle is attached to the end of the hose, the water

▲ Figure 42.10 **The structure of blood vessels.**

will exit the nozzle at a much greater velocity. Because water doesn't compress under pressure, the volume of water moving through the nozzle in a given time must be the same as the volume moving through the rest of the hose. The cross-sectional area of the nozzle is smaller than that of the hose, so the water speeds up in the nozzle.

An analogous situation exists in the circulatory system, but blood *slows* as it moves from arteries to arterioles to capillaries. Why? The reason is that the number of capillaries is enormous. Each artery conveys blood to so many capillaries that the *total* cross-sectional area is much greater in capillary beds than in the arteries or any other part of the circulatory system (Figure 42.11). The result is a dramatic decrease in velocity from the arteries to the capillaries: Blood travels 500 times slower in the capillaries (about 0.1 cm/sec) than in the aorta (about 48 cm/sec).

The reduced velocity of blood flow in capillaries is essential to the function of the circulatory system. The ex-

change of substances between the blood and interstitial fluid occurs only in capillaries because only capillaries have walls thin enough to permit this transfer. Diffusion, however, is not instantaneous. The slower flow of blood through capillaries is thus necessary to provide time for exchange to occur. After passing through the capillaries, the blood speeds up as it enters the venules and veins, which have smaller *total* cross-sectional areas than the capillaries.

Blood Pressure

Blood, like all fluids, flows from areas of higher pressure to areas of lower pressure. Contraction of a heart ventricle generates blood pressure, which exerts a force in all directions. The force directed lengthwise in an artery causes the blood to flow away from the heart, the site of highest pressure. The force exerted against the elastic wall of an artery stretches the wall, and the recoil of arterial walls plays a critical role in maintaining blood pressure, and hence blood flow, throughout the cardiac cycle. Once the blood enters the millions of tiny arterioles and capillaries, the narrow diameter of these vessels generates substantial resistance to flow. This resistance dissipates much of the pressure generated by the pumping heart by the time the blood enters the veins.

Changes in Blood Pressure During the Cardiac Cycle

Arterial blood pressure is highest when the heart contracts during ventricular systole. The pressure at this time is called **systolic pressure** (see Figure 42.11). The spikes in blood pressure caused by the powerful contractions of the ventricles stretch the arteries. By placing your fingers on the inside of your wrist, you can feel a **pulse**—the rhythmic bulging of the artery walls with each heartbeat. The surge of pressure is partly due to the narrow openings of arterioles impeding the exit of blood from the arteries. Thus, when the heart contracts, blood enters the arteries faster than it can leave, and the vessels stretch from the rise in pressure.

During diastole, the elastic walls of the arteries snap back. As a consequence, there is a lower but still substantial blood pressure when the ventricles are relaxed (**diastolic pressure**). Before enough blood has flowed into the arterioles to completely relieve pressure in the arteries, the heart contracts again. Because the arteries remain pressurized throughout the cardiac cycle (see Figure 42.11), blood continuously flows into arterioles and capillaries.

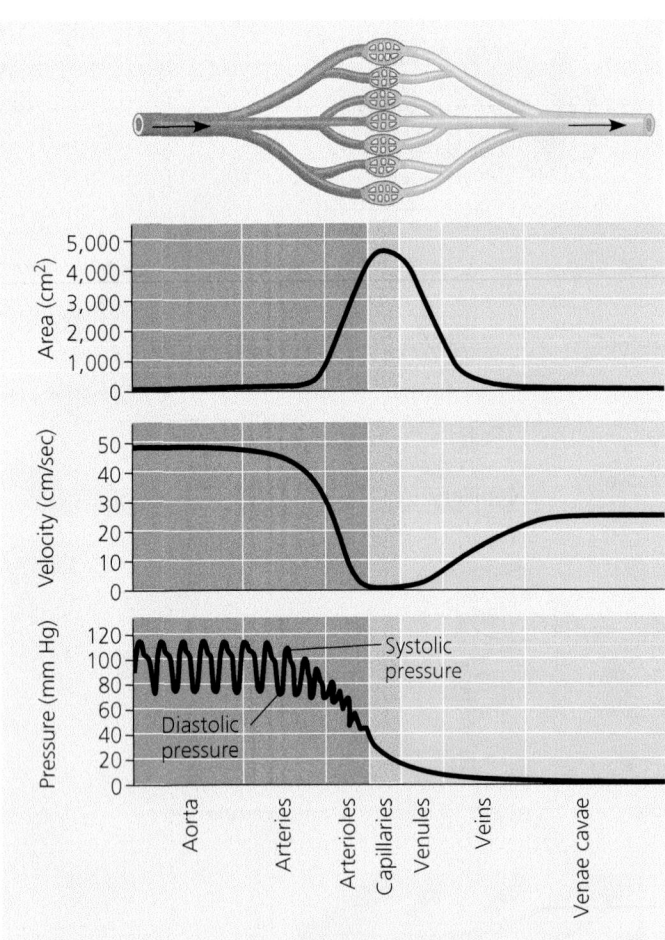

▲ **Figure 42.11 The interrelationship of cross-sectional area of blood vessels, blood flow velocity, and blood pressure.** Owing to an increase in total cross-sectional area, blood flow velocity decreases markedly in the arterioles and is lowest in the capillaries. Blood pressure, the main force driving blood from the heart to the capillaries, is highest in the aorta and other arteries.

Regulation of Blood Pressure

Changes in arterial blood pressure are not limited to the oscillation during each cardiac cycle. Blood pressure also fluctuates on a longer time scale in response to signals that change the state of smooth muscles in arteriole walls. For example, physical or emotional stress can trigger nervous and hormonal responses that cause smooth muscles in arteriole walls to contract. When that happens, the arterioles narrow, a process called **vasoconstriction**. Narrowing of the arterioles increases blood pressure upstream in the arteries. When the smooth muscles relax, the arterioles undergo **vasodilation**, an increase in diameter that causes blood pressure in the arteries to fall.

Researchers have identified a gas, nitric oxide (NO), as a major inducer of vasodilation and a peptide, endothelin, as the most potent inducer of vasoconstriction. Both NO and endothelin are signaling molecules produced in blood vessels in response to cues from the nervous and endocrine systems. Each kind of molecule binds to a specific receptor, activating a signal transduction pathway that alters smooth muscle contraction and thus changes blood vessel diameter.

Vasoconstriction and vasodilation are often coupled to changes in cardiac output that also affect blood pressure. This coordination of regulatory mechanisms maintains adequate blood flow as the body's demands on the circulatory system change. During heavy exercise, for example, the arterioles in working muscles dilate, causing a greater flow of oxygen-rich blood to the muscles. By itself, this increased flow to the muscles would cause a drop in blood pressure (and therefore blood flow) in the body as a whole. However, cardiac output increases at the same time, maintaining blood pressure and supporting the necessary increase in blood flow.

Blood Pressure and Gravity

Blood pressure is generally measured for an artery in the arm at the same height as the heart **(Figure 42.12)**. For a healthy 20-year-old human at rest, arterial blood pressure in the systemic circuit is typically about 120 millimeters of mercury (mm Hg) at systole and 70 mm Hg at diastole, expressed as 120/70. (Arterial blood pressure in the pulmonary circuit is six to ten times lower.)

Gravity has a significant effect on blood pressure. When you are standing, for example, your head is roughly 0.35 m higher than your chest, and the arterial blood pressure in your brain is about 27 mm Hg less than that near your heart. If the blood pressure in your brain is too low to provide adequate blood flow, you will likely faint. By causing your body to collapse to the ground, fainting effectively places your head at the level of your heart, quickly increasing blood flow to your brain.

The challenge of pumping blood against gravity is particularly great for animals with very long necks. A giraffe, for example, requires a systolic pressure of more than 250 mm Hg near the heart to get blood to its head. When a giraffe lowers its head to drink, one-way valves and sinuses, along with feedback mechanisms that reduce cardiac output, prevent this high pressure from damaging its brain. We can calculate that a dinosaur with a neck nearly 10 m long would have required even greater systolic pressure—nearly 760 mm Hg—to pump blood to its brain when its head was fully raised. However, calculations based on anatomy and inferred metabolic rate suggest that dinosaurs did not have a heart powerful enough to generate such high pressure. Based on this evidence as well as studies of neck bone structure, some biologists have concluded that the long-necked dinosaurs fed close to the ground rather than on high foliage.

Gravity is also a consideration for blood flow in veins, especially those in the legs. Although blood pressure in veins is relatively low, several mechanisms assist the return of venous blood to the heart. First, rhythmic contractions of smooth muscles in the walls of venules and veins aid in the movement of the blood. Second, and more important, the contraction of skeletal muscles during exercise squeezes blood through the

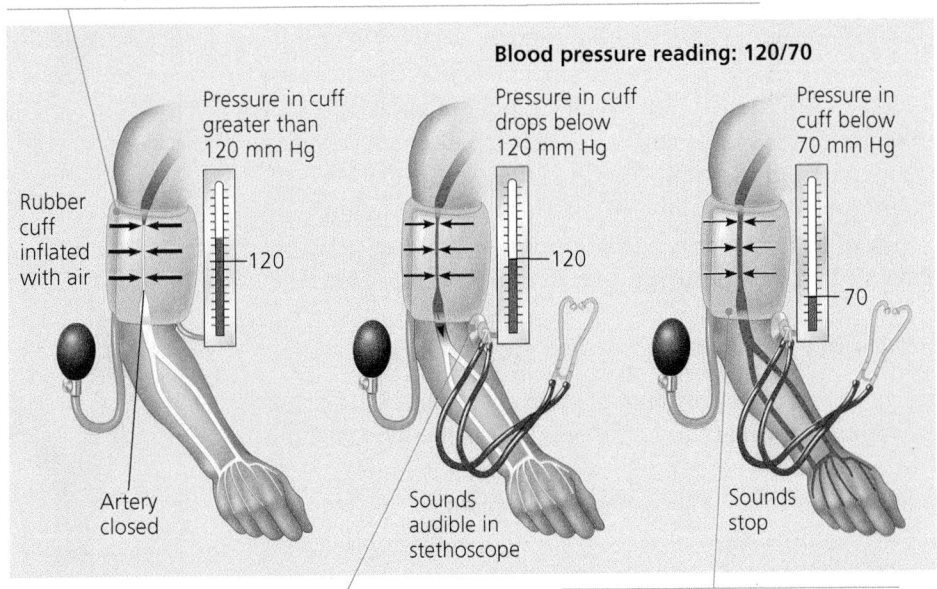

❶ A sphygmomanometer, an inflatable cuff attached to a pressure gauge, measures blood pressure in an artery. The cuff is inflated until the pressure closes the artery, so that no blood flows past the cuff. When this occurs, the pressure exerted by the cuff exceeds the pressure in the artery.

Blood pressure reading: 120/70

Pressure in cuff greater than 120 mm Hg

Rubber cuff inflated with air

120

Artery closed

Pressure in cuff drops below 120 mm Hg

120

Sounds audible in stethoscope

Pressure in cuff below 70 mm Hg

70

Sounds stop

❷ The cuff is allowed to deflate gradually. When the pressure exerted by the cuff falls just below that in the artery, blood pulses into the forearm, generating sounds that can be heard with the stethoscope. The pressure measured at this point is the systolic pressure.

❸ The cuff is allowed to deflate further, just until the blood flows freely through the artery and the sounds below the cuff disappear. The pressure at this point is the diastolic pressure.

▲ **Figure 42.12 Measurement of blood pressure.** Blood pressure is recorded as two numbers separated by a slash. The first number is the systolic pressure; the second is the diastolic pressure.

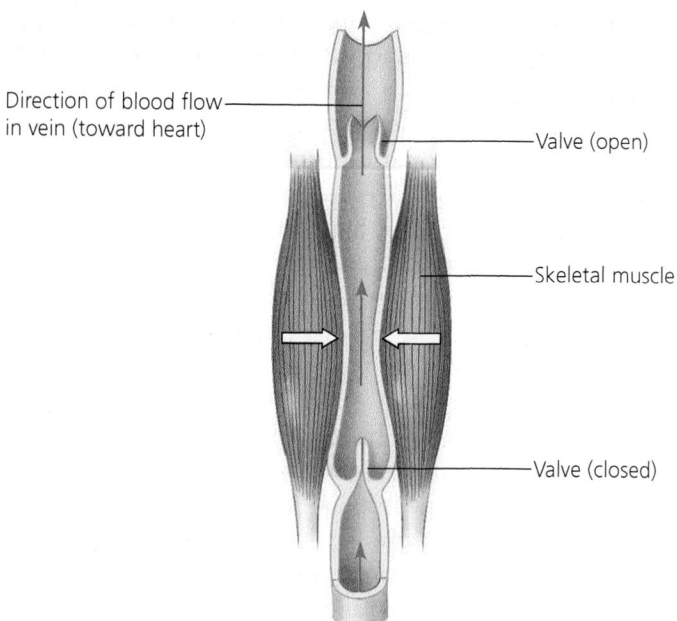

Direction of blood flow in vein (toward heart)

Valve (open)

Skeletal muscle

Valve (closed)

▲ **Figure 42.13 Blood flow in veins.** Skeletal muscle contraction squeezes and constricts veins. Flaps of tissue within the veins act as one-way valves that keep blood moving only toward the heart. If you sit or stand too long, the lack of muscular activity may cause your feet to swell as blood pools in your veins.

veins toward the heart **(Figure 42.13)**. Third, the change in pressure within the thoracic (chest) cavity during inhalation causes the venae cavae and other large veins near the heart to expand and fill with blood.

In rare instances, runners and other athletes can suffer heart failure if they stop vigorous exercise abruptly. When the leg muscles suddenly cease contracting and relaxing, less blood returns to the heart, which continues to beat rapidly. If the heart is weak or damaged, this inadequate blood flow may cause the heart to malfunction. To reduce the risk of stressing the heart excessively, athletes are encouraged to follow hard exercise with moderate activity, such as walking, to "cool down" until their heart rate approaches its resting level.

Capillary Function

At any given time, only about 5–10% of the body's capillaries have blood flowing through them. However, each tissue has many capillaries, so every part of the body is supplied with blood at all times. Capillaries in the brain, heart, kidneys, and liver are usually filled to capacity, but at many other sites the blood supply varies over time as blood is diverted from one destination to another. For example, blood flow to the skin is regulated to help control body temperature, and blood supply to the digestive tract increases after a meal. During strenuous exercise, blood is diverted from the digestive tract and supplied more generously to skeletal muscles and skin. This is one reason why exercising heavily immediately after eating a big meal may cause indigestion.

Given that capillaries lack smooth muscle, how is blood flow in capillary beds altered? There are two mechanisms, both of which rely on signals that regulate the flow into capillaries. One mechanism involves contraction of the smooth muscle in the wall of an arteriole, which reduces the vessel's diameter and decreases blood flow to the adjoining capillary beds. When the smooth muscle relaxes, the arterioles dilate, allowing blood to enter the capillaries. The other mechanism for altering flow, shown in **Figure 42.14**, involves the action of *precapillary sphincters*, rings of smooth muscle located at the entrance to capillary beds. The signals that regulate blood flow include nerve impulses, hormones traveling throughout the bloodstream, and chemicals produced locally. For example, the chemical histamine released by cells at a wound site causes smooth muscle relaxation, dilating blood vessels and increasing blood flow. The dilated vessels also give disease-fighting white blood cells greater access to invading microorganisms.

As you have read, the critical exchange of substances between the blood and interstitial fluid takes place across the

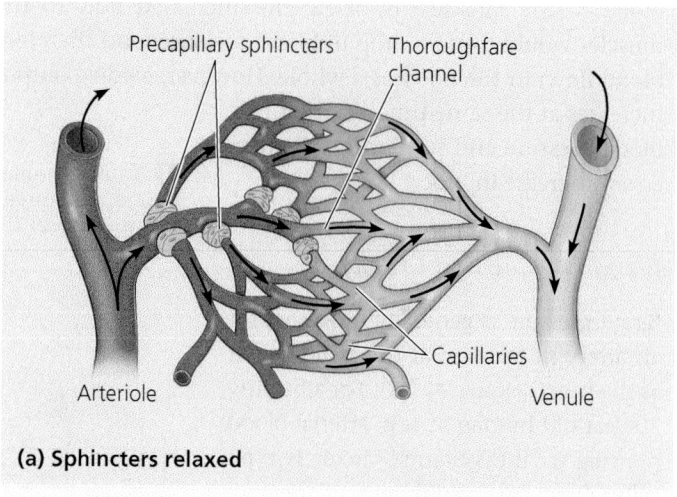

Precapillary sphincters

Thoroughfare channel

Capillaries

Arteriole

Venule

(a) Sphincters relaxed

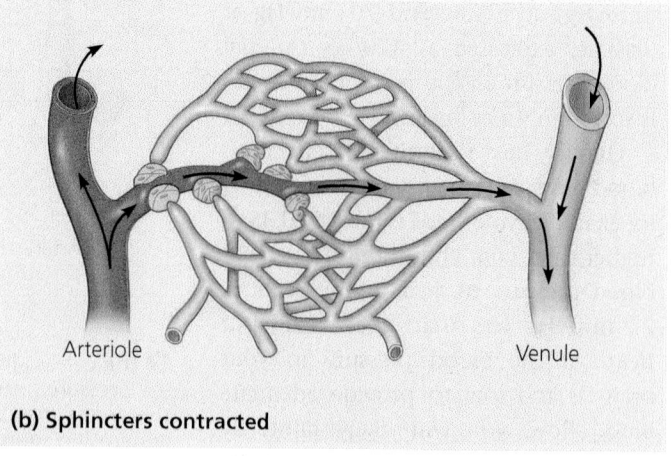

Arteriole

Venule

(b) Sphincters contracted

▲ **Figure 42.14 Blood flow in capillary beds.** Precapillary sphincters regulate the passage of blood into capillary beds. Some blood flows directly from arterioles to venules through capillaries called thoroughfare channels, which are always open.

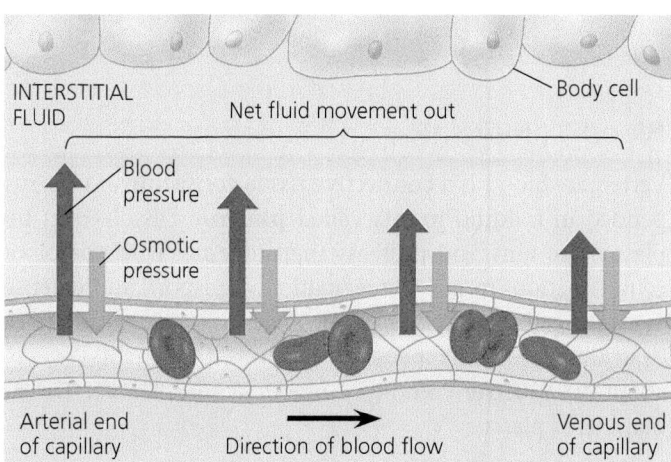

▲ **Figure 42.15 Fluid exchange between capillaries and the interstitial fluid.** This diagram shows a hypothetical capillary in which blood pressure exceeds osmotic pressure throughout the entire length of the capillary. In other capillaries, blood pressure may be lower than osmotic pressure along all or part of the capillary.

Labels in figure:
- INTERSTITIAL FLUID
- Net fluid movement out
- Body cell
- Blood pressure
- Osmotic pressure
- Arterial end of capillary
- Direction of blood flow
- Venous end of capillary

thin endothelial walls of the capillaries. Some substances are carried across the endothelium in vesicles that form on one side by endocytosis and release their contents on the opposite side by exocytosis. Small molecules, such as O_2 and CO_2, simply diffuse across the endothelial cells or, in some tissues, through microscopic pores in the capillary wall. These openings also provide the route for transport of small solutes such as sugars, salts, and urea, as well as for bulk flow of fluid into tissues driven by blood pressure within the capillary.

Two opposing forces control the movement of fluid between the capillaries and the surrounding tissues: Blood pressure tends to drive fluid out of the capillaries, and the presence of blood proteins tends to pull fluid back (Figure 42.15). Many blood proteins (and all blood cells) are too large to pass readily through the endothelium, and they remain in the capillaries. These dissolved proteins are responsible for much of the blood's *osmotic pressure* (the pressure produced by the difference in solute concentration across a membrane). The difference in osmotic pressure between the blood and the interstitial fluid opposes fluid movement out of the capillaries. On average, blood pressure is greater than the opposing forces, leading to a net loss of fluid from capillaries. The net loss is generally greatest at the arterial end of these vessels, where blood pressure is highest.

Fluid Return by the Lymphatic System

Each day, the adult human body loses approximately 4–8 L of fluid from capillaries to the surrounding tissues. There is also some leakage of blood proteins, even though the capillary wall is not very permeable to large molecules. The lost fluid and proteins return to the blood via the **lymphatic system**, which includes a network of tiny vessels intermingled among capillaries of the cardiovascular system.

After entering the lymphatic system by diffusion, the fluid lost by capillaries is called **lymph**; its composition is about the same as that of interstitial fluid. The lymphatic system drains into large veins of the circulatory system at the base of the neck (see Figure 43.7). As you read in Chapter 41, this joining of the lymphatic and circulatory systems functions in the transfer of lipids from the small intestine to the blood.

The movement of lymph from peripheral tissues to the heart relies on much the same mechanisms that assist blood flow in veins. Lymph vessels, like veins, have valves that prevent the backflow of fluid. Rhythmic contractions of the vessel walls help draw fluid into the small lymphatic vessels. In addition, skeletal muscle contractions play a role in moving lymph.

Disorders that interfere with the lymphatic system highlight its role in maintaining proper fluid distribution in the body. Disruptions in the movement of lymph often cause edema, swelling resulting from the excessive accumulation of fluid in tissues. Severe blockage of lymph flow, as occurs when certain parasitic worms lodge in lymph vessels, results in extremely swollen limbs or other body parts, a condition known as elephantiasis.

Along a lymph vessel are organs called **lymph nodes** (Figure 42.16). By filtering the lymph and by housing cells that attack viruses and bacteria, lymph nodes play an important role in the body's defense. Inside each lymph node is a honeycomb of connective tissue with spaces filled by white blood cells. When the body is fighting an infection, these cells multiply rapidly, and the lymph nodes become swollen and tender (which is why your doctor may check for swollen lymph nodes in your neck, armpits, or groin when you feel sick). Because lymph nodes have filtering and surveillance functions, doctors may examine the lymph nodes of cancer patients to detect the spread of diseased cells.

In recent years, evidence has surfaced demonstrating that the lymphatic system also plays a role in harmful immune responses, such as those responsible for asthma. Because of these and other findings, the lymphatic system, largely ignored until the 1990s, has become a very active and promising area of biomedical research.

▶ **Figure 42.16 Human lymph nodes and vessels.** In this colorized X-ray image of the groin, lymph nodes and vessels (yellow) are visible next to the upper thigh bone (femur).

1. What is the primary cause of the low velocity of blood flow through capillaries?
2. What short-term changes in cardiovascular function might best enable skeletal muscles to help an animal escape from a dangerous situation?
3. **WHAT IF?** If you had additional hearts distributed throughout your body, what would be one likely advantage and one likely disadvantage?

For suggested answers, see Appendix A.

CONCEPT **42.4**

Blood components function in exchange, transport, and defense

As we discussed earlier, the fluid transported by an open circulatory system is continuous with the fluid that surrounds all of the body cells and therefore has the same composition. In contrast, the fluid in a closed circulatory system can be much more highly specialized, as is the case for the blood of vertebrates.

Blood Composition and Function

Vertebrate blood is a connective tissue consisting of cells suspended in a liquid matrix called **plasma**. Dissolved in the plasma are ions and proteins that, together with the blood cells, function in osmotic regulation, transport, and defense. Separating the components of blood using a centrifuge reveals that cellular elements (cells and cell fragments) occupy about 45% of the volume of blood (**Figure 42.17**). The remainder is plasma.

Plasma

Among the many solutes in plasma are inorganic salts in the form of dissolved ions, sometimes referred to as blood electrolytes (see Figure 42.17). Although plasma is about 90% water, the dissolved salts are an essential component of the blood. Some of these ions buffer the blood, which in humans normally has a pH of 7.4. Salts are also important in maintaining the osmotic balance of the blood. In addition, the concentration of ions in plasma directly affects the composition of

Plasma 55%	
Constituent	**Major functions**
Water	Solvent for carrying other substances
Ions (blood electrolytes) Sodium Potassium Calcium Magnesium Chloride Bicarbonate	Osmotic balance, pH buffering, and regulation of membrane permeability
Plasma proteins Albumin	Osmotic balance, pH buffering
Fibrinogen	Clotting
Immunoglobulins (antibodies)	Defense
Substances transported by blood Nutrients (such as glucose, fatty acids, vitamins) Waste products of metabolism Respiratory gases (O_2 and CO_2) Hormones	

Separated blood elements

Cellular elements 45%		
Cell type	**Number** per μL (mm^3) of blood	**Functions**
Leukocytes (white blood cells) Basophils Lymphocytes Eosinophils Neutrophils Monocytes	5,000–10,000	Defense and immunity
Platelets	250,000–400,000	Blood clotting
Erythrocytes (red blood cells)	5–6 million	Transport of O_2 and some CO_2

▲ **Figure 42.17 The composition of mammalian blood.**

the interstitial fluid, where many of these ions have a vital role in muscle and nerve activity. To serve all of these functions, plasma electrolytes must be kept within narrow concentration ranges, a homeostatic function we will explore in Chapter 44.

Plasma proteins act as buffers against pH changes, help maintain the osmotic balance between blood and interstitial fluid, and contribute to the blood's viscosity (thickness). Particular plasma proteins have additional functions. The immunoglobulins, or antibodies, help combat viruses and other foreign agents that invade the body (see Chapter 43). Others are escorts for lipids, which are insoluble in water and can travel in blood only when bound to proteins. A third group of plasma proteins are clotting factors that help plug leaks when blood vessels are injured. (The term *serum* refers to blood plasma from which these clotting factors have been removed.)

Plasma also contains a wide variety of other substances in transit from one part of the body to another, including nutrients, metabolic wastes, respiratory gases, and hormones. Plasma has a much higher protein concentration than interstitial fluid, although the two fluids are otherwise similar. (Capillary walls, remember, are not very permeable to proteins.)

Cellular Elements

Blood contains two classes of cells: red blood cells, which transport O_2, and white blood cells, which function in defense (see Figure 42.17). Also suspended in blood plasma are **platelets**, fragments of cells that are involved in the clotting process.

Erythrocytes Red blood cells, or **erythrocytes**, are by far the most numerous blood cells. Each microliter (μL, or mm³) of human blood contains 5–6 million red cells, and there are about 25 trillion of these cells in the body's 5 L of blood. Their main function is O_2 transport, and their structure is closely related to this function. Human erythrocytes are small disks (7–8 μm in diameter) that are biconcave—thinner in the center than at the edges. This shape increases surface area, enhancing the rate of diffusion of O_2 across their plasma membranes. Mature mammalian erythrocytes lack nuclei. This unusual characteristic leaves more space in these tiny cells for **hemoglobin**, the iron-containing protein that transports O_2 (see Figure 5.20). Erythrocytes also lack mitochondria and generate their ATP exclusively by anaerobic metabolism. Oxygen transport would be less efficient if erythrocytes were aerobic and consumed some of the O_2 they carry.

Despite its small size, an erythrocyte contains about 250 million molecules of hemoglobin. Because each molecule of hemoglobin binds up to four molecules of O_2, one erythrocyte can transport about a billion O_2 molecules. As erythrocytes pass through the capillary beds of lungs, gills, or other respiratory organs, O_2 diffuses into the erythrocytes and binds to hemoglobin. In the systemic capillaries, O_2 dissociates from hemoglobin and diffuses into body cells.

In **sickle-cell disease**, an abnormal form of hemoglobin (Hb^S) polymerizes into aggregates. Because the concentration of hemoglobin in erythrocytes is so high, these aggregates are large enough to distort the erythrocyte into an elongated, curved shape that resembles a sickle. As you learned in Chapter 5, this abnormality results from an alteration in the amino acid sequence of hemoglobin at a single position (see Figure 5.21).

Sickle-cell disease significantly impairs the function of the circulatory system. Sickled cells often lodge in arterioles and capillaries, preventing delivery of O_2 and nutrients and removal of CO_2 and wastes. Blood vessel blockage and resulting organ swelling often result in severe pain. In addition, sickled cells frequently rupture, reducing the number of red blood cells available for transporting O_2. The average life span of a sickled erythrocyte is only 20 days—one-sixth that of a normal erythrocyte. The rate of erythrocyte loss outstrips the replacement capacity of the bone marrow. Short-term therapy includes replacement of erythrocytes by blood transfusion; long-term treatments are generally aimed at inhibiting aggregation of Hb^S.

Leukocytes The blood contains five major types of white blood cells, or **leukocytes**. Their function is to fight infections. Some are phagocytic, engulfing and digesting microorganisms as well as debris from the body's own dead cells. As we will see in Chapter 43, other leukocytes, called lymphocytes, develop into specialized B cells and T cells that mount immune responses against foreign substances. Normally, 1 μL of human blood contains about 5,000–10,000 leukocytes; their numbers increase temporarily whenever the body is fighting an infection. Unlike erythrocytes, leukocytes are also found outside the circulatory system, patrolling both interstitial fluid and the lymphatic system.

Platelets Platelets are pinched-off cytoplasmic fragments of specialized bone marrow cells. They are about 2–3 μm in diameter and have no nuclei. Platelets serve both structural and molecular functions in blood clotting.

Blood Clotting

The occasional cut or scrape is not life-threatening because blood components seal the broken blood vessels. A break in a blood vessel wall exposes proteins that attract platelets and initiate coagulation, the conversion of liquid components of blood to a solid clot. The coagulant, or sealant, circulates in an inactive form called *fibrinogen*. In response to a broken blood vessel, platelets release clotting factors that trigger reactions leading to the formation of *thrombin*, an enzyme that converts fibrinogen to *fibrin*. Newly formed fibrin aggregates into threads that form the framework of the clot. Thrombin also activates a factor that catalyzes the formation of more thrombin, driving clotting to completion through positive feedback (see Chapter 40). The steps in the production of a

① The clotting process begins when the endothelium of a vessel is damaged, exposing connective tissue in the vessel wall to blood. Platelets adhere to collagen fibers in the connective tissue and release a substance that makes nearby platelets sticky.

② The platelets form a plug that provides emergency protection against blood loss.

③ This plug is reinforced by a fibrin clot when vessel damage is severe.

Collagen fibers

Platelet

Platelet plug

Fibrin clot

Red blood cell

5 μm

Clotting factors from:
→ Platelets
→ Damaged cells
→ Plasma (factors include calcium, vitamin K)

Enzymatic cascade

Prothrombin → Thrombin ⊕

Fibrinogen → Fibrin

Fibrin clot formation
Clotting factors released from the clumped platelets or damaged cells mix with clotting factors in the plasma, forming an enzymatic cascade that converts a plasma protein called prothrombin to its active form, thrombin. Thrombin itself is an enzyme that catalyzes the final step of the clotting process, the conversion of fibrinogen to fibrin. The threads of fibrin become interwoven into a clot (see colorized SEM above).

▲ **Figure 42.18 Blood clotting.**

blood clot are diagrammed in **Figure 42.18**. Any genetic mutation that blocks a step in the clotting process can cause hemophilia, a disease characterized by excessive bleeding and bruising from even minor cuts and bumps (see Chapter 15).

Anticlotting factors in the blood normally prevent spontaneous clotting in the absence of injury. Sometimes, however, clots form within a blood vessel, blocking the flow of blood. Such a clot is called a **thrombus**. We will explore how a thrombus forms and the danger that it poses later in this chapter.

Stem Cells and the Replacement of Cellular Elements

Erythrocytes, leukocytes, and platelets all develop from a common source: multipotent **stem cells** that are dedicated to replenishing the body's blood cell populations (**Figure 42.19**). The stem cells that produce blood cells are located in the red marrow of bones, particularly the ribs, vertebrae, sternum, and pelvis. Multipotent stem cells are so named because they have the ability to form multiple types of cells—in this case, the myeloid and lymphoid cell lineages. When a stem cell divides, one daughter cell remains a stem cell while the other takes on a specialized function.

Throughout a person's life, erythrocytes, leukocytes, and platelets arising from stem cell divisions replace the worn-out

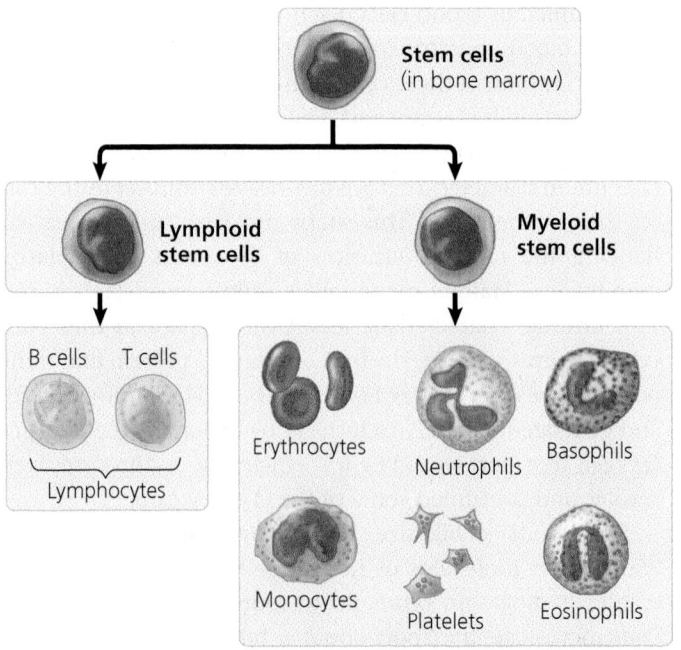

Stem cells (in bone marrow)

Lymphoid stem cells

Myeloid stem cells

B cells   T cells

Lymphocytes

Erythrocytes

Neutrophils

Basophils

Monocytes

Platelets

Eosinophils

▲ **Figure 42.19 Differentiation of blood cells.** Some of the multipotent stem cells differentiate into lymphoid stem cells, which then develop into B cells and T cells, two types of lymphocytes that function in immunity (see Chapter 43). All other blood cells and platelets arise from myeloid stem cells.

cellular elements of blood. Erythrocytes, for example, circulate for only 120 days on average before being replaced; the old cells are consumed by phagocytic cells in the liver and spleen. The production of new erythrocytes involves recycling of materials, such as the use of iron scavenged from old erythrocytes in new hemoglobin molecules.

A negative-feedback mechanism, sensitive to the amount of O_2 reaching the body's tissues via the blood, controls erythrocyte production. If the tissues do not receive enough O_2, the kidneys synthesize and secrete a hormone called **erythropoietin (EPO)** that stimulates erythrocyte production. If the blood is delivering more O_2 than the tissues can use, the level of EPO falls and erythrocyte production slows. Physicians use synthetic EPO to treat people with health problems such as *anemia*, a condition of lower-than-normal erythrocyte or hemoglobin levels that lowers the oxygen-carrying capacity of the blood. Some athletes inject themselves with EPO to increase their erythrocyte levels, although this practice, a form of blood doping, has been banned by the International Olympic Committee and other sports organizations. In recent years, a number of well-known runners and cyclists have tested positive for EPO-related drugs and have forfeited both their records and their right to participate in future competitions.

Cardiovascular Disease

More than half of all human deaths in the United States are caused by cardiovascular diseases—disorders of the heart and blood vessels. Cardiovascular diseases range from a minor disturbance of vein or heart valve function to a life-threatening disruption of blood flow to the heart or brain.

Cholesterol metabolism plays a central role in cardiovascular disease. As you learned in Chapter 7, the presence of this steroid in animal cell membranes helps maintain normal membrane fluidity. Cholesterol travels in blood plasma mainly in particles that consist of thousands of cholesterol molecules and other lipids bound to a protein. One type of particle—**low-density lipoprotein (LDL)**—delivers cholesterol to cells for membrane production. Another type—**high-density lipoprotein (HDL)**—scavenges excess cholesterol for return to the liver. Individuals with a high ratio of LDL to HDL are at substantially increased risk for heart disease.

Another factor in cardiovascular disease is *inflammation*, the body's reaction to injury. As you will learn in the next chapter, tissue damage leads to recruitment of two types of circulating immune cells, macrophages and leukocytes. Signals released by these cells trigger a flow of fluid out of blood vessels at the site of injury, resulting in the tissue swelling characteristic of inflammation (see Figure 43.8). Although inflammation is often a normal and healthy response to injury, it can significantly disrupt circulatory function, as explained in the next section.

Atherosclerosis, Heart Attacks, and Stroke

Circulating cholesterol and inflammation can act together to produce a cardiovascular disease called **atherosclerosis**, the hardening of the arteries by accumulation of fatty deposits (Figure 42.20). Healthy arteries have a smooth inner lining

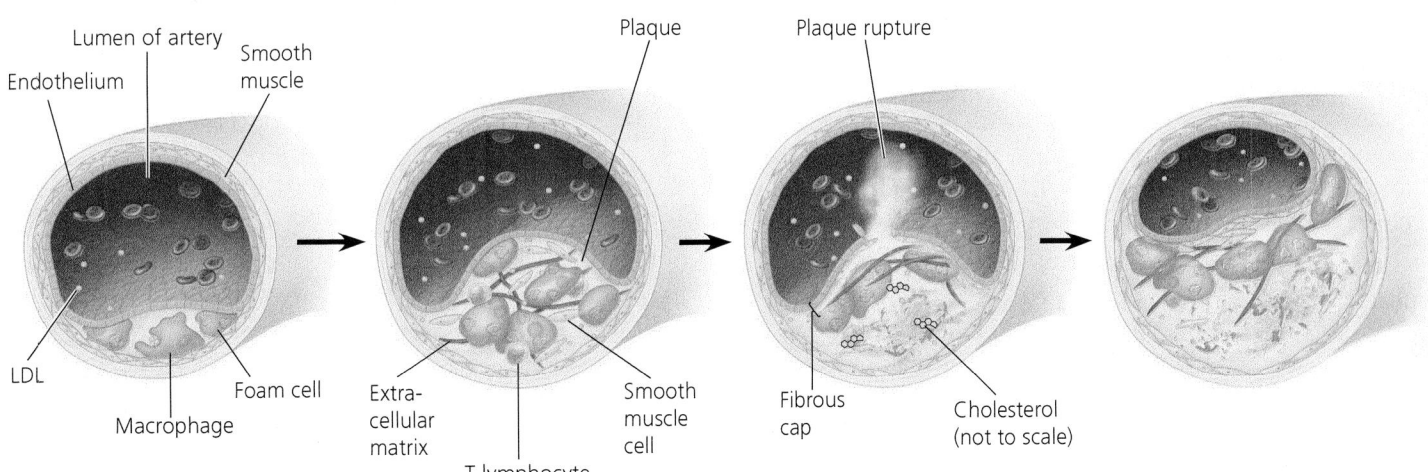

1 Lipoproteins such as LDL enter the lining of the artery and aggregate, leading to engulfment by immune cells called *macrophages*. Uptake of these lipoproteins by macrophages leads to the generation of lipid-rich *foam cells*.

2 Secretion of extracellular matrix components increases lipoprotein aggregation. T lymphocytes enter the growing *plaque*, causing chronic inflammation. Smooth muscle cells from the lining of the artery also enter the plaque.

3 Smooth muscle cells form a fibrous cap separating the plaque from the blood. Within the plaque, foam cells die, releasing cellular debris and cholesterol. If the plaque ruptures, a blood clot can form within the artery.

4 If the plaque continues to grow but does not rupture, the artery becomes increasingly obstructed.

▲ **Figure 42.20 Atherosclerosis.** In atherosclerosis, thickening of an arterial wall by plaque formation can restrict blood flow through the artery. Fragments of a ruptured plaque can travel via the bloodstream and become lodged in other arteries. If those arteries supply the heart or brain, the resulting obstruction could cause a heart attack or stroke, respectively.

that reduces resistance to blood flow. Damage or infection can roughen the lining and lead to inflammation. Leukocytes are attracted to the damaged lining and begin to take up lipids, including cholesterol. A fatty deposit, called a plaque, grows steadily, incorporating fibrous connective tissue and additional cholesterol. As the plaque grows, the walls of the artery become thick and stiff, and the obstruction of the artery increases.

The result of untreated atherosclerosis is often a heart attack or a stroke. A **heart attack**, also called a *myocardial infarction*, is the damage or death of cardiac muscle tissue resulting from blockage of one or more coronary arteries, which supply oxygen-rich blood to the heart muscle. Because the coronary arteries are small in diameter, they are especially vulnerable to obstruction. Such blockage can destroy cardiac muscle quickly because the constantly beating heart muscle cannot survive long without O_2. If the heart stops beating, the victim may nevertheless survive if a heartbeat is restored by cardiopulmonary resuscitation (CPR) or some other emergency procedure within a few minutes of the attack. A **stroke** is the death of nervous tissue in the brain due to a lack of O_2. Strokes usually result from rupture or blockage of arteries in the head. The effects of a stroke and the individual's chance of survival depend on the extent and location of the damaged brain tissue. Rapid administration of a clot-dissolving drug may reduce the effects of a stroke or heart attack.

Although atherosclerosis often isn't detected until critical blood flow is disrupted, there can be warning signs. Partial blockage of the coronary arteries may cause occasional chest pain, a condition known as angina pectoris. The pain is most likely to be felt when the heart is laboring hard during physical or emotional stress, and it signals that part of the heart is not receiving enough O_2. An obstructed coronary artery may be treated surgically, either by inserting a metal mesh tube called a stent to expand the artery or by transplanting a healthy blood vessel from the chest or a limb to bypass the blockage.

Risk Factors and Treatment of Cardiovascular Disease

Although the tendency to develop particular cardiovascular diseases is inherited, it is also strongly influenced by lifestyle. Smoking and consumption of certain processed vegetable oils called *trans fats* (see Chapter 5) increase the ratio of LDL to HDL, raising the risk of cardiovascular disease. In contrast, exercise decreases the LDL/HDL ratio.

There has been considerable progress in the last decade in preventing cardiovascular disease. Many individuals at high risk are now treated with drugs called statins, which lower LDL levels and thereby reduce the risk of heart attacks. A recent discovery highlighted in Figure 42.21 may lead to the development of additional drugs effective at lowering LDL levels in the blood.

The recognition that inflammation plays a central role in atherosclerosis and thrombus formation is also changing the

▼ Figure 42.21

INQUIRY

Can inactivating a liver enzyme lower plasma LDL levels?

EXPERIMENT In 2003, French researchers found that plasma LDL levels are higher in people who have mutations that increase the activity of a human liver enzyme called PCSK9. Helen Hobbs and co-workers in Dallas, Texas, then asked whether mutations that *inactivate* the *PCSK9* gene could *lower* LDL levels. By screening 15,000 participants in a 15-year study of cardiovascular disease, they discovered that 2% of individuals of African descent have mutations that inactivate one copy of the *PCSK9* gene. They then measured plasma LDL levels in individuals with one of these mutations and in control individuals.

RESULTS

Individuals with two functional copies of *PCSK9* gene (control group)

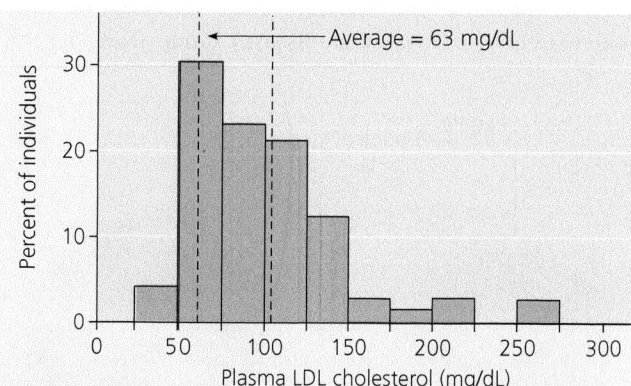

Individuals with an inactivating mutation in one copy of *PCSK9* gene

CONCLUSION Inactivating one copy of the *PCSK9* gene lowers the average plasma LDL level by 40%. Based on this result, Hobbs and colleagues hypothesized that decreasing PCSK9 activity reduces the risk for heart disease. Further analysis of data from the 15-year study supported this hypothesis: Individuals carrying *PCSK9* mutations had an 88% lower risk for heart disease compared with the control group. A search is now under way for molecules that inhibit PCSK9 as potential drugs to prevent heart disease.

SOURCE J. Cohen, A. Pertsemlidis, I. Kotowski, R. Graham, C. Garcia, and H. Hobbs, Low LDL cholesterol in individuals of African descent resulting from frequent nonsense mutations in *PCSK9*, *Nature Genetics* 37:161–165 (2005).

WHAT IF? Suppose you could measure the activity of PCSK9 in blood samples. How would you expect the activity to compare for the individuals studied by the French researchers and by Dr. Hobbs's team?

treatment of cardiovascular disease. For example, aspirin, which inhibits the inflammatory response, has been found to help prevent the recurrence of heart attacks and stroke. Researchers have also focused on C-reactive protein (CRP), which is produced by the liver and found in the blood during episodes of acute inflammation. Like a high level of LDL cholesterol, the presence of significant amounts of CRP in blood is a useful risk indicator for cardiovascular disease.

Hypertension (high blood pressure) is yet another contributor to heart attack and stroke as well as other health problems. According to one hypothesis, chronic high blood pressure damages the endothelium that lines the arteries, promoting plaque formation. The usual definition of hypertension in adults is a systolic pressure above 140 mm Hg or a diastolic pressure above 90 mm Hg. Fortunately, hypertension is simple to diagnose and can usually be controlled by dietary changes, exercise, medication, or a combination of these approaches.

CONCEPT CHECK 42.4

1. Explain why a physician might order a white cell count for a patient with symptoms of an infection.
2. Clots in arteries can cause heart attacks and strokes. Why, then, does it make sense to treat hemophiliacs by introducing clotting factors into their blood?
3. **WHAT IF?** Nitroglycerin (the key ingredient in dynamite) is sometimes prescribed for heart disease patients. Within the body, the nitroglycerin is converted to nitric oxide. Why would you expect nitroglycerin to relieve chest pain in these patients?
4. **MAKE CONNECTIONS** The allele that encodes Hb^S is codominant with the allele encoding normal hemoglobin (Hb) (see Concept 14.4, pp. 277–278). What can you deduce about the properties of Hb and Hb^S with regard to aggregate formation and sickling?
5. **MAKE CONNECTIONS** How do stem cells from the bone marrow of an adult differ from embryonic stem cells (see Concept 20.3, p. 415–416)?

For suggested answers, see Appendix A.

CONCEPT 42.5

Gas exchange occurs across specialized respiratory surfaces

In the remainder of this chapter, we will focus on the process of **gas exchange**. Although this process is often called respiratory exchange or respiration, it should not be confused with the energy transformations of cellular respiration. Gas exchange is the uptake of molecular O_2 from the environment and the discharge of CO_2 to the environment.

Partial Pressure Gradients in Gas Exchange

To understand the driving forces for gas exchange, we must calculate **partial pressure**, which is simply the pressure exerted by a particular gas in a mixture of gases. To do so, we need to know the pressure that the mixture exerts and the fraction of the mixture represented by a particular gas. Let's consider O_2 as an example. At sea level, the atmosphere exerts a downward force equal to that of a column of mercury (Hg) 760 mm high. Therefore, atmospheric pressure at sea level is 760 mm Hg. Since the atmosphere is 21% O_2 by volume, the partial pressure of O_2 is 0.21 × 760, or about 160 mm Hg. This value is called the *partial pressure* of O_2 (abbreviated P_{O_2}) because it is the part of atmospheric pressure contributed by O_2. The partial pressure of CO_2 (abbreviated P_{CO_2}) is much less, only 0.29 mm Hg at sea level.

Partial pressures also apply to gases dissolved in a liquid, such as water. When water is exposed to air, an equilibrium is reached in which the partial pressure of each gas in the water equals the partial pressure of that gas in the air. Thus, water exposed to air at sea level has a P_{O_2} of 160 mm Hg, the same as in the atmosphere. However, the *concentrations* of O_2 in the air and water differ substantially because O_2 is much less soluble in water than in air.

Once we have calculated partial pressures, we can readily predict the net result of diffusion at gas exchange surfaces: A gas always diffuses from a region of higher partial pressure to a region of lower partial pressure.

Respiratory Media

The conditions for gas exchange vary considerably, depending on whether the respiratory medium—the source of O_2—is air or water. As already noted, O_2 is plentiful in air, making up about 21% of Earth's atmosphere by volume. Compared to water, air is much less dense and less viscous, so it is easier to move and to force through small passageways. As a result, breathing air is relatively easy and need not be particularly efficient. Humans, for example, extract only about 25% of the O_2 in inhaled air.

Gas exchange with water as the respiratory medium is much more demanding. The amount of O_2 dissolved in a given volume of water varies but is always less than in an equivalent volume of air: Water in many marine and freshwater habitats contains only 4–8 mL of dissolved O_2 per liter, a concentration roughly 40 times less than in air. The warmer and saltier the water is, the less dissolved O_2 it can hold. Water's lower O_2 content, greater density, and greater viscosity mean that aquatic animals such as fishes and lobsters must expend considerable energy to carry out gas exchange. In the context of these challenges, adaptations have evolved that enable most aquatic animals to be very efficient in gas exchange. Many of these adaptations involve the organization of the surfaces dedicated to exchange.

Respiratory Surfaces

Specialization for gas exchange is apparent in the structure of the respiratory surface, the part of an animal's body where gas exchange occurs. Like all living cells, the cells that carry out gas exchange have a plasma membrane that must be in contact with an aqueous solution. Respiratory surfaces are therefore always moist.

The movement of O_2 and CO_2 across moist respiratory surfaces takes place entirely by diffusion. The rate of diffusion is proportional to the surface area across which it occurs and inversely proportional to the square of the distance through which molecules must move. In other words, gas exchange is fast when the area for diffusion is large and the path for diffusion is short. As a result, respiratory surfaces tend to be large and thin.

In some relatively simple animals, such as sponges, cnidarians, and flatworms, every cell in the body is close enough to the external environment that gases can diffuse quickly between all cells and the environment. In many animals, however, the bulk of the body's cells lack immediate access to the environment. The respiratory surface in these animals is a thin, moist epithelium that constitutes a respiratory organ.

The skin serves as a respiratory organ in some animals, including earthworms and some amphibians. Just below the skin, a dense network of capillaries facilitates the exchange of gases between the circulatory system and the environment. Because the respiratory surface must remain moist, earthworms and many other skin-breathers can survive for extended periods only in damp places.

The general body surface of most animals lacks sufficient area to exchange gases for the whole organism. The evolutionary solution to this limitation is a respiratory organ that is extensively folded or branched, thereby enlarging the available surface area for gas exchange. Gills, tracheae, and lungs are three such organs.

Gills in Aquatic Animals

Gills are outfoldings of the body surface that are suspended in the water. As illustrated in **Figure 42.22**, the distribution of gills over the body can vary considerably. Regardless of their distribution, gills often have a total surface area much greater than that of the rest of the body's exterior.

Movement of the respiratory medium over the respiratory surface, a process called **ventilation**, maintains the partial pressure gradients of O_2 and CO_2 across the gill that

(a) Marine worm. Many polychaetes (marine worms of the phylum Annelida) have a pair of flattened appendages called parapodia on each body segment. The parapodia serve as gills and also function in crawling and swimming.

Parapodium (functions as gill)

Gills

(b) Crayfish. Crayfish and other crustaceans have long, feathery gills covered by the exoskeleton. Specialized body appendages drive water over the gill surfaces.

Coelom

Gills

Tube foot

(c) Sea star. The gills of a sea star are simple tubular projections of the skin. The hollow core of each gill is an extension of the coelom (body cavity). Gas exchange occurs by diffusion across the gill surfaces, and fluid in the coelom circulates in and out of the gills, aiding gas transport. The surfaces of a sea star's tube feet also function in gas exchange.

▲ **Figure 42.22 Diversity in the structure of gills, external body surfaces that function in gas exchange**.
MAKE CONNECTIONS *As shown in Figure 32.11, animals with bilateral symmetry are divided into three main lineages. What are those lineages? How many are represented by the gilled animals shown above?*

are necessary for gas exchange. To promote ventilation, most gill-bearing animals either move their gills through the water or move water over their gills. For example, crayfish and lobsters have paddle-like appendages that drive a current of water over the gills, whereas mussels and clams move water with cilia. Octopuses and squids ventilate their gills by taking in and ejecting water, with the side benefit of locomotion by jet propulsion. Fishes use the motion of swimming or coordinated movements of the mouth and gill covers to ventilate their gills. In both cases, a current of water enters the mouth, passes through slits in the pharynx, flows over the gills, and then exits the body (Figure 42.23).

The arrangement of capillaries in a fish gill allows for **countercurrent exchange**, the exchange of a substance or heat between two fluids flowing in opposite directions. In a fish gill, this process maximizes gas exchange efficiency. Because blood flows in the direction opposite to that of water passing over the gills, at each point in its travel blood is less saturated with O_2 than the water it meets (see Figure 42.23). As blood enters a gill capillary, it encounters water that is completing its passage through the gill. Depleted of much of its dissolved O_2, this water nevertheless has a higher P_{O_2} than the incoming blood, and O_2 transfer takes place. As the blood continues its passage, its P_{O_2} steadily increases, but so does that of the water it encounters, since each successive position in the blood's travel corresponds to an earlier position in the water's passage over the gills. Thus, a partial pressure gradient favoring the diffusion of O_2 from water to blood exists along the entire length of the capillary.

Countercurrent exchange mechanisms are remarkably efficient. In the fish gill, more than 80% of the O_2 dissolved in the water is removed as it passes over the respiratory surface. In other settings, countercurrent exchange contributes to temperature regulation (see Chapter 40) and to the functioning of the mammalian kidney, as we will see in Chapter 44.

Gills are generally unsuitable for an animal living on land. An expansive surface of wet membrane exposed directly to air currents in the environment would lose too much water by evaporation. Furthermore, the gills would collapse as their fine filaments, no longer supported by water, stuck together. In most terrestrial animals, respiratory surfaces are enclosed within the body, exposed to the atmosphere only through narrow tubes.

Tracheal Systems in Insects

Although the most familiar respiratory structure among terrestrial animals is the lung, the most common is actually the **tracheal system** of insects. Made up of air tubes that branch throughout the body, this system is one variation on the theme of an internal respiratory surface. The largest

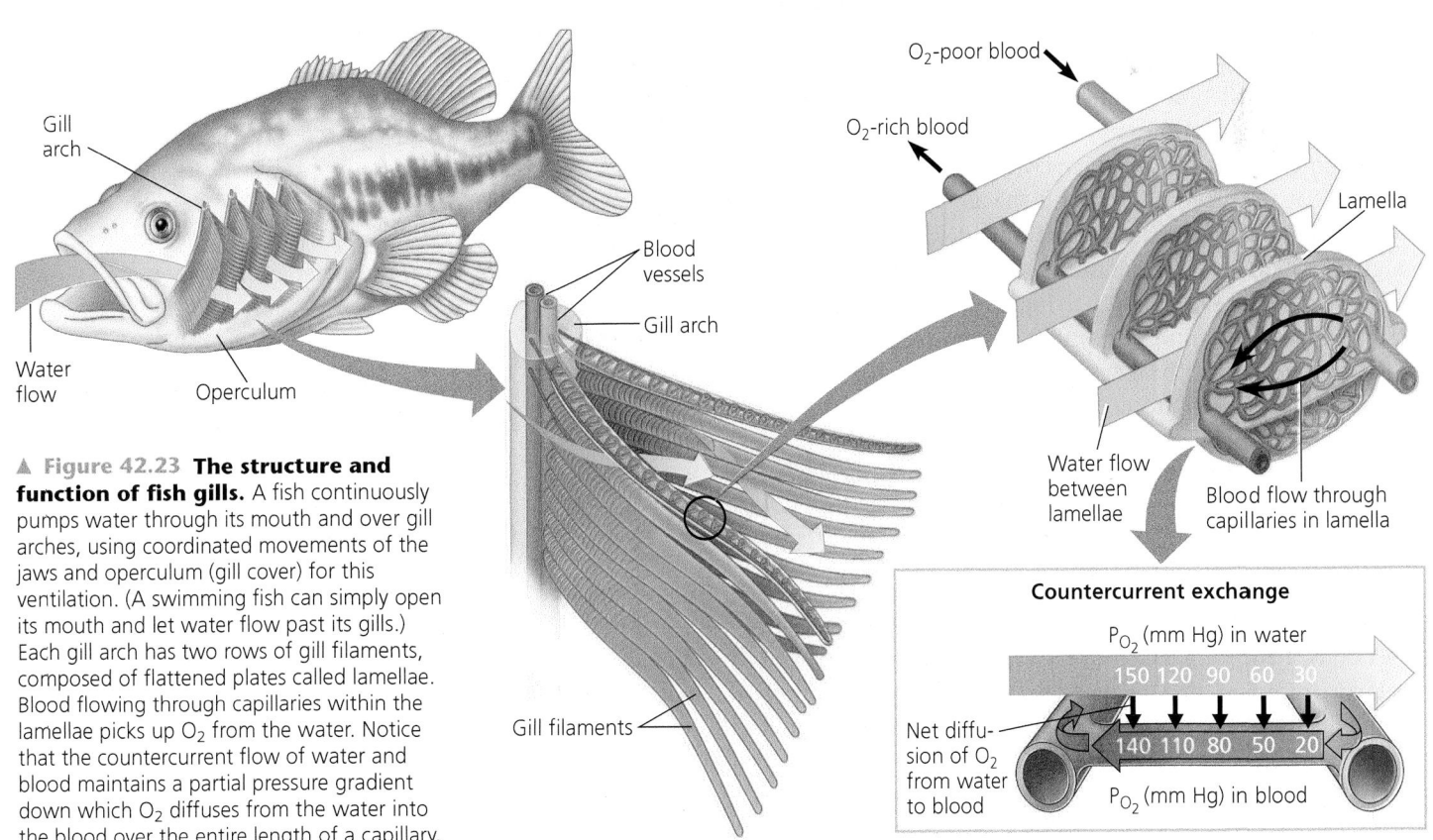

▲ **Figure 42.23 The structure and function of fish gills.** A fish continuously pumps water through its mouth and over gill arches, using coordinated movements of the jaws and operculum (gill cover) for this ventilation. (A swimming fish can simply open its mouth and let water flow past its gills.) Each gill arch has two rows of gill filaments, composed of flattened plates called lamellae. Blood flowing through capillaries within the lamellae picks up O_2 from the water. Notice that the countercurrent flow of water and blood maintains a partial pressure gradient down which O_2 diffuses from the water into the blood over the entire length of a capillary.

Gill arch

Water flow

Operculum

Blood vessels

Gill arch

Gill filaments

O_2-poor blood

O_2-rich blood

Lamella

Water flow between lamellae

Blood flow through capillaries in lamella

Countercurrent exchange

P_{O_2} (mm Hg) in water

150 120 90 60 30

Net diffusion of O_2 from water to blood

140 110 80 50 20

P_{O_2} (mm Hg) in blood

(a) The respiratory system of an insect consists of branched internal tubes. The largest tubes, called tracheae, connect to external openings spaced along the insect's body surface. Air sacs formed from enlarged portions of the tracheae are found near organs that require a large supply of oxygen.

(b) Rings of chitin keep the tracheae open, allowing air to enter and pass into smaller tubes called tracheoles. The branched tracheoles deliver air directly to cells throughout the body. Tracheoles have closed ends filled with fluid (blue-gray). When the animal is active and using more O_2, most of the fluid is withdrawn into the body. This increases the surface area of air-filled tracheoles in contact with cells.

(c) The TEM above shows cross sections of tracheoles in a tiny piece of insect flight muscle. Each of the numerous mitochondria in the muscle cells lies within about 5 μm of a tracheole.

▲ **Figure 42.24 Tracheal systems.**

tubes, called tracheae, open to the outside (**Figure 42.24a**). The finest branches extend close to the surface of nearly every cell, where gas is exchanged by diffusion across the moist epithelium that lines the tips of the tracheal branches (**Figure 42.24b**). Because the tracheal system brings air within a very short distance of virtually every body cell in an insect, it can transport O_2 and CO_2 without the participation of the animal's open circulatory system.

For small insects, diffusion through the tracheae brings in enough O_2 and removes enough CO_2 to support cellular respiration. Larger insects meet their higher energy demands by ventilating their tracheal systems with rhythmic body movements that compress and expand the air tubes like bellows. For example, consider an insect in flight, which has a very high metabolic rate, consuming 10 to 200 times more O_2 than it does at rest. In many flying insects, alternating contraction and relaxation of the flight muscles pumps air rapidly through the tracheal system. The flight muscle cells are packed with mitochondria that support the high metabolic rate, and the tracheal tubes supply these ATP-generating organelles with ample O_2 (**Figure 42.24c**). Thus, adaptations of tracheal systems are directly related to bioenergetics.

Lungs

Unlike tracheal systems, which branch throughout the insect body, **lungs** are localized respiratory organs. Representing an infolding of the body surface, they are typically subdivided into numerous pockets. Because the respiratory surface of a lung is not in direct contact with all other parts of the body, the gap must be bridged by the circulatory system, which transports gases between the lungs and the rest of the body. Lungs have evolved in organisms with open

circulatory systems, such as spiders and land snails, as well as in vertebrates.

Among vertebrates that lack gills, the use of lungs for gas exchange varies. Amphibian lungs, when present, are relatively small and lack an extensive surface for exchange. Amphibians instead rely heavily on diffusion across other body surfaces, such as the skin, to carry out gas exchange. In contrast, most reptiles (including all birds) and all mammals depend entirely on lungs for gas exchange. Turtles are an exception; they supplement lung breathing with gas exchange across moist epithelial surfaces continuous with their mouth or anus. Lungs and air breathing have evolved in a few aquatic vertebrates (including lungfishes) as adaptations to living in oxygen-poor water or to spending part of their time exposed to air (for instance, when the water level of a pond recedes).

Mammalian Respiratory Systems: A Closer Look

In mammals, a system of branching ducts conveys air to the lungs, which are located in the thoracic cavity (**Figure 42.25**). Air enters through the nostrils and is then filtered by hairs, warmed, humidified, and sampled for odors as it flows through a maze of spaces in the nasal cavity. The nasal cavity leads to the pharynx, an intersection where the paths for air and food cross. When food is swallowed, the **larynx** (the upper part of the respiratory tract) moves upward and tips the epiglottis over the glottis (the opening of the **trachea**, or windpipe). This allows food to go down the esophagus to the stomach (see Figure 41.11). The rest of the time, the glottis is open, enabling breathing.

From the larynx, air passes into the trachea. Cartilage reinforcing the walls of both the larynx and the trachea keeps this part of the airway open. Within the larynx of most mammals,

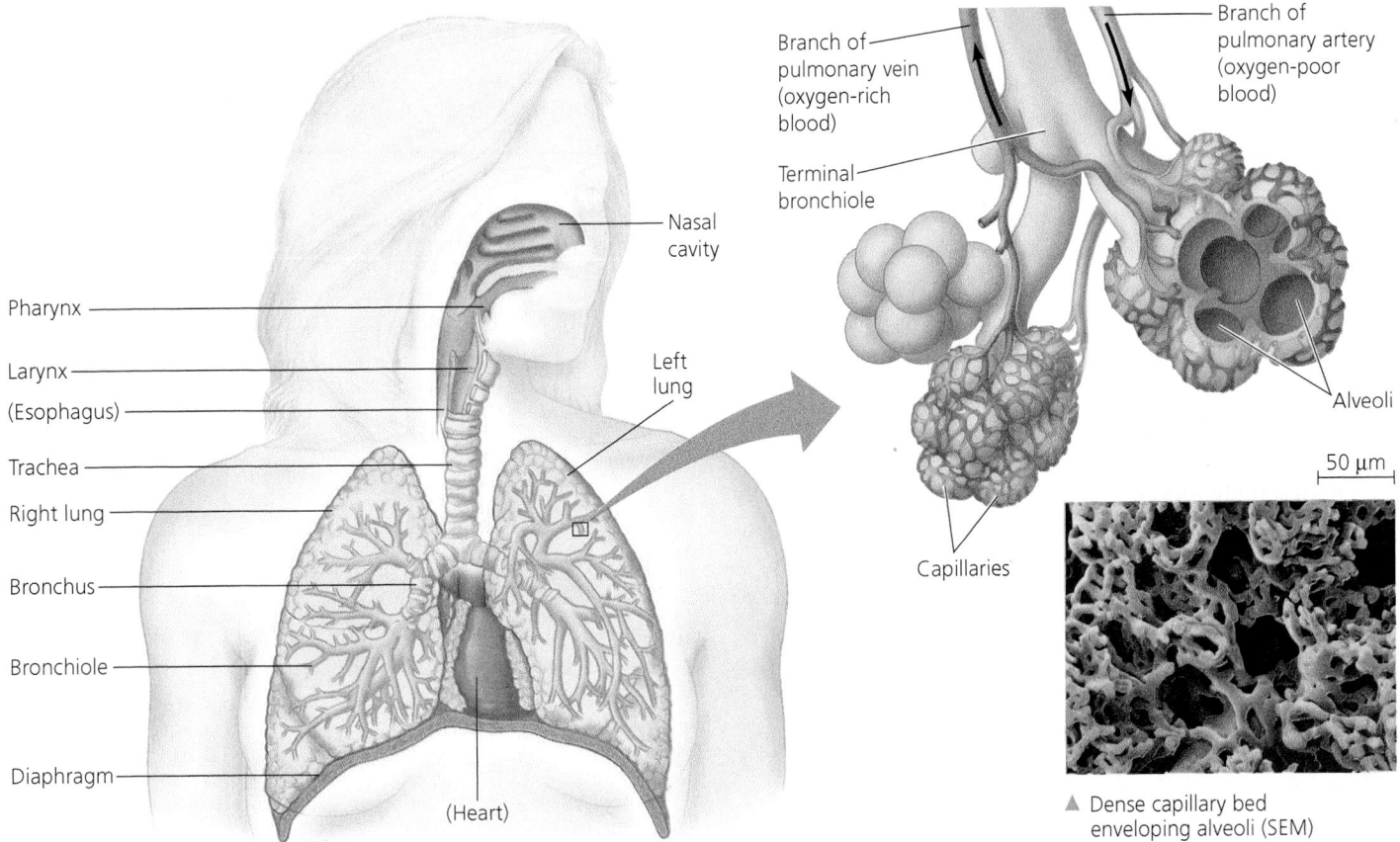

Branch of pulmonary vein (oxygen-rich blood)

Branch of pulmonary artery (oxygen-poor blood)

Terminal bronchiole

Alveoli

Capillaries

50 μm

▲ Dense capillary bed enveloping alveoli (SEM)

Nasal cavity

Pharynx

Larynx

(Esophagus)

Trachea

Right lung

Bronchus

Bronchiole

Diaphragm

Left lung

(Heart)

▲ **Figure 42.25 The mammalian respiratory system.** From the nasal cavity and pharynx, inhaled air passes through the larynx, trachea, and bronchi to the bronchioles, which end in microscopic alveoli lined by a thin, moist epithelium. Branches of the pulmonary arteries convey oxygen-poor blood to the alveoli; branches of the pulmonary veins transport oxygen-rich blood from the alveoli back to the heart.

exhaled air rushes by a pair of elastic bands of muscle called *vocal folds*, or, in humans, *vocal cords*. Sounds are produced when muscles in the larynx are tensed, stretching the cords so they vibrate. High-pitched sounds result from tightly stretched cords vibrating rapidly; low-pitched sounds come from less tense cords vibrating slowly.

The trachea branches into two **bronchi** (singular, *bronchus*), one leading to each lung. Within the lung, the bronchi branch repeatedly into finer and finer tubes called **bronchioles**. The entire system of air ducts has the appearance of an inverted tree, the trunk being the trachea. The epithelium lining the major branches of this respiratory tree is covered by cilia and a thin film of mucus. The mucus traps dust, pollen, and other particulate contaminants, and the beating cilia move the mucus upward to the pharynx, where it can be swallowed into the esophagus. This process, sometimes referred to as the "mucus escalator," plays a crucial role in cleansing the respiratory system.

Gas exchange in mammals occurs in **alveoli** (singular, *alveolus*; see Figure 42.25), air sacs clustered at the tips of the tiniest bronchioles. Human lungs contain millions of alveoli, which together have a surface area of about 100 m², 50 times

that of the skin. Oxygen in the air entering the alveoli dissolves in the moist film lining their inner surfaces and rapidly diffuses across the epithelium into a web of capillaries that surrounds each alveolus. Net diffusion of carbon dioxide occurs in the opposite direction, from the capillaries across the epithelium of the alveolus and into the air space.

Lacking cilia or significant air currents to remove particles from their surface, alveoli are highly susceptible to contamination. White blood cells patrol alveoli, engulfing foreign particles. However, if too much particulate matter reaches the alveoli, the defenses can be overwhelmed, leading to inflammation and irreversible damage. For example, particulates from cigarette smoke that enter alveoli can cause a permanent reduction in lung capacity. For coal miners, inhalation of large amounts of coal dust can lead to silicosis, a disabling, irreversible, and sometimes fatal lung disease.

The film of liquid that lines alveoli is subject to surface tension, an attractive force that acts to minimize the surface area of a liquid (see Chapter 3). Given their tiny diameter (about 0.25 mm), why don't alveoli collapse under high surface tension? Researchers reasoned that alveoli must be coated with a material that reduces surface tension. In 1955, English biophysicist Richard Pattle obtained experimental evidence for such a material, now called a **surfactant**, for *surface-active* agent. In addition, he proposed that the absence of surfactant might cause *respiratory distress syndrome (RDS)*, a disease common among preterm infants born 6 weeks or more before their due dates. In the 1950s, RDS killed 10,000 infants annually in the United States alone.

In the late 1950s, Mary Ellen Avery carried out the first experiment linking RDS to a surfactant deficiency (**Figure 42.26**). Subsequent studies revealed that surfactant contains a mixture of phospholipids and proteins and typically appears in the lungs after 33 weeks of development. (The average full-term pregnancy lasts 38 weeks in humans.) Artificial surfactants are now used routinely to treat early preterm infants. Treated babies with a body mass over 900 g (2 pounds) at birth usually survive without long-term health problems. For her contributions, Avery received the National Medal of Science in 1991.

Having surveyed the route that air follows when we breathe, we will turn next to the process of breathing itself.

▼ **Figure 42.26**

INQUIRY

What causes respiratory distress syndrome?

EXPERIMENT Mary Ellen Avery, a research fellow working with Jere Mead at Harvard University Medical School, wondered whether a lack of surfactant caused respiratory distress syndrome (RDS) in preterm infants. She obtained autopsy samples of lungs from infants that had died of RDS and from infants that had died of other causes. She extracted material from the samples and allowed it to form a film on a water surface. Then Dr. Avery measured the tension (in dynes per centimeter) across the surface of the water and recorded the lowest surface tension observed for each sample.

RESULTS

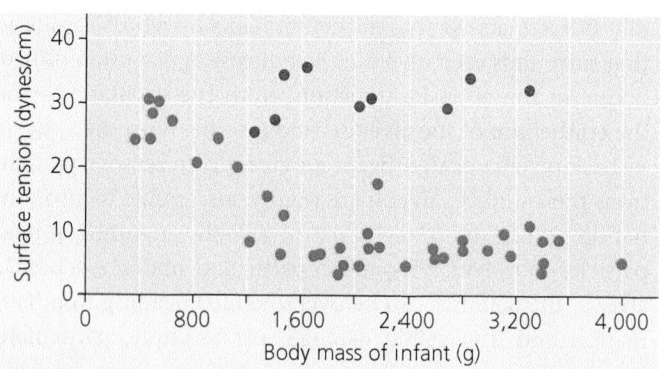

- RDS deaths
- Deaths from other causes

CONCLUSION The lungs of infants with a body mass over 1,200 g (2.7 pounds) contain a substance that reduces surface tension. That substance is absent in the lungs of infants with RDS.

SOURCE M. E. Avery and J. Mead, Surface properties in relation to atelectasis and hyaline membrane disease, *American Journal of Diseases of Children* 97:517–523 (1959).

WHAT IF? Suppose you repeated this experiment but instead measured the amount of surfactant in lung samples. Describe the graph you would expect if you plotted the amount of surfactant versus infant weight.

CONCEPT 42.6

Breathing ventilates the lungs

Like fishes, terrestrial vertebrates rely on ventilation to maintain high O_2 and low CO_2 concentrations at the gas exchange surface. The process that ventilates lungs is **breathing**, the alternating inhalation and exhalation of air. A variety of mechanisms for moving air in and out of lungs have evolved, as we will see by considering breathing in amphibians, mammals, and birds.

How an Amphibian Breathes

An amphibian such as a frog ventilates its lungs by **positive pressure breathing**, inflating the lungs with forced airflow. During the first stage of inhalation, muscles lower the floor of an amphibian's oral cavity, drawing in air through its nostrils. Next, with the nostrils and mouth closed, the floor of the oral cavity rises, forcing air down the trachea. During exhalation, air is forced back out by the elastic recoil of the lungs and by compression of the muscular body wall. When male frogs puff themselves up in aggressive or courtship displays, they disrupt this breathing cycle, taking in air several times without allowing any release.

How a Bird Breathes

Two features of ventilation in birds make it highly efficient. First, when birds breathe, they pass air over the gas exchange surface in only one direction. Second, incoming fresh air does not mix with air that has already carried out gas exchange.

To bring fresh air to their lungs, birds use eight or nine air sacs situated on either side of the lungs (**Figure 42.27**). The air sacs do not function directly in gas exchange but act as bellows that keep air flowing through the lungs. Instead of alveoli, which are dead ends, the sites of gas exchange in bird lungs are tiny channels called *parabronchi*. Passage of air through the entire system—lungs and air sacs—requires two cycles of inhalation and exhalation. In some passageways, the direction in

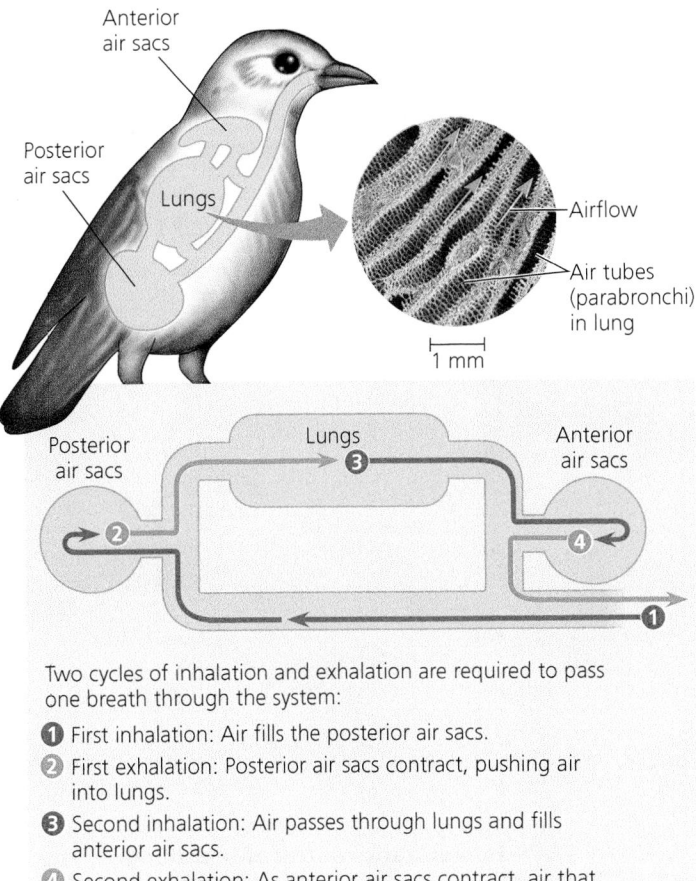

Two cycles of inhalation and exhalation are required to pass one breath through the system:

❶ First inhalation: Air fills the posterior air sacs.

❷ First exhalation: Posterior air sacs contract, pushing air into lungs.

❸ Second inhalation: Air passes through lungs and fills anterior air sacs.

❹ Second exhalation: As anterior air sacs contract, air that entered body at first inhalation is pushed out of body.

▲ **Figure 42.27 The avian respiratory system.** This diagram traces a breath of air through the respiratory system of a bird. As shown, two cycles of inhalation and exhalation are required for the air to pass all the way through the system and out of the bird.

which air moves alternates (see Figure 42.27). Within the parabronchi, however, air always flows in the same direction.

How a Mammal Breathes

Unlike amphibians and birds, mammals employ **negative pressure breathing**—pulling, rather than pushing, air into their lungs (**Figure 42.28**). Using muscle contraction to actively expand the thoracic cavity, mammals lower air pressure in their lungs below that of the air outside their body. Because gas flows from a region of higher pressure to a region of lower pressure, air rushes through the nostrils and mouth and down the breathing tubes to the alveoli. During exhalation, the muscles controlling the thoracic cavity relax, and the volume of the cavity is reduced. The increased air pressure in the alveoli forces air up the breathing tubes and out of the body. Thus, inhalation is always active and requires work, whereas exhalation is usually passive.

Expanding the thoracic cavity during inhalation involves the animal's rib muscles and the **diaphragm**, a sheet of skeletal muscle that forms the bottom wall of the cavity. Contracting the rib muscles expands the rib cage, the front wall of the thoracic cavity, by pulling the ribs upward and the sternum outward. At the same time, the diaphragm contracts, expanding the thoracic cavity downward. The effect of the descending diaphragm is similar to that of a plunger being drawn out of a syringe.

Within the thoracic cavity, a double membrane surrounds the lungs. The inner layer of this membrane adheres to the outside of the lungs, and the outer layer adheres to the wall of the thoracic cavity. A thin space filled with fluid separates the two layers. Surface tension in the fluid causes the two layers to stick together like two plates of glass separated by a film of water: The layers can slide smoothly past each other, but they cannot be pulled apart easily. Consequently, the volume of the thoracic cavity and the volume of the lungs change in unison.

Depending on activity level, additional muscles may be recruited to aid breathing. The rib muscles and diaphragm are sufficient to change lung volume when a mammal is at rest. During exercise, other muscles of the neck, back, and chest increase the volume of the thoracic cavity by raising the rib cage. In kangaroos and some other species, locomotion causes a rhythmic movement of organs in the abdomen, including the stomach and liver. The result is a piston-like pumping motion that pushes and pulls on the diaphragm, further increasing the volume of air moved in and out of the lungs.

Rib cage expands as rib muscles contract.

Air inhaled.

Lung

Diaphragm

❶ Inhalation: Diaphragm contracts (moves down).

Rib cage gets smaller as rib muscles relax.

Air exhaled.

❷ Exhalation: Diaphragm relaxes (moves up).

▲ **Figure 42.28 Negative pressure breathing.** A mammal breathes by changing the air pressure within its lungs relative to the pressure of the outside atmosphere.

WHAT IF? *The walls of alveoli contain elastic fibers that allow the alveoli to expand and contract with each breath. If alveoli lost their elasticity, how would that affect gas exchange in the lungs?*

The volume of air inhaled and exhaled with each breath is called **tidal volume**. It averages about 500 mL in resting humans. The tidal volume during maximal inhalation and exhalation is the **vital capacity**, which is about 3.4 L and 4.8 L for college-age women and men, respectively. The air that remains after a forced exhalation is called the **residual volume**. As we age, our lungs lose their resilience, and residual volume increases at the expense of vital capacity.

Because the lungs in mammals do not completely empty with each breath, and because inhalation occurs through the same airways as exhalation, each inhalation mixes fresh air with oxygen-depleted residual air. As a result, the maximum P_{O_2} in alveoli is always considerably less than in the atmosphere. The maximum P_{O_2} in lungs is also less for mammals than for birds, which renew the air in their lungs with every exhalation. This is one reason mammals function less well than birds at high altitude. For example, humans have great difficulty obtaining enough O_2 when climbing Earth's highest peaks, such as Mount Everest (8,850 m), in the Himalayas. However, bar-headed geese and several other bird species easily fly over the Himalayas during their migrations.

Control of Breathing in Humans

Although you can voluntarily hold your breath or breathe faster and deeper, most of the time your breathing is regulated by involuntary mechanisms. These control mechanisms ensure that gas exchange is coordinated with blood circulation and with metabolic demand.

The neurons mainly responsible for regulating breathing are in the medulla oblongata, near the base of the brain (**Figure 42.29**). Neural circuits in the medulla form a *breathing control center* that establishes the breathing rhythm. When you breathe deeply, a negative-feedback mechanism prevents the lungs from overexpanding: During inhalation, sensors that detect stretching of the lung tissue send nerve impulses to the control circuits in the medulla, inhibiting further inhalation.

In regulating breathing, the medulla uses the pH of the surrounding tissue fluid as an indicator of blood CO_2 concentration. The reason pH can be used in this way is that blood CO_2 is the main determinant of the pH of *cerebrospinal fluid*, the fluid surrounding the brain and spinal cord. Carbon dioxide diffuses from the blood to the cerebrospinal fluid, where it reacts with water and forms carbonic acid (H_2CO_3). The H_2CO_3 can then dissociate into a bicarbonate ion (HCO_3^-) and a hydrogen ion (H^+):

$$CO_2 + H_2O \rightleftharpoons H_2CO_3 \rightleftharpoons HCO_3^- + H^+$$

Increased metabolic activity, such as occurs during exercise, lowers pH by increasing the concentration of CO_2 in the blood. Sensors in blood vessels and the medulla detect this pH change. In response, the medulla's control circuits increase the depth and rate of breathing. Both remain high until the excess CO_2 is eliminated in exhaled air and pH returns to a normal value.

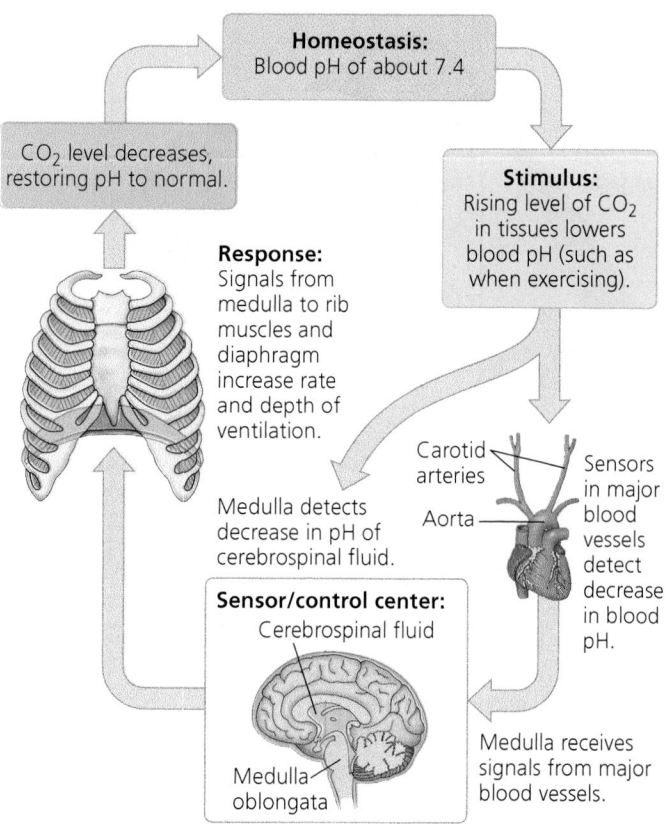

▲ **Figure 42.29 Homeostatic control of breathing.**

WHAT IF? *Suppose a person began breathing very rapidly while resting. Describe the effect on blood CO_2 levels and the steps by which the negative feedback circuit in this figure would restore homeostasis.*

The blood O_2 level usually has little effect on the breathing control centers. However, when the O_2 level drops very low (at high altitudes, for instance), O_2 sensors in the aorta and the carotid arteries in the neck send signals to the breathing control centers, which respond by increasing the breathing rate.

The pons, a part of the brain next to the medulla, also regulates breathing, although its exact role remains an open question. The pons may act in the regulatory circuit with the medulla or modulate the output of that circuit.

Breathing control is effective only if ventilation is matched to blood flow through alveolar capillaries. During exercise, for instance, such coordination couples an increased breathing rate, which enhances O_2 uptake and CO_2 removal, with an increase in cardiac output.

CONCEPT CHECK 42.6

1. How does an increase in the CO_2 concentration in the blood affect the pH of cerebrospinal fluid?
2. A drop in blood pH causes an increase in heart rate. What is the function of this control mechanism?
3. **WHAT IF?** If an injury tore a small hole in the membranes surrounding your lungs, what effect on lung function would you expect?

For suggested answers, see Appendix A.

Adaptations for gas exchange include pigments that bind and transport gases

The high metabolic demands of many animals necessitate the exchange of large quantities of O_2 and CO_2. Here we'll examine how blood molecules called respiratory pigments facilitate this exchange through their interaction with O_2 and CO_2. We will also investigate physiological adaptations that enable animals to be active under conditions of high metabolic load or very limiting P_{O_2}. As a basis for exploring these topics, let's summarize the basic gas exchange circuit in humans.

Coordination of Circulation and Gas Exchange

The partial pressures of O_2 and CO_2 in the blood vary at different points in the circulatory system, as shown in **Figure 42.30**. Blood flowing through the alveolar capillaries has a lower P_{O_2} and a higher P_{CO_2} than the air in the alveoli. As a result, CO_2 diffuses down its partial pressure gradient from the blood to the air in the alveoli. Meanwhile, O_2 in the air dissolves in the fluid that coats the alveolar epithelium and diffuses into the blood. By the time the blood leaves the lungs in the pulmonary veins, its P_{O_2} has been raised and its P_{CO_2} has been lowered. After returning to the heart, this blood is pumped through the systemic circuit.

In the tissue capillaries, gradients of partial pressure favor the diffusion of O_2 out of the blood and CO_2 into the blood. These gradients exist because cellular respiration in the mitochondria of cells near each capillary removes O_2 from and adds CO_2 to the surrounding interstitial fluid. After the blood unloads O_2 and loads CO_2, it is returned to the heart and pumped to the lungs again.

Although this description faithfully characterizes the driving forces for gas exchange in different tissues, it omits the critical role of the specialized carrier proteins we will discuss next.

Respiratory Pigments

The low solubility of O_2 in water (and thus in blood) poses a problem for animals that rely on the circulatory system to deliver O_2. For example, a person requires almost 2 L of O_2 per minute during intense exercise, and all of it must be carried in the blood from the lungs to the active tissues. At normal body temperature and air pressure, however, only 4.5 mL of O_2 can dissolve into a liter of blood in the lungs. Even if 80% of the dissolved O_2 were delivered to the tissues (an unrealistically high percentage), the heart would still need to pump 555 L of blood per minute!

In fact, animals transport most of their O_2 bound to proteins called **respiratory pigments**. Respiratory pigments circulate with the blood or hemolymph and are often contained within specialized cells. The pigments greatly increase the amount of O_2 that can be carried in the circulatory fluid (to about 200 mL of O_2 per liter in mammalian blood).

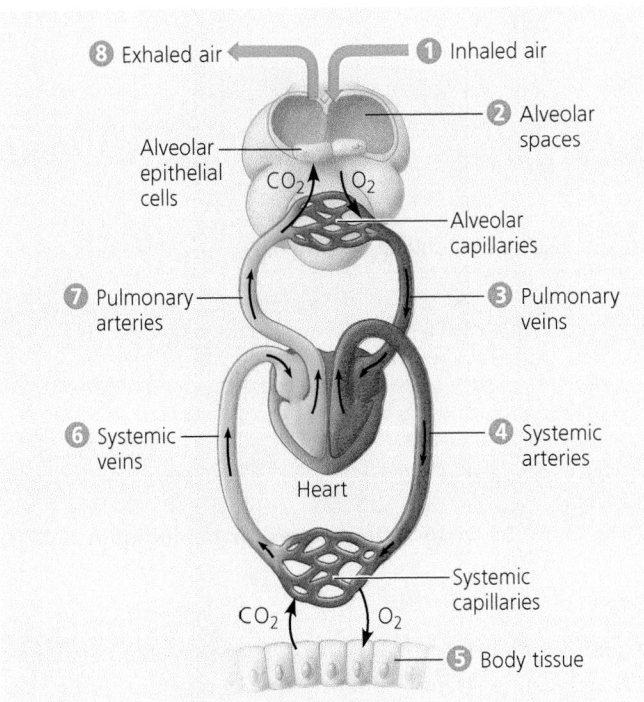

(a) The path of respiratory gases in the circulatory system

(b) Partial pressure of O_2 and CO_2 at different points in the circulatory system numbered in (a)

▲ **Figure 42.30 Loading and unloading of respiratory gases.**

WHAT IF? *If you consciously forced more air out of your lungs each time you exhaled, how would that affect the values shown in (b)?*

In our example of an exercising human with an O_2 delivery rate of 80%, the presence of a respiratory pigment reduces the cardiac output necessary for O_2 transport to a manageable 12.5 L of blood per minute.

A variety of respiratory pigments have evolved among the animal taxa. With a few exceptions, these molecules have a distinctive color (hence the term *pigment*) and consist of a protein bound to a metal. One example is the blue pigment *hemocyanin*, which has copper as its oxygen-binding component and is found in arthropods and many molluscs. The respiratory pigment of almost all vertebrates and many invertebrates is hemoglobin. In vertebrates, it is contained in the erythrocytes.

Hemoglobin

Hemoglobin

Vertebrate hemoglobin consists of four subunits (polypeptide chains), each with a cofactor called a heme group that has an iron atom at its center. Each iron atom binds one molecule of O_2; hence, a single hemoglobin molecule can carry four molecules of O_2. Like all respiratory pigments, hemoglobin binds O_2 reversibly, loading O_2 in the lungs or gills and unloading it in other parts of the body. This process depends on cooperativity between the hemoglobin subunits (see pp. 158–159). When O_2 binds to one subunit, the others change shape slightly, increasing their affinity for O_2. When four O_2 molecules are bound and one subunit unloads its O_2, the other three subunits more readily unload O_2, as an associated shape change lowers their affinity for O_2.

Cooperativity in O_2 binding and release is evident in the dissociation curve for hemoglobin (**Figure 42.31a**). Over the range of P_{O_2} where the dissociation curve has a steep slope, even a slight change in P_{O_2} causes hemoglobin to load or unload a substantial amount of O_2. Notice that the steep part of the curve corresponds to the range of P_{O_2} found in body tissues. When cells in a particular location begin working harder—during exercise, for instance—P_{O_2} dips in their vicinity as the O_2 is consumed in cellular respiration. Because of the effect of subunit cooperativity, a slight drop in P_{O_2} causes a relatively large increase in the amount of O_2 the blood unloads.

The production of CO_2 during cellular respiration promotes the unloading of O_2 by hemoglobin in active tissues. As we have seen, CO_2 reacts with water, forming carbonic acid, which lowers the pH of its surroundings. Low pH, in turn, decreases the affinity of hemoglobin for O_2, an effect called the **Bohr shift** (**Figure 42.31b**). Thus, where CO_2 production is greater, hemoglobin releases more O_2, which can then be used to support more cellular respiration.

(a) P_{O_2} and hemoglobin dissociation at pH 7.4. The curve shows the relative amounts of O_2 bound to hemoglobin exposed to solutions with different P_{O_2}. At a P_{O_2} of 100 mm Hg, typical in the lungs, hemoglobin is about 98% saturated with O_2. At a P_{O_2} of 40 mm Hg, common in the vicinity of tissues at rest, hemoglobin is about 70% saturated. Hemoglobin can release additional O_2 to metabolically very active tissues, such as muscle tissue during exercise.

(b) pH and hemoglobin dissociation. Because hydrogen ions affect the shape of hemoglobin, a drop in pH shifts the O_2 dissociation curve toward the right (the Bohr shift). At a given P_{O_2}, say 40 mm Hg, hemoglobin gives up more O_2 at pH 7.2 than at pH 7.4, the normal pH of human blood. The pH decreases in very active tissues because the CO_2 produced by cellular respiration reacts with water, forming carbonic acid. Hemoglobin then releases more O_2, which supports the increased cellular respiration in the active tissues.

▲ **Figure 42.31 Dissociation curves for hemoglobin at 37°C.**

Carbon Dioxide Transport

In addition to its role in O_2 transport, hemoglobin helps transport CO_2 and assists in buffering the blood—that is, preventing harmful changes in pH. Only about 7% of the CO_2

released by respiring cells is transported in solution in blood plasma. Another 23% binds to the amino ends of the hemoglobin polypeptide chains, and about 70% is transported in the blood in the form of bicarbonate ions (HCO_3^-).

As shown in **Figure 42.32**, carbon dioxide from respiring cells diffuses into the blood plasma and then into erythrocytes. There the CO_2 reacts with water (assisted by the enzyme carbonic anhydrase) and forms H_2CO_3, which dissociates into H^+ and HCO_3^-. Most of the H^+ binds to hemoglobin and other proteins, minimizing the change in blood pH. The HCO_3^- diffuses into the plasma.

When blood flows through the lungs, the relative partial pressures of CO_2 favor the diffusion of CO_2 out of the blood. As CO_2 diffuses into alveoli, the amount of CO_2 in the blood decreases. This decrease shifts the chemical equilibrium in favor of the conversion of HCO_3^- to CO_2, enabling further net diffusion of CO_2 into alveoli. Overall, the P_{CO_2} gradient is sufficient to reduce P_{CO_2} by roughly 15% during passage of blood through the lungs.

Respiratory Adaptations of Diving Mammals

EVOLUTION Animals vary greatly in their ability to temporarily inhabit environments in which there is no access to their normal respiratory medium—for example, when an air-breathing mammal swims underwater. Whereas most humans, even well-trained divers, cannot hold their breath longer than 2 or 3 minutes or swim deeper than 20 m, the Weddell seal of Antarctica routinely plunges to 200–500 m and remains there for about 20 minutes (and sometimes for more than an hour). (Humans can remain submerged for comparable periods, but only with the aid of specialized gear and compressed air tanks.) Some whales and other species of seals make even more impressive dives. Elephant seals can reach depths of 1,500 m—almost a mile—and stay submerged for as long as 2 hours! One elephant seal carrying a recording device spent 40 days at sea,

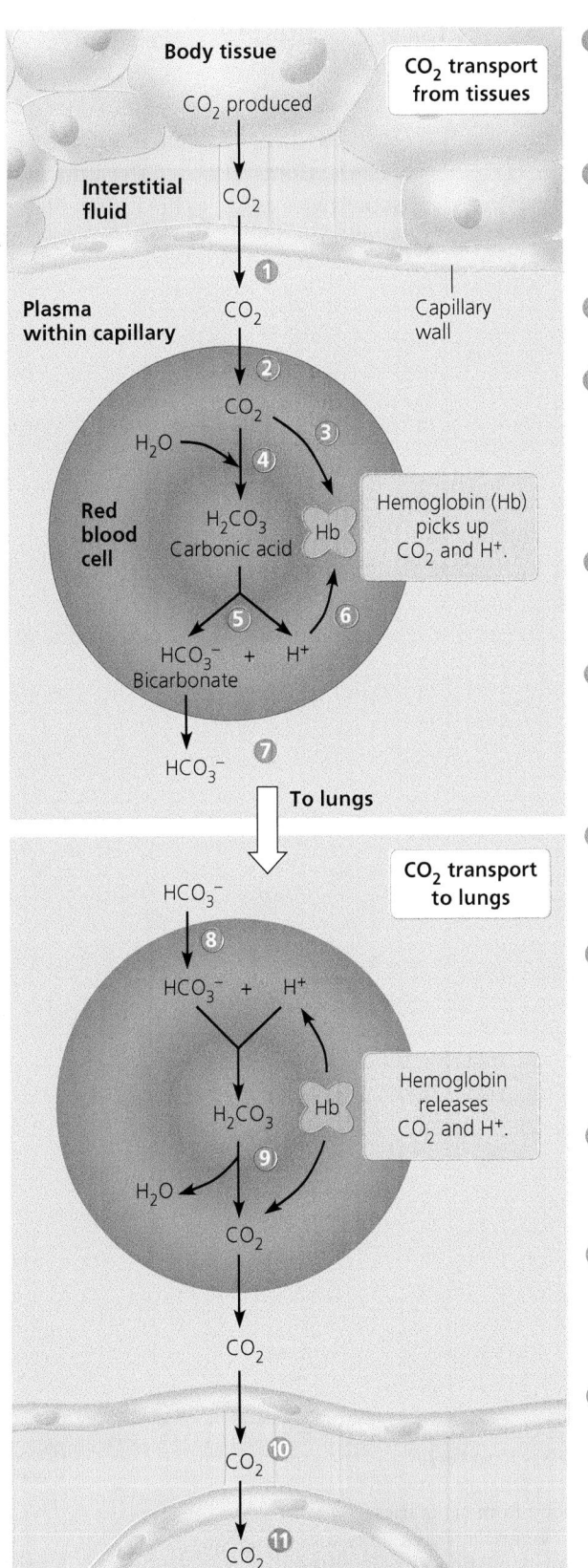

▲ Figure 42.32 Carbon dioxide transport in the blood.

? *In what three forms is CO_2 transported in the bloodstream?*

① Carbon dioxide produced by body tissues diffuses into the interstitial fluid and the plasma.

② Over 90% of the CO_2 diffuses into red blood cells, leaving only 7% in the plasma as dissolved CO_2.

③ Some CO_2 is picked up and transported by hemoglobin.

④ However, most CO_2 reacts with water in red blood cells, forming carbonic acid (H_2CO_3), a reaction catalyzed by carbonic anhydrase contained within red blood cells.

⑤ Carbonic acid dissociates into a bicarbonate ion (HCO_3^-) and a hydrogen ion (H^+).

⑥ Hemoglobin binds most of the H^+ from H_2CO_3, preventing the H^+ from acidifying the blood and thus preventing the Bohr shift.

⑦ Most of the HCO_3^- diffuses into the plasma, where it is carried in the bloodstream to the lungs.

⑧ In the lungs, HCO_3^- diffuses from the plasma into red blood cells, combining with H^+ released from hemoglobin and forming H_2CO_3.

⑨ Carbonic acid is converted back to CO_2 and water. CO_2 is also unloaded from hemoglobin.

⑩ CO_2 diffuses into the plasma and the interstitial fluid.

⑪ CO_2 diffuses into the alveolar space, from which it is expelled during exhalation. The reduction of CO_2 concentration in the plasma drives the breakdown of H_2CO_3 into CO_2 and water in the red blood cells (see ⑨), a reversal of the reaction that occurs near body tissues (see ④).

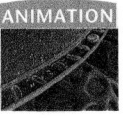

ANIMATION **BioFlix** Visit the Study Area at www.masteringbiology.com for the BioFlix® 3-D Animation on Gas Exchange.

diving almost continuously with no surface period longer than 6 minutes. What evolutionary adaptations enable these animals to perform such amazing feats?

One adaptation of diving mammals to prolonged stays underwater is an ability to store large amounts of O_2. Compared with humans, the Weddell seal can store about twice as much O_2 per kilogram of body mass. About 36% of our total O_2 is in our lungs, and 51% is in our blood. In contrast, the Weddell seal holds only about 5% of its O_2 in its relatively small lungs (and may exhale before diving, which reduces buoyancy), stockpiling 70% in the blood. And the seal has about twice the volume of blood per kilogram of body mass as a human. Diving mammals also have a high concentration of an oxygen-storing protein called **myoglobin** in their muscles. The Weddell seal can store about 25% of its O_2 in muscle, compared with only 13% in humans.

Diving mammals not only have a relatively large O_2 stockpile but also have adaptations that conserve O_2. They swim with little muscular effort and glide passively upward or downward by changing their buoyancy. Their heart rate and O_2 consumption rate decrease during a dive. At the same time, regulatory mechanisms route most blood to the brain, spinal cord, eyes, adrenal glands, and, in pregnant seals, the placenta. Blood supply to the muscles is restricted or, during the longest dives, shut off altogether. During dives of more than about 20 minutes, a Weddell seal's muscles deplete the O_2 stored in myoglobin and then derive their ATP from fermentation instead of respiration (see Chapter 9).

The unusual abilities of the Weddell seal and other air-breathing divers to power their bodies during long dives showcase two related themes in our study of organisms—the response to environmental challenges over the short term by physiological adjustments and over the long term as a result of natural selection.

42 CHAPTER REVIEW

SUMMARY OF KEY CONCEPTS

CONCEPT 42.1

Circulatory systems link exchange surfaces with cells throughout the body (pp. 897–902)

- In animals with simple body plans, gastrovascular cavities mediate exchange between the environment and cells that can be reached by diffusion. Because diffusion is slow over long distances, most complex animals have a circulatory system that moves fluid between cells and the organs that carry out exchange with the environment. Arthropods and most molluscs have an **open circulatory system**, in which **hemolymph** bathes organs directly. Vertebrates have a **closed circulatory system**, in which **blood** circulates in a closed network of pumps and vessels.
- The closed circulatory system of vertebrates consists of blood, **blood vessels**, and a two- to four-chambered **heart**. Blood pumped by a heart **ventricle** passes to **arteries** and then to **capillaries**, the sites of chemical exchange between blood and interstitial fluid. **Veins** return blood from capillaries to an **atrium**, which passes blood to a ventricle. Fishes, rays, and sharks have a single pump in their circulation. Air-breathing vertebrates have two pumps combined in a single heart. Variations in ventricle number and separation reflect adaptations to different environments and metabolic needs.

> ? *How does the flow of a fluid in a closed circulatory system differ from the movement of molecules between cells and their environment with regard to distance traveled, direction traveled, and driving force?*

CONCEPT 42.2

Coordinated cycles of heart contraction drive double circulation in mammals (pp. 902–904)

- The right ventricle pumps blood to the lungs, where it loads O_2 and unloads CO_2. Oxygen-rich blood from the lungs enters the heart at the left atrium and is pumped to the body tissues by the left ventricle. Blood returns to the heart through the right atrium.

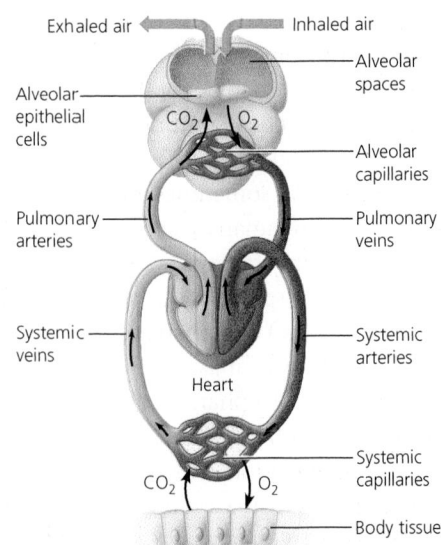

- The **cardiac cycle**, one complete sequence of the heart's pumping and filling, consists of a period of contraction, called **systole**, and a period of relaxation, called **diastole**. Heart function can be assessed by measuring the **pulse** (number of times the heart beats each minute) and **cardiac output** (volume of blood pumped by each ventricle per minute).
- The heartbeat originates with impulses at the **sinoatrial (SA) node** (pacemaker) of the right atrium. The impulses trigger contraction of both atria before passing to the **atrioventricular (AV) node**, where the impulses are temporarily delayed. They are then conducted along the bundle branches and Purkinje fibers, triggering contraction of the ventricles. The nervous system, hormones, and body temperature influence pacemaker activity.

? *What changes in cardiac function might you expect after surgical replacement of a defective heart valve?*

CONCEPT 42.3

Patterns of blood pressure and flow reflect the structure and arrangement of blood vessels (pp. 905–910)

- Blood vessels have structures well adapted to function. Capillaries have narrow diameters and thin walls that facilitate exchange. Arteries contain thick elastic walls that maintain blood pressure. Veins contain one-way valves that contribute to the return of blood to the heart.
- Physical laws governing the movement of fluids through pipes influence blood flow and blood pressure. The velocity of blood flow varies in the circulatory system, being lowest in the capillary beds as a result of their large total cross-sectional area. Blood pressure is altered by changes in cardiac output and by variable constriction of arterioles.
- Fluid leaks out of capillaries and is returned to blood by the **lymphatic system**. This system parallels the circulatory system in its extent and its mechanisms for fluid flow under low hydrostatic pressure. It also plays a vital role in defense against infection.

? *If you placed your forearm on your head, how, if at all, would the blood pressure in that arm change? Explain.*

CONCEPT 42.4

Blood components function in exchange, transport, and defense (pp. 910–915)

- Whole blood consists of cells and cell fragments (**platelets**) suspended in a liquid matrix called **plasma**. Plasma proteins influence blood pH, osmotic pressure, and viscosity, and they function in lipid transport, immunity (antibodies), and blood clotting (fibrinogen). Red blood cells, or **erythrocytes**, transport O_2. Five types of white blood cells, or **leukocytes**, function in defense against microbes and foreign substances in the blood. Platelets function in blood clotting, a cascade of reactions that converts plasma fibrinogen to fibrin.
- A variety of diseases impair function of the circulatory system. In **sickle-cell disease**, an aberrant form of **hemoglobin** disrupts erythrocyte shape and function, leading to blockage of small blood vessels and a decrease in the oxygen-carrying capacity of the blood. In cardiovascular disease, inflammation caused by damage to the lining of arteries enhances deposition of lipids and cells, resulting in the potential for life-threatening damage to the heart or brain.

? *In the absence of infection, what percentage of cells in human blood are leukocytes?*

CONCEPT 42.5

Gas exchange occurs across specialized respiratory surfaces (pp. 915–920)

- At all sites of **gas exchange**, a gas diffuses from where its **partial pressure** is higher to where it is lower. Air is more conducive to gas exchange than water because air has a higher O_2 content, lower density, and lower viscosity. Regardless of whether the respiratory medium is air or water, adequate diffusion of O_2 and CO_2 between the medium and an animal's cells requires large, moist respiratory surfaces.
- The structure and organization of respiratory surfaces differ among animal species. Gills are outfoldings of the body surface specialized for gas exchange in water. The effectiveness of gas exchange in some gills, including those of fishes, is increased by **ventilation** and **countercurrent exchange** between blood and water. Gas exchange in insects relies on a **tracheal system** consisting of tiny, branching tubes that penetrate the body, bringing O_2 directly to cells. Spiders, land snails, and most terrestrial vertebrates have internal **lungs**. In mammals, air inhaled through the nostrils passes through the pharynx into the **trachea, bronchi, bronchioles**, and dead-end **alveoli**, where gas exchange occurs.

? *Why does altitude have almost no effect on an animal's ability to rid itself of CO_2 through gas exchange?*

CONCEPT 42.6

Breathing ventilates the lungs (pp. 920–922)

- Breathing mechanisms vary substantially among vertebrates. An amphibian ventilates its lungs by **positive pressure breathing**, which forces air down the trachea. Birds use a system of air sacs as bellows to keep air flowing through the lungs in one direction only. Every exhalation completely renews the air in the lungs. Mammals ventilate their lungs by **negative pressure breathing**, which pulls air into the lungs. Lung volume increases as the rib muscles and **diaphragm** contract. Incoming and outgoing air mix, decreasing the efficiency of ventilation.
- Control centers in the medulla oblongata and pons of the human brain regulate the rate and depth of breathing. Sensors detect the pH of cerebrospinal fluid (reflecting CO_2 concentration in the blood), and the medulla adjusts breathing rate and depth to match metabolic demands. Secondary control over breathing is exerted by sensors in the aorta and carotid arteries that monitor blood levels of O_2 as well as CO_2 (via blood pH).

? *How does tidal volume differ from the volume of fresh air that enters the body during inspiration?*

CONCEPT 42.7

Adaptations for gas exchange include pigments that bind and transport gases (pp. 923–926)

- In the lungs, gradients of partial pressure favor the diffusion of O_2 into the blood and CO_2 out of the blood. The opposite situation exists in the rest of the body. **Respiratory pigments** transport O_2, greatly increasing the amount of O_2 that blood or hemolymph can carry. Many arthropods and molluscs have copper-containing hemocyanin; vertebrates and a wide variety of invertebrates have hemoglobin. Hemoglobin also helps transport CO_2 and assists in buffering the blood.

- Evolutionary adaptations enable some animals to satisfy extraordinary O_2 demands. Deep-diving air-breathers stockpile O_2 in blood and other tissues and deplete it slowly.

> **?** *In what way is the role of a respiratory pigment like that of an enzyme?*

TEST YOUR UNDERSTANDING

LEVEL 1: KNOWLEDGE/COMPREHENSION

1. Which of the following respiratory systems is not closely associated with a blood supply?
   a. the lungs of a vertebrate
   b. the gills of a fish
   c. the tracheal system of an insect
   d. the skin of an earthworm
   e. the parapodia of a polychaete worm

2. Blood returning to the mammalian heart in a pulmonary vein drains first into the
   a. vena cava.
   b. left atrium.
   c. right atrium.
   d. left ventricle.
   e. right ventricle.

3. Pulse is a direct measure of
   a. blood pressure.
   b. stroke volume.
   c. cardiac output.
   d. heart rate.
   e. breathing rate.

4. When you hold your breath, which of the following blood gas changes first leads to the urge to breathe?
   a. rising O_2
   b. falling O_2
   c. rising CO_2
   d. falling CO_2
   e. rising CO_2 and falling O_2

5. One feature that amphibians and humans have in common is
   a. the number of heart chambers.
   b. the type of gas exchange tissues.
   c. a complete separation of circuits for circulation.
   d. the number of circuits for circulation.
   e. a low blood pressure in the systemic circuit.

LEVEL 2: APPLICATION/ANALYSIS

6. If a molecule of CO_2 released into the blood in your left toe is exhaled from your nose, it must pass through all of the following except
   a. the pulmonary vein.
   b. an alveolus.
   c. the trachea.
   d. the right atrium.
   e. the right ventricle.

7. Compared with the interstitial fluid that bathes active muscle cells, blood reaching these cells in arteries has a
   a. higher P_{O_2}.
   b. higher P_{CO_2}.
   c. greater bicarbonate concentration.
   d. lower pH.
   e. lower osmotic pressure.

8. Which of the following reactions prevails in red blood cells traveling through alveolar capillaries? (Hb = hemoglobin)
   a. $Hb + 4 O_2 \rightarrow Hb(O_2)_4$
   b. $Hb(O_2)_4 \rightarrow Hb + 4 O_2$
   c. $CO_2 + H_2O \rightarrow H_2CO_3$
   d. $H_2CO_3 \rightarrow H^+ + HCO_3^-$
   e. $Hb + 4 CO_2 \rightarrow Hb(CO_2)_4$

LEVEL 3: SYNTHESIS/EVALUATION

9. **DRAW IT** Plot blood pressure against time for one cardiac cycle in humans, drawing separate lines for the pressure in the aorta, the left ventricle, and the right ventricle. Below the

time axis, add a vertical arrow pointing to the time when you expect a peak in atrial blood pressure.

10. **EVOLUTION CONNECTION**
    One of the many mutant opponents that the movie monster Godzilla contends with is Mothra, a giant mothlike creature with a wingspan of several dozen meters. Science fiction creatures like these can be critiqued on the grounds of biomechanical and physiological principles. What problems of respiration and gas exchange would Mothra face? The largest insects that have ever lived are Paleozoic dragonflies with half-meter wingspans. Why do you think truly giant insects are improbable?

11. **SCIENTIFIC INQUIRY**
    The hemoglobin of a human fetus differs from adult hemoglobin. Compare the dissociation curves of the two hemoglobins in the graph at right. Propose a hypothesis to explain the benefit of this difference between these two hemoglobins.

12. **SCIENCE, TECHNOLOGY, AND SOCIETY**
    Hundreds of studies have linked smoking with cardiovascular and lung disease. According to most health authorities, smoking is the leading cause of preventable, premature death in the United States. Antismoking groups have proposed that cigarette advertising in all media be banned entirely. What are some arguments in favor of a total ban on cigarette advertising? What are arguments in opposition? Do you favor or oppose such a ban? Defend your position.

13.

    Environmental Interactions Some athletes prepare for competition at sea level by sleeping in a tent in which P_{O_2} is kept artificially low. When climbing very high peaks, some mountaineers breathe from bottles of pure O_2. In a short essay (100–150 words), relate these behaviors to the mechanism of O_2 transport in the human body and to our physiological interactions with our gaseous environment.

For selected answers, see Appendix A.

Mastering**BIOLOGY**   www.masteringbiology.com

1. MasteringBiology® Assignments
   BioFlix **Tutorial** Gas Exchange
   Tutorial Gas Transport in Blood
   Activities Mammalian Cardiovascular System Structure • The Human Heart • Path of Blood Flow in Mammals • Mammalian Cardiovascular System Function • Discovery Channel Video: Blood • The Human Respiratory System • Gas Exchange in the Lungs and Tissues • Transport of Respiratory Gases
   Questions Student Misconceptions • Reading Quiz • Multiple Choice • End-of-Chapter

2. eText
   Read your book online, search, take notes, highlight text, and more.

3. The Study Area
   Practice Tests • Cumulative Test • **BioFlix** 3-D Animations • MP3 Tutor Sessions • Videos • Activities • Investigations • Lab Media • Audio Glossary • Word Study Tools • Art

43

The Immune System

▲ **Figure 43.1 How do an animal's immune cells recognize foreign cells?**

KEY CONCEPTS

43.1 In innate immunity, recognition and response rely on traits common to groups of pathogens

43.2 In adaptive immunity, receptors provide pathogen-specific recognition

43.3 Adaptive immunity defends against infection of body fluids and body cells

43.4 Disruptions in immune system function can elicit or exacerbate disease

OVERVIEW

Recognition and Response

Pathogens, agents that cause disease, infect a wide range of animals. For a virus, bacterium, fungus, or other pathogen, the internal environment of an animal is a nearly ideal habitat. The animal body offers a ready source of nutrients, a protected setting for growth and reproduction, and a means of transport to new environments. From the perspective of a cold or flu virus, we are wonderful hosts. From our vantage point, things are not so ideal. Fortunately, adaptations have arisen over the course of evolution that protect animals against many invaders.

Dedicated immune cells in the body fluids and tissues of most animals specifically interact with and destroy pathogens. As shown in Figure 43.1 (a colorized scanning electron micrograph), an immune cell called a macrophage (blue) can engulf a yeast cell (green). Additional responses to infection take many forms, including proteins that punch holes in bacterial membranes or block viruses from entering body cells. These and other defenses make up the **immune system**, which enables an animal to avoid or limit many infections. A foreign molecule or cell doesn't have to be pathogenic to elicit an immune response, but we'll focus here on the immune system's role in defending against pathogens.

All animals have **innate immunity**, a defense that is active immediately upon infection and is the same whether or not the pathogen has been encountered previously. Innate immunity includes an outer covering, such as a skin or shell, that provides a significant barrier to entry by microbes. Sealing off the entire body surface is impossible, however, because gas exchange, nutrition, and reproduction require openings to the environment. Chemical secretions that trap or kill microbes guard the body's entrances and exits, while the linings of the digestive tract, airway, and other exchange surfaces provide additional barriers to infection.

If a pathogen breaches barrier defenses and enters the body, the problem of how to fend off attack changes substantially. Housed within the body fluids and tissues, the invader is no longer an outsider. To fight infections, an animal's immune system must detect foreign particles and cells within the body. In other words, a properly functioning immune system distinguishes nonself from self. Detection of nonself is accomplished by *molecular recognition*, in which receptor molecules bind specifically to molecules from foreign cells or viruses.

In innate immunity, a small preset group of receptor proteins bind to molecules or structures that are absent from animal bodies but common to a group of viruses, bacteria, or other microbes. Binding of an innate immune receptor to a foreign molecule activates internal defenses, enabling responses to a very broad range of pathogens.

A different type of molecular recognition provides the basis for **adaptive immunity**, a defense found only in vertebrates. Animals with adaptive immunity produce a vast arsenal of receptors, each of which recognizes a feature typically found only on a particular part of a particular molecule in a particular pathogen. As a result, recognition and response in adaptive immunity occur with tremendous specificity.

The adaptive immune response, also known as the acquired immune response, is activated after the innate immune response and develops more slowly. The names *adaptive* and

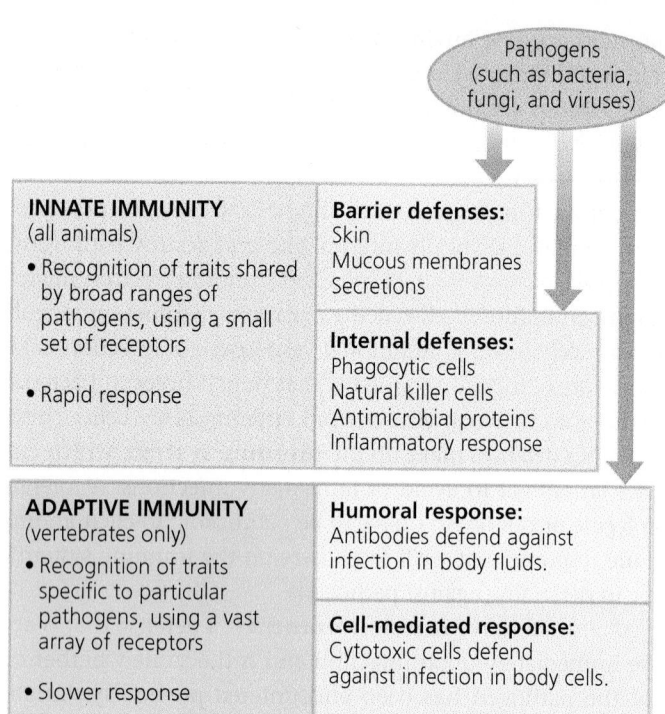

INNATE IMMUNITY (all animals)	Barrier defenses:
• Recognition of traits shared by broad ranges of pathogens, using a small set of receptors • Rapid response	Skin Mucous membranes Secretions
	Internal defenses: Phagocytic cells Natural killer cells Antimicrobial proteins Inflammatory response

ADAPTIVE IMMUNITY (vertebrates only)	Humoral response:
• Recognition of traits specific to particular pathogens, using a vast array of receptors • Slower response	Antibodies defend against infection in body fluids.
	Cell-mediated response: Cytotoxic cells defend against infection in body cells.

▲ Figure 43.2 **Overview of animal immunity.** Immune responses in animals can be divided into innate and adaptive immunity. Some components of innate immunity contribute to activation of adaptive immune defenses.

acquired reflect the fact that this immune response is enhanced by previous exposure to the infecting pathogen. Examples of adaptive responses include the synthesis of proteins that inactivate a bacterial toxin and the targeted killing of a virus-infected body cell.

Figure 43.2 provides an overview of the basic components of innate and adaptive immunity. In this chapter, you will learn how each type of immunity protects animals from disease. You will also examine how pathogens can avoid or overwhelm the immune system and how defects in the immune system can imperil an animal's health.

CONCEPT 43.1

In innate immunity, recognition and response rely on traits common to groups of pathogens

Innate immunity is found in all animals (as well as in plants). In exploring innate immunity, we'll begin with invertebrates, which repel and fight infection with only this type of immunity. We'll then turn to vertebrates, in which innate immunity serves both as an immediate defense against infection and as the foundation for adaptive immune defenses.

Innate Immunity of Invertebrates

The great success of insects in terrestrial and freshwater habitats teeming with diverse microbes highlights the effectiveness of invertebrate innate immunity. In each of these environments, insects rely on their exoskeleton as a first line of defense against infection. Composed largely of the polysaccharide chitin, the exoskeleton provides an effective barrier defense against most pathogens. A chitin-based barrier is also present in the insect intestine, where it blocks infection by many pathogens ingested with food. **Lysozyme**, an enzyme that breaks down bacterial cell walls, further protects the insect digestive system.

Any pathogen that breaches an insect's barrier defenses encounters a number of internal immune defenses. Immune cells called *hemocytes* travel throughout the body in the hemolymph, the insect circulatory fluid. Some hemocytes carry out a defense called **phagocytosis**, the cellular ingestion and digestion of bacteria and other foreign substances (**Figure 43.3**). Other hemocytes trigger the production of chemicals that kill pathogens and help entrap large parasites, such as *Plasmodium*, the parasite of mosquitoes that causes malaria. In addition, encounters with pathogens in the hemolymph cause hemocytes and certain other cells to secrete *antimicrobial peptides*, which are short chains of amino acids. The antimicrobial peptides circulate throughout the body of the insect (**Figure 43.4**) and inactivate or kill fungi and bacteria by disrupting their plasma membranes.

Immune cells of insects bind to molecules found only in the outer layers of fungi or bacteria. Fungal cell walls contain certain unique polysaccharides, whereas bacterial cell walls have polymers containing combinations of sugars and amino

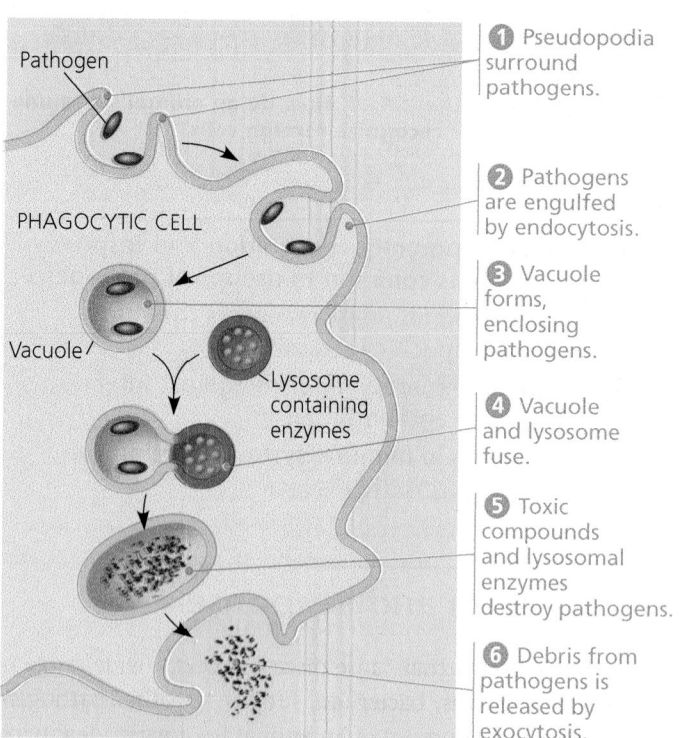

① Pseudopodia surround pathogens.

② Pathogens are engulfed by endocytosis.

③ Vacuole forms, enclosing pathogens.

④ Vacuole and lysosome fuse.

⑤ Toxic compounds and lysosomal enzymes destroy pathogens.

⑥ Debris from pathogens is released by exocytosis.

▲ Figure 43.3 **Phagocytosis.** This schematic depicts events in the ingestion and destruction of a microbe by a typical phagocytic cell.

▲ **Figure 43.4 An inducible innate immune response.** These fruit flies were engineered to express the green fluorescent protein (GFP) gene upon activation of the innate immune response. The fly on the top was injected with bacteria; the fly on the bottom was not. Only the infected fly activates antimicrobial peptide genes, produces GFP, and glows a bright green under fluorescent light.

acids not found in animal cells. Such macromolecules serve as identity tags in the process of pathogen recognition. Insect immune cells secrete specialized recognition proteins, each of which binds to a macromolecule characteristic of fungi or a broad class of bacteria.

Innate immune responses are distinct for different classes of pathogens. For example, when the fungus *Neurospora crassa* infects a fruit fly, pieces of the fungal cell wall bind a recognition protein. Together, the complex activates the protein Toll, a receptor on the surface of hemocytes. Signal transduction from the Toll receptor to the cell nucleus leads to synthesis of a set of antimicrobial peptides active against fungi. If the fly is instead infected by the bacterium *Micrococcus luteus*, a different recognition protein is activated, and the fly produces a different set of antimicrobial peptides effective against *M. luteus* and many related bacteria.

Because fruit flies secrete many distinct antimicrobial peptides in response to a single infection, it is difficult to study the activity of any one peptide. To get around this problem, Bruno Lemaitre and fellow researchers used modern genetic techniques to reprogram the fly immune system (Figure 43.5). They found that the synthesis of a single type of antimicrobial peptide in the fly's body could provide an effective immune defense. They also showed that particular antimicrobial peptides act against different kinds of pathogens.

▼ Figure 43.5

INQUIRY

Can a single antimicrobial peptide protect fruit flies against infection?

EXPERIMENT In 2002, Bruno Lemaitre and colleagues in France devised a novel strategy to test the function of a single antimicrobial peptide. They began with a mutant fruit fly strain in which pathogens are recognized but the signaling that would normally trigger innate immune responses is blocked. As a result, the mutant flies do not make any antimicrobial peptides. The researchers then genetically engineered some of the mutant fruit flies to express significant amounts of a single antimicrobial peptide, either drosomycin or defensin. The scientists infected the various flies with the fungus *Neurospora crassa* and monitored survival over a five-day period. They repeated the procedure for infection by the bacterium *Micrococcus luteus*.

RESULTS

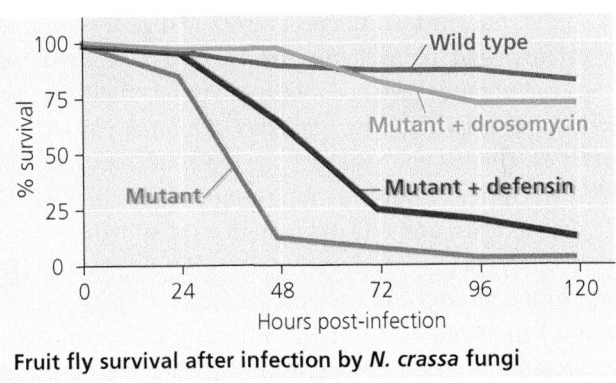

Fruit fly survival after infection by *N. crassa* fungi

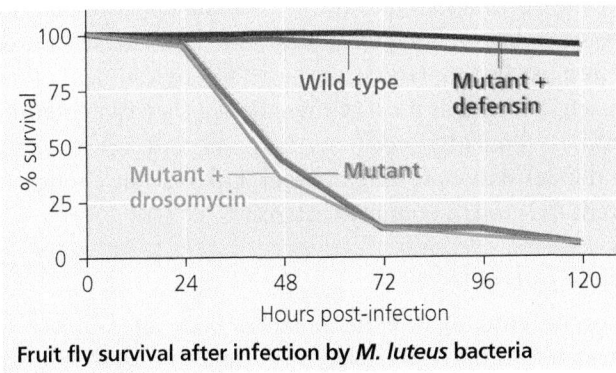

Fruit fly survival after infection by *M. luteus* bacteria

CONCLUSION Each of the two antimicrobial peptides provided a protective immune response. Furthermore, the different peptides defended against different pathogens. Drosomycin was effective against *N. crassa*, and defensin was effective against *M. luteus*.

SOURCE P. Tzou, J. Reichhart, and B. Lemaitre, Constitutive expression of a single antimicrobial peptide can restore wild-type resistance to infection in immunodeficient *Drosophila* mutants, *Proceedings of the National Academy of Sciences USA* 99:2152–2157 (2002).

WHAT IF? Even if a particular antimicrobial peptide showed no beneficial effect in such an experiment, why might it still be beneficial to flies?

Innate Immunity of Vertebrates

Among vertebrates, innate immune defenses coexist with the more recently evolved system of adaptive immunity. Because most of the recent discoveries regarding vertebrate innate immunity have come from studies of mice and humans, we'll focus here on mammals. We'll consider the innate defenses that are similar to those found among invertebrates: barrier defenses, phagocytosis, and antimicrobial peptides. We'll also examine some unique aspects of vertebrate innate immunity, such as natural killer cells, interferons, and the inflammatory response.

Barrier Defenses

In mammals, epithelial tissues block the entry of many pathogens. These barrier defenses include not only the skin but also the mucous membranes lining the digestive, respiratory, urinary, and reproductive tracts. Certain cells of the mucous membranes produce *mucus*, a viscous fluid that enhances defenses by trapping microbes and other particles. In the trachea, ciliated epithelial cells sweep mucus and any entrapped microbes upward, helping prevent infection of the lungs. Saliva, tears, and mucous secretions that bathe various exposed epithelia provide a washing action that also inhibits colonization by fungi and bacteria.

Beyond their physical role in inhibiting microbial entry, body secretions create an environment that is hostile to many microbes. Lysozyme in tears, saliva, and mucous secretions destroys the cell walls of susceptible bacteria as they enter the openings around the eyes or the upper respiratory tract. Microbes in food or water and those in swallowed mucus must also contend with the acidic environment of the stomach, which kills most of them before they can enter the intestines. Similarly, secretions from oil and sweat glands give human skin a pH ranging from 3 to 5, acidic enough to prevent the growth of many bacteria.

Cellular Innate Defenses

Pathogens entering the mammalian body are subject to phagocytosis. Phagocytic cells detect fungal or bacterial components using several types of receptors, some of which are very similar to the Toll receptor of insects. Each mammalian **Toll-like receptor (TLR)** binds to fragments of molecules characteristic of a set of pathogens **(Figure 43.6)**. For example, TLR3, on the inner surface of vesicles formed by endocytosis, is the sensor for double-stranded RNA, a form of nucleic acid characteristic of certain viruses. Similarly, TLR4, located on immune cell plasma membranes, recognizes lipopolysaccharide, a type of molecule found on the surface of many bacteria; and TLR5 recognizes flagellin, the main protein of bacterial flagella. In each case, the recognized macromolecule is normally absent from the vertebrate body and is an essential component of certain groups of pathogens.

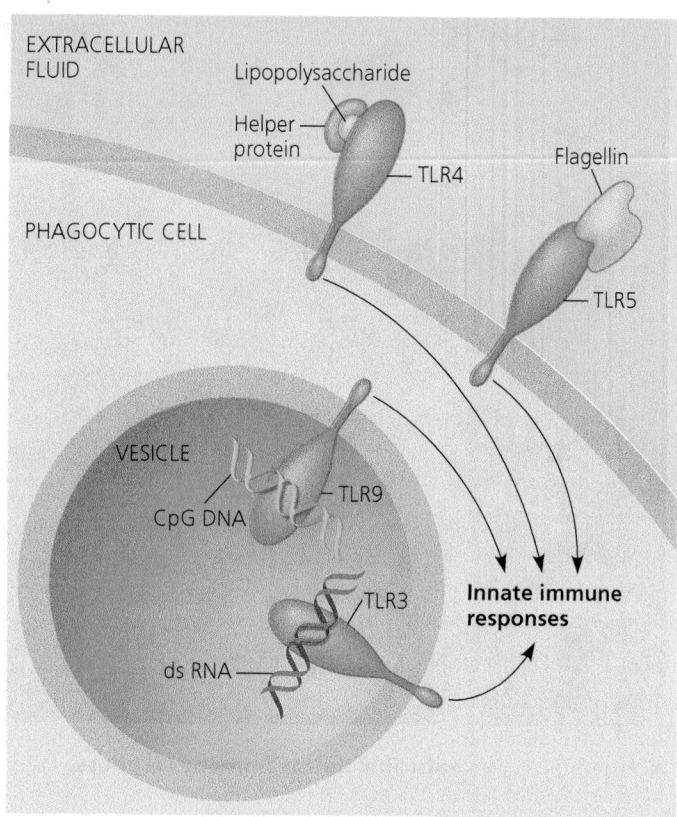

▲ **Figure 43.6 TLR signaling.** Each mammalian Toll-like receptor (TLR) recognizes a molecular pattern characteristic of a group of pathogens. Lipopolysaccharide, flagellin, CpG DNA (DNA containing unmethylated CG sequences), and double-stranded (ds) RNA are all found in bacteria, fungi, or viruses, but not in animal cells. Together with other recognition and response factors, TLR proteins trigger internal innate immune defenses.

? *Some TLR proteins are on the cell surface, whereas others are inside vesicles. Suggest a possible benefit of this distribution.*

After detecting invading pathogens, a phagocytic cell engulfs them, trapping them in a vacuole. The vacuole then fuses with a lysosome (see Figure 43.3), leading to destruction of the invaders in two ways. First, gases produced in the lysosome poison the engulfed pathogens. Second, lysozyme and other enzymes in the lysosome degrade the components of the pathogens.

The two main types of phagocytic cells in the mammalian body are neutrophils and macrophages. **Neutrophils**, which circulate in the blood, are attracted by signals from infected tissues and then engulf and destroy the infecting pathogens. **Macrophages** ("big eaters"), like the one shown in Figure 43.1, are larger phagocytic cells. Some migrate throughout the body, whereas others reside permanently in organs and tissues where they are likely to encounter pathogens. For example, some macrophages are located in the spleen, where pathogens in the blood become trapped.

Two other types of phagocytic cells—dendritic cells and eosinophils—provide additional functions in innate defense. **Dendritic cells** mainly populate tissues, such as skin, that contact the environment. They stimulate adaptive immunity against pathogens they encounter and engulf, as we'll explore shortly. *Eosinophils*, often found beneath mucosal surfaces, have low phagocytic activity but are important in defending against multicellular invaders, such as parasitic worms. Upon encountering such parasites, eosinophils discharge destructive enzymes.

Cellular innate defenses in vertebrates also involve **natural killer cells**. These cells circulate through the body and detect the abnormal array of surface proteins characteristic of some virus-infected and cancerous cells. Natural killer cells do not engulf stricken cells. Instead, they release chemicals that lead to cell death, inhibiting further spread of the virus or cancer.

Many cellular innate defenses of vertebrates involve the lymphatic system, a network that distributes the fluid called lymph throughout the body **(Figure 43.7)**. Some macrophages reside in the structures called lymph nodes, where they engulf pathogens that have flowed from the interstitial fluid into the lymph. Dendritic cells reside outside the lymphatic system but migrate to lymph nodes after interaction with pathogens. Within the lymph nodes, dendritic cells interact with other immune cells, stimulating adaptive immunity.

Antimicrobial Peptides and Proteins

In mammals, pathogen recognition triggers the production and release of a variety of peptides and proteins that attack pathogens or impede their reproduction. Some of these defense molecules function like the antimicrobial peptides of insects, damaging broad groups of pathogens by disrupting membrane integrity. Others, including the interferons and complement proteins, are unique to vertebrate immune systems.

Interferons are proteins that provide innate defense by interfering with viral infections. Virus-infected body cells secrete interferons, which induce nearby uninfected cells to produce substances that inhibit viral reproduction. In this way, interferons limit the cell-to-cell spread of viruses in the body, helping control viral infections such as colds and influenza. Some white blood cells secrete a different type of interferon that helps activate macrophages, enhancing their phagocytic ability. Pharmaceutical companies now use recombinant DNA technology to mass-produce interferons to help treat certain viral infections, such as hepatitis C.

The infection-fighting **complement system** consists of roughly 30 proteins in blood plasma. These proteins circulate in an inactive state and are activated by substances on the surface of many microbes. Activation results in a cascade of biochemical reactions that can lead to lysis (bursting) of invading cells. The complement system also functions in the inflammatory response, our next topic, as well as in the adaptive defenses discussed later in the chapter.

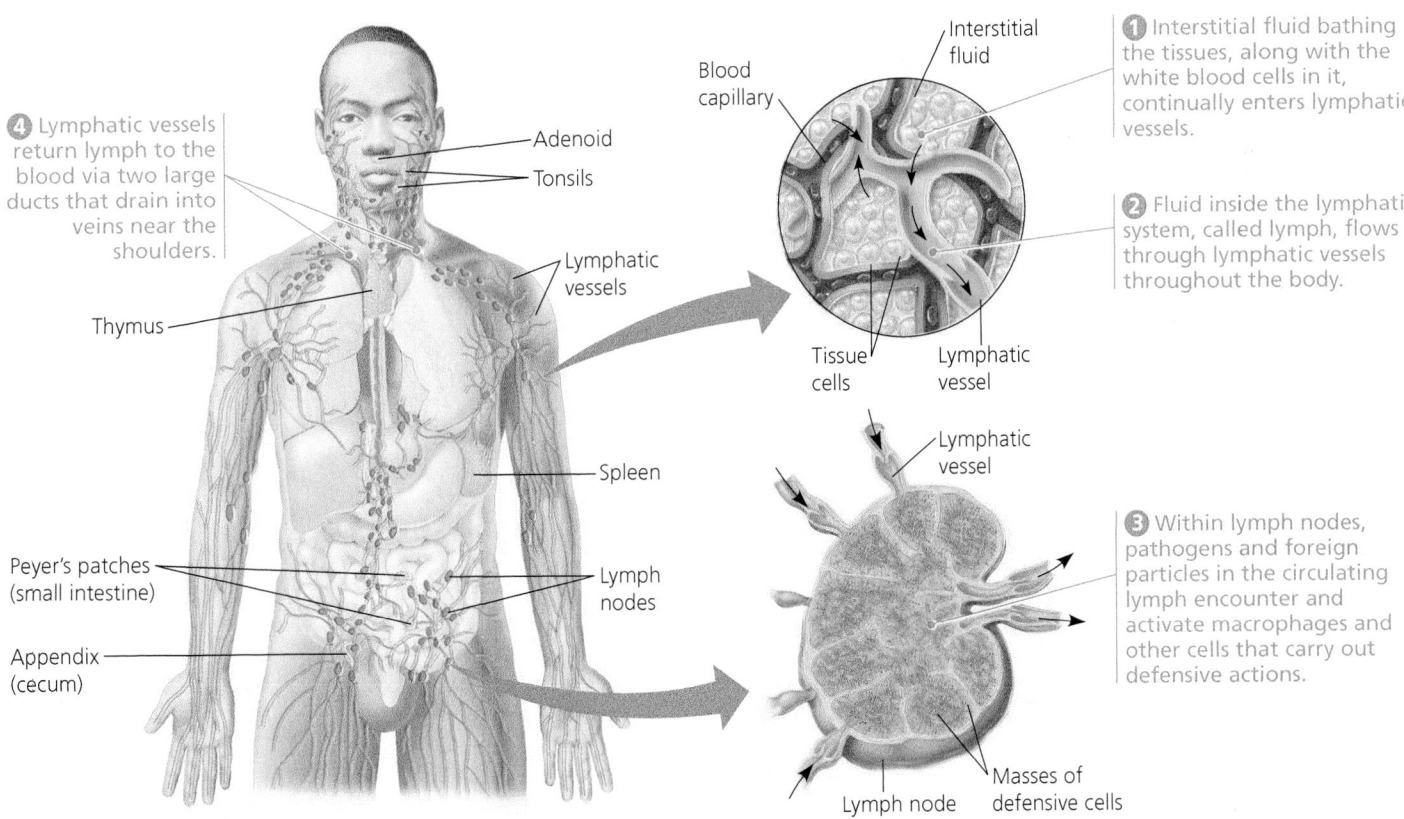

▲ **Figure 43.7 The human lymphatic system.** The lymphatic system consists of lymphatic vessels (shown in green), through which lymph travels, and structures that trap foreign substances. These structures include lymph nodes (orange) and lymphoid organs (yellow): the adenoids, tonsils, spleen, Peyer's patches, and appendix. Steps 1–4 trace the flow of lymph and illustrate the critical role of lymph nodes in activating adaptive immunity. (See also p. 909 for a description of the relationship between the lymphatic and circulatory systems.)

Inflammatory Response

The pain and swelling that alert you to a splinter under your skin are the result of a local **inflammatory response**, the changes brought about by signaling molecules released upon injury or infection (**Figure 43.8**). One important inflammatory signaling molecule is **histamine**, which is stored in the granules (vesicles) of **mast cells**, found in connective tissue. Histamine released at sites of damage triggers nearby blood vessels to dilate and become more permeable. Activated macrophages and neutrophils discharge **cytokines**, signaling molecules that enhance an immune response. These cytokines promote blood flow to the site of injury or infection. The increase in local blood supply causes the redness and increased skin temperature typical of the inflammatory response (from the Latin *inflammare*, to set on fire). Blood-engorged capillaries leak fluid into neighboring tissues, causing swelling.

During inflammation, cycles of signaling and response transform the site. Activated complement proteins promote further release of histamine, attracting more phagocytic cells that enter injured tissues (see Figure 43.8) and carry out additional phagocytosis. At the same time, enhanced blood flow to the site helps deliver antimicrobial peptides. The result is an accumulation of *pus*, a fluid rich in white blood cells, dead pathogens, and cell debris from damaged tissue.

A minor injury or infection causes a local inflammatory response, but severe tissue damage or infection may lead to a response that is systemic (throughout the body). Cells in injured or infected tissue often secrete molecules that stimulate the release of additional neutrophils from the bone marrow. In a severe infection, such as meningitis or appendicitis, the number of white blood cells in the blood may increase several-fold within a few hours.

Another systemic inflammatory response is fever. In response to certain pathogens, substances released by activated macrophages cause the body's thermostat to reset to a higher temperature (see Chapter 40). The benefits of the resulting fever are still a subject of debate. One of several competing hypotheses is that an elevated body temperature may enhance phagocytosis and, by speeding up chemical reactions, accelerate tissue repair.

Certain bacterial infections can induce an overwhelming systemic inflammatory response, leading to a life-threatening condition called *septic shock*. Characterized by very high fever, low blood pressure, and poor blood flow through capillaries, septic shock occurs most often in the very old and the very young. It is fatal in more than one-third of cases and kills more than 90,000 people each year in the United States alone.

Chronic (ongoing) inflammation can also threaten human health. For example, millions of individuals worldwide suffer from Crohn's disease and ulcerative colitis, often debilitating disorders in which an unregulated inflammatory response disrupts intestinal function.

Evasion of Innate Immunity by Pathogens

Adaptations have evolved in some pathogens that enable them to avoid destruction by phagocytic cells. For example, the outer capsule that surrounds certain bacteria interferes with molecular recognition and phagocytosis. One such bacterium, *Streptococcus pneumoniae*, played a critical role in the discovery that DNA can convey genetic information (see

① At the injury site, mast cells release histamines, and macrophages secrete cytokines. These signaling molecules cause nearby capillaries to dilate.

② Capillaries widen and become more permeable, allowing fluid containing antimicrobial peptides to enter the tissue. Signals released by immune cells attract neutrophils.

③ Neutrophils digest pathogens and cell debris at the site, and the tissue heals.

▲ **Figure 43.8 Major events in a local inflammatory response.**

Figure 16.2). Some bacteria, after being engulfed by a host cell, resist breakdown within lysosomes. An example is the bacterium that causes tuberculosis (TB). Rather than being destroyed within host cells, this bacterium grows and reproduces, effectively hidden from the body's innate immune defenses. These and other mechanisms that prevent destruction by the innate immune system make certain fungi and bacteria substantial pathogenic threats. Indeed, TB kills more than a million people a year worldwide.

CONCEPT CHECK 43.1

1. Although pus is often seen simply as a sign of infection, it is also an indicator of immune defenses in action. Explain.
2. **MAKE CONNECTIONS** How do the molecules that activate the vertebrate TLR signal transduction pathway differ from the ligands in most other pathways, such as those shown in Concept 11.2 (pp. 210–214)?
3. **WHAT IF?** Suppose humans were the major host for a bacterial species. What temperature would you predict would be optimal for growth of this species? Explain.

For suggested answers, see Appendix A.

CONCEPT 43.2

In adaptive immunity, receptors provide pathogen-specific recognition

Vertebrates are unique in having adaptive immunity in addition to innate immunity. The adaptive response relies on T cells and B cells, which are types of white blood cells called **lymphocytes**. Like all blood cells, lymphocytes originate from stem cells in the bone marrow. Some lymphocytes migrate from the bone marrow to the **thymus**, an organ in the thoracic cavity above the heart (see Figure 43.7). These lymphocytes mature into **T cells**. Lymphocytes that remain and mature in the bone marrow develop as **B cells**. (Lymphocytes of a third type remain in the blood and become the natural killer cells active in innate immunity.)

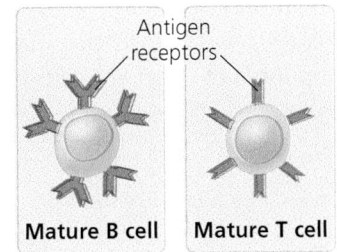

Mature B cell   Mature T cell

Any substance that elicits a response from a B cell or T cell is called an **antigen**. In adaptive immunity, recognition occurs when a B cell or T cell binds to an antigen, such as a bacterial or viral protein, via a protein called an **antigen receptor**. An antigen receptor is specific enough to bind to just one part of one molecule from a particular pathogen, such as a species of bacteria or strain of virus. Although the cells of the immune system produce millions of different antigen receptors, all of the antigen receptors made by a single B or T cell are identical. Infection by a virus, bacterium, or other pathogen triggers activation of B and T cells with antigen receptors specific for parts of that pathogen. B and T cells are shown here with only a few antigen receptors, but there are actually about 100,000 antigen receptors on the surface of a single B or T cell.

Antigens are usually foreign and are typically large molecules, either proteins or polysaccharides. Many antigens protrude from the surface of foreign cells or viruses. Other antigens, such as toxins secreted by bacteria, are released into the extracellular fluid.

The small, accessible portion of an antigen that binds to an antigen receptor is called an **epitope**, or *antigenic determinant*. An example is a group of amino acids in a particular protein. A single antigen usually has several different epitopes, each binding a receptor with a different specificity. Because all antigen receptors produced by a single B cell or T cell are identical, they bind to the same epitope. Each B cell or T cell thus displays *specificity* for a particular epitope, enabling it to respond to any pathogen that produces molecules containing that same epitope.

The antigen receptors of B cells and T cells have similar components, but they encounter antigens in different ways. We'll consider the two processes in turn.

Antigen Recognition by B Cells and Antibodies

Each B cell antigen receptor is a Y-shaped molecule consisting of four polypeptide chains: two identical **heavy chains** and two identical **light chains**, with disulfide bridges linking the chains together (Figure 43.9). A transmembrane region near one end of each heavy chain anchors the receptor in the cell's plasma membrane. A short tail region at the end of the heavy chain extends into the cytoplasm.

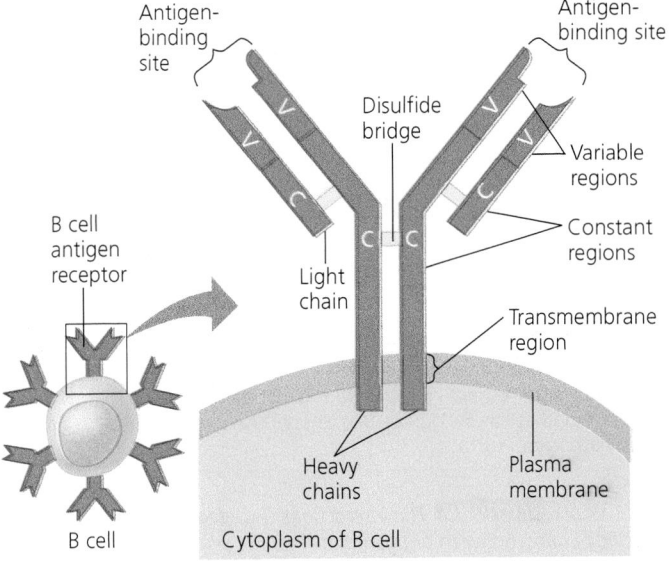

▲ Figure 43.9 **The structure of a B cell antigen receptor.**

The light and heavy chains each have a *constant (C) region*, where amino acid sequences vary little among the receptors on different B cells. The C region includes the cytoplasmic tail and transmembrane region of the heavy chain and all of the disulfide bridges. Within the two tips of the Y shape, the light and heavy chains each have a *variable (V) region*, so named because its amino acid sequence varies extensively from one B cell to another. Together, parts of a heavy-chain V region and a light-chain V region form an asymmetrical binding site for an antigen. As shown in Figure 43.9, each B cell antigen receptor has two identical antigen-binding sites.

The binding of a B cell antigen receptor to an antigen is an early step in B cell activation, leading eventually to formation of cells that secrete a soluble form of the receptor (Figure 43.10a). This secreted protein is called an **antibody**, or **immunoglobulin (Ig)**. Antibodies have the same Y-shaped organization as B cell antigen receptors, but they are secreted rather than membrane bound. It is the antibodies, rather than the B cells themselves, that actually help defend against pathogens. Antibodies have distinct functions, as we'll see later.

The antigen-binding site of a membrane-bound receptor or antibody has a unique shape that provides a lock-and-key fit for a particular epitope. Many noncovalent bonds between an epitope and the binding surface provide a stable and specific interaction. Differences in the amino acid sequences of variable regions provide the variation in binding surfaces that enables this highly specific binding.

B cell antigen receptors and antibodies bind to intact antigens in the blood and lymph. As illustrated in Figure 43.10b for antibodies, they can bind to antigens on the surface of pathogens or free in body fluids. The antigen receptors of T cells function quite differently, as we'll see next.

Antigen Recognition by T Cells

For a T cell, the antigen receptor consists of two different polypeptide chains, an α *chain* and a β *chain*, linked by a disulfide bridge (Figure 43.11). Near the base of the T cell antigen receptor (often called simply a T cell receptor) is a transmembrane region that anchors the molecule in the cell's plasma membrane. At the outer tip of the molecule, the variable (V) regions of α and β chains together form a single antigen-binding site. The remainder of the molecule is made up of the constant (C) regions.

Although T cell and B cell antigen receptors have many features in common, they function in fundamentally different ways. Whereas the antigen receptors of B cells bind to epitopes of intact antigens circulating in body fluids, those of

▼ Figure 43.10 **Antigen recognition by B cells and antibodies.**

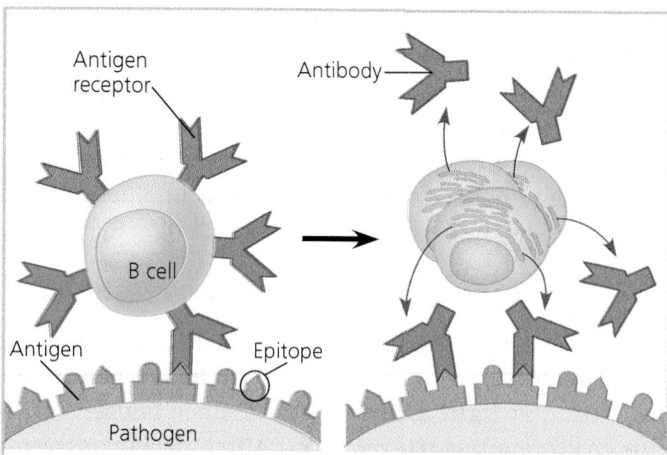

(a) B cell antigen receptors and antibodies. An antigen receptor of a B cell binds to an epitope, a particular part of an antigen. Following binding, the B cell gives rise to cells that secrete a soluble form of the antigen receptor. This soluble receptor, called an antibody, is specific for the same epitope as the original B cell.

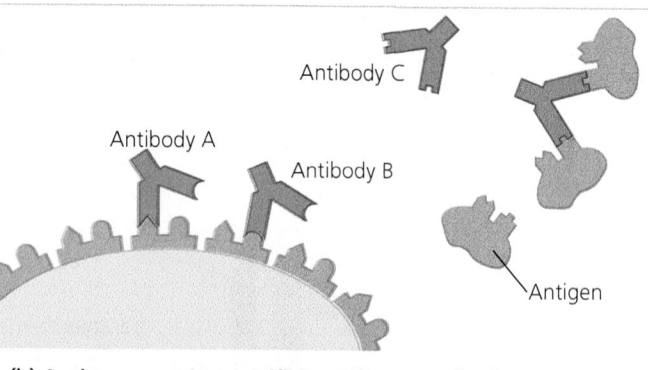

(b) Antigen receptor specificity. Different antibodies can recognize distinct epitopes on the same antigen. Furthermore, antibodies can recognize free antigens as well as antigens on a pathogen's surface.

MAKE CONNECTIONS *The interactions depicted here involve a highly specific binding between antigen and receptor, as shown in Figure 5.19 (p. 81). How is this similar to the enzyme-substrate interaction shown in Figure 8.14 (p. 154)?*

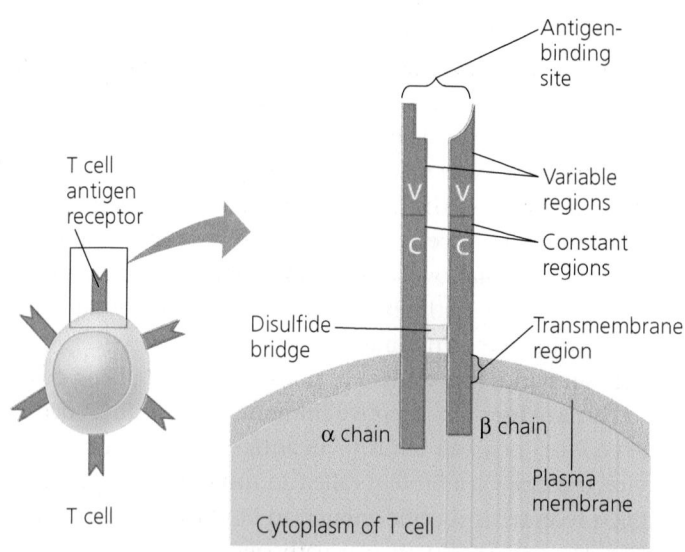

▲ Figure 43.11 **The structure of a T cell antigen receptor.**

T cells bind only to fragments of antigens that are displayed, or *presented*, on the surface of host cells. The host protein that displays the antigen fragment on the cell surface is called an **MHC (major histocompatibility complex) molecule**.

Recognition of protein antigens by T cells begins when a pathogen or part of a pathogen either infects or is taken in by a host cell (Figure 43.12a). Inside the host cell, enzymes in the cell cleave the antigen into smaller peptides. Each peptide, called an *antigen fragment*, then binds to an MHC molecule inside the cell. Movement of the MHC molecule and bound antigen fragment to the cell surface results in **antigen presentation**, the display of the antigen fragment in an exposed groove of the MHC protein. Figure 43.12b shows a close-up view of antigen presentation, which

advertises the fact that a host cell contains a foreign substance. If the cell displaying an antigen fragment encounters a T cell with the right specificity, the antigen receptor on the T cell can bind to both the antigen fragment and the MHC molecule. This interaction of an MHC molecule, an antigen fragment, and an antigen receptor is necessary for a T cell to participate in an adaptive immune response, as we'll see later.

B Cell and T Cell Development

Now that you know how B cells and T cells recognize antigens, let's consider four major characteristics of adaptive immunity. First, there is an immense diversity of lymphocytes and receptors, enabling the immune system to detect pathogens never before encountered. Second, adaptive immunity normally has self-tolerance, the lack of reactivity against an animal's own molecules and cells. Third, cell proliferation triggered by activation greatly increases the number of B and T cells specific for an antigen. Fourth, there is a stronger and more rapid response to an antigen encountered previously, due to a feature known as *immunological memory*.

Receptor diversity and self-tolerance arise as a lymphocyte matures. Proliferation of cells and the formation of immunological memory occur later, after a mature lymphocyte encounters and binds to a specific antigen. We'll consider these four characteristics in the order in which they develop.

Generation of B and T Cell Diversity

Each person makes more than 1 million different B cell antigen receptors and 10 million different T cell antigen receptors. Yet there are only about 20,000 protein-coding genes in the human genome. How, then, do we generate such remarkable diversity in antigen receptors? The answer lies in combinations. Think of selecting a car with a choice of three interior colors and six exterior colors. There are 18 (3 × 6) color combinations to consider. Similarly, by combining variable elements, the immune system assembles many different receptors from a much smaller collection of parts.

To understand the origin of receptor diversity, let's consider an immunoglobulin (Ig) gene that encodes the light chain of both secreted antibodies (immunoglobulins) and membrane-bound B cell antigen receptors. Although we'll analyze only a single Ig light-chain gene, all B and T cell antigen receptor genes undergo very similar transformations.

The capacity to generate diversity is built into the structure of Ig genes. A receptor light chain is encoded by three gene segments: a variable (*V*) segment, a joining (*J*) segment, and a constant (*C*) segment. The *V* and *J* segments together encode the variable region of the receptor chain, while the *C* segment encodes the constant region. The light-chain gene contains a single *C* segment, 40 different *V* segments, and 5 different *J* segments. These alternative copies of the *V* and *J* segments are arranged within the gene in a

▼ Figure 43.12 **Antigen recognition by T cells.**

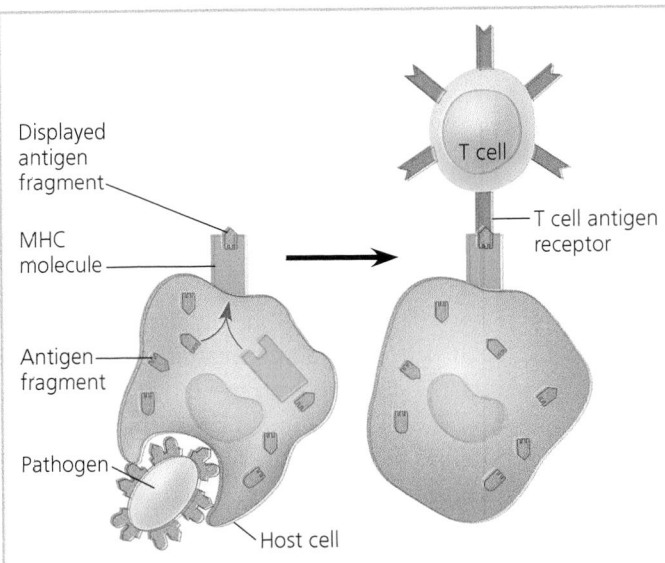

(a) **Antigen recognition by a T cell.** Inside the host cell, an antigen fragment from a pathogen binds to an MHC molecule and is brought up to the cell surface, where it is displayed. The combination of MHC molecule and antigen fragment is recognized by a T cell.

(b) **A closer look at antigen presentation.** As shown in this ribbon model, the top of the MHC molecule cradles an antigen fragment, like a bun holding a hot dog. An MHC molecule can display many different antigen fragments, but the antigen receptor of a T cell is specific for a single antigen fragment.

DNA of undifferentiated B cell

V_{37} V_{38} V_{39} V_{40} J_1 J_2 J_3 J_4 J_5 Intron C

① Recombination deletes DNA between randomly selected V segment and J segment

DNA of differentiated B cell

V_{37} V_{38} V_{39} J_5 Intron C

Functional gene

② Transcription of permanently rearranged, functional gene

pre-mRNA V_{39} J_5 Intron C

③ RNA processing (removal of intron; addition of cap and poly-A tail)

mRNA Cap V_{39} J_5 C Poly-A tail

④ Translation

Light-chain polypeptide V C

Variable region   Constant region

Antigen receptor

B cell

◄ **Figure 43.13**

Immunoglobulin (antibody) gene rearrangement. The joining of randomly selected V and J gene segments (V_{39} and J_5 in this example) results in a functional gene that encodes the light-chain polypeptide of a B cell antigen receptor. Transcription, splicing, and translation result in a light chain that combines with a polypeptide produced from an independently rearranged heavy-chain gene to form a functional receptor. Mature B cells (and T cells) are exceptions to the generalization that all nucleated cells in the body have exactly the same DNA.

MAKE CONNECTIONS

Both alternative splicing (see Figure 18.13 on p. 363) and joining of V and J segments by recombination generate diverse gene products from a limited set of gene segments. How do these processes differ?

series **(Figure 43.13)**. Because a functional gene is built from one copy of each type of segment, the pieces can be combined in 200 different ways (40 V × 5 J × 1 C). The number of different heavy-chain combinations is even greater, resulting in even more diversity.

Assembling a functional Ig gene requires rearranging the DNA. Early in B cell development, an enzyme complex called *recombinase* links one light-chain V gene segment to one J gene segment. This recombination event eliminates the long stretch of DNA between the segments, forming a single exon that is part V and part J. Because there is only an intron between the J and C DNA segments, no further DNA rearrangement is required. Instead, the J and C segments of the RNA transcript will be joined when splicing removes the intervening RNA (see Figure 17.11 to review RNA splicing).

Recombinase acts randomly, linking any one of the 40 V gene segments to any one of the 5 J gene segments. Heavy-chain genes undergo a similar rearrangement. In any given cell, however, only one allele of a light-chain gene and one allele of a heavy-chain gene are rearranged. Furthermore, the rearrangements are permanent and are passed on to the daughter cells when the lymphocyte divides.

After both the light- and heavy-chain genes have rearranged, antigen receptors can be synthesized. The rearranged genes are transcribed, and the transcripts are processed for translation. Following translation, the light chain and heavy chain assemble together, forming an antigen receptor (see Figure 43.13). Each pair of randomly rearranged heavy and light chains results in a different antigen-binding site. For the total population of B cells in a human body, the number of such combinations has been calculated as 3.5×10^6. Furthermore, mutations introduced during VJ recombination add additional variation, making the number of possible antigen-binding specificities even greater.

Origin of Self-Tolerance

How does adaptive immunity distinguish self from nonself? Because antigen receptor genes are randomly rearranged, some immature lymphocytes produce receptors specific for epitopes on the organism's own molecules. If these self-reactive lymphocytes were not eliminated or inactivated, the immune system could not distinguish self from nonself and would attack body proteins, cells, and tissues. Instead, as lymphocytes mature in the bone marrow or thymus, their antigen receptors are tested for self-reactivity. Some B and T cells with receptors specific for the body's own molecules are destroyed by *apoptosis*, which is a programmed cell death (see Chapter 11). The remaining self-reactive lymphocytes are typically rendered nonfunctional, leaving only those that react to foreign molecules. Since the body normally lacks mature lymphocytes that can react against its own components, the immune system is said to exhibit *self-tolerance*.

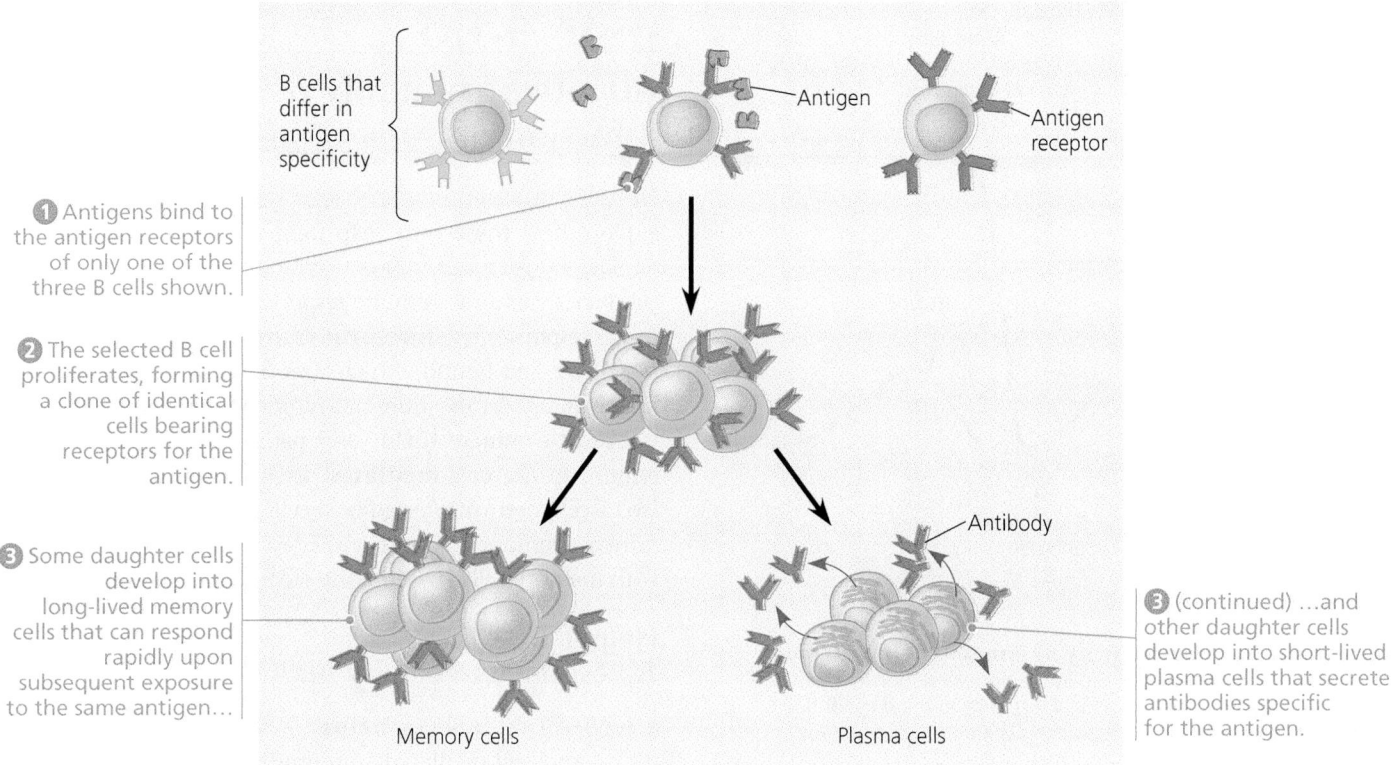

B cells that differ in antigen specificity

Antigen

Antigen receptor

① Antigens bind to the antigen receptors of only one of the three B cells shown.

② The selected B cell proliferates, forming a clone of identical cells bearing receptors for the antigen.

③ Some daughter cells develop into long-lived memory cells that can respond rapidly upon subsequent exposure to the same antigen...

Antibody

③ (continued) ...and other daughter cells develop into short-lived plasma cells that secrete antibodies specific for the antigen.

Memory cells

Plasma cells

▲ **Figure 43.14 Clonal selection.** This figure illustrates clonal selection, using B cells as an example. In response to a specific antigen and to immune cell signals (not shown), one B cell divides and forms a clone of cells. The remaining B cells, which have antigen receptors specific for other antigens, do not respond. The clone of cells formed by the selected B cell gives rise to memory B cells and antibody-secreting plasma cells. T cells also undergo clonal selection, generating memory T cells and effector T cells (cytotoxic T cells and helper T cells).

Proliferation of B Cells and T Cells

Despite the enormous variety of antigen receptors, only a tiny fraction are specific for a given epitope. So how is adaptive immunity so effective? To begin with, an antigen is presented to a steady stream of lymphocytes in the lymph nodes (see Figure 43.7) until a match is made. A successful match then triggers changes in cell number and activity for the lymphocyte to which an antigen has bound.

The binding of an antigen receptor to an epitope initiates events that activate the lymphocyte. Once activated, a B cell or T cell undergoes multiple cell divisions. For each activated cell, the result of this proliferation is a clone, a population of cells that are identical to the original cell. Some cells from this clone become **effector cells**, short-lived cells that take effect immediately against the antigen and any pathogens producing that antigen. The effector forms of B cells are plasma cells, which secrete antibodies. The effector forms of T cells are helper T cells and cytotoxic T cells, whose roles we'll explore in Concept 43.3. The remaining cells in the clone become **memory cells**, long-lived cells that can give rise to effector cells if the same antigen is encountered later in the animal's life.

Figure 43.14 summarizes the proliferation of a lymphocyte into a clone of cells in response to binding to an antigen, using B cells as an example. This process is called **clonal selection** because an encounter with an antigen *selects* which lymphocyte will divide to produce a *clonal* population of thousands of cells specific for a particular epitope.

Immunological Memory

Immunological memory is responsible for the long-term protection that a prior infection or vaccination provides against many diseases, such as chickenpox. This type of protection was noted almost 2,400 years ago by the Greek historian Thucydides. He observed that individuals who had recovered from the plague could safely care for those who were sick or dying, "for the same man was never attacked twice—never at least fatally."

Prior exposure to an antigen alters the speed, strength, and duration of the immune response. The production of effector cells from a clone of lymphocytes during the first exposure to an antigen is the basis for the **primary immune response**. The primary response peaks about 10–17 days after the initial exposure. During this time, selected B cells and T cells give rise to their effector forms. If an individual is exposed again to the same antigen, the response is faster (typically peaking only 2–7 days after exposure), of greater magnitude, and more prolonged. This is the **secondary immune response**, a hallmark of adaptive, or acquired, immunity. Because selected B cells give

Primary immune response to antigen A produces antibodies to A.

Secondary immune response to antigen A produces antibodies to A; primary immune response to antigen B produces antibodies to B.

Antibodies to A

Antibodies to B

Exposure to antigen A

Exposure to antigens A and B

Time (days)

▲ Figure 43.15 **The specificity of immunological memory.** Long-lived memory cells generated in the primary response to antigen A give rise to a heightened secondary response to the same antigen, but do not affect the primary response to a different antigen (B).

rise to antibody-secreting effector cells, measuring the concentrations of specific antibodies in blood over time distinguishes the primary and secondary immune responses (Figure 43.15).

The secondary immune response relies on the reservoir of T and B memory cells generated following initial exposure to an antigen. Because these cells are long-lived, they provide the basis for immunological memory, which can span many decades. (Effector cells have much shorter life spans, which is why the immune response diminishes after an infection is overcome.) If an antigen is encountered again, memory cells specific for that antigen enable the rapid formation of clones of thousands of effector cells also specific for that antigen, thus generating a greatly enhanced immune defense.

Although the processes for antigen recognition, clonal selection, and immunological memory are similar for B cells and T cells, these two classes of lymphocytes fight infection in different ways and in different settings, as we'll explore next.

CONCEPT CHECK 43.2

1. **DRAW IT** Sketch a B cell antigen receptor. Label the V and C regions of the light and heavy chains. Label the antigen-binding sites, disulfide bridges, and transmembrane region. Where are these features located relative to the V and C regions?

2. Explain two advantages of having memory cells when a pathogen is encountered for a second time.

3. **WHAT IF?** If both copies of a light-chain gene and a heavy-chain gene recombined in each (diploid) B cell, how would this affect B cell development?

For suggested answers, see Appendix A.

CONCEPT 43.3

Adaptive immunity defends against infection of body fluids and body cells

Having considered how clones of lymphocytes arise, we now explore how these cells help fight infections and minimize damage by pathogens. The activities of B and T lymphocytes produce a humoral immune response and a cell-mediated immune response. The **humoral immune response** occurs in the blood and lymph, which were long ago called body humors (fluids). In the humoral response, antibodies help neutralize or eliminate toxins and pathogens in the blood and lymph. In the **cell-mediated immune response**, specialized T cells destroy infected host cells. Both responses include a primary immune response and a secondary immune response, with memory cells enabling the secondary response.

Helper T Cells: A Response to Nearly All Antigens

A type of T cell called a **helper T cell** triggers both the humoral and cell-mediated immune responses. Helper T cells themselves do not carry out those responses. Instead, signals from helper T cells initiate production of antibodies that neutralize pathogens and activate T cells that kill infected cells.

Two requirements must be met for a helper T cell to activate adaptive immune responses. First, a foreign molecule must be present that can bind specifically to the antigen receptor of the T cell. Second, this antigen must be displayed on the surface of an **antigen-presenting cell**. The antigen-presenting cell can be a dendritic cell, macrophage, or B cell.

When host cells are infected, they too display antigens on their surface. What then distinguishes an antigen-presenting cell? The answer lies in the existence of two classes of MHC molecules. Most body cells have only class I MHC molecules, but antigen-presenting cells have both class I and class II MHC molecules. The class II molecules provide a molecular signature by which an antigen-presenting cell is recognized.

A helper T cell and the antigen-presenting cell displaying its specific epitope have a complex interaction (Figure 43.16). The antigen receptors on the surface of the helper T cell bind to the antigen fragment and to the class II MHC molecule displaying that fragment on the antigen-presenting cell. At the same time, an accessory protein on the helper T cell surface binds to the class II MHC molecule, helping keep the cells joined. As the two cells interact, signals in the form of cytokines are exchanged in both directions. For example, the cytokines secreted from a dendritic cell act in combination with the antigen to stimulate the helper T cell, causing it to produce its own set of cytokines. Also, extensive contact between the cell surfaces enables further information exchange.

The different types of antigen-presenting cells interact with helper T cells in distinct contexts. Antigen presentation

① After an antigen-presenting cell engulfs and degrades a pathogen, it displays antigen fragments complexed with class II MHC molecules on the cell surface. A specific helper T cell binds to a displayed complex via its antigen receptor and an accessory protein (called CD4). This interaction promotes secretion of cytokines by the antigen-presenting cell.

Antigen-presenting cell

Pathogen

Antigen fragment

Class II MHC molecule
Accessory protein
Antigen receptor
Helper T cell

② Proliferation of the helper T cell, stimulated by cytokines from both the antigen-presenting cell and the helper T cell itself, gives rise to a clone of activated helper T cells (not shown), all with receptors for the same MHC–antigen fragment complex.

Cytokines

Humoral immunity (secretion of antibodies by plasma cells)

B cell

Cytotoxic T cell

Cell-mediated immunity (attack on infected cells)

③ Following proliferation, helper T cells secrete other cytokines, which help activate B cells and cytotoxic T cells.

▲ **Figure 43.16** **The central role of helper T cells in humoral and cell-mediated immune responses.** In this example, a helper T cell responds to a dendritic cell displaying a microbial antigen.

by a dendritic cell or macrophage activates a helper T cell. The helper T cell then proliferates, forming a clone of activated helper T cells. The B cells present antigens to *already* activated helper T cells, which in turn activate the B cells themselves. Activated helper T cells also help stimulate cytotoxic T cells, as we'll discuss next.

Cytotoxic T Cells: A Response to Infected Cells

In the cell-mediated immune response, **cytotoxic T cells** are the effector cells. The term *cytotoxic* refers to their use of toxic gene products to kill infected cells. To become active,

they require signaling molecules from helper T cells as well as interaction with a cell that presents an antigen. Once activated, cytotoxic T cells can eliminate cells that are infected by viruses or other intracellular pathogens.

Fragments of foreign proteins produced in infected host cells associate with class I MHC molecules and are displayed on the cell surface, where they can be recognized by cytotoxic T cells **(Figure 43.17)**. As with helper T cells, cytotoxic T cells have an accessory protein that binds to the MHC molecule, helping keep the two cells in contact while the T cell is activated.

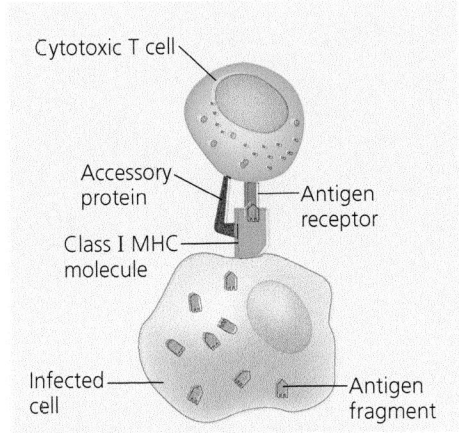

① An activated cytotoxic T cell binds to a class I MHC–antigen fragment complex on an infected cell via its antigen receptor and an accessory protein (called CD8).

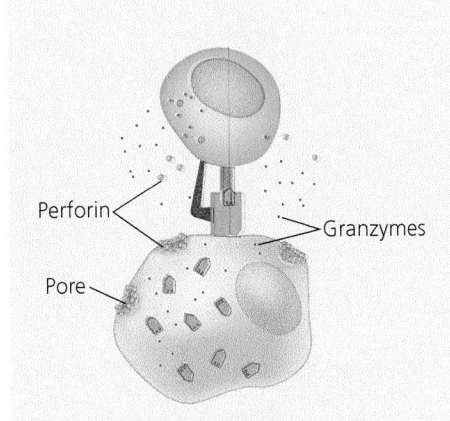

② The T cell releases perforin molecules, which form pores in the infected cell membrane, and granzymes, enzymes that break down proteins. Granzymes enter the infected cell by endocytosis.

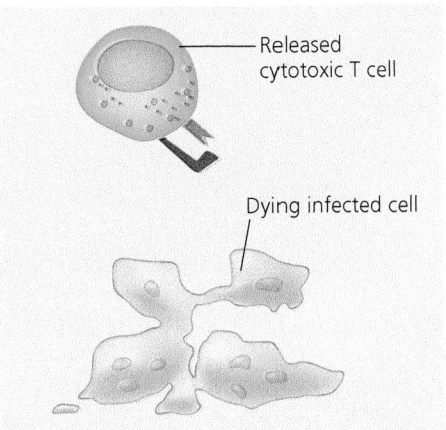

③ The granzymes initiate apoptosis within the infected cell, leading to fragmentation of the nucleus and cytoplasm and eventual cell death. The released cytotoxic T cell can attack other infected cells.

▲ **Figure 43.17** **The killing action of cytotoxic T cells on an infected host cell.** An activated cytotoxic T cell releases molecules that make pores in an infected cell's membrane and enzymes that break down proteins, promoting the cell's death.

The targeted destruction of an infected host cell by a cyto-toxic T cell involves the secretion of proteins that disrupt membrane integrity and trigger apoptosis (see Figure 43.17). The death of the infected cell not only deprives the pathogen of a place to reproduce, but also exposes cell contents to circulating antibodies, which mark them for disposal. After destroying an infected cell, the cytotoxic T cell can move on and kill other cells infected with the same pathogen.

B Cells and Antibodies: A Response to Extracellular Pathogens

The secretion of antibodies by clonally selected B cells is the hallmark of the humoral immune response. We'll explore how B cells become activated before investigating how antibodies function.

Activation of B Cells

Activation of the humoral immune response typically involves B cells and helper T cells as well as proteins on the surface of pathogens. As depicted in **Figure 43.18**, B cell activation by an antigen is aided by cytokines secreted from helper T cells that have encountered the same antigen. Stimulated by both an antigen and cytokines, the B cell proliferates and differentiates into memory B cells and antibody-secreting effector cells called **plasma cells**.

The pathway for antigen processing and display in B cells differs from that in other antigen-presenting cells. A macrophage or dendritic cell can present fragments from a wide variety of protein antigens, whereas a B cell presents only the antigen to which it specifically binds. When an antigen first binds to receptors on the surface of a B cell, the cell takes in a few foreign molecules by receptor-mediated endocytosis (see Figure 7.22). The class II MHC protein of the B cell then presents an antigen fragment to a helper T cell. This direct cell-to-cell contact is usually critical to B cell activation (see step 2 in Figure 43.18).

B cell activation leads to a robust humoral immune response: An activated B cell gives rise to thousands of identical plasma cells. These plasma cells stop expressing a membrane-bound antigen receptor and begin producing and secreting antibodies (see step 3 in Figure 43.18). Each plasma cell secretes approximately 2,000 antibodies every second of the cell's 4- to 5-day life span. Furthermore, most antigens recognized by B cells contain multiple epitopes. An exposure to a single antigen therefore normally activates a variety of B cells, with different plasma cells producing antibodies directed against different epitopes on the common antigen.

Antibody Function

Antibodies do not kill pathogens, but by binding to antigens, they mark pathogens in various ways for inactivation or

❶ After an antigen-presenting cell engulfs and degrades a pathogen, it displays an antigen fragment complexed with a class II MHC molecule. A helper T cell that recognizes the complex is activated with the aid of cytokines secreted from the antigen-presenting cell.

❷ When a B cell with receptors for the same epitope internalizes the antigen, it displays an antigen fragment on the cell surface in a complex with a class II MHC molecule. An activated helper T cell bearing receptors specific for the displayed fragment binds to the B cell. This interaction, with the aid of cytokines from the T cell, activates the B cell.

❸ The activated B cell proliferates and differentiates into memory B cells and antibody-secreting plasma cells. The secreted antibodies are specific for the same antigen that initiated the response.

▲ **Figure 43.18 Activation of a B cell in the humoral immune response.** Most protein antigens require activated helper T cells to trigger a humoral response. A macrophage (shown here) or a dendritic cell can activate a helper T cell, which in turn can activate a B cell to give rise to antibody-secreting plasma cells.

? *What function do cell-surface antigen receptors play for memory B cells?*

Neutralization	Opsonization	Activation of complement system and pore formation
		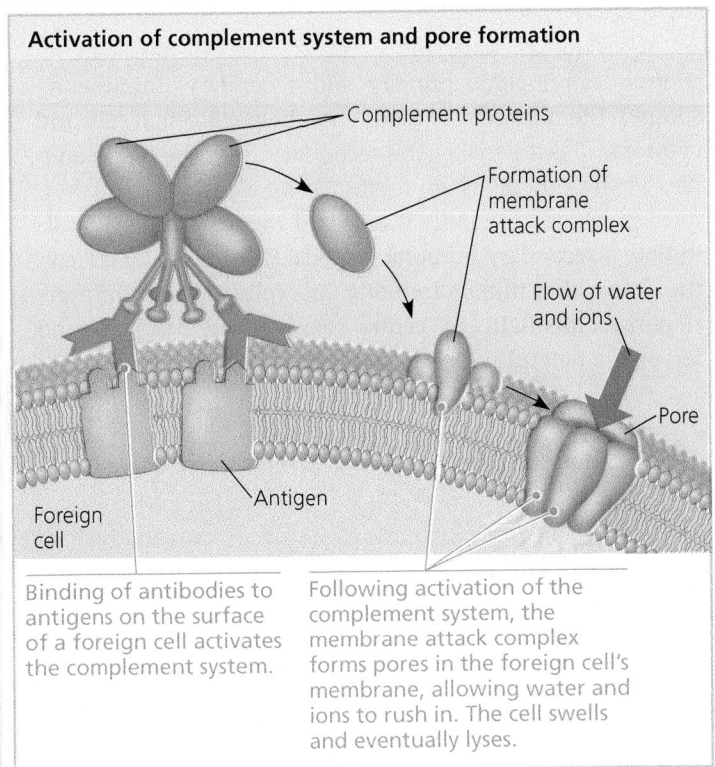
Antibodies bound to antigens on the surface of a virus neutralize it by blocking its ability to bind to a host cell.	Binding of antibodies to antigens on the surface of bacteria promotes phagocytosis by macrophages and neutrophils.	Binding of antibodies to antigens on the surface of a foreign cell activates the complement system. / Following activation of the complement system, the membrane attack complex forms pores in the foreign cell's membrane, allowing water and ions to rush in. The cell swells and eventually lyses.

destruction. In the simplest of these activities, *neutralization*, antibodies bind to viral surface proteins (Figure 43.19, left). The bound antibodies prevent infection of a host cell, thus neutralizing the virus. Similarly, antibodies sometimes bind to toxins released in body fluids, preventing the toxins from entering body cells. In another process, called *opsonization*, antibodies bound to antigens on bacteria present a readily recognized structure for macrophages or neutrophils and therefore increase phagocytosis (Figure 43.19, middle). Because each antibody has two antigen-binding sites, antibodies sometimes also facilitate phagocytosis by linking bacterial cells, virus particles, or other foreign substances into aggregates.

Antibodies sometimes work together with the proteins of the complement system to dispose of pathogens. (The name *complement* reflects the fact that these proteins increase the effectiveness of antibody-directed attacks on bacteria.) Binding of a complement protein to an antigen-antibody complex on a foreign cell (or an enveloped virus) triggers a cascade in which each protein of the complement system activates the next protein. Ultimately, activated complement proteins generate a *membrane attack complex* that forms a pore in the membrane of the foreign cell. Ions and water rush into the cell, causing it to swell and lyse (Figure 43.19, right). Whether activated as part of innate defenses or as part of adaptive defenses, this cascade of complement protein activity results in the lysis of foreign cells and produces factors that promote inflammation or stimulate phagocytosis.

When antibodies facilitate phagocytosis (see Figure 43.19, middle), they also help fine-tune the humoral immune response. Recall that phagocytosis enables macrophages and dendritic cells to present antigens to and stimulate helper T cells, which in turn stimulate the very B cells whose antibodies contribute to phagocytosis. This positive feedback between innate and adaptive immunity contributes to a coordinated, effective response to infection.

Although antibodies are the cornerstone of the response in body fluids, there is also a mechanism by which they can bring about the death of infected body cells. When a virus uses a cell's biosynthetic machinery to produce viral proteins, these viral products can appear on the cell surface. If antibodies specific for epitopes on these viral proteins bind to the exposed proteins, the presence of bound antibody at the cell surface can recruit a natural killer cell. The natural killer cell then releases proteins that cause the infected cell to undergo apoptosis.

B cells can express five different forms of immunoglobulin (Ig). For a given B cell, each form or *class* has an identical antigen-binding specificity, but a distinct heavy-chain C region. The B cell antigen receptor, known as IgD, is membrane bound. The other four classes consist of soluble antibodies. IgM is the first class of soluble antibody produced. IgG, which follows next, is the most abundant antibody in blood. We will learn more about the function of IgG, as well as the two remaining antibody classes (IgA and IgE), as we further explore the role of antibodies in immunity and disease.

Summary of the Humoral and Cell-Mediated Immune Responses

As noted earlier, both the humoral and cell-mediated responses can include primary and secondary immune responses. Memory cells of each type—helper T cell, B cell, and cytotoxic T cell—enable the secondary response. For example, when body fluids are reinfected by a pathogen encountered previously, memory B cells and memory helper T cells initiate a secondary humoral response. **Figure 43.20** reviews the events that initiate humoral and cell-mediated immune responses, highlights the central role of the helper T cell, and serves as a helpful summary of adaptive immunity.

Active and Passive Immunization

Our discussion of adaptive immunity has to this point focused on **active immunity**, the defenses that arise when a pathogen infects the body and prompts a primary or secondary immune response. In contrast, a different type of immunity results when the IgG antibodies in the blood of a pregnant female cross the placenta to her fetus. The transferred antibodies can immediately react with any pathogens for which they are specific. This protection is called **passive immunity** because the antibodies provided by the mother guard against pathogens that have never infected the newborn. Because passive immunity does not involve the recipient's

Humoral (antibody-mediated) immune response | Cell-mediated immune response

Key
- + → Stimulates
- ⟹ Gives rise to

Antigen (1st exposure)

Engulfed by

Antigen-presenting cell

B cell

Helper T cell

Cytotoxic T cell

Memory helper T cells

Antigen (2nd exposure)

Plasma cells

Memory B cells

Memory cytotoxic T cells

Active cytotoxic T cells

Secreted antibodies

Defend against extracellular pathogens in blood and lymph by binding to antigens, thereby neutralizing pathogens or making them better targets for phagocytic cells and complement proteins.

Defend against intracellular pathogens and cancer by binding to and lysing the infected cells or cancer cells.

▲ **Figure 43.20 An overview of the adaptive immune response.**

? *Identify each black or brown arrow as representing part of the primary or secondary response.*

ANIMATION **BioFlix** Visit the Study Area at **www.masteringbiology.com** for the BioFlix® 3-D Animation on Immunology.

B and T cells, it persists only as long as the transferred antibodies last (a few weeks to a few months).

After giving birth, a nursing mother continues to transfer protection against disease to her infant. IgA antibodies present in breast milk provide additional passive immunity to the infant's digestive tract while the infant's immune system develops. Later in life, IgA functions in active immunity: IgA antibodies secreted in tears, saliva, and mucus protect the mucous membranes of both males and females.

Both active immunity and passive immunity can be induced artificially. Active immunity can develop from the introduction of antigens into the body through **immunization**. In 1796, Edward Jenner noted that milkmaids who had cowpox, a mild disease usually seen only in cows, did not contract smallpox, a far more dangerous disease. In the first documented immunization (or **vaccination**, from the Latin *vacca*, cow), Jenner used the cowpox virus to induce adaptive immunity against the closely related smallpox virus. Today, many sources of antigen are used to make vaccines, including inactivated bacterial toxins, killed pathogens, parts of pathogens, weakened pathogens that generally do not cause illness, and even genes encoding microbial proteins. Because all of these agents induce a primary immune response and immunological memory, an encounter with the pathogen from which the vaccine was derived triggers a rapid and strong secondary immune response (see Figure 43.15).

Vaccination programs have been successful against many infectious diseases that once killed or incapacitated large numbers of people. A worldwide vaccination campaign led to eradication of smallpox in the late 1970s. In industrialized nations, routine active immunization of infants and children has dramatically reduced the incidence of sometimes devastating diseases, such as polio, measles, and whooping cough. Unfortunately, not all pathogens are easily managed by vaccination. Furthermore, some vaccines are not readily available in impoverished areas of the globe.

Misinformation about vaccine safety and disease risk has led some parents to refuse to immunize their children with available, effective vaccines. The consequence has been a substantial and growing public health problem. Consider measles as just one example. Side effects of immunization are remarkably rare: Fewer than one in a million children suffer a significant allergic reaction to the measles vaccine. The disease, however, is quite dangerous: Roughly one out of every 1,000 patients develop *encephalitis*, an inflammation of the brain. Worldwide, measles kills more than 200,000 people each year. Sadly, declines in measles vaccination rates in parts of the United Kingdom, Russia, and the United States have recently resulted in a number of measles outbreaks and significant numbers of preventable deaths.

In artificial passive immunization, antibodies from an immune animal are injected into a nonimmune animal. For example, humans bitten by venomous snakes are sometimes treated with antivenin, serum from sheep or horses that have been immunized against the venom of one or more species of venomous snakes. When injected immediately after a snakebite, the antibodies in antivenin can neutralize toxins in the venom before the toxins do massive damage.

Antibodies as Tools

The power of antibody specificity and antigen-antibody binding has been harnessed in research, diagnosis, and therapy. Some antibody tools are *polyclonal*: They are the products of many different clones of plasma cells, each specific for a different epitope (Figure 43.21). Antibodies that an animal produces after exposure to a microbial antigen are polyclonal. In contrast, other antibody tools are *monoclonal*: They are prepared from a single clone of B cells grown in culture. The **monoclonal antibodies** produced by such a culture are identical and specific for the same epitope on an antigen.

Monoclonal antibodies have provided the basis for many recent advances in medical diagnosis and treatment. For example, home pregnancy kits use monoclonal antibodies to detect human chorionic gonadotropin (hCG). Because hCG is produced as soon as an embryo implants in the uterus (see Chapter 46), the presence of this hormone in a woman's urine is a reliable indicator for a very early stage of pregnancy. In the clinic, monoclonal antibodies are being used to

Endoplasmic reticulum of plasma cell

2 μm

▲ **Figure 43.21 A plasma cell.** A plasma cell contains abundant endoplasmic reticulum, a common feature of cells dedicated to making proteins for secretion (TEM).

treat many human diseases. For this type of therapy, researchers use mouse B cell clones to identify antibodies specific for an epitope on diseased cells. Next, the mouse antibody genes are altered to code for antibodies that appear less foreign to the human adaptive immune defenses. Scientists then use the "humanized" genes to produce large amounts of antibody for injecting into patients.

Immune Rejection

Like pathogens, cells from another person can be recognized as foreign and attacked by immune defenses. For example, skin transplanted from one person to a genetically nonidentical person will look healthy for a week or so but will then be destroyed (rejected) by the recipient's immune response. Keep in mind that the body's rejection of transplanted tissues or organs or of an incompatible blood transfusion is the expected reaction of a healthy immune system exposed to foreign antigens. (It remains a largely unanswered question why a pregnant woman does not reject her fetus as nonself tissue.)

Blood Groups

To avoid a blood transfusion being recognized as foreign by the recipient's immune system, the ABO blood groups of the donor and recipient must be taken into account. As discussed in Chapter 14, red blood cells are designated as type A if they have the type A carbohydrate on their surface. Similarly, the type B carbohydrate is found on type B red blood cells; both A and B carbohydrates are found on type AB red blood cells; and neither carbohydrate is found on type O red blood cells (see Figure 14.11).

To understand how ABO blood groups affect transfusions, let's consider the immune response of someone with type A blood. It turns out that certain bacteria normally present in the body have epitopes very similar to the A and B carbohydrates. By responding to the bacterial epitope similar to the B carbohydrate, a person with type A blood makes antibodies that will react with the type B carbohydrate. No antibodies are made against the bacterial epitope similar to the type A carbohydrate because lymphocytes reactive with the body's own molecules are inactivated or eliminated during development. If the person with type A blood receives a transfusion of type B blood, that person's anti-B antibodies cause an immediate and devastating transfusion reaction. The transfused red blood cells undergo lysis, which can lead to chills, fever, shock, and kidney malfunction. By the same token, anti-A antibodies in the donated type B blood will act against the recipient's type A red blood cells. Although such interactions prevent type O individuals from receiving transfusions of any other blood type, the recent discovery of enzymes that can cleave the A and B carbohydrates from red blood cells may eliminate this problem.

Tissue and Organ Transplants

In the case of tissue and organ transplants, or grafts, MHC molecules stimulate the immune response that leads to rejection. Each vertebrate species has many alleles for each MHC gene, enabling presentation of antigen fragments that vary in shape and net electrical charge. This diversity of MHC molecules almost guarantees that no two people, except identical twins, will have exactly the same set. Thus, in the vast majority of graft and transplant recipients, some MHC molecules on the donated tissue are foreign to the recipient. To minimize rejection, physicians use donor tissue bearing MHC molecules that match those of the recipient as closely as possible. In addition, the recipient takes medicines that suppress immune responses (but also leave the recipient more susceptible to infections).

Transplants of bone marrow from one person to another can also cause an immune reaction, but for a different reason. Bone marrow transplants are used to treat leukemia and other cancers as well as various hematological (blood cell) diseases. Prior to receiving transplanted bone marrow, the recipient is typically treated with radiation to eliminate his or her own bone marrow cells, thus destroying the source of abnormal cells. This treatment effectively obliterates the recipient's immune system, leaving little chance of graft rejection. However, lymphocytes in the donated marrow may react against the recipient. This *graft versus host reaction* is limited if the MHC molecules of the donor and recipient are well matched. Bone marrow donor programs continually seek volunteers because the great variability of MHC molecules makes a diverse pool of donors essential.

CONCEPT CHECK 43.3

1. If a child were born without a thymus, what cells and functions would be deficient? Explain.
2. Treatment of antibodies with a particular protease clips the heavy chains in half, releasing the two arms of the Y-shaped molecule. How might the antibodies continue to function?
3. **WHAT IF?** Suppose that a snake handler bitten by a particular venomous snake species was treated with antivenin. Why might the same treatment for a second such bite have different results?

For suggested answers, see Appendix A.

CONCEPT 43.4

Disruptions in immune system function can elicit or exacerbate disease

Although adaptive immunity offers significant protection against a wide range of pathogens, it is not fail-safe. In this last section of the chapter, we'll first examine the problems that arise when adaptive immunity is blocked or misregulated. We'll then turn to some of the evolutionary adaptations of pathogens that diminish the effectiveness of host immune responses.

Exaggerated, Self-Directed, and Diminished Immune Responses

The highly regulated interplay among lymphocytes, other body cells, and foreign substances generates an immune response that provides extraordinary protection against many pathogens. When allergic, autoimmune, or immunodeficiency disorders disrupt this delicate balance, the effects are frequently severe and sometimes life-threatening.

Allergies

Allergies are exaggerated (hypersensitive) responses to certain antigens called **allergens**. The most common allergies involve antibodies of the IgE class. Hay fever, for instance, occurs when plasma cells secrete IgE antibodies specific for antigens on the surface of pollen grains (Figure 43.22). Some IgE antibodies attach by their base to mast cells in connective tissues. Pollen grains that enter the body later attach to the antigen-binding sites of these IgE antibodies. This attachment links adjacent IgE molecules, inducing the mast cell to release histamine and other inflammatory chemicals from granules (vesicles). Acting on a variety of cell types, these signals bring about the typical allergy symptoms: sneezing, runny nose, teary eyes, and smooth muscle contractions that can result in breathing difficulty. Drugs called antihistamines diminish allergy symptoms (and inflammation) by blocking receptors for histamine.

An acute allergic response sometimes leads to *anaphylactic shock*, a whole-body, life-threatening reaction that can occur within seconds of exposure to an allergen. Anaphylactic shock develops when widespread release of mast cell contents triggers abrupt dilation of peripheral blood vessels, causing a precipitous drop in blood pressure, as well as constriction of bronchioles. Death may occur within minutes due to lack of blood flow and the inability to breathe. Allergic responses to bee venom or penicillin can lead to anaphylactic shock in people who are extremely allergic to these substances. Likewise, people very allergic to peanuts, fish, or shellfish can die from ingesting only tiny amounts of these allergens, which trigger reactions through interactions with mast cells on the surface of the digestive tract. People with severe hypersensitivities often carry syringes containing the hormone epinephrine, which counteracts this allergic response (see Figure 45.8).

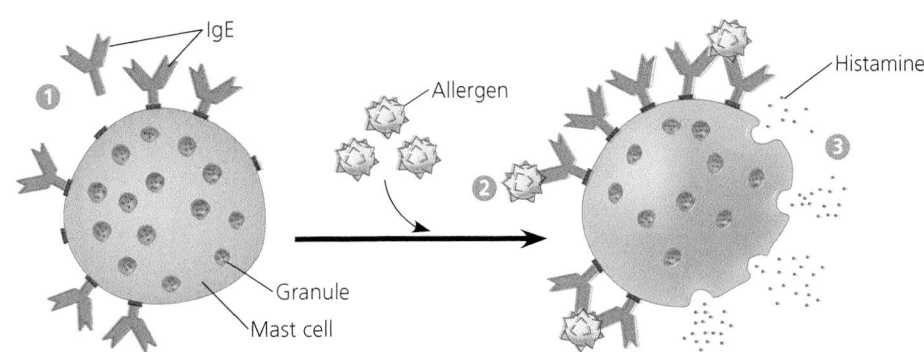

① IgE antibodies produced in response to initial exposure to an allergen bind to receptors on mast cells.

② On subsequent exposure to the same allergen, IgE molecules attached to a mast cell recognize and bind the allergen.

③ Cross-linking of adjacent IgE molecules triggers release of histamine and other chemicals, leading to allergy symptoms.

▲ **Figure 43.22 Mast cells, IgE, and the allergic response.** In this example, pollen grains act as the allergen.

Autoimmune Diseases

In some people, the immune system is active against particular molecules of the body, causing an **autoimmune disease**. Such a loss of self-tolerance has many forms. In *systemic lupus erythematosus*, commonly called *lupus*, the immune system generates antibodies against histones and DNA released by the normal breakdown of body cells. These self-reactive antibodies cause skin rashes, fever, arthritis, and kidney dysfunction. Another autoimmune disease,

▲ **Figure 43.23 X-ray of hands deformed by rheumatoid arthritis.**

rheumatoid arthritis, leads to damage and painful inflammation of the cartilage and bone of joints (Figure 43.23). In *type 1 diabetes mellitus*, the insulin-producing beta cells of the pancreas are the targets of autoimmune cytotoxic T cells. The most common chronic neurological disorder in developed countries is the autoimmune disease *multiple sclerosis*. In this disease, T cells infiltrate the central nervous system. The result is destruction of the myelin sheath that surrounds parts of many neurons (see Figure 48.12), leading to muscle paralysis through a disruption in neuron function.

Gender, genetics, and environment all influence susceptibility to autoimmune disorders. For example, members of certain families show an increased susceptibility to particular autoimmune disorders. In addition, many autoimmune diseases afflict females more often than males. Women are two to three times more likely than men to suffer from multiple sclerosis and rheumatoid arthritis and nine times more likely to develop lupus. The cause of this sex bias, as well as the rise in autoimmune disease frequency in industrialized countries, is an area of active research and debate. Clearly, much remains to be learned about these often devastating disorders.

Exertion, Stress, and the Immune System

Many forms of exertion and stress influence immune system function. Consider, for example, susceptibility to the common cold and other infections of the upper respiratory tract. Moderate exercise improves immune system function and significantly reduces the risk of these infections. In contrast, exercise to the point of exhaustion leads to more frequent infections and to more severe symptoms. Studies of marathon runners support the conclusion that exercise intensity is the critical variable. On average, such runners get sick less often than their more sedentary peers during training, a time of moderate exertion, but have a marked increase in illness in the period immediately following the grueling race itself. Similarly, psychological stress has been shown to disrupt immune system regulation by altering the interplay of the hormonal, nervous, and immune systems (see Figure 45.21). Recent research also confirms that rest is important for immunity: Adults who averaged fewer than 7 hours of sleep a night got sick three times as often when exposed to a cold virus as individuals who averaged at least 8 hours of sleep.

Immunodeficiency Diseases

A disorder in which an immune system response to antigens is defective or absent is called an **immunodeficiency**. An *inborn immunodeficiency* results from a genetic or developmental defect in the immune system. An *acquired immunodeficiency* develops later in life following exposure to chemical or biological agents. Whatever its cause and nature, an immunodeficiency can lead to frequent and recurrent infections and increased susceptibility to certain cancers.

Inborn immunodeficiencies result from defects in the development of various immune system cells or defects in the production of specific proteins, such as antibodies or the proteins of the complement system. Depending on the specific genetic defect, either innate or adaptive defenses—or both—may be impaired. In severe combined immunodeficiency (SCID), functional lymphocytes are rare or absent. Lacking an adaptive immune response, SCID patients are susceptible to infections, such as pneumonia and meningitis, that can cause death in infancy. Treatments include bone marrow and stem cell transplantation.

Exposure to certain agents can cause immunodeficiencies that develop later in life. Drugs used to fight autoimmune diseases or prevent transplant rejection suppress the immune system, leading to an immunodeficient state. Certain cancers also suppress the immune system, especially Hodgkin's disease, which damages the lymphatic system. Acquired immunodeficiencies range from temporary states that may arise from physiological stress to the devastating **acquired immunodeficiency syndrome (AIDS)**, which is caused by the human immunodeficiency virus (HIV). We will discuss AIDS further in the next section, which focuses on how pathogens escape the adaptive immune response.

Evolutionary Adaptations of Pathogens That Underlie Immune System Avoidance

EVOLUTION Just as immune systems that ward off pathogens have evolved in animals, mechanisms that thwart immune responses have evolved in pathogens. Using human pathogens as examples, we'll examine some common mechanisms: antigenic variation, latency, and direct attack on the immune system.

Antigenic Variation

One mechanism for escaping the body's defenses is for a pathogen to alter how it appears to the immune system. Immunological memory is a record of the foreign epitopes an animal has encountered. If the pathogen that expressed those epitopes no longer does so, it can reinfect or remain in a host without triggering the rapid and robust response that memory cells provide. Such changes in epitope expression, which are called *antigenic variation*, are regular events for some viruses and parasites. The parasite that causes sleeping sickness (trypanosomiasis) provides one example. By periodically switching at random among 1,000 different versions of the protein found over its entire surface, this pathogen can persist in the body without facing an effective adaptive immune response (Figure 43.24).

Antigenic variation is the major reason the influenza, or "flu," virus remains a major public health problem. As it replicates in one human host after another, the human influenza virus mutates. Because any change that lessens recognition by the immune system provides a selective advantage, the virus steadily accumulates such alterations. These changes in the surface proteins of the influenza virus are the reason that a new flu vaccine must be manufactured and distributed each year. Of much greater danger, however, is the fact that the human virus occasionally exchanges genes with influenza viruses that infect domesticated animals, such as pigs or chickens. When this occurs, influenza can take on such a radically different appearance that none of the memory cells in

▲ Figure 43.24 **Antigenic variation in the parasite that causes sleeping sickness.** Blood samples taken from a patient during a chronic infection of sleeping sickness reveal cyclic variation in the surface coat protein of the parasite. The infection has become chronic because this weekly variation allows the parasite to evade the adaptive immune response.

the human population recognize the new strain. Such an event led to the influenza outbreak of 1918–1919, which killed more than half a million people in the United States (see Figure 19.9). Worldwide more than 20 million people died, a greater number than had died in World War I.

In 2009, an influenza virus called H1N1 appeared that contained a novel combination of genes from flu viruses that normally circulate in pigs, birds, and humans. The rapid spread of this flu across the human population caused a *pandemic*, an outbreak of worldwide proportions. Fortunately, a rapidly developed H1N1 vaccine soon provided public health officials with an excellent means of slowing the spread of this virus and reducing the impact of the outbreak.

Latency

After infecting a host, some viruses enter a largely inactive state called *latency*. Because such dormant viruses cease making most viral proteins and typically produce no free virus particles, they do not trigger an adaptive immune response. Nevertheless, the viral genome persists in the nuclei of infected cells, either as a separate small DNA molecule or as a copy integrated into the host genome. Latency typically persists until conditions arise that are favorable for viral transmission or unfavorable for host survival, such as when the host is infected by another pathogen. Such circumstances trigger the synthesis and release of virus particles that can infect new hosts.

Herpes simplex viruses, which establish themselves in human sensory neurons, provide a good example of latency. The type 1 virus causes most oral herpes infections, whereas the type 2 virus is responsible for most cases of genital herpes. Because sensory neurons express relatively few MHC I molecules, the infected cells are inefficient at presenting viral antigens to circulating lymphocytes. Stimuli such as fever, emotional stress, or menstruation reactivate the virus to reproduce and infect surrounding epithelial tissues. Activation of the type 1 virus can result in blisters around the mouth that are inaccurately called "cold" sores. The type 2 virus can cause genital sores, but people infected with either type 1 or type 2 virus often lack any apparent symptoms. Infections of the type 2 virus, which is sexually transmitted, pose a serious threat to the babies of infected mothers and can increase transmission of HIV, the virus that causes AIDS.

Attack on the Immune System: HIV

The human immunodeficiency virus (HIV), the pathogen that causes AIDS, both escapes and attacks the adaptive immune response. Once introduced into the body, HIV infects helper T cells with high efficiency. To infect these cells, the virus binds specifically to the CD4 accessory protein (see Figure 43.16). However, HIV also infects some cell types that have low levels of CD4, such as macrophages and brain cells. In the cell, the HIV RNA genome is reverse-transcribed,

and the product DNA is integrated into the host cell's genome (see Figure 19.8). In this form, the viral genome can direct production of new virus particles.

Although the body responds to HIV with an immune response sufficient to eliminate most viral infections, some HIV invariably escapes. One reason HIV persists is antigenic variation. The virus mutates at a very high rate during replication. Altered proteins on the surface of some mutated viruses reduce interaction with antibodies and cytotoxic T cells. Such viruses survive, proliferate, and mutate further. The virus thus evolves within the body. The continued presence of HIV is also helped by latency. When the viral DNA integrates into the chromosome of a host cell but does not produce new virus proteins or particles, it is shielded from the immune system by the host cell. This inactive, or latent, viral DNA is also protected from antiviral agents currently used against HIV because they attack only actively replicating viruses.

Over time, an untreated HIV infection not only avoids the adaptive immune response but also abolishes it **(Figure 43.25)**. Viral reproduction and cell death triggered by the virus lead to loss of helper T cells, impairing both humoral and cell-mediated immune responses. The result is a progression to AIDS, characterized by a susceptibility to infections and cancers that a healthy immune system would usually defeat. For example, *Pneumocystis carinii*, a common fungus that does not cause disease in healthy individuals, can result in severe pneumonia in people with AIDS. Likewise, the Kaposi's sarcoma herpesvirus causes a cancer among AIDS patients that is extremely rare in individuals not infected with HIV. Such opportunistic diseases, as well as nerve damage and body wasting, are the primary causes of death in AIDS patients, not the HIV virus itself.

At present, HIV infection cannot be cured, although certain drugs can slow HIV reproduction and the progression to

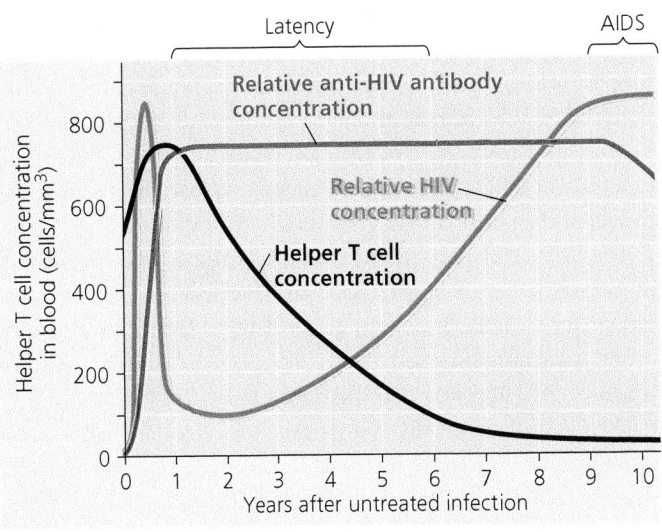

▲ **Figure 43.25 The progress of an untreated HIV infection.**

AIDS. Unfortunately, mutations that occur in each round of viral reproduction can generate strains of HIV that are drug resistant. The impact of such viral drug resistance can be reduced by the use of a combination of drugs; viruses newly resistant to one drug can be defeated by another. However, the appearance of strains resistant to multiple drugs reduces the effectiveness of such multidrug "cocktails" in some patients. Frequent mutations in genes for HIV surface antigens also have hampered efforts to develop an effective vaccine. Worldwide, the AIDS epidemic continues to grow. In 2008, approximately 2 million people died of AIDS, and the disease is now the leading cause of death in Africa.

Transmission of HIV requires the transfer of virus particles or infected cells from person to person via body fluids such as semen, blood, or breast milk. Unprotected sex (that is, without a condom) and transmission via HIV-contaminated needles (typically among intravenous drug users) account for the vast majority of HIV infections. The virus can enter the body through the mucosal linings of the vagina, vulva, penis, or rectum during intercourse or via the mouth during oral sex. The likelihood of transmission is increased by factors that may damage these linings, especially other sexually transmitted infections that cause ulcers or inflammation.

People infected with HIV can transmit the disease in the first few weeks of infection, *before* they express HIV-specific antibodies that can be detected in a blood test (see Figure 43.25). Currently, 10–50% of all new HIV infections appear to be caused by recently infected individuals.

Cancer and Immunity

When adaptive immunity is inactivated, the frequency of certain cancers increases dramatically. For example, the risk of developing Kaposi's sarcoma is 20,000 times greater for untreated AIDS patients than for healthy people. This observation was unanticipated. If the immune system recognizes only nonself, it should fail to recognize the uncontrolled growth of self cells that is the hallmark of cancer. It turns out, however, that viruses are involved in about 15–20% of all human cancers. Because the immune system can recognize viral proteins as foreign, it can act as a defense against viruses that can cause cancer and against cancer cells that harbor viruses.

Scientists have identified six viruses that can cause cancer in humans. The Kaposi's sarcoma herpesvirus is one such virus. Hepatitis B virus, which can trigger liver cancer, is another. A vaccine directed against hepatitis B virus that was introduced in 1986 was demonstrated to be the first vaccine to help prevent a specific human cancer. Rapid progress on virus-induced cancers continues. In 2006, the release of a vaccine against cervical cancer, specifically human papillomavirus (HPV), marked a major victory against a disease that afflicts more than half a million women worldwide every year **(Figure 43.26)**.

▼ Figure 43.26

IMPACT

Vaccinating Against Cervical Cancer

In the 1970s, Harald zur Hausen, working in Heidelberg, Germany, proposed that human papillomavirus (HPV) causes cervical cancer. Many scientists were skeptical that cancer could result from infection by HPV, the most common sexually transmitted pathogen. However, after more than a decade of work, zur Hausen isolated two particular types of HPV from patients with cervical cancer. He quickly made samples available to other scientists, leading to development of highly effective vaccines against cervical cancer. In 2008, zur Hausen shared the Nobel Prize in Physiology or Medicine for his discovery. This computer graphic image of an HPV particle illustrates the abundant copies of the capsid protein (yellow) that is used as the antigen in vaccination.

WHY IT MATTERS Cervical cancer kills more than 4,000 women annually in the United States and is the fifth-most common cause of cancer deaths among women worldwide. Administering an HPV vaccine, either Gardasil or Cervarix, to preteen girls and young women greatly reduces their chance of being infected with the HPV viruses that cause most cervical cancers.

FURTHER READING L. R. Badenet et al., Human papillomavirus vaccine: Opportunity and challenge, *New England Journal of Medicine* 356:1990–1991 (2007).

WHAT IF? Suppose you tracked the health of women infected with the types of HPV that cause cancer. Why might only a fraction of such women develop cervical cancer? (*Hint*: Refer to Figure 18.25 on p. 376 and the accompanying text.)

CONCEPT CHECK 43.4

1. In myasthenia gravis, antibodies bind to and block certain receptors on muscle cells, preventing muscle contraction. Is this disease best classified as an immunodeficiency disease, an autoimmune disease, or an allergic reaction? Explain.

2. People with herpes simplex type 1 viruses often get mouth sores when they have a cold or similar infection. How might this location benefit the virus?

3. **WHAT IF?** How would a macrophage deficiency likely affect a person's innate and adaptive defenses?

For suggested answers, see Appendix A.

CONCEPT 43.1

In innate immunity, recognition and response rely on traits common to groups of pathogens (pp. 930–935)

- In both invertebrates and vertebrates, **innate immunity** is mediated by physical and chemical barriers as well as cell-based defenses. Activation of innate immune responses relies on recognition proteins specific for broad classes of **pathogens**. In insects, pathogens that penetrate barrier defenses are ingested by cells in the hemolymph that also release antimicrobial peptides.
- In vertebrates, intact skin and mucous membranes form barriers to pathogens. Mucus produced by membrane cells, the low pH of the skin and stomach, and degradation by **lysozyme** also deter pathogens. Microbes that penetrate barrier defenses are ingested by phagocytic cells, including **macrophages** and **dendritic cells**. Additional cellular defenses include **natural killer cells**, which can induce the death of virus-infected cells. **Complement system** proteins, **interferons**, and other antimicrobial peptides also act against microbes. In the **inflammatory response**, **histamine** and other chemicals released from cells at the injury site promote changes in blood vessels that allow fluid, more phagocytic cells, and antimicrobial peptides to enter tissues.
- Pathogens sometimes evade innate immune defenses. For example, some bacteria have an outer capsule that prevents recognition, while others are resistant to breakdown within lysosomes.

? *In what ways does innate immunity protect the mammalian digestive tract?*

CONCEPT 43.2

In adaptive immunity, receptors provide pathogen-specific recognition (pp. 935–940)

- **Adaptive immunity** relies on **lymphocytes** that arise from stem cells in the bone marrow and complete their maturation in the bone marrow (**B cells**) or in the **thymus** (**T cells**). Lymphocytes have cell-surface **antigen receptors** for foreign molecules. All receptor proteins on a single B or T cell are the same, but there are millions of B and T cells in the body that differ in the foreign molecules that their receptors recognize. Upon infection, B and T cells specific for the pathogen are activated. Some T cells help other lymphocytes; others kill infected host cells. B cells called **plasma cells** produce soluble receptor proteins called **antibodies**, which bind to foreign molecules and cells. The activated lymphocytes called **memory cells** defend against future infections by the same pathogen.
- Recognition of foreign molecules involves the binding of variable regions of receptors to an **epitope**, a small region of an antigen. B cells and antibodies recognize epitopes on the surface of antigens circulating in the blood or lymph. T cells recognize protein epitopes in small antigen fragments (peptides) that are presented on the surface of host cells, complexed with cell-surface proteins called **MHC (major histocompatibility complex) molecules**.
- The four major characteristics of B and T cell development are the generation of cell diversity, self-tolerance, proliferation, and immunological memory.

The following figure uses B cells to illustrate clonal selection:

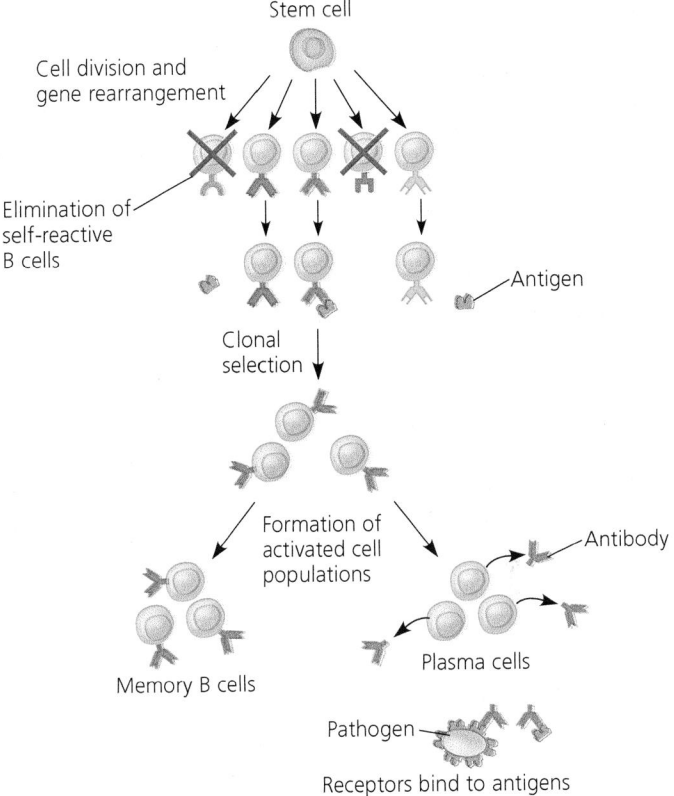

? *Why is the adaptive immune response to an initial infection slower than the innate response?*

CONCEPT 43.3

Adaptive immunity defends against infection of body fluids and body cells (pp. 940–946)

- **Helper T cells** interact with antigen fragments displayed by class II MHC molecules on the surface of dendritic cells, macrophages, and B cells (**antigen-presenting cells**). Activated helper T cells secrete **cytokines** that stimulate other lymphocytes as part of the response to nearly all antigens. **Cytotoxic T cells** bind to a complex of an antigen fragment and a class I MHC molecule on infected host cells. In the **cell-mediated immune response**, activated cytotoxic T cells secrete proteins that initiate destruction of infected cells. All T cells have an accessory protein that enhances binding to MHC–antigen fragment complexes.

  In the **humoral immune response**, B cell antigen receptors and antibodies bind to extracellular foreign substances in blood and lymph. The binding of antibodies helps eliminate antigens by phagocytosis and complement-mediated lysis. The five major antibody classes differ in distribution and function.
- **Active immunity** develops in response to infection or to immunization with a nonpathogenic form or part of a pathogen. Active immunity includes a response to and immunological memory for that pathogen. **Passive immunity**, which provides immediate, short-term protection, is conferred naturally when IgG crosses the placenta from mother to fetus or when IgA passes from mother to infant in breast milk. It also can be conferred artificially by injecting antibodies into a nonimmune person.

- Tissues or cells transferred from one person to another are subject to immune rejection. In tissue grafts and organ transplants, MHC molecules stimulate rejection. Lymphocytes in bone marrow transplants may cause a graft versus host reaction.

? *Is immunological memory after a natural infection fundamentally different from immunological memory after vaccination? Explain.*

CONCEPT 43.4

Disruptions in immune system function can elicit or exacerbate disease (pp. 946–950)

- Disruption of normal immune system regulation or function can result in an exaggerated, self-directed, or diminished response. In localized allergies, IgE attached to **mast cells** induces the cells to release histamine and other mediators that cause vascular changes and allergic symptoms. Loss of self-tolerance can lead to **autoimmune diseases**, such as multiple sclerosis. Inborn **immunodeficiencies** result from defects that interfere with innate, humoral, or cell-mediated defenses. **AIDS** is an acquired immunodeficiency caused by HIV.
- Antigenic variation, latency, and direct assault on the immune system allow some pathogens to thwart immune responses. HIV infection destroys helper T cells, leaving the patient prone to disease. Immune defense against cancer appears to primarily involve action against viruses that can cause cancer, as well as against cancer cells that harbor viruses.

? *Is being infected with HIV the same as having AIDS? Explain.*

TEST YOUR UNDERSTANDING

LEVEL 1: KNOWLEDGE/COMPREHENSION

1. Which of these is *not* part of insect immunity?
   a. enzyme activation of microbe-killing chemicals
   b. activation of natural killer cells
   c. phagocytosis by hemocytes
   d. production of antimicrobial peptides
   e. a protective exoskeleton

2. An epitope associates with which part of an antigen receptor or antibody?
   a. the disulfide bridge
   b. the heavy-chain constant regions only
   c. variable regions of a heavy chain and light chain combined
   d. the light-chain constant regions only
   e. the tail

3. Which statement best describes the difference in responses of effector B cells (plasma cells) and cytotoxic T cells?
   a. B cells confer active immunity; cytotoxic T cells confer passive immunity.
   b. B cells kill pathogens directly; cytotoxic T cells kill host cells.
   c. B cells secrete antibodies against a pathogen; cytotoxic T cells kill pathogen-infected host cells.
   d. B cells carry out the cell-mediated response; cytotoxic T cells carry out the humoral response.
   e. B cells respond the first time a pathogen is present; cytotoxic T cells respond subsequent times.

LEVEL 2: APPLICATION/ANALYSIS

4. Which of the following statements is *not* true?
   a. An antibody has more than one antigen-binding site.
   b. An antigen can have different epitopes.
   c. A pathogen makes more than one antigen.
   d. A lymphocyte has receptors for multiple different antigens.
   e. A liver cell makes one class of MHC molecule.

5. Which of the following should be the same in identical twins?
   a. the set of antibodies produced
   b. the set of MHC molecules produced
   c. the set of T cell antigen receptors produced
   d. the susceptibility to a particular virus
   e. the set of immune cells eliminated as self-reactive

LEVEL 3: SYNTHESIS/EVALUATION

6. Vaccination increases the number of
   a. different receptors that recognize a pathogen.
   b. lymphocytes with receptors that can bind to the pathogen.
   c. epitopes that the immune system can recognize.
   d. macrophages specific for a pathogen.
   e. MHC molecules that can present an antigen.

7. Which of the following would *not* help a virus avoid triggering an adaptive immune response?
   a. having frequent mutations in genes for surface proteins
   b. infecting cells that produce very few MHC molecules
   c. producing proteins very similar to those of other viruses
   d. infecting and killing helper T cells
   e. building the viral shell from host proteins

8. **DRAW IT** Consider a pencil-shaped protein with two epitopes, Y (the "eraser" end) and Z (the "point" end). They are recognized by antibodies A1 and A2, respectively. Draw and label a picture showing the antibodies linking proteins into a complex that could trigger endocytosis by a macrophage.

9. **MAKE CONNECTIONS** Contrast Lamarck's idea for the inheritance of acquired characteristics, discussed on pp. 454–455 of Concept 22.1, with the clonal selection of lymphocytes.

10. **EVOLUTION CONNECTION**
    Describe one invertebrate defense mechanism and discuss how it is an evolutionary adaptation retained in vertebrates.

11. **SCIENTIFIC INQUIRY**
    A diagnostic test for tuberculosis (TB) involves injecting antigen (from the bacterium that causes TB) under the skin and then waiting a few days for a reaction to appear. This test is *not* useful for diagnosing TB in AIDS patients. Why?

12. **WRITE ABOUT A THEME**
    The Genetic Basis of Life Among all nucleated body cells, only B and T cells lose DNA during their development and maturation. In a short essay (100–150 words), discuss the relationship between this loss and the theme of DNA as heritable biological information, focusing on similarities between cellular and organismal generations.

For selected answers, see Appendix A.

MasteringBIOLOGY® **www.masteringbiology.com**

1. MasteringBiology® Assignments
Tutorial Acquired Immunity
Activities The Inflammatory Response • Immune Responses • The Adaptive Immune Response • Discovery Channel Video: Vaccines • HIV Reproductive Cycle • Discovery Channel Video: Fighting Cancer
Questions Student Misconceptions • Reading Quiz • Multiple Choice • End-of-Chapter

2. eText
Read your book online, search, take notes, highlight text, and more.

3. The Study Area
Practice Tests • Cumulative Test • *BioFlix* 3-D Animations • MP3 Tutor Sessions • Videos • Activities • Investigations • Lab Media • Audio Glossary • Word Study Tools • Art

44

Osmoregulation and Excretion

▲ Figure 44.1 **How does an albatross drink salt water without ill effect?**

KEY CONCEPTS

44.1 Osmoregulation balances the uptake and loss of water and solutes

44.2 An animal's nitrogenous wastes reflect its phylogeny and habitat

44.3 Diverse excretory systems are variations on a tubular theme

44.4 The nephron is organized for stepwise processing of blood filtrate

44.5 Hormonal circuits link kidney function, water balance, and blood pressure

OVERVIEW

A Balancing Act

With a wingspan that can reach 3.5 m, the largest of any living bird, a wandering albatross (*Diomedea exulans*) soaring over the ocean is hard to miss (Figure 44.1). Yet the albatross commands attention for more than just its size. This massive bird remains at sea day and night throughout the year, returning to land only to reproduce. A human with only seawater to drink would die of dehydration, but faced with the same conditions, the albatross thrives.

For both albatross and human, maintaining the fluid environment of their cells, tissues, and organs requires keeping relative concentrations of water and solutes within fairly narrow limits. In addition, ions such as sodium and calcium must be maintained at concentrations that permit normal activity of muscles, neurons, and other body cells. Homeostasis thus requires **osmoregulation**, the general term for the processes by which animals control solute concentrations and balance water gain and loss.

A number of strategies for water and solute control have arisen during evolution, reflecting the varied and often severe osmoregulatory challenges presented by an animal's surroundings. The arid environment of a desert, for instance, can quickly deplete an animal of body water. Despite a quite different environment, albatrosses and other marine animals also face potential dehydration. The success of animals in an ocean environment depends critically on conserving water and, for marine birds and fishes, eliminating excess salts. In contrast, freshwater animals live in an environment that threatens to flood and dilute their body fluids. These organisms survive by conserving solutes and absorbing salts from their surroundings.

In safeguarding their internal fluid environment, animals must also deal with a hazardous metabolite produced by the dismantling of proteins and nucleic acids. Breakdown of *nitrogenous* (nitrogen-containing) molecules releases ammonia, a very toxic compound. Several different mechanisms have evolved for **excretion**, the process that rids the body of nitrogenous metabolites and other metabolic waste products. Because systems for excretion and osmoregulation are structurally and functionally linked in many animals, we will consider both of these processes in this chapter.

CONCEPT 44.1

Osmoregulation balances the uptake and loss of water and solutes

Just as thermoregulation depends on balancing heat loss and gain (see Chapter 40), regulating the chemical composition of body fluids depends on balancing the uptake and loss of water and solutes. This process of osmoregulation is based largely on the controlled movement of solutes between internal fluids and the external environment. Because solute movement results in the movement of water by osmosis, the net effect is to regulate both solutes and water.

Osmosis and Osmolarity

All animals—regardless of habitat or type of waste produced—face the same need to balance water uptake and loss. If water

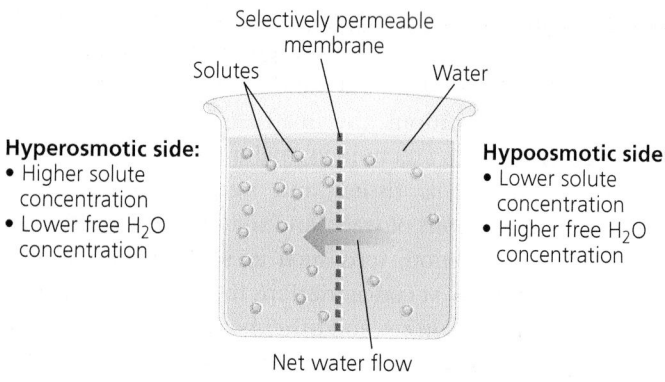

Selectively permeable
membrane

Solutes   Water

Hyperosmotic side:
• Higher solute
  concentration
• Lower free H$_2$O
  concentration

Hypoosmotic side:
• Lower solute
  concentration
• Higher free H$_2$O
  concentration

Net water flow

▲ **Figure 44.2 Solute concentration and osmosis.**

MAKE CONNECTIONS *Review types of membrane proteins and their functions in Concepts 7.1 and 7.2 (pp. 129–132). Which membrane proteins allow water, but not solutes, to diffuse across a lipid bilayer?*

uptake is excessive, animal cells swell and burst; if water loss is substantial, they shrivel and die (see Figure 7.15).

Water enters and leaves cells by osmosis. Recall from Chapter 7 that osmosis, a special case of diffusion, is the movement of water across a selectively permeable membrane. It occurs whenever two solutions separated by the membrane differ in osmotic pressure, or **osmolarity** (total solute concentration expressed as molarity, that is, moles of solute per liter of solution). The unit of measurement for osmolarity used in this chapter is milliOsmoles per liter (mOsm/L). Seawater has an osmolarity of about 1,000 mOsm/L (equivalent to a total solute concentration of 1 *M*), while the osmolarity of human blood is about 300 mOsm/L.

If two solutions separated by a selectively permeable membrane have the same osmolarity, they are said to be *isoosmotic*. Water molecules continually cross the membrane, but under these conditions they do so at equal rates in both directions. Thus, there is no *net* movement of water by osmosis between isoosmotic solutions. When two solutions differ in osmolarity, the one with the greater concentration of solutes is said to be *hyperosmotic*, and the more dilute solution is said to be *hypoosmotic* **(Figure 44.2)**. Water flows by osmosis from a hypoosmotic solution to a hyperosmotic one.*

Osmotic Challenges

Given the chemical principles that govern osmotic flow, an animal can maintain water balance in two ways. One is to be an **osmoconformer**: to be isoosmotic with its surroundings. The second is to be an **osmoregulator**: to control internal osmolarity independent of that of its environment.

All osmoconformers are marine animals. Because an osmoconformer's internal osmolarity is the same as that of its environment, there is no tendency to gain or lose water.

---

*In this chapter, we use the terms *isoosmotic*, *hypoosmotic*, and *hyperosmotic*, which refer specifically to osmolarity, instead of *isotonic*, *hypotonic*, and *hypertonic*. The latter set of terms applies to the response of animal cells— whether they swell or shrink—in solutions of known solute concentrations.

Many osmoconformers live in water that has a stable composition and hence have a constant internal osmolarity.

Osmoregulation enables animals to live in environments that are uninhabitable for osmoconformers, such as freshwater and terrestrial habitats. To survive in a hypoosmotic environment, an osmoregulator must discharge excess water. In a hyperosmotic environment, an osmoregulator must instead take in water to offset osmotic loss. Osmoregulation also allows many marine animals to maintain an internal osmolarity different from that of seawater.

Most animals, whether osmoconformers or osmoregulators, cannot tolerate substantial changes in external osmolarity and are said to be *stenohaline* (from the Greek *stenos*, narrow, and *halos*, salt). In contrast, *euryhaline* animals (from the Greek *eurys*, broad) can survive large fluctuations in external osmolarity. Euryhaline osmoconformers include many barnacles and mussels, which are continually covered and uncovered by ocean tides; examples of euryhaline osmoregulators are the striped bass and the various species of salmon.

Next we'll examine some adaptations for osmoregulation that have evolved in marine, freshwater, and terrestrial animals.

Marine Animals

Most marine invertebrates are osmoconformers. Their osmolarity is the same as that of seawater. They therefore face no substantial challenges in water balance. However, because these animals differ considerably from seawater in the concentrations of *specific* solutes, they must actively transport these solutes to maintain homeostasis. For example, although the concentration of magnesium ions (Mg^{2+}) in seawater is 50 m*M* (millimolar, or 10^{-3} mol/L), homeostatic mechanisms in the Atlantic lobster (*Homarus americanus*) result in a Mg^{2+} concentration of less than 9 m*M* in this animal's hemolymph (circulatory fluid).

Many marine vertebrates and some marine invertebrates are osmoregulators. For most of these animals, the ocean is a strongly dehydrating environment. For example, marine fishes, such as the cod in **Figure 44.3a**, constantly lose water by osmosis. Such fishes balance the water loss by drinking large amounts of seawater. In ridding themselves of salts, they make use of both their gills and kidneys. In the gills, specialized *chloride cells* actively transport chloride ions (Cl$^-$) out and allow sodium ions (Na$^+$) to follow passively. In the kidneys, excess calcium, magnesium, and sulfate ions are excreted with the loss of only small amounts of water.

A distinct osmoregulatory strategy evolved in marine sharks and most other chondrichthyans (cartilaginous animals; see Chapter 34). Like "bony fishes" (as we'll refer collectively to ray-finned and lobe-finned fishes in this chapter), sharks have an internal salt concentration much lower than that of seawater. Thus, salt tends to diffuse into their bodies from the water, especially across their gills. Unlike bony fishes, however, marine sharks are not hypoosmotic to seawater. The explanation

(a) Osmoregulation in a marine fish

Gain of water and salt ions from food

Excretion of salt ions from gills

Osmotic water **loss** through gills and other parts of body surface

SALT WATER

Gain of water and salt ions from drinking seawater

Excretion of salt ions and small amounts of water in scanty urine from kidneys

(b) Osmoregulation in a freshwater fish

Gain of water and some ions in food

Uptake of salt ions by gills

Osmotic water **gain** through gills and other parts of body surface

FRESH WATER

Excretion of salt ions and large amounts of water in dilute urine from kidneys

Key

⇨ Water

➡ Salt

▲ **Figure 44.3 Osmoregulation in marine and freshwater bony fishes: a comparison.**

is that shark tissue contains high concentrations of urea, a nitrogenous waste product of protein and nucleic acid metabolism (see Figure 44.8). A shark's body fluids also contain trimethylamine oxide (TMAO), an organic molecule that protects proteins from damage by urea. Together, the salts, urea, TMAO, and other compounds maintained in the body fluids of sharks result in an osmolarity very close to that of seawater. For this reason, sharks are often considered osmoconformers. However, because the solute concentration in their body fluids is actually somewhat higher than 1,000 mOsm/L, water slowly *enters* the shark's body by osmosis and in food (sharks do not drink). This small influx of water is disposed of in urine produced by the shark's kidneys. The urine also removes some of the salt that diffuses into the shark's body; the rest is lost in feces or is secreted from a specialized gland.

Freshwater Animals

The osmoregulatory problems of freshwater animals are the opposite of those of marine animals. The body fluids of freshwater animals must be hyperosmotic because animal cells cannot tolerate salt concentrations as low as that of lake or river water. Having internal fluids with an osmolarity higher than that of their surroundings, freshwater animals face the problem of gaining water by osmosis and losing salts by diffusion. Many freshwater animals, including bony fishes, solve the problem of water balance by drinking almost no water and excreting large amounts of very dilute urine. At the same time, salts lost by diffusion and in the urine are replenished by eating. Freshwater fishes, such as the perch in **Figure 44.3b**, also replenish salts by uptake across the gills. Chloride cells in the gills of the fish actively transport Cl⁻ into the body, and Na⁺ follows.

Salmon and other euryhaline fishes that migrate between fresh water and seawater undergo dramatic changes in osmoregulatory status **(Figure 44.4)**. When living in rivers and streams, salmon osmoregulate like other freshwater fishes,

▲ **Figure 44.4 Sockeye salmon (*Oncorhynchus nerka*), euryhaline osmoregulators.**

producing large amounts of dilute urine and taking up salt from the dilute environment through their gills. When they migrate to the ocean, salmon acclimatize. They produce more of the steroid hormone cortisol, which increases the number and size of salt-secreting chloride cells. As a result of these and other physiological changes, salmon in salt water excrete excess salt from their gills and produce only small amounts of urine—just like bony fishes that spend their entire lives in salt water.

Animals That Live in Temporary Waters

Extreme dehydration, or *desiccation*, is fatal for most animals. However, a few aquatic invertebrates that live in temporary ponds and in films of water around soil particles can lose almost all their body water and survive. These animals enter a dormant state when their habitats dry up, an adaptation called **anhydrobiosis** ("life without water"). Among the

(a) Hydrated tardigrade   (b) Dehydrated tardigrade

▲ **Figure 44.5 Anhydrobiosis.** SEM images of tardigrades (water bears), which inhabit temporary ponds as well as droplets of water in soil and on moist plants.

most striking examples are the tardigrades, or water bears (Figure 44.5). Less than 1 mm long, these tiny invertebrates are found in marine, freshwater, and moist terrestrial environments. In their active, hydrated state, they contain about 85% water by weight, but they can dehydrate to less than 2% water and survive in an inactive state, dry as dust, for a decade or more. Just add water, and within hours the rehydrated tardigrades are moving about and feeding.

Anhydrobiosis requires adaptations that keep cell membranes intact. Researchers are just beginning to learn how tardigrades survive drying out, but studies of anhydrobiotic roundworms (phylum Nematoda; see Chapter 33) show that desiccated individuals contain large amounts of sugars. In particular, a disaccharide called trehalose seems to protect the cells by replacing the water that is normally associated with proteins and membrane lipids. Many insects that survive freezing in the winter also use trehalose as a membrane protectant, as do some plants resistant to desiccation.

Land Animals

The threat of dehydration is a major regulatory problem for terrestrial plants and animals. Humans, for example, die if they lose as little as 12% of their body water (desert camels can withstand approximately twice that level of dehydration). Adaptations that reduce water loss are key to survival on land. Much as a waxy cuticle contributes to the success of land plants, the body coverings of most terrestrial animals help prevent dehydration. Examples are the waxy layers of insect exoskeletons, the shells of land snails, and the layers of dead, keratinized skin cells covering most terrestrial vertebrates, including humans. Many terrestrial animals, especially desert-dwellers, are nocturnal, which reduces evaporative water loss because of the lower temperature and higher humidity of night air.

Despite these and other adaptations, most terrestrial animals lose water through many routes: in urine and feces, across their skin, and from the surfaces of gas exchange organs. Land animals maintain water balance by drinking and

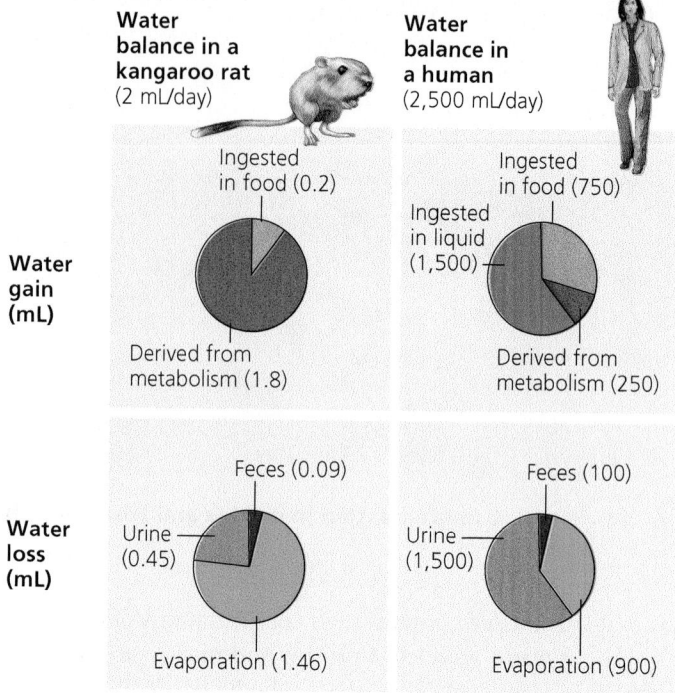

▲ **Figure 44.6 Water balance in two terrestrial mammals.** Kangaroo rats, which live in the American Southwest, eat mostly dry seeds and do not drink water. A kangaroo rat gains water mainly from cellular metabolism and loses water mainly by evaporation during gas exchange. In contrast, a human gains water in food and drink and loses the largest fraction of it in urine.

eating moist foods and by producing water metabolically through cellular respiration. A number of desert animals, including many insect-eating birds and other reptiles, are well enough adapted for minimizing water loss that they can survive for long periods of time without drinking. A noteworthy example is the kangaroo rat: It typically loses so little water that 90% is replaced by water it generates metabolically (Figure 44.6); the remaining 10% comes from the small amount of water in its diet of seeds. During particularly hot periods, kangaroo rats supplement their diet with juicy insects, thereby maintaining their water balance.

Energetics of Osmoregulation

Maintaining an osmolarity difference between an animal's body and its external environment carries an energy cost. Because diffusion tends to equalize concentrations in a system, osmoregulators must expend energy to maintain the osmotic gradients that cause water to move in or out. They do so by using active transport to manipulate solute concentrations in their body fluids.

The energy cost of osmoregulation depends on how different an animal's osmolarity is from its surroundings, how easily water and solutes can move across the animal's surface, and how much work is required to pump solutes across the membrane. Osmoregulation accounts for 5% or more of the resting metabolic rate of many freshwater and marine bony fishes. For brine shrimp, small crustaceans that live in extremely salty lakes, the gradient between internal and external osmolarity is very large, and the cost of osmoregulation is correspondingly high—as much as 30% of the resting metabolic rate.

The energy cost to an animal of maintaining water and salt balance is minimized by having body fluids that are adapted to the salinity of the animal's habitat. Thus, the body fluids of most animals that live in fresh water (which has an osmolarity of 0.5–15 mOsm/L) have lower solute concentrations than the body fluids of their closest relatives that live in seawater (1,000 mOsm/L). For instance, whereas marine molluscs have body fluids with solute concentrations of approximately 1,000 mOsm/L, some freshwater molluscs maintain the osmolarity of their body fluids at just 40 mOsm/L. In each case, minimizing the osmotic difference between body fluids and the surrounding environment decreases the energy the animal expends for osmoregulation.

Transport Epithelia in Osmoregulation

The ultimate function of osmoregulation is to control solute concentrations in cells, but most animals do this indirectly by managing the solute content of an internal body fluid that bathes the cells. In insects and other animals with an open circulatory system, the fluid surrounding cells is hemolymph. In vertebrates and other animals with a closed circulatory system, the cells are bathed in an interstitial fluid that contains a mixture of solutes controlled indirectly by the blood. Maintaining the composition of such fluids depends on structures ranging from individual cells that regulate solute movement to complex organs such as the vertebrate kidney.

In most animals, osmoregulation and metabolic waste disposal rely on **transport epithelia**—one or more layers of epithelial cells specialized for moving particular solutes in controlled amounts in specific directions. Transport epithelia are typically arranged into complex tubular networks with extensive surface areas. Some transport epithelia face the outside environment directly, while others line channels connected to the outside by an opening on the body surface.

The transport epithelium that enables the albatross to survive on seawater remained undiscovered for many years. Some scientists suggested that marine birds do not actually drink water, asserting that although the birds take water into their mouths, they do not swallow. Questioning this idea, Knut Schmidt-Nielsen and colleagues at the Mount Desert Island Laboratory, in Maine, gave captive marine birds only seawater to drink. The researchers found that while very little salt appeared in the birds' urine, fluid dripping from the tip of their beaks was a concentrated solution of salt (NaCl). Where did this fluid come from? As Schmidt-Nielsen demonstrated, the salt solution was produced by a pair of structures called the nasal glands. Similar structures, called salt glands, eliminate excess salt from the bodies of sea turtles and marine iguanas.

As shown in **Figure 44.7**, the nasal gland removes excess NaCl (in the form of Na^+ and Cl^-) from the blood

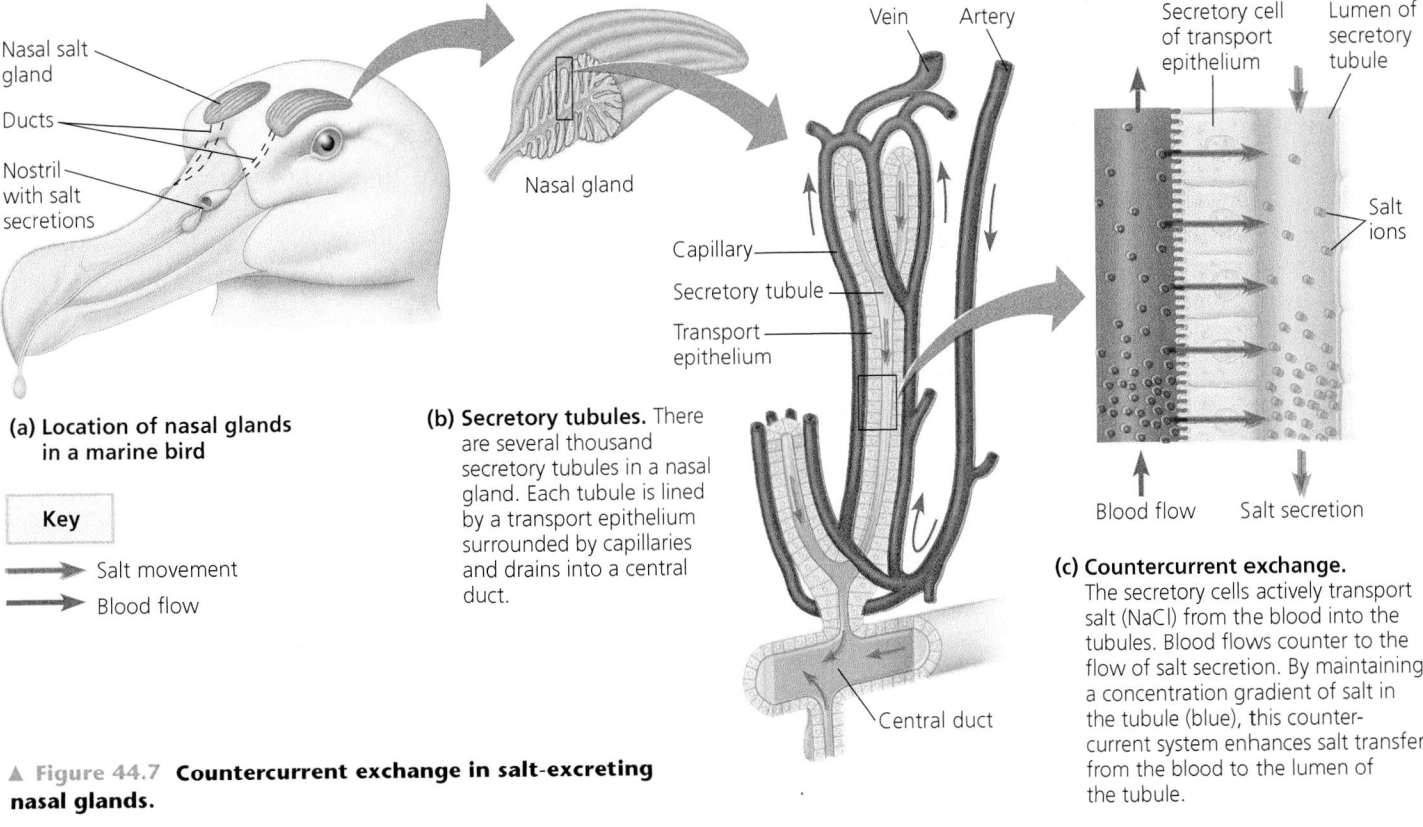

(a) Location of nasal glands in a marine bird

Key
→ Salt movement
→ Blood flow

(b) Secretory tubules. There are several thousand secretory tubules in a nasal gland. Each tubule is lined by a transport epithelium surrounded by capillaries and drains into a central duct.

(c) Countercurrent exchange. The secretory cells actively transport salt (NaCl) from the blood into the tubules. Blood flows counter to the flow of salt secretion. By maintaining a concentration gradient of salt in the tubule (blue), this countercurrent system enhances salt transfer from the blood to the lumen of the tubule.

▲ **Figure 44.7 Countercurrent exchange in salt-excreting nasal glands.**

by countercurrent exchange. Recall from Chapter 40 that countercurrent exchange occurs between two fluids separated by one or more membranes and flowing in opposite directions. In the albatross's nasal gland, the net result is the secretion of fluid much saltier than the ocean. Thus, even though drinking seawater brings in a lot of salt, the bird achieves a net gain of water. By contrast, humans who drink a given volume of seawater must use a *greater* volume of water to excrete the salt load, with the result that they become dehydrated.

Transport epithelia that function in maintaining water balance also often function in disposal of metabolic wastes. We will see examples of this coordinated function in our upcoming consideration of earthworm and insect excretory systems as well as the vertebrate kidney.

CONCEPT CHECK 44.1

1. The movement of salt from the surrounding water to the blood of a freshwater fish requires the expenditure of energy in the form of ATP. Why?
2. Why aren't any freshwater animals osmoconformers?
3. **WHAT IF?** Researchers found that a camel standing in the sun required much more water when its fur was shaved off, although its body temperature remained the same. What can you conclude about the relationship between osmoregulation and the insulation provided by fur?

For suggested answers, see Appendix A.

CONCEPT 44.2

An animal's nitrogenous wastes reflect its phylogeny and habitat

Because most metabolic wastes must be dissolved in water to be excreted from the body, the type and quantity of an animal's waste products may have a large impact on its water balance. In this regard, some of the most significant waste products are the nitrogenous breakdown products of proteins and nucleic acids (**Figure 44.8**). When proteins and nucleic acids are broken apart for energy or converted to carbohydrates or fats, enzymes remove nitrogen in the form of **ammonia** (NH_3). Ammonia is very toxic, in part because its ion, ammonium (NH_4^+), interferes with oxidative phosphorylation. Although some animals excrete ammonia directly, many species expend energy to convert it to less toxic compounds prior to excretion.

Forms of Nitrogenous Waste

Animals excrete nitrogenous wastes as ammonia, urea, or uric acid. These different forms vary significantly in their toxicity and the energy costs of producing them.

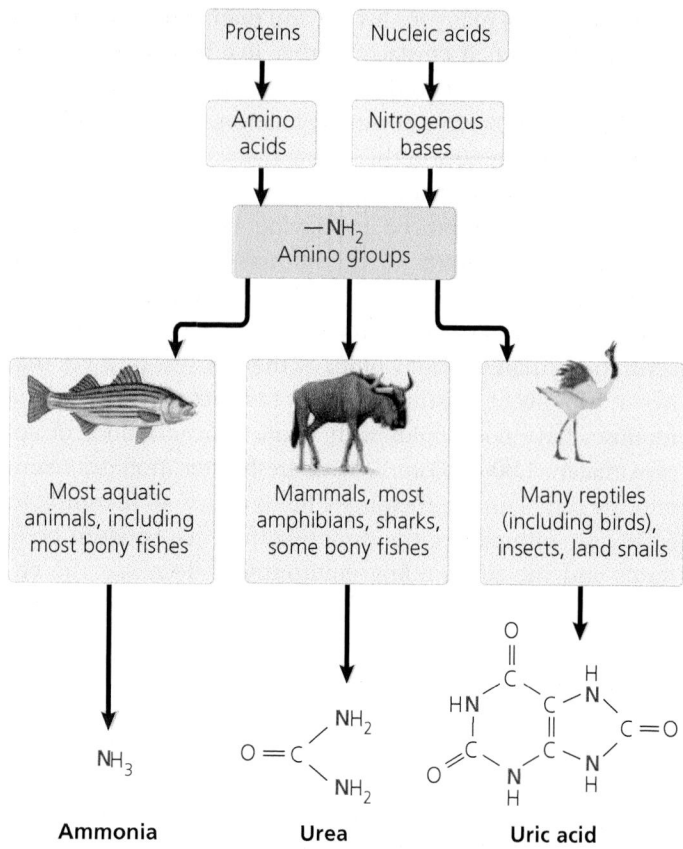

▲ Figure 44.8 **Forms of nitrogenous waste.**

Ammonia

Because ammonia can be tolerated only at very low concentrations, animals that excrete nitrogenous wastes as ammonia need access to lots of water. Therefore, ammonia excretion is most common in aquatic species. Being highly soluble, ammonia molecules easily pass through membranes and are readily lost by diffusion to the surrounding water. In many invertebrates, ammonia release occurs across the whole body surface. In fishes, most of the ammonia is lost as NH_4^+ across the epithelium of the gills; the kidneys excrete only minor amounts of nitrogenous waste.

Urea

Although ammonia excretion works well in many aquatic species, it is much less suitable for land animals. Ammonia is so toxic that it can be transported and excreted only in large volumes of very dilute solutions. As a result, most terrestrial animals and many marine species (principally those that tend to lose water to their environment by osmosis) simply do not have access to sufficient water to routinely excrete ammonia. Instead, mammals, most adult amphibians, sharks, and some marine bony fishes and turtles mainly excrete a different nitrogenous waste, **urea**. Produced in the vertebrate liver, urea is the product of a metabolic cycle that combines ammonia with carbon dioxide.

The main advantage of urea is its very low toxicity. Animals can transport urea in the circulatory system and store it safely at high concentrations. Furthermore, much less water is lost when a given quantity of nitrogen is excreted in a concentrated solution of urea rather than a dilute solution of ammonia.

The main disadvantage of urea is its energy cost: Animals must expend energy to produce urea from ammonia. From a bioenergetic standpoint, we would predict that animals that spend part of their lives in water and part on land would switch between excreting ammonia (thereby saving energy) and excreting urea (reducing excretory water loss). Indeed, many amphibians excrete mainly ammonia when they are aquatic tadpoles and switch largely to urea excretion when they become land-dwelling adults.

Uric Acid

Insects, land snails, and many reptiles, including birds, excrete **uric acid** as their primary nitrogenous waste. (Bird droppings, or *guano*, are a mixture of white uric acid and brown feces.) Uric acid is relatively nontoxic and does not readily dissolve in water. It therefore can be excreted as a semisolid paste with very little water loss. This is a great advantage for animals with little access to water, but there is a cost: Uric acid is even more energetically expensive to produce than urea, requiring considerable ATP for synthesis from ammonia.

Because uric acid releases nitrates to soil, bird guano can be used as fertilizer in agriculture. Before synthetic fertilizers were developed, this "waste" was so valued that nations fought wars over South American islands covered with piles of seabird guano as tall as 12-story buildings! Recently, interest in organic fertilizers has revived the commercial trade in guano (**Figure 44.9**).

While not primarily uric acid producers, humans and some other animals generate a small amount of uric acid as a product of purine breakdown. Diseases that alter this process reflect the problems that can arise when a metabolic product is insoluble. For example, a genetic defect in purine metabolism predisposes Dalmatian dogs to form uric acid stones in their bladder. In humans, adult males are particularly susceptible to *gout*, a painful joint inflammation caused by deposits of uric acid crystals. Meals containing purine-rich animal tissues can increase the inflammation. Some dinosaurs appear to have been similarly affected: Fossilized bones of *Tyrannosaurus rex* exhibit joint damage characteristic of gout.

The Influence of Evolution and Environment on Nitrogenous Wastes

EVOLUTION In general, the kind of nitrogenous wastes an animal excretes depends on both the species' evolutionary history (phylogeny) and its habitat, especially the availability of water. For example, terrestrial turtles (which often live in dry areas) excrete mainly uric acid, whereas aquatic turtles excrete both urea and ammonia. Another factor affecting the primary type of nitrogenous waste produced by a particular group of animals is the immediate environment of the animal egg. For example, soluble wastes can diffuse out of a shell-less amphibian egg or be carried away from a mammalian embryo by the mother's blood. However, the shelled eggs produced by birds and other reptiles (see Figure 34.25) are permeable to gases but not to liquids, which means that soluble nitrogenous wastes released by an embryo would be trapped within the egg and could accumulate to dangerous levels. (Although urea is much less harmful than ammonia, it is toxic at very high concentrations.) Using uric acid as a waste product conveys a selective advantage because it precipitates out of solution and can be stored within the egg as a harmless solid left behind when the animal hatches.

Regardless of the type of nitrogenous waste, the amount produced is coupled to the animal's energy budget. Endotherms, which use energy at high rates, eat more food and produce more nitrogenous waste than ectotherms. The amount of nitrogenous waste is also linked to diet. Predators, which derive much of their energy from protein, excrete more nitrogen than animals that rely mainly on lipids or carbohydrates as energy sources.

Having surveyed the forms of nitrogenous waste and their interrelationship with evolutionary lineage, habitat, and energy consumption, we will turn next to the processes and systems animals use to excrete these and other wastes.

▼ **Figure 44.9 Recycling nitrogenous waste.** Seabirds nesting on islands off Peru annually produce 12,000 tons of guano, which workers collect for sale as organic fertilizer.

CONCEPT CHECK 44.2

1. What advantage does uric acid offer as a nitrogenous waste in arid environments?
2. **WHAT IF?** Suppose a bird and a human both have gout. Why might reducing purine in their diets help the human much more than the bird?

For suggested answers, see Appendix A.

Diverse excretory systems are variations on a tubular theme

Whether an animal lives on land, in salt water, or in fresh water, water balance depends on the regulation of solute movement between internal fluids and the external environment. Much of this movement is handled by excretory systems. These systems are central to homeostasis because they dispose of metabolic wastes and control body fluid composition. Before we describe particular excretory systems, let's consider a generalized version of the process of excretion.

Excretory Processes

Animals across a wide range of species produce a fluid waste called urine through the basic steps shown in **Figure 44.10**. In the first step, body fluid (blood, coelomic fluid, or hemolymph) is brought in contact with the selectively permeable membrane of a transport epithelium. In most cases, hydrostatic pressure (blood pressure in many animals) drives a process of **filtration**. Cells, as well as proteins and other large molecules, cannot cross the epithelial membrane and

remain in the body fluid. In contrast, water and small solutes, such as salts, sugars, amino acids, and nitrogenous wastes, cross the membrane, forming a solution called the **filtrate**.

The filtrate is converted to a waste fluid by the specific transport of materials into or out of the filtrate. The process of selective **reabsorption** recovers useful molecules and water from the filtrate and returns them to the body fluids. Valuable solutes—including glucose, certain salts, vitamins, hormones, and amino acids—are reabsorbed by active transport. Nonessential solutes and wastes are left in the filtrate or are added to it by selective **secretion**, which also occurs by active transport. The pumping of various solutes adjusts the osmotic movement of water into or out of the filtrate. In the last step—excretion—the processed filtrate containing nitrogenous wastes is released from the body as urine.

Survey of Excretory Systems

The systems that perform the basic excretory functions vary widely among animal groups. However, they are generally built on a complex network of tubules that provide a large surface area for the exchange of water and solutes, including nitrogenous wastes. We'll examine the excretory systems of flatworms, earthworms, insects, and vertebrates as examples of evolutionary variations on tubule networks.

Protonephridia

Flatworms (phylum Platyhelminthes) have excretory systems called **protonephridia** (singular, *protonephridium*), which form a network of dead-end tubules (**Figure 44.11**). The

❶ Filtration. The excretory tubule collects a filtrate from the blood. Water and solutes are forced by blood pressure across the selectively permeable membranes of a cluster of capillaries and into the excretory tubule.

❷ Reabsorption. The transport epithelium reclaims valuable substances from the filtrate and returns them to the body fluids.

❸ Secretion. Other substances, such as toxins and excess ions, are extracted from body fluids and added to the contents of the excretory tubule.

❹ Excretion. The altered filtrate (urine) leaves the system and the body.

Capillary

Filtrate

Excretory tubule

Urine

▲ **Figure 44.10 Key steps of excretory system function: an overview.** Most excretory systems produce a filtrate by pressure-filtering body fluids and then modify the filtrate's contents. This diagram is modeled after the vertebrate excretory system.

▶ **Figure 44.11 Protonephridia: the flame bulb system of a planarian.** Protonephridia are branching internal tubules that function mainly in osmoregulation.

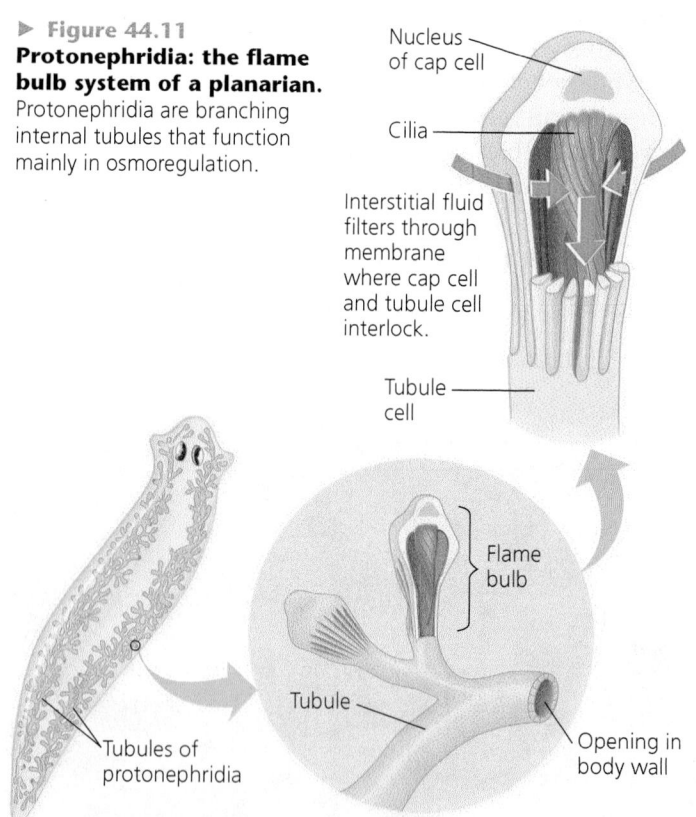

Nucleus of cap cell

Cilia

Interstitial fluid filters through membrane where cap cell and tubule cell interlock.

Tubule cell

Flame bulb

Tubule

Tubules of protonephridia

Opening in body wall

tubules, which are connected to external openings, branch throughout the flatworm body, which lacks a coelom or body cavity. Cellular units called flame bulbs cap the branches of each protonephridium. Consisting of a tubule cell and a cap cell, each flame bulb has a tuft of cilia projecting into the tubule. During filtration, the beating of the cilia draws water and solutes from the interstitial fluid through the flame bulb, releasing filtrate into the tubule network. (The moving cilia resemble a flickering flame, hence the name *flame bulb*.) The processed filtrate then moves outward through the tubules and empties as urine into the external environment. The urine excreted by freshwater flatworms has a low solute concentration, helping to balance the osmotic uptake of water from the environment.

Protonephridia are also found in rotifers, some annelids, mollusc larvae, and lancelets (see Figure 34.4). Among these animals, the function of the protonephridia varies. In the freshwater flatworms, protonephridia serve chiefly in osmoregulation. Most metabolic wastes diffuse out of the animal across the body surface or are excreted into the gastrovascular cavity and eliminated through the mouth (see Figure 33.10). However, in some parasitic flatworms, which are isoosmotic to the surrounding fluids of their host organisms, the main function of protonephridia is the disposal of nitrogenous wastes. Natural selection has thus adapted protonephridia to different tasks in different environments.

Metanephridia

Most annelids, such as earthworms, have **metanephridia** (singular, *metanephridium*), excretory organs that collect fluid directly from the coelom (Figure 44.12). Each segment of a worm has a pair of metanephridia, which are immersed in coelomic fluid and enveloped by a capillary network. A ciliated funnel surrounds the internal opening. As the cilia beat, fluid is drawn into a collecting tubule, which includes a storage bladder that opens to the outside.

The metanephridia of an earthworm have both excretory and osmoregulatory functions. As urine moves along the tubule, the transport epithelium bordering the lumen reabsorbs most solutes and returns them to the blood in the capillaries. Nitrogenous wastes remain in the tubule and are excreted to the outside. Earthworms inhabit damp soil and usually experience a net uptake of water by osmosis through their skin. Their metanephridia balance the water influx by producing urine that is dilute (hypoosmotic to body fluids).

Malpighian Tubules

Insects and other terrestrial arthropods have organs called **Malpighian tubules** that remove nitrogenous wastes and that also function in osmoregulation (Figure 44.13). The Malpighian tubules extend from dead-end tips immersed in hemolymph (circulatory fluid) to openings into the digestive tract. The filtration step common to other excretory systems is absent. Instead, the transport epithelium that lines the tubules secretes certain solutes, including nitrogenous wastes, from the hemolymph into the lumen of the tubule. Water follows the solutes into the tubule by osmosis, and the fluid then passes into the rectum. There, most solutes are pumped back into the hemolymph, and water reabsorption by osmosis follows. The nitrogenous wastes—mainly insoluble

▲ Figure 44.12 Metanephridia of an earthworm. Each segment of the worm contains a pair of metanephridia, which collect coelomic fluid from the adjacent anterior segment. The region highlighted in yellow illustrates the organization of one metanephridium of a pair; the other would be behind it.

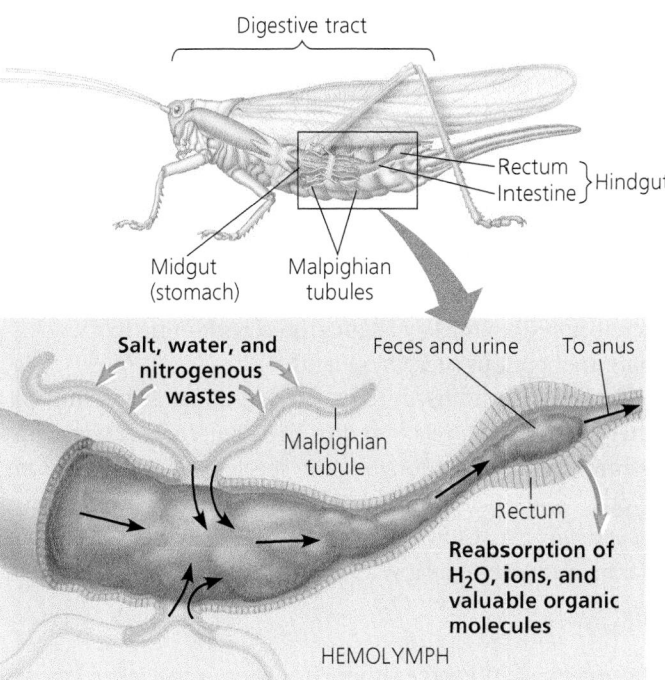

▲ Figure 44.13 Malpighian tubules of insects. Malpighian tubules are outpocketings of the digestive tract that remove nitrogenous wastes and function in osmoregulation.

Exploring the Mammalian Excretory System

Excretory Organs

Posterior vena cava
Renal artery and vein
Aorta
Ureter
Urinary bladder
Urethra
Kidney

In humans, the excretory system consists of a pair of **kidneys**, bean-shaped organs about 10 cm in length, as well as organs for transporting and storing urine. Urine produced by each kidney exits through a duct called the **ureter**; the two ureters drain into a common sac called the **urinary bladder**. During urination, urine is expelled from the bladder through a tube called the **urethra**, which empties to the outside near the vagina in females and through the penis in males. Sphincter muscles near the junction of the urethra and bladder regulate urination.

Kidney Structure

Renal cortex
Renal medulla
Renal artery
Renal vein
Ureter
Renal pelvis

Each kidney has an outer **renal cortex** and an inner **renal medulla**. Both regions are supplied with blood by a renal artery and drained by a renal vein. Within the cortex and medulla lie tightly packed excretory tubules and associated blood vessels. The inner **renal pelvis** collects urine from the excretory tubules and passes it to the urinary bladder.

Nephron Types

Cortical nephron
Juxtamedullary nephron
Renal cortex
Renal medulla

Weaving back and forth across the renal cortex and medulla are the **nephrons**, the functional units of the vertebrate kidney. Of the roughly 1 million nephrons in a human kidney, 85% are **cortical nephrons**, which reach only a short distance into the medulla. The remainder, the **juxtamedullary nephrons**, extend deep into the medulla. Juxtamedullary nephrons are essential for production of urine that is hyperosmotic to body fluids, a key adaptation for water conservation in mammals.

---

uric acid—are eliminated as nearly dry matter along with the feces. Capable of conserving water very effectively, the insect excretory system is a key adaptation contributing to these animals' tremendous success on land.

Some terrestrial insects have an additional adaptation for water balance: The rectal end of their gut enables water uptake from the air. Although some species absorb water from air only when it is very humid, others, such as fleas (genus *Xenopsylla*), can capture water from the atmosphere when relative humidity is as low as 50%.

Kidneys

In vertebrates and some other chordates, a specialized organ called the kidney functions in both osmoregulation and excretion. Like the excretory organs of most animal phyla, kidneys consist of tubules. The numerous tubules of these compact organs are arranged in a highly organized manner and are closely associated with a network of capillaries. The vertebrate excretory system also includes ducts and other structures that carry urine from the tubules out of the kidney and, eventually, the body.

Vertebrate kidneys are typically nonsegmented. However, hagfishes, which are invertebrate chordates, have kidneys with segmentally arranged excretory tubules. This suggests that the excretory structures of vertebrate ancestors also may have been segmented.

Because kidney organization is integral to kidney function, we begin with **Figure 44.14**, an exploration of the anatomy of the mammalian kidney and associated structures. Familiarizing yourself with the terms and diagrams in this figure will provide you with a solid foundation for learning about filtrate processing in the kidney, our focus in the next concept.

Nephron Organization

Afferent arteriole from renal artery
Glomerulus
Bowman's capsule
Proximal tubule
Distal tubule
Peritubular capillaries
Efferent arteriole from glomerulus
Branch of renal vein
Vasa recta
Descending limb
Loop of Henle
Collecting duct
Ascending limb

Each nephron consists of a single long tubule as well as a ball of capillaries called the **glomerulus**. The blind end of the tubule forms a cup-shaped swelling, called **Bowman's capsule**, which surrounds the glomerulus. Filtrate is formed when blood pressure forces fluid from the blood in the glomerulus into the lumen of Bowman's capsule. Processing occurs as the filtrate passes through three major regions of the nephron: the **proximal tubule**, the **loop of Henle** (a hairpin turn with a descending limb and an ascending limb), and the **distal tubule**. A **collecting duct** receives processed filtrate from many nephrons and transports it to the renal pelvis.

Each nephron is supplied with blood by an *afferent arteriole*, an offshoot of the renal artery that branches and forms the capillaries of the glomerulus. The capillaries converge as they leave the glomerulus, forming an *efferent arteriole*. Branches of this vessel form the **peritubular capillaries**, which surround the proximal and distal tubules. Other branches extend downward and form the **vasa recta**, hairpin-shaped capillaries that serve the renal medulla, including the long loop of Henle of juxtamedullary nephrons.

▶ In this SEM of densely packed blood vessels from a human kidney, arterioles and peritubular capillaries appear pink; the glomeruli appear yellow.

200 μm

CONCEPT CHECK 44.3

1. Compare and contrast the different ways that metabolic waste products enter the excretory systems of flatworms, earthworms, and insects.
2. What is the function of the filtration step in excretory systems?
3. **WHAT IF?** Kidney failure is often treated by hemodialysis, in which blood diverted out of the body is filtered and then allowed to flow on one side of a semipermeable membrane. Fluid called dialysate flows in the opposite direction on the other side of the membrane. In replacing the reabsorption and secretion of solutes in a functional kidney, the makeup of the starting dialysate is critical. What initial solute composition would work well?

For suggested answers, see Appendix A.

CONCEPT 44.4

The nephron is organized for stepwise processing of blood filtrate

We'll continue our exploration of the nephron with a discussion of filtrate processing. We will then focus on how tubules, capillaries, and surrounding tissue function together.

The porous capillaries and specialized cells of Bowman's capsule are permeable to water and small solutes, but not blood cells or large molecules, such as plasma proteins. Thus, the filtrate produced in the capsule contains salts, glucose, amino acids, vitamins, nitrogenous wastes, and other small molecules. Because such molecules pass freely between glomerular capillaries and Bowman's capsule, the concentrations of these substances in the initial filtrate are the same as those in blood plasma.

From Blood Filtrate to Urine: *A Closer Look*

In this section, we will follow filtrate along its path in the nephron and collecting duct, examining how each region contributes to the stepwise processing of filtrate into urine. The circled numbers correspond to the numbers in **Figure 44.15.**

❶ Proximal tubule. Reabsorption in the proximal tubule is critical for the recapture of ions, water, and valuable nutrients from the huge volume of initial filtrate. NaCl (salt) in the filtrate diffuses into the cells of the transport epithelium, where Na^+ is actively transported into the interstitial fluid. This transfer of positive charge out of the tubule drives the passive transport of Cl^-, as well as the movement of more Na^+ from the lumen into the cells of the tubule wall by facilitated diffusion and cotransport mechanisms (see Figures 7.17 and 7.21).

As salt moves from the filtrate to the interstitial fluid, water follows by osmosis. The salt and water then diffuse from the interstitial fluid into the peritubular capillaries. Glucose, amino acids, potassium ions (K^+), and other essential substances are also actively or passively transported from the filtrate to the interstitial fluid and then into the peritubular capillaries.

Processing of filtrate in the proximal tubule helps maintain a relatively constant pH in body fluids. Cells of the transport epithelium secrete H^+ into the lumen of the tubule but also synthesize and secrete ammonia, which acts as a buffer to trap H^+ in the form of ammonium ions (NH_4^+). The more acidic the filtrate, the more ammonia the cells produce and secrete, and a mammal's urine usually contains some ammonia from this source (even though most nitrogenous waste is excreted as urea). The proximal tubules also reabsorb about 90% of the buffer bicarbonate (HCO_3^-) from the filtrate, contributing further to pH balance in body fluids.

As the filtrate passes through the proximal tubule, materials to be excreted become concentrated. Many wastes leave the body fluids during the nonselective filtration process and remain in the filtrate while water and salts are reabsorbed. Urea, for example, is reabsorbed at a much lower rate than are salt and water. Some other toxic materials are actively secreted into filtrate from surrounding tissues. For example, drugs and toxins that have been processed in the liver pass from the peritubular capillaries into the interstitial fluid. These molecules then enter the proximal tubule, where they are actively secreted from the transport epithelium into the lumen.

▲ Figure 44.15 The nephron and collecting duct: regional functions of the transport epithelium. The numbered regions in this diagram are keyed to the circled numbers in the text discussion of kidney function.

? *Some cells lining tubules in the kidney synthesize organic solutes to maintain normal cell volume. Where in the kidney would you find these cells? Explain.*

② Descending limb of the loop of Henle. Reabsorption of water continues as the filtrate moves into the descending limb of the loop of Henle. Here numerous water channels formed by **aquaporin** proteins make the transport epithelium freely permeable to water. In contrast, there are almost no channels for salt and other small solutes, resulting in very low permeability for these substances.

For water to move out of the tubule by osmosis, the interstitial fluid bathing the tubule must be hyperosmotic to the filtrate. This condition is met along the entire length of the descending limb, because the osmolarity of the interstitial fluid increases progressively from the outer cortex to the inner medulla of the kidney. As a result, the filtrate loses water—and therefore its solute concentration increases—all along its journey down the descending limb.

③ Ascending limb of the loop of Henle. The filtrate reaches the tip of the loop and then travels within the ascending limb as it returns to the cortex. Unlike the descending limb, the ascending limb has a transport epithelium studded with ion channels, but not water channels. Indeed, this membrane is impermeable to water. Impermeability to water is very rare among biological membranes and is critical to the function of the ascending limb.

The ascending limb has two specialized regions: a thin segment near the loop tip and a thick segment adjacent to the distal tubule. As filtrate ascends in the thin segment, NaCl, which became concentrated in the descending limb, diffuses out of the permeable tubule into the interstitial fluid. This movement of NaCl out of the tubule helps maintain the osmolarity of the interstitial fluid in the medulla. In the thick segment of the ascending limb, the movement of NaCl out of the filtrate continues. Here, however, the epithelium actively transports NaCl into the interstitial fluid. As a result of losing salt but not water, the filtrate becomes progressively more dilute as it moves up to the cortex in the ascending limb of the loop.

④ Distal tubule. The distal tubule plays a key role in regulating the K^+ and NaCl concentration of body fluids. This regulation involves variation in the amount of K^+ secreted into the filtrate as well as the amount of NaCl reabsorbed from the filtrate. Like the proximal tubule, the distal tubule contributes to pH regulation by the controlled secretion of H^+ and reabsorption of HCO_3^-.

⑤ Collecting duct. The collecting duct carries the filtrate through the medulla to the renal pelvis. The transport epithelium of the nephron and collecting duct processes the filtrate, forming the urine. One of this epithelium's most important tasks is reabsorption of solutes and water. Under normal conditions, approximately 1,600 L of blood flows through a pair of human kidneys each day, about 300 times the total volume of blood in the body. From this enormous traffic of blood, the nephrons and collecting ducts process about 180 L of initial filtrate. Of this, about 99% of the water and nearly all of the sugars, amino acids, vitamins, and other organic nutrients are reabsorbed into the blood, leaving only about 1.5 L of urine to be transported to the bladder.

As filtrate passes along the transport epithelium of the collecting duct, hormonal control of permeability and transport determines the extent to which the urine becomes concentrated.

When the kidneys are conserving water, aquaporin channels in the collecting duct allow water molecules to cross the epithelium. At the same time, the epithelium remains impermeable to salt and, in the renal cortex, to urea. As the collecting duct traverses the gradient of osmolarity in the kidney, the filtrate becomes increasingly concentrated, losing more and more water by osmosis to the hyperosmotic interstitial fluid. In the inner medulla, the duct becomes permeable to urea. Because of the high urea concentration in the filtrate at this point, some urea diffuses out of the duct and into the interstitial fluid. Along with NaCl, this urea contributes to the high osmolarity of the interstitial fluid in the medulla. The net result is urine that is hyperosmotic to the general body fluids.

In producing dilute rather than concentrated urine, the kidney actively reabsorbs salts without allowing water to follow by osmosis. At these times, the epithelium lacks water channels, and NaCl is actively transported out of filtrate. As we will see shortly, the state of the collecting duct epithelium is controlled by hormones that together maintain homeostasis for osmolarity, blood pressure, and blood volume.

Solute Gradients and Water Conservation

The mammalian kidney's ability to conserve water is a key terrestrial adaptation. In humans, the osmolarity of blood is about 300 mOsm/L, but the kidney can excrete urine up to four times as concentrated—about 1,200 mOsm/L. Some mammals can do even better: Australian hopping mice, small marsupials that live in dry desert regions, can produce urine with an osmolarity of 9,300 mOsm/L, 25 times as concentrated as the animal's blood.

In a mammalian kidney, the production of hyperosmotic urine is possible only because considerable energy is expended for the active transport of solutes against concentration gradients. The nephrons—particularly the loops of Henle—can be thought of as energy-consuming machines that produce an osmolarity gradient suitable for extracting water from the filtrate in the collecting duct. The two primary solutes affecting osmolarity are NaCl, which is deposited in the renal medulla by the loop of Henle, and urea, which passes across the epithelium of the collecting duct in the inner medulla.

The Two-Solute Model

To better understand the physiology of the mammalian kidney as a water-conserving organ, let's retrace the flow of filtrate through the excretory tubule. This time, let's focus on how the juxtamedullary nephrons maintain an osmolarity gradient in the tissues that surround the loop of Henle and how they use that gradient to excrete a hyperosmotic urine (Figure 44.16). Filtrate passing from Bowman's capsule to the proximal tubule has an osmolarity of about 300 mOsm/L, the same as blood. A large amount of water *and* salt is reabsorbed from the filtrate as it flows through the proximal tubule in the renal cortex. As a result, the filtrate's volume decreases substantially, but its osmolarity remains about the same.

As the filtrate flows from cortex to medulla in the descending limb of the loop of Henle, water leaves the tubule by osmosis. Solutes, including NaCl, become more concentrated, increasing the osmolarity of the filtrate. The highest osmolarity (about 1,200 mOsm/L) occurs at the elbow of the loop of Henle. This maximizes the diffusion of salt out of the tubule as the filtrate rounds the curve and enters the ascending limb, which is permeable to salt but not to water. NaCl diffusing from the ascending limb helps maintain a high osmolarity in the interstitial fluid of the renal medulla.

Notice that the loop of Henle has several qualities of a countercurrent system, such as the mechanisms that maximize oxygen absorption by fish gills (see Figure 42.22) or reduce heat loss in endotherms (see Figure 40.12). In those cases, the countercurrent mechanisms involve passive movement along either an oxygen concentration gradient or a heat gradient. In contrast, the countercurrent system involving the loop of Henle expends energy to actively transport NaCl from the filtrate in the upper part of the ascending limb of the loop. Such countercurrent systems, which expend energy to create concentration gradients, are called **countercurrent multiplier systems**. The countercurrent multiplier system involving the loop of Henle maintains a high salt concentration in the interior of the kidney, enabling the kidney to form concentrated urine.

What prevents the capillaries of the vasa recta from dissipating the gradient by carrying away the high concentration of NaCl in the medulla's interstitial fluid? As shown in Figure 44.14, the descending and ascending vessels of the vasa recta carry blood in opposite directions through the kidney's osmolarity gradient. As the descending vessel conveys blood toward the inner medulla, water is lost from the blood and NaCl is gained by diffusion. These fluxes are reversed as blood flows back toward the cortex in the ascending vessel, with water reentering the blood and salt diffusing out. Thus,

▶ **Figure 44.16 How the human kidney concentrates urine: the two-solute model.** Two solutes contribute to the osmolarity of the interstitial fluid: NaCl (used as shorthand here to refer collectively to Na^+ and Cl^-) and urea. The loop of Henle maintains the interstitial gradient of NaCl, which increases continuously in concentration from the cortex to the inner medulla. Urea diffuses into the interstitial fluid of the medulla from the collecting duct (most of the urea in the filtrate remains in the collecting duct and is excreted). The filtrate makes three trips between the cortex and medulla: first down, then up, and then down again in the collecting duct. As the filtrate flows in the collecting duct past interstitial fluid of increasing osmolarity, more water moves out of the duct by osmosis. The loss of water concentrates the solutes, including urea, that will be excreted in the urine.

WHAT IF? The drug furosemide blocks the cotransporters for Na^+ and Cl^- in the ascending limb of the loop of Henle. What effect would you expect this drug to have on urine volume?

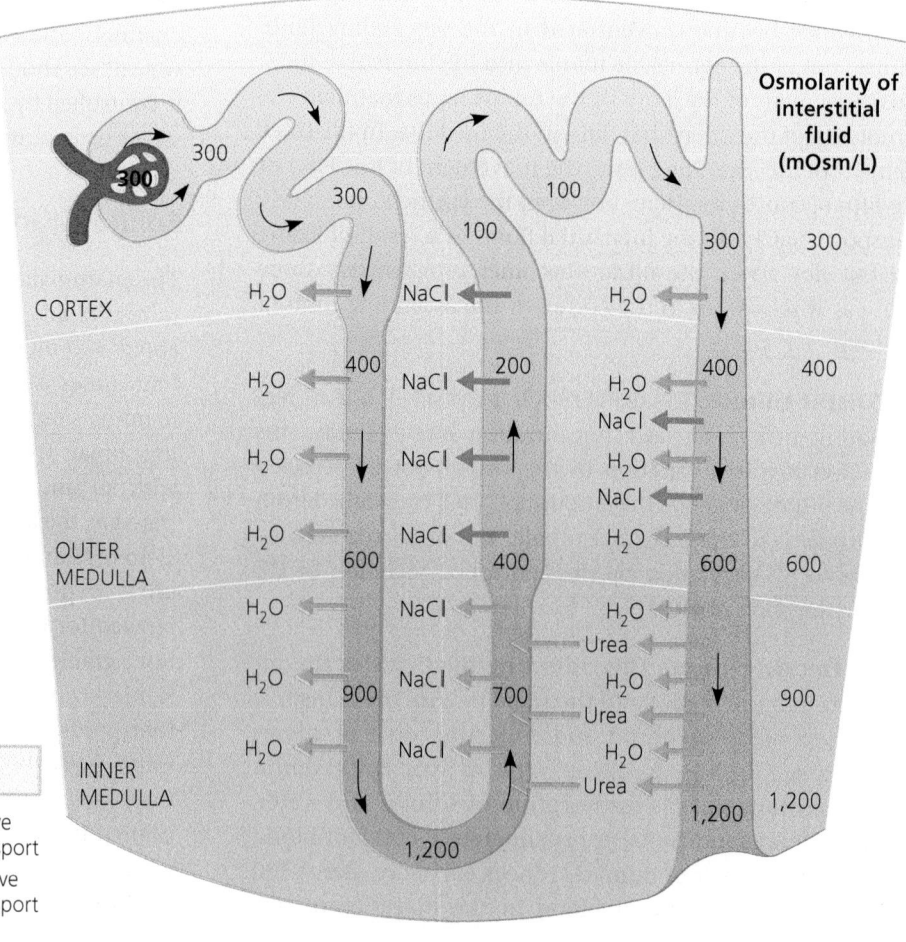

Key
→ Active transport
→ Passive transport

the vasa recta can supply the kidney with nutrients and other important substances carried by the blood without interfering with the osmolarity gradient in the inner and outer medulla.

The countercurrent-like characteristics of the loop of Henle and the vasa recta help to generate the steep osmotic gradient between the medulla and cortex. However, diffusion will eventually eliminate any osmotic gradient within animal tissue unless gradient formation is supported by an expenditure of energy. In the kidney, this expenditure largely occurs in the thick segment of the ascending limb of the loop of Henle, where NaCl is actively transported out of the tubule. Even with the benefits of countercurrent exchange, this process—along with other renal active transport systems—consumes considerable ATP. Thus, for its size, the kidney has one of the highest metabolic rates of any organ.

As a result of active transport of NaCl out of the thick segment of the ascending limb, the filtrate is actually hypoosmotic to body fluids by the time it reaches the distal tubule. Next the filtrate descends again toward the medulla, this time in the collecting duct, which is permeable to water but not to salt. Therefore, osmosis extracts water from the filtrate as it passes from cortex to medulla and encounters interstitial fluid of increasing osmolarity. This process concentrates salt, urea, and other solutes in the filtrate. Some urea passes out of the lower portion of the collecting duct and contributes to the high interstitial osmolarity of the inner medulla. (This urea is recycled by diffusion into the loop of Henle, but continual leakage from the collecting duct maintains a high interstitial urea concentration.) When the kidney concentrates urine maximally, the urine reaches 1,200 mOsm/L, the osmolarity of the interstitial fluid in the inner medulla. Although *isoosmotic* to the inner medulla's interstitial fluid, the urine is *hyperosmotic* to blood and interstitial fluid elsewhere in the body. This high osmolarity allows the solutes remaining in the urine to be excreted from the body with minimal water loss.

Adaptations of the Vertebrate Kidney to Diverse Environments

EVOLUTION Vertebrate animals occupy habitats ranging from rain forests to deserts and from some of the saltiest bodies of water to the nearly pure waters of high mountain lakes. Variations in nephron structure and function equip the kidneys of different vertebrates for osmoregulation in their various habitats. The adaptations of the vertebrate kidney are made apparent by comparing species that inhabit a wide range of environments or by comparing the responses of different vertebrate groups to similar environmental conditions.

Mammals

The juxtamedullary nephron, with its urine-concentrating features, is a key adaptation to terrestrial life, enabling mammals to get rid of salts and nitrogenous wastes without squandering

water. As we have seen, the remarkable ability of the mammalian kidney to produce hyperosmotic urine depends on the precise arrangement of the tubules and collecting ducts in the renal cortex and medulla. In this respect, the kidney is one of the clearest examples of how natural selection links the function of an organ to its structure.

Mammals that excrete the most hyperosmotic urine, such as Australian hopping mice, North American kangaroo rats, and other desert mammals, have loops of Henle that extend deep into the medulla. Long loops maintain steep osmotic gradients in the kidney, resulting in urine becoming very concentrated as it passes from cortex to medulla in the collecting ducts.

In contrast, beavers, muskrats, and other aquatic mammals that spend much of their time in fresh water and rarely face problems of dehydration have nephrons with relatively short loops, resulting in a much lower ability to concentrate urine. Terrestrial mammals living in moist conditions have loops of Henle of intermediate length and the capacity to produce urine intermediate in concentration to that produced by freshwater and desert mammals.

Birds and Other Reptiles

Most birds, including the albatross (see Figure 44.1) and the roadrunner (Figure 44.17), live in environments that are dehydrating. Like mammals, birds have kidneys with juxtamedullary nephrons that specialize in conserving water. However, the nephrons of birds have loops of Henle that extend less far into the medulla than those of mammals. Thus, bird kidneys cannot concentrate urine to the high osmolarities achieved by mammalian kidneys. Although birds can produce hyperosmotic urine, their main water conservation adaptation is having uric acid as the nitrogen waste molecule. Since uric acid can be excreted as a paste, it reduces urine volume.

The kidneys of other reptiles, which have only cortical nephrons, produce urine that is isoosmotic or hypoosmotic to body fluids. However, the epithelium of the chamber from

▲ **Figure 44.17 The roadrunner (*Geococcyx californianus*), an animal well adapted to its dry environment.**

which urine and feces leave the body (the cloaca) helps conserve fluid by reabsorbing water from these wastes. Also like birds, most other reptiles excrete their nitrogenous wastes as uric acid.

Freshwater Fishes and Amphibians

Freshwater fishes are hyperosmotic to their surroundings, so they must excrete excess water continuously. In contrast to mammals and birds, freshwater fishes produce large volumes of very dilute urine. Their kidneys, which contain many nephrons, produce filtrate at a high rate. Freshwater fishes conserve salts by reabsorbing ions from the filtrate in their distal tubules, leaving water behind.

Amphibian kidneys function much like those of freshwater fishes. When in fresh water, the kidneys of frogs excrete dilute urine while the skin accumulates certain salts from the water by active transport. On land, where dehydration is the most pressing problem of osmoregulation, frogs conserve body fluid by reabsorbing water across the epithelium of the urinary bladder.

Marine Bony Fishes

The tissues of marine bony fishes gain excess salts from their surroundings and lose water. These environmental challenges are opposite to those faced by their freshwater relatives. Compared with freshwater fishes, marine fishes have fewer and smaller nephrons, and their nephrons lack a distal tubule. In addition, their kidneys have small glomeruli or lack glomeruli entirely. In keeping with these features, filtration rates are low and very little urine is excreted.

The main function of kidneys in marine bony fishes is to get rid of divalent ions (those with a charge of 2+ or 2−) such as calcium (Ca^{2+}), magnesium (Mg^{2+}), and sulfate (SO_4^{2-}). Marine fishes take in divalent ions by incessantly drinking seawater. They rid themselves of these ions by secreting them into the proximal tubules of the nephrons and excreting them in urine. Secretion by the gills maintains proper levels of monovalent ions (charge of 1+ or 1−) such as Na^+ and Cl^-.

CONCEPT CHECK 44.4

1. What do the number and length of nephrons in a fish's kidney indicate about the fish's habitat? How do they correlate with urine production?
2. Many medications make the epithelium of the collecting duct less permeable to water. How would taking such a drug affect kidney output?
3. **WHAT IF?** If blood pressure in the afferent arteriole leading to a glomerulus decreased, how would the rate of blood filtration within Bowman's capsule be affected? Explain.

For suggested answers, see Appendix A.

CONCEPT 44.5

Hormonal circuits link kidney function, water balance, and blood pressure

In mammals, both the volume and osmolarity of urine are adjusted according to an animal's water and salt balance and its rate of urea production. In situations of high salt intake and low water availability, a mammal can excrete urea and salt in small volumes of hyperosmotic urine with minimal water loss. If salt is scarce and fluid intake is high, the kidney can instead get rid of the excess water with little salt loss by producing large volumes of hypoosmotic urine. At such times, the urine can be as dilute as 70 mOsm/L, compared with an osmolarity of 300 mOsm/L for human blood.

The South American vampire bat shown in **Figure 44.18** illustrates the versatility of the mammalian kidney. Bats of this species feed at night on the blood of large birds and mammals. The bats use their sharp teeth to make a small incision in the prey's skin and then lap up blood from the wound (the prey animal is typically not seriously harmed). Anticoagulants in the bat's saliva prevent the blood from clotting. Because vampire bats often search for hours and fly long distances to locate a suitable victim, they benefit from consuming as much blood as possible when they do find prey—so much that after feeding, a bat could be too heavy to fly. However, the bat's kidneys offload much of the water absorbed from a blood meal by excreting large volumes of dilute urine as it feeds, up to 24% of body mass per hour. Having lost enough weight to take off, the bat can fly back to its roost in a cave or hollow tree, where it spends the day.

In the roost, the bat faces a different regulatory problem. Most of the nutrition it derives from blood comes in the form of protein. Digesting proteins generates large quantities of urea, but roosting bats lack access to the drinking water necessary to

▲ Figure 44.18 **A vampire bat (*Desmodus rotundas*), a mammal with a unique excretory situation.**

dilute it. Instead, their kidneys shift to producing small quantities of highly concentrated urine (up to 4,600 mOsm/L), an adjustment that disposes of the urea load while conserving as much water as possible. The vampire bat's ability to alternate rapidly between producing large amounts of dilute urine and small amounts of very hyperosmotic urine is an essential part of its adaptation to an unusual food source.

Antidiuretic Hormone

A combination of nervous and hormonal controls manages the osmoregulatory function of the mammalian kidney. One key hormone in this regulatory circuitry is **antidiuretic hormone (ADH)**, also called *vasopressin*. ADH is produced in the hypothalamus of the brain and stored in the posterior pituitary gland, located just below the hypothalamus. Osmoreceptor cells in the hypothalamus monitor the osmolarity of blood and regulate release of ADH from the posterior pituitary.

To understand the role of ADH, let's consider what occurs when blood osmolarity rises, such as after eating salty food or losing water through sweating **(Figure 44.19)**. In response to an

increase in osmolarity above the set point of 300 mOsm/L, more ADH is released into the bloodstream. When ADH reaches the kidney, its main targets are the collecting ducts. There, ADH brings about changes that make the epithelium more permeable to water. The resulting increase in water reabsorption concentrates urine, reduces urine volume, and lowers blood osmolarity back toward the set point. (Only the gain of additional water in food and drink can fully restore osmolarity to 300 mOsm/L.) As the osmolarity of the blood subsides, a negative-feedback mechanism reduces the activity of osmoreceptor cells in the hypothalamus, and ADH secretion is reduced (not shown in figure).

A reduction in blood osmolarity below the set point has the opposite set of effects. For example, intake of a large volume of water leads to a decrease in ADH secretion to a very low level. The resulting decrease in permeability of the collecting ducts reduces water reabsorption, resulting in discharge of large volumes of dilute urine. (Diuresis refers to increased urination, and ADH is called *anti*diuretic hormone because it opposes this state.)

ADH influences water uptake in the kidney's collecting ducts by regulating the water-selective channels formed by aquaporins. Binding of ADH to receptor molecules leads to a temporary increase in the number of aquaporin proteins in the membranes of collecting duct cells **(Figure 44.20)**. Additional channels recapture more water, reducing urine volume.

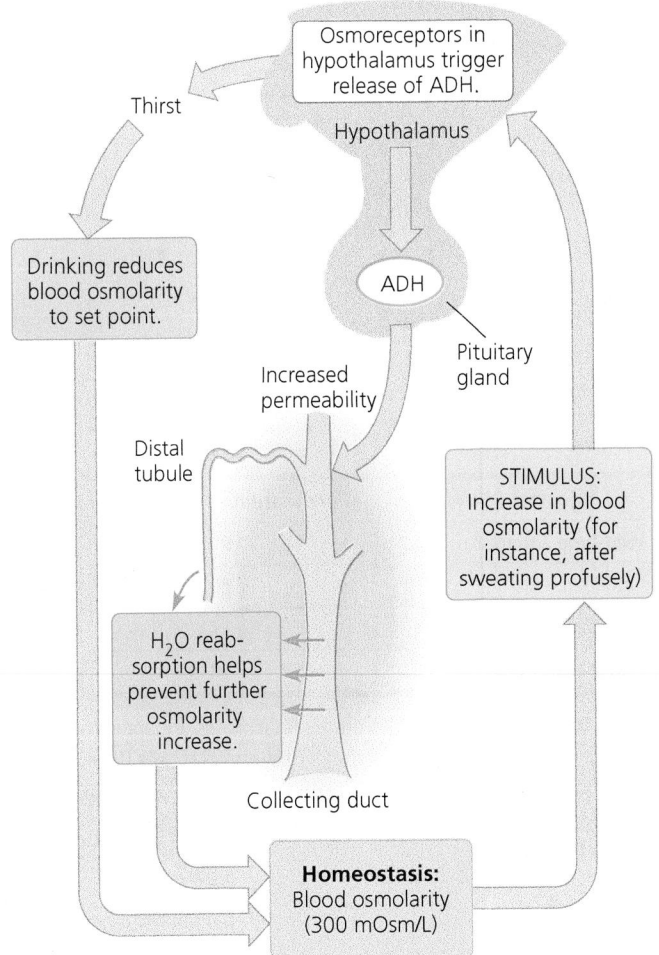

▲ **Figure 44.19 Regulation of fluid retention in the kidney by antidiuretic hormone (ADH).**

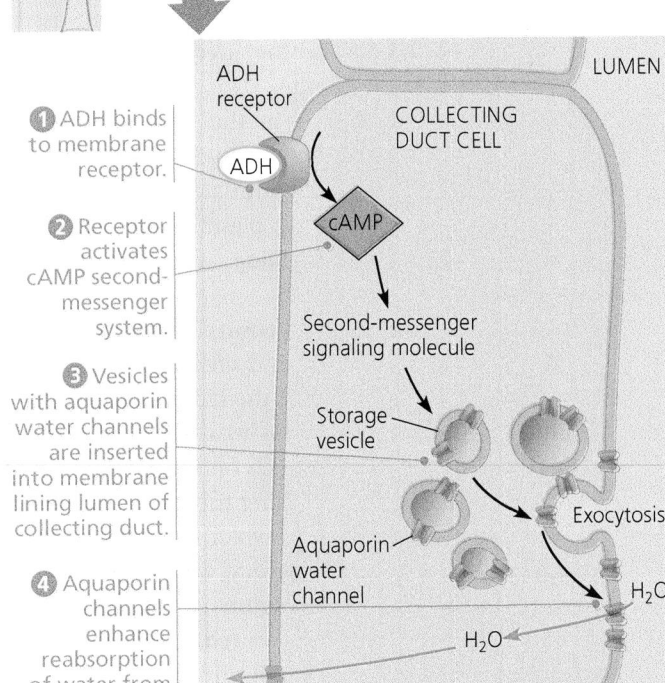

▲ **Figure 44.20 ADH response pathway in the collecting duct.**

Mutations that prevent ADH production or that inactivate the ADH receptor gene block the increase in channel number and thus the ADH response. The resulting disorder can cause severe dehydration and solute imbalance due to production of urine that is abnormally large in volume and very dilute. These symptoms give the condition its name: *diabetes insipidus* (from the Greek for "to pass through" and "having no flavor").

Researchers in the Netherlands wondered whether mutations in an aquaporin gene itself might also cause diabetes insipidus. Having found aquaporin gene mutations in a patient, they set out to determine whether the alterations led to nonfunctional water channels (**Figure 44.21**).

Taken together with previous studies, the experiment described in Figure 44.21 demonstrated that a wide variety of genetic defects can disrupt ADH regulation of water balance in the body. Even in the absence of such genetic changes, certain substances can alter the regulation of osmolarity. For example, alcohol can disturb water balance by inhibiting ADH release, leading to excessive urinary water loss and dehydration (which may cause some of the symptoms of a hangover). Normally, blood osmolarity, ADH release, and water reabsorption in the kidney are all linked in a feedback loop that contributes to homeostasis.

The Renin-Angiotensin-Aldosterone System

A second regulatory mechanism that helps maintain homeostasis by acting on the kidney is the **renin-angiotensin-aldosterone system (RAAS)**. The RAAS involves the **juxtaglomerular apparatus (JGA)**, a specialized tissue consisting of cells of and around the afferent arteriole that supplies blood to the glomerulus (**Figure 44.22**). When blood pressure or blood volume in the afferent arteriole drops (for instance, as a result of dehydration), the JGA releases the enzyme renin. Renin initiates a sequence of chemical reactions that cleave a plasma protein called angiotensinogen, ultimately yielding a peptide called **angiotensin II**.

Functioning as a hormone, angiotensin II raises blood pressure by constricting arterioles, which decreases blood flow to many capillaries, including those of the kidney. Angiotensin II also stimulates the adrenal glands to release a hormone called **aldosterone**. This hormone acts on the nephrons' distal tubules and collecting duct, making them reabsorb more Na^+ and water, thus increasing blood volume and pressure.

Because angiotensin II acts in several ways that increase blood pressure, drugs that block angiotensin II production are widely used to treat hypertension (chronic high blood pressure). Many of these drugs are specific inhibitors of angiotensin converting enzyme (ACE), which catalyzes the second step in the production of angiotensin II. As shown in Figure 44.21, renin released from the JGA acts on

▼ Figure 44.21

INQUIRY

Can aquaporin mutations cause diabetes insipidus?

EXPERIMENT Bernard van Oost and colleagues at the University of Nijmegen were studying a patient with diabetes insipidus but a normal ADH receptor gene. Sequencing of the patient's DNA revealed two different mutations, one in each copy of an aquaporin gene. To determine whether each mutation blocked channel formation, they studied the mutant proteins in a cell that could be manipulated and studied outside the body. The cell they chose was the frog oocyte, which can be collected in large numbers from an adult female and will express foreign genes. The researchers synthesized messenger RNA from clones of the wild-type and mutant aquaporin genes and injected the synthetic mRNA into oocytes. Within the oocytes, the cellular machinery translated the mRNA into aquaporin proteins. To determine if the mutant aquaporin proteins made functional water channels in the plasma membrane, the investigators transferred the oocytes from a 200-mOsm to a 10-mOsm solution. They then measured swelling by light microscopy and calculated the permeability of the oocytes to water.

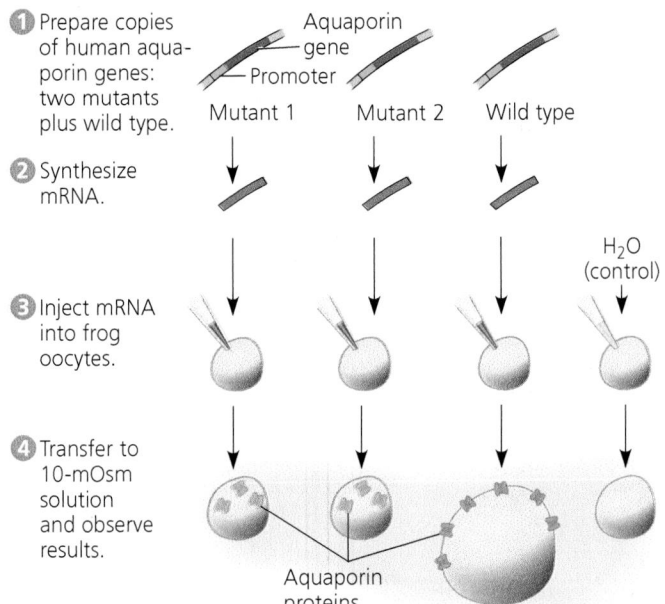

1. Prepare copies of human aquaporin genes: two mutants plus wild type.

2. Synthesize mRNA.

3. Inject mRNA into frog oocytes.

4. Transfer to 10-mOsm solution and observe results.

Aquaporin gene

Promoter

Mutant 1   Mutant 2   Wild type

H_2O (control)

Aquaporin proteins

RESULTS

Injected RNA	Permeability (μm/sec)
Wild-type aquaporin	196
None	20
Aquaporin mutant 1	17
Aquaporin mutant 2	18

CONCLUSION Because each mutation inactivates aquaporin as a water channel, the patient's disorder can be attributed to these mutations.

SOURCE P. M. Deen, M. A. Verdijk, N. V. Knoers, B. Wieringa, L. A. Monnens, C. H. van Os, and B. A. van Oost, Requirement of human renal water channel aquaporin-2 for vasopressin-dependent concentration of urine, *Science* 264:92–95 (1994).

WHAT IF? If you measured ADH levels in patients with ADH receptor mutations and in patients with aquaporin mutations, what would you expect to find, compared with wild-type subjects?

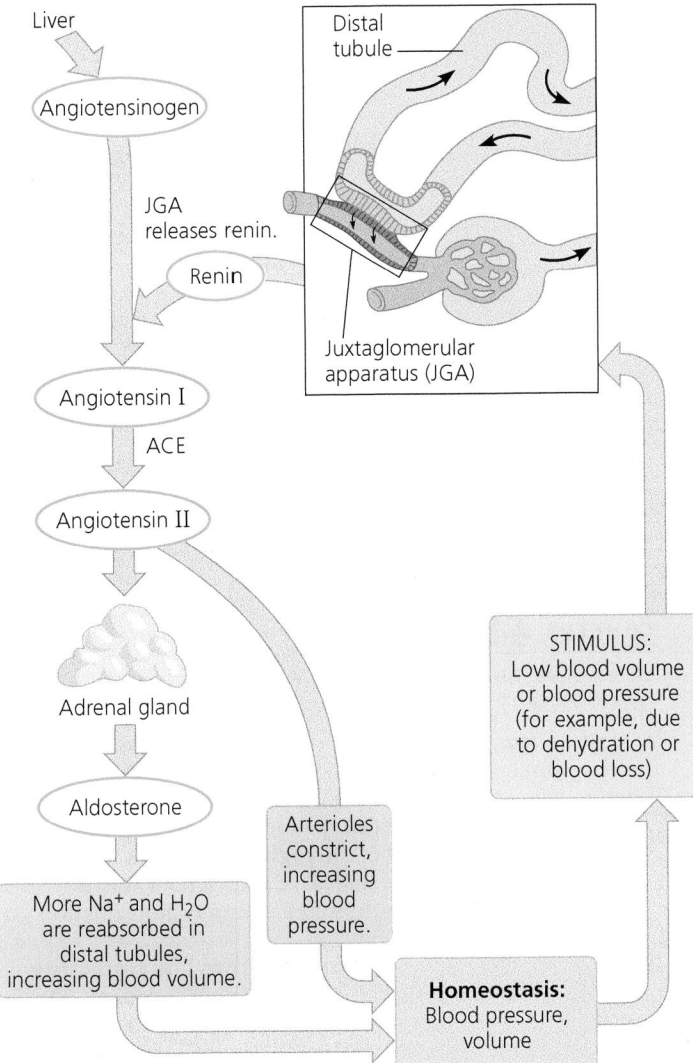

Liver

Angiotensinogen

JGA
releases renin.

Renin

Distal
tubule

Juxtaglomerular
apparatus (JGA)

Angiotensin I

ACE

Angiotensin II

Adrenal gland

Aldosterone

More Na⁺ and H₂O
are reabsorbed in
distal tubules,
increasing blood volume.

Arterioles
constrict,
increasing
blood
pressure.

STIMULUS:
Low blood volume
or blood pressure
(for example, due
to dehydration or
blood loss)

Homeostasis:
Blood pressure,
volume

▲ Figure 44.22 **Regulation of blood volume and blood pressure by the renin-angiotensin-aldosterone system (RAAS).**

angiotensinogen (in the blood), forming angiotensin I. ACE in vascular endothelium, particularly in the lungs, then splits off two amino acids from angiotensin I, forming active angiotensin II. Blocking ACE activity with drugs prevents angiotensin II production and often lowers blood pressure into the normal range.

Homeostatic Regulation of the Kidney

The renin-angiotensin-aldosterone system operates as part of a complex feedback circuit that results in homeostasis. A drop in blood pressure and blood volume triggers renin release from the JGA. In turn, the rise in blood pressure and volume resulting from the various actions of angiotensin II and aldosterone reduces the release of renin.

The functions of ADH and the RAAS may seem to be redundant, but this is not the case. Both increase water reabsorption

in the kidney, but they counter different osmoregulatory problems. The release of ADH is a response to an increase in blood osmolarity, as when the body is dehydrated from excessive water loss or inadequate water intake. However, a situation that causes an excessive loss of both salt and body fluids—a major wound, for example, or severe diarrhea—will reduce blood volume *without* increasing osmolarity. This will not affect ADH release, but the RAAS will respond to the drop in blood volume and pressure by increasing water and Na⁺ reabsorption. Thus, ADH and the RAAS are partners in homeostasis. ADH alone would lower blood Na⁺ concentration by stimulating water reabsorption in the kidney, but the RAAS helps maintain the osmolarity of body fluids at the set point by stimulating Na⁺ reabsorption.

Another hormone, **atrial natriuretic peptide (ANP)**, opposes the RAAS. The walls of the atria of the heart release ANP in response to an increase in blood volume and pressure. ANP inhibits the release of renin from the JGA, inhibits NaCl reabsorption by the collecting ducts, and reduces aldosterone release from the adrenal glands. These actions lower blood volume and pressure. Thus, ADH, the RAAS, and ANP provide an elaborate system of checks and balances that regulate the kidney's ability to control the osmolarity, salt concentration, volume, and pressure of blood. The precise regulatory role of ANP is an area of active research.

In all animals, certain of the intricate physiological machines we call organs work continuously in maintaining solute and water balance and excreting nitrogenous wastes. The details that we have reviewed in this chapter only hint at the great complexity of the neural and hormonal mechanisms involved in regulating these homeostatic processes.

CONCEPT CHECK 44.5

1. How does alcohol affect regulation of water balance in the body?
2. Why could it be dangerous to drink a very large amount of water in a short period of time?
3. **WHAT IF?** Conn's syndrome is a condition caused by tumors of the adrenal cortex that secrete high amounts of aldosterone in an unregulated manner. What would you expect to be the major symptom of this disorder?
4. **MAKE CONNECTIONS** Compare the activity of renin and ACE in the renin-angiotensin-aldosterone system with that of the protein kinases in a phosphorylation cascade, such as the one shown in Figure 11.10 (p. 215). How are the roles of these enzymes similar and different in the two regulated response pathways?

For suggested answers, see Appendix A.

SUMMARY OF KEY CONCEPTS

CONCEPT 44.1

Osmoregulation balances the uptake and loss of water and solutes (pp. 953–958)

- Cells balance water gain and loss through **osmoregulation**, a process based on the controlled movement of solutes between internal fluids and the external environment and on the movement of water, which follows by osmosis. **Osmoconformers** are isoosmotic with their marine environment and do not regulate their **osmolarity**. In contrast, **osmoregulators** control water uptake and loss in a hypoosmotic or hyperosmotic environment, respectively. Water-conserving excretory organs help terrestrial animals to avoid desiccation. Animals that live in temporary waters may be **anhydrobiotic** for one stage of life.

Animal	Inflow/Outflow	Urine
Freshwater fish. Lives in water less concentrated than body fluids; fish tends to gain water, lose salt	Does not drink water Salt in (active transport by gills) H₂O in Salt out	▶ Large volume of urine ▶ Urine is less concentrated than body fluids
Marine bony fish. Lives in water more concentrated than body fluids; fish tends to lose water, gain salt	Drinks water Salt in H₂O out Salt out (active transport by gills)	▶ Small volume of urine ▶ Urine is slightly less concentrated than body fluids
Terrestrial vertebrate. Terrestrial environment; tends to lose body water to air	Drinks water Salt in (by mouth) H₂O and salt out	▶ Moderate volume of urine ▶ Urine is more concentrated than body fluids

- **Transport epithelia** contain specialized epithelial cells that regulate the solute movements required for waste disposal and for tempering changes in body fluids.

? *Under what environmental conditions does water move into a cell by osmosis?*

CONCEPT 44.2

An animal's nitrogenous wastes reflect its phylogeny and habitat (pp. 958–959)

- Protein and nucleic acid metabolism generates **ammonia**. Most aquatic animals excrete ammonia. Mammals and most adult amphibians convert ammonia to the less toxic **urea**, which is excreted with a minimal loss of water. Insects and many reptiles, including birds, convert ammonia to **uric acid**, a mostly insoluble waste excreted in a paste-like urine.
- The kind of nitrogenous waste excreted depends on an animal's evolutionary history and habitat. The amount of nitrogenous waste produced is coupled to the animal's energy budget and amount of dietary protein.

DRAW IT *Construct a table summarizing the three major types of nitrogenous wastes and their relative toxicity, energy content, and associated water loss during excretion.*

CONCEPT 44.3

Diverse excretory systems are variations on a tubular theme (pp. 960–963)

- Most excretory systems carry out **filtration, reabsorption, secretion,** and **excretion**. The **protonephridia** of the flatworm flame bulb excrete a dilute **filtrate**. An earthworm has pairs of open-ended **metanephridia** in each segment that produce urine. In insects, **Malpighian tubules** function in osmoregulation and removal of nitrogenous wastes. **Kidneys** function in both excretion and osmoregulation in vertebrates.
- Excretory tubules (consisting of **nephrons** and **collecting ducts**) and blood vessels pack the mammalian kidney. Blood pressure forces fluid from blood in the **glomerulus** into the lumen of **Bowman's capsule**. Following reabsorption and secretion, filtrate flows into a collecting duct. The **ureter** conveys urine from the **renal pelvis** to the **urinary bladder**.

? *Given that a typical excretory system selectively absorbs and secretes materials, what function does filtration serve?*

CONCEPT 44.4

The nephron is organized for stepwise processing of blood filtrate (pp. 963–968)

- Within the nephron, selective secretion and reabsorption in the **proximal tubule** alter filtrate volume and composition. The *descending limb* of the **loop of Henle** is permeable to water but not salt; water moves by osmosis into the interstitial fluid. The *ascending limb* is permeable to salt but not water; as the filtrate ascends, salt leaves by diffusion and by active transport. The **distal tubule** and collecting duct regulate K⁺ and NaCl levels in body fluids. The collecting duct can respond to hormonal signals to reabsorb more water.
- In a mammalian kidney, a **countercurrent multiplier system** involving the loop of Henle maintains the gradient of salt concentration in the kidney interior. In response to hormonal signals, urine can be concentrated in the collecting duct. Urea, which leaves the collecting duct within the inner medulla, contributes to the osmotic gradient of the kidney.
- Natural selection has shaped the form and function of nephrons in various vertebrates to the osmoregulatory challenges of the animals' habitats. For example, desert mammals, which excrete

the most hyperosmotic urine, have loops of Henle that extend deep into the **renal medulla**, whereas mammals in moist habitats have shorter loops and excrete more dilute urine.

? *How do cortical and juxtamedullary nephrons differ with respect to reabsorbing nutrients and concentrating urine?*

CONCEPT 44.5

Hormonal circuits link kidney function, water balance, and blood pressure (pp. 968–971)

- The posterior pituitary gland releases **antidiuretic hormone (ADH)** when blood osmolarity rises above a set point, such as when water intake is inadequate. ADH increases permeability to water in collecting ducts through an increase in the number of epithelial water channels. When blood pressure or blood volume in the afferent arteriole drops, the **juxtaglomerular apparatus (JGA)** releases renin. **Angiotensin II** formed in response to **renin** constricts arterioles and triggers release of the hormone **aldosterone**, raising blood pressure and reducing the release of renin. This **renin-angiotensin-aldosterone system (RAAS)** has functions that overlap with those of ADH and are opposed by **atrial natriuretic peptide (ANP)**.

? *Why can only some patients with diabetes insipidus be treated effectively with ADH?*

TEST YOUR UNDERSTANDING

LEVEL 1: KNOWLEDGE/COMPREHENSION

1. *Unlike* an earthworm's metanephridia, a mammalian nephron
   a. is intimately associated with a capillary network.
   b. forms urine by changing fluid composition inside a tubule.
   c. functions in both osmoregulation and excretion.
   d. receives filtrate from blood instead of coelomic fluid.
   e. has a transport epithelium.

2. Which process in the nephron is *least* selective?
   a. filtration
   b. reabsorption
   c. active transport
   d. secretion
   e. salt pumping by the loop of Henle

3. Which of the following animals generally has the lowest volume of urine production?
   a. a vampire bat
   b. a salmon in fresh water
   c. a marine bony fish
   d. a freshwater bony fish
   e. a shark inhabiting freshwater Lake Nicaragua

LEVEL 2: APPLICATION/ANALYSIS

4. The high osmolarity of the renal medulla is maintained by all of the following *except*
   a. diffusion of salt from the thin segment of the ascending limb of the loop of Henle.
   b. active transport of salt from the upper region of the ascending limb.
   c. the spatial arrangement of juxtamedullary nephrons.
   d. diffusion of urea from the collecting duct.
   e. diffusion of salt from the descending limb of the loop of Henle.

5. Natural selection should favor the highest proportion of juxtamedullary nephrons in which of the following species?
   a. a river otter
   b. a mouse species living in a tropical rain forest
   c. a mouse species living in a temperate broadleaf forest
   d. a mouse species living in a desert
   e. a beaver

6. African lungfish, which are often found in small stagnant pools of fresh water, produce urea as a nitrogenous waste. What is the advantage of this adaptation?
   a. Urea takes less energy to synthesize than ammonia.
   b. Small stagnant pools do not provide enough water to dilute the toxic ammonia.
   c. The highly toxic urea makes the pool uninhabitable to potential competitors.
   d. Urea forms an insoluble precipitate.
   e. Urea makes lungfish tissue hypoosmotic to the pool.

LEVEL 3: SYNTHESIS/EVALUATION

7. **DRAW IT** Using Figure 44.3 as an example, sketch the exchange of salt (NaCl) and water between a shark and its marine environment.

8. **EVOLUTION CONNECTION**
   Merriam's kangaroo rats (*Dipodomys merriami*) live in North American habitats ranging from moist, cool woodlands to hot deserts. Assuming that natural selection has resulted in differences in water conservation between *D. merriami* populations, propose a hypothesis concerning the relative rates of evaporative water loss by populations that live in moist versus dry environments. Using a humidity sensor to detect evaporative water loss by kangaroo rats, how could you test your hypothesis?

9. **SCIENTIFIC INQUIRY**
   You are exploring kidney function in kangaroo rats. You measure urine volume and osmolarity, as well as the amount of chloride (Cl^-) and urea in the urine. If the water source provided to the animals were switched from tap water to a 2% NaCl solution, what change in urine osmolarity would you expect? How would you determine if this change was more likely due to a change in the excretion of Cl^- or urea?

10. **WRITE ABOUT A THEME**
    Structure and Function In a short essay (100–150 words), compare how membrane structures in the loop of Henle and collecting duct of the mammalian kidney enable water to be recovered from filtrate in the process of osmoregulation.

For selected answers, see Appendix A.

Mastering BIOLOGY www.masteringbiology.com

1. MasteringBiology® Assignments
   Make Connections Tutorial Kidney Function (Chapter 44) and Passive and Active Transport (Chapter 7)
   Tutorial Kidney Structure and Function
   Activities Structure of the Human Excretory System • The Mammalian Kidney • Nephron Function • Control of Water Reabsorption
   Questions Student Misconceptions • Reading Quiz • Multiple Choice • End-of-Chapter

2. eText
   Read your book online, search, take notes, highlight text, and more.

3. The Study Area
   Practice Tests • Cumulative Test • *BioFlix* 3-D Animations • MP3 Tutor Sessions • Videos • Activities • Investigations • Lab Media • Audio Glossary • Word Study Tools • Art

45

Hormones and the Endocrine System

▲ Figure 45.1 **What signals caused this butterfly to grow within the body of a caterpillar?**

KEY CONCEPTS

45.1 Hormones and other signaling molecules bind to target receptors, triggering specific response pathways

45.2 Feedback regulation and antagonistic hormone pairs are common in endocrine systems

45.3 The hypothalamus and pituitary are central to endocrine regulation

45.4 Endocrine glands respond to diverse stimuli in regulating homeostasis, development, and behavior

OVERVIEW

The Body's Long-Distance Regulators

To say that a butterfly, such as the anise swallowtail (*Papilio zelicaon*) in **Figure 45.1**, was once a caterpillar is only partly true. The adult cells that form the butterfly begin growing in

the embryo. Within the larval caterpillar, they are nourished as islands of tissues that will eventually become the eyes, wings, brain, and other structures of the butterfly. Once the plump, crawling caterpillar becomes a stationary pupa, the adult cells take over. They complete their program of development, while many larval tissues undergo programmed cell death. The end result is a butterfly, a delicate, free-flying adult that bears little resemblance to the larval and pupal forms from which it arose.

What brings about such a complete change of body form, or *metamorphosis*? The answer for this and many other biological processes is a type of molecule called a **hormone** (from the Greek *horman*, to excite). In animals, hormones are secreted into the extracellular fluid, circulate in the hemolymph or blood, and communicate regulatory messages throughout the body. In the case of the caterpillar, a hormone called **ecdysteroid** stimulates the growth of adult cells, the programmed death of larval cells, and even the behaviors that bring about the motionless pupal stage. Communication within the body by ecdysteroid and other hormones also regulates the timing of metamorphosis and ensures that different parts of the swallowtail's adult body develop in unison.

Each hormone has specific receptors in the body. Although a given hormone can reach all cells of the body, only some cells have receptors for that hormone. A hormone elicits a response—such as a change in metabolism—only from specific *target cells*, those that have the matching receptor. Cells lacking a receptor for that particular hormone are unaffected.

Chemical signaling by hormones is the function of the **endocrine system**, one of the two basic systems of communication and regulation throughout the body. Hormones secreted by endocrine cells regulate reproduction, development, energy metabolism, growth, and behavior. The other major communication and control system is the **nervous system**, a network of specialized cells—neurons—that transmit signals along dedicated pathways. These signals in turn regulate neurons, muscle cells, and endocrine cells. Because signaling by neurons can regulate the release of hormones, the nervous and endocrine systems often overlap in function.

In this chapter, we'll begin with an overview of the different types of chemical signaling in animals and the ways in which the activities of the endocrine and nervous systems are coordinated. We will then explore how hormones regulate target cells, how hormone secretion is regulated, and how hormones help maintain homeostasis. We'll conclude by examining the role of hormones in regulating growth, development, and reproduction, topics we'll return to in Chapters 46 and 47.

Hormones and other signaling molecules bind to target receptors, triggering specific response pathways

Endocrine signaling is just one of several ways information is transmitted between animal cells. Let's consider the similarities and differences in these various signaling processes.

Intercellular Communication

The ways in which signals are transmitted between animal cells are often classified by two criteria: the type of secreting cell and the route taken by the signal in reaching its target.

Endocrine Signaling

As illustrated in **Figure 45.2a**, hormones secreted into extracellular fluids by endocrine cells reach target cells via the bloodstream (or hemolymph). Endocrine signaling maintains homeostasis, mediates responses to environmental stimuli, and regulates growth and development. For example, hormones coordinate the body's responses to stress, dehydration, and low blood glucose levels. They also trigger behavioral and physical changes underlying sexual maturity and reproduction.

Paracrine and Autocrine Signaling

Many types of cells produce and secrete **local regulators**, molecules that act over short distances and reach their target cells solely by diffusion. Cytokines, for example, are local regulators that enable communication between immune cells (see Figures 43.16 and 43.18). Depending on the target cell, signaling by local regulators can be either paracrine or autocrine. In **paracrine** signaling (from the Greek *para*, to one side of), target cells lie near the secreting cell (**Figure 45.2b**). In **autocrine** signaling (from the Greek *auto*, self), the target cell is the secreting cell itself (**Figure 45.2c**). As we will discuss later in this chapter, paracrine and autocrine signaling play roles in many physiological processes, including blood pressure regulation, nervous system function, and reproduction.

Synaptic and Neuroendocrine Signaling

Secreted molecules are crucial for two types of signaling by neurons. In *synaptic signaling*, neurons form specialized junctions called synapses with target cells, such as other neurons and muscle cells. At synapses, neurons secrete molecules called **neurotransmitters** that diffuse a very short distance to bind to receptors on the target cells (**Figure 45.2d**). Neurotransmitters are central to sensation, memory, cognition, and movement, as we will explore in Chapters 48–50.

In *neuroendocrine signaling*, specialized neurons called neurosecretory cells secrete molecules that diffuse from nerve cell

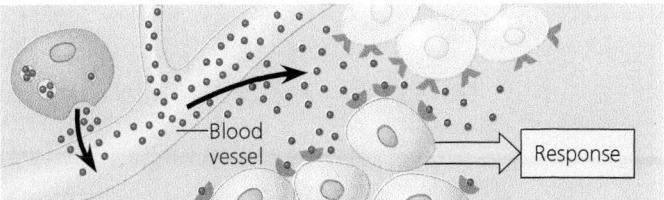

(a) In **endocrine signaling**, secreted molecules diffuse into the bloodstream and trigger responses in target cells anywhere in the body.

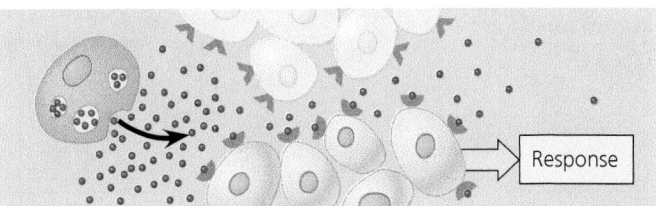

(b) In **paracrine signaling**, secreted molecules diffuse locally and trigger a response in neighboring cells.

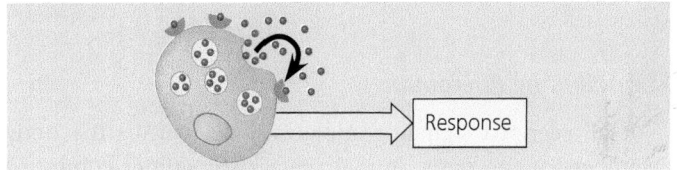

(c) In **autocrine signaling**, secreted molecules diffuse locally and trigger a response in the cells that secrete them.

(d) In **synaptic signaling**, neurotransmitters diffuse across synapses and trigger responses in cells of target tissues (neurons, muscles, or glands).

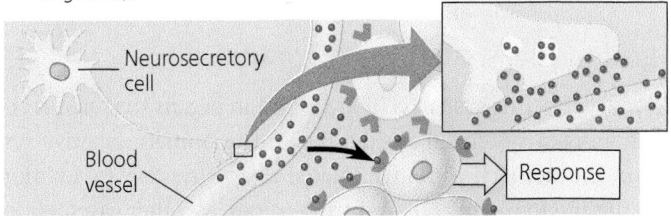

(e) In **neuroendocrine signaling**, neurohormones diffuse into the bloodstream and trigger responses in target cells anywhere in the body.

▲ **Figure 45.2 Intercellular communication by secreted molecules.** In each type of signaling, secreted molecules (•) bind to a specific receptor protein (⌣) expressed by target cells. Some receptors are located inside cells, but for simplicity here, all are drawn on the cell surface.

endings into the bloodstream (**Figure 45.2e**). These molecules, which travel through the bloodstream to target cells, are a class of hormone called **neurohormones**. One example is antidiuretic hormone, also known as vasopressin, a hormone essential to kidney function and water balance (see Chapter 44).

▲ Figure 45.3 **Signaling by pheromones.** Using their lowered antennae, these Asian army ants (*Leptogenys distinguenda*) follow a pheromone-marked trail as they carry pupae and larvae to a new nest site.

Signaling by Pheromones

Not all secreted signaling molecules act within the body. Members of the same animal species sometimes communicate via **pheromones**, chemicals that are released into the external environment. For example, when a foraging ant discovers a new food source, it marks its path back to the nest with a pheromone. Ants also use pheromones for guidance when a colony migrates to a new location (**Figure 45.3**).

Pheromones serve a wide range of functions that include defining territories, warning of predators, and attracting potential mates. The giant silk moth (*Antheraea polyphemus*) provides a noteworthy example: The sex pheromone released into the air by a female enables her to attract a male of the species from up to 4.5 km away.

Endocrine Tissues and Organs

Some endocrine system cells are found in organs that are part of other organ systems. For example, in the human digestive system, the stomach contains isolated endocrine cells in addition to the predominant cell and tissue types. In other cases, endocrine cells are grouped in ductless organs called **endocrine glands**, such as the thyroid and parathyroid glands of the neck. The various human glands and organs with endocrine function are illustrated in **Figure 45.4**, which will serve as a useful point of reference as you move through the chapter.

Note that endocrine glands secrete hormones directly into the surrounding fluid. Endocrine glands thus contrast with *exocrine glands*, such as salivary glands, which have ducts that carry secreted substances onto body surfaces or into body cavities. This distinction is reflected in their names: The Greek *endo* ("within") and *exo* ("out of") reflect secretion into or out of body fluids, while *crine* (from the Greek for "separate") reflects movement away from the secreting cell.

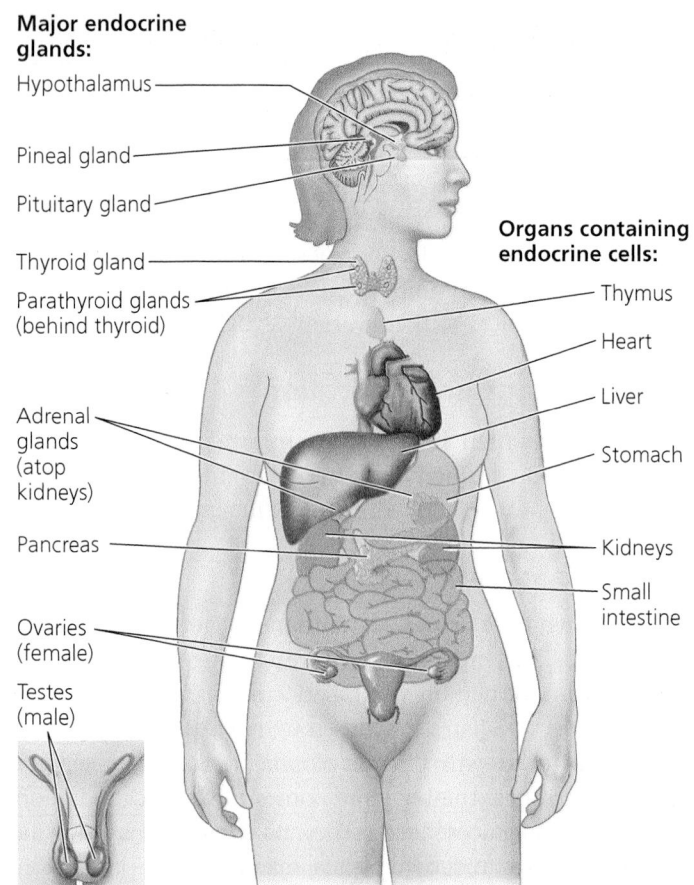

Major endocrine glands:
Hypothalamus
Pineal gland
Pituitary gland
Thyroid gland
Parathyroid glands (behind thyroid)
Adrenal glands (atop kidneys)
Pancreas
Ovaries (female)
Testes (male)

Organs containing endocrine cells:
Thymus
Heart
Liver
Stomach
Kidneys
Small intestine

▲ Figure 45.4 **Major human endocrine glands.**

Chemical Classes of Hormones

Hormone molecules vary substantially in size and chemical properties. Some of these differences are apparent in examples drawn from the three major chemical classes of hormones: polypeptides (proteins and peptides), steroids, and amines (**Figure 45.5**). The polypeptide hormone insulin is made up of two polypeptide chains. Like most hormones in this group, insulin is formed by cleavage of one long polypeptide chain. Steroid hormones, such as cortisol and ecdysteroid, are lipids that contain four fused carbon rings. All are derived from the steroid cholesterol (see Figure 5.14). Epinephrine and thyroxine are amine hormones, each synthesized from a single amino acid, either tyrosine or tryptophan.

As Figure 45.5 indicates, hormones vary in their solubility in aqueous and lipid-rich environments. Polypeptides and most amine hormones are water-soluble. Being insoluble in lipids, these hormones cannot pass through the plasma membranes of cells. Instead, they bind to cell-surface receptors that relay information to the nucleus through intracellular pathways. In contrast, steroid hormones, as well as other largely nonpolar (hydrophobic) hormones, such as thyroxine, are lipid-soluble and can pass through cell membranes readily. Receptors for lipid-soluble hormones typically reside in the cytoplasm or nucleus.

Water-soluble (hydrophilic)	Lipid-soluble (hydrophobic)
Polypeptides	**Steroids**
Insulin	Cortisol

0.8 nm

Amines

Epinephrine

Thyroxine

▲ Figure 45.5 **Hormones differ in structure and solubility.**

MAKE CONNECTIONS *The biosynthesis of epinephrine involves breaking just one carbon-carbon bond in the amino acid tyrosine (see Figure 5.16, p. 79). Which bond is it?*

Cellular Response Pathways

There are several differences between the response pathways for water-soluble and lipid-soluble hormones. One difference is the location of the target cells' signal receptors **(Figure 45.6)**. Water-soluble hormones are secreted by exocytosis, travel freely in the bloodstream, and bind to cell-surface signal receptors. Binding of such hormones to receptors induces changes in cytoplasmic molecules and sometimes alters gene transcription (synthesis of messenger RNA molecules). In contrast, lipid-soluble hormones diffuse out across the membranes of endocrine cells. Outside the cell, they bind to transport proteins that keep them soluble in the aqueous environment of the bloodstream. Upon leaving the bloodstream, they diffuse into target cells, bind to intracellular signal receptors, and trigger changes in gene transcription.

To follow the distinct cellular responses to water-soluble and lipid-soluble hormones, we'll examine the two response pathways in turn.

Pathway for Water-Soluble Hormones

The binding of a water-soluble hormone to a signal receptor protein triggers events at the plasma membrane that result in a cellular response. The response may be the activation of an enzyme, a change in the uptake or secretion of specific molecules,

(a) Receptor in plasma membrane

(b) Receptor in cell nucleus

▲ Figure 45.6 **Receptor location varies with hormone type.**
(a) A water-soluble hormone binds to a signal receptor protein on the surface of a target cell. This interaction triggers events that lead to either a change in cytoplasmic function or a change in gene transcription in the nucleus. **(b)** A lipid-soluble hormone penetrates the target cell's plasma membrane and binds to an intracellular signal receptor, either in the cytoplasm or in the nucleus (shown here). The hormone-receptor complex acts as a transcription factor, typically activating gene expression.

? *Suppose you were studying a cell's response to a particular hormone, and you observed that the cell continued to respond to the hormone even when treated with a chemical that blocks transcription. What could you surmise about the hormone and its receptor?*

or a rearrangement of the cytoskeleton. In addition, some cell-surface receptors cause proteins in the cytoplasm to move into the nucleus and alter transcription of specific genes.

The series of changes in cellular proteins that converts the extracellular chemical signal to a specific intracellular response is called **signal transduction**. As described in Chapter 11, a signal transduction pathway typically involves multiple steps, each involving specific molecular interactions.

To explore the role of signal transduction in hormone signaling, consider one response to short-term stress. When you find yourself in a stressful situation, perhaps running to catch a bus, your adrenal glands secrete **epinephrine**, a hormone also

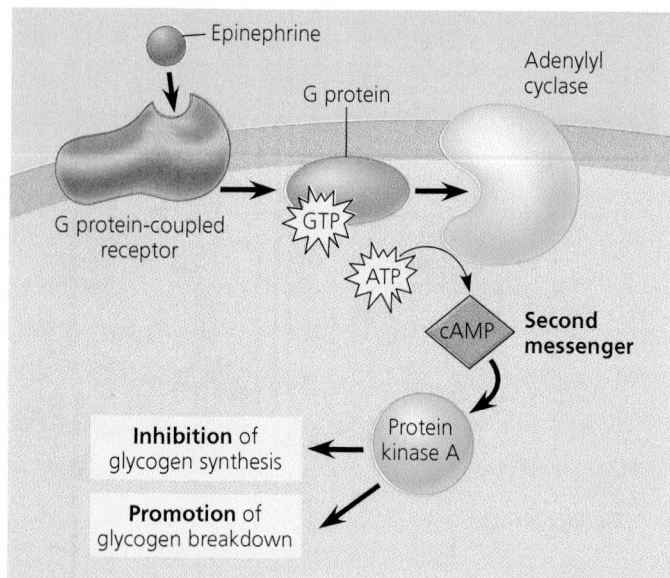

▲ **Figure 45.7 Cell-surface hormone receptors trigger signal transduction.**

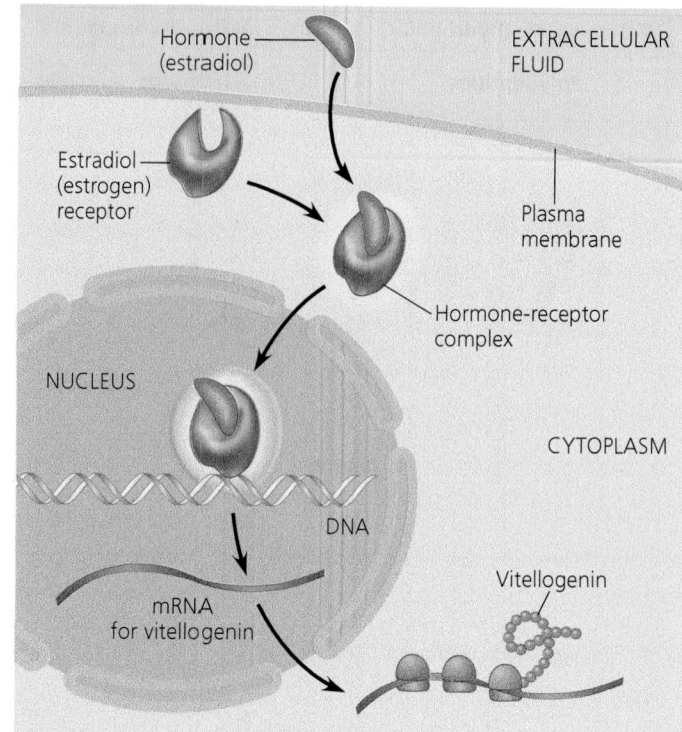

▲ **Figure 45.8 Steroid hormone receptors directly regulate gene expression.**

called *adrenaline*. When epinephrine reaches the liver, it binds to a G protein-coupled receptor in the plasma membrane of target cells, as discussed in Chapter 11 and reviewed in **Figure 45.7**. The binding of hormone to receptor triggers a cascade of events involving synthesis of cyclic AMP (cAMP) as a short-lived *second messenger*. Activation of protein kinase A by cAMP leads to activation of an enzyme required for glycogen breakdown and inactivation of an enzyme necessary for glycogen synthesis. The net result is that the liver releases glucose into the bloodstream, providing the fuel you need to chase the departing bus.

Pathway for Lipid-Soluble Hormones

Intracellular receptors for lipid-soluble hormones perform the entire task of transducing a signal within a target cell. The hormone activates the receptor, which then directly triggers the cell's response. In most cases, the response to a lipid-soluble hormone is a change in gene expression.

Steroid hormone receptors are located in the cytosol prior to binding to a hormone. When a steroid hormone binds to its cytosolic receptor, a hormone-receptor complex forms, which moves into the nucleus. There, the receptor portion of the complex alters transcription of particular genes by interacting with a specific DNA-binding protein or response element in the DNA (see Figure 18.9). Consider, for example, estrogens, steroid hormones necessary for female reproductive function in vertebrates. In female birds and frogs, estradiol, a form of estrogen, has a specific receptor in liver cells. Binding of estradiol to this receptor activates transcription of the gene for the protein vitellogenin **(Figure 45.8)**. Following translation of the messenger RNA, vitellogenin is secreted and transported in the blood to the reproductive system, where it is used to produce egg yolk.

Thyroxine, vitamin D, and other lipid-soluble hormones that are not steroid hormones have receptors that are typically located in the nucleus. These receptors bind hormone molecules that diffuse from the bloodstream across both the plasma membrane and nuclear envelope. Once bound by a hormone, the receptor binds to specific sites in the cell's DNA and stimulates the transcription of specific genes.

There is now substantial evidence that estrogens and some other lipid-soluble hormones sometimes trigger responses at the cell surface without entering the nucleus. How and when these responses arise are currently the subjects of active study.

Multiple Effects of Hormones

Many hormones elicit more than one type of response in the body. The effects brought about by a particular hormone can vary if target cells differ in the molecules that receive or produce the response to that hormone. Consider the effects of epinephrine in mediating the body's response to short-term stress **(Figure 45.9)**. Epinephrine simultaneously triggers glycogen breakdown in the liver, increased blood flow to major skeletal muscles, and decreased blood flow to the digestive tract. These varied effects enhance the rapid reactions of the body in emergencies.

Tissues vary in their response to epinephrine because they vary in their receptors or in their signal transduction pathways. Target cell recognition of epinephrine involves G protein-coupled receptors. Liver cells have a β-type epinephrine receptor that activates the enzyme protein kinase A, which in turn regulates enzymes in glycogen metabolism (Figure 45.9a). In blood vessels supplying skeletal muscle, the same kinase activated by the same epinephrine receptor inactivates a muscle-specific enzyme. The result is smooth muscle relaxation and hence increased blood flow (Figure 45.9b). In contrast, intestinal blood vessels have an α-type epinephrine receptor (Figure 45.9c). Rather than activate protein kinase A, the α receptor triggers a distinct signaling pathway involving a different G protein and different enzymes. The result is smooth muscle contraction and restricted blood flow to the intestines.

Lipid-soluble hormones often exert different effects on different target cells as well. For example, the estrogen that stimulates a bird's liver to synthesize the yolk protein vitellogenin also stimulates its reproductive system to synthesize proteins that form the egg white.

Signaling by Local Regulators

Recall that local regulators are secreted molecules that link neighboring cells (paracrine signaling) or directly regulate the secreting cell (autocrine signaling). Once secreted, local regulators act on their target cells within seconds or even milliseconds, eliciting responses more quickly than do hormones. Nevertheless, the pathways by which local regulators trigger responses are the same as those activated by hormones. (Although the definition of hormones is sometimes broadened to include local regulators, in this chapter we use *hormone* to refer to chemicals that reach target cells through the bloodstream or hemolymph.)

Several types of chemical compounds function as local regulators. Polypeptide local regulators include cytokines, as mentioned, and also most **growth factors**, which stimulate cell proliferation and differentiation. Many types of cells grow, divide, and develop normally only when growth factors are present in their extracellular environment.

The gas **nitric oxide (NO)** functions in the body as both a neurotransmitter and a local regulator. When the level of oxygen (O_2) in the blood falls, endothelial cells in blood vessel walls synthesize and release NO. Nitric oxide activates an enzyme that relaxes the surrounding smooth muscle cells, resulting in vasodilation, which improves blood flow to tissues. Highly reactive and potentially toxic, NO usually triggers changes in a target cell within a few seconds of contact and then breaks down. In human males, NO's ability to promote vasodilation enables sexual function by increasing blood flow into the penis, producing an erection. The drug Viagra (sildenafil citrate), a treatment for male erectile dysfunction, sustains an erection by prolonging activity of the NO response pathway.

A group of local regulators called **prostaglandins** are modified fatty acids. They are so named because they were first discovered in prostate gland secretions that contribute to semen. Prostaglandins are produced by many cell types and have varied activities. In semen that reaches the reproductive tract of a female, prostaglandins stimulate the smooth muscles of the female's uterine wall to contract, helping sperm reach an egg. At the onset of childbirth, prostaglandin-secreting cells of the placenta cause the nearby muscles of the uterus to become more excitable, helping to induce labor (see Figure 46.18).

In the immune system, prostaglandins promote fever and inflammation and also intensify the sensation of pain. The anti-inflammatory and pain-relieving effects of aspirin and ibuprofen are due to the inhibition of prostaglandin synthesis by these drugs. Prostaglandins also help regulate the aggregation of platelets, one step in the formation of blood clots. Because blood clots can cause a heart attack by blocking blood flow in vessels that supply the heart (see Chapter 42), some physicians recommend that people at risk for a heart attack take aspirin on a regular basis. However, because prostaglandins also help maintain a protective lining in the stomach, long-term aspirin therapy can cause debilitating stomach irritation.

▲ Figure 45.9 **One hormone, different effects.** Epinephrine, the primary "fight-or-flight" hormone, produces different responses in different target cells. Target cells with the same receptor exhibit different responses if they have different signal transduction pathways and/or effector proteins; compare (a) with (b). Responses of target cells may also differ if they have different receptors for the hormone; compare (b) with (c).

Coordination of Neuroendocrine and Endocrine Signaling

In all animals but the simplest invertebrates, the endocrine and nervous systems act coordinately to control reproduction and development. As an example, we'll explore the life cycle of the butterfly, a process highlighted earlier in the chapter.

A butterfly larva grows in stages. Because its exoskeleton cannot stretch, the larva must periodically molt, shedding the old exoskeleton and secreting a new one. The signals that direct molting originate in the brain (Figure 45.10). There, neurosecretory cells produce *prothoracicotropic hormone (PTTH)*, a polypeptide neurohormone. In response to PTTH, a pair of endocrine glands behind the brain release ecdysteroid. Ecdysteroid triggers each successive molt, as well as the metamorphosis of larva into butterfly during the final molt.

Given that ecdysteroid triggers both molting and metamorphosis, what determines when metamorphosis takes place? The answer is a third molecule, *juvenile hormone*, secreted by another pair of endocrine glands behind the brain. As its name suggests, one of the many functions of juvenile hormone is to maintain larval (juvenile) characteristics. Juvenile hormone modulates the activity of ecdysteroid. As long as the level of juvenile hormone is high, ecdysteroid stimulates larval molting. When the juvenile hormone level drops, ecdysteroid-induced molting instead produces the pupal form, within which metamorphosis occurs.

Knowledge of endocrine signaling in insects has important applications for agricultural pest control. For example, synthetic chemicals that can bind to the ecdysteroid receptor cause insect larvae to molt prematurely and die.

CONCEPT CHECK 45.1

1. How do response mechanisms in target cells differ for water-soluble and lipid-soluble hormones?
2. In what way does one activity described for prostaglandins resemble that of a pheromone?
3. **MAKE CONNECTIONS** What parallels in properties and effects can you identify between epinephrine and the plant hormone auxin (see Concept 39.2, pp. 827–829)?

For suggested answers, see Appendix A.

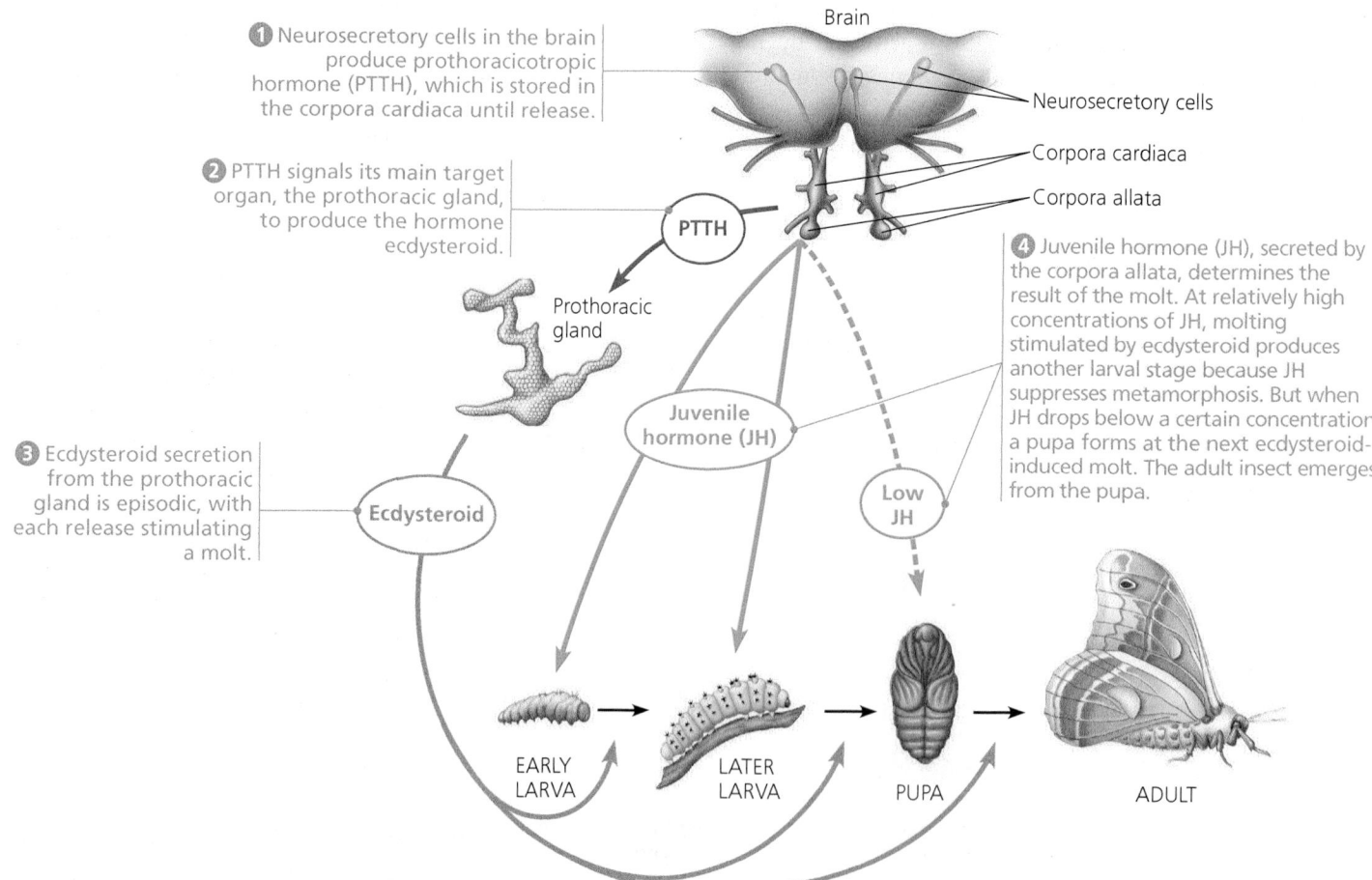

1 Neurosecretory cells in the brain produce prothoracicotropic hormone (PTTH), which is stored in the corpora cardiaca until release.

2 PTTH signals its main target organ, the prothoracic gland, to produce the hormone ecdysteroid.

3 Ecdysteroid secretion from the prothoracic gland is episodic, with each release stimulating a molt.

4 Juvenile hormone (JH), secreted by the corpora allata, determines the result of the molt. At relatively high concentrations of JH, molting stimulated by ecdysteroid produces another larval stage because JH suppresses metamorphosis. But when JH drops below a certain concentration, a pupa forms at the next ecdysteroid-induced molt. The adult insect emerges from the pupa.

Brain — Neurosecretory cells — Corpora cardiaca — Corpora allata

PTTH — Prothoracic gland — Ecdysteroid — Juvenile hormone (JH) — Low JH

EARLY LARVA → LATER LARVA → PUPA → ADULT

▲ Figure 45.10 **Regulation of insect development and metamorphosis.** As shown here for a moth, most insects go through a series of larval stages, with each molt (shedding of the old exoskeleton) leading to a larger larva. Molting of the final larval stage gives rise to a pupa, in which metamorphosis produces the adult form of the insect. Neurohormones and hormones control the progression of stages.

CONCEPT 45.2

Feedback regulation and antagonistic hormone pairs are common in endocrine systems

So far, we have explored forms of intercellular signaling as well as hormone structure, recognition, and response. We turn now to considering how regulatory pathways that control hormone secretion are organized.

Simple Hormone Pathways

In examining the regulation of hormone secretion, we begin with two basic types of organization—simple endocrine and simple neuroendocrine pathways. In a *simple endocrine pathway*, endocrine cells respond directly to an internal or environmental stimulus by secreting a particular hormone (Figure 45.11). The hormone travels in the bloodstream to target cells, where it interacts with its specific receptors. Signal transduction within target cells brings about a physiological response.

In the example of a simple endocrine pathway shown in Figure 45.11, the stimulus is the release of the acidic contents of the stomach into the duodenum (the first part of the small intestine). Low pH in the duodenum stimulates certain endocrine cells there, called S cells, to secrete the hormone *secretin*. Secretin enters the bloodstream and travels to the **pancreas**, a gland located behind the stomach (see Figure 45.4). Target cells in the pancreas then release bicarbonate into ducts leading to the duodenum, where it raises the pH.

In a *simple neuroendocrine pathway*, the stimulus is received by a sensory neuron, which stimulates a neurosecretory cell (Figure 45.12). The neurosecretory cell then secretes a neurohormone, which diffuses into the bloodstream and travels to target cells. Such a pathway regulates milk release during nursing in mammals. Suckling by an infant stimulates sensory neurons in the nipples, generating signals in the nervous system that reach the hypothalamus. Nerve impulses from the hypothalamus then trigger the release of the neurohormone **oxytocin** from the posterior pituitary gland. In response to circulating oxytocin, the mammary glands secrete milk.

▲ **Figure 45.11 A simple endocrine pathway.** Endocrine cells respond to a change in some internal or external variable—the stimulus—by secreting hormone molecules that trigger a specific response by target cells. In the case of secretin signaling, the simple endocrine pathway is self-limiting because the response to secretin (bicarbonate release) reduces the stimulus (low pH) through negative feedback.

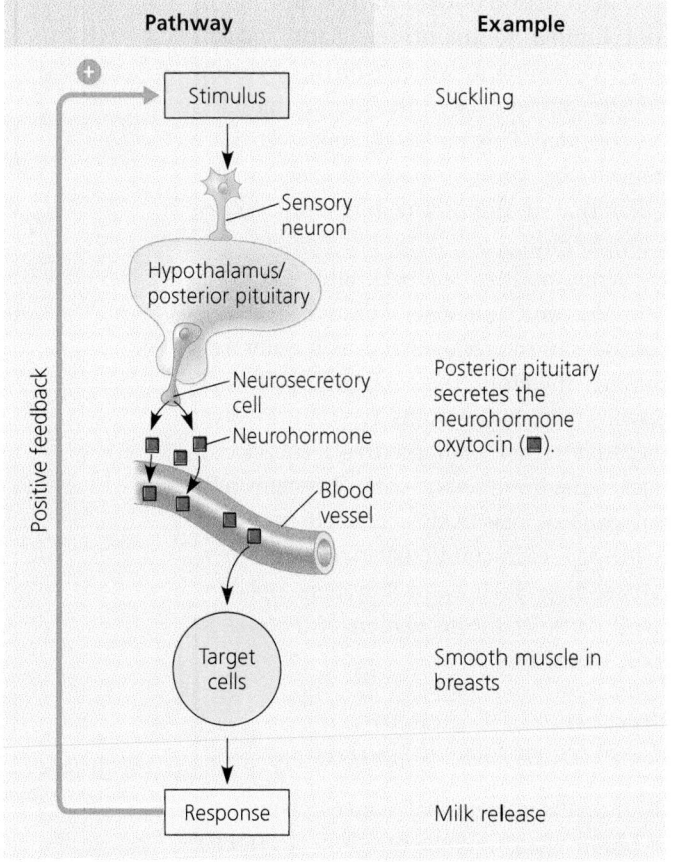

▲ **Figure 45.12 A simple neuroendocrine pathway.** Sensory neurons respond to a stimulus by sending nerve impulses to a neurosecretory cell, triggering secretion of a neurohormone. Upon reaching its target cells via the bloodstream, the neurohormone binds to its receptor, triggering signal transduction that results in a specific response. In the neuroendocrine pathway for oxytocin signaling, the response increases the stimulus, forming a positive-feedback loop that amplifies signaling in the pathway.

Feedback Regulation

A feedback loop linking the response back to the initial stimulus is characteristic of control pathways. For many hormones, the response pathway involves **negative feedback**, a loop in which the response reduces the initial stimulus. In the case of secretin signaling (see Figure 45.11), the release of bicarbonate by the pancreas increases pH in the intestine, eliminating the stimulus and thereby shutting off the pathway. By decreasing or abolishing hormone signaling, negative-feedback regulation prevents excessive pathway activity.

Whereas negative feedback dampens a stimulus, **positive feedback** reinforces a stimulus, leading to an even greater response. Consider, for instance, the oxytocin pathway outlined in Figure 45.12. In response to the circulating oxytocin, the mammary glands secrete milk. Milk released in response to the oxytocin leads to more suckling and therefore more stimulation. Activation of the pathway is sustained until the baby stops suckling.

The role of oxytocin in reproduction is not limited to mammary gland regulation. When mammals give birth, oxytocin induces target cells in the uterine muscles to contract. This pathway, too, is characterized by positive-feedback regulation, such that it drives the birth process to completion.

While positive feedback amplifies both stimulus and response, negative feedback helps restore a preexisting state. It is not surprising, therefore, that hormone pathways involved in homeostasis typically involve negative rather than positive feedback. In fact, some homeostatic control systems rely on pairs of negatively regulated hormone pathways, each counterbalancing the other. To see how such control systems operate, we'll consider the regulation of blood glucose levels.

Insulin and Glucagon: Control of Blood Glucose

In humans, metabolic balance depends on a blood glucose concentration of 70–110 mg/100 mL. Because glucose is a major fuel for cellular respiration and a key source of carbon skeletons for biosynthesis, maintaining blood glucose concentrations near this normal range is critical.

Two antagonistic (opposing) hormones, insulin and glucagon, regulate the concentration of glucose in the blood (**Figure 45.13**). Each of these hormones operates in a simple endocrine pathway regulated by negative feedback. When blood glucose rises above the normal range, release of **insulin** triggers uptake of glucose from the blood into body cells, decreasing the blood glucose concentration. When blood glucose drops below the normal range, the release of **glucagon** promotes the release of glucose into the blood from energy stores, such as liver glycogen, increasing the blood glucose concentration. Because insulin and glucagon have opposing effects, the combined activity of these two hormones tightly controls the concentration of glucose in the blood.

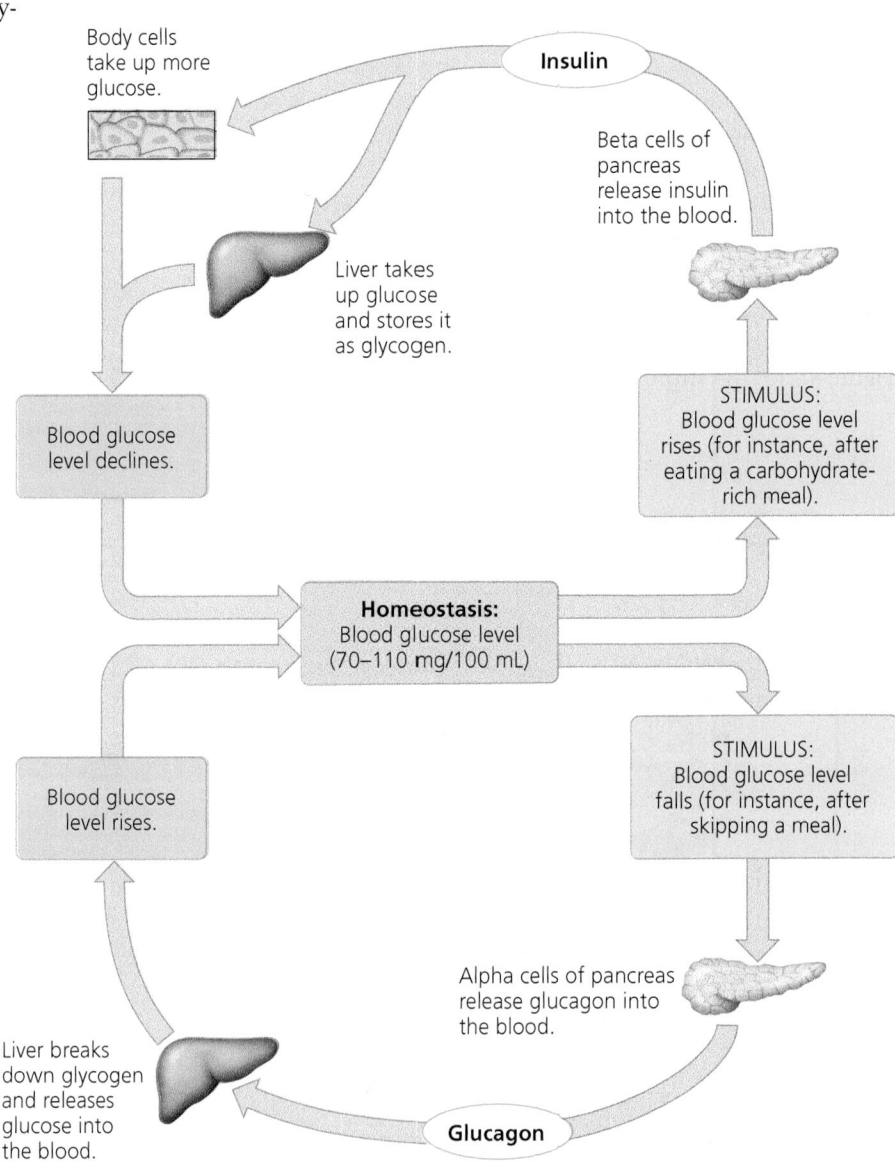

▲ Figure 45.13 Maintenance of glucose homeostasis by insulin and glucagon. The antagonistic effects of insulin and glucagon help keep blood glucose levels in the normal range.

 BioFlix Visit the Study Area at **www.masteringbiology.com** for the BioFlix® 3-D Animation on Homeostasis: Regulating Blood Sugar.

Glucagon and insulin are produced in the pancreas. Scattered throughout this organ are clusters of endocrine cells called pancreatic islets. Each pancreatic islet has *alpha cells*, which make glucagon, and *beta cells*, which make insulin. Like all hormones, insulin and glucagon are secreted into the interstitial fluid and enter the circulatory system.

Overall, hormone-secreting cells make up only 1–2% of the mass of the pancreas. Other cells in the pancreas produce and secrete bicarbonate ions and digestive enzymes. These exocrine secretions are released into small ducts that empty into the pancreatic duct, which leads to the small intestine. Thus, the pancreas is both an endocrine gland and an exocrine gland and has functions in both the endocrine and digestive systems.

Target Tissues for Insulin and Glucagon

Insulin lowers blood glucose levels by stimulating nearly all body cells outside the brain to take up glucose from the blood. (Brain cells can take up glucose without insulin, so the brain almost always has access to circulating fuel.) Insulin also decreases blood glucose by slowing glycogen breakdown in the liver and inhibiting the conversion of glycerol (from fats) and amino acids to glucose.

Glucagon influences blood glucose levels mainly through its effects on target cells in the liver. The liver, skeletal muscles, and adipose tissues store large amounts of fuel. The liver and muscles store sugar as glycogen, whereas cells in adipose tissue convert sugars to fats. When the blood glucose level decreases to a level at or below the normal range (70–110 mg/100 mL), a primary effect of glucagon is to signal liver cells to increase glycogen hydrolysis, convert amino acids and glycerol to glucose, and release glucose into the bloodstream. The net result is a return of the blood glucose level to the normal range.

The antagonistic effects of glucagon and insulin are vital to managing fuel storage and consumption by body cells. For both hormones, as we've mentioned, the liver is a critical target. Recall from Chapter 41 that nutrients absorbed by blood vessels of the small intestine are transported directly to the liver by the hepatic portal vein. Within the liver, glucagon and insulin regulate nutrient processing in ways that support glucose homeostasis. However, glucose homeostasis also relies on responses to glucagon and insulin elsewhere in the body as well as responses to other hormones—growth hormone and glucocorticoids—discussed later in this chapter.

In discussing the role of insulin and glucagon in glucose homeostasis, we have focused exclusively on a healthy metabolic state. However, a number of disorders can disrupt glucose homeostasis with potentially serious consequences, especially for the heart, blood vessels, eyes, and kidneys. We'll discuss the best known and most prevalent of these disorders—diabetes mellitus—next.

Diabetes Mellitus

The disease **diabetes mellitus** is caused by a deficiency of insulin or a decreased response to insulin in target tissues. Blood glucose levels rise, but cells are unable to take up enough glucose to meet metabolic needs. Instead, fat becomes the main substrate for cellular respiration. In severe cases, acidic metabolites formed during fat breakdown accumulate in the blood, threatening life by lowering blood pH and depleting sodium and potassium ions from the body.

In people with diabetes mellitus, the level of glucose in blood may exceed the capacity of the kidneys to reabsorb this nutrient. Glucose that remains in the kidney filtrate is excreted. For this reason, the presence of sugar in urine is one test for this disorder. As glucose is concentrated in the urine, more water is excreted along with it, resulting in excessive volumes of urine. *Diabetes* (from the Greek *diabainein*, to pass through) refers to this copious urination; and *mellitus* (from the Greek *meli*, honey) refers to the presence of sugar in urine. (*Diabetes insipidus*, discussed in Chapter 44, is a rare disorder of kidney function that results in large volumes of dilute urine but no major disruption in glucose metabolism.)

There are two main types of diabetes mellitus. Each is marked by high blood glucose, but with very different causes. *Type 1 diabetes*, or insulin-dependent diabetes, is an autoimmune disorder in which the immune system destroys the beta cells of the pancreas. Type 1 diabetes, which usually appears during childhood, destroys the person's ability to produce insulin. Treatment consists of insulin, typically injected several times daily. In the past, insulin was extracted from animal pancreases, but now human insulin can be obtained from genetically engineered bacteria, a relatively inexpensive source (see Figure 20.2). Stem cell research may someday provide a cure for type 1 diabetes by generating replacement beta cells that restore insulin production by the pancreas.

Type 2 diabetes, or non-insulin-dependent diabetes, is characterized by a failure of target cells to respond normally to insulin. Insulin is produced, but target cells fail to take up glucose from the blood, and blood glucose levels remain elevated. Although heredity can play a role in type 2 diabetes, excess body weight and lack of exercise significantly increase the risk. This form of diabetes generally appears after age 40, but even children who are overweight and sedentary can develop the disease. More than 90% of people with diabetes have type 2. Many can control their blood glucose levels with regular exercise and a healthy diet; some require medications. Nevertheless, type 2 diabetes is the seventh most common cause of death in the United States and a growing public health problem worldwide.

The resistance to insulin signaling in type 2 diabetes is sometimes due to a genetic defect in the insulin receptor or the insulin response pathway. In many cases, however, events in target cells suppress activity of an otherwise functional response pathway. One source of this suppression appears to be inflammatory signals generated by the innate immune system (see Chapter 43). How obesity and inactivity relate to this suppression is being studied in both humans and laboratory animals.

CONCEPT CHECK 45.2

1. In a glucose tolerance test, periodic measurements of blood glucose level are taken after a person drinks a glucose-rich solution. In a healthy individual, blood glucose rises moderately at first but falls to near normal within 2–3 hours. Predict the results of this test in a person with diabetes mellitus. Explain your answer.
2. If a hormone pathway provides a transient response to a stimulus, how would shortening the stimulus duration affect the need for negative feedback?
3. **WHAT IF?** Consider a diabetes patient who has a family history of type 2 diabetes but is active and not obese. To identify genes that might be defective in the patient, which genes would you examine first?

For suggested answers, see Appendix A.

CONCEPT 45.3

The hypothalamus and pituitary are central to endocrine regulation

Having reviewed the organization of hormone pathways, we return to the role of the nervous system in regulating endocrine pathways. In particular, we now turn our focus to the vertebrate brain and endocrine system.

Coordination of Endocrine and Nervous Systems in Vertebrates

In vertebrates, the **hypothalamus** plays a central role in integrating the endocrine and nervous systems. One of several endocrine glands located in the brain (**Figure 45.14**), the hypothalamus receives information from nerves throughout the body, including the brain. In response, the hypothalamus initiates endocrine signaling appropriate to environmental conditions. In many vertebrates, for example, nerve signals from the brain pass sensory information to the hypothalamus about seasonal changes. The hypothalamus, in turn, regulates the release of reproductive hormones required during the breeding season.

Signals from the hypothalamus travel to the **pituitary gland**, a gland located at its base (see Figure 45.14). Roughly the size and shape of a lima bean, the pituitary has discrete posterior and anterior parts, or lobes, that secrete different sets of hormones.

The **posterior pituitary** is an extension of the hypothalamus. Hypothalamic axons that reach into the posterior

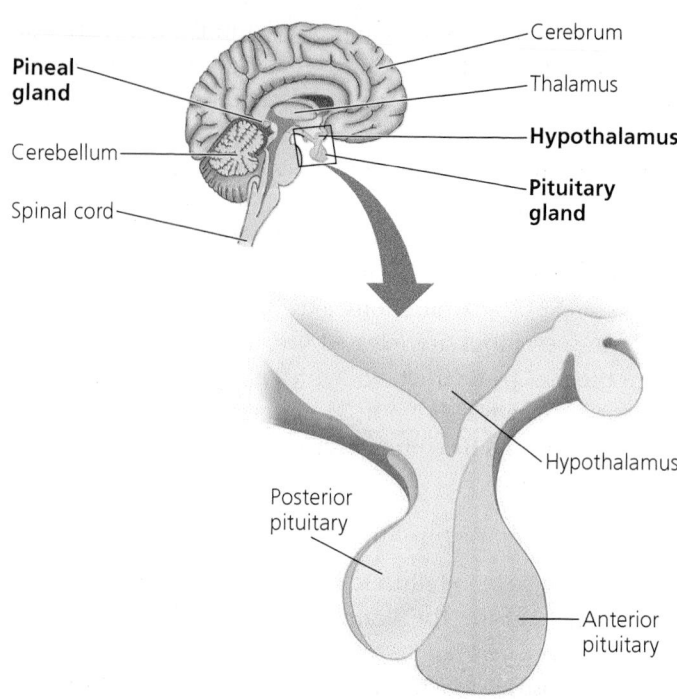

▲ **Figure 45.14 Endocrine glands in the human brain.** This side view of the brain indicates the position of the hypothalamus, the pituitary gland, and the pineal gland. (The pineal gland plays a role in regulating biorhythm.)

pituitary secrete neurohormones synthesized in the hypothalamus. In contrast, the **anterior pituitary** is an endocrine gland that synthesizes and secretes hormones in response to signals from the hypothalamus. Many anterior pituitary hormones act as **tropic hormones**, meaning that they regulate the function of other endocrine cells or glands.

Posterior Pituitary Hormones

Neurosecretory cells of the hypothalamus synthesize the two posterior pituitary hormones: oxytocin and antidiuretic hormone. After traveling to the posterior pituitary within the long axons of the neurosecretory cells, the hormones are stored in pituitary cells, to be released in response to nerve impulses transmitted by the hypothalamus (**Figure 45.15**).

As discussed in Concept 45.2 (see Figure 45.12), oxytocin regulates milk secretion by the mammary glands and also contractions of the uterus during birthing. In addition, oxytocin has targets in the brain, where it influences behaviors related to maternal care, pair bonding, and sexual activity.

Like oxytocin, **antidiuretic hormone (ADH)**, or *vasopressin*, regulates both physiology and behavior. As you read in Chapter 44, ADH is one of several hormones that regulate kidney function. In particular, ADH increases water retention in the kidneys, thus decreasing urine volume. The net result is to help maintain blood osmolarity within a normal range. ADH also plays an important role in social behavior, as detailed in Chapter 51.

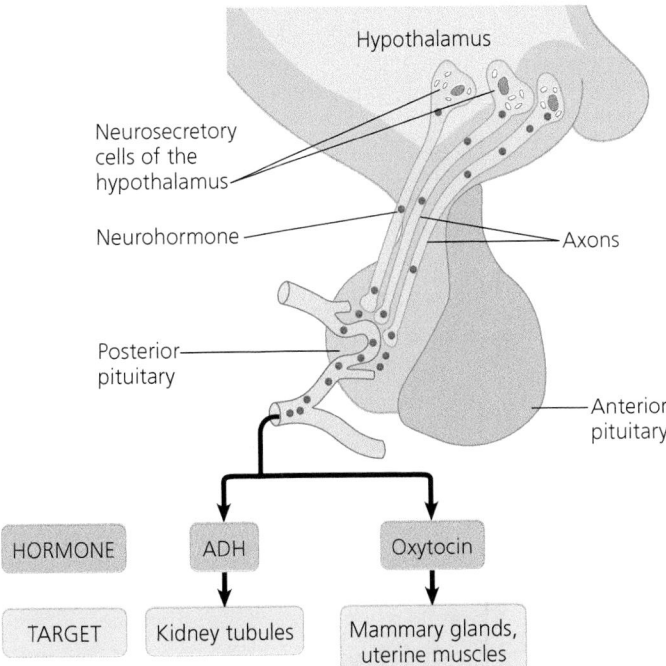

HORMONE: ADH | Oxytocin
TARGET: Kidney tubules | Mammary glands, uterine muscles

▲ **Figure 45.15 Production and release of posterior pituitary hormones.** The posterior pituitary gland is an extension of the hypothalamus. Certain neurosecretory cells in the hypothalamus make antidiuretic hormone (ADH) and oxytocin, which are transported to the posterior pituitary, where they are stored. Nerve signals from the brain trigger release of these neurohormones.

Anterior Pituitary Hormones

Endocrine signals generated by the hypothalamus regulate hormone secretion by the anterior pituitary (Figure 45.16). Each hypothalamic hormone is either a *releasing hormone* or an *inhibiting hormone*, reflecting its role in promoting or inhibiting release of one or more specific hormones by the anterior pituitary. *Prolactin-releasing hormone*, for example, is a hypothalamic hormone that stimulates the anterior pituitary to secrete **prolactin**, which has activities that include stimulating milk production. Every anterior pituitary hormone is controlled by at least one releasing hormone. Some, such as prolactin, have both a releasing hormone and an inhibiting hormone.

The hypothalamic releasing and inhibiting hormones are secreted near capillaries at the base of the hypothalamus. The capillaries drain into short blood vessels, called portal vessels, which subdivide into a second capillary bed within the anterior pituitary. In this way, the releasing and inhibiting hormones have direct access to the gland they control.

Hormones secreted by the anterior pituitary regulate a diverse set of processes in the human body, including metabolism, osmoregulation, and reproductive activity. We turn next to an exploration of these hormones and the processes they govern, beginning with the hormones of the thyroid gland. Table 45.1 (on the next page), which provides an overview of the major hormones of the endocrine system and their physiological functions, will serve as a useful point of reference for this discussion.

Tropic effects only:
FSH (follicle-stimulating hormone)
LH (luteinizing hormone)
TSH (thyroid-stimulating hormone)
ACTH (adrenocorticotropic hormone)

Nontropic effects only:
Prolactin
MSH (melanocyte-stimulating hormone)

Nontropic and tropic effects:
GH (growth hormone)

◀ **Figure 45.16**
Production and release of anterior pituitary hormones. The release of hormones synthesized in the anterior pituitary gland is controlled by hypothalamic releasing and inhibiting hormones. The hypothalamic hormones are secreted by neurosecretory cells and enter a capillary network within the hypothalamus. These capillaries drain into portal vessels that connect with a second capillary network in the anterior pituitary.

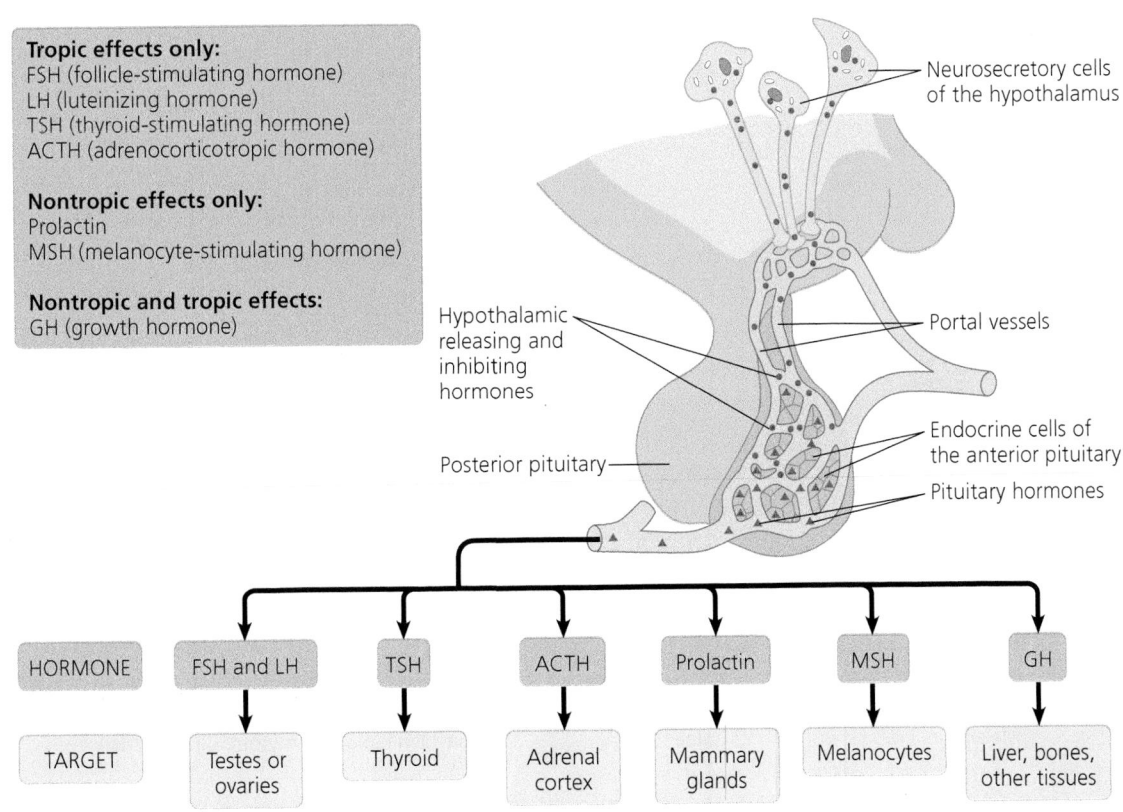

HORMONE: FSH and LH | TSH | ACTH | Prolactin | MSH | GH
TARGET: Testes or ovaries | Thyroid | Adrenal cortex | Mammary glands | Melanocytes | Liver, bones, other tissues

Table 45.1 Major Human Endocrine Glands and Some of Their Hormones

Gland	Hormone	Chemical Class	Representative Actions	Regulated By
Hypothalamus	Hormones released from the posterior pituitary and hormones that regulate the anterior pituitary (see below)			
Posterior pituitary gland (releases neurohormones made in hypothalamus)	Oxytocin	Peptide	Stimulates contraction of uterus and mammary gland cells	Nervous system
	Antidiuretic hormone (ADH)	Peptide	Promotes retention of water by kidneys	Water/salt balance
Anterior pituitary gland	Growth hormone (GH)	Protein	Stimulates growth (especially bones) and metabolic functions	Hypothalamic hormones
	Prolactin	Protein	Stimulates milk production and secretion	Hypothalamic hormones
	Follicle-stimulating hormone (FSH)	Glycoprotein	Stimulates production of ova and sperm	Hypothalamic hormones
	Luteinizing hormone (LH)	Glycoprotein	Stimulates ovaries and testes	Hypothalamic hormones
	Thyroid-stimulating hormone (TSH)	Glycoprotein	Stimulates thyroid gland	Hypothalamic hormones
	Adrenocorticotropic hormone (ACTH)	Peptide	Stimulates adrenal cortex to secrete glucocorticoids	Hypothalamic hormones
Thyroid gland	Triiodothyronine (T_3) and thyroxine (T_4)	Amines	Stimulate and maintain metabolic processes	TSH
	Calcitonin	Peptide	Lowers blood calcium level	Calcium in blood
Parathyroid glands	Parathyroid hormone (PTH)	Peptide	Raises blood calcium level	Calcium in blood
Pancreas	Insulin	Protein	Lowers blood glucose level	Glucose in blood
	Glucagon	Protein	Raises blood glucose level	Glucose in blood
Adrenal glands Adrenal medulla	Epinephrine and norepinephrine	Amines	Raise blood glucose level; increase metabolic activities; constrict certain blood vessels	Nervous system
Adrenal cortex	Glucocorticoids	Steroids	Raise blood glucose level	ACTH
	Mineralocorticoids	Steroids	Promote reabsorption of Na^+ and excretion of K^+ in kidneys	K^+ in blood; angiotensin II
Gonads Testes	Androgens	Steroids	Support sperm formation; promote development and maintenance of male secondary sex characteristics	FSH and LH
Ovaries	Estrogens	Steroids	Stimulate uterine lining growth; promote development and maintenance of female secondary sex characteristics	FSH and LH
	Progestins	Steroids	Promote uterine lining growth	FSH and LH
Pineal gland	Melatonin	Amine	Involved in biological rhythms	Light/dark cycles

Thyroid Regulation: A Hormone Cascade Pathway

Sets of hormones from the hypothalamus, the anterior pituitary, and a target endocrine gland are often organized into a *hormone cascade pathway* (**Figure 45.17**). Signals to the brain stimulate the hypothalamus to secrete a hormone that stimulates or inhibits release of a tropic anterior pituitary hormone. The anterior pituitary hormone in turn acts on a target endocrine tissue, stimulating secretion of yet another hormone that exerts systemic metabolic or developmental effects.

To learn more about how a hormone cascade pathway works, let's consider activation of the thyroid gland when an infant is exposed to cold (see Figure 45.17). When a young child's body temperature drops, the hypothalamus secretes thyrotropin-releasing hormone (TRH). The anterior pituitary responds to TRH by secreting thyroid-stimulating hormone (TSH), also known as thyrotropin. TSH stimulates release of thyroid hormone by the **thyroid gland**, an organ consisting of two lobes on the ventral surface of the trachea (see Figure 42.24). As thyroid hormone accumulates, it increases metabolic rate, resulting in the release of thermal energy, which raises body temperature.

Like simple hormone pathways, hormone cascade pathways typically involve negative feedback. In the case of the thyroid hormone pathway, thyroid hormone itself carries out negative feedback. Because thyroid hormone blocks TSH release from the anterior pituitary and TRH release from the hypothalamus, the negative-feedback loop prevents overproduction of thyroid hormone. Overall, the hormone cascade pathway brings about a self-limiting response to the original stimulus in the target cells.

In humans and other mammals, thyroid hormone regulates bioenergetics; helps maintain normal blood pressure, heart rate, and muscle tone; and regulates digestive and reproductive functions. Too much or too little thyroid hormone in the blood can result in serious metabolic disorders.

Disorders of Thyroid Function and Regulation

In humans, hypothyroidism, a condition of too little thyroid function, can produce symptoms such as weight gain, lethargy, and intolerance to cold in adults. Excessive secretion of thyroid hormone, known as hyperthyroidism, can lead to high body temperature, profuse sweating, weight loss, irritability, and high blood pressure.

The most common form of hyperthyroidism is Graves' disease. Protruding eyes, caused by fluid accumulation behind the eyes, are a typical symptom. In this autoimmune disorder, the body produces antibodies that bind to and activate the receptor for TSH. The result is sustained thyroid hormone production.

▲ **Figure 45.17 A hormone cascade pathway.** In response to the stimulus, the hypothalamus secretes a releasing hormone that targets the anterior pituitary. The anterior pituitary responds by secreting a second tropic hormone, which travels through the bloodstream to an endocrine gland. In response to this tropic hormone, the endocrine gland secretes a hormone that travels to target cells, where it induces a response. In the example of thyroid hormone regulation, thyroid hormone exerts negative feedback on the hypothalamus and anterior pituitary. This feedback inhibits release of TRH and TSH, preventing overreaction to the stimulus (such as low temperature in the case of a human infant).

? *Suppose a lab test of two patients, each diagnosed with excessive thyroid hormone production, revealed elevated levels of TSH in one but not the other. Was the diagnosis of one patient necessarily incorrect? Explain.*

Malnutrition can also alter thyroid hormone production. The specific link between diet and thyroid hormone synthesis reflects the chemical nature of thyroid hormone. The term *thyroid hormone* actually refers to a pair of very similar hormones derived from the amino acid tyrosine. **Triiodothyronine (T_3)** contains three iodine atoms, whereas tetraiodothyronine, or **thyroxine (T_4)**, contains four iodine atoms (see Figure 45.5). In mammals, the same receptor binds both hormones. The thyroid gland secretes mainly T_4, but target cells convert most of it to T_3 by removing one iodine atom.

Although iodine is readily obtained from seafood or iodized salt, people in many parts of the world suffer from inadequate iodine in their diet. Without sufficient iodine, the thyroid gland cannot synthesize adequate amounts of T_3 and T_4, and the resulting low blood levels of T_3 and T_4 cannot exert the usual negative feedback on the hypothalamus and anterior pituitary (see Figure 45.17). As a consequence, the pituitary continues to secrete TSH. Elevated TSH levels cause an enlargement of the thyroid gland resulting in goiter, a characteristic swelling of the neck.

Humans and other vertebrates require thyroid hormones for the normal functioning of bone-forming cells, as well as for the branching of nerve cells during embryonic development of the brain. In humans, congenital hypothyroidism, an inherited condition of thyroid deficiency, results in markedly retarded skeletal growth and poor mental development. These defects can often be avoided, at least partially, if treatment with thyroid hormones begins early in life. Iodine deficiency in childhood causes the same defects, but it is fully preventable if iodized salt is used in food preparation.

The fact that iodine in the body is dedicated to the production of thyroid hormone provides a novel diagnostic tool for disorders of thyroid function: Radioactive forms of iodine enable specific imaging of the thyroid gland (Figure 45.18).

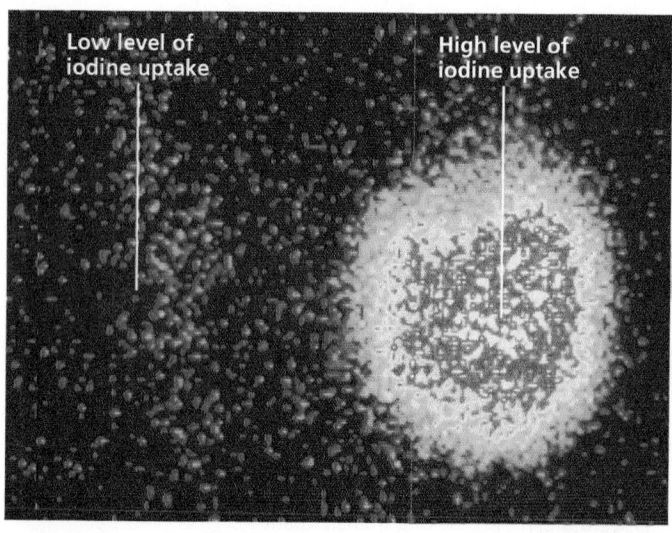

▲ **Figure 45.18 Thyroid scan.** Radioactive iodine enables doctors to identify abnormal patterns of iodine uptake that could indicate a thyroid disorder.

Evolution of Hormone Function

EVOLUTION Over the course of evolution, the functions of a given hormone often diverge between species. An example is thyroid hormone, which plays a role in regulating metabolism across many evolutionary lineages. In frogs, however, thyroid hormone (thyroxine) has taken on an apparently unique function: stimulating resorption of the tadpole's tail during metamorphosis (Figure 45.19).

Diverse functions have also evolved for many other vertebrate hormones. Prolactin, a product of the anterior pituitary, has an especially broad range of activities. Prolactin stimulates mammary gland growth and milk synthesis in mammals, regulates fat metabolism and reproduction in birds, delays metamorphosis in amphibians, and regulates salt and water balance in freshwater fishes. These varied roles suggest that prolactin is an ancient hormone with functions that have diversified during the evolution of vertebrate groups.

Melanocyte-stimulating hormone (MSH) is another example of an anterior pituitary hormone with distinct functions in different evolutionary lineages. In amphibians, fishes, and reptiles, MSH regulates skin color by controlling pigment distribution in skin cells called melanocytes. In mammals, MSH functions in hunger and metabolism in addition to coloration.

The specialized action of MSH that has evolved in the mammalian brain may prove to be of particular medical importance. Many patients with late-stage cancer, AIDS, tuberculosis, and certain aging disorders suffer from a devastating wasting

▲ **Tadpole**

▲ **Adult frog**

▲ Figure 45.19 **Specialized role of a hormone in frog metamorphosis.** The hormone thyroxine is responsible for the resorption of the tadpole's tail as the frog develops into its adult form.

condition called cachexia. Characterized by weight loss, muscle atrophy, and loss of appetite, cachexia is only poorly responsive to existing therapies. However, it turns out that activation of one brain receptor for MSH stimulates metabolism of fat and severely decreases appetite, changes also seen in cachexia. This fact led scientists to hypothesize that activation of this MSH receptor causes cachexia. To test this idea, they studied mice with mutations that cause cancerous tumors to develop, triggering cachexia. When the mice were treated with drugs that inhibit the brain MSH receptor, tumors occurred, but not cachexia! Whether such drugs can be used to treat cachexia in humans is an area of active study.

Tropic and Nontropic Hormones

As we have seen, thyroid-stimulating hormone (TSH) regulates the thyroid gland. This activity makes TSH an example of a tropic hormone. Although MSH and prolactin don't regulate endocrine cells or glands and are thus nontropic, three other anterior pituitary hormones act primarily or exclusively as tropic hormones: **follicle-stimulating hormone (FSH)**, **luteinizing hormone (LH)**, and **adrenocorticotropic hormone (ACTH)**.

FSH and LH stimulate the activities of both the male and female gonads, the testes and ovaries. For this reason, FSH and LH are also known as *gonadotropins*, and they are both regulated by hypothalamic *gonadotropin-releasing hormone* (*GnRH*). In Chapter 46, we will discuss how gonadotropins regulate reproductive functions.

ACTH stimulates the production and secretion of steroid hormones by the adrenal cortex. We will take a closer look at the hormone pathway involving ACTH later in this chapter.

Growth hormone (GH), which is secreted by the anterior pituitary, stimulates growth through both tropic and nontropic effects. A major target, the liver, responds to GH by releasing *insulin-like growth factors* (*IGFs*), which circulate in the blood and directly stimulate bone and cartilage growth. (IGFs also appear to play a key role in aging in many animal species.) In the absence of GH, the skeleton of an immature animal stops growing. GH also exerts diverse metabolic effects that tend to raise blood glucose levels, thus opposing the effects of insulin.

Abnormal production of GH in humans can result in several disorders, depending on when the problem occurs and whether it involves hypersecretion (too much) or hyposecretion (too little). Hypersecretion of GH during childhood can lead to gigantism, in which the person grows unusually tall—as tall as 2.4 m (8 feet)—though body proportions remain relatively normal. Excessive GH production in adulthood stimulates bony growth in the few tissues that are still responsive to the hormone. Because remaining target cells are predominantly in the face, hands, and feet, the result is an overgrowth of the extremities called acromegaly (from the Greek *acros*, extreme, and *mega*, large).

Hyposecretion of GH in childhood retards long-bone growth and can lead to pituitary dwarfism. Individuals with this disorder are for the most part properly proportioned but generally reach a height of only about 1.2 m (4 feet). If diagnosed before puberty, pituitary dwarfism can be treated successfully with human GH (also called HGH). Since the mid-1980s, scientists have used recombinant DNA technology to produce HGH in bacteria (see Chapter 20). Treatment with this genetically engineered HGH is now fairly routine for affected children.

CONCEPT CHECK 45.3

1. How do the two fused glands of the pituitary gland differ in function?
2. Why does hypothalamic control of oxytocin not require a releasing factor?
3. **WHAT IF?** Propose an explanation for why people with defects in specific endocrine pathways typically have defects in the final gland in the pathway rather than in the hypothalamus or pituitary.

For suggested answers, see Appendix A.

CONCEPT 45.4

Endocrine glands respond to diverse stimuli in regulating homeostasis, development, and behavior

Now that we've seen how endocrine glands in the brain initiate hormone cascade pathways, we return to the broader question of how endocrine signaling regulates animal physiology. We'll focus on homeostasis, development, and behavior, leaving the topic of reproduction largely for later chapters. This section presents more examples of hormone regulation by metabolic stimuli, by nervous system input, and by hormones of the anterior pituitary. First we'll examine another simple hormone pathway, the regulation of calcium ion concentration in the circulatory system.

Parathyroid Hormone and Vitamin D: Control of Blood Calcium

Because calcium ions (Ca^{2+}) are essential to the normal functioning of all cells, homeostatic control of blood calcium level is critical. If the blood Ca^{2+} level falls substantially, skeletal muscles begin to contract convulsively, a potentially fatal condition called tetany. If the blood Ca^{2+} level rises substantially, precipitates of calcium phosphate can form in body tissues, leading to widespread organ damage.

In mammals, the **parathyroid glands**, a set of four small structures embedded in the posterior surface of the thyroid (see Figure 45.4), play a major role in blood Ca^{2+} regulation. When

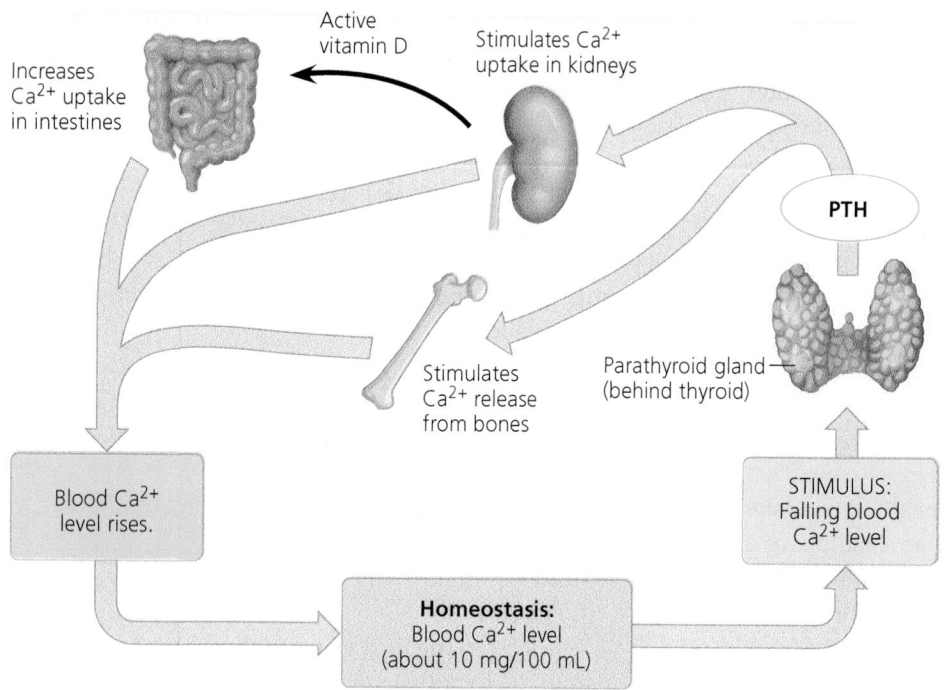

▲ **Figure 45.20 The roles of parathyroid hormone (PTH) in regulating blood calcium levels in mammals.**

blood Ca^{2+} falls below a set point of about 10 mg/100 mL, these glands release **parathyroid hormone (PTH)**.

PTH raises the level of blood Ca^{2+} by direct and indirect effects (Figure 45.20). In bone, PTH causes the mineralized matrix to decompose and release Ca^{2+} into the blood. In the kidneys, PTH directly stimulates reabsorption of Ca^{2+} through the renal tubules. PTH also has an indirect effect on the kidneys, promoting the conversion of vitamin D to an active hormone. An inactive form of vitamin D, a steroid-derived molecule, is obtained from food or synthesized in the skin when exposed to sunlight. Vitamin D activation begins in the liver and is completed in the kidneys, the process stimulated by PTH. The active form of vitamin D acts directly on the intestines, stimulating the uptake of Ca^{2+} from food and thus augmenting the effect of PTH. As blood Ca^{2+} rises, a negative-feedback loop inhibits further release of PTH from the parathyroid glands (not shown in figure).

The thyroid gland can also contribute to calcium homeostasis. If blood Ca^{2+} rises above the set point, the thyroid gland releases **calcitonin**, a hormone that inhibits bone resorption and enhances Ca^{2+} release by the kidney. In fishes, rodents, and some other animals, calcitonin is required for Ca^{2+} homeostasis. In humans, however, it is apparently needed only during the extensive bone growth of childhood.

Adrenal Hormones: Response to Stress

The **adrenal glands** of vertebrates are associated with the kidneys (the *renal* organs). In mammals, each adrenal gland is actually made up of two glands with different cell types, functions, and embryonic origins: the *adrenal cortex*, the outer portion, and the *adrenal medulla*, the central portion. The adrenal cortex consists of true endocrine cells, whereas the secretory cells of the adrenal medulla derive from neural tissue during embryonic development. Thus, like the pituitary gland, each adrenal gland is a fused endocrine and neuroendocrine gland.

Catecholamines from the Adrenal Medulla

Imagine that while walking in the woods at night you hear a growling noise nearby. "A bear?" you wonder. Your heart beats faster, your breath quickens, your muscles tense, and your thoughts speed up. These and other rapid responses to perceived danger comprise the "fight-or-flight," or acute stress, response. This coordinated set of physiological changes is triggered by two hormones of the adrenal medulla, **norepinephrine** (also known as noradrenaline) and epinephrine (adrenaline). Both are **catecholamines**, a class of amine hormones synthesized from the amino acid tyrosine.

The adrenal medulla secretes epinephrine and norepinephrine in response to stress—whether extreme pleasure or life-threatening danger. A major activity of these hormones is to increase the amount of chemical energy available for immediate use. Both epinephrine and norepinephrine increase the rate of glycogen breakdown in the liver and skeletal muscles, promote glucose release by liver cells, and stimulate the release of fatty acids from fat cells. The released glucose and fatty acids circulate in the blood and can be used by body cells as fuel.

In addition to increasing the availability of energy sources, norepinephrine and epinephrine exert profound effects on the cardiovascular and respiratory systems. For example, they increase both the heart rate and stroke volume and dilate the bronchioles in the lungs, actions that raise the rate of oxygen delivery to body cells. For this reason, doctors may prescribe epinephrine as a heart stimulant or to open the airways during an asthma attack. The catecholamines also alter blood flow, causing constriction of some blood vessels and dilation of others (see Figure 45.9). The overall effect is to shunt blood away from the skin, digestive organs, and kidneys, while increasing the blood supply to the heart, brain, and skeletal muscles. Epinephrine generally has a stronger effect on heart and metabolic rates, while the primary role of norepinephrine is in modulating blood pressure.

Nerve signals carried from the brain via involuntary (autonomic) neurons regulate secretion by the adrenal medulla. In response to a stressful stimulus, nerve impulses travel to the adrenal medulla, where they trigger the

▼ **Figure 45.21 Stress and the adrenal gland.**

(a) Short-term stress response and the adrenal medulla

1 Stressful stimuli cause the hypothalamus to activate the adrenal medulla via nerve impulses.

Spinal cord (cross section)

Nerve signals

Nerve cell

Adrenal medulla

Nerve cell

2 Adrenal medulla secretes epinephrine and norepinephrine.

(b) Long-term stress response and the adrenal cortex

Stress

Hypothalamus

Releasing hormone

Nerve cell

Anterior pituitary

Blood vessel

ACTH

1 Stressful stimuli cause the hypothalamus to activate the adrenal cortex via hormonal signals.

2 Adrenal cortex secretes mineralo-corticoids and glucocorticoids.

Adrenal gland

Kidney

Adrenal cortex

Effects of epinephrine and norepinephrine:

- Glycogen broken down to glucose; increased blood glucose
- Increased blood pressure
- Increased breathing rate
- Increased metabolic rate
- Change in blood flow patterns, leading to increased alertness and decreased digestive, excretory, and reproductive system activity

Effects of mineralocorticoids:

- Retention of sodium ions and water by kidneys
- Increased blood volume and blood pressure

Effects of glucocorticoids:

- Proteins and fats broken down and converted to glucose, leading to increased blood glucose
- Partial suppression of immune system

release of catecholamines from neurosecretory cells (Figure 45.21a). Acting on target tissues, epinephrine and norepinephrine each function in a simple neurohormone pathway. As you will read in Chapter 48, epinephrine and norepinephrine also function as neurotransmitters.

Steroid Hormones from the Adrenal Cortex

Hormones from the adrenal cortex also function in the body's response to stress. But in contrast to the adrenal medulla, which reacts to nervous input, the adrenal cortex responds to endocrine signals. Stressful stimuli cause the hypothalamus to secrete a releasing hormone that stimulates the anterior pituitary to release the tropic hormone ACTH. When ACTH reaches the adrenal cortex via the bloodstream, it stimulates the endocrine cells to synthesize and secrete a family of steroids called **corticosteroids** (Figure 45.21b). The two main types of corticosteroids in humans are glucocorticoids and mineralocorticoids.

As reflected in their name, **glucocorticoids** have a primary effect on glucose metabolism. Augmenting the fuel-mobilizing

effects of glucagon from the pancreas, glucocorticoids promote glucose synthesis from noncarbohydrate sources, such as proteins, making more glucose available as fuel. Glucocorticoids, such as cortisol (see Figure 45.5), act on skeletal muscle, causing the breakdown of muscle proteins. The resulting amino acids are transported to the liver and kidneys, where they are converted to glucose and released into the blood. The synthesis of glucose from muscle proteins provides circulating fuel when the body requires more glucose than the liver can mobilize from its glycogen stores.

When glucocorticoids are introduced into the body at levels above those normally present, they suppress certain components of the body's immune system. Because of this anti-inflammatory effect, glucocorticoids are sometimes used to treat inflammatory diseases such as arthritis. However, long-term use can have serious side effects, reflecting the potent activity of glucocorticoids on metabolism. For these reasons, nonsteroidal anti-inflammatory drugs (NSAIDs), such as aspirin or ibuprofen, generally are preferred for treating chronic inflammatory conditions.

Mineralocorticoids, named for their effects on mineral metabolism, act principally in maintaining salt and water balance. For example, the mineralocorticoid *aldosterone* functions in ion and water homeostasis of the blood. Low blood volume or pressure leads to production of angiotensin II, which stimulates the secretion of aldosterone (see Figure 44.22). Aldosterone, in turn, stimulates cells in the kidneys to reabsorb sodium ions and water from filtrate, raising blood pressure and volume. Aldosterone also functions in the body's response to severe stress. In these circumstances, a rise in blood ACTH levels increases the rate at which the adrenal cortex secretes aldosterone as well as glucocorticoids.

The corticosteroid products of the adrenal cortex include small amounts of steroid hormones that function as sex hormones. Small structural differences between these steroid hormones (see p. 63) are associated with major differences in effects. The sex hormones produced by the adrenal cortex are mainly "male" hormones (androgens), with small amounts of "female" hormones (estrogens and progestins). There is evidence that adrenal androgens account for the sex drive in adult females, but otherwise the physiological roles of the adrenal sex hormones are not well understood.

Gonadal Sex Hormones

Sex hormones affect growth, development, reproductive cycles, and sexual behavior. Whereas the adrenal glands secrete small quantities of these hormones, the testes of males and ovaries of females are their principal sources. The gonads produce and secrete three major categories of steroid hormones: androgens, estrogens, and progestins. All three types are found in both males and females but in significantly different proportions.

The testes primarily synthesize **androgens**, the main one being **testosterone**. Testosterone first functions before birth, as shown in the 1940s by French researcher Alfred Jost. He was interested in how hormones determine whether an individual develops as a male or female. Working with rabbits, Jost carried out a surgical study that provided a simple and unexpected answer **(Figure 45.22)**. His studies established that for mammals (but not all animals), female development is the default process in embryos.

Androgens have a major role again at human puberty, when they are responsible for the development of human male secondary sex characteristics. High concentrations of androgen lead to a low voice and male patterns of hair growth, as well as increases in muscle and bone mass. The muscle-building, or anabolic, action of testosterone and related steroids has enticed some athletes to take them as supplements, despite prohibitions against their use in nearly all sports. Use of anabolic steroids, while effective in increasing muscle mass, can cause severe acne outbreaks and liver damage, as well as significant decreases in sperm count and testicular size.

Estrogens, of which the most important is **estradiol**, are responsible for the maintenance of the female reproductive

system and for the development of female secondary sex characteristics. In mammals, **progestins**, which include **progesterone**, are primarily involved in preparing and maintaining tissues of the uterus required to support the growth and development of an embryo.

Estrogens and other gonadal sex hormones are components of hormone cascade pathways. Synthesis of these hormones is controlled by gonadotropins (FSH and LH) from the anterior pituitary gland (see Figure 45.16). FSH and LH secretion is in turn controlled by GnRH (gonadotropin-releasing hormone), a releasing hormone from the hypothalamus. We will examine the feedback relationships that regulate gonadal steroid secretion in detail in Chapter 46.

Endocrine Disruptors

Between 1938 and 1971, some pregnant women at risk for complications were prescribed a synthetic estrogen called diethylstilbestrol (DES). What was not known until 1971 was that exposure to DES can alter reproductive system development in the fetus. Collectively, daughters of women who took DES are more frequently afflicted with certain reproductive abnormalities, including a form of vaginal and cervical cancer, structural changes in the reproductive organs, and increased risk of miscarriage (spontaneous abortion). DES is now recognized as an *endocrine disruptor*, a foreign molecule that interrupts the normal function of a hormone pathway.

In recent years, it has been hypothesized that molecules in the environment also act as endocrine disruptors. Some estrogen-like molecules, such as those present in soybeans and other edible plant products, have been suggested to lower breast cancer risk. Others, such as bisphenol A, a chemical used in making some plastics, have been studied for potential interference with normal reproduction and development. Sorting out such effects has proved quite difficult, however, in part because enzymes in the liver change the properties of any such molecules entering the body through the digestive system.

Melatonin and Biorhythms

We conclude our discussion of the vertebrate endocrine system with the **pineal gland**, a small mass of tissue near the center of the mammalian brain (see Figure 45.14). The pineal gland is a primary source of the hormone **melatonin**, a modified amino acid.

Melatonin regulates functions related to light and to seasons marked by changes in day length. Although melatonin affects skin pigmentation in many vertebrates, its primary functions relate to biological rhythms associated with reproduction and with daily activity levels. Melatonin is secreted at night, and the amount released depends on the length of the night. In winter, for example, when days are short and nights are long, more melatonin is secreted. There is also good evidence that nightly increases in the levels of melatonin play a significant role in promoting sleep.

The release of melatonin by the pineal gland is controlled by a group of neurons in the hypothalamus called the suprachiasmatic nucleus (SCN). The SCN functions as a biological clock and receives input from specialized light-sensitive neurons in the retina of the eye. Although the SCN regulates melatonin production during the 24-hour light/dark cycle, melatonin also influences SCN activity. We will consider biological rhythms further in Chapter 49, where we analyze experiments on SCN function.

In the next chapter, we will look at reproduction in both vertebrates and invertebrates. There we will see that the endocrine system is central not only to the survival of the individual, but also to the propagation of the species.

CONCEPT CHECK 45.4

1. How does the fact that two adrenal hormones act as neurotransmitters relate to the developmental origin of the adrenal gland?
2. How would a decrease in the number of corticosteroid receptors in the hypothalamus affect levels of corticosteroids in the blood?
3. **WHAT IF?** Suppose you receive an injection of cortisone, a glucocorticoid, in an inflamed joint. What aspects of glucocorticoid activity would you be exploiting? If a glucocorticoid pill were also effective at treating the inflammation, why would it still be preferable to introduce the drug locally?

For suggested answers, see Appendix A.

45 CHAPTER REVIEW

SUMMARY OF KEY CONCEPTS

CONCEPT 45.1

Hormones and other signaling molecules bind to target receptors, triggering specific response pathways (pp. 975–980)

- The forms of communication between animal cells differ in the type of secreting cell and the route taken by the signal to its target. **Endocrine** signals, or **hormones**, are secreted into extracellular fluids by endocrine cells or ductless glands and reach target cells via circulatory fluids. **Paracrine** signals act on neighboring cells, whereas **autocrine** signals act on the secreting cell itself. **Neurotransmitters** also act locally, but **neurohormones** can act throughout the body. **Pheromones** are released into the environment for communication between animals of the same species.
- In insects, molting and development are controlled by PTTH; **ecdysteroid**, whose release is triggered by PTTH; and juvenile hormone. Coordination of signals from the nervous and endocrine systems and modulation of one hormone activity by another bring about the precise series of developmental stages that lead to an adult form.

- Distinct cellular responses are associated with water-soluble and lipid-soluble hormones. Polypeptide hormones and most amine hormones are water-soluble and bind to receptors embedded in the plasma membrane. Binding of water-soluble hormones to cell-surface receptors triggers intracellular **signal transduction**, leading to specific responses in the cytoplasm or changes in gene expression. In contrast, steroid and thyroid hormones are lipid-soluble and readily enter target cells. There they bind to specific protein receptors in the cytosol or nucleus. These complexes of a lipid-soluble hormone and its receptor act in the nucleus to regulate transcription of specific genes. The same hormone may have different effects on target cells that have different receptors for the hormone or different signal transduction pathways.
- **Local regulators**, which carry out paracrine and autocrine signaling, include cytokines and **growth factors** (proteins/peptides), **nitric oxide** (a gas), and **prostaglandins** (modified fatty acids).

? *Predict what would happen if you injected a water-soluble hormone directly into the cytosol of a target cell.*

CONCEPT 45.2

Feedback regulation and antagonistic hormone pairs are common in endocrine systems (pp. 981–984)

Pathway	Example
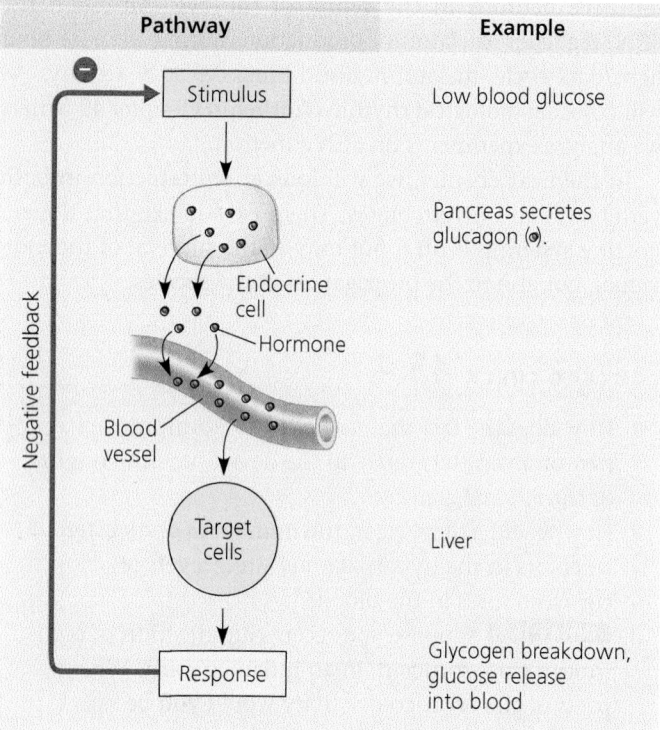	Low blood glucose
	Pancreas secretes glucagon (•).
	Liver
	Glycogen breakdown, glucose release into blood

- Hormone pathways may be regulated by **negative feedback**, which dampens the stimulus, or **positive feedback**, which amplifies the stimulus and drives the response to completion. Negative-feedback pathways sometimes occur in antagonistic pairs, such as the maintainance of glucose homeostasis by **glucagon** (from alpha cells of the **pancreas**) and **insulin** (from beta cells of the pancreas). Insulin reduces blood glucose levels by promoting cellular uptake of glucose, glycogen formation in the liver, protein synthesis, and fat storage. The disorder **diabetes mellitus**, which is marked by elevated blood glucose levels, results from inadequate production of insulin (type 1) or loss of responsiveness of target cells to insulin (type 2).

? *Would taking a drug that blocks the action of glucagon lessen the symptoms of diabetes or make them worse? Explain.*

CONCEPT 45.3

The hypothalamus and pituitary are central to endocrine regulation (pp. 984–989)

- Some neurosecretory cells in the **hypothalamus** produce hormones secreted by the **posterior pituitary**. Other hypothalamic cells produce hormones that are transported by portal vessels to the **anterior pituitary**, where they stimulate or inhibit the release of particular hormones.
- The two hormones released from the **posterior pituitary** act directly on nonendocrine tissues. **Oxytocin** induces uterine contractions and release of milk from mammary glands, and **antidiuretic hormone** (ADH) enhances water reabsorption in the kidneys.
- Often, anterior pituitary hormones act in a cascade. In the case of thyrotropin, or thyroid-stimulating hormone (TSH), TSH secretion is regulated by thyrotropin-releasing hormone (TRH).

TSH in turn induces the **thyroid gland** to secrete **thyroid hormone**, a combination of the iodine-containing hormones T_3 and T_4. Thyroid hormone stimulates metabolism and influences development and maturation.

- Hormones sometimes acquire distinct roles in different species over the course of evolution. **Prolactin** stimulates milk production in mammals but has diverse effects in different vertebrates. **Melanocyte-stimulating hormone** (MSH) influences skin pigmentation in some vertebrates and fat metabolism in mammals.
- Although prolactin and MSH act on nonendocrine targets, most anterior pituitary hormones are tropic, acting on endocrine tissues or glands to regulate hormone secretion. **Tropic hormones** of the anterior pituitary include TSH, **follicle-stimulating hormone** (FSH), **luteinizing hormone** (LH), and **adrenocorticotropic hormone** (ACTH). **Growth hormone** (GH) has both tropic and nontropic effects. It promotes growth directly, has diverse metabolic effects, and stimulates the production of growth factors by other tissues.

? *Which major endocrine organs are regulated independently of the hypothalamus and pituitary? Explain.*

CONCEPT 45.4

Endocrine glands respond to diverse stimuli in regulating homeostasis, development, and behavior (pp. 989–993)

- **Parathyroid hormone** (PTH), secreted by the **parathyroid glands**, causes bone to release Ca^{2+} into the blood and stimulates reabsorption of Ca^{2+} in the kidneys. PTH also stimulates the kidneys to activate vitamin D, which promotes intestinal uptake of Ca^{2+} from food. **Calcitonin**, secreted by the thyroid, has the opposite effects in bones and kidneys as PTH. Calcitonin is important for calcium homeostasis in adults of some vertebrates, but not humans.
- In response to stress, neurosecretory cells in the adrenal medulla release **epinephrine** and **norepinephrine**, which mediate various fight-or-flight responses. The adrenal cortex releases **glucocorticoids**, such as cortisol, which influence glucose metabolism and the immune system, as well as **mineralocorticoids**, primarily aldosterone, which help regulate salt and water balance.
- Although the adrenal cortex produces small amounts of sex hormones, the gonads—testes and ovaries—produce most of the body's sex hormones. All three types—**androgens**, **estrogens**, and **progestins**—are produced in males and females, but in different proportions.
- The **pineal gland**, located within the brain, secretes **melatonin**, which functions in biological rhythms related to reproduction and sleep. Release of melatonin is controlled by the SCN, the region of the brain that functions as a biological clock.

? *ADH and epinephrine act as hormones when released into the bloodstream and as neurotransmitters when released in synapses between neurons. What is similar about the endocrine glands that produce these two molecules?*

TEST YOUR UNDERSTANDING

LEVEL 1: KNOWLEDGE/COMPREHENSION

1. Which of the following is *not* an accurate statement?
   a. Hormones are chemical messengers that travel to target cells through the circulatory system.
   b. Hormones often regulate homeostasis through antagonistic functions.
   c. Hormones of the same chemical class usually have the same function.

d. Hormones are secreted by specialized cells usually located in endocrine glands.

e. Hormones are often regulated through feedback loops.

2. An example of antagonistic hormones controlling homeostasis is
   a. thyroxine and parathyroid hormone in calcium balance.
   b. insulin and glucagon in glucose metabolism.
   c. progestins and estrogens in sexual differentiation.
   d. epinephrine and norepinephrine in fight-or-flight responses.
   e. oxytocin and prolactin in milk production.

3. Growth factors are local regulators that
   a. are produced by the anterior pituitary.
   b. are modified fatty acids that stimulate bone and cartilage growth.
   c. are found on the surface of cancer cells and stimulate abnormal cell division.
   d. bind to cell-surface receptors and stimulate growth and development of target cells.
   e. convey messages between nerve cells.

4. Which hormone is *incorrectly* paired with its action?
   a. oxytocin—stimulates uterine contractions during childbirth
   b. thyroxine—stimulates metabolic processes
   c. insulin—stimulates glycogen breakdown in the liver
   d. ACTH—stimulates the release of glucocorticoids by the adrenal cortex
   e. melatonin—affects biological rhythms, seasonal reproduction

LEVEL 2: APPLICATION/ANALYSIS

5. Steroid and peptide hormones typically have in common
   a. the building blocks from which they are synthesized.
   b. their solubility in cell membranes.
   c. their requirement for travel through the bloodstream.
   d. the location of their receptors.
   e. their reliance on signal transduction in the cell.

6. Which of the following is the most likely explanation for hypothyroidism in a patient whose iodine level is normal?
   a. greater production of T_3 than of T_4
   b. hyposecretion of TSH
   c. hypersecretion of TSH
   d. hypersecretion of MSH
   e. a decrease in the thyroid secretion of calcitonin

7. Shortly after ingesting a big plate of carbohydrate-rich pasta, you measure your blood's hormone levels. What results would you expect, compared to before the meal?
   a. high insulin, low glucagon
   b. low insulin, low glucagon
   c. high insulin, high glucagon
   d. low insulin, high glucagon
   e. low insulin, no change in glucagon

8. The relationship between the insect hormones ecdysteroid and PTTH is an example of
   a. an interaction of the endocrine and nervous systems.
   b. homeostasis achieved by positive feedback.
   c. how peptide-derived hormones have more widespread effects than steroid hormones.
   d. homeostasis maintained by antagonistic hormones.
   e. competitive inhibition of a hormone receptor.

9. **DRAW IT** In mammals, milk production by mammary glands is controlled by prolactin and prolactin-releasing hormone. Draw a simple sketch of this pathway, including glands and tissues, hormones, routes for hormone movement, and effects.

LEVEL 3: SYNTHESIS/EVALUATION

10. **EVOLUTION CONNECTION**
    The intracellular receptors used by all the steroid and thyroid hormones are similar enough in structure that they are all considered members of one "superfamily" of proteins. Propose a hypothesis for how the genes encoding these receptors may have evolved. (*Hint*: See Figure 21.13.) How could you test your hypothesis using DNA sequence data?

11. **SCIENTIFIC INQUIRY**
    Chronically high levels of glucocorticoids can result in obesity, muscle weakness, and depression, a combination of symptoms called Cushing's syndrome. Excessive activity of either the pituitary or the adrenal gland can be the cause. To determine which gland has abnormal activity in a particular patient, doctors use the drug dexamethasone, a synthetic glucocorticoid that blocks ACTH release. Based on the graph, which gland is affected in patient X?

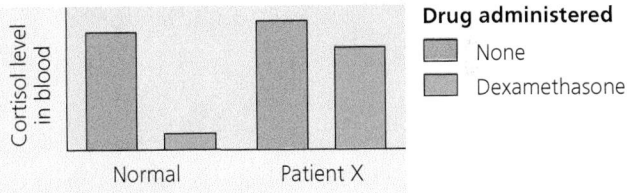

12. **WRITE ABOUT A THEME**
    Environmental Interactions In a short essay (100–150 words), use specific examples to discuss the role of hormones in an animal's responses to changes in its environment.

For selected answers, see Appendix A.

46

Animal Reproduction

▲ **Figure 46.1 How can each of these sea slugs be both male and female?**

KEY CONCEPTS

46.1 Both asexual and sexual reproduction occur in the animal kingdom

46.2 Fertilization depends on mechanisms that bring together sperm and eggs of the same species

46.3 Reproductive organs produce and transport gametes

46.4 The interplay of tropic and sex hormones regulates mammalian reproduction

46.5 In placental mammals, an embryo develops fully within the mother's uterus

OVERVIEW

Pairing Up for Sexual Reproduction

The sea slugs, or nudibranchs (*Nembrotha rutilans*), in Figure 46.1 are mating. If not disturbed, these marine molluscs may remain joined for hours. Sperm will be transferred and will fertilize eggs. A few weeks later, sexual reproduction

will be complete. New individuals will hatch, but which parent is the mother? The answer is simple yet probably unexpected: both. In fact, each sea slug produces eggs *and* sperm.

As humans, we tend to think of reproduction in terms of the mating of males and females and the fusion of sperm and eggs. Animal reproduction, however, takes many forms. In some species, individuals change their sex during their lifetime; in other species, such as sea slugs, an individual is both male and female. There are animals that can fertilize their own eggs, as well as others that can reproduce without any form of sex. For certain species, such as honeybees, only a few individuals within a large population reproduce.

A population outlives its members only by reproduction, the generation of new individuals from existing ones. In this chapter, we will compare the diverse reproductive mechanisms that have evolved in the animal kingdom. We will then examine details of mammalian reproduction, particularly that of humans. We will focus on the physiology of reproduction mostly from the parents' perspective, deferring the details of embryonic development until the next chapter.

CONCEPT 46.1

Both asexual and sexual reproduction occur in the animal kingdom

There are two modes of animal reproduction—sexual and asexual. In **sexual reproduction**, the fusion of haploid gametes forms a diploid cell, the **zygote**. The animal that develops from a zygote can in turn give rise to gametes by meiosis (see Figure 13.8). The female gamete, the **egg**, is a large, nonmotile cell. The male gamete, the **sperm**, is generally a much smaller, motile cell. **Asexual reproduction** is the generation of new individuals without the fusion of egg and sperm. In most asexual animals, reproduction relies entirely on mitotic cell division.

For the vast majority of animals, reproduction is primarily or exclusively sexual. However, there are species that have a primarily asexual mode of reproduction, including a few all-female species for which reproduction is exclusively asexual. These include the microscopic bdelloid rotifer (see p. 677), as well as certain species of whiptail lizard (*Aspidoscelis*), which we will discuss shortly.

Mechanisms of Asexual Reproduction

Several forms of asexual reproduction are found only among invertebrates. One of these is **fission**, the separation of a parent organism into two individuals of approximately equal size (Figure 46.2). Also common among invertebrates is **budding**, in which new individuals arise from outgrowths of existing ones (see Figure 13.2). In stony corals, for example, buds form and remain attached to the parent. The eventual result is a

▲ Figure 46.2 **Asexual reproduction of a sea anemone** (***Anthopleura elegantissima***). The large individual in the center of this photograph is undergoing fission, a type of asexual reproduction. Two smaller individuals will form as the parent divides approximately in half. Each offspring will be a genetic copy of the parent.

colony more than 1 m across, consisting of thousands of connected individuals. In another form of asexual reproduction, some invertebrates, including certain sponges, release specialized groups of cells that can grow into new individuals.

Another process of asexual reproduction involves two steps: *fragmentation*, the breaking of the body into several pieces, followed by *regeneration*, the regrowth of lost body parts. If more than one piece grows and develops into a complete animal, the net effect is reproduction. For example, certain annelid worms can split their body into several fragments, each regenerating a complete worm in less than a week. Numerous sponges, cnidarians, bristle worms, and sea squirts also reproduce by fragmentation and regeneration.

Parthenogenesis is asexual reproduction in which an egg develops without being fertilized. Among invertebrates, parthenogenesis occurs in certain species of bees, wasps, and ants. The progeny can be either haploid or diploid. If haploid, the offspring develop into adults that produce eggs or sperm without meiosis. In the case of honeybees, males (drones) are fertile haploid adults that arise by parthenogenesis. (In contrast, female honeybees, including both the sterile workers and the fertile queens, are diploid adults that develop from fertilized eggs.) Among vertebrates, parthenogenesis has been observed in about one in every thousand species. Recently, zookeepers discovered parthenogenesis in the Komodo dragon and in a species of hammerhead shark. In both cases, females had been kept completely isolated from males of their species but nevertheless produced offspring.

Sexual Reproduction: An Evolutionary Enigma

EVOLUTION Sex must enhance reproductive success or survival because it would otherwise rapidly disappear. To see why, consider an animal population in which half the females reproduce sexually and half reproduce asexually (Figure 46.3). We'll assume that the number of offspring per female is a constant, two in this case. The two offspring of an asexual female will both be daughters that will each give birth to two more reproductive daughters. In contrast, half of a sexual female's offspring will be male. The number of sexual offspring will remain the same at each generation, because both a male and a female are required to reproduce. Thus, the asexual condition will increase in frequency at each generation. Yet despite this "twofold cost," sex is maintained even in animal species that can also reproduce asexually.

What advantage does sex provide? The answer remains elusive. Most hypotheses focus on the unique combinations of parental genes formed during meiotic recombination and fertilization. By producing offspring of varied genotypes, sexual reproduction may enhance the reproductive success of parents when environmental factors, such as pathogens, change relatively rapidly. In contrast, asexual reproduction is expected to be most advantageous in stable, favorable environments because it perpetuates successful genotypes faithfully and precisely.

There are a number of reasons why the unique gene combinations formed during sexual reproduction might be advantageous. One is that beneficial gene combinations arising through recombination might speed up adaptation. Although this idea appears straightforward, the theoretical advantage is significant only when the rate of beneficial mutations is high and population size is small. Another idea is that the shuffling of genes during sexual reproduction might allow a population to rid itself of sets of harmful genes

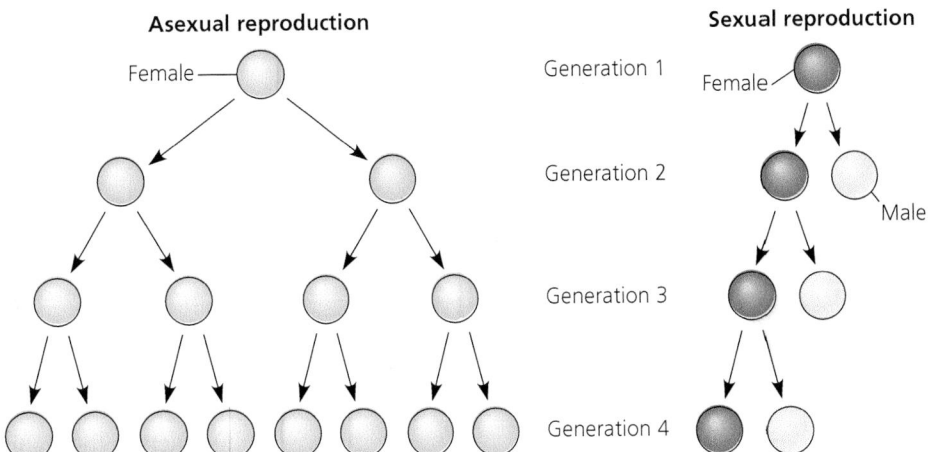

▲ Figure 46.3 **The "reproductive handicap" of sex.** These diagrams contrast the reproductive output of females (blue spheres) over four generations for asexual versus sexual reproduction, assuming two surviving offspring per female. The asexual population rapidly outgrows the sexual one.

more readily. Experiments to test these and other hypotheses are ongoing in many laboratories.

Reproductive Cycles

Most animals exhibit cycles in reproductive activity, often related to changing seasons. In this way, animals conserve resources, reproducing only when sufficient energy sources or stores are available and when environmental conditions favor the survival of offspring. For example, ewes (female sheep) have a reproductive cycle lasting 15–17 days. **Ovulation**, the release of mature eggs, occurs at the midpoint of each cycle. A ewe's cycle generally occurs only during fall and early winter, and the length of any resulting pregnancy is 5 months. Thus, most lambs are born in the early spring, when their chances of survival are optimal. Reproductive cycles are controlled by hormones, which in turn are regulated by environmental cues. Common environmental cues are changes in day length, seasonal temperature, rainfall, and lunar cycles.

Because seasonal temperature is often an important cue for reproduction, climate change can decrease reproductive success. Researchers in Denmark have demonstrated just such an effect on caribou (wild reindeer). In spring, caribou migrate to calving grounds to eat sprouting green plants, give birth, and care for their new calves (**Figure 46.4**). Changes in the length of daylight trigger the migration, while the seasonal rise in temperature that thaws the tundra causes plants to sprout. Prior to 1993, the arrival of the caribou at the calving grounds coincided with the brief period during which the plants were nutritious and digestible. Between 1993 and 2006, average spring temperatures in the calving grounds increased by more than 4°C, and the plants now sprout two weeks earlier. Since the length of daylight is unaffected by climate change, the timing

of the caribou migration has not changed. The result is a timing mismatch between new plant growth and caribou birthing. Without adequate nutrition for the nursing females, production of caribou offspring has declined by 75%.

Reproductive cycles are also found among animals that can reproduce both sexually and asexually. Consider, for instance, the water flea (genus *Daphnia*). A *Daphnia* female can produce eggs of two types. One type of egg requires fertilization to develop, but the other type does not and develops instead by parthenogenesis. Asexual reproduction occurs when environmental conditions are favorable, whereas sexual reproduction occurs during times of environmental stress. As a result, the switch between sexual and asexual reproduction is roughly linked to season.

A very different type of reproductive cycle is found among animals that only reproduce asexually. Several genera of fishes, amphibians, and reptiles engage in a complex form of parthenogenesis that involves the doubling of chromosomes after meiosis, producing diploid offspring. Among these are about 15 species of whiptail lizards in the genus *Aspidoscelis*. There are no males, but courtship and mating behaviors are typical of sexual species of the same genus. During the breeding season, one female of each mating pair mimics a male (**Figure 46.5a**). Each member of the pair alternates roles two or three times during the season. An individual adopts female behavior prior to ovulation, when the level of the female sex hormone estradiol is high, then switches to male-like behavior after ovulation, when the level of progesterone is highest (**Figure 46.5b**). Ovulation is more likely to occur if the individual is mounted during the critical time of the hormone cycle; isolated lizards lay fewer eggs than those that go through the motions of sex. These observations support the hypothesis that these parthenogenetic lizards evolved from species having two sexes and still require certain sexual stimuli for maximum reproductive success.

Variation in Patterns of Sexual Reproduction

For many animals, finding a partner for sexual reproduction can be challenging. Adaptations that arose during the evolution of some species meet this challenge in a novel way—by blurring the strict distinction between male and female. One such adaptation arose among sessile (stationary) animals, such as barnacles; burrowing animals, such as clams; and some parasites, including tapeworms. Lacking locomotion, these animals have a very limited opportunity to find a mate. An evolutionary solution to this problem is **hermaphroditism**, in which each individual has both male and female reproductive systems (the term *hermaphrodite* merges the names Hermes and Aphrodite, a Greek god and goddess). Because each hermaphrodite reproduces as both a male and a female, *any* two individuals can mate. Each animal donates and receives sperm during mating, as the sea slugs in Figure 46.1 are doing. In some species, hermaphrodites are

▲ **Figure 46.4 Caribou (*Rangifer tarandus*) mother and calf.** As a result of warming due to global climate change, the number of caribou offspring in a West Greenland study site has fallen fourfold.

(a) Both lizards in this photograph are *A. uniparens* females. The one on top is playing the role of a male. Every two or three weeks during the breeding season, individuals switch sex roles.

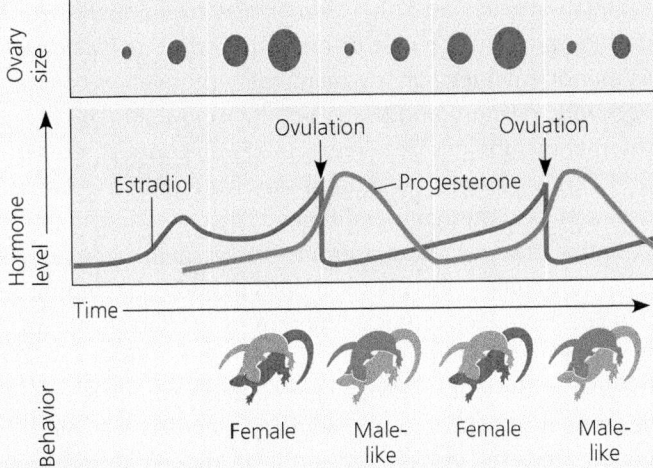

(b) The sexual behavior of *A. uniparens* is correlated with the cycle of ovulation mediated by sex hormones. As the blood level of estradiol rises, the ovaries grow, and the lizard behaves as a female. After ovulation, the estradiol level drops abruptly, and the progesterone level rises; these hormone levels correlate with male-like behavior.

▲ **Figure 46.5 Sexual behavior in parthenogenetic lizards.** The desert-grassland whiptail lizard (*Aspidoscelis uniparens*) is an all-female species. These reptiles reproduce by parthenogenesis, the development of an unfertilized egg. Nevertheless, ovulation is stimulated by mating behavior.

also capable of self-fertilization, allowing a form of sexual reproduction that doesn't require any partner.

The bluehead wrasse (*Thalassoma bifasciatum*), a coral reef fish, provides a well-studied example of a quite different variation in sexual reproduction. These wrasses live in harems, each consisting of a single male and several females. When the lone male dies, the opportunity for sexual reproduction would appear lost. Instead, a female wrasse undergoes sex reversal, a change in sex. Within a week, the transformed individual is producing sperm instead of eggs. Scientists have observed that it is the largest (and usually oldest) female in the harem that undergoes sex reversal. What advantage did this offer in the evolution of this wrasse? Because it is the male that defends a harem against intruders, a larger size may be more important for males than females in ensuring successful reproduction.

Certain oyster species also undergo sex reversal. In this case, individuals reproduce as males and then later as females, when their size is greatest. Since the number of gametes produced generally increases with size much more for females than for males, sex reversal in this direction maximizes gamete production. The result is enhanced reproductive success: Because oysters are sedentary animals and release their gametes into the surrounding water rather than mating directly, releasing more gametes tends to result in more offspring.

CONCEPT CHECK 46.1

1. Compare and contrast the outcomes of asexual and sexual reproduction.
2. Parthenogenesis is the most common form of asexual reproduction in animals that at other times reproduce sexually. What characteristic of parthenogenesis might explain this observation?
3. **WHAT IF?** If a hermaphrodite self-fertilizes, will the offspring be identical to the parent? Explain.
4. **MAKE CONNECTIONS** What examples of plant reproduction are most similar to asexual reproduction in animals? (See Concept 38.2, p. 812.)

For suggested answers, see Appendix A.

CONCEPT 46.2

Fertilization depends on mechanisms that bring together sperm and eggs of the same species

The union of sperm and egg—**fertilization**—can be either external or internal. In species with **external fertilization**, the female releases eggs into the environment, where the male then fertilizes them. Other species have **internal fertilization**: Sperm are deposited in or near the female reproductive tract, and fertilization occurs within the tract. (We'll discuss the cellular and molecular details of fertilization in Chapter 47.)

A moist habitat is almost always required for external fertilization, both to prevent the gametes from drying out and to allow the sperm to swim to the eggs. Many aquatic invertebrates simply shed their eggs and sperm into the surroundings, and fertilization occurs without the parents making physical contact. However, timing is crucial to ensure that mature sperm and eggs encounter one another.

Among some species with external fertilization, individuals clustered in the same area release their gametes into the water at the same time, a process known as *spawning*. In some cases, chemical signals that one individual generates in releasing gametes trigger others to release gametes. In other cases, environmental cues, such as temperature or day length, cause a whole population to release gametes at one time. For example, the palolo worm, native to coral reefs of the South Pacific, times its spawning to both the season and the lunar cycle. In spring, when the moon is in its last quarter, palolo worms break in half, releasing tail segments engorged with sperm or eggs. These packets rise to the ocean surface and burst in such vast numbers that the sea appears milky with gametes. The sperm quickly fertilize the floating eggs, and within hours, the palolo's once-a-year reproductive frenzy is complete.

When external fertilization is not synchronous across a population, individuals may exhibit specific mating behaviors leading to the fertilization of the eggs of one female by one male (Figure 46.6). Such "courtship" behavior has two important benefits: It allows mate choice (see Chapter 23) and, by triggering the release of both sperm and eggs, increases the probability of successful fertilization.

Internal fertilization is an adaptation that enables sperm to reach an egg efficiently, even when the environment is dry. It typically requires cooperative behavior that leads to copulation, as well as sophisticated and compatible reproductive systems. The male copulatory organ delivers sperm, and the female reproductive tract often has receptacles for storage and delivery of sperm to mature eggs.

No matter how fertilization occurs, the mating animals may make use of *pheromones*, chemicals released by one organism that can influence the physiology and behavior of other individuals of the same species. Pheromones are small, volatile or water-soluble molecules that disperse into the environment and, like hormones, are active in tiny amounts (see Chapter 45). Many pheromones function as mate attractants, enabling some female insects to be detected by males from as far away as a mile. (We will discuss mating behavior and pheromones further in Chapter 51.)

Ensuring the Survival of Offspring

Comparing internal and external fertilization across many species reveals that internal fertilization is typically associated with the production of fewer gametes but the survival of a higher fraction of zygotes. Better zygote survival is due in part to the fact that eggs fertilized internally are sheltered from potential predators. However, internal fertilization is also more often associated with mechanisms that provide greater protection of the embryos and parental care of the young. For example, the internally fertilized eggs of many species of terrestrial animals exhibit adaptations that protect against water loss and physical damage during their external development. In the case of birds and other reptiles, as well as monotremes (egg-laying mammals), the zygotes consist of eggs with calcium- and protein-containing shells and several internal membranes (see Figure 34.25). In contrast, the fertilized eggs of fishes and amphibians have only a gelatinous coat and lack internal membranes.

Rather than secreting a protective eggshell, some animals retain the embryo for a portion of its development within the female's reproductive tract. Embryos of marsupial mammals, such as kangaroos and opossums, spend only a short period in the uterus; the embryos then crawl out and complete fetal development attached to a mammary gland in the mother's pouch. However, embryos of eutherian (placental) mammals, such as humans, remain in the uterus throughout fetal development. There they are nourished by the mother's blood supply through a temporary organ, the placenta. The embryos of some fishes and sharks also complete development internally, although typically the embryo and mother in such species lack a connection dedicated to nutrient exchange.

When a baby eagle hatches out of an egg or when a human is born, the newborn is not yet capable of independent existence. Instead, adult birds feed their young and mammals nurse their offspring. Parental care is in fact much more widespread than you might suspect. For example, there are many invertebrates that provide parental care (Figure 46.7). Among vertebrates, the gastric brooding frogs (genus *Rheobatrachus*) of Australia provided a particularly unusual example prior to their extinction in the 1980s. During reproduction, the female frog would carry the tadpoles in her stomach until they underwent metamorphosis and hopped out of her mouth as young frogs.

Gamete Production and Delivery

Sexual reproduction in animals relies on sets of cells that are precursors for eggs and sperm. A group of cells dedicated to this purpose is often established very early in the formation of the embryo and remains in an inactive state while the body plan

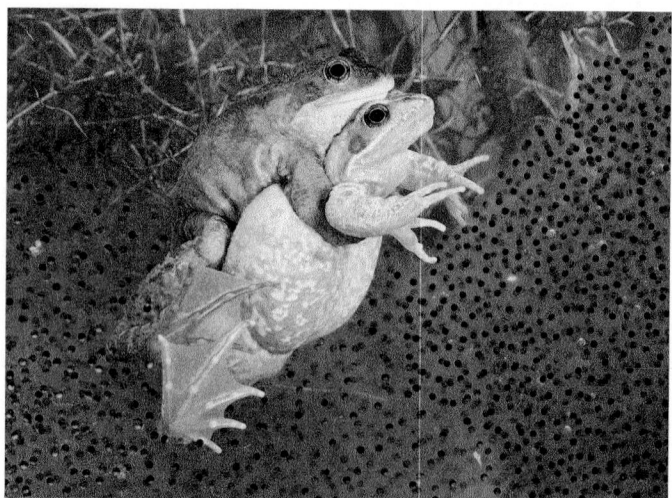

▲ Figure 46.6 **External fertilization.** Many species of amphibians reproduce by external fertilization. In most of these species, behavioral adaptations ensure that a male is present when the female releases eggs. Here, a female frog (on bottom) has released a mass of eggs in response to being clasped by a male. The male released sperm (not visible) at the same time, and external fertilization has already occurred in the water.

▲ **Figure 46.7 Parental care in an invertebrate.** Compared with many other insects, giant water bugs of the genus *Belostoma* produce relatively few offspring, but offer much greater parental protection. Following internal fertilization, the female glues her fertilized eggs to the back of the male (shown here). The male carries them for days, frequently fanning water over them to keep the eggs moist, aerated, and free of parasites.

develops. Cycles of growth and mitosis then increase, or *amplify*, the number of cells available for making eggs or sperm.

In producing gametes from the amplified precursor cells and making them available for fertilization, animals employ a variety of reproductive systems. The simplest systems do not even include discrete **gonads**, the organs that produce gametes in most animals. The palolo and most other polychaete worms (phylum Annelida) have separate sexes but do not have distinct gonads; rather, the eggs and sperm develop from undifferentiated cells lining the coelom (body cavity). As the gametes mature, they are released from the body wall and fill the coelom. Depending on the species, mature gametes may be shed through the excretory opening, or the swelling mass of eggs may split a portion of the body open, spilling the eggs into the environment.

More elaborate reproductive systems include sets of accessory tubes and glands that carry, nourish, and protect the gametes and sometimes the developing embryos. Most insect species, for example, have separate sexes with complex reproductive systems **(Figure 46.8)**. In the males, sperm develop in a pair of testes and are passed along a coiled duct to two seminal vesicles for storage. During mating, sperm are ejaculated into the female reproductive system. There, eggs develop in a pair of ovaries and are conveyed through ducts to the uterus. Eggs are fertilized in the uterus and then expelled for development outside the body. In many insect species, the female reproductive system includes one or more **spermathecae** (singular, spermatheca), sacs in which sperm may be stored for extended periods, a year or more in some species. Because the female releases male gametes from the spermatheca only in response to the appropriate stimuli, fertilization occurs

(a) Male fruit fly. Sperm form in the testes, pass through the sperm ducts (vas deferens), and are stored in the seminal vesicles. The male ejaculates sperm along with fluid from the accessory glands. (Males of some species of insects and other arthropods have appendages called claspers that grasp the female during copulation.)

(b) Female fruit fly. Eggs develop in the ovaries and then travel through the oviducts to the uterus. After mating, sperm are stored in the spermathecae, which are connected to the uterus by short ducts. The female uses a stored sperm to fertilize each egg as it enters the uterus before she passes the egg out through the vulva.

▲ **Figure 46.8 Insect reproductive anatomy.** Circled numbers indicate sequences of sperm and egg movement.

under conditions likely to be well suited to embryonic development. Even more complex reproductive systems can be found in some animals whose body plans are otherwise fairly simple, such as parasitic flatworms.

The basic plans of all vertebrate reproductive systems are quite similar, but there are some important variations. In many nonmammalian vertebrates, the digestive, excretory, and reproductive systems have a common opening to the outside, the **cloaca**, a structure that was probably also present in the ancestors of all vertebrates. In contrast, mammals generally lack a cloaca and have a separate opening for the digestive tract. In addition, most female mammals have separate openings for the excretory and reproductive systems. Among most vertebrates, the uterus is partly or completely divided into two chambers. However, in humans and other mammals that produce only one or a few young at a time, as well as in birds and many snakes, the uterus is a single structure. Male reproductive systems differ mainly in the copulatory organs. Many nonmammalian vertebrates, including all reptiles and amphibians, lack a well-developed penis and instead ejaculate sperm by turning the cloaca inside out.

Although fertilization involves the union of a single egg and sperm, animals often mate with more than one member of the other sex. Indeed, monogamy, the sustained sexual partnership of two individuals, is relatively rare among animals, including most mammals. Mechanisms have evolved, however, that enhance the reproductive success of a male with a particular female and diminish the chance of that female mating successfully with another partner. For example, some male insects transfer secretions that make a female less receptive to courtship, thereby reducing the likelihood of her mating again.

Can females also influence the relative reproductive success of their mates? This question intrigued two scientific collaborators working in Europe. Studying female fruit flies that copulated with one male and then another, the researchers traced the fate of sperm transferred in the first mating. As shown in Figure 46.9, they found that female fruit flies play a major role in determining the reproductive outcome of multiple matings. Nevertheless, the processes by which gametes and individuals compete during reproduction are only partly understood and remain a vibrant research area.

CONCEPT CHECK 46.2

1. How does internal fertilization facilitate life on land?
2. What mechanisms have evolved in animals with (a) external fertilization and (b) internal fertilization that help ensure that offspring survive to adulthood?
3. **MAKE CONNECTIONS** What are the shared and distinct functions of the uterus of an insect and the ovary of a flowering plant? (See Figure 38.6, p. 806.)

For suggested answers, see Appendix A.

▼ Figure 46.9

INQUIRY

Why is sperm usage biased when female fruit flies mate twice?

EXPERIMENT When a female fruit fly mates twice, 80% of the offspring result from the second mating. Scientists had postulated that ejaculate from the second mating displaces stored sperm. To test this hypothesis, Rhonda Snook, at the University of Sheffield, and David Hosken, at the University of Zurich, used mutant males with altered reproductive systems. "No-ejaculate" males mate, but do not transfer sperm or fluid to females. "No-sperm" males mate and ejaculate, but make no sperm. The researchers allowed females to mate with wild-type males and then mate with wild-type males, no-sperm males, or no-ejaculate males. As a control, some females were mated only once. The scientists then dissected each female under a microscope and recorded whether sperm were absent from the spermatheca, the major sperm storage organ.

RESULTS

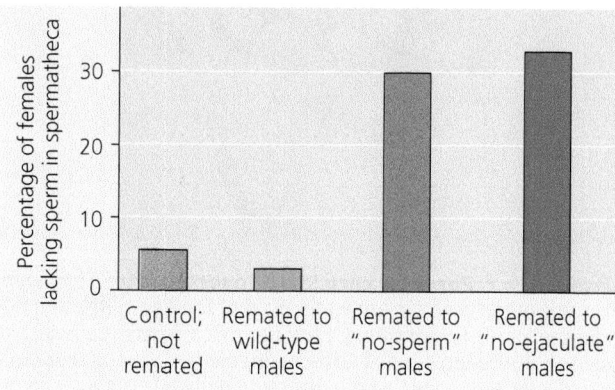

CONCLUSION Because remating reduces sperm storage when no sperm or fluids are transferred, the hypothesis that ejaculate from a second mating displaces stored sperm is incorrect. Instead, it appears that females sometimes get rid of stored sperm in response to remating. This might represent a way for females to replace stored sperm, possibly of diminished fitness, with fresh sperm.

SOURCE R. R. Snook and D. J. Hosken, Sperm death and dumping in *Drosophila, Nature* 428:939–941 (2004).

WHAT IF? Suppose males in the first mating had a mutant allele for the dominant trait of smaller eyes. What fraction of the females would produce some offspring with smaller eyes?

CONCEPT 46.3

Reproductive organs produce and transport gametes

Having surveyed some of the general features of animal reproduction, we will focus the rest of the chapter on humans, beginning with the anatomy of the reproductive system in each sex.

Female Reproductive Anatomy

The female's external reproductive structures are the clitoris and two sets of labia, which surround the clitoris and vaginal opening. The internal organs are the gonads, which produce both eggs and reproductive hormones, and a system of ducts and chambers, which receive and carry gametes and house the embryo and fetus **(Figure 46.10)**.

Ovaries

The female gonads are a pair of ovaries that flank the uterus and are held in place in the abdominal cavity by ligaments. The outer layer of each ovary is packed with **follicles**, each consisting of an **oocyte**, a partially developed egg, surrounded by a group of support cells. The surrounding cells nourish and protect the oocyte during much of the formation and development of an egg. Although at birth the ovaries together contain about 1–2 million follicles, only about 500 follicles fully mature between puberty and menopause. During a typical 4-week menstrual cycle, one follicle matures and expels its egg, a process called ovulation. Prior to ovulation, cells of the follicle produce the primary female sex hormone, estradiol (a type of estrogen). After ovulation, the residual follicular tissue grows within the ovary, forming a mass called the **corpus luteum** ("yellow body"). The corpus luteum secretes additional estradiol, as well as progesterone, a hormone that helps maintain the uterine lining during pregnancy. If the egg cell is not fertilized, the corpus luteum degenerates, and a new follicle matures during the next cycle.

Oviducts and Uterus

An **oviduct**, or fallopian tube, extends from the uterus toward each ovary. The dimensions of this tube vary along its length, with the inside diameter near the uterus being as narrow as a human hair. At ovulation, the egg is released into the abdominal cavity near the funnel-like opening of the oviduct. Cilia on the epithelial lining of the duct help collect the egg by drawing fluid from the body cavity into the oviduct. Together with wavelike contractions of the oviduct, the cilia convey the egg down the duct to the **uterus**, also known as the womb. The uterus is a thick, muscular organ that can expand during pregnancy to accommodate a 4-kg fetus. The inner lining of the uterus, the **endometrium**, is richly supplied with blood vessels. The neck of the uterus, called the **cervix**, opens into the vagina.

Vagina and Vulva

The **vagina** is a muscular but elastic chamber that is the site for insertion of the penis and deposition of sperm during copulation. The vagina, which also serves as the birth canal through which a baby is born, opens to the outside at the **vulva**, the collective term for the external female genitalia.

A pair of thick, fatty ridges, the **labia majora**, encloses and protects the rest of the vulva. The vaginal opening and the separate opening of the urethra are located within a cavity bordered by a pair of slender skin folds, the **labia minora**. A thin piece of

▲ **Figure 46.10 Reproductive anatomy of the human female.** Some nonreproductive structures are labeled in parentheses for orientation purposes.

tissue called the **hymen** partly covers the vaginal opening in humans at birth and usually until sexual intercourse or vigorous physical activity ruptures it. Located at the top of the labia minora, the **clitoris** consists of erectile tissue supporting a rounded **glans**, or head, covered by a small hood of skin, the **prepuce**. During sexual arousal, the clitoris, vagina, and labia minora all engorge with blood and enlarge. Richly supplied with nerve endings, the clitoris is one of the most sensitive points of sexual stimulation. Sexual arousal also induces the vestibular glands near the vaginal opening to secrete lubricating mucus, thereby facilitating intercourse.

Mammary Glands

The **mammary glands** are present in both sexes, but they normally produce milk only in females. Though not part of the reproductive system, the female mammary glands are important to reproduction. Within the glands, small sacs of epithelial tissue secrete milk, which drains into a series of ducts that open at the nipple. The breasts contain connective and fatty (adipose) tissue in addition to the mammary glands. Because the low level of estradiol in males limits the development of the fat deposits, male breasts usually remain small.

Male Reproductive Anatomy

The human male's external reproductive organs are the scrotum and penis. The internal reproductive organs consist of gonads that produce both sperm and reproductive hormones, accessory glands that secrete products essential to sperm movement, and ducts that carry the sperm and glandular secretions (**Figure 46.11**).

Testes

The male gonads, or **testes** (singular, *testis*), produce sperm in highly coiled tubes called **seminiferous tubules**. The **Leydig cells**, scattered in connective tissue between the tubules, produce testosterone and other androgens (see Chapter 45).

Most mammals produce sperm properly only when the testes are cooler than normal body temperature. In humans and many other mammals, the **scrotum**, a fold of the body wall, maintains testis temperature about 2°C below that of the rest of the body. The testes develop in the abdominal cavity and descend into the scrotum just before birth (a testis within a scrotum is a *testicle*). In many rodents, the testes are drawn back into the cavity between breeding seasons, interrupting sperm maturation. Some mammals whose body temperature is low enough to allow sperm maturation—such as whales and elephants—retain the testes in the abdominal cavity.

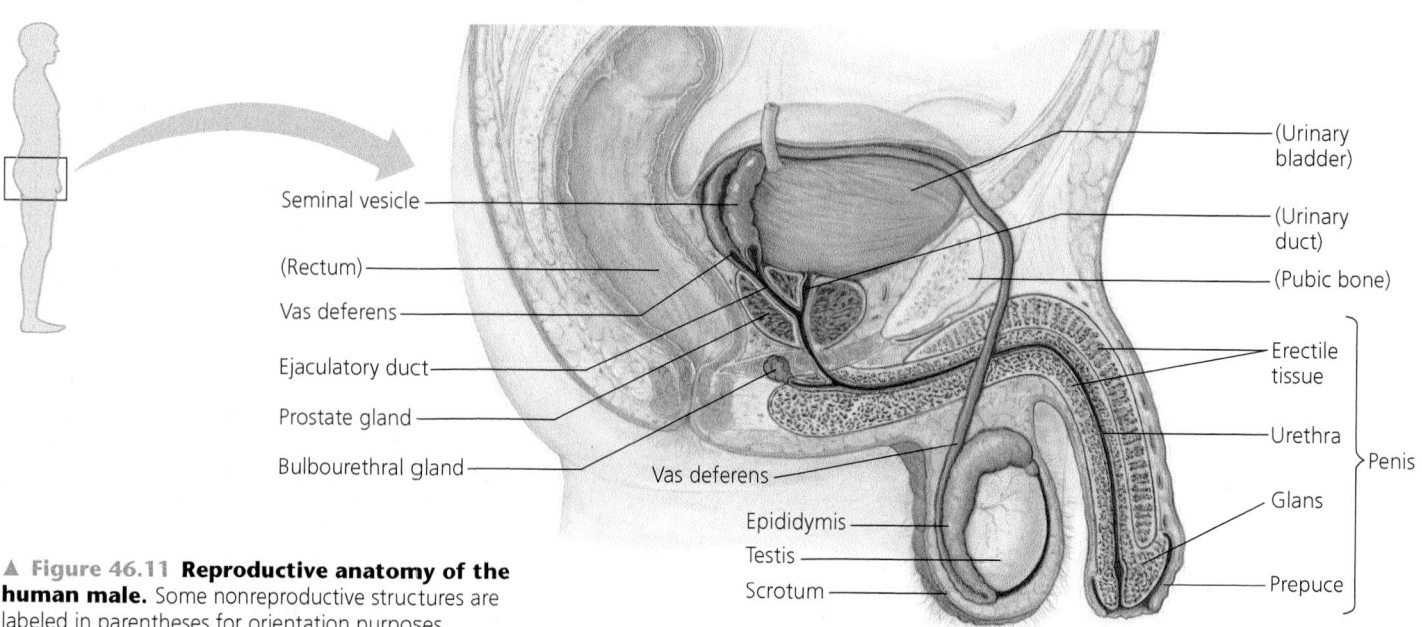

▲ **Figure 46.11 Reproductive anatomy of the human male.** Some nonreproductive structures are labeled in parentheses for orientation purposes.

Ducts

From the seminiferous tubules of a testis, the sperm pass into the coiled duct of an **epididymis**. In humans, it takes 3 weeks for sperm to pass through this 6-m-long duct. During this passage through the epididymis, the sperm complete maturation and become motile, although they acquire the ability to fertilize an egg only upon exposure to the chemical environment of the female reproductive system. During **ejaculation**, the sperm are propelled from each epididymis through a muscular duct, the **vas deferens**. Each vas deferens (one from each epididymis) extends around and behind the urinary bladder, where it joins a duct from the seminal vesicle, forming a short **ejaculatory duct**. The ejaculatory ducts open into the **urethra**, the outlet tube for both the excretory system and the reproductive system. The urethra runs through the penis and opens to the outside at the tip of the penis.

Accessory Glands

Three sets of accessory glands—the seminal vesicles, the prostate gland, and the bulbourethral glands—produce secretions that combine with sperm to form **semen**, the fluid that is ejaculated. Two **seminal vesicles** contribute about 60% of the volume of semen. The fluid from the seminal vesicles is thick, yellowish, and alkaline. It contains mucus, the sugar fructose (which provides most of the sperm's energy), a coagulating enzyme, ascorbic acid, and local regulators called prostaglandins (see Chapter 45).

The **prostate gland** secretes its products directly into the urethra through several small ducts. This fluid is thin and milky; it contains anticoagulant enzymes and citrate (a sperm nutrient). The prostate gland is the source of some of the most common medical problems of men over age 40. Benign (noncancerous) enlargement of the prostate occurs in more than half of all men in this age-group and in almost all men over 70. In addition, prostate cancer, which most often afflicts men 65 and older, is one of the most common human cancers.

The *bulbourethral glands* are a pair of small glands along the urethra below the prostate. Before ejaculation, they secrete clear mucus that neutralizes any acidic urine remaining in the urethra. Bulbourethral fluid also carries some sperm released before ejaculation, which is one reason for the high failure rate of the withdrawal method of birth control (coitus interruptus).

Penis

The human **penis** contains the urethra, as well as three cylinders of spongy erectile tissue. During sexual arousal, the erectile tissue, which is derived from modified veins and capillaries, fills with blood from the arteries. As this tissue fills, the increasing pressure seals off the veins that drain the penis, causing it to engorge with blood. The resulting erection enables the penis to be inserted into the vagina. Alcohol consumption, certain drugs, emotional issues, and aging all can cause a temporary inability to achieve an erection (erectile dysfunction). For individuals with long-term erectile dysfunction, drugs such as Viagra promote the vasodilating action of the local regulator nitric oxide (NO; see Chapter 45); the resulting relaxation of smooth muscles in the blood vessels of the penis enhances blood flow into the erectile tissues. Although all mammals rely on penile erection for mating, the penis of rodents, raccoons, walruses, whales, and several other mammals also contains a bone, the baculum, which probably further stiffens the penis for mating.

The main shaft of the penis is covered by relatively thick skin. The head, or glans, of the penis has a much thinner covering and is consequently more sensitive to stimulation. The human glans is covered by a fold of skin called the prepuce, or foreskin, which is removed if a male is circumcised.

Gametogenesis

Many of the differences in reproductive anatomy between males and females reflect the distinct structures and functions of the two types of gametes. Sperm are small and motile and must pass from the male to the female. In contrast, eggs, which provide the initial food stores for the embryo, are typically much larger and carry out their function within the female reproductive system. There they must mature in synchrony with the tissues that will support the embryo. Reflecting these differences, egg development and sperm development involve different patterns of meiotic division. We will highlight these differences as we explore **gametogenesis**, the production of gametes.

Spermatogenesis, the formation and development of sperm, is continuous and prolific in adult males. To produce hundreds of millions of sperm each day, cell division and maturation occur throughout the seminiferous tubules coiled within the two testes. For a single sperm, the process takes about 7 weeks from start to finish.

Oogenesis, the development of mature oocytes (eggs), is a prolonged process in the human female. Immature eggs form in the ovary of the female embryo but do not complete their development until years, and often decades, later.

Spermatogenesis differs from oogenesis in three significant ways. First, only in spermatogenesis do all four products of meiosis develop into mature gametes. In oogenesis, cytokinesis during meiosis is unequal, with almost all the cytoplasm segregated to a single daughter cell. This large cell is destined to become the egg; the other products of meiosis, smaller cells called polar bodies, degenerate. Second, spermatogenesis occurs throughout adolescence and adulthood. During oogenesis in human females, mitotic divisions are thought to be complete before birth, and the production of mature gametes ceases at about age 50. Third, spermatogenesis produces mature sperm from precursor cells in a continuous sequence, whereas oogenesis has long interruptions. **Figure 46.12**, on the next two pages, compares and contrasts the steps and organization of spermatogenesis and oogenesis in humans.

Exploring Human Gametogenesis

Spermatogenesis

These drawings correlate the mitotic and meiotic divisions in sperm development with the microscopic structure of seminiferous tubules.

The initial or *primordial* germ cells of the embryonic testes divide and differentiate into stem cells that divide mitotically to form **spermatogonia**, which in turn generate spermatocytes, also by mitosis. Each spermatocyte gives rise to four spermatids through meiotic cell divisions that reduce the chromosome number from diploid ($2n = 46$ in humans) to haploid ($n = 23$). Spermatids undergo extensive changes in cell shape and organization in differentiating into sperm.

Within the seminiferous tubules, there is a concentric organization of the steps of spermatogenesis. Stem cells are situated near the outer edge of the tubules. As spermatogenesis proceeds, cells move steadily inward as they pass through the spermatocyte stage and the spermatid stage. In the last step, mature sperm are released into the lumen (fluid-filled cavity) of the tubule. The sperm travel along the tubule into the epididymis, where they become motile.

The structure of a sperm cell fits its function. In humans, as in most species, a head containing the haploid nucleus is tipped with a special vesicle, the **acrosome**, which contains enzymes that help the sperm penetrate an egg. Behind the head, the sperm cell contains large numbers of mitochondria (or one large mitochondrion in some species) that provide ATP for movement of the tail, which is a flagellum.

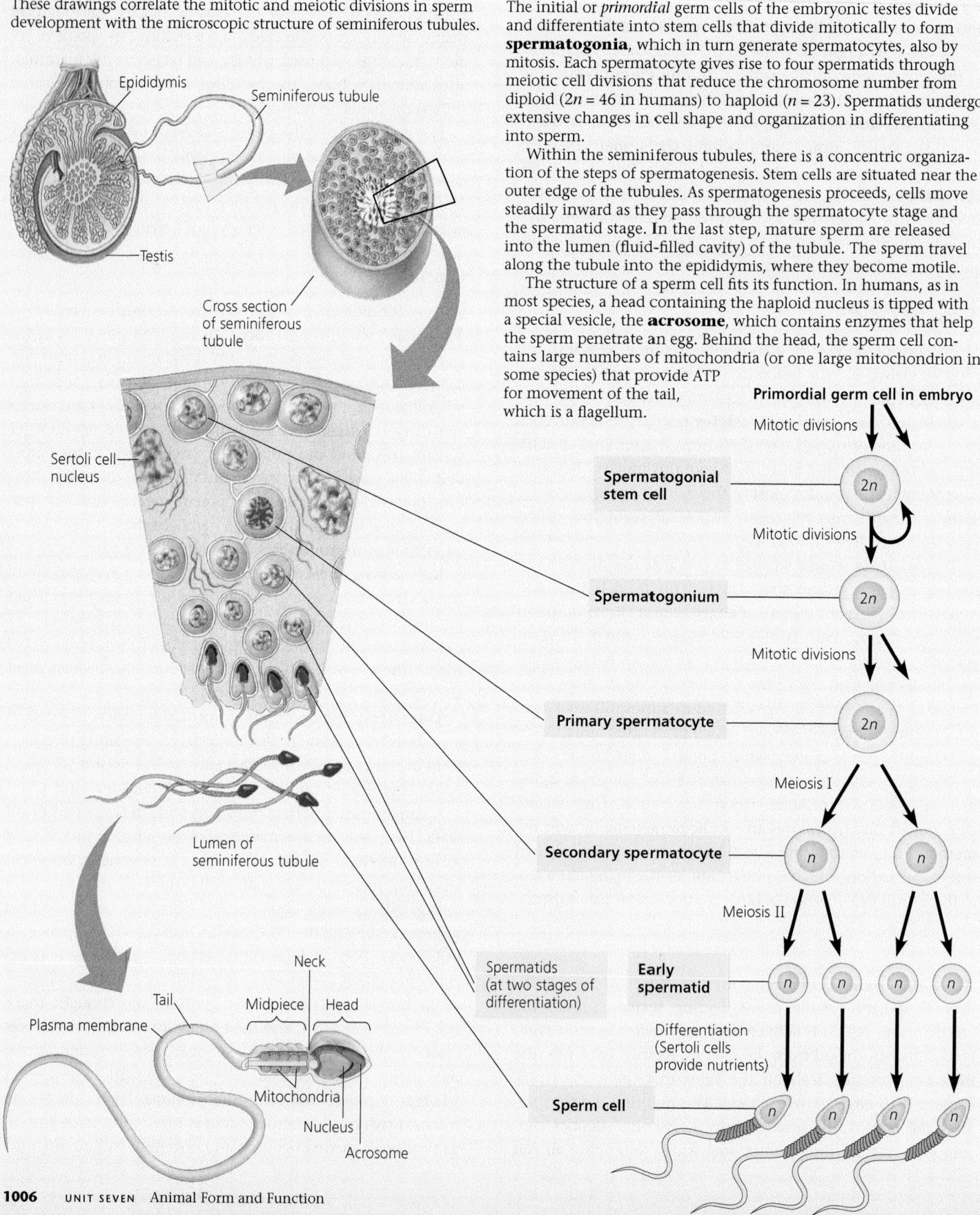

Oogenesis

Oogenesis begins in the female embryo with the production of **oogonia** from primordial germ cells. The oogonia divide by mitosis to form cells that begin meiosis, but stop the process at prophase I before birth. These developmentally arrested cells, called **primary oocytes**, each reside within a small follicle, a cavity lined with protective cells. Beginning at puberty, follicle-stimulating hormone (FSH) periodically stimulates a small group offollicles to resume growth and development. Typically, only one follicle fully matures each month, with its primary oocyte completing meiosis I. The second meiotic division begins, but stops at metaphase. Thus arrested in meiosis II, the **secondary oocyte** is released at ovulation, when its follicle breaks open. Only if a sperm penetrates the oocyte does meiosis II resume. (In other animal species, the sperm may enter the oocyte at the same stage, earlier, or later.) Each of the two meiotic divisions involves unequal cytokinesis, with the smaller cells becoming polar bodies that eventually degenerate (the first polar body may or may not divide again). Thus, the functional product of complete oogenesis is a single mature egg already containing a sperm head; fertilization is defined strictly as the fusion of the haploid nuclei of the sperm and secondary oocyte, although we often use it loosely to mean the entry of the sperm head into the egg.

The ruptured follicle left behind after ovulation develops into the corpus luteum. If the released oocyte is not fertilized and does not complete oogenesis, the corpus luteum degenerates.

To the best of our current knowledge, women are born with all the primary oocytes they will ever have. It is worth noting, however, that a similar conclusion regarding most other mammals was overturned by the discovery in 2004 of multiplying oogonia in the ovaries of adult mice that develop into oocytes. If the same turned out to be true of humans, it might be that the marked decline in fertility that occurs as women age results from both a depletion of oogonia and the degeneration of aging oocytes.

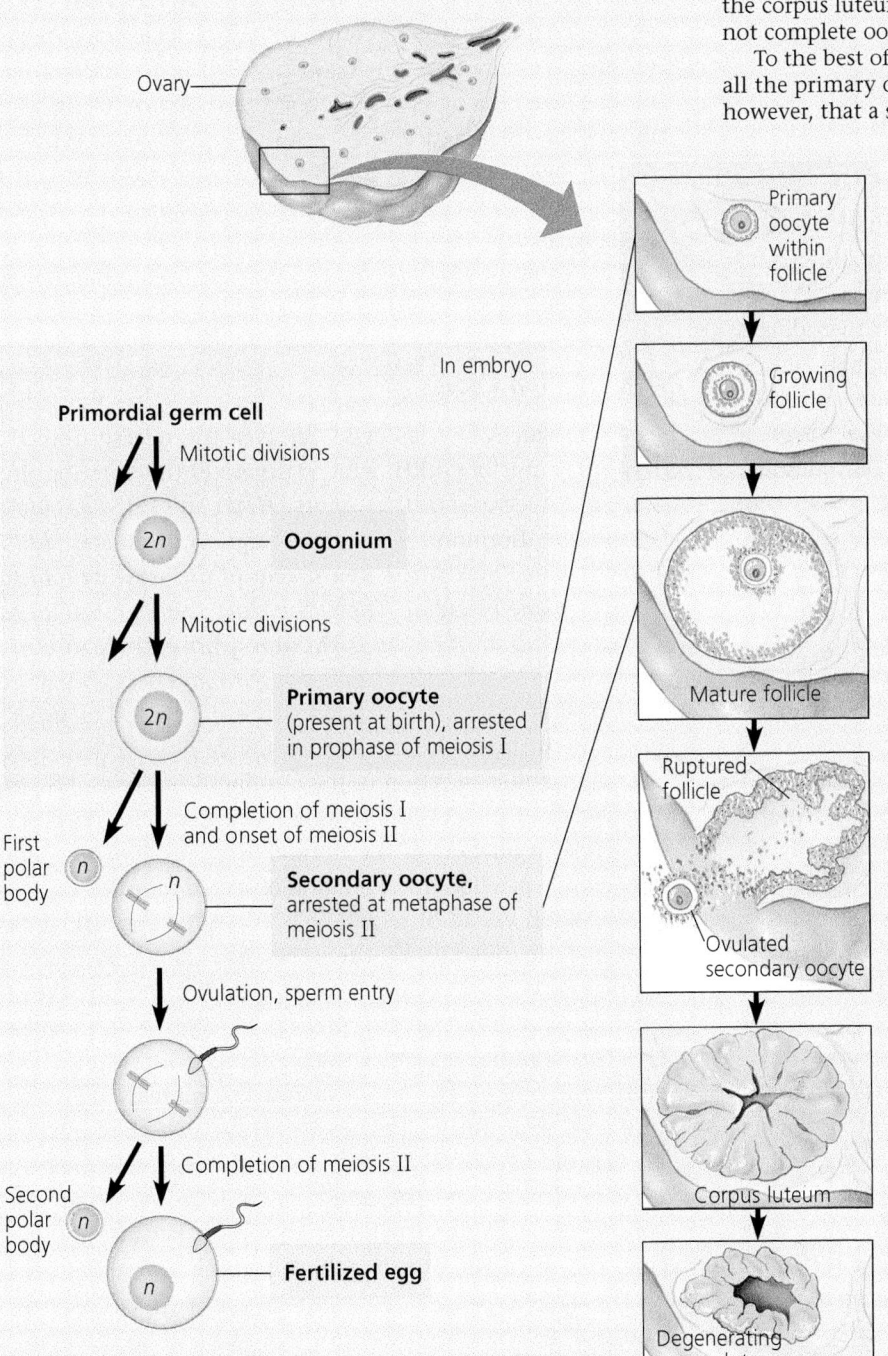

WHAT IF? Suppose you are analyzing the DNA from the polar bodies formed during human oogenesis. If the mother has a mutation in a known disease gene, would analyzing the polar body DNA allow you to infer whether the mutation is present in the mature oocyte? Explain.

CONCEPT 46.4

The interplay of tropic and sex hormones regulates mammalian reproduction

In both male and female humans, the coordinated actions of hormones from the hypothalamus, anterior pituitary, and gonads govern reproduction. The hypothalamus secretes gonadotropin-releasing hormone (GnRH), which then directs the anterior pituitary to secrete the gonadotropins, follicle-stimulating hormone (FSH) and luteinizing hormone (LH) (see Figure 45.16). These two hormones regulate gametogenesis directly, by targeting tissues in the gonads, as well as indirectly, by regulating sex hormone production. The principal sex hormones are steroid hormones: in males, androgens, especially testosterone; in females, estrogens, especially estradiol, and progesterone. Like the gonadotropins, the sex hormones regulate gametogenesis both directly and indirectly.

Sex hormones serve many functions in addition to promoting gamete production. In many vertebrates, androgens are responsible for male vocalizations, such as the territorial songs of birds and the mating calls of frogs. During development of the human embryo, androgens promote the appearance of the primary sex characteristics of males, the structures directly involved in reproduction. These include the seminal vesicles and associated ducts, as well as external reproductive anatomy. At puberty, sex hormones in both males and females induce formation of secondary sex characteristics, the physical and behavioral features that are not directly related to the reproductive system. In males, androgens cause the voice to deepen, facial and pubic hair to develop, and muscles to grow (by stimulating protein synthesis). Androgens also promote specific sexual behaviors and sex drive, as well as an increase in general aggressiveness. Estrogens similarly have multiple effects in females. At puberty, estradiol stimulates breast and pubic hair development. Estradiol also influences female sexual behavior, induces fat deposition in the breasts and hips, increases water retention, and alters calcium metabolism.

Hormonal Control of Female Reproductive Cycles

Upon reaching sexual maturity, human males carry out gametogenesis continuously, whereas human females produce gametes in cycles. Ovulation occurs only after the endometrium (lining of the uterus) has started to thicken and develop a rich blood supply, preparing the uterus for the possible implantation of an embryo. If pregnancy does not occur, the uterine lining is sloughed off, and another cycle begins. The cyclic shedding of the blood-rich endometrium from the uterus, a process that occurs in a flow through the cervix and vagina, is called **menstruation**.

There are two closely linked reproductive cycles in human females. Changes in the uterus define the **menstrual cycle**, also called the **uterine cycle**. Menstrual cycles average 28 days (although cycles vary, ranging from about 20 to 40 days). The cyclic events in the ovaries define the **ovarian cycle**. Hormone activity links the two cycles to one another, synchronizing ovarian follicle growth and ovulation with the establishment of a uterine lining that can support embryonic development.

Let's examine the reproductive cycle of the human female (Figure 46.13).

The Ovarian Cycle

The reproductive cycle begins ❶ with the release from the hypothalamus of GnRH, which stimulates the anterior pituitary to ❷ secrete small amounts of FSH and LH. ❸ Follicle-stimulating hormone (as its name implies) stimulates follicle growth, aided by LH, and ❹ the cells of the growing follicles start to make estradiol. There is a slow rise in estradiol secreted during most of the **follicular phase**, the part of the ovarian cycle during which follicles grow and oocytes mature. (Several follicles begin to grow with each cycle, but usually only one matures; the others disintegrate.) The low levels of estradiol inhibit secretion of the pituitary hormones, keeping the levels of FSH and LH relatively low. During this portion of the cycle, regulation of the hormones controlling reproduction closely parallels the regulation observed in males.

❺ When estradiol secretion by the growing follicle begins to rise steeply, ❻ the FSH and LH levels increase markedly. Whereas a low level of estradiol inhibits the secretion of pituitary gonadotropins, a high concentration has the opposite effect: It stimulates gonadotropin secretion by acting on the hypothalamus to increase its output of GnRH. The effect is greater for LH because the high concentration of estradiol increases the GnRH sensitivity of LH-releasing cells in the pituitary. In addition, follicles respond more strongly to LH at this stage because more of their cells have receptors for this hormone.

The increase in LH concentration caused by increased estradiol secretion from the growing follicle is an example of positive feedback. The result is final maturation of the follicle. ❼ The maturing follicle, containing a fluid-filled cavity, enlarges, forming a bulge near the surface of the ovary. The follicular phase ends at ovulation, about a day after the LH surge. In response to the peak in LH levels, the follicle and adjacent wall of the ovary rupture, releasing the secondary oocyte. There is sometimes a distinctive pain in the lower abdomen at or near the time of ovulation; this pain is felt on the left or right side, corresponding to whichever ovary has matured a follicle during that cycle.

The **luteal phase** of the ovarian cycle follows ovulation. ❽ LH stimulates the follicular tissue left behind in the ovary to transform into a corpus luteum, a glandular structure. Under continued stimulation by LH, the corpus luteum secretes progesterone and estradiol. As progesterone and estradiol levels rise, the combination of these steroid hormones exerts negative feedback on the hypothalamus and pituitary, reducing the secretion of LH and FSH to very low levels. This negative feedback prevents another egg from maturing when a pregnancy may already be under way.

Near the end of the luteal phase, low gonadotropin levels cause the corpus luteum to disintegrate, triggering a sharp decline in estradiol and progesterone concentrations. The decreasing levels of ovarian steroid hormones liberate the hypothalamus and pituitary from the negative-feedback effect of these hormones. The pituitary can then begin to secrete enough FSH to stimulate the growth of new follicles in the ovary, initiating the next ovarian cycle.

The Uterine (Menstrual) Cycle

Prior to ovulation, ovarian steroid hormones stimulate the uterus to prepare for support of an embryo. Estradiol secreted in increasing amounts by growing follicles signals the endometrium to thicken. In this way, the follicular phase of the ovarian cycle is coordinated with the **proliferative phase** of the uterine cycle. After ovulation, ❾ estradiol and

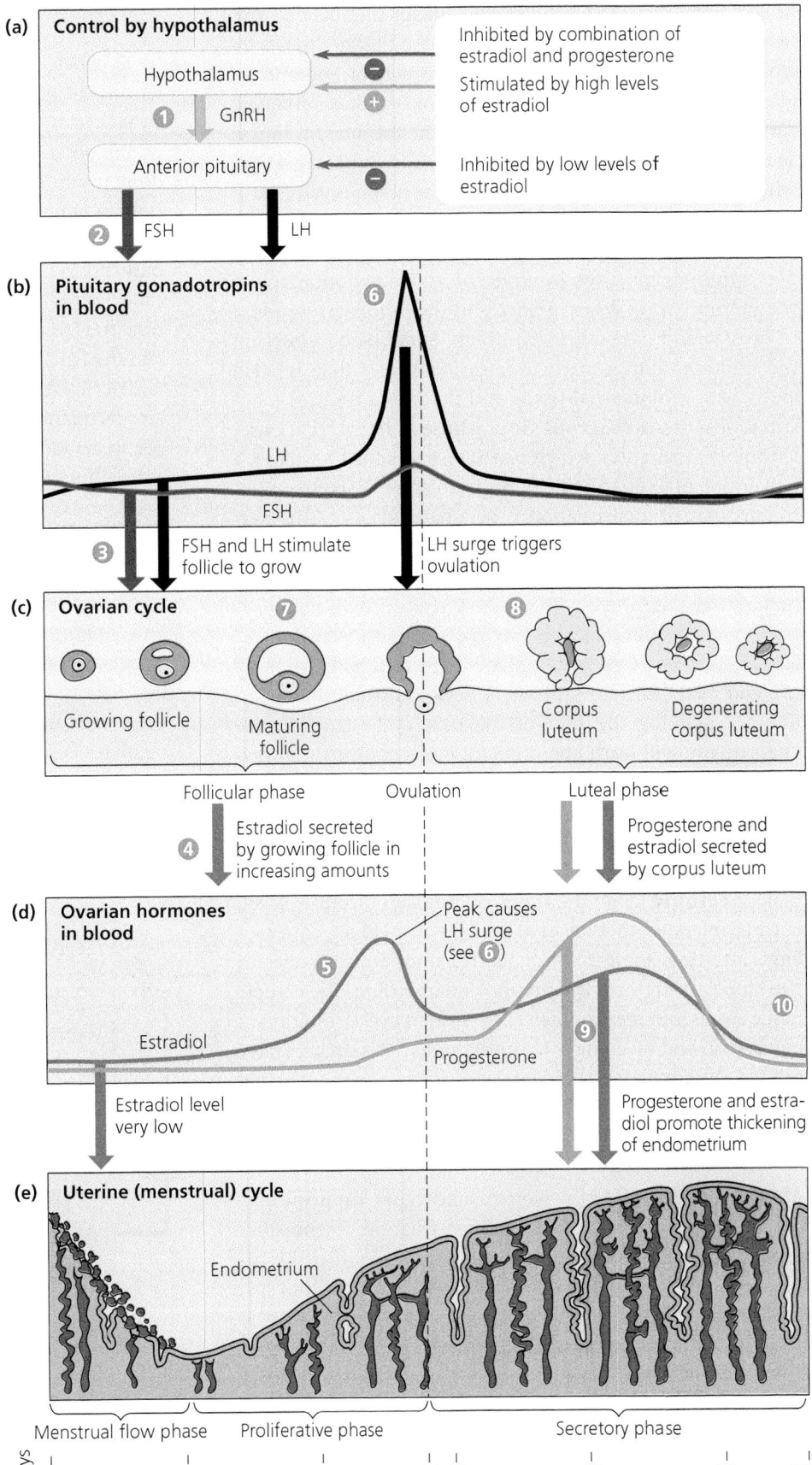

▲ **Figure 46.13 The reproductive cycle of the human female.** This figure shows how **(c)** the ovarian cycle and **(e)** the uterine (menstrual) cycle are regulated by changing hormone levels in the blood, depicted in parts **(a)**, **(b)**, and **(d)**. The time scale at the bottom of the figure applies to parts **(b)–(e)**.

progesterone secreted by the corpus luteum stimulate continued development and maintenance of the uterine lining, including enlargement of arteries and growth of endometrial glands. These glands secrete a nutrient fluid that can sustain an early embryo even before it implants in the uterine lining. Thus, the luteal phase of the ovarian cycle is coordinated with what is called the **secretory phase** of the uterine cycle.

Upon disintegration of the corpus luteum, the rapid drop in ovarian hormone levels causes arteries in the endometrium to constrict. Deprived of its circulation, much of the uterine lining disintegrates, and the uterus, in response to prostaglandin secretion, contracts. Small blood vessels in the endometrium constrict, releasing blood that is shed along with endometrial tissue and fluid. The result is menstruation—the **menstrual flow phase** of the uterine cycle. During menstruation, which usually persists for a few days, a new group of ovarian follicles begin to grow. By convention, the first day of menstruation is designated day 1 of the new uterine (and ovarian) cycle.

Overall, the hormonal cycles in females coordinate egg maturation and release with changes in the uterus, the organ that must accommodate an embryo if the egg cell is fertilized. If an embryo has not implanted in the endometrium by the end of the secretory phase, a new menstrual flow commences, marking the start of the next cycle. Later in the chapter, you will learn about override mechanisms that prevent disintegration of the endometrium in pregnancy.

About 7% of women of reproductive age suffer from **endometriosis**, a disorder in which some cells of the uterine lining migrate to an abdominal location that is abnormal, or **ectopic** (from the Greek *ektopos*, away from a place). Having migrated to a location such as an oviduct, ovary, or large intestine, the ectopic tissue responds to hormones in the bloodstream. Like the uterine endometrium, the ectopic tissue swells and breaks down each ovarian cycle, resulting in pelvic pain and bleeding into the abdomen. Researchers have not yet determined why endometriosis occurs, but hormonal therapy or surgery can be used to lessen discomfort.

Menopause

After about 500 cycles, a woman undergoes **menopause**, the cessation of ovulation and menstruation. Menopause usually occurs between the ages of 46 and 54. During this interval, the ovaries lose their responsiveness to FSH and LH, resulting in a decline in estradiol production.

Menopause is an unusual phenomenon. In most other species, females and males retain their reproductive capacity throughout life. Is there an evolutionary explanation for menopause? One intriguing hypothesis proposes that during early human evolution, undergoing menopause after bearing several children allowed a mother to provide better care for her children and grandchildren, thereby increasing the survival of individuals who share much of her genetic makeup.

Menstrual Versus Estrous Cycles

In all female mammals, the endometrium thickens before ovulation, but only humans and some other primates have menstrual cycles. Other mammals have **estrous cycles**, in which in the absence of a pregnancy, the uterus reabsorbs the endometrium and no extensive fluid flow occurs. Whereas human females may engage in sexual activity throughout the menstrual cycle, mammals with estrous cycles usually copulate only during the period surrounding ovulation. This period, called estrus (from the Latin *oestrus*, frenzy, passion), is the only time the female is receptive to mating. It is often called "heat," and the female's temperature does increase slightly.

The length and frequency of estrous cycles vary widely among mammals. Bears and wolves have one estrous cycle per year; elephants have several. Rats have estrous cycles throughout the year, each lasting only 5 days.

Hormonal Control of the Male Reproductive System

In males, the FSH and LH secreted in response to GnRH are both required for normal spermatogenesis. Each acts on a distinct type of cell in the testis **(Figure 46.14)**. FSH promotes the activity of Sertoli cells. Within the seminiferous tubules, these cells nourish developing sperm (see Figure 46.12). LH regulates Leydig cells, located in the interstitial space between

▲ **Figure 46.14 Hormonal control of the testes.** Gonadotropin-releasing hormone (GnRH) from the hypothalamus stimulates the anterior pituitary to secrete follicle-stimulating hormone (FSH) and luteinizing hormone (LH). FSH acts on Sertoli cells, which nourish developing sperm. LH acts on Leydig cells, which produce androgens, chiefly testosterone. Negative feedback by testosterone on the hypothalamus and anterior pituitary regulates blood levels of GnRH, LH, and FSH. FSH secretion is also subject to negative feedback by a hormone called inhibin, secreted by Sertoli cells.

the seminiferous tubules. In response to LH, Leydig cells secrete testosterone and other androgens, which promote spermatogenesis in the tubules. Both androgen secretion and spermatogenesis occur continuously from puberty onward.

Two negative-feedback mechanisms control sex hormone production in males (see Figure 46.14). Testosterone regulates blood levels of GnRH, FSH, and LH through inhibitory effects on the hypothalamus and anterior pituitary. In addition, **inhibin**, a hormone that in males is produced by Sertoli cells, acts on the anterior pituitary gland to reduce FSH secretion. Together, these negative-feedback circuits maintain androgen production at optimal levels.

Human Sexual Response

Whereas there is a wealth of information regarding the hormonal regulation of human oogenesis and spermatogenesis, comparable data regarding sexual desire and responses are scanty. Testosterone, prolactin, and oxytocin each appear to influence sexual function in males and females, but their precise roles have yet to be defined. Instead, the study of human sexual response has largely focused on the physiological changes associated with sexual activity.

As mentioned earlier, many animals exhibit elaborate mating behavior. The arousal of sexual interest in humans is particularly complex, involving a variety of psychological as well as physical factors. Reproductive structures in the male and female that are quite different in appearance often serve similar functions, reflecting their shared developmental origin. For example, the same embryonic tissues give rise to the glans of the penis and the clitoris, the scrotum and the labia majora, and the skin on the penis and the labia minora.

The general pattern of human sexual response is similar in males and females. Two types of physiological reactions predominate in both sexes: **vasocongestion**, the filling of a tissue with blood, and **myotonia**, increased muscle tension. Both skeletal and smooth muscle may show sustained or rhythmic contractions, including those associated with orgasm.

The sexual response cycle can be divided into four phases: excitement, plateau, orgasm, and resolution. An important function of the excitement phase is to prepare the vagina and penis for **coitus** (sexual intercourse). During this phase, vasocongestion is particularly evident in erection of the penis and clitoris; enlargement of the testicles, labia, and breasts; and vaginal lubrication. Myotonia may occur, resulting in nipple erection or tension of the arms and legs.

In the plateau phase, these responses continue as a result of direct stimulation of the genitalia. In females, the outer third of the vagina becomes vasocongested, while the inner two-thirds slightly expands. This change, coupled with the elevation of the uterus, forms a depression for receiving sperm at the back of the vagina. Breathing increases and heart rate rises, sometimes to 150 beats per minute—not only in response to the physical effort of sexual activity, but also as

an involuntary response to stimulation of the autonomic nervous system (see Figure 49.8).

Orgasm is characterized by rhythmic, involuntary contractions of the reproductive structures in both sexes. Male orgasm has two stages. The first, emission, occurs when the glands and ducts of the reproductive tract contract, forcing semen into the urethra. Expulsion, or ejaculation, occurs when the urethra contracts and the semen is expelled. During female orgasm, the uterus and outer vagina contract, but the inner two-thirds of the vagina does not. Orgasm is the shortest phase of the sexual response cycle, usually lasting only a few seconds. In both sexes, contractions occur at about 0.8-second intervals and may also involve the anal sphincter and several abdominal muscles.

The resolution phase completes the cycle and reverses the responses of the earlier stages. Vasocongested organs return to their normal size and color, and muscles relax. Most of the changes of resolution are completed within 5 minutes, but some may take as long as an hour. Following orgasm, the male typically enters a refractory period, lasting anywhere from a few minutes to hours, during which erection and orgasm cannot be achieved. Females do not have a refractory period, making possible multiple orgasms within a short period of time.

CONCEPT CHECK 46.4

1. FSH and LH get their names from events of the female reproductive cycle, but they also function in males. How are their functions in females and males similar?
2. How does an estrous cycle differ from a menstrual cycle, and in what animals are the two types of cycles found?
3. **WHAT IF?** If a human female begins taking estradiol and progesterone immediately after the start of a new menstrual cycle, how will ovulation be affected? Explain.
4. **MAKE CONNECTIONS** A coordination of developmental events is characteristic of the reproductive cycles of a human female and an enveloped RNA virus (see Figure 19.7, p. 388). What is the nature of the coordination in each of these cycles?

For suggested answers, see Appendix A.

CONCEPT 46.5

In placental mammals, an embryo develops fully within the mother's uterus

Having surveyed the ovarian and uterine cycles of human females, we turn now to reproduction itself, beginning with the events that transform an egg into a developing embryo.

Conception, Embryonic Development, and Birth

During human copulation, 2–5 mL of semen is transferred, with 70–130 million sperm in each milliliter. The alkalinity of the semen helps neutralize the acidic environment of the vagina, protecting the sperm and increasing their motility. When first ejaculated, the semen coagulates, which may serve to keep the ejaculate in place until sperm reach the cervix. Soon after, anticoagulants liquefy the semen, and the sperm begin swimming through the uterus and oviducts.

Fertilization—also called **conception** in humans—occurs when a sperm fuses with an egg (mature oocyte) in the oviduct (Figure 46.15a). About 24 hours later, the resulting zygote begins dividing, a process called **cleavage**. After another 2–3 days, the embryo typically arrives at the uterus as a ball of 16 cells. By about 5 days after fertilization, cleavage has produced an embryonic stage called the **blastocyst**, a sphere of cells surrounding a central cavity.

Several days after blastocyst formation, the embryo implants into the endometrium (Figure 46.15b). Only after implantation can an embryo develop into a fetus. The implanted embryo secretes hormones that signal its presence and regulate the mother's reproductive system. One embryonic hormone, **human chorionic gonadotropin (hCG)**, acts like pituitary LH in maintaining secretion of progesterone and estrogens by the corpus luteum through the first few months of pregnancy. In the absence of this hormonal override during pregnancy, the corpus luteum would deteriorate and progesterone levels would drop, resulting in menstruation and loss of the embryo. Levels of hCG in the maternal blood are so high that some is excreted in the urine, where its presence is the basis of many early pregnancy tests.

The condition of carrying one or more embryos in the uterus is called **pregnancy**, or **gestation**. Human pregnancy averages 266 days (38 weeks) from fertilization of the egg, or 40 weeks from the start of the last menstrual cycle. Duration of pregnancy in other placental mammals correlates with body size and the maturity of the young at birth. Many rodents have gestation periods of about 21 days, whereas those of dogs are closer to 60 days. In cows, gestation averages 270 days (almost the same as in humans), while in elephants it lasts more than 600 days.

❸ Cleavage (cell division) begins in the oviduct as the embryo is moved toward the uterus by peristalsis and the movements of cilia.

❷ Fertilization occurs: A sperm enters the oocyte; meiosis of the oocyte is completed; and the nuclei of the oocyte and the sperm fuse, producing a zygote.

❶ Ovulation releases a secondary oocyte, which enters the oviduct.

Ovary

Uterus

Endometrium

❹ Cleavage continues. By the time the embryo reaches the uterus, it is a ball of cells. It floats in the uterus for several days, nourished by endometrial secretions. It becomes a blastocyst.

❺ The blastocyst implants in the endometrium about 7 days after conception.

(a) From ovulation to implantation

Endometrium Inner cell mass

Cavity

Blastocyst

Trophoblast

(b) Implantation of blastocyst

▲ Figure 46.15 **Formation of the zygote and early postfertilization events.**

Not all fertilized eggs are capable of completing development. Many pregnancies terminate spontaneously as a result of chromosomal or developmental abnormalities. Much less often, a fertilized egg lodges in the oviduct (fallopian tube), resulting in a tubal, or ectopic, pregnancy. Such pregnancies cannot be sustained and may rupture the oviduct, resulting in serious internal bleeding. A number of conditions, including endometriosis, increase the likelihood of tubal pregnancy. Bacterial infections arising during childbirth, from medical procedures, or as a *sexually transmitted disease (STD)* can scar the oviduct, making ectopic pregnancy more likely.

STDs are the most significant preventable causes of infertility. For women who are between 15 and 24 years of age, approximately 700,000 cases of chlamydia and gonorrhea are reported annually in the United States. The number of women infected is actually significantly higher because most women with these STDs have no symptoms and are therefore unaware of their infection. Among women who remain untreated for either chlamydia or gonorrhea, up to 40% develop an inflammatory disorder that can lead to infertility or to potentially fatal ectopic pregnancies.

First Trimester

Human gestation can be divided for convenience into three **trimesters** of about three months each. The first trimester is the time of most radical change for both the mother and the embryo. Upon implantation, the endometrium grows over the blastocyst. Cells and tissues of the embryo begin to differentiate into specialized body structures. (You will learn much more about embryonic development in Chapter 47.)

During its first 2–4 weeks of development, the embryo obtains nutrients directly from the endometrium. Meanwhile, the outer layer of the blastocyst, called the **trophoblast**, grows outward and mingles with the endometrium, eventually helping form the **placenta**. This disk-shaped organ, containing both embryonic and maternal blood vessels, can weigh close to 1 kg. Material diffusing between the maternal and embryonic circulatory systems supplies nutrients, provides immune protection, exchanges respiratory gases, and disposes of metabolic wastes for the embryo. Blood from the embryo travels to the placenta through the arteries of the umbilical cord and returns via the umbilical vein (Figure 46.16).

▲ **Figure 46.16 Placental circulation.** From the 4th week of development until birth, the placenta, a combination of maternal and embryonic tissues, transports nutrients, respiratory gases, and wastes between the embryo or fetus and the mother. Maternal blood enters the placenta in arteries, flows through blood pools in the endometrium, and leaves via veins. Embryonic or fetal blood, which remains in vessels, enters the placenta through arteries and passes through capillaries in finger-like chorionic villi, where oxygen and nutrients are acquired. As indicated in the drawing, the fetal (or embryonic) capillaries and villi project into the maternal portion of the placenta. Fetal blood leaves the placenta through veins leading back to the fetus. Materials are exchanged by diffusion, active transport, and selective absorption between the fetal capillary bed and the maternal blood pools.

? *In a rare genetic disorder, the absence of a particular enzyme leads to increased testosterone production. When the fetus has this disorder, the mother develops a male-like pattern of body hair during the pregnancy. Explain.*

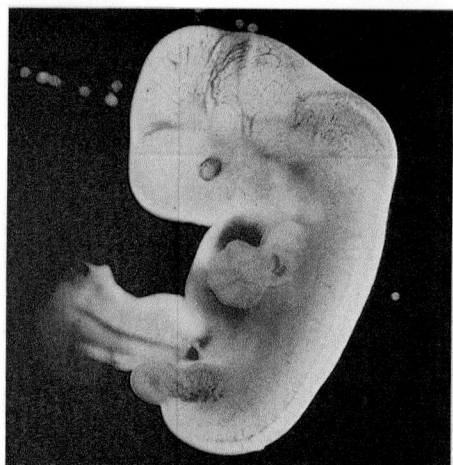

(a) **5 weeks.** Limb buds, eyes, the heart, the liver, and rudiments of all other organs have started to develop in the embryo, which is only about 1 cm long.

(b) **14 weeks.** Growth and development of the offspring, now called a fetus, continue during the second trimester. This fetus is about 6 cm long.

(c) **20 weeks.** Growth to nearly 20 cm in length requires adoption of the fetal position (head at knees) due to the limited space available.

▲ Figure 46.17 **Human fetal development.**

Splitting of the embryo during the first month of development can result in identical, or *monozygotic* (one-egg), twins. Fraternal, or *dizygotic*, twins arise in a very different way: Two follicles mature in a single cycle, followed by independent fertilization and implantation of two genetically distinct embryos.

The first trimester is the main period of **organogenesis**, the development of the body organs **(Figure 46.17)**. During organogenesis, the embryo is particularly susceptible to damage, such as from radiation or drugs, that can lead to birth defects. At 8 weeks, all the major structures of the adult are present in rudimentary form, and the embryo is called a **fetus**. The heart begins beating by the 4th week; a heartbeat can be detected at 8–10 weeks. At the end of the first trimester, the fetus, although well differentiated, is only 5 cm long.

Meanwhile, the mother is also undergoing rapid changes. High levels of progesterone initiate changes in her reproductive system: Increased mucus in the cervix forms a plug to protect against infection, the maternal part of the placenta grows, the uterus gets larger, and (by negative feedback on the hypothalamus and pituitary) ovulation and menstrual cycling stop. The breasts also enlarge rapidly and are often quite tender. About three-fourths of all pregnant women experience nausea, misleadingly called "morning sickness," during the first trimester.

The connection between mother and developing fetus via the placenta allows harmful as well as beneficial substances to pass between them. For this reason, consuming alcohol during pregnancy poses a major risk. Alcohol that reaches the developing central nervous system of the fetus can cause fetal alcohol syndrome, a disorder that can result in mental retardation and other serious birth defects. Similarly, smoking during pregnancy is associated with high risk of low birth weight and other health problems.

Second Trimester

During the second trimester, the uterus grows enough for the pregnancy to become apparent. The fetus itself grows to about 30 cm in length and is very active. The mother may feel fetal movements as early as one month into the second trimester; fetal activity is typically visible through the abdominal wall one to two months later. Hormone levels stabilize as hCG declines; the corpus luteum deteriorates; and the placenta completely takes over the production of progesterone, the hormone that maintains the pregnancy.

Third Trimester

During the final trimester, the fetus grows to about 3–4 kg in weight and 50 cm in length. Fetal activity may decrease as the fetus fills the available space. As the fetus grows and the uterus expands around it, the mother's abdominal organs become compressed and displaced, leading to frequent urination and digestive blockages.

Childbirth begins with **labor**, a series of strong, rhythmic uterine contractions that push the fetus and placenta out of the body. Recent studies suggest that labor begins when the fully developed fetus produces hormones and certain lung proteins that initiate an inflammatory response (see Chapter 43) in the mother. However, further study is needed to determine if inflammation does in fact trigger labor.

Once labor begins, a complex interplay of local regulators (prostaglandins) and hormones (chiefly estradiol and oxytocin) induces and regulates further contractions of the uterus **(Figure 46.18)**. The action of oxytocin forms a positive-feedback loop (see Chapter 45), with uterine contractions stimulating secretion of oxytocin, which in turn stimulates further contractions.

▲ Figure 46.18 Positive feedback in labor.

? *Predict the effect of a single dose of oxytocin on a pregnant woman at the end of 39 weeks gestation.*

Labor is typically described as having three stages (Figure 46.19). The first stage is the thinning and opening up (dilation) of the cervix. The second stage is the expulsion, or delivery, of the baby. Continuous strong contractions force the fetus out of the uterus and through the vagina. The final stage of labor is delivery of the placenta.

One aspect of postnatal care unique to mammals is **lactation**, the production of mother's milk. In response to suckling by the newborn, as well as changes in estradiol levels after birth, the hypothalamus signals the anterior pituitary to secrete prolactin, which stimulates the mammary glands to produce milk. Suckling also stimulates the secretion of oxytocin from the posterior pituitary, which triggers release of milk from the mammary glands (see Figure 45.15).

Maternal Immune Tolerance of the Embryo and Fetus

Pregnancy is an immunological puzzle. Half of the embryo's genes are inherited from the father; thus, many of the chemical markers present on the surface of the embryo are foreign to the mother. Why, then, does the mother not reject the embryo as a foreign body, as she would a tissue or organ graft from another person? One intriguing clue comes from the relationship between certain autoimmune disorders and pregnancy. For example, the symptoms of rheumatoid arthritis, an autoimmune disease of the joints, become less severe during pregnancy. Thus, the overall regulation of the immune system appears to be altered by the reproductive process. Sorting out these changes and how they might protect the developing fetus is an active area of research for immunologists.

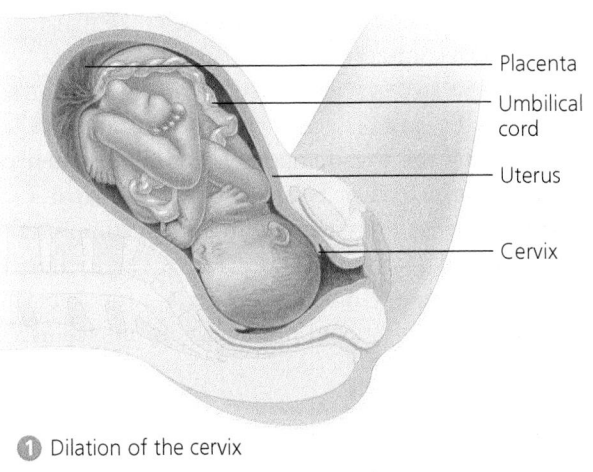

1 Dilation of the cervix

2 Expulsion: delivery of the infant

3 Delivery of the placenta

▲ Figure 46.19 The three stages of labor.

Contraception and Abortion

Contraception, the deliberate prevention of pregnancy, can be achieved in a number of ways. Some contraceptive methods prevent gamete development or release from female or male gonads; others prevent fertilization by keeping sperm and egg apart; and still others prevent implantation of an embryo. For complete information on contraceptive methods, you should consult a health-care provider. The following brief introduction to the biology of the most common methods and the corresponding diagram in **Figure 46.20** make no pretense of being a contraception manual.

Fertilization can be prevented by abstinence from sexual intercourse or by any of several barriers that keep live sperm from contacting the egg. Temporary abstinence, often called the **rhythm method** of birth control or **natural family planning**, depends on refraining from intercourse when conception is most likely. Because the egg can survive in the oviduct for 24–48 hours and sperm for up to 5 days, a couple practicing temporary abstinence should not engage in intercourse for a number of days before and after ovulation. The most effective methods for determining the time of ovulation combine several indicators, including changes in cervical mucus and body temperature during the menstrual cycle. Thus, natural family planning requires that the couple be knowledgeable about these physiological signs. Note that a pregnancy rate of 10–20% is typically reported for couples practicing natural family planning. (Pregnancy rate is the average number of women who become pregnant during a year for every 100 women using a particular pregnancy prevention method, expressed as a percentage.) Some couples use ovulation-timing methods to *increase* the probability of conception.

As a method of preventing fertilization, *coitus interruptus*, or withdrawal (removal of the penis from the vagina before ejaculation), is unreliable. Sperm from a previous ejaculate may be transferred in secretions that precede ejaculation. Furthermore, a split-second lapse in timing or willpower can result in tens of millions of sperm being transferred before withdrawal.

The several barrier methods of contraception that block the sperm from meeting the egg have pregnancy rates of less than 10%. The **condom** is a thin, latex rubber or natural membrane sheath that fits over the penis to collect the semen. For sexually active individuals, latex condoms are the only contraceptives that are highly effective in preventing the spread of sexually transmitted diseases, including AIDS. (This protection is, however, not absolute.) Another common barrier device is the **diaphragm**, a dome-shaped rubber cap inserted into the upper portion of the vagina before intercourse. Both of these devices have lower pregnancy rates when used in conjunction with a spermicidal (sperm-killing) foam or jelly. Other barrier devices include the vaginal pouch, or "female condom."

Except for complete abstinence from sexual intercourse, the most effective means of birth control are sterilization, intrauterine devices (IUDs), and hormonal contraceptives. Sterilization (discussed later) is almost 100% effective. The IUD has a pregnancy rate of 1% or less and is the most commonly used reversible method of birth control outside the United States. Placed in the uterus by a doctor, the IUD interferes with fertilization and implantation. Hormonal contraceptives, most often in the form of **birth control pills**, also have pregnancy rates of 1% or less.

The most commonly prescribed birth control pills are a combination of a synthetic estrogen and a synthetic progestin (progesterone-like hormone). This combination mimics negative feedback in the ovarian cycle, stopping the release of GnRH by the hypothalamus and thus of FSH and LH by the pituitary. The prevention of LH release blocks ovulation. In addition, the inhibition of FSH secretion by the low dose of estrogens in the pills prevents follicles from developing. A similar combination of hormones is also available as an injection, as a ring inserted into the vagina, and as a skin

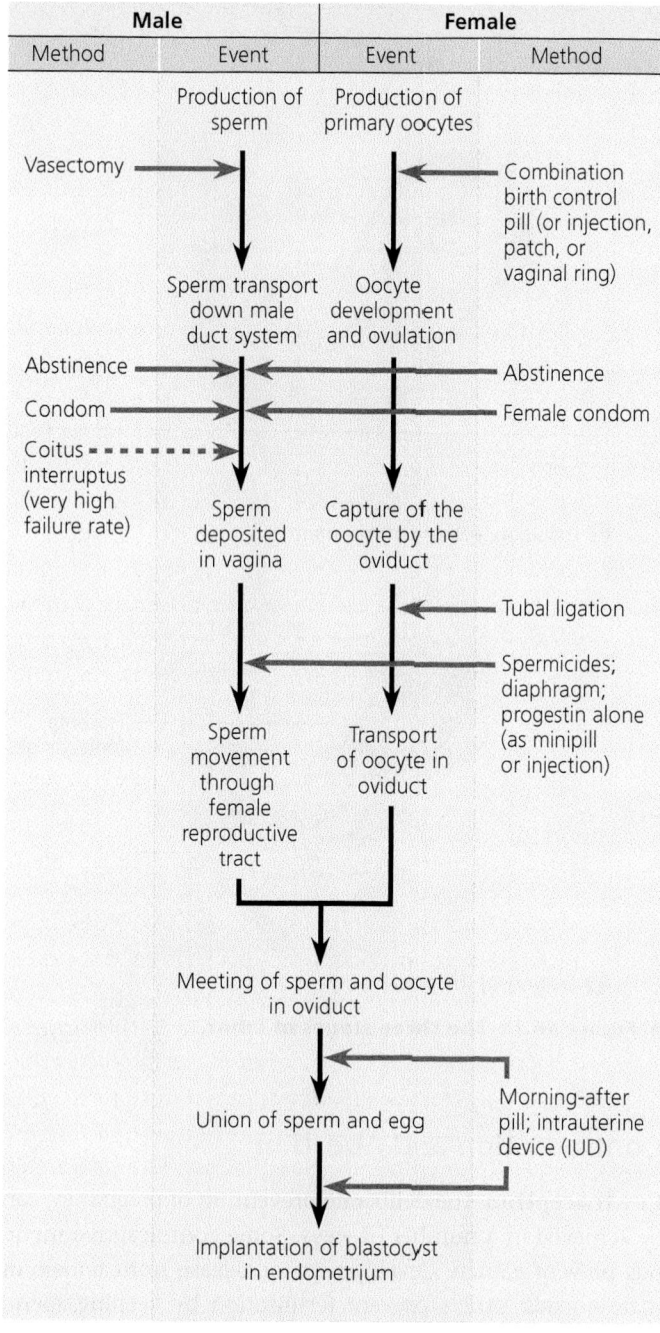

▲ **Figure 46.20 Mechanisms of several contraceptive methods.** Red arrows indicate where these methods, devices, or products interfere with events from the production of sperm and primary oocytes to an implanted, developing embryo.

patch. Combination birth control pills can also be used in high doses as "morning-after" pills. Taken within 3 days after unprotected intercourse, they prevent fertilization or implantation with an effectiveness of about 75%.

A different type of hormone-based contraceptive contains only progestin. Progestin causes thickening of a woman's cervical mucus so that it blocks sperm from entering the uterus. Progestin also decreases the frequency of ovulation and causes changes in the endometrium that may interfere with implantation if fertilization occurs. Progestin can be administered as injections that last for three months or as a tablet ("minipill") taken daily. Pregnancy rates for progestin treatment are very low.

Hormone-based contraceptives have both beneficial and harmful side effects. For women taking a combination pill, cardiovascular problems are the most serious concern. Women who regularly smoke cigarettes face a three to ten times greater risk of dying from cardiovascular disease if they also use oral contraceptives. Among nonsmokers, birth control pills slightly raise a woman's risk of abnormal blood clotting, high blood pressure, heart attack, and stroke. Although oral contraceptives increase the risk for these cardiovascular disorders, they eliminate the dangers of pregnancy; women on birth control pills have mortality rates about one-half those of pregnant women. Also, the pill decreases the risk of ovarian and endometrial cancers.

One elusive research goal has been a reversible chemical contraceptive for men. Recent strategies have focused on hormone combinations that suppress gonadotropin release and thereby block spermatogenesis. Testosterone included in such combinations has two desirable effects: inhibiting reproductive functions of the hypothalamus and pituitary and maintaining secondary sex characteristics. Although there have been some promising results, hormonal male contraceptives are still in the testing stage.

Sterilization is the permanent prevention of gamete production or release. **Tubal ligation** in women usually involves sealing shut or tying off (ligating) a section of each oviduct to prevent eggs from traveling into the uterus. Similarly, **vasectomy** in men is the cutting and tying off of each vas deferens to prevent sperm from entering the urethra. Both male and female sterilization procedures are relatively safe and free from harmful effects. Sex hormone secretion and sexual function are unaffected by both procedures, with no change in menstrual cycles in females or ejaculate volume in males. Although tubal ligation or vasectomy are considered permanent, both procedures can in many cases be reversed by microsurgery.

The termination of a pregnancy in progress is called **abortion**. Spontaneous abortion, or *miscarriage*, is very common; it occurs in as many as one-third of all pregnancies, often before the woman is even aware she is pregnant. In addition, each year about 850,000 women in the United States choose to have an abortion performed by a physician.

A drug called mifepristone, or RU486, can terminate a pregnancy nonsurgically within the first 7 weeks. RU486 blocks progesterone receptors in the uterus, thus preventing progesterone from maintaining the pregnancy. It is taken with a small amount of prostaglandin to induce uterine contractions.

Modern Reproductive Technologies

Recent scientific and technological advances have made it possible to address many reproductive problems, including genetic diseases and infertility.

Detecting Disorders During Pregnancy

Many genetic diseases and developmental problems can now be diagnosed while the fetus is in the uterus. Ultrasound imaging, which generates images using sound frequencies above the normal hearing range, is commonly used to analyze the fetus's size and condition. Amniocentesis and chorionic villus sampling are techniques in which a needle is used to obtain fetal cells from fluid or tissue surrounding the embryo; these cells then provide the basis for genetic analysis (see Figure 14.19). An alternative technique for obtaining fetal tissue relies on the fact that a few fetal blood cells leak across the placenta into the mother's bloodstream. A blood sample from the mother yields fetal cells that can be identified with specific antibodies (which bind to proteins on the surface of fetal cells) and then tested for genetic disorders.

Diagnosing genetic diseases in a fetus poses ethical questions. To date, almost all detectable disorders remain untreatable in the uterus, and many cannot be corrected even after birth. Parents may be faced with difficult decisions about whether to terminate a pregnancy or to raise a child who may have profound defects and a short life expectancy. These are complex issues that demand careful, informed thought and competent genetic counseling.

Treating Infertility

Infertility—an inability to conceive offspring—is quite common, affecting about one in ten couples both in the United States and worldwide. The causes of infertility are varied, and the likelihood of a reproductive defect is nearly the same for men and women. For women, however, the risk of reproductive difficulties, as well as genetic abnormalities of the fetus, increases steadily past age 35. Evidence suggests that the prolonged period of time oocytes spend in meiosis is largely responsible for this increased risk.

Reproductive technology can help with a number of fertility problems. Hormone therapy can sometimes increase sperm or egg production, and surgery can often correct ducts that have failed to form properly or have become blocked. Many infertile couples turn to **assisted reproductive technologies**, procedures that generally involve surgically removing eggs (secondary oocytes) from a woman's ovaries after hormonal stimulation, fertilizing the eggs, and returning early embryos to the woman's body. Unused eggs, sperm, and embryos are sometimes frozen for later pregnancy attempts.

The technique of *in vitro* fertilization **(IVF)** involves mixing oocytes and sperm in culture dishes. Fertilized eggs are incubated until they have formed at least eight cells and are then typically transferred to the woman's uterus for implantation. If mature sperm are defective, low in number (less than 20 million per milliliter of ejaculate), or even absent, fertility is often restored by a technique called **intracytoplasmic sperm injection (ICSI)**. In this form of IVF, the head of a spermatid or sperm is drawn up into a needle and injected directly into an oocyte to achieve fertilization.

Though costly, IVF procedures have enabled more than a million couples to conceive children. In some cases, these procedures are carried out with sperm or eggs from donors. To date, evidence indicates that abnormalities arising as a consequence of IVF procedures are rare.

By whatever means fertilization occurs, a developmental program follows that transforms the single-celled zygote into a multicellular organism. The mechanisms of this remarkable program of development in humans and other animals are the subject of Chapter 47.

CONCEPT CHECK 46.5

1. Why does testing for hCG (human chorionic gonadotropin) work as a pregnancy test early in pregnancy but not late in pregnancy? What is the function of hCG in pregnancy?
2. In what ways are tubal ligation and vasectomy similar?
3. **WHAT IF?** If a spermatid nucleus is used for ICSI, what steps of gametogenesis and conception are bypassed?

For suggested answers, see Appendix A.

46 CHAPTER REVIEW

SUMMARY OF KEY CONCEPTS

CONCEPT 46.1

Both asexual and sexual reproduction occur in the animal kingdom (pp. 996–999)

- Animals reproduce either asexually or sexually. **Sexual reproduction** requires the fusion of male and female gametes, forming a diploid **zygote**. **Asexual reproduction** is the production of offspring without gamete fusion. Fission, budding, fragmentation with regeneration, and **parthenogenesis** are mechanisms of asexual reproduction in various invertebrates. Facilitating selection for or against sets of genes may explain why sexual reproduction is widespread among animal species.
- Although most animals reproduce exclusively sexually or asexually, some alternate between the two. Variations on these two modes are made possible through parthenogenesis, **hermaphroditism**, and sex reversal. Hormones and environmental cues control reproductive cycles.

? *Would a pair of haploid offspring produced by parthenogenesis be genetically identical?*

CONCEPT 46.2

Fertilization depends on mechanisms that bring together sperm and eggs of the same species (pp. 999–1002)

- Fertilization can occur externally or internally with regard to the mother's body. In either case, fertilization requires coordinated timing, which may be mediated by environmental cues, pheromones, or courtship behavior. Internal fertilization is typically often associated both with relatively fewer offspring and with greater protection of offspring by the parents. Systems for

gamete production and delivery range from undifferentiated cells in the body cavity to complex **gonads** with accessory tubes and glands that carry and protect gametes and embryos. Although sexual reproduction involves a partnership, it also provides an opportunity for competition between individuals and between gametes.

? *Identify which of the following are unique to mammals: a female uterus and a male vas deferens, extended internal development, parental care of newborns.*

CONCEPT 46.3

Reproductive organs produce and transport gametes (pp. 1002–1008)

- The reproductive system of the human female consists principally of the **labia** and the **glans** of the **clitoris** externally and the **vagina**, **uterus**, **oviducts**, and **ovaries** internally. Eggs are produced in the ovaries and upon fertilization develop in the uterus. In males, sperm are produced in **testes**, which are suspended outside the body in the **scrotum**. Ducts extending from the scrotum connect the testes to internal accessory glands and to the opening of the **penis**. Both males and females have **mammary glands**, but milk production occurs only in females. During intercourse, males and females each experience the erection of certain body tissues due to **vasocongestion** and **myotonia**, culminating in **orgasm**.
- Gametogenesis, or gamete production, consists of **oogenesis** in females and **spermatogenesis** in males. Meiosis generates one large egg in oogenesis, but four sperm in spermatogenesis. In humans, sperm develop continuously, whereas oocyte maturation is discontinuous and cyclic.

Human gametogenesis

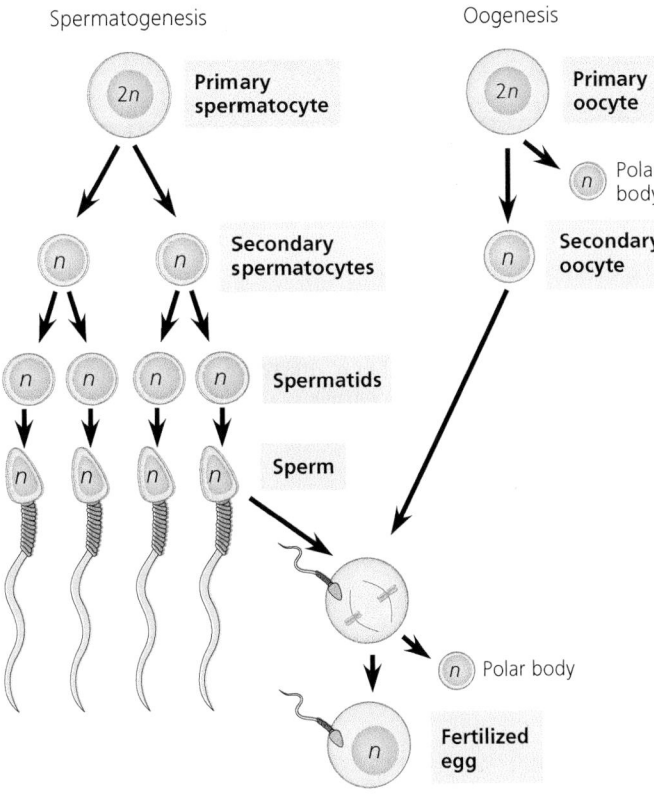

Spermatogenesis   Oogenesis

? *How does the difference in size and cellular contents between sperm and eggs relate to their specific functions in reproduction?*

CONCEPT 46.4

The interplay of tropic and sex hormones regulates mammalian reproduction (pp. 1008–1011)

- In human males, androgens (chiefly testosterone) from the testes cause the development of primary and secondary sex characteristics. Androgen secretion and sperm production are both controlled by hypothalamic and pituitary hormones.
- In human females, cyclic secretion of GnRH from the hypothalamus and FSH and LH from the anterior pituitary orchestrates the reproductive cycle. FSH and LH bring about changes in the ovary and uterus via estrogens, primarily estradiol, and progesterone. The developing follicle and the corpus luteum also secrete hormones, with positive and negative feedback coordinating the uterine and ovarian cycles.
- **Estrous cycles** differ from **menstrual cycles** in that the endometrial lining is reabsorbed rather than shed and sexual receptivity is limited to a heat period.

? *Why do anabolic steroids lead to reduced sperm count?*

CONCEPT 46.5

In placental mammals, an embryo develops fully within the mother's uterus (pp. 1011–1018)

- After fertilization and the completion of meiosis in the oviduct, the zygote undergoes cleavage and develops into a blastocyst before implantation in the endometrium. All major organs start developing by 8 weeks. A pregnant woman's acceptance of her "foreign" offspring likely reflects partial suppression of the maternal immune response.

- Contraceptive methods may prevent release of mature gametes from the gonads, fertilization, or implantation of the embryo. Reproductive technologies can assist infertile couples by hormonal methods or *in vitro* fertilization and can also help detect problems before birth.

? *What route would oxygen in the mother's blood follow to arrive at a body cell of the fetus?*

TEST YOUR UNDERSTANDING

LEVEL 1: KNOWLEDGE/COMPREHENSION

1. Which of the following characterizes parthenogenesis?
   a. An individual may change its sex during its lifetime.
   b. Specialized groups of cells grow into new individuals.
   c. An organism is first a male and then a female.
   d. An egg develops without being fertilized.
   e. Both mates have male and female reproductive organs.

2. In male mammals, excretory and reproductive systems share
   a. the testes.
   b. the urethra.
   c. the seminal vesicle.
   d. the vas deferens.
   e. the prostate.

3. Which of the following is *not* properly paired?
   a. seminiferous tubule—cervix
   b. Sertoli cells—follicle cells
   c. testosterone—estradiol
   d. scrotum—labia majora
   e. vas deferens—oviduct

4. Peaks of LH and FSH production occur during
   a. the menstrual flow phase of the uterine cycle.
   b. the beginning of the follicular phase of the ovarian cycle.
   c. the period just before ovulation.
   d. the end of the luteal phase of the ovarian cycle.
   e. the secretory phase of the menstrual cycle.

5. During human gestation, rudiments of all organs develop
   a. in the first trimester.
   b. in the second trimester.
   c. in the third trimester.
   d. while the embryo is in the oviduct.
   e. during the blastocyst stage.

LEVEL 2: APPLICATION/ANALYSIS

6. Which of the following is a true statement?
   a. All mammals have menstrual cycles.
   b. The endometrial lining is shed in menstrual cycles but reabsorbed in estrous cycles.
   c. Estrous cycles are more frequent than menstrual cycles.
   d. Estrous cycles are not controlled by hormones.
   e. Ovulation occurs before the endometrium thickens in estrous cycles.

7. For which of the following is the number the same in spermatogenesis and oogenesis?
   a. interruptions in meiotic divisions
   b. functional gametes produced by meiosis
   c. meiotic divisions required to produce each gamete
   d. gametes produced in a given time period
   e. different cell types produced by meiosis

8. Which statement about human reproduction is false?
   a. Fertilization occurs in the oviduct.
   b. Effective hormonal contraceptives are currently available only for females.
   c. An oocyte completes meiosis after a sperm penetrates it.
   d. The earliest stages of spermatogenesis occur closest to the lumen of the seminiferous tubules.
   e. Spermatogenesis and oogenesis require different temperatures.

LEVEL 3: SYNTHESIS/EVALUATION

9. **DRAW IT** In human spermatogenesis, mitosis of a stem cell gives rise to one cell that remains a stem cell and one cell that becomes a spermatogonium. (a) Draw four rounds of mitosis for a stem cell, and label the daughter cells. (b) For one spermatogonium, draw the cells it would produce from one round of mitosis followed by meiosis. Label the cells, and label mitosis and meiosis. (c) What would happen if stem cells divided like spermatogonia?

10. **EVOLUTION CONNECTION**
    Hermaphroditism is often found in animals that are fixed to a surface. Motile species are less often hermaphroditic. Why?

11. **SCIENTIFIC INQUIRY**
    You discover a new egg-laying worm species. You dissect four adults and find both oocytes and sperm in each. Cells outside the gonad contain five chromosome pairs. Lacking genetic variants, how would you determine whether the worms can self-fertilize?

12. **WRITE ABOUT A THEME**

    Energy Transfer In reproducing, animals transfer energy to their offspring. In a short essay (100–150 words), discuss how distinct investments of energy by females contribute to the reproductive success of a frog, a chicken, and a human.

For selected answers, see Appendix A.

 MasteringBIOLOGY® www.masteringbiology.com

1. MasteringBiology® Assignments
Tutorial Sex Hormones and Mammalian Reproduction
Activities Reproductive System of the Human Female • Reproductive System of the Human Male • Human Gametogenesis • Human Reproduction
Questions Student Misconceptions • Reading Quiz • Multiple Choice • End-of-Chapter

2. eText
Read your book online, search, take notes, highlight text, and more.

3. The Study Area
Practice Tests • Cumulative Test • *BioFlix* 3-D Animations • MP3 Tutor Sessions • Videos • Activities • Investigations • Lab Media • Audio Glossary • Word Study Tools • Art

47

Animal Development

▲ **Figure 47.1 How did a single cell develop into this intricately detailed embryo?**

1 mm

KEY CONCEPTS

47.1 Fertilization and cleavage initiate embryonic development

47.2 Morphogenesis in animals involves specific changes in cell shape, position, and survival

47.3 Cytoplasmic determinants and inductive signals contribute to cell fate specification

OVERVIEW

A Body-Building Plan

The 7-week-old human embryo in Figure 47.1 has already achieved a remarkable number of milestones in its development. Its heart—the red spot in the center—is beating, and a digestive tract traverses the length of its body. Its

brain is forming (at the upper left in the photo), while the blocks of tissue that will give rise to the vertebrae are lined up along its back.

Development occurs at many points in the life cycle of an animal (Figure 47.2). In a frog, for example, a major developmental period is metamorphosis, when the larva (tadpole) is transformed into an adult. Other developmental events in the adult gonads produce sperm and eggs (gametes). In this chapter, our focus is on embryonic development.

Across a range of animal species, embryonic development involves common stages that occur in a set order. As shown in Figure 47.2, the first is fertilization, the fusion of sperm and egg, which forms a zygote. Development proceeds with the cleavage stage, during which a series of cell divisions divide, or cleave, the zygote into a many-celled embryo. These cleavage divisions, which typically are rapid and lack accompanying cell growth, convert the embryo to a hollow ball of cells called a blastula. Next, the blastula folds in on itself, rearranging into a three-layered embryo, the gastrula, in a process called gastrulation. During organogenesis, the last major stage of embryonic development, local changes in cell shape and large-scale changes in cell location generate the rudimentary organs from which adult structures grow.

By combining molecular genetics with classical embryology, developmental biologists have learned a great deal about the transformation of a fertilized egg into an adult. As an embryo develops, specific patterns of gene expression direct cells to adopt distinct fates. Although animals display

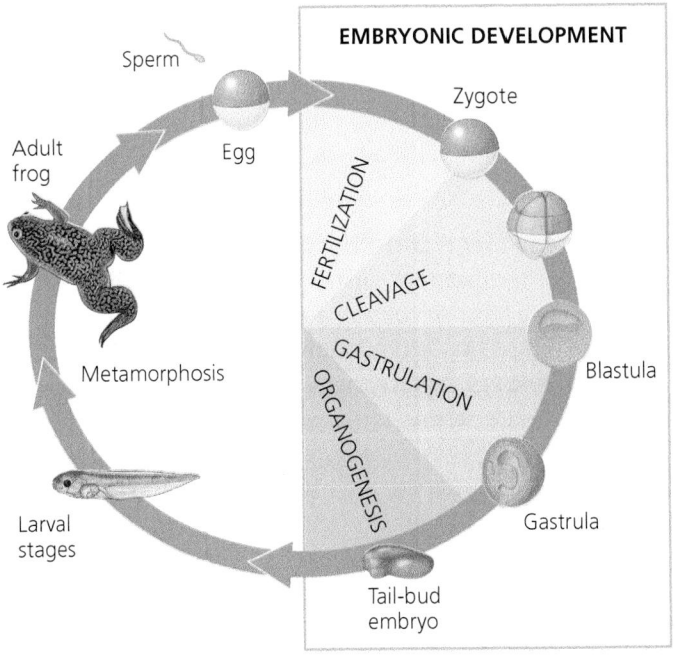

▲ **Figure 47.2 Developmental events in the life cycle of a frog.**

widely differing body plans, they share many basic mechanisms of development and use a common set of regulatory genes. For example, the gene that specifies heart location in a human embryo (such as the one in Figure 47.1) has a close counterpart with a nearly identical function in the fruit fly, *Drosophila*. (Noting that the fly heart fails to develop when this gene is defective, researchers named the *Drosophila* gene *tinman*, after the similarly affected character from *The Wizard of Oz*.)

In studying development, biologists frequently make use of **model organisms**, species chosen for the ease with which they can be studied in the laboratory. *Drosophila* is a useful model organism: Its life cycle is short, and mutants can be readily identified and studied (see Chapters 15 and 18). In this chapter, we will concentrate on four other model organisms: the sea urchin, the frog, the chick, and the nematode (roundworm). We will also explore some aspects of human embryonic development. Even though humans are not model organisms, we are, of course, intensely interested in our own species.

Our exploration of embryonic development will begin with a description of the basic stages common to most animals. We will then look at some of the cellular mechanisms that generate body form. Finally, we will consider how a cell becomes committed to a particular specialized role.

CONCEPT 47.1

Fertilization and cleavage initiate embryonic development

With the preceding overview of embryonic development in mind, let's take a closer look at the events surrounding **fertilization**, the formation of a diploid zygote from a haploid egg and sperm.

Fertilization

Molecules and events at the egg surface play a crucial role in each step of fertilization. First, sperm dissolve or penetrate any protective layer surrounding the egg to reach the plasma membrane. Next, molecules on the sperm surface bind to receptors on the egg surface, helping ensure that a sperm of the same species fertilizes the egg. Finally, changes at the surface of the egg prevent *polyspermy*, the entry of multiple sperm nuclei into the egg. If polyspermy were to occur, the resulting abnormal number of chromosomes in the embryo would be lethal.

The cell surface events that take place during fertilization have been studied most extensively in sea urchins (members of the phylum Echinodermata; see Figure 33.43). Sea urchin gametes are easy to collect, and fertilization is external.

As a result, researchers can observe fertilization and subsequent events simply by combining eggs and sperm in seawater in the laboratory. Furthermore, fertilization in sea urchins provides a good general model for the same process in vertebrates.

The Acrosomal Reaction

When sea urchins release their gametes into the water, the jelly coat that surrounds the egg exudes soluble molecules that attract the sperm, which swim toward the egg. As soon as the head of a sea urchin sperm contacts the jelly coat of a sea urchin egg, molecules in the jelly coat trigger the **acrosomal reaction** in the sperm (**Figure 47.3**). This reaction begins with the discharge of hydrolytic enzymes from the **acrosome**, a specialized vesicle at the tip of the sperm. These enzymes partially digest the jelly coat, enabling a sperm structure called the *acrosomal process* to elongate and penetrate the coat. Protein molecules on the tip of the extended acrosomal process bind to specific receptor proteins that jut out from the egg plasma membrane. This "lock-and-key" recognition is especially important for sea urchins and other species with external fertilization because the surrounding water may contain gametes of other species.

Contact between the tip of the acrosomal process and the receptors on the egg leads to the fusion of the sperm and egg plasma membranes. The sperm nucleus then enters the egg cytoplasm as ion channels open in the egg's plasma membrane. Sodium ions diffuse into the egg and cause *depolarization*, a decrease in the membrane potential (see Chapter 7). The depolarization occurs within about 1–3 seconds after a sperm binds to an egg. By preventing additional sperm from fusing with the egg's plasma membrane, this depolarization acts as a **fast block to polyspermy**.

The Cortical Reaction

Membrane depolarization lasts for only a minute or so. A longer-lasting block to polyspermy is established by vesicles that lie just beneath the egg plasma membrane, in the rim of cytoplasm known as the *cortex*. Within seconds after a sperm binds to the egg, these vesicles, called cortical granules, fuse with the egg plasma membrane (see Figure 47.3, ❹). The contents of the cortical granules are released into the space between the plasma membrane and the surrounding *vitelline layer*, a structure formed by the extracellular matrix of the egg. Enzymes and other macromolecules from the granules trigger a cortical reaction, which lifts the vitelline layer away from the egg and hardens the layer into a protective fertilization envelope. Additional enzymes clip off and release the external portions of the remaining receptor proteins, along with any attached sperm. Together, the fertilization envelope

2 **Acrosomal reaction.** Hydrolytic enzymes released from the acrosome make a hole in the jelly coat. Growing actin filaments form the acrosomal process, which protrudes from the sperm head and penetrates the jelly coat. Proteins on the surface of the acrosomal process bind to receptors in the egg plasma membrane.

3 **Contact and fusion of sperm and egg membranes.** Fusion triggers depolarization of the membrane, which acts as a fast block to polyspermy.

4 **Cortical reaction.** Cortical granules in the egg fuse with the plasma membrane. The secreted contents clip off sperm-binding receptors and cause the fertilization envelope to form. This acts as a slow block to polyspermy.

1 **Contact.** The sperm contacts the egg's jelly coat, triggering exocytosis of the sperm's acrosome.

5 **Entry of sperm nucleus.**

Sperm plasma membrane

Sperm nucleus

Acrosomal process

Basal body (centriole)

Sperm head

Actin filament

Fertilization envelope

Acrosome

Cortical granule

Fused plasma membranes

Hydrolytic enzymes

Perivitelline space

Jelly coat

Vitelline layer

Sperm-binding receptors

Egg plasma membrane

EGG CYTOPLASM

▲ **Figure 47.3 The acrosomal and cortical reactions during sea urchin fertilization.** The events following contact of a single sperm and egg ensure that the nucleus of only one sperm enters the egg cytoplasm.

The icon above is a simplified drawing of an adult sea urchin. Throughout the chapter, this and other icons of an adult frog, chicken, nematode, and human indicate the animals whose embryos are featured in certain figures.

and other changes in the egg's surface impede the entry of additional sperm nuclei and thus act as a longer-term **slow block to polyspermy**.

Formation of the fertilization envelope requires a high concentration of calcium ions (Ca^{2+}) in the egg. Does a change in the Ca^{2+} concentration trigger the cortical reaction? To answer this question, researchers at the University of California, Berkeley, used a calcium-sensitive dye to assess the amount and distribution of Ca^{2+} in the egg during fertilization. As described in **Figure 47.4**, on the next page, they found that Ca^{2+} spread across the egg in a wave that correlated with the appearance of the fertilization envelope. Further studies demonstrated that release of Ca^{2+} into the cytosol from the endoplasmic reticulum is controlled by a signal transduction pathway activated by sperm binding. The resulting increase in Ca^{2+} levels causes cortical granules to fuse with the plasma membrane. Although understood in greatest detail in sea urchins, the cortical reaction triggered by Ca^{2+} also occurs in vertebrates such as fishes and mammals.

Egg Activation

A major function of fertilization is the combining of haploid sets of chromosomes from two individuals into a single diploid cell, the zygote. However, the events of fertilization also initiate metabolic reactions that trigger the onset of embryonic development, thus "activating" the egg. There is, for example, a marked increase in the rates of cellular respiration and protein synthesis in the egg following fertilization.

What triggers egg activation? Studies show that injecting Ca^{2+} into an unfertilized egg activates egg metabolism in many species, despite the absence of sperm. Researchers therefore conclude that the rise in Ca^{2+} concentration that causes the cortical reaction also causes egg activation. Further experiments have revealed that artificial activation is possible even if the nucleus has been removed from the egg. This finding indicates that egg activation requires only the proteins and mRNAs already present in the egg cytoplasm.

INQUIRY

Does the distribution of Ca²⁺ in an egg correlate with formation of the fertilization envelope?

EXPERIMENT During fertilization, fusion of cortical granules with the egg plasma membrane causes the fertilization envelope to rise and spread around the egg from the point of sperm binding.

10 sec after fertilization	25 sec	35 sec	1 min

500 µm

Calcium ion (Ca²⁺) signaling is involved in fusion of vesicles with the plasma membrane during neurotransmitter release, insulin secretion, and plant pollen tube formation. Rick Steinhardt, Gerald Schatten, and colleagues, then at the University of California at Berkeley, hypothesized that an increase in Ca²⁺ levels similarly triggers cortical granule fusion. To test this hypothesis, they tracked the release of free Ca²⁺ in sea urchin eggs after sperm binding to see if it correlated with formation of the fertilization envelope. A fluorescent dye that glows when it binds free Ca²⁺ was injected into unfertilized eggs. The researchers then added sea urchin sperm and observed the eggs with a fluorescence microscope. Schatten and colleagues later repeated the experiment using a more sensitive dye, producing the results shown here.

RESULTS A rise in cytosolic Ca²⁺ concentration began at the point of sperm entry and spread in a wave to the other side of the egg. Soon after the wave passed, the fertilization envelope rose.

1 sec before fertilization	10 sec after fertilization	20 sec	30 sec

500 µm

CONCLUSION The researchers concluded that Ca²⁺ release is correlated with the cortical reaction and formation of the fertilization envelope, supporting their hypothesis that an increase in Ca²⁺ levels triggers cortical granule fusion.

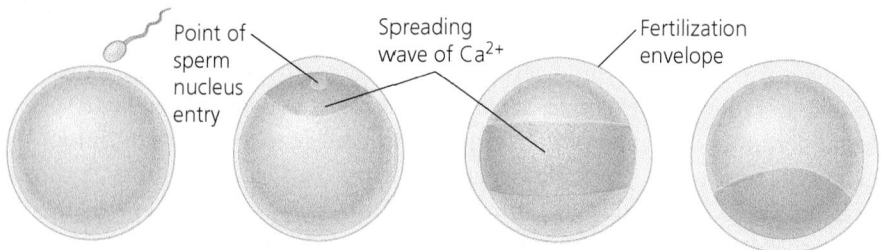

Point of sperm nucleus entry

Spreading wave of Ca²⁺

Fertilization envelope

SOURCE R. Steinhardt et al., Intracellular calcium release at fertilization in the sea urchin egg, *Developmental Biology* 58:185–197 (1977). M. Hafner et al., Wave of free calcium at fertilization in the sea urchin egg visualized with Fura-2, *Cell Motility and the Cytoskeleton* 9:271–277 (1988).

(MB) See the related Experimental Inquiry Tutorial in MasteringBiology.

WHAT IF? Suppose you were given a chemical compound that could enter the egg and bind to Ca²⁺, blocking its function. How would you use this compound to further test the hypothesis that a rise in Ca²⁺ levels triggers cortical granule fusion?

About 20 minutes after the sperm nucleus enters the sea urchin egg, the sperm and egg nuclei fuse. DNA synthesis begins, and the first cell division occurs after about 90 minutes, marking the end of the fertilization stage.

Fertilization in other species shares many features with the process in sea urchins. However, the timing of events differs, as does the stage of meiosis the egg has reached by the time it is fertilized. Sea urchin eggs have already completed meiosis when they are released from the female. In other species, eggs are arrested at a specific stage of meiosis and do not complete the meiotic divisions until fertilization occurs. Human eggs, for example, are arrested at metaphase of meiosis II prior to fertilization (see Figure 46.12).

Fertilization in Mammals

Unlike sea urchins and most other marine invertebrates, terrestrial animals, including mammals, fertilize eggs internally. Secretions in the mammalian female reproductive tract not only provide a moist environment for the sperm, but also bring about changes in sperm motility and structure. Only after these changes occur do sperm have the capacity to fertilize an egg. In humans, this process of *capacitation* occurs during the first 6 hours after the sperm enter the female reproductive tract.

Support cells of the developing follicle surround the mammalian egg and remain with it during and after ovulation (see Figure 46.12). A sperm must travel through this layer of follicle cells before it reaches the **zona pellucida**, the extracellular matrix of the egg. Within the zona pellucida is a component that functions as a receptor for sperm. Binding of a sperm to this receptor induces an acrosomal reaction, facilitating sperm passage through the zona pellucida to the egg. This binding also exposes a protein on the sperm that binds with the egg plasma membrane. At this point, the two cells fuse (**Figure 47.5**).

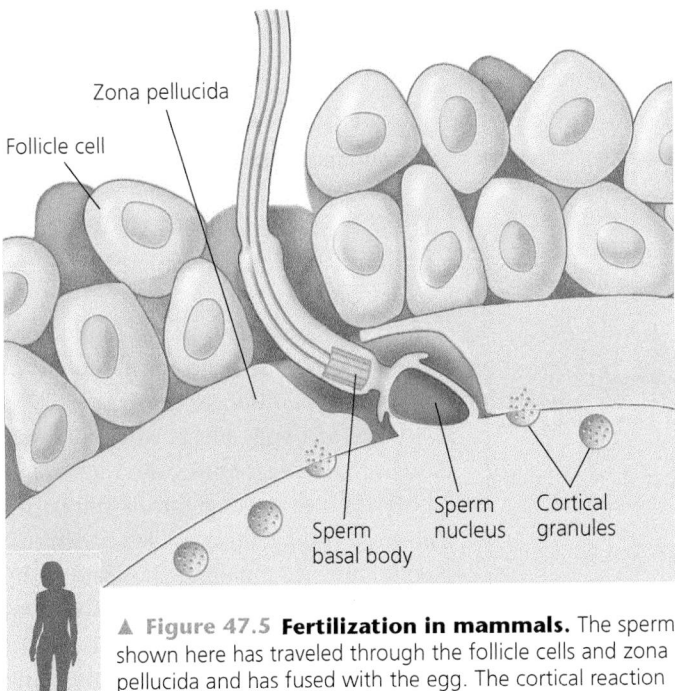

Zona pellucida

Follicle cell

Sperm basal body

Sperm nucleus

Cortical granules

▲ Figure 47.5 **Fertilization in mammals.** The sperm shown here has traveled through the follicle cells and zona pellucida and has fused with the egg. The cortical reaction has begun, initiating events that ensure that only one sperm nucleus enters the egg.

As in sea urchin fertilization, sperm binding triggers changes within the mammalian egg that lead to a cortical reaction, the release of enzymes from cortical granules to the outside of the cell. These enzymes catalyze changes in the zona pellucida, which then functions as the slow block to polyspermy. (No fast block to polyspermy has been identified in mammals.)

After the egg and sperm membranes fuse, the whole sperm is taken into the egg. Once the envelopes of both haploid nuclei have dispersed, the sperm and egg chromosomes are organized onto a single mitotic spindle. Only after the first division is there a true diploid nucleus with a nuclear membrane.

Overall, fertilization is much slower in mammals than in sea urchins: The first cell division occurs 12–36 hours after sperm binding in mammals, compared with about 90 minutes in sea urchins. This cell division marks the end of fertilization and the beginning of the next stage, cleavage.

Cleavage

Once fertilization is complete, many animal species undergo a succession of rapid cell divisions that characterize the **cleavage** stage of early development. During cleavage, the cell cycle consists primarily of the S (DNA synthesis) and M (mitosis) phases. Cells essentially skip the G_1 and G_2 (gap) phases, and little or no protein synthesis occurs (see Figure 12.6 for a review of the cell cycle). As a result, cleavage partitions the cytoplasm of the large fertilized egg into many smaller cells called **blastomeres**, as shown in Figure 47.6.

The first five to seven cleavage divisions produce a hollow ball of cells, the **blastula**, surrounding a fluid-filled cavity called the **blastocoel** (see Figure 47.6).

Cleavage Patterns

In frogs and many other animals, the distribution of **yolk** (stored nutrients) is a key factor influencing the pattern of cleavage. Yolk is often concentrated toward one pole of the egg, called the **vegetal pole**. The yolk concentration decreases significantly toward the opposite pole, the **animal pole**. This difference in yolk distribution results

(a) Fertilized egg. Shown here is the zygote shortly before the first cleavage division, surrounded by the fertilization envelope.

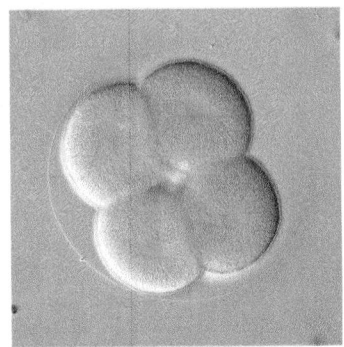

(b) Four-cell stage. Remnants of the mitotic spindle can be seen between the two pairs of cells that have just completed the second cleavage division.

(c) Early blastula. After further cleavage divisions, the embryo is a multicellular ball that is still surrounded by the fertilization envelope. The blastocoel has begun to form in the center.

(d) Later blastula. A single layer of cells surrounds a large blastocoel. Although not visible here, the fertilization envelope is still present; the embryo will soon hatch from it and begin swimming.

50 μm

▲ Figure 47.6 **Cleavage in an echinoderm embryo.** Cleavage is a series of mitotic cell divisions that transform the fertilized egg into a blastula, a hollow ball composed of cells called blastomeres. These light micrographs show the cleavage stages of a sand dollar embryo, which are virtually identical to those of a sea urchin.

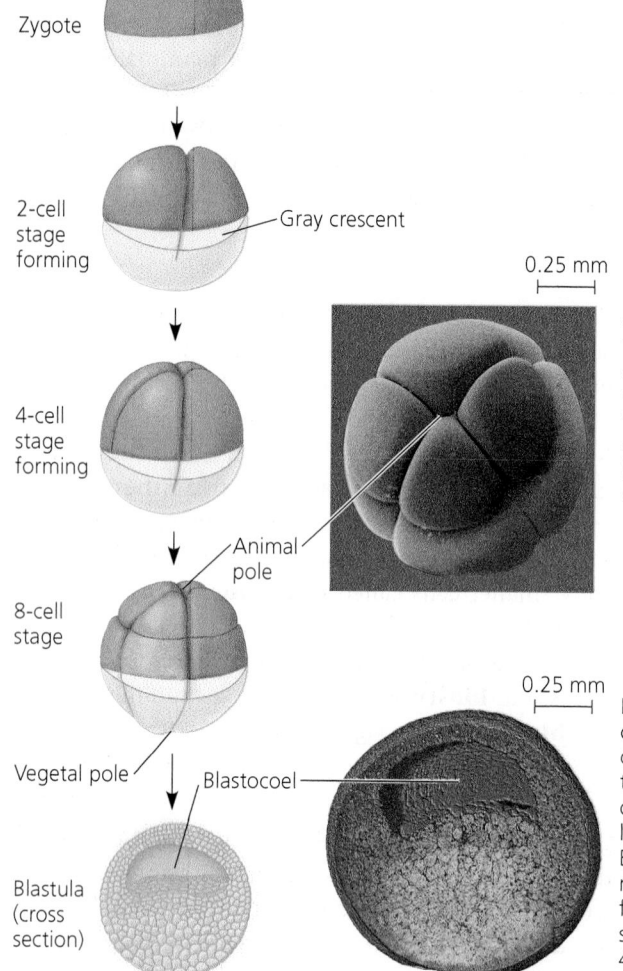

Zygote

2-cell stage forming — Gray crescent

4-cell stage forming

Animal pole

8-cell stage

Vegetal pole — Blastocoel

Blastula (cross section)

0.25 mm

8-cell stage (viewed from the animal pole). The large amount of yolk displaces the third cleavage toward the animal pole, forming two tiers of cells. The four cells near the animal pole (closer, in this view) are smaller than the other four cells (colorized SEM).

0.25 mm

Blastula (at least 128 cells). As cleavage continues, a fluid-filled cavity, the blastocoel, forms within the embryo. Because of unequal cell division, the blastocoel is located in the animal hemisphere. Both the drawing and the micrograph (assembled from fluorescence images) show cross sections of a blastula with about 4,000 cells.

▲ **Figure 47.7 Cleavage in a frog embryo.** The cleavage planes in the first and second divisions extend from the animal pole to the vegetal pole, but the third cleavage is perpendicular to the polar axis. In some species, the first division bisects the gray crescent, a lighter-colored region that appears opposite the site of sperm entry.

in animal and vegetal hemispheres that differ in appearance (Figure 47.7).

During cell division, an indentation called a *cleavage furrow* forms in the cell surface as cytokinesis divides the cell in half. As shown in Figure 47.7, the first two cleavage furrows in the frog lie parallel to the line (or meridian) connecting the two poles. The second cell division begins before the first is complete, so the second cleavage furrow further divides the animal hemisphere while the first furrow is dividing the yolky cytoplasm of the vegetal hemisphere. Nevertheless, the first two divisions eventually produce four blastomeres of equal size, each extending from the animal pole to the vegetal pole.

During the third division of the frog egg, the asymmetric distribution of yolk in the embryo affects the relative size of cells produced in the two hemispheres. This division is equatorial (perpendicular to the line connecting the poles) and produces an eight-celled embryo. However, as each of the four blastomeres begins this division, the high concentration of yolk around the

vegetal pole displaces the mitotic apparatus toward the animal pole. Consequently, the cleavage furrow is also displaced from the egg equator toward the animal pole, yielding smaller blastomeres in the animal hemisphere than in the vegetal hemisphere. The displacing effect of the yolk persists in the subsequent divisions that produce a blastula. In frogs, these unequal cell divisions cause the blastocoel to form entirely in the animal hemisphere (see Figure 47.7).

Although yolk affects where division occurs in the eggs of frogs and other amphibians, the cleavage furrow still passes entirely through the egg. Cleavage in amphibian development is thus said to be **holoblastic** (from the Greek *holos*, complete). Holoblastic cleavage is also seen in many other groups of animals, including echinoderms, mammals, and annelids. The orientation of the cleavage furrows varies within these groups, resulting in blastulas that vary considerably in appearance. In those animals whose eggs contain relatively little yolk, the blastocoel forms centrally and the blastomeres are often of similar size, particularly during the first few divisions (see Figure 47.6). This is the case for humans, whose embryos complete three divisions in the first 3 days after fertilization.

Yolk is most plentiful and has its most pronounced effect on cleavage in the eggs of birds, other reptiles, many fishes, and insects. In these animals, the volume of yolk is so great that cleavage furrows cannot pass through it, and only the region of the egg lacking yolk undergoes cleavage. This incomplete cleavage of a yolk-rich egg is said to be **meroblastic** (from the Greek *meros*, partial).

In birds, the part of the egg commonly called the yolk is actually the entire egg cell, swollen with yolk nutrients. Cell divisions are limited to a small whitish area at the animal pole. These divisions produce a cap of cells that sort into upper and lower layers. The cavity between these two layers is the avian version of the blastocoel.

In the eggs of *Drosophila* and most other insects, the sperm and egg nuclei fuse *within* a mass of yolk. Multiple rounds of mitosis occur without cytokinesis. In other words, no cell membranes form around the early nuclei. The first several hundred nuclei spread throughout the yolk and later migrate to the outer edge of the embryo. After several more rounds of mitosis, a plasma membrane forms around each nucleus, and the embryo, now the equivalent of a blastula, consists of a single layer of about 6,000 cells surrounding a mass of yolk (see Figure 18.22).

Regulation of Cleavage

The number of cleavage divisions varies among animals but appears to be controlled by a shared mechanism. Experimental results support the hypothesis that an animal embryo finishes the cleavage stage when the ratio of material in each nucleus to that in the cytoplasm is sufficiently large. One line of evidence comes from experiments in which researchers changed the starting amount of cytoplasm and then counted the cleavage divisions that occurred. For example, when half the normal amount of cytoplasm surrounds the newly formed zygotic nucleus, one fewer cleavage division occurs, consistent with the nuclear-cytoplasmic ratio reaching the threshold after one fewer cell cycle.

What is the adaptive advantage of linking the duration of the cleavage stage to the ratio of material in the nucleus and cytoplasm? The single nucleus in a newly fertilized egg has too little DNA to produce the amount of messenger RNA required to meet the cell's need for new proteins. Instead, the initial stages of development are carried out by RNA and proteins deposited in the egg during oogenesis. After cleavage, the egg cytoplasm has been divided among the many blastomeres, each with its own nucleus. Because each blastomere is much smaller than the entire egg or embryo, its nucleus can make enough RNA to program the cell's metabolism and its further development. The increase in the number of cells also sets the stage for morphogenesis, the transformation of embryo organization and shape.

CONCEPT CHECK **47.1**

1. How does the fertilization envelope form in sea urchins? What is its function?
2. **WHAT IF?** Predict what would happen if you injected Ca^{2+} into an unfertilized sea urchin egg.
3. **MAKE CONNECTIONS** Review Figure 12.17 on page 240. Would you expect MPF activity to fluctuate or remain steady during cleavage? Explain your logic.

For suggested answers, see Appendix A.

CONCEPT **47.2**

Morphogenesis in animals involves specific changes in cell shape, position, and survival

After cleavage, the rate of cell division slows considerably as the normal cell cycle is restored. The last two stages of embryonic

development are responsible for **morphogenesis**, the cellular and tissue-based processes by which the animal body takes shape. During **gastrulation**, a set of cells at or near the surface of the blastula moves to an interior location, cell layers are established, and a primitive digestive tube is formed. Further transformation occurs during **organogenesis**, the formation of organs. We will discuss these two stages in turn, focusing in each case on the development of a few model organisms.

Gastrulation

Gastrulation is a dramatic reorganization of the hollow blastula into a two-layered or three-layered embryo called a **gastrula**. The cell layers produced by gastrulation are collectively called the embryonic **germ layers** (from the Latin *germen*, to sprout or germinate). In the late gastrula, **ectoderm** forms the outer layer and **endoderm** lines the embryonic digestive compartment or tract. In cnidarians and a few other radially symmetrical animals, only these two germ layers form during gastrulation. Such animals are called diploblasts (see Chapter 32). In contrast, animals with bilateral symmetry are triploblasts, having a third germ layer, the **mesoderm**, between the ectoderm and the endoderm.

Each germ layer contributes to a distinct set of structures in the adult animal **(Figure 47.8)**. Note that some organs and many organ systems of the adult derive from more than one germ layer. For example, the adrenal gland has both ectodermal and mesoderm tissue, and many other endocrine glands contain endodermal tissue.

ECTODERM (outer layer of embryo)

- Epidermis of skin and its derivatives (including sweat glands, hair follicles)
- Nervous and sensory systems
- Pituitary gland, adrenal medulla
- Jaws and teeth
- Germ cells

MESODERM (middle layer of embryo)

- Skeletal and muscular systems
- Circulatory and lymphatic systems
- Excretory and reproductive systems (except germ cells)
- Dermis of skin
- Adrenal cortex

ENDODERM (inner layer of embryo)

- Epithelial lining of digestive tract and associated organs (liver, pancreas)
- Epithelial lining of respiratory, excretory, and reproductive tracts and ducts
- Thymus, thyroid, and parathyroid glands

▲ Figure 47.8 **Major derivatives of the three embryonic germ layers in vertebrates.**

► **Figure 47.9 Gastrulation in a sea urchin embryo.** The movement of cells during gastrulation forms an embryo with a primitive digestive tube and three germ layers. Some of the mesodermal mesenchyme cells that migrate inward (step ❶) will eventually secrete calcium carbonate and form a simple internal skeleton. Embryos in steps ❶–❸ are viewed from the front, those in ❹ and ❺ from the side.

Animal pole

Blastocoel
Mesenchyme cells
Vegetal plate
Vegetal pole

❶ Once the blastula is formed, gastrulation begins with the migration of mesenchyme cells from the vegetal pole into the blastocoel.

❷ The vegetal plate invaginates. Mesenchyme cells migrate throughout the blastocoel.

Blastocoel
Filopodia pulling archenteron tip
Archenteron
Mesenchyme cells
Blastopore
50 μm

❸ Endoderm cells form the archenteron (future digestive tube). New mesenchyme cells at the tip of the tube send out thin extensions (filopodia) toward the blastocoel wall (left, LM).

❹ The filopodia then contract, dragging the archenteron across the blastocoel.

Blastocoel
Archenteron
Blastopore

❺ Fusion of the archenteron with the blastocoel wall forms the digestive tube, which now has a mouth and an anus. The gastrula has three germ layers and is covered with cilia, which will function later in feeding and movement.

Ectoderm
Mouth
Mesenchyme (mesoderm forms future skeleton)
Digestive tube (endoderm)
Anus (from blastopore)

Key

■ Future ectoderm
■ Future mesoderm
□ Future endoderm

Gastrulation in Sea Urchins

Gastrulation in the sea urchin begins at the vegetal pole of the blastula (**Figure 47.9**). There, cells called *mesenchyme cells* individually detach from the blastocoel wall and enter the blastocoel. The remaining cells near the vegetal pole flatten slightly and cause that end of the embryo to buckle inward as a result of cell shape changes we will discuss later. This process—the infolding of a sheet of cells into the embryo—is called *invagination*. Extensive rearrangement of cells transforms the shallow depression into a deeper, narrower, blind-ended tube called the **archenteron**. The open end of the archenteron, which will become the anus, is called the **blastopore**. A second opening, which will become the mouth, forms when the opposite end of the archenteron touches the inside of the ectoderm and the two layers fuse, producing a rudimentary digestive tube.

As you learned in Chapter 32, animals can be categorized by whether the mouth develops from the first opening that forms in the embryo (protostomes) or the second (deuterostomes).

Sea urchins and other echinoderms are deuterostomes, as are chordates like ourselves and other vertebrates.

Upon completing gastrulation, sea urchin embryos develop into ciliated larvae that drift in ocean surface waters as zooplankton, feeding on bacteria and unicellular algae. Eventually, each larva metamorphoses into the adult form of the sea urchin, which takes up residence on the ocean floor.

Gastrulation in Frogs

The frog blastula contains large, yolk-laden cells in the vegetal hemisphere and a blastocoel wall that in most species is more than one cell thick. Recall from Chapter 32 that frogs and other bilaterally symmetrical animals have a dorsal (top) side and a ventral (bottom) side, a left side and a right side, and an anterior (front) end and a posterior (back) end. As shown in **Figure 47.10**, frog gastrulation begins when a group of cells on the dorsal side of the blastula begins to invaginate. This process forms a crease along the region where the gray crescent formed (see Figure 47.7). It may help to

1 Gastrulation begins when a small indented crease, the blastopore, appears on the dorsal side of the late blastula. The crease is formed by cells changing shape and invaginating. Sheets of outer cells then roll inward over the dorsal lip (involution) and move into the interior (shown by the dashed arrow), where they will form endoderm and mesoderm. Meanwhile, cells at the animal pole change shape and begin spreading over the outer surface.

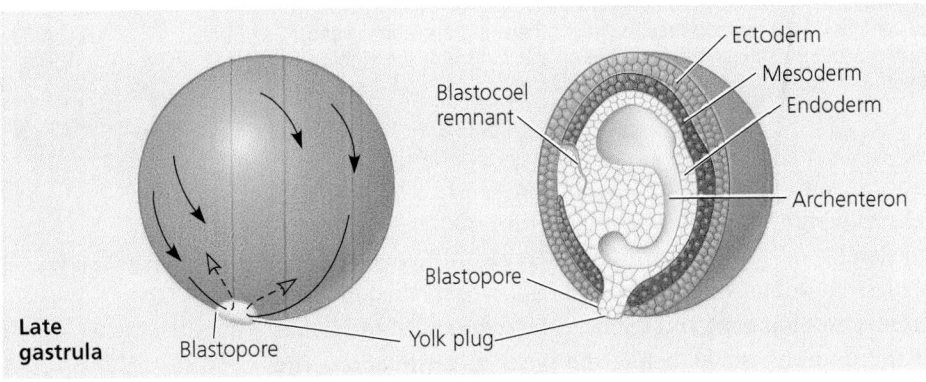

Animal pole

Blastocoel

Dorsal lip of blasto-pore

Dorsal lip of blastopore

Blastopore

Early gastrula   Vegetal pole

2 The blastopore extends around both sides of the embryo (red arrows) as more cells invaginate. When the ends meet, the blastopore forms a circle that becomes smaller as ectoderm spreads downward over the surface. Internally, continued involution expands the endoderm and mesoderm, and the archenteron begins to form; as a result, the blastocoel becomes smaller.

Blastocoel shrinking

Archenteron

3 Late in gastrulation, the endoderm-lined archenteron has completely replaced the blastocoel and the three germ layers are in place. The circular blastopore surrounds a plug of yolk-filled cells.

Ectoderm

Mesoderm

Endoderm

Blastocoel remnant

Archenteron

Key	
	Future ectoderm
	Future mesoderm
	Future endoderm

Blastopore

Late gastrula   Blastopore   Yolk plug

▲ **Figure 47.10 Gastrulation in a frog embryo.** In the frog blastula, the blastocoel is displaced toward the animal pole and is surrounded by a wall several cells thick. The cell movements that begin gastrulation occur on the dorsal side of the blastula, opposite where the sperm entered the egg.

think of this crease as the site where two thin lips are pressed together. The part above the crease becomes the dorsal side of the blastopore, called the **dorsal lip**.

As the blastopore is forming, a sheet of cells begins to spread out of the animal hemisphere. Some of these cells roll over the edge of the lip into the interior of the embryo, a process called *involution*. Once inside the embryo, these cells move away from the blastopore toward the animal pole and become organized into layers of endoderm and mesoderm, with the endoderm on the inside. Cells continue to spread over the gastrula surface, shifting and shrinking the blastopore. In the interior of the embryo, an archenteron forms and grows as the blastocoel shrinks and eventually disappears.

At the end of gastrulation, the cells remaining on the surface make up the ectoderm, the tube of endoderm is the innermost layer, and the mesoderm lies between them. As in the sea urchin, the frog's anus develops from the blastopore, and the mouth eventually breaks through at the opposite end of the archenteron.

Gastrulation in Chicks

The starting point for gastrulation in chicks is an embryo consisting of upper and lower layers—the *epiblast* and *hypoblast*—lying atop a yolk mass. All the cells that will form the embryo come from the epiblast. During gastrulation, some epiblast cells move toward the midline of the blastoderm, detach, and

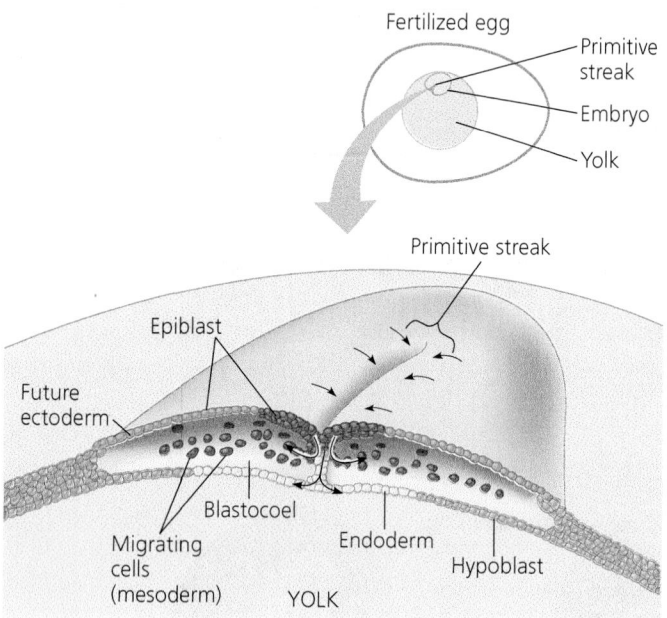

Fertilized egg

- Primitive streak
- Embryo
- Yolk

Primitive streak

- Epiblast
- Future ectoderm
- Blastocoel
- Migrating cells (mesoderm)
- Endoderm
- Hypoblast
- YOLK

▲ **Figure 47.11 Gastrulation in a chick embryo.** The chick blastula consists of an upper layer of cells, the epiblast, and a lower layer, the hypoblast, with a space (the blastocoel) between them. This is a cross section at a right angle to the primitive streak, looking toward the anterior end of a gastrulating embryo. During gastrulation, some cells of the epiblast migrate (arrows) into the interior of the embryo through the primitive streak. Some of these cells move downward and form endoderm, pushing aside the hypoblast cells, while others migrate laterally and form mesoderm. The cells left behind on the surface of the embryo at the end of gastrulation will become ectoderm.

move inward toward the yolk (**Figure 47.11**). The pileup of cells moving inward at the blastoderm's midline produces a thickening called the **primitive streak**. Although the hypoblast contributes no cells to the embryo, it is required for normal development and seems to help direct the formation of the primitive streak before the onset of gastrulation. The hypoblast cells later segregate from the endoderm and eventually form part of the sac that surrounds the yolk and also part of the stalk that connects the yolk mass to the embryo.

Gastrulation in Humans

Unlike the large, yolky eggs of many vertebrates, human eggs are quite small, storing little in the way of food reserves. Fertilization takes place in the oviduct, and the earliest stages of development occur while the embryo completes its journey down the oviduct to the uterus (see Figure 46.15). Knowledge about gastrulation in humans is therefore largely based on what we can extrapolate from other mammals, such as the mouse, and on observation of very early human development following *in vitro* fertilization.

Figure 47.12 depicts development of the human embryo starting about 6 days after fertilization. The description on page 1031 follows the numbered stages in the figure.

Uterus

- Endometrial epithelium (uterine lining)
- Inner cell mass
- Trophoblast
- Blastocoel

❶ Blastocyst reaches uterus.

- Maternal blood vessel
- Expanding region of trophoblast
- Epiblast
- Hypoblast
- Trophoblast

❷ Blastocyst implants (7 days after fertilization).

- Expanding region of trophoblast
- Amniotic cavity
- Epiblast
- Hypoblast
- Yolk sac (from hypoblast)
- Extraembryonic mesoderm cells (from epiblast)
- Chorion (from trophoblast)

❸ Extraembryonic membranes start to form (10–11 days), and gastrulation begins (13 days).

- Amnion
- Chorion
- Ectoderm
- Mesoderm
- Endoderm
- Yolk sac
- Extraembryonic mesoderm
- Allantois

❹ Gastrulation has produced a three-layered embryo with four extraembryonic membranes.

▲ **Figure 47.12 Four stages in the early embryonic development of a human.**

1 At the end of cleavage, the embryo has more than 100 cells arranged around a central cavity and has traveled down the oviduct to the uterus. At this stage of development, the embryo is called a **blastocyst**, the mammalian version of a blastula. Clustered at one end of the blastocyst cavity is a group of cells called the **inner cell mass**, which will develop into the embryo proper. It is the cells of the very early blastocyst stage that are the source of embryonic stem cell lines.

2 The **trophoblast**, the outer epithelium of the blastocyst, does not contribute to the embryo itself but instead supports embryo growth in a number of ways. It initiates implantation by secreting enzymes that break down molecules of the endometrium, the lining of the uterus. This allows the blastocyst to invade the endometrium. As the trophoblast thickens through cell division, it extends finger-like projections into the surrounding maternal tissue. Invasion by the trophoblast leads to erosion of capillaries in the endometrium, causing blood to spill out and bathe trophoblast tissues. Around the time of implantation, the inner cell mass of the blastocyst forms a flat disk with an upper layer of cells, the *epiblast*, and a lower layer, the *hypoblast*. As in birds, the human embryo develops almost entirely from epiblast cells.

3 Following implantation, the trophoblast continues to expand into the endometrium, and four new membranes appear. Although these **extraembryonic membranes** are formed by the embryo, they enclose specialized structures located outside the embryo. As implantation is completed, gastrulation begins. Cells move inward from the epiblast through a primitive streak and form mesoderm and endoderm, just as in the chick (see Figure 47.11).

4 By the end of gastrulation, the embryonic germ layers have formed. Extraembryonic mesoderm and the four extraembryonic membranes now surround the embryo. As development proceeds, the invading trophoblast, cells from the epiblast, and adjacent endometrial tissue will all contribute to formation of the placenta. This vital organ mediates exchange of nutrients, gases, and nitrogenous wastes between the embryo and the mother (see Figure 46.16).

Developmental Adaptations of Amniotes

EVOLUTION As you read in Chapter 34, birds and other reptiles, like mammals, form four extraembryonic membranes. In all these groups, such membranes provide a "life-support system" for further embryonic development. Why, then, did this adaptation appear in the evolutionary history of reptiles and mammals but not other vertebrates, such as fishes and amphibians? We can formulate a reasonable hypothesis by considering a few basic facts about embryonic development. All vertebrate embryos require an aqueous environment for their development. The embryos of fishes and amphibians usually develop in the surrounding sea or pond and need no specialized water-filled enclosure. However, the extensive colonization of land by vertebrates was possible only after the evolution of structures that would allow reproduction in dry environments. Two such structures exist today: (1) the shelled egg of birds and other reptiles as well as a few mammals (the monotremes) and (2) the uterus of marsupial and eutherian mammals. Inside the shell or uterus, the embryos of these animals are surrounded by fluid within a sac formed by one of the extraembryonic membranes, the amnion. Mammals and reptiles, including birds, are therefore called **amniotes** (see Chapter 34).

We can explore the evolution of extraembryonic membranes by comparing their functions in different groups of amniotes. For the purposes of this discussion, you may find it useful to refer to Figure 34.26, which describes the functions of the extraembryonic membranes in the egg of a reptile.

For the most part, the extraembryonic membranes have similar functions in mammals and reptiles, consistent with a common evolutionary origin. The chorion is the site of gas exchange, and the fluid within the amnion physically protects the developing embryo. (This amniotic fluid is released from the vagina when a pregnant woman's "water breaks" just before childbirth.) The allantois, which disposes of wastes in the reptilian egg, is incorporated into the umbilical cord in mammals. There it forms blood vessels that transport oxygen and nutrients from the placenta to the embryo and rid the embryo of carbon dioxide and nitrogenous wastes. The fourth extraembryonic membrane, the yolk sac, encloses yolk in the eggs of reptiles. In mammals it is a site of early formation of blood cells, which later migrate into the embryo proper. Thus, although the extraembryonic membranes of reptiles were conserved in mammals in the course of evolution, modifications appeared that were adapted to development within the uterus of the mother.

After gastrulation is complete and any extraembryonic membranes are formed, the next stage of embryonic development begins: organ formation.

Organogenesis

During organogenesis, regions of the three embryonic germ layers develop into the rudiments of organs. Whereas gastrulation involves mass movements of cells, organogenesis involves

Neural folds

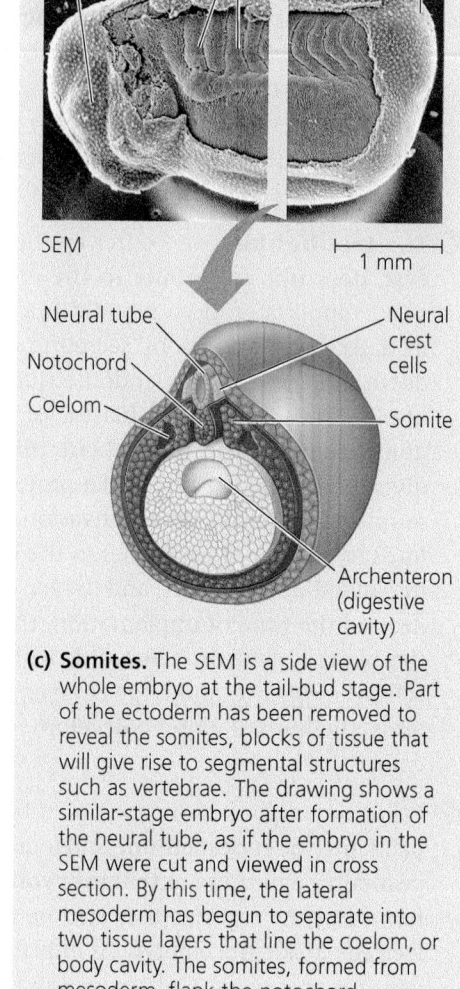

├─── 1 mm ───┤

Neural fold — Neural plate

Notochord
Ectoderm
Mesoderm
Endoderm
Archenteron

(a) Neural plate formation. By this stage, the notochord has developed from dorsal mesoderm, and the dorsal ectoderm has thickened, forming the neural plate, in response to signals from other embryonic tissues. The neural folds are the two ridges that form the lateral edges of the neural plate. These folds are visible in the LM of a whole embryo.

Neural fold — Neural plate

Neural crest cells

Outer layer of ectoderm

Neural crest cells

Neural tube

(b) Neural tube formation. Infolding and pinching off of the neural plate generates the neural tube. Note the neural crest cells, which will migrate and give rise to numerous structures. (See also Figure 34.7.)

Eye — Somites — Tail bud

SEM ├─── 1 mm ───┤

Neural tube — Neural crest cells
Notochord
Coelom — Somite

Archenteron (digestive cavity)

(c) Somites. The SEM is a side view of the whole embryo at the tail-bud stage. Part of the ectoderm has been removed to reveal the somites, blocks of tissue that will give rise to segmental structures such as vertebrae. The drawing shows a similar-stage embryo after formation of the neural tube, as if the embryo in the SEM were cut and viewed in cross section. By this time, the lateral mesoderm has begun to separate into two tissue layers that line the coelom, or body cavity. The somites, formed from mesoderm, flank the notochord.

▲ **Figure 47.13 Neurulation in a frog embryo.**

more localized changes. To illustrate the basic principles of this process, we'll focus on *neurulation*, the first steps in the formation of the brain and spinal cord in vertebrates.

Neurulation begins as cells from the dorsal mesoderm come together to form the **notochord**, the rod that extends along the dorsal side of the chordate embryo, seen in **Figure 47.13a** for the frog. Signaling molecules secreted by these mesodermal cells and other tissues induce the ectoderm above the notochord to become the *neural plate*. Next, the cells of the neural plate change shape, curving the neural plate inward. In this way, the neural plate rolls itself into the **neural tube**, which runs along the anterior-posterior axis of the embryo **(Figure 47.13b)**. The neural tube will become the brain in the head and the spinal cord along the rest of the body.

In vertebrate embryos, two sets of cells develop near the neural tube and then migrate elsewhere in the body. The first

set is a band of cells called the **neural crest**, which develops along the borders where the neural tube pinches off from the ectoderm. Neural crest cells subsequently migrate to many parts of the embryo, forming a variety of tissues that include peripheral nerves as well as parts of the teeth and skull bones. The second set of migratory cells is formed when groups of cells located in strips of mesoderm lateral to the notochord separate into blocks called **somites** **(Figure 47.13c)**. The somites are arranged serially on both sides along the length of the notochord. Parts of the somites dissociate into mesenchyme cells, which migrate individually to new locations.

Somites play a major role in organizing the segmented structure of the vertebrate body. One of the major functions of the mesenchyme cells that leave the somites is formation of the vertebrae. Although the notochord disappears before birth, parts of the notochord persist as the inner portions of

▶ **Figure 47.14**
Organogenesis in a chick embryo.

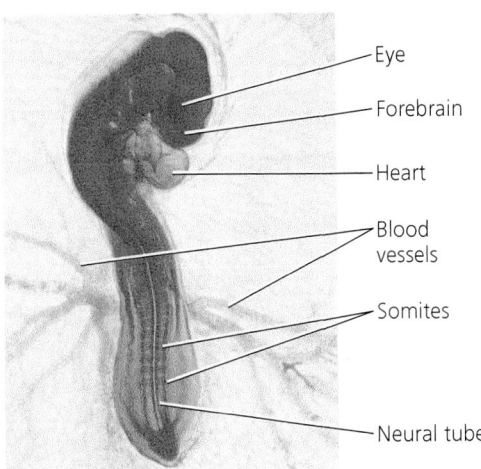

(a) Early organogenesis. The archenteron forms when lateral folds pinch the embryo away from the yolk. The embryo remains open to the yolk, attached by the yolk stalk, about midway along its length, as shown in this cross section. The notochord, neural tube, and somites subsequently develop much as they do in the frog. The germ layers lateral to the embryo itself form extraembryonic membranes.

(b) Late organogenesis. Rudiments of most major organs have already formed in this chick embryo, which is 3 days old and about 2–3 mm long. The extraembryonic membranes eventually are supplied by blood vessels extending from the embryo; several major blood vessels are seen here (LM).

the vertebral disks in adults. (These are the disks that can herniate or rupture, causing back pain.) Somite cells that become mesenchymal later form the muscles associated with the vertebral column and the ribs. Through these processes, serially repeating structures of the embryo (somites) form repeated structures in the adult. Chordates can thus be described as segmented animals, although the segmentation becomes less obvious later in development. Lateral to the somites, the mesoderm splits into two layers that form the lining of the body cavity, or coelom (see Figure 32.8).

Early organogenesis in other vertebrates is quite similar to that in the frog. In the chick, for example, the borders of the blastoderm fold downward and come together, pinching the embryo into a three-layered tube joined under the middle of the body to the yolk (Figure 47.14a). By the time the chick embryo is 3 days old, rudiments of the major organs, including the brain, eyes, and heart, are readily apparent (Figure 47.14b).

In humans, an error in neural tube formation results in *spina bifida*, the most common disabling birth defect in the United States. In spina bifida, a portion of the neural tube fails to develop or close properly, leaving an opening in the spinal column and causing nerve damage. Although the opening can be surgically repaired shortly after birth, the nerve damage is permanent, resulting in varying degrees of leg paralysis.

Organogenesis is somewhat different in invertebrates, which is not surprising, given that their body plans diverge significantly from those of vertebrates. The underlying mechanisms, however, involve many of the same cellular activities: cell migration, cell signaling between different tissues, and cell shape changes generating new organs. In insects, for example, tissues of the nervous system form when ectoderm

along the anterior-posterior axis rolls into a tube inside the embryo, similar to the vertebrate neural tube. Interestingly, the tube is on the ventral side of the insect embryo rather than the dorsal side, where it is in vertebrates. In spite of the different locations, the molecular signaling pathways that bring about the events in the two groups are very similar, underscoring their ancient shared evolutionary history.

As we have seen in our consideration of gastrulation and organogenesis, changes in cell shape and location are essential to early development. We will turn now to an exploration of how these changes take place.

Mechanisms of Morphogenesis

Morphogenesis is a major stage of development in both animals and plants, but only in animals does it involve the *movement* of cells. The rigid cell wall that surrounds plant cells prevents complex movements like those that occur during gastrulation and organogenesis. In animals, movement of parts of a cell can bring about changes in cell shape or enable a cell to migrate from one place to another within the embryo. Here we will consider some of the cellular components that contribute to these events. We'll begin with the roles of the microtubules and microfilaments that make up the cytoskeleton (see Table 6.1).

The Cytoskeleton in Morphogenesis

Reorganization of the cytoskeleton is a major force in changing cell shape during development. As an example, let's return to the topic of neurulation. At the onset of neural tube formation, microtubules oriented from dorsal to ventral in a sheet of ectodermal cells help lengthen the cells along that

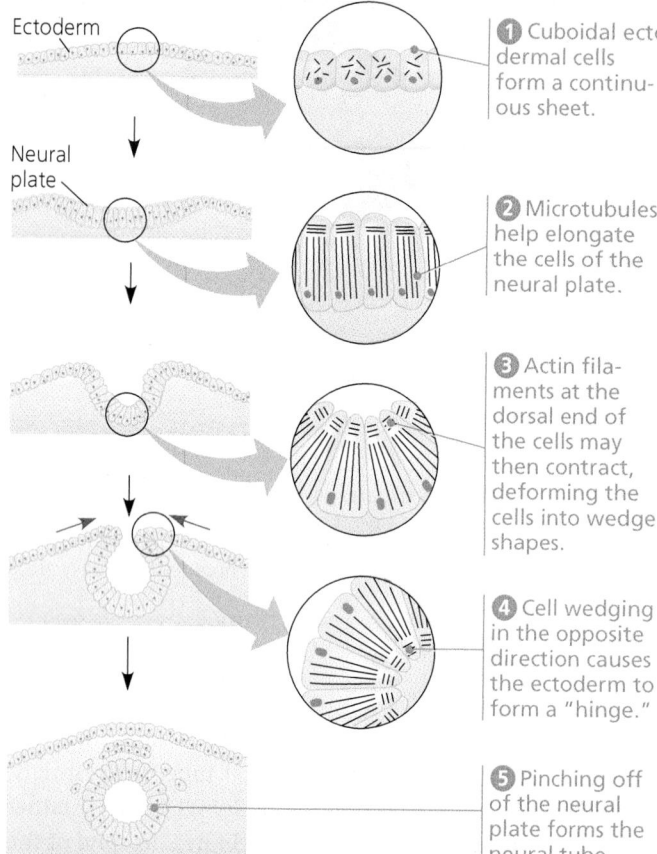

1 Cuboidal ecto-dermal cells form a continuous sheet.

2 Microtubules help elongate the cells of the neural plate.

3 Actin filaments at the dorsal end of the cells may then contract, deforming the cells into wedge shapes.

4 Cell wedging in the opposite direction causes the ectoderm to form a "hinge."

5 Pinching off of the neural plate forms the neural tube.

▲ **Figure 47.15 Change in cell shape during morphogenesis.** Reorganization of the cytoskeleton is associated with morphogenetic changes in embryonic tissues, as shown here for the formation of the neural tube in vertebrates.

axis (**Figure 47.15**). At the dorsal end of each cell is a bundle of actin filaments (microfilaments) oriented crosswise. These actin filaments contract, giving the cells a wedge shape that bends the ectoderm layer inward. Similar changes in cell shape occur at the hinge regions where the neural tube is pinching off from the ectoderm. However, the generation of wedge-shaped cells is not limited to neurulation or even to vertebrates. In *Drosophila* gastrulation, for instance, the formation of wedge-shaped cells along the ventral surface is responsible for invagination of a tube of cells that form the mesoderm.

The cytoskeleton directs a different type of morphogenetic movement in promoting elongation of the archenteron in the sea urchin embryo (see Figure 47.9). In this case, cytoskeletal changes direct **convergent extension**, a rearrangement of the cells of a tissue layer that causes the sheet to become narrower (converge) while it becomes longer (extends). It's as if a crowd of people waiting to

enter a theater for a concert began to form a single-file line; the line would become much longer as it narrowed. In the embryo, the cells elongate, with their ends pointing in the direction they will move, and they wedge between each other into fewer columns of cells (**Figure 47.16**). Convergent extension is also important in other developmental settings, such as involution in the frog gastrula. There, convergent extension changes the gastrulating embryo from a spherical shape to the rounded rectangular shape seen in Figure 47.13c.

The cytoskeleton is responsible not only for cell shape changes but also for cell migration. During organogenesis in vertebrates, cells from the neural crest and from somites migrate to locations throughout the embryo. Cells "crawl" within the embryo by using cytoskeletal fibers to extend and retract cellular protrusions. This type of motility is akin to the amoeboid movement described in Figure 6.27b. Transmembrane glycoproteins called *cell adhesion molecules* play a key role in cell migration by promoting interaction between pairs of cells. Cell migration also involves the *extracellular matrix (ECM)*, the meshwork of secreted glycoproteins and other macromolecules lying outside the plasma membranes of cells (see Figure 6.30). The ECM helps to guide cells in many types of movements, such as migration of individual cells and shape changes of cell sheets. Cells that line migration pathways regulate movement of migrating cells by secreting specific molecules into the ECM.

Programmed Cell Death

Just as certain cells of the embryo are programmed to change shape or location, others are programmed to die. A type of *programmed cell death* called **apoptosis** is in fact a common feature of animal development. At various times in development, individual cells, sets of cells, or whole tissues cease to develop and are engulfed by neighboring cells. In some cases, a structure functions in a larval or other immature form of the organism and then is eliminated during later development. One familiar example is provided by the cells in the tail of a tadpole, which undergo apoptosis during frog metamorphosis (see Figure 45.19). Apoptosis can also occur when cells compete with one another for survival. For instance, many more neurons are produced during development of the vertebrate nervous system than exist in the adult. In general, neurons survive if they make functional connections with other neurons and die if they do not.

Some cells that undergo apoptosis don't seem to have any function in the developing embryo. Why do such cells form? The answer can be found by considering the evolution of

▶ **Figure 47.16 Convergent extension of a sheet of cells.** In this simplified diagram, the cells elongate in a particular direction and crawl between each other (convergence) as the sheet becomes longer and narrower (extension).

Convergence

Extension

amphibians, birds, and mammals. When these groups began to diverge during evolution, the developmental program for making a vertebrate body was already in place. The differences in present-day body forms arose through modification of that common developmental program (which is why the early embryos of all vertebrates look so similar). As these groups evolved, many structures produced by the ancestral program that no longer offered a selective advantage were targeted for cell death. For example, the shared developmental program generates webbing between the embryonic digits, but in many birds and mammals the webbing is eliminated by apoptosis (see Figure 11.22).

As you have seen, cell behavior and the molecular mechanisms underlying it are crucial to the morphogenesis of the embryo. In the next section, you'll learn that a shared set of cellular and genetic processes ensure that the various types of cells end up in the right places in each embryo.

CONCEPT CHECK 47.2

1. In the frog embryo, convergent extension elongates the notochord. Explain how the words *convergent* and *extension* apply to this process.
2. **WHAT IF?** Predict what would happen if, just before neural tube formation, you treated embryos with a drug that blocks the function of microfilaments.
3. **MAKE CONNECTIONS** Unlike some other types of birth defects, neural tube defects are largely preventable. Explain (see Figure 41.4, p. 879).

For suggested answers, see Appendix A.

CONCEPT 47.3

Cytoplasmic determinants and inductive signals contribute to cell fate specification

During embryonic development, cells arise by division, take up particular locations in the body, and become specialized in structure and function. Where a cell resides, how it appears, and what it does define its development fate. Developmental biologists use the terms **determination** to refer to the process by which a cell or group of cells becomes committed to a particular fate and **differentiation** to refer to the resulting specialization in structure and function.

Every diploid cell formed during an animal's development has the same genome. With the exception of certain mature immune cells, the collection of genes present is the same throughout the cell's life. How, then, do cells acquire different fates? As discussed in Concept 18.4, particular tissues, and often cells within a tissue, differ from one another by expressing distinct sets of genes from their shared genome.

A major focus of developmental biology is to uncover the mechanisms that direct the differences in gene expression underlying developmental fates. As one step toward this goal, scientists often seek to trace tissues and cell types back to their origins in the early embryo.

Fate Mapping

One way to trace the ancestry of embryonic cells is direct observation through the microscope. Such studies produced the first **fate maps**, diagrams showing the structures arising from each region of an embryo. In the 1920s, German embryologist Walther Vogt used this approach to determine where groups of cells from the blastula end up in the gastrula (Figure 47.17a). Later researchers developed techniques that allowed them to mark an individual blastomere during cleavage and then follow the marker as it was distributed to all the mitotic descendants of that cell (Figure 47.17b).

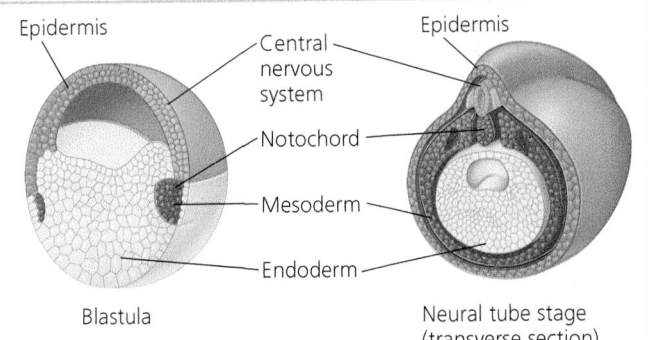

(a) **Fate map of a frog embryo.** The fates of groups of cells in a frog blastula (left) were determined in part by marking different regions of the blastula surface with nontoxic dyes of various colors. The embryos were sectioned at later stages of development, such as the neural tube stage shown on the right, and the locations of the dyed cells determined. The two embryonic stages shown here represent the result of numerous such experiments.

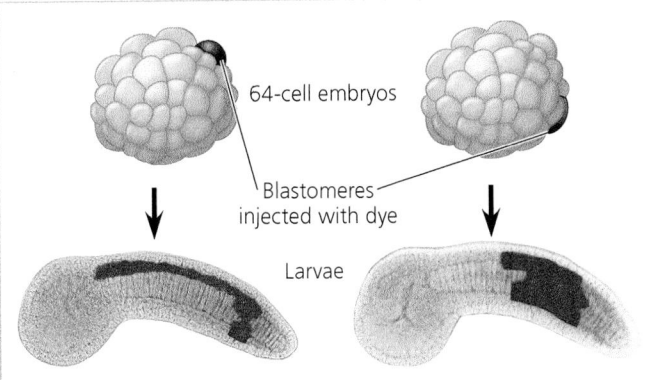

(b) **Cell lineage analysis in a tunicate.** In lineage analysis, an individual blastomere is injected with a dye during cleavage, as indicated in the drawings of 64-cell embryos of a tunicate, an invertebrate chordate (top). The dark regions in the light micrographs of larvae (bottom) correspond to the cells that developed from the two different blastomeres indicated in the drawings.

▲ Figure 47.17 **Fate mapping for two chordates.**

A much more comprehensive approach to fate mapping has been carried out on the soil-dwelling nematode *Caenorhabditis elegans*. This roundworm is about 1 mm long, has a simple, transparent body with only a few types of cells, and develops into a mature adult hermaphrodite in only 3½ days in the laboratory. These attributes allowed Sydney Brenner, Robert Horvitz, and John Sulston to determine the complete cell lineage of *C. elegans*. They found that every adult hermaphrodite has exactly 959 somatic cells, which arise from the fertilized egg in virtually the same way for every individual. Careful microscopic observations of worms at all stages of development, coupled with experiments in which particular cells or groups of cells were destroyed by a laser beam or through mutations, resulted in the cell lineage diagram shown in **Figure 47.18**.

As an example of a particular cell fate, we'll consider *germ cells*, the specialized cells that give rise to eggs or sperm. In all animals studied, complexes of RNA and protein are involved in the specification of germ cell fate. In *C. elegans*, such complexes, called *P granules*, persist throughout development and can be detected in the germ cells of the adult gonad (**Figure 47.19**).

▲ **Figure 47.19 Determination of germ cell fate in C. elegans.** Labeling with an antibody specific for a *C. elegans* P granule protein (green) reveals the specific incorporation of P granules into the cells of the adult worm that will produce sperm or eggs.

Tracing the position of the P granules provides a dramatic illustration of cell fate specification during development. The P granules are distributed throughout the newly fertilized egg but move to the posterior end of the zygote before the first cleavage division (**Figure 47.20 ❶** and **❷**). As a result, only the posterior of the two cells formed by the first division contains P granules (**Figure 47.20 ❸**). The P granules continue to be asymmetrically partitioned during subsequent divisions (**Figure 47.20 ❹**). Thus, the P granules act as cytoplasmic determinants (see Concept 18.4), fixing germ cell fate at the earliest stage of *C. elegans* development.

Fate mapping in *C. elegans* paved the way for major discoveries about programmed cell death. Lineage analysis demonstrated that exactly 131 cells die during normal *C. elegans* development. In the 1980s, researchers found that a mutation inactivating a single gene allows all 131 cells to live. Further research revealed that this gene is part of a pathway that controls and carries out apoptosis in a wide range of animals, including humans. In 2002, Brenner, Horvitz, and Sulston shared a Nobel Prize for their use of the *C. elegans* fate map in studies of programmed cell death and organogenesis.

Having established fate maps for early development, scientists were positioned to answer questions about underlying mechanisms, such as how the basic axes of the embryo are established, a process known as axis formation.

Axis Formation

A body plan with bilateral symmetry is found across a range of animals, including nematodes, echinoderms, and vertebrates (see Chapter 32). As shown for a frog tadpole in **Figure 47.21a**, this body plan exhibits asymmetry along the dorsal-ventral and anterior-posterior axes. The right-left axis is largely symmetrical, as

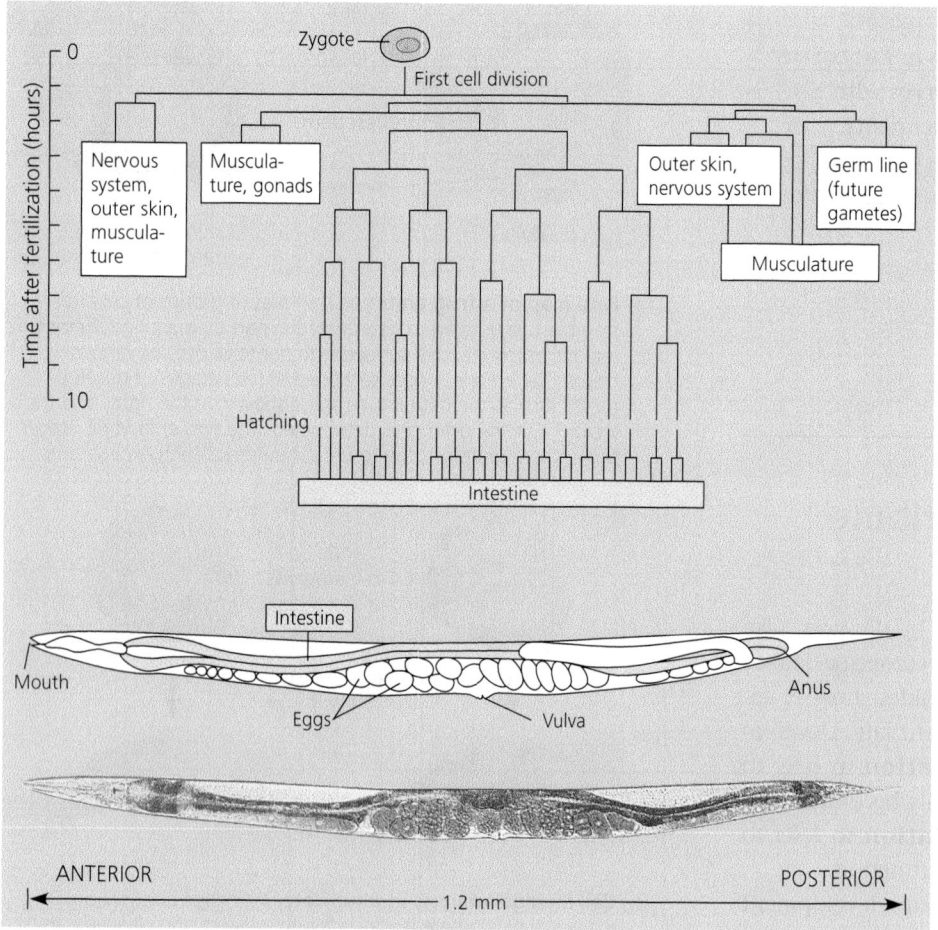

▲ **Figure 47.18 Cell lineage in *Caenorhabditis elegans*.** The *C. elegans* embryo is transparent, making it possible for researchers to trace the lineage of every cell, from the zygote to the adult worm (LM). The diagram shows a detailed lineage only for the intestine, which is derived exclusively from one of the first four cells formed from the zygote. The eggs will be fertilized internally and released through the vulva.

1 Newly fertilized egg

2 Zygote prior to first division

3 Two-cell embryo

4 Four-cell embryo

▲ **Figure 47.20 Partitioning of P granules during *C. elegans* development.** The differential interference contrast micrographs (left) highlight the boundaries of nuclei and cells through the first two cell divisions. The immunofluorescence micrographs (right) show identically staged embryos stained with a labeled antibody specific for a P granule protein.

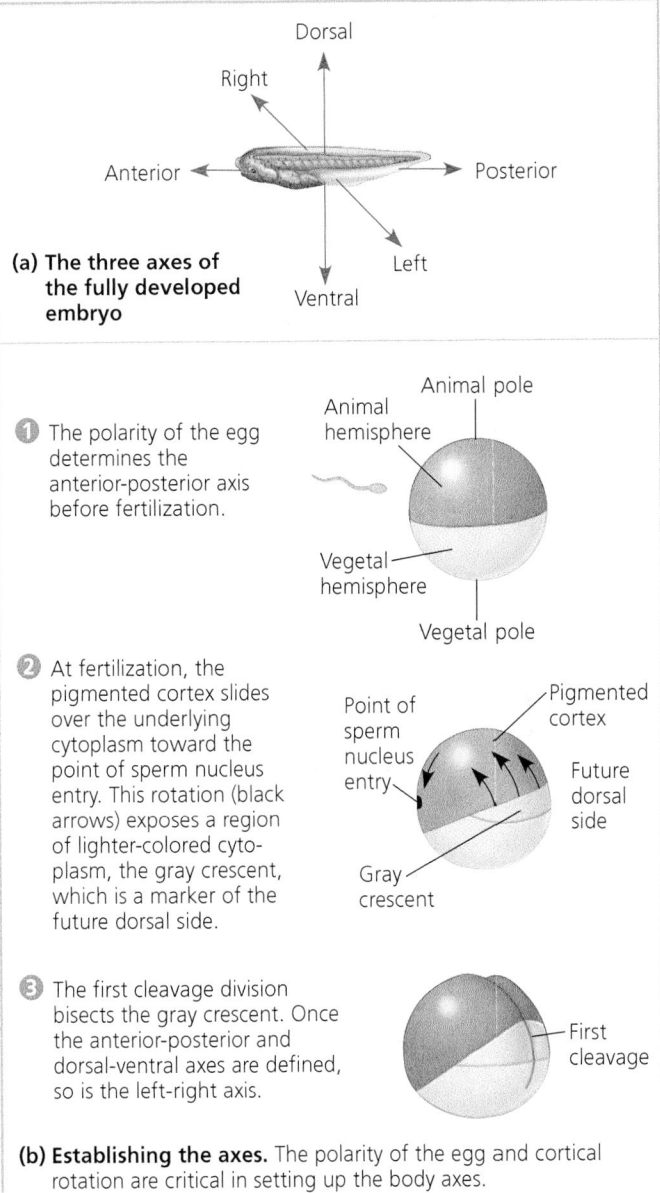

(a) The three axes of the fully developed embryo

1 The polarity of the egg determines the anterior-posterior axis before fertilization.

2 At fertilization, the pigmented cortex slides over the underlying cytoplasm toward the point of sperm nucleus entry. This rotation (black arrows) exposes a region of lighter-colored cytoplasm, the gray crescent, which is a marker of the future dorsal side.

3 The first cleavage division bisects the gray crescent. Once the anterior-posterior and dorsal-ventral axes are defined, so is the left-right axis.

(b) Establishing the axes. The polarity of the egg and cortical rotation are critical in setting up the body axes.

▲ **Figure 47.21 The body axes and their establishment in an amphibian.** All three axes are established before the zygote begins to undergo cleavage.

WHAT IF? *To study axis establishment, researchers can block cortical rotation or force it to occur in a specific direction. One such study resulted in a two-headed embryo because the "back" developed on both sides. What do you think the researchers did to obtain such an embryo?*

the two sides are roughly mirror images of each other. These three body axes are established early in development.

The anterior-posterior axis of the frog embryo is determined during oogenesis. Asymmetry is apparent in the formation of two distinct hemispheres: Dark melanin granules are embedded in the cortex of the animal hemisphere, whereas a yellow yolk fills the vegetal hemisphere. This animal-vegetal asymmetry dictates where the anterior-posterior axis forms in the embryo. Note, however, that the anterior-posterior and animal-vegetal axes are not the same; that is, the head of the embryo does not form at the animal pole.

The dorsal-ventral axis of the frog embryo is not determined until fertilization. Upon fusion of the egg and the sperm, the egg surface—the plasma membrane and associated cortex—rotates with respect to the inner cytoplasm, a movement called *cortical rotation*. From the perspective of the animal pole, this rotation is always toward the point of sperm entry **(Figure 47.21b)**.

How does cortical rotation establish the dorsal-ventral axis? Cortical rotation allows molecules in one portion of the vegetal cortex to interact with molecules in the inner cytoplasm of the animal hemisphere. These inductive interactions activate regulatory factors in specific portions of the vegetal cortex, leading to expression of different sets of genes in dorsal and ventral regions of the embryo.

In chicks, gravity is apparently involved in establishing the anterior-posterior axis as the egg travels down the hen's oviduct before being laid. Later, pH differences between the two sides of the blastoderm cells establish the dorsal-ventral axis. If the pH is artificially reversed above and below the blastoderm, the cells' fates will be reversed: The side facing the egg white will become the ventral part of the embryo, whereas the side facing the yolk will become the dorsal part.

In mammals, no polarity is obvious until after cleavage. However, the results of recent experiments suggest that the orientation of the egg and sperm nuclei before they fuse influences the location of the first cleavage plane and thus may play a role in establishing the embryonic axes. In insects, morphogen gradients establish both the anterior-posterior and dorsal-ventral axes (see Chapter 18).

Once the anterior-posterior and dorsal-ventral axes are established, the position of the left-right axis is fixed. Nevertheless, specific molecular mechanisms must establish which side is left and which is right. In vertebrates, there are marked left-right differences in the location of internal organs as well as in the organization and structure of the heart and brain. Recent research has revealed that cilia are involved in setting up this left-right asymmetry. We will discuss this and other developmental roles of cilia at the end of this chapter.

Restricting Developmental Potential

Earlier we described determination in terms of commitment to a particular cell fate. Is cell fate commitment immediately irreversible, or is there a period of time during which cell fate can be modified? The German zoologist Hans Spemann addressed this question in 1938. By manipulating embryos to perturb normal development and then examining cell fate after the manipulation, he was able to assay a

cell's *developmental potential*, the range of structures to which it can give rise (**Figure 47.22**). Spemann found that the fates of embryonic cells are affected by both the distribution of determinants and the pattern of cleavage relative to this distribution. Furthermore, the work of Spemann and others demonstrated that the first two blastomeres of the frog embryo are **totipotent**, meaning that they can each develop into all the different cell types of that species.

In mammals, embryonic cells remain totipotent through the eight-cell stage, much longer than in many other animals. Recent work, however, indicates that the very early cells (even the first two) are not actually equivalent in a normal embryo. Rather, their totipotency when isolated likely

▼ **Figure 47.22**

INQUIRY

How does distribution of the gray crescent affect the developmental potential of the first two daughter cells?

EXPERIMENT Hans Spemann, at the University of Freiburg-im-Breisgau, in Germany, carried out the following experiment in 1938 to test whether substances were located asymmetrically in the gray crescent.

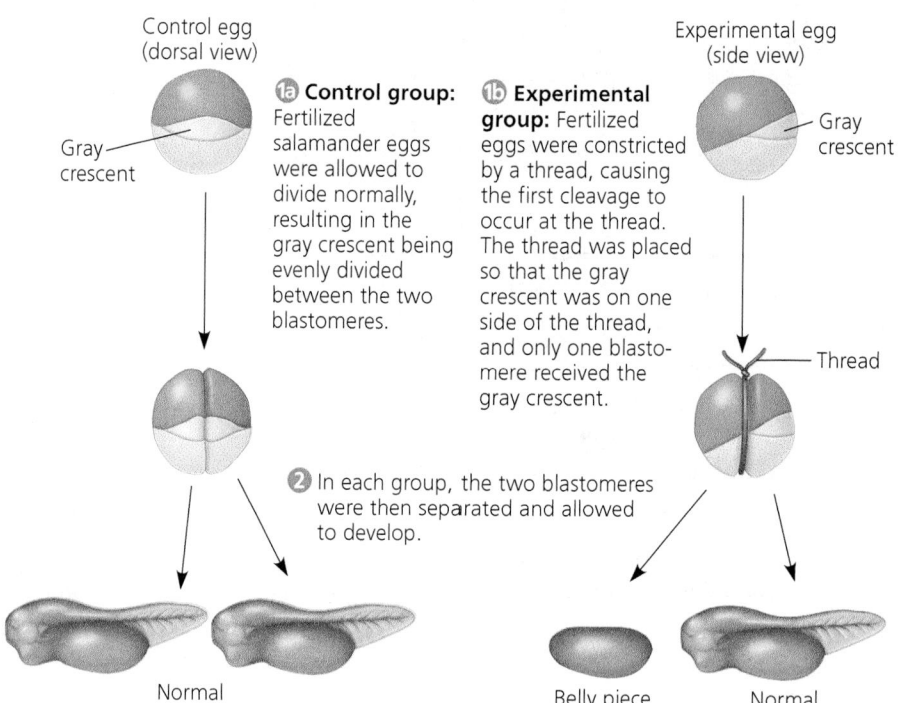

1a Control group: Fertilized salamander eggs were allowed to divide normally, resulting in the gray crescent being evenly divided between the two blastomeres.

1b Experimental group: Fertilized eggs were constricted by a thread, causing the first cleavage to occur at the thread. The thread was placed so that the gray crescent was on one side of the thread, and only one blastomere received the gray crescent.

2 In each group, the two blastomeres were then separated and allowed to develop.

RESULTS Blastomeres that received half or all of the material in the gray crescent developed into normal embryos, but a blastomere that received none of the gray crescent gave rise to an abnormal embryo without dorsal structures. Spemann called it a "belly piece."

CONCLUSION The developmental potential of the two blastomeres normally formed during the first cleavage division depends on their acquisition of cytoplasmic determinants localized in the gray crescent.

SOURCE H. Spemann, *Embryonic Development and Induction*, Yale University Press, New Haven, CT (1938).

WHAT IF? In a similar experiment 40 years earlier, embryologist Hans Roux allowed the first cleavage to occur and then used a needle to kill just one blastomere. The embryo that developed from the remaining blastomere (plus remnants of the dead cell) was abnormal, resembling a half-embryo. Propose a hypothesis to explain why Roux's result differed from the control result in Spemann's experiment.

means that the cells can regulate their fate in response to their embryonic environment. Once the 16-cell stage is reached, mammalian cells are determined to form the trophoblast or the inner cell mass. Although the cells have a limited developmental potential from this point onward, their nuclei remain totipotent, as demonstrated in cloning experiments like that described in Figure 20.19.

As you learned in Chapter 46, identical (monozygotic) twins can develop when embryonic cells become separated. If the separation occurs before the trophoblast and inner cell mass become differentiated, two embryos grow, each with its own chorion and amnion. This is the case for about a third of identical twins. For the rest, the two embryos that develop share a chorion and, in very rare cases where separation is particularly late, an amnion as well.

Regardless of how uniform or varied early embryonic cells are in a particular species, the progressive restriction of developmental potential is a general feature of development in all animals. In general, the tissue-specific fates of cells are fixed in a late gastrula, but not always so in an early gastrula. For example, if the dorsal ectoderm of an early amphibian gastrula is experimentally replaced with ectoderm from some other location in the same gastrula, the transplanted tissue forms a neural plate. But if the same experiment is performed on a late-stage gastrula, the transplanted ectoderm does not respond to its new environment and does not form a neural plate.

Cell Fate Determination and Pattern Formation by Inductive Signals

As embryonic cells acquire distinct fates, the cells begin to influence each other's fates by induction. At the molecular level, the response to an inductive signal is usually to switch on a set of genes that make the receiving cells differentiate into a specific tissue. Here we will examine two examples of induction, an essential process in the development of many tissues in most animals.

The "Organizer" of Spemann and Mangold

Before his studies of totipotency in the fertilized frog egg, Spemann had investigated cell fate determination during gastrulation. In these experiments, he and his student Hilde Mangold transplanted tissues between early gastrulas. In their most famous such experiment, summarized in Figure 47.23, they made a remarkable discovery. Not only did a transplanted dorsal lip of the blastopore continue to be a blastopore lip, but it also triggered gastrulation of the surrounding tissue. They concluded that the dorsal lip of the blastopore in the early gastrula functions as an "organizer" of the embryo's body plan, inducing changes in surrounding tissue that direct formation of the notochord, the neural tube, and other organs.

Nearly a century later, developmental biologists are still actively studying the basis of induction by *Spemann's organizer*. An important clue has come from studies of a growth factor called

▼ Figure 47.23 | INQUIRY

Can the dorsal lip of the blastopore induce cells in another part of the amphibian embryo to change their developmental fate?

EXPERIMENT In 1924, Hans Spemann and Hilde Mangold, at the University of Freiburg-im-Breisgau, in Germany, transplanted a piece of the dorsal lip from a pigmented newt gastrula to the ventral side of a nonpigmented newt gastrula to investigate the inductive ability of the dorsal lip. Cross sections of the gastrulas are shown here.

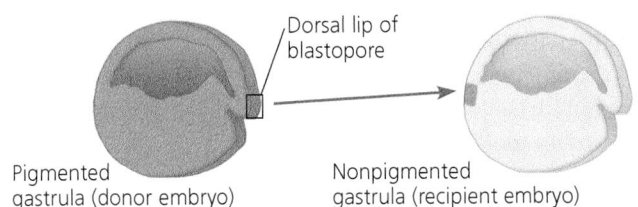

Dorsal lip of blastopore

Pigmented gastrula (donor embryo)

Nonpigmented gastrula (recipient embryo)

RESULTS The recipient embryo formed a second notochord and neural tube in the region of the transplant, and eventually most of a second embryo developed. Examination of the interior of the double embryo revealed that the secondary structures were formed partly, but not wholly, from recipient tissue.

Primary embryo

Secondary (induced) embryo

Primary structures:
Neural tube
Notochord

Secondary structures:
Notochord (pigmented cells)
Neural tube (mostly nonpigmented cells)

CONCLUSION The transplanted dorsal lip was able to induce cells in a different region of the recipient to form structures different from their normal fate. In effect, the transplanted dorsal lip "organized" the later development of an entire extra embryo.

SOURCE H. Spemann and H. Mangold, Induction of embryonic primordia by implantation of organizers from a different species, Trans. V. Hamburger (1924). Reprinted in *International Journal of Developmental Biology* 45:13–38 (2001).

WHAT IF? Because the transplanted dorsal lip caused the recipient tissue to become something it would not otherwise have become, a signal of some sort must have passed from the dorsal lip. If you identified a protein candidate for the signaling molecule, how could you test whether it actually functions in signaling?

bone morphogenetic protein 4 (BMP-4). (Bone morphogenetic proteins, a family of related proteins with a variety of developmental roles, derive their name from members of the family that are important in bone formation.) One major function of the cells of the organizer seems to be to *inactivate* BMP-4 on the dorsal side of the embryo. Inactivation of BMP-4 allows cells on the dorsal side to make dorsal structures, such as the notochord and neural tube. Proteins related to BMP-4 and its inhibitors are also found in other animals, including invertebrates such as the fruit fly, where they also regulate the dorsal-ventral axis.

Formation of the Vertebrate Limb

Inductive signals play a major role in **pattern formation**, the development of an animal's spatial organization, the arrangement of organs and tissues in their characteristic places in three-dimensional space. The molecular cues that control pattern formation, called **positional information**, tell a cell where it is with respect to the animal's body axes and help to determine how the cell and its descendants will respond to molecular signaling.

In Chapter 18, we discussed pattern formation in the development of *Drosophila*. For the study of pattern formation in vertebrates, a classic model system has been limb development in the chick. The wings and legs of chicks, like all vertebrate limbs, begin as limb buds, bumps of mesodermal tissue covered by a layer of ectoderm **(Figure 47.24a)**. Each component of a chick limb, such as a specific bone or muscle, develops with a precise location and orientation relative to three axes: the proximal-distal axis (the "shoulder-to-fingertip" axis), the anterior-posterior axis (the "thumb-to-little finger" axis), and the dorsal-ventral axis (the "knuckle-to-palm" axis). The embryonic cells within a limb bud respond to positional information indicating location along these three axes **(Figure 47.24b)**.

Two regions in a limb bud have profound effects on the limb's development. These regions are present in all vertebrate limb buds, including those that will develop into forelimbs (such as wings or arms) and those destined to become hind limbs. The cells of these regions secrete proteins that provide key positional information to the other cells of the bud.

One region regulating limb-bud development is the **apical ectodermal ridge (AER)**, a thickened area of ectoderm at the tip of the bud (see Figure 47.24a). Removing the AER blocks outgrowth of the limb along the proximal-distal axis. The cells of the AER secrete several protein signals in the fibroblast growth factor (FGF) family that promote limb-bud outgrowth. If the AER is surgically removed and beads soaked with FGF are put in its place, a nearly normal limb will develop. In 2006, researchers identified an FGF-secreting AER that appears to be responsible for building a shark's unpaired (median) fins. This finding suggests that the specific function of the AER predated the appearance of paired limbs in the vertebrate lineage.

The second major limb-bud regulatory region is the **zone of polarizing activity (ZPA)**, a block of mesodermal tissue located underneath the ectoderm where the posterior side of the bud is attached to the body (see Figure 47.24a). The ZPA is necessary for proper pattern formation along the anterior-posterior axis of the limb. Cells nearest the ZPA give rise to the posterior structures, such as the most posterior of the chick's three digits (positioned like our little finger); cells

(a) Organizer regions. Vertebrate limbs develop from protrusions called limb buds, each consisting of mesoderm cells covered by a layer of ectoderm. Two regions in each limb bud, the apical ectodermal ridge (AER, shown in this SEM) and the zone of polarizing activity (ZPA), play key roles as organizers in limb pattern formation.

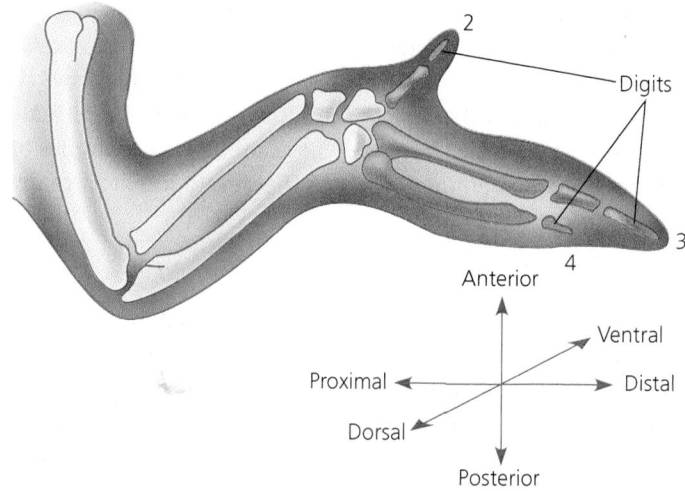

(b) Wing of chick embryo. As the bud develops into a limb, a specific pattern of tissues emerges. In the chick wing, for example, the digits are always present in the arrangement shown here. Pattern formation requires each embryonic cell to receive some kind of positional information indicating location along the three axes of the limb. The AER and ZPA secrete molecules that help provide this information. (Numbers are assigned to the digits based on a convention established for vertebrate limbs. The chicken wing has only four digits; the first digit points backward and is not shown in the diagram.)

▲ **Figure 47.24 Vertebrate limb development.**

farthest from the ZPA form anterior structures, including the most anterior digit (like our thumb).

The tissue transplantation experiment outlined in Figure 47.25 supports the hypothesis that the inductive signal produced by the ZPA conveys positional information indicating "posterior." Indeed, researchers have discovered that the cells of the ZPA secrete a growth factor called Sonic hedgehog. (Sonic hedgehog gets its name from two sources: its similarity to a *Drosophila* protein called Hedgehog, which is involved in segmentation of the fly embryo, and a video game character.) If cells genetically engineered to produce large amounts of Sonic hedgehog are implanted in the anterior region of a normal limb bud, a mirror-image limb results—just as if a ZPA had been grafted there. Studies of the mouse version of Sonic hedgehog suggest that extra toes in mice—and perhaps also in humans—can result when this protein is produced in part of the limb bud where it is normally absent. Sonic hedgehog and other similar Hedgehog proteins function in many developmental settings and organisms, including pattern formation in *Drosophila* and regulation of cell fate and number in the vertebrate nervous system.

Signaling by Sonic hedgehog plays a vital role in limb-bud development, but what determines whether a limb bud develops into a forelimb or a hind limb? It turns out that the cells receiving the Hedgehog signals from the AER and ZPA respond according to their developmental histories. Before the AER or ZPA issues its signals, earlier developmental signaling sets up specific spatial patterns of *Hox* gene expression (see Figure 21.18). Differences in *Hox* gene expression cause cells of the forelimb and hind limb buds—and cells in different parts of each limb bud—to react differently to the same positional cues.

Hedgehog, FGF, and BMP-4 are examples of a much larger set of signaling molecules that govern cell fates in animals. Having mapped out many of the basic functions of these molecules in embryonic development, researchers are now addressing their role in organogenesis, focusing in particular on the development of the brain.

Cilia and Cell Fate

For many years, developmental biologists largely ignored the cellular organelles known as cilia. That is no longer the case. There is now good experimental evidence that ciliary function is essential for proper specification of cell fate in the human embryo.

Like other mammals, humans have stationary and motile cilia (see Figure 6.24). Stationary primary cilia, or *monocilia*, exist as a single projection on the surface of nearly all cells. Motile cilia are found on cells that propel fluid over their surface, such as the epithelial cells of airways, and on sperm (in the form of flagella that propel sperm movement). Both stationary and motile cilia play vital roles in development.

In 2003, geneticists discovered that certain mutations disrupting development of the mouse nervous system affect

INQUIRY

▼ Figure 47.25

What role does the zone of polarizing activity (ZPA) play in limb pattern formation in vertebrates?

EXPERIMENT In 1985, Dennis Summerbell and Lawrence Honig, then at the National Institute for Medical Research in Mill Hill, near London, were eager to investigate the nature of the zone of polarizing activity. They transplanted ZPA tissue from a donor chick embryo under the ectoderm in the anterior margin of a limb bud in another chick (the host).

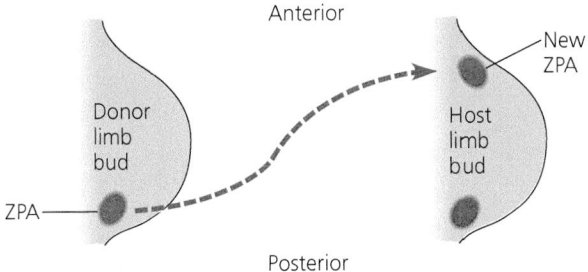

RESULTS The host limb bud developed extra digits from host tissue in a mirror-image arrangement to the normal digits, which also formed (compare with Figure 47.24b, which shows a normal chick wing).

CONCLUSION The mirror-image duplication observed in this experiment suggests that ZPA cells secrete a signal that diffuses from its source and conveys positional information indicating "posterior." As the distance from the ZPA increases, the signal concentration decreases, and hence more anterior digits develop.

SOURCE L. S. Honig and D. Summerbell, Maps of strength of positional signaling activity in the developing chick wing bud, *Journal of Embryology and Experimental Morphology* 87:163–174 (1985).

WHAT IF? Suppose you learned that the ZPA forms after the AER, leading you to develop the hypothesis that the AER is necessary for formation of the ZPA. Given what you know about molecules expressed in the AER and ZPA (see the text), how could you test your hypothesis?

genes that function in the assembly of monocilia. Other researchers found that mutations responsible for a severe kidney disease in mice alter a gene important for the transport of materials up and down monocilia. Mutations that block the function of monocilia have also been linked to cystic kidney disease in humans.

Given that monocilia are stationary, how do they function in development? The answer is that each acts as an antenna on the cell surface, receiving signals from multiple signaling

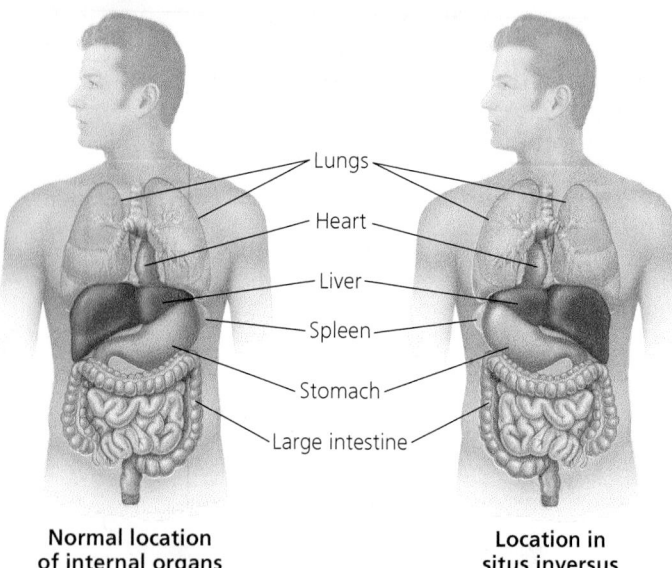

Lungs
Heart
Liver
Spleen
Stomach
Large intestine

Normal location
of internal organs

Location in
situs inversus

▲ Figure 47.26 **Situs inversus, a reversal of normal left-right asymmetry in the chest and abdomen.**

proteins, including Sonic hedgehog. When the monocilia are defective, signaling is disrupted.

Research on the role of motile cilia in development grew from the observation that certain individuals share a particular set of medical conditions, later named Kartagener's syndrome. Such individuals are prone to infections of the nasal sinuses and bronchi. Males with Kartagener's syndrome also produce immotile sperm. But the most intriguing feature of this syndrome is *situs inversus*, a reversal of the normal left-right asymmetry of the organs in the chest and abdomen (Figure 47.26). For example, in situs inversus, the heart is on the right side rather than the left. (About one in 10,000 individuals have situs inversus, which causes no significant medical problems by itself.)

The conditions associated with Kartagener's syndrome all result from a defect that makes cilia immotile. Without motility, sperm tails cannot beat and airway cells cannot sweep mucus and microbes out of the airway. But what causes situs inversus in these individuals? The current model proposes that ciliary motion in a particular part of the embryo is essential for normal development. Evidence indicates that movement of the cilia generates a leftward fluid flow, breaking the symmetry between left and right sides. Without that flow, asymmetry along the left-right axis arises randomly, and half of the affected embryos develop situs inversus.

If we step back from the specification of particular cell fates to consider development as a whole, we see a sequence of events marked by cycles of signaling and differentiation. Initial cell asymmetries allow different types of cells to influence each other, resulting in the expression of specific sets of genes. The products of these genes then direct cells to differentiate into specific types. Through pattern formation and morphogenesis, differentiated cells ultimately produce a complex arrangement of tissues and organs, each functioning in its appropriate location and in coordination with other cells, tissues, and organs throughout the organism.

CONCEPT CHECK 47.3

1. How do axis formation and pattern formation differ?
2. **MAKE CONNECTIONS** How does a morphogen gradient differ from cytoplasmic determinants and inductive interactions with regard to the set of cells it affects (see Concept 18.4, p. 367)?
3. **WHAT IF?** If the ventral cells of an early frog gastrula are experimentally induced to express large amounts of a protein that inhibits BMP-4, could a second embryo develop? Explain.
4. **WHAT IF?** If you removed the ZPA from a limb bud and then placed a bead soaked in Sonic hedgehog in the middle of the limb bud, what would be the most likely result?

For suggested answers, see Appendix A.

---

47 CHAPTER REVIEW

SUMMARY OF KEY CONCEPTS

CONCEPT 47.1

Fertilization and cleavage initiate embryonic development (pp. 1022–1027)

- **Fertilization** brings together the nuclei of sperm and egg, forming a diploid zygote, and activates the egg, initiating embryonic development. The **acrosomal reaction**, which is triggered when the sperm meets the egg, releases hydrolytic enzymes that digest material surrounding the egg. Gamete contact and/or fusion depolarizes the egg cell membrane and sets up a **fast block to polyspermy** in many animals. Sperm-egg fusion also initiates the cortical reaction.

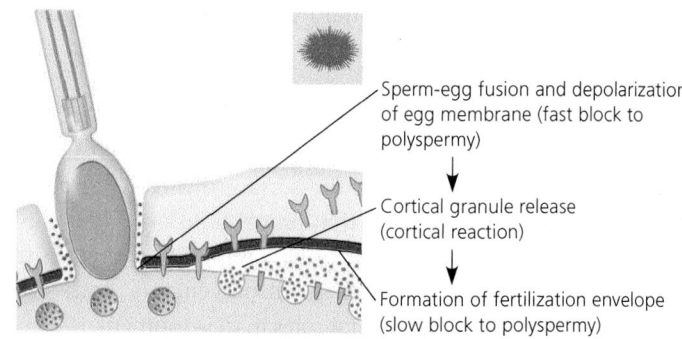

Sperm-egg fusion and depolarization of egg membrane (fast block to polyspermy)

Cortical granule release (cortical reaction)

Formation of fertilization envelope (slow block to polyspermy)

In mammalian fertilization, the cortical reaction modifies the zona pellucida as a **slow block to polyspermy**.

- Fertilization is followed by **cleavage**, a period of rapid cell division without growth, which results in the production of a large number of cells called **blastomeres**. In many species, cleavage creates a multicellular ball called the **blastula**, which contains a fluid-filled cavity, the **blastocoel**. **Holoblastic** cleavage (division of the entire egg) occurs in species whose eggs have little or moderate amounts of **yolk** (as in sea urchins, frogs, and mammals). **Meroblastic** cleavage (incomplete division of the egg) occurs in species with yolk-rich eggs (as in birds and other reptiles).

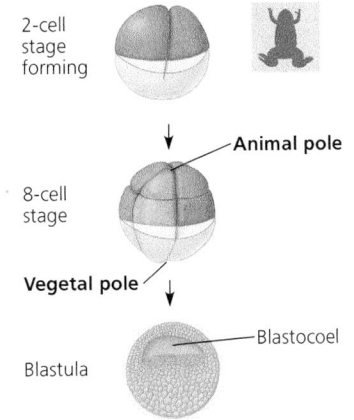

2-cell stage forming

Animal pole

8-cell stage

Vegetal pole

Blastocoel

Blastula

? *What cell-surface barrier prevents fertilization of an egg by a sperm of a different species?*

CONCEPT 47.2

Morphogenesis in animals involves specific changes in cell shape, position, and survival (pp. 1027–1035)

- **Gastrulation** converts the blastula to a **gastrula**, which has a primitive digestive cavity and three **germ layers**: **ectoderm** (blue), **mesoderm** (red), and **endoderm** (yellow).

- Mammalian eggs are small, store few nutrients, exhibit holoblastic cleavage, and show no obvious polarity. However, gastrulation and organogenesis in mammals resemble the processes in birds and other reptiles. After fertilization and early cleavage in the oviduct, the **blastocyst** implants in the uterus. The **trophoblast** initiates formation of the fetal portion of the placenta, and the embryo proper develops from a single layer of cells, the epiblast, within the blastocyst.
- The embryos of birds, other reptiles, and mammals develop within a fluid-filled sac that is contained within a shell or the uterus. In these organisms, the three germ layers give rise not only to embryonic tissue but also to the four **extraembryonic membranes**: the amnion, chorion, yolk sac, and allantois.
- The organs of the animal body develop from specific portions of the three embryonic germ layers. Early events in **organogenesis** in vertebrates include neurulation: formation of the **notochord** by cells of the dorsal mesoderm and development of the **neural tube** from infolding of the ectodermal neural plate.

Neural tube
Notochord
Coelom

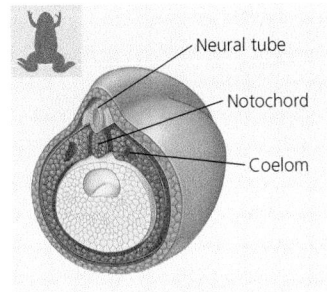

Neural tube
Notochord
Coelom

- Cytoskeletal rearrangements are responsible for changes in the shape of cells that underlie cell movements in gastrulation and organogenesis, including invaginations and **convergent extension**. The cytoskeleton is also involved in cell migration, which relies on cell adhesion molecules and the extracellular matrix to help cells reach specific destinations.

? *How does the neural tube form? How do neural crest cells arise?*

CONCEPT 47.3

Cytoplasmic determinants and inductive signals contribute to cell fate specification (pp. 1035–1042)

- Experimentally derived **fate maps** of embryos show that specific regions of the zygote or blastula develop into specific parts of older embryos. The complete cell lineage has been worked out for *C. elegans*. Mechanisms for establishing cellular asymmetries include morphogen gradients, localized determinants, and inductive interactions. As embryonic development proceeds, the developmental potential of cells becomes progressively more limited in all species.
- Cells in a developing embryo receive and respond to **positional information** that varies with location. This information is often in the form of signaling molecules secreted by cells in specific regions of the embryo, such as the dorsal lip of the blastopore in the amphibian gastrula and the **apical ectodermal ridge** and **zone of polarizing activity** of the vertebrate limb bud. The signaling molecules influence gene expression in the cells that receive them, leading to **differentiation** and the development of particular structures.

? *Suppose you found two classes of mouse mutations, one that affected limb development only and one that affected both limb and kidney development. Which class would be more likely to alter the function of monocilia? Explain.*

TEST YOUR UNDERSTANDING

LEVEL 1: KNOWLEDGE/COMPREHENSION

1. The cortical reaction of sea urchin eggs functions directly in
   a. the formation of a fertilization envelope.
   b. the production of a fast block to polyspermy.
   c. the release of hydrolytic enzymes from the sperm.
   d. the generation of an electrical impulse by the egg.
   e. the fusion of egg and sperm nuclei.

2. Which of the following is common to the development of both birds and mammals?
   a. holoblastic cleavage
   b. epiblast and hypoblast
   c. trophoblast
   d. yolk plug
   e. gray crescent

3. The archenteron develops into
   a. the mesoderm.   d. the placenta.
   b. the blastocoel.   e. the lumen of the
   c. the endoderm.   digestive tract.

4. What structural adaptation in chickens allows them to lay their eggs in arid environments rather than in water?
   a. extraembryonic membranes
   b. yolk
   c. cleavage
   d. gastrulation
   e. development of the brain from ectoderm

LEVEL 2: APPLICATION/ANALYSIS

5. In an egg cell treated with EDTA, a chemical that binds calcium and magnesium ions,
   a. the acrosomal reaction would be blocked.
   b. the fusion of sperm and egg nuclei would be blocked.
   c. the fast block to polyspermy would not occur.
   d. the fertilization envelope would not form.
   e. the zygote would not contain maternal and paternal chromosomes.

6. In humans, identical twins are possible because
   a. cytoplasmic determinants are distributed unevenly in unfertilized eggs.
   b. extraembryonic cells interact with the zygote nucleus.
   c. convergent extension occurs.
   d. early blastomeres can form a complete embryo if isolated.
   e. the gray crescent divides the dorsal-ventral axis into new cells.

7. Cells transplanted from the neural tube of a frog embryo to the ventral part of another embryo develop into nervous system tissues. This result indicates that the transplanted cells were
   a. totipotent.
   b. determined.
   c. differentiated.
   d. mesenchymal.
   e. apoptotic.

8. **DRAW IT** Fill in the blanks in the figure below, and draw arrows showing the movement of ectoderm, mesoderm, and endoderm.

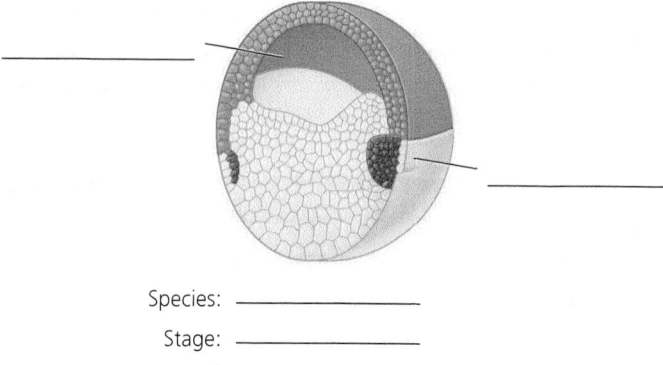

Species: _____

Stage: _____

LEVEL 3: SYNTHESIS/EVALUATION

9. **EVOLUTION CONNECTION**
   Evolution in insects and vertebrates has involved the repeated duplication of body segments, followed by fusion of some segments and specialization of their structure and function. What parts of vertebrate anatomy reflect the vertebrate segmentation pattern?

10. **SCIENTIFIC INQUIRY**
    The "snout" of a frog tadpole bears a sucker. A salamander tadpole has a mustache-shaped structure called a balancer in the same area. Suppose that you perform an experiment in which you transplant ectoderm from the side of a young salamander embryo to the snout of a frog embryo. The tadpole that develops has a balancer. When you transplant ectoderm from the side of a slightly older salamander embryo to the snout of a frog embryo, the frog tadpole ends up with a patch of salamander skin on its snout. Suggest a hypothesis to explain these results in terms of developmental mechanisms. How might you test your hypothesis?

11. **SCIENCE, TECHNOLOGY, AND SOCIETY**
    Many scientists think that fetal tissue transplants offer great potential for treating Parkinson's disease, epilepsy, diabetes, Alzheimer's disease, and spinal cord injuries. Why might tissues from a fetus be particularly useful for replacing diseased or damaged cells in patients with such conditions? Some people would allow only tissues from miscarriages to be used in fetal transplant research. However, most researchers prefer to use tissues from surgically aborted fetuses. Why? Explain your position on this controversial issue.

12. **WRITE ABOUT A THEME**
    Emergent Properties In a short essay (100–150 words), describe how the emergent properties of the cells of the gastrula direct embryonic development.

For selected answers, see Appendix A.

Mastering BIOLOGY   www.masteringbiology.com

1. MasteringBiology® Assignments
   Experimental Inquiry Tutorial How Do Calcium Ions Help to Prevent Polyspermy During Egg Fertilization?
   Tutorial Embryonic Development
   Activities Early Stages of Animal Development • Sea Urchin Development • Frog Development
   Questions Student Misconceptions • Reading Quiz • Multiple Choice • End-of-Chapter

2. eText
   Read your book online, search, take notes, highlight text, and more.

3. The Study Area
   Practice Tests • Cumulative Test • *BioFlix* 3-D Animations • MP3 Tutor Sessions • Videos • Activities • Investigations • Lab Media • Audio Glossary • Word Study Tools • Art

48

Neurons, Synapses, and Signaling

▲ Figure 48.1 **What makes this snail such a deadly predator?**

KEY CONCEPTS

48.1 Neuron organization and structure reflect function in information transfer

48.2 Ion pumps and ion channels establish the resting potential of a neuron

48.3 Action potentials are the signals conducted by axons

48.4 Neurons communicate with other cells at synapses

OVERVIEW

Lines of Communication

The tropical cone snail (*Conus geographus*) in **Figure 48.1** is both beautiful and dangerous. A carnivore, this marine snail hunts, kills, and dines on fish. Injecting venom with a hollow, harpoon-like part of its mouth, the cone snail paralyzes its free-swimming prey in seconds. The venom is so deadly that unlucky scuba divers have died from just a single injection. What makes cone snail venom so fast acting and lethal? As Baldomero Olivera discusses in the interview opening the unit (pp. 850–851), the answer is a mixture of molecules that disable **neurons**, the nerve cells that transfer information within the body. Because the venom almost instantaneously disrupts neuronal control of locomotion and respiration, an animal attacked by the cone snail can neither defend itself nor escape.

Communication by neurons largely consists of long-distance electrical signals and short-distance chemical signals. The specialized structure of neurons allows them to use pulses of electrical current to receive, transmit, and regulate the flow of information over long distances within the body. In transferring information from one cell to another, neurons often rely on chemical signals that act over very short distances. The cone snail's venom is particularly potent because it interferes with both electrical and chemical signaling by neurons.

Neurons transmit sensory information, control heart rate, coordinate hand and eye movement, record memories, generate dreams, and much more. All of this information is transmitted within neurons as an electrical signal. The identity of the type of information being transmitted is encoded by the connections made by the active neuron. Interpreting signals in the nervous system therefore involves sorting a complex set of neuronal paths and connections. In more complex animals, this higher-order processing is carried out largely in groups of neurons organized into a **brain** or into simpler clusters called **ganglia**.

In this chapter, we examine the structure of a neuron and explore the molecules and physical principles that govern signaling by neurons. In Chapter 49, we will look at the organization of nervous systems and at higher-order information processing in vertebrates. In Chapter 50, we will investigate systems that detect environmental stimuli and systems that carry out the body's responses to those stimuli. Finally, in Chapter 51, we will consider how these nervous system functions are integrated into the activities and interactions that make up animal behavior.

CONCEPT 48.1

Neuron organization and structure reflect function in information transfer

Before delving into the activity of an individual neuron, let's take an overall look at how neurons function in the flow of information through the animal body. We'll use as our example the squid, an organism that has some extraordinarily large nerve cells that played a crucial role in the discovery of how neurons transmit signals.

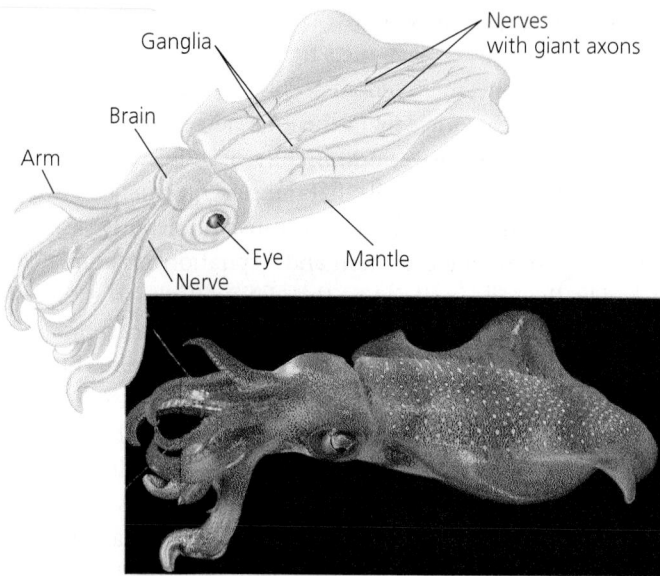

▲ **Figure 48.2 Overview of the squid nervous system.**
Signals travel from the brain to the muscular mantle along *giant axons*, nerve cell extensions of unusually large diameter.

Introduction to Information Processing

Like the cone snail in Figure 48.1, the squid in **Figure 48.2** is an active predator. Using its brain to process information captured by its image-forming eyes, the squid surveys its environment. When the squid spots prey, signals travel from its brain to neurons in its mantle, causing muscle contractions that propel the squid forward.

Information processing by a nervous system occurs in three stages: sensory input, integration, and motor output **(Figure 48.3)**. In many animals, the neurons that carry out integration are organized in a **central nervous system (CNS)**, which includes the brain and a longitudinal nerve cord. The neurons that carry information into and out of the CNS constitute the **peripheral nervous system (PNS)**. When bundled together, such neurons form **nerves**.

In all but the simplest animals, specialized populations of neurons handle each stage of information processing. **Sensory neurons** transmit information from eyes and other sensors that detect external stimuli (light, sound, touch, heat, smell, and taste) or internal conditions (such as blood pressure, blood carbon dioxide level, and muscle tension). This information is sent to processing centers in the brain or ganglia. Neurons in the brain or ganglia integrate (analyze and interpret) the sensory input, taking into account the immediate context and the animal's experience. The vast majority of neurons in the brain are **interneurons**, which form the local circuits connecting neurons in the brain. Motor output relies on neurons that extend out of the processing centers and trigger muscle or gland activity. For example, **motor neurons** transmit signals to muscle cells, causing them to contract. In exploring how this transmission of information flows within the nervous system, we'll begin with the unique structure of neurons.

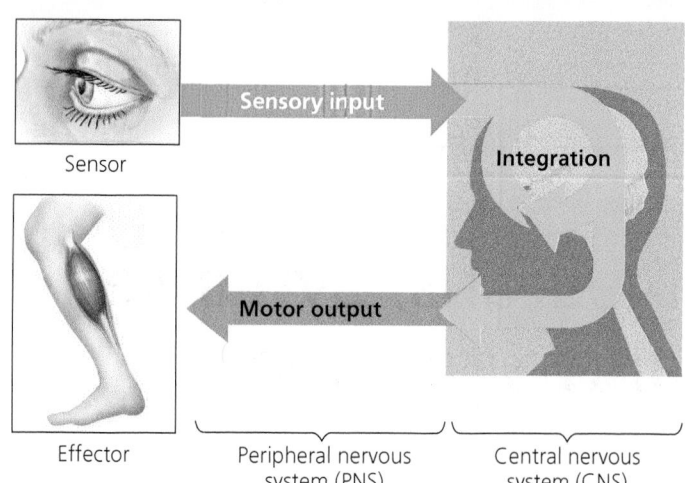

▲ **Figure 48.3 Summary of information processing.**

Neuron Structure and Function

The ability of a neuron to receive and transmit information is based on a highly specialized cellular organization **(Figure 48.4)**. Most of a neuron's organelles, including its nucleus, are located in the **cell body**. A typical neuron has numerous highly branched extensions called **dendrites** (from the Greek *dendron*, tree). Together with the cell body, the dendrites *receive* signals from other neurons. A neuron also has a single **axon**, an extension that *transmits* signals to other cells. Axons are often much longer than dendrites, and some, such as those that reach from the spinal cord of a giraffe to the muscle cells in its feet, are over a meter long. The cone-shaped base of an axon, the *axon hillock*, is typically where signals that travel down the axon are generated. Near its other end, an axon usually divides into many branches.

Each branched end of an axon transmits information to another cell at a junction called a **synapse** (see Figure 48.4). The part of each axon branch that forms this specialized junction is a *synaptic terminal*. At most synapses, chemical messengers called **neurotransmitters** pass information from the transmitting neuron to the receiving cell. In describing a synapse, we refer to the transmitting neuron as the *presynaptic cell* and the neuron, muscle, or gland cell that receives the signal as the *postsynaptic cell*.

Depending on the number of synapses a neuron has with other cells, its shape can vary from simple to quite complex **(Figure 48.5)**. Highly branched axons can transmit information to many target cells. Similarly, neurons with highly branched dendrites can receive input through large numbers of synapses, as many as 100,000 in the case of some interneurons.

The neurons of vertebrates and most invertebrates require supporting cells called **glial cells**, or **glia** (from a Greek word meaning "glue") **(Figure 48.6)**. Glia nourish neurons, insulate the axons of neurons, and regulate the extracellular fluid surrounding neurons. Overall, glia outnumber neurons in the mammalian brain 10- to 50-fold. We will examine the functions of specific glia later in this chapter and in Chapter 49.

▲ Figure 48.4 Neuron structure and organization.

CONCEPT CHECK 48.1

1. Describe the basic pathway of information flow through neurons that causes you to turn your head when someone calls your name.
2. **WHAT IF?** How might increased branching of an axon help coordinate responses to signals communicated by the nervous system?
3. **MAKE CONNECTIONS** Consider how communication occurs in a colony of bacteria (see Figure 11.3, p. 207). In what general ways is that communication similar to and different from transmission of a nerve impulse by a neuron?

For suggested answers, see Appendix A.

Dendrites

Axon

Cell body

Portion of axon

Sensory neuron   **Interneurons**   **Motor neuron**

▲ Figure 48.5 Structural diversity of neurons. Cell bodies and dendrites are black in these diagrams; axons are red. In the sensory neuron, unlike the other neurons here, the cell body is located partway along the axon that conveys signals from the dendrites to the axon's terminal branches.

80 μm

Glia

Cell bodies of neurons

▲ Figure 48.6 Glia in the mammalian brain. This micrograph (a fluorescently labeled laser confocal image) shows a region of the rat brain packed with glia and interneurons. The glia are labeled red, the DNA in nuclei is labeled blue, and the dendrites of neurons are labeled green.

Ion pumps and ion channels establish the resting potential of a neuron

As you read in Chapter 7, ions are unequally distributed between the interior of cells and the fluid that surrounds them. As a result, the inside of a cell is negatively charged relative to the outside. Because the attraction of opposite charges across the plasma membrane is a source of potential energy, this charge difference, or voltage, is called the **membrane potential**. The membrane potential of a resting neuron—one that is not sending a signal—is its **resting potential** and is typically between −60 and −80 mV (millivolts).

Inputs from other neurons or specific stimuli cause changes in the neuron's membrane potential that act as signals, transmitting and processing information. Rapid changes in membrane potential are what enable us to see a flower, read a book, or climb a tree. Thus, to understand how neurons function, we first need to examine how chemical and electrical forces form, maintain, and alter membrane potentials.

Formation of the Resting Potential

Potassium ions (K^+) and sodium ions (Na^+) play an essential role in the formation of the resting potential. Each type of ion has a concentration gradient across the plasma membrane of a neuron (Table 48.1). In the case of mammalian neurons, the concentration of K^+ is highest inside the cell, while the concentration of Na^+ is highest outside. These Na^+ and K^+ gradients are maintained by *sodium-potassium pumps* in the plasma membrane. As discussed in Chapter 7, these ion pumps use the energy of ATP hydrolysis to actively transport Na^+ out of the cell and K^+ into the cell (Figure 48.7). There are also concentration gradients for chloride ions (Cl^-) and other anions, as shown in Table 48.1, but we will ignore these for the moment.

A sodium-potassium pump transports three sodium ions out of the cell for every two potassium ions that it transports in. Although this pumping generates a net export of positive

Key

 Na^+ Sodium-potassium pump

 K^+ Potassium channel

 Sodium channel

▲ **Figure 48.7 The basis of the membrane potential.** The sodium-potassium pump generates and maintains the ionic gradients of Na^+ and K^+ shown in Table 48.1. The pump uses ATP to actively transport Na^+ out of the cell and K^+ into the cell. Although there is a substantial concentration gradient of sodium across the membrane, very little net diffusion of Na^+ occurs because there are very few open sodium channels. In contrast, the large number of open potassium channels allow a significant net outflow of K^+. Because the membrane is only weakly permeable to chloride and other anions, this outflow of K^+ results in a net negative charge inside the cell.

charge, the resulting voltage difference is only a few millivolts. Why, then, is there a voltage difference of 60–80 mV in a resting neuron? The answer lies in ion movement through **ion channels**, pores formed by clusters of specialized proteins that span the membrane. Ion channels allow ions to diffuse back and forth across the membrane. As ions diffuse through channels, they carry with them units of electrical charge. Any resulting *net* movement of positive or negative charge will generate a membrane potential, or voltage across the membrane.

The concentration gradients of K^+ and Na^+ across the plasma membrane represent a chemical form of potential energy. The ion channels that convert this chemical potential energy to electrical potential energy can do so because they have *selective permeability*, allowing only certain ions to pass. For example, a potassium channel allows K^+ to diffuse freely across the membrane, but not other ions, such as Na^+.

Table 48.1 Ion Concentrations Inside and Outside of Mammalian Neurons

Ion	Intracellular Concentration (mM)	Extracellular Concentration (mM)
Potassium (K^+)	140	5
Sodium (Na^+)	15	150
Chloride (Cl^-)	10	120
Large anions (A^-) inside cell, such as proteins	100	(not applicable)

Diffusion of K⁺ through open potassium channels is critical for formation of the resting potential. The K⁺ concentration is 140 m*M* inside the cell, but only 5 m*M* outside. The chemical concentration gradient thus favors a net outflow of K⁺. Furthermore, a resting neuron has many open potassium channels, but very few open sodium channels (see Figure 48.7). Because Na⁺ and other ions can't readily cross the membrane, K⁺ outflow leads to a net negative charge inside the cell. This buildup of negative charge within the neuron is the major source of the membrane potential.

What stops the buildup of negative charge? The excess negative charges inside the cell exert an attractive force that opposes the flow of additional positively charged potassium ions out of the cell. The separation of charge (voltage) thus results in an electrical gradient that counterbalances the chemical concentration gradient of K⁺.

Modeling the Resting Potential

The net flow of K⁺ out of a neuron proceeds until the chemical and electrical forces are in balance. How well do these two forces account for the resting potential in a mammalian neuron? To answer this question, let's consider a simple model consisting of two chambers separated by an artificial membrane (Figure 48.8a). To begin, imagine that the membrane contains many open ion channels, all of which allow only K⁺ to diffuse across. To produce a K⁺ concentration gradient like that of a mammalian neuron, we place a solution of 140 m*M* potassium chloride (KCl) in the inner chamber and 5 m*M* KCl in the outer chamber. The K⁺ will diffuse down its concentration gradient into the outer chamber. But because the chloride ions (Cl⁻) lack a means of crossing the membrane, there will be an excess of negative charge in the inner chamber.

When our model neuron reaches equilibrium, the electrical gradient will exactly balance the chemical gradient, so that no further net diffusion of K⁺ occurs across the membrane. The magnitude of the membrane voltage at equilibrium for a particular ion is called that ion's **equilibrium potential (E_{ion})**. For a membrane permeable to a single type of ion, E_{ion} can be calculated using a formula called the Nernst equation. At human body temperature (37°C) and for an ion with a net charge of 1+, such as K⁺ or Na⁺, the Nernst equation is

$$E_{ion} = 62 \text{ mV} \left(\log \frac{[\text{ion}]_{outside}}{[\text{ion}]_{inside}} \right)$$

Plugging in the K⁺ concentrations reveals that the equilibrium potential for K⁺ (E_K) is −90 mV (see Figure 48.8a). The minus sign indicates that K⁺ is at equilibrium when the inside of the membrane is 90 mV more negative than the outside.

Although the equilibrium potential for K⁺ is −90 mV, the resting potential of a mammalian neuron is somewhat less negative. This difference reflects the small but steady movement of Na⁺ across the few open sodium channels in a resting neuron. The concentration gradient of Na⁺ has a direction opposite to that of K⁺ (see Table 48.1). Na⁺ therefore diffuses into the cell, making the inside of the cell less negative. If we model a membrane in which the only open channels are selectively permeable to Na⁺, we find that a tenfold higher concentration of Na⁺ in the outer chamber results in an equilibrium potential (E_{Na}) of +62 mV (Figure 48.8b). In an actual neuron, the resting potential (−60 to −80 mV) is much closer to E_K than to E_{Na} because there are many open potassium channels but only a small number of open sodium channels.

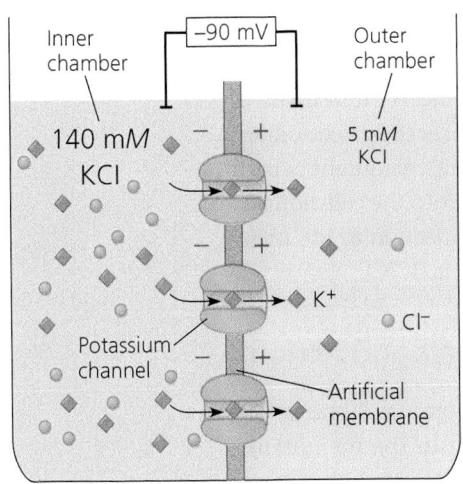

(a) **Membrane selectively permeable to K⁺**

Nernst equation for K⁺ equilibrium potential at 37°C:

$$E_K = 62 \text{ mV} \left(\log \frac{5 \text{ m}M}{140 \text{ m}M} \right) = -90 \text{ mV}$$

(b) **Membrane selectively permeable to Na⁺**

Nernst equation for Na⁺ equilibrium potential at 37°C:

$$E_{Na} = 62 \text{ mV} \left(\log \frac{150 \text{ m}M}{15 \text{ m}M} \right) = +62 \text{ mV}$$

◀ **Figure 48.8 Modeling a mammalian neuron.** Each container is divided into two chambers by an artificial membrane. Ion channels allow free diffusion for particular ions, resulting in the net ion flow represented by arrows. **(a)** The presence of open potassium channels makes the membrane selectively permeable to K⁺, and the inner chamber contains a 28-fold higher concentration of K⁺ than the outer chamber; at equilibrium, the inside of the membrane is −90 mV relative to the outside. **(b)** The membrane is selectively permeable to Na⁺, and the inner chamber contains a tenfold lower concentration of Na⁺ than the outer chamber; at equilibrium, the inside of the membrane is +62 mV relative to the outside.

WHAT IF? Adding channels specific for one type of ion to the membrane in (b) would alter the membrane potential. Which ion would pass through these channels, and in what direction would the membrane potential change?

Because neither K^+ nor Na^+ is at equilibrium in a resting neuron, each ion has a net flow (a current) across the membrane. The resting potential remains steady, which means that the K^+ and Na^+ currents are equal and opposite. Ion concentrations on either side of the membrane also remain steady. Keep in mind that the extent of ion movement required to generate the resting potential is extremely small (about 10^{-12} mole/cm^2 of membrane), far less than would be required to alter the chemical concentration gradient.

Under conditions that allow Na^+ to cross the membrane more readily, the membrane potential will move toward E_{Na} and away from E_K. As we will see in the next section, this is precisely what happens during the generation of a nerve impulse.

CONCEPT CHECK 48.2

1. Under what circumstances could ions flow through ion channels from regions of low ion concentration to regions of high ion concentration?
2. **WHAT IF?** Suppose a cell's membrane potential shifts from -70 mV to -50 mV. What changes in the cell's permeability to K^+ or Na^+ could cause such a shift?
3. **WHAT IF?** Ouabain, a plant substance used in some cultures to poison hunting arrows, disables the sodium-potassium pump. What change in the resting potential would you expect to see if you treated a neuron with ouabain? Explain.
4. **MAKE CONNECTIONS** Figure 7.13, on page 132, illustrates diffusion by dye molecules. Could diffusion eliminate the concentration gradient of a dye that has a net charge? Explain.

For suggested answers, see Appendix A.

CONCEPT 48.3

Action potentials are the signals conducted by axons

The membrane potential of a neuron changes in response to a variety of stimuli. Using the technique of intracellular recording, researchers can record and graph these changes as a function of time (Figure 48.9). Changes in the membrane potential occur because neurons contain **gated ion channels**, ion channels that open or close in response to stimuli. The opening or closing of gated ion channels alters the membrane's permeability to particular ions, which in turn alters the membrane potential.

Hyperpolarization and Depolarization

To explore how the membrane potential changes, let's consider what happens when gated potassium channels that are closed in a resting neuron are stimulated to open. Opening

▼ **Figure 48.9** **RESEARCH METHOD**

Intracellular Recording

APPLICATION Electrophysiologists use intracellular recording to measure the membrane potential of neurons and other cells.

TECHNIQUE A microelectrode is made from a glass capillary tube filled with an electrically conductive salt solution. One end of the tube tapers to an extremely fine tip (diameter < 1 μm). While looking through a microscope, the experimenter uses a micropositioner to insert the tip of the microelectrode into a cell. A voltage recorder (usually an oscilloscope or a computer-based system) measures the voltage between the microelectrode tip inside the cell and a reference electrode placed in the solution outside the cell.

these potassium channels increases the membrane's permeability to K^+. Net diffusion of K^+ out of the neuron increases, shifting the membrane potential toward E_K (-90 mV at 37°C). This increase in the magnitude of the membrane potential, called a **hyperpolarization**, makes the inside of the membrane more negative (Figure 48.10a). In a resting neuron, hyperpolarization results from any stimulus that increases the outflow of positive ions or the inflow of negative ions.

Although opening potassium channels in a resting neuron causes hyperpolarization, opening some other types of ion channels has an opposite effect, making the inside of the membrane less negative (Figure 48.10b). A reduction in the magnitude of the membrane potential is called a **depolarization**. Depolarization in neurons often involves gated sodium channels. If a stimulus causes the gated sodium channels in a resting neuron to open, the membrane's permeability to Na^+ increases. Na^+ diffuses into the cell along its concentration gradient, causing a depolarization as the membrane potential shifts toward E_{Na} ($+62$ mV at 37°C).

Graded Potentials and Action Potentials

Sometimes, the response to hyperpolarization or depolarization is simply a shift in the membrane potential. This shift, called a **graded potential**, has a magnitude that varies with the strength of the stimulus, with a larger stimulus causing a greater change in the membrane potential. Graded potentials induce a small electrical current that leaks out of the neuron as it flows along the membrane. Graded potentials

(a) Graded hyperpolarizations produced by two stimuli that increase membrane permeability to K⁺. The larger stimulus produces a larger hyperpolarization.

(b) Graded depolarizations produced by two stimuli that increase membrane permeability to Na⁺. The larger stimulus produces a larger depolarization.

(c) Action potential triggered by a depolarization that reaches the threshold.

▲ **Figure 48.10 Graded potentials and an action potential in a neuron.**

DRAW IT *Redraw the graph in part (c), extending the y-axis. Then label the positions of E_K and E_{Na}.*

thus decay with distance from their source. Although graded potentials are not the nerve signals that travel along axons, they have a major effect on the generation of nerve signals.

If a depolarization shifts the membrane potential sufficiently, the result is a massive change in membrane voltage called an **action potential**. Unlike graded potentials, action potentials have a constant magnitude and can regenerate in adjacent regions of the membrane. Action potentials can therefore spread along axons, making them well suited for transmitting a signal over long distances.

Action potentials arise because some of the ion channels in neurons are **voltage-gated ion channels**, opening or closing when the membrane potential passes a particular level. If a depolarization opens voltage-gated sodium channels, the resulting flow of Na⁺ into the neuron results in further depolarization. Because the sodium channels are voltage gated, an increased depolarization causes more sodium channels to open, leading to an even greater flow of current. The result is a process of *positive feedback* (see Figure 1.13) that triggers a very rapid opening of all voltage-gated sodium channels and the marked change in membrane potential that defines an action potential (**Figure 48.10c**).

Action potentials occur whenever a depolarization increases the membrane voltage to a particular value, called the **threshold**. For mammalian neurons, the threshold is a membrane potential of about −55 mV. Once initiated, the action potential has a magnitude that is independent of the strength of the triggering stimulus. Because action potentials

occur fully or not at all, they represent an *all-or-none* response to stimuli. This all-or-none property reflects the fact that depolarization opens voltage-gated sodium channels, and the opening of sodium channels causes further depolarization. The positive-feedback loop of depolarization and channel opening triggers an action potential whenever the membrane potential reaches the threshold.

The discovery of how action potentials are generated dates to the 1940s and 1950s, with the work of British scientists Andrew Huxley and Alan Hodgkin. Because no techniques were available for studying electrical events in small cells, they took electrical recordings from the giant neurons of the squid (see Figure 48.2). Their experiments led to a model, presented in the next section, that earned them a Nobel Prize in 1963.

Generation of Action Potentials: *A Closer Look*

The characteristic shape of the graph of an action potential (see Figure 48.10c) reflects the large change in membrane potential resulting from ion movement through voltage-gated sodium and potassium channels. Membrane depolarization opens both types of channels, but they respond independently and sequentially. Sodium channels open first, initiating the action potential. As the action potential proceeds, the sodium channels become inactivated: A loop of the channel protein moves, blocking ion flow through the opening. Sodium channels remain inactivated until after the membrane returns to the resting potential and the channels close. Potassium channels open more slowly than sodium channels, but remain open and functional until the end of the action potential.

To understand further how voltage-gated channels shape the action potential, we'll consider the process as a series of stages (Figure 48.11). ❶ When the membrane of the axon is at the resting potential, most voltage-gated sodium channels are closed. Some potassium channels are open, but most voltage-gated potassium channels are closed. ❷ When a stimulus depolarizes the membrane, some gated sodium channels open, allowing more Na^+ to diffuse into the cell. The Na^+ inflow causes further depolarization, which opens still more gated sodium channels, allowing even more Na^+ to diffuse into the cell. ❸ Once the threshold is crossed, the positive-feedback cycle rapidly brings the membrane potential close to E_{Na}. This stage of the action potential is called the *rising phase*. ❹ Two events prevent the membrane potential from actually reaching E_{Na}: Voltage-gated sodium channels inactivate soon after opening, halting Na^+ inflow; and most voltage-gated potassium channels open, causing a rapid outflow of K^+. Both events quickly bring the membrane potential back toward E_K. This stage is called the *falling phase*. ❺ In the final phase of an action potential, called the *undershoot*, the membrane's permeability to K^+ is higher than at rest, so the membrane potential is closer to E_K than it is at the resting potential. The gated potassium channels eventually close, and the membrane potential returns to the resting potential.

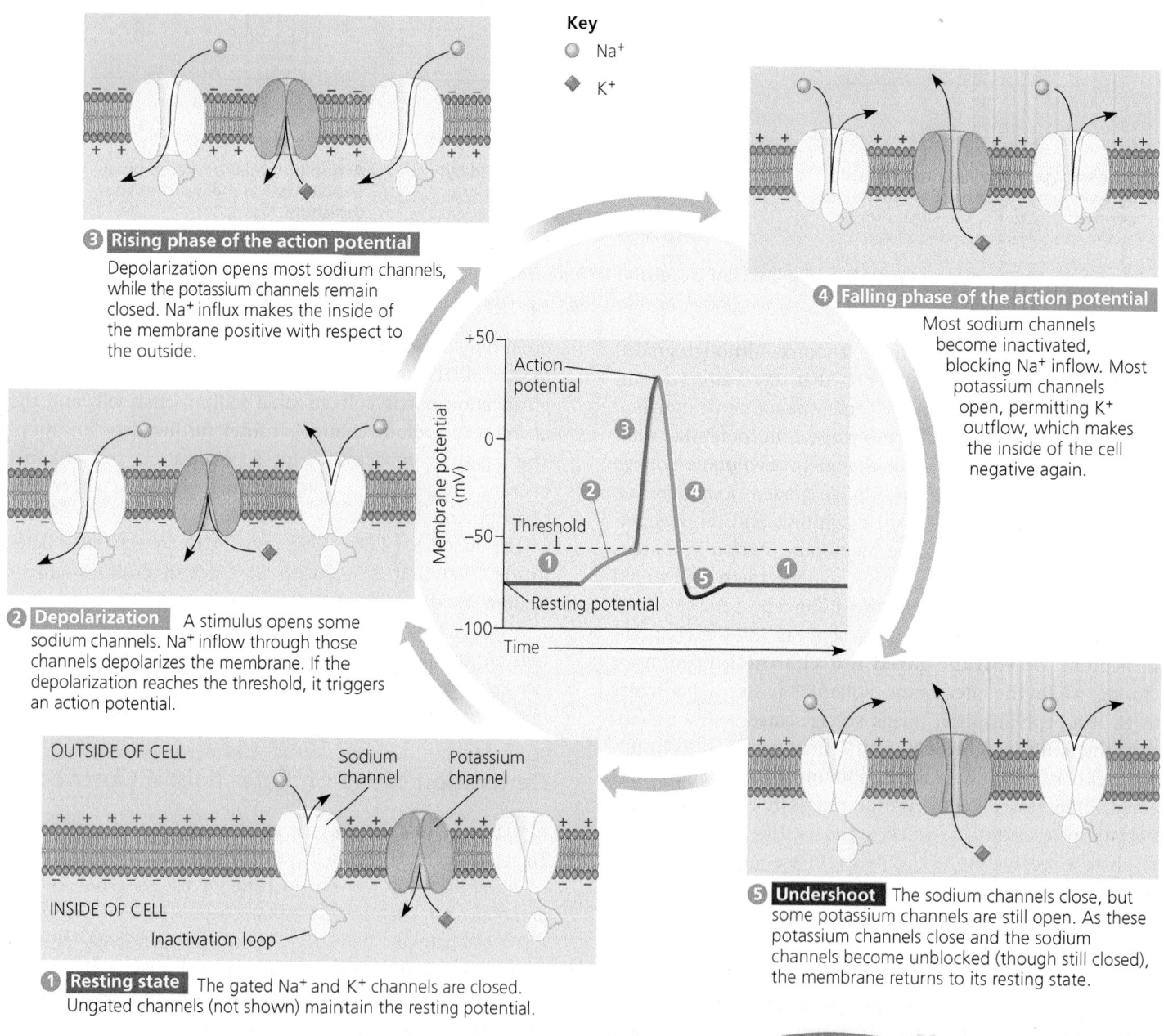

Key
○ Na^+
◆ K^+

❸ **Rising phase of the action potential**
Depolarization opens most sodium channels, while the potassium channels remain closed. Na^+ influx makes the inside of the membrane positive with respect to the outside.

❹ **Falling phase of the action potential**
Most sodium channels become inactivated, blocking Na^+ inflow. Most potassium channels open, permitting K^+ outflow, which makes the inside of the cell negative again.

❷ **Depolarization** A stimulus opens some sodium channels. Na^+ inflow through those channels depolarizes the membrane. If the depolarization reaches the threshold, it triggers an action potential.

OUTSIDE OF CELL
Sodium channel
Potassium channel
INSIDE OF CELL
Inactivation loop

❶ **Resting state** The gated Na^+ and K^+ channels are closed. Ungated channels (not shown) maintain the resting potential.

❺ **Undershoot** The sodium channels close, but some potassium channels are still open. As these potassium channels close and the sodium channels become unblocked (though still closed), the membrane returns to its resting state.

Action potential
Threshold
Resting potential
Membrane potential (mV)
+50
0
−50
−100
Time

▲ **Figure 48.11 The role of voltage-gated ion channels in the generation of an action potential.** The circled numbers on the graph in the center and the colors of the action potential phases correspond to the five diagrams showing voltage-gated sodium and potassium channels in a neuron's plasma membrane. (Ungated ion channels are not illustrated.)

ANIMATION **BioFlix** Visit the Study Area at **www.masteringbiology.com** for the BioFlix® 3-D Animation on How Neurons Work.

The sodium channels remain inactivated during the falling phase and the early part of the undershoot. As a result, if a second depolarizing stimulus occurs during this period, it will be unable to trigger an action potential. The "downtime" when a second action potential cannot be initiated is called the **refractory period**. This interval sets a limit on the maximum frequency at which action potentials can be generated. As we will discuss shortly, the refractory period also ensures that all signals in an axon travel in one direction, from the cell body to the axon terminals.

Note that the refractory period is due to the inactivation of sodium channels, not to a change in the ion gradients across the plasma membrane. The flow of charged particles during an action potential involves far too few ions to change the concentration on either side of the membrane significantly.

For most neurons, the interval between the onset of an action potential and the end of the refractory period is only 1–2 milliseconds (msec). Because action potentials are so brief, a neuron can produce hundreds per second. Furthermore, the frequency with which a neuron generates action potentials varies in response to input. Such differences in action potential frequency convey information about signal strength. In hearing, for example, louder sounds result in more frequent action potentials in neurons connecting the ear to the brain. Differences in the time interval between action potentials are in fact the only variable in transmission of information by an axon.

Gated ion channels and action potentials have a central role in all nervous system function. As a consequence, mutations in genes that encode ion channel proteins can cause disorders affecting the nerves, muscles, brain, or heart. The type of disorder depends largely on where in the body the gene for the ion channel protein is expressed. For example, mutations affecting voltage-gated sodium channels in skeletal muscle cells can cause myotonia, a periodic spasming of those muscles; and mutations affecting sodium channels in the brain can cause epilepsy, in which excessive synchronized firing of groups of nerve cells causes seizures.

Conduction of Action Potentials

At the site where an action potential is initiated (usually the axon hillock), Na$^+$ inflow during the rising phase creates an electrical current that depolarizes the neighboring region of the axon membrane (Figure 48.12). The depolarization in the neighboring region is large enough to reach the threshold, causing the action potential to be reinitiated there. This process is repeated many times along the length of the axon. Because an action potential is an all-or-none event, the magnitude and duration of the action potential remain constant at each position along the axon. The result is the movement of a nerve impulse from the cell body to the synaptic terminals, much like the cascade of events triggered by knocking over the first domino in a line.

1 An action potential is generated as Na$^+$ flows inward across the membrane at one location.

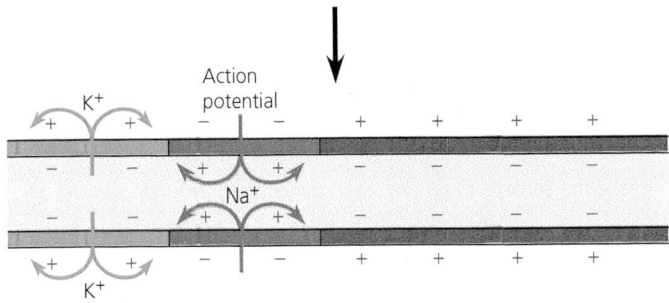

2 The depolarization of the action potential spreads to the neighboring region of the membrane, reinitiating the action potential there. To the left of this region, the membrane is repolarizing as K$^+$ flows outward.

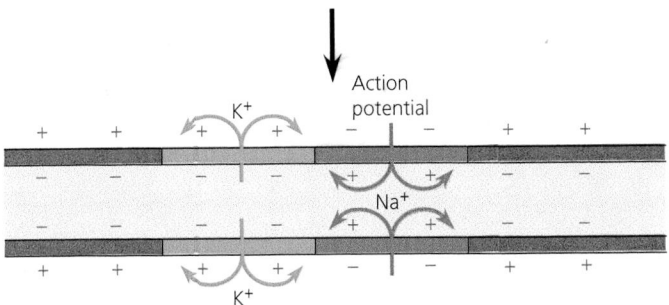

3 The depolarization-repolarization process is repeated in the next region of the membrane. In this way, local currents of ions *across* the plasma membrane cause the action potential to be propagated *along* the length of the axon.

▲ **Figure 48.12 Conduction of an action potential.** This figure shows events at three successive times as an action potential passes from left to right. At each point along the axon, voltage-gated ion channels go through the sequence of changes in Figure 48.10. Membrane colors correspond to the action potential phases in Figure 48.10.

An action potential that starts at the axon hillock moves along the axon only toward the synaptic terminals. Why? Immediately behind the traveling zone of depolarization caused by Na$^+$ inflow is a zone of repolarization caused by K$^+$ outflow. In the repolarized zone, the sodium channels remain inactivated. Consequently, the inward current that depolarizes the axon membrane *ahead* of the action potential cannot produce another action potential *behind* it. This prevents action potentials from traveling back toward the cell body.

Evolutionary Adaptations of Axon Structure

EVOLUTION Axon diameter is a major factor affecting the speed at which action potentials are conducted. One adaptation that increases conductance speed is an increased axon width. Resistance to electrical current flow is inversely proportional to the cross-sectional area of a conductor (such as a wire or an axon). In the same way that a wide hose offers less resistance to the flow of water than does a narrow hose, a wide axon provides less resistance to the current associated with an action potential than does a narrow axon.

In invertebrates, conduction speed varies from several centimeters per second in very narrow axons to about 30 m/sec in the giant axons of some arthropods and molluscs (see Figure 48.2). These giant axons (up to 1 mm wide) function in rapid behavioral responses, such as the muscle contraction that propels a squid toward its prey.

Vertebrate axons have narrow diameters but can still conduct action potentials at high speed. How is this possible? The evolutionary adaptation that enables fast conduction in vertebrate axons is electrical insulation, analogous to the plastic insulation that covers many electrical wires. Insulation causes the depolarizing current associated with an action potential to spread farther along the axon interior, bringing more distant regions to the threshold sooner.

The electrical insulation that surrounds vertebrate axons is called a **myelin sheath** (Figure 48.13). Myelin sheaths are produced by two types of glia—**oligodendrocytes** in the CNS and **Schwann cells** in the PNS. During development, these specialized glia wrap axons in many layers of membrane. The membranes forming these layers are mostly lipid, which is a poor conductor of electrical current.

In myelinated axons, voltage-gated sodium channels are restricted to gaps in the myelin sheath called **nodes of Ranvier** (see Figure 48.13). The extracellular fluid is in contact with the axon membrane only at the nodes. As a result, action potentials are not generated in the regions between the nodes. Rather, the inward current produced during the rising phase of the action potential at a node travels all the way to the next node, where it depolarizes the membrane and regenerates the action potential **(Figure 48.14)**. Thus, the time-consuming process of opening and closing of ion channels occurs at only a limited number of positions along the axon. This mechanism for action potential propagation is called **saltatory conduction** (from the Latin *saltare*, to leap) because the action potential appears to jump along the axon from node to node.

The major selective advantage of myelination is its space efficiency. A myelinated axon 20 μm in diameter has a conduction speed faster than that of a squid giant axon with a diameter 40 times greater. Furthermore, more than 2,000 of those myelinated axons can be packed into the space occupied by just one giant axon.

0.1 μm

▲ **Figure 48.13 Schwann cells and the myelin sheath.** In the PNS, glia called Schwann cells wrap themselves around axons, forming layers of myelin. Gaps between adjacent Schwann cells are called nodes of Ranvier. The TEM shows a cross section through a myelinated axon.

▶ Figure 48.14 **Saltatory conduction.**
In a myelinated axon, the depolarizing current during an action potential at one node of Ranvier spreads along the interior of the axon to the next node (blue arrows), where voltage-gated sodium channels enable reinitiation. Thus, the action potential jumps from node to node as it travels along the axon (red arrows).

1. How do action potentials and graded potentials differ?
2. In multiple sclerosis (from the Greek *skleros*, hard), myelin sheaths harden and deteriorate. How would this affect nervous system function?
3. **WHAT IF?** Suppose a mutation caused gated sodium channels to remain inactivated longer after an action potential. How would this affect the frequency at which action potentials could be generated? Explain.

For suggested answers, see Appendix A.

CONCEPT 48.4

Neurons communicate with other cells at synapses

In most cases, action potentials are not transmitted from neurons to other cells. However, information is transmitted, and this transmission occurs at the synapses. Some synapses, called *electrical synapses*, contain gap junctions (see Figure 6.32), which *do* allow electrical current to flow directly from one neuron to another. In both vertebrates and invertebrates, electrical synapses synchronize the activity of neurons responsible for certain rapid, unvarying behaviors. For example, electrical synapses associated with the giant axons of squids and lobsters facilitate the swift execution of escape responses. There are also many electrical synapses in the vertebrate brain.

The majority of synapses are *chemical synapses*, which involve the release of a chemical neurotransmitter by the presynaptic neuron. At each terminal, the presynaptic neuron synthesizes the neurotransmitter and packages it in multiple membrane-bounded compartments called *synaptic vesicles*. The arrival of an action potential at a synaptic terminal depolarizes the plasma membrane, opening voltage-gated channels that allow Ca^{2+} to diffuse into the terminal (Figure 48.15). The resulting rise in Ca^{2+} concentration in the terminal causes some of the synaptic vesicles to fuse with the terminal membrane, releasing the neurotransmitter.

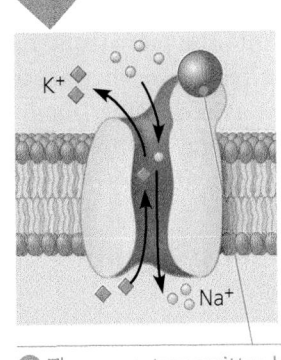

◀ **Figure 48.15 A chemical synapse.** This figure illustrates the sequence of events that transmits a nerve impulse across a chemical synapse. In response to binding of neurotransmitter, ligand-gated ion channels in the postsynaptic membrane open (as shown here) or, less commonly, close. Synaptic transmission ends when the neurotransmitter diffuses out of the synaptic cleft, is taken up by the synaptic terminal or by another cell, or is degraded by an enzyme.

WHAT IF? *If all the Ca^{2+} in the fluid surrounding a neuron were removed, how would this affect the transmission of information within and between neurons?*

ANIMATION **BioFlix** Visit the Study Area at www.masteringbiology.com for the BioFlix® 3-D Animation on How Synapses Work.

Presynaptic cell

Postsynaptic cell

Axon

Synaptic vesicle containing neurotransmitter

Synaptic cleft

Postsynaptic membrane

Presynaptic membrane

Ca^{2+}

K^+

Na^+

Voltage-gated Ca^{2+} channel

Ligand-gated ion channels

❶ An action potential arrives, depolarizing the presynaptic membrane.

❷ The depolarization opens voltage-gated channels, triggering an influx of Ca^{2+}.

❸ The elevated Ca^{2+} concentration causes synaptic vesicles to fuse with the presynaptic membrane, releasing neurotransmitter into the synaptic cleft.

❹ The neurotransmitter binds to ligand-gated ion channels in the postsynaptic membrane. In this example, binding triggers opening, allowing Na^+ and K^+ to diffuse through.

Once released, the neurotransmitter diffuses across the *synaptic cleft*, the gap that separates the presynaptic neuron from the postsynaptic cell. Diffusion time is very short because the gap is less than 50 nm across. Upon reaching the postsynaptic membrane, the neurotransmitter binds to and activates a specific receptor in the membrane.

Information transfer is much more readily modified at chemical synapses than at electrical synapses. A variety of factors can affect the amount of neurotransmitter that is released or the responsiveness of the postsynaptic cell. Such modifications underlie an animal's ability to alter its behavior in response to change and form the basis for learning and memory, as you will learn in Chapter 49.

Generation of Postsynaptic Potentials

At many chemical synapses, the receptor protein that binds and responds to neurotransmitters is a **ligand-gated ion channel**, often called an *ionotropic receptor*. These receptors are clustered in the membrane of the postsynaptic cell, directly opposite the synaptic terminal. Binding of the neurotransmitter (the receptor's ligand) to a particular part of the receptor opens the channel and allows specific ions to diffuse across the postsynaptic membrane. The result is a *postsynaptic potential*, a graded potential in the postsynaptic cell.

At some synapses, the ligand-gated ion channel is permeable to both K^+ and Na^+ (see Figure 48.15). When this channel opens, the membrane potential depolarizes toward a value roughly midway between E_K and E_{Na}. Because such a depolarization brings the membrane potential toward threshold, it is called an **excitatory postsynaptic potential (EPSP)**.

At other synapses, the ligand-gated ion channel is selectively permeable for only K^+ or Cl^-. When such a channel opens, the postsynaptic membrane hyperpolarizes. A hyperpolarization produced in this manner is an **inhibitory postsynaptic potential (IPSP)** because it moves the membrane potential further from threshold.

Various mechanisms that rapidly clear neurotransmitter molecules from the synaptic cleft limit the duration of postsynaptic potentials. Some neurotransmitters are actively transported back into the presynaptic neuron, to be repackaged into synaptic vesicles, or they are transported into glia, to be metabolized as fuel. Other neurotransmitters are removed from the synaptic cleft by simple diffusion or by an enzyme that catalyzes hydrolysis of the neurotransmitter.

Summation of Postsynaptic Potentials

The cell body and dendrites of one postsynaptic neuron may receive inputs from chemical synapses with hundreds or even thousands of synaptic terminals (**Figure 48.16**). The magnitude of the postsynaptic potential at any one synapse varies

▲ **Figure 48.16** **Synaptic terminals on the cell body of a postsynaptic neuron** (colorized SEM).

with a number of factors, including the amount of neurotransmitter released by the presynaptic neuron. As a graded potential, a postsynaptic potential becomes smaller with distance from the synapse. Therefore, by the time a single EPSP reaches the axon hillock, it is usually too small to trigger an action potential in a postsynaptic neuron (**Figure 48.17a**).

On some occasions, two EPSPs occur at a single synapse in such rapid succession that the postsynaptic neuron's membrane potential has not returned to the resting potential before the arrival of the second EPSP. When that happens, the EPSPs add together, an effect called **temporal summation** (**Figure 48.17b**). Moreover, EPSPs produced nearly simultaneously by *different* synapses on the same postsynaptic neuron can also add together, an effect called **spatial summation** (**Figure 48.17c**). Through spatial and temporal summation, several EPSPs can combine to depolarize the membrane at the axon hillock to the threshold, causing the postsynaptic neuron to produce an action potential. Summation applies as well to IPSPs: Two or more IPSPs occurring nearly simultaneously at synapses in the same region or in rapid succession at the same synapse have a larger hyperpolarizing effect than a single IPSP. Through summation, an IPSP can also counter the effect of an EPSP (**Figure 48.17d**).

The interplay between multiple excitatory and inhibitory inputs is the essence of integration in the nervous system. The axon hillock is the neuron's integrating center, the region where the membrane potential at any instant represents the summed effect of all EPSPs and IPSPs. Whenever the membrane potential at the axon hillock reaches the threshold, an action potential is generated and travels along the axon to its synaptic terminals. After the refractory period, the neuron may produce another action potential, provided the membrane potential at the axon hillock once again reaches the threshold.

▲ Figure 48.17 Summation of postsynaptic potentials. These graphs trace changes in the membrane potential at a postsynaptic neuron's axon hillock. The arrows indicate times when postsynaptic potentials occur at two excitatory synapses (E_1 and E_2, green in the diagrams above the graphs) and at one inhibitory synapse (I, red). Like most EPSPs, those produced at E_1 or E_2 do not reach the threshold at the axon hillock without summation.

Modulated Signaling at Synapses

So far, we have focused on synapses where a neurotransmitter binds directly to an ion channel, causing the channel to open. However, there are also synapses in which the receptor for the neurotransmitter is *not* part of an ion channel. At these synapses, the neurotransmitter binds to a *metabotropic receptor*, so called because the resulting opening or closing of ion channels depends on one or more metabolic steps. Binding of a neurotransmitter to a metabotropic receptor activates a signal transduction pathway in the postsynaptic cell involving a second messenger (see Chapter 11). Compared with the postsynaptic potentials produced by ligand-gated channels, the effects of these second-messenger systems have a slower onset but last longer (minutes or even hours). Second messengers modulate the responsiveness of postsynaptic neurons to inputs in diverse ways, such as by altering the number of open potassium channels.

A variety of signal transduction pathways play a role in modulating synaptic transmission. One of the best-studied pathways involves cyclic AMP (cAMP) as a second messenger. For example, when the neurotransmitter norepinephrine binds to its metabotropic receptor, the neurotransmitter-receptor complex activates a G protein, which in turn activates adenylyl cyclase, the enzyme that converts ATP to cAMP (see Figure 11.11). Cyclic AMP activates protein kinase A, which phosphorylates specific ion channel proteins in the postsynaptic membrane, causing them to open or close. Because of the amplifying effect of the signal transduction pathway, the binding of a neurotransmitter molecule to a metabotropic receptor can open or close many channels.

Neurotransmitters

Researchers have identified more than 100 neurotransmitters belonging to five groups: acetylcholine, amino acids, biogenic amines, neuropeptides, and gases (Table 48.2, on the next page). The response triggered depends on the particular kind of receptor expressed by the postsynaptic cell. A single neurotransmitter may bind specifically to more than a dozen different receptors, including ionotropic and metabotropic types. Indeed, a particular neurotransmitter can excite postsynaptic cells expressing one receptor and inhibit postsynaptic cells expressing a different receptor. As an example, let's examine **acetylcholine**, a common neurotransmitter in both invertebrates and vertebrates.

Acetylcholine

Acetylcholine is vital for nervous system functions that include muscle stimulation, memory formation, and learning. In vertebrates, there are two major classes of acetylcholine receptor. One type is a ligand-gated ion channel. We know the most about its function at the *neuromuscular junction*, the site where motor neurons synapse with skeletal muscle cells. When acetylcholine released by motor neurons binds this receptor,

Table 48.2 Major Neurotransmitters

Neurotransmitter	Structure
Acetylcholine	$H_3C-\overset{\displaystyle O}{\overset{\|}{C}}-O-CH_2-CH_2-\overset{\displaystyle CH_3}{\overset{\|}{\underset{\|}{N^+}}}-CH_3$ $\quad CH_3$
Amino Acids	
GABA (gamma-aminobutyric acid)	$H_2N-CH_2-CH_2-CH_2-COOH$
Glutamate	$H_2N-\overset{\displaystyle}{\underset{\|}{CH}}-CH_2-CH_2-COOH$ $\qquad COOH$
Glycine	H_2N-CH_2-COOH
Biogenic Amines	
Norepinephrine	
Dopamine	
Serotonin	
Neuropeptides (a very diverse group, only two of which are shown)	
Substance P	Arg—Pro—Lys—Pro—Gln—Gln—Phe—Phe—Gly—Leu—Met
Met-enkephalin (an endorphin)	Tyr—Gly—Gly—Phe—Met
Gases	
Nitric oxide	$N=O$

the ion channel opens, producing an EPSP. This excitatory activity is soon terminated by acetylcholinesterase, an enzyme in the synaptic cleft that hydrolyzes the neurotransmitter.

The acetylcholine receptor active at the neuromuscular junction is also found elsewhere in the PNS, as well as in the CNS. There this ionotropic receptor can bind nicotine, a chemical found in tobacco and tobacco smoke. Nicotine's effects as a physiological and psychological stimulant result from its binding to this receptor.

A metabotropic acetylcholine receptor is found at locations that include the vertebrate CNS and heart. In heart muscle, acetylcholine released by neurons activates a signal transduction pathway. The G proteins in the pathway inhibit adenylyl cyclase and open potassium channels in the muscle cell membrane. Both effects reduce the rate at which the heart pumps. Thus, the effect of acetylcholine in heart muscle is inhibitory rather than excitatory.

A number of natural and synthetic toxins disrupt neurotransmission by acetylcholine. For example, the nerve gas

sarin inhibits acetylcholinesterase, causing a buildup of acetylcholine to levels that trigger paralysis and typically death. In contrast, certain bacteria produce a toxin that inhibits presynaptic release of acetylcholine. This toxin causes a rare but severe form of food poisoning called botulism. Untreated botulism is typically fatal because muscles required for breathing fail to contract when acetylcholine release is blocked. Today, the same botulinum toxin is commonly used in cosmetic procedures. Injections of the toxin, known by the trade name Botox, minimize wrinkles around the eyes or mouth by blocking transmission at synapses that control particular facial muscles.

Amino Acids

Amino acid neurotransmitters are active in the vertebrate CNS and PNS. In the CNS, the amino acid **glutamate** is the most common neurotransmitter. When glutamate binds to any of several types of ligand-gated ion channels, it has an excitatory effect on postsynaptic cells. Synapses at which glutamate is the neurotransmitter have a key role in the formation of long-term memory, as we will discuss in Chapter 49.

The amino acid **gamma-aminobutyric acid (GABA)** is the neurotransmitter at most inhibitory synapses in the brain. Binding of GABA to receptors in postsynaptic cells increases membrane permeability to Cl^-, resulting in an IPSP. The widely prescribed drug diazepam (Valium) reduces anxiety through binding to a site on a GABA receptor.

A third amino acid, glycine, acts at inhibitory synapses in parts of the CNS that lie outside of the brain. There, glycine binds to an ionotropic receptor that is inhibited by strychnine, a chemical often used as a rat poison.

Biogenic Amines

The neurotransmitters grouped as **biogenic amines** are synthesized from amino acids and include **norepinephrine**, which is made from tyrosine. Norepinephrine is an excitatory neurotransmitter in the autonomic nervous system, a branch of the PNS discussed in Chapter 49. Outside the nervous system, norepinephrine has distinct but related functions as a hormone, as does the related biogenic amine *epinephrine* (see Chapter 45).

The biogenic amines **dopamine**, made from tyrosine, and **serotonin**, made from tryptophan, are released at many sites in the brain and affect sleep, mood, attention, and learning. Some psychoactive drugs, including LSD and mescaline, apparently produce their hallucinatory effects by binding to brain receptors for these neurotransmitters.

Biogenic amines have a central role in a number of nervous system disorders and treatments (see Chapter 49). The degenerative illness Parkinson's disease is associated with a lack of dopamine in the brain. In addition, depression is often treated with drugs that increase the brain concentrations of biogenic amines. Prozac, for instance, enhances the effect of serotonin by inhibiting its reuptake after release.

Neuropeptides

Several **neuropeptides**, relatively short chains of amino acids, serve as neurotransmitters that operate via metabotropic receptors. Such peptides are typically produced by cleavage of much larger protein precursors. The neuropeptide *substance P* is a key excitatory neurotransmitter that mediates our perception of pain, while other neuropeptides, called **endorphins**, function as natural analgesics, decreasing pain perception.

In the 1970s, Candace Pert, then a graduate student at Johns Hopkins University, and her research supervisor, Solomon Snyder, discovered endorphins as an outcome of their research on the biochemistry of behavior. Previous studies had suggested that the brain contains receptors for opiates, painkilling drugs such as morphine and heroin. To find these receptors, Pert and Snyder had the insight to apply existing knowledge about the activity of different drugs in the brain (**Figure 48.18**). In a single, straightforward experiment, they provided the first demonstration that specific opiate receptors exist. Setting out to identify molecules normally present in the brain that could also activate these receptors, they discovered endorphins.

Endorphins are produced in the brain during times of physical or emotional stress, such as childbirth. In addition to relieving pain, they decrease urine output, depress respiration, and produce euphoria, as well as other emotional effects. Because opiates bind to the same receptor proteins as endorphins, opiates mimic endorphins and produce many of the same physiological effects (see Figure 2.18).

Gases

In common with many other types of cells, some neurons in vertebrates release dissolved gases, notably nitric oxide (NO), that act as local regulators. For example, during sexual arousal, certain neurons in human males release NO into the erectile tissue of the penis. In response, smooth muscle cells in the blood vessel walls of the erectile tissue relax, which causes the blood vessels to dilate and fill the spongy erectile tissue with blood, producing an erection. As you read in Chapter 45, the erectile dysfunction drug Viagra increases the ability to achieve and maintain an erection by inhibiting an enzyme that terminates the action of NO.

Unlike most neurotransmitters, NO is not stored in cytoplasmic vesicles but is instead synthesized on demand. NO

▼ **Figure 48.18**   **INQUIRY**

Does the brain have a specific protein receptor for opiates?

EXPERIMENT In 1973, Candace Pert and Solomon Snyder, of Johns Hopkins University, were searching for an opiate receptor in the mammalian brain. It was known that the drug naloxone antagonizes (opposes) the narcotic effect of opiates. Pert and Snyder reasoned that naloxone acts as an opiate antagonist by binding tightly to the opiate receptor without activating the receptor. They prepared radioactive naloxone and then incubated it with a protein mixture prepared from rodent brains. If proteins that could bind naloxone were present, the radioactivity would become stably associated with the protein mixture. Furthermore, the researchers could determine whether a specific receptor was present by comparing the ability of opiates and non-opiates to interfere with the binding activity.

① Radioactive naloxone and a test drug are incubated with a protein mixture.

② Proteins are trapped on a filter. Bound naloxone is detected by measuring radioactivity.

RESULTS

Drug	Opiate	Concentration That Blocked Naloxone Binding
Morphine	Yes	$6 \times 10^{-9}\ M$
Methadone	Yes	$2 \times 10^{-8}\ M$
Levorphanol	Yes	$2 \times 10^{-9}\ M$
Phenobarbital	No	No effect at $10^{-4}\ M$
Atropine	No	No effect at $10^{-4}\ M$
Serotonin	No	No effect at $10^{-4}\ M$

CONCLUSION Because opiates interfered with naloxone binding, but unrelated drugs did not, Pert and Snyder concluded that the binding activity had the specificity expected of the opiate receptor. They also found that the binding activity was present in tissue from regions of the brain involved in the sensation of pain, but not in tissue from the cerebellum, a brain region that coordinates motor activity.

SOURCE C. B. Pert and S. H. Snyder, Opiate receptor: demonstration in nervous tissue, *Science* 179:1011–1014 (1973).

WHAT IF? Suppose you found a drug that blocks naloxone binding at a concentration of $10^{-8}\ M$ but has no narcotic effect on animals. What are some possible explanations for this finding?

diffuses into neighboring target cells, produces a change, and is broken down—all within a few seconds. In many of its targets, including smooth muscle cells, NO works like many hormones, stimulating an enzyme to synthesize a second messenger that directly affects cellular metabolism.

Although inhaling air containing the gas carbon monoxide (CO) can be deadly, the vertebrate body produces small amounts of CO, some of which acts as a neurotransmitter. Carbon monoxide is generated by the enzyme heme oxygenase, one form of which is found in certain populations of neurons in the brain and PNS. In the brain, CO regulates the release of hypothalamic hormones. In the PNS, it acts as an inhibitory neurotransmitter that hyperpolarizes the plasma membrane of intestinal smooth muscle cells.

In the next chapter, we will consider how the cellular and biochemical mechanisms we have discussed contribute to nervous system function on the system level.

CONCEPT CHECK 48.4

1. How is it possible for a particular neurotransmitter to produce opposite effects in different tissues?
2. Organophosphate pesticides work by inhibiting acetylcholinesterase, the enzyme that breaks down the neurotransmitter acetylcholine. Explain how these toxins would affect EPSPs produced by acetylcholine.
3. **WHAT IF?** If a drug mimicked the activity of GABA in the CNS, what general effect on behavior might you expect? Explain.
4. **MAKE CONNECTIONS** A change in the concentration of calcium ions is important for fertilization in sea urchins and other animals (see Figure 47.3, on p. 1023). What membrane activity is common to fertilization and neurotransmitter release?

For suggested answers, see Appendix A.

48 CHAPTER REVIEW

SUMMARY OF KEY CONCEPTS

CONCEPT 48.1

Neuron organization and structure reflect function in information transfer (pp. 1045–1047)

- A **central nervous system (CNS)** and a **peripheral nervous system (PNS)** process information in three stages: sensory input, integration, and motor output to effector cells.
- Most neurons have branched **dendrites** that receive signals from other neurons and an **axon** that transmits signals to other cells at **synapses**. Neurons rely on **glia** for functions that include nourishment, insulation, and regulation.

? *How would severing an axon affect the flow of information in a neuron?*

CONCEPT 48.2

Ion pumps and ion channels establish the resting potential of a neuron (pp. 1048–1050)

- Ionic gradients generate a voltage difference, or **membrane potential**, across the plasma membrane of cells. The concentration of Na^+ is higher outside than inside; the reverse is true for K^+. In resting neurons, the plasma membrane has many open potassium channels but few open sodium channels. Diffusion of ions, principally K^+, through channels generates a **resting potential**, with the inside more negative than the outside.

? *Suppose you placed an isolated neuron in a solution similar to extracellular fluid and later transferred the neuron to a solution lacking any sodium ions. What change would you expect in the resting potential?*

CONCEPT 48.3

Action potentials are the signals conducted by axons (pp. 1050–1055)

- Neurons have gated ion channels that open or close in response to stimuli, leading to changes in the membrane potential. An

increase in the magnitude of the membrane potential is a **hyperpolarization**; a decrease is a **depolarization**. Changes in membrane potential that vary continuously with the strength of a stimulus are known as **graded potentials**.
- An **action potential** is a brief, all-or-none depolarization of a neuron's plasma membrane. When a graded depolarization brings the membrane potential to the threshold, many **voltage-gated ion channels** open, triggering an inflow of Na^+ that rapidly brings the membrane potential to a positive value. A negative membrane potential is restored by the inactivation of sodium channels and by the opening of many voltage-gated potassium channels, which increases K^+ outflow. A **refractory period** follows, corresponding to the interval when the sodium channels are inactivated.

- A nerve impulse travels from the axon hillock to the synaptic terminals by propagation of a series of action potentials along the axon. The speed of conduction increases with the diameter of the axon and, in many vertebrate axons, with **myelination**. Action potentials in myelinated axons jump between the **nodes of Ranvier**, a process called **saltatory conduction**.

? *In what ways do both positive and negative feedback contribute to the shape of an action potential?*

CONCEPT 48.4

Neurons communicate with other cells at synapses (pp. 1055–1060)

- In an electrical **synapse**, electrical current flows directly from one cell to another. In a chemical synapse, depolarization causes synaptic vesicles to fuse with the terminal membrane and release **neurotransmitter** into the synaptic cleft.
- At many synapses, the neurotransmitter binds to **ligand-gated ion channels** in the postsynaptic membrane, producing an **excitatory** or **inhibitory postsynaptic potential** (**EPSP** or **IPSP**). The neurotransmitter then diffuses out of the cleft, is taken up by surrounding cells, or is degraded by enzymes. **Temporal** and **spatial summation** at the axon hillock determines whether a neuron generates an action potential.
- Different receptors for the same neurotransmitter produce different effects. Some neurotransmitter receptors activate signal transduction pathways, which can produce long-lasting changes in postsynaptic cells. Major neurotransmitters include acetylcholine; the amino acids GABA, glutamate, and glycine; biogenic amines; neuropeptides; and gases such as NO.

> **?** *Why are many drugs used to treat nervous system diseases or affect brain function targeted to specific receptors rather than particular neurotransmitters?*

TEST YOUR UNDERSTANDING

LEVEL 1: KNOWLEDGE/COMPREHENSION

1. What happens when a resting neuron's membrane depolarizes?
   a. There is a net diffusion of Na^+ out of the cell.
   b. The equilibrium potential for K^+ (E_K) becomes more positive.
   c. The neuron's membrane voltage becomes more positive.
   d. The neuron is less likely to generate an action potential.
   e. The cell's inside is more negative than the outside.

2. A common feature of action potentials is that they
   a. cause the membrane to hyperpolarize and then depolarize.
   b. can undergo temporal and spatial summation.
   c. are triggered by a depolarization that reaches the threshold.
   d. move at the same speed along all axons.
   e. require the diffusion of Na^+ and K^+ through ligand-gated channels to propagate.

3. Where are neurotransmitter receptors located?
   a. the nuclear membrane
   b. the nodes of Ranvier
   c. the postsynaptic membrane
   d. synaptic vesicle membranes
   e. the myelin sheath

4. Temporal summation always involves
   a. both inhibitory and excitatory inputs.
   b. synapses at more than one site.
   c. inputs that are not simultaneous.
   d. electrical synapses.
   e. multiple inputs at a single synapse.

LEVEL 2: APPLICATION/ANALYSIS

5. Why are action potentials usually conducted in one direction?
   a. The nodes of Ranvier conduct potentials in one direction.
   b. The brief refractory period prevents reopening of voltage-gated Na^+ channels.
   c. The axon hillock has a higher membrane potential than the terminals of the axon.
   d. Ions can flow along the axon in only one direction.
   e. Voltage-gated channels for both Na^+ and K^+ open in only one direction.

6. Which of the following is a *direct* result of depolarizing the presynaptic membrane of an axon terminal?
   a. Voltage-gated calcium channels in the membrane open.
   b. Synaptic vesicles fuse with the membrane.
   c. The postsynaptic cell produces an action potential.
   d. Ligand-gated channels open, allowing neurotransmitters to enter the synaptic cleft.
   e. An EPSP or IPSP is generated in the postsynaptic cell.

LEVEL 3: SYNTHESIS/EVALUATION

7. **DRAW IT** Suppose a researcher inserts a pair of electrodes at two different positions along the middle of an axon dissected out of a squid. By applying a depolarizing stimulus, the researcher brings the plasma membrane at both positions to threshold. Using the drawing below as a model, create one or more drawings that illustrate where each action potential would terminate.

8. **EVOLUTION CONNECTION**
   An action potential is an all-or-none event. This on/off signaling is an evolutionary adaptation of animals that must sense and act in a complex environment. It is possible to imagine a nervous system in which the action potentials are graded, with the amplitude depending on the size of the stimulus. What evolutionary advantage might on/off signaling have over a graded (continuously variable) kind of signaling?

9. **SCIENTIFIC INQUIRY**
   From what you know about action potentials and synapses, propose two or three hypotheses for how various anesthetics might block pain.

10. **WRITE ABOUT A THEME**
    The Cellular Basis of Life In a short essay (100–150 words), describe how the structure and electrical properties of vertebrate neurons reflect similarities and differences with other animal cells.

For selected answers, see Appendix A.

Mastering BIOLOGY www.masteringbiology.com

1. MasteringBiology® Assignments

BioFlix **Tutorials** How Neurons Work: Neuron Structure and Resting Potential • The Action Potential • Conduction of an Action Potential; How Synapses Work: Chemical Synapses • Postsynaptic Potentials
Activities Neuron Structure • Membrane Potentials • Action Potentials • Nerve Signals: Action Potentials • Signal Transmission at a Chemical Synapse • Discovery Channel Video: Novelty Gene
Questions Student Misconceptions • Reading Quiz • Multiple Choice • End-of-Chapter

2. eText

Read your book online, search, take notes, highlight text, and more.

3. The Study Area

Practice Tests • Cumulative Test • *BioFlix* 3-D Animations • MP3 Tutor Sessions • Videos • Activities • Investigations • Lab Media • Audio Glossary • Word Study Tools • Art

49

Nervous Systems

▲ Figure 49.1 **How do scientists identify individual neurons in the brain?**

KEY CONCEPTS

49.1 Nervous systems consist of circuits of neurons and supporting cells

49.2 The vertebrate brain is regionally specialized

49.3 The cerebral cortex controls voluntary movement and cognitive functions

49.4 Changes in synaptic connections underlie memory and learning

49.5 Many nervous system disorders can be explained in molecular terms

OVERVIEW

Command and Control Center

What happens in your brain when you solve a math problem or listen to music? Until quite recently, scientists had little hope of answering that question. The human brain contains an estimated 10^{11} (100 billion) neurons. Interconnecting

these brain cells are circuits more complex than those of even the most powerful supercomputers. Yet the circuitry of the brain has been largely hidden from view. That's no longer the case, thanks in part to several exciting new technologies.

One recent advance in exploring the brain relies on a method for expressing random combinations of colored proteins in brain cells—such that each cell shows up in a different color. The result is a "brainbow" like the one in **Figure 49.1**, which highlights neurons in the brain of a mouse. In this image, each neuron expresses one of more than 90 different color combinations of four fluorescent proteins. Using the brainbow technology, neuroscientists hope to develop detailed maps of the connections that transfer information between particular regions of the brain.

Another breakthrough came with the development of powerful imaging techniques that reveal activity in the working brain. Researchers can monitor multiple areas of the human brain while a subject is performing various tasks, such as speaking, looking at pictures, or forming a mental image of a person's face. They can use these techniques to look for a correlation between a particular task and activity in specific brain areas.

In this chapter, we will discuss the organization and evolution of animal nervous systems, exploring how groups of neurons function in specialized circuits dedicated to specific tasks. First we'll focus on specialization in regions of the vertebrate brain. We will then turn to the ways in which brain activity makes information storage and organization possible. Finally, we'll consider several disorders of the nervous system that are the subject of intense research today.

CONCEPT 49.1

Nervous systems consist of circuits of neurons and supporting cells

The ability to sense and react originated billions of years ago with prokaryotes that could detect changes in their environment and respond in ways that enhanced their survival and reproductive success. For example, bacteria keep moving in a particular direction as long as they encounter increasing concentrations of a food source. Later in evolution, modification of simple recognition and response processes provided multicellular organisms with a mechanism for communication between cells of the body. By the time of the Cambrian explosion more than 500 million years ago (see Chapter 32), systems of neurons allowing animals to sense and move rapidly were present in essentially their current forms.

Hydras, jellies, and other cnidarians are the simplest animals with nervous systems. As you read in Chapters 33 and 41, these animals have radially symmetrical bodies organized around a central digestive compartment, the gastrovascular cavity. In most cnidarians, interconnected nerve cells form a diffuse **nerve net** (Figure 49.2a), which controls the contraction and expansion of the gastrovascular cavity. Unlike the nervous systems of other animals, the nerve net of cnidarians lacks clusters of neurons that perform specialized functions.

In more complex animals, the axons of multiple nerve cells are often bundled together, forming **nerves**. These fibrous structures channel and organize information flow along specific routes through the nervous system. For example, sea stars have a set of radial nerves connecting to a central nerve ring (Figure 49.2b). Within each arm of a sea star, the radial nerve is linked to a nerve net from which it receives input and to which it sends signals controlling muscle contraction.

Animals that have elongated, bilaterally symmetrical bodies have even more specialized nervous systems. Such animals exhibit cephalization, an evolutionary trend toward a clustering of sensory neurons and interneurons at the anterior (front) end of the body. These anterior neurons communicate with cells elsewhere in the body, including neurons located in one or more nerve cords extending toward the posterior (rear) end. In nonsegmented worms, such as the planarian shown in Figure 49.2c, a small brain and longitudinal nerve cords constitute the simplest clearly defined *central nervous system* (*CNS*). In some such animals, the entire nervous system is constructed from only a small number of cells, as shown by studies of another nonsegmented worm, the nematode *Caenorhabditis elegans*. In this species, an adult worm (hermaphrodite) has exactly 302 neurons, no more and no fewer. More complex invertebrates, such as segmented worms

(annelids; Figure 49.2d) and arthropods (Figure 49.2e), have many more neurons. The behavior of such invertebrates is regulated by more complicated brains and by ventral nerve cords containing ganglia, segmentally arranged clusters of neurons.

Within an animal group, nervous system organization often correlates with lifestyle. Among the molluscs, for example, sessile and slow-moving species, such as clams and chitons, have relatively simple sense organs and little or no cephalization (Figure 49.2f). In contrast, active predatory molluscs, such as octopuses and squids (Figure 49.2g), have the most sophisticated nervous systems of any invertebrates, rivaling those of some vertebrates. With their large, image-forming eyes and a brain containing millions of neurons, octopuses can learn to discriminate between visual patterns and to perform complex tasks.

In vertebrates (Figure 49.2h), the brain and the spinal cord form the CNS; nerves and ganglia form the *peripheral nervous system* (*PNS*). Regional specialization is a hallmark of both systems, as we will see throughout the remainder of this chapter.

Organization of the Vertebrate Nervous System

In the vertebrate CNS, the functions of the brain and spinal cord are tightly coordinated. The brain provides the integrative power that underlies the complex behavior of vertebrates. The spinal cord, which runs lengthwise inside the vertebral column (spine), conveys information to and from the brain

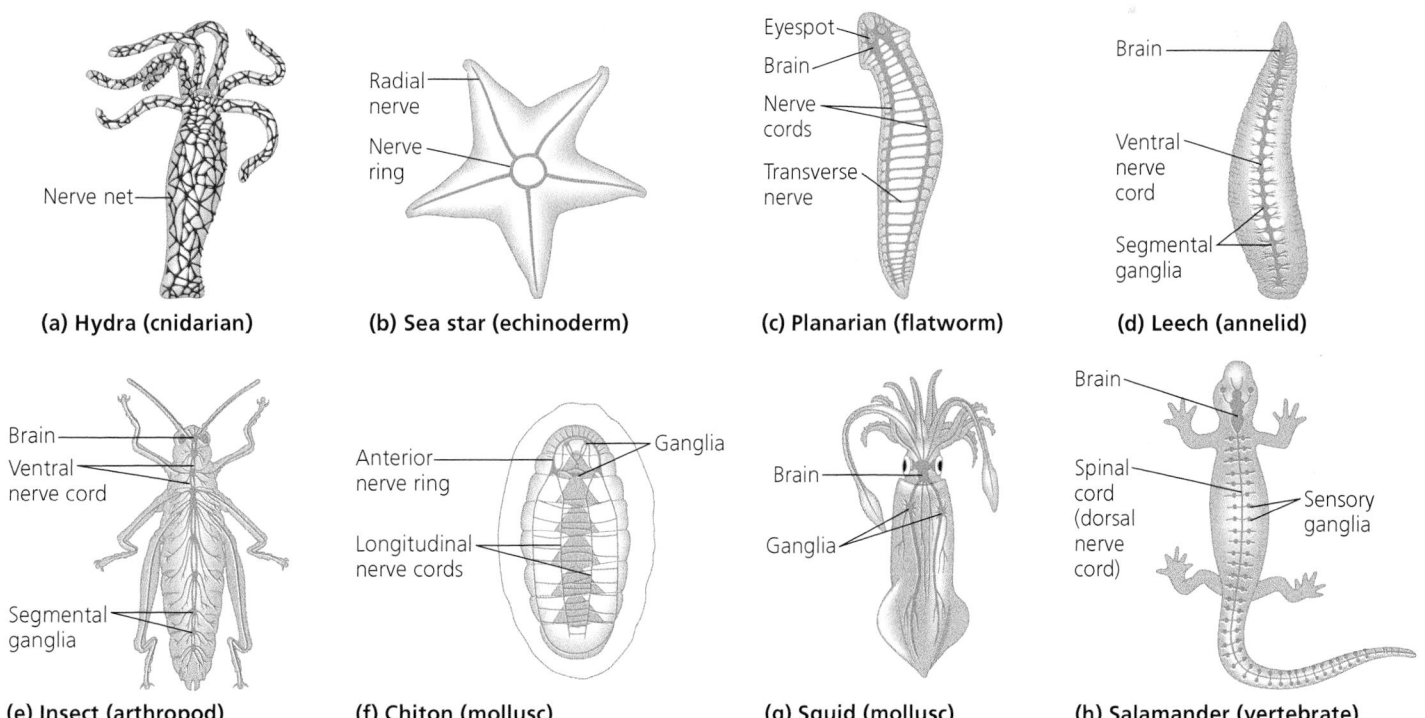

(a) Hydra (cnidarian) (b) Sea star (echinoderm) (c) Planarian (flatworm) (d) Leech (annelid)

(e) Insect (arthropod) (f) Chiton (mollusc) (g) Squid (mollusc) (h) Salamander (vertebrate)

▲ **Figure 49.2 Nervous system organization. (a)** A hydra contains individual neurons (purple) organized in a diffuse nerve net. **(b–h)** Animals with more sophisticated nervous systems contain groups of neurons (blue) organized into nerves and often ganglia and a brain.

❷ Sensors detect a sudden stretch in the quadriceps.

❸ Sensory neurons convey the information to the spinal cord.

❹ In response to signals from the sensory neurons, **motor neurons** convey signals to the quadriceps, causing it to contract and jerking the lower leg forward.

Cell body of sensory neuron in dorsal root ganglion

Gray matter

Quadriceps muscle

❶ The reflex is initiated artificially by tapping the tendon connected to the quadriceps muscle.

White matter

❺ Sensory neurons also communicate with **interneurons** in the spinal cord.

❻ The interneurons inhibit motor neurons that lead to the hamstring muscle. This inhibition prevents contraction of the hamstring, which would resist the action of the quadriceps.

Hamstring muscle

Spinal cord (cross section)

● Sensory neuron
● Motor neuron
● Interneuron

▲ **Figure 49.3 The knee-jerk reflex.** Many neurons are involved in the reflex, but for simplicity, only a few neurons are shown.

MAKE CONNECTIONS *Using the nerve signals to the hamstring and quadriceps in this reflex as an example, propose a model for regulation of smooth muscle activity in the esophagus during the swallowing reflex (see Figure 41.10, p. 884).*

and generates basic patterns of locomotion. The spinal cord also acts independently of the brain as part of the simple nerve circuits that produce **reflexes**, the body's automatic responses to certain stimuli.

A reflex protects the body by triggering a rapid, involuntary response to a particular stimulus. If you put your hand on a hot burner, a reflex begins to pull your hand back well before the sensation of pain has been processed in your brain. Similarly, if your knees buckle when you pick up a heavy object, the tension across your knees triggers a reflex that contracts the thigh muscles, helping you stay upright and support the load. During a physical exam, your doctor may trigger this knee-jerk reflex with a mallet to help assess nervous system function **(Figure 49.3)**.

Whereas the nerve cord of many invertebrates is located ventrally, the spinal cord of vertebrates runs along the dorsal side of the body **(Figure 49.4)**. An underlying segmental organization is apparent in the arrangement of neurons within the spinal cord and in the distribution of spinal nerves and ganglia just outside the spinal cord.

During embryonic development in vertebrates, the central nervous system develops from the hollow dorsal nerve cord—a hallmark of chordates (see Chapter 34). The cavity

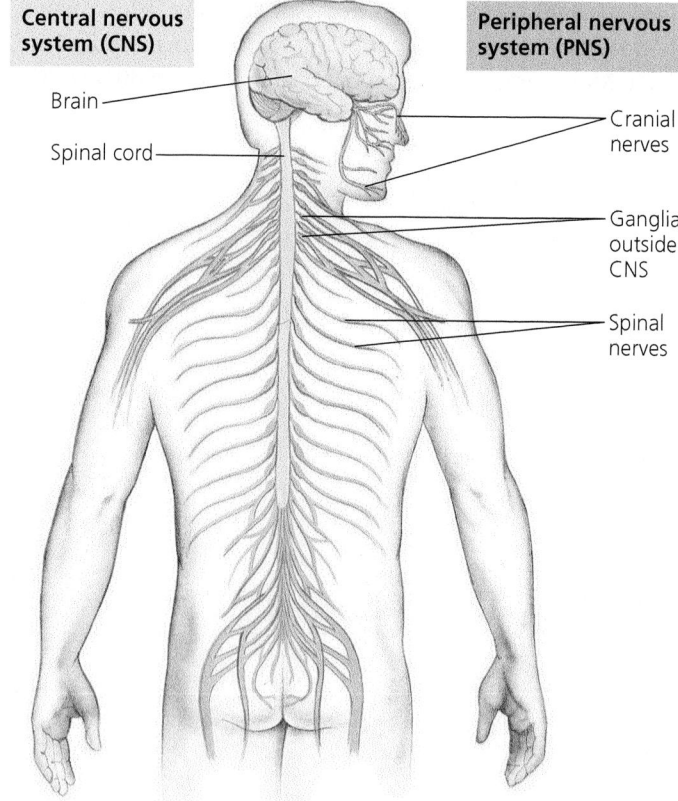

Central nervous system (CNS)

Peripheral nervous system (PNS)

Brain

Spinal cord

Cranial nerves

Ganglia outside CNS

Spinal nerves

▲ **Figure 49.4 The vertebrate nervous system.** The central nervous system consists of the brain and spinal cord (yellow). Left-right pairs of cranial nerves, spinal nerves, and ganglia make up most of the peripheral nervous system (dark gold).

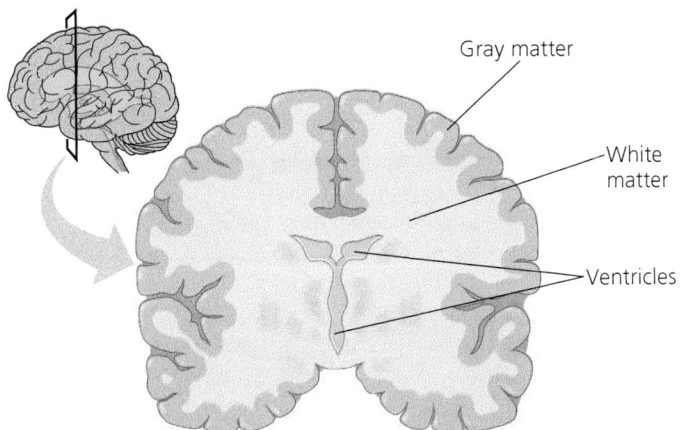

▲ Figure 49.5 Ventricles, gray matter, and white matter.
Ventricles deep in the brain's interior contain cerebrospinal fluid. Most of the gray matter is on the surface of the brain, surrounding the white matter.

of the nerve cord gives rise to the narrow **central canal** of the spinal cord as well as the **ventricles** of the brain (Figure 49.5). Both the canal and ventricles fill with **cerebrospinal fluid**, which is formed in the brain by filtration of arterial blood. The cerebrospinal fluid circulates slowly through the central canal and ventricles and then drains into the veins. This circulation supplies the brain with nutrients and hormones and carries away wastes. In mammals, the cerebrospinal fluid also cushions the brain and spinal cord by circulating between layers of connective tissue that surround the CNS.

In addition to these fluid-filled spaces, the brain and spinal cord contain gray matter and white matter (see Figure 49.5). **Gray matter** consists mainly of neuron cell bodies, dendrites, and unmyelinated axons. In contrast, **white matter** consists of bundled axons that have myelin sheaths, which give the axons a whitish appearance. White matter in the spinal cord lies on the outside, consistent with its function in linking the CNS to sensory and motor neurons of the PNS. White matter in the brain is predominantly on the inside, reflecting the role of signaling between neurons of the brain in learning, feeling emotions, processing sensory information, and generating commands.

Glia

The glia present throughout the vertebrate brain and spinal cord carry out functions crucial for the activity of the nervous system. Figure 49.6 illustrates the major types of glia in the adult nervous system and provides an overview of the ways in which they nourish, support, and regulate the functioning of neurons.

Ependymal cells line the ventricles and have cilia that promote circulation of the cerebrospinal fluid.

Oligodendrocytes myelinate axons in the CNS. Myelination greatly increases the conduction speed of action potentials.

Schwann cells myelinate axons in the PNS.

Microglia are immune cells that protect against pathogens.

Astrocytes (from the Greek *astron*, star) facilitate information transfer at synapses and in some instances release neurotransmitters. Astrocytes next to active neurons cause nearby blood vessels to dilate, increasing blood flow and enabling the neurons to obtain oxygen and glucose more quickly. Astrocytes also regulate extracellular concentrations of ions and neurotransmitters.

The green cells in this mammalian brain tissue are astrocytes labeled with a fluorescent antibody.

A blue dye that binds DNA in the nuclei of all cells reveals the intermingling of astrocytes with other cells, predominantly neurons.

▲ Figure 49.6 Glia in the vertebrate nervous system.

Glia also have an essential role in development of the nervous system. In embryos, cells called *radial glia* form tracks along which newly formed neurons migrate from the neural tube, the structure that gives rise to the CNS (see Figure 47.13). Later, astrocytes induce cells that line the capillaries in the CNS to form tight junctions (see Figure 6.32). The result is the *blood-brain barrier*, which controls the extracellular environment of the CNS by restricting the entry of most substances from the blood.

Both radial glia and astrocytes can also act as stem cells, generating new neurons and glia. Researchers view these multipotent precursors as a potential means for replacing neurons and glia that are lost to injury or disease, a topic we'll explore further in Concept 49.4.

The Peripheral Nervous System

The PNS transmits information to and from the CNS and plays a large role in regulating an animal's movement and internal environment (**Figure 49.7**). Sensory information reaches the CNS along PNS neurons designated as *afferent* (from the Latin, meaning "to carry toward"). Following information processing within the CNS, instructions then travel to muscles, glands, and endocrine cells along PNS neurons designated as *efferent* (from the Latin, meaning "to carry away"). Most nerves contain both afferent and efferent neurons. One exception is the olfactory nerve, which conveys only sensory information from the nose to the brain.

The PNS has two efferent components: the motor system and the autonomic nervous system (see Figure 49.7). The **motor system** consists of neurons that carry signals to skeletal muscles. This control of skeletal muscles can be voluntary, as when you raise your hand to ask a question, or involuntary, as in the knee-jerk reflex controlled by the spinal cord. In contrast, regulation of smooth and cardiac muscles by the **autonomic nervous system** is generally involuntary. The three divisions of the autonomic nervous system—sympathetic, parasympathetic, and enteric—together control the organs of the digestive, cardiovascular, excretory, and endocrine systems.

The sympathetic and parasympathetic divisions of the autonomic nervous system have largely antagonistic (opposite) functions in regulating organ function (**Figure 49.8**). Activation of

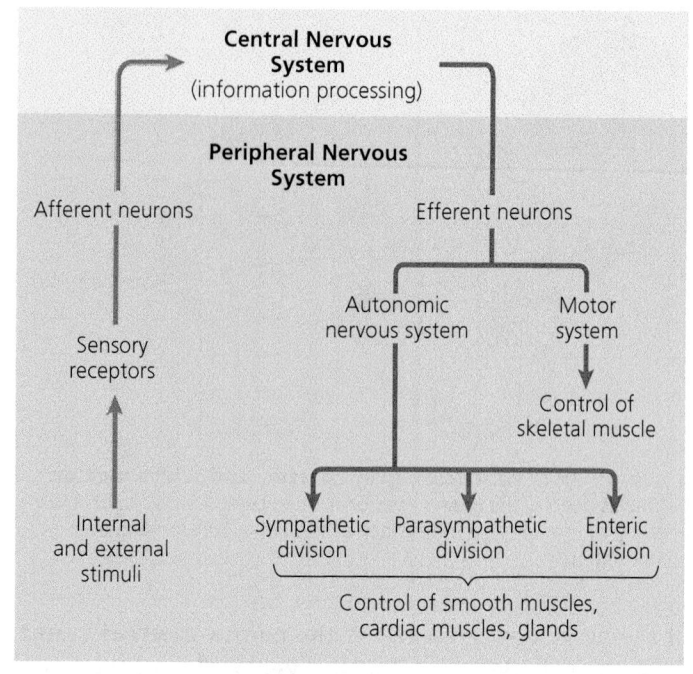

▲ **Figure 49.7 Functional hierarchy of the vertebrate peripheral nervous system.**

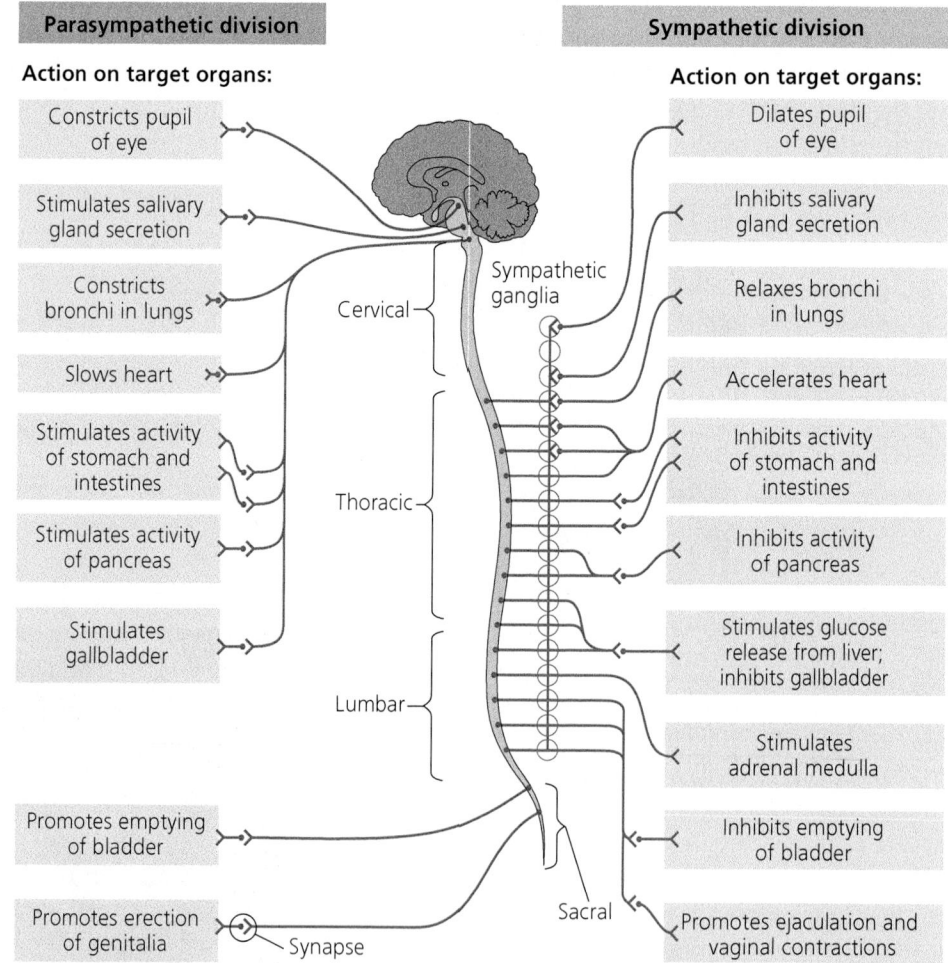

▲ **Figure 49.8 The parasympathetic and sympathetic divisions of the autonomic nervous system.** Most pathways in each division consist of preganglionic neurons (having cell bodies in the CNS) and postganglionic neurons (having cell bodies in ganglia in the PNS).

the **sympathetic division** corresponds to arousal and energy generation (the "fight-or-flight" response). For example, the heart beats faster, digestion is inhibited, the liver converts glycogen to glucose, and the adrenal medulla increases secretion of epinephrine (adrenaline) and norepinephrine. Activation of the **parasympathetic division** generally causes opposite responses that promote calming and a return to self-maintenance functions ("rest and digest"). Thus, heart rate decreases, digestion is enhanced, and glycogen production increases. In regulating reproductive activity, however, the parasympathetic division complements rather than antagonizes the sympathetic division (see Figure 49.8).

Networks of neurons that form the **enteric division** of the PNS are active in the digestive tract, pancreas, and gallbladder. Within these organs, the enteric division regulates secretion and peristalsis (see Chapter 41). The sympathetic and parasympathetic divisions normally regulate the enteric division, although it is capable of independent activity.

Homeostasis often relies on cooperation between the motor and autonomic nervous systems. In response to a drop in body temperature, for example, the hypothalamus signals the motor system to cause shivering, which increases heat production. At the same time, the hypothalamus signals the autonomic nervous system to constrict surface blood vessels, reducing heat loss.

CONCEPT CHECK 49.1

1. Which division of the autonomic nervous system would likely be activated if a student learned that an exam she had forgotten about would start in 5 minutes? Explain your answer.
2. The parasympathetic and sympathetic divisions of the PNS (see Figure 49.8) use the same neurotransmitters at the axon terminals of preganglionic neurons, but different neurotransmitters at the axon terminals of postganglionic neurons. How does this difference correlate with the function of the axons bringing signals into and out of the ganglia in the two divisions?
3. **WHAT IF?** Suppose a person had an accident that severed a small nerve required to move some of the fingers of the right hand. Would you also expect an effect on sensation from those fingers?
4. **MAKE CONNECTIONS** Most tissues regulated by the autonomic nervous system receive both sympathetic and parasympathetic input from postganglionic neurons. Responses are typically local. In contrast, the adrenal medulla receives input only from the sympathetic division and only from preganglionic neurons, yet responses are observed throughout the body. Explain why (see Figure 45.21, p. 991).

For suggested answers, see Appendix A.

The vertebrate brain is regionally specialized

Having considered some of the basic functions of the PNS, we turn now to the brain. Images of the human brain in popular culture almost always focus on the cerebrum, the part of the brain whose surface lies just beneath the skull. The cerebrum is responsible for many activities we commonly associate with the brain, such as calculation, contemplation, and memory. Underneath the cerebrum, however, are additional brain structures with important and diverse activities, including homeostasis, coordination, and information transfer.

Figure 49.9, on pages 1068–1069, explores the origin, form, and function of major regions of the human brain. It outlines how brain structures arise during embryonic development, illustrates their size, shape, and location in the adult, and summarizes their best-understood functions. Figure 49.9 will serve as an introduction to the regional specialization in the brain and provide a useful point of reference for later discussions of specific brain functions.

To learn more about how brain organization relates to brain function, we'll first consider activity cycles of the brain and the physiological basis of emotion. Then, in Concept 49.3, we'll shift our attention to regional specialization within the cerebrum.

Arousal and Sleep

If you've ever drifted off to sleep while listening to a lecture (or reading a book), you know that your attentiveness and mental alertness can change rapidly. Such transitions are regulated by the brainstem and cerebrum, which control arousal and sleep. Arousal is a state of awareness of the external world. Sleep is a state in which external stimuli are received but not consciously perceived.

Contrary to appearances, sleep is an active state, at least for the brain. By placing electrodes at multiple sites on the scalp, we can record patterns of electrical activity called brain waves in an electroencephalogram (EEG). These recordings reveal that brain wave frequencies change as the brain progresses through distinct stages of sleep.

Although sleep is essential for survival, we still know very little about its function. One hypothesis is that sleep and dreams are involved in consolidating learning and memory. This hypothesis is supported by the finding that test subjects who are kept awake for 36 hours have a reduced ability to remember when particular events occurred, even if they first "perk up" with caffeine. Other experiments show that regions of the brain that are activated during a learning task can become active again during sleep.

Exploring The Organization of the Human Brain

The brain is the most complex organ in the human body. Surrounded by the thick bones of the skull, the brain is divided into a set of distinctive structures, some of which are visible in the magnetic resonance image (MRI) of an adult's head shown at right. The diagram below traces the development of these structures in the embryo. Their major functions are explained on the facing page.

Human Brain Development

As a human embryo develops, the neural tube forms three anterior bulges—the **forebrain**, **midbrain**, and **hindbrain**—that together produce the adult brain. The midbrain and a part of the hindbrain give rise to the **brainstem**, a stalk that joins with the spinal cord at the base of the brain. The rest of the hindbrain gives rise to the **cerebellum**, which lies behind the brainstem. The third anterior bulge, the forebrain, develops into the diencephalon, including the neuroendocrine tissues of the brain, and the telencephalon, which becomes the **cerebrum**. Rapid, expansive growth of the telencephalon during the second and third months causes the outer portion, or cortex, of the cerebrum to extend over and around much of the rest of the brain.

Embryonic brain regions

Forebrain
- Telencephalon
- Diencephalon

Midbrain
- Mesencephalon

Hindbrain
- Metencephalon
- Myelencephalon

Brain structures in child and adult

- Cerebrum (includes cerebral cortex, white matter, basal nuclei)
- Diencephalon (thalamus, hypothalamus, epithalamus)
- Midbrain (part of brainstem)
- Pons (part of brainstem), cerebellum
- Medulla oblongata (part of brainstem)

Midbrain
Hindbrain
Forebrain

Embryo at 1 month

Mesencephalon
Metencephalon
Diencephalon
Myelencephalon
Spinal cord
Telencephalon

Embryo at 5 weeks

Cerebrum
Diencephalon
Midbrain
Pons
Medulla oblongata
Cerebellum
Spinal cord

Child

The Cerebrum

The cerebrum controls skeletal muscle contraction and is the center for learning, emotion, memory, and perception. It is divided into right and left **cerebral hemispheres**. The **cerebral cortex** is vital for perception, voluntary movement, and learning. Like the rest of the cerebrum, the cerebral cortex is divided into right and left sides. The left side receives information from, and controls the movement of, the right side of the body, and vice versa. A thick band of axons known as the **corpus callosum** enables the right and left cerebral cortices to communicate. Deep within the white matter, clusters of neurons called *basal nuclei* serve as centers for planning and learning movement sequences. Damage to these sites during fetal development can result in cerebral palsy, a disorder resulting from a disruption in the transmission of motor commands to the muscles.

The Cerebellum

The cerebellum coordinates movement and balance and helps in learning and remembering motor skills. The cerebellum receives sensory information about the positions of the joints and the lengths of the muscles, as well as input from the auditory (hearing) and visual systems. It also monitors motor commands issued by the cerebrum. The cerebellum integrates this information as it carries out coordination and error checking during motor and perceptual functions. Hand-eye coordination is an example of cerebellar control; if the cerebellum is damaged, the eyes can follow a moving object, but they will not stop at the same place as the object. Hand movement toward the object will also be erratic.

Left cerebral hemisphere
Right cerebral hemisphere
Cerebral cortex
Corpus callosum
Cerebrum
Basal nuclei
Cerebellum

Adult brain viewed from the rear

The Diencephalon

The diencephalon gives rise to the thalamus, hypothalamus, and epithalamus. The **thalamus** is the main input center for sensory information going to the cerebrum. Incoming information from all the senses is sorted in the thalamus and sent to the appropriate cerebral centers for further processing. The thalamus is formed by two masses, each roughly the size and shape of a walnut. A much smaller structure, the **hypothalamus**, contains the body's thermostat as well as the central biological clock. Through its control of the pituitary gland, the hypothalamus regulates hunger and thirst, plays a role in sexual and mating behaviors, and controls the fight-or-flight response. The hypothalamus is also the source of posterior pituitary hormones and of releasing hormones that act on the anterior pituitary (see Figures 45.15 and 45.17). The *epithalamus* includes the pineal gland, the source of melatonin. It also contains one of several clusters of capillaries that generate cerebrospinal fluid from blood.

Diencephalon
Thalamus
Pineal gland
Hypothalamus
Pituitary gland
Spinal cord

The Brainstem

The brainstem consists of the midbrain, the **pons**, and the **medulla oblongata** (commonly called the *medulla*). The midbrain receives and integrates several types of sensory information and sends it to specific regions of the forebrain. All sensory axons involved in hearing either terminate in the midbrain or pass through it on their way to the cerebrum. In addition, the midbrain coordinates visual reflexes, such as the peripheral vision reflex: The head turns toward an object approaching from the side without the brain having formed an image of the object.

A major function of the pons and medulla is to transfer information between the PNS and the midbrain and forebrain. The pons and medulla also help coordinate large-scale body movements, such as running and climbing. Most axons that carry instructions about these movements cross from one side of the CNS to the other in the medulla. As a result, the right side of the brain controls much of the movement of the left side of the body, and vice versa. An additional function of the medulla is the control of several automatic, homeostatic functions, including breathing, heart and blood vessel activity, swallowing, vomiting, and digestion. The pons also participates in some of these activities; for example, it regulates the breathing centers in the medulla.

Brainstem
Midbrain
Pons
Medulla oblongata

Eye
Reticular formation
Input from touch, pain, and temperature receptors
Input from nerves of ears

▲ **Figure 49.10 The reticular formation.** This system of neurons distributed throughout the core of the brainstem filters sensory input (blue arrows), blocking familiar and repetitive information that constantly enters the nervous system. It sends the filtered input to the cerebral cortex (green arrows).

Key

∧∧ Low-frequency waves characteristic of sleep

∿∿ High-frequency waves characteristic of wakefulness

Location	Time: 0 hours	Time: 1 hour
Left hemisphere	∿∧∧∧∿∿	∿∿∿∿
Right hemisphere	∿∿∿	∧∧∧∧∧∧

▲ **Figure 49.11 Dolphins can be asleep and awake at the same time.** EEG recordings were made separately for the two sides of a dolphin's brain. Low-frequency activity was recorded in one hemisphere while higher-frequency activity typical of being awake was recorded in the other hemisphere.

Arousal and sleep are controlled in part by the **reticular formation**, a diffuse network of neurons in the core of the brainstem (**Figure 49.10**). Acting as a sensory filter, the reticular formation determines which incoming information reaches the cerebrum. The more information the cerebrum receives, the more alert and aware a person is, although the brain often ignores certain stimuli while actively processing other inputs. Besides the diffuse reticular formation, there are also specific parts of the brainstem that regulate sleep and wakefulness: The pons and medulla contain centers that cause sleep when stimulated, and the midbrain has a center that causes arousal.

All birds and mammals show characteristic sleep/wake cycles. Melatonin, a hormone produced by the pineal gland, appears to play an important role in these cycles. As you read in Chapter 45, peak melatonin secretion occurs at night.

Some animals display evolutionary adaptations that allow for substantial activity during sleep. Bottlenose dolphins, for example, swim while sleeping, rising to the surface to breathe air on a regular basis. How do they manage this feat? A critical clue came from American physiologist John Lilly, who in 1964 observed that dolphins sleep with one eye open and one closed. As in humans and other mammals, the forebrain of dolphins is physically and functionally divided into two halves, the right and left hemispheres. Lilly suggested that a dolphin sleeping with one eye closed could mean that just one side of the brain was asleep. In 1977, Russian scientist Lev Mukhametov set out to test Lilly's hypothesis by collecting EEG recordings from each hemisphere of sleeping dolphins (**Figure 49.11**). Mukhametov's findings demonstrate that dolphins do in fact sleep with one brain hemisphere at a time.

Biological Clock Regulation

Cycles of sleep and wakefulness are just one example of a circadian rhythm, a daily cycle of biological activity. Such cycles occur in organisms ranging from bacteria to fungi, plants, insects, birds, and humans. As in other organisms, circadian rhythms in mammals rely on a **biological clock**, a molecular mechanism that directs periodic gene expression and cellular activity. Although biological clocks are typically synchronized to the cycles of light and dark in the environment, they can maintain a roughly 24-hour cycle even in the absence of environmental cues (see Figure 40.9). For example, humans kept in a constant environment exhibit a cycle length of 24.2 hours, with very little variation among individuals.

What normally links an animal's biological clock to environmental cycles of light and dark? In mammals, circadian rhythms are coordinated by a group of neurons in the hypothalamus called the **suprachiasmatic nucleus**, or **SCN**. (Certain clusters of neurons in the CNS are referred to as "nuclei.") In response to transmission of sensory information by the eyes, the SCN acts as a pacemaker, synchronizing the biological clock in cells throughout the body to the natural cycles of day length. By surgically removing the SCN from laboratory animals and then observing their behavior, scientists demonstrated that the SCN is required for circadian rhythms: Animals without an SCN lack rhythmicity in behaviors and in electrical activity of the brain. These experiments did not, however, reveal whether rhythms originate in the SCN or elsewhere. In 1990, researchers answered this question with the aid of a mutation that changes the circadian rhythm of hamsters (**Figure 49.12**). By transplanting brain tissue between normal and mutant hamsters, these scientists demonstrated that the SCN determines the circadian rhythm of the whole animal.

INQUIRY

Which cells control the circadian rhythm in mammals?

EXPERIMENT The τ (tau) mutation alters the period of the circadian rhythm in Syrian (golden) hamsters (*Mesocricetus auratus*). Whereas wild-type hamsters have a circadian cycle lasting 24 hours in the absence of external cues, hamsters homozygous for the τ mutation have a cycle lasting only about 20 hours. To determine if the SCN controls the circadian rhythm, Michael Menaker and colleagues at the University of Virginia surgically removed the SCN from wild-type and τ hamsters. Several weeks later, each of these hamsters received a transplant of an SCN from a hamster of the opposite genotype. The researchers then measured the circadian cycle period of the transplant recipients.

RESULTS In 80% of the hamsters in which the SCN had been removed, transplanting an SCN from another hamster restored rhythmic activity. For hamsters in which an SCN transplant restored a circadian rhythm, the net effect of the two procedures (SCN destruction and replacement) on circadian rhythm is graphed below. Each of the eight lines represents the change in the observed circadian cycle period for an individual hamster.

● Wild-type hamster
▲ Wild-type hamster with SCN from τ hamster
● τ hamster
▲ τ hamster with SCN from wild-type hamster

CONCLUSION Because the circadian rhythm of the animal that received the transplant was that of the donor animal, regardless of whether the recipient was wild-type or τ mutant, cells associated with the suprachiasmatic nucleus must determine the period of the circadian rhythm.

SOURCE M. R. Ralph, R. G. Foster, F. C. Davis, and M. Menaker, Transplanted suprachiasmatic nucleus determines circadian period, *Science* 247:975–978 (1990).

WHAT IF? Suppose in the course of your research you identified a hamster mutant that lacked rhythmic activity. How might you use this mutant in transplant experiments with wild-type or τ mutant hamsters to demonstrate that the mutation affected the pacemaker function of the SCN?

Emotions

Whereas a single structure in the brain controls the biological clock, the generation and experience of emotions depend on many brain structures, including the amygdala, hippocampus, and parts of the thalamus (Figure 49.13). These structures border the brainstem in mammals and are therefore grouped as the *limbic system* (from the Latin *limbus*, border). The limbic system, however, is not dedicated solely to emotion. It also functions in motivation, olfaction (the sense of smell), behavior, and memory.

Generating emotion and experiencing emotion require parts of the brain in addition to the limbic system. For example, emotions that manifest themselves in behaviors such as laughing and crying involve an interaction of parts of the limbic system with sensory areas of the cerebrum. Structures in the forebrain also attach emotional "feelings" to basic, survival-related functions controlled by the brainstem, including aggression, feeding, and sexuality.

Emotional experiences are often stored as memories that can be recalled by similar circumstances. In the case of fear, emotional memory is stored separately from the memory system that supports explicit recall of events. The brain structure with the most important role in storage of emotional memory is the **amygdala**, an almond-shaped mass of nuclei (clusters of neurons) located near the base of the cerebrum.

To study the function of the human amygdala, researchers sometimes present adult subjects with an image followed by an unpleasant experience, such as a mild electrical shock. After several trials, study participants experience *autonomic arousal*—as measured by increased heart rate or sweating—if they see the image again. Subjects with brain damage confined to the amygdala can recall the image because their explicit memory is intact. However, they do not exhibit autonomic arousal, indicating that damage to the amygdala has resulted in a reduced capacity for emotional memory.

▲ Figure 49.13 **The limbic system.**

Today, the amygdala and other brain structures are being studied with functional imaging methods that are transforming our understanding of the normal and diseased brain (Figure 49.14).

▼ Figure 49.14

IMPACT

Using Functional Brain Imaging to Map Activity in the Working Brain

Techniques for mapping brain activity have transformed the study of human brain function. The first widely used technique was positron-emission tomography (PET; see Figure 2.7). After injecting radioactive glucose into the blood of a subject, researchers can use PET scans to monitor metabolic activity across the brain. Further progress has come with functional magnetic resonance imaging (fMRI). In fMRI, the subject lies with his or her head in the center of a large, doughnut-shaped magnet. When the brain is scanned with electromagnetic waves, changes in blood oxygen concentration in active parts of the brain generate a signal that can be recorded.

Functional brain imaging has been applied to the study of human cognition, consciousness, and emotion. For example, functional imaging suggests that consciousness may be an emergent property of the brain based on activity in many areas of the cortex. In the experiment shown here, researchers explored differences in brain activity associated with music that listeners described as happy or sad. Listening to happy music activated the *nucleus accumbens*, a brain structure important for the perception of pleasure. In contrast, subjects who heard sad music had increased activity in the amygdala, a brain structure that serves as a center for emotional memory.

Nucleus accumbens   Amygdala

Happy music   Sad music

WHY IT MATTERS Functional brain imaging is aiding the investigation of recovery from stroke and other brain traumas, as well as helping map abnormalities in migraine headaches, dyslexia, and many psychiatric disorders. Functional imaging is also having a major impact on brain surgery. For example, for patients with epilepsy that is not responsive to drug therapy, functional imaging can pinpoint the region of abnormal function, increasing the effectiveness of surgery and enhancing recovery. Finally, functional imaging has been used to explore sex-based differences in the CNS, demonstrating, for instance, that cerebral blood flow is higher on average in women than in men.

FURTHER READING R. C. deCharms, Applications of real-time fMRI, *Nature Reviews Neuroscience* 9:720–729 (2008).

WHAT IF? In the experiment illustrated above, some regions of the brain showed activity under all conditions. What function might such regions carry out?

CONCEPT CHECK 49.2

1. When you wave your right hand, what part of your brain initiates the action?
2. When a police officer stops a driver for driving erratically and suspects that the person is intoxicated, the officer may ask the driver to close his or her eyes and touch his or her nose. What can you deduce from this test about one of the brain regions affected by alcohol?
3. **WHAT IF?** Suppose you examine individuals with damage to the CNS that has resulted in either coma (a prolonged state of unconsciousness) or general paralysis (a loss of skeletal muscle function throughout the body). Relative to the position of the reticular formation, where would you predict the site of injury to lie in each group of patients? Explain.

For suggested answers, see Appendix A.

CONCEPT 49.3

The cerebral cortex controls voluntary movement and cognitive functions

We turn now to the cerebrum, the part of the brain essential for awareness of our surroundings, language, cognition, memory, and consciousness. As shown in Figure 49.9, the cerebrum is the largest structure in the human brain. Like the brain overall, it exhibits regional specialization. For the most part, cognitive functions reside in the cortex, the outer layer of the cerebrum. Within the cortex, sensory areas receive and process sensory information, association areas integrate the information, and motor areas transmit instructions to other parts of the body.

In discussing the location of particular functions in the cerebral cortex, neurobiologists often use four regions, or *lobes*, as physical landmarks. As shown in Figure 49.15, each side of the cerebral cortex has a frontal, temporal, occipital, and parietal lobe (each is named for a nearby bone of the skull).

Language and Speech

The mapping of higher cognitive functions to specific brain areas began in the 1800s when physicians learned that damage to particular regions of the cortex by injuries, strokes, or tumors can produce distinctive changes in a person's behavior. The French physician Pierre Broca conducted postmortem (after death) examinations of patients who had been able to understand language but unable to speak. He discovered that many of these patients had defects in a small region of the left frontal lobe, now known as *Broca's area*, that controls muscles in the face. The German physician Karl Wernicke found that damage to a posterior portion of the left temporal lobe, now

Motor cortex (control of skeletal muscles)

Somatosensory cortex (sense of touch)

Frontal lobe

Parietal lobe

Prefrontal cortex (decision making, planning)

Sensory association cortex (integration of sensory information)

Broca's area (forming speech)

Visual association cortex (combining images and object recognition)

Temporal lobe

Occipital lobe

Auditory cortex (hearing)

Visual cortex (processing visual stimuli and pattern recognition)

Wernicke's area (comprehending language)

Cerebellum

◀ **Figure 49.15 The human cerebral cortex.** Each side of the cerebral cortex is divided into four lobes, and each lobe has specialized functions, some of which are listed here. Some areas on the left side of the brain (shown here) have different functions from those on the right side (not shown).

called *Wernicke's area*, abolished the ability to comprehend speech but not the ability to speak.

More than a century after the discoveries of Broca and Wernicke, functional imaging studies confirmed that Broca's area is active during speech generation (Figure 49.16, lower left image) and Wernicke's area is active when speech is heard (Figure 49.16, upper left image). In addition, researchers have found that these areas belong to a much larger network of brain regions involved in language. Reading a printed word without speaking activates the visual cortex (Figure 49.16, upper right image), whereas reading a printed word out loud activates both the visual cortex and Broca's area. Frontal and temporal areas become active when meaning must be attached to words, such as when a person generates verbs to go

▲ **Figure 49.16 Mapping language areas in the cerebral cortex.** These PET images show regions with different activity levels in one person's brain during four activities, all related to speech.

with nouns or groups related words or concepts (Figure 49.16, lower right image).

Lateralization of Cortical Function

Both Broca's area and Wernicke's area reside in the left cortical hemisphere, reflecting a significantly greater role with regard to language for the left side of the cerebrum than for the right side. The two hemispheres also make distinct contributions to some other brain functions, although to a lesser degree than for language. For example, the left hemisphere is more adept at math and logical operations. In contrast, the right hemisphere appears to be dominant in the recognition of faces and patterns, spatial relations, and nonverbal thinking. The establishment of these differences in hemisphere function in humans is called **lateralization**.

At least some lateralization relates to handedness, the preference for using one hand for certain motor activities. Across human populations, roughly 90% of individuals are more skilled with their right hand than with their left hand. Studies using fMRI have revealed how language processing differs in relation to handedness. When subjects thought of words without speaking out loud, brain activity was localized to the left hemisphere in 96% of right-handed subjects but in only 76% of left-handed subjects.

The two hemispheres normally work together harmoniously, trading information back and forth through the fibers of the corpus callosum. The importance of this exchange is revealed in patients whose corpus callosum has been surgically severed (a treatment of last resort for the most extreme forms of epilepsy, a seizure disorder). Individuals with a severed corpus callosum exhibit a "split-brain" effect. When a familiar word appears in their left field of vision, they cannot read the word: The sensory information that travels from the left field of vision to the right hemisphere cannot reach the language centers in the left hemisphere. Each hemisphere in such patients functions independently of the other.

Information Processing

As you will learn further in Chapter 50, some of the sensory input to the cerebral cortex comes from groups of receptors clustered in dedicated sensory organs, such as the eyes and nose. Other sensory input originates in individual receptors in the hands, scalp, and elsewhere in the body. These somatic sensory, or *somatosensory*, receptors (from the Greek *soma*, body) provide information about touch, pain, pressure, temperature, and the position of muscles and limbs.

Most sensory information coming into the cortex is directed via the thalamus to primary sensory areas within the brain lobes. The thalamus directs different types of input to distinct locations. For example, visual information is sent to the occipital lobe, whereas auditory input is directed to the temporal lobe (see Figure 49.15).

Information received at the primary sensory areas is passed along to nearby association areas, which process particular features in the sensory input. In the occipital lobe, for instance, some groups of neurons in the primary visual area are specifically sensitive to rays of light oriented in a particular direction. In the visual association area, information related to such features is combined in a region dedicated to recognizing complex images, such as faces.

Integrated sensory information passes to the prefrontal cortex, which helps plan actions and movement. The cerebral cortex may then generate motor commands that cause particular behaviors—moving a limb or saying hello, for example. These commands consist of action potentials produced by neurons in the motor cortex, which lies at the rear of the frontal lobe (see Figure 49.15). The action potentials travel along axons to the brainstem and spinal cord, where they excite motor neurons, which in turn excite skeletal muscle cells.

In the somatosensory cortex and motor cortex, neurons are arranged according to the part of the body that generates the sensory input or receives the motor commands (Figure 49.17). For example, neurons that process sensory information from the legs and feet lie in the region of the somatosensory cortex closest to the midline. Neurons that control muscles in the

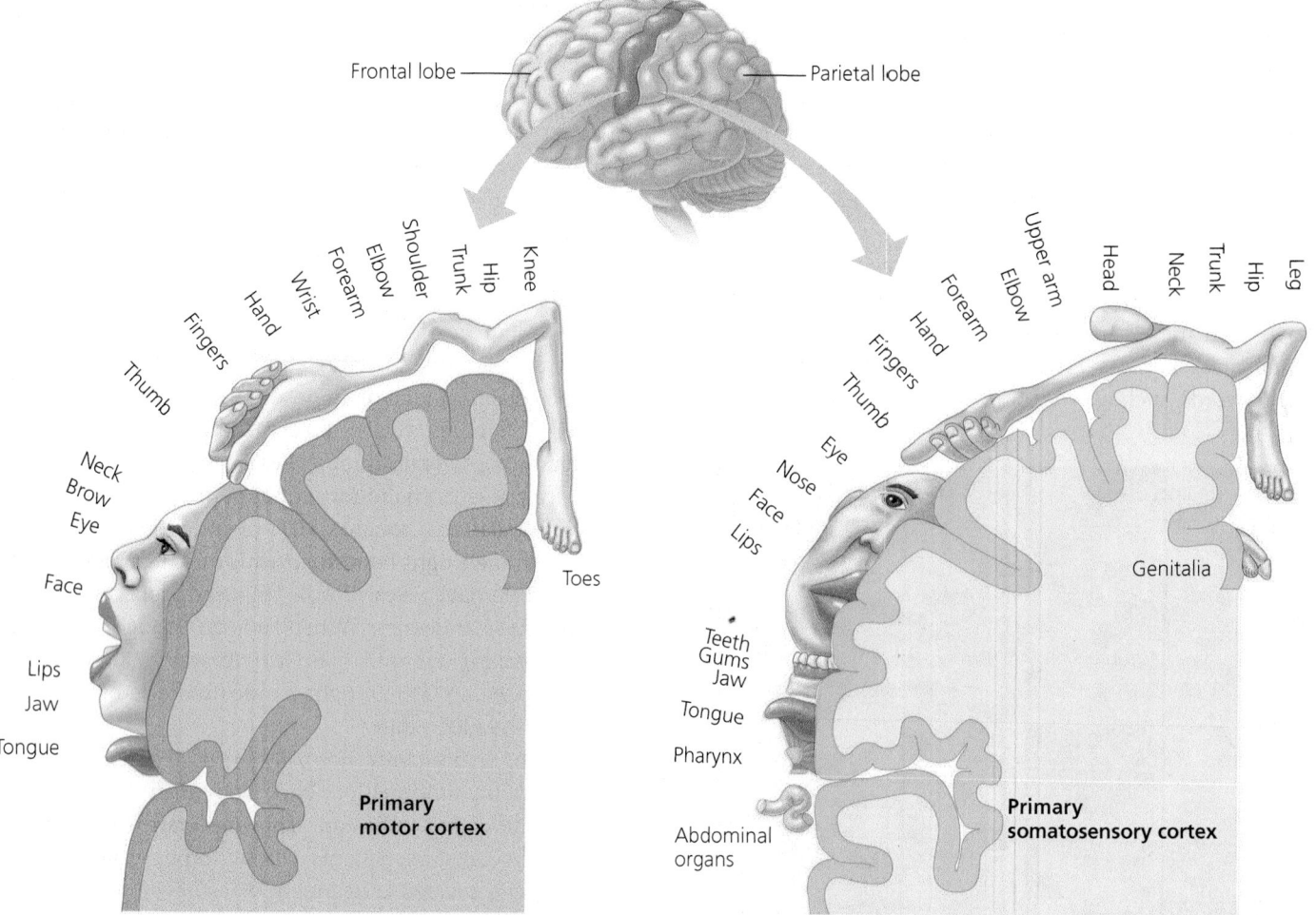

▲ **Figure 49.17 Body part representation in the primary motor and primary somatosensory cortices.** In these cross-sectional maps of the cortices, the cortical surface area devoted to each body part is represented by the relative size of that part in the cartoons.

legs and feet are located in the corresponding region of the motor cortex. Notice in Figure 49.17 that the cortical surface area devoted to each body part is not proportional to the size of the part. Instead, surface area correlates with the extent of neuronal control needed (for the motor cortex) or with the number of sensory neurons that extend axons to that part (for the somatosensory cortex). Thus, the surface area of the motor cortex devoted to the face is much larger than that devoted to the trunk, reflecting the extensive involvement of facial muscles in communication.

Frontal Lobe Function

In 1848, a horrific workplace accident pointed to the role of the prefrontal cortex in temperament and decision making. Phineas Gage was working as the foreman of a railroad construction crew when an explosion drove a meter-long iron rod through his head. The rod, which was more than 3 cm in diameter at one end, entered his skull just below his left eye and exited through the top of his head, damaging large portions of his frontal lobe. Astonishingly, Gage recovered. His personality, however, changed dramatically. He became emotionally detached, impatient, and erratic in his behavior.

Although the connection between Gage's brain injury and his personality change is a subject of debate, some tumors that develop in the frontal lobe cause symptoms that are similar to those of Gage. Intellect and memory seem intact, but decision making is flawed and emotional responses are diminished. In the 20th century, the same problems were observed as a result of frontal lobotomy, a surgical procedure that severs the connection between the prefrontal cortex and the limbic system. Together, these observations provide evidence that the frontal lobes have a substantial influence on what are often called "executive functions."

Frontal lobotomy was once a common treatment for severe behavioral disorders but later was abandoned as a medical practice. Behavioral disorders are now typically treated with medications, as discussed later in this chapter.

Evolution of Cognition in Vertebrates

EVOLUTION In humans, the cerebral cortex accounts for about 80% of total brain mass and is highly convoluted (see Figure 49.9). The convolutions allow the cerebral cortex to have a large surface area and still fit inside the skull: Less than 5 mm thick, it has a surface area of approximately 1,000 cm². The outermost part of the human cerebral cortex forms the *neocortex*, six parallel layers of neurons arranged tangential to the brain surface.

It was long thought that a highly convoluted neocortex was required for advanced *cognition*, the perception and reasoning that constitute knowledge. Primates and cetaceans (whales, dolphins, and porpoises) possess an extensively convoluted neocortex. However, birds lack such a structure and were thought to have much lower intellectual capacity. Experiments in recent years have refuted this idea. Western scrub jays (*Aphelocoma californica*) can remember the relative period of time that has passed after they stored and hid specific food items. New Caledonian crows (*Corvus moneduloides*) are highly skilled at making and using tools, an ability otherwise well documented only for humans and some other apes. African gray parrots (*Psittacus erithacus*) understand numerical and abstract concepts, distinguishing between "same" and "different" and grasping the idea of "none."

The anatomical basis for sophisticated information processing in birds appears to be the grouping of nuclei within the *pallium*, the top or outer portion of the brain (Figure 49.18). This arrangement is different from that in the human pallium—the cerebral cortex—which contains flat sheets of cells in six layers. Thus, there are two types of pallium, each of which supports complex and flexible brain function.

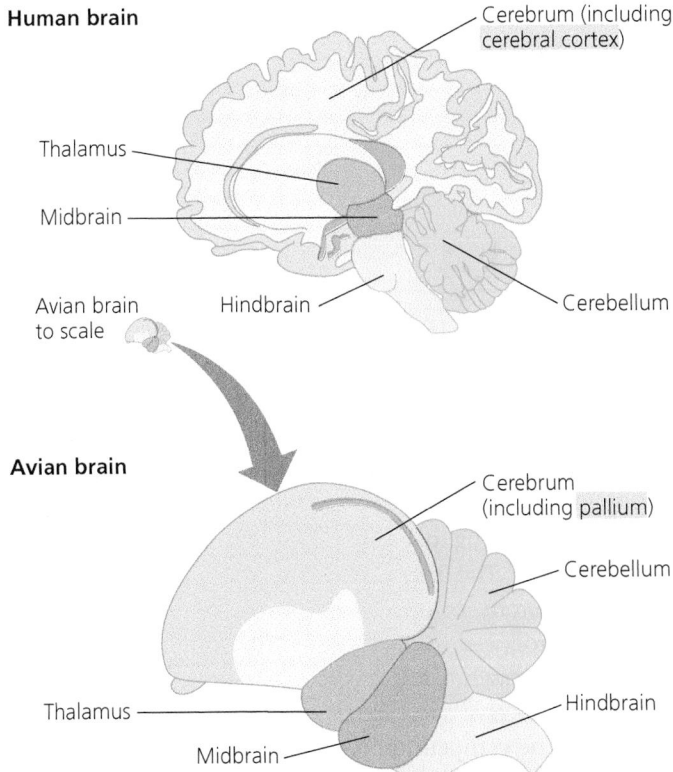

▲ Figure 49.18 **Comparison of regions for higher cognition in avian and human brains.** Although structurally different, the cerebral cortex of the human brain (top cross section) and the pallium of a songbird brain (bottom cross section) have similar roles in higher cognitive activities and make many similar connections with other brain structures.

How did the differences between the bird pallium and human pallium arise during evolution? The current consensus is that the common ancestor of birds and mammals had a pallium in which neurons were organized into nuclei, as is still found in birds. Early in mammalian evolution, this nuclear (clustered) organization of neurons was transformed into a layered one. Connectivity was maintained during this transformation such that, for example, the thalamus relays sensory input relating to sights, sounds, and touch to the pallium in both birds and mammals.

Sophisticated information processing depends not only on the overall organization of a brain but also on the very small-scale changes that enable learning and encode memory. We'll turn to these changes in the context of humans in the next section.

CONCEPT CHECK 49.3

1. How can studying individuals with damage to a particular brain region provide insight into the normal function of that region?
2. Two brain areas important in the generation or perception of speech are Broca's area and Wernicke's area. How is the function of each area related to the activity of the surrounding portion of the cerebral cortex?
3. **WHAT IF?** If a woman with a severed corpus callosum viewed a photograph of a familiar face, first in her left field of vision and then in her right field, why would she find it difficult to put a name to the face in either field?

For suggested answers, see Appendix A.

CONCEPT 49.4

Changes in synaptic connections underlie memory and learning

During embryonic development, regulated gene expression and signal transduction establish the overall structure of the nervous system (see Chapter 47). Two processes then dominate the remaining development and remodeling of the nervous system. The first is a competition among neurons for survival. Neurons compete for growth-supporting factors, which are produced in limited quantities by tissues that direct neuron growth. Cells that don't reach the proper locations fail to receive such factors and undergo programmed cell death. The competition is so severe that half of the neurons formed in the embryo are eliminated. The net effect is the preferential survival of neurons that are located properly within the nervous system.

Synapse elimination is the second major process that shapes the nervous system. A developing neuron forms numerous synapses, more than are required for its proper function. The

activity of that neuron then stabilizes some synapses and destabilizes others. By the end of embryonic development, neurons on average have lost more than half of their initial synapses, leaving behind the connections that survive into adulthood.

Together, neuron death and synapse elimination set up the basic network of cells and connections within the nervous system required throughout life.

Neural Plasticity

Although the overall organization of the CNS is established during embryonic development, it can change after birth. This capacity for the nervous system to be remodeled, especially in response to its own activity, is called **neural plasticity**.

Much of the reshaping of the nervous system occurs at synapses. When the activity of a synapse correlates with that of other synapses, changes may occur that reinforce that synaptic connection. Conversely, when the activity of a synapse fails to correlate with that of other synapses, the synaptic connection sometimes becomes weaker. In this way, synapses belonging to circuits that link information in useful ways are maintained, whereas those that convey bits of information lacking any context may be lost.

Figure 49.19a illustrates how these processes can result in either the addition or loss of a synapse. If you think of signals

(a) Connections between neurons are strengthened or weakened in response to activity. High-level activity at the synapse of the postsynaptic neuron with presynaptic neuron N_1 leads to recruitment of additional axon terminals from that neuron. Lack of activity at the synapse with presynaptic neuron N_2 leads to loss of functional connections with that neuron.

(b) If two synapses on the same postsynaptic cell are often active at the same time, the strength of the postsynaptic response may increase at both synapses.

▲ **Figure 49.19 Neural plasticity.** Synaptic connections can change over time, depending on the activity level at the synapse.

in the nervous system as traffic on a highway, such changes are comparable to adding or removing an entrance ramp. The net effect is to increase signaling between particular pairs of neurons and decrease signaling between other pairs. As shown in Figure 49.19b, changes can also strengthen or weaken signaling at a synapse. In our traffic analogy, this would be equivalent to widening or narrowing an entrance ramp.

Research indicates that *autism*, a developmental disorder that first appears early in childhood, involves a disruption of activity-dependent remodeling at synapses. Children affected with autism display impaired communication and social interaction, as well as stereotyped and repetitive behaviors.

Although the underlying causes of autism are unknown, there is a strong genetic contribution to this and related disorders. Extensive research has ruled out a link to vaccine preservatives, once proposed as a potential risk factor. Further understanding of the autism-associated disruption in synaptic plasticity may help efforts to better understand and treat this disorder.

Remodeling and refining of the nervous system occur in many contexts. For instance, soon after birth, the visual cortex of the mammalian brain undergoes reorganization in response to input from the optic nerve triggered by visual stimuli. Experiments have shown that this remodeling is a necessary step in the development of normal visual ability.

Remodeling of functional brain circuitry also occurs in diseases and injuries to the nervous system from which significant recovery is possible. One example is the treatment for a condition called phantom limb syndrome, in which a person feels pain or discomfort that seems to originate from an arm or leg that has been amputated. Having the patient view a reflection of the remaining limb in a mirrored box can reorganize the brain's neural connections in a way that eliminates the unpleasant feelings from the lost limb.

Memory and Learning

The formation of memories is another example of neural plasticity. Though we may not be aware of it, we are constantly checking what is happening against what just happened a few moments ago. We hold information for a time in **short-term memory** locations and then release it if it becomes irrelevant. If we wish to retain knowledge of a name, phone number, or other fact, the mechanisms of **long-term memory** are activated. If we later need to recall the name or number, we fetch it from long-term memory and return it to short-term memory.

Scientists have long wondered where in the brain short-term and long-term memories are located. We now know that both types of memory involve the storage of information in the cerebral cortex. In short-term memory, this information is accessed via temporary links formed in the hippocampus. When memories are made long-term, the links in the hippocampus are replaced by more permanent connections within the cerebral cortex itself. Some of this consolidation of memory is thought to occur during sleep. Furthermore, the reactivation of the hippocampus that is required for memory consolidation likely forms the basis for at least some of our dreams.

According to our current understanding of memory, the hippocampus is essential for acquiring new long-term memories but not for maintaining them. This hypothesis readily explains the symptoms of some individuals who suffer damage to the hippocampus: They cannot form any new lasting memories but can freely recall events from before their injury. In effect, their lack of normal hippocampal function traps them in their past.

What evolutionary advantage might be offered by organizing short-term and long-term memories differently? Current thinking is that the delay in forming connections in the cerebral cortex allows long-term memories to be integrated gradually into the existing store of knowledge and experience, providing a basis for more meaningful associations. Consistent with this idea, the transfer of information from short-term to long-term memory is enhanced by the association of new data with data previously learned and stored in long-term memory. For example, it's easier to learn a new card game if you already have "card sense" from playing other card games.

Motor skills, such as walking, tying your shoes, or writing, are usually learned by repetition. You can perform these skills without consciously recalling the individual steps required to do these tasks correctly. Learning skills and procedures, such as those required to ride a bicycle, appears to involve cellular mechanisms very similar to those responsible for brain growth and development. In such cases, neurons actually make new connections. In contrast, memorizing phone numbers, facts, and places—which can be very rapid and may require only one exposure to the relevant item—may rely mainly on changes in the strength of existing neuronal connections. Next we will consider one way that such changes in strength can take place.

Long-Term Potentiation

In searching for the physiological basis of memory, researchers have concentrated their attention on processes that can alter a synaptic connection, making the flow of communication either more efficient or less efficient. We will focus here on **long-term potentiation (LTP)**, a lasting increase in the strength of synaptic transmission.

First characterized in tissue slices from the hippocampus, LTP involves a presynaptic neuron that releases the excitatory neurotransmitter glutamate. For LTP to occur, there must be a high-frequency series of action potentials in this presynaptic neuron. In addition, these action potentials must arrive at the synaptic terminal at the same time that the postsynaptic cell receives a depolarizing stimulus at another synapse.

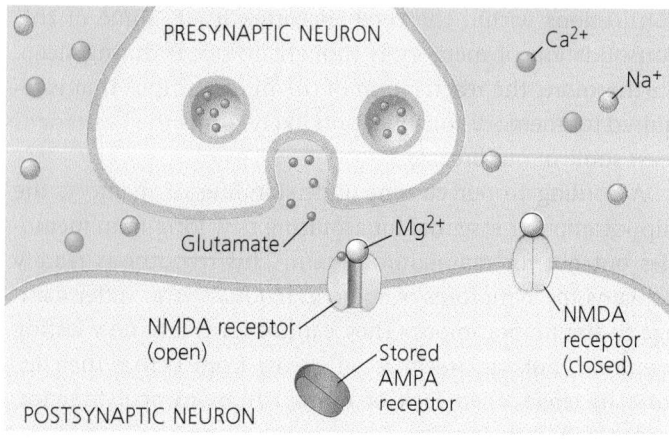

(a) Synapse prior to long-term potentiation (LTP). The NMDA glutamate receptors open in response to glutamate but are blocked by Mg^{2+}.

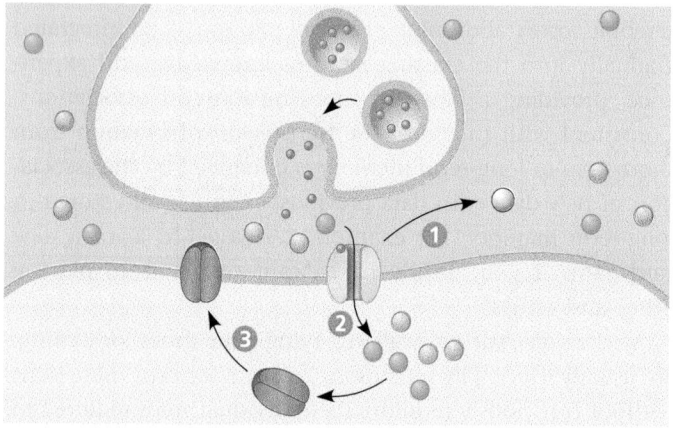

(b) Establishing LTP. Activity at nearby synapses (not shown) depolarizes the postsynaptic membrane, causing ❶ Mg^{2+} release from NMDA receptors. The unblocked receptors respond to glutamate by allowing ❷ an influx of Na^+ and Ca^{2+}. The Ca^{2+} influx triggers ❸ insertion of stored AMPA glutamate receptors into the postsynaptic membrane.

(c) Synapse exhibiting LTP. Glutamate release activates ❶ AMPA receptors that trigger ❷ depolarization. The depolarization unblocks ❸ NMDA receptors. Together, the AMPA and NMDA receptors trigger postsynaptic potentials strong enough to initiate ❹ action potentials without input from other synapses. Additional mechanisms (not shown) contribute to LTP, including receptor modification by protein kinases.

▲ Figure 49.20 **Long-term potentiation in the brain.**

LTP involves two types of glutamate receptors, each named for a molecule—NMDA or AMPA—that artificially activates that particular receptor. As shown in **Figure 49.20**, the set of receptors present on the postsynaptic membrane changes in response to an active synapse and a depolarizing stimulus. The result is LTP—a stable increase in the size of the postsynaptic potentials at the synapse. Because LTP can last for days or weeks in dissected tissue, it is thought to represent one of the fundamental processes by which memories are stored and learning takes place.

Stem Cells in the Brain

In 1998, Fred Gage, at the Salk Institute in California, and Peter Ericksson, at the Sahlgrenska University Hospital in Sweden, discovered that the adult human brain contains neural stem cells. Recall from Chapters 20 and 46 that stem cells retain the ability to divide indefinitely. While some of their progeny remain undifferentiated, others differentiate into specialized cells. Studies with mice reveal that stem cells in the brain give rise to neurons that mature, migrate to particular locations in the hippocampus, and become incorporated into the circuitry of the adult nervous system (**Figure 49.21**). Evidence from other studies indicates that such neurons play an essential role in learning and memory. In this manner, adult neural stem cells contribute to the plasticity that enables remodeling of brain circuitry in response to experience.

Researchers are now tackling the challenge of finding a way to use neural stem cells as a means of replacing brain tissue

▲ Figure 49.21 **Newly born neurons in the hippocampus of an adult mouse.** In this light micrograph, new neurons derived from adult stem cells are labeled with green fluorescent protein (GFP), and all neurons are labeled with a red dye that binds DNA.

that has ceased to function properly. Unlike the PNS, the mammalian CNS cannot fully repair itself when damaged or diseased. Surviving neurons in the brain can make new connections and sometimes compensate for damage, as occurs in the remarkable recoveries of some stroke victims. Generally, however, brain and spinal cord injuries, strokes, and disorders that destroy CNS neurons, such as Alzheimer's disease and Parkinson's disease, have devastating and irreversible effects.

Although stem cell therapy for the brain is likely to be a long way off, the recent discovery that expression of just four particular genes converts differentiated adult cells to stem cells (see Chapter 20) represents significant progress in this endeavor.

CONCEPT CHECK 49.4

1. Outline two mechanisms by which the flow of information between two neurons in adults can increase.
2. Individuals with localized brain damage have been very useful in the study of many brain functions. Why is this unlikely to be true for consciousness?
3. **WHAT IF?** Suppose that a person with damage to the hippocampus is unable to acquire new long-term memories. Why might the acquisition of short-term memories also be impaired?

For suggested answers, see Appendix A.

CONCEPT 49.5

Many nervous system disorders can be explained in molecular terms

Disorders of the nervous system, including schizophrenia, depression, drug addiction, Alzheimer's disease, and Parkinson's disease, are a major public health problem. Together, they result in more hospitalizations in the United States than do heart disease or cancer. Until recently, hospitalization was typically the only available treatment, and many affected individuals were institutionalized for the rest of their lives. Today, many disorders that alter mood or behavior can be treated with medication, reducing average hospital stays for these disorders to only a few weeks. At the same time, societal attitudes are changing as awareness grows that nervous system disorders often result from chemical or anatomical changes in the brain. Many challenges remain, however, especially for Alzheimer's and other diseases that lead to nervous system degeneration.

Major research efforts are under way to identify genes that cause or contribute to disorders of the nervous system. Identifying such genes offers hope for identifying causes, predicting outcomes, and developing effective treatments. For most nervous system disorders, however, genetic contributions only partially account for which individuals are affected. The other significant contribution to disease comes from environmental factors. Unfortunately, environmental contributions are typically very difficult to identify.

To distinguish between genetic and environmental variables, scientists often carry out family studies. In such studies, researchers track how family members are related genetically, which individuals are affected, and which family members grew up in the same household. These studies are especially informative when one of the affected individuals has either an identical twin or an adopted sibling who is genetically unrelated. The results of family studies indicate that certain nervous system disorders, such as schizophrenia, have a very strong genetic component (Figure 49.22).

Schizophrenia

About 1% of the world's population suffer from **schizophrenia**, a severe mental disturbance characterized by psychotic episodes in which patients have a distorted perception of reality. People with schizophrenia typically experience hallucinations (such as "voices" that only they can hear) and delusions (for example, the idea that others are plotting to harm them). Despite the commonly held notion,

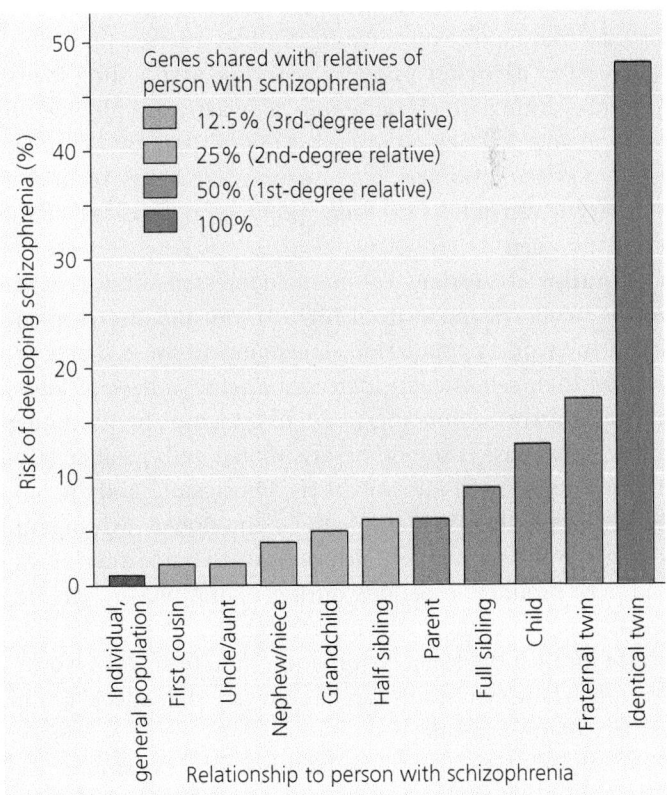

▲ **Figure 49.22 Genetic contribution to schizophrenia.** First cousins, uncles, and aunts of a person with schizophrenia have twice the risk of unrelated members of the population of developing the disease. The risks for closer relatives are many times greater.

schizophrenia does not necessarily result in multiple personalities. Rather, the name *schizophrenia* (from the Greek *schizo*, split, and *phren*, mind) refers to the fragmentation of what are normally integrated brain functions.

Two lines of evidence suggest that schizophrenia affects neuronal pathways that use dopamine as a neurotransmitter. First, the drug amphetamine ("speed"), which stimulates dopamine release, can produce the same set of symptoms as schizophrenia. Second, many of the drugs that alleviate the symptoms of schizophrenia block dopamine receptors. Schizophrenia may also alter glutamate signaling, since the street drug "angel dust," or PCP, blocks glutamate receptors and induces strong schizophrenia-like symptoms.

Fortunately, medications frequently can alleviate the major symptoms of schizophrenia. Although the first treatments developed often had substantial negative side effects, newer medications are equally effective and much safer to use. Ongoing research aimed at identifying the genetic mutations that contribute to schizophrenia may yield new insights about the causes of the disease and lead to even more effective therapies.

Depression

Depression is a disorder characterized by depressed mood, as well as abnormalities in sleep, appetite, and energy level. Two broad forms of depressive illness are known: major depressive disorder and bipolar disorder. Individuals affected by **major depressive disorder** undergo periods—often lasting many months—during which once enjoyable activities provide no pleasure and provoke no interest. One of the most common nervous system disorders, major depression affects about one in every seven adults at some point, and twice as many women as men.

Bipolar disorder, or manic-depressive disorder, involves swings of mood from high to low and affects about 1% of the world's population. The manic phase is characterized by high self-esteem, increased energy, a flow of ideas, overtalkativeness, and increased risk taking. In its milder forms, this phase is sometimes associated with great creativity, and some well-known artists, musicians, and literary figures (including Vincent Van Gogh, Robert Schumann, Virginia Woolf, and Ernest Hemingway, to name a few) have had very productive periods during manic phases. The depressive phase comes with lowered ability to feel pleasure, loss of motivation, sleep disturbances, and feelings of worthlessness. These symptoms can be so severe that affected individuals attempt suicide.

Major depressive and bipolar disorders are among the nervous system disorders for which available therapies are most effective. Many drugs used to treat depressive illness, including fluoxetine (Prozac), increase the activity of biogenic amines in the brain.

Drug Addiction and the Brain's Reward System

Drug addiction is a disorder characterized by compulsive consumption of a drug and loss of control in limiting intake. Addictive drugs include stimulants, such as cocaine and amphetamine, and sedatives, such as heroin. However, all of these drugs, as well as alcohol and nicotine, are addictive for the same reason: Each increases activity of the brain's reward system, neural circuitry that normally functions in pleasure, motivation, and learning.

In the absence of drug addiction, the reward system of the brain provides motivation for activities that enhance survival and reproduction, such as eating in response to hunger, drinking when thirsty, and engaging in sexual activity when aroused. In addicted individuals, "wanting" is instead directed toward further drug consumption.

As shown in **Figure 49.23**, inputs to the reward system are received by neurons in a region near the base of the brain called the *ventral tegmental area (VTA)*. When activated, these neurons release dopamine from their synaptic terminals in

Nicotine stimulates dopamine-releasing VTA neuron.

Inhibitory neuron

Dopamine-releasing VTA neuron

Opium and heroin decrease activity of inhibitory neuron.

Cocaine and amphetamines block removal of dopamine from synaptic cleft.

Cerebral neuron of reward pathway

Reward system response

▲ **Figure 49.23 Effects of addictive drugs on the reward system of the mammalian brain.** Addictive drugs alter the transmission of signals in the pathway formed by neurons of the ventral tegmental area (VTA).

MAKE CONNECTIONS *Based on what you learned in Concept 48.3 (pp. 1050–1051), what effect would you expect if you depolarized the neurons in the VTA? Explain.*

specific regions of the cerebrum, including the *nucleus accumbens* (see Figure 49.14).

Addictive drugs affect the reward system in several ways. First, each drug has an immediate and direct effect that enhances the activity of the dopamine pathway (see Figure 49.23). As addiction develops, there are also long-lasting changes in the reward circuitry. The result is a craving for the drug independent of any pleasure associated with consumption.

Laboratory animals have proved especially useful in teaching us how the brain's reward system works and how particular drugs affect its function. Rats, for example, will provide themselves with cocaine, heroin, or amphetamine when given a dispensing system linked to a lever in their cage. Furthermore, they exhibit addictive behavior in such circumstances, continuing to self-administer the drug rather than seek food, even to the point of starvation.

As scientists expand their knowledge about the brain's reward system and the various forms of addiction, there is hope that the insights will lead to more effective prevention and treatment.

Alzheimer's Disease

Alzheimer's disease is a mental deterioration, or dementia, characterized by confusion and memory loss. Its incidence is age related, rising from about 10% at age 65 to about 35% at age 85. The disease is progressive, with patients gradually becoming less able to function and eventually needing to be dressed, bathed, and fed by others. Moreover, patients with Alzheimer's disease often lose their ability to recognize people, including their immediate family, and may treat them with suspicion and hostility.

Alzheimer's disease leads to the death of neurons in many areas of the brain, including the hippocampus and cerebral cortex. As a result, there is often massive shrinkage of brain tissue. Postmortem examination of the remaining brain tissue reveals two characteristic features—amyloid plaques and neurofibrillary tangles **(Figure 49.24)**.

The plaques are aggregates of β-amyloid, an insoluble peptide that is cleaved from the extracellular portion of a membrane protein found in neurons. Membrane enzymes, called secretases, catalyze the cleavage, causing β-amyloid to accumulate in plaques outside the neurons. It is these plaques that appear to trigger the death of surrounding neurons.

The neurofibrillary tangles observed in Alzheimer's disease are primarily made up of the tau protein. (This protein is unrelated to the tau mutation that affects circadian rhythm in hamsters.) The tau protein normally helps assemble and maintain microtubules that transport nutrients along axons. In Alzheimer's disease, tau undergoes changes that cause it to bind to itself, resulting in neurofibrillary tangles. There is evidence that changes in tau are associated with the appearance

Amyloid plaque   Neurofibrillary tangle   20 μm

▲ **Figure 49.24 Microscopic signs of Alzheimer's disease.** A hallmark of Alzheimer's disease is the presence in brain tissue of neurofibrillary tangles surrounding plaques made of β-amyloid (LM).

of early-onset Alzheimer's disease, a much less common disorder that affects relatively young individuals.

There is currently no cure for Alzheimer's disease, but an enormous effort has led to the recent development of drugs that are partially effective in relieving some of the symptoms. Doctors are also beginning to use functional brain imaging to diagnose Alzheimer's disease in patients exhibiting early signs of dementia.

Parkinson's Disease

Symptoms of **Parkinson's disease**, a motor disorder, include muscle tremors, poor balance, a flexed posture, and a shuffling gait. Facial muscles become rigid, limiting the ability of patients to vary their expressions. Like Alzheimer's disease, Parkinson's disease is a progressive brain illness and is more common with advancing age. The incidence of Parkinson's disease is about 1% at age 65 and about 5% at age 85. In the U.S. population, approximately 1 million people are afflicted.

The symptoms of Parkinson's disease result from the death of neurons in the midbrain that normally release dopamine at synapses in the basal nuclei. As with Alzheimer's disease, protein aggregates accumulate. Most cases of Parkinson's disease lack an identifiable cause; however, a rare form of the disease that appears in relatively young adults has a clear genetic basis. Molecular studies of mutations linked to this early-onset Parkinson's disease reveal disruption of genes required for certain mitochondrial functions. Researchers are investigating whether mitochondrial defects also contribute to the more common and later-onset form of the disease.

At present there is no cure for Parkinson's disease. Approaches used to manage the symptoms include brain surgery, deep-brain stimulation, and drugs such as L-dopa, a molecule that can cross the blood-brain barrier and be converted to dopamine in the CNS. One potential cure is to implant dopamine-secreting neurons, either in the midbrain or in the basal nuclei. Laboratory studies of this strategy show promise: In rats with an experimentally induced condition that mimics Parkinson's disease, implanting dopamine-secreting neurons can lead to a recovery of motor control. Whether this regenerative approach can also work in humans is one of many important questions in modern brain research.

49 CHAPTER REVIEW

SUMMARY OF KEY CONCEPTS

CONCEPT 49.1

Nervous systems consist of circuits of neurons and supporting cells (pp. 1062–1067)

- Invertebrate nervous systems range in complexity from simple **nerve nets** to highly centralized nervous systems having complicated brains and ventral nerve cords.

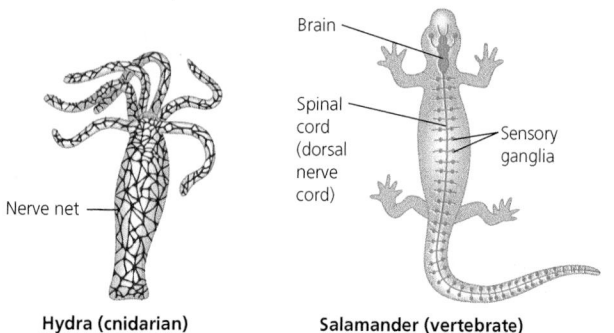

Hydra (cnidarian)   **Salamander (vertebrate)**

In vertebrates, the central nervous system (CNS), consisting of the brain and the spinal cord, integrates information, while the **nerves** of the peripheral nervous system (PNS) transmit sensory and motor signals between the CNS and the rest of the body. The simplest circuits in the vertebrate nervous system control **reflex** responses, in which sensory input is linked to motor output without involvement of the brain. Vertebrate neurons are supported by several types of glia, including **astrocytes**, oligodendrocytes, Schwann cells, and ependymal cells.

- Afferent neurons carry sensory signals to the CNS. Efferent neurons function in either the **motor system**, which carries signals to skeletal muscles, or the **autonomic nervous system**, which regulates smooth and cardiac muscles. The **sympathetic** and **parasympathetic divisions** of the autonomic nervous system have antagonistic effects on a diverse set of target organs, while the **enteric division** controls the activity of many digestive organs.

? *How does the circuitry of a reflex facilitate a rapid response?*

CONCEPT 49.2

The vertebrate brain is regionally specialized (pp. 1067–1072)

- The cerebrum has two hemispheres, each of which consists of cortical **gray matter** overlying **white matter** and basal nuclei, which are important in planning and learning movements. A thick band of axons, the **corpus callosum**, provides communication between the right and left cerebral cortices.
- Within each region of the brain, particular structures have specialized functions. The **pons** and **medulla oblongata** are relay stations for information traveling between the PNS and the cerebrum. The **reticular formation**, a network of neurons within the **brainstem**, regulates sleep and arousal. The **cerebellum** helps coordinate motor, perceptual, and cognitive functions. It is also involved in learning and remembering

motor skills. The **thalamus** is the main center through which sensory and motor information passes to the **cerebrum**. The **hypothalamus** regulates homeostasis and basic survival behaviors. Within the hypothalamus, the **suprachiasmatic nucleus (SCN)** acts as the pacemaker for circadian rhythms.

- The generation and experience of emotions involve many regions of the brain. However, the **amygdala** plays a key role in recognizing and recalling a number of emotions.

 What role do particular regions of the brain play in vision and responses to visual input?

CONCEPT 49.3

The cerebral cortex controls voluntary movement and cognitive functions (pp. 1072–1076)

- Each side of the **cerebral cortex** has four lobes—frontal, temporal, occipital, and parietal—that contain primary sensory areas and association areas. Specific types of sensory input enter the primary sensory areas. Association areas integrate information from different sensory areas.
- Portions of the frontal and temporal lobes, including Broca's area and Wernicke's area, are essential for generating and understanding language. These functions are concentrated in the left **cerebral hemisphere**, as are math and logic operations. The right hemisphere appears to be stronger at pattern recognition and nonverbal thinking. At least some of this **lateralization** of functions relates to handedness.
- In the somatosensory cortex and the motor cortex, neurons are distributed according to the part of the body that generates sensory input or receives motor commands.
- Primates and cetaceans, which are capable of higher cognition, have an extensively convoluted neocortex, the outermost part of the cerebral cortex. In birds, a brain region called the pallium contains clustered nuclei that carry out functions similar to those performed by the cerebral cortex of mammals. Some birds can solve problems and understand abstractions in a manner indicative of higher cognition.

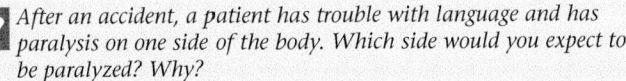 *After an accident, a patient has trouble with language and has paralysis on one side of the body. Which side would you expect to be paralyzed? Why?*

CONCEPT 49.4

Changes in synaptic connections underlie memory and learning (pp. 1076–1079)

- During development, more neurons and synapses form than will exist in the adult. The programmed death of neurons and elimination of synapses in embryos establish the basic structure of the nervous system. In the adult, reshaping of the nervous system can involve the loss or addition of synapses or the strengthening or weakening of signaling at synapses. This capacity for remodeling is termed **neural plasticity**. Defective remodeling of synapses is partly responsible for the developmental abnormalities of autism.
- **Short-term memory** relies on temporary links in the hippocampus. In **long-term memory**, these temporary links are replaced by connections within the cerebral cortex. This transfer of information from short-term to long-term memory is enhanced by the association of new data with that already in long-term memory. **Long-term potentiation (LTP)** is a lasting increase in the strength of synaptic transmission and appears to be an important process in memory storage and learning.

- The adult human brain contains stem cells that can differentiate into mature neurons. Therapy based on stem cells offers a potential method for replacing neurons lost to injury or disease.

Learning multiple languages is typically easier earlier in childhood than later in life. How does this fit with our understanding of neural development?

CONCEPT 49.5

Many nervous system disorders can be explained in molecular terms (pp. 1079–1082)

- Research has identified the biochemical basis of a number of nervous system disorders. **Schizophrenia**, which is characterized by hallucinations, delusions, and other symptoms, affects neuronal pathways that use dopamine as a neurotransmitter. Drugs that increase the activity of biogenic amines in the brain can be used to treat **bipolar disorder** and **major depressive disorder**. The compulsive drug use that characterizes addiction reflects altered activity of the brain's reward system, which normally provides motivation for actions that enhance survival or reproduction.
- **Alzheimer's disease** and **Parkinson's disease** are neurodegenerative and typically age related. Alzheimer's disease is a dementia in which neurofibrillary tangles and amyloid plaques form in the brain. Parkinson's disease is a motor disorder caused by the death of dopamine-secreting neurons and associated with the presence of protein aggregates.

The fact that both amphetamines and PCP have effects similar to the symptoms of schizophrenia suggests a potentially complex basis for this disease. Explain.

TEST YOUR UNDERSTANDING

LEVEL 1: KNOWLEDGE/COMPREHENSION

1. Wakefulness is regulated by the reticular formation, which is present in the
   a. basal nuclei.
   b. cerebral cortex.
   c. brainstem.
   d. limbic system.
   e. spinal cord.

2. Which of the following structures or regions is *incorrectly* paired with its function?
   a. limbic system—motor control of speech
   b. medulla oblongata—homeostatic control
   c. cerebellum—coordination of movement and balance
   d. corpus callosum—communication between the left and right cerebral cortices
   e. amygdala—emotional memory

3. Patients with damage to Wernicke's area have difficulty
   a. coordinating limb movement.
   b. generating speech.
   c. recognizing faces.
   d. understanding language.
   e. experiencing emotion.

4. The cerebral cortex plays a major role in all of the following *except*
   a. short-term memory.
   b. long-term memory.
   c. circadian rhythm.
   d. foot-tapping rhythm.
   e. breath holding.

LEVEL 2: APPLICATION/ANALYSIS

5. After suffering a stroke, a patient can see objects anywhere in front of him but pays attention only to objects in his right field of vision. When asked to describe these objects, he has difficulty judging their size and distance. What part of the brain was likely damaged by the stroke?
   a. the left frontal lobe
   b. the right frontal lobe
   c. the left parietal lobe
   d. the right parietal lobe
   e. the corpus callosum

6. Injury localized to the hypothalamus would most likely disrupt
   a. short-term memory.
   b. coordination during locomotion.
   c. executive functions, such as decision making.
   d. sorting of sensory information.
   e. regulation of body temperature.

7. **DRAW IT** The reflex that pulls your hand away when you prick your finger on a sharp object relies on a simple neuronal circuit with two synapses in the spinal cord. (a) Using a circle to represent a cross section of the spinal cord, draw the circuit, labeling the types of neurons, the direction of information flow in each, and the locations of synapses. (b) Draw a simple diagram of the brain indicating where pain would eventually be perceived.

LEVEL 3: SYNTHESIS/EVALUATION

8. **EVOLUTION CONNECTION**
   Scientists often use measures of "higher-order thinking" to assess intelligence in other animals. For example, birds are judged to have sophisticated thought processes because they can use tools and make use of abstract concepts. What problems do you see in defining intelligence in these ways?

9. **SCIENTIFIC INQUIRY**
   Consider an individual who had been fluent in American Sign Language before suffering damage to the left cerebral hemisphere. After the injury, this person could still understand signs, but could not readily generate signs that represented his thoughts. What two hypotheses could explain this finding, and how might you distinguish between them?

10. **SCIENCE, TECHNOLOGY, AND SOCIETY**
    With increasingly sophisticated methods for scanning brain activity, scientists are rapidly developing the ability to detect an individual's particular emotions and thought processes from outside the body. What benefits and problems do you envision when such technology becomes readily available?

11. **WRITE ABOUT A THEME**
    The Genetic Basis of Life In a short essay (100–150 words), explain how specification of the adult nervous system by the genome is incomplete.

For selected answers, see Appendix A.

1. MasteringBiology® Assignments
Tutorial The Vertebrate Nervous System
Activities Discovery Channel Video: Teen Brains
Questions Student Misconceptions • Reading Quiz • Multiple Choice • End-of-Chapter

2. eText
Read your book online, search, take notes, highlight text, and more.

3. The Study Area
Practice Tests • Cumulative Test • *BioFlix* 3-D Animations • MP3 Tutor Sessions • Videos • Activities • Investigations • Lab Media • Audio Glossary • Word Study Tools • Art

50

Sensory and Motor Mechanisms

▲ Figure 50.1 **Is a star-shaped nose merely decorative?**

KEY CONCEPTS

50.1 Sensory receptors transduce stimulus energy and transmit signals to the central nervous system

50.2 The mechanoreceptors responsible for hearing and equilibrium detect moving fluid or settling particles

50.3 Visual receptors in diverse animals depend on light-absorbing pigments

50.4 The senses of taste and smell rely on similar sets of sensory receptors

50.5 The physical interaction of protein filaments is required for muscle function

50.6 Skeletal systems transform muscle contraction into locomotion

Sensing and Acting

The face of the star-nosed mole (*Condulura cristata*) is, in a word, astounding (Figure 50.1). Eleven pairs of appendages protrude from its nose, forming a prominent pink star. Although they look a bit like fingers, these appendages are not used in grasping. Nor is the nose used to detect odors. Is the star, then, simply ornamental? No—it has a highly specialized function. Just below its surface lie 25,000 touch-sensitive receptors, more than are found in your whole hand.

Tunneling beneath the wetlands of eastern North America, the virtually blind mole lives in almost total darkness. But as 100,000 neurons relay tactile information from its nose to its brain, the mole finds and captures food with remarkable rapidity: A star-nosed mole can detect and eat prey in as little as 120 milliseconds (msec).

Detecting and processing sensory information and generating motor responses provide the physiological basis for all animal behavior. In this chapter, we will explore the processes of sensing and acting in both vertebrates and invertebrates. We will start with sensory processes that convey information about an animal's external and internal environment to its brain. We will then consider the structure and function of muscles and skeletons that carry out movements as instructed by the brain. Finally, we will investigate various mechanisms of animal movement. These topics will lead us naturally to our discussion of animal behavior in Chapter 51.

CONCEPT 50.1

Sensory receptors transduce stimulus energy and transmit signals to the central nervous system

All sensory processes begin with stimuli, and all stimuli represent forms of energy. A sensory receptor converts stimulus energy to a change in membrane potential and thereby regulates the output of action potentials to the central nervous system (CNS). Activating a sensory receptor does not necessarily require a large amount of stimulus energy. Indeed, some sensory receptors can detect the smallest possible unit of stimulus; most light receptors, for example, can detect a single quantum (photon) of light.

When a stimulus is received and processed by the nervous system, a motor response may be generated. One of the simplest stimulus-response circuits is a reflex, such as the knee-jerk reflex shown in Figure 49.3. Many other behaviors rely on more elaborate processing that involves integration of sensory input. As an example, consider how the star-nosed mole

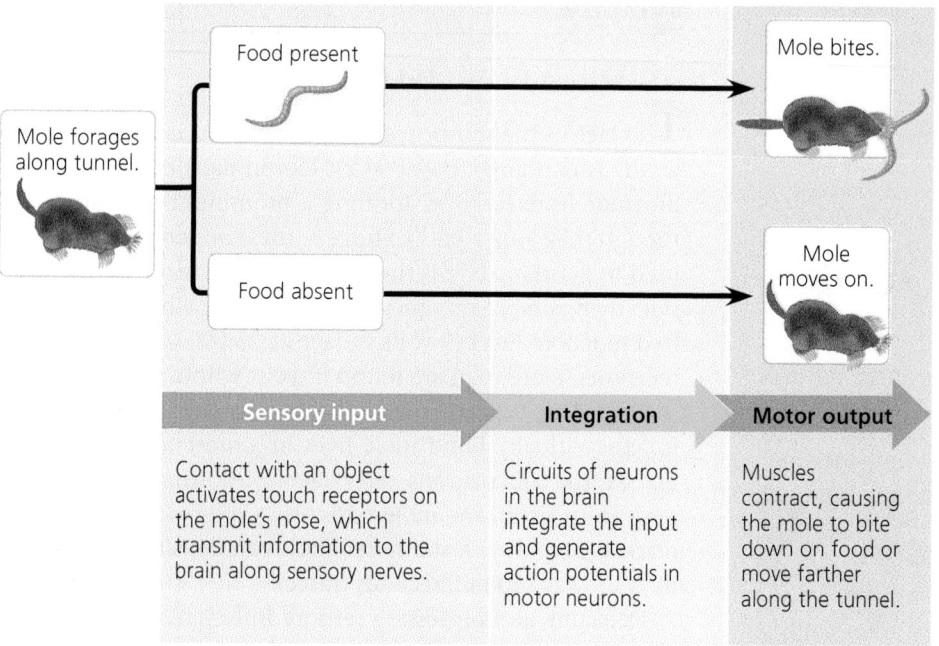

Sensory input	Integration	Motor output
Contact with an object activates touch receptors on the mole's nose, which transmit information to the brain along sensory nerves.	Circuits of neurons in the brain integrate the input and generate action potentials in motor neurons.	Muscles contract, causing the mole to bite down on food or move farther along the tunnel.

▲ **Figure 50.2 A simple response pathway: foraging by a star-nosed mole.**

forages for food in its tunnel environment **(Figure 50.2)**. When the mole's nose contacts an object in its tunnel, touch receptors in the nose are activated. These receptors transmit sensory information about the object to the mole's brain. Circuits in the brain integrate the input and initiate one of two response pathways, depending on whether food was detected. Motor output commands from the brain sent to skeletal muscles in the body cause the mole either to bite down with its teeth or to continue moving along the tunnel.

With this overview in mind, let's examine the general organization and activity of animal sensory systems.

Sensory Pathways

Sensory pathways have in common four basic functions: sensory reception, transduction, transmission, and perception.

Sensory Reception and Transduction

A sensory pathway begins with **sensory reception**, the detection of a stimulus by sensory cells. Most sensory cells are specialized neurons or epithelial cells. Some exist singly; others are collected in sensory organs, such as eyes and ears. The term **sensory receptor** is used to describe a sensory cell or organ, as well as the subcellular structure that interacts directly with stimuli. Many sensory receptors detect stimuli from outside the body, such as heat, light, pressure, and chemicals, but there are also receptors for stimuli from within the body, such as blood pressure and body position.

Although animals use a range of sensory receptors to detect widely varying stimuli, the effect in all cases is to open or close ion channels. Thus, for example, ion channels open or close when a substance outside the cell binds to a chemical receptor

in the plasma membrane. The resulting flow of ions across the membrane changes the membrane potential.

The conversion of a physical or chemical stimulus to a change in the membrane potential of a sensory receptor is called **sensory transduction**, and the change in membrane potential itself is known as a **receptor potential**. Receptor potentials are graded potentials; their magnitude varies with the strength of the stimulus.

Transmission

Sensory information travels through the nervous system as nerve impulses, or action potentials. For many sensory receptors, transducing the energy in a stimulus into a receptor potential initiates **transmission** of action potentials to the CNS.

Some sensory receptors are themselves specialized neurons, whereas others are specialized cells that regulate neurons **(Figure 50.3)**. Neurons that act directly as sensory receptors produce action potentials and have an axon that extends into the CNS. Non-neuronal sensory receptor cells form chemical synapses with sensory (afferent) neurons and typically respond to stimuli by increasing the rate at

▼ **Figure 50.3 Classes of sensory receptors.**

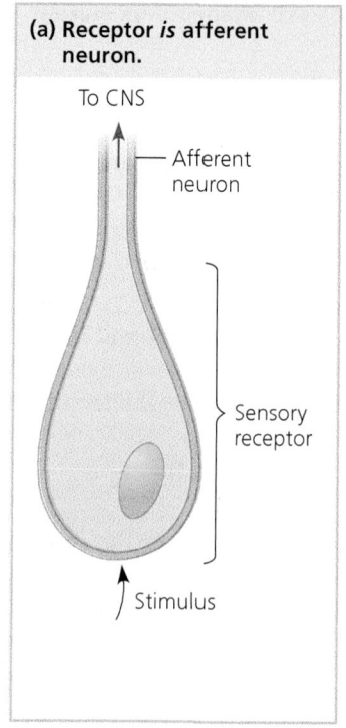

(a) Receptor *is* afferent neuron.

To CNS

Afferent neuron

Sensory receptor

Stimulus

(b) Receptor *regulates* afferent neuron.

To CNS

Afferent neuron

Receptor protein

Neurotransmitter

Stimulus leads to neurotransmitter release.

Sensory receptor cell

Stimulus

(a) Single sensory receptor activated

(b) Multiple receptors activated

which the afferent neurons produce action potentials. (One exception is in the vertebrate visual system, discussed in Concept 50.3.)

The response of a sensory receptor varies with stimuli of different intensities. The primary difference is the magnitude of the receptor potential, which controls the rate at which action potentials are produced. If the receptor is a sensory neuron, a larger receptor potential results in more frequent action potentials (**Figure 50.4a**). If the receptor is not a sensory neuron, a larger receptor potential causes more neurotransmitter to be released, which usually increases the production of action potentials by the postsynaptic neuron.

Many sensory neurons spontaneously generate action potentials at a low rate. In these neurons, a stimulus does not switch the production of action potentials on or off, but it does change *how often* an action potential is produced. In this manner, such neurons are also able to alert the nervous system to changes in stimulus intensity.

A difference in stimulus strength may not only alter the activity of individual receptors, but also affect the number of receptors that are activated (**Figure 50.4b**). If a stronger stimulus triggers a response by more receptors, more axons transmit action potentials. This increase in the number of axons transmitting action potentials is then decoded by the nervous system as a stronger stimulus.

Processing of sensory information can occur before, during, and after transmission of action potentials to the CNS. In many cases, the *integration* of sensory information begins as soon as the information is received. Receptor potentials produced by stimuli delivered to different parts of a sensory receptor cell are integrated through summation, as are postsynaptic potentials in sensory neurons that form synapses with multiple receptors (see Figure 48.16). As we will discuss shortly, sensory structures such as eyes also provide higher levels of integration, and the brain further processes all incoming signals.

Perception

When action potentials reach the brain via sensory neurons, circuits of neurons process this input, generating the **perception** of the stimuli. Perceptions—such as colors, smells, sounds, and tastes—are constructions formed in the brain and do not exist outside it. So, if a tree falls and no animal is present to hear it, is there a sound? The falling tree certainly produces pressure waves in the air, but if sound is defined as a perception, then there is none unless an animal senses the waves and its brain perceives them.

Action potentials are all-or-none events (see Figure 48.10c). An action potential triggered by light striking the eye has the same properties as an action potential triggered by air vibrating in the ear. How, then, do we distinguish sights, sounds, and other stimuli? The answer lies in the connections that link sensory receptors to the brain. Action potentials from sensory receptors travel along neurons that are dedicated to a particular stimulus; these dedicated neurons synapse with particular neurons in the brain or spinal cord. As a result, the brain distinguishes sensory stimuli such as sight or sound solely by the path to the brain along which the action potentials have traveled.

Amplification and Adaptation

The transduction of stimuli by sensory receptors is subject to two types of modification—amplification and adaptation. **Amplification** refers to the strengthening of a sensory signal during transduction. The effect can be considerable. For example, an action potential conducted from the eye to the human brain has about 100,000 times as much energy as the few photons of light that triggered it.

Amplification that occurs in sensory receptor cells often requires signal transduction pathways involving second messengers. Because these pathways include enzyme-catalyzed reactions, they amplify signal strength through the formation of many product molecules by a single enzyme molecule.

Amplification may also take place in accessory structures of a complex sense organ, as when the pressure associated with sound waves is enhanced by a factor of more than 20 before reaching receptors in the innermost part of the ear.

Upon continued stimulation, many receptors undergo a decrease in responsiveness termed **sensory adaptation** (not to be confused with the evolutionary term *adaptation*). Without sensory adaptation, you would be constantly aware of feeling every beat of your heart and every bit of clothing on your body. Adaptation also enables you to see, hear, and smell changes in the environment that vary widely in stimulus intensity.

Types of Sensory Receptors

A sensory cell typically has a single type of receptor specific for a particular stimulus, such as light or cold. Often, distinct cells and receptors are responsible for particular qualities of a sensation, such as distinguishing red from blue. Before exploring these specializations, let's consider sensory receptor function at a more basic level. We can classify sensory receptors into five categories based on the nature of the stimuli they transduce: mechanoreceptors, chemoreceptors, electromagnetic receptors, thermoreceptors, and pain receptors.

Mechanoreceptors

Mechanoreceptors sense physical deformation caused by forms of mechanical energy such as pressure, touch, stretch, motion, and sound. Mechanoreceptors typically consist of ion channels that are linked to structures that extend outside the cell, such as "hairs" (cilia), as well as internal cell structures, such as the cytoskeleton. Bending or stretching of the external structure generates tension that alters the permeability of the ion channels. This change in ion permeability alters the membrane potential, resulting in a depolarization or hyperpolarization (see Chapter 48).

The familiar knee-jerk reflex (see Figure 49.3) is triggered by the vertebrate stretch receptor, a mechanoreceptor that detects muscle movement. Vertebrate stretch receptors are dendrites of sensory neurons that spiral around the middle of certain small skeletal muscle fibers. Groups of about 2 to 12 of these fibers, formed into a spindle shape and surrounded by connective tissue, are distributed throughout the muscle, parallel to other muscle fibers. When the muscle is stretched, the spindle fibers are stretched, depolarizing sensory neurons and triggering action potentials that are transmitted to the spinal cord.

The mammalian sense of touch also relies on mechanoreceptors that are the dendrites of sensory neurons. Touch receptors, such as those illustrated in Figure 50.4, are often embedded in layers of connective tissue. The structure of the connective tissue and the location of the receptors dramatically affect the type of mechanical energy (light touch, vibration, or strong pressure) that best stimulates them **(Figure 50.5)**. Receptors that detect a light touch or vibration are close to the surface of the skin; they transduce very slight inputs of mechanical energy into receptor

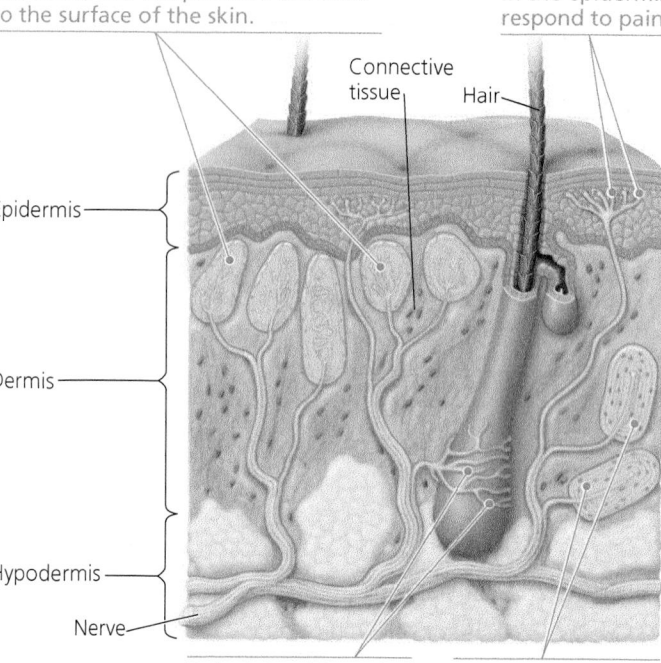

Receptors that detect gentle pressure, vibration, and temperature are close to the surface of the skin.

Naked dendrites in the epidermis respond to pain.

Connective tissue
Hair
Epidermis
Dermis
Hypodermis
Nerve

Naked dendrites wind around the base of hairs and detect hair movement.

Receptors that respond to strong pressure are in deep skin layers.

▲ **Figure 50.5 Sensory receptors in human skin.** Most receptors in the dermis are encapsulated by connective tissue. Receptors in the epidermis are naked dendrites, as are hair movement receptors that wind around the base of hairs in the dermis.

potentials. Receptors that respond to stronger pressure and vibrations are in deep skin layers.

Some animals use mechanoreceptors to literally get a feel for their environment. For example, cats as well as many rodents have extremely sensitive mechanoreceptors at the base of their whiskers. Because deflection of different whiskers triggers action potentials that reach different cells in the brain, an animal's whiskers provide detailed information about nearby objects.

Chemoreceptors

Chemoreceptors include both general receptors—those that transmit information about total solute concentration—and specific receptors—those that respond to individual kinds of molecules. Osmoreceptors in the mammalian brain, for example, detect changes in the total solute concentration of the blood and stimulate thirst when osmolarity increases (see Figure 44.19). Most animals also have receptors for specific molecules, including glucose, oxygen, carbon dioxide, and amino acids.

Two of the most sensitive and specific chemoreceptors known are found in the antennae of the male silkworm moth **(Figure 50.6)**; they detect the two chemical components of the female moth sex pheromone. For pheromones and other molecules detected by chemoreceptors, the stimulus molecule binds to the specific receptor on the membrane of the sensory cell and initiates changes in ion permeability.

▲ **Figure 50.6 Chemoreceptors in an insect.** The antennae of the male silkworm moth *Bombyx mori* are covered with sensory hairs, visible in the SEM enlargement. The hairs have chemoreceptors that are highly sensitive to the sex pheromone released by the female.

Electromagnetic Receptors

Electromagnetic receptors detect various forms of electromagnetic energy, such as visible light, electricity, and magnetism. For example, snakes have very sensitive infrared receptors that detect the body heat of prey (**Figure 50.7a**). Similarly, the platypus, a monotreme mammal (see Chapter 34), has electroreceptors on its bill that are thought to detect the electric field generated by the muscles of crustaceans, frogs, small fish, and other prey. In a few cases, the animal detecting an electromagnetic stimulus is also its source: Some fishes generate electric currents and then use their electroreceptors to locate prey or other objects that disturb those currents.

Many animals appear to use Earth's magnetic field lines to orient themselves as they migrate (**Figure 50.7b**). The iron-containing mineral magnetite is found in many vertebrates (including salmon, pigeons, sea turtles, and humans), in bees, in some molluscs, and in certain protists and prokaryotes that orient to Earth's magnetic field. Once collected by sailors to make compasses for navigation, magnetite may be part of an orienting mechanism in many animals (see Chapter 51).

Thermoreceptors

Thermoreceptors detect heat and cold. Located in the skin and in the anterior hypothalamus, thermoreceptor cells send information to the body's thermostat in the posterior hypothalamus. Our understanding of thermoreception has increased substantially recently, thanks to scientists with an appreciation for fiery foods. Jalapeno and cayenne peppers

(a) This rattlesnake and other pit vipers have a pair of infrared receptors, one anterior to and just below each eye. These organs are sensitive enough to detect the infrared radiation emitted by a warm mouse a meter away. The snake moves its head from side to side until the radiation is detected equally by the two receptors, indicating that the mouse is straight ahead.

(b) Some migrating animals, such as these beluga whales, apparently sense Earth's magnetic field and use the information, along with other cues, for orientation.

▲ **Figure 50.7 Specialized electromagnetic receptors.**

taste "hot" because they contain a natural product called capsaicin. It turns out that exposing sensory neurons to capsaicin triggers an influx of calcium ions. When scientists identified the receptor protein that binds capsaicin, they made a fascinating discovery: The receptor opens a calcium channel in response not only to capsaicin, but also to high temperatures (42°C or higher). In essence, spicy foods taste "hot" because they activate the same receptors as hot soup and coffee.

Mammals have a number of kinds of thermoreceptors, each specific for a particular temperature range. The capsaicin receptor and at least five other types of thermoreceptors belong to the TRP (transient receptor potential) family of ion channel proteins. Just as the TRP-type receptor specific for high temperature is sensitive to capsaicin, the receptor for temperatures below 28°C can be activated by menthol, a plant product that we perceive to have a "cool" flavor.

Pain Receptors

Extreme pressure or temperature, as well as certain chemicals, can damage animal tissues. To detect stimuli that reflect such noxious (or harmful) conditions, animals rely on **nociceptors** (from the Latin *nocere*, to hurt), also called **pain receptors**. By triggering defensive reactions, such as withdrawal from danger, the perception of pain serves an important function.

In humans, certain naked dendrites act as nociceptors by detecting noxious thermal, mechanical, or chemical stimuli. The capsaicin receptor is thus a thermoreceptor and also a nociceptor. Although nociceptor density is highest in skin, some pain receptors are associated with other organs.

Chemicals produced in an animal's body sometimes enhance the perception of pain. For example, damaged tissues produce prostaglandins, which act as local regulators of inflammation (see Chapter 45). Prostaglandins worsen pain by increasing nociceptor sensitivity to noxious stimuli. Aspirin and ibuprofen reduce pain by inhibiting the synthesis of prostaglandins.

Next we'll turn our focus to sensory systems, beginning with systems for maintaining balance and detecting sound.

CONCEPT CHECK 50.1

1. Which one of the five categories of sensory receptors is primarily dedicated to external stimuli?
2. Why can eating "hot" peppers cause a person to sweat?
3. **WHAT IF?** If you stimulated a sensory neuron electrically, how would that stimulation be perceived?

For suggested answers, see Appendix A.

CONCEPT 50.2

The mechanoreceptors responsible for hearing and equilibrium detect moving fluid or settling particles

Hearing and the perception of body equilibrium, or balance, are related in most animals. For both senses, mechanoreceptor cells produce receptor potentials when settling particles or moving fluid causes deflection of cell-surface structures.

Sensing of Gravity and Sound in Invertebrates

To sense gravity and maintain equilibrium, most invertebrates rely on mechanoreceptors located in organs called **statocysts** (Figure 50.8). In a typical statocyst, a layer of ciliated receptor cells surrounds a chamber that contains one or more **statoliths**, which are grains of sand or other dense granules. When statoliths settle to the low point in the chamber, they stimulate mechanoreceptors in that location. In experiments in which statoliths were replaced with metal shavings, researchers "tricked" crayfish into swimming upside down by using magnets to pull the shavings to the upper end of the statocysts located at the base of their antennae.

Many (perhaps most) insects have body hairs that vibrate in response to sound waves. Hairs of different stiffnesses and lengths vibrate at different frequencies. For example, fine hairs on the antennae of a male mosquito vibrate in a specific way in response to the hum produced by the beating wings

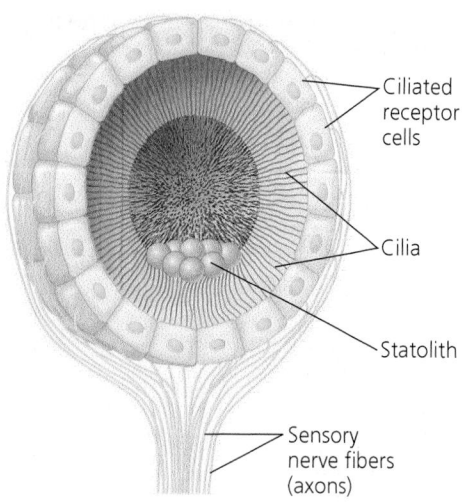

▶ **Figure 50.8**
The statocyst of an invertebrate. The settling of statoliths to the low point in the chamber bends cilia on receptor cells in that location, providing the brain with information about the orientation of the body with respect to gravity.

Ciliated receptor cells

Cilia

Statolith

Sensory nerve fibers (axons)

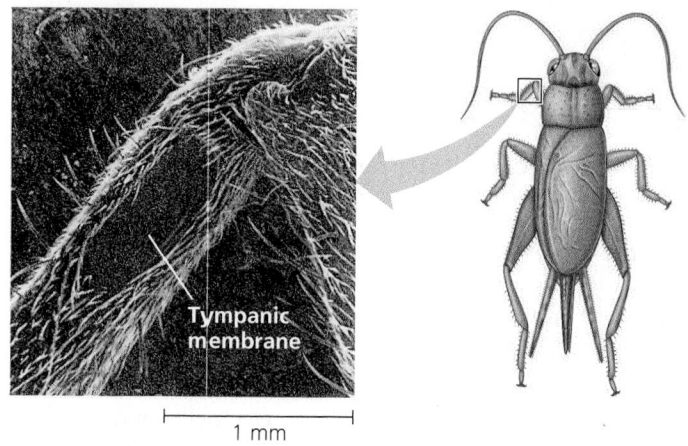

Tympanic membrane

1 mm

▲ **Figure 50.9 An insect's "ear"—on its leg.** The tympanic membrane, visible in this SEM of a cricket's front leg, vibrates in response to sound waves. The vibrations stimulate mechanoreceptors attached to the inside of the tympanic membrane.

of flying females. The importance of this sensory system in the attraction of males to a potential mate can be demonstrated very simply: A tuning fork vibrating at the same frequency as that of a female's wings will itself attract males.

Many insects also detect sound by means of "ears" consisting of a tympanic membrane (eardrum) stretched over an internal air chamber (Figure 50.9). Sound waves vibrate the tympanic membrane, stimulating receptor cells attached to the inside of the membrane and resulting in nerve impulses that are transmitted to the brain. Cockroaches lack such a tympanic membrane, but instead have vibration-sensitive organs located in each leg. These organs can provide enough warning for the insect to avoid being crushed by a descending human foot.

Hearing and Equilibrium in Mammals

In mammals, as in most other terrestrial vertebrates, the sensory organs for hearing and equilibrium are closely associated. Figure 50.10 explores the structure and function of these organs in the human ear.

Exploring The Structure of the Human Ear

1 Overview of Ear Structure

The **outer ear** consists of the external pinna and the auditory canal, which collect sound waves and channel them to the **tympanic membrane** (eardrum), which separates the outer ear from the middle ear. In the **middle ear**, three small bones—the malleus (hammer), incus (anvil), and stapes (stirrup)—transmit vibrations to the **oval window**, which is a membrane beneath the stapes. The middle ear also opens into the **Eustachian tube**, which connects to the pharynx and equalizes pressure between the middle ear and the atmosphere. The **inner ear** consists of fluid-filled chambers, including the **semicircular canals**, which function in equilibrium, and the coiled **cochlea** (from the Latin meaning "snail"), a bony chamber that is involved in hearing.

2 The Cochlea

The cochlea has two large canals—an upper vestibular canal and a lower tympanic canal—separated by a smaller cochlear duct. Both canals are filled with fluid.

Outer ear — Middle ear — Inner ear
Skull bone, Stapes, Incus, Malleus, Semicircular canals, Auditory nerve to brain, Pinna, Auditory canal, Tympanic membrane, Oval window, Round window, Cochlea, Eustachian tube, Cochlear duct, Vestibular canal, Bone, Auditory nerve, Tympanic canal, Organ of Corti

Tectorial membrane

1 μm

▲ Bundled hairs projecting from a single mammalian hair cell (SEM). Two shorter rows of hairs lie behind the tall hairs in the foreground.

Basilar membrane, Hair cells, Axons of sensory neurons, To auditory nerve

4 Hair Cell

Projecting from each hair cell is a bundle of rod-shaped "hairs," each containing a core of actin filaments. Vibration of the basilar membrane in response to sound raises and lowers the hair cells, bending the hairs against the surrounding fluid and the tectorial membrane. When the hairs within the bundle are displaced, mechanoreceptors are activated, changing the membrane potential of the hair cell.

3 The Organ of Corti

The floor of the cochlear duct, the basilar membrane, bears the **organ of Corti**, which contains the mechanoreceptors of the ear, hair cells with hairs projecting into the cochlear duct. Many of the hairs are attached to the tectorial membrane, which hangs over the organ of Corti like an awning. Sound waves make the basilar membrane vibrate, which results in bending of the hairs and depolarization of the hair cells.

Hearing

Vibrating objects, such as a plucked guitar string or the vocal cords of your instructor, create pressure waves in the surrounding air. In *hearing*, the ear transduces this mechanical stimulus (pressure waves) into nerve impulses that the brain perceives as sound. To hear music, speech, or other sounds in our environment, we rely on **hair cells**, sensory receptors with hair-like projections on the cell surface that detect motion. Before the vibration waves reach the hair cells, however, they are amplified and transformed by several accessory structures.

The first steps in hearing involve structures in the ear that convert the vibrations of moving air to pressure waves in fluid. Upon reaching the outer ear, moving air causes the tympanic membrane to vibrate. The three bones of the middle ear transmit the vibrations to the oval window, a membrane on the cochlea's surface. When one of those bones, the stapes, vibrates against the oval window, it creates pressure waves in the fluid (called perilymph) inside the cochlea.

Upon entering the vestibular canal, the pressure waves push down on the cochlear duct and basilar membrane. In response, the basilar membrane and attached hair cells vibrate up and down. The hairs projecting from the moving hair cells are deflected by the tectorial membrane, which lies immediately above in a fixed position (see Figure 50.10). With each vibration, the hairs bend first in one direction and then the other. Mechanoreceptors in the hair cells respond by opening or closing ion channels. As shown in **Figure 50.11**, bending in one direction depolarizes hair cells, increasing neurotransmitter release and the frequency of action potentials directed to the

brain along the auditory nerve. Bending the hairs in the other direction hyperpolarizes hair cells, reducing neurotransmitter release and the frequency of auditory nerve sensations.

What prevents pressure waves from reverberating within the ear and causing prolonged sensation? Once pressure waves travel through the vestibular canal, they pass around the apex (tip) of the cochlea. The waves then continue through the tympanic canal, dissipating as they strike the **round window** (Figure 50.12a). This damping of sound waves resets the apparatus for the next vibrations that arrive.

The ear conveys information to the brain about two important sound variables: volume and pitch. *Volume* (loudness) is determined by the amplitude, or height, of the sound wave. A large-amplitude sound wave causes more vigorous vibration of the basilar membrane, greater bending of the hairs on hair cells, and more action potentials in the sensory neurons. *Pitch* is a function of a sound wave's frequency, the number of vibrations per unit time. High-frequency waves produce high-pitched sounds, whereas low-frequency waves produce low-pitched sounds. Pitch is commonly expressed in cycles per second, or hertz (Hz). Healthy young humans can hear in the range of 20–20,000 Hz; dogs can hear sounds as high as 40,000 Hz; and bats can emit and hear clicking sounds at frequencies above 100,000 Hz, using this ability to locate objects.

The cochlea can distinguish pitch because the basilar membrane is not uniform along its length: It is relatively narrow and stiff at the base of the cochlea near the oval window and wider and more flexible at the apex. Each region of the basilar membrane is tuned to a particular vibration frequency (Figure 50.12b). At any instant, the region of the membrane

(a) No bending of hairs

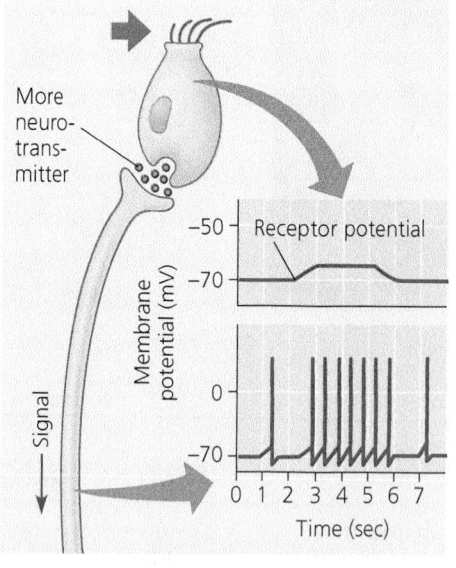

(b) Bending of hairs in one direction

(c) Bending of hairs in other direction

▲ **Figure 50.11 Sensory reception by hair cells.** Vertebrate hair cells required for hearing and balance have "hairs" formed into a bundle that bends when surrounding fluid moves. Each hair cell releases an excitatory neurotransmitter at a synapse with a sensory neuron, which conducts action potentials to the CNS. Bending of the bundle in one direction depolarizes the hair cell, causing it to release more neurotransmitter and increasing the frequency of action potentials in the sensory neuron. Bending in the other direction has the opposite effect.

(a) Vibrations of the stapes against the oval window produce pressure waves (black arrows) in the fluid (perilymph; blue) of the cochlea. (For purposes of illustration, the cochlea on the right is drawn partially uncoiled.) The waves travel to the apex via the vestibular canal and back towards the base via the tympanic canal. The energy in the waves causes the basilar membrane (pink) to vibrate, stimulating hair cells (not shown). Because the basilar membrane varies in stiffness along its length, each point along the membrane vibrates maximally in response to waves of a particular frequency.

(b) These graphs show the patterns of vibration along the basilar membrane for three different frequencies, high (top), medium (middle), and low (bottom). The higher the frequency, the closer the vibration to the oval window.

▲ **Figure 50.12 Transduction in the cochlea.**

? *A musical chord consists of several notes, each formed by a sound wave of different frequency. When you hear a chord, where in your body are these notes combined?*

vibrating most vigorously triggers the highest frequency of action potentials in the neuronal pathway leading to the brain. There, within the cerebral cortex, the actual perception of pitch occurs. Axons in the auditory nerve project into auditory areas of the cerebral cortex according to the region of the basilar membrane in which the signal originated. When a particular site in our cortex is stimulated, we perceive the sound of a particular pitch.

Equilibrium

Several organs in the inner ear of humans and most other mammals detect body movement, position, and balance.

Situated in a vestibule behind the oval window, the chambers called the **utricle** and **saccule** allow us to perceive position with respect to gravity or linear movement **(Figure 50.13)**. Each of these chambers contains a sheet of hair cells that project into a gelatinous material. Embedded in this gel are many small calcium carbonate particles called otoliths ("ear stones"). When you tilt your head, the otoliths press on the hairs protruding into the gel. Through the hair cell receptors, this deflection of the hairs is transformed into a change in the output of sensory neurons, signaling the brain that your head is at an angle. The otoliths are also responsible for

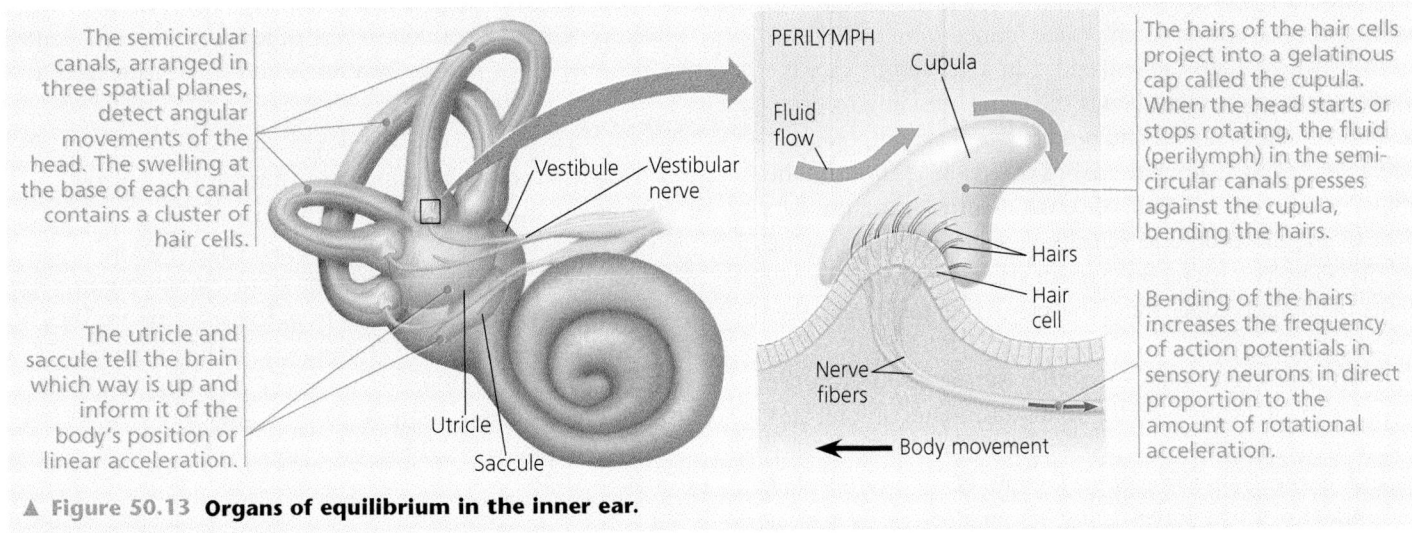

▲ **Figure 50.13 Organs of equilibrium in the inner ear.**

your ability to perceive acceleration, as, for example, when a stationary car in which you are sitting pulls forward. Because the utricle is oriented horizontally and the saccule is positioned vertically, you can detect motion in either the forward-and-back or up-and-down direction.

Three semicircular canals connected to the utricle detect turning of the head and other forms of angular acceleration (see Figure 50.11). Within each canal the hair cells form a single cluster, with the hairs projecting into a gelatinous cap called the cupula. Because the three canals are arranged in the three spatial planes, they can detect angular motion of the head in any direction. For example, if you turn your head to the left or right, the fluid within the horizontal canal pushes against the cupula, deflecting the hairs. The brain interprets the resulting changes in impulse production by the sensory neurons as turning of the head. If you spin in place, the fluid and canal eventually come to equilibrium and remain in that state until you stop. At that point, the moving fluid encounters a stationary cupula, triggering the false sensation of angular motion that we call dizziness.

Hearing and Equilibrium in Other Vertebrates

Unlike the mammalian hearing apparatus, the ear of a fish does not open to the outside of the body and has no eardrum or cochlea. The vibrations of the water caused by sound waves are conducted through the skeleton of the head to a pair of inner ears, setting otoliths in motion and stimulating hair cells. The fish's air-filled swim bladder (see Figure 34.16) also vibrates in response to sound. Some fishes, including catfishes and minnows, have a series of bones that conduct vibrations from the swim bladder to the inner ear.

As discussed in Chapter 34, most fishes and aquatic amphibians have a **lateral line system** along both sides of their body (**Figure 50.14**). The system contains mechanoreceptors that detect low-frequency waves by a mechanism similar to that of the mammalian inner ear. Water from the animal's surroundings enters the lateral line system through numerous pores and flows along a tube past the mechanoreceptors. As in our semicircular canals, receptors are formed from a cluster of hair cells whose hairs are embedded in a gelatinous cap, the cupula. Water movement bends the cupula, leading to depolarization of the hair cells and production of action potentials that are transmitted along the axons of sensory neurons to the brain. In this way, the fish perceives its movement through water or the direction and velocity of water currents flowing over its body. The lateral line system also detects water movements or vibrations generated by prey, predators, and other moving objects.

In terrestrial vertebrates, the inner ear has evolved as the main organ of hearing and equilibrium. Some amphibians have a lateral line system as juveniles, but not as adults living on land. In the ear of a frog or toad, sound vibrations in the air are conducted to the inner ear by a tympanic membrane on

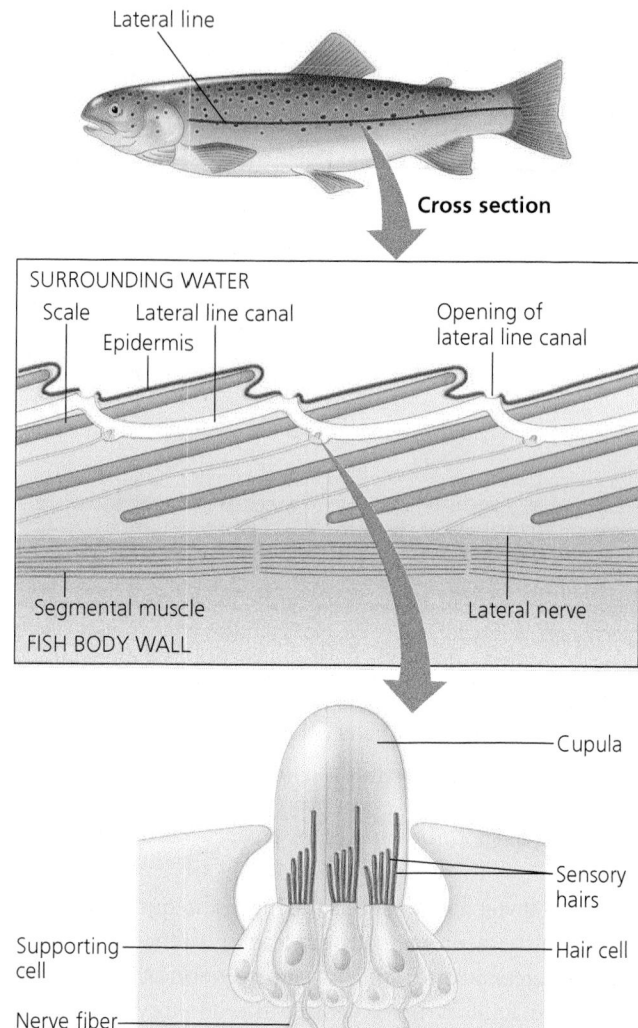

▲ Figure 50.14 **The lateral line system in a fish.** Water flowing through the system bends hair cells. The hair cells transduce the energy into receptor potentials, triggering action potentials that are conveyed to the brain. The lateral line system enables a fish to monitor water currents, pressure waves produced by moving objects, and low-frequency sounds conducted through the water.

the body surface and a single middle ear bone. Like mammals, birds and other reptiles have a cochlea. However, as in amphibians, sound is conducted from the tympanic membrane to the inner ear of reptiles by a single bone (see Figure 34.37).

CONCEPT CHECK 50.2

1. How are statocysts adaptive for animals that burrow underground or live deep in the ocean?
2. **WHAT IF?** Suppose a series of pressure waves in your cochlea caused a vibration of the basilar membrane that moves gradually from the apex toward the base. How would your brain interpret this stimulus?
3. **WHAT IF?** If the stapes became fused to the other middle ear bones or to the oval window, how would this condition affect hearing? Explain.

For suggested answers, see Appendix A.

CONCEPT 50.3

Visual receptors in diverse animals depend on light-absorbing pigments

The ability to detect light has a central role in the interaction of nearly all animals with their environment. Although animals use a diverse set of organs for vision, the underlying mechanism for capturing light is the same, suggesting a common evolutionary origin.

Evolution of Visual Perception

EVOLUTION Light detectors in the animal kingdom range from simple clusters of cells that detect only the direction and intensity of light to complex organs that form images. These diverse light detectors all contain **photoreceptors**, cells that contain light-absorbing pigment molecules. Furthermore, the genes that specify where and when photoreceptors arise during embryonic development are shared among animals as diverse as flatworms, annelids, arthropods, and vertebrates. It is thus very probable that the genetic underpinnings of all photoreceptors were already present in the earliest bilaterian animals.

Light-Detecting Organs

Most invertebrates have some kind of light-detecting organ. One of the simplest is that of planarians (**Figure 50.15**). A pair of ocelli (singular, *ocellus*), which are sometimes called eyespots,

are located in the head region. A layer of darkly pigmented cells surrounds the ocelli on three sides, blocking light. Photoreceptors in each ocellus receive light only through the opening where there are no pigmented cells. Because the opening of one ocellus faces left and slightly forward and that of the other ocellus faces right and forward, light shining from one side of the planarian stimulates only the ocellus on that side. The planarian brain compares the rate of action potentials coming from the two ocelli and directs turning movements that minimize the stimulation of both ocelli. The result is that the planarian moves away from the light source until it reaches a shaded location, where a rock or other object is likely to hide the animal from predators.

Compound Eyes

Insects and crustaceans (phylum Arthropoda) have compound eyes, as do some polychaete worms (phylum Annelida). A **compound eye** consists of up to several thousand light detectors called **ommatidia** (the "facets" of the eye), each with its own light-focusing lens (**Figure 50.16**). Each ommatidium detects light from a tiny portion of the visual field. A compound eye is very effective at detecting movement, an important adaptation for flying insects and small animals constantly threatened with predation. Whereas the

(a) The planarian's brain directs the body to turn until the sensations from the two ocelli are equal and minimal, causing the animal to move away from light.

(b) Whereas light striking the front of an ocellus excites the photoreceptors, light striking the back is blocked by the screening pigment. In this way, the ocelli indicate the direction of a light source, triggering the light avoidance behavior.

▲ **Figure 50.15 Ocelli and orientation behavior of a planarian.**

(a) The faceted eyes on the head of a fly form a repeating pattern visible in this photomicrograph.

(b) The cornea and crystalline cone of each ommatidium together function as a lens that focuses light on the rhabdom, an organelle formed by and extending inward from a circle of photoreceptors. The rhabdom traps light, serving as the photosensitive part of the ommatidium. Information gathered from different intensities of light entering the many ommatidia from different angles is used to form a visual image.

▲ **Figure 50.16 Compound eyes.**

human eye can distinguish only about 50 flashes of light per second, the compound eyes of some insects can detect flickering at six times that rate. (If they slipped into a movie theater, these insects could easily resolve each frame of the film being projected as a separate still image.) Insects also have excellent color vision, and some (including bees) can see into the ultraviolet (UV) range of the electromagnetic spectrum. Because UV light is invisible to humans, we miss seeing differences in the environment that bees and other insects detect. In studying animal behavior, we cannot simply extrapolate our sensory world to other species; different animals have different sensitivities and different brain organizations.

Single-Lens Eyes

Among invertebrates, **single-lens eyes** are found in some jellies and polychaete worms, as well as in spiders and many molluscs. A single-lens eye works somewhat like a camera. The eye of an octopus or squid, for example, has a small opening, the **pupil**, through which light enters. Like a camera's adjustable aperture, the **iris** contracts or expands, changing the

▼ Figure 50.17

Exploring The Structure of the Human Eye

1 Overview of Eye Structure

Starting from the outside, the human eye is surrounded by the conjunctiva, a mucous membrane (not shown); the sclera, a connective tissue; and the choroid, a thin, pigmented layer. At the front, the sclera forms the transparent *cornea* and the choroid forms the colored *iris*. By changing size, the iris regulates the amount of light entering the pupil, the hole in the center of the iris. Just inside the choroid, the neurons and photoreceptors of the **retina** form the innermost layer of the eyeball. The optic nerve exits the eye at the optic disk.

The **lens**, a transparent disk of protein, divides the eye into two cavities. In front of the lens lies the *aqueous humor*, a clear watery substance. Blockage of ducts that drain this fluid can produce glaucoma, a condition in which increased pressure in the eye damages the optic nerve, causing vision loss. Behind the lens lies the jellylike *vitreous humor* (illustrated here in the lower portion of the eyeball).

2 The Retina

Light (coming from left in the above view) strikes the retina, passing through largely transparent layers of neurons before reaching the rods and cones, two types of photoreceptors that differ in shape and in function. The neurons of the retina then relay visual information captured by the photoreceptors to the optic nerve and brain along the pathways shown with red arrows. Each *bipolar cell* receives information from several rods or cones, and each *ganglion cell* gathers input from several bipolar cells. *Horizontal* and *amacrine cells* integrate information across the retina.

One region of the retina, the optic disk, lacks photoreceptors. As a result, this region forms a "blind spot" where light is not detected.

diameter of the pupil to let in more or less light. Behind the pupil, a single lens focuses light on a layer of photoreceptors. Similar to a camera's focusing action, muscles in an invertebrate's single-lens eye move the lens forward or backward, focusing on objects at different distances.

The eyes of all vertebrates have a single lens. In fishes, focusing is as in invertebrates, with the lens moving forward or backward. In other species, including mammals, focusing is achieved by changing the shape of the lens. We will learn about this mechanism, as well as explore visual perception in much more detail, as we shift our attention to the vertebrate visual system.

The Vertebrate Visual System

The human eye will serve as our model of vision in vertebrates. As detailed in **Figure 50.17,** vision begins when photons of light enter the eye and strike the rods and cones. There the energy of each photon is captured by a shift in configuration of a single chemical bond in retinal.

3 Photoreceptor Cells

Humans have two main types of photoreceptor cells: rods and cones. Within the outer segment of a rod or cone is a stack of membranous disks in which *visual pigments* are embedded. **Rods** are more sensitive to light but do not distinguish colors; they enable us to see at night, but only in black and white. **Cones** provide color vision, but, being less sensitive, contribute very little to night vision. There are three types of cones. Each has a different sensitivity across the visible spectrum, providing an optimal response to red, green, or blue light.

In the colorized SEM shown above, cones (green), rods (light tan), and adjacent neurons (purple) are visible. The pigmented epithelium, which was removed in this preparation, would be to the right.

4 Visual Pigments

Vertebrate visual pigments consist of a light-absorbing molecule called **retinal** (a derivative of vitamin A) bound to a membrane protein called an **opsin**. Seven α helices of each opsin molecule span the disk membrane. The visual pigment of rods, shown here, is called **rhodopsin**.

Retinal exists as two isomers. Absorption of light shifts one bond in retinal from a *cis* to a *trans* arrangement, converting the molecule from an angled shape to a straight shape. This change in configuration destabilizes and activates the opsin protein to which retinal is bound.

Although light detection in the eye is the first stage in vision, remember that it is actually the brain that "sees." Thus, to understand vision, we must examine how the capture of light by retinal changes the production of action potentials and then follow these signals to the visual centers of the brain, where images are perceived.

Sensory Transduction in the Eye

The transduction of visual information to the nervous system begins with the light-induced conversion of *cis*-retinal to *trans*-retinal. As shown in **Figure 50.18**, this conversion activates rhodopsin, which activates a G protein, which in turn activates an enzyme that can hydrolyze cyclic GMP. In the dark, cyclic GMP in photoreceptor cells binds to sodium ion (Na^+) channels and keeps them open. When the G protein-dependent pathway is activated, cyclic GMP is broken down, Na^+ channels close, and the cell becomes hyperpolarized.

The signal transduction pathway in photoreceptor cells normally shuts off as enzymes convert retinal back to the *cis* form, returning rhodopsin to its inactive state. In very bright light, however, rhodopsin remains active, and the response in the rods becomes saturated. If the amount of light entering the eyes decreases abruptly, the rods do not regain full responsiveness for several minutes. This is why you are temporarily blinded if you pass quickly from the bright sunshine into a movie theater or other dark environment. (Because light activation changes the color of rhodopsin from purple to yellow, rods in which the light response is saturated are often described as "bleached.")

Processing of Visual Information in the Retina

The processing of visual information begins in the retina itself, where both rods and cones form synapses with bipolar cells **(Figure 50.19)**. In the dark, rods and cones are depolarized and continually release the neurotransmitter glutamate at these synapses (see Table 48.2). Some bipolar cells depolarize in response to glutamate, whereas others hyperpolarize. Which of the two responses a bipolar cell exhibits depends on the type of glutamate receptor on its surface at the synapse. When light strikes the rods and cones, they hyperpolarize, shutting off their release of glutamate. In response, the bipolar cells that are depolarized by glutamate hyperpolarize, and those that are hyperpolarized by glutamate depolarize.

In addition to bipolar cells, information processing in the retina requires three other types of neurons—ganglion, horizontal, and amacrine cells (see Figure 50.17).

Signals from rods and cones can follow several different pathways in the retina. Some information passes directly from photoreceptors to bipolar cells to ganglion cells. In other cases, horizontal cells carry signals from one rod or cone to other photoreceptors and to several bipolar cells. When an illuminated rod or cone stimulates a horizontal cell, the horizontal cell inhibits more distant photoreceptors and bipolar cells that are not illuminated. The result is

▲ **Figure 50.18 Production of the receptor potential in a rod cell.** In rods (and cones), the receptor potential triggered by light is a hyperpolarization, not a depolarization.

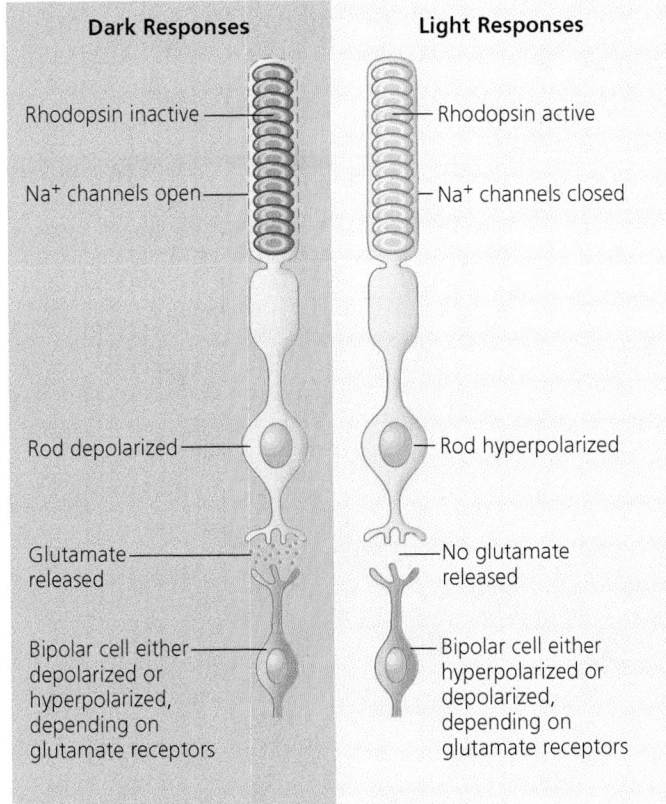

Dark Responses	Light Responses
Rhodopsin inactive	Rhodopsin active
Na+ channels open	Na+ channels closed
Rod depolarized	Rod hyperpolarized
Glutamate released	No glutamate released
Bipolar cell either depolarized or hyperpolarized, depending on glutamate receptors	Bipolar cell either hyperpolarized or depolarized, depending on glutamate receptors

▲ Figure 50.19 **Synaptic activity of rod cells in light and dark.**

[?] *Like rods, cone cells are depolarized when rhodopsin is inactive. In the case of a cone, why might it be misleading to call this a dark response?*

that the region receiving light appears lighter and the dark surroundings even darker. This form of integration, called **lateral inhibition,** sharpens edges and enhances contrast in the image. Amacrine cells distribute some information from one bipolar cell to several ganglion cells. Lateral inhibition is repeated by the interactions of the amacrine cells with the ganglion cells and occurs at all levels of visual processing in the brain.

A single ganglion cell receives information from an array of rods and cones, each of which responds to light coming from a particular location. Together, the rods or cones that feed information to one ganglion cell define a *receptive field*—the part of the visual field to which the ganglion can respond. The fewer rods or cones that supply a single ganglion cell, the smaller the receptive field. A smaller receptive field results in a sharper image, because the information as to where light has struck the retina is more precise. The ganglion cells of the fovea have very small receptive fields, so visual acuity (sharpness) in the fovea is high.

Processing of Visual Information in the Brain

Axons of ganglion cells form the optic nerves that transmit sensations from the eyes to the brain (Figure 50.20). The two

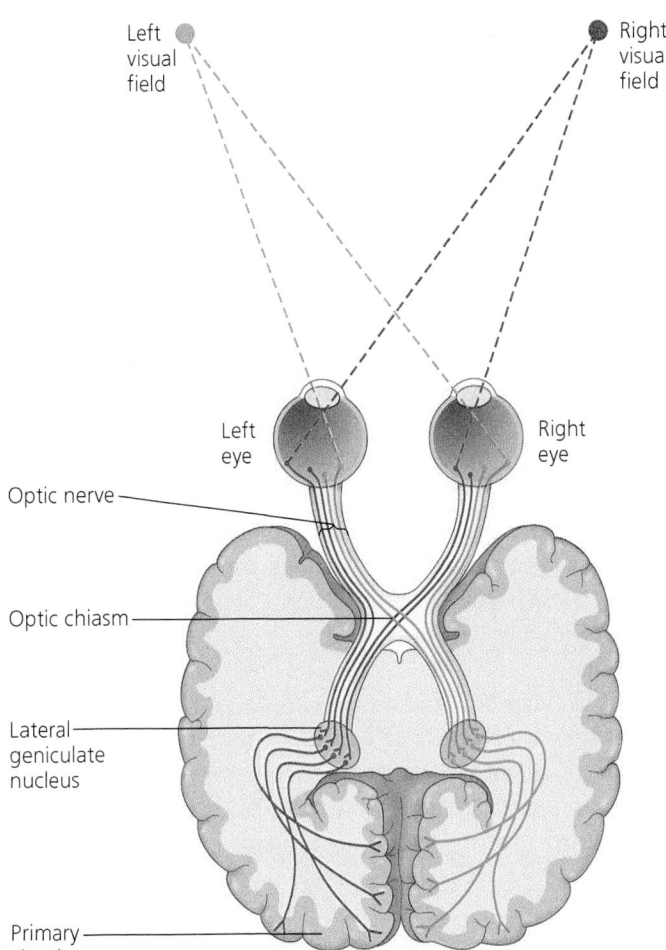

▲ Figure 50.20 **Neural pathways for vision.** Each optic nerve contains about a million axons that synapse with interneurons in the lateral geniculate nuclei. The nuclei relay sensations to the primary visual cortex, one of many brain centers that cooperate in constructing our visual perceptions.

optic nerves meet at the **optic chiasm** near the center of the base of the cerebral cortex. Axons in the optic nerves are routed at the optic chiasm such that sensations from the left visual field of both eyes are transmitted to the right side of the brain, and sensations from the right visual field are transmitted to the left side of the brain. (Note that each visual field, whether right or left, involves input from both eyes.)

Within the brain, most ganglion cell axons lead to the **lateral geniculate nuclei,** which have axons that reach the **primary visual cortex** in the cerebrum. Additional neurons carry the information to higher-order visual processing and integrating centers elsewhere in the cortex.

Point-by-point information in the visual field is projected along neurons onto the visual cortex. How does the cortex convert a complex set of action potentials representing two-dimensional images focused on the retina to three-dimensional perceptions of our surroundings? Researchers estimate that at least 30% of the cerebral cortex, comprising hundreds of millions of neurons in perhaps dozens of integrating centers, takes part in formulating what we actually "see." Determining how these centers integrate such components of our vision as color, motion, depth, shape, and detail is the focus of much exciting research.

Color Vision

Among vertebrates, most fishes, amphibians, and reptiles, including birds, have very good color vision. Humans and other primates also see color well, but are among the minority of mammals with this ability. Many mammals are nocturnal, and having a high proportion of rods in the retina is an adaptation that gives these animals keen night vision. Cats, for instance, are usually most active at night; they have limited color vision and probably see a pastel world during the day.

In humans, the perception of color is based on three types of cones, each with a different visual pigment—red, green, or blue. The three visual pigments, called *photopsins*, are formed from the binding of retinal to three distinct opsin proteins. Slight differences in the opsin proteins are sufficient for each photopsin to absorb light optimally at a different wavelength. Although the visual pigments are designated as red, green, or blue, their absorption spectra in fact overlap. For this reason, the brain's perception of intermediate hues depends on the differential stimulation of two or more classes of cones. For example, when both red and green cones are stimulated, we may see yellow or orange, depending on which class is more strongly stimulated.

Abnormal color vision typically results from alterations in the genes for one or more photopsin proteins. Because the human genes for the red and green pigments are located on the X chromosome, a single defective copy of either gene can disrupt color vision in males (see Figure 15.7 to review the genetics of sex-linked traits). For this reason, color blindness is more common in males than in females (5–8% of males, fewer than 1% of females) and nearly always disrupts perception of red or green (the gene for blue pigment is on human chromosome 7).

Color blindness is also more common among males than females in squirrel monkeys (*Saimiri sciureus*), providing a good experimental model for studying this disorder. In 2009, researchers studying color blindness in squirrel monkeys made a significant breakthrough in the field of gene therapy (**Figure 50.21**).

The Visual Field

The brain not only processes visual information, but also controls what information is captured. One important type of control is focusing, which, as noted earlier and illustrated in **Figure 50.22**, occurs by changing the shape of the lens. When you focus on a close object, your lens becomes almost spherical. When you view a distant object, your lens is flattened. By turning your head and pointing your eyes in a particular direction, your brain also determines what lies in your field of vision.

▼ **Figure 50.21**
IMPACT

Gene Therapy for Vision

Seeking to learn whether a defect in color vision could be remedied in an adult animal, researchers chose to study squirrel monkeys, which have only two opsin genes. The opsin encoded by one gene is sensitive to blue light, while the other opsin is sensitive to either red or green light, depending on the allele. Because the red/green opsin gene is X-linked, all males have only the red-sensitive or the green-sensitive version and are red-green color-blind. In a gene therapy experiment, researchers injected a virus containing the gene for the missing version into the retina of adult male monkeys. After 20 weeks, the new opsin allele was being expressed in cones and the monkeys had begun to distinguish red from green in a field of colored dots.

WHY IT MATTERS These experiments demonstrate that the neural circuits required to process visual information can be generated or activated even in adults, opening up the possibility for treating a range of vision disorders by gene therapy. Indeed, gene therapy has already been used to treat Leber's congenital amaurosis (LCA), an inherited retinal degenerative disease that causes severe loss of vision at birth. After using gene therapy to restore vision in dogs and mice with LCA, researchers successfully treated the disease in humans by injecting the functional LCA gene in a viral vector.

FURTHER READING F. P. M. Cremers and R. W. J. Collin, Promises and challenges of genetic therapy for blindness, *The Lancet* 374:1569–1570 (2009).

MAKE CONNECTIONS Red-green color blindness is X-linked in squirrel monkeys and humans (see Figure 15.7, p. 291). Why is the inheritance pattern in humans not apparent in squirrel monkeys?

Although our peripheral vision allows us to see objects over a nearly 180° range, the distribution of photoreceptors across the eye limits both what we see and how well we see it. Overall, the human retina contains about 125 million rods and about 6 million cones. At the **fovea**, the center of the visual field, there are no rods but a very high density of cones—about 150,000 cones per square millimeter. The ratio of rods to cones increases with distance from the fovea, with the peripheral regions having only rods. In daylight, you achieve your sharpest vision by looking directly at an object, such that light shines on the tightly packed cones in your fovea.

▼ Figure 50.22 **Focusing in the mammalian eye.** Ciliary muscles control the shape of the lens, which bends light and focuses it on the retina. The thicker the lens, the more sharply the light is bent.

(a) Near vision (accommodation)

Ciliary muscles contract, pulling border of choroid toward lens.

Suspensory ligaments relax.

Lens becomes thicker and rounder, focusing on nearby objects.

Choroid

Retina

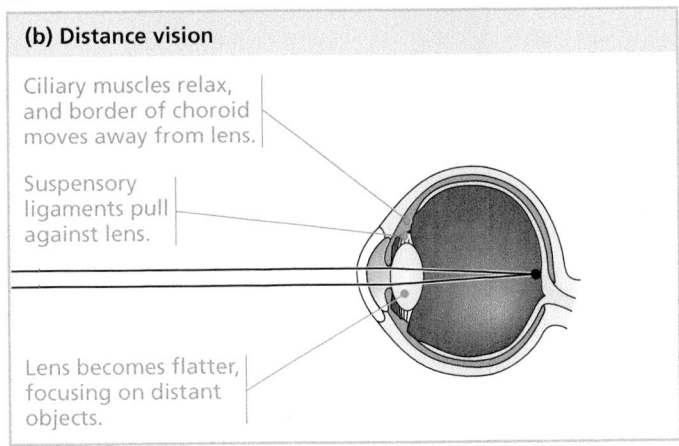

(b) Distance vision

Ciliary muscles relax, and border of choroid moves away from lens.

Suspensory ligaments pull against lens.

Lens becomes flatter, focusing on distant objects.

At night, looking directly at a dimly lit object is ineffective, since the rods—the more sensitive light receptors—are found outside the fovea. Thus, for example, you see a dim star best by focusing on a point just to one side of it.

CONCEPT CHECK 50.3

1. Contrast the light-detecting organs of planarians and flies. How is each organ adaptive for the lifestyle of the animal?
2. In a condition called presbyopia, the eyes' lenses lose much of their elasticity and maintain a flat shape. Explain how this condition affects a person's vision.
3. **WHAT IF?** If you perceive an object floating across your field of view, how might you determine whether the image represents a real object rather than a disturbance in your eye or in a neural circuit of your brain?
4. **MAKE CONNECTIONS** Compare the function of retinal in the eye with that of the pigment chlorophyll in a plant photosystem (see Concept 10.2, pp. 190–194).

For suggested answers, see Appendix A.

The senses of taste and smell rely on similar sets of sensory receptors

Many animals use their chemical senses to find mates (as when male silk moths respond to pheromones emitted by females), to recognize territory that has been marked by some chemical substance (as when dogs and cats sniff boundaries that have been staked out by their spraying neighbors), and to help navigate during migration (as when salmon use the unique scent of their streams of origin to return there for breeding). Animals such as ants and bees that live in large social groups rely extensively on chemical "conversation." In all animals, chemical senses are important in feeding behavior. For example, a hydra retracts its tentacles toward its mouth when it detects the compound glutathione, which is released from prey captured by the tentacles.

The perceptions of **gustation** (taste) and **olfaction** (smell) both depend on chemoreceptors that detect specific chemicals in the environment. In the case of terrestrial animals, taste is the detection of chemicals called **tastants** that are present in a solution, and smell is the detection of **odorants** that are carried through the air. There is no distinction between taste and smell in aquatic animals.

The taste receptors of insects are located within sensory hairs located on the feet and in mouthparts. These animals use their sense of taste to select food. A tasting hair contains several chemoreceptors, each especially responsive to a particular class of tastant, such as sugar or salt. Insects are also capable of smelling airborne odorants using olfactory hairs, usually located on their antennae (see Figure 50.6). The chemical DEET (*N,N*-diethyl-meta-toluamide), sold as an insect "repellant," actually protects against bites by blocking the olfactory receptor in mosquitoes that detects human scent.

Taste in Mammals

Humans and other mammals recognize five types of tastants. Four represent the familiar taste perceptions—sweet, sour, salty, and bitter. The fifth, called umami (Japanese for "delicious"), is elicited by the amino acid glutamate. Often used as a flavor enhancer, monosodium glutamate (MSG) occurs naturally in foods such as meat and aged cheese, imparting a quality sometimes described as savory. Researchers have identified the receptor proteins for all of the tastes except salty.

For decades, many researchers assumed that a taste cell could have more than one type of receptor. An alternative idea is that each taste cell has a single receptor type, programming the cell to recognize only one of the five tastes. Which hypothesis is correct? In 2005, scientists at the University of California, San Diego, used a cloned bitter taste receptor to genetically

How do mammals detect different tastes?

EXPERIMENT To investigate the basis of mammalian taste perception, Ken Mueller, Nick Ryba, and Charles Zuker used a chemical called phenyl-β-D-glucopyranoside (PBDG). Humans find the taste of PBDG extremely bitter. Mice, however, appear to lack a receptor for PBDG. Whereas mice avoid drinking water containing other bitter tastants, they show no aversion to water that contains PBDG.

Using a molecular cloning strategy, Mueller generated mice that made the human PBDG receptor in cells that normally make either a sweet receptor or a bitter receptor. The mice were given a choice of two bottles, one filled with pure water and one filled with water containing PBDG at varying concentrations. The researchers then observed whether the mice had an attraction or an aversion to PBDG.

RESULTS

Relative consumption = (Fluid intake from bottle containing PBDG ÷ Total fluid intake) × 100%

CONCLUSION The researchers found that the presence of a bitter receptor in sweet taste cells is sufficient to cause mice to be attracted to a bitter chemical. They concluded that the mammalian brain must therefore perceive sweet or bitter taste solely on the basis of which sensory neurons are activated.

SOURCE K. L. Mueller et al., The receptors and coding logic for bitter taste, *Nature* 434:225–229 (2005).

WHAT IF? Suppose instead of the PBDG receptor the researchers had used a receptor specific for a sweetener that humans crave but mice ignore. How would the results of the experiment have differed?

reprogram gustation in a mouse **(Figure 50.23)**. Based on these and other studies, the researchers concluded that an individual taste cell expresses a single receptor type and detects tastants representing only one of the five tastes.

The receptor cells for taste in mammals are modified epithelial cells organized into **taste buds**, which are scattered in several areas of the tongue and mouth **(Figure 50.24)**. Most taste buds on the tongue are associated with nipple-shaped projections called papillae. Any region of the tongue with taste buds can detect any of the five types of taste. (The frequently reproduced "taste maps" of the tongue are thus not accurate.)

Taste receptors fall into two categories, each evolutionarily related to receptors for other senses. The sensation of sweet,

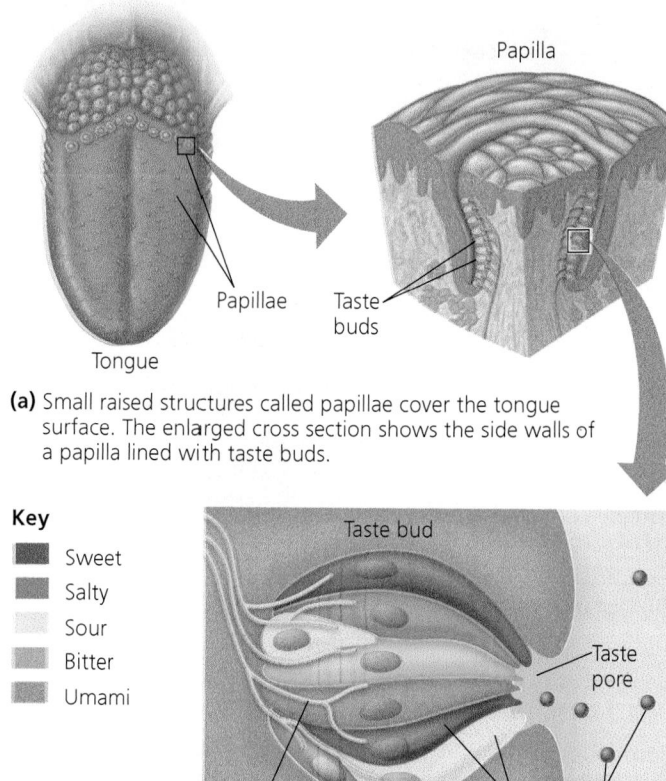

(a) Small raised structures called papillae cover the tongue surface. The enlarged cross section shows the side walls of a papilla lined with taste buds.

Key
- Sweet
- Salty
- Sour
- Bitter
- Umami

(b) Taste buds in all regions of the tongue contain sensory receptor cells specific for each of the five taste types.

▲ **Figure 50.24 Human taste receptors.**

umami, and bitter tastes requires a G protein-coupled receptor, or GPCR (see Figure 11.7). In humans, there are more than 30 different receptors for bitter taste, each able to recognize multiple bitter tastants. In contrast, humans have one type of sweet receptor and one type of umami receptor, each assembled from a different pair of GPCR proteins. Other GPCR proteins are critical for the sense of smell, as we will discuss shortly.

Unlike the other identified taste receptors, the receptor for sour tastants belongs to the TRP family (see p. 1089). Formed from a pair of TRP proteins, the sour receptor is similar to the capsaicin receptor and other thermoreceptor proteins. In taste buds, the TRP proteins of the sour receptor assemble into a channel in the plasma membrane of the taste cell. Binding of an acid or other sour-tasting substance to the receptor triggers a change in the ion channel. Depolarization occurs, activating a sensory neuron.

Smell in Humans

In olfaction, unlike gustation, the sensory cells are neurons. Olfactory receptor cells line the upper portion of the nasal cavity and send impulses along their axons directly to the olfactory bulb of the brain **(Figure 50.25)**. The receptive ends

▲ **Figure 50.25 Smell in humans.** Odorant molecules bind to specific receptor proteins in the plasma membrane of olfactory receptor cells, triggering action potentials.

WHAT IF? *If you spray an "air freshener" in a musty room, would you be affecting detection, transmission, or perception of the odorants responsible for the musty smell?*

of the cells contain cilia that extend into the layer of mucus coating the nasal cavity. When an odorant diffuses into this region, it binds to a specific GPCR protein called an odorant receptor (OR) on the plasma membrane of the olfactory cilia. These events trigger signal transduction leading to the production of cyclic AMP. In olfactory cells, cyclic AMP opens channels in the plasma membrane that are permeable to both Na^+ and Ca^{2+}. The flow of these ions into the receptor cell leads to depolarization of the membrane, generating action potentials.

Humans can distinguish thousands of different odors, each caused by a structurally distinct odorant. This level of sensory discrimination requires many different ORs. In 1991, Richard Axel and Linda Buck, working at Columbia University, discovered a family of more than 1,000 OR genes—about 3% of all human genes. Each olfactory receptor cell appears to express one OR gene. Cells selective for different odorants are interspersed in the nasal cavity. Those cells that express the same OR gene transmit action potentials to the same small region of the olfactory bulb. In 2004, Axel and Buck shared a Nobel Prize for their studies of the gene family and receptors that function in olfaction.

Although the receptors and brain pathways for taste and smell are independent, the two senses do interact. Indeed, much of the complex flavor humans experience when eating is due to our sense of smell. If the olfactory system is blocked, as occurs when you have a head cold, the perception of taste is sharply reduced.

CONCEPT CHECK 50.4

1. Explain why some taste receptor cells and all olfactory receptor cells use G protein-coupled receptors, yet only olfactory receptor cells produce action potentials.
2. Pathways involving G proteins provide an opportunity for an increase in signal strength in the course of signal transduction, a change referred to as amplification. How might this be beneficial in olfaction?
3. **WHAT IF?** If you discovered a mutation in mice that disrupted the ability to taste sweet, bitter, and umami, but not sour or salty, what might you predict about where this mutation acts in the signaling pathways used by these receptors?

For suggested answers, see Appendix A.

CONCEPT 50.5

The physical interaction of protein filaments is required for muscle function

Throughout our discussion of sensory mechanisms, we have seen how sensory inputs to the nervous system result in specific behaviors: the touch-guided foraging of a star-nosed mole, the upside-down swimming of a crayfish with manipulated statocysts, and the light-avoiding maneuvers of planarians. Underlying the diverse forms of behavior in animals are common fundamental mechanisms: Feeding, swimming, and crawling all require muscle activity in response to nervous system input.

Muscle cell function relies on microfilaments, which are the actin components of the cytoskeleton. Recall from Chapter 6 that microfilaments, like microtubules, function in cell motility. Muscle contraction is the product of microfilament movement powered by chemical energy; muscle extension occurs only passively. To understand how microfilaments contribute to muscle contraction, we must analyze the structure of muscles and muscle fibers. We will begin by examining vertebrate skeletal muscle and then turn our attention to other types of muscle.

Vertebrate Skeletal Muscle

Vertebrate **skeletal muscle**, which moves bones and body, is characterized by a hierarchy of smaller and smaller units (**Figure 50.26**). Most skeletal muscles consist of a bundle of long fibers running parallel to the length of the muscle. Each fiber is a single cell. A muscle fiber, or cell, contains multiple nuclei, reflecting its formation by the fusion of many embryonic cells. Inside the fiber lies a bundle of smaller **myofibrils** arranged longitudinally. The myofibrils, in turn, are composed of thin filaments and thick filaments. **Thin filaments** consist of two strands of actin and two strands of a regulatory protein (not shown here) coiled around one another. **Thick filaments** are staggered arrays of myosin molecules.

Skeletal muscle is also called **striated muscle** because the regular arrangement of the filaments creates a pattern of light and dark bands. Each repeating unit is a **sarcomere**, the basic contractile unit of the muscle. The borders of the sarcomere are lined up in adjacent myofibrils and contribute to the striations visible with a light microscope. Thin filaments are attached at the Z lines and project toward the center of the sarcomere, while thick filaments are attached at the M lines centered in the sarcomere. In a muscle fiber at rest, thick and thin filaments only partially overlap. Near the edge of the sarcomere there are only thin filaments, whereas the zone in the center contains only thick filaments. This arrangement is the key to how the sarcomere, and hence the whole muscle, contracts.

The Sliding-Filament Model of Muscle Contraction

We can explain much of what happens during the contraction of a whole muscle by focusing on the contraction of a single sarcomere (**Figure 50.27**). According to the **sliding-filament model**, the filaments do not change in length when the sarcomere shortens. Instead, the thin and thick filaments slide past each other, increasing their overlap.

The longitudinal sliding of the filaments relies on the interaction of actin and myosin. Each myosin molecule has a long "tail" region and a globular "head" region. The tail adheres to the tails of other myosin molecules that form the thick filament. The head, which extends to the side, can bind

▲ Figure 50.26 **The structure of skeletal muscle.**

ATP and hydrolyze it to ADP and inorganic phosphate. As shown in **Figure 50.28**, hydrolysis of ATP converts myosin to a high-energy form. This form of myosin binds to actin, forms a cross-bridge, and pulls the thin filament toward the center of the sarcomere. The cross-bridge is broken when a new molecule of ATP binds to the myosin head.

Muscle contraction requires repeated cycles of binding and release. In each cycle, the myosin head freed from a cross-bridge cleaves the newly bound ATP and binds again to actin. Because the thin filament moved toward the center of

The sliding-filament model of muscle contraction. The drawings on the left show that the lengths of the thick (myosin) filaments (purple) and thin (actin) filaments (orange) remain the same as a muscle fiber contracts.

Relaxed muscle

Contracting muscle

Fully contracted muscle

Thick filament

Thin filaments

① Starting here, the myosin head is bound to ATP and is in its low-energy configuration.

Thin filament

Myosin head (low-energy configuration)

ATP

Thick filament

② The myosin head hydrolyzes ATP to ADP and inorganic phosphate (P_i) and is in its high-energy configuration.

⑤ Binding of a new molecule of ATP releases the myosin head from actin, and a new cycle begins.

Thin filament moves toward center of sarcomere.

Myosin head (low-energy configuration)

Actin

Myosin-binding sites

ADP
P_i

Myosin head (high-energy configuration)

ADP + P_i

ADP
P_i
Cross-bridge

③ The myosin head binds to actin, forming a cross-bridge.

④ Releasing ADP and P_i, myosin returns to its low-energy configuration, sliding the thin filament.

▲ Figure 50.28 **Myosin-actin interactions underlying muscle fiber contraction.**

? *When ATP binds, what prevents the filaments from sliding back into their original positions?*

 ANIMATION ***BioFlix*** Visit the Study Area at **www.masteringbiology.com** for the BioFlix® 3-D Animation on Muscle Contraction.

the sarcomere in the previous cycle, the myosin head now attaches to a new binding site farther along the thin filament. Each of the approximately 350 heads of a thick filament forms and re-forms about five cross-bridges per second, driving filaments past each other.

A typical muscle fiber at rest contains only enough ATP for a few contractions. To power repetitive contractions, the muscle cell relies on two other storage compounds: creatine phosphate and glycogen. Transfer of a phosphate group from creatine phosphate to ADP in an enzyme-catalyzed reaction synthesizes additional ATP. In this way, the resting supply of creatine phosphate can sustain contractions for about 15 seconds. ATP stores are also replenished when glycogen is broken down to glucose, which can be used to generate ATP, by either aerobic respiration or glycolysis (and lactic acid fermentation; see Chapter 9). Using a typical muscle fiber's glycogen store, glycolysis can support about 1 minute of sustained contraction, whereas aerobic respiration can power contractions for nearly an hour.

The Role of Calcium and Regulatory Proteins

Calcium ions (Ca^{2+}) and proteins bound to actin play crucial roles in both muscle cell contraction and relaxation. **Tropomyosin**, a regulatory protein, and the **troponin complex**, a set of additional regulatory proteins, are bound to the actin strands of thin filaments. In a muscle fiber at rest, tropomyosin covers the myosin-binding sites along the thin filament, preventing actin and myosin from interacting **(Figure 50.29a)**. When Ca^{2+} accumulates in the cytosol, it binds to the troponin complex, causing tropomyosin bound along the actin strands to shift position and expose the myosin-binding sites on the thin filament **(Figure 50.29b)**. Thus, when the Ca^{2+} concentration rises in the cytosol, the thin and thick filaments slide past each other, and the muscle fiber contracts. When the Ca^{2+} concentration falls, the binding sites are covered, and contraction stops.

Motor neurons cause muscle contraction by triggering the release of Ca^{2+} into the cytosol of muscle cells with which they form synapses. This regulation of Ca^{2+} concentration is a multistep process involving a network of membranes and compartments within the muscle cell. As you read the following description, refer to the overview and diagram in **Figure 50.30**.

The arrival of an action potential at the synaptic terminal of a motor neuron causes release of the neurotransmitter acetylcholine. Binding of acetylcholine to receptors on the muscle fiber leads to a depolarization, triggering an action potential. Within the muscle fiber, the action potential spreads deep into the interior, following infoldings of the plasma membrane called **transverse (T) tubules**. The T tubules make close contact with the **sarcoplasmic reticulum (SR)**, a specialized endoplasmic reticulum. As the action potential spreads along the T tubules, it triggers changes in the SR, opening Ca^{2+} channels. Calcium ions stored in the interior of the SR flow through these open channels into the cytosol and bind to the troponin complex, initiating contraction of the muscle fiber.

When motor neuron input stops, the muscle cell relaxes. As it relaxes, the filaments slide back to their starting position. During this phase, proteins in the cell reset the muscle for the next cycle of contraction. Relaxation begins as transport proteins in the SR pump Ca^{2+} in from the cytosol. When the Ca^{2+} concentration in the cytosol drops to a low level, the regulatory proteins bound to the thin filament shift back to their starting position, once again blocking the myosin-binding sites. At the same time, the Ca^{2+} pumped from the cytosol accumulates in the SR, providing the stores needed to respond to the next action potential.

Several diseases cause paralysis by interfering with the excitation of skeletal muscle fibers by motor neurons. In amyotrophic lateral sclerosis (ALS), also called Lou Gehrig's disease, motor neurons in the spinal cord and brainstem degenerate, and the muscle fibers with which they synapse atrophy. ALS is progressive and usually fatal within five years after symptoms appear; currently there is no cure or treatment. Myasthenia gravis is an autoimmune disease in which a person produces antibodies to the acetylcholine receptors on skeletal muscle fibers. As the number of these receptors decreases, synaptic transmission between motor neurons and muscle fibers declines. Fortunately, effective treatments are available for mysathenia gravis.

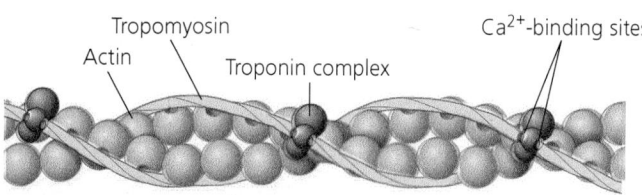

Tropomyosin
Actin
Troponin complex
Ca^{2+}-binding sites

(a) Myosin-binding sites blocked

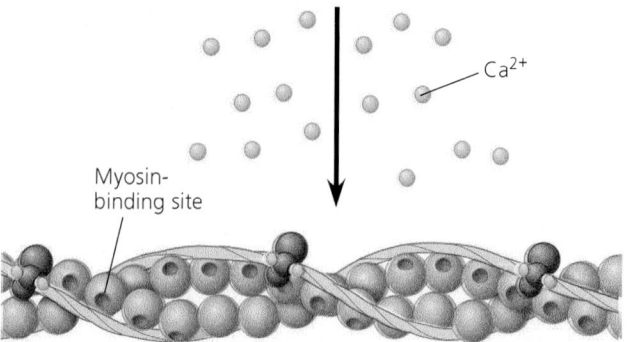

Ca^{2+}

Myosin-binding site

(b) Myosin-binding sites exposed

▲ **Figure 50.29 The role of regulatory proteins and calcium in muscle fiber contraction.** Each thin filament consists of two strands of actin, tropomyosin, and the troponin complex.

Exploring The Regulation of Skeletal Muscle Contraction

The electrical, chemical, and molecular events regulating skeletal muscle contraction are shown in a cutaway view of a muscle cell and in the enlarged diagram below. Action potentials (red arrows) **t**riggered by the motor neuron sweep across the muscle fiber and into it along the transverse (T) tubules, initiating the movements of calcium (green dots) that regulate muscle activity.

Synaptic terminal

Axon of motor neuron

T tubule

Mitochondrion

Sarcoplasmic reticulum (SR)

Myofibril

Plasma membrane of muscle fiber

Ca^{2+} released from SR

Sarcomere

Synaptic terminal of motor neuron

1 Acetylcholine (ACh) released at synaptic terminal diffuses across synaptic cleft and binds to receptor proteins on muscle fiber's plasma membrane, triggering an action potential in muscle fiber.

Synaptic cleft

T tubule

Plasma membrane

ACh

2 Action potential is propagated along plasma membrane and down T tubules.

Sarcoplasmic reticulum (SR)

3 Action potential triggers Ca^{2+} release from SR.

Ca^{2+} pump

Ca^{2+}

ATP

CYTOSOL

Ca^{2+}

4 Calcium ions bind to troponin in thin filament; myosin-binding sites exposed.

7 Tropomyosin blockage of myosin-binding sites is restored; contraction ends, and muscle fiber relaxes.

6 Cytosolic Ca^{2+} is removed by active transport into SR after action potential ends.

5 Cycles of myosin cross-bridge formation and breakdown, coupled with ATP hydrolysis, slide thin filament toward center of sarcomere.

Nervous Control of Muscle Tension

Whereas contraction of a single skeletal muscle fiber is a brief all-or-none twitch, contraction of a whole muscle, such as the biceps in your upper arm, is graded; you can voluntarily alter the extent and strength of its contraction. There are two basic mechanisms by which the nervous system produces graded contractions of whole muscles: (1) by varying the number of muscle fibers that contract and (2) by varying the rate at which muscle fibers are stimulated. Let's consider each mechanism in turn.

In vertebrates, each branched motor neuron may form synapses with many skeletal muscle fibers, although each fiber is controlled by only one motor neuron. For the whole muscle, there may be hundreds of motor neurons, each with its own pool of muscle fibers. A **motor unit** consists of a single motor neuron and all the muscle fibers it controls **(Figure 50.31)**. When a motor neuron produces an action potential, all the muscle fibers in its motor unit contract as a group. The strength of the resulting contraction depends on how many muscle fibers the motor neuron controls.

In most muscles, the number of muscle fibers in different motor units ranges from a few to hundreds. The nervous system can thus regulate the strength of contraction in a muscle by determining how many motor units are activated at a given instant and by selecting large or small motor units to activate. The force (tension) developed by a muscle progressively increases as more and more of the motor neurons controlling the muscle are activated, a process called *recruitment* of motor neurons. Depending on the number of motor neurons your brain recruits and the size of their motor units, you can lift a fork or something much heavier, like your biology textbook.

Some muscles, especially those that hold up the body and maintain posture, are almost always partially contracted. In such muscles, the nervous system may alternate activation among the motor units, reducing the length of time any one set of fibers is contracted. Prolonged contraction can result in muscle fatigue due to the depletion of ATP and dissipation of ion gradients required for normal electrical signaling. Although accumulation of lactate (see Figure 9.17) may also contribute to muscle fatigue, recent research actually points to a beneficial effect of lactate on muscle function.

The nervous system regulates muscle contraction not only by controlling which motor units are activated, but also by varying the rate of muscle fiber stimulation. A single action potential produces a twitch lasting about 100 msec or less. If a second action potential arrives before the muscle fiber has completely relaxed, the two twitches add together, resulting in greater tension **(Figure 50.32)**. Further summation occurs as the rate of stimulation increases. When the rate is so high that the muscle fiber cannot relax at all between stimuli, the twitches fuse into one smooth, sustained

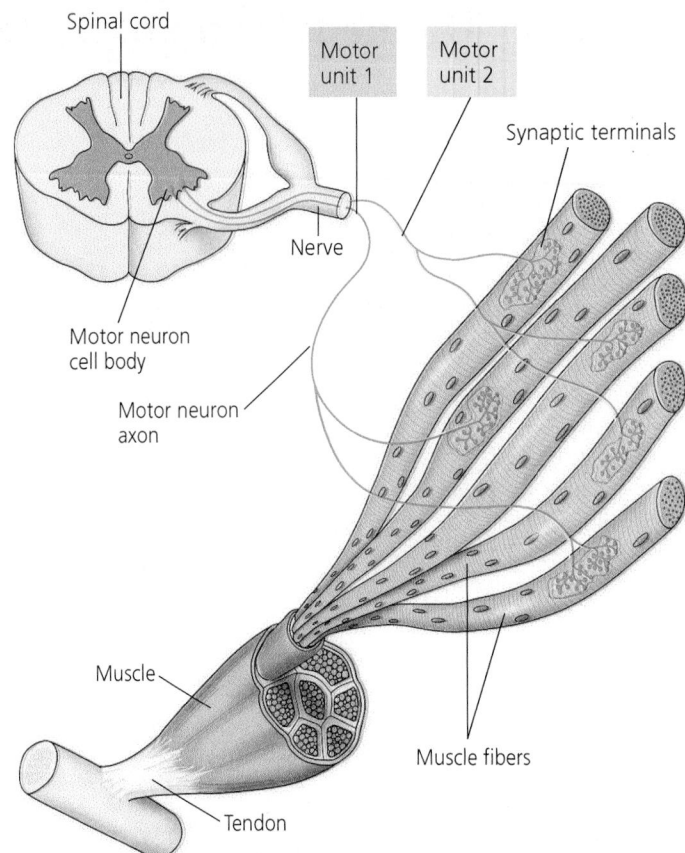

▲ **Figure 50.31 Motor units in a vertebrate skeletal muscle.** Each muscle fiber (cell) forms synapses with only one motor neuron, but each motor neuron typically synapses with many muscle fibers. A motor neuron and all the muscle fibers it controls constitute a motor unit.

contraction called **tetanus**. Motor neurons usually deliver their action potentials in rapid-fire volleys, and the resulting summation of tension results in the smooth contraction typical of tetanus rather than the jerky actions of individual twitches. (Although a smooth, sustained contraction is part of normal muscle function, tetanus is also the name of a disease of uncontrolled muscle contraction caused by a bacterial toxin.)

The increase in tension during summation and tetanus occurs because skeletal muscle fibers are connected to bones via tendons and connective tissues. When a muscle fiber contracts, it stretches these elastic structures, which then transmit tension to the bones. In a single twitch, the muscle fiber begins to relax before the elastic structures are fully stretched. During summation, however, the high-frequency action potentials maintain an elevated concentration of Ca^{2+} in the muscle fiber's cytosol, prolonging cross-bridge cycling and causing greater stretching of the elastic structures. During tetanus, the elastic structures are fully stretched, and all of the tension generated by the muscle fiber is transmitted to the bones.

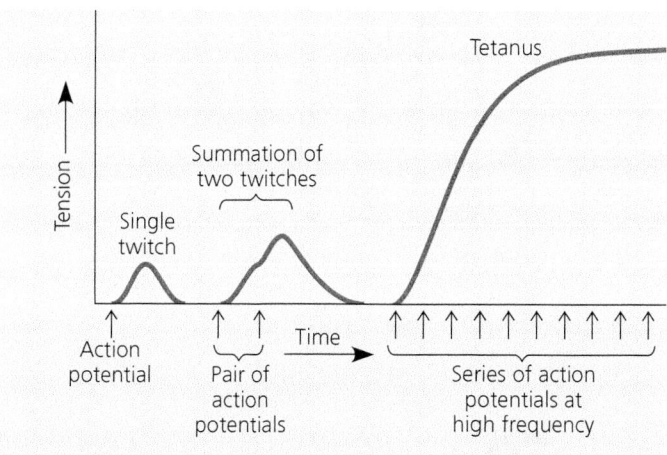

▲ **Figure 50.32 Summation of twitches.** This graph illustrates how the number of action potentials in a short period of time influences the tension developed in a muscle fiber.

? *How could the nervous system cause a skeletal muscle to produce the most forceful contraction it is capable of?*

Types of Skeletal Muscle Fibers

Our discussion to this point has focused on the general properties of vertebrate skeletal muscles. There are, however, several distinct types of skeletal muscle fibers, each of which is adapted to a particular set of functions. Scientists typically classify these varied fiber types either by the source of ATP used to power muscle activity or by the speed of muscle contraction. We'll consider each of the two classification schemes.

Oxidative and Glycolytic Fibers Fibers that rely mostly on aerobic respiration are called oxidative fibers. Such fibers are specialized in ways that enable them to make use of a steady energy supply: They have many mitochondria, a rich blood supply, and a large amount of an oxygen-storing protein called **myoglobin**. A brownish red pigment, myoglobin binds oxygen more tightly than does hemoglobin, enabling oxidative fiber to extract oxygen from the blood efficiently. In contrast to oxidative fibers, glycolytic fibers use glycolysis as their primary source of ATP. They have a larger diameter and less myoglobin than oxidative fibers and thus fatigue much more readily. These different fiber types are readily apparent in the muscle of poultry and fish: The dark meat is made up of oxidative fibers rich in myoglobin, and the light meat is composed of glycolytic fibers.

Fast-Twitch and Slow-Twitch Fibers Muscle fibers vary in the speed with which they contract: **Fast-twitch fibers** develop tension two to three times faster than **slow-twitch fibers**. Fast fibers enable brief, rapid, powerful contractions. Slow fibers, often found in muscles that maintain posture, can sustain long contractions. A slow fiber has less sarcoplasmic reticulum and pumps Ca^{2+} more slowly than a fast fiber. Because

Ca^{2+} remains in the cytosol longer, a muscle twitch in a slow fiber lasts about five times as long as one in a fast fiber.

The difference in contraction speed between slow-twitch and fast-twitch fibers mainly reflects the rate at which their myosin heads hydrolyze ATP. However, there isn't a one-to-one relationship between contraction speed and ATP source. Whereas all slow-twitch fibers are oxidative, fast-twitch fibers can be either glycolytic or oxidative.

Most human skeletal muscles contain both fast- and slow-twitch fibers, although the muscles of the eye and hand are exclusively fast-twitch. In a muscle that has a mixture of fast and slow fibers, the relative proportions of each are genetically determined. However, if such a muscle is used repeatedly for activities requiring high endurance, some fast glycolytic fibers can develop into fast oxidative fibers. Because fast oxidative fibers fatigue more slowly than fast glycolytic fibers, the result will be a muscle that is more resistant to fatigue.

Some vertebrates have skeletal muscle fibers that twitch at rates far faster than any human muscle. For example, superfast muscles produce a rattlesnake's rattle and a dove's coo. The fastest such muscles, however, surround the gas-filled swim bladder inside the male toadfish **(Figure 50.33)**. In producing its characteristic "boat whistle" mating call, the toadfish can contract and relax these muscles more than 200 times per second!

Other Types of Muscle

Although all muscles share the same fundamental mechanism of contraction—actin and myosin filaments sliding past each other—there are many different types of muscle. Vertebrates, for example, have cardiac muscle and smooth muscle in addition to skeletal muscle (see Figure 40.5).

▲ **Figure 50.33 Specialization of skeletal muscles.** The male toadfish (*Opsanus tau*) uses superfast muscles to produce its mating call.

Vertebrate **cardiac muscle** is found in only one part of the body: the heart. Like skeletal muscle, cardiac muscle is striated. However, structural differences between skeletal and cardiac muscle fibers result in differences in their electrical and membrane properties. Whereas skeletal muscle fibers do not produce action potentials unless stimulated by a motor neuron, cardiac muscle cells have ion channels in their plasma membrane that cause rhythmic depolarizations, triggering action potentials without input from the nervous system. Action potentials of cardiac muscle cells last up to 20 times longer than those of the skeletal muscle fibers. Plasma membranes of adjacent cardiac muscle cells interlock at specialized regions called **intercalated disks**, where gap junctions (see Figure 6.32) provide direct electrical coupling between the cells. Thus, the action potential generated by specialized cells in one part of the heart spreads to all other cardiac muscle cells, causing the whole heart to contract. A long refractory period prevents summation and tetanus.

Smooth muscle in vertebrates is found mainly in the walls of hollow organs, such as blood vessels and organs of the digestive tract. Smooth muscle cells lack striations because their actin and myosin filaments are not regularly arrayed along the length of the cell. Instead, the thick filaments are scattered throughout the cytoplasm, and the thin filaments are attached to structures called dense bodies, some of which are tethered to the plasma membrane. There is less myosin than in striated muscle fibers, and the myosin is not associated with specific actin strands. Some smooth muscle cells contract only when stimulated by neurons of the autonomic nervous system. Others can generate action potentials without input from neurons—they are electrically coupled to one another. Smooth muscles contract and relax more slowly than striated muscles.

Although Ca^{2+} regulates smooth muscle contraction, the mechanism for regulation is different from that in skeletal and cardiac muscle. Smooth muscle cells have no troponin complex or T tubules, and their sarcoplasmic reticulum is not well developed. During an action potential, Ca^{2+} enters the cytosol mainly through the plasma membrane. Calcium ions cause contraction by binding to the protein calmodulin, which activates an enzyme that phosphorylates the myosin head, enabling cross-bridge activity.

Invertebrates have muscle cells similar to vertebrate skeletal and smooth muscle cells, and arthropod skeletal muscles are nearly identical to those of vertebrates. However, because the flight muscles of insects are capable of independent, rhythmic contraction, the wings of some insects can actually beat faster than action potentials can arrive from the central nervous system. Another interesting evolutionary adaptation has been discovered in the muscles that hold a clam's shell closed. The thick filaments in these muscles contain a protein called paramyosin that enables the muscles to remain contracted for as long as a month with only a low rate of energy consumption.

CONCEPT 50.6

Skeletal systems transform muscle contraction into locomotion

Converting muscle contraction to movement requires a skeleton—a rigid structure to which muscles can attach. An animal changes its rigidity, shape, or location by contracting muscles connecting two parts of its skeleton.

Because muscles exert force only during contraction, moving a body part back and forth typically requires two muscles attached to the same section of the skeleton. We can see such an arrangement of muscles in the upper portion of a human arm or grasshopper leg (**Figure 50.34**). Although we call such

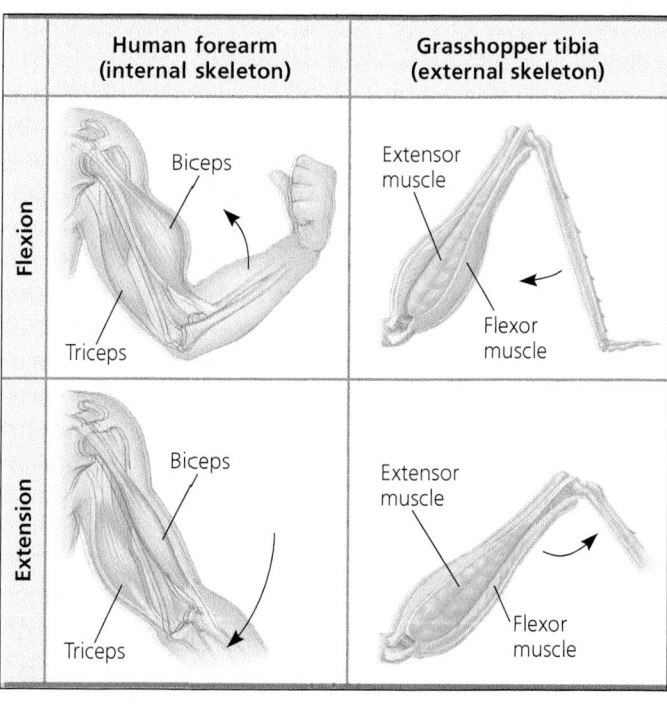

Human forearm (internal skeleton)	Grasshopper tibia (external skeleton)
Flexion — Biceps, Triceps	Extensor muscle, Flexor muscle
Extension — Biceps, Triceps	Extensor muscle, Flexor muscle

Key ■ Contracting muscle ■ Relaxing muscle

▲ **Figure 50.34 The interaction of muscles and skeletons in movement.** Back-and-forth movement of a body part is generally accomplished by antagonistic muscles. This arrangement works with either an internal skeleton, as in mammals, or an external skeleton, as in insects.

muscles an antagonistic pair, their function is actually cooperative, coordinated by the nervous system. For example, when you extend your arm, motor neurons trigger your triceps muscle to contract while the absence of neuronal input allows your biceps to relax.

Vital for movement, the skeletons of animals also function in support and protection. Most land animals would collapse if they had no skeleton to support their mass. Even an animal living in water would be formless without a framework to maintain its shape. In many animals, a hard skeleton also protects soft tissues. For example, the vertebrate skull protects the brain, and the ribs of terrestrial vertebrates form a cage around the heart, lungs, and other internal organs.

Types of Skeletal Systems

Although we tend to think of skeletons only as interconnected sets of bones, skeletons come in many different forms. Hardened support structures can be external (as in exoskeletons), internal (as in endoskeletons), or even absent (as in fluid-based, or hydrostatic, skeletons).

Hydrostatic Skeletons

A **hydrostatic skeleton** consists of fluid held under pressure in a closed body compartment. This is the main type of skeleton in most cnidarians, flatworms, nematodes, and annelids (see Chapter 33). These animals control their form and movement by using muscles to change the shape of fluid-filled compartments. Among the cnidarians, for example, a hydra elongates by closing its mouth and using contractile cells in its body wall to constrict its central gastrovascular cavity. Because water cannot be compressed very much, decreasing the diameter of the cavity forces the cavity to become longer.

Worms use hydrostatic skeletons in diverse ways to move through their environment. In planarians and other flatworms, movement results mainly from muscles in the body wall exerting localized forces against the interstitial fluid. In nematodes (roundworms), longitudinal muscles contracting around the fluid-filled body cavity move the animal forward by undulations, or wavelike motions. In earthworms and many other annelids, circular and longitudinal muscles act together to change the shape of individual fluid-filled segments, which are divided by septa. These shape changes bring about **peristalsis**, a movement produced by rhythmic waves of muscle contractions passing from front to back **(Figure 50.35)**.

Hydrostatic skeletons are well suited for life in aquatic environments. On land, they provide support for crawling and burrowing and may cushion internal organs from shocks. However, a hydrostatic skeleton cannot support walking or running, in which an animal's body is held off the ground.

Exoskeletons

The clam shell you find on a beach once served as an **exoskeleton**, a hard encasement deposited on an animal's

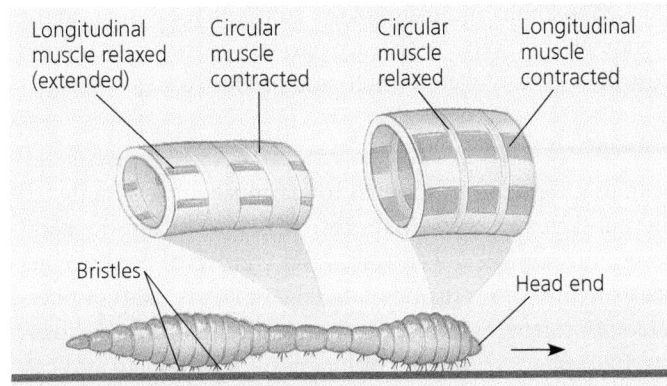

❶ At the moment depicted, body segments at the earthworm's head end and just in front of the rear end are short and thick (longitudinal muscles contracted; circular muscles relaxed) and are anchored to the ground by bristles. The other segments are thin and elongated (circular muscles contracted; longitudinal muscles relaxed).

❷ The head has moved forward because circular muscles in the head segments have contracted. Segments behind the head and at the rear are now thick and anchored, thus preventing the worm from slipping backward.

❸ The head segments are thick again and anchored in their new positions. The rear segments have released their hold on the ground and have been pulled forward.

▲ **Figure 50.35 Crawling by peristalsis.** Contraction of the longitudinal muscles thickens and shortens the earthworm; contraction of the circular muscles constricts and elongates it.

surface. The shells of clams and most other molluscs are made of calcium carbonate secreted by the mantle, a sheet-like extension of the body wall (see Figure 33.15). Clams and other bivalves close their hinged shell using muscles attached to the inside of this exoskeleton. As the animal grows, it enlarges its shell by adding to the outer edge.

Insects and other arthropods have a jointed exoskeleton called a cuticle, a nonliving coat secreted by the epidermis. About 30–50% of the arthropod cuticle consists of **chitin**, a polysaccharide similar to cellulose (see Figure 5.9). Fibrils of chitin are embedded in a protein matrix, forming a composite material that combines strength and flexibility. The cuticle may be hardened with organic compounds that cross-link the proteins of the matrix, and in crustaceans such as lobsters, calcium salts may also be added. In body parts that must be flexible, such as leg joints, the cuticle remains unhardened. Muscles are attached to knobs and plates of the cuticle that extend into the interior of the body. With each growth spurt, an arthropod must shed its exoskeleton (molt) and produce a larger one.

Endoskeletons

Animals ranging from sponges to mammals have a hardened internal skeleton, or **endoskeleton**, buried within their soft tissues. In sponges, the endoskeleton consists of hard needle-like structures of inorganic material (see Figure 33.4) or fibers made of protein. Echinoderms' bodies are reinforced by ossicles, hard plates composed of magnesium carbonate and calcium carbonate crystals. Whereas the ossicles of sea urchins

are tightly bound, the ossicles of sea stars are more loosely linked, allowing a sea star to change the shape of its arms.

Chordates have an endoskeleton consisting of cartilage, bone, or some combination of these materials (see Figure 40.5). The mammalian skeleton is built from more than 200 bones, some fused together and others connected at joints by ligaments that allow freedom of movement (**Figures 50.36** and **50.37**).

Size and Scale of Skeletons

An exoskeleton needs to cover and protect an animal's body, but how thick does an endoskeleton need to be? We can begin to answer this question by applying ideas from civil

▼ Figure 50.36 **Bones and joints of the human skeleton.**

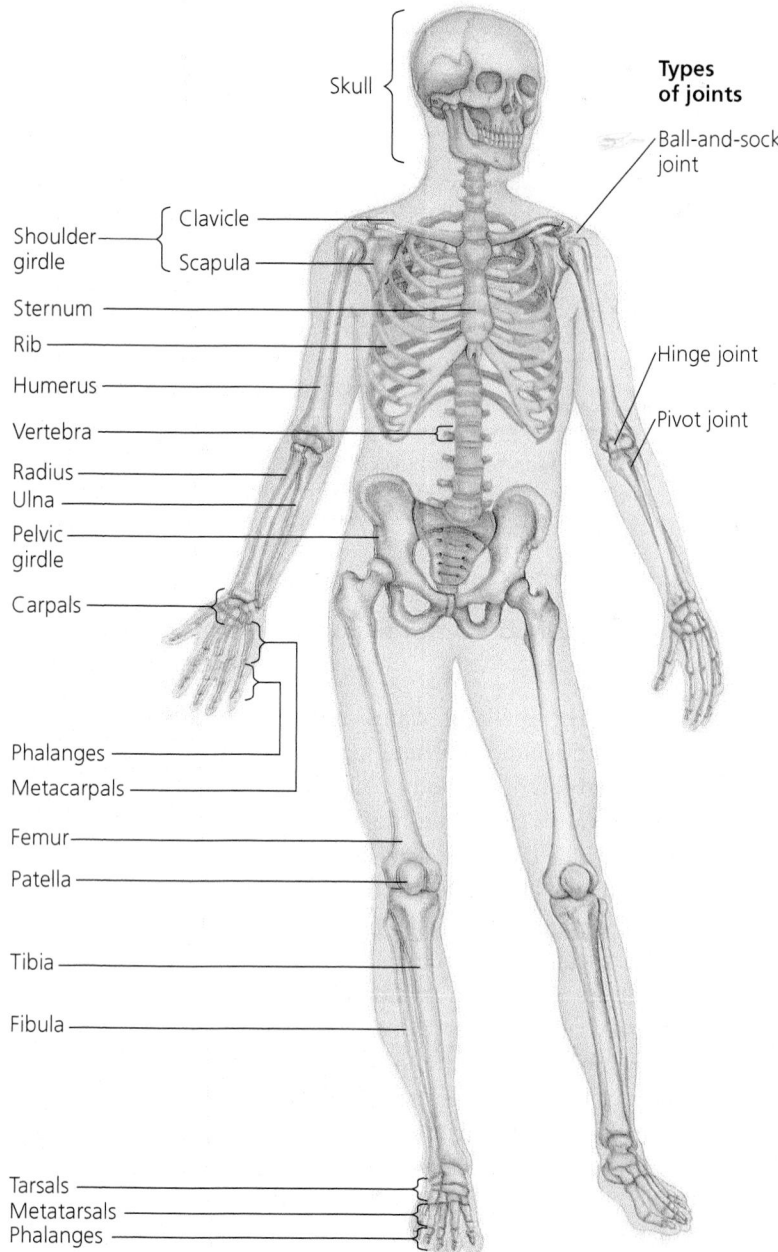

Skull
Shoulder girdle { Clavicle, Scapula }
Sternum
Rib
Humerus
Vertebra
Radius
Ulna
Pelvic girdle
Carpals
Phalanges
Metacarpals
Femur
Patella
Tibia
Fibula
Tarsals
Metatarsals
Phalanges

Types of joints
Ball-and-socket joint
Hinge joint
Pivot joint

▼ Figure 50.37 **Types of joints.**

Ball-and-socket joint

Head of humerus
Scapula

Ball-and-socket joints are found where the humerus contacts the shoulder girdle and where the femur contacts the pelvic girdle. These joints enable the arms and legs to rotate and move in several planes.

Hinge joint

Humerus
Ulna

Hinge joints, such as between the humerus and the head of the ulna, restrict movement to a single plane.

Pivot joint

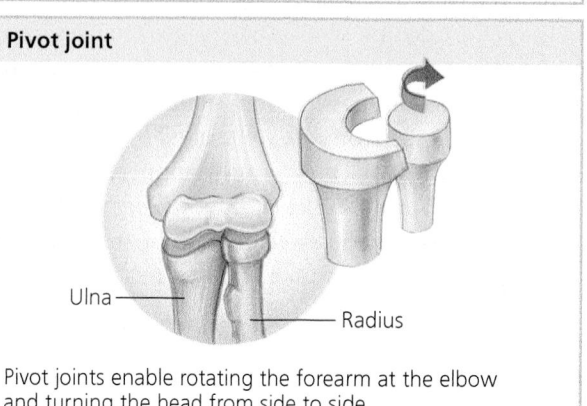

Ulna
Radius

Pivot joints enable rotating the forearm at the elbow and turning the head from side to side.

engineering. For example, the weight of a building increases with the cube of its dimensions. However, the strength of a building support depends on its cross-sectional area, which only increases with the square of its diameter. We can thus predict that if we scaled up a mouse to the size of an elephant, the legs of the giant mouse would be too thin to support its weight. Indeed, large animals do have very different body proportions from those of small animals.

In applying the building analogy, we might also predict that the size of leg bones should be directly proportional to the strain imposed by body weight. However, our prediction would be inaccurate, in part because animal bodies are complex and nonrigid. In supporting body weight, it turns out that body posture—the position of the legs relative to the main body—is more important than leg size, at least in mammals and birds. Muscles and tendons (connective tissue that joins muscle to bone) hold the legs of large mammals relatively straight and positioned under the body and actually bear most of the load.

Types of Locomotion

Movement is a hallmark of animals. Even animals fixed to a surface move their body parts: Sponges use beating flagella to generate water currents that draw and trap small food particles, and sessile cnidarians wave tentacles that capture prey (see Chapter 33). Most animals, however, are mobile and spend a considerable portion of their time and energy actively searching for food, escaping from danger, and seeking mates. These activities involve **locomotion**, or active travel from place to place.

Friction and gravity tend to keep an animal stationary and thus oppose locomotion. To move, an animal must expend energy to overcome these two forces. As we will see next, the amount of energy required to oppose friction or gravity is often reduced by an animal body plan adapted for movement in a particular environment.

Locomotion on Land

On land, a walking, running, hopping, or crawling animal must be able to support itself and move against gravity, but air poses relatively little resistance, at least at moderate speeds. When a land animal walks, runs, or hops, its leg muscles expend energy both to propel it and to keep it from falling down. With each step, the animal's leg muscles must overcome inertia by accelerating a leg from a standing start. For moving on land, powerful muscles and strong skeletal support are more important than a streamlined shape.

Diverse adaptations for traveling on land have evolved in various vertebrates. For example, kangaroos have large, powerful muscles in their hind legs, suitable for locomotion by hopping (**Figure 50.38**). As a kangaroo lands after each leap, tendons in its hind legs momentarily store energy. The farther the animal hops, the more energy its tendons store. Analogous to the energy in a compressed spring, the energy stored in the tendons is available for the next jump and

▲ **Figure 50.38 Energy-efficient locomotion on land.** Members of the kangaroo family travel from place to place mainly by leaping on their large hind legs. Kinetic energy momentarily stored in tendons after each leap provides a boost for the next leap. In fact, a large kangaroo hopping at 30 km/hr uses no more energy per minute than it does at 6 km/hr. The large tail helps balance the kangaroo when it leaps as well as when it sits.

reduces the total amount of energy the animal must expend to travel. The legs of an insect, dog, or human also retain some energy during walking or running, although a considerably smaller share than those of a kangaroo.

Maintaining balance is another prerequisite for walking, running, or hopping. A kangaroo's large tail helps balance its body during leaps and also forms a stable tripod with its hind legs when the animal sits or moves slowly. Illustrating the same principle, a walking cat, dog, or horse keeps three feet on the ground. Bipedal animals, such as humans and birds, keep part of at least one foot on the ground when walking. When an animal runs, all four feet (or both feet for bipeds) may be off the ground briefly, but at running speeds it is momentum more than foot contact that keeps the body upright.

Crawling poses a very different situation. Because much of its body is in contact with the ground, a crawling animal must exert considerable effort to overcome friction. You have read how earthworms crawl by peristalsis. Many snakes crawl by undulating their entire body from side to side. Assisted by large, movable scales on its underside, a snake's body pushes against the ground, propelling the animal forward. Boa constrictors and pythons creep straight forward, driven by muscles that lift belly scales off the ground, tilt the scales forward, and then push them backward against the ground.

Swimming

Because most animals are reasonably buoyant in water, overcoming gravity is less of a problem for swimming animals than for species that move on land or through the air. On the other hand, water is a much denser and more viscous medium than air, and thus drag (friction) is a major problem for aquatic animals. A sleek, fusiform (torpedo-like) shape is a common adaptation of fast swimmers (see Figure 40.2).

Although most animal phyla include species that swim, swimming occurs in diverse ways. For instance, many insects and four-legged vertebrates use their legs as oars to push against the water. Squids, scallops, and some cnidarians are jet-propelled, taking in water and squirting it out in bursts. Sharks and bony fishes swim by moving their body and tail from side to side, while whales and dolphins move by undulating their body and tail up and down.

Flying

Active flight (in contrast to gliding downward from a tree) has evolved in only a few animal groups: insects, reptiles (including birds), and, among the mammals, bats. One group of flying reptiles, the pterosaurs, died out millions of years ago, leaving birds and bats as the only flying vertebrates.

Gravity poses a major problem for a flying animal because its wings must develop enough lift to overcome gravity's downward force. The key to flight is wing shape. All wings are airfoils—structures whose shape alters air currents in a way that helps animals or airplanes stay aloft. As for the body to which the wings attach, a fusiform shape helps reduce drag in air as it does in water.

Flying animals are relatively light, with body masses ranging from less than a gram for some insects to about 20 kg for the largest flying birds. Many flying animals have structural adaptations that contribute to low body mass. Birds, for example, have no urinary bladder or teeth and have relatively large bones with air-filled regions that help lessen the bird's weight (see Chapter 34).

Energy Costs of Locomotion

During the 1960s, three scientists at Duke University became interested in the bioenergetics of locomotion. Physiologists typically determine an animal's rate of energy use during locomotion by measuring oxygen consumption or carbon dioxide production (see Chapter 40). To apply such a strategy to flight, Vance Tucker trained parakeets to fly in a wind tunnel while wearing a face mask (**Figure 50.39**). By connecting

▲ **Figure 50.39 Measuring energy usage during flight.**
The tube connected to the plastic face mask collects the gases this parakeet exhales during flight in a wind tunnel.

the mask to a tube that collected the air the bird exhaled as it flew, he could measure rates of gas exchange and calculate energy expenditure. In the meantime, Dick Taylor and Knut Schmidt-Nielsen measured energy consumption at rest and during locomotion for animals of widely varying body sizes. Schmidt-Nielsen then calculated an energy cost for locomotion: the amount of fuel it takes to transport a given amount of body weight over a set distance.

Schmidt-Nielsen's analysis demonstrated that the energy cost of locomotion depends on the mode of locomotion and the environment (**Figure 50.40**). Swimming is the most energy-efficient mode of locomotion (assuming that an animal has adaptations that facilitate swimming). Running animals generally expend more energy per meter traveled than equivalently sized swimming animals, partly because running and walking require energy to overcome gravity. If we compare

▼ **Figure 50.40** ┃ **INQUIRY**

What are the energy costs of locomotion?

EXPERIMENT Knut Schmidt-Nielsen wondered whether there were general principles governing the energy costs of different types of locomotion among diverse animal species. To answer this question, he drew on his own studies as well as the scientific literature for measurements made when animals swam in water flumes, ran on treadmills, or flew in wind tunnels. He converted all of these data to a common set of units and graphed the results.

RESULTS

This graph plots the energy cost, in calories per kilogram of body mass per meter traveled, against body mass for animals specialized for running, flying, and swimming. Note that both axes are plotted on logarithmic scales.

CONCLUSION For most animals of a given body mass, swimming is the most energy-efficient and running the least energy-efficient mode of locomotion. In addition, a small animal typically expends more energy per kilogram of body mass than a large animal, regardless of the type of locomotion used.

SOURCE K. Schmidt-Nielsen, Locomotion: Energy cost of swimming, flying, and running, *Science* 177:222–228 (1972).

WHAT IF? If you plotted the efficiency of a duck as a swimmer on this graph, where might you expect it to fall, and why?

the energy consumption per minute rather than per meter, we find that flying animals use more energy than swimming or running animals with the same body mass.

Figure 50.40 also reveals that a larger animal travels more efficiently than a smaller animal adapted to the same mode of transport. This relationship of size to energy expenditure during locomotion is apparent in the downward slope of each line on the graph. For example, a 450-kg horse expends less energy *per kilogram of body mass* than a 4-kg cat running the same distance. Of course, the total amount of energy expended in locomotion is greater for the larger animal.

Energy from food that is used for locomotion is unavailable for other activities, such as growth and reproduction. Thus, structural and behavioral adaptations that maximize the efficiency of locomotion increase an organism's evolutionary fitness.

Although we have discussed sensory receptors and muscles separately in this chapter, they are part of a single integrated system linking brain, body, and the external world. An animal's behavior is the product of this system. In Chapter 51, we'll discuss behavior in the context of animal form and function and also link it to ecology, the study of how organisms interact with their environment.

CONCEPT CHECK 50.6

1. In what way are septa an important feature of the earthworm skeleton?
2. Contrast swimming and flying in terms of the main problems they pose and the adaptations that allow animals to overcome those problems.
3. **WHAT IF?** When using your arms to lower yourself into a chair, you bend your arms without using your biceps. Explain how this is possible. (*Hint:* Think about gravity as an antagonistic force.)

For suggested answers, see Appendix A.

50 CHAPTER REVIEW

SUMMARY OF KEY CONCEPTS

CONCEPT 50.1

Sensory receptors transduce stimulus energy and transmit signals to the central nervous system (pp. 1085–1090)

- **Sensory receptors** are usually specialized neurons or epithelial cells that detect external or internal stimuli. The detection of a stimulus by sensory cells precedes **sensory transduction**, the change in the membrane potential of a sensory receptor in response to a stimulus. The resulting receptor potential controls **transmission** of action potentials to the CNS, where sensory information is integrated to generate perceptions. The frequency of action potentials in an axon and the number of axons activated determine stimulus strength. The identity of the axon carrying the signal encodes the nature or quality of the stimulus. Signal transduction pathways in receptor cells often amplify the signal, which causes the receptor cell either to produce action potentials or to release neurotransmitter at a synapse with a sensory neuron.
- There are five basic types of sensory receptors. **Mechanoreceptors** respond to stimuli such as pressure, touch, stretch, motion, and sound. **Chemoreceptors** detect either total solute concentrations or specific molecules. **Electromagnetic receptors** detect different forms of electromagnetic radiation. Various types of **thermoreceptors** signal surface and core temperatures of the body. Pain is detected by a group of **nociceptors** that respond to excess heat, pressure, or specific classes of chemicals.

? *To simplify the classification of sensory receptors, why might it make sense to eliminate nociceptors as a distinct class?*

CONCEPT 50.2

The mechanoreceptors responsible for hearing and equilibrium detect moving fluid or settling particles (pp. 1090–1094)

- Most invertebrates sense their orientation with respect to gravity by means of **statocysts**. Specialized **hair cells** form the basis for hearing and balance in mammals and for detection of water movement in fishes and aquatic amphibians. In mammals, the **tympanic membrane** (eardrum) transmits sound waves to three small bones of the middle ear, which transmit the waves through the oval window to the fluid in the coiled **cochlea** of the inner ear. Pressure waves in the fluid vibrate the **basilar membrane**, depolarizing hair cells and triggering action potentials that travel via the auditory nerve to the brain. Each region of the basilar membrane vibrates most vigorously at a particular frequency and leads to excitation of a specific auditory area of the cerebral cortex. Receptors in the inner ear function in balance and equilibrium.

? *What quality of sound determines the direction of displacement of a particular hair cell in the ear, and how is that quality encoded in signals sent to the brain?*

CONCEPT 50.3

Visual receptors in diverse animals depend on light-absorbing pigments (pp. 1095–1101)

- Invertebrates have varied light detectors, including simple light-sensitive eyespots, image-forming compound eyes, and single-lens eyes. In the vertebrate eye, a single lens is used to focus light on **photoreceptors** in the **retina**. Both **rods** and **cones** contain a pigment, **retinal**, bonded to a protein (opsin).

Absorption of light by retinal triggers a signal transduction pathway that hyperpolarizes the photoreceptors, causing them to release less neurotransmitter. Synapses transmit information from photoreceptors to cells that integrate information and convey it to the brain along axons that form the optic nerve.

> ? *How does processing of sensory information sent to the vertebrate brain in vision differ from that in hearing or olfaction?*

CONCEPT 50.4

The senses of taste and smell rely on similar sets of sensory receptors (pp. 1101–1103)

- Both taste (**gustation**) and smell (**olfaction**) depend on the stimulation of chemoreceptors by small dissolved molecules that bind to proteins on the plasma membrane. In humans, sensory cells within taste buds express a single receptor type specific for one of the five taste perceptions—sweet, sour, salty, bitter, and umami (elicited by glutamate). Olfactory receptor cells line the upper part of the nasal cavity and extend axons to the olfactory bulb of the brain. More than 1,000 genes code for membrane proteins that bind to specific classes of odorants, and each receptor cell appears to express only one of those genes.

> ? *Why do foods taste bland when you have a head cold?*

CONCEPT 50.5

The physical interaction of protein filaments is required for muscle function (pp. 1103–1110)

- The muscle cells (fibers) of vertebrate skeletal muscle contain myofibrils composed of **thin filaments** of (mostly) actin and **thick filaments** of myosin. Together with accessory proteins, these filaments are organized into repeating units called **sarcomeres**. Myosin heads, energized by the hydrolysis of ATP, bind to the thin filaments, forming cross-bridges, then release upon binding ATP anew. As this cycle repeats, the thick and thin filaments slide past each other, shortening the sarcomere and contracting the muscle fiber.

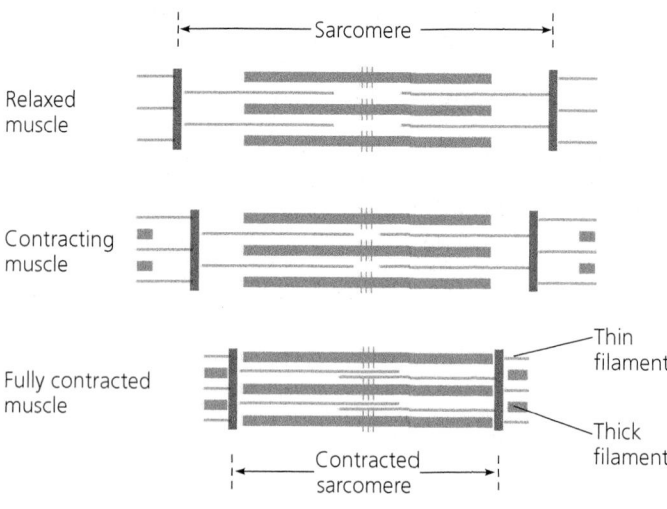

- Motor neurons release acetylcholine, triggering action potentials that penetrate the muscle fiber along the T tubules and stimulate the release of Ca^{2+} from the **sarcoplasmic reticulum**. When the Ca^{2+} binds the **troponin complex**, **tropomyosin** repositions on the thin filaments, exposing the myosin-binding sites on actin and thus initiating cross-bridge formation. A **motor unit** consists of a motor neuron and the muscle fibers it controls. Recruiting multiple motor units results in stronger contractions. A twitch results from a single action potential in a motor neuron. Skeletal muscle fibers can be slow-twitch or fast-twitch and oxidative or glycolytic.

- Cardiac muscle, found only in the heart, consists of striated cells that are electrically connected by intercalated disks and that can generate action potentials without input from neurons. In smooth muscles, contractions are slow and may be initiated by the muscles themselves or by stimulation from neurons in the autonomic nervous system.

> ? *What are two major functions of ATP hydrolysis in skeletal muscle activity?*

CONCEPT 50.6

Skeletal systems transform muscle contraction into locomotion (pp. 1110–1115)

- Skeletal muscles, often in antagonistic pairs, bring about movement by contracting and pulling against the skeleton. Skeletons may be **hydrostatic** and maintained by fluid pressure, as in worms; hardened into **exoskeletons**, as in insects; or in the form of **endoskeletons**, as in vertebrates.

- Each form of **locomotion**—swimming, movement on land, or flying—presents a particular challenge. For example, swimmers need to overcome friction, but face less of a challenge from gravity than do animals that move on land or fly. Animals specialized for swimming expend less energy per distance traveled than similarly sized animals specialized for flying or running. For any of the three major modes of locomotion, larger animals are more efficient than smaller ones.

> ? *Explain how microscopic and macroscopic anchoring of muscle filaments enables you to bend your elbow.*

TEST YOUR UNDERSTANDING

LEVEL 1: KNOWLEDGE/COMPREHENSION

1. Which of the following sensory receptors is *incorrectly* paired with its category?
   a. hair cell—mechanoreceptor
   b. muscle spindle—mechanoreceptor
   c. taste receptor—chemoreceptor
   d. rod—electromagnetic receptor
   e. olfactory receptor—electromagnetic receptor

2. The middle ear converts
   a. air pressure waves to fluid pressure waves.
   b. fluid pressure waves to air pressure waves.
   c. air pressure waves to nerve impulses.
   d. fluid pressure waves to nerve impulses.
   e. pressure waves to hair cell movements.

3. During the contraction of a vertebrate skeletal muscle fiber, calcium ions
   a. break cross-bridges by acting as a cofactor in the hydrolysis of ATP.
   b. bind with troponin, changing its shape so that the myosin-binding sites on actin are exposed.
   c. transmit action potentials from the motor neuron to the muscle fiber.
   d. spread action potentials through the T tubules.
   e. re-establish the polarization of the plasma membrane following an action potential.

LEVEL 2: APPLICATION/ANALYSIS

4. Which sensory distinction is *not* encoded by a difference in neuron identity?
- a. white and red
- b. red and green
- c. loud and faint
- d. salty and sweet
- e. spicy and cool

5. The transduction of sound waves into action potentials takes place
- a. within the tectorial membrane as it is stimulated by the hair cells.
- b. when hair cells are bent against the tectorial membrane, causing them to depolarize and release neurotransmitter that stimulates sensory neurons.
- c. as the basilar membrane becomes more permeable to sodium ions and depolarizes, initiating an action potential in a sensory neuron.
- d. as the basilar membrane vibrates at different frequencies in response to the varying volume of sounds.
- e. within the middle ear as the vibrations are amplified by the malleus, incus, and stapes.

LEVEL 3: SYNTHESIS/EVALUATION

6. Although some sharks close their eyes just before they bite, their bites are on target. Researchers have noted that sharks often misdirect their bites at metal objects and that they can find batteries buried under sand. This evidence suggests that sharks keep track of their prey during the split second before they bite in the same way that
- a. a rattlesnake finds a mouse in its burrow.
- b. a male silkworm moth locates a mate.
- c. a bat finds moths in the dark.
- d. a platypus locates its prey in a muddy river.
- e. a flatworm avoids light places.

7. **DRAW IT** Based on the information in the text, fill in the following graph. Use one line for rods and another line for cones.

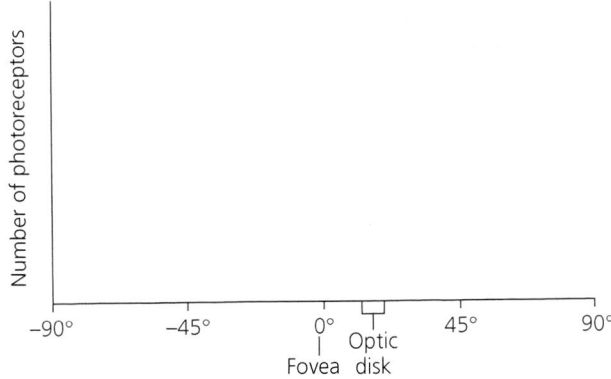

Position along retina (in degrees away from fovea)

8. EVOLUTION CONNECTION

In general, locomotion on land requires more energy than locomotion in water. By integrating what you have learned about animal form and function in Unit 7, discuss some of the evolutionary adaptations of mammals that support the high energy requirements for moving on land.

9. SCIENTIFIC INQUIRY

Although skeletal muscles generally fatigue fairly rapidly, clam shell muscles have a protein called paramyosin that allows them to sustain contraction for up to a month. From your knowledge of the cellular mechanism of contraction, propose a hypothesis to explain how paramyosin might work. How would you test your hypothesis experimentally?

10. **WRITE ABOUT A THEME**

Structure and Function In a short essay (100–150 words), describe at least three ways in which the structure of the lens of the human eye is well adapted to its function in vision.

For selected answers, see Appendix A.

MasteringBIOLOGY® www.masteringbiology.com

1. MasteringBiology® Assignments

BioFlix **Tutorial** Muscle Contraction: Muscle Cells and Action Potentials • The Sarcomere and the Sliding-Filament Model
Activities The Vertebrate Eye • Structure and Function of the Eye • Structure and Contraction of Muscle Fibers • Skeletal Muscle Structure • Muscle Contraction • Discovery Channel Video: Muscles and Bones • Human Skeleton
Questions Student Misconceptions • Reading Quiz • Multiple Choice • End-of-Chapter

2. eText
Read your book online, search, take notes, highlight text, and more.

3. The Study Area
Practice Tests • Cumulative Test • *BioFlix* 3-D Animations • MP3 Tutor Sessions • Videos • Activities • Investigations • Lab Media • Audio Glossary • Word Study Tools • Art

51

Animal Behavior

▲ Figure 51.1 **What prompts a fiddler crab to wave its giant claw?**

KEY CONCEPTS

51.1 Discrete sensory inputs can stimulate both simple and complex behaviors

51.2 Learning establishes specific links between experience and behavior

51.3 Selection for individual survival and reproductive success can explain most behaviors

51.4 Inclusive fitness can account for the evolution of behavior, including altruism

OVERVIEW

The How and Why of Animal Activity

Unlike most animals, male fiddler crabs (genus *Uca*) are highly asymmetrical: One claw grows to giant proportions, half the mass of the entire body (**Figure 51.1**). The name *fiddler* comes from the crab's appearance as it feeds on algae from the mudflats where it lives: The smaller front claw moves to and from the mouth in front of the enlarged claw.

Sometimes, however, the male waves his large claw in the air. What triggers this behavior? What purpose does it serve?

Claw waving by a male fiddler crab has two functions. Waving the claw, which can be used as a weapon, helps the crab *repel* other males wandering too close to his burrow. Vigorous claw waving also helps him *attract* females, who wander through the crab colony in search of a mate. After the male fiddler crab lures a female to his burrow, he seals her in with mud or sand in preparation for mating.

Animal behavior, be it solitary or social, fixed or variable, is based on physiological systems and processes. An individual **behavior** is an action carried out by muscles under control of the nervous system in response to a stimulus. Examples include an animal using its chest and throat muscles to produce a song, releasing a scent to mark its territory, or simply waving a claw. Behavior is an essential part of acquiring nutrients for digestion and finding a partner for sexual reproduction. Behavior also contributes to homeostasis, as in honeybees huddling to conserve heat (see Chapter 40). In short, all of animal physiology contributes to behavior, and animal behavior influences all of physiology.

Being essential for survival and reproduction, behavior is subject to substantial natural selection over time. This evolutionary process of selection also affects anatomy because the recognition and communication that underlie many behaviors depend on body form and appearance. Thus, the enlarged claw of the male fiddler crab is an adaptation that enables the display essential for recognition by other members of the species. Similarly, the positioning of the eyes on stalks held well above the crab's head enables him to see intruders from far off.

In this chapter, we'll examine how behavior is controlled, how it develops during an animal's life, and how it is influenced by genes and the environment. We'll also explore the ways in which behavior evolves over many generations. In moving from our study of an animal's inner workings to its interactions with the outside world, we will also provide a transition to ecology, the focus of Unit Eight.

CONCEPT 51.1

Discrete sensory inputs can stimulate both simple and complex behaviors

What approach do biologists use to determine how behaviors arise and what functions they serve? The Dutch scientist Niko Tinbergen, a pioneer in the study of animal behavior, suggested that understanding any behavior requires answering four questions, which can be summarized as follows:

1. What stimulus elicits the behavior, and what physiological mechanisms mediate the response?
2. How does the animal's experience during growth and development influence the response?

3. How does the behavior aid survival and reproduction?

4. What is the behavior's evolutionary history?

Tinbergen's first two questions ask about *proximate causation*: "how" a behavior occurs or is modified. The last two questions ask about *ultimate causation*: "why" a behavior occurs in the context of natural selection.

Today, Tinbergen's questions and the associated ideas of causation underlie **behavioral ecology**, the study of the ecological and evolutionary basis for animal behavior. As we explore this vibrant area of modern biological research, we will also review studies by Tinbergen and two other early researchers—Karl von Frisch and Konrad Lorenz—that earned the three scientists a Nobel Prize in 1973.

In addressing Tinbergen's first question, the nature of the stimuli that trigger behavior, we'll begin with behavioral responses to well-defined stimuli, starting with an example from Tinbergen's own experiments.

Fixed Action Patterns

As part of his research, Tinbergen kept fish tanks containing three-spined sticklebacks (*Gasterosteus aculeatus*). Male sticklebacks, which have red bellies, attack other males that invade their nesting territories. Tinbergen noticed that his male sticklebacks also behaved aggressively when a red truck passed in front of their tank. Inspired by this chance observation, he carried out experiments showing that the red color of an intruder's underside is what provokes the attack behavior. A male stickleback will not attack a fish lacking red coloration (note that female sticklebacks never have red bellies), but will attack even unrealistic models if they contain areas of red color **(Figure 51.2)**.

The territorial response of male sticklebacks is an example of a **fixed action pattern**, a sequence of unlearned acts directly linked to a simple stimulus. Fixed action patterns are essentially unchangeable and, once initiated, usually carried to completion. The trigger for the behavior is an external cue called a **sign stimulus**, such as a red object prompting the male stickleback's aggressive behavior.

Migration

Environmental stimuli not only trigger behaviors but also provide cues that animals use to carry out those behaviors. For example, a wide variety of birds, fishes, and other animals use environmental cues to guide **migration**—a regular, long-distance change in location **(Figure 51.3)**.

Many migrating animals pass through environments they have not previously encountered. How, then, do they find their way in these foreign settings?

Some migrating animals track their position relative to the sun, even though the sun's position relative to Earth changes throughout the day. Animals can adjust for these changes by means of a *circadian clock*, an internal mechanism that maintains a 24-hour activity rhythm or cycle (see Chapter 49). For

(a) A male stickleback fish attacks other male sticklebacks that invade its nesting territory. The red belly of the intruding male (left) acts as the sign stimulus that releases the aggressive behavior.

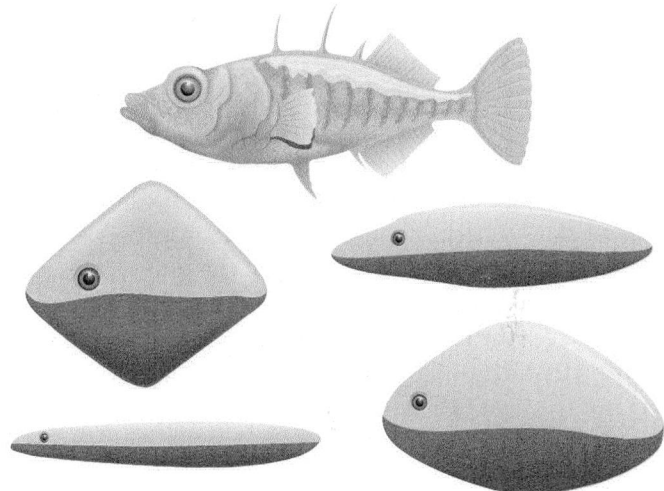

(b) The realistic model at the top, without a red underside, produces no aggressive response in a male three-spined stickleback. The other models, with red undersides, produce strong responses.

▲ **Figure 51.2 Sign stimuli in a classic fixed action pattern.**

? *Suggest an explanation for why this behavior evolved (its ultimate causation).*

▲ **Figure 51.3 Migration.** Each spring, snow geese (*Chen caerulescens*) migrate from their wintering grounds, which may be as far south as Mexico, to their breeding grounds in Greenland, Canada, and Alaska. In the autumn, they return to their wintering grounds.

example, experiments have shown that migrating birds orient differently relative to the sun at distinct times of the day. Nocturnal animals can instead use the North Star, which has a constant position in the night sky.

Although the sun and stars can provide useful clues for navigation, these landmarks can be obscured by clouds. How do migrating animals overcome this problem? A simple experiment with homing pigeons provides one answer. On an overcast day, placing a small magnet on the head of a homing pigeon prevents it from returning efficiently to its roost. Researchers concluded that pigeons can sense their position relative to Earth's magnetic field and thereby navigate without solar or celestial cues.

The way in which animals detect Earth's magnetic field remains a matter of debate. It is known that the heads of migrating fishes and birds contain bits of magnetite, a magnetic iron mineral. This fact leads some scientists to hypothesize that Earth's pull on magnetite-containing structures triggers transmission of nerve impulses to the brain. Others propose that migrating animals are guided by the effects of Earth's magnetic field on photoreceptors in the eye. The idea that animals "see" the magnetic field is supported by experiments showing that light of particular wavelengths must be present for birds to orient in a magnetic field during the day or night.

Behavioral Rhythms

Although the circadian clock plays a small but significant role in navigation by some migrating species, it has a major role in the daily activity of all animals. As discussed in Chapters 40 and 49, the output of the clock is a circadian rhythm, a daily cycle of rest and activity with far-reaching effects on behavioral physiology. The clock is normally synchronized with the light and dark cycles of the environment but can maintain rhythmic activity under constant environmental conditions, such as during hibernation.

Some behaviors, such as migration and reproduction, reflect biological rhythms with a longer cycle, or period, than the circadian rhythm. Behavioral rhythms linked to the yearly cycle of seasons are called *circannual rhythms*. Although migration and reproduction typically correlate with food availability, these behaviors are not a direct response to changes in food intake. Instead, circannual rhythms, like circadian rhythms, are influenced by the periods of daylight and darkness in the environment. For example, studies with several bird species have shown that an artificial environment with extended daylight can induce out-of-season migratory behavior.

Not all biological rhythms are linked to the light and dark cycles in the environment. Consider, for instance, the fiddler crab shown in Figure 51.1. The male's claw-waving courtship behavior is linked not to day length but to the timing of the new and full moon. Why? Fiddler crabs begin their lives as plankton, settling in the mudflats after several larval stages. By courting at the time of the new or full moon, crabs link their reproduction to the times of greatest tidal movement. The tides disperse larvae to deeper waters, where they complete early development in relative safety before returning to the tidal flats.

Animal Signals and Communication

Claw waving by fiddler crabs during courtship is an example of one animal (the male crab) generating the stimulus that guides the behavior of another animal (the female crab). A stimulus transmitted from one animal to another is called a **signal**. The transmission and reception of signals constitute animal **communication**, an essential element of interactions between individuals.

Forms of Animal Communication

Let's consider the courtship behavior of *Drosophila melanogaster*, the fruit fly **(Figure 51.4)**, as an introduction to the four

Male visually recognizes female.

Female releases chemicals detected by the male's sense of smell.

(a) Orienting

Male taps female's abdomen with a foreleg.

(b) Tapping

Male extends and vibrates wing, producing a courtship song.

(c) "Singing"

▲ **Figure 51.4 Courtship behavior of the fruit fly.** Fruit fly courtship involves a fixed set of behaviors that follow one another in a fixed order.

common modes of animal communication: visual, chemical, tactile, and auditory.

Fruit fly courtship constitutes a *stimulus-response chain*, in which the response to each stimulus is itself the stimulus for the next behavior. In the first step, a male identifies a female of the same species and then orients his body toward hers. When the male sees and turns toward the female, he relies on *visual communication*. In addition, the male's sense of smell, or olfactory system, detects chemicals released into the air by the female. This is an example of *chemical communication*, the transmission and reception of signals in the form of specific molecules. Having recognized the female, the male approaches and taps the female with a foreleg. This touching, or *tactile communication*, alerts the female to the male's presence. In the process, chemicals on her abdomen are transferred to the male, providing further chemical confirmation of her species identity. In the third stage of courtship, the male extends and vibrates his wing, producing a specific courtship song. This singing, an example of *auditory communication*, informs the female that the male is of the same species. Only if all of these forms of communication are successful will a female allow the male to attempt copulation.

The information content of animal communication varies considerably. One of the most remarkable examples is the symbolic language of the European honeybee (*Apis mellifera*), discovered in the early 1900s by Austrian researcher Karl von Frisch. Using glass-walled observation hives, he and his students spent several decades observing these bees. Methodical recordings of bee movements enabled von Frisch to decipher a "dance language" that returning foragers use to inform other bees about the distance and direction of travel to food sources.

As illustrated in **Figure 51.5**, a returning bee quickly becomes the center of attention for other bees, called followers. If the food source is close to the hive (less than 50 m away), the returning bee moves in tight circles while waggling its abdomen from side to side. This behavior, called the "round dance," motivates the follower bees to leave the hive and search for nearby food.

When the food source is farther from the nest, the returning bee instead performs a "waggle dance." This dance, consisting of a half-circle swing in one direction, a straight run during which the bee waggles its abdomen, and a half-circle swing in the other direction, communicates to the follower bees both the direction and distance of the food source in relation to the hive. The angle of the straight run relative to the hive's vertical surface is the same as the horizontal angle of the food in relation to the sun. For example, if the returning bee runs at a 30° angle to the right of vertical, the follower bees leaving the hive fly 30° to the right of the horizontal direction of the sun. A dance with a longer straight run, and

(a) Worker bees cluster around a bee that recently returned from a foraging trip.

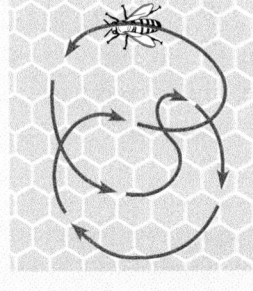

(b) The round dance indicates that food is near.

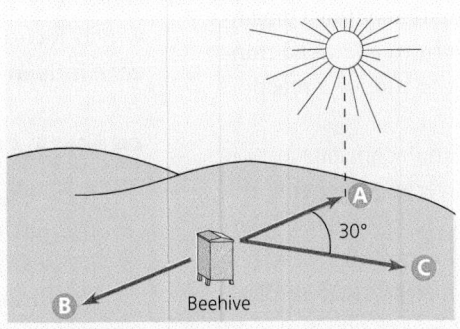

(c) The waggle dance, performed when food is distant, resembles a figure eight (below). Distance is indicated by the number of abdominal waggles performed in the straight-run part of the dance. Direction is indicated by the angle (in relation to the vertical surface of the hive) of the straight run.

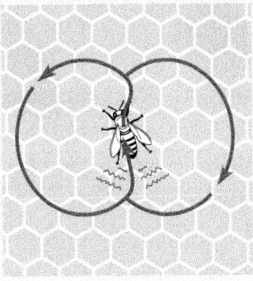

Location **A**: Food source is in same direction as sun.

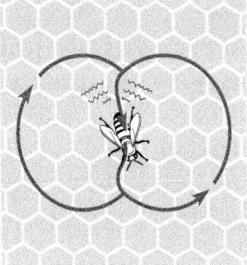

Location **B**: Food source is in direction opposite sun.

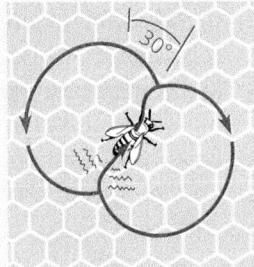

Location **C**: Food source is 30° to right of sun.

▲ **Figure 51.5 Honeybee dance language.** Honeybees returning to the hive communicate the location of food sources through the symbolic language of a dance.

therefore more abdominal waggles per run, indicates a greater distance to the food source. As follower bees exit the hive, they fly almost directly to the area indicated by the waggle dance. By using flower odor and other clues, they locate the food source within this area.

Pheromones

Animals that communicate through odors or tastes emit chemical substances called **pheromones**. Pheromones are especially common among mammals and insects and often relate to reproductive behavior. For example, pheromones are the basis for the chemical communication in fruit fly courtship (see Figure 51.4). Pheromones are not limited to short-distance signaling, however. Male silkworm moths have receptors that can detect the pheromone from a female moth from several kilometers away (see Figure 50.6). After the moths are together, pheromones also trigger specific courtship behaviors.

In a honeybee colony, pheromones produced by the queen and her daughters, the workers, maintain the hive's complex social order. One pheromone (once called the queen substance) has a particularly wide range of effects. It attracts workers to the queen, inhibits development of ovaries in workers, and attracts males (drones) to the queen during her mating flights out of the hive.

Pheromones can also serve as alarm signals. For example, when a minnow or catfish is injured, a substance released from the fish's skin disperses in the water, inducing a fright response in other fish. These nearby fish become more vigilant and often form tightly packed schools near the river or lake bottom, where they are safer from attack **(Figure 51.6)**. Pheromones can be very effective at remarkably low concentrations. For instance, just 1 cm² of skin from a fathead minnow contains sufficient alarm substance to induce a reaction in 58,000 L of water.

As we have seen, the forms of animal communication used to convey information are quite diverse. In general, the form of communication that evolves is closely related to an animal's lifestyle and environment. For example, most terrestrial mammals are nocturnal, which makes visual displays relatively ineffective. Instead, these species use olfactory and auditory signals, which work as well in the dark as in the light. In contrast, most birds are diurnal (active mainly in daytime) and communicate primarily by visual and auditory signals. Humans are also diurnal and, like birds, use primarily visual and auditory communication. We can thus detect and appreciate the songs and bright colors used by birds to communicate but miss many chemical cues on which other mammals base their behavior.

So far in this chapter, we have explored the types of stimuli that elicit behaviors—the first part of Tinbergen's first question. The second part of that question—the physiological mechanisms that mediate responses—was the focus of

(a) Minnows are widely dispersed in an aquarium before an alarm substance is introduced.

(b) Within seconds of the alarm substance being introduced, minnows aggregate near the bottom of the aquarium and reduce their movement.

▲ Figure 51.6 **Minnows responding to the presence of an alarm substance.**

Chapters 49 and 50. Stimuli activate sensory systems, are processed in the central nervous system, and result in motor outputs that constitute behavior. You may want to review those two chapters before proceeding to the next concept, which focuses on Tinbergen's second question—how experience influences behavior.

CONCEPT CHECK 51.1

1. If an egg rolls out of the nest, a mother graylag goose will retrieve it by nudging it with her beak and head. If researchers remove the egg or substitute a ball during this process, the goose continues to bob her beak and head while she moves back to the nest. Explain how and why this behavior occurs.
2. **MAKE CONNECTIONS** How is the seasonal timing of plant flowering similar in mechanism and function to the lunar-linked rhythm of fiddler crab courtship? (See pp. 839–841 of Concept 39.3.)
3. **WHAT IF?** Suppose you exposed various fish species to the alarm substance from minnows. Based on what you know about natural selection, suggest why some species might respond like minnows, some might increase activity, and some might show no change.

For suggested answers, see Appendix A.

Learning establishes specific links between experience and behavior

For many behaviors—such as a fixed action pattern, a courtship stimulus-response chain, and pheromone signaling—nearly all individuals in a population exhibit virtually the same behavior, despite internal and environmental differences during development and throughout life. Behavior that is developmentally fixed in this way is known as **innate behavior**. In other cases, behavior is variable, depending on experience.

Experience and Behavior

Tinbergen's second question asks how an animal's experiences during growth and development influence the response to stimuli. How do researchers answer this question? One informative approach is a **cross-fostering study**, in which the young of one species are placed in the care of adults from another species. The extent to which the offspring's behavior changes in such a situation provides one measure of how the social and physical environment influences behavior.

The males of certain mouse species have behavioral differences that are well suited for cross-fostering experiments. Males of the species *Peromyscus californicus*, commonly called California mice, are highly aggressive toward other mice and provide extensive parental care. In contrast, male white-footed mice (*Peromyscus leucopus*) are less aggressive and engage in little parental care. When the pups of each species were placed in the nests of the other species, the cross-fostering altered some behaviors of both species (Table 51.1). For instance, male California mice raised by white-footed mice were less aggressive toward intruders. Thus, experience during development can strongly influence aggressive behavior in these rodents.

Table 51.1 Influence of Cross-Fostering on Male Mice*

Species	Aggression Toward an Intruder	Aggression in Neutral Situation	Paternal Behavior
California mice fostered by white-footed mice	Reduced	No difference	Reduced
White-footed mice fostered by California mice	No difference	Increased	No difference

*Comparisons are with mice raised by parents of their own species.

One of the most important findings of the cross-fostering experiments with mice was that the influence of experience on behavior can be passed on to progeny: When the cross-fostered California mice became parents, they spent less time retrieving offspring who wandered off than did California mice raised by their own species. Thus, experience during development can modify physiology in a way that alters parental behavior, extending the influence of environment to a subsequent generation.

For humans, the influence of genetics and environment on behavior can be explored by a **twin study**, in which researchers compare the behavior of identical twins raised apart with the behavior of those raised in the same household. Twin studies have been instrumental in studying human behavioral disorders, such as schizophrenia, anxiety disorders, and alcoholism. As discussed in Chapter 49, these investigations have revealed that both genetics and environment (nature *and* nurture) contribute significantly to the behaviors that characterize these disorders in humans.

Learning

One of the most powerful ways that environmental conditions can influence behavior is through **learning**, the modification of behavior based on specific experiences. We will now consider a number of different types of learning, beginning with a form of learning first explored by Austrian biologist Konrad Lorenz.

Imprinting

A type of behavior that includes both learned and innate components is **imprinting**, the formation at a specific stage in life of a long-lasting behavioral response to a particular individual or object. Imprinting is distinguished from other types of learning by having a **sensitive period**, also called a critical period, a limited developmental phase when this type of learning can occur. During the sensitive period, the young imprint on their parent and learn the basic behaviors of their species, while the parent learns to recognize its offspring. Among gulls, for instance, the sensitive period for a parent to bond with its young lasts one to two days. If bonding does not occur, the parent will not care for the infant, leading to death for the offspring and a decrease in reproductive success for the parent.

But how do the young know on whom—or what—to imprint? For example, how do young birds know that they should follow their mother? The tendency to respond is innate in the birds; the outside world provides the *imprinting stimulus*, something to which the response will be directed. Experiments with many species of waterfowl indicate that they have no innate recognition of "mother." Rather, they identify with the first object they encounter that has certain key characteristics. In classic experiments done in the 1930s, Lorenz showed that the principal imprinting stimulus in graylag geese (*Anser anser*) is a nearby object that is moving away from the young. When incubator-hatched goslings spent their first few hours with Lorenz rather than with a goose, they imprinted on him and steadfastly followed him from then on **(Figure 51.7a)**. Furthermore, they showed no

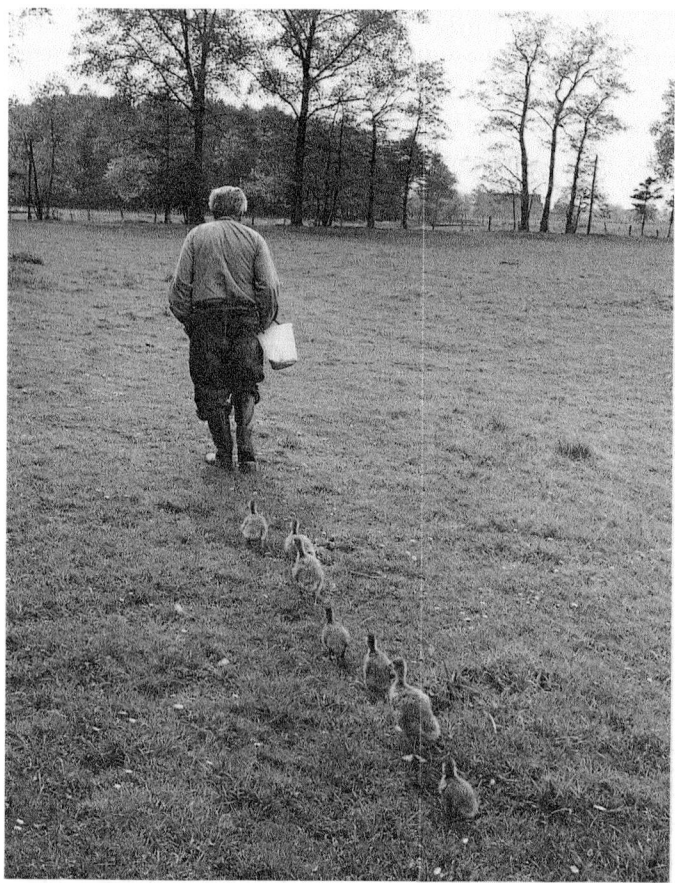

(a) These young greylag geese imprinted on ethologist Konrad Lorenz.

(b) A pilot wearing a crane suit and flying an ultralight plane acts as a surrogate parent to direct the migration of whooping cranes.

▲ **Figure 51.7 Imprinting.** Imprinting can be altered to **(a)** investigate animal behavior or **(b)** direct animal behavior.

WHAT IF? *Suppose the geese following Lorenz were bred to each other. How might their imprinting on Lorenz affect their offspring? Explain.*

recognition of their biological mother or other adults of their own species.

Imprinting has become an important component of efforts to save endangered species, such as the whooping crane (*Grus americana*). Scientists tried raising whooping cranes in captivity by using sandhill cranes (*Grus canadensis*) as foster parents. However, because the whooping cranes imprinted on their foster parents, none formed a *pair-bond* (strong attachment) with a whooping crane mate. To avoid such problems, captive breeding programs now isolate young cranes, exposing them to the sights and sounds of members of their own species.

Scientists have made further use of imprinting to teach cranes born in captivity to migrate along safe routes. Young whooping cranes are imprinted on humans in "crane suits" and then allowed to follow these "parents" as they fly ultralight aircraft along selected migration routes **(Figure 51.7b)**. Importantly, these cranes still form mating pair-bonds with other whooping cranes, indicating that the crane costumes have the features required to direct "normal" imprinting.

Spatial Learning and Cognitive Maps

Every natural environment has spatial variation, as in locations of nest sites, hazards, food, and prospective mates. Therefore, an organism's fitness may be enhanced by the capacity for **spatial learning**, the establishment of a memory that reflects the environment's spatial structure.

The idea of spatial learning intrigued Tinbergen while he was a graduate student in the Netherlands. At that time, he was studying the female digger wasp (*Philanthus triangulum*), which nests in small burrows dug into sand dunes. Tinbergen noticed that when a wasp left her nest to go hunting, she hid the entrance from potential intruders by covering it with sand. Upon her return, she flew directly to her hidden nest, despite the presence of hundreds of other burrows in the area. Tinbergen hypothesized that a wasp locates her nest by learning its position relative to visible landmarks, or location indicators. To test this hypothesis, he carried out an experiment in the wasps' natural habitat **(Figure 51.8)**. By manipulating objects around nest entrances, he demonstrated that digger wasps engage in spatial learning. This experiment was so simple and informative that it could be summarized very concisely. In fact, at 32 pages, Tinbergen's Ph.D. thesis from 1932 is still the shortest ever approved at Leiden University.

In many animal species, spatial learning can be quite sophisticated. Some animals guide their activity by a **cognitive map**, a representation in the nervous system of the spatial relationships between objects in an animal's surroundings. Rather than relying solely on moving from landmark to landmark, animals using cognitive maps can navigate more flexibly and efficiently by relating landmark positions to one another.

One striking example of cognitive mapping is found in the Clark's nutcracker (*Nucifraga columbiana*). Nutcrackers are corvids, the bird family that also includes ravens, crows, and jays. In the fall, a single nutcracker stores as many as 30,000 pine seeds in thousands of hiding places called caches, distributed over an area as large as 35 km². During the winter, the birds relocate many of their caches. By experimentally varying the distance between landmarks, researchers demonstrated that birds could identify the halfway point between landmarks. This behavior suggests that nutcrackers employ an abstract geometric rule, which we can approximate as "Seed caches are found halfway between particular landmarks." Such rules, a fundamental property of cognitive maps, reduce the amount of detail required to remember an object's location. As we discussed in Chapter 49, corvids also display other forms of higher nervous system function.

Associative Learning

Learning often involves making associations between experiences. Consider, for example, a blue jay (*Cyanocitta cristata*) that ingests a brightly colored monarch butterfly (*Danaus plexippus*). Substances that the monarch accumulates from milkweed plants cause the blue jay to vomit almost immediately (Figure 51.9). Following such experiences, blue jays avoid attacking monarchs and similar-looking butterflies. The ability to associate one environmental feature (such as a color) with another (such as a foul taste) is called **associative learning**.

Among animal behaviors, associative learning is particularly suited to laboratory studies because they typically involve either classical conditioning or operant conditioning. In *classical conditioning*, an arbitrary stimulus becomes associated with a particular outcome. Russian physiologist Ivan Pavlov carried out early experiments in classical conditioning, demonstrating that if he always rang a bell just before feeding a dog, the dog would eventually salivate when the bell sounded, anticipating food. In *operant conditioning*, also called trial-and-error learning, an animal first learns to associate one of its behaviors with a reward or punishment and then tends to repeat or avoid that behavior (see Figure 51.9). B. F. Skinner, an American pioneer in the study of operant conditioning, explored this process in the laboratory by, for example, having a rat learn through trial-and-error to obtain food by pressing a lever.

▼ Figure 51.8

INQUIRY

Does a digger wasp use landmarks to find her nest?

EXPERIMENT A female digger wasp covers the entrance to her nest while foraging for food, but finds the correct wasp nest reliably upon her return 30 minutes or more later. Niko Tinbergen wanted to test the hypothesis that a wasp learns visual landmarks that mark her nest before she leaves on hunting trips. First, he marked one nest with a ring of pinecones while the wasp was in the burrow. After leaving the nest to forage, the wasp returned to the nest successfully.

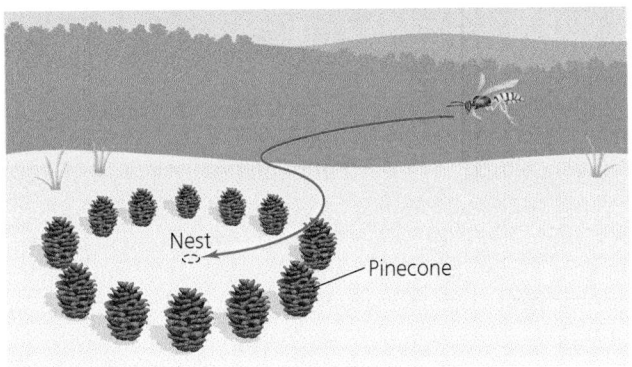

Nest

Pinecone

Two days later, after the wasp had again left, Tinbergen shifted the ring of pinecones away from the nest. Then he waited to observe the wasp's behavior.

RESULTS When the wasp returned, she flew to the center of the pinecone circle instead of to the nearby nest. Repeating the experiment with many wasps, Tinbergen obtained the same results.

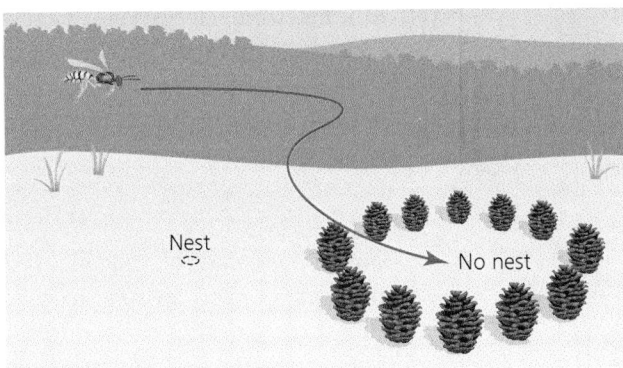

Nest

No nest

CONCLUSION The experiment supported the hypothesis that digger wasps use visual landmarks to keep track of their nests.

SOURCE N. Tinbergen, *The Study of Instinct*, Clarendon Press, Oxford (1951).

WHAT IF? Suppose the digger wasp had returned to her original nest site, despite the pinecones having been moved. What alternative hypotheses might you propose regarding how the wasp finds her nest and why the pinecones didn't misdirect the wasp?

▲ Figure 51.9 **Associative learning.** Having ingested and vomited a monarch butterfly, a blue jay has probably learned to avoid this species.

Studies reveal that animals can learn to link many pairs of features of their environment, but not all. For example, pigeons can learn to associate danger with a sound but not with a color. However, they can learn to associate a color with food. What does this mean? The development and organization of the pigeon's nervous system apparently restrict the associations that can be formed. Moreover, such restrictions are not limited to birds. Rats, for example, can learn to avoid illness-inducing foods on the basis of smells, but not on the basis of sights or sounds.

If we take into account the evolution of behavior, the fact that some animals can't learn to make particular associations appears logical. The associations an animal can readily form typically reflect relationships likely to occur in nature. Conversely, associations that can't be formed are those unlikely to be of selective advantage in a native environment. In the case of a rat's diet in the wild, for example, a harmful food is far more likely to have a certain odor than to be associated with a particular sound.

Cognition and Problem Solving

The most complex forms of learning involve **cognition**—the process of knowing that involves awareness, reasoning, recollection, and judgment. Although it was once argued that only primates and certain marine mammals have high-level thought processes, many other groups of animals, including insects, appear to exhibit cognition in controlled laboratory studies. For example, an experiment using Y-shaped mazes tested whether honeybees can distinguish between "same" and "different." One maze had different colors, and one had different black-and-white striped patterns, either vertical or horizontal bars. Two groups of honeybees were trained in the color maze.

Upon entering, a bee would see a sample color and could then choose between an arm of the maze with the same color or an arm with a different color. Only one arm contained a food reward. The first group of bees were rewarded for flying into the arm with the *same* color as the sample **(Figure 51.10a)**; the second group were rewarded for choosing the arm with the *different* color. Next, they were tested in the bar maze, which had no food reward. After encountering a sample black-and-white pattern of bars, a bee could choose between an arm with the same pattern or an arm with a different pattern. The bees in the first group most often chose the arm with the same pattern **(Figure 51.10b)**, whereas those in the second group typically chose the arm with the different pattern.

The maze experiments provide strong experimental support for the hypothesis that honeybees can distinguish on the basis of "same" and "different." Remarkably, research published in 2010 indicates that honeybees can also learn to distinguish between human faces.

The information-processing ability of a nervous system can also be revealed in **problem solving**, the cognitive activity of devising a method to proceed from one state to another in the face of real or apparent obstacles. For example, if a chimpanzee is placed in a room with several boxes on the floor and a banana hung high out of reach, the chimp can assess the situation and stack the boxes, enabling it to reach the food. Such problem-solving behavior is highly developed in some mammals, especially primates and dolphins. Notable examples have also been observed in some bird species, especially corvids. In one study, ravens were confronted with food hanging from a branch by a string. After failing to grab the food in flight, one raven flew to the branch and alternately pulled up and stepped on the string until the food was within reach. A number of other ravens eventually arrived at similar solutions. Nevertheless, some ravens failed to solve the problem, indicating that problem-solving success in this species, as in others, varies with individual experience and abilities.

Development of Learned Behaviors

Most of the learned behaviors we have discussed develop over a relatively short time. Some behaviors develop more gradually. For example, some bird species learn songs in stages.

In the case of the white-crowned sparrow (*Zonotrichia leucophrys*), the first stage of song learning takes place early in life, when the fledgling sparrow first hears the song. If a fledgling is prevented from hearing real sparrows or recordings of sparrow songs during the first 50 days of its life, it fails to

(a) Bees were trained in a color maze. As shown here, one group were rewarded for choosing the same color as the stimulus.

(b) Bees were tested in a pattern maze. If previously rewarded for choosing the same color, bees most often chose lines oriented the same way as the stimulus.

▲ **Figure 51.10 A maze test of abstract thinking by honeybees.** These mazes are designed to test whether honeybees can distinguish "same" from "different."

develop the adult song of its species. Although the young bird does not sing during the sensitive period, it memorizes the song of its species by listening to other white-crowned sparrows sing. During the sensitive period, fledglings chirp more in response to songs of their own species than to songs of other species. Thus, although young white-crowned sparrows learn the songs they will sing as adults, learning appears to be bounded by genetically controlled preferences.

The sensitive period when a white-crowned sparrow memorizes its species' song is followed by a second learning phase when the juvenile bird sings tentative notes called a subsong. The juvenile bird hears its own singing and compares it with the song memorized during the sensitive period. Once a sparrow's own song matches the one it memorized, the song "crystallizes" as the final song, and the bird sings only this adult song for the rest of its life.

The song-learning process is quite different for canaries than for white-crowned sparrows. Canaries, for example, do not have a single sensitive period for song learning. A young canary begins with a subsong, but the full song does not crystallize in the same way as in white-crowned sparrows. Between breeding seasons, the song becomes flexible again, and an adult male may learn new song "syllables" each year, adding to the song it already sings.

Song learning is one of many examples of how animals learn from other members of their species. In finishing our exploration of learning, we'll look at several more examples that reflect the more general phenomenon of social learning.

Social Learning

Many animals learn to solve problems by observing the behavior of other individuals. Young wild chimpanzees, for example, learn how to crack open oil palm nuts with two stones by copying experienced chimpanzees **(Figure 51.11)**. This type of learning through observing others is called **social learning**.

▲ **Figure 51.11 A young chimpanzee learning to crack oil palm nuts by observing an experienced elder.**

Another example of how social learning can modify behavior comes from studies of the vervet monkeys (*Cercopithecus aethiops*) in Amboseli National Park, Kenya. Vervet monkeys, which are about the size of a domestic cat, produce a complex set of alarm calls. Amboseli vervets give distinct alarm calls for leopards, eagles, or snakes, all of which prey on vervets. When a vervet sees a leopard, it gives a loud barking sound; when it sees an eagle, it gives a short double-syllable cough; and the snake alarm call is a "chutter." Upon hearing a particular alarm call, other vervets in the group behave in an appropriate way: They run up a tree on hearing the alarm for a leopard (vervets are nimbler than leopards in the trees); look up on hearing the alarm for an eagle; and look down on hearing the alarm for a snake **(Figure 51.12)**.

Infant vervet monkeys give alarm calls, but in a relatively undiscriminating way. For example, they give the "eagle" alarm on seeing any bird, including harmless birds such as bee-eaters. With age, the monkeys improve their accuracy. In fact, adult vervet monkeys give the eagle alarm only on seeing an eagle belonging to either of the two species that eat vervets. Infants probably learn how to give the right call by observing other members of the group and receiving social confirmation. For instance, if the infant gives the call on the right occasion— say, an eagle alarm when there is an eagle overhead—another member of the group will also give the eagle call. But if the infant gives the call when a bee-eater flies by, the adults in the group are silent. Thus, vervet monkeys have an initial, unlearned tendency to give calls upon seeing potentially threatening objects in the environment. Learning fine-tunes the call so that adult vervets give calls only in response to genuine danger and can fine-tune the alarm calls of the next generation.

▲ Figure 51.12 **Vervet monkeys learning correct use of alarm calls.** On seeing a python (foreground), vervet monkeys give a distinct "snake" alarm call (inset), and the members of the group stand upright and look down.

Social learning forms the roots of **culture**, which can be defined as a system of information transfer through social learning or teaching that influences the behavior of individuals in a population. Cultural transfer of information can alter behavioral phenotypes and thereby influence the fitness of individuals.

Changes in behavior that result from natural selection occur on a much longer time scale than does learning. In Concept 51.3, we'll examine the relationship between particular behaviors and the processes of selection related to survival and reproduction.

CONCEPT CHECK 51.2

1. How might associative learning explain why different species of distasteful or stinging insects have similar colors?
2. **WHAT IF?** How might you position and manipulate a few objects in a lab to test whether an animal can use a cognitive map to remember the location of a food source?
3. **MAKE CONNECTIONS** How can a learned behavior contribute to speciation? (See Concept 24.1, pp. 488–492.)

For suggested answers, see Appendix A.

CONCEPT 51.3

Selection for individual survival and reproductive success can explain most behaviors

We turn now from the physiology of behavior (how animals behave) to the benefits to a species from a particular behavior (why animals behave the way they do). In particular, we will address Tinbergen's third question—how behavior enhances survival and reproductive success in a population. We'll begin with an activity essential for both types of success: gathering food.

Foraging Behavior

Because adequate nutrition is essential to an animal's survival and reproductive success, we should expect natural selection to refine behaviors that enhance the efficiency of feeding. Food-obtaining behavior, or **foraging**, includes not only eating but also any activities an animal uses to search for, recognize, and capture food items.

Evolution of Foraging Behavior

The fruit fly (*Drosophila melanogaster*) has provided an opportunity to examine how foraging behavior might have evolved. Variation in a gene called *forager* (*for*) dictates the food-search behavior of fruit fly larvae. On average, larvae carrying the *for^R* ("Rover") allele travel nearly twice as far while feeding as do larvae with the *for^s* ("sitter") allele. Experiments have shown

that the enzyme encoded by the *forager* locus is more active in *for^R* larvae than in *for^s* larvae and has properties typical of an enzyme in a signal transduction pathway (see Chapter 45).

Both the *for^R* and *for^s* alleles are present in natural populations. What circumstances might favor one or the other allele? The answer became apparent in experiments when flies were kept for many generations at either low or high population densities. The larvae from the two samples clearly diverged in behavior, as measured by differences in average length of their foraging paths (**Figure 51.13**). Larvae maintained for many generations at a low density foraged over shorter distances than those kept at high density. Furthermore, genetic tests indicated that the *for^s* allele had increased in frequency in the low-density populations, whereas the *for^R* allele had increased in frequency in the high-density group. These changes make sense. At low population density, short-distance foraging yields sufficient food, while long-distance foraging would result in unnecessary energy expenditure. Under crowded conditions, however, long-distance foraging could enable larvae to move beyond areas of food depletion. In summary, there was an observable and interpretable evolutionary change in behavior in the laboratory populations.

Optimal Foraging Model

To study the proximate and ultimate causation of diverse foraging strategies, biologists sometimes apply a type of cost-benefit analysis used in economics. This idea proposes that foraging behavior is a compromise between the benefits of nutrition and the costs of obtaining food. These costs might include the energy expenditure of foraging as well as the risk of being eaten while foraging. According to this **optimal foraging model**, natural selection should favor a foraging behavior that minimizes the costs of foraging and maximizes the benefits.

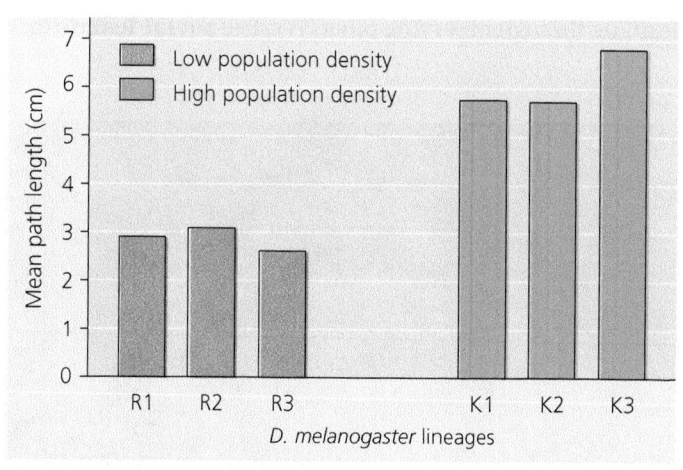

▲ **Figure 51.13 Evolution of foraging behavior by laboratory populations of *Drosophila melanogaster*.** After 74 generations of living at low population density, *D. melanogaster* larvae (populations R1–R3) followed foraging paths significantly shorter than those of *D. melanogaster* larvae that had lived at high density (populations K1–K3).

As an example of how the optimal foraging model can be applied, let's consider the feeding behavior of the Northwestern crow (*Corvus caurinus*). On islands off British Columbia, these crows search rocky tide pools for sea snails called whelks. After spotting a whelk, the crow picks the whelk up in its beak, flies upward, and drops the whelk onto the rocks. If the drop is successful, the shell breaks and the crow can dine on the whelk's soft parts. If not, the crow flies up and drops the whelk again and again until the shell breaks. What determines how high the crow flies? The higher the crow flies, the greater the force with which the whelk strikes the rocks, increasing the chance the shell will break. Flying higher, however, means consuming more energy.

If energetic considerations dominated selection for the crow's foraging behavior, the average drop height might reflect a trade-off between the cost of flying higher and the benefit of more frequent success. To test this idea, researchers dropped whelks from different heights and noted the number of drops required to break a shell. For each height, they calculated the average number of drops and the average *total flight height*, the drop height times the average number of drops (**Figure 51.14**). A drop height of about 5 m turned out to be optimal, breaking the shells with the lowest total flight height—in other words, with the least work. The actual average flight height for crows in their whelk-eating behavior is 5.23 m, very close to the prediction based on an optimal trade-off between energy gained (food) and energy expended.

The close agreement between the predicted and actual flight heights suggests that the optimal foraging model reflects the selective forces shaping the evolution of this behavior. However, other models could explain the findings equally well. For example, the average flight height could minimize the average *time* necessary to break open a whelk. Further experiments are needed to evaluate these possibilities.

Balancing Risk and Reward

One of the most significant potential costs to a forager is risk of predation. Maximizing energy gain and minimizing energy costs are of little benefit if the behavior makes the forager a likely meal for a predator. It seems logical, therefore, that predation risk would influence foraging behavior. Such appears to be the case for the mule deer (*Odocoileus hemionus*), which lives in the mountains of western North America. Researchers found that the food available for mule deer was fairly uniform across the potential foraging areas, although somewhat lower in open, nonforested areas. In contrast, the risk of predation differed greatly; mountain lions (*Puma concolor*), the major predator, killed large numbers of mule deer at forest edges and only a small number in open areas and forest interiors.

How does mule deer foraging behavior reflect the differences in predation risk in particular areas? Mule deer feed predominantly in open areas. Thus, it appears that mule deer foraging behavior reflects the large variation in predation risk and not the smaller variation in food availability. This result underscores the point that behavior typically reflects a compromise between competing selective pressures.

Mating Behavior and Mate Choice

Just as foraging is crucial for individual survival, mating behavior and mate choice play a major role in determining reproductive success. These behaviors include seeking or attracting mates, choosing among potential mates, competing for mates, and caring for offspring. Although we tend to think of mating simply as the union of a male and female, the mating relationship between males and females varies greatly from species to species, defining a number of distinct mating systems.

Mating Systems and Sexual Dimorphism

Mating systems vary with regard to both the length and number of relationships. In many animal species, mating is **promiscuous**, with no strong pair-bonds. In species in which the mates remain together for a longer period, the relationship may be **monogamous** (one male mating with one female) or **polygamous** (an individual of one sex mating with several of the other). Polygamous relationships most often involve a single male and many females, a system called *polygyny*, though some species exhibit *polyandry*, in which a single female mates with several males.

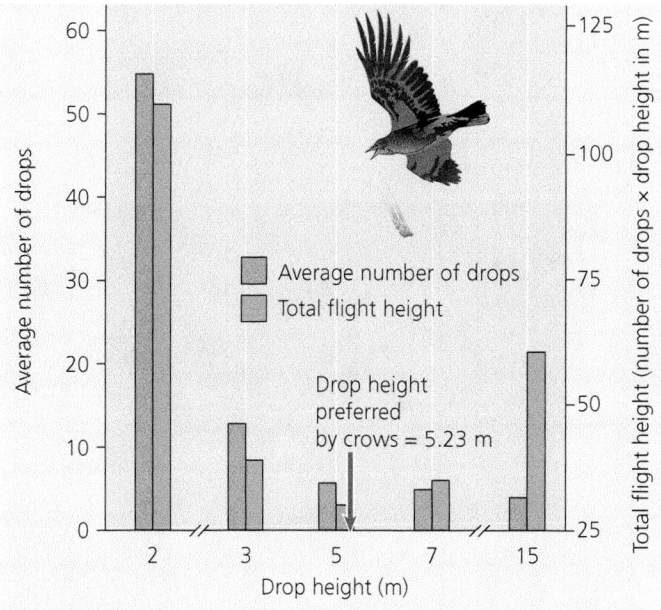

▲ **Figure 51.14 Energy costs and benefits in foraging behavior.** Experimental results indicate that dropping shells from a height of 5 m results in breakage with the least amount of work. The actual drop height preferred by crows corresponds almost exactly to the height that minimizes total flight height.

The extent to which males and females differ in appearance, a characteristic known as *sexual dimorphism*, typically varies with the type of mating system (Figure 51.15). Among monogamous species, males and females are often so much alike morphologically that they may be difficult or impossible to distinguish based on external characteristics. In contrast, polygynous species are generally dimorphic, with males being showier and often larger than females. Polyandrous species are also dimorphic, but the females are generally more ornamented and larger than the males.

Mating Systems and Parental Care

The needs of the young are an important factor constraining the evolution of mating systems. Most newly hatched birds, for instance, cannot care for themselves. Rather, they require a large, continuous food supply, a need that is difficult for a single parent to meet. In such cases, a male that stays with and helps a single mate may ultimately have more viable offspring than it would by going off to seek additional mates. This may explain why most birds are monogamous. In contrast, for birds with young that can feed and care for themselves almost immediately after hatching, the males derive less benefit from staying with their partner. Males of these species, such as pheasants and quail, can maximize their reproductive success by seeking other mates, and polygyny is relatively common in such birds. In the case of mammals, the lactating female is often the only food source for the young; males usually play no role in raising the young. In mammalian species where males protect the females and young, such as lions, a male or small group of males typically takes care of a harem of many females at the same time.

Another factor influencing mating behavior and parental care is *certainty of paternity*. Young born to or eggs laid by a female definitely contain that female's genes. However, even within a normally monogamous relationship, a male other than the female's usual mate may have fathered that female's offspring. The certainty of paternity is relatively low in most species with internal fertilization because the acts of mating and birth (or mating and egg laying) are separated over time. This could explain why exclusively male parental care is rare in bird and mammal species. However, the males of many species with internal fertilization engage in behaviors that appear to increase their certainty of paternity. These behaviors include guarding females, removing any sperm from the female reproductive tract before copulation, and introducing large quantities of sperm that displace the sperm of other males.

Certainty of paternity is high when egg laying and mating occur together, as in external fertilization. This may explain why parental care in aquatic invertebrates, fishes, and amphibians, when it occurs at all, is at least as likely to be by males as

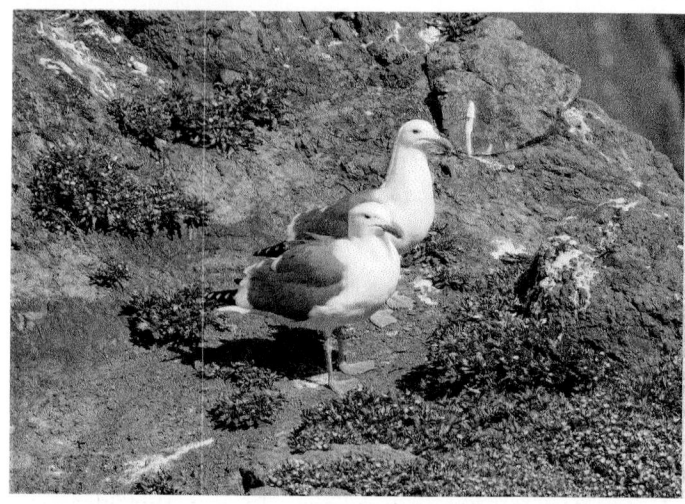

(a) In monogamous species, such as these western gulls, males and females are difficult to distinguish using external characteristics only.

(b) Among polygynous species, such as elk, the male (right) is often highly ornamented.

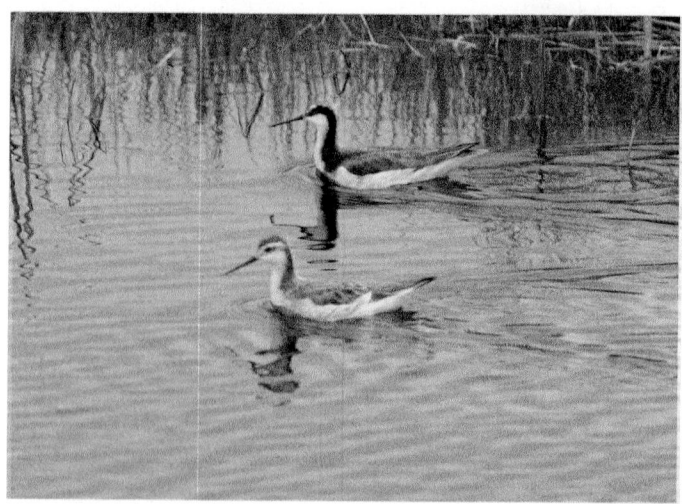

(c) In polyandrous species, such as these Wilson's phalaropes, females (top) are generally more ornamented than males.

▲ Figure 51.16 **Paternal care by a male jawfish.** The male jawfish, which lives in tropical marine environments, holds the eggs it has fertilized in its mouth, keeping them aerated and protecting them from egg predators until the young hatch.

▲ Figure 51.17 **Male stalk-eyed flies.** Male eye span plays a role in mate selection by females and, as shown here, in ritualized contests between males. In such contests, two males face off, with the male whose eye span is smaller very often retreating without any combat taking place.

by females (**Figure 51.16**; see also Figure 46.7). Among fishes and amphibians, parental care occurs in only 7% of species with internal fertilization but in 69% of species with external fertilization.

It is important to point out that certainty of paternity does not mean that animals are aware of those factors when they behave a certain way. Parental behavior correlated with certainty of paternity exists because it has been reinforced over generations by natural selection. Nevertheless, the relationship between certainty of paternity and male parental care remains an area of active research, enlivened by controversy.

Sexual Selection and Mate Choice

As you read in Chapter 23, the degree of sexual dimorphism within a species results from sexual selection, a form of natural selection in which differences in reproductive success among individuals are a consequence of differences in mating success. Recall from that chapter that sexual selection can take the form of *intersexual selection*, in which members of one sex choose mates on the basis of characteristics of the other sex, such as courtship songs, or *intrasexual selection*, which involves competition between members of one sex for mates. Let's look at some experimental evidence for sexual selection.

Mate Choice by Females Mate preferences of females may play a central role in the evolution of male behavior and anatomy through intersexual selection. As an example, let's consider the courtship behavior of stalk-eyed flies. The eyes of these insects are at the tips of stalks, which are longer in males than in females (**Figure 51.17**). During courtship, a male approaches the female headfirst. Researchers have shown that females are more likely to mate with males that have relatively long eyestalks. Why would females favor this seemingly arbitrary trait? As discussed in Chapter 23, ornaments such as long

eyestalks in these flies and bright coloration in male birds correlate in general with the male's health and vitality. A female whose mate choice is a healthy male is likely to produce more offspring that survive to reproduce.

Mate choice can also be influenced by imprinting, as revealed by experiments carried out with zebra finches. Both male and female zebra finches normally lack any feather crest on their head (**Figure 51.18**). To explore whether parental appearance affects mate preference in offspring independent of any genetic influence, researchers provided zebra finches with artificial ornamentation. A 2.5-cm-long red feather was taped to the forehead feathers of either or both zebra finch parents when their chicks were 8 days old, approximately 2 days before they opened their eyes. A control group of zebra finches were raised by unadorned parents. When the chicks matured,

▲ Figure 51.18 **Appearance of zebra finches in nature.** The male zebra finch (left) is more patterned and colorful than the female zebra finch.

they were presented with prospective mates that were either artificially ornamented with a red feather or non-ornamented (Figure 51.19). Males showed no preference. Females also showed no preference if they were raised by a male parent that was not ornamented. However, females raised by an ornamented male parent preferred ornamented males as their own mates. Thus, female finches apparently take cues from their fathers in choosing mates.

Mate-choice copying, a behavior in which individuals in a population copy the mate choice of others, has been studied in the guppy *Poecilia reticulata*. When a female guppy chooses between males with no other females present, the female almost always chooses the male with more orange coloration. To explore if the behavior of other females could influence this preference, an experiment was set up using both living females and artificial model females (Figure 51.20). If a female guppy observed the model "courting" a male with less extensive orange markings, she often copied the preference of the model female. That is, the female chose the male that had been presented in association with a model female rather than a more orange alternative. The exceptions were also informative. Mate-choice behavior typically did not change when the difference in coloration was particularly large. Mate-choice copying can thus mask genetically controlled female preference below a certain threshold of difference, in this case for male color.

Mate-choice copying, a form of social learning, has also been observed in several other fish and bird species. What is the selective pressure for such a mechanism? One possibility is that a female that mates with males that are attractive to other females increases the probability that her male offspring will also be attractive and have high reproductive success.

Male Competition for Mates The previous examples show how female choice can select for one best type of male in a given situation, resulting in low variation among males. Male competition for mates also can reduce variation among males.

▶ Figure 51.20 **Mate choice copying by female guppies (*Poecilia reticulata*).** Female guppies generally choose the males with more orange coloration. But when males were matched for orange or differed in the amount of orange by 12% or 24%, the females in the experimental group chose the *less* orange male that was presented with a model female. Females ignored the apparent choice of the model female only where the alternative male had 40% more orange coloration.

Experimental Groups of Parental Pairs			Control Group
Both parents ornamented	Males ornamented	Females ornamented	Parents not ornamented

Offspring — Offspring

Mate preference of female offspring: ornamented male

Mate preference of female offspring: none

▲ Figure 51.19 **Sexual selection influenced by imprinting.** Experiments demonstrated that female zebra finch chicks that had imprinted on artificially ornamented fathers preferred ornamented males as adult mates. For all experimental groups, male offspring showed no preference for either ornamented or non-ornamented female mates.

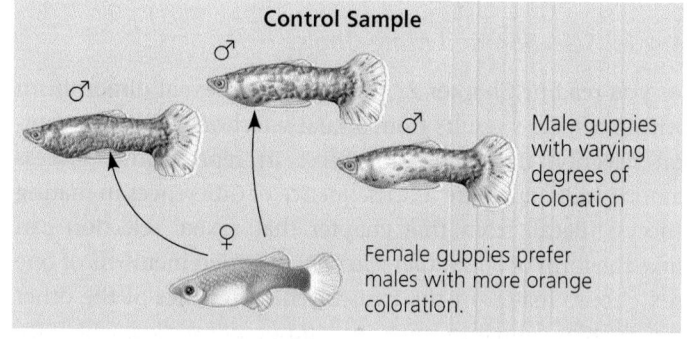

Control Sample

Male guppies with varying degrees of coloration

Female guppies prefer males with more orange coloration.

Experimental Sample

Female model in mock courtship with less orange male

Female guppies prefer males that are associated with another female.

Such competition may involve *agonistic behavior*, an often-ritualized contest that determines which competitor gains access to a resource, such as food or mates (Figure 51.21). The outcomes of such contests are often determined by strength or size, but the consequences may nevertheless be psychological rather than physical (see Figure 51.17).

Despite the potential for male competition to select for reduced variation, behavioral and morphological variation in males is extremely high in some vertebrate species, including species of fish and deer, as well as in a wide variety of invertebrates. In some species, sexual selection has led to the evolution of alternative male mating behavior and morphology. How do scientists analyze situations where more than one mating behavior can result in successful reproduction? One approach relies on the rules that govern games.

Applying Game Theory

Often, the fitness of a particular behavioral phenotype is influenced by other behavioral phenotypes in the population. In studying such situations, behavioral ecologists use a range of tools, including game theory. Developed by American mathematician John Nash and others to model human economic behavior, **game theory** evaluates alternative strategies in situations where the outcome depends on the strategies of all the individuals involved.

▲ **Figure 51.21 Agonistic interaction.** Male eastern grey kangaroos (*Macropus giganteus*) often "box" in contests that determine which male is most likely to mate with an available female. Typically, one male snorts loudly before striking the other around the head and throat with his forelimbs. Further snorting and cuffing, as well as grappling, often follow. If the male under attack does not retreat, the fight may escalate, with each male balancing on his tail while attempting to kick his rival with the sharp toenails of a hind leg.

▲ **Figure 51.22 Male polymorphism in the side-blotched lizard (*Uta stansburiana*).** An orange-throat male, left; a blue-throat male, center; a yellow-throat male, right.

As an example of applying game theory to mating behavior, let's consider the side-blotched lizard (*Uta stansburiana*) of California. Males can have orange, blue, or yellow throats (Figure 51.22). Each throat color is associated with a different pattern of behavior. Orange-throat males are the most aggressive and defend large territories that contain many females. Blue-throat males are also territorial but defend smaller territories and fewer females. Yellow-throats are nonterritorial males that mimic females and use "sneaky" tactics to gain the chance to mate.

Evidence indicates that the mating success of each male lizard type is influenced by the relative abundance of the other types, an example of frequency-dependent selection. In one study population, the most frequent throat coloration changed over a period of several years from blue to orange to yellow and back to blue.

By comparing the competition between side-blotched lizard males to the children's game of rock-paper-scissors, scientists devised an explanation for the cycles of variation in the lizard population. In the game, paper defeats rock, rock defeats scissors, and scissors defeats paper. Each hand symbol thus wins one matchup but loses the other. Similarly, each type of male lizard has an advantage over one of the other two types. When blue-throats are abundant, they can defend the few females in their territories from the advances of the sneaky yellow-throat males. However, blue-throats cannot defend their territories against the hyperaggressive orange-throats. Once the orange-throats become the most abundant, the larger number of females in each territory provides the opportunity for the yellow-throats to have greater mating success. The yellow-throats become more frequent, but then give way to the blue-throats, whose tactic of guarding small territories once again allows them the most success.

Game theory provides a way to think about complex evolutionary problems in which relative performance (reproductive success relative to other phenotypes), not absolute performance, is the key to understanding the evolution of behavior. This makes game theory an important tool because the relative performance of one phenotype compared with others is a measure of Darwinian fitness.

1. Why does the mode of fertilization correlate with the presence or absence of male parental care?
2. **MAKE CONNECTIONS** Balancing selection can maintain variation at a locus (see Concept 23.4, pp. 483–484). Based on the foraging experiments described in this chapter, devise a simple hypothesis to explain the presence of both *for^R* and *for^s* alleles in natural fly populations.
3. **WHAT IF?** Suppose an infection in a side-blotched lizard population killed many more males than females. What would be the immediate effect on male competition for reproductive success?

For suggested answers, see Appendix A.

CONCEPT **51.4**

Inclusive fitness can account for the evolution of behavior, including altruism

EVOLUTION We'll now explore issues related to the focus of Tinbergen's fourth question—the evolutionary history of behaviors. We will first look at examples that reveal the genetic underpinnings of behavior. Next, we will examine the genetic variation underlying the evolution of particular behaviors. Finally, we will see how expanding the definition of fitness beyond individual survival can help explain "selfless" behavior.

Genetic Basis of Behavior

In exploring the behavioral basis of behavior, we'll begin with the courtship behavior of the male fruit fly, diagrammed in Figure 51.4. During courtship, the male fly carries out a complex series of actions in response to multiple sensory stimuli. Genetic studies have revealed that a single gene called *fru* controls this entire courtship ritual. If the *fru* gene is mutated to an inactive form, males do not court or mate with females. (The name *fru* is short for *fruitless*, reflecting the absence of offspring from the mutant males.) Normal male and female flies express distinct forms of the *fru* gene. When females are genetically manipulated to express the male form of *fru*, they court other females, performing the role normally played by the male. How can a single gene control so many behaviors and actions? Experiments carried out cooperatively in several laboratories demonstrated that *fru* is a master regulatory gene that directs the expression and activity of many genes with narrower functions. Together, genes that are controlled by the *fru* gene bring about sex-specific development of the fly nervous system. In effect, *fru* programs the fly for male courtship behavior by overseeing a male-specific wiring of the central nervous system.

Researchers have also used insect courtship to explore genetic variation underlying differences in behavior. One well-studied example involves the courtship song of the green lacewing (**Figure 51.23**). Found throughout central to northern Eurasia and North America, these insects include at least

▼ **Figure 51.23**

INQUIRY

Are the songs of green lacewing species under the control of multiple genes?

EXPERIMENT Charles Henry, Lucía Martínez, and Kent Holsinger crossed males and females of *Chrysoperla plorabunda* and *Chrysoperla johnsoni*, two morphologically identical species of lacewings that sing different courtship songs.

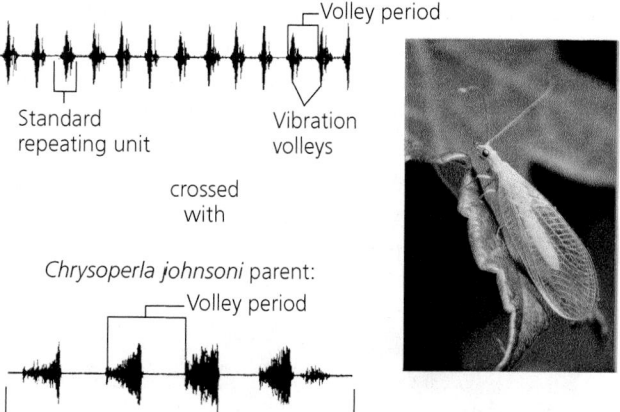

SOUND RECORDINGS
Chrysoperla plorabunda parent:

crossed with

Chrysoperla johnsoni parent:

The researchers compared the songs of the male and female parents with those of the hybrid offspring that had been raised in isolation from other lacewings.

RESULTS The F₁ hybrid offspring sang a song in which the length of the standard repeating unit was similar to that sung by the *Chrysoperla plorabunda* parent, but the volley period—the interval between vibration volleys—was more similar to that of the *Chrysoperla johnsoni* parent.

F₁ hybrids, typical phenotype:

CONCLUSION Since the song of the hybrid offspring has features of the songs of both parents, the results indicate that the songs sung by *Chrysoperla plorabunda* and *Chrysoperla johnsoni* are under the control of more than one gene.

SOURCE C. S. Henry et al., The inheritance of mating songs in two cryptic, sibling lacewing species, *Genetica* 116:269–289 (2002).

WHAT IF? Suppose the hybrids generated in this experiment were fertile. Would the appearance of the hybrid song shown in the figure be likely to lead to the formation of a new species? Explain your answer.

15 species, identical in appearance but having different courtship songs. When researchers at the University of Connecticut reared lacewings in isolation in the laboratory, they found that the lacewings performed the song specific to their species. Thus, they concluded, the courtship song must be genetically controlled. They then crossed different green lacewing species in the laboratory and analyzed the songs produced by the hybrid offspring. These experiments demonstrated that a different gene governs each component or property of the courtship song. Furthermore, the distinct courtship song of each green lacewing species reflects genetic differences at multiple, independent loci.

Whereas variation in multiple genes can bring about distinct behaviors, as is true for the lacewing courtship song, variation in a single locus is sometimes sufficient to bring about dramatic differences in behavior. One striking example is the behavior of two closely related species of voles, which are small, mouse-like rodents. Male meadow voles (*Microtus pennsylvanicus*) are solitary and do not form lasting relationships with mates. Following mating, they pay little attention to their pups. In contrast, male prairie voles (*Microtus ochrogaster*) form a pair-bond with a single female after they mate (**Figure 51.24**). Male prairie voles hover over their young pups, licking them and carrying them, while acting aggressively toward intruders.

Research suggested that a neurotransmitter released during mating is critical for the partnering and parental behavior of male voles. Known as ADH or vasopressin (see Chapter 44), this peptide binds to a specific receptor in the central nervous system. When male prairie voles are treated with a drug that inhibits the brain receptor for vasopressin, they fail to form pair-bonds after mating. Scientists have also observed that the vasopressin receptor gene of prairie voles is highly expressed in the brain, whereas that of meadow voles is not.

To test whether the amount of the vasopressin receptor present in the brain regulates the postmating behavior of voles, researchers inserted the vasopressin receptor gene from prairie voles into male meadow voles. The meadow voles carrying this gene not only developed brains with higher levels of the vasopressin receptor but also showed many of the same mating behaviors as male prairie voles, such as pair-bonding. Thus, although many genes influence pair-bond formation and parenting among voles, the level of the vasopressin receptor alone determines which behavioral pattern develops.

Genetic Variation and the Evolution of Behavior

Behavioral differences between closely related species, such as meadow and prairie voles, are common. Significant differences in behavior can also be found *within* a species but are often less obvious. When behavioral variation between populations of a species corresponds to variation in environmental conditions, it may be evidence of past evolution.

Case Study: Variation in Prey Selection

An example of genetically based behavioral variation within a species involves prey selection by the western garter snake (*Thamnophis elegans*). The natural diet of this species differs widely across its range in California. Coastal populations feed predominantly on banana slugs (*Ariolimus californicus*) (**Figure 51.25**). Inland populations feed on frogs, leeches, and fish, but not on banana slugs. In fact, banana slugs are rare or absent in the inland habitats.

◀ **Figure 51.24 A pair of prairie voles (*Microtus ochrogaster*) huddling.** Male North American prairie voles associate closely with their mates, as shown here, and contribute substantially to the care of young.

▲ **Figure 51.25 Western garter snake from a coastal habitat eating a banana slug.** Experiments indicate that the preference of these snakes for banana slugs may be influenced mainly by genetics rather than by environment.

When researchers offered banana slugs to snakes from each wild population, most coastal snakes readily ate them, whereas inland snakes tended to refuse. To what extent does genetic variation contribute to a snake's fondness for banana slugs? To answer this question, researchers collected pregnant snakes from each wild population and housed them in separate cages in the laboratory. While still very young, the offspring were offered a small piece of banana slug on each of ten days. More than 60% of the young snakes from coastal mothers ate banana slugs on eight or more of the ten days. In contrast, fewer than 20% of the young snakes from inland mothers ate a piece of banana slug even once. Perhaps not surprisingly, banana slugs thus appear to be a genetically acquired taste.

How did a genetically determined difference in feeding preference come to match the snakes' habitats so well? It turns out that the coastal and inland populations also vary with respect to their ability to recognize and respond to odor molecules produced by banana slugs. Researchers hypothesize that when inland snakes colonized coastal habitats more than 10,000 years ago, some of them could recognize banana slugs by scent. Because these snakes took advantage of this food source, they had higher fitness than snakes in the population that ignored the slugs. Over hundreds or thousands of generations, the capacity to recognize the slugs as prey increased in frequency in the coastal population. The marked variation in behavior observed today between the coastal and inland populations may be evidence of this past evolutionary change.

Case Study: Variation in Migratory Patterns

Another species suited to the study of behavioral variation is the blackcap (*Sylvia atricapilla*), a small migratory warbler. Blackcaps that breed in Germany generally migrate southwest to Spain and then south to Africa for the winter. In the 1950s, a few blackcaps began to spend their winters in Britain, and over time the population of blackcaps wintering in Britain grew to many thousands. Leg bands showed that some of these birds had migrated westward from central Germany. Why were there now two patterns of migration from Germany? To answer this question, researchers at the Max Planck Research Center in Radolfzell, Germany, devised a strategy to study migratory orientation in the laboratory (Figure 51.26). The results demonstrated that the two patterns of migration reflect genetic differences between the two populations.

The study of western European blackcaps indicated that the change in their migratory behavior occurred both recently and rapidly. Before the year 1950, there were no known westward-migrating blackcaps in Germany. By the 1990s, westward migrants made up 7–11% of the blackcap populations of Germany. Once westward migration began, it persisted and increased in frequency, perhaps due to the widespread use of winter bird feeders in Britain, as well as shorter migration distances.

▼ Figure 51.26

INQUIRY

Are differences in migratory orientation within a species genetically determined?

EXPERIMENT Peter Berthold and colleagues in southern Germany raised two sets of young birds for their study. One group consisted of the offspring of blackcaps captured while wintering in Britain and then bred in Germany in an outdoor cage. The other group consisted of young birds collected from nests near the laboratory and then raised in cages. In the autumn, Berthold's team placed the blackcaps captured in Britain and the young birds raised in cages in large, glass-covered funnel cages lined with carbon-coated paper for 1.5–2 hours. When the funnels were placed outside at night, the birds moved around, making marks on the paper that indicated the direction in which they were trying to "migrate."

Scratch marks

RESULTS The wintering adult birds captured in Britain and their laboratory-raised offspring both attempted to migrate to the west. In contrast, the young birds collected from nests in southern Germany attempted to migrate to the southwest.

Adults from Britain and offspring of British adults

Young from SW Germany

CONCLUSION The young of the British blackcaps and the young birds from Germany (the control group) were raised under similar conditions but showed very different migratory orientations, indicating that migratory orientation has a genetic basis.

SOURCE P. Berthold et al., Rapid microevolution of migratory behavior in a wild bird species, *Nature* 360:668–690 (1992).

WHAT IF? Suppose the birds had not shown a difference in orientation in these experiments. Could you conclude that the behavior was not genetically based? Explain.

Altruism

Reconstructing the evolutionary basis of a behavior requires an understanding of the behavior's genetic basis and of the selective advantage conferred by the behavior. Typically, we assume that behaviors are selfish; that is, they benefit the individual at the expense of others, especially competitors. For example, superior foraging ability by one individual may leave less food for others. The problem comes, however, with "unselfish" behaviors. How can such behaviors arise through natural selection? To answer this question, let's look more closely at some examples of unselfish behavior and then consider how such behaviors might arise.

In discussing selflessness, we will use the term **altruism** to describe a behavior that reduces an animal's individual fitness but increases the fitness of other individuals in the population. Consider the Belding's ground squirrel, which lives in some mountainous regions of the western United States and is vulnerable to predators such as coyotes and hawks. A squirrel that sees a predator approach often gives a high-pitched alarm call that alerts unaware individuals to retreat to their burrows. Note that for the squirrel that warns others, the conspicuous alarm behavior increases the risk of being killed because it brings attention to the caller's location.

Another example of altruistic behavior occurs in honeybee societies, in which the workers are sterile. The workers themselves never reproduce, but they labor on behalf of a single fertile queen. Furthermore, the workers sting intruders, a behavior that helps defend the hive but results in the death of those workers.

Altruism is also observed in naked mole rats (*Heterocephalus glaber*), highly social rodents that live in underground chambers and tunnels in southern and northeastern Africa. The naked mole rat, which is almost hairless and nearly blind, lives in colonies of 75 to 250 or more individuals (**Figure 51.27**). Each colony has only one reproducing female, the queen, who mates with one to three males, called kings. The rest of the colony consists of nonreproductive females and males who

▲ **Figure 51.27 Naked mole rats, a species of colonial mammal that exhibits altruistic behavior.** Pictured here is a queen nursing offspring while surrounded by other members of the colony.

forage for underground roots and tubers and care for the queen, the kings, and new offspring. The nonreproductive individuals may sacrifice their own lives in trying to protect the queen or kings from snakes or other predators that invade the colony.

Inclusive Fitness

How can a Belding's ground squirrel, a worker honeybee, or a naked mole rat enhance its fitness by aiding members of the population that may be its closest competitors? How can altruistic behavior be maintained by evolution if it does not enhance the survival and reproductive success of the self-sacrificing individuals?

The selection for altruistic behavior is most readily apparent in the case of parents sacrificing for their offspring. When parents sacrifice their own well-being to produce and aid offspring, this actually increases the fitness of the parents because it maximizes their genetic representation in the population. However, individuals sometimes help others who are not their offspring.

Biologist William Hamilton proposed that an animal could increase its genetic representation in the next generation by "altruistically" helping close relatives other than its own offspring. Like parents and offspring, full siblings have half their genes in common. Therefore, selection might also favor helping siblings or helping one's parents produce more siblings. This idea led to Hamilton's idea of **inclusive fitness**, the total effect an individual has on proliferating its genes by producing its own offspring *and* by providing aid that enables other close relatives, who share many of those genes, to produce offspring.

Hamilton's Rule and Kin Selection

According to Hamilton, the three key variables in an act of altruism are the benefit to the recipient, the cost to the altruist, and the coefficient of relatedness. The benefit, B, is the average number of *extra* offspring that the beneficiary of an altruistic act produces. The cost, C, is how many *fewer* offspring the altruist produces. The **coefficient of relatedness**, r, equals the fraction of genes that, on average, are shared. Natural selection favors altruism when the benefit to the recipient multiplied by the coefficient of relatedness exceeds the cost to the altruist—in other words, when $rB > C$. This statement is called **Hamilton's rule**.

To better understand Hamilton's rule, let's apply it to a human population in which the average individual has two children. We'll imagine that a young man is close to drowning in heavy surf, and his sister risks her life to swim out and pull her sibling to safety. If the young man had drowned, his reproductive output would have been zero; but now, if we use the average, he can father two children. The benefit to the brother is thus two offspring ($B = 2$). What about the risk taken by his sister? Let's say that the sister has a 25% chance of drowning in attempting to rescue her brother. We can then calculate the cost of the altruistic act to the sister as 0.25 times 2, the number of offspring she would be expected to have if she had stayed on shore ($C = 0.25 \times 2 = 0.5$). Finally, we note that a brother and sister share half their genes on average ($r = 0.5$). One way to see this is in terms of the segregation of homologous chromosomes that occurs during meiosis of gametes (**Figure 51.28**; see also Chapter 13).

We can now use our values of B, C, and r to evaluate whether natural selection would favor the altruistic act in our imaginary scenario. For the surf rescue, $rB = 0.5 \times 2 = 1$, whereas $C = 0.5$. Because rB is greater than C, Hamilton's rule is satisfied; thus, natural selection would favor this altruistic act of the sister attempting to save her brother. Averaging over many individuals and generations, any particular gene in a sister faced with this situation will be passed on to more offspring if she risks the rescue than if she does not. Furthermore, among genes propagated in this way may be some that contribute to altruistic behavior. The natural selection that favors altruistic behavior by enhancing reproductive success of relatives is called **kin selection**.

Kin selection weakens with hereditary distance. Siblings have an r of 0.5, but between an aunt and her niece, $r = 0.25$ (¼), and between first cousins, $r = 0.125$ (⅛). Notice that as the degree of relatedness decreases, the rB term in the Hamilton inequality also decreases. Would natural selection favor rescuing a cousin? Not unless the surf were less treacherous. For the original conditions, $rB = 0.125 \times 2 = 0.25$, which is

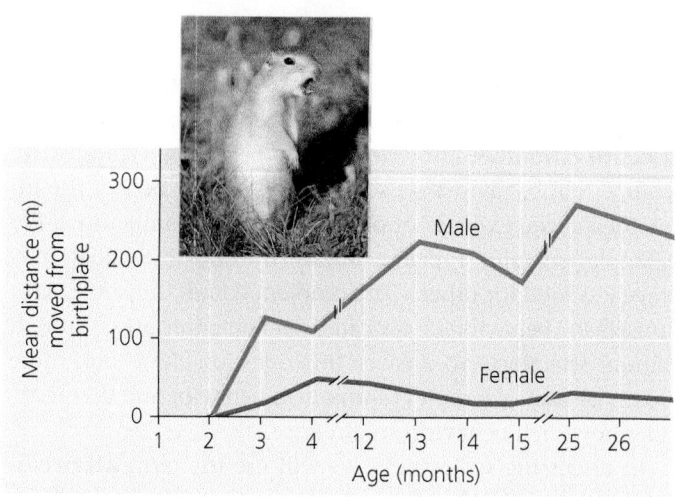

▲ **Figure 51.29 Kin selection and altruism in Belding's ground squirrels.** This graph helps explain the male-female difference in altruistic behavior of ground squirrels. Once weaned (pups are nursed for about one month), females are more likely than males to live near close relatives. Alarm calls that warn these relatives increase the inclusive fitness of the female altruist.

only half the value of C (0.5). British geneticist J. B. S. Haldane appears to have anticipated these ideas when he jokingly stated that he would not lay down his life for one brother, but would do so for two brothers or eight cousins.

If kin selection explains altruism, then the examples of unselfish behavior we observe among diverse animal species should involve close relatives. This is apparently the case, but often in complex ways. Like most mammals, female Belding's ground squirrels settle close to their site of birth, whereas males settle at distant sites (**Figure 51.29**). Since nearly all alarm calls are given by females, they are most likely aiding close relatives. In the case of worker bees, who are all sterile, anything they do to help the entire hive benefits the only permanent member who is reproductively active—the queen, who is their mother.

In the case of naked mole rats, DNA analyses have shown that all the individuals in a colony are closely related. Genetically, the queen appears to be a sibling, daughter, or mother of the kings, and the nonreproductive mole rats are the queen's direct descendants or her siblings. Therefore, when a nonreproductive individual enhances a queen's or king's chances of reproducing, the altruist increases the chance that some genes identical to its own will be passed to the next generation.

Reciprocal Altruism

Some animals occasionally behave altruistically toward others who are not relatives. A baboon may help an unrelated companion in a fight, or a wolf may offer food to another wolf even though they share no kinship. Such behavior can be adaptive if the aided individual returns the favor in the future. This sort of exchange of aid, called **reciprocal altruism**, is commonly invoked to explain altruism that occurs between

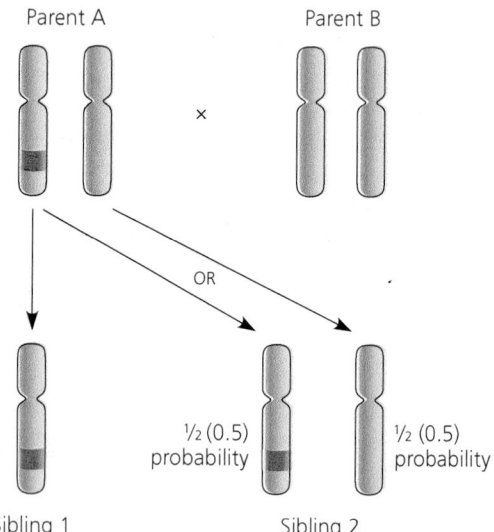

Parent A   **Parent B**

OR

½ (0.5) probability   ½ (0.5) probability

Sibling 1   Sibling 2

▲ **Figure 51.28 The coefficient of relatedness between siblings.** The red band indicates a particular allele (version of a gene) present on one chromosome, but not its homolog, in parent A. Sibling 1 has inherited the allele from parent A. There is a probability of ½ that sibling 2 will also inherit this allele from parent A. Any allele present on one chromosome of either parent will behave similarly. The coefficient of relatedness between the two siblings is thus ½, or 0.5.

WHAT IF? *The coefficient of relatedness of an individual to a full (nontwin) sibling or to either parent is the same, 0.5. Does this value also hold true in the cases of polyandry and polygyny?*

unrelated humans. Reciprocal altruism is rare in other animals; it is limited largely to species (such as chimpanzees) with social groups stable enough that individuals have many chances to exchange aid. It is generally thought to occur when individuals are likely to meet again and when there would be negative consequences associated with not returning favors to individuals who had been helpful in the past, a pattern of behavior that behavioral ecologists refer to as "cheating."

Since cheating may benefit the cheater substantially, how could reciprocal altruism evolve? Game theory provides a possible answer in the form of a behavioral strategy called *tit for tat*. In the tit-for-tat strategy, an individual treats another in the same way it was treated the last time they met. Individuals adopting this behavior are always altruistic, or cooperative, on the first encounter with another individual and will remain so as long as their altruism is reciprocated. When their cooperation is not reciprocated, however, individuals employing tit for tat will retaliate immediately but return to cooperative behavior as soon as the other individual becomes cooperative. The tit-for-tat strategy has been used to explain the few apparently reciprocal altruistic interactions observed in animals—ranging from blood sharing between nonrelated vampire bats to social grooming in primates.

Evolution and Human Culture

Human culture is related to evolutionary theory in the discipline of **sociobiology**. The main premise of sociobiology is that certain behavioral characteristics exist because they are expressions of genes that have been perpetuated by natural selection. In his seminal 1975 book *Sociobiology: The New Synthesis*, E. O. Wilson speculated about the evolutionary basis of certain kinds of social behavior. By including a few examples from human culture, he sparked a debate that remains heated today.

The spectrum of human social behaviors may be influenced by our genetic makeup, but this is very different from saying that genes are rigid determinants of behavior. This distinction is at the core of the debate about evolutionary perspectives on human behavior. Skeptics fear that evolutionary interpretations of human behavior could be used to justify the status quo in human society, thus rationalizing current social injustices. Evolutionary biologists argue that this is a gross oversimplification and misunderstanding of what the data tell us about human biology. Evolutionary explanations of human behavior do not reduce us to robots stamped out of rigid genetic molds. Just as individuals vary extensively in anatomical features, we should expect inherent variations in behavior as well. Environment intervenes in the pathway from genotype to phenotype for physical traits and even more so for behavioral traits. And because of our capacity for learning and our versatility, human behavior is probably more plastic than that of any other animal. Over our recent evolutionary history, we have built up a diversity of structured societies with governments, laws, cultural values, and religions that define what is acceptable behavior and what is not, even when unacceptable behavior might enhance an individual's Darwinian fitness. Perhaps it is our social and cultural institutions that make us distinct and that provide those qualities in which there is the least continuum between humans and other animals.

CONCEPT CHECK 51.4

1. Explain why geographic variation in garter snake prey choice might indicate that the behavior evolved by natural selection.
2. **WHAT IF?** If an animal were unable to distinguish close from distant relatives, would the concept of inclusive fitness still be applicable? Explain.
3. **WHAT IF?** Suppose you applied Hamilton's logic to a situation in which one individual is past reproductive age. Could there still be a selection for an altruistic act?

For suggested answers, see Appendix A.

51 CHAPTER REVIEW

SUMMARY OF KEY CONCEPTS

CONCEPT 51.1

Discrete sensory inputs can stimulate both simple and complex behaviors (pp. 1118–1122)

- **Behavior** is the sum of responses to external and internal stimuli and includes muscular as well as nonmuscular activity. Tinbergen developed a set of questions that highlight the complementary nature of two perspectives. Proximate, or "how," questions focus on the environmental stimuli, if any, that trigger a behavior, as well as the genetic, physiological, and anatomical mechanisms underlying a behavioral act. Ultimate, or "why," questions address the evolutionary significance of a behavior.
- A **fixed action pattern** is a largely invariant behavior triggered by a simple cue known as a **sign stimulus**. Migratory movements involve navigation, which can be based on orientation relative to the sun, the stars, or Earth's magnetic field. Animal behavior is sometimes synchronized to the daily, or circadian, cycle of light and dark in the environment or to environmental cues that cycle over the seasons.

- The transmission and reception of signals constitute animal **communication**. Animals use visual, auditory, chemical (usually olfactory), and tactile signals, sometimes as part of a stimulus-response chain that governs a complex behavior. Chemical substances called pheromones transmit species-specific information through the environment in behaviors ranging from foraging to courtship.

? *How is migration based on circannual rhythms poorly suited for adaptation to global climate change?*

CONCEPT 51.2

Learning establishes specific links between experience and behavior (pp. 1123–1128)

- Cross-fostering studies can be used to measure the influence of social environment and experience on behavior.
- **Learning**, the modification of behavior based on experience, can take many forms:

Imprinting

Learning and problem solving

Spatial learning

Cognition

Associative learning

Social learning

? *How do imprinting in geese and song development in sparrows differ with regard to the resulting behavior?*

CONCEPT 51.3

Selection for individual survival and reproductive success can explain most behaviors (pp. 1128–1134)

- An **optimal foraging model** is based on the idea that natural selection should favor foraging behavior that minimizes the costs of foraging and maximizes the benefits.
- Sexual dimorphism correlates with the type of mating relationship between males and females. These include **monogamous** and **polygamous** mating systems. Variation in mating system and variation in the mode of fertilization affect certainty of paternity, which in turn has a significant influence on mating behavior and parental care.

- Game theory provides a way of thinking about evolution in situations where the fitness of a particular behavioral phenotype is influenced by other behavioral phenotypes in the population.

? *In some spider species, the female eats the male immediately after copulation. How might you explain this behavior from an evolutionary perspective?*

CONCEPT 51.4

Inclusive fitness can account for the evolution of behavior, including altruism (pp. 1134–1139)

- Genetic studies in insects have revealed the existence of master regulatory genes that control complex behaviors. Within the underlying hierarchy, multiple genes influence specific behaviors, such as a courtship song. Research with two species of voles has revealed that variation in a single gene can determine differences in complex behaviors involved in both mating and parenting.
- When behavioral variation within a species corresponds to variation in environmental conditions, it may be evidence of past evolution. Field and laboratory studies have documented the genetic basis for a change in migratory behavior of certain birds and revealed behavioral differences in snakes that correlate with geographic variation in prey availability.
- On occasion, animals exhibit **altruism**. This behavior can be explained by the concept of **inclusive fitness**, the total effect an individual has on proliferating its genes by producing its own offspring *and* by providing aid that enables close relatives to produce offspring. **The coefficient of relatedness** and **Hamilton's rule** provide a way of measuring the strength of the selective forces favoring altruism against the potential cost of the "selfless" behavior. Kin selection favors altruistic behavior by enhancing the reproductive success of relatives. Altruistic behavior toward unrelated individuals can be adaptive if the aided individual returns the favor in the future, an exchange of aid called reciprocal altruism.

? *Suppose you studied the genetics of the lacewing courtship song, but not the effects of courtship mutations in flies or of variation in the vasopressin receptor gene of voles. What insight about the genetic basis of behavior would you likely have missed?*

TEST YOUR UNDERSTANDING

LEVEL 1: KNOWLEDGE/COMPREHENSION

1. Which of the following is true of innate behaviors?
   a. Their expression is only weakly influenced by genes.
   b. They occur with or without environmental stimuli.
   c. They are limited to invertebrate animals.
   d. They are expressed in most individuals in a population.
   e. They occur in invertebrates and some vertebrates but not mammals.

2. According to Hamilton's rule,
   a. natural selection does not favor altruistic behavior that causes the death of the altruist.
   b. natural selection favors altruistic acts when the resulting benefit to the beneficiary, corrected for relatedness, exceeds the cost to the altruist.
   c. natural selection is more likely to favor altruistic behavior that benefits an offspring than altruistic behavior that benefits a sibling.
   d. the effects of kin selection are larger than the effects of direct natural selection on individuals.
   e. altruism is always reciprocal.

3. Female spotted sandpipers aggressively court males and, after mating, leave the clutch of young for the male to incubate. This sequence may be repeated several times with different males until no available males remain, forcing the female to incubate her last clutch. Which of the following terms best describes this behavior?
   a. monogamy
   b. polygyny
   c. polyandry
   d. promiscuity
   e. certainty of paternity

LEVEL 2: APPLICATION/ANALYSIS

4. A region of the canary forebrain shrinks during the nonbreeding season and enlarges when breeding season begins. This change is probably associated with the annual
   a. addition of new syllables to a canary's song repertoire.
   b. crystallization of subsong into adult songs.
   c. sensitive period in which canary parents imprint on new offspring.
   d. renewal of mating and nest-building behaviors.
   e. elimination of the memorized template for songs sung the previous year.

5. Although many chimpanzees live in environments containing oil palm nuts, members of only a few populations use stones to crack open the nuts. The likely explanation is that
   a. the behavioral difference is caused by genetic differences between populations.
   b. members of different populations have different nutritional requirements.
   c. the cultural tradition of using stones to crack nuts has arisen in only some populations.
   d. members of different populations differ in learning ability.
   e. members of different populations differ in manual dexterity.

6. Which of the following is *not* required for a behavioral trait to evolve by natural selection?
   a. In each individual, the form of the behavior is determined entirely by genes.
   b. The behavior varies among individuals.
   c. An individual's reproductive success depends in part on how the behavior is performed.
   d. Some component of the behavior is genetically inherited.
   e. An individual's genotype influences its behavioral phenotype.

LEVEL 3: SYNTHESIS/EVALUATION

7. **DRAW IT** You are considering two optimal foraging models for the behavior of a mussel-feeding shorebird, the oystercatcher. In model A, the energetic reward increases solely with mussel size. In model B, you take into consideration that larger mussels are more difficult to open. Draw a graph of reward (energy benefit on a scale of 0–10) versus mussel length (scale of 0–70 mm) for each model. Assume that mussels under 10 mm provide no benefit and are ignored by the birds. Also assume that mussels start becoming difficult to open

when they reach 40 mm in length and impossible to open when 70 mm long. Considering the graphs you have drawn, how could you distinguish between the models by observation and measurement in the oystercatcher's habitat?

8. **EVOLUTION CONNECTION**
   We often explain our behavior in terms of subjective feelings, motives, or reasons, but evolutionary explanations are based on reproductive fitness. What is the relationship between the two kinds of explanation? For instance, is a human explanation for behavior, such as "falling in love," incompatible with an evolutionary explanation?

9. **SCIENTIFIC INQUIRY**
   Scientists studying scrub jays found that "helpers" often assist mated pairs of birds in raising their young. The helpers lack territories and mates of their own. Instead, they help the territory owners gather food for their offspring. Propose a hypothesis to explain what advantage there might be for the helpers to engage in this behavior instead of seeking their own territories and mates. How would you test your hypothesis? If it is correct, what results would you expect your tests to yield?

10. **SCIENCE, TECHNOLOGY, AND SOCIETY**
    Researchers are very interested in studying identical twins separated at birth and raised apart. So far, the data reveal that such twins frequently have similar personalities, mannerisms, habits, and interests. What general question do you think researchers hope to answer by studying such twins? Why do identical twins make good subjects for this research? What are the potential pitfalls of this research? What abuses might occur if the studies are not evaluated critically?

11. **WRITE ABOUT A THEME**
    The Genetic Basis of Life Learning is defined as a change in behavior based on experience. In a short essay (100–150 words), describe the role of heritable information in the acquisition of learning, using some examples from imprinting and associative learning.

For selected answers, see Appendix A.

UNIT 8

Ecology

An Interview with
Camille Parmesan

Camille Parmesan planned to be a doctor when she first enrolled at the University of Texas in Austin in 1979. Three decades later, she's never regretted her decision to study butterflies around the world instead.

Dr. Parmesan's research expertise is on the ecology, evolution, and behavior of butterflies and their plant hosts, particularly how climate change is affecting them today. As an expert on climate change, she has testified before the U.S. Congress and been a lead author to the United Nations Intergovernmental Panel on Climate Change. She also advises many conservation groups, including The Nature Conservancy, World Wildlife Fund, and the National Wildlife Federation. Having earned both undergraduate and doctoral degrees from the University of Texas in Austin, she is currently an Associate Professor in the Section of Integrative Biology there.

What inspired you to go into science, and ecology in particular?
My mother had studied geology and botany, and as soon as I could walk, she started taking me on hikes through the forest or into the mountains and telling me what every rock and every plant and every bird was. She would have all her field guides with her, and if she didn't know something we would look it up together. So nature was always something that fascinated me. I loved being outdoors; I loved camping out; I loved hiking.

In high school, though, I felt that I really wanted to do something relevant for society, so I decided I wanted to be a medical doctor. I was premed throughout my undergraduate career until my last semester, and it was only because of some independent research projects that I changed my mind. I did one on honeybees, and I did one with primates. Then, the summer before graduation, I went out to the mountains of California and worked with butterflies for the summer. At that point, I asked myself, "Can I get paid to do this? I don't want to sit in an office or a hospital all day, every day, when I could be out here for three months of the year." So I switched my plans for my last semester. I wanted to do research in the mountains the rest of my life.

What did you do right out of college?
I took a break and worked as a research technician. It took me a couple of years before I was ready—refreshed enough—to enter grad school. As a technician, I was continuing to study the ecology and evolution of butterflies, following up on the research I did as an undergrad. But it can be frustrating to be doing this research and knowing it's not your own project; you're not really able to pursue what you're most interested in. I wanted to be working for excitement and satisfaction, not just for the pay.

What was your research in graduate school?
Ecology, evolution, and behavior. I started out working in the tropics, in Costa Rica, still studying interactions between butterflies and their host plants. So that theme was still there. But I was ready to learn a new system, and the tropics are absolutely amazing for a biologist. When you're working in the California mountains, you get to know the butterfly species in about 15 minutes because there are only about a dozen of them. Then you go to Costa Rica, and every single thing you see is a new species, and you're seeing dozens in a day. It was incredible. So I started a project down there and combined it with a study colony of butterflies I was growing back here in Texas as well. We had a little tropical greenhouse in the lab and a humidifier.

But you switched back to studying butterflies in temperate areas?
I absolutely loved the tropics, but I got very sick there, and so I went back to doing research in the temperate zone. When I started studying climate change, the need for really good historical records led me to study sites in Europe. Now I work in the European Alps and the Pyrenees, and I've gotten to know Sweden and Finland as well. My study site in the Alps is only a few hundred meters from the route taken by the Tour de France.

Why are butterflies useful for studying climate change?
Although I personally think butterflies are incredibly beautiful, and a lot of people agree with me, that is not the main reason we study them. The reason they are so important, especially to the study of climate change, is that they are extremely sensitive to very small variations in climate. Climate affects the development times of both the insects and their host plants, and changes in climate can alter how in sync the interacting species are. Species adjust their ranges so that they remain in a particular climate space, and thus act as indicators of change.

We don't know exactly what populations are responding to when they change their ranges. It's not just mean annual temperature. It's something much more complex, probably having to do with the timing of short bursts of heat, snowfalls, and other unusual events that affect how well butterfly populations do in any given year. If there are several years in a row with these kinds of extreme events, the populations could either boom, if they are good extreme events, or become extinct. We're just starting to understand how very tiny changes in the number of days in a row of, say, warm temperatures above a certain threshold can affect their survival.

One year when we arrived at our work site, we found that the snow pack was really light. Although the site was at an elevation of 8,000 feet, the snow melted in early April—really early—and the temperatures were unusually warm. The butterflies we were studying, called Edith's checkerspots (*Euphydryas editha*), started their flight season two months early, in April instead of in June. But the plants hadn't responded to the unusual weather and were still dormant. So when the butterflies came out, there was no nectar available for them, and they died. I remember going out to the hillside and seeing orange specks all over the hill. When I moved closer, I found that the specks were dead butterflies. They had emerged from their cocoons, but there was nothing for them to feed on.

So are butterflies a first warning signal for climate change?
Exactly, but you need a long record, over many years, to understand the signal. In Sweden, Finland, and Britain, for example, there are sites that have been monitored every year for 140 years. I have sites where either I or another butterfly researcher has been working nearly every year for the last 40 years. When Paul Ehrlich first started working with the Edith's checkerspot butterfly in the late 1950s, he reported how sensitive this species is to yearly climate variability, changes in temperature and rainfall. My husband, Mike Singer, studied the checkerspot for his dissertation under Ehrlich in the 1960s, and he found even more evidence for sensitivity to climate variability. This was long before any awareness of global warming. When I started studying the butterflies in the 1980s, I found the same thing, the most dramatic example being that horrible false spring when all the butterflies died. So the sensitivity of these butterflies to climate changes has been documented over 50 years of research. All butterflies are sensitive to climate change, but *Euphydryas editha* is especially so.

How did you first realize that your butterfly data suggested that climate change was already occurring?
In order to demonstrate the likelihood that climate change was affecting my butterfly, I was expecting to have to do a very complex analysis of my data, separating out all the different types of butterflies and their locations and figuring out what aspects of climate affected the butterflies each year. The dynamics of the coastal butterflies might be driven by winter precipitation, for example, in order for their host plants to grow. But when I put my data together, I said to my husband, "You know, I'm getting something really simple here. It looks like the butterflies in the south are going extinct, and the ones in the north are doing really well. Also, the ones at low elevation are going extinct, and the ones at high elevation are doing well. I think the butterfly is just shifting its range."

What kinds of species are most at risk from climate change and other environmental problems?
We're not too worried about the common species that live everywhere. It's the rarer ones with smaller distributions that are most at risk. Think about how many of our conservation programs are based on being able to preserve an area for habitat. As long as you keep invasive species and other threats out, you can usually maintain what the area was set up to protect. Climate change alters all of that. Suddenly your preserve is not climatically suitable. So a species may go extinct in your preserve, and yet outside of the preserve all you've got are cornfields and urban sprawl. Where are you going to put the species next?

Why is it important to study and maintain biodiversity on Earth?
For me, there are two reasons why biodiversity is important. First, there is what I call the spiritual component. Species are important because they give us a grounding in this world; they connect us to the rest of life. But biodiversity is also important because of the services that different species provide. Plants and microorganisms produce breathable air and purify our lakes and streams; wild animals and plants provide food and new genes for healthy crops. We are relying on lands outside of cities to provide us with those things.

> "The sensitivity of these butterflies to climate changes has been documented over 50 years of research."

What are some of the important, unanswered questions in ecology for climate change research?
I think that climate change in general is a field where we don't understand the responses well enough to know exactly where things are going. We're pretty sure of some processes occurring in the Arctic—the sea ice is melting, for instance. What we really don't understand is what's happening in the tropics. Will tropical rain forests expand as Earth warms, or are we going to be having extreme climates emerge at the equator like a few models project, even to the extent of the Amazon rain forest drying up? Will we have coral reefs in another hundred years? Or are they going to disappear as an entire ecosystem? We don't know at what point such processes may occur and be unstoppable.

What would you say to a student considering a career in ecology?
Many biology students entering college are interested in medicine or biotechnology. It's often not till their senior year that they realize that ecology is so interesting. In the career lecture I give in class, I tell students about all the different careers you can have with degrees in ecology and environmental sciences. Most students don't realize how many options there are. You can work for a large company or do consulting work. You can work for government agencies such as the Department of Agriculture, the Environmental Protection Agency, and the Fish and Wildlife Service. Every state has different natural resource agencies that need good biologists, too. You can also work internationally for groups such as the World Health Organization. There are so many useful opportunities beyond becoming a faculty member.

Why is ecology important for the general public?
An undergraduate working in my lab is a premed, yet this summer he's doing an ecological project on the Barton Springs salamander. I asked him if he could see links between human health and ecology, and he said, "Well, humans need clean water, and this salamander does too, so keeping the salamander healthy keeps us healthy." I was thrilled that a summer's field work has given someone in the health sciences the insight that for us to be healthy we need to have a healthy environment. Ecologists are one of the only groups of people who study how environmental health relates to climate change and nitrogen pollution from cars and other things that humans are doing that affect the environment. What specific impacts do those changes have? Ecologists are the scientists answering that important question.

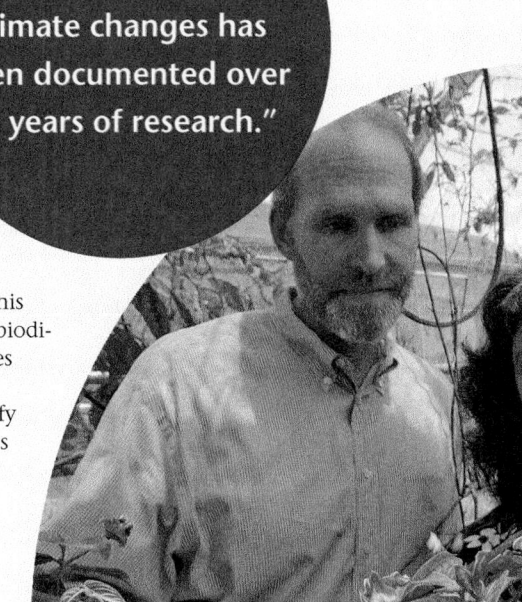

Camille Parmesan (center) with Rob Jackson (left) and Jane Reece

52

An Introduction to Ecology and the Biosphere

▲ **Figure 52.1 What threatens this amphibian's survival?**

KEY CONCEPTS

52.1 Earth's climate varies by latitude and season and is changing rapidly

52.2 The structure and distribution of terrestrial biomes are controlled by climate and disturbance

52.3 Aquatic biomes are diverse and dynamic systems that cover most of Earth

52.4 Interactions between organisms and the environment limit the distribution of species

OVERVIEW

Discovering Ecology

When University of Delaware undergraduate Justin Yeager spent his summer abroad in Costa Rica, all he wanted was to see the tropical rain forest and to practice his Spanish. Instead, he rediscovered the variable harlequin toad (*Atelopus varius*), a species thought to be extinct in the mountain slopes of Costa

Rica and Panama where it once lived (**Figure 52.1**). During the 1980s and 1990s, roughly two-thirds of the 82 known species of harlequin toads vanished. Scientists think that a disease-causing chytrid fungus, *Batrachochytrium dendrobatidis* (see Figure 31.26), contributed to many of these extinctions. Why was the fungus suddenly thriving in the rain forest? Cloudier days and warmer nights associated with global warming appear to have created an environment ideal for its success. As of 2009, the species that Yeager found was surviving as a single known population of fewer than 100 individuals.

What environmental factors limit the geographic distribution of harlequin toads? How do variations in their food supply or interactions with other species, such as pathogens, affect the size of their population? Questions like these are the subject of **ecology** (from the Greek *oikos*, home, and *logos*, study), the scientific study of the interactions between organisms and the environment. Ecological interactions occur at a hierarchy of scales that ecologists study, from single organisms to the globe (**Figure 52.2**).

Ecology's roots are in our basic human interest in observing other organisms. Naturalists, including Aristotle and Darwin, have long studied the living world and systematically recorded their observations. However, modern ecology involves more than observation. It is a rigorous experimental science that requires a breadth of biological knowledge. Ecologists generate hypotheses, manipulate environmental variables, and observe the outcome. In this unit, you will encounter many examples of ecological experiments, whose complex challenges have made ecologists innovators in experimental design and statistical inference.

In addition to providing a conceptual framework for understanding the field of ecology, Figure 52.2 provides the organizational framework for our final unit. In this chapter, we first describe Earth's climate and the importance of climate and other physical factors in determining the location of major life zones on land and in the oceans. We then examine how ecologists determine what controls the distribution and abundance of individual species. The next three chapters investigate population, community, and ecosystem ecology in detail, including approaches for restoring degraded ecosystems. The final chapter explores conservation biology and global ecology as we consider how ecologists apply biological knowledge to predict the global consequences of human activities and to conserve Earth's biodiversity.

CONCEPT 52.1

Earth's climate varies by latitude and season and is changing rapidly

The most significant influence on the distribution of organisms on land and in the oceans is **climate**, the long-term, prevailing weather conditions in a given area. Four physical

Exploring The Scope of Ecological Research

Ecologists work at different levels of the biological hierarchy, from individual organisms to the planet. Here we present a sample research question for each level of the hierarchy.

Global Ecology

The **biosphere** is the global ecosystem—the sum of all the planet's ecosystems and landscapes. **Global ecology** examines how the regional exchange of energy and materials influences the functioning and distribution of organisms across the biosphere.

◄ How does ocean circulation affect the global distribution of crustaceans?

Landscape Ecology

A **landscape** (or seascape) is a mosaic of connected ecosystems. Research in **landscape ecology** focuses on the factors controlling exchanges of energy, materials, and organisms across multiple ecosystems.

◄ To what extent do the trees lining a river serve as corridors of dispersal for animals?

Ecosystem Ecology

An **ecosystem** is the community of organisms in an area and the physical factors with which those organisms interact. **Ecosystem ecology** emphasizes energy flow and chemical cycling between organisms and the environment.

◄ What factors control photosynthetic productivity in a temperate grassland ecosystem?

Community Ecology

A **community** is a group of populations of different species in an area. **Community ecology** examines how interactions between species, such as predation and competition, affect community structure and organization.

◄ What factors influence the diversity of species that make up a forest?

Population Ecology

A **population** is a group of individuals of the same species living in an area. **Population ecology** analyzes factors that affect population size and how and why it changes through time.

◄ What environmental factors affect the reproductive rate of locusts?

Organismal Ecology

Organismal ecology, which includes the subdisciplines of physiological, evolutionary, and behavioral ecology, is concerned with how an organism's structure, physiology, and behavior meet the challenges posed by its environment.

◄ How do hammerhead sharks select a mate?

Exploring Global Climate Patterns

Latitudinal Variation in Sunlight Intensity

Earth's curved shape causes latitudinal variation in the intensity of sunlight. Because sunlight strikes the **tropics** (those regions that lie between 23.5° north latitude and 23.5° south latitude) most directly, more heat and light per unit of surface area are delivered there. At higher latitudes, sunlight strikes Earth at an oblique angle, and thus the light energy is more diffuse on Earth's surface.

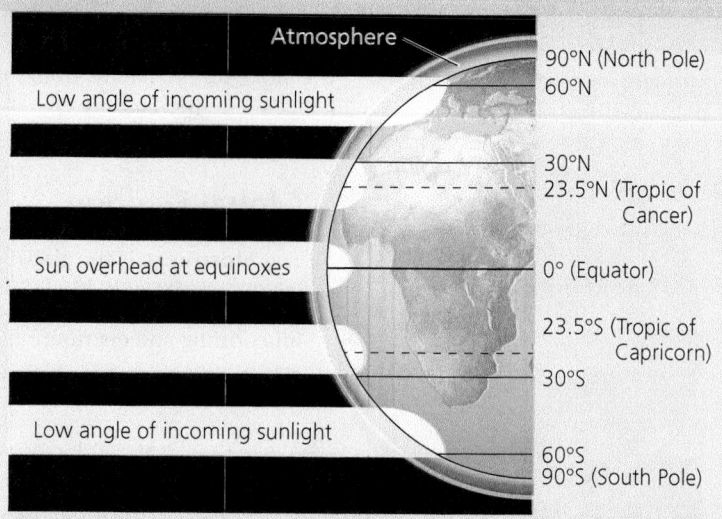

Global Air Circulation and Precipitation Patterns

Intense solar radiation near the equator initiates a global pattern of air circulation and precipitation. High temperatures in the tropics evaporate water from Earth's surface and cause warm, wet air masses to rise (blue arrows) and flow toward the poles. The rising air masses release much of their water content, creating abundant precipitation in tropical regions. The high-altitude air masses, now dry, descend (tan arrows) toward Earth around 30° north and south, absorbing moisture from the land and creating an arid climate conducive to the development of the deserts that are common at those latitudes. Some of the descending air then flows toward the poles. At latitudes around 60° north and south, the air masses again rise and release abundant precipitation (though less than in the tropics). Some of the cold, dry rising air then flows to the poles, where it descends and flows back toward the equator, absorbing moisture and creating the comparatively rainless and bitterly cold climates of the polar regions.

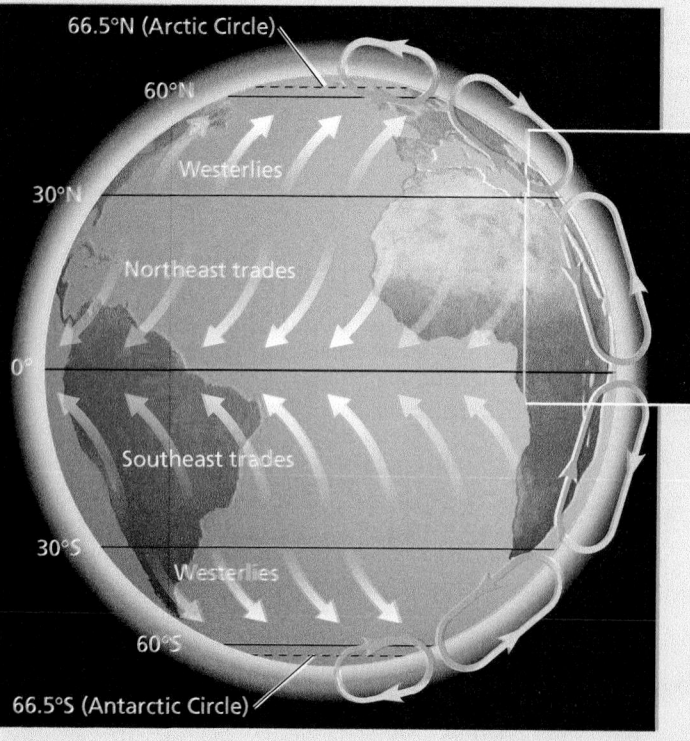

Air flowing close to Earth's surface creates predictable global wind patterns. As Earth rotates on its axis, land near the equator moves faster than that at the poles, deflecting the winds from the vertical paths shown above and creating the more easterly and westerly flows shown at left. Cooling trade winds blow from east to west in the tropics; prevailing westerlies blow from west to east in the temperate zones, defined as the regions between the Tropic of Cancer and the Arctic Circle and between the Tropic of Capricorn and the Antarctic Circle.

factors—temperature, precipitation, sunlight, and wind—are particularly important components of climate. In this section, we will describe climate patterns at two scales: **macroclimate**, patterns on the global, regional, and landscape level; and **microclimate**, very fine, localized patterns, such as those encountered by the community of organisms that live in the microhabitat beneath a fallen log. First let's examine Earth's macroclimate.

Global Climate Patterns

Global climate patterns are determined largely by the input of solar energy and Earth's movement in space. The sun warms the atmosphere, land, and water. This warming establishes the temperature variations, cycles of air and water movement, and evaporation of water that cause dramatic latitudinal variations in climate. **Figure 52.3** summarizes Earth's climate patterns and how they are formed.

Regional and Local Effects on Climate

Climate patterns can be modified by many factors, including seasonal variation in climate, large bodies of water, and mountain ranges. We will examine each of these factors in more detail.

Seasonality

As described in **Figure 52.4**, Earth's tilted axis of rotation and its annual passage around the sun cause strong seasonal cycles in middle to high latitudes. In addition to these global changes in day length, solar radiation, and temperature, the changing angle of the sun over the course of the year affects local environments. For example, the belts of wet and dry air on either side of the equator move slightly northward and southward with the changing angle of the sun, producing marked wet and dry seasons around 20° north and 20° south latitude, where many tropical deciduous forests grow. In addition, seasonal changes in wind patterns alter ocean currents, sometimes causing the upwelling of cold water from deep ocean layers. This nutrient-rich water stimulates the growth of surface-dwelling phytoplankton and the organisms that feed on them.

Bodies of Water

Ocean currents influence climate along the coasts of continents by heating or cooling overlying air masses that pass across the land. Coastal regions are also generally wetter than inland areas at the same latitude. The cool, misty climate produced by the cold California Current that flows southward

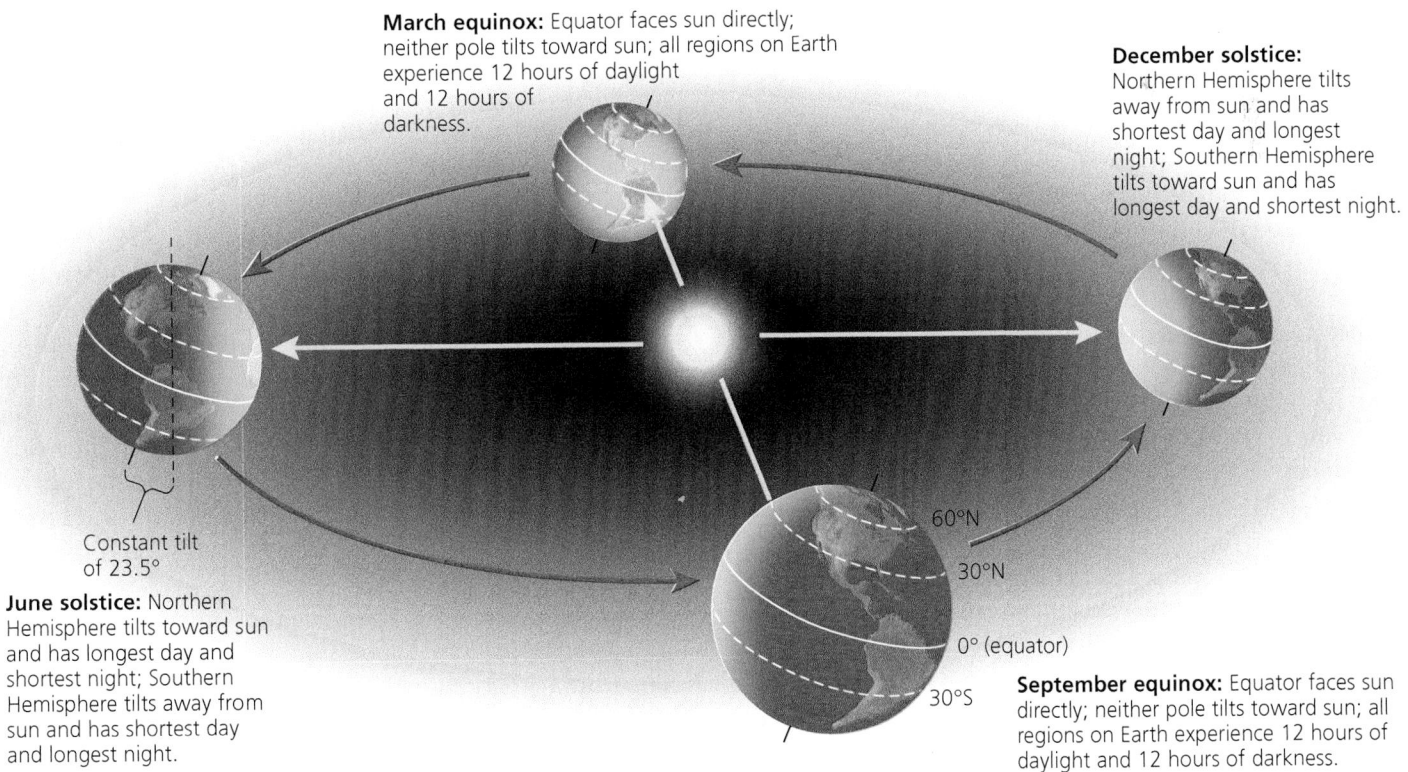

March equinox: Equator faces sun directly; neither pole tilts toward sun; all regions on Earth experience 12 hours of daylight and 12 hours of darkness.

December solstice: Northern Hemisphere tilts away from sun and has shortest day and longest night; Southern Hemisphere tilts toward sun and has longest day and shortest night.

Constant tilt of 23.5°

June solstice: Northern Hemisphere tilts toward sun and has longest day and shortest night; Southern Hemisphere tilts away from sun and has shortest day and longest night.

60°N
30°N
0° (equator)
30°S

September equinox: Equator faces sun directly; neither pole tilts toward sun; all regions on Earth experience 12 hours of daylight and 12 hours of darkness.

▲ **Figure 52.4 Seasonal variation in sunlight intensity.** Because Earth is tilted on its axis relative to its plane of orbit around the sun, the intensity of solar radiation varies seasonally. This variation is smallest in the tropics and increases toward the poles.

▲ **Figure 52.5 Global circulation of surface water in the oceans.** Water is warmed at the equator and flows north and south toward the poles, where it cools. Note the similarities between the direction of water circulation in the gyres and the direction of the trade winds in Figure 52.3.

along western North America supports a coniferous rain forest ecosystem along much of the continent's Pacific coast and large redwood groves farther south. Conversely, the west coast of northern Europe has a mild climate because the Gulf Stream carries warm water from the equator to the North Atlantic **(Figure 52.5)**. As a result, northwestern Europe is warmer during winter than southeastern Canada, which is farther south but is cooled by the Labrador Current flowing south from the coast of Greenland.

Because of the high specific heat of water (see Chapter 3), oceans and large lakes tend to moderate the climate of nearby land. During a hot day, when land is warmer than the water, air over the land heats up and rises, drawing a cool breeze from the water across the land **(Figure 52.6)**. In contrast, because temperatures drop more quickly over land than over water at night, air over the now warmer water rises, drawing cooler air from the land back out over the water and replacing it with warmer air from offshore. This local moderation of climate can be limited to the coast itself, however. In regions such as southern California and southwestern Australia, cool, dry ocean breezes in summer are warmed when they contact the land, absorbing moisture and creating a hot, arid climate just a few kilometers inland (see Figure 3.5). This

climate pattern also occurs around the Mediterranean Sea, which gives it the name *Mediterranean climate*.

Mountains

Like large bodies of water, mountains influence air flow over land. When warm, moist air approaches a mountain, the air rises and cools, releasing moisture on the windward side of the peak (see Figure 52.6). On the leeward side, cooler, dry air descends, absorbing moisture and producing a "rain shadow." This leeward rain shadow determines where many deserts are found, including the Great Basin and the Mojave Desert of western North America, the Gobi Desert of Asia, and the small deserts found in the southwest corners of some Caribbean islands.

Mountains also affect the amount of sunlight reaching an area and thus the local temperature and rainfall. South-facing slopes in the Northern Hemisphere receive more sunlight than north-facing slopes and are therefore warmer and drier. These physical differences influence species distributions locally. In many mountains of western North America, spruce and other conifers grow on the cooler north-facing slopes, but shrubby, drought-resistant plants inhabit the south-facing slopes. In addition, every 1,000-m increase in elevation

② Air that encounters mountains flows upward, cools at higher altitudes, and releases water as rain and snow.

◀ **Figure 52.6 How large bodies of water and mountains affect climate.** This figure illustrates what can happen on a hot summer day.

① Cool air flows inland from the water, moderating temperatures near the shore.

③ Less moisture is left in the air reaching the leeward side, which therefore has little precipitation. This rain shadow can create a desert on the back side of the mountain range.

Leeward side of mountains

Mountain range

Ocean

produces an average temperature drop of approximately 6°C, equivalent to that produced by an 880-km increase in latitude. This is one reason that high-elevation communities at one latitude can be similar to those at lower elevations much farther from the equator.

Microclimate

Many features in the environment influence microclimate by casting shade, altering evaporation from soil, or changing wind patterns. Forest trees often moderate the microclimate below them. Cleared areas therefore typically experience greater temperature extremes than the forest interior because of greater solar radiation and wind currents that arise from the rapid heating and cooling of open land. Within a forest, low-lying ground is usually wetter than higher ground and tends to be occupied by different tree species. A log or large stone can shelter organisms such as salamanders, worms, and insects, buffering them from the extremes of temperature and moisture. Every environment on Earth is characterized by a mosaic of small-scale differences in **abiotic**, or nonliving, factors, the chemical and physical attributes, such as temperature, light, water, and nutrients, that influence the distribution and abundance of organisms. Later in this chapter, we will also examine how all of the **biotic**, or living, factors—the other organisms that are part of an individual's environment—similarly influence the distribution and abundance of life on Earth.

Global Climate Change

Because climatic variables affect the geographic ranges of most plants and animals, any large-scale change in Earth's climate profoundly affects the biosphere. In fact, such a large-scale climate "experiment" is already under way, a topic we will examine in more detail in Chapter 56. The burning of

fossil fuels and deforestation are increasing the concentrations of carbon dioxide and other greenhouse gases in the atmosphere. As a result, Earth has warmed an average of 0.8°C (1.4°F) since 1900 and is projected to warm 1–6°C (2–11°F) more by the year 2100.

One way to predict the possible effects of future climate change on geographic ranges is to look back at the changes that have occurred in temperate regions since the last ice age ended. Until about 16,000 years ago, continental glaciers covered much of North America and Eurasia. As the climate warmed and the glaciers retreated, tree distributions expanded northward. A detailed record of these changes is captured in fossil pollen deposited in lakes and ponds. (Recall from Chapter 38 that wind and animals sometimes disperse pollen and seeds over great distances.) If researchers can determine the climatic limits of current distributions of organisms, they can make predictions about how those distributions may change with continued climatic warming.

A fundamental question when applying this approach to plants is whether seeds can disperse quickly enough to sustain the range shift of each species as climate changes. Fossil pollen shows that species with winged seeds that disperse relatively far from a parent tree, such as the sugar maple (*Acer saccharum*), expanded rapidly into the northeastern United States and Canada after the last ice age ended. In contrast, the northward range expansion of the eastern hemlock (*Tsuga canadensis*), whose seeds lack wings, was delayed nearly 2,500 years compared with the shift in suitable habitat.

Will plants and other species be able to keep up with the much more rapid warming projected for this century? Ecologists have attempted to answer this question for the American beech (*Fagus grandifolia*). Their models predict that the northern limit of the beech's range may move 700–900 km northward in the next century, and its southern range limit will

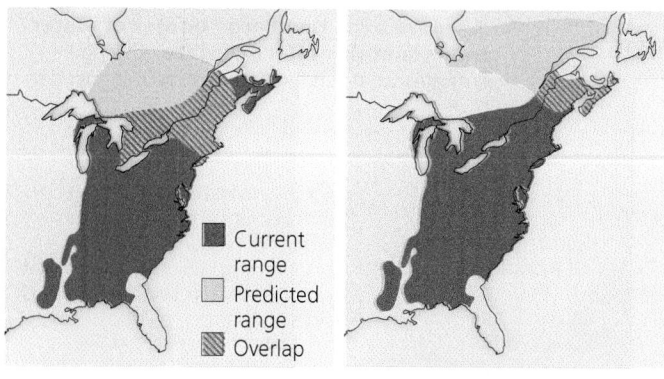

(a) 4.5°C warming over next century

(b) 6.5°C warming over next century

- ■ Current range
- ░ Predicted range
- ▨ Overlap

▲ **Figure 52.7 Current range and predicted range for the American beech under two climate-change scenarios.**

? *The predicted range in each scenario is based on climate factors alone. What other factors might alter the distribution of this species?*

shift even more. The current and predicted geographic ranges of this species under two different climate-change scenarios are illustrated in **Figure 52.7.** If these predictions are even approximately correct, the beech's range must shift 7–9 km northward per year to keep pace with the warming climate. However, since the end of the last ice age, the beech has moved at a rate of only 0.2 km per year. Without human help in moving to new habitats, species such as the American beech may have much smaller ranges or even become extinct.

Changes in the distributions of species are already evident in many well-studied groups of terrestrial, marine, and freshwater organisms, consistent with the signature of a warmer world. Ecologist Camille Parmesan (see interview on pp. 1142–1143) has studied range changes in European butterfly species, including the silver-washed fritillary (*Argynnis paphia*; see **Figure 52.8**). Parmesan and her colleagues found that the

- ■ Expanded range in 1997
- ░ Range in 1970

▲ **Figure 52.8 Northward range expansion of the silver-washed fritillary in Sweden and Finland.** This butterfly is one of many European species whose northern range limits have moved farther north in recent decades.

northern range limits of 22 of the 35 butterfly species studied had shifted farther north by 35–240 km over the time periods for which records exist, in some cases beginning in 1900. And other scientists have reported that a Pacific diatom species, *Neodenticula seminae*, recently has colonized the Atlantic Ocean for the first time in 800,000 years. As Arctic sea ice has receded in the past decade, the increased flow of water from the Pacific has swept these diatoms around Canada and into the Atlantic, where they quickly became established. The observation that many species are on the move in the face of climate change illustrates the importance of climate in determining species distributions, a topic we will explore further in the next section.

CONCEPT CHECK 52.1

1. Explain how the sun's unequal heating of Earth's surface leads to the development of deserts around 30° north and south of the equator.
2. What are some of the differences in microclimate between an unplanted agricultural field and a nearby stream corridor with trees?
3. **WHAT IF?** Changes in Earth's climate at the end of the last ice age happened gradually, taking centuries to thousands of years. If the current global warming happens very quickly, as predicted, how may this rapid climate change affect the ability of long-lived trees to evolve, compared with annual plants, which have much shorter generation times?
4. **MAKE CONNECTIONS** In Concept 10.4 (pp. 199–201), you learned about the important differences between C_3 and C_4 plants. Focusing just on the effects of temperature, would you expect the global distribution of C_4 plants to expand or contract as Earth becomes warmer? Why?

For suggested answers, see Appendix A.

CONCEPT 52.2

The structure and distribution of terrestrial biomes are controlled by climate and disturbance

Throughout this book, you have seen many examples of how climate and other factors influence where individual species are found on Earth (see Figure 30.5, for instance). We turn now to the role of climate in determining the nature and location of Earth's **biomes**, major life zones characterized by vegetation type (in terrestrial biomes) or by the physical environment (in aquatic biomes). We first examine the influence of climate on terrestrial biomes, surveying aquatic systems later in the chapter.

▲ **Figure 52.9 The distribution of major terrestrial biomes.** Although biomes are mapped here with sharp boundaries, biomes actually grade into one another, sometimes over large areas.

Legend:
- Tropical forest
- Savanna
- Desert
- Chaparral
- Temperate grassland
- Temperate broadleaf forest
- Northern coniferous forest
- Tundra
- High mountains
- Polar ice

Climate and Terrestrial Biomes

Because of the latitudinal patterns of climate described in Figure 52.3, terrestrial biomes show strong latitudinal patterns in where they are found (Figure 52.9). One way to highlight the importance of climate on the distribution of biomes is to construct a **climograph**, a plot of the annual mean temperature and precipitation in a particular region. Figure 52.10 is a climograph for some of the biomes found in North America. Notice, for instance, that the range of precipitation in northern coniferous and temperate forests is similar but that temperate forests are generally warmer. Grasslands are typically drier than either kind of forest, and deserts are drier still.

Factors other than mean temperature and precipitation also play a role in determining where biomes exist. For example, some areas in North America with a particular combination of temperature and precipitation support a temperate broadleaf forest, but other areas with similar values for these variables support a coniferous forest (see the overlap in Figure 52.10). How might we explain this variation? First, remember that the climograph is based on annual *averages*. Often, however, the *pattern* of climatic variation is as important as the average climate. Some areas may receive regular precipitation throughout the year, whereas other areas may have distinct wet and dry seasons. A similar phenomenon may occur for temperature. In addition, other abiotic characteristics, such as the type of bedrock in an area, may greatly affect mineral nutrient availability and soil structure, which in turn affect the kind of vegetation that can grow.

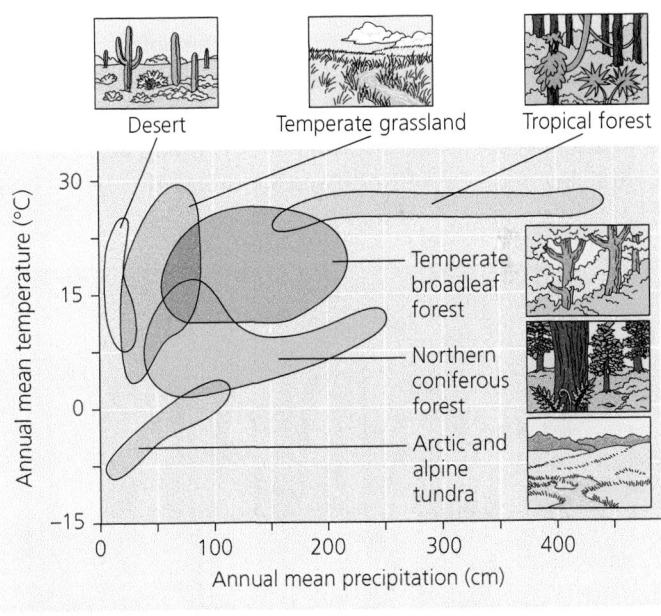

▲ **Figure 52.10 A climograph for some major types of biomes in North America.** The areas plotted here encompass the ranges of annual mean temperature and precipitation in the biomes.

General Features of Terrestrial Biomes

Most terrestrial biomes are named for major physical or climatic features and for their predominant vegetation. Temperate grasslands, for instance, are generally found in middle latitudes, where the climate is more moderate than in the tropics or polar regions, and are dominated by various grass species (see Figure 52.9). Each biome is also characterized by microorganisms, fungi, and animals adapted to that particular environment. Temperate grasslands are usually more likely than temperate forests to be populated by large grazing mammals and to have arbuscular mycorrhizal fungi (see Figure 37.13).

Although Figure 52.9 shows distinct boundaries between the biomes, terrestrial biomes usually grade into each other without sharp boundaries. The area of intergradation, called an **ecotone**, may be wide or narrow.

Vertical layering is an important feature of terrestrial biomes, and the shapes and sizes of plants largely define that layering. In many forests, the layers from top to bottom consist of the upper **canopy**, the low-tree layer, the shrub understory, the ground layer of herbaceous plants, the forest floor (litter layer), and the root layer. Nonforest biomes have similar, though usually less pronounced, layers. Grasslands have an herbaceous layer of grasses and forbs (small broadleaf plants), a litter layer, and a root layer. Layering of vegetation provides many different habitats for animals, which sometimes exist in well-defined feeding groups, from the insectivorous birds and bats that feed above canopies to the small mammals, numerous worms, and arthropods that search for food in the litter and root layers below.

The species composition of each kind of biome varies from one location to another. For instance, in the northern coniferous forest (taiga) of North America, red spruce is common in the east but does not occur in most other areas, where black spruce and white spruce are abundant. As Figure 52.11 shows, cacti living in deserts of North and South America appear very similar to plants called euphorbs found in African deserts. But since cacti and euphorbs belong to different evolutionary lineages, their similarities are due to convergent evolution (see Concept 22.3).

Disturbance and Terrestrial Biomes

Biomes are dynamic, and disturbance rather than stability tends to be the rule. In ecological terms, **disturbance** is an event such as a storm, fire, or human activity that changes a community, removing organisms from it and altering resource availability. For instance, frequent fires can kill woody plants and keep a savanna from becoming the woodland that climate alone would support. Hurricanes and other storms create openings for new species in many tropical and temperate forests. Fires and outbreaks of pests, such as pine beetles and spruce budworms, produce gaps in northern coniferous forests that allow deciduous species, including aspen and birch, to grow. As a result of disturbances, biomes often exhibit extensive patchiness, with several different communities represented in a single area.

In many biomes, even the dominant plants depend on periodic disturbance. Natural wildfires are an integral component of grasslands, savannas, chaparral, and many coniferous forests. In North America, fires are no longer common across much of the Great Plains because tallgrass prairie ecosystems have been converted to agricultural fields that rarely burn. Before agricultural and urban development, much of the southeastern United States was dominated by a single conifer species, the longleaf pine. Without periodic burning, broadleaf trees tended to replace the pines. Forest managers now use fire as a tool to help maintain many coniferous forests.

Figure 52.12, on the next four pages, summarizes the major features of terrestrial biomes. As you read about the characteristics of each biome, remember that humans have altered much of Earth's surface, replacing natural communities with urban and agricultural ones. Most of the eastern United States, for example, is classified as temperate broadleaf forest, but little of that original forest remains.

▲ *Euphorbia canariensis*

◀ *Cereus peruvianus*

▲ Figure 52.11 **Convergent evolution in a cactus and a euphorb.** *Cereus peruvianus*, a cactus, is found in the Americas; *Euphorbia canariensis*, a euphorb, is native to the Canary Islands, off the northwest coast of Africa.

CONCEPT CHECK 52.2

1. Based on the climograph in Figure 52.10, what mainly differentiates temperate grassland from temperate broadleaf forest?
2. Identify the natural biome in which you live, and summarize its abiotic and biotic characteristics. Do these reflect your actual surroundings? Explain.
3. **WHAT IF?** If global warming increases average temperatures on Earth by 4°C in this century, predict which biome is most likely to replace tundra in some locations as a result. Explain your answer.

For suggested answers, see Appendix A.

Exploring Terrestrial Biomes

Tropical Forest

Distribution Equatorial and subequatorial regions

Precipitation In **tropical rain forests**, rainfall is relatively constant, about 200–400 cm annually. In **tropical dry forests**, precipitation is highly seasonal, about 150–200 cm annually, with a six- to seven-month dry season.

Temperature High year-round, averaging 25–29°C with little seasonal variation

Plants Tropical forests are vertically layered, and competition for light is intense. Layers in rain forests include emergent trees that grow above a closed canopy, the canopy trees, one or two layers of subcanopy trees, and layers of shrubs and herbs (small, nonwoody plants). There are generally fewer layers in tropical dry forests. Broadleaf evergreen trees are dominant in tropical rain forests, whereas many tropical dry forest trees drop their leaves during the dry season.

Epiphytes such as bromeliads and orchids generally cover tropical forest trees but are less abundant in dry forests. Thorny shrubs and succulent plants are common in some tropical dry forests.

Animals Earth's tropical forests are home to millions of species, including an estimated 5–30 million still undescribed species of insects, spiders, and other arthropods. In fact, animal diversity is higher in tropical forests than in any other terrestrial biome. The animals, including amphibians, birds and other reptiles, mammals, and arthropods, are adapted to the vertically layered environment and are often inconspicuous.

Human Impact Humans long ago established thriving communities in tropical forests. Rapid population growth leading to agriculture and development is now destroying many tropical forests.

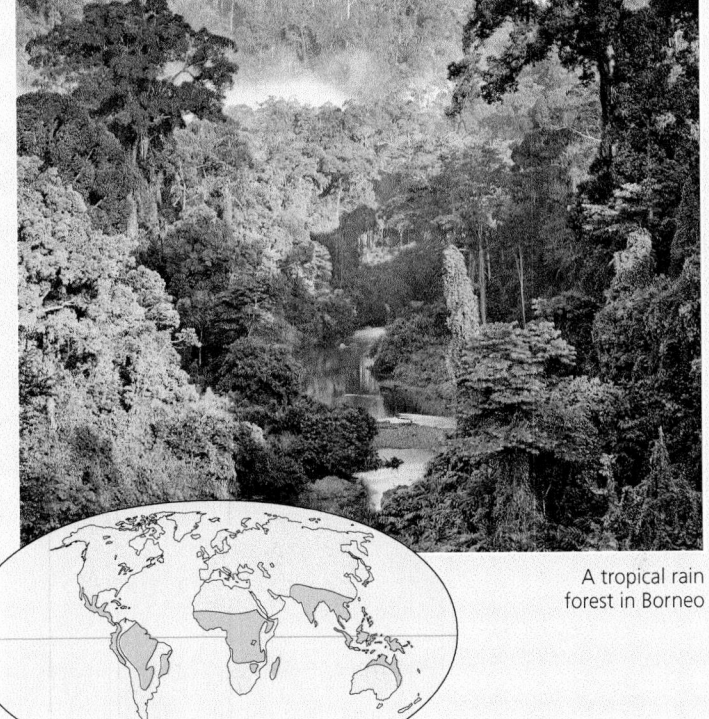

A tropical rain forest in Borneo

Desert

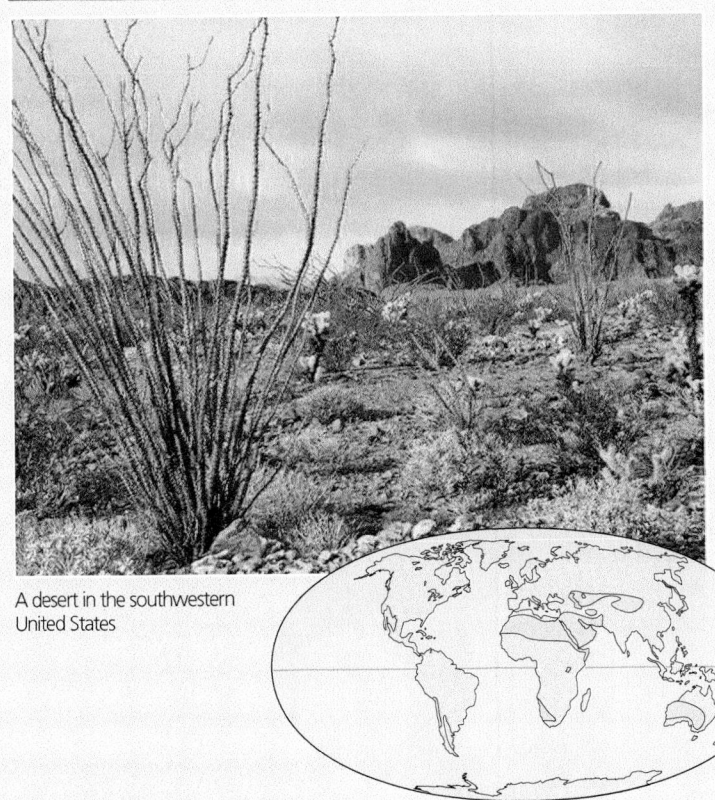

A desert in the southwestern United States

Distribution **Deserts** occur in bands near 30° north and south latitude or at other latitudes in the interior of continents (for instance, the Gobi Desert of north-central Asia).

Precipitation Precipitation is low and highly variable, generally less than 30 cm per year.

Temperature Temperature is variable seasonally and daily. Maximum air temperature in hot deserts may exceed 50°C; in cold deserts air temperature may fall below –30°C.

Plants Desert landscapes are dominated by low, widely scattered vegetation; the proportion of bare ground is high compared with other terrestrial biomes. The plants include succulents such as cacti or euphorbs, deeply rooted shrubs, and herbs that grow during the infrequent moist periods. Desert plant adaptations include heat and desiccation tolerance, water storage, and reduced leaf surface area. Physical defenses, such as spines, and chemical defenses, such as toxins in the leaves of shrubs, are common. Many of the plants exhibit C_4 or CAM photosynthesis (see Chapter 10).

Animals Common desert animals include snakes and lizards, scorpions, ants, beetles, migratory and resident birds, and seed-eating rodents. Many species are nocturnal. Water conservation is a common adaptation, with some species surviving solely on water from breaking down carbohydrates in seeds.

Human Impact Long-distance transport of water and deep groundwater wells have allowed humans to maintain substantial populations in deserts. Urbanization and conversion to irrigated agriculture have reduced the natural biodiversity of some deserts.

Exploring Terrestrial Biomes

Savanna

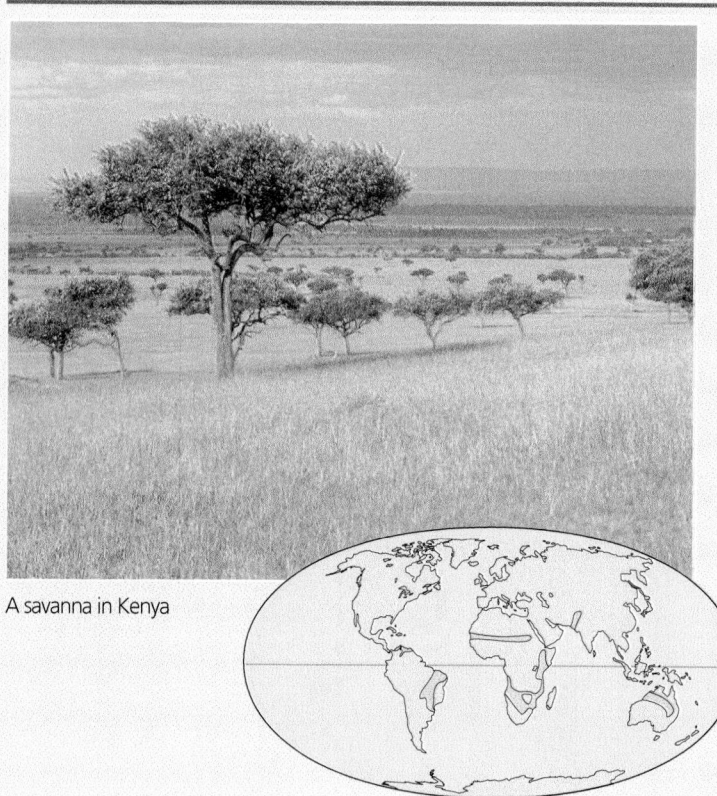

A savanna in Kenya

Distribution Equatorial and subequatorial regions

Precipitation Rainfall, which is seasonal, averages 30–50 cm per year. The dry season can last up to eight or nine months.

Temperature The **savanna** is warm year-round, averaging 24–29°C, but with somewhat more seasonal variation than in tropical forests.

Plants The scattered trees found at different densities in the savanna often are thorny and have small leaves, an apparent adaptation to the relatively dry conditions. Fires are common in the dry season, and the dominant plant species are fire-adapted and tolerant of seasonal drought. Grasses and small nonwoody plants called forbs, which make up most of the ground cover, grow rapidly in response to seasonal rains and are toler-ant of grazing by large mammals and other herbivores.

Animals Large plant-eating mammals, such as wildebeests and zebras, and predators, including lions and hyenas, are common inhabitants. However, the dominant herbivores are actually insects, especially termites. During seasonal droughts, grazing mammals often migrate to parts of the savanna with more forage and scattered watering holes.

Human Impact There is evidence that the earliest humans lived in savannas. Fires set by humans may help maintain this biome, though overly frequent fires reduce tree regeneration by killing the seedlings and saplings. Cattle ranching and overhunting have led to declines in large-mammal populations.

Chaparral

Distribution This biome occurs in midlatitude coastal regions on several continents, and its many names reflect its far-flung distribution: **chaparral** in North America, *matorral* in Spain and Chile, *garigue* and *maquis* in southern France, and *fynbos* in South Africa.

Precipitation Precipitation is highly seasonal, with rainy winters and dry summers. Annual precipitation generally falls within the range of 30–50 cm.

Temperature Fall, winter, and spring are cool, with average temperatures in the range of 10–12°C. Average summer temperature can reach 30°C, and daytime maximum temperature can exceed 40°C.

Plants Chaparral is dominated by shrubs and small trees, along with many kinds of grasses and herbs. Plant diversity is high, with many species confined to a specific, relatively small geo-graphic area. Adaptations to drought include the tough evergreen leaves of woody plants, which reduce water loss. Adaptations to fire are also prominent. Some of the shrubs produce seeds that will germinate only after a hot fire; food reserves stored in their fire-resistant roots enable them to resprout quickly and use nutrients released by the fire.

Animals Native mammals include browsers, such as deer and goats, that feed on twigs and buds of woody vegetation, and a high diversity of small mammals. Chaparral areas also support many species of amphibians, birds and other reptiles, and insects.

Human Impact Chaparral areas have been heavily settled and reduced through conversion to agriculture and urbanization. Humans contribute to the fires that sweep across the chaparral.

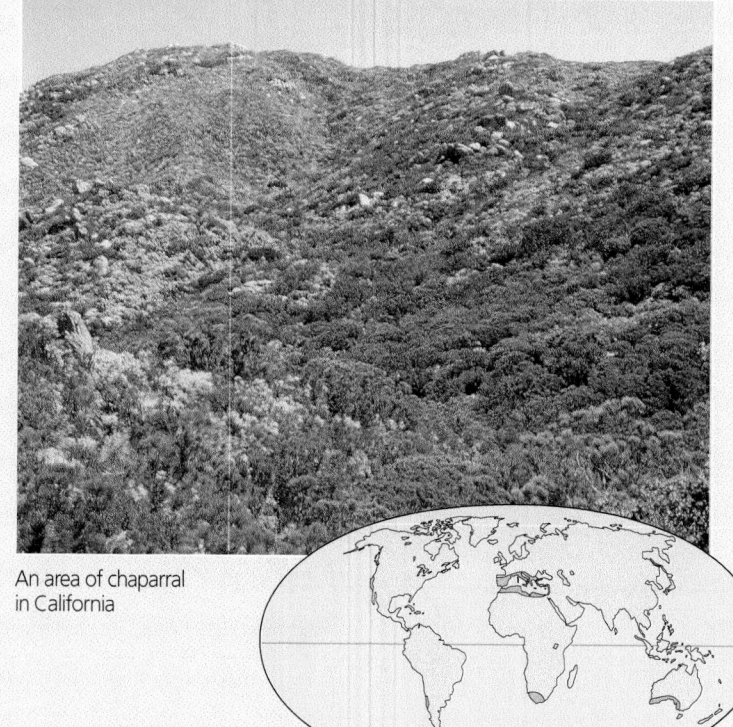

An area of chaparral in California

Temperate Grassland

Distribution The veldts of South Africa, the *puszta* of Hungary, the pampas of Argentina and Uruguay, the steppes of Russia, and the plains and prairies of central North America are examples of **temperate grasslands**.

Precipitation Precipitation is often highly seasonal, with relatively dry winters and wet summers. Annual precipitation generally averages between 30 and 100 cm. Periodic drought is common.

Temperature Winters are generally cold, with average temperatures frequently falling well below –10°C. Summers, with average temperatures often approaching 30°C, are hot.

Plants The dominant plants are grasses and forbs, which vary in height from a few centimeters to 2 m in tallgrass prairie. Many grassland plants have adaptations that help them survive periodic, protracted droughts and fire. For example, grasses can sprout quickly following fire. Grazing by large mammals helps prevent establishment of woody shrubs and trees.

Animals Native mammals include large grazers such as bison and wild horses. Temperate grasslands are also inhabited by a wide variety of burrowing mammals, such as prairie dogs in North America.

Human Impact Deep, fertile soils make temperate grasslands ideal places for agriculture, especially for growing grains. As a consequence, most grassland in North America and much of Eurasia has been converted to farmland. In some drier grasslands, cattle and other grazers have turned parts of the biome into desert.

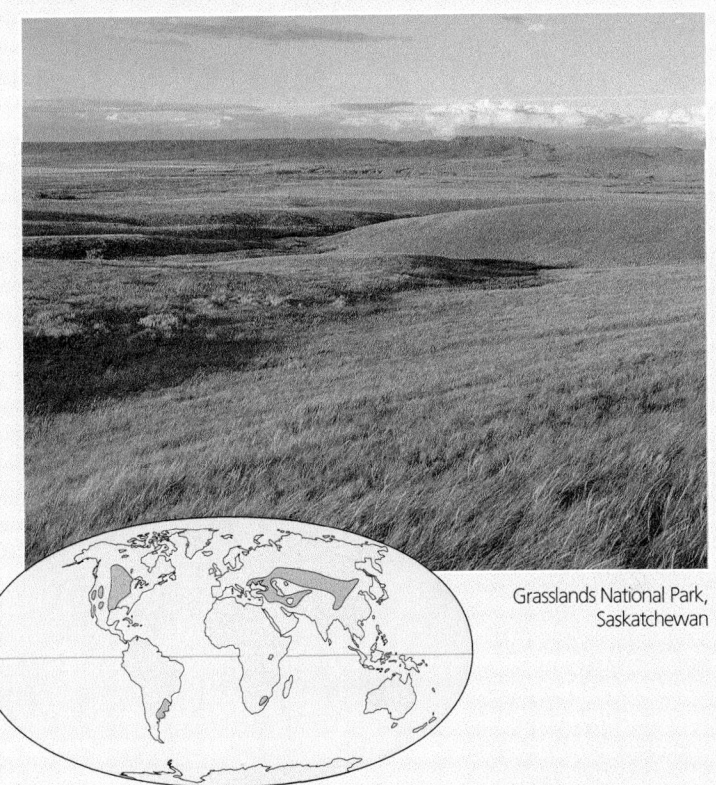

Grasslands National Park, Saskatchewan

Northern Coniferous Forest

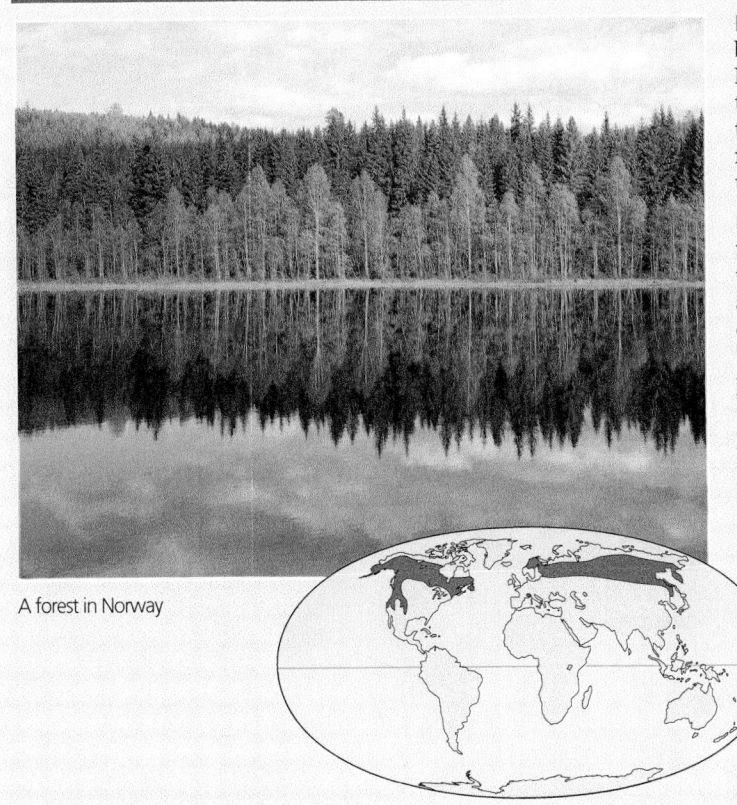

A forest in Norway

Distribution Extending in a broad band across northern North America and Eurasia to the edge of the arctic tundra, the **northern coniferous forest**, or *taiga*, is the largest terrestrial biome on Earth.

Precipitation Annual precipitation generally ranges from 30 to 70 cm, and periodic droughts are common. However, some coastal coniferous forests of the U.S. Pacific Northwest are temperate rain forests that may receive over 300 cm of annual precipitation.

Temperature Winters are usually cold; summers may be hot. Some areas of coniferous forest in Siberia typically range in temperature from –50°C in winter to over 20°C in summer.

Plants Northern coniferous forests are dominated by cone-bearing trees, such as pine, spruce, fir, and hemlock, some of which depend on fire to regenerate. The conical shape of many conifers prevents too much snow from accumulating and breaking their branches, and their needle- or scale-like leaves reduce water loss. The diversity of plants in the shrub and herb layers of these forests is lower than in temperate broadleaf forests.

Animals While many migratory birds nest in northern coniferous forests, other species reside there year-round. The mammals of this biome, which include moose, brown bears, and Siberian tigers, are diverse. Periodic outbreaks of insects that feed on the dominant trees can kill vast tracts of trees.

Human Impact Although they have not been heavily settled by human populations, northern coniferous forests are being logged at an alarming rate, and the old-growth stands of these trees may soon disappear.

Exploring Terrestrial Biomes

Temperate Broadleaf Forest

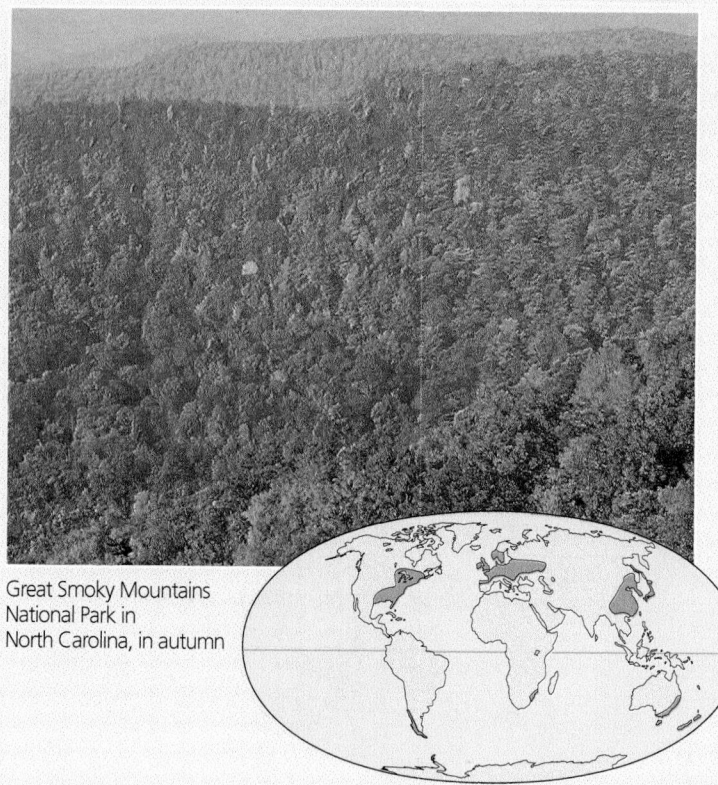

Great Smoky Mountains National Park in North Carolina, in autumn

Distribution Found mainly at midlatitudes in the Northern Hemisphere, with smaller areas in Chile, South Africa, Australia, and New Zealand

Precipitation Precipitation can average from about 70 to over 200 cm annually. Significant amounts fall during all seasons, including summer rain and, in some forests, winter snow.

Temperature Winter temperatures average around 0°C. Summers, with maximum temperatures near 35°C, are hot and humid.

Plants A mature **temperate broadleaf forest** has distinct vertical layers, including a closed canopy, one or two strata of understory trees, a shrub layer, and an herb layer. There are few epiphytes. The dominant plants in the Northern Hemisphere are deciduous trees, which drop their leaves before winter, when low temperatures would reduce photosynthesis and make water uptake from frozen soil difficult. In Australia, evergreen eucalyptus trees dominate these forests.

Animals In the Northern Hemisphere, many mammals hibernate in winter, while many bird species migrate to warmer climates. Mammals, birds, and insects make use of all the vertical layers of the forest.

Human Impact Temperate broadleaf forest has been heavily settled on all continents. Logging and land clearing for agriculture and urban development have destroyed virtually all the original deciduous forests in North America. However, owing to their capacity for recovery, these forests are returning over much of their former range.

Tundra

Distribution **Tundra** covers expansive areas of the Arctic, amounting to 20% of Earth's land surface. High winds and low temperatures produce similar plant communities, called *alpine tundra*, on very high mountaintops at all latitudes, including the tropics.

Precipitation Precipitation averages from 20 to 60 cm annually in arctic tundra but may exceed 100 cm in alpine tundra.

Temperature Winters are cold, with averages in some areas below –30°C. Summer temperatures generally average less than 10°C.

Plants The vegetation of tundra is mostly herbaceous, consisting of a mixture of mosses, grasses, and forbs, along with some dwarf shrubs and trees and lichens. A permanently frozen layer of soil called permafrost restricts the growth of plant roots.

Animals Large grazing musk oxen are resident, while caribou and reindeer are migratory. Predators include bears, wolves, and foxes. Many bird species migrate to the tundra for summer nesting.

Human Impact Tundra is sparsely settled but has become the focus of significant mineral and oil extraction in recent years.

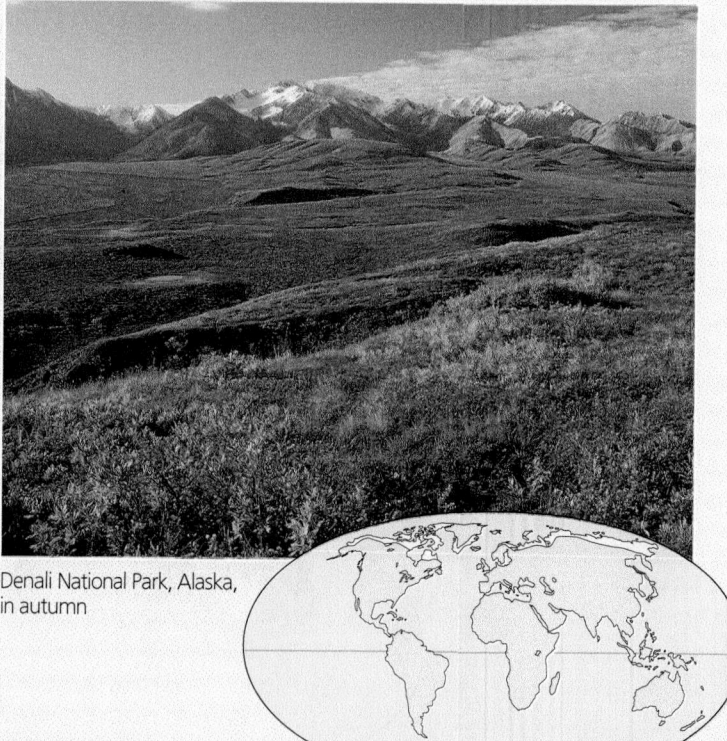

Denali National Park, Alaska, in autumn

CONCEPT 52.3

Aquatic biomes are diverse and dynamic systems that cover most of Earth

Now that we have examined terrestrial biomes, let's turn to aquatic biomes. Unlike terrestrial biomes, aquatic biomes are characterized primarily by their physical environment. They also show far less latitudinal variation, with all types found across the globe. Ecologists distinguish between freshwater and marine biomes on the basis of physical and chemical differences. Marine biomes generally have salt concentrations that average 3%, whereas freshwater biomes are usually characterized by a salt concentration of less than 0.1%.

The oceans make up the largest marine biome, covering about 75% of Earth's surface. Because of their vast size, they greatly impact the biosphere. Water evaporated from the oceans provides most of the planet's rainfall, and ocean temperatures have a major effect on global climate and wind patterns (see Figure 52.3). Marine algae and photosynthetic bacteria also supply a substantial portion of the world's oxygen and consume large amounts of atmospheric carbon dioxide.

Freshwater biomes are closely linked to the soils and biotic components of the surrounding terrestrial biome. The particular characteristics of a freshwater biome are also influenced by the patterns and speed of water flow and the climate to which the biome is exposed.

Zonation in Aquatic Biomes

Many aquatic biomes are physically and chemically stratified (layered), vertically and horizontally, as illustrated for both a lake and a marine environment in **Figure 52.13**. Light is absorbed by the water itself and by photosynthetic organisms, so its intensity decreases rapidly with depth. Ecologists distinguish between the upper **photic zone**, where there is sufficient light for photosynthesis, and the lower **aphotic zone**, where little light penetrates. The photic and aphotic zones together make up the **pelagic zone**. Deep in the aphotic zone lies the **abyssal zone**, the part of the ocean 2,000–6,000 m below the surface. At the bottom of all aquatic biomes, deep or shallow, is the **benthic zone**. Made up of sand and organic and inorganic sediments, the benthic zone is occupied by communities of organisms collectively called the **benthos**. A major source of food for many benthic species is dead organic matter called **detritus**, which "rains" down from the productive surface waters of the photic zone.

Thermal energy from sunlight warms surface waters to whatever depth the sunlight penetrates, but the deeper waters remain quite cold. In the ocean and in most lakes, a narrow layer of abrupt temperature change called a **thermocline**

▼ Figure 52.13 **Zonation in aquatic environments.**

(a) Zonation in a lake

The lake environment is generally classified on the basis of three physical criteria: light penetration (photic and aphotic zones), distance from shore and water depth (littoral and limnetic zones), and whether the environment is open water (pelagic zone) or bottom (benthic zone).

(b) Marine zonation

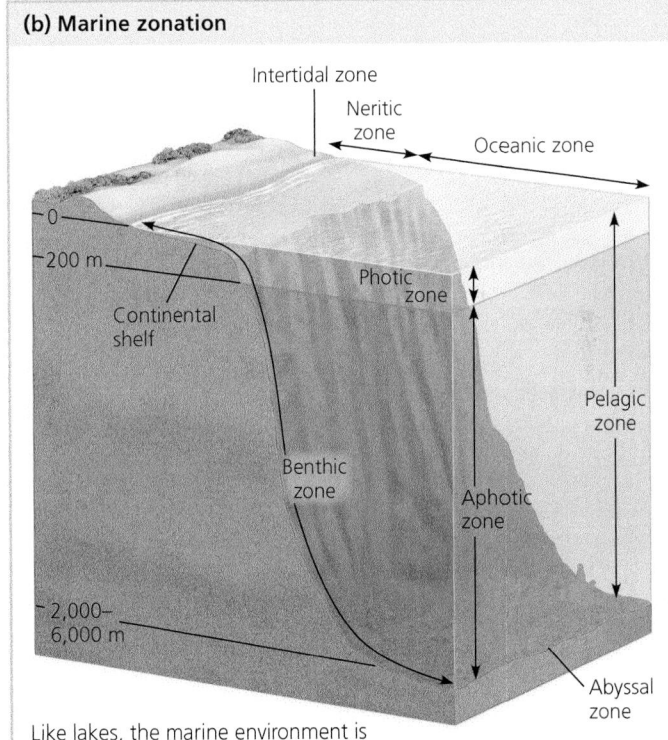

Like lakes, the marine environment is generally classified on the basis of light penetration (photic and aphotic zones), distance from shore and water depth (intertidal, neritic, and oceanic zones), and whether the environment is open water (pelagic zone) or bottom (benthic and abyssal zones).

separates the more uniformly warm upper layer from more uniformly cold deeper waters. Lakes tend to be particularly layered with respect to temperature, especially during summer and winter, but many temperate lakes undergo a semiannual mixing of their waters as a result of changing temperature

① In winter, the coldest water in the lake (0°C) lies just below the surface ice; water becomes progressively warmer at deeper levels of the lake, typically 4°C at the bottom.

② In spring, as the ice melts, the surface water warms to 4°C and mixes with the formerly cooler layers below, eliminating thermal stratification. Spring winds help mix the water, bringing oxygen to the bottom waters and nutrients to the surface.

③ In summer, the lake regains a distinctive thermal profile, with warm surface water separated from cold bottom water by a narrow vertical zone of abrupt temperature change, called a thermocline.

④ In autumn, as surface water cools rapidly, it sinks beneath the underlying layers, remixing the water until the surface begins to freeze and the winter temperature profile is reestablished.

▲ **Figure 52.14** **Seasonal turnover in lakes with winter ice cover.** Because of the seasonal turnover shown here, lake waters are well oxygenated at all depths in spring and autumn; in winter and summer, when the lake is stratified by temperature, oxygen concentrations are lower in deeper waters and higher near the surface of the lake.

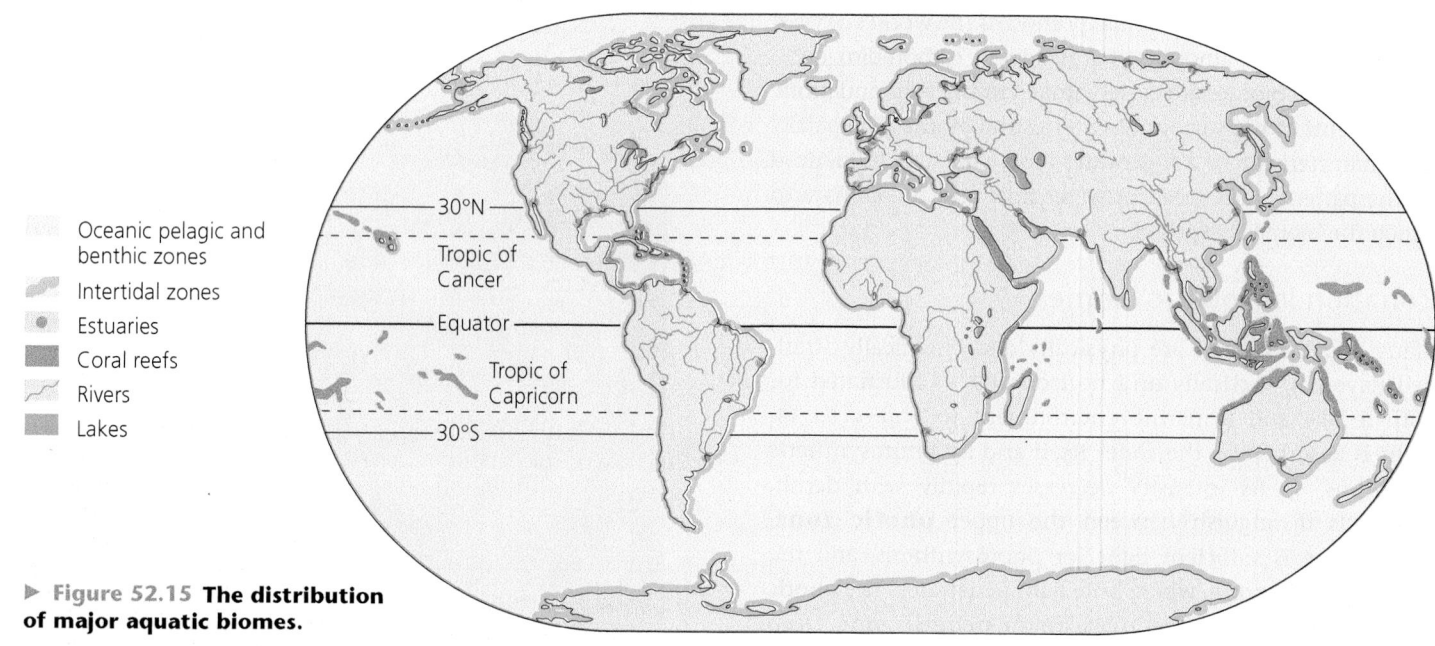

▢ Oceanic pelagic and benthic zones
▨ Intertidal zones
⬤ Estuaries
▮ Coral reefs
⟋ Rivers
▬ Lakes

▶ **Figure 52.15** **The distribution of major aquatic biomes.**

profiles **(Figure 52.14).** This **turnover**, as it is called, sends oxygenated water from a lake's surface to the bottom and brings nutrient-rich water from the bottom to the surface in both spring and autumn. These cyclic changes in the abiotic properties of lakes are essential for the survival and growth of organisms at all levels within this ecosystem.

In both freshwater and marine environments, communities are distributed according to water depth, degree of light penetration, distance from shore, and whether they are found in open water or near the bottom. Marine communities, in particular, illustrate the limitations on species distribution that result from these abiotic factors. Plankton and many fish species occur in the relatively shallow photic zone (see Figure 52.13b). Because water absorbs light so well and the ocean is so deep, most of the ocean volume is virtually devoid of light (the aphotic zone) and harbors relatively little life, except for microorganisms and relatively sparse populations of fishes and invertebrates. Similar factors limit species distribution in deep lakes as well.

Figure 52.15 shows the locations of Earth's major aquatic biomes. **Figure 52.16,** on the next four pages, explores their main characteristics.

Exploring Aquatic Biomes

Lakes

Physical Environment
Standing bodies of water range from ponds a few square meters in area to lakes covering thousands of square kilometers. Light decreases with depth, creating stratification (see Figure 52.13a). Temperate lakes may have a seasonal thermocline (see Figure 52.14); tropical lowland lakes have a thermocline year-round.

Chemical Environment
The salinity, oxygen concentration, and nutrient content differ greatly among lakes and can vary with season. **Oligotrophic lakes** are nutrient-poor and generally oxygen-rich; **eutrophic lakes** are nutrient-rich and often depleted of oxygen in the deepest zone in summer and if covered with ice in winter. The amount of decomposable organic matter in bottom sediments is low in oligotrophic lakes and high in eutrophic lakes; high rates of decomposition in deeper layers of eutrophic lakes cause periodic oxygen depletion.

Geologic Features
Oligotrophic lakes may become more eutrophic over time as runoff adds sediments and nutrients. They tend to have less surface area relative to their depth than eutrophic lakes.

Photosynthetic Organisms
Rooted and floating aquatic plants live in the **littoral zone**, the shallow, well-lit waters close to shore. Farther from shore, where water is too deep to support rooted aquatic plants, the **limnetic zone** is inhabited by a variety of phytoplankton, including cyanobacteria.

Heterotrophs
In the limnetic zone, small drifting heterotrophs, or zooplankton, graze on the phytoplankton. The benthic zone is inhabited by assorted invertebrates whose species composition depends partly on oxygen levels. Fishes live in all zones with sufficient oxygen.

Human Impact
Runoff from fertilized land and dumping of wastes lead to nutrient enrichment, which can produce algal blooms, oxygen depletion, and fish kills.

An oligotrophic lake in Grand Teton National Park, Wyoming

A eutrophic lake in the Okavango Delta, Botswana

Wetlands

Physical Environment
A **wetland** is a habitat that is inundated by water at least some of the time and that supports plants adapted to water-saturated soil. Some wetlands are inundated at all times, whereas others flood infrequently.

Chemical Environment
Because of high organic production by plants and decomposition by microbes and other organisms, both the water and the soils are periodically low in dissolved oxygen. Wetlands have a high capacity to filter dissolved nutrients and chemical pollutants.

Geologic Features
Basin wetlands develop in shallow basins, ranging from upland depressions to filled-in lakes and ponds. *Riverine wetlands* develop along shallow and periodically flooded banks of rivers and streams. *Fringe wetlands* occur along the coasts of large lakes and seas, where water flows back and forth because of rising lake levels or tidal action. Thus, fringe wetlands include both freshwater and marine biomes.

Photosynthetic Organisms
Wetlands are among the most productive biomes on Earth. Their water-saturated soils favor the growth of plants such as floating pond lilies and emergent cattails, many sedges, tamarack, and black spruce, which have adaptations enabling them to grow in water or in soil that is periodically anaerobic owing to the presence of unaerated water. Woody plants dominate the vegetation of swamps, while bogs are dominated by sphagnum mosses.

Heterotrophs
Wetlands are home to a diverse community of invertebrates, birds, and many other organisms. Herbivores, from crustaceans and aquatic insect larvae to muskrats, consume algae, detritus, and plants. Carnivores are also varied and may include dragonflies, otters, frogs, alligators, and herons.

Human Impact
Draining and filling have destroyed up to 90% of wetlands, which help purify water and reduce peak flooding.

A basin wetland in the United Kingdom

Exploring Aquatic Biomes

Streams and Rivers

Physical Environment The most prominent physical characteristic of streams and rivers is their current. Headwater streams are generally cold, clear, turbulent, and swift. Farther downstream, where numerous tributaries may have joined, forming a river, the water is generally warmer and more turbid because of suspended sediment. Streams and rivers are stratified into vertical zones.

Chemical Environment The salt and nutrient content of streams and rivers increases from the headwaters to the mouth. Headwaters are generally rich in oxygen. Downstream water may also contain substantial oxygen, except where there has been organic enrichment. A large fraction of the organic matter in rivers consists of dissolved or highly fragmented material that is carried by the current from forested streams.

Geologic Features Headwater stream channels are often narrow, have a rocky bottom, and alternate between shallow sections and deeper pools. The downstream stretches of rivers are generally wide and meandering. River bottoms are often silty from sediments deposited over long periods of time.

Photosynthetic Organisms Headwater streams that flow through grasslands or deserts may be rich in phytoplankton or rooted aquatic plants.

Heterotrophs A great diversity of fishes and invertebrates inhabit unpolluted rivers and streams, distributed according to, and throughout, the vertical zones. In streams flowing through temperate or tropical forests, organic matter from terrestrial vegetation is the primary source of food for aquatic consumers.

Human Impact Municipal, agricultural, and industrial pollution degrade water quality and kill aquatic organisms. Damming and flood control impair the natural functioning of stream and river ecosystems and threaten migratory species such as salmon.

A headwater stream in the Great Smoky Mountains

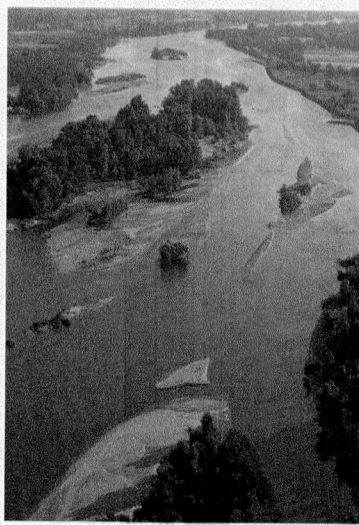

The Loire River (in France) far from its headwaters

Estuaries

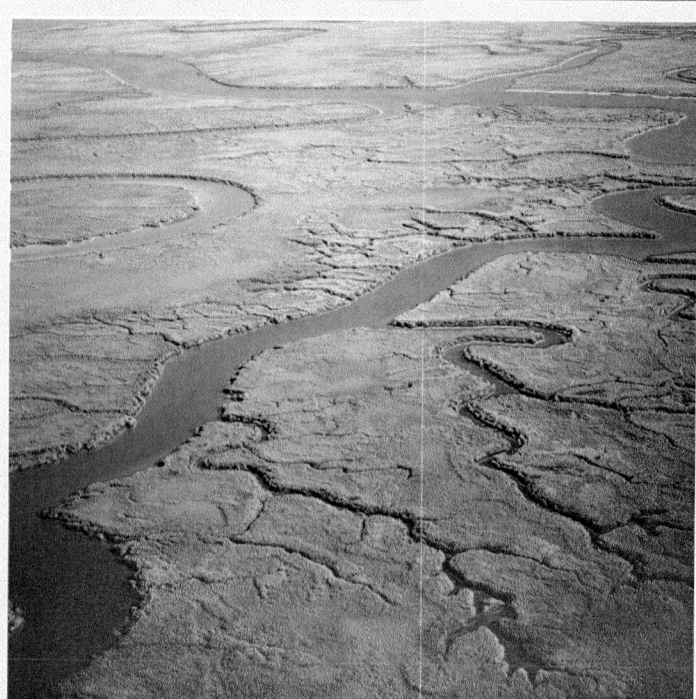

An estuary in the southeastern United States

Physical Environment An **estuary** is a transition area between river and sea. Seawater flows up the estuary channel during a rising tide and flows back down during the falling tide. Often, higher-density seawater occupies the bottom of the channel and mixes little with the lower-density river water at the surface.

Chemical Environment Salinity varies spatially within estuaries, from nearly that of fresh water to that of seawater. Salinity also varies with the rise and fall of the tides. Nutrients from the river make estuaries, like wetlands, among the most productive biomes.

Geologic Features Estuarine flow patterns combined with the sediments carried by river and tidal waters create a complex network of tidal channels, islands, natural levees, and mudflats.

Photosynthetic Organisms Saltmarsh grasses and algae, including phytoplankton, are the major producers in estuaries.

Heterotrophs Estuaries support an abundance of worms, oysters, crabs, and many fish species that humans consume. Many marine invertebrates and fishes use estuaries as a breeding ground or migrate through them to freshwater habitats upstream. Estuaries are also crucial feeding areas for waterfowl and some marine mammals.

Human Impact Filling, dredging, and pollution from upstream have disrupted estuaries worldwide.

Intertidal Zones

Physical Environment An **intertidal zone** is periodically submerged and exposed by the tides, twice daily on most marine shores. Upper zones experience longer exposures to air and greater variations in temperature and salinity. Changes in physical conditions from the upper to the lower intertidal zones limit the distributions of many organisms to particular strata, as shown in the photograph.

Chemical Environment Oxygen and nutrient levels are generally high and are renewed with each turn of the tides.

Geologic Features The substrates of intertidal zones, which are generally either rocky or sandy, select for particular behavior and anatomy among intertidal organisms. The configuration of bays or coastlines influences the magnitude of tides and the relative exposure of intertidal organisms to wave action.

Photosynthetic Organisms A high diversity and biomass of attached marine algae inhabit rocky intertidal zones, especially in the lower zone. Sandy intertidal zones exposed to vigorous wave action generally lack attached plants or algae, while sandy intertidal zones in protected bays or lagoons often support rich beds of seagrass and algae.

Heterotrophs Many of the animals in rocky intertidal environments have structural adaptations that enable them to attach to the hard substrate. The composition, density, and diversity of animals change markedly from the upper to the lower intertidal zones. Many of the animals in sandy or muddy intertidal zones, such as worms, clams, and predatory crustaceans, bury themselves and feed as the tides bring sources of food. Other common animals are sponges, sea anemones, echinoderms, and small fishes.

Human Impact Oil pollution has disrupted many intertidal areas. The construction of rock walls and barriers to reduce erosion from waves and storm surges has disrupted this zone in some locations.

Rocky intertidal zone on the Oregon coast

Oceanic Pelagic Zone

Physical Environment The **oceanic pelagic zone** is a vast realm of open blue water, constantly mixed by wind-driven oceanic currents. Because of higher water clarity, the photic zone extends to greater depths than in coastal marine waters.

Chemical Environment Oxygen levels are generally high. Nutrient concentrations are generally lower than in coastal waters. Because they are thermally stratified year-round, some tropical areas of the oceanic pelagic zone have lower nutrient concentrations than temperate oceans. Turnover between fall and spring renews nutrients in the photic zones of temperate and high-latitude ocean areas.

Geologic Features This biome covers approximately 70% of Earth's surface and has an average depth of nearly 4,000 m. The deepest point in the ocean is more than 10,000 m beneath the surface.

Photosynthetic Organisms The dominant photosynthetic organisms are phytoplankton, including photosynthetic bacteria, that drift with the oceanic currents. Spring turnover renews nutrients in temperate oceans producing a surge of phytoplankton growth. Because of the large extent of this biome, photosynthetic plankton account for about half of the photosynthetic activity on Earth.

Heterotrophs The most abundant heterotrophs in this biome are zooplankton. These protists, worms, copepods, shrimp-like krill, jellies, and small larvae of invertebrates and fishes graze on photosynthetic plankton. The oceanic pelagic zone also includes free-swimming animals, such as large squids, fishes, sea turtles, and marine mammals.

Human Impact Overfishing has depleted fish stocks in all Earth's oceans, which have also been polluted by waste dumping.

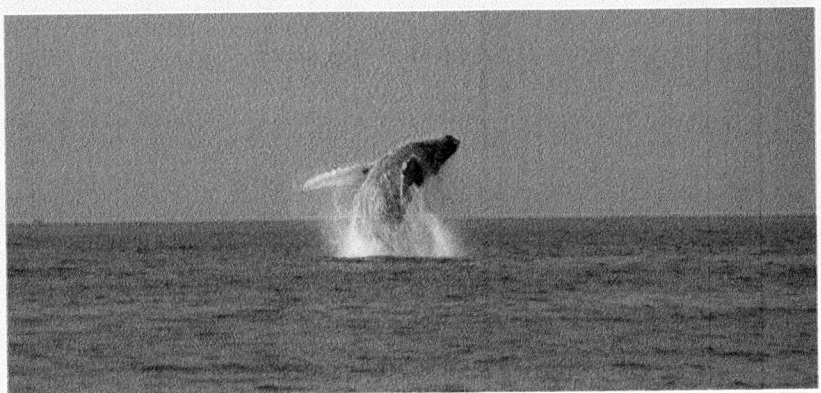

Open ocean off the island of Hawaii

Exploring Aquatic Biomes

Coral Reefs

Physical Environment **Coral reefs** are formed largely from the calcium carbonate skeletons of corals. Shallow reef-building corals live in the photic zone of relatively stable tropical marine environments with high water clarity, primarily on islands and along the edge of some continents. They are sensitive to temperatures below about 18–20°C and above 30°C. Deep-sea coral reefs, found between 200 and 1,500 m deep, are less known than their shallow counterparts but harbor as much diversity as many shallow reefs do.

Chemical Environment Corals require high oxygen levels and are excluded by high inputs of fresh water and nutrients.

Geologic Features Corals require a solid substrate for attachment. A typical coral reef begins as a *fringing reef* on a young, high island, forming an offshore *barrier reef* later in the history of the island and becoming a *coral atoll* as the older island submerges.

Photosynthetic Organisms Unicellular algae live within the tissues of the corals, forming a mutualistic relationship that provides the corals with organic molecules. Diverse multicellular red and green algae growing on the reef also contribute substantial amounts of photosynthesis.

Heterotrophs Corals, a diverse group of cnidarians (see Chapter 33), are themselves the predominant animals on coral reefs. However, fish and invertebrate diversity is exceptionally high. Overall animal diversity on coral reefs rivals that of tropical forests.

Human Impact Collecting of coral skeletons and overfishing have reduced populations of corals and reef fishes. Global warming and pollution may be contributing to large-scale coral death. Development of coastal mangroves for aquaculture has also reduced spawning grounds for many species of reef fishes.

A coral reef in the Red Sea

Marine Benthic Zone

A deep-sea hydrothermal vent community

Physical Environment The **marine benthic zone** consists of the seafloor below the surface waters of the coastal, or **neritic**, zone and the offshore, pelagic zone (see Figure 52.13b). Except for shallow, near-coastal areas, the marine benthic zone receives no sunlight. Water temperature declines with depth, while pressure increases. As a result, organisms in the very deep benthic, or abyssal, zone are adapted to continuous cold (about 3°C) and very high water pressure.

Chemical Environment Except in areas of organic enrichment, oxygen is usually present at sufficient concentrations to support diverse animal life.

Geologic Features Soft sediments cover most of the benthic zone. However, there are areas of rocky substrate on reefs, submarine mountains, and new oceanic crust.

Autotrophs Photosynthetic organisms, mainly seaweeds and filamentous algae, are limited to shallow benthic areas with sufficient light to support them. Unique assemblages of organisms, such as those shown in the photo, are found near **deep-sea hydrothermal vents** on mid-ocean ridges. In these dark, hot environments, the food producers are chemoautotrophic prokaryotes (see Chapter 27) that obtain energy by oxidizing H_2S formed by a reaction of the hot water with dissolved sulfate (SO_4^{2-}).

Heterotrophs Neritic benthic communities include numerous invertebrates and fishes. Beyond the photic zone, most consumers depend entirely on organic matter raining down from above. Among the animals of the deep-sea hydrothermal vent communities are giant tube worms (pictured at left), some more than 1 m long. They are nourished by chemoautotrophic prokaryotes that live as symbionts within their bodies. Many other invertebrates, including arthropods and echinoderms, are also abundant around the hydrothermal vents.

Human Impact Overfishing has decimated important benthic fish populations, such as the cod of the Grand Banks off Newfoundland. Dumping of organic wastes has created oxygen-deprived benthic areas.

The first two questions refer to Figure 52.16.

1. Why are phytoplankton, and not benthic algae or rooted aquatic plants, the dominant photosynthetic organisms of the oceanic pelagic zone?

2. **MAKE CONNECTIONS** Many organisms living in estuaries experience freshwater and saltwater conditions each day with the rising and falling of tides. Based on what you learned in Concept 44.1 (pp. 953–958), explain how these changing conditions challenge the survival of these organisms.

3. **WHAT IF?** Water leaving a reservoir behind a dam is often taken from deep layers of the reservoir. Would you expect fish found in a river below a dam in summer to be species that prefer colder or warmer water than fish found in an undammed river? Explain.

For suggested answers, see Appendix A.

CONCEPT **52.4**

Interactions between organisms and the environment limit the distribution of species

So far in this chapter we've examined Earth's climate and the characteristics of terrestrial and aquatic biomes. We've also introduced the range of biological levels at which ecologists work (see Figure 52.2). In this section, we will examine how ecologists determine what factors control the distribution of species, such as the harlequin toad shown in Figure 52.1.

Species distributions are a consequence of both ecological and evolutionary interactions through time. The differential survival and reproduction of individuals that lead to evolution occur in *ecological time*, the minute-to-minute time frame of interactions between organisms and the environment. Through natural selection, organisms adapt to their environment over the time frame of many generations, in *evolutionary time*. One example of how events in ecological time have led to evolution is the selection for beak depth in Galápagos finches (see Figures 23.1 and 23.2). On the island of Daphne Major, finches with larger, deeper beaks were better able to survive during a drought because they could eat the large, hard seeds that were available. Finches with shallower beaks, which required smaller, softer seeds that were in short supply, were less likely to survive and reproduce. Because beak depth is hereditary in this species, the generation of finches born after the drought had beaks that were deeper than those of previous generations.

Biologists have long recognized global and regional patterns in the distribution of organisms (see the discussion of biogeography in Chapter 22). Kangaroos, for instance, are found in Australia but nowhere else on Earth. Ecologists ask not only *where* species occur, but also *why* species occur where they do: What factors determine their distribution? In seeking to answer this question, ecologists focus on both biotic and abiotic factors that influence the distribution and abundance of organisms.

Figure 52.17 presents an example of how both kinds of factors might affect the distribution of a species, in this case the red kangaroo (*Macropus rufus*). As the figure shows, red kangaroos are most abundant in a few areas in the interior of Australia, where precipitation is relatively sparse and variable. They are not found around most of the periphery of the continent,

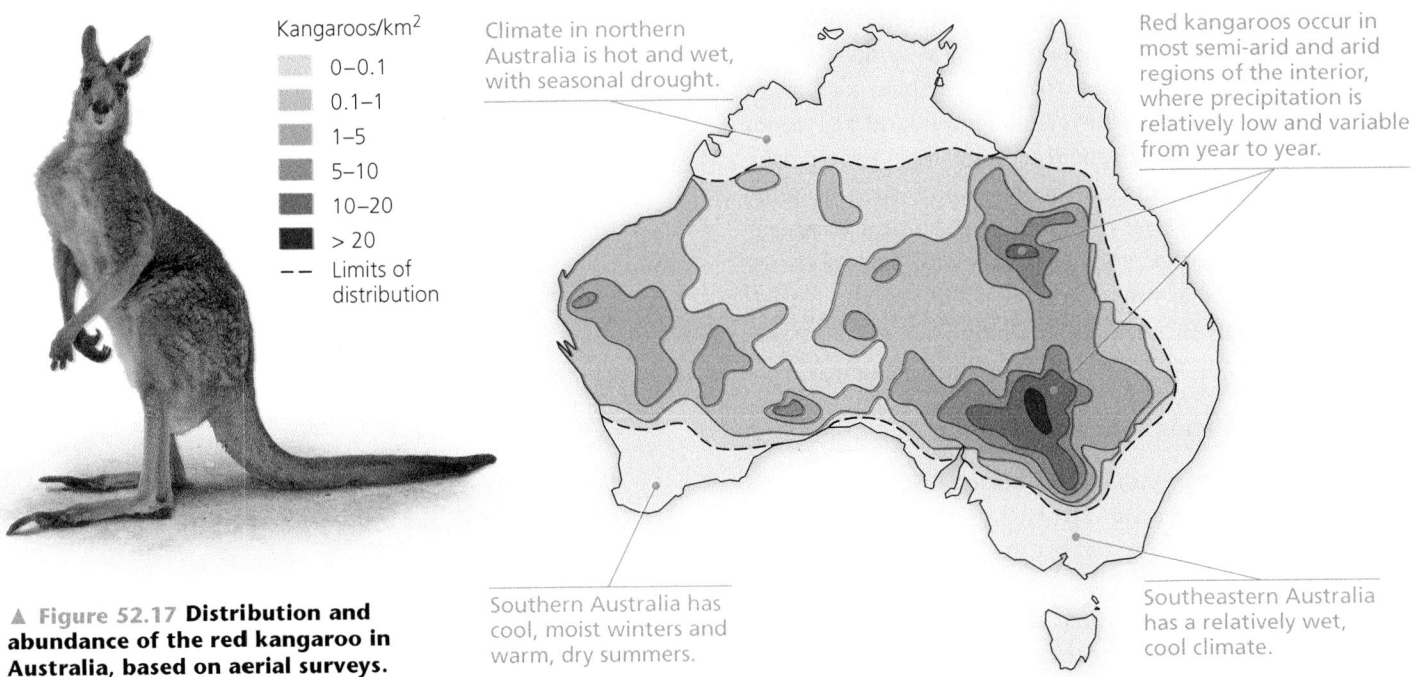

Kangaroos/km²

- ░ 0–0.1
- ▒ 0.1–1
- ▓ 1–5
- 5–10
- 10–20
- > 20
- – – Limits of distribution

Climate in northern Australia is hot and wet, with seasonal drought.

Red kangaroos occur in most semi-arid and arid regions of the interior, where precipitation is relatively low and variable from year to year.

Southern Australia has cool, moist winters and warm, dry summers.

Southeastern Australia has a relatively wet, cool climate.

▲ **Figure 52.17 Distribution and abundance of the red kangaroo in Australia, based on aerial surveys.**

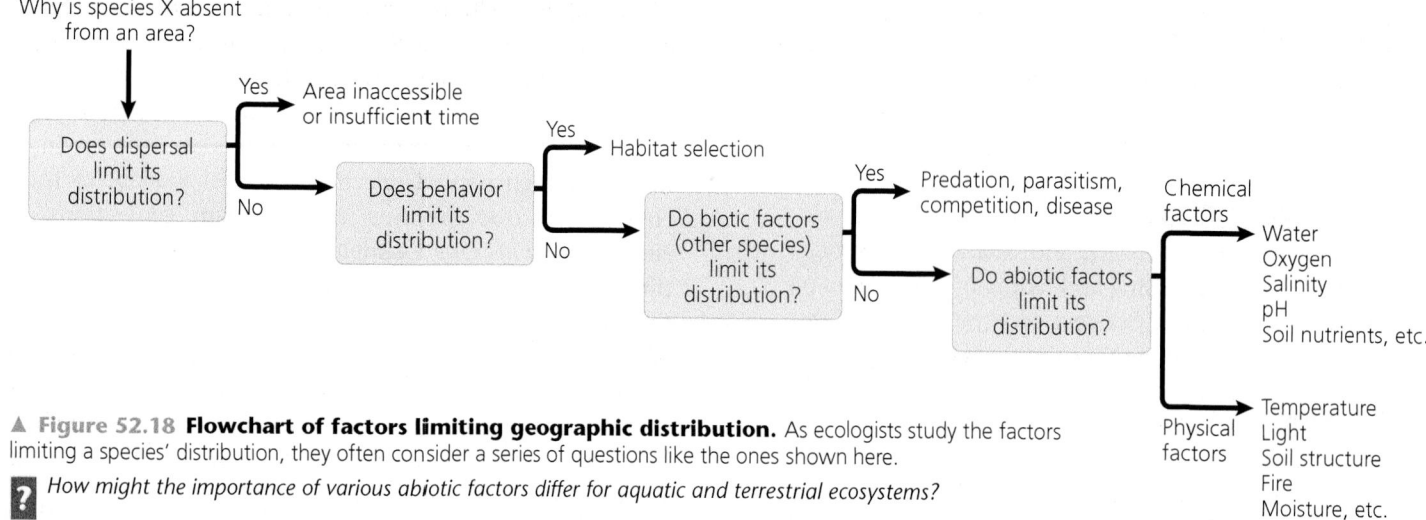

▲ **Figure 52.18 Flowchart of factors limiting geographic distribution.** As ecologists study the factors limiting a species' distribution, they often consider a series of questions like the ones shown here.

❓ *How might the importance of various abiotic factors differ for aquatic and terrestrial ecosystems?*

where the climate is wetter. At first glance, this distribution might suggest that an abiotic factor—the amount and variability of precipitation—directly determines where red kangaroos live. However, climate may also influence red kangaroo populations indirectly through biotic factors, such as pathogens, parasites, predators, competitors, and food availability. Ecologists generally need to consider multiple factors and alternative hypotheses when attempting to explain the distribution of species.

To see how ecologists might arrive at such an explanation, let's work our way through the series of questions in the flowchart in **Figure 52.18**.

Dispersal and Distribution

One factor that contributes greatly to the global distribution of organisms is **dispersal**, the movement of individuals or gametes away from their area of origin or from centers of high population density. A biogeographer who studies the distributions of species in the context of evolutionary theory might consider dispersal in hypothesizing why there are no kangaroos in North America: A barrier may have kept them from reaching the continent. While land-bound kangaroos have not reached North America under their own power, other organisms that disperse more readily, such as some birds, have. The dispersal of organisms is critical to understanding the role of geographic isolation in evolution (see Chapter 24) as well as the broad patterns of species distribution we see today, including that of the Pacific diatom discussed earlier in this chapter.

Natural Range Expansions and Adaptive Radiation

EVOLUTION The importance of dispersal is most evident when organisms reach an area where they did not exist previously. For instance, 200 years ago, the cattle egret (*Bubulcus ibis*) was found only in Africa and southwestern Europe. But in the late 1800s, some of these birds managed to cross the Atlantic Ocean and colonize northeastern South America.

From there, cattle egrets gradually spread southward and also northward through Central America and into North America, reaching Florida by 1960 **(Figure 52.19)**. Today they have breeding populations as far west as the Pacific coast of the United States and as far north as southern Canada.

In rare cases, such long-distance dispersal can lead to adaptive radiation, the rapid evolution of an ancestral species into new species that fill many ecological niches (see Chapter 25). The incredible diversity of Hawaiian silverswords is an example of adaptive radiation that was possible only with the long-distance dispersal of an ancestral tarweed from North America (see Figure 25.20).

▶ **Figure 52.19 Dispersal of the cattle egret in the Americas.** Native to Africa, cattle egrets were first reported in South America in 1877.

Natural range expansions clearly show the influence of dispersal on distribution. However, opportunities to observe such dispersal directly are rare, so ecologists often turn to experimental methods to better understand the role of dispersal in limiting the distribution of species.

Species Transplants

To determine if dispersal is a key factor limiting the distribution of a species, ecologists may observe the results of intentional or accidental transplants of the species to areas where it was previously absent. For a transplant to be considered successful, some of the organisms must not only survive in the new area but also reproduce there sustainably. If a transplant is successful, then we can conclude that the *potential* range of the species is larger than its *actual* range; in other words, the species *could* live in certain areas where it currently does not.

Species introduced to new geographic locations often disrupt the communities and ecosystems to which they have been introduced and spread far beyond the area of introduction (see Chapter 56). Consequently, ecologists rarely move species to new geographic regions. Instead, they document the outcome when a species has been transplanted for other purposes, such as to introduce game animals or predators of pest species, or when a species has been accidentally transplanted.

Behavior and Habitat Selection

As transplant experiments show, some organisms do not occupy all of their potential range, even though they may be physically able to disperse into the unoccupied areas. To follow our line of questioning from Figure 52.18, does behavior play a role in limiting distribution in such cases? When individuals seem to avoid certain habitats, even when the habitats are suitable, the organism's distribution may be limited by habitat selection behavior.

Although habitat selection is one of the least understood of all ecological processes, some instances in insects have been closely studied. Female insects often deposit eggs only in response to a very narrow set of stimuli, which may restrict distribution of the insects to certain host plants. Larvae of the European corn borer, for example, can feed on a wide variety of plants but are found almost exclusively on corn (maize) because egg-laying females are attracted by odors produced by the plant. Habitat selection behavior clearly restricts this insect to geographic locations where corn is found.

Biotic Factors

If behavior does not limit the distribution of a species, our next question is whether biotic factors—other species—are responsible. Often, negative interactions with predators (organisms that kill their prey) or herbivores (organisms that eat plants or algae) restrict the ability of a species to survive and reproduce. **Figure 52.20** describes a specific case of an herbivore, a sea urchin, limiting the distribution of a food species.

▼ **Figure 52.20**

INQUIRY

Does feeding by sea urchins limit seaweed distribution?

EXPERIMENT W. J. Fletcher, of the University of Sydney, Australia, reasoned that if sea urchins are a limiting biotic factor in a particular ecosystem, then more seaweeds should invade an area from which sea urchins have been removed. To isolate the effect of sea urchins from that of a seaweed-eating mollusc, the limpet, he removed only urchins, only limpets, or both from study areas adjacent to a control site.

RESULTS Fletcher observed a large difference in seaweed growth between areas with and without sea urchins.

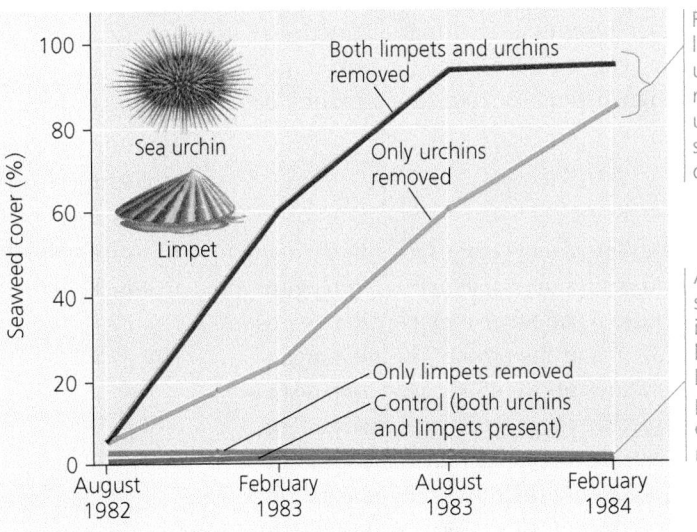

CONCLUSION Removing both limpets and urchins resulted in the greatest increase in seaweed cover, indicating that both species have some influence on seaweed distribution. But since removing only urchins greatly increased seaweed growth while removing only limpets had little effect, Fletcher concluded that sea urchins have a much greater effect than limpets in limiting seaweed distribution.

SOURCE W. J. Fletcher, Interactions among subtidal Australian sea urchins, gastropods, and algae: effects of experimental removals, *Ecological Monographs* 57:89–109 (1989).

WHAT IF? Seaweed cover increased the most when both urchins *and* limpets were removed. How might you explain this result?

In certain marine ecosystems, there is often an inverse relationship between the abundance of sea urchins and seaweeds (multicellular algae, such as kelp). Where urchins that graze on seaweeds and other algae are common, large stands of seaweeds do not become established. As described in Figure 52.20, Australian researchers have tested the hypothesis that sea urchins are a biotic factor limiting seaweed distribution. When sea urchins were removed from experimental plots, seaweed cover increased dramatically, showing that urchins limited the distribution of seaweeds.

In addition to predation and herbivory, the presence or absence of pollinators, food resources, parasites, pathogens, and competing organisms can act as a biotic limitation on species distribution. Some of the most striking cases of limitation occur when humans accidentally or intentionally introduce exotic predators or pathogens into new areas and wipe out native species. You will encounter examples of these impacts in Chapter 56, where we discuss conservation biology.

Abiotic Factors

The last question in the flowchart in Figure 52.18 considers whether abiotic factors, such as temperature, water, oxygen, salinity, sunlight, or soil, might be limiting a species' distribution. If the physical conditions at a site do not allow a species to survive and reproduce, then the species will not be found there. Throughout this discussion, keep in mind that most abiotic factors vary substantially in space and time. Daily and annual fluctuations of abiotic factors may either blur or accentuate regional distinctions. Furthermore, organisms can avoid some stressful conditions temporarily through behaviors such as dormancy or hibernation.

Temperature

Environmental temperature is an important factor in the distribution of organisms because of its effect on biological processes. Cells may rupture if the water they contain freezes (at temperatures below 0°C), and the proteins of most organisms denature at temperatures above 45°C. Most organisms function best within a specific range of environmental temperature. Temperatures outside that range may force some animals to expend energy regulating their internal temperature, as mammals and birds do (see Chapter 40). Extraordinary adaptations enable certain organisms, such as thermophilic prokaryotes (see Chapter 27), to live outside the temperature range habitable by other life.

Water and Oxygen

The dramatic variation in water availability among habitats is another important factor in species distribution. Species

living at the seashore or in tidal wetlands can desiccate (dry out) as the tide recedes. Terrestrial organisms face a nearly constant threat of desiccation, and the distribution of terrestrial species reflects their ability to obtain and conserve water. Many amphibians, such as the harlequin toad in Figure 52.1, are particularly vulnerable to drying because they use their moist, delicate skin for gas exchange. Desert organisms exhibit a variety of adaptations for acquiring and conserving water in dry environments, as described in Chapter 44.

Water affects oxygen availability in aquatic environments and in flooded soils. Because oxygen diffuses slowly in water, its concentration can be low in certain aquatic systems and soils, limiting cellular respiration and other physiological processes. Oxygen concentrations can be particularly low in both deep ocean and deep lake waters and sediments where organic matter is abundant. Flooded wetland soils may also have low oxygen content. Mangroves and other trees have specialized roots that project above the water and help the root system obtain oxygen (see Figure 35.4). Unlike many flooded wetlands, the surface waters of streams and rivers tend to be well oxygenated because of rapid exchange of gases with the atmosphere.

Salinity

As you learned in Chapter 7, the salt concentration of water in the environment affects the water balance of organisms through osmosis. Most aquatic organisms are restricted to either freshwater or saltwater habitats by their limited ability to osmoregulate (see Chapter 44). Although most terrestrial organisms can excrete excess salts from specialized glands or in feces or urine, salt flats and other high-salinity habitats typically have few species of plants or animals.

Salmon that migrate between freshwater streams and the ocean use both behavioral and physiological mechanisms to osmoregulate. They adjust the amount of water they drink to help balance their salt content, and their gills switch from taking up salt in fresh water to excreting salt in the ocean.

Sunlight

Sunlight absorbed by photosynthetic organisms provides the energy that drives most ecosystems, and too little sunlight can limit the distribution of photosynthetic species. In forests, shading by leaves in the treetops makes competition for light especially intense, particularly for seedlings growing on the forest floor. In aquatic environments, every meter of water depth selectively absorbs about 45% of the red light and about 2% of the blue light passing through it. As a result, most photosynthesis in aquatic environments occurs relatively near the surface.

▲ **Figure 52.21 Alpine tree line in Banff National Park, Canada.** Organisms living at high elevations are exposed not only to high levels of ultraviolet radiation but also to freezing temperatures, moisture deficits, and strong winds. Above the tree line, the combination of such factors restricts the growth and survival of trees.

Too much light can also limit the survival of organisms. In some ecosystems, such as deserts, high light levels can increase temperature stress if animals and plants are unable to avoid the light or to cool themselves through evaporation (see Chapter 40). At high elevations, the sun's rays are more likely to damage DNA and proteins because the atmosphere is thinner, absorbing less ultraviolet (UV) radiation. Damage from UV radiation, combined with other abiotic stresses, prevents trees from surviving above a certain elevation, resulting in the appearance of a tree line on mountain slopes (**Figure 52.21**).

Rocks and Soil

In terrestrial environments, the pH, mineral composition, and physical structure of rocks and soil limit the distribution of plants and thus of the animals that feed on them, contributing to the patchiness of terrestrial ecosystems. The pH of soil can limit the distribution of organisms directly, through extreme acidic or basic conditions, or indirectly, by affecting the solubility of nutrients and toxins.

In a river, the composition of the rocks and soil that make up the substrate (riverbed) can affect water chemistry, which in turn influences the resident organisms. In freshwater and marine environments, the structure of the substrate determines the organisms that can attach to it or burrow into it.

Throughout this chapter, you have seen how the distributions of biomes and organisms depend on abiotic and biotic factors. In the next chapter, we continue to work our way through the hierarchy outlined in Figure 52.2, focusing on how abiotic and biotic factors influence the ecology of populations.

CONCEPT CHECK 52.4

1. Give examples of human actions that could expand a species' distribution by changing its (a) dispersal or (b) biotic interactions.
2. **WHAT IF?** You suspect that deer are restricting the distribution of a tree species by preferentially eating the seedlings of the tree. How might you test this hypothesis?
3. **MAKE CONNECTIONS** As you saw in Figure 25.20 (p. 525), Hawaiian silverswords underwent a remarkable adaptive radiation after their ancestor reached Hawaii, while the islands were still young. Would you expect the cattle egret to undergo a similar adaptive radiation in the Americas (see Figure 52.19)? Explain.

For suggested answers, see Appendix A.

52 CHAPTER REVIEW

SUMMARY OF KEY CONCEPTS

CONCEPT 52.1

Earth's climate varies by latitude and season and is changing rapidly (pp. 1144–1150)

- Global **climate** patterns are largely determined by the input of solar energy and Earth's revolution around the sun.
- The changing angle of the sun over the year, bodies of water, and mountains exert seasonal, regional, and local effects on **macroclimate**.
- Fine-scale differences in **abiotic** (nonliving) factors, such as sunlight and temperature, determine **microclimate**.
- Increasing greenhouse gas concentrations in the air are warming Earth and altering the distributions of many species. Some species will not be able to shift their ranges quickly enough to reach suitable habitat in the future.

> **?** *Suppose global air circulation suddenly reversed, with most air ascending at 30° north and south latitude and descending at the equator. At what latitude would you most likely find deserts in this scenario?*

The structure and distribution of terrestrial biomes are controlled by climate and disturbance (pp. 1150–1156)

- **Climographs** show that temperature and precipitation are correlated with **biomes**. Because other factors also play roles in biome location, biomes overlap.
- Terrestrial biomes are often named for major physical or climatic factors and for their predominant vegetation. Vertical layering is an important feature of terrestrial biomes.
- **Disturbance**, both natural and human-induced, influences the type of vegetation found in biomes. Humans have altered much of Earth's surface, replacing the natural terrestrial communities described and depicted in Figure 52.12 with urban and agricultural ones.

> **?** *Some arctic tundra ecosystems receive as little rainfall as deserts but have much more dense vegetation. Based on Figure 52.10, what climatic factor might explain this difference? Explain.*

CONCEPT **52.3**

Aquatic biomes are diverse and dynamic systems that cover most of Earth (pp. 1157–1163)

- Aquatic biomes are characterized primarily by their physical environment rather than by climate and are often layered with regard to light penetration, temperature, and community structure. Marine biomes have a higher salt concentration than freshwater biomes.
- In the ocean and in most lakes, an abrupt temperature change called a **thermocline** separates a more uniformly warm upper layer from more uniformly cold deeper waters.

> **?** *In which aquatic biomes might you find an aphotic zone?*

CONCEPT **52.4**

Interactions between organisms and the environment limit the distribution of species (pp. 1163–1167)

- Ecologists want to know not only *where* species occur but also *why* those species occur where they do.

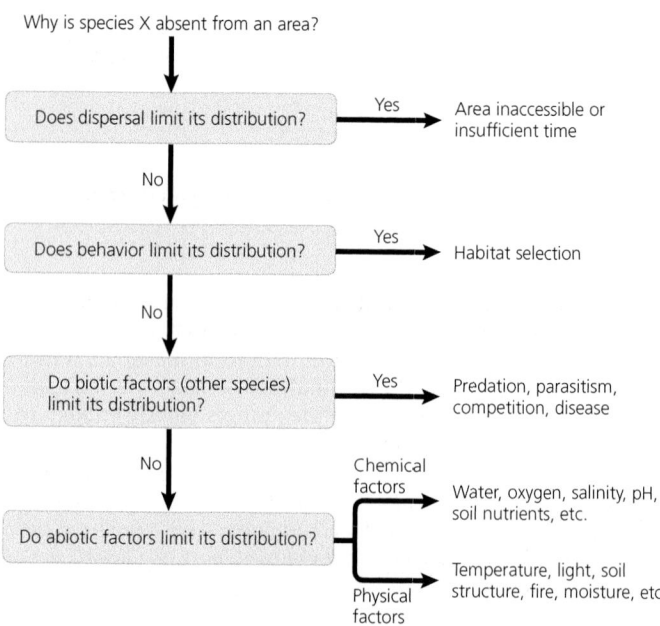

- The distribution of species may be limited by **dispersal**, the movement of individuals away from their area of origin; behavior; **biotic** (living) factors; and abiotic factors, such as temperature extremes, salinity, and water availability.

> **?** *If you were an ecologist studying the chemical and physical limits to the distributions of species, how might you rearrange the flowchart preceding this question?*

TEST YOUR UNDERSTANDING

LEVEL 1: KNOWLEDGE/COMPREHENSION

1. Which of the following areas of study focuses on the exchange of energy, organisms, and materials between ecosystems?
   a. population ecology
   b. organismal ecology
   c. landscape ecology
   d. ecosystem ecology
   e. community ecology

2. Which lake zone would be absent in a very shallow lake?
   a. benthic zone
   b. aphotic zone
   c. pelagic zone
   d. littoral zone
   e. limnetic zone

3. Which of the following is true with respect to oligotrophic lakes and eutrophic lakes?
   a. Oligotrophic lakes are more subject to oxygen depletion.
   b. Rates of photosynthesis are lower in eutrophic lakes.
   c. Eutrophic lake water contains lower concentrations of nutrients.
   d. Eutrophic lakes are richer in nutrients.
   e. Sediments in oligotrophic lakes contain larger amounts of decomposable organic matter.

4. Which of the following biomes is correctly paired with the description of its climate?
   a. savanna—low temperature, precipitation uniform during the year
   b. tundra—long summers, mild winters
   c. temperate broadleaf forest—relatively short growing season, mild winters
   d. temperate grasslands—relatively warm winters, most rainfall in summer
   e. tropical forests—nearly constant day length and temperature

LEVEL 2: APPLICATION/ANALYSIS

5. Which of the following is characteristic of most terrestrial biomes?
   a. annual average rainfall in excess of 250 cm
   b. a distribution predicted almost entirely by rock and soil patterns
   c. clear boundaries between adjacent biomes
   d. vegetation demonstrating vertical layering
   e. cold winter months

6. The oceans affect the biosphere in all of the following ways *except*
   a. producing a substantial amount of the biosphere's oxygen.
   b. removing carbon dioxide from the atmosphere.
   c. moderating the climate of terrestrial biomes.
   d. regulating the pH of freshwater biomes and terrestrial groundwater.
   e. being the source of most of Earth's rainfall.

7. Which statement about dispersal is *false*?
   a. Dispersal is a common component of the life cycles of plants and animals.
   b. Colonization of devastated areas after floods or volcanic eruptions depends on dispersal.
   c. Dispersal occurs only on an evolutionary time scale.
   d. Seeds are important dispersal stages in the life cycles of most flowering plants.
   e. The ability to disperse can expand the geographic distribution of a species.

8. When climbing a mountain, we can observe transitions in biological communities that are analogous to the changes
   a. in biomes at different latitudes.
   b. at different depths in the ocean.
   c. in a community through different seasons.
   d. in an ecosystem as it evolves over time.
   e. across the United States from east to west.

9. Suppose that the number of bird species is determined mainly by the number of vertical strata found in the environment. If so, in which of the following biomes would you find the greatest number of bird species?
   a. tropical rain forest
   b. savanna
   c. desert
   d. temperate broadleaf forest
   e. temperate grassland

LEVEL 3: SYNTHESIS/EVALUATION

10. **WHAT IF?** If the direction of Earth's rotation reversed, the most predictable effect would be
   a. no more night and day.
   b. a big change in the length of the year.
   c. winds blowing from west to east along the equator.
   d. a loss of seasonal variation at high latitudes.
   e. the elimination of ocean currents.

11. **DRAW IT** After reading about the experiment of W. J. Fletcher described in Figure 52.20, you decide to study feeding relationships among sea otters, sea urchins, and kelp on your own. You know that sea otters prey on sea urchins and that urchins eat kelp. At four coastal sites, you measure kelp abundance. Then you spend one day at each site and mark whether otters are present or absent every 5 minutes during daylight hours. Make a graph that shows how otter density depends on kelp abundance, using the data shown below. Then formulate a hypothesis to explain the pattern you observed.

Site	Kelp Abundance (% cover)	Otter Density (# sightings per day)
1	75	98
2	15	18
3	60	85
4	25	36

12. EVOLUTION CONNECTION
Discuss how the concept of time applies to ecological situations and evolutionary changes. Do ecological time and evolutionary time ever overlap? If so, what are some examples?

13. SCIENTIFIC INQUIRY
Jens Clausen and colleagues, at the Carnegie Institution of Washington, studied how the size of yarrow plants (*Achillea lanulosa*) growing on the slopes of the Sierra Nevada varied with elevation. They found that plants from low elevations were generally taller than plants from high elevations, as shown below:

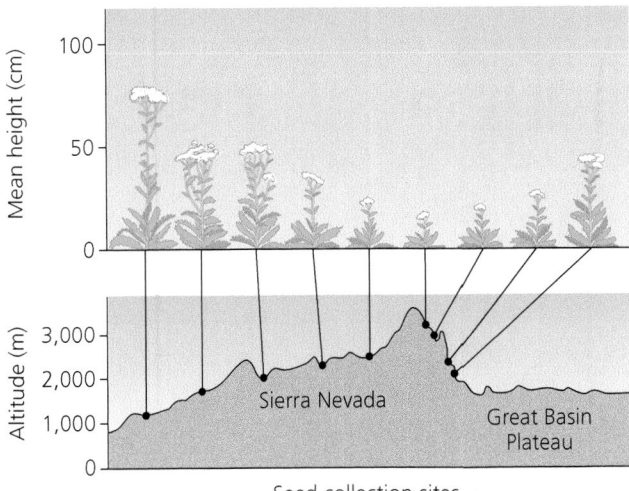

Source: J. Clausen et al., Experimental studies on the nature of species. III. Environmental responses of climatic races of *Achillea*, Carnegie Institution of Washington Publication No. 581 (1948).

Clausen and colleagues proposed two hypotheses to explain this variation within a species: (1) There are genetic differences between populations of plants found at different elevations. (2) The species has developmental flexibility and can assume tall or short growth forms, depending on local abiotic factors. If you had seeds from yarrow plants found at low and high elevations, what experiments would you perform to test these hypotheses?

14. **WRITE ABOUT A THEME**
Feedback Regulation Global warming is occurring rapidly in Arctic marine and terrestrial ecosystems, including tundra and northern coniferous forests. In such locations, reflective white snow and ice cover are melting more quickly and extensively, uncovering darker-colored ocean water, plants, and rocks. In a short essay (100–150 words), explain how this process might represent a positive-feedback loop.

For selected answers, see Appendix A.

1. MasteringBiology® Assignments
Tutorial Aquatic Biomes
Activities Tropical Atmospheric Circulation • Terrestrial Biomes • Adaptations to Biotic and Abiotic Factors • Discovery Channel Video: Trees
Questions Student Misconceptions • Reading Quiz • Multiple Choice • End-of-Chapter

2. eText
Read your book online, search, take notes, highlight text, and more.

3. The Study Area
Practice Tests • Cumulative Test • *BioFlix* 3-D Animations • MP3 Tutor Sessions • Videos • Activities • Investigations • Lab Media • Audio Glossary • Word Study Tools • Art

53

Population Ecology

▲ Figure 53.1 **What causes a sheep population to fluctuate in size?**

KEY CONCEPTS

53.1 Dynamic biological processes influence population density, dispersion, and demographics

53.2 The exponential model describes population growth in an idealized, unlimited environment

53.3 The logistic model describes how a population grows more slowly as it nears its carrying capacity

53.4 Life history traits are products of natural selection

53.5 Many factors that regulate population growth are density dependent

53.6 The human population is no longer growing exponentially but is still increasing rapidly

Counting Sheep

On the rugged Scottish island of Hirta, ecologists have been studying a population of Soay sheep for more than 50 years **(Figure 53.1)**. What makes these animals worth studying for such a long time? Soay sheep are a rare and ancient breed, the closest living relative of the domesticated sheep that lived in Europe thousands of years ago. To help preserve the breed, conservationists captured sheep in 1932 on Soay Island, at the time the animals' only home, and released them on nearby Hirta. There, the sheep became valuable for a second reason: They provided an ideal opportunity to study how an isolated population of animals changes in size when food is plentiful and predators are absent. Surprisingly, ecologists found that the number of sheep on Hirta swung dramatically under these conditions, sometimes changing by more than 50% from one year to the next.

Why do populations of some species fluctuate greatly while populations of other species do not? To answer this question, we turn to the field of population ecology, the study of populations in relation to their environment. Population ecology explores how biotic and abiotic factors influence the density, distribution, size, and age structure of populations.

Our earlier study of populations in Chapter 23 emphasized the relationship between population genetics—the structure and dynamics of gene pools—and evolution. Populations evolve as natural selection acts on heritable variations among individuals, changing the frequencies of alleles and traits over time. Evolution remains a central theme as we now view populations in the context of ecology.

In this chapter, we will first examine some of the structural and dynamic aspects of populations. We will then explore the tools and models ecologists use to analyze populations and the factors that regulate the abundance of organisms. Finally, we will apply these basic concepts as we examine recent trends in the size and makeup of the human population.

CONCEPT 53.1

Dynamic biological processes influence population density, dispersion, and demographics

A **population** is a group of individuals of a single species living in the same general area. Members of a population rely on the same resources, are influenced by similar environmental factors, and are likely to interact and breed with one another.

Populations are often described by their boundaries and size (the number of individuals living within those boundaries). Ecologists usually begin investigating a population by defining boundaries appropriate to the organism under study and to the questions being asked. A population's boundaries may be natural ones, as in the case of Hirta Island and its Soay sheep, or they may be arbitrarily defined by an investigator—for example, a specific county in Minnesota for a study of oak trees.

Density and Dispersion

The **density** of a population is the number of individuals per unit area or volume: the number of oak trees per square kilometer in the Minnesota county or the number of *Escherichia coli* bacteria per milliliter in a test tube. **Dispersion** is the pattern of spacing among individuals within the boundaries of the population.

Density: A Dynamic Perspective

In rare cases, population size and density can be determined by counting all individuals within the boundaries of the population. We could count all the Soay sheep on Hirta Island or all the sea stars in a tide pool, for instance. Large mammals that live in herds, such as buffalo or elephants, can sometimes be counted accurately from airplanes. In most cases, however, it is impractical or impossible to count all individuals in a population. Instead, ecologists use a variety of sampling techniques to estimate densities and total population sizes. For example, they might count the number of oak trees in several randomly located 100 × 100 m plots, calculate the average density in the plots, and then extend the estimate to the population size in the entire area. Such estimates are most accurate when there are many sample plots and when the habitat is fairly homogeneous. In other cases, instead of counting single organisms, population ecologists estimate density from an indicator of population size, such as the number of nests, burrows, tracks, or fecal droppings. Ecologists also use the **mark-recapture method** to estimate the size of wildlife populations (Figure 53.2).

Density is not a static property but changes as individuals are added to or removed from a population (Figure 53.3).

▼ Figure 53.2

RESEARCH METHOD

Determining Population Size Using the Mark-Recapture Method

APPLICATION Ecologists cannot count all the individuals in a population if the organisms move too quickly or are hidden from view. In such cases, researchers often use the mark-recapture method to estimate population size. Andrew Gormley and his colleagues at the University of Otago applied this method to a population of endangered Hector's dolphins (*Cephalorhynchus hectori*) near Banks Peninsula, in New Zealand.

Hector's dolphins

TECHNIQUE Scientists typically begin by capturing a random sample of individuals in a population. They tag, or "mark," each individual and then release it. With some species, researchers can identify individuals without physically capturing them. For example, Gormley and colleagues identified 180 Hector's dolphins by photographing their distinctive dorsal fins from boats.

After waiting for the marked or otherwise identified individuals to mix back into the population, usually a few days or weeks, scientists capture or sample a second set of individuals. At Banks Peninsula, Gormley's team encountered 44 dolphins in their second sampling, 7 of which they had photographed before. The number of marked animals captured in the second sampling (*x*) divided by the total number of animals captured in the second sampling (*n*) should equal the number of individuals marked and released in the first sampling (*s*) divided by the estimated population size (*N*):

$$\frac{x}{n} = \frac{s}{N} \qquad \text{or, solving for population size,} \qquad N = \frac{sn}{x}$$

The method assumes that marked and unmarked individuals have the same probability of being captured or sampled, that the marked organisms have mixed completely back into the population, and that no individuals are born, die, immigrate, or emigrate during the resampling interval.

RESULTS Based on these initial data, the estimated population size of Hector's dolphins at Banks Peninsula would be 180 × 44/7 = 1,131 individuals. Repeated sampling by Gormley and colleagues suggested a true population size closer to 1,100.

SOURCE A. M. Gormley et al., Capture-recapture estimates of Hector's dolphin abundance at Banks Peninsula, New Zealand, *Marine Mammal Science* 21:204–216 (2005).

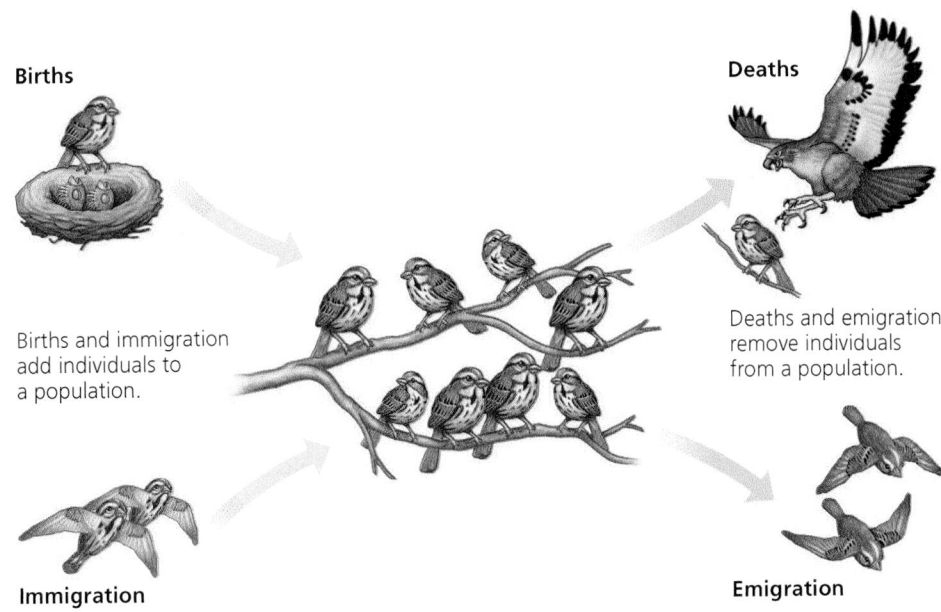

Births

Births and immigration add individuals to a population.

Immigration

Deaths

Deaths and emigration remove individuals from a population.

Emigration

▲ Figure 53.3 **Population dynamics.**

Additions occur through birth (which we define here to include all forms of reproduction) and **immigration**, the influx of new individuals from other areas. The factors that remove individuals from a population are death (mortality) and **emigration**, the movement of individuals out of a population and into other locations

While birth and death rates influence the density of all populations, immigration and emigration also alter the density of many populations. Long-term studies of Belding's ground squirrels (*Spermophilus beldingi*) in the vicinity of Tioga Pass, in the Sierra Nevada of California, showed that some of the squirrels moved nearly 2 km from where they were born. This long-distance movement made them immigrants to other populations. In fact, immigrants made up 1–8% of the males and 0.7–6% of the females in the study population. Although these percentages may seem small, such immigration is a meaningful biological exchange between populations over time.

Patterns of Dispersion

Within a population's geographic range, local densities may differ substantially, creating contrasting patterns of dispersion. Differences in local density are among the most important characteristics for a population ecologist to study, since they provide insight into the environmental associations and social interactions of individuals in the population.

The most common pattern of dispersion is *clumped*, in which individuals are aggregated in patches. Plants and fungi are often clumped where soil conditions and other environmental factors favor germination and growth. Mushrooms, for instance, may be clumped within and on top of a rotting log. Insects and salamanders may be clumped under the same log because of the higher humidity there. Clumping of animals may also be associated with mating behavior. Mayflies, which survive only a day or two as mating adults, often swarm in great numbers, a behavior that increases their chance of mating. Sea stars group together in tide pools, where food is readily available and where they can breed successfully **(Figure 53.4a)**. Forming groups may also increase the effectiveness of predation or defense; for example, a wolf pack is more likely than a single wolf to subdue a moose, and a flock of birds is more likely than a single bird to warn of a potential attack.

A *uniform*, or evenly spaced, pattern of dispersion may result from direct interactions between individuals in the population. Some plants secrete chemicals that inhibit the germination and growth of nearby individuals that could compete for resources. Animals often exhibit uniform dispersion as a result of antagonistic social interactions, such as **territoriality**—the defense of a bounded physical space against encroachment by other individuals **(Figure 53.4b)**. Uniform patterns are rarer than clumped patterns.

▼ **Figure 53.4 Patterns of dispersion within a population's geographic range.**

(a) Clumped

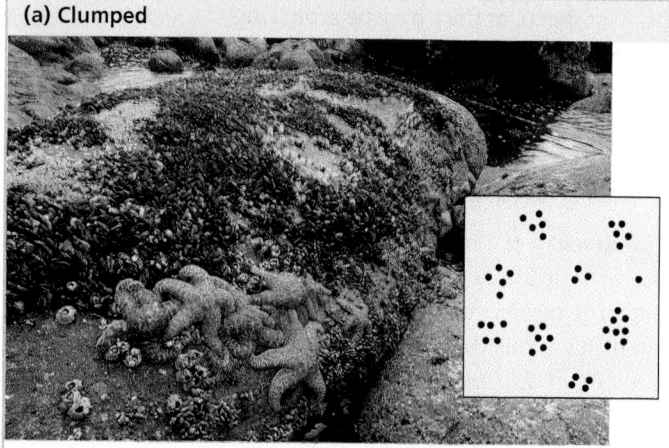

Many animals, such as these sea stars, group together where food is abundant.

(b) Uniform

Birds nesting on small islands, such as these king penguins in the Falkland Islands, near the southern tip of South America, often exhibit uniform spacing, maintained by aggressive interactions between neighbors.

(c) Random

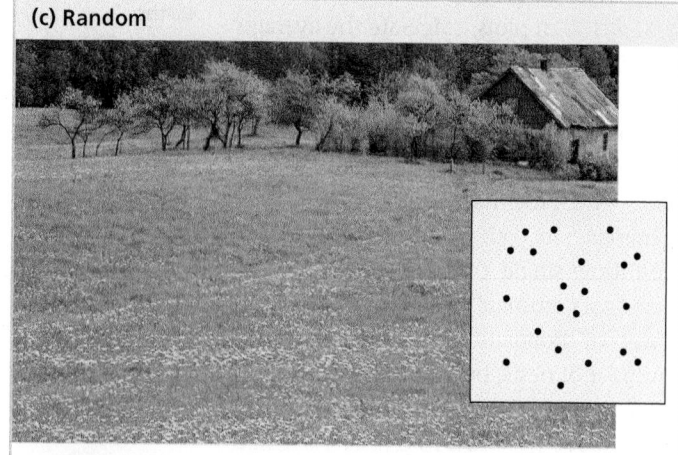

Many plants, such as these dandelions, grow from windblown seeds that land at random and later germinate.

WHAT IF? *Patterns of dispersion can depend on scale. How might the penguin dispersion look from an airplane over the ocean?*

In *random* dispersion (unpredictable spacing), the position of each individual in a population is independent of other individuals. This pattern occurs in the absence of strong attractions or repulsions among individuals or where key physical or chemical factors are relatively constant across the study area. Plants established by windblown seeds, such as dandelions, may be randomly distributed in a fairly uniform habitat (Figure 53.4c). Random patterns are not as common in nature as one might expect; most populations show at least a tendency toward a clumped distribution.

Demographics

The factors that influence population density and dispersion patterns—ecological needs of a species, structure of the environment, and interactions among individuals within the population—also influence other characteristics of populations. **Demography** is the study of the vital statistics of populations and how they change over time. Of particular interest to demographers are birth rates and death rates. A useful way to summarize some of the vital statistics of a population is to make a life table.

Life Tables

About a century ago, when life insurance first became available, insurance companies began to estimate how long, on average, people of a given age could be expected to live. To do this, demographers developed **life tables**, age-specific summaries of the survival pattern of a population. Population ecologists adapted this approach to the study of populations in general.

The best way to construct a life table is to follow the fate of a **cohort**, a group of individuals of the same age, from birth until all of the individuals are dead. To build the life table, we need to determine the number of individuals that die in each age-group and to calculate the proportion of the cohort surviving from one age class to the next. Studies of the Belding's ground squirrels near Tioga Pass produced the life table in Table 53.1. The table reveals many things about the population. For instance, the third and eighth columns list, respectively, the proportions of females and males in the cohort that are still alive at each age. A comparison of the fifth and tenth columns reveals that males have higher death rates than females.

Survivorship Curves

A graphic method of representing some of the data in a life table is a **survivorship curve**, a plot of the proportion or numbers in a cohort still alive at each age. As an example, let's use the data for Belding's ground squirrels in Table 53.1 to draw a survivorship curve for this population. Generally, a survivorship curve begins with a cohort of a convenient size—say, 1,000 individuals. To obtain the other points in the curve for the Belding's ground squirrel population, we multiply the proportion alive at the start of each year (the third and eighth columns of Table 53.1) by 1,000 (the hypothetical beginning cohort). The result is the number alive at the start

Table 53.1 Life Table for Belding's Ground Squirrels (*Spermophilus beldingi*) at Tioga Pass, in the Sierra Nevada of California*

| Age (years) | FEMALES | | | | | MALES | | | | |
	Number Alive at Start of Year	Proportion Alive at Start of Year	Number of Deaths During Year	Death Rate[†]	Average Additional Life Expectancy (years)	Number Alive at Start of Year	Proportion Alive at Start of Year	Number of Deaths During Year	Death Rate[†]	Average Additional Life Expectancy (years)
0–1	337	1.000	207	0.61	1.33	349	1.000	227	0.65	1.07
1–2	252[‡]	0.386	125	0.50	1.56	248[‡]	0.350	140	0.56	1.12
2–3	127	0.197	60	0.47	1.60	108	0.152	74	0.69	0.93
3–4	67	0.106	32	0.48	1.59	34	0.048	23	0.68	0.89
4–5	35	0.054	16	0.46	1.59	11	0.015	9	0.82	0.68
5–6	19	0.029	10	0.53	1.50	2	0.003	2	1.00	0.50
6–7	9	0.014	4	0.44	1.61	0				
7–8	5	0.008	1	0.20	1.50					
8–9	4	0.006	3	0.75	0.75					
9–10	1	0.002	1	1.00	0.50					

Source: P. W. Sherman and M. L. Morton, Demography of Belding's ground squirrel, *Ecology* 65:1617–1628 (1984).
*Females and males have different mortality schedules, so they are tallied separately.
[†]The death rate is the proportion of individuals dying during the specific time interval.
[‡]Includes 122 females and 126 males first captured as 1-year-olds and therefore not included in the count of squirrels age 0–1.

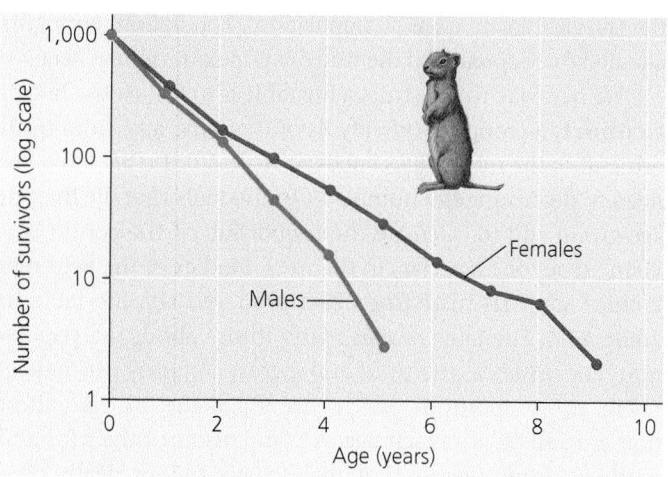

▲ **Figure 53.5 Survivorship curves for male and female Belding's ground squirrels.** The logarithmic scale on the y-axis allows the number of survivors to be visible across the entire range (2–1,000 individuals) on the graph.

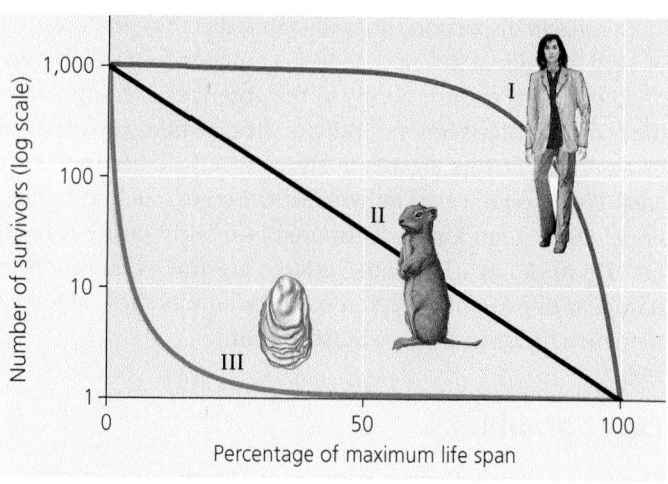

▲ **Figure 53.6 Idealized survivorship curves: Types I, II, and III.** The y-axis is logarithmic and the x-axis is on a relative scale, so that species with widely varying life spans can be presented together on the same graph.

of each year. Plotting these numbers versus age for female and male Belding's ground squirrels yields **Figure 53.5**. The relatively straight lines of the plots indicate relatively constant rates of death; however, male Belding's ground squirrels have a lower survival rate than females.

Figure 53.5 represents just one of many patterns of survivorship exhibited by natural populations. Though diverse, survivorship curves can be classified into three general types **(Figure 53.6)**. A Type I curve is flat at the start, reflecting low death rates during early and middle life, and then drops steeply as death rates increase among older age-groups. Many large mammals, including humans, that produce few offspring but provide them with good care exhibit this kind of curve. In contrast, a Type III curve drops sharply at the start, reflecting very high death rates for the young, but flattens out as death rates decline for those few individuals that survive the early period of die-off. This type of curve is usually associated with organisms that produce very large numbers of offspring but provide little or no care, such as long-lived plants, many fishes, and most marine invertebrates. An oyster, for example, may release millions of eggs, but most larvae hatched from fertilized eggs die from predation or other causes. Those few offspring that survive long enough to attach to a suitable substrate and begin growing a hard shell tend to survive for a relatively long time. Type II curves are intermediate, with a constant death rate over the organism's life span. This kind of survivorship occurs in Belding's ground squirrels (see Figure 53.5) and some other rodents, various invertebrates, some lizards, and some annual plants.

Many species fall somewhere between these basic types of survivorship or show more complex patterns. In birds, mortality is often high among the youngest individuals (as in a Type III curve) but fairly constant among adults (as in a Type

II curve). Some invertebrates, such as crabs, may show a "stair-stepped" curve, with brief periods of increased mortality during molts, followed by periods of lower mortality when their protective exoskeleton is hard.

In populations not experiencing immigration or emigration, survivorship is one of the two key factors determining changes in population size. The other key factor determining population trends is reproductive rate.

Reproductive Rates

Demographers who study sexually reproducing species generally ignore the males and concentrate on the females in a population because only females produce offspring. Therefore, demographers view populations in terms of females giving rise to new females. The simplest way to describe the reproductive pattern of a population is to ask how reproductive output varies with the ages of females.

A **reproductive table**, or fertility schedule, is an age-specific summary of the reproductive rates in a population. It is constructed by measuring the reproductive output of a cohort from birth until death. For a sexual species, the reproductive table tallies the number of female offspring produced by each age-group. **Table 53.2** illustrates a reproductive table for Belding's ground squirrels. Reproductive output for sexual organisms such as birds and mammals is the product of the proportion of females of a given age that are breeding and the number of female offspring of those breeding females. Multiplying these numbers gives the average number of female offspring for each female in a given age-group (the last column in Table 53.2). For Belding's ground squirrels, which begin to reproduce at age 1 year, reproductive output rises to a peak at 4 years of age and then falls off in older females.

Table 53.2 Reproductive Table for Belding's Ground Squirrels at Tioga Pass				
Age (years)	Proportion of Females Weaning a Litter	Mean Size of Litters (Males + Females)	Mean Number of Females in a Litter	Average Number of Female Offspring*
0–1	0.00	0.00	0.00	0.00
1–2	0.65	3.30	1.65	1.07
2–3	0.92	4.05	2.03	1.87
3–4	0.90	4.90	2.45	2.21
4–5	0.95	5.45	2.73	2.59
5–6	1.00	4.15	2.08	2.08
6–7	1.00	3.40	1.70	1.70
7–8	1.00	3.85	1.93	1.93
8–9	1.00	3.85	1.93	1.93
9–10	1.00	3.15	1.58	1.58

Source: P. W. Sherman and M. L. Morton, Demography of Belding's ground squirrel, *Ecology* 65:1617–1628 (1984).
*The average number of female offspring is the proportion weaning a litter multiplied by the mean number of females in a litter.

Reproductive tables vary considerably by species. Squirrels, for example, have a litter of two to six young once a year for less than a decade, whereas oak trees drop thousands of acorns each year for tens or hundreds of years. Mussels and other invertebrates may release millions of eggs and sperm in a spawning cycle. However, a high reproductive rate will not lead to rapid population growth unless conditions are near ideal for the growth and survival of offspring, as you'll learn in the next section.

CONCEPT CHECK 53.1

1. **DRAW IT** Each female of a particular fish species produces millions of eggs per year. Draw and label the most likely survivorship curve for this species, and explain your choice.

2. **WHAT IF?** As noted in Figure 53.2, an important assumption of the mark-recapture method is that marked individuals have the same probability of being captured as unmarked individuals. Describe a situation where this assumption might not be valid, and explain how the estimate of population size would be affected.

3. **MAKE CONNECTIONS** As shown in Figure 51.2a (p. 1119), a male stickleback fish attacks other males that invade its nesting territory. Predict the likely pattern of dispersion for male sticklebacks, and explain your reasoning.

For suggested answers, see Appendix A.

CONCEPT 53.2

The exponential model describes population growth in an idealized, unlimited environment

Populations of all species have the potential to expand greatly when resources are abundant. To appreciate the potential for population increase, consider a bacterium that can reproduce by fission every 20 minutes under ideal laboratory conditions. There would be 2 bacteria after 20 minutes, 4 after 40 minutes, and 8 after 60 minutes. If reproduction continued at this rate for a day and a half without mortality, there would be enough bacteria to form a layer 30 cm deep over the entire globe. At the other extreme, an elephant may produce only 6 offspring in a 100-year life span. Still, Charles Darwin once estimated that the descendants of a single pair of mating elephants would number 19 million within only 750 years. Darwin's estimate may not have been precisely correct, but such analyses led him to recognize the tremendous capacity for growth in all populations. Although unlimited growth does not occur for long in nature, studying population growth in an ideal, unlimited environment reveals how fast a population is capable of growing and the conditions under which rapid growth might actually occur.

Per Capita Rate of Increase

Imagine a population consisting of a few individuals living in an ideal, unlimited environment. Under these conditions, there are no external restrictions on the abilities of individuals to harvest energy, grow, and reproduce. The population will increase in size with every birth and with the immigration of individuals from other populations, and it will decrease in size with every death and with the emigration of individuals out of the population. We can thus define a change in population size during a fixed time interval with the following verbal equation:

$$\text{Change in population size} = \text{Births} + \text{Immigrants entering population} - \text{Deaths} - \text{Emigrants leaving population}$$

For simplicity here, we will ignore the effects of immigration and emigration, although a more complex formulation would certainly include these factors. We can also use mathematical notation to express this simplified relationship more concisely. If N represents population size and t represents time, then ΔN is the change in population size and Δt is the time interval (appropriate to the life span or generation time of the species) over which we are evaluating population growth. (The Greek letter delta, Δ, indicates change, such as change in time.) Using B for the number of births in the population during the time interval and D for the number of deaths, we can rewrite the verbal equation:

$$\frac{\Delta N}{\Delta t} = B - D$$

Next, we can convert this simple model to one in which births and deaths are expressed as the average number of births and deaths per individual (per capita) during the specified time interval. The *per capita birth rate* is the number of offspring produced per unit time by an average member of the population. If, for example, there are 34 births per year in a population of 1,000 individuals, the annual per capita birth rate is 34/1,000, or 0.034. If we know the annual per capita birth rate (symbolized by b), we can use the formula $B = bN$ to calculate the expected number of births per year in a population of any size. For example, if the annual per capita birth rate is 0.034 and the population size is 500,

$$B = bN$$
$$B = 0.034 \times 500$$
$$B = 17 \text{ per year}$$

Similarly, the *per capita death rate* (symbolized by m, for mortality) allows us to calculate the expected number of deaths per unit time in a population of any size, using the formula $D = mN$. If $m = 0.016$ per year, we would expect 16 deaths per year in a population of 1,000 individuals. For natural populations or those in the laboratory, the per capita birth and death rates can be calculated from estimates of population size and data in life tables and reproductive tables (for example, Tables 53.1 and 53.2).

Now we can revise the population growth equation again, this time using per capita birth and death rates rather than the numbers of births and deaths:

$$\frac{\Delta N}{\Delta t} = bN - mN$$

One final simplification is in order. Population ecologists are most interested in the *difference* between the per capita birth rate and the per capita death rate. This difference is the *per capita rate of increase*, or r:

$$r = b - m$$

The value of r indicates whether a given population is growing ($r > 0$) or declining ($r < 0$). **Zero population growth (ZPG)** occurs when the per capita birth and death rates are equal ($r = 0$). Births and deaths still occur in such a population, of course, but they balance each other exactly.

Using the per capita rate of increase, we can now rewrite the equation for change in population size as

$$\frac{\Delta N}{\Delta t} = rN$$

Remember that this equation is for a discrete, or fixed, time interval (often one year, as in the previous example) and does

not include immigration or emigration. Most ecologists prefer to use differential calculus to express population growth *instantaneously*, as growth rate at a particular instant in time:

$$\frac{dN}{dt} = r_{inst}N$$

In this case r_{inst} is simply the instantaneous per capita rate of increase. If you have not yet studied calculus, don't be intimidated by the form of the last equation; it is similar to the previous one, except that the time intervals Δt are very short and are expressed in the equation as dt. In fact, as Δt becomes shorter, the discrete r approaches the instantaneous r_{inst} in value.

Exponential Growth

Earlier we described a population whose members all have access to abundant food and are free to reproduce at their physiological capacity. Population increase under these ideal conditions is called **exponential population growth**, also known as geometric population growth. Under these conditions, the per capita rate of increase may assume the maximum rate for the species, denoted as r_{max}. The equation for exponential population growth is

$$\frac{dN}{dt} = r_{max}N$$

The size of a population that is growing exponentially increases at a constant rate, resulting eventually in a J-shaped growth curve when population size is plotted over time (Figure 53.7). Although the maximum *rate* of increase is constant, the population accumulates more new individuals per unit of time when it is large than when it is small; thus, the

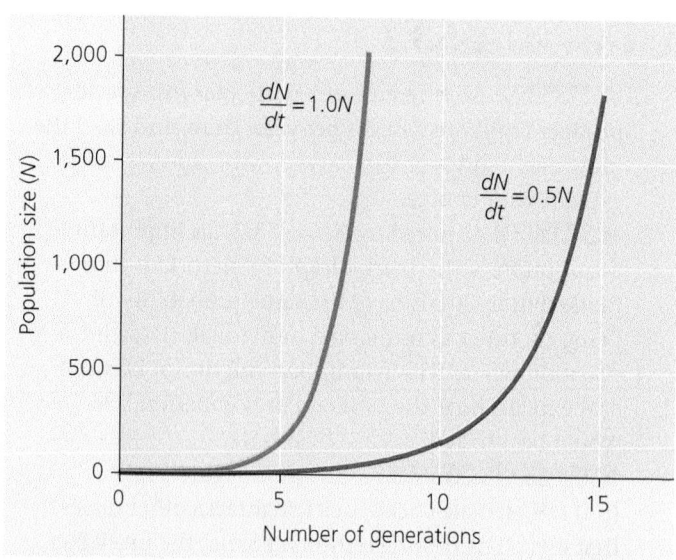

▲ Figure 53.7 **Population growth predicted by the exponential model.** This graph compares growth in two populations with different values of r_{max}. Increasing the value of r_{max} from 0.5 to 1.0 increases the rate of rise in population size over time, as reflected by the relative slopes of the curves at any given population size.

Figure 53.8 Exponential growth in the African elephant population of Kruger National Park, South Africa.

curves in Figure 53.7 get progressively steeper over time. This occurs because population growth depends on N as well as r_{max}, and larger populations experience more births (and deaths) than small ones growing at the same per capita rate. It is also clear from Figure 53.7 that a population with a higher maximum rate of increase ($dN/dt = 1.0N$) will grow faster than one with a lower rate of increase ($dN/dt = 0.5N$).

The J-shaped curve of exponential growth is characteristic of some populations that are introduced into a new environment or whose numbers have been drastically reduced by a catastrophic event and are rebounding. For example, the population of elephants in Kruger National Park, South Africa, grew exponentially for approximately 60 years after they were first protected from hunting (Figure 53.8). The increasingly large number of elephants eventually caused enough damage to vegetation in the park that a collapse in their food supply was likely. To protect other species and the park ecosystem before that happened, park managers began limiting the elephant population by using birth control and exporting elephants to other countries.

CONCEPT CHECK 53.2

1. Explain why a constant rate of increase (r_{max}) for a population produces a growth graph that is J-shaped.
2. Where is exponential growth by a plant population more likely—in an area where a forest was destroyed by fire or in a mature, undisturbed forest? Why?
3. **WHAT IF?** In 2009, the United States had a population of about 307 million people. If there were 14 births and 8 deaths per 1,000 people, what was the country's net population growth that year (ignoring immigration and emigration, which are substantial)? Do you think the United States is currently experiencing exponential population growth? Explain.

For suggested answers, see Appendix A.

The logistic model describes how a population grows more slowly as it nears its carrying capacity

The exponential growth model assumes that resources are unlimited, which is rarely the case in the real world. As population density increases, each individual has access to fewer resources. Ultimately, there is a limit to the number of individuals that can occupy a habitat. Ecologists define **carrying capacity**, symbolized by K, as the maximum population size that a particular environment can sustain. Carrying capacity varies over space and time with the abundance of limiting resources. Energy, shelter, refuge from predators, nutrient availability, water, and suitable nesting sites can all be limiting factors. For example, the carrying capacity for bats may be high in a habitat with abundant flying insects and roosting sites, but lower where there is abundant food but fewer suitable shelters.

Crowding and resource limitation can have a profound effect on population growth rate. If individuals cannot obtain sufficient resources to reproduce, the per capita birth rate (b) will decline. If they cannot consume enough energy to maintain themselves or if disease or parasitism increases with density, the per capita death rate (m) may increase. A decrease in b or an increase in m results in a lower per capita rate of increase (r).

The Logistic Growth Model

We can modify our mathematical model to incorporate changes in growth rate as the population size nears the carrying capacity. In the **logistic population growth** model, the per capita rate of increase approaches zero as the carrying capacity is reached.

To construct the logistic model, we start with the exponential population growth model and add an expression that reduces the per capita rate of increase as N increases. If the maximum sustainable population size (carrying capacity) is K, then $K - N$ is the number of additional individuals the environment can support, and $(K - N)/K$ is the fraction of K that is still available for population growth. By multiplying the exponential rate of increase $r_{max}N$ by $(K - N)/K$, we modify the change in population size as N increases:

$$\frac{dN}{dt} = r_{max}N \frac{(K - N)}{K}$$

When N is small compared to K, the term $(K - N)/K$ is close to 1, and the per capita rate of increase, $r_{max}(K - N)/K$, approaches the maximum rate of increase. But when N is large and resources are limiting, then $(K - N)/K$ is close to 0, and the per capita rate of increase is small. When N equals K, the population stops

Table 53.3 Logistic Growth of a Hypothetical Population (K = 1,500)				
Population Size (N)	Maximum Rate of Increase (r_{max})	$\dfrac{K - N}{K}$	Per Capita Rate of Increase: $r_{max}\left(\dfrac{K - N}{K}\right)$	Population Growth Rate:* $r_{max}N\left(\dfrac{K - N}{K}\right)$
25	1.0	0.98	0.98	+25
100	1.0	0.93	0.93	+93
250	1.0	0.83	0.83	+208
500	1.0	0.67	0.67	+333
750	1.0	0.50	0.50	+375
1,000	1.0	0.33	0.33	+333
1,500	1.0	0.00	0.00	0

*Rounded to the nearest whole number.

growing. **Table 53.3** shows calculations of population growth rate for a hypothetical population growing according to the logistic model, with r_{max} = 1.0 per individual per year. Notice that the overall population growth rate is highest, +375 individuals per year, when the population size is 750, or half the carrying capacity. At a population size of 750, the per capita rate of increase remains relatively high (one-half the maximum rate), but there are more reproducing individuals (N) in the population than at lower population sizes.

As shown in **Figure 53.9**, the logistic model of population growth produces a sigmoid (S-shaped) growth curve when N

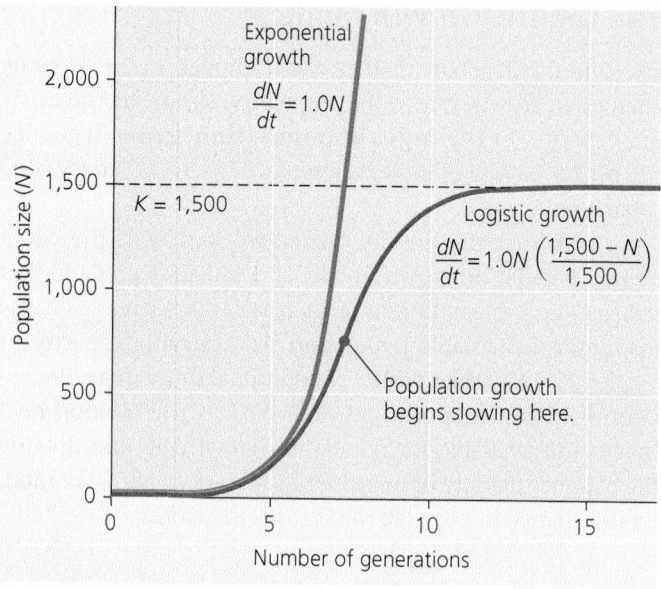

▲ **Figure 53.9 Population growth predicted by the logistic model.** The rate of population growth decreases as population size (N) approaches the carrying capacity (K) of the environment. The red line shows logistic growth in a population where r_{max} = 1.0 and K = 1,500 individuals. For comparison, the blue line illustrates a population continuing to grow exponentially with the same r_{max}.

is plotted over time (the red line). New individuals are added to the population most rapidly at intermediate population sizes, when there is not only a breeding population of substantial size, but also lots of available space and other resources in the environment. The population growth rate decreases dramatically as N approaches K.

Note that we haven't said anything yet about *why* the population growth rate decreases as N approaches K. For a population's growth rate to decrease, the birth rate b must decrease, the death rate m must increase, or both. Later in the chapter, we will consider some of the factors affecting these rates, including the presence of disease, predation, and limited amounts of food and other resources.

The Logistic Model and Real Populations

The growth of laboratory populations of some small animals, such as beetles and crustaceans, and of some microorganisms, such as bacteria, *Paramecium*, and yeasts, fits an S-shaped curve fairly well under conditions of limited resources (**Figure 53.10a**). These populations are grown in a constant environment lacking predators and competing species that may reduce growth of the populations, conditions that rarely occur in nature.

Some of the basic assumptions built into the logistic model clearly do not apply to all populations. The logistic model assumes that populations adjust instantaneously to growth and approach carrying capacity smoothly. In reality, there is often a delay before the negative effects of an increasing population are realized. If food becomes limiting for a population, for instance, reproduction will decline eventually, but females may use their energy reserves to continue reproducing for a short time. This may cause the population to overshoot its carrying capacity temporarily, as shown for the water fleas in **Figure 53.10b**. If the population then drops below carrying capacity, there will be a delay in population growth until the increased number of offspring are actually born. Still other populations fluctuate greatly, making it difficult even to define carrying capacity. We will examine some possible reasons for such fluctuations later in the chapter.

In addition to the assumption that populations adjust instantaneously to growth, the logistic model is based on another assumption—that regardless of population density, each individual added to a population has the same negative effect on population growth rate. However, some populations show an *Allee effect* (named after W. C. Allee, of the University of Chicago, who first described it), in which individuals may have a more difficult time surviving or reproducing if the population size is too small. For example, a single plant may be damaged by excessive wind if it is standing alone, but it would be protected in a clump of individuals.

(a) A *Paramecium* population in the lab. The growth (black dots) of *Paramecium aurelia* in a small culture closely approximates logistic growth (red curve) if the researcher maintains a constant environment.

(b) A *Daphnia* population in the lab. The growth (black dots) of a population of water fleas (*Daphnia*) in a small laboratory culture does not correspond well to the logistic model (red curve). This population overshoots the carrying capacity of its artificial environment before it settles down to an approximately stable population size.

The logistic model is a useful starting point for thinking about how populations grow and for constructing more complex models. The model is also important in conservation biology for predicting how rapidly a particular population might increase in numbers after it has been reduced to a small size and for estimating sustainable harvest rates for wildlife populations. Conservation biologists can use the model to estimate the critical size below which populations of certain organisms, such as the northern subspecies of the white rhinoceros (*Ceratotherium simum*), may become extinct **(Figure 53.11)**. Like any useful starting hypothesis, the logistic model has stimulated research that has led to a better understanding of the subject: in this case, the factors affecting population growth.

▲ **Figure 53.11 White rhinoceros mother and calf.** The two animals pictured here are members of the southern subspecies, which has a population of more than 10,000 individuals. The northern subspecies is critically endangered, with a population of fewer than 15 known individuals.

CONCEPT CHECK 53.3

1. Explain why a population that fits the logistic growth model increases more rapidly at intermediate size than at relatively small and large sizes.

2. **WHAT IF?** Add rows to Table 53.3 for three cases where $N > K$, specifically, $N = 1,600, 1,750$, and $2,000$. What is the population growth rate in each case? In which portion of Figure 53.10b is the *Daphnia* population changing in a way that corresponds to the values you calculated?

3. **MAKE CONNECTIONS** Concept 19.3, pp. 390–393, discusses viruses that are pathogens of animals and plants. How might the presence of such pathogens alter the carrying capacity of a population? Explain.

For suggested answers, see Appendix A.

CONCEPT 53.4

Life history traits are products of natural selection

EVOLUTION Natural selection favors traits that improve an organism's chances of survival and reproductive success. In every species, there are trade-offs between survival and reproductive traits such as frequency of reproduction, number of offspring (number of seeds produced by plants; litter or clutch size for animals), and investment in parental care. The traits that affect an organism's schedule of reproduction and survival make up its **life history**. A life history entails three main variables: when reproduction begins (the age at first reproduction or age at maturity), how often the organism reproduces, and how many offspring are produced per reproductive episode.

With the important exception of humans, which we will consider later in the chapter, organisms do not choose consciously when to reproduce or how many offspring to have. Rather, organisms' life history traits are evolutionary outcomes reflected in their development, physiology, and behavior.

Evolution and Life History Diversity

The fundamental idea that evolution accounts for the diversity of life is manifest in a broad range of life histories found in nature. The Pacific salmon, for example, hatches in the headwaters of a stream and then migrates to the open ocean, where it requires one to four years to mature. The salmon eventually returns to the freshwater stream to spawn, producing thousands of eggs in a single reproductive opportunity before it dies. This "one-shot" pattern of big-bang reproduction, or **semelparity** (from the Latin *semel*, once, and *parere*, to beget), also occurs in some plants, such as the agave, or "century plant" (**Figure 53.12**). Agaves generally grow in arid climates with unpredictable rainfall and poor soils. An agave grows for years, accumulating nutrients in its tissues, until there is an unusually wet year. It then sends up a large flowering stalk, produces seeds, and dies. This life history is an adaptation to the agave's harsh desert environment.

In contrast to semelparity is **iteroparity** (from the Latin *iterare*, to repeat), or repeated reproduction. In iteroparity, organisms produce relatively few but large offspring each time they reproduce, and they provision the offspring better. Some lizards, for example, produce a few large, nutrient-containing eggs annually beginning in their second year of life.

What factors contribute to the evolution of semelparity versus iteroparity? A current hypothesis suggests that there are two critical factors: the survival rate of the offspring and the likelihood that the adult will survive to reproduce again. Where the survival rate of offspring is low, typically in highly variable or unpredictable environments, the prediction is that semelparity will be favored. Adults are also less likely to survive in such environments, so producing large numbers of offspring should increase the probability that at least some of those offspring will survive. Iteroparity may be favored in more dependable environments, where adults are more likely to survive to breed again and where competition for resources may be intense. In such cases, a few relatively large, well-provisioned offspring should have a better chance of surviving until they can reproduce.

Nature abounds with life histories that are intermediate between the two extremes of semelparity and iteroparity. Oak trees and sea urchins, for example, can live a long time but repeatedly produce relatively large numbers of offspring.

"Trade-offs" and Life Histories

No organism could produce as many offspring as a semelparous species and provision them as well as an iteroparous species. There is a trade-off between reproduction and survival. **Figure 53.13** describes a study of European kestrels that demonstrated a survival cost to parents that care for a large

▼ **Figure 53.13** | INQUIRY

How does caring for offspring affect parental survival in kestrels?

EXPERIMENT Cor Dijkstra and colleagues in the Netherlands studied the effects of parental caregiving in European kestrels over five years. The researchers transferred chicks among nests to produce reduced broods (three or four chicks), normal broods (five or six), and enlarged broods (seven or eight). They then measured the percentage of male and female parent birds that survived the following winter. (Both males and females provide care for chicks.)

RESULTS

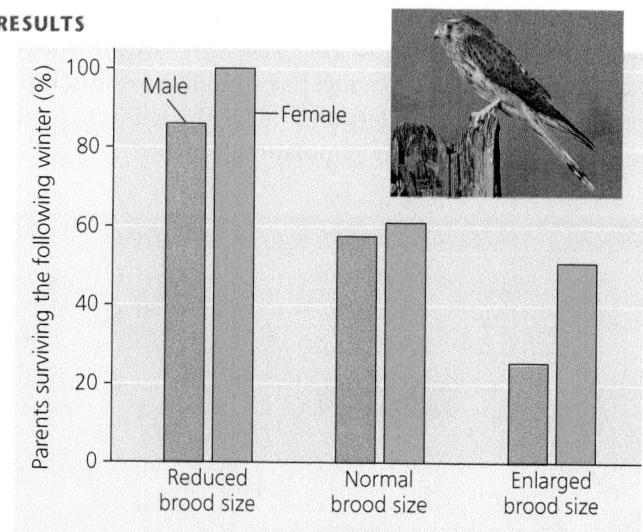

CONCLUSION The lower survival rates of kestrels with larger broods indicate that caring for more offspring negatively affects survival of the parents.

SOURCE C. Dijkstra et al., Brood size manipulations in the kestrel (*Falco tinnunculus*): effects on offspring and parent survival, *Journal of Animal Ecology* 59:269–285 (1990).

WHAT IF? The males of some bird species provide no parental care. If this were true for the European kestrel, how would the experimental results differ from those shown above?

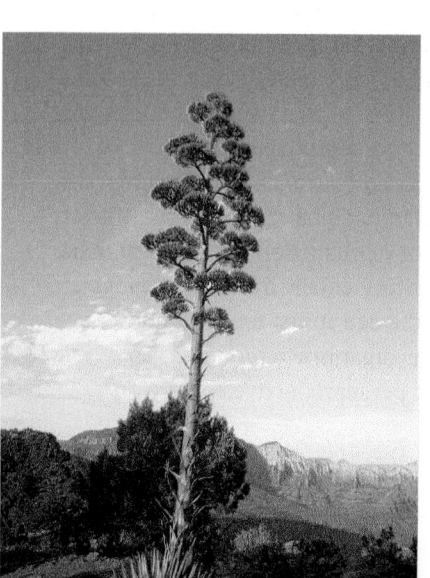

◀ **Figure 53.12 An agave (*Agave americana*), an example of big-bang reproduction.** The leaves of the plant are visible at the base of the giant flowering stalk, which is produced only at the end of the agave's life.

number of young. In another study, in Scotland, researchers found that female red deer that reproduced in a given summer were more likely to die the next winter than were females that did not reproduce.

Selective pressures influence the trade-off between the number and size of offspring. Plants and animals whose young are subject to high mortality rates often produce large numbers of relatively small offspring. Plants that colonize disturbed environments, for example, usually produce many small seeds, only a few of which may reach a suitable habitat. Small size may also increase the chance of seedling establishment by enabling the seeds to be carried longer distances to a broader range of habitats (Figure 53.14a). Animals that suffer high predation rates, such as quail, sardines, and mice, also tend to produce large numbers of offspring.

In other organisms, extra investment on the part of the parent greatly increases the offspring's chances of survival. Walnut and Brazil nut trees provision large seeds with nutrients that help the seedlings become established (Figure 53.14b). Primates generally bear only one or two offspring at a time; parental care and an extended period of learning in the first several years of life are very important to offspring fitness. Such provisioning and extra care can be especially important in habitats with high population densities.

Ecologists have attempted to connect differences in favored traits at different population densities with the logistic growth model discussed in Concept 53.3. Selection for traits that are sensitive to population density and are favored at high densities is known as *K*-selection, or density-dependent selection. In contrast, selection for traits that maximize reproductive success in uncrowded environments (low densities) is called *r*-selection, or density-independent selection. These names follow from the variables of the logistic equation. *K*-selection is said to operate in populations living at a density near the limit imposed by their resources (the carrying capacity, *K*), where competition among individuals is stronger. Mature trees growing in an old-growth forest are an example of *K*-selected organisms. In contrast, *r*-selection is said to maximize *r*, the per capita rate of increase, and occurs in environments in which population densities are well below carrying capacity or individuals face little competition. Such conditions are often found in disturbed habitats. Weeds growing in an abandoned agricultural field are an example of *r*-selected organisms.

The concepts of *K*- and *r*-selection represent two extremes in a range of actual life histories. The framework of *K*- and *r*-selection, grounded in the idea of carrying capacity, has helped ecologists to propose alternative hypotheses of life history evolution. These alternative hypotheses, in turn, have stimulated more thorough study of how factors such as disturbance, stress, and the frequency of opportunities for successful reproduction affect the evolution of life histories. They have also forced ecologists to address the important question we alluded to earlier: *Why* does population growth

(a) Dandelions grow quickly and release a large number of tiny fruits, each containing a single seed. Producing numerous seeds ensures that at least some will grow into plants that eventually produce seeds themselves.

(b) Some plants, such as the Brazil nut tree (right), produce a moderate number of large seeds in pods (above). Each seed's large endosperm provides nutrients for the embryo, an adaptation that helps a relatively large fraction of offspring survive.

▲ Figure 53.14 **Variation in the size of seed crops in plants.**

rate decrease as population size approaches carrying capacity? Answering this question is the focus of the next section.

CONCEPT CHECK 53.4

1. Consider two rivers: One is spring fed and has a constant water volume and temperature year-round; the other drains a desert landscape and floods and dries out at unpredictable intervals. Which river would you predict is more likely to support many species of iteroparous animals? Why?

2. In the fish called the peacock wrasse (*Symphodus tinca*), females disperse some of their eggs widely and lay other eggs in a nest. Only the latter receive parental care. Explain the trade-offs in reproduction that this behavior illustrates.

3. **WHAT IF?** Mice that experience stress such as a food shortage will sometimes abandon their young. Explain how this behavior might have evolved in the context of reproductive trade-offs and life history.

For suggested answers, see Appendix A.

CONCEPT 53.5

Many factors that regulate population growth are density dependent

What environmental factors keep populations from growing indefinitely? Why are some populations fairly stable in size, while others, such as the Soay sheep on Hirta Island, are not?

Population regulation is an area of ecology that has many practical applications. Farmers may want to reduce the abundance of insect pests or stop the growth of an invasive weed that is spreading rapidly. Conservation ecologists need to know what environmental factors create favorable feeding or breeding habitats for endangered species, such as the white rhinoceros and the whooping crane. Management programs based on population-regulating factors have helped prevent the extinction of many endangered species.

Population Change and Population Density

To understand why a population stops growing, ecologists study how the rates of birth, death, immigration, and emigration change as population density rises. If immigration and emigration offset each other, then a population grows when the birth rate exceeds the death rate and declines when the death rate exceeds the birth rate.

A birth rate or death rate that does *not* change with population density is said to be **density independent**. In a classic study of population regulation, Andrew Watkinson and John Harper, of the University of Wales, found that the mortality of dune fescue grass (*Vulpia membranacea*) is mainly due to physical factors that kill similar proportions of a local population, regardless of its density. For example, drought stress that arises when the roots of the grass are uncovered by shifting sands is a density-independent factor. In contrast, a death rate that rises as population density rises is said to be **density dependent**, as is a birth rate that falls with rising density. Watkinson and Harper found that reproduction by dune fescue declines as population density increases, in part because water or nutrients become more scarce. Thus, the key factors regulating birth rate in this population are density-dependent, while death rate is largely regulated by density-independent factors. **Figure 53.15** shows how the combination of density-dependent reproduction and density-independent mortality can stop population growth, leading to an equilibrium population density in species such as dune fescue.

Mechanisms of Density-Dependent Population Regulation

Biology's unifying theme of *feedback regulation* (see Chapter 1) applies to population dynamics. Without some type of negative feedback between population density and the rates of

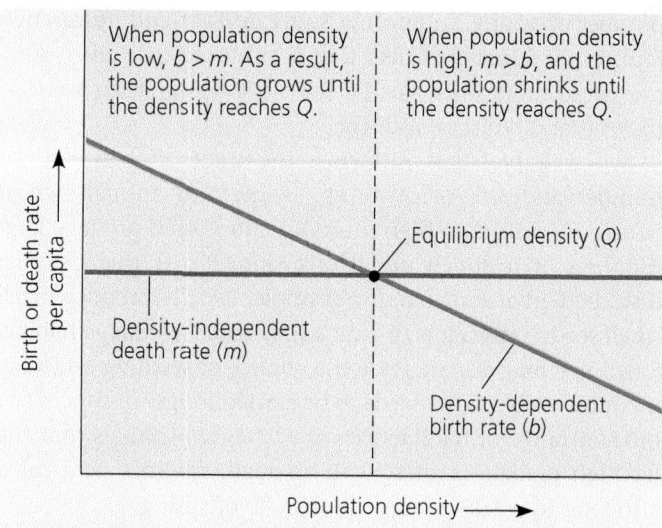

When population density is low, $b > m$. As a result, the population grows until the density reaches Q.

When population density is high, $m > b$, and the population shrinks until the density reaches Q.

Equilibrium density (Q)

Density-independent death rate (m)

Density-dependent birth rate (b)

Population density ⟶

▲ **Figure 53.15 Determining equilibrium for population density.** This simple model considers only birth and death rates. (Immigration and emigration rates are assumed to be either zero or equal.) In this example, the birth rate changes with population density, while the death rate is constant. At the equilibrium density (Q), the birth and death rates are equal.

DRAW IT *Redraw this figure for the case where the birth and death rates are both density dependent, as occurs for many species.*

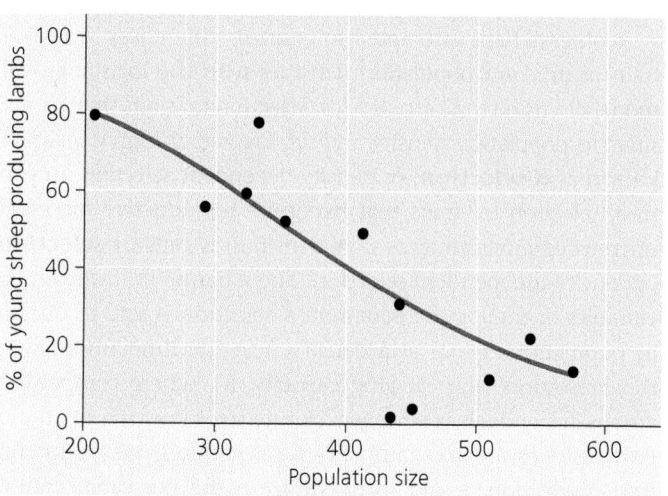

▲ **Figure 53.16 Decreased reproduction at high population densities.** Reproduction by young Soay sheep on Hirta Island drops dramatically as population size increases.

birth and death, a population would never stop growing. Density-dependent regulation provides that feedback, halting population growth through mechanisms that reduce birth rates or increase death rates For example, on Hirta Island, Soay sheep compete for food and other resources. Ecologists have closely monitored sheep density and reproduction for many years. The strongest density-dependent reduction in birth rates appears in young sheep, typically 1-year-olds giving birth for the first time (**Figure 53.16**). Competition and several other mechanisms of density-dependent population regulation are described in **Figure 53.17**, on pages 1183–1184.

Exploring Mechanisms of Density-Dependent Regulation

As population density increases, many density-dependent mechanisms slow or stop population growth by decreasing birth rates or increasing death rates.

Competition for Resources

Increasing population density intensifies competition for nutrients and other resources, reducing reproductive rates. Farmers minimize the effect of resource competition on the growth of grains such as wheat (*Triticum aestivum*) and other crops by applying fertilizers to reduce nutrient limitations on crop yield.

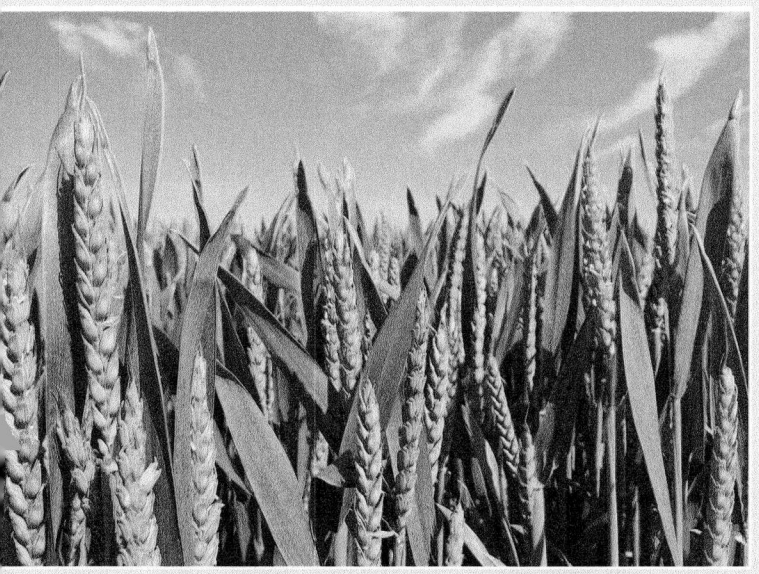

Predation

Predation can be an important cause of density-dependent mortality if a predator captures more food as the population density of the prey increases. As a prey population builds up, predators may also feed preferentially on that species. Some fish species, such as the cutthroat trout (*Oncorhynchus clarkii*), concentrate for a few days on a particular insect species that is emerging from its aquatic larval stage and then switch to another prey species when it becomes more abundant.

Toxic Wastes

Yeasts, such as the brewer's yeast *Saccharomyces cerevisiae*, are used to convert carbohydrates to ethanol in wine making. The ethanol that accumulates in the wine is toxic to yeasts and contributes to density-dependent regulation of yeast population size. The alcohol content of wine is usually less than 13% because that is the maximum concentration of ethanol that most wine-producing yeast cells can tolerate.

5 μm

Intrinsic Factors

Intrinsic physiological factors sometimes regulate population size. Reproductive rates of white-footed mice (*Peromyscus leucopus*) in a field enclosure can drop even when food and shelter are abundant. This drop in reproduction at high population density is associated with aggressive interactions and hormonal changes that delay sexual maturation and depress the immune system. In this species, high density causes a decrease in the birth rate and an increase in the death rate.

Exploring Mechanisms of Density-Dependent Regulation

Territoriality

Territoriality can limit population density when space becomes the resource for which individuals compete. Cheetahs (*Acinonyx jubatus*) use a chemical marker in urine to warn other cheetahs of their territorial boundaries. Australasian gannets (*Morus serrator*) defend their territories when nesting by calling and pecking at one another. Maintaining a territory increases the likelihood that an animal will capture enough food to reproduce. The presence of surplus, or nonbreeding, individuals is a good indication that territoriality is restricting population growth.

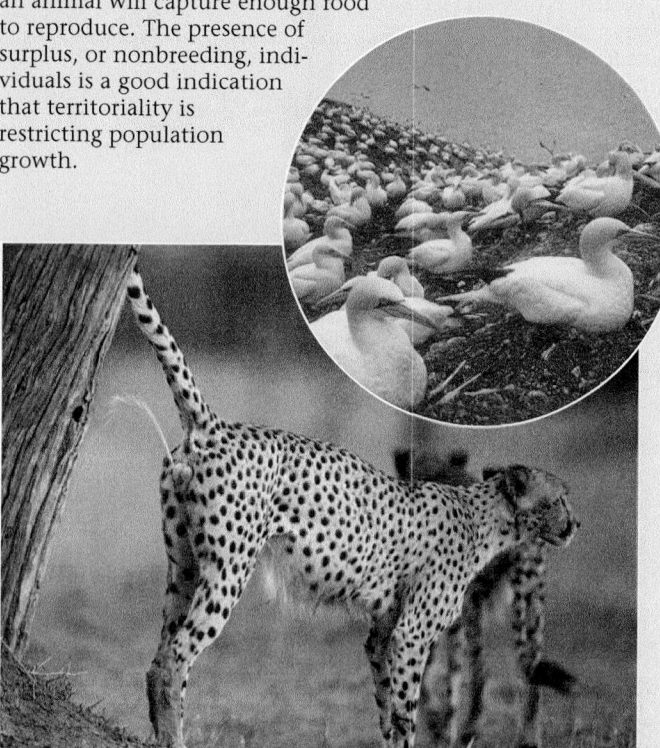

Disease

If the transmission rate of a particular disease depends on a certain level of crowding in a population, then the disease's impact is density dependent. In humans, respiratory diseases such as influenza (flu) and tuberculosis are caused by pathogens that spread through the air when an infected person sneezes or coughs. Both diseases strike a greater percentage of people in densely populated cities than in rural areas.

These various examples of population regulation by negative feedback show how increased densities cause population growth rates to decline by affecting reproduction, growth, and survival. But though negative feedback helps explain why populations stop growing, it does not address why some populations fluctuate dramatically while others remain relatively stable. That is the topic we address next.

Population Dynamics

All populations for which we have long-term data show some fluctuation in size. Such population fluctuations from year to year or place to place, called **population dynamics**, are influenced by many factors and in turn affect other species, including our own. For example, fluctuations in fish populations influence seasonal harvests of commercially important species. The study of population dynamics focuses on the complex interactions between biotic and abiotic factors that cause variation in population sizes.

Stability and Fluctuation

Populations of large mammals were once thought to remain relatively stable over time, but long-term studies have challenged that idea. The number of Soay sheep on Hirta Island fluctuates greatly, rising or falling by more than half from one year to the next. What causes the size of this population to change so dramatically? Harsh weather, particularly cold, wet winters, can weaken the sheep and reduce food availability, decreasing the size of the population. When sheep numbers are high, other factors, such as an increase in the density of parasites, also cause the population to shrink. Conversely, when sheep numbers are low and the weather is mild, food is readily available and the population grows quickly.

Like the Soay sheep population on Hirta, the moose population on Isle Royale in Lake Superior also fluctuates over time. In the case of the moose, predation is an additional factor that regulates the population. Moose from the mainland colonized

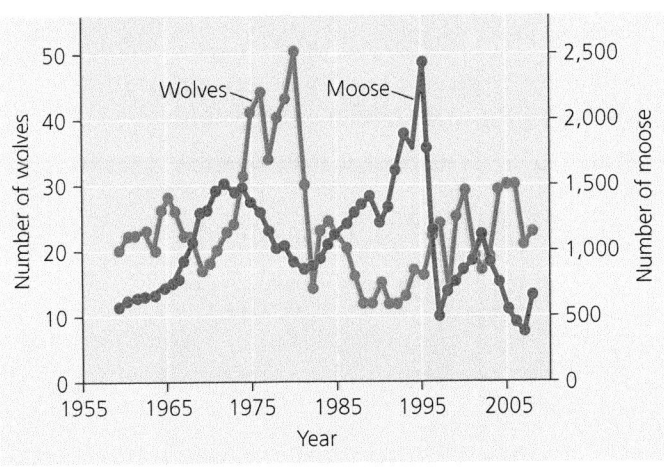

▲ **Figure 53.18 Fluctuations in moose and wolf populations on Isle Royale, 1959–2008.**

 ANIMATION **BioFlix** Visit the Study Area at **www.masteringbiology.com** for the BioFlix® 3-D Animation on Population Ecology.

the island around 1900 by walking across the frozen lake. Wolves, which rely on moose for most of their food, followed around 1950. Because the lake has not frozen over in recent years, both populations have been isolated from immigration and emigration. Despite this isolation, the moose population experienced two major increases and collapses during the last 50 years **(Figure 53.18)**. The first collapse coincided with a peak in the numbers of wolves from 1975 to 1980. The second collapse, around 1995, coincided with harsh winter weather, which increased the energy needs of the animals and made it harder for the moose to find food under the deep snow.

Population Cycles: Scientific Inquiry

While many populations fluctuate at unpredictable intervals, others undergo regular boom-and-bust cycles. Some small herbivorous mammals, such as voles and lemmings, tend to have 3- to 4-year cycles, and some birds, such as ruffed grouse and ptarmigans, have 9- to 11-year cycles.

One striking example of population cycles is the roughly 10-year cycling of snowshoe hares (*Lepus americanus*) and lynx (*Lynx canadensis*) in the far northern forests of Canada and Alaska. Lynx are predators that specialize in preying on snowshoe hares, so lynx numbers might be expected to rise and fall with the numbers of hares **(Figure 53.19)**. But why do hare numbers rise and fall in approximately 10-year cycles? Three main hypotheses have been proposed. First, the cycles may be caused by food shortage during winter. Hares eat the terminal twigs of small shrubs such as willow and birch in winter, although why this food supply might cycle in 10-year intervals is uncertain. Second, the cycles may be due to predator-prey interactions. Many predators other than lynx

▲ **Figure 53.19 Population cycles in the snowshoe hare and lynx.** Population counts are based on the number of pelts sold by trappers to the Hudson Bay Company.

? *What do you observe about the relative timing of the peaks in lynx numbers and hare numbers? What might explain this observation?*

eat hares, and they may overexploit their prey. Third, the size of the hare population may vary with sunspot activity, which also undergoes cyclic changes. When sunspot activity is low, slightly less atmospheric ozone is produced, and slightly more UV radiation reaches Earth's surface. In response, plants produce more UV-blocking chemicals and fewer chemicals that deter herbivores, increasing the quality of the hares' food.

Let's consider the evidence for these three hypotheses. If hare cycles are due to winter food shortage, then they should stop if extra food is provided to a field population. Researchers conducted such experiments in the Yukon for 20 years—over two hare cycles. They found that hare populations in the areas with extra food increased about threefold in density but continued to cycle in the same way as the unfed control populations. Thus, food supplies alone do not cause the hare cycle shown in Figure 53.19, so we can reject the first hypothesis.

Using radio collars, ecologists tracked individual hares to determine why they died. Predators killed almost 90% of the hares in such studies, and none of the hares appeared to have died of starvation. These data support the second hypothesis. When ecologists excluded predators from one area with electric fences and also excluded predators *and* provided food in another area, they found that the hare cycle is driven largely by excessive predation but that food availability also plays an important role, particularly in the winter. Better-fed hares may be more likely to escape from predators.

To test the third hypothesis, ecologists compared the timing of hare cycles with sunspot activity, which has a cycle of approximately 11 years. As predicted, periods of low sunspot activity were followed by peaks in the hare population. The results of all of these experiments suggest that both predation and sunspot activity regulate the cycling of hare numbers and that food availability plays a less important role.

The availability of prey is the major factor influencing population changes for predators such as lynx, great-horned owls, and weasels, each of which depends heavily on a single prey species. When prey become scarce, predators often turn on one another. Coyotes kill both foxes and lynx, and great-horned owls kill smaller birds of prey as well as weasels, accelerating the collapse of the predator populations. Long-term experimental studies help to unravel the causes of such population cycles.

Immigration, Emigration, and Metapopulations

So far, our discussion of population dynamics has focused mainly on the contributions of births and deaths. However, immigration and emigration also influence populations. When a population becomes crowded and resource competition increases (see Figure 53.16), emigration often increases. In the slime mold *Dictyostelium discoideum*, single-celled individuals (called amoebas) group together when food is scarce and form a "slug" containing thousands of cells (see Figure 28.25). This multicellularity likely evolved in part because slugs can produce a fruiting body that is raised off the forest floor, allowing the spores to disperse relatively long distances. New work shows an additional advantage of multicellularity in *Dictyostelium* (Figure 53.20). Aggregating improved emigration and foraging: *Dictyostelium* slugs traveled across stretches of soil much better than single amoebas did, and amoebas that separated from slugs reached soil patches and food that solitary amoebas did not.

Immigration and emigration are particularly important when a number of local populations are linked, forming a **metapopulation**. Immigration and emigration link the Belding's ground squirrel population we discussed earlier to other populations of the species, all of which make up a metapopulation.

Local populations in a metapopulation can be thought of as occupying discrete patches of suitable habitat in a sea of otherwise unsuitable habitat. Such patches vary in size, quality, and isolation from other patches, factors that influence how many individuals move among the populations. Patches with many individuals can supply more emigrants to other patches. If one population becomes extinct, the patch it occupied can be recolonized by immigrants from another population.

The Glanville fritillary (*Melitaea cinxia*) illustrates the movement of individuals between populations. This butterfly is found in about 500 meadows across the Åland Islands of Finland, but its potential habitat in the islands is much

INQUIRY

How does food availability affect emigration and foraging in a cellular slime mold?

EXPERIMENT Jennie Kuzdzal-Fick and colleagues at Rice University, in Texas, examined whether multicellular "slugs" of the protist *Dictyostelium discoideum* were more successful than single cells (called amoebas) of that species at crossing soil and finding bacteria to feed on.

Dictyostelium discoideum slug

The researchers placed a 6-cm-wide layer of sterilized topsoil on a dish containing agar, pipetted *Dictyostelium* amoebas onto the agar on one side of the topsoil, and added bacteria to the other side.

In one set of dishes, the amoebas were wild-type cells, which are capable of aggregating into slugs; in another set of dishes, the amoebas were mutants that cannot aggregate.

RESULTS Slugs traveled farther across the soil than amoebas did. The researchers also found that amoebas that sloughed off (separated from) the slugs reached areas that solitary amoebas could not reach.

CONCLUSION An advantage of multicellularity in *Dictyostelium* is improved emigration and foraging.

SOURCE J. J. Kuzdzal-Fick et al., Exploiting new terrain: an advantage to sociality in the slime mold *Dictyostelium discoideum*, *Behavioral Ecology* 18:433–437 (2007).

WHAT IF? Even in cases of severe resource depletion, *Dictyostelium* amoebas do not always aggregate into slugs. Suggest one potential disadvantage of aggregation for a *Dictyostelium* population.

larger, approximately 4,000 suitable patches. New populations of the butterfly regularly appear and existing populations become extinct, constantly shifting the locations of the 500 colonized patches (Figure 53.21). The species persists in a balance of extinctions and recolonizations.

The metapopulation concept underscores the significance of immigration and emigration in the butterfly populations. It also helps ecologists understand population dynamics and gene flow in patchy habitats, providing a framework for the conservation of species living in a network of habitat fragments and reserves.

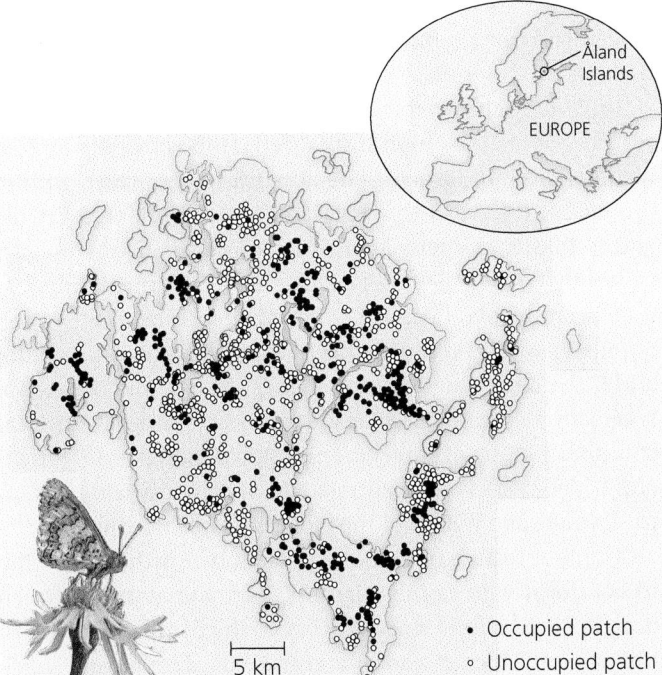

▲ **Figure 53.21 The Glanville fritillary: a metapopulation.** On the Åland Islands, local populations of this butterfly (filled circles) are found in only a fraction of the suitable habitat patches (open circles) at any given time. Individuals can move between local populations and colonize unoccupied patches.

• Occupied patch
◦ Unoccupied patch

5 km

CONCEPT CHECK 53.5

1. Describe three attributes of habitat patches that could affect population density and rates of immigration and emigration.
2. **WHAT IF?** Suppose you were studying a species that has a population cycle of about ten years. How long would you need to study the species to determine if its population size were declining? Explain.
3. **MAKE CONNECTIONS** Concept 40.2, p. 861, describes negative feedback as a process that regulates biological systems. Explain how the density-dependent birth rate of dune fescue grass exemplifies negative feedback.

For suggested answers, see Appendix A.

CONCEPT 53.6

The human population is no longer growing exponentially but is still increasing rapidly

In the last few centuries, the human population has grown at an unprecedented rate, more like the elephant population in Kruger National Park (see Figure 53.8) than the fluctuating populations we considered in Concept 53.5. No population can grow indefinitely, however. In this section of the chapter, we'll apply the concepts of population dynamics to the specific case of the human population.

The Global Human Population

The exponential growth model in Figure 53.7 approximates the human population explosion over the last four centuries (Figure 53.22). Ours is a singular case; no other population of large animals has likely ever sustained so much growth for so long. The human population increased relatively slowly until about 1650, at which time approximately 500 million people inhabited Earth. Our population doubled to 1 billion within the next two centuries, doubled again to 2 billion by 1930, and doubled still again by 1975 to more than 4 billion. The global population is now more than 6.8 billion people and is increasing by about 79 million each year. Currently the population grows by more than 200,000 people each day, the equivalent of adding a city the size of Amarillo, Texas, or Kitchener, Ontario. At this rate, it takes only about four years to add the equivalent of another United States to the world population. Population ecologists predict a population of 7.8–10.8 billion people on Earth by the year 2050.

Though the global population is still growing, the *rate* of growth did begin to slow during the 1960s (Figure 53.23, on the next page). The annual rate of increase in the global population peaked at 2.2% in 1962; by 2009, it had declined to 1.2%. Current models project a continued decline in the annual growth rate to roughly 0.5% by 2050, a rate that would still add 45 million more people per year if the population climbs to a projected 9 billion. The reduction in growth rate over the past four decades shows that the human population has departed from true exponential growth, which assumes a constant rate. This departure is the result of fundamental changes in population dynamics due to diseases, including AIDS, and to voluntary population control.

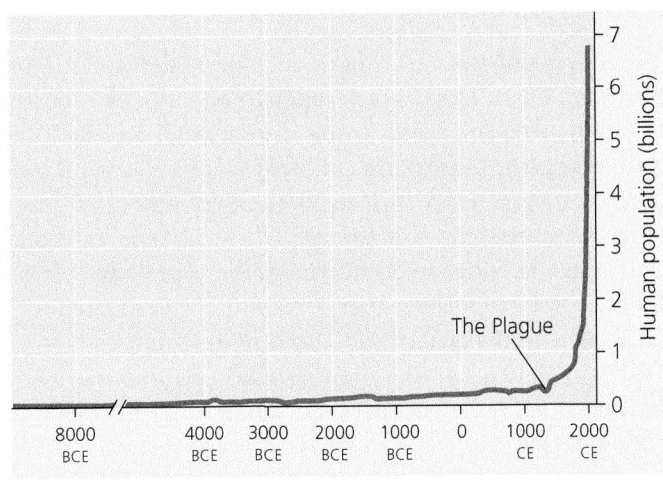

▲ **Figure 53.22 Human population growth (data as of 2009).** The global human population has grown almost continuously throughout history, but it skyrocketed after the Industrial Revolution. Though it is not apparent at this scale, the rate of population growth has slowed in recent decades, mainly as a result of decreased birth rates throughout the world.

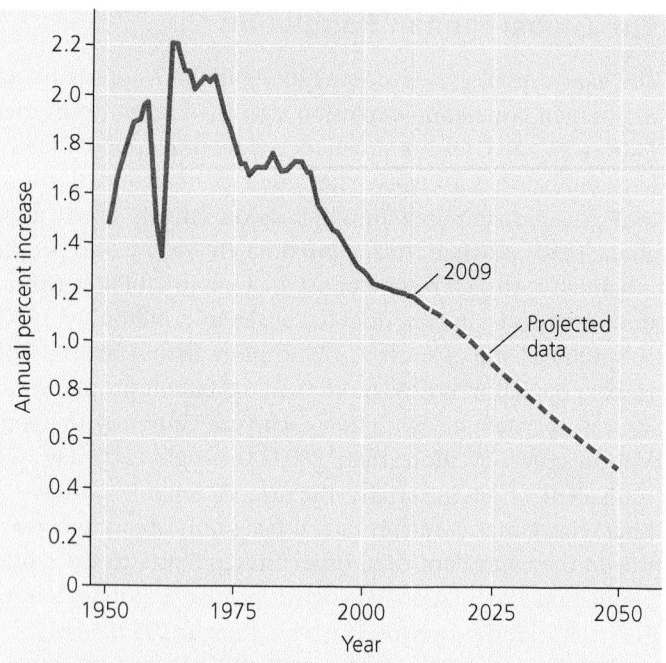

▲ **Figure 53.23** **Annual percent increase in the global human population (data as of 2009).** The sharp dip in the 1960s is due mainly to a famine in China in which about 60 million people died.

Regional Patterns of Population Change

We have described changes in the global population, but population dynamics vary widely from region to region. In a stable regional human population, birth rate equals death rate (disregarding the effects of immigration and emigration). Two possible configurations for a stable population are

Zero population growth = High birth rate − High death rate

or

Zero population growth = Low birth rate − Low death rate

The movement from high birth and death rates toward low birth and death rates, which tends to accompany industrialization and improved living conditions, is called the **demographic transition**. In Sweden, this transition took about 150 years, from 1810 to 1960, when birth rates finally approached death rates. In Mexico, where the human population is still growing rapidly, the transition is projected to take until at least 2050. Demographic transition is associated with an increase in the quality of health care and sanitation as well as improved access to education, especially for women.

After 1950, death rates declined rapidly in most developing countries, but birth rates have declined in a more variable manner. The fall in birth rate has been most dramatic in China. In 1970, the Chinese birth rate predicted an average of 5.9 children per woman per lifetime (total fertility rate); by 2009, largely because of the government's strict one-child policy, the expected total fertility rate was 1.8 children. In some countries of Africa, the transition to lower birth rates has also

been rapid, though birth rates remain high in most of sub-Saharan Africa. In India, birth rates have fallen more slowly.

How do such variable birth rates affect the growth of the world's population? In industrialized nations, populations are near equilibrium (growth rate about 0.1% per year), with reproductive rates near the replacement level (total fertility rate = 2.1 children per female). In many industrialized countries, including Canada, Germany, Japan, and the United Kingdom, total reproductive rates are in fact *below* replacement. These populations will eventually decline if there is no immigration and if the birth rate does not change. In fact, the population is already declining in many eastern and central European countries. Most of the current global population growth (1.2% per year) is concentrated in less industrialized countries, where about 80% of the world's people now live.

A unique feature of human population growth is our ability to control it with family planning and voluntary contraception. Reduced family size is the key to the demographic transition. Social change and the rising educational and career aspirations of women in many cultures encourage women to delay marriage and postpone reproduction. Delayed reproduction helps to decrease population growth rates and to move a society toward zero population growth under conditions of low birth rates and low death rates. However, there is a great deal of disagreement as to how much support should be provided for global family planning efforts.

Age Structure

Another important demographic variable in present and future growth trends is a country's **age structure**, the relative number of individuals of each age in the population. Age structure is commonly graphed as "pyramids" like those in **Figure 53.24**. For Afghanistan, the pyramid is bottom-heavy, skewed toward young individuals who will grow up and perhaps sustain the explosive growth with their own reproduction. The age structure for the United States is relatively even until the older, postreproductive ages, except for a bulge that corresponds to the "baby boom" that lasted for about two decades after the end of World War II. Even though couples born during those years have had an average of fewer than two children, the nation's overall birth rate still exceeds the death rate because some "boomers" and most of the boomers' offspring are still of reproductive age. Moreover, although the current total reproductive rate in the United States is 2.1 children per woman—approximately replacement rate—the population is projected to grow slowly through 2050 as a result of immigration. For Italy, the pyramid has a small base, indicating that individuals younger than reproductive age are relatively underrepresented in the population. This situation contributes to the projection of a population decrease in Italy.

Age-structure diagrams not only predict a population's growth trends but can also illuminate social conditions. Based on the diagrams in Figure 53.24, we can predict, for

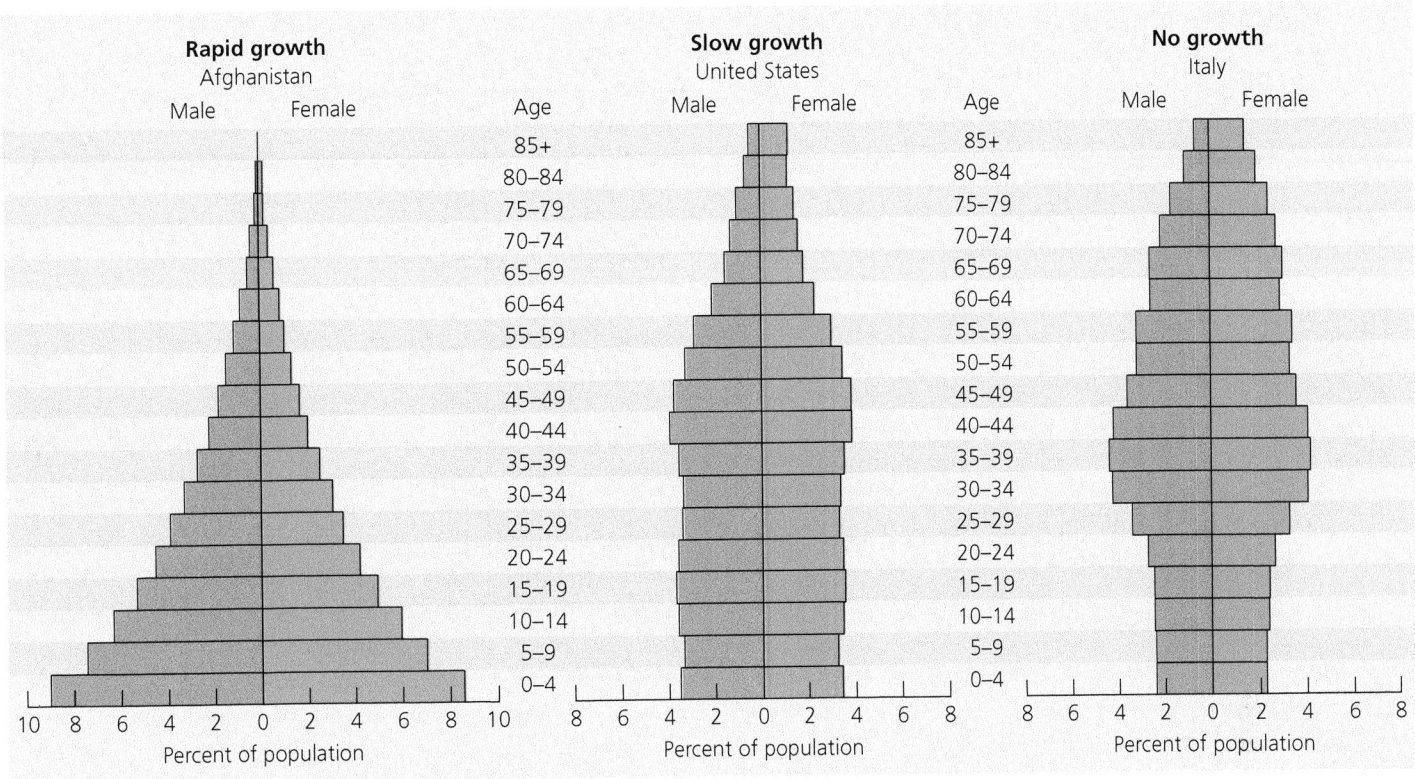

▲ **Figure 53.24 Age-structure pyramids for the human population of three countries (data as of 2009).** The annual growth rate was approximately 2.6% in Afghanistan, 1.0% in the United States, and 0.0% in Italy.

instance, that employment and education opportunities will continue to be a significant problem for Afghanistan in the foreseeable future. The large number of young people entering the Afghan population could also be a source of continuing social and political unrest, particularly if their needs and aspirations are not met. In Italy and the United States, a decreasing proportion of younger working-age people will soon be supporting an increasing population of retired "boomers." In the United States, this demographic feature has made the future of Social Security and Medicare a major political issue. Understanding age structures can help us plan for the future.

Infant Mortality and Life Expectancy

Infant mortality, the number of infant deaths per 1,000 live births, and *life expectancy at birth*, the predicted average length of life at birth, vary widely among different human populations. These differences reflect the quality of life faced by children at birth and influence the reproductive choices parents make. If infant mortality is high, then parents are likely to have more children to ensure that some reach adulthood. **Figure 53.25** contrasts average infant mortality and life expectancy in the industrialized and less industrialized countries of the world in 2008. While these averages are markedly different, they do not capture the broad range of the human condition. In 2008, for example, the infant mortality rate was 155 (15.5%) in Afghanistan but only 3 (0.3%) in Japan, while

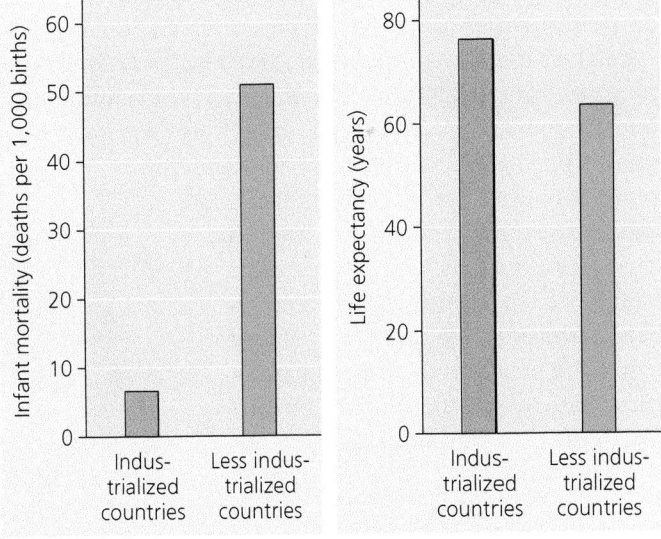

▲ **Figure 53.25 Infant mortality and life expectancy at birth in industrialized and less industrialized countries (data as of 2008).**

life expectancy at birth was 44 years in Afghanistan and 82 years in Japan. Although global life expectancy has been increasing since about 1950, it has recently dropped in a number of regions, including countries of the former Soviet Union and in sub-Saharan Africa. In these regions, social upheaval, decaying infrastructure, and infectious diseases such as AIDS and tuberculosis are reducing life expectancy. In the African country of Angola, for instance, life expectancy in 2008 was approximately 38 years, about half of that in Japan, Sweden, Italy, and Spain.

Global Carrying Capacity

No ecological question is more important than the future size of the human population. The projected worldwide population size depends on assumptions about future changes in birth and death rates. As we noted earlier, population ecologists project a global population of approximately 7.8–10.8 billion people in 2050. In other words, without some catastrophe, an estimated 1–4 billion people will be added to the population in the next four decades because of the momentum of population growth. But just how many humans can the biosphere support? Will the world be overpopulated in 2050? Is it *already* overpopulated?

Estimates of Carrying Capacity

For over three centuries, scientists have attempted to estimate the human carrying capacity of Earth. The first known estimate, 13.4 billion people, was made in 1679 by Anton van Leeuwenhoek, the discoverer of protists (see Chapter 28). Since then, estimates have varied from less than 1 billion to more than 1,000 billion (1 trillion), with an average of 10–15 billion.

Carrying capacity is difficult to estimate, and scientists use different methods to produce their estimates. Some current researchers use curves like that produced by the logistic equation (see Figure 53.9) to predict the future maximum of the human population. Others generalize from existing "maximum" population density and multiply this number by the area of habitable land. Still others base their estimates on a single limiting factor, such as food, and consider variables such as the amount of available farmland, the average yield of crops, the prevalent diet—vegetarian or meat based—and the number of calories needed per person per day.

Limits on Human Population Size

A more comprehensive approach to estimating the carrying capacity of Earth is to recognize that humans have multiple constraints: We need food, water, fuel, building materials, and other resources, such as clothing and transportation. The **ecological footprint** concept summarizes the aggregate land and water area required by each person, city, or nation to produce all the resources it consumes and to absorb all the waste it generates. One way to estimate the eco-

logical footprint of the entire human population is to add up all the ecologically productive land on the planet and divide by the population. This calculation yields approximately 2 hectares (ha) per person (1 ha = 2.47 acres). Reserving some land for parks and conservation means reducing this allotment to 1.7 ha per person—the benchmark for comparing actual ecological footprints. Anyone who consumes resources that require more than 1.7 ha to produce is said to be using an unsustainable share of Earth's resources. A typical ecological footprint for a person in the United States is about 10 ha.

Ecologists sometimes calculate ecological footprints using other currencies besides land area, such as energy use. Average energy use differs greatly for a person in developed and developing nations (Figure 53.26). A typical person in the United States, Canada, or Norway consumes roughly 30 times the energy that a person in central Africa does. Moreover, fossil fuels, such as oil, coal, and natural gas, are the source of 80% or more of the energy used in most developed nations. As you will see in Chapter 56, this unsustainable reliance on fossil fuels is changing Earth's climate and increasing the amount of waste that each of us produces. Ultimately, the combination of resource use per person and population density determines our global ecological footprint.

We can only speculate about Earth's ultimate carrying capacity for the human population and about what factors will eventually limit our growth. Perhaps food will be the main limiting factor. Malnutrition and famine are common in some regions, but they result mainly from the unequal distribution of food rather than from inadequate production. So far, technological improvements in agriculture have allowed

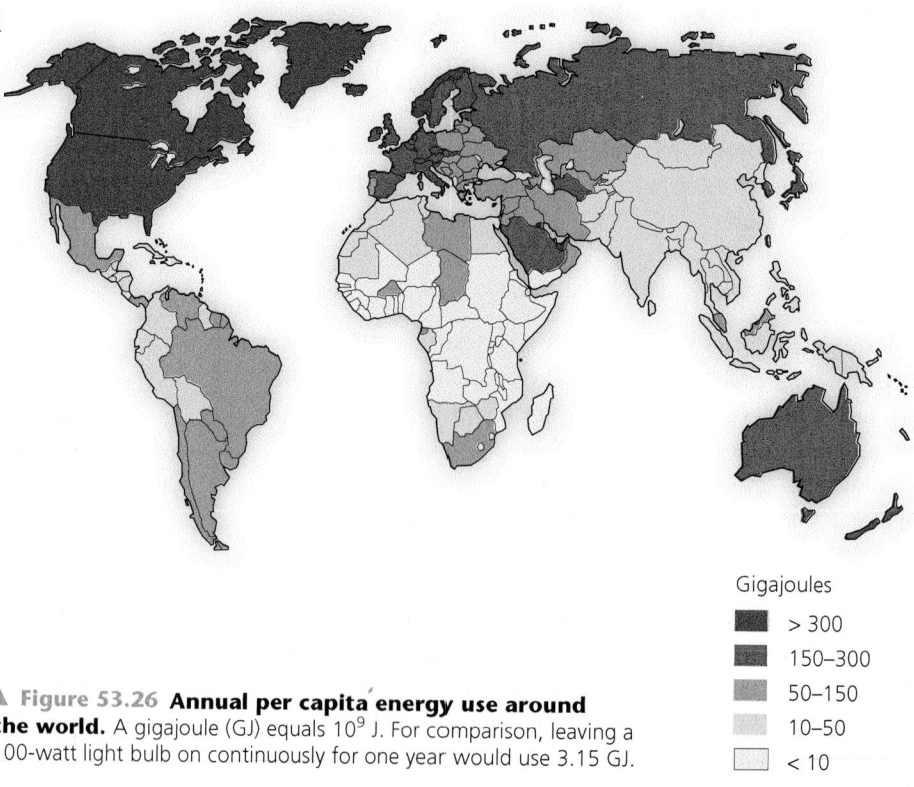

▲ Figure 53.26 **Annual per capita energy use around the world.** A gigajoule (GJ) equals 10⁹ J. For comparison, leaving a 100-watt light bulb on continuously for one year would use 3.15 GJ.

Gigajoules
- > 300
- 150–300
- 50–150
- 10–50
- < 10

food supplies to keep up with global population growth. However, the principles of energy flow through ecosystems (which you read about in Chapter 55) tell us that environments can support a larger number of herbivores than carnivores. If everyone ate as much meat as the wealthiest people in the world, less than half of the present world population could be fed by current food harvests.

Perhaps we humans will eventually be limited by suitable space. Certainly, as our population grows, the conflict over how space is utilized will intensify, and agricultural land will be developed for housing. There seem to be few limits, however, on how closely humans can be crowded together, as long as adequate food and water are provided to us and space is available to dispose of our wastes.

Humans could also run out of nonrenewable resources, such as certain metals and fossil fuels. The demands of many populations have already far exceeded the local and even regional supplies of one renewable resource—fresh water. More than 1 billion people do not have access to sufficient water to meet their basic sanitation needs. The human population may also be limited by the capacity of the environment to absorb its wastes. If so, then Earth's current human occupants could lower the planet's long-term carrying capacity for future generations.

Technology has undoubtedly increased Earth's carrying capacity for humans, but no population can continue to grow indefinitely. After reading this chapter, you should realize that there is no single carrying capacity for the human population on Earth. How many people our planet can sustain depends on the quality of life each of us enjoys and the distribution of wealth across people and nations, topics of great concern and political debate. Unlike other organisms, we can decide whether zero population growth will be attained through social changes based on human choices or, instead, through increased mortality due to resource limitation, plagues, war, and environmental degradation.

CONCEPT CHECK 53.6

1. How does a human population's age structure affect its growth rate?
2. How has the growth of Earth's human population changed in recent decades? Answer in terms of growth rate and the number of people added each year.
3. **WHAT IF?** What choices can you make to influence your own ecological footprint?

For suggested answers, see Appendix A.

53 CHAPTER REVIEW

SUMMARY OF KEY CONCEPTS

CONCEPT 53.1

Dynamic biological processes influence population density, dispersion, and demographics (pp. 1170–1175)

- Population **density**—the number of individuals per unit area or volume—reflects the interplay of births, deaths, immigration, and emigration. Environmental and social factors influence the **dispersion** of individuals.

Patterns of dispersion

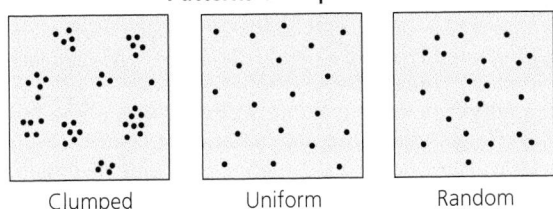

Clumped   Uniform   Random

- Populations increase from births and **immigration** and decrease from deaths and **emigration**. **Life tables**, **survivorship curves**, and **reproductive tables** summarize specific trends in **demography**.

 ? *Gray whales* (Eschrichtius robustus) *gather each winter near Baja California to give birth. How might such behavior make it easier for ecologists to estimate birth and death rates for the species?*

CONCEPT 53.2

The exponential model describes population growth in an idealized, unlimited environment (pp. 1175–1177)

- If immigration and emigration are ignored, a population's growth rate (the per capita rate of increase) equals its birth rate minus its death rate.
- The **exponential growth** equation $dN/dt = r_{max}N$ represents a population's potential growth in an unlimited environment, where r_{max} is the maximum per capita rate of increase and N is the number of individuals in the population.

$$\frac{dN}{dt} = r_{max} N$$

Population size (N) vs. Number of generations

 ? *Suppose one population has an r_{max} that is twice as large as the r_{max} of another population. What is the maximum size that both populations will reach over time, based on the exponential model?*

CONCEPT 53.3

The logistic model describes how a population grows more slowly as it nears its carrying capacity (pp. 1177–1179)

- Exponential growth cannot be sustained for long in any population. A more realistic population model limits growth by incorporating **carrying capacity** (K), the maximum population size the environment can support.
- According to the **logistic growth** equation $dN/dt = r_{max}N(K - N)/K$, growth levels off as population size approaches the carrying capacity.

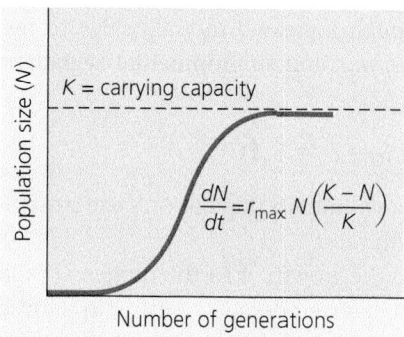

- The logistic model fits few real populations perfectly, but it is useful for estimating possible growth.

> **?** As an ecologist who manages a wildlife preserve, you want to increase the preserve's carrying capacity for a particular endangered species. How might you go about accomplishing this?

CONCEPT 53.4

Life history traits are products of natural selection (pp. 1179–1181)

- **Life history** traits are evolutionary outcomes reflected in the development, physiology, and behavior of organisms.
- Big-bang, or **semelparous**, organisms reproduce once and die. **Iteroparous** organisms produce offspring repeatedly.
- Life history traits such as brood size, age at maturity, and parental caregiving represent trade-offs between conflicting demands for time, energy, and nutrients. Two hypothetical life history patterns are **K-selection**, or density-dependent selection, and **r-selection**, or density-independent selection.

> **?** What two factors likely contribute to the evolution of semelparity versus iteroparity?

CONCEPT 53.5

Many factors that regulate population growth are density dependent (pp. 1182–1187)

- In **density-dependent** population regulation, death rates rise and birth rates fall with increasing density. In **density-independent** population regulation, birth and death rates do not vary with density.
- Density-dependent changes in birth and death rates curb population increase through negative feedback and can eventually stabilize a population near its carrying capacity. Density-dependent limiting factors include intraspecific competition for limited food or space, increased predation, disease, stress due to crowding, and buildup of toxic substances.
- Because changing environmental conditions periodically disrupt them, all populations exhibit some size fluctuations. Many

populations undergo regular boom-and-bust cycles that are influenced by complex interactions between biotic and abiotic factors. A **metapopulation** is a group of populations linked by immigration and emigration.

> **?** Give an example of one biotic and one abiotic factor that contribute to yearly fluctuations in the size of the human population.

CONCEPT 53.6

The human population is no longer growing exponentially but is still increasing rapidly (pp. 1187–1191)

- Since about 1650, the global human population has grown exponentially, but within the last 50 years, the rate of growth has fallen by nearly half. Differences in **age structure** show that while some nations' populations are growing rapidly, those of others are stable or declining in size. Infant mortality rates and life expectancy at birth differ markedly between industrialized and less industrialized countries.
- The carrying capacity of Earth for humans is uncertain. **Ecological footprint** is the aggregate land and water area needed to produce all the resources a person or group of people consume and to absorb all of their wastes. It is one measure of how close we are to the carrying capacity of Earth. With a world population of more than 6.8 billion people, we are already using many resources in an unsustainable manner.

> **?** How are humans different from other species in the ability to "choose" a carrying capacity for their environment?

TEST YOUR UNDERSTANDING

LEVEL 1: KNOWLEDGE/COMPREHENSION

1. Population ecologists follow the fate of same-age cohorts to
   a. determine a population's carrying capacity.
   b. determine the birth rate and death rate of each group in a population.
   c. determine if a population is regulated by density-dependent processes.
   d. determine the factors that regulate the size of a population.
   e. determine if a population's growth is cyclic.

2. A population's carrying capacity
   a. may change as environmental conditions change.
   b. can be accurately calculated using the logistic growth model.
   c. generally remains constant over time.
   d. increases as the per capita growth rate (r) decreases.
   e. can never be exceeded.

3. Scientific study of the population cycles of the snowshoe hare and its predator, the lynx, has revealed that
   a. the prey population is controlled by predators alone.
   b. hares and lynx are so mutually dependent that each species cannot survive without the other.
   c. multiple biotic and abiotic factors contribute to the cycling of the hare and lynx populations.
   d. both hare and lynx populations are regulated mainly by abiotic factors.
   e. the hare population is r-selected and the lynx population is K-selected.

4. Based on current growth rates, Earth's human population in 2012 will be closest to
   a. 2 million.   d. 7 billion.
   b. 3 billion.   e. 10 billion.
   c. 4 billion.

5. A recent study of ecological footprints concluded that
   a. Earth's carrying capacity for humans is about 10 billion.
   b. Earth's carrying capacity would increase if per capita meat consumption increased.
   c. current demand by industrialized countries for resources is much smaller than the ecological footprint of those countries.
   d. it is not possible for technological improvements to increase Earth's carrying capacity for humans.
   e. the ecological footprint of the United States is large because per capita resource use is high.

LEVEL 2: APPLICATION/ANALYSIS

6. The observation that members of a population are uniformly distributed suggests that
   a. the size of the area occupied by the population is increasing.
   b. resources are distributed unevenly.
   c. the members of the population are competing for access to a resource.
   d. the members of the population are neither attracted to nor repelled by one another.
   e. the density of the population is low.

7. According to the logistic growth equation

$$\frac{dN}{dt} = r_{max}N \frac{(K - N)}{K}$$

   a. the number of individuals added per unit time is greatest when N is close to zero.
   b. the per capita growth rate (r) increases as N approaches K.
   c. population growth is zero when N equals K.
   d. the population grows exponentially when K is small.
   e. the birth rate (b) approaches zero as N approaches K.

8. Which pair of terms most accurately describes life history traits for a stable population of wolves?
   a. semelparous; r-selected
   b. semelparous; K-selected
   c. iteroparous; r-selected
   d. iteroparous; K-selected
   e. iteroparous; N-selected

9. During exponential growth, a population always
   a. grows by thousands of individuals.
   b. grows at its maximum per capita rate.
   c. quickly reaches its carrying capacity.
   d. cycles through time.
   e. loses some individuals to emigration.

10. Which of the following statements about human population in industrialized countries is *incorrect*?
    a. Life history is r-selected.
    b. Average family size is relatively small.
    c. The population has undergone the demographic transition.
    d. The survivorship curve is Type I.
    e. Age distribution is relatively uniform.

LEVEL 3: SYNTHESIS/EVALUATION

11. **DRAW IT** To estimate which age cohort in a population of females produces the most female offspring, you need information about the number of offspring produced per capita within that cohort and the number of individuals alive in the cohort. Make this estimate for Belding's ground squirrels by multiplying the number of females alive at the start of the year (column 2 in Table 53.1) by the average number of female offspring produced per female (column 5 in Table 53.2). Draw a bar graph with female age in years on the x-axis (0–1, 1–2, and so on) and total number of female offspring produced for each age cohort on the y-axis. Which cohort of female Belding's ground squirrels produces the most female young?

12. **EVOLUTION CONNECTION**
    Write a paragraph contrasting the conditions that favor the evolution of semelparous (one-time) reproduction versus iteroparous (repeated) reproduction.

13. **SCIENTIFIC INQUIRY**
    You are testing the hypothesis that increased population density of a particular plant species increases the rate at which a pathogenic fungus infects the plant. Because the fungus causes visible scars on the leaves, you can easily determine whether a plant is infected. Design an experiment to test your hypothesis. Describe your experimental and control groups, how you would collect data, and what results you would see in the data you will collect, and the results expected if your hypothesis is correct.

14. **SCIENCE, TECHNOLOGY, AND SOCIETY**
    Many people regard the rapid population growth of less industrialized countries as our most serious environmental problem. Others think that the population growth in industrialized countries, though smaller, is actually a greater environmental threat. What problems result from population growth in (a) less industrialized countries and (b) industrialized nations? Which do you think is a greater threat, and why?

15. **WRITE ABOUT A THEME**
    Environmental Interactions In a short essay (100–150 words), identify the factor or factors in Figure 53.17 that you think may ultimately be most important for density-dependent population regulation in humans, and explain your reasoning.

For selected answers, see Appendix A.

54

Community Ecology

▲ **Figure 54.1 Which species benefits from this interaction?**

KEY CONCEPTS

54.1 Community interactions are classified by whether they help, harm, or have no effect on the species involved

54.2 Diversity and trophic structure characterize biological communities

54.3 Disturbance influences species diversity and composition

54.4 Biogeographic factors affect community diversity

54.5 Pathogens alter community structure locally and globally

OVERVIEW

Communities in Motion

Deep in the Lembeh Strait of Indonesia, a crab in the family Homolidae scuttles across the ocean floor holding a large sea urchin on its back (**Figure 54.1**). When a predatory fish arrives, the crab settles quickly into the sediments and puts

its living shield to use. The fish darts in and tries to bite the crab. In response, the crab tilts the spiny sea urchin toward whichever side the fish attacks. The fish eventually gives up and swims away.

The "carrier crab" in Figure 54.1 clearly benefits from having the sea urchin on its back. But how does the sea urchin fare in this relationship? Its association with the crab might harm it, help it, or have no effect on its survival and reproduction. Additional observations or experiments would be needed before ecologists could answer this question.

In Chapter 53, you learned how individuals within a population can affect other individuals of the same species. This chapter will examine ecological interactions between populations of different species. A group of populations of different species living close enough to interact is called a biological **community**. Ecologists define the boundaries of a particular community to fit their research questions: They might study the community of decomposers and other organisms living on a rotting log, the benthic community in Lake Superior, or the community of trees and shrubs in Banff National Park in Alberta.

We begin this chapter by exploring the kinds of interactions that occur between species in a community, such as the crab and sea urchin in Figure 54.1. We'll then consider several of the factors that are most significant in structuring a community—in determining how many species there are, which particular species are present, and the relative abundance of these species. Finally, we will apply some of the principles of community ecology to the study of human disease.

CONCEPT 54.1

Community interactions are classified by whether they help, harm, or have no effect on the species involved

Some key relationships in the life of an organism are its interactions with individuals of other species in the community. These **interspecific interactions** include competition, predation, herbivory, symbiosis (including parasitism, mutualism, and commensalism), and facilitation. In this section, we will define and describe each of these interactions, recognizing that ecologists do not always agree on the precise boundaries of each type of interaction.

We will use the symbols + and − to indicate how each interspecific interaction affects the survival and reproduction of the two species engaged in the interaction. For example, predation is a +/− interaction, with a positive effect on the survival and reproduction of the predator population and a negative effect on that of the prey population. Mutualism is a +/+ interaction because the survival and reproduction of both species are increased in the presence of the other. A 0 indicates that a population is not affected by the interaction in any known way.

Historically, most ecological research has focused on interactions that have a negative effect on at least one species, such as competition and predation. However, positive interactions are ubiquitous, and their contributions to community structure are the subject of considerable study today.

Competition

Interspecific competition is a −/− interaction that occurs when individuals of different species compete for a resource that limits their growth and survival. Weeds growing in a garden compete with garden plants for soil nutrients and water. Grasshoppers and bison in the Great Plains compete for the grass they both eat. Lynx and foxes in the northern forests of Alaska and Canada compete for prey such as snowshoe hares. In contrast, some resources, such as oxygen, are rarely in short supply; thus, although most species use this resource, they do not usually compete for it.

Competitive Exclusion

What happens in a community when two species compete for limited resources? In 1934, Russian ecologist G. F. Gause studied this question using laboratory experiments with two closely related species of ciliated protists, *Paramecium aurelia* and *Paramecium caudatum*. He cultured the species under stable conditions, adding a constant amount of food each day. When Gause grew the two species separately, each population grew rapidly and then leveled off at the apparent carrying capacity of the culture (see Figure 53.10a for an illustration of the logistic growth of *P. aurelia*). But when Gause grew the two species together, *P. caudatum* became extinct in the culture. Gause inferred that *P. aurelia* had a competitive edge in obtaining food. He concluded that two species competing for the same limiting resources cannot coexist permanently in the same place. In the absence of disturbance, one species will use the resources more efficiently and reproduce more rapidly than the other. Even a slight reproductive advantage will eventually lead to local elimination of the inferior competitor, an outcome called **competitive exclusion**.

Ecological Niches and Natural Selection

EVOLUTION The sum of a species' use of the biotic and abiotic resources in its environment is called its **ecological niche**. American ecologist Eugene Odum used the following analogy to explain the niche concept: If an organism's habitat is its "address," the niche is the organism's "profession." The niche of a tropical tree lizard, for instance, includes the temperature range it tolerates, the size of branches on which it perches, the time of day when it is active, and the sizes and kinds of insects it eats. Such factors define the lizard's niche, or ecological role—how it fits into an ecosystem.

We can use the niche concept to restate the principle of competitive exclusion: Two species cannot coexist permanently in a community if their niches are identical. However, ecologically similar species *can* coexist in a community if one or more significant differences in their niches arise through time. Evolution by natural selection can result in one of the species using a different set of resources. The differentiation of niches that enables similar species to coexist in a community is called **resource partitioning** (Figure 54.2). You can think of resource partitioning in a community as "the ghost of competition past"—the indirect evidence of earlier interspecific competition resolved by the evolution of niche differentiation.

As a result of competition, a species' *fundamental niche*, which is the niche potentially occupied by that species, is often different from its *realized niche*, the portion of its fundamental niche that it actually occupies in a particular environment. Ecologists can identify the fundamental niche of a species by testing the range of conditions in which it grows and reproduces in the absence of competitors. They can also test whether a potential competitor limits a species' realized niche by removing the competitor and seeing if the first species expands into the newly available space. The classic experiment depicted in **Figure 54.3**, on the next page, clearly showed that competition between two barnacle species kept one species from occupying part of its fundamental niche.

A. *distichus* perches on fence posts and other sunny surfaces.

A. *insolitus* usually perches on shady branches.

A. *ricordii*

A. *insolitus*

A. *aliniger*
A. *distichus*

A. *christophei*

A. *cybotes*
A. *etheridgei*

▲ **Figure 54.2 Resource partitioning among Dominican Republic lizards.** Seven species of *Anolis* lizards live in close proximity, and all feed on insects and other small arthropods. However, competition for food is reduced because each lizard species has a different preferred perch, thus occupying a distinct niche.

▲ **The golden spiny mouse**
(*Acomys russatus*)

Figure 54.3

INQUIRY

Can a species' niche be influenced by interspecific competition?

EXPERIMENT Ecologist Joseph Connell studied two barnacle species—*Chthamalus stellatus* and *Balanus balanoides*—that have a stratified distribution on rocks along the coast of Scotland. *Chthamalus* is usually found higher on the rocks than *Balanus*. To determine whether the distribution of *Chthamalus* is the result of interspecific competition with *Balanus*, Connell removed *Balanus* from the rocks at several sites.

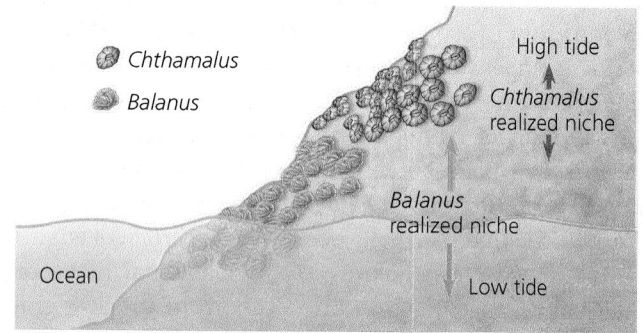

RESULTS *Chthamalus* spread into the region formerly occupied by *Balanus*.

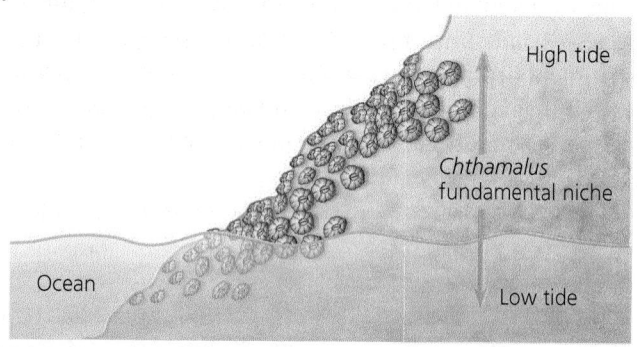

CONCLUSION Interspecific competition makes the realized niche of *Chthamalus* much smaller than its fundamental niche.

SOURCE J. H. Connell, The influence of interspecific competition and other factors on the distribution of the barnacle *Chthamalus stellatus*, *Ecology* 42:710–723 (1961).

(MB) See the related Experimental Inquiry Tutorial in MasteringBiology.

WHAT IF? Other observations showed that *Balanus* cannot survive high on the rocks because it dries out during low tides. How would *Balanus*'s realized niche compare with its fundamental niche?

Species can partition their niches not just in space, as lizards and barnacles do, but in time as well. The common spiny mouse (*Acomys cahirinus*) and the golden spiny mouse (*A. russatus*) live in rocky habitats of the Middle East and Africa, sharing similar microhabitats and food sources. Where they coexist, *A. cahirinus* is nocturnal (active at night), while *A. russatus* is diurnal (active during the day). Surprisingly, laboratory research showed that *A. russatus* is naturally nocturnal. To be active during the day, it must override its biological clock in the presence of *A. cahirinus*. When researchers in Israel removed all *A. cahirinus* individuals from a site in the species'

natural habitat, *A. russatus* individuals at that site became nocturnal, consistent with the laboratory results. This change in behavior suggests that competition exists between the species and that partitioning of their active time helps them coexist.

Character Displacement

Closely related species whose populations are sometimes allopatric (geographically separate; see Chapter 24) and sometimes sympatric (geographically overlapping) provide more evidence for the importance of competition in structuring communities. In some cases, the allopatric populations of such species are morphologically similar and use similar resources. By contrast, sympatric populations, which would potentially compete for resources, show differences in body structures and in the resources they use. This tendency for characteristics to diverge more in sympatric than in allopatric populations of two species is called **character displacement**. An example of character displacement in Galápagos finches is shown in **Figure 54.4**.

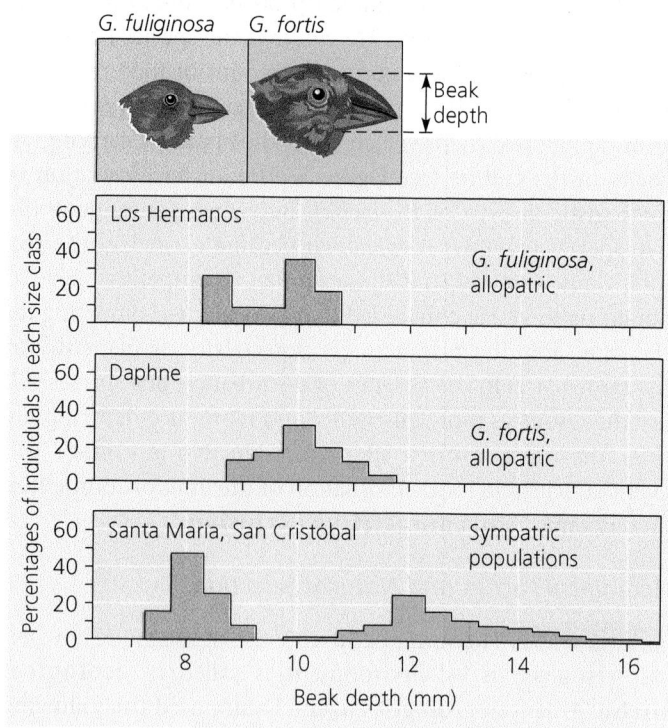

▲ **Figure 54.4 Character displacement: indirect evidence of past competition.** Allopatric populations of *Geospiza fuliginosa* and *Geospiza fortis* on Los Hermanos and Daphne Islands have similar beak morphologies (top two graphs) and presumably eat similarly sized seeds. However, where the two species are sympatric on Santa María and San Cristóbal, *G. fuliginosa* has a shallower, smaller beak and *G. fortis* a deeper, larger one (bottom graph), adaptations that favor eating different-sized seeds.

Predation

Predation refers to a +/− interaction between species in which one species, the predator, kills and eats the other, the prey. Though the term *predation* generally elicits such images as a lion attacking and eating an antelope, it applies to a wide range of interactions. An animal that kills a plant by eating the plant's tissues can also be considered a predator. Because eating and avoiding being eaten are prerequisite to reproductive success, the adaptations of both predators and prey tend to be refined through natural selection.

Many important feeding adaptations of predators are obvious and familiar. Most predators have acute senses that enable them to find and identify potential prey. Many predators also have adaptations such as claws, teeth, fangs, stingers, or poison that help them catch and subdue their food.

▼ **Figure 54.5 Examples of defensive coloration in animals.**

(a) Cryptic coloration

▶ Canyon tree frog

(b) Aposematic coloration

▶ Poison dart frog

(c) Batesian mimicry: A harmless species mimics a harmful one.

◀ Hawkmoth larva

▼ Green parrot snake

Rattlesnakes and other pit vipers, for example, find their prey with a pair of heat-sensing organs located between their eyes and nostrils (see Figure 50.7a), and they kill small birds and mammals by injecting them with toxins through their fangs. Predators that pursue their prey are generally fast and agile, whereas those that lie in ambush are often disguised in their environments.

Just as predators possess adaptations for capturing prey, prey animals have adaptations that help them avoid being eaten. Some common behavioral defenses are hiding, fleeing, and forming herds or schools. Active self-defense is less common, though some large grazing mammals vigorously defend their young from predators such as lions. Other behavioral defenses include alarm calls that summon many individuals of the prey species, which then mob the predator.

Animals also display a variety of morphological and physiological defensive adaptations. **Cryptic coloration**, or camouflage, makes prey difficult to see (Figure 54.5a). Mechanical or chemical defenses protect species such as porcupines and skunks. Some animals, including the European fire salamander, can synthesize toxins, whereas others accumulate toxins passively from the plants they eat. Animals with effective chemical defenses often exhibit bright **aposematic coloration**, or warning coloration, such as that of the poison dart frog (Figure 54.5b). Aposematic coloration seems to be adaptive because predators often avoid prey that have bright color patterns (see Chapter 1).

Some prey species are protected by their resemblance to other species. In **Batesian mimicry**, a palatable or harmless species mimics an unpalatable or harmful one. The larva of the hawkmoth *Hemeroplanes ornatus* puffs up its head and thorax when disturbed, looking like the head of a small poisonous snake (Figure 54.5c). In this case, the mimicry even involves behavior; the larva weaves its head back and forth and hisses like a snake. In **Müllerian mimicry**, two or more unpalatable species, such as the cuckoo bee and yellow jacket, resemble each other (Figure 54.5d). Presumably, the more unpalatable prey there are, the more quickly predators learn

(d) Müllerian mimicry: Two unpalatable species mimic each other.

◀ Cuckoo bee

▼ Yellow jacket

to avoid prey with that particular appearance. The shared appearance thus becomes a kind of aposematic coloration. In an example of convergent evolution, unpalatable animals in several different taxa have similar patterns of coloration: Black and yellow or red stripes characterize unpalatable animals as diverse as yellow jackets and coral snakes (see Figure 1.25).

Many predators also use mimicry. Alligator snapping turtles have tongues that resemble a wriggling worm, thus luring small fish. Any fish that tries to eat the "bait" is itself quickly consumed as the turtle's strong jaws snap closed. Anglerfish also lure prey with their own bait, in this case a modified bone of the dorsal fin that luminesces in some species.

Herbivory

Ecologists use the term **herbivory** to refer to a +/− interaction in which an organism eats parts of a plant or alga. While large mammalian herbivores such as cattle, sheep, and water buffalo may be most familiar, most herbivores are actually invertebrates, such as grasshoppers and beetles. In the ocean, herbivores include snails, sea urchins, some tropical fishes, and certain mammals, including the manatee **(Figure 54.6)**.

Like predators, herbivores have many specialized adaptations. Many herbivorous insects have chemical sensors on their feet that enable them to distinguish between toxic and nontoxic plants as well as between more nutritious and less nutritious plants. Some mammalian herbivores, such as goats, use their sense of smell to examine plants, rejecting some and eating others. They may also eat just a specific part of a plant, such as the flowers. Many herbivores also have specialized teeth or digestive systems adapted for processing vegetation (see Chapter 41).

Unlike prey animals, plants cannot run away to avoid being eaten. Instead, a plant's arsenal against herbivores may feature chemical toxins or structures such as spines and thorns.

▲ **Figure 54.6 A West Indies manatee (*Trichechus manatus*) in Florida.** The animal in this photo is feeding on hydrilla, an introduced species.

Among the plant compounds that serve as chemical weapons are the poison strychnine, produced by the tropical vine *Strychnos toxifera*; nicotine, from the tobacco plant; and tannins, from a variety of plant species. Plants in the genus *Astragalus* accumulate selenium; they are known as "locoweeds" because the cattle and sheep that eat them wander aimlessly in circles and may even die. Compounds that are not toxic to humans but may be distasteful to many herbivores are responsible for the familiar flavors of cinnamon, cloves, and peppermint. Certain plants produce chemicals that cause abnormal development in some insects that eat them.

Symbiosis

When individuals of two or more species live in direct and intimate contact with one another, their relationship is called **symbiosis**. In this book, we adopt a general definition of symbiosis that includes all such interactions, whether they are harmful, helpful, or neutral. Some biologists define symbiosis more narrowly as a synonym for mutualism, an interaction in which both species benefit.

Parasitism

Parasitism is a +/− symbiotic interaction in which one organism, the **parasite**, derives its nourishment from another organism, its **host**, which is harmed in the process. Parasites that live within the body of their host, such as tapeworms, are called **endoparasites**; parasites that feed on the external surface of a host, such as ticks and lice, are called **ectoparasites**. In one particular type of parasitism, parasitoid insects—usually small wasps—lay eggs on or in living hosts. The larvae then feed on the body of the host, eventually killing it. Some ecologists have estimated that at least one-third of all species on Earth are parasites.

Many parasites have complex life cycles involving multiple hosts. The blood fluke, which currently infects approximately 200 million people around the world, requires two hosts at different times in its development: humans and freshwater snails (see Figure 33.11). Some parasites change the behavior of their hosts in a way that increases the probability of the parasite being transferred from one host to another. For instance, the presence of parasitic acanthocephalan (spiny-headed) worms leads their crustacean hosts to engage in a variety of atypical behaviors, including leaving protective cover and moving into the open. As a result of their modified behavior, the crustaceans have a greater chance of being eaten by the birds that are the second host in the parasitic worm's life cycle.

Parasites can significantly affect the survival, reproduction, and density of their host population, either directly or indirectly. For example, ticks that live as ectoparasites on moose weaken their hosts by withdrawing blood and causing hair breakage and loss. In their weakened condition, the moose have a greater chance of dying from cold stress or predation by wolves (see Figure 53.18).

Mutualism

Mutualistic symbiosis, or **mutualism**, is an interspecific interaction that benefits both species (+/+). We have described many examples of mutualism in previous chapters: nitrogen fixation by bacteria in the root nodules of legumes; the digestion of cellulose by microorganisms in the digestive systems of termites and ruminant mammals; the exchange of nutrients in mycorrhizae, associations of fungi and the roots of plants; and photosynthesis by unicellular algae in corals. The interaction between termites and the microorganisms in their digestive system is an example of *obligate mutualism*, in which at least one species has lost the ability to survive without its partner. In *facultative mutualism*, as in the acacia-ant example shown in **Figure 54.7**, both species can survive alone.

Mutualistic relationships sometimes involve the coevolution of related adaptations in both species, with changes in either species likely to affect the survival and reproduction of the other. For example, most flowering plants have adaptations such as nectar or fruit that attract animals that function in pollination or seed dispersal (see Chapter 38). In turn, many animals have adaptations that help them find and consume nectar.

Commensalism

An interaction between species that benefits one of the species but neither harms nor helps the other (+/0) is called **commensalism**. Commensal interactions are difficult to document in nature because any close association between species likely affects both species, even if only slightly. For instance, "hitchhiking" species, such as algae that live on the shells of aquatic turtles or barnacles that attach to whales, are sometimes considered commensal. The hitchhikers gain a place to grow while having seemingly little effect on their ride. However, the hitchhikers may in fact slightly decrease the reproductive success of their hosts by reducing the hosts' efficiency of movement in searching for food or escaping from predators. Conversely, the hitchhikers may provide a benefit in the form of camouflage.

Some associations that are possibly commensal involve one species obtaining food that is inadvertently exposed by another. Cowbirds and cattle egrets feed on insects flushed out of the grass by grazing bison, cattle, horses, and other herbivores. Because the birds increase their feeding rates when following the herbivores, they clearly benefit from the association. Much of the time, the herbivores may be unaffected by the relationship (**Figure 54.8**). However, they, too, may sometimes derive some benefit; the birds tend to be opportunistic feeders that occasionally remove and eat ticks and other ectoparasites from the herbivores. They may also warn the herbivores of a predator's approach.

(a) Certain species of acacia trees in Central and South America have hollow thorns that house stinging ants of the genus *Pseudomyrmex*. The ants feed on nectar produced by the tree and on protein-rich swellings (orange in the photograph) at the tips of leaflets.

(b) The acacia benefits because the pugnacious ants, which attack anything that touches the tree, remove fungal spores, small herbivores, and debris. They also clip vegetation that grows close to the acacia.

▲ **Figure 54.7 Mutualism between acacia trees and ants.**

▲ **Figure 54.8 A possible example of commensalism between cattle egrets and water buffalo.**

(a) Salt marsh with *Juncus* (foreground)

(b)

▲ Figure 54.9 **Facilitation by black rush (*Juncus gerardi*) in New England salt marshes.** Black rush increases the number of plant species that can live in the upper middle zone of the marsh.

Facilitation

Species can have positive effects (+/+ or 0/+) on the survival and reproduction of other species without necessarily living in the direct and intimate contact of a symbiosis. This type of interaction, called **facilitation**, is particularly common in plant ecology. For instance, the black rush *Juncus gerardi* makes the soil more hospitable for other plant species in some zones of New England salt marshes **(Figure 54.9a)**. *Juncus* helps prevent salt buildup in the soil by shading the soil surface, which reduces evaporation. *Juncus* also prevents the salt marsh soils from becoming oxygen depleted as it transports oxygen to its belowground tissues. In one study, when *Juncus* was removed from areas in the upper middle intertidal zone, those areas supported 50% fewer plant species **(Figure 54.9b)**.

All five types of interactions that we have discussed so far—competition, predation, herbivory, symbiosis, and facilitation—strongly influence the structure of communities. You will see other examples of these interactions throughout this chapter.

CONCEPT CHECK 54.1

1. Explain how interspecific competition, predation, and mutualism differ in their effects on the interacting populations of two species.
2. According to the principle of competitive exclusion, what outcome is expected when two species with identical niches compete for a resource? Why?
3. **MAKE CONNECTIONS** Figure 24.14 (p. 499) illustrates the formation of and possible outcomes for a hybrid zone over time. Imagine that two finch species colonize a new island and are capable of hybridizing. The island contains two plant species, one with large seeds and one with small, growing in isolated habitats. If the two finch species specialize in eating different plant species, would reproductive barriers be reinforced, weakened, or unchanged in this hybrid zone? Explain.

For suggested answers, see Appendix A.

Diversity and trophic structure characterize biological communities

Along with the specific interactions described in the previous section, communities are also characterized by more general attributes, including how diverse they are and the feeding relationships of their species. In this section, you will read why such ecological attributes are important. You will also learn how a few species sometimes exert strong control on a community's structure, particularly on the composition, relative abundance, and diversity of its species.

Species Diversity

The **species diversity** of a community—the variety of different kinds of organisms that make up the community—has two components. One is **species richness**, the number of different species in the community. The other is the **relative abundance** of the different species, the proportion each species represents of all individuals in the community.

Imagine two small forest communities, each with 100 individuals distributed among four tree species (A, B, C, and D) as follows:

Community 1: 25A, 25B, 25C, 25D
Community 2: 80A, 5B, 5C, 10D

The species richness is the same for both communities because they both contain four species of trees, but the relative abundance is very different **(Figure 54.10)**. You would easily notice the four types of trees in community 1, but without looking carefully, you might see only the abundant species A in the second forest. Most observers would intuitively describe community 1 as the more diverse of the two communities.

Ecologists use many tools to quantitatively compare the diversity of different communities across time and space. They often calculate indexes of diversity based on species richness and relative abundance. One widely used index is **Shannon diversity** (*H*):

$$H = -(p_A \ln p_A + p_B \ln p_B + p_C \ln p_C + \ldots)$$

where A, B, C . . . are the species in the community, *p* is the relative abundance of each species, and ln is the natural logarithm. A higher value of *H* indicates a more diverse community. Let's use this equation to calculate the Shannon diversity index of the two communities in Figure 54.10. For community 1, *p* = 0.25 for each species, so

$$H = -4(0.25 \ln 0.25) = 1.39.$$

For community 2,

$$H = -[0.8 \ln 0.8 + 2(0.05 \ln 0.05) + 0.1 \ln 0.1] = 0.71.$$

These calculations confirm our intuitive description of community 1 as more diverse.

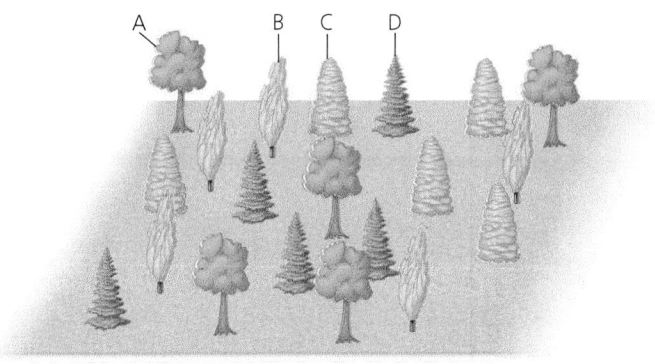

Community 1
A: 25% B: 25% C: 25% D: 25%

Community 2
A: 80% B: 5% C: 5% D: 10%

▲ **Figure 54.10 Which forest is more diverse?** Ecologists would say that community 1 has greater species diversity, a measure that includes both species richness and relative abundance.

Determining the number and relative abundance of species in a community is easier said than done. Many sampling techniques can be used, but since most species in a community are relatively rare, it may be hard to obtain a sample size large enough to be representative. It is also difficult to census the highly mobile or less visible or accessible members of communities, such as microorganisms, nematodes, deep-sea creatures, and nocturnal species. The small size of microorganisms makes them particularly difficult to sample, so ecologists now use molecular tools to help determine microbial diversity (**Figure 54.11**). Measuring species diversity is often challenging but is essential for understanding community structure and for conserving diversity, as you will read in Chapter 56.

Diversity and Community Stability

In addition to measuring species diversity, ecologists manipulate diversity in experimental communities in nature and in the laboratory. They do this to examine the potential benefits of diversity, including increased productivity and stability of biological communities.

Researchers at the Cedar Creek Natural History Area, in Minnesota, have been manipulating plant diversity in

▼ Figure 54.11 **RESEARCH METHOD**

Determining Microbial Diversity Using Molecular Tools

APPLICATION Ecologists are increasingly using molecular techniques, such as the analysis of restriction fragment length polymorphisms (RFLPs), to determine microbial diversity and richness in environmental samples. As used in this application, RFLP analysis produces a DNA profile for microbial taxa based on sequence variations in the DNA that encodes the small subunit of ribosomal RNA. Noah Fierer and Rob Jackson, of Duke University, used this method to compare the diversity of soil bacteria in 98 habitats across North and South America to help identify environmental variables associated with high bacterial diversity.

TECHNIQUE Researchers first extract and purify DNA from the microbial community in each sample. They use the polymerase chain reaction (PCR) to amplify the ribosomal DNA and label the DNA with a fluorescent dye (see Chapter 20). Restriction enzymes then cut the amplified, labeled DNA into fragments of different lengths, which are separated by gel electrophoresis. The number and abundance of these fragments characterize the DNA profile of the sample.

Based on their RFLP analysis, Fierer and Jackson calculated the Shannon diversity (H) of each sample. They then looked for a correlation between H and several environmental variables, including vegetation type, mean annual temperature and rainfall, and acidity and quality of the soil at each site.

RESULTS The diversity of bacterial communities in soils across North and South America was related almost exclusively to soil pH, with the Shannon diversity being highest in neutral soils and lowest in acidic soils. Amazonian rain forests, which have extremely high plant and animal diversity, had the most acidic soils and the lowest bacterial diversity of the samples tested.

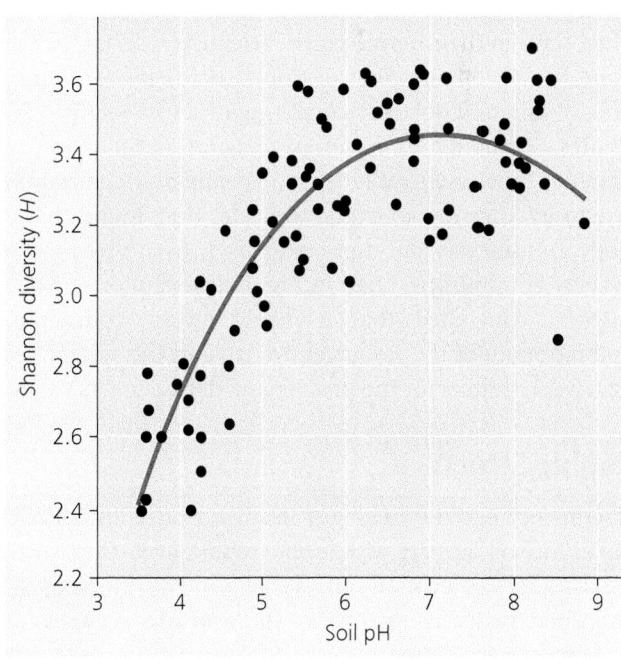

SOURCE N. Fierer and R. B. Jackson, The diversity and biogeography of soil bacterial communities, *Proceedings of the National Academy of Sciences USA* 103:626–631 (2006).

▲ **Figure 54.12 Study plots at the Cedar Creek Natural History Area, site of long-term experiments on manipulating plant diversity.**

experimental communities for two decades (Figure 54.12). Higher-diversity communities generally are more productive and are better able to withstand and recover from environmental stresses, such as droughts. More diverse communities are also more stable year to year in their productivity. In one decade-long experiment, for instance, researchers at Cedar Creek created 168 plots, each containing 1, 2, 4, 8, or 16 perennial grassland species. The most diverse plots were 70% more stable than the single-species plots in the amount of plant mass produced each year.

Higher-diversity communities are often more resistant to **invasive species**, which are organisms that become established outside their native range. Scientists working in Long Island Sound, off the coast of Connecticut, created communities of different diversity consisting of sessile marine invertebrates, including tunicates (see Figure 34.5). They then examined how vulnerable these experimental communities were to invasion by an exotic tunicate. They found that the exotic tunicate was four times more likely to survive in lower-diversity communities than in higher-diversity ones. The researchers concluded that relatively diverse communities captured more of the resources available in the system, leaving fewer resources for the invader and decreasing its survival.

Trophic Structure

Experiments like the ones just described often examine the importance of diversity within one trophic level. The structure and dynamics of a community also depend on the feeding relationships between organisms—the **trophic structure** of the community. The transfer of food energy up the trophic levels from its source in plants and other autotrophic organisms (primary producers) through herbivores (primary consumers) to carnivores (secondary, tertiary, and quaternary consumers) and eventually to decomposers is referred to as a **food chain** (Figure 54.13).

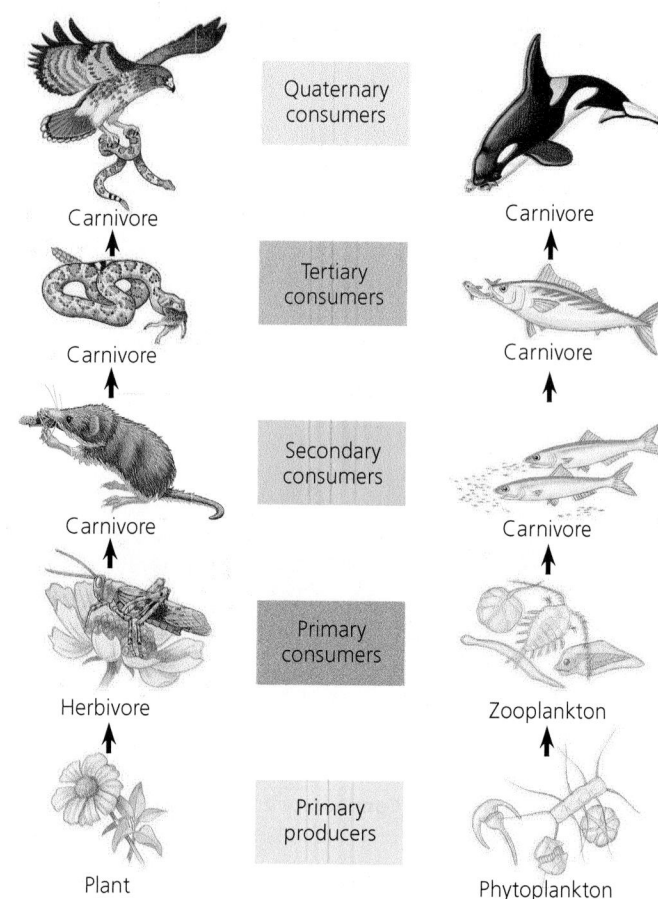

A terrestrial food chain

A marine food chain

▲ **Figure 54.13 Examples of terrestrial and marine food chains.** The arrows trace energy and nutrients that pass through the trophic levels of a community when organisms feed on one another. Decomposers, which "feed" on organisms from all trophic levels, are not shown here.

Food Webs

In the 1920s, Oxford University biologist Charles Elton recognized that food chains are not isolated units but are linked together in **food webs**. Ecologists summarize the trophic relationships of a community by diagramming a food web with arrows linking species according to who eats whom. In an Antarctic pelagic community, for example, the primary producers are phytoplankton, which serve as food for the dominant grazing zooplankton, especially euphausids (krill) and copepods, both of which are crustaceans (Figure 54.14). These zooplankton species are in turn eaten by various carnivores, including other plankton, penguins, seals, fishes, and baleen whales. Squids, which are carnivores that feed on fish and zooplankton, are another important link in these food webs, as they are in turn eaten by seals and toothed whales. During the time when whales were commonly hunted for food, humans became the top predator in this food web. Having hunted many whale species to low numbers, humans are now harvesting at lower trophic levels, catching krill as well as fishes for food.

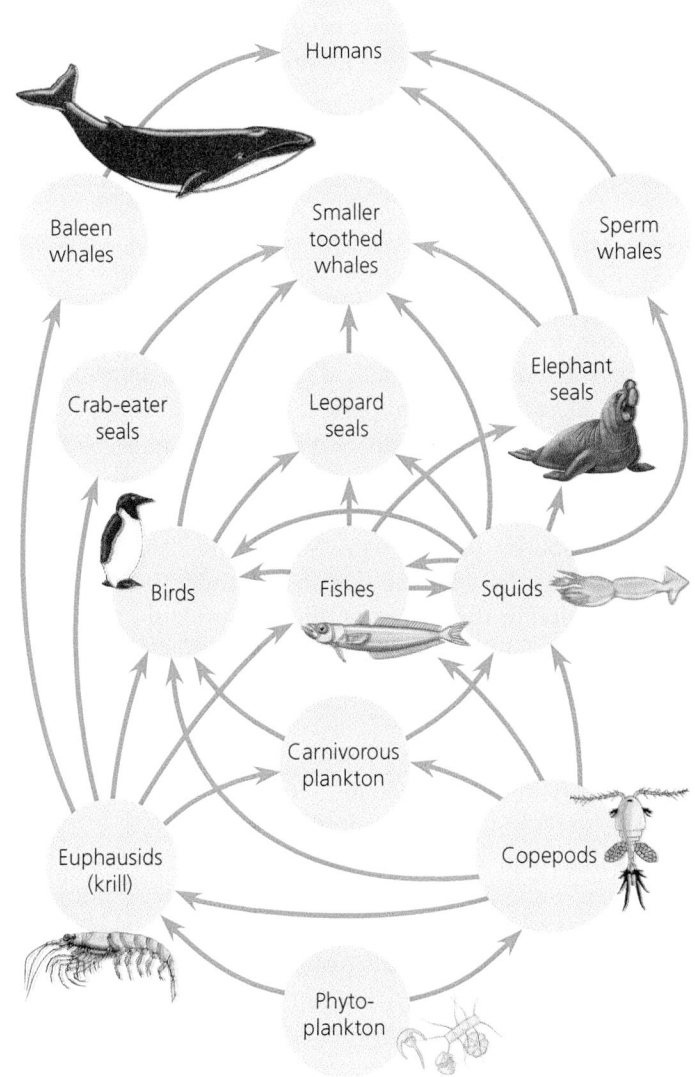

▲ **Figure 54.14 An Antarctic marine food web.** Arrows follow the transfer of food from the producers (phytoplankton) up through the trophic levels. For simplicity, this diagram omits decomposers.

How are food chains linked into food webs? A given species may weave into the web at more than one trophic level. In the food web shown in Figure 54.14, euphausids feed on phytoplankton as well as on other grazing zooplankton, such as copepods. Such "nonexclusive" consumers are also found in terrestrial communities. For instance, foxes are omnivores whose diet includes berries and other plant materials, herbivores such as mice, and other predators, such as weasels. Humans are among the most versatile of omnivores.

Complicated food webs can be simplified in two ways for easier study. First, species with similar trophic relationships in a given community can be grouped into broad functional groups. In Figure 54.14, more than 100 phytoplankton species are grouped as the primary producers in the food web. A second way to simplify a food web for closer study is to isolate a portion of the web that interacts very little with

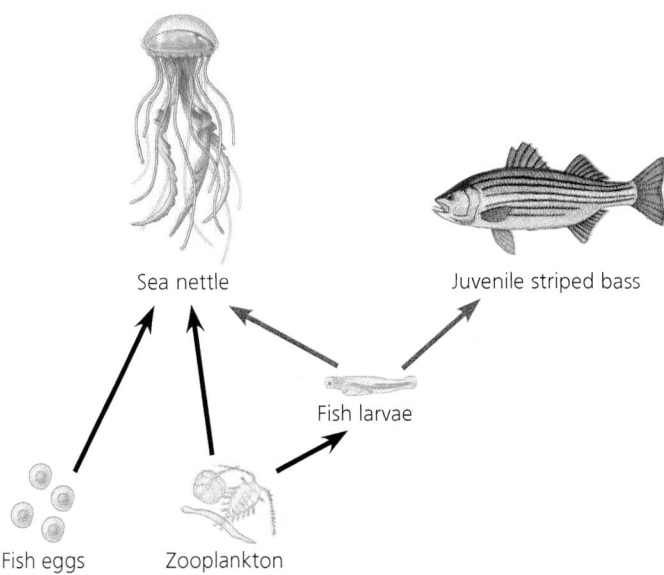

▲ **Figure 54.15 Partial food web for the Chesapeake Bay estuary on the U.S. Atlantic coast.** The sea nettle (*Chrysaora quinquecirrha*) and juvenile striped bass (*Morone saxatilis*) are the main predators of fish larvae (bay anchovy and several other species). Note that sea nettles are secondary consumers (black arrows) when they eat zooplankton, but tertiary consumers (red arrows) when they eat fish larvae, which are themselves secondary consumers of zooplankton.

the rest of the community. **Figure 54.15** illustrates a partial food web for sea nettles (a type of cnidarian) and juvenile striped bass in Chesapeake Bay.

Limits on Food Chain Length

Each food chain within a food web is usually only a few links long. In the Antarctic web of Figure 54.14, there are rarely more than seven links from the producers to any top-level predator, and most chains in this web have fewer links. In fact, most food webs studied to date have chains consisting of five or fewer links.

Why are food chains relatively short? There are two main hypotheses. One, the **energetic hypothesis**, suggests that the length of a food chain is limited by the inefficiency of energy transfer along the chain. As you will read in Chapter 55, only about 10% of the energy stored in the organic matter of each trophic level is converted to organic matter at the next trophic level. Thus, a producer level consisting of 100 kg of plant material can support about 10 kg of herbivore **biomass** (the total mass of all individuals in a population) and 1 kg of carnivore biomass. The energetic hypothesis predicts that food chains should be relatively longer in habitats of higher photosynthetic production, since the starting amount of energy is greater than in habitats with lower photosynthetic production.

A second hypothesis, the **dynamic stability hypothesis**, proposes that long food chains are less stable than short chains. Population fluctuations at lower trophic levels are magnified at higher levels, potentially causing the local extinction of top

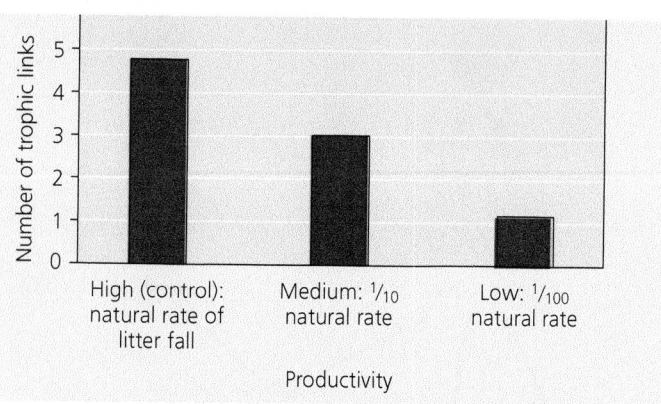

▲ **Figure 54.16 Test of the energetic hypothesis for the restriction of food chain length.** Researchers manipulated the productivity of tree-hole communities in Queensland, Australia, by providing leaf litter input at three levels. Reducing energy input reduced food chain length, a result consistent with the energetic hypothesis.

? *According to the dynamic stability hypothesis, which productivity treatment should have the most stable food chain? Explain.*

predators. In a variable environment, top predators must be able to recover from environmental shocks (such as extreme winters) that can reduce the food supply all the way up the food chain. The longer a food chain is, the more slowly top predators can recover from environmental setbacks. This hypothesis predicts that food chains should be shorter in unpredictable environments.

Most of the data available support the energetic hypothesis. For example, ecologists have used tree-hole communities in tropical forests as experimental models to test the energetic hypothesis. Many trees have small branch scars that rot, forming holes in the tree trunk. The holes hold water and provide a habitat for tiny communities consisting of microorganisms and insects that feed on leaf litter, as well as predatory insects. **Figure 54.16** shows the results of experiments in which researchers manipulated productivity by varying the amount of leaf litter in tree holes. As predicted by the energetic hypothesis, holes with the most leaf litter, and hence the greatest total food supply at the producer level, supported the longest food chains.

Another factor that may limit food chain length is that carnivores in a food chain tend to be larger at successive trophic levels. The size of a carnivore and its feeding mechanism put some upper limit on the size of food it can take into its mouth. And except in a few cases, large carnivores cannot live on very small food items because they cannot procure enough food in a given time to meet their metabolic needs. Among the exceptions are baleen whales, huge suspension feeders with adaptations that enable them to consume enormous quantities of krill and other small organisms (see Figure 41.6).

Species with a Large Impact

Certain species have an especially large impact on the structure of entire communities because they are highly abundant or play a pivotal role in community dynamics. The impact of these species occurs through trophic interactions and their influence on the physical environment.

Dominant Species

Dominant species in a community are the species that are the most abundant or that collectively have the highest biomass. As a result, dominant species exert a powerful control over the occurrence and distribution of other species. For example, the dominance of sugar maples in an eastern North American forest community has a major impact on abiotic factors such as shading and soil nutrient availability, which in turn affect which other species live there.

There is no single explanation for why a species becomes dominant in a community. One hypothesis suggests that dominant species are competitively superior in exploiting limited resources such as water or nutrients. Another explanation is that dominant species are most successful at avoiding predation or the impact of disease. This latter idea could explain the high biomass attained in some environments by invasive species. Such species may not face the natural predators and agents of disease that would otherwise hold their populations in check.

One way to discover the impact of a dominant species is to remove it from the community. The American chestnut was a dominant tree in deciduous forests of eastern North America before 1910, making up more than 40% of mature trees. Then humans accidentally introduced the fungal disease chestnut blight to New York City via nursery stock imported from Asia. Between 1910 and 1950, this fungus killed almost all of the chestnut trees in eastern North America. In this case, removing the dominant species had a relatively small impact on some species but severe effects on others. Oaks, hickories, beeches, and red maples that were already present in the forest increased in abundance and replaced the chestnuts. No mammals or birds seemed to have been harmed by the loss of the chestnut, but seven species of moths and butterflies that fed on the tree became extinct.

Keystone Species and Ecosystem Engineers

In contrast to dominant species, **keystone species** are not usually abundant in a community. They exert strong control on community structure not by numerical might but by their pivotal ecological roles, or niches. **Figure 54.17** highlights the importance of a keystone species, a sea star, in maintaining the diversity of an intertidal community.

The sea otter, a keystone predator in the North Pacific, offers another example. Sea otters feed on sea urchins, and sea urchins feed mainly on kelp. In areas where sea otters are abundant, sea urchins are rare and kelp forests are well developed. Where sea otters are rare, sea urchins are common and kelp is almost absent. Over the last 20 years, orcas have been preying on sea otters as the orcas' usual prey has

INQUIRY

Is *Pisaster ochraceus* a keystone predator?

EXPERIMENT In rocky intertidal communities of western North America, the relatively uncommon sea star *Pisaster ochraceus* preys on mussels such as *Mytilus californianus*, a dominant species and strong competitor for space.

Robert Paine, of the University of Washington, removed *Pisaster* from an area in the intertidal zone and examined the effect on species richness.

RESULTS In the absence of *Pisaster*, species richness declined as mussels monopolized the rock face and eliminated most other invertebrates and algae. In a control area where *Pisaster* was not removed, species richness changed very little.

CONCLUSION *Pisaster* acts as a keystone species, exerting an influence on the community that is not reflected in its abundance.

SOURCE R. T. Paine, Food web complexity and species diversity, *American Naturalist* 100:65–75 (1966).

WHAT IF? Suppose that an invasive fungus killed most individuals of *Mytilus* at these sites. Predict how species richness would be affected if *Pisaster* were then removed.

(a) Sea otter abundance

(b) Sea urchin biomass

(c) Total kelp density

▲ **Figure 54.18 Sea otter as a keystone predator in the North Pacific.** The graphs correlate changes over time in sea otter abundance **(a)** with changes in sea urchin biomass **(b)** and changes in kelp density **(c)** in kelp forests at Adak Island (part of the Aleutian Island chain). The vertical diagram on the right represents the food chain after orcas (top) entered the chain.

▲ **Figure 54.19 Beavers as ecosystem engineers.** By felling trees, building dams, and creating ponds, beavers can transform large areas of forest into flooded wetlands.

declined. As a result, sea otter populations have plummeted in large areas off the coast of western Alaska, sometimes at rates as high as 25% per year. The loss of this keystone species has allowed sea urchin populations to increase, resulting in the loss of kelp forests **(Figure 54.18)**.

Other organisms exert their influence on a community not through trophic interactions but by changing their physical environment. Species that dramatically alter their environment are called **ecosystem engineers** or, to avoid implying conscious intent, "foundation species." A familiar ecosystem engineer is the beaver **(Figure 54.19)**. The effects of ecosystem engineers on other species can be positive or negative, depending on the needs of the other species.

Bottom-Up and Top-Down Controls

Simplified models based on relationships between adjacent trophic levels are useful for discussing community organization. For example, let's consider the three possible relationships between plants (*V* for vegetation) and herbivores (*H*):

$$V \rightarrow H \quad V \leftarrow H \quad V \leftrightarrow H$$

The arrows indicate that a change in the biomass of one trophic level causes a change in the other trophic level. $V \rightarrow H$ means that an increase in vegetation will increase the numbers or biomass of herbivores, but not vice versa. In this situation, herbivores are limited by vegetation, but vegetation is not limited by herbivory. In contrast, $V \leftarrow H$ means that an increase in herbivore biomass will decrease the abundance of vegetation, but not vice versa. A double-headed arrow indicates that feedback flows in both directions, with each trophic level sensitive to changes in the biomass of the other.

Two models of community organization are common: the bottom-up model and the top-down model. The $V \rightarrow H$ linkage suggests a **bottom-up model**, which postulates a unidirectional influence from lower to higher trophic levels. In this case, the presence or absence of mineral nutrients (*N*) controls plant (*V*) numbers, which control herbivore (*H*) numbers, which in turn control predator (*P*) numbers. The simplified bottom-up model is thus $N \rightarrow V \rightarrow H \rightarrow P$. To change the community structure of a bottom-up community, you need to alter biomass at the lower trophic levels, allowing those changes to propagate up through the food web. For example, if you add mineral nutrients to stimulate growth of vegetation, then the higher trophic levels should also increase in biomass. If you add predators to or remove predators from a bottom-up community, however, the effect should not extend down to the lower trophic levels.

In contrast, the **top-down model** postulates the opposite: Predation mainly controls community organization because predators limit herbivores, herbivores limit plants, and plants limit nutrient levels through nutrient uptake. The simplified top-down model, $N \leftarrow V \leftarrow H \leftarrow P$, is also called the *trophic cascade model*. In a lake community with four trophic levels, the model predicts that removing the top carnivores will increase the abundance of primary carnivores, in turn decreasing the number of herbivores, increasing phytoplankton abundance, and decreasing concentrations of mineral nutrients. If there were only three trophic levels in a lake, removing primary carnivores would increase the number of herbivores and decrease phytoplankton abundance, causing nutrient levels to increase. The effects thus move down the trophic structure as alternating +/− effects.

The top-down model has practical applications. For example, ecologists have applied the top-down model to improve water quality in polluted lakes. This approach, called **biomanipulation**, attempts to prevent algal blooms and eutrophication by altering the density of higher-level consumers in lakes instead of using chemical treatments. In lakes with three trophic levels, removing fish should improve water quality by increasing zooplankton density and thereby decreasing algal populations. In lakes with four trophic levels, adding top predators should have the same effect. We can summarize the scenario of three trophic levels with the following diagram:

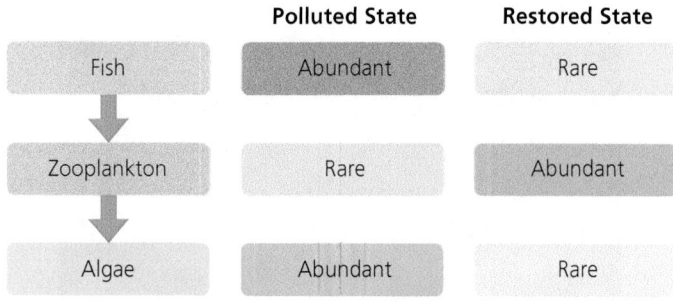

Ecologists in Finland used biomanipulation to help purify Lake Vesijärvi, a large lake that was polluted with city sewage and industrial wastewater until 1976. After pollution controls reduced these inputs, the water quality of the lake began to improve. By 1986, however, massive blooms of cyanobacteria started to occur in the lake. These blooms coincided with an increase in the population of roach, a fish that had benefited from the mineral nutrients that the pollution provided over many years. Roach eat zooplankton, which otherwise keep the cyanobacteria and algae in check. To reverse these changes, ecologists removed nearly a million kilograms of fish from Lake Vesijärvi between 1989 and 1993, reducing roach abundance by about 80%. At the same time, they added a fourth trophic level by stocking the lake with pike perch, a predatory fish that eats roach. The water became clear, and the last cyanobacterial bloom was in 1989. The lake remains clear even though roach removal ended in 1993.

As these examples show, communities vary in their degree of bottom-up and top-down control. To manage agricultural landscapes, parks, reservoirs, and fisheries, we need to understand each particular community's dynamics.

CONCEPT CHECK 54.2

1. What two components contribute to species diversity? Explain how two communities that contain the same number of species can differ in species diversity.
2. Describe two hypotheses that explain why food chains are usually short, and state a key prediction of each hypothesis.
3. **WHAT IF?** Consider a grassland with five trophic levels: plants, grasshoppers, snakes, raccoons, and bobcats. If you released additional bobcats into the grassland, how would plant biomass change if the bottom-up model applied? If the top-down model applied?

For suggested answers, see Appendix A.

Disturbance influences species diversity and composition

Decades ago, most ecologists favored the traditional view that biological communities are at equilibrium, a more or less stable balance, unless seriously disturbed by human activities. The "balance of nature" view focused on interspecific competition as a key factor determining community composition and maintaining stability in communities. *Stability* in this context refers to a community's tendency to reach and maintain a relatively constant composition of species.

One of the earliest proponents of this view, F. E. Clements, of the Carnegie Institution of Washington, argued in the early 1900s that the community of plants at a site had only one state of equilibrium, controlled solely by climate. According to Clements, biotic interactions caused the species in this *climax community* to function as an integrated unit—in effect, as a superorganism. His argument was based on the observation that certain species of plants are consistently found together, such as the oaks, maples, birches, and beeches in deciduous forests of the northeastern United States.

Other ecologists questioned whether most communities were at equilibrium or functioned as integrated units. A. G. Tansley, of Oxford University, challenged the concept of a climax community, arguing that differences in soils, topography, and other factors created many potential communities that were stable within a region. H. A. Gleason, of the University of Chicago, saw communities not as superorganisms but more as chance assemblages of species found together because they happen to have similar abiotic requirements—for example, for temperature, rainfall, and soil type. Gleason and other ecologists also realized that disturbance keeps many communities from reaching a state of equilibrium in species diversity or composition. A **disturbance** is an event, such as a storm, fire, flood, drought, overgrazing, or human activity, that changes a community by removing organisms from it or altering resource availability.

This recent emphasis on change has produced the **nonequilibrium model**, which describes most communities as constantly changing after being affected by disturbances. Even where relatively stable communities do exist, they can be rapidly transformed into nonequilibrium communities. Let's now take a look at the ways disturbances influence community structure and composition.

Characterizing Disturbance

The types of disturbances and their frequency and severity vary among communities. Storms disturb almost all communities, even those in the oceans, through the action of waves. Fire is a significant disturbance in most terrestrial communities; in fact, chaparral and some grassland biomes require regular burning to maintain their structure and species composition. Freezing is a frequent occurrence in many rivers, lakes, and ponds, and many streams and ponds are disturbed by spring flooding and seasonal drying. A high level of disturbance is generally the result of a high intensity *and* high frequency of disturbance, while low disturbance levels can result from either a low intensity or low frequency of disturbance.

The **intermediate disturbance hypothesis** states that moderate levels of disturbance foster greater species diversity than do low or high levels of disturbance. High levels of disturbance reduce diversity by creating environmental stresses that exceed the tolerances of many species or by disturbing the community so often that slow-growing or slow-colonizing species are excluded. At the other extreme, low levels of disturbance can reduce species diversity by allowing competitively dominant species to exclude less competitive ones. Meanwhile, intermediate levels of disturbance can foster greater species diversity by opening up habitats for occupation by less competitive species. Such intermediate disturbance levels rarely create conditions so severe that they exceed the environmental tolerances or recovery rates of potential community members.

The intermediate disturbance hypothesis is supported by many terrestrial and aquatic studies. In one such study, ecologists in New Zealand compared the richness of invertebrate taxa living in the beds of streams exposed to different frequencies and intensities of flooding (Figure 54.20). When floods occurred either very frequently or rarely, invertebrate richness was low. Frequent floods made it difficult for some species to become established in the streambed, while rare floods resulted in species being displaced by superior competitors. Invertebrate richness peaked in streams that had an intermediate frequency or intensity of flooding, as predicted by the hypothesis.

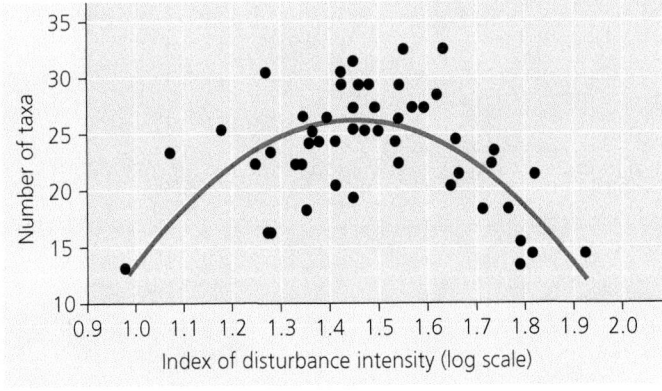

▲ Figure 54.20 **Testing the intermediate disturbance hypothesis.** Researchers identified the taxa (species or genera) of invertebrates at two locations in each of 27 New Zealand streams. They assessed the intensity of flooding at each location using an index of streambed disturbance. The number of invertebrate taxa peaked where the intensity of flooding was at intermediate levels.

Although moderate levels of disturbance appear to maximize species diversity, small and large disturbances often have important effects on community structure. Small-scale disturbances can create patches of different habitats across a landscape, which help maintain diversity in a community. Large-scale disturbances are also a natural part of many communities. Much of Yellowstone National Park, for example, is dominated by lodgepole pine, a tree that requires the rejuvenating influence of periodic fires. Lodgepole cones remain closed until exposed to intense heat. When a forest fire burns the trees, the cones open and the seeds are released. The new generation of lodgepole pines can then thrive on nutrients released from the burned trees and in the sunlight that is no longer blocked by taller trees.

In the summer of 1988, extensive areas of Yellowstone burned during a severe drought. By 1989, burned areas in the park were largely covered with new vegetation, suggesting that the species in this community are adapted to rapid recovery after fire (**Figure 54.21**). In fact, large-scale fires have periodically swept through the lodgepole pine forests of Yellowstone and other northern areas for thousands of years. In contrast, more southerly pine forests were historically affected by frequent but low-intensity fires. In these forests, a century of human intervention to suppress small fires has allowed an unnatural buildup of fuels in some places and elevated the risk of large, severe fires to which the species are not adapted.

Studies of the Yellowstone forest community and many others indicate that they are nonequilibrium communities, changing continually because of natural disturbances and the internal processes of growth and reproduction. Mounting evidence suggests that nonequilibrium conditions resulting from disturbance are in fact the norm for most communities.

Ecological Succession

Changes in the composition and structure of terrestrial communities are most apparent after some severe disturbance, such as a volcanic eruption or a glacier, strips away all the existing vegetation. The disturbed area may be colonized by a variety of species, which are gradually replaced by other species, which are in turn replaced by still other species—a process called **ecological succession**.

When this process begins in a virtually lifeless area where soil has not yet formed, such as on a new volcanic island or on the rubble (moraine) left by a retreating glacier, it is called **primary succession**. Often the only life-forms initially present are autotrophic prokaryotes and heterotrophic prokaryotes and protists. Lichens and mosses, which grow from wind-blown spores, are commonly the first macroscopic photosynthesizers to colonize such areas. Soil develops gradually as rocks weather and organic matter accumulates from the decomposed remains of the early colonizers. Once soil is present, the lichens and mosses are usually overgrown by grasses, shrubs, and trees that sprout from seeds blown in from nearby areas or carried in by animals. Eventually, an area is colonized by plants that become the community's prevalent form of vegetation. Producing such a community through primary succession may take hundreds or thousands of years.

Secondary succession occurs when an existing community has been cleared by some disturbance that leaves the soil intact, as in Yellowstone following the 1988 fires (see Figure 54.21). Sometimes the area begins to return to something like its original state. For instance, in a forested area that has been cleared for farming and later abandoned, the earliest plants to recolonize are often herbaceous species that

(a) Soon after fire. The fire has left a patchy landscape. Note the unburned trees in the far distance.

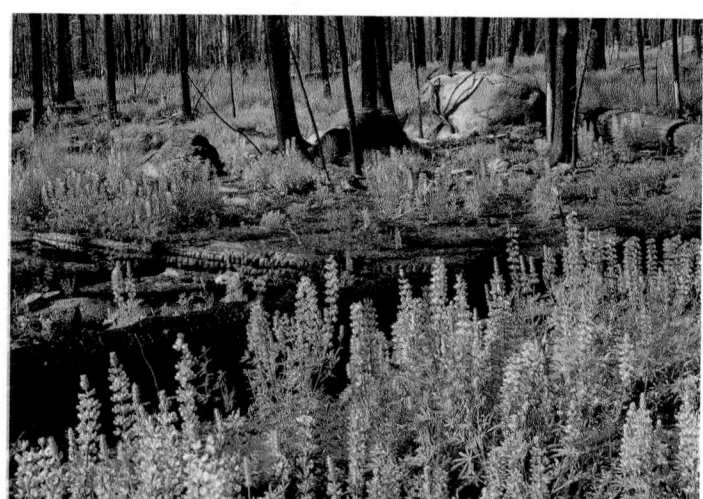

(b) One year after fire. The community has begun to recover. A variety of herbaceous plants, different from those in the former forest, cover the ground.

▲ **Figure 54.21 Recovery following a large-scale disturbance.** The 1988 Yellowstone National Park fires burned large areas of forests dominated by lodgepole pines.

grow from windblown or animal-borne seeds. If the area has not been burned or heavily grazed, woody shrubs may in time replace most of the herbaceous species, and forest trees may eventually replace most of the shrubs.

Early arrivals and later-arriving species may be linked in one of three key processes. The early arrivals may *facilitate* the appearance of the later species by making the environment more favorable—for example, by increasing the fertility of the soil. Alternatively, the early species may *inhibit* establishment of the later species, so that successful colonization by later species occurs in spite of, rather than because of, the activities of the early species. Finally, the early species may be completely independent of the later species, which *tolerate* conditions created early in succession but are neither helped nor hindered by early species.

Let's look at how these various processes contribute to primary succession on glacial moraines. Ecologists have conducted the most extensive research on moraine succession at Glacier Bay in southeastern Alaska, where glaciers have retreated more than 100 km since 1760 **(Figure 54.22)**. By studying the communities on moraines at different distances

from the mouth of the bay, ecologists can examine different stages in succession. ❶ The exposed moraine is colonized first by pioneering species that include liverworts, mosses, fireweed, scattered *Dryas* (a mat-forming shrub), willows, and cottonwood. ❷ After about three decades, *Dryas* dominates the plant community. ❸ A few decades later, the area is invaded by alder, which forms dense thickets up to 9 m tall. ❹ In the next two centuries, these alder stands are overgrown first by Sitka spruce and later by a combination of western hemlock and mountain hemlock. In areas of poor drainage, the forest floor of this spruce-hemlock forest is invaded by sphagnum moss, which holds large amounts of water and acidifies the soil, eventually killing the trees. Thus, by about 300 years after glacial retreat, the vegetation consists of sphagnum bogs on the poorly drained flat areas and spruce-hemlock forest on the well-drained slopes.

How is succession on glacial moraines related to the environmental changes caused by transitions in the vegetation? The bare soil exposed as the glacier retreats is quite basic, with a pH of 8.0–8.4 due to the carbonate compounds in the parent rocks. The soil pH falls rapidly as vegetation develops.

❶ Pioneer stage, with fireweed dominant

❷ *Dryas* stage

❹ Spruce stage

❸ Alder stage

▲ **Figure 54.22 Glacial retreat and primary succession at Glacier Bay, Alaska.** The different shades of blue on the map show retreat of the glacier since 1760, based on historical descriptions.

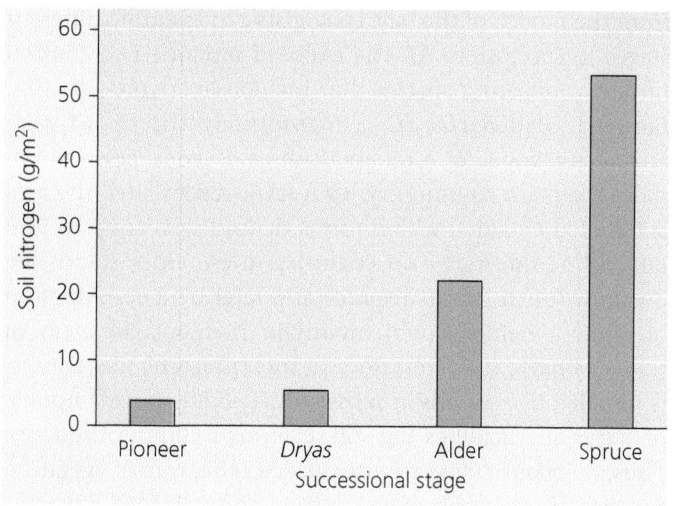

▲ **Figure 54.23 Changes in soil nitrogen content during succession at Glacier Bay.**

MAKE CONNECTIONS *Figures 37.10 and 37.11 illustrate two types of atmospheric nitrogen fixation by prokaryotes. At the earliest stages of primary succession, before any plants are present at a site, which type of nitrogen fixation would occur, and why?*

▲ **Figure 54.24 Disturbance of the ocean floor by trawling.** These photos show the seafloor off northwestern Australia before (top) and after (bottom) deep-sea trawlers have passed.

Decomposition of acidic spruce needles in particular reduces the pH of the soil from 7.0 to approximately 4.0. The soil concentrations of mineral nutrients also change with time. Because the bare soil after glacial retreat is low in nitrogen content, almost all the pioneer plant species begin succession with poor growth and yellow leaves due to inadequate nitrogen supply. The exceptions are *Dryas* and, particularly, alder; these species have symbiotic bacteria that fix atmospheric nitrogen (see Chapter 37). Soil nitrogen content increases rapidly during the alder stage of succession and continues to increase during the spruce stage **(Figure 54.23)**. By altering soil properties, pioneer plant species permit new plant species to grow, and the new plants in turn alter the environment in different ways, contributing to succession.

Human Disturbance

Ecological succession is a response to disturbance of the environment, and the strongest agent of disturbance today is human activity. Agricultural development has disrupted what were once the vast grasslands of the North American prairie. Logging and clearing for urban development, mining, and farming have reduced large tracts of forests to small patches of disconnected woodlots in many parts of the United States and throughout Europe. After forests are clear-cut, weedy and shrubby vegetation often colonizes the area and dominates it for many years. This type of vegetation is also found in agricultural fields that are no longer under cultivation and in vacant lots and construction sites.

Human disturbance of communities is not limited to the United States and Europe, nor is it a recent problem. Tropical rain forests are quickly disappearing as a result of clear-cutting for lumber, cattle grazing, and farmland. Centuries of overgrazing and agricultural disturbance have contributed to famine in parts of Africa by turning seasonal grasslands into vast barren areas.

Humans disturb marine ecosystems as well as terrestrial ones. The effects of ocean trawling, where boats drag weighted nets across the seafloor, are similar to those of clear-cutting a forest or plowing a field **(Figure 54.24)**. The trawls scrape and scour corals and other life on the seafloor and in its sediments. In a typical year, ships trawl 15 million km² of ocean floor, an area about the size of South America and 150 times larger than the area of forests that are clear-cut annually.

Because disturbance by human activities is often severe, it reduces species diversity in many communities. In Chapter 56, we will take a closer look at how human-caused disturbance is affecting the diversity of life.

CONCEPT CHECK 54.3

1. Why do high and low levels of disturbance usually reduce species diversity? Why does an intermediate level of disturbance promote species diversity?
2. During succession, how might the early species facilitate the arrival of other species?
3. **WHAT IF?** Most prairies experience regular fires, typically every few years. If these disturbances were relatively modest, how would the species diversity of a prairie likely be affected if no burning occurred for 100 years? Explain your answer.

For suggested answers, see Appendix A.

CONCEPT 54.4

Biogeographic factors affect community diversity

So far, we have examined relatively small-scale or local factors that influence the diversity of communities, including the effects of species interactions, dominant species, and many types of disturbances. Ecologists also recognize that large-scale biogeographic factors contribute to the tremendous range of diversity observed in biological communities. The contributions of two biogeographic factors in particular—the latitude of a community and the area it occupies—have been investigated for more than a century.

Latitudinal Gradients

In the 1850s, both Charles Darwin and Alfred Wallace pointed out that plant and animal life was generally more abundant and diverse in the tropics than in other parts of the globe. Since that time, many researchers have confirmed this observation. One study found that a 6.6-hectare (1 ha = 10,000 m²) plot in tropical Malaysia contained 711 tree species, while a 2-ha plot of deciduous forest in Michigan typically contained just 10 to 15 tree species. Moreover, there are only 50 tree species in all of western Europe north of the Alps. Many groups of animals show similar latitudinal gradients. There are more than 200 species of ants in Brazil but only 7 in Alaska, for instance.

The two key factors in latitudinal gradients of species richness are probably evolutionary history and climate. Over the course of evolutionary time, species richness may increase in a community as more speciation events occur (see Chapter 24). Tropical communities are generally older than temperate or polar communities because temperate and polar communities have repeatedly "started over" after major disturbances from glaciations. Another factor is that the growing season in tropical forests is about five times as long as in the tundra communities of high latitudes. In effect, biological time runs about five times as fast in the tropics as near the poles, so intervals between speciation events are shorter in the tropics.

Climate is likely the primary cause of the latitudinal gradient in richness and diversity. In terrestrial communities, the two main climatic factors correlated with diversity are solar energy input and water availability, both of which are relatively high in the tropics. These factors can be considered together by measuring a community's rate of **evapotranspiration**, the evaporation of water from soil plus the transpiration of water from plants. Evapotranspiration, a function of solar radiation, temperature, and water availability, is much higher in hot areas with abundant rainfall than in areas with low temperatures or low precipitation. *Potential evapotranspiration*, a measure of potential water loss that assumes that water is readily available, is determined by the amount of solar radiation

(a) Trees

(b) Vertebrates

▲ **Figure 54.25 Energy, water, and species richness. (a)** Species richness of North American trees increases most predictably with actual evapotranspiration, while **(b)** vertebrate species richness in North America increases most predictably with potential evapotranspiration. Evapotranspiration values are expressed as rainfall equivalents.

and temperature and is highest in regions where both are plentiful. The species richness of plants and animals correlates with both measures of evapotranspiration (**Figure 54.25**).

Area Effects

In 1807, naturalist and explorer Alexander von Humboldt described one of the first patterns of species richness to be recognized, the **species-area curve**: All other factors being equal, the larger the geographic area of a community, the

▲ **Figure 54.26 Species-area curve for North American breeding birds.** Both area and number of species are plotted on a logarithmic scale. The data points range from a 0.2-ha plot with 3 species in Pennsylvania to the whole United States and Canada (1.9 billion ha) with 625 species.

more species it has. The likely explanation for this pattern is that larger areas offer a greater diversity of habitats and microhabitats than smaller areas. In conservation biology, developing species-area curves for the key taxa in a community helps ecologists predict how the potential loss of a certain area of habitat is likely to affect the community's diversity.

Figure 54.26 is a species-area curve for North American breeding birds (birds with breeding populations in the mapped area, as opposed to migrant populations). The slope indicates the extent to which species richness increases with community area. While the slopes of different species-area curves vary, the basic concept of diversity increasing with increasing area applies in a variety of situations, from surveys of ant diversity in New Guinea to the number of plant species on islands of different sizes. In fact, island biogeography provides some of the best examples of species-area curves, as we will discuss next.

Island Equilibrium Model

Because of their isolation and limited size, islands provide excellent opportunities for studying the biogeographic factors that affect the species diversity of communities. By "islands," we mean not only oceanic islands, but also habitat islands on land, such as lakes, mountain peaks separated by lowlands, or natural woodland fragments surrounded by areas disturbed by humans—in other words, any patch surrounded by an environment not suitable for the "island" species. In the 1960s, American ecologists Robert MacArthur and E. O. Wilson developed a general model of island biogeography, identifying the key determinants of species diversity on an island with a given set of physical characteristics (Figure 54.27).

Consider a newly formed oceanic island that receives colonizing species from a distant mainland. Two factors that determine the number of species on the island are the rate at which new species immigrate to the island and the rate at which species become extinct on the island. At any given time, an island's immigration and extinction rates are affected by the number of species already present. As the number of species on the island increases, the immigration rate of new species decreases, because any individual reaching the island is less likely to represent a species that is not already present. At the same time, as more species inhabit an island, extinction rates on the island increase because of the greater likelihood of competitive exclusion.

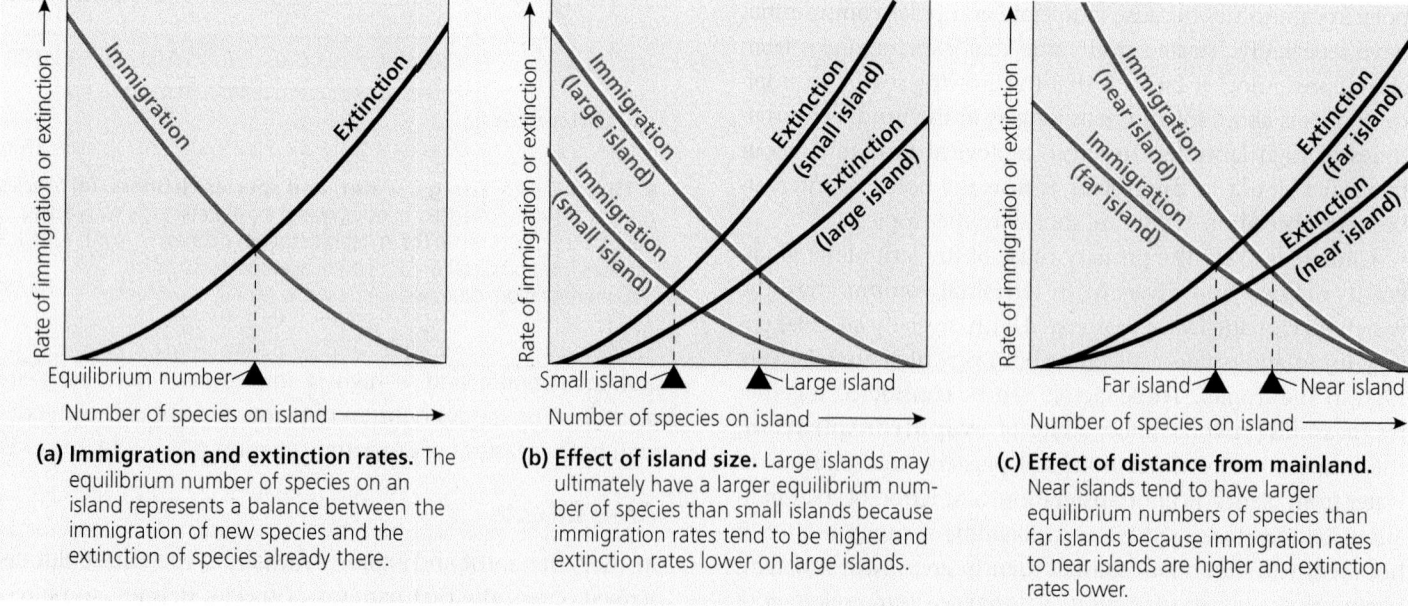

(a) Immigration and extinction rates. The equilibrium number of species on an island represents a balance between the immigration of new species and the extinction of species already there.

(b) Effect of island size. Large islands may ultimately have a larger equilibrium number of species than small islands because immigration rates tend to be higher and extinction rates lower on large islands.

(c) Effect of distance from mainland. Near islands tend to have larger equilibrium numbers of species than far islands because immigration rates to near islands are higher and extinction rates lower.

▲ **Figure 54.27 The equilibrium model of island biogeography.** Black triangles represent equilibrium numbers of species.

Two physical features of the island further affect immigration and extinction rates: its size and its distance from the mainland. Small islands generally have lower immigration rates because potential colonizers are less likely to reach a small island. For instance, birds blown out to sea by a storm are more likely to land by chance on a large island than on a small one. Small islands also have higher extinction rates because they generally contain fewer resources, have less diverse habitats, and have smaller population sizes. Distance from the mainland is also important; for two islands of equal size, a closer island generally has a higher immigration rate than one farther away. Because of their higher immigration rates, closer islands tend to have lower extinction rates, as arriving colonists help sustain the presence of a species on a near island and prevent its extinction.

MacArthur and Wilson's model is called the *island equilibrium model* because an equilibrium will eventually be reached where the rate of species immigration equals the rate of species extinction. The number of species at this equilibrium point is correlated with the island's size and distance from the mainland. Like any ecological equilibrium, this species equilibrium is dynamic; immigration and extinction continue, and the exact species composition may change over time.

MacArthur and Wilson's studies of the diversity of plants and animals on many island chains support the prediction that species richness increases with island size, in keeping with the island equilibrium model (Figure 54.28). Species counts also fit the prediction that the number of species decreases with increasing remoteness of the island.

Predictions of species composition based on the island equilibrium model may apply in only a limited number of cases and over relatively short periods, where colonization is the main process affecting species composition. Over longer periods, abiotic disturbances such as storms, adaptive evolutionary changes, and speciation generally alter the species composition and community structure on islands. Nonetheless, the model is widely applied in conservation biology, particularly for the design of habitat reserves and for providing a starting point for predicting the effects of habitat loss on species diversity.

CONCEPT CHECK 54.4

1. Describe two hypotheses that explain why species diversity is greater in tropical regions than in temperate and polar regions.
2. Describe how an island's size and distance from the mainland affect the island's species richness.
3. **WHAT IF?** Based on MacArthur and Wilson's model of island biogeography, how would you expect the richness of birds on islands to compare with the richness of snakes and lizards? Explain.

For suggested answers, see Appendix A.

▼ Figure 54.28 | **INQUIRY**

How does species richness relate to area?

FIELD STUDY Ecologists Robert MacArthur and E. O. Wilson studied the number of plant species on the Galápagos Islands in relation to the area of the different islands.

RESULTS

CONCLUSION Plant species richness increases with island size, supporting the island equilibrium model.

SOURCE R. H. MacArthur and E. O. Wilson, *The Theory of Island Biogeography*, Princeton University Press, Princeton, NJ (1967).

WHAT IF? Four islands in this study ranging in area from about 40 to 10,000 ha each contained about 50 plant species. What does such variation tell you about the simple assumptions of the island equilibrium model?

CONCEPT 54.5

Pathogens alter community structure locally and globally

Now that we have examined several important factors that structure biological communities, we will finish the chapter by examining community interactions involving **pathogens**—disease-causing microorganisms, viruses, viroids, or prions. (Viroids and prions are infectious RNA molecules and proteins, respectively; see Chapter 19.) Scientists have only recently come to appreciate how universal the effects of pathogens are in communities.

As you will read, pathogens can alter community structure quickly and extensively. They produce especially clear effects when they are introduced into new habitats, as in the case of chestnut blight and the fungus that causes it (see Concept 54.2). A pathogen can be particularly virulent in a new habitat because new hosts have not had a chance to become resistant to the pathogen through natural selection. The invasive chestnut blight fungus had far stronger effects on the American chestnut, for instance, than it had on Asian chestnut species in the fungus's native habitat. Humans are similarly vulnerable to the effects of emerging diseases spread by our increasingly global economy. Ecologists are applying ecological knowledge to help track and control the pathogens that cause such diseases.

Pathogens and Community Structure

In spite of the potential of pathogens to limit populations, pathogens have until recently been the subject of relatively few ecological studies. This imbalance is now being addressed as events highlight the ecological importance of disease.

Coral reef communities are increasingly susceptible to the influence of newly discovered pathogens. White-band disease, caused by an unknown pathogen, has resulted in dramatic changes in the structure and composition of Caribbean reefs. The disease kills corals by causing their tissue to slough off in a band from the base to the tip of the branches. Because of the disease, staghorn coral (*Acropora cervicornis*) has virtually disappeared from the Caribbean since the 1980s. In the same region, populations of elkhorn coral (*Acropora palmata*) have also been decimated. Such corals provide key habitat for lobsters as well as snappers and other fish species. When the corals die, they are quickly overgrown by algae. Surgeonfish and other herbivores that feed on algae come to dominate the fish community. Eventually, the corals topple because of damage from storms and other disturbances. The complex, three-dimensional structure of the reef disappears, and diversity plummets.

Pathogens also influence community structure in terrestrial ecosystems. In the forests and savannas of California, trees of several species are dying from sudden oak death (SOD). This recently discovered disease is caused by the fungus-like protist *Phytophthora ramorum* (see Chapter 28). SOD was first described in California in 1995, when hikers noticed trees dying around San Francisco Bay. By 2010, it had spread more than 800 km. During that time, it killed more than a million oaks and other trees from the central California coast to southern Oregon. The loss of these oaks has led to the decreased abundance of at least five bird species, including the acorn woodpecker and the oak titmouse, that rely on the oaks for food and habitat. Although there is currently no cure for SOD, scientists recently sequenced the genome of *P. ramorum* in hopes of finding a way to fight the pathogen.

Human activities are transporting pathogens around the world at unprecedented rates. Genetic analyses using simple sequence DNA (see Chapter 21) suggest that *P. ramorum* likely came to North America from Europe through the horticulture trade. Similarly, the pathogens that cause human diseases are spread by our global economy. H1N1, the virus that causes "swine flu" in humans, was first detected in Veracruz, Mexico, in early 2009. It quickly spread around the world when infected individuals flew on airplanes to other countries. By mid-2010, the world's first flu pandemic in 40 years had killed more than 17,000 people.

▼ **Figure 54.29**

IMPACT

Identifying Lyme Disease Host Species

A student researcher collects ticks from a white-footed mouse.

For years, scientists thought that the white-footed mouse was the primary host for the Lyme pathogen because mice are heavily parasitized by young ticks. When researchers vaccinated mice against Lyme disease and released them into the wild, however, the number of infected ticks hardly changed. That result prompted biologists in New York to look for other hosts for the Lyme pathogen. They first trapped individuals of 11 potential host species in the field and measured the density of larval ticks on the animals. They showed that each host species transmitted to the ticks a unique set of alleles of a gene that encodes a protein on the pathogen's outer surface. The researchers then collected ticks in the field that were no longer attached to any host and used the genetic database to identify their former hosts. They were surprised to learn that two inconspicuous shrew species had been the hosts of more than half the ticks examined.

WHY IT MATTERS By identifying the species that host a pathogen and determining their abundance and distribution, community ecologists obtain information that can be used to control the hosts most responsible for spreading diseases.

FURTHER READING D. Brisson et al., Conspicuous impacts of inconspicuous hosts on the Lyme disease epidemic, *Proceedings of the Royal Society B* 275:227–235 (2008).

MAKE CONNECTIONS Concept 23.1 (p. 470) describes genetic variation between populations. How might genetic variation between shrew populations in different locations affect the results of this study?

Community Ecology and Zoonotic Diseases

Three-quarters of emerging human diseases and many of the most devastating diseases are caused by **zoonotic pathogens**. Zoonotic pathogens are defined as those that are transferred to humans from other animals, either through direct contact with an infected animal or by means of an intermediate species, called a **vector**. The vectors that spread zoonotic diseases are often parasites, including ticks, lice, and mosquitoes. Identifying the community of hosts and vectors for a pathogen can help prevent disease (**Figure 54.29**).

Ecologists also use their knowledge of community interactions to track the spread of zoonotic diseases. One example, avian flu, is caused by highly contagious viruses transmitted through the saliva and feces of birds (see Chapter 19). Most of these viruses affect wild birds mildly, but they often cause stronger symptoms in domesticated birds, the most common source of human infections. Since 2003, one particular viral strain, called H5N1, has killed hundreds of millions of poultry and more than 250 people. Millions more people are at risk of infection.

Control programs that quarantine domestic birds or monitor their transport may be ineffective if avian flu spreads naturally through the movements of wild birds. From 2003 to 2006, the H5N1 strain spread rapidly from southeast Asia into Europe and Africa, but by mid-2010, it had not appeared in Australia or the Americas. The most likely place for infected wild birds to enter the Americas is Alaska, the entry point for ducks, geese, and shorebirds that migrate across the Bering Sea from Asia every year. Ecologists are studying the spread of the virus by trapping and testing migrating and resident birds in Alaska (Figure 54.30). These ecological detectives are trying to catch the first wave of the disease entering North America.

Community ecology provides the foundation for understanding the life cycles of pathogens and their interactions with hosts. Pathogen interactions are also greatly influenced by changes in the physical environment. To control pathogens and the diseases they cause, scientists need an ecosystem perspective—an intimate knowledge of how the pathogens interact with other species and with all aspects of their environment. Ecosystems are the subject of Chapter 55.

▲ Figure 54.30 **Tracking avian flu.** Graduate student Travis Booms, of Boise State University, bands a young gyrfalcon as part of a project to monitor the spread of the disease.

CONCEPT CHECK 54.5

1. What are pathogens?
2. **WHAT IF?** Rabies, a viral disease in mammals, is not currently found in the British Isles. If you were in charge of disease control there, what practical approaches might you employ to keep the rabies virus from reaching these islands?

For suggested answers, see Appendix A.

54 CHAPTER REVIEW

SUMMARY OF KEY CONCEPTS

CONCEPT 54.1

Community interactions are classified by whether they help, harm, or have no effect on the species involved (pp. 1194–1200)

- A variety of **interspecific interactions** affect the survival and reproduction of the species that engage in them. These interactions include **interspecific competition, predation, herbivory, symbiosis,** and **facilitation. Parasitism, mutualism,** and **commensalism** are types of symbiotic interactions.
- **Competitive exclusion** states that two species competing for the same resource cannot coexist permanently in the same place. **Resource partitioning** is the differentiation of species **niches** that enables species to coexist in a community.

> ? *Give an example of a pair of species that exhibit each interaction listed in the table at right.*

Interspecific Interaction	Description
Competition (−/−)	Two or more species compete for a resource that is in short supply.
Predation (+/−)	One species, the predator, kills and eats the other, the prey. Predation has led to diverse adaptations, including mimicry.
Herbivory (+/−)	An herbivore eats part of a plant or alga. Plants have various chemical and mechanical defenses against herbivory, and herbivores have specialized adaptations for feeding.
Symbiosis	Individuals of two or more species live in close contact with one another. Symbiosis includes parasitism, mutualism, and commensalism.
Parasitism (+/−)	The **parasite** derives its nourishment from a second organism, its **host,** which is harmed.
Mutualism (+/+)	Both species benefit from the interaction.
Commensalism (+/0)	One species benefits from the interaction, while the other is unaffected by it.
Facilitation (+/+ or 0/+)	Species have positive effects on the survival and reproduction of other species without the intimate contact of a symbiosis.

CONCEPT 54.2

Diversity and trophic structure characterize biological communities (pp. 1200–1206)

- **Species diversity** measures the number of species in a community—its **species richness**—and their **relative abundance**. A community with similar abundances of species is more diverse than one in which one or two species are abundant and the remainder are rare.
- More diverse communities typically produce more **biomass** and show less year-to-year variation in growth than less diverse communities and are more resistant to invasion by exotic species.
- **Trophic structure** is a key factor in community dynamics. **Food chains** link the trophic levels from producers to top carnivores. Branching food chains and complex trophic interactions form **food webs**. The **energetic hypothesis** suggests that the length of a food chain is limited by the inefficiency of energy transfer along the chain.
- **Dominant species** are the most abundant species in a community and possess high competitive abilities. **Keystone species** are usually less abundant species that exert a disproportionate influence on community structure because of their ecological niche. **Ecosystem engineers** influence community structure through their effects on the physical environment.
- The **bottom-up model** proposes a unidirectional influence from lower to higher trophic levels, in which nutrients and other abiotic factors primarily determine community structure, including the abundance of primary producers. **The top-down model** proposes that control of each trophic level comes from the trophic level above, with the result that predators control herbivores, which in turn control primary producers.

? *Based on indexes such as Shannon diversity, is a community of higher species richness always more diverse than a community of lower species richness? Explain.*

CONCEPT 54.3

Disturbance influences species diversity and composition (pp. 1207–1210)

- Increasing evidence suggests that **disturbance** and lack of equilibrium, rather than stability and equilibrium, are the norm for most communities. According to the **intermediate disturbance hypothesis**, moderate levels of disturbance can foster higher species diversity than can low or high levels of disturbance.
- **Ecological succession** is the sequence of community and ecosystem changes after a disturbance. **Primary succession** occurs where no soil exists when succession begins; **secondary succession** begins in an area where soil remains after a disturbance. Mechanisms that produce community change during succession include facilitation and inhibition.
- Humans are the most widespread agents of disturbance, and their effects on communities often reduce species diversity. Humans also prevent some naturally occurring disturbances, such as fire, which can be important to community structure.

? *Is the disturbance pictured in Figure 54.24 more likely to initiate primary or secondary succession? Explain.*

CONCEPT 54.4

Biogeographic factors affect community diversity (pp. 1211–1213)

- Species richness generally declines along a latitudinal gradient from the tropics to the poles. The greater age of tropical environments may account for the greater species richness of the tropics. Climate also influences the diversity gradient through energy (heat and light) and water.
- Species richness is directly related to a community's geographic size, a principle formalized in the **species-area curve**.
- Species richness on islands depends on island size and distance from the mainland. The island equilibrium model maintains that species richness on an ecological island reaches an equilibrium where new immigrations are balanced by extinctions. This model may not apply over long periods, during which abiotic disturbances, evolutionary changes, and speciation may alter community structure.

? *How have periods of glaciation influenced latitudinal patterns of diversity?*

CONCEPT 54.5

Pathogens alter community structure locally and globally (pp. 1213–1215)

- Recent work has highlighted the role that **pathogens** play in structuring terrestrial and marine communities.
- **Zoonotic pathogens** are transferred from other animals to humans and cause the largest class of emerging human diseases. Community ecology provides the framework for identifying key species interactions associated with such pathogens and for helping us track and control their spread.

? *In what way can a vector of a zoonotic pathogen differ from a host of the pathogen?*

TEST YOUR UNDERSTANDING

LEVEL 1: KNOWLEDGE/COMPREHENSION

1. The feeding relationships among the species in a community determine the community's
   a. secondary succession.
   b. ecological niche.
   c. species richness.
   d. species-area curve.
   e. trophic structure.

2. The principle of competitive exclusion states that
   a. two species cannot coexist in the same habitat.
   b. competition between two species always causes extinction or emigration of one species.
   c. competition in a population promotes survival of the best-adapted individuals.
   d. two species that have exactly the same niche cannot coexist in a community.
   e. two species will stop reproducing until one species leaves the habitat.

3. Based on the intermediate disturbance hypothesis, a community's species diversity is increased by
   a. frequent massive disturbance.
   b. stable conditions with no disturbance.
   c. moderate levels of disturbance.
   d. human intervention to eliminate disturbance.
   e. intensive disturbance by humans.

4. According to the equilibrium model of island biogeography, species richness would be greatest on an island that is
   a. large and close to a mainland.
   b. large and remote.
   c. small and remote.
   d. small and close to a mainland.
   e. environmentally homogeneous.

LEVEL 2: APPLICATION/ANALYSIS

5. Keystone predators can maintain species diversity in a community if they
   a. competitively exclude other predators.
   b. prey on the community's dominant species.
   c. allow immigration of other predators.
   d. reduce the number of disruptions in the community.
   e. prey only on the least abundant species in the community.

6. Food chains are sometimes short because
   a. only a single species of herbivore feeds on each plant species.
   b. local extinction of a species causes extinction of the other species in its food chain.
   c. most of the energy in a trophic level is lost as it passes to the next higher level.
   d. predator species tend to be less diverse and less abundant than prey species.
   e. most producers are inedible.

7. Which of the following could qualify as a top-down control on a grassland community?
   a. limitation of plant biomass by rainfall amount
   b. influence of temperature on competition among plants
   c. influence of soil nutrients on the abundance of grasses versus wildflowers
   d. effect of grazing intensity by bison on plant species diversity
   e. effect of humidity on plant growth rates

8. The most plausible hypothesis to explain why species richness is higher in tropical than in temperate regions is that
   a. tropical communities are younger.
   b. tropical regions generally have more available water and higher levels of solar radiation.
   c. higher temperatures cause more rapid speciation.
   d. diversity increases as evapotranspiration decreases.
   e. tropical regions have very high rates of immigration and very low rates of extinction.

9. Community 1 contains 100 individuals distributed among four species (A, B, C, and D). Community 2 contains 100 individuals distributed among three species (A, B, and C).

   Community 1: 5A, 5B, 85C, 5D
   Community 2: 30A, 40B, 30C

   Calculate the Shannon diversity (H) for each community. Which community is more diverse?

LEVEL 3: SYNTHESIS/EVALUATION

10. **DRAW IT** Another important species in the Chesapeake Bay estuary (see Figure 54.15) is the blue crab (*Callinectes sapidus*). It is an omnivore, eating eelgrass and other primary producers as well as clams. It is also a cannibal. In turn, the crabs are eaten by humans and by the endangered Kemp's Ridley sea turtle. Based on this information, draw a food web that includes the blue crab. Assuming that the top-down model holds for this system, what would happen to the abundance of eelgrass if humans stopped eating blue crabs?

11. **EVOLUTION CONNECTION**
    Explain why adaptations of particular organisms to interspecific competition may not necessarily represent instances of character displacement. What would a researcher have to demonstrate about two competing species to make a convincing case for character displacement?

12. **SCIENTIFIC INQUIRY**
    An ecologist studying plants in the desert performed the following experiment. She staked out two identical plots, each of which included a few sagebrush plants and numerous small annual wildflowers. She found the same five wildflower species in roughly equal numbers on both plots. She then enclosed one of the plots with a fence to keep out kangaroo rats, the most common grain-eaters of the area. After two years, four of the wildflower species were no longer present in the fenced plot, but one species had increased drastically. The control plot had not changed in species diversity. Using the principles of community ecology, propose a hypothesis to explain her results. What additional evidence would support your hypothesis?

13. **SCIENCE, TECHNOLOGY, AND SOCIETY**
    By 1935, hunting and trapping had eliminated wolves from the United States except for Alaska. Wolves have since been protected as an endangered species, and they have moved south from Canada and become reestablished in the Rocky Mountains and northern Great Lakes region. Conservationists who would like to speed up wolf recovery have reintroduced wolves into Yellowstone National Park. Local ranchers are opposed to bringing back the wolves because they fear predation on their cattle and sheep. What are some reasons for reestablishing wolves in Yellowstone National Park? What effects might the reintroduction of wolves have on the biological communities in the region? What might be done to mitigate the conflict between ranchers and wolves?

14. **WRITE ABOUT A THEME**

    Genetic Basis of Life In Batesian mimicry, a palatable species gains protection by mimicking an unpalatable one. Imagine that several individuals of a palatable, brightly colored fly species are carried by the wind to three remote islands. The first island has no predators of that species; the second has predators but no similarly colored, unpalatable species; and the third has both predators and a similarly colored, unpalatable species. In a short essay (100–150 words), predict what might happen to the coloration of the palatable species on each of the islands through evolutionary time if coloration is a genetically controlled trait. Explain your predictions.

For selected answers, see Appendix A.

MasteringBIOLOGY®   www.masteringbiology.com

1. MasteringBiology® Assignments
Make Connections Tutorial Character Displacement (Chapter 54) and Modes of Selection (Chapter 23)
Experimental Inquiry Tutorial Can a Species' Niche Be Influenced by Interspecific Competition?
Tutorial Interspecific Interactions
Activities Interspecific Interactions • Food Webs • Primary Succession • Exploring Island Biogeography • GraphIt!: Species Area Effect and Island Biogeography
Questions Student Misconceptions • Reading Quiz • Multiple Choice • End-of-Chapter

2. eText
Read your book online, search, take notes, highlight text, and more.

3. The Study Area
Practice Tests • Cumulative Test • *BioFlix* 3-D Animations • MP3 Tutor Sessions • Videos • Activities • Investigations • Lab Media • Audio Glossary • Word Study Tools • Art

55

Ecosystems and Restoration Ecology

▲ Figure 55.1 **Why is this Antarctic ice blood red?**

KEY CONCEPTS

55.1 Physical laws govern energy flow and chemical cycling in ecosystems

55.2 Energy and other limiting factors control primary production in ecosystems

55.3 Energy transfer between trophic levels is typically only 10% efficient

55.4 Biological and geochemical processes cycle nutrients and water in ecosystems

55.5 Restoration ecologists help return degraded ecosystems to a more natural state

OVERVIEW

Cool Ecosystem

Three hundred meters below Taylor Glacier, in Antarctica, an unusual community of bacteria lives on sulfur- and iron-containing ions. These organisms thrive in harsh conditions, without light or oxygen and at a temperature of −10°C, so low that the water would freeze if it weren't three times as salty as the ocean. How has this community survived, isolated from Earth's surface for at least 1.5 million years? The bacteria are chemoautotrophs, which obtain energy by oxidizing sulfur taken up from their sulfate-rich environment (see Chapter 27). They use iron as a final electron acceptor in their reactions. When the water flows from the base of the glacier and comes into contact with air, the reduced iron in the water is oxidized and turns red before the water freezes. The distinctive color gives this area of the glacier its name—Blood Falls **(Figure 55.1)**.

Together, the bacterial community and surrounding environment make up an **ecosystem**, the sum of all the organisms living in a given area and the abiotic factors with which they interact. An ecosystem can encompass a vast area, such as a lake or forest, or a microcosm, such as the space under a fallen log or a desert spring **(Figure 55.2)**. As with populations and communities, the boundaries of ecosystems are not always discrete. Many ecologists view the entire biosphere as a global ecosystem, a composite of all the local ecosystems on Earth.

Regardless of an ecosystem's size, its dynamics involve two processes that cannot be fully described by population or community phenomena: energy flow and chemical cycling. Energy enters most ecosystems as sunlight. It is converted to chemical energy by autotrophs, passed to heterotrophs in the organic compounds of food, and dissipated as heat. Chemical elements, such as carbon and nitrogen, are cycled among abiotic and biotic components of the ecosystem. Photosynthetic and chemosynthetic organisms assimilate these elements in inorganic form from the air, soil, and water and incorporate them into their biomass, some of which is consumed by animals. The elements are returned in inorganic form to the environment by the metabolism of plants and animals and by organisms such as bacteria and fungi that break down organic wastes and dead organisms.

Both energy and matter are transformed in ecosystems through photosynthesis and feeding relationships. But unlike matter, energy cannot be recycled. An ecosystem must be powered by a continuous influx of energy from an external source—in most cases, the sun. Energy flows through ecosystems, whereas matter cycles within and through them.

Resources critical to human survival and welfare, ranging from the food we eat to the oxygen we breathe, are products of ecosystem processes. In this chapter, we will explore the dynamics of energy flow and chemical cycling, emphasizing the results of ecosystem experiments. One way to study ecosystem processes is to alter environmental factors, such as temperature or the abundance of nutrients, and study how ecosystems respond. We will also consider some of the impacts of human activities on energy flow and chemical cycling. Finally, we will explore the growing science of restoration ecology, which focuses on returning degraded ecosystems to a more natural state.

▲ Figure 55.2 **A desert spring ecosystem.**

CONCEPT **55.1**

Physical laws govern energy flow and chemical cycling in ecosystems

In Unit Two, you learned how cells transform energy and matter, subject to the laws of thermodynamics. Like cell biologists, ecosystem ecologists study the transformations of energy and matter within a system and measure the amounts of both that cross the system's boundaries. By grouping the species in a community into trophic levels of feeding relationships (see Chapter 54), we can follow the transformations of energy in an ecosystem and map the movements of chemical elements.

Conservation of Energy

Because ecosystem ecologists study the interactions of organisms with the physical environment, many ecosystem approaches are based on laws of physics and chemistry. The first law of thermodynamics, which we discussed in Chapter 8, states that energy cannot be created or destroyed but only transferred or transformed. Thus, we can potentially account for the transfer of energy through an ecosystem from its input as solar radiation to its release as heat from organisms. Plants and other photosynthetic organisms convert solar energy to chemical energy, but the total amount of energy does not change: The amount of energy stored in organic molecules must equal the total solar energy intercepted by the plant, minus the amounts reflected and dissipated as heat. One area of ecosystem ecology involves computing energy budgets and tracing energy flow through ecosystems in order to understand the factors that control these energy transfers. Such transfers help determine how many organisms a habitat can support and the amount of food humans can harvest from a site.

One implication of the second law of thermodynamics, which states that every exchange of energy increases the entropy of the universe, is that energy conversions are inefficient; some energy is always lost as heat (see Chapter 8). We

can measure the efficiency of ecological energy conversions just as we measure the efficiency of light bulbs and car engines. Energy flowing through ecosystems is ultimately dissipated into space as heat, so if the sun were not continuously providing energy to Earth, most ecosystems would vanish.

Conservation of Mass

Matter, like energy, cannot be created or destroyed. This **law of conservation of mass** is as important for ecosystems as the laws of thermodynamics are. Because mass is conserved, we can determine how much of a chemical element cycles within an ecosystem or is gained or lost by that ecosystem over time.

Unlike energy, chemical elements are continually recycled within ecosystems. A carbon atom in CO_2 is released from the soil by a decomposer, taken up by a grass through photosynthesis, consumed by a bison or other grazer, and returned to the soil in the bison's waste. The measurement and analysis of chemical cycling within ecosystems and in the biosphere as a whole are an important aspect of ecosystem ecology.

Although elements are not significantly gained or lost on a global scale, they can be gained by or lost from a particular ecosystem. In a forest ecosystem, most mineral nutrients—the essential elements that plants obtain from soil—enter as dust or as solutes dissolved in rainwater or leached from rocks in the ground. Nitrogen is also supplied through the biological process of nitrogen fixation (see Figure 37.10). In terms of losses, some elements return to the atmosphere as gases, and others are carried out of the ecosystem by moving water. Like organisms, ecosystems are open systems, absorbing energy and mass and releasing heat and waste products.

In nature, most gains and losses to ecosystems are small compared to the amounts recycled within them. Still, the balance between inputs and outputs determines whether an ecosystem is a source or a sink for a given element. If a mineral nutrient's outputs exceed its inputs, it will eventually limit production in that system. Human activities often change the balance of inputs and outputs considerably, as we will see later in this chapter and in Chapter 56.

Energy, Mass, and Trophic Levels

As you read in Chapter 54, ecologists assign species to trophic levels based on their main source of nutrition and energy. The trophic level that ultimately supports all others consists of autotrophs, also called the **primary producers** of the ecosystem. Most autotrophs are photosynthetic organisms that use light energy to synthesize sugars and other organic compounds, which they then use as fuel for cellular respiration and as building material for growth. Plants, algae, and photosynthetic prokaryotes are the biosphere's main autotrophs, although chemosynthetic prokaryotes are the primary producers in ecosystems such as deep-sea hydrothermal vents (see Figure 52.16) and places deep under the ground or ice (see Figure 55.1).

Organisms in trophic levels above the primary producers are heterotrophs, which depend directly or indirectly on the outputs of primary producers for their source of energy. Herbivores, which eat plants and other primary producers, are **primary consumers**. Carnivores that eat herbivores are **secondary consumers**, and carnivores that eat other carnivores are **tertiary consumers**.

Another group of heterotrophs is the **detritivores,** or **decomposers**, terms we use synonymously in this text to refer to consumers that get their energy from detritus. **Detritus** is nonliving organic material, such as the remains of dead organisms, feces, fallen leaves, and wood. Many detritivores are in turn eaten by secondary and tertiary consumers. Two important groups of detritivores are prokaryotes and fungi (Figure 55.3). These organisms secrete enzymes that digest organic material; they then absorb the breakdown products, linking the consumers and primary producers in an ecosystem. In a forest, for instance, birds eat earthworms that have been feeding on leaf litter and its associated prokaryotes and fungi.

Detritivores also play a critical role in recycling chemical elements back to primary producers. Detritivores convert organic matter from all trophic levels to inorganic compounds usable by primary producers, closing the loop of an ecosystem's chemical cycling. Producers can then recycle these elements into organic compounds. If decomposition stopped, life would cease as detritus piled up and the

▲ Figure 55.3 **Fungi decomposing a dead tree.**

supply of ingredients needed to synthesize new organic matter was exhausted. **Figure 55.4** summarizes the trophic relationships in an ecosystem.

CONCEPT CHECK 55.1

1. Why is the transfer of energy in an ecosystem referred to as energy flow, not energy cycling?
2. **WHAT IF?** You are studying nitrogen cycling on the Serengeti Plain in Africa. During your experiment, a herd of migrating wildebeests grazes through your study plot. What would you need to know to measure their effect on nitrogen balance in the plot?
3. **MAKE CONNECTIONS** Review the discussion of the second law of thermodynamics in Concept 8.1 (p. 144). How does this physical law explain why an ecosystem's energy supply must be continually replenished?

For suggested answers, see Appendix A.

CONCEPT 55.2

Energy and other limiting factors control primary production in ecosystems

As you read in Chapter 1, the theme of energy transfer underlies all biological interactions. In most ecosystems, the amount of light energy converted to chemical energy—in the form of organic compounds—by autotrophs during a given time period is the ecosystem's **primary production**. These photosynthetic products are the starting point for most studies of ecosystem metabolism and energy flow. In ecosystems where the primary producers are chemoautotrophs, as described in the Overview on page 1218, the initial energy input is chemical,

▶ **Figure 55.4 An overview of energy and nutrient dynamics in an ecosystem.** Energy enters, flows through, and exits an ecosystem, whereas chemical nutrients cycle primarily within it. In this generalized scheme, energy (dark orange arrows) enters from the sun as radiation, moves as chemical energy transfers through the food web, and exits as heat radiated into space. Most transfers of nutrients (blue arrows) through the trophic levels lead eventually to detritus; the nutrients then cycle back to the primary producers.

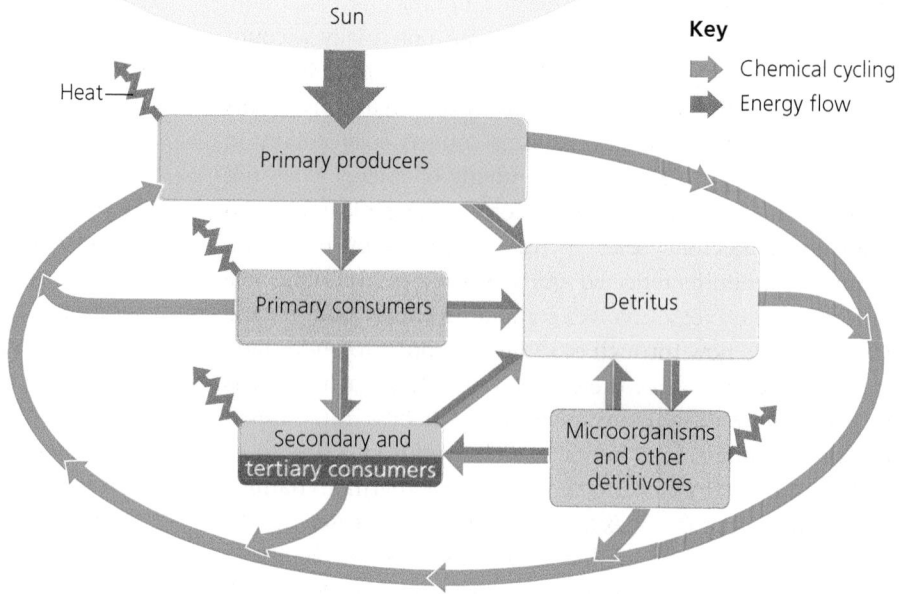

Key
➡ Chemical cycling
➡ Energy flow

Sun

Heat

Primary producers

Primary consumers

Detritus

Secondary and tertiary consumers

Microorganisms and other detritivores

and the initial products are the organic compounds synthesized by the microorganisms.

Ecosystem Energy Budgets

Since most primary producers use light energy to synthesize energy-rich organic molecules, consumers acquire their organic fuels secondhand (or even third- or fourthhand) through food webs such as that in Figure 54.15. Therefore, the total amount of photosynthetic production sets the spending limit for the entire ecosystem's energy budget.

The Global Energy Budget

Each day, Earth's atmosphere is bombarded by about 10^{22} joules of solar radiation (1 J = 0.239 cal). This is enough energy to supply the demands of the entire human population for approximately 25 years at 2009 energy consumption levels. As described in Chapter 52, the intensity of the solar energy striking Earth varies with latitude, with the tropics receiving the greatest input. Most incoming solar radiation is absorbed, scattered, or reflected by clouds and dust in the atmosphere. The amount of solar radiation that ultimately reaches Earth's surface limits the possible photosynthetic output of ecosystems.

Only a small fraction of the sunlight that reaches Earth's surface is actually used in photosynthesis. Much of the radiation strikes materials that don't photosynthesize, such as ice and soil. Of the radiation that does reach photosynthetic organisms, only certain wavelengths are absorbed by photosynthetic pigments (see Figure 10.9); the rest is transmitted, reflected, or lost as heat. As a result, only about 1% of the visible light that strikes photosynthetic organisms is converted to chemical energy. Nevertheless, Earth's primary producers create about 150 billion metric tons (1.50×10^{14} kg) of organic material each year.

Gross and Net Production

Total primary production in an ecosystem is known as that ecosystem's **gross primary production (GPP)**—the amount of energy from light (or chemicals, in chemoautotrophic systems) converted to the chemical energy of organic molecules per unit time. Not all of this production is stored as organic material in the primary producers because they use some of the molecules as fuel in their own cellular respiration. **Net primary production (NPP)** is equal to gross primary production minus the energy used by the primary producers for their "autotrophic respiration" (R_a):

$$NPP = GPP - R_a$$

On average, NPP is about one-half of GPP. To ecologists, net primary production is the key measurement because it represents the storage of chemical energy that will be available to consumers in the ecosystem.

Net primary production can be expressed as energy per unit area per unit time ($J/m^2 \cdot yr$) or as biomass (mass of vegetation) added per unit area per unit time ($g/m^2 \cdot yr$). (Note that biomass is usually expressed in terms of the dry mass of organic material.) An ecosystem's NPP should not be confused with the total biomass of photosynthetic autotrophs present, a measure called the *standing crop*. Net primary production is the amount of *new* biomass added in a given period of time. Although a forest has a large standing crop, its net primary production may actually be less than that of some grasslands; grasslands do not accumulate as much biomass as forests because animals consume the plants rapidly and because grasses and herbs decompose more quickly than trees do.

Satellites provide a powerful tool for studying global patterns of primary production (Figure 55.5). Images produced from satellite data show that different ecosystems vary considerably in their net primary production. Tropical rain forests are among the most productive terrestrial ecosystems and contribute a large portion of the planet's net primary production. Estuaries and coral reefs also have very high net primary production, but their contribution to the global total is small because these ecosystems cover only about one-tenth the area covered by tropical rain forests. In contrast, while

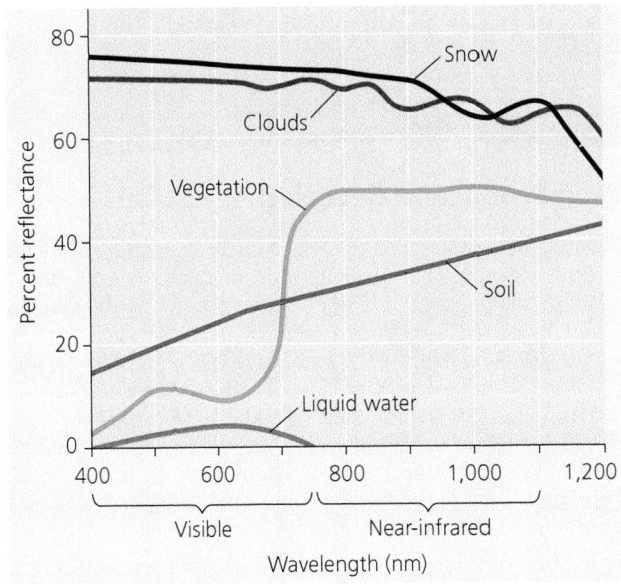

▼ Figure 55.5   **RESEARCH METHOD**

Determining Primary Production with Satellites

APPLICATION Because chlorophyll captures visible light (see Figure 10.9), photosynthetic organisms absorb more light at visible wavelengths (about 380–750 nm) than at near-infrared wavelengths (750–1,100 nm). Scientists use this difference in absorption to estimate the rate of photosynthesis in different regions of the globe using satellites.

TECHNIQUE Most satellites determine what they "see" by comparing the ratios of wavelengths reflected back to them. Vegetation reflects much more near-infrared radiation than visible radiation, producing a reflectance pattern very different from that of snow, clouds, soil, and liquid water.

RESULTS Scientists use the satellite data to help produce maps of primary production like the one in Figure 55.6.

► **Figure 55.6 Global net primary production.** The map is based on data collected by satellites, such as amount of sunlight absorbed by vegetation. Note that tropical land areas have the highest rates of production (yellow and red on the map).

Net primary production (kg carbon/m²·yr)

? *Does this global map accurately reflect the importance of some highly productive habitats, such as wetlands, coral reefs, and coastal zones? Explain.*

the oceans are relatively unproductive **(Figure 55.6)**, their vast size means that together they contribute as much global net primary production as terrestrial systems do.

Whereas net primary production can be stated as the amount of new biomass added in a given period of time, **net ecosystem production (NEP)** is a measure of the *total biomass accumulation* during that time. Net ecosystem production is defined as gross primary production minus the total respiration of all organisms in the system (R_T)—not just primary producers, as for the calculation of NPP, but decomposers and other heterotrophs as well:

$$NEP = GPP - R_T$$

NEP is useful to ecologists because its value determines whether an ecosystem is gaining or losing carbon over time. A forest may have a positive NPP but still lose carbon if heterotrophs release it as CO_2 more quickly than primary producers incorporate it into organic compounds.

The most common way to estimate NEP is to measure the net flux (flow) of CO_2 or O_2 entering or leaving the ecosystem. If more CO_2 enters than leaves, the system is storing carbon. Because O_2 release is directly coupled to photosynthesis and respiration (see Figure 9.2), a system that is giving off O_2 is also storing carbon. On land, ecologists typically measure only the net flux of CO_2 from ecosystems; detecting small changes in O_2 in a large atmospheric O_2 pool is difficult. In the oceans, researchers use both approaches. New marine research using O_2 measurements has revealed surprisingly high NEP in some of the nutrient-poor waters that cover much of the open ocean **(Figure 55.7)**. This result is causing biologists to reevaluate regional and global estimates of ocean productivity and to examine the constraints to marine productivity.

What limits production in ecosystems? To ask this question another way, what factors could we change to increase production for a given ecosystem? We'll address this question first for aquatic ecosystems.

▼ **Figure 55.7**

IMPACT

Ocean Production Revealed

Net ecosystem production (NEP) is difficult to measure in the low-nutrient regions that make up most of Earth's oceans. Rates of primary production and total respiration are low, and the difference between them—NEP—is even lower. In principle, scientists could estimate NEP by measuring the amounts of O_2 present in the water. Until recently, though, they lacked a means of obtaining the necessary data. But in 2008, researchers were able to measure NEP in parts of the Pacific Ocean using high-resolution oxygen sensors deployed on floats. The floats were "parked" about 1,000 m deep and, after drifting for 9 days, automatically rose to the surface, measuring O_2 concentrations as they went. Overall, the researchers observed an average NEP of 25 g C/m² over the three-year study.

WHY IT MATTERS Phytoplankton communities in extensive regions of the oceans are more productive than scientists believed even a few years ago. Biologists have a new understanding of Earth's carbon cycle and what limits marine productivity around the world.

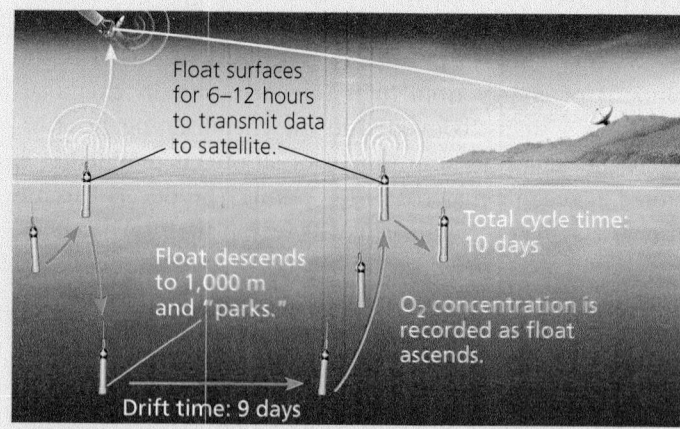

Float surfaces for 6–12 hours to transmit data to satellite.

Float descends to 1,000 m and "parks."

Total cycle time: 10 days

O_2 concentration is recorded as float ascends.

Drift time: 9 days

FURTHER READING S. C. Riser and K. S. Johnson, Net production of oxygen in the subtropical ocean, *Nature* 451:323–325(2008).

MAKE CONNECTIONS Review the discussion in Concept 28.7 (p. 597) of the role of photosynthetic protists as producers in aquatic ecosystems. What factors in addition to light availability are likely to limit primary production in the oceans?

Primary Production in Aquatic Ecosystems

In aquatic (marine and freshwater) ecosystems, both light and nutrients are important in controlling primary production.

Light Limitation

Because solar radiation drives photosynthesis, you would expect light to be a key variable in controlling primary production in oceans. Indeed, the depth of light penetration affects primary production throughout the photic zone of an ocean or lake (see Figure 52.13). About half of the solar radiation is absorbed in the first 15 m of water. Even in "clear" water, only 5–10% of the radiation may reach a depth of 75 m.

If light were the main variable limiting primary production in the ocean, we would expect production to increase along a gradient from the poles toward the equator, which receives the greatest intensity of light. However, you can see in Figure 55.6 that there is no such gradient. Another factor must strongly influence primary production in the ocean.

Nutrient Limitation

More than light, nutrients limit primary production in most oceans and lakes. A **limiting nutrient** is the element that must be added for production to increase. The nutrient most often limiting marine production is either nitrogen or phosphorus. Concentrations of these nutrients are typically low in the photic zone because they are rapidly taken up by phytoplankton and because detritus tends to sink.

As detailed in **Figure 55.8**, nutrient enrichment experiments confirmed that nitrogen was limiting phytoplankton growth off the south shore of Long Island, New York. One practical application of this work is in preventing algal "blooms" caused by excess nitrogen runoff that fertilizes the phytoplankton. Prior to this research, phosphate contamination was thought to cause many such blooms in the ocean, but eliminating phosphates alone may not help unless nitrogen pollution is also controlled.

The macronutrients nitrogen and phosphorus are not the only nutrients that limit aquatic production. Several large areas of the ocean have low phytoplankton densities despite relatively high nitrogen concentrations. The Sargasso Sea, a subtropical region of the Atlantic Ocean, has some of the clearest water in the world because of its low phytoplankton density. Nutrient enrichment experiments have revealed that the availability of the micronutrient iron limits primary production there (Table 55.1). Windblown dust from land supplies most of the iron to the oceans but is relatively scarce in this and certain other regions compared to the oceans as a whole.

The finding that iron limits production in some oceanic ecosystems encouraged marine ecologists to carry out recent large-scale ocean fertilization experiments in the Pacific Ocean—research that might also shed light on ocean fertilization as a tool to remove the greenhouse gas carbon dioxide from the atmosphere. In one study, researchers spread low concentrations of dissolved iron over 72 km² of ocean and

INQUIRY

Which nutrient limits phytoplankton production along the coast of Long Island?

EXPERIMENT Pollution from duck farms concentrated near Moriches Bay adds both nitrogen and phosphorus to the coastal water off Long Island, New York. To determine which nutrient limits phytoplankton growth in this area, John Ryther and William Dunstan, of the Woods Hole Oceanographic Institution, cultured the phytoplankton *Nannochloris atomus* with water collected from several sites, identified as A–G. They added either ammonium (NH_4^+) or phosphate (PO_4^{3-}) to some of the cultures.

RESULTS The addition of ammonium caused heavy phytoplankton growth in the cultures, but the addition of phosphate did not.

CONCLUSION Since adding phosphorus, which was already in rich supply, did not increase *Nannochloris* growth, whereas adding nitrogen increased phytoplankton density dramatically, the researchers concluded that nitrogen is the nutrient that limits phytoplankton growth in this ecosystem.

SOURCE J. H. Ryther and W. M. Dunstan, Nitrogen, phosphorus, and eutrophication in the coastal marine environment, *Science* 171:1008–1013 (1971).

WHAT IF? How would you expect the results of this experiment to change if new duck farms substantially increased the amount of pollution in the water? Explain your reasoning.

Table 55.1 Nutrient Enrichment Experiment for Sargasso Sea Samples

Nutrients Added to Experimental Culture	Relative Uptake of ^{14}C by Cultures*
None (controls)	1.00
Nitrogen (N) + phosphorus (P) only	1.10
N + P + metals (excluding iron)	1.08
N + P + metals (including iron)	12.90
N + P + iron	12.00

*^{14}C uptake by cultures measures primary production.

Source: D. W. Menzel and J. H. Ryther, Nutrients limiting the production of phytoplankton in the Sargasso Sea, with special reference to iron, *Deep Sea Research* 7:276–281 (1961).

then measured the change in phytoplankton density over a seven-day period. A massive phytoplankton bloom occurred, as indicated by increased chlorophyll concentration in the water. Adding iron had stimulated growth of cyanobacteria that fix additional atmospheric nitrogen (see Chapter 27), and the extra nitrogen stimulated proliferation of phytoplankton.

As a tool to remove carbon dioxide from air, iron fertilization remains controversial. There is little evidence from iron fertilization experiments that organic carbon sinks into deep-ocean water and sediments. Instead, it tends to be recycled by secondary consumers and decomposers in shallow waters, returning eventually to the atmosphere. Ecologists also have concerns about the overall effects of large-scale fertilization on marine communities. Iron fertilization is therefore unlikely to be widely applied anytime soon.

Areas of upwelling, where deep, nutrient-rich waters circulate to the ocean surface, have exceptionally high primary production. This fact supports the hypothesis that nutrient availability determines marine primary production. Because upwelling stimulates growth of the phytoplankton that form the base of marine food webs, upwelling areas typically host highly productive, diverse ecosystems and are prime fishing locations. The largest areas of upwelling occur in the Southern Ocean (also called the Antarctic Ocean), along the equator, and in the coastal waters off Peru, California, and parts of western Africa.

In freshwater lakes, nutrient limitation is also common. During the 1970s, scientists showed that sewage and fertilizer runoff from farms and lawns added large amounts of nutrients to lakes. Cyanobacteria and algae grow rapidly in response to these added nutrients, ultimately reducing the oxygen concentration and clarity of the water. The ecological impacts of this process, known as **eutrophication** (from the Greek *eutrophos*, well nourished), include the loss of many fish species from the lakes (see Figure 52.16).

Controlling eutrophication requires knowing which polluting nutrient is responsible. While nitrogen rarely limits primary production in lakes, a series of whole-lake experiments showed that phosphorus availability limited cyanobacterial growth. This and other ecological research led to the use of phosphate-free detergents and other important water quality reforms.

Primary Production in Terrestrial Ecosystems

At regional and global scales, temperature and moisture are the main factors controlling primary production in terrestrial ecosystems. Tropical rain forests, with their warm, wet conditions that promote plant growth, are the most productive of all terrestrial ecosystems (see Figure 55.6). In contrast, low-productivity systems are generally hot and dry, like many deserts, or cold and dry, like arctic tundra. Between these extremes lie the temperate forest and grassland ecosystems, which have moderate climates and intermediate productivity.

The climate variables of moisture and temperature are very useful for predicting NPP in terrestrial ecosystems. Pri-

▲ Figure 55.9 **A global relationship between net primary production and mean annual precipitation for terrestrial ecosystems.**

mary production is greater in wetter ecosystems, as shown for the plot of NPP and annual precipitation in **Figure 55.9**. Along with mean annual precipitation, a second useful predictor is *actual evapotranspiration*, the total amount of water transpired by plants and evaporated from a landscape. Evapotranspiration increases with the temperature and amount of solar energy available to drive evaporation and transpiration.

Nutrient Limitations and Adaptations That Reduce Them

EVOLUTION Mineral nutrients in the soil also limit primary production in terrestrial ecosystems. As in aquatic systems, nitrogen and phosphorus are the nutrients that most commonly limit terrestrial production. Globally, nitrogen limits plant growth most. Phosphorus limitations are common in older soils where phosphate molecules have been leached away by water, such as in many tropical ecosystems. Phosphorus availability is also often low in soils of deserts and other ecosystems with a basic pH, where some phosphorus precipitates and becomes unavailable to plants. Adding a nonlimiting nutrient, even one that is scarce, will not stimulate production. Conversely, adding more of the limiting nutrient will increase production until some other nutrient becomes limiting.

Various adaptations have evolved in plants that can increase their uptake of limiting nutrients. One important mutualism that you have already studied is the symbiosis between plant roots and nitrogen-fixing bacteria. Another important mutualism is mycorrhizal association between plant roots and fungi that supply phosphorus and other limiting elements to plants (see Chapters 36 and 37). Plants have root hairs and other anatomical features that increase the area of the soil that roots contact (see Chapter 35). Also, many plants release enzymes and other substances into the soil that increase the availability of limiting nutrients; examples include phosphatases, enzymes that cleave a phosphate group from larger molecules, and chelating agents that make micronutrients such as iron more soluble in the soil.

Studies relating nutrients to terrestrial primary production have practical applications in agriculture. Farmers maximize their crop yields by using fertilizers with the right balance of nutrients for the local soil and type of crop. This knowledge of limiting nutrients helps us feed billions of people on Earth today.

CONCEPT CHECK 55.2

1. Why is only a small portion of the solar energy that strikes Earth's atmosphere stored by primary producers?
2. How can ecologists experimentally determine the factor that limits primary production in an ecosystem?
3. **MAKE CONNECTIONS** Concept 10.3 (pp. 198–199) describes the Calvin cycle of photosynthesis. Explain how nitrogen and phosphorus, the nutrients that most often limit primary production, are necessary for the Calvin cycle to function.

For suggested answers, see Appendix A.

CONCEPT 55.3

Energy transfer between trophic levels is typically only 10% efficient

The amount of chemical energy in consumers' food that is converted to their own new biomass during a given period is called the **secondary production** of the ecosystem. Consider the transfer of organic matter from primary producers to herbivores, the primary consumers. In most ecosystems, herbivores eat only a small fraction of plant material produced; globally, they consume only about one-sixth of total plant production. Moreover, they cannot digest all the plant material that they *do* eat, as anyone who has walked through a dairy farm will attest. The vast majority of an ecosystem's production is eventually consumed by detritivores. Let's analyze the process of energy transfer and cycling more closely.

Production Efficiency

First we'll examine secondary production in an individual organism—a caterpillar. When a caterpillar feeds on a plant leaf, only about 33 J out of 200 J (48 cal), or one-sixth of the potential energy in the leaf, is used for secondary production, or growth **(Figure 55.10)**. The caterpillar uses some of the remaining energy (stored in organic compounds) for cellular respiration and passes the rest in its feces. The energy contained in the feces remains in the ecosystem temporarily, but most of it is lost as heat after the feces are consumed by detritivores. The energy used for the caterpillar's respiration is also eventually lost from the

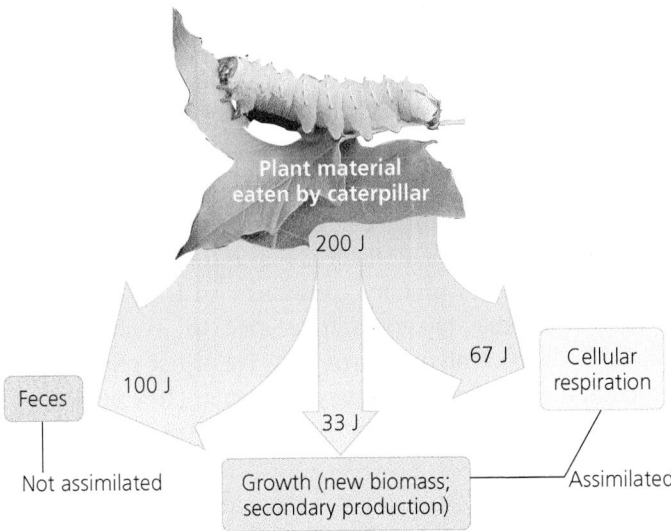

▲ **Figure 55.10 Energy partitioning within a link of the food chain.** Less than 17% of the caterpillar's food is actually used for secondary production (growth).

ecosystem as heat. This is why energy is said to flow through, not cycle within, ecosystems. Only the chemical energy stored by herbivores as biomass, through growth or the production of offspring, is available as food to secondary consumers.

We can measure the efficiency of animals as energy transformers using the following equation:

$$\text{Production efficiency} = \frac{\text{Net secondary production} \times 100\%}{\text{Assimilation of primary production}}$$

Net secondary production is the energy stored in biomass represented by growth and reproduction. Assimilation consists of the total energy taken in, not including losses in feces, used for growth, reproduction, and respiration. **Production efficiency**, therefore, is the percentage of energy stored in assimilated food that is *not* used for respiration. For the caterpillar in Figure 55.10, production efficiency is 33%; 67 J of the 100 J of assimilated energy is used for respiration. (The 100 J of energy lost as undigested material in feces does not count toward assimilation.) Birds and mammals typically have low production efficiencies, in the range of 1–3%, because they use so much energy in maintaining a constant, high body temperature. Fishes, which are ectotherms (see Chapter 40), have production efficiencies around 10%. Insects and microorganisms are even more efficient, with production efficiencies averaging 40% or more.

Trophic Efficiency and Ecological Pyramids

Let's scale up now from the production efficiencies of individual consumers to the flow of energy through trophic levels.

Trophic efficiency is the percentage of production transferred from one trophic level to the next. Trophic efficiencies must always be less than production efficiencies because they take into account not only the energy lost through respiration and contained in feces, but also the energy in organic material in a lower trophic level that is not consumed by the next trophic level. Trophic efficiencies are generally only about 10% and range from approximately 5% to 20%, depending on the type of ecosystem. In other words, 90% of the energy available at one trophic level typically is *not* transferred to the next. This loss is multiplied over the length of a food chain. For example, if 10% of available energy is transferred from primary producers to primary consumers, such as caterpillars, and 10% of that energy is transferred to secondary consumers, called carnivores, then only 1% of net primary production is available to secondary consumers (10% of 10%).

The progressive loss of energy along a food chain severely limits the abundance of top-level carnivores that an ecosystem can support. Only about 0.1% of the chemical energy fixed by photosynthesis can flow all the way through a food web to a tertiary consumer, such as a snake or a shark. This explains why most food webs include only about four or five trophic levels (see Chapter 54).

The loss of energy with each transfer in a food chain can be represented by a *pyramid of net production*, in which the trophic levels are arranged in tiers (**Figure 55.11**). The width of each tier is proportional to the net production, expressed in joules, of each trophic level. The highest level, which represents top-level predators, contains relatively few individuals. The small population size typical of top predator species is one reason they tend to be vulnerable to extinction (as well as to the evolutionary consequences of small population size, discussed in Chapter 23).

One important ecological consequence of low trophic efficiencies is represented in a *biomass pyramid*, in which each tier represents the standing crop (the total dry mass of all organisms) in one trophic level. Most biomass pyramids narrow sharply from primary producers at the base to top-level carnivores at the apex because energy transfers between trophic

levels are so inefficient (**Figure 55.12a**). Certain aquatic ecosystems, however, have inverted biomass pyramids: Primary consumers outweigh the producers (**Figure 55.12b**). Such inverted biomass pyramids occur because the producers—phytoplankton—grow, reproduce, and are consumed so quickly by the zooplankton that they never develop a large population size, or standing crop. In other words, the phytoplankton have a short **turnover time**, which means they have a small standing crop compared to their production:

$$\text{Turnover time} = \frac{\text{Standing crop (g/m}^2)}{\text{Production (g/m}^2 \cdot \text{day)}}$$

Because the phytoplankton continually replace their biomass at such a rapid rate, they can support a biomass of zooplankton bigger than their own biomass. Nevertheless, because phytoplankton have much higher production than zooplankton, the pyramid of *production* for this ecosystem is still bottom-heavy, like the one in Figure 55.11.

The dynamics of energy flow through ecosystems have important implications for humans. Eating meat is a relatively inefficient way of tapping photosynthetic production. The same pound of soybeans that a person could eat for protein produces only a fifth of a pound of beef or less when fed to a cow. Worldwide agriculture could, in fact, successfully feed many more people and require less cultivated land if humans all fed more efficiently—as primary consumers, eating plant material. Consequently, estimates of Earth's human carrying capacity (see Chapter 53) depend greatly on our diet and on the amount of resources each of us consumes.

In the next section, we will look at how the transfer of nutrients and energy through food webs is part of a larger picture of chemical cycling in ecosystems.

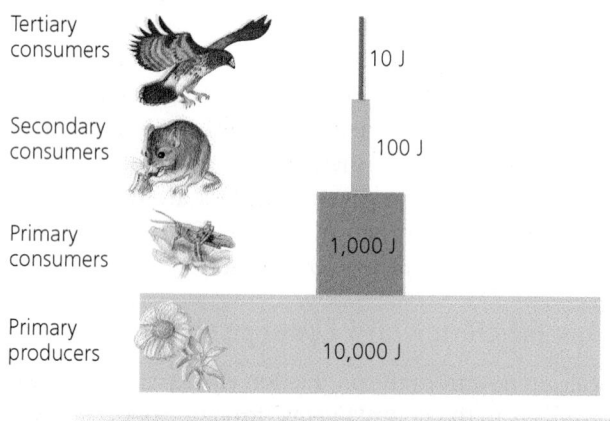

▲ Figure 55.11 An idealized pyramid of net production. This example assumes a trophic efficiency of 10% for each link in the food chain. Notice that primary producers convert only about 1% of the energy available to them to net primary production.

(a) Most biomass pyramids show a sharp decrease in biomass at successively higher trophic levels, as illustrated by data from a Florida bog.

(b) In some aquatic ecosystems, such as the English Channel, a small standing crop of primary producers (phytoplankton) supports a larger standing crop of primary consumers (zooplankton).

▲ Figure 55.12 Pyramids of biomass (standing crop). Numbers denote the dry mass of all organisms at each trophic level.

CONCEPT CHECK 55.3

1. If an insect that eats plant seeds containing 100 J of energy uses 30 J of that energy for respiration and excretes 50 J in its feces, what is the insect's net secondary production? What is its production efficiency?

2. Tobacco leaves contain nicotine, a poisonous compound that is energetically expensive for the plant to make. What advantage might the plant gain by using some of its resources to produce nicotine?

3. **MAKE CONNECTIONS** Figure 40.20 describes relative energy budgets for four animals. What are some ways in which the energy expenditures of the caterpillar described in Figure 55.10 would differ from the woman pictured in Figure 40.20?

For suggested answers, see Appendix A.

CONCEPT 55.4

Biological and geochemical processes cycle nutrients and water in ecosystems

Although most ecosystems receive an abundant supply of solar energy, chemical elements are available only in limited amounts. Life on Earth therefore depends on the recycling of essential chemical elements. Much of an organism's chemical stock is replaced continuously as nutrients are assimilated and waste products released. When the organism dies, the atoms in its complex molecules are returned in simpler compounds to the atmosphere, water, or soil by the action of decomposers. Decomposition replenishes the pools of inorganic nutrients that plants and other autotrophs use to build new organic matter. Because nutrient cycles involve both biotic and abiotic components, they are called **biogeochemical cycles**.

Biogeochemical Cycles

An element's specific route through a biogeochemical cycle depends on the element and the trophic structure of the ecosystem. For convenience, however, we can recognize two general categories of biogeochemical cycles: global and local. Gaseous forms of carbon, oxygen, sulfur, and nitrogen occur in the atmosphere, and cycles of these elements are essentially global. For example, some of the carbon and oxygen atoms a plant acquires from the air as CO_2 may have been released into the atmosphere by the respiration of an organism in a distant locale. Other elements, including phosphorus, potassium, and calcium, are too heavy to occur as gases at Earth's surface, although they are transported in dust. In terrestrial ecosystems, these elements cycle more locally, absorbed from the soil by plant roots and eventually returned to the soil by decomposers. In aquatic systems, however, they cycle more broadly as dissolved forms carried in currents.

Let's first look at a general model of nutrient cycling that includes the main reservoirs of elements and the processes that transfer elements between reservoirs (Figure 55.13). Each reservoir is defined by two characteristics: whether it contains organic or inorganic materials and whether or not the materials are directly available for use by organisms.

The nutrients in living organisms and in detritus (reservoir A in Figure 55.13) are available to other organisms when consumers feed and when detritivores consume nonliving organic matter. Some living organic material moved to the fossilized organic reservoir (reservoir B) long ago, when dead organisms were converted to coal, oil, or peat (fossil fuels). Nutrients in these deposits generally cannot be assimilated directly.

Inorganic materials (elements and compounds) that are dissolved in water or present in soil or air (reservoir C) are available for use. Organisms assimilate materials from this reservoir directly and return chemicals to it through the relatively rapid processes of cellular respiration, excretion, and decomposition. Although most organisms cannot directly tap into the inorganic elements tied up in rocks (reservoir D), these nutrients may slowly become available through weathering and erosion. Similarly, unavailable organic materials move into the available reservoir of inorganic nutrients when fossil fuels are burned, releasing exhaust into the atmosphere.

Figure 55.14, on the next two pages, provides a detailed look at the cycling of water, carbon, nitrogen, and phosphorus.

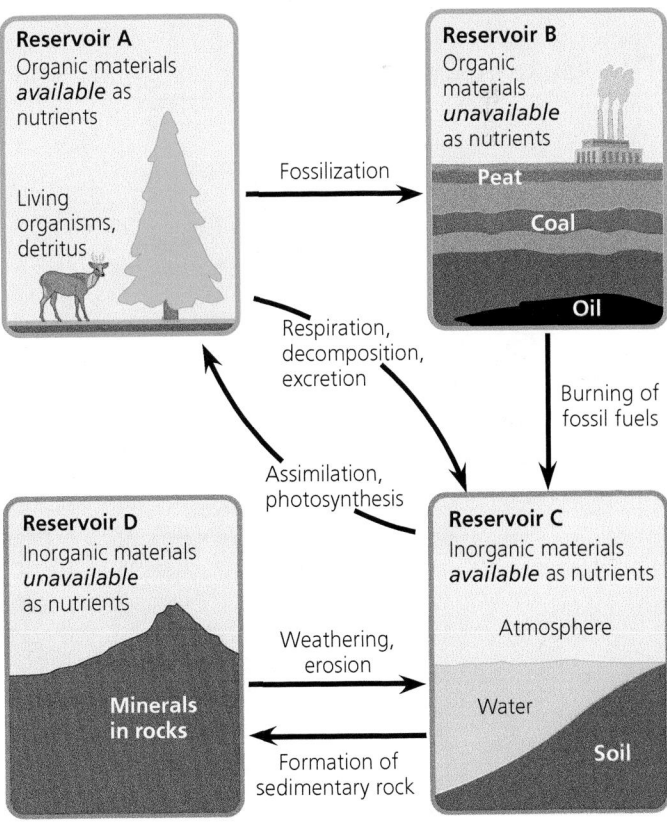

▲ **Figure 55.13 A general model of nutrient cycling.** Arrows indicate the processes that move nutrients between reservoirs.

Exploring Water and Nutrient Cycling

Examine each cycle closely, considering the major reservoirs of water, carbon, nitrogen, and phosphorus and the processes that drive each cycle. The widths of the arrows in the diagrams approximately reflect the relative contribution of each process to the movement of water or a nutrient in the biosphere.

The Water Cycle

Biological importance   Water is essential to all organisms (see Chapter 3), and its availability influences the rates of ecosystem processes, particularly primary production and decomposition in terrestrial ecosystems.

Forms available to life   Liquid water is the primary physical phase in which water is used, though some organisms can harvest water vapor. Freezing of soil water can limit water availability to terrestrial plants.

Reservoirs   The oceans contain 97% of the water in the biosphere. Approximately 2% is bound in glaciers and polar ice caps, and the remaining 1% is in lakes, rivers, and groundwater, with a negligible amount in the atmosphere.

Key processes   The main processes driving the water cycle are evaporation of liquid water by solar energy, condensation of water vapor into clouds, and precipitation. Transpiration by terrestrial plants also moves large volumes of water into the atmosphere. Surface and groundwater flow can return water to the oceans, completing the water cycle.

Movement over land by wind

Precipitation over ocean

Evaporation from ocean

Evapotranspiration from land

Precipitation over land

Percolation through soil

Runoff and groundwater

The Carbon Cycle

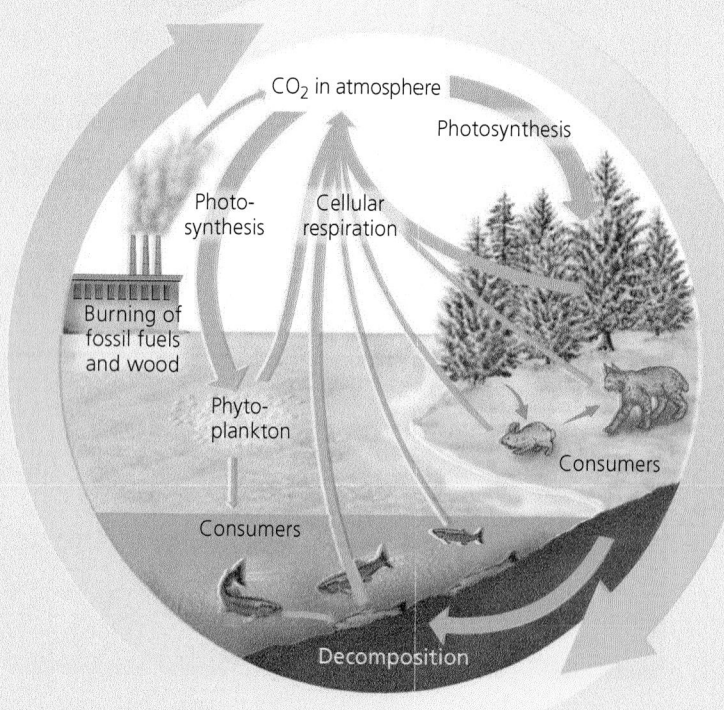

CO$_2$ in atmosphere

Photosynthesis

Photo-synthesis

Cellular respiration

Burning of fossil fuels and wood

Phyto-plankton

Consumers

Consumers

Decomposition

Biological importance   Carbon forms the framework of the organic molecules essential to all organisms.

Forms available to life   Photosynthetic organisms utilize CO$_2$ during photosynthesis and convert the carbon to organic forms that are used by consumers, including animals, fungi, and heterotrophic protists and prokaryotes.

Reservoirs   The major reservoirs of carbon include fossil fuels, soils, the sediments of aquatic ecosystems, the oceans (dissolved carbon compounds), plant and animal biomass, and the atmosphere (CO$_2$). The largest reservoir is sedimentary rocks such as limestone; however, this pool turns over very slowly.

Key processes   Photosynthesis by plants and phytoplankton removes substantial amounts of atmospheric CO$_2$ each year. This quantity is approximately equaled by CO$_2$ added to the atmosphere through cellular respiration by producers and consumers. The burning of fossil fuels and wood is adding significant amounts of additional CO$_2$ to the atmosphere. Over geologic time, volcanoes are also a substantial source of CO$_2$.

ANIMATION   **BioFlix**   Visit the Study Area at **www.masteringbiology.com** for the BioFlix® 3-D Animation on The Carbon Cycle.

The Nitrogen Cycle

Biological importance   Nitrogen is part of amino acids, proteins, and nucleic acids and is often a limiting plant nutrient.

Forms available to life   Plants can assimilate (use) two inorganic forms of nitrogen—ammonium (NH_4^+) and nitrate (NO_3^-)—and some organic forms, such as amino acids. Various bacteria can use all of these forms as well as nitrite (NO_2^-). Animals can use only organic forms of nitrogen.

Reservoirs   The main reservoir of nitrogen is the atmosphere, which is 80% free nitrogen gas (N_2). The other reservoirs of inorganic and organic nitrogen compounds are soils and the sediments of lakes, rivers, and oceans; surface water and groundwater; and the biomass of living organisms.

Key processes   The major pathway for nitrogen to enter an ecosystem is via *nitrogen fixation*, the conversion of N_2 to forms that can be used to synthesize organic nitrogen compounds. Certain bacteria, as well as lightning, fix nitrogen naturally. Nitrogen inputs from human activities now outpace natural inputs on land. Two major contributors are industrially produced fertilizers and legume crops that fix nitrogen via bacteria in their root nodules. Other bacteria in soil convert nitrogen to different forms (see also Figure 37.9). Some bacteria carry out *denitrification*, the reduction of nitrate to nitrogen gases. Human activities also release large quantities of reactive nitrogen gases, such as nitrogen oxides, to the atmosphere.

The Phosphorus Cycle

Biological importance   Organisms require phosphorus as a major constituent of nucleic acids, phospholipids, and ATP and other energy-storing molecules and as a mineral constituent of bones and teeth.

Forms available to life   The most biologically important inorganic form of phosphorus is phosphate (PO_4^{3-}), which plants absorb and use in the synthesis of organic compounds.

Reservoirs   The largest accumulations of phosphorus are in sedimentary rocks of marine origin. There are also large quantities of phosphorus in soil, in the oceans (in dissolved form), and in organisms. Because soil particles bind PO_4^{3-}, the recycling of phosphorus tends to be quite localized in ecosystems.

Key processes   Weathering of rocks gradually adds PO_4^{3-} to soil; some leaches into groundwater and surface water and may eventually reach the sea. Phosphate taken up by producers and incorporated into biological molecules may be eaten by consumers. Phosphate is returned to soil or water by either decomposition of biomass or excretion by consumers. Because there are no significant phosphorus-containing gases, only relatively small amounts of phosphorus move through the atmosphere, usually in the forms of dust and sea spray.

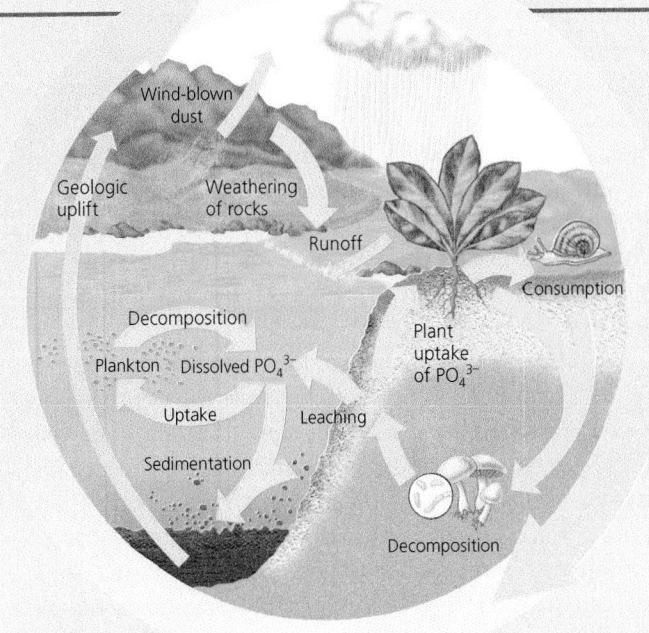

How have ecologists worked out the details of chemical cycling in various ecosystems? Two common methods use isotopes. One method is to follow the movement of naturally occurring, nonradioactive isotopes through the biotic and abiotic components of an ecosystem. The other method involves adding tiny amounts of radioactive isotopes of specific elements and tracing their progress. Scientists have also been able to make use of radioactive carbon (^{14}C) released into the atmosphere during atom bomb testing in the 1950s and early 1960s. Scientists use this "spike" of ^{14}C to trace where and how quickly carbon flows into ecosystem components, including plants, soils, and ocean water.

Decomposition and Nutrient Cycling Rates

The diagrams in Figure 55.14 illustrate the essential role that decomposers (detritivores) play in recycling carbon, nitrogen, and phosphorus. The rates at which these nutrients cycle in different ecosystems are extremely variable, mostly as a result of differences in rates of decomposition.

Decomposition is controlled by the same factors that limit primary production in aquatic and terrestrial ecosystems (see Concept 55.2). These factors include temperature, moisture, and nutrient availability. Decomposers usually grow faster and decompose material more quickly in warmer ecosystems (Figure 55.15). In tropical rain forests, for instance, most organic material decomposes in a few months to a few years, while in temperate forests, decomposition takes four to six years, on average. The difference is largely the result of the higher temperatures and more abundant precipitation in tropical rain forests.

Because decomposition in a tropical rain forest is rapid, relatively little organic material accumulates as leaf litter on the forest floor; about 75% of the nutrients in the ecosystem is present in the woody trunks of trees, and only about 10% is contained in the soil. Thus, the relatively low concentrations of some nutrients in the soil of tropical rain forests result from a short cycling time, not from a lack of these elements in the ecosystem. In temperate forests, where decomposition is much slower, the soil may contain as much as 50% of all the organic material in the ecosystem. The nutrients that are present in temperate forest detritus and soil may remain there for fairly long periods before plants assimilate them.

Decomposition on land is also slower when conditions are either too dry for decomposers to thrive or too wet to supply them with enough oxygen. Ecosystems that are both cold and wet, such as peatlands, store large amounts of organic matter (see Figure 29.11). Decomposers grow poorly there, and net primary production greatly exceeds decomposition.

In aquatic ecosystems, decomposition in anaerobic muds can take 50 years or longer. Bottom sediments are

How does temperature affect litter decomposition in an ecosystem?

EXPERIMENT Researchers with the Canadian Forest Service placed identical samples of organic material—litter—on the ground in 21 sites across Canada (marked by letters on the map below). Three years later, they returned to see how much of each sample had decomposed.

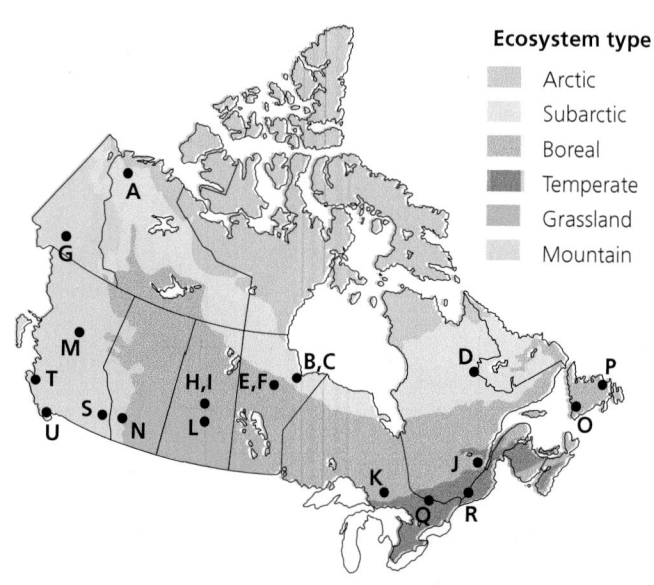

Ecosystem type
- Arctic
- Subarctic
- Boreal
- Temperate
- Grassland
- Mountain

RESULTS The mass of litter decreased four times faster in the warmest ecosystem than in the coldest ecosystem.

CONCLUSION Decomposition rate increases with temperature across much of Canada.

SOURCE T. R. Moore et al., Litter decomposition rates in Canadian forests, *Global Change Biology* 5:75–82 (1999).

WHAT IF? What factors other than temperature might also have varied across these 21 sites? How might this variation have affected the interpretation of the results?

comparable to the detritus layer in terrestrial ecosystems; however, algae and aquatic plants usually assimilate nutrients directly from the water. Thus, the sediments often constitute a nutrient sink, and aquatic ecosystems are very productive only when there is interchange between the bottom layers of water and the water at the surface (as occurs in the upwelling regions described earlier).

Case Study: Nutrient Cycling in the Hubbard Brook Experimental Forest

Since 1963, ecologists Herbert Bormann, Eugene Likens, and their colleagues have been studying nutrient cycling at the Hubbard Brook Experimental Forest in the White Mountains of New Hampshire. Their research site is a deciduous forest that grows in six small valleys, each drained by a single creek. Impenetrable bedrock underlies the soil of the forest.

The research team first determined the mineral budget for each of six valleys by measuring the input and outflow of several key nutrients. They collected rainfall at several sites to measure the amount of water and dissolved minerals added to the ecosystem. To monitor the loss of water and minerals, they constructed a small concrete dam with a V-shaped spillway across the creek at the bottom of each valley (Figure 55.16a). They found that about 60% of the water added to the ecosystem as rainfall and snow exits through the stream, and the remaining 40% is lost by evapotranspiration.

Preliminary studies confirmed that internal cycling conserved most of the mineral nutrients in the system. For example, only about 0.3% more calcium (Ca^{2+}) leaves a valley via its creek than is added by rainwater, and this small net loss is probably replaced by chemical decomposition of the bedrock. During most years, the forest even registers small net gains of a few mineral nutrients, including nitrogen.

Experimental deforestation of a watershed dramatically increased the flow of water and minerals leaving the watershed (Figure 55.16b and c). Over three years, water runoff

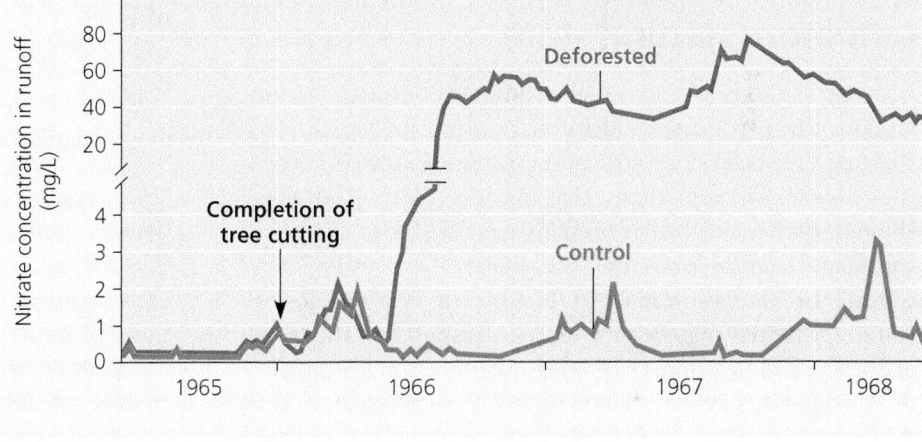

(a) Concrete dams and weirs built across streams at the bottom of watersheds enabled researchers to monitor the outflow of water and nutrients from the ecosystem.

(b) One watershed was clear-cut to study the effects of the loss of vegetation on drainage and nutrient cycling. All of the original plant material was left in place to decompose.

(c) The concentration of nitrate in runoff from the deforested watershed was 60 times greater than in a control (unlogged) watershed.

▲ **Figure 55.16 Nutrient cycling in the Hubbard Brook Experimental Forest: an example of long-term ecological research.**

(MB) See the related Experimental Inquiry Tutorial in MasteringBiology.

from the newly deforested watershed was 30–40% greater than in a control watershed, apparently because there were no plants to absorb and transpire water from the soil. The concentration of Ca^{2+} in the creek increased 4-fold, and the concentration of K^+ increased by a factor of 15. Most remarkable was the loss of nitrate, whose concentration in the creek increased 60-fold, reaching levels considered unsafe for drinking water (Figure 55.16c). The Hubbard Brook deforestation study showed that the amount of nutrients leaving an intact forest ecosystem is controlled mainly by the plants. Retaining nutrients in ecosystems helps to maintain the productivity of the systems and, in some cases, to avoid problems cause by excess nutrient runoff (see Figure 55.8).

1. **DRAW IT** For each of the four biogeochemical cycles detailed in Figure 55.14, draw a simple diagram that shows one possible path for an atom of that chemical from abiotic to biotic reservoirs and back.
2. Why does deforestation of a watershed increase the concentration of nitrates in streams draining the watershed?
3. **WHAT IF?** Why is nutrient availability in a tropical rain forest particularly vulnerable to logging?

For suggested answers, see Appendix A.

CONCEPT 55.5

Restoration ecologists help return degraded ecosystems to a more natural state

Ecosystems can recover naturally from most disturbances (including the experimental deforestation at Hubbard Brook) through the stages of ecological succession that we discussed in Chapter 54. Sometimes that recovery takes centuries, though, particularly when humans have degraded the environment. Tropical areas that are cleared for farming may quickly become unproductive because of nutrient losses. Mining activities may last for several decades, and the lands are often abandoned in a degraded state. Ecosystems can also be damaged by salts that build up in soils from irrigation and by toxic chemicals or oil spills. Biologists increasingly are called on to help restore and repair ecosystem damage.

Restoration ecologists seek to initiate or speed up the recovery of degraded ecosystems. One of the basic assumptions is that environmental damage is at least partly reversible.

This optimistic view must be balanced by a second assumption—that ecosystems are not infinitely resilient. Restoration ecologists therefore work to identify and manipulate the processes that most limit recovery of ecosystems from disturbances. Where disturbance is so severe that restoring all of a habitat is impractical, ecologists try to reclaim as much of a habitat or ecological process as possible, within the limits of the time and money available to them.

In extreme cases, the physical structure of an ecosystem may need to be restored before biological restoration can occur. If a stream was straightened to channel water quickly through a suburb, restoration ecologists may reconstruct a meandering channel to slow down the flow of water eroding the stream bank. To restore an open-pit mine, engineers may first grade the site with heavy equipment to reestablish a gentle slope, spreading topsoil when the slope is in place (Figure 55.17).

Once physical reconstruction of the ecosystem is complete—or when it is not needed—biological restoration is the next step. Two key strategies in biological restoration are bioremediation and biological augmentation.

Bioremediation

Using organisms—usually prokaryotes, fungi, or plants—to detoxify polluted ecosystems is known as **bioremediation** (see Chapter 27). Some plants and lichens adapted to soils containing heavy metals can accumulate high concentrations of potentially toxic metals such as zinc, nickel, lead, and cadmium in their tissues. Restoration ecologists can introduce such species to sites polluted by mining and other human activities and then harvest these organisms to remove the metals from the ecosystem. For instance, researchers in the United Kingdom have discovered a lichen species that grows on soil polluted with uranium dust left over from mining. The lichen concentrates uranium in a dark

(a) In 1991, before restoration

(b) In 2000, near the completion of restoration

▲ Figure 55.17 **A gravel and clay mine site in New Jersey before and after restoration.**

▲ **Figure 55.18 Bioremediation of groundwater contaminated with uranium at Oak Ridge National Laboratory, Tennessee.** Wastes containing uranium were dumped in four unlined pits (inset) for more than 30 years, contaminating soils and groundwater. After ethanol was added, microbial activity decreased the concentration of soluble uranium in groundwater near the pits.

pigment, making it useful as a biological monitor and potentially as a remediator.

Ecologists already use the abilities of many prokaryotes to carry out bioremediation of soils and water. Scientists have sequenced the genomes of at least ten prokaryotic species specifically for their bioremediation potential. One of the species, the bacterium *Shewanella oneidensis*, appears particularly promising. It can metabolize a dozen or more elements under aerobic and anaerobic conditions. In doing so, it converts soluble forms of uranium, chromium, and nitrogen to insoluble forms that are less likely to leach into streams or groundwater. Researchers at Oak Ridge National Laboratory, in Tennessee, stimulated the growth of *Shewanella* and other uranium-reducing bacteria by adding ethanol to groundwater contaminated with uranium; the bacteria can use ethanol as an energy source. In just five months, the concentration of soluble uranium in the ecosystem dropped by 80% **(Figure 55.18)**. In the future, genetic engineering could be increasingly useful as a tool for improving the performance of prokaryotes and other organisms as bioremediators.

Biological Augmentation

In contrast to bioremediation, which is a strategy for removing harmful substances from an ecosystem, **biological augmentation** uses organisms to *add* essential materials to a degraded ecosystem. To augment ecosystem processes, restoration ecologists need to determine which factors, such as chemical nutrients, have been lost from a system and are limiting its recovery.

Encouraging the growth of plants that thrive in nutrient-poor soils often speeds up succession and ecosystem recovery. In alpine ecosystems of the western United States, nitrogen-fixing plants such as lupines are often planted to raise nitrogen concentrations in soils disturbed by mining and other activities. Once these nitrogen-fixing plants become established, other native species are better able to obtain enough soil nitrogen to survive. In other systems where the soil has been severely disturbed or where topsoil is missing entirely, plant roots may lack the mycorrhizal symbionts that help them meet their nutritional needs (see Chapter 31). Ecologists restoring a tallgrass prairie in Minnesota recognized this limitation and enhanced the recovery of native species by adding mycorrhizal symbionts to the soil they seeded.

Restoring the physical structure and plant community of an ecosystem does not necessarily ensure that animal species will recolonize a site and persist there. Because animals aid critical ecosystem services, including pollination, seed dispersal, and herbivory, restoration ecologists sometimes help wildlife reach and use restored ecosystems. They might release animals at a site or establish habitat corridors that connect a restored site to other places where the animals are found. They sometimes establish artificial perches for birds or dig burrows for other animals to use at the site. These and other efforts can improve the biodiversity of restored ecosystems and help the community persist.

Restoration Projects Worldwide

Because restoration ecology is a relatively new discipline and because ecosystems are complex, restoration ecologists generally learn as they go. Many restoration ecologists advocate adaptive management: experimenting with several promising types of management to learn what works best.

The long-term objective of restoration is to return an ecosystem as much as possible to its predisturbance state. **Figure 55.19**, on the next two pages, identifies several ambitious and successful restoration projects around the world. The great number of such projects, the dedication of the people engaged in them, and the successes that have been achieved suggest that restoration ecology will continue to grow as a discipline for many years.

CONCEPT CHECK 55.5

1. Identify the main goal of restoration ecology.
2. How do bioremediation and biological augmentation differ?
3. **WHAT IF?** In what way is the Kissimmee River project a more complete ecological restoration than the Maungatautari project (see Figure 55.19)?

For suggested answers, see Appendix A.

Exploring Restoration Ecology Worldwide

The examples highlighted on these pages are just a few of the many restoration ecology projects taking place around the world. The color-coded dots on the map indicate the locations of the projects.

■ Kissimmee River, Florida

The Kissimmee River was converted from a meandering river to a 90-km canal, threatening many fish and wetland bird populations. Kissimmee River restoration has filled 12 km of drainage canal and reestablished 24 km of the original 167 km of natural river channel. Pictured here is a section of the Kissimmee canal that has been plugged (wide, light strip on the right side of the photo), diverting flow into remnant river channels (center of the photo). The project will also restore natural flow patterns, which will foster self-sustaining populations of wetland birds and fishes.

■ Truckee River, Nevada

Damming and water diversions during the 20th century reduced flow in the Truckee River, leading to declines in riparian (riverside) forests. Restoration ecologists worked with water managers to ensure that sufficient water would be released during the short season of seed release by the native cottonwood and willow trees for seedlings to become established. Nine years of controlled-flow release led to the result shown here: a dramatic recovery of cottonwood-willow riparian forest.

■ Tropical dry forest, Costa Rica

Clearing for agriculture, mainly for livestock grazing, eliminated approximately 98% of tropical dry forest in Central America and Mexico. Reversing this trend, tropical dry forest restoration in Costa Rica has used domestic livestock to disperse the seeds of native trees into open grasslands. The photo shows one of the first trees (right center), dispersed as seed by livestock, to colonize former pastureland. This project is a model for joining restoration ecology with the local economy and educational institutions.

Rhine River, Europe

Centuries of dredging and channeling for navigation (see the barges in the wide, main channel on the right side of the photo) have straightened the once-meandering Rhine River and disconnected it from its floodplain and associated wetlands. The countries along the Rhine, particularly France, Germany, Luxembourg, the Netherlands, and Switzerland, are cooperating to reconnect the river to side channels, such as the one shown on the left side of the photo. Such side channels increase the diversity of habitats available to aquatic organisms, improve water quality, and provide flood protection.

Succulent Karoo, South Africa

In this desert region of southern Africa, as in many arid regions, overgrazing by livestock has damaged vast areas. Private landowners and government agencies in South Africa are restoring large areas of this unique region, revegetating the land and employing more sustainable resource management. The photo shows a small sample of the exceptional plant diversity of the Succulent Karoo; its 5,000 plant species include the highest diversity of succulent plants in the world.

Coastal Japan

Seaweed and seagrass beds are important nursery grounds for a wide variety of fishes and shellfish. Once extensive but now reduced by development, these beds are being restored in the coastal areas of Japan. Techniques include constructing suitable seafloor habitat, transplanting from natural beds using artificial substrates, and hand seeding (shown in this photograph).

Maungatautari, New Zealand

Weasels, rats, pigs, and other introduced species pose a serious threat to New Zealand's native plants and animals, including kiwis, a group of flightless, ground-dwelling bird species. The goal of the Maungatautari restoration project is to exclude all exotic mammals from a 3,400-ha reserve located on a forested volcanic cone. A specialized fence around the reserve eliminates the need to continue setting traps and using poisons that can harm native wildlife. In 2006, a pair of critically endangered takahe (a species of flightless rail) were released into the reserve in hopes of reestablishing a breeding population of this colorful bird on New Zealand's North Island.

55 CHAPTER REVIEW

SUMMARY OF KEY CONCEPTS

CONCEPT 55.1

Physical laws govern energy flow and chemical cycling in ecosystems (pp. 1219–1220)

- An **ecosystem** consists of all the organisms in a community and all the abiotic factors with which they interact. The laws of physics and chemistry apply to ecosystems, particularly in regard to the conservation of energy. Energy is conserved but degraded to heat during ecosystem processes.
- Based on the **law of conservation of mass**, ecologists study how much of a chemical element enters and leaves an ecosystem and cycles within it. Inputs and outputs are generally small compared to recycled amounts, but their balance determines whether the ecosystem gains or loses an element over time.

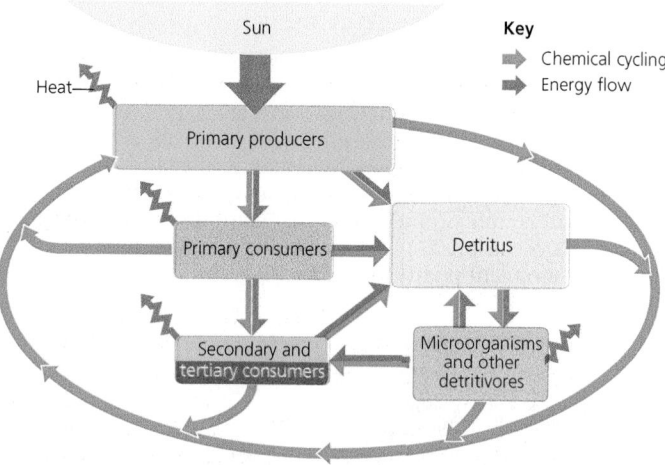

Key
→ Chemical cycling
→ Energy flow

? *Based on the second law of thermodynamics, would you expect the typical biomass of primary producers in an ecosystem to be greater than or less than the biomass of secondary producers in the same ecosystem? Explain your reasoning.*

CONCEPT 55.2

Energy and other limiting factors control primary production in ecosystems (pp. 1220–1225)

- **Primary production** sets the spending limit for the global energy budget. **Gross primary production** is the total energy assimilated by an ecosystem in a given period. **Net primary production**, the energy accumulated in autotroph biomass, equals gross primary production minus the energy used by the primary producers for respiration. **Net ecosystem production** is the total biomass accumulation of an ecosystem, defined as the difference between gross primary production and total ecosystem respiration.
- In aquatic ecosystems, light and nutrients limit primary production.
- In terrestrial ecosystems, climatic factors such as temperature and moisture affect primary production on a large geographic scale. More locally, a soil nutrient is often the limiting factor in primary production.

? *What additional variable do you need to know the value of in order to estimate NEP from NPP? Why might measuring this variable be difficult, for instance, in a sample of ocean water?*

CONCEPT 55.3

Energy transfer between trophic levels is typically only 10% efficient (pp. 1225–1227)

- The amount of energy available to each trophic level is determined by the net primary production and the **production efficiency**, the efficiency with which food energy is converted to biomass at each link in the food chain.
- The percentage of energy transferred from one trophic level to the next, called **trophic efficiency**, is generally 5–20%, with 10% being the typical value. Pyramids of net production and biomass reflect low trophic efficiency.

? *Why would a long-distance runner typically have a lower production efficiency than a more sedentary person?*

CONCEPT 55.4

Biological and geochemical processes cycle nutrients and water in ecosystems (pp. 1227–1232)

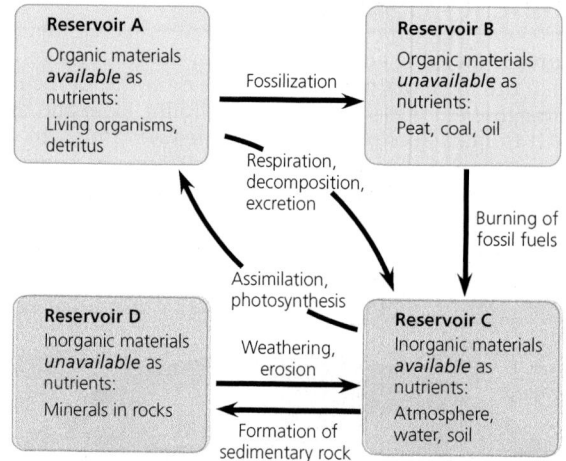

- Water moves in a global cycle driven by solar energy. The carbon cycle primarily reflects the reciprocal processes of photosynthesis and cellular respiration. Nitrogen enters ecosystems through atmospheric deposition and nitrogen fixation by prokaryotes, but most of the nitrogen cycling in natural ecosystems involves local cycles between organisms and soil or water. The phosphorus cycle is relatively localized.
- The proportion of a nutrient in a particular form and its cycling in that form vary among ecosystems, largely because of differences in the rate of decomposition.
- Nutrient cycling is strongly regulated by vegetation. The Hubbard Brook case study showed that logging increases water runoff and can cause large losses of minerals. It also demonstrated the importance of long-term ecological measurements in documenting the occurrence of and recovery from environmental problems.

? *If decomposers usually grow faster and decompose material more quickly in warmer ecosystems, why is decomposition in hot deserts so slow?*

CONCEPT 55.5

Restoration ecologists help return degraded ecosystems to a more natural state (pp. 1232–1235)

- Restoration ecologists harness organisms to detoxify polluted ecosystems through the process of **bioremediation**.

- In **biological augmentation**, ecologists use organisms to add essential materials to ecosystems.

> **?** *In preparing a site for surface mining and later restoration, what would be the advantage of removing the shallow topsoil first and setting it aside separately from the deeper soil, rather than removing all soil at once and mixing it in a single pile?*

TEST YOUR UNDERSTANDING

LEVEL 1: KNOWLEDGE/COMPREHENSION

1. Which of the following organisms is *incorrectly* paired with its trophic level?
   a. cyanobacterium—primary producer
   b. grasshopper—primary consumer
   c. zooplankton—primary producer
   d. eagle—tertiary consumer
   e. fungus—detritivore

2. Which of these ecosystems has the *lowest* net primary production per square meter?
   a. a salt marsh
   b. an open ocean
   c. a coral reef
   d. a grassland
   e. a tropical rain forest

3. The discipline that applies ecological principles to returning degraded ecosystems to a more natural state is known as
   a. population viability analysis.
   b. landscape ecology.
   c. conservation ecology.
   d. restoration ecology.
   e. resource conservation.

LEVEL 2: APPLICATION/ANALYSIS

4. Nitrifying bacteria participate in the nitrogen cycle mainly by
   a. converting nitrogen gas to ammonia.
   b. releasing ammonium from organic compounds, thus returning it to the soil.
   c. converting ammonia to nitrogen gas, which returns to the atmosphere.
   d. converting ammonium to nitrate, which plants absorb.
   e. incorporating nitrogen into amino acids and organic compounds.

5. Which of the following has the greatest effect on the rate of chemical cycling in an ecosystem?
   a. the ecosystem's rate of primary production
   b. the production efficiency of the ecosystem's consumers
   c. the rate of decomposition in the ecosystem
   d. the trophic efficiency of the ecosystem
   e. the location of the nutrient reservoirs in the ecosystem

6. The Hubbard Brook watershed deforestation experiment yielded all of the following results *except*:
   a. Most minerals were recycled within a forest ecosystem.
   b. The flow of minerals out of a natural watershed was offset by minerals flowing in.
   c. Deforestation increased water runoff.
   d. The nitrate concentration in waters draining the deforested area became dangerously high.
   e. Calcium levels remained high in the soil of deforested areas.

7. Which of the following would be considered an example of bioremediation?
   a. adding nitrogen-fixing microorganisms to a degraded ecosystem to increase nitrogen availability
   b. using a bulldozer to regrade a strip mine
   c. dredging a river bottom to remove contaminated sediments
   d. reconfiguring the channel of a river
   e. adding seeds of a chromium-accumulating plant to soil contaminated by chromium

8. If you applied a fungicide to a cornfield, what would you expect to happen to the rate of decomposition and net ecosystem production (NEP)?
   a. Both decomposition rate and NEP would decrease.
   b. Both decomposition rate and NEP would increase.
   c. Neither would change.
   d. Decomposition rate would increase and NEP would decrease.
   e. Decomposition rate would decrease and NEP would increase.

LEVEL 3: SYNTHESIS/EVALUATION

9. **DRAW IT** Draw a simplified global water cycle showing ocean, land, atmosphere, and runoff from the land to the ocean. Add these annual water fluxes to the figure: ocean evaporation, 425 km^3; ocean evaporation that returns to the ocean as precipitation, 385 km^3; ocean evaporation that falls as precipitation on land, 40 km^3; evapotranspiration from plants and soil that falls as precipitation on land, 70 km^3; runoff to the oceans, 40 km^3. Based on these global numbers, how much precipitation falls on land in a typical year?

10. **EVOLUTION CONNECTION**
    Some biologists have suggested that ecosystems are emergent, "living" systems capable of evolving. One manifestation of this idea is environmentalist James Lovelock's Gaia hypothesis, which views Earth itself as a living, homeostatic entity—a kind of superorganism. If ecosystems are capable of evolving, would this be a form of Darwinian evolution? Why or why not?

11. **SCIENTIFIC INQUIRY**
    Using two neighboring ponds in a forest as your study site, design a controlled experiment to measure the effect of falling leaves on net primary production in a pond.

12. **WRITE ABOUT A THEME**
    Energy Transfer As described in Concept 55.4, decomposition typically occurs quickly in moist tropical forests. However, waterlogging in the soil of some moist tropical forests results in a buildup of organic matter ("peat"; see Figure 29.11) over time. In a short essay (100–150 words), discuss the relationship of net primary production, net ecosystem production, and decomposition for such an ecosystem. Are NPP and NEP likely to be positive? What do you think would happen to NEP if a landowner drained the water from a tropical peatland, exposing the organic matter to air?

For selected answers, see Appendix A.

Mastering BIOLOGY   www.masteringbiology.com

1. MasteringBiology® Assignments

Make Connections Tutorial Pyramid of Net Production (Chapter 55) and Bioenergetics (Chapter 40)
Experimental Inquiry Tutorial What Factors Influence the Loss of Nutrients from a Forest Ecosystem?
 BioFlix Tutorial The Carbon Cycle
Tutorial Energy Flow Through Ecosystems
Activities Pyramids of Production • GraphIt!: Animal Food Production Efficiency and Food Policy • Energy Flow and Chemical Cycling • The Carbon Cycle • The Nitrogen Cycle • The Global Carbon Cycle
Questions Student Misconceptions • Reading Quiz • Multiple Choice • End-of-Chapter

2. eText

Read your book online, search, take notes, highlight text, and more.

3. The Study Area

Practice Tests • Cumulative Test • *BioFlix* 3-D Animations • MP3 Tutor Sessions • Videos • Activities • Investigations • Lab Media • Audio Glossary • Word Study Tools • Art

56

Conservation Biology and Global Change

▲ **Figure 56.1 What will be the fate of this newly described bird species?**

KEY CONCEPTS

56.1 Human activities threaten Earth's biodiversity

56.2 Population conservation focuses on population size, genetic diversity, and critical habitat

56.3 Landscape and regional conservation help sustain biodiversity

56.4 Earth is changing rapidly as a result of human actions

56.5 Sustainable development can improve human lives while conserving biodiversity

OVERVIEW

Striking Gold

Tucking its wings, a bird lands on a branch deep inside a tropical jungle. Sensing the motion, a conservation biologist scans the branch through binoculars, a glimpse of golden orange stopping her short. Staring back is a wattled smoky

honeyeater (*Melipotes carolae*), a species that had never been described before (Figure 56.1). In 2005, a team of American, Indonesian, and Australian biologists experienced many moments like this as they spent a month cataloging the living riches hidden in a remote mountain range in Indonesia. In addition to the honeyeater, they discovered dozens of new frog, butterfly, and plant species, including five new palms.

To date, scientists have described and formally named about 1.8 million species of organisms. Some biologists think that about 10 million more species currently exist; others estimate the number to be as high as 100 million. Some of the greatest concentrations of species are found in the tropics. Unfortunately, tropical forests are being cleared at an alarming rate to make room for and support a burgeoning human population. Rates of deforestation in Indonesia are among the highest in the world (Figure 56.2). What will become of the smoky honeyeater and other newly discovered species in Indonesia if such deforestation continues unchecked?

Throughout the biosphere, human activities are altering trophic structures, energy flow, chemical cycling, and natural disturbance—ecosystem processes on which we and all other species depend (see Chapter 55). We have physically altered nearly half of Earth's land surface, and we use over half of all accessible surface fresh water. In the oceans, stocks of most major fisheries are shrinking because of overharvesting. By some estimates, we may be pushing more species toward extinction than the large asteroid that triggered the mass extinctions at the close of the Cretaceous period 65.5 million years ago (see Figure 25.16).

Biology is the science of life. Thus, it is fitting that our final chapter focuses on a discipline that seeks to preserve life. **Conservation biology** integrates ecology, physiology, molecular biology, genetics, and evolutionary biology to conserve

▲ **Figure 56.2 Tropical deforestation in West Kalimantan, an Indonesian province.**

biological diversity at all levels. Efforts to sustain ecosystem processes and stem the loss of biodiversity also connect the life sciences with the social sciences, economics, and humanities.

In this chapter, we will take a closer look at the biodiversity crisis and examine some of the conservation strategies being adopted to slow the rate of species loss. We will also examine how human activities are altering the environment through climate change, ozone depletion, and other global processes, and we will consider how these alterations could affect life on Earth.

CONCEPT 56.1

Human activities threaten Earth's biodiversity

Extinction is a natural phenomenon that has been occurring since life first evolved; it is the high *rate* of extinction that is responsible for today's biodiversity crisis (see Chapter 25). Because we can only estimate the number of species currently existing, we cannot determine the exact rate of species loss. However, we do know that the extinction rate is high and that human activities threaten Earth's biodiversity at all levels.

Three Levels of Biodiversity

Biodiversity—short for biological diversity—can be considered at three main levels: genetic diversity, species diversity, and ecosystem diversity (Figure 56.3).

Genetic Diversity

Genetic diversity comprises not only the individual genetic variation *within* a population, but also the genetic variation *between* populations that is often associated with adaptations to local conditions (see Chapter 23). If one population becomes extinct, then a species may have lost some of the genetic diversity that makes microevolution possible. This erosion of genetic diversity in turn reduces the adaptive potential of the species.

Species Diversity

Public awareness of the biodiversity crisis centers on species diversity—the variety of species in an ecosystem or across the biosphere (see Chapter 54). As more species are lost to extinction, species diversity decreases. The U.S. Endangered Species Act (ESA) defines an **endangered species** as one that is "in danger of extinction throughout all or a significant portion of its range." **Threatened species** are those that are considered likely to become endangered in the near future. The following are just a few statistics that illustrate the problem of species loss:

- According to the International Union for Conservation of Nature and Natural Resources (IUCN), 12% of the 10,000 known species of birds and 21% of the 5,500 known species of mammals are threatened.

Genetic diversity in a vole population

Species diversity in a coastal redwood ecosystem

Community and ecosystem diversity across the landscape of an entire region

▲ Figure 56.3 **Three levels of biodiversity.** The oversized chromosomes in the top diagram symbolize the genetic variation within the population.

- A survey by the Center for Plant Conservation showed that of the nearly 20,000 known plant species in the United States, 200 have become extinct since such records have been kept, and 730 are endangered or threatened.
- More than 30% of the known species of fishes in the world either have become extinct during historical times or are seriously threatened.
- In North America, at least 123 freshwater animal species have become extinct since 1900, and hundreds more species are threatened. The extinction rate for North American freshwater fauna is about five times as high as that for terrestrial animals.
- According to a 2004 report in the journal *Science* that was based on a global assessment of amphibians by more than

500 scientists, 32% of all known amphibian species are endangered, with many species very near extinction.

Extinction of species may also be local; for example, a species may be lost in one river system but survive in an adjacent one. Global extinction of a species means that it is lost from *all* the ecosystems in which it lived, leaving them permanently impoverished (Figure 56.4).

Ecosystem Diversity

The variety of the biosphere's ecosystems is a third level of biological diversity. Because of the many interactions between populations of different species in an ecosystem, the local extinction of one species can have a negative impact on other species in the ecosystem (see Figure 54.17). For instance, bats called "flying foxes" are important pollinators and seed dis-

persers in the Pacific Islands, where they are increasingly hunted as a luxury food (Figure 56.5). Conservation biologists fear that the extinction of flying foxes would also harm the native plants of the Samoan Islands, where four-fifths of the tree species depend on flying foxes for pollination or seed dispersal.

Some ecosystems have already been heavily affected by humans, and others are being altered at a rapid pace. Since European colonization, more than half of the wetlands in the contiguous United States have been drained and converted to agricultural and other uses. In California, Arizona, and New Mexico, roughly 90% of native riparian (streamside) communities have been affected by overgrazing, flood control, water diversions, lowering of water tables, and invasion by non-native plants.

Biodiversity and Human Welfare

Why should we care about the loss of biodiversity? One reason is what the Harvard biologist E. O. Wilson calls *biophilia*, our sense of connection to nature and all life. The belief that other species are entitled to life is a pervasive theme of many religions and the basis of a moral argument that we should protect biodiversity. There is also a concern for future human generations. Paraphrasing an old proverb, G. H. Brundtland, a former prime minister of Norway, said: "We must consider our planet to be on loan from our children, rather than being a gift from our ancestors." In addition to such philosophical and moral justifications, species and genetic diversity bring us many practical benefits.

Benefits of Species and Genetic Diversity

Many species that are threatened could potentially provide food, fibers, and medicines for human use, making biodiversity a crucial natural resource. If we lose wild populations of plants closely related to agricultural species, we lose genetic resources

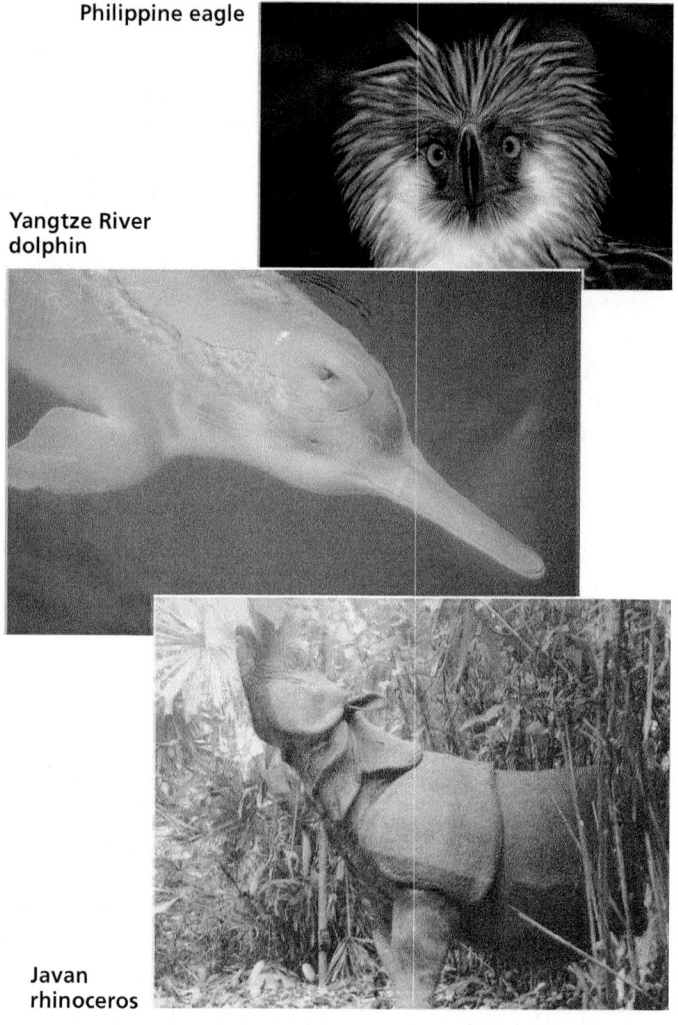

Philippine eagle

Yangtze River dolphin

Javan rhinoceros

▲ **Figure 56.4 A hundred heartbeats from extinction.** These are just three members of what E. O. Wilson calls the Hundred Heartbeat Club, species with fewer than 100 individuals remaining on Earth. The Yangtze River dolphin was even thought to be extinct, but a few individuals were reportedly sighted in 2007.

? *To document that a species has actually become extinct, what spatial and temporal factors would you need to consider?*

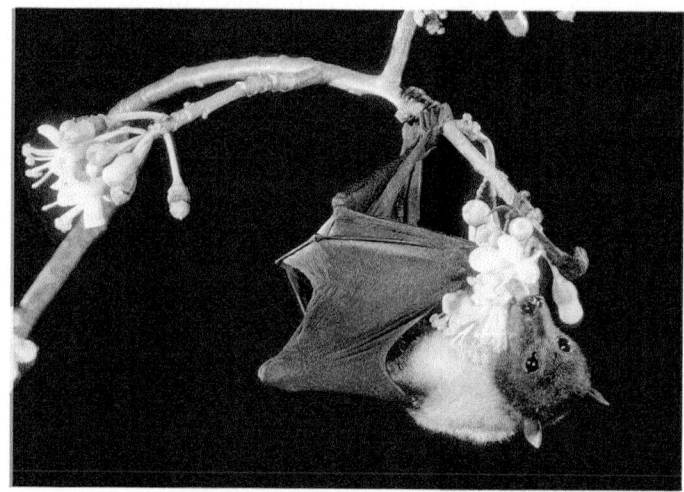

▲ **Figure 56.5 The endangered Marianas "flying fox" bat (*Pteropus mariannus*), an important pollinator.**

that could be used to improve crop qualities, such as disease resistance. For instance, plant breeders responded to devastating outbreaks of the grassy stunt virus in rice (*Oryza sativa*) by screening 7,000 populations of this species and its close relatives for resistance to the virus. One population of a single relative, Indian rice (*Oryza nivara*), was found to be resistant to the virus, and scientists succeeded in breeding the resistance trait into commercial rice varieties. Today, the original disease-resistant population has apparently become extinct in the wild.

In the United States, about 25% of the prescriptions dispensed from pharmacies contain substances originally derived from plants. In the 1970s, researchers discovered that the rosy periwinkle, which grows on the island of Madagascar, off the coast of Africa, contains alkaloids that inhibit cancer cell growth (Figure 56.6). This discovery led to treatments for two deadly forms of cancer, Hodgkin's lymphoma and childhood leukemia, resulting in remission in most cases. Madagascar is also home to five other species of periwinkles, one of which is approaching extinction. The loss of these species would mean the loss of any possible medicinal benefits they might offer.

Each loss of a species means the loss of unique genes, some of which may code for enormously useful proteins. The enzyme Taq polymerase was first extracted from a bacterium, *Thermus aquaticus*, found in hot springs at Yellowstone National Park. This enzyme is essential for the polymerase chain reaction (PCR) because it is stable at the high temperatures required for automated PCR (see Figure 20.8). DNA from many other species of prokaryotes, living in a variety of environments, is used in the mass production of proteins for new medicines, foods, petroleum substitutes, other industrial chemicals, and other products. However, because millions of species may become extinct before we discover them, we stand to lose the valuable genetic potential held in their unique libraries of genes.

Ecosystem Services

The benefits that individual species provide to humans are substantial, but saving individual species is only part of the reason for preserving ecosystems. Humans evolved in Earth's ecosystems, and we rely on these systems and their inhabitants for our survival. **Ecosystem services** encompass all the processes through which natural ecosystems help sustain human life. Ecosystems purify our air and water. They detoxify and decompose our wastes and reduce the impacts of extreme weather and flooding. The organisms in ecosystems pollinate our crops, control pests, and create and preserve our soils. Moreover, these diverse services are provided for free.

Perhaps because we don't attach a monetary value to the services of natural ecosystems, we generally undervalue them. In 1997, ecologist Robert Costanza and his colleagues estimated the value of Earth's ecosystem services at $33 trillion per year, nearly twice the gross national product of all the countries on Earth at the time ($18 trillion). It may be more realistic to do the accounting on a smaller scale. In 1996, New York City invested more than $1 billion to buy land and restore habitat in the Catskill Mountains, the source of much of the city's fresh water. This investment was spurred by increasing pollution of the water by sewage, pesticides, and fertilizers. By harnessing ecosystem services to purify its water naturally, the city saved $8 billion it would have otherwise spent to build a new water-treatment plant and $300 million a year to run the plant.

There is growing evidence that the functioning of ecosystems, and hence their capacity to perform services, is linked to biodiversity. As human activities reduce biodiversity, we are reducing the capacity of the planet's ecosystems to perform processes critical to our own survival.

Threats to Biodiversity

Many different human activities threaten biodiversity on local, regional, and global scales. The threats posed by these activities are of four major types: habitat loss, introduced species, overharvesting, and global change.

Habitat Loss

Human alteration of habitat is the single greatest threat to biodiversity throughout the biosphere. Habitat loss has been brought about by agriculture, urban development, forestry, mining, and pollution. Global climate change is already altering habitats today and will have an even larger effect later this century (discussed shortly). When no alternative habitat is available or a species is unable to move, habitat loss may mean extinction. The IUCN implicates destruction of physical habitat for 73% of the species that have become extinct, endangered, vulnerable, or rare in the last few hundred years.

Habitat loss and fragmentation may occur over immense regions. Approximately 98% of the tropical dry forests of Central America and Mexico have been cleared (cut down). Clearing of tropical rain forest in the state of Veracruz, Mexico,

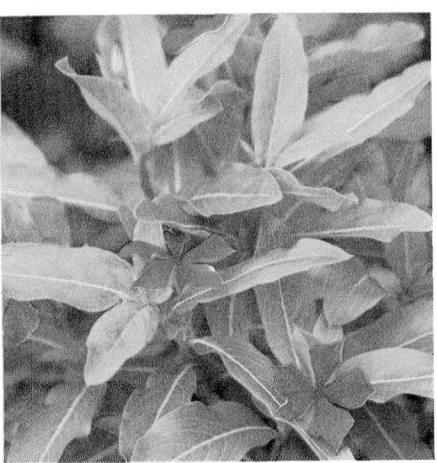

◀ **Figure 56.6 The rosy periwinkle (*Catharanthus roseus*), a plant that saves lives.**

▲ Figure 56.7 **Habitat fragmentation in the foothills of Los Angeles.** Development in the valleys may confine the organisms that inhabit the narrow strips of hillside.

mostly for cattle ranching, has resulted in the loss of more than 90% of the original forest, leaving relatively small, isolated patches of forest. Other natural habitats have also been fragmented by human activities (**Figure 56.7**).

In almost all cases, habitat fragmentation leads to species loss because the smaller populations in habitat fragments have a higher probability of local extinction. Prairie covered about 800,000 hectares of southern Wisconsin when Europeans first arrived in North America but now occupies less than 0.1% of its original area. Plant diversity surveys of 54 Wisconsin prairie remnants conducted in 1948–1954 and repeated in 1987–1988 showed that the remnants lost between 8% and 60% of their plant species in the time between the two surveys.

Habitat loss is also a major threat to aquatic biodiversity. About 93% of coral reefs, among Earth's most species-rich aquatic communities, have been damaged by human activities. At the current rate of destruction, 40–50% of the reefs, home to one-third of marine fish species, could disappear in the next 30 to 40 years. Freshwater habitats are also being lost, often as a result of the dams, reservoirs, channel modification, and flow regulation now affecting most of the world's rivers. For example, the more than 30 dams and locks built along the Mobile River basin in the southeastern United States changed river depth and flow and helped drive more than 40 species of mussels and snails to extinction.

Introduced Species

Introduced species, also called non-native or exotic species, are those that humans move intentionally or accidentally from the species' native locations to new geographic regions. Human travel by ship and airplane has accelerated the transplant of species. Free from the predators, parasites, and

pathogens that limit their populations in their native habitats, such transplanted species may spread rapidly through a new region.

Some introduced species disrupt their new community, often by preying on native organisms or outcompeting them for resources. The brown tree snake was accidentally introduced to the island of Guam from other parts of the South Pacific after World War II: It was a "stowaway" in military cargo (**Figure 56.8a**). Since then, 12 species of birds and 6 species of lizards that the snakes ate have become extinct on Guam, which had no native snakes. The devastating zebra mussel, a filter-feeding mollusc, was introduced into the Great Lakes of North America in 1988, most likely in the ballast water of ships arriving from Europe. Zebra mussels form dense colonies and have disrupted freshwater ecosystems, threatening native aquatic species. They have also clogged water intake structures, causing billions of dollars in damage to domestic and industrial water supplies.

Humans have deliberately introduced many species with good intentions but disastrous effects. An Asian plant called kudzu, which the U.S. Department of Agriculture once introduced in the southern United States to help control erosion, has taken over large areas of the landscape there

(a) Brown tree snake, introduced to Guam in cargo

(b) Introduced kudzu thriving in South Carolina

▲ Figure 56.8 **Two introduced species.**

(Figure 56.8b). The European starling was brought intentionally into New York's Central Park in 1890 by a citizens' group intent on introducing all the plants and animals mentioned in Shakespeare's plays. It quickly spread across North America, where its population now exceeds 100 million, displacing many native songbirds.

Introduced species are a worldwide problem, contributing to approximately 40% of the extinctions recorded since 1750 and costing billions of dollars each year in damage and control efforts. There are more than 50,000 introduced species in the United States alone.

Overharvesting

The term *overharvesting* refers generally to the human harvesting of wild organisms at rates exceeding the ability of populations of those species to rebound. Species with restricted habitats, such as small islands, are particularly vulnerable to overharvesting. One such species was the great auk, a large, flightless seabird found on islands in the North Atlantic Ocean. By the 1840s, humans had hunted the great auk to extinction to satisfy demand for its feathers, eggs, and meat.

Also susceptible to overharvesting are large organisms with low reproductive rates, such as elephants, whales, and rhinoceroses. The decline of Earth's largest terrestrial animals, the African elephants, is a classic example of the impact of overhunting. Largely because of the trade in ivory, elephant populations have been declining in most of Africa for the last 50 years. An international ban on the sale of new ivory resulted in increased poaching (illegal hunting), so the ban had little effect in much of central and eastern Africa. Only in South Africa, where once-decimated herds have been well protected for nearly a century, have elephant populations been stable or increasing (see Figure 53.8).

Conservation biologists increasingly use the tools of molecular genetics to track the origins of tissues harvested from endangered species. Researchers at the University of Washington have constructed a DNA reference map for the African elephant using DNA isolated from elephant dung. By comparing this reference map with DNA isolated from samples of ivory harvested either legally or by poachers, they can determine to within a few hundred kilometers where the elephants were killed (Figure 56.9). Similarly, biologists using phylogenetic analyses of mitochondrial DNA (mtDNA) showed that some whale meat sold in Japanese fish markets came from illegally harvested species, including fin and humpback whales, which are endangered (see Figure 26.6).

Many commercially important fish populations, once thought to be inexhaustible, have been decimated by overfishing. Demands for protein-rich food from an increasing human population, coupled with new harvesting technologies, such as long-line fishing and modern trawlers, have reduced these fish populations to levels that cannot sustain further

▼ **Figure 56.9**
IMPACT

Forensic Ecology and Elephant Poaching

This array of severed tusks is part of an illegal shipment of 6,000 kg of ivory intercepted on its way from Africa to Singapore in 2002. Investigators wondered whether the elephants slaughtered for the ivory—perhaps as many as 6,500—were killed in the area where the shipment originated, primarily Zambia, or instead were killed across Africa, indicating a broader smuggling ring. Samuel Wasser, of the University of Washington, and colleagues amplified specific segments of DNA from the tusks using the polymerase chain reaction (PCR). These segments included stretches of DNA containing short tandem repeats (STRs; see Concept 20.4, pp. 420–421), the number of which varies among different elephant populations. The researchers then compared alleles at seven or more loci with a reference DNA database they had generated for elephants of known geographic origin. Their results showed conclusively that the elephants came from a narrow east-west band centered on Zambia rather than from across Africa.

WHY IT MATTERS The DNA analyses suggested that poaching rates were 30 times higher in Zambia than previously estimated. This news led to improved antipoaching efforts by the Zambian government. Techniques like those used in this study are being employed by conservation biologists to track the harvesting of many endangered species, including whales, sharks, and orchids.

FURTHER READING S. K. Wasser et al., Forensic tools battle ivory poachers, *Scientific American* 399:68–76 (2009); S. K. Wasser et al., Using DNA to track the origin of the largest ivory seizure since the 1989 trade ban, *Proceedings of the National Academy of Sciences USA* 104:4228–4233 (2007).

MAKE CONNECTIONS Figure 26.6 (p. 539) describes another example in which conservation biologists used DNA analyses to compare harvested samples with a reference DNA database. How are these examples similar, and how are they different? What limitations might there be to using such forensic methods in other suspected cases of poaching?

exploitation. Until the past few decades, the North Atlantic bluefin tuna was considered a sport fish of little commercial value—just a few cents per pound for use in cat food. In the 1980s, however, wholesalers began airfreighting fresh, iced bluefin to Japan for sushi and sashimi. In that market, the fish

▲ **Figure 56.10 Overharvesting.** North Atlantic bluefin tuna are auctioned in a Japanese fish market.

▲ **Figure 56.11 Changes in the pH of precipitation at Hubbard Brook, New Hampshire.** Although still very acidic, the precipitation in this northeastern U.S. forest has been increasing in pH for more than three decades.

now brings up to $100 per pound **(Figure 56.10)**. With increased harvesting spurred by such high prices, it took just ten years to reduce the western North Atlantic bluefin population to less than 20% of its 1980 size. The collapse of the northern cod fishery off Newfoundland in the 1990s is another example of the overharvesting of a once-common species.

Global Change

The fourth threat to biodiversity, global change, alters the fabric of Earth's ecosystems at regional to global scales. Global change includes alterations in climate, atmospheric chemistry, and broad ecological systems that reduce the capacity of Earth to sustain life.

One of the first types of global change to cause concern was *acid precipitation*, which is rain, snow, sleet, or fog with a pH less than 5.2. The burning of wood and fossil fuels releases oxides of sulfur and nitrogen that react with water in air, forming sulfuric and nitric acids. The acids eventually fall to Earth's surface, harming some aquatic and terrestrial organisms.

In the 1960s, ecologists determined that lake-dwelling organisms in eastern Canada were dying because of air pollution from factories in the midwestern United States. Newly hatched lake trout, for instance, die when the pH drops below 5.4. Lakes and streams in southern Norway and Sweden were losing fish because of pollution generated in Great Britain and central Europe. By 1980, the pH of precipitation in large areas of North America and Europe averaged 4.0–4.5 and sometimes dropped as low as 3.0. (To review pH, see Concept 3.3.)

Environmental regulations and new technologies have enabled many countries to reduce sulfur dioxide emissions in recent decades. In the United States, sulfur dioxide emissions decreased more than 40% between 1993 and 2008, gradually reducing the acidity of precipitation **(Figure 56.11)**. However, ecologists estimate that it will take decades for aquatic

ecosystems to recover. Meanwhile, emissions of nitrogen oxides are increasing in the United States, and emissions of sulfur dioxide and acid precipitation continue to damage forests in central and eastern Europe.

We will explore the importance of global change for Earth's biodiversity in more detail in Concept 56.4, where we examine such factors as global climate change and ozone depletion.

CONCEPT CHECK 56.1

1. Explain why it is too narrow to define the biodiversity crisis as simply a loss of species.
2. Identify the four main threats to biodiversity and explain how each damages diversity.
3. **WHAT IF?** Imagine two populations of a fish species, one in the Mediterranean Sea and one in the Caribbean Sea. Now imagine two scenarios: (1) The populations breed separately, and (2) adults of both populations migrate yearly to the North Atlantic to interbreed. Which scenario would result in a greater loss of genetic diversity if the Mediterranean population were harvested to extinction? Explain your answer.

For suggested answers, see Appendix A.

CONCEPT 56.2

Population conservation focuses on population size, genetic diversity, and critical habitat

Biologists who work on conservation at the population and species levels use two main approaches: the small-population approach and the declining-population approach.

Small-Population Approach

Small populations are particularly vulnerable to overharvesting, habitat loss, and the other threats to biodiversity that you read about in Concept 56.1. After such factors have reduced a population's size, the small size itself can push the population to extinction. Conservation biologists who adopt the small-population approach study the processes that cause extinctions once population sizes have been severely reduced.

The Extinction Vortex: Evolutionary Implications of Small Population Size

EVOLUTION A small population is vulnerable to inbreeding and genetic drift, which draw the population down an **extinction vortex** toward smaller and smaller population size until no individuals survive **(Figure 56.12)**. A key factor driving the extinction vortex is the loss of the genetic variation that enables evolutionary responses to environmental change, such as the appearance of new strains of pathogens. Both inbreeding and genetic drift can cause a loss of genetic variation (see Chapter 23), and their effects become more harmful as a population shrinks. Inbreeding often reduces fitness because offspring are more likely to be homozygous for harmful recessive traits.

Not all small populations are doomed by low genetic diversity, and low genetic variability does not automatically lead to permanently small populations. For instance, overhunting of northern elephant seals in the 1890s reduced the species to only 20 individuals—clearly a bottleneck with reduced

genetic variation. Since that time, however, the northern elephant seal populations have rebounded to about 150,000 individuals today, though their genetic variation remains relatively low. A number of plant species also seem to have inherently low genetic variability. Many populations of cordgrass (*Spartina anglica*), which thrives in salt marshes, are genetically uniform at many loci. *Spartina anglica* arose from a few parent plants only about a century ago by hybridization and allopolyploidy (see Figure 24.11). Having spread by natural cloning, this species now dominates large areas of tidal mudflats in Europe and Asia. Thus, low genetic diversity does not always impede population growth.

Case Study: The Greater Prairie Chicken and the Extinction Vortex

When Europeans arrived in North America, the greater prairie chicken (*Tympanuchus cupido*) was common from New England to Virginia and across the western prairies of the continent. As you read in Chapter 23, land cultivation for agriculture fragmented the populations of this species, and its abundance decreased rapidly. Illinois had millions of greater prairie chickens in the 19th century but fewer than 50 by 1993. Researchers found that the decline in the Illinois population was associated with a decrease in fertility. As a test of the extinction vortex hypothesis, scientists increased genetic variation by importing 271 birds from larger populations elsewhere **(Figure 56.13**, on the next page). The Illinois population rebounded, confirming that it had been on its way to extinction until rescued by the transfusion of genetic variation.

Minimum Viable Population Size

How small does a population have to be before it starts down an extinction vortex? The answer depends on the type of organism and other factors. Large predators that feed high on the food chain usually require extensive individual ranges, resulting in low population densities. Therefore, not all rare species concern conservation biologists. All populations, however, require some minimum size to remain viable.

The minimal population size at which a species is able to sustain its numbers is known as the **minimum viable population (MVP)**. MVP is usually estimated for a given species using computer models that integrate many factors. The calculation may include, for instance, an estimate of how many individuals in a small population are likely to be killed by a natural catastrophe such as a storm. Once in the extinction vortex, two or three consecutive years of bad weather could finish off a population that is already below its MVP.

Effective Population Size

Genetic variation is the key issue in the small-population approach. The *total* size of a population may be misleading

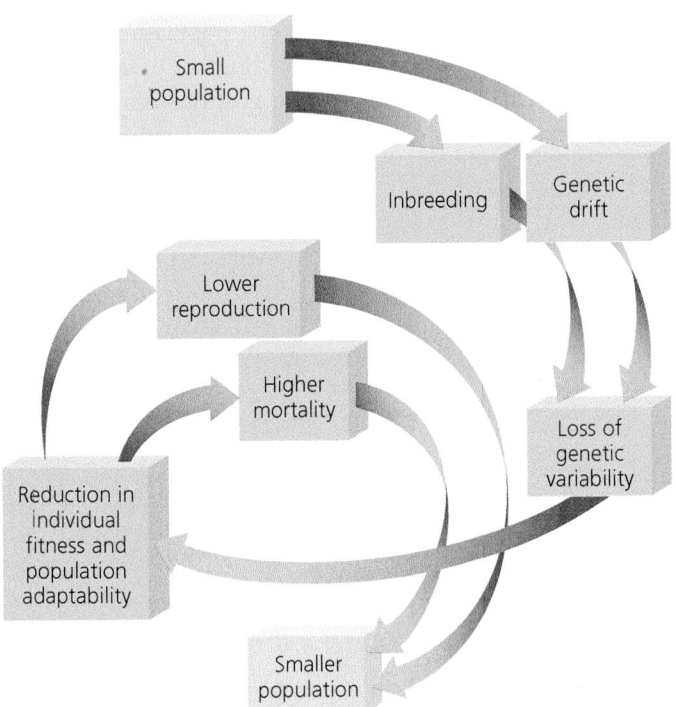

▲ **Figure 56.12 Processes driving an extinction vortex.**

▼ Figure 56.13

What caused the drastic decline of the Illinois greater prairie chicken population?

EXPERIMENT Researchers had observed that the population collapse of the greater prairie chicken was mirrored in a reduction in fertility, as measured by the hatching rate of eggs. Comparison of DNA samples from the Jasper County, Illinois, population with DNA from feathers in museum specimens showed that genetic variation had declined in the study population (see Figure 23.11). In 1992, Ronald Westemeier, Jeffrey Brawn, and colleagues began translocating prairie chickens from Minnesota, Kansas, and Nebraska in an attempt to increase genetic variation.

RESULTS After translocation (blue arrow), the viability of eggs rapidly increased, and the population rebounded.

(a) Population dynamics

(b) Hatching rate

CONCLUSION Reduced genetic variation had started the Jasper County population of prairie chickens down the extinction vortex.

SOURCE R. L. Westemeier et al., Tracking the long-term decline and recovery of an isolated population, *Science* 282:1695–1698 (1998).

INQUIRY IN ACTION Read and analyze the original paper in *Inquiry in Action: Interpreting Scientific Papers.*

WHAT IF? Given the success of using transplanted birds as a tool for increasing the percentage of hatched eggs in Illinois, why wouldn't you transplant *additional* birds immediately to Illinois?

---

because only certain members of the population breed successfully and pass their alleles on to offspring. Therefore, a meaningful estimate of MVP requires the researcher to determine the **effective population size**, which is based on the breeding potential of the population.

The following formula incorporates the sex ratio of breeding individuals into the estimate of effective population size, abbreviated N_e:

$$N_e = \frac{4N_f N_m}{N_f + N_m}$$

where N_f and N_m are, respectively, the number of females and the number of males that successfully breed. If we apply this formula to an idealized population whose total size is 1,000 individuals, N_e will also be 1,000 if every individual breeds and the sex ratio is 500 females to 500 males. In this case, $N_e = (4 \times 500 \times 500)/(500 + 500) = 1,000$. Any deviation from these conditions (not all individuals breed or there is not a 1:1 sex ratio) reduces N_e. For instance, if the total population size is 1,000 but only 400 females and 400 males breed, then $N_e = (4 \times 400 \times 400)/(400 + 400) = 800$, or 80% of the total population size. Numerous life history traits can influence N_e, and alternative formulas for estimating N_e take into account factors such as family size, age at maturation, genetic relatedness among population members, the effects of gene flow between geographically separated populations, and population fluctuations.

In actual study populations, N_e is always some fraction of the total population. Thus, simply determining the total number of individuals in a small population does not provide a good measure of whether the population is large enough to avoid extinction. Whenever possible, conservation programs attempt to sustain total population sizes that include at least the minimum viable number of *reproductively active* individuals. The conservation goal of sustaining effective population size (N_e) above MVP stems from the concern that populations retain enough genetic diversity to adapt as their environment changes.

The MVP of a population is often used in population viability analysis. The objective of this analysis is to predict a population's chances for survival, usually expressed as a specific probability of survival, such as a 95% chance, over a particular time interval, perhaps 100 years. Such modeling approaches allow conservation biologists to explore the potential consequences of alternative management plans. Because modeling depends on accurate information for the populations under study, conservation biology is most effective when theoretical modeling is combined with field studies of the managed populations.

Case Study: *Analysis of Grizzly Bear Populations*

One of the first population viability analyses was conducted in 1978 by Mark Shaffer, of Duke University, as part of a long-term study of grizzly bears in Yellowstone National Park and

▲ **Figure 56.14 Long-term monitoring of a grizzly bear population.** The ecologist is fitting this tranquilized bear with a radio collar so that the bear's movements can be compared with those of other grizzlies in the Yellowstone National Park population.

its surrounding areas **(Figure 56.14)**. A threatened species in the United States, the grizzly bear (*Ursus arctos horribilis*) is currently found in only 4 of the 48 contiguous states. Its populations in those states have been drastically reduced and fragmented. In 1800, an estimated 100,000 grizzlies ranged over about 500 million hectares of habitat, while today only about 1,000 individuals in six relatively isolated populations range over less than 5 million hectares.

Shaffer attempted to determine viable sizes for the Yellowstone grizzly population. Using life history data obtained for individual Yellowstone bears over a 12-year period, he simulated the effects of environmental factors on survival and reproduction. His models predicted that, given a suitable habitat, a Yellowstone grizzly bear population of 70–90 individuals would have about a 95% chance of surviving for 100 years. A slightly larger population of only 100 bears would have a 95% chance of surviving for twice as long, about 200 years.

How does the actual size of the Yellowstone grizzly population compare with Shaffer's predicted MVP? A current estimate puts the total grizzly bear population in the greater Yellowstone ecosystem at about 400 individuals. The relationship of this estimate to the effective population size, N_e, depends on several factors. Usually, only a few dominant males breed, and it may be difficult for them to locate females, since individuals inhabit such large areas. Moreover, females may reproduce only when there is abundant food. As a result, N_e is only about 25% of the total population size, or about 100 bears.

Because small populations tend to lose genetic variation over time, a number of research teams have analyzed proteins, mtDNA, and short tandem repeats (see Chapter 21) to assess genetic variability in the Yellowstone grizzly bear population. All results to date indicate that the Yellowstone population has less genetic variability than other grizzly bear populations in North America. However, the isolation and

decline in genetic variability in the Yellowstone grizzly bear population were gradual during the 20th century and not as severe as feared: Museum specimens collected in the early 1900s demonstrate that genetic variability among the Yellowstone grizzly bears was low even then.

How might conservation biologists increase the effective size and genetic variation of the Yellowstone grizzly bear population? Migration between isolated populations of grizzlies could increase both effective and total population sizes. Computer models predict that introducing only two unrelated bears each decade into a population of 100 individuals would reduce the loss of genetic variation by about half. For the grizzly bear, and probably for many other species with small populations, finding ways to promote dispersal among populations may be one of the most urgent conservation needs.

This case study and that of the greater prairie chicken bridge small-population models and practical applications in conservation. Next, we look at an alternative approach to understanding the biology of extinction.

Declining-Population Approach

The declining-population approach focuses on threatened and endangered populations that show a downward trend, even if the population is far above its minimum viable population. The distinction between a declining population (which is not always small) and a small population (which is not always declining) is less important than the different priorities of the two approaches. The small-population approach emphasizes smallness itself as an ultimate cause of a population's extinction, especially through the loss of genetic diversity. In contrast, the declining-population approach emphasizes the environmental factors that caused a population decline in the first place. If, for instance, an area is deforested, then species that depend on trees will decline in abundance and become locally extinct, whether or not they retain genetic variation.

Steps for Analysis and Intervention

The declining-population approach requires that population declines be evaluated on a case-by-case basis, with researchers carefully dissecting the causes of a decline before taking steps to correct it. If an invasive species such as the brown tree snake in Guam (see Figure 56.8a) is harming a native bird species, then managers need to reduce or eliminate the invader to restore vulnerable populations of the bird. Although most situations are more complex, we can use the following steps for analyzing declining populations:

1. Confirm, using population data, that the species was more widely distributed or abundant in the past.
2. Study the natural history of this and related species, including reviewing the research literature, to determine the species' environmental needs.

3. Develop hypotheses for all possible causes of the decline, including human activities and natural events, and list the predictions of each hypothesis.

4. Because many factors may be correlated with the decline, test the most likely hypothesis first. For example, remove the suspected agent of decline to see if the experimental population rebounds compared to a control population.

5. Apply the results of the diagnosis to manage the threatened species and monitor its recovery.

The following case study is one example of how the declining-population approach has been applied to the conservation of an endangered species.

Case Study: *Decline of the Red-Cockaded Woodpecker*

The red-cockaded woodpecker (*Picoides borealis*) is found only in the southeastern United States. It requires mature pine forests, preferably ones dominated by the longleaf pine, for its habitat. Most woodpeckers nest in dead trees, but the red-cockaded woodpecker drills its nest holes in mature, living pine trees. It also drills small holes around the entrance to its nest cavity, which causes resin from the tree to ooze down the trunk. The resin seems to repel predators, such as corn snakes, that eat bird eggs and nestlings.

Another critical habitat factor for the red-cockaded woodpecker is that the undergrowth of plants around the pine trunks must be low (**Figure 56.15a**). Breeding birds tend to abandon nests when vegetation among the pines is thick and higher than about 4.5 m (**Figure 56.15b**). Apparently, the birds need a

clear flight path between their home trees and the neighboring feeding grounds. Periodic fires have historically swept through longleaf pine forests, keeping the undergrowth low.

One factor leading to decline of the red-cockaded woodpecker has been the destruction or fragmentation of suitable habitats by logging and agriculture. By recognizing key habitat factors, protecting some longleaf pine forests, and using controlled fires to reduce forest undergrowth, conservation managers have helped restore habitat that can support viable populations.

A successful recovery program for red-cockaded woodpeckers was hindered, however, by the birds' social organization. Red-cockaded woodpeckers live in groups of one breeding pair and up to four "helpers," mostly males (an example of altruism; see Chapter 51). Helpers are offspring that do not disperse to breed but remain behind to help incubate eggs and feed nestlings of the breeding pair. Helpers may eventually attain breeding status within the flock when older birds die, but the wait may take years, and helpers must still compete to breed. Young birds that do disperse as members of new groups also have a tough path to reproductive success. New groups usually occupy abandoned territories or start at a new site, where they must excavate nesting cavities, which can take months. Individuals generally have a better chance of reproducing by remaining behind than by dispersing and excavating cavities in new territories.

To test the hypothesis that this social behavior was contributing to the decline of the red-cockaded woodpecker, researchers constructed cavities in pine trees at 20 sites. The

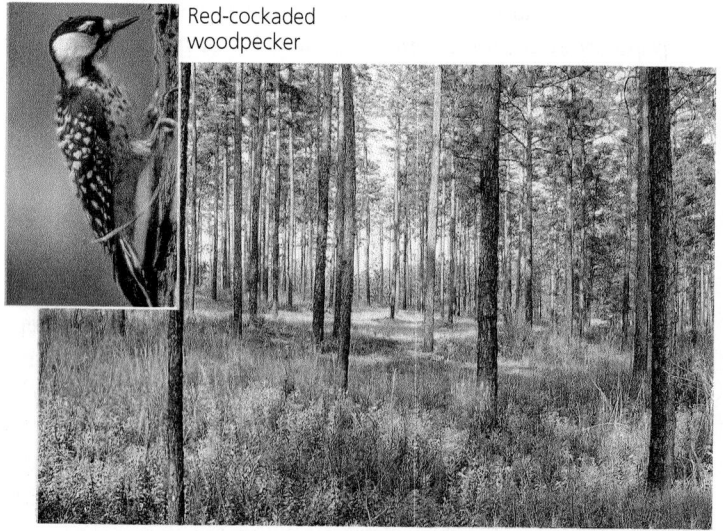

Red-cockaded woodpecker

(a) Forests that can sustain red-cockaded woodpeckers have low undergrowth.

(b) Forests that cannot sustain red-cockaded woodpeckers have high, dense undergrowth that interferes with the woodpeckers' access to feeding grounds.

▲ Figure 56.15 **A habitat requirement of the red-cockaded woodpecker.**

? *How is habitat disturbance absolutely necessary for the long-term survival of the woodpecker?*

results were dramatic. Cavities in 18 of the 20 sites were colonized by red-cockaded woodpeckers, and new breeding groups formed only in these sites. The experiment supported the hypothesis that this woodpecker species had been avoiding suitable habitat because of a lack of breeding cavities. Based on this experiment, conservationists initiated a habitat maintenance program that included controlled burning and excavation of new breeding cavities, enabling this endangered species to begin to recover.

Weighing Conflicting Demands

Determining population numbers and habitat needs is only part of a strategy to save species. Scientists also need to weigh a species' needs against other conflicting demands. Conservation biology often highlights the relationship between science, technology, and society. For example, an ongoing, sometimes bitter debate in the western United States pits habitat preservation for wolf, grizzly bear, and bull trout populations against job opportunities in the grazing and resource extraction industries. Programs to restock wolves in Yellowstone National Park were opposed by some recreationists concerned for human safety and by many ranchers concerned with potential loss of livestock outside the park.

Large, high-profile vertebrates are not always the focal point in such conflicts, but habitat use is almost always the issue. Should work proceed on a new highway bridge if it destroys the only remaining habitat of a species of freshwater mussel? If you were the owner of a coffee plantation growing varieties that thrive in bright sunlight, would you be willing to change to shade-tolerant varieties that produce less coffee per hectare but can grow beneath trees that support large numbers of songbirds?

Another important consideration is the ecological role of a species. Because we cannot save every endangered species, we must determine which species are most important for conserving biodiversity as a whole. Identifying keystone species and finding ways to sustain their populations can be central to maintaining communities and ecosystems.

Management aimed at conserving a single species carries with it the possibility of harming populations of other species. For example, management of open pine forests for the red-cockaded woodpecker might impact migratory birds that use later-successional broadleaf forests. To test this idea, ecologists compared bird communities near clusters of nest cavities in managed pine forests with communities in forests not managed for the woodpeckers. Contrary to expectations, the managed sites supported higher numbers and a higher diversity of other birds than the control forests did. In this case, managing for one bird species increased the diversity of an entire bird community. In most situations, conservation must look beyond single species and consider the whole community and ecosystem as an important unit of biodiversity.

CONCEPT CHECK 56.2

1. How does the reduced genetic diversity of small populations make them more vulnerable to extinction?
2. If there was a total of 50 individuals in the two Illinois populations of greater prairie chickens in 1993, what was the effective population size if 15 females and 5 males bred?
3. **WHAT IF?** In 2005, at least ten grizzly bears in the greater Yellowstone ecosystem were killed through contact with people. Three things caused most of these deaths: collisions with automobiles, hunters (of other animals) shooting when charged by a female grizzly bear with cubs nearby, and conservation managers killing bears that attacked livestock repeatedly. If you were a conservation manager, what steps might you take to minimize such encounters in Yellowstone?

For suggested answers, Appendix A.

CONCEPT 56.3

Landscape and regional conservation help sustain biodiversity

Although conservation efforts historically focused on saving individual species, efforts today often seek to sustain the biodiversity of entire communities, ecosystems, and landscapes. Such a broad view requires applying not just the principles of community, ecosystem, and landscape ecology but aspects of human population dynamics and economics as well. The goals of landscape ecology (see Chapter 52) include projecting future patterns of landscape use and making biodiversity conservation part of land-use planning.

Landscape Structure and Biodiversity

The biodiversity of a given landscape is in large part a function of the structure of the landscape. Understanding landscape structure is critically important in conservation because many species use more than one kind of ecosystem, and many live on the borders between ecosystems.

Fragmentation and Edges

The boundaries, or *edges*, between ecosystems—such as between a lake and the surrounding forest or between cropland and suburban housing tracts—are defining features of

(a) Natural edges. Grasslands give way to forest ecosystems in Yellowstone National Park.

(b) Edges created by human activity. Pronounced edges (roads) surround clear-cut areas in this photograph of a heavily logged rain forest in Malaysia.

▲ **Figure 56.16** **Edges between ecosystems.**

▲ **Figure 56.17** **Amazon rain forest fragments created as part of the Biological Dynamics of Forest Fragments Project.**

The proliferation of edge species can have positive or negative effects on biodiversity. A 1997 study in Cameroon comparing edge and interior populations of the little greenbul (a tropical rain forest bird) suggested that forest edges may be important sites of speciation. On the other hand, ecosystems in which edges arise from human alterations often have reduced biodiversity and a preponderance of edge-adapted species. For example, the brown-headed cowbird (*Molothrus ater*) is an edge-adapted species that lays its eggs in the nests of other birds, often migratory songbirds. Cowbirds need forests, where they can parasitize the nests of other birds, and open fields, where they forage on insects. Thus, their populations are growing where forests are being cut and fragmented, creating more edge habitat and open land. Increasing cowbird parasitism and habitat loss are correlated with declining populations of several of the cowbird's host species.

The influence of fragmentation on the structure of communities has been explored since 1979 in the long-term Biological Dynamics of Forest Fragments Project. Located in the heart of the Amazon River basin, the study area consists of isolated fragments of tropical rain forest separated from surrounding continuous forest by distances of 80–1,000 m (Figure 56.17). Numerous researchers working on this project have clearly documented the effects of this fragmentation on organisms ranging from bryophytes to beetles to birds. They have consistently found that species adapted to forest interiors show the greatest declines when patches are the smallest, suggesting that landscapes dominated by small fragments will support fewer species.

Corridors That Connect Habitat Fragments

In fragmented habitats, the presence of a **movement corridor**, a narrow strip or series of small clumps of habitat

landscapes (**Figure 56.16**). An edge has its own set of physical conditions, which differ from those on either side of it. The soil surface of an edge between a forest patch and a burned area receives more sunlight and is usually hotter and drier than the forest interior, but it is cooler and wetter than the soil surface in the burned area.

Some organisms thrive in edge communities because they gain resources from both adjacent areas. The ruffed grouse (*Bonasa umbellus*) is a bird that needs forest habitat for nesting, winter food, and shelter, but it also needs forest openings with dense shrubs and herbs for summer food. White-tailed deer also thrive in edge habitats, where they can browse on woody shrubs; deer populations often expand when forests are logged and more edges are generated.

▲ **Figure 56.18 An artificial corridor.** This bridge in Banff National Park, Canada, helps animals cross a human-created barrier.

connecting otherwise isolated patches, can be extremely important for conserving biodiversity. Riparian habitats often serve as corridors, and in some nations, government policy prohibits altering these habitats. In areas of heavy human use, artificial corridors are sometimes constructed. Bridges or tunnels, for instance, can reduce the number of animals killed trying to cross highways (Figure 56.18).

Movement corridors can also promote dispersal and reduce inbreeding in declining populations. Corridors have been shown to increase the exchange of individuals among populations of many organisms, including butterflies, voles, and aquatic plants. Corridors are especially important to species that migrate between different habitats seasonally. However, a corridor can also be harmful—for example, by allowing the spread of disease. In a 2003 study, a scientist at the University of Zaragoza, Spain, showed that habitat corridors facilitate the movement of disease-carrying ticks among forest patches in northern Spain. All the effects of corridors are not yet understood, and their impact is an area of active research in conservation biology.

Establishing Protected Areas

Conservation biologists are applying their understanding of landscape dynamics in establishing protected areas to slow biodiversity loss. Currently, governments have set aside about 7% of the world's land in various forms of reserves. Choosing where to place nature reserves and how to design them poses many challenges. Should the reserve be managed to minimize the risks of fire and predation to a threatened species? Or should the reserve be left as natural as possible, with such processes as fires ignited by lightning allowed to play out on their own? This is just one of the debates that arise among people who share an interest in the health of national parks and other protected areas.

Preserving Biodiversity Hot Spots

In deciding which areas are of highest conservation priority, biologists often focus on hot spots of biodiversity. A **biodiversity hot spot** is a relatively small area with numerous endemic species (species found nowhere else in the world) and a large number of endangered and threatened species (Figure 56.19). Nearly 30% of all bird species can be found in hot spots that make up only about 2% of Earth's land area. Approximately 50,000 plant species, or about one-sixth of all known plant species, inhabit just 18 hot spots covering 0.5% of the global land surface. Together, the "hottest" of the terrestrial biodiversity hot spots total less than 1.5% of Earth's land but are home to more than a third of all species of plants, amphibians, reptiles (including birds), and mammals. Aquatic ecosystems also have hot spots, such as coral reefs and certain river systems.

Biodiversity hot spots are good choices for nature reserves, but identifying them is not always simple. One problem is that a hot spot for one taxonomic group, such as butterflies, may not be a hot spot for some other taxonomic group, such as birds. Designating an area as a biodiversity hot spot is often biased toward saving vertebrates and plants, with less attention paid to invertebrates and microorganisms. Some biologists are

◀ Figure 56.19 **Earth's terrestrial and marine biodiversity hot spots.**

■ Terrestrial biodiversity hot spots

▲ Marine biodiversity hot spots

Equator

also concerned that the hot-spot strategy places too much emphasis on such a small fraction of Earth's surface.

Global change makes the task of preserving hot spots even more challenging because the conditions that favor a particular community may not be found in the same location in the future. The biodiversity hot spot in the southwest corner of Australia (see Figure 56.19) holds thousands of species of endemic plants and numerous endemic vertebrates. Researchers recently concluded that between 5% and 25% of the plant species they examined may become extinct by 2080 because the plants will be unable to tolerate the increased dryness predicted for this region.

Philosophy of Nature Reserves

Nature reserves are biodiversity islands in a sea of habitat degraded by human activity. Protected "islands" are not isolated from their surroundings, however, and the nonequilibrium model we described in Chapter 54 applies to nature reserves as well as to the larger landscapes around them.

An earlier policy—that protected areas should be set aside to remain unchanged forever—was based on the concept that ecosystems are balanced, self-regulating units. As we saw in Chapter 54, however, disturbance is common in all ecosystems, and management policies that ignore natural disturbances or attempt to prevent them have generally failed. For instance, setting aside an area of a fire-dependent community, such as a portion of a tallgrass prairie, chaparral, or dry pine forest, with the intention of saving it is unrealistic if periodic burning is excluded. Without the dominant disturbance, the fire-adapted species are usually outcompeted and biodiversity is reduced.

Because human disturbance and fragmentation are increasingly common, understanding the dynamics of disturbances, populations, edges, and corridors is essential for designing and managing protected areas. An important conservation question is whether to create fewer large reserves or more numerous small reserves. One argument for large reserves is that large, far-ranging animals with low-density populations, such as the grizzly bear, require extensive habitats. Large reserves also have proportionately smaller perimeters than small reserves and are therefore less affected by edges.

As conservation biologists have learned more about the requirements for achieving minimum viable populations for endangered species, they have realized that most national parks and other reserves are far too small. The area needed for the long-term survival of the Yellowstone grizzly bear population is more than ten times the combined area of Yellowstone and Grand Teton National Parks (Figure 56.20). Given political and economic realities, many existing parks will not be enlarged, and most newly created reserves will also be too small. Areas of private and public land surrounding reserves will likely have to contribute to biodiversity conservation. On the other side of the argument, smaller, unconnected reserves may slow the spread of disease between populations.

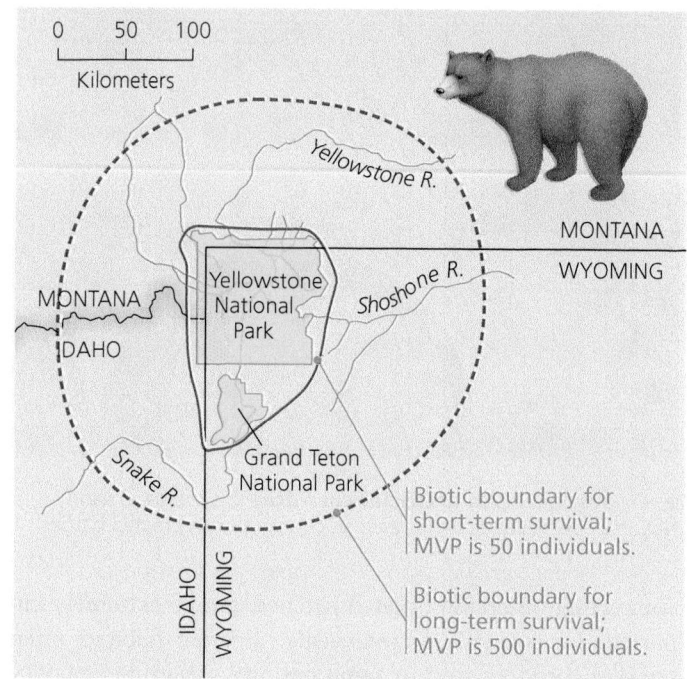

▲ Figure 56.20 **Biotic boundaries for grizzly bears in Yellowstone and Grand Teton National Parks.** The biotic boundaries (solid and dashed red lines) surround the areas needed to support minimum viable populations of 50 and 500 bears. Even the smaller of these areas is larger than the two parks.

In practical terms, land use by humans may outweigh all other considerations and ultimately dictate the size and shape of protected areas. Much of the land left for conservation efforts is useless for exploitation by agriculture or forestry. But in some cases, as when reserve land is surrounded by commercially valuable property, the use of land for agriculture or forestry must be integrated into conservation strategies.

Zoned Reserves

Several nations have adopted a zoned reserve approach to landscape management. A **zoned reserve** is an extensive region that includes areas relatively undisturbed by humans surrounded by areas that have been changed by human activity and are used for economic gain. The key challenge of the zoned reserve approach is to develop a social and economic climate in the surrounding lands that is compatible with the long-term viability of the protected core. These surrounding areas continue to support human activities, but regulations prevent the types of extensive alterations likely to harm the protected area. As a result, the surrounding habitats serve as buffer zones against further intrusion into the undisturbed area.

The small Central American nation of Costa Rica has become a world leader in establishing zoned reserves (Figure 56.21). An agreement initiated in 1987 reduced Costa Rica's international debt in return for land preservation there. The agreement resulted in eight zoned reserves, called "conservation areas," that contain designated national park land. Costa Rica is making progress toward managing its zoned reserves, and the buffer

(a) Boundaries of the zoned reserves are indicated by black outlines.

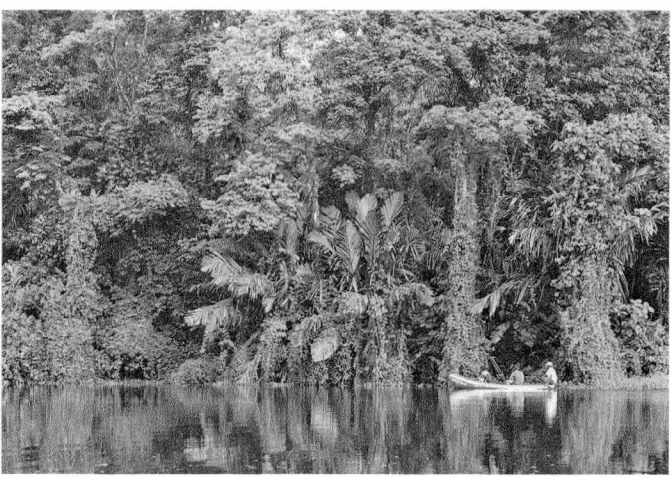

(b) Tourists marvel at the diversity of life in one of Costa Rica's zoned reserves.

▲ Figure 56.21 **Zoned reserves in Costa Rica.**

zones provide a steady, lasting supply of forest products, water, and hydroelectric power while also supporting sustainable agriculture and tourism.

An important goal of zoned reserves is to provide a stable economic base for people living there. As University of Pennsylvania ecologist Daniel Janzen, a leader in tropical conservation, has said, "The likelihood of long-term survival of a conserved wildland area is directly proportional to the economic health and stability of the society in which that wildland is embedded." Destructive practices that are not compatible with long-term ecosystem conservation and from which there is often little local profit, such as massive logging, large-scale single-crop agriculture, and extensive mining, are ideally confined to the outermost fringes of the buffer zones in Costa Rica and are gradually being discouraged.

Costa Rica relies on its zoned reserve system to maintain at least 80% of its native species, but the system is not without problems. A 2003 analysis of land cover change between 1960 and 1997 showed negligible deforestation within Costa Rica's national parks and a gain in forest cover in the 1-km buffer around the parks. However, significant losses in forest cover were discovered in the 10-km buffer zones around all national parks, threatening to turn the parks into isolated habitat islands.

Although marine ecosystems have also been heavily affected by human exploitation, reserves in the ocean are far less common than reserves on land. Many fish populations around the world have collapsed as increasingly sophisticated equipment puts nearly all potential fishing grounds within human reach. In response, scientists at the University of York, England, have proposed establishing marine reserves around the world that would be off limits to fishing. They present strong evidence that a patchwork of marine reserves can serve as a means of both increasing fish populations within the reserves and improving fishing success in nearby areas. Their proposed system is a modern application of a centuries-old practice in the Fiji Islands in which some areas have historically remained closed to fishing—a traditional example of the zoned reserve concept.

The United States adopted such a system in creating a set of 13 national marine sanctuaries, including the Florida Keys National Marine Sanctuary, which was established in 1990 (Figure 56.22). Populations of marine organisms, including fishes and lobsters, recovered quickly after harvests were banned in the 9,500-km² reserve. Larger and more abundant fish now produce larvae that help repopulate reefs and improve fishing outside the sanctuary. The increased marine life within the sanctuary also makes it a favorite for recreational divers, increasing the economic value of this zoned reserve.

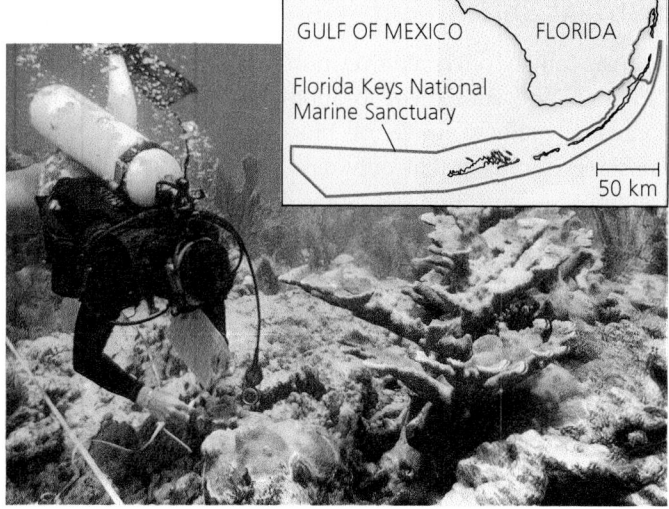

▲ Figure 56.22 **A diver measuring coral in the Florida Keys National Marine Sanctuary.**

CONCEPT CHECK 56.3

1. What is a biodiversity hot spot?
2. How do zoned reserves provide economic incentives for long-term conservation of protected areas?
3. **WHAT IF?** Suppose a developer proposes to clear-cut a forest that serves as a corridor between two parks. To compensate, the developer also proposes to add the same area of forest to one of the parks. As a professional ecologist, how might you argue for retaining the corridor?

For suggested answers, see Appendix A.

CONCEPT 56.4

Earth is changing rapidly as a result of human actions

As we've discussed, landscape and regional conservation help protect habitats and preserve species. However, environmental changes that result from human activities are creating new challenges. As a consequence of human-caused climate change, for example, the place where a vulnerable species is found today may not be the same as the one needed for preservation in the future. What would happen if *many* habitats on Earth changed so quickly that the locations of preserves today were unsuitable for their species in 10, 50, or 100 years? Such a scenario is increasingly possible.

The rest of this section describes four types of environmental change that humans are bringing about: nutrient enrichment, toxin accumulation, climate change, and ozone depletion. The impacts of these and other changes are evident not just in human-dominated ecosystems, such as cities and farms, but also in the most remote ecosystems on Earth.

Nutrient Enrichment

Human activity often removes nutrients from one part of the biosphere and adds them to another. On the simplest level, someone eating a piece of broccoli in Washington, DC, consumes nutrients that only days before were in the soil in California; a short time later, some of these nutrients will be in the Potomac River, having passed through the person's digestive system and a local sewage treatment facility. On a larger scale, nutrients in farm soil may run off into streams and lakes, depleting nutrients in one area, increasing them in another, and altering chemical cycles in both. Furthermore, humans have added entirely novel materials—some of them toxic—to ecosystems.

Farming is an example of how, even with the best of intentions, human activities are altering the environment through the enrichment of nutrients, particularly ones containing nitrogen. After natural vegetation is cleared from an area, the existing reserve of nutrients in the soil is sufficient to grow crops for some time. In agricultural ecosystems, however, a substantial fraction of these nutrients is exported from the area in crop biomass. The "free" period for crop production—when there is no need to add nutrients to the soil—varies greatly. When some of the early North American prairie lands were first tilled, good crops could be produced for decades because the large store of organic materials in the soil continued to decompose and provide nutrients. By contrast, some cleared land in the tropics can be farmed for only one or two years because so little of the ecosystems' nutrient load is contained in the soil. Despite such variations, in any area under intensive agriculture, the natural store of nutrients eventually becomes exhausted.

Nitrogen is the main nutrient element lost through agriculture (see Figure 55.14). Plowing mixes the soil and speeds up decomposition of organic matter, releasing nitrogen that is then removed when crops are harvested. Applied fertilizers make up for the loss of usable nitrogen from agricultural ecosystems (Figure 56.23). In addition, as we saw in the case of Hubbard Brook (see Figure 55.16), without plants to take up nitrates from the soil, the nitrates are likely to be leached from the ecosystem.

Recent studies indicate that human activities have more than doubled Earth's supply of fixed nitrogen available to primary producers. Industrial fertilizers provide the largest additional nitrogen source. Fossil fuel combustion also releases nitrogen oxides, which enter the atmosphere and dissolve in rainwater; the nitrogen ultimately enters ecosystems as nitrate. Increased cultivation of legumes, with their nitrogen-fixing symbionts, is a third way in which humans increase the amount of fixed nitrogen in the soil.

A problem arises when the nutrient level in an ecosystem exceeds the **critical load**, the amount of added nutrient, usually nitrogen or phosphorus, that can be absorbed by plants without damaging ecosystem integrity. For example, nitrogenous minerals in the soil that exceed the critical load

▲ **Figure 56.23 Fertilization of a corn (maize) crop.** To replace the nutrients removed in crops, farmers must apply fertilizers—either organic, such as manure or mulch, or synthetic, as shown here.

Winter

Summer

▲ **Figure 56.24 A phytoplankton bloom arising from nitrogen pollution in the Mississippi basin that leads to a dead zone.** In these satellite images from 2004, red and orange represent high concentrations of phytoplankton in the Gulf of Mexico. This dead zone extends much farther from land in summer than in winter.

eventually leach into groundwater or run off into freshwater and marine ecosystems, contaminating water supplies and killing fish. Nitrate concentrations in groundwater are increasing in most agricultural regions, sometimes reaching levels that are unsafe for drinking.

Many rivers contaminated with nitrates and ammonium from agricultural runoff and sewage drain into the Atlantic Ocean, with the highest inputs coming from northern Europe and the central United States. The Mississippi River carries nitrogen pollution to the Gulf of Mexico, fueling a phytoplankton bloom each summer. When the phytoplankton die, their decomposition by oxygen-using organisms creates an extensive "dead zone" of low oxygen levels along the coast (Figure 56.24). Fish and other marine animals disappear from some of the most economically important waters in the United States. To reduce the size of the dead zone, farmers have begun using fertilizers more efficiently, and managers are restoring wetlands in the Mississippi watershed, two changes stimulated by the results of ecosystem experiments.

Nutrient runoff can also lead to the eutrophication of lakes, as you learned in Concept 55.2. The bloom and subsequent die-off of algae and cyanobacteria and the ensuing depletion of oxygen are similar to what occurs in a marine dead zone. Such conditions threaten the survival of organisms. For example, eutrophication of Lake Erie coupled with overfishing wiped out commercially important fishes such as blue pike, whitefish, and lake trout by the 1960s. Since then, tighter regulations on waste dumping into the lake have enabled some fish populations to rebound, but many native species of fish and invertebrates have not recovered.

Toxins in the Environment

Humans release an immense variety of toxic chemicals, including thousands of synthetic compounds previously unknown in nature, with little regard for the ecological consequences. Organisms acquire toxic substances from the environment along with nutrients and water. Some of the poisons are metabolized or excreted, but others accumulate in specific tissues, often fat.

One of the reasons accumulated toxins are particularly harmful is that they become more concentrated in successive trophic levels of a food web. This phenomenon, called **biological magnification**, occurs because the biomass at any given trophic level is produced from a much larger biomass ingested from the level below (see Concept 55.3). Thus, top-level carnivores tend to be most severely affected by toxic compounds in the environment.

One class of industrially synthesized compounds that have demonstrated biological magnification are the chlorinated hydrocarbons, which include the industrial chemicals called PCBs (polychlorinated biphenyls) and many pesticides, such as DDT. Current research implicates many of these compounds in endocrine system disruption in a large number of animal species, including humans (see pp. 992–993). Biological magnification of PCBs has been found in the food web of the Great Lakes, where the concentration of PCBs in herring gull eggs, at the top of the food web, is nearly 5,000 times that in phytoplankton, at the base of the food web (Figure 56.25).

Concentration of PCBs

Herring gull eggs 124 ppm

Lake trout 4.83 ppm

Smelt 1.04 ppm

Zooplankton 0.123 ppm

Phytoplankton 0.025 ppm

▲ **Figure 56.25 Biological magnification of PCBs in a Great Lakes food web.**

An infamous case of biological magnification that harmed top-level carnivores involved DDT, a chemical used to control insects such as mosquitoes and agricultural pests. In the decade after World War II, the use of DDT grew rapidly; its ecological consequences were not yet fully understood. By the 1950s, scientists were learning that DDT persists in the environment and is transported by water to areas far from where it is applied. One of the first signs that DDT was a serious environmental problem was a decline in the populations of pelicans, ospreys, and eagles, birds that feed at the top of food webs. The accumulation of DDT (and DDE, a product of its breakdown) in the tissues of these birds interfered with the deposition of calcium in their eggshells. When the birds tried to incubate their eggs, the weight of the parents broke the shells of affected eggs, resulting in catastrophic declines in the birds' reproduction rates. Rachel Carson's book *Silent Spring* helped bring the problem to public attention in the 1960s (Figure 56.26), and DDT was banned in the United States in 1971. A dramatic recovery in populations of the affected bird species followed.

In much of the tropics, DDT is still used to control the mosquitoes that spread malaria and other diseases. Societies there face a trade-off between saving human lives and protecting other species. The best approach seems to be to apply DDT sparingly and to couple its use with mosquito netting and other low-technology solutions. The complicated history of DDT illustrates the importance of understanding the ecological connections between diseases and communities (see Concept 54.5).

Many toxins cannot be degraded by microorganisms and persist in the environment for years or even decades. In other cases, chemicals released into the environment may be relatively harmless but are converted to more toxic products by reaction with other substances, by exposure to light, or by the metabolism of microorganisms. Mercury, a by-product of plastic production and coal-fired power generation, has been routinely expelled into rivers and the sea in an insoluble form. Bacteria in the bottom mud convert the waste to methylmercury (CH_3Hg^+), an extremely toxic water-soluble compound that accumulates in the tissues of organisms, including humans, who consume fish from the contaminated waters.

Greenhouse Gases and Global Warming

Human activities release a variety of gaseous waste products. People once thought that the vast atmosphere could absorb these materials indefinitely, but we now know that such additions can cause fundamental changes to the atmosphere and to its interactions with the rest of the biosphere. In this section, we will examine how increasing atmospheric carbon dioxide concentration and global warming affect species and ecosystems.

Rising Atmospheric CO_2 Levels

Since the Industrial Revolution, the concentration of CO_2 in the atmosphere has been increasing as a result of the burning of fossil fuels and deforestation. Scientists estimate that the average CO_2 concentration in the atmosphere before 1850 was about 274 ppm. In 1958, a monitoring station began taking very accurate measurements on Hawaii's Mauna Loa peak, a location far from cities and high enough for the atmosphere to be well mixed. At that time, the CO_2 concentration was 316 ppm (Figure 56.27). Today, it exceeds 385 ppm, an increase of more than 40% since the mid-19th century. If CO_2 emissions continue to increase at the present rate, by the year 2075 the atmospheric concentration of this gas will be more than double what it was in 1850.

Increased productivity by plants is one predictable consequence of increasing CO_2 levels. In fact, when CO_2 concentrations are raised in experimental chambers such as greenhouses, most plants grow faster. Because C_3 plants are more limited than C_4 plants by CO_2 availability (see Concept 10.4), one effect of increasing global CO_2 concentration may be the spread of C_3 species into terrestrial habitats that currently favor C_4 plants. Such changes could influence whether corn (maize), a C_4 plant and the most important grain crop in the United States, will be replaced by wheat and soybeans, C_3 crops that could outproduce corn in a CO_2-enriched environment. To predict the gradual and complex effects of rising CO_2 levels on productivity and species composition, scientists are turning to long-term field experiments.

How Elevated CO_2 Levels Affect Forest Ecology: The FACTS-I Experiment

To assess how the increasing atmospheric concentration of CO_2 might affect temperate forests, scientists at Duke University began the Forest-Atmosphere Carbon Transfer and Storage (FACTS-I) experiment in 1995. The researchers are manipulating the concentration of CO_2 to which trees are exposed. The FACTS-I experiment includes six plots in an 80-hectare (200-acre) tract of loblolly pine within the university's experimental forest. Each plot consists of a circular area, approximately 30 m in diameter, ringed by 16 towers

► **Figure 56.26**
Rachel Carson.
Through her writing and her testimony before the U.S. Congress, biologist and author Carson helped promote a new environmental ethic. Her efforts led to a ban on DDT use in the United States and stronger controls on the use of other chemicals.

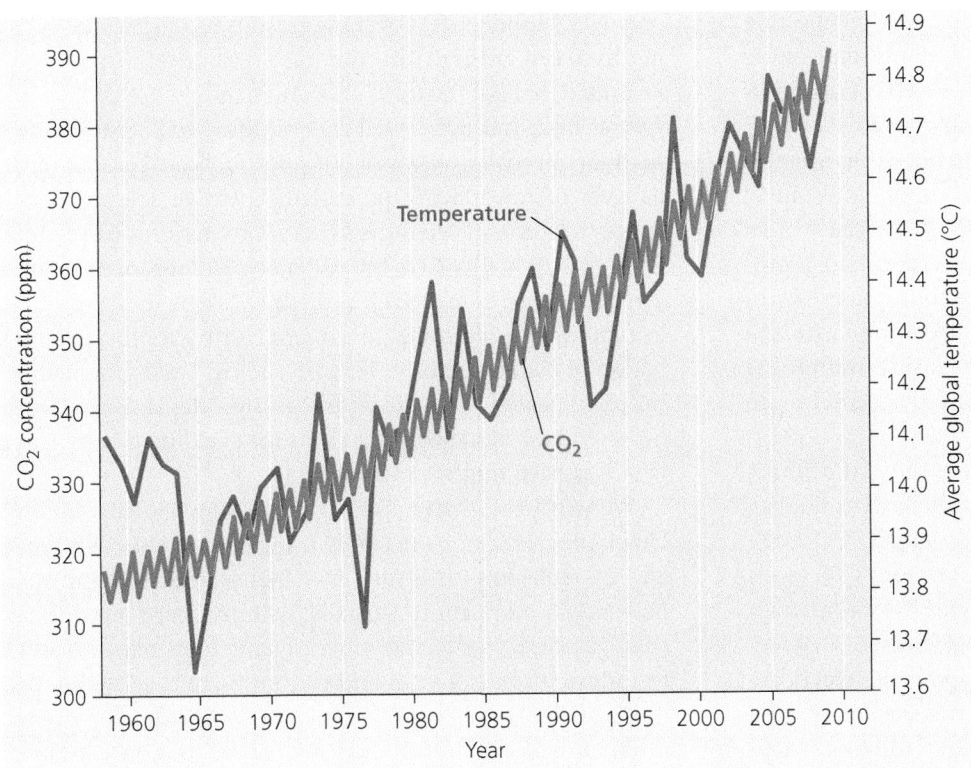

(Figure 56.28). In three of the six plots, the towers produce air containing about 1½ times present-day CO_2 concentrations. Instruments on a tall tower in the center of each plot measure the direction and speed of the wind, adjusting the distribution of CO_2 to maintain a stable CO_2 concentration. All other factors, such as temperature, precipitation, and wind speed and direction, vary normally for both experimental plots and adjacent control plots exposed to atmospheric CO_2.

The FACTS-I study is testing how elevated CO_2 levels influence tree growth, carbon concentration in soils, insect populations, soil moisture, the growth of plants in the forest understory, and other factors. After 12 years, trees in the experimental plots produced about 15% more wood each year than those in the control plots. This increased growth is important for timber production and carbon storage but is far lower than predicted from the results of greenhouse experiments. The availability of nitrogen and other nutrients apparently limits the ability of the trees to use the extra CO_2. Researchers at FACTS-I began removing this limitation in 2005 by fertilizing half of each plot with ammonium nitrate.

In most of the world's ecosystems, nutrients limit ecosystem productivity and fertilizers are unavailable. The results of FACTS-I and other experiments suggest that increased atmospheric CO_2 levels will increase plant production somewhat, but far less than scientists predicted even a decade ago.

The Greenhouse Effect and Climate

Rising concentrations of long-lived greenhouse gases such as CO_2 are also changing Earth's heat budget. Much of the solar

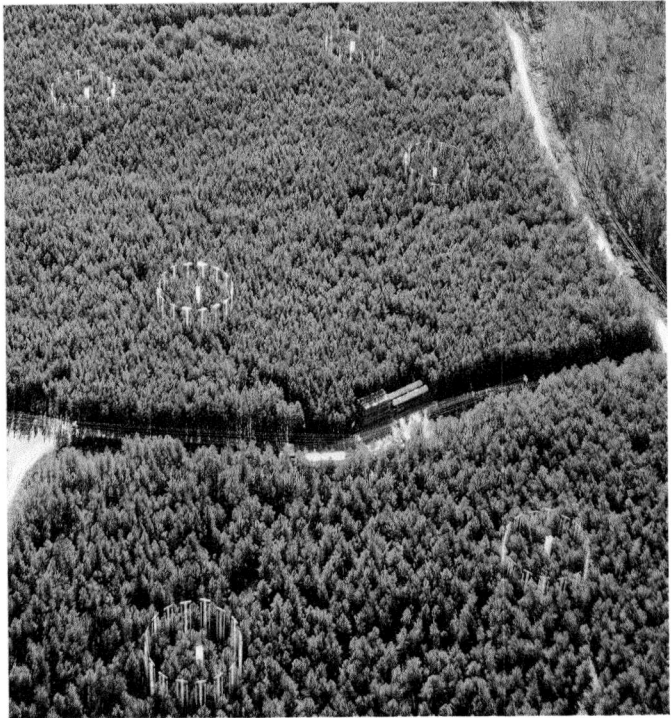

▲ Figure 56.28 **Large-scale experiment on the effects of elevated CO_2 concentration.** Rings of towers in the Duke University Experimental Forest emit enough carbon dioxide to raise and maintain CO_2 levels 200 ppm above present-day concentrations in half of the experimental plots.

radiation that strikes the planet is reflected back into space. Although CO_2, water vapor, and other greenhouse gases in the atmosphere are transparent to visible light, they intercept and absorb much of the infrared radiation Earth emits, re-reflecting some of it back toward Earth. This process retains some of the solar heat. If it were not for this **greenhouse effect**, the average air temperature at Earth's surface would be a frigid $-18°C$ ($-0.4°F$), and most life as we know it could not exist.

The marked increase in the concentration of atmospheric CO_2 over the last 150 years concerns scientists because of its link to increased global temperature. For more than a century, scientists have studied how greenhouse gases warm Earth and how fossil fuel burning could contribute to the warming. Most scientists are convinced that such warming is already occurring and will increase rapidly this century (see Figure 56.27).

Global models predict that by the end of the 21st century, the atmospheric CO_2 concentration will more than double, increasing average global temperature by about 3°C (5°F). Supporting these models is a correlation between CO_2 levels and temperatures in prehistoric times. One way climatologists estimate past CO_2 concentrations is to measure CO_2 levels in bubbles trapped in glacial ice, some of which are 700,000 years old. Prehistoric temperatures are inferred by several methods, including analysis of past vegetation based on fossils and the chemical isotopes in sediments and corals. An increase of only 1.3°C would make the world warmer than at any time in the past 100,000 years. A warming trend would also alter the geographic distribution of precipitation, likely making agricultural areas of the central United States much drier, for example.

The ecosystems where the largest warming has *already* occurred are those in the far north, particularly northern coniferous forests and tundra. As snow and ice melt and uncover darker, more absorptive surfaces, these systems reflect less radiation back to the atmosphere and warm further. Arctic sea ice in the summer of 2007 covered the smallest area on record. Climate models suggest that there may be no summer ice there within a few decades, decreasing habitat for polar bears, seals, and seabirds. Higher temperatures also increase the likelihood of fires. In boreal forests of western North America and Russia, fires have burned twice the usual area in recent decades.

By studying how past periods of global warming and cooling affected plant communities, ecologists are trying to predict the consequences of future changes in temperature and precipitation. Analysis of fossilized pollen indicates that plant communities change dramatically with changes in temperature. Past climate changes occurred gradually, though, and most plant and animal populations had time to migrate into areas where abiotic conditions allowed them to survive.

Many organisms, especially plants that cannot disperse rapidly over long distances, may not be able to survive the rapid climate change projected to result from global warming. Furthermore, many habitats today are more fragmented than ever (see Concept 56.3), further limiting the ability of many organisms to migrate. For these reasons, ecologists are debating **assisted migration**, the translocation of a species to a favorable habitat beyond its native range to protect the species from human-caused threats. Most ecologists consider such an approach only as a last resort, in part because of the dangers of introducing potentially invasive species to new regions. Although scientists have yet to perform assisted migration, activists in 2008 transplanted seedlings of the endangered tree *Torreya taxifolia* hundreds of kilometers north from its native range in Florida to western North Carolina in anticipation of climate change. This "rewilding," as it is sometimes called, appeared to be driven in part by a desire for publicity; no ecological framework yet exists for deciding if, when, and where assisted migration is desirable.

We will need many approaches to slow global warming. Quick progress can be made by using energy more efficiently and by replacing fossil fuels with renewable solar and wind power and, more controversially, with nuclear power. Today, coal, gasoline, wood, and other organic fuels remain central to industrialized societies and cannot be burned without releasing CO_2. Stabilizing CO_2 emissions will require concerted international effort and changes in both personal lifestyles and industrial processes. Many ecologists think that effort suffered a major setback in 2001, when the United States pulled out of the Kyoto Protocol, a 1997 pledge by industrialized nations to reduce their CO_2 output by about 5%. Such a reduction would be a first step in the journey to stabilize atmospheric CO_2 concentrations. Recent international negotiations, including a 2009 meeting in Copenhagen, Denmark, have yet to reach a global consensus on how to reduce greenhouse gas emissions.

Another important approach to slowing global warming is to reduce deforestation around the world, particularly in the tropics. Deforestation currently accounts for about 12% of greenhouse gas emissions. Recent research shows that paying countries *not* to cut forests could decrease the rate of deforestation by half within 10 to 20 years. Reduced deforestation would not only slow the buildup of greenhouse gases in our atmosphere, but would sustain native forests and preserve biodiversity, a positive outcome for all.

Depletion of Atmospheric Ozone

Like carbon dioxide and other greenhouse gases, atmospheric ozone (O_3) has also changed in concentration because of human activities. Life on Earth is protected from the damaging effects of ultraviolet (UV) radiation by a layer of ozone located in the stratosphere 17–25 km above Earth's surface. However, satellite studies of the atmosphere show that the springtime ozone layer over Antarctica has thinned substantially since the mid-1970s (Figure 56.29). As Susan Solomon discussed in the interview opening Unit 1, the destruction of atmospheric ozone results primarily from the

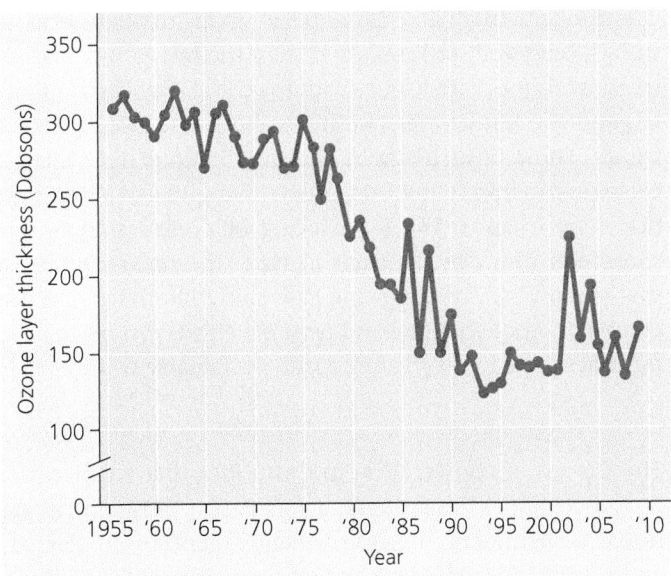

▲ Figure 56.29 Thickness of the October ozone layer over Antarctica in units called Dobsons.

September 1979   September 2009

▲ Figure 56.31 Erosion of Earth's ozone shield. The ozone hole over Antarctica is visible as the dark blue patch in these images based on atmospheric data.

accumulation of chlorofluorocarbons (CFCs), chemicals once widely used in refrigeration and manufacturing. In the stratosphere, chlorine atoms released from CFCs react with ozone, reducing it to molecular O_2 **(Figure 56.30)**. Subsequent chemical reactions liberate the chlorine, allowing it to react with other ozone molecules in a catalytic chain reaction.

The thinning of the ozone layer is most apparent over Antarctica in spring, where cold, stable air allows the chain reaction to continue. The magnitude of ozone depletion and the size of the ozone hole have generally increased in recent years, and the hole sometimes extends as far as the southernmost portions of Australia, New Zealand, and South America **(Figure 56.31)**. At the more heavily populated middle latitudes, ozone levels have decreased 2–10% during the past 20 years.

Decreased ozone levels in the stratosphere increase the intensity of UV rays reaching Earth's surface. The consequences of ozone depletion for life on Earth may be severe for plants, animals, and microorganisms. Some scientists expect increases in both lethal and nonlethal forms of skin cancer and in cataracts among humans, as well as unpredictable effects on crops and natural communities, especially the phytoplankton that are responsible for a large proportion of Earth's primary production.

To study the consequences of ozone depletion, ecologists have conducted field experiments in which they use filters to decrease or block the UV radiation in sunlight. One such experiment, performed on a scrub ecosystem near the tip of South America, showed that when the ozone hole passed over the area, the amount of UV radiation reaching the ground increased sharply, causing more DNA damage in plants that were not protected by filters. Scientists have shown similar DNA damage and a reduction in phytoplankton growth when the ozone hole opens over the Southern Ocean each year.

The good news about the ozone hole is how quickly many countries have responded to it. Since 1987, more than 190 nations, including the United States, have signed the Montreal Protocol, a treaty that regulates the use of ozone-depleting chemicals. Most nations, again including the United States, have ended the production of CFCs. As a consequence of these actions, chlorine concentrations in the stratosphere have stabilized and ozone depletion is slowing. Even though CFC emissions are close to zero today, however, chlorine molecules already in the atmosphere will continue to influence stratospheric ozone levels for at least 50 years.

The partial destruction of Earth's ozone shield is one more example of how much humans have been able to disrupt the dynamics of ecosystems and the biosphere. It also highlights our ability to solve environmental problems when we set our minds to it.

❶ Chlorine from CFCs interacts with ozone (O_3), forming chlorine monoxide (ClO) and oxygen (O_2).

Chlorine atom

Chlorine O_3

O_2

O_2

ClO

ClO

❸ Sunlight causes Cl_2O_2 to break down into O_2 and free chlorine atoms. The chlorine atoms can begin the cycle again.

Sunlight

Cl_2O_2

❷ Two ClO molecules react, forming chlorine peroxide (Cl_2O_2).

▲ Figure 56.30 How free chlorine in the atmosphere destroys ozone.

1. How can the addition of excess mineral nutrients to a lake threaten its fish population?
2. **MAKE CONNECTIONS** There are vast stores of organic matter in the soils of northern coniferous forests and tundra around the world. Based on what you learned about decomposition from Figure 55.15 (p. 1230), suggest an explanation for why scientists who study global warming are closely monitoring these stores.
3. **MAKE CONNECTIONS** Concept 17.5 (p. 346) describes the action of mutagens, chemical and physical agents that induce mutations in DNA. How does reduced ozone concentration in the atmosphere increase the likelihood of mutations in various organisms?

For suggested answers, see Appendix A.

CONCEPT 56.5

Sustainable development can improve human lives while conserving biodiversity

With the increasing loss and fragmentation of habitats and changes in Earth's climate and physical environment, we face difficult trade-offs in managing the world's resources. Preserving all habitat patches isn't feasible, so biologists must help societies set conservation priorities by identifying which habitat patches are most crucial. Ideally, implementing these priorities should also improve the quality of life for local people. Ecologists use the concept of *sustainability* as a tool to establish long-term conservation priorities.

Sustainable Biosphere Initiative

We need to understand the interconnections of the biosphere if we are to protect species from extinction and improve the quality of human life. To this end, many nations, scientific societies, and other groups have embraced the concept of **sustainable development**, economic development that meets the needs of people today without limiting the ability of future generations to meet their needs. The forward-looking Ecological Society of America, the world's largest organization of professional ecologists, endorses a research agenda called the Sustainable Biosphere Initiative. The goal of this initiative is to define and acquire the basic ecological information needed to develop, manage, and conserve Earth's resources as responsibly as possible. The research agenda includes studies of global change, including interactions between climate and ecological processes; biological diversity and its role in maintaining ecological processes; and the ways in which the productivity of natural and artificial ecosystems can be sustained. This initiative requires a strong commitment of human and economic resources.

Achieving sustainable development is an ambitious goal. To sustain ecosystem processes and stem the loss of biodiversity, we must connect life science with the social sciences, economics, and the humanities. We must also reassess our personal values. Those of us living in wealthier nations have a larger ecological footprint than do people living in developing nations (see Chapter 53). By reducing our orientation toward short-term gain, we can learn to value the natural processes that sustain us. The following case study illustrates how the combination of scientific and personal efforts can make a significant difference in creating a truly sustainable world.

Case Study: *Sustainable Development in Costa Rica*

The success of conservation in Costa Rica that we discussed in Concept 56.3 has required a partnership between the national government, nongovernment organizations (NGOs), and private citizens. Many nature reserves established by individuals have been recognized by the government as national wildlife reserves and given significant tax benefits. However, conservation and restoration of biodiversity make up only one facet of sustainable development; the other key facet is improving the human condition.

How have the living conditions of the Costa Rican people changed as the country has pursued its conservation goals? As we discussed in Chapter 53, two of the most fundamental indicators of living conditions are infant mortality rate and life expectancy. From 1930 to 2009, the infant mortality rate in Costa Rica declined from 170 to 9 per 1,000 live births; over the same period, life expectancy increased from about 43 years to 78 years **(Figure 56.32)**. Another indicator of living conditions is the literacy rate. The 2004 literacy rate in Costa Rica was 96%, compared to 97% in the United States. Such statistics show that living conditions in Costa Rica have

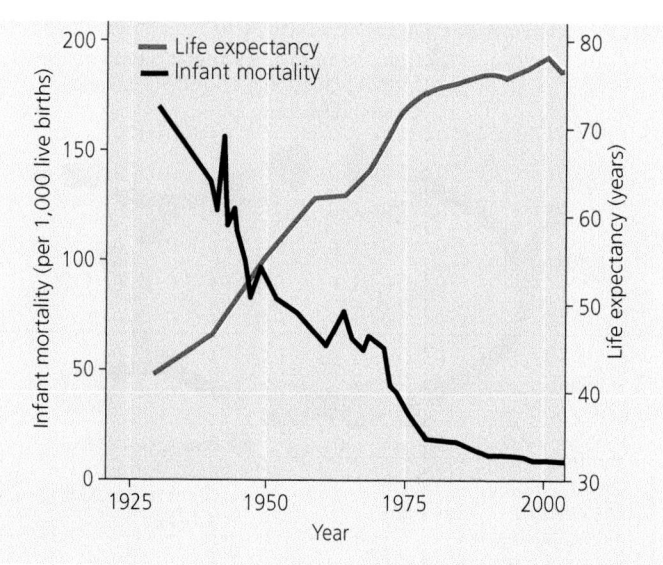

▲ **Figure 56.32 Infant mortality and life expectancy at birth in Costa Rica.**

improved greatly over the period in which the country has dedicated itself to conservation and restoration. While this result does not prove that conservation *causes* an improvement in human welfare, we can say with certainty that development in Costa Rica has attended to both nature *and* people.

Despite the successes in Costa Rica, many problems remain. One of the challenges that Costa Rica faces is maintaining its commitment to conservation while its population grows. Costa Rica is in the middle of a rapid demographic transition (see Chapter 53), and even though birth rates are dropping rapidly, its population is growing at about 1.5% annually. The population, which is currently about 4 million, is predicted to continue to grow until the middle of this century, when it is projected to level off at approximately 6 million. If recent success is any guide, the people of Costa Rica will overcome the challenge of population growth in their quest for sustainable development.

(a) Detail of animals in a 36,000-year-old cave painting, Lascaux, France

(b) A 30,000-year-old ivory carving of a water bird, found in Germany

(c) Nature lovers on a wildlife-watching expedition

▲ **Figure 56.33 Biophilia, past and present.**

The Future of the Biosphere

Our modern lives are very different from those of early humans, who hunted and gathered to survive. Their reverence for the natural world is evident in the early murals of wildlife they painted on cave walls **(Figure 56.33a)** and in the stylized visions of life they sculpted from bone and ivory **(Figure 56.33b)**.

Our lives reflect remnants of our ancestral attachment to nature and the diversity of life—the concept of *biophilia* that was introduced early in this chapter. We evolved in natural environments rich in biodiversity, and we still have an affinity for such settings **(Figure 56.33c, d)**. E. O. Wilson makes the case that our biophilia is innate, an evolutionary product of natural selection acting on a brainy species whose survival depended on a close connection to the environment and a practical appreciation of plants and animals.

Our appreciation of life guides the field of biology today. We celebrate life by deciphering the genetic code that makes each species unique. We embrace life by using fossils and DNA to chronicle evolution through time. We preserve life through our efforts to classify and protect the millions of species on Earth. We respect life by using nature responsibly and reverently to improve human welfare.

Biology is the scientific expression of our desire to know nature. We are most likely to protect what we appreciate, and we are most likely to appreciate what we understand. By learning about the processes and diversity of life, we also become more aware of ourselves and our place in the biosphere. We hope this book has served you well in this lifelong adventure.

CONCEPT CHECK 56.5

1. What is meant by the term *sustainable development*?
2. How might biophilia influence us to conserve species and restore ecosystems?
3. **WHAT IF?** Suppose a new fishery is discovered, and you are put in charge of developing it sustainably. What ecological data might you want on the fish population? What criteria would you apply for the fishery's development?

For suggested answers, see Appendix A.

(d) A young biologist holding a songbird

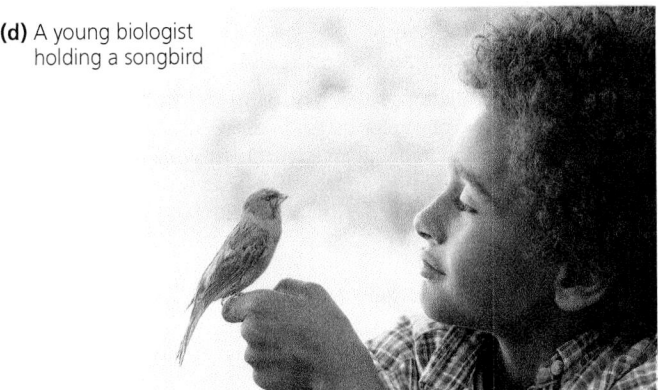

SUMMARY OF KEY CONCEPTS

CONCEPT 56.1

Human activities threaten Earth's biodiversity (pp. 1239–1244)

- Biodiversity can be considered at three main levels:

Genetic diversity: source of variations that enable populations to adapt to environmental changes

Species diversity: important in maintaining structure of communities and food webs

Ecosystem diversity: provides life-sustaining services such as nutrient cycling and waste decomposition

- Our biophilia enables us to recognize the value of biodiversity for its own sake. Other species also provide humans with food, fiber, medicines, and **ecosystem services**.
- Four major threats to biodiversity are habitat loss, **introduced species**, overharvesting, and global change.

> ? *Give at least three examples of key ecosystem services that nature provides for people.*

CONCEPT 56.2

Population conservation focuses on population size, genetic diversity, and critical habitat (pp. 1244–1249)

- When a population drops below a **minimum viable population (MVP)** size, its loss of genetic variation due to nonrandom mating and genetic drift can trap it in an **extinction vortex**.
- The declining-population approach focuses on the environmental factors that cause decline, regardless of absolute population size. It follows a step-by-step conservation strategy.
- Conserving species often requires resolving conflicts between the habitat needs of **endangered species** and human demands.

> ? *Why is the minimum viable population size smaller for a population that is more genetically diverse than it is for a less genetically diverse population?*

CONCEPT 56.3

Landscape and regional conservation help sustain biodiversity (pp. 1249–1254)

- The structure of a landscape can strongly influence biodiversity. As habitat fragmentation increases and edges become more extensive, biodiversity tends to decrease. **Movement corridors** can promote dispersal and help sustain populations.
- **Biodiversity hot spots** are also hot spots of extinction and thus prime candidates for protection. Sustaining biodiversity in parks and reserves requires management to ensure that human activities in the surrounding landscape do not harm the protected habitats. The **zoned reserve** model recognizes that conservation efforts often involve working in landscapes that are greatly affected by human activity.

> ? *Give two examples that show how habitat fragmentation can harm species in the long term.*

CONCEPT 56.4

Earth is changing rapidly as a result of human actions (pp. 1254–1260)

- Agriculture removes plant nutrients from ecosystems, so large supplements are usually required. The nutrients in fertilizer can pollute groundwater and surface-water aquatic ecosystems, where they can stimulate excess algal growth (eutrophication).
- The release of toxic wastes has polluted the environment with harmful substances that often persist for long periods and become increasingly concentrated in successively higher trophic levels of food webs (**biological magnification**).
- Because of the burning of wood and fossil fuels and other human activities, the atmospheric concentration of CO_2 and other greenhouse gases has been steadily increasing. The ultimate effects include significant global warming and other changes in climate.
- The ozone layer reduces the penetration of UV radiation through the atmosphere. Human activities, notably the release of chlorine-containing pollutants, have eroded the ozone layer, but government policies are helping to solve the problem.

> ? *In the face of biological magnification of toxins, is it healthier to feed at a lower or higher trophic level? Explain.*

CONCEPT 56.5

Sustainable development can improve human lives while conserving biodiversity (pp. 1260–1261)

- The goal of the Sustainable Biosphere Initiative is to acquire the ecological information needed for the development, management, and conservation of Earth's resources.
- Costa Rica's success in conserving tropical biodiversity has involved a partnership among the government, other organizations, and private citizens. Human living conditions in Costa Rica have improved along with ecological conservation.
- By learning about biological processes and the diversity of life, we become more aware of our close connection to the environment and the value of other organisms that share it.

> ? *Why is sustainability such an important goal for conservation biologists?*

LEVEL 1: KNOWLEDGE/COMPREHENSION

1. One characteristic that distinguishes a population in an extinction vortex from most other populations is that
   a. its habitat is fragmented.
   b. it is a rare, top-level predator.
   c. its effective population size is much lower than its total population size.
   d. its genetic diversity is very low.
   e. it is not well adapted to edge conditions.

2. The main cause of the increase in the amount of CO_2 in Earth's atmosphere over the past 150 years is
   a. increased worldwide primary production.
   b. increased worldwide standing crop.
   c. an increase in the amount of infrared radiation absorbed by the atmosphere.
   d. the burning of larger amounts of wood and fossil fuels.
   e. additional respiration by the rapidly growing human population.

3. What is the single greatest threat to biodiversity?
   a. overharvesting of commercially important species
   b. introduced species that compete with native species
   c. pollution of Earth's air, water, and soil
   d. disruption of trophic relationships as more and more prey species become extinct
   e. habitat alteration, fragmentation, and destruction

LEVEL 2: APPLICATION/ANALYSIS

4. Which of the following is a consequence of biological magnification?
   a. Toxic chemicals in the environment pose greater risk to top-level predators than to primary consumers.
   b. Populations of top-level predators are generally smaller than populations of primary consumers.
   c. The biomass of producers in an ecosystem is generally higher than the biomass of primary consumers.
   d. Only a small portion of the energy captured by producers is transferred to consumers.
   e. The amount of biomass in the producer level of an ecosystem decreases if the producer turnover time increases.

5. Which of the following strategies would most rapidly increase the genetic diversity of a population in an extinction vortex?
   a. Capture all remaining individuals in the population for captive breeding followed by reintroduction to the wild.
   b. Establish a reserve that protects the population's habitat.
   c. Introduce new individuals transported from other populations of the same species.
   d. Sterilize the least fit individuals in the population.
   e. Control populations of the endangered population's predators and competitors.

6. Of the following statements about protected areas that have been established to preserve biodiversity, which one is *not* correct?
   a. About 25% of Earth's land area is now protected.
   b. National parks are one of many types of protected areas.
   c. Most protected areas are too small to protect species.
   d. Management of a protected area should be coordinated with management of the land surrounding the area.
   e. It is especially important to protect biodiversity hot spots.

LEVEL 3: SYNTHESIS/EVALUATION

7. **DRAW IT** Using Figure 56.27 as a starting point, extend the *x*-axis to the year 2100. Then extend the CO_2 curve, assuming that the CO_2 concentration continues to rise as fast as it did from 1974 to 2009. What will be the approximate CO_2 concentration in 2100? What ecological factors and human decisions will influence the actual rise in CO_2 concentration? How might additional scientific data help societies predict this value?

8. **EVOLUTION CONNECTION**
   Concept 25.4 (pp. 521–523) described five mass extinction events in Earth's history. Many ecologists think we are currently entering a sixth mass extinction event because of the threats to biodiversity described in this chapter. Briefly discuss the history of mass extinctions and the length of time it typically takes for species diversity to recover through the process of evolution. Explain why this should motivate us to slow the loss of biodiversity today.

9. **SCIENTIFIC INQUIRY**
   DRAW IT Suppose that you are managing a forest reserve, and one of your goals is to protect local populations of woodland birds from parasitism by the brown-headed cowbird. You know that female cowbirds usually do not venture more than about 100 m into a forest and that nest parasitism is reduced when woodland birds nest away from forest edges. The reserve you manage extends about 6,000 m from east to west and 1,000 m from north to south. It is surrounded by a deforested pasture on the west, an agricultural field for 500 m in the southwest corner, and intact forest everywhere else. You must build a road, 10 m by 1,000 m, from the north to the south side of the reserve and construct a maintenance building that will take up 100 m² in the reserve. Draw a map of the reserve, showing where you would put the road and the building to minimize cowbird intrusion along edges. Explain your reasoning.

10. **WRITE ABOUT A THEME**

    Feedback Regulation One factor favoring rapid population growth by an introduced species is the absence of the predators, parasites, and pathogens that controlled its population in the region where it evolved. In a short essay (100–150 words), explain how evolution by natural selection would influence the rate at which native predators, parasites, and pathogens in a region of introduction attack an introduced species.

For selected answers, see Appendix A.

www.masteringbiology.com

1. MasteringBiology® Assignments

Tutorial Biodiversity
Activities Habitat Fragmentation • Madagascar and the Biodiversity Crisis • Introduced Species: Fire Ants • Discovery Channel Video: Introduced Species • GraphIt!: Forestation Change; Global Fisheries and Overfishing; Municipal Solid Waste Trends in the U.S. • Discovery Channel Video: Rain Forests • Water Pollution from Nitrates • The Greenhouse Effect • GraphIt!: Global Fresh Water Resources; Atmospheric CO_2 and Temperature Changes; Prospects for Renewable Energy • Conservation Biology Review
Questions Student Misconceptions • Reading Quiz • Multiple Choice • End-of-Chapter

2. eText
Read your book online, search, take notes, highlight text, and more.

3. The Study Area
Practice Tests • Cumulative Test • **BioFlix** 3-D Animations • MP3 Tutor Sessions • Videos • Activities • Investigations • Lab Media • Audio Glossary • Word Study Tools • Art

A Short Guide to Writing about Biology, Seventh Edition

by Jan A. Pechenik

GENERAL ADVICE ON READING AND NOTE-TAKING

The truth is that badly written papers are most often written by people who are not clear in their own minds what they want to say.

JOHN MADDOX

That is one of the worst feelings I can think of, to have had a wonderful moment or insight or vision or phrase, to know you had it, and then to lose it. So now I use index cards.

ANNE LAMOTT

WHY READ AND WHAT TO READ

The **primary literature** is based on original observations and experiments, and includes detailed information about how those observations or experiments were made or conducted. Articles encompassing this primary literature are published (after being reviewed and evaluated by other scientists—a process called "peer review") in formal research journals such as *Science*, *Ecology*, *Genome Biology*, and *BMC Neuroscience*. The **secondary literature**, in contrast, is based on summaries of the primary literature. Textbooks, magazine articles, encyclopedia entries, and review articles are examples of the secondary literature.

Reading secondary sources is an excellent way to get up to speed in a new area, but you will generally be learning more about what is known than about what remains to be found out. For most assignments in upper-level biology courses, you will be asked to go beyond the factual foundation of the field and to interpret, evaluate, synthesize, ask new questions, and maybe even design experiments to address some of those questions. To see the basis for—and often the limits of—our current knowledge, you will need to explore the primary research literature. Reading that literature is very different from reading the secondary literature. It's a skill that requires some practice and a bit of guidance.

EFFECTIVE READING

Too many students think of reading as the mechanical act of moving the eyes left to right, line by line, to the end of a page, and repeating the process page after page to the end of a chapter or an assignment. I call this "brain-off" reading. When the last page has been "read," the task is over and it's on to something else. This is, after all, the way we typically watch television: We sit transfixed before the television until the program has ended, and then either change the channel or turn the set off; we've "seen" the program. In the same way, students typically "listen" to a lecture by furiously copying whatever the instructor writes or says, without really thinking about the information as it is presented.

However, **if you hope to develop something worth saying in your writing**, **you must *interact* intellectually with the material**; you must become what I call a "brain-on" reader, wrestling thoughtfully with every sentence, every graph, every illustration, and every table *as you read*. If you don't fully understand some element of what you are reading (including your lecture notes), you must work through the problem until it is resolved rather than skipping over the difficult material and moving along to something more accessible.

This is inevitably a time-consuming process, but you can do a number of things to smooth the way. Whether you are writing an essay or a review paper, the Introduction or Discussion section of a laboratory report or research article, or the introduction to an oral presentation, always begin by carefully reading the appropriate sections of your textbook and class notes to get a solid overview of your general subject. It is usually wise to then consult 1 or 2 additional textbooks before venturing into the primary literature to read about the results of original research; a solid construction requires a firm foundation. Your instructor may have placed a number of pertinent textbooks on reserve in your college library. Alternatively, you can consult the library on-line catalog, looking for books listed under the topic you are investigating. Science encyclopedias, such as the *McGraw-Hill Encyclopedia of Science and Technology*, are also excellent sources of factual information. Wikipedia articles can be good sources of background information, but you should always be skeptical of their accuracy since you don't know the source of the information.

Armed with this background information, you are now prepared to tackle the primary research literature.

Reading a formal scientific paper is unlike reading a work of fiction or even a textbook or review article. The primary scientific literature must be read slowly, thoughtfully, and patiently, and a single paper must usually be reread several times before it can be thoroughly understood. Don't become discouraged after only 1 or 2 readings. As with playing tennis or sight-reading music, reading the primary literature gets easier with practice. If, after several rereadings of the paper, and if, after consulting several textbooks, you are still baffled by something in the paper you are reading, ask your instructor for help.

As you carefully read each paper, pay special attention to the following:

- What specific questions were asked?
- How was the study designed, and how does the design of the study address the question posed?
- What are the controls for each experiment?
- What are the specific results of the study? How convincing are they? Are any of the results surprising?
- What assumptions were made? Do they seem reasonable?
- What contribution does the study make toward answering the original question?
- What aspects of the original question remain unanswered?

You can answer many of these questions just by studying the figures and tables in the Results section, as described below.

If you are planning to write a research proposal, you should ask one additional question:

- What question(s) would I ask next?

As discussed below, you should spend most of your time looking at the original data presented in the papers you read.

READING DATA: PLUMBING THE DEPTHS OF FIGURES AND TABLES

Data—the most important parts of any book or journal article—are displayed either in figures or in tables; both must be examined critically. Your goal here is to come to your own interpretation of the data so that you can better understand or evaluate the author's interpretation. To do this, **you must study the data and ask yourself some questions about how the study was done, why it was done, and what the major findings were**.

Consider the example shown in Figure 1, modified from a review paper by David E. Cochrane entitled "Peptide regulation of mast-cell function." From your background reading or class lecture notes, you would probably know that mast cells release into the blood a variety of substances involved in provoking allergic and inflammatory responses. If you didn't already know this, you would do some background reading in your textbook before proceeding.

Looking at Figure 1, let us see if we can figure out what the researchers did to collect their data. By reading the axis labels, we learn that the graph shows how blood histamine concentrations changed over time, and we learn from the figure caption that these changes were provoked by a particular peptide called neurotensin. The study was done on anesthetized rats and all the action seems to have occurred rather quickly, since the x-axis extends only to 30 minutes. Looking more closely, we see that histamine concentrations were initially quite low (less than 1 nanogram° per 10 microliters°° of blood plasma), as indicated by the arrow (at the lower left side of the graph), and that they rose impressively by the time the first blood sample was taken 1 minute into the study. Other blood samples were taken 3, 15, and 30 minutes after neurotensin was administered, and 3 to 8 separate samples were taken at each time period. Even without reading the figure caption and without seeing the numbers alongside each data point, we would know that replicate samples were taken, because the thin lines extending vertically from each point indicate the amount of variation seen about the mean value recorded for each sampling time; obviously, one can see variation about a mean value only when multiple samples were taken.

°1 nanogram (ng) = 10^{-9} gram.
°°1 microliter (µl) = 10^{-6} liter.

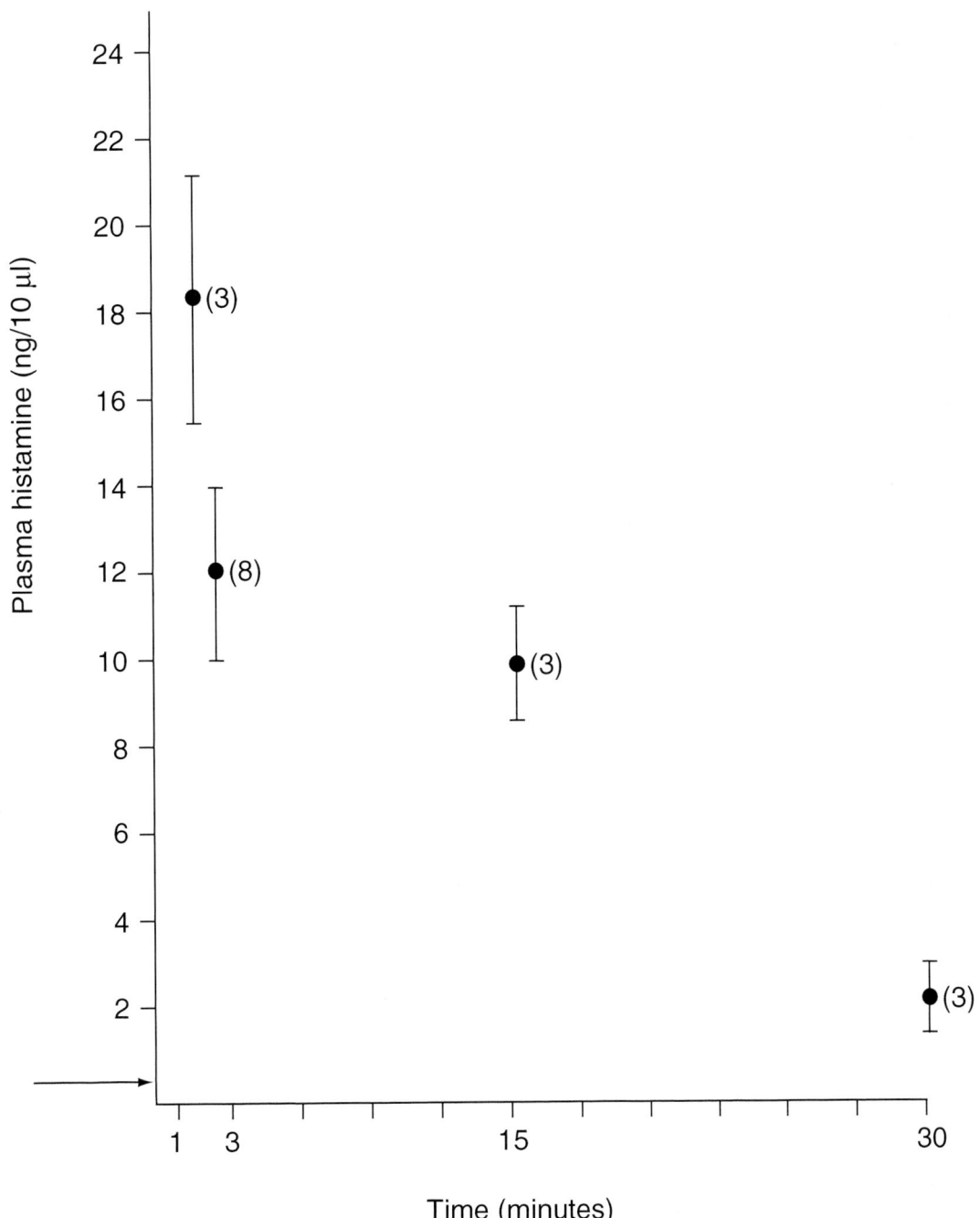

Figure 1. Plasma histamine concentrations in response to neurotensin (NT) given at t = 0. Rats were anesthetized and given NT (5 nmol/kg) or saline (0.3 ml) intravenously. Blood samples were collected at the indicated times. Each point represents the mean (±one standard error about the mean) of n values (given in parentheses). The horizontal arrow (lower left) shows the mean histamine concentration before addition of NT. Intravenous injection of saline did not alter this concentration over the 30-minute observation period.

Source: From Cochrane, D.E., 1990. Peptide regulation of mast-cell function. In *Progr. Medicinal Chemistry*, Vol. 27; G.P. Ellis and G.B. West, eds.; Elsevier Science Publ. (Biomedical Division), pp. 143–188.

　　What were the controls for this experiment? Apparently, a number of rats were injected with a saline solution instead of with neurotensin, and blood samples were also taken from these rats at appropriate times.

　　So, we know quite a bit about how this aspect of the study was conducted just by scrutinizing the graph. It helps considerably that the graph and figure caption were carefully constructed. What additional information might you wish to have? Here are a few questions that might arise as you think about the figure.

1. How did Dr. Cochrane decide to inject neurotensin at a concentration of 5 nmol/kg? Is this a physiologically realistic concentration?
2. How was histamine concentration determined?
3. How many rats served as controls for each time interval?
4. How old were the rats? What sex were they? Where did Dr. Cochrane get them?
5. How were the rats anesthetized, and might this pretreatment have affected their response to neurotensin?
6. With regard to the replicate samples, were 3 to 8 blood samples taken simultaneously from a single rat at each sampling time, or were blood samples taken from 3 to 8 different rats each time? Blood samples were *probably* taken from a number of different individual rats, but we can't be sure from the graph.
7. Were different rats sampled at each time interval, or were the same individuals sampled repeatedly—for example, at 15 minutes and again at 30 minutes? One might guess that the same individuals were sampled repeatedly. On the other hand, there may be technical limitations to drawing blood from any individual rat more than once. Suppose, for instance, that a very large volume of blood was required to determine the histamine concentration. This issue leads to my last 3 questions.
8. What volume of blood was withdrawn for each sample?
9. How were the blood samples obtained? How was the plasma separated from the blood cells before analysis?
10. Does drawing blood influence the production of histamine? How could one tell?

Asking such questions puts you in a good position to interpret the results illustrated and provides a framework for your later reading of the Materials and Methods section of the report; you can now enter the methodology section of the paper looking for the answers to specific questions.

If asked to describe how this aspect of the study was conducted and why the study was probably undertaken, how might you respond? Even without reading anything else in the paper, **you could write the following summary**:

> This study was apparently undertaken to determine the ability of the peptide neurotensin to elicit histamine secretion from mast cells. A number of rats were anesthetized and then injected intravenously with 5 nmol/kg of neurotensin, whereas others (control rats) received intravenous injections of saline solution to control for the possibility that the act of injection itself provoked histamine release. Some quantity of blood was withdrawn from a number of rats 1, 3, 15, or 30 minutes after injections were made, and the histamine concentration in each blood sample was somehow determined.

Now, in a few short sentences, let us try to summarize the results, beginning with the most general statements we can make.

1. Neurotensin had a dramatic and rapid effect on histamine concentrations in the blood of laboratory rats, with histamine concentration increasing by about 20 times within 1 minute after injection.
2. The effect seems rather short-lived; only 2 minutes into the study, the histamine concentrations had already fallen considerably from the peak level recorded 1 minute earlier.
3. By 30 minutes after the injection, the mean histamine concentration approached initial levels.
4. The effect shown is clearly due to the peptide rather than the procedure itself, because histamine concentrations in the blood of control rats receiving saline injections did not change appreciably during the study.

Summarizing information as you read is one of the best ways to digest the material and generate new ideas, as discussed in the next section.

You can approach tabular data in the same way, first reading the accompanying legend and column headings and then asking yourself *how* the study was done, *why* it might have been undertaken, and *what* the key general results seem to be. If the tables were prepared with as much care as the figure we just looked at, you should be able to answer each of those questions.

For example, take a look at Table 1. For some reason, the authors wanted to know if 3 types of predatory cat in Peru ate the same foods, and they came up with an ingenious way of addressing that question. I'll let you think about why they might have asked the question. Reading the table legend, you know where the study was conducted, what the data represent, and what "n" stands for. Looking at the table, you know what predators were of interest and the 7 categories of prey found in their feces. How do you think the study was done? Looking now at the data, how much did the predators overlap in diet? Did each predator specialize on any one type of prey? Did all 3 predators specialize on the same prey? Did each predator eat at least some prey from each category? The more you look at the data, the more you will see, and the more questions you will ask. What questions would you like to ask the authors? What question would you ask next if you were going to continue this study?

Apply the same procedure figure by figure, table by table, until you reach the last bit of data. Now it is safe to actually read the text of the paper. Perhaps you will find the author reaching conclusions different from your own. You may have missed some crucial element in studying the data yourself, or perhaps you will learn something crucial in the text of the paper that was not made clear in the figure. If so, you can then happily leave your own opinion behind and embrace the author's. On the other hand, you may genuinely disagree with the conclusion reached by the paper's author (or authors), or you may object to the author's interpretation

Table 1. The diets of 3 predatory cats from Rio Manu, Peru, inferred from fecal samples collected in nature. An entry of 5% (top left) means that fish, in this case, made up 5% of all the prey items found in the feces from that predator. The data are based on the minimum number of prey that must have been eaten to have obtained the number of bones of each type collected. n = number of feces examined from each kind of predator.

Kind of prey eaten	Name of predator			Total from all predators
	Jaguar (n = 40)	Puma (n = 12)	Ocelot (n = 177)	
Fish	5%	0%	2%	7%
Reptiles	33%	17%	12%	62%
Small rodents and opossums	8%	17%	66%	91%
Large rodents	15%	58%	5%	78%
Other large mammals	23%	0%	0%	23%
Birds	10%	0%	11%	21%
Bats	5%	8%	5%	18%
Total	99%	100%	101%	

Based on Emmons, L.H. 1987. *Behav. Ecol. Sociobiol.* 20: 271–283.

because of some concern you have about the method used. This is, in fact, how new questions often get asked in science, and how new studies get designed, with each new step building on the work of others. Most of us will never have the final say in any particular research area, but we can each contribute a valuable next step, even if our individual interpretation of that step turns out to be mildly— or even dramatically—wrong.

Thinking about figures and tables in these ways, you may be on your way to a productive scientific career, research project in hand. At the very least, you will be in an excellent position to *discuss* the paper, either on its own or in relationship to other studies that you will go on to scrutinize just as thoroughly.

If you don't go through these steps in "reading" the data, you will be all too accepting of the author's interpretation. In consequence, you will have considerable difficulty avoiding the book report format in your writing, simply repeating what others did and what they say they found. You can move your work to a higher, more interesting plane (more interesting for you and for the reader) by becoming a brain-on reader. It's tough slogging, and although it becomes considerably easier with practice, it never becomes trivial. But it does become enjoyable, and satisfying, in the same way that a good tennis game can be enjoyable and satisfying, even when played in hot, humid weather.

READING TEXT: SUMMARIZE AS YOU GO

Resist the temptation to copy your source's words verbatim, or simply to highlight them. Instead, try to summarize chunks of material as you read along, as in the neurotensin example discussed earlier (p. 1270). In that way, you will be processing information as you read it, which moves you one major step closer to having something interesting to write about later.

To summarize effectively, you must first determine the most important points in the material you wish to summarize. Consider the following paragraph from Rachel Carson's landmark book *Silent Spring*.° For many people, this book, first published in 1962, marks the start of the environmental movement.

> Water, soil, and the earth's green mantle of plants make up the world that supports the animal life of the earth. Although modern man seldom remembers the fact, he could not exist without the plants that harness the sun's energy and manufacture the basic foodstuffs he depends upon for life. Our attitude toward plants is a singularly narrow one. If we see any immediate utility in a plant we foster it. If for any reason we find its presence undesirable or merely a matter of indifference, we may condemn it to destruction forthwith. Besides the various plants that are poisonous to man or his livestock, or crowd out food plants, many are marked for destruction merely because, according to our narrow view, they happen to be in the wrong place at the wrong time. Many others are destroyed merely because they happen to be associates of the unwanted plants.

° I have not altered the original wording, with its anachronistic use of what is now generally considered to be sexist writing. If Rachel Carson were writing this today, she would most likely replace "modern man" with "people," and "he" with "we." This would actually strengthen the paragraph, by pointing the finger clearly at all of us.

What are the key points in this paragraph? What information would Ms. Carson be unhappy to see left out?

- All animals, including people, depend on plants for food.
- People think little about the consequences of destroying plants that annoy them or don't seem to do anything useful.

Here is a possible one-sentence summary that incorporates both of these points:

> People destroy any plant that happens to annoy them or doesn't seem to do anything useful, forgetting the extent to which all animal life ultimately depends on photosynthesis.

This summary is (1) **accurate**, (2) **complete**—it incorporates all major points, (3) **self-sufficient**—it makes good sense even if the reader has never read the original text, and (4) **in my own words**. Get in the habit of writing such summaries as you read and as you take notes in lecture. It is a real challenge, but one that gets easier with practice. Persist: The eventual payoff is tremendous. Moreover, summarizing in your own words is an excellent way to avoid plagiarism, as discussed below.

PLAGIARISM AND NOTE-TAKING

Plagiarism

The paper or report you submit for evaluation must be original: It must be *your* work. **Submitting anyone else's work under your own name is plagiarism**, even if you alter some words or reorder some sentences. **Presenting someone else's ideas as your own is also plagiarism.** Consider the following 2 paragraphs:

> Smith (1991) suggests that this discrepancy in feeding rates may reflect differences in light intensities used in the two different experiments. Jones (1994), however, found that light intensity did not influence the feeding rates of these animals and suggested that the rate differences reflect differences in the density at which the animals were held during the two experiments.

> This discrepancy in feeding rates might reflect differences in light intensities. Jones (1994), however, found that light level did not influence feeding rates. Perhaps the difference in rates reflects differences in the density at which the animals were held during the two experiments.

The first example is fine: Every idea is clearly associated with its source. In the second example, however, the writer takes credit for the ideas of Smith and Jones; the writer has plagiarized.

As another example, consider this student's summary sentence based on the Rachel Carson passage presented on p. 1271:

> The world that supports the animal life on planet earth is made up of water, soil, and a green mantle of plants.

That's plagiarism in action. This is not:

> Rachel Carson (1962) stresses that animal life on our planet could not exist without plants.

The second student has *processed* information; the first student has not.

Plagiarism is theft. It is one of the most serious offenses that can be committed in academia, where original thought is the major product of one's work—often months, sometimes years of physical and mental work. At the very least, an act of plagiarism will result in an F on the assignment, or for the entire course. Repeated plagiarism (but sometimes even a single offense) can get you expelled from college.

And now for the really bad news: **Plagiarism is getting easier to detect.** Computer programs designed to detect plagiarism are now being used at more and more colleges and universities (and by more scientific journal editors). Such programs, like Turnitin, search enormous databases that include millions of pages from books and journals, millions of Web sites, and tens of millions of papers previously submitted by college students across the country.

Doing a Google search on the phrase "avoiding plagiarism" brought back over 360,000 entries, so plagiarism is clearly a problem of great concern to many people. Intentional plagiarism (e.g., copying text directly from a Web site, or putting your own name on a paper written by someone else) is easy to avoid: Just don't do it! But some plagiarism is unintentional; how do you avoid that? One approach is to read widely. If all you know about a particular topic is what you have read in your laboratory manual or textbook, your options for original thinking will be limited. The more you read, the more you will have to draw on in expressing your own thoughts.

Plagiarism can also occur unintentionally through bad note-taking practices. **Take notes in ways that minimize the likelihood of plagiarism**, as discussed below. An added benefit of these note-taking techniques is that you will come away with a much greater understanding of what you read, and you will have much more substantive things to talk about and write about.

Another way to help avoid unintentional plagiarism is to write your first draft without looking at your notes. If you can't do this, you're probably not ready to write anyway.

Take Notes in Your Own Words

Photocopying an article or book chapter does not constitute note-taking; neither does highlighting or even copying a passage by hand, occasionally substituting a synonym for a word used by the source's author. Take notes using your own words; you must get away from being awed by other people's words and move toward building confidence in your own thoughts and phrasings.

Note-taking involves critical evaluation; as you read, you must decide either that particular facts or ideas are relevant to your topic or that they are irrelevant. As Sylvan Barnet says in *A Short Guide to Writing about Art* (2003, Pearson Longman, seventh edition, p. 251), "You are not doing stenography; rather, you are assimilating knowledge and you are thinking, and so for the most part your source should be digested rather than engorged whole." If an idea is relevant, you should **jot down a summary using your own words** (see p. 1272). Try not to write complete sentences as you take notes; this will help you to avoid unintentional plagiarism later and will encourage you to see through to the essence of a statement while note-taking. For the same reason, **do not take notes or write while you are looking at the source**.

Sometimes an author's words seem so perfect that you cannot see how they might be revised to best advantage for your paper. In this case, you may wish to copy a phrase or a sentence or two verbatim, but be sure to enclose this material in quotation marks as you write, and clearly indicate the source and page number from which the quotation derives. If you modify the original wording slightly as you take notes, you should indicate this as well, perhaps by using modified quotation marks: ⚡. . . ⚡. If your notes on a particular passage are in your own words, you should also indicate this as you write. I precede such notes, reflecting my own ideas or my own choice of words, with the word *Me* and a colon. If you take notes in this manner, you will avoid the unintentional plagiarism that occurs when you later forget who is actually responsible for the wording of your notes or for the origin of an idea.

If you find yourself copying verbatim or paraphrasing your source, be sure it is not simply because you do not understand what you are reading. Be honest with yourself. **It is always best to summarize in your own words as you read along**; at the very least, you should think your way to some good questions about what you are reading, and then write those questions down. Sooner or later, serious intellectual engagement is required; there are no shortcuts available here, I'm afraid.

Here is an example of some notes taken using the suggested system of notation. These notes are based on a paper by William Biggers and Hans Laufer. Figure 2 shows an excerpt from the paper, and Figure 3 shows some notes based on that excerpt. Note that **the student has avoided using complete sentences**, focusing instead on distilling the basic points and pinning down a few words and phrases that might be useful later. Notice also that **the student has taken notes selectively**, has found it unnecessary to quote any of the material directly, and **has clearly distinguished his or her own thoughts** from those of the original authors (by preceding such thoughts with "Me:"). Similarly, the student has distinguished between what the authors did and what the student thinks could be done later or might have influenced the results. Perhaps the most important points are that the note-taker clearly *thought* while reading and took notes in his or her own words. This student will not have to worry about accidental plagiarism when writing a paper based on these notes.

You cannot take notes selectively or in your own words if you do not understand what you are reading. I suggest that you first consult at least one general reference textbook and read that material carefully, as recommended earlier. Once you have located a particularly promising scientific article, read the entire paper at least once without taking any notes. **Resist the (strong) temptation to annotate and take notes during this first reading**, even though you may feel that without a pen in your hand you are accomplishing nothing. Put your pencils, pens, note cards, paper, or laptop computer away, and just read. **Read slowly and with care.** Read to understand. Study the illustrations, figure captions, tables, and graphs carefully, and try to develop your own interpretations before reading those of the author(s). Don't be frustrated by not understanding the paper at the first reading; understanding scientific literature takes time and patience—and often many rereadings, even for practicing biologists. Concentrate not only on the results reported in the paper but also on the reason the study was undertaken and the way the data were obtained. **The results of a study are real; the interpretation of the results is always open to question.** And the interpretation is largely influenced by the way the study was conducted. Read with a critical, questioning eye. Many of the interpretations and conclusions in today's journals will be modified in the future. It is difficult, if not impossible, to have the last word in biology; progress is made by continually building on and modifying the work of others.

Once you have completed your first reading of the paper, you may find that the article is not really relevant to your topic after all, or is of little help in developing your theme. If so, the preliminary read-through will have saved you from wasted note-taking.

People differ in their note-taking styles. Some people suggest taking notes on index cards, with one idea per card so that the notes can be sorted readily into categories at a later stage of the paper's development. If you prefer taking notes on full-size paper, begin a separate page for each new source, and write on only one side of each page to facilitate sorting into categories later. Similarly, if you enter notes directly into a computer, be sure to leave a few lines of space above and below each entry. Whatever system works best for you, that's the one to use. If your present system of note-taking is not working, experiment until you find one that does.

Introduction

The chemoreception by marine invertebrate larvae of chemical "cues" that are present in the ocean environment and induce settlement and metamorphosis is important for the recognition of habitats that favor growth and reproduction (Chia and Rice, 1978; Rittschof and Bonaventura, 1986; Scheuer, 1990). These settlement signals appear to be specific for different species, as evidenced by findings that larvae of the abalone *Haliotis rufescens* respond to specific chemicals in red algae (Morse *et al.*, 1984), larvae of the nudibranch *Phestilla sibogae* respond to chemicals in corals (Hadfield, 1978, 1984), larvae of the polychaete annelid *Phragmatopoma californica* respond to chemicals present in the burrows of adult worms (Pawlik, 1988, 1990; Jensen and Morse, 1990), and larvae of the sand dollars *Dendraster excentricus* (Burke, 1984) and *Echinarachnius parma* (Pearce and Scheibling, 1990) respond to chemicals produced by adult sand dollars. | **1** **2**

In previous studies, we have found that juvenile hormones (JH), which are known morphogens that regulate reproduction and development of insects and crustaceans (Laufer and Borst, 1983, 1988; Laufer *et al.*, 1987), as well as chemicals with juvenile hormone activity in insect cuticle bioassays, are able to induce settlement and metamorphosis of metatrochophore larvae of the polychaete annelid *Capitella* sp. I (Biggers and Laufer, 1992, 1996). In nature, larvae of *Capitella* sp. I are stimulated to settle and metamorphose when they come into contact with chemical inducers present in sediments (Butman *et al.*, 1988); although the identity of these chemicals remains in debate (Cuomo, 1985; Dubilier, 1987), they appear to have JH-activity (Biggers, 1994). | **3**

We have now investigated the signal transduction process through which the *Capitella* larvae respond to JH-active compounds. Our results presented in this paper indicate that JH-active compounds stimulate settlement and metamorphosis of these larvae through the activation of protein kinase C (PKC) and subsequent modulation of ion channels. | **4**

Materials and Methods

Capitella larval settlement bioassays

Stock cultures of *Capitella* sp. I were maintained at 18°C in artificial seawater (Utikem Co.) and washed sea sand (Fisher Scientific) and were fed Tetramin fish food flakes. Brood tubes containing adult females along with their developing eggs and larvae were then separated from the cultures and placed into 60-mm glass Petri dishes containing seawater. The dishes were checked daily for hatched, swimming larvae to be used for bioassays. Stock solutions of juvenile hormone III (JH III), MF, phorbol-12,13 dibutyrate (PDBU), 1-(5-isoquinolinyl-sulfonyl)-2-methylpiperazine (H-7), arachidonic acid, elaidic acid, verapamil, 4-aminopyridine, and nigericin were prepared in 95% ethanol. Settlement and metamorphosis bioassays were conducted at 18°C using 60-mm glass Petri dishes that were pre-baked at 250°C to remove contaminants (Biggers and Laufer, 1996). For the assays, 10 to 100 μl of the test chemical stock solutions were added by micropipette into Petri dishes containing 10 metatrochophore larvae less than 1 day old (1 day post-release), and 10 ml of artificial seawater. The dishes were then observed. After 1 h, the amount of settlement and metamorphosis was assessed by placing each dish under a dissecting microscope and counting the number of settled larvae crawling on the bottom of the dish. Metamorphosis after 1 hour was also more critically assessed by using a compound microscope and noting the loss of cilia, elongation, and development of capillary setae. | **5**

Protein kinase C assays

Assays for the presence of protein kinase C were carried out essentially as described by Yasuda *et al.* (1990), by measuring phosphorylation of an 11-residue synthetic peptide from myelin basic protein (MBP$_{4-14}$). This method is specific for measurement of PKC, and permits selective measurement in crude tissue prepar-

Figure 2. Modified excerpt from "Settlement and metamorphosis of *Capitella* larvae induced by juvenile hormone-active compounds is mediated by protein kinase C and ion channels," by William J. Biggers and Hans Laufer (pp. 187–188), as reprinted from *The Biological Bulletin* 196 (1999): 187–198. Reprinted with permission of *The Biological Bulletin* and the authors, William J. Biggers and Hans Laufer.

1. Marine larvae do not metamorphose until contact chemicals that indicate juveniles will do well here.

2. Larvae of different species respond to different chemicals.
   Me: How many diff. species have been looked at?
   Do we know what the chemical cues are? How (and where?) do the larvae sense them?

3. Larvae of the polychaete <u>Capitella</u> sp. I metamorphose in response to a juvenile hormone-like chemical in mud.
   Me: odd that same chemical works on both insects and worms?
   What distinguishes polych. from other annelids?
   And how big are these larvae? Microscopic I think . . .

   Purpose of this study: How does the juvenile hormone make the larvae metamorphose?

4. Apparently the chem. cue activates "protein kinase C," which then either opens or closes ion channels somewhere (Me: calcium channels maybe?).

5. Methods: Collect larvae $\rightarrow$ expose to very small amounts of chemical ($\leq 100 \mu1*!$) $\xrightarrow[1hr]{}$ count number of larvae that have metam.'d.
   Nine chemicals tested (Me: must find out what each one does).
   * microliters

Figure 3. Handwritten notes based on the article by Biggers and Laufer (see Fig. 2). Numbers in the margin correspond to the indicated portions of Figure 2.

Split-Page Note-Taking: A Can't-Fail System

Perfectly organized notes that cover everything are beautiful, but they live on paper, not in your mind.

PETER ELBOW

If you have trouble taking notes in your own words and thinking as you read, try split-page note-taking. With this system, you divide a piece of paper into left and right halves, either by folding the paper in half lengthwise or by drawing a line down the middle. On the left side of the page, write factual information as you read—preferably in your own words, but it's also okay to quote directly. Then, on the right side of the page, write your response to the entry you just made on the left side. Try to respond to everything that you write on the left as you read. Your response could be a simple question ("What on earth is protein kinase C?"), a more thoughtful question ("How can they know that? First they would have had to measure . . ."), a reminiscence ("That reminds me of what Professor Bolker said in lecture last week about . . ."), or a comparison ("Interesting: The freshwater species have very different life histories"). Write whatever you happen to think of when you look at what you wrote on the left. See Figure 4 for an example of split-page note-taking in action, based on the first few paragraphs of the material presented in Figure 2.

Split-page note-taking may seem like a gimmick. Well, actually it *is* a gimmick, but it's a gimmick that *works*. It works by slowing you down, forcing you to think as you read. Split-page note-taking is also a very effective way to read tables and figures. Try it, for example, in looking at Figure 1 and its caption. Even experienced note-takers often find that they learn something new by taking notes this way.

<u>Facts</u>   <u>Responses</u>

marine invert. larvae are induced   True for <u>all</u> larvae? How many
to metam. by chemical cues   species have been studied?
                                           The larvae are awfully tiny —
                                           what body parts "smell" the
                                           cues? What <u>are</u> the cues?

Different species respond to   Must be pretty widespread.
diff. chem. cues   Examples given incl. a variety
                                           of species from very different
                                           groups.

Juvenile hormone (JH) regulates   Why would juvenile hormone be
insect development, but also   floating around in seawater?
makes polychaete annelid   Maybe it's not—maybe it's
larvae metamorphose   not the chem. cue discussed
                                           in first paragr. but rather
                                           something that acts inside
                                           the larva? Why would an
                                           insect chemical work on a
                                           worm? Are worms and in-
                                           sects closely related?

Figure 4. An example of split-page note-taking, based on the first 2 paragraphs of material presented in Figure 2. The student has recorded factual information on the left side of the page and her response to that information on the right.

Final Thoughts on Note-Taking: Document Your Sources

As you take notes, be sure to make a complete record of each source used: author(s), year of publication, volume and page numbers (if consulting a scientific journal), title of article or book, publisher, and total number of pages (if consulting a book). It is not always easy to relocate a source once it has been returned to the library stacks; in fact, the source you forgot to record completely is always the one that vanishes as soon as you realize that you need it again. Finally, before you finish with a source, it is good practice to read through that source one last time to be sure that your notes accurately reflect the content of what you have read.

SUMMARY

1. Become a brain-on reader: Work to understand your sources fully, sentence by sentence, figure by figure, and table by table.

2. Take notes thoughtfully. In particular, practice summarizing information as you go along. Your summary must be accurate, complete, self-sufficient, and in your own words.

3. In your note-taking, be careful to distinguish your words and thoughts from those of the author(s) to avoid unintentional plagiarism. Be sure to record the complete citation information for everything on which you take notes.

2

CITING SOURCES AND LISTING REFERENCES

As described briefly in previous chapters, **all statements of fact and opinion require support** to be convincing to the thoughtful, critical reader. The firmer the statement, and the more important it is to your argument, the greater the need for support. In research reports (including lab reports), review papers ("term papers"), and theses, factual statements are often supported by reference to the source (or sources) of the facts presented. Therefore, in a separate section at the end of your manuscript, you must list the books, research articles, and Web sites referred to so that they can be located by interested (or skeptical) readers.

In general, your instructor will expect you to cite textbooks, research articles, and review papers published in "peer-reviewed" journals. Articles from some magazines and newspapers may also be acceptable in introductory courses, but you should check with your instructor before including such citations.

CITING SOURCES

Here are a few general rules to follow when citing sources to back up factual statements. These rules apply to review papers, essays, theses, and research reports, and to citations throughout the research report:

1. **Don't footnote: Cite by author and year of publication.** In most published research papers, references are cited directly in the text by author and year of publication, as in the following example:

   > A variety of organic molecules are commonly used to maintain or adjust the osmotic concentration of intracellular fluids (Hochachka and Somero, 1984; Schmidt-Nielsen, 1990).

   Note that the period, both here and in the examples that follow, appears at the end of the closing parenthesis since the reference, including the publication date, is part of the sentence.

   - Where appropriate, you may instead **incorporate the authors' names directly into a sentence**:

     > Kim (1976) demonstrated that magnetic fields established by direct current can alter the rates of enzyme-mediated reactions in cell-free systems.

   or

     > The ability of magnetic fields established by direct current to alter the activity of certain liver enzymes was first demonstrated by Kim (1976).

   - Try to **make the relevance of the cited reference clear** to the reader. For example, rather than writing:

     > Temperature tolerances have been determined for gastropods, bivalves, annelids, and insects (Merz, 1988; Heibert Burch, 1998; Merz and Heibert Burch, 1993 a, b).

   it would be clearer to write

     > Temperature tolerances have been determined for gastropods (Merz, 1988), bivalves and annelids (Heibert Burch, 1998), and insects (Merz and Heibert Burch, 1993 a, b).

   - When **more than 2 authors** have collaborated on a single publication, a shortcut is standard practice:

     > A mutation is defined as any change occurring in the nitrogenous base sequence of DNA (Tortora *et al.*, 1982).

The *et al.* **is an abbreviation for** *et alii*, meaning "and others." The words are underlined or italicized, even when abbreviated, because they are in a foreign language, Latin; underlining tells a printer to set the designated words or letters in italics. Note that there is no period after the "*et*".

- If you cite **2 papers published in a single year by the same author**, use letters to distinguish between them: (Asmodeus and Li, 1998 a, b) or (Asmodeus *et al.*, 1999 a, b).

- You can **cite your laboratory manual** by its author (e.g., Professor S. Heibert Burch, 1999) or as follows:

  Preparation of buffers and other solutions is described elsewhere (Biology 1 Laboratory Manual, Swarthmore College, 1999).

- If your information comes from a **lecture or from a conversation** with a particular individual, support your statement as follows:

  California gray whales migrate up to 18,000 km yearly (Professor Chuck Booth, personal communication, September 2005).

- **In some biological journals, the "author–year" format for citing references has been replaced by a more compact "number-sequence" format.** In the number-sequence format, each reference cited in the paper is represented by a unique number. The first paper to be cited is assigned the number 1, the second paper to be cited is assigned the number 2, and so forth, as in the following example:

  Substantial declines in amphibian populations have been documented from numerous locations around the world over the past 40 years (3,5, 8–12).

  The numerals 3 and 5 represent the 3rd and 5th references to have been cited in the student's paper. Earlier in the paper, the author must have cited references 1 through 7. References 3 and 5, although cited earlier in the paper, are relevant here and so are cited again using the same numbers.

  Unless your instructor asks you to adopt the number-sequence format in your own work, use the author–year format discussed earlier. For one thing, it is a nuisance for readers to have to keep turning to the back of a paper to see whose work is being cited. Moreover, biologists commonly refer to particular papers by their author(s) and year of publication ("Have you read Booth and Gable, 2002, yet?"), and using the author–year format of citing references helps you remember who did what, and when. But perhaps most importantly, research papers are written by real people, and as you become more familiar with the literature in any particular field, you will find yourself coming across many of the same names repeatedly. Using the author–year format is a good way to learn which people are best associated with your field of interest. Perhaps you will decide to do graduate work with one of these people in the future.

2. **Be concise in citing references.** Avoid writing:

   In his classic work, *The Biology of Marine Animals*, published in 1967, Colin Nicol reviewed the literature on invertebrate bioluminescence.

   Instead, write:

   The phenomenon of invertebrate bioluminescence was carefully reviewed by Nicol (1967).

   Again, the period follows the parenthesis.

3. **Cite only those sources you have actually read and would feel confident discussing with your instructor.** Don't list references simply to add bulk to this section of your report; your instructor is perfectly justified in expecting you to be able to discuss any material you cite. Listing a few references you have thoughtfully incorporated into your paper should do more for your grade than an attempt to create the illusion that you have read everything in the library.

   You may occasionally have to cite a source that you have not actually read. For example, results reported by Hendler (1999) may be cited in a book or article written by Dufus (2003), and you have read only the work by Dufus. Your citation should then read "(Hendler, 1999, as cited by Dufus, 2003)." Let Dufus take the blame if he or she has misinterpreted something. In the Literature Cited section of your report, you would include both sources.

4. If **citing a review paper that does not include the original data supporting a particular statement** that you wish to make, cite the reference as "... (reviewed by Furhman, 2004)."

5. **Avoid citation overkill.** When discussing a series of facts from a single source or group of sources, it is not necessary to cite the same source(s) in every sentence. There are many ways of informing the reader that a series of sentences is based on a single source of information, as in the following example:

> Hochachka and Somero (1984) discuss the physiological adaptations of diving mammals in considerable detail. In particular, they note that diving Weddell seals exhibit a pronounced decline in both rate of metabolism and ATP turnover rate. In one experiment, ATP turnover rates were reduced by as much as 50% during a 20-minute dive.

6. When citing an on-line journal, use the same format (author, year of "publication") as for a hard-copy journal.

7. Don't cite personal Web sites, or any other Web sites (e.g., Wikipedia) that publish information without verifiable authoritative review.

   Information posted on Web sites is ephemeral and has usually not been peer-reviewed: Avoid using Web pages as sources of information unless you are fully confident of the accuracy of the material presented. In general, this means relying only on peer-reviewed electronic journals or Web sites maintained by recognized scientific authorities, such as those associated with major museums and research institutions, or by government organizations, such as the U.S. Department of Agriculture (USDA), the National Oceanic and Atmospheric Administration (NOAA), and the World Health Organization (WHO). Such Web sites will include ".edu", ".gov", or ".org" in their URLs. If you have any questions about whether a Web site is valid, ask your instructor.

SUMMARY OF CITATION FORMAT RULES

- **Use the author–year format** for citing references unless you are told otherwise by your instructor or unless you are submitting a manuscript to a journal using a different (number-citation) format.
- **Cite authors only by their last names** unless you include in your paper citations by 2 authors sharing a last name (e.g., Bilbo Baggins and Frodo Baggins). In such a case, distinguish between the 2 authors by using the first letter of the first name (e.g., B. Baggins, 1946).
- Cite **work by 2 authors** using the last names of both (e.g., Fraga and Iyengar, 2000).
- Cite **work by 3 or more authors** using only the last name of the first author, followed by *et al.* (meaning, "and others").
- **If you must cite a reference that you have not read**, do it as follows: (Tankersly, 1995, as cited by Rittschof, 2006).
- Cite information provided directly by your instructor (orally or through e-mail) as follows: (J. Bolker, personal communication, Oct. 2008).

PREPARING THE LITERATURE CITED SECTION

Whenever you cite sources to support statements, you must provide a separate Literature Cited section, giving the full citations for each source cited. This presentation enables the interested reader—including, perhaps, you, at a later date—to locate and examine the basis for factual statements made in your report. It occasionally happens that a reference is used incorrectly; your interpretation or recollection of what was said in a textbook, lecture, or journal article may be wrong. By giving the source of your information, the reader can more easily recognize such errors. If the reader is your instructor, this list of references may provide an opportunity for him or her to correct any misconceptions you have acquired. If you fail to provide the source of your information, your instructor will have more difficulty in determining where you went wrong. Proper referencing is even more crucial in scientific publications. Misstatements of fact are readily propagated in the literature by others; the Literature Cited section of a report enables readers to verify all factual statements made. The careful scientist consults the listed references before accepting statements made by other authors.

Listing the References—General Rules

Include only those references that you have actually read (see p. 1278 for one exception to this rule) **and that you specifically mention in your report or paper**, and **include all of the references that you cite**. Unless you are told otherwise by your instructor, list references in alphabetical order according to the last name of the first author of each publication. If you cite several papers written by the same author, list those papers chronologically. If one author has published 2 papers in the same year, list those papers as, for example, "Hentschel, B. 1995a," and "Hentschel, B. 1995b."

Each listing must include the names of all authors, the year of publication, and the full title of the paper, article, or book.

In addition, **when citing books**, you must report the publisher, the place of publication, and the pages referred to, or the total number of pages in the book.

When citing journal articles, you must include the name of the journal, the volume number of the journal, and the page numbers of the article consulted.

When listing an article from a hard-copy journal that you accessed on-line, use the standard hard-copy journal format; there is no need to include a URL, for example.

When citing exclusively on-line journals and other Internet sources, you must include the date that the material was posted (or the most recent revision date), the date that you accessed the material, the full URL for the Web site, and an indication (in brackets: []) that the medium is the Internet. See p. 1282 for examples of correct citations. Standards are still being established; with Internet sources, it is sometimes difficult, or impossible, to determine the author of the material, the publication date, the publisher, and even the title of the article! The most recent and detailed advice for citing Internet sources is available through the Council of Science Editors and the National Library of Medicine (see Appendix F for the Web sites).

Listing the References—Using the Correct Format

Here are a few general rules followed by most journals:

- List references in alphabetical order and then chronologically.
- Spell out only the last names of authors; initials are used for first and middle names.
- Include the names of all authors, even though the names of only 1 or, at most, 2 authors (e.g., Woodin *et al.*, 1995; Svane and Havenhand, 1994) are cited in the text of the report.
- Latin names, including species names, are italicized, or they are underlined to indicate italics.
- Titles of journal articles are not enclosed within quotation marks, and only the first word is capitalized.
- For book titles, capitalize the first letter of each word other than *the, and*, or *or*.
- Journal names are usually abbreviated. In particular, the word *Journal* is abbreviated as *J.*, and words ending in *-ology* are usually abbreviated as *-ol*. The *Journal of Zoology* thus becomes *J. Zool.* Do not abbreviate the names of journals whose titles are single words (for example, *Science* or *Evolution*). Acceptable abbreviations for the titles of journals can usually be found within the journals themselves.

Unfortunately, formats differ from journal to journal, despite the best efforts of the Council of Science Editors. Consider, for example, how one particular citation would be formatted for 4 different journals:

For Biological Bulletin **Contakos, S.P., C.M. Gaydos, E.C. Pfeil, and K.A. McLaughlin. 2006.** Subdividing the embryo: A role for Notch signaling during germ layer patterning in *Xenopus laevis. Devel. Biol.* **288**: 122–134.

For Developmental Biology Contakos, S.P., Gaydos, C.M., Pfeil, E.C., McLaughlin, K.A., 2006. Subdividing the embryo: A role for Notch signaling during germ layer patterning in *Xenopus laevis.* Dev. Biol. 288, 122–134.

For Ecology Contakos, S.P., C.M. Gaydos, E.C. Pfeil, and K.A. McLaughlin. 2006. Subdividing the embryo: A role for Notch signaling during germ layer patterning in *Xenopus laevis.* Developmental Biology **288**:122–134.

For Science Contakos, S.P., C.M. Gaydos, E.C. Pfeil, K.A. McLaughlin. *Devel. Biol.* **288**, 122 (2006).

List all the differences you can find! Why do citation formats differ so much among journals? I have no idea, and I wish they wouldn't. But they do. The following examples should help you to prepare your own Literature Cited sections, but check to see if your instructor wants you to follow a particular format, or the format used by a particular journal.

The most important rule in preparing the Literature Cited section is to provide all the information required and to be consistent in the manner in which you present it. If you are using bibliographic management software (see Technology Tip 3 p. 1281), this can be specified at the touch of a button.

When preparing a paper for publication, follow the format used by the journal to which you are submitting the paper, and follow it to the last detail.

Note in the following examples that the citation begins at the far left, and that subsequent lines are indented several spaces to the right. This format is called a "hanging indent" (see Technology Tip 4, p. 1281, to learn how to do this automatically in Microsoft Word). A sample Literature Cited section appears at the end of this chapter.

TECHNOLOGY TIP 3

Bibliographic management software

As you start accumulating large numbers of references, you might want to start putting them into a bibliographic database manager, such as ProCite, EndNote, or Refworks. You have to buy ProCite and EndNote and install them on your desktop. Refworks is Web-based, and it may be available for free through your college or university library. Bibliographic management software allows you to retrieve references by keyword searching, and it also allows you to print your references in any desired format.

TECHNOLOGY TIP 4

Producing hanging indents

To produce the "hanging indent" format shown in the examples below, open the Format menu in the Word tool bar, and then click on Paragraph, and then on the arrow associated with the term Special toward the right side of the layout. Then, select "hanging" or "hanging indent," depending on your version of Word, and specify how much you would like to indent (0.300 works well). Click OK to leave the menu and you're ready to roll—I mean, indent. Alternatively, you can type all the references first and then highlight them. Next, open the Format menu, select Paragraph, open Special, and then choose the hanging indent option and specify the amount of indenting that you want.

Format for Journal References

Jarrett, J.N. 1997. Temporal variation in substratum specificity of *Semibalanus balanoides* (Linnaeus) cyprids. *J. Exp. Mar. Biol. Ecol.* 211: 103–114.

Twombly, S., Burns, C.W. 1996. Effects of food quality on individual growth and development in the freshwater copepod *Boeckella triarticulata. J. Plankton Res.* 18: 75–82.

Woodin, S.A., Lindsay, S.M., Wethey, D.S. 1995. Process-specific recruitment cues in marine sedimentary systems. *Biol. Bull.* 189: 49–58.

Format for Book References

Nybakken, J.W., Bertness, M.D. 2005. *Marine Biology: An Ecological Approach*, 6th ed. Pearson Education, Inc., CA, pp. 25–31.

Format for an Article from a Book

Thompson, S.N. 1997. Physiology and biochemistry of snail-larval trematode relationships. In: *Advances in Trematode Biology* (Fried, B., Graczyk, T.K., eds.). CRC Press, NY, pp. 149–195.

Format for a Laboratory Manual or Handout

Biology 13 Laboratory Manual. 2005. Exercise in enzyme kinetics, pp. 16–23. Tufts University, Medford, MA.

Bernheim, H. 2002. Principles of physiology, using insects as models. II. Excretion of organic compounds by Malpighian tubules. Biology 50 Laboratory Handout. Tufts University, Medford, MA.

Format for Items from the World Wide Web

Lawrence, R.A. A review of the medical benefits and contraindications to breastfeeding in the United States [Internet]. Arlington (VA): National Center for Education in Maternal and Child Health; 1997 Oct [cited 2005 Oct 27]. 40 p. Available from http://www.ncemch.org/pubs/PDFs/breastfeedingTIB.pdf
Note that there is no period at the end of the URL.

A SAMPLE LITERATURE CITED SECTION

A sample Literature Cited section follows, with items arranged alphabetically and chronologically. Your instructor may specify a different format for this section of your report, so check first if you are uncertain.

Literature Cited

Journal, >2 authors

Bayne, B.L., Livingstone, D.R., Moore, M.N., Widdows, J. 1976. A cytochemical and biochemical index of stress in *Mytilus edulis* L. *Mar. Poll. Bull.* 7: 221–224. Biology 220 Laboratory Manual. 2005. Exercise in enzyme kinetics, pp. 16–23. College of Wooster, OH.

Journal, 2 authors

Finch, C.E., Rose, M.R. 1995. Hormones and the physiological architecture of life history evolution. *Q. Rev. Biol.* 70: 1–52.

Web journal

Fox, D.S., Heitman, J. 2002. Good fungi gone bad: the corruption of calcineurin. BioEssays [Internet] 2002 [cited 2005 Dec 18]; 24 (10): 894–903. Available from http://www3.interscience.wiley.com/cgi-bin/abstract/98518344/ABSTRACT

Book, 2 authors

Haas, W., Haberl, B. 1997. Host recognition by trematode miracidia and cercariae. In: *Advances in Trematode Biology* (B. Fried and T. L. Graczyk, eds.), CRC Press, NY, pp. 197–227.

2 papers by same author in same year

McVey, M., LaRocque, J.R., Adams, M.D., Sekelsky, J.J. 2004a. Formation of deletions during double-strand break repair in *Drosophila* DmBlm mutants occurs after strand invasion. *Proc. Nat. Acad. Sci. USA* 101: 15694–15699.

McVey, M., Radut, D., Sekelsky, J.J. 2004b. End-joining repair of double-strand breaks in *Drosophila melanogaster* is largely DNA ligase IV independent. *Genetics* 168: 2067–2076.

Journal, 1 author

Orians, C. 2005. Herbivores, vascular pathways, and systemic induction: facts and artifacts. *J. Chem. Ecol.* 31: 2231–2241.

Book, 4 authors

Purves, W.K., Sadava, D., Orians, G.H., Heller, H.C. 2000. *Life: The Science of Biology*, 6th ed. Sinauer Assoc., Sunderland, MA, pp. 374–379.

Book, 2 authors

Quinn, G.P., Keough, M.J. 2002. *Experimental design and data analysis for biologists.* Cambridge University Press, NY, 537 pp.

Web site

Wray, G.A. Echinodermata. [Internet]. 1999 Dec 14 [cited 2006 Jan 12]. The Tree of Life Web Project. Available from http://tolweb.org/tree?group=Echinodermata&congroup=Metazoa/

WRITING LABORATORY AND OTHER RESEARCH REPORTS

Inside every practical scientist the same pleasure in competing against nature lurks below the surface, the same enthusiasm for experiment, the same satisfaction in dreaming up new gambits and thrusts that can trick or tease the natural world into revealing its secrets.

JANET BROWNE

WHY ARE YOU DOING THIS?

It is no accident that most biology courses include laboratory components in addition to lecture sessions. Doing biology involves making observations, asking questions, formulating hypotheses, devising experiments to test the hypotheses, presenting data, analyzing and interpreting data, and formulating new questions and hypotheses. **The so-called facts you learn from lectures and textbooks are primarily interpretations of data**. By participating in the acquisition and interpretation of data, you glimpse the true nature of the scientific process.

If you are contemplating a career in research, be assured that learning to write effective research reports now is an investment in your future. As a laboratory technician or research assistant, you will often be asked to analyze, summarize, and graph data so that the future path of the research can be decided. If you eventually pursue a research M.S. or Ph.D., you will find that a graduate thesis is essentially a very large lab report. Writing up your research for publication, either as a graduate student or as a researcher with a laboratory of your own, you will quickly find that you are again following exactly the procedures you used in preparing good laboratory reports in college biology courses; it can't hurt to learn the tools of your trade now.

You can also benefit from writing good research reports even if you do not expect to go on in the field of biology. Preparing such reports develops the ability to organize ideas logically, think clearly, and express yourself accurately and concisely. It is difficult to imagine a career in which the mastery of such skills is not a great asset.

THE PURPOSE OF LABORATORY AND FIELD NOTEBOOKS

The first step in preparing a good research report is to keep a detailed notebook. Research notebooks function to:

1. Record the design and specific goals of your studies.
2. Record and organize your thoughts and questions about the work you are doing or planning to do.
3. Record your observations and numerical data.
4. Help you organize your activities in the laboratory or field so that you can work efficiently and accurately.

Keeping a detailed notebook will make the task of writing your report much easier, and you will end up producing a better report; after all, every product benefits from the use of quality materials. Moreover, the skills you learn in keeping the notebook could really pay off later in life. The Nobel Prize for the isolation of insulin would probably have gone to J. B. Collip instead of to Frederick Banting and C. H. Best had Dr. Collip learned to keep a more careful record of his work as a student. Collip was apparently the first to purify the hormone, but his notes were incomplete and he was therefore unable to repeat the procedure successfully in subsequent studies.

Similarly, Charles Darwin neglected to make careful field notes about the birds he collected among the Galapagos Islands. Not realizing at the time that the birds collected on the different islands represented different species of finch, all of which were new to science, Darwin didn't even keep the specimens from different islands in separate packages. Fortunately, Captain FitzRoy and some of the crew members aboard the *Beagle* (including Darwin's much underacknowledged servant, Syms Covington) made their own bird collections during the voyage and *did* keep track of which birds came from which islands. Without their help, Darwin would never have been able to put the now-famous finch story together at all.

You might not be so lucky: Take notes carefully and in detail.

Figure 10. A page from a student's laboratory notebook. The flowchart is based on more-detailed information provided by the instructor.

Taking Notes

In keeping your research notebook, assume that you are doing something worthwhile, that you might well discover something remarkable (it does happen), and that you will suffer complete amnesia while you sleep that night. In other words, take the time to write down—in your own words—everything you are about to do, everything you actually do, and every reason why you do it. You can't always tell what will turn out to be important later on.

Record your data clearly, with each number identified by the appropriate units. Many of the details that seem too obvious to write down—for example, today's date (including the year), the name and location of your field site, the name of the species you are working with, or the units of measurements—are forgotten surprisingly quickly upon leaving the laboratory or field. You *can* write down too little, but it's difficult to write down too much.

Write so legibly and clearly that, should you be run over by a truck on your way to class the next day, other students in the course would have no difficulty reconstructing your study and following your results. Similarly, if you use abbreviations in your notebook, be sure to indicate what each stands for. These procedures will greatly facilitate the writing of your research report. They are, in fact, crucial in any functioning research laboratory, because anyone in the lab must be able to pick up or interpret your work where you left off if you are unable to come in some day or if you leave that laboratory permanently.

October 4, 2008

Goal—To determine rate at which the marine bivalve Mercenaria mercenaria (hardshell clam) moves water across its gills.

Approach—Use unicellular alga (phytoplankton) Dunaliella tertiolecta.

Determine initial cells $\cdot$ ml^{-1}, final cells $\cdot$ ml^{-1}. If know elapsed time and volume of seawater in container, can calculate cells eaten per hour per clam, and ml of sea H_2O cleared of cells/h/clam.

Weight of clam (incl. shell): 9.4g [Fisher/Ainsworth balance, Model MX-200]

Find initial concentration of algal cells:
1. 1 ml of culture + drop of Lugol's iodine to kill cells.
2. Load hemacytometer for cell counts—finally got it right on 5th try!
   Helps to tilt pipet at about 45° angle.

because of dilution w/0.05ml Lugol's sol'n

Data: (multiply by 1.05 and then by 10^4 ⟶ cells ml^{-1})

Note: ask Prof. Scully why 10^4.

counts per section of hemacytom slide

Sample 1	Sample 2
22	18
2) 13	21
18	20
4) 22	20
26	16
6) 21	12
20	18
8) 16	22
22	19

$\overline{X}$ = 20.0 (× 1.05) ⟶   18.4 (× 1.05) ⟶
⟶ 21.0 × 10^4 cells ml^{-1} 19.4 × 10^4 cells ml^{-1}

good agreement!

Put clam in 150 ml of this solution at 2:10 PM; H_2O = 21.4°C

Figure 11. A sample page from a student's laboratory notebook.

Some of this writing can be done before the laboratory session. Whenever possible, read about the day's study ahead of time, being sure (through writing in your notebook) that you understand its goals, and plan exactly how you will record your data. You will get more out of the exercise and will undoubtedly finish your work in the lab or field more quickly if you arrive prepared. **It often helps to sketch a simple flowchart of your planned activities ahead of time**, as shown in Figure 10. (You can use this flowchart again later, in writing the Materials and Methods section of your report [p. 1288].

Your research notebook should contain any thoughts, observations, or questions you have about what you are doing, along with the actual protocol and data. A sample page from a model notebook is shown in Figure 11. Note that the notebook entry begins by stating the date and a specific goal. With such clear, well-organized, and well-thought-out notes, this student is well on his or her way to preparing a fine report.

September 17, 2008. 1-3 PM. Sunny, 27°C air temp.; 17°C water.
Goal: Investigate size distribution of L. littorea shells at
different distances from high tide line.
ME: Might expect shells to get larger as get closer to water,
since these are marine snails and so should be able to feed more
hours per day if spend more time under water. (What do they
eat? Can they only eat in water?)

– – – –

Note: Many of the empty shells have large round holes made by a
drilling predator—probably Nucella lapillus or Lunatia heros,
which seem to be the only carnivorous gastropods living here.
——→ Should calc. % of dead snails (empty shells) that have drill
holes. Drill holes seem to be in exact same location on each shell.
How is this possible?

– – – –

Note: Most of the rocks in this area are almost completely
covered by very tiny (young) barnacles. Covering = so dense in
some places can't even see the rock surface.
Question: Why no big, adult barnacles on these rocks?
Perhaps all die off during the summer for some reason.
There are many large barnacles on rocks much farther down the
beach. Same species? If so, why only die here? Would be
interesting to come back and monitor survival of young
barnacles here and down the beach a few times during the
summer and fall—perhaps once a month?
SAMPLING: 0.25 m² around each transect point, every 2 m from
high tide (HT) mark.
DATA: No snails found from 0-3 meters (m) below high tide mark.
D = DRILLED

Distance from high tide (m)	Shell lengths (cm)	
	Live snails	Empty shells
4m	1.6, 1.4, 0.5	1.4
	1.7, 0.9, 2.1	
6m	1.7, 1.9, 1.1	1.8D
	2.0, 1.8, 1.8	1.4
		1.4

etc.

Figure 12. A sample page from a student's field notebook.

A notebook recording field observations (a "field notebook") would look similar to that shown in Figure 12, which records part of a study investigating the size distributions of the common marine intertidal snail *Littorina littorea* along a Massachusetts beach. Again, the quality of the entries suggests that this student is not simply trying to "get it over with," or simply writing down textbook facts and paraphrases of lecture notes; the student is clearly looking around and thinking—every instructor's dream.

Making Drawings

In both laboratory and field work, it is often necessary to draw what you are seeing, particularly when working with living organisms. And perhaps the most important benefit is that, **done properly, the act of drawing forces you to look more carefully at the object or organism before you**. As you draw, pay special attention to the relative sizes, shapes, and textures of different parts. Is part *A* connected to part *B*, or are they only adjacent to each other? Are the widths of parts *A* and *B* similar, or is one part wider than the other and, if so, how much wider? Is part *A* twice as wide as part *B* or 3 times as wide? The closer you look, the more you will see.

If possible, draw using a hard-lead pencil so that you can modify your drawings easily while you work. If you must use a pen, be sure the ink does not smear when wet. Try to figure out what things are as you draw, and label them as you go along. Be sure to indicate the approximate size of what you are drawing, and include a scale bar if appropriate. Most important, make your drawings *big* so that they can accommodate plenty of detail. Most beginning students make their drawings much too small; **think big**. Even if you are looking at something through a microscope, your drawing of that something should fill a 4-by-6-inch space. Remember, the goal is not to become a great artist; rather, the goal is to learn how to observe closely and how to record those observations accurately and in sufficient detail.

COMPONENTS OF THE RESEARCH REPORT

A research report is typically divided into 6 major sections:

1. *Abstract.* In the Abstract, you summarize the problem addressed, why the problem was addressed, your approach to the problem, and the major findings and conclusions of your study. This is probably the most difficult part of the report to write well; it summarizes the entire report, so save it for last.
2. *Introduction.* The Introduction, often only 1 or 2 paragraphs long, tells why the study was undertaken; a brief summary of relevant background facts leads to a statement of the specific problem being addressed. If appropriate, also describe the specific hypotheses that you set out to test.
3. *Materials and Methods.* This section is *your* reminder of what you did, and it also serves as a set of instructions for anyone wishing to repeat your study in the future.
4. *Results.* **This is the centerpiece of your report.** What were the major findings of the study? Present the data or summarize your observations using graphs and tables to reveal any trends you found. Point out major trends to the reader. If you make good use of your tables and graphs, the results can usually be presented in only 1 or 2 paragraphs of text; one picture is worth quite a few words. Avoid interpreting the data in this section.
5. *Discussion.* How do your results relate to the goals of the study, as stated in your Introduction, and how do they relate to the results that might have been expected from background information obtained in lectures, textbooks, or outside reading? Do your results support or argue against the hypotheses presented in your Introduction? What new hypotheses might now be formulated, and how might these hypotheses be tested? This section is typically the longest part of the report.
6. *Literature Cited ("References").* This section includes the full citations for any references (including textbooks, laboratory handouts, and Web sites) that you have cited in your report. Double-check your sources to be certain they are listed correctly; this list of citations will permit the interested reader to confirm the accuracy of any factual statements you make and, often, to understand the basis for your interpretations of the data. With only one exception (p. 1278), cite only material you have actually read. The proper formats for citing literature and presenting citations are described in Chapter 2.

You may also be asked to include an Acknowledgments section, in which you formally thank particular people for their contributions to the project or to the report. And of course, your report will need an informative title.

Before writing your report, first study a few short papers in a relevant biological journal, such as *Biological Bulletin, Developmental Biology,* or *Ecology.* Your instructor may provide you with a few especially good models. Reading these journal articles for content is unnecessary; you don't need to understand the topic of a paper to appreciate how the article is crafted. But do pay attention to the way the Introduction is constructed, the amount of detail included in the Materials and Methods section, and the material that is—and is not—included in the Results section.

While studying an article or two, note that figures and tables are always accompanied by explanatory captions (for figures) and legends (for tables), and that the axes of graphs and the columns and rows of tables are clearly labeled, with units of measure indicated. Note the location of figure captions and table legends. Study the captions and legends carefully, and imitate them (or improve them) in crafting your own.

WHERE TO START

Beginnings are hardest. . . . How can you write the beginning of something till you know what it's the beginning of?

PETER ELBOW

Strangely enough, you should begin writing your report with neither the title, the Abstract, nor the Introduction. It is far easier to write the Introduction—and the title—toward the end of the job, after you have fully digested what it is that you have done. And since the Abstract should be a tight summary of the entire report, this would be the worst section to begin with: How can you summarize something you haven't yet written? Save the Abstract (and the title) for later. **Start work with either the Materials and Methods section or the Results section.** Better still, you may profitably work on the two in tandem: Working on the Results section sometimes helps clarify what should be included in the Materials and Methods section, and working on this section sometimes clarifies the order in which results should be presented in the Results section.

Because the Materials and Methods section requires the least mental effort, completing it is a good way to overcome inertia. You may not know why you did the experiment or what you found out by doing it, but you can probably reconstruct what you did without much difficulty. Moreover, reminiscing carefully about what you did puts you in the right frame of mind to consider *why* you did it.

WHEN TO START

Start as soon as you can, preferably within 24 hours of finishing the study. In particular, start writing the Materials and Methods section while what you did is still fresh in your mind. Allow time for at least one major revision of each section.

WRITING THE MATERIALS AND METHODS SECTION

Results are meaningful in science only if they can be obtained over and over, whenever the experiment is repeated. Unfortunately, the results of any study depend to a large extent on the way the study was done. It is therefore essential that you describe your methods so that your experiment can be repeated in all its essential details. Perhaps the best reason for writing a detailed Materials and Methods section is that it helps you review what you have done in an organized way and starts you thinking about why you have done it. Developing a good Materials and Methods section also puts you in the right frame of mind to do an equally good job on the other sections of the report.

The difficulty in writing this section of a research report (or journal manuscript) is in selecting the right level of detail, as discussed below. Students commonly give too little information; when informed of this defect, they may then give too much information. It's hard to hit it just right, but keeping your audience in mind (yourself and your fellow students) will help.

Determining the Correct Level of Detail

Many students begin with a one-sentence Materials and Methods section: "Methods were as described in the lab manual." Although this sentence meets the criterion of brevity, it is unacceptable as a stand-alone Materials and Methods section. For one thing, studies are rarely performed exactly as described in a laboratory manual or handout. Your instructions may call for the use of 15 animals, for example, but only 12 animals might be available for use on the day of your experiment. In addition, many details of a study will vary from year to year, from week to week, or from place to place and must therefore be omitted from your set of instructions.

Don't get carried away, however. Consider the following overly detailed description of a study involving the growth of radish seedlings:

> On January 5, I obtained 4 paper cups, 400 g of potting soil, and 12 radish seeds. I labeled the cups A, B, C, D and planted 3 seeds per cup, using a plastic spoon to cover each seed with about 1/4 inch of soil.

The author has used the first sentence simply to list the materials; whenever possible, it is far better to **mention each new material as you discuss what you did with it.** Furthermore, why do we need to know the weight of the soil obtained, or that the cups were labeled A–D rather than 1–4, or that a plastic spoon was used to add soil? Omitting the excess details and starting right in with what was done, we obtain:

> On January 5, I planted 3 radish seeds in each of 4 individually marked paper cups, covering the seeds with about 1 cm of potting soil.

Note that the essential details—individually marked cups, 3 seeds per cup, 1 cm of soil—not only survive in the edited version but now stand out clearly. The trick, then, is to determine which details are essential and which details are not. Happily, I've come up with a can't-fail method for getting this right.

Begin by listing all the factors that might have influenced your results. If, for example, you measured the feeding rates of caterpillars on several different diets, your list might look something like this:

Species of caterpillar used
Diets used
Amount of food provided per caterpillar
Time of year
Time of day
Air temperature in room
Manufacturer and model number of any specialized equipment used (e.g., balances, centrifuges, or spectrophotometers)
Size and age of caterpillars
Duration of the experiment
Container size or volume
Number of animals per container
Total number of individuals in the study
Precision of measurements made

Sometimes you will need to think carefully about whether a particular methodological detail might have influenced your results. Do you need to tell readers that you wore a red shirt the day you conducted the experiment? Not if you were studying the effect of different fertilizer concentrations on the growth rates of radish seedlings, but could the shirt have influenced your results if you were observing mating displays among sparrows? Possibly.

This list, which you do not turn in with your report, contains the bricks with which you will construct the Materials and Methods section. Each of the listed details must find its way into your report (but not necessarily in the order in which you jotted them down), because each gives information essential for later replication of the experiment. Some of this information may also help you explain why your results differed from those of others who have gone before you, a topic that will deserve some attention later, in the Discussion section of your report. Details that do not merit inclusion in the list are superfluous and should not appear in your Materials and Methods section.

In describing the procedures followed, **you must say what you did, but you should freely refer to your laboratory manual or handouts in describing how you did it**. For example, you might write:

The 3 different diets were distributed to the caterpillars in random fashion, as described in the laboratory manual (Lynch, 2009).

The important point here is that the diets were distributed at random; the outcome might be quite different if the largest caterpillars were to receive one diet and the smallest caterpillars another. The interested reader (including you, perhaps, at some later date) can refer to the stated source (Lynch, 2009) for detailed instruction in the method of randomization. You might want to append the relevant portion of your handout or manual at the end of your report as an appendix; this is a fine way to keep everything together for later use.

Be sure to note any departures from the given instructions. Suppose you were told to weigh the caterpillars individually but found that your balance was not sensitive enough to record the weight of a single animal. Your laboratory instructor, never at a loss for good ideas, probably suggested that you weigh the individuals in each container as a group. Your report might then include the following information:

Determining the weight gained by each caterpillar over the 3-hour period of the experiment required that both initial and final weights be determined. The caterpillars were too small to be weighed individually. Therefore, similar sized caterpillars were weighed in groups of 3 at a time, to the nearest 0.1 g. The average weight of each caterpillar in the group was then calculated.

Giving Rationales

Mention, for your own benefit as well as that of your reader, why particular steps were taken whenever you think it might not be obvious. Imagine yourself explaining things to a classmate who has not yet performed the study. We might, for example, profitably rewrite the sentence given above:

To avoid prejudicing the results by distributing food according to size of caterpillar, the 3 different diets were distributed to the caterpillars in random fashion as described by Lynch (2001).

A similar strategy can be used in writing about studies in molecular genetics:

To test the sensitivity of *lig4* mutants to ionizing radiation, *lig4*[169]/*FM7w* females were crossed to *lig4*[169]/Y males.*

---

*Modified from McVey *et al.*, 2004. *Genetics* 168: 2067–2076.

Describing Data Analysis

It is also usually appropriate to include any formulas used in analyzing your data. The following sentences, for example, would belong in a Materials and Methods section:

> The data were analyzed by a series of chi-square tests. The rate at which food was eaten was calculated by dividing the weight loss of the food by 3 hours, according to the following formula: Feeding rate = (Initial food weight − final food weight) ÷ 3 h.

Often this information is presented in a separate subsection at the end of the Materials and Methods section (see below).
Note in this example that **"rates" always have units of "per time."** If it doesn't have units of "per time," it is not a rate.

Use of Subheadings

Unless your Materials and Methods section is very short (e.g., a single paragraph), **use informative subheadings to help organize and present your material by topic**. The emphasis here is on the word *informative*. Below are some uninformative subheadings, relating to a study of shell choice by hermit crabs, followed by more substantive revisions on the same topic:

Uninformative: Field experiment

Informative: Occupancy of damaged and intact shells in the field

Uninformative: Shell choice

Informative: Effect of shell condition on shell choice in the laboratory

Two subsections commonly included at the end of the Materials and Methods section are "Data analysis" and a description of your study system or organism. An example of a Data Analysis subsection is given on p. 1291. Here is a sample subsection describing the study organism, from a paper* reporting the role of environmental cues in stimulating larval metamorphosis:

Study Organism

> *Hydroides dianthus* is a tube-dwelling serpulid polychaete found from New England through the West Indies, commonly on the underside of rocks (Hartman, 1969). Individuals are gonochoristic (i.e., they have separate sexes) and release gametes into seawater every 2–4 wk at 23°C (Zuraw and Leone, 1968). The larvae begin feeding 18–24 h after eggs are fertilized, and become capable of metamorphosing after about 5 d at 23°C (Scheltema *et al.*, 1981; Bryan and Qian, 1997). The larvae undergo rapid and substantial morphological changes during metamorphosis that readily distinguish metamorphosed individuals from attached larvae (Scheltema *et al.*, 1981).

Alternatively, particularly if the organism or study site was chosen for specific attributes related to the nature of the research question, you could include this sort of information at the end of the Introduction (see p. 1315).
Notice how the use of references in this example increases the author's credibility.

A Model Materials and Methods Section

The Materials and Methods section of your report should be brief but informative. The following example completely describes an experiment designed to test the influence of decreased salinity on the body weight of a marine worm. **Note that it is written in the past tense.**

Obtaining and Maintaining Worms

> The polychaete worms used in this study were *Nereis virens*, freshly collected from Nahant, MA, and ranging in length between 10 and 12 cm. All treatments were performed at room temperature, approximately 21°C, on April 15, 2009. One hundred ml of full-strength seawater was added to each of six 200-ml glass jars; these jars served as controls, to monitor worm weight in the absence of any salinity change. Another 6 jars were filled with 100 ml of seawater diluted by 50% with distilled water.

Monitoring Water Gain and Loss

> Twelve polychaetes were quickly blotted with paper towels to remove adhering water, and were then weighed to the nearest 0.1 g using a Model MX-200 Fisher/Ainsworth balance. Each worm was then added to one of the jars of seawater. Blotted worm weights were later determined 30, 60, and 120 minutes after the initial weights were taken.

Determining Osmotic Concentration

> The initial and final osmotic concentrations of all test solutions were determined using a Wescor VAPRO vapor pressure osmometer, following instructions provided in the handout (Gaudette, 1998).

---

*Modified from Toonen, R., Pawlik, J.R., 2001. *Mar. Ecol. Progr. Ser.* 224: 103–114.

`Data Analysis`

The rate of weight gain over time was examined by linear regression analysis, after log-transforming the independent variable (time). A series of Student's *t*-tests were used to assess the effect of salinity on rate of weight gain, by comparing mean weights of worms in the 2 treatment groups at 30, 60, and 120 minutes.

Note that all essential details have been included: temperature, species used, size of animals used, number of animals used per treatment, number of animals per container, volume of fluid in the containers, type and size of containers, time of year, equipment used, and how the data were analyzed. After reading this Materials and Methods section, you could repeat the study if you wanted to (or had to). Note, too, that **the writer has made clear why certain steps were taken**; 3 jars of full-strength seawater served as controls, for example, and worms were blotted dry to remove external water. The fact that worms were blotted dry before they were weighed was mentioned because that's a procedural detail that would obviously influence the results. On the other hand, the author does not describe how the balance or osmometer were operated since these techniques are standard, and the author does not tell us whether he or she used a clock or a stopwatch to monitor the passage of time because that choice could not have influenced the results obtained. The author has written a report that might be useful to someone in the future—and ends up with a top grade.

On to the Results!

WRITING THE RESULTS SECTION

The Results section is the most important part of any research report. Other parts of the report reflect the author's *interpretation* of the data. Interpretations necessarily reflect the author's biases, hopes, and opinions, and they are always subject to change, particularly as new information becomes available. In contrast, as long as a study was conducted carefully, and as long as the data were collected carefully, analyzed correctly, and presented accurately, the results are valid regardless of how interpretations change over time. Our understanding about how immune systems work has changed remarkably over the past decade, for example, and the current interpretation of older data differs considerably from the original interpretation. But the older data are still valid. The *results* of any study are real; the *interpretations* often change. That's why the Results section is indeed the centerpiece of your report.

In this section, you summarize your findings, using tables, graphs, and words. The Results section is:

1. Not the place to discuss why the experiment was performed.
2. Not the place to discuss how the experiment was performed.
3. Not the place to discuss whether the results were expected, unexpected, disappointing, or interesting.

Simply present the results, drawing the reader's attention to the major observations and key trends in the data. Don't interpret them here. Most of the work in preparing this section of the report involves constructing a clear and well-organized presentation of data.

Summarizing Data Using Tables and Graphs

Before you even think about writing your Results section, you must work with your data. The observations you've made and the data you've collected most likely contain a story that is crying out for recognition. Contrary to popular opinion, the purpose of showing data in tables and graphs is not to add bulk to laboratory reports. Rather, **you wish to arrange the data in tables and graphs to reveal trends** and to make the most important points stand out, not only to your instructor but, more importantly, to yourself. The trick now is to organize the data so that (1) the underlying story is revealed and (2) the task of revealing the story to your reader is simplified.

There is no single right way to present data summaries; use any system that illustrates the trends clearly. First decide what relationships might be worth examining. Suppose we return to the experiment in which caterpillars fed for 3 hours on 3 different diets. We determined both the initial weight of food provided and the weight of food remaining after the 3-hour period so that we can calculate the weight of food eaten per caterpillar per hour. In your report, you should provide a sample calculation so that if you make a mistake your instructor can see where you went wrong. We also know the initial and final weights of the caterpillars for each diet and the initial and final weights of dishes of food in the absence of caterpillars; these control dishes will tell us the amount of water lost from the food by evaporation.

What relationships in the data might be especially worth examining? The first step in answering this question is to **make a list of specific questions that might be worth asking**, as follows:

1. Did the caterpillars feed at different rates on the different diets? That is, did feeding rate vary with diet?
2. Did larger caterpillars eat faster than smaller caterpillars? That is, did feeding rate vary with caterpillar size?
3. How does the weight gained by a caterpillar relate to the weight lost by the food?
4. Did the weight of the control dishes change, and, if so, by how much?

Table 3. Summary of raw data.

Diet	Initial Caterpillar Wt. (g)	Final Caterpillar Wt. (g)	Caterpillar Wt. Change (g)	Wt. of Food Lost (g) over 3 h	Feeding Rate (g food lost/h) of Caterpillar
A (Wheatgerm)	8.05	9.55	+1.55	3.65	15.2×10^{-2}
A	4.80	5.80	+1.00	1.74	7.2×10^{-2}
A	5.50	7.00	+1.50	3.33	13.9×10^{-2}
A	5.50	4.70	~~−0.80~~	~~0.00~~	0
A	5.90	6.95	+1.05	1.35	5.6×10^{-2}
Average	5.95	6.80	+1.28	2.52	8.4×10^{-2}
B (sinigrin 10^{-5} M)	4.40	5.11	+0.71	2.19	9.1×10^{-2}
B	5.20	5.60	+0.40	1.25	5.2×10^{-2}
.	.	.	.	.	.
.	.	.	.	.	.
.	.	.	.	.	.
Control 1	—	—	—	0.22	—
2 (no caterpillars)	—	—	—	0.10	—
3	—	—	—	0.16	—

Table 4. The effect of sinigrin (allyl glucosinolate) added to a basic wheatgerm diet, on food consumption of *Manduca sexta* caterpillars over 24 hours.

Diet	No. Caterpillars	(mean g food eaten/caterpillar/h)
Wheatgerm control	4°	8.4×10^{-2}
Sinigrin (10^{-5} M)	5	7.9×10^{-2}
Sinigrin (10^{-3} M)	5	3.8×10^{-2}

°One individual died during the study without eating any food.

The first question on this list was inspired by the null hypothesis established at the start of the study (in this case, H_0 = diet has no effect on feeding rate). But the other issues arose only after the data were collected and examined. **In scrutinizing your data, do not limit yourself to the questions and hypotheses posed at the start of your study.**

As in preparing the Materials and Methods section, this list of questions is for your own use and is not to be included in your report. Don't take any shortcuts here. Write these questions in complete sentences. Once you have this list of questions, it is easy to list the relationships that must be examined in your Results section:

1. Feeding rate as a function of diet
2. Feeding rate as a function of caterpillar size
3. Caterpillar weight gain versus food weight loss for each caterpillar
4. Food weight loss in the presence of caterpillars versus food weight loss in controls

Constructing a Summary Table

Now you must organize your data into a summary table in a way that will let you examine each of these relationships. Consider Table 3. This rough draft lists all the data obtained in the experiment. This summary table is for your own use; it is not usually something to be submitted as a formal part of your report. **Your goal is to tidy up your data so that you can work with it more easily.**

For the first relationship in our list (feeding rate as a function of diet), a simple table will tell the entire story. For your report, you can simply present an abbreviated summary table, with explanatory caption, as in Table 4. Note that one of the caterpillars offered diet A ate no food and lost weight during the experiment. This individual died during the study, and the associated data were therefore omitted from Table 4. (The weight loss for this caterpillar probably reflects evaporation of body water.)

To Graph or Not to Graph

Finally, the time has come to reveal more subtle trends that may be lurking in the data. These trends may not be readily apparent from the summary table (Table 3); the trends may be made visible, however, both to you and your reader, through carefully designed and executed graphing. A word of caution: **Do not automatically assume that your data must be graphed.** If you can tell your story clearly using only a table—for example, if you are not interested in visualizing trends—a graph is superfluous. In other cases, you may be able to summarize some aspects of the data without using any graphs or tables at all. You might write, for example, "No animals ate at temperatures below 15°C," and then present data only for animals held at higher temperatures. **In any event, never present the same data in both a graph and a table**.

See Technology Tip 7 at the end of this chapter if you will be using Excel to plot graphs.

Graphs in biology generally take one of two basic forms: scatter plots (point graphs) or histograms and bar graphs. For the second relationship we wish to examine using the caterpillar data—feeding rate versus caterpillar size—a scatter graph, like the one shown in Figure 13, will be especially appropriate.

In examining Figure 13, note that:

1. Each axis of the graph is clearly labeled and includes units of measurement.
2. Tick marks on both axes are at intervals frequent enough to allow readers to estimate the value of each data point.
3. The meaning of each symbol is clearly indicated.
4. **The symbols chosen facilitate interpretation of the graph**: Darker symbols represent increasing concentrations of sinigrin in the diet.
5. **The symbols are large and easy to tell apart.** Avoid using squares and circles of the same type (e.g., open square and open circle) on the same graph since these symbols can be difficult to tell apart.
6. A detailed explanatory caption (figure legend) is below the figure.

All of your graphs should exhibit these 6 characteristics. In Figure 13, it would be insufficient to simply label the y-axis "Feeding Rate." Feeding rates can be expressed as per minute, per hour, per day, or per year and as per animal, per group of animals, or per gram of body weight. Similarly, it is unacceptable to label the x-axis as "Weight," or even as "Caterpillar Weight." Don't make readers guess what you have done. From the figure caption, the axis labels, and the graph itself, the reader should be able to determine the question being asked, get a good idea of how the study was done, and be able to interpret the figure without referring to the text (see pp. 1268 and 1303). Never make the reader back up; **a good graph is self-contained**.

In this chapter, a "thumbs up" symbol indicates a well-constructed, model graph, whereas a "thumbs down" symbol indicates a graph that suffers one or more major defects.

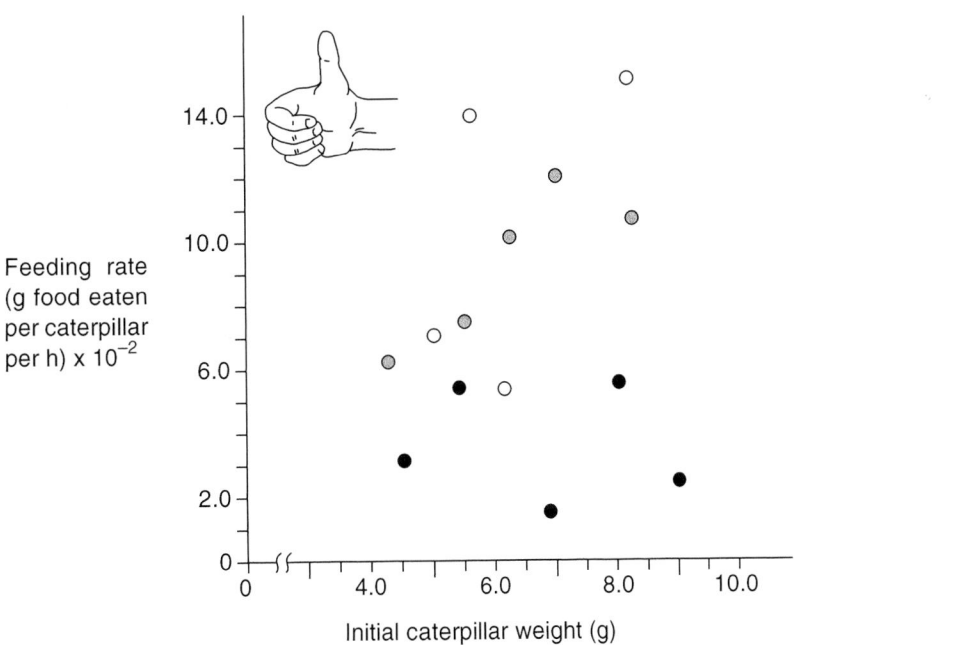

Figure 13. The relationship between initial caterpillar weight and rates of food consumption for *Manduca sexta* feeding for 3 hours on 1 of 3 different diets at 24°C. Each point represents data from a different individual. Feeding rates varied from about 0.01 to 0.15 g eaten per caterpillar^{-1} h^{-1}. ° = wheatgerm control diet; • = 10^{-5} M sinigrin; • = 10^{-3} M sinigrin.

The third relationship (animal weight gain versus food weight loss) might well be left in table form since in this case the trend is readily discernible; caterpillars always gained less weight than that lost by the food (Table 3). The same trend could be revealed more dramatically (or, let us say, more graphically) with a scatter plot, as shown in Figure 14, but a graph is not essential here. Again, note the steps taken to avoid ambiguity: Axes are labeled, units of measurement are indicated, symbols are interpreted on the graph, and the figure is accompanied by an informative figure legend. Note also that the symbols used in the student's Figure 14 are consistent with their usage in Figure 13. **Always use the same system of symbols throughout a report** so as not to confuse your reader; if filled circles are used to represent data obtained on diet *A* in one graph, filled circles should be used to represent data obtained on diet *A* in all other graphs. And, as mentioned earlier, **try to use symbols that make sense whenever possible**. In Figures 13 and 14, increasing concentrations of sinigrin are represented by increasingly dark symbols. Similarly, if you were comparing metabolic rates at different times of day, you could help readers interpret your data, for example, by representing daytime measurements with open symbols and nighttime measurements with solid symbols. Note also that the order of symbols in the key corresponds to their placement in the figure, in which most of the open symbols lie above most of the filled symbols. Do whatever you can do to ease interpretation for the reader.

The fourth relationship in our list considers food weight loss in control dishes (no caterpillars). No graphs or tables are needed here; 2 sentences will do:

> Control containers exhibited less than a 3% weight loss (N = 3 containers) during the 24-h period. In contrast, food in containers with caterpillars lost at least 23% of initial weight.

If the weight loss had been substantial, perhaps 5 to 10% or more of initial weight, you might wish to adjust all the data in your tables accordingly before making other calculations:

> Control containers lost 7.6% of their initial weight (N = 3 containers) over the 24-h period. We therefore adjusted weight loss in other containers for this 7.6% evaporative loss before calculating feeding rates.

You would then provide a sample calculation, both for your instructor to examine and so that you will remember what you did if you consult your report again at a later date. A less desirable but nevertheless acceptable alternative would be to state the magnitude of the evaporative weight loss in your Results section and then bring this point up again when interpreting your results in the Discussion section. In this case, you would label appropriate portions of graphs and tables as "Apparent Feeding Rates" rather than "Feeding Rates." Again, although there are many wrong ways to present the data, there is no single right way; you must simply be complete, logical, consistent, and clear.

Note that in Figure 14, the student has defined the symbols directly in the graph rather than in the figure caption (compare with Fig. 13). When appropriate, you can also use empty space to report the results of statistical analyses, as in Figure 15, thus making the figure even more self-sufficient. Don't do this, however, if it will make the graph cluttered and difficult to read; instead, put the information in the caption and/or in the text of the Results section.

If the slope of the regression line had not been significantly different from zero, by the way, the student would have included neither the line nor the equation of the line in the figure (or elsewhere in the report).

So far, we have looked only at examples of tables and point plots. If you were studying the differences in species composition of insect populations trapped in the light fixtures on 4 different floors of your biology building, a bar graph, as in Figure 16, might be more suitable. Note again that the axes are clearly labeled, including units of measurement, and that an explanatory legend accompanies the figure. Don't make the reader back up; make each figure self-sufficient. Note also that the graph tells an interesting story; given that *A* is the fruit fly *Drosophila melanogaster*, it is not difficult to guess where the genetics laboratory is located!

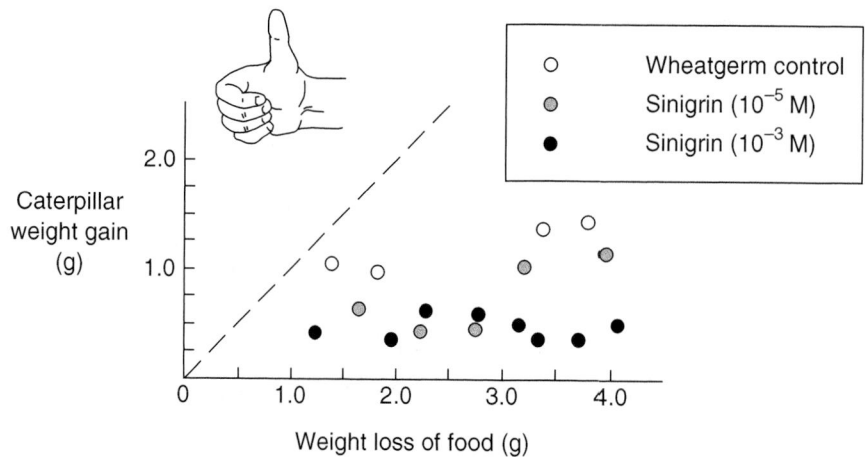

Figure 14. Caterpillar weight gain as a function of food consumption for *Manduca sexta* fed for 3 hours on 1 of 3 diets at 24°C. Points falling on the dotted line would indicate equality between weight gained and food eaten. Each point represents data from a different individual.

Use tables and graphs only if they make your data work for you; if a table or graph fails to help you summarize some trend in your results, it contributes nothing to your report and should be left out. Be selective. Don't include a drawing, graph, or table unless you plan to discuss it, and include only those illustrations that best help you tell your story.

Figure 15. Relationship between wet weight (mg) of the hermit crab *Pagurus longicarpus* and the size of the periwinkle shells (*Littorina littorea*) occupied at Nahant, MA, on September 23, 2008 (N = 12). Each point represents a measurement on a single individual.

Figure 16. The distribution of insect species collected from light fixtures on 4 floors of the biology building on May 5, 2007. The number to the right of each bar gives the total number of insects collected on each floor.

Preparing Graphs

Graphs may be constructed with the aid of a computer (see Technology Tip 7), but unless your instructor suggests otherwise, don't feel that you *must* submit computer-generated graphs to earn a top grade. Most instructors would rather see a carefully thought-out, neatly executed graph done by hand than a poorly thought-out, neatly executed piece of computer graphics. To emphasize the point, I have retained many hand-drawn graphs in this book. I have seen some gorgeous pieces of complete garbage prepared using computers, but I would rather see beginning students spend less time learning to use software and more time thinking about what they present, how they present it, and why they present it.

On the other hand, once you have mastered the key principles of graphing data, learning to use a good software package is certainly worthwhile, particularly since it allows you to quickly examine a variety of relationships in your data and determine which aspects of the data merit graphical presentation. But don't get carried away with all the bells and whistles; once the graphs are plotted, for example, it is sometimes faster to type or hand-print the axis labels or legends than to figure out how to have the computer execute these steps for you.

When preparing graphs by hand, always use graph paper, which can be purchased in your campus bookstore. The most useful sort of graph paper has heavier lines at uniform intervals—at every 4 or 5 divisions, for example, as shown in Figures 17 through 21. These heavy lines facilitate the plotting of data and reduce eyestrain, since every individual line need not be counted in locating data points.

By convention, the independent variable is plotted on the x-axis, and the dependent variable is plotted on the y-axis: y is a function of x. For example, if you examined feeding rates as a function of temperature (Fig. 17), you would plot temperature on the x-axis and feeding rate on the y-axis; feeding rate *depends* on temperature. On the other hand, temperature is not controlled by feeding rate; that is, temperature varies independently of feeding rate. Temperature is the independent variable and is plotted on the x-axis. Note that each point in Figure 17 represents data averaged from 5 individuals so that each point is an average value, or a "mean" value. This is clearly indicated in the y-axis label and in the figure caption.

It is a good practice to label the axes of graphs beginning with zero. To avoid generating graphs with lots of empty, wasted space, breaks can be put in along one or both axes, as in Figure 17 (see also Fig. 13 and Figs. 20–22). If a break had not been inserted in the y-axis of Figure 17, for example, the graph would have been less compact, with much wasted space, as in Figure 18.

(Not) Falsifying Data

You cannot move, add, or delete data points to improve or create trends in your data. Report the data you actually collected. **Falsifying data is, perhaps even more than plagiarism, an unforgivable offense**, and one that can get you into very serious trouble. Biologists build on the work of others, and that involves a lot of trust. Believe in the data that you collected, and present it unaltered. Sometimes unusual or unexpected results lead to interesting new questions or discoveries.

Figure 17. Feeding rate of *Manduca sexta* caterpillars on standard wheatgerm diet as a function of environmental temperature. Each point represents the mean feeding rate of 5 individuals measured over 24 hours.

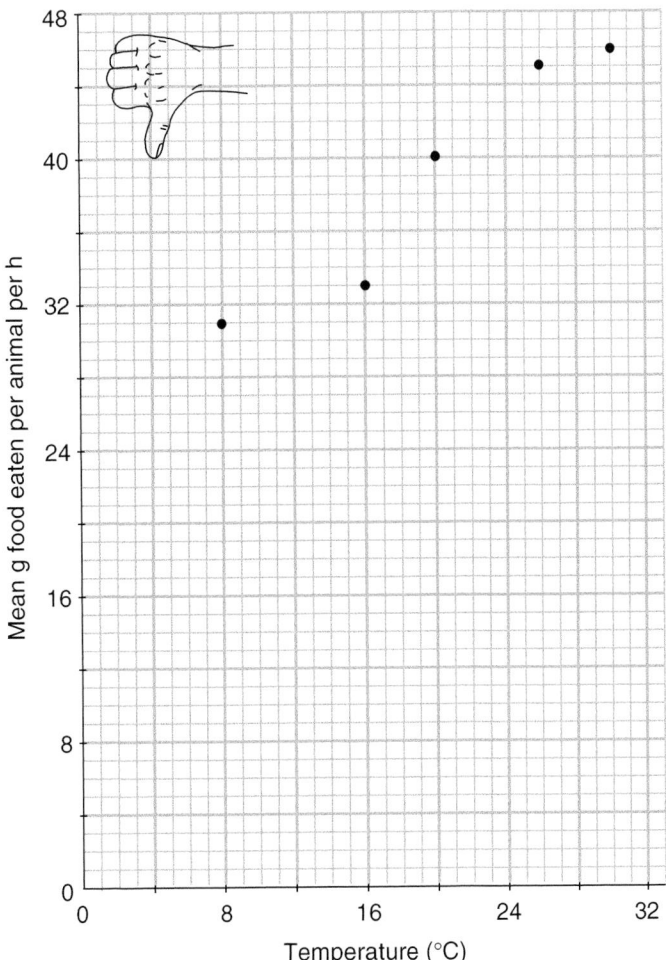

Figure 18. Feeding rate of *Manduca sexta* caterpillars on standard wheatgerm diet as a function of environmental temperature. Each point represents the mean feeding rate of 5 individuals measured over 24 hours.

The Question: To Connect or Not to Connect the Dots?

After plotting data points, lines are often added to graphs to clarify trends in the data. It is especially important to add such lines if data from several different treatments are plotted on a single graph, as in Figure 19. Note that this graph has been made easier to interpret by using different symbols for the data obtained at each temperature, and that the zero point on the x-axis has been displaced to the right, to prevent the first data point from lying on the y-axis, where it might be overlooked (compare with Figure 20, in which the first point does lie on the y-axis). Note also that each line is labeled. Using a key instead would have required readers to work a little harder in interpreting the graph.

In some cases, it makes more sense to draw smooth curves than to simply connect the dots. For example, suppose we have monitored the increase in height of tomato seedlings over some period of time in the laboratory. Every week we randomly selected 15 to 20 seedlings, from the laboratory population of several hundred, to measure so that different seedlings were usually measured at each sampling period. After about 2 months, the data were plotted as in Figure 20.

Connecting the dots would not be the most sensible way to reveal trends in the data of Figure 20, because we know that the seedlings did not really shrink between days 20 and 28, or between days 36 and 44; simply connecting the points would suggest that shrinkage had occurred. The apparent decline in seedling height reflects the considerable variability in individual growth rates found within the same population, as well as the fact that we did not measure every seedling in the population on every sampling day. In this case, the trend in growth is best revealed by drawing a smooth curve, as shown in Figure 21.

When plotting average values (usually called arithmetic means) on a graph, **always include a visual summary of the amount of variation** present in the data by adding bars extending vertically from each point plotted (Figure 21). You may, for example, choose to simply illustrate the range of values obtained in a given sample. More commonly, you would plot "error bars" (typically the standard error or standard deviation about the mean), giving a visual impression of how much individual data points differed from the calculated mean values, as in Figure 21. The less overlap there is between error bars, the more likely it is that differences between mean values reflect real, biologically meaningful differences.

Figure 19. Rate of tomato seedling growth at 3 different temperatures. Each point represents the mean height of 15 to 17 individuals.

Figure 20. Rate of tomato seedling growth at 20°C. Fifteen to 20 seedlings, out of 205 seedlings in the population, were measured on each day of sampling.

Plots of standard deviations or standard errors are always symmetrical about the mean value and so convey only partial information about the range of values obtained. If more of your individual values are above the mean than below the mean, the error bars will give a misleading impression about how the data are actually distributed. If your graph is fairly simple, you may be able to achieve the best of both worlds, indicating both the range and standard deviation (or standard error), as shown in Figure 22. In Figure 22, the vertical bars extending from the point at day 30 indicate that although the average seedling height was about 37 mm on that day, at least 1 seedling in the sample was as small as 25 mm, and at least 1 seedling was as large as 48 mm. Seedlings meas-

Figure 21. Rate of tomato seedling growth at 20°C. On each day of sampling, 15 to 20 seedlings were randomly sampled from a group of 205 seedlings and measured. Error bars represent one standard deviation about the mean.

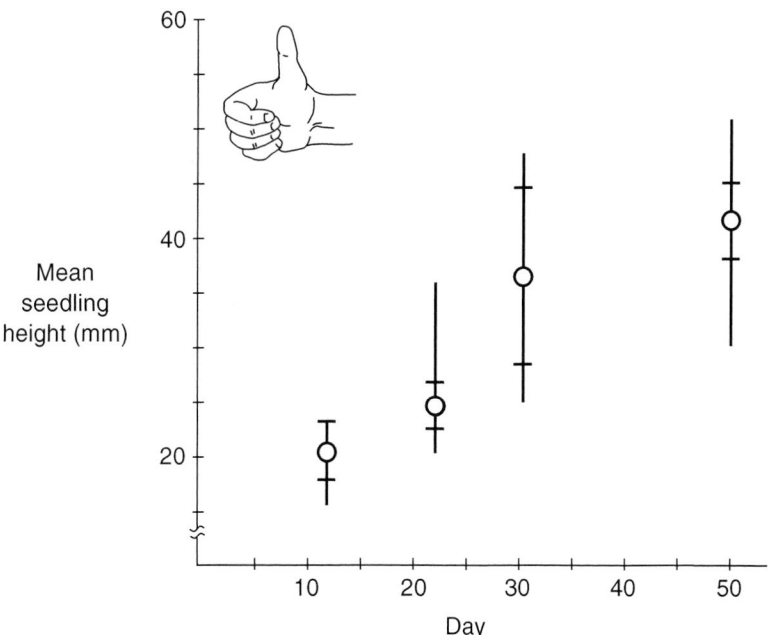

Figure 22. Mean height of tomato plant seedlings over a 50-day period. Each point represents the mean height of 18 seedlings raised at 20°C, with a photoperiod of 12L:12D. Vertical bars represent the range of heights; cross-bars represent 1 standard deviation about the mean.

ured on day 50 also differed in height by somewhat more than 20 mm. But we also see that the error bars are much larger for day 30 than for day 50, even though the range of lengths measured was similar for both samples. This tells us that most seedlings were close to the mean length on day 50, about 42 mm long, but that many of the seedlings measured on day 30 were substantially larger or smaller than the mean value measured on that day.

Whether you choose to plot standard deviations, standard errors, ranges, or some other indicator of variation, **be sure to indicate in your figure caption what you have plotted, along with the number of measurements associated with each mean**.

Making Bar Graphs and Histograms

When the variable along the *x*-axis (the independent variable) is numerical and continuous, points can be plotted and trends can be indicated by lines or curves, as we have seen in Figures 13 through 21. In Figure 17, for example, the *x*-axis shows temperature rising continuously from 0°C to 32°C, with each centimeter along the *x*-axis corresponding to a 4°C rise in temperature. Similarly, the *x*-axes of Figures 20 and 21 reflect the march of time, from 0 to 60 days, with each centimeter along the *x*-axis reflecting 10 additional days.

When the independent variable is nonnumerical or discontinuous, or when the independent variable represents a range of measurements rather than a single measurement, the data are represented by bars, as shown in Figures 23 and 24. The *x*-axis of Figure 23 (a bar graph) is labeled with the names of different mammals. In contrast to the *x*-axes of Figures 13 through 22, the *x*-axis of Figure 23 does not represent a continuum: No particular quantity continually increases or decreases as one moves along the *x*-axis, and a line connecting the data for sea lion and Weddell seal would be meaningless. In Figure 24 (a histogram), the data for shell length are numerical but are grouped together (e.g., all shells 25.0–29.9 mm in length are treated as a single data point). Note also that the magnitude of the size categories represented by the different bars varies: The leftmost bar represents the percentage of shells found within a range of about 0.1 to 21 mm in length, whereas each of the next several bars to the right represents the percentage of shells found within a range of only about 5 mm in length. The size range of shells represented by the bar at the extreme right side of the graph is unknown. We know that all shells found in this category exceeded 45 mm in length, but the graph does not indicate the size of the largest shell.

Use a single color or fill pattern for all bars unless there is a logical reason not to do so. In Figures 23 and 24, for example, all bars should be the same color or fill pattern.

Figure 23. Breath-holding abilities of humans and selected marine mammals. *Data from Sumich, J.L. 1999.* An Introduction to the Biology of Marine Life, *seventh ed. WCB/McGraw-Hill, Publishers.*

Figure 24. Size distribution of snail shells (*Littorina littorea*) collected from the low intertidal zone at Blissful Beach, Massachusetts, on August 15, 2008. Only living animals were measured. A total of 197 snails were included in the survey.

Learning to Love Logarithms

Logarithmic scales make excellent sense when the data presented cover 2 or more powers of 10. Consider the following example: We wish to explore the relationship between the size of hermit crabs and the mass of the snail shells that they choose to live in. The relationship for the tropical hermit crab species *Clibanarius longitarsus* is presented using a standard linear scale in Figure 25*a*. The crabs measured ranged in mass from 0.3 g to nearly 40 g (2 powers of 10). Notice that data points for many quite small crabs are crowded together at the lower left side of the graph so it is difficult to tell the actual values for either crab mass or shell mass, or even to tell how many data points are represented. In addition, the data point for the largest (heaviest) crab is easily overlooked, since it is the only data point for any crab heavier than about 10 g (grams). Plotting logarithms (base 10) of the same data on the *x*-axis (Figure 25*b*) creates a more uniform distribution of data points. Individual data points are now much easier to see. However, this representation is still somewhat difficult to interpret, because it requires you either to know how to decode logarithms or to refer to Table 5. Alternatively, we can replot the data of Figure 25*a* using a log base 10 scale on the *x*-axis, with each major tick now representing 10 times the value of the preceding numbered tick. The value 0 on the *x*-axis of Figure 25*b* corresponds to the value 1 on the *x*-axis of Figure 25*c*, while the value 1.0 on the *x*-axis of Figure 25*b* corresponds to the value 10 on the *x*-axis of Figure 25*c* (see Table 5).

Figure 25. The relationship between the mass of hermit crabs (*Clibanarius longitarsus*) from Mozambique and the mass of the shells they choose to occupy. (a) The data are plotted on a normal, linear scale. Note the large number of data points crowded together in the lower left corner of the graph. (b) The same data replotted after taking the log (base 10) of hermit crab mass. A value of 1 represents 10 g (grams) (see Table 5). (c) The same data plotted using a logarithmic scale (base 10) for the *x*-axis. Hermit crab mass increases 10-fold from one numbered tick mark to the next. In both (b) and (c), note the more even distribution of points.

Based on data of Barnes, D.K.A., 1999. Ecology of tropical hermit crabs at Quirimba Island, Mozambique: shell characteristics and utilization. Mar. Ecol. Progr. Ser. 183: 241–251.

Table 5. Understanding logarithms. (a) In log base 10, each successive whole number is 10 times larger than the preceding whole number. Log base 10 scales are especially useful in presenting data that cover many powers of 10. (b) In log base 2, each successive whole number is twice as large as the preceding whole number. Log base 2 scales are especially useful for visualizing doublings of quantities. Note that in both systems, the log of a number is simply the exponent to which the base (10 in "a," 2 in "b") must be raised to obtain that number.

(a) Number	Log base 10	(b) Number	Log base 2
$0.01 = 1/100 = 10^{-2}$	-2	$1/4 = 2^{-2}$	-2
$0.1 = 1/10 = 10^{-1}$	-1	$1/2 = 2^{-1}$	-1
$1 = 10^0$	0	$1 = 2^0$	0
$10 = 10^1$	1	$2 = 2^1$	1
$100 = 10^2$	$4 = 2^2$	2	
$1,000 = 10^3$	3	$8 = 2^3$	3
$10,000 = 10^4$	4	$16 = 2^4$	4
$100,000 = 10^5$	5	$32 = 2^5$	5

Similarly, compare the clarity of Figure 26a with that of the inset (Figure 26b). In this case, the data extend through 4 powers of 10. Note how most of the data form a difficult-to-decipher mess in the lower left corner of the inset but are spread out evenly using a scale of log base 10 on the x-axis of the main graph.

Although logarithmic graphs are usually plotted using scales in base 10, base 2 scales can also be useful. The hermit crab data of Figure 25a are replotted using this log base 2 scale for both axes in Figure 27; now each numbered major tick represents a doubling of crab or shell mass. A quick visual inspection of this graph shows that as the mass of the hermit crab approximately doubles, the mass of the shell it prefers to inhabit also doubles, something not so obvious in the previous plots of the same data (see Figure 25).

In some cases, logarithms can also be useful in forcing data into straight lines. Figure 28 shows the relationship between the basal diameter of barnacles (*Balanus amphitrite*) and the dry weight of their tissues. Plotted on a linear scale (Figure 28a), tissue weight increases exponentially with increases in barnacle length. Replotting the same data using a double-log scale (base 10), we have essentially bent the data into a straight line (inset) so that the relationship can be represented by a simple equation of the form $y = mx + b$.

Preparing Tables

Tables should always be organized with the data related to a given characteristic being presented vertically rather than horizontally. Tables 6 and 7 present the same information, but in different formats. Table 6 correctly places all information about a single species in one row so that readers can view the information for each species by scanning from left to right and can compare data among different species by scanning up and down a single column. Note also that the independent variable ("species" in this case) is presented vertically in the first column.

Table 7 is incorrectly organized and so is more difficult to read. Like graphs, tables should be self-sufficient; note how much useful information the author has packed into the legend and column headings of Table 6. Note also that the table legend is placed above the table.

As mentioned earlier (p. 1293), do not present the same data in both a graph and a table: choose the format that makes it easiest for you to get your findings across to readers.

Making Your Graphs and Tables Self-Sufficient

A properly executed graph or table is largely self-sufficient: Snipped out of your report along with its accompanying legend or caption, it should make perfectly good sense to any biology major you hand it to. By examining only the axes of a graph and reading the figure caption, for example, the reader should be able to determine the specific question that was asked, how the study was done, and what the main findings are, as discussed in Chapter 1 (pp. 1268–1271). Consider, for example, Figure 21. We can tell quite a lot about how and why this study was done just by carefully studying the figure and its caption. The study was apparently undertaken to determine how fast tomato seedlings grow at one particular temperature, 20°C. We know that the growth of 205 seedlings was followed over nearly 2 months, and that seedlings were measured 9 times over that period, approximately once each week. We also know that not all 205 seedlings were measured every time; instead, the researchers subsampled 15 to 20 each time so that different

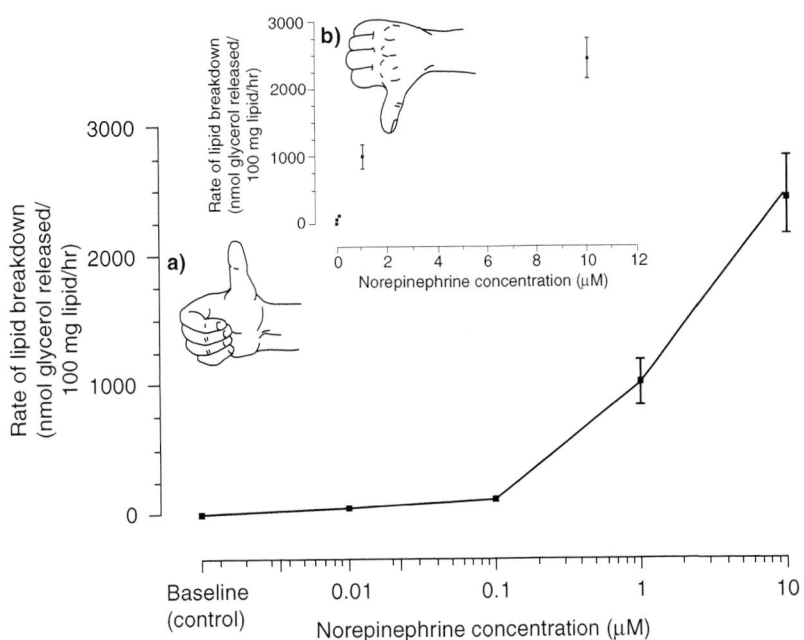

Figure 26. Influence of the neurotransmitter norepinephrine (= noradrenaline) on rate of lipid breakdown in the subcutaneous fatty tissue of hibernating marmots (*Marmota marmota*). Each point represents the mean of 11 determinations, and error bars represent 1 standard deviation about the mean. Note that the norepinephrine concentrations used in the study encompass 4 powers of 10, a situation that typically calls out for logarithmic data representation. (a) The data plotted using a log base 10 scale on the x-axis. (b) (inset) The same data plotted much less effectively, using a normal linear scale.

Based on data of N. Cochet et al., 1999. Regional variation of white adipocyte lipolysis during the annual cycle of the alpine marmot. Comp. Biochem. Physiol. C 123: 225–232.

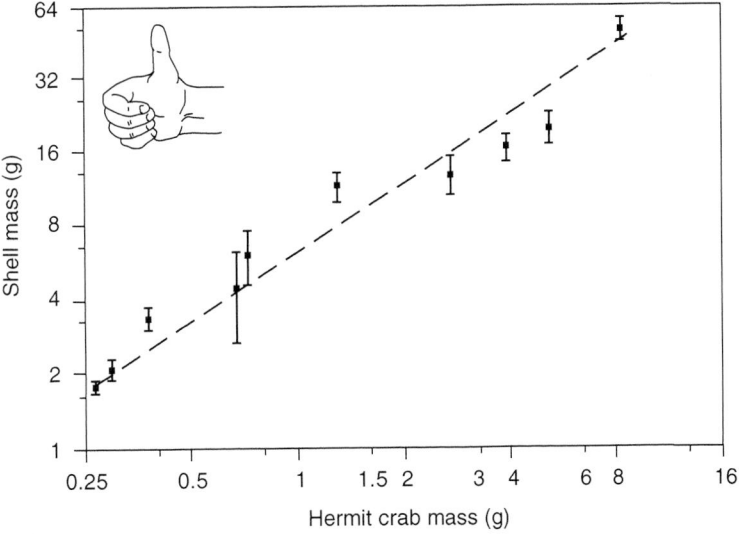

Figure 27. The hermit crab data of Figure 25 plotted using a log base 2 scale on each axis. Such scales are very helpful when you are interested in the effects of doublings, or in how much of a change in x is required to produce a doubling of y.

seedlings were probably measured each time. Finally, we see that each point represents a mean value and that the vertical bars represent 1 standard deviation about the mean.

Similarly, from Figure 17 we know what species was studied and for how long. We also know that caterpillars were maintained at 1 of 5 temperatures, and we know what those temperatures were. Furthermore, we know the number of caterpillars maintained at each temperature.

Try to make your data presentations as self-sufficient as these examples are. In particular, **always indicate the species studied, the sample size** (e.g., Figure 28), **and the number of replicates** (e.g., Table 6). The easier you make it for readers to understand your data, the more likely it is that your work will be read and that you will get your point across intact. Additional advice about constructing good graphs and tables is given in books by W.S. Cleveland and by J. Quinn and M.J. Keough.

Table 6. Characteristics of 4 snail populations sampled at Nahant, MA, on October 13, 2008. Data are means of 4 replicate samples ± 1 standard error.

Species	Average Shell Length (cm)	Sample Size	Average No. Animals per m²
Crepidula fornicata	1.63 ± 0.21	122 indiv.	32.1 ± 4.7
C. plana	1.01 ± 0.34	116	20.8 ± 10.6
Littorina littorea	0.87 ± 0.11	447	113.6 ± 29.1
L. saxatilis	0.40 ± 0.10	60	8.2 ± 5.2

Figure 28. Relationship between barnacle size (in micrometers) and dry tissue weight (micrograms) for juveniles of *Balanus amphitrite*. Each point represents measurements on a single individual. (a) The data plotted on a normal linear scale. (b) The same data replotted using log base 10 scales for both axes. Notice that the exponential curve depicted in (a) becomes a straight line in (b).

Data from Pechenik et al., 1993. Influence of delayed metamorphosis on survival and growth of juvenile barnacles Balanus amphitrite. Mar. Biol. 115: 287–294.

Table 7. Characteristics of 4 snail populations sampled at Nahant, MA, on October 13, 2008. Data are means of 4 replicate samples ± 1 standard error.

Species	*Crepidula fornicata*	*C. plana*	*Littorina littorea*	*L. saxatilis*
Av. shell length (cm)	1.63 ± 0.21	1.01 ± 0.34	0.87 ± 0.11	0.40 ± 0.10
Sample size	122 indiv.	116	447	60
Av. no. animals per m²	32.1 ± 4.7	20.8 ± 10.6	113.6 ± 29.1	8.2 ± 5.2

Putting Your Graphs and Tables in Order

Once you have your graphs (and other figures like drawings or photographs) and tables prepared, you need to decide in what order to present them. **Arrange them logically, in the order that you will discuss them.** The first figure that you refer to in the text of your report will be Figure 1, the second will be Figure 2, and so forth. Order your tables in the same way, with Table 1 the first table that you refer to, in order to facilitate a logical presentation of the data.

Incorporating Figures and Tables into Your Report (or Not)

Ask your instructor whether you should incorporate your graphs and tables into the text of the Results section, as they would appear in a published journal article, or whether you should print the figures and tables on separate pages and include them at the end of your report.

To incorporate figures directly into your report, click on the figure to be inserted, and then use the cut and paste function. Alternatively, you can use the Insert function in the Word menu.

Do not insert figures into the text unless your instructor asks you to. Many of us would prefer to see each figure on a separate page at the end of your report; larger figures are much easier to read and comment on.

Verbalizing Results: General Principles

One-sentence Results sections are common in student reports: "The results are shown in the following tables and graphs." However, *common* does not mean *acceptable*. **You must use words to draw the reader's attention to the key patterns in your data. But do not simply redraw the graphs in words**, as in this description of Figure 19:

> At 20°C, the seedlings showed negligible growth for the first 8 days of study. However, between days 8 and 16, the average seedling grew nearly 5 mm, from about 8 mm to about 13 mm. Growth continued over the next 16 days, with the seedlings reaching an average height of 24 mm by day 24, and 30 mm by day 32.

Let the graph do this work for you; **your task is to summarize the most important findings displayed by the graph** and then to indicate briefly the basis for the statements you make.

First, **decide exactly what you want your reader to see when looking at each graph or table, and then stick the reader's nose right in it**. For example, you might write:

> Temperature had a pronounced effect on seedling growth rates (Figure 19). In particular, seedlings at 25°C consistently grew more rapidly than those at 20°C. . . .

Remember, in scientific writing every statement of fact or opinion must be backed up with evidence. In the example just given, a general statement was supported by reference to a figure, followed by a specific detail that illustrates the point particularly well. In some cases, only a single sentence is required:

> Caterpillars generally fed more slowly on the diet of 10^{-3} M sinigrin than on the wheatgerm controls (Fig. 13).

Readers can then look at Figure 13 and decide whether they see the same trend you do: One sentence and a figure say it all.

Note the use of the past tense in the statement about caterpillar feeding rates:

> Caterpillars generally fed at faster rates on diet *A*.

This statement is quite different from the following one, which uses the present tense:

> Caterpillars feed at faster rates on diet *A*.

By using the present tense, you would be making a broad generalization extending to all caterpillars, or at least to all caterpillars of the species tested. Before one can make such a broad statement, the experiment must be repeated many, many times, and similar results must be obtained each time. After all, the writer is making a statement about all caterpillars under all conditions. By sticking with the past tense here, you are clearly referring only to the results of your study. Be cautious: **Always present your results in the past tense.**

Note also that the authors of these examples **do not make the reader interpret the data**. You must tell your readers exactly what you want them to see when they look at your table or graph. Consider the following 2 examples. The data concern the shell lengths of a particular snail species collected along a rocky coastline, from 2 regions between the high-tide level and the low-tide level. I have not included any figures or tables from this survey, so I refer to them only as "xx" in these examples:

> Although individual specimens of *Littorina littorea* varied considerably in shell length at each tidal height (Figure xx), there was a significant ($t = 26.3$; d.f. = 47; $p < 0.05$) distributional effect of shore position on mean size (Table xx).

> Although individual specimens of *Littorina littorea* varied considerably in shell length at each tidal height (Figure xx), the mean shell length was significantly greater ($t = 26.3$; d.f. = 47; $p < 0.05$) for snails collected higher up in the intertidal zone (Table xx); high shore animals were, on average, 26% larger than low-shore animals.

In the first of these examples, the author expects the readers to figure out what specific information is important in the data. Sometimes this is because the author has not taken the time to think carefully enough about the data. The modified version conveys quite a different impression: We know exactly what the author wants us to see, and we can then decide whether we agree with the author's statements.

Note that in the model example just presented, the lead factual statement was supported both by reference to a figure and by the results of statistical analyses. **Note also that the author provided not just the p-value associated with the result (to indicate how convincing the difference among means is) but also the name of the test statistic (a t-statistic in this example, resulting from a t-test) and the number of degrees of freedom associated with the analysis.** This allows readers to check the validity of the statistical test performed and the validity of the results obtained. Also note that the author correctly refers to the observed differences in shell length as being "significant." **Saying that differences are "significant" (or "not significant") implies that you have subjected your data to rigorous statistical testing.** If you have not conducted statistical analyses, it is perfectly fair to write "Temperature had a pronounced effect on seedling growth rates," or "Seedlings treated with nutrients appeared to grow at slightly faster rates than those treated with distilled water," referring readers to the appropriate table or figure. But if you cannot provide statistical support, you *cannot* say that seedlings in one treatment grew *significantly* faster than those in another treatment. Note also that the author of this example indicates the magnitude of the effect observed; the size differences are not just statistically significant but are, in fact, quite large (26%).

Even if you analyze your data statistically, you must nevertheless be cautious in drawing conclusions. Your data may support one hypothesis more than another, but they cannot *prove* that any hypothesis is true or false. As biologists in training, the *why* of statistical analysis is more important to you than the *how*.

Verbalizing Results: Turning Principles into Action

Let us apply these principles to the caterpillar study discussed earlier in this chapter. First, is there anything about the general response of the animals worth drawing attention to? You might, for example, be able to write:

> All the caterpillars were observed to eat throughout the experiment.

More likely, living things behaving as they do, you will say something like:

> One of the animals offered diet A and 2 of the animals offered diet B were not observed to eat during the 3 h experiment, and the results from these animals were therefore excluded from analysis.

Such a decision to exclude data from further analysis is fine, by the way—it won't be considered data falsification—as long as you indicate the reason for the decision, and as long as the decision is made objectively; as discussed earlier, **you cannot exclude data simply because they violate a trend that would otherwise be apparent, or because the data contradict a favored hypothesis.**

Next, **go back to your initial list, and reword each question as a statement.** For example, the first question posed on p. 1291 ("Did the caterpillars feed at different rates on the different diets?") might be reworded as:

> Caterpillars generally fed at slower rates on the 10^{-3} M sinigrin diet than on the wheatgerm controls (Fig. 13).

or:

> Caterpillars fed at significantly slower rates on the 10^{-3} M sinigrin diet than on either the lower-concentration sinigrin diet or the wheatgerm controls (Fig. 13) ($F = 30.3$, d.f. = 2, 11; $p < 0.0001$).

If you follow this procedure for each question on your list, your Results section will be complete. The written part will generally be quite short.

What Is a "Figure"?

Note that in all of the examples given in this chapter, data summaries are formally referred to as either tables or figures. **"Figures" include graphs of all types; photographs of all types, whether of organisms or of electrophoretic gels; drawings; and flowcharts. Anything and everything, in fact, that is not a "table" is a "figure."**

Writing about Negative Results

An experiment that was correctly performed always "works." The results may not be what you had expected or hoped for, but this does not mean that the experiment has been a waste of time. If biologists threw away their data every time something unexpected happened, we would rarely learn anything new. The data you collect are real; only the interpretation of those data is open to question. Therefore, always treat your data with respect. The lack of a trend, or the presence of a trend contrary to expectation, is itself a story worth telling.

Writing about Numbers

According to the Council of Science Editors (*Scientific Style and Format: The CSE Manual for Authors, Editors, and Publishers*, seventh edition), you should **use numerals rather than words when writing about counted or measured items, percentages, decimals, magnifications, and abbreviated units of measurement**: 6 larvae, 18 seedlings, 25 drops, 25%, 1.5 times greater, 50× magnification, a 3:1 ratio, 0.7 g, 18 ml.

All rules, however, have exceptions. Use words rather than numerals if beginning a sentence with a number or percentage:

Twenty grams of NaCl were added to each of 4 flasks.

Thirty percent of the tadpoles metamorphosed by the end of the second week.

Or, avoid starting sentences with numbers, as in this rewrite of the first example:

To each of 4 flasks we added 20 g of NaCl.

When 2 numbers are written adjacent to each other without being separated by words or a comma, write one of the numbers in words:

The sample was divided into five 25-seedling groups.

Better still, that sentence could easily be rewritten so that numerals are appropriate for both numbers:

The samples were divided into 5 groups of 25 seedlings each.

Zero and one present special problems: a "0" is easily mistaken for the letter "O," and the numeral "1" is easily mistaken for the letters "l" (as in the abbreviation for "liters") or "I." Plus, it just looks odd to read, "I know that 1 day my prince will come." The Council of Science Editors has recently clarified its position on these issues. In most cases, unless the zero or one is followed by units of measure (e.g., "I added 1 mg of sucrose to the solution"), or is part of an equation (e.g., "$n = 1$"), or is part of a series that includes larger numbers ("1, 8, and 25 individuals . . ."), use words rather than numerals for zero and one.

When writing about numbers smaller than zero, precede the decimal point with a zero:

. . . and we then added 0.25 g NaCl to each flask.

When using ordinal numbers (e.g., first, fifth), the Council of Science Editors suggests using words for the first 9 numbers and numerals for the others ("the 25th replicate . . ."). However, you should be consistent within a series ("first, fifth, ninth" and "13th, 14th, 15th"; but "5th, 9th, 15th," rather than "fifth, ninth, 15th").

When writing about very large or very small numbers, particularly in association with concentrations or rates, **use scientific notation**. It is preferable, for example, to write about solute concentrations of 5.6×10^{-3} g/ml rather than 0.0056 g/ml, and about cell concentrations being approximately 1.8×10^5 cells/ml rather than about 180,000 cells/ml. Note that I could have avoided both scientific notation and commas in the first example by describing the solute concentration as 5.6 mg/ml. By the way, the word *per*, as in "cells per ml" or "distance per second," may be indicated using either a slash or an exponent: "1.8×10^5 cells/ml" and "1.8×10^5 cells ml^{-1}" are equally acceptable forms of expression.

Finally, the Council of Science Editors recommends **using commas** only when numerals contain 5 or more numbers, as in the following example:

Only 1073 of the original 12,450 frog tadpoles died during the study.

Date and time started: _____
Date and time ended: _____

Caterpillar No.	Diet	Caterpillar wt. (g) Initial	Caterpillar wt. (g) Final	Weight Change (g)	Food wt. (g) Initial	Food wt. (g) Final	Food wt. Change (g)	Feeding rate g eaten/caterp./h
X	X	X	X		X	X		

Figure 29. Sample format for a laboratory data sheet.

In Anticipation—Preparing in Advance for Data Collection

Much of the work involved in putting together a good research report goes into preparing the Results section. You can save yourself considerable effort and frustration by planning ahead before you enter the laboratory to do the experiment. Be prepared to record your data in a format that will enable you to make your calculations easily. For the caterpillar experiment referred to previously, come to the laboratory with a data sheet set up like the one shown in Figure 29. Using this data sheet, the data are recorded in the *x* areas during the laboratory period; the blank spaces will be filled in later, as you make your calculations. If possible, leave a few blank columns at the right to accommodate unanticipated needs discovered as you record or work up your data.

In introductory laboratory exercises, students are often provided with data sheets already set up in a useful format. Take a careful look at those data sheets to understand how they are organized and why they appear as they do; in more advanced laboratory courses, you will be responsible for organizing your own data sheets. As mentioned earlier, always follow any number you write down with the appropriate units, such as mg (milligrams), cm (centimeters), or mm/min (millimeters per minute, often written as $mm \cdot min^{-1}$). This will avoid potential confusion later.

You can also enter your data directly into a computer if you set up a data sheet in advance (see Technology Tip 6).

Following the advice of the previous paragraph can save you hours of work later on. Even so, it takes time and care to put together an effective Results section. But this section is the heart of your report. Craft it properly, and the remainder of the work will be relatively easy.

TECHNOLOGY TIP 6

Using computer spreadsheets for data collection

One advantage of entering data directly into a spreadsheet (e.g., Excel) is that you can preprogram automatic calculations into the spreadsheet. Consider, for example, Table 3 (p. 1292). If we enter data into columns 2, 3, and 5 (Initial Caterpillar Wt., Final Caterpillar Wt., and Wt. of Food Lost), we can enter formulas into columns 4 and 6 so that Caterpillar Wt. Change and Feeding Rate will be calculated automatically. Before entering formulas in Excel, remember to first click on the appropriate box and then click "=" to indicate that a formula is on its way.

Whenever you enter formulas into a spreadsheet, make one sample calculation by hand or with a calculator to be sure that the formula you entered is correct. Also check to be sure that the formula is correctly applied to all entries in each column.

Especially useful operators include SUM, AVG, and STDEV. For example "= AVG(B3:B21)" calculates the average of the numbers in columns B3 through B21 of the spreadsheet, whereas "= STDEV(B3:B21)" returns the standard deviation about the mean.

CITING SOURCES

The next sections to prepare are the Discussion section and the Introduction. In both sections, you will be making statements of fact that require support, often from written sources. As stated in previous chapters and discussed more fully in Chapter 2, **every statement of fact or opinion must be supported with a reference to its source**. Read Chapter 2 (pp. 1277–1279) for specific instructions on citing sources.

WHAT TO DO NEXT?

I usually draft my Discussion section next, although you might instead try drafting your Introduction (p. 1312). See what works best for you. The key is to undertake neither one until you have your Materials and Methods section and your Results section in good order.

WRITING THE DISCUSSION SECTION

The scientific method does not require researchers to be unbiased observers of nature. Scientists almost always have a theory in mind when they perform an experiment. But the method does require that scientists be willing to change their views about nature when the data demand it.

R.M. Hazen and J. Trefil

In the Discussion section of the report, you must interpret your results in the context of the specific questions you set out to address during your experiment and in the context of any relevant broader issues that have been raised in lectures, textbook readings, previous coursework, and possibly, your library research. You will consider the following issues:

1. What did you expect to find, and why?
2. How did your actual results compare with the results you expected? If you set out to test specific hypotheses, do your data support one hypothesis more than another, or allow you to eliminate one or more of them? Explain your logic.
3. How might you explain any unexpected results?
4. How might you test those potential explanations?
5. Based on your results, what question or questions might you logically want to ask next?

Clearly, if your results coincide exactly with those expected from prior knowledge, your Discussion section will be rather short, but such a high level of agreement is rarely obtained in 3- or 4-hour laboratory studies. Indeed, high degrees of variability characterize many aspects of research in biology, especially at the level of the whole organism. After all, genetically based variation in traits is the raw material of evolution: Without such variation, evolution by natural selection would not be possible. Often a study will need to be repeated many times, with very large sample sizes, before convincing trends emerge. A short paper in a biological journal may well represent years of work by several competent, hardworking individuals. Even the simplest of questions are often not easily answered. Nevertheless, every experiment that was carried out properly tells you *something*, even if that something is not what you specifically intended to find out.

Expectations

State your expectations explicitly, and back up your statements with a reference. Scientific hypotheses are not simply random guesses. Your expectations must be based on facts, not opinions; these facts could come from lectures, laboratory manuals or handouts, textbooks, or any other traceable source. In discussing a study on the effectiveness of different wavelengths of light in promoting photosynthesis, for example, you might write something like:

> All wavelengths of light are not equally effective in promoting photosynthesis: green light is said to be especially ineffective (Ellmore and Feldberg, 2003). This is because green light tends to be reflected rather than absorbed by plant pigments, which is why most plants look green (Ellmore and Feldberg, 2003). Our results supported this expectation. In particular . . .

Alternatively, a Discussion section might profitably begin:

> The results of our experiment failed to support the hypothesis (McClaughlin and McVey, 2001) that caterpillars of *Manduca sexta* reared on one uniquely flavored diet will prefer that diet when subsequently given a choice of foods.

Here we have managed to state our expectations and compare them with our results in a single sentence. In both cases, we have begun our discussion on firm ground—with facts rather than unsupported opinions.

Note that in this last example, the expectations were based on previously published research. Your expectations might instead be based on a hypothesis stated in your Introduction and tested in your Results section.

Explaining Unexpected Results

When results refuse to meet expectations, students commonly blame the equipment, the laboratory instructor, their laboratory partners, or themselves. Generally, more scientifically interesting possibilities than experimenter incompetence are the culprits. A few years ago, I did an experiment with 2 colleagues to see if dopamine receptors were involved in the pathway that led to metamorphosis in a particular marine animal. The idea was to add to seawater a chemical known to disable dopamine receptors and then see if the larvae could nevertheless be made to metamorphose. Every time we did the experiment, we got a different result. Sometimes the chemical blocked metamorphosis, but in other experiments it actually stimulated larvae to metamorphose! What on earth was going on? It turned out that the response of competent larvae to the chemical changes predictably as larvae age—something never reported before. The paper we ended up publishing[*] was very different from the paper we had originally envisioned. Yes, dopamine receptors are involved in the metamorphic pathway of this species, but this turned out to be, in my view, the least interesting aspect of the work.

---

[*]Pechenik, J.A., Cochrane, D.E., Li, W. 2002. Timing is everything: The effects of putative dopamine antagonists on metamorphosis vary with larval age and experimental duration in the prosobranch gastropod *Crepidula fornicata*. *Biol. Bull.* 202: 137–147.

Don't be too hard on yourself if your results don't fit your expectations, or if they don't disprove your null hypothesis when you expected them to. **Base your discussion on the data you obtain.** And don't limit yourself to assessing *a priori* hypotheses: Probe your data thoroughly, expect the unexpected, and consider all potential aspects of, and reasonable explanations for, your data. Take another look at the list of factors you wrote when beginning to work on your Materials and Methods section. Could any of these factors be sufficiently different from the normal or standard conditions under which the experiment is performed to account for the difference in results? Look again at your laboratory manual or handout. Are any of the conditions under which your experiment was performed substantially different from those assumed in the instruction manual? If you discover no obvious differences in the experimental conditions, or if the differences cannot account for your results, include this point in your report, as in this example:

> The discrepancy in results cannot be explained by the unusually low temperature in the laboratory on the day of the experiment, since the control animals were subjected to the same conditions and yet behaved as expected.

If potentially important differences are noted, put this ammunition to good use:

> In prior years, these experiments have been performed using species *X* (Professor E. Iyengar, personal communication). It is possible that species *Y* simply behaves differently under the same experimental conditions.

Note that the writer does not *conclude* that species *X* and species *Y* behave differently; the writer merely *suggests* this explanation as a possibility. **Always be careful to distinguish possibility from fact.** Suggesting a logical possibility won't get you into any trouble. Stating your idea as though it was an accepted fact, on the other hand, is sticking your neck out far enough to get your head chopped off.

Continue your discussion by indicating possible ways that the differences in behavioral responses **might be tested**. For example:

> This possibility can be examined by simultaneously exposing individuals of both species to the same experimental conditions. If species *X* behaves as expected and species *Y* behaves as it did in our experiment, then the hypothesis of species-specific behavioral differences will be supported. If species *X* and species *Y* both respond as species *Y* did in the present study, then some other explanation will be called for.

Continue in this vein, evaluating all the reasonable, testable possibilities you can think of. An instructor enjoys reading these sorts of analyses, because they indicate that students have been thinking about what they've done.

Notice that in the preceding example the writer did not say, "If species *X* behaves as expected and species *Y* behaves as it did in the present experiment, then the hypothesis will be supported." This writer remembers rule number 14: **Never make the reader back up.** Notice, too, that the writer did not say, "then the hypothesis will be true," or "then the hypothesis will be proven." **Experiments cannot *prove* anything; they can only support or not support specific hypotheses.** As scientists, our interpretations of phenomena may make excellent sense based on what we know at the moment, but those interpretations are not necessarily correct. New information often changes our interpretations of previously acquired data.

Analysis of Specific Examples

EXAMPLE 1

In this study, tobacco hornworm caterpillars were raised for 4 days on one diet, and then tested over a 3-hour period to see if they preferred that food when given a choice of diets.

STUDENT PRESENTATION

The data indicate that the choice of food was not related to the food upon which the caterpillars had been reared. These data run counter to the hypothesis (Back and Reese, 1976) that hornworms are conditioned to respond to certain specific foods. Only 1 set of data out of the 4 gave any indication of a preference for the original diet, and that indication was rather weak.

There are many possible explanations for data that are so contrary to previous experimental results. Inexperience of the experimenters, combined with the fact that 3 different people were recording data about the caterpillars, may account for part of the error. Keeping track of many worms and attempting to interpret their actions as having chosen a food or having merely been passing by may have proven to be too much for first-time hornworm watchers. The mere fact that each of 3 people will interpret actions differently and will have somewhat different methods of recording information introduces bias into the data.

ANALYSIS

This Discussion section starts out well, with a comparison between the results expected and the results obtained. The hypothesis being discussed is clearly stated, and a supporting reference is given. The student even recognizes that "data are" rather than "data is." The second paragraph, however, betrays a total lack of confidence in the data obtained; the results could not possibly have turned out this way unless the researchers were incompetent, writes the student. Although inexperience can certainly contribute to suspicious results, are there no other possible explanations? Does it really take years of training to determine whether a caterpillar ate food *A* or food *B*?

Compare this report with the one in the next example. This Discussion section deals with the same experiment. In fact, the 2 students were laboratory partners.

EXAMPLE 2

Contrary to expectation, our results suggest that caterpillars of this species showed no preference in the diet they touched first and the diet they spent the most time feeding on. This unexpected finding may be due to the fact that the caterpillars were not reared on the original diets long enough to acquire a lasting feeding preference. They were reared on the original diets for only 4 days, whereas the laboratory handout had suggested a pre-feeding period of 5–10 days (Orians and Starks, 2003). This possibility may be tested by performing the same experiment but varying the amount of time that the caterpillars are reared on the original diets. Such an experiment would determine whether there is a critical time that caterpillars should be reared on a particular diet before they will show a preference for that diet. Another possible explanation for our results may be that the caterpillars used in our study were very young, weighing only 3–6 mg. Finally, this experiment lasted only 3 hours. Perhaps different results would have been obtained had the organisms been given more time to adjust to the test conditions. We suggest conducting an identical experiment for a longer period of time, such as 10–12 hours.

The author of this report produced a paper that clearly indicates thought. Which report do you suppose received the higher grade?

EXAMPLE 3

In this experiment, several hundred milliliters (ml) of filtered pond water were inoculated with a small population of the ciliated protozoan *Paramecium multimicronucleatum* and then distributed among 3 small flasks. Over the next 5 days, changes in the numbers of individuals per ml of water in each flask were monitored.

STUDENT PRESENTATION

The large variation observed between the groups of 3 replicate populations suggests that the experimental technique was imperfect. The sampling error was high because it was difficult to be precise in counting the numbers of individuals. Some animals may have been missed while others were counted repeatedly. More accurate data may be obtained if the number of samples taken is increased, especially at the higher population densities. In addition, more than 3 replicate populations of each treatment could be established. Finally, extremely precise microscopes and pipets could be used by experienced operators to reduce sampling error.

ANALYSIS

This writer, like the writer of Example 1, starts out by assuming that the experiment was a failure, and then spends the rest of the report making excuses for this failure. The quality of the microscopes was certainly adequate to recognize moving objects, and *P. multimicronucleatum* was the only organism moving in the water: The author is grasping at straws. If the author had more confidence in his or her abilities, the paper might have been far different. Isn't there some chance that the experiment was performed correctly? Lacking confidence in the data, the student took the easy way out and looked no further, even though he or she actually had access to data that would have allowed several of the stated hypotheses to be assessed. On each day, for example, several sets of samples were taken from each flask, and each set gave similar estimates for the numbers of organisms per milliliter: This consistency of results suggests that the variation in population density from flask to flask was real, and not due to experimenter incompetence. In addition, although the student stated correctly that larger sample sizes would have been helpful, he or she should have supported that statement with additional data analysis. Fifteen drops were sampled from each flask for each set of samples. The student could have calculated the mean number of individuals in the first 3 drops, the first 6 drops, the first 9 drops, the first 12 drops, and then the full 15 drops, to see how the estimates of population size changed as the sample size increased. With such calculations, the student would probably have found that larger sample sizes are especially important when population density is low. (Why might this be so?)

EXAMPLE 4

In this last study, a group of students went seining for fish in a local pond. Every fish was then identified to species. It turned out that 91% of the fish in the sample of 73 individuals belonged to a single species. The remaining fish were distributed among only 2 additional species.

STUDENT PRESENTATION

I find the small number of species represented in our sample surprising, since the pond is fed by several streams that might be expected to introduce a variety of different species into it, assuming that the streams are not polluted. The lab manual states that 12 fish species have been found in the adjacent streams. It appears that the conditions in the pond at the time of our sampling were especially suitable for one species in particular out of all those that most likely have access to it. Perhaps the physical nature of the pond is such that the number of niches is small, in which case competition would become very keen; only one species can occupy a given niche at any one time (Ricklefs and Miller, 2000). The reproductive pattern of the fishes might also contribute to the observed results. Possibly *Lepomis macrochirus*, the dominant species, lays more eggs than the others, or perhaps the young of this species survive better, or prey on the young of other species.

Another possible explanation for our findings is that we sampled only the perimeter of the pond, since our seining was limited to a depth of water not exceeding the heights of the seiners. The species distribution could be very different in the middle of the pond at a greater depth.

ANALYSIS

I have not reproduced the entire Discussion section of the student's paper, but even this excerpt demonstrates that a little thinking goes a long way. Note that the student did not require much specialized knowledge to write this Discussion section, only a bit of confidence in the data. Another student might well have written:

Most likely, the fish were incorrectly identified; more species were probably present than could be recognized by our inexperienced team. It is also possible that the net had a large tear, which let the members of other species escape. I didn't notice this rip in the fabric, but my glasses were probably dirty, and then again, I'm not very observant.

WRITING THE INTRODUCTION SECTION

The Introduction section establishes the framework for the entire report. In this section, **you briefly present background information that leads to a clear statement of the specific issue or issues that will be addressed in the remainder of the report**; by the time you have finished writing the Materials and Methods, Results, and Discussion sections of your laboratory report, you should be in a good position to know what these issues are. In 1 or 2 paragraphs, then, you must present an argument explaining why the study was undertaken. More to the point, perhaps, the Introduction provides you with your first opportunity to convince your instructor that you understand why you have been asked to do the exercise.

Every topic that appears in later sections of your report should be anticipated clearly in the Introduction, and the Introduction should contain only information that is directly relevant to the rest of the report.

Stating the Question

Even though the statement of questions posed, or of issues addressed, generally concludes the Introduction section of a report, it is useful to deal with this issue first. What was the *specific* issue or question addressed in this study?

First, write the following words: "In this study" or "In this experiment." Then complete the sentence as specifically as possible. Three examples follow:

In this study, the oxygen consumption of mice and rats was measured to investigate the relationships between metabolic rate, body weight, and body surface area.

In this study, we collected fish from 2 local ponds and classified each fish into its proper taxonomic category.

In this experiment, we asked the following question: Do the larvae of *Manduca sexta* prefer the diet upon which they have been reared when offered a choice of diets?

Note that each statement of intent is phrased in the past tense since the students are describing studies that have now been completed.

The strong points of these statements are best revealed by examining a few unsatisfactory alternatives:

In this study, we measured the metabolic rate of rats and mice.

In this study, we worked with freshwater fish.

In this experiment, the feeding habits of *Manduca sexta* larvae were studied.

Each of these 3 unsatisfactory statements is vague; readers will assume, perhaps correctly, that you are as much in the dark about what you've done as your writing implies. **Be specific.** Here, in one sentence, you must come fully to grips with the goals of your study. There *was* some point to the time that you were asked to spend in the laboratory; find it.

If you go on to state specific expectations, or to present specific hypotheses that you set out to test, **make the source of those hypotheses clear**, as in the following example:

> We expected larger mice to respire faster than smaller mice, since larger mice support a greater biomass. However, we also predicted that respiration rates per gram of tissue would be similar in large and small individuals, since dividing by weight should adjust for size differences.

As mentioned earlier (p. 1309), you must provide a rationale (e.g., logical argument or results from prior studies) for any expectations or specific hypotheses that you state.

An Aside: Studies Versus Experiments

An experiment always involves manipulating something, such as an organism, an enzyme, or the environment, in a way that will permit specific relationships to be examined or hypotheses to be tested. Containers of protozoans in pond water could be distributed among 3 different temperatures, for example, to test the influence of temperature on the reproductive rate of the particular species under study. The ability of salivary amylase to function over a range of pHs might be examined to test the hypothesis that the activity of this enzyme is pH-sensitive. In the field, a population of marine snails from one location might be transplanted to another location and the subsequent survival and growth of the transplanted population studied so as to test the hypothesis that conditions in the new location are less hospitable for that species than in the location from which the original population was obtained. As a control, of course, the survival and growth of animals not transplanted would also have to be monitored over the same period. Note that an experiment may be conducted in the laboratory or in the field.

It is permissible to refer to experiments as "studies," but not all studies are "experiments." In contrast to the preceding experiments, some exercises require you to collect, observe, enumerate, or describe. You should avoid referring to such studies as experiments; **where there are no manipulations, there are no experiments**. You might, for example, collect insects from light fixtures located at several different locations within the biology building and identify them to the species level, enabling you to examine the distribution of insect species within the building. Or you might be asked to provide a detailed description of the feeding activities of an insect. Or you might spend an afternoon documenting the depth to which light penetrates in various areas of a lake, and then correlate that information with data on the distribution of aquatic plants in the different areas. In each case, you should refer to your work as a study, not as an experiment. For example:

> In this study, insects were collected from all light fixtures on floors 1, 3, and 5 of the Dana building, and the distribution of species among the different locations was determined.

Providing the Background

Having posed, in a single sentence, the question or issue that was addressed, it will now be easier to fill in the background needed to understand why the question was asked. A few general rules should be kept in mind:

1. **Support all statements of fact with a reference to your textbook, laboratory manual, outside reading, or lecture notes.** Unless you are told otherwise by your instructor, do not use footnotes. Rather, refer to your reference within the text, giving the author of the source and the year of publication, as in the following example:

   > Many marine gastropods enclose their fertilized eggs within complex encapsulating structures (Hunt, 1966; Tamarin and Carriker, 1968).

   Note that the period concluding the sentence comes after the closing parenthesis.

2. **Define specialized terminology.** Your instructor probably knows the meaning of the terms you will use in your report, but by defining them in your own words, you can convince the instructor that you, too, know what these words mean. Write to illuminate, not to impress. As always, if you write with your future self in mind as the audience, you will usually come out on top; write an Introduction you will be able to understand 5 years from now. The following examples obey this and the preceding rule:

    A number of caterpillar species are known to exhibit induction of preference, a phenomenon in which an organism develops a preference for the particular flavor on which it has been reared (Westneat and Sesterhenn, 1983).

    The development of mature female gametes, a process termed oogenesis, is regulated by changing hormonal levels in the blood (Gilbert, 2006; McVey, 2008).

3. **Never set out to prove, verify, or demonstrate the truth of something.** Rather, set out to test, document, or describe. In biology (and science in general), truth is elusive; it is important to keep an open mind when you begin a study and when you write up the results of that study. It is not uncommon to repeat someone else's experiment or observations and obtain a different result or description. Responses will differ with species, time of year, and other, often subtle changes in the conditions under which the study is conducted. To show that you had an open mind when you undertook your study, you would want to revise the following sentences before submitting them to your instructor:

    In this experiment, we attempted to demonstrate induction of preference in larvae of *Manduca sexta*.

This experiment was designed to show that pepsin, an enzyme promoting protein degradation in the vertebrate stomach, functions best at a pH of 2, as commonly reported (Bernheim and Cochrane, 1983).

The first example might be modified to read:

In this experiment, we tested the hypothesis that young caterpillars of *Manduca sexta* demonstrate the phenomenon of induction of preference.

4. **Be brief.** The Introduction must not be a series of interesting but random facts about the topic you have investigated. Rather, **every sentence should be designed to directly prepare the reader for the statement of intent**, which will appear at the end of the Introduction section, as already discussed. If, for example, your study was undertaken to determine which wavelengths of light are most effective in promoting photosynthesis, there is no need to describe the detailed biochemical reactions that characterize photosynthesis. As another example of what not to do, consider these few sentences taken from a report describing an induction-of-preference study. Caterpillars were reared on one diet for 5 days and tested later to see if they chose that food over foods that the caterpillars had never before experienced.

    In this experiment, we explored the possibility that larvae of *Manduca sexta* could be induced to prefer a particular diet when later offered a choice of diets. The results of this experiment are important because induction of preference is apparently linked to (1) the release of electrophysiological signals by sensory cells in the animal's mouth and (2) the release of particular enzymes, produced during the period of induction, that facilitate the digestion and metabolism of secondary plant compounds (laboratory handout, 2001).

The entire last sentence does not belong in the Introduction. The work referred to in this example was a simple behavioral study: Students did not make electrophysiological recordings, nor did they isolate and characterize any enzymes. Although a consideration of these 2 topics might profitably be incorporated into a discussion of the results obtained, these issues should be excluded from the Introduction, because they do not explain why this particular study was undertaken. **Include in your Introduction section only information that prepares the reader for the final statement of intent.** You might, on a separate piece of paper, jot down other ideas that occur to you for possible use in revising your Discussion section, but if they don't contribute to your Introduction, don't let them intrude. Be firm. Stay focused.

5. **Write an Introduction for the study that you ended up doing.** Sometimes it is necessary to modify a study for a particular set of conditions, with the result that the observations actually made no longer relate to the questions originally posed in your laboratory handout or laboratory manual. For example, the pH meter might not have been working on the day of your laboratory experience, and your instructor modified the experiment accordingly. Perhaps the experiment you actually performed dealt with the influence of temperature, rather than pH, on enzymatic reaction rates. In such an instance, you would not mention pH in your Introduction section since the work you ended up doing dealt only with the effects of temperature.

6. Once you have written a first draft of your Introduction, idea mapping can help you decide which ideas to keep, and help you to organize those ideas to best advantage.

A Sample Introduction

The following paragraphs satisfy all the requirements of a valid Introduction. This Introduction section is brief but complete—and effective:

It is well known that plants can use sunlight as an energy source for carbon fixation (Ellmore and Reed, 1993). However, all wavelengths of light need not be equally effective in promoting such photosynthesis. Indeed, the green coloration of most leaves suggests that wavelengths of approximately 550 nm are reflected rather than absorbed so that this wavelength would not be expected to produce much carbon fixation by green plants.

During photosynthesis, oxygen is liberated in proportion to the rate at which carbon dioxide is fixed (Ellmore and Reed, 1993). Thus, relative rates of photosynthesis can be determined either by monitoring rates of oxygen production or by monitoring rates of carbon dioxide uptake. In this experiment, we monitored rates of oxygen production to test the hypothesis that wavelengths of light differ in their ability to promote carbon fixation by the aquatic plant *Elodea canadensis*.

Note how, in this Introduction, the material progressed from a rather general statement (plants photosynthesize) to more specific statements and, finally, to the specific research objectives of the study. You will see the same progression in the Introduction sections of most published studies. Your instructor should also see it in yours. Note also that every sentence leads the reader logically to the final sentence.

TALKING ABOUT YOUR STUDY ORGANISM OR FIELD SITE

If your study organism or field site was deliberately chosen because it was ideally suited to investigating the particular problem that you addressed, conclude your Introduction with a brief paragraph explaining your choice. Otherwise, that information would be more appropriate in your Materials and Methods section, as on p. 1290. Here is an example of how the material presented on p. 1290 could be rewritten as a fine ending to an Introduction:

> *Hydroides dianthus* is an excellent organism for such a study, as its larvae can be obtained in great numbers almost year-round and reared in the laboratory with greater than 90% survival (Qian, 2000; Toonen and Pawlik, 2001). Moreover, the larvae become capable of metamorphosing within 4–6 days at 25°C (Scheltema, 1981; Bryan and Qian, 1997) and can be readily induced to metamorphose by simply elevating the potassium concentration of seawater by 15 mM* (Bryan and Qian, 1997).

DECIDING ON A TITLE

A good title summarizes, as specifically as possible, what lies within the Introduction and Results sections of the report. For this reason, **write your title after you have written the rest of your report**. Your instructor is a captive audience. In the real world of publications, however, your article will vie for attention with many other articles written by many other people; the busy potential reader of your paper will glance at the title of your report and promptly decide whether to stay or move on. The more revealing your title, the more easily potential readers can assess the relevance of your paper to their interests. A paper that delivers something other than what is promised by the title can lose you considerable good will when read by the wrong audience, and it may be overlooked by the very readers for whom the paper was intended. Indeed, many potential readers will miss your paper entirely, because indexing services, such as *Biological Abstracts* and *ISI Web of Science,* use keywords from a paper's title in preparing their subject indexes.

Here is a list of mediocre titles, each followed by 1 or 2 more revealing counterparts:

1. **No:** Metabolic rate determinations

   Yes: Exploring the relationship between body size and oxygen consumption in mice

2. **No:** The role of a homeobox gene

   Yes: The homeobox gene *Irx5* is needed for retinal cell development in mice

3. **No:**

   a. Measuring the feeding behavior of caterpillars

   b. Food preferences of *Manduca sexta* larvae

   Yes:

   a. Measurements of feeding preferences in tobacco hornworm larvae (*Manduca sexta*) reared on 3 different diets

   b. Can larvae of *Manduca sexta* (Arthropoda: Insecta) be induced to prefer a particular diet?

4. **No:** Effects of pollutants on sea urchin development

   Yes: Influence of Cu^{2+} on fertilization success and gastrulation in the sea urchin *Strongylocentrotus purpuratus*

The original titles are too vague to be compelling. Why go out of your way to give potentially interested readers an excuse to ignore your paper? Of more immediate concern in writing up laboratory reports rather than journal articles is this suggestion: Why not use a title that demonstrates to your instructor that you have understood the point of the exercise? Win your reader's confidence right at the start of your report. (By the way, the title should appear on a separate page, along with your name and the date on which your report is submitted.)

---

*millimolar = 10^{-3} moles per liter.

WRITING AN ABSTRACT

The Abstract, if requested by your instructor, is placed at the beginning of your report, immediately following the title page. Yet it should be the last thing that you write, other than the title, since it must completely summarize the entire report: why the experiment was undertaken, what problem was addressed, how the problem was approached, what major results were found, and what major conclusions were drawn. And it should do all this in a single paragraph.

Despite its unimpressive length, a successful abstract is notoriously difficult to write. **In compact form, your abstract must present a complete and accurate summary of your work, and that summary must be fully self-contained**—that is, it must make perfect sense to someone who has not read any other part of your report, as in the following example:

> This study was undertaken to determine the wavelengths of light that are most effective in promoting photosynthesis in the aquatic plant *Elodea canadensis* since some wavelengths are generally more effective than others. Rate of photosynthesis was determined at 25°C, using wavelengths of 400, 450, 500, 550, 600, 650, and 700 nm and measuring the rate of oxygen production for 1-h periods at each wavelength. Oxygen production was estimated from the rate of bubble production by the submerged plant. We tested 4 plants at each wavelength. The rate of oxygen production at 450 nm (approximately 2.5 ml O_2/mg wet weight of plant/h) was nearly 1.5× greater than that at any other wavelength tested, suggesting that light of this wavelength (blue) is most readily absorbed by the chlorophyll pigments. In contrast, light of 550 nm (green) produced no detectable photosynthesis, suggesting that light of this wavelength is reflected rather than absorbed by the chlorophyll.

Note also that the sample Abstract is informative. The author does not simply say that "Oxygen consumption varied with wavelength. These results are discussed in terms of the wavelengths that chlorophyll absorbs and reflects." Rather, the author provides a specific summary of the results and what they mean. Be sure that your Abstract is equally informative. Clearly, this section of your report will be easiest to write if you save it for last.

PREPARING AN ACKNOWLEDGMENTS SECTION

Most biologists are aided by colleagues in various aspects of their research, and it is customary to thank those helpful people in an Acknowledgments section, the penultimate section of the report. Here is an example that might be found in a typical student report:

> I am happy to thank Casey Deiderich and Steve Untersee for sharing their data with me, and Olivia Ambrogio for late-night discussions concerning the effects of temperature on metabolic rate. Professor C. Orians made me aware of the crucial Lesser and Schick (1989) reference. Finally, I am also indebted to Jean-François Vilain for lending me his graphics software, and to Regina Campbell for teaching me how to use it.

As in the example above, you must include the last names of the people you are acknowledging and indicate the specific assistance that you received from each person named.

PREPARING THE LITERATURE CITED SECTION

In the Literature Cited section, the final section of your paper, you present the complete citations (in alphabetical order, according to last name of the first author of each paper or book) for all the factual material you refer to in the text of your report. This presentation provides a convenient way for readers to obtain additional information about a particular topic, as well as a means of verifying what you have written as fact. Detailed directions for preparing this section are given in Chapter 2 (pp. 1279–1282).

PREPARING A PAPER FOR FORMAL PUBLICATION

Papers submitted to an editor for possible publication must conform exactly to the requirements of the specific journal you have targeted. Before beginning a manuscript, you must determine which is the most appropriate journal for your work and then read carefully that journal's Instructions for Authors, typically found at the front or back of each issue or, in some cases, at the front or back of several issues each year. Many journals also make this material available on-line. **It also helps to study similar papers published in recent issues of the targeted journal.** How are references cited in the text? How are they listed in the Literature Cited section? Does the journal permit (or require) subheadings in the Materials and Methods or Results section? If you fail to follow the relevant instructions, your paper may be returned unreviewed; at the least, you will annoy the editor and reviewers.

Do not incorporate figures and tables into the text of the manuscript unless you are required to do so (as for some on-line journals). Instead, put tables (in numerical order, and including the table legends) after the Literature Cited and Acknowledgments sections. Then insert a page of figure captions (in numerical order, with multiple captions per page), and finally, include the figures themselves. These days, manuscripts—including the figures—are usually submitted on-line; follow the specific instructions given by the targeted journal.

Before submitting your manuscript to the journal's editor, go through your work one last time, and be certain that every reference cited in the text is listed (and correctly so) in the Literature Cited section, and that the Literature Cited section contains no references not actually mentioned in the text.

If submitted by mail, your manuscript should be accompanied by the correct number of copies, as specified in the Instructions for Authors section of the journal, along with a brief cover letter, which should read something like this:

> Dear Dr. Schachinger:
>
> Please consider the enclosed manuscript entitled "Effects of salinity on spawning and early development of the tube-building polychaete *Hydroides elegans* in Hong Kong: Not just the sperm's fault," by J.A. Pechenik, J.S. Pearse, and P.-Y. Qian, for publication in *The Biological Bulletin*. Drs. David Epel (Hopkins Marine Station, Stanford University) and John Havenhand (Tjärnö Marine Biological Laboratory Sweden) would be especially suitable reviewers for this manuscript. I can send the original figures and photographs immediately upon request.
>
> My contact information follows:
>
> > phone (617-627-9999)
> >
> > fax (617-627-3805)
> >
> > e-mail: jan.pechenik@tufts.edu
>
> Thank you for your attention.

Note that in the example above, the author recommends specific reviewers for the submitted article. Although editors are happy to have you suggest appropriate reviewers, they won't necessarily take all of your suggestions. Recommend experienced people who will give honest and carefully considered reviews—if the manuscript has problems, you want them found out before publication. Once the paper is published, it's out there forever.

CHECKLIST FOR THE FINAL DRAFT

Title

❑ Title gives a specific indication of what the study is about (p. 1315)

Abstract

❑ Background stated in 1 or 2 sentences (p. 1316)

❑ Clear statement of specific question addressed and of specific hypotheses tested (p. 1316)

❑ Methods summarized in no more than 3 or 4 sentences (p. 1316)

❑ Major findings reported in no more than 2 or 3 sentences (p. 1316)

❑ Concluding sentence relates to statement of specific question addressed (pp. 1316)

❑ Abstract is a single paragraph; if not, can it be rewritten as one paragraph? (p. 1316)

Introduction

❑ Clear statement of specific question or issue addressed (p. 1312)

❑ Logical argument provided as to why the question or issue was addressed (pp. 1313–1314)

❑ Specific hypotheses are indicated, if appropriate, and a rationale for those expectations is provided (pp. 1309, 1312–1313)

❑ Every sentence leads to the statement of what was done in this study (pp. 1312, 1314)

❑ All statements of fact or opinion are supported with a reference or example (p. 1313)

❑ If appropriate, the rationale for choosing the study system or organism is given (p. 1315)

Materials and Methods

❑ Methods are presented in the past tense (p. 1290)

❑ Design of study or experiment is clear and complete (pp. 1288–1291)

❑ Rationale for each step is self-evident or clearly indicated (pp. 1289, 1291)

❑ Each factor mentioned is likely to have influenced the outcome of this study, and all factors likely to have influenced the outcome are mentioned (pp. 1289, 1291)

- ❑ Precision of all measurements is indicated (p. 1289)
- ❑ Includes brief description of how data were analyzed (calculations made, statistical tests used) (p. 1290)
- ❑ If appropriate, the field site or study organism is described (p. 1290)

Results

- ❑ Text summarizes important findings in the data and does not simply repeat raw data from the graphs or tables (p. 1304–1305)
- ❑ Results are presented in the past tense (p. 1305)
- ❑ Results are presented in active terms whenever possible (e.g., in terms of what organisms or enzymes did)
- ❑ All general statements are supported with reference to data (and by results of statistical analysis when possible) (pp. 1304–1306)
- ❑ Major results are presented in words, but their implications are not discussed (pp. 1287–1291, 1305–1306)
- ❑ No raw data are presented (p. 1292)
- ❑ Figures are referred to as "Figures" and not as graphs, drawings, or photographs (pp. 1304, 1306)
- ❑ The same data are not presented in both tabular and graphical form within the same report (pp. 1293,1302)
- ❑ Every table or graph makes an important and unique contribution to the report (pp.1293-1294)
- ❑ Each figure or table has an informative caption or legend, correctly placed (below figure, above table) (pp. 1293, 1294)
- ❑ Symbols are used consistently in all figures and are chosen to facilitate interpretation when possible (p. 1293)
- ❑ Tables and figures are numbered in the order in which they are first referred to in the paper (p. 1304)
- ❑ Each figure or table is self-sufficient; readers can tell what question is being asked, what the major aspects of how the question was addressed are, and what the most important results are without reference to the rest of the paper (pp. 1268–1270, 1293, 1302)
- ❑ Numbers of individuals and numbers of replicates are clearly indicated in the graph, table, caption, or legend (pp. 1299, 1302-1304)
- ❑ The meaning of error bars on figures is clearly indicated in the caption (e.g., 1 standard error about the mean) (pp. 1297–1299)

Discussion

- ❑ Data are clearly related to the expectations and hypotheses raised in the Introduction (p. 1309)
- ❑ Facts are carefully distinguished from speculation (p. 1310)
- ❑ Unusual or unexpected findings are discussed logically, based on biology rather than apology (pp. 1309-1312)
- ❑ All statements of fact or opinion are supported with references to the literature, data, or an example (pp. 1309, 1311)
- ❑ Section suggests further studies that should be conducted, additional questions that should be posed, or ways that the present study should be modified in the future (pp. 1311-1312)

Literature Cited

- ❑ Citations are provided for every reference cited in the report and are in the correct format (pp. 1277–1279, 1316)
- ❑ Section includes no references that are not cited in the report (pp. 1279, 1317)
- ❑ Each citation includes names of all authors, title of paper, name of journal, year of publication, volume number, and page numbers (pp. 1280–1282)

Acknowledgments

- ❑ People are mentioned by first and last names, and their specific contributions are noted (p. 1316)

General

- ❑ Text of report is double-spaced
- ❑ First page shows name of author, name of lab section or instructor, and date submitted
- ❑ All information is presented in the appropriate section of the report (p. 1287)
- ❑ All pages are numbered

TECHNOLOGY TIP 7

Graphing with Excel

Excel was designed for businesspeople, not biologists, and for graphing it is less flexible and intuitive than some other programs, such as GraphPad Prism. However, Excel is so widely used (and misused) by students in biology courses that it is worth pointing out some tips for using it effectively. I assume here that you already have some familiarity with the program.

Entering data. Enter your data in a new spreadsheet. For bar charts, enter the treatment names (the independent variable; e.g., human, dolphin, sea lion, and so on if you were plotting Figure 23) in the first row. Enter your data starting with the second row.

If you are plotting data for a scatter plot (e.g., Figs. 13, 15, and 17), enter data for your x-axis (usually the independent variable, e.g., temperature in Fig. 17) in the first column. In Figure 17, feeding rate data would then be entered in the adjacent column. For Figure 13, you would enter feeding rate data for each of the 3 treatments in adjacent columns. Do not leave space between columns.

Save your worksheet frequently. I recommend including the date on which the study was conducted as part of the title you give the project.

Transforming data. You may wish to transform your data before plotting it. For example, you may need to convert your measurements to different units, or you may wish to plot the logarithms of the data collected. To transform a column of data, first click on an empty column. Click in the first box of the new column and type an equal sign, which tells the program that you are about to enter a formula. Then, select Function within the Insert command on the menu bar. The transform functions you need are found under the Math option. Once you select the desired function, specify the row and values to be transformed. For example, suppose you have 8 values in Column B of your spreadsheet. To take the log (base 10) of those 8 data points and put those new values in Column D, first click in space D1 and type an equal sign. Then, select the Log10 function, enter A1 within the parentheses, and click OK. Next, click on the button in the lower right of the rectangle around space D1, and drag down to space D8. You should see the transformed values in all 8 rows of column D.

Calculating statistics. First, click on an empty rectangle below the column of numbers you wish to work with, and type an equal sign in the box, which instructs the program that you are about to insert a formula. Then, select Function within the Insert command on the menu bar, and choose the correct option (e.g., Average, for calculating the mean, or StDev, for calculating the standard deviation). Next, specify the range of values to use (e.g., B1:B8), and click OK. Once you have calculated your statistic for one column of data, drag the calculation into adjacent columns to calculate the same statistics for those columns.

Making graphs. One of the many endearing idiosyncrasies of Excel is the terminology it uses, which agrees hardly at all with that used by biologists. I present an Excel decoder in Table 8.

Note the tool bar above the worksheet that contains your data. To plot a graph, first highlight the data you wish to plot. Usually you will highlight all the numbers entered (by holding the left mouse button and dragging over the screen), but sometimes you will want to select certain columns (e.g., columns of transformed data). Then, alert Chart Wizard (hereafter

Table 8. The Excel decoder

What It Means	What Excel Calls It
Graph	Chart
x-axis	Category axis
y-axis	Value axis
Area inside the axes of the graph	Plot area
Area outside the axes of the graph but inside the frame	Chart area
Scatter plot (a point graph)	XY (Scatter)
Don't use this!	Line (under Chart Type)
Key (for on-graph explanation of symbols used in graph)	Legend

(Continued)

referred to as CW) of your intentions to plot a graph by clicking on the CW icon (a small but colorful bar chart) toward the right side of the tool bar. When working with the CW, keep the following in mind:

- If you wish to plot a bar graph or histogram, select the Column option. Do not plot three-dimensional graphs, which can be difficult to read.

- If you wish to produce a scatter plot (e.g., Figs. 13 and 17), choose XY Scatter.

- Do not select Line even when you wish to plot a line graph. Your x-axis values will not be properly spaced.

- For scatter plots, you have several suboptions to choose from. Usually you will want to just plot the points without any lines (you can add a regression line later), or to connect the points with straight lines. Occasionally you will want to include smooth curves. **Never choose the options for plotting curves without data points.**

- To add a regression line to a scatter plot, first click on any point in the graph to identify the data set, and then select Add Trendline.

- Use white as a background color for all graphs to maximize contrast and clarity. To do so, double-click anywhere inside the graph, and select the white icon (the default option is gray!). At the same time, select None for Area, and also select None for Border (to remove the frame that Excel otherwise draws around each graph).

- If you will include a key to symbols used in your graph (i.e., if you are displaying more than one treatment, requiring the use of at least 2 symbols), use white as the background color for that as well. Double-click anywhere within the key area, and follow the instructions given above.

- If space is available in the figure, move the key into the figure by clicking on it once and then dragging it into the figure.

- In the Chart Options of the Chart menu, leave Chart Title blank. You will enter your title as part of your figure caption later. Be sure to enter the units (in parentheses) after the labels for the x- and y-axes.

- To add error bars to a point or bar, double-click on the point or bar to obtain the Format Data Series menu, and then select the Y Error Bars option. Enter the values of the error bars to be added (e.g., the standard errors, calculated on the spreadsheet using the Function button), in sequence and separated by commas (e.g., 8.4, 12.5, and 5.5), in the Custom rectangle on the menu. Choose the type of display you want, at the top of the menu (usually "plus" for bars, and "both" for points).

- To change the size of the points plotted in a scatter plot, double-click on any point, and change the size in the Patterns part of the menu.

- To modify a graph at a later time, click anywhere inside the graph, and then select the desired option from the Chart item in the menu bar. If you wish to add or remove particular data points, do so first on the spreadsheet, and then use either the Add Data or Source Data options in the Chart menu.

- If you correct a data entry in the spreadsheet, the correction will appear automatically in your graph.

Chapter 1

Figure Questions

Figure 1.7 The arrangement of fingers and opposable thumb in the human hand, combined with fingernails and a complex system of nerves and muscles, allows the hand to grasp and manipulate objects with great dexterity. **Figure 1.13** Substance B would be made continuously and would accumulate in large amounts. Neither C nor D would be made, so D would not be able to inhibit Enzyme 1 and regulate the pathway. **Figure 1.27** The percentage of brown artificial snakes attacked would probably be higher than the percentage of artificial kingsnakes attacked in all areas (whether or not inhabited by coral snakes).

Concept Check 1.1

1. Examples: A molecule consists of *atoms* bonded together. Each organelle has an orderly arrangement of *molecules*. Photosynthetic plant cells contain *organelles* called chloroplasts. A tissue consists of a group of similar *cells*. Organs such as the heart are constructed from several *tissues*. A complex multicellular organism, such as a plant, has several types of *organs*, such as leaves and roots. A population is a set of *organisms* of the same species. A community consists of *populations* of the various species inhabiting a specific area. An ecosystem consists of a biological *community* along with the nonliving factors important to life, such as air, soil, and water. The biosphere is made up of all of Earth's *ecosystems*. **2.** (a) Structure and function are correlated. (b) Cells are an organism's basic units, *and* the continuity of life is based on heritable information in the form of DNA. (c) Organisms interact with other organisms and with the physical environment, *and* life requires energy transfer and transformation. **3.** Some possible answers: *Emergent properties*: The ability of a human heart to pump blood requires an intact heart; it is not a capability of any of the heart's tissues or cells working alone. *Environmental interactions*: A mouse eats food, such as nuts or grasses, and deposits some of the food material as feces and urine. Construction of a nest rearranges the physical environment and may hasten degradation of some of its components. The mouse may also act as food for a predator. *Energy transfer*: A plant, such as a grass, absorbs energy from the sun and transforms it into molecules that act as stored fuel. Animals can eat parts of the plant and use the food for energy to carry out their activities. *Structure and function*: The strong, sharp teeth of a wolf are well suited to grasping and dismembering its prey. *The cellular basis of life*: The digestion of food is made possible by chemicals (chiefly enzymes) made by cells of the digestive tract. *The genetic basis of life*: Human eye color is determined by the combination of genes inherited from the two parents. *Feedback regulation*: When your stomach is full, it signals your brain to decrease your appetite. *Evolution*: All plants have chloroplasts, indicating their descent from a common ancestor.

Concept Check 1.2

1. An address pinpoints a location by tracking from broader to narrower categories—a state, city, zip, street, and building number. This is analogous to the groups-subordinate-to-groups structure of biological taxonomy. **2.** The naturally occurring heritable variation in a population is "edited" by natural selection because individuals with heritable traits better suited to the environment survive and reproduce more successfully than others. Over time, better-suited individuals persist and their percentage in the population increases, while less suited individuals become less prevalent—a type of population editing.
3.

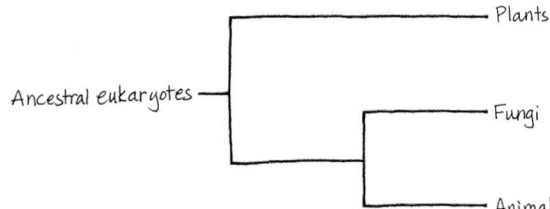

Concept Check 1.3

1. Inductive reasoning derives generalizations from specific cases; deductive reasoning predicts specific outcomes from general premises. **2.** The coloration pattern on the snakes **3.** Compared to a hypothesis, a scientific theory is usually more general and substantiated by a much greater amount of evidence. Natural selection is an explanatory idea that applies to all kinds of organisms and is supported by vast amounts of evidence of various kinds. **4.** Based on the results shown in Figure 1.27, you might predict that the colorful artificial snakes would be attacked more often than the brown ones, simply because they are easier to see. This prediction assumes that the area in Virginia where you are working has predators that attack snakes but no venomous snakes that resemble the colorful artificial snakes.

Concept Check 1.4

1. Science aims to understand natural phenomena and how they work, while technology involves application of scientific discoveries for a particular purpose or to solve a specific problem. **2.** Natural selection could be operating. Malaria is present in sub-Saharan Africa, so there might be an advantage to people with the sickle-cell disease form of the gene that makes them more able to survive and pass on their genes to offspring. Among those of African descent living in the United States, where malaria is absent, there would be no advantage, so they would be selected against more strongly, resulting in fewer individuals with the sickle-cell disease form of the gene.

Summary of Key Concepts Questions

1.1 Evolution explains the most fundamental aspects of all life on earth. It accounts for the common features shared by all forms of life due to descent from a common ancestor, while also providing an explanation for how the great diversity of living organisms on the planet has arisen. **1.2** Ancestors of this plant may have exhibited variation in how well their leaves conserved water. Because not much soil is present in the crevices where these plants are found, the variant plants that could conserve water may have survived better and been able to produce more offspring. Over time, a higher and higher proportion of individuals in the population would have had the adaptation of thick, water-conserving leaves. **1.3** Inductive reasoning is used in forming hypotheses, while deductive reasoning leads to predictions that are used to test hypotheses. **1.4** Different approaches taken by scientists studying natural phenomena at different levels complement each other, so more is learned about each problem being studied. A diversity of backgrounds among scientists may lead to fruitful ideas in the same way that important innovations have often arisen where a mix of cultures coexist.

Test Your Understanding

1. b **2.** d **3.** a **4.** c **5.** c **6.** c **7.** b **8.** c **9.** c **10.** d
11. Your figure should show: (1) For the biosphere, the Earth with an arrow coming out of a tropical ocean; (2) for the ecosystem, a distant view of a coral reef; (3) for the community, a collection of reef animals and algae, with corals, fishes, some seaweed, and any other organisms you can think of; (4) for the population, a group of fish of the same species; (5) for the organism, one fish from your population; (6) for the organ, the fish's stomach, and for the organ system, the whole digestive tract (see Chapter 41 for help); (7) for a tissue, a group of similar cells from the stomach; (8) for a cell, one cell from the tissue, showing its nucleus and a few other organelles; (9) for an organelle, the nucleus, where most of the cell's DNA is located; and (10) for a molecule, a DNA double helix. Your sketches can be very rough!

Chapter 2

Figure Questions

Figure 2.2 The most significant difference in the results would be that the two *Cedrela* saplings inside each garden would show similar amounts of dying leaf tissue because a poisonous chemical released from the *Duroia* trees would presumably reach the saplings via the air or soil and would not be blocked by the insect barrier. The *Cedrela* saplings planted outside the gardens would not show damage unless *Duroia* trees were nearby. Also, any ants present on the unprotected *Cedrela* saplings would probably not be observed making injections into the leaves. However, formic acid would likely still be found in the ants' glands, as it is for most species of ants. **Figure 2.9** Atomic number = 12; 12 protons, 12 electrons; 3 electron shells; 2 valence electrons **Figure 2.16** One possible answer:

Figure 2.19 The plant is submerged in water (H_2O), in which the CO_2 is dissolved. The sun's energy is used to make sugar, which is found in the plant and can act as food for the plant itself, as well as for animals that eat the plant. The oxygen (O_2) is present in the bubbles.

Concept Check 2.1

1. Table salt (sodium chloride) is made up of sodium and chlorine. We are able to eat the compound, showing that it has different properties from those of a metal (sodium) and a poisonous gas (chlorine). **2.** Yes, because an organism requires trace elements, even though only in small amounts **3.** A person with an iron deficiency will probably show fatigue and other effects of a low oxygen level in the blood. (The condition is called anemia and can also result from too few red blood cells or abnormal hemoglobin.) **4.** Variant ancestral plants that could tolerate the toxic elements could grow and reproduce in serpentine soils. (Plants that were well adapted to nonserpentine soils would not be expected to survive in serpentine areas.) The offspring of the variants would also vary, with those most capable of thriving under serpentine conditions growing best and reproducing most. Over many generations, this probably led to the serpentine-adapted species we see today.

Concept Check 2.2
1. 7 **2.** $^{15}_{7}$N **3.** 9 electrons; two electron shells; 1s, 2s, 2p (three orbitals); 1 electron is needed to fill the valence shell. **4.** The elements in a row all have the same number of electron shells. In a column, all the elements have the same number of electrons in their valence shells.

Concept Check 2.3
1. Each carbon atom has only three covalent bonds instead of the required four. **2.** The attraction between oppositely charged ions, forming ionic bonds **3.** If you could synthesize molecules that mimic these shapes, you might be able to treat diseases or conditions caused by the inability of affected individuals to synthesize such molecules.

Concept Check 2.4
1.

2. At equilibrium, the forward and reverse reactions occur at the same rate. **3.** $C_6H_{12}O_6 + 6 O_2 \rightarrow 6 CO_2 + 6 H_2O + $ Energy. Glucose and oxygen react to form carbon dioxide and water, releasing energy. We breathe in oxygen because we need it for this reaction to occur, and we breathe out carbon dioxide because it is a by-product of this reaction. (This reaction is called cellular respiration, and you will learn more about it in Chapter 9.)

Summary of Key Concepts Questions
2.1 Iodine (part of a thyroid hormone) and iron (part of hemoglobin in blood) are both trace elements, required in minute quantities. Calcium and phosphorus (components of bones and teeth) are needed by the body in much greater quantities.
2.2

Both neon and argon have completed valence shells, containing 8 electrons. They do not have unpaired electrons that could participate in chemical bonds. **2.3** Electrons are shared equally between the two atoms in a nonpolar covalent bond. In a polar covalent bond, the electrons are drawn closer to the more electronegative atom. In the formation of ions, an electron is completely transferred from one atom to a much more electronegative atom. **2.4** The concentration of products would increase as the added reactants were converted to products. Eventually, an equilibrium would again be reached in which the forward and reverse reactions were proceeding at the same rate and the relative concentrations of reactants and products returned to where they were before the addition of more reactants.

Test Your Understanding
1. a **2.** e **3.** b **4.** a **5.** d **6.** b **7.** c **8.** e

9. a. Ö::C:H   This structure doesn't make sense because the valence shell of carbon is incomplete; carbon can form 4 bonds.

b. H:Ö:C:C::Ö   This structure makes sense because all valence shells are complete, and all bonds have the correct number of electrons.

c. H:C:H.C::Ö   This structure doesn't make sense because H has only 1 electron to share, so it cannot form bonds with 2 atoms.

d. This structure doesn't make sense for several reasons:
The valence shell of oxygen is incomplete; oxygen can form 2 bonds.
:Ö:
H:N..H   H has only 1 electron to share, so it cannot form a double bond.
Nitrogen usually makes only 3 bonds. It does not have enough electrons to make 2 single bonds, make a double bond, and complete its valence shell.

Chapter 3

Figure Questions
Figure 3.2 One possible answer:

Figure 3.6 Without hydrogen bonds, water would behave like other small molecules, and the solid phase (ice) would be denser than liquid water. The ice would sink to the bottom and would no longer insulate the whole body of water, which would eventually freeze because the average annual temperature at the South Pole is –50°C. The krill could not survive. **Figure 3.7** Heating the solution would cause the water to evaporate faster than it is evaporating at room temperature. At a certain point, there wouldn't be enough water molecules to dissolve the salt ions. The salt would start coming out of solution and re-forming crystals. Eventually, all the water would evaporate, leaving behind a pile of salt like the original pile. **Figure 3.12** By causing the loss of coral reefs, a decrease in the ocean's carbonate concentration would have a ripple effect on noncalcifying organisms. Some of these organisms depend on the reef structure for protection, while others feed on species associated with reefs.

Concept Check 3.1
1. Electronegativity is the attraction of an atom for the electrons of a covalent bond. Because oxygen is more electronegative than hydrogen, the oxygen atom in H_2O pulls electrons toward itself, resulting in a partial negative charge on the oxygen atom and partial positive charges on the hydrogen atoms. Atoms in neighboring water molecules with opposite partial charges are attracted to each other, forming a hydrogen bond. **2.** The hydrogen atoms of one molecule, with their partial positive charges, would repel the hydrogen atoms of the adjacent molecule. **3.** The covalent bonds of water molecules would not be polar, and water molecules would not form hydrogen bonds with each other.

Concept Check 3.2
1. Hydrogen bonds hold neighboring water molecules together. This cohesion helps the chain of water molecules move upward against gravity in water-conducting cells as water evaporates from the leaves. Adhesion between water molecules and the walls of the water-conducting cells also helps counter gravity. **2.** High humidity hampers cooling by suppressing the evaporation of sweat. **3.** As water freezes, it expands because water molecules move farther apart in forming ice crystals. When there is water in a crevice of a boulder, expansion due to freezing may crack the boulder. **4.** A liter of blood would contain 7.8×10^{13} molecules of ghrelin (1.3×10^{-10} moles per liter $\times 6.02 \times 10^{23}$ molecules per mole). **5.** The hydrophobic substance repels water, perhaps helping to keep the ends of the legs from becoming coated with water and breaking through the surface. If the legs were coated with a hydrophilic substance, water would be drawn up them, possibly making it more difficult for the water strider to walk on water.

Concept Check 3.3
1. 10^5, or 100,000 **2.** $[H^+] = 0.01 M = 10^{-2}M$, so pH = 2. **3.** $CH_3COOH \rightarrow CH_3COO^- + H^+$. CH_3COOH is the acid (the H^+ donor), and CH_3COO^- is the base (the H^+ acceptor). **4.** The pH of the water should decrease from 7 to about 2; the pH of the acetic acid solution will decrease only a small amount, because the reaction shown for question 3 will shift to the left, with CH_3COO^- accepting the influx of H^+ and becoming CH_3COOH molecules.

Summary of Key Concepts Questions
3.1

Each water molecule can make four hydrogen bonds with neighboring molecules. **3.2** Ions dissolve in water when polar water molecules form a hydration shell around them. Polar molecules dissolve as water molecules form hydrogen bonds with them and surround them. Solutions are homogeneous mixtures of solute and solvent. Colloids form when particles that are too large to dissolve remain suspended in a liquid. **3.3** CO_2 reacts with H_2O to form carbonic acid (H_2CO_3), which dissociates into H^+ and bicarbonate (HCO_3^-). Although the carbonic acid–bicarbonate reaction is a buffering system, adding CO_2 drives the reaction to the right, releasing more H^+ and lowering pH. The excess protons combine with CO_3^{2-} to form bicarbonate, lowering the concentration of carbonate available for the formation of calcium carbonate (calcification) by corals.

Test Your Understanding
1. d 2. b 3. c 4. e 5. c 6. a 7. e 8. d
9.

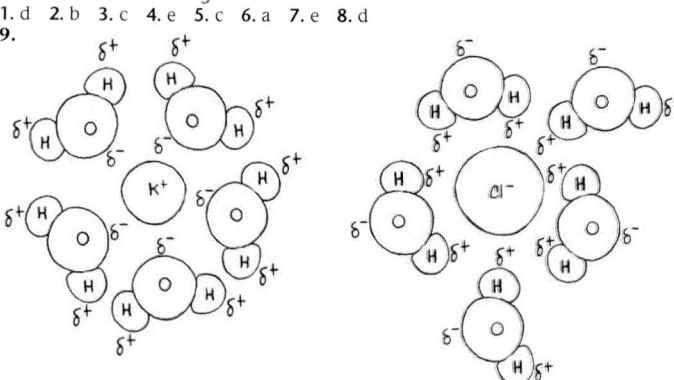

10. Both global warming and ocean acidification are caused by increasing levels of carbon dioxide in the atmosphere, the result of burning fossil fuels. **11.** Due to intermolecular hydrogen bonds, water has a high specific heat (the amount of heat required to increase the temperature of water by 1°C). When water is heated, much of the heat is absorbed in breaking hydrogen bonds before the water molecules increase their motion and the temperature increases. Conversely, when water is cooled, many H bonds are formed, which releases a significant amount of heat. This release of heat can provide some protection against freezing of the plants' leaves, thus protecting the cells from damage.

Chapter 4

Figure Questions
Figure 4.2 Because the concentration of the reactants influences the equilibrium (as discussed in Chapter 2), there might have been more HCN relative to CH_2O, since there would have been a higher concentration of the reactant gas containing nitrogen.
Figure 4.4

$$Na\cdot \quad \cdot\overset{\cdot\cdot}{P}\cdot \quad \cdot\overset{\cdot\cdot}{\underset{\cdot\cdot}{S}}\cdot \quad \cdot\overset{\cdot\cdot}{\underset{\cdot\cdot}{C}l\colon}$$

Figure 4.6 The tails of fats contain only carbon-hydrogen bonds, which are relatively nonpolar. Because the tails occupy the bulk of a fat molecule, they make the molecule as a whole nonpolar and therefore incapable of forming hydrogen bonds with water.
Figure 4.7

```
              H
              |
          H - C - H
       H    |    H
       |    |    |
   H - C -  C  - C - H
       |    |    |
       H    |    H
          H - C - H
              |
              H
```

Figure 4.9 Molecule b, because there are not only the two electronegative oxygens of the carboxyl group, but also an oxygen on the next (carbonyl) carbon. All of these oxygens help make the bond between the O and H of the —OH group more polar, thus making the dissociation of H^+ more likely.

Concept Check 4.1
1. Prior to Wöhler's experiment, the prevailing view was that only living organisms could synthesize "organic" compounds. Wöhler made urea, an organic compound, without the involvement of living organisms. **2.** The spark provided energy needed for the inorganic molecules in the atmosphere to react with each other. (You'll learn more about energy and chemical reactions in Chapter 8.)

Concept Check 4.2
1.

```
   H            H
    \          /
     C  =  C
    /          \
   H            H
```

2. The forms of C_4H_{10} in (b) are structural isomers, as are the butenes in (c).
3. Both consist largely of hydrocarbon chains. **4.** No. There is not enough diversity in the atoms. It can't form structural isomers because there is only one way for three carbons to attach to each other (in a line). There are no double bonds, so *cis-trans* isomers are not possible. Each carbon has at least two hydrogens attached to it, so the molecule is symmetrical and cannot have enantiomers.

Concept Check 4.3
1. It has both an amino group (—NH_2), which makes it an amine, and a carboxyl group (—COOH), which makes it a carboxylic acid. **2.** The ATP molecule loses a phosphate, becoming ADP. **3.** A chemical group that can act as a base has been replaced with a group that can act as an acid, increasing the acidic properties of the molecule. The shape of the molecule would also change, likely changing the molecules with which it can interact. The original cysteine molecule has an asymmetric carbon in the center. After replacement of the amino group with a carboxyl group, this carbon is no longer asymmetric.

```
   O       H       O
   ‖       |       ‖
   C   -   C   -   C
  /        |        \
HO        CH₂        OH
           |
           SH
```

Summary of Key Concepts Questions
4.1 Miller showed that organic molecules could form under the physical and chemical conditions estimated to have been present on early Earth. This abiotic synthesis of organic molecules would have been a first step in the origin of life.
4.2 Acetone and propanal are structural isomers. Acetic acid and glycine have no asymmetric carbons, whereas glycerol phosphate has one. Therefore, glycerol phosphate can exist as forms that are enantiomers, but acetic acid and glycine cannot. **4.3** The methyl group is nonpolar and not reactive. The other six groups are called functional groups. They are each hydrophilic, increasing the solubility of organic compounds in water, and can participate in chemical reactions.

Test Your Understanding
1. b 2. b 3. d 4. d 5. a 6. b 7. a 8. The molecule on the right; the middle carbon is asymmetric.
9. $\cdot\overset{\cdot}{\underset{\cdot}{Si}}\cdot$ Si has 4 valence electrons, the same number as carbon. Therefore, silicon would be able to form long chains, including branches, that could act as skeletons for large molecules. It would clearly do this much better than neon (with no valence electrons) or aluminum (with 3 valence electrons).

Chapter 5

Figure Questions
Figure 5.3 Glucose and fructose are structural isomers.
Figure 5.4

Linear form   Ring forming   Ring form

Note that the oxygen on carbon 5 lost its proton and that the oxygen on carbon 2, which used to be the carbonyl oxygen, gained a proton. Four carbons are in the fructose ring, and two are not. (The latter two carbons are attached to carbons 2 and 5, which are in the ring.) The fructose ring differs from the glucose ring, which has five carbons in the ring and one that is not. (Note that the orientation of this fructose molecule is flipped relative to that of the one in Figure 5.5b.)

Figure 5.5

Glucose Glucose → Maltose
(with H₂O below)

Glucose Fructose → Sucrose
(1–4 glycosidic linkage, 1–2 glycosidic linkage; H₂O below)

Figure 5.12

Figure 5.14

Figure 5.17

Peptide bond Carboxyl group Amino group (H₂O)

Figure 5.21 The R group on glutamic acid is acidic and hydrophilic, whereas that on valine is nonpolar and hydrophobic. Therefore, it is unlikely that valine can participate in the same intramolecular interactions that glutamic acid can. A change in these interactions causes a disruption of molecular structure.
Figure 5.24 The spirals are α helices.

Concept Check 5.1
1. The four main classes are proteins, carbohydrates, lipids, and nucleic acids. Lipids are not polymers. **2.** Nine, with one water molecule required to hydrolyze each connected pair of monomers **3.** The amino acids in the fish protein must be released in hydrolysis reactions and incorporated into other proteins in dehydration reactions.

Concept Check 5.2
1. $C_3H_6O_3$ **2.** $C_{12}H_{22}O_{11}$ **3.** The antibiotic treatment is likely to have killed the cellulose-digesting prokaryotes in the cow's stomach. The absence of these prokaryotes would hamper the cow's ability to obtain energy from food and could lead to weight loss and possibly death. Thus, prokaryotic species are reintroduced, in appropriate combinations, in the gut culture given to treated cows.

Concept Check 5.3
1. Both have a glycerol molecule attached to fatty acids. The glycerol of a fat has three fatty acids attached, whereas the glycerol of a phospholipid is attached to two fatty acids and one phosphate group. **2.** Human sex hormones are steroids, a type of hydrophobic compound. **3.** The oil droplet membrane could consist of

a single layer of phospholipids rather than a bilayer, because an arrangement in which the hydrophobic tails of the membrane phospholipids were in contact with the hydrocarbon regions of the oil molecules would be more stable.

Concept Check 5.4
1. The function of a protein is a consequence of its specific shape, which is lost when a protein becomes denatured. **2.** Secondary structure involves hydrogen bonds between atoms of the polypeptide backbone. Tertiary structure involves interactions between atoms of the side chains of the amino acid subunits. **3.** These are all nonpolar amino acids, so you would expect this region to be located in the interior of the folded polypeptide, where it would not contact the aqueous environment inside the cell.

Concept Check 5.5
1.

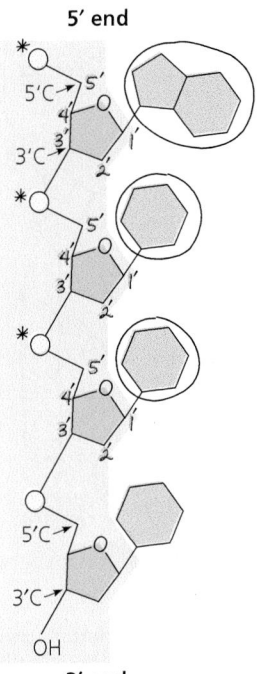

5' end

3' end

2. 5'–T A G G C C T–3'
3'–A T C C G G A–5'

3. a. Mismatch
5'–T A A G C C T–3'
3'–A T C C G G A–5'

b. 3'–A T T C G G A–5'

Summary of Key Concepts Questions
Concept 5.1 The polymers of carbohydrates, proteins, and nucleic acids are built from three different types of monomers: monosaccharides, amino acids, and nucleotides, respectively. **Concept 5.2** Both starch and cellulose are polymers of glucose, but the glucose monomers are in the α configuration in starch and the β configuration in cellulose. The glycosidic linkages thus have different geometries, giving the polymers different shapes and thus different properties. Starch is an energy-storage compound in plants; cellulose is a structural component of plant cell walls. Humans can hydrolyze starch to provide energy but cannot hydrolyze cellulose. Cellulose aids in the passage of food through the digestive tract. **Concept 5.3** Lipids are not polymers because they do not exist as a chain of linked monomers. They are not considered macromolecules because they do not reach the giant size of many polysaccharides, proteins, and nucleic acids. **Concept 5.4** A polypeptide, which may consist of hundreds of amino acids in a specific sequence (primary structure), has regions of coils and pleats (secondary structure), which are then folded into irregular contortions (tertiary structure) and may be noncovalently associated with other polypeptides (quaternary structure). The linear order of amino acids, with the varying properties of their side chains (R groups), determines what secondary and tertiary structures will form to produce a protein. The resulting three-dimensional shapes of proteins are key to their specific and diverse functions. **Concept 5.5** The complementary base pairing of the two strands of DNA makes possible the precise replication of DNA every time a cell divides, ensuring that genetic information is faithfully transmitted. In some types of RNA, complementary base pairing enables

RNA molecules to assume specific three-dimensional shapes that facilitate diverse functions.

Test Your Understanding

1. d   2. a   3. b   4. a   5. b   6. c   7. d

8.

	Monomers or Components	Polymer or larger molecule	Type of linkage
Carbohydrates	Monosaccharides	Polysaccharides	Glycosidic linkages
Lipids	Fatty acids	Triacylglycerols	Ester linkages
Proteins	Amino acids	Polypeptides	Peptide bonds
Nucleic acids	Nucleotides	Polynucleotides	Phosphodiester linkages

9.

Original Strand   Complementary Strand

Chapter 6

Figure Questions

Figure 6.6 A phospholipid is a lipid, consisting of a glycerol molecule joined to two fatty acids and one phosphate group. Together, the glycerol and phosphate end of the phospholipid form the "head," which is hydrophilic, while the hydrocarbon chains on the fatty acids form hydrophobic "tails." The presence in a single molecule of both a hydrophilic and a hydrophobic region makes the molecule ideal as the main building block of a membrane. **Figure 6.9** The DNA in a chromosome dictates synthesis of a messenger RNA (mRNA) molecule, which then moves out to the cytoplasm. There, the information is used for the production, on ribosomes, of proteins that carry out cellular functions. **Figure 6.10** Any of the bound ribosomes (attached to the endoplasmic reticulum) could be circled, because any could be making a protein that will be secreted. **Figure 6.22** Each centriole has 9 sets of 3 microtubules, so the entire centrosome (two centrioles) has 54 microtubules. Each microtubule consists of a helical array of tubulin dimers (as shown in Table 6.1).

1 microtubule

Triplet of microtubules

Figure 6.24

Central pair of microtubules

They terminate here

The two central microtubules terminate above the basal body, so they aren't present at the level of the cross section through the basal body, indicated by the lower red rectangle in (a). **Figure 6.29** The microtubules would reorient, and based on the earlier results, the cellulose synthase proteins would also change their path, orienting along the repositioned microtubules. (This is, in fact, what was observed.)

Concept Check 6.1

1. Stains used for light microscopy are colored molecules that bind to cell components, affecting the light passing through, while stains used for electron microscopy involve heavy metals that affect the beams of electrons passing through. **2.** (a) Light microscope, (b) scanning electron microscope

Concept Check 6.2

1. See Figure 6.8.
2.

This cell would have the same volume as the cells in columns 2 and 3 but proportionally more surface area than that in column 2 and less than that in column 3. Thus, the surface-to-volume ratio should be greater than 1.2 but less than 6. To obtain the surface area, you would add the area of the six sides (the top, bottom, sides, and ends): 125 + 125 + 125 + 125 + 1 + 1 = 502. The surface-to-volume ratio equals 502 divided by a volume of 125, or 4.0.

Concept Check 6.3

1. Ribosomes in the cytoplasm translate the genetic message, carried from the DNA in the nucleus by mRNA, into a polypeptide chain. **2.** Nucleoli consist of DNA and the ribosomal RNA (rRNA) made according to its instructions, as well as proteins imported from the cytoplasm. Together, the rRNA and proteins are assembled into large and small ribosomal subunits. (These are exported through nuclear pores to the cytoplasm, where they will participate in polypeptide synthesis.) **3.** No. Each chromosome is present whether its chromatin is relatively diffuse (when the cell is not dividing) or condensed (when the cell is dividing).

Concept Check 6.4

1. The primary distinction between rough and smooth ER is the presence of bound ribosomes on the rough ER. Both types of ER make phospholipids, but membrane proteins and secretory proteins are all produced on the ribosomes of the rough ER. The smooth ER also functions in detoxification, carbohydrate metabolism, and storage of calcium ions. **2.** Transport vesicles move membranes and substances they enclose between other components of the endomembrane system. **3.** The mRNA is synthesized in the nucleus and then passes out through a nuclear pore to be translated on a bound ribosome, attached to the rough ER. The protein is synthesized into the lumen of the ER and perhaps modified there. A transport vesicle carries the protein to the Golgi apparatus. After further modification in the Golgi, another transport vesicle carries it back to the ER, where it will perform its cellular function.

Concept Check 6.5

1. Both organelles are involved in energy transformation, mitochondria in cellular respiration and chloroplasts in photosynthesis. They both have multiple membranes that separate their interiors into compartments. In both organelles, the innermost membranes—cristae, or infoldings of the inner membrane, in mitochondria, and the thylakoid membranes in chloroplasts—have large surface areas with embedded enzymes that carry out their main functions. **2.** Yes. Plant cells are able to make their own sugar by photosynthesis, but mitochondria in these eukaryotic cells are the organelles that are able to generate energy from sugars, a function required in all cells. **3.** Mitochondria and chloroplasts are not derived from the ER, nor are they connected physically or via transport vesicles to organelles of the endomembrane system. Mitochondria and chloroplasts are structurally quite different from vesicles derived from the ER, which are bounded by a single membrane.

Concept Check 6.6

1. Both systems of movement involve long filaments that are moved in relation to each other by motor proteins that grip, release, and grip again adjacent polymers. **2.** Dynein arms, powered by ATP, move neighboring doublets of microtubules relative to each other. Because they are anchored within the organelle and with respect to one another, the doublets bend instead of sliding past each other. Synchronized bending of the nine microtubule doublets brings about bending of both structures. **3.** Such individuals have defects in the microtubule-based movement of cilia and flagella. Thus, the sperm can't move because of malfunctioning or nonexistent flagella, and the airways are compromised because cilia that line the trachea malfunction or don't exist, and so mucus cannot be cleared from the lungs.

Concept Check 6.7

1. The most obvious difference is the presence of direct cytoplasmic connections between cells of plants (plasmodesmata) and animals (gap junctions). These connections result in the cytoplasm being continuous between adjacent cells. **2.** The cell would not be able to function properly and would probably soon die, as the cell wall or ECM must be permeable to allow the exchange of matter between the cell and its external environment. Molecules involved in energy production and use must be allowed entry, as well as those that provide information about the cell's environment. Other molecules, such as products synthesized by the cell for export and the by-products of cellular respiration, must be allowed to exit. **3.** The parts of the protein that face aqueous regions would be expected to have polar or charged (hydrophilic) amino acids, while the parts that go through the membrane would be expected to have nonpolar (hydrophobic) amino acids. You would predict polar or charged amino acids at each end (tail), in the region of the cytoplasmic loop, and in the regions of the two extracellular loops. You would predict nonpolar amino acids in the four regions that go through the membrane between the tails and loops.

Summary of Key Concepts Questions

6.1 Both light and electron microscopy allow cells to be studied visually, thus helping us understand internal cellular structure and the arrangement of cell components. Cell fractionation techniques separate out different groups of cell components, which can then be analyzed biochemically to determine their function. Performing microscopy on the same cell fraction helps to correlate the biochemical function of the cell with the cell component responsible. **6.2** The separation of different functions in different organelles has several advantages. Reactants and enzymes can be concentrated in one area instead of spread throughout the cell. Reactions that require specific conditions, such as a lower pH, can be compartmentalized. And enzymes for specific reactions are often embedded in the membranes that enclose or partition an organelle. **6.3** The nucleus contains the genetic material of the cell in the form of DNA, which codes for messenger RNA, which in turn provides instructions for the synthesis of proteins (including the proteins that make up part of the ribosomes). DNA also codes for ribosomal RNA, which is combined with proteins in the nucleolus into the subunits of ribosomes. Within the cytoplasm, ribosomes join with mRNA to build polypeptides, using the genetic information in the mRNA. **6.4** Transport vesicles move proteins and membranes synthesized by the rough ER to the Golgi for further processing and then to the plasma membrane, lysosomes, or other locations in the cell, including back to the ER. **6.5** According to the endosymbiont theory, mitochondria originated from an oxygen-using prokaryotic cell that was engulfed by an ancestral eukaryotic cell. Over time, the host and endosymbiont evolved into a single organism. Chloroplasts originated when at least one of these eukaryotic cells containing mitochondria engulfed and then retained a photosynthetic prokaryote. **6.6** Inside the cell, motor proteins interact with components of the cytoskeleton to move cellular parts. Motor proteins may "walk" vesicles along microtubules. The movement of cytoplasm within a cell involves interactions of the motor protein myosin and microfilaments (actin filaments). Whole cells can be moved by the rapid bending of flagella or cilia, which is caused by the motor-protein-powered sliding of microtubules within these structures. Cell movement can also occur when pseudopodia form at one end of a cell (caused by actin polymerization into a filamentous network), followed by contraction of the cell toward that end; this is powered by interactions of microfilaments with myosin. Interactions of motor proteins and microfilaments in muscle cells can propel whole organisms. **6.7** A plant cell wall is primarily composed of microfibrils of cellulose embedded in other polysaccharides and proteins. The ECM of animal cells is primarily composed of collagen and other protein fibers, such as the glycoprotein fibronectins. These fibers are embedded in a network of carbohydrate-rich proteoglycans. A plant cell wall provides structural support for the cell and, collectively, for the plant body. In addition to giving support, the ECM of an animal cell allows for communication of environmental changes into the cell.

Test Your Understanding

1. b **2.** d **3.** b **4.** e **5.** a **6.** d **7.** c **8.** See Figure 6.8.

Chapter 7

Figure Questions

Figure 7.2

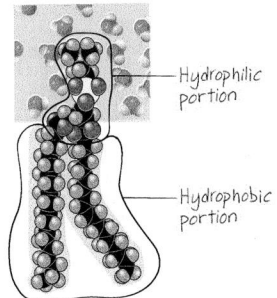

The hydrophilic portion is in contact with an aqueous environment (cytosol or extracellular fluid), and the hydrophobic portion is in contact with the hydrophobic portions of other phospholipids in the interior of the bilayer. **Figure 7.7** You couldn't rule out movement of proteins within membranes of the same species. You might propose that the membrane lipids and proteins from one species weren't able to mingle with those from the other species because of some incompatibility. **Figure 7.10** A transmembrane protein like the dimer in (f) might change its shape upon binding to a particular ECM molecule. The new shape might enable the interior portion of the protein to bind to a second, cytoplasmic protein that would relay the message to the inside of the cell, as shown in (c). **Figure 7.11** The shape of a protein on the HIV surface is likely to be complementary to the shape of the receptor (CD4) and also to that of the co-receptor (CCR5). A molecule that was a similar shape to the HIV surface protein could bind CCR5, blocking HIV binding. (Another alternative would be a molecule that bound to CCR5 and changed the shape of CCR5 so it could no longer bind HIV.)

Figure 7.12

The protein would contact the extracellular fluid. **Figure 7.14** The orange dye would be evenly distributed throughout the solution on both sides of the membrane. The solution levels would not be affected because the orange dye can diffuse through the membrane and equalize its concentration. Thus, no additional osmosis would take place in either direction. **Figure 7.19** The diamond solutes are moving into the cell (down), and the round solutes are moving out of the cell (up); both are moving against their concentration gradient.

Concept Check 7.1

1. They are on the inner side of the transport vesicle membrane. **2.** The grasses living in the cooler region would be expected to have more unsaturated fatty acids in their membranes because those fatty acids remain fluid at lower temperatures. The grasses living immediately adjacent to the hot springs would be expected to have more saturated fatty acids, which would allow the fatty acids to "stack" more closely, making the membranes less fluid and therefore helping them to stay intact at higher temperatures. (Cholesterol could not be used to moderate the effects of temperature on membrane fluidity because it is not found within plant cell membranes.)

Concept Check 7.2

1. O_2 and CO_2 are both nonpolar molecules that can easily pass through the hydrophobic interior of a membrane. **2.** Water is a polar molecule, so it cannot pass very rapidly through the hydrophobic region in the middle of a phospholipid bilayer. **3.** The hydronium ion is charged, while glycerol is not. Charge is probably more significant than size as a basis for exclusion by the aquaporin channel.

Concept Check 7.3

1. CO_2 is a nonpolar molecule that can diffuse through the plasma membrane. As long as it diffuses away so that the concentration remains low outside the cell, it will continue to exit the cell in this way. (This is the opposite of the case for O_2, described in this section.) **2.** The water is hypotonic to the plant cells, so the plant cells take up water. Thus, the cells of the vegetable remain turgid rather than plasmolyzing, and the vegetable (for example, lettuce or spinach) remains crisp and not wilted. **3.** The activity of *Paramecium caudatum*'s contractile vacuole will decrease. The vacuole pumps out excess water that accumulates in the cell; this accumulation occurs only in a hypotonic environment.

Concept Check 7.4

1. The pump uses ATP. To establish a voltage, ions have to be pumped against their gradients, which requires energy. **2.** Each ion is being transported against its electrochemical gradient. If either ion were transported down its electrochemical gradient, this *would* be considered cotransport. **3.** The internal environment of a lysosome is acidic, so it has a higher concentration of H^+ than does the cytoplasm. Therefore, you might expect the membrane of the lysosome to have a proton pump such as that shown in Figure 7.20 to pump H^+ into the lysosome.

Concept Check 7.5

1. Exocytosis. When a transport vesicle fuses with the plasma membrane, the vesicle membrane becomes part of the plasma membrane.
2.

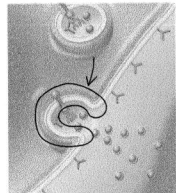

3. The glycoprotein would be synthesized in the ER lumen, move through the Golgi apparatus, and then travel in a vesicle to the plasma membrane, where it would undergo exocytosis and become part of the ECM.

Summary of Key Concepts Questions

7.1 Plasma membranes define the cell by separating the cellular components from the external environment. This allows conditions inside cells to be controlled by membrane proteins, which regulate entry and exit of molecules and even cell function (see Figure 7.10). The processes of life can be carried out inside the controlled environment of the cell, so membranes are crucial. In eukaryotes, membranes also function to subdivide the cytoplasm into different compartments where distinct processes can occur, even under differing conditions such as pH.   **7.2** Aquaporins are channel proteins that greatly increase the permeability of a membrane to water molecules, which are polar and therefore do not readily diffuse through the hydrophobic interior of the membrane.   **7.3** There will be a net diffusion of water out of a cell into a hypertonic solution. The free water concentration is higher inside the cell than in the solution (where water molecules are not free, but are clustered around the higher concentration of solute particles).   **7.4** One of the solutes moved by the cotransporter is actively transported against its concentration gradient. The energy for this transport comes from the concentration gradient of the other solute, which was established by an electrogenic pump that used energy to transport the other solute across the membrane.   **7.5** In receptor-mediated endocytosis, specific molecules act as ligands when they bind to receptors on the plasma membrane. The cell can acquire bulk quantities of those molecules when a coated pit forms a vesicle and carries the bound molecules into the cell.

Test Your Understanding

1. b **2.** c **3.** a **4.** d **5.** b
6. (a)

(b) The solution outside is hypotonic. It has less sucrose, which is a nonpenetrating solute. (c) See answer for (a). (d) The artificial cell will become more turgid. (e) Eventually, the two solutions will have the same solute concentrations. Even though sucrose can't move through the membrane, water flow (osmosis) will lead to isotonic conditions.

Chapter 8

Figure Questions

Figure 8.12   **Figure 8.16**

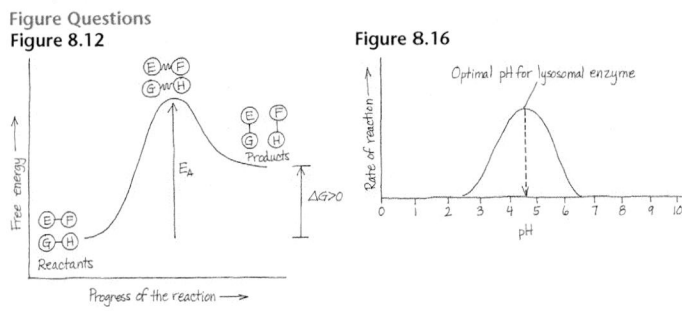

Figure 8.20 Because the affinity of the caspase for the inhibitor is very low (as is expected of an allosterically inhibited enzyme), the inhibitor is likely to diffuse away. Because no additional source of the inhibitory compound is present and the concentration of inhibitor is very low, the inhibitor is unlikely to bind again to the allosteric binding site once the covalent linkage is broken. Therefore, the activity of the enzyme would most likely be normal. (In fact, this is what the researchers observed when they broke the disulfide linkage.)

Concept Check 8.1

1. The second law is the trend toward randomization, or increasing entropy. When the concentrations of a substance on both sides of a membrane are equal, the distribution is more random than when they are unequal. Diffusion of a substance to a region where it is initially less concentrated increases entropy, making it an energetically favorable (spontaneous) process as described by the second law. This explains the process seen in Figure 7.13.   **2.** The apple has potential energy in its position hanging on the tree, and the sugars and other nutrients it contains have chemical energy. The apple has kinetic energy as it falls from the tree to the ground. Finally, when the apple is digested and its molecules broken down, some of the chemical energy is used to do work, and the rest is lost as thermal energy.   **3.** The sugar crystals become less ordered (entropy increases) as they dissolve and become randomly spread out in the water. Over time, the water evaporates, and the crystals form again because the water volume is insufficient to keep them in solution. While the reappearance of sugar crystals may represent a "spontaneous" increase in order (decrease in entropy), it is balanced by the decrease in order (increase in entropy) of the water molecules, which changed from a relatively compact arrangement as liquid water to a much more dispersed and disordered form as water vapor.

Concept Check 8.2

1. Cellular respiration is a spontaneous and exergonic process. The energy released from glucose is used to do work in the cell or is lost as heat.   **2.** When the H^+ concentrations are the same, the system is at equilibrium and can do no work. Hydrogen ions can perform work only if their concentrations on each side of a membrane differ—in other words, when a gradient is present. This is consistent with Figure 7.20, which shows that an energy input (provided by ATP hydrolysis) is required to establish the concentration gradient (the H^+ gradient) that can in turn perform work.   **3.** The reaction is exergonic because it releases energy—in this case, in the form of light. (This is a nonbiological version of the bioluminescence seen in Figure 8.1.)

Concept Check 8.3

1. ATP usually transfers energy to endergonic processes by phosphorylating (adding phosphate groups to) other molecules. (Exergonic processes phosphorylate ADP to regenerate ATP.)   **2.** A set of coupled reactions can transform the first combination into the second. Since this is an exergonic process overall, ΔG is negative and the first combination must have more free energy (see Figure 8.9).   **3.** Active transport: The solute is being transported against its concentration gradient, which requires energy, provided by ATP hydrolysis.

Concept Check 8.4

1. A spontaneous reaction is a reaction that is exergonic. However, if it has a high activation energy that is rarely attained, the rate of the reaction may be low.   **2.** Only the specific substrate(s) will fit properly into the active site of an enzyme, the part of the enzyme that carries out catalysis.   **3.** In the presence of malonate, increase the concentration of the normal substrate (succinate) and see whether the rate of reaction increases. If it does, malonate is a competitive inhibitor.   **4.** If lactose wasn't present in the environment as a source of food and the fucose-containing disaccharide was available, bacteria that could digest the latter would be better able to grow and multiply than those that could not.

Concept Check 8.5

1. The activator binds in such a way that it stabilizes the active form of an enzyme, whereas the inhibitor stabilizes the inactive form.   **2.** An inhibitor that binds to the active site of the enzyme you want to inhibit could also bind to and block the enzymes with similar structures, causing significant side effects. For this reason, you would be better off choosing to screen chemical compounds that bind allosterically to the enzyme in question, because allosteric regulatory sites are less likely to share similarity with other enzymes.

Summary of Key Concepts Questions

8.1 The process of "ordering" a cell's structure is accompanied by an increase in the entropy or disorder of the universe. For example, an animal cell takes in highly ordered organic molecules as the source of matter and energy used to build and maintain its structures. In the same process, however, the cell releases heat and the simple molecules of carbon dioxide and water to the surroundings. The increase in entropy of the latter process offsets the entropy decrease in the former.   **8.2** A spontaneous reaction has a negative ΔG and is exergonic. For a chemical reaction to proceed with a net release of free energy ($-\Delta G$), the enthalpy or total energy of the system must decrease ($-\Delta H$), and/or the entropy or disorder must increase (yielding a more negative term, $-T\Delta S$). Spontaneous reactions supply the energy to perform cellular work.   **8.3** The free energy released from the hydrolysis of ATP may drive endergonic reactions through the transfer of a phosphate group to a reactant molecule, forming a more reactive phosphorylated intermediate. ATP hydrolysis also powers the mechanical and transport work of a cell, often by powering shape changes in the relevant motor proteins. Cellular respiration, the catabolic breakdown of glucose, provides the energy for the endergonic regeneration of ATP from ADP and P_i.   **8.4** Activation energy barriers prevent the complex molecules of the cell, which are rich in free energy, from spontaneously breaking down to less ordered, more stable molecules. Enzymes permit a regulated metabolism by binding to specific substrates and forming enzyme-substrate complexes that selectively lower the E_A for the chemical reactions in a cell.   **8.5** A cell tightly regulates its metabolic pathways in response to fluctuating needs for energy and materials. The binding of activators or inhibitors to regulatory sites on allosteric enzymes stabilizes either the active or inactive form of the subunits. For example, the binding of ATP to a catabolic enzyme in a cell with excess ATP would inhibit that pathway. Such types of feedback inhibition preserve chemical resources within a cell. If ATP supplies are depleted, binding of ADP to the regulatory site of catabolic enzymes would activate that pathway.

Test Your Understanding

1. b **2.** c **3.** b **4.** a **5.** c **6.** e **7.** c

9.

A. The substrate molecules are entering the cells, so no product is made yet.

B. There is sufficient substrate, so the reaction is proceeding at a maximum rate.

C. As the substrate is used up, the rate decreases (the slope is less steep).

D. The line is flat because no new substrate remains and thus no new product appears.

Chapter 9

Figure Questions

Figure 9.7 Because there is no external source of energy for the reaction, it must be exergonic, and the reactants must be at a higher energy level than the products. **Figure 9.9** The removal would probably stop glycolysis, or at least slow it down, since it would push the equilibrium for step 5 toward the left. If less (or no) glyceraldehyde 3-phosphate were available, step 6 would slow down (or be unable to occur). **Figure 9.15** At first, some ATP could be made, since electron transport could proceed as far as complex III, and a small H^+ gradient could be built up. Soon, however, no more electrons could be passed to complex III because it could not be reoxidized by passing its electrons to complex IV. **Figure 9.16** First, there are 2 NADH from the oxidation of pyruvate plus 6 NADH from the citric acid cycle (CAC); 8 NADH × 2.5 ATP/NADH = 20 ATP. Second, there are 2 $FADH_2$ from the CAC; 2 $FADH_2$ × 1.5 ATP/$FADH_2$ = 3 ATP. Third, the 2 NADH from glycolysis enter the mitochondrion through one of two types of shuttle. They pass their electrons either to 2 FAD, which become $FADH_2$ and result in 3 ATP, or to 2 NAD^+, which become NADH and result in 5 ATP. Thus, 20 + 3 + 3 = 26 ATP, or 20 + 3 + 5 = 28 ATP from all NADH and $FADH_2$.

Concept Check 9.1

1. Both processes include glycolysis, the citric acid cycle, and oxidative phosphorylation. In aerobic respiration, the final electron acceptor is molecular oxygen (O_2); in anaerobic respiration, the final electron acceptor is a different substance. **2.** $C_4H_6O_5$ would be oxidized and NAD^+ would be reduced.

Concept Check 9.2

1. NAD^+ acts as the oxidizing agent in step 6, accepting electrons from glyceraldehyde 3-phosphate, which thus acts as the reducing agent. **2.** Since the overall process of glycolysis results in net production of ATP, it would make sense for the process to slow down when ATP levels have increased substantially. Thus, we would expect ATP to allosterically inhibit phosphofructokinase.

Concept Check 9.3

1. NADH and $FADH_2$; they will donate electrons to the electron transport chain. **2.** CO_2 is released from the pyruvate that is the end product of glycolysis, and CO_2 is also released during the citric acid cycle. **3.** In both cases, the precursor molecule loses a CO_2 molecule and then donates electrons to an electron carrier in an oxidation step. Also, the product has been activated due to the attachment of a CoA group.

Concept Check 9.4

1. Oxidative phosphorylation would eventually stop entirely, resulting in no ATP production by this process. Without oxygen to "pull" electrons down the electron transport chain, H^+ would not be pumped into the mitochondrion's intermembrane space and chemiosmosis would not occur. **2.** Decreasing the pH means addition of H^+. This would establish a proton gradient even without the function of the electron transport chain, and we would expect ATP synthase to function and synthesize ATP. (In fact, it was experiments like this that provided support for chemiosmosis as an energy-coupling mechanism.) **3.** One of the components of the electron transport chain, ubiquinone (Q), must be able to diffuse within the membrane. It could not do so if the membrane were locked rigidly into place.

Concept Check 9.5

1. A derivative of pyruvate, such as acetaldehyde during alcohol fermentation, or pyruvate itself during lactic acid fermentation; oxygen **2.** The cell would need to consume glucose at a rate about 16 times the consumption rate in the aerobic environment (2 ATP are generated by fermentation versus up to 32 ATP by cellular respiration).

Concept Check 9.6

1. The fat is much more reduced; it has many —CH_2— units, and in all these bonds the electrons are equally shared. The electrons present in a carbohydrate molecule are already somewhat oxidized (shared unequally in bonds), as quite a few of them are bound to oxygen. **2.** When we consume more food than necessary for metabolic processes, our body synthesizes fat as a way of storing energy for later use. **3.** Glycogen is a storage polysaccharide in liver and muscle cells. When energy is needed, glucose units are hydrolyzed from glycogen. Glycolysis in the cytosol breaks down glucose to two pyruvate molecules, which are transported into the mitochondrion. Here they are further oxidized, ultimately producing the needed ATP. **4.** AMP will accumulate, stimulating phosphofructokinase, and thus increasing the rate of glycolysis. Since oxygen is not present, the cell will convert pyruvate to lactate in lactic acid fermentation, providing a supply of ATP. **5.** When oxygen is present, the fatty acid chains containing most of the energy of a fat are oxidized and fed into the citric acid cycle and the electron transport chain. During intense exercise, however, oxygen is scarce in muscle cells, so ATP must be generated by glycolysis alone. A very small part of the fat molecule, the glycerol backbone, can be oxidized via glycolysis, but the amount of energy released by this portion is insignificant compared to that released by the fatty acid chains. (This is why moderate exercise, staying below 70% maximum heart rate, is better for burning fat—because enough oxygen remains available to the muscles.)

Summary of Key Concepts Questions

9.1 Most of the ATP produced in cellular respiration comes from oxidative phosphorylation, in which the energy released from redox reactions in an electron transport chain is used to produce ATP. In substrate-level phosphorylation, an enzyme directly transfers a phosphate group to ADP from an intermediate substrate. All ATP production in glycolysis occurs by substrate-level phosphorylation; this form of ATP production also occurs at one step in the citric acid cycle. **9.2** The oxidation of the three-carbon sugar, glyceraldehyde 3-phosphate, yields energy. In this oxidation, electrons and H^+ are transferred to NAD^+, forming NADH, and a phosphate group is attached to the oxidized substrate. ATP is then formed by substrate-level phosphorylation when this phosphate group is transferred to ADP. **9.3** The release of six molecules of CO_2 represents the complete oxidation of glucose. During the processing of two pyruvates to acetyl CoA, the fully oxidized carboxyl group (—COO^-) is given off as CO_2. The remaining four carbons are released as CO_2 in the citric acid cycle as citrate is oxidized back to oxaloacetate. **9.4** The flow of H^+ through the ATP synthase complex causes the rotor and attached rod to rotate, exposing catalytic sites in the knob portion that produce ATP from ADP and $\circled{P}_i$. ATP synthases are found in the inner mitochondrial membrane, the plasma membrane of prokaryotes, and membranes within chloroplasts. **9.5** Anaerobic respiration yields more ATP. The 2 ATP produced by substrate-level phosphorylation in glycolysis represent the total energy yield of fermentation. NADH passes its "high-energy" electrons to pyruvate or a derivative of pyruvate, recycling NAD^+ and allowing glycolysis to continue. Anaerobic respiration uses an electron transport chain to capture the energy of the electrons in NADH via a series of redox reactions; ultimately, the electrons are transferred to an electronegative molecule other than oxygen. And additional molecules of NADH are produced in anaerobic respiration as pyruvate is oxidized. **9.6** The ATP produced by catabolic pathways is used to drive anabolic pathways. Also, many of the intermediates of glycolysis and the citric acid cycle are used in the biosynthesis of a cell's molecules.

Test Your Understanding

1. d **2.** c **3.** c **4.** a **5.** e **6.** a **7.** b
8.

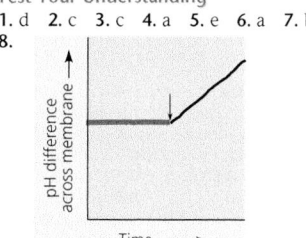

Chapter 10

Figure Questions

Figure 10.3 Situating containers of algae near sources of CO_2 emissions makes sense because algae need CO_2 to carry out photosynthesis. The higher their rate of photosynthesis, the more plant oil they will produce. At the same time, algae would be absorbing the CO_2 emitted from industrial plants or from car engines, reducing the amount of CO_2 entering the atmosphere. **Figure 10.10** Red, but not violet-blue, wavelengths would pass through the filter, so the bacteria would not congregate where the violet-blue light normally comes through. Therefore, the left "peak" of bacteria would not be present, but the right peak would be observed because the red wavelengths passing through the filter would be used for photosynthesis. **Figure 10.12** In the leaf, most of the chlorophyll electrons excited by photon absorption are used to power the reactions of photosynthesis. **Figure 10.16** The person at the top of the photosystem I tower would not turn and throw his electron into the bucket. Instead, he would throw it onto the top of the ramp right next to the photosystem II tower. The electron would then roll down the ramp, get energized by a photon, and return to him. This cycle would continue as long as light was available. (This is why it's called cyclic electron flow.) **Figure 10.19**

$$3 \times 1 (=3)$$
$$3 \times 6 (=18)$$
$$3 \times 5 (=15)$$
$$6 \times 3 (=18)$$
$$6 \times 3 (=18)$$
$$5 \times 3 (=15)$$
$$6 \times 3 (=18)$$
$$1 \times 3 (=3)$$

Three carbon atoms enter the cycle, one by one, as individual CO_2 molecules, and leave the cycle in one three-carbon molecule (G3P) per three turns of the cycle. **Figure 10.22**

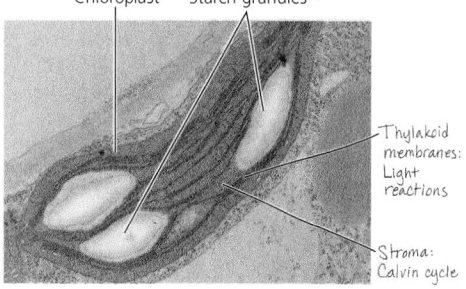

Chloroplast Starch granules

Thylakoid membranes: Light reactions

Stroma: Calvin cycle

The photosystems that carry out the light reactions are embedded in the thylakoid membranes, and the ATP and NADPH that are formed are released into the stroma. There, they are used for the reactions of the Calvin cycle, which produces G3P. Excess sugar molecules that are not used by the plant can be converted to glucose, then stored in the form of starch.

Concept Check 10.1

1. CO$_2$ enters leaves via stomata, and water enters via roots and is carried to leaves through veins. **2.** Using ^{18}O, a heavy isotope of oxygen, as a label, researchers were able to confirm van Niel's hypothesis that the oxygen produced during photosynthesis originates in water, not in carbon dioxide. **3.** The light reactions could *not* keep producing NADPH and ATP without the NADP$^+$, ADP, and ℗$_i$ that the Calvin cycle generates. The two cycles are interdependent.

Concept Check 10.2

1. Green, because green light is mostly transmitted and reflected—not absorbed—by photosynthetic pigments **2.** In chloroplasts, light-excited electrons are trapped by a primary electron acceptor, which prevents them from dropping back to the ground state. In isolated chlorophyll, there is no electron acceptor, so the photoexcited electrons immediately drop back down to the ground state, with the emission of light and heat. **3.** Water (H$_2$O) is the initial electron donor; NADP$^+$ accepts electrons at the end of the electron transport chain, becoming reduced to NADPH. **4.** In this experiment, the rate of ATP synthesis would slow and eventually stop. Because the added compound would not allow a proton gradient to build up across the membrane, ATP synthase could not catalyze ATP production.

Concept Check 10.3

1. 6, 18, 12 **2.** The more potential energy a molecule stores, the more energy and reducing power is required for the formation of that molecule. Glucose is a valuable energy source because it is highly reduced, storing lots of potential energy in its electrons. To reduce CO$_2$ to glucose, much energy and reducing power are required in the form of large numbers of ATP and NADPH molecules, respectively. **3.** The light reactions require ADP and NADP$^+$, which would not be formed in sufficient quantities from ATP and NADPH if the Calvin cycle stopped. **4.** In glycolysis, G3P acts as an intermediate. The 6-carbon sugar fructose 1,6-bisphosphate is cleaved into two 3-carbon sugars, one of which is G3P. The other is an isomer called dihydroxyacetone phosphate, which can be converted to G3P by an isomerase. Because G3P is the substrate for the next enzyme, it is constantly removed, and the reaction equilibrium is pulled in the direction of conversion of dihydroxyacetone phosphate to more G3P. In the Calvin cycle, G3P acts as both an intermediate and a product. For every three CO$_2$ molecules that enter the cycle, six G3P molecules are formed, five of which must remain in the cycle and become rearranged to regenerate three 5-carbon RuBP molecules. The one remaining G3P is a product, which can be thought of as the result of "reducing" the three CO$_2$ molecules that entered the cycle into a 3-carbon sugar that can later be used to generate energy.

Concept Check 10.4

1. Photorespiration decreases photosynthetic output by adding oxygen, instead of carbon dioxide, to the Calvin cycle. As a result, no sugar is generated (no carbon is fixed), and O$_2$ is used rather than generated. **2.** Without PS II, no O$_2$ is generated in bundle-sheath cells. This avoids the problem of O$_2$ competing with CO$_2$ for binding to rubisco in these cells. **3.** Both problems are caused by a drastic change in Earth's atmosphere due to burning of fossil fuels. The increase in CO$_2$ concentration affects ocean chemistry by decreasing pH, thus affecting calcification by marine organisms. On land, CO$_2$ concentration and air temperature are conditions that plants have become adapted to, and changes in these characteristics have a strong effect on photosynthesis by plants. Thus, alteration of these two fundamental factors could have critical effects on organisms all around the planet, in all different habitats. **4.** C$_4$ and CAM species would replace many of the C$_3$ species.

Summary of Key Concepts Questions

10.1 CO$_2$ and H$_2$O are the products of respiration; they are the reactants in photosynthesis. In respiration, glucose is oxidized to CO$_2$ as electrons are passed through an electron transfer chain from glucose to O$_2$, producing H$_2$O. In photosynthesis, H$_2$O is the source of electrons, which are energized by light, temporarily stored in NADPH, and used to reduce CO$_2$ to carbohydrate. **10.2** The action spectrum of photosynthesis shows that some wavelengths of light that are not absorbed by chlorophyll *a* are still effective at promoting photosynthesis. The light-harvesting complexes of photosystems contain accessory pigments such as chlorophyll *b* and carotenoids, which absorb different wavelengths and pass the energy to chlorophyll *a*, broadening the spectrum of light useful for photosynthesis.
10.3

In the reduction phase of the Calvin cycle, ATP phosphorylates a 3-carbon compound, and NADPH then reduces this compound to G3P. ATP is also used in the regeneration phase, when five molecules of G3P are converted to three molecules of the 5-carbon compound RuBP. Rubisco catalyzes the first step of carbon fixation—the addition of CO$_2$ to RuBP. **10.4** Both C$_4$ and CAM photosynthesis involve initial fixation of CO$_2$ to produce a 4-carbon compound (in mesophyll cells in C$_4$ plants and at night in CAM plants). These compounds are then broken down to release CO$_2$ (in the bundle-sheath cells in C$_4$ plants and during the day in CAM plants). These pathways avoid the photorespiration that consumes ATP and reduces the photosynthetic output of C$_3$ plants when they close stomata on hot, dry, bright days. Thus, hot, arid climates would favor C$_4$ and CAM plants.

Test Your Understanding
1. d **2.** b **3.** c **4.** d **5.** c **6.** b **7.** d
9.

The ATP would end up outside the thylakoid. The thylakoids were able to make ATP in the dark because the researchers set up an artificial proton concentration gradient across the thylakoid membrane; thus, the light reactions were not necessary to establish the H$^+$ gradient required for ATP synthesis by ATP synthase.

Chapter 11

Figure Questions
Figure 11.6 Epinephrine is a signaling molecule; presumably, it binds to a cell-surface receptor protein. **Figure 11.7** Figure 7.1 shows a potassium channel, which, according to the description on p. 135, opens in response to an electrical stimulus, allowing potassium ions to rush out of the cell. Thus, it is a voltage-gated ion channel. **Figure 11.8** When the receptor is actively transmitting a signal to the inside of the cell, it is bound to a G protein. To determine a structure corresponding to that state, it might work to crystallize the receptor in the presence of many copies of the G protein. (In fact, the researchers planned to try this approach next. Another research group also used this approach successfully with a related G protein-coupled receptor the following year.) **Figure 11.9** The testosterone molecule is hydrophobic and can therefore pass directly through the lipid bilayer of the plasma membrane into the cell. (Hydrophilic molecules cannot do this.) **Figure 11.10** The active form of protein kinase 2 **Figure 11.11** The signaling molecule (cAMP) would remain in its active form and would continue to signal. **Figure 11.17** In the model, the directionality of growth is determined by the association of Fus3 with the membrane near the site of receptor activation. Thus, the development of shmoos would be severely compromised, and the affected cell would likely resemble the ΔFus3 and Δformin cells. **Figure 11.18** The signaling pathway shown in Figure 11.14 leads to the splitting of PIP$_2$ into the second messengers DAG and IP$_3$, which produce different responses. (The response elicited by DAG is mentioned but not shown.) The pathway shown for cell B is similar in that it branches and leads to two responses.

Concept Check 11.1
1. The two cells of opposite mating type (**a** and **α**) each secrete a certain signaling molecule, which can only be bound by receptors carried on cells of the opposite mating type. Thus, the **a** mating factor cannot bind to another **a** cell and cause it to grow toward the first **a** cell. Only an **α** cell can "receive" the signaling molecule and respond by directed growth (see Figure 11.17 for more information). **2.** The secretion of neurotransmitter molecules at a synapse is an example of local signaling. The electrical signal that travels along a very long nerve cell and is passed to the next nerve cell can be considered an example of long-distance signaling. (Note, however, that local signaling at the synapse between two cells is necessary for the signal to pass from one cell to the next.) **3.** Glucose 1-phosphate is not generated, because the activation of the enzyme requires an intact cell, with an intact receptor in the membrane and an intact signal transduction pathway. The enzyme cannot be activated directly by interaction with the signaling molecule in the test tube. **4.** Glycogen phosphorylase acts in the third stage, the response to epinephrine signaling.

Concept Check 11.2
1. NGF is water-soluble (hydrophilic), so it cannot pass through the lipid membrane to reach intracellular receptors, as steroid hormones can. Therefore, you'd expect the NGF receptor to be in the plasma membrane—which is, in fact, the case. **2.** The cell with the faulty receptor would not be able to respond appropriately to the signaling molecule when it was present. This would most likely have dire consequences for the cell, since regulation of the cell's activities by this receptor would not occur appropriately. **3.** Binding of a ligand to a receptor changes the shape of the receptor, altering the ability of the receptor to transmit a signal. Binding of an allosteric regulator to an enzyme changes the shape of the enzyme, either promoting or inhibiting enzyme activity.

Concept Check 11.3

1. A protein kinase is an enzyme that transfers a phosphate group from ATP to a protein, usually activating that protein (often a second type of protein kinase). Many signal transduction pathways include a series of such interactions, in which each phosphorylated protein kinase in turn phosphorylates the next protein kinase in the series. Such phosphorylation cascades carry a signal from outside the cell to the cellular protein(s) that will carry out the response. **2.** Protein phosphatases reverse the effects of the kinases. **3.** The signal that is being transduced is the information that a signaling molecule is bound to the cell-surface receptor. Information is transduced by way of sequential protein-protein interactions that change protein shapes, causing them to function in a way that passes the signal along. **4.** The IP_3-gated channel opens, allowing calcium ions to flow out of the ER, which raises the cytosolic Ca^{2+} concentration.

Concept Check 11.4

1. At each step in a cascade of sequential activations, one molecule or ion may activate numerous molecules functioning in the next step. **2.** Scaffolding proteins hold molecular components of signaling pathways in a complex with each other. Different scaffolding proteins would assemble different collections of proteins, leading to different cellular responses in the two cells. **3.** A malfunctioning protein phosphatase would not be able to dephosphorylate a particular receptor or relay protein. As a result, the signaling pathway, once activated, would not be able to be terminated. (In fact, one study found altered protein phosphatases in cells from 25% of colorectal tumors.)

Concept Check 11.5

1. In formation of the hand or paw in mammals, cells in the regions between the digits are programmed to undergo apoptosis. This serves to shape the digits of the hand or paw so that they are not webbed. **2.** If a receptor protein for a death-signaling molecule were defective such that it was activated even in the absence of the death signal, this would lead to apoptosis when it wouldn't normally occur. Similar defects in any of the proteins in the signaling pathway, which would activate these relay or response proteins in the absence of interaction with the previous protein or second messenger in the pathway, would have the same effect. Conversely, if any protein in the pathway were defective in its ability to respond to an interaction with an early protein or other molecule or ion, apoptosis would not occur when it normally should. For example, a receptor protein for a death-signaling ligand might not be able to be activated, even when ligand was bound. This would stop the signal from being transduced into the cell.

Summary of Key Concepts Questions

11.1 A cell is able to respond to a hormone only if it has a receptor protein on the cell surface or inside the cell that can bind to the hormone. The response to a hormone depends on the specific cellular activity that a signal transduction pathway triggers within the cell. The response can vary for different types of cells. **11.2** Both GPCRs and RTKs have an extracellular binding site for a signaling molecule (ligand) and an α helix region of the polypeptide that spans the membrane. GPCRs usually trigger a single transduction pathway, whereas the multiple activated tyrosines on an RTK dimer may trigger several different transduction pathways at the same time. **11.3** A protein kinase is an enzyme that adds a phosphate group to another protein. Protein kinases are often part of a phosphorylation cascade that transduces a signal. A second messenger is a small, nonprotein molecule or ion that rapidly diffuses and relays a signal throughout a cell. Both protein kinases and second messengers can operate in the same pathway. For example, the second messenger cAMP often activates protein kinase A, which then phosphorylates other proteins. **11.4** In G protein-coupled pathways, the GTPase portion of a G protein converts GTP to GDP and inactivates the G protein. Protein phosphatases remove phosphate groups from activated proteins, thus stopping a phosphorylation cascade of protein kinases. Phosphodiesterase converts cAMP to AMP, thus reducing the effect of cAMP in a signal transduction pathway. **11.5** The basic mechanism of controlled cell suicide evolved early in eukaryotic evolution, and the genetic basis for these pathways has been conserved during animal evolution. Such a mechanism is essential to the development and maintenance of all animals.

Test Your Understanding

1. c **2.** d **3.** a **4.** b **5.** a **6.** d **7.** c **8.** c **9.** This is one possible drawing of the pathway. (Similar drawings would also be correct.)

Chapter 12

Figure Questions

Figure 12.4

Circling the other chromatid instead would also be correct. **Figure 12.5** The chromosome has four arms. **Figure 12.7** 12; 2; 2; 1

Figure 12.8

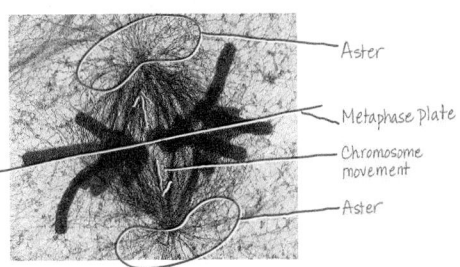

Figure 12.9 The mark would have moved toward the nearer pole. The lengths of fluorescent microtubules between that pole and the mark would have decreased, while the lengths between the chromosomes and the mark would have remained the same. **Figure 12.14** In both cases, the G_1 nucleus would have remained in G_1 until the time it normally would have entered the S phase. Chromosome condensation and spindle formation would not have occurred until the S and G_2 phases had been completed. **Figure 12.16** The cell would divide under conditions where it was inappropriate to do so. If the daughter cells and their descendants also ignored the checkpoint and divided, there would soon be an abnormal mass of cells. (This type of inappropriate cell division can contribute to the development of cancer.) **Figure 12.17** Passing the G_2 checkpoint in the diagram corresponds to the beginning of the "Time" axis of the graph, and entry into the mitotic phase (yellow background on the diagram) corresponds to the peaks of MPF activity and cyclin concentration on the graph (see the yellow M banner over the peaks). During G_1 and S phase in the diagram, Cdk is present without cyclin, so on the graph both cyclin concentration and MPF activity are low. The curved purple arrow in the diagram shows increasing cyclin concentration, seen on the graph during the end of S phase and throughout G_2 phase. Then the cell cycle begins again. **Figure 12.18** The cells in the vessel with PDGF would not be able to respond to the growth factor signal and thus would not divide. The culture would resemble that without the added PDGF. **Figure 12.21** The intracellular estrogen receptor, once activated, would be able to act as a transcription factor in the nucleus, turning on genes that may cause the cell to pass a checkpoint and divide. The HER2 receptor, when activated by a ligand, would form a dimer, and each subunit of the dimer would phosphorylate the other. This would lead to a series of signal transduction steps, ultimately turning on genes in the nucleus. As in the case of the estrogen receptor, the genes would code for proteins necessary to commit the cell to divide.

Concept Check 12.1

1. 2 **2.** 39; 39; 78

Concept Check 12.2

1. 6 chromosomes, duplicated; 12 chromatids **2.** Following mitosis, cytokinesis results in two genetically identical daughter cells in both plant cells and animal cells. However, the mechanism of dividing the cytoplasm is different in animals and plants. In an animal cell, cytokinesis occurs by cleavage, which divides the parent cell in two with a contractile ring of actin filaments. In a plant cell, a cell plate forms in the middle of the cell and grows until its membrane fuses with the plasma membrane of the parent cell. Material inside the cell plate thus becomes the new cell wall. **3.** They elongate the cell during anaphase. **4.** During eukaryotic cell division, tubulin is involved in spindle formation and chromosome movement, while actin functions during cytokinesis. In bacterial binary fission, it's the opposite: Tubulin-like molecules are thought to act in daughter cell separation, and actin-like molecules are thought to move the daughter bacterial chromosomes to opposite ends of the cell. **5.** Microtubules made up of tubulin in the cell provide "rails" along which vesicles and other organelles can travel, based on interactions of motor proteins with tubulin in the microtubules. In muscle cells, actin in microfilaments interacts with myosin filaments to cause muscle contraction. **6.** From the end of S phase in interphase through the end of metaphase in mitosis

Concept Check 12.3

1. The nucleus on the right was originally in the G_1 phase; therefore, it had not yet duplicated its chromosome. The nucleus on the left was in the M phase, so it had already duplicated its chromosome. **2.** A sufficient amount of MPF has to exist for a cell to pass the G_2 checkpoint; this occurs through the accumulation of cyclin proteins, which combine with Cdk to form MPF. **3.** Most body cells are in a nondividing state called G_0. **4.** Both types of tumors consist of abnormal cells, but their characteristics are different. A benign tumor stays at the original site and can usually be surgically removed; the cells have some genetic and cellular changes from normal, non-tumor cells. Cancer cells from a malignant tumor have more significant genetic and cellular changes, can spread from the original site by metastasis, and may impair the functions of one or more organs.   **5.** The cells might divide even in the absence of PDGF. In addition, they would not stop when the surface of the culture vessel was covered; they would continue to divide, piling on top of one another.

Summary of Key Concepts Questions
12.1 The DNA of a eukaryotic cell is packaged into structures called *chromosomes*. Each chromosome is a long molecule of DNA, which carries hundreds to thousands of genes, with associated proteins that maintain chromosome structure and help control gene activity. This DNA-protein complex is called *chromatin*. The chromatin of each chromosome is long and thin when the cell is not dividing. Prior to cell division, each chromosome is duplicated, and the resulting sister *chromatids* are attached to each other by proteins at the centromeres and, for many species, all along their lengths (sister chromatid cohesion).   **12.2** Chromosomes exist as single DNA molecules in G_1 of interphase and in anaphase and telophase of mitosis. During S phase, DNA replication produces sister chromatids, which persist during G_2 of interphase and through prophase, prometaphase, and metaphase of mitosis. **12.3** Checkpoints allow cellular surveillance mechanisms to determine whether the cell is prepared to go to the next stage. Internal and external signals move a cell past these checkpoints. The G_1 checkpoint, called the "restriction point" in mammalian cells, determines whether a cell will complete the cell cycle and divide or switch into the G_0 phase. The signals to pass this checkpoint often are external—such as growth factors. Passing the G_2 checkpoint requires sufficient numbers of active MPF complexes, which in turn orchestrate several mitotic events. MPF also initiates degradation of its cyclin component, terminating the M phase. The M phase will not begin again until sufficient cyclin is produced during the next S and G_2 phases. The signal to pass the M phase checkpoint is not activated until all chromosomes are attached to kinetochore fibers and are aligned at the metaphase plate. Only then will sister chromatid separation occur.

Test Your Understanding
1. b   **2.** a   **3.** c   **4.** c   **5.** a   **6.** b
7. See Figure 12.7 for a description of major events.

Only one cell is indicated for each stage, but other correct answers are also present in this micrograph.
8. a   **9.** e
10.

Chapter 13

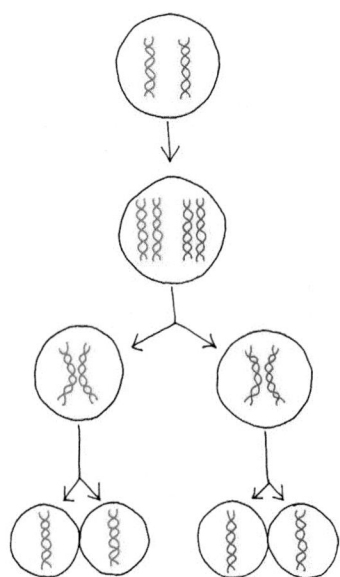

(A short strand of DNA is shown here for simplicity, but each chromosome or chromatid contains a very long coiled and folded DNA molecule.)
Figure 13.8 If the two cells in Figure 12.7 underwent another round of mitosis, each of the four resulting cells would have six chromosomes, while the four cells resulting from meiosis in Figure 13.8 each have three chromosomes. In mitosis, DNA replication (and thus chromosome duplication) precedes each prophase, ensuring that daughter cells have the same number of chromosomes as the parent cell. In meiosis, in contrast, DNA replication occurs only before prophase I (not prophase II). Thus, in two rounds of mitosis, the chromosomes duplicate twice and divide twice, while in meiosis, the chromosomes duplicate once and divide twice.   **Figure 13.9** Yes. Each of the six chromosomes (three per cell) shown in telophase I has one nonrecombinant chromatid and one recombinant chromatid. Therefore, eight possible sets of chromosomes can be generated for the cell on the left and eight for the cell on the right.

Concept Check 13.1
1. Parents pass genes to their offspring; the genes program cells to make specific enzymes and other proteins, whose cumulative action produces an individual's inherited traits.   **2.** Such organisms reproduce by mitosis, which generates offspring whose genomes are exact copies of the parent's genome (in the absence of mutation).   **3.** She should clone it. Cross-breeding it with another plant would generate offspring that have additional variation, which she no longer desires now that she has obtained her ideal orchid.

Concept Check 13.2
1. Each of the six chromosomes is duplicated, so each contains two DNA double helices. Therefore, there are 12 DNA molecules in the cell.   **2.** In meiosis, the chromosome count is reduced from diploid to haploid; the union of two haploid gametes in fertilization restores the diploid chromosome count.   **3.** The haploid number (*n*) is 7; the diploid number (2*n*) is 14.   **4.** This organism has the life cycle shown in Figure 13.6c. Therefore, it must be a fungus or a protist, perhaps an alga.

Concept Check 13.3
1. The chromosomes are similar in that each is composed of two sister chromatids, and the individual chromosomes are positioned similarly at the metaphase plate. The chromosomes differ in that in a mitotically dividing cell, sister chromatids of each chromosome are genetically identical, but in a meiotically dividing cell, sister chromatids are genetically distinct because of crossing over in meiosis I. Moreover, the chromosomes in metaphase of mitosis can be a diploid set or a haploid set, but the chromosomes in metaphase of meiosis II always consist of a haploid set.   **2.** If crossing over did not occur, the two homologs would not be associated in any way. This might result in incorrect arrangement of homologs during metaphase I and ultimately in formation of gametes with an abnormal number of chromosomes.

Concept Check 13.4
1. Mutations in a gene lead to the different versions (alleles) of that gene.
2. Without crossing over, independent assortment of chromosomes during meiosis I theoretically can generate 2^n possible haploid gametes, and random fertilization can produce $2^n \times 2^n$ possible diploid zygotes. Because the haploid number (*n*) of grasshoppers is 23 and that of fruit flies is 4, two grasshoppers would be expected to produce a greater variety of zygotes than would two fruit flies.   **3.** If the segments of the maternal and paternal chromatids that undergo

crossing over are genetically identical and thus have the same two alleles for every gene, then the recombinant chromosomes will be genetically equivalent to the parental chromosomes. Crossing over contributes to genetic variation only when it involves the rearrangement of different alleles.

Summary of Key Concepts Questions

13.1 Genes program specific traits, and offspring inherit their genes from each parent, accounting for similarities in their appearance to one or the other parent. Humans reproduce sexually, which ensures new combinations of genes (and thus traits) in the offspring. Consequently, the offspring are not clones of their parents (which would be the case if humans reproduced asexually). **13.2** Animals and plants both reproduce sexually, alternating meiosis with fertilization. Both have haploid gametes that unite to form a diploid zygote, which then goes on to divide mitotically, forming a diploid multicellular organism. In animals, haploid cells become gametes and don't undergo mitosis, while in plants, the haploid cells resulting from meiosis undergo mitosis to form a haploid multicellular organism, the gametophyte. This organism then goes on to generate haploid gametes. (In plants such as trees, the gametophyte is quite reduced in size and not obvious to the casual observer.) **13.3** At the end of meiosis I, the two members of a homologous pair end up in different cells, so they cannot pair up and undergo crossing over. **13.4** First, during independent assortment in metaphase I, each pair of homologous chromosomes lines up independent of each other pair at the metaphase plate, so a daughter cell of meiosis I randomly inherits either a maternal or paternal chromosome. Second, due to crossing over, each chromosome is not exclusively maternal or paternal, but includes regions at the ends of the chromatid from a nonsister chromatid (a chromatid of the other homolog). (The nonsister segment can also be in an internal region of the chromatid if a second crossover occurs beyond the first one before the end of the chromatid.) This provides much additional diversity in the form of new combinations of alleles. Third, random fertilization ensures even more variation, since any sperm of a large number containing many possible genetic combinations can fertilize any egg of a similarly large number of possible combinations.

Test Your Understanding

1. a **2.** d **3.** b **4.** a **5.** d **6.** c **7.** d
8. (a)

The chromosomes of one color make up a haploid set.
All red and blue chromosomes together make up a diploid set.

(b) The chromosomes of one color make up a haploid set. (In cases where crossovers have occurred, a haploid set of one color may include segments of chromatids of the other color.) All red and blue chromosomes together make up a diploid set.
(c) Metaphase I **9.** This cell must be undergoing meiosis because homologous chromosomes are associated with each other at the metaphase plate; this does not occur in mitosis.

Chapter 14

Figure Questions

Figure 14.3 All offspring would have purple flowers. (The ratio would be one purple to zero white.) The P generation plants are true-breeding, so mating two purple-flowered plants produces the same result as self-pollination: All the offspring have the same trait.

Figure 14.8

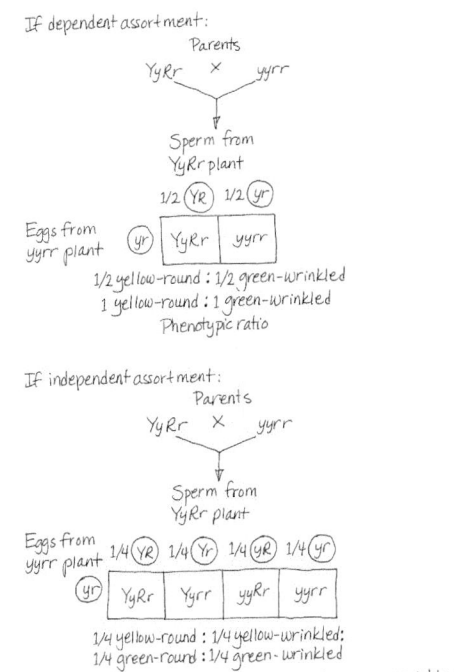

Yes, this cross would also have allowed Mendel to make different predictions for the two hypotheses, thereby allowing him to distinguish the correct one.
Figure 14.10 Your classmate would probably point out that the F_1 generation hybrids show an intermediate phenotype between those of the homozygous parents, which supports the blending hypothesis. You could respond that crossing the F_1 hybrids results in the reappearance of the white phenotype, rather than identical pink offspring, which fails to support the idea of traits blending during inheritance.
Figure 14.11 Both the I^A and I^B alleles are dominant to the i allele, which results in no attached carbohydrate. The I^A and I^B alleles are codominant; both are expressed in the phenotype of $I^A I^B$ heterozygotes, who have type AB blood.
Figure 14.13

The majority of individuals have intermediate phenotypes (skin color in the middle range), while fewer individuals have phenotypes at either end (very dark or very light skin). (As you may know, this is called a "bell curve" and represents a "normal distribution.") **Figure 14.16** In the Punnett square, two of the three individuals with normal coloration are carriers, so the probability is ⅔. (Note that you must take into account everything you know when you calculate probability: You know she is not aa, so there are only three possible genotypes to consider.) **Figure 14.18** If one parent tests negative for the recessive allele, then the probability is zero that the offspring will have the disease and ½ that the offspring will be a carrier. If the first child is a carrier, the probability of the next child being a carrier is still ½ because the two births are independent events.

1. According to the law of independent assortment, 25 plants (¹/₁₆ of the offspring) are predicted to be *aatt*, or recessive for both characters. The actual result is likely to differ slightly from this value.

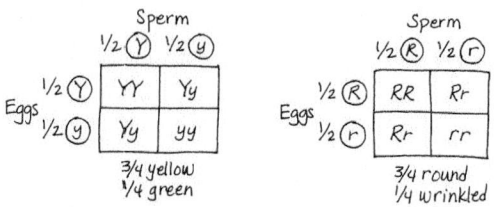

2. The plant could make eight different gametes (*YRI, YRi, YrI, Yri, yRI, yRi, yrI,* and *yri*). To fit all the possible gametes in a self-pollination, a Punnett square would need 8 rows and 8 columns. It would have spaces for the 64 possible unions of gametes in the offspring.   **3.** Self-pollination is sexual reproduction because meiosis is involved in forming gametes, which unite during fertilization. As a result, the offspring in self-pollination are genetically different from the parent. (As mentioned in the footnote on p. 263, we have simplified the explanation in referring to the single pea plant as a parent. Technically, the gametophytes in the flower are the two "parents.")

Concept Check 14.2

1. ½ homozygous dominant (*AA*), 0 homozygous recessive (*aa*), and ½ heterozygous (*Aa*)   **2.** ¼ *BBDD*; ¼ *BbDD*; ¼ *BBDd*; ¼ *BbDd*   **3.** The genotypes that fulfill this condition are *ppyyIi, ppYyii, Ppyyii, ppYYii,* and *ppyyii.* Use the multiplication rule to find the probability of getting each genotype, and then use the addition rule to find the overall probability of meeting the conditions of this problem:

ppyy Ii	½ (probability of *pp*) × ¼ (*yy*) × ½ (*Ii*)	= $\frac{1}{16}$
pp Yy ii	½ (*pp*) × ½ (*Yy*) × ½ (*ii*)	= $\frac{2}{16}$
Pp yy ii	½ (*Pp*) × ¼ (*yy*) × ½ (*ii*)	= $\frac{1}{16}$
pp YY ii	½ (*pp*) × ¼ (*YY*) × ½ (*ii*)	= $\frac{1}{16}$
pp yy ii	½ (*pp*) × ¼ (*yy*) × ½ (*ii*)	= $\frac{1}{16}$

Fraction predicted to have at least = $\frac{6}{16}$ or ⅜
two recessive traits

Concept Check 14.3

1. Incomplete dominance describes the relationship between two alleles of a single gene, whereas epistasis relates to the genetic relationship between two genes (and the respective alleles of each).   **2.** Half of the children would be expected to have type A blood and half type B blood.   **3.** The black and white alleles are incompletely dominant, with heterozygotes being gray in color. A cross between a gray rooster and a black hen should yield approximately equal numbers of gray and black offspring.

Concept Check 14.4

1. ⅙ (Since cystic fibrosis is caused by a recessive allele, Beth and Tom's siblings who have CF must be homozygous recessive. Therefore, each parent must be a carrier of the recessive allele. Since neither Beth nor Tom has CF, this means they each have a ⅔ chance of being a carrier. If they are both carriers, there is a ¼ chance that they will have a child with CF. ⅔ × ⅔ × ¼ = ⅑); 0 (Both Beth and Tom would have to be carriers to produce a child with the disease.)   **2.** In normal hemoglobin, the sixth amino acid is glutamic acid (Glu), which is acidic (has a negative charge on its side chain). In sickle-cell hemoglobin, Glu is replaced by valine (Val), which is a nonpolar amino acid, very different from Glu. The primary structure of a protein (its amino acid sequence) ultimately determines the shape of the protein and thus its function. The substitution of Val for Glu enables the hemoglobin molecules to interact with each other and form long fibers, leading to the protein's deficient function and the deformation of the red blood cell.   **3.** Joan's genotype is *Dd*. Because the allele for polydactyly (*D*) is dominant to the allele for five digits per appendage (*d*), the trait is expressed in people with either the *DD* or *Dd* genotype. But because Joan's father does not have polydactyly, his genotype must be *dd*, which means that Joan inherited a *d* allele from him. Therefore Joan, who does have the trait, must be heterozygous.   **4.** In the monohybrid cross involving flower color, the ratio is 3.15 purple : 1 white, while in the human family in the pedigree, the ratio in the third generation is 1 free : 1 attached earlobe. The difference is due to the small sample size (two offspring) in the human family. If the second-generation couple in this pedigree were able to have 929 offspring as in the pea plant cross, the ratio would likely be closer to 3:1. (Note that none of the pea plant crosses in Table 14.1 yielded *exactly* a 3:1 ratio.)

Summary of Key Concepts Questions

14.1 Alternative versions of genes, called alleles, are passed from parent to offspring during sexual reproduction. In a cross between purple- and white-flowered

homozygous parents, the F₁ offspring are all heterozygous, each inheriting a purple allele from one parent and a white allele from the other. Because the purple allele is dominant, it determines the phenotype of the F₁ offspring to be purple, and the expression of the white allele is masked. Only in the F₂ generation is it possible for a white allele to exist in a homozygous state, which causes the white trait to be expressed.
14.2

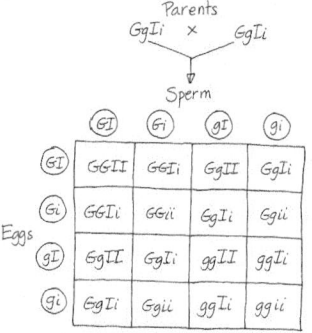

¾ yellow × ¾ round   = 9/16 yellow-round
¾ yellow × ¼ wrinkled = 3/16 yellow-wrinkled
¼ green × ¾ round   = 3/16 green-round
¼ green × ¼ wrinkled = 1/16 green-wrinkled

= 9 yellow-round : 3 yellow-wrinkled : 3 green-round : 1 green-wrinkled

14.3 The ABO blood group is an example of multiple alleles because this single gene has more than two alleles (I^A, I^B, and *i*). Two of the alleles, I^A and I^B, exhibit codominance, since both carbohydrates (A and B) are present when these two alleles exist together in a genotype. I^A and I^B each exhibit complete dominance over the *i* allele. This situation is not an example of incomplete dominance because each allele affects the phenotype in a distinguishable way, so the result is not intermediate between the two phenotypes. Because this situation involves a single gene, it is not an example of epistasis or polygenic inheritance.   **14.4** The chance of the fourth child having cystic fibrosis is ¼, as it was for each of the other children, because each birth is an independent event. We already know both parents are carriers, so whether their first three children are carriers or not has no bearing on the probability that their next child will have the disease. The parents' genotypes provide the only relevant information.

Test Your Understanding

1. Gene, l. Allele, e. Character, g. Trait, b. Dominant allele, j. Recessive allele, a. Genotype, k. Phenotype, h. Homozygous, c. Heterozygous, f. Testcross, i. Monohybrid cross, d.
2.

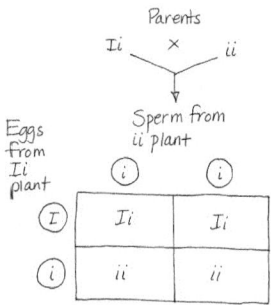

9 green-inflated : 3 green-constricted :
3 yellow-inflated : 1 yellow-constricted

3. Parental cross is $AAC^RC^R \times aaC^WC^W$. F₁ genotype is AaC^RC^W, phenotype is all axial-pink. F₂ genotypes are 1 AAC^RC^R : 2 AAC^RC^W : 1 AAC^WC^W : 2 AaC^RC^R : 4 AaC^RC^W : 2 AaC^WC^W : 1 aaC^RC^R : 2 aaC^RC^W : 1 aaC^WC^W. F₂ phenotypes are 3 axial-red : 6 axial-pink : 3 axial-white : 1 terminal-red : 2 terminal-pink : 1 terminal-white.   **4.** Man I^Ai; woman I^Bi; child *ii*. Genotypes for future children are predicted to be ¼ I^AI^B, ¼ I^Ai, ¼ I^Bi, ¼ *ii*.   **5.** ½   **6.** A cross of *Ii* × *ii* would yield offspring with a genotypic ratio of 1 *Ii* : 1 *ii* (2:2 is an equivalent answer) and a phenotypic ratio of 1 inflated : 1 constricted (2:2 is equivalent).

Parents

Ii   ×   *ii*

Sperm from
ii plant

Eggs from *Ii* plant

	i	*i*
I	*Ii*	*Ii*
i	*ii*	*ii*

Genotypic ratio 1 *Ii* : 1 *ii*
(2:2 is equivalent)

Phenotypic ratio 1 inflated : 1 constricted
(2:2 is equivalent)

7. (a) ¼₄; (b) ¾₄; (c) ⅛; (d) ½₂ **8.** Albino (*b*) is a recessive trait; black (*B*) is dominant. First cross: parents *BB* × *bb*; gametes *B* and *b*; offspring all *Bb* (black coat).
The black guinea pig in the second cross is a heterozygote. Second cross: parents
Bb × *bb*; gametes ½ *B* and ½ *b* (heterozygous parent) and *b*; offspring ½ *Bb* and ½ *bb*.
9. (a) *PPLl* × *PPLl*, *PPLl* × *PpLl*, or *PPLl* × *ppLl*; (b) *ppLl* × *ppLl*; (c) *PPLL* × any of
the 9 possible genotypes or *PPll* × *ppLL*; (d) *PpLl* × *Ppll*; (e) *PpLl* × *PpLl* **10.** (a) ¾ ×
¾ × ¾ = ²⁷⁄₆₄; (b) 1 − ²⁷⁄₆₄ = ³⁷⁄₆₄; (c) ¼ × ¼ × ¼ = ¹⁄₆₄; (d) 1 − ¹⁄₆₄ = ⁶³⁄₆₄ **11.** (a) ½₅₆; (b) ¹⁄₁₆;
(c) ½₅₆; (d) ¼₄; (e) ½₅₆ **12.** (a) ¹⁄₁₆; (b) ½₂; (c) ⅛; (d) ⅛ **13.** ⅛ **14.** Matings of the original mutant cat with true-breeding noncurl cats will produce both curl and non-
curl F₁ offspring if the curl allele is dominant, but only noncurl offspring if the
curl allele is recessive. You would obtain some true-breeding offspring homozygous for the curl allele from matings between the F₁ cats resulting from the original curl × noncurl crosses whether the curl trait is dominant or recessive. You
know that cats are true-breeding when curl × curl matings produce only curl offspring. As it turns out, the allele that causes curled ears is dominant. **15.** ¹⁄₁₆
16. 25%, or ¼, will be cross-eyed; all (100%) of the cross-eyed offspring will also
be white. **17.** The dominant allele *I* is epistatic to the *P/p* locus, and thus the
genotypic ratio for the F₁ generation will be 9 *I_P_* (colorless) : 3 *I_pp* (colorless) :
3 *iiP_* (purple) : 1 *iipp* (red). Overall, the phenotypic ratio is 12 colorless : 3 purple :
1 red. **18.** Recessive. All affected individuals (Arlene, Tom, Wilma, and Carla) are
homozygous recessive *aa*. George is *Aa*, since some of his children with Arlene are
affected. Sam, Ann, Daniel, and Alan are each *Aa*, since they are all unaffected
children with one affected parent. Michael also is *Aa*, since he has an affected
child (Carla) with his heterozygous wife Ann. Sandra, Tina, and Christopher can
each have either the *AA* or *Aa* genotype. **19.** ⅛ **20.** 9 *B_A_* (agouti) : 3 *B_aa*
(black) : 3 *bbA_* (white) : 1 *bbaa* (white). Overall, 9 agouti : 3 black : 4 white.

Chapter 15

Figure Questions
Figure 15.2 The ratio would be 1 yellow-round : 1 green-round : 1 yellow-wrinkled :
1 green-wrinkled. **Figure 15.4** About ¾ of the F₂ offspring would have red eyes and
about ¼ would have white eyes. About half of the white-eyed flies would be female
and half would be male; similarly, about half of the red-eyed flies would be female
and half would be male. **Figure 15.7** All the males would be color-blind, and all
the females would be carriers. **Figure 15.9** The two largest classes would still be the
parental-type offspring (offspring with the phenotypes of the true-breeding P generation flies), but now they would be gray-vestigial and black-normal because those
were the specific allele combinations in the P generation. **Figure 15.10** The two
chromosomes below, left, are like the two chromosomes inherited by the F₁ female, one from each P generation fly. They are passed by the F₁ female intact to
the offspring and thus could be called "parental" chromosomes. The other two
chromosomes result from crossing over during meiosis in the F₁ female. Because
they have combinations of alleles not seen in either of the F₁ female's chromosomes, they can be called "recombinant" chromosomes. (Note that in this example, the alleles on the recombinant chromosomes, *b⁺ vg⁺* and *b vg*, are the allele
combinations that were on the parental chromosomes in the cross shown in
Figures 15.9 and 15.10. The basis for calling them parental chromosomes is the
combination of alleles that was present on the P generation chromosomes.)

Parental chromosomes   Recombinant chromosomes

Concept Check 15.1
1. The law of segregation relates to the inheritance of alleles for a single character.
The law of independent assortment of alleles relates to the inheritance of alleles for
two characters. **2.** The physical basis for the law of segregation is the separation of
homologs in anaphase I. The physical basis for the law of independent assortment
is the alternative arrangements of homologous chromosome pairs in metaphase I.
3. To show the mutant phenotype, a male needs to possess only one mutant allele.
If this gene had been on a pair of autosomes, *two* mutant alleles would have had to
be present for an individual to show the recessive mutant phenotype, a much less
probable situation.

Concept Check 15.2
1. Because the gene for this eye-color character is located on the X chromosome, all
female offspring will be red-eyed and heterozygous (*X^{w⁺} X^w*); all male offspring will
inherit a Y chromosome from the father and be white-eyed (*X^w Y*). **2.** ¼ (½ chance
that the child will inherit a Y chromosome from the father and be male × ½ chance
that he will inherit the X carrying the disease allele from his mother) If the child is a
boy, there is a ½ chance he will have the disease; a female would have zero chance
(but ½ chance of being a carrier). **3.** With a disorder caused by a dominant allele,
there is no such thing as a "carrier," since those with the allele have the disorder.
Because the allele is dominant, the females lose any "advantage" in having two X
chromosomes, since one disorder-associated allele is sufficient to result in the disorder. All fathers who have the dominant allele will pass it along to *all* their daughters, who will also have the disorder. A mother who has the allele (and thus the
disorder) will pass it to half of her sons and half of her daughters.

Concept Check 15.3
1. Crossing over during meiosis I in the heterozygous parent produces some gametes with recombinant genotypes for the two genes. Offspring with a recombi-

nant phenotype arise from fertilization of the recombinant gametes by homozygous recessive gametes from the double-mutant parent. **2.** In each case, the alleles contributed by the female parent determine the phenotype of the offspring
because the male in this cross contributes only recessive alleles. **3.** No. The order
could be *A-C-B* or *C-A-B*. To determine which possibility is correct, you need to
know the recombination frequency between *B* and *C*.

Concept Check 15.4
1. In meiosis, a combined 14-21 chromosome will behave as one chromosome. If
a gamete receives the combined 14-21 chromosome and a normal copy of chromosome 21, trisomy 21 will result when this gamete combines with a normal gamete during fertilization. **2.** No. The child can be either *I^A I^A i* or *I^A ii*. A sperm of
genotype *I^A I^A i* could result from nondisjunction in the father during meiosis II,
while an egg with the genotype *ii* could result from nondisjunction in the mother
during either meiosis I or meiosis II. **3.** Activation of this gene could lead to the
production of too much of this kinase. If the kinase is involved in a signaling
pathway that triggers cell division, too much of it could trigger unrestricted cell
division, which in turn could contribute to the development of a cancer (in this
case, a cancer of one type of white blood cell).

Concept Check 15.5
1. Inactivation of an X chromosome in females and genomic imprinting. Because of
X inactivation, the effective dose of genes on the X chromosome is the same in
males and females. As a result of genomic imprinting, only one allele of certain
genes is phenotypically expressed. **2.** The genes for leaf coloration are located in
plastids within the cytoplasm. Normally, only the maternal parent transmits plastid
genes to offspring. Since variegated offspring are produced only when the female
parent is of the B variety, we can conclude that variety B contains both the wild-
type and mutant alleles of pigment genes, producing variegated leaves. (Variety A
contains only the wild-type allele of pigment genes.) **3.** The situation is similar to
that for chloroplasts. Each cell contains numerous mitochondria, and in affected individuals, most cells contain a variable mixture of normal and mutant mitochondria. The normal mitochondria carry out enough cellular respiration for survival.

Summary of Key Concepts Questions
15.1 Because the sex chromosomes are different from each other and because they
determine the sex of the offspring, Morgan could use the sex of the offspring as a
phenotypic characteristic to follow the parental chromosomes. (He could also have
followed them under a microscope, as the X and Y chromosomes look different.) At
the same time, he could record eye color to follow the eye-color alleles. **15.2** Males
have only one X chromosome, along with a Y chromosome, while females have two
X chromosomes. The Y chromosome has very few genes on it, while the X has about
1,000. When a recessive X-linked allele that causes a disorder is inherited by a male
on the X from his mother, there isn't a second allele present on the Y (males are
hemizygous), so the male has the disorder. Because females have two X chromosomes, they must inherit two recessive alleles in order to have the disorder, a rarer
occurrence. **15.3** Crossing over results in new combinations of alleles. Crossing over
is a random occurrence, and the more distance there is between two genes, the more
chances there are for crossing over to occur, leading to a new allele combination.
15.4 In inversions and reciprocal translocations, the same genetic material is present
in the same relative amount but just organized differently. In aneuploidy, duplications, deletions, and nonreciprocal translocations, the balance of genetic material is
upset, as large segments are either missing or present in more than one copy. Apparently, this type of imbalance is very damaging to the organism. (Although it isn't
lethal in the developing embryo, the reciprocal translocation that produces the
Philadelphia chromosome can lead to a serious condition, cancer, by altering the expression of important genes.) **15.5** In these cases, the sex of the parent contributing
an allele affects the inheritance pattern. For imprinted genes, either the paternal or
the maternal allele is expressed, depending on the imprint. For mitochondrial and
chloroplast genes, only the maternal contribution will affect offspring phenotype because the offspring inherit these organelles from the mother, via the egg cytoplasm.

Test Your Understanding
1. 0; ½; ¹⁄₁₆ **2.** Recessive; if the disorder were dominant, it would affect at least
one parent of a child born with the disorder. The disorder's inheritance is sex-
linked because it is seen only in boys. For a girl to have the disorder, she
would have to inherit recessive alleles from *both* parents. This would be very
rare, since males with the recessive allele on their X chromosome die in their
early teens. **3.** 17% **4.** The disorder would always be inherited from the
mother. **5.** Between *T* and *A*, 12%; between *A* and *S*, 5% **6.** Between *T* and
S, 18%; sequence of genes is *T–A–S* **7.** ¼ for each daughter (½ chance
that child will be female × ½ chance of a homozygous recessive genotype);
½ for first son. **8.** 6%; wild-type heterozygous for normal wings and red
eyes) × recessive homozygous for vestigial wings and purple eyes
9.

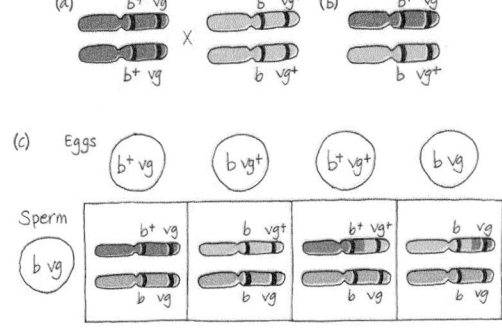

(d) 41.5% gray body, vestigial wings
   41.5% black body, normal wings
   8.5% gray body, normal wings
   8.5% black body, vestigial wings
10. The inactivation of two X chromosomes in XXX women would leave them with one genetically active X, as in women with the normal number of chromosomes. Microscopy should reveal two Barr bodies in XXX women. **11.** *D–A–B–C*   **12.** Fifty percent of the offspring will show phenotypes resulting from crossovers. These results would be the same as those from a cross where *A* and *B* were *not* on the same chromosome. Further crosses involving other genes on the same chromosome would reveal the genetic linkage and map distances.   **13.** 450 each of blue-oval and white-round (parentals) and 50 each of blue-round and white-oval (recombinants)   **14.** About one-third of the distance from the vestigial-wing locus to the brown-eye locus   **15.** Because bananas are triploid, homologous pairs cannot line up during meiosis. Therefore, it is not possible to generate gametes that can fuse to produce a zygote with the triploid number of chromosomes.

Chapter 16

Figure Questions
Figure 16.2 The living S cells found in the blood sample were able to reproduce to yield more S cells, indicating that the S trait is a permanent, heritable change, rather than just a one-time use of the dead S cells' capsules. **Figure 16.4** The radioactivity would have been found in the pellet when proteins were labeled (batch 1) because proteins would have had to enter the bacterial cells to program them with genetic instructions. It's hard for us to imagine now, but the DNA might have played a structural role that allowed some of the proteins to be injected while it remained outside the bacterial cell (thus no radioactivity in the pellet in batch 2). **Figure 16.11** The tube from the first replication would look the same, with a middle band of hybrid ^{15}N-^{14}N DNA, but the second tube would not have the upper band of two light blue strands. Instead it would have a bottom band of two dark blue strands, like the bottom band in the result predicted after one replication in the conservative model. **Figure 16.12** In the bubble at the top in (b), arrows should be drawn pointing left and right to indicate the two replication forks. **Figure 16.14** Looking at any of the DNA strands, we see that one end is called the 5' end and the other the 3' end. If we proceed from the 5' end to the 3' end on the left-most strand, for example, we list the components in this order: phosphate group → 5' C of the sugar → 3' C → phosphate → 5' C → 3' C. Going in the opposite direction on the same strand, the components proceed in the reverse order: 3' C → 5' C → phosphate. Thus, the two directions are distinguishable, which is what we mean when we say that the strands have directionality. (Review Figure 15.5 if necessary.)
Figure 16.17

Figure 16.23 The two members of a homologous pair (which would be the same color) would be associated tightly together at the metaphase plate. In metaphase of mitosis, however, each chromosome would be lined up individually, so the two chromosomes of the same color would be in different places at the metaphase plate.

Concept Check 16.1
1. Chargaff's rule about base ratios states that in DNA, the percentages of A and T are essentially the same, as are those of G and C. The fly data are consistent with that rule. (Slight variations are most likely due to limitations of analytical technique.)   **2.** You can't tell which end is the 5' end. You need to know which end has a phosphate group on the 5' carbon (the 5' end) or which end has an —OH group on the 3' carbon (the 3' end).   **3.** He was expecting that the mouse injected with the mixture of heat-killed S cells and living R cells would survive, since neither type of cell alone would kill the mouse.

Concept Check 16.2
1. Complementary base pairing ensures that the two daughter molecules are exact copies of the parental molecule. When the two strands of the parental molecule separate, each serves as a template on which nucleotides are arranged, by the base-pairing rules, into new complementary strands.

2.

Protein	Function
Helicase	Unwinds parental double helix at replication forks
Single-strand binding protein	Binds to and stabilizes single-stranded DNA until it can be used as a template
Topoisomerase	Relieves "overwinding" strain ahead of replication forks by breaking, swiveling, and rejoining DNA strands
Primase	Synthesizes an RNA primer at 5' end of leading strand and at 5' end of each Okazaki fragment of lagging strand
DNA pol III	Using parental DNA as a template, synthesizes new DNA strand by covalently adding nucleotides to 3' end of a pre-existing DNA strand or RNA primer
DNA pol I	Removes RNA nucleotides of primer from 5' end and replaces them with DNA nucleotides
DNA ligase	Joins 3' end of DNA that replaces primer to rest of leading strand and joins Okazaki fragments of lagging strand

3. In the cell cycle, DNA synthesis occurs during the S phase, between the G_1 and G_2 phases of interphase. DNA replication is therefore complete before the mitotic phase begins.   **4.** Synthesis of the leading strand is initiated by an RNA primer, which must be removed and replaced with DNA, a task that could not be performed if the cell's DNA pol I were nonfunctional. In the overview box in Figure 16.17, just to the left of the top origin of replication, a functional DNA pol I would replace the RNA primer of the leading strand (shown in red) with DNA nucleotides (blue).

Concept Check 16.3
1. A nucleosome is made up of eight histone proteins, two each of four different types, around which DNA is wound. Linker DNA runs from one nucleosome to the next.   **2.** Euchromatin is chromatin that becomes less compacted during interphase and is accessible to the cellular machinery responsible for gene activity. Heterochromatin, on the other hand, remains quite condensed during interphase and contains genes that are largely inaccessible to this machinery.   **3.** The nuclear lamina is a netlike array of protein filaments that provides mechanical support just inside the nuclear envelope and thus maintains the shape of the nucleus. Considerable evidence also supports the existence of a nuclear matrix, a framework of protein fibers extending throughout the nuclear interior.

Summary of Key Concepts Questions
16.1 Each strand in the double helix has polarity, the end with a phosphate group on the 5' carbon of the sugar being called the 5' end, and the end with an —OH group on the 3' carbon of the sugar being called the 3' end. The two strands run in opposite directions, so each end of the molecule has both a 5' and a 3' end. This arrangement is called "antiparallel." If the strands were parallel, they would both run 5' → 3' in the same direction, so an end of the molecule would have either two 5' ends or two 3' ends.   **16.2** On both the leading and lagging strands, DNA polymerase adds onto the 3' end of an RNA primer synthesized by primase, synthesizing DNA in the 5' → 3' direction. Because the parental strands are antiparallel, however, only on the leading strand does synthesis proceed continuously into the replication fork. The lagging strand is synthesized bit by bit in the direction away from the fork as a series of shorter Okazaki fragments, which are later joined together by DNA ligase. Each fragment is initiated by synthesis of an RNA primer by primase as soon as a given stretch of single-stranded template strand is opened up. Although both strands are synthesized at the same rate, synthesis of the lagging strand is delayed because initiation of each fragment begins only when sufficient template strand is available.   **16.3** Most of the chromatin in an interphase nucleus is uncondensed. Much is present as the 30-nm fiber, with some in the form of the 10-nm fiber and some as looped domains of the 30-nm fiber. (These different levels of chromatin packing may reflect differences in gene expression occurring in these regions.) Also, a small percentage of the chromatin, such as that at the centromeres and telomeres, is highly condensed heterochromatin.

Test Your Understanding
1. c **2.** c **3.** b **4.** d **5.** c **6.** d **7.** b **8.** a
9. Like histones, the *E. coli* proteins would be expected to contain many basic (positively charged) amino acids, such as lysine and arginine, which can form weak bonds with the negatively charged phosphate groups on the sugar-phosphate backbone of the DNA molecule.   **10.** Each species' DNA has a slightly different percentage of a given base. For example, the percentage of A ranges from 24.7% for *E. coli* to 32.8% for sea urchin. This illustrates Chargaff's rule that the DNA of different species varies in its base composition. Chargaff's other rule states

that in any given species, the percentage of A is roughly equal to that of T, and the percentage of C is roughly equal to that of G. For example, sea urchins have about 32–33% each of A and T and about 17% of G and C. (Your answer may use any similar examples from the table.)

12.

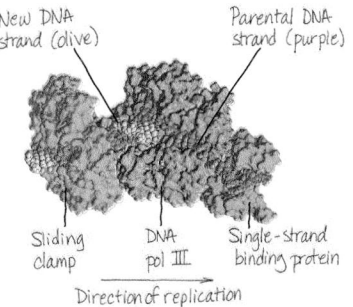

New DNA strand (olive)
Parental DNA strand (purple)
Sliding clamp
DNA pol III
Single-strand binding protein
Direction of replication

Chapter 17

Figure Questions

Figure 17.2 The previously presumed pathway would have been wrong. The new results would support this pathway: precursor → citrulline → ornithine → arginine. They would also indicate that class I mutants have a defect in the second step and class II mutants have a defect in the first step. **Figure 17.4** The mRNA sequence (5'-UGGUUUGGCUCA-3') is the same as the nontemplate DNA strand sequence (5'-TGGTTTGGCTCA-3'), except there is U in the mRNA and T in the DNA. **Figure 17.7** The processes are similar in that polymerases form polynucleotides complementary to an antiparallel DNA template strand. In replication, however, both strands act as templates, whereas in transcription, only one DNA strand acts as a template. **Figure 17.8** The RNA polymerase would bind directly to the promoter, rather than depending on the previous binding of other factors. **Figure 17.25** The RNA polymerase on the right (associated with the longest mRNA) started transcribing first. The ribosome at the top, closest to the DNA, started translating first and thus has the longest polypeptide.

Concept Check 17.1

1. Recessive **2.** A polypeptide made up of 10 Gly (glycine) amino acids

3. Template sequence
(from problem): 3'-TTCAGTCGT-5'

Nontemplate sequence: 5'-AAGTCAGCA-3'

mRNA sequence: 5'-AAGUCAGCA-3'

The nontemplate and mRNA nucleotide sequences are the same except that there is T in the nontemplate strand of DNA wherever there is U in the mRNA.

4. "Template sequence" (from nontemplate sequence in problem, written 3' → 5'): 3'-ACGACTGAA-5'

mRNA sequence: 5'-UGCUGACUU-3'

Translated: Cys-STOP-Leu

(Remember that the mRNA is antiparallel to the DNA strand.) A protein translated from the nontemplate sequence would have a completely different amino acid sequence and would most likely be nonfunctional. (It would also be shorter because of the stop signal shown in the mRNA sequence above—and possibly others earlier in the mRNA sequence.)

Concept Check 17.2

1. Both assemble nucleic acid chains from monomer nucleotides whose order is determined by complementary base pairing to a template strand. Both synthesize in the 5' → 3' direction, antiparallel to the template. DNA polymerase requires a primer, but RNA polymerase can start a nucleotide chain from scratch. DNA polymerase uses nucleotides with the sugar deoxyribose and the base T, whereas RNA polymerase uses nucleotides with the sugar ribose and the base U. **2.** The promoter is the region of DNA to which RNA polymerase binds to begin transcription, and it is at the upstream end of the gene (transcription unit). **3.** In a bacterial cell, RNA polymerase recognizes the gene's promoter and binds to it. In a eukaryotic cell, transcription factors mediate the binding of RNA polymerase to the promoter. In both cases, sequences in the promoter bind precisely to the RNA polymerase, so the enzyme is in the right location and orientation. **4.** The transcription factor that recognizes the TATA sequence would be unable to bind, so RNA polymerase could not bind and transcription of that gene probably would not occur.

Concept Check 17.3

1. Due to alternative splicing of exons, each gene can result in multiple different mRNAs and can thus direct synthesis of multiple different proteins. **2.** In editing a video, segments are cut out and discarded (like introns), and the remaining segments are joined together (like exons) so that the regions of joining ("splicing") are not noticeable. **3.** Once the mRNA has exited the nucleus, the cap

prevents it from being degraded by hydrolytic enzymes and facilitates its attachment to ribosomes. If the cap were removed from all mRNAs, the cell would no longer be able to synthesize any proteins and would probably die.

Concept Check 17.4

1. First, each aminoacyl-tRNA synthetase specifically recognizes a single amino acid and attaches it only to an appropriate tRNA. Second, a tRNA charged with its specific amino acid binds only to an mRNA codon for that amino acid. **2.** The structure and function of the ribosome seem to depend more on the rRNAs than on the ribosomal proteins. Because it is single-stranded, an RNA molecule can hydrogen-bond with itself and with other RNA molecules. RNA molecules make up the interface between the two ribosomal subunits, so presumably RNA-RNA binding helps hold the ribosome together. The binding site for mRNA in the ribosome includes rRNA that can bind the mRNA. Also, complementary bonding within an RNA molecule allows it to assume a particular three-dimensional shape and, along with the RNA's functional groups, presumably enables rRNA to catalyze peptide bond formation during translation. **3.** A signal peptide on the leading end of the polypeptide being synthesized is recognized by a signal-recognition particle that brings the ribosome to the ER membrane. There the ribosome attaches and continues to synthesize the polypeptide, depositing it in the ER lumen. **4.** Because of wobble, the tRNA could bind to either 5'-GCA-3' or 5'-GCG-3', both of which code for alanine (Ala). Alanine would be attached to the tRNA.

Ala
3' CGU 5'
GCA
5' 3'
GCG
5' 3'

Concept Check 17.5

1. In the mRNA, the reading frame downstream from the deletion is shifted, leading to a long string of incorrect amino acids in the polypeptide, and in most cases, a stop codon will arise, leading to premature termination. The polypeptide will most likely be nonfunctional. **2.** Heterozygous individuals, said to have sickle-cell trait, have a copy each of the wild-type allele and the sickle-cell allele. Both alleles will be expressed, so these individuals will have both normal and sickle-cell hemoglobin molecules. Apparently, having a mix of the two forms of β-globin has no effect under most conditions, but during prolonged periods of low blood oxygen (such as at higher altitudes), these individuals can show some signs of sickle-cell disease.

3.

Normal DNA sequence
(template strand is on top): 3'-TACTTGTCCGATATC-5'
5'-ATGAACAGGCTATAG-3'

mRNA sequence: 5'-AUGAACAGGCUAUAG-3'

Amino acid sequence: Met-Asn-Arg-Leu-STOP

Mutated DNA sequence
(template strand is on top): 3'-TACTTGTCCAATATC-5'
5'-ATGAACAGGTTATAG-3'

mRNA sequence: 5'-AUGAACAGGUUAUAG-3'

Amino acid sequence: Met-Asn-Arg-Leu-STOP

No effect: The amino acid sequence is Met-Asn-Arg-Leu both before and after the mutation because the mRNA codons 5'-CUA-3' and 5'-UUA-3' both code for Leu. (The fifth codon is a stop codon.)

Concept Check 17.6

1. No, transcription and translation are separated in space and time in a eukaryotic cell, a result of the eukaryotic cell's nuclear compartment. **2.** When one ribosome terminates translation and dissociates, the two subunits would be very close to the cap. This could facilitate their rebinding and initiating synthesis of a new polypeptide, thus increasing the efficiency of translation.

Summary of Key Concepts Questions

17.1 A gene contains genetic information in the form of a nucleotide sequence. The gene is first transcribed into an RNA molecule, and a messenger RNA molecule is ultimately translated into a polypeptide. The polypeptide makes up part or all of a protein, which performs a function in the cell and contributes to the phenotype of the organism. **17.2** Both bacterial and eukaryotic genes have promoters, regions where RNA polymerase ultimately binds and begins transcription. In bacteria, RNA polymerase binds directly to the promoter; in eukaryotes, transcription factors bind first to the promoter, and then RNA polymerase binds to the transcription factors and promoter together. **17.3** Both the 5′ cap and the poly-A tail help the mRNA exit from the nucleus and then, in the cytoplasm, help ensure mRNA stability and allow it to bind to ribosomes. **17.4** tRNAs function as translators between the nucleotide-based language of mRNA and the amino-acid-based language of polypeptides. A tRNA carries a specific amino acid, and the anticodon on the tRNA is complementary to the codon on the mRNA that codes for that amino acid. In the ribosome, the tRNA binds to the A site, where the polypeptide being synthesized is joined to the new amino acid, which becomes the new (C-terminal) end of the polypeptide. Next, the tRNA moves to the P site. When the next amino acid is added via transfer of the polypeptide to the new tRNA, the now empty tRNA moves to the E site, where it exits the ribosome. **17.5** When a nucleotide base is altered chemically, its base-pairing characteristics may be changed. When that happens, an incorrect nucleotide is likely to be incorporated into the complementary strand during the next replication of the DNA, and successive rounds of replication will perpetuate the mutation. Once the gene is transcribed, the mutated codon may code for a different amino acid that inhibits or changes the function of a protein. If the chemical change in the base is detected and repaired by the DNA repair system before the next replication, no mutation will result. **17.6** The presence of a nuclear envelope in eukaryotes means that transcription and translation are separated in space and therefore in time. This separation allows other processes (specifically, RNA processing) to occur and provides other steps at which gene expression can be regulated.

Test Your Understanding

1. b **2.** d **3.** a **4.** a **5.** b **6.** d **7.** e
8.

Type of RNA	Functions
Messenger RNA (mRNA)	Carries information specifying amino acid sequences of proteins from DNA to ribosomes
Transfer RNA (tRNA)	Serves as translator molecule in protein synthesis; translates mRNA codons into amino acids
Ribosomal RNA (rRNA)	Plays catalytic (ribozyme) roles and structural roles in ribosomes
Primary transcript	Is a precursor to mRNA, rRNA, or tRNA, before being processed; some intron RNA acts as a ribozyme, catalyzing its own splicing
Small nuclear RNA (snRNA)	Plays structural and catalytic roles in spliceosomes, the complexes of protein and RNA that splice pre-mRNA

Chapter 18

Figure Questions

Figure 18.3 As the concentration of tryptophan in the cell falls, eventually there will be none bound to repressor molecules. These will then take on their inactive shapes and dissociate from the operator, allowing transcription of the operon to resume. The enzymes for tryptophan synthesis will be made, and they will begin to synthesize tryptophan again in the cell. **Figure 18.11** The albumin gene enhancer has the three control elements colored yellow, gray, and red. The sequences in the liver and lens cells would be identical, since the cells are in the same organism. **Figure 18.18** Even if the mutant MyoD protein couldn't activate the *myoD* gene, it could still turn on genes for the other proteins in the pathway (other transcription factors, which would turn on the genes for muscle-specific proteins, for example). Therefore, some differentiation would occur. But unless there were other activators that could compensate for the loss of the MyoD protein's activation of the *myoD* gene, the cell would not be able to maintain its differentiated state. **Figure 18.22** Normal Bicoid protein would be made in the anterior end and compensate for the presence of mutant *bicoid* mRNA put into the egg by the mother. Development should be normal, with a head present. **Figure 18.24** The mutation is likely to be recessive because it is more likely to have an effect if both copies of the gene are mutated and code for nonfunctional proteins. If one normal copy of the gene is present, its product could inhibit the cell cycle. (However, there are also known cases of dominant *p53* mutations.)

Concept Check 18.1

1. Binding by the *trp* corepressor (tryptophan) activates the *trp* repressor, shutting off transcription of the *trp* operon; binding by the *lac* inducer (allolactose) inactivates the *lac* repressor, leading to transcription of the *lac* operon. **2.** When glucose is scarce, cAMP is bound to CAP and CAP is bound to the promoter, favoring the binding of RNA polymerase. However, in the absence of lactose, the repressor is bound to the operator, blocking RNA polymerase binding to the promoter. Therefore, the operon genes are not transcribed. **3.** The cell would continuously

produce β-galactosidase and the two other enzymes for lactose utilization, even in the absence of lactose, thus wasting cell resources.

Concept Check 18.2

1. Histone acetylation is generally associated with gene expression, while DNA methylation is generally associated with lack of expression. **2.** General transcription factors function in assembling the transcription initiation complex at the promoters for all genes. Specific transcription factors bind to control elements associated with a particular gene and, once bound, either increase (activators) or decrease (repressors) transcription of that gene. **3.** The three genes should have some similar or identical sequences in the control elements of their enhancers. Because of this similarity, the same specific transcription factors in muscle cells could bind to the enhancers of all three genes and stimulate their expression coordinately. **4.** Degradation of the mRNA, regulation of translation, activation of the protein (by chemical modification, for example), and protein degradation **5.** Expression of the gene encoding the yellow activator (YA) must be regulated at one of the steps shown in Figure 18.6. The YA gene might be transcribed only in liver cells because the necessary activators for the enhancer of the YA gene are found only in liver cells.

Concept Check 18.3

1. Both miRNAs and siRNAs are small, single-stranded RNAs that associate with a complex of proteins and then can base-pair with mRNAs that have a complementary sequence. This base pairing leads to either degradation of the mRNA or blockage of its translation. Some siRNAs, in association with other proteins, can bind back to the chromatin in a certain region, causing chromatin changes that affect transcription. Both miRNAs and siRNAs are processed from double-stranded RNA precursors by the enzyme Dicer. All miRNAs are specified by genes in the cell's genome, and the single transcript folds back on itself to form one or more double-stranded hairpins, each of which is processed into an miRNA. In contrast, siRNAs arise from a longer stretch of linear double-stranded RNA, which may be introduced into the cell by a virus or an experimenter. Alternatively, in some cases, a cellular gene specifies one RNA strand of the precursor molecule, and an enzyme then synthesizes the complementary strand. **2.** The mRNA would persist and be translated into the cell division–promoting protein, and the cell would probably divide. If the intact miRNA is necessary for inhibition of cell division, then division of this cell might be inappropriate. Uncontrolled cell division could lead to formation of a mass of cells (tumor) that prevents proper functioning of the organism and could contribute to the development of cancer. **3.** The *XIST* RNA is transcribed from the *XIST* gene on the X chromosome that will be inactivated. It then binds to that chromosome and induces heterochromatin formation. A likely model is that the *XIST* RNA somehow recruits chromatin modification enzymes that lead to formation of heterochromatin.

Concept Check 18.4

1. Cells undergo differentiation during embryonic development, becoming different from each other; in the adult organism, there are many highly specialized cell types. **2.** By binding to a receptor on the receiving cell's surface and triggering a signal transduction pathway, involving intracellular molecules such as second messengers and transcription factors that affect gene expression **3.** Because their products, made and deposited into the egg by the mother, determine the head and tail ends, as well as the back and belly, of the embryo (and eventually the adult fly) **4.** The lower cell is synthesizing signaling molecules because the gene encoding them is activated, meaning that the appropriate specific transcription factors are binding to the gene's enhancer. The genes encoding these specific transcription factors are also being expressed in this cell because the transcriptional activators that can turn them on were expressed in the precursor to this cell. A similar explanation also applies to the cells expressing the receptor proteins. This scenario began with specific cytoplasmic determinants localized in specific regions of the egg. These cytoplasmic determinants were distributed unevenly to daughter cells, resulting in cells going down different developmental pathways.

Concept Check 18.5

1. Apoptosis is signaled by p53 protein when a cell has extensive DNA damage, so apoptosis plays a protective role in eliminating a cell that might contribute to cancer. If mutations in the genes in the apoptotic pathway blocked apoptosis, a cell with such damage could continue to divide and might lead to tumor formation. **2.** When an individual has inherited an oncogene or a mutant allele of a tumor-suppressor gene **3.** A cancer-causing mutation in a proto-oncogene usually makes the gene product overactive, whereas a cancer-causing mutation in a tumor-suppressor gene usually makes the gene product nonfunctional.

Summary of Key Concepts Questions

18.1 A corepressor and an inducer are both small molecules that bind to the repressor protein in an operon, causing the repressor to change shape. In the case of a corepressor (like tryptophan), this shape change allows the repressor to bind to the operator, blocking transcription. In contrast, an inducer causes the repressor to dissociate from the operator, allowing transcription to begin. **18.2** The chromatin must not be tightly condensed because it must be accessible to transcription factors. The appropriate specific transcription factors (activators) must bind to the control elements in the enhancer of the gene, while repressors must not be bound. The DNA must be bent by a bending protein so the activators can contact the mediator proteins and form a complex with general transcription factors at the promoter. Then RNA polymerase must bind and begin transcription. **18.3** miRNAs do not "code" for the amino acids of a protein—they are never translated. Each miRNA is cleaved from its hairpin RNA structure and then trimmed by Dicer. Next, one strand is degraded while the other associates with a group of proteins to form a complex. Binding of the complex to an mRNA with a complementary sequence causes that mRNA to be degraded or blocks its translation. This is considered gene regulation because it controls the amount of a particular mRNA that can be translated into a functional protein. **18.4** The first process involves cytoplasmic determinants, including mRNAs and proteins, placed into specific locations in the egg by the mother. The cells that are formed from different regions in the egg during early cell divisions will have different proteins in them, which will direct different programs of gene expression. The second process involves the cell in question responding to signaling molecules secreted by neighboring cells. The signaling pathway in the responding cell also leads to a different pattern of gene expression. The coordination of these two processes results in each cell following a unique pathway in the developing embryo. **18.5** The protein product of a proto-oncogene is usually involved in a pathway that stimulates cell division. The protein product of a tumor-suppressor gene is usually involved in a pathway that inhibits cell division.

Test Your Understanding
1. d **2.** a **3.** a **4.** a **5.** c **6.** d **7.** c **8.** e **9.** b **10.** b
11. a.

The purple, blue, and red activator proteins would be present.
b.

Only gene 4 would be transcribed.
c. In nerve cells, the orange, blue, green, and black activators would have to be present, thus activating transcription of genes 1, 2, and 4. In skin cells, the red, black, purple, and blue activators would have to be present, thus activating genes 3 and 5.

Chapter 19

Figure Questions
Figure 19.2 Beijerinck might have concluded that the agent was a toxin produced by the plant that was able to pass through a filter but that became more and more dilute. In this case, he would have concluded that the infectious agent could not replicate. **Figure 19.4** Top vertical arrow: Infection. Left upper arrow: Replication. Right upper arrow: Transcription. Right middle arrow: Translation. Lower left and right arrows: Self-assembly. Bottom middle arrow: Exit. **Figure 19.7** Any class V virus, including the viruses that cause influenza (flu), measles, and mumps **Figure 19.8** The main protein on the cell surface that HIV binds to is called CD4. However, HIV also requires a "co-receptor," which in many cases is a protein called CCR5. HIV binds to both of these proteins together and then is taken into the cell. Researchers discovered this requirement by studying individuals who seemed to be resistant to HIV infection, despite multiple exposures. These individuals turned out to have mutations in the gene that encodes CCR5 such that the protein apparently cannot act as a co-receptor, and so HIV can't enter and infect cells.

Concept Check 19.1
1. TMV consists of one molecule of RNA surrounded by a helical array of proteins. The influenza virus has eight molecules of RNA, each surrounded by a helical array of proteins, similar to the arrangement of the single RNA molecule in TMV. Another difference between the viruses is that the influenza virus has an outer envelope and TMV does not. **2.** The T2 phages were an excellent choice for use in the Hershey-Chase experiment because they consist of only DNA surrounded by a protein coat, and DNA and protein were the two candidates for macromolecules that carried genetic information. Hershey and Chase were able to radioactively label each type of molecule alone and follow it during separate infections of *E. coli* cells with T2. Only the DNA entered the bacterial cell during infection, and only labeled DNA showed up in some of the progeny phage.

Hershey and Chase concluded that the DNA must carry the genetic information necessary for the phage to reprogram the cell and produce progeny phages.

Concept Check 19.2
1. Lytic phages can only carry out lysis of the host cell, whereas lysogenic phages may either lyse the host cell or integrate into the host chromosome. In the latter case, the viral DNA (prophage) is simply replicated along with the host chromosome. Under certain conditions, a prophage may exit the host chromosome and initiate a lytic cycle. **2.** Both the viral RNA polymerase and the RNA polymerase in Figure 17.9 synthesize an RNA molecule complementary to a template strand. However, the RNA polymerase in Figure 17.9 uses one of the strands of the DNA double helix as a template, whereas the viral RNA polymerase uses the RNA of the viral genome as a template. **3.** Because it synthesizes DNA from its RNA genome. This is the reverse ("retro") of the usual DNA → RNA information flow. **4.** There are many steps that could be interfered with: binding of the virus to the cell, reverse transcriptase function, integration into the host cell chromosome, genome synthesis (in this case, transcription of RNA from the integrated provirus), assembly of the virus inside the cell, and budding of the virus. (Many of these, if not all, are targets of actual medical strategies to block progress of the infection in HIV-infected people.)

Concept Check 19.3
1. Mutations can lead to a new strain of a virus that can no longer be effectively fought by the immune system, even if an animal had been exposed to the original strain; a virus can jump from one species to a new host; and a rare virus can spread if a host population becomes less isolated. **2.** In horizontal transmission, a plant is infected from an external source of virus, which could enter through a break in the plant's epidermis due to damage by herbivores. In vertical transmission, a plant inherits viruses from its parent either via infected seeds (sexual reproduction) or via an infected cutting (asexual reproduction). **3.** Humans are not within the host range of TMV, so they can't be infected by the virus.

Summary of Key Concepts Questions
19.1 Viruses are generally considered nonliving, because they are not capable of replicating outside of a host cell. To replicate, they depend completely on host enzymes and resources. **19.2** Single-stranded RNA viruses require an RNA polymerase that can make RNA using an RNA template. (Cellular RNA polymerases make RNA using a DNA template.) Retroviruses require reverse transcriptases to make DNA using an RNA template. (Once the first DNA strand has been made, the same enzyme can promote synthesis of the second DNA strand.) **19.3** The mutation rate of RNA viruses is higher than that of DNA viruses because RNA polymerase has no proofreading function, so errors in replication are not corrected. Their higher mutation rate means that RNA viruses change faster than DNA viruses, leading to their being able to have an altered host range and to evade immune defenses in possible hosts.

Test Your Understanding
1. c **2.** d **3.** c **4.** d **5.** b
6. As shown below, the viral genome would be translated into capsid proteins and envelope glycoproteins directly, rather than after a complementary RNA copy was made. A complementary RNA strand would still be made, however, that could be used as a template for many new copies of the viral genome.

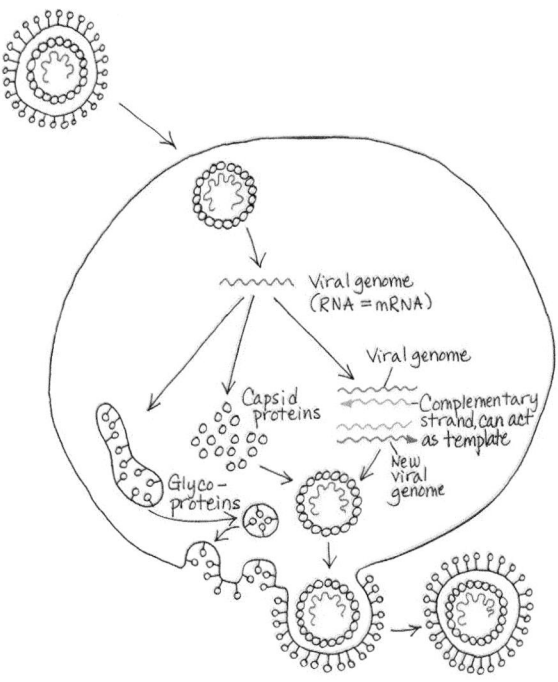

Chapter 20

Figure Questions
Figure 20.3

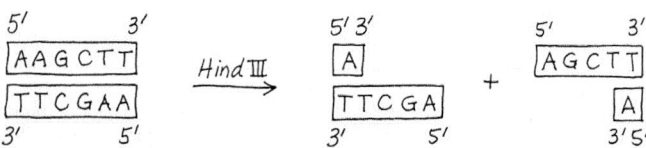

Figure 20.4 Cells containing no plasmid at all would be able to grow; these colonies would be white because they would lack functional *lacZ* genes. **Figure 20.10** Grow each clone of cells in culture. Isolate the plasmids from each and cut them with the restriction enzyme originally used to make the clone (see Figure 20.4). Run each sample on an electrophoretic gel, and recover the DNA of the insert from the gel band. **Figure 20.16** Crossing over, which causes recombination, is a random event. The chance of crossing over occurring between two loci increases as the distance between them increases. The SNP is located very close to an unknown disease-causing allele, and therefore crossing over rarely occurs between the SNP and the allele, so the SNP is a genetic marker indicating the presence of the particular allele. **Figure 20.18** None of the eggs with the transplanted nuclei from the four-cell embryo at the upper left would have developed into a tadpole. Also, the result might include only some of the tissues of a tadpole, which might differ, depending on which nucleus was transplanted. (This assumes that there was some way to tell the four cells apart, as one can in some frog species.) **Figure 20.22** Using converted iPS cells would not carry the same risk, which is its major advantage. Because the donor cells would come from the patient, they would be perfectly matched. The patient's immune system would recognize them as "self" cells and would not mount an attack (which is what leads to rejection).

Concept Check 20.1
1. The covalent sugar-phosphate bonds of the DNA strands **2.** Yes, *Pvu*I will cut the molecule.

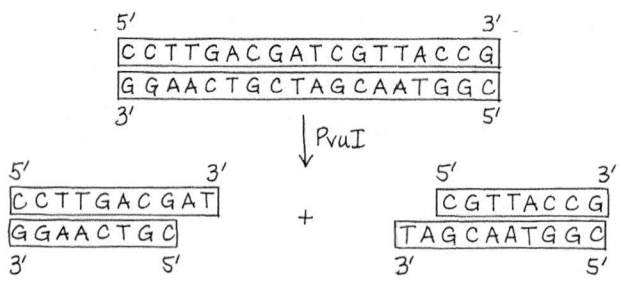

3. Some human genes are too large to be incorporated into bacterial plasmids. Bacterial cells lack the means to process RNA transcripts into mRNA, and even if the need for RNA processing is avoided by using cDNA, bacteria lack enzymes to catalyze the post-translational processing that many human proteins require to function properly. **4.** During the replication of the ends of linear DNA molecules (see Figure 16.20), an RNA primer is used at the 5' end of each new strand. The RNA must be replaced by DNA nucleotides, but DNA polymerase is incapable of starting from scratch at the 5' end of a new DNA strand. During PCR, the primers are made of DNA nucleotides already, so they don't need to be replaced—they just remain as part of each new strand. Therefore, there is no problem with end replication during PCR, and the fragments don't shorten with each replication.

Concept Check 20.2
1. Any restriction enzyme will cut genomic DNA in many places, generating such a large number of fragments that they would appear as a smear rather than distinct bands when the gel is stained after electrophoresis. **2.** In Southern blotting, Northern blotting, and microarray analysis, the labeled probe binds only to the specific target sequence owing to complementary nucleic acid hybridization (DNA-DNA hybridization in Southern blotting and microarray analysis, DNA-RNA hybridization in Northern blotting). In DNA sequencing, primers base-pair to the template, allowing DNA synthesis to start. In RT-PCR, the primers must base-pair with their target sequences in the DNA mixture, locating one specific region among many. **3.** A SNP is a single nucleotide that varies in the population, existing in two or more variations. A RFLP is a type of SNP that occurs in a restriction site, leading to a difference in restriction fragment length when cutting two variants with a restriction enzyme. **4.** If a spot is green, the gene represented on that spot is expressed only in normal tissue. If red, the gene is expressed only in cancerous tissue. If yellow, the gene is expressed in both. And if black, the gene is expressed in neither type of tissue. As a researcher interested in cancer development, you would want to study genes represented by spots that are green or red because these are genes for which the expression level differs between the two types of tissues. Some of these genes may be expressed differently as a result of cancer, but others might play a role in causing cancer.

Concept Check 20.3
1. The state of chromatin modification in the nucleus from the intestinal cell was undoubtedly less similar to that of a nucleus from a fertilized egg, explaining why many fewer of these nuclei were able to be reprogrammed. In contrast, the chromatin in a nucleus from a cell at the four-cell stage would have been much more like that of a nucleus in a fertilized egg and therefore much more easily programmed to direct development. **2.** No, primarily because of subtle (and perhaps not so subtle)

differences in their environments **3.** A technique would have to be worked out for turning a human iPS cell into a pancreatic cell (probably by inducing expression of pancreas-specific regulatory genes in the cell). **4.** The carrot cell has much more potential. The cloning experiment shows that an individual carrot cell can generate all the tissues of an adult plant. The muscle cell, on the other hand, will always remain a muscle cell because of its genetic program (it expresses the *myoD* gene, which ensures continued differentiation). The muscle cell is like other fully differentiated animal cells: It will remain fully differentiated on its own unless it is reprogrammed into an iPS cell using the new techniques described here. (This would be quite difficult to accomplish because a muscle cell has multiple nuclei.)

Concept Check 20.4
1. Stem cells continue to reproduce themselves. **2.** Herbicide resistance, pest resistance, disease resistance, salinity resistance, and delayed ripening **3.** Because hepatitis A is an RNA virus, you could isolate RNA from the blood and try to detect copies of hepatitis A RNA by one of three methods. First, you could run the RNA on a gel and then do a Northern blot using probes complementary to hepatitis A genome sequences. A second approach would be to use reverse transcriptase to make cDNA from the RNA in the blood, run the cDNA on a gel, and do a Southern blot using the same probe. However, neither of these methods would be as sensitive as RT-PCR, in which you would reverse-transcribe the blood RNA into cDNA and then use PCR to amplify the cDNA, using primers specific to hepatitis A sequences. If you then ran the products on an electrophoretic gel, the presence of a band would support your hypothesis.

Summary of Key Concepts Questions
20.1 A plasmid vector and a source of foreign DNA to be cloned are both cut with the same restriction enzyme, generating restriction fragments with sticky ends. These fragments are mixed together, ligated, and reintroduced into bacterial cells, which are then grown on the antibiotic ampicillin. The plasmid has two genes that allow selection of recombinant clones. The first is a gene for ampicillin resistance, which only allows cells to grow if they have taken up a plasmid. The second is a gene for β-galactosidase, which can generate a blue product if the gene is intact. The cloning site is within this gene, so only nonrecombinant colonies will be blue, and recombinant plasmids will be found in cells that are in white colonies. **20.2** Many techniques used to analyze genes and their expression involve nucleic acid hybridization: Southern and Northern blotting, DNA sequencing, PCR, *in situ* hybridization, and DNA microarray analysis. The base pairing between the two strands of a DNA molecule or between a DNA strand and an RNA strand is the key to finding specific nucleic acid sequences in all of these techniques. **20.3** Cloning a mouse involves transplanting a nucleus from a differentiated mouse cell into a mouse egg cell that has had its own nucleus removed. Fertilizing the egg cell and promoting its development into an embryo in a surrogate mother results in a mouse that is genetically identical to the mouse that donated the nucleus. In this case, the differentiated nucleus has been reprogrammed by factors in the egg cytoplasm. Mouse ES cells are generated from inner cells in mouse blastocysts, so in this case the cells are "naturally" reprogrammed by the process of reproduction and development. (Cloned mouse embryos can also be used as a source of ES cells.) iPS cells can be generated without the use of embryos from a differentiated adult mouse cell, by adding certain transcription factors into the cell. In this case, the transcription factors are reprogramming the cells to become pluripotent. **20.4** First, the disease must be caused by a single gene, and the molecular basis of the problem must be understood. Second, the cells that are going to be introduced into the patient must be cells that will integrate into body tissues and continue to multiply (and provide the needed gene product). Third, the gene must be able to be introduced into the cells in question in a safe way, as there have been instances of cancer resulting from some gene therapy trials. (Note that this will require testing the procedure in mice; moreover, the factors that determine a safe vector are not yet well understood. Maybe one of you will go on to solve this problem!)

Test Your Understanding
1. b **2.** c **3.** b **4.** c **5.** d **6.** b **7.** a **8.** c
9.

10. A cDNA library, made using mRNA from human lens cells, which would be expected to contain many copies of mRNA for the crystallin of interest

Chapter 21

Figure Questions

Figure 21.3 The fragments in stage 2 of this figure are like those in stage 2 of Figure 21.2, but in this figure their order relative to each other is not known and will be determined later by computer. The order of the fragments in Figure 21.2 is completely known before sequencing begins. (Determining the order takes longer but makes the eventual sequence assembly much easier.) **Figure 21.9** The transposon would be cut out of the DNA at the original site rather than copied, so the figure would show the original stretch of DNA without the transposon after the mobile transposon had been cut out. **Figure 21.11** The RNA transcripts extending from the DNA in each transcription unit are shorter on the left and longer on the right. This means that RNA polymerase must be starting on the left end of the unit and moving toward the right.
Figure 21.13

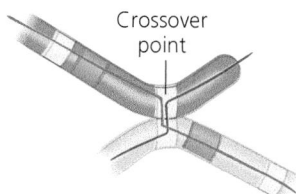
Crossover point

Figure 21.14 Pseudogenes are nonfunctional. They could have arisen by any mutations in the second copy that made the gene product unable to function. Examples would be base changes that introduce stop codons in the sequence, alter amino acids, or change a region of the gene promoter so that the gene can no longer be expressed. **Figure 21.15** Let's say a transposable element (TE) existed in the intron to the left of the indicated EGF exon in the EGF gene, and the same TE was present in the intron to the right of the indicated F exon in the fibronectin gene. During meiotic recombination, these TEs could cause nonsister chromatids on homologous chromosomes to pair up incorrectly, as seen in Figure 21.13. One gene might end up with an F exon next to an EGF exon. Further mistakes in pairing over many generations might result in these two exons being separated from the rest of the gene and placed next to a single or duplicated K exon. In general, the presence of repeated sequences in introns and between genes facilitates these processes because it allows incorrect pairing of nonsister chromatids, leading to novel exon combinations. **Figure 21.17** Since you know that chimpanzees do not speak but humans do, you'd probably want to know how many amino acid differences there are between the human wild-type FOXP2 protein and that of the chimpanzee and whether these changes affect the function of the protein. (As we explain later in the text, there are two amino acid differences.) You know that humans with mutations in this gene have severe language impairment. You would want to learn more about the human mutations by checking whether they affect the same amino acids in the gene product that the chimpanzee sequence differences affect. If so, those amino acids might play an important role in the function of the protein in language. Going further, you could analyze the differences between the chimpanzee and mouse FOXP2 proteins. You might ask: Are they more similar than the chimpanzee and human proteins? (It turns out that the chimpanzee and mouse proteins have only one amino acid difference and thus are more similar than the chimpanzee and human proteins, which have two differences, and more similar than the human and mouse proteins, which have three differences.)

Concept Check 21.1

1. In a linkage map, genes and other markers are ordered with respect to each other, but only the relative distances between them are known. In a physical map, the actual distances between markers, expressed in base pairs, are known. 2. The three-stage approach employed in the Human Genome Project involves linkage mapping, physical mapping, and then sequencing of short, overlapping fragments that previously have been ordered relative to each other (see Figure 21.2). The whole-genome shotgun approach eliminates the linkage mapping and physical mapping stages; instead, short fragments generated by multiple restriction enzymes are sequenced and then ordered by computer programs that identify overlapping regions (see Figure 21.3).

Concept Check 21.2

1. The Internet allows centralization of databases such as GenBank and software resources such as BLAST, making them freely accessible. Having all the data in a central database, easily accessible on the Internet, minimizes the possibility of errors and of researchers working with different data. It streamlines the process of science, since all researchers are able to use the same software programs, rather than each having to obtain their own, possibly different, software. It speeds up dissemination of data and ensures as much as possible that errors are corrected in a timely fashion. There are just a few answers; you can probably think of more. 2. Cancer is a disease caused by multiple factors. To focus on a single gene or a single defect would ignore other factors that may influence the cancer and even the behavior of the single gene being studied. The systems approach, because it takes into account many factors at the same time, is more likely to lead to an understanding of the causes and most useful treatments for cancer. 3. Some of the transcribed region is accounted for by introns. The rest is transcribed into noncoding RNAs, including small RNAs, such as microRNAs (miRNAs). These RNAs help regulate gene expression by blocking translation, causing degradation of mRNA, binding to the promoter and repressing transcription, or causing remodeling of chromatin structure.

The functions of the remainder are not yet known. 4. Genome-wide association studies use the systems biology approach in that they consider the correlation of many single nucleotide polymorphisms (SNPs) with particular diseases, such as heart disease and diabetes, in an attempt to find patterns of SNPs that correlate with each disease.

Concept Check 21.3

1. Alternative splicing of RNA transcripts from a gene and post-translational processing of polypeptides 2. The total number of completed genomes is found by clicking on "Published Complete Genomes." Add the figures for bacterial, archaeal, and eukaryotic "ongoing genomes" to get the number "in progress." Finally, look at the top of the Published Complete Genomes page to get numbers of completed genomes for each domain. (*Note:* You can click on the "Size" column and the table will be resorted by genome size. Scroll down to get an idea of relative sizes of genomes in the three domains. Remember, though, that most of the sequenced genomes are bacterial.) 3. Prokaryotes are generally smaller cells than eukaryotic cells, and they reproduce by binary fission. The evolutionary process involved is natural selection for more quickly reproducing cells: The faster they can replicate their DNA and divide, the more likely they will be able to dominate a population of prokaryotes. The less DNA they have to replicate, then, the faster they will reproduce.

Concept Check 21.4

1. The number of genes is higher in mammals, and the amount of noncoding DNA is greater. Also, the presence of introns in mammalian genes makes them larger, on average, than prokaryotic genes. 2. In the copy-and-paste transposon mechanism and in retrotransposition 3. In the rRNA gene family, identical transcription units for the three different RNA products are present in long, tandemly repeated arrays. The large number of copies of the rRNA genes enable organisms to produce the rRNA for enough ribosomes to carry out active protein synthesis, and the single transcription unit ensures that the relative amounts of the different rRNA molecules produced are correct. Each globin gene family consists of a relatively small number of nonidentical genes. The differences in the globin proteins encoded by these genes result in production of hemoglobin molecules adapted to particular developmental stages of the organism. 4. The exons would be classified as exons (1.5%); the enhancer region containing the distal control elements, the region closer to the promoter containing the proximal control elements, and the promoter itself would be classified as regulatory sequences (5%); and the introns would be classified as introns (20%).

Concept Check 21.5

1. If meiosis is faulty, two copies of the entire genome can end up in a single cell. Errors in crossing over during meiosis can lead to one segment being duplicated while another is deleted. During DNA replication, slippage backward along the template strand can result in segment duplication. 2. For either gene, a mistake in crossing over during meiosis could have occurred between the two copies of that gene, such that one ended up with a duplicated exon. This could have happened several times, resulting in the multiple copies of a particular exon in each gene. 3. Homologous transposable elements scattered throughout the genome provide sites where recombination can occur between different chromosomes. Movement of these elements into coding or regulatory sequences may change expression of genes. Transposable elements also can carry genes with them, leading to dispersion of genes and in some cases different patterns of expression. Transport of an exon during transposition and its insertion into a gene may add a new functional domain to the originally encoded protein, a type of exon shuffling. (For any of these changes to be heritable, they must happen in germ cells, cells that will give rise to gametes.) 4. Because more offspring are born to women who have this inversion, it must provide some advantage. It would be expected to persist and spread in the population. (In fact, evidence in the study allowed the researchers to conclude that it has been increasing in proportion in the population. You'll learn more about population genetics in the next unit.)

Concept Check 21.6

1. Because both humans and macaques are primates, their genomes are expected to be more similar than the macaque and mouse genomes are. The mouse lineage diverged from the primate lineage before the human and macaque lineages diverged. 2. Homeotic genes differ in their *non*homeobox sequences, which determine the interactions of homeotic gene products with other transcription factors and hence which genes are regulated by the homeotic genes. These nonhomeobox sequences differ in the two organisms, as do the expression patterns of the homeobox genes. 3. *Alu* elements must have undergone transposition more actively in the human genome for some reason. Their increased numbers may have then allowed more recombination errors in the human genome, resulting in more or different duplications. The divergence of the organization and content of the two genomes presumably made the chromosomes of each genome less homologous to those of the other, thus accelerating divergence of the two species by making matings less and less likely to result in fertile offspring.

Summary of Key Concepts Questions

21.1 Considering the sequencing of the human genome as an example, less time was required to sequence the first human genome using the whole-genome shotgun approach. Although this approach relied in part on data resulting from the three-stage approach used by the public consortium, the whole-genome shotgun approach was (and still is) faster and more efficient than the more labor-intensive three-stage process. The whole-genome shotgun approach was facilitated in large part by significant advances in computing power. **21.2** The most significant finding was that more than 90% of the human genomic region studied was transcribed, which suggested that the transcribed RNA (and thus the DNA from which it was produced) was performing some unknown functions. The project has been expanded to include other species because to determine the functions of these transcribed DNA elements, it is necessary to carry out this type of analysis on the genomes of species that can be used in laboratory experiments. **21.3** (a) In general, bacteria and archaea have smaller genomes, lower numbers of genes, and higher gene density than eukaryotes. (b) Among eukaryotes, there is no apparent systematic relationship between genome size and phenotype. The number of genes is often lower than would be expected from the size of the genome—in other words, the gene density is often lower in larger genomes. (Humans are an example.) **21.4** Transposable element-related sequences can move from place to place in the genome, and a subset of these sequences make a new copy of themselves when they do so. Thus, it is not surprising that they make up a significant percentage of the genome, and this percentage might be expected to increase over evolutionary time. **21.5** Chromosomal rearrangements within a species lead to some individuals having different chromosomal arrangements. Each of these individuals could still undergo meiosis and produce gametes, and fertilization involving gametes with different chromosomal arrangements could result in viable offspring. However, during meiosis in the offspring, the maternal and paternal chromosomes might not be able to pair up, causing gametes with incomplete sets of chromosomes to form. Most often, when zygotes are produced from such gametes, they do not survive. Ultimately, a new species could form if two different chromosomal arrangements became prevalent within a population and individuals could mate successfully only with other individuals having the same arrangement. **21.6** Comparing the genomes of two closely related species can reveal information about more recent evolutionary events, perhaps events that resulted in the distinguishing characteristics of the two species. Comparing the genomes of very distantly related species can tell us about evolutionary events that occurred a very long time ago. For example, genes that are shared between two distantly related species must have arisen before the two species diverged.

Test Your Understanding
1. c   2. a   3. a   4. c
5.

```
1. ATETI...PKSSD...TSSTT...NARRD

2. ATETI...PKSSE...TSSTT...NARRD

3. ATETI...PKSSD...TSSTT...NARRD

4. ATETI...PKSSD...TSSNT...SARRD

5. ATETI...PKSSD...TSSTT...NARRD

6. VTETI...PKSSD...TSSTT...NARRD
```

(a) Lines 1, 3, and 5 are the C, G, R species. (b) Line 4 is the human sequence. (c) Line 6 is the orangutan sequence. (d) There is one amino acid difference between the mouse (the E on line 2) and the C, G, R species (which have a D in that position). There are three amino acid differences between the mouse and the human. (The E, T, and N in the mouse sequence are instead D, N, and S, respectively, in the human sequence.) (e) Because only one amino acid difference arose during the 60–100 million years since the mouse and C, G, R species diverged, it is somewhat surprising that two additional amino acid differences resulted during the 6 million years since chimpanzees and humans diverged. This indicates that the *FOXP2* gene has been evolving faster in the human lineage than in the lineages of other primates.

Chapter 22

Figure Questions

Figure 22.6 The cactus-eater is more closely related to the seed-eater; Figure 1.22 shows that they share a more recent common ancestor (a seed-eater) than the cactus-eater shares with the insect-eater. **Figure 22.8** More than 5.5 million years ago. **Figure 22.12** The colors and body forms of these mantids allow them to blend into their surroundings, providing an example of how organisms are well matched to life in their environments. The mantids also share features with one another (and with all other mantids), such as six legs, grasping forelimbs, and large eyes. These shared features illustrate another key observation about life: the unity of life that results from descent from a common ancestor. Over time, as these mantids diverged from a common ancestor, they accumulated different adaptations that made them well suited for life in their different environments. Eventually, these differences became large enough that new species were formed, thus contributing to the great diversity of life. **Figure 22.13** These results show that being reared from the egg stage on one plant species or the other did not result in the adult having a beak length appropriate for that host; instead, adult beak lengths were determined primarily by the population from which the eggs were obtained. Because an egg from a balloon vine population likely had long-beaked parents, while an egg from a goldenrain tree population likely had short-beaked parents, these results indicate that beak length is an inherited trait. **Figure 22.14** Both strategies should increase the time it takes *S. aureus* to become resistant to a new drug. If a drug that harms *S. aureus* does not harm other bacteria, natural selection will not favor resistance to that drug in the other species. This would decrease the chance that *S. aureus* would acquire resistance genes from other bacteria—thus slowing the evolution of resistance. Similarly, selection for resistance to a drug that slows the growth but does not kill *S. aureus* is much weaker than selection for resistance to a drug the kills *S. aureus*—again slowing the evolution of resistance. **Figure 22.17** Based on this evolutionary tree, crocodiles are more closely related to birds than to lizards because they share a more recent common an-

cestor with birds (ancestor ⑤) than with lizards (ancestor ④). **Figure 22.20** Hind limb structure changed first. *Rodhocetus* lacked flukes, but its pelvic bones and hind limbs had changed substantially from how those bones were shaped and arranged in *Pakicetus*. For example, in *Rodhocetus*, the pelvis and hind limbs appear to be oriented for paddling, whereas they were oriented for walking in *Pakicetus*.

Concept Check 22.1

1. Hutton and Lyell proposed that events in the past were caused by the same processes operating today. This principle suggested that Earth must be much older than a few thousand years, the age that was widely accepted at that time. Hutton and Lyell also thought that geologic change occurs gradually, stimulating Darwin to reason that the slow accumulation of small changes could ultimately produce the profound changes documented in the fossil record. In this context, the age of Earth was important to Darwin, because unless Earth was very old, he could not envision how there would have been enough time for evolution to occur.   **2.** By these criteria, Cuvier's explanation of the fossil record and Lamarck's hypothesis of evolution are both scientific. Cuvier thought that species did not evolve over time. He also suggested that catastrophes and the resulting extinctions were usually confined to local regions and that such regions were later repopulated by a different set of species that immigrated from other areas. These assertions can be tested against the fossil record, and his assertion that species do not evolve has been found to be false. With respect to Lamarck, his principle of use and disuse can be used to make testable predictions for fossils of groups such as whale ancestors as they adapted to a new habitat. Lamarck's principle of use and disuse and his associated principle of the inheritance of acquired characteristics can also be tested directly in living organisms (these principles have been found to be false).

Concept Check 22.2

1. Organisms share characteristics (the unity of life) because they share common ancestors; the great diversity of life occurs because new species have repeatedly formed when descendant organisms gradually adapted to different environments, becoming different from their ancestors.   **2.** The fossil mammal species (or its ancestors) would most likely have colonized the Andes from within South America, whereas ancestors of mammals currently found in African mountains would most likely have colonized those mountains from other parts of Africa. As a result, the Andes fossil species would share a more recent common ancestor with South American mammals than with mammals in Africa. Thus, for many of its traits, the fossil mammal species would probably more closely resemble mammals that live in South American jungles than mammals that live on African mountains. It is also possible, however, that the fossil mammal species could resemble the African mountain mammals by convergent evolution (even though they were only distantly related to one another).   **3.** As long as the white phenotype (encoded by the genotype *pp*) continues to be favored by natural selection, the frequency of the *p* allele will likely increase over time in the population. The explanation is that if the proportion of white individuals increases relative to purple individuals, the frequency of the recessive *p* allele will also increase relative to that of the *P* allele, which only appears in purple individuals (some of whom also carry a *p* allele).

Concept Check 22.3

1. An environmental factor such as a drug does not create new traits, such as drug resistance, but rather selects for traits among those that are already present in the population.   **2.** (a) Despite their different functions, the forelimbs of different mammals are structurally similar because they all represent modifications of a structure found in the common ancestor. (b) Convergent evolution: The similarities between the sugar glider and flying squirrel indicate that similar environments selected for similar adaptations despite different ancestry.   **3.** At the time that dinosaurs originated, Earth's landmasses formed a single large continent, Pangaea. Because many dinosaurs were large and mobile, it is likely that early members of these groups lived on many different parts of Pangaea. When Pangaea broke apart, fossils of these organisms would have moved with the rocks in which they were deposited. As a result, we would predict that fossils of early dinosaurs would have a broad geographic distribution (this prediction has been upheld).

Summary of Key Concepts Questions

Concept 22.1 Darwin thought that descent with modification occurred as a gradual, steplike process. The age of Earth was important to him because if Earth were only a few thousand years old (as conventional wisdom suggested), there wouldn't have been sufficient time for major evolutionary change. **Concept 22.2** All species have the potential to produce more offspring (overproduce) than can be supported by the environment. This ensures that there will be what Darwin called a "struggle for existence" in which many of the offspring are eaten, starved, diseased, or unable to reproduce for a variety of other reasons. Members of a population exhibit a range of heritable variations, some of which make it likely that their bearers will leave more offspring than other individuals (for example, the bearer may escape predators more effectively or be more tolerant of the physical conditions of the environment). Over time, natural selection resulting from factors such as predators, lack of food, or the physical conditions of the environment can increase the proportion of individuals with favorable traits in a population (evolutionary adaptation). **Concept 22.3** The hypothesis that cetaceans originated from a terrestrial mammal and are closely related to even-toed ungulates is supported by several lines of evidence. For example, fossils document that early cetaceans had hind limbs, as expected for organisms that descended from a land mammal; these fossils also show that cetacean hind limbs became reduced over time. Other fossils show that early cetaceans had a type of ankle bone that is otherwise found only in even-toed ungulates, providing strong evidence that even-toed ungulates are the land mammals to which cetaceans are most closely related. DNA sequence data also indicate that even-toed ungulates are the land mammals to which cetaceans are most closely related.

Test Your Understanding
1. b **2.** d **3.** d **4.** c **5.** a
7. (a)

(b) The rapid rise in the percentage of mosquitoes resistant to DDT was most likely caused by natural selection in which mosquitoes resistant to DDT could survive and reproduce while other mosquitoes could not. (c) In India—where DDT resistance first appeared—natural selection would have caused the frequency of resistant mosquitoes to increase over time. If resistant mosquitoes then migrated from India (for example, transported by wind or in planes, trains, or ships) to other parts of the world, the frequency of DDT resistance would increase there as well.

Chapter 23

Figure Questions

Figure 23.8 The predicted frequencies are 36% $C^R C^R$, 48% $C^R C^W$, and 16% $C^W C^W$. **Figure 23.12** Local survival should increase in both populations. The increase would probably occur more rapidly among birds born into the central population because gene flow from the mainland is higher in that population. **Figure 23.13** Directional selection. Goldenrain tree has smaller fruit than does the native host, balloon vine. Thus, in soapberry bug populations feeding on goldenrain tree, bugs with shorter beaks had an advantage, resulting in directional selection for shorter beak length. **Figure 23.16** Crossing a single female's eggs with both an SC and an LC male's sperm allowed the researchers to directly compare the effects of the males' contribution to the next generation, since both batches of offspring had the same maternal contribution. This isolation of the male's impact enabled researchers to draw conclusions about differences in genetic "quality" between the SC and LC males. **Figure 23.18** The researchers measured the percentages of successfully reproducing adults in the breeding adult population that had each phenotype. This approach of determining which phenotype was favored by selection assumes that reproduction was a sufficient indicator of relative fitness (as opposed to counting the number of eggs laid or offspring hatched, for example) and that mouth phenotype was the driving factor determining the fish's ability to reproduce.

Concept Check 23.1

1. (a) Within a population, genetic differences among individuals provide the raw material on which natural selection and other mechanisms can act. Without such differences, allele frequencies could not change over time—and hence the population could not evolve. (b) Genetic differences between separate populations can result from natural selection if different alleles are favored in different populations; this might occur, for example, if the different populations experienced different environmental conditions (as in Figure 23.4). Genetic differences between populations can also result from chance events (genetic drift) if the genetic changes have few or no phenotypic effects (as in Figure 23.3). **2.** Many mutations occur in somatic cells, which do not produce gametes and so are lost when the organism dies. Of mutations that do occur in cell lines that produce gametes, many do not have a phenotypic effect on which natural selection can act. Others have a harmful effect and are thus unlikely to increase in frequency because they decrease the reproductive success of their bearers. **3.** Its genetic variation (whether measured at the level of genes or at the level of nucleotide sequences) would probably drop over time. During meiosis, crossing over and the independent assortment of chromosomes produce many new combinations of alleles. In addition, a population contains a vast number of possible mating combinations, and fertilization brings together the gametes of individuals with different genetic backgrounds. Thus, via crossing over, independent assortment of chromosomes, and fertilization, sexual reproduction reshuffles alleles into fresh combinations each generation. Without sexual reproduction, the rate of forming new combinations of alleles would be vastly reduced, causing the overall amount of genetic variation to drop.

Concept Check 23.2

1. 30,000. Half the loci (10,000) are fixed, meaning only one type of allele exists for each locus: $10,000 \times 1 = 10,000$. There are two types of alleles each for the other loci: $10,000 \times 2 = 20,000$. $10,000 + 20,000 = 30,000$. **2.** $p^2 + 2pq$; p^2 represents homozygotes with two A alleles, and $2pq$ represents heterozygotes with one A allele. **3.** There are 120 individuals in the population, so there are 240 alleles. Of these, there are 124 A alleles—32 from the 16 AA individuals and 92 from the 92 Aa individuals. Thus, the frequency of the A allele is $p = 124/240 = 0.52$; hence, the frequency of the a allele is $q = 0.48$. Based on the Hardy-Weinberg equation, if the population were not evolving, the frequency of genotype AA should be $p^2 = 0.52 \times 0.52 = 0.27$; the frequency of genotype Aa should be $2pq = 2 \times 0.52 \times 0.48 = 0.5$; and the frequency of genotype aa should be $q^2 = 0.48 \times 0.48 = 0.23$. In a population of 120 individuals, these expected genotype frequencies lead us to predict that there would be 32 AA individuals (0.27×120), 60 Aa individuals (0.5×120), and 28 aa individuals (0.23×120). The actual numbers for the population (16 AA, 92 Aa, 12 aa) deviate from these expectations (fewer homozygotes and more heterozygotes than expected). This indicates that the population is not in Hardy-Weinberg equilibrium and hence may be evolving at this locus.

Concept Check 23.3

1. Natural selection is more "predictable" in that it alters allele frequencies in a nonrandom way: It tends to increase the frequency of alleles that increase the organism's reproductive success in its environment and decrease the frequency of alleles that decrease the organism's reproductive success. Alleles subject to genetic drift increase or decrease in frequency by chance alone, whether or not they are advantageous. **2.** Genetic drift results from chance events that cause allele frequencies to fluctuate at random from generation to generation; within a population, this process tends to decrease genetic variation over time. Gene flow is the exchange of alleles between populations, a process that can introduce new alleles to a population and hence may increase its genetic variation (albeit slightly, since rates of gene flow are often low). **3.** Selection is not important at this locus; furthermore, the populations are not small, and hence the effects of genetic drift should not be pronounced. Gene flow is occurring via the movement of pollen and seeds. Thus, allele and genotype frequencies in these populations should become more similar over time as a result of gene flow.

Concept Check 23.4

1. Zero, because fitness includes reproductive contribution to the next generation, and a sterile mule cannot produce offspring. **2.** Although both gene flow and genetic drift can increase the frequency of advantageous alleles in a population, they can also decrease the frequency of advantageous alleles or increase the frequency of harmful alleles. Only natural selection *consistently* results in an increase in the frequency of alleles that enhance survival or reproduction. Thus, natural selection is the only mechanism that consistently causes adaptive evolution. **3.** The three modes of natural selection (directional, stabilizing, and disruptive) are defined in terms of the selective advantage of different *phenotypes*, not different genotypes. Thus, the type of selection represented by heterozygote advantage depends on the phenotype of the heterozygotes. In this question, because heterozygous individuals have a more extreme phenotype than either homozygote, heterozygote advantage represents directional selection. **4.** Under prolonged low-oxygen conditions, some of the red blood cells of a heterozygote may sickle, leading to harmful effects (see Chapter 14). This does not occur in individuals with two normal hemoglobin alleles, suggesting that there may be selection against heterozygotes in malaria-free regions (where heterozygote advantage does not occur). However, since heterozygotes are healthy under most conditions, selection against them is unlikely to be strong.

Summary of Key Concepts Questions

23.1 One reason biologists estimate gene variability and nucleotide variability is to assess whether populations have enough genetic variation for evolution to occur. Gene variability indicates the extent to which individuals differ genetically at the whole-gene level. Nucleotide variability provides a measure of genetic variation at the DNA sequence level. **23.2** No, this is not an example of circular reasoning. Calculating p and q from observed genotype frequencies does not imply that those genotype frequencies must be in Hardy-Weinberg equilibrium. Consider a population that has 195 individuals of genotype AA, 10 of genotype Aa, and 195 of genotype aa. Calculating p and q from these values yields $p = q = 0.5$. Using the Hardy-Weinberg equation, the predicted equilibrium frequencies are $p^2 = 0.25$ for genotype AA, $2pq = 0.5$ for genotype Aa, and $q^2 = 0.25$ for genotype aa. Since there are 400 individuals in the population, these predicted genotype frequencies indicate there should be 100 AA individuals, 200 Aa individuals, and 100 aa individuals—numbers that differ greatly from the values that we used to calculate p and q. **23.3** It is unlikely that two such populations would evolve in similar ways. Since their environments are very different, the alleles favored by natural selection would probably differ between the two populations; although genetic drift may have important effects in each of these small populations, drift causes unpredictable changes in allele frequencies, so it is unlikely that drift would cause the populations to evolve in similar ways; both populations are geographically isolated, suggesting that little gene flow will occur between them (again making it less likely that they will evolve in similar ways). **23.4** Compared to males, it is likely that the females of such species would be larger, more colorful, endowed with more elaborate ornamentation (for example, a large morphological feature such as the peacock's tail), and more apt to engage in behaviors intended to attract mates or prevent other members of their sex from obtaining mates.

Test Your Understanding

1. e **2.** c **3.** e **4.** b **5.** a **6.** d

7. Although natural selection can improve the match between organisms and their environments, the evolutionary process can also lead to imperfections in organisms. A central reason for this is that evolution does not design organisms from scratch to match their environments and ways of life but works instead by a process of descent with modification: Organisms inherit a basic form from their ancestors, and that form is modified by natural selection over time. As a result, a flying mammal such as a bat has wings that are not perfectly designed, but rather represent modifications of forelimbs that bat ancestors used for walking. Imperfections in organisms result from a variety of other constraints, such as a lack of genetic variation for the trait in question, and the fact that adaptations often represent compromises (since organisms must do many different things, and a "perfect" design for one activity might impair the performance of another activity). **8.** The frequency of the *lap⁹⁴* allele forms a cline, decreasing as one moves from southwest to northeast across Long Island Sound.

A hypothesis that explains the cline and accounts for the observations stated in the question is that the cline is maintained by an interaction between selection and gene flow. Under this hypothesis, in the southwest portion of the Sound, salinity is relatively low, and selection against the *lap⁹⁴* allele is strong. Moving toward the northeast and into the open ocean, where salinity is relatively high, selection favors a high frequency of the *lap⁹⁴* allele. However, because mussel larvae disperse long distances, gene flow prevents the *lap⁹⁴* allele from becoming fixed in the open ocean or from declining to zero in the southwestern portion of Long Island Sound.

Chapter 24

Figure Questions
Figure 24.10 This was done to remove the possibility that the flies could differentiate among potential mates by detecting what those potential mates had eaten as larvae. If this had not been done, the strong preference of "starch flies" and "maltose flies" to mate with like-adapted flies could have occurred simply because the flies could detect (for example, by sense of smell) what their potential mates had eaten as larvae—and they preferred to mate with flies that had a similar smell to their own. **Figure 24.12** Such results would suggest that mate choice based on coloration does not provide a reproductive barrier between these two cichlid species. **Figure 24.13** The graph suggests there has been gene flow of some fire-bellied toad alleles into the range of the yellow-bellied toad. Otherwise, all individuals located to the left of the hybrid zone portion of the graph would have allele frequencies close to 1.0. **Figure 24.14** Because the populations had only just begun to diverge from one another at this point in the process, it is likely that any existing barriers to reproduction would weaken over time. **Figure 24.19** No. Over time, the chromosomes of the experimental hybrids came to resemble those of *H. anomalus*. This occurred even though conditions in the laboratory differed greatly from conditions in the field, where *H. anomalus* is found, suggesting that selection for laboratory conditions was not strong. Thus, it is unlikely that the observed rise in the fertility of the experimental hybrids was due to selection for life under laboratory conditions. **Figure 24.20** The presence of *M. cardinalis* plants that carry the *M. lewisii yup* allele would make it more likely that bumblebees would transfer pollen between the two monkey flower species. As a result, we would expect the number of hybrid offspring to increase.

Concept Check 24.1
1. (a) All except the biological species concept can be applied to both asexual and sexual species because they define species on the basis of characteristics other than ability to reproduce. In contrast, the biological species concept can be applied only to sexual species. (b) The easiest species concept to apply in the field would be the morphological species concept because it is based only on the appearance of the organism. Additional information about its ecological habits, evolutionary history, and reproduction are not required. **2.** Because these birds live in fairly similar environments and can breed successfully in captivity, the reproductive barrier in nature is probably prezygotic; given the species' differences in habitat preference, this barrier could result from habitat isolation.

Concept Check 24.2
1. In allopatric speciation, a new species forms while in geographic isolation from its parent species; in sympatric speciation, a new species forms in the absence of geographic isolation. Geographic isolation greatly reduces gene flow between populations, whereas ongoing gene flow is more likely in sympatric populations. As a result, sympatric speciation is less common than allopatric speciation. **2.** Gene flow between subsets of a population that live in the same area can be reduced in a variety of ways. In some species—especially plants—changes in chromosome number can block gene flow and establish reproductive isolation in a single generation. Gene flow can also be reduced in sympatric populations by habitat differentiation (as seen in the apple maggot fly, *Rhagoletis*) and sexual selection (as seen in Lake Victoria cichlids). **3.** Allopatric speciation would be less likely to occur on a nearby island than on an isolated island of the same size. The reason we expect this result is that continued gene flow between mainland populations and those on a nearby island reduces the chance that enough genetic divergence will take place for allopatric speciation to occur. **4.** If all of the homologs failed to separate during anaphase I of meiosis, some gametes would end up with an extra set of chromosomes (and others would end up with no chromosomes). If a gamete with an extra set of chromosomes fused with a normal gamete, a triploid would result; if two gametes with an extra set of chromosomes fused with each other, a tetraploid would result.

Concept Check 24.3
1. Hybrid zones are regions in which members of different species meet and mate, producing some offspring of mixed ancestry. Such regions can be viewed as "natural laboratories" in which to study speciation because scientists can directly observe factors that cause (or fail to cause) reproductive isolation. **2.** (a) If hybrids consistently survive and reproduce poorly compared to the offspring of intraspecific matings, reinforcement could occur. If it did, natural selection would cause prezygotic barriers to reproduction between the parent species to strengthen over time, decreasing the production of unfit hybrids and leading to a completion of the speciation process. (b) If hybrid offspring survived and reproduced as well as the offspring of intraspecific matings, indiscriminate mating between the parent species would lead to the production of large numbers of hybrid offspring. As these hybrids mated with each other and with members of both parent species, the gene pools of the parent species could fuse over time, reversing the speciation process.

Concept Check 24.4
1. The time between speciation events includes (1) the length of time that it takes for populations of a newly formed species to begin diverging reproductively from one another and (2) the time it takes for speciation to be complete once this divergence begins. Although speciation can occur rapidly once populations have begun to diverge from one another, it may take millions of years for that divergence to begin. **2.** Investigators transferred alleles at the *yup* locus (which influences flower color) from each parent species to the other. *M. lewisii* plants with an *M. cardinalis yup* allele received many more visits from hummingbirds than usual; hummingbirds usually pollinate *M. cardinalis* but avoid *M. lewisii*. Similarly, *M. cardinalis* plants with an *M. lewisii yup* allele received many more visits from bumblebees than usual; bumblebees usually pollinate *M. lewisii* and avoid *M. cardinalis*. Thus, alleles at the *yup* locus can influence pollinator choice, which in these species provides the primary barrier to interspecific mating. Nevertheless, the experiment does not prove that the *yup* locus alone controls barriers to reproduction between *M. lewisii* and *M. cardinalis*; other genes might enhance the effect of the *yup* locus (by modifying flower color) or cause entirely different barriers to reproduction (for example, gametic isolation or a postzygotic barrier). **3.** Crossing over. If crossing over did not occur, each chromosome in an experimental hybrid would remain as in the F₁ generation: composed entirely of DNA from one parent species or the other.

Summary of Key Concepts Questions
24.1 According to the biological species concept, a species is a group of populations whose members interbreed and produce viable, fertile offspring; thus, gene flow occurs between populations of a species. In contrast, members of different species do not interbreed and hence no gene flow occurs between their populations. Overall, then, in the biological species concept, species can be viewed as designated by the *absence* of gene flow—making gene flow of central importance to the biological species concept. **24.2** Sympatric speciation can be promoted by factors such as polyploidy, habitat shifts, and sexual selection, all of which can reduce gene flow between the subpopulations of a larger population. But such factors can also occur in allopatric populations and hence can also promote allopatric speciation. **24.3** If the hybrids are selected against, the hybrid zone could persist if individuals from the parent species regularly travel into the zone, where they mate to produce hybrid offspring. If hybrids are not selected against, there is no cost to the continued production of hybrids, and large numbers of hybrid offspring may be produced. However, natural selection for life in different environments may keep the gene pools of the two parent species distinct—thus preventing the loss (by fusion) of the parent species and once again causing the hybrid zone to be stable over time. **24.4** As the goatsbeard plant, Bahamas mosquitofish, and apple maggot fly examples illustrate, speciation continues to happen today. A new species can begin to form whenever gene flow is reduced between populations of the parent species. Such reductions in gene flow can occur in many ways: A new, geographically isolated population may be founded by a few colonists; some members of the parent species may begin to utilize new habitat; and sexual selection may isolate formerly connected populations or subpopulations. These and many other such events are happening today.

1. b **2.** c **3.** c **4.** a **5.** e **6.** d **7.** e

10. Here is one possibility:

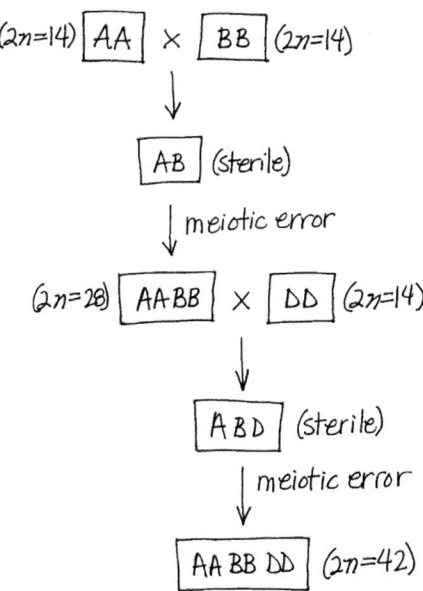

Chapter 25

Figure Questions

Figure 25.2 Proteins are almost always composed of the 20 amino acids shown in Figure 5.16. However, many other amino acids could potentially form in this or any other experiment. For example, any molecule that had a different R group than those listed in Figure 5.16 (yet still contained an α carbon, an amino group, and a carboxyl group) would be an amino acid—yet it would not be one of the 20 amino acids commonly found in nature. **Figure 25.5** Because uranium-238 has a half-life of 4.5 billion years, the x-axis would be relabeled (in billions of years) as 4.5, 9, 13.5, and 18. **Figure 25.10** You should have circled the node, shown in the tree diagram at approximately 580 million years ago (mya), that leads to the echinoderm/chordate lineage and to the lineage that gave rise to brachiopods, annelids, molluscs, and arthropods. Although the 580 mya date is estimated, this common ancestor must be at least as old as any of its descendants. Since fossil molluscs date to about 555 mya, the common ancestor represented by the circled branch point must be at least 555 million years old. **Figure 25.15** The blue curve is for marine animal families. Families often contain many species, so we would expect the percentage of families that became extinct to be lower than the percentage of species that became extinct. **Figure 25.25** The coding sequence of the *Pitx1* gene would differ between the marine and lake populations, but patterns of gene expression would not.

Concept Check 25.1

1. The hypothesis that conditions on early Earth could have permitted the synthesis of organic molecules from inorganic ingredients **2.** In contrast to random mingling of molecules in an open solution, segregation of molecular systems by membranes could concentrate organic molecules, assisting biochemical reactions. **3.** Today, genetic information usually flows from DNA to RNA, as when the DNA sequence of a gene is used as a template to synthesize the mRNA encoding a particular protein. However, the life cycle of retroviruses such as HIV shows that genetic information can flow in the reverse direction (from RNA to DNA). In these viruses, the enzyme reverse transcriptase uses RNA as a template for DNA synthesis, suggesting that a similar enzyme could have played a key role in the transition from an RNA world to a DNA world.

Concept Check 25.2

1. 22,920 years (four half-lives: 5,730 × 4) **2.** The fossil record shows that different groups of organisms dominated life on Earth at different points in time and that many organisms once alive are now extinct; specific examples of these points can be found in Figure 25.4. The fossil record also indicates that new groups of organisms can arise via the gradual modification of previously existing organisms, as illustrated by fossils that document the origin of mammals from their cynodont ancestors. **3.** The discovery of such a (hypothetical) fossil organism would indicate that aspects of our current understanding of the origin of mammals are not correct because mammals are thought to have originated much more recently (see Figure 25.6). For example, such a discovery could suggest that the dates of previous fossil discoveries are not correct or that the lineages shown in Figure 25.6 shared features with mammals but were not their direct ancestors. Such a discovery would also suggest that radical changes in multiple aspects of the skeletal structure of organisms could arise suddenly—an idea that is not supported by the known fossil record.

Concept Check 25.3

1. Free oxygen attacks chemical bonds and can inhibit enzymes and damage cells. As a result, prokaryotes that had thrived in anaerobic environments would have survived and reproduced poorly in oxygen-rich environments, driving many species to extinction. **2.** All eukaryotes have mitochondria or remnants of these organelles, but not all eukaryotes have plastids. **3.** A fossil record of life today would include many organisms with hard body parts (such as vertebrates and many marine invertebrates), but might not include some species we are very familiar with, such as those that have small geographic ranges and/or small population sizes (for example, endangered species such as the giant panda, tiger, and several rhinoceros species).

Concept Check 25.4

1. Continental drift alters the physical geography and climate of Earth, as well as the extent to which organisms are geographically isolated. Because these factors affect extinction and speciation rates, continental drift has a major impact on life on Earth. **2.** Mass extinctions; major evolutionary innovations; the diversification of another group of organisms (which can provide new sources of food); migration to new locations where few competitor species exist **3.** In principle, fossils of both common and rare species would be present right up to the time of the catastrophic event, then disappear. Reality is more complicated because the fossil record is not perfect. So the most recent fossil for a species might be a million years before the mass extinction—even though the species did not become extinct *until* the mass extinction. This complication is especially likely for rare species because few of their fossils will form and be discovered. Hence, for many rare species, the fossil record would not document that the species was alive immediately before the extinction (even if it was).

Concept Check 25.5

1. Heterochrony can cause a variety of morphological changes. For example, if the onset of sexual maturity changes, a retention of juvenile characteristics (paedomorphosis) may result. Paedomorphosis can be caused by small genetic changes that result in large changes in morphology, as seen in the axolotl salamander. **2.** In animal embryos, *Hox* genes influence the development of structures such as limbs and feeding appendages. As a result, changes in these genes—or in the regulation of these genes—are likely to have major effects on morphology. **3.** From genetics, we know that gene regulation is altered by how well transcription factors bind to noncoding DNA sequences called control elements. Thus, if changes in morphology are often caused by changes in gene regulation, portions of noncoding DNA that contain control elements are likely to be strongly affected by natural selection.

Concept Check 25.6

1. Complex structures do not evolve all at once, but in increments, with natural selection selecting for adaptive variants of the earlier versions. **2.** Although the myxoma virus is highly lethal, initially some of the rabbits are resistant (0.2% of infected rabbits are not killed). Thus, assuming resistance is an inherited trait, we would expect the rabbit population to show a trend for increased resistance to the virus. We would also expect the virus to show an evolutionary trend toward reduced lethality. We would expect this trend because a rabbit infected with a less lethal virus would be more likely to live long enough for a mosquito to bite it and hence potentially transmit the virus to another rabbit. (A virus that kills its rabbit host before a mosquito transmits the virus to another rabbit dies with its host.)

Summary of Key Concepts Questions

Concept 25.1 Particles of montmorillonite clay may have provided surfaces on which organic molecules became concentrated and hence were more likely to react with one another. Montmorillonite clay particles may also have facilitated the transport of key molecules, such as short strands of RNA, into vesicles. These vesicles can form spontaneously from simple precursor molecules, "reproduce" and "grow" on their own, and maintain internal concentrations of molecules that differ from those in the surrounding environment. These features of vesicles represent key steps in the emergence of protocells and (ultimately) the first living cells. **Concept 25.2** One challenge is that organisms do not use radioisotopes that have long half-lives to build their bones or shells. As a result, fossils older than 75,000 years cannot be dated directly. Fossils are often found in sedimentary rock, but those rocks typically contain sediments of different ages, again posing a challenge when trying to date old fossils. To circumvent these challenges, geologists date layers of volcanic rock that surround old fossils and that use radioisotopes with long half-lives. This approach provides minimum and maximum estimates for the ages of fossils sandwiched between two layers of volcanic rock. **Concept 25.3** The "Cambrian explosion" refers to a relatively short interval of time (535–525 million years ago) during which large forms of many present-day animal phyla first appear in the fossil record. The evolutionary changes that occurred during this time, such as the appearance of large predators and well-defended prey, were important because they set the stage for many of the key events in the history of life over the last 500 million years. **Concept 25.4** The broad evolutionary changes documented by the fossil record reflect the rise and fall of major groups of organisms. In turn, the rise or fall of any particular group results from a balance between speciation and extinction rates: A group increases in size when the rate at which its members produce new species is greater than the rate at which its member species are lost to extinction, while a group shrinks in size if extinction rates are greater than speciation rates. **Concept 25.5** Yes. A change to the sequence or regulation of a developmental gene can produce major morphological changes. In some cases, such morphological changes may enable organisms to perform new functions or live in new environments—thus potentially leading to an adaptive radiation and the formation of a new group of organisms. **Concept 25.6** Evolutionary change results from interactions between organisms and their current environments. No goal is involved in this process. As environments change over time, the features of organisms favored by natural selection may also change. When this happens, what once may have seemed like a "goal" of evolution (for example, improvements in the function of a feature previously favored by natural selection) may cease to be beneficial or may even be harmful.

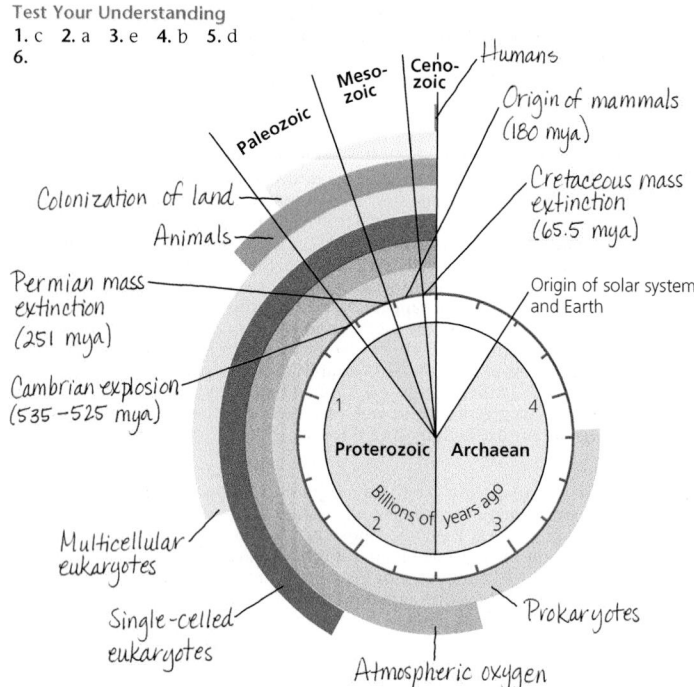

7. c **8.** b

Chapter 26

Figure Questions

Figure 26.5 This new version does not alter any of the evolutionary relationships shown in Figure 26.5. For example, B and C remain sister taxa, taxon A is still as closely related to taxon B as it is to taxon C, and so on.

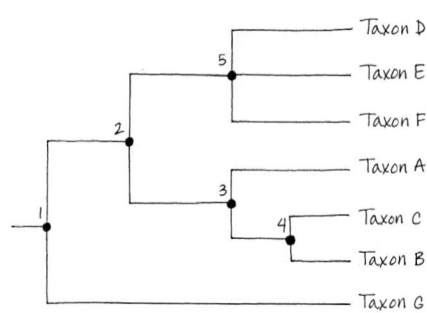

Figure 26.6 Unknown 1b (a portion of sample 1) and Unknowns 9–13 all would have to be located on the branch of the tree that currently leads to Minke (Southern Hemisphere) and Unknowns 1a and 2–8. **Figure 26.9** There are four possible bases (A, C, G, T) at each nucleotide position. If the base at each position depends on chance, not common descent, we would expect roughly one out of four (25%) of them to be the same. **Figure 26.11** You should have drawn a box around the frog, turtle, and leopard lineages, along with their most recent common ancestor. **Figure 26.12** The zebrafish lineage; of the five vertebrate lineages shown, its branch is the longest. **Figure 26.16** The lizard and snake lineage is the most basal taxon shown (closest to the root of the tree). Among the descendants of the common ancestor indicated by the blue dot, the crocodilian lineage is the most basal. **Figure 26.19** The molecular clock indicates that the divergence time is roughly 45–50 million years. **Figure 26.21** As shown in this diagram, Bacteria was the first to emerge and Archaea is the sister domain to Eukarya.

Concept Check 26.1

1. We are classified the same from the domain level to the class level; both the leopard and human are mammals. Leopards belong to order Carnivora, whereas humans do not.   **2.** The branching pattern of the tree indicates that the badger and the wolf share a common ancestor that is more recent than the ancestor that these two animals share with the leopard.   **3.** The tree in (c) shows a different pattern of evolutionary relationships. In (c), C and B are sister taxa, whereas C and D are sister taxa in (a) and (b).

4.

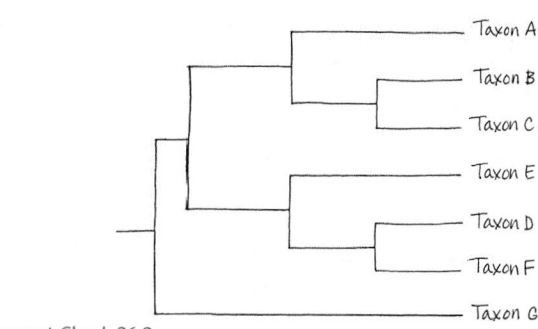

Concept Check 26.2

1. (a) Analogy, since porcupines and cacti are not closely related and since most other animals and plants do not have similar structures; (b) homology, since cats and humans are both mammals and have homologous forelimbs, of which the hand and paw are the lower part; (c) analogy, since owls and hornets are not closely related and since the structure of their wings is very different   **2.** Species 2 and 3 are more likely to be closely related. Small genetic changes (as between species 2 and 3) can produce divergent physical appearances, but if many genes have diverged greatly (as in species 1 and 2), then the lineages have probably been separate for a long time.

Concept Check 26.3

1. No; when comparing groups of mammals, hair is a shared ancestral character common to all mammals and thus is not helpful in distinguishing different mammalian subgroups.   **2.** The principle of maximum parsimony states that the hypothesis about nature we investigate first should be the simplest explanation found to be consistent with the facts. Actual evolutionary relationships may differ from those inferred by parsimony owing to complicating factors such as convergent evolution.   **3.** The traditional classification provides a poor match to evolutionary history, thus violating the basic principle of cladistics—that classification should be based on common descent. Both birds and mammals originated from groups traditionally designated as reptiles, making reptiles (as traditionally delineated) a paraphyletic group. These problems can be addressed by removing *Dimetrodon* and cynodonts from the reptiles and by considering birds as a group of reptiles (specifically, as a group of dinosaurs).

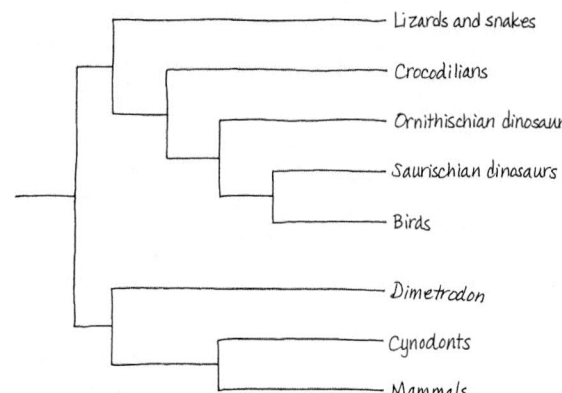

Concept Check 26.4

1. Proteins are gene products. Their amino acid sequences are determined by the nucleotide sequences of the DNA that codes for them. Thus, differences between comparable proteins in two species reflect underlying genetic differences that have accumulated as the species diverged from one another. As a result, differences between the proteins can reflect the evolutionary history of the species.   **2.** In RNA processing, the exons or coding regions of a gene can be spliced together in different ways, yielding different mRNAs and hence different protein products. As a result, different proteins could potentially be produced from the same gene in different tissues, thereby enabling the gene to perform different functions in these different tissues.   **3.** These observations suggest that the evolutionary lineages leading to species 1 and species 2 diverged from one another before a gene duplication event in species 1 produced gene B from gene A.

Concept Check 26.5

1. A molecular clock is a method of estimating the actual time of evolutionary events based on numbers of base changes in orthologous genes. It is based on the assumption that the regions of genomes being compared evolve at constant rates.   **2.** There are many portions of the genome that do not code for genes; many base changes in these regions could accumulate through drift without affecting an organism's fitness. Even in coding regions of the genome, some mutations may not have a critical effect on genes or proteins.   **3.** The gene (or genes) used for the molecular clock may have evolved more slowly in these two taxa than in the species used to calibrate the clock; as a result, the clock would underestimate the time at which the taxa diverged from each other.

Concept Check 26.6

1. The kingdom Monera included bacteria and archaea, but we now know that these organisms are in separate domains. Kingdoms are subsets of domains, so a single kingdom (like Monera) that includes taxa from different domains is not valid. **2.** Because of horizontal gene transfer, some genes in eukaryotes are more closely related to bacteria, while others are more closely related to archaea; thus, depending on which genes are used, phylogenetic trees constructed from DNA data can yield conflicting results.

3.

The fossil record indicates that prokaryotes originated long before eukaryotes. This suggests that the third tree, in which the eukaryotic lineage diverged first, is not accurate and hence is not likely to receive support from genetic data.

Summary of Key Concepts Questions

26.1 The fact that humans and chimpanzees are sister species indicates that we share a more recent common ancestor with chimpanzees than we do with any other living primate species. But that does not mean that humans evolved from chimpanzees, or vice versa; instead, it indicates that both humans and chimpanzees are descendants of that common ancestor. **26.2** Homologous characters result from shared ancestry. As organisms diverge over time, some of their homologous characters will also diverge. The homologous characters of organisms that diverged long ago typically differ more than do the homologous characters of organisms that diverged more recently. As a result, differences in homologous characters can be used to infer phylogeny. In contrast, analogous characters result from convergent evolution, not shared ancestry, and hence can give misleading estimates of phylogeny. **26.3** All features of organisms arose at some point in the history of life. In the group in which a new feature first arises, that feature is a shared derived character that is unique to that clade. The group in which each shared derived character first appears can be determined, and the resulting nested pattern can be used to infer evolutionary history. **26.4** Orthologous genes should be used; for such genes, the homology results from speciation and hence reflects evolutionary history. **26.5** A key assumption of molecular clocks is that nucleotide substitutions occur at fixed rates and hence the number of nucleotide differences between two DNA sequences is proportional to the time since the sequences diverged from each other. Some limitations of molecular clocks: No gene marks time with complete precision; natural selection can favor certain DNA changes over others; nucleotide substitution rates can change over long periods of time (causing molecular clocks estimates of when events in the distant past occurred to be highly uncertain); and the same gene can evolve at different rates in different organisms **26.6** Genetic data indicated that many prokaryotes differed as much from each other as they did from eukaryotes. This indicated that organisms should be grouped into three "super-kingdoms," or domains (Archaea, Bacteria, Eukarya). These data also indicated that the previous kingdom Monera (which had contained all the prokaryotes) did not make biological sense and should be abandoned. Later genetic and morphological data also indicated that the former kingdom Protista (which had primarily contained single-celled organisms) should be abandoned because it was polyphyletic.

Test Your Understanding

1. b **2.** d **3.** a **4.** d **5.** d **6.** c **7.** d
9. (a)

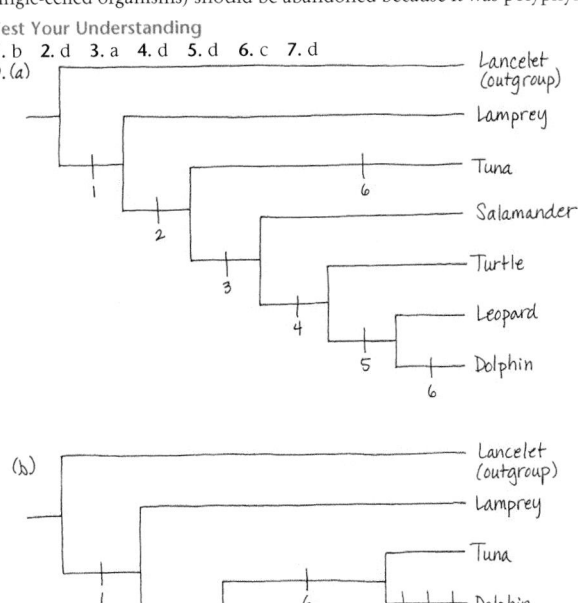

(c) The tree in (a) requires seven evolutionary changes, while the tree in (b) requires nine evolutionary changes. Thus, the tree in (a) is more parsimonious, since it requires fewer evolutionary changes.

Chapter 27

Figure Questions

Figure 27.10 It is likely that the expression or sequence of genes that affect glucose metabolism may have changed; genes for metabolic processes no longer needed by the cell also may have changed. **Figure 27.11** Transduction results in horizontal gene transfer when the host and recipient cells are members of different species. **Figure 27.16** Thermophiles live in very hot environments, so it is likely that their enzymes can continue to function normally at much higher temperatures than do the enzymes of other organisms. At low temperatures, however, the enzymes of thermophiles may not function as well as the enzymes of other organisms. **Figure 27.18** From the graph, plant uptake can be estimated as 0.7, 0.6, and 0.95 (mg K) for strains 1, 2, and 3, respectively. These values average to 0.75 mg K. If bacteria had no effect, the average plant uptake of potassium for strains 1, 2, and 3 should be close to 0.5 mg K, the value observed for plants grown in bacteria-free soil.

Concept Check 27.1

1. Adaptations include the capsule (shields prokaryotes from host's immune system) and endospores (enable cells to survive harsh conditions and to revive when the environment becomes favorable). **2.** Prokaryotic cells generally lack the internal compartmentalization of eukaryotic cells. Prokaryotic genomes have much less DNA than eukaryotic genomes, and most of this DNA is contained in a single ring-shaped chromosome located in the nucleoid rather than within a true membrane-bounded nucleus. In addition, many prokaryotes also have plasmids, small ring-shaped DNA molecules containing a few genes. **3.** Plastids such as chloroplasts are thought to have evolved from an endosymbiotic photosynthetic prokaryote. More specifically, the phylogenetic tree shown in Figure 26.21 indicates that plastids are closely related to cyanobacteria. Hence, we can hypothesize that the thylakoid membranes of chloroplasts resemble those of cyanobacteria because chloroplasts evolved from a cyanobacterium endosymbiont.

Concept Check 27.2

1. Prokaryotes have extremely large population sizes, in part because they have short generation times. The large number of individuals in prokaryotic populations makes it likely that in each generation there will be thousands of individuals that have new mutations at any particular gene, thereby adding considerable genetic diversity to the population. **2.** In transformation, naked, foreign DNA from the environment is taken up by a bacterial cell. In transduction, phages carry bacterial genes from one bacterial cell to another. In conjugation, a bacterial cell directly transfers plasmid or chromosomal DNA to another cell via a mating bridge that temporarily connects the two cells. **3.** The population that includes individuals capable of conjugation would probably be more successful, since some of its members could form recombinant cells whose new gene combinations might be advantageous in a novel environment. **4.** Yes. Genes for antibiotic resistance could be transferred (by transformation, transduction, or conjugation) from the nonpathogenic bacterium to a pathogenic bacterium; this could make the pathogen an even greater threat to human health. In general, transformation, transduction, and conjugation tend to increase the spread of resistance genes.

Concept Check 27.3

1. A phototroph derives its energy from light, while a chemotroph gets its energy from chemical sources. An autotroph derives its carbon from a form of CO_2, while a heterotroph gets its carbon from organic nutrients such as glucose. Thus, there are four nutritional modes: photoautotrophic, photoheterotrophic (unique to prokaryotes), chemoautotrophic (unique to prokaryotes), and chemoheterotrophic. **2.** Chemoheterotrophy; the bacterium must rely on chemical sources of energy, since it is not exposed to light, and it must be a heterotroph if it requires a source of carbon other than CO_2 (or a related compound, such as bicarbonate). **3.** If humans could fix nitrogen, we could build proteins using atmospheric N_2 and hence would not need to eat high-protein foods such as meat, fish, or soy. Our diet would, however, need to include a source of carbon, along with minerals and water. Thus, a typical meal might consist of carbohydrates as a carbon source, along with fruits and vegetables to provide essential minerals (and additional carbon).

Concept Check 27.4

1. Before molecular systematics, taxonomists classified prokaryotes according to phenotypic characters that did not clarify evolutionary relationships. Molecular comparisons—of DNA in particular—indicate key divergences in prokaryotic lineages. **2.** By not requiring that organisms be cultured in the laboratory, genetic prospecting has revealed an immense diversity of previously unknown prokaryotic species. Over time, the ongoing discovery of new species by genetic prospecting is likely to alter our understanding of prokaryotic phylogeny greatly. **3.** At present, all known methanogens are archaea in the clade Euryarchaeota; this suggests that this unique metabolic pathway probably arose in ancestral species within Euryarchaeota. Since Bacteria and Archaea have been separate evolutionary lineages for billions of years, the discovery of a methanogen from the domain Bacteria would suggest that adaptations that enabled the use of CO_2 to oxidize H_2 may have evolved twice—once in Archaea (within Euryarchaeota) and once in Bacteria. (It is also possible that a newly discovered bacterial methanogen could have acquired the genes for this metabolic pathway by horizontal gene transfer from a methanogen in domain Archaea. However, horizontal gene transfer is not a likely explanation because of the large number of genes involved and because gene transfers between species in different domains are rare.)

Concept Check 27.5

1. Although prokaryotes are small, their large numbers and metabolic abilities enable them to play key roles in ecosystems by decomposing wastes, recycling chemicals, and affecting the concentrations of nutrients available to other organisms   2. Cyanobacteria produce oxygen when water is split in the light reactions of photosynthesis. The Calvin cycle incorporates CO_2 from the air into organic molecules, which are then converted to sugars.

Concept Check 27.6

1. Sample answers: eating fermented foods such as yogurt, sourdough bread, or cheese; receiving clean water from sewage treatment; taking medicines produced by bacteria   2. No. If the poison is secreted as an exotoxin, live bacteria could be transmitted to another person. But the same is true if the poison is an endotoxin—only in this case, the live bacteria that are transmitted may be descendants of the (now-dead) bacteria that produced the poison.   3. Some of the many different species of prokaryotes that live in the human gut compete with one another for resources (in the food you eat). Because different prokaryotic species have different adaptations, a change in diet may alter which species can grow most rapidly, thus altering species abundance.

Summary of Key Concepts Questions

27.1. Prokaryotes are small, they have short generation times, and their populations can consist of trillions of individuals. As a result, populations of prokaryotes can evolve substantially in short periods of time, enabling them to adapt to a wide range of environments. Specific structural features that enable prokaryotes to thrive in diverse environments include their cell walls (which provide shape and protection), flagella (which function in directed movement), and ability to form endospores (which enable tolerance of harsh conditions). Prokaryotes also possess biochemical adaptations for growth in varied conditions, such as those that enable them to tolerate extremely hot or salty environments.   **27.2** Prokaryotes reproduce extremely rapidly, and their populations can number in the trillions. As a result, even though mutations are rare, every day thousands of offspring are produced that have new mutations at particular gene loci. In addition, even though prokaryotes reproduce asexually and hence the vast majority of offspring are genetically identical to their parent, the genetic variation of their populations can be increased by transduction, transformation, and conjugation. Each of these (nonreproductive) processes can increase genetic variation by transferring DNA from one cell to another—even among cells that are of different species.   **27.3** Prokaryotes have an exceptionally broad range of metabolic adaptations. As a group, prokaryotes perform all four modes of nutrition (photoautotrophy, chemoautotrophy, photoheterotrophy, and chemoheterotrophy), whereas eukaryotes perform only two of these (photoautotrophy and chemoheterotrophy). Prokaryotes are also able to metabolize nitrogen in a wide variety of forms (again unlike eukaryotes), and they frequently cooperate with other prokaryotic cells of the same or different species.   **27.4** Phenotypic criteria such as shape, motility, and nutritional mode do not provide a clear picture of the evolutionary history of the prokaryotes. In contrast, molecular data have elucidated relationships among major groups of prokaryotes. Molecular data have also allowed researchers to sample genes directly from the environment; using such genes to construct phylogenies has led to the discovery of major new groups of prokaryotes.   **27.5** Prokaryotes play key roles in the chemical cycles on which life depends. For example, prokaryotes are important decomposers, breaking down corpses and waste materials, thereby releasing nutrients to the environment where they can be used by other organisms. Prokaryotes also convert inorganic compounds to forms that other organisms can use. With respect to their ecological interactions, many prokaryotes form life-sustaining mutualisms with other species. In some cases, such as hydrothermal vent communities, the metabolic activities of prokaryotes provide an energy source on which hundreds of other species depend; in the absence of the prokaryotes, the community collapses.   **27.6** Human well-being depends on our associations with mutualistic prokaryotes, such as the many species that live in our intestines and digest food that we cannot. Humans also can harness the remarkable metabolic capabilities of prokaryotes to produce a wide range of useful products. Negative effects of prokaryotes result primarily from bacterial pathogens that cause disease.

Test Your Understanding

1. e 2. a 3. d 4. d 5. b 6. a
8. (a)

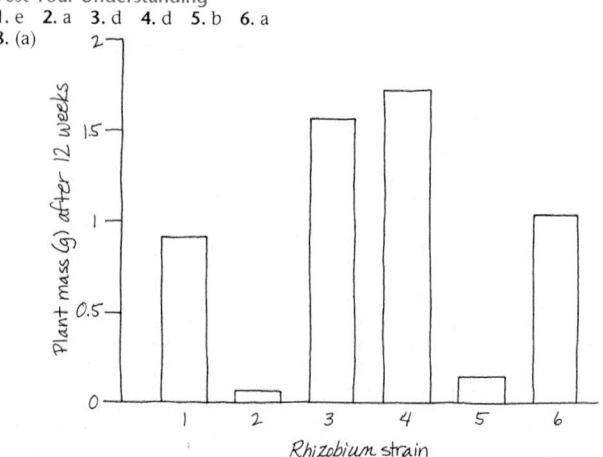

(b) Some *Rhizobium* strains are much more effective at promoting plant growth than other *Rhizobium* strains; the most ineffective strains have little positive effect (plant growth with these strains differs little from plant growth in the absence of *Rhizobium*). The ineffective strains may transfer relatively little nitrogen to their plant host, limiting plant growth.

Chapter 28

Figure Questions

Figure 28.10 Merozoites are produced by the asexual (mitotic) cell division of haploid sporozoites; similarly, gametocytes are produced by the asexual cell division of merozoites. Hence, it is likely that individuals in these three stages have the same complement of genes and that morphological differences between them result from changes in gene expression. **Figure 28.16** The sperm cells in the diagram are produced by the asexual (mitotic) division of cells in a single male gametophyte, which was itself produced by the asexual (mitotic) division of a single zoospore. Thus, the sperm cells are all derived from a single zoospore and so are genetically identical to one another. However, the male gametophyte that produced the sperm developed from one zoospore, while the female gametophyte that produced the egg developed from a different zoospore. Zoospores are produced by meiosis, so each zoospore differs genetically from the others. Hence, the sperm cells (which can be traced back to one zoospore) differ genetically from the egg cell (which can be traced back to another zoospore). **Figure 28.22** The following stage should be circled: step 6, where a mature cell undergoes mitosis and forms four or more daughter cells. In step 7, the zoospores eventually grow into mature haploid cells, but they do not produce new daughter cells. Likewise, in step 2, a mature cell develops into a gamete, but it does not produce new daughter cells. **Figure 28.23** If the assumption is correct, then their results indicate that the DHFR-TS gene fusion may be a derived trait shared by members of four supergroups of eukaryotes (Excavata, Chromalveolata, Rhizaria, and Archaeplastida). However, if the assumption is not correct, the presence or absence of the gene fusion may tell little about phylogenetic history. For example, if the genes fused multiple times, groups could share the trait because of convergent evolution rather than common descent. If the genes were secondarily split, a group with such a split could be placed (incorrectly) in Unikonta rather than its correct placement in one of the other four supergroups. **Figure 28.28** If diatom populations decrease in size as global temperatures warm, less carbon dioxide would be "pumped" from surface waters to the deep ocean floor. Atmospheric carbon dioxide levels might increase as a result, thereby potentially causing further warming. If this process continues, a positive-feedback loop would result in which warming causes diatom populations to drop, thereby causing additional warming, further drops in diatom populations, and so on.

Concept Check 28.1

1. Sample response: Protists include unicellular, colonial, and multicellular organisms; photoautotrophs, heterotrophs, and mixotrophs; species that reproduce asexually, sexually, or both ways; and organisms with diverse physical forms and adaptations.   2. Strong evidence shows that eukaryotes acquired mitochondria after an early eukaryote first engulfed and then formed an endosymbiotic association with an alpha proteobacterium. Similarly, chloroplasts in red and green algae appear to have descended from a photosynthetic cyanobacterium that was engulfed by an ancient heterotrophic eukaryote. Secondary endosymbiosis also played an important role: Various protist lineages acquired plastids by engulfing unicellular red or green algae.   3. The modified tree would look as follows:

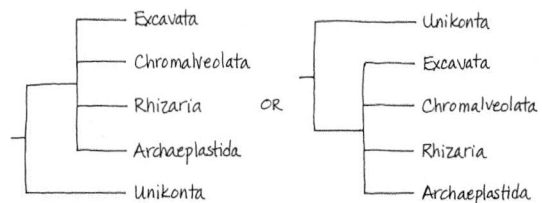

Concept Check 28.2

1. Their mitochondria do not have an electron transport chain and so cannot function in aerobic respiration.   2. Since the unknown protist is more closely related to diplomonads than to euglenids, it must have originated after the diplomonads and parabasalids diverged from the euglenozoans. In addition, since the unknown species has fully functional mitochondria—yet both diplomonads and parabasalids do not—it is likely that the unknown species originated *before* the last common ancestor of the diplomonads and parabasalids.

Concept Check 28.3

1. Some DNA data indicate that Chromalveolata is a monophyletic group, but other DNA data fail to support this result. In support of monophyly, for many species in the group, the structure of their plastids and the sequence of their plastid DNA suggest that the group originated by a secondary endosymbiosis event (in which a red alga was engulfed). However, other species in the group lack plastids entirely, making the secondary endosymbiosis hypothesis difficult to test.   2. The plastid DNA would likely be more similar to the chromosomal DNA of cyanobacteria based on the well-supported hypothesis that eukaryotic plastids (such as those found in the eukaryotic groups listed) originated by an endosymbiosis event in which a eukaryote engulfed a cyanobacterium. If the plastid is derived from the cyanobacterium, its DNA would be derived from the bacterial DNA.   3. Figure 13.6b. Algae and plants with alternation

of generations have a multicellular haploid stage *and* a multicellular diploid stage. In the other two life cycles, either the haploid stage or the diploid stage is unicellular.

Concept Check 28.4

1. Because foram tests are hardened with calcium carbonate, they form long-lasting fossils in marine sediments and sedimentary rocks. **2.** Convergent evolution. The different organisms have come to display similar morphological adaptations over time owing to their similar lifestyles. **3.** During photosynthesis, aerobic algae produce O_2 and use CO_2. O_2 is produced as a by-product of the light reactions, while CO_2 is used as an input to the Calvin cycle (the end products of which are sugars). Aerobic algae also perform cellular respiration, which uses O_2 as an input and produces CO_2 as a waste product.

Concept Check 28.5

1. Many red algae contain an accessory pigment called phycoerythrin, which gives them a reddish color and allows them to carry out photosynthesis in relatively deep coastal water. Also unlike brown algae, red algae have no flagellated stages in their life cycle and must depend on water currents to bring gametes together for fertilization. **2.** *Ulva*'s thallus contains many cells and is differentiated into leaflike blades and a rootlike holdfast. *Caulerpa*'s thallus is composed of multinucleate filaments without cross-walls, so it is essentially one large cell. **3.** Red algae have no flagellated stages in their life cycle and hence must depend on water currents to bring their gametes together. This feature of their biology might increase the difficulty of reproducing on land. In contrast, the gametes of green algae are flagellated, making it possible for them to swim in thin films of water. In addition, a variety of green algae contain compounds in their cytoplasm, cell wall, or zygote coat that protect against intense sunlight and other terrestrial conditions. Such compounds may have increased the chance that descendants of green algae could survive on land.

Concept Check 28.6

1. Amoebozoans have lobe-shaped pseudopodia, whereas forams have threadlike pseudopodia. **2.** Slime molds are fungus-like in that they produce fruiting bodies that aid in the dispersal of spores, and they are animal-like in that they are motile and ingest food. However, slime molds are more closely related to gymnamoebas and entamoebas than to fungi or animals. **3.** Support. Unikonts lack the unique cytoskeletal features shared by many excavates (see Concept 28.2). Thus, if the unikonts were the first group of eukaryotes to diverge from other eukaryotes (as shown in Figure 28.23), it would be unlikely that the eukaryote common ancestor had the cytoskeletal features found today in many excavates. Such a result would strengthen the case that many excavates share cytoskeletal features because they are members of a monophyletic group, the Excavata.

Concept Check 28.7

1. Because photosynthetic protists constitute the base of aquatic food webs, many aquatic organisms depend on them for food, either directly or indirectly. (In addition, a substantial percentage of the oxygen produced in photosynthesis on Earth is made by photosynthetic protists.) **2.** Protists form mutualistic and parasitic associations with other organisms. Examples include photosynthetic dinoflagellates that form a mutualistic symbiosis with coral polyps, parabasalids that form a mutualistic symbiosis with termites, and the oomycete *Phytophthora ramorum*, a parasite of oak trees. **3.** Corals depend on their dinoflagellate symbionts for nourishment, so coral bleaching would be expected to cause the corals to die. As the corals die, less food will be available for fishes and other species that eat coral. As a result, populations of these species may decline, and that, in turn, might cause populations of their predators to decline.

Summary of Key Concepts Questions

28.1 Sample response: Protists, plants, animals, and fungi are similar in that their cells have a nucleus and other membrane-bounded organelles, unlike the cells of prokaryotes. These membrane-bounded organelles make the cells of eukaryotes more complex than the cells of prokaryotes. With respect to differences between protists and other eukaryotes, most protists are unicellular, unlike animals, plants, and most fungi. Protists also have greater nutritional diversity than other eukaryotes. **28.2** Unique cytoskeletal features are shared by many excavates. In addition, some members of Excavata have an "excavated" feeding groove for which the group was named. DNA evidence does not strongly support or refute Excavata as a group. Overall, evidence for the group is relatively weak. **28.3** We can infer that the common ancestor of the group had a plastid, in this case of red algal origin. Thus, we would expect that members of Chromalveolata either would have plastids or would have lost their plastids over the course of evolution. **28.4** The main subgroups are the radiolarians, the forams, and the cercozoans. They are united as a clade by DNA similarities. **28.5** Red algae, green algae, and land plants are placed in the same supergroup because considerable evidence indicates that these organisms all descended from the same ancestor, an ancient heterotrophic protist that acquired a cyanobacterial endosymbiont. **28.6** The unikonts are a diverse group of eukaryotes that includes many protists, along with animals and fungi. Most of the protists in Unikonta are amoebozoans, a clade of amoebas that have lobe- or tube-shaped pseudopodia (as opposed to the threadlike pseudopodia of rhizarians). Other protists in Unikonta include several groups that are closely related to fungi and several other groups that are closely related to animals. **28.7** Sample response: Ecologically important protists include photosynthetic dinoflagellates that provide essential sources of energy to their symbiotic partners, the corals that build coral reefs. Other important protistan symbionts include those that enable termites to digest wood and *Plasmodium*, the pathogen that causes malaria. Photosynthetic protists such as diatoms are among the most important producers in aquatic communities; as such, many other species in aquatic environments depend on them for food.

Test Your Understanding

1. d **2.** b **3.** c **4.** e **5.** d **6.** d

7.

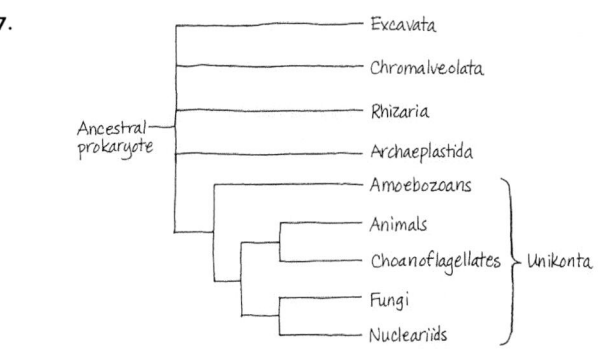

Pathogens that share a relatively recent common ancestor with humans should also share metabolic and structural characteristics with humans. Because drugs target the pathogen's metabolism or structure, developing drugs that harm the pathogen but not the patient should be most difficult for pathogens with whom we share the most recent evolutionary history. Working backward in time, we can use the phylogenetic tree to determine the order in which humans shared a common ancestor with pathogens in different taxa. This process leads to the prediction that it should be hardest to develop drugs to combat animal pathogens, followed by choanoflagellate pathogens, fungal and nucleariid pathogens, amoebozoans, other protists, and finally prokaryotes.

Chapter 29

Figure Questions

Figure 29.5 The life cycle in Figure 13.6b has alternation of generations; the others do not. Unlike the animal life cycle (Figure 13.6a), in alternation of generations, meiosis produces spores, not gametes. These spores then divide repeatedly by mitosis, ultimately forming a multicellular haploid individual that produces gametes. There is no multicellular haploid stage in the animal life cycle. An alternation of generations life cycle also has a multicellular diploid stage, whereas the life cycle shown in Figure 13.6c does not. **Figure 29.8** Yes. As shown in the diagram, the sperm cell and the egg cell that fuse each resulted from the mitotic division of spores produced by the same sporophyte. However, these spores would differ genetically from one another because they were produced by meiosis, a cell division process that generates genetic variation among the offspring cells. **Figure 29.10** Because the moss reduces nitrogen loss from the ecosystem, species that typically colonize the soils after the moss probably experience higher soil nitrogen levels than they otherwise would. The resulting increased availability of nitrogen may benefit these species because nitrogen is an essential nutrient that often is in short supply. **Figure 29.13** A fern that had wind-dispersed sperm would not require water for fertilization, thus removing a difficulty that ferns face when they live in arid environments. The fern would also be under strong selection to produce sperm above ground (as opposed to the current situation, where some fern gametophytes are located below ground). **Figure 29.16** When not reproducing, the lycophyte trees that dominate this forest would resemble poles covered by short leaves (microphylls). Since the trees would not have a branched canopy at their tops, the forest would be very open, and a considerable amount of light would reach the ground level.

Concept Check 29.1

1. Land plants share some key traits only with charophytes: rings of cellulose-synthesizing complexes, presence of peroxisome enzymes, similarity in sperm structure, and the formation of a phragmoplast in cell division. Comparisons of nuclear and chloroplast genes also point to a common ancestry. **2.** Spore walls toughened by sporopollenin (protects against harsh environmental conditions); multicellular, dependent embryos (provides nutrients and protection to the developing embryo); cuticle (reduces water loss) **3.** The multicellular diploid stage of the life cycle would not produce gametes. Instead, both males and females would produce haploid spores by meiosis. These spores would give rise to multicellular male and female haploid stages—a major change from the single-celled haploid stages (sperm and eggs) that we actually have. The multicellular haploid stages would produce gametes and reproduce sexually. An individual at the multicellular haploid stage of the human life cycle might look like us, or it might look completely different. **4.** Land plants, vascular plants, and seed plants are monophyletic because each of these groups includes the common ancestor of the group and all of the descendants of that common ancestor. The other two categories of plants, the nonvascular plants and the seedless vascular plants, are paraphyletic: These groups do not include all of the descendants of the group's most recent common ancestor.

Concept Check 29.2

1. Bryophytes do not have a vascular transport system, and their life cycle is dominated by gametophytes rather than sporophytes. **2.** Answers may include the following: Large surface area of protonema enhances absorption of water and minerals; the vase-shaped archegonia protect eggs during fertilization and transport nutrients to the embryos via placental transfer cells; the stalk-like seta conducts nutrients from the gametophyte to the capsule, where spores are produced; the peristome enables gradual spore discharge; stomata enable CO_2/O_2 exchange while minimizing water loss; lightweight spores are readily dispersed by wind.

3.

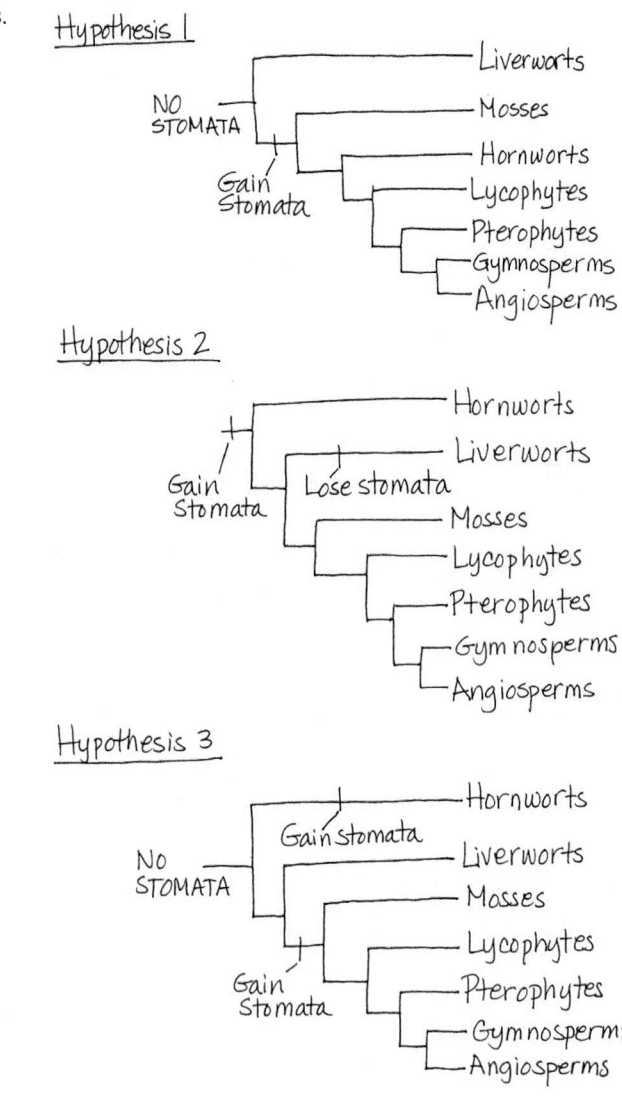

Hypothesis 1

NO STOMATA — Gain Stomata
- Liverworts
- Mosses
- Hornworts
- Lycophytes
- Pterophytes
- Gymnosperms
- Angiosperms

Hypothesis 2

Gain Stomata — Lose stomata
- Hornworts
- Liverworts
- Mosses
- Lycophytes
- Pterophytes
- Gymnosperms
- Angiosperms

Hypothesis 3

NO STOMATA — Gain stomata — Gain Stomata
- Hornworts
- Liverworts
- Mosses
- Lycophytes
- Pterophytes
- Gymnosperms
- Angiosperms

Concept Check 29.3

1. Lycophytes have microphylls, whereas seed plants and pterophytes (ferns and their relatives) have megaphylls. Pterophytes and seed plants also share other traits not found in lycophytes, such as overtopping growth and the initiation of new root branches at various points along the length of an existing root. **2.** Both seedless vascular plants and bryophytes have flagellated sperm that require moisture for fertilization; this shared similarity poses challenges for these species in arid regions. With respect to key differences, seedless vascular plants have lignified, well-developed vascular tissue, a trait that enables the sporophyte to grow tall and that has transformed life on Earth (via the formation of forests). Seedless vascular plants also have true leaves and roots, which, when compared with bryophytes, provide increased surface area for photosynthesis and improve their ability to extract nutrients from soil. **3.** If lycophytes and pterophytes formed a clade, the traits shared by pterophytes and seed plants might have been present in the common ancestor of all vascular plants, but lost in the lycophytes. Alternatively, the common ancestor of all vascular plants may have lacked the traits shared by pterophytes and seed plants; in this case, pterophytes and seed plants would share these traits as a result of convergent evolution. **4.** Three mechanisms contribute to the production of genetic variation in sexual reproduction: independent assortment of chromosomes, crossing over, and random fertilization. If fertilization were to occur between gametes from the same gametophyte, all of the offspring would be genetically identical. This would be the case because all of the cells produced by a gametophyte—including its sperm and egg cells—are the descendants of a single spore and hence are genetically identical. Genetic variation would continue to be generated by the first two mechanisms mentioned, but overall, the amount of genetic variation produced by sexual reproduction would drop.

Summary of Key Concepts Questions
29.1

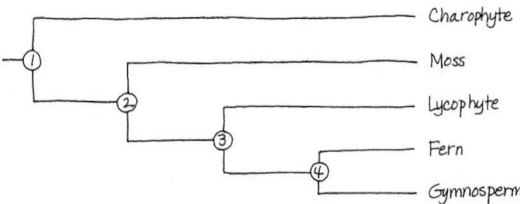

Multicellular gametangia — COMMON ANCESTOR OF ALL LAND PLANTS — Vascular tissue — Seeds
- Liverworts
- Mosses
- Hornworts
- Lycophytes
- Pterophytes
- Gymnosperms
- Angiosperms

29.2 Some mosses colonize bare, sandy soils, leading to the increased retention of nitrogen in these otherwise low-nitrogen environments. Other mosses harbor nitrogen-fixing cyanobacteria that increase the availability of nitrogen in the ecosystem. The moss *Sphagnum* is often a major component of deposits of peat (partially decayed organic material). Boggy regions with thick layers of peat, known as peatlands, cover broad geographic regions and contain large reservoirs of carbon. By storing large amounts of carbon—in effect, removing CO_2 from the atmosphere—peatlands affect the global climate, making them of considerable ecological importance.
29.3 Lignified vascular tissue provided the strength needed to support a tall plant against gravity, as well as a means to transport water and nutrients to plant parts located high above ground. Roots were another key trait, anchoring the plant to the ground and providing additional structural support for plants that grew tall. Tall plants could shade shorter plants, thereby outcompeting them for light. Because the spores of a tall plant disperse farther than the spores of a short plant, it is also likely that tall plants could colonize new habitats more rapidly than short plants.

Test Your Understanding
1. b **2.** e **3.** d **4.** c **5.** a **6.** a. diploid; b. haploid; c. haploid; d. diploid; e. haploid **7.** c
8. Based on our current understanding of the evolution of major plant groups, the phylogeny has the four branch points shown here:

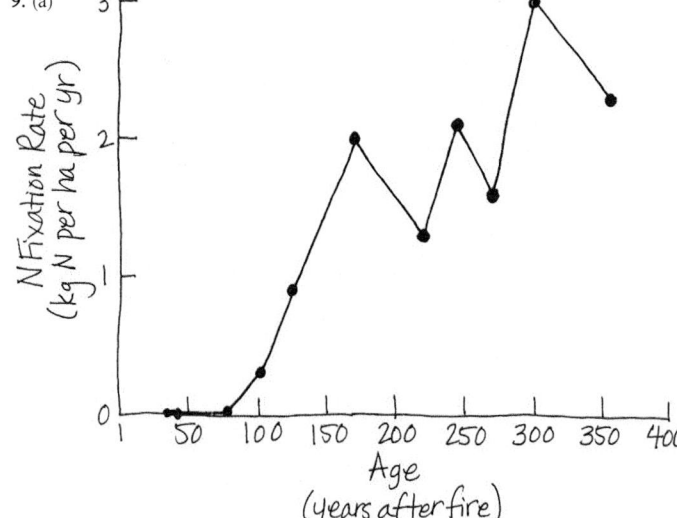

① ② ③ ④
- Charophyte
- Moss
- Lycophyte
- Fern
- Gymnosperm

Derived characters unique to the charophyte and land plant clade (indicated by branch point 1) include rings of cellulose-synthesizing complexes, peroxisome enzymes, flagellated sperm structure, and a phragmoplast. Derived characters unique to the land plant clade (branch point 2) include apical meristems, alternation of generations, walled spores produced in sporangia, and multicellular gametangia. Derived characters unique to the vascular plant clade (branch point 3) include life cycles with dominant sporophytes, complex vascular systems (xylem and phloem), and well-developed roots and leaves. Derived characters unique to the pterophyte and seed plant clade (branch point 4) include megaphylls and overtopping growth.
9. (a)

[graph: N Fixation Rate (kg N per ha per yr) vs. Age (years after fire)]

(b) In the first 40 years after a fire, nitrogen fixation rates were below 0.01 kg per ha per yr, which was less than 1% of the amount of nitrogen deposited from the atmosphere. Thus, in the initial decades after a fire, the moss *Pleurozium* and the nitrogen-fixing bacteria it harbors had relatively little effect on the amount of nitrogen added to the forest. With time, however, *Pleurozium* and its symbiotic, nitrogen-fixing bacteria became increasingly important. By 170 years after a fire, the percentage of the ground surface covered by the moss had increased to about 70%, leading to a corresponding increase in populations of the symbiotic bacteria. As would be predicted from this result, in older forests considerably more nitrogen (130–300%) was added by nitrogen fixation than was deposited from the atmosphere.

Chapter 30

Figure Questions

Figure 30.2 Retaining the gametophyte within the sporophyte shields the egg-containing gametophyte from UV radiation. UV radiation is a mutagen. Hence, we would expect fewer mutations to occur in the egg cells produced by a gametophyte retained within the body of a sporophyte. Most mutations are harmful. Thus, the fitness of embryos should increase because fewer embryos would carry harmful mutations. **Figure 30.3** Three generations: (1) the current sporophyte (cells of ploidy 2n, found in the seed coat and in the megasporangium remnant that surrounds the spore wall); (2) the female gametophyte (cells of ploidy n, found in the food supply); and (3) the sporophyte of the next generation (cells of ploidy 2n, found in the embryo) **Figure 30.6** Mitosis. A single haploid megaspore divides by mitosis to produce a multicellular, haploid female gametophyte. (Likewise, a single haploid microspore divides by mitosis to produce a multicellular male gametophyte.) **Figure 30.12** No. The branching order shown could still be correct if *Amborella* and other early angiosperms had originated prior to 150 million years ago, but angiosperm fossils of that age had not yet been discovered. In such a situation, the 140-million-year-old date for the origin of the angiosperms shown on the phylogeny would be incorrect. **Figure 30.16** Temperatures and the amount of sunlight striking the forest floor would both be likely to increase, whereas rainfall would likely decrease. Each of these changes could have dramatic effects on forest species that live near the edges of remaining forest fragments.

Concept Check 30.1

1. To reach the eggs, the flagellated sperm of seedless plants must swim through a film of water, usually over a distance of no more than a few centimeters. In contrast, the sperm of seed plants do not require water because they are produced within pollen grains that can be transported long distances by wind or by animal pollinators. Although flagellated in some species, the sperm of seed plants do not require mobility because pollen tubes convey them from the point at which the pollen grain is deposited (near the ovules) directly to the eggs. **2.** The reduced gametophytes of seed plants are nurtured by sporophytes and protected from stress, such as drought conditions and UV radiation. Pollen grains, with walls containing sporopollenin, provide protection during transport by wind or animals. Seeds have one or two layers of protective tissue, the seed coat, that improve survival by providing more protection from environmental stresses than do the walls of spores. Seeds also contain a stored supply of food, which provides nourishment for growth after dormancy is broken and the embryo emerges as a seedling. **3.** If a seed could not enter dormancy, the embryo would continue to grow after it was fertilized. As a result, the embryo might rapidly become too large to be dispersed, thus limiting its transport. The embryo's chance of survival might also be reduced because it could not delay growth until conditions become favorable.

Concept Check 30.2

1. Although gymnosperms are similar in not having their seeds enclosed in ovaries and fruits, their seed-bearing structures vary greatly. For instance, cycads have large cones, whereas some gymnosperms, such as *Ginkgo* and *Gnetum*, have small cones that look somewhat like berries, even though they are not fruits. Leaf shape also varies greatly, from the needles of many conifers to the palmlike leaves of cycads to *Gnetum* leaves that look like those of flowering plants. **2.** The pine life cycle illustrates heterospory, as ovulate cones produce megaspores and pollen cones produce microspores. The reduced gametophytes are evident in the form of the microscopic pollen grains that develop from microspores and the microscopic female gametophyte that develops from the megaspore. The egg is shown developing within an ovule, and a pollen tube is shown conveying the sperm. The figure also shows the protective and nutritive features of a seed. **3.** No. Fossil evidence indicates that gymnosperms originated at least 305 million years ago, but this does not mean that angiosperms are that old—only that the most recent common ancestor of gymnosperms and angiosperms must be that old.

Concept Check 30.3

1. In the oak's life cycle, the tree (the sporophyte) produces flowers, which contain gametophytes in pollen grains and ovules; the eggs in ovules are fertilized, and the mature ovaries develop into dry fruits called acorns. We can view the oak's life cycle as starting when the acorn seeds germinate, resulting in embryos giving rise to seedlings and finally to mature trees, which produce flowers—and then more acorns. **2.** Pine cones and flowers both have sporophylls, modified leaves that produce spores. Pine trees have separate pollen cones (with pollen grains) and ovulate cones (with ovules inside cone scales). In flowers, pollen grains are produced by the anthers of stamens, and ovules are within the ovaries of carpels. Unlike pine cones, many flowers produce both pollen and ovules. **3.** The fact that the clade with bilaterally symmetrical flowers had more species establishes a correlation between flower shape and the rate of plant speciation. Flower shape is not necessarily responsible for the result because the shape (that is, bilateral or radial symmetry) may have been correlated with another

factor that was the actual cause of the observed result. Note, however, that flower shape was associated with increased speciation rates when averaged across 19 different pairs of plant lineages. Since these 19 lineage pairs were independent of one another, this association suggests—but does not establish—that differences in flower shape cause differences in speciation rates. In general, strong evidence for causation can come from controlled, manipulative experiments, but such experiments are usually not possible for studies of past evolutionary events.

Concept Check 30.4

1. Plant diversity can be considered a resource because plants provide many important benefits to humans; as a resource, plant diversity is nonrenewable because if a species is lost to extinction, that loss is permanent. **2.** A detailed phylogeny of the seed plants would identify many different monophyletic groups of seed plants. Using this phylogeny, researchers could look for clades that contained species in which medicinally useful compounds had already been discovered. Identification of such clades would allow researchers to concentrate their search for new medicinal compounds among clade members—as opposed to searching for new compounds in species that were selected at random from the more than 250,000 existing species of seed plants.

Summary of Key Concepts Questions

30.1 The integument of an ovule develops into the protective seed coat of a seed. The ovule's megaspore develops into a haploid female gametophyte, and two parts of the seed are derived from this gametophyte: The food supply of the seed is derived from haploid gametophyte cells, and the embryo of the seed develops after the female gametophyte's egg cell is fertilized by a sperm cell. A remnant of the ovule's megasporangium surrounds the spore wall that encloses the seed's food supply and embryo. **30.2** Gymnosperms arose about 305 million years ago, making them a successful group in terms of their evolutionary longevity. Gymnosperms have the five derived traits common to all seed plants (reduced gametophytes, heterospory, ovules, pollen, and seeds), making them well adapted for life on land. Finally, because gymnosperms dominate immense geographic regions today, the group is also highly successful in geographic distribution. **30.3** The origin of flowering plants is puzzling because their distinctive features, flowers and fruits, bear little resemblance to structures in living gymnosperms. This makes it difficult to infer how flowers and fruits arose, leading Darwin to refer to the origin of flowering plants as an "abominable mystery." Progress has been made toward solving this mystery, particularly in our understanding of angiosperm phylogeny, but the mystery has yet to be solved. We still do not know, for example, which extinct group of seed plants is most closely related to flowering plants. **30.4** The loss of tropical forests could contribute to global warming (which would have negative effects on many human societies) and reduce agricultural production in some of the world's poorest regions. People also depend on Earth's biodiversity for many products and services and hence would be harmed by the loss of species that would occur if the world's remaining tropical forests were cut down. With respect to a possible mass extinction, tropical forests harbor at least 50% of the species on Earth. If the remaining tropical forests were destroyed, large numbers of these species could be driven to extinction, thus rivaling the losses that occurred in the five mass extinction events documented in the fossil record.

Test Your Understanding

1. d **2.** a **3.** b **4.** a **5.** d
6.

8. (a)

(b) The phylogeny indicates that basal angiosperms differed from other angiosperms in terms of the number of cells in female gametophytes and the ploidy of the endosperm. The ancestral state of the angiosperms cannot be determined from these data alone. It is possible that the common ancestor of angiosperms had seven-celled female gametophytes and triploid endosperm and hence that the eight-celled and four-celled conditions found in basal angiosperms represent derived traits for those lineages. Alternatively, either the eight-celled or four-celled condition may represent the ancestral state.

Chapter 31

Figure Questions

Figure 31.2 DNA from each of these mushrooms would be identical if each mushroom is part of a single hyphal network, as is likely. **Figure 31.16** One or both of the following would apply to each species: DNA analyses would reveal that it is a member of the ascomycete clade, or aspects of its sexual life cycle would indicate that it is an ascomycete (for example, it would produce asci and ascospores). **Figure 31.21** Two possible controls would be E−P− and E+P−. Results from an E−P− control could be compared with results from the E−P+ experiment, and results from an E+P− control could be compared with results from the E+P+ experiment. Together, these two comparisons would indicate whether the addition of the pathogen causes an increase in leaf mortality. Results from an E−P− experiment could also be compared with results from the second control (E+P−) to determine whether adding the endophytes has a negative effect on the plant. **Figure 31.26** The correspondence between when the chytrid fungi arrived to the region and when frog populations decreased greatly suggests that the chytrid was the cause of the decline, not just correlated to it. The fact that by 2009, the only surviving frogs were in the two lakes treated with fungicides provides additional support for causation.

Concept Check 31.1

1. Both a fungus and a human are heterotrophs. Many fungi digest their food externally by secreting enzymes into the food and then absorbing the small molecules that result from digestion. Other fungi absorb such small molecules directly from their environment. In contrast, humans (and most other animals) ingest relatively large pieces of food and digest the food within their bodies. **2.** The ancestors of such a mutualist most likely secreted powerful enzymes to digest the body of their insect host. Since such enzymes would harm a living host, it is likely that the mutualist would not produce such enzymes or would restrict their secretion and use. **3.** Carbon that enters the plant through stomata is fixed into sugar through photosynthesis. Some of these sugars are absorbed by the fungus that partners with the plant to form mycorrhizae; others are transported within the plant body and used in the plant. Thus, the carbon may be deposited in either the body of the plant or the body of the fungus.

Concept Check 31.2

1. The majority of the fungal life cycle is spent in the haploid stage, whereas the majority of the human life cycle is spent in the diploid stage. **2.** The two mushrooms might be reproductive structures of the same mycelium (the same organism). Or they might be parts of two separate organisms that have arisen from a single parent organism through asexual reproduction and thus carry the same genetic information.

Concept Check 31.3

1. DNA evidence indicates that fungi, animals, and their protistan relatives form a clade, the opisthokonts. Furthermore, an early-diverging fungal lineage, the chytrids, have posterior flagella, as do most other opisthokonts. This suggests that other fungal lineages lost their flagella after diverging from chytrids. **2.** This indicates that fungi had already established mutualistic relationships with plants by the date the fossils of the earliest vascular plants had formed. **3.** Fungi are heterotrophs. Prior to the colonization of land by plants, terrestrial fungi would have lived where other organisms (or their remains) were present and provided a source of food. Thus, if fungi had colonized land before plants, they could have fed on any prokaryotes or protists that lived on land or by the water's edge—but not on the plants or animals on which many fungi feed today.

Concept Check 31.4

1. Flagellated spores; molecular evidence also suggests that chytrids are an early-diverging fungal lineage. **2.** Possible answers include the following: In zygomycetes, the sturdy, thick-walled zygosporangium can withstand harsh conditions and then undergo karyogamy and meiosis when the environment is favorable for reproduction. In glomeromycetes, the hyphae have a specialized morphology that enables the fungi to form arbuscular mycorrhizae with plant roots. In ascomycetes, the asexual spores (conidia) are often produced in chains or clusters at the tips of conidiophores, where they are easily dispersed by wind. The often cup-shaped ascocarps house the sexual spore-forming asci. In basidiomycetes, the basidiocarp supports and protects a large surface area of basidia, from which spores are dispersed. **3.** Such a change to the life cycle of an ascomycete would reduce the number and genetic diversity of ascospores that result from a mating event. Ascospore number would drop because a mating event would lead to the formation of only one ascus. Ascospore genetic diversity would also drop because in ascomycetes, one mating event leads to the formation of asci by many different dikaryotic cells. As a result, genetic recombination and meiosis occur independently many different times—which could not happen if only a single ascus was formed. It is also likely that if such an ascomycete formed an ascocarp, the shape of the ascocarp would differ considerably from that found in its close relatives.

Concept Check 31.5

1. A suitable environment for growth, retention of water and minerals, protection from intense sunlight, and protection from being eaten **2.** A hardy spore stage enables dispersal to host organisms through a variety of mechanisms; their ability to grow rapidly in a favorable new environment enables them to capitalize on the host's resources. **3.** Many different outcomes might have occurred. Organisms that currently form mutualisms with fungi might have gained the ability to perform the tasks currently done by their fungal partners, or they might have formed similar mutualisms with other organisms (such as bacteria). Alternatively, organisms that currently form mutualisms with fungi might be less effective at living in their present environments. For example, the colonization of land by plants might have been more difficult. And if plants did eventually colonize land without fungal mutualists, natural selection might have favored plants that formed more highly divided and extensive root systems (in part replacing mycorrhizae).

31.1 The body of a multicellular fungus typically consists of thin filaments called hyphae. These filaments form an interwoven mass (mycelium) that penetrates the substrate on which the fungus grows and feeds. Because the individual filaments are thin, the surface-to-volume ratio of the mycelium is maximized, making nutrient absorption highly efficient.

31.2

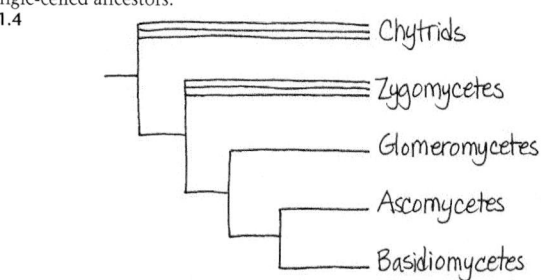

31.3 Phylogenetic analyses show that fungi and animals are more closely related to each other than either is to other multicellular eukaryotes (such as plants or multicellular algae). These analyses also show that fungi are more closely related to single-celled protists called nucleariids than they are to animals, whereas animals are more closely related to a different group of single-celled protists, the choanoflagellates, than they are to fungi. In combination, these results indicate that multicellularity evolved in fungi and animals independently, from different single-celled ancestors.

31.4

Chytrids

Zygomycetes

Glomeromycetes

Ascomycetes

Basidiomycetes

31.5 As decomposers, fungi break down the bodies of dead organisms, thereby recycling elements between the living and nonliving environments. Without the activities of fungi and bacterial decomposers, essential nutrients would remain tied up in organic matter, and life would cease. As an example of their key role as mutualists, fungi form mycorrhizal associations with plants. These associations improve the growth and survival of plants, thereby indirectly affecting the many other species (humans included) that depend on plants. As pathogens, fungi harm other species. In some cases, fungal pathogens have caused their host populations to decline across broad geographic regions, as seen for the American chestnut.

Test Your Understanding
1. b **2.** c **3.** d **4.** b **5.** a **6.** e
7.

☐ No endophytes (E−)
▨ Endophyte present (E+)

Plant mass (g) vs. Temperature (°C)

As indicated by the raw data and bar graph, grass plants with endophytes (E+) produced more new shoots and had greater biomass than did grass plants that lacked endophytes (E−). These differences were especially pronounced at the highest soil temperature, where E− grass plants produced no new shoots and had a biomass of zero (indicating they were dead).

Chapter 32

Figure Questions

Figure 32.3 As described in ❶ and ❷, choanoflagellates and a broad range of animals have collar cells. Since collar cells have never been observed in plants, fungi, or non-choanoflagellate protists, this suggests that choanoflagellates may be more closely related to animals than to other eukaryotes. If choanoflagellates are more closely related to animals than to any other group of eukaryotes, choanoflagellates and animals should share other traits that are not found in other eukaryotes. The data described in ❸ are consistent with this prediction. **Figure 32.6** The sea anemone embryos could be infused with a protein that can bind to β-catenin's DNA-binding site, thereby limiting the extent to which β-catenin activates the transcription of genes necessary for gastrulation. Such an experiment would provide an independent check of the results shown in step 4. **Figure 32.9** The cells of an early embryo with deuterostome development typically are not committed to a particular developmental fate, whereas the cells of an early embryo with protostome development typically are committed to a particular developmental fate. As a result, an embryo with deuterostome development would be more likely to contain stem cells that could give rise to cells of any type. **Figure 32.10** Ctenophora is the sister phylum in this figure, while Cnidaria is the sister phylum in Figure 32.11.

Concept Check 32.1

1. In most animals, the zygote undergoes cleavage, which leads to the formation of a blastula. Next, in gastrulation, one end of the embryo folds inward, producing layers of embryonic tissue. As the cells of these layers differentiate, a wide variety of animal forms result. Despite the diversity of animal forms, animal development is controlled by a similar set of *Hox* genes across a broad range of taxa. **2.** The imaginary plant would require tissues composed of cells that were analogous to the muscle and nerve cells found in animals: "Muscle" tissue would be necessary for the plant to chase prey, and "nerve" tissue would be required for the plant to coordinate its movements when chasing prey. To digest captured prey, the plant would need to either secrete enzymes into one or more digestive cavities (which could be modified leaves, as in a Venus flytrap) or secrete enzymes outside of its body and feed by absorption. To extract nutrients from the soil—yet be able to chase prey—the plant would need something other than fixed roots, perhaps retractable "roots" or a way to ingest soil. To conduct photosynthesis, the plant would require chloroplasts. Overall, such an imaginary plant would be very similar to an animal that had chloroplasts and retractable roots. **3.** As described in Chapter 18, miRNAs help regulate gene expression by binding to and hence blocking the translation of particular mRNA molecules, their "target mRNAs." Because each miRNA can bind to many target mRNAs, an increase in the number of miRNA molecules could potentially add many layers of control to the regulation of gene expression. As a result of a more varied and complex control of gene expression, the construction of a complex body form would be more likely in an organism with many miRNAs than in an organism with few miRNAs, even though both organisms had roughly the same total number of genes.

Concept Check 32.2

1. c, b, a, d **2.** We cannot infer whether animals originated before or after fungi. If correct, the date provided for the most recent common ancestor of fungi and animals would indicate that animals originated some time within the last billion years. The fossil record indicates that animals originated at least 565 million years ago. Thus, we could conclude only that animals originated sometime between 1 billion years ago and 565 million years ago.

Concept Check 32.3

1. Grade-level characteristics are those that multiple lineages share regardless of evolutionary history. Some grade-level characteristics may have evolved multiple times independently. Features that unite clades are derived characteristics that originated in a common ancestor and were passed on to the various descendants. **2.** A snail has a spiral and determinate cleavage pattern; a human has radial, indeterminate cleavage. In a snail, the coelomic cavity is formed by splitting of mesoderm masses; in a human, the coelom forms from folds of archenteron. In a snail, the mouth forms from the blastopore; in a human, the anus develops from the blastopore. **3.** Most coelomate triploblasts have two openings to their digestive tract, a mouth and an anus. As such, their bodies have a structure that is analogous to that of a doughnut: The digestive tract (the hole of the doughnut) runs from the mouth to the anus and is surrounded by various tissues (the solid part of the doughnut). The doughnut analogy is most obvious at early stages of development (see Figure 32.9c).

Concept Check 32.4

1. Cnidarians possess true tissues, while sponges do not. Also unlike sponges, cnidarians exhibit body symmetry, though it is radial and not bilateral as in other animal phyla. **2.** The morphology-based tree divides Bilateria into two major clades: Deuterostomia and Protostomia. The molecular-based tree recognizes three major clades: Deuterostomia, Ecdysozoa, and Lophotrochozoa. **3.** The phylogeny in Figure 32.11 indicates that molluscs are members of Lophotrochozoa, one the three main groups of bilaterians (the others being Deuterostomia and Ecdysozoa). As seen in Figure 25.10, the fossil record shows that molluscs were present tens of millions of years before the Cambrian explosion. Thus, long before the Cambrian explosion, the lophotrochoan clade had formed and was evolving independently of the evolutionary lineages leading to Deuterostomia and Ecdysozoa. Based on the phylogeny in Figure 32.11, we can also conclude that the lineages leading to Deuterostomia and Ecdysozoa were independent of one another before the Cambrian explosion. Since the lineages leading to the three main clades of bilaterians were evolving independently of one another prior to the Cambrian explosion, that explosion could be viewed as consisting of three "explosions," not one.

Summary of Key Concepts Questions

Concept 32.1 Unlike animals, which are heterotrophs that ingest their food, plants are autotrophs, and fungi are heterotrophs that grow on their food and feed by absorption. Animals lack cell walls, which are found in both plants and fungi. Animals also have muscle tissue and nerve tissue, which are not found in either plants or fungi. In addition, the sperm and egg cells of animals are produced by meiotic divi-

sion, unlike what occurs in plants and fungi (where reproductive cells such as sperm and eggs are produced by mitotic division). Finally, animals regulate the development of body form with *Hox* genes, a unique group of genes that is not found in either plants or fungi. **Concept 32.2** Current hypotheses about the cause of the Cambrian explosion include new predator-prey relationships, an increase in atmospheric oxygen, and an increase in developmental flexibility provided by the origin of *Hox* genes and other genetic changes. **Concept 32.3** Body plans provide a helpful way to compare and contrast key features of organisms. However, phylogenetic analyses show that similar body plans have arisen independently in different groups of organisms. As such, similar body plans may have arisen by convergent evolution and hence may not be informative about evolutionary relationships. **Concept 32.4** To reconstruct the evolutionary history of animal life, researchers collect morphological and molecular data and use cladistic methods to analyze that data. In a cladistic approach, shared derived (morphological and molecular) characters are used to place organisms into a nested hierarchy of monophyletic clades.

Test Your Understanding
1. a **2.** d **3.** e **4.** c **5.** b
7.

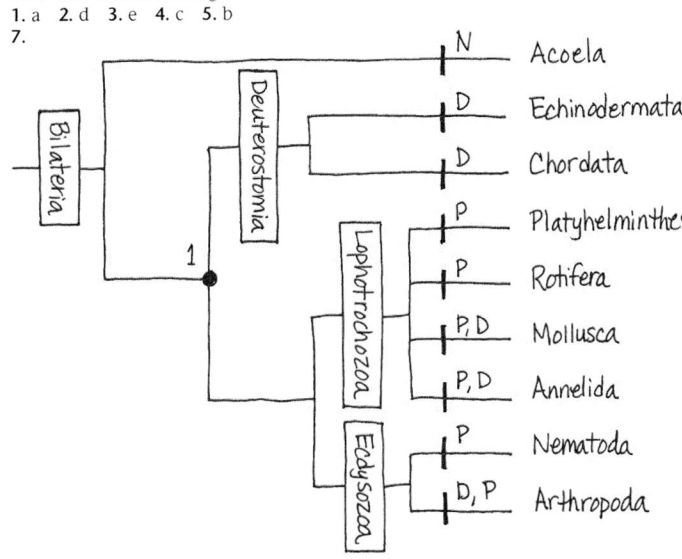

Based on the phylogeny, the ancestral condition in bilaterians may have been similar to that in Acoela, where the blastopore closes and the mouth forms elsewhere (N); however, it is also possible that blastopore fate in Acoela is a derived trait and hence is not informative about the ancestral condition. Although the phylogeny indicates that blastopore fate has changed multiple times over the course of evolution, a precise estimate cannot be made. For example, if we assume that the common ancestor of all non-Acoela bilaterians (marked with a 1 on the tree) exhibited protostomy, then blastopore fate has changed at least five times: once in common ancestor 1, once in Deuterostomia, at least once in Mollusca, at least once in Annelida, and at least once in Arthropoda. Other assumptions would lead to different estimates.

Chapter 33

Figure Questions

Figure 33.8 Within a reproductive polyp, a cell that gives rise to a medusa would have to divide by meiosis. A resulting haploid cell would then divide repeatedly (by mitosis), forming a haploid medusa. Later, cells in the medusa's gonads would divide by mitosis, forming the haploid eggs and sperm. **Figure 33.11** Adding fertilizer to the water supply would probably increase the abundance of algae, and that, in turn, would likely increase the abundance of snails (which eat algae). If the water was also contaminated with infected human feces, an increase in the number of snails would likely lead to an increase in the abundance of blood flukes (which require snails as an intermediate host). As a result, the occurrence of schistosomiasis might increase. **Figure 33.22** The extinctions of freshwater bivalves might lead to an increase in the abundance of photosynthetic protists and bacteria. Because these organisms are at the base of aquatic food webs, increases in their abundance could have major effects on aquatic communities (including both increases and decreases in the abundance of other species). **Figure 33.29** Such a result would be consistent with the *Ubx* and *abd-A Hox* genes having played a major role in the evolution of increased body segment diversity in arthropods. However, by itself, such a result would simply show that the presence of the *Ubx* and *abd-A Hox* genes was *correlated with* an increase in body segment diversity in arthropods; it would not provide direct experimental evidence that the acquisition of the *Ubx* and *adb-A* genes *caused* an increase in arthropod body segment diversity.

Concept Check 33.1

1. The flagella of choanocytes draw water through their collars, which trap food particles. The particles are engulfed by phagocytosis and digested, either by choanocytes or by amoebocytes. **2.** The collar cells of sponges (and some other animals—see Chapter 32) bear a striking resemblance to a choanoflagellate cell. This suggests that the last common ancestor of animals and their protist sister group may have resembled a choanoflagellate. Nevertheless, mesomycetozoans could still be the sister group of animals. If this is the case, the lack of collar cells in mesomycetozoans would indicate that over time their structure evolved in ways that caused it to no longer resemble a choanoflagellate cell. It is also possible that choanoflagellates and sponges share similar-looking collar cells as a result of convergent evolution.

Concept Check 33.2

1. Both the polyp and the medusa are composed of an outer epidermis and an inner gastrodermis separated by a gelatinous layer, the mesoglea. The polyp is a cylindrical form that adheres to the substrate by its aboral end; the medusa is a flattened, mouth-down form that moves freely in the water. 2. Cnidarian stinging cells (cnidocytes) function in defense and prey capture. They contain capsule-like organelles (cnidae), which in turn contain coiled threads. The threads either inject poison or stick to and entangle small prey. 3. Evolution is not goal oriented; hence, it would not be correct to argue that cnidarians were not "highly evolved" simply because their form had changed relatively little over the past 560 million years. Instead, the fact that cnidarians have persisted for hundreds of millions of years indicates that the cnidarian body plan is a highly successful one.

Concept Check 33.3

1. Tapeworms can absorb food from their environment and release ammonia into their environment through their body surface because their body is very flat, due in part to the lack of a coelom. 2. The inner tube is the alimentary canal, which runs the length of the body. The outer tube is the body wall. The two tubes are separated by the coelom. 3. All molluscs have inherited a foot from their common ancestor. However, in different groups of molluscs, the structure of the foot has been modified over time (by natural selection) in ways that reflect how the foot is used in locomotion by members of each clade. In gastropods, the foot is used as a holdfast or to move slowly on the substrate. In cephalopods, the foot has been modified into part of the tentacles and into an excurrent siphon, through which water is propelled (resulting in movement in the opposite direction).

Concept Check 33.4

1. Nematodes lack body segments and a true coelom; annelids have both. 2. The arthropod exoskeleton, which had already evolved in the ocean, allow terrestrial species to retain water and support their bodies on land. Wings allow them to disperse quickly to new habitats and to find food and mates. The tracheal system allows for efficient gas exchange despite the presence of an exoskeleton. 3. Arthropod mouthparts are modified appendages, which are bilaterally paired. As a result, the mouthparts come into contact by moving laterally, not up and down. 4. Yes. Under the traditional hypothesis, we would expect body segmentation to be controlled by similar *Hox* genes in annelids and arthropods. However, if annelids are in Lophotrochozoa and arthropods are in Ecdysozoa, body segmentation may have evolved independently in these two groups. In such a case, we might expect that different *Hox* genes would control the development of body segmentation in the two clades.

Concept Check 33.5

1. Each tube foot consists of an ampulla and a podium. When the ampulla squeezes, it forces water into the podium, which causes the podium to expand and contact the substrate. Adhesive chemicals are then secreted from the base of the podium, thereby attaching the podium to the substrate. 2. Both insects and nematodes are members of Ecdysozoa, one of the three major clades of bilaterians. Therefore, a characteristic shared by *Drosophila* and *Caenorhabditis* may be informative for other members of their clade—but not necessarily for members of Deuterostomia. Instead, Figure 33.2 suggests that a species within Echinodermata or Chordata might be a more appropriate invertebrate model organism from which to draw inferences about humans and other vertebrates. 3. Echinoderms include species with a wide range of body forms, some of which are shown in Figure 33.40. However, even echinoderms that look very different from one another, such as sea stars and sea cucumbers, share characteristics unique to their phylum, including a water vascular system and tube feet. The differences between echinoderm species illustrate the diversity of life, while the characteristics they share illustrate the unity of life. The match between organisms and their environments can be seen in such echinoderm features as the eversible stomachs of sea stars (enabling them to digest prey that are larger than their mouth) and the complex, jaw-like structure that sea urchins use to eat seaweed.

Summary of Key Concepts Questions

Concept 33.1 The sponge body consists of two layers of cells, both of which are in contact with water. As a result, gas exchange and waste removal occur as substances diffuse into and out of the cells of the body. Choanocytes and amoebocytes ingest food particles from the surrounding water. Choanocytes also release food particles to amoebocytes, which then digest the food particles and deliver nutrients to other cells. **Concept 33.2** The cnidarian body plan consists of a sac with a central digestive compartment, the gastrovascular cavity. The single opening to this compartment serves as both a mouth and an anus. The two main variations on this body plan are sessile polyps (which adhere to the substrate at the end of the body opposite to the mouth/anus) and motile medusae (which move freely through the water and resemble flattened, mouth-down versions of polyps). **Concept 33.3** No. Some lophotrochozoans have a crown of ciliated tentacles that function in feeding (called a lophophore), while others go through a distinctive developmental stage known as trochophore larvae. Many other lophotrochozoans do not have either of these features. As a result, the clade is defined primarily by DNA similarities, not morphological similarities. **Concept 33.4** Many nematode species live in soil and in sediments on the bottom of bodies of water. These free-living species play important roles in decomposition and nutrient cycling. Other nematodes are parasites, including many species that attack the roots of plants and some that attack animals (including humans). Arthropods have profound effects on all aspects of ecology. In aquatic

environments, crustaceans play key roles as grazers (of algae), scavengers, and predators, and some species, such as krill, are important sources of food for whales and other vertebrates. On land, it is difficult to think of features of the natural world that are not affected in some way by insects and other arthropods, such as spiders and ticks. There are more than 1 million species of insects, many of which have enormous ecological effects as herbivores, predators, parasites, decomposers, and vectors of disease. Insects are also key sources of food for many organisms, including humans in some regions of the world. **Concept 33.5** Echinoderms and chordates are both members of Deuterostomia, one of the three main clades of bilaterian animals. As such, chordates (including humans) are more closely related to echinoderms than we are to animals in any of the other phyla covered in this chapter. Nevertheless, echinoderms and chordates have evolved independently for over 500 million years. This statement does not contradict the close relationship of echinoderms and chordates, but it does make clear that "close" is a relative term indicating that these two phyla are more closely related to each other than either is to animal phyla not in Deuterostomia.

Test Your Understanding

1. a 2. d 3. b 4. e 5. c 6. d
7.

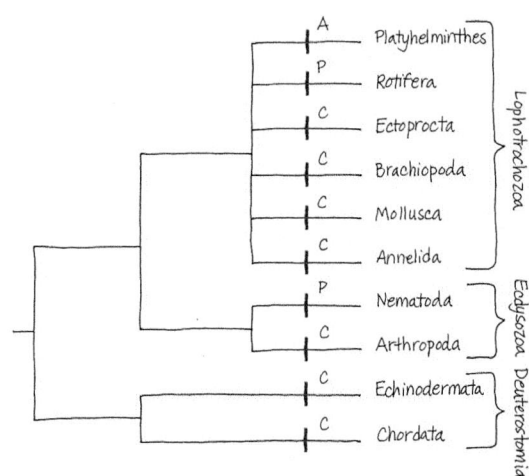

(a) Both phyla in Deuterostomia are coelomates, suggesting that their most recent common ancestor had a true coelom. Lophotrochozoa contains one phylum of acoelomates (Platyhelminthes), one phylum of pseudocoelomates (Rotifera), and four phyla of coelomates (Ectoprocta, Brachiopoda, Mollusca, Annelida); thus, we cannot, from this information alone, infer the condition of the most recent common ancestor shared by these phyla. Similarly, since Ecdysozoa contains one phylum of pseudocoelomates (Nematoda) and one phylum of coelomates (Arthropoda), we cannot infer whether their most recent common ancestor had a true coelom or not. (b) Depending on whether or not the last common ancestor of Bilateria had a true coelom, the presence of a true coelom has either been lost or gained multiple times during the evolutionary history of bilaterians. Thus, the presence of a true coelom appears to have changed over the course of evolution.

Chapter 34

Figure Questions

Figure 34.6 Results in these figures suggest that specific *Hox* genes, as well as the order in which they are expressed, have been highly conserved over the course of evolution. **Figure 34.20** *Tiktaalik* was a lobe-fin fish that had both fish and tetrapod characters. Like a fish, *Tiktaalik* had fins, scales, and gills. As described by Darwin's concept of descent with modification, such shared characters can be attributed to descent from ancestral species—in this case, *Tiktaalik*'s descent from fish ancestors. *Tiktaalik* also had traits that were unlike a fish, but like a tetrapod, including a flat skull, a neck, a full set of ribs, and the skeletal structure of its fin. These characters illustrate the second part of descent with modification, showing how ancestral features had become modified over time. **Figure 34.21** Sometime between 380 mya and 340 mya. We can infer this because amphibians must have originated after the most recent common ancestor of *Tulerpeton* and living tetrapods (and that ancestor originated 380 mya), but no later than the date of the earliest known fossils of amphibians (shown in the figure as 340 mya). **Figure 34.25** Crocodilians. Among extant amniotes, crocodilians are the sister group of birds. Hence, it is likely that DNA sequences in birds are more similar to those in crocodilians than they are to those of more distantly related amniotes. **Figure 34.37** In general, the process of exaptation occurs as a structure that had one function acquires a different function via a series of intermediate stages. Each of these intermediate stages typically has some function in the organism in which it is found. The incorporation of articular and quadrate bones into the mammalian ear illustrates exaptation because these bones originally evolved as part of the jaw, where they functioned as the jaw hinge, but over time they became co-opted for another function, namely the transmission of sound. **Figure 34.43** The phylogeny shows humans as the sister group to the lineage that contains chimpanzees and bonobos. This relationship is not consistent with humans as having descended from either chimpanzees or bonobos. If humans had descended from chimpanzees, for example, the human lineage would be nested within the chimpanzee lineage, much as birds are nested within the reptile clade (see Figure 34.25). **Figure 34.50** No. The phylogeny shown in RESULTS does not include any information on when the branch points occurred, nor is it scaled by time. Thus, although the phylogeny shows the relative order in which lineages diverged, we cannot infer when those events took place.

Concept Check 34.1

1. The four characters are a notochord; a dorsal, hollow nerve chord; pharyngeal slits or clefts; and a muscular, post-anal tail. **2.** In humans, these characters are present only in the embryo. The notochord becomes disks between the vertebrae, the tail is almost completely lost, and the pharyngeal clefts develop into various adult structures. **3.** Not necessarily. It would be possible that the chordate common ancestor had this gene, which was then lost in the lancelet lineage and retained in other chordates. However, it would also be possible that the chordate common ancestor lacked this gene; this could occur if the gene originated after lancelets diverged from other chordates but before tunicates diverged from other chordates.

Concept Check 34.2

1. Hagfishes have a head and skull made of cartilage, plus a small brain, sensory organs, and tooth-like structures. They have a neural crest, gill slits, and more extensive organ systems. In addition, hagfishes have slime glands that ward off predators and may repel competing scavengers. **2.** *Myllokunmingia*. Fossils of this organism provide evidence of ear capsules and eye capsules; these structures are part of the skull. Thus, *Myllokunmingia* is considered a craniate, as are humans. *Haikouella* did not have a skull. **3.** Such a finding suggests that early organisms with a head were favored by natural selection in several different evolutionary lineages. However, while a logical argument can be made that having a head was advantageous, fossils alone do not constitute proof.

Concept Check 34.3

1. Lampreys have a round, rasping mouth, which they use to attach to fish. Conodonts had two sets of mineralized dental elements, which may have been used to impale prey and cut it into smaller pieces. **2.** In armored jawless vertebrates, bone served as external armor that may have provided protection from predators. Some species also had mineralized mouthparts, which could be used for either predation or scavenging. Still others had mineralized fin rays, which may have enabled them to swim more rapidly and with greater steering control.

Concept Check 34.4

1. Both are gnathostomes and have jaws, four clusters of *Hox* genes, enlarged forebrains, and lateral line systems. Shark skeletons consist mainly of cartilage, whereas tuna have bony skeletons. Sharks also have a spiral valve. Tuna have an operculum and a swim bladder, as well as flexible rays supporting their fins. **2.** Aquatic gnathostomes have jaws (an adaptation for feeding) and paired fins and a tail (adaptations for swimming). Aquatic gnathostomes also typically have streamlined bodies for efficient swimming and swim bladders or other mechanisms (such as oil storage in sharks) for buoyancy. **3.** Yes, that could have happened. The paired appendages of aquatic gnathostomes other than the lobe-fins could have served as a starting point for the evolution of limbs. The colonization of land by aquatic gnathostomes other than the lobe-fins might have been facilitated in lineages that possessed lungs, as that would have enabled those organisms to breathe air.

Concept Check 34.5

1. Tetrapods are thought to have originated about 365 million years ago when the fins of some lobe-fins evolved into the limbs of tetrapods. In addition to their four limbs with digits—a key derived trait for which the group is named—other derived traits of tetrapods include a neck (consisting of vertebrae that separate the head from the rest of the body), a pelvic girdle that is fused to the backbone, and a lack of gill slits. **2.** Some fully aquatic species are paedomorphic, retaining larval features for life in water as adults. Species that live in dry environments may avoid dehydration by burrowing or living under moist leaves, and they protect their eggs with foam nests, viviparity, and other adaptations. **3.** Many amphibians spend part of their life cycle in aquatic environments and part on land. Thus, they may be exposed to a wide range of environmental problems, including water and air pollution and the loss or degradation of aquatic and/or terrestrial habitats. In addition, amphibians have highly permeable skin, providing relatively little protection from external conditions, and their eggs do not have a protective shell.

Concept Check 34.6

1. The amniotic egg provides protection to the embryo and allows the embryo to develop on land, eliminating the necessity of a watery environment for reproduction. Another key adaptation is rib cage ventilation, which improves the efficiency of air intake and may have allowed early amniotes to dispense with breathing through their skin. Finally, not breathing through their skin allowed amniotes to develop relatively impermeable skin, thereby conserving water. **2.** Yes. Although snakes lack limbs, they descended from lizards with legs. Some snakes retain vestigial pelvic and leg bones, providing evidence of their descent from an ancestor with legs. **3.** Birds have weight-saving modifications, including the absence of teeth, a urinary bladder, and a second ovary in females. The wings and feathers are adaptations that facilitate flight, and so are efficient respiratory and circulatory systems that support a high metabolic rate.

4.

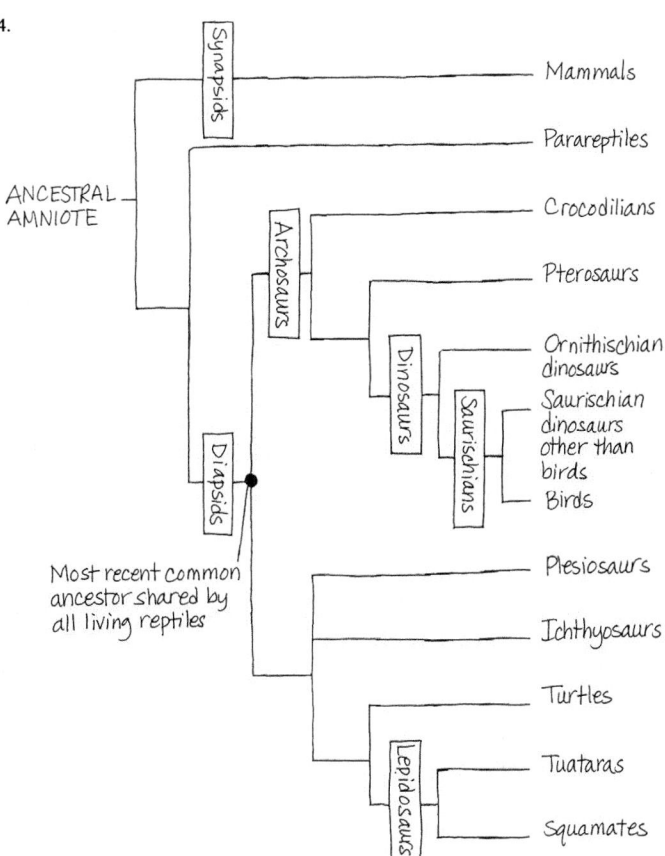

Under this convention, the reptiles would consist of all groups in Figure 34.25 except parareptiles and mammals.

Concept Check 34.7

1. Monotremes lay eggs. Marsupials give birth to very small live young that attach to a nipple in the mother's pouch, where they complete development. Eutherians give birth to more developed live young. **2.** Hands and feet adapted for grasping, flat nails, large brain, forward-looking eyes on a flat face, parental care, and movable big toe and thumb **3.** Mammals are endothermic, enabling them to live in a wide range of habitats. Milk provides young with a balanced set of nutrients, and hair and a layer of fat under the skin help mammals retain heat. Mammals have differentiated teeth, enabling them to eat many different kinds of food. Mammals also have relatively large brains, and many species are capable learners. Following the mass extinction at the end of the Cretaceous period, the absence of large terrestrial dinosaurs may have opened many new ecological niches to mammals, promoting their adaptive radiation. Continental drift also isolated many groups of mammals from one another, promoting the formation of many new species.

Concept Check 34.8

1. Hominins are a clade within the ape clade that includes humans and all species more closely related to humans than other apes. The derived characters of hominins include bipedal locomotion and relatively larger brains. **2.** In hominins, bipedal locomotion evolved long before large brain size. *Homo ergaster*, for example, was fully upright, bipedal, and as tall as modern humans, but its brain was significantly smaller than that of modern humans. **3.** Yes, both can be correct. *Homo sapiens* may have established populations outside of Africa as early as 115,000 years ago, as indicated by the fossil record. However, those populations may have left few or no descendants today. Instead, all living humans may have descended from Africans that spread from Africa roughly 50,000 years ago, as indicated by genetic data.

Summary of Key Concepts Questions

Concept 34.1 Lancelets are the most basal group of living chordates, and as adults they have key derived characters of chordates. This suggests that the chordate common ancestor may have resembled a lancelet in having an anterior end with a mouth along with the following four derived characters: a notochord; a dorsal, hollow nerve cord; pharyngeal slits or clefts; and a muscular, post-anal tail. **Concept 34.2** Craniates have a head and a more extensive muscular system than lancelets or tunicates. These features enable craniates to coordinate and perform more complex behaviors than found in lancelets and tunicates. Basal craniates (the hagfishes), for example, are scavengers that locate and feed on worms and dead or sick fishes. In contrast, lancelets and tunicates feed by filtering food items from the water. **Concept 34.3** Conodonts, among the earliest vertebrates in the fossil record, were very abundant for over 300 million years. While jawless, their well-developed teeth provide early signs of bone formation. Other species of jawless vertebrates developed armor on the outside of their bodies, which probably helped protect them from predators. Like lampreys, these species had paired fins for locomotion and an inner ear with semicircular canals that provided a sense of balance. There were many species of these armored jawless vertebrates, but they all became extinct by the close of the Devonian period, 359 million years ago. **Concept 34.4** The origin of jaws altered how fossil gnathostomes obtained food, which in turn had large effects on ecological interactions. Predators could use their jaws to grab prey or remove chunks of flesh, stimulating the evolution of increasingly sophisticated means of defense in prey species. Evidence for these changes can be found in the fossil record, which includes fossils of 10-m-long predators with remarkably powerful jaws, as well as lineages of well-defended prey species whose bodies were covered by armored plates. **Concept 34.5** Amphibians require water for reproduction; their bodies can lose water rapidly through their moist, highly permeable skin; and amphibian eggs do not have a shell and hence are vulnerable to desiccation. **Concept 34.6** Birds are descended from theropod dinosaurs, and dinosaurs are nested within the archosaur lineage, one of the two main reptile lineages. Thus, the other living archosaur reptiles, the crocodilians, are more closely related to birds than they are to non-archosaur reptiles such as lizards. As a result, birds are considered reptiles. (Note that if reptiles were defined as excluding birds, the reptiles would not form a clade; instead, the reptiles would be a paraphyletic group.) **Concept 34.7** Mammals are members of a group of amniotes called synapsids. Early (nonmammalian) synapsids laid eggs and had a sprawling gait. Fossil evidence shows that mammalian features arose gradually over a period of more than 100 million years. For example, the jaw was modified over time in non-mammalian synapsids, eventually coming to resemble that of a mammal. By 180 million years ago, the first mammals had appeared. There were many species of early mammals, but most of them were small, and they were not abundant or dominant members of their community. Mammals did not rise to ecological dominance until after the extinction of the dinosaurs. **Concept 34.8** The fossil record shows that from 4.5 to 2.5 million years ago, a wide range of hominin species walked upright but had relatively small brain sizes. About 2.5 million years ago, the first members of genus *Homo* emerged. These species used tools and had larger brains than those of earlier hominins. Fossil evidence indicates that multiple members of our genus were alive at any given point in time. Furthermore, until about 1.3 million years ago, these various *Homo* species also coexisted with members of earlier hominin lineages, such as *Paranthropus*. The different hominins alive at the same periods of time varied in body size, body shape, brain size, dental morphology, and the capacity for tool use. Ultimately, except for *Homo sapiens*, all of these species became extinct. Thus, human evolution is viewed not as an evolutionary path leading to *H. sapiens*, but rather as an evolutionary tree with many branches—the only surviving lineage of which is our own.

Test Your Understanding
1. e   2. c   3. a   4. b   5. c   6. c   8. (a) Because brain size tends to increase consistently in such lineages, we can conclude that natural selection favored the evolution of larger brains and hence that the benefits outweighed the costs. (b) As long as the benefits of brains that are large relative to body size are greater than the costs, large brains can evolve. Natural selection might favor the evolution of brains that are large relative to body size because such brains confer an advantage in obtaining mates and/or an advantage in survival.
(c)

Adult mortality tends to be lower in birds with larger brains.

Chapter 35

Figure Questions
Figure 35.9 The finding might suggest that the tan-colored trichomes deter the beetles by some means other than physically obstructing the beetles. Perhaps they contain a chemical that is harmful or distasteful to the beetles. **Figure 35.17** Pith and cortex are defined, respectively, as ground tissue that is internal and ground tissue that is external to vascular tissue. Since vascular bundles of monocot stems are scattered throughout the ground tissue, there is no clear distinction between internal and external relative to the vascular tissue. **Figure 35.19** The vascular cambium produces growth that increases the diameter of a stem or root. The tissues that are exterior to the vascular cambium cannot keep pace with the growth because their cells no longer divide. As a result, these tissues rupture. **Figure 35.31** Every root epidermal cell would develop a root hair. **Figure 35.33** Another example of homeotic gene mutation is the *Drosophila* mutation depicted in Figure 18.20, in which a mutation in a *Hox* gene causes legs to form in place of antennae. **Figure 35.34** The flower would consist of nothing but carpels.

Concept Check 35.1
1. The vascular tissue system connects leaves and roots, allowing sugars to move from leaves to roots in the phloem and allowing water and minerals to move to the leaves in the xylem.   2. (a) large axillary buds; (b) petioles; (c) a bulb, an underground shoot with a small stem and large storage leaves; (d) storage roots   3. To get sufficient energy from photosynthesis, we would need lots of surface area exposed to the sun. This large surface-to-volume ratio, however, would create a new problem—evaporative water loss. We would have to be permanently connected to a water source—the soil, also our source of minerals. In short, we would probably look and behave very much like plants.   4. As plant cells enlarge, they typically form a huge central vacuole that contains a dilute watery sap. Central vacuoles enable plant cells to become large with only a minimal investment of new cytoplasm. The orientation of the cellulose microfibrils in plant cell walls affects the growth pattern of cells.

Concept Check 35.2
1. Primary growth arises from apical meristems and involves production and elongation of organs. Secondary growth arises from lateral meristems and adds to the girth of roots and stems.   2. Your dividing cells are normally limited in the types of cells they can form. In contrast, the products of cell division in a plant meristem can differentiate into all the types of plant cells.   3. The largest, oldest leaves would be lowest on the shoot. Since they would probably be heavily shaded, they would not photosynthesize much regardless of their size.   4. No, the carrot roots will probably be smaller at the end of the second year because the food stored in the root will be used to produce flowers, fruits, and seeds.

Concept Check 35.3
1. In roots, primary growth occurs in three successive stages, moving away from the tip of the root: the zones of cell division, elongation, and differentiation. In shoots, it occurs at the tip of apical buds, with leaf primordia arising along the sides of an apical meristem. Most growth in length occurs in older internodes below the shoot tip.   2. No. Because vertically oriented leaves, such as maize, can capture light equally on both sides of the leaf, you would expect them to have mesophyll cells that are not differentiated into palisade and spongy layers. This is typically the case. Also, vertical leaves usually have stomata on both leaf surfaces.   3. Root hairs are cellular extensions that increase the surface area of the root epidermis, thereby enhancing the absorption of minerals and water. Microvilli are extensions that increase the absorption of nutrients by increasing the surface area of the gut.

Concept Check 35.4
1. The sign will still be 2 m above the ground because this part of the tree is no longer growing in length (primary growth); it is now growing only in thickness (secondary growth).   2. Stomata must be able to close because evaporation is much more intensive from leaves than from the trunks of woody trees as a result of the higher surface-to-volume ratio in leaves.   3. Since there is little temperature variation in the tropics, the growth rings of a tree from the tropics would be difficult to discern unless the tree came from an area that had pronounced wet and dry seasons.   4. Girdling removes an entire ring of secondary phloem (part of the bark), completely preventing transport of sugars and starches from the shoots to the roots.

Concept Check 35.5
1. Although all the living vegetative cells of a plant have the same genome, they differentiate to have different forms and functions because of differential gene expression.   2. Plants show indeterminate growth; juvenile and mature phases are found on the same individual plant; cell differentiation in plants is more dependent on final position than on lineage.   3. In theory, tepals could arise if *B* gene activity was present in all three of the outer whorls of the flower.

Summary of Key Concepts Questions
35.1 Here are a few examples: The cuticle of leaves and stems protects these structures from desiccation. Collenchyma and sclerenchyma cells have thick walls that provide support for plants. Strong, branching root systems help anchor the plant in the soil.   **35.2** All plant organs and tissues are ultimately derived by meristematic activity.   **35.3** Lateral roots emerge from the pericycle and destroy plant cells as they emerge. In stems, branches arise from axillary buds and do not destroy any cells.   **35.4** With the evolution of secondary growth, plants were able to grow taller and shade competitors.   **35.5** The orientation of cellulose microfibrils in the innermost layers of the cell wall causes this growth along one axis. Microtubules play a key role in regulating the plane of cell expansion. It is the orientation of microtubules in the cell's outermost cytoplasm that determines the orientation of cellulose microfibrils.

Test Your Understanding
1. d   2. c   3. c   4. a   5. b   6. e   7. d
8.

Chapter 36

Figure Questions

Figure 36.3 The leaves are being produced in a counterclockwise spiral. **Figure 36.4** A higher leaf area index will not necessarily increase photosynthesis because of upper leaves shading lower leaves. **Figure 36.7** A proton pump inhibitor would depolarize the membrane potential because fewer H^+ ions would be pumped out across the plasma membrane. The immediate effect of an inhibitor of the H^+/sucrose transporter would be to hyperpolarize the membrane potential because fewer H^+ ions would be leaking back into the cell through these co-transporters. An inhibitor of the H^+/NO_3^- cotransporter would have no effect on the membrane potential because the simultaneous cotransport of a positively charged ion and a negatively charged ion has no net effect on charge difference across the membrane. An inhibitor of the K^+ ion channels would decrease the membrane potential because additional positively charged ions would not be accumulating outside the cell. **Figure 36.10** The Casparian strip blocks water and minerals from moving between endodermal cells or moving around an endodermal cell via the cell's wall. Therefore, water and minerals must pass through an endodermal cell's plasma membrane. **Figure 36.19** Because the xylem is under negative pressure (tension), excising a stylet that had been inserted into a tracheid or vessel element would probably introduce air into the cell. No xylem sap would exude unless positive root pressure was predominant.

Concept Check 36.1

1. Vascular plants must transport minerals and water absorbed by the roots to all the other parts of the plant. They must also transport sugars from sites of production to sites of use.   2. Many features of plant architecture affect self-shading, including leaf arrangement, leaf and stem orientation, and leaf area index.   3. Increased stem elongation would raise the plant's upper leaves. Erect leaves and reduced lateral branching would make the plant less subject to shading by the encroaching neighbors.   4. As discussed in Chapter 35 (p. 741), pruning shoot tips removes apical dominance, resulting in axillary buds growing into lateral shoots (branches). This branching produces a bushier plant with a higher leaf area index.   5. Fungal hyphae are long, thin filaments that form a large interwoven network in the soil. Their high surface-to-volume ratio is an adaptation that enhances the absorption of materials from the soil.

Concept Check 36.2

1. The cell's ψ_P is 0.7 MPa. In a solution with a ψ of –0.4 MPa, the cell's ψ_P at equilibrium would be 0.3 MPa.   2. The cells would still adjust to changes in their osmotic environment, but their responses would be slower. Although aquaporins do not affect the water potential gradient across membranes, they allow for more rapid osmotic adjustments.   3. If tracheids and vessel elements were alive at maturity, their cytoplasm would impede water movement, preventing rapid long-distance transport.   4. The protoplasts would burst. Because the cytoplasm has many dissolved solutes, water would enter the protoplast continuously without reaching equilibrium. (When present, the cell wall prevents rupturing by excessive expansion of the protoplast.)

Concept Check 36.3

1. Because water-conducting xylem cells are dead at maturity and form essentially hollow tubes, they offer little resistance to water flow, and their thick walls prevent the cells from collapsing from the negative pressure inside.   2. At dawn, a drop is exuded because the xylem is under positive pressure due to root pressure. At noon, the xylem is under negative pressure tension when it is cut and the xylem sap is pulled away from the cut surface up into the stem. Root pressure cannot keep pace with the increased rate of transpiration at noon.   3. The endodermis regulates the passage of water-soluble solutes by requiring all such molecules to cross a selectively permeable membrane. Presumably, the inhibitor never reaches the plant's photosynthetic cells.   4. Perhaps greater root mass helps compensate for the lower water permeability of the plasma membranes.   5. The Casparian strip and tight junctions both prevent movement of fluid between cells.

Concept Check 36.4

1. Stomatal opening at dawn is controlled mainly by light, CO_2 concentrations, and a circadian rhythm. Environmental stresses such as drought, high temperature, and wind can stimulate stomata to close during the day. Water deficiency can trigger release of the plant hormone abscisic acid, which signals guard cells to close stomata.   2. The activation of the proton pump of stomatal cells would cause the guard cells to take up K^+. The increased turgor of the guard cells would lock the stomata open and lead to extreme evaporation from the leaf.   3. After the flowers are cut, transpiration from any leaves and from the petals (which are modified leaves) will continue to draw water up the xylem. If cut flowers are transferred directly to a vase, air pockets in xylem vessels prevent delivery of water from the vase to the flowers. Cutting stems again underwater, a few centimeters from the original cut, will sever the xylem above the air pocket. The water droplets prevent another air pocket from forming while placing the flowers in a vase.   4. Water molecules are in constant motion, traveling at different rates. The average speed of these particles depends on the water's temperature. If water molecules gain enough energy, the most energetic molecules near the liquid's surface will impart sufficient speed, and therefore sufficient kinetic energy, to cause water molecules to propel away from the liquid in the form of gaseous molecules or, more simply, as water vapor. As the particles with the highest kinetic energy levels evaporate, the average kinetic energy of the remaining liquid decreases. Because a liquid's temperature is directly related to the average kinetic energy of its molecules, the liquid cools as it evaporates.

Concept Check 36.5

1. In both cases, the long-distance transport is a bulk flow driven by a pressure difference at opposite ends of tubes. Pressure is generated at the source end of a sieve tube by the loading of sugar and resulting osmotic flow of water into the phloem, and this pressure *pushes* sap from the source end to the sink end of the tube. In contrast, transpiration generates a negative pressure potential (tension) as a force that *pulls* the ascent of xylem sap.   2. The main sources are fully grown leaves (by photosynthesis) and fully developed storage organs (by breakdown of starch). Roots, buds, stems, expanding leaves, and fruits are powerful sinks because they are actively growing. A storage organ may be a sink in the summer when accumulating carbohydrates, but a source in the spring when breaking down starch into sugar for growing shoot tips.   3. Positive pressure, whether it be in the xylem when root pressure predominates or in the sieve-tube elements of the phloem, requires active transport. Most long-distance transport in the xylem depends on bulk flow driven by negative pressure potential generated ultimately by the evaporation of water from the leaf and does not require living cells.   4. The spiral slash prevents optimal bulk flow of the phloem sap to the root sinks. Therefore, more phloem sap can move from the source leaves to the fruit sinks, making them sweeter.

Concept Check 36.6

1. Plasmodesmata, unlike gap junctions, have the ability to pass RNA, proteins, and viruses from cell to cell.   2. Long-distance signaling is critical for the integrated functioning of all large organisms, but the speed of such integration is much less critical to plants because their responses to the environment, unlike those of animals, do not typically involve rapid movements.   3. Although this strategy would eliminate the systemic spread of viral infections, it would also severely impact the development of the plants.

Summary of Key Concepts Questions

36.1 Plants with tall shoots and elevated leaf canopies generally had an advantage over shorter competitors. A consequence of the selective pressure for tall shoots was the further separation of leaves from roots. This separation created problems for the transport of materials between root and shoot systems. Plants with xylem cells were more successful at supplying their shoot systems with soil resources (water and minerals). Similarly, those with phloem cells were more successful at supplying sugar sinks with carbohydrates. **36.2** Xylem sap is usually pulled up the plant by transpiration, much more often than it is pushed up the plant by root pressure. **36.3** Hydrogen bonds are necessary for the cohesion of water molecules to each other and for the adhesion of water to other materials, such as cell walls. Both adhesion and cohesion of water molecules are involved in the ascent of xylem sap under conditions of negative pressure. **36.4** Although stomata account for most of the water lost from plants, they are necessary for exchange of gases—for example, for the uptake of carbon dioxide needed for photosynthesis. **36.5** Although the movement of phloem sap depends on bulk flow, the pressure gradient that drives phloem transport depends on the osmotic uptake of water in response to the loading of sugars into sieve-tube elements at sugar sources. Phloem loading depends on H^+ cotransport processes that ultimately depend on H^+ gradients established by active H^+ pumping. **36.6** Voltage between cells, cytoplasmic pH, cytoplasmic calcium concentration, and viral movement proteins all affect symplastic communication, as do developmental changes in the number of plasmodesmata.

Test Your Understanding

1. c 2. a 3. b 4. b 5. c 6. e 7. c 8. a 9. d
10.

Chapter 37

Figure Questions

Figure 37.3 Anions. Because cations are bound to soil particles, they are less likely to be lost from the soil following heavy rains. **Table 37.1** Fluorine, selenium, and chromium. Plants may contain more than 50 elements, but only a few are essential for the plant to complete its life cycle. The others, including fluorine, selenium and chromium, are present but not essential for survival. **Figure 37.11** The legume plants benefit because the bacteria fix nitrogen that is absorbed by their roots. The bacteria benefit because they acquire photosynthetic products from the plants. **Figure 37.12** All three plant tissue systems are affected. Root hairs (dermal tissue) are modified to allow *Rhizobium* penetration. The cortex (ground tissue) and pericycle (vascular tissue) proliferate during nodule formation. The vascular tissue of the nodule connects to the vascular cylinder of the root to allow for efficient nutrient exchange. **Figure 37.14** If phosphate were the only limiting mineral, then native tree growth would be less severely impacted by the reduction in mycorrhizal associations caused by garlic mustard. Consequently, the competitive advantage of garlic mustard would be reduced by the addition of phosphate to the soil.

Concept Check 37.1

1. Overwatering deprives roots of oxygen. Overfertilizing is wasteful and can lead to soil salinization and water pollution. **2.** As lawn clippings decompose, they restore mineral nutrients to the soil. If they are removed, the minerals lost from the soil must be replaced by fertilization. **3.** Because of their small size and negative charge, clay particles would increase the number of binding sites for cations and water molecules and would therefore increase cation exchange and water retention in the soil. **4.** Due to hydrogen bonding between water molecules, water expands when it freezes, and this causes mechanical fracturing of rocks. Water also coheres to many objects, and this cohesion combined with other forces, such as gravity, can help tug particles from rock. Finally, water, because it is polar, is an excellent solvent that allows many substances, including ions, to become dissolved in solution.

Concept Check 37.2

1. Table 37.1 shows that CO_2 is the source of 90% of a plant's dry weight, supporting Hales's view that plants are nourished mostly by air. **2.** No, because even though macronutrients are required in greater amounts, all essential elements are necessary for the plant to complete its life cycle. **3.** No. The fact that the addition of an element results in an increase in the growth rate of a crop does not mean that the element is strictly required for the plant to complete its life cycle. **4.** Waterlogging displaces air from the soil, leading to low O_2 conditions. Such conditions promote the anaerobic process of alcoholic fermentation in plants, the end product of which is ethanol.

Concept Check 37.3

1. The rhizosphere is a narrow zone in the soil immediately adjacent to living roots. This zone is especially rich in both organic and inorganic nutrients and has a microbial population that is many times greater than the bulk of the soil. **2.** Soil bacteria and mycorrhizae enhance plant nutrition by making certain minerals more available to plants. For example, many types of soil bacteria are involved in the nitrogen cycle, and the hyphae of mycorrhizae provide a large surface area for the absorption of nutrients, particularly phosphate ions. **3.** Saturating rainfall may deplete the soil of oxygen. A lack of soil oxygen would inhibit nitrogen fixation by the peanut root nodules and decrease the nitrogen available to the plant. Alternatively, heavy rain may leach nitrate from the soil. A symptom of nitrogen deficiency is yellowing of older leaves.

Summary of Key Concepts Questions

37.1 The term *ecosystem* refes to the communities of organisms within a given area and their interactions with the physical environment around them. Soil is teeming with many communities of organisms, including bacteria, fungi, animals, and the root systems of plants. The vigor of these individual communities depends on nonliving factors in the soil environment, such as minerals, oxygen, and water, as well as on interactions, both positive and negative, between different communities of organisms. **37.2** No, plants can complete their life cycle when grown hydroponically, that is, in aerated salt solutions containing the proper ratios of all the minerals needed by plants. **37.3** No, some parasitic plants obtain their energy by siphoning off carbon nutrients from other organisms.

Test Your Understanding

1. b **2.** b **3.** a **4.** e **5.** b **6.** b **7.** d **8.** c **9.** d
10.

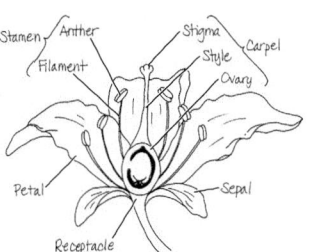

Chapter 38

Figure Questions

Figure 38.4 Having a specific pollinator is more efficient because less pollen gets delivered to flowers of the wrong species. However, it is also a risky strategy: If the pollinator population suffers to an unusual degree from predation, disease, or climate change, then the plant may not be able to produce seeds. **Figure 38.8** In addition to having a single cotyledon, monocots have leaves with parallel leaf venation, scattered vascular bundles in their stems, a fibrous root system, floral parts in threes or multiples of threes, and pollen grains with only one opening. In contrast, dicots have two cotyledons, netlike leaf venation, vascular bundles in a ring, taproots, floral parts in fours or fives or multiples thereof, and pollen grains with three openings. **Figure 38.9** Beans use a hypocotyl hook to push through the soil. The delicate leaves and shoot apical meristem are also protected by being sandwiched between two large cotyledons. The coleoptile of maize seedlings helps protect the emerging leaves. **Figure 38.17** The crown gall bacterium (*Agrobacterium tumefaciens*) normally causes cancer-like growths in susceptible plants. *Agrobacterium* inserts its own genes into plant cells by means of plasmids. These plasmids have been genetically engineered to retain their ability to insert genes into plant cells without causing cancerous growth.

Concept Check 38.1

1. In angiosperms, pollination is the transfer of pollen from an anther to a stigma. Fertilization is the fusion of the egg and sperm to form the zygote; it cannot occur until after the growth of the pollen tube from the pollen grain. **2.** Seed dormancy prevents the premature germination of seeds. A seed will germinate only when the environmental conditions are optimal for the survival of its embryo as a young seedling. **3.** Long styles help to weed out pollen grains that are genetically inferior and not capable of successfully growing long pollen tubes. **4.** No. The haploid (gametophyte) generation of plants is multicellular and arises from spores. The haploid phase of the animal life cycles is a single-celled gamete (egg or sperm) that arises directly from meiosis: There are no spores.

Concept Check 38.2

1. Asexually propagated crops lack genetic diversity. Genetically diverse populations are less likely to become extinct in the face of an epidemic because there is a greater likelihood that a few individuals in the population are resistant. **2.** In the short term, selfing may be advantageous in a population that is so dispersed and sparse that pollen delivery is unreliable. In the long term, however, selfing is an evolutionary dead end because it leads to a loss of genetic diversity that may preclude adaptive evolution. **3.** This might be possible, but satisfactory results would be very unlikely. Both tubers and fruits are tremendous energy sinks. Each plant has only a finite amount of energy to divide between sexual and asexual reproduction. Although a tomato-potato hybrid could, in theory, produce an offspring that makes fruits and tubers equally, these fruits and tubers would be of inferior quality or low yielding.

Concept Check 38.3

1. Traditional breeding and genetic engineering both involve artificial selection for desired traits. However, genetic engineering techniques facilitate faster gene transfer and are not limited to transferring genes between closely related varieties or species. **2.** GM crops may be more nutritious and less susceptible to insect damage or pathogens that invade insect-damaged plants. They also may not require as much chemical spraying. However, unknown risks may include adverse effects on human health and nontarget organisms and the possibility of transgene escape. **3.** *Bt* maize suffers less insect damage; therefore, *Bt* maize plants are less likely to be infected by fumonisin-producing fungi that infect plants through wounds. **4.** In such species, engineering the transgene into the chloroplast DNA would not prevent its escape in pollen; such a method requires that the chloroplast DNA be found only in the egg. An entirely different method of preventing transgene escape would therefore be needed, such as male sterility, apomixis, or self-pollinating closed flowers.

Summary of Key Concepts Questions

38.1 After pollination, a flower typically changes into a fruit. The petals, sepals, and stamens typically fall off the flower. The stigma of the pistil withers and the ovary begins to swell. The ovules (embryonic seeds) inside the ovary begin to mature. **38.2** Asexual reproduction can be advantageous in a stable environment because individual plants that are well suited to that environment pass on all their genes to offspring. Also, asexual reproduction generally results in offspring that are less fragile than the seedlings produced by sexual reproduction. However, sexual reproduction offers the advantage of dispersal of tough seeds. Moreover, sexual reproduction produces genetic variety, which may be advantageous in an unstable environment. The likelihood is better that at least one offspring of sexual reproduction will survive in a changed environment. **38.3** "Golden Rice" has been engineered to produce more vitamin A, thereby raising the nutritional value of rice. A protoxin gene from a soil bacterium has been engineered into *Bt* maize. This protoxin is lethal to invertebrates but harmless to vertebrates. *Bt* crops require less pesticide spraying and have lower levels of fungal infection. The nutritional value of cassava is being increased in many ways by genetic engineering. Enriched levels of protein, iron, and beta-carotene (a vitamin A precursor) have been achieved, and cyanide-producing chemicals have been almost eliminated from the roots.

Test Your Understanding

1. c **2.** a **3.** c **4.** e **5.** c **6.** d **7.** d **8.** c **9.** d
10.

Chapter 39

Figure Questions

Figure 39.4 Panel B in Figure 11.18 shows a branching signal transduction pathway that resembles the branching phytochrome-dependent pathway involved in de-etiolation. **Figure 39.5** To determine which wavelengths of light are most effective in phototropism, you could use a glass prism to split white light into its component colors and see which colors cause the quickest bending (the answer is blue; see Figure 39.16). **Figure 39.6** More auxin would move down the side without the TIBA-containing agar bead, causing greater elongation on this side and, consequently, bending of the coleoptile toward the side with the bead. **Figure 39.7** No. Polar auxin transport depends on the distribution of auxin transport proteins at the basal ends of cells. **Figure 39.17** Yes. The white light, which contains red light, would stimulate seed germination in all treatments. **Figure 39.22** The short-day plant would not flower. The long-day plant would flower. **Figure 39.23** If this were true, florigen would be an inhibitor of flowering, not an inducer.

Concept Check 39.1

1. Dark-grown seedlings are etiolated: They have long stems, underdeveloped root systems, and unexpanded leaves, and their shoots lack chlorophyll. Etiolated growth is beneficial to seeds sprouting under the dark conditions they would encounter underground. By devoting more energy to stem elongation and less to leaf expansion and root growth, a plant increases the likelihood that the shoot will reach the sunlight before its stored foods run out. **2.** Cycloheximide should inhibit de-etiolation by preventing the synthesis of new proteins necessary for de-etiolation. **3.** No. Applying Viagra, like injecting cyclic GMP as described in the text, should cause only a partial de-etiolation response. Full de-etiolation would require activation of the calcium branch of the signal transduction pathway.

Concept Check 39.2
1. Because cytokinins delay leaf senescence and floral parts are modified leaves, cytokinins also delay the senescence of cut flowers. **2.** Fusicoccin's ability to cause an increase in plasma H^+ pump activity has an auxin-like effect and promotes stem cell elongation. **3.** The plant will exhibit a constitutive triple response. Because the kinase that normally prevents the triple response is dysfunctional, the plant will undergo the triple response regardless of whether ethylene is present or the ethylene receptor is functional. **4.** Since ethylene often stimulates its own synthesis, it is under positive-feedback regulation.

Concept Check 39.3
1. Not necessarily. Many environmental factors, such as temperature and light, change over a 24-hour period in the field. To determine whether the enzyme is under circadian control, a scientist would have to demonstrate that its activity oscillates even when environmental conditions are held constant. **2.** Flowering of the species may have been day-neutral or required multiple exposures to short nights. **3.** You might determine which wavelengths of light are most effective and plot an action spectrum. If the action spectrum indicates phytochrome, you could do further experiments to test for red/far-red photosensitivity. **4.** It is impossible to say. To establish that this species is a short-day plant, it would be necessary to establish the critical night length for flowering and that this species only flowers when the night is longer than the critical night length. **5.** According to the action spectrum of photosynthesis, red and blue light are the most effective in photosynthesis. Thus, it is not surprising that plants assess their light environment using blue- and red-light-absorbing photoreceptors.

Concept Check 39.4
1. A plant that overproduces ABA would undergo less evaporative cooling because its stomata would not open as widely. **2.** Plants close to the aisles may be more subject to mechanical stresses caused by passing workers and air currents. The plants nearer to the center of the bench may also be taller as a result of shading and less evaporative stress. **3.** No. Because root caps are involved in sensing gravity, roots that have their root caps removed are almost completely insensitive to gravity.

Concept Check 39.5
1. Some insects increase plants' productivity by eating harmful insects or aiding in pollination. **2.** Mechanical damage breaches a plant's first line of defense against infection, its protective dermal tissue. **3.** No. Pathogens that kill their hosts would soon run out of victims and might themselves go extinct. **4.** Perhaps the breeze dilutes the local concentration of a volatile defense compound that the plants produce.

Summary of Key Concepts Questions
39.1 Signal transduction pathways often activate protein kinases, enzymes that phosphorylate other proteins. Protein kinases can directly activate certain preexisting enzymes by phosphorylating them, or they can regulate gene transcription (and enzyme production) by phosphorylating specific transcription factors. **39.2** Yes, there is truth to the old adage that one bad apple spoils the whole bunch. Ethylene, a gaseous hormone that stimulates ripening, is produced by damaged, infected, or overripe fruits. Ethylene can diffuse to healthy fruit in the "bunch" and stimulate their rapid ripening. **39.3** Plant physiologists proposed the existence of a floral-promoting factor (florigen) based on the fact that a plant induced to flower could induce flowering in a second plant to which it was grafted, even though the second plant was not in an environment that would normally induce flowering in that species. **39.4** Plants subjected to drought stress are often even more resistant to freezing stress because the two types of stress are quite similar. Freezing of water in the extracellular spaces causes free water concentrations outside the cell to decrease. This, in turn, causes free water to leave the cell by osmosis, leading to the dehydration of cytoplasm, much like what is seen in drought stress. **39.5** Chewing insects make plants more susceptible to pathogen invasion by disrupting the waxy cuticle of shoots, thereby creating an opening for infection. Moreover, substances released from damaged cells can serve as nutrients for the invading pathogens.

Test Your Understanding
1. e **2.** c **3.** d **4.** e **5.** b **6.** b **7.** c **8.** e
9.

Chapter 40

Figure Questions
Figure 40.4 Such exchange surfaces are internal in the sense that they are inside the body. However, they are also continuous with openings on the external body surface that contact the environment. **Figure 40.8** The air conditioner would form a second control circuit, cooling the house when air temperature exceeded the set point. Such opposing, or antagonistic, pairs of control circuits increase the effectiveness of a homeostatic mechanism. **Figure 40.14** If a female Burmese python were not incubating eggs, her oxygen consumption would decrease with decreasing temperature, as for any other ectotherm. **Figure 40.17** The transport of nutrients across membranes and the synthesis of RNA and protein are coupled to ATP hydrolysis. These processes proceed spontaneously because there is an overall drop in free energy, with the excess energy given off as heat. Similarly, less than half of the free energy in glucose is captured in the coupled reactions of cellular respiration. The remainder of the energy is released as heat. **Figure 40.21** Nothing. Although genes that show a circadian variation in expression during euthermia exhibit constant RNA levels during hibernation, a gene that shows constant expression during hibernation might also show constant expression during euthermia.

Concept Check 40.1
1. All types of epithelia consist of cells that line a surface, are tightly packed, are situated on top of a basal lamina, and form an active and protective interface with the external environment. **2.** By flattening its ears along its body, the jackrabbit can reduce the exposed surface area of its body and hence the amount of heat lost. However, by placing its ears flat, the jackrabbit reduces its ability to detect potential predators. **3.** You need the nervous system to perceive the danger and provoke a split-second muscular response to keep from falling. The nervous system, however, does not make a direct connection with blood vessels or glucose-storing cells in the liver. Instead, the nervous system triggers the release of a hormone (called epinephrine, or adrenaline) by the endocrine system, bringing about a change in these tissues in just a few seconds.

Concept Check 40.2
1. In the enzyme-catalyzed biosynthetic process, the product of a pathway (in this case, isoleucine) inhibits the pathway that generated it. In thermoregulation, the product of the pathway (a change in temperature) decreases pathway activity by reducing the stimulus. **2.** You would want to put the thermostat close to where you would be spending time, where it would be protected from environmental perturbations, such as direct sunshine, and not right in the path of the output of the heating system. Similarly, the sensors for homeostasis located in the human brain are separated from environmental influences and can monitor conditions in a vital and sensitive tissue. **3.** In convergent evolution, the same biological trait arises independently in two or more species. Gene analysis can provide evidence for an independent origin. In particular, if the genes responsible for the trait in one species lack significant sequence similarity to the corresponding genes in another species, scientists conclude that there is a separate genetic basis for the trait in the two species and thus an independent origin. In the case of circadian rhythms, the clock genes in cyanobacteria appear unrelated to those in humans.

Concept Check 40.3
1. "Wind chill" involves heat loss through convection, as the moving air contributes to heat loss from the skin surface. **2.** The hummingbird, being a very small endotherm, has a very high metabolic rate. If by absorbing sunlight certain flowers warm their nectar, a hummingbird feeding on these flowers is saved the metabolic expense of warming the nectar to its body temperature. **3.** The ice water would cool tissues in your head, including blood that would then circulate throughout your body. This effect would accelerate the return to a normal body temperature. If, however, the ice water reached the eardrum and cooled the blood vessel that supplies the hypothalamus, the hypothalamic thermostat would respond by inhibiting sweating and constricting blood vessels in the skin, slowing cooling elsewhere in the body.

Concept Check 40.4
1. The mouse would consume oxygen at a higher rate because it is an endotherm, so its basal metabolic rate is higher than the ectothermic lizard's standard metabolic rate. **2.** The house cat; smaller animals have a higher metabolic rate per unit body mass and a greater demand for food per unit body mass. **3.** Although penguins do not grow as adults, they increase and decrease in size as they repeatedly form and use energy stores. A significant amount of energy might be stored in fat during part of the year but be used later in the year. Monitoring energy allocation only during the period when energy is stored in fat would lead to the erroneous conclusion that the penguin is growing.

Summary of Key Concepts Questions
40.1 Animals exchange materials with their environment across their body surface, and a spherical shape has the minimum surface area per unit volume. As body size increases, the ratio of surface area to body volume decreases. **40.2** No; even though an animal regulates some aspects of its internal environment, the internal environment fluctuates slightly around set points. Homeostasis is a dynamic state. Furthermore, there are sometimes programmed changes in set points, such as those resulting in radical increases in hormone levels at particular times in development. **40.3** Heat exchange across the skin is a primary mechanism for the regulation of body core temperature, with the result that the skin is cooler than the body core. **40.4** Because small animals have the highest ratio of BMR per unit mass, they have the greatest energetic savings per unit mass during hibernation. Consequently, the selective pressure favoring hibernation during evolution is especially strong for small animals.

Test Your Understanding
1. b **2.** c **3.** a **4.** b **5.** d **6.** c **7.** e

8.

Chapter 41

Figure Questions

Figure 41.2 Just as penguin muscle protein provides amino acids for regrowth of large numbers of feathers, ovalbumin and casein provide amino acids for growth of a fertilized egg or nursing mammal. Thus, the common circumstance is a period of rapid developmental growth. **Figure 41.4** As in the described study, they needed a sample size large enough that they could expect a significant number of neural tube defects in the control group. The information needed to determine the appropriate sample size was the frequency of neural tube defects in first-time pregnancies in the general population. **Figure 41.12** Since enzymes are proteins, and proteins are hydrolyzed in the small intestine, the digestive enzymes in that compartment need to be resistant to enzymatic cleavage other than the cleavage required to activate them. **Figure 41.13** None. Since digestion is completed in the small intestine, tapeworms simply absorb predigested nutrients through their large body surface. **Figure 41.20** Both insulin and glucagon are involved in negative feedback circuits. **Figure 41.22** The wild-type mouse produces leptin after a meal. As the mouse depletes its fat stores, leptin production drops. The mouse eventually regains its appetite, eats another meal, and makes another burst of leptin. Thus, leptin levels would oscillate during the day. Because the *db* mouse cannot respond to leptin, its fat stores are constantly built up through excessive consumption. As a result, leptin is produced continuously and builds up to a high, steady concentration in the blood.

Concept Check 41.1

1. The only essential amino acids are those that an animal cannot synthesize from other molecules. **2.** Many vitamins serve as enzyme cofactors, which, like enzymes themselves, are unchanged by the chemical reactions in which they participate. Therefore, only very small amounts of vitamins are needed. **3.** To identify the essential nutrient missing from an animal's diet, a researcher could supplement the diet with individual nutrients and determine which nutrient eliminates the signs of malnutrition.

Concept Check 41.2

1. A gastrovascular cavity is a digestive pouch with a single opening that functions in both ingestion and elimination; an alimentary canal is a digestive tube with a separate mouth and anus at opposite ends. **2.** As long as nutrients are within the cavity of the alimentary canal, they are in a compartment that is continuous with the outside environment via the mouth and anus and have not yet crossed a membrane to enter the body. **3.** Just as food remains outside the body in a digestive tract, gasoline moves from the fuel tank to the engine, and waste products exit through the exhaust without ever entering the passenger compartment of the automobile. In addition, gasoline, like food, is broken down in a specialized compartment, so that the rest of the automobile (or body) is protected from disassembly. In both cases, high-energy fuels are consumed, complex molecules are broken down into simpler ones, and waste products are eliminated.

Concept Check 41.3

1. By peristalsis, which can squeeze food through the esophagus even without the help of gravity. **2.** Because parietal cells in the stomach pump hydrogen ions to produce HCl, a proton pump inhibitor reduces the acidity of chyme and thus the irritation that occurs when chyme enters the esophagus. **3.** Proteins would be denatured and digested into peptides. Further digestion, to individual amino acids, would require enzymatic secretions found in the small intestine. No digestion of carbohydrates or lipids would occur.

Concept Check 41.4

1. The increased time for transit through the alimentary canal allows for more extensive processing, and the increased surface of the canal area provides greater

opportunity for absorption. **2.** A mammal's digestive system provides mutualistic microbes with an environment that is protected against other microbes by saliva and gastric juice, that is held at a constant temperature conducive to enzyme action, and that provides a steady source of nutrients. **3.** For the yogurt treatment to be effective, the bacteria from yogurt would have to establish a mutualistic relationship with the small intestine, where disaccharides are broken down and sugars are absorbed. Conditions in the small intestine are likely to be very different from those in a yogurt culture. The bacteria might be killed before they reach the small intestine, or they might not be able to grow there in sufficient numbers to aid in digestion.

Concept Check 41.5

1. Over the long term, the body stores excess calories in fat, whether those calories come from fat, carbohydrate, or protein in food. **2.** Both hormones have appetite-suppressing effects on the brain's satiety center. During the course of a day, PYY, secreted by the intestine, suppresses appetite after meals. Over the longer term, leptin, produced by adipose tissue, normally reduces appetite as fat storage increases. **3.** In normal individuals, leptin levels decline during fasting. Individuals in the group with low levels of leptin are likely to be defective in leptin production, so leptin levels would remain low regardless of food intake. Individuals in the group with high leptin levels are likely to be defective in responding to leptin, but they still should shut off leptin production as fat stores are used up.

Summary of Key Concepts Questions

41.1 Since collagen is found in all mammals, a likely explanation is that mammals other than primates and guinea pigs can synthesize vitamin C from other organic molecules. **41.2** A liquid diet containing glucose, amino acids, and other building blocks could be ingested and absorbed without the need for mechanical or chemical digestion. **41.3** The small intestine has a much larger surface area than the stomach. **41.4** The assortment of teeth in our mouth and the short length of our cecum suggest that our ancestors' digestive systems were not specialized for digesting plant material. **41.5** When mealtime arrives, nervous inputs from the brain signal the stomach to prepare to digest food through secretions and churning.

Test Your Understanding

1. a **2.** c **3.** c **4.** d **5.** d **6.** b
7.

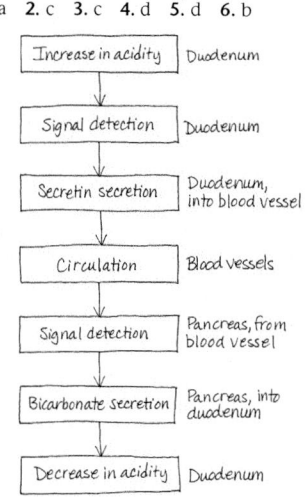

Chapter 42

Figure Questions

Figure 42.2 Although gas exchange might be improved by a steady, one-way flow of fluid, there would likely be inadequate time for food to be digested and nutrients absorbed if fluid flowed through the cavity in this manner. **Figure 42.9** Each feature of the ECG recording, such as the sharp upward spike, occurs once per cardiac cycle. Using the *x*-axis to measure the time in seconds between successive spikes and dividing that number into 60 would yield the heart rate as the number of cycles per minute. **Figure 42.21** The mutations studied by Dr. Hobbs's team inactivate the enzyme. Carriers for these mutations should have roughly half the normal level of PCSK9 activity. The mutations studied by the French researchers have the opposite effect on LDL levels as the inactivating mutations. It is therefore likely that individuals carrying these mutations would have increased PCSK9 activity. **Figure 42.22** The three main lineages are Deuterostomia, Lophotrochozoa, and Ecdysozoa. All three are represented by the animals shown in Figure 42.22: Polychaetes (phylum Annelida) are lophotrochozoans, crayfish (phylum Arthropoda) are ecdysozoans, and sea stars (phylum Echinodermata) are deuterostomes. **Figure 42.26** The reduction in surface tension results from the presence of surfactant. Therefore, for all the infants that had died of RDS, you would expect the amount of surfactant to be near zero. For infants that had died of other causes, you would expect the amount of surfactant to be near zero for weights less than 1,200 g but much greater than zero for weights above 1,200 g. **Figure 42.28** Since exhalation is largely passive, the recoil of the elastic fibers in alveoli helps force air out of the lungs. When alveoli lose their elasticity, as occurs in the disease emphysema, less air is exhaled. Because more air is left in the lungs, less fresh air can be inhaled. With a smaller volume of air exchanged, there is a decrease in the partial pressure gradient that drives gas exchange. **Figure 42.29** Breathing at a rate greater than that needed to meet metabolic demand (hyperventilation) would lower blood CO_2 levels. Sensors in major blood vessels and the medulla would signal the breathing control centers to decrease the rate of contraction of the diaphragm and rib muscles, decreasing the breathing rate and restoring normal CO_2 levels in the blood and other tissues. **Figure 42.30** The resulting increase in tidal volume would enhance ventilation within the lungs, increasing P_{O_2} and decreasing P_{CO_2} in the alveoli. **Figure 42.32** Some CO_2 is dissolved in plasma, some is bound to hemoglobin, and some is converted to bicarbonate ion (HCO_3^-), which is dissolved in plasma.

Concept Check 42.1

1. In both an open circulatory system and a fountain, fluid is pumped through a tube and then returns to the pump after collecting in a pool. **2.** The ability to shut off blood supply to the lungs when the animal is submerged **3.** The O_2 content would be abnormally low because some oxygen-depleted blood returned to the right atrium from the systemic circuit would mix with the oxygen-rich blood in the left atrium.

Concept Check 42.2

1. The pulmonary veins carry blood that has just passed through capillary beds in the lungs, where it accumulated O_2. The venae cavae carry blood that has just passed through capillary beds in the rest of the body, where it lost O_2 to the tissues. **2.** The delay allows the atria to empty completely, filling ventricles fully before they contract. **3.** The heart, like any other muscle, becomes stronger through regular exercise. You would expect a stronger heart to have a greater stroke volume, which would allow for the decrease in heart rate.

Concept Check 42.3

1. The large total cross-sectional area of the capillaries **2.** An increase in blood pressure and cardiac output combined with the diversion of more blood to the skeletal muscles would increase the capacity for action by increasing the rate of blood circulation and delivering more O_2 and nutrients to the skeletal muscles. **3.** Additional hearts could be used to improve blood return from the legs. However, it might be difficult to coordinate the activity of multiple hearts and to maintain adequate blood flow to hearts far from the gas exchange organs.

Concept Check 42.4

1. An increase in the number of white blood cells (leukocytes) may indicate that the person is combating an infection. **2.** Clotting factors do not initiate clotting but are essential steps in the clotting process. Also, the clots that form a thrombus typically result from an inflammatory response to an atherosclerotic plaque, not from clotting at a wound site. **3.** The chest pain results from inadequate blood flow in coronary arteries. Vasodilation promoted by nitric oxide from nitroglycerin increases blood flow, providing the heart muscle with additional oxygen and thus relieving the pain. **4.** When a mutant allele is codominant with the wild-type allele, the phenotype of heterozygotes is intermediate between that of wild-type and mutant homozygotes. Therefore, in the presence of wild-type Hb, the aggregation of Hb^S that causes sickling must be significantly reduced. Based on this fact, some therapies for sickle-cell disease are aimed at boosting adult expression of another hemoglobin gene in the body, such as that normally expressed only in the fetus. **5.** Embryonic stem cells are pluripotent rather than multipotent, meaning that they can give rise to many rather than a few different cell types.

Concept Check 42.5

1. Their interior position helps them stay moist. If the respiratory surfaces of lungs extended out into the terrestrial environment, they would quickly dry out, and diffusion of O_2 and CO_2 across these surfaces would stop. **2.** Earthworms need to keep their skin moist for gas exchange, but they need air outside this moist layer. If they stay in their waterlogged tunnels after a heavy rain, they will suffocate because they cannot get as much O_2 from water as from air. **3.** In the extremities of some vertebrates, blood flows in opposite directions in neighboring veins and arteries; this countercurrent arrangement maximizes the recapture of heat from blood leaving the body core in arteries, which is important for thermoregulation in cold environments. Similarly, in the gills of fish, water passes over the gills in the direction opposite to that of blood flowing through the gill capillaries, maximizing the extraction of oxygen from the water along the length of the exchange surface.

Concept Check 42.6

1. An increase in blood CO_2 concentration causes an increase in the rate of CO_2 diffusion into the cerebrospinal fluid, where the CO_2 combines with water to form carbonic acid. Dissociation of carbonic acid releases hydrogen ions, decreasing the pH of the cerebrospinal fluid. **2.** Increased heart rate increases the rate at which CO_2-rich blood is delivered to the lungs, where CO_2 is removed. **3.** A hole would allow air to enter the space between the inner and outer layers of the double membrane, resulting in a condition called a pneumothorax. The two layers would no longer stick together, and the lung on the side with the hole would collapse and cease functioning.

Concept Check 42.7

1. Differences in partial pressure; gases diffuse from a region of higher partial pressure to a region of lower partial pressure. **2.** The Bohr shift causes hemoglobin to release more O_2 at a lower pH, such as found in the vicinity of tissues with high rates of cellular respiration and CO_2 release. **3.** The doctor is assuming that the rapid breathing is the body's response to low blood pH. Metabolic acidosis, the lowering of blood pH, can have many causes, including complications of certain types of diabetes, shock (extremely low blood pressure), and poisoning.

Summary of Key Concepts Questions

42.1 In a closed circulatory system, an ATP-driven muscular pump generally moves fluids in one direction on a scale of millimeters to meters. Exchange between cells and their environment relies on diffusion, which involves random movements of molecules. Concentration gradients of molecules across exchange surfaces can drive rapid

net diffusion on a scale of 1 mm or less. **42.2** Replacement of a defective valve should increase stroke volume. A lower heart rate would therefore be sufficient to maintain the same cardiac output. **42.3** Blood pressure in the arm would fall by 25–30 mm Hg, the same difference as is normally seen between your heart and your brain. **42.4.** One microliter of blood contains about 5 million erythrocytes and 5,000 leukocytes, so leukocytes make up only about 0.1% of the cells in the absence of infection. **42.5.** Because CO_2 is such a small fraction of atmospheric gas (0.29 mm Hg/760 mm Hg, or less than 0.04%), the partial pressure gradient of CO_2 between the respiratory surface and the environment always strongly favors the release of CO_2 to the atmosphere. **42.6.** Because the lungs do not empty completely with each breath, incoming and outgoing air mix, so not all of the tidal volume represents fresh air. **42.7.** An enzyme speeds up a reaction without changing the equilibrium and without being consumed. Similarly, a respiratory pigment speeds up the movement of gases in the body without changing the equilibrium and without being consumed.

Test Your Understanding
1. c **2.** b **3.** d **4.** c **5.** d **6.** a **7.** a **8.** a
9.

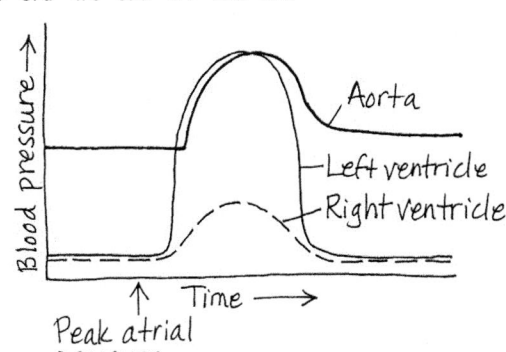

Chapter 43

Figure Questions

Figure 43.5 The seemingly inactive peptides might offer protection against pathogens other than those studied. Also, some antimicrobial peptides might work best in combination. **Figure 43.6** Cell-surface TLRs recognize pathogens identifiable by surface molecules, whereas TLRs in vesicles recognize pathogens identifiable by internal molecules after the pathogens are broken down. **Figure 43.10** Part of the enzyme or antigen receptor provides a structural "backbone" that maintains overall shape, while interaction occurs at a surface with a close fit to the substrate or antigen. The combined effect of multiple noncovalent interactions at the active site or binding site is a high-affinity interaction of tremendous specificity. **Figure 43.13** After gene rearrangement, a lymphocyte and its daughter cells make a single version of the antigen receptor. In contrast, alternative splicing is not heritable and can give rise to diverse gene products in a single cell. **Figure 43.18** These receptors enable memory cells to present antigen on their cell surface to a helper T cell. This presentation of antigen is required to activate memory cells in a secondary immune response.
Figure 43.20 Primary response: arrows extending from Antigen (1st exposure), Antigen-presenting cell, Helper T cell, B cell, Plasma cells, Cytotoxic T cell, and Active cytotoxic T cells; secondary response: arrows extending from Antigen (2nd exposure), Memory helper T cells, Memory B cells, and Memory cytotoxic T cells. **Figure 43.26** The loss of growth control that characterizes cancer involves many changes in gene regulation. HPV and other viruses can bring about some of these changes, but other mutations must occur in an infected cell to transform the cell to a cancerous state.

Concept Check 43.1

1. Because pus contains white blood cells, fluid, and cell debris, it indicates an active and at least partially successful inflammatory response against invading microbes. **2.** Whereas the ligand for the TLR receptor is a foreign molecule, the ligand for many signal transduction pathways is a molecule produced by the animal itself. **3.** Bacteria with a human host would be likely to grow optimally at normal body temperature or, if fever were often induced, at a temperature a few degrees higher.

Concept Check 43.2

1. See Figure 43.9. The transmembrane regions lie within the C regions, which also form the disulfide bridges. In contrast, the antigen-binding sites are in the V regions. **2.** Generating memory cells ensures both that a receptor specific for a particular epitope will be present and that there will be more lymphocytes with this specificity than in a host that had never encountered the antigen. **3.** If each B cell produced two different light and heavy chains for its antigen receptor, different combinations would make four different receptors. If any one was self-reactive, the lymphocyte would be eliminated in the generation of self-tolerance. For this reason, many more B cells would be eliminated, and those that could respond to a foreign antigen would be less effective at doing so due to the variety of receptors (and antibodies) they express.

Concept Check 43.3

1. A child lacking a thymus would have no functional T cells. Without helper T cells to help activate B cells, the child would be unable to produce antibodies against extracellular bacteria. Furthermore, without cytotoxic T cells or helper T cells, the child's immune system would be unable to kill virus-infected cells. **2.** Since the antigen-binding site is intact, the antibody fragments could neutralize viruses and opsonize bacteria. **3.** If the handler developed immunity to proteins in the antivenin, another injection could provoke a severe immune response. The handler's immune system might also now produce antibodies that could neutralize the venom.

Concept Check 43.4
1. Myasthenia gravis is considered an autoimmune disease because the immune system produces antibodies against self molecules (certain receptors on muscle cells). **2.** A person with a cold is likely to produce oral and nasal secretions that facilitate viral transfer. In addition, since sickness can cause incapacitation or death, a virus that is programmed to exit the host when there is a physiological stress has the opportunity to find a new host at a time when the current host may cease to function. **3.** A person with a macrophage deficiency would have frequent infections. The causes would be poor innate responses, due to diminished phagocytosis and inflammation, and poor adaptive responses, due to the lack of macrophages to present antigens to helper T cells.

Summary of Key Concepts Questions
43.1 Lysozyme in saliva destroys bacterial cell walls; the viscosity of mucus helps trap bacteria; acidic pH in the stomach kills many bacteria; and the tight packing of cells lining the gut provides a physical barrier to infection. **43.2** Sufficient numbers of cells to mediate an innate immune response are always present, whereas an adaptive response requires selection and proliferation of an initially very small cell population specific for the infecting pathogen. **43.3** No. Immunological memory after a natural infection and after vaccination are very similar. There may be minor differences in the particular antigens that can be recognized in a subsequent infection. **43.4** No. AIDS refers to a loss of immune function that can occur over time in an individual infected with HIV, not to the viral infection itself. For individuals infected with HIV, certain multidrug combinations ("cocktails") or rare genetic variations usually prevent progression to AIDS.

Test Your Understanding
1. b **2.** c **3.** c **4.** d **5.** b **6.** b **7.** c
8. One possible answer:

Chapter 44

Figure Questions
Figure 44.2 Aquaporins, which act as water channels **Figure 44.15** You would expect to find these cells lining tubules where they pass through the renal medulla. Because the extracellular fluid of the renal medulla has a very high osmolarity, production of solutes by tubule cells in this region keeps intracellular osmolarity high, with the result that these cells maintain normal volume. **Figure 44.16** Furosemide increases urine volume. The absence of ion transport in the ascending limb leaves the filtrate too concentrated for substantial volume reduction in the distal tubule and collecting duct. **Figure 44.21** The ADH levels would likely be elevated in both sets of patients with mutations because either defect prevents the recapture of water that restores blood osmolarity to normal levels.

Concept Check 44.1
1. Because the salt is moved against its concentration gradient, from low concentration (fresh water) to high concentration (blood) **2.** A freshwater osmoconformer would have body fluids too dilute to carry out life's processes. **3.** Without a layer of insulating fur, the camel must use the cooling effect of evaporative water loss to maintain body temperature, thus linking thermoregulation and osmoregulation.

Concept Check 44.2
1. Because uric acid is largely insoluble in water, it can be excreted as a semisolid paste, thereby reducing an animal's water loss. **2.** Humans produce uric acid from purine breakdown, and reducing purines in the diet often lessens the severity of gout. Birds, however, produce uric acid as a waste product of general nitrogen metabolism. They would therefore need a diet low in all nitrogen-containing compounds, not just purines.

Concept Check 44.3
1. In flatworms, ciliated cells draw interstitial fluids containing waste products into protonephridia. In earthworms, waste products pass from interstitial fluids into the coelom. From there the cilia move the wastes into metanephridia via a funnel surrounding an internal opening to the metanephridia. In insects, the Malpighian tubules pump fluids from the hemolymph, which receives waste products during exchange with interstitial fluids in the course of circulation. **2.** Filtration produces a fluid for exchange processes that is free of cells and large molecules, which are of benefit to the animal and could not readily be reabsorbed. **3.** The presence of Na^+ and other ions (electrolytes) in the dialysate would limit the extent to which they would be removed from the filtrate during dialysis. Adjusting the electrolytes in the starting dialysate can thus lead to the restoration of proper electrolyte concentrations in the plasma. Similarly, the absence of urea and other waste products in the starting dialysate results in their efficient removal from the filtrate.

Concept Check 44.4
1. The numerous nephrons and well-developed glomeruli of freshwater fishes produce urine at a high rate, while the small numbers of nephrons and smaller glomeruli of marine fishes produce urine at a low rate. **2.** The kidney medulla would absorb less water; thus, the drug would increase the amount of water lost

in the urine. **3.** A decline in blood pressure in the afferent arteriole would reduce the rate of filtration by moving less material through the vessels.

Concept Check 44.5
1. Alcohol inhibits the release of ADH, causing an increase in urinary water loss and increasing the chance of dehydration. **2.** The consumption of a large amount of water in a very short period of time, coupled with an absence of solute intake, can reduce sodium levels in the blood below tolerable levels. This condition, called hyponatremia, leads to disorientation and, sometimes, respiratory distress. It has occurred in some marathon runners who drink water rather than sports drinks. (It has also caused the death of a fraternity pledge as a consequence of a water hazing ritual and the death of a contestant in a water-drinking competition.) **3.** High blood pressure **4.** Each molecule of renin or ACE activates multiple molecules of the next protein in the pathway. The same is true for the protein kinases. The proteases differ from the protein kinases in at least two ways. First, their action is irreversible. Second, they do not require activation by another enzyme molecule.

Summary of Key Concepts Questions
44.1 Water moves into a cell by osmosis when the fluid outside the cells is hypoosmotic (has a lower solute concentration than the cytosol).
44.2

Waste Attribute	Ammonia	Urea	Uric Acid
Toxicity	High	Very low	Low
Energy content	Low	Moderate	High
Water loss in excretion	High	Moderate	Low

44.3 Filtration retains large molecules that would be difficult to transport across membranes. **44.4** Both types of nephrons have proximal tubules that can reabsorb nutrients, but only juxtamedullary nephrons have loops of Henle that extend deep into the renal medulla. Thus, only kidneys containing juxtamedullary nephrons can produce urine that is more concentrated than the blood. **44.5** Patients who don't produce ADH have symptoms relieved by treatment with the hormone, but many patients with diabetes insipidus lack functional receptors for ADH.

Test Your Understanding
1. d **2.** a **3.** c **4.** e **5.** d **6.** b
7.

Water and salt in food
Osmotic water gain through gills and other surfaces
Uptake of salt ions by gills
Ions and water lost in urine
Salt excreted by rectal gland

Chapter 45

Figure Questions
Figure 45.5 Synthesizing epinephrine requires breaking the bond between the carboxyl group ($-COOH$) and the α-carbon in tyrosine. **Figure 45.6** The hormone is water-soluble and has a cell-surface receptor. Such receptors, unlike those for lipid-soluble hormones, can cause observable changes in cells without hormone-dependent gene transcription. **Figure 45.17** Both diagnoses could be correct. In one case, the thyroid gland may produce excess thyroid hormone despite normal hormonal input from the hypothalamus and anterior pituitary. In the other, abnormally elevated hormonal input may be the cause of the overactive thyroid gland. **Figure 45.22** The result of the surgery would have been the same for both sexes—an absence of sexual differentiation in the genitalia.

Concept Check 45.1
1. Water-soluble hormones, which cannot penetrate the plasma membrane, bind to cell-surface receptors. This interaction triggers an intracellular signal transduction pathway that ultimately alters the activity of a preexisting protein in the cytoplasm and/or changes transcription of specific genes in the nucleus. Steroid hormones are lipid-soluble and can cross the plasma membrane into the cell interior, where they bind to receptors located in the cytosol or nucleus. The hormone-receptor complex then functions directly as a transcription factor that changes transcription of specific genes. **2.** Prostaglandins in semen that induce contractions in the uterus are acting as signaling molecules that are transferred from one individual to another of the same species (like pheromones), thus aiding in reproduction. **3.** Epinephrine in animals and auxin in plants act as hormones that trigger specific cellular responses that vary among different tissues of the organism.

Concept Check 45.2
1. In a healthy person, insulin released in response to the initial rise in blood glucose stimulates uptake of glucose by body cells. In a person with diabetes, however, inadequate production of insulin or nonresponsiveness of target cells decreases the body's ability to clear excess glucose from the blood. The initial increase in blood glucose is therefore greater in a person with diabetes, and it remains high for a prolonged period. **2.** If the function of the pathway is to provide a transient response, a short-lived stimulus would be less dependent on negative feedback. **3.** Since patients with type 2 diabetes produce insulin but fail to maintain normal glucose levels, you might predict that there could be

mutations in the genes for the insulin receptor or the signal transduction pathway it activates. Such mutations have in fact been found in type 2 patients.

Concept Check 45.3

1. The posterior pituitary, an extension of the hypothalamus that contains the axons of neurosecretory cells, is the storage and release site for two neurohormones, oxytocin and antidiuretic hormone (ADH). The anterior pituitary contains endocrine cells that make at least six different hormones. Secretion of anterior pituitary hormones is controlled by hypothalamic hormones that travel via portal vessels to the anterior pituitary. **2.** Because oxytocin responses involve positive feedback (via nerve cells) from suckling, the pathway does not require a sustained hormonal input stimulus. **3.** The hypothalamus and pituitary glands function in many different endocrine pathways. Many defects in these glands, such as those affecting growth or organization, would therefore disrupt many hormone pathways. Only a very specific defect, such as a mutation affecting a particular hormone receptor, would alter just one endocrine pathway. The situation is quite different for the final gland in a pathway, such as the thyroid gland. In this case, a wide range of defects that disrupt gland function would disrupt only the one pathway or small set of pathways in which that gland functions.

Concept Check 45.4

1. The adrenal medulla is derived from neural tissue during development. Reflecting this origin, it is an endocrine organ that produces two molecules—epinephrine and norepinephrine—that act both as hormones and as neurotransmitters. **2.** The levels of these hormones in the blood would become very high. This would be due to the diminished negative feedback on the hypothalamic neurons that secrete the releasing hormone that stimulates the secretion of ACTH by the anterior pituitary. **3.** By applying glucocorticoids to tissue by local injection, you exploit their anti-inflammatory activity. Local injection avoids the effects on glucose metabolism that would occur if glucocorticoids were taken orally and transported throughout the body in the bloodstream.

Summary of Key Concepts Questions

45.1 Because receptors for water-soluble hormones are located on the cell surface, facing the extracellular space, injecting the hormone into the cytoplasm would not trigger a response. **45.2** It would lessen the symptoms. Glucagon acts antagonistically with insulin, so lowering the effects of glucagon would be similar to increasing the levels or activity of insulin. **45.3** The pancreas, parathyroid glands, and pineal gland **45.4** Both the pituitary and the adrenal glands are formed by fusion of neural and nonneural tissue. ADH is secreted by the neurosecretory portion of the pituitary gland, and epinephrine is secreted by the neurosecretory portion of the adrenal gland.

Test Your Understanding

1. c   2. b   3. d   4. c   5. c   6. b   7. a   8. a

9.

Chapter 46

Figure Questions

Figure 46.9 According to the graph, about one-third of the females rid themselves of all sperm from the first mating. Thus, two-thirds retain some sperm from the first mating. We would therefore predict that two-thirds of the females would have some offspring exhibiting the small-eye phenotype of the dominant mutation carried by the males with which they mated first. **Figure 46.12** The analysis would be informative because the polar bodies contain all of the maternal chromosomes that don't end up in the mature egg. For example, finding two copies of the disease gene in the polar bodies would indicate its absence in the egg. This method of genetic testing is sometimes carried out when oocytes collected from a female are fertilized with sperm in a laboratory dish. **Figure 46.16** Testosterone can pass from fetal blood to maternal blood via the placental circulation, temporarily

upsetting the hormonal balance in the mother. **Figure 46.18** Oxytocin would most likely induce labor, starting a positive-feedback loop that would direct labor to completion. Synthetic oxytocin is in fact frequently used to induce labor when prolonged pregnancy might endanger the mother or fetus.

Concept Check 46.1

1. The offspring of sexual reproduction are more genetically diverse. However, asexual reproduction can produce more offspring over multiple generations. **2.** Unlike other forms of asexual reproduction, parthenogenesis involves gamete production. By controlling whether or not haploid eggs are fertilized, species such as honeybees can readily switch between asexual and sexual reproduction. **3.** No. Owing to random assortment of chromosomes during meiosis, the offspring may receive the same copy or different copies of a particular parental chromosome from the sperm and the egg. Furthermore, genetic recombination during meiosis will result in reassortment of genes between pairs of parental chromosomes. **4.** Both fragmentation and budding in animals have direct counterparts in the asexual reproduction of plants.

Concept Check 46.2

1. Internal fertilization allows the sperm to reach the egg without either gamete drying out. **2.** (a) Animals with external fertilization tend to release many gametes at once, resulting in the production of enormous numbers of zygotes. This increases the chances that some will survive to adulthood. (b) Animals with internal fertilization produce fewer offspring but generally exhibit greater care of the embryos and the young. **3.** Like the uterus of an insect, the ovary of a plant is the site of fertilization. Unlike the plant ovary, the uterus is not the site of egg production, which occurs in the insect ovary. In addition, the fertilized insect egg is expelled from the uterus, whereas the plant embryo develops within a seed in the ovary.

Concept Check 46.3

1. Spermatogenesis occurs normally only when the testicles are cooler than normal body temperature. Extensive use of a hot tub (or of very tight-fitting underwear) can cause a decrease in sperm quality and number. **2.** In humans, the secondary oocyte combines with a sperm before it finishes the second meiotic division. Thus, oogenesis is completed after, not before, fertilization. **3.** The only effect of sealing off each vas deferens is an absence of sperm in the ejaculate. Sexual response and ejaculate volume are unchanged. The cutting and sealing off of these ducts, a *vasectomy*, is a common surgical procedure for men who do not wish to produce any (more) offspring.

Concept Check 46.4

1. In the testis, FSH stimulates the Sertoli cells, which nourish developing sperm. LH stimulates the production of androgens (mainly testosterone), which in turn stimulate sperm production. In both females and males, FSH encourages the growth of cells that support and nourish developing gametes (follicle cells in females and Sertoli cells in males), and LH stimulates the production of sex hormones that promote gametogenesis (estrogens, primarily estradiol, in females and androgens, especially testosterone, in males). **2.** In estrous cycles, which occur in most female mammals, the endometrium is reabsorbed (rather than shed) if fertilization does not occur. Estrous cycles often occur just one or a few times a year, and the female is usually receptive to copulation only during the period around ovulation. Menstrual cycles are found only in humans and some other primates. **3.** The combination of estradiol and progesterone would have a negative-feedback effect on the hypothalamus, blocking release of GnRH. This would interfere with LH secretion by the pituitary, thus preventing ovulation. This is in fact one basis of action of the most common hormonal contraceptives. **4.** In the viral reproductive cycle, the production of new viral genomes is coordinated with capsid protein expression and with the production of phospholipids for viral coats. In the case of the human female, there is hormonally based coordination of egg maturation with the development of support tissues of the uterus.

Concept Check 46.5

1. hCG secreted by the early embryo stimulates the corpus luteum to make progesterone, which helps maintain the pregnancy. During the second trimester, however, hCG production drops, the corpus luteum disintegrates, and the placenta completely takes over progesterone production. **2.** Both tubal ligation and vasectomy block the movement of gametes from the gonads to a site where fertilization could take place. **3.** By introducing a spermatid nucleus directly into an oocyte, ICSI bypasses the sperm's acquisition of motility in the epididymis, its swimming to meet the egg in the oviduct, and its fusion with the egg.

Summary of Key Concepts Questions

46.1 No. Because parthenogenesis involves meiosis, the mother would pass on to each offspring a random and therefore typically distinct combination of the chromosomes she inherited from her mother and father. **46.2** None **46.3** The small size and lack of cytoplasm characteristic of a sperm are adaptations well suited to its function as a delivery vehicle for DNA. The large size and rich cytoplasmic contents of eggs support the growth and development of the embryo. **46.4** Circulating anabolic steroids mimic the feedback regulation of testosterone, turning off pituitary signaling to the testes and thereby blocking release of signals required for spermatogenesis. **46.5** Oxygen-rich blood in maternal arteries flows into pools in the endometrium, passes into fetal capillaries in the chorionic villi of the placenta, and from there travels throughout the circulatory system of the fetus.

Test Your Understanding

1. d   2. b   3. a   4. c   5. a   6. b   7. c   8. d

9.

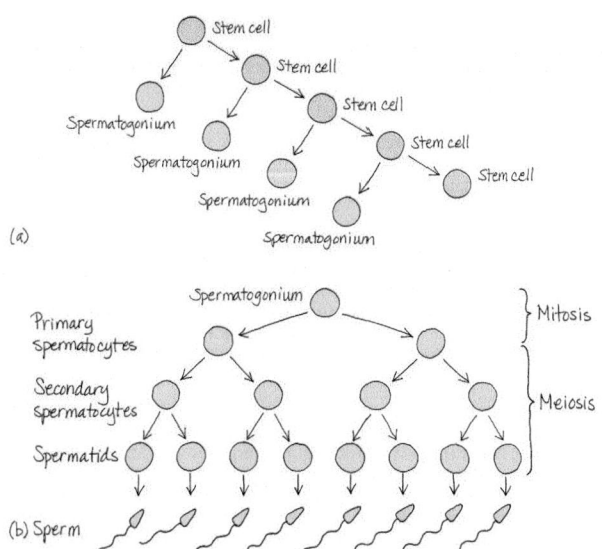

(c) The supply of stem cells would be used up and spermatogenesis would not be able to continue.

Chapter 47

Figure Questions
Figure 47.4 You could inject the compound into an unfertilized egg, expose the egg to sperm, and see whether the fertilization envelope forms. **Figure 47.21** The researchers allowed normal cortical rotation to occur, resulting in activation of the "back-forming" determinants. Then they forced the opposite rotation to occur, which established the back on the opposite side as well. Because the molecules on the normal side were already activated, forcing the opposite rotation apparently did not "cancel out" the establishment of the back side by the first rotation. **Figure 47.22** In Spemann's control, the two blastomeres were physically separated, and each grew into a whole embryo. In Roux's experiment, remnants of the dead blastomere were still contacting the live blastomere, which developed into a half-embryo. Therefore, molecules present in the dead cell's remnants may have been signaling to the live cell, inhibiting it from making all the embryonic structures. **Figure 47.23** You could inject the isolated protein or an mRNA encoding it into ventral cells of an earlier gastrula. If dorsal structures form on the ventral side, that would support the idea that the protein is the signaling molecule secreted or presented by the dorsal lip. You should also do a control experiment to make sure the injection process alone did not cause dorsal structures to form. **Figure 47.25** You could remove the AER and look for Sonic hedgehog mRNA or protein as a marker of the ZPA. If either was absent, that would support your hypothesis. You could also block FGF function and see whether the ZPA formed (by looking for Sonic hedgehog).

Concept Check 47.1
1. The fertilization envelope forms after cortical granules release their contents outside the egg, causing the vitelline membrane to rise and harden. The fertilization envelope serves as a barrier to fertilization by more than one sperm.
2. The increased Ca^{2+} concentration in the egg would cause the cortical granules to fuse with the plasma membrane, releasing their contents and causing a fertilization envelope to form, even though no sperm had entered. This would prevent fertilization. **3.** You would expect it to fluctuate. The fluctuation of MPF drives the transition between DNA replication (S phase) and mitosis (M phase), which is still required in the abbreviated cleavage cell cycle.

Concept Check 47.2
1. The cells of the notochord migrate toward the midline of the embryo (converge), rearranging themselves so there are fewer cells across the notochord, which thus becomes longer overall (extends; see Figure 47.16). **2.** Because microfilaments would not be able to contract and decrease the size of one end of the cell, both the inward bending in the middle of the neural tube and the outward bending of the hinge regions at the edges would be blocked. Therefore, the neural tube probably would not form. **3.** Dietary intake of the vitamin folic acid dramatically reduces the frequency of neural tube defects.

Concept Check 47.3
1. Axis formation establishes the location and polarity of the three axes that provide the coordinates for development. Pattern formation positions particular tissues and organs in the three-dimensional space defined by those coordinates. **2.** Morphogen gradients act by specifying cell fates across a field of cells through variation in the level of a determinant. Morphogen gradients thus act more globally than cytoplasmic determinants or inductive interactions between pairs of cells. **3.** Yes, a second embryo could develop because inhibiting BMP-4 activity would have the same effect as transplanting an organizer. **4.** The limb that developed probably would have a mirror-image duplication, with the most posterior digits in the middle and the most anterior digits at either end.

Summary of Key Concepts Questions
47.1 The binding of a sperm to a receptor on the egg surface is very specific and likely would not occur if the two gametes were from different species. Without

sperm binding, the sperm and egg membranes would not fuse. **47.2** The neural tube forms when the neural plate, a band of ectodermal tissue oriented along the anterior-posterior axis on the dorsal side of the embryo, rolls into a tube and pinches off from the rest of the ectoderm. Neural crest cells arise as groups of cells in the regions between the edges of the neural tube and the surrounding ectoderm migrate away from the neural tube. **47.3** Mutations that affected both limb and kidney development would be more likely to alter the function of monocilia because these organelles are important in several signaling pathways. Mutations that affected limb development but not kidney development would more likely alter a single pathway, such as Hedgehog signaling.

Test Your Understanding
1. a **2.** b **3.** e **4.** a **5.** d **6.** d **7.** b
8.

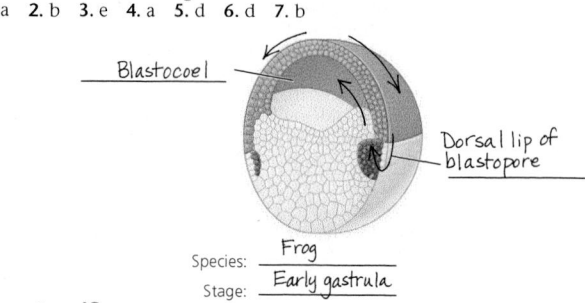

Species: ___Frog___
Stage: ___Early gastrula___

Chapter 48

Figure Questions
Figure 48.8 Adding chloride channels makes the membrane potential less positive. Adding sodium or potassium channels would have no effect, because sodium movement is already at equilibrium and there are no potassium ions present. **Figure 48.10**

Figure 48.15 The production and transmission of action potentials would be unaffected. However, action potentials arriving at chemical synapses would be unable to trigger release of neurotransmitter. Signaling at such synapses would thus be blocked. **Figure 48.18** The drug might be destroyed very quickly in the body, not reach the central nervous system, or bind to but not activate the receptor.

Concept Check 48.1
1. Sensors in your ear transmit information to your brain. There the activity of interneurons in processing centers enables you to recognize your name. In response, signals transmitted via motor neurons cause contraction of muscles that turn your neck. **2.** Increased branching would allow control of a greater number of postsynaptic cells, enhancing coordination of responses to nervous system signals. **3.** Communication by bacteria involves all the cells in a colony, whereas communication by neurons involves just a few cells in the animal body. In addition, neurons direct signals from one location to another, whereas bacterial cells communicate in all directions.

Concept Check 48.2
1. Ions can flow against a chemical concentration gradient if there is an opposing electrical gradient of greater magnitude. **2.** A decrease in permeability to K^+, an increase in permeability to Na^+, or both **3.** The activity of the sodium-potassium pump is essential to maintain the resting potential. With the pump inactivated, the sodium and potassium concentration gradients would gradually disappear, resulting in a greatly reduced resting potential. **4.** Charged dye molecules could equilibrate only if other charged molecules could also cross the membrane. If not, a membrane potential would develop that would counterbalance the chemical gradient.

Concept Check 48.3
1. A graded potential has a magnitude that varies with stimulus strength, whereas an action potential has an all-or-none magnitude that is independent of stimulus strength. **2.** Loss of the insulation provided by myelin sheaths leads to a disruption of action potential propagation along axons. Voltage-gated sodium channels are restricted to the nodes of Ranvier, and without the insulating effect of myelin, the inward current produced at one node during an action potential

cannot depolarize the membrane to the threshold at the next node. **3.** The maximum frequency would decrease because the refractory period would be extended.

Concept Check 48.4

1. It can bind to different types of receptors, each triggering a specific response in postsynaptic cells. **2.** These toxins would prolong the EPSPs that acetylcholine produces because the neurotransmitter would remain longer in the synaptic cleft. **3.** Since GABA is an inhibitory neurotransmitter in the CNS, this drug would be expected to decrease brain activity. A decrease in brain activity might be expected to slow down or reduce behavioral activity. Many sedative drugs act in this fashion. **4.** Membrane fusion

Summary of Key Concepts Questions

48.1 It would prevent information from being transmitted away from the cell body along the axon. **48.2** There are very few open sodium channels in a resting neuron, so the resting potential either would not change or would become slightly more negative (hyperpolarization). **48.3** Positive feedback is responsible for the rapid opening of many voltage-gated sodium channels, causing the rapid outflow of sodium ions responsible for the rising phase of the action potential. As the membrane potential becomes positive, voltage-gated potassium channels open in a form of negative feedback that helps bring about the falling phase of the action potential. **48.4** A given neurotransmitter can have many receptors that differ in their location and activity. Drugs that target receptor activity rather than neurotransmitter release or stability are therefore likely to exhibit greater specificity and potentially have fewer undesirable side effects.

Test Your Understanding

1. c **2.** c **3.** c **4.** e **5.** b **6.** a **7.** As shown in this pair of drawings, a pair of action potentials would move outward in both directions from each electrode. (Action potentials are unidirectional only if they begin at one end of an axon.) However, because of the refractory period, the two action potentials between the electrodes both stop where they meet. Thus, only one action potential reaches the synaptic terminals.

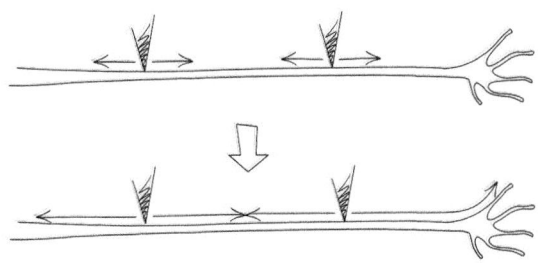

Chapter 49

Figure Questions

Figure 49.3 During swallowing, muscles along the esophagus alternately contract and relax, resulting in peristalsis. One model to explain this alternation is that each section of muscle receives nerve impulses that alternate between excitation and inhibition, just as the quadriceps and hamstring receive opposing signals in the knee-jerk reflex. **Figure 49.12** If the new mutation disrupted only pacemaker function, you should be able to restore rhythmic activity by removing the SCN and replacing it with an SCN transplant from either a wild-type or τ mutant hamster. Using the new mutant as the donor would not be as informative, since both failed transplants and successful ones would result in a lack of rhythmic activity. **Figure 49.14** Regions you would expect to be active regardless of the type of music played would include ones that are important for processing and interpreting sounds. **Figure 49.23** If the depolarization brings the membrane potential to or past threshold, it should initiate action potentials that cause dopamine release from the VTA neurons. This should mimic natural stimulation of the brain reward system, resulting in positive and perhaps pleasurable sensations.

Concept Check 49.1

1. The sympathetic division would likely be activated. It mediates the "fight-or-flight" response in stressful situations. **2.** The preganglionic neurons use the same neurotransmitter and function similarly in each division (to stimulate postganglionic neurons). The postganglionic neurons use different neurotransmitters that generally bring about opposing functions in the same target tissues. **3.** Nerves contain bundles of axons, some that belong to motor neurons, which send signals outward from the CNS, and some that belong to sensory neurons, which bring signals into the CNS. Therefore, you would expect effects on both motor control and sensation. **4.** Neurosecretory cells of the adrenal medulla secrete the hormones epinephrine and norepinephrine in response to preganglionic input from sympathetic neurons. These hormones travel in the circulation throughout the body, triggering responses in many tissues.

Concept Check 49.2

1. The cerebral cortex on the left side of the brain initiates voluntary movement of the right side of the body. **2.** Alcohol diminishes function of the cerebellum. **3.** Paralysis reflects an inability to carry out motor commands transmitted from the cerebrum to the spinal cord. You would expect these patients to have injuries in the portion of the CNS extending from the spinal cord up to but not including the reticular formation. A coma reflects a disruption in the cycles of sleep and arousal regulated by communication between the reticular formation and the cerebrum. You would expect these patients to have injuries in the reticular formation or in the portion of the brain on the opposite side of the reticular formation from the spinal cord.

Concept Check 49.3

1. Brain damage that disrupts behavior, cognition, memory, or other functions provides evidence that the portion of the brain affected by the damage is important for the normal activity that is blocked or altered. **2.** Broca's area, which is active during the generation of speech, is located near the part of the primary motor cortex that controls muscles in the face. Wernicke's area, which is active when speech is heard, is located near the part of the temporal lobe that is involved in hearing. **3.** Each cerebral hemisphere is specialized for different parts of this task—the right for face recognition and the left for language. Without an intact corpus callosum, neither hemisphere can take advantage of the other's processing abilities.

Concept Check 49.4

1. There can be an increase in the number of synapses between the neurons or an increase in the strength of existing synaptic connections. **2.** If consciousness is an emergent property resulting from the interaction of many different regions of the brain, then it is unlikely that localized brain damage will have a discrete effect on consciousness. **3.** The hippocampus is responsible for organizing newly acquired information. Without hippocampal function, the links necessary to retrieve information from the neocortex will be lacking, and no functional memory, short- or long-term, will be formed.

Concept Check 49.5

1. Both are progressive brain diseases whose risk increases with advancing age. Both result from the death of brain neurons and are associated with the accumulation of peptide or protein aggregates. **2.** The symptoms of schizophrenia can be mimicked by a drug that stimulates dopamine-releasing neurons. The brain's reward system, which is involved in drug addiction, is composed of dopamine-releasing neurons that connect the ventral tegmental area to regions in the cerebrum. Parkinson's disease results from the death of dopamine-releasing neurons. **3.** Not necessarily. It might be that the plaques, tangles, and missing regions of the brain seen at death reflect secondary effects, the consequence of other unseen changes that are actually responsible for the alterations in brain function.

Summary of Key Concepts Questions

49.1 Because reflex circuits involve only a few neurons—the simplest consist of a sensory neuron and a motor neuron—the path for information transfer is short and simple, increasing the speed of the response. **49.2** The pons and medulla (the midbrain) coordinate visual reflexes; the cerebellum controls coordination of movement that depends on visual input; the thalamus serves as a routing center for visual information; and the cerebrum is essential for converting visual input to a visual image. **49.3** You would expect the right side of the body to be paralyzed because it is controlled by the left cerebral hemisphere, where language generation and interpretation are localized. **49.4** Learning a new language likely requires the maintenance of synapses that are formed during early development but are otherwise lost prior to adulthood. **49.5** Whereas amphetamines stimulate dopamine release, PCP blocks glutamate receptors, suggesting that schizophrenia does not reflect a defect in the function of just one neurotransmitter.

Test Your Understanding

1. c **2.** a **3.** d **4.** c **5.** d **6.** e

7.

Chapter 50

Figure Questions

Figure 50.12 In the brain. Each note is detected separately in the ear, with each causing vibration of the basilar membrane and deflection of hair cells in a distinct location. Sensory neurons in each location provide output in the form of action potentials that travel along distinct axons in the auditory nerve. It is not until the information reaches the brain that the individual notes are detected and the perception of the chord is generated. **Figure 50.19** Each of the three types of cones is most sensitive to a different wavelength of light. A cone might be fully depolarized when there is light present if the light is of a wavelength far from its optimum. **Figure 50.21** In humans, an X chromosome with a defect in the red or green opsin gene is much less common than a wild-type X chromosome. Color blindness therefore typically skips a generation as the defective allele passes from an affected male to a carrier daughter and back to an affected grandson. In squirrel monkeys, no X chromosome can confer full color vision. As a result, all males are color-blind and no unusual inheritance pattern is observed. **Figure 50.23** The results of the experiment would have been identical. What matters is the activation of particular sets of neurons, not the manner in which they are activated. Any signal from a bitter cell will be interpreted by the brain as a bitter taste, regardless of the nature of the compound and the receptor involved. **Figure 50.25** Only perception. Binding of an odorant to its receptor will cause action potentials to be sent to the brain. Although an excess of that odorant might cause a diminished response through adaptation, another odorant can mask the first only at the level of perception in the brain. **Figure 50.28** Hundreds of myosin heads participate in sliding each pair of thick and thin filaments past each other. Because cross-bridge formation and breakdown are not synchronized, many myosin heads are exerting force on the thin filaments at all times during muscle contraction. **Figure 50.32** By causing all of the motor neurons that control the muscle to generate action potentials at a rate high enough to produce tetanus in all of the muscle fibers. **Figure 50.40** Since a duck is more specialized for flying than for swimming, you might expect that it would consume more energy per unit body mass and distance in swimming than would, for example, a fish. (In fact, if the value for a 10^3-g swimming duck were plotted on this graph, it would appear well above the line for swimmers and just above the line for runners.)

Concept Check 50.1

1. Electromagnetic receptors in general detect only external stimuli. Nonelectromagnetic receptors, such as chemoreceptors or mechanoreceptors, can act as either internal or external sensors. **2.** The capsaicin present in the peppers activates the thermoreceptor for high temperatures. In response to the perceived high temperature, the nervous system triggers sweating to achieve evaporative cooling. **3.** You would perceive the electrical stimulus as if the sensory receptors that regulate that neuron had been activated. For example, electrical stimulation of the sensory neuron controlled by the thermoreceptor activated by menthol would likely be perceived as a local cooling.

Concept Check 50.2

1. Statocysts detect the animal's orientation with respect to gravity, providing information that is essential in environments such as these, where light cues are absent. **2.** As a sound that changes gradually from a very low to a very high pitch **3.** The stapes and the other middle ear bones transmit vibrations from the tympanic membrane to the oval window. Fusion of these bones (as occurs in a disease called otosclerosis) would block this transmission and result in hearing loss.

Concept Check 50.3

1. Planarians have ocelli that cannot form images but can sense the intensity and direction of light, providing enough information to enable the animals to find protection in shaded places. Flies have compound eyes that form images and excel at detecting movement. **2.** The person can focus on distant objects but not close objects (without glasses) because close focusing requires the lens to become almost spherical. This problem is common after age 50. **3.** Close each eye in turn. An object floating on the surface of an eyeball will appear only when that eye is open. **4.** Absorption of light by retinal converts a structure isomer in the *cis* configuration to the isomer in the *trans* configuration, initiating the process of light detection. In contrast, a photon absorbed by chlorophyll does not bring about isomerization, but instead boosts an electron to a higher energy orbital, initiating the electron flow that generates ATP and NADPH.

Concept Check 50.4

1. Both taste cells and olfactory cells have receptor proteins in their plasma membrane that bind certain substances, leading to membrane depolarization through a signal transduction pathway involving a G protein. However, olfactory cells are sensory neurons, whereas taste cells are not. **2.** Since animals rely on chemical signals for behaviors that include finding mates, marking territories, and avoiding dangerous substances, it is adaptive for the olfactory system to have a robust response to a very small number of molecules of a particular odorant. **3.** Because the sweet, bitter, and umami tastes involve GPCR proteins but the sour taste does not, you might predict that the mutation is in a molecule that acts in the signal transduction pathway common to the different GPCRs.

Concept Check 50.5

1. In a skeletal muscle fiber, Ca^{2+} binds to the troponin complex, which moves tropomyosin away from the myosin-binding sites on actin and allows cross-bridges to form. In a smooth muscle cell, Ca^{2+} binds to calmodulin, which activates an enzyme that phosphorylates the myosin head and thus enables cross-bridge formation. **2.** *Rigor mortis*, a Latin phrase meaning "stiffness of death," results from the complete depletion of ATP in skeletal muscle. Since ATP is required to release myosin from actin and to pump Ca^{2+} out of the cytosol, muscles become chronically contracted beginning about 3–4 hours after death. **3.** A competitive inhibitor binds to the same site as the substrate for the enzyme. In contrast, the troponin and tropomyosin complex masks, but does not bind to, the myosin-binding sites on actin.

Concept Check 50.6

1. Septa provide the divisions of the coelom that allow for peristalsis, a form of locomotion requiring independent control of different body segments. **2.** The main problem in swimming is drag; a fusiform body minimizes drag. The main problem in flying is overcoming gravity; wings shaped like airfoils provide lift, and adaptations such as air-filled bones reduce body mass. **3.** When you grasp the sides of the chair, you are using a contraction of the triceps to keep your arms extended against the pull of gravity on your body. As you lower yourself slowly into the chair, you gradually decrease the number of motor units in the triceps that are contracted. Contracting your biceps would jerk you down, since you would no longer be opposing gravity.

Summary of Key Concepts Questions

50.1 Nociceptors overlap with other classes of receptors in the type of stimulus they detect. They differ from other receptors only in how a particular stimulus is perceived. **50.2** The direction of displacement of a hair cell is determined by stimulus intensity, which is encoded by the frequency of action potentials transmitted to the brain. **50.3** Our olfactory sense is responsible for most of what we describe as distinct tastes. A head cold or other source of congestion blocks odorant access to receptors lining portions of the nasal cavity. **50.4** The major difference is that neurons in the retina integrate information from multiple sensory receptors (photoreceptors) before transmitting information to the central nervous system. **50.5** Hydrolysis of ATP is required to convert myosin to a high-energy configuration for binding to actin and to power the Ca^{2+} pump that removes cytosolic Ca^{2+} during muscle relaxation. **50.6** Human body movements rely on the contraction of muscles anchored to a rigid endoskeleton. Tendons attach muscles to bones, which in turn are composed of fibers built up from a basic organizational unit, the sarcomere. The thin and thick filaments have separate points of attachment within the sarcomere. In response to nervous system motor output, the formation and breakdown of cross-bridges between myosin heads and actin ratchet the thin and thick filaments past each other. Because the filaments are anchored, this sliding movement shortens the muscle fibers. Furthermore, because the fibers themselves are part of the muscles attached at each end to bones, muscle contraction moves bones of the body relative to each other. In this way, the structural anchoring of muscles and filaments enables muscle function, such as the bending of an elbow by contraction of the biceps.

Test Your Understanding

1. e **2.** a **3.** b **4.** c **5.** b **6.** d
7.

Position along retina (in degrees away from fovea)

The answer shows the actual distribution of rods and cones in the human eye. Your graph may differ but should have the following properties: Only cones at the fovea; fewer cones and more rods at both ends of the x-axis; no photoreceptors in the optic disk.

Chapter 51

Figure Questions

Figure 51.2 The fixed action pattern based on the sign stimulus of a red belly ensures that the male will chase away any invading males of his species. By chasing away such males, the defender decreases the chance that another male will fertilize eggs laid in his nesting territory. **Figure 51.7** There should be no effect. Imprinting is an innate behavior that is carried out anew in each generation. Assuming the nest was not disturbed, the offspring of the Lorenz followers would imprint on the mother goose. **Figure 51.8** Perhaps the wasp doesn't use visual cues. It might also be that wasps recognize objects native to their environment, but not foreign objects, such as the pinecones. Tinbergen addressed these ideas before carrying out the pinecone study. When he swept away the pebbles and sticks around the nest, the wasps could no longer find their nests. If he shifted the natural objects in their natural arrangement, the shift in the landmarks caused a shift in the site to which the wasps returned. Finally, if natural objects around the nest site were replaced with pinecones while the wasp was in the burrow, the wasp nevertheless found her way back to the nest site. **Figure 51.23** Courtship song generation must be coupled to courtship song recognition. Unless the genes that control generation of particular song elements also control recognition, the hybrids might be unlikely to find mating partners, depending on what aspects of the songs are important for mate recognition and acceptance. **Figure 51.26** It might be that the birds require stimuli during flight to exhibit their migratory preference. If this were true, the birds would show the same orientation in the funnel experiment despite their distinct genetic programming. **Figure 51.28** It holds true for some, but not all individuals. If a parent has more than one reproductive partner, the offspring of different partners will have a coefficient of relatedness less than 0.5.

Concept Check 51.1

1. The proximate explanation for this fixed action pattern might be that nudging and rolling are released by the sign stimulus of an object outside the nest, and the behavior is carried to completion once initiated. The ultimate explanation might be that ensuring that eggs remain in the nest increases the chance of producing healthy offspring. **2.** In both cases, the detection of periodic variation in the environment results in a reproductive cycle timed to environmental conditions that optimize the opportunity for success. **3.** There might be selective pressure for other prey fish to detect an injured fish because the source of the injury might threaten them as well. Among predators, there might be selection for those that are attracted to the alarm substance because they would be more likely to encounter crippled prey. Fish with adequate defenses might show no change because they have a selective advantage if they do not waste energy responding to the alarm substance.

Concept Check 51.2

1. Natural selection would tend to favor convergence in color pattern because a predator learning to associate a pattern with a sting or bad taste would avoid all other individuals with that same color pattern, regardless of species. **2.** You might move objects around to establish an abstract rule, such as "past landmark A, the same distance as A is from the starting point," while maintaining a minimum of fixed metric relationships, that is, avoiding having the food directly adjacent to or a set distance from a landmark. As you might surmise, designing an informative experiment of this kind is not easy. **3.** Learned behavior, just like innate behavior, can contribute to reproductive isolation and thus to speciation. For example, learned bird songs contribute to species recognition during courtship, thereby helping ensure that only members of the same species mate.

Concept Check 51.3

1. Certainty of paternity is higher with external fertilization. **2.** Balancing selection could maintain the two alleles at the *forager* locus if population density fluctuated from one generation to another. At times of low population density, the energy-conserving sitter larvae (carrying the *for^s* allele) would be favored, while at higher population density, the more mobile Rover larvae (*for^R* allele) would have a selective advantage. **3.** Because females would now be present in much larger numbers than males, all three types of males should have some reproductive success. Nevertheless, since the advantage that the blue-throats rely on—a limited number of females in their territory—will be absent, the yellow-throats are likely to increase in frequency in the short term.

Concept Check 51.4

1. Because this geographic variation corresponds to differences in prey availability between two garter snake habitats, it seems likely that snakes with characteristics enabling them to feed on the abundant prey in their locale would have had increased survival and reproductive success. In this way, natural selection would have resulted in the divergent foraging behaviors. **2.** Yes. Kin selection does not require any recognition or awareness of relatedness. **3.** The older individual cannot be the beneficiary because he or she cannot have extra offspring. However, the cost is low for an older individual performing the altruistic act because that individual has already reproduced (but perhaps is still caring for a child or grandchild). There can therefore be selection for an altruistic act by a postreproductive individual that benefits a young relative.

Summary of Key Concepts Questions

51.1 Circannual rhythms are typically based on the cycles of light and dark in the environment. As the global climate changes, animals that migrate in response to these rhythms may shift to a location before or after local environmental conditions are optimal for reproduction and survival. **51.2** For the goose, all that is acquired is an object at which the behavior is directed. In the case of the sparrow, learning takes place that will give shape to the behavior itself. **51.3** Because feeding the female is likely to improve her reproductive success, the genes from the sacrificed male are likely to appear in a greater number of progeny. **51.4** You would likely have missed the idea that changes in a single gene can have large-scale effects on even complex behaviors.

Test Your Understanding

1. d **2.** b **3.** c **4.** a **5.** c **6.** a
7.

You could measure the size of mussels that oystercatchers successfully open and compare that with the size distribution in the habitat.

Chapter 52

Figure Questions

Figure 52.7 Dispersal limitations, the activities of people (such as a broad-scale conversion of forests to agriculture or selective harvesting), or many other factors, including those discussed later in the chapter (see Figure 52.18) **Figure 52.18** Some factors, such as fire, are relevant only for terrestrial systems. At first glance, water availability is primarily a terrestrial factor, too. However, species living along the intertidal zone of oceans or along the edge of lakes also suffer desiccation. Salinity stress is important for species in some aquatic and terrestrial

systems. Oxygen availability is an important factor primarily for species in some aquatic systems and in soils and sediments. **Figure 52.20** When only urchins were removed, limpets may have increased in abundance and reduced seaweed cover somewhat (the difference between the purple and blue lines on the graph).

Concept Check 52.1

1. In the tropics, high temperatures evaporate water and cause warm, moist air to rise. The rising air cools and releases much of its water as rain over the tropics. The remaining dry air descends at approximately 30° north and south, causing deserts to occur in those regions. **2.** The microclimate around the stream will be cooler, moister, and shadier than that around the unplanted agricultural field. **3.** Trees that require a long time to reach reproductive age are likely to evolve more slowly than annual plants in response to climate change, constraining the potential ability of such trees to respond to rapid climate change. **4.** Plants with C_4 photosynthesis are likely to expand their range globally as Earth's climate warms. As described in Concept 10.4, C_4 photosynthesis minimizes photorespiration and enhances sugar production, an advantage that is especially useful in warmer regions where C_4 plants are found today.

Concept Check 52.2

1. Temperate broadleaf forests have higher mean annual precipitation. **2.** Answers will vary by location but should be based on the information and maps in Figure 52.12. How much your local area has been altered from its natural state will influence how much it reflects the expected characteristics of your biome, particularly the expected plants and animals. **3.** Northern coniferous forest is likely to replace tundra along the boundary between these biomes. To see why, note that northern coniferous forest is adjacent to tundra throughout North America, northern Europe, and Asia (see Figure 52.9) and that the temperature range for northern coniferous forest is just above that for tundra (see Figure 52.10).

Concept Check 52.3

1. In the oceanic pelagic zone, the ocean bottom lies below the photic zone, so there is too little light to support benthic algae or rooted plants. **2.** As explained in Concept 44.1, aquatic organisms either gain or lose water by osmosis if the osmolarity of their environment differs from their internal osmolarity. Water gain can cause cells to swell, and water loss can cause them to shrink. To avoid excessive changes in cell volume, organisms that live in estuaries must be able to compensate for both water gain (under freshwater conditions) and water loss (under saltwater conditions). **3.** In a river below a dam, the fish are more likely to be species that prefer colder water. In summer, the deep layers of a reservoir are colder than the surface layers, so a river below a dam will be colder than an undammed river.

Concept Check 52.4

1. (a) Humans might transplant a species to a new area that it could not previously reach because of a geographic barrier. (b) Humans might eliminate a predator or herbivore species, such as sea urchins, from an area. **2.** One test would be to build a fence around a plot of land in an area that has trees of that species, excluding all deer from the plot. You could then compare the abundance of tree seedlings inside and outside the fenced plot over time. **3.** Because the ancestor of the silverswords reached isolated Hawaii early in the islands' existence, it likely faced little competition and was able to occupy many unfilled niches. The cattle egret, in contrast, arrived in the Americas only recently and has to compete with a well-established group of species. Thus, its opportunities for adaptive radiation have probably been much more limited.

Summary of Key Concepts Questions

52.1 Because dry air would descend at the equator instead of at 30° north and south latitude (where deserts exist today), deserts would be more likely to exist along the equator (see Figure 52.3). **52.2** Because tundra is much cooler than deserts (see Figure 52.10), less water evaporates during the growing season and the tundra stays more moist. **52.3** An aphotic zone is most likely to be found in the deep waters of a lake, the oceanic pelagic zone, or the marine benthic zone. **52.4** You could arrange a flowchart that begins with abiotic limitations—first determining the physical and chemical conditions under which a species could survive—and then moves through the other factors listed in the flowchart.

Test Your Understanding

1. c **2.** b **3.** d **4.** e **5.** d **6.** d **7.** c **8.** a **9.** a **10.** c
11.

Based on what you learned from Figure 52.20 and on the positive relationship you observed in the field between kelp abundance and otter density, you could hypothesize that otters lower sea urchin density, reducing feeding of the urchins on kelp.

Chapter 53

Figure Questions

Figure 53.4 The dispersion of the penguins would likely appear clumped as you flew over densely populated islands and sparsely populated ocean. **Figure 53.13** If male European kestrels provided no parental care, brood size should not affect their survival. Therefore, the three bars representing male survival in Figure 53.13 should have similar heights. In contrast, female survival should still decline with increasing brood size, as shown in the current figure.
Figure 53.15

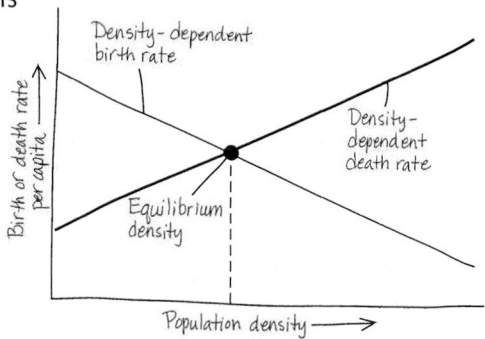

Figure 53.19 Hare numbers typically peaked slightly before lynx numbers did. The lynx depend on the hares for food, but there is a delay between increased food availability and increased reproduction by the lynx. **Figure 53.20** *Dictyostelium* slugs are more vulnerable to predation by animals than are amoebas.

Concept Check 53.1

1.

A type III survivorship curve is most likely because very few of the young probably survive. **2.** If an animal is captured by attracting it with food, it may be more likely to be recaptured if it seeks the same food. The number of marked animals captured (x) would be an overestimate, and because the population size (N) is equal to sn/x, N would be an underestimate. Alternatively, if an animal has a negative experience during capture and learns from that experience, it may be less likely to be recaptured. In this case, x would be an underestimate and N would be an overestimate. **3.** Male sticklebacks would likely have a uniform pattern of dispersion, with antagonistic interactions maintaining a relatively constant spacing between them.

Concept Check 53.2

1. Though r_{max} is constant, N, the population size, is increasing. As r_{max} is applied to an increasingly large N, population growth ($r_{max}N$) accelerates, producing the J-shaped curve. **2.** Exponential growth is more likely in the area where a forest was destroyed by fire. The first plants that found suitable habitat there would encounter an abundance of space, nutrients, and light. In the undisturbed forest, competition among plants for these resources would be intense. **3.** The net population growth is $\Delta N/\Delta t = bN - mN$. The annual per capita birth rate, b, equals 14/1,000, or 0.014, and the per capita death rate, m, equals 8/1,000, or 0.008. Therefore, the net population growth in 2009 was

$$\frac{\Delta N}{\Delta t} = (0.014 \times 307,000,000) - (0.008 \times 307,000,000)$$

or 1.84 million people. A population is growing exponentially only if its per capita rate of increase equals its maximum rate. That is not the case for the United States currently.

Concept Check 53.3

1. When N (population size) is small, there are relatively few individuals producing offspring. When N is large, near the carrying capacity, the per capita growth rate is relatively small because it is limited by available resources. The steepest part of the logistic growth curve corresponds to a population with a number of reproducing individuals that is substantial but not yet near carrying capacity. **2.** Using a population size of 1,600 as an example,

$$\frac{dN}{dt} = r_{max}N\frac{(K-N)}{K} = \frac{1(1,600)(1,500 - 1,600)}{1,500}$$

and the population "growth" rate is –107 individuals per year. The population shrinks even faster when N is farther from the carrying capacity; when N equals 1,750 and 2,000 individuals, the population shrinks by 292 and 667 individuals per

year, respectively. These negative growth rates correspond most closely to the time when the *Daphnia* population has overshot its carrying capacity and is shrinking, about days 65–100 in Figure 53.10b. **3.** If a population becomes too crowded, the likelihood of disease and mortality may increase because of the effects of pathogens. Thus, pathogens can reduce the long-term carrying capacity of a population.

Concept Check 53.4

1. The constant, spring-fed stream. In more constant physical conditions, populations are more stable and competition for resources is more likely. In such conditions, larger, well-provisioned young typical of iteroparous species have a better chance of surviving. **2.** By preferentially investing in the eggs it lays in the nest, the peacock wrasse increases their probability of survival. The eggs it disperses widely and does not provide care for are less likely to survive, at least some of the time, but require a lower investment by the adults. (In this sense, the adults avoid the risk of placing all their eggs in one basket.) **3.** If a parent's survival is compromised greatly by bearing young during times of stress, the animal's fitness may increase if it abandons its current young and survives to produce healthier young at a later time.

Concept Check 53.5

1. Three attributes are the size, quality, and isolation of patches. A patch that is larger or of higher quality is more likely to attract individuals and to be a source of individuals for other patches. A patch that is relatively isolated will undergo less exchange of individuals with other patches. **2.** You would need to study the population for more than one cycle (longer than 10 years and probably at least 20) before having sufficient data to examine changes through time. Otherwise, it would be impossible to know whether an observed decrease in the population size reflected a long-term trend or was part of the normal cycle. **3.** In negative feedback, the output, or product, of a process slows that process. In populations that have a density-dependent birth rate, such as dune fescue grass, an accumulation of product (more individuals, resulting in a higher population density) slows the process (population growth) by decreasing the birth rate.

Concept Check 53.6

1. A bottom-heavy age structure, with a disproportionate number of young people, portends continuing growth of the population as these young people begin reproducing. In contrast, a more evenly distributed age structure predicts a more stable population size, and a top-heavy age structure predicts a decrease in population size because relatively fewer young people are reproducing. **2.** The growth rate of Earth's human population has dropped by half since the 1960s, from 2.2% in 1962 to 1.2% today. Nonetheless, growth has not slowed much because the smaller growth rate is counterbalanced by increased population size; the number of extra people on Earth each year remains enormous—approximately 79 million. **3.** Each of us influences our ecological footprint by how we live—what we eat, how much energy we use, and the amount of waste we generate—as well as by how many children we have. Making choices that reduce our demand for resources makes our ecological footprint smaller.

Summary of Key Concepts Questions

53.1 Ecologists can potentially estimate birth rates by counting the number of young born each year, and they can estimate death rates by seeing how the number of adults changes each year. **53.2** Under the exponential model, both populations will continue to grow to infinite size, regardless of the specific value of r_{max} (see Figure 53.7). **53.3** There are many things you can do to increase the carrying capacity of the species, including increasing its food supply, protecting it from predators, and providing more sites for nesting or reproduction. **53.4** Two key factors appear to be the survival rate of the offspring and the chance that adults will live long enough to reproduce again. **53.5** An example of a biotic factor would be disease caused by a pathogen; natural disasters, such as floods and storms, are examples of abiotic factors. **53.6** Humans are unique in our potential ability to reduce global population through contraception and family planning. Humans also are capable of consciously choosing their diet and personal lifestyle, and these choices influence the number of people Earth can support.

Test Your Understanding

1. b **2.** a **3.** c **4.** d **5.** e **6.** c **7.** c **8.** d **9.** b **10.** a
11.

The total number of female offspring produced is greatest in females 1–2 years of age. Sample calculation for females of this age group: 252 indiv. × 1.07 female offspring/indiv. = 270 female offspring.

Chapter 54

Figure Questions

Figure 54.3 Its realized and fundamental niches would be similar, unlike those of *Chthamalus*. **Figure 54.16** The low-productivity treatment had the shortest food chain, so that food chain should be the most stable. **Figure 54.17** The death of individuals of *Mytilus*, a dominant species, should open up space for other species and increase species richness even in the absence of *Pisaster*. **Figure 54.23** At the earliest stages of primary succession, free-living prokaryotes in the soil would reduce atmospheric N_2 to NH_3. Symbiotic nitrogen fixation could not occur until plants were present at the site. **Figure 54.28** Other factors not included in the model must contribute to the number of species. **Figure 54.29** Shrew populations in different locations and habitats might show substantial genetic variation in their susceptibility to the Lyme pathogen. Further studies would be needed to test the generality of the results shown in Figure 54.29.

Concept Check 54.1

1. Interspecific competition has negative effects on both species $(-/-)$. In predation, the predator population benefits at the expense of the prey population $(+/-)$. Mutualism is a symbiosis in which both species benefit $(+/+)$. 2. One of the competing species will become locally extinct because of the greater reproductive success of the more efficient competitor. 3. By specializing in eating seeds of a single plant species, individuals of the two finch species may be less likely to come into contact in the separate habitats, reinforcing a reproductive barrier to hybridization.

Concept Check 54.2

1. Species richness, the number of species in the community, and relative abundance, the proportions of the community represented by the various species, both contribute to species diversity. Compared to a community with a very high proportion of one species, one with a more even proportion of species is considered more diverse. 2. The energetic hypothesis suggests that the length of a food chain is limited by the inefficiency of energy transfer along the chain, while the dynamic stability hypothesis proposes that long food chains are less stable than short chains. The energetic hypothesis predicts that food chains will be longer in habitats with higher primary productivity. The dynamic stability hypothesis predicts that food chains will be longer in more predictable environments. 3. According to the bottom-up model, adding extra predators would have little effect on lower trophic levels, particularly vegetation. If the top-down model applied, increased bobcat numbers would decrease raccoon numbers, increase snake numbers, decrease grasshopper numbers, and increase plant biomass.

Concept Check 54.3

1. High levels of disturbance are generally so disruptive that they eliminate many species from communities, leaving the community dominated by a few tolerant species. Low levels of disturbance permit competitively dominant species to exclude other species from the community. But moderate levels of disturbance can facilitate coexistence of a greater number of species in a community by preventing competitively dominant species from becoming abundant enough to eliminate other species from the community. 2. Early successional species can facilitate the arrival of other species in many ways, including increasing the fertility or water-holding capacity of soils or providing shelter to seedlings from wind and intense sunlight. 3. The absence of fire for 100 years would represent a change to a low level of disturbance. According to the intermediate disturbance hypothesis, this change should cause diversity to decline as competitively dominant species gain sufficient time to exclude less competitive species.

Concept Check 54.4

1. Ecologists propose that the greater species richness of tropical regions is the result of their longer evolutionary history and the greater solar energy input and water availability in tropical regions. 2. Immigration of species to islands declines with distance from the mainland and increases with island area. Extinction of species is lower on larger islands and on less isolated islands. Since the number of species on islands is largely determined by the difference between rates of immigration and extinction, the number of species will be highest on large islands near the mainland and lowest on small islands far from the mainland. 3. Because of their greater mobility, birds disperse to islands more often than snakes and lizards, so birds should have greater richness.

Concept Check 54.5

1. Pathogens are microorganisms, viruses, viroids, or prions that cause disease. 2. To keep the rabies virus out, you could ban imports of all mammals, including pets. Potentially, you could also attempt to vaccinate all dogs in the British Isles against the virus. A more practical approach might be to quarantine all pets brought into the country that are potential carriers of the disease, the approach the British government actually takes.

Summary of Key Concepts Questions

54.1 Competition: a fox and a bobcat competing for prey. Predation: an orca eating a sea otter. Herbivory: a bison grazing in a prairie. Parasitism: a parasitoid wasp that lays its eggs on a caterpillar. Mutualism: a fungus and an alga that make up a lichen. Commensalism: a remora attached to a whale. Facilitation: a flowering plant and its pollinator. **54.2** Not necessarily if the more species-rich community is dominated by only one or a few species **54.3** Because of the presence of species initially, the disturbance would initiate secondary succession in spite of its severe appearance. **54.4** Glaciations have severely reduced diversity in northern temperate, boreal, and Arctic ecosystems, compared to tropical ecosystems. **54.5** A host is required to complete the pathogen's life cycle, but a vector is not. Vectors are intermediate species that merely transport a pathogen to its host.

Test Your Understanding

1. e 2. d 3. c 4. a 5. b 6. c 7. d 8. b 9. Community 1: $H = -(0.05 \ln 0.05 + 0.05 \ln 0.05 + 0.85 \ln 0.85 + 0.05 \ln 0.05) = 0.59$. Community 2: $H = -(0.30 \ln 0.30 + 0.40 \ln 0.40 + 0.30 \ln 0.30) = 1.1$. Community 2 is more diverse.

10. Crab numbers should increase, reducing the abundance of eelgrass.

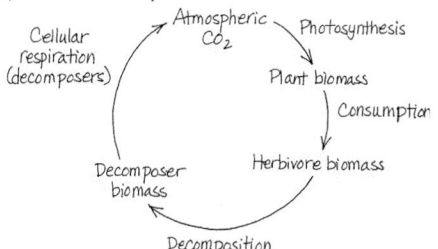

Chapter 55

Figure Questions

Figure 55.6 Wetlands, coral reefs, and coastal zones cover areas too small to show up clearly on global maps. **Figure 55.7** The availability of nutrients, particularly nitrogen, phosphorus, and iron, as well as temperature, is likely to limit primary production in the oceans. **Figure 55.8** If the new duck farms made nitrogen available in rich supply, as phosphorus already is, then adding extra nitrogen in the experiment would not increase phytoplankton density. **Figure 55.15** Water availability is probably another factor that varied across the sites. Such factors not included in the experimental design could make the results more difficult to interpret. Multiple factors can also covary in nature, so ecologists must be careful that the factor they are studying is actually causing the observed response and is not just correlated with it.

Concept Check 55.1

1. Energy passes through an ecosystem, entering as sunlight and leaving as heat. It is not recycled within the ecosystem. 2. You would need to know how much biomass the wildebeests ate from your plot and how much nitrogen was contained in that biomass. You would also need to know how much nitrogen they deposited in urine or feces. 3. The second law states that in any energy transfer or transformation, some of the energy is dissipated to the surroundings as heat. This "escape" of energy from an ecosystem is offset by the continuous influx of solar radiation.

Concept Check 55.2

1. Only a fraction of solar radiation strikes plants or algae, only a portion of that fraction is of wavelengths suitable for photosynthesis, and much energy is lost as a result of reflection or heating of plant tissue. 2. By manipulating the level of the factors of interest, such as phosphorus availability or soil moisture, and measuring responses by primary producers 3. The enzyme rubisco, which catalyzes the first step in the Calvin cycle, is the most abundant protein on Earth. Photosynthetic organisms require considerable nitrogen to make rubisco. Phosphorus is also needed as a component of several metabolites in the Calvin cycle and as a component of both ATP and NADPH (see Figure 10.19).

Concept Check 55.3

1. 20 J; 40% 2. Nicotine protects the plant from herbivores. 3. Unlike for the woman pictured in Figure 40.20, the caterpillar would have no energy devoted to thermoregulation or to reproduction. Its relative contribution to growth, however, would be much higher than for the woman.

Concept Check 55.4

1. For example, for the carbon cycle:

Cycling of a carbon atom

2. Removal of the trees stops nitrogen uptake from the soil, allowing nitrate to accumulate there. The nitrate is washed away by precipitation and enters the streams. 3. Most of the nutrients in a tropical rain forest are contained in the trees, so removing the trees by logging rapidly depletes nutrients from the ecosystem. The nutrients that remain in the soil are quickly carried away into streams and groundwater by the abundant precipitation.

Concept Check 55.5

1. The main goal is to restore degraded ecosystems to a more natural state. 2. Bioremediation uses organisms, generally prokaryotes, fungi, or plants, to detoxify or remove pollutants from ecosystems. Biological augmentation uses organisms, such as nitrogen-fixing plants, to add essential materials to degraded ecosystems. 3. The Kissimmee River project returns the flow of water to the original channel and restores natural flow, a self-sustaining outcome. Ecologists at the Maungatautari reserve will need to maintain the integrity of the fence indefinitely, an outcome that is not self-sustaining in the long term.

Summary of Key Concepts Questions

55.1 Because energy conversions are inefficient, with some energy inevitably lost as heat, you would expect that a given mass of primary producers would support a smaller biomass of secondary producers. **55.2** For estimates of NEP, you need to measure the respiration of all organisms in an ecosystem, not just the respiration of primary producers. In a sample of ocean water, primary producers and other organisms are usually mixed together, making their respective respirations hard to separate. **55.3** The runner would typically burn many more calories through respiration, reducing his or her production efficiency. **55.4** Factors other than temperature, including a shortage of water and nutrients, slow decomposition in hot deserts. **55.5** If the topsoil and deeper soil are kept separate, you could return the deeper soil to the site first and then apply the more fertile topsoil to improve the success of revegetation and other restoration efforts.

Test Your Understanding
1. c 2. b 3. d 4. d 5. c 6. e 7. a 8. e
9.

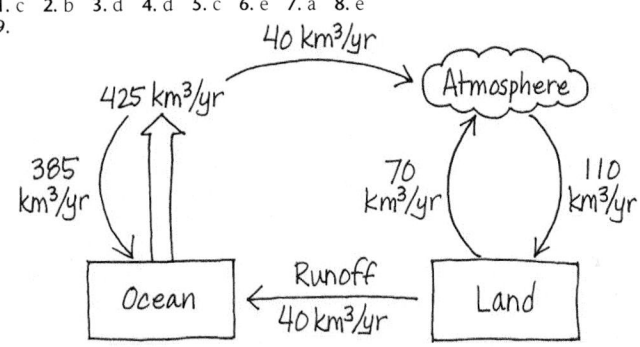

Based on these global numbers, approximately 110 km³ of precipitation falls over land each year.

Chapter 56

Figure Questions
Figure 56.4 You would need to know the complete range of the species and that it is missing across all of that range. You would also need to be certain that the species isn't hidden, as might be the case for an animal that is hibernating underground or a plant that is present in the form of seeds or spores. **Figure 56.9** The two examples are similar in that segments of DNA from the harvested samples were analyzed and compared with segments from specimens of known origin. One difference is that the whale researchers investigated relatedness at species and population levels to determine whether illegal activity had occurred, whereas the elephant investigators determined relatedness at the population level to determine the precise location of the poaching. Another difference is that mtDNA was used for the whale study, whereas STRs were used for the elephant study. The primary limitations of such approaches are the need to have (or generate) a reference database and the requirement that the organisms have sufficient variation in their DNA to reveal the relatedness of samples. **Figure 56.13** Because the population of Illinois birds has a different genetic makeup than birds in other regions, you would want to maintain to the greatest extent possible the frequency of beneficial genes or alleles found only in that population. In restoration, preserving genetic diversity in a species is as important as increasing organism numbers. **Figure 56.15** The natural disturbance regime in this habitat includes frequent fires that clear undergrowth but do not kill mature pine trees. Without these fires, the undergrowth quickly fills in and the habitat becomes unsuitable for red-cockaded woodpeckers.

Concept Check 56.1
1. In addition to species loss, the biodiversity crisis includes the loss of genetic diversity within populations and species and the degradation of entire ecosystems. 2. Habitat destruction, such as deforestation, channelizing of rivers, or conversion of natural ecosystems to agriculture or cities, deprives species of places to live. Introduced species, which are transported by humans to regions outside their native range, where they are not controlled by their natural pathogens or predators, often reduce the population sizes of native species through competition or predation. Overharvesting has reduced populations of plants and animals or driven them to extinction. Finally, global change is altering the environment to the extent that it reduces the capacity of Earth to sustain life. 3. If both populations breed separately, then gene flow between the populations would not occur and genetic differences between them would be greater. As a result, the loss of genetic diversity would be greater than if the populations interbreed.

Concept Check 56.2
1. Reduced genetic variation decreases the capacity of a population to evolve in the face of change. 2. The effective population size, N_e, was $4(15 \times 5)/(15 + 5) = 15$ birds. 3. Because millions of people use the greater Yellowstone ecosystem each year, it would be impossible to eliminate all contact between people and bears. Instead, you might try to reduce the kinds of encounters where bears are killed. You might recommend lower speed limits on roads in the park, adjust the timing or location of hunting seasons (where hunting is allowed outside the park) to minimize contact with mother bears and cubs, and provide financial incentives for livestock owners to try alternative means of protecting livestock, such as using guard dogs.

Concept Check 56.3
1. A small area supporting numerous endemic species as well as a large number of endangered and threatened species 2. Zoned reserves may provide sustained supplies of forest products, water, hydroelectric power, educational opportunities, and income from tourism. 3. Habitat corridors can increase the rate of movement or dispersal of organisms between habitat patches and thus the rate of gene flow between subpopulations. They thus help prevent a decrease in fitness attributable to inbreeding. They can also minimize interactions between organisms and humans as the organisms disperse; in cases involving potential predators, such as bears or large cats, minimizing such interactions is desirable.

Concept Check 56.4
1. Adding nutrients causes population explosions of algae and the organisms that feed on them. Increased respiration by algae and consumers, including detritivores, depletes the lake's oxygen, which the fish require. 2. Because higher temperatures lead to faster decomposition, organic matter in these soils could be quickly decomposed to CO_2, speeding up global warming. 3. Reduced concentrations of ozone in the atmosphere increase the amount of UV radiation that reaches Earth's surface and the organisms living there. UV radiation can cause mutations by producing disruptive thymine dimers in DNA.

Concept Check 56.5
1. Sustainable development is an approach to development that works toward the long-term prosperity of human societies and the ecosystems that support them, which requires linking the biological sciences with the social sciences, economics, and humanities. 2. Biophilia, our sense of connection to nature and all forms of life, may act as a significant motivation for the development of an environmental ethic that resolves not to allow species to become extinct or ecosystems to be destroyed. Such an ethic is necessary if we are to become more attentive and effective custodians of the environment. 3. At a minimum, you would want to know the size of the population and the average reproductive rate of individuals in it. To develop the fishery sustainably, you would seek a harvest rate that maintains the population near its original size and maximizes its harvest in the long term rather than the short term.

Summary of Key Concepts Questions
56.1. Nature provides us with many beneficial services, including a supply of reliable, clean water, the production of food and fiber, and the dilution and detoxification of our pollutants. **56.2.** A more genetically diverse population is better able to withstand pressures from disease or environmental change, making it less likely to become extinct over a given period of time. **56.3.** Habitat fragmentation can isolate populations, leading to inbreeding and genetic drift, and it can make populations more susceptible to local extinctions resulting from the effects of pathogens, parasites, or predators. **56.4.** It's healthier to feed at a lower trophic level because biological magnification increases the concentration of toxins at higher levels. **56.5.** One goal of conservation biology is to preserve as many species as possible. Sustainable approaches that maintain the quality of habitats are required for the long-term survival of organisms.

Test Your Understanding
1. d 2. d 3. e 4. a 5. c 6. a
7.

Between 1974 and 2009, Earth's atmospheric CO_2 concentration increased from approximately 330 ppm to 390 ppm. If this rate of increase of 1.7 ppm/yr continues, the concentration in 2 ATP and NADPH (see 0 will be about 540 ppm. The actual rise in CO_2 concentration could be larger or smaller, depending on Earth's human population, per capita energy use, and the extent to which societies take steps to reduce CO_2 emissions, including replacing fossil fuels with renewable or nuclear fuels. Additional scientific data will be important for many reasons, including determining how quickly greenhouse gases such as CO_2 are removed from the atmosphere by the biosphere.
9.

To minimize the area of forest into which the cowbirds penetrate, you should locate the road along one edge of the reserve. Any other location would increase the area of affected habitat. Similarly, the maintenance building should be in a corner of the reserve to minimize the area susceptible to cowbirds.

Periodic Table of the Elements

Name (Symbol)	Atomic Number	Name (Symbol)	Atomic Number	Name (Symbol)	Atomic Number	Name (Symbol)	Atomic Number	Name (Symbol)	Atomic Number
Actinium (Ac)	89	Copernicium (Cn)	112	Iridium (Ir)	77	Palladium (Pd)	46	Sodium (Na)	11
Aluminum (Al)	13	Copper (Cu)	29	Iron (Fe)	26	Phosphorus (P)	15	Strontium (Sr)	38
Americium (Am)	95	Curium (Cm)	96	Krypton (Kr)	36	Platinum (Pt)	78	Sulfur (S)	16
Antimony (Sb)	51	Darmstadtium (Ds)	110	Lanthanum (La)	57	Plutonium (Pu)	94	Tantalum (Ta)	73
Argon (Ar)	18	Dubnium (Db)	105	Lawrencium (Lr)	103	Polonium (Po)	84	Technetium (Tc)	43
Arsenic (As)	33	Dysprosium (Dy)	66	Lead (Pb)	82	Potassium (K)	19	Tellurium (Te)	52
Astatine (At)	85	Einsteinium (Es)	99	Lithium (Li)	3	Praseodymium (Pr)	59	Terbium (Tb)	65
Barium (Ba)	56	Erbium (Er)	68	Lutetium (Lu)	71	Promethium (Pm)	61	Thallium (Tl)	81
Berkelium (Bk)	97	Europium (Eu)	63	Magnesium (Mg)	12	Protactinium (Pa)	91	Thorium (Th)	90
Beryllium (Be)	4	Fermium (Fm)	100	Manganese (Mn)	25	Radium (Ra)	88	Thulium (Tm)	69
Bismuth (Bi)	83	Fluorine (F)	9	Meitnerium (Mt)	109	Radon (Rn)	86	Tin (Sn)	50
Bohrium (Bh)	107	Francium (Fr)	87	Mendelevium (Md)	101	Rhenium (Re)	75	Titanium (Ti)	22
Boron (B)	5	Gadolinium (Gd)	64	Mercury (Hg)	80	Rhodium (Rh)	45	Tungsten (W)	74
Bromine (Br)	35	Gallium (Ga)	31	Molybdenum (Mo)	42	Roentgenium (Rg)	111	Uranium (U)	92
Cadmium (Cd)	48	Germanium (Ge)	32	Neodymium (Nd)	60	Rubidium (Rb)	37	Vanadium (V)	23
Calcium (Ca)	20	Gold (Au)	79	Neon (Ne)	10	Ruthenium (Ru)	44	Xenon (Xe)	54
Californium (Cf)	98	Hafnium (Hf)	72	Neptunium (Np)	93	Rutherfordium (Rf)	104	Ytterbium (Yb)	70
Carbon (C)	6	Hassium (Hs)	108	Nickel (Ni)	28	Samarium (Sm)	62	Yttrium (Y)	39
Cerium (Ce)	58	Helium (He)	2	Niobium (Nb)	41	Scandium (Sc)	21	Zinc (Zn)	30
Cesium (Cs)	55	Holmium (Ho)	67	Nitrogen (N)	7	Seaborgium (Sg)	106	Zirconium (Zr)	40
Chlorine (Cl)	17	Hydrogen (H)	1	Nobelium (No)	102	Selenium (Se)	34		
Chromium (Cr)	24	Indium (In)	49	Osmium (Os)	76	Silicon (Si)	14		
Cobalt (Co)	27	Iodine (I)	53	Oxygen (O)	8	Silver (Ag)	47		

The Metric System

Measurement	Unit and Abbreviation	Metric Equivalent	Metric-to-English Conversion Factor	English-to-Metric Conversion Factor
Length	1 kilometer (km)	= 1,000 (10^3) meters	1 km = 0.62 mile	1 mile = 1.61 km
	1 meter (m)	= 100 (10^2) centimeters	1 m = 1.09 yards	1 yard = 0.914 m
		= 1,000 millimeters	1 m = 3.28 feet	1 foot = 0.305 m
			1 m = 39.37 inches	
	1 centimeter (cm)	= 0.01 (10^{-2}) meter	1 cm = 0.394 inch	1 foot = 30.5 cm
				1 inch = 2.54 cm
	1 millimeter (mm)	= 0.001 (10^{-3}) meter	1 mm = 0.039 inch	
	1 micrometer (μm) (formerly micron, μ)	= 10^{-6} meter (10^{-3} mm)		
	1 nanometer (nm) (formerly millimicron, mμ)	= 10^{-9} meter (10^{-3} μm)		
	1 angstrom (Å)	= 10^{-10} meter (10^{-4} μm)		
Area	1 hectare (ha)	= 10,000 square meters	1 ha = 2.47 acres	1 acre = 0.405 ha
	1 square meter (m²)	= 10,000 square centimeters	1 m² = 1.196 square yards	1 square yard = 0.8361 m²
			1 m² = 10.764 square feet	1 square foot = 0.0929 m²
	1 square centimeter (cm²)	= 100 square millimeters	1 cm² = 0.155 square inch	1 square inch = 6.4516 cm²
Mass	1 metric ton (t)	= 1,000 kilograms	1 t = 1.103 tons	1 ton = 0.907 t
	1 kilogram (kg)	= 1,000 grams	1 kg = 2.205 pounds	1 pound = 0.4536 kg
	1 gram (g)	= 1,000 milligrams	1 g = 0.0353 ounce	1 ounce = 28.35 g
			1 g = 15.432 grains	
	1 milligram (mg)	= 10^{-3} gram	1 mg = approx. 0.015 grain	
	1 microgram (μg)	= 10^{-6} gram		
Volume (solids)	1 cubic meter (m³)	= 1,000,000 cubic centimeters	1 m³ = 1.308 cubic yards	1 cubic yard = 0.7646 m³
			1 m³ = 35.315 cubic feet	1 cubic foot = 0.0283 m³
	1 cubic centimeter (cm³ or cc)	= 10^{-6} cubic meter	1 cm³ = 0.061 cubic inch	1 cubic inch = 16.387 cm³
	1 cubic millimeter (mm³)	= 10^{-9} cubic meter = 10^{-3} cubic centimeter		
Volume (liquids and gases)	1 kiloliter (kL or kl)	= 1,000 liters	1 kL = 264.17 gallons	
	1 liter (L or l)	= 1,000 milliliters	1 L = 0.264 gallons	1 gallon = 3.785 L
			1 L = 1.057 quarts	1 quart = 0.946 L
	1 milliliter (mL or ml)	= 10^{-3} liter	1 mL = 0.034 fluid ounce	1 quart = 946 mL
		= 1 cubic centimeter	1 mL = approx. ¼ teaspoon	1 pint = 473 mL
			1 mL = approx. 15–16 drops (gtt.)	1 fluid ounce = 29.57 mL
				1 teaspoon = approx. 5 mL
	1 microliter (μL or μl)	= 10^{-6} liter (10^{-3} milliliters)		
Time	1 second (s or sec)	= ⅟₆₀ minute		
	1 millisecond (ms or msec)	= 10^{-3} second		
Temperature	Degrees Celsius (°C) (Absolute zero, when all molecular motion ceases, is −273.15°C. The Kelvin [K] scale, which has the same size degrees as Celsius, has its zero point at absolute zero. Thus, 0 K = −273.15°C.)		°F = ⅘°C + 32	°C = ⅚ (°F − 32)

A Comparison of the Light Microscope and the Electron Microscope

Light Microscope

In light microscopy, light is focused on a specimen by a glass condenser lens; the image is then magnified by an objective lens and an ocular lens, for projection on the eye, digital camera, digital video camera, or photographic film.

Electron Microscope

In electron microscopy, a beam of electrons (top of the microscope) is used instead of light, and electromagnets are used instead of glass lenses. The electron beam is focused on the specimen by a condenser lens; the image is magnified by an objective lens and a projector lens for projection on a digital detector, fluorescent screen, or photographic film.

Classification of Life

This appendix presents a taxonomic classification for the major extant groups of organisms discussed in this text; not all phyla are included. The classification presented here is based on the three-domain system, which assigns the two major groups of prokaryotes, bacteria and archaea, to separate domains (with eukaryotes making up the third domain).

Various alternative classification schemes are discussed in Unit Five of the text. The taxonomic turmoil includes debates about the number and boundaries of kingdoms and about the alignment of the Linnaean classification hierarchy with the findings of modern cladistic analysis. In this review, asterisks (*) indicate currently recognized phyla thought by some systematists to be paraphyletic.

DOMAIN BACTERIA

- Proteobacteria
- Chlamydia
- Spirochetes
- Gram-positive Bacteria
- Cyanobacteria

DOMAIN ARCHAEA

- **Korarchaeota**
- **Euryarchaeota**
- **Crenarchaeota**
- **Nanoarchaeota**

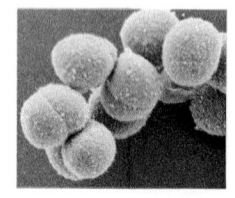

DOMAIN EUKARYA

In the phylogenetic hypothesis we present in Chapter 28, major clades of eukaryotes are grouped together in the five "supergroups" listed below in blue type. Formerly, all the eukaryotes generally called protists were assigned to a single kingdom, Protista. However, advances in systematics have made it clear that Protista is in fact polyphyletic: Some protists are more closely related to plants, fungi, or animals than they are to other protists. As a result, the kingdom Protista has been abandoned.

Excavata
- Diplomonadida (diplomonads)
- Parabasala (parabasalids)
- Euglenozoa (euglenozoans)
    Kinetoplastida (kinetoplastids)
    Euglenophyta (euglenids)

Chromalveolata
- Alveolata (alveolates)
    Dinoflagellata (dinoflagellates)
    Apicomplexa (apicomplexans)
    Ciliophora (ciliates)
- Stramenopila (stramenopiles)
    Bacillariophyta (diatoms)
    Chrysophyta (golden algae)
    Phaeophyta (brown algae)
    Oomycota (water molds)

Archaeplastida
- Rhodophyta (red algae)
- Chlorophyta (green algae: chlorophytes)
- Charophyta (green algae: charophytes)
- Plantae
    Phylum Hepatophyta (liverworts)
    Phylum Bryophyta (mosses) } Nonvascular plants (bryophytes)
    Phylum Anthocerophyta (hornworts)
    Phylum Lycophyta (lycophytes)
    Phylum Pterophyta (ferns, horsetails, whisk ferns) } Seedless vascular plants
    Phylum Ginkgophyta (ginkgo)
    Phylum Cycadophyta (cycads)
    Phylum Gnetophyta (gnetophytes) } Gymnosperms
    Phylum Coniferophyta (conifers)
    Phylum Anthophyta (flowering plants) } Angiosperms

Gymnosperms and Angiosperms = Seed plants

Rhizaria
- Radiolaria (radiolarians)
- Foraminifera (forams)
- Cercozoa (cercozoans)

Unikonta

- Amoebozoa (amoebozoans)
  - Myxogastrida (plasmodial slime molds)
  - Dictyostelida (cellular slime molds)
  - Gymnamoeba (gymnamoebas)
  - Entamoeba (entamoebas)
- Nucleariida (nucleariids)
- Fungi
  - *Phylum Chytridiomycota (chytrids)
  - *Phylum Zygomycota (zygomycetes)
  - Phylum Glomeromycota (glomeromycetes)
  - Phylum Basidiomycota (club fungi)
  - Phylum Ascomycota (sac fungi)

- Choanoflagellata (choanoflagellates)
- Animalia
  - Phylum Porifera (sponges)
  - Phylum Ctenophora (comb jellies)
  - Phylum Cnidaria (cnidarians)
    - Hydrozoa (hydrozoans)
    - Scyphozoa (jellies)
    - Cubozoa (box jellies and sea wasps)
    - Anthozoa (sea anemones and most corals)
  - Phylum Acoela (acoel flatworms)
  - Phylum Placozoa (placozoans)

Lophotrochozoa (lophotrochozoans)
  - Phylum Kinorhyncha (kinorhynchs)
  - Phylum Platyhelminthes (flatworms)
    - Catenulida (chain worms)
    - Rhabditophora (planarians, flukes, tapeworms)
  - Phylum Nemertea (proboscis worms)
  - Phylum Ectoprocta (ectoprocts)
  - Phylum Brachiopoda (brachiopods)
  - Phylum Phoronida (phoronids)
  - Phylum Rotifera (rotifers)
  - Phylum Cycliophora (cycliophorans)
  - Phylum Mollusca (molluscs)
    - Polyplacophora (chitons)
    - Gastropoda (gastropods)
    - Bivalvia (bivalves)
    - Cephalopoda (cephalopods)

Phylum Annelida (segmented worms)
  - Polychaeta (polychaetes)
  - Oligochaeta (oligochaetes)
Phylum Acanthocephala (spiny-headed worms)
Ecdysozoa (ecdysozoans)
  - Phylum Loricifera (loriciferans)
  - Phylum Priapula (priapulans)
  - Phylum Nematoda (roundworms)
  - Phylum Arthropoda (This survey groups arthropods into a single phylum, but some zoologists now split the arthropods into multiple phyla.)
    - Subphylum Chelicerata (horseshoe crabs, arachnids)
    - Subphylum Myriapoda (millipedes, centipedes)
    - Subphylum Hexapoda (insects, springtails)
    - Subphylum Crustacea (crustaceans)
  - Phylum Tardigrada (tardigrades)
  - Phylum Onychophora (velvet worms)
Deuterostomia (deuterostomes)
  - Phylum Hemichordata (hemichordates)
  - Phylum Echinodermata (echinoderms)
    - Asteroidea (sea stars, sea daisies)
    - Ophiuroidea (brittle stars)
    - Echinoidea (sea urchins and sand dollars)
    - Crinoidea (sea lilies)
    - Holothuroidea (sea cucumbers)
  - Phylum Chordata (chordates)
    - Subphylum Cephalochordata (cephalochordates: lancelets)
    - Subphylum Urochrodata (urochordates: tunicates)
    - Subphylum Craniata (craniates)
      - Myxini (hagfishes)
      - Petromyzontida (lampreys)
      - Chondrichthyes (sharks, rays, chimaeras)
      - Actinopterygii (ray-finned fishes)
      - Actinistia (coelacanths)
      - Dipnoi (lungfishes)
      - Amphibia (amphibians)
      - Reptilia (tuataras, lizards, snakes, turtles, crocodilians, birds)
      - Mammalia (mammals)

} Vertebrates

Credits

Photo Credits

Cover Image "Succulent I" © 2005 Amy Lamb, www.amylamb.com

Unit Opening Interviews **UNIT 1** Justina Thorsen, Showcase Reflections; **UNIT 2** Brian Wilson, Princeton University; **UNIT 3** William K. Sacco, Yale ITS Photo + Design Services; **UNIT 4** Steve Bonnel, Bonnel Photography; **UNIT 5** Jacob Mailman; **UNIT 6** Michael Starghill, Michael Starghill Photography; **UNIT 7** River Healey, Rusty Healey Photography; **UNIT 8** Marsha Miller, Director of Photography, University of Texas at Austin.

About the Author Photos River Healey, Rusty Healey Photography.

Detailed Contents **UNIT I** Photo by T. Naeser, from Patrick Cramer Laboratory, Gene Center Munich, Ludwig-Maximilians-Universität München, Munich, Germany; **UNIT II** Biophoto Associates/Photo Researchers; **UNIT III** From: Multicolor Spectral Karyotyping of Human Chromosomes. E. Schröck, S. du Manoir, T. Veldman, B. Schoell, J. Wienberg, M. A. Ferguson-Smith, Y. Ning, D. H. Ledbetter, I. Bar-Am, D. Soenksen, Y. Garini, T. Ried. *Science*. 1996 Jul 26;273(5274):494-7.; **UNIT IV** © Ted Daeschler/Academy of Natural Sciences/VIREO; **UNIT V** Yufeng Zhou/iStockphoto; **UNIT VI** PD photo: John Walker (www.fourmilab.ch); **UNIT VII** David Wall/Alamy; David Doubilet/Getty Images; Kenneth Catania; **UNIT VIII** Daniel Mosquin.

Chapter 1 **1.1** Amy Lamb Studio; **1.2** Walter Teague; **1.3.2** R.Dirscherl/FLPA; **1.3.3** Kim Taylor and Jane Burton/Dorling Kindersley; **1.3.4** Malcolm Schuyl/FLPA; **1.3.5** Frans Lanting/Corbis; **1.3.6** Michael & Patricia Fogden/Corbis; **1.3.7** Joe McDonald/Corbis; **1.3.8** ImageState/International Stock Photography Ltd.; **1.4.2** WorldSat International/Photo Researchers, Inc.; **1.4.3** Bill Brooks/Alamy; **1.4.4** Linda Freshwaters Arndt/Alamy; **1.4.5** Michael Orton/Photographer's Choice/Getty Images; **1.4.6** Ross M. Horowitz/Getty Images; **1.4.7** Photodisc/Getty Images; **1.4.9** Jeremy Burgess/SPL/Photo Researchers; **1.4.11** John Durham/Photo Researchers; **1.4.13** Electron micrograph by Wm. P. Wergin, courtesy of E. H. Newcomb, University of Wisconsin; **1.5.2** James Balog/Aurora Creative/Getty Images; **1.6.2** Anup Shah/Nature Picture Library; **1.6.3** Anup Shah/Nature Picture Library; **1.7.2** Photodisc/Getty Images; **1.7.3** Janice Sheldon; **1.8.2** S. C. Holt/Biological Photo Service; **1.8.3** Steve Gschmeissner/Photo Researchers; **1.9.2** Conly L. Rieder; **1.9.3** Conly L. Rieder; **1.10.2** Camille Tokerud/Stone/Getty Images; **1.11.2** Photodisc/Getty Images; **1.12** Roy Kaltschmidt, Lawrence Berkeley National Laboratory; **1.15.2** Oliver Meckes/Nicole Ottawa/Photo Researchers; **1.15.3** Eye of Science/Photo Researchers; **1.15.4** Kunst & Scheidulin/AGE Fotostock; **1.15.5** Peter Lilja/Taxi/Getty Images; **1.15.6** Anup Shah/Nature Picture Library; **1.15.7** D. P. Wilson/Photo Researchers; **1.16.2** VVG/SPL/Photo Researchers; **1.16.3** W. L. Dentler/Biological Photo Service; **1.16.4** OMIKRON/Photo Researchers; **1.17** Photo by Dede Randrianarisata, from Kristi Curry Rogers, Macalester College, St. Paul, MN; **1.18** ARCHIV/Photo Researchers; **1.19.2** Michael P. Fogden/Bruce Coleman/Alamy; **1.19.3** Matt T. Lee; **1.19.4** Hal Horwitz/Corbis; **1.21** Frank Greenaway/Dorling Kindersley; **1.23.2** Karl Ammann/Corbis; **1.23.3** Tim Ridley/Dorling Kindersley, Courtesy of the Jane Goodall Institute, Clarendon Park, Hampshire; **1.25.2** Breck P. Kent; **1.25.3** Photo Researchers; **1.26.2** David Pfennig; **1.26.3** David Pfennig; **1.28** Gary L. Firestone's Lab researchers meeting in the Dept. of Molecular and Cell Biology, University of California at Berkeley. Photo: Seelevel.com, Pearson Science; **1.29** Tim Sharp/AP Images; **p. 25, top right** James Balog/Aurora Creative/Getty Images; **p. 25, bottom left** Anup Shah/Nature Picture Library; **p. 25, bottom right** Anup Shah/Nature Picture Library; **p.26, top** PhotoDisc/Getty Images; **p. 26, 2nd from top** S. C. Holt/Biological Photo Service; **p. 26, 3rd from top** Steve Gschmeissner/Photo Researchers.

Chapter 2 **2.1** Martin Dohrn/BBC Natural History Unit; **2.2.3** Martin Dohrn/BBC Natural History Unit; **2.3.2** Chip Clark; **2.4.2** C. Michael Hogan; **2.4.3** Rick York and California Native Plant Society (www.cnps.org); **2.4.4** Andrew Alden; **2.6.2** Clayton T. Hamilton, Stanford University; **2.7.2** National Library of Medicine; **p. 41, left** Jerry Young/Dorling Kindersley; **2.19** Nigel Cattlin/Photo Researchers; **p. 45** Rolf Nussbaumer/Nature Picture Library.

Chapter 3 **3.1** Alexander/Fotoloia; **3.3.2** N.C. Brown Center for Ultrastructure Studies, SUNY-Environmental Science & Forestry, Syracuse, NY; **3.4** iStockphoto; **3.6.2** Jan van Franeker, IMARES, Alfred Wegener Institute for Polar and Marine Research; **3.9** NASA/JPL-Caltech/University of Arizona/Texas A&M University; **3.10.2** Jakub Semeniuk/iStockphoto; **3.10.3** Feng Yu/iStockphoto; **3.10.4** Monika Wisniewska/iStockphoto; **3.10.5** Beth Van Trees/Shutterstock; **3.12.2** From "Coral Reefs Under Rapid Climate Change and Ocean Acidification." O. Hoegh-Guldberg, et al. *Science* 14 December 2007: 318 (5857):1737–1742. Photos by Ove Hoegh-Guldberg, Centre for Marine Studies, The University of Queensland; **3.12.3** From "Coral Reefs Under Rapid Climate Change and Ocean Acidification." O. Hoegh-Guldberg, et al. *Science* 14 December 2007: 318 (5857):1737–1742. Photos by Ove Hoegh-Guldberg, Centre for Marine Studies, The University of Queensland; **3.12.4** From "Coral Reefs Under Rapid Climate Change and Ocean Acidification." O. Hoegh-Guldberg, et al. *Science* 14 December 2007: 318 (5857):1737–1742. Photos by Ove Hoegh-Guldberg, Centre for Marine Studies, The University of Queensland.

Chapter 4 **4.1** Shutterstock; **4.6.2** David M. Phillips/Photo Researchers.

Chapter 5 **5.1** Photo by T. Naeser, from Patrick Cramer Laboratory, Gene Center Munich, Ludwig-Maximilians-Universität München, Munich, Germany; **5.6.2** John N. A. Lott/Biological Photo Service; **5.6.3** H. Shio and P. B. Lazarow; **5.8.2** Alexey Repka/iStockphoto; **5.8.3** John Durham/Photo Researchers; **5.8.4** Biophoto Associates/Photo Researchers; **5.9.2** F. Collet/Photo Researchers; **5.9.3** Corbis; **5.11.2** Dorling Kindersley; **5.11.3** Dorling Kindersley; **5.15.2** Andrey Stratilatov/Shutterstock; **5.15.3** Nina Zanetti; **5.15.4** Nina Zanetti; **5.19.2** Reproduced by permission from Tulip WR, Varghese JN, Laver WG, Webster RG, Colman PM. Refined crystal structure of the influenza virus N9 neuraminidase-NC41 Fab complex. *J Mol Biol.* September 5; 227(1):122–48. Copyright © 1992 by Elsevier Science Ltd. **5.20.3** Dieter Hopf/AGE Fotostock; **5.20.8** Monika Wisniewska/iStockphoto; **5.21.2** Eye of Science/Photo Researchers; **5.21.3** Eye of Science/Photo Researchers; **5.23.2** Reprinted by permission from *Nature*. P. B. Sigler from Z. Xu, A. L. Horwich, and P. B. Sigler. 388:741–750 Copyright © 1997 Macmillan Magazines Limited; **5.24.2** Dave Bushnell; **5.24.4** Dave Bushnell; **p. 90** Dorling Kindersley.

Chapter 6 **6.1** Eye of Science/Photo Researchers; **6.3.2** Elisabeth Pierson, FNWI-Radboud University Nijmegen, Pearson Science; **6.3.3** Elisabeth Pierson, FNWI-Radboud University Nijmegen, Pearson Science; **6.3.4** Elisabeth Pierson, FNWI-Radboud University Nijmegen, Pearson Science; **6.3.5** Elisabeth Pierson, FNWI-Radboud University Nijmegen, Pearson Science; **6.3.6** Michael W. Davidson/The Florida State University Research Foundation; **6.3.7** Karl Garsha, Beckman Institute for Advanced Science and Technology, University of Illinois; **6.3.9** Macrophage fluorescently stained for tubulin (yellow), actin (red) and the nucleus (DAPI, blue). Top part of the image: data recorded with a widefield microscope and visualized with the Simulated Fluorescence Process (SFP) volume rendering algorithm. Bottom part: the same dataset, deconvolved using Huygens Professional (Scientific Volume Imaging, Hilversum, The Netherlands) and again rendered with the SFP algorithm. Data courtesy Dr. James G. Evans, Whitehead Institute, MIT Boston MA, USA; **6.3.11** From "Motile Cilia of Human Airway Epithelia Are Chemosensory." Alok S. Shah, Yehuda Ben-Shahar, T.s O. Moninger, J. N. Kline, M. J. Welsh. Science Express on 23 July 2009. *Science* 28 August 2009:325 (5944): 1131–1134 (cover). Pseudocolored scanning electron micrograph by Tom Moninger (epithelia generated by Phil Karp); **6.3.12** William Dentler/Biological Photo Service; **6.3.13** From "STED microscopy reveals that synaptotagmin remains clustered after synaptic vesicle exocytosis." Katrin I. Willig, Silvio O. Rizzoli, Volker Westphal, Reinhard Jahn & . . . Stefan W. Hell. *Nature*, 440 (13) April 2006. doi:10.1038/nature04592, Letters; **6.5.2** S. C. Holt/Biological Photo Service; **6.6.2** Daniel Friend; **6.8.4** S. Cinti/Photo Researchers; **6.8.6** SPL/Photo Researchers; **6.8.8** A. Barry Dowsett/Photo Researchers; **6.8.10** Biophoto Associates/Photo Researchers; **6.8.12** SPL/Photo Researchers; **6.8.14** From "Flagellar Microtubule Dynamics in *Chlamydomonas*: Cytochalasin D Induces Periods of Microtubule Shortening and Elongation; and Colchicine Induces Disassembly of the Distal, but Not Proximal, Half of the Flagellum." W. L. Dentler and C. Adams. *The Journal of Cell Biology*, 117(6): 1289–1298, Copyright © 1992 by The Rockefeller University Press; **6.9.2** Reproduced by permission from L.Orci and A.Perelet, Freeze-Etch Histology. (Heidelberg: Springer-Verlag, 1975). Copyright ©1975 by Springer-Verlag GmbH & Co KG; **6.9.3** Reproduced by permission from A. C. Faberge, *Cell Tiss. Res.* 151 Copyright © 1974 by Springer-Verlag GmbH & Co KG; **6.9.4** Reprinted by permission from *Nature* 323. U. Aebi et al. Copyright © 1996: 560–564, figure 1a. Used with permission. Macmillan Magazines Limited; **6.10.2** D. W. Fawcett/Photo Researchers; **6.11.2** R. Bolender, D. Fawcett/Photo Researchers; **6.12.2** Don W. Fawcett/Photo Researchers; **6.13.2** Daniel S. Friend; **6.13.3** Daniel S. Friend; **6.14.2** E. H. Newcomb; **6.17.2** Daniel S. Friend; **6.17.3** From "The shape of mitochondria and the number of mitochondrial nucleoids during the cell cycle of *Euglena gracilis*." Y. Hayashi and K. Ueda. *Journal of Cell Science*, 93:565–570, Copyright © 1989 by Company of Biologists; **6.18.2** Courtesy of W.P. Wergin and E.H. Newcomb, University of Wisconsin/Biological Photo Service; **6.18.3** Franz Grolig, Philipps-University Marburg, Germany. Image acquired with the confocal microscope Leica TCS SP2; **6.19.2** From S. E. Fredrick and E. H. Newcomb, *The Journal of Cell Biology* 43 (1969):343. Provided by E. H. Newcomb; **6.20** Albert Tousson, High Resolution Imaging Facility, University of Alabama at Birmingham; **6.21.2** Dr. Bruce J. Schnapp; **p. 113, left** Mary Osborn; **p. 113, middle** Frank Solomon; **p. 113, right** Mark S. Ladinsky and J. Richard McIntosh, University of Colorado; **6.22.2** Kent L. McDonald; **6.23.2** Biophoto Associates/Photo Researchers; **6.23.3** Oliver Meckes & Nicole Ottawa/Eye of Science/Photo Researchers; **6.24.2** OMIKRON/Science Source/Photo Researchers; **6.24.3** W. L. Dentler/Biological Photo Service; **6.24.4** Linck RW, Stephens RE. Functional protofilament numbering of ciliary, flagellar, and centriolar microtubules. *Cell Motil Cytoskeleton.* 2007 Jul;64(7):489–95; cover. Micrograph by D. Woodrum Hensley; **6.26.2** From Hirokawa Nobutaka, *The Journal of Cell Biology* 94 (1982):425 by copyright permission of The Rockefeller University Press; **6.27.2** Clara Franzini-Armstrong, University of Pennsylvania; **6.27.3** M. I. Walker/Photo Researchers; **6.27.4** Michael Clayton, University of Wisconsin-Madison; **6.28.2** G. F. Leedale/Photo Researchers; **6.29.2** David Ehrhardt; **6.29.3** From "Visualization of cellulose synthase demonstrates functional association with microtubules." A. R. Paredez, C. R. Somerville, D. W. Ehrhardt. *Science.* 2006 Jun 9;312(5779):1491–5. Epub 2006 Apr 20; **6.31.2** Micrograph by W. P. Wergin, provided by E. H. Newcomb; **6.32.2** From Douglas J. Kelly, *The Journal of Cell Biology* 28 (1966): 51. Fig.17. Reproduced by copyright permission of The Rockefeller University Press; **6.32.3** From Douglas J. Kelly, *The Journal of Cell Biology* 28 (1966):51 by copyright permission of The Rockefeller University Press; **6.32.5** Reproduced by permission from L. Orci and A. Perrelet, Freeze-Etch Histology. (Heidelberg: Springer-Verlag). Copyright © 1975 by Springer-Verlag GmbH & Co KG; **6.32.7** From C. Peracchia and A. F. Dulhunty, *The Journal of Cell Biology* 70 (1976):419 by copyright permission of The Rockefeller University Press; **6.33.2** Lennart Nilsson/Scanpix; **p. 123, top** Courtesy E. H. Newcomb; **p. 123, bottom** From S. E. Fredrick and E. H. Newcomb, *The Journal of Cell Biology* 43 (1969): 343.

Chapter 7 **7.1** Roderick Mackinnon; **7.4.3** D. W. Fawcett/Photo Researchers; **7.4.4** D. W. Fawcett/Photo Researchers; **7.16.2.** Michael Abbey/Photo Researchers; **7.22.3** H. S. Pankratz, T.C. Beaman & P. Gerhardt/Biological Photo Service; **7.22.6** D. W. Fawcett/Photo Researchers; **7.22.9** M. M. Perry and A. B. Gilbert, *J. Cell Science* 39 (1979) 257. Copyright 1979 by The Company of Biologists Ltd. **7.22.10** M. M. Perry and A. B. Gilbert, *J. Cell Science* 39 (1979) 257. Copyright 1979 by The Company of Biologists Ltd.

Chapter 8 **8.1** Photoshot/NHPA; **8.2.2** Jupiter Images; **8.3.2** Robert N. Johnson/RnJ Photography; **8.3.3** Robert N. Johnson/RnJ Photography; **8.4.1** Brandon Blinken-

Plant Research Laboratory, Michigan State University; **39.14.3** Joe Kieber, University of North Carolina; **39.15.2** Ed Reschke; **39.16.3** Malcolm B. Wilkins, University of Glasgow, Glasgow, Scotland, U.K. **39.16.4** Malcolm B. Wilkins, University of Glasgow, Glasgow, Scotland, U.K. **39.17.2** Malcolm B. Wilkins, University of Glasgow, Glasgow, Scotland, U.K. **39.17.3** Malcolm B. Wilkins, University of Glasgow, Glasgow, Scotland, U.K. **39.17.4** Malcolm B. Wilkins, University of Glasgow, Glasgow, Scotland, U.K. **39.17.5** Malcolm B. Wilkins, University of Glasgow, Glasgow, Scotland, U.K. **39.17.6** Malcolm B. Wilkins, University of Glasgow, Glasgow, Scotland, U.K. **39.20.2** Malcolm B. Wilkins, University of Glasgow, Glasgow, Scotland, U.K. **39.20.3** Malcolm B. Wilkins, University of Glasgow, Glasgow, Scotland, U.K. **39.24.2** Michael Evans, Ohio State University; **39.24.3** Michael Evans, Ohio State University; **39.24.4** Michael Evans, Ohio State University; **39.24.5** Michael Evans, Ohio State University; **39.25** Reproduced by permission from Janet Braam, *Cell* 60 (9 February 1990): Cover. Copyright © 1990 Cell Press. Image courtesy of Elsevier Sciences Ltd. **39.26.2** Martin Shields/Photo Researchers; **39.26.3** Martin Shields/Photo Researchers; **39.26.4** From K. Esau. "Anatomy of Seed Plants," 2nd ed. (New York: John Wiley and Sons, 1977), fig. 19.4, p.358; **39.26.5** From K. Esau. "Anatomy of Seed Plants," 2nd ed. (New York: John Wiley and sons, 1977), fig. 19.4, p.358; **39.27.2** J. L. Basq and M. C. Drew; **39.27.3** J. L. Basq and M. C. Drew; **39.29.2** New York State Agricultural Experiment Station (NYSAES)/Cornell.

Chapter 40 **40.1** JOEL SARTORE/National Geographic Stock; **40.2.2** Peter Aitken/ Peter Arnold Images/ PhotoLibrary; **40.2.3** Duncan Usher/Alamy; **40.2.4** Frank Greenaway/Dorling Kindersley/Getty Images; **40.4.2** Susumu Nishinaga/Photo Researchers; **40.4.3** Eye of Science/Photo Researchers; **40.4.4** Susumu Nishinaga/Photo Researchers; **40.5.7** CNRI/SPL/Photo Researchers; **40.5.11** Dr. Gopal Murti/SPL/Photo Researchers; **40.5.13** Chuck Brown/Photo Researchers; **40.5.15** Nina Zanetti; **40.5.17** Nina Zanetti; **40.5.19** Nina Zanetti; **40.5.21** Alamy; **40.5.24** Nina Zanetti; **40.5.26** Ed Reschke/Peter Arnold Images/PhotoLibrary; **40.5.28** Manfred Kage/Peter Arnold/PhotoLibrary; **40.5.31** Ulrich Gartner; **40.5.33** Thomas Deerinck/National Center for Microscopy and Imaging Research, University of California, San Diego; **40.10.2** Patricio Robles Gil/ naturepl.com; **40.10.3** Matt T. Lee; **40.13** Robert Ganz; **40.18** Jeff Rotman/Alamy.

Chapter 41 **41.1** Michael deYoung/Corbis; **41.2** Roland Seitre/Peter Arnold/ PhotoLibrary; **41.3** Stefan Huwiler/Rolf Nussbaumer Photography/Alamy; **41.5.2** camelia/Shutterstock; **41.6.2** Hervey Bay Whale Watch (www.herveybaywhalewatch .com.au); **41.6.4** Thomas Eisner; **41.6.5** Photo Lennart Nilsson/Scanpix; **41.6.6** Gunter Ziesler/Peter Arnold/PhotoLibrary; **41.11.2** Visuals Unlimited/Corbis; **41.17.2** Fritz Polking/Peter Arnold, Inc./Alamy; **41.17.3** EyeWire Collection/ Photodisc/Getty Images; **41.22** Photo courtesy of The Jackson Laboratory, Bar Harbor, Maine; **41.23** Wolfgang Kaehler/Corbis.

Chapter 42 **42.1** Stephen Dalton/Photo Researchers; **42.2.2** Reinhard dirscheri/ PhotoLibrary; **42.2.3** Eric Grave/Photo Researchers; **42.10.2** From "Human Histology Photo CD." Image courtesy Indigo Instruments (www.indigo.com); **42.10.3** Photo Lennart Nilsson/Scanpix; **42.16** Biophoto Associates/Photo Researchers; **42.18.2** Eye of Science/Photo Researchers; **42.22.2** Peter Batson/Image Quest Marine; **42.22.3** Olgysha/Shutterstock; **42.22.4** Jez Tryner/Image Quest Marine; **42.24.2** Prepared by Dr. Hong Y. Yan, University of Kentcky and Dr. Peng Chai, University of Texas; **42.25.2** Motta & Macchiarelli/Anatomy Dept., Univ. La Sapienza, Rome/Photo Researchers; **42.27.2** Hans-Rainer Duncker, University of Giessen, Germany.

Chapter 43 **43.1** Biology Media/Science Source/Photo Researchers; **43.4** Dominique Ferrandon; **43.21.2** Steve Gschmeissner/Photo Researchers; **43.23** CNRI/Photo Researchers; **43.26** The Laboratory of Structural Cell Biology, headed by Stephen C. Harrison, Harvard Medical School/HHMI.

Chapter 44 **44.1** David Wall/Alamy; **44.4** Mark Conlin/Image Quest Marine; **44.5.2** Dr. John Crowe, University of California, Davis; **44.5.3** Dr. John Crowe, University of California, Davis; **44.9** AFP/Getty Images; **44.14.5** Steve Gschmeissner/Photo Researchers; **44.17** Jim Cancalosi/Peter Arnold Images/PhotoLibrary; **44.18** Michael Fodgen/OSF/PhotoLibrary.

Chapter 45 **45.1** Ralph A. Clevenger/Corbis; **p. 974** Stuart Wilson/Photo Researchers; **45.3** Volker Witte; **45.18.2** Astier/BSIP/Photo Researchers; **45.19.2** Photoshot Holdings Ltd/Alamy; **45.19.3** Jurgen & Christine Sohns/FLPA.

Chapter 46 **46.1** David Doubilet/Getty Images; **46.2** David Wrobel; **46.4** Chris Wallace Photography, photographersdirect.com; **46.5.2** P. de Vries, courtesy of David Crews; **46.6** Andy Sands/naturepl.com; **46.7** John Cancalosi/Peter Arnold Images/PhotoLibrary; **46.17.2** Photo Lennart Nilsson/Scanpix; **46.17.3** Photo Lennart Nilsson/Scanpix; **46.17.4** Photo Lennart Nilsson/Scanpix.

Chapter 47 **47.1** Photo Lennart Nilsson/Scanpix; **47.4.2** Vacquier VD, Payne JE. Methods for quantitating sea urchin sperm-egg binding. *Exp Cell Res.* 1973 Nov;82(1):227–35; **47.4.3** Vacquier VD, Payne JE. Methods for quantitating sea urchin sperm-egg binding. *Exp Cell Res.* 1973 Nov;82(1):227–35; **47.4.4** Vacquier VD, Payne JE. Methods for quantitating sea urchin sperm-egg binding. *Exp Cell Res.* 1973 Nov;82(1):227–35; **47.4.5** Vacquier VD, Payne JE. Methods for quantitating sea urchin sperm-egg binding. *Exp Cell Res.* 1973 Nov;82(1):227–35; **47.4.7** Hafner, M., Petzelt, C., Nobiling, R., Pawley, J., Kramp, D. and G. Schatten. Wave of Free Calcium at Fertilization in the Sea Urchin Egg Visualized with Fura-2. *Cell Motil. Cytoskel.*, 9:271–277 (1988); **47.4.8** Hafner, M., Petzelt, C., Nobiling, R., Pawley, J., Kramp, D. and G. Schatten. Wave of Free Calcium at Fertilization in the Sea Urchin Egg Visualized with Fura-2. *Cell Motil. Cytoskel.*, 9:271–277 (1988); **47.4.9** Hafner, M., Petzelt, C., Nobiling, R., Pawley, J., Kramp, D. and G. Schatten. Wave of Free Calcium at Fertilization in the Sea Urchin Egg Visualized with Fura-2. *Cell Motil. Cytoskel.*, 9:271–277 (1988); **47.4.10** Hafner, M., Petzelt, C., Nobiling, R., Pawley, J., Kramp, D. and G. Schatten. Wave of Free Calcium at Fertilization in the Sea Urchin Egg Visualized with Fura-2. *Cell Motil. Cytoskel.*, 9:271–277 (1988); **47.6.2** George von Dassow; **47.6.3** George von Dassow; **47.6.4** George von Dassow; **47.6.5** George von Dassow; **47.7.2** Jürgen Berger/Max Planck Institute for Developmental Biology, Tübingen, Germany; **47.7.3** Andrew J. Ewald, Johns Hopkins Medical School; **47.9.2** Charles A. Ettensohn; **47.13.2** Huw Williams; **47.13.3** Thomas Poole, SUNY Health Science Center; **47.14.2** Dr. Keith Wheeler/Photo Researchers; **47.17.2** Hiroki Nishida, *Developmental Biology* 121 (1987): 526. Reprinted by permission of Academic Press; **47.17.3** Hiroki Nishida, *Developmental Biology* 121 (1987): 526. Reprinted by permission of Academic Press; **47.18.2** J. E. Sulston and H. R. Horvitz, *Dev. Biol.* 56 (1977):110–156; **47.19.2** Adapted from Strome (International Review of Cytology 114: 81–123, 1989); **47.20.2** Adapted from Strome (International Review of Cytology 114: 81–123, 1989); **47.20.3** Adapted from Strome (International Review of Cytology 114: 81–123, 1989); **47.20.4** Adapted from Strome (International Review of Cytology 114: 81–123, 1989); **47.20.5** Adapted from Strome (International Review of Cytology 114: 81–123, 1989); **47.24.2** Kathryn W. Tosney, University of Michigan; **47.25.2** Dennis Summerbell.

Chapter 48 **48.1** Marinethemes; **48.2.2** David Fleetham/Alamy; **48.6.2** Thomas Deerinck; **48.13.2** Bear, Connors, and Paradiso, "Neuroscience: Exploring the Brain" © 1996, p. 43; **48.16.2** Edwin R. Lewis, University of California at Berkeley.

Chapter 49 **49.1** Brainbow mouse cerebellum. Image by Tamily Weissman, Harvard University. The Brainbow mouse was produced by Livet J, Weissman TA, Kang H, Draft RW, Lu J, Bennis RA, Sanes JR, Lichtman JW. *Nature* (2007) 450:56–62; **49.6.2** N. Kedersha/Photo Researchers; **49.9** Larry Mulvehill/Corbis; **49.14.2** From "A functional MRI study of happy and sad affective states induced by classical music.";... M. T. Mitterschiffthaler et al. *Hum Brain Mapp.* 2007 Nov;28(11):1150–62; **49.16.2** Marcus E. Raichle, M.D., Washington University Medical Center; **p. 1075** From "Dr. Harlow's Case of Recovery from the passage of an Iron Bar through the Head." H. Bigelow. *Am. Journal of the Med. Sci.* July 1850;XXXIX. Images from the History of Medicine (NLM); **49.21** Image by Sebastian Jessberger. Fred H. Gage, Laboratory of Genetics LOG-G, The Salk Institute for Biological Studies; **49.24.2** Martin M. Rotker/ Photo Researchers.

Chapter 50 **50.1** Kenneth Catania; **50.6.1** CSIRO; **50.6.2** R. A. Steinbrecht; **50.7.2** James Gerholdt/Photolibrary; **50.7.3** Splashdown Direct/ OSF/Photolibrary; **50.9.2** From Richard Elzinga, "Fundamentals of Entomology" 3rd. © 1987, p. 185. Reprinted by permission of Prentice-Hall, Upper Saddle River, NJ; **50.10.2** SPL/Photo Researchers; **50.16.2** USDA/APHIS Animal and Plant Health Inspection Service; **50.17.3** STEVE GSCHMEISSNER/SPL/Photo Researchers; **50.21** From "Gene therapy for red-green colour blindness in adult primates.";... K. Mancuso et al. *Nature.* 2009 Oct 8; 461(7265):784–7. Photo: Neitz Laboratory; **50.26.2** Clara Franzini-Armstrong, University of Pennsylvania; **50.27.2** Courtesy of Dr. H. E. Huxley; **50.27.3** Courtesy of Dr. H. E. Huxley; **50.27.4** Courtesy of Dr. H. E. Huxley; **50.33** George Cathcart Photography, photographersdirect.com; **50.38** Dave Watts/NHPA/Photo Researchers; **50.39** Vance A. Tucker.

Chapter 51 **51.1** Michael Nichols/National Geographic/Getty Images; **51.3** Susan Lee Powell; **51.5.2** Kenneth Lorenzen, UC Davis; **51.7.2** Thomas McAvoy/Life Magazine/Getty Images; **51.7.3** Operation Migration Inc.; **51.9.2** Lincoln Brower, Sweet Briar College; **51.9.3** Lincoln Brower, Sweet Briar College; **51.9.4** Lincoln Brower, Sweet Briar College; **51.11** Clive Bromhall/OSF/Photolibrary; **51.12.2** Alissa Crandall/Corbis; **51.12.3** Richard Wrangham; **51.15.2** Matt T. Lee; **51.15.3** David Osborn/Alamy; **51.15.4** Bill Schmoker; **51.16.2** James D Watt/Image Quest Marine; **51.17** Courtesy of Gerald S. Wilkinson; from G.S. Wilkinson and G. N. Dodson, in J. Choe and B. Crespi (eds)., "The Evolution of Mating Systems in Insects and Arachnids," Cambridge University Press, Cambridge (1997), pp. 310–328; **51.18** Cyril Laubscher/Dorling Kindersley; **51.21** Martin Harvey/Peter Arnold Images/ PhotoLibrary; **51.22** Erik Svensson, Lund University, Sweden; **51.23.2** Robert Pickett/ Corbis; **51.24** Lowell L. Getz and Lisa Davis; **51.25** Rory Doolin; **51.27** Jennifer Jarvis; **51.29.2.** Stephen J. Krasemann/Peter Arnold/PhotoLibrary.

Chapter 52 **52.1** Dr. Paul A. Zahl/Photo Researchers; **52.2.2** James D. Watt/ Stephen Frink Collection/Alamy; **52.2.3** Gianni Tortoli/Photo Researchers; **52.2.4** Tom Bean/Corbis; **52.2.5** B. Tharp/Photo Researchers; **52.2.6** Yann Arthus-Bertrand/ Corbis; **52.2.7** NASA/Goddard Space Flight Center; **52.11.1** JTB Photo Communications, Inc./Alamy; **52.11.2** imagebroker/Alamy; **52.12.2** Frans Lanting/Corbis; **52.12.4** Gordon Whitten/Corbis; **52.12.6** Wolfgang Kaehler/Corbis; **52.12.8** The California Chaparral Institute (http://californiachaparral.net). Photo supplied by Richard Halsey; **52.12.10** Tom Bean/Image Bank/ Getty Images; **52.12.12** Shutterstock; **52.12.14** Kennan Ward/Corbis; **52.12.16** Darrell Gulin/Corbis; **52.16.1** Allen Russell/PhotoLibrary; **52.16.2** AfriPics.com/Alamy; **52.16.3** David Tipling/ Nature Picture Library; **52.16.4** Ron Watts/Corbis; **52.16.5** Photononstop/SuperStock; **52.16.6** James Randklev/Image Bank/Getty Images; **52.16.7** Stuart Westmorland/ Corbis; **52.16.8** Stuart Westmorland/Corbis; **52.16.9** Digital Vision/Getty Images; **52.16.10** William Lange/Woods Hole Oceanographic Institution; **52.17.2** Geoff Dann/ Dorling Kindersley; **52.19.2** Peter Llewellyn/Alamy; **52.21** Daniel Mosquin.

Chapter 53 **53.1** Arpat Ozgul; **53.2** Todd Pusser/Naturepl.com; **53.4.2** Bernard Castelein/ Nature Picture Library/Alamy; **53.4.3** Frans Lanting/Corbis; **53.4.4** Niall Benvie/Corbis; **53.8.2** Hansjoerg Richter/iStockphoto; **53.11** Photodisc/White/PhotoLibrary; **53.12** Tom Bean/Corbis; **53.13.2** H. Willcox/Wildlife Picture/Peter Arnold/Photolibrary; **53.14.2** Jean Louis Batt/Taxi/Getty Images; **53.14.3** Christine Osborne/ Corbis; **53.14.4** Edward Parker/Alamy; **53.17.2** fotoVoyager/iStockphoto; **53.17.3** Adrian Bailey/Aurora Photos; **53.17.4** Joe Raedle/Getty Images; **53.17.5** Patrick Clayton, www.fisheyeguyphotography.com; **53.17.6** JOZSEF SZENTPETERI/NGS Image Collection; **53.17.7** Andrew Syred/Photo Researchers; **53.17.8** Nicholas Bergkessel, Jr./ Photo Researchers; **53.19.2** Joe McDonald/Corbis; **53.20.2** Robert Kay; **53.21.2** Niclas Fritzén.

Chapter 54 **54.1** Hal Beral VWPics/SuperStock; **54.2.2** Joseph T. Collins/Photo Researchers; **54.2.3** National Museum of Natural History/Smithsonian Institution; **p. 1196** Frank W Lane/FLPA; **54.5.2** Barry Mansell/Nature Picture Library; **54.5.3** Fogden/Corbis; **54.5.4** Stephen J. Krasemann/Photo Researchers; **54.5.5** Robert Pickett/ Papilio/Alamy; **54.5.6** Edward S. Ross, California Academy of Sciences; **54.5.7** © James K. Lindsey; **54.6** Douglas Faulkner/Photo Researchers; **54.7.2** Fogden/ Corbis; **54.7.3** Dan Janzen, Department of Biology, University of Pennsylvania; **54.8** Peter Johnson/Corbis; **54.9.2** Sally D. Hacker; **54.12** Cedar Creek Ecosystem Science Reserve, University of Minnesota; **54.17.2** Genny Anderson; **54.19** SuperStock; **54.21.2** Ron Landis Photography, www.ronlandisphotography.co; **54.21.3** Scott T. Smith/Corbis; **54.22.2** Charles Mauzy/Corbis; **54.22.3** Keith Boggs; **54.22.4** Glacier Bay National Park Photo/Glacier Bay National Park and Preserve; **54.22.5** Terry Donnelly, Mary Liz Austin; **54.24.2** R. Grant Gilmore, Dynamac Corporation; **54.24.3** Lance Horn, National Undersea Research Center, University of North Carolina-Wilmington; **54.29** Nelish Pradhan, Bates College, Lewiston, ME; **54.30** Josh Spice.

Chapter 55 **55.1** Hassan Basagic; **55.2** Stone Nature Photography/Alamy; **55.3** Justus de Cuveland/AGE Fotostock; **55.16.2** Hubbard Brook Research Foundation/ USDA Forest Service; **55.16.3** USDA Forest Service; **55.17.2** Mark Gallagher;

55.17.3 Mark Gallagher; **55.18.2** U.S. Department of Energy; **55.19.2** Stewart Rood, University of Lethbridge; **55.19.3** Photo provided by Kissimmee Division staff, South Florida Water Management District (WPB); **55.19.4** Tim Day, Xcluder Pest Proof Fencing Company; **55.19.5** Daniel H. Janzen, University of Pennsylvania; **55.19.6** Bert Boekhoven; **55.19.7** Jean Hall/Holt Studios/Photo Researchers; **55.19.8** Kenji Morita/Environment Division, Tokyo Kyuei Co., Ltd.

Chapter 56 **56.1** Stephen J Richards; **56.2** Wayne Lawler/Ecoscene/Corbis; **56.4.2** Neil Lucas/Nature Picture Library; **56.4.3** Mark Carwardine/Still Pictures/Peter Arnold/ PhotoLibrary; **56.4.4** Nazir Foead; **56.5** Merlin D. Tuttle, Bat Conservation International, www.batcon.org; **56.6** Scott Camazine/Photo Researchers; **56.7** Michael Edwards/Getty Images; **56.8.2** Bruce Cowell, www.brucecowellphotographer .com; **56.8.3** Robert Ginn/PhotoEdit Inc. **56.9** Benezeth Mutayoba, photo provided by the University of Washington; **56.10** Richard Vogel/Liaison/Getty Images; **56.13.2** William Ervin/SPL/Photo Researchers; **56.14** Craighead Environmental Research Institute; **56.15.2** Tim Thompson/Getty Images; **56.15.3** Chuck Bargeron, University of Georgia; **56.15.4** William D. Boyer, USDA Forest Service; **56.16.2** Yann Arthus-Bertrand/Corbis; **56.16.3** James P. Blair/National Geographic Image Collection; **56.17** R. O. Bierregaard, Jr., Biology Dept., University of North Carolina, Charlotte; **56.18** SPL/Photo Researchers; **56.21.2** Edwin Giesbers/naturepl.com; **56.22.2** Mark Chiappone and Steven Miller, Center for Marine Science, University of North Carolina-Wilmington, Key Largo, FL; **56.23** Nigel Cattlin/Photo Researchers; **56.24.2** NASA; **56.24.3** NASA; **56.26** Erich Hartmann/Magnum Photos; **56.28** Prof. William H. Schlesinger; **56.31.2** NASA; **56.31.3** NASA; **56.33.2** Serge de Sazo/ Photo Researchers; **56.33.3** Hilde Jensen, University of Tubingen/Nature Magazine/ AP Photo; **56.33.4** Gabriel Rojo/Nature Picture Library; **56.33.5** Titus Lacoste/Getty Images. Appendix A **p. A-5** OMIKRON/Science Source/Photo Researchers; **p. A-8** John N. A. Lott/Biological Photo Service; **p. A-10, top** Biophoto/Photo Researchers; **p. A-10, 2nd from top** Conly L. Rieder; **p. A-11** USDA/ARS/Agricultural Research Service; **p. A-35** Peter Kitin; Appendix E **p. E-1, top left** Dr. Kari Lounatmaa/ Photo Researchers; **p. E-1, bottom left** Eye of Science/Photo Researchers; **p. E-1, middle** M. I. Walker/NHPA/Photoshot; **p. E-1 right** Kathy Piper/iStockphoto; **p. E-2, left** Douglas Adams/iStockphoto; **p. E-2, right** McPHOTO/AGE Fotostock.

Illustration and Text Credits

4.6b, 9.9, 17.17b and **c** are adapted from C. K. Matthews and K. E. van Holde, *Biochemistry*, 2nd ed. Copyright © 1996 Pearson Education, Inc., publishing as Pearson Benjamin Cummings. **4.7, 6.6b, 11.7, 11.12, 17.11, 18.25, 20.8, 21.9, and 21.10** are adapted from W. M. Becker, J. B. Reece, and M. F. Poenie, *The World of the Cell*, 3rd ed. Copyright © 1996 Pearson Education, Inc., publishing as Pearson Benjamin Cummings. **Table 6.1a** Adapted from W. M. Becker, L. J. Kleinsmith, and J. Hardin, *The World of the Cell*, 4th ed. p. 753. Copyright © 2000 Pearson Education, Inc., publishing as Pearson Benjamin Cummings. **6.8** and **6.23a** and cell organelle drawings in **6.11** and **6.12** are adapted from illustrations by Tomo Narashima in E. N. Marieb, *Human Anatomy and Physiology*, 5th ed. Copyright © 2001 Pearson Education, Inc., publishing as Pearson Benjamin Cummings. **6.9a, 50.12,** and **50.13** are also from *Human Anatomy and Physiology*, 5th ed. Copyright © 2001 Pearson Education, Inc., publishing as Pearson Benjamin Cummings. **30.4, 30.13i,** and **39.13** are adapted from M. W. Nabors, *Introduction to Botany*, Copyright © 2004 Pearson Education, Inc., publishing as Pearson Benjamin Cummings. **42.30a, 46.16, 49.8, 49.10, 50.26, and 50.30** are adapted from E. N. Marieb, *Human Anatomy and Physiology*, 4th ed. Copyright © 1998 Pearson Education, Inc., publishing as Pearson Benjamin Cummings. **42.30a** From Campbell et al., *Biology: Concepts and Connections*, 6th ed., fig. 22.10, p. 462. Copyright © 2009 Pearson Education, Inc., publishing as Pearson Benjamin Cummings. **43.8** Adapted from Gerard J. Tortora, Berdell R. Funke, and Christine L. Case. 1998. *Microbiology: An Introduction*, 6th ed. Copyright © 1998 Pearson Education, Inc., publishing as Pearson Benjamin Cummings. **44.8** and **51.8** are adapted from L. G. Mitchell, J. A. Mutchmor, and W. D. Dolphin. *Zoology*. Copyright © 1988 Pearson Education, Inc., publishing as Pearson Benjamin Cummings.

Chapter 1 **1.25** Map provided courtesy of David W. Pfennig, University of North Carolina at Chapel Hill; **1.27** Data in bar graph based on D. W. Pfennig et al. 2001. Frequency-dependent Batesian mimicry. *Nature* 410:323.

Chapter 2 **2.2 (bottom)** Reprinted by permission of Macmillan Publishers Ltd. *Nature*. M.E. Frederickson et al. 'Devil's gardens' bedeviled by ants, *437*:495, 9/22/05. Copyright © 2005.

Chapter 3 **3.8a** Adapted from *Scientific American*, Nov. 1998, p.102.

Chapter 5 **5.12** Adapted from *Biology: The Science of Life*, 3rd ed. by Robert Wallace et al. Copyright © 1991. Reprinted by permission of Pearson Education, Inc; **5.15** and **5.20F** PDB ID 1CGD: J. Bella, B. Brodsky, and H. M. Berman. 1995. Hydration structure of a collagen peptide. *Structure* 3: 893–906; **5.18** Adapted from D. W. Heinz et al. 1993. How amino-acid insertions are allowed in an alpha-helix of T4 lysozyme. *Nature* 361:561; **5.20D** PDB ID 3GSO: Palaninathan, S.K., Mohamedmohaideen, N.N., Orlandini, E., Ortore, G., Nencetti, S., Lapucci, A., Rossello, A., Freundlich, J.S., Sacchettini, J.C. 2009. Novel transthyretin amyloid fibril formation inhibitors: synthesis, biological evaluation, and X-ray structural analysis. *Public Library of Science One* 4: e6290–e6290; **5.20G, 21.10b, Un42.1** PDB ID 2HHB: G. Fermi, M. F. Perutz, B. Shaanan, R. Fourme. 1984. The crystal structure of human deoxyhaemoglobin at 1.74 A resolution. *J.Mol.Biol. 175*: 159–174.

Chapter 7 **7.9** PDB ID 3HAO: N. H. Joh, A. Oberai, D. Yang, J. P. Whitelegge, J. U. Bowie. 2009. Similar energetic contributions of packing in the core of membrane and water-soluble proteins. *J. Am.Chem.Soc. 131*: 10846–10847.

Chapter 8 **8.18** PDB ID 3e1f: D H. Juers, B. Rob, M. L. Dugdale, N. Rahimzadeh, C. Giang, M. Lee, B. W. Matthews, R.E. Huber. 2009. Direct and indirect roles of His-418 in metal binding and in the activity of beta-galactosidase (E. coli). *Protein Sci. 18*: 1281–1292; **8.19** PDB ID 1MDY: P. C. Ma, M.A. Rould, H. Weintraub, C.O. Pabo. 1994. Crystal structure of MyoD bHLH domain-DNA complex: perspectives on DNA recognition and implications for transcriptional activation. *Cell* (Cambridge, Mass.) 77: 451–459; **8.20** Figures 4a and 4e from "A common allosteric site and mechanism in caspases" by J.M. Scheer et al., in *Proceedings of the National Academy of Sciences*,

103, no. 20: 7595–7600, May 16, 2006. Copyright © 2006 National Academy of Sciences, U.S.A. Used by permission.

Chapter 9 **9.5** From *Molecular Biology of the Cell*, 4th edition, by Bruce Alberts et al., fig. 2.69, p. 92. Copyright © 2002 by Bruce Alberts, Alexander Johnson, Julian Lewis, Martin Raff, Keith Roberts, and Peter Walter. Used by permission

Chapter 10 **10.13b** Figure 1a from "Architecture of the photosynthetic Oxygen-evolving center" by K.N. Ferreira et al., in *Science*, 303, No. 5665: 1831–1838, March 19, 2004. Copyright © 2004, The American Association for the Advancement of Science. Reprinted with permission from AAAS; **10.15** Adapted from Richard and David Walker. Energy, Plants, and Man, fig. 4.1, p. 69. Sheffield: University of Sheffield. Oxygraphics http:// www.oxygraphics.co.uk. © Richard Walker. Used with permission.

Chapter 12 **12.13** From *Molecular Biology of the Cell*, 4th edition, by Bruce Alberts et al., fig. 18.41, p. 1059. Copyright © 2002 by Bruce Alberts, Alexander Johnson, Julian Lewis, Martin Raff, Keith Roberts, and Peter Walter. Used by permission.

Chapter 17 **17.13** Figure 10-45 from *Principles of Cell and Molecular Biology*, 2nd edition, by Valerie M. Kish and Lewis J. Kleinsmith. Copyright © 1995 HarperCollins College Publishers. Reprinted by permission of Pearson Education.

Chapter 18 **18.15a** Figure 1d from "An Abundant Class of Tiny RNAs with Probable Regulatory Roles in *Caenorhabditis elegans*" by N.C. Lau et al., in *Science*, 294, No. 5543: 858–862, Oct. 1, 2001. Copyright © 2001, The American Association for the Advancement of Science. Reprinted with permission from AAAS.

Chapter 20 **20.10** Figure 15.24, p. 481, from *Genetics*, 5th ed., by Peter Russell. Copyright © 1998 Pearson Education, Inc., publishing as Pearson Benjamin Cummings. Used by permission of the publisher.

Chapter 21 **21.2** Adapted from a figure by Chris A. Kaiser and Erica Beade; **21.5b** Figure 2B from "The Genetic Landscape of a Cell" by M. Costanzo et al., in *Science*, 327, No. 5964: 425–431, Jan. 22, 2010. Copyright © 2010, The American Association for the Advancement of Science. Reprinted with permission from AAAS; **21.17** Adapted from an illustration by William McGinnis in Peter Radetsky, "The homeobox: Something very precious that we share with flies, from egg to adult." Bethesda, MD: Howard Hughes Medical Institute, 1992, p. 92. Reprinted by permission of William McGinnis; **21.18** Adapted from M. Akam, "Hox genes and the evolution of diverse body plans," *Philosophical Transactions of the Royal Society B*, 1995, 349: 313–319, fig. 3. © Royal Society of London. Reprinted by permission.

Chapter 22 **22.8** © Utako Kikutani 2007. Used with permission; **22.13** Figure 4a from "Host Race Radiation in the Soapberry Bug: Natural History with the History" by S.P. Carroll and C. Boyd, in Evolution, Vol. 46 No. 4, p. 1060, Aug. 1992. Reproduced with permission of Blackwell Publishing Ltd.; **22.14** Reprinted from *Trends in Microbiology*, 16, Issue 8: 361–369. B.A. Diep and M. Otto, "The role of virulence determinants in community-associated MRSA pathogenesis," Copyright © 2008, with permission from Elsevier.

Chapter 23 **23.5** Figure 3 from "Genetic mechanisms for adapting to a changing environment" by D.A. Powers et al., from *Annual Review of Genetics*, 25, Dec. 1991. Copyright © 1991 by Annual Reviews. Reprinted by permission; **23.11** Figure 20.6 (maps only) from *Discover Biology*, Second Edition by Michael L. Cain, Hans Damman, Robert A. Lue & Carol Kaesuk Loon, Editors. Copyright © 2002 by Sinauer Associates, Inc. Used by permission of W.W. Norton & Company, Inc.; **23.12** Reprinted by permission from Macmillan Publishers Ltd.: *Nature*. E. Postma and A. J. van Noordijk, Gene flow maintains a large genetic difference in clutch size at a small spatial scale, *433*, 1/6/05. Copyright © 2005; **23.14** Adapted from many sources including D. J. Futuyma. 2005. *Evolution*, fig. 11.3. Sunderland, MA: Sinauer Associates and from R. L. Carroll, 1988. *Vertebrate Paleontology and Evolution*. W.H. Freeman & Co.; **23.16** Adapted from A. M. Welch et al. 1998. Call duration as an indicator of genetic quality in male gray tree frogs. *Science* 280:1928–1930; **23.17** Adapted from A. C. Allison. 1961. Abnormal hemoglobin and erythrocyte enzyme-deficiency traits. In *Genetic Variation in Human Populations*, ed. G.A. Harrison. Oxford: Elsevier Science and from S. I. Hay et al., A world malaria map: *Plasmodium falciparum* endemicity in 2007. *PLoS Medicine 6*: fig. 3, p. 291; **23.18** Figure 2a from "Frequency-Dependent Natural Selection in the Handedness of Scale-Eating Cichlid Fish" by Michio Hori in *Science*, 260, No. 5105: 216–219, April 9, 1993. Copyright © 1993, The American Association for the Advancement of Science. Reprinted with permission from AAAS; **Un 23.2** Data from R. K. Koehn and T. J. Hilbish. 1987. The adaptive importance of genetic variation. *American Scientist* 75: 134–141.

Chapter 24 **24.7** Figure 3 from "Ecological Speciation in *Gambusia* Fishes" by R.B. Langerhans et al., from *Evolution*, 61, No. 9, July 2007, published by The Society for the Study of Evolution. Copyright © 2007 R.B. Langerhans, M.E. Gifford, E.O. Joseph. Reprinted by permission; **24.9** From figure 2 in "Correspondence between sexual isolation and allozyme differentiation" *Proceedings of the National Academy of Science*, 87: 2715–2719, 1990, p. 2718. Copyright © 1990 Stephen G. Tilley, Paul A. Verrell, Steven J. Arnold. Used with permission; **24.10a** Adapted from D. M. B. Dodd, 1989. Reproductive isolation as a consequence of adaptive divergence in *Drosophila pseudoobscura*. *Evolution* 43: 1308–1311; **24.13** *Hybrid Zone and the Evolutionary Process* edited by R.G. Harrison (1993): Map of Bombina hybrid zone (p. 263) and figure 10.1 (p. 278) from chapter "Analysis of hybrid zones with bombina" by J. M. Szymura. By permission of Oxford University Press; **24.15** Reprinted by permission of Macmillan Publishers Ltd.: *Nature*. G. P. Saetre et al. A sexually selected character displacement in flycatchers reinforces premating isolation, *387*:589–591, fig. 2, 6/5/97. Copyright © 1997; **24.19b** From fig. 2 in L. H. Rieseberg et al. 1996. Role of Gene Interactions in Hybrid Speciation: Evidence from Ancient and Experimental Hybrids. *Science* 272: 741–745. Copyright © 1996. Reprinted with permission from AAAS.

Chapter 25 **25.3a** Graph from "Experimental Models of Primitive Cellular Compartments Encapsulation Growth and Division" by M.M. Hanczyc et al., in *Science*, 302, No. 5645: 618–622. Oct. 24, 2003. Copyright © 2003, The American Association for the Advancement of Science. Reprinted with permission from AAAS; **25.5** From Don L. Eicher, *Geologic Time*, 1st edition, © 1968. Printed and Electronically reproduced by permission of Pearson Education, Inc., Upper Saddle River, New Jersey; **25.6a–d** Adapted from many sources including D. J. Futuyma. 2005. *Evolution*, fig. 4.10. Sunderland, MA: Sinauer Associates and from R. L. Carroll, 1988. *Vertebrate*

Paleontology and Evolution. W.H. Freeman & Co.; **25.6e** Adapted from Luo et al. 2001. A new mammalia form from the Early Jurassic and evolution of mammalian characteristics. *Science* 292: 1535; **25.7** Adapted from D. J. Des Marais. September 8, 2000. When did photosynthesis emerge on Earth? *Science* 289: 1703–1705; **25.8** Reprinted by permission from Macmillan Publishers Ltd.: *Nature.* L. R. Kump. The rise of atmospheric oxygen, *451*:277–278, 1/17/08. Copyright © 2008; **25.13** Map adapted from http://gelology.er.usgs.gov/eastern/plates.html; **25.15** Graph created from D. M. Raup and J. J. Sepkoski, Jr. 1982. Mass extinctions in the marine fossil record. *Science*. 215: 1501–1503 and J. J. Sepkoski, Jr. 1984. A kinetic model of Phanerozoic taxonomic diversity. III. Post-Paleozoic families and mass extinctions. *Paleobiology.* Vol 10, No. 2, pp. 246–267 in D. J. Futuyma, fig. 7.3a, p. 143 and fig. 7.6, p. 145, Sunderland, MA: Sinauer Associates; **25.17** From Mayhew, P. J. et al. 2008. A long-term association between global temperature and biodiversity, origination and extinction in the fossil record. *Proceedings of the Royal Society B, 275:* 47–53, fig. 3b. Reprinted by permission; **25.18** Figure 3 from "Anatomical and ecological constraints on Phanerozoic animal diversity in the marine realm" by R.K. Bambach et al., in *Proceedings of the National Academy of Sciences, 99,* no. 10: 6854–6859, May 14, 2002. Copyright © 2002 National Academy of Sciences, U.S.A. Used by permission; **25.19** Adapted from Hickman, Roberts, and Larson.1997, *Zoology,* 10th ed, Wm. C. Brown, fig. 31.1; **25.24** Reprinted by permission from Macmillan Publishers Ltd: *Nature.* M. Ronshaugen et al. Hox protein mutation and macroevolution of the insect body plan, *415*:914–917, fig. 1a. Copyright © 2002; **25.26** Adapted from M. Strickberger, 1990. *Evolution,* Boston: Jones & Bartlett.

Chapter 26 26.6 Figure 1 from "Which Whales Are Hunted? A Molecular Genetic Approach to Monitoring Whaling" by C.S. Baker and S.R. Palumbi, in *Science, 265,* No. 5178:1538–1539, Sep. 9, 1994. Copyright © 1994, The American Association for the Advancement of Science. Reprinted with permission from AAAS; **26.12** With kind permission from Springer Science+Business Media: *Development Genes and Evolution,* "The evolution of the hedgehog gene family in chordates: insights from amphioxus hedgehog," vol. 209, 1999, pp. 40–47, Jan. 1999, S.M. Shimeld, fig. 3; **26.19** Figure 4.3c, p. 124 from *Molecular Markers, Natural History, and Evolution,* 2nd edition, by John Avise. Copyright © 2004 Sinauer Associates. Used by permission; **26.20** Figure from "Timing the Ancestor of the HIV-1 Pandemic Strains" by B. Korber et al., in *Science, 288,* No. 5472: 1789–1796, Jun 9, 2000. Copyright © 2000, The American Association for the Advancement of Science. Reprinted with permission from AAAS; **26.21** Figure 4.1, p. 45, "The three domains of life" by S.L. Baldauf et al., from *Assembling the Tree of Life,* edited by Joel Cracraft and Michael Donoghue. By permission of Oxford University Press, Inc. **26.22** Adapted from S. Blair Hedges. The origin and evolution of model organisms. *Nature Reviews Genetics* 3:838–848, fig. 1, p. 840.

Chapter 27 27.10 Reprinted by permission from Macmillan Publishers Ltd.: *Nature.* V.S. Cooper and R.E. Lenski. The population genetics of ecological specialization in evolving *E. coli* populations, *407*:736–739, fig. 1. Copyright © 2000; **27.18** Graph created from data in C. Calvaruso et al. 2006. Root-associated bacteria contribute to mineral weathering and to mineral nutrition in trees: A budgeting analysis. *Applied and Environmental Microbiology* 72: 1258–1266.

Chapter 28 28.2 Reprinted from *Trends in Genetics,18,* No. 11, J.M. Archibald and P.J. Keeling, "Recycled plastids: a 'green movement' in eukaryotic evolution," Copyright © 2002, with permission from Elsevier; **28.11** Figure 12.7, p. 350, from *Microbiology,* by R. W. Bauman. Copyright © 2004 Pearson Education, Inc., publishing as Benjamin Cummings; **28.23** Data from A. Stechman and T. Cavalier-Smith. 2002. Rooting the eukaryote tree by using a derived gene fusion, *Science* 297: 89–91; **28.28** Reprinted by permission from Macmillan Publishers Ltd.: *Nature.* M.J. Behrenfeld et al. Climate-driven trends in contemporary ocean productivity, *44*: 752–755, fig. 3. Copyright © 2006.

Chapter 29 29.10 Source: R. D. Bowden. 1991. Inputs, outputs and accumulation of nitrogen in an early successional moss *(Polytrichum)* ecosystem. *Ecological Monographs* 61: 207–223; **29.14** Adapted from Raven et al. *Biology of Plants,* 6th ed., fig. 19.7, W. H. Freeman & Co.

Chapter 30 30.12a From P. R. Crane. 1985. Phylogenetic analysis of seed plants and the origin of angiosperms. *Annals of the Missouri Botanical Garden, 72:*716–793, fig. 11a, p. 738. Used by permission of Missouri Botanical Garden Press; **30.12b** Figure 2.3, p. 28, from *Phylogeny and Evolution of Angiosperms* by Douglas E. Soltis et al. Copyright © 2005 Sinauer Associates. Used by permission. **Table 30.1** Adapted from Randy Moore et al., *Botany,* 2nd ed. Dubuque, IA: Brown, 1998, Table 2.2, p. 37.

Chapter 31 31.21 Figures 4 and 5 from "Fungal endophytes limit pathogen damage in a tropical tree" by A.E. Arnold et al., in *Proceedings of the National Academy of Sciences, 100,* no. 26: 15652–15653, December 23, 2003. Copyright © 2003 National Academy of Sciences, U.S.A. Used by permission; **31.26** Figure 1 from "Reversing introduced species effects: Experimental removal of introduced fish leads to rapid recovery of a declining frog" by Vance T. Vredenburg from *Proceedings of the National Academy of Sciences 101:* 7646–7650. Copyright © 2004 National Academy of Sciences, U.S.A. Used by permission.

Chapter 33 33.22 C. Lydeard et al., The Global Decline of Nonmarine Mollusks, *BioScience,* Vol. 54, No. 4: 321–330. © 2004, American Institute of Biological Sciences. Used by permission. All rights reserved. (Updated data are from International Union for Conservation of Nature, 2008.); **33.29a** Reprinted from *Current Biology, 7,* Issue 8, J.K. Grenier, S. Carroll et al., "Evolution of the entire arthropod *Hox* gene set predated the origin and radiation of the onychophoran/arthropod clade," p. 551, fig. 2a, Copyright © 1987, with permission from Elsevier.

Chapter 34 34.8b From "Fossil sister group of craniates: Predicted and found" by J. Mallatt and J. Chen, from *Journal of Morphology, 258,* Issue 1, May 15, 2003. Copyright © 2003 Wiley-Liss, Inc. Reprinted with permission; **34.12** From *Vertebrates: Comparative Anatomy, Function, Evolution,* 3/e by Kenneth Kardong. © 2002 McGraw-Hill Science/Engineering/Mathematics. Reprinted by permission of The McGraw-Hill Companies, Inc. **34.18 (bottom)** Reprinted by permission of Macmillan Publishers Ltd.: *Nature.* M. Zhu et al. The oldest articulated osteichthyan reveals mosaic gnathostome characters, *458*:469–474. Copyright © 2009; **34.21 (left)** Reproduced by permission of the Royal Society of Edinburgh from Transactions of the Roya Society of Edinburgh: Earth Sciences, volume 87 (1996), pp. 363–421;

34.21 (right) Reprinted by permission of Macmillan Publishers Ltd.: *Nature.* N.H. Shubin et al. The pectoral fin of *Tiktaalik roseae* and the origin of the tetrapod limb, *440*:768, fig. 4. Copyright © 2006; **34.37a** Adapted from many sources including D. J. Futuyma. 2005. *Evolution,* 1/e, fig. 4.10. Sunderland, MA: Sinauer Associates and from R. L. Carroll, 1988. *Vertebrate Paleontology and Evolution.* W.H. Freeman & Co. **34.47** Drawn from many photos of fossils. Some sources are *O. tugenensis* photo in Michael Balter, Early hominid sows division, *ScienceNow,* Feb. 22, 2001, © 2001 American Association for the Advancement of Science. *A. garhi,* and *H. neanderthalensis* adapted from *The Human Evolution Coloring Book.* *K platyops* drawn from photo in Meave Leakey et al., New hominid genus from eastern Africa shows diverse middle Pliocene lineages, *Nature,* March 22, 2001, 410: 433. *P. boisei* drawn from a photo by David Bill. *H. ergaster* drawn from a photo at www.inhandmuseum.com. *S. tchadensis* drawn from a photo in Michel Brunet et al., A new hominid from the Upper Miocene of Chad, Central Africa, *Nature,* July 11, 2002, 418: 147, fig. 1b; **34.50 (a/b)** Reprinted by permission of Macmillan Publishers Ltd.: *Nature.* I.V. Ovchinnikov et al. Molecular analysis of Neanderthal DNA from the northern Caucasus, *404*: 492, fig.3a and b. Copyright © 2000.

Chapter 35 35.21 Figure 2b from "Mongolian Tree Rings and 20th-Century Warming" by G.C. Jacoby et al., in *Science, 273,* No. 5276: 771–773, Aug. 9, 1996. Copyright © 1996, The American Association for the Advancement of Science. Reprinted with permission from AAAS.

Chapter 39 39.16 (top) Adapted from M. Wilkins. 1988. *Plant Watching,* Facts of File Publ. **39.28** Figure "No Free Lunch" from "Plant Biology: New fatty acid-based signals: A lesson from the plant world" by Edward Farmer in *Science, 276,* No. 5314: 912–913, May 9, 1997. Copyright © 1997, The American Association for the Advancement of Science. Reprinted with permission from AAAS.

Chapter 40 40.14 Figure 2 from "Thermoregulation in a brooding female Indian python, Python molurus bivittatus" by V.H. Hutchison et al., in *Science, 151,* No. 3711: 694–695, Feb. 11, 1966. Copyright © 1966, The American Association for the Advancement of Science. Reprinted with permission from AAAS; **40.15** Figure 7 from "Thermoregulation in Endothermic Insects" by Bernd Heinrich, in *Science, 185,* No. 4153: 747–756, August 30, 1974. Copyright © 1974, The American Association for the Advancement of Science. Reprinted with permission from AAAS; **40.21** Adapted from figures 2b and 2c from "The circadian clock stops ticking during deep hibernation in the European hamster" by F.G. Revel et al., in *Proceedings of the National Academy of Sciences, 104,* no. 34: 13816–13820, Aug. 21, 2007. Copyright © 2007 National Academy of Sciences, U.S.A. Used by permission.

Chapter 41 41.9a Figure 23.1 from *Human Anatomy and Physiology,* 8e, by Elaine Marieb and Katja Hoehn. Copyright © 2010 Pearson Education, Inc., publishing as Pearson Benjamin Cummings. Used by permission of the publisher; **41.9b** Figure 22-1 from Rhoades, *Human Physiology,* 3e. © 1996 Brooks/Cole, a part of Cengage Learning, Inc. Reproduced by permission. www.cengage.com/permissions; **41.21** Figure "Appetite Controllers" from "Cellular Warriors at the Battle of the Bulge" by Jean Marx, from *Science, 299:* p. 86, Feb. 7, 2003. Illustration by Kathleen Sutliff. Copyright © 2003, The American Association for the Advancement of Science. Reprinted with permission from AAAS.

Chapter 42 42.20 Reprinted by permission from Macmillan Publishers Ltd.: *Nature.* D.J. Rader and A. Daugherty. Translating molecular discoveries into new therapies for atherosclerosis, *451*:904–913, fig. 1, 2/21/08. Copyright © 2008; **42.21** From J.C. Cohen et al., "Sequence variations in PCSK9, low LDL, and protection against coronary heart disease," *New England Journal of Medicine.* 2006 Mar 23; *354*:1264–72, fig. 1A. Copyright © 2006 Massachusetts Medical Society. Used by permission. All rights reserved; **42.26** Adapted from "Surface properties in relation to atelectasis and hyaline membrane disease" by M.E. Avery and J. Mead, from A.M.A. *American Journal of Diseases of Children 97:*517–523 (June 1959). Copyright © 1959 American Medical Association. Used by permission. All rights reserved.

Chapter 43 43.5 From figures 2a and 4a in Phoebe Tzou et al., "Constitutive expression of a single antimicrobial peptide can restore wild-type resistance to infection in immuno-deficient *Drosophila* mutants," *PNAS,* 99: 2152–2157. Copyright © 2002 National Academy of Sciences, U.S.A. Used with permission; **43.7** Figures 20.4 and 20.5 from *Human Anatomy and Physiology,* 8e, by Elaine Marieb and Katja Hoehn. Copyright © 2010 Pearson Education, Inc., publishing as Pearson Benjamin Cummings. Used by permission of the publisher.

Chapter 44 44.6 Kangaroo rat data adapted from K. B. Schmidt-Nielson. 1990. *Animal Physiology: Adaptation and Environment,* 4th ed., p. 339. Cambridge: Cambridge University Press; **44.7a** Adapted from K. B. Schmidt-Nielsen et al. 1958. Extrarenal salt excretion in birds. *American Journal of Physiology* 193: 101–107; **44.14B and 44.15** Figure 25.3b from *Human Anatomy and Physiology,* 8e, by Elaine Marieb and Katja Hoehn. Copyright © 2010 Pearson Education, Inc., publishing as Pearson Benjamin Cummings. Used by permission of the publisher; **44.21** Table 1 from "Requirement of human renal water channel aquaporin-2 for vasopressin-dependent concentration in urine" by P.M. Deen et al., in *Science, 264,* No. 5155: 92–95, April 1, 1994. Copyright © 1994, The American Association for the Advancement of Science. Reprinted with permission from AAAS; **44EOC** From W.S. Beck et al., *Life: An Introduction to Biology,* 3rd edition, copyright © 1991. Reprinted and electronically reproduced by permission of Pearson Education, Inc., Upper Saddle River, New Jersey.

Chapter 46 46.9 Reprinted by permission of Macmillan Publishers Ltd.: *Nature.* R.R. Snook and D.J. Hosken, "Sperm death and dumping in Drosophila," *428*:939–941, fig. 2. Copyright © 2004.

Chapter 47 47.16 Figures 1.10 and 8.25 from *Principles of Development* by Lewis Wolpert (1998). By permission of Oxford University Press, Inc. **47.17a** Figure 21-70 from *Molecular Biology of the Cell,* 4th ed, by Bruce Alberts, used with permission from Garland Science - Books, permission conveyed through Copyright Clearance Center, Inc. Adapted for use from "Cell commitment and gene expression in the axolotl embryo" by T.J. Mohun from *Cell 22:* 9–15 (1980), by permission of the author; **47.17b** Reprinted from *Developmental Biology, 121,* Issue 2, Hiroki Nishida, "Cell lineage analysis in ascidian embryos by intracellular injection of a tracer enzyme: III. Up to the tissue restricted stage," p. 526, Copyright © 1987, with permission from Elsevier; **47.18** From *Molecular Biology of the Cell,* 4th edition, by Bruce Alberts et al., fig. 21.17, p. 1172. Copyright © 2002 by Bruce Alberts, Alexander Johnson, Julian Lewis, Martin Raff, Keith Roberts, and Peter Walter. Used by permission; **47.23 (experiment, results left)** Figures 1.10 and 8.25 from *Principles of Development* by Lewis Wolpert (1998). By permission of Oxford University Press, Inc. **47.23 (results, right)** Figure 15.12, p. 604, from *Developmental Biology*, 5th edition, by Gilbert et al. Copyright © 1997 Sinauer Associates. Used by permission; **47.26** Figure 23.1 from *Human Anatomy and Physiology*, 8e, by Elaine Marieb and Katja Hoehn. Copyright © 2010 Pearson Education, Inc., publishing as Pearson Benjamin Cummings. Used by permission of the publisher.

Chapter 48 **48.11** Adapted from G. Matthews, 2003. *Cellular Physiology of Nerve and Muscle*, 4th edition, fig. 6-2d, p. 61. Cambridge, MA: Blackwell Scientific Publications. Reprinted by permission of Wiley Blackwell; **48.18** Table 1 from "Opiate Receptor: Demonstration in nervous tissue" by C.B. Pert and S.H. Snyder in *Science, 179*, No. 4077: 1011–1014, March 9, 1973. Copyright © 1973, The American Association for the Advancement of Science. Reprinted with permission from AAAS.

Chapter 49 **49.11** Adapted from L. M. Mukhametov. 1984. Sleep in marine mammals. In *Sleep Mechanisms*, by A. A. Borbély and J. L. Valatx (eds.). Munich: Springer-Verlag, pp 227–238; **49.12** Figure 2a from "Transplanted suprachiasmatic nucleus determines circadian period" by M.R. Ralph et al., in *Science, 247*, No. 4945: 975–978, Feb. 23, 1990. Copyright © 1990, The American Association for the Advancement of Science. Reprinted with permission from AAAS; **49.18** Adapted from E. D. Jarvis et al. 2005. Avian brains and a new understanding of vertebrate brain evolution. *Nature Reviews Neuroscience* 6: 151–159, fig. 1c; **49.22** From *Schizophrenia Genesis: The Origins of Madness* by I. I. Gottesman, and D. Wolfgram, fig. 10, p. 96. New York: Freeman. © 1991 by Irving I. Gottesman. Used with the permission of Worth Publishers.

Chapter 50 **50.17A** Figure 15.4(a) from *Human Anatomy and Physiology*, 8e, by Elaine Marieb and Katja Hoehn. Copyright © 2010 Pearson Education, Inc., publishing as Pearson Benjamin Cummings. Used by permission of the publisher; **50.17B** Figure 15.15 from *Human Anatomy and Physiology*, 8e, by Elaine Marieb and Katja Hoehn. Copyright © 2010 Pearson Education, Inc., publishing as Pearson Benjamin Cummings. Used by permission of the publisher; **50.23** Reprinted by permission from Macmillan Publishers Ltd.: *Nature*. K.L. Mueller et al. The receptors and coding logic for bitter taste, *434*:225–229, fig. 4b. Copyright © 2005; **50.24a** Figure 15.23(a) and (b) from *Human Anatomy and Physiology*, 8e, by Elaine Marieb and Katja Hoehn. Copyright © 2010 Pearson Education, Inc., publishing as Pearson Benjamin Cummings. Used by permission of the publisher; **50.34** Grasshopper adapted from Hickman et al. 1993. *Integrated Principles of Zoology*, 9th ed., Fig. 22.6, p. 518. New York: McGraw-Hill Higher Education. © 1993 The McGraw-Hill Companies; **50.40** Figure 4 from "Locomotion: Energy Cost of Swimming, Flying, and Running" by K. Schmidt-Nielsen, in *Science, 177*, No. 4045: 222–228, July 21, 1972. Copyright © 1972, The American Association for the Advancement of Science. Reprinted with permission from AAAS.

Chapter 51 **51.2b** Figure 20, p. 28, from *Study of Instinct* by N. Tinbergen (1989). By permission of Oxford University Press, Inc.; **51.4** Reprinted by permission from Macmillan Publishing Ltd.: *Nature Reviews: Genetics*: M.B. Sokolowski. Drosophila: Genetics meets behavior, *2*:881, fig. 1. Copyright © 2001; **51.10** Figure 3a from "Prospective and retrospective learning in honeybees" by M. Biurfa and J. Benard, in *International Journal of Comparative Psychology, 19*, Issue 3: 358–367, 2006; Reprinted with permission; **51.13** Figure 2a from "Evolution of foraging behavior in Drosophila by density-dependent selection" by M.B. Sokolowski et al., in *Proceedings of the National Academy of Sciences, 94*, no. 14: 7373–7377, July 8, 1997. Copyright © 2007 National Academy of Sciences, U.S.A. Used by permission; **51.19** K. Witte and N. Sawka. 2003. Sexual imprinting on a novel trait in the dimorphic zebra finch: sexes differ. *Animal Behaviour* 65: 195–203. Art adapted from http://www.uni-bielefeld.de/biologue/vhf/KW/Forschungsprojekte2.html; **51.23 (left, bottom)** With kind permission from Springer Science+Business Media: *Genetica*, "The inheritance of mating songs in two cryptic, sibling lacewing species," vol. 116, 2002, pp. 269–289, C. S. Henry, fig. 2; **51.26 (top)** Adapted from a photograph by Jonathan Blair in Alcock, 2002. *Animal Behavior*, 7th ed. Sinauer Associates, Inc., Publiishers; **51.26 (bottom)** Reprinted by permission from Macmillan Publishers Ltd.: *Nature*. P. Berthold et al. Rapid microevolution of migratory behaviour in a wild bird species, *360*:668, fig. 1, 12/17/92. Copyright © 1992.

Chapter 52 **52.7** Adapted from L. Roberts. 1989. How fast can trees migrate? *Science* 243: 736, fig. 2. © 1989 by the American Association for the Advancement of Science; fig; **52.8** Reprinted by permission from Macmillan Publishers Ltd.: *Nature*. C. Parmesan et al. Poleward shift of butterfly species' ranges associated with regional warming, *399*:579–583, fig. 3. Copyright © 1999; **52.9** Adapted from Heinrich Walter and Siegmar-Walter Breckle. 2003. *Walter's Vegetation of the Earth*, fig. 16, p. 36. Springer-Verlag, © 2003; **52.17** Figure 1.7, p. 9 from *Kangaroos, Their Ecology and Management in the Sheep Rangelands of Australia*, edited by Graeme Caughley, Neil Shepherd, Jeff Short. © Cambridge University Press 1987. Reprinted with the permission of Cambridge University Press; **52.19** Map adapted from R. L. Smith. 1974. *Ecology and Field Biology*, fig. 11.19, p. 353. Harper and Row Publishers. Map updated from D. A. Sibley. 2000. National Audubon Society *The Sibley Guide to Birds*, Alfred A. Knopf: New York; **52.20** Data from W. J. Fletcher. 1987. Interactions among subtidal Australian sea urchins, gastropods and algae: effects of experimental removals. *Ecological Monographs* 57: 89–109; **Un. 52.2** Data from J. Clausen, D. D. Keck, and W. M. Hiesey. 1948. Experimental studies on the nature of species. III. Environmental responses of climatic races of *Achillea*. Carnegie Institution of Washington Publication 581.

Chapter 53 **53.5** Adapted from P. W. Sherman and M. L. Morton. 1984. "Demography of Belding's ground squirrels," *Ecology*, Vol. 65, No. 5, p. 1622, fig. 1a, 1984. Copyright © 1984 Ecological Society of America. Used by permission; **53.15** Adapted from J. T. Enright. 1976. Climate and population regulation: The biogeographer's

dilemma. *Oecologia* 24: 295–310; **53.16** Figure 3.5b, page 59, from *Soay Sheep: Dynamics and Selection in an Island Population* edited by T.H. Clutton-Brock and J.M. Pemberton. Copyright © Cambridge University Press 2004. Reprinted with the permission of Cambridge University Press; **53.18** Data courtesy of Rolf O. Peterson, Michigan Technological University; **53.23** Data from U. S. Census Bureau International Data Base; **53.24** Data from U. S. Census Bureau International Data Base; **53.25** Data from U. S. Census Bureau International Data Base 2008; **53.26** Source: Used courtesy of UNEP/GRID-Arendel at http://maps.grida.no/go/graphic/energy_consumption_per_capita_2004; **Tables 53.1** and **53.2** Data from P. W. Sherman and M. L. Morton, "Demography of Belding's ground squirrels," *Ecology*, Vol. 65, No. 5, p. 1622, fig. 1a, 1984. Copyright © 1984 Ecological Society of America.

Chapter 54 **54.2** From "The anoles of La Palma: aspects of their ecological relationships" by A.S. Rand and E. E. Williams in *Breviora 327*: 1–19, 1969. Copyright © 1969 by the President and Fellows of Harvard College. Used with permission from the Museum of Comparative Zoology, Harvard University; **54.9** Data for graph from S. D. Hacker and M. D. Bertness. 1999. Experimental evidence for factors maintaining plant species diversity in a New England salt marsh. *Ecology* 80: 2064–2073; **54.11** Adapted from N. Fierer and R. B. Jackson. 2006. The diversity and biogeography of soil bacterial communities. *Proceedings of the National Academy of Sciences USA 103*: 626–631 fig. 1a; **54.14** Adapted from E. A. Knox. 1970. Antarctic marine ecosystems. In *Antarctic Ecology*, ed. M. W. Holdgate, 69–96. London: Academic Press; **54.15** Adapted from D. L. Breitburg et al. 1997. Varying effects of low dissolved oxygen on trophic interactions in an estuarine food web. *Ecological Monographs* 67: 490. Copyright © 1997 Ecological Society of America; **54.16** Adapted from B. Jenkins. 1992. Productivity, disturbance and food web structure at a local spatial scale in experimental container habitats. *Oikos* 65: 252. Copyright © 1992 Oikos, Sweden; **54.17** Adapted from R. T. Paine. 1966. Food web complexity and species diversity. *American Naturalist* 100: 65–75; **54.18** From J. A. Estes et al. 1998. Killer whale predation on sea otters linking oceanic and nearshore ecosystems. *Science 282*: 474, fig. 1. Copyright © 1998 by the American Association for the Advancement of Science; **54.20** Graph adapted from A. R. Townsend et al. 1997. The intermediate disturbance hypothesis, refugia, and diversity in streams. *Limnology and Oceanography* 42:938–949. **54.22** Adapted from R. L. Crocker and J. Major. 1955. Soil Development in relation to vegetation and surface age at Glacier Bay, Alaska. *Journal of Ecology* 43: 427–448; **54.23** Data from F. S. Chapin, III, et al. 1994. Mechanisms of primary succession following deglaciation at Glacier Bay, Alaska. *Ecological Monographs* 64: 149–175; **54.25** Adapted from D. J. Currie. 1991. Energy and large-scale patterns of animal- and plant-species richness. *American Naturalist* 137: 27–49; **54.26** Adapted from F. W. Preston. 1960. Time and space and the variation of species. *Ecology* 41: 611–627; **54.28** Adapted from F. W. Preston. 1962. The canonical distribution of commonness and rarity. *Ecology* 43:185–215, 410–432.

Chapter 55 **55.4** and **Un 55.1** Adapted from D. L. DeAngelis. 1992. *Dynamics of Nutrient Cycling and Food Webs*. New York: Chapman & Hall; **55.7** Adapted from National Oceanic and Atmospheric Administration's National Data Buoy Center Voluntary Observing Ship Project, www.vos.noaa.gov/MWL/dec_06/Images/OCP_fig4.jpg; **55.8** Figure 2 from "Nitrogen, phosphorus, and eutrophication in the coastal marine environment" by J.H. Ryther, in *Science, 171*, No. 3975: 1008–1013, Mar. 12, 1971. Copyright © 1971, The American Association for the Advancement of Science. Reprinted with permission from AAAS; **55.9** Fig. 4.1 p. 82 from *Communities and Ecosystems*, 1e by Robert H. Whittaker. Copyright © 1970 Robert H. Whittaker. Reprinted by permission of Pearson Education; **55.14** From *The Economy of Nature*, 5th edition by Robert E. Ricklefs. © 2001 by W. H. Freeman and Company. Used with the permission of Worth Publishers. **55.15a** Adapted from J.A. Trofymow et al., *The Canadian Intersite Decomposition Experiment: Project and Site Establishment Report*, Information Report BC-X-378, page 2, Natural Resources Canada, Canadian Forest Service (1998). Reproduced with permission from the Minister of Public Works and Government Services, Canada, 2010; **55.15b** Adapted from: T.R. Moore et al., Litter decomposition rates in Canadian forests, *Global Change Biology* 5: 75–82 (1999), copyright © 2001, 1998 Blackwell Science Ltd. Reproduced with permission from the Minister of Public Works and Government Services, Canada, 2010 and Wiley Blackwell; **55.18b** Data adapted from Wu, W-M et al. 2006. Pilot-scale in situ bioremediation of uranium in a highly contaminated aquifer. 2. Reduction of U(VI) and geochemical control of a U(VI) bioavailability. *Environ. Sci. Technol.* 40: 3986–3995, fig. 1D; **Table 55.1** Data from Menzel and Ryther. 1961. *Deep Sea Ranch* 7: 276–281.

Chapter 56 **56.12** Figure 19.1 from *Ecology*, 5e by C.J. Krebs. Copyright © 2001 Pearson Education, Inc. Reprinted by permission; **56.13** Figure 2 from "Tracking the Long-Term Decline and Recovery of an Isolated Population" by R.L. Westemeier et al., in *Science, 282*, No. 5394: 1695–1698, Nov. 27, 1998. Copyright © 1998, The American Association for the Advancement of Science. Reprinted with permission from AAAS; **56.19** Reprinted by permission from Macmillan Publishers, Ltd.: *Nature*. N. Myers et al. Biodiversity hotspots for conservation priorities, *403*: 853–858, fig. 1, 2/24/00. Copyright © 2000; **56.20** Reprinted from W. D. Newmark, 1985. Legal and biotic boundaries of western North American national parks: a problem of congruence. *Biological Conservation* 33: 197–208, fig. 1, p. 199. © 1985, with permission from Elsevier; **56.21a** Map adapted from W. Purves and G. Orians, *Life, The Science of Biology*, 5th ed., fig. 55.23, p. 1239. © 1998 by Sinauer Associates, Inc. Reprinted with permission; **56.27** CO_2 data from www.esrl.noaa.gov/gmd/ccgg/trends. Temperature data from www.giss.nasa.gov/gistemp/graphs/Fig.A.lrg.gif; **56.29** Data from ozonewatch.gsfc.nasa.gov/facts/history/html; **56.32** Data from Instituto Nacional de Estadistica y Censos de Costa Rica and Centro Centroamericano de Poblacion, Universidad de Costa Rica.

Glossary

Pronunciation Key

Pronounce

ā	as in	ace
a/ah		ash
ch		chose
ē		meet
e/eh		bet
g		game
ī		ice
i		hit
ks		box
kw		quick
ng		song
ō		robe
o		ox
oy		boy
s		say
sh		shell
th		thin
ū		boot
u/uh		up
z		zoo

ʹ = primary accent

ʹ = secondary accent

5ʹ cap A modified form of guanine nucleotide added onto the 5ʹ end of a pre-mRNA molecule.

A site One of a ribosome's three binding sites for tRNA during translation. The A site holds the tRNA carrying the next amino acid to be added to the polypeptide chain. (A stands for aminoacyl tRNA.)

ABC hypothesis A model of flower formation identifying three classes of organ identity genes that direct formation of the four types of floral organs.

abiotic (ā'-bī-ot'-ik) Nonliving; referring to the physical and chemical properties of an environment.

abortion The termination of a pregnancy in progress.

abscisic acid (ABA) (ab-sis'-ik) A plant hormone that slows growth, often antagonizing the actions of growth hormones. Two of its many effects are to promote seed dormancy and facilitate drought tolerance.

absorption The third stage of food processing in animals: the uptake of small nutrient molecules by an organism's body.

absorption spectrum The range of a pigment's ability to absorb various wavelengths of light; also a graph of such a range.

abyssal zone (uh-bis'-ul) The part of the ocean's benthic zone between 2,000 and 6,000 m deep.

acanthodian (ak'-an-thō'-dē-un) Any of a group of ancient jawed aquatic vertebrates from the Silurian and Devonian periods.

accessory fruit A fruit, or assemblage of fruits, in which the fleshy parts are derived largely or entirely from tissues other than the ovary.

acclimatization (uh-klī'-muh-tī-zā'-shun) Physiological adjustment to a change in an environmental factor.

acetyl CoA Acetyl coenzyme A; the entry compound for the citric acid cycle in cellular respiration, formed from a fragment of pyruvate attached to a coenzyme.

acetylcholine (as'-uh-til-kō'-lēn) One of the most common neurotransmitters; functions by binding to receptors and altering the permeability of the postsynaptic membrane to specific ions, either depolarizing or hyperpolarizing the membrane.

acid A substance that increases the hydrogen ion concentration of a solution.

acid precipitation Rain, snow, or fog that is more acidic than pH 5.2.

acoelomate (uh-sē'-lō-māt) A solid-bodied animal lacking a cavity between the gut and outer body wall.

acrosomal reaction (ak'-ruh-sōm'-ul) The discharge of hydrolytic enzymes from the acrosome, a vesicle in the tip of a sperm, when the sperm approaches or contacts an egg.

acrosome (ak'-ruh-sōm) A vesicle in the tip of a sperm containing hydrolytic enzymes and other proteins that help the sperm reach the egg.

actin (ak'-tin) A globular protein that links into chains, two of which twist helically about each other, forming microfilaments (actin filaments) in muscle and other kinds of cells.

action potential An electrical signal that propagates (travels) along the membrane of a neuron or other excitable cell as a nongraded (all-or-none) depolarization.

action spectrum A graph that profiles the relative effectiveness of different wavelengths of radiation in driving a particular process.

activation energy The amount of energy that reactants must absorb before a chemical reaction will start; also called free energy of activation.

activator A protein that binds to DNA and stimulates gene transcription. In prokaryotes, activators bind in or near the promoter; in eukaryotes, activators generally bind to control elements in enhancers.

active immunity Long-lasting immunity conferred by the action of B cells and T cells and the resulting B and T memory cells specific for a pathogen. Active immunity can develop as a result of natural infection or immunization.

active site The specific region of an enzyme that binds the substrate and that forms the pocket in which catalysis occurs.

active transport The movement of a substance across a cell membrane against its concentration or electrochemical gradient, mediated by specific transport proteins and requiring an expenditure of energy.

adaptation Inherited characteristic of an organism that enhances its survival and reproduction in a specific environment.

adaptive immunity A vertebrate-specific defense that is mediated by B lymphocytes (B cells) and T lymphocytes (T cells). It exhibits specificity, memory, and self-nonself recognition. Also called acquired immunity.

adaptive radiation Period of evolutionary change in which groups of organisms form many new species whose adaptations allow them to fill different ecological roles in their communities.

addition rule A rule of probability stating that the probability of any one of two or more mutually exclusive events occurring can be determined by adding their individual probabilities.

adenosine triphosphate *See* ATP (adenosine triphosphate).

adenylyl cyclase (uh-den'-uh-lil) An enzyme that converts ATP to cyclic AMP in response to an extracellular signal.

adhesion The clinging of one substance to another, such as water to plant cell walls by means of hydrogen bonds.

adipose tissue A connective tissue that insulates the body and serves as a fuel reserve; contains fat-storing cells called adipose cells.

adrenal gland (uh-drē'-nul) One of two endocrine glands located adjacent to the kidneys in mammals. Endocrine cells in the outer portion (cortex) respond to adrenocorticotropic hormone (ACTH) by secreting steroid hormones that help maintain homeostasis during long-term stress. Neurosecretory cells in the central portion (medulla) secrete epinephrine and norepinephrine in response to nerve signals triggered by short-term stress.

adrenocorticotropic hormone (ACTH) A tropic hormone that is produced and secreted by the anterior pituitary and that stimulates the production and secretion of steroid hormones by the adrenal cortex.

aerobic respiration A catabolic pathway for organic molecules, using oxygen (O_2) as the final electron acceptor in an electron transport chain and ultimately producing ATP. This is the most efficient catabolic pathway and is carried out in most eukaryotic cells and many prokaryotic organisms.

age structure The relative number of individuals of each age in a population.

aggregate fruit A fruit derived from a single flower that has more than one carpel.

AIDS (acquired immunodeficiency syndrome) The symptoms and signs present during the late stages of HIV infection, defined by a specified reduction in the number of T cells and the appearance of characteristic secondary infections.

alcohol fermentation Glycolysis followed by the reduction of pyruvate to ethyl alcohol, regenerating NAD^+ and releasing carbon dioxide.

aldosterone (al-dos'-tuh-rōn) A steroid hormone that acts on tubules of the kidney to regulate the transport of sodium ions (Na$^+$) and potassium ions (K$^+$).

algae A diverse grade of photosynthetic protists, including unicellular and multicellular forms. Algal species are included in three of the five eukaryote supergroups (Chromalveolata, Rhizaria, and Archaeplastida).

alimentary canal (al'-uh-men'-tuh-rē) A complete digestive tract, consisting of a tube running between a mouth and an anus.

allele (uh-lē'-ul) Any of the alternative versions of a gene that may produce distinguishable phenotypic effects.

allergen An antigen that triggers an exaggerated immune response.

allopatric speciation (al'-uh-pat'-rik) The formation of new species in populations that are geographically isolated from one another.

allopolyploid (al'-ō-pol'-ē-ployd) A fertile individual that has more than two chromosome sets as a result of two different species interbreeding and combining their chromosomes.

allosteric regulation The binding of a regulatory molecule to a protein at one site that affects the function of the protein at a different site.

alpha (α) helix (al'-fuh hē'-liks) A coiled region constituting one form of the secondary structure of proteins, arising from a specific pattern of hydrogen bonding between atoms of the polypeptide backbone (not the side chains).

alternation of generations A life cycle in which there is both a multicellular diploid form, the sporophyte, and a multicellular haploid form, the gametophyte; characteristic of plants and some algae.

alternative RNA splicing A type of eukaryotic gene regulation at the RNA-processing level in which different mRNA molecules are produced from the same primary transcript, depending on which RNA segments are treated as exons and which as introns.

altruism (al'-trū-iz-um) Selflessness; behavior that reduces an individual's fitness while increasing the fitness of another individual.

alveolate (al-vē'-uh-let) A protist with membrane-bounded sacs (alveoli) located just under the plasma membrane.

alveolus (al-vē'-uh-lus) (plural, **alveoli**) One of the dead-end air sacs where gas exchange occurs in a mammalian lung.

Alzheimer's disease (alts'-hī-merz) An age-related dementia (mental deterioration) characterized by confusion and memory loss.

amacrine cell (am'-uh-krin) A neuron of the retina that helps integrate information before it is sent to the brain.

amino acid (uh-mēn'-ō) An organic molecule possessing both a carboxyl and an amino group. Amino acids serve as the monomers of polypeptides.

amino group A chemical group consisting of a nitrogen atom bonded to two hydrogen atoms; can act as a base in solution, accepting a hydrogen ion and acquiring a charge of 1+.

aminoacyl-tRNA synthetase An enzyme that joins each amino acid to the appropriate tRNA.

ammonia A small, toxic molecule (NH$_3$) produced by nitrogen fixation or as a metabolic waste product of protein and nucleic acid metabolism.

ammonite A member of a group of shelled cephalopods that were important marine predators for hundreds of millions of years until their extinction at the end of the Cretaceous period (65.5 million years ago).

amniocentesis (am'-nē-ō-sen-tē'-sis) A technique associated with prenatal diagnosis in which amniotic fluid is obtained by aspiration from a needle inserted into the uterus. The fluid and the fetal cells it contains are analyzed to detect certain genetic and congenital defects in the fetus.

amniote (am'-nē-ōt) Member of a clade of tetrapods named for a key derived character, the amniotic egg, which contains specialized membranes, including the fluid-filled amnion, that protect the embryo. Amniotes include mammals as well as birds and other reptiles.

amniotic egg An egg that contains specialized membranes that function in protection, nourishment, and gas exchange. The amniotic egg was a major evolutionary innovation, allowing embryos to develop on land in a fluid-filled sac, thus reducing the dependence of tetrapods on water for reproduction.

amoeba (uh-mē'-buh) A protist grade characterized by the presence of pseudopodia.

amoebocyte (uh-mē'-buh-sīt') An amoeba-like cell that moves by pseudopodia and is found in most animals. Depending on the species, it may digest and distribute food, dispose of wastes, form skeletal fibers, fight infections, or change into other cell types.

amoebozoan (uh-mē'-buh-zō'-an) A protist in a clade that includes many species with lobe- or tube-shaped pseudopodia.

amphibian Member of the tetrapod class Amphibia, including salamanders, frogs, and caecilians.

amphipathic (am'-fē-path'-ik) Having both a hydrophilic region and a hydrophobic region.

amplification The strengthening of stimulus energy during transduction.

amygdala (uh-mig'-duh-luh) A structure in the temporal lobe of the vertebrate brain that has a major role in the processing of emotions.

amylase (am'-uh-lās') An enzyme that hydrolyzes starch (a glucose polymer from plants) and glycogen (a glucose polymer from animals) into smaller polysaccharides and the disaccharide maltose.

anabolic pathway (an'-uh-bol'-ik) A metabolic pathway that consumes energy to synthesize a complex molecule from simpler molecules.

anaerobic respiration (an-er-ō'-bik) A catabolic pathway in which inorganic molecules other than oxygen accept electrons at the "downhill" end of electron transport chains.

analogous Having characteristics that are similar because of convergent evolution, not homology.

analogy (an-al'-uh-jē) Similarity between two species that is due to convergent evolution rather than to descent from a common ancestor with the same trait.

anaphase The fourth stage of mitosis, in which the chromatids of each chromosome have separated and the daughter chromosomes are moving to the poles of the cell.

anatomy The structure of an organism.

anchorage dependence The requirement that a cell must be attached to a substratum in order to initiate cell division.

androgen (an'-drō-jen) Any steroid hormone, such as testosterone, that stimulates the development and maintenance of the male reproductive system and secondary sex characteristics.

aneuploidy (an'-yū-ploy'-dē) A chromosomal aberration in which one or more chromosomes are present in extra copies or are deficient in number.

angiosperm (an'-jē-ō-sperm) A flowering plant, which forms seeds inside a protective chamber called an ovary.

angiotensin II A peptide hormone that stimulates constriction of precapillary arterioles and increases reabsorption of NaCl and water by the proximal tubules of the kidney, increasing blood pressure and volume.

anhydrobiosis (an-hī'-drō-bī-ō'-sis) A dormant state involving loss of almost all body water.

animal pole The point at the end of an egg in the hemisphere where the least yolk is concentrated; opposite of vegetal pole.

anion (an'-ī-on) A negatively charged ion.

anterior Pertaining to the front, or head, of a bilaterally symmetrical animal.

anterior pituitary A portion of the pituitary that develops from nonneural tissue; consists of endocrine cells that synthesize and secrete several tropic and nontropic hormones.

anther In an angiosperm, the terminal pollen sac of a stamen, where pollen grains containing sperm-producing male gametophytes form.

antheridium (an-thuh-rid'-ē-um) (plural, **antheridia**) In plants, the male gametangium, a moist chamber in which gametes develop.

anthropoid (an'-thruh-poyd) Member of a primate group made up of the monkeys and the apes (gibbons, orangutans, gorillas, chimpanzees, bonobos, and humans).

antibody A protein secreted by plasma cells (differentiated B cells) that binds to a particular antigen; also called immunoglobulin. All antibodies have the same Y-shaped structure and in their monomer form consist of two identical heavy chains and two identical light chains.

anticodon (an'-tī-kō'-don) A nucleotide triplet at one end of a tRNA molecule that base-pairs with a particular complementary codon on an mRNA molecule.

antidiuretic hormone (ADH) (an'-tī-dī-yū-ret'-ik) A peptide hormone, also known as vasopressin, that promotes water retention by the kidneys. Produced in the hypothalamus and released from the posterior pituitary, ADH also functions in the brain.

antigen (an'-ti-jen) A substance that elicits an immune response by binding to receptors of B cells, antibodies, or of T cells.

antigen presentation The process by which an MHC molecule binds to a fragment of an intracellular protein antigen and carries it to the cell surface, where it is displayed and can be recognized by a T cell.

antigen receptor The general term for a surface protein, located on B cells and T cells, that binds to antigens, initiating adaptive immune responses. The antigen receptors on B cells are called B cell receptors, and the antigen receptors on T cells are called T cell receptors.

antigen-presenting cell A cell that upon ingesting pathogens or internalizing pathogen proteins generates peptide fragments that are bound by class II MHC molecules and subsequently displayed on the cell surface to T cells. Macrophages, dendritic cells, and B cells are the primary antigen-presenting cells.

antiparallel Referring to the arrangement of the sugar-phosphate backbones in a DNA double helix (they run in opposite $5' \rightarrow 3'$ directions).

aphotic zone (ā'-fō'-tik) The part of an ocean or lake beneath the photic zone, where light does not penetrate sufficiently for photosynthesis to occur.

apical bud (ā'-pik-ul) A bud at the tip of a plant stem; also called a terminal bud.

apical dominance (ā'-pik-ul) Tendency for growth to be concentrated at the tip of a plant shoot, because the apical bud partially inhibits axillary bud growth.

apical ectodermal ridge (AER) A thickened area of ectoderm at the tip of a limb bud that promotes outgrowth of the limb bud.

apical meristem (ā'-pik-ul mār'-uh-stem) Embryonic plant tissue in the tips of roots and buds of shoots. The dividing cells of an apical meristem enable the plant to grow in length.

apicomplexan (ap'-ē-kom-pleks'-un) A protist in a clade that includes many species that parasitize animals. Some apicomplexans cause human disease.

apomixis (ap'-uh-mik'-sis) The ability of some plant species to reproduce asexually through seeds without fertilization by a male gamete.

apoplast (ap'-ō-plast) Everything external to the plasma membrane of a plant cell, including cell walls, intercellular spaces, and the space within dead structures such as xylem vessels and tracheids.

apoptosis (ā-puh-tō'-sus) A type of programmed cell death, which is brought about by activation of enzymes that break down many chemical components in the cell.

aposematic coloration (ap'-ō-si-mat'-ik) The bright warning coloration of many animals with effective physical or chemical defenses.

appendix A small, finger-like extension of the vertebrate cecum; contains a mass of white blood cells that contribute to immunity.

aquaporin A channel protein in the plasma membrane of a plant, animal, or microorganism cell that specifically facilitates osmosis, the diffusion of free water across the membrane.

aqueous solution (ā'-kwē-us) A solution in which water is the solvent.

arachnid A member of a major arthropod group, the chelicerates. Arachnids include spiders, scorpions, ticks, and mites.

arbuscular mycorrhiza (ar-bus'-kyū-lur mī'-kō-rī'-zuh) Association of a fungus with a plant root system in which the fungus causes the

invagination of the host (plant) cells' plasma membranes.

arbuscular mycorrhizal fungus A symbiotic fungus whose hyphae grow through the cell wall of plant roots and extend into the root cell (enclosed in tubes formed by invagination of the root cell plasma membrane).

Archaea (ar'-kē'-uh) One of two prokaryotic domains, the other being Bacteria.

Archaeplastida (ar'-kē-plas'-tid-uh) One of five supergroups of eukaryotes proposed in a current hypothesis of the evolutionary history of eukaryotes. This monophyletic group, which includes red algae, green algae, and land plants, descended from an ancient protist ancestor that engulfed a cyanobacterium. *See also* Excavata, Chromalveolata, Rhizaria, and Unikonta.

archegonium (ar-ki-gō'-nē-um) (plural, **archegonia**) In plants, the female gametangium, a moist chamber in which gametes develop.

archenteron (ar-ken'-tuh-ron) The endoderm-lined cavity, formed during gastrulation, that develops into the digestive tract of an animal.

archosaur (ar'-kō-sōr) Member of the reptilian group that includes crocodiles, alligators and dinosaurs, including birds.

arteriole (ar-ter'-ē-ōl) A vessel that conveys blood between an artery and a capillary bed.

artery A vessel that carries blood away from the heart to organs throughout the body.

arthropod A segmented ecdysozoan with a hard exoskeleton and jointed appendages. Familiar examples include insects, spiders, millipedes, and crabs.

artificial selection The selective breeding of domesticated plants and animals to encourage the occurrence of desirable traits.

ascocarp The fruiting body of a sac fungus (ascomycete).

ascomycete (as'-kuh-mī'-sēt) Member of the fungal phylum Ascomycota, commonly called sac fungus. The name comes from the saclike structure in which the spores develop.

ascus (plural, **asci**) A saclike spore capsule located at the tip of a dikaryotic hypha of a sac fungus.

asexual reproduction The generation of offspring from a single parent that occurs without the fusion of gametes (by budding, division of a single cell, or division of the entire organism into two or more parts). In most cases, the offspring are genetically identical to the parent.

assisted migration The translocation of a species to a favorable habitat beyond its native range for the purpose of protecting the species from human-caused threats.

assisted reproductive technology A fertilization procedure that generally involves surgically removing eggs (secondary oocytes) from a woman's ovaries after hormonal stimulation, fertilizing the eggs, and returning them to the woman's body.

associative learning The acquired ability to associate one environmental feature (such as a color) with another (such as danger).

aster A radial array of short microtubules that extends from each centrosome toward the

plasma membrane in an animal cell undergoing mitosis.

astrocyte A glial cell with diverse functions, including providing structural support for neurons, regulating the interstitial environment, facilitating synaptic transmission, and assisting in regulating the blood supply to the brain.

atherosclerosis A cardiovascular disease in which fatty deposits called plaques develop in the inner walls of the arteries, obstructing the arteries and causing them to harden.

atom The smallest unit of matter that retains the properties of an element.

atomic mass The total mass of an atom, which is the mass in grams of 1 mole of the atom.

atomic nucleus An atom's dense central core, containing protons and neutrons.

atomic number The number of protons in the nucleus of an atom, unique for each element and designated by a subscript to the left of the elemental symbol.

ATP (adenosine triphosphate) (a-den'-ō-sēn trī-fos'-fāt) An adenine-containing nucleoside triphosphate that releases free energy when its phosphate bonds are hydrolyzed. This energy is used to drive endergonic reactions in cells.

ATP synthase A complex of several membrane proteins that functions in chemiosmosis with adjacent electron transport chains, using the energy of a hydrogen ion (proton) concentration gradient to make ATP. ATP synthases are found in the inner mitochondrial membranes of eukaryotic cells and in the plasma membranes of prokaryotes.

atrial natriuretic peptide (ANP) (ā'-trē-ul na'-trē-yū-ret'-ik) A peptide hormone secreted by cells of the atria of the heart in response to high blood pressure. ANP's effects on the kidney alter ion and water movement and reduce blood pressure.

atrioventricular (AV) node A region of specialized heart muscle tissue between the left and right atria where electrical impulses are delayed for about 0.1 second before spreading to both ventricles and causing them to contract.

atrioventricular (AV) valve A heart valve located between each atrium and ventricle that prevents a backflow of blood when the ventricle contracts.

atrium (ā'-trē-um) (plural, **atria**) A chamber of the vertebrate heart that receives blood from the veins and transfers blood to a ventricle.

autocrine Referring to a secreted molecule that acts on the cell that secreted it.

autoimmune disease An immunological disorder in which the immune system turns against self.

autonomic nervous system (ot'-ō-nom'-ik) An efferent branch of the vertebrate peripheral nervous system that regulates the internal environment; consists of the sympathetic, parasympathetic, and enteric divisions.

autopolyploid (ot'-ō-pol'-ē-ployd) An individual that has more than two chromosome sets that are all derived from a single species.

autosome (ot'-ō-sōm) A chromosome that is not directly involved in determining sex; not a sex chromosome.

autotroph (ot'-ō-trōf) An organism that obtains organic food molecules without eating other organisms or substances derived from other organisms. Autotrophs use energy from the sun or from oxidation of inorganic substances to make organic molecules from inorganic ones.

auxin (ôk'-sin) A term that primarily refers to indoleacetic acid (IAA), a natural plant hormone that has a variety of effects, including cell elongation, root formation, secondary growth, and fruit growth.

average heterozygosity (het'-er-ō-zī-gō'-si-tē) The percentage, on average, of a population's loci that are heterozygous in members of the population.

avirulent Describing a pathogen that can mildly harm, but not kill, the host.

axillary bud (ak'-sil-ār-ē) A structure that has the potential to form a lateral shoot, or branch. The bud appears in the angle formed between a leaf and a stem.

axon (ak'-son) A typically long extension, or process, of a neuron that carries nerve impulses away from the cell body toward target cells.

B cells The lymphocytes that complete their development in the bone marrow and become effector cells for the humoral immune response.

Bacteria One of two prokaryotic domains, the other being Archaea.

bacterial artificial chromosome (BAC) A large plasmid that acts as a bacterial chromosome and can carry inserts of 100,000 to 300,000 base pairs (100–300 kb).

bacteriophage (bak-tēr'-ē-ō-fāj) A virus that infects bacteria; also called a phage.

bacteroid A form of the bacterium *Rhizobium* contained within the vesicles formed by the root cells of a root nodule.

balancing selection Natural selection that maintains two or more phenotypic forms in a population.

bark All tissues external to the vascular cambium, consisting mainly of the secondary phloem and layers of periderm.

Barr body A dense object lying along the inside of the nuclear envelope in cells of female mammals, representing a highly condensed, inactivated X chromosome.

basal angiosperm A member of one of three clades of early-diverging lineages of flowering plants. Examples are *Amborella*, water lilies, and star anise and its relatives.

basal body (bā'-sul) A eukaryotic cell structure consisting of a "9 + 0" arrangement of microtubule triplets. The basal body may organize the microtubule assembly of a cilium or flagellum and is structurally very similar to a centriole.

basal metabolic rate (BMR) The metabolic rate of a resting, fasting, and nonstressed endotherm at a comfortable temperature.

basal taxon In a specified group of organisms, a taxon whose evolutionary lineage diverged early in the history of the group.

base A substance that reduces the hydrogen ion concentration of a solution.

basidiocarp Elaborate fruiting body of a dikaryotic mycelium of a club fungus.

basidiomycete (buh-sid'-ē-ō-mī'-sēt) Member of the fungal phylum Basidiomycota, commonly called club fungus. The name comes from the club-like shape of the basidium.

basidium (plural, **basidia**) (buh-sid'-ē-um, buh-sid'-ē-ah) A reproductive appendage that produces sexual spores on the gills of mushrooms (club fungi).

Batesian mimicry (bāt'-zē-un mim'-uh-krē) A type of mimicry in which a harmless species looks like a species that is poisonous or otherwise harmful to predators.

behavior Individually, an action carried out by muscles or glands under control of the nervous system in response to a stimulus; collectively, the sum of an animal's responses to external and internal stimuli.

behavioral ecology The study of the evolution of and ecological basis for animal behavior.

benign tumor A mass of abnormal cells with specific genetic and cellular changes such that the cells are not capable of surviving at a new site and generally remain at the site of the tumor's origin.

benthic zone The bottom surface of an aquatic environment.

benthos (ben'-thōz) The communities of organisms living in the benthic zone of an aquatic biome.

beta (β) pleated sheet One form of the secondary structure of proteins in which the polypeptide chain folds back and forth. Two regions of the chain lie parallel to each other and are held together by hydrogen bonds between atoms of the polypeptide backbone (not the side chains).

beta oxidation A metabolic sequence that breaks fatty acids down to two-carbon fragments that enter the citric acid cycle as acetyl CoA.

bicoid A maternal effect gene that codes for a protein responsible for specifying the anterior end in *Drosophila melanogaster*.

bilateral symmetry Body symmetry in which a central longitudinal plane divides the body into two equal but opposite halves.

bilaterian (bī'-luh-ter'-ē-uhn) Member of a clade of animals with bilateral symmetry and three germ layers.

bile A mixture of substances that is produced in the liver and stored in the gallbladder; enables formation of fat droplets in water as an aid in the digestion and absorption of fats.

binary fission A method of asexual reproduction by "division in half." In prokaryotes, binary fission does not involve mitosis, but in single-celled eukaryotes that undergo binary fission, mitosis is part of the process.

binomial The two-part, latinized format for naming a species, consisting of the genus and specific epithet; a binomen.

biodiversity hot spot A relatively small area with numerous endemic species and a large number of endangered and threatened species.

bioenergetics (1) The overall flow and transformation of energy in an organism. (2) The study of how energy flows through organisms.

biofilm A surface-coating colony of one or more species of prokaryotes that engage in metabolic cooperation.

biofuel A fuel produced from dry organic matter or combustible oils produced by plants.

biogenic amine A neurotransmitter derived from an amino acid.

biogeochemical cycle Any of the various chemical cycles, which involve both biotic and abiotic components of ecosystems.

biogeography The study of the past and present geographic distribution of species.

bioinformatics The use of computers, software, and mathematical models to process and integrate biological information from large data sets.

biological augmentation An approach to restoration ecology that uses organisms to add essential materials to a degraded ecosystem.

biological clock An internal timekeeper that controls an organism's biological rhythms. The biological clock marks time with or without environmental cues but often requires signals from the environment to remain tuned to an appropriate period. *See also* circadian rhythm.

biological magnification A process in which retained substances become more concentrated at each higher trophic level in a food chain.

biological species concept Definition of a species as a group of populations whose members have the potential to interbreed in nature and produce viable, fertile offspring, but do not produce viable, fertile offspring with members of other such groups.

biology The scientific study of life.

biomanipulation An approach that applies the top-down model of community organization to alter ecosystem characteristics. For example, ecologists can prevent algal blooms and eutrophication by altering the density of higher-level consumers in lakes instead of by using chemical treatments.

biomass The total mass of organic matter comprising a group of organisms in a particular habitat.

biome (bī'-ōm) Any of the world's major ecosystem types, often classified according to the predominant vegetation for terrestrial biomes and the physical environment for aquatic biomes and characterized by adaptations of organisms to that particular environment.

bioremediation The use of organisms to detoxify and restore polluted and degraded ecosystems.

biosphere The entire portion of Earth inhabited by life; the sum of all the planet's ecosystems.

biotechnology The manipulation of organisms or their components to produce useful products.

biotic (bī-ot'-ik) Pertaining to the living factors—the organisms—in an environment.

bipolar cell A neuron that relays information between photoreceptors and ganglion cells in the retina.

bipolar disorder A depressive mental illness characterized by swings of mood from high to low; also called manic-depressive disorder.

birth control pill A chemical contraceptive that inhibits ovulation, retards follicular development, or alters a woman's cervical mucus to prevent sperm from entering the uterus.

blade (1) A leaflike structure of a seaweed that provides most of the surface area for photosynthesis. (2) The flattened portion of a typical leaf.

blastocoel (blas'-tuh-sēl) The fluid-filled cavity that forms in the center of a blastula.

blastocyst (blas'-tuh-sist) The blastula stage of mammalian embryonic development, consisting of an inner cell mass, a cavity, and an outer layer, the trophoblast. In humans, the blastocyst forms 1 week after fertilization.

blastomere An early embryonic cell arising during the cleavage stage of an early embryo.

blastopore (blas'-tō-pōr) In a gastrula, the opening of the archenteron that typically develops into the anus in deuterostomes and the mouth in protostomes.

blastula (blas'-tyū-luh) A hollow ball of cells that marks the end of the cleavage stage during early embryonic development in animals.

blood A connective tissue with a fluid matrix called plasma in which red blood cells, white blood cells, and cell fragments called platelets are suspended.

blue-light photoreceptor A type of light receptor in plants that initiates a variety of responses, such as phototropism and slowing of hypocotyl elongation.

body cavity A fluid- or air-filled space between the digestive tract and the body wall.

body plan In multicellular eukaryotes, a set of morphological and developmental traits that are integrated into a functional whole—the living organism.

Bohr shift A lowering of the affinity of hemoglobin for oxygen, caused by a drop in pH. It facilitates the release of oxygen from hemoglobin in the vicinity of active tissues.

bolus A lubricated ball of chewed food.

bone A connective tissue consisting of living cells held in a rigid matrix of collagen fibers embedded in calcium salts.

book lung An organ of gas exchange in spiders, consisting of stacked plates contained in an internal chamber.

bottleneck effect Genetic drift that occurs when the size of a population is reduced, as by a natural disaster or human actions. Typically, the surviving population is no longer genetically representative of the original population.

bottom-up model A model of community organization in which mineral nutrients influence community organization by controlling plant or phytoplankton numbers, which in turn control herbivore numbers, which in turn control predator numbers.

Bowman's capsule (bō'-munz) A cup-shaped receptacle in the vertebrate kidney that is the initial, expanded segment of the nephron where filtrate enters from the blood.

brachiopod (bra'-kē- uh-pod') A marine lophophorate with a shell divided into dorsal and ventral halves; also called a lamp shell.

brain Organ of the central nervous system where information is processed and integrated.

brainstem A collection of structures in the vertebrate brain, including the midbrain, the pons, and the medulla oblongata; functions in homeostasis, coordination of movement, and conduction of information to higher brain centers.

branch point The representation on a phylogenetic tree of the divergence of two or more taxa from a common ancestor. A branch point is usually shown as a dichotomy in which a branch representing the ancestral lineage splits (at the branch point) into two branches, one for each of the two descendant lineages.

brassinosteroid A steroid hormone in plants that has a variety of effects, including inducing cell elongation, retarding leaf abscission, and promoting xylem differentiation.

breathing Ventilation of the lungs through alternating inhalation and exhalation.

bronchiole (brong'-kē-ōl') A fine branch of the bronchi that transports air to alveoli.

bronchus (brong'-kus) (plural, **bronchi**) One of a pair of breathing tubes that branch from the trachea into the lungs.

brown alga A multicellular, photosynthetic protist with a characteristic brown or olive color that results from carotenoids in its plastids. Most brown algae are marine, and some have a plantlike body (thallus).

bryophyte (brī'-uh-fīt) An informal name for a moss, liverwort, or hornwort; a nonvascular plant that lives on land but lacks some of the terrestrial adaptations of vascular plants.

budding Asexual reproduction in which outgrowths from the parent form and pinch off to live independently or else remain attached to eventually form extensive colonies.

buffer A solution that contains a weak acid and its corresponding base. A buffer minimizes changes in pH when acids or bases are added to the solution.

bulk feeder An animal that eats relatively large pieces of food.

bulk flow The movement of a fluid due to a difference in pressure between two locations.

bundle-sheath cell In C_4 plants, a type of photosynthetic cell arranged into tightly packed sheaths around the veins of a leaf.

C_3 plant A plant that uses the Calvin cycle for the initial steps that incorporate CO_2 into organic material, forming a three-carbon compound as the first stable intermediate.

C_4 plant A plant in which the Calvin cycle is preceded by reactions that incorporate CO_2 into a four-carbon compound, the end product of which supplies CO_2 for the Calvin cycle.

calcitonin (kal'-si-tō'-nin) A hormone secreted by the thyroid gland that lowers blood calcium levels by promoting calcium deposition in bone and calcium excretion from the kidneys; nonessential in adult humans.

callus A mass of dividing, undifferentiated cells growing in culture.

calorie (cal) The amount of heat energy required to raise the temperature of 1 g of water by 1°C; also the amount of heat energy that 1 g of water releases when it cools by 1°C. The Calorie (with a capital C), usually used to indicate the energy content of food, is a kilocalorie.

Calvin cycle The second of two major stages in photosynthesis (following the light reactions), involving fixation of atmospheric CO_2 and reduction of the fixed carbon into carbohydrate.

CAM plant A plant that uses crassulacean acid metabolism, an adaptation for photosynthesis in arid conditions. In this process, carbon dioxide entering open stomata during the night is converted to organic acids, which release CO_2 for the Calvin cycle during the day, when stomata are closed.

Cambrian explosion A relatively brief time in geologic history when many present-day phyla of animals first appeared in the fossil record. This burst of evolutionary change occurred about 535–525 million years ago and saw the emergence of the first large, hard-bodied animals.

cAMP *See* cyclic AMP (cAMP).

canopy The uppermost layer of vegetation in a terrestrial biome.

capillary (kap'-il-ār'-ē) A microscopic blood vessel that penetrates the tissues and consists of a single layer of endothelial cells that allows exchange between the blood and interstitial fluid.

capillary bed A network of capillaries in a tissue or organ.

capsid The protein shell that encloses a viral genome. It may be rod-shaped, polyhedral, or more complex in shape.

capsule (1) In many prokaryotes, a dense and well-defined layer of polysaccharide or protein that surrounds the cell wall and is sticky, protecting the cell and enabling it to adhere to substrates or other cells. (2) The sporangium of a bryophyte (moss, liverwort, or hornwort).

carbohydrate (kar'-bō-hī'-drāt) A sugar (monosaccharide) or one of its dimers (disaccharides) or polymers (polysaccharides).

carbon fixation The initial incorporation of carbon from CO_2 into an organic compound by an autotrophic organism (a plant, another photosynthetic organism, or a chemoautotrophic prokaryote).

carbonyl group (kar-buh-nēl') A chemical group present in aldehydes and ketones and consisting of a carbon atom double-bonded to an oxygen atom.

carboxyl group (kar-bok'-sil) A chemical group present in organic acids and consisting of a single carbon atom double-bonded to an oxygen atom and also bonded to a hydroxyl group.

cardiac cycle (kar'-dē-ak) The alternating contractions and relaxations of the heart.

cardiac muscle A type of striated muscle that forms the contractile wall of the heart. Its cells are joined by intercalated disks that relay the electrical signals underlying each heartbeat.

cardiac output The volume of blood pumped per minute by each ventricle of the heart.

cardiovascular system A closed circulatory system with a heart and branching network of arteries, capillaries, and veins. The system is characteristic of vertebrates.

carnivore An animal that mainly eats other animals.

carotenoid (kuh-rot'-uh-noyd' An accessory pigment, either yellow or orange, in the chloroplasts of plants and in some prokaryotes. By absorbing wavelengths of light that chlorophyll cannot, carotenoids broaden the spectrum of colors that can drive photosynthesis.

carpel (kar'-pul) The ovule-producing reproductive organ of a flower, consisting of the stigma, style, and ovary.

carrier In genetics, an individual who is heterozygous at a given genetic locus for a recessively inherited disorder. The heterozygote is generally phenotypically normal for the disorder but can pass on the recessive allele to offspring.

carrying capacity The maximum population size that can be supported by the available resources, symbolized as *K*.

cartilage (kar'-til-ij) A flexible connective tissue with an abundance of collagenous fibers embedded in chondroitin sulfate.

Casparian strip (ka-spar'-ē-un) A water-impermeable ring of wax in the endodermal cells of plants that blocks the passive flow of water and solutes into the stele by way of cell walls.

catabolic pathway (kat'-uh-bol'-ik) A metabolic pathway that releases energy by breaking down complex molecules to simpler molecules.

catalyst (kat'-uh-list) A chemical agent that selectively increases the rate of a reaction without being consumed by the reaction.

catastrophism (kuh-tas'-truh-fiz'-um) The principle that events in the past occurred suddenly and were caused by different mechanisms than those operating today. *See* uniformitarianism.

catecholamine (kat'-uh-kōl'-uh-mēn) Any of a class of neurotransmitters and hormones, including the hormones epinephrine and norepinephrine, that are synthesized from the amino acid tyrosine.

cation (cat'-ī-on) A positively charged ion.

cation exchange A process in which positively charged minerals are made available to a plant when hydrogen ions in the soil displace mineral ions from the clay particles.

cDNA library A gene library containing clones that carry complementary DNA (cDNA) inserts. The library includes only the genes that were transcribed in the cells whose mRNA was isolated to make the cDNA.

cecum (sē'-kum) (plural, **ceca**) The blind pouch forming one branch of the large intestine.

cell body The part of a neuron that houses the nucleus and most other organelles.

cell cycle An ordered sequence of events in the life of a cell, from its origin in the division of a parent cell until its own division into two. The eukaryotic cell cycle is composed of interphase (including G_1, S, and G_2 subphases) and M phase (including mitosis and cytokinesis).

cell cycle control system A cyclically operating set of molecules in the eukaryotic cell that both triggers and coordinates key events in the cell cycle.

cell division The reproduction of cells.

cell fractionation The disruption of a cell and separation of its parts by centrifugation at successively higher speeds.

cell plate A membrane-bounded, flattened sac located at the midline of a dividing plant cell, inside which the new cell wall forms during cytokinesis.

cell wall A protective layer external to the plasma membrane in the cells of plants, prokaryotes, fungi, and some protists. Polysaccharides such as cellulose (in plants and some protists), chitin (in fungi), and peptidoglycan (in bacteria) are important structural components of cell walls.

cell-mediated immune response The branch of adaptive immunity that involves the activation of cytotoxic T cells, which defend against infected cells.

cellular respiration The catabolic pathways of aerobic and anaerobic respiration, which break down organic molecules and use an electron transport chain for the production of ATP.

cellular slime mold A type of protist characterized by unicellular amoeboid cells and aggregated reproductive bodies in its life cycle.

cellulose (sel'-yū-lōs) A structural polysaccharide of plant cell walls, consisting of glucose monomers joined by β glycosidic linkages.

Celsius scale (sel'-sē-us) A temperature scale (°C) equal to $\frac{5}{9}$(°F − 32) that measures the freezing point of water at 0°C and the boiling point of water at 100°C.

central canal The narrow cavity in the center of the spinal cord that is continuous with the fluid-filled ventricles of the brain.

central nervous system (CNS) The portion of the nervous system where signal integration occurs; in vertebrate animals, the brain and spinal cord.

central vacuole In a mature plant cell, a large membranous sac with diverse roles in growth, storage, and sequestration of toxic substances.

centriole (sen'-trē-ōl) A structure in the centrosome of an animal cell composed of a cylinder of microtubule triplets arranged in a 9 + 0 pattern. A centrosome has a pair of centrioles.

centromere (sen'-trō-mēr) In a duplicated chromosome, the region on each sister chromatid where they are most closely attached to each other by proteins that bind to specific DNA sequences; this close attachment causes a constriction in the condensed chromosome. (An uncondensed, unduplicated chromosome has a single centromere, identified by its DNA sequence.)

centrosome (sen'-trō-sōm) A structure present in the cytoplasm of animal cells that functions as a microtubule-organizing center and is important during cell division. A centrosome has two centrioles.

cephalization (sef'-uh-luh-zā'-shun) An evolutionary trend toward the concentration of sensory equipment at the anterior end of the body.

cercozoan An amoeboid or flagellated protist that feeds with threadlike pseudopodia.

cerebellum (sār'-ruh-bel'-um) Part of the vertebrate hindbrain located dorsally; functions in unconscious coordination of movement and balance.

cerebral cortex (suh-rē'-brul) The surface of the cerebrum; the largest and most complex part of the mammalian brain, containing nerve cell bodies of the cerebrum; the part of the vertebrate brain most changed through evolution.

cerebral hemisphere The right or left side of the cerebrum.

cerebrospinal fluid (suh-rē'-brō-spī'-nul) Blood-derived fluid that surrounds, protects against infection, nourishes, and cushions the brain and spinal cord.

cerebrum (suh-rē'-brum) The dorsal portion of the vertebrate forebrain, composed of right and left hemispheres; the integrating center for memory, learning, emotions, and other highly complex functions of the central nervous system.

cervix (ser'-viks) The neck of the uterus, which opens into the vagina.

chaparral A scrubland biome of dense, spiny evergreen shrubs found at midlatitudes along coasts where cold ocean currents circulate offshore; characterized by mild, rainy winters and long, hot, dry summers.

chaperonin (shap'-er-ō'-nin) A protein complex that assists in the proper folding of other proteins.

character An observable heritable feature that may vary among individuals.

character displacement The tendency for characteristics to be more divergent in sympatric populations of two species than in allopatric populations of the same two species.

checkpoint A control point in the cell cycle where stop and go-ahead signals can regulate the cycle.

chelicera (kē-lih'-suh-ruh) (plural, **chelicerae**) One of a pair of clawlike feeding appendages characteristic of chelicerates.

chelicerate (kē-lih-suh'-rāte) An arthropod that has chelicerae and a body divided into a cephalothorax and an abdomen. Living chelicerates include sea spiders, horseshoe crabs, scorpions, ticks, and spiders.

chemical bond An attraction between two atoms, resulting from a sharing of outer-shell electrons or the presence of opposite charges on the atoms. The bonded atoms gain complete outer electron shells.

chemical energy Energy available in molecules for release in a chemical reaction; a form of potential energy.

chemical equilibrium In a chemical reaction, the state in which the rate of the forward reaction equals the rate of the reverse reaction, so that the relative concentrations of the reactants and products do not change with time.

chemical reaction The making and breaking of chemical bonds, leading to changes in the composition of matter.

chemiosmosis (kem'-ē-oz-mō'-sis) An energy-coupling mechanism that uses energy stored in the form of a hydrogen ion gradient across a membrane to drive cellular work, such as the synthesis of ATP. Under aerobic conditions, most ATP synthesis in cells occurs by chemiosmosis.

chemoautotroph (kē'-mō-ot'-ō-trōf) An organism that obtains energy by oxidizing inorganic substances and needs only carbon dioxide as a carbon source.

chemoheterotroph (kē′-mō-het′-er-ō-trōf) An organism that requires organic molecules for both energy and carbon.

chemoreceptor A sensory receptor that responds to a chemical stimulus, such as a solute or an odorant.

chiasma (plural, **chiasmata**) (kī-az′-muh, kī-az′-muh-tuh) The X-shaped, microscopically visible region where crossing over has occurred earlier in prophase I between homologous nonsister chromatids. Chiasmata become visible after synapsis ends, with the two homologs remaining associated due to sister chromatid cohesion.

chitin (kī′-tin) A structural polysaccharide, consisting of amino sugar monomers, found in many fungal cell walls and in the exoskeletons of all arthropods.

chlorophyll (klōr′-ō-fil) A green pigment located in membranes within the chloroplasts of plants and algae and in the membranes of certain prokaryotes. Chlorophyll *a* participates directly in the light reactions, which convert solar energy to chemical energy.

chlorophyll *a* A photosynthetic pigment that participates directly in the light reactions, which convert solar energy to chemical energy.

chlorophyll *b* An accessory photosynthetic pigment that transfers energy to chlorophyll *a*.

chloroplast (klōr′-ō-plast) An organelle found in plants and photosynthetic protists that absorbs sunlight and uses it to drive the synthesis of organic compounds from carbon dioxide and water.

choanocyte (kō-an′-uh-sīt) A flagellated feeding cell found in sponges. Also called a collar cell, it has a collar-like ring that traps food particles around the base of its flagellum.

cholesterol (kō-les′-tuh-rol) A steroid that forms an essential component of animal cell membranes and acts as a precursor molecule for the synthesis of other biologically important steroids, such as many hormones.

chondrichthyan (kon-drik′-thē-an) Member of the class Chondrichthyes, vertebrates with skeletons made mostly of cartilage, such as sharks and rays.

chordate Member of the phylum Chordata, animals that at some point during their development have a notochord; a dorsal, hollow nerve cord; pharyngeal slits or clefts; and a muscular, post-anal tail.

chorionic villus sampling (CVS) (kōr′-ē-on′-ik vil′-us) A technique associated with prenatal diagnosis in which a small sample of the fetal portion of the placenta is removed for analysis to detect certain genetic and congenital defects in the fetus.

Chromalveolata One of five supergroups of eukaryotes proposed in a current hypothesis of the evolutionary history of eukaryotes. Chromalveolates may have originated by secondary endosymbiosis and include two large protist clades, the alveolates and the stramenopiles. *See also* Excavata, Rhizaria, Archaeplastida, and Unikonta.

chromatin (krō′-muh-tin) The complex of DNA and proteins that makes up eukaryotic chromosomes. When the cell is not dividing, chromatin exists in its dispersed form, as a mass of very long, thin fibers that are not visible with a light microscope.

chromosome (krō′-muh-sōm) A cellular structure carrying genetic material, found in the nucleus of eukaryotic cells. Each chromosome consists of one very long DNA molecule and associated proteins. (A bacterial chromosome usually consists of a single circular DNA molecule and associated proteins. It is found in the nucleoid region, which is not membrane bounded.) *See also* chromatin.

chromosome theory of inheritance A basic principle in biology stating that genes are located at specific positions (loci) on chromosomes and that the behavior of chromosomes during meiosis accounts for inheritance patterns.

chylomicron (kī′-lō-mī′-kron) A lipid transport globule composed of fats mixed with cholesterol and coated with proteins.

chyme (kīm) The mixture of partially digested food and digestive juices formed in the stomach.

chytrid (kī′-trid) Member of the fungal phylum Chytridiomycota, mostly aquatic fungi with flagellated zoospores that represent an early-diverging fungal lineage.

ciliate (sil′-ē-it) A type of protist that moves by means of cilia.

cilium (sil′-ē-um) (plural, **cilia**) A short appendage containing microtubules in eukaryotic cells. A motile cilium is specialized for locomotion or moving fluid past the cell; it is formed from a core of nine outer doublet microtubules and two inner single microtubules (the "9 + 2" arrangement) ensheathed in an extension of the plasma membrane. A primary cilium is usually nonmotile and plays a sensory and signaling role; it lacks the two inner microtubules (the "9 + 0" arrangement).

circadian rhythm (ser-kā′-dē-un) A physiological cycle of about 24 hours that persists even in the absence of external cues.

***cis-trans* isomer** One of several compounds that have the same molecular formula and covalent bonds between atoms but differ in the spatial arrangements of their atoms owing to the inflexibility of double bonds; formerly called a geometric isomer.

citric acid cycle A chemical cycle involving eight steps that completes the metabolic breakdown of glucose molecules begun in glycolysis by oxidizing acetyl CoA (derived from pyruvate) to carbon dioxide; occurs within the mitochondrion in eukaryotic cells and in the cytosol of prokaryotes; together with pyruvate oxidation, the second major stage in cellular respiration.

clade (klayd) A group of species that includes an ancestral species and all of its descendants.

cladistics (kluh-dis′-tiks) An approach to systematics in which organisms are placed into groups called clades based primarily on common descent.

class In Linnaean classification, the taxonomic category above the level of order.

cleavage (1) The process of cytokinesis in animal cells, characterized by pinching of the plasma membrane. (2) The succession of rapid cell divisions without significant growth during early embryonic development that converts the zygote to a ball of cells.

cleavage furrow The first sign of cleavage in an animal cell; a shallow groove around the cell in the cell surface near the old metaphase plate.

climate The long-term prevailing weather conditions at a given place.

climograph A plot of the temperature and precipitation in a particular region.

cline A graded change in a character along a geographic axis.

clitoris (klit′-uh-ris) An organ at the upper intersection of the labia minora that engorges with blood and becomes erect during sexual arousal.

cloaca (klō-ā′-kuh) A common opening for the digestive, urinary, and reproductive tracts found in many nonmammalian vertebrates but in few mammals.

clonal selection The process by which an antigen selectively binds to and activates only those lymphocytes bearing receptors specific for the antigen. The selected lymphocytes proliferate and differentiate into a clone of effector cells and a clone of memory cells specific for the stimulating antigen.

clone (1) A lineage of genetically identical individuals or cells. (2) In popular usage, an individual that is genetically identical to another individual. (3) As a verb, to make one or more genetic replicas of an individual or cell. *See also* gene cloning.

cloning vector In genetic engineering, a DNA molecule that can carry foreign DNA into a host cell and replicate there. Cloning vectors include plasmids and bacterial artificial chromosomes (BACs), which move recombinant DNA from a test tube back into a cell, and viruses that transfer recombinant DNA by infection.

closed circulatory system A circulatory system in which blood is confined to vessels and is kept separate from the interstitial fluid.

cnidocyte (nī′-duh-sīt) A specialized cell unique to the phylum Cnidaria; contains a capsule-like organelle housing a coiled thread that, when discharged, explodes outward and functions in prey capture or defense.

cochlea (kok′-lē-uh) The complex, coiled organ of hearing that contains the organ of Corti.

codominance The situation in which the phenotypes of both alleles are exhibited in the heterozygote because both alleles affect the phenotype in separate, distinguishable ways.

codon (kō′-don) A three-nucleotide sequence of DNA or mRNA that specifies a particular amino acid or termination signal; the basic unit of the genetic code.

coefficient of relatedness The fraction of genes that, on average, are shared by two individuals.

coelom (sē′-lōm) A body cavity lined by tissue derived only from mesoderm.

coelomate (sē′-lō-māt) An animal that possesses a true coelom (a body cavity lined by tissue completely derived from mesoderm).

coenocytic fungus (sē′-no-si′-tic) A fungus that lacks septa and hence whose body is made up of a continuous cytoplasmic mass that may contain hundreds or thousands of nuclei.

coenzyme (kō-en′-zīm) An organic molecule serving as a cofactor. Most vitamins function as coenzymes in metabolic reactions.

coevolution The joint evolution of two interacting species, each in response to selection imposed by the other.

cofactor Any nonprotein molecule or ion that is required for the proper functioning of an enzyme. Cofactors can be permanently bound to the active site or may bind loosely and reversibly, along with the substrate, during catalysis.

cognition The process of knowing that may include awareness, reasoning, recollection, and judgment.

cognitive map A neural representation of the abstract spatial relationships between objects in an animal's surroundings.

cohesion The linking together of like molecules, often by hydrogen bonds.

cohesion-tension hypothesis The leading explanation of the ascent of xylem sap. It states that transpiration exerts pull on xylem sap, putting the sap under negative pressure or tension, and that the cohesion of water molecules transmits this pull along the entire length of the xylem from shoots to roots.

cohort A group of individuals of the same age in a population.

coitus (kō′-uh-tus) The insertion of a penis into a vagina; also called sexual intercourse.

coleoptile (kō′-lē-op′-tul) The covering of the young shoot of the embryo of a grass seed.

coleorhiza (kō′-lē-uh-rī′-zuh) The covering of the young root of the embryo of a grass seed.

collagen A glycoprotein in the extracellular matrix of animal cells that forms strong fibers, found extensively in connective tissue and bone; the most abundant protein in the animal kingdom.

collecting duct The location in the kidney where processed filtrate, called urine, is collected from the renal tubules.

collenchyma cell (kō-len′-kim-uh) A flexible plant cell type that occurs in strands or cylinders that support young parts of the plant without restraining growth.

colloid A mixture made up of a liquid and particles that (because of their large size) remain suspended rather than dissolved in that liquid.

colon (kō′-len) The largest section of the vertebrate large intestine; functions in water absorption and formation of feces.

commensalism (kuh-men′-suh-lizm) A symbiotic relationship in which one organism benefits but the other is neither helped nor harmed.

communication In animal behavior, a process involving transmission of, reception of, and response to signals. The term is also used in connection with other organisms, as well as individual cells of multicellular organisms.

community All the organisms that inhabit a particular area; an assemblage of populations of different species living close enough together for potential interaction.

community ecology The study of how interactions between species affect community structure and organization.

companion cell A type of plant cell that is connected to a sieve-tube element by many plasmodesmata and whose nucleus and ribosomes may serve one or more adjacent sieve-tube elements.

competitive exclusion The concept that when populations of two similar species compete for the same limited resources, one population will use the resources more efficiently and have a reproductive advantage that will eventually lead to the elimination of the other population.

competitive inhibitor A substance that reduces the activity of an enzyme by entering the active site in place of the substrate, whose structure it mimics.

complement system A group of about 30 blood proteins that may amplify the inflammatory response, enhance phagocytosis, or directly lyse extracellular pathogens.

complementary DNA (cDNA) A double-stranded DNA molecule made *in vitro* using mRNA as a template and the enzymes reverse transcriptase and DNA polymerase. A cDNA molecule corresponds to the exons of a gene.

complete digestive tract A digestive tube that runs between a mouth and an anus; also called an alimentary canal.

complete dominance The situation in which the phenotypes of the heterozygote and dominant homozygote are indistinguishable.

complete flower A flower that has all four basic floral organs: sepals, petals, stamens, and carpels.

complete metamorphosis The transformation of a larva into an adult that looks very different, and often functions very differently in its environment, than the larva.

compound A substance consisting of two or more different elements combined in a fixed ratio.

compound eye A type of multifaceted eye in insects and crustaceans consisting of up to several thousand light-detecting, focusing ommatidia.

concentration gradient A region along which the density of a chemical substance increases or decreases.

conception The fertilization of an egg by a sperm in humans.

condom A thin, latex rubber or natural membrane sheath that fits over the penis to collect semen.

conduction The direct transfer of thermal motion (heat) between molecules of objects in direct contact with each other.

cone A cone-shaped cell in the retina of the vertebrate eye, sensitive to color.

conformer An animal for which an internal condition conforms to (changes in accordance with) changes in an environmental variable.

conidium (plural, **conidia**) A haploid spore produced at the tip of a specialized hypha in ascomycetes during asexual reproduction.

conifer Member of the largest gymnosperm phylum. Most conifers are cone-bearing trees, such as pines and firs.

conjugation (kon′-jū-gā′-shun) (1) In prokaryotes, the direct transfer of DNA between two cells that are temporarily joined. When the two cells are members of different species, conjugation results in horizontal gene transfer. (2) In ciliates, a sexual process in which two cells exchange haploid micronuclei but do not reproduce.

connective tissue Animal tissue that functions mainly to bind and support other tissues, having a sparse population of cells scattered through an extracellular matrix.

conodont An early, soft-bodied vertebrate with prominent eyes and dental elements.

conservation biology The integrated study of ecology, evolutionary biology, physiology, molecular biology, and genetics to sustain biological diversity at all levels.

contraception The deliberate prevention of pregnancy.

contractile vacuole A membranous sac that helps move excess water out of certain freshwater protists.

control element A segment of noncoding DNA that helps regulate transcription of a gene by serving as a binding site for a transcription factor. Multiple control elements are present in a eukaryotic gene's enhancer.

controlled experiment An experiment in which an experimental group is compared with a control group that varies only in the factor being tested.

convection The mass movement of warmed air or liquid to or from the surface of a body or object.

convergent evolution The evolution of similar features in independent evolutionary lineages.

convergent extension A process in which the cells of a tissue layer rearrange themselves in such a way that the sheet of cells becomes narrower (converges) and longer (extends).

cooperativity A kind of allosteric regulation whereby a shape change in one subunit of a protein caused by substrate binding is transmitted to all the other subunits, facilitating binding of additional substrate molecules to those subunits.

copepod (kō′-puh-pod) Any of a group of small crustaceans that are important members of marine and freshwater plankton communities.

coral reef Typically a warm-water, tropical ecosystem dominated by the hard skeletal structures secreted primarily by corals. Some coral reefs also exist in cold, deep waters.

corepressor A small molecule that binds to a bacterial repressor protein and changes the protein's shape, allowing it to bind to the operator and switch an operon off.

cork cambium (kam′-bē-um) A cylinder of meristematic tissue in woody plants that replaces the epidermis with thicker, tougher cork cells.

corpus callosum (kor′-pus kuh-lō′-sum) The thick band of nerve fibers that connects the right and left cerebral hemispheres in mammals, enabling the hemispheres to process information together.

corpus luteum (kor'-pus lū'-tē-um) A secreting tissue in the ovary that forms from the collapsed follicle after ovulation and produces progesterone.

cortex (1) The outer region of cytoplasm in a eukaryotic cell, lying just under the plasma membrane, that has a more gel-like consistency than the inner regions due to the presence of multiple microfilaments. (2) In plants, ground tissue that is between the vascular tissue and dermal tissue in a root or eudicot stem.

cortical nephron In mammals and birds, a nephron with a loop of Henle located almost entirely in the renal cortex.

corticosteroid Any steroid hormone produced and secreted by the adrenal cortex.

cotransport The coupling of the "downhill" diffusion of one substance to the "uphill" transport of another against its own concentration gradient.

cotyledon (kot'-uh-lē'-dun) A seed leaf of an angiosperm embryo. Some species have one cotyledon, others two.

countercurrent exchange The exchange of a substance or heat between two fluids flowing in opposite directions. For example, blood in a fish gill flows in the opposite direction of water passing over the gill, maximizing diffusion of oxygen into and carbon dioxide out of the blood.

countercurrent multiplier system A countercurrent system in which energy is expended in active transport to facilitate exchange of materials and generate concentration gradients.

covalent bond (kō-vā'-lent) A type of strong chemical bond in which two atoms share one or more pairs of valence electrons.

craniate A chordate with a head.

crassulacean acid metabolism (CAM) An adaptation for photosynthesis in arid conditions, first discovered in the family Crassulaceae. In this process, a plant takes up CO_2 and incorporates it into a variety of organic acids at night; during the day, CO_2 is released from organic acids for use in the Calvin cycle.

crista (plural, **cristae**) (kris'-tuh, kris'-tē) An infolding of the inner membrane of a mitochondrion. The inner membrane houses electron transport chains and molecules of the enzyme catalyzing the synthesis of ATP (ATP synthase).

critical load The amount of added nutrient, usually nitrogen or phosphorus, that can be absorbed by plants without damaging ecosystem integrity.

crop rotation The practice of planting nonlegumes one year and legumes in alternating years to restore concentrations of fixed nitrogen in the soil.

cross-fostering study A behavioral study in which the young of one species are placed in the care of adults from another species.

crossing over The reciprocal exchange of genetic material between nonsister chromatids during prophase I of meiosis.

cross-pollination In angiosperms, the transfer of pollen from an anther of a flower on one plant to the stigma of a flower on another plant of the same species.

crustacean (kruh-stā'-shun) A member of a subphylum of mostly aquatic arthropods that includes lobsters, crayfishes, crabs, shrimps, and barnacles.

cryptic coloration Camouflage that makes a potential prey difficult to spot against its background.

culture A system of information transfer through social learning or teaching that influences the behavior of individuals in a population.

cuticle (kyū'-tuh-kul) (1) A waxy covering on the surface of stems and leaves that prevents desiccation in terrestrial plants. (2) The exoskeleton of an arthropod, consisting of layers of protein and chitin that are variously modified for different functions. (3) A tough coat that covers the body of a nematode.

cyclic AMP (cAMP) Cyclic adenosine monophosphate, a ring-shaped molecule made from ATP that is a common intracellular signaling molecule (second messenger) in eukaryotic cells. It is also a regulator of some bacterial operons.

cyclic electron flow A route of electron flow during the light reactions of photosynthesis that involves only photosystem I and that produces ATP but not NADPH or O_2.

cyclin (sī'-klin) A cellular protein that occurs in a cyclically fluctuating concentration and that plays an important role in regulating the cell cycle.

cyclin-dependent kinase (Cdk) A protein kinase that is active only when attached to a particular cyclin.

cystic fibrosis (sis'-tik fī-brō'-sis) A human genetic disorder caused by a recessive allele for a chloride channel protein; characterized by an excessive secretion of mucus and consequent vulnerability to infection; fatal if untreated.

cytochrome (sī'-tō-krōm) An iron-containing protein that is a component of electron transport chains in the mitochondria and chloroplasts of eukaryotic cells and the plasma membranes of prokaryotic cells.

cytogenetic map A map of a chromosome that locates genes with respect to chromosomal features distinguishable in a microscope.

cytokine (sī'-tō-kīn') Any of a group of small proteins secreted by a number of cell types, including macrophages and helper T cells, that regulate the function of other cells.

cytokinesis (sī'-tō-kuh-nē'-sis) The division of the cytoplasm to form two separate daughter cells immediately after mitosis, meiosis I, or meiosis II.

cytokinin (sī'-tō-kī'-nin) Any of a class of related plant hormones that retard aging and act in concert with auxin to stimulate cell division, influence the pathway of differentiation, and control apical dominance.

cytoplasm (sī'-tō-plaz'-um) The contents of the cell bounded by the plasma membrane; in eukaryotes, the portion exclusive of the nucleus.

cytoplasmic determinant A maternal substance, such as a protein or RNA, that when placed into an egg influences the course of early development by regulating the expression of genes that affect the developmental fate of cells.

cytoplasmic streaming A circular flow of cytoplasm, involving interactions of myosin and actin filaments, that speeds the distribution of materials within cells.

cytoskeleton A network of microtubules, microfilaments, and intermediate filaments that extend throughout the cytoplasm and serve a variety of mechanical, transport, and signaling functions.

cytosol (sī'-tō-sol) The semifluid portion of the cytoplasm.

cytotoxic T cell A type of lymphocyte that, when activated, kills infected cells as well as certain cancer cells and transplanted cells.

dalton A measure of mass for atoms and subatomic particles; the same as the atomic mass unit, or amu.

data Recorded observations.

day-neutral plant A plant in which flower formation is not controlled by photoperiod or day length.

decapod A member of the group of crustaceans that includes lobsters, crayfishes, crabs, and shrimps.

decomposer An organism that absorbs nutrients from nonliving organic material such as corpses, fallen plant material, and the wastes of living organisms and converts them to inorganic forms; a detritivore.

deductive reasoning A type of logic in which specific results are predicted from a general premise.

deep-sea hydrothermal vent A dark, hot, oxygen-deficient environment associated with volcanic activity on or near the seafloor. The producers in a vent community are chemoautotrophic prokaryotes.

de-etiolation The changes a plant shoot undergoes in response to sunlight; also known informally as greening.

dehydration reaction A chemical reaction in which two molecules become covalently bonded to each other with the removal of a water molecule.

deletion (1) A deficiency in a chromosome resulting from the loss of a fragment through breakage. (2) A mutational loss of one or more nucleotide pairs from a gene.

demographic transition In a stable population, a shift from high birth and death rates to low birth and death rates.

demography The study of changes over time in the vital statistics of populations, especially birth rates and death rates.

denaturation (dē-nā'-chur-ā'-shun) In proteins, a process in which a protein loses its native shape due to the disruption of weak chemical bonds and interactions, thereby becoming biologically inactive; in DNA, the separation of the two strands of the double helix. Denaturation occurs under extreme (noncellular) conditions of pH, salt concentration, or temperature.

dendrite (den'-drīt) One of usually numerous, short, highly branched extensions of a neuron that receive signals from other neurons.

dendritic cell An antigen-presenting cell, located mainly in lymphatic tissues and skin, that is particularly efficient in presenting antigens to helper T cells, thereby initiating a primary immune response.

density The number of individuals per unit area or volume.

density dependent Referring to any characteristic that varies with population density.

density independent Referring to any characteristic that is not affected by population density.

density-dependent inhibition The phenomenon observed in normal animal cells that causes them to stop dividing when they come into contact with one another.

deoxyribonucleic acid (DNA) (dē-ok′-sē-rī-bō-nū-klā′-ik) A nucleic acid molecule, usually a double-stranded helix, in which each polynucleotide strand consists of nucleotide monomers with a deoxyribose sugar and the nitrogenous bases adenine (A), cytosine (C), guanine (G), and thymine (T); capable of being replicated and determining the inherited structure of a cell's proteins.

deoxyribose (dē-ok′-si-rī′-bōs) The sugar component of DNA nucleotides, having one fewer hydroxyl group than ribose, the sugar component of RNA nucleotides.

depolarization A change in a cell's membrane potential such that the inside of the membrane is made less negative relative to the outside. For example, a neuron membrane is depolarized if a stimulus decreases its voltage from the resting potential of −70 mV in the direction of zero voltage.

dermal tissue system The outer protective covering of plants.

desert A terrestrial biome characterized by very low precipitation.

desmosome A type of intercellular junction in animal cells that functions as a rivet, fastening cells together.

determinate cleavage A type of embryonic development in protostomes that rigidly casts the developmental fate of each embryonic cell very early.

determinate growth A type of growth characteristic of most animals and some plant organs, in which growth stops after a certain size is reached.

determination The progressive restriction of developmental potential in which the possible fate of each cell becomes more limited as an embryo develops. At the end of determination, a cell is committed to its fate.

detritivore (deh-trī′-tuh-vōr) A consumer that derives its energy and nutrients from nonliving organic material such as corpses, fallen plant material, and the wastes of living organisms; a decomposer.

detritus (di-trī′-tus) Dead organic matter.

deuteromycete (dū′-tuh-rō-mī′-sēt) Traditional classification for a fungus with no known sexual stage.

deuterostome development (dū′-tuh-rō-stōm′) In animals, a developmental mode distinguished by the development of the anus from the blastopore; often also characterized by radial cleavage and by the body cavity forming as outpockets of mesodermal tissue.

development The events involved in an organism's changing gradually from a simple to a more complex or specialized form.

diabetes mellitus (dī′-uh-bē′-tis mel′-uh-tus) An endocrine disorder marked by an inability to maintain glucose homeostasis. The type 1 form results from autoimmune destruction of insulin-secreting cells; treatment usually requires daily insulin injections. The type 2 form most commonly results from reduced responsiveness of target cells to insulin; obesity and lack of exercise are risk factors.

diacylglycerol (DAG) (dī-a′-sil-glis′-er-ol) A second messenger produced by the cleavage of the phospholipid PIP$_2$ in the plasma membrane.

diaphragm (dī′-uh-fram′) (1) A sheet of muscle that forms the bottom wall of the thoracic cavity in mammals. Contraction of the diaphragm pulls air into the lungs. (2) A dome-shaped rubber cup fitted into the upper portion of the vagina before sexual intercourse. It serves as a physical barrier to the passage of sperm into the uterus.

diapsid (dī-ap′-sid) Member of an amniote clade distinguished by a pair of holes on each side of the skull. Diapsids include the lepidosaurs and archosaurs.

diastole (dī-as′-tō-lē) The stage of the cardiac cycle in which a heart chamber is relaxed and fills with blood.

diastolic pressure Blood pressure in the arteries when the ventricles are relaxed.

dicot A term traditionally used to refer to flowering plants that have two embryonic seed leaves, or cotyledons. Recent molecular evidence indicates that dicots do not form a clade; species once classified as dicots are now grouped into eudicots, magnoliids, and several lineages of basal angiosperms.

differential gene expression The expression of different sets of genes by cells with the same genome.

differentiation The process by which a cell or group of cells become specialized in structure and function.

diffusion The spontaneous movement of a substance down its concentration or electrochemical gradient, from a region where it is more concentrated to a region where it is less concentrated.

digestion The second stage of food processing in animals: the breaking down of food into molecules small enough for the body to absorb.

dihybrid (dī′-hī′-brid) An organism that is heterozygous with respect to two genes of interest. All the offspring from a cross between parents doubly homozygous for different alleles are dihybrids. For example, parents of genotypes *AABB* and *aabb* produce a dihybrid of genotype *AaBb*.

dihybrid cross A cross between two organisms that are each heterozygous for both of the characters being followed (or the self-pollination of a plant that is heterozygous for both characters).

dikaryotic (dī′-kār-ē-ot′-ik) Referring to a fungal mycelium with two haploid nuclei per cell, one from each parent.

dinoflagellate (dī′-nō-flaj′-uh-let) Member of a group of mostly unicellular photosynthetic algae with two flagella situated in perpendicular grooves in cellulose plates covering the cell.

dinosaur Member of an extremely diverse clade of reptiles varying in body shape, size, and habitat. Birds are the only extant dinosaurs.

dioecious (dī-ē′-shus) In plant biology, having the male and female reproductive parts on different individuals of the same species.

diploblastic Having two germ layers.

diploid cell (dip′-loyd) A cell containing two sets of chromosomes (2*n*), one set inherited from each parent.

diplomonad A protist that has modified mitochondria, two equal-sized nuclei, and multiple flagella.

directional selection Natural selection in which individuals at one end of the phenotypic range survive or reproduce more successfully than do other individuals.

disaccharide (dī-sak′-uh-rīd) A double sugar, consisting of two monosaccharides joined by a glycosidic linkage formed by a dehydration reaction.

dispersal The movement of individuals or gametes away from their parent location. This movement sometimes expands the geographic range of a population or species.

dispersion The pattern of spacing among individuals within the boundaries of a population.

disruptive selection Natural selection in which individuals on both extremes of a phenotypic range survive or reproduce more successfully than do individuals with intermediate phenotypes.

distal tubule In the vertebrate kidney, the portion of a nephron that helps refine filtrate and empties it into a collecting duct.

disturbance A natural or human-caused event that changes a biological community and usually removes organisms from it. Disturbances, such as fires and storms, play a pivotal role in structuring many communities.

disulfide bridge A strong covalent bond formed when the sulfur of one cysteine monomer bonds to the sulfur of another cysteine monomer.

DNA (deoxyribonucleic acid) (dē-ok′-sē-rī-bō-nū-klā′-ik) A double-stranded, helical nucleic acid molecule, consisting of nucleotide monomers with a deoxyribose sugar and the nitrogenous bases adenine (A), cytosine (C), guanine (G), and thymine (T); capable of being replicated and determining the inherited structure of a cell's proteins.

DNA ligase (lī′-gās) A linking enzyme essential for DNA replication; catalyzes the covalent bonding of the 3′ end of one DNA fragment (such as an Okazaki fragment) to the 5′ end of another DNA fragment (such as a growing DNA chain).

DNA methylation The presence of methyl groups on the DNA bases (usually cytosine) of plants, animals, and fungi. (The term also refers to the process of adding methyl groups to DNA bases.)

DNA microarray assay A method to detect and measure the expression of thousands of genes at one time. Tiny amounts of a large number of single-stranded DNA fragments representing different genes are fixed to a glass slide and tested for hybridization with samples of labeled cDNA.

DNA polymerase (puh-lim'-er-ās) An enzyme that catalyzes the elongation of new DNA (for example, at a replication fork) by the addition of nucleotides to the 3' end of an existing chain. There are several different DNA polymerases; DNA polymerase III and DNA polymerase I play major roles in DNA replication in *E. coli*.

DNA replication The process by which a DNA molecule is copied; also called DNA synthesis.

domain (1) A taxonomic category above the kingdom level. The three domains are Archaea, Bacteria, and Eukarya. (2) A discrete structural and functional region of a protein.

dominant allele An allele that is fully expressed in the phenotype of a heterozygote.

dominant species A species with substantially higher abundance or biomass than other species in a community. Dominant species exert a powerful control over the occurrence and distribution of other species.

dopamine A neurotransmitter that is a catecholamine, like epinephrine and norepinephrine.

dormancy A condition typified by extremely low metabolic rate and a suspension of growth and development.

dorsal Pertaining to the top of an animal with radial or bilateral symmetry.

dorsal lip The region above the blastopore on the dorsal side of the amphibian embryo.

double bond A double covalent bond; the sharing of two pairs of valence electrons by two atoms.

double circulation A circulatory system consisting of separate pulmonary and systemic circuits, in which blood passes through the heart after completing each circuit.

double fertilization A mechanism of fertilization in angiosperms in which two sperm cells unite with two cells in the female gametophyte (embryo sac) to form the zygote and endosperm.

double helix The form of native DNA, referring to its two adjacent antiparallel polynucleotide strands wound around an imaginary axis into a spiral shape.

Down syndrome A human genetic disease usually caused by the presence of an extra chromosome 21; characterized by developmental delays and heart and other defects that are generally treatable or non-life-threatening.

Duchenne muscular dystrophy (duh-shen') A human genetic disease caused by a sex-linked recessive allele; characterized by progressive weakening and a loss of muscle tissue.

duodenum (dū'-uh-dēn'-um) The first section of the small intestine, where chyme from the stomach mixes with digestive juices from the pancreas, liver, and gallbladder as well as from gland cells of the intestinal wall.

duplication An aberration in chromosome structure due to fusion with a fragment from a homologous chromosome, such that a portion of a chromosome is duplicated.

dynamic stability hypothesis The concept that long food chains are less stable than short chains.

dynein (dī'-nē-un) In cilia and flagella, a large motor protein extending from one microtubule doublet to the adjacent doublet. ATP hydrolysis drives changes in dynein shape that lead to bending of cilia and flagella.

E site One of a ribosome's three binding sites for tRNA during translation. The E site is the place where discharged tRNAs leave the ribosome. (E stands for exit.)

ecdysozoan Member of a group of animal phyla identified as a clade by molecular evidence. Many ecdysozoans are molting animals.

ecdysteroid A steroid hormone, secreted by the prothoracic glands, that triggers molting in arthropods.

echinoderm (i-kī'-nō-derm) A slow-moving or sessile marine deuterostome with a water vascular system and, in larvae, bilateral symmetry. Echinoderms include sea stars, brittle stars, sea urchins, feather stars, and sea cucumbers.

ecological footprint The aggregate land and water area required by a person, city, or nation to produce all of the resources it consumes and to absorb all of the wastes it generates.

ecological niche (nich) The sum of a species' use of the biotic and abiotic resources in its environment.

ecological species concept A definition of species in terms of ecological niche, the sum of how members of the species interact with the nonliving and living parts of their environment.

ecological succession Transition in the species composition of a community following a disturbance; establishment of a community in an area virtually barren of life.

ecology The study of how organisms interact with each other and their environment.

ecosystem All the organisms in a given area as well as the abiotic factors with which they interact; one or more communities and the physical environment around them.

ecosystem ecology The study of energy flow and the cycling of chemicals among the various biotic and abiotic components in an ecosystem.

ecosystem engineer An organism that influences community structure by causing physical changes in the environment.

ecosystem service A function performed by an ecosystem that directly or indirectly benefits humans.

ecotone The transition from one type of habitat or ecosystem to another, such as the transition from a forest to a grassland.

ectoderm (ek'-tō-durm) The outermost of the three primary germ layers in animal embryos; gives rise to the outer covering and, in some phyla, the nervous system, inner ear, and lens of the eye.

ectomycorrhiza (ek'-tō-mī'-kō-rī'-zuh) Association of a fungus with a plant root system in which the fungus surrounds the roots but does not cause invagination of the host (plant) cells' plasma membranes.

ectomycorrhizal fungus A symbiotic fungus that forms sheaths of hyphae over the surface of plant roots and also grows into extracellular spaces of the root cortex.

ectoparasite A parasite that feeds on the external surface of a host.

ectopic Occurring in an abnormal location.

ectoproct A sessile, colonial lophophorate; also called a bryozoan.

ectothermic Referring to organisms for which external sources provide most of the heat for temperature regulation.

Ediacaran biota (ē'-dē-uh-keh'-run bī-ō'-tuh) An early group of soft-bodied, multicellular eukaryotes known from fossils that range in age from 565 million to 550 million years old.

effective population size An estimate of the size of a population based on the numbers of females and males that successfully breed; generally smaller than the total population.

effector cell (1) A muscle cell or gland cell that performs the body's response to stimuli as directed by signals from the brain or other processing center of the nervous system. (2) A lymphocyte that has undergone clonal selection and is capable of mediating an adaptive immune response.

egg The female gamete.

egg-polarity gene A gene that helps control the orientation (polarity) of the egg; also called a maternal effect gene.

ejaculation The propulsion of sperm from the epididymis through the muscular vas deferens, ejaculatory duct, and urethra.

ejaculatory duct In mammals, the short section of the ejaculatory route formed by the convergence of the vas deferens and a duct from the seminal vesicle. The ejaculatory duct transports sperm from the vas deferens to the urethra.

electrocardiogram (ECG or EKG) A record of the electrical impulses that travel through heart muscle during the cardiac cycle.

electrochemical gradient The diffusion gradient of an ion, which is affected by both the concentration difference of an ion across a membrane (a chemical force) and the ion's tendency to move relative to the membrane potential (an electrical force).

electrogenic pump An active transport protein that generates voltage across a membrane while pumping ions.

electromagnetic receptor A receptor of electromagnetic energy, such as visible light, electricity, or magnetism.

electromagnetic spectrum The entire spectrum of electromagnetic radiation, ranging in wavelength from less than a nanometer to more than a kilometer.

electron A subatomic particle with a single negative electrical charge and a mass about 1/2,000 that of a neutron or proton. One or more electrons move around the nucleus of an atom.

electron microscope (EM) A microscope that uses magnets to focus an electron beam on or through a specimen, resulting in a practical resolution of a hundredfold greater than that of a light microscope using standard techniques. A transmission electron microscope (TEM) is used to study the internal structure of thin sections of cells. A scanning electron microscope (SEM) is used to study the fine details of cell surfaces.

electron shell An energy level of electrons at a characteristic average distance from the nucleus of an atom.

electron transport chain A sequence of electron carrier molecules (membrane proteins) that shuttle electrons down a series of redox reactions that release energy used to make ATP.

electronegativity The attraction of a given atom for the electrons of a covalent bond.

electroporation A technique to introduce recombinant DNA into cells by applying a brief electrical pulse to a solution containing the cells. The pulse creates temporary holes in the cells' plasma membranes, through which DNA can enter.

element Any substance that cannot be broken down to any other substance by chemical reactions.

elimination The fourth and final stage of food processing in animals: the passing of undigested material out of the body.

embryo sac (em'-brē-ō) The female gametophyte of angiosperms, formed from the growth and division of the megaspore into a multicellular structure that typically has eight haploid nuclei.

embryonic lethal A mutation with a phenotype leading to death of an embryo or larva.

embryophyte Alternate name for land plants that refers to their shared derived trait of multicellular, dependent embryos.

emergent properties New properties that arise with each step upward in the hierarchy of life, owing to the arrangement and interactions of parts as complexity increases.

emigration The movement of individuals out of a population.

enantiomer (en-an'-tē-ō-mer) One of two compounds that are mirror images of each other and that differ in shape due to the presence of an asymmetric carbon.

endangered species A species that is in danger of extinction throughout all or a significant portion of its range.

endemic (en-dem'-ik) Referring to a species that is confined to a specific geographic area.

endergonic reaction (en'-der-gon'-ik) A nonspontaneous chemical reaction, in which free energy is absorbed from the surroundings.

endocrine gland (en'-dō-krin) A ductless gland that secretes hormones directly into the interstitial fluid, from which they diffuse into the bloodstream.

endocrine system The internal system of communication involving hormones, the ductless glands that secrete hormones, and the molecular receptors on or in target cells that respond to hormones; functions in concert with the nervous system to effect internal regulation and maintain homeostasis.

endocytosis (en'-dō-sī-tō'-sis) Cellular uptake of biological molecules and particulate matter via formation of vesicles from the plasma membrane.

endoderm (en'-dō-durm) The innermost of the three primary germ layers in animal embryos; lines the archenteron and gives rise to the liver, pancreas, lungs, and the lining of the digestive tract in species that have these structures.

endodermis In plant roots, the innermost layer of the cortex that surrounds the vascular cylinder.

endomembrane system The collection of membranes inside and surrounding a eukaryotic cell, related either through direct physical contact or by the transfer of membranous vesicles; includes the plasma membrane, the nuclear envelope, the smooth and rough endoplasmic reticulum, the Golgi apparatus, lysosomes, vesicles, and vacuoles.

endometriosis (en'-dō-mē-trē-ō'-sis) The condition resulting from the presence of endometrial tissue outside of the uterus.

endometrium (en'-dō-mē'-trē-um) The inner lining of the uterus, which is richly supplied with blood vessels.

endoparasite A parasite that lives within a host.

endophyte A fungus that lives inside a leaf or other plant part without causing harm to the plant.

endoplasmic reticulum (ER) (en'-dō-plaz'-mik ruh-tik'-yū-lum) An extensive membranous network in eukaryotic cells, continuous with the outer nuclear membrane and composed of ribosome-studded (rough) and ribosome-free (smooth) regions.

endorphin (en-dōr'-fin) Any of several hormones produced in the brain and anterior pituitary that inhibit pain perception.

endoskeleton A hard skeleton buried within the soft tissues of an animal.

endosperm In angiosperms, a nutrient-rich tissue formed by the union of a sperm with two polar nuclei during double fertilization. The endosperm provides nourishment to the developing embryo in angiosperm seeds.

endospore A thick-coated, resistant cell produced by some bacterial cells when they are exposed to harsh conditions.

endosymbiont theory The theory that mitochondria and plastids, including chloroplasts, originated as prokaryotic cells engulfed by an ancestral eukaryotic cell. The engulfed cell and its host cell then evolved into a single organism.

endosymbiosis A process in which a unicellular organism (the "host") engulfs another cell, which lives within the host cell and ultimately becomes an organelle in the host cell. *See also* endosymbiont theory.

endothelium (en'-dō-thē'-lē-um) The simple squamous layer of cells lining the lumen of blood vessels.

endothermic Referring to organisms that are warmed by heat generated by their own metabolism. This heat usually maintains a relatively stable body temperature higher than that of the external environment.

endotoxin A toxic component of the outer membrane of certain gram-negative bacteria that is released only when the bacteria die.

energetic hypothesis The concept that the length of a food chain is limited by the inefficiency of energy transfer along the chain.

energy The capacity to cause change, especially to do work (to move matter against an opposing force).

energy coupling In cellular metabolism, the use of energy released from an exergonic reaction to drive an endergonic reaction.

enhancer A segment of eukaryotic DNA containing multiple control elements, usually located far from the gene whose transcription it regulates.

enteric division One of three divisions of the autonomic nervous system; consists of networks of neurons in the digestive tract, pancreas, and gallbladder; normally regulated by the sympathetic and parasympathetic divisions of the autonomic nervous system.

entropy A measure of disorder, or randomness.

enzymatic hydrolysis The process in digestion that splits macromolecules from food by the enzymatic addition of water.

enzyme (en'-zīm) A macromolecule serving as a catalyst, a chemical agent that increases the rate of a reaction without being consumed by the reaction. Most enzymes are proteins.

enzyme-substrate complex A temporary complex formed when an enzyme binds to its substrate molecule(s).

epicotyl (ep'-uh-kot'-ul) In an angiosperm embryo, the embryonic axis above the point of attachment of the cotyledon(s) and below the first pair of miniature leaves.

epidemic A general outbreak of a disease.

epidermis (1) The dermal tissue system of nonwoody plants, usually consisting of a single layer of tightly packed cells. (2) The outermost layer of cells in an animal.

epididymis (ep'-uh-did'-uh-mus) A coiled tubule located adjacent to the mammalian testis where sperm are stored.

epigenetic inheritance Inheritance of traits transmitted by mechanisms not directly involving the nucleotide sequence of a genome.

epinephrine (ep'-i-nef'-rin) A catecholamine that, when secreted as a hormone by the adrenal medulla, mediates "fight-or-flight" responses to short-term stresses; also released by some neurons as a neurotransmitter; also known as adrenaline.

epiphyte (ep'-uh-fīt) A plant that nourishes itself but grows on the surface of another plant for support, usually on the branches or trunks of trees.

epistasis (ep'-i-stā'-sis) A type of gene interaction in which the phenotypic expression of one gene alters that of another independently inherited gene.

epithelial tissue (ep'-uh-thē'-lē-ul) Sheets of tightly packed cells that line organs and body cavities as well as external surfaces.

epithelium An epithelial tissue.

epitope A small, accessible region of an antigen to which an antigen receptor or antibody binds; also called an antigenic determinant.

EPSP *See* excitatory postsynaptic potential.

equilibrium potential (E_{ion}) The magnitude of a cell's membrane voltage at equilibrium; calculated using the Nernst equation.

erythrocyte (eh-rith´-ruh-sīt) A blood cell that contains hemoglobin, which transports oxygen; also called a red blood cell.

erythropoietin (EPO) (eh-rith´-rō-poy´-uh-tin) A hormone that stimulates the production of erythrocytes. It is secreted by the kidney when body tissues do not receive enough oxygen.

esophagus (eh-sof´-uh-gus) A muscular tube that conducts food, by peristalsis, from the pharynx to the stomach.

essential amino acid An amino acid that an animal cannot synthesize itself and must be obtained from food in prefabricated form.

essential element A chemical element required for an organism to survive, grow, and reproduce.

essential fatty acid An unsaturated fatty acid that an animal needs but cannot make.

essential nutrient A substance that an organism cannot synthesize from any other material and therefore must absorb in preassembled form.

estradiol (es´-truh-dī´-ol) A steroid hormone that stimulates the development and maintenance of the female reproductive system and secondary sex characteristics; the major estrogen in mammals.

estrogen (es´-trō-jen) Any steroid hormone, such as estradiol, that stimulates the development and maintenance of the female reproductive system and secondary sex characteristics.

estrous cycle (es´-trus) A reproductive cycle characteristic of female mammals except humans and certain other primates, in which the nonpregnant endometrium is reabsorbed rather than shed, and sexual response occurs only during mid-cycle at estrus.

estuary The area where a freshwater stream or river merges with the ocean.

ethylene (eth´-uh-lēn) A gaseous plant hormone involved in responses to mechanical stress, programmed cell death, leaf abscission, and fruit ripening.

etiolation Plant morphological adaptations for growing in darkness.

euchromatin (yū-krō´-muh-tin) The less condensed form of eukaryotic chromatin that is available for transcription.

eudicot (yū-dī´-kot) Member of a clade that contains the vast majority of flowering plants that have two embryonic seed leaves, or cotyledons.

euglenid (yū´-glen-id) A protist, such as *Euglena* or its relatives, characterized by an anterior pocket from which one or two flagella emerge.

euglenozoan Member of a diverse clade of flagellated protists that includes predatory heterotrophs, photosynthetic autotrophs, and pathogenic parasites.

Eukarya (yū-kar´-ē-uh) The domain that includes all eukaryotic organisms.

eukaryotic cell (yū´-ker-ē-ot´-ik) A type of cell with a membrane-enclosed nucleus and membrane-enclosed organelles. Organisms with eukaryotic cells (protists, plants, fungi, and animals) are called eukaryotes.

eumetazoan (yū´-met-uh-zō´-un) Member of a clade of animals with true tissues. All animals except sponges and a few other groups are eumetazoans.

eurypterid (yur-ip´-tuh-rid) An extinct carnivorous chelicerate; also called a water scorpion.

Eustachian tube (yū-stā´-shun) The tube that connects the middle ear to the pharynx.

eutherian (yū-thēr´-ē-un) Placental mammal; mammal whose young complete their embryonic development within the uterus, joined to the mother by the placenta.

eutrophic lake (yū-trōf´-ik) A lake that has a high rate of biological productivity supported by a high rate of nutrient cycling.

eutrophication A process by which nutrients, particularly phosphorus and nitrogen, become highly concentrated in a body of water, leading to increased growth of organisms such as algae or cyanobacteria.

evaporation The process by which a liquid changes to a gas.

evaporative cooling The process in which the surface of an object becomes cooler during evaporation, a result of the molecules with the greatest kinetic energy changing from the liquid to the gaseous state.

evapotranspiration The total evaporation of water from an ecosystem, including water transpired by plants and evaporated from a landscape, usually measured in millimeters and estimated for a year.

evo-devo Evolutionary developmental biology; a field of biology that compares developmental processes of different multicellular organisms to understand how these processes have evolved and how changes can modify existing organismal features or lead to new ones.

evolution Descent with modification; the idea that living species are descendants of ancestral species that were different from the present-day ones; also defined more narrowly as the change in the genetic composition of a population from generation to generation.

evolutionary tree A branching diagram that reflects a hypothesis about evolutionary relationships among groups of organisms.

Excavata One of five supergroups of eukaryotes proposed in a current hypothesis of the evolutionary history of eukaryotes. Excavates have unique cytoskeletal features, and some species have an "excavated" feeding groove on one side of the cell body. *See also* Chromalveolata, Rhizaria, Archaeplastida, and Unikonta.

excitatory postsynaptic potential (EPSP) An electrical change (depolarization) in the membrane of a postsynaptic cell caused by the binding of an excitatory neurotransmitter from a presynaptic cell to a postsynaptic receptor; makes it more likely for a postsynaptic cell to generate an action potential.

excretion The disposal of nitrogen-containing metabolites and other waste products.

exergonic reaction (ek´-ser-gon´-ik) A spontaneous chemical reaction, in which there is a net release of free energy.

exocytosis (ek´-sō-sī-tō´-sis) The cellular secretion of biological molecules by the fusion of vesicles containing them with the plasma membrane.

exon A sequence within a primary transcript that remains in the RNA after RNA processing; also refers to the region of DNA from which this sequence was transcribed.

exoskeleton A hard encasement on the surface of an animal, such as the shell of a mollusc or the cuticle of an arthropod, that provides protection and points of attachment for muscles.

exotoxin (ek´-sō-tok´-sin) A toxic protein that is secreted by a prokaryote or other pathogen and that produces specific symptoms, even if the pathogen is no longer present.

expansin Plant enzyme that breaks the cross-links (hydrogen bonds) between cellulose microfibrils and other cell wall constituents, loosening the wall's fabric.

exponential population growth Growth of a population in an ideal, unlimited environment, represented by a J-shaped curve when population size is plotted over time.

expression vector A cloning vector that contains a highly active bacterial promoter just upstream of a restriction site where a eukaryotic gene can be inserted, allowing the gene to be expressed in a bacterial cell. Expression vectors are also available that have been genetically engineered for use in specific types of eukaryotic cells.

external fertilization The fusion of gametes that parents have discharged into the environment.

extinction vortex A downward population spiral in which inbreeding and genetic drift combine to cause a small population to shrink and, unless the spiral is reversed, become extinct.

extracellular digestion The breakdown of food in compartments that are continuous with the outside of an animal's body.

extracellular matrix (ECM) The meshwork surrounding animal cells, consisting of glycoproteins, polysaccharides, and proteoglycans synthesized and secreted by the cells.

extraembryonic membrane One of four membranes (yolk sac, amnion, chorion, and allantois) located outside the embryo that support the developing embryo in reptiles and mammals.

extreme halophile An organism that lives in a highly saline environment, such as the Great Salt Lake or the Dead Sea.

extreme thermophile An organism that thrives in hot environments (often 60–80°C or hotter).

extremophile An organism that lives in environmental conditions so extreme that few other species can survive there. Extremophiles include extreme halophiles ("salt lovers") and extreme thermophiles ("heat lovers").

F factor In bacteria, the DNA segment that confers the ability to form pili for conjugation and associated functions required for the transfer of DNA from donor to recipient. The F factor may exist as a plasmid or be integrated into the bacterial chromosome.

F plasmid The plasmid form of the F factor.

F₁ generation The first filial, hybrid (heterozygous) offspring arising from a parental (P generation) cross.

F₂ generation The offspring resulting from interbreeding (or self-pollination) of the hybrid F₁ generation.

facilitated diffusion The passage of molecules or ions down their electrochemical gradient across a biological membrane with the assistance of specific transmembrane transport proteins, requiring no energy expenditure.

facilitation An interaction in which one species has a positive effect on the survival and reproduction of another species without the intimate association of a symbiosis.

facultative anaerobe (fak′-ul-tā′-tiv an′-uh-rōb) An organism that makes ATP by aerobic respiration if oxygen is present but that switches to anaerobic respiration or fermentation if oxygen is not present.

family In Linnaean classification, the taxonomic category above genus.

fast block to polyspermy The depolarization of the egg plasma membrane that begins within 1–3 seconds after a sperm binds to an egg membrane protein. The depolarization lasts about 1 minute and prevents additional sperm from fusing with the egg during that time.

fast-twitch fiber A muscle fiber used for rapid, powerful contractions.

fat A lipid consisting of three fatty acids linked to one glycerol molecule; also called a triacylglycerol or triglyceride.

fate map A territorial diagram of embryonic development that displays the future derivatives of individual cells and tissues.

fatty acid A carboxylic acid with a long carbon chain. Fatty acids vary in length and in the number and location of double bonds; three fatty acids linked to a glycerol molecule form a fat molecule, also known as a triacylglycerol or triglyceride.

feces (fē′-sēz) The wastes of the digestive tract.

feedback inhibition A method of metabolic control in which the end product of a metabolic pathway acts as an inhibitor of an enzyme within that pathway.

fermentation A catabolic process that makes a limited amount of ATP from glucose (or other organic molecules) without an electron transport chain and that produces a characteristic end product, such as ethyl alcohol or lactic acid.

fertilization (1) The union of haploid gametes to produce a diploid zygote. (2) The addition of mineral nutrients to the soil.

fetus (fē′-tus) A developing mammal that has all the major structures of an adult. In humans, the fetal stage lasts from the 9th week of gestation until birth.

fiber A lignified cell type that reinforces the xylem of angiosperms and functions in mechanical support; a slender, tapered sclerenchyma cell that usually occurs in bundles.

fibroblast (fī′-brō-blast) A type of cell in loose connective tissue that secretes the protein ingredients of the extracellular fibers.

fibronectin An extracellular glycoprotein secreted by animal cells that helps them attach to the extracellular matrix.

filament In an angiosperm, the stalk portion of the stamen, the pollen-producing reproductive organ of a flower.

filtrate Cell-free fluid extracted from the body fluid by the excretory system.

filtration In excretory systems, the extraction of water and small solutes, including metabolic wastes, from the body fluid.

fimbria (plural, **fimbriae**) A short, hairlike appendage of a prokaryotic cell that helps it adhere to the substrate or to other cells.

first law of thermodynamics The principle of conservation of energy: Energy can be transferred and transformed, but it cannot be created or destroyed.

fission The separation of an organism into two or more individuals of approximately equal size.

fixed action pattern In animal behavior, a sequence of unlearned acts that is essentially unchangeable and, once initiated, usually carried to completion.

flaccid (flas′-id) Limp. Lacking turgor (stiffness or firmness), as in a plant cell in surroundings where there is a tendency for water to leave the cell. (A walled cell becomes flaccid if it has a higher water potential than its surroundings, resulting in the loss of water.)

flagellum (fluh-jel′-um) (plural, **flagella**) A long cellular appendage specialized for locomotion. Like motile cilia, eukaryotic flagella have a core with nine outer doublet microtubules and two inner single microtubules (the "9 + 2" arrangement) ensheathed in an extension of the plasma membrane. Prokaryotic flagella have a different structure.

florigen A flowering signal, probably a protein, that is made in leaves under certain conditions and that travels to the shoot apical meristems, inducing them to switch from vegetative to reproductive growth.

flower In an angiosperm, a specialized shoot with up to four sets of modified leaves, bearing structures that function in sexual reproduction.

fluid feeder An animal that lives by sucking nutrient-rich fluids from another living organism.

fluid mosaic model The currently accepted model of cell membrane structure, which envisions the membrane as a mosaic of protein molecules drifting laterally in a fluid bilayer of phospholipids.

follicle (fol′-uh-kul) A microscopic structure in the ovary that contains the developing oocyte and secretes estrogens.

follicle-stimulating hormone (FSH) A tropic hormone that is produced and secreted by the anterior pituitary and that stimulates the production of eggs by the ovaries and sperm by the testes.

follicular phase That part of the ovarian cycle during which follicles are growing and oocytes maturing.

food chain The pathway along which food energy is transferred from trophic level to trophic level, beginning with producers.

food vacuole A membranous sac formed by phagocytosis of microorganisms or particles to be used as food by the cell.

food web The interconnected feeding relationships in an ecosystem.

foot (1) The portion of a bryophyte sporophyte that gathers sugars, amino acids, water, and minerals from the parent gametophyte via transfer cells. (2) One of the three main parts of a mollusc; a muscular structure usually used for movement. *See also* mantle, visceral mass.

foraging The seeking and obtaining of food.

foram (foraminiferan) An aquatic protist that secretes a hardened shell containing calcium carbonate and extends pseudopodia through pores in the shell.

forebrain One of three ancestral and embryonic regions of the vertebrate brain; develops into the thalamus, hypothalamus, and cerebrum.

fossil A preserved remnant or impression of an organism that lived in the past.

founder effect Genetic drift that occurs when a few individuals become isolated from a larger population and form a new population whose gene pool composition is not reflective of that of the original population.

fovea (fō′-vē-uh) The place on the retina at the eye's center of focus, where cones are highly concentrated.

fragmentation A means of asexual reproduction whereby a single parent breaks into parts that regenerate into whole new individuals.

frameshift mutation A mutation occurring when nucleotides are inserted in or deleted from a gene and the number inserted or deleted is not a multiple of three, resulting in the improper grouping of the subsequent nucleotides into codons.

free energy The portion of a biological system's energy that can perform work when temperature and pressure are uniform throughout the system. The change in free energy of a system (ΔG) is calculated by the equation $\Delta G = \Delta H - T\Delta S$, where ΔH is the change in enthalpy (in biological systems, equivalent to total energy), T is the absolute temperature, and ΔS is the change in entropy.

frequency-dependent selection Selection in which the fitness of a phenotype depends on how common the phenotype is in a population.

fruit A mature ovary of a flower. The fruit protects dormant seeds and often aids in their dispersal.

functional group A specific configuration of atoms commonly attached to the carbon skeletons of organic molecules and involved in chemical reactions.

G protein A GTP-binding protein that relays signals from a plasma membrane signal receptor, known as a G protein-coupled receptor, to other signal transduction proteins inside the cell.

G protein-coupled receptor (GPCR) A signal receptor protein in the plasma membrane that responds to the binding of a signaling molecule by activating a G protein. Also called a G protein-linked receptor.

G₀ phase A nondividing state occupied by cells that have left the cell cycle, sometimes reversibly.

G₁ phase The first gap, or growth phase, of the cell cycle, consisting of the portion of interphase before DNA synthesis begins.

G₂ phase The second gap, or growth phase, of the cell cycle, consisting of the portion of interphase after DNA synthesis occurs.

gallbladder An organ that stores bile and releases it as needed into the small intestine.

game theory An approach to evaluating alternative strategies in situations where the outcome of a particular strategy depends on the strategies used by other individuals.

gametangium (gam′-uh-tan′-jē-um) (plural, **gametangia**) Multicellular plant structure in which gametes are formed. Female gametangia are called archegonia, and male gametangia are called antheridia.

gamete (gam′-ēt) A haploid reproductive cell, such as an egg or sperm. Gametes unite during sexual reproduction to produce a diploid zygote.

gametogenesis The process by which gametes are produced.

gametophore (guh-mē′-tō-fōr) The mature gamete-producing structure of a moss gametophyte.

gametophyte (guh-mē′-tō-fīt) In organisms (plants and some algae) that have alternation of generations, the multicellular haploid form that produces haploid gametes by mitosis. The haploid gametes unite and develop into sporophytes.

gamma-aminobutyric acid (GABA) An amino acid that functions as a CNS neurotransmitter in the central nervous system of vertebrates.

ganglia (gang′-glē-uh) (singular, **ganglion**) Clusters (functional groups) of nerve cell bodies in a centralized nervous system.

ganglion cell A type of neuron in the retina that synapses with bipolar cells and transmits action potentials to the brain via axons in the optic nerve.

gap junction A type of intercellular junction in animal cells, consisting of proteins surrounding a pore that allows the passage of materials between cells.

gas exchange The uptake of molecular oxygen from the environment and the discharge of carbon dioxide to the environment.

gastric juice A digestive fluid secreted by the stomach.

gastrovascular cavity A central cavity with a single opening in the body of certain animals, including cnidarians and flatworms, that functions in both the digestion and distribution of nutrients.

gastrula (gas′-trū-luh) An embryonic stage in animal development encompassing the formation of three layers: ectoderm, mesoderm, and endoderm.

gastrulation (gas′-trū-lā′-shun) In animal development, a series of cell and tissue movements in which the blastula-stage embryo folds inward, producing a three-layered embryo, the gastrula.

gated channel A transmembrane protein channel that opens or closes in response to a particular stimulus.

gated ion channel A gated channel for a specific ion. The opening or closing of such channels may alter a cell's membrane potential.

gel electrophoresis (ē-lek′-trō-fōr-ē′-sis) A technique for separating nucleic acids or proteins on the basis of their size and electrical charge, both of which affect their rate of movement through an electric field in a gel made of agarose or another polymer.

gene A discrete unit of hereditary information consisting of a specific nucleotide sequence in DNA (or RNA, in some viruses).

gene annotation Analysis of genomic sequences to identify protein-coding genes and determine the function of their products.

gene cloning The production of multiple copies of a gene.

gene expression The process by which information encoded in DNA directs the synthesis of proteins or, in some cases, RNAs that are not translated into proteins and instead function as RNAs.

gene flow The transfer of alleles from one population to another, resulting from the movement of fertile individuals or their gametes.

gene pool The aggregate of all copies of every type of allele at all loci in every individual in a population. The term is also used in a more restricted sense as the aggregate of alleles for just one or a few loci in a population.

gene therapy The introduction of genes into an afflicted individual for therapeutic purposes.

gene-for-gene recognition A widespread form of plant disease resistance involving recognition of pathogen-derived molecules by the protein products of specific plant disease resistance genes.

genetic drift A process in which chance events cause unpredictable fluctuations in allele frequencies from one generation to the next. Effects of genetic drift are most pronounced in small populations.

genetic engineering The direct manipulation of genes for practical purposes.

genetic map An ordered list of genetic loci (genes or other genetic markers) along a chromosome.

genetic profile An individual's unique set of genetic markers, detected most often today by PCR or, previously, by electrophoresis and nucleic acid probes.

genetic recombination General term for the production of offspring with combinations of traits that differ from those found in either parent.

genetic variation Differences among individuals in the composition of their genes or other DNA segments.

genetically modified (GM) organism An organism that has acquired one or more genes by artificial means; also known as a transgenic organism.

genetics The scientific study of heredity and hereditary variation.

genome (jē′-nōm) The genetic material of an organism or virus; the complete complement of an organism's or virus's genes along with its noncoding nucleic acid sequences.

genome-wide association study A large-scale analysis of the genomes of many people having a certain phenotype or disease, with the aim of finding genetic markers that correlate with that phenotype or disease.

genomic imprinting A phenomenon in which expression of an allele in offspring depends on whether the allele is inherited from the male or female parent.

genomic library A set of cell clones containing all the DNA segments from a genome, each within a plasmid, BAC, or other cloning vector.

genomics (juh-nō′-miks) The study of whole sets of genes and their interactions within a species, as well as genome comparisons between species.

genotype (jē′-nō-tīp) The genetic makeup, or set of alleles, of an organism.

genus (jē′-nus) (plural, **genera**) A taxonomic category above the species level, designated by the first word of a species' two-part scientific name.

geographic variation Differences between the gene pools of geographically separate populations or population subgroups.

geologic record The division of Earth's history into time periods, grouped into three eons—Archaean, Proterozoic, and Phanerozoic—and further subdivided into eras, periods, and epochs.

germ layer One of the three main layers in a gastrula that will form the various tissues and organs of an animal body.

gestation (jes-tā′-shun) Pregnancy; the state of carrying developing young within the female reproductive tract.

gibberellin (jib′-uh-rel′-in) Any of a class of related plant hormones that stimulate growth in the stem and leaves, trigger the germination of seeds and breaking of bud dormancy, and (with auxin) stimulate fruit development.

glans The rounded structure at the tip of the clitoris or penis that is involved in sexual arousal.

glia (glial cells) Cells of the nervous system that support, regulate, and augment the functions of neurons.

global climate change Increase in temperature and change in weather patterns all around the planet, due mostly to increasing atmospheric CO_2 levels from the burning of fossil fuels. The increase in temperature, called global warming, is a major aspect of global climate change.

global ecology The study of the functioning and distribution of organisms across the biosphere and how the regional exchange of energy and materials affects them.

glomeromycete (glō′-mer-ō-mī′-sēt) Member of the fungal phylum Glomeromycota, characterized by a distinct branching form of mycorrhizae called arbuscular mycorrhizae.

glomerulus (glō-mār′-yū-lus) A ball of capillaries surrounded by Bowman's capsule in the nephron and serving as the site of filtration in the vertebrate kidney.

glucagon (glū′-kuh-gon) A hormone secreted by pancreatic alpha cells that raises blood glucose levels. It promotes glycogen breakdown and release of glucose by the liver.

glucocorticoid A steroid hormone that is secreted by the adrenal cortex and that influences glucose metabolism and immune function.

glutamate An amino acid that functions as a neurotransmitter in the central nervous system.

glyceraldehyde 3-phosphate (G3P) (glis'-er-al'-de-hīd) A three-carbon carbohydrate that is the direct product of the Calvin cycle; it is also an intermediate in glycolysis.

glycogen (glī'-kō-jen) An extensively branched glucose storage polysaccharide found in the liver and muscle of animals; the animal equivalent of starch.

glycolipid A lipid with one or more covalently attached carbohydrates.

glycolysis (glī-kol'-uh-sis) A series of reactions that ultimately splits glucose into pyruvate. Glycolysis occurs in almost all living cells, serving as the starting point for fermentation or cellular respiration.

glycoprotein A protein with one or more covalently attached carbohydrates.

glycosidic linkage A covalent bond formed between two monosaccharides by a dehydration reaction.

gnathostome (na'-thu-stōm) Member of the vertebrate subgroup possessing jaws.

golden alga A biflagellated, photosynthetic protist named for its color, which results from its yellow and brown carotenoids.

Golgi apparatus (gol'-jē) An organelle in eukaryotic cells consisting of stacks of flat membranous sacs that modify, store, and route products of the endoplasmic reticulum and synthesize some products, notably noncellulose carbohydrates.

gonads (gō'-nadz) The male and female sex organs; the gamete-producing organs in most animals.

grade A group of organisms that share the same level of organizational complexity or share a key adaptation.

graded potential In a neuron, a shift in the membrane potential that has an amplitude proportional to signal strength and that decays as it spreads.

Gram stain A staining method that distinguishes between two different kinds of bacterial cell walls; may be used to help determine medical response to an infection.

gram-negative Describing the group of bacteria that have a cell wall that is structurally more complex and contains less peptidoglycan than the cell wall of gram-positive bacteria. Gram-negative bacteria are often more toxic than gram-positive bacteria.

gram-positive Describing the group of bacteria that have a cell wall that is structurally less complex and contains more peptidoglycan than the cell wall of gram-negative bacteria. Gram-positive bacteria are usually less toxic than gram-negative bacteria.

granum (gran'-um) (plural, **grana**) A stack of membrane-bounded thylakoids in the chloroplast. Grana function in the light reactions of photosynthesis.

gravitropism (grav'-uh-trō'-pizm) A response of a plant or animal to gravity.

gray matter Regions of dendrites and clustered neuron cell bodies within the CNS.

green alga A photosynthetic protist, named for green chloroplasts that are similar in structure and pigment composition to those of land plants. Green algae are a paraphyletic group,

some of whose members are more closely related to land plants than they are to other green algae.

greenhouse effect The warming of Earth due to the atmospheric accumulation of carbon dioxide and certain other gases, which absorb reflected infrared radiation and reradiate some of it back toward Earth.

gross primary production (GPP) The total primary production of an ecosystem.

ground tissue system Plant tissues that are neither vascular nor dermal, fulfilling a variety of functions, such as storage, photosynthesis, and support.

growth An irreversible increase in size or biomass.

growth factor (1) A protein that must be present in the extracellular environment (culture medium or animal body) for the growth and normal development of certain types of cells. (2) A local regulator that acts on nearby cells to stimulate cell proliferation and differentiation.

growth hormone (GH) A hormone that is produced and secreted by the anterior pituitary and that has both direct (nontropic) and tropic effects on a wide variety of tissues.

guard cells The two cells that flank the stomatal pore and regulate the opening and closing of the pore.

gustation The sense of taste.

guttation The exudation of water droplets from leaves, caused by root pressure in certain plants.

gymnosperm (jim'-nō-sperm) A vascular plant that bears naked seeds—seeds not enclosed in protective chambers.

hair cell A mechanosensory cell that alters output to the nervous system when hairlike projections on the cell surface are displaced.

half-life The amount of time it takes for 50% of a sample of a radioactive isotope to decay.

Hamilton's rule The principle that for natural selection to favor an altruistic act, the benefit to the recipient, devalued by the coefficient of relatedness, must exceed the cost to the altruist.

haploid cell (hap'-loyd) A cell containing only one set of chromosomes (*n*).

Hardy-Weinberg principle The principle that frequencies of alleles and genotypes in a population remain constant from generation to generation, provided that only Mendelian segregation and recombination of alleles are at work.

haustorium (plural, **haustoria**) (ho-stōr'-ē-um, ho-stōr'-ē-uh) In certain symbiotic fungi, a specialized hypha that can penetrate the tissues of host organisms.

heart A muscular pump that uses metabolic energy to elevate the hydrostatic pressure of the circulatory fluid (blood or hemolymph). The fluid then flows down a pressure gradient through the body and eventually returns to the heart.

heart attack The damage or death of cardiac muscle tissue resulting from prolonged blockage of one or more coronary arteries.

heart murmur A hissing sound that most often results from blood squirting backward through a leaky valve in the heart.

heart rate The frequency of heart contraction (in beats per minute).

heat The total amount of kinetic energy due to the random motion of atoms or molecules in a body of matter; also called thermal energy. Heat is energy in its most random form.

heat of vaporization The quantity of heat a liquid must absorb for 1 g of it to be converted from the liquid to the gaseous state.

heat-shock protein A protein that helps protect other proteins during heat stress. Heat-shock proteins are found in plants, animals, and microorganisms.

heavy chain One of the two types of polypeptide chains that make up an antibody molecule and B cell receptor; consists of a variable region, which contributes to the antigen-binding site, and a constant region.

helicase An enzyme that untwists the double helix of DNA at replication forks, separating the two strands and making them available as template strands.

helper T cell A type of T cell that, when activated, secretes cytokines that promote the response of B cells (humoral response) and cytotoxic T cells (cell-mediated response) to antigens.

hemoglobin (hē'-mō-glō'-bin) An iron-containing protein in red blood cells that reversibly binds oxygen.

hemolymph (hē'-mō-limf') In invertebrates with an open circulatory system, the body fluid that bathes tissues.

hemophilia (hē'-muh-fil'-ē-uh) A human genetic disease caused by a sex-linked recessive allele resulting in the absence of one or more blood-clotting proteins; characterized by excessive bleeding following injury.

hepatic portal vein A large vessel that conveys nutrient-laden blood from the small intestine to the liver, which regulates the blood's nutrient content.

herbivore (hur'-bi-vōr') An animal that mainly eats plants or algae.

herbivory An interaction in which an organism eats parts of a plant or alga.

heredity The transmission of traits from one generation to the next.

hermaphrodite (hur-maf'-ruh-dīt') An individual that functions as both male and female in sexual reproduction by producing both sperm and eggs.

hermaphroditism (hur-maf'-rō-dī-tizm) A condition in which an individual has both female and male gonads and functions as both a male and female in sexual reproduction by producing both sperm and eggs.

heterochromatin (het'-er-ō-krō'-muh-tin) Eukaryotic chromatin that remains highly compacted during interphase and is generally not transcribed.

heterochrony (het'-uh-rok'-ruh-nē) Evolutionary change in the timing or rate of an organism's development.

heterocyst (het'-er-ō-sist) A specialized cell that engages in nitrogen fixation in some filamentous cyanobacteria; also called a *heterocyte*.

heterokaryon (het′-er-ō-kār′-ē-un) A fungal mycelium that contains two or more haploid nuclei per cell.

heteromorphic (het′-er-ō-mōr′-fik) Referring to a condition in the life cycle of plants and certain algae in which the sporophyte and gametophyte generations differ in morphology.

heterosporous (het-er-os′-pōr-us) Referring to a plant species that has two kinds of spores: microspores, which develop into male gametophytes, and megaspores, which develop into female gametophytes.

heterotroph (het′-er-ō-trōf) An organism that obtains organic food molecules by eating other organisms or substances derived from them.

heterozygote advantage Greater reproductive success of heterozygous individuals compared with homozygotes; tends to preserve variation in a gene pool.

heterozygous (het′-er-ō-zī′-gus) Having two different alleles for a given gene.

hexapod An insect or closely related wingless, six-legged arthropod.

hibernation A long-term physiological state in which metabolism decreases, the heart and respiratory system slow down, and body temperature is maintained at a lower level than normal.

high-density lipoprotein (HDL) A particle in the blood made up of thousands of cholesterol molecules and other lipids bound to a protein. HDL scavenges excess cholesterol.

hindbrain One of three ancestral and embryonic regions of the vertebrate brain; develops into the medulla oblongata, pons, and cerebellum.

histamine (his′-tuh-mēn) A substance released by mast cells that causes blood vessels to dilate and become more permeable in inflammatory and allergic responses.

histone (his′-tōn) A small protein with a high proportion of positively charged amino acids that binds to the negatively charged DNA and plays a key role in chromatin structure.

histone acetylation The attachment of acetyl groups to certain amino acids of histone proteins.

HIV (human immunodeficiency virus) The infectious agent that causes AIDS. HIV is a retrovirus.

holdfast A rootlike structure that anchors a seaweed.

holoblastic (hō′-lō-blas′-tik) Referring to a type of cleavage in which there is complete division of the egg; occurs in eggs that have little yolk (such as those of the sea urchin) or a moderate amount of yolk (such as those of the frog).

homeobox (hō′-mē-ō-boks′) A 180-nucleotide sequence within homeotic genes and some other developmental genes that is widely conserved in animals. Related sequences occur in plants and yeasts.

homeostasis (hō-mē-ō-stā′-sis) The steady-state physiological condition of the body.

homeotic gene (hō-mē-o′-tik) Any of the master regulatory genes that control placement and spatial organization of body parts in animals, plants, and fungi by controlling the developmental fate of groups of cells.

hominin (hō′-mi-nin) A member of the human branch of the evolutionary tree. Hominins include *Homo sapiens* and our ancestors, a group of extinct species that are more closely related to us than to chimpanzees.

homologous chromosomes (hō-mol′-uh-gus) A pair of chromosomes of the same length, centromere position, and staining pattern that possess genes for the same characters at corresponding loci. One homologous chromosome is inherited from the organism's father, the other from the mother. Also called homologs, or a homologous pair.

homologous structures Structures in different species that are similar because of common ancestry.

homology (hō-mol′-ō-jē) Similarity in characteristics resulting from a shared ancestry.

homoplasy (hō′-muh-play′-zē) A similar (analogous) structure or molecular sequence that has evolved independently in two species.

homosporous (hō-mos′-puh-rus) Referring to a plant species that has a single kind of spore, which typically develops into a bisexual gametophyte.

homozygous (hō′-mō-zī′-gus) Having two identical alleles for a given gene.

horizontal cell A neuron of the retina that helps integrate the information that is sent to the brain.

horizontal gene transfer The transfer of genes from one genome to another through mechanisms such as transposable elements, plasmid exchange, viral activity, and perhaps fusions of different organisms.

hormone In multicellular organisms, one of many types of secreted chemicals that are formed in specialized cells, travel in body fluids, and act on specific target cells in other parts of the body, changing the target cells' functioning. Hormones are thus important in long-distance signaling.

hornwort A small, herbaceous, nonvascular plant that is a member of the phylum Anthocerophyta.

host The larger participant in a symbiotic relationship, often providing a home and food source for the smaller symbiont.

host range The limited number of species whose cells can be infected by a particular virus.

human chorionic gonadotropin (hCG) (kōr′-ē-on′-ik gō-na′-dō-trō′-pin) A hormone secreted by the chorion that maintains the corpus luteum of the ovary during the first three months of pregnancy.

Human Genome Project An international collaborative effort to map and sequence the DNA of the entire human genome.

humoral immune response (hyū′-mer-ul) The branch of adaptive immunity that involves the activation of B cells and that leads to the production of antibodies, which defend against bacteria and viruses in body fluids.

humus (hyū′-mus) Decomposing organic material that is a component of topsoil.

Huntington's disease A human genetic disease caused by a dominant allele; characterized by uncontrollable body movements and degeneration of the nervous system; usually fatal 10 to 20 years after the onset of symptoms.

hybrid Offspring that results from the mating of individuals from two different species or from two true-breeding varieties of the same species.

hybrid zone A geographic region in which members of different species meet and mate, producing at least some offspring of mixed ancestry.

hybridization In genetics, the mating, or crossing, of two true-breeding varieties.

hydration shell The sphere of water molecules around a dissolved ion.

hydrocarbon An organic molecule consisting only of carbon and hydrogen.

hydrogen bond A type of weak chemical bond that is formed when the slightly positive hydrogen atom of a polar covalent bond in one molecule is attracted to the slightly negative atom of a polar covalent bond in another molecule or in another region of the same molecule.

hydrogen ion A single proton with a charge of 1+. The dissociation of a water molecule (H_2O) leads to the generation of a hydroxide ion (OH^-) and a hydrogen ion (H^+); in water, H^+ is not found alone but associates with a water molecule to form a hydronium ion.

hydrolysis (hī-drol′-uh-sis) A chemical reaction that breaks bonds between two molecules by the addition of water; functions in disassembly of polymers to monomers.

hydronium ion A water molecule that has an extra proton bound to it; H_3O^+, commonly represented as H^+.

hydrophilic (hī′-drō-fil′-ik) Having an affinity for water.

hydrophobic (hī′-drō-fō′-bik) Having no affinity for water; tending to coalesce and form droplets in water.

hydrophobic interaction A type of weak chemical interaction caused when molecules that do not mix with water coalesce to exclude water.

hydroponic culture A method in which plants are grown in mineral solutions rather than in soil.

hydrostatic skeleton A skeletal system composed of fluid held under pressure in a closed body compartment; the main skeleton of most cnidarians, flatworms, nematodes, and annelids.

hydroxide ion A water molecule that has lost a proton; OH^-.

hydroxyl group (hī-drok′-sil) A chemical group consisting of an oxygen atom joined to a hydrogen atom. Molecules possessing this group are soluble in water and are called alcohols.

hymen A thin membrane that partly covers the vaginal opening in the human female. The hymen is ruptured by sexual intercourse or other vigorous activity.

hyperpolarization A change in a cell's membrane potential such that the inside of the membrane becomes more negative relative to the outside. Hyperpolarization reduces the chance that a neuron will transmit a nerve impulse.

hypersensitive response A plant's localized defense response to a pathogen, involving the death of cells around the site of infection.

hypertension A disorder in which blood pressure remains abnormally high.

hypertonic Referring to a solution that, when surrounding a cell, will cause the cell to lose water.

hypha (plural, **hyphae**) (hī′-fuh, hī′-fē) One of many connected filaments that collectively make up the mycelium of a fungus.

hypocotyl (hī′-puh-cot′-ul) In an angiosperm embryo, the embryonic axis below the point of attachment of the cotyledon(s) and above the radicle.

hypothalamus (hī′-pō-thal′-uh-mus) The ventral part of the vertebrate forebrain; functions in maintaining homeostasis, especially in coordinating the endocrine and nervous systems; secretes hormones of the posterior pituitary and releasing factors that regulate the anterior pituitary.

hypothesis (hī-poth′-uh-sis) A testable explanation for a set of observations based on the available data and guided by inductive reasoning. A hypothesis is narrower in scope than a theory.

hypotonic Referring to a solution that, when surrounding a cell, will cause the cell to take up water.

imbibition The physical adsorption of water onto the internal surfaces of structures.

immigration The influx of new individuals into a population from other areas.

immune system An animal body's system of defenses against agents that cause disease.

immunization The process of generating a state of immunity by artificial means. In active immunization, also called vaccination, an inactive or weakened form of a pathogen is administered, inducing B and T cell responses and immunological memory. In passive immunization, antibodies specific for a particular microbe are administered, conferring immediate but temporary protection.

immunodeficiency A disorder in which the ability of an immune system to protect against pathogens is defective or absent.

immunoglobulin (Ig) (im′-yū-nō-glob′-yū-lin) Any of the class of proteins that function as antibodies. Immunoglobulins are divided into five major classes that differ in their distribution in the body and antigen disposal activities.

imprinting In animal behavior, the formation at a specific stage in life of a long-lasting behavioral response to a specific individual or object. *See also* genomic imprinting.

***in situ* hybridization** A technique using nucleic acid hybridization with a labeled probe to detect the location of a specific mRNA in an intact organism.

***in vitro* fertilization (IVF)** (vē′-trō) Fertilization of oocytes in laboratory containers followed by artificial implantation of the early embryo in the mother's uterus.

***in vitro* mutagenesis** A technique used to discover the function of a gene by cloning it, introducing specific changes into the cloned gene's sequence, reinserting the mutated gene into a cell, and studying the phenotype of the mutant.

inclusive fitness The total effect an individual has on proliferating its genes by producing its own offspring and by providing aid that enables other close relatives to increase production of their offspring.

incomplete dominance The situation in which the phenotype of heterozygotes is intermediate between the phenotypes of individuals homozygous for either allele.

incomplete flower A flower in which one or more of the four basic floral organs (sepals, petals, stamens, or carpels) are either absent or nonfunctional.

incomplete metamorphosis A type of development in certain insects, such as grasshoppers, in which the young (called nymphs) resemble adults but are smaller and have different body proportions. The nymph goes through a series of molts, each time looking more like an adult, until it reaches full size.

indeterminate cleavage A type of embryonic development in deuterostomes in which each cell produced by early cleavage divisions retains the capacity to develop into a complete embryo.

indeterminate growth A type of growth characteristic of plants, in which the organism continues to grow as long as it lives.

induced fit Caused by entry of the substrate, the change in shape of the active site of an enzyme so that it binds more snugly to the substrate.

inducer A specific small molecule that binds to a bacterial repressor protein and changes the repressor's shape so that it cannot bind to an operator, thus switching an operon on.

induction The process in which one group of embryonic cells influences the development of another, usually by causing changes in gene expression.

inductive reasoning A type of logic in which generalizations are based on a large number of specific observations.

inflammatory response An innate immune defense triggered by physical injury or infection of tissue involving the release of substances that promote swelling, enhance the infiltration of white blood cells, and aid in tissue repair and destruction of invading pathogens.

inflorescence A group of flowers tightly clustered together.

ingestion The first stage of food processing in animals: the act of eating.

ingroup A species or group of species whose evolutionary relationships we seek to determine.

inhibin A hormone produced in the male and female gonads that functions in part by regulating the anterior pituitary by negative feedback.

inhibitory postsynaptic potential (IPSP) An electrical change (usually hyperpolarization) in the membrane of a postsynaptic neuron caused by the binding of an inhibitory neuro-transmitter from a presynaptic cell to a postsynaptic receptor; makes it more difficult for a postsynaptic neuron to generate an action potential.

innate behavior Animal behavior that is developmentally fixed and under strong genetic control. Innate behavior is exhibited in virtually the same form by all individuals in a population despite internal and external environmental differences during development and throughout their lifetimes.

innate immunity A form of defense common to all animals that is active immediately upon exposure to pathogens and that is the same whether or not the pathogen has been encountered previously.

inner cell mass An inner cluster of cells at one end of a mammalian blastocyst that subsequently develops into the embryo proper and some of the extraembryonic membranes.

inner ear One of three main regions of the vertebrate ear; includes the cochlea (which in turn contains the organ of Corti) and the semicircular canals.

inositol trisphosphate (IP$_3$) (in-ō′-suh-tol) A second messenger that functions as an intermediate between certain signaling molecules and a subsequent second messenger, Ca^{2+}, by causing a rise in cytoplasmic Ca^{2+} concentration.

inquiry The search for information and explanation, often focusing on specific questions.

insertion A mutation involving the addition of one or more nucleotide pairs to a gene.

insulin (in′-suh-lin) A hormone secreted by pancreatic beta cells that lowers blood glucose levels. It promotes the uptake of glucose by most body cells and the synthesis and storage of glycogen in the liver and also stimulates protein and fat synthesis.

integral protein A transmembrane protein with hydrophobic regions that extend into and often completely span the hydrophobic interior of the membrane and with hydrophilic regions in contact with the aqueous solution on one or both sides of the membrane (or lining the channel in the case of a channel protein).

integrin In animal cells, a transmembrane receptor protein with two subunits that interconnects the extracellular matrix and the cytoskeleton.

integument (in-teg′-yū-ment) Layer of sporophyte tissue that contributes to the structure of an ovule of a seed plant.

integumentary system The outer covering of a mammal's body, including skin, hair, and nails, claws, or hooves.

intercalated disk (in-ter′-kuh-lā′-ted) A specialized junction between cardiac muscle cells that provides direct electrical coupling between the cells.

interferon (in′-ter-fēr′-on) A protein that has antiviral or immune regulatory functions. Interferon-α and interferon-β, secreted by virus-infected cells, help nearby cells resist viral infection; interferon-γ, secreted by T cells, helps activate macrophages.

intermediate disturbance hypothesis The concept that moderate levels of disturbance can foster greater species diversity than low or high levels of disturbance.

intermediate filament A component of the cytoskeleton that includes filaments intermediate in size between microtubules and microfilaments.

internal fertilization The fusion of eggs and sperm within the female reproductive tract. The sperm are typically deposited in or near the tract.

interneuron An association neuron; a nerve cell within the central nervous system that forms synapses with sensory and/or motor neurons and integrates sensory input and motor output.

internode A segment of a plant stem between the points where leaves are attached.

interphase The period in the cell cycle when the cell is not dividing. During interphase, cellular metabolic activity is high, chromosomes and organelles are duplicated, and cell size may increase. Interphase often accounts for about 90% of the cell cycle.

intersexual selection Selection whereby individuals of one sex (usually females) are choosy in selecting their mates from individuals of the other sex; also called mate choice.

interspecific competition Competition for resources between individuals of two or more species when resources are in short supply.

interspecific interaction A relationship between individuals of two or more species in a community.

interstitial fluid The fluid filling the spaces between cells in most animals.

intertidal zone The shallow zone of the ocean adjacent to land and between the high- and low-tide lines.

intracytoplasmic sperm injection (ICSI) The fertilization of an egg in the laboratory by the direct injection of a single sperm.

intrasexual selection Selection in which there is direct competition among individuals of one sex for mates of the opposite sex.

introduced species A species moved by humans, either intentionally or accidentally, from its native location to a new geographic region; also called non-native or exotic species.

intron (in'-tron) A noncoding, intervening sequence within a primary transcript that is removed from the transcript during RNA processing; also refers to the region of DNA from which this sequence was transcribed.

invasive species A species, often introduced by humans, that takes hold outside its native range.

inversion An aberration in chromosome structure resulting from reattachment of a chromosomal fragment in a reverse orientation to the chromosome from which it originated.

invertebrate An animal without a backbone. Invertebrates make up 95% of animal species.

ion (ī'-on) An atom or group of atoms that has gained or lost one or more electrons, thus acquiring a charge.

ion channel A transmembrane protein channel that allows a specific ion to diffuse across the membrane down its concentration or electro-chemical gradient.

ionic bond (ī-on'-ik) A chemical bond resulting from the attraction between oppositely charged ions.

ionic compound A compound resulting from the formation of an ionic bond; also called a salt.

IPSP *See* inhibitory postsynaptic potential.

iris The colored part of the vertebrate eye, formed by the anterior portion of the choroid.

isomer (ī'-sō-mer) One of several compounds with the same molecular formula but different structures and therefore different properties. The three types of isomers are structural isomers, *cis-trans* isomers, and enantiomers.

isomorphic Referring to alternating generations in plants and certain algae in which the sporophytes and gametophytes look alike, although they differ in chromosome number.

isopod A member of one of the largest groups of crustaceans, which includes terrestrial, fresh-water, and marine species. Among the terrestrial isopods are the pill bugs, or wood lice.

isotonic (ī'-sō-ton'-ik) Referring to a solution that, when surrounding a cell, causes no net movement of water into or out of the cell.

isotope (ī'-sō-tōp') One of several atomic forms of an element, each with the same number of protons but a different number of neutrons, thus differing in atomic mass.

iteroparity Reproduction in which adults produce offspring over many years; also known as repeated reproduction.

joule (J) A unit of energy: 1 J = 0.239 cal; 1 cal = 4.184 J.

juxtaglomerular apparatus (JGA) (juks'-tuh-gluh-mār'-yū-ler) A specialized tissue in nephrons that releases the enzyme renin in response to a drop in blood pressure or volume.

juxtamedullary nephron In mammals and birds, a nephron with a loop of Henle that extends far into the renal medulla.

karyogamy (kār'-ē-og'-uh-mē) In fungi, the fusion of haploid nuclei contributed by the two parents; occurs as one stage of sexual reproduction, preceded by plasmogamy.

karyotype (kār'-ē-ō-tīp) A display of the chromosome pairs of a cell arranged by size and shape.

keystone species A species that is not necessarily abundant in a community yet exerts strong control on community structure by the nature of its ecological role or niche.

kidney In vertebrates, one of a pair of excretory organs where blood filtrate is formed and processed into urine.

kilocalorie (kcal) A thousand calories; the amount of heat energy required to raise the temperature of 1 kg of water by 1°C.

kin selection Natural selection that favors altruistic behavior by enhancing the reproductive success of relatives.

kinetic energy (kuh-net'-ik) The energy associated with the relative motion of objects. Moving matter can perform work by imparting motion to other matter.

kinetochore (kuh-net'-uh-kōr) A structure of proteins attached to the centromere that links each sister chromatid to the mitotic spindle.

kinetoplastid A protist, such as a trypanosome, that has a single large mitochondrion that houses an organized mass of DNA.

kingdom A taxonomic category, the second broadest after domain.

***K*-selection** Selection for life history traits that are sensitive to population density; also called density-dependent selection.

labia majora A pair of thick, fatty ridges that encloses and protects the rest of the vulva.

labia minora A pair of slender skin folds that surrounds the openings of the vagina and urethra.

labor A series of strong, rhythmic contractions of the uterus that expels a baby out of the uterus and vagina during childbirth.

lactation The continued production of milk from the mammary glands.

lacteal (lak'-tē-ul) A tiny lymph vessel extending into the core of an intestinal villus and serving as the destination for absorbed chylomicrons.

lactic acid fermentation Glycolysis followed by the reduction of pyruvate to lactate, regenerating NAD^+ with no release of carbon dioxide.

lagging strand A discontinuously synthesized DNA strand that elongates by means of Okazaki fragments, each synthesized in a $5' \rightarrow 3'$ direction away from the replication fork.

lancelet Member of the clade Cephalochordata, small blade-shaped marine chordates that lack a backbone.

landscape An area containing several different ecosystems linked by exchanges of energy, materials, and organisms.

landscape ecology The study of how the spatial arrangement of habitat types affects the distribution and abundance of organisms and ecosystem processes.

large intestine The portion of the vertebrate alimentary canal between the small intestine and the anus; functions mainly in water absorption and the formation of feces.

larva (lar'-vuh) (plural, **larvae**) A free-living, sexually immature form in some animal life cycles that may differ from the adult animal in morphology, nutrition, and habitat.

larynx (lār'-inks) The portion of the respiratory tract containing the vocal cords; also called the voice box.

lateral geniculate nucleus One of a pair of structures in the brain that are the destination for most of the ganglion cell axons that form the optic nerves.

lateral inhibition A process that sharpens the edges and enhances the contrast of a perceived image by inhibiting receptors lateral to those that have responded to light.

lateral line system A mechanoreceptor system consisting of a series of pores and receptor units along the sides of the body in fishes and aquatic amphibians; detects water movements made by the animal itself and by other moving objects.

lateral meristem (mār'-uh-stem) A meristem that thickens the roots and shoots of woody plants. The vascular cambium and cork cambium are lateral meristems.

lateral root A root that arises from the pericycle of an established root.

lateralization Segregation of functions in the cortex of the left and right cerebral hemispheres.

law of conservation of mass A physical law stating that matter can change form but cannot be created or destroyed. In a closed system, the mass of the system is constant.

law of independent assortment Mendel's second law, stating that each pair of alleles segregates, or assorts, independently of each other pair during gamete formation; applies when genes for two characters are located on different pairs of homologous chromosomes or when they are far enough apart on the same chromosome to behave as though they are on different chromosomes.

law of segregation Mendel's first law, stating that the two alleles in a pair segregate (separate from each other) into different gametes during gamete formation.

leading strand The new complementary DNA strand synthesized continuously along the template strand toward the replication fork in the mandatory $5' \rightarrow 3'$ direction.

leaf The main photosynthetic organ of vascular plants.

leaf primordium A finger-like projection along the flank of a shoot apical meristem, from which a leaf arises.

learning The modification of behavior based on specific experiences.

lens The structure in an eye that focuses light rays onto the photoreceptors.

lenticel (len'-ti-sel) A small raised area in the bark of stems and roots that enables gas exchange between living cells and the outside air.

lepidosaur (leh-pid'-uh-sōr) Member of the reptilian group that includes lizards, snakes, and two species of New Zealand animals called tuataras.

leptin A hormone produced by adipose (fat) cells that acts as a satiety factor in regulating appetite.

leukocyte (lū'-kō-sīt') A blood cell that functions in fighting infections; also called a white blood cell.

Leydig cell (lī'-dig) A cell that produces testosterone and other androgens and is located between the seminiferous tubules of the testes.

lichen The mutualistic association between a fungus and a photosynthetic alga or cyanobacterium.

life cycle The generation-to-generation sequence of stages in the reproductive history of an organism.

life history The traits that affect an organism's schedule of reproduction and survival.

life table An age-specific summary of the survival pattern of a population.

ligament A fibrous connective tissue that joins bones together at joints.

ligand (lig'-und) A molecule that binds specifically to another molecule, usually a larger one.

ligand-gated ion channel A transmembrane protein containing a pore that opens or closes as it changes shape in response to a signaling molecule (ligand), allowing or blocking the flow of specific ions; also called an ionotropic receptor.

light chain One of the two types of polypeptide chains that make up an antibody molecule and B cell receptor; consists of a variable region, which contributes to the antigen-binding site, and a constant region.

light microscope (LM) An optical instrument with lenses that refract (bend) visible light to magnify images of specimens.

light reactions The first of two major stages in photosynthesis (preceding the Calvin cycle). These reactions, which occur on the thylakoid membranes of the chloroplast or on membranes of certain prokaryotes, convert solar energy to the chemical energy of ATP and NADPH, releasing oxygen in the process.

light-harvesting complex A complex of proteins associated with pigment molecules (including chlorophyll *a*, chlorophyll *b*, and carotenoids) that captures light energy and transfers it to reaction-center pigments in a photosystem.

lignin (lig'-nin) A hard material embedded in the cellulose matrix of vascular plant cell walls that provides structural support in terrestrial species.

limiting nutrient An element that must be added for production to increase in a particular area.

limnetic zone In a lake, the well-lit, open surface waters far from shore.

linear electron flow A route of electron flow during the light reactions of photosynthesis that involves both photosystems (I and II) and produces ATP, NADPH, and O_2. The net electron flow is from H_2O to $NADP^+$.

linkage map A genetic map based on the frequencies of recombination between markers during crossing over of homologous chromosomes.

linked genes Genes located close enough together on a chromosome that they tend to be inherited together.

lipid (lip'-id) Any of a group of large biological molecules, including fats, phospholipids, and steroids, that mix poorly, if at all, with water.

littoral zone In a lake, the shallow, well-lit waters close to shore.

liver A large internal organ in vertebrates that performs diverse functions, such as producing bile, maintaining blood glucose level, and detoxifying poisonous chemicals in the blood.

liverwort A small, herbaceous, nonvascular plant that is a member of the phylum Hepatophyta.

loam The most fertile soil type, made up of roughly equal amounts of sand, silt, and clay.

lobe-fin Member of the vertebrate clade Sarcopterygii, osteichthyans with rod-shaped muscular fins, including coelacanths, lungfishes, and tetrapods.

local regulator A secreted molecule that influences cells near where it is secreted.

locomotion Active motion from place to place.

locus (lō'-kus) (plural, **loci**) A specific place along the length of a chromosome where a given gene is located.

logistic population growth Population growth that levels off as population size approaches carrying capacity.

long-day plant A plant that flowers (usually in late spring or early summer) only when the light period is longer than a critical length.

long-term memory The ability to hold, associate, and recall information over one's lifetime.

long-term potentiation (LTP) An enhanced responsiveness to an action potential (nerve signal) by a receiving neuron.

loop of Henle The hairpin turn, with a descending and ascending limb, between the proximal and distal tubules of the vertebrate kidney; functions in water and salt reabsorption.

lophophore (lof'-uh-fōr) In some lophotrochozoan animals, including brachiopods, a crown of ciliated tentacles that surround the mouth and function in feeding.

lophotrochozoan Member of a group of animal phyla identified as a clade by molecular evidence. Lophotrochozoans include organisms that have lophophores or trochophore larvae.

low-density lipoprotein (LDL) A particle in the blood made up of thousands of cholesterol molecules and other lipids bound to a protein. LDL transports cholesterol from the liver for incorporation into cell membranes.

lung An infolded respiratory surface of a terrestrial vertebrate, land snail, or spider that connects to the atmosphere by narrow tubes.

luteal phase That portion of the ovarian cycle during which endocrine cells of the corpus luteum secrete female hormones.

luteinizing hormone (LH) (lū'-tē-uh-nī'-zing) A tropic hormone that is produced and secreted by the anterior pituitary and that stimulates ovulation in females and androgen production in males.

lycophyte (lī'-kuh-fīt) An informal name for a member of the phylum Lycophyta, which includes club mosses, spike mosses, and quillworts.

lymph The colorless fluid, derived from interstitial fluid, in the lymphatic system of vertebrates.

lymph node An organ located along a lymph vessel. Lymph nodes filter lymph and contain cells that attack viruses and bacteria.

lymphatic system A system of vessels and nodes, separate from the circulatory system, that returns fluid, proteins, and cells to the blood.

lymphocyte A type of white blood cell that mediates immune responses. The two main classes are B cells and T cells.

lysogenic cycle (lī'-sō-jen'-ik) A type of phage replicative cycle in which the viral genome becomes incorporated into the bacterial host chromosome as a prophage, is replicated along with the chromosome, and does not kill the host.

lysosome (lī'-suh-sōm) A membrane-enclosed sac of hydrolytic enzymes found in the cytoplasm of animal cells and some protists.

lysozyme (lī'-sō-zīm) An enzyme that destroys bacterial cell walls; in mammals, found in sweat, tears, and saliva.

lytic cycle (lit'-ik) A type of phage replicative cycle resulting in the release of new phages by lysis (and death) of the host cell.

macroclimate Large-scale patterns in climate; the climate of an entire region.

macroevolution Evolutionary change above the species level. Examples of macro-evolutionary change include the origin of a new group of organisms through a series of speciation events and the impact of mass extinctions on the diversity of life and its subsequent recovery.

macromolecule A giant molecule formed by the joining of smaller molecules, usually by a dehydration reaction. Polysaccharides, proteins, and nucleic acids are macromolecules.

macronutrient An essential element that an organism must obtain in relatively large amounts. *See also* micronutrient.

macrophage (mak'-rō-fāj) A phagocytic cell present in many tissues that functions in innate immunity by destroying microbes and in acquired immunity as an antigen-presenting cell.

magnoliid Member of the angiosperm clade that is most closely related to the combined eudicot and monocot clades. Extant examples are magnolias, laurels, and black pepper plants.

major depressive disorder A mood disorder characterized by feelings of sadness, lack of self-worth, emptiness, or loss of interest in nearly all things.

major histocompatibility complex (MHC) molecule A host protein that functions in antigen presentation. Foreign MHC molecules on transplanted tissue can trigger T cell responses that may lead to rejection of the transplant.

malignant tumor A cancerous tumor containing cells that have significant genetic and cellular changes and are capable of invading and surviving in new sites. Malignant tumors can impair the functions of one or more organs.

Malpighian tubule (mal-pig'-ē-un) A unique excretory organ of insects that empties into the digestive tract, removes nitrogenous wastes from the hemolymph, and functions in osmoregulation.

mammal Member of the class Mammalia, amniotes that have hair and mammary glands (glands that produce milk).

mammary gland An exocrine gland that secretes milk to nourish the young. Mammary glands are characteristic of mammals.

mandible One of a pair of jaw-like feeding appendages found in myriapods, hexapods, and crustaceans.

mantle One of the three main parts of a mollusc; a fold of tissue that drapes over the mollusc's visceral mass and may secrete a shell. *See also* foot, visceral mass.

mantle cavity A water-filled chamber that houses the gills, anus, and excretory pores of a mollusc.

map unit A unit of measurement of the distance between genes. One map unit is equivalent to a 1% recombination frequency.

marine benthic zone The ocean floor.

mark-recapture method A sampling technique used to estimate the size of animal populations.

marsupial (mar-sū'-pē-ul) A mammal, such as a koala, kangaroo, or opossum, whose young complete their embryonic development inside a maternal pouch called the marsupium.

mass extinction The elimination of a large number of species throughout Earth, the result of global environmental changes.

mass number The sum of the number of protons and neutrons in an atom's nucleus.

mast cell A vertebrate body cell that produces histamine and other molecules that trigger inflammation in response to infection and in allergic reactions.

mate-choice copying Behavior in which individuals in a population copy the mate choice of others, apparently as a result of social learning.

maternal effect gene A gene that, when mutant in the mother, results in a mutant phenotype in the offspring, regardless of the offspring's genotype. Maternal effect genes, also called egg-polarity genes, were first identified in *Drosophila melanogaster*.

matter Anything that takes up space and has mass.

maximum likelihood As applied to molecular systematics, a principle that states that when considering multiple phylogenetic hypotheses, one should take into account the hypothesis that reflects the most likely sequence of evolutionary events, given certain rules about how DNA changes over time.

maximum parsimony A principle that states that when considering multiple explanations for an observation, one should first investigate the simplest explanation that is consistent with the facts.

mechanoreceptor A sensory receptor that detects physical deformation in the body's environment associated with pressure, touch, stretch, motion, or sound.

medulla oblongata (meh-dul'-uh ōb'-long-go'-tuh) The lowest part of the vertebrate brain, commonly called the medulla; a swelling of the hindbrain anterior to the spinal cord that controls autonomic, homeostatic functions, including breathing, heart and blood vessel activity, swallowing, digestion, and vomiting.

Medusa (plural, **medusae**) (muh-dū'-suh) The floating, flattened, mouth-down version of the cnidarian body plan. The alternate form is the polyp.

megapascal (MPa) (meg'-uh-pas-kal') A unit of pressure equivalent to about 10 atmospheres of pressure.

megaphyll (meh'-guh-fil) A leaf with a highly branched vascular system, characteristic of the vast majority of vascular plants. *See* microphyll.

megaspore A spore from a heterosporous plant species that develops into a female gametophyte.

meiosis (mī-ō'-sis) A modified type of cell division in sexually reproducing organisms consisting of two rounds of cell division but only one round of DNA replication. It results in cells with half the number of chromosome sets as the original cell.

meiosis I The first division of a two-stage process of cell division in sexually reproducing organisms that results in cells with half the number of chromosome sets as the original cell.

meiosis II The second division of a two-stage process of cell division in sexually reproducing organisms that results in cells with half the number of chromosome sets as the original cell.

melanocyte-stimulating hormone (MSH) A hormone produced and secreted by the anterior pituitary with multiple activities, including regulating the behavior of pigment-containing cells in the skin of some vertebrates.

melatonin A hormone that is secreted by the pineal gland and that is involved in the regulation of biological rhythms and sleep.

membrane potential The difference in electrical charge (voltage) across a cell's plasma membrane due to the differential distribution of ions. Membrane potential affects the activity of excitable cells and the transmembrane movement of all charged substances.

memory cell One of a clone of long-lived lymphocytes, formed during the primary immune response, that remains in a lymphoid organ until activated by exposure to the same antigen that triggered its formation. Activated memory cells mount the secondary immune response.

menopause The cessation of ovulation and menstruation marking the end of a human female's reproductive years.

menstrual cycle (men'-strū-ul) In humans and certain other primates, a type of reproductive cycle in which the nonpregnant endometrium is shed through the cervix into the vagina; also called the uterine cycle.

menstrual flow phase That portion of the uterine (menstrual) cycle when menstrual bleeding occurs.

menstruation The shedding of portions of the endometrium during a uterine (menstrual) cycle.

meristem (mār'-uh-stem) Plant tissue that remains embryonic as long as the plant lives, allowing for indeterminate growth.

meristem identity gene A plant gene that promotes the switch from vegetative growth to flowering.

meroblastic (mār'-ō-blas'-tik) Referring to a type of cleavage in which there is incomplete division of a yolk-rich egg, characteristic of avian development.

mesoderm (mez'-ō-derm) The middle primary germ layer in a triploblastic animal embryo; develops into the notochord, the lining of the coelom, muscles, skeleton, gonads, kidneys, and most of the circulatory system in species that have these structures.

mesohyl (mez'-ō-hīl) A gelatinous region between the two layers of cells of a sponge.

mesophyll (mez'-ō-fil) Leaf cells specialized for photosynthesis. In C_3 and CAM plants, mesophyll cells are located between the upper and lower epidermis; in C_4 plants, they are located between the bundle-sheath cells and the epidermis.

messenger RNA (mRNA) A type of RNA, synthesized using a DNA template, that attaches to ribosomes in the cytoplasm and specifies the primary structure of a protein. (In eukaryotes, the primary RNA transcript must undergo RNA processing to become mRNA.)

metabolic pathway A series of chemical reactions that either builds a complex molecule (anabolic pathway) or breaks down a complex molecule to simpler molecules (catabolic pathway).

metabolic rate The total amount of energy an animal uses in a unit of time.

metabolism (muh-tab'-uh-lizm) The totality of an organism's chemical reactions, consisting of catabolic and anabolic pathways, which manage the material and energy resources of the organism.

metagenomics The collection and sequencing of DNA from a group of species, usually an environmental sample of microorganisms. Computer software sorts partial sequences and assembles them into genome sequences of individual species making up the sample.

metamorphosis (met'-uh-mōr'-fuh-sis) A developmental transformation that turns an animal larva into either an adult or an adult-like stage that is not yet sexually mature.

metanephridium (met'-uh-nuh-frid'-ē-um) (plural, **metanephridia**) An excretory organ found in many invertebrates that typically consists of tubules connecting ciliated internal openings to external openings.

metaphase The third stage of mitosis, in which the spindle is complete and the chromosomes, attached to microtubules at their kinetochores, are all aligned at the metaphase plate.

metaphase plate An imaginary structure located at a plane midway between the two poles of a cell in metaphase on which the centromeres of all the duplicated chromosomes are located.

metapopulation A group of spatially separated populations of one species that interact through immigration and emigration.

metastasis (muh-tas'-tuh-sis) The spread of cancer cells to locations distant from their original site.

methanogen (meth-an'-ō-jen) An organism that produces methane as a waste product of the way it obtains energy. All known methanogens are in domain Archaea.

methyl group A chemical group consisting of a carbon bonded to three hydrogen atoms. The methyl group may be attached to a carbon or to a different atom.

microclimate Climate patterns on a very fine scale, such as the specific climatic conditions underneath a log.

microevolution Evolutionary change below the species level; change in the allele frequencies in a population over generations.

microfilament A cable composed of actin proteins in the cytoplasm of almost every eukaryotic cell, making up part of the cytoskeleton and acting alone or with myosin to cause cell contraction; also known as an actin filament.

micronutrient An essential element that an organism needs in very small amounts. *See also* macronutrient.

microphyll (mī'-krō-fil) In lycophytes, a small leaf with a single unbranched vein. *See* megaphyll.

micropyle A pore in the integuments of an ovule.

microRNA (miRNA) A small, single-stranded RNA molecule, generated from a hairpin structure on a precursor RNA transcribed from a particular gene. The miRNA associates with one or more proteins in a complex that can degrade or prevent translation of an mRNA with a complementary sequence.

microspore A spore from a heterosporous plant species that develops into a male gametophyte.

microtubule A hollow rod composed of tubulin proteins that makes up part of the cytoskeleton in all eukaryotic cells and is found in cilia and flagella.

microvillus (plural, **microvilli**) One of many fine, finger-like projections of the epithelial cells in the lumen of the small intestine that increase its surface area.

midbrain One of three ancestral and embryonic regions of the vertebrate brain; develops into sensory integrating and relay centers that send sensory information to the cerebrum.

middle ear One of three main regions of the vertebrate ear; in mammals, a chamber containing three small bones (the malleus, incus, and stapes) that convey vibrations from the eardrum to the oval window.

middle lamella (luh-mel'-uh) In plants, a thin layer of adhesive extracellular material, primarily pectins, found between the primary walls of adjacent young cells.

migration A regular, long-distance change in location.

mineral In nutrition, a simple nutrient that is inorganic and therefore cannot be synthesized in the body.

mineralocorticoid A steroid hormone secreted by the adrenal cortex that regulates salt and water homeostasis.

minimum viable population (MVP) The smallest population size at which a species is able to sustain its numbers and survive.

mismatch repair The cellular process that uses specific enzymes to remove and replace incorrectly paired nucleotides.

missense mutation A nucleotide-pair substitution that results in a codon that codes for a different amino acid.

mitochondrial matrix The compartment of the mitochondrion enclosed by the inner membrane and containing enzymes and substrates for the citric acid cycle, as well as ribosomes and DNA.

mitochondrion (mī'-tō-kon'-drē-un) (plural, **mitochondria**) An organelle in eukaryotic cells that serves as the site of cellular respiration; uses oxygen to break down organic molecules and synthesize ATP.

mitosis (mī-tō'-sis) A process of nuclear division in eukaryotic cells conventionally divided into five stages: prophase, prometaphase, metaphase, anaphase, and telophase. Mitosis conserves chromosome number by allocating replicated chromosomes equally to each of the daughter nuclei.

mitotic (M) phase The phase of the cell cycle that includes mitosis and cytokinesis.

mitotic spindle An assemblage of microtubules and associated proteins that is involved in the movement of chromosomes during mitosis.

mixotroph An organism that is capable of both photosynthesis and heterotrophy.

model organism A particular species chosen for research into broad biological principles because it is representative of a larger group and usually easy to grow in a lab.

molarity A common measure of solute concentration, referring to the number of moles of solute per liter of solution.

mold Informal term for a fungus that grows as a filamentous fungus, producing haploid spores by mitosis and forming a visible mycelium.

mole (mol) The number of grams of a substance that equals its molecular weight in daltons and contains Avogadro's number of molecules.

molecular clock A method for estimating the time required for a given amount of evolutionary change, based on the observation that some regions of genomes evolve at constant rates.

molecular mass The sum of the masses of all the atoms in a molecule; sometimes called molecular weight.

molecular systematics A scientific discipline that uses nucleic acids or other molecules to infer evolutionary relationships between different species.

molecule Two or more atoms held together by covalent bonds.

molting A process in ecdysozoans in which the exoskeleton is shed at intervals, allowing growth by the production of a larger exoskeleton.

monoclonal antibody (mon'-ō-klōn'-ul) Any of a preparation of antibodies that have been produced by a single clone of cultured cells and thus are all specific for the same epitope.

monocot Member of a clade consisting of flowering plants that have one embryonic seed leaf, or cotyledon.

monogamous (muh-nog'-uh-mus) Referring to a type of relationship in which one male mates with just one female.

monohybrid An organism that is heterozygous with respect to a single gene of interest. All the offspring from a cross between parents homozygous for different alleles are monohybrids. For example, parents of genotypes *AA* and *aa* produce a monohybrid of genotype *Aa*.

monohybrid cross A cross between two organisms that are heterozygous for the character being followed (or the self-pollination of a heterozygous plant).

monomer (mon'-uh-mer) The subunit that serves as the building block of a polymer.

monophyletic (mon'-ō-fī-let'-ik) Pertaining to a group of taxa that consists of a common ancestor and all of its descendants. A monophyletic taxon is equivalent to a clade.

monosaccharide (mon'-ō-sak'-uh-rīd) The simplest carbohydrate, active alone or serving as a monomer for disaccharides and polysaccharides. Also known as simple sugars, monosaccharides have molecular formulas that are generally some multiple of CH_2O.

monosomic Referring to a diploid cell that has only one copy of a particular chromosome instead of the normal two.

monotreme An egg-laying mammal, such as a platypus or echidna. Like all mammals, monotremes have hair and produce milk, but they lack nipples.

morphogen A substance, such as Bicoid protein in *Drosophila*, that provides positional information in the form of a concentration gradient along an embryonic axis.

morphogenesis (mōr'-fō-jen'-uh-sis) The cellular and tissue-based processes by which an animal body takes shape.

morphological species concept A definition of species in terms of measurable anatomical criteria.

moss A small, herbaceous, nonvascular plant that is a member of the phylum Bryophyta.

motor neuron A nerve cell that transmits signals from the brain or spinal cord to muscles or glands.

motor protein A protein that interacts with cytoskeletal elements and other cell components, producing movement of the whole cell or parts of the cell.

motor system An efferent branch of the vertebrate peripheral nervous system composed of motor neurons that carry signals to skeletal muscles in response to external stimuli.

motor unit A single motor neuron and all the muscle fibers it controls.

movement corridor A series of small clumps or a narrow strip of quality habitat (usable by organisms) that connects otherwise isolated patches of quality habitat.

MPF Maturation-promoting factor (or M-phase-promoting factor); a protein complex required for a cell to progress from late interphase to mitosis. The active form consists of cyclin and a protein kinase.

mucus A viscous and slippery mixture of glycoproteins, cells, salts, and water that moistens and protects the membranes lining body cavities that open to the exterior.

Müllerian mimicry (myū-lār'-ē-un) Reciprocal mimicry by two unpalatable species.

multifactorial Referring to a phenotypic character that is influenced by multiple genes and environmental factors.

multigene family A collection of genes with similar or identical sequences, presumably of common origin.

multiple fruit A fruit derived from an entire inflorescence.

multiplication rule A rule of probability stating that the probability of two or more independent events occurring together can be determined by multiplying their individual probabilities.

muscle tissue Tissue consisting of long muscle cells that can contract, either on its own or when stimulated by nerve impulses.

mutagen (myū'-tuh-jen) A chemical or physical agent that interacts with DNA and can cause a mutation.

mutation (myū-tā'-shun) A change in the nucleotide sequence of an organism's DNA or in the DNA or RNA of a virus.

mutualism (myū'-chū-ul-izm) A symbiotic relationship in which both participants benefit.

mycelium (mī-sē'-lē-um) The densely branched network of hyphae in a fungus.

mycorrhiza (mī'-kō-rī'-zuh) (plural, **mycorrhizae**) A mutualistic association of plant roots and fungus.

mycosis (mī-kō'-sis) General term for a fungal infection.

myelin sheath (mī'-uh-lin) Wrapped around the axon of a neuron, an insulating coat of cell membranes from Schwann cells or oligodendrocytes. It is interrupted by nodes of Ranvier, where action potentials are generated.

myofibril (mī'-ō-fī'-bril) A longitudinal bundle in a muscle cell (fiber) that contains thin filaments of actin and regulatory proteins and thick filaments of myosin.

myoglobin (mī'-uh-glō'-bin) An oxygen-storing, pigmented protein in muscle cells.

myosin (mī'-uh-sin) A type of motor protein that associates into filaments that interact with actin filaments to cause cell contraction.

myotonia (mī'-uh-tō'-nī-uh) Increased muscle tension, characteristic of sexual arousal in certain human tissues.

myriapod (mir'-ē-uh-pod') A terrestrial arthropod with many body segments and one or two pairs of legs per segment. Millipedes and centipedes are the two major groups of living myriapods.

NAD$^+$ Nicotinamide adenine dinucleotide, a coenzyme that cycles easily between oxidized (NAD$^+$) and reduced (NADH) states, thus acting as an electron carrier.

NADP$^+$ Nicotinamide adenine dinucleotide phosphate, an electron acceptor that, as NADPH, temporarily stores energized electrons produced during the light reactions.

natural family planning A form of contraception that relies on refraining from sexual intercourse when conception is most likely to occur; also called the rhythm method.

natural killer cell A type of white blood cell that can kill tumor cells and virus-infected cells as part of innate immunity.

natural selection A process in which individuals that have certain inherited traits tend to survive and reproduce at higher rates than other individuals *because of* those traits.

negative feedback A form of regulation in which accumulation of an end product of a process slows the process; in physiology, a primary mechanism of homeostasis, whereby a change in a variable triggers a response that counteracts the initial change.

negative pressure breathing A breathing system in which air is pulled into the lungs.

nematocyst (nem'-uh-tuh-sist') In a cnidocyte of a cnidarian, a capsule-like organelle containing a coiled thread that when discharged can penetrate the body wall of the prey.

nephron (nef'-ron) The tubular excretory unit of the vertebrate kidney.

neritic zone The shallow region of the ocean overlying the continental shelf.

nerve A fiber composed primarily of the bundled axons of PNS neurons.

nerve net A weblike system of neurons, characteristic of radially symmetrical animals, such as hydras.

nervous system The fast-acting internal system of communication involving sensory receptors, networks of nerve cells, and connections to muscles and glands that respond to nerve signals; functions in concert with the endocrine system to effect internal regulation and maintain homeostasis.

nervous tissue Tissue made up of neurons and supportive cells.

net ecosystem production (NEP) The gross primary production of an ecosystem minus the energy used by all autotrophs and heterotrophs for respiration.

net primary production (NPP) The gross primary production of an ecosystem minus the energy used by the producers for respiration.

neural crest In vertebrates, a region located along the sides of the neural tube where it pinches off from the ectoderm. Neural crest cells migrate to various parts of the embryo and form pigment cells in the skin and parts of the skull, teeth, adrenal glands, and peripheral nervous system.

neural plasticity The capacity of a nervous system to change with experience.

neural tube A tube of infolded ectodermal cells that runs along the anterior-posterior axis of a vertebrate, just dorsal to the notochord. It will give rise to the central nervous system.

neurohormone A molecule that is secreted by a neuron, travels in body fluids, and acts on specific target cells, changing their functioning.

neuron (nyūr'-on) A nerve cell; the fundamental unit of the nervous system, having structure and properties that allow it to conduct signals by taking advantage of the electrical charge across its plasma membrane.

neuropeptide A relatively short chain of amino acids that serves as a neurotransmitter.

neurotransmitter A molecule that is released from the synaptic terminal of a neuron at a chemical synapse, diffuses across the synaptic cleft, and binds to the postsynaptic cell, triggering a response.

neutral theory The hypothesis that much evolutionary change in genes and proteins has no effect on fitness and therefore is not influenced by natural selection.

neutral variation Genetic variation that does not provide a selective advantage or disadvantage.

neutron A subatomic particle having no electrical charge (electrically neutral), with a mass of about 1.7×10^{-24} g, found in the nucleus of an atom.

neutrophil The most abundant type of white blood cell. Neutrophils are phagocytic and tend to self-destruct as they destroy foreign invaders, limiting their life span to a few days.

nitric oxide (NO) A gas produced by many types of cells that functions as a local regulator and as a neurotransmitter.

nitrogen cycle The natural process by which nitrogen, either from the atmosphere or from decomposed organic material, is converted by soil bacteria to compounds assimilated by plants. This incorporated nitrogen is then taken in by other organisms and subsequently released, acted on by bacteria, and made available again to the nonliving environment.

nitrogen fixation The conversion of atmospheric nitrogen (N_2) to ammonia (NH_3). Biological nitrogen fixation is carried out by certain prokaryotes, some of which have mutualistic relationships with plants.

nociceptor (nō'-si-sep'-tur) A sensory receptor that responds to noxious or painful stimuli; also called a pain receptor.

node A point along the stem of a plant at which leaves are attached.

node of Ranvier (ron'-vē-ā') Gap in the myelin sheath of certain axons where an action potential may be generated. In saltatory conduction, an action potential is regenerated at each node, appearing to "jump" along the axon from node to node.

nodule A swelling on the root of a legume. Nodules are composed of plant cells that contain nitrogen-fixing bacteria of the genus *Rhizobium*.

noncompetitive inhibitor A substance that reduces the activity of an enzyme by binding to a location remote from the active site, changing the enzyme's shape so that the active site no longer effectively catalyzes the conversion of substrate to product.

nondisjunction An error in meiosis or mitosis in which members of a pair of homologous chromosomes or a pair of sister chromatids fail to separate properly from each other.

nonequilibrium model A model that maintains that communities change constantly after being buffeted by disturbances.

nonpolar covalent bond A type of covalent bond in which electrons are shared equally between two atoms of similar electronegativity.

nonsense mutation A mutation that changes an amino acid codon to one of the three stop codons, resulting in a shorter and usually non-functional protein.

norepinephrine A catecholamine that is chemically and functionally similar to epinephrine and acts as a hormone or neurotransmitter; also known as noradrenaline.

norm of reaction The range of phenotypes produced by a single genotype, due to environmental influences.

Northern blotting A technique that enables specific nucleotide sequences to be detected in samples of mRNA. It involves gel electrophoresis of RNA molecules and their transfer to a membrane (blotting), followed by nucleic acid hybridization with a labeled probe.

northern coniferous forest A terrestrial biome characterized by long, cold winters and dominated by cone-bearing trees.

no-till agriculture A plowing technique that minimally disturbs the soil, thereby reducing soil loss.

notochord (nō'-tuh-kord') A longitudinal, flexible rod made of tightly packed mesodermal cells that runs along the anterior-posterior axis of a chordate in the dorsal part of the body.

nuclear envelope In a eukaryotic cell, the double membrane that surrounds the nucleus, perforated with pores that regulate traffic with the cytoplasm. The outer membrane is continuous with the endoplasmic reticulum.

nuclear lamina A netlike array of protein filaments that lines the inner surface of the nuclear envelope and helps maintain the shape of the nucleus.

nucleariid Member of a group of unicellular, amoeboid protists that are more closely related to fungi than they are to other protists.

nuclease An enzyme that cuts DNA or RNA, either removing one or a few bases or hydrolyzing the DNA or RNA completely into its component nucleotides.

nucleic acid (nū-klā'-ik) A polymer (polynucleotide) consisting of many nucleotide monomers; serves as a blueprint for proteins and, through the actions of proteins, for all cellular activities. The two types are DNA and RNA.

nucleic acid hybridization The process of base pairing between a gene and a complementary sequence on another nucleic acid molecule.

nucleic acid probe In DNA technology, a labeled single-stranded nucleic acid molecule used to locate a specific nucleotide sequence in a nucleic acid sample. Molecules of the probe hydrogen-bond to the complementary sequence wherever it occurs; radioactive, fluorescent, or other labeling of the probe allows its location to be detected.

nucleoid (nū'-klē-oyd) A non-membrane-bounded region in a prokaryotic cell where the DNA is concentrated.

nucleolus (nū-klē'-ō-lus) (plural, **nucleoli**) A specialized structure in the nucleus, consisting of chromosomal regions containing ribosomal RNA (rRNA) genes along with ribosomal proteins imported from the cytoplasm; site of rRNA synthesis and ribosomal subunit assembly. *See also* ribosome.

nucleosome (nū'-klē-ō-sōm') The basic, bead-like unit of DNA packing in eukaryotes, consisting of a segment of DNA wound around a protein core composed of two copies of each of four types of histone.

nucleotide (nū'-klē-ō-tīd') The building block of a nucleic acid, consisting of a five-carbon sugar covalently bonded to a nitrogenous base and one or more phosphate groups.

nucleotide excision repair A repair system that removes and then correctly replaces a damaged segment of DNA using the undamaged strand as a guide.

nucleotide-pair substitution A type of point mutation in which one nucleotide in a DNA strand and its partner in the complementary strand are replaced by another pair of nucleotides.

nucleus (1) An atom's central core, containing protons and neutrons. (2) The organelle of a eukaryotic cell that contains the genetic material in the form of chromosomes, made up of chromatin. (3) A cluster of neurons.

nutrition The process by which an organism takes in and makes use of food substances.

obligate aerobe (ob'-lig-et ār'-ōb) An organism that requires oxygen for cellular respiration and cannot live without it.

obligate anaerobe (ob'-lig-et an'-uh-rōb) An organism that only carries out fermentation or anaerobic respiration. Such organisms cannot use oxygen and in fact may be poisoned by it.

ocean acidification Decreasing pH of ocean waters due to absorption of excess atmospheric CO_2 from the burning of fossil fuels.

oceanic pelagic zone Most of the ocean's waters far from shore, constantly mixed by ocean currents.

odorant A molecule that can be detected by sensory receptors of the olfactory system.

Okazaki fragment (ō'-kah-zah'-kē) A short segment of DNA synthesized away from the replication fork on a template strand during DNA replication. Many such segments are joined together to make up the lagging strand of newly synthesized DNA.

olfaction The sense of smell.

oligodendrocyte A type of glial cell that forms insulating myelin sheaths around the axons of neurons in the central nervous system.

oligotrophic lake A nutrient-poor, clear lake with few phytoplankton.

ommatidium (ōm'-uh-tid'-ē-um) (plural, **ommatidia**) One of the facets of the compound eye of arthropods and some polychaete worms.

omnivore An animal that regularly eats animals as well as plants or algae.

oncogene (on'-kō-jēn) A gene found in viral or cellular genomes that is involved in triggering molecular events that can lead to cancer.

oocyte A cell in the female reproductive system that differentiates to form an egg.

oogenesis (ō'-uh-jen'-uh-sis) The process in the ovary that results in the production of female gametes.

oogonium (ō'-uh- gō'-nē-em) (plural, **oogonia**) A cell that divides mitotically to form oocytes.

oomycete (ō'-uh-mī'-sēt) A protist with flagellated cells, such as a water mold, white rust, or downy mildew, that acquires nutrition mainly as a decomposer or plant parasite.

open circulatory system A circulatory system in which fluid called hemolymph bathes the tissues and organs directly and there is no distinction between the circulating fluid and the interstitial fluid.

operator In bacterial and phage DNA, a sequence of nucleotides near the start of an operon to which an active repressor can attach. The binding of the repressor prevents RNA polymerase from attaching to the promoter and transcribing the genes of the operon.

operculum (ō-per'-kyuh-lum) In aquatic osteichthyans, a protective bony flap that covers and protects the gills.

operon (op'-er-on) A unit of genetic function found in bacteria and phages, consisting of a promoter, an operator, and a coordinately regulated cluster of genes whose products function in a common pathway.

opisthokont (uh-pis'-thuh-kont') Member of the diverse clade Opisthokonta, organisms that descended from an ancestor with a posterior flagellum, including fungi, animals, and certain protists.

opposable thumb A thumb that can touch the ventral surface of the fingertips of all four fingers.

opsin A membrane protein bound to a light-absorbing pigment molecule.

optic chiasm The place where the two optic nerves meet and axons representing distinct sides of the visual field are segregated from one another before reaching the brain.

optimal foraging model The basis for analyzing behavior as a compromise between feeding costs and feeding benefits.

oral cavity The mouth of an animal.

orbital The three-dimensional space where an electron is found 90% of the time.

order In Linnaean classification, the taxonomic category above the level of family.

organ A specialized center of body function composed of several different types of tissues.

organ identity gene A plant homeotic gene that uses positional information to determine which emerging leaves develop into which types of floral organs.

organ of Corti The actual hearing organ of the vertebrate ear, located in the floor of the cochlear duct in the inner ear; contains the receptor cells (hair cells) of the ear.

organ system A group of organs that work together in performing vital body functions.

organelle (ōr-guh-nel') Any of several membrane-enclosed structures with specialized functions, suspended in the cytosol of eukaryotic cells.

organic chemistry The study of carbon compounds (organic compounds).

organismal ecology The branch of ecology concerned with the morphological, physiological, and behavioral ways in which individual organisms meet the challenges posed by their biotic and abiotic environments.

organogenesis (ōr-gan'-ō-jen'-uh-sis) The process in which organ rudiments develop from the three germ layers after gastrulation.

orgasm Rhythmic, involuntary contractions of certain reproductive structures in both sexes during the human sexual response cycle.

origin of replication Site where the replication of a DNA molecule begins, consisting of a specific sequence of nucleotides.

orthologous genes Homologous genes that are found in different species because of speciation.

osculum (os'-kyuh-lum) A large opening in a sponge that connects the spongocoel to the environment.

osmoconformer An animal that is isoosmotic with its environment.

osmolarity (oz'-mō-lār'-uh-tē) Solute concentration expressed as molarity.

osmoregulation Regulation of solute concentrations and water balance by a cell or organism.

osmoregulator An animal that controls its internal osmolarity independent of the external environment.

osmosis (oz-mō'-sis) The diffusion of free water across a selectively permeable membrane.

osteichthyan (os'-tē-ik'-thē-an) Member of a vertebrate clade with jaws and mostly bony skeletons.

outer ear One of three main regions of the ear in reptiles (including birds) and mammals; made up of the auditory canal and, in many birds and mammals, the pinna.

outgroup A species or group of species from an evolutionary lineage that is known to have diverged before the lineage that contains the group of species being studied. An outgroup is selected so that its members are closely related to the group of species being studied, but not as closely related as any study-group members are to each other.

oval window In the vertebrate ear, a membrane-covered gap in the skull bone, through which sound waves pass from the middle ear to the inner ear.

ovarian cycle (ō-vār'-ē-un) The cyclic recurrence of the follicular phase, ovulation, and the luteal phase in the mammalian ovary, regulated by hormones.

ovary (ō'-vuh-rē) (1) In flowers, the portion of a carpel in which the egg-containing ovules develop. (2) In animals, the structure that produces female gametes and reproductive hormones.

oviduct (ō'-vuh-duct) A tube passing from the ovary to the vagina in invertebrates or to the uterus in vertebrates, where it is also known as a fallopian tube.

oviparous (ō-vip'-uh-rus) Referring to a type of development in which young hatch from eggs laid outside the mother's body.

ovoviviparous (ō'-vō-vī-vip'-uh-rus) Referring to a type of development in which young hatch from eggs that are retained in the mother's uterus.

ovulation The release of an egg from an ovary. In humans, an ovarian follicle releases an egg during each uterine (menstrual) cycle.

ovule (o'-vyūl) A structure that develops within the ovary of a seed plant and contains the female gametophyte.

oxidation The complete or partial loss of electrons from a substance involved in a redox reaction.

oxidative phosphorylation (fos'-fōr-uh-lā'-shun) The production of ATP using energy derived from the redox reactions of an electron transport chain; the third major stage of cellular respiration.

oxidizing agent The electron acceptor in a redox reaction.

oxytocin (ok'-si-tō'-sen) A hormone produced by the hypothalamus and released from the posterior pituitary. It induces contractions of the uterine muscles during labor and causes the mammary glands to eject milk during nursing.

P generation The true-breeding (homozygous) parent individuals from which F_1 hybrid offspring are derived in studies of inheritance; P stands for "parental."

P site One of a ribosome's three binding sites for tRNA during translation. The P site holds the tRNA carrying the growing polypeptide chain. (P stands for peptidyl tRNA.)

p53 gene A tumor-suppressor gene that codes for a specific transcription factor that promotes the synthesis of proteins that inhibit the cell cycle.

paedomorphosis (pē'-duh-mōr'-fuh-sis) The retention in an adult organism of the juvenile features of its evolutionary ancestors.

pain receptor A sensory receptor that responds to noxious or painful stimuli; also called a nociceptor.

paleoanthropology The study of human origins and evolution.

paleontology (pā-lē-un-tol'-ō-jē) The scientific study of fossils.

pancreas (pan'-krē-us) A gland with exocrine and endocrine tissues. The exocrine portion functions in digestion, secreting enzymes and an alkaline solution into the small intestine via a duct; the ductless endocrine portion functions in homeostasis, secreting the hormones insulin and glucagon into the blood.

pandemic A global epidemic.

Pangaea (pan-jē'-uh) The supercontinent that formed near the end of the Paleozoic era, when plate movements brought all the landmasses of Earth together.

parabasalid A protist, such as a trichomonad, with modified mitochondria.

paracrine Referring to a secreted molecule that acts on a neighboring cell.

paralogous genes Homologous genes that are found in the same genome as a result of gene duplication.

paraphyletic (pār'-uh-fī-let'-ik) Pertaining to a group of taxa that consists of a common ancestor and some, but not all, of its descendants.

parareptile A basal group of reptiles, consisting mostly of large, stocky quadrupedal herbivores. Parareptiles died out in the late Triassic period.

parasite (pār'-uh-sīt) An organism that feeds on the cell contents, tissues, or body fluids of another species (the host) while in or on the host organism. Parasites harm but usually do not kill their host.

parasitism (pār'-uh-sit-izm) A symbiotic relationship in which one organism, the parasite, benefits at the expense of another, the host, by living either within or on the host.

parasympathetic division One of three divisions of the autonomic nervous system; generally enhances body activities that gain and conserve energy, such as digestion and reduced heart rate.

parathyroid gland One of four small endocrine glands, embedded in the surface of the thyroid gland, that secrete parathyroid hormone.

parathyroid hormone (PTH) A hormone secreted by the parathyroid glands that raises blood calcium level by promoting calcium release from bone and calcium retention by the kidneys.

parenchyma cell (puh-ren'-ki-muh) A relatively unspecialized plant cell type that carries out most of the metabolism, synthesizes and stores organic products, and develops into a more differentiated cell type.

parental type An offspring with a phenotype that matches one of the true-breeding parental (P generation) phenotypes; also refers to the phenotype itself.

Parkinson's disease A progressive brain disease characterized by difficulty in initiating movements, slowness of movement, and rigidity.

parthenogenesis (par´-thuh-nō´-jen´-uh-sis) A form of asexual reproduction in which females produce offspring from unfertilized eggs.

partial pressure The pressure exerted by a particular gas in a mixture of gases (for instance, the pressure exerted by oxygen in air).

passive immunity Short-term immunity conferred by the transfer of antibodies, as occurs in the transfer of maternal antibodies to a fetus or nursing infant.

passive transport The diffusion of a substance across a biological membrane with no expenditure of energy.

pathogen An organism, virus, viroid, or prion that causes disease.

pattern formation The development of a multicellular organism's spatial organization, the arrangement of organs and tissues in their characteristic places in three-dimensional space.

peat Extensive deposits of partially decayed organic material often formed primarily from the wetland moss *Sphagnum*.

pedigree A diagram of a family tree with conventional symbols, showing the occurrence of heritable characters in parents and offspring over multiple generations.

pelagic zone The open-water component of aquatic biomes.

penis The copulatory structure of male mammals.

PEP carboxylase An enzyme that adds CO_2 to phosphoenolpyruvate (PEP) to form oxaloacetate in mesophyll cells of C_4 plants. It acts prior to photosynthesis.

pepsin An enzyme present in gastric juice that begins the hydrolysis of proteins.

pepsinogen The inactive form of pepsin secreted by chief cells located in gastric pits of the stomach.

peptide bond The covalent bond between the carboxyl group on one amino acid and the amino group on another, formed by a dehydration reaction.

peptidoglycan (pep´-tid-ō-glī´-kan) A type of polymer in bacterial cell walls consisting of modified sugars cross-linked by short polypeptides.

perception The interpretation of sensory system input by the brain.

pericycle The outermost layer in the vascular cylinder, from which lateral roots arise.

periderm (pār´-uh-derm´) The protective coat that replaces the epidermis in woody plants during secondary growth, formed of the cork and cork cambium.

peripheral nervous system (PNS) The sensory and motor neurons that connect to the central nervous system.

peripheral protein A protein loosely bound to the surface of a membrane or to part of an integral protein and not embedded in the lipid bilayer.

peristalsis (pār´-uh-stal´-sis) (1) Alternating waves of contraction and relaxation in the smooth muscles lining the alimentary canal that push food along the canal. (2) A type of movement on land produced by rhythmic waves of muscle contractions passing from front to back, as in many annelids.

peristome A ring of interlocking, tooth-like structures on the upper part of a moss capsule (sporangium), often specialized for gradual spore discharge.

peritubular capillary One of the tiny blood vessels that form a network surrounding the proximal and distal tubules in the kidney.

permafrost A permanently frozen soil layer.

peroxisome (puh-rok´-suh-sōm´) An organelle containing enzymes that transfer hydrogen atoms from various substrates to oxygen (O_2), producing and then degrading hydrogen peroxide (H_2O_2).

petal A modified leaf of a flowering plant. Petals are the often colorful parts of a flower that advertise it to insects and other pollinators.

petiole (pet´-ē-ōl) The stalk of a leaf, which joins the leaf to a node of the stem.

pH A measure of hydrogen ion concentration equal to $-\log [H^+]$ and ranging in value from 0 to 14.

phage (fāj) A virus that infects bacteria; also called a bacteriophage.

phagocytosis (fag´-ō-sī-tō´-sis) A type of endocytosis in which large particulate substances or small organisms are taken up by a cell. It is carried out by some protists and by certain immune cells of animals (in mammals, mainly macrophages, neutrophils, and dendritic cells).

pharyngeal cleft (fuh-rin´-jē-ul) In chordate embryos, one of the grooves that separate a series of pouches along the sides of the pharynx and may develop into a pharyngeal slit.

pharyngeal slit (fuh-rin´-jē-ul) In chordate embryos, one of the slits that form from the pharyngeal clefts and communicate to the outside, later developing into gill slits in many vertebrates.

pharynx (fār´-inks) (1) An area in the vertebrate throat where air and food passages cross. (2) In flatworms, the muscular tube that protrudes from the ventral side of the worm and ends in the mouth.

phase change A shift from one developmental phase to another.

phenotype (fē´-nō-tīp) The observable physical and physiological traits of an organism, which are determined by its genetic makeup.

pheromone (fār´-uh-mōn) In animals and fungi, a small molecule released into the environment that functions in communication between members of the same species. In animals, it acts much like a hormone in influencing physiology and behavior.

phloem (flō´-em) Vascular plant tissue consisting of living cells arranged into elongated tubes that transport sugar and other organic nutrients throughout the plant.

phloem sap The sugar-rich solution carried through a plant's sieve tubes.

phosphate group A chemical group consisting of a phosphorus atom bonded to four oxygen atoms; important in energy transfer.

phospholipid (fos´-fō-lip´-id) A lipid made up of glycerol joined to two fatty acids and a phosphate group. The hydrocarbon chains of the fatty acids act as nonpolar, hydrophobic tails, while the rest of the molecule acts as a polar, hydrophilic head. Phospholipids form bilayers that function as biological membranes.

phosphorylated intermediate A molecule (often a reactant) with a phosphate group covalently bound to it, making it more reactive (less stable) than the unphosphorylated molecule.

photic zone (fō´-tic) The narrow top layer of an ocean or lake, where light penetrates sufficiently for photosynthesis to occur.

photoautotroph (fō´-tō-ot´-ō-trōf) An organism that harnesses light energy to drive the synthesis of organic compounds from carbon dioxide.

photoheterotroph (fō´-tō-het´-er-ō-trōf) An organism that uses light to generate ATP but must obtain carbon in organic form.

photomorphogenesis Effects of light on plant morphology.

photon (fō´-ton) A quantum, or discrete quantity, of light energy that behaves as if it were a particle.

photoperiodism (fō´-tō-pēr´-ē-ō-dizm) A physiological response to photoperiod, the relative lengths of night and day. An example of photoperiodism is flowering.

photophosphorylation (fō´-tō-fos´-fōr-uh-lā´-shun) The process of generating ATP from ADP and phosphate by means of chemiosmosis, using a proton-motive force generated across the thylakoid membrane of the chloroplast or the membrane of certain prokaryotes during the light reactions of photosynthesis.

photoreceptor An electromagnetic receptor that detects the radiation known as visible light.

photorespiration A metabolic pathway that consumes oxygen and ATP, releases carbon dioxide, and decreases photosynthetic output. Photorespiration generally occurs on hot, dry, bright days, when stomata close and the O_2/CO_2 ratio in the leaf increases, favoring the binding of O_2 rather than CO_2 by rubisco.

photosynthesis (fō´-tō-sin´-thi-sis) The conversion of light energy to chemical energy that is stored in sugars or other organic compounds; occurs in plants, algae, and certain prokaryotes.

photosystem A light-capturing unit located in the thylakoid membrane of the chloroplast or in the membrane of some prokaryotes, consisting of a reaction-center complex surrounded by numerous light-harvesting complexes. There are two types of photosystems, I and II; they absorb light best at different wavelengths.

photosystem I (PS I) A light-capturing unit in a chloroplast's thylakoid membrane or in the membrane of some prokaryotes; it has two molecules of P700 chlorophyll *a* at its reaction center.

photosystem II (PS II) One of two light-capturing units in a chloroplast's thylakoid membrane or in the membrane of some prokaryotes; it has two molecules of P680 chlorophyll *a* at its reaction center.

phototropism (fō'-tō-trō'-pizm) Growth of a plant shoot toward or away from light.

phragmoplast (frag'-mō-plast') An alignment of cytoskeletal elements and Golgi-derived vesicles that forms across the midline of a dividing plant cell.

phyllotaxy (fil'-uh-tak'-sē) The pattern of leaf attachment to the stem of a plant.

PhyloCode Proposed system of classification of organisms based on evolutionary relationships: Only groups that include a common ancestor and all of its descendants are named.

phylogenetic species concept A definition of species as the smallest group of individuals that share a common ancestor, forming one branch on the tree of life.

phylogenetic tree A branching diagram that represents a hypothesis about the evolutionary history of a group of organisms.

phylogeny (fī-loj'-uh-nē) The evolutionary history of a species or group of related species.

phylum (fī'-lum) (plural, **phyla**) In Linnaean classification, the taxonomic category above class.

physical map A genetic map in which the actual physical distances between genes or other genetic markers are expressed, usually as the number of base pairs along the DNA.

physiology The processes and functions of an organism.

phytochrome (fī'-tuh-krōm) A type of light receptor in plants that mostly absorbs red light and regulates many plant responses, such as seed germination and shade avoidance.

phytoremediation An emerging technology that seeks to reclaim contaminated areas by taking advantage of some plant species' ability to extract heavy metals and other pollutants from the soil and to concentrate them in easily harvested portions of the plant.

pilus (plural, **pili**) (pī'-lus, pī'-lī) In bacteria, a structure that links one cell to another at the start of conjugation; also known as a sex pilus or conjugation pilus.

pineal gland (pī'-nē-ul) A small gland on the dorsal surface of the vertebrate forebrain that secretes the hormone melatonin.

pinocytosis (pī'-nō-sī-tō'-sis) A type of endocytosis in which the cell ingests extracellular fluid and its dissolved solutes.

pistil A single carpel or a group of fused carpels.

pith Ground tissue that is internal to the vascular tissue in a stem; in many monocot roots, parenchyma cells that form the central core of the vascular cylinder.

pituitary gland (puh-tū'-uh-tār'-ē) An endocrine gland at the base of the hypothalamus; consists of a posterior lobe, which stores and releases two hormones produced by the hypothalamus, and an anterior lobe, which produces and secretes many hormones that regulate diverse body functions.

placenta (pluh-sen'-tuh) A structure in the pregnant uterus for nourishing a viviparous fetus with the mother's blood supply; formed from the uterine lining and embryonic membranes.

placental transfer cell A plant cell that enhances the transfer of nutrients from parent to embryo.

placoderm A member of an extinct group of fishlike vertebrates that had jaws and were enclosed in a tough outer armor.

planarian A free-living flatworm found in ponds and streams.

plasma (plaz'-muh) The liquid matrix of blood in which the blood cells are suspended.

plasma cell The antibody-secreting effector cell of humoral immunity. Plasma cells arise from antigen-stimulated B cells.

plasma membrane The membrane at the boundary of every cell that acts as a selective barrier, regulating the cell's chemical composition.

plasmid (plaz'-mid) A small, circular, double-stranded DNA molecule that carries accessory genes separate from those of a bacterial chromosome; in DNA cloning, used as vectors carrying up to about 10,000 base pairs (10 kb) of DNA. Plasmids are also found in some eukaryotes, such as yeasts.

plasmodesma (plaz'-mō-dez'-muh) (plural, **plasmodesmata**) An open channel through the cell wall that connects the cytoplasm of adjacent plant cells, allowing water, small solutes, and some larger molecules to pass between the cells.

plasmodial slime mold (plaz-mō'-dē-ul) A type of protist that has amoeboid cells, flagellated cells, and a plasmodial feeding stage in its life cycle.

plasmodium A single mass of cytoplasm containing many diploid nuclei that forms during the life cycle of some slime molds.

plasmogamy (plaz-moh'-guh-mē) In fungi, the fusion of the cytoplasm of cells from two individuals; occurs as one stage of sexual reproduction, followed later by karyogamy.

plasmolysis (plaz-mol'-uh-sis) A phenomenon in walled cells in which the cytoplasm shrivels and the plasma membrane pulls away from the cell wall; occurs when the cell loses water to a hypertonic environment.

plastid One of a family of closely related organelles that includes chloroplasts, chromoplasts, and amyloplasts. Plastids are found in cells of photosynthetic eukaryotes.

plate tectonics The theory that the continents are part of great plates of Earth's crust that float on the hot, underlying portion of the mantle. Movements in the mantle cause the continents to move slowly over time.

platelet A pinched-off cytoplasmic fragment of a specialized bone marrow cell. Platelets circulate in the blood and are important in blood clotting.

pleiotropy (plī'-o-truh-pē) The ability of a single gene to have multiple effects.

pluripotent Describing a cell that can give rise to many, but not all, parts of an organism.

point mutation A change in a single nucleotide pair of a gene.

polar covalent bond A covalent bond between atoms that differ in electronegativity. The shared electrons are pulled closer to the more electronegative atom, making it slightly negative and the other atom slightly positive.

polar molecule A molecule (such as water) with an uneven distribution of charges in different regions of the molecule.

polarity A lack of symmetry; structural differences in opposite ends of an organism or structure, such as the root end and shoot end of a plant.

pollen grain In seed plants, a structure consisting of the male gametophyte enclosed within a pollen wall.

pollen tube A tube that forms after germination of the pollen grain and that functions in the delivery of sperm to the ovule.

pollination (pol'-uh-nā'-shun) The transfer of pollen to the part of a seed plant containing the ovules, a process required for fertilization.

poly-A tail A sequence of 50–250 adenine nucleotides added onto the 3' end of a pre-mRNA molecule.

polygamous Referring to a type of relationship in which an individual of one sex mates with several of the other.

polygenic inheritance (pol'-ē-jen'-ik) An additive effect of two or more genes on a single phenotypic character.

polymer (pol'-uh-mer) A long molecule consisting of many similar or identical monomers linked together by covalent bonds.

polymerase chain reaction (PCR) (puh-lim'-uh-rās) A technique for amplifying DNA *in vitro* by incubating it with specific primers, a heat-resistant DNA polymerase, and nucleotides.

polynucleotide (pol'-ē-nū'-klē-ō-tīd) A polymer consisting of many nucleotide monomers in a chain. The nucleotides can be those of DNA or RNA.

polyp The sessile variant of the cnidarian body plan. The alternate form is the medusa.

polypeptide (pol'-ē-pep'-tīd) A polymer of many amino acids linked together by peptide bonds.

polyphyletic (pol'-ē-fī-let'-ik) Pertaining to a group of taxa derived from two or more different ancestors.

polyploidy (pol'-ē-ploy'-dē) A chromosomal alteration in which the organism possesses more than two complete chromosome sets. It is the result of an accident of cell division.

polyribosome (polysome) (pol'-ē-rī'-buh-sōm') A group of several ribosomes attached to, and translating, the same messenger RNA molecule.

polysaccharide (pol'-ē-sak'-uh-rīd) A polymer of many monosaccharides, formed by dehydration reactions.

polytomy (puh-lit'-uh-mē) In a phylogenetic tree, a branch point from which more than two descendant taxa emerge. A polytomy indicates that the evolutionary relationships between the descendant taxa are not yet clear.

pons A portion of the brain that participates in certain automatic, homeostatic functions, such as regulating the breathing centers in the medulla.

population A group of individuals of the same species that live in the same area and interbreed, producing fertile offspring.

population dynamics The study of how complex interactions between biotic and abiotic factors influence variations in population size.

population ecology The study of populations in relation to their environment, including environmental influences on population density and distribution, age structure, and variations in population size.

positional information Molecular cues that control pattern formation in an animal or plant embryonic structure by indicating a cell's location relative to the organism's body axes. These cues elicit a response by genes that regulate development.

positive feedback A form of regulation in which an end product of a process speeds up that process; in physiology, a control mechanism in which a change in a variable triggers a response that reinforces or amplifies the change.

positive pressure breathing A breathing system in which air is forced into the lungs.

posterior Pertaining to the rear, or tail end, of a bilaterally symmetrical animal.

posterior pituitary An extension of the hypothalamus composed of nervous tissue that secretes oxytocin and antidiuretic hormone made in the hypothalamus; a temporary storage site for these hormones.

postzygotic barrier (pōst′-zī-got′-ik) A reproductive barrier that prevents hybrid zygotes produced by two different species from developing into viable, fertile adults.

potential energy The energy that matter possesses as a result of its location or spatial arrangement (structure).

predation An interaction between species in which one species, the predator, eats the other, the prey.

pregnancy The condition of carrying one or more embryos in the uterus.

prepuce (prē′-pyūs) A fold of skin covering the head of the clitoris or penis.

pressure potential (Ψ_P) A component of water potential that consists of the physical pressure on a solution, which can be positive, zero, or negative.

prezygotic barrier (prē′-zī-got′-ik) A reproductive barrier that impedes mating between species or hinders fertilization if interspecific mating is attempted.

primary cell wall In plants, a relatively thin and flexible layer that surrounds the plasma membrane of a young cell.

primary consumer An herbivore; an organism that eats plants or other autotrophs.

primary electron acceptor In the thylakoid membrane of a chloroplast or in the membrane of some prokaryotes, a specialized molecule that shares the reaction-center complex with a pair of chlorophyll *a* molecules and that accepts an electron from them.

primary growth Growth produced by apical meristems, lengthening stems and roots.

primary immune response The initial adaptive immune response to an antigen, which appears after a lag of about 10 to 17 days.

primary oocyte (ō′-uh-sīt) An oocyte prior to completion of meiosis I.

primary producer An autotroph, usually a photosynthetic organism. Collectively, autotrophs make up the trophic level of an ecosystem that ultimately supports all other levels.

primary production The amount of light energy converted to chemical energy (organic compounds) by the autotrophs in an ecosystem during a given time period.

primary structure The level of protein structure referring to the specific linear sequence of amino acids.

primary succession A type of ecological succession that occurs in an area where there were originally no organisms present and where soil has not yet formed.

primary transcript An initial RNA transcript from any gene; also called pre-mRNA when transcribed from a protein-coding gene.

primary visual cortex The destination in the occipital lobe of the cerebrum for most of the axons from the lateral geniculate nuclei.

primase An enzyme that joins RNA nucleotides to make a primer during DNA replication, using the parental DNA strand as a template.

primer A short stretch of RNA with a free 3′ end, bound by complementary base pairing to the template strand and elongated with DNA nucleotides during DNA replication.

primitive streak A thickening along the future anterior-posterior axis on the surface of an early avian or mammalian embryo, caused by a piling up of cells as they congregate at the midline before moving into the embryo.

prion An infectious agent that is a misfolded version of a normal cellular protein. Prions appear to increase in number by converting correctly folded versions of the protein to more prions.

problem solving The cognitive activity of devising a method to proceed from one state to another in the face of real or apparent obstacles.

producer An organism that produces organic compounds from CO_2 by harnessing light energy (in photosynthesis) or by oxidizing inorganic chemicals (in chemosynthetic reactions carried out by some prokaryotes).

product A material resulting from a chemical reaction.

production efficiency The percentage of energy stored in assimilated food that is not used for respiration or eliminated as waste.

progesterone A steroid hormone that prepares the uterus for pregnancy; the major progestin in mammals.

progestin Any steroid hormone with progesterone-like activity.

progymnosperm (prō′-jim′-nō-sperm) An extinct seedless vascular plant that may be ancestral to seed plants.

prokaryotic cell (prō′-kār′-ē-ot′-ik) A type of cell lacking a membrane-enclosed nucleus and membrane-enclosed organelles. Organisms with prokaryotic cells (bacteria and archaea) are called prokaryotes.

prolactin A hormone produced and secreted by the anterior pituitary with a great diversity of effects in different vertebrate species. In mammals, it stimulates growth of and milk production by the mammary glands.

proliferative phase That portion of the uterine (menstrual) cycle when the endometrium regenerates and thickens.

prometaphase The second stage of mitosis, in which the nuclear envelope fragments and the spindle microtubules attach to the kinetochores of the chromosomes.

promiscuous Referring to a type of relationship in which mating occurs with no strong pair-bonds or lasting relationships.

promoter A specific nucleotide sequence in the DNA of a gene that binds RNA polymerase, positioning it to start transcribing RNA at the appropriate place.

prophage (prō′-fāj) A phage genome that has been inserted into a specific site on a bacterial chromosome.

prophase The first stage of mitosis, in which the chromatin condenses into discrete chromosomes visible with a light microscope, the mitotic spindle begins to form, and the nucleolus disappears but the nucleus remains intact.

prostaglandin (pros′-tuh-glan′-din) One of a group of modified fatty acids secreted by virtually all tissues and performing a wide variety of functions as local regulators.

prostate gland (pros′-tāt) A gland in human males that secretes an acid-neutralizing component of semen.

protease An enzyme that digests proteins by hydrolysis.

proteasome A giant protein complex that recognizes and destroys proteins tagged for elimination by the small protein ubiquitin.

protein (prō′-tēn) A biologically functional molecule consisting of one or more polypeptides folded and coiled into a specific three-dimensional structure.

protein kinase An enzyme that transfers phosphate groups from ATP to a protein, thus phosphorylating the protein.

protein phosphatase An enzyme that removes phosphate groups from (dephosphorylates) proteins, often functioning to reverse the effect of a protein kinase.

proteoglycan (prō′-tē-ō-glī′-kan) A large molecule consisting of a small core protein with many carbohydrate chains attached, found in the extracellular matrix of animal cells. A proteoglycan may consist of up to 95% carbohydrate.

proteomics (prō′-tē-ō′-miks) The systematic study of the full protein sets (proteomes) encoded by genomes.

protist An informal term applied to any eukaryote that is not a plant, animal, or fungus. Most protists are unicellular, though some are colonial or multicellular.

protocell An abiotic precursor of a living cell that had a membrane-like structure and that maintained an internal chemistry different from that of its surroundings.

proton (prō′-ton) A subatomic particle with a single positive electrical charge, with a mass of about 1.7×10^{-24} g, found in the nucleus of an atom.

proton pump An active transport protein in a cell membrane that uses ATP to transport hydrogen ions out of a cell against their concentration gradient, generating a membrane potential in the process.

protonema (plural, **protonemata**) A mass of green, branched, one-cell-thick filaments produced by germinating moss spores.

protonephridium (prō′-tō-nuh-frid′-ē-uhm) (plural, **protonephridia**) An excretory system, such as the flame bulb system of flatworms, consisting of a network of tubules lacking internal openings.

proton-motive force The potential energy stored in the form of a proton electrochemical gradient, generated by the pumping of hydrogen ions (H^+) across a biological membrane during chemiosmosis.

proto-oncogene (prō′-tō-on′-kō-jēn) A normal cellular gene that has the potential to become an oncogene.

protoplast The living part of a plant cell, which also includes the plasma membrane.

protoplast fusion The fusing of two protoplasts from different plant species that would otherwise be reproductively incompatible.

protostome development In animals, a developmental mode distinguished by the development of the mouth from the blastopore; often also characterized by spiral cleavage and by the body cavity forming when solid masses of mesoderm split.

provirus A viral genome that is permanently inserted into a host genome.

proximal tubule In the vertebrate kidney, the portion of a nephron immediately downstream from Bowman's capsule that conveys and helps refine filtrate.

pseudocoelomate (sū′-dō-sē′-lō-māt) An animal whose body cavity is lined by tissue derived from mesoderm and endoderm.

pseudogene (sū′-dō-jēn) A DNA segment very similar to a real gene but which does not yield a functional product; a DNA segment that formerly functioned as a gene but has become inactivated in a particular species because of mutation.

pseudopodium (sū′-dō-pō′-dē-um) (plural, **pseudopodia**) A cellular extension of amoeboid cells used in moving and feeding.

pterophyte (ter′-uh-fīt) An informal name for a member of the phylum Pterophyta, which includes ferns, horsetails, and whisk ferns and their relatives.

pterosaur Winged reptile that lived during the Mesozoic era.

pulmocutaneous circuit A branch of the circulatory system in many amphibians that supplies the lungs and skin.

pulmonary circuit The branch of the circulatory system that supplies the lungs.

pulse The rhythmic bulging of the artery walls with each heartbeat.

punctuated equilibria In the fossil record, long periods of apparent stasis, in which a species undergoes little or no morphological change, interrupted by relatively brief periods of sudden change.

Punnett square A diagram used in the study of inheritance to show the predicted genotypic results of random fertilization in genetic crosses between individuals of known genotype.

pupil The opening in the iris, which admits light into the interior of the vertebrate eye. Muscles in the iris regulate its size.

purine (pyū′-rēn) One of two types of nitrogenous bases found in nucleotides, characterized by a six-membered ring fused to a five-membered ring. Adenine (A) and guanine (G) are purines.

pyrimidine (puh-rim′-uh-dēn) One of two types of nitrogenous bases found in nucleotides, characterized by a six-membered ring. Cytosine (C), thymine (T), and uracil (U) are pyrimidines.

quantitative character A heritable feature that varies continuously over a range rather than in an either-or fashion.

quaternary structure (kwot-er-nār-ē) The particular shape of a complex, aggregate protein, defined by the characteristic three-dimensional arrangement of its constituent subunits, each a polypeptide.

R plasmid A bacterial plasmid carrying genes that confer resistance to certain antibiotics.

radial cleavage A type of embryonic development in deuterostomes in which the planes of cell division that transform the zygote into a ball of cells are either parallel or perpendicular to the vertical axis of the embryo, thereby aligning tiers of cells one above the other.

radial symmetry Symmetry in which the body is shaped like a pie or barrel (lacking a left side and a right side) and can be divided into mirror-imaged halves by any plane through its central axis.

radiation The emission of electromagnetic waves by all objects warmer than absolute zero.

radicle An embryonic root of a plant.

radioactive isotope An isotope (an atomic form of a chemical element) that is unstable; the nucleus decays spontaneously, giving off detectable particles and energy.

radiolarian A protist, usually marine, with a shell generally made of silica and pseudopodia that radiate from the central body.

radiometric dating A method for determining the absolute age of rocks and fossils, based on the half-life of radioactive isotopes.

radula A straplike scraping organ used by many molluscs during feeding.

ras **gene** A gene that codes for Ras, a G protein that relays a growth signal from a growth factor receptor on the plasma membrane to a cascade of protein kinases, ultimately resulting in stimulation of the cell cycle.

ratite (rat′-īt) Member of the group of flightless birds.

ray-finned fish Member of the class Actinopterygii, aquatic osteichthyans with fins supported by long, flexible rays, including tuna, bass, and herring.

reabsorption In excretory systems, the recovery of solutes and water from filtrate.

reactant A starting material in a chemical reaction.

reaction-center complex A complex of proteins associated with a special pair of chlorophyll *a* molecules and a primary electron acceptor. Located centrally in a photosystem, this complex triggers the light reactions of photosynthesis. Excited by light energy, the pair of chlorophylls donates an electron to the primary electron acceptor, which passes an electron to an electron transport chain.

reading frame On an mRNA, the triplet grouping of ribonucleotides used by the translation machinery during polypeptide synthesis.

receptacle The base of a flower; the part of the stem that is the site of attachment of the floral organs.

receptor potential An initial response of a receptor cell to a stimulus, consisting of a change in voltage across the receptor membrane proportional to the stimulus strength.

receptor tyrosine kinase (RTK) A receptor protein spanning the plasma membrane, the cytoplasmic (intracellular) part of which can catalyze the transfer of a phosphate group from ATP to a tyrosine on another protein. Receptor tyrosine kinases often respond to the binding of a signaling molecule by dimerizing and then phosphorylating a tyrosine on the cytoplasmic portion of the other receptor in the dimer. The phosphorylated tyrosines on the receptors then activate other signal transduction proteins within the cell.

receptor-mediated endocytosis (en′-dō-sī-tō′-sis) The movement of specific molecules into a cell by the inward budding of vesicles containing proteins with receptor sites specific to the molecules being taken in; enables a cell to acquire bulk quantities of specific substances.

recessive allele An allele whose phenotypic effect is not observed in a heterozygote.

reciprocal altruism Altruistic behavior between unrelated individuals, whereby the altruistic individual benefits in the future when the beneficiary reciprocates.

recombinant chromosome A chromosome created when crossing over combines DNA from two parents into a single chromosome.

recombinant DNA A DNA molecule made *in vitro* with segments from different sources.

recombinant type (recombinant) An offspring whose phenotype differs from that of the true-breeding P generation parents; also refers to the phenotype itself.

rectum The terminal portion of the large intestine, where the feces are stored prior to elimination.

red alga A photosynthetic protist, named for its color, which results from a red pigment that masks the green of chlorophyll. Most red algae are multicellular and marine.

redox reaction (rē′-doks) A chemical reaction involving the complete or partial transfer of one or more electrons from one reactant to another; short for **red**uction-**ox**idation reaction.

reducing agent The electron donor in a redox reaction.

reduction The complete or partial addition of electrons to a substance involved in a redox reaction.

reflex An automatic reaction to a stimulus, mediated by the spinal cord or lower brain.

refractory period (rē-frakt′-ōr-ē) The short time immediately after an action potential in which the neuron cannot respond to another stimulus, owing to the inactivation of voltage-gated sodium channels.

regulator An animal for which mechanisms of homeostasis moderate internal changes in a particular variable in the face of external fluctuation of that variable.

regulatory gene A gene that codes for a protein, such as a repressor, that controls the transcription of another gene or group of genes.

reinforcement In evolutionary biology, a process in which a process in which natural selection strengthens prezygotic barriers to reproduction, thus reducing the chances of hybrid formation. Such a process is likely to occur only if hybrid offspring are less fit than members of the parent species.

relative abundance The proportional abundance of different species in a community.

relative fitness The contribution an individual makes to the gene pool of the next generation, relative to the contributions of other individuals in the population.

renal cortex The outer portion of the vertebrate kidney.

renal medulla The inner portion of the vertebrate kidney, beneath the renal cortex.

renal pelvis The funnel-shaped chamber that receives processed filtrate from the vertebrate kidney's collecting ducts and is drained by the ureter.

renin-angiotensin-aldosterone system (RAAS) A hormone cascade pathway that helps regulate blood pressure and blood volume.

repetitive DNA Nucleotide sequences, usually noncoding, that are present in many copies in a eukaryotic genome. The repeated units may be short and arranged tandemly (in series) or long and dispersed in the genome.

replication fork A Y-shaped region on a replicating DNA molecule where the parental strands are being unwound and new strands are being synthesized.

repressor A protein that inhibits gene transcription. In prokaryotes, repressors bind to the DNA in or near the promoter. In eukaryotes, repressors may bind to control elements within enhancers, to activators, or to other proteins in a way that blocks activators from binding to DNA.

reproductive isolation The existence of biological factors (barriers) that impede members of two species from producing viable, fertile offspring.

reproductive table An age-specific summary of the reproductive rates in a population.

reptile Member of the clade of amniotes that includes tuataras, lizards, snakes, turtles, crocodilians, and birds.

residual volume The amount of air that remains in the lungs after forceful exhalation.

resource partitioning The division of environmental resources by coexisting species such that the niche of each species differs by one or more significant factors from the niches of all coexisting species.

respiratory pigment A protein that transports oxygen in blood or hemolymph.

response (1) In cellular communication, the change in a specific cellular activity brought about by a transduced signal from outside the cell. (2) In feedback regulation, a physiological activity triggered by a change in a variable.

resting potential The membrane potential characteristic of a nonconducting excitable cell, with the inside of the cell more negative than the outside.

restriction enzyme An endonuclease (type of enzyme) that recognizes and cuts DNA molecules foreign to a bacterium (such as phage genomes). The enzyme cuts at specific nucleotide sequences (restriction sites).

restriction fragment A DNA segment that results from the cutting of DNA by a restriction enzyme.

restriction fragment length polymorphism (RFLP) A single nucleotide polymorphism (SNP) that exists in the restriction site for a particular enzyme, thus making the site unrecognizable by that enzyme and changing the lengths of the restriction fragments formed by digestion with that enzyme. A RFLP can be in coding or noncoding DNA.

restriction site A specific sequence on a DNA strand that is recognized and cut by a restriction enzyme.

reticular formation (re-tik'-yū-ler) A diffuse network of neurons in the core of the brainstem that filters information traveling to the cerebral cortex.

retina (ret'-i-nuh) The innermost layer of the vertebrate eye, containing photoreceptor cells (rods and cones) and neurons; transmits images formed by the lens to the brain via the optic nerve.

retinal The light-absorbing pigment in rods and cones of the vertebrate eye.

retrotransposon (re'-trō-trans-pō'-zon) A transposable element that moves within a genome by means of an RNA intermediate, a transcript of the retrotransposon DNA.

retrovirus (re'-trō-vī'-rus) An RNA virus that replicates by transcribing its RNA into DNA and then inserting the DNA into a cellular chromosome; an important class of cancer-causing viruses.

reverse transcriptase (tran-skrip'-tās) An enzyme encoded by certain viruses (retroviruses) that uses RNA as a template for DNA synthesis.

reverse transcriptase–polymerase chain reaction (RT-PCR) A technique for determining expression of a particular gene. It uses reverse transcriptase and DNA polymerase to synthesize cDNA from all the mRNA in a sample and then subjects the cDNA to PCR amplification using primers specific for the gene of interest.

Rhizaria (rī-za'-rē-uh) One of five supergroups of eukaryotes proposed in a current hypothesis of the evolutionary history of eukaryotes; a morphologically diverse protist clade that is defined by DNA similarities. *See also* Excavata, Chromalveolata, Archaeplastida, and Unikonta.

rhizobacterium A soil bacterium whose population size is much enhanced in the rhizosphere, the soil region close to a plant's roots.

rhizoid (rī'-zoyd) A long, tubular single cell or filament of cells that anchors bryophytes to the ground. Unlike roots, rhizoids are not composed of tissues, lack specialized conducting cells, and do not play a primary role in water and mineral absorption.

rhizosphere The soil region close to plant roots and characterized by a high level of microbiological activity.

rhodopsin (rō-dop'-sin) A visual pigment consisting of retinal and opsin. Upon absorbing light, the retinal changes shape and dissociates from the opsin.

rhythm method A form of contraception that relies on refraining from sexual intercourse when conception is most likely to occur; also called natural family planning.

ribonucleic acid (RNA) (rī'-bō-nū-klā'-ik) A type of nucleic acid consisting of a polynucleotide made up of nucleotide monomers with a ribose sugar and the nitrogenous bases adenine (A), cytosine (C), guanine (G), and uracil (U); usually single-stranded; functions in protein synthesis, gene regulation, and as the genome of some viruses.

ribose The sugar component of RNA nucleotides.

ribosomal RNA (rRNA) (rī'-buh-sō'-mul) RNA molecules that, together with proteins, make up ribosomes; the most abundant type of RNA.

ribosome (rī'-buh-sōm') A complex of rRNA and protein molecules that functions as a site of protein synthesis in the cytoplasm; consists of a large and a small subunit. In eukaryotic cells, each subunit is assembled in the nucleolus. *See also* nucleolus.

ribozyme (rī'-buh-zīm) An RNA molecule that functions as an enzyme, such as an intron that catalyzes its own removal during RNA splicing.

RNA interference (RNAi) A technique used to silence the expression of selected genes. RNAi uses synthetic double-stranded RNA molecules that match the sequence of a particular gene to trigger the breakdown of the gene's messenger RNA.

RNA polymerase An enzyme that links ribonucleotides into a growing RNA chain during transcription, based on complementary binding to nucleotides on a DNA template strand.

RNA processing Modification of RNA primary transcripts, including splicing out of introns, joining together of exons, and alteration of the 5' and 3' ends.

RNA splicing After synthesis of a eukaryotic primary RNA transcript, the removal of portions of the transcript (introns) that will not be included in the mRNA and the joining together of the remaining portions (exons).

rod A rodlike cell in the retina of the vertebrate eye, sensitive to low light intensity.

root An organ in vascular plants that anchors the plant and enables it to absorb water and minerals from the soil.

root cap A cone of cells at the tip of a plant root that protects the apical meristem.

root hair A tiny extension of a root epidermal cell, growing just behind the root tip and increasing surface area for absorption of water and minerals.

root pressure Pressure exerted in the roots of plants as the result of osmosis, causing exudation from cut stems and guttation of water from leaves.

root system All of a plant's roots, which anchor it in the soil, absorb and transport minerals and water, and store food.

rooted Describing a phylogenetic tree that contains a branch point (often, the one farthest to the left) representing the most recent common ancestor of all taxa in the tree.

rough ER That portion of the endoplasmic reticulum with ribosomes attached.

round window In the mammalian ear, the point of contact where vibrations of the stapes create a traveling series of pressure waves in the fluid of the cochlea.

r-selection Selection for life history traits that maximize reproductive success in uncrowded environments; also called density-independent selection.

rubisco (rū-bis'-kō) Ribulose bisphosphate (RuBP) carboxylase, the enzyme that catalyzes the first step of the Calvin cycle (the addition of CO_2 to RuBP).

ruminant (rū'-muh-nent) An animal, such as a cow or a sheep, with multiple stomach compartments specialized for an herbivorous diet.

S phase The synthesis phase of the cell cycle; the portion of interphase during which DNA is replicated.

saccule In the vertebrate ear, a chamber in the vestibule behind the oval window that participates in the sense of balance.

salicylic acid (sal'-i-sil'-ik) A signaling molecule in plants that may be partially responsible for activating systemic acquired resistance to pathogens.

salivary gland A gland associated with the oral cavity that secretes substances that lubricate food and begin the process of chemical digestion.

salt A compound resulting from the formation of an ionic bond; also called an ionic compound.

saltatory conduction (sol'-tuh-tōr'-ē) Rapid transmission of a nerve impulse along an axon, resulting from the action potential jumping from one node of Ranvier to another, skipping the myelin-sheathed regions of membrane.

sarcomere (sar'-kō-mēr) The fundamental, repeating unit of striated muscle, delimited by the Z lines.

sarcoplasmic reticulum (SR) (sar'-kō-plaz'-mik ruh-tik'-yū-lum) A specialized endoplasmic reticulum that regulates the calcium concentration in the cytosol of muscle cells.

saturated fatty acid A fatty acid in which all carbons in the hydrocarbon tail are connected by single bonds, thus maximizing the number of hydrogen atoms that are attached to the carbon skeleton.

savanna A tropical grassland biome with scattered individual trees and large herbivores and maintained by occasional fires and drought.

scaffolding protein A type of large relay protein to which several other relay proteins are simultaneously attached, increasing the efficiency of signal transduction.

scanning electron microscope (SEM) A microscope that uses an electron beam to scan the surface of a sample, coated with metal atoms, to study details of its topography.

schizophrenia (skit'-suh-frē'-nē-uh) A severe mental disturbance characterized by psychotic episodes in which patients have a distorted perception of reality.

Schwann cell A type of glial cell that forms insulating myelin sheaths around the axons of neurons in the peripheral nervous system.

science An approach to understanding the natural world.

scion (sī'-un) The twig grafted onto the stock when making a graft.

sclereid (sklār'-ē-id) A short, irregular sclerenchyma cell in nutshells and seed coats. Sclereids are scattered throughout the parenchyma of some plants.

sclerenchyma cell (skluh-ren'-kim-uh) A rigid, supportive plant cell type usually lacking a protoplast and possessing thick secondary walls strengthened by lignin at maturity.

scrotum A pouch of skin outside the abdomen that houses the testes; functions in maintaining the testes at the lower temperature required for spermatogenesis.

second law of thermodynamics The principle stating that every energy transfer or transformation increases the entropy of the universe. Usable forms of energy are at least partly converted to heat.

second messenger A small, nonprotein, water-soluble molecule or ion, such as a calcium ion (Ca^{2+}) or cyclic AMP, that relays a signal to a cell's interior in response to a signaling molecule bound by a signal receptor protein.

secondary cell wall In plant cells, a strong and durable matrix that is often deposited in several laminated layers around the plasma membrane and provides protection and support.

secondary consumer A carnivore that eats herbivores.

secondary endosymbiosis A process in eukaryotic evolution in which a heterotrophic eukaryotic cell engulfed a photosynthetic eukaryotic cell, which survived in a symbiotic relationship inside the heterotrophic cell.

secondary growth Growth produced by lateral meristems, thickening the roots and shoots of woody plants.

secondary immune response The adaptive immune response elicited on second or subsequent exposures to a particular antigen. The secondary immune response is more rapid, of greater magnitude, and of longer duration than the primary immune response.

secondary oocyte (ō'-uh-sīt) An oocyte that has completed the first of the two meiotic divisions.

secondary production The amount of chemical energy in consumers' food that is converted to their own new biomass during a given time period.

secondary structure Regions of repetitive coiling or folding of the polypeptide backbone of a protein due to hydrogen bonding between constituents of the backbone (not the side chains).

secondary succession A type of succession that occurs where an existing community has been cleared by some disturbance that leaves the soil or substrate intact.

secretion (1) The discharge of molecules synthesized by a cell. (2) The discharge of wastes from the body fluid into the filtrate.

secretory phase That portion of the uterine (menstrual) cycle when the endometrium continues to thicken, becomes more vascularized, and develops glands that secrete a fluid rich in glycogen.

seed An adaptation of some terrestrial plants consisting of an embryo packaged along with a store of food within a protective coat.

seed coat A tough outer covering of a seed, formed from the outer coat of an ovule. In a flowering plant, the seed coat encloses and protects the embryo and endosperm.

seedless vascular plant An informal name for a plant that has vascular tissue but lacks seeds. Seedless vascular plants form a paraphyletic group that includes the phyla Lycophyta (club mosses and their relatives) and Pterophyta (ferns and their relatives).

selective permeability A property of biological membranes that allows them to regulate the passage of substances across them.

self-incompatibility The ability of a seed plant to reject its own pollen and sometimes the pollen of closely related individuals.

semelparity Reproduction in which an organism produces all of its offspring in a single event; also known as big-bang reproduction.

semen (sē'-mun) The fluid that is ejaculated by the male during orgasm; contains sperm and secretions from several glands of the male reproductive tract.

semicircular canals A three-part chamber of the inner ear that functions in maintaining equilibrium.

semiconservative model Type of DNA replication in which the replicated double helix consists of one old strand, derived from the parental molecule, and one newly made strand.

semilunar valve A valve located at each exit of the heart, where the aorta leaves the left ventricle and the pulmonary artery leaves the right ventricle.

seminal vesicle (sem'-i-nul ves'-i-kul) A gland in males that secretes a fluid component of semen that lubricates and nourishes sperm.

seminiferous tubule (sem'-i-nif'-er-us) A highly coiled tube in the testis in which sperm are produced.

senescence (se-nes'-ens) The growth phase in a plant or plant part (as a leaf) from full maturity to death.

sensitive period A limited phase in an animal's development when learning of particular behaviors can take place; also called a critical period.

sensor In homeostasis, a receptor that detects a stimulus.

sensory adaptation The tendency of sensory neurons to become less sensitive when they are stimulated repeatedly.

sensory neuron A nerve cell that receives information from the internal or external environment and transmits signals to the central nervous system.

sensory reception The detection of a stimulus by sensory cells.

sensory receptor An organ, cell, or structure within a cell that responds to specific stimuli from an organism's external or internal environment.

sensory transduction The conversion of stimulus energy to a change in the membrane potential of a sensory receptor cell.

sepal (sē′-pul) A modified leaf in angiosperms that helps enclose and protect a flower bud before it opens.

septum (plural, **septa**) One of the cross-walls that divide a fungal hypha into cells. Septa generally have pores large enough to allow ribosomes, mitochondria, and even nuclei to flow from cell to cell.

serial endosymbiosis A hypothesis for the origin of eukaryotes consisting of a sequence of endosymbiotic events in which mitochondria, chloroplasts, and perhaps other cellular structures were derived from small prokaryotes that had been engulfed by larger cells.

serotonin (ser′-uh-tō′-nin) A neurotransmitter, synthesized from the amino acid tryptophan, that functions in the central nervous system.

set point In homeostasis in animals, a value maintained for a particular variable, such as body temperature or solute concentration.

seta (sē′-tuh) (plural, **setae**) The elongated stalk of a bryophyte sporophyte.

sex chromosome A chromosome responsible for determining the sex of an individual.

sex-linked gene A gene located on either sex chromosome. Most sex-linked genes are on the X chromosome and show distinctive patterns of inheritance; there are very few genes on the Y chromosome.

sexual dimorphism (dī-mōr′-fizm) Differences between the secondary sex characteristics of males and females.

sexual reproduction A type of reproduction in which two parents give rise to offspring that have unique combinations of genes inherited from both parents via the gametes.

sexual selection A form of selection in which individuals with certain inherited characteristics are more likely than other individuals to obtain mates.

Shannon diversity An index of community diversity symbolized by H and represented by the equation $H = -(p_A \ln p_A + p_B \ln p_B + p_C \ln p_C + \ldots)$, where A, B, C . . . are species, p is the relative abundance of each species, and ln is the natural logarithm.

shared ancestral character A character, shared by members of a particular clade, that originated in an ancestor that is not a member of that clade.

shared derived character An evolutionary novelty that is unique to a particular clade.

shoot system The aerial portion of a plant body, consisting of stems, leaves, and (in angiosperms) flowers.

short tandem repeat (STR) Simple sequence DNA containing multiple tandemly repeated units of two to five nucleotides. Variations in STRs act as genetic markers in STR analysis, used to prepare genetic profiles.

short-day plant A plant that flowers (usually in late summer, fall, or winter) only when the light period is shorter than a critical length.

short-term memory The ability to hold information, anticipations, or goals for a time and then release them if they become irrelevant.

sickle-cell disease A recessively inherited human blood disorder in which a single nucleotide change in the β-globin gene causes hemoglobin to aggregate, changing red blood cell shape and causing multiple symptoms in afflicted individuals.

sieve plate An end wall in a sieve-tube element, which facilitates the flow of phloem sap in angiosperm sieve tubes.

sieve-tube element A living cell that conducts sugars and other organic nutrients in the phloem of angiosperms; also called a sieve-tube member. Connected end to end, they form sieve tubes.

sign stimulus An external sensory cue that triggers a fixed action pattern by an animal.

signal In animal behavior, transmission of a stimulus from one animal to another. The term is also used in the context of communication in other kinds of organisms and in cell-to-cell communication in all multicellular organisms.

signal peptide A sequence of about 20 amino acids at or near the leading (amino) end of a polypeptide that targets it to the endoplasmic reticulum or other organelles in a eukaryotic cell.

signal transduction The linkage of a mechanical, chemical, or electromagnetic stimulus to a specific cellular response.

signal transduction pathway A series of steps linking a mechanical, chemical, or electrical stimulus to a specific cellular response.

signal-recognition particle (SRP) A protein-RNA complex that recognizes a signal peptide as it emerges from a ribosome and helps direct the ribosome to the endoplasmic reticulum (ER) by binding to a receptor protein on the ER.

silent mutation A nucleotide-pair substitution that has no observable effect on the phenotype; for example, within a gene, a mutation that results in a codon that codes for the same amino acid.

simple fruit A fruit derived from a single carpel or several fused carpels.

simple sequence DNA A DNA sequence that contains many copies of tandemly repeated short sequences.

single bond A single covalent bond; the sharing of a pair of valence electrons by two atoms.

single circulation A circulatory system consisting of a single pump and circuit, in which blood passes from the sites of gas exchange to the rest of the body before returning to the heart.

single nucleotide polymorphism (SNP) A single base-pair site in a genome where nucleotide variation is found in at least 1% of the population.

single-lens eye The camera-like eye found in some jellies, polychaete worms, spiders, and many molluscs.

single-strand binding protein A protein that binds to the unpaired DNA strands during DNA replication, stabilizing them and holding them apart while they serve as templates for the synthesis of complementary strands of DNA.

sinoatrial (SA) node A region in the right atrium of the heart that sets the rate and timing at which all cardiac muscle cells contract; the pacemaker.

sister chromatids Two copies of a duplicated chromosome attached to each other by proteins at the centromere and, sometimes, along the arms. While joined, two sister chromatids make up one chromosome. Chromatids are eventually separated during mitosis or meiosis II.

sister taxa Groups of organisms that share an immediate common ancestor and hence are each other's closest relatives.

skeletal muscle A type of striated muscle that is generally responsible for the voluntary movements of the body.

sliding-filament model The idea that muscle contraction is based on the movement of thin (actin) filaments along thick (myosin) filaments, shortening the sarcomere, the basic unit of muscle organization.

slow block to polyspermy The formation of the fertilization envelope and other changes in an egg's surface that prevent fusion of the egg with more than one sperm. The slow block begins about 1 minute after fertilization.

slow-twitch fiber A muscle fiber that can sustain long contractions.

small interfering RNA (siRNA) One of multiple small, single-stranded RNA molecules generated by cellular machinery from a long, linear, double-stranded RNA molecule. The siRNA associates with one or more proteins in a complex that can degrade or prevent translation of an mRNA with a complementary sequence. In some cases, siRNA can also block transcription by promoting chromatin modification.

small intestine The longest section of the alimentary canal, so named because of its small diameter compared with that of the large intestine; the principal site of the enzymatic hydrolysis of food macromolecules and the absorption of nutrients.

smooth ER That portion of the endoplasmic reticulum that is free of ribosomes.

smooth muscle A type of muscle lacking the striations of skeletal and cardiac muscle because of the uniform distribution of myosin filaments in the cells; responsible for involuntary body activities.

social learning Modification of behavior through the observation of other individuals.

sociobiology The study of social behavior based on evolutionary theory.

sodium-potassium pump A transport protein in the plasma membrane of animal cells that actively transports sodium out of the cell and potassium into the cell.

soil horizon A soil layer with physical characteristics that differ from those of the layers above or beneath.

solute (sol'-yūt) A substance that is dissolved in a solution.

solute potential (Ψ_S) A component of water potential that is proportional to the molarity of a solution and that measures the effect of solutes on the direction of water movement; also called osmotic potential, it can be either zero or negative.

solution A liquid that is a homogeneous mixture of two or more substances.

solvent The dissolving agent of a solution. Water is the most versatile solvent known.

somatic cell (sō-mat'-ik) Any cell in a multicellular organism except a sperm or egg or their precursors.

somite One of a series of blocks of mesoderm that exist in pairs just lateral to the notochord in a vertebrate embryo.

soredium (plural, **soredia**) In lichens, a small cluster of fungal hyphae with embedded algae.

sorus (plural, **sori**) A cluster of sporangia on a fern sporophyll. Sori may be arranged in various patterns, such as parallel lines or dots, which are useful in fern identification.

Southern blotting A technique that enables specific nucleotide sequences to be detected in samples of DNA. It involves gel electrophoresis of DNA molecules and their transfer to a membrane (blotting), followed by nucleic acid hybridization with a labeled probe.

spatial learning The establishment of a memory that reflects the environment's spatial structure.

spatial summation A phenomenon of neural integration in which the membrane potential of the postsynaptic cell is determined by the combined effect of EPSPs or IPSPs produced nearly simultaneously by different synapses.

speciation (spē'-sē-ā'-shun) An evolutionary process in which one species splits into two or more species.

species (spē'-sēz) A population or group of populations whose members have the potential to interbreed in nature and produce viable, fertile offspring, but do not produce viable, fertile offspring with members of other such groups.

species diversity The number and relative abundance of species in a biological community.

species richness The number of species in a biological community.

species-area curve The biodiversity pattern that shows that the larger the geographic area of a community is, the more species it has.

specific heat The amount of heat that must be absorbed or lost for 1 g of a substance to change its temperature by 1°C.

spectrophotometer An instrument that measures the proportions of light of different wavelengths absorbed and transmitted by a pigment solution.

sperm The male gamete.

spermatheca (sper'-muh-thē'-kuh) In many insects, a sac in the female reproductive system where sperm are stored.

spermatogenesis The continuous and prolific production of mature sperm cells in the testis.

spermatogonium (plural, **spermatogonia**) A cell that divides mitotically to form spermatocytes.

sphincter (sfink'-ter) A ringlike band of muscle fibers that controls the size of an opening in the body, such as the passage between the esophagus and the stomach.

spiral cleavage A type of embryonic development in protostomes in which the planes of cell division that transform the zygote into a ball of cells are diagonal to the vertical axis of the embryo. As a result, the cells of each tier sit in the grooves between cells of adjacent tiers.

spliceosome (splī'-sō-sōm) A large complex made up of proteins and RNA molecules that splices RNA by interacting with the ends of an RNA intron, releasing the intron and joining the two adjacent exons.

spongocoel (spon'-jō-sēl) The central cavity of a sponge.

spontaneous process A process that occurs without an overall input of energy; a process that is energetically favorable.

sporangium (spōr-an'-jē-um) (plural, **sporangia**) A multicellular organ in fungi and plants in which meiosis occurs and haploid cells develop.

spore (1) In the life cycle of a plant or alga undergoing alternation of generations, a haploid cell produced in the sporophyte by meiosis. A spore can divide by mitosis to develop into a multicellular haploid individual, the gametophyte, without fusing with another cell. (2) In fungi, a haploid cell, produced either sexually or asexually, that produces a mycelium after germination.

sporocyte A diploid cell, also known as a spore mother cell, that undergoes meiosis and generates haploid spores.

sporophyll (spō'-ruh-fil) A modified leaf that bears sporangia and hence is specialized for reproduction.

sporophyte (spō-ruh-fīt') In organisms (plants and some algae) that have alternation of generations, the multicellular diploid form that results from the union of gametes. The sporophyte produces haploid spores by meiosis that develop into gametophytes.

sporopollenin (spōr-uh-pol'-eh-nin) A durable polymer that covers exposed zygotes of charophyte algae and forms the walls of plant spores, preventing them from drying out.

stabilizing selection Natural selection in which intermediate phenotypes survive or reproduce more successfully than do extreme phenotypes.

stamen (stā'-men) The pollen-producing reproductive organ of a flower, consisting of an anther and a filament.

standard metabolic rate (SMR) Metabolic rate of a resting, fasting, and nonstressed ectotherm at a particular temperature.

starch A storage polysaccharide in plants, consisting entirely of glucose monomers joined by α glycosidic linkages.

start point In transcription, the nucleotide position on the promoter where RNA polymerase begins synthesis of RNA.

statocyst (stat'-uh-sist') A type of mechanoreceptor that functions in equilibrium in invertebrates by use of statoliths, which stimulate hair cells in relation to gravity.

statolith (stat'-uh-lith') (1) In plants, a specialized plastid that contains dense starch grains and may play a role in detecting gravity. (2) In invertebrates, a dense particle that settles in response to gravity and is found in sensory organs that function in equilibrium.

stele (stēl) The vascular tissue of a stem or root.

stem A vascular plant organ consisting of an alternating system of nodes and internodes that support the leaves and reproductive structures.

stem cell Any relatively unspecialized cell that can produce, during a single division, one identical daughter cell and one more specialized daughter cell that can undergo further differentiation.

steroid A type of lipid characterized by a carbon skeleton consisting of four fused rings with various chemical groups attached.

sticky end A single-stranded end of a double-stranded restriction fragment.

stigma (plural, **stigmata**) The sticky part of a flower's carpel, which receives pollen grains.

stimulus In feedback regulation, a fluctuation in a variable that triggers a response.

stipe A stemlike structure of a seaweed.

stock The plant that provides the root system when making a graft.

stoma (stō'-muh) (plural, **stomata**) A microscopic pore surrounded by guard cells in the epidermis of leaves and stems that allows gas exchange between the environment and the interior of the plant.

stomach An organ of the digestive system that stores food and performs preliminary steps of digestion.

stramenopile A protist in which a "hairy" flagellum (one covered with fine, hairlike projections) is paired with a shorter, smooth flagellum.

stratum (strah'-tum) (plural, **strata**) A rock layer formed when new layers of sediment cover older ones and compress them.

striated muscle Muscle in which the regular arrangement of filaments creates a pattern of light and dark bands.

strigolactones A class of plant hormone that inhibits shoot branching, triggers the germination of parasitic plant seeds, and stimulates the association of plant roots with mycorrhizal fungi.

strobilus (strō-bī'-lus) (plural, **strobili**) The technical term for a cluster of sporophylls known commonly as a cone, found in most gymnosperms and some seedless vascular plants.

stroke The death of nervous tissue in the brain, usually resulting from rupture or blockage of arteries in the head.

stroke volume The volume of blood pumped by a heart ventricle in a single contraction.

stroma (strō'-muh) The dense fluid within the chloroplast surrounding the thylakoid membrane and containing ribosomes and DNA; involved in the synthesis of organic molecules from carbon dioxide and water.

stromatolite Layered rock that results from the activities of prokaryotes that bind thin films of sediment together.

structural isomer One of several compounds that have the same molecular formula but differ in the covalent arrangements of their atoms.

style The stalk of a flower's carpel, with the ovary at the base and the stigma at the top.

substrate The reactant on which an enzyme works.

substrate feeder An animal that lives in or on its food source, eating its way through the food.

substrate-level phosphorylation The enzyme-catalyzed formation of ATP by direct transfer of a phosphate group to ADP from an intermediate substrate in catabolism.

sugar sink A plant organ that is a net consumer or storer of sugar. Growing roots, shoot tips, stems, and fruits are examples of sugar sinks supplied by phloem.

sugar source A plant organ in which sugar is being produced by either photosynthesis or the breakdown of starch. Mature leaves are the primary sugar sources of plants.

sulfhydryl group A chemical group consisting of a sulfur atom bonded to a hydrogen atom.

suprachiasmatic nucleus (SCN) A group of neurons in the hypothalamus of mammals that functions as a biological clock.

surface tension A measure of how difficult it is to stretch or break the surface of a liquid. Water has a high surface tension because of the hydrogen bonding of surface molecules.

surfactant A substance secreted by alveoli that decreases surface tension in the fluid that coats the alveoli.

survivorship curve A plot of the number of members of a cohort that are still alive at each age; one way to represent age-specific mortality.

suspension feeder An aquatic animal, such as a sponge, clam, or baleen whale, that feeds by sifting small organisms or food particles from the water.

sustainable agriculture Long-term productive farming methods that are environmentally safe.

sustainable development Development that meets the needs of people today without limiting the ability of future generations to meet their needs.

swim bladder In aquatic osteichthyans, an air sac that enables the animal to control its buoyancy in the water.

symbiont (sim'-bē-ont) The smaller participant in a symbiotic relationship, living in or on the host.

symbiosis An ecological relationship between organisms of two different species that live together in direct and intimate contact.

sympathetic division One of three divisions of the autonomic nervous system; generally increases energy expenditure and prepares the body for action.

sympatric speciation (sim-pat'-rik) The formation of new species in populations that live in the same geographic area.

symplast In plants, the continuum of cytoplasm connected by plasmodesmata between cells.

synapse (sin'-aps) The junction where a neuron communicates with another cell across a narrow gap via a neurotransmitter or an electrical coupling.

synapsid Member of an amniote clade distinguished by a single hole on each side of the skull. Synapsids include the mammals.

synapsis (si-nap'-sis) The pairing and physical connection of duplicated homologous chromosomes during prophase I of meiosis.

systematics A scientific discipline focused on classifying organisms and determining their evolutionary relationships.

systemic acquired resistance A defensive response in infected plants that helps protect healthy tissue from pathogenic invasion.

systemic circuit The branch of the circulatory system that supplies oxygenated blood to and carries deoxygenated blood away from organs and tissues throughout the body.

systems biology An approach to studying biology that aims to model the dynamic behavior of whole biological systems based on a study of the interactions among the system's parts.

systole (sis'-tō-lē) The stage of the cardiac cycle in which a heart chamber contracts and pumps blood.

systolic pressure Blood pressure in the arteries during contraction of the ventricles.

T cells The class of lymphocytes that mature in the thymus; they include both effector cells for the cell-mediated immune response and helper cells required for both branches of adaptive immunity.

taproot A main vertical root that develops from an embryonic root and gives rise to lateral (branch) roots.

tastant Any chemical that stimulates the sensory receptors in a taste bud.

taste bud A collection of modified epithelial cells on the tongue or in the mouth that are receptors for taste in mammals.

TATA box A DNA sequence in eukaryotic promoters crucial in forming the transcription initiation complex.

taxis (tak'-sis) An oriented movement toward or away from a stimulus.

taxon (plural, **taxa**) A named taxonomic unit at any given level of classification.

taxonomy (tak-son'-uh-mē) A scientific discipline concerned with naming and classifying the diverse forms of life.

Tay-Sachs disease A human genetic disease caused by a recessive allele for a dysfunctional enzyme, leading to accumulation of certain lipids in the brain. Seizures, blindness, and degeneration of motor and mental performance usually become manifest a few months after birth, followed by death within a few years.

technology The application of scientific knowledge for a specific purpose, often involving industry or commerce but also including uses in basic research.

telomerase An enzyme that catalyzes the lengthening of telomeres in eukaryotic germ cells.

telomere (tel'-uh-mēr) The tandemly repetitive DNA at the end of a eukaryotic chromosome's DNA molecule. Telomeres protect the organism's genes from being eroded during successive rounds of replication. See also repetitive DNA.

telophase The fifth and final stage of mitosis, in which daughter nuclei are forming and cytokinesis has typically begun.

temperate broadleaf forest A biome located throughout midlatitude regions where there is sufficient moisture to support the growth of large, broadleaf deciduous trees.

temperate grassland A terrestrial biome that exists at midlatitude regions and is dominated by grasses and forbs.

temperate phage A phage that is capable of replicating by either a lytic or lysogenic cycle.

temperature A measure of the intensity of heat in degrees, reflecting the average kinetic energy of the molecules.

template strand The DNA strand that provides the pattern, or template, for ordering, by complementary base pairing, the sequence of nucleotides in an RNA transcript.

temporal summation A phenomenon of neural integration in which the membrane potential of the postsynaptic cell in a chemical synapse is determined by the combined effect of EPSPs or IPSPs produced in rapid succession.

tendon A fibrous connective tissue that attaches muscle to bone.

terminator In bacteria, a sequence of nucleotides in DNA that marks the end of a gene and signals RNA polymerase to release the newly made RNA molecule and detach from the DNA.

territoriality A behavior in which an animal defends a bounded physical space against encroachment by other individuals, usually of its own species.

tertiary consumer (ter-shē-ār'-ē) A carnivore that eats other carnivores.

tertiary structure The overall shape of a protein molecule due to interactions of amino acid side chains, including hydrophobic interactions, ionic bonds, hydrogen bonds, and disulfide bridges.

testcross Breeding an organism of unknown genotype with a homozygous recessive individual to determine the unknown genotype. The ratio of phenotypes in the offspring reveals the unknown genotype.

testis (plural, **testes**) The male reproductive organ, or gonad, in which sperm and reproductive hormones are produced.

testosterone A steroid hormone required for development of the male reproductive system, spermatogenesis, and male secondary sex characteristics; the major androgen in mammals.

tetanus (tet'-uh-nus) The maximal, sustained contraction of a skeletal muscle, caused by a very high frequency of action potentials elicited by continual stimulation.

tetrapod A vertebrate clade whose members have limbs with digits. Tetrapods include mammals, amphibians, and birds and other reptiles.

thalamus (thal'-uh-mus) An integrating center of the vertebrate forebrain. Neurons with cell bodies in the thalamus relay neural input to specific areas in the cerebral cortex and regulate what information goes to the cerebral cortex.

thallus (plural, **thalli**) A seaweed body that is plantlike, consisting of a holdfast, stipe, and blades, yet lacks true roots, stems, and leaves.

theory An explanation that is broader in scope than a hypothesis, generates new hypotheses, and is supported by a large body of evidence.

thermal energy *See* heat.

thermocline A narrow stratum of abrupt temperature change in the ocean and in many temperate-zone lakes.

thermodynamics (ther'-mō-dī-nam'-iks) The study of energy transformations that occur in a collection of matter. *See* first law of thermodynamics; second law of thermodynamics.

thermoreceptor A receptor stimulated by either heat or cold.

thermoregulation The maintenance of internal body temperature within a tolerable range.

theropod Member of a group of dinosaurs that were bipedal carnivores.

thick filament A filament composed of staggered arrays of myosin molecules; a component of myofibrils in muscle fibers.

thigmomorphogenesis A response in plants to chronic mechanical stimulation, resulting from increased ethylene production. An example is thickening stems in response to strong winds.

thigmotropism (thig-mo'-truh-pizm) A directional growth of a plant in response to touch.

thin filament A filament consisting of two strands of actin and two strands of regulatory protein coiled around one another; a component of myofibrils in muscle fibers.

threatened species A species that is considered likely to become endangered in the foreseeable future.

threshold The potential that an excitable cell membrane must reach for an action potential to be initiated.

thrombus A fibrin-containing clot that forms in a blood vessel and blocks the flow of blood.

thylakoid (thī'-luh-koyd) A flattened, membranous sac inside a chloroplast. Thylakoids often exist in stacks called grana that are interconnected; their membranes contain molecular "machinery" used to convert light energy to chemical energy.

thymus (thī'-mus) A small organ in the thoracic cavity of vertebrates where maturation of T cells is completed.

thyroid gland An endocrine gland, located on the ventral surface of the trachea, that secretes two iodine-containing hormones, triiodothyronine (T_3) and thyroxine (T_4), as well as calcitonin.

thyroxine (T_4) One of two iodine-containing hormones that are secreted by the thyroid gland and that help regulate metabolism, development, and maturation in vertebrates.

Ti plasmid A plasmid of a tumor-inducing bacterium (the plant pathogen *Agrobacterium*) that integrates a segment of its DNA (T DNA) into a chromosome of a host plant. The Ti plasmid is frequently used as a vector for genetic engineering in plants.

tidal volume The volume of air a mammal inhales and exhales with each breath.

tight junction A type of intercellular junction between animal cells that prevents the leakage of material through the space between cells.

tissue An integrated group of cells with a common structure, function, or both.

tissue system One or more tissues organized into a functional unit connecting the organs of a plant.

Toll-like receptor (TLR) A membrane receptor on a phagocytic white blood cell that recognizes fragments of molecules common to a set of pathogens.

tonicity The ability of a solution surrounding a cell to cause that cell to gain or lose water.

top-down model A model of community organization in which predation influences community organization by controlling herbivore numbers, which in turn control plant or phytoplankton numbers, which in turn control nutrient levels; also called the trophic cascade model.

topoisomerase A protein that breaks, swivels, and rejoins DNA strands. During DNA replication, topoisomerase helps to relieve strain in the double helix ahead of the replication fork.

topsoil A mixture of particles derived from rock, living organisms, and decaying organic material (humus).

torpor A physiological state in which activity is low and metabolism decreases.

torsion In gastropods, a developmental process in which the visceral mass rotates up to 180°, causing the animal's anus and mantle cavity to be positioned above its head.

totipotent (tō'-tuh-pōt'-ent) Describing a cell that can give rise to all parts of the embryo and adult, as well as extraembryonic membranes in species that have them.

trace element An element indispensable for life but required in extremely minute amounts.

trachea (trā'-kē-uh) The portion of the respiratory tract that passes from the larynx to the bronchi; also called the windpipe.

tracheal system In insects, a system of branched, air-filled tubes that extends throughout the body and carries oxygen directly to cells.

tracheid (trā'-kē-id) A long, tapered water-conducting cell found in the xylem of nearly all vascular plants. Functioning tracheids are no longer living.

trait One of two or more detectable variants in a genetic character.

trans fat An unsaturated fat, formed artificially during hydrogenation of oils, containing one or more *trans* double bonds.

transcription The synthesis of RNA using a DNA template.

transcription factor A regulatory protein that binds to DNA and affects transcription of specific genes.

transcription initiation complex The completed assembly of transcription factors and RNA polymerase bound to a promoter.

transcription unit A region of DNA that is transcribed into an RNA molecule.

transduction (1) A process in which phages (viruses) carry bacterial DNA from one bacterial cell to another. When these two cells are members of different species, transduction results in horizontal gene transfer. (2) In cellular communication, the conversion of a signal from outside the cell to a form that can bring about a specific cellular response; also called *signal transduction*.

transfer RNA (tRNA) An RNA molecule that functions as a translator between nucleic acid and protein languages by carrying specific amino acids to the ribosome, where they recognize the appropriate codons in the mRNA.

transformation (1) The conversion of a normal animal cell to a cancerous cell. (2) A change in genotype and phenotype due to the assimilation of external DNA by a cell. When the external DNA is from a member of a different species, transformation results in horizontal gene transfer.

transgenic Pertaining to an organism whose genome contains a gene introduced from another organism of the same or a different species.

translation The synthesis of a polypeptide using the genetic information encoded in an mRNA molecule. There is a change of "language" from nucleotides to amino acids.

translocation (1) An aberration in chromosome structure resulting from attachment of a chromosomal fragment to a nonhomologous chromosome. (2) During protein synthesis, the third stage in the elongation cycle, when the RNA carrying the growing polypeptide moves from the A site to the P site on the ribosome. (3) The transport of organic nutrients in the phloem of vascular plants.

transmission The passage of a nerve impulse along axons.

transmission electron microscope (TEM) A microscope that passes an electron beam through very thin sections stained with metal atoms and is primarily used to study the internal ultrastructure of cells.

transpiration The evaporative loss of water from a plant.

transport epithelium One or more layers of specialized epithelial cells that carry out and regulate solute movement.

transport protein A transmembrane protein that helps a certain substance or class of closely related substances to cross the membrane.

transport vesicle A small membranous sac in a eukaryotic cell's cytoplasm carrying molecules produced by the cell.

transposable element A segment of DNA that can move within the genome of a cell by means of a DNA or RNA intermediate; also called a transposable genetic element.

transposon A transposable element that moves within a genome by means of a DNA intermediate.

transverse (T) tubule An infolding of the plasma membrane of skeletal muscle cells.

triacylglycerol (trī-as'-ul-glis'-uh-rol) A lipid consisting of three fatty acids linked to one glycerol molecule; also called a fat or triglyceride.

triiodothyronine (T$_3$) (trī′-ī-ō′-dō-thī′-rō-nēn) One of two iodine-containing hormones that are secreted by the thyroid gland and that help regulate metabolism, development, and maturation in vertebrates.

trimester In human development, one of three 3-month-long periods of pregnancy.

triple response A plant growth maneuver in response to mechanical stress, involving slowing of stem elongation, thickening of the stem, and a curvature that causes the stem to start growing horizontally.

triplet code A genetic information system in which a set of three-nucleotide-long words specify the amino acids for polypeptide chains.

triploblastic Possessing three germ layers: the endoderm, mesoderm, and ectoderm. Most eumetazoans are triploblastic.

trisomic Referring to a diploid cell that has three copies of a particular chromosome instead of the normal two.

trochophore larva (trō′-kuh-fōr) Distinctive larval stage observed in some lophotrochozoan animals, including some annelids and molluscs.

trophic efficiency The percentage of production transferred from one trophic level to the next.

trophic structure The different feeding relationships in an ecosystem, which determine the route of energy flow and the pattern of chemical cycling.

trophoblast The outer epithelium of a mammalian blastocyst. It forms the fetal part of the placenta, supporting embryonic development but not forming part of the embryo proper.

tropic hormone A hormone that has an endocrine gland or cells as a target.

tropical dry forest A terrestrial biome characterized by relatively high temperatures and precipitation overall but with a pronounced dry season.

tropical rain forest A terrestrial biome characterized by relatively high precipitation and temperatures year-round.

tropics Latitudes between 23.5° north and south.

tropism A growth response that results in the curvature of whole plant organs toward or away from stimuli due to differential rates of cell elongation.

tropomyosin The regulatory protein that blocks the myosin-binding sites on actin molecules.

troponin complex The regulatory proteins that control the position of tropomyosin on the thin filament.

true-breeding Referring to organisms that produce offspring of the same variety over many generations of self-pollination.

tubal ligation A means of sterilization in which a woman's two oviducts (fallopian tubes) are tied closed to prevent eggs from reaching the uterus. A segment of each oviduct is removed.

tube foot One of numerous extensions of an echinoderm's water vascular system. Tube feet function in locomotion and feeding.

tumor-suppressor gene A gene whose protein product inhibits cell division, thereby preventing the uncontrolled cell growth that contributes to cancer.

tundra A terrestrial biome at the extreme limits of plant growth. At the northernmost limits, it is called arctic tundra, and at high altitudes, where plant forms are limited to low shrubby or matlike vegetation, it is called alpine tundra.

tunicate Member of the clade Urochordata, sessile marine chordates that lack a backbone.

turgid (ter′-jid) Swollen or distended, as in plant cells. (A walled cell becomes turgid if it has a lower water potential than its surroundings, resulting in entry of water.)

turgor pressure The force directed against a plant cell wall after the influx of water and swelling of the cell due to osmosis.

turnover The mixing of waters as a result of changing water-temperature profiles in a lake.

turnover time The time required to replace the standing crop of a population or group of populations (for example, of phytoplankton), calculated as the ratio of standing crop to production.

twin study A behavioral study in which researchers compare the behavior of identical twins raised apart with that of identical twins raised in the same household.

tympanic membrane Another name for the eardrum, the membrane between the outer and middle ear.

uniformitarianism The principle that mechanisms of change are constant over time. *See* catastrophism.

Unikonta (yū′-ni-kon′-tuh) One of five supergroups of eukaryotes proposed in a current hypothesis of the evolutionary history of eukaryotes. This clade, which is supported by studies of myosin proteins and DNA, consists of amoebozoans and opisthokonts. *See also* Excavata, Chromalveolata, Rhizaria, and Archaeplastida.

unsaturated fatty acid A fatty acid that has one or more double bonds between carbons in the hydrocarbon tail. Such bonding reduces the number of hydrogen atoms attached to the carbon skeleton.

urea A soluble nitrogenous waste produced in the liver by a metabolic cycle that combines ammonia with carbon dioxide.

ureter (yū-rē′-ter) A duct leading from the kidney to the urinary bladder.

urethra (yū-rē′-thruh) A tube that releases urine from the mammalian body near the vagina in females and through the penis in males; also serves in males as the exit tube for the reproductive system.

uric acid A product of protein and purine metabolism and the major nitrogenous waste product of insects, land snails, and many reptiles. Uric acid is relatively nontoxic and largely insoluble.

urinary bladder The pouch where urine is stored prior to elimination.

uterine cycle The changes that occur in the uterus during the reproductive cycle of the human female; also called the menstrual cycle.

uterus A female organ where eggs are fertilized and/or development of the young occurs.

utricle In the vertebrate ear, a chamber in the vestibule behind the oval window that opens into the three semicircular canals.

vaccination *See* immunization.

vaccine A harmless variant or derivative of a pathogen that stimulates a host's immune system to mount defenses against the pathogen.

vacuole (vak′-yū-ōl′) A membrane-bounded vesicle whose specialized function varies in different kinds of cells.

vagina Part of the female reproductive system between the uterus and the outside opening; the birth canal in mammals. During copulation, the vagina accommodates the male's penis and receives sperm.

valence The bonding capacity of a given atom; usually equals the number of unpaired electrons required to complete the atom's outermost (valence) shell.

valence electron An electron in the outermost electron shell.

valence shell The outermost energy shell of an atom, containing the valence electrons involved in the chemical reactions of that atom.

van der Waals interactions Weak attractions between molecules or parts of molecules that result from transient local partial charges.

variation Differences between members of the same species.

vas deferens In mammals, the tube in the male reproductive system in which sperm travel from the epididymis to the urethra.

vasa recta The capillary system in the kidney that serves the loop of Henle.

vascular cambium A cylinder of meristematic tissue in woody plants that adds layers of secondary vascular tissue called secondary xylem (wood) and secondary phloem.

vascular plant A plant with vascular tissue. Vascular plants include all living plant species except liverworts, mosses, and hornworts.

vascular tissue Plant tissue consisting of cells joined into tubes that transport water and nutrients throughout the plant body.

vascular tissue system A transport system formed by xylem and phloem throughout a vascular plant. Xylem transports water and minerals; phloem transports sugars, the products of photosynthesis.

vasectomy The cutting and sealing of each vas deferens to prevent sperm from entering the urethra.

vasocongestion The filling of a tissue with blood, caused by increased blood flow through the arteries of that tissue.

vasoconstriction A decrease in the diameter of blood vessels caused by contraction of smooth muscles in the vessel walls.

vasodilation An increase in the diameter of blood vessels caused by relaxation of smooth muscles in the vessel walls.

vector An organism that transmits pathogens from one host to another.

vegetal pole The point at the end of an egg in the hemisphere where most yolk is concentrated; opposite of animal pole.

vegetative reproduction Cloning of plants by asexual means.

vein (1) In animals, a vessel that carries blood toward the heart. (2) In plants, a vascular bundle in a leaf.

ventilation The flow of air or water over a respiratory surface.

ventral Pertaining to the underside, or bottom, of an animal with radial or bilateral symmetry.

ventricle (ven'-tri-kul) (1) A heart chamber that pumps blood out of the heart. (2) A space in the vertebrate brain, filled with cerebrospinal fluid.

venule (ven'-yūl) A vessel that conveys blood between a capillary bed and a vein.

vernalization The use of cold treatment to induce a plant to flower.

vertebrate A chordate animal with a backbone, including sharks and rays, ray-finned fishes, coelacanths, lungfishes, amphibians, reptiles, and mammals.

vesicle (ves'-i-kul) A membranous sac in the cytoplasm of a eukaryotic cell.

vessel A continuous water-conducting micropipe found in most angiosperms and a few nonflowering vascular plants.

vessel element A short, wide water-conducting cell found in the xylem of most angiosperms and a few nonflowering vascular plants. Dead at maturity, vessel elements are aligned end to end to form micropipes called vessels.

vestigial structure A feature of an organism that is a historical remnant of a structure that served a function in the organism's ancestors.

villus (plural, **villi**) (1) A finger-like projection of the inner surface of the small intestine. (2) A finger-like projection of the chorion of the mammalian placenta. Large numbers of villi increase the surface areas of these organs.

viral envelope A membrane, derived from membranes of the host cell, that cloaks the capsid, which in turn encloses a viral genome.

viroid (vī'-royd) A plant pathogen consisting of a molecule of naked, circular RNA a few hundred nucleotides long.

virulent Describing a pathogen against which an organism has little specific defense.

virulent phage A phage that replicates only by a lytic cycle.

virus An infectious particle incapable of replicating outside of a cell, consisting of an RNA or DNA genome surrounded by a protein coat (capsid) and, for some viruses, a membranous envelope.

visceral mass One of the three main parts of a mollusc; the part containing most of the internal organs. *See also* foot, mantle.

visible light That portion of the electromagnetic spectrum that can be detected as various colors by the human eye, ranging in wavelength from about 380 nm to about 750 nm.

vital capacity The maximum volume of air that a mammal can inhale and exhale with each breath.

vitamin An organic molecule required in the diet in very small amounts. Many vitamins serve as coenzymes or parts of coenzymes.

viviparous (vī-vip'-uh-rus) Referring to a type of development in which the young are born alive after having been nourished in the uterus by blood from the placenta.

voltage-gated ion channel A specialized ion channel that opens or closes in response to changes in membrane potential.

vulva Collective term for the female external genitalia.

water potential (Ψ) The physical property predicting the direction in which water will flow, governed by solute concentration and applied pressure.

water vascular system A network of hydraulic canals unique to echinoderms that branches into extensions called tube feet, which function in locomotion and feeding.

wavelength The distance between crests of waves, such as those of the electromagnetic spectrum.

wetland A habitat that is inundated by water at least some of the time and that supports plants adapted to water-saturated soil.

white matter Tracts of axons within the CNS.

wild type The phenotype most commonly observed in natural populations; also refers to the individual with that phenotype.

wilting The drooping of leaves and stems as a result of plant cells becoming flaccid.

wobble Flexibility in the base-pairing rules in which the nucleotide at the 5' end of a tRNA anticodon can form hydrogen bonds with more than one kind of base in the third position (3' end) of a codon.

xerophyte A plant adapted to an arid climate.

X-linked gene A gene located on the X chromosome; such genes show a distinctive pattern of inheritance.

X-ray crystallography A technique used to study the three-dimensional structure of molecules. It depends on the diffraction of an X-ray beam by the individual atoms of a crystallized molecule.

xylem (zī'-lum) Vascular plant tissue consisting mainly of tubular dead cells that conduct most of the water and minerals upward from the roots to the rest of the plant.

xylem sap The dilute solution of water and dissolved minerals carried through vessels and tracheids.

yeast Single-celled fungus. Yeasts reproduce asexually by binary fission or by the pinching of small buds off a parent cell. Many fungal species can grow both as yeasts and as a network of filaments; relatively few species grow only as yeasts.

yolk Nutrients stored in an egg.

zero population growth (ZPG) A period of stability in population size, when additions to the population through births and immigration are balanced by subtractions through deaths and emigration.

zona pellucida The extracellular matrix surrounding a mammalian egg.

zone of polarizing activity (ZPA) A block of mesoderm located just under the ectoderm where the posterior side of a limb bud is attached to the body; required for proper pattern formation along the anterior-posterior axis of the limb.

zoned reserve An extensive region that includes areas relatively undisturbed by humans surrounded by areas that have been changed by human activity and are used for economic gain.

zoonotic pathogen A disease-causing agent that is transmitted to humans from other animals.

zoospore Flagellated spore found in chytrid fungi and some protists.

zygomycete (zī'-guh-mī'-sēt) Member of the fungal phylum Zygomycota, characterized by the formation of a sturdy structure called a zygosporangium during sexual reproduction.

zygosporangium (zī'-guh-spōr-an'-jē-um) In zygomycete fungi, a sturdy multinucleate structure in which karyogamy and meiosis occur.

zygote (zī'-gōt) The diploid cell produced by the union of haploid gametes during fertilization; a fertilized egg.

Index

10-nm fibers, 320*f*
1 nucleotide-pair deletions, 345*f*
1 nucleotide-pair insertions, 345*f*
3′ end (sugar-phosphate backbone), 88, 334
300-nm fibers, 321*f*
30-nm fibers, 321*f*, 322
3 nucleotide-pair deletions, 345*f*
3-phosphoglycerate, 199
5′ cap, **334**
5′ end (sugar-phosphate backbone), 88
5-methyl cytidine, **65***f*

A
α chain, 936
α-globin gene family, 437–38
α-helix, **82***f*
α-lactalbumin, 440–41
ABC hypothesis, flower formation, **760**–61
abd-A gene, 685*f*
Abdomen, insect, 688*f*
Abiotic factors, **1149**
    climate and, 1149
    in pollination, 804*f*
    in species distributions, 1163–64, 1166–67
Abiotic stresses, plant, **843**–45
Abiotic synthesis, organic molecule, 58–59, 508, 509
Abnormal chromosome numbers, 297–98
ABO blood groups, 272–73, 946
Abomasum, 891*f*
Abortion, 297, **1017**
Abscisic acid (ABA), **778**, 827*t*, **831**–32, 843
Abscission, leaf, 831–32, 834
Absorption, **880**
    animal food processing and, 880
    fungal nutrition and, 14
    in large intestine, 888–89
    in small intestine, 887–88
    of water and minerals by root cells, 772
Absorption spectrum, **190**–91
Abstinence, 1016
Abyssal zone, **1157**
Acacia trees, 1199*f*
Acanthocephala, 668*f*
Acanthodians, **705**
Accessory fruits, **810**
Accessory glands, male reproductive, 1005
Acclimatization, **862**, 867
Accommodation, visual, 1101*f*
Acetic acid, 59, **64***f*
Acetone, **64***f*
Acetylation, histone, 357
Acetylcholine, **1057**–58, 1106–7*f*
Acetylcholinesterase, 1058
Acetyl CoA (acetyl coenzyme A), **170**
Acetylsalicylic acid, 633
Achondroplasia, 278
Acid growth hypothesis, 828, 829*f*
Acidic soils, 736–37
Acidification, ocean, 55–56
Acid precipitation, **55**–56, 1244
Acid reflux, 886
Acids, **53**
    amino acids as, 79*f*
    buffers and, 54–55
    carboxylic, 64*f*
    hydrogen ions and, 53

ocean acidification, acid precipitation, and, 29, 55–56, 1244
    pH scale and, 53–54
Acoela, 667*f*
Acoelomates, **660**
Acorn worms, 669*f*
Acquired immunity. *See* Adaptive immunity
Acquired immunodeficiency, 948. *See also* AIDS (acquired immunodeficiency syndrome)
Acromegaly, 989
Acrosomal reaction, **1022**, 1023*f*
Acrosome, **1006***f*, **1022**
Actin, 78*f*, **116**, 234, 858*f*
Actin filaments. *See also* Microfilaments
    cell motility and, 112–13
    cytoskeleton structure and function and, 113*t*
    in morphogenesis, 1034
    in vertebrate muscle, 1104–6
Actinopterygii, 707
Action potentials, neuron, **842**, **1051**
    conduction of, 1053–54
    evolution of axon myelination for conduction of, 1054
    generation of, 1051–53
    graded potentials and, 1050–51
    hyperpolarization and depolarization of membrane and, 1050, 1051*f*
    in long-term potentiation, 1077–78
    in muscle contraction, 1108–9*f*
    in plant thigmotropism, 842–43
    in sensory systems, 1086–87
Action spectrum, **190**–91, **835**–36
Activation, allosteric, 158–59
Activation domains, 359–60
Activation energy, **152**–53
Activator proteins, 359–61
Activators, 158, **355**, 359–61, 824
Active immunity, **944**–45
Active sites, enzyme, **154**–55
Active transport, **135**
    across cellular membranes, 135–38
    ATP as energy for, 135–36
    cotransport in, 137–38
    maintenance of membrane potential by ion pumps, 136–37
    passive transport vs., 136*f*
    of solutes across plant plasma membranes, 768, 769*f*
Activity, animal metabolic rate and, 870
Actual evapotranspiration, 1224
Actual range, 1165
Acyclovir, 391
Adaptation, sensory, 1088
Adaptations, **456**. *See also* Evolution; Natural selection
    adaptive radiations and, 16–17
    in amniote development, 1031
    animal thermoregulatory, 864–67
    artificial selection, natural selection, and, 458–59
    of axon width and myelination, 1054
    C. Darwin on natural selection and, 15–16
    C. Darwin's research focus on, 456–57
    evolution and, 4
    floral, that prevent self-fertilization, 813*f*
    herbivore, 1198
    of multicellular slime mold slugs, 1186
    of muscles, 1110
    mycorrhizae as plant, 796
    of pathogens, 948–50
    of plants to global climate change, 201
    of plants to toxic elements, 32
    prokaryotic, 556–61*f*
    as property of life, 2*f*
    respiratory, of diving mammals, 925–26
    sexual reproduction patterns as, 998–99
    structural and functional, of prokaryotes, 556–61*f*
    terrestrial, of fungi and land plants, 601, 641
    terrestrial, of seed plants, 618–21

to terrestrial life, 199–202
    that reduce terrestrial nutrient limitations, 1224–25
    of vertebrate digestive systems, 889–91
Adaptive evolution, 476, 480–85
Adaptive immunity, **929**, 935–46
    active and passive immunity, immunization, and, 944–45
    antibodies as tools in research, diagnosis, and therapy, 945
    antigen recognition by B cells and antibodies in, 935–36
    antigen recognition by T cells in, 936–37
    B cell and T cell development in, 937–40
    B cell and T cell diversity in, 937–38
    B cells and antibodies as responses to extracellular pathogens in, 942–43
    cytotoxic T cells as responses to infected cells in, 941–42
    elements of, 935
    helper T cells as responses to antigens in, 940–41
    humoral and cell-mediated immune responses in, 940–46
    immune rejection and, 945–46
    immunological memory in, 937, 939–40
    innate immunity vs., 929–30
    origin of self-tolerance in, 938
    overview of, 944
    pathogen evasion of, 948–50
    proliferation of B cells and T cells in, 939
Adaptive management, 1233
Adaptive radiations, **524**–25*f*
    natural selection and, 16–17
    regional, 524–25*f*
    of reptiles, 715–16
    in species distributions, 1164–65
    worldwide, 524
Addition rule, **269**–71
Adenine, 87*f*–88, 308, 829
Adenoma, 376*f*
Adenomatous polyposis coli (APC), 376*f*, 377
Adenosine triphosphate (ATP). *See* ATP (adenosine triphosphate)
Adenoviruses, 383
Adenylyl cyclase, **217**
Adhesion, 47–**48**, 775–76
Adhesive chemicals, echinoderm, 692
Adipose cells, 76
Adipose tissue, animal, **857***f*, 892
ADP (adenosine diphosphate)
    as enzyme activator, 158–59
    hydrolysis of ATP to, 149–50
    regeneration of ATP from, 151
    synthesis of ATP from, 168, 173–74
Adrenal cortex, 986*t*, 990–92
Adrenal glands, 986*t*, **990**–92
    catecholamines produced by, 990–91
    epinephrine and, 977–78
    rough ER and, 105
    steroid hormones produced by, 991–92
Adrenaline. *See* Epinephrine
Adrenal medulla, 986*t*, 990–91
Adrenocorticotropic hormone (ACTH), 985*f*, 986*t*, **989**, 991–92
Adult stem cells, 416
Adventitious roots, 739, 757
Adventitious shoots, 812
Adventitious stems, 757
Aerial roots, 740*f*
Aerobic prokaryotes, 559*f*
Aerobic respiration, **164**. *See also* Cellular respiration
    as catabolic pathway, 164
    fermentation vs., 178–79
    oxidative muscle fibers and, 1109
Afferent neurons, 1066, 1086–87
Afghanistan, age-structure pyramid for, 1188–89*f*
Aflatoxins, 650

African-Americans, sickle-cell disease in, 277–78
African elephants, 457–58, 1177, 1243
Africans
    genomes of, 445
    sickle-cell disease in, 277–78
African sleeping sickness, 691
Agave, 1180
Age structure, human population, **1188**–89
Aggregate fruits, **810**
Aging, telomeric DNA and, 319
Agonistic behavior, 1133
Agriculture
    allopolyploidy in crops, 496
    applications of DNA technology for, 421–22f
    C$_3$ plants in, 200
    community disturbances by, 1210
    fertilizing in, 1225
    fungi as food products of, 651
    global climate change and, 28–29
    global human population size and, 1190–91
    impact of oomycetes on, 588–89
    importance of insects to, 691
    nematode pests in, 684
    nitrogen fixation and, 795
    no-till, 789
    nutrient pollution from, 1254–55
    plant biotechnology and genetic engineering in,
        816–19
    seed plants as crop plants for, 633
    slash-and-burn, 634
    sustainable, 787–89, 1253
    transgenic plants in, 736–37
    vegetative propagation of plants in, 814–15
Agrobacterium tumefaciens, 403, 421–22f, 568f, 572,
        736, 756
A horizon, 786f
AIDS (acquired immunodeficiency syndrome), **388**,
        948–50. *See also* HIV (human immunodefi-
        ciency virus)
    cell-surface proteins and blocking HIV entry into
        cells, 130
    drug cocktails in treatment of, 472
    HIV and, 388–90
    mycoses and, 650
    specificity of virus of, 384
Ailuropoda melanoleuca (giant panda), 433t
Ain, Michael C., 278f
Air circulation patterns, global, 1146f
Air pollution, lichens and, 650
Air roots, 740f
Air sacs, 920–21
Alanine, 79f
Alarm calls, 1127
Alarm signals, 1122
Albatross, 953, 957–58
Albinism, 277f, 325
Albumin, 361f, 714f
Albuterol, 63f
Alcohol fermentation, **178**
Alcoholic beverages, 651
Alcohols, **64**f
Aldehydes, **64**f
Alder, 1209–10
Aldoses, 70
Aldosterone, **970**–71, 992
Algae, **576**
    alternation of generations in, 252
    biofuels from, 185f
    brown, 586, 587f
    chloroplasts in, 110–11
    diatoms, 585
    as earliest multicellular eukaryotes, 517–18
    evolution of, 576, 577f
    evolution of land plants from green, 600–601
    fossils, 511f
    fungi and, as lichens, 645, 649–50

golden, 586
green, 576, 577f, 579f, 591–92
photosynthesis in, 184
preventing blooms of, 1223–24
red, 576, 577f, 579f, 590–91
stramenopiles as marine, 585–89
Algin, 586
Alimentary canals, 667f, **676**, 683, **882**–83, 890–91
Alkalinity, semen, 1012
Alkaptonuria, 326
Allantois, 714f, 1031
Allee, W. C., 1178
Allee effect, 1178
Alleles, **265**
    as alternative versions of genes, 265
    behavior of recessive, 276–77
    correlating behavior of chromosome pairs with,
        288–89
    degrees of dominance of, 271–72
    dominant, and phenotype, 272
    dominant vs. recessive, 265–66
    frequencies of, in populations, 473–76
    genetic variation and, 257
    genetic variation preserved in recessive, 483
    genomic imprinting of maternal or paternal, 358
    homologous chromosomes and, 253
    homozygous vs. heterozygous organisms and,
        266–67
    microevolution as alteration in frequencies of, in
        populations, 469, 476–80
    multiple, and pleiotropy, 272–73
    as mutations, 259
    mutations as sources of new, 472
    recombination of (*see* Genetic recombination)
    sexual life cycles and, 257
Allergens, 818, **947**
Allergies, 947–48
Alligators, 716f, 717
Alligator snapping turtles, 1198
Allolactose, 354
Allopatric speciation, **493**–95
    continental drift and, 521
    evidence of, 494–95
    process of, 493–94
    sympatric speciation vs., 493f
Allopolyploids, **496**
All-or-none responses, 1051
Allosteric regulation, **158**–60
Alpha cells, 983
Alpha proteobacteria, 568f
Alpine pennycress, 789
Alpine tundra, 1156f
Alpine woodsorrel, 813f
Alternate phyllotaxy, 766
Alternation of generations, **252**, **586–87**, **602**
Alternative RNA splicing, **336**, **362**–63, 433
Altman, Sidney, 509
Altruism, **1137**–39
Alu elements, 436, 443
Aluminum, bioremediation of, 1232–33
Aluminum toxicity, plant, 788, 792
Alvarez, Luis, 522
Alvarez, Walter, 522
Alveolates, **582**–85
    apicomplexans, 583–84
    ciliates, 584–85
    dinoflagellates, 582–83
Alveoli, 582, **919**–20
Alzheimer's disease, 85, 225, **1081**
Amacrine cells, 1096f, 1098–99
Amanita muscaria, 642f
Amazon rain forest, 1250
Amborella, 629–30
Amebic (amoebic) dysentery, 596
American alligator, 716f
American beech trees, 1148–49

American black bears, 12f
American chestnut trees, 1204
American Dust Bowl, 787
Amine hormones, 976–77f
Amines, **65**f
Amino acids, **78**. *See also* Proteins
    abiotic synthesis of, 508–9
    activation of, in eukaryotic cells, 348f
    deamination of, for catabolism, 180
    essential, for animal nutrition, 876
    genetic code and, 328–31
    from meteorites, 508
    as monomers of polypeptides and proteins, 78–80
    neurotransmitters as, 1058
    as polypeptide polymers, 80
    proteins as built from, 69
    sequence of, in human globin proteins, 440t
    sickle-cell disease and, 84
    specified by triplets of nucleotides, 329–30, 337
    twenty, of proteins, 79f
Aminoacyl-tRNA synthetases, **338–39**
Amino group, **65**f. *See also* Amino acids
Amionoacyl tRNA, 339
Amitochondriate protists, 577
Ammonia, **958**
    as base, 53
    excretion of, 953
    hydrogen bonds and, 41f
    nephron processing of, 964–65
    as nitrogenous waste, 958
Ammonifying bacteria, 793
Ammonites, **680**
Amniocentesis, **280**, 281f
Amnion, 464, 714f, 1031
Amniotes, **713**–20, **1031**
    derived characters of, 713–14
    developmental adaptations of, 1031
    early, 714
    evolution of, 658
    mammals as, 720
    phylogenetic tree of, 713f
    reptiles, 715–20
Amniotic egg, **713**–14
Amoebas, 117–18, 228f, 433, 579f, **589**, 853f
Amoebocytes, **670**
Amoeboid movement, 117–18
Amoebozoans, **593**–96
    entamoebas, 596
    gymnamoebas, 596
    slime molds or mycetozoans, 594–96
AMP (adenosine monophosphate), 181, 338f
Amphibians (Amphibia), **710**–12
    breathing in, 920
    cell fate and developmental potential of cells of, 1038f
    cleavage in, 1026
    decline and extinction of, 712
    double circulatory system of, 901f
    embryo body plan, 1039f
    endangered or threatened, 1239–40
    evolution of, 658
    external fertilization in, 999f
    fungal infection of, 650–51f
    gastrulation in, 1028–29
    hearing and equilibrium in, 1094
    kidney adaptations in, 968
    parental care in, 1131
Amphipathic molecules, **125**
Ampicillin resistance, 399–400
Amplification, cancer gene, 373–74
Amplification, sensory, **1087**–88
Amplification, signal, 214, 220
amp^k gene, 399–400
Ampulla, sea star, 693f
Amygdala, **1071**–72
Amylase, **884**
Amyloid plaques, 1081

Amylopectin, 72–73*f*
Amyloplasts, 111
Amylose, 72–73*f*, 111
Amyotrophic lateral sclerosis (ALS), 1106
Anabolic pathways, **143**, 180. *See also* Protein synthesis
Anabrus simplex (cricket), 433
Anaerobic respiration, 164, 177, 178–79, **564**
Analgesics, 1059
Analogies, **540**–42
Analogous structures, **465**
Anaphase, **231**, 233*f*, 235*f*
Anaphase I, 254*f*
Anaphase II, 255*f*
Anaphylactic shock, 947
Anatomical homologies, 463
Anatomy, **852**. *See also* Animal form and function; Morphology; Plant structure
Ancestral characters, shared, **543**
Ancestry, common, 16, 462–65, 538–39, 542–43, 629
Anchorage, roots and, 766–67
Anchorage dependence, **241**–42
Anchoring junctions, 121*f*
Androgens, 986*t*, **992**, 1008
Anemia, 913
Aneuploidies, **298**, 299–300
Angina pectoris, 914
Angiosperms (Anthophyta), **606**, 625–32, 801–20. *See also* Crop plants
  agriculture and breeding of, 815–16
  agriculture and vegetative propagation of, 814–15
  asexual reproduction in, 812–15
  biotechnology and genetic engineering of, 815–19
  bulk flow by positive pressure in sugar translocation in, 780–81
  characteristics of, 625–30
  diversity of, 630–31*f*
  double fertilization in, 806–7
  evolutionary links between animals and, 632
  evolution of, 628–30
  flowers of, 625–26, 801–6 (*see also* Flowers)
  fruit and seed dispersal in, 811*f*
  fruits of, 625, 626, 809–10, 811*f* (*see also* Fruits)
  gametophyte-sporophyte relationships in, 619*f*
  life cycles of, 627–28, 802*f*, 803*f*
  phylogeny of, 605*t*, 629*f*
  review of, 819
  seeds of, 807–9, 811*f* (*see also* Seeds)
  sexual reproduction in, 801–11*f*
  structure of (*see* Plant structure)
Angiotensin II, **970**–71
Angraecum sesquipedale, 806*f*
Anhydrobiosis, **955**–56
Animal(s), 654–65
  apoptosis in, 224–25
  aquatic (*see* Aquatic animals)
  asexual reproduction in, 259–60
  body plans of, 658–61
  cardiovascular systems (*see* Cardiovascular systems)
  cell junctions in, 121
  cells of (*see* Animal cells)
  cellular respiration in hibernating, 177
  circulatory systems (*see* Circulatory systems)
  cloning of, 413–15
  development (*see* Animal development)
  diseases in (*see* Diseases, animal; Diseases and disorders, human; Pathogens)
  diversity of, 654
  in domain Eukarya and kingdom Animalia, 13–14
  endocrine signaling in, 208*f*–9
  energy flow and, 7
  as eukaryotes, 8
  evolutionary history of, 656–58
  evolutionary links between plants and, 632
  excretory systems (*see* Excretory systems)
  flower pollination by, 804*f*–5*f*, 806
  form and function of (*see* Animal form and function)

fruit and seed dispersal by, 811*f*
fungi as pathogens of, 650–51*f*
gas exchange (*see* Gas exchange)
glycogen as storage polysaccharide for, 71–72
herbivore adaptations in, 461
immune systems (*see* Immune systems)
land colonization by, 518–19
nutritional mode of, 654 (*see also* Animal nutrition)
as opisthokonts, 596, 640
osmoregulation in (*see* Osmoregulation; Water balance)
phylogeny of, 662–64, 666*f*
plant recruitment of predator, as herbivore defense, 845
protein production by transgenic "pharm", 419–20
relationship of, to unikont protists, 593
reproduction and development of (*see* Animal development; Animal reproduction)
review of, 664–65
seed dispersal by, 626
symbioses with fungi, 648–49
viruses of (*see* Animal viruses)
Animal behavior. *See* Behavior, animal
Animal cells, 100*f*, 654–55. *See also* Eukaryotic cells
  cytokinesis in, 234–35*f*
  endocytosis in, 139*f*
  extracellular matrix of, 119–20
  fate of (*see* Cell fate)
  local and long-distance cell signaling in, 208–9
  nuclear transplantation of differentiated, and organismal development, 413*f*
  reproductive cloning by nuclear transplantation from, 414*f*
  stem cells, 415–17*f*
  structure and specialization of, 654–55
  water balance of, 133–34
Animal development, 1021–44. *See also* Development
  animal phylogeny and, 662–63
  cell fate specification by cytoplasmic determinants and inductive signals, 1035–42
  comparing plant development and, 447
  comparing processes of, 445–47
  developmental biology and, 1021–22
  embryonic, 655*f*, 1021–27 (*see also* Embryonic development)
  Hox genes and (*see Hox* genes)
  morphogenesis in, 1027–35
  nuclear transplantation of differentiated cells and, 413*f*
  protostome vs. deuterostome, 660–61
  reproduction and, 655
  review of, 1042–43
Animal form and function, 850–74
  anatomy, physiology, and, 852
  body plans, 658–61
  coordination and control in, by endocrine and nervous systems, 859
  energy requirements and bioenergetics in, 868–72
  exchange with environment in, 853–55
  feedback control and maintenance of internal environment in, 860–62
  hierarchical organization of body plans in, 855
  homeostatic processes for thermoregulation in, 862–68
  levels of organization in, 852–60
  mammalian organ systems in, 855*t*
  B. M. Olivera's work on, 850–51
  physical laws constraining evolution of body size and shape in, 853
  review of, 873
  tissue structure and function in, 856*f*–58*f*
Animalia, kingdom, 13–14, 551–52. *See also* Eukarya, domain
Animal nutrition, **875**–96
  diets and requirements for, 875–80 (*see also* Diets)
  digestion and (*see* Digestion)

evolutionary adaptations of vertebrate digestive systems and diets in, 889–91
feedback control of digestion, energy storage, and appetite in, 891–95
feeding mechanisms in, 881*f*
food processing stages in, 880–83
mammalian digestive systems and, 883–89
review of, 895–96
Animal pole, **1025**
Animal reproduction, 996–1020
  amphibian, 712
  asexual, 996–97
  development and, 655–56
  embryonic development in mammalian, 1011–18 (*see also* Embryonic development; Embryonic development, human)
  fertilization mechanisms in, 999–1002
  of fish, 707
  hormonal regulation of mammalian, 1008–11
  human gametogenesis in, 1005–8
  human sexual response in, 1011
  parthenogenesis in, 997
  reproductive cycles in, 998, 999*f*
  review of, 1018–19
  sexual, as evolutionary enigma, 997–98
  sexual life cycles in, 252
  sexual reproductive organs in, 1002–8
  of sharks and rays, 707
  variations in patterns of, 998–99
Animal viruses
  as cause of disease, 390–94
  classes of, 387*t*
  replicative cycles of, 387–90
Anions, **40**, 787
Ankle bones, 465*f*
Annelids (Annelida), 668*f*, 681–83, 961, 1063*f*
Annual human population growth rates, 1187–88*f*
Annuals, 747
Antagonistic functions, autonomic nervous system, 1066–67
Antagonistic hormones, 982–84
Antagonistic muscle pairs, 1110–11
Antarctica, 28, 507, 1203*f*, 1218, 1258–59
Antelope squirrels, 493*f*
Antennae, 691, 1088, 1101
Anterior end, **658**
Anterior pituitary gland, **984**
  hormones of, 985–86*t*
  in mammalian reproduction, 1008
Anterior-posterior axis, 1036–38, 1040
Antheridia, **603***f*
Anthers, **626**, **802**
Anthocerophyta, 606, 608*f*. *See also* Bryophytes
Anthoceros, 608*f*
Anthophyta, 625. *See also* Angiosperms (Anthophyta)
Anthozoans (Anthozoa), 672*f*, 673
Anthrax, 569*f*, 572
Anthropoids, **726**–27
Antibiotic drugs
  bacterial resistance to, 564, 572
  for cystic fibrosis, 277
  as enzyme inhibitors, 157
  evolution of resistance to, 461–62
  fungal production of, 651
  gram-positive bacteria and, 569*f*
  peptidoglycan and, 558
  prokaryotic ribosomes and, 560
  viruses and, 391
Antibodies, **936**
  antigen recognition by, 935–36
  gene rearrangement by, 937–38
  in humoral immune response, 940–41, 942–43
  as proteins, 9, 78*f*, 81
  as research, diagnosis, and therapy tools, 945
  role of, in immunity, 944–45
Anticodons, **337**

Antidiuretic hormone (ADH), **969**–70, 971, 975, **984**–85f, 986t, 1135
Antifreeze proteins, 845
Antigenic determinant, 936
Antigenic variation, 948–49
Antigen presentation, **937**
Antigen-presenting cells, **940**
Antigen receptors, **935**
  of B cells and antibodies, 935–36
  of T cells, 936–37
Antigens, **935**
  epitopes of, 935
  helper T cells as responses to, 940–41
  recognition of, by B cells and antibodies, 935–36
  variations in, and immune system evasion, 948–49
Antihistamines, 947
Antimicrobial peptides, 930–31, 934f
Antioxidant properties, 192
Antiparallel DNA sugar-phosphate backbones, **88**, **310**, 314–16, 317f
Antithrombin, 419
Antivenin, 945
Antiviral drugs, 391
Ants, 30–31f, 290f, 648–49, 690f, 811f, 1199f
Anurans, 710–12
Anus, 889
Apes, 726–27
Aphotic zone, **1157**–58
Apical buds, **740**–41
Apical dominance, **740**–41, 830
Apical ectodermal ridge (AER), **1040**–41
Apical meristems, 603f, **746**. See also Primary growth, plant
Apical surface, epithelial, 856f
Apicomplexans, **583**–84
Apicoplast, 583–84
Apodans, 710–12
Apomixis, **812**, 818
Apoplast, **767**–68
Apoplastic route, 768, 773f
Apoptosis, **223**, **830**, **1034**
  blebbing in, 223
  caspases in, 159
  cytokinins in, 830
  cytotoxic T cell response and, 941f
  integration of cell-signaling pathways in, 223–25
  in morphogenesis, 1034–35
  p53 gene and, 376
  as plant response to flooding, 843–44
  self-tolerance vs., 938
  senescence and, 834
  signals triggering pathways of, 224–25
  in soil worm *Caenorhabditis elegans*, 224
Aposematic coloration, **1197**
Appendages, arthropod, 685
Appendix, **889**
Appetite, 893–94
Apple fruit, 810f
Apple maggot flies, 496–97
Applications, DNA technology, 417–23
  agricultural, 421–22f
  environmental cleanup, 421
  forensic, 420–21
  medical, 417–20
  safety and ethical issues of, 422–23
A-protein, 246
Aquaporins, **132**, **771**, **965**
  cellular membrane selective permeability and, 132
  facilitated diffusion and, 135
  kidney nephron function and role of, 965
  mutations in, as causes of diabetes insipidus, 970f
  role of, in kidney function, 969–70
  water diffusion and role of, 771
Aquatic animals. *See also* Fishes
  gills for gas exchange in, 916–17
  kidney adaptations in, 968

  nitrogenous wastes of, 958–59
  osmoregulation in, 954–56
Aquatic biomes, 1157–63
  acid precipitation and, 1244
  coral reefs, 1162f
  determining net ecosystem production in oceans, 1222f
  estuaries, 1160f
  global distribution of, 1158f
  habitat loss and, 1242
  hot spots of, 1251
  intertidal zones, 1161f
  inverted biomass pyramids of, 1226
  lakes, 1159f
  locomotion in, 1113–14
  marine benthic zones, 1162f
  marine vs. freshwater, 1157
  nutrient cycling in, 1230–31
  oceanic pelagic zones, 1161f
  primary production in, 1223–24
  protists as producers in, 597
  streams and rivers, 1160f
  wetlands, 1159f
  zonation in, 1157–58
Aqueous humor, 1096f
Aqueous solutions, **50**
  acidic and basic conditions of, 52–56
  hydrophilic and hydrophobic substances and, 51
  solute concentration in, 51–52
  solvents, solutes, and, 50–51
Aquifers, 788
Arabidopsis thaliana (mustard plant), 433t
  altering gene expression by touch, 842f
  genome of, 835
  MADS-box genes in, 447
  as model organism, 24, 755–56
  studying evolution of secondary growth in, 755
  triple response in, 833
Arachnids, 669f, **686**–87
Arbuscular mycorrhizae, **638**, 642f, 644, **796**–97
Archaea
  domain Archaea and, 13f (*see also* Archaea, domain)
  genome size and number of genes in, 432–33
  as prokaryotes, 8, 98 (*see also* Prokaryotes)
Archaea, domain, **13**, 551–52. *See also* Archaea; Prokaryotes
  compared to Bacteria and Eukarya, 566t
  gene expression in, compared to other domains, 346–47
  genome size in, 433t
  phylogeny of, 566–67
  as prokaryotic, 13
Archaean eon, 514, 515t
Archaefructus, 628–29
Archaeoglobus fulgidus, 433t
Archaeognatha, 690f
Archaeology, peat moss and, 610f
Archaeopteryx, 719
Archaeplastida, 579f, **590**–92
  green algae, 591–92
  red algae, 590–91
Archegonia, 603f
Archenterons, **661**, **1028**
Architeuthis dux, 680
Archosaurs, **715**
Arctic, 50, 1258
Ardipithecus ramidus, 728f–29
Arginine, 79f, 326, 327f
Arid conditions, 199–202
Aristotle, 453, 789
Arms, chromatid, 230
Arms race, evolutionary, 450–51
Arnold, A. Elizabeth, 648f
Arousal
  autonomic, 1071

  brain functions and, 1067–70
  human sexual, 1059
Arsenic, 32
Art, humans and, 733
Arteries, **899**–900, 905, 907, 913–14
Arterioles, **899**–900, 905f
Arthrophytes, 614f
Arthropods (Arthropoda), 669f, **684**–92, 1063f
  chelicerates, 686–87
  chitin as structural polysaccharide for, 74
  compound eyes of, 1095–96
  crustaceans, 691–92
  evolution of, 657–58
  exoskeletons of, 1111–12
  external anatomy of, 685f
  general characteristics of, 685–86
  Hox genes and body plan of, 684–85
  insects, 688–91 (*see also* Insects (Hexapoda))
  land colonization by, 519
  Malpighian tubules of, 961–62
  myriapods, 687–88
  origins of, 684–85
Artificial corridors, 1250–51
Artificial selection, **458**–59f, 633, 801, 815–16
Artiodactyls, 725f
Ascending limb, loop of Henle, **965**
Asci, **644**
Ascocarps, 642f, **644**
Ascomycetes (Ascomycota), 642f, **644**–46
Asexual reproduction, **249**, **812**, **996**
  in angiosperms, 812–15
  angiosperm sexual reproduction vs., 812–13
  bryophyte, 609
  evolution and, in animals, 259–60
  fungal, 639–40
  inheritance and, 249
  of lichens, 649–50
  mechanisms of, 996–97
  protist, 576
  rotifer, 676–77
  sexual reproduction vs., 996–97 (*see also* Sexual reproduction)
  of single-cell eukaryotes, 236
Asian elephant, 457–58
A site (aminoacyl-tRNA binding site), 339f, **340**, 341f
Asparagine, 79f
Aspartic acid, 79f
Aspen trees, 812
Aspergillus, 650, 651
Aspirin, 633, 847, 979, 1090
Assassin bugs, 690f
Assembly stage, phage lytic cycle, 385f
Assisted migration, **1258**
Assisted reproductive technologies, **1017**–18
Associative learning, **1125**–26
Asteroidea, 692–93f
Asters, **231**, 232f
Asthma, 63f, 213f, 909
Astragalus bones, 465f
Astrobiologists, 52
Astrocytes, 1065f, 1066
Asymmetrical cell division, 757
Asymmetric carbon, 62–63, 70, 78
Asymmetry, body, 1036–38, 1042
Atherosclerosis, 76, 77, 138, **913**–14
Athletes, blood doping by, 913
Athlete's foot, 650
Atmosphere
  chemistry of, 28–29
  Earth's early, 507–8
  ozone in, 1258–59
  photosynthesis and development of oxygen in, 516
Atomic mass, **33**
Atomic mass unit (amu), 33
Atomic nucleus, **33**
Atomic number, **33**

Atoms, **33**
    properties of elements and structure of, 33–37
    tracking, through photosynthesis, 187–88
ATP (adenosine triphosphate), **66**, **149**
    aminoacyl-tRNA synthetases and, 338f
    in animal metabolism, 869
    conversion of, to cyclic AMP, 216–17
    in DNA replication, 314
    energy coupling and, 149
    as energy for active transport, 136
    as energy source for cellular processes, 66
    in feedback regulation, 10–11, 181
    hydrolysis of, and work of, 150–51
    regeneration of, 151
    regulation of regeneration of, 158–59
    in sliding-filament model of muscle contraction,
        1104–6
    structure and hydrolysis of, 149–50
    synthesis of, by cellular respiration, 163, 174–77 (see
        also Cellular respiration)
    synthesis of, by fermentation, 177–79
    synthesis of, in light reactions of photosynthesis,
        188, 193–95
ATP cycle, 151f
ATP synthase, **173**–74
Atria, heart, **900**, 902–3
Atrial natriuretic peptide (ANP), **971**
Atrioventricular (AV) nodes, **904**
Atrioventricular (AV) valves, **903**
Attached earlobes pedigree analysis case, 275–76
Attachment function, membrane protein, 129f
Attachment stage, phage lytic cycle, 385f
Auditory communication, 1121
Auditory nerve, 1093
Aurea mutant tomato, 822
Australia, 464–65, 521, 1163–64, 1252
Australian moles, 540–41
Australian scaly-foot lizard, 536
Australian thorny devil lizard, 716f
Australopithecus afarensis, 729–30
Australopithecus anamensis, 729
Australopiths, 729–30
Autism, 1077
Autocrine signaling, **975**, 979
Autoimmune diseases, 247, **947**
Automatic DNA-sequencing machines, 10
Autonomic arousal, 1071
Autonomic nervous system, **1066**–67
Autophagy, 107
Autopolyploids, **495**–96
Autosomal trisomies, 299
Autosomes, **250**, 300–301
Autotrophs, **184**, 564, 565f, 570, 1219
Auxin, **827**–29
    in cell differentiation, 830
    in control of apical dominance, 830
    in de-etiolation (greening) responses, 824
    discovery of, 826
    in embryo sacs, 804
    ethylene and, 833
    overview of, 827t
    in plant development, 828–29
    in plant gravitropism, 842
    polar transport and, 827–28
    practical uses of, 829
    role of, in cell elongation, 828, 829f
Average heterozygosity, **470**–71
Avery, Mary Ellen, 920
Avery, Oswald, 306
Avian flu, 392, 1215. *See also* Birds
Avirulent pathogens, **846**, 847f
Avogadro's number, 51–52
Avr (avirulence) genes, 846
Axel, Richard, 1103
Axial polarity, 757f
Axillary buds, **740**–41

Axis formation, 371–73, 1036–38
Axolotls, 526f, 897
Axon hillocks, 1046, 1053
Axons, 858f, **1046**, 1054, 1065
Azidothymidine (AZT), 391

B
β₂-adrenergic receptor, 213f
β-amyloid, 1081
β-catenin, animal gastrulation control and, 659f
β chain, 936
β-galactosidase, 157, 354, 399–400
β-globin gene, 399–400, 406, 437–38
β-keratin, bird feathers and, 718
β pleated sheat, **82**f
Baby boom, U. S., 1188–89
Bacillus anthracis, 572
Bacillus thuringiensis, 816
Backbone, polypetide, 80
Backbone, sugar-phosphate, 88–89f
Backbones
    invertebrate lack of, 666
    vertebrate, 703–4
Bacteria
    alcohol fermentation and, 178
    anaerobic respiration in, 177
    antibiotic drugs and, 339
    antibiotic resistance in, 461–62, 564
    B. L. Bassler's work on, 92–93
    binary fission in, 236–37f
    bioremediation using, 1233
    cell signaling in, 92–93, 207
    cell structure of, 98f
    cellular integration and, 122
    chemoautotrophs in Antarctica, 1218
    cholera, 217
    conjugation in, 562–64
    DNA packing in chromosomes of, 320–21
    DNA replication in, 312–16, 317f
    domain Bacteria and, 13f (see also Bacteria, domain)
    evidence for DNA and, 305–8
    expressing cloned eukaryotic genes in, 402–3
    gene expression in, 346–47
    genome size and number of genes in, 432–33
    glycolysis and ancient, 179
    Gram staining of, 557–58
    as model organisms (see Escherichia coli (E. coli)
        bacteria)
    mutualistic, and vertebrate digestion, 890–91
    mutualistic and pathogenic, 571–72
    origins of mitochondria and chloroplasts in, 109–10
    origins of photosynthesis in, 186
    in Permian mass extinction, 522
    photosynthesis and, 195
    phylogeny of, 567–70
    in plant nutrition mutualisms, 793–95
    plasmids of (see Plasmids)
    polymerase chain reaction and, 403–4
    as prokaryotes, 8, 98 (see also Prokaryotes)
    regulation of transcription in, 351–56
    soil, 787, 1201f
    transcription and translation in, 329f, 347f
    viruses in (see Bacteriophages (phages))
Bacteria, domain, **13**. *See also* Bacteria
    compared to Archaea and Eukarya, 566t
    gene expression in, compared to other domains,
        346–47
    genome size in, 433t
    phylogeny of, 567–70
    as prokaryotic, 13 (see also Prokaryotes)
Bacterial artificial chromosome (BAC), **400**–401, 427–28
Bacteriophages (phages), **306**, **383**–87, 562. *See also*
        Phages
Bacteriorhodopsin, 129f
Bacteroides thetaiotaomicron, 571
Bacteroids, **794**–95

Bait-and-switch defense, 581
Baker, C. S., 539f
Baker's yeast, 651. *See also* Yeasts
Balance, body, 1090–94, 1113
Balance of nature view, 1207
Balancing selection, **483**–84, 485f
Baleen, 881f
Ball-and-socket joints, 1112f
Ball-and-stick models, 41f, 60f
Ballooning, spider, 687
Bandicoots, 722
Barbiturates, 105
Barbs, 626f
Bark, **754**
Barley, 631f, 831f
Barnacles, 691–92, 1196f
Barr, Murray, 291
Barr body, **291**–92
Barrier contraceptives, 1016
Barrier defenses, 930f, 932
Barrier reefs, 1162f
Basal angiosperms, **630**
Basal animals, sponges as, 662
Basal body, 115f, **116**
Basal lamina, epithelial, 856f
Basal metabolic rate (BMR), **869**–70
Basal surface, epithelial, 856f
Basal taxon, **539**
Base pairing
    in DNA and RNA structure, 88–89f
    in DNA double helix structure, 310
    in DNA replication, 311–12
Base-pair sites, 411–12
Bases, **53**
    amino acids as, 79f
    buffers and, 54–55
    hydrogen ions and, 53
    pH scale and, 53–54
Bases, nitrogenous. *See* Nitrogenous bases; Nucleotides
Basidiocarps, **646**
Basidiomycetes (Basidiomycota), 642f, **646**–48
Basidiospores, 646–47
Basidium, **646**
Basilar membrane, 1091f, 1092–93
Basin wetlands, 1159f
Basophils, 910f, 912f
Bassler, Bonnie L., 92–93, 207
Bates, Henry, 21
Batesian mimicry, **1197**
Batrachochytrium dendrobatidis, 650–51f
Bats, 16, 541, 805f, 968–69, 1240
B cells, **935**
    activation of, in humoral immune response, 942
    antigen recognition by, 935–36
    development of, 937–40
    diversity of, 937–38
    proliferation of, 939
Bdelloidea, 677
Bdelloid rotifers, 259–60, 677
Beadle, George, 326, 327f
Beagle, Charles Darwin's voyage on H.M.S., 455–56
Beaks
    finch, 456–57f, 469
    shapes of bird, 720
    soapberry bug, 461
Beans, 808f, 809f, 838, 876
Bears, 12f, 46, 144f, 492, 500, 875, 1246–47, 1252
Beavers, 1205
Bed bugs, 690f
Beech trees, 1148–49
Bees, 290f, 690f, 804f. *See also* Honeybees
Beetles, 452, 690f
Behavior, animal, **1118**–41
    altruism and inclusive fitness in, 1137–39
    animal signals and communication and, 1120–22
    applying game theory to, 1133

behavioral ecology and causation questions about, 1118–19
cerebral cortex information processing and, 1074–75
experience and, 1123
fixed action patterns, 1119
foraging, 1128–29
genetic basis of, 1134–35
genetic variation and evolution of, 1135–36
human culture and evolution of, 1139
innate vs. variable, 1123
learning and, 1123–28
mating, 1129–34
migration, 1119–20
natural selection and evolution of, 1118
review of, 1139–40
rhythms of, 1120
sensory inputs as stimuli for simple and complex, 1118–22
species distributions and habitat selection, 1165
survival, reproductive success, and, 1128–34
thermoregulatory responses in, 866
Behavioral ecology, **1119**
Behavioral isolation, 490*f*
Beijerinck, Martinus, 382
Belding's ground squirrels, 1137–38, 1172–75*t*
Beluga whales, 1089
Benign tumors, **242**
Benthic zone, **1157**
Benthos, **1157**
Berries, 626*f*
Berthold, Peter, 1136*f*
Berzelius, Jöns Jakob, 58
Beta-carotene, 816, 817, 878–79
Beta cells, 983
Beta oxidation, **180**
Beta proteobacteria, 568*f*
BGI (formerly Beijing Genome Institute), 429
B horizon, 786*f*
bicoid gene, **372**–73, 445
Biennials, 747
Big-bang reproduction, 1180
Bilateral symmetry, 632, **658**–59, 662, 1036–38
Bilaterians (Bilateria), **662**–64, 674, 697
Bilayers, phospholipid, 76–77, 99, 125–27, 131. *See also* Cellular membranes; Plasma membranes
Bile, **887**
Binary fission, **236**, 560–61*f*, 585
Binding sites, ribosome, 339*f*
Binomial nomenclature, 453–54, **537**
Biochemical pathways, 327*f*
Biochemistry, 97
Biodiesel, 185*f*
Biodiversity, 452
angiosperm, 630–31*f*
animal (*see* Animal(s))
bacteria and archaea and prokaryotic (*see* Prokaryotes)
branching phylogeny and, 733
colonization of land by plants (*see* Land plants)
W. F. Doolittle's work on evolution of, 534–35
ecosystem and community diversity, 1240
effects of mass extinctions on, 521*f*, 522–24
evolution and, 14–16, 457 (*see also* Darwin, Charles; Evolution; Natural selection)
evolutionary developmental biology and (*see* Evolutionary developmental biology (evo-devo))
fungal (*see* Fungi)
genetic diversity, 1239
global change and, 1244
habitat loss and fragmentation and, 1241–42
human welfare and, 1240–41
importance of, 1143
introduced species and, 1242–43
invertebrate (*see* Invertebrates)
landscape ecology and, 1249–54
levels of, 1239–40

microbial, 535
overharvesting and, 1243–44
phylogenies of (*see* Phylogenetic trees; Phylogenies)
plant (*see* Plant(s))
protist (*see* Protists)
seed plant (*see* Seed plants)
species diversity, 1239–40
of species in communities (*see* Species diversity)
taxonomy and classification of, 12–14 (*see also* Taxonomy)
threats to, 1241–44
tree of life and, 16–17 (*see also* Tree of life)
unity in, 14, 15*f*, 16
of venomous molluscs, 851
vertebrate (*see* Vertebrates)
Biodiversity hot spots, **1251**–52
Bioenergetics, **143**, **868**–72
energy allocation and use in, 868–69
energy budgets in, 871
influences on metabolic rate in, 870
of locomotion, 1114–15
of osmoregulation, 956–57
overview of animal, 869*f*
quantifying energy use in, 869
thermoregulation and minimum metabolic rate in, 869–70
thyroid hormones and, 987–88
torpor, hibernation, and energy conservation in, 871–72
of urea and uric acid, 959
Bioethanol, 185*f*
Biofilms, 93, 207, **565**
Biofuels, 185*f*, **817**
Biogenic amines, **1058**–59, 1080
Biogeochemical cycles, **1227**–32
Biogeographic factors, community, 1211–13
island equilibrium model and, 1212–13
latitudinal gradients and, 1211
species-area curve, area effects, and, 1211–12
Biogeography, **466**, 1163–67
Bioinformatics, **10**, **426**
analysis of genomes using, 10, 426, 429–32
centralized resources for, 429, 430*f*
identifying protein-coding genes and their functions using gene annotation, 429–30
protein structure analysis in, 85
systems biology, proteomics and, in study of genes and gene expression, 430–32 (*see also* Systems biology)
Biological augmentation, **1233**
Biological clocks, 838–39, **1070**–71*f*. *See also* Circadian clocks
Biological communities. *See* Communities
Biological diversity. *See* Biodiversity
Biological Dynamics of Forest Fragments Project, 1250
Biological magnification, **1255**
Biological molecules, 68–91
carbohydrates, 69–74
emergent properties in, 89
four classes of, 68
lipids, 74–77
macromolecules as polymers built from monomers, 68–69
nucleic acids, 86–89
proteins, 77–86*f*
review of, 90
Biological species concept, **489**. *See also* Species
limitations of, and alternatives to, 492
morphology and, 488
reproductive isolation and, 489–91*f*
Biology, **1**
astrobiology, 52
biophilia and, 1261
carbon, organic compounds, organic chemistry, and (*see* Organic compounds)

careers in, 93, 535, 851, 1143
cells (*see* Cell(s))
connection of, to chemistry, 30–31*f* (*see also* Chemistry)
conservation (*see* Conservation biology)
emergent properties in systems biology, 3–6 (*see also* Emergent properties)
evolution as core theme of, 1, 11–18 (*see also* Evolution)
genetics in, 248 (*see also* Genetics)
genomics and bioinformatics in, 10 (*see also* Bioinformatics; Genomics)
large biological molecules (*see* Biological molecules)
levels of organization and themes of this book about, 2–11
molecular (*see* Molecular biology)
review of themes of, 25–26
scientific method and inquiry in, 18–25 (*see also* Inquiry, scientific; Inquiry studies; Research methods; Science)
as scientific study of life, 1–2 (*see also* Life)
taxonomy in, 12–14
Bioluminescence, 92, 142, 838
Biomanipulation, **1206**
Biomass, **1203**
biofuels and, 817
pyramid of, and standing crop, 1226
standing crop measure of, 1221
total biomass accumulation, 1222
Biomass pyramid, 1226
Biomes, **1150**. *See also* Aquatic biomes; Terrestrial biomes
Biophilia, 1240, 1261
Bioremediation, 572*f*, **573**, 648, 789, **1232**–33
Biorhythms, melatonin and, 993. *See also* Biological clocks; Circadian rhythms
Biosphere, **1145***f*. *See also* Earth
biophilia and future of, 1261
ecological role of prokaryotes in, 570–71
global climate change of, 1148–49
human carrying capacity of, 1190–91
human impacts on (*see* Human environmental impacts)
importance of seedless vascular plants to, 615
as level of biological organization, 4*f*
photosynthesis as process that feeds, 184–85
Biosynthetic pathways, 143, 180
Biotechnology, **396**–425. *See also* DNA technology; Genetics
agricultural applications of, 421–22*f*
analyzing gene expression, 409–10
determining gene function, 410–12
DNA cloning, 396–405
DNA sequencing, 10, 407–9
environmental cleanup applications of, 421
forensic applications of, 420–21
gel electrophoresis and Southern blotting, 405–7
genetic engineering and, 816–19
genetic testing and, 279–81
medical applications of, 417–20
organismal cloning, 412–17*f*
phytoremediation, 789
plant, 814–15
practical applications of, 417–23
prokaryotes in, 572–73
recombinant DNA, genetic engineering, and, 396
review of, 423–24
safety and ethical issues of, 422–23
science, society, and, 24–25
society and plant, 819
techniques of, 405–12
Bioterrorism, 572
Biotic factors, **1149**
climate and, 1149
in pollination, 804*f*–5*f*

in species distributions, 1163–64, 1165–66
Biotic stresses, plants and, **843**, 845–47
Bipedal animals, 730, 1113
Bipolar cells, 1096*f*, 1098
Bipolar disorder, 20, **1080**
Birds
    alimentary canals in, 882*f*
    avian flu in, 1215
    breathing by, 920–21
    DDT and, 1256
    derived characters of, 717–18
    as descended from dinosaurs, 547–48
    discovery of new species of, 1238
    double circulation in, 901*f*
    endangered or threatened, 1239
    evolution of, 658
    evolution of cognition and brains of, 1075–76
    evolution of genes in, 440–41
    fat hoarding in, 894–95
    flight adaptations of, 1114
    flower pollination by, 805*f*
    gastrulation in, 1029–30
    gene flow in great tits, 479–80
    global climate change and migration of, 29
    greater prairie chicken, 478–79, 1245–46
    kidney adaptations in, 967–68
    limb formation in, 1040–41
    living, 719–20
    nitrogenous wastes of, 958–59
    organogenesis in, 1033*f*
    origin of, 718–19
    problem solving of, 1126
    red-cockaded woodpecker decline, 1248–49
    as reptiles, 715
    salt excretion in marine, 957–58
    sex determination of, 290*f*
    species-area curve of North American breeding, 1212
    thermoregulation in, 866
    wings of, 7*f*, 541, 718*f*
Birth control, human, 1015–17
Birth control pills, **1016**–17
Birth defects, human, 879, 1014
Births, human
    demographics and rates of, 1173–75, 1188
    effects of vitamin supplementation on neural tube
        defects in, 879
    labor and, 1014–15
    newborn screening, 280–81
    population density and rates of, 1182
    population dynamics and, 1171*f*–72, 1175–76
Bisphenol A, 993
Bitter taste, 1101–2
Bivalves, 679, 680–81*f*
Black bears, 12*f*
Black bread mold, 643–44
Blackcap warblers, 1136
Black rush plants, 1200
Blacktip reef sharks, 706*f*
Blades, **586**, **741**
Blastocoel, **1025**
Blastocysts, 415, **1012**, **1031**
Blastomeres, **1025**
Blastopores, **661**, **1028**, 1039*f*
BLAST program, 429, 430*f*
Blastula, **655**, 1021, **1025**
Blebbing, 223
Blending hypothesis in heredity, 262
Blindness, 301, 477–78, 569*f*, 878–79
Blind spot, 1096*f*
Blood, **857***f*, **899**. *See also* Blood vessels; Circulatory
        systems
    apoptosis of human white blood cells, 223*f*
    blood groups of, 272–73, 946
    bone marrow cells and, 228*f*
    cellular elements in, 910*f*, 911

cholesterol in, and atherosclerosis, 77
in closed circulatory systems, 686, 899–901
clotting of, 11, 291, 397*f*, 683, 911–12, 979
composition of mammalian, 910*f*
filtration of, by nephrons, 963–65
flow of, in mammalian excretory system, 962*f*
flow velocity of, 905–6
glycoproteins and types of human, 130
homeostasis of glucose levels in, 982–84
hormonal regulation of volume and pressure of,
        970–71
human blood groups, 272–73
immune rejection of transfusions of, 946
melatonin concentrations in human, 862*f*
pH of human, 54–55
plasma, 910–11
pressure of (*see* Blood pressure)
regulation of calcium levels in, by parathyroid
        glands, 989–90
respiratory pigments in, 923–25
sickle-cell disease and, 84
stem cells and replacement of cellular elements in,
        912–13
thermoregulation and, 864–65
vampire bat digestion of, 968–69
Blood-brain barrier, 1066
Blood clotting, 11, 291, 397*f*, 683, 911–12, 979
Blood doping, 913
Blood Falls, 1218*f*
Blood flukes, 675–76, 1198
Blood groups, 272–73, 946
Bloodletting, 683
Blood poisoning, 568*f*
Blood pressure, 906–8
    changes in, during cardiac cycle, 906
    in closed circulatory systems, 899
    gravity and, 907–8
    hypertension and, 914, 915
    measurement of, 907*f*
    regulation of, 906–7
    renin-angiotensin-aldosterone system (RAAS) and,
        970–71
Blood vessels
    blood flow velocity in, 905–6
    blood pressure in, 906–8
    capillary function, 908–9
    in circulatory systems, 898
    dilation of, 217
    mammalian excretory system and, 962*f*
    structure and function of, 905
Blooms
    diatom, 585
    dinoflagellate, 583
    nitrogen pollution and phytoplankton, 1255
    preventing algal, 1223–24
Blowfly, 805*f*
Bluefin tuna, 1243–44
Blue-footed boobies, 490*f*
Bluehead wrasse, 999
Blue jays, 1125
Blue-light photoreceptors, **836**, 839
Body axes, 1036–38
Body cavities, **660**
Body cells. *See* Somatic cells
Body hairs, insect, 1090
Body plans, **658**. *See also* Animal form and function
    angiosperm, 629
    animal, 658–61, 853, 855
    arthropod, 684–85
    axis formation and, 1036–38
    body cavities, 660
    cell fate specification and (*see* Cell fate)
    evolutionary effect of developmental genes on,
        525–26, 527*f*
    fungal, 637–38

homeotic genes and, 445–47
insect, 527
lichen, 649*f*
mollusc, 678*f*
organizer of, 1039–40
pattern formation and setting up of, 369–73
protostome and deuterostome development of,
        660–61
symmetry in, 658–59
tissues and, 659–60
totipotency, developmental potential, and, 1038–39
Body size, metabolic rate and, 870
Body temperature regulation, animal, 861–64. *See also*
        Thermoregulation
Bog mummy, 610*f*
Bohr shift, **924**
Bolivar, Francisco, 736
Bolting, 831
Bolus, **884**
Bombina toads, 498–99, 501
Bonds, chemical. *See* Chemical bonds
Bone, animal, 704, **857***f*
Bone marrow cells, 228*f*
Bone marrow transplants, 946
Bone morphogenetic protein 4 (BMP-4), 1039–40
Bones
    of human skeleton, 1112*f*
    mammalian ear, 721
Bonobos, 726–27*f*
Bony fishes, 954–55, 968
Book lungs, **687**
Boom-and-bust population cycles, 1185
Boren, Linda, 534
Borisy, Gary, 235*f*
Bormann, Herbert, 1231
Botox, 1058
Bottleneck effect, **478**–79
Bottlenose dolphins, 865*f*, 1070
Bottom-up model, trophic control, **1206**
Botulism, 387, 569*f*, 572, 1058
Boundaries
    community, 1194
    ecosystem, 1218, 1249–50
    population, 1170–71
Bound ribosomes, 102–4, 343
Bouzat, Juan, 478–79
Boveri, Theodor, 286
Bowden, Richard, 609*f*
Bowman's capsule, **963***f*
Boysen-Jensen, Peter, 825
Brachiopods (Brachiopoda), 667*f*, **677**
Bracts, 742*f*
Brain cells, 94
Brains, **1045**
    arousal and sleep functions of, 1067–70
    biological clock regulation by, 1070–71*f*
    breathing control centers in human, 922
    in central nervous systems, 1063–65
    cerebral cortex functions in, 1072–76
    cognition and human, 1075–76
    cortical frontal lobe function of, 1075
    drug addiction and reward system of, 1080–81
    emotion functions of, 1071–72
    endocrine glands in human, 984–86*t*
    evolution of chordate and vertebrate, 700–701
    evolution of pallium of avian and human, 1075–76
    functional imaging of, 1072*f*
    glioblastoma cancer of, 432
    hominin, 728–29
    information processing in, 1074–75
    language and speech functions of, 1072–73
    lateralization of cortical function in, 1073–74
    mammalian, 720, 1046–47*f*
    Neanderthal, 731
    neurons in human, 1062

opiate receptors in, 1059
organization of human, 1068f–69f
in sensory systems, 1085–87
strokes in, 914
structure and function of, 1067–76
thermostatic role of hypothalamus of human, 867–68
visual information processing in, 1099–1100
Brainstem, 1067, **1068**f
Brain waves, 1067
Branching, carbon skeleton, 61
Branching, plant, 749
Branching evolution, 530
Branch length, phylogenetic tree, 544, 545f
Branch points, **538**–39
Brassinosteroids, 824, 827t, **831**
Brawn, Jeffrey, 1246f
Brazil nut trees, 1181f
BRCA1 and *BRCA2* genes, 377
Bread mold (*Neurospora crassa*), 326, 327f, 645–46
Bread yeast, 651. *See also* Yeasts
Breakdown pathways, 143
Breast cancer, 213, 242f, 243f, 377, 418
Breasts, 1004
Breathing, **920**–22
in amphibians, 920
in birds, 920–21
control of, in humans, 922
in mammals, 921–22
Breathing control centers, 922
Breeding, plant, 815–16
Breeding, selective, 458–59f
Breeding birds, 1212
Brenner, Sydney, 1036
Brewer's yeast, 651, 1183f. *See also* Yeasts
Briggs, Robert, 413
Brightfield (unstained specimen) microscopy, **96**f
Brightfield (stained specimen) microscopy, **96**f
Brine shrimp, 446f, 527
Bristlecone pine tree, 623f
Bristletails, 690f
Brittle stars, 693
Broca, Pierre, 1073–74
Broca's area, 1073–74
Bronchi, **919**
Bronchioles, **919**
Brood bodies, 609
Brooding, 547–48
Brown algae, 579f, **586**, 587f
Brown bears, 144f
Brown fat, 177, 866
Brown-headed cowbird, 1250
Brown tree snake, 1242
Brundtland, G. H., 1240
Brush border, 887f, 888
Brushtail possum, 722f
Bryophytes (Bryophyta), **604**, 606–10
ecological and economic importance of, 609–10
gametophytes of, 606–9
gametophyte-sporophyte relationships in, 619f
as nonvascular plants, 604–5
phylogeny of, 605t, 608f
sporophytes of, 609
Bryozoans, 667f, 677
Bt toxin, 816–18
Buck, Linda, 1103
Budding, 100f, 249f, 640, **996**–97
Buffers, **54**–55
Bugs, 690f
Bulbourethral glands, 1005
Bulbs, 741f
Bulk feeders, **881**f
Bulk flow, **771**, 772–76, 780–81
Bundle-sheath cells, **200**, 750
Burgess Shale fossil bed, 511f
Burkitt's lymphoma, 377

Burmese python, 867f
Bush babies, 726
Butterflies, 689f, 690f, 805f, 818, 974, 980, 1142–43, 1149
Buttress roots, 740f
Buxbaum, Joseph, 444f

C

C_3 plants, **199–200**
C_4 plants, **200**, 202f
Cabomba caroliniana, 755
Cacao tree, 648f
Caches, food, 1125
Cachexia, 988–89
Cactus, 779f, 805f, 1152
Cadang-cadang, 393
Caecilians, 710–12
Caenorhabditis elegans (soil worm)
apoptosis in, 224
complete genome sequence for, 426
DNA microarray assays on, 410
fate mapping for, 1036
as model organism, 24, 684
nervous system of, 1063
size of and number of genes in genome of, 433
Cain, Michael, 451f, 535f
Calcitonin, 986t, **990**
Calcium, 32, 989–90
Calcium carbonate, 589
Calcium channels, 851
Calcium ions, 105, 217–18, 822–23, 1057–58, 1106–7f, 1109–10
California Current, 1147–48
California poppy, 631f
Callus, **814**
Calorie (cal), **48**, 869
Calories, food, 48
Calorimeters, 869
Calvin, Melvin, 188–89
Calvin cycle, **188**–89, 198–99
Cambrian explosion, **518**, **657**
Cambrian period, 697
Camels, 956
Camouflage, 460f, 1197
cAMP. *See* Cyclic AMP
CAM (crassulacean acid metabolism) plants, 201–**2**, 778
Canada goose, 865f
Canavanine, 845
Cancer
abnormal cell cycle control systems in, 242–43
abnormal protein kinases and, 216
breast and colorectal, 376, 377
carcinogen screening and, 346
chromosomal translocations and, 300
density-dependent inhibition, anchorage dependence, and, 241f
DNA microarray detection of, 396
due to faulty apoptosis, 225
due to faulty cell cycle control, 373–77
endocrine disruptors and, 992–93
HIV and, 949
inherited predisposition and other factors contributing to, 376–77
interferences with normal cell-signaling pathways and development of, 374–76
mismatch repair and colon, 317
multistep developmental model of, 376
obesity and, 893
ozone depletion, UV radiation, and, 1259
personalized treatments for, 376, 418
PET scanners and, 34–35f
receptor tyrosine kinase malfunctions and, 213
skin, 28, 318, 1259
species and genetic diversity and treatments for, 1241
systems biology approach to, 432
telomeres and prevention of, 319
tumor-suppressor genes and, 374

types of genes associated with, 373–74
ultraviolet radiation and, 28
vaccines, 950
Cancer Genome Atlas, 432
Candida albicans, 650
Canopy, **1152**
Canyon tree frog, 1197f
Capacitation, 1024
Capecchi, Mario, 410
Capillaries, **899**–900, 905, 908–9
Capillary beds, **899**–900, 908–9
Capsaicin, 1089, 1090
Capsids, **383**–84
Capsomeres, 383
Capsule, 98f, **558**, **609**
Carbohydrates, **69**–74
cell-cell recognition role of membrane, 130
digestion of, 886f
as fuel for catabolism, 179–80
as macromolecules, 68
monosaccharides and disaccharides, 69–70, 71f
in plant composition, 789
polysaccharides as, 70–74
as product of photosynthesis, 203
Carbon
in amino acids, 78
atoms of, in organic compounds, 60–63
as essential element, 32, 58, 66
fixation (*see* Carbon fixation)
isotopes of, 34–35f
net ecosystem production and, 1222
in organic compounds, 58, 66 (*see also* Organic compounds)
in peatlands, 610
in plant composition, 789
Carbon-12, 512
Carbon-14, 512
Carbonate ions, 55
Carbon cycle, 1228f
Carbon dioxide
in alternative carbon fixation mechanisms, 199–202
in capillaries, 908–9
in circulation and gas exchange, 923–25
conversion of, to carbohydrate by Calvin cycle of photosynthesis, 189
covalent bonding of carbon atoms in, 60–61
diatoms and capture of, 585
fossil fuels, ocean acidification, acid precipitation, and, 55–56
gas exchange and, 915–16 (*see also* Gas exchange)
global climate change and, 6, 50, 1148
greenhouse effect and, 28–29, 50
inhibition of fruit ripening with, 834
iron fertilization of oceans to remove, 1223–24
in mammalian circulation, 902
metabolic rate as production of, 869
net ecosystem production and, 1222
in photosynthesis, 43
photosynthetic processing of, by marine protists, 597
rising levels of atmospheric, 1256–58
rubisco as acceptor for, 199
seedless vascular plants and, 615
as stimulus for stomatal opening and closing, 777–78
tropical rain forest deforestation and, 633f
Carbon fixation, **189**. *See also* Carbon
alternative mechanisms of, 199–202
C_4 plants and C_4 pathway of, 200–201
in Calvin cycle of photosynthesis, 188–89, 199
CAM plants and crassulacean acid metabolism mode of, 201–2
in photorespiration, 199–200
Carbonic acid, 53, 54–56
Carbon monoxide, 1060
Carbon skeletons, 61–63
Carbonyl group, **64**f

Carboxyl group, **64**f
Carboxylic acids, **64**f
Carcinoma, 376f
Cardiac cycle, **903**, 906
Cardiac muscle, **858**f, **1110**
Cardiac output, **903**
Cardiovascular diseases, 76, 893, 913–15
Cardiovascular systems, **899**–902
 blood composition and function in, 910–15 (see also Blood)
 blood vessels, blood flow, and blood pressure in, 905–10
 as closed circulatory systems, 899
 hearts in mammalian, 902–4
 human diseases of, 913–15
 lymphatic systems and, 909
 vertebrate, 899–902
Caribou, 473f, 878f, 998
Carnivores (Carnivora), 538f, 725f
Carnivores, **875**
 dentition and diet in, 889f
 in ecosystems, 1220
 energetic hypothesis and biomass of, 1203–4
 herbivore alimentary canals vs., 890f
Carnivorous plants, 785, 797, 798f
Carotenoids, 190–**91**, 583
Carpellate flowers, 813
Carpels, 263, **626**, **802**
Carrier crabs, 1194
Carrier proteins
 in active transport, 135–36
 cellular membrane selective permeability and, 132
 facilitated diffusion and, 134–35
Carriers, **276**, 279–80
Carrion flower, 805f
Carroll, Scott, 461f
Carroll, Sean, 685f
Carrots, 412f, 814f
Carrying capacity, **1177**
 for human population, 1190–91
 logistic population growth model and, 1177–79
Carson, Rachel, 1256
Cartilage, **857**f
Cartilage skeleton, 703, 705–6
Casein, 78f
Casparian strip, **772**
Caspase, 159
Cassava, 633, 816–17
Castor bean seeds, 808f
Catabolic pathways, **143**
 ATP production by, 164
 cellular respiration as, 143, 164–68 (see also Cellular respiration)
 metabolism, cellular respiration, and, 179–80
 redox reactions in, 164–67
 regulation of, 181
Catabolite activator protein (CAP), 355
Catalysts, **77**, **152**. See also Enzymatic catalysis; Enzymes
Catalytic cycle, 154–55
Cataracts, 28, 1259
Catastrophism, **454**
Catecholamines, **990**–91
Catenulida, 674
Caterpillars, 470f, 845, 881f, 974, 980, 1225
Cation exchange, **786**–87
Cations, **40**
Cats, 292, 414
Cattle egrets, 1164, 1199
Caulerpa, 592
Causation, behavioral, 1118–19
Cavalier-Smith, Thomas, 593
CC (Carbon Copy, cloned cat), 414
CCR5 protein, 130f
cDNA libraries, **401**
Cech, Thomas, 509
Cecum, **888**–89

Cedar Creek Natural History Area, 1201–2
Celera Genomics, 428–29
Cell(s), 92–124
 animal (see Animal cells)
 auxin in differentiation of, 830
 auxin in elongation of, 828, 829f
 B. L. Bassler's work on, 92–93
 cell fractionation for studying, 97
 cellular elements in blood, 910f, 911, 912–13
 cellular integration of, 122
 circulatory systems, gas exchange surfaces, and, 897–98
 communication between (see Cell signaling)
 cytokinins in division and differentiation of, 829–30
 division of (see Cell cycle; Cell division)
 energy metabolism of (see Cellular respiration; Fermentation; Metabolism; Photosynthesis)
 eukaryotic vs. prokaryotic, 98–99 (see also Eukaryotic cells; Prokaryotic cells)
 fate of (see Cell fate)
 as fundamental units of life, 8, 94, 228
 as level of biological organization, 5f
 membranes of (see Cellular membranes; Cell walls)
 metabolism and (see Metabolism)
 microscopy for studying, 94–97
 motility of (see Cell motility)
 photosynthesis in (see Photosynthesis)
 plant (see Plant cells)
 producing clones of, to carry recombinant plasmids, 399–400
 programmed cell death (see Apoptosis)
 prokaryotic, 557–58
 protein folding in, 85–86f
 protocells as first, 509
 review of, 122–24
 sequential regulation of gene expression during differentiation of, 367–69
 size range of, 95f
 stem (see Stem cells)
 transcription specific to type of, 361f
 water and, 46
Cell adhesion molecules, 1034
Cell body, neuron, 858f, **1046**, 1056
Cell-cell communication. See Cell signaling
Cell-cell recognition
 in local cell signaling, 208
 membrane carbohydrates and, 130
 membrane proteins and, 129f
Cell cycle, **228**–45. See also Cell division; Cell(s)
 binary fission in bacteria, 236–37f
 cell division process in, 228
 cellular organization of genetic material in, 229
 cytokinesis in, 234–36
 distribution of chromosomes during eukaryotic cell division, 229–30
 evolution of mitosis, 237–38
 genetic changes affecting, and cancer development, 373–77
 mitotic phases alternating with interphase in, 230–38
 mitotic spindle in, 231–34, 235f
 phases of, 231
 phases of, in animal cells, 232f–33f
 phases of, in plant cells, 236f
 regulation of eukaryotic, by cell cycle control system, 238–43
 review of, 244
Cell cycle control system, **238**–43
 breast cancer treatments and, 243f
 checkpoints in, 238–39
 cyclins and cyclin-dependent kinases in, 239–40
 evidence for cytoplasmic signals in, 238
 genetic changes affecting, and cancer development, 373–77
 internal and external signals at checkpoints of, as stop and go signs, 240–42
 loss of, in cancer cells, 242–43

Cell cycle-inhibiting pathway, 375f
Cell cycle-stimulating pathway, 375f
Cell death. See Apoptosis
Cell differentiation, 366–**67**
 cytokinins and, 829–30
 gene expression and control of, 759
 plant development and, 755
Cell division, **228**. See also Cell cycle
 bacterial, 236–37f
 cell cycle and, 228 (see also Cell cycle)
 cell-signaling pathways that regulate, 375f
 cytokinins and, 829–30
 distribution of chromosomes during eukaryotic, 229–30
 embryonic development and, 366–67
 evolution of, 237
 in meiosis, 253–57 (see also Meiosis)
 in mitosis, 256f–57 (see also Mitosis)
 newt lung cell, 8f
 plane and symmetry of, in plants, 756–57
 prokaryotic, 560
Cell fate, 1035–42
 axis formation in, 1036–38
 determination, differentiation, and, 1035
 determination and pattern formation of, by inductive signals, 1039–42
 developmental potential and, 1038–39
 fate maps and, 1035–39
 of germ cells, 1036
Cell fractionation, **97**
Cell junctions
 in local cell signaling, 208
 plasmodesmata in plants, 120–21
 tight junctions, desmosomes, and gap junctions in animals, 121
Cell-mediated immune response, 930f, **940**–42
Cell motility
 in animal morphogenesis, 1033–34
 cilia, flagella, and, 114–16
 cytoskeletons and, 112–13
 microfilaments and, 116–18
 in morphogenesis, 1034
Cell plate, **236**
Cell signaling, 206–27. See also Cell(s)
 in animal endocrine and nervous systems, 859
 apoptosis as integration of, 223–25
 B. L. Bassler's work on quorum sensing, 92–93
 cancer and interference with normal, 374–76
 cell cycle control system, 238–43 (see also Cell cycle control system)
 cellular membrane selective permeability and, 125
 cilia in, 114
 evolution of, 206–7
 fight-or-flight responses and types of, 206
 hormones and types of, 975–76
 local and long-distance, 208–9
 local regulators and, 979
 in plants (see Plant responses)
 reception stage of, 210–14
 response stage of, 219–23
 review of, 225–26
 symplastic electrical signaling in phloem, 782
 three stages of, 209–10
 transduction stage of, 214–19
Cell-surface proteins, 120, 130, 243f
Cell-surface transmembrane receptors, 210–13, 243f
Cell-type specific transcription, 361f
Cellular innate immune defenses, 932–33
Cellular membranes, 125–41. See also Cell(s)
 active transport across, 135–38
 animal, 654
 bulk transport across, by exocytosis and endocytosis, 138–39f
 development of fluid mosaic model of, 125–27
 evolution of differences in lipid composition of, 128
 fluidity of, 127–28

as fluid mosaics of lipids and proteins, 125–31*f*
of mitochondria, 110
nuclear envelopes, 102, 103*f*
organelles and internal, 99 (*see also* Organelles)
passive transport as diffusion across, 132–35
phospholipids in, 76–77
in plant response to cold stress, 844–45
plasma membrane selective permeability of, 125
review of, 140
specialized prokaryotic, 559
structure of, and selective permeability of, 131–32
synthesis and sidedness of, 130–31*f*
Cellular respiration, 163–83. *See also* Cell(s)
ATP synthesis yield at each stage of, 174–77
biosynthesis in anabolic pathways and, 180
as catabolic pathway, 143
catabolic pathways, ATP production, and, 164
citric acid cycle in, 170–72
defined, **164**
energy flow and, 7, 163
fermentation vs., 177–79
glycolysis in, 168–69*f*
measuring energy use in, 869
mitochondria in, 109, 110
monosaccharides in, 70
origin of, 516
overall reaction for, 147–48
oxidation of organic fuel molecules during, 165
oxidative phosphorylation in, 172–77
oxygen diffusion and, 133
photosynthesis, energy flow, and, 163
photosynthesis vs., 188
redox reactions and, 164–67
regulation of, via feedback mechanisms, 181
review of, 182–83
stages of, 167–68
using cell fractionation to study, 97
versatility of catabolic pathways and, 179–80
Cellular slime molds, **595**–96, 1186
Cellulose, **72**
in plant cell walls, 72–74, 118–19
as product of photosynthesis, 203
proteins synthesizing, 600–601*f*
Cellulose synthase, 118–19
Cell walls, **118**
cellulose in land plant, 600–601*f*
fungal cell, 100*f*
osmosis, water balance, and, 133–34
plant cell, 101*f*, 118–19
prokaryotic cell, 98*f*, 557–58
Celsius scale, **48**
Cenozoic era, 514, 515*t*, 658
Center for Plant Conservation, 1239
Centipedes, 687–88
Central canal, **1065**
Central disk, sea star, 693*f*
Central dogma, DNA, 328
Central nervous system (CNS), **1046**
brain and (*see* Brains)
neural plasticity of, 1076–77
neural stem cells and repair of, 1078–79
neurotransmitters and, 1058
peripheral nervous system and, 1063, 1064*f*
in sensory systems, 1085, 1087
structure and function of vertebrate, 1063–66
Central vacuoles, 101*f*, **108**
Centrifuge, 97
Centrioles, **114**, 231
Centromeres, **229**–30
Centromeric DNA, 437
Centrosomes, 100*f*, **114**, **231**–35*f*
Century plants, 1180
Cephalization, **658**, 1063
Cephalochordata, 698, 699–701
Cephalopods, 680
Cercozoans, **590**

Cerebellum, **1068***f*–69*f*
Cerebral cortex, **1069***f*
evolution of pallium of avian and human, 1075–76
frontal lobe function of, 1075
hearing and, 1093
information processing of, 1074–75
language and speech functions of, 1072–73
lateralization of function in, 1073–74
long-term memory and, 1077
structure of human, 1074*f*
Cerebral ganglia
earthworm, 682*f*
insect, 688*f*
Cerebral hemispheres, **1069***f*
Cerebrospinal fluid, 922, **1065**
Cerebrum, 1067, **1068***f*–69*f*. *See also* Cerebral cortex
Certainty of paternity, 1130–31
Cervical cancer, 950*f*
Cervix, **1003**
Cetaceans, 465–66, 725*f*
Cetartiodactyla, 725*f*
Chaetae, 681
Chagas' disease, 580–81
Chain worms, 674
Chambered nautilus, 680*f*
Chance, natural selection and, 485. *See also* Probability
Channel proteins
cellular membrane selective permeability and, 131–32
facilitated diffusion and, 134–35
Chaparral, **1154***f*
Chaperonins, **85**, 342, 844
Character displacement, **1196**
Characters, **263**
construction of phylogenetic trees from shared, 542–48
discrete vs. quantitative, 470
multifactorial, 275
taxonomy and, 538
traits and, 263 (*see also* Traits)
Character tables, 543*f*
Chargaff, Edwin, 308
Chargaff's rules, 308, 310
Charged tRNA, 339
Charophytes, 591, 600–601
Chase, Martha, 307–8
Chatman, Charles, 24*f*
Cheating behavior, 1139
Checkerspot butterflies, 1142–43
Checkpoints, cell cycle control system, **239**–42
Cheetahs, 1184*f*
Chelicerates, **686**–87
Chemical bonds, **38**–42
carbon atoms and, 60–61
covalent, 38–39
ionic, 39–40
making and breaking of, by chemical reactions, 42–43
shape and function of molecules and, 41–42
weak hydrogen and van der Waals, 40–41*f*
Chemical cycling. *See* Nutrient cycling
Chemical digestion, 885–86
Chemical energy, **143**, 184, 186. *See also* Cellular respiration; Photosynthesis
Chemical equilibrium, **43**
buffers and, 54–55
free energy and, 146–47*f*
metabolism and, 148–49
Chemical groups. *See* Functional groups
Chemical mutagens, 346
Chemical reactions, **42**–43
activation energy barrier of, 152–53
chemical energy in, 143
free energy and, 147*f*
making and breaking of chemical bonds by, 42–43
metabolism and, 142 (*see also* Metabolism)

in photosynthesis, 187–88
speeding up (*see* Enzymatic catalysis)
Chemical signals. *See also* Cell signaling; Endocrine systems; Hormones
in animals, 859
B. L. Bassler's work on, 92–93
hormones as, 206, 214, 220, 974
neurons and, 1045 (*see also* Neurons)
plant early warning systems and, 846
Chemical structure, DNA, 309*f*
Chemical synapses, neurotransmitters and, 1057–58
Chemical work, 149, 150–51
Chemiosmosis, **173**
in chloroplasts vs. in mitochondria, 196–97*f*
as energy-coupling mechanism, 173–75*f*
in light reactions of photosynthesis, 188
Chemistry, 28–45
atomic structure and properties of elements in, 33–37
connection of, to biology, 30–31*f* (*see also* Biology)
emergent properties as theme in, 89 (*see also* Emergent properties)
formation of molecules through chemical bonding between atoms in, 38–42
of large biological molecules (*see* Biological molecules)
making and breaking of chemical bonds through chemical reactions, 42–43
matter as elements and compounds in, 31–32
organic, as study of carbon compounds, 58–59 (*see also* Carbon; Organic compounds)
review of, 44–45
S. Solomon's work in, 28–29
of water (*see* Water)
Chemoautotrophs, 565*f*, 1218, 1219
Chemoheterotrophs, 565*f*
Chemoreceptors, 850, **1088**–89*f*, 1101–3
Chemosynthetic prokaryotes, 1219
Chemotaxis, 92, 558
Chemotherapy, 243
Chemotrophs, 564
Chesapeake Bay estuary food web, 1203*f*
Chestnut blight, 650, 1204, 1213–14
Chiasmata, **254***f*, 257
Chicken pox, 939
Chicks, 1029–30
Chicxulub crater, 522
Chief cells, 885
Childbirth, human, 1014–15. *See also* Births, human
Chimpanzees
cellular respiration and energy for, 163
comparison of chromosome sequences of humans and, 438, 439*f*
comparison of human genome with genome of, 443
complete genome sequence for, 426
J. Goodall's research on, 18–19
heterochrony and differential growth rates in skulls of, 525–26
HIV in, 550–51
hominins vs., 728–29
as living primates, 726–27*f*
problem solving of, 1126
skulls of humans vs., 541
social learning in, 1127
tool use, 731
China, 1188
Chips, human gene microarray, 432
Chiroptera, 725*f*
Chitin, **74**, **637**, 686, **1111**–12
Chitons, 678, 1063*f*
Chlamydias, 569*f*
Chlamydomonas, 101*f*, 591–92*f*
Chlorarachniophytes, 576, 590
Chloride cells, 954–55
Chloride ions, 1048*t*
Chloride transport channels, 277
Chlorinated hydrocarbons, 1255
Chlorine, 28, 32*t*, 1259

Chlorofluorocarbons (CFCs), 28–29, 1259
Chlorophyll, 5f, **186**–87, 191f, 192
Chlorophyll a, **190**, 192–93
Chlorophyll b, 190–**91**
Chlorophytes, 591–92
Chloroplasts, **109**
  chemiosmosis in, 174, 196–97f
  evolutionary origins of, 109–10
  light energy capture by, 110–11
  light reactions in thylakoids of, 189
  as organelles, 5f
  pigments of, 190–92
  plant cell, 101f
  as sites of photosynthesis, 186–87
  transgenic crops and DNA in, 818
Chlorosis, 790
Choanocytes, **670**
Choanoflagellates, 596, 656
Cholecystokinin (CCK), **892**f
Cholera, 217, 568f, 572
Cholesterol, **77**
  and cardiovascular disease, 913–14f
  in cellular membranes, 128
  receptor-mediated endocytosis and, 138
  as steroid lipid, 77
Chondrichthyans (Chondrichthyes), **705**–7
Chondrocytes, 857f
Chondroitin sulfate, 857f
Chordates (Chordata), **697**
  craniates as, 701–3
  derived characters of, 698–99
  endoskeletons of, 1112
  evolution of, 700–701
  fate mapping for, 1035f
  invertebrate, 663, 669f, 694 (see also Invertebrates)
  kidneys of, 962–63
  lancelets, 699–701
  phylogeny of living, 698f
  tunicates, 700
  vertebrate, 697–701 (see also Vertebrates)
Chorion, 714f, 1031
Chorionic villus sampling (CVS), **280**, 281f
C horizon, 786f
Choroid, 1096f
Christmas tree worms, 666, 681
Chromalveolates (Chromalveolata), 579f, **582**–89
  alveolates, 582–85
  ciliates, 584–85
  stramenopiles, 585–89
Chromatid. See Sister chromatid
Chromatin, **102**, **229**, **321**
  animal cell, 100f
  cell division and, 229–30
  in eukaryotic cell nucleus, 102, 103f
  packing of, in chromosomes, 320–22 (see also
    Chromosomes)
  plant cell, 101f
  regulation of structure of, 357–58
  remodeling of, by siRNAs, 366
Chromatophores, 590f
Chromophores, 837
Chromoplasts, 111
Chromosomal alterations, 297–300
  abnormal chromosome numbers, 297–98
  of chromosome structure, 298–99
  human disorders due to, 299–300
Chromosomal basis of inheritance, 286–304. See also
    Genetics
  behavior of chromosomes as physical basis of
    Mendelian inheritance, 286–89
  chromosomal alterations and genetic disorders,
    297–300
  evolution of gene concept from, 347
  exceptions to Mendelian inheritance in, 300–302
  genomic imprinting and, 300–301
  inheritance of organelle genes and, 301–2

linked genes and linkage in, 292–97
G. Mendel's hereditary factors as genes along
    chromosomes, 286
review of, 302–3
sex-linked genes in, 289–92
Chromosomal breakage points, 439
Chromosomes, **102**, **229**
  alteration of structure of, and genome evolution,
    438–39
  alterations of, 297–300 (see also Chromosomal
    alterations)
  bacterial, 236
  behavior of, as physical basis of Mendelian
    inheritance, 286–89
  behavior of, in human life cycle, 251–52
  in cancer cells, 242–43
  cell division and, 228
  correlating behavior of alleles with pairs of, 288–89
  describing, 251f
  distribution of, during eukaryotic cell division,
    229–30
  DNA, genes, and, 8–10 (see also DNA (deoxyribonu-
    cleic acid); Gene(s))
  DNA and chromatin packing in, 320–22
  duplication of sets of, and genome evolution, 438
  eukaryotic, 229f
  in eukaryotic cell nucleus, 102
  evidence in, for evolution of land plants from green
    algae, 601
  gene expression and interaction of, in interphase
    nucleus, 362
  genes in, 249
  genetic variation due to mutations in, 472
  human, 229f, 249, 250–51
  independent assortment of, 257–58
  karyotypes of, 250f
  linked genes on (see Linked genes)
  locating genes along, 286 (see also Chromosomal
    basis of inheritance)
  mapping distance between genes on, 296–97
  G. Mendel's deductions and, 265
  molecular tags and karyotypes of human, 322f
  movement of, on kinetochore microtubules,
    234, 235f
  number of, in human cells, 229–30
  in prokaryotic and eukaryotic cells, 98
  in prokaryotic cells, 559–60
  prokaryotic conjugation and gene transfer between,
    562–64
  recombinant, 258, 259f
  reduction of number of, by meiosis, 253f
Chromosome theory of inheritance, **286**–89. See also
    Chromosomal basis of inheritance
Chronic inflammation, 934
Chronic myelogenous leukemia (CML), 300, 419
Chrysanthemums, 840
Chylomicrons, **888**
Chyme, **885**
Chytrids (Chytridiomycota), **641**, 642f, 650–51f, 712
Cichlid fish, 497, 500–501f
Cigarette smoke, cancer and, 377
Cilia, **114**
  bronchial, 919
  cell fate and, 1041–42
  ciliates and, 584–85
  as example of unity in diversity of life, 14f
  flagella vs., 115f
  as microtubules, 114–16
Ciliates, **584**–85
Cilium-based signaling, 114
Circadian clocks, 1119–20. See also Biological clocks
Circadian rhythms, **778**, **838**, **861**–62, 871, 993,
    1070–71f, 1119–20, See also Biological clocks
Circannual rhythms, 1120
Circulatory systems, 897–915
  blood in, 910–15 (see also Blood)

blood vessels, blood flow, and blood pressure in,
    905–10
cells and exchange surfaces of, 897–98
closed cephalopod, 680
evolutionary variation in, 898–99
gas exchange and, 897, 923–26 (see also Gas
    exchange)
gastrovascular cavities and, 898
general properties of, 898
hearts in mammalian, 902–4
human diseases of, 913–15
lymphatic systems and, 909
open and closed, 899
review of, 926–28
single and double circulation in vertebrate, 899–902
thermoregulatory adaptations of animal, 864–65
cis face, Golgi apparatus, 105–6
cis isomers, 62
Cisternae, 104, 105–6
Cisternal maturation model, 106
Cisternal space, 104
cis-trans isomers, **62**
Citrate synthase gene, 792
Citric acid cycle, **167**–68, 170–72
Citrulline, 327f
Clades (taxonomy), **542**–43, 605, 660, 661
Cladistics, **542**–43
Clams, 677, 679f
Clark, Craig, 851
Clark's nutcracker, 1124–25
Classes (taxonomy), **537**
Classical conditioning, 1125
Classification of life. See Taxonomy
Claw waving behavior, 1118, 1120
Clean Air Act, 56
Cleavage, **234**, **655**, 660–61, **1012**, **1025**–27
Cleavage furrows, 233f, **234**
Clements, F. E., 1207
Climate, **1144**–50
  community equilibrium and, 1207
  continental drift and changes in, 520–21
  effect of large bodies of water on, 49
  global climate change, 1149–50 (see also Global cli-
    mate change)
  global patterns of, 1146f–47
  greenhouse gases, global warming, and, 1256–58 (see
    also Global warming)
  latitudinal gradients of species diversity and, 1211
  microclimate, 1147, 1149
  mountains and, 1148–49
  population fluctuations and, 1184–85
  regional and local effects on, 1147–49
  seasonality and, 1147
  seedless vascular plants and ancient, 615
  terrestrial biomes and, 1151
  using dendrochronolgy to study, 753f
  water bodies and, 1147–48, 1149f
Climax communities, 1207
Climographs, **1151**
Clines, **471**
Clitellum, 682
Clitoris, **1004**, 1011
Cloaca, **707**, **1002**
Clock, floral, 821
Clock genes, 838
Clocks, biological. See Biological clocks; Circadian clocks
Clonal selection, **939**
Cloned genes, 397–98
Clones, **249**. See also DNA cloning; Organismal cloning
  asexual reproduction and, 249
  from cuttings, 814
  fragmentation and, 812
  meaning of term, 412
  test-tube or in vitro, 814–15
Cloning, DNA. See DNA cloning
Cloning, organismal. See Organismal cloning

Cloning, therapeutic. *See* Therapeutic cloning
Cloning vectors, **398**–402
Closed circulatory systems, 680, **899**, 957
Clostridium botulinum, 572
Clotting, blood. *See* Blood clotting
Club fungi, 646–48
Club mosses (Lycophyta), 613, 614*f*
Clumped dispersion, 1172
Clutch size, 1179
Cnidarians (Cnidaria), 518, 659*f*, 667*f*, 671–73, 898*f*, 1062–63
Cnidocytes, **671**–72
Coal, 615
Coal gas, 832
Coastal Japan restoration project, 1235*f*
Cob, corn, 815
Coccidioidomycosis, 650
Cochlea, **1091***f*, 1092–93
Cochlear duct, 1091*f*
Cocklebur, 839–40
Cocktails, drug, 391, 472, 949–50
Cod, 708, 954–55*f*, 1244
Codominance, **272**
Codons, **330**
    anticodons, 337
    codon recognition, 341*f*
    genetic code and, 329–30
Coefficient of relatedness (*r*), **1137**–38
Coelacanths, 709
Coelom, **660**, 661, 682*f*
Coelomates, **660**
Coenocytic fungi, **637**–38
Coenzymes, **156**
Coevolution, **806**
Cofactors, **156**, 790
Coffee, 633
Cognition, 1075, **1126**
Cognitive maps, **1124**–25
Cohesins, 229, 233*f*, 257
Cohesion, **47**–48, 775–76
Cohesion-tension hypothesis, **774**–76
Cohorts, **1173**
Coitus, **1011**
Coitus interruptus, 1016
Cold
    plant response to, 844–45
    thermoreceptors and, 1089
Cold viruses, 384
Coleman, Doug, 893–94
Coleoptera, 690*f*
Coleoptiles, **808**, 825–26
Coleorhiza, **808**
Collagen, 78*f*, 83*f*, **119**–20, 654
Collagenous fibers, 857*f*
Collar cells, 656*f*
Collared flycatchers, 500
Collecting duct, 963*f*, 964*f*, **965**, 969
Collenchyma cells, **744***f*, 750
Colloids, **51**
Colon, **888**–89
Colon cancer, 317
Colonial algae, 586, 591–92
Coloration
    chromosome, 322*f*
    predation and, 1197–98
    skin, 988
Color blindness, 291, 1100
Colorectal cancer, 376, 377
Color vision, 1096, 1100
Columnar cells, 856*f*
Columnar epithelium, 856*f*
Combinatorial gene expression regulation, 360–61
Comb jellies, 667*f*
Comet collision, mass extinction by, 522
Commensalism, **570**, 642*f*, 643, **1199**
Commercial applications

DNA technology and development of pharmaceutical
        products, 419–20
    of fungi, 651–52
    of mosses, 609–10
Common arrowhead, 813*f*
Common juniper, 623*f*
Common scaly-foot lizard, 536
Communicating junctions, 121*f*
Communication, animal, 859, **1120**–22
Communication, cell. *See* Cell signaling
Communication, symplastic. *See* Symplastic
        communication
Communities, **1145***f*, **1194**
    diversity of, 1239*f*, 1240
    as level of biological organization, 4*f*
    species diversity and stability of, 1201–2 (*see also*
        Species diversity)
Community ecology, **1145***f*, 1194–1217
    biogeographic factors affecting community diversity
        in, 1211–13
    communities and, 1194
    community disturbances in, 1207–10
    interspecific interactions in, 1194–1200
    pathogens in, 1213–15
    review of, 1215–16
    species diversity and trophic structure in,
        1200–1206
Companion cells, **745***f*
Competition
    density-dependent population regulation
        through, 1183*f*
    interspecific (*see* Interspecific competition)
    marine molluscs and, 450–51
    sexual, 482, 1132–33
Competitive exclusion, **1195**
Competitive inhibitors, **156**–57
Complementary base pairing, DNA and RNA, 88–89*f*
Complementary DNA (cDNA), **401**, 409*f*
Complementary RNA, 246
Complement systems, **933**, 943
Complete digestive tracts, 882–83
Complete dominance, **271**
Complete flowers, **802**
Complete growth medium, 326
Complete metamorphosis, **689**, 690*f*
Complete proteins, 876
Complex eyes, 529–30
Compound eyes, 690*f*, **1095**–96
Compound leaves, 741*f*
Compounds, **31**. *See also* Molecules
    carbon and small organic (*see* Organic compounds)
    elements and, 31
    ionic, 40
    land plant secondary, 604
    large biological (*see* Biological molecules)
    pure elements vs., 39
Compromises, evolutionary, 485
Computational tools, 10, 339*f*, 430–32, 541–42, 756
Concentration gradients, **132**–33, 135–38
Concentrations, chemical reactions and, 43
Conception, human, **1012**
Condoms, **1016**
Conduction, **864***f*
Conduction, neuron action potential, 1053–54
Cones, **1097***f*, 1098–99, 1100–1101
Cones, gymnosperm, 621, 623*f*, 624*f*
Cone snails, 850–51, 1045*f*
Confocal microscopy, **96***f*, 97
Conformer animals, **860**
Congenital disorders, 250*f*
Conidia, **645**
Coniferophyta, 623*f*
Conifers, 606, **621**, 623*f*, 624*f*, 625
Conjugation, 562–64, 584*f*–85
Connective tissue, animal, 78*f*, **857***f*
Connell, Joseph, 1196*f*

Conodonts, **703**–4
Consanguineous mating, human, 277
Conservation biology, **1238**–63
    biodiversity and, 1238–44
    conservation of mollusc species, 680–81*f*
    global change and, 1254–60
    landscape ecology and regional conservation in,
        1249–54
    population conservation in, 1244–49
    review of, 1262
    soil conservation (*see* Soil conservation)
    sustainable development in, 1260–61
Conservation of energy, 144, 1219
Conservation of mass, 1219
Conservative model, DNA replication, 311–12*f*
Conserved Domain Database (CDD), 430*f*
Constant (C) region, light and heavy chain, 936
Constipation, 889
Consumers
    energy flow and, 6–7
    heterotrophs as, 184
Consumption, regulation of animal, 893–94
Continental drift, 466, 519–21
Contour tillage, 788*f*
Contraception, human, **1015**–17, 1188
Contractile proteins, 78*f*
Contractile vacuoles, **108**, 134
Contraction, muscle, 1104–9
Contrast, 95
Control elements, **358**, 360–61
Control groups, 21–22
Controlled experiments, **22**–23
Convection, **864***f*
Convergent evolution, **464**–65. *See also* Evolution
    analogies and, 540–41
    in cacti and euphorbs, 1152
    of fast swimmers, 853*f*
    of marsupials and eutherians, 722–23*f*
Convergent extension, **1034**
Cooling, evaporative, 49, 865–66
Cooper, Vaughn, 561*f*
Cooperation
    evolution and, 451
    science and, 23–24
Cooperativity, 158*f*, **159**, 565
Coordinately controlled genes, 352, 361–62
Coordination, cell-signaling response, 220–22
Copepods, **691**
Coprophagy, 890
Copulatory organs, 1002
Copying, DNA. *See* DNA replication
Copy-number variants (CNVs), 445
CoQ (coenzyme Q), 172–73
Coral atolls, 1162*f*
Coral reefs, 55, 596, 673, **1162***f*, 1214, 1242
Corals, 673
Coral snake case study, 20–23
Cord grass, 1245
Corepressors, **353**
Cork cambium, **746**, 754
Cormorant, flightless, 488, 493
Corn (*Zea mays*), 426, 433*t*, 633. *See also* Maize (corn)
Corn, Indian, 435
Cornea, 1096*f*
Corn smut, 650*f*
Coronavirus, 391
Corpus callosum, **1069***f*, 1073–74
Corpus luteum, **1003**
Correns, Karl, 300–301
Cortex, **117**, **743**, 750*f*, 1022
Cortical granules, 1022
Cortical microfilaments, 117
Cortical nephrons, 962*f*, 967–68
Cortical reactions, 1022–23, 1024*f*
Cortical rotation, 1037–38
Corticosteroids, **991**–92

Cortisol, 976–77f
Corvids, 1126
Costanza, Robert, 1241
Costa Rica
    sustainable development in, 1260–61
    tropical dry forest restoration project in, 1234f
    zoned reserves in, 1252–53
Cost-benefit behavior analysis, 1128–29
Cotransport, **137**–38
Cotransport proteins, 137–38
Cotyledons, **628**, 807–8
Counseling, genetic, 279
Countercurrent exchange, **865**, **917**, 957–58
Countercurrent heat exchangers, 865
Countercurrent multiplier systems, **966**–67
Courtship rituals
    behavioral isolation and, 490f
    external fertilization and, 1000
    forms of animal communication in, 1120–21
    genetic basis of, 1134
    sexual selection and, 482–83
    sexual selection and female mate choice in,
        1131–32
Covalent bonds, **38**
    of disaccharides, 70
    in organic compounds, 60–61, 66
    protein tertiary structure and, 83f
Cowbirds, 1199
Coyotes, 890
Crabs, 691, 1194
Cranes, 1124
Craniates, **701**–3. See also Vertebrates
    derived characters of, 701–2
    hagfishes, 702
    origin of, 702
"Crank" drug, 63
Crassulacean acid metabolism (CAM) plants, 201–**2**, 778
Crawling, 1111, 1113
Crayfish, 916f, 1090
C-reactive protein (CRP), 914, 915
Creatine phosphate, 1106
Crenarchaeota, 567, 570
Cretaceous mass extinction, 522
Creutzfeldt-Jakob disease, 393
Creuzot, John, 24f
Crick, Francis
    central dogma of, 328
    discovery of DNA molecular structure by, 3, 24, 305,
        308–10
    J. A. Steitz's work with, 246–47
    model of DNA replication of, 311–12
Crickets, 433, 690f
Cri du chat, 300
Crime scene investigation. See Forensic science
Crinoidea, 694
Cristae, **110**
Critical load, **1254**
Critical period, 1123
Crocodiles, 547, 717
Crop plants, 815–19. See also Angiosperms (Anthophyta);
        Plant(s)
    artificial selection and breeding of, 815–16
    biotechnology and genetic engineering of, 816–19
    debate over transgenic, 817–19
    domestication, artificial selection, and genetic
        engineering of, 801
    impact of oomycetes on, 588–89
    seed plants as, 633
    transgenic and genetically modified, 421–23
Crop rotation, **795**
Cross-fostering studies, **1123**
Crossing over, 254f, **294**
    gene duplication due to unequal, 439
    in meiosis, 254f
    in recombination of linked genes, 294–95f
    in sexual life cycles, 257, 258, 259f

Cross-pollination, **627**
    angiosperm, 627–28
    G. Mendel's techniques of, 263–64
    of plants, 815–16
Cross-talk, cell-signaling, 221–22
Crown gall disease, 736
Crows, 1129
Crustaceans, 446f, 527, 669f, **686**, 691–92
Crustose lichens, 649f
Cryolophosaurus, 507, 507f
Cryptic coloration, **1197**
Cryptochromes, 836
Crypts, 779f
Crystallin, 361f
Crystals, ice, 50f
Ctenophora, 667f
C-terminus, 80, 340
Cuboidal epithelium, 856f
Cubozoans (Cubozoa), 672
Cuckoo bee, 1197f
Culex pipiens (mosquito), 480
Culture, **1128**
    evolution of human social behavior
        and, 1139
    social learning and, 1128
Cupula, 1094
Cuticle, **604**, **683**, 686, **742**
Cutthroat trout, 1183f
Cuttings, plant, 814, 829
Cuttlefish, 482
Cuvier, Georges, 453f, 454–55
Cyanide, 817f
Cyanobacteria
    as bacterial group, 569f
    blooms of, 1224
    bryophytes and, 608f, 609
    chemical recycling by, 570
    W. F. Doolittle's work on, 534–35
    endosymbiosis and, 576, 590
    fungi and, as lichens, 645, 649–50
    glycolysis and ancient, 179
    land colonization by, 518
    metabolic cooperation in, 565
    photosynthesis of, 195, 516
    terrestrial, 600
Cycadophyta, 622f
Cycads (Cycadophyta), 622f
Cyclic AMP (cyclic adenosine monophosphate, cAMP),
        216–17, **355**, 978, 1057
Cyclic electron flow, **195**
Cyclic GMP (cGMP), 217, 822–23
Cyclin, **239**–40
Cyclin-dependent kinases (cdks), **239**–40
Cycliophora, 668f
Cyclosporine, 651
Cynodonts, 513f
Cysteine, 65f, 79f
Cystic fibrosis, 273, **276**, 277
Cystic kidney disease, 1041
Cystinuria, 135
Cytochrome *c*, 224, 548
Cytochromes, **173**, 196
Cytogenetic maps, **296**–97, 427–28
Cytokines, **934**, 975, 979
Cytokinesis, **230**, 233f, 254f–55f
Cytokinins, 827t, **829**–30
Cytology, 97, 286
Cytoplasm, **98**
    cell cycle control signals in, 238
    cell-signaling responses in, 219–20
    cytokinesis and division of, 230
    of prokaryotic and eukaryotic cells, 98
Cytoplasmic determinants, **367**, 368f, 1036
Cytoplasmic genes, 300–301
Cytoplasmic responses, cell-signaling, 219–20
Cytoplasmic streaming, 117f–**18**, 589, 594

Cytosine, 87f–88, 308
Cytoskeletons, **112**–18
    actin microfilaments of, 116–18
    animal cell, 100f
    ATP mechanical work and, 151
    intermediate filaments of, 118
    membrane proteins and attachment to, 129f
    microtubules of, 113–16
    in morphogenesis, 1033–34
    plant cell, 101f
    support, motility, and regulation roles of,
        112–13
Cytosol, **98**
Cytosolic calcium, 822–23
Cytotoxic T cells, **941**–42

D

dalton (atomic mass unit), **33**, 52
Dalton, John, 33
Dance language, honeybee, 1121–22
Dandelions, 804f, 811f, 1181f
Danio rerio (zebrafish), 24
Daphnia, 998, 1179f
Darkness
    flowering in long-night plants and, 839–40
    plant etiolation response to, 821–22
Dark responses, rod cell, 1099f
D'Arrigo, Rosanne, 753f
Darwin, Charles
    barnacles and, 692
    Beagle voyage and field research of, on adaptations,
        455–57
    on earthworms, 682
    evidence supporting theory of, 460–67
    in flower pollination mutualism, 806
    on grandeur of evolutionary process, 467
    historical context of life and ideas of, 453–55
    on island species, 466
    on lung evolution from swim bladders, 707
    on mystery of speciation, 488
    on natural selection and differential reproductive
        success, 259–60
    on natural selection and inheritance, 469–70
    publication of *The Origin of Species* by, 452
    on speciation, 457–60
    on species diversity of tropics, 1211
    study by, of phototropism in grass coleoptiles, 825
    theory of descent with modification by, 14–16 (see
        also Descent with modification theory; Evolu-
        tion; Natural selection)
    timeline of work of, 453f
Darwin, Erasmus, 454
Darwin, Francis, 825
Darwinism, 14. See also Darwin, Charles; Descent
        with modification theory; Evolution; Natural
        selection
Data, **18**–19
Databases, genome-sequence, 429, 430f
Dating, fossil record, 512
dATP, 314
Daughter cells, 228, 229–30
Davidson, Norman, 850
Davson, Hugh, 126
Day-neutral plants, **839**
db gene, 893–94
DDT pesticide, 157, 1256
Dead zone, 1255
Death, cell. See Apoptosis
Deaths
    demographics and rates of, 1173–75
    high rates of, and reproductive rates, 1181
    population density and rates of, 1182
    population dynamics and, 1171f–72, 1175–76
    rate of human, 1188
Death signals, apoptosis, 224–25. See also Apoptosis

Decapods, **691**
December solstice, 1147f
Deciduous forest, nutrient cycling in, 1231
Declining-population approach, population conservation, 1247–49
Decomposers, **570**, **1220**
    fungi as, 637, 639f, 642f, 645, 646, 648
    gymnamoebas, 596
    lichens as, 650
    methanogens as, 567
    soil bacteria as, 793
Decomposition
    effects of temperature on, 1230f
    fungal nutrition and, 14
    nutrient cycling and, 1227
    nutrient cycling rates and, 1230–31
Deconvolution microscopy, **96**f, 97
Deductive reasoning, **19**–20
Deep-sea hydrothermal vents, 508, **1162**f, 1219
Deer albinism, 325
Deer mouse, 871
DEET insect repellant, 1101
De-etiolation (greening), **822**, 823f, 824
Defense adaptations, predation and, 1197–98
Defensive proteins, 78f
Deficiencies
    mycorrhizae and plant, 797
    plant mineral, 790–91
    smart plants and nutrient, 792
Deforestation
    as community disturbance, 1210
    experimental, and nutrient cycling, 1231
    global climate change and, 1149, 1256–58
    greenhouse gases and, 1258
    loss of species from, 1238
    of tropical rain forests, 633–34
    zoned reserves and, 1253
Degenerative diseases, human, 225
Degradation
    mRNA, 363
    protein, 363–64
Dehydration, 199–202, 518–19, 955–56, 970
Dehydration reactions, **68**–69
Dehydrogenases, 165–66, 167
Deinococcus radiodurans, 556
Delayed reproduction, 1188
Deleted in colorectal cancer (*DCC*) gene, 376f
Deletions (mutations), **298**–99, 300, **345**–46
Delta proteobacteria, 568f
Dementia, 1081
Demographics, population, 1173–75
    life tables in, 1173
    reproductive rates in, 1174–75
    survivorship curves in, 1173–74
Demographic transition, **1188**, 1261
Demography, **1173**
Denaturation, **84**–85
Dendrites, 858f, **1046**, 1056, 1088, 1090
Dendritic cells, **932**–33
Dendrochronology, 753
Density, population, **1171**, 1182–84
    as dynamic, 1171–72
    equilibrium, 1182
    natural selection of traits sensitive to, 1181
    population change and, 1182
    population regulation mechanisms and, 1182–84
Density-dependent inhibition, **241**–42
Density-dependent population change, **1182**
Density-dependent selection, 1181
Density-independent population change, **1182**
Density-independent selection, 1181
Dentition
    diet and adaptations of, 889–90
    mammalian, 512–13f
Deoxyribonucleic acid. *See* DNA (deoxyribonucleic acid)
Deoxyribose, 87f–**88**, 308

Dephosphorylation, 215–16
Depolarization, 1022, **1050**–53, 1110
Depolymerization, 231
Depression, 1059, 1080
Derivatives, cell, 746
Derived characters, shared, **543**
Derived traits, 601–4
Dermal tissue system, plant, **742**–43
DES (diethylstilbestrol), 993–94
Descent with modification theory, 14–16, 452, 456–60.
    See also Evolution; Natural selection
Desert camels, 956
Desert iguana, 868
Deserts, 778–79f, 1148–49, **1153**f
Desiccation, 955–56, 1166
Desmosomes, **121**f
Desynchronization, 838–39
Determinate cleavage, **660**
Determinate growth, **746**
Determination, **368**–69, **1035**
Detoxification, 105, 111, 789
Detritivores, **1220**, 1227
Detritus, **1157**, **1220**, 1227
Deuteromycetes, **640**
Deuterostome development, **660**–64
Deuterostomes (Deuterostomia), 663, 669f, 692–94, 697–98
Development, **755**
    angiosperms, 629–30
    as cell division function, 228f
    comparing animal, 445–47
    comparing animal and plant, 447 (*see also* Animal development; Plant development)
    embryonic, of different cell types in multicellular organisms, 366–73 (*see also* Embryonic development)
    gene expression and brain, in lancelets and vertebrates, 700–701
    in human life cycle, 251f
    macroevolution of, 525–29
    postzygotic barriers and, 489, 491f
    as property of life, 2f
Developmental biology, 1021–22
Developmental plasticity, 755
Developmental potential, cell fate and, 1038–39
Devil's gardens case study, 30–31f
Diabetes
    aquaporin mutations as causes of diabetes insipidus, 970f
    diabetes insipidus, 983
    diabetes mellitus, 947, **983**–84
    obesity and, 893
    transgenic insulin for, 419
Diacylglycerol (DAG), **218**
Diagnosis. *See also* Medicine(s)
    antibodies as tools in, 945
    DNA technology for, 417–18
Diaphragm, birth control, 1016
Diaphragm, breathing and, **921**
Diapsids, **715**
Diarrhea, 137–38, 217, 572, 578f, 889
Diastole phase, **903**
Diastolic pressure, **906**, 907f
Diatomaceous earth, 585
Diatoms, 237f, 579f, **585**, 1150
Diazepam, 1058
Dicer enzyme, 365f
Dickie, Margaret, 894f
Dicots, **630**
Dictyostelium discoideum, 595f, 1186
Dideoxyribonucleotide (dideoxy) chain termination method of DNA sequencing, 407–9
Diets. *See also* Animal nutrition; Food; Nutrition
    assessing nutritional needs in, 879
    catabolism and human, 179–80

    deficiencies in, 878–79
    evolutionary adaptions of vertebrate digestive systems correlated with, 889–91
    genetic variation in prey selection and, 1135–36
    nonheritable variation and, 470f
    nutritional requirements and, 875–80
    phenylketonuria and, 475–76
Differential centrifugation, 97f
Differential gene expression, **356**, 366–73
    cellular differentiation and sequential regulation of, 367–69
    cytoplasmic determinants and inductive signals in, 367, 368f
    embryonic development processes and, 366–67
    pattern formation, body plan, and, 369–73
    regulation of, 361
Differential-interference microscopy, **96**f
Differential reproductive success, 259–60
Differential speciation success, 530
Differentiation, **367**–69, **755**, **1035**
Diffusion, **132**
    effect of distance rate of, 898
    effects of osmosis on water balance, 133–34
    free energy and, 147f
    as passive transport, 132–33
    proteins and facilitated, 134–35
    of water across plant plasma membranes, 768–71
    of water and minerals into root cells, 772
Digestion, **880**. *See also* Animal nutrition
    animal food processing and, 880
    digestive compartments in, 882–84
    digestive systems and, 854f (*see also* Digestive systems)
    endocrine system hormonal control of, 892
    extracellular, 882–83
    feeding mechanisms and, 881f
    fungal, 636–37, 648–49
    hydrolysis in, 69
    intracellular, 880–82
    lysosomes in intracellular, 106–7
    regulation of animal, 891–92
    sea star, 692–93f
    in small intestine, 886f, 887–88
    in stomach, 885–86
    vertebrate adaptations for, 889–91
Digestive enzymes, 78f
Digestive glands, sea star, 693f
Digestive systems, 883–89
    evolutionary adaptations of, 889–91
    human, 883f, 884f, 886f
    internal exchange surfaces and, 854f
    large intestine in, 888–89
    oral cavity, pharynx, and esophagus in, 883–84
    small intestine in, 886f, 887–88
    stomach in, 885–86
Digger wasps, 1124, 1125f
Dihybrid crosses, **268**–71
Dihybrids, **268**–69
Dihydrofolate reductase (DHFR), 593f
Dihydroxyacetone, 70f
Dijkstra, Cor, 1180f
Dikaryotic mycelia, **639**
Dimers, tubulin, 113–14
Dimetrodon fossil, 511f
Dimorphism, sexual, 1130
Dinoflagellates, 237f, **582**–83
Dinosaurs, **715**
    blood pressure of, 907
    disappearance of, 658
    as early reptiles, 715–16
    flying, 1114
    in fossil record, 15f, 507, 511f, 547–48
    mass extinction of, 522, 524
    in Mesozoic era, 514
Dioecious species, **813**
Diphtheria, 387
Diploblastic animals, **659**–60

Diploid cells, **251**
    genetic variation preserved in recessive alleles of, 483
    mitosis vs. meiosis in, 256*f*–57
    in sexual life cycles, 252–53
Diploidy, 483
Diplomonads, **580**
Diptera, 690*f*
Direct contact, cell signaling and, 208
Direct inhibition hypothesis, 830
Directionality, DNA replication, 314–16, 317*f*
Directional natural selection, 550
Directional selection, **481**
Disaccharides, 69–**70**, 71*f*
Discoveries vs. inventions, 24
Discrete characters, 470
Diseases, animal
    density-dependent population regulation
        through, 1184*f*
    ecological importance of pathogens and,
        1213–15
    human (*see* Diseases and disorders, human)
    movement corridors and spread of, 1251
Diseases, plant
    epidemics of, 847
    plant defenses against, 846–47
    plant pathogens and, 1213–14
    viral, 381–82, 383*f*, 393
Diseases and disorders, human
    allergies, 947
    Alzheimer's disease, 1081
    amebic (amoebic) dysentery, 596
    aneuploidy of sex chromosomes and, 299–300
    apoptosis in degenerative, 225
    asthma and lymphatic system, 63*f*, 909
    atherosclerosis, 76, 77, 138
    autism, 1077
    autoimmune, 947
    biogenic amines and, 1058–59
    cachexia, 988–89
    cancer (*see* Cancer)
    cardiovascular diseases, 913–15
    from cell-surface receptor malfunctions, 210, 213
    cholera, 217
    color blindness, 291, 1100
    community ecology, pathogens, and, 1214–15
    cri du chat and chronic myelogenous leukemia
        (CML), 300
    cystic fibrosis, 273, 277
    cystic kidney disease, 1041
    cystinuria, 135
    depression, 1059
    detecting fetal, during pregnancy, 1017
    diabetes (*see* Diabetes)
    diagnosis and treatment of, 417–18
    diarrhea, 137–38
    dominantly inherited, 278–79
    Down syndrome, 250*f*, 299
    drug addiction, 1080–81
    drug-resistance and, 461–62
    Duchenne muscular dystrophy, 291
    due to chromosomal alterations, 299–300
    epilepsy, 1073–74
    erectile dysfunction, 1059
    flesh-eating disease, 462
    fungal, 650
    gastric ulcers and acid reflux, 886
    goiter, 32, 988
    gonorrhea, 558
    gout, 959
    growth-related, 989
    heart murmurs, 903
    hemophilia, 291, 912
    Huntington's disease, 278–79
    hypercholesterolemia, 138
    hypertension, 915
    immune system disruptions and, 946–50

    immunization against, 945, 950*f*
    immunodeficiency, 948 (*see also* AIDS (acquired
        immunodeficiency syndrome); HIV (human
        immunodeficiency virus))
    insects as carriers of, 691
    Kartagener's syndrome, 1042
    Klinefelter syndrome, 299–300
    Lou Gehrig's disease, 1106
    lupus, 247
    major depressive disorder and bipolar disorder, 1080
    mitochondrial, 301
    mosaicism, 292
    multifactorial, 279
    myasthenia gravis, 1106
    myotonia and epilepsy, 1053
    nematode parasites and trichinosis, 684
    of nervous system, 1079–82
    parasites and, 675–76
    Parkinson's disease, 1059, 1081–82
    pathogenic bacteria and, 571–72
    phenylketonuria, 475–76
    pleiotropy and, 273
    polydactyly, 272
    population density-dependent transmission of, 1184*f*
    population dynamics and, 1187
    prophages and bacterial, 387
    protein misfolding and, 85
    protists and, 578*f*–79*f*
    recessively inherited, 276–78
    respiratory distress syndrome (RDS), 920
    retinitis pigmentosa, 477–78
    schizophrenia, 1079–80
    sexually transmitted diseases (STDs), 1013, 1016
    sickle-cell disease (*see* Sickle-cell disease)
    spina bifida, 1033
    Tay-Sachs disease and lysosomal storage, 107, 272
    thyroid, 987–88
    Turner syndrome, 300
    viral, 387–94
    Vitamin A deficiency, 878–79
    Wiskott-Aldrich syndrome (WAS), 223
    xeroderma pigmentosum, 318
    x-linked disorders, 291
Disorder, entropy and, 144–45
Disparity, vertebrate, 697
Dispersal, **1164**
    fruit and seed, 811*f*
    seed, 626
    in species distributions, 1164–65
Dispersion, population, **1171**, 1172–73
Dispersive model, DNA replication, 311–12*f*
Disruptive selection, **481**
Dissociation, water, 53
Distal control elements, 359–60
Distal tubule, **963***f*, 964*f*, **965**
Distance vision, 1101*f*
Distant hybridization, 815–16
Disturbances, **1152**, **1207**–10
    characterizing, 1207
    ecological succession and, 1208–10
    human, 1210
    in nature reserves, 1252
    in terrestrial biomes, 1152
Disulfide bridges, **83***f*
Diurnal animals, 1122
Divergence
    allopatric speciation and, 493–95
    of angiosperms, 628–29
    of animals and fungi, 640
    of closely related species, 443–45
    morphological, 540
    in phylogenetic trees, 538–39
    speciation tempo after, 503
    of unikonts from other eukaryotes, 593
Diversity
    B cell and T cell, 937–38

    biological (*see* Biodiversity)
    molecular (*see* Organic compounds)
    of scientific viewpoints, 25
    within species, 489*f* (*see also* Species diversity)
    vertebrate disparity vs., 697
Diving mammals, respiratory adaptations of, 925–26
Division, cell. *See* Cell cycle
Dizygotic twins, 1014
Dlx gene family, 702
DNA (deoxyribonucleic acid), **8**, **86**
    amplification of, using polymerase chain reaction,
        403–4
    analysis of Neanderthal mitochondrial, 732*f*
    in bacteria, 236
    cell division and distribution of, 229–30
    cell reproduction and (*see* Cell cycle)
    Chargaff's rules on structure of, 308
    complementary (cDNA), 401
    components of, 87–88
    damage to, from ultraviolet (UV) radiation, 28,
        1167, 1259
    discovery of structure of, 3, 24, 305, 308–10
    DNA technology to study, 405–7
    elevation and UV damage to, 1167
    in eukaryotic vs. prokaryotic cells, 8, 98, 102, 103*f*
    evidence for, as genetic material, 305–8
    evolutionary significance of mutations of, 318 (*see*
        also Mutations)
    evolution of genomes from changes in, 438–42
    forensic ecology and, 1243
    gene density and noncoding, 434
    genes, chromosomes, gene expression, and (*see also*
        Chromosomes; Gene expression; Gene(s))
    genomics, bioinformatics, genomes, and sequencing
        of, 10 (*see also* Bioinformatics; DNA sequences;
        DNA sequencing; Genomes; Genomics)
    homeoboxes in, 445–47
    horizontal gene transfer and, 534–35
    human gene microarray chips containing, 432
    identification (fingerprints) based on, 420–21
    in inheritance of genes, 249
    as measure of evolution, 89
    methylation, 358
    microarray assays, 410, 411*f*
    as molecular homology, 463
    B. M. Olivera's work on, 850–51
    ozone depletion and damage to, 1259
    p53 gene and repair of, 376
    packing of proteins and, into chromosomes, 320–22
    phylogenies based on, 536*f*
    programming of cells by viral, 306–8
    prokaryotic, 559–60
    prokaryotic genetic recombination of, 561–64
    proofreading and repairing of, 316–18
    recombinant, 396
    repetitive noncoding, 434–37
    replication of, 311–19 (*see also* DNA cloning; DNA
        replication)
    roles of RNA vs., 86–87
    simple sequence and short-tandem repeat (STR),
        436–37
    Southern blotting of fragments of, 407*f*
    species identity in mitochondrial, 539*f*
    J. A. Steitz's work on, 246–47
    structure and function of, 8–10
    structure of, 88–89*f*
    technology (*see* Biotechnology; DNA technology)
    transformation of bacteria by, 305–6
    viral, 382, 384–85, 387*t* (*see also* Viruses)
DNA bending, 360*f*, 435
DNA chips, 410, 411*f*
DNA cloning, 396–405. *See also* DNA replication
    amplifying DNA *in vitro* using polymerase chain
        reaction, 403–4
    of eukaryotic genes in bacterial plasmids, 398–402
    expressing cloned eukaryotic genes in, 402–3

gene cloning and applications of, 397–98
screening libraries for specific genes, 401–2
storing cloned genes in DNA libraries, 400–401
using restriction enzymes to make recombinant DNA, 398
DNA Data Bank of Japan, 429
DNA ligase, **316**, 318, **398**
DNA methylation, **358**, 415
DNA microarray assay, 396, **410**, 411*f*
DNA polymerases, **314**–18
DNA replication, **305**, 311–19. *See also* DNA cloning
antiparallel elongation of DNA strands in, 314–16, 317*f*
DNA replication complex of, 316, 317*f*
errors in, and genome evolution, 439–41
evolutionary significance of mutations during, 318
inheritance and, 8–10
proofreading and repairing of DNA during, 316–18
semiconservative model of, 311–12
start of, at origins of replication, 313–14
steps of, 312–16
synthesis of new DNA strands, 314, 315*f*
of telomeres at ends of molecules, 318–19
DNA replication complex, 316, 317*f*
DNA sequences
animal phylogeny and, 662–64
constructing phylogenetic trees using, 544–47
detecting specific, using nucleic acid probe, 401–2
determining, 407–9
evaluating molecular homologies in, 541–42
exon and intron, 335
genes as, 347
genetic variation due to mutations in, 472
noncoding, 433–37
polymorphisms as variations in, 417–18
promoter and terminator, 332
types of, in human genome, 435*f*
DNA sequencing
and advances in breast cancer treatment, 243*f*
dideoxyribonucleotide (dideoxy) chain-termination method, 407–9
genetic testing and, 280*f*, 377*f*
genome sequencing and, 427–28 (*see also* Genomes)
genomics, bioinformatics, and, 10 (*see also* Bioinformatics; Genomics)
machines, 428
personalized treatments for cancer and, 376
three-domain taxonomy system and, 13
DNA strands, 9*f*, 308, 329, 330, 398
DNA technology, 396–425. *See also* Biotechnology
advances in treatment of breast cancer by, 243*f*
DNA cloning, 396–405
gel electrophoresis and Southern blotting, 405–7
organismal cloning as, 412–16
practical applications of, 417–23
recombinant DNA, genetic engineering, biotechnology and, 396
review of, 423–24
science, society, and, 24–25
to study gene sequence, expression, and function, 405–12
Dobzhansky, Theodosius, 11
Dodd, Diane, 495*f*
Dodder, 798*f*
Dog rose, 631*f*
Dolly (cloned lamb), 413–14
Dolphins, 465–66, 1070, 1171*f*, 1240*f*
Domains, protein, **336**
Domains, taxonomy, 13–14, 442*f*, **537**, 551–52, 566*t. See also* Archaea, domain; Bacteria, domain; Eukarya, domain
Domestication, plant, 618, 633, 801, 815
Dominance, degrees of, 271–72
Dominant alleles, **265**–66, 272
Dominantly inherited diseases, human, 278–79
Dominant species, **1204**

Dominant traits, 264, 265*t*
Doolittle, W. Ford, 534–35, 553
Dopamine, **1058**–59
in drug addiction, 1080–81
Parkinson's disease and, 1081–82
schizophrenia and, 1080
Doppler, Christian, 263
Dormancy, **808**
abscisic acid in, 832
prokaryotic endospores and, 560
seed, 620–21, 808–9
Dorsal lips, blastopore, **1029**, 1039*f*
Dorsal sides, **658**
Dorsal-ventral axis, 1036–38, 1040
Double bonds, **38**, 61
Double circulation, **900**–901
Double fertilization, **628**, 806–**7**
Double helix, DNA, 9, **88**–89*f*, 305, **309**–10, 320*f. See also* DNA (deoxyribonucleic acid)
Double-stranded DNA (dsDNA) viruses, 387*t*
Double-stranded RNA (dsRNA) viruses, 387*t*
Doubly compound leaves, 741*f*
Douglas fir, 623*f*
Dowling, Herndon, 866–67
Down syndrome, 250*f*, 280, 298, **299**
Dragonflies, 689, 866*f*
Drip irrigation, 788
Drosophila melanogaster (fruit fly)
axis establishment in development of body plan in, 371–73
body plan regulatory gene of, 1022
changes in developmental genes of, 527
complete genome sequence for, 426
courtship behaviors of, 1120–21
crossing over in, 294–95*f*
diploid and haploid numbers of, 251
eye color of, 326
female bias in sperm usage in, 1002*f*
foraging genes of, 1128
genetic analysis of early development in, 371
genetic basis of behavior in, 1134
genetic variability of, 470–71
genome size of, 433
homeotic genes in, 445–46, 447
life cycle and developmental events of, 370–71
linked genes and, 292–94
as model organism, 24, 288–89, 1022
pattern formation and body plan of, 370–73
phylogenetic tree of, 544*f*
protecting, against infection using antimicrobial peptide, 931*f*
regulation of gene expression in, 351
reproductive anatomy of, 1001*f*
Drosophila pseudoobscura (fruit fly), 495*f*, 504
Drosophila species (fruit flies), molecular clocks of, 550
Drought
abscisic acid in plant tolerance to, 832
American Dust Bowl and, 787
plant responses to, 843
Drugs. *See also* Pharmaceutical products
addiction to, 1080–81
cocktails of, in AIDS treatment, 472, 949–50
enantiomers in, 63
evolution of resistance to, 461–62
fungal production of antibiotic, 651
G protein-coupled receptors (GPCRs) and, 213*f*
molecular shape and, 42, 81
species and genetic diversity and, 1241
synthesis of small molecules for use as, 419
tolerance of, 105
Dryas, 1209–10
Dry fruits, 626, 810
Duchenne muscular dystrophy, **291**
Duckweed, 101*f*
Ducts, male reproductive, 1005
Dunstan, William, 1223*f*

Duodenum, **887**
Duplications, chromosome, **298**–99, 438–41
Duplications, gene, 472, 548, 549*f*, 702
Duroia hirsuta case study, 30–31*f*
Dusky salamanders, 494–95
Dust Bowl, American, 787
Dust mites, 687*f*
Dwarfism, 278, 989
Dynamic stability hypothesis, **1203**–4
Dyneins, **116**
Dysentery, 564, 596
Dystrophin, 291

E
Eagles, 718*f*, 1000, 1240*f*
Ear bones, mammalian, 512–13*f*, 721
Eardrums, 1090
Early warning systems, plant, 846
Ears
bones of mammalian, 512–13*f*, 721
human, 1091*f*
insect, 1090
thermoregulation in jackrabbit, 852
Earth. *See also* Biosphere
abiotic synthesis of organic molecules as origin of life on, 59
conditions on early, and development of life, 507–10
development of photosynthesis and atmospheric oxygen on, 516
history of life on (*see* Evolution)
importance of water on, 46
mass extinctions of life on, 521–24 (*see also* Mass extinctions)
plate tectonics of, 519–21
Earthquakes, 520
Earthworms, 681–82, 787, 882*f*, 899*f*, 961
Eastern box turtle, 716*f*
Eastern indigo snake, 871
Ebola virus, 391
Ecdysis, 663–64, 683
Ecdysozoans (Ecdysozoa), **663**–64, 668*f*–69*f*, 683–92
arthropods, 684–92
nematodes, 683–84
Ecdysteroid, **974**, 980
Echidnas, 722*f*
Echinoderms (Echinodermata), 669*f*, **692**–94, 1023*f*, 1063*f*, 1112
Echinoidea, 694
E. coli. See Escherichia coli (E. coli) bacteria
Ecological footprint, **1190**–91
Ecological niches, **1195**–96
Ecological pyramids, 1225–26
Ecological Society of America, 1260
Ecological species concept, **492**
Ecological succession, **1208**–10
Ecological time, 1163
Ecology, **1144**–69
aquatic biomes and, 1157–63
climate and, 1144–50
of communities, 1145*f*
of ecosystems, 1145*f*
fungi in, 648–51*f*
global, of biosphere, 1145*f*
as interactions between organisms and environment, 1144
of landscapes, 1145*f*
mosses in, 609–10
of organisms, 1145*f*
C. Parmesan's work in, 1142–43
of populations, 1145*f*
prokaryotes in global, 570–71
of prokaryotes, 566–70
review of, 1167–68
scope and fields of, 1145*f*
seedless vascular plants in, 615

species distributions and, 1163–67
terrestrial biomes and, 1150–56f
Ecosystem ecology, **1145f**
Ecosystem engineers, **1205**
Ecosystems, **1145f**, **1218**–37. *See also* Biomes
   communities of species in (*see* Communities)
   coral reefs (*see* Coral reefs)
   diversity of, 1239f, 1240
   dynamics of, 1218
   edges between, 1249–50
   effects of mass extinctions on, 523–24
   energy and nutrient dynamics for, 1220f
   energy budgets of, 1221–22
   energy dynamics in, 1219
   energy flow and chemical (nutrient) cycling in, 163f, 1219–20
   energy flow in, 6–7
   importance of mosses to, 609–10
   importance of seedless vascular plants to, 615
   interactions in, 6
   as level of biological organization, 4f
   metagenomics and genome sequencing of groups of species in, 428–29
   nutrient cycling and biogeochemical cycles in, 1227–32
   primary production in, 1220–25
   prokaryotic chemical recycling in, 570
   prokaryotic interactions in, 570–71
   restoration ecology and restoration of degraded, 1232–35
   review of, 1236–37
   roles of fungi in, 648–51f
   roles of protists in, 596–97
   secondary production in, 1225–27
   trophic levels of, 1219–20
Ecosystem services, 1143, **1241**
Ecotones, **1152**
Ectoderm, **659**, **1027**
Ectomycorrhizae, **638**, 642f, **796**–97
Ectoparasites, **1198**
Ectopic cells and tissue, **1010**
Ectopic pregnancies, 1013
Ectoprocts (Ectoprocta), 664f, 667f, **677**
Ectothermic organisms, **715**, **863**, 866, 870
Edges, ecosystem, 1249–50
Ediacaran biota, 511f, 517–18, 526–27, **656**–57
Edidin, Michael, 128
Effective population size, 1245–**46**
Effector cells, **939**
Effectors, 846, 1046f
Efferent neurons, 1066
Efficiency, cell-signaling, 222–23
Egg-polarity genes, **371**, **372**
Eggs, **996**
   amniotic, 713–14
   amphibian, 712
   of birds and dinosaurs, 547–48
   Burmese python heat generation for incubation of, 867f
   chromosomes in human, 229–30
   conception and, 1012
   development of angiosperm, 629–30
   egg activation in embryonic development, 1023–24
   as female gametes, 996, 1001–2
   fertilization of (*see* Fertilization, reproductive)
   human oogenesis and, 1005, 1007f
   nitrogenous wastes and, 959
   ovules and production of, in seed plants, 619–20
Ehrhardt, David, 119f
Ehrlich, Paul, 1143
Eisner, Thomas, 691
Ejaculation, **1005**
Ejaculatory duct, **1005**
Elastic fibers, 857f
Elastin, 78f
Eldredge, Niles, 503

Electrically charged side chains, 79f
Electrical signaling
   neurons and, 1045 (*see also* Neurons)
   phloem and symplastic, 782
Electrical synapses, 1057
Electrocardiogram (ECG or EKG), **904**
Electrochemical gradients, 136–**37**
Electroencephalogram (EEG), 1067
Electrogenic pump, **137**
Electrolytes, 910–11
Electromagnetic energy or radiation, 189. *See also* Light energy
Electromagnetic receptors, **1089**
Electromagnetic spectrum, **189**
Electron distribution diagrams, 37f, 38f
Electronegativity, **39**
Electron microscope (EM), **95**
Electron microscopy (EM), **96f**
Electrons, **33**
   in carbon atoms, 60–61
   chemical properties and distribution of, 36
   energy levels of, 35
   linear electron flow in light reactions of photosynthesis, 193–95
   orbitals of, 37
   redox reactions and, 164–65
   as subatomic particles, 33
Electron shells, **35**–37
Electron transport chains, **167**
   in anaerobic respiration vs. in fermentation, 177
   chemiosmosis and, 173–75f
   NAD^+ as electron carrier for, 165–67
   in oxidative phosphorylation, 172–73
Electrophysiologists, 1050f
Electroporation, **403**
Elements, **31**
   atomic structure and properties of, 33–37
   compounds of, 31
   essential, for plant nutrition (*see* Essential elements, plant)
   essential and trace, 32
   evolution of tolerance to toxic, 32
   in plant composition, 789
Elephantiasis, 909
Elephants, 457–58, 1177, 1243
Elephant seals, 925, 1245
Elevation
   climate and, 1148–49
   ultraviolet (UV) light damage and, 1167
Elimination, **880**, 888–89.
Elk, 58f
Elodea, 43f, 744f
Elongation, antiparallel DNA, 314–16, 317f
Elongation factors, 340
Elongation stage
   transcription, 332f
   translation, 340–41
Elton, Charles, 1202
Embryo(s). *See also* Embryonic development
   anatomical similarities in vertebrate, 463
   development of plant, 807–8
   ensuring survival of, 1000, 1001f
   hybrid embryonic mortality rates, 299
   land plant, 602f
   maternal immune tolerance of, 1015
   monocot vs. eudicot, 631f
Embryology, 1021
Embryonic development, 1021–27. *See also* Embryo(s)
   animal, 655f
   cleavage in, 1025–27
   developmental biology and, 1021–22
   differential gene expression in, 366–73 (*see also* Differential gene expression)
   fertilization in, 1022–25
   genomic imprinting and, 301

Embryonic development, human
   brain in, 1068f
   conception, pregnancy, and birth in, 1011–15
   maternal immune tolerance of embryo and fetus in, 1015
   neuron competition in, 1076
Embryonic lethals, **371**
Embryonic stem (ES) cells, 415
Embryophytes, 601, **602f**. *See also* Land plants
Embryo sacs, **627**, **803**–4
Emergent properties, **3**
   in chemistry of life, 30, 89
   of compounds, 31
   integration of Mendelian inheritance with, 275
   levels of biological organization and, 3–6
   meaning and purpose as, 451
   of water, 47–52
   weak chemical bonds and, 40
Emerging diseases, 1213–15
Emerging viruses, 391–93
Emigration, 1171f, **1172**, 1175–76, 1186–87
Emotions, 1071–72
Emu, 719f
Enantiomers, **62**–63
Encephalitis, 391, 945
ENCODE (Encyclopedia of DNA Elements), 431
Endangered species, **1239**–40, 1251
Endangered Species Act (ESA), 1239
Endemic species, **466**
Endergonic reactions, 147–**48**
Endocarp, 811f
Endocrine disruptors, 992–93, 1255
Endocrine glands, **976**, 986t
   adrenal gland, 990–92
   hypothalamus and pituitary gland, 984–86t
   major human, 986t
   parathyroid glands, 989–90
   pineal gland, 993
   thyroid, 987–88
Endocrine signaling, 208f–9, 975, 981
Endocrine systems, **974**–95
   coordination of nervous systems and, 984–86t
   disruption of, 992–93, 1255
   evolution of hormone function in, 988–99
   feedback regulation and antagonistic hormone pairs in, 981–84
   hormonal control of digestion by animal, 892
   hormones and cell signaling in animal, 859
   hormones as chemical signals in, 974–80
   major glands and hormones of human, 976f, 984f, 986t
   regulation of, 984–89
   regulation of blood calcium levels by, 989–90
   regulatory functions of, 989–93
   review of, 994
   thyroid regulation of, 987–88
   tissues and organs of, 976
   tropic and nontropic hormones in, 989
Endocytosis, **138**–39f
Endoderm, **659**, **1027**
Endodermis, **749**, **772**, 773f
Endomembrane system, **104**–9
   bound ribosomes and, 343
   endoplasmic reticulum (ER) as biosynthetic factory in, 104–5
   Golgi apparatus in, 105–6
   lysosomes in, 106–7
   overview of, 108–9
   signal mechanism for targeting proteins to, 343f
   vacuoles in, 107–8
   vesicles in, 104
Endometriosis, **1010**
Endometrium, **1003**
Endomycorrhizae, 796–97
Endoparasites, **1198**

Endophytes, **648**
Endoplasmic reticulum (ER), **104**
    animal cell, 100*f*
    as biosynthetic factory, 104–5
    cellular membrane synthesis and, 131*f*
    ribosomes and, 102–4
    targeting polypeptides to, 343*f*
Endorphins, 42, 81, **1059**
Endoskeletons, 692, 1110*f*, **1112**
Endosperm, **628**, **807**
Endospores, **560**
Endosymbiont theory, **109**–10, 186, **516**–17, 534
Endosymbiosis, **576**
    cercozoan, 590
    in eukaryotic evolution, 109–10, 576, 577*f*
    serial, and origin of eukaryotes, 516–17
Endothelin, 907
Endothelium, **905**
Endothermic organisms, **715**, **863**, 870
Endotoxins, **572**
Energetic hypothesis, **1203**–4
Energy, **35**, **143**. *See also* Bioenergetics
    alternatives to fossil fuels, 1258
    animal bioenergetics and (*see* Bioenergetics)
    animal energy budgets, 871
    ATP energy coupling, 149–51
    biofuel technology to reduce dependence on fossil
        fuels for, 817
    chemical recycling and flow of, in ecosystems, 163*f*
    chemiosmosis as energy-coupling mechanism,
        173–75*f*
    conservation of, 1219
    costs of, for osmoregulation, 956–57
    costs of, for urea and uric acid, 959
    ecosystem energy budgets, 1219, 1221–22
    energy levels of electrons, 35
    fats and storage of, 76
    foraging and costs of, 1129
    forms of, 143–44
    global human use of, 1190
    heat as, 48 (*see also* Heat)
    locomotion and, 1113–15
    metabolism and cellular, 142 (*see also* Cellular respira-
        tion; Fermentation; Metabolism; Photosynthesis)
    regulation of storage of, in animal nutrition, 892–93*f*
    solar (*see* Solar energy)
    torpor, hibernation, and conservation of, in animals,
        871–72
    transfer and transformation of, as theme in biology,
        6–7
    transfer of, between ecosystem trophic levels,
        1225–27
    transformation of, by mitochondria and chloroplasts
        in eukaryotic cells, 109–12
Energy coupling, **149**–51
Energy flow, ecosystem, 1218–20
Energy processing, as property of life, 2*f*
Engelmann, Theodor W., 190–91
Enhancers, **359**–61
Entamoebas, 596
Enteric division, peripheral nervous system, 892,
    1066–**67**
Enthalpy, 146
Entropy, **144**–45
Entry stage, phage lytic cycle, 385*f*
Enveloped viruses, 387–88
Environment
    adaptive evolution as fitness to, 476, 480–85
    animal exchanges with, 853–55, 864–67
    aquatic biomes and physical, 1150, 1157
    behavior and stimuli from, 1119–20
    bottleneck effect and changes in, 477–79
    cell cycle control system and factors of, 240–42
    cellular membranes and factors of, 128
    C. Darwin on adaptations to, 15–16
    Earth's early, and origin of life, 507–10

enzymatic catalysis and factors of, 155–56
evolution of adaptations to (*see* Adaptations;
    Evolution)
evolution of plant response to stimuli from, 841
genetics vs., 1123
habitat and (*see* Habitat)
human impacts on (*see* Human environmental
    impacts)
impact of, on phenotypes, 274–75
induction in differential gene expression and,
    367, 368*f*
influence of, on nitrogenous wastes, 959
interaction of chance, natural selection, and, 485
interaction with, as theme in biology, 6
metagenomics and genome sequencing of groups of
    species in, 428–29
as organisms and their surroundings, 452
plant responses to abiotic stresses from, 777–78,
    843–45
post-transcriptional regulation of gene expression
    and changes in, 362
prokaryotic adaptations to extreme conditions in, 556
protein structure and factors of, 84–85
reproductive cycles and cues from, 998
response to, as property of life, 2*f*
strength of ionic bonds and factors in, 40
vertebrate kidney adaptations to diverse, 967–68
Environmental issues. *See also* Human environmental
    impacts
    cancer and, 377
    decline in amphibian populations, 712
    DNA technology for environmental cleanup,
        397*f*, 421
    ecology and, 1144
    global change (*see* Global change; Global climate
        change; Global warming)
    honeybee population decline, 804*f*
    invasive exotic plants, 797
    overharvesting (*see* Overharvesting)
    prokaryotes and biotechnology, 572–73
    threats to seed plant diversity, 633–34
Environmental science. *See* Ecology
Enzymatic catalysis, **152**–57. *See also* Enzymes
    activation energy barrier and, 152–53
    of cellular respiration, 181
    cofactors and, 156
    effects of environmental factors on, 155–57
    effects of temperature and pH on, 155–56
    in enzyme active sites, 154–55
    enzyme inhibitors and, 156–57
    evolution of enzymes and, 157
    in feedback regulation, 10–11
    lowering of activation energy by, 153
    metabolism and, 152–57
    substrate specificity of enzymes in, 153–54
Enzymatic hydrolysis, 880, 886*f*
Enzymatic proteins, 78*f*
Enzymes, **68**, **152**
    allosteric regulation of, 158–60
    as catalysts, 152 (*see also* Enzymatic catalysis)
    cell-signaling nuclear responses and, 219
    in DNA replication (*see* DNA replication)
    evolution of, 157
    facilitation of synthesis and breakdown of polymers
        by, 68–69
    in feedback regulation, 10–11
    fungal, 637
    in gastric juice, 885–86
    gene relationship with, in protein synthesis, 326
    in human chemical digestion, 886*f*
    inducible, 354–55
    locations of, in organelles, 160
    lowering plasma LDL levels by inactivating liver, 914*f*
    lysosomes and, 106–7
    membrane proteins as, 129*f*
    pancreatic, 887

peroxisome, 600–601
as proteins, 9, 77, 78*f*
regulation of activity of, 352
restriction, 385 (*see also* Restriction enzymes)
RNA molecules functioning as (*see* Ribozymes)
in saliva, 884
small intestine, 887
smooth ER and rough ER, 105
Enzyme-substrate complexes, **153**–54
Eosinophils, 910*f*, 912*f*, 933
Ependymal cells, 1065*f*
Ephedra, 622*f*
Ephedrine, 622*f*
Ephrussi, Boris, 326
Epiblast cells, 1029–30, 1031
Epicotyl, **808**
Epidemics, **391**, 847
Epidemiology, 535, 879
Epidermis, **742**, 846
Epididymis, **1005**
Epigenetic inheritance, **358**
Epiglottis, 884
Epilepsy, 1053, 1073–74
Epinephrine, **977**
    adrenal glands and, 986*t*, 990–91
    as amine hormone, 976–77*f*
    as biogenic amine, 1058
    in fight-or-flight responses, 206, 904
    multiple effects of, 978–79
    second messenger of, 216–17
    signal transduction pathway of, 209–10, 219, 220*f*
    as water-soluble hormone, 977–78
Epiphytes, 614*f*, 615, 797, **798***f*
Epistasis, **273**–74
Epithelial tissue (epithelia), **856***f*
    animal, 856*f*
    as barrier defense, 932
    cell junctions in, 121
    in small intestine, 887*f*, 888
    transport, in osmoregulation, 957–58
Epitopes, **935**, 945
Epsilon proteobacteria, 568*f*
Epstein-Barr virus, 377
Equational division, 257
Equilibrium
    chemical (*see* Chemical equilibrium)
    mechanoreceptors for, in vertebrate and mammal
        bodies, 1090–94
    population density and population, 1182
Equilibrium model, community, 1207
Equilibrium potential (E_{ion}), **1049**–50
Equisetum, 614*f*, 615
Erectile dysfunction, 1005, 1059
Ergots, 650, 651
Ericksson, Peter, 1078
ER lumen, 104
Erosion, controlling soil, 788–89
Errors, DNA replication, 316–18
Erythrocytes, 857*f*, 910*f*, **911**, 912–13
Erythropoietin (EPO), **913**
Escherichia coli (*E. coli*) bacteria
    binary fission in, 236–37*f*
    complete genome sequence for, 426
    DNA replication using, 312–16, 317*f*
    genetic recombination and conjugation in, 562–64
    genome size of, 432–33*t*
    in human digestive system, 889
    lac operon in, 354*f*, 355*f*
    metabolic pathway regulation in, 352
    as model organism, 24
    pathogenic strains of, 572
    phages and, 306–8
    rapid adaptive evolution of, 560–61*f*
    trp operon in, 353*f*
    viral infection of, 381, 383, 385*f*
E site (exit site), 339*f*, **340**

Esophagus, **884**, 886
Essential amino acids, **876**
Essential elements, **790**. *See also* Essential nutrients
for humans, 32*t*
for life, **32**
plant, 789–92
Essential fatty acids, 76, **876**
Essential nutrients, **876**–78*t*
amino acids, 876
assessing needs for, 879
deficiencies in, 878–79
fatty acids, 876
minerals, 877–78*t*
vitamins, 876–77
Estivation, 872
Estrada-Peña, Agustin, 1251
Estradiol, 63, 976, 978, **992**, 1008, 1014–15*f*
Estrogens, 63, 976, 986*t*, **992**–93, 1008, 1016–17
Estrous cycles, **1010**
Estuaries, **1160***f*
Ethane, 60*f*
Ethanol (ethyl alcohol), **64***f*, 178, 572*f*, 573, 1183*f*
Ethene (ethylene), 60*f*
Ethical issues
on diagnosing fetal genetic diseases, 1017
on DNA technology, 24–25, 422–23
on gene therapy, 418–19
on plant biotechnology, 817–19
seed plant extinctions as, 634
Ethylene, 209, 827*t*, **832**–34, 843–44
Etiolation, **821**. *See also* De-etiolation
Euchromatin, **322**
Eudicots, **630**, 631*f*
embryo development in, 807*f*
roots of, 748
seed structure of, 808*f*
shoots of, 750
Eugenics, 419
Euglenids, **581**
Euglenozoans, **580**–81
euglenids, 581
kinetoplastids, 580–81
Eukarya, domain, **13**, 551–52. *See also* Eukaryotes
compared to Bacteria and Archaea, 566*t*
gene expression in, compared to other domains,
346–47
genome size in, 433*t*
kingdoms of, 13–14
protists in, 575–79*f* (*see also* Protists)
Eukaryotes. *See also* Eukarya, domain
animals as, 654–56
cell division in, 237*f*
cells of (*see* Eukaryotic cells)
chromatin packing in chromosomes of, 320–22
coordinately controlled genes in, 361–62
electron transport chains in, 167, 172
endosymbiosis in evolution of, 576, 577*f*
gene expression in, 346–47
genome size and number of genes in, 432–33 (*see
also* Eukaryotic genes; Eukaryotic genomes)
organization of typical gene in, 358, 359*f*
origins of first, 516–17
origins of multicellular, 517–18
phylogenetic tree of, 593*f*
plants and animals as, 8 (*see also* Animal(s); Plant(s))
protists as single-celled, 575–79*f* (*see also* Protists)
replication of ends of DNA molecules of, 318–19
as single-celled organisms, 575–76
taxonomy of, 551–52
unikonts as first, to diverge, 593
Eukaryotic cells, **8**, **98**–124. *See also* Animal cells; Cell(s);
Plant cells
animal cell, 100*f*
cell cycle control system of (*see* Cell cycle control
system)
cell cycle of (*see* Cell cycle)

cell division in, 229–30
cellular integration of, 122
cytoskeletons of, 112–18
differential gene expression in, 356–57, 366–73
distribution of chromosomes in cell division of,
229–30
DNA replication in, 313–14
endomembrane system of, 104–9
expressing cloned eukaryotic genes in, 403
extracellular components and connections between,
118–22
genetic instructions in, 102–4
initiation of transcription in, 333*f*
internal membranes and organelles of, 99,
100*f*, 101*f*
mechanisms of post-transcriptional regulation of
gene expression in, 362–64
microsporidia infecting, 641*f*
mitochondria, chloroplasts, and peroxisomes of,
109–12
noncoding RNAs in regulation of gene expression in,
364–66
nucleus as information center of, 102, 103*f*
post-transcription modification of RNA in, 334–36
prokaryotic cells vs., 8, 98–99 (*see also*
Prokaryotic cells)
regulation of chromatin structure in, 357–58
regulation of gene expression in, 356–64
regulation of transcription initiation in, 358–62
ribosomes as protein factories of, 102–4
J. A. Steitz's work with, 247
transcription and translation in, 329*f*, 331–34,
337–44, 348*f*
Eukaryotic genes
cloning of, 398–402
expression of cloned, 402–3
making complementary DNA for, 401*f*
Eukaryotic genomes, 434–38. *See also* Genomes
evolution of, from DNA changes, 438–42
gene expression in (*see* Gene expression)
genes and multigene families in, 437–38
human (*see* Human genome)
noncoding repetitive DNA sequences in, 434–37
Eulipotyphla, 725*f*
Eumetazoans (Eumetazoa), **662**, 666, 671
Euphorbs, 1152
Euphydryas editha, 1142–43
Europe, 1188, 1235*f*
European butterflies, 1149
European flycatchers, 500
European honeybees, 1121–22
European kestrels, 1180–81
European larch, 623*f*
European Molecular Biology Laboratory, 429
European starling, 1243
Euryarchaeota, clade, 567
Euryhaline animals, 954
Eurypterids, **686**
Eustachian tube, **1091***f*
Eutherians (placental mammals), **723**–28
convergent evolution of, 464–65, 722–23*f*
phylogeny of, 724*f*–25*f*
primates, 723–28
Euthermia, 871*f*
Eutrophication, **1224**, 1255
Eutrophic lakes, **1159***f*
Evans, Martin, 410
Evaporation, 47–48, **864***f*
Evaporative cooling, **49**, 865–66
Evapotranspiration, **1211**
Even-toed ungulates, 465–66
Evergreen trees, 624*f*
Evidence
fossils as, for evolution, 14
scientific data as, 18–19
theories and, 23

Evo-devo (evolutionary developmental biology),
445–47, 525–29
Evolution, **1**, **452**. *See also* Adaptations; Darwin, Charles;
Natural selection
abiotic synthesis of organic molecules as origin of
life on Earth, 59
of adaptations that reduce terrestrial nutrient limitations, 1224–25
of altered DNA nucleotides as mutations, 318
of alternative carbon fixation mechanisms in plants,
199–202
of amniotes, 714
angiosperm, 628–30
of animal obesity, 894–95
of animals, 656–58
of animal size and shape, 853
of arthropods, 684–85
associative learning and, 1126
of axon diameter and myelination, 1054
of biodiversity (*see* Biodiversity)
of biological order, 145
of bryophyte stomata, 609
of butterflies, 1142–43
of cell signaling, 206–7
chordate, 700–701
of circulatory systems, 898–99
classification of biodiversity and, 12–14
coevolution of flowers and pollinators, 806
of cognition and vertebrate brains, 1075–76
comparing genome sequences to study, 442–47
convergent, 464–65, 540–41, 722–23*f*, 1152
as core theme of biology, 1, 11–18
craniate, 702
Darwinian, 450–68
C. Darwin's field research on adaptations and,
455–57
C. Darwin's theory of descent with modification
and, 14–16 (*see also* Descent with modification
theory)
C. Darwin's theory on speciation, 457–60
of development, 525–29
of differences in cellular membrane lipid
composition, 128
DNA and proteins as measures of, 89
W. F. Doolittle's work on, of biodiversity, 534–35
of ecological niches, 1195–96
endosymbiosis in eukaryotic, 576, 577*f*
of enzymes, 157
evidence for, in direct observations of evolutionary
change, 460–62
evidence for, in fossil record, 465–66
evidence for, in geographical distribution of
species, 466
evidence for, in homologies, 462–65
evidence supporting C. Darwin's theory of, 460–67
evolutionary adaptations as property of life, 1, 2*f*
evolutionary advantage of seeds for seed plants,
620–21
of extraembryonic membranes in amniote
development, 1031
of fishes, 708–9
of foraging behaviors, 1129
of fungi, 640–41
of genes and genomes, 548–49
genetic variation and, of behavior, 1135–36
of genetic variation from genetic recombination and
natural selection, 295
of genetic variation in populations, 259–60
of genomes from DNA changes, 438–42
of glycolysis, 179
of gnathostomes and jaws, 704–5
gymnosperm, 621
historical context of Darwinian revolution in,
453–55
hominin, 728–32
of hormone function, 988–89

human, 549, 729f, 732–33
of introns, 336
J.-B. de Lamarck's theory of, 454–55
land plant, 600–601, 604–6
life history diversity and, 1179–80
of life on Earth (*see* Macroevolution)
mammal, 721
of mitochondria and chloroplasts, 109–10
of mitosis, 237
molecular clocks and rates of, 549–51
of muscles, 1110
mycorrhizae in plant, 796
of nitrogenous wastes, 959
of pathogens, 948–50
of patterns of sexual reproduction, 998–99
phylogenies and relationships in, 537–40
of plant defense systems, 845
of plant responses to environmental stimuli, 841
of plant secondary growth, 754–55
of populations (*see* Microevolution)
possible, of life on planets with water, 52
of prokaryotic flagella, 558–59
rapid prokaryotic, in response to environmental
    change, 560–61f
of reptiles, 715–16
respiratory adaptations of diving mammals, 925–26
review of, 467–68
of roots, 612
as scientific theory, 467
sexual reproduction as enigma of, 997–98
of short-term and long-term memory, 1077
significance of cross-species gene expression and, 403
of small ncRNAs, 366
of species (*see* Speciation; Species)
species dispersal and, 1164–65
of tolerance to toxic elements, 32
of toxin diversity in cone snails, 851
tree of life and, 16–17
of vascular plant resource acquistion adaptations,
    764–65
of vascular plant roots and leaves, 612, 613f
of vascular plants, 610–13
G. J. Vermeij's work on mechanisms of, 450–51
of vertebrate digestive systems, 889–91
of viruses, 390
of visual perception, 1095–97
Evolutionary biology, 452, 1139
Evolutionary developmental biology (evo-devo),
    445–47, 525–29
Evolutionary time, 1163
Evolutionary trees, 457–58f, **464**, 534–35. *See also* Phylo-
    genetic trees
Exaptations, 530
Excavata (excavates), 578f, **580**–81
    diplomonads and parabasalids, 580
    euglenozoans, 580–81
Exchange surfaces, animal, 853–55
Excitatory postsynaptic potential (EPSP), **1056**–57f
Excretion, **953**, 960. *See also* Excretory systems;
    Nitrogenous wastes
    by aquatic animals, 954–56
    by marine birds, 957–58
    by terrestrial animals, 956
Excretory systems, 953–73. *See also* Osmoregulation
    excretion, osmoregulation, and, 953
    excretory processes of, 960
    hormonal regulation of, 968–71
    internal exchange surfaces and, 854f
    kidneys in, 962–63
    Malpighian tubules in, 961–62
    mammalian and human, 962f–63f
    metanephridia in, 961
    nitrogenous wastes and, 958–59
    osmoregulation and, 953–58
    processing of blood filtrate by nephrons in, 963–68
    protonephridia in, 960–61

review of, 972–73
survey of, 960–63
Executive functions, brain, 1075
Exercise, immune systems and, 947–48
Exergonic reactions, **147**–48, 164
Exhalation, 920–22
Exit tunnel, ribosome, 340
Exocrine glands, 976
Exocytosis, **138**
Exons, **335**, 336, 433, 441
Exon shuffling, 336
Exoskeletons, **677**, **1111**
    animal, 663
    arthropod, 686
    chitin as structural polysaccharide in, 74
    ectoproct, 677
    locomotion and, 1111–12
Exotic species, 1242–43
Exotoxins, **572**
Expansins, **828**
Experience, animal behavior and, 1123
Experimental groups, 21–22
Experiments
    controlled, 22–23
    designing, 20
    G. Mendel's, 262–64
Exponential population growth, **1176**–77, 1187
Exponential population growth model, 1175–77
Expressed sequence tags (ESTs), 429–30
Expression vectors, **402**
Extension, muscle, 1110f
External factors, cell cycle control system, 240–42
External fertilization, **999**–1000, 1130–31
Extinctions
    amphibian, 712
    current rate of, 1239
    deforestation and, 1238
    extinction vortex and, 1245
    in fossil record, 465, 510–11f
    global and local, 1240
    global temperature and, 523
    introduced species and, 1243
    island equilibrium model and, 1212–13
    mass, 521–24 (*see also* Mass extinctions)
    mollusc, 680–81f
    of seed plant species, 633–34
    speciation, macroevolution, and, 504
Extinction vortex, **1245**
Extracellular digestion, 882–83
Extracellular matrix (ECM), **119**–20, 129f, 1034
Extraembryonic membranes, 713–14, **1031**
Extranuclear genes, 300–301
Extreme halophiles, **567**
Extreme thermophiles, **567**
Extremophiles, **567**
Eyes
    color of fruit fly, 288–89, 326
    complexity of mollusc, 529f
    compound, 1095–96
    euglenid eyespot as, 581f, 1095
    evolution of, 529–30
    insect compound, 690f
    single-lens, 1096–97
    visual information processing in vertebrate, 1098–99
Eyespots, 581f, 1095

F

F_1 (first filial) generations, **264**
F_2 (second filial) generations, **264**
Faceted eyes, arthropod, 1095–96
Facilitated diffusion, **134**
Facilitation, **1200**
FACTS-I (Forest-Atmosphere Carbon Transfer and
    Storage) experiment, 1256–57
Facultative anaerobes, **179**, **564**
Facultative mutualism, 1199

FAD (flavin adenine dinucleotide), 171–72
$FADH_2$, 171–72, 173
Fahrenheit scale, 48
Fairy ring, mushroom, 646–47f
Falling phase, action potential, 1052
Falsifiable hypotheses, 20
Families (taxonomy), **537**
Family histories, 275–76
Family planning, 1188
Family studies, 1079
Fangs, 890
Fan worms, 681
Fanwort, 755
Far-red light, plant response to, 836–37
Fast block to polyspermy, **1022**
Fast-twitch fibers, **1109**
Fate maps, **1035**–39
    axis formation and, 1036–38
    developmental potential and, 1038–39
Fatigue, muscle, 1108
Fats, **74**. *See also* Lipids
    absorption of, in small intestine, 888
    as animal insulation, 864
    in cardiovascular diseases, 913–15
    digestion of, 886f
    as energy source, 892
    evolution of hoarding of, 894–95
    as fuel for catabolism, 180
    hydrocarbons in, 61–62f
    as lipids, 74–76
    overnourishment, obesity, and, 893–95
    trans fats, 62
Fat-soluble vitamins, 876–77t
Fatty acids, **74**
    beta oxidation of, for catabolism, 180
    essential, for animal nutrition, 876
    fats and, 74–76
Feathers, 718
Feather stars, 694
Feces, **889**
    production efficiency and, 1225
    seed dispersal in, 811f
    tapeworms and, 676
Feedback inhibition, **160**, 181, 352
Feedback regulation. *See also* Regulation; Positive feed-
    back; Negative feedback
    of animal digestion, energy storage, and appetite,
        891–95
    as biological theme, 10–11, 1182
    of endocrine systems, 982
    homeostasis in, 860–62
    maintenance of animal internal environments by,
        860–62
    population dynamics and, 1182–84
    regulators and conformers in, 860
Feeding mechanisms, 636–37, **881**f
Feeding relationships. *See* Trophic structure
Feet, bird, 720
Female gametophytes, angiosperm, 803–4
Females
    autoimmune diseases in human, 947
    energy budgets for female animals, 871
    fruit fly bias in sperm usage by, 1002f
    hormonal control of reproductive systems of,
        1008–10
    inactivation of x-linked genes in mammals,
        291–92
    mate choice by, 482–83, 1131–32
    maternal immune tolerance of embryo and fetus
        during pregnancy, 1015
    oogenesis in human, 1005, 1007f
    parental care and, 1130–31
    parthenogenesis by, 676–77
    reproductive anatomy of human, 1002–4
    reproductive rates and, 1174–75
    sex determination of, 289–90

Fermentation, **164**, 177–79. *See also* Cell(s); Cellular
respiration
anaerobic and aerobic respiration vs., 178–79
as catabolic, 164
types of, 177–78
Fern galls, 657–58
Ferns (Pterophyta), 611*f*, 613–15. *See also* Seedless vascular plants
Ferrodoxin, 195
Fertility schedules, 1174–75
Fertilization, reproductive, **251**, **788**, **802**,
999–1002, **1022**
acrosomal reactions in, 1022, 1023*f*
angiosperm, 802
angiosperm double, 806–7
brown algae, 587
cortical reactions in, 1022–23, 1024*f*
double, 628
egg activation in, 1023–24
in embryonic development, 1022–25
ensuring offspring survival following, 1000, 1001*f*
external versus internal, 999–1000
gamete production and delivery in, 1000–1002
human conception as, 1012
in mammals, 1024–25
mechanisms preventing angiosperm
self-fertilization, 813
meiosis and, 230, 251–52
G. Mendel's techniques of, 263–64
parental care and internal vs. external, 1130–31
parthenogenic self-fertilization, 996, 998–99
prezygotic barriers and, 489–91*f*
random, 258–59
reproductive organs and (*see* Reproductive organs,
human)
in three types of sexual life cycles, 252–53
in vitro fertilization (IVF), 1018
Fertilization, soil, **788**, 959, 1183*f*, 1225, 1254
Fescue grass, 1182
Fetal alcohol syndrome, 1014
Fetal testing, 280, 281*f*, 1017
Fetoscopy, 280
Fetus, **1014**
detecting disorders of, during pregnancy, 1017
gestation of, 1012–15
maternal immune tolerance of, 1015
Fever, 867–68, 934, 946, 979
F factor, **563**
Fibers, **744***f*
Fibrin, 911–12*f*
Fibrinogen, 911
Fibroblast growth factor (FGF), 1040
Fibroblasts, 113*t*, 241, **857***f*
Fibronectin, **120**
Fibrous connective tissue, 857*f*
Fibrous proteins, 81
Fibrous root systems, 739
Fiddler crabs, 1118, 1120
Fierer, Noah, 1201*f*
Fight-or-flight responses, 206, 904, 1067
Filamentous fungi, 639–40
Filaments, flagellum, 558–59
Filaments, flower, **626**, 802
Filter feeders, **881***f*
Filtrates, **960**, 963–65
Filtration, **960**
Fimbriae, 98*f*, **558**, 558*f*
Finches, 16–17, 23, 456–57*f*, 469, 1163
Finland, 1206
Fin whales, 539*f*–40
Fire, 1152, 1207, 1208–9
Fireflies, 838
Firefly squid, 142
First law of thermodynamics, **144**
First trimester, 1013–14
"Fishapod" discovery, 709–10

Fishes
allopatric speciation in, 493–94
animal diets and, 875
changes in gene regulation in, 527–29
discovery of "fishapod" *Tiktaalik*, 709–10
endangered or threatened, 1239
frequency-dependent selection and, 484, 485*f*
gills for gas exchange in, 916–17*f*
hearing and equilibrium in, 1094
kidney adaptations in, 968
mummichog, and temperature clines, 471
osmoregulation in, 954–56
parental care in, 1131
pheromones as alarm signals for, 1122
population density and predation by, 1183*f*
protists as pathogens of, 596
ray-finned, and lobe-finned, 707–9
sex determination of, 290*f*
sex reversal in, 999
single circulation in, 898*f*
Fisk, Jack, Madison, and Schuyler, 248
Fission, **996**–97
Fitness
neutral theory on natural selection and, 550
relative, 480
Fitness of the Environment, The (book), 46
FitzRoy, Robert, 455
Fixed action patterns, **1119**
Fixed alleles, 473
Flaccid cells, **134**, **770**
Flagella, **114**
animal cell, 100*f*
cilia vs., 115*f*
dinoflagellates and, 582–83
euglenozoan, 580, 581*f*
evolutionary origins of bacterial, 558–59*f*
flagellated sperm, 601
as microtubules, 114–16
prokaryotic, 558–59*f*
prokaryotic cell, 98*f*
protistan cell, 101*f*
stramenopile, 585
Flagellated sperm, 601
Flame bulbs, 674, 960–61
Flamingos, 720
Flatworms (Platyhelminthes), 667*f*, 674–76, 898*f*,
960–61, 1063*f*
Flavin mononucleotide (FMN), 172
Flavoproteins, 172
Fleas, 962
Flemming, Walther, 230
Flesh-eating disease, 462
Fleshy fruits, 626, 810
Fletcher, W. J., 1165*f*
Flexion, muscle, 1110*f*
Flies, 632*f*, 690*f*, 805*f*. *See also Drosophila melanogaster*
(fruit fly)
Flight, 688–89, 717–18, 1114–15
Flightless birds, 719
Flightless cormorant, 488, 493
Flight muscles, 1110
Floating of ice, 49–50
Flooding, 792, 843–44, 1207–8
Floral clock, 821
Florida, 1234*f*
Florida Keys National Marine Sanctuary, 1253
Florigen, **840**–41
FLOWERING LOCUS T (FT) gene, 841
Flowers, **625**–26. *See also* Angiosperms (Anthophyta)
adaptations of, that prevent self-fertilization, 813*f*
coevolution of pollinators and, 806
genetic control of formation and flowering of,
760–61
hormonal control of flowering of, 840–41
monocot vs. eudicot, 631*f*
photoperiodism and flowering of, 839–40

pollination of, 801, 804*f*–5*f*
preventing transgene escape with genetically
engineered, 818
shape of, and insect pollination of, 632
structure and function of, 802–6
Flu. *See* Influenza viruses
Fluctuation, population, 1184–85
Fluid feeders, **881***f*
Fluid mosaic model, **125**–27
Fluid retention, kidney, 969–70
Fluorescence, 192, 411*f*
Fluorescence *in situ* hybridization (FISH), 427
Fluorescence microscopy, **96***f*, 97, 236
Fluoxetine, 1080
Fly agaric, 642*f*
Flycatchers, European, 500
Flying. *See* Flight
Flying fox bats, 1240
Flying squirrels, 465
fMRI. *See* Functional magnetic resonance imaging
Focusing, visual, 1100–1101
Folding, protein, 85–86*f*
Folic acid, 879
Foliose lichens, 649*f*
Follicles, **1003**
Follicle-stimulating hormone (FSH), 985*f*, 986*t*, **989**,
1007*f*, 1008–11
Follicular phase, **1008**
Food. *See also* Diets; Nutrition
animal processing of, 880–83
availability of, as limiting factor for human population size, 1190–91
bioenergetics and animal energy from, 868–69
brown algae as human, 586
calories, 48
as fuel for cellular respiration, 164
fungi as human, 651
genetically modified organisms (GMOs) as,
422–23, 818
population cycles and shortages of, 1185–86
ray-finned fishes as human, 708
seed plants as human, 633
Food chains, 1202–4, 1225–26
Food poisoning, 387, 568*f*, 569*f*, 572, 1058
Food vacuoles, 107, **108**, 584*f*, 880
Food webs, 597, **1202**–3
Foolish seedling disease, 830
Foot, mollusc, **677**, 678*f*
Foot, sporophyte, **609**
Foraging, **1128**–29
balancing risk and reward in, 1129
cellular slime mold, 1186
evolution of, 1128
optimal foraging model, 1128–29
Foraminiferans (forams), 579*f*, **589**
Forebrain, **1068***f*
Forelimbs, mammalian, 463
Forensic ecology, 1243*f*
Forensic science
DNA analysis in, 24*f*
DNA technology and, 420–21
phylogenetic trees in, 535
Forest-Atmosphere Carbon Transfer and Storage (FACTS-I)
experiment, 1256–57
Forest fires, 1208
Forests, northern coniferous, 1155*f*
Forests, temperate broadleaf, 1156*f*
Forests, tropical, 1153*f*
Form and function. *See* Structure and function
Formic acid, 30–31*f*
Fossil fuels
biofuels as alternatives to, 185*f*
biofuel technology to reduce dependence on, 817
global climate change and, 6, 201, 1256–58
global human use of, 1190
greenhouse effect and, 28–29

hydrocarbons as, 61
ocean acidification, acid precipitation, and, 55–56
photosynthesis as source of, 184–85
seedless vascular plants and, 615
Fossil record, 510–14
angiosperms in, 628–29
animals in, 656–58
biogeography and, 466
diatoms in, 585
evidence for evolutionary change found in, 14, 15f, 16, 458, 465–66
evidence in, of dinosaurs as ancestors of birds, 547–48
evolutionary trends in, 530–31f
forams in, 589–90
geologic record and, 514, 515f
gymnosperms in, 621
insects in, 688
land plant origin and diversification in, 604
origin of mammals in, 512–14
seedless vascular plants in, 610–11
speciation patterns in, 501–3
strata in, 510–11f
Fossils, 454
amniote, 714
arthropod, 684
Australopiths, 729–30
bird, 718–19
dating, 34, 512
dinosaur, 507, 716
of early craniates, 702
of early *Homo* species, 731
of early vertebrates, 703–4
fungal, 640, 641
of gnathostomes, 705
hominin, 728–29
Homo sapiens, 732–33
horseshoe crabs as living, 686f
human, 727
of marine molluscs, 450–51
reptile, 715
seedless vascular plant, 611f
tetrapod, 709–10
whisk ferns as living, 615
Founder effect, 477–78
Fovea, 1099, 1100–1101
FOXP2 gene, 443–44
F plasmids, 563
Fragmentation, habitat, 1241–42, 1250
Fragmentation, reproductive, 812, 997
Frameshift mutations, 345f, 346
Franklin, Rosalind, 308–10
Frederickson, Megan, 31f
Free energy, 146
free-energy change and, 146
metabolism and, 147–49
stability, equilibrium, and, 146–47f
Free energy of activation, 152–53
Free ribosomes, 102–4, 343
Freeze-fractured method, 126–27
Freezing, 844–45, 1207
Frequency-dependent selection, 484, 485f
Freshwater animals
endangered or threatened, 1239
kidney adaptations in, 968
osmoregulation in, 955–56
Freshwater biomes, 1157–58. *See also* Aquatic biomes
Friction, locomotion and, 1113–14
Fringe wetlands, 1159f
Fringing reefs, 1162f
Fritillaria assyriaca (lily), 433
Fritillaries, 1149, 1186–87f
Frogs
as amphibians, 710–12
cleavage in, 1026

coloration of, 1197f
evolutionary compromise in Túngara, 485f
external fertilization of, 999f, 1000
fate mapping for, 1035f
fungal infection of, 650–51f
gastrulation in, 1028–29
intersexual selection and mate choice among tree, 483f
metamorphosis of, 988
neurulation in, 1032f
nuclear transplantation in, 413f
polyploidy in, 495
Fronds, 614f
Frontal lobe, 1074f, 1075
Frontal lobotomy, 1075
Frost-tolerant plants, 844–45
Fructose, 70
Fruit flies. *See Drosophila melanogaster* (fruit fly)
Fruiting bodies, 207f
cellular slime mold, 595
fungal, 642f, 644
Fruitlets, 810
Fruits, 626, 809
angiosperm, 625, 626
dispersal of, 811f
form and function of, 809–10
role of auxin in growth of, 829
role of ethylene in ripening of, 834
role of gibberellins in growth of, 831
Fruticose lichens, 649f
Frye, Larry, 128
Fuels. *See also* Biofuels; Fossil fuels
peat, 610, 615
seed plants as, 633
Fumonisin, 818
Function, structure and. *See* Structure and function
Functional brain imaging, 1072f
Functional groups, 63–65f
Functional magnetic resonance imaging (fMRI), 1072f
Fundamental niches, 1195
Fungi, 636–53
amphibian population declines due to, 712
ascomycetes, 642f, 644–46
basidiomycetes, 642f, 646–48
body structure of, 637–38
cells of, 100f (*see also* Eukaryotic cells)
chytrids, 641, 642f
as decomposers, 648, 1220
diversity of, 636
in domain Eukarya and kingdom Fungi, 13–14
ecological roles of, 636, 637, 648–52
fungal plant toxin, 818
glomeromycetes, 642f, 644
land colonization by, 518–19
life cycles of, 639f, 643f, 645f, 647f
microsporidia as possible, 641
as mutualists, 648–50
mycorrhizal, 604, 638, 767, 795–97
nutrition and ecological roles of, 636–37
as opisthokonts, 596
origin of, in protists, 640
as pathogens and parasites, 650–51f
phylogeny of, 641–48
practical uses of, for humans, 651–52
relationship of, to humans, 536f
relationship of, to unikont protists, 593
review of, 652–53
sexual and asexual reproduction of, 638–40
sexual life cycles of, 252
terrestrial adaptations of land plants and, 641
zygomycetes, 642f, 643–44
Fungi, kingdom, 13–14, 551–52. *See also* Eukarya, domain
Fusarium, 818
Fusion, hybrid zone species, 500–501f
Fynbos, 1154f

G

G_0 phase, 239
G_1 checkpoint, 239
G_1 phase, 231
G_2 checkpoint, 240
G_2 phase, 231
Gage, Fred, 1078
Gage, Phineas, 1075
Galactose, 70f
Galápagos Islands, 16–17, 23, 456–57f, 488, 1163
Gall, Joe, 246
Gallbladders, 887
Gälweiler, Leo, 828f
Gametangia, 603f, 607
Gametes, 229, 249
chromosomes in human, 229–30
as haploid cells, 251
human gametogenesis and, 1005–8
inheritance of genes in, 249
law of segregation of, 265–66
production and delivery of, in animal reproduction, 1000–1002 (*see also* Reproductive organs, human)
Game theory, 1133, 1139
Gametic isolation, 491f
Gametogenesis, 1005–8
Gametophores, 606
Gametophytes, 602f
advantage of reduced, in seed plants, 618–19
brown algae, 587
of bryophytes, 606–9
development of male and female, in angiosperms, 803–4
of land plants, 602f
plant fertilization and, 263
sporophyte relationships with, in plants, 619f
Gamma-aminobutyric acid (GABA), 1058
Gamma proteobacteria, 568f
Ganglia, 675f, 1045
Ganglion cells, 1096f, 1098–99
Gannets, 1184f
Gap junctions, 121f, 1110
Garden peas, G. Mendel's, 262–69. *See also* Mendelian inheritance
Garigue, 1154f
Garlic mustard, 797f
Garrod, Archibald, 326
Garter snakes, 490f, 1135–36
Gas chromatography, 832
Gases
as neurotransmitters, 1058t, 1059–60
water vapor, 46
Gas exchange, 915–26
arthropod, 686
breathing, lung ventilation, and, 920–22
chordate, 699
circulatory systems and, 897, 923–26 (*see also* Circulatory systems)
fish, 707
gills for, in aquatic animals, 916–17
insect, 688f
lungs for, in vertebrates and mammals, 918–20
partial pressure gradients in, 915
respiratory media in, 915
respiratory surfaces in, 916
review of, 926–28
shark, 706
spider, 687
tracheal systems for, in insects, 917–18
Gastric glands, 885
Gastric juices, 885–86
Gastric ulcers, 886
Gastrin, 892f
Gastrodermis, 671f, 882
Gastropods, 523–24, 678–79, 680–81f
Gastrovascular cavity, 671, 882–83, 898

Gastrula, **655**, 1021, **1027**
Gastrulation, **655**, **1027**–31
 animal, 658, 659*f*
 in chicks, 1029–30
 coelom formation, 661
 in frogs, 1028–29
 germ layers in, 659–60
 in humans, 1030–31
 process of, 1027
 in sea urchins, 1028
Gated channels, **135**
Gated ion channels, **1050**–53
Gause, G. F., 1195
Gazelles, 206
Geese, 1124
Gel electrophoresis, **405**–7, 409*f*, 470–71
Genbank, 429
Gene(s), **8**, **86**, **249**
 alleles as alternative versions of, 265 (*see also* Alleles)
 animal behavior and, 1134–35
 apoptosis, 224
 B cell and T cell diversity and rearrangement of, 937–38
 bicoid, 372–73
 calibrating molecular clocks of, 549–50
 cloning of (*see* DNA cloning; Gene cloning)
 for color vision, 1100
 coordinately controlled, in eukaryotes, 361–62
 density of, in genomes, 434
 developmental, 525–26, 527*f*
 DNA, chromosomes, gene expression, and, 8–10 (*see also* Chromosomes; DNA (deoxyribonucleic acid); Gene expression)
 DNA technology to study function of, 410–12
 duplication of, due to unequal crossing over, 439
 egg-polarity, 371
 enzyme relationship with, in protein synthesis, 326, 327*f*
 epistasis of, 273–74
 evolution of, with novel functions, 440–41
 evolution of *FOXP2*, 443–44
 evolution of homologous, 548, 549*f*
 evolution of related-function, 440
 extending Mendelian inheritance for multiple, 273–74
 extending Mendelian inheritance for single, 271–73
 flower formation, 760–61
 foraging, 1128
 gene expression and concept of, 347
 genetic diversity and, 1241
 genetic variation due to alterations of number or position of, 472
 genomes, genomics, and, 10 (*see also* Genomes; Genomics)
 genomic imprinting and, **300**–301
 homeotic, 371, 445–47, 526, 527*f*
 homologies and, 541
 homologous, 463
 horizontal gene transfer of, 553
 Hox genes, 445–47, 1041
 identifying protein-coding, 429–30
 inheritance of, 248–49
 inheritance of organelle, 300–301
 jumping, 435 (*see also* Transposable elements)
 linked (*see* Linked genes)
 locating, along chromosomes, 286
 long-term inactivation of, 358
 macroevolution due to changes in developmental, 527
 mapping distance between, on chromosomes, 296–97
 maternal effect, 371–73
 G. Mendel's hereditary factors as, 262
 meristem identity and organ identity, 760
 multigene families and, in genomes, 437–38
 notation systems for, 288
 nucleic acids and, 86

 number of, in genomes, 433
 ob and *db* genes and appetite regulation in mice, 893–94
 olfactory, 1103
 organization of typical eukaryotic, 358, 359*f*
 pattern formation, 371
 protein synthesis and (*see* Protein synthesis)
 pseudogenes, 434, 463
 ras and *p53*, 374–76
 rearrangement of parts of, 441
 regulatory, 353
 sex-linked, 290–92
 speciation and, 503–4
 split, 334–36
 study of, by systems biology, 430–32
 transplanting, into different species, 331*f*
 types of, associated with cancer, 373–74
 vertebrate development and mutations of, 702
Genealogy, molecular, 89
Gene annotation, **429**–30
Gene cloning, **397**–98
 of eukaryotic genes in bacterial plasmids, 398–400
 polymerase chain reaction vs., 404
 screening DNA libraries for specific cloned genes, 401–2
 storing cloned genes in DNA libraries, 400*f*, 401
Gene expression, **9**, **325**–50. *See also* Genetics; Protein synthesis; Transcription; Translation
 analysis of, 409–10, 411*f*
 auxin and, 828
 of brain development genes in lancelets and vertebrates, 700–701
 in cell fate specification, 1035–42
 of cloned eukaryotic genes, 402–3
 control of plant cell differentiation and, 759
 DNA, RNA, genes, and, 9–10 (*see also* DNA (deoxyribonucleic acid); Gene(s); RNA (ribonucleic acid))
 DNA technology to silence, 410–11
 DNA technology to study, 409–10
 in domains Bacteria, Archaea, and Eukarya, 346–47
 evolutionary significance of cross-species, 403
 evolution due to changes in, 527–29
 faulty genes and, 325
 flowering and, 841
 flow of genetic information and, 325
 gene concept and, 347
 gene specification of proteins via transcription and translation as, 325–31
 genetic code and, 328–31
 mutations and, 344–46
 nematode parasite control of host, 684
 nucleic acids in, 86–87
 polypeptide synthesis via RNA-directed translation as, 337–44
 regulation of (*see* Gene expression, regulation of)
 review of, 349–50
 RNA modification after transcription by eukaryotic cells, 334–36
 RNA synthesis via DNA-directed transcription, 331–34
 study of, by systems biology, 430–32
 summary of eukaryotic transcription and translation in, 348*f*
 as transcription, 357
 transgenic, 331*f*
Gene expression, regulation of, 351–80. *See also* Genetics
 in bacterial transcription, 351–56
 cancer due to faulty, 373–77
 control of plant cell differentiation and, 759
 differential gene expression in multicellular organisms and, 366–73
 in eukaryotic cells, 356–64
 nuclear architecture and, 362
 in plant signal transduction pathways, 824
 review of, 378–79
 role of noncoding RNAs in, 364–66
 steroid hormones and, 978

 Gene families, 548, 549*f*
Gene flow, **479**
 biological species concept and, 489, 492
 as cause of microevolution, 479–80
 speciation and, 503
Gene-for-gene recognition, **846**
Gene notation systems, 288
Gene pools, **473**–76
General transcription factors, 358–59
Generative cells, 627, 803
Gene therapy, 381, **418**–19, 1100*f*
Genetically modified (GM) organisms, **422**–23. *See also* Transgenic organisms
 fungi as, 652
 Golden Rice, 572, 816, 878–79
 L. Herrera-Estrella's work with, 736–37
 plant biotechnology and issues about, 816–19
 transgenic organisms as, 814–15
Genetic code, 328–31
 codons and triplet code of, 329–30
 deciphering, 330–31
 dictionary of, 330*f*
 evolution of, 331
 as molecular homology, 463
 mutations and, 344–46
 nucleotides and, 9
 reading frame for, 331
 as sequence of nitrogenous bases, 88
 universality of, 17
Genetic counseling, 279
Genetic disorders, 276–81
 alkaptonuria, 326
 counseling for, 279
 diagnosing fetal, 1017
 DNA technology applications for, 417–20
 dominantly inherited, 278–79
 multifactorial, 279
 mutations and, 344–46
 recessively inherited, 276–78
 sickle-cell disease (*see* Sickle-cell disease)
 testing for, 279–81
Genetic diversity, 561–64, 1239, 1240–41. *See also* Genetic variation
Genetic drift, **477**
 bottleneck effect in, 478–79
 as cause of microevolution, 477–79
 effects of, 479
 founder effect in, 477–78
 greater prairie chicken case study of, 478–79
Genetic engineering, **396**. *See also* DNA technology
 of angiosperms, 801
 of antifreeze proteins, 845
 biotechnology and, 816
 of crop plants, 801, 816–19
 of ethylene signal transduction pathways, 834
 of fruit flies to express infection, 931*f*
 fungi and, 652
 L. Herrera-Estrella's work in, 736–37
 of plants, 792
 prokaryotes in, 572–73
 of transgenic animals, 419–20
 of transgenic organisms, 814–15
 of transgenic plants, 421–22*f*
Genetic Information Nondiscrimination Act, 279
Genetic maps, **296**–97
Genetic markers, 411–12, 417–18, 420–21
Genetic profiles, **420**–21
Genetic prospecting, 566, 575
Genetic recombination, **294**–95
 of linked genes and crossing over, 294–95*f*
 natural selection and genetic variation from, 295
 in prokaryotes, 561–64
 transposable elements and, 441–42
 of unlinked genes and independent assortment of chromosomes, 294

Genetics, **248**. *See also* Heredity; Inheritance
  asexual vs. sexual reproduction and, 249
  B. L. Bassler's work in, 92–93
  biotechnology (*see* Biotechnology)
  chromosomal basis of inheritance (*see* Chromosomal basis of inheritance)
  cytology and, 286
  DNA technology (*see* DNA technology)
  environment vs., 1123
  forensic ecology, elephant poaching, and, 1243
  gene expression (*see* Gene expression; Gene expression, regulation of)
  genetic basis of animal behavior, 1134–35
  genetic basis of human culture, 1139
  genomes (*see* Genomes)
  heredity, hereditary variation, and, 248
  human (*see* Human genetics)
  inheritance of genes, 249 (*see also* Gene(s))
  meiosis, sexual life cycles, and (*see* Meiosis; Sexual life cycles)
  Mendelian inheritance (*see* Mendel, Gregor; Mendelian inheritance)
  molecular basis of inheritance (*see* Molecular basis of inheritance)
  Punnett square as tool in, 266
  rules of probability and, 270–71
  of speciation, 503–4
  J. A. Steitz's work in, 246–47
  variation in (*see* Genetic variation)
  viruses and (*see* Viruses)
Genetic testing
  for breast cancer, 377f
  fetal, 280
  identifying carriers, 279–80
  newborn, 280–81
Genetic variation, 257–60, 469–73, 1246–47
  crossing over, recombinant chromosomes, and, 258, 259f
  defined, **248**, **470**
  evolutionary significance of, within populations, 259–60
  evolution of, from recombinant chromosomes and natural selection, 295
  extinction vortex and loss of, 1245–**47**
  genetic diversity and, 1239
  genetic drift and loss of, 478–79
  independent assortment of chromosomes and, 257–58
  in migratory patterns, 1136
  molecular clocks and rates of, 549–50
  natural selection, inheritance, and, 469–70
  origins of, among offspring, 257–59
  phenotype, genotype, and, 470
  phylogenetic tree branch lengths and, 544
  within populations, 470–71
  between populations, 471
  preservation of, 483–84, 485f
  in prey selection, 1135–36
  random fertilization and, 258–59
  sources of, 471–73
Gene trees, 539f
Gene variability, 470–71
Genomes, **10**, **229**, 426–49. *See also* Genetics
  analyzing, using bioinformatics, 429–32
  Arabidopsis thaliana gene functions, 756t
  cell division and, 229
  comparing developmental processes and, 442–47
  complete, 571, 646, 701, 754–56, 835, 1233
  differential gene expression for identical, 356
  eukaryotic, 434–38
  evolutionary history in, 548–49
  evolution of, 438–42, 535, 549
  of fungi, 652
  gene density and noncoding DNA in, 434
  genome sequencing approaches, 427–29

genome-wide association studies of, 411, 417–18
  genomics, bioinformatics, and study of, 10, 426 (*see also* Bioinformatics; Genomics)
  horizontal gene transfer between, 553
  human (*see* Human genome)
  number of genes in, 433
  p53 gene in, 376
  prokaryotic, 559–60
  review of, 447–49
  simple tree of life based on, 552–53
  size and estimated number of genes in, for bacteria, archaea, and eukaryotes, 433t
  size of, 432–33
  species with complete sequences available, 426, 432
  vertebrate, 701
  viral, 382
Genome sequencing, 427–29. *See also* Genomes
  three-stage approach to, 427–28
  whole-genome shotgun approach to, 428–29
Genome-wide association studies, **411**, 417–18
Genomic equivalence, 412
Genomic imprinting, **300–301**, 358
Genomic libraries, **400**–401
Genomics, **10**, **426**. *See also* Genomes
Genotypes, **266**
  gene expression as link between phenotypes and, 325 (*see also* Gene expression)
  genetic variability and, 470
  heterozygote advantage and, 484
  phenotypes and norms of reaction of, 274–75
  phenotypes vs., 266–67, 275
  relative fitness and, 480
  transformation and, 306
Genus, **537**
Geographical barriers, speciation with and without, 493–98
Geographical hybrid zones. *See* Hybrid zones
Geographic distribution. *See* Species distributions
Geographic variation, **471**
Geologic record, **514**, 515t
Geometric isomers, 62
Germ cells
  fate maps and, 1036
  human, 251–52, 1006f–7f
  lengthening of telomeres in, 319
Germination
  gibberellins in seed, 831
  phytochromes and, 836–37
  seed, 809
  strigolactones in seed, 832
Germ layers, 659–60, **1027**
Gestation, **1012**–15
Ghost crabs, 691f
Ghost plant, 1
Ghrelin, 893f
Giant panda, 433t
Giant squids, 680
Giardia, 578f, 580
Gibberellins, 827t, **830**–31
Gibbons, 726–27f
Gibbs, J. Willard, 146
Gibbs free energy, 146. *See also* Free energy
Gigantism, 989
Gill filaments, 917
Gills, 916f–917f
  arthropod, 686
  of axolotls, 897
  crustacean, 691, 916f
  fish, 917f
  mollusc, 679
  osmoregulation by, 954–55
  polychaete, 916f
  sea star, 916f
  structure and function of, 916f–917f
Gill slits, 699, 701–2

Ginkgo (Ginkgophyta), 622f
Giraffes, 907
Glabra-2 gene, 759
Glaciation
  ecological succession after, 1209–10
  seedless vascular plants and, 615
Glacier Bay, Alaska, 1209–10
Glans, **1004**
Glanville fritillaries, 1186–87f
Gleason, H. A., 1207
Glia (glial cells), **858**, **1046**, 1047f, 1054, 1065–66
Glioblastoma (brain cancer), 432
Global biogeochemical cycles, 1227
Global change, 1254–60
  biodiversity and, 1244
  biodiversity hot spots and, 1252
  depletion of atmospheric ozone, 1258–59
  environmental toxins, 1255–56
  greenhouse gases and global warming, 1256–58
  human impacts on (*see* Human environmental impacts)
  nutrient enrichment, 1254–55
  Sustainable Biosphere Initiative and, 1260
Global climate change, 6
  butterflies as warning signals of, 1142–43
  ecology and, 1149–50
  habitat loss and, 1241
  as human impact on environment, 6 (*see also* Human environmental impacts)
  melting of Arctic sea ice by, 50
  C. Parmesan's work on, 1142–43
  plant adaptations to, 201
  S. Solomon's work on atmospheric ozone hole and, 28–29
  as topic at different levels of biology, 24
  using dendrochronology to study, 753f
Global climate patterns, 1146f–47
Global cooling, 615
Global ecology, 55–56, 522–523, 597, 633–634, **1145**f, 1238–39, 1244, 1254–1259
Global energy budget, 1221
Global extinctions, 1240
Global net primary production, 1222f
Global temperatures, extinction rates and, 523
Global warming. *See also* Global climate change
  coral reefs and, 673
  effects of, on photosynthetic marine protists, 597
  extinction rates and, 523
  greenhouse effect and, 1257–58
  human impact on, 6, 50, 1256–57 (*see also* Human environmental impacts)
  overharvesting of peat moss and, 610
  seedless vascular plants and, 615
  tropical rain forest deforestation and, 633f
  using dendrochronology to study, 753f
  volcanism and, 522
Globigerina, 579f
Globin genes and proteins, 437–38, 440
Globular proteins, 81
Glomeromycetes (Glomeromycota), 642f, **644**
Glomerulus, **963**f
Glottis, 884
Glucagon, 892–93f, **982**–84, 986t
Glucocorticoids, 986t, **991**–92
Glucose
  as fuel for cellular respiration, 164–67
  glucocorticoids and metabolism of, 991
  homeostasis, 892–93f, 982–84
  as monosaccharide, 69–70, 71f
  oxidation of, to pyruvate by glycolysis, 168–69f
  in photosynthesis, 43, 187, 203
  in signal transduction pathways, 209
Glucose transporter protein, 132, 135
Glutamate, **1058**, 1077–78, 1098
Glutamic acid, 79f, 150f, 330
Glutamine, 79f, 150f

Glyceraldehyde, 70f
Glyceraldehyde 3-phosphate (G3P), **198**–99
Glycerol phosphate, 65f
Glycine, **65f**, 79f, 1058
Glycogen, **72**, 209, 219, 220f, 892–93f, 1106
Glycogen phosphorylase, 209–10
Glycolipids, **130**
Glycolysis, **167**
    evolutionary significance of, 179
    fermentation and, 177
    glycolytic muscle fibers and, 1109
    oxidation of glucose to pyruvate by, 168–69f
    as stage of cellular respiration, 167–68
Glycolytic muscle fibers, 1109
Glycoproteins, **105**, **130**
    in animal morphogenesis, 1034
    in cellular membranes, 126–27
    in extracellular matrix, 119–20
    fungus-produced, 652
    viruses and, 383, 388f
Glycosidic linkages, **70**
Glyoxysomes, 111
Gnathostomes, **704**–9
    chondrichthyans (sharks, rays), 705–7
    derived characters of, 704–5
    fossil, 705
    ray-finned fishes and lobe-fins, 707–9
    tetrapods as, 709
Gnetophytes (Gnetophyta), 622f, 623f, 628
Gnetum, 622f
Goatsbeard plants, 496
Goiter, 32, 988
Golden algae, **586**
Golden Rice, 572, 816, 878–79
Golgi apparatus, 100f, **105**–6, 131f
Gonadotropin-releasing hormone (GnRH), 989, 1008–11
Gonadotropins, 989, 992, 1008–11
Gonads, 230, 251–52, 986t, 989, **1001**–2
Gonorrhea, 558
Goodall, Jane, 18–19
Goodwin, William, 732f
Gordon, Deborah, 31f
Gorillas, 726–27f
Gormley, Andrew, 1171f
Gould, Stephen Jay, 503
Gout, 959
G protein-coupled receptors (GPCRs), **211f**, 213f, 217, 978–79, 1102–3
G proteins, **211f**, 217
Graded muscle contraction, 1108–9f
Graded potentials, **1050**–**51**, 1056
Grades (taxonomy), **605**, 660
Gradients, solute, 965–67
Grafting, plant, 814
Graft versus host reaction, 946
Gram (unit), 52
Gram, Hans Christian, 557
Gram-negative bacteria, **557**–58, 568f
Gram-positive bacteria, **557**–58, 569f
Gram stain technique, **557f**–58
Grant, Peter and Rosemary, 23, 469
Granum, **110**–11, 186
Grapefruit, 626f
Grapes, 831f, 835
Grapes of Wrath, The (book), 787
Grass, phototropism in coleoptiles of, 825–26
Grasshoppers, 446f, 688f, 690f, 882f, 899f, 917f, 1110f
Grasslands, temperate, 1155f
Grassy stunt virus, 1239
Graves' disease, 987
Gravitational motion, free energy and, 147f
Gravitropism, **841**–42
Gravity
    axis formation and, 1038
    blood pressure and, 907–8
    locomotion and, 1113–14

mechanoreceptors for sensing, in humans, 1093–94
mechanoreceptors for sensing, in invertebrates, 1090
plant responses to, 841–42
Graylag geese, 1124
Gray matter, **1065**
Gray tree frogs, 495
Great auk, 1243
Greater prairie chickens, 478–79, 1245–46
Great Salt Lake, 556, 567
Green algae, 101f, 576, 577f, 579f, **591**–92, 600–601
Greene, Michael, 31f
Greenhouse effect, **1258**. *See also* Global climate change; Global warming
    carbon dioxide, greenhouse gases, and, 50
    fossil fuels and, 28–29
    global climate change and, 6, 1257–58
    prokaryotic metabolic cooperation and, 565
Greenhouse gases, 1148, 1256–58
Greening, plant, 822, 823f
Green lacewings, 1134–35
Green manure, 795
Green parrot snake, 1197f
Griffith, Frederick, 306
Grizzly bears, 492f, 500, 1246–47, 1252
"Grolar" bears, 492f, 500
Gross primary production (GPP), **1221**–22
Ground tissue system, plant, 742f, **743**
Growth, **755**
    as cell division function, 228f
    growth hormone and, 985f, 986t, 989
    heterochrony and differential rates of, 525–26
    as property of life, 2f
Growth factors, **240**, **979**
    in cell cycle control system, 240–41
    cell fate and, 1039–40, 1041
    in cell-signaling nuclear responses, 219
    induction and, 367
    as local regulators in cell signaling, 208
Growth hormone (GH), 985f, 986t, **989**
Growth inhibitors, 826
GTP (guanosine triphosphate), 172, 211f, 340, 341f
GTPase, 223
Guanine, 87f–88, 308
Guano, 959
Guard cells, **750**, 777–78
Gulf of Mexico dead zone, 1255
Gulf Stream, 1148
Gulls, 7f, 1130f
Guppies, 1132
Gurdon, John, 413
Gustation, **1101**–2
Gutenberg, Johannes, 25
Guttation, **773**–74
Gymnamoebas, 596
Gymnosperms, **606**, 621–25
    double fertilization in, 628
    evolution of, 621
    gametophyte-sporophyte relationships in, 619f
    life cycle of pine and, 624f, 625
    ovules and production of seeds in, 620f
    phylogeny of, 605t, 622f–23f
Gyres, ocean, 1148f

H

H1N1 virus, 392, 949, 1214
H5N1 virus, 392, 1215
Habitat. *See also* Environment
    carrying capacity of, 1177–79
    destruction of, in tropical rain forests, 634
    fragmented, 1241–42, 1250
    island habitat, 1212–13
    loss of, as threat to biodiversity, 1241–42
    nitrogenous wastes and, 959
    requirements for red-cockaded woodpecker, 1248–49
    sympatric speciation and differentiation of, 496–98
Habitat corridors, 1233

Habitat isolation, 490f, 491f
Habitat selection behavior, 1165
Haemophilus influenzae, 433t
Hagfishes (Myxini), 702
Haikouella, 702
Hair, mammalian, 720
Hair cells, 1090, **1092**–94
Hairy-cap moss, 608f
Haldane, J. B. S., 508
Hales, Stephen, 789
Half-life, **512**
Halobacterium, 556, 567
Hamilton, William, 1137
Hamilton's rule, **1137**–38
Hamsters, 871
Haplo-diploid sex determination system, 290f
Haploid cells, **251**, 252–53
Harcombe, William, 21–23
Hardy-Weinberg equilibrium, 474–75
Hardy-Weinberg principle, **474**
    applying, 475–76
    Hardy-Weinberg equilibrium and, 474–75
    testing population evolution using, 473–76
Hares, 1185–86
Harlequin toads, 1144, 1166
Harper, John, 1182
Haustoria, **638**
Hawaiian Islands, 494, 524–25f
Hawaiian silversword plants, 524–25f, 540, 1164
Hawkmoth, 806f, 867f, 1197f
Hazel, 804f
Hazelnut, 626f
Heads
    craniate, 701
    insect, 688f
Headstander beetle, evolution and, 452
Head structure morphogen, 372–73
Health, ecology and human, 1143. *See also* Diseases and disorders, human
Hearing, 1090–94
Heart, **898**
    atrial natriuretic peptide hormone released by, 971
    blood pressure and, 906–8
    in circulatory systems, 898
    control of rhythmic beating of, 904
    craniate, 702
    failure, 213f
    fetal, 1013
    insect, 688f
    mammalian, 902–4
    mollusc, 678f
Heart attacks, 913–**14**, 979
Heartbeat rhythm, 904
Heartburn, 886
Heart murmurs, **903**
Heart rate, **903**, 904
Heartwood, 754
Heat, **48**, **143**. *See also* Specific heat
    as by-product of cellular respiration, 177
    diffusion and, 132
    metabolic rate calculation and, 869
    plant response to, 844
    temperature vs., 48
    thermophiles and, 566–67
    thermoreceptors and, 1089
    thermoregulation and (*see* Thermoregulation)
Heat exchanges, animal environmental, 864–67
    adjustment of metabolic heat production in, 866–67
    behavioral responses in, 866
    circulatory adaptations for, 864–65
    cooling by evaporative heat loss in, 865–66
    insulation and, 864
Heat of vaporization, **49**
Heat-shock proteins, **844**
Heavy chains, **935**–36
Hector's dolphins, 1171f

Hedgehog growth factor, 1041
Heimlich maneuver, 884
HeLa cancer cells, 242
Helical viruses, 383
Helicases, **314**
Helicobacter pylori, 886
Helium, 33*f*
Helper T cells, **940**–41
Heme group, 173
Heme oxygenase, 1060
Hemichordata, 669*f*
Hemiptera, 690*f*
Hemispheres, brain, 1069*f*, 1070, 1073–74
Hemizygous organisms, 291
Hemocoel, 686
Hemocyanin, 924
Hemocytes, 930
Hemoglobin, **911**
    α-globin and β-globin gene families of, 437–38, 440
    cooperativity as allosteric regulation in, 159
    in gas exchange, 924
    as measure of evolution, 89
    as protein, 78*f*
    protein quaternary structure and, 83*f*
    sickle-cell disease and, 84, 277–78 (*see also* Sickle-cell
        disease)
Hemolymph, 686, **899**, 957, 961–62
Hemophilia, **291**, 912
Hemorrhagic fever, 391
Henderson, Lawrence, 46
Henry, Charles, 1134*f*
Henslow, John, 455
Hepatic portal veins, **888**
Hepatitis B virus, 950
Hepatophyta, 606, 608*f. See also* Bryophytes
HER2 receptor tyrosine kinase, 243*f*
Herbicides
    auxin in, 829
    transgenic, 816–17
Herbivores, **875**
    as biotic factors limiting species distribution, 1165–66
    carnivore alimentary canals vs., 890*f*
    dentition and diet in, 889*f*
    in ecosystems, 1220
    energetic hypothesis and biomass of, 1203–4
    evolutionary links between plants and, 632
    insects as, 690*f*
    mutualistic digestive adaptations of, 890–91
    plant defenses against, 845–46
    soybean pod trichome deterrence of, 743*f*
Herbivory, **1198**
Herceptin, 213, 243*f*
Hereditary factors, genes as, 262, 286. *See also* Gene(s)
Hereditary variation. *See* Genetic variation
Heredity, **248**. *See also* DNA (deoxyribonucleic acid);
    Genetics; Inheritance
Hermaphrodites, **671**, 682
Hermaphroditism, 996, **998**–99
Heroin, 42, 81
Herpesviruses, 387–88, 391, 949
Herrera-Estrella, Luis, 736–37, 792, 815
Hershey, Alfred, 307–8
Heterochromatin, **322**, 357, 366
Heterochrony, **525**–26
Heterocysts, **565**
Heterocytes, **565**
Heterokaryon, **639**
Heteromorphic generations, **587**
Heterosporous species, **612–13**, 619
Heterotrophs, **184**
    animals as, 654
    in ecosystems, 1220
    fungi as, 636–37
    prokaryotic, 564, 565*f*
    protist, 576
Heterozygote advantage, **484**

Heterozygous organisms, **266**
Hexapods (Hexapoda), **686**, 688–91. *See also* Insects
    (Hexapoda)
Hexoses, 70
Hfr cells, 563
Hibernation, 177, **872**
Hierarchical classification, 537–38. *See also* Taxonomy
High-density lipoproteins (HDLs), **913**
Highly conserved genes, 443
High-resolution oxygen sensors, 1222*f*
High-throughput technology, 10, 428
Hindbrain, **1068***f*
Hinge joints, 1112*f*
Hippocampus, 1071, 1077
Hirta Island, 1170, 1182, 1185
Hirudin, 683
Histamine, **934**, 947
Histone acetylation, **357**
Histone code hypothesis, 357
Histones, **320***f*, 357
Hitchhiking commensalism, 1199
HIV (human immunodeficiency virus), **388**. *See also*
    AIDS (acquired immunodeficiency syndrome)
    AIDS and, 388–90
    antiviral drugs and, 391
    applying molecular clock to origin of, 550–51
    attacks on immune system by, 949–50
    cell-surface proteins and blocking HIV entry into
        cells, 130
    diagnosing, 417
    as emerging virus, 391
    rapid reproduction of, 472
    replicative cycle of, 389*f*
HIV-1 M strain, 551
Hoatzin, 890
Hobbs, Helen, 914*f*
Hodgkin, Alan, 1051
Hodgkin's disease, 1241
Holdfasts, **586**
Holoblastic cleavage, **1026**
Holothuroidea, 694
Holsinger, Kent, 1134*f*
Homeoboxes, **445**–47, 655
Homeodomains, 445
Homeostasis, **860**–62
    alterations in, 861–62
    of blood calcium levels, 989–90
    of blood glucose levels, 892–93*f*, 982–84
    excretory systems and (*see* Excretory systems)
    feedback control in, 861
    hormonal regulation of kidneys for, 968–71
    of human breathing, 922
    mechanisms of, 860–61
    osmoregulation and (*see* Osmoregulation)
    peripheral nervous system and, 1067
    thermoregulation and, 862–68
    thyroid regulation and, 987–88
Homeotherms, 863
Homeotic genes, **371**, 445–47, **526**, 527*f*, 758
Homing pigeons, 1120
Hominins, **728**–33
    Australopiths, 729–30
    bipedalism in, 730
    derived characters of, 728
    earliest, 728–29
    early *Homo*, 731
    evolutionary timeline of, 729*f*
    Homo sapiens, 732–33 (*see also* Human(s))
    Neanderthals, 731–32
    tool use in, 730–31
Homo erectus, 731
Homo ergaster, 731
Homo floresiensis, 733
Homogenization, 97*f*
Homo, genus, 726, 731
Homo habilis, 731

Homologies, **462**
    analogies vs., 540–42
    anatomical and molecular, 463
    convergent evolution and analogies vs., 464–65
    evaluating molecular, 541–42
    as evidence for evolution, 462–65
    in evolutionary trees, 464
    morphological and molecular, 540
Homologous chromosomes (homologs), **250**
    alleles in, 253
    behavior of as basis of law of segregation, 286–87*f*
    human, 250–51
    in meiosis I, 254*f*, 257
Homologous genes, 548, 549*f*
Homologous structures, 249, **463**
Homo neanderthalensis, 731–32
Homoplasies, **541**, 542
Homo sapiens, 537, 728, 729*f*, 732–33. *See also* Human(s)
Homosporous species, **612–13**, 619
Homozygous organisms, **266**
Honeybees, 804*f*, 866–67, 1121–22, 1126, 1137, 1138.
    See also Bees
Honey mushrooms, 636
Honig, Lawrence, 1041*f*
Hook, flagellum, 558–59
Hooke, Robert, 94
Hookworms, 684
Horizontal cells, 1096*f*, 1098–99
Horizontal gene transfer, **553**
    in asexual reproduction of bdelloid rotifers, 259–60
    W. F. Doolittle's work on, 534–35
    pathogenic bacteria and, 572
    in prokaryote evolution, 566
Horizontal transmission, 393
Hormonal proteins, 78*f*
Hormone cascade pathway, 987
Hormones, **209**, **824**, **859**, **974**–80
    adrenal gland, 990–92
    animal endocrine system, 859
    antagonistic pairs of, 982–84
    birth control, 1016–17
    cellular response pathways for, 977–78
    chemical classes of, 976–77*t*
    coordinate control by, 361–62
    coordination of neuroendocrine and endocrine sig-
        naling and, 980
    embryonic, 1012
    endocrine systems and, 892, 974 (*see also* Endocrine
        systems)
    endocrine tissues and organs and, 976
    in fight-or-flight responses, 206
    gonadal sex hormones, 992–93 (*see also* Sex
        hormones)
    inducing labor, 1014–15*f*
    intercellular communication processes and, 975–76
    as intracellular chemical signals, 214
    kidney regulation by, 968–71
    local regulators and, 979
    in long-distance cell signaling, 209
    major human endocrine glands and, 986*t*
    melatonin, 993
    multiple effects of, 978–79
    nervous systems and, 984–86*t*
    parathyroid, 989–90
    pituitary, 984–86*t*
    plant (*see* Plant hormones)
    regulation of appetite by, 893–94
    regulation of human sexual response by, 1011
    regulation of mammalian reproduction by, 1008–11
    review of, 994
    simple regulatory pathways for, 981
    thyroid, 987–88
    tropic and nontropic, 989
Hornworts (Anthocerophyta), **606**, 608*f. See also*
    Bryophytes
Horowitz, Norman, 326, 327*f*

Horses, 530–31*f*, 890
Horseshoe crabs, 686*f*
Horsetails (Pterophyta), 613–15
Horvitz, Robert, 1036
Hosken, David, 1002*f*
Host cells, 516–17
Host ranges, viral, **384**
Hosts, **570**, **1198**, 1214*f*
Hot spots, biodiversity, 1251–52
House mouse. *See Mus musculus* (mouse)
Hox genes
    as animal development genes, 445–47, 655
    animal evolution and origin of, 657
    arthropod body plan and, 685
    craniate, 701
    as development genes, 526, 527*f*
    gene expression of, 1041
    jaws and, 705
    lancelet and vertebrate, 700–701
    in plants, 758
    tunicate, 700
HTLV-1 virus, 377
Hubbard Brook Experimental Forest, 1231
Human(s)
    as anthropoid apes, 726
    behavior of chromosome sets in life cycle of, 251–52
    biodiversity and welfare of, 1240–41
    blood pH of, 54–55
    blood pressure of, 907*f*
    body of (*see* Human body)
    brain and nerve cells of, 94
    brown algae as food for, 586
    catabolism and diets of, 179–80 (*see also* Diets)
    chromosome number of, 102
    chromosome sets in cells of, 250–51
    chromosomes in somatic cells and gametes of, 229–30
    cilia of windpipe cells of, 14*f*
    cloning of, 414–15
    control of breathing in, 922
    derived characters of, 728
    development of (*see* Human development)
    diseases and disorders of (*see* Diseases and disorders, human)
    diversity within, 489*f*
    ecology and health of, 1143
    environmental impacts of, 1152, 1210
    essential elements and trace elements for, 32
    evolution of culture in, 1139
    family tree of, 536*f*
    first appearance of, 519
    flatworms as parasites of, 675–76
    gene therapy for, 418–19
    genetics of (*see* Human genetics)
    glycoproteins and blood types of, 130
    hearts in circulatory systems of, 902–4
    importance of insects to, 691
    importance of seed plants to welfare of, 618, 632–34
    inactivated olfactory receptor genes of, 472
    inherited DNA and development of, 9*f*
    karyotypes of chromosomes of, 250*f*
    lymphatic systems of, 909
    molecular tags and karyotypes of chromosomes of, 322*f*
    mutualistic bacterial and, 571
    nutrition (*see* Human nutrition)
    origin of, in hominins, 728–29 (*see also* Hominins)
    pathogenic bacteria and, 571–72
    pathogenic prokaryotes and, 570–72
    population dynamics of (*see* Human population)
    primate phylogenetic tree and, 726*f*
    reducing hunger and malnutrition in, with transgenic crops, 816–17
    relationship of Neanderthals and, 732*f*

reproduction of (*see* Human reproduction)
sequencing of genome of, 10 (*see also* Human genome)
sex chromosomes of, 289–90
skulls of chimpanzees vs., 541
spread of pathogens by, 1214–15
sustainable development in Costa Rica and living conditions of, 1260–61
transgenic crops and health of, 818
Human body
    brain in, 1068*f*–69*f* (*see also* Brains)
    circadian rhythms and thermoregulation in, 862
    colon of, 888–89
    digestive system of (*see* Digestive systems)
    endocrine glands in, 986*t*
    energy budget for female, 871
    evolution of human eye, 529
    excretory systems of, 962–71
    glucose homeostasis in, 892–93*f*
    heterochrony and differential growth rates in skulls of, 525–26
    hormonal regulation of growth in, 989
    hypothalamus as physiological thermostat in thermoregulation of, 867–68
    interaction of muscles and skeletons in locomotion in, 1110–11 (*see also* Locomotion; Skeletal systems)
    lymphatic system of, 933*f*
    overnourishment, obesity, and, 894–96
    skeleton of, 1112*f*
    skin of, 1088*f*
    structure of ears of, 1091*f*
    structure of eyes of, 1096*f*–97
    two-solute model of kidney function, 966*f*
    water balance in, 956
Human chorionic gonadotropin (hCG), 945, **1012**
Human development
    cilia and cell fate in, 1041–42
    embryonic (*see also* Embryonic development)
    gastrulation in, 1030–31
Human environmental impacts. *See also* Environmental issues; Global change; Global climate change; Global warming
    biodiversity crisis, 1238–39
    biome disturbances, 1152
    community disturbances, 1210
    global change, 1244, 1254–60
    global climate change, 6
    habitat loss and fragmentation, 1241–42
    introduced species, 1242–43
    ocean acidification, acid precipitation, and, 55–56
    overharvesting, 1243–44
    threats to biodiversity from, 1241–44
Human genetics, 275–81
    dominantly inherited diseases, 278–79
    genetic testing and counseling in, 279–81
    multifactorial disorders, 279
    pedigree analysis in, 275–76
    recessively inherited diseases, 276–78
Human genome
    α-globin and β-globin gene families in, 437–38, 440
    comparing genomes of other species to, 442–45
    comparison of chromosome sequences of chimpanzee and mouse with, 439*f*
    complete sequence for, 426
    evolution of, 549
    evolution of globin genes in, 440
    function of *FOXP2* gene in, 443–44
    microarray chips containing, 432
    size and number of genes in, 433
    size of, 433*t*
    types of DNA sequences in, 435*f*
Human Genome Project, 336, **427**–29, 430
Human growth hormone (HGH), 397*f*, 419, 989
Human immunodeficiency virus. *See* HIV (human immunodeficiency virus)

Human nutrition
    assessing nutritional needs for, 879
    dietary deficiencies in, 878–79
    digestive system in (*see* Digestive systems)
    effect of vitamin supplementation on birth defect frequencies in, 879
    essential nutrients for, 876–78*t*
    evolutionary role of fat hoarding in, 895
    mineral requirements for, 877–78*t*
    vitamin requirements for, 876–77
Human papillomavirus (HPV), 950
Human population, 1187–91
    age structure of, 1188–89
    characteristics of global, 1187–90
    factors limiting size of global, 1190–91
    global carrying capacity for, 1190–91
    infant mortality and life expectancy in, 1189–90
    regional patterns of change in, 1188
    voluntary control of, 1187
Human reproduction. *See also* Animal reproduction
    detecting disorders of, during pregnancy, 1017
    embryonic development in, 1011–15 (*see also* Embryonic development, human)
    female reproductive anatomy, 1002–4
    female reproductive cycles in, 1008–10
    gametogenesis in, 1005–8
    hormonal regulation of, 1008–11
    human sexual response in, 1011
    infertility in, 1017–18
    male reproductive anatomy, 1004–5
    modern reproductive technologies and, 1017–18
    prevention of, 1015–17
    reproductive organs in, 1002–8
    review of, 1018–19
Hummel, Katherine, 894*f*
Hummingbird hawkmoth, 690*f*
Hummingbirds, 399–400, 719–20, 805*f*
Humoral immune response, 930*f*, **940**–43
Humpback whales, 539*f*–40, 881*f*
Humus, **786**, 787
Hundred Heartbeat Club, 1240*f*
Hunger, transgenic crops and reducing human, 816–17
Huntington's disease, **278**–79, 416
Hutchison, Victor, 867*f*
Hutton, James, 453*f*, 454
Huxley, Andrew, 1051
Hybrid breakdown, 491*f*
Hybridization, **264**, 815–16, 818
Hybrid orbitals, 41–42
Hybrids, **489**
    bears, 492
    reproductive barriers and sterility of, 491*f*
    sterility of, 504
Hybrid zones, **498**–501
    patterns within, 498–99
    reproductive barriers of, over time, 499–501
Hydrangea, 274*f*
Hydras, 249*f*, 672, 853*f*, 882, 1063*f*, 1111
Hydration shells, **50**
Hydrocarbons, **61**–62*f*. *See also* Fossil fuels
Hydrocarbon tail, chlorophyll, 191*f*
Hydrochloric acid (HCl), 53, 885–86
Hydrogen
    covalent bonding and, 38–39
    as essential element, 32, 58, 66
    oxidation of organic molecules containing, 165
    in plant composition, 789
    saturated and unsaturated fats and, 75–76
Hydrogen bonds, **40**
    in DNA structure, 88–89*f*
    floating of ice and, 49–50
    in water molecules, 46–47
    as weak chemical bonds, 40, 41*f*
Hydrogen ions, **52**–54
Hydrogenosomes, 580

Hydrogen peroxide, 111
Hydrogen sulfide gas, 522
Hydrolysis, **68–69**
  of ATP, 149–50
  disassembling of polymers to monomers by, 68–69
  enzymatic, 880
  by lysosomes, 106–7
Hydrolytic enzymes, fungal, 637
Hydronium ions, **52**–53
Hydrophilic substances, **51**, 79f, 125
Hydrophobic interaction, **83**f
Hydrophobic substances, **51**, 79f, 125
Hydroponic culture, **790**
Hydrostatic skeletons, **1111**
Hydrothermal vents, 508, 566–67, 571, 890–91
Hydroxide ions, **52**–53
Hydroxyl group, **64**f, 88
Hydrozoans (Hydrozoa), 672, 673f
Hylobates, 726
Hymen, **1004**
Hymenoptera, 690f
Hypercholesterolemia, 138
Hypermastigote, 596f
Hyperosmotic solutions, 954, 967
Hyperpolarization, **1050**, 1051f
Hypersensitive response, plant, **846**, 847f
Hypertension, 213f, **915**
Hypertonic solutions, **133**, 954
Hyphae, fungal, **637**, 638, 640f, 797
Hypoblast cells, 1029–30, 1031
Hypocotyl, **808**
Hypoosmotic solutions, 954
Hypothalamus, **867**, **984**, **1069**f
  blood osmolarity and, 969–70
  endocrine regulation by, 984–85, 989, 993
  in homeostasis, 1067
  regulation of mammalian reproduction by, 1008–11
  suprachiasmatic nucleus (SCN) in, 1070–71f
  thermoregulation by, 867–68
Hypotheses, **19**
  phylogenetic trees as, 547–48
  science and testing of, 18, 19–20
  theories vs., 23, 467
Hypothyroidism, 987
Hypotonic solutions, **134**, 954
Hyracoidea, 725f

I

Ibuprofen, 63f
Ice
  floating of, on liquid water, 49–50
  on Mars, 52
  as solid water, 46
Ice ages, 517–18, 1148
Icosahedral viruses, 383
Identical DNA sequences, 437
IgE antibodies, 947
Ileum, 887
Imaging techniques, fetal testing, 280
Imatinib, 419
Imbibition, **809**
Immigration, 1171f, **1172**, 1175–76, 1186–87, 1212–13
Immune response
  primary and secondary, 939–40
  trypanosome evasion of, 581
Immune systems, **929**–52
  adaptive immunity in, 935–46
  cancer and, 950
  diabetes mellitus and, 983–84
  diseases of, 223
  disruptions in, 946–50
  evolutionary adaptations of pathogens that evade, 948–50
  exaggerated, self-directed, and diminished immune responses by, 946–48
  immune rejection by, 945–46

immunization and, 944–45, 950f
innate immunity in, 930–35
leukocytes in, 911
lymphatic systems and, 909
lymphocytes and (*see also* Lymphocytes)
membrane carbohydrate cell-cell recognition in, 130
overview of innate and adaptive immunity in, 929–30
review of, 951–52
trematode camouflage and, 675–76
Immunity
  active and passive, and immunization, 944–45
  maternal tolerance of embryo and fetus, 1015
Immunization, **945**, 950f
Immunodeficiency, **948**. *See also* AIDS (acquired immunodeficiency syndrome); HIV (human immunodeficiency virus)
Immunoglobulin (Ig), **936**, 937–38
Immunological memory, 937, 939–40
Impact figures
  advances in treatment of breast cancer, 243f
  amphibian population declines due to fungal infection, 651f
  biofuels from plants and algae, 185f
  blocking HIV entry into cells as medical treatment, 130f
  cervical cancer vaccination, 950f
  clear-cutting of tropical forests, 633f
  determining the structure of G protein-coupled receptors, 213f
  discovery of "fishapod" *Tiktaalik*, 710f
  effects of global warming on photosynthetic marine protists, 597f
  forensic ecology and elephant poaching, 1243f
  functional brain imaging, 1072f
  gene therapy for vision, 1100f
  genetic testing, 280f
  identification of Lyme disease hosts, 1214f
  mollusc extinctions, 681f
  reducing human hunger with transgenic cassava, 817f
  rise of MRSA, 462f
  threat of ocean acidification to coral reef ecosystems, 55f
  treating chromosomes to display in different colors, 322f
Imprinting, **1123**–24, 1131–32
Imprinting stimulus, 1122–23
Inactivation, cell-signaling, 223
Inborn immunodeficiency, 948
Inclusive fitness, **1137**–39
Incomplete dominance, **271**–72
Incomplete flowers, **802**
Incomplete metamorphosis, **689**, 690f
Incomplete proteins, 876
Independent assortment, law of, 267–**69**, 286–87f
Independent assortment of chromosomes, 257–58, 295
Indeterminate cleavage, **661**
Indeterminate growth, **746**
Indian corn, 435
Indian Ocean Subtropical Gyre, 1148f
Indian pipe, 798f
Indian rice, 1241
Indoleacetic acid (IAA), 826, 827. *See also* Auxin
Indolebutyric acid (IBA), 829. *See also* Auxin
Indonesia, 1238
Induced fit, **154**
Induced pluripotent stem cells, 416–17f
Inducers, **354**–55
Inducible enzymes, 354–55
Inducible innate immune response, 930–31
Inducible operons, 353–55
Induction, **367**, 368f
Inductive reasoning, **19**
Inductive signals, cell fate and, 1039–42
  cilia and, 1041–42

Spemann's organizer and, 1039–40
  vertebrate limb formation and, 1040–41
Industrialization, 1188, 1189
Inertia, 1113
Infant mortality, human, 1189–90, 1260
Infection. *See also* Pathogens
  cytotoxic T cell response to, 941–42
  fungal, 650–51f
  inflammatory response and, 934
  plant response to, 846
Infection thread, bacterial, 794–95
Infertility, 1013, 1017–18
Inflammation. *See* Inflammatory response
Inflammatory response, 159, 568f, 913–15, **934**, 991, 1090
Inflorescences, **802**
Influenza viruses, 81, 383, 391–93, 948–49, 1184f, 1214–15
Information processing
  cerebral cortex and, 1074–75
  neurons and, 1046
  problem solving and, 1126
  vertebrate visual, 1098–1100
Infrared receptors, 1089f
Ingestion, 14, **880**
Ingroups, **543**
Inhalation, 920–22
Inheritance. *See also* Genetics; Heredity
  blending hypothesis of, 262
  of cancer predisposition, 376–77
  chromosome theory of, 286–89 (*see also* Chromosomal basis of inheritance)
  C. Darwin on, 15–16, 458–60
  DNA and, 8–10 (*see also* DNA (deoxyribonucleic acid))
  epigenetic, 358
  of genes, 248–49
  genetic variability and, 469–70
  genomic imprinting and, 300–301
  heredity as, 248
  meiosis, sexual life cycles, and (*see* Meiosis; Sexual life cycles)
  Mendelian (*see* Mendel, Gregor; Mendelian inheritance)
  molecular basis of (*see* Molecular basis of inheritance)
  nonheritable variation, 470f
  nucleic acids and, 86–89
  of organelle genes, 301–2
  particulate hypothesis on, 262
  of x-linked genes, 290–91
Inheritance of acquired characteristics principle, Lamarck's, 455
Inhibin, **1011**
Inhibiting hormones, 985
Inhibition, allosteric, 158–59
Inhibitors, enzyme, 156–57
Inhibitory postsynaptic potential (IPSP), **1056**–57f
Initials, cell, 746
Initiation
  transcription, 332f, 358–62
  translation, 340, 340f, 363
Initiation factors, 340
Innate behavior, **1123**
Innate immunity, **929**–35
  adaptive immunity vs., 929–30
  antimicrobial peptides and proteins in, 933
  barrier defenses as, 932
  cellular innate defenses as, 932–33
  evasion of, by pathogens, 934–35
  inflammatory response in, 934
  invertebrate, 930–32
  vertebrate, 932–34
Inner cell mass, **1031**
Inner ear, **1091**f
Innocence Project, 420
Inorganic components, topsoil, 786–87
Inositol trisphosphate (IP$_3$), **218**

Inquiry, scientific, **18**. *See also* Science
  on cellular membrane models, 125–27
  discovery of viruses, 381–82
  on gene-enzyme relationship in protein synthesis, 326, 327*f*
  genetic analysis of fruit fly early development, 371
  T. Morgan's experimental evidence for chromosome theory of inheritance, 288–89
  process of, 18–20
  on snake mimicry case, 20–23
  tracking atoms through photosynthesis, 187–88
Inquiry figures
  on abiotic synthesis of organic molecules as origin of life on Earth, 59*f*
  on allosteric inhibitors of caspase enzymes, 159*f*
  on aquaporin mutations as causes of diabetes insipidus, 970*f*
  on benefits of endophytes to woody plants, 648*f*
  on *bicoid* gene and body plan determination in fruit flies, 372*f*
  on blastopore dorsal lips as organizers of embryo body plans, 1039*f*
  on bryophyte reduction of nitrogen leaching from soil, 609*f*
  on Burmese python heat generation for egg incubation, 867*f*
  on calcium ion release during formation of fertilization envelope, 1024*f*
  on causes of greater prairie chicken decline, 1246*f*
  on cell cycle regulation by cytoplasmic signals, 238*f*
  on cell fate and developmental potential of cells, 1038*f*
  on changes in gene regulation of stickleback fish, 528*f*
  on circadian clocks during hibernation, 871*f*
  on control of mammalian circadian rhythms, 1071*f*
  on creation of devil's gardens in rain forest, 31*f*
  on determining cause of tobacco mosaic disease, 382*f*
  on determining root of eukaryotic phylogenetic tree, 593*f*
  on diet and birth defects, 879*f*
  on digger wasp spatial learning, 1125*f*
  on disruption of mutalistic plant and fungi associations by garlic mustard, 797*f*
  on DNA replication models, 312*f*
  on effect of vitamin supplementation on human birth defect frequencies, 879*f*
  on effects of food availability on cellular slime mold emigration and foraging, 1186*f*
  on effects of order of red and far-red illumination on seed germination, 836*f*
  on effects of temperature on litter decomposition, 1230*f*
  on energy costs of locomotion, 1114*f*
  on evolution by natural selection due to food source changes, 461*f*
  on eye color after crosses between wild-type and mutant fruit flies, 289*f*
  on female fruit fly bias in sperm usage, 1002*f*
  on function of *FOXP2* gene in human genome, 444*f*
  on gene specification of enzymes in biochemical pathways, 327*f*
  on genetic basis of migratory orientation, 1136*f*
  on genetic control of green lacewing songs, 1134*f*
  on growth-promoting chemical (auxin) effect on phototropism in grass coleoptiles, 826*f*
  on how signals induce directional cell growth during yeast mating, 221*f*
  on identifying species of whales sold as meat, 539*f*
  on intersexual selection and mate choice in tree frogs, 483*f*
  on interspecific competition and realized niches, 1196*f*
  on lack of surfactants in respiratory distress syndrome, 920*f*

  on linkage between genes and inheritance of characters, 293*f*
  on lowering plasma LDL levels by inactivating liver enzymes, 914*f*
  on mammalian taste detection, 1102*f*
  on membrane protein movement, 128*f*
  on microtubule role in depositing cellulose in cell walls, 119*f*
  on most effective light wavelengths for photosynthesis, 191*f*
  on nitrogen limitation of phytoplankton production, 1223*f*
  on nuclear transplantation of differentiated animal cells and organismal development, 413*f*
  on opiate receptors, 1059*f*
  on phototropism in grass coleoptiles, 825*f*
  on polar movement of auxin in plant shoots, 828*f*
  on pressure-flow hypothesis about phloem sap sugar content near sources, 781*f*
  on protecting fruit flies against infection with antimicrobial peptides, 931*f*
  on protein vs. DNA as genetic material of T2 phages, 307*f*
  on rapid prokaryotic evolution, 561*f*
  on relationship between Neanderthals and *Homo sapiens*, 732*f*
  on reproductive isolation from divergence of allopatric populations, 495*f*
  on role of β-catenin in molecular control of animal gastrulation, 659*f*
  on role of *Hox* genes in arthropod body plan, 685*f*
  on role of sex hormones in mammalian sex determination, 992*f*
  on role of zone of polarizing activity (ZPA) on vertebrate limb formation, 1041*f*
  on roles of *ob* and *db* genes in appetite regulation, 894*f*
  on sea stars as keystone predators, 1205*f*
  on sea urchin feeding as limiting seaweed distribution, 1165*f*
  on sexual selection and reproductive isolation, 497*f*
  on soybean pod trichome deterrence of herbivores, 743*f*
  on speciation from hybridization in sunflowers, 503*f*
  on survival costs of parental care in kestrels, 1180*f*
  on transfer of genetic trait between different bacterial strains, 306*f*
  on using X-ray crystallography to determine 3-D shape of RNA polymerase II, 86*f*
  on venomous snake mimicry and predation rates, 22*f*
  on whether alleles for two characters assort into gametes dependently or independent of each other, 268*f*
  on which end of kinetochore microtubules shortens during anaphase, 235*f*
  on which traits appear when hybrid pea plants self- or cross-pollinate, 264*f*
Insecticide resistance, 480
Insects (Hexapoda)
  body plans of, 527
  camouflage in, 460*f*
  compound eyes of, 1095–96
  endocrine signaling in, 980
  evolution by natural selection in, due to food source changes, 461
  exoskeletons of, 1111–12
  flower pollination by, 632, 804*f*, 805*f*
  gamete production and delivery in, 1001–2
  general features of, 688–91
  Hox genes in, 446*f*
  insecticide resistance in, 480
  as invertebrates, 669*f*
  malaria and, 583–84
  malpighian tubules of, 961–62
  nervous systems of, 1063*f*

  nonheritable variation in, 470*f*
  parasitism of, 1198
  plant response to herbivores and, 845
  sex determination of, 290*f*
  taste and smell in, 1101
  thermogenesis in, 866–67
  tracheal systems for gas exchange in, 917–18
  transgenic crops and pests, 816
Insertions (mutations), **345**–46
In situ hybridization, **410**
Instability, free energy and, 146–47*f*
Instantaneous per capita rate of increase, 1176
Insulation, animal thermoregulatory, 864
Insulin, **982**
  amino acid sequence for, 409
  control of blood glucose by, 982–84
  discovery of amino acid sequence of, 80
  exocytosis and, 138
  glucose homeostasis and, 892–93*f*
  manufacturing, 419
  pancreas and, 986*t*
  as protein, 78*f*
  rough ER and, 105
  size of, 209
  as water-soluble hormone, 976–77*f*
Insulin-like growth factors (IGFs), 989
Integral proteins, **129**
Integration
  cellular, 122
  sensory, 1086, 1087
Integrins, **120**, 129
Integument, **620**, 803
Integumentary systems, **864**
Interactions
  mutualistic (*see* Mutualism)
  plant and animal, 632
  prokaryotic ecological, 570–71
  systems biology and hormone, 834–35
  as theme in biology, 6
Intercalary meristems, 749
Intercalated disks, **1110**
Intercellular joining function, membrane protein, 129*f*
Interdisciplinary research teams, 10
Interferons, **933**
Intergovernmental Panel on Climate Change (IPCC), 28–29, 1142–43
Intergradation, terrestrial biome, 1152
Intermediate disturbance hypothesis, **1207**–8
Intermediate filaments, 100*f*, 101*f*, 113*t*, **118**
Intermembrane space, 110
Internal defenses, 930*f*
Internal environments, animal
  exchange surfaces in, 853–55
  feedback control and maintenance of, 860–62
Internal factors, cell cycle control system, 240–42
Internal fertilization, **999**–1000, 1130–31
International Union for Conservation of Nature and Natural Resources (IUCN), 1239
Internet resources, genome-sequence, 429, 430*f*
Interneurons, **1046**, 1047*f*, 1064*f*
Internodes, **740**
Interphase, **231**, 232*f*
Interphase nucleus transcription factories, 362
Intersexual selection, **482**–83, 1131
Interspecific competition, **1195**–96
  character displacement in, 1196
  competitive exclusion in, 1195
  natural selection, ecological niches, and resource partitioning in, 1195–96
Interspecific interactions, **1194**–1200
  competition, 1195–96
  facilitation, 1200
  herbivory, 1198
  predation, 1197–98
  symbiosis, 1198–99
  symbols of, 1194–95

Interspecific mating, 489
Interstitial fluid, **854**, 899, 908–9, 957, 966–67
Intertidal zones, **1161**f
Intestinal bacteria, 571
Intestines. See Large intestine; Small intestine
Intracellular digestion, 880–82
Intracellular receptors, cell-signaling, 214
Intracellular recording, 1050f
Intracytoplasmic sperm injection (ICSI), **1018**
Intrasexual selection, **482**, 1131
Intrauterine devices (IUDs), 1016
Intrinsic (physiological) factors, density-dependent
        population regulation due to, 1183f
Introduced species, **1242**–43
Introns, 247, **335**, 336, 434
Invagination, 1028
Invasive species, 797, **1202**, 1204, 1213–14
Inventions vs. discoveries, 24
Inversions, **298**–99
Invertebrates, **666**–96
        action potential conduction speed in, 1054
        arthropods, 684–92
        chordates, 669f, 694
        cnidarians, 667f, 671–73
        deuterostomes, 669f
        deuterostomes, echinoderms, and chordates,
                692–94
        diversity of, 666
        ecdysozoans, 668f–69f, 683–92
        echinoderms, 669f
        gamete production and delivery in, 1001–2
        hydrostatic skeletons of, 1111
        innate immunity in, 930–32
        life cycles of, 673f, 675f
        lophotrochozoans, 667f–68f, 674–82
        mechanoreceptors for sensing gravity and sound
                in, 1090
        nervous systems of, 1062–63
        organogenesis in, 1033
        osmoregulation in, 955–56
        parental care among, 1000, 1001f
        phylogeny of, 666–69f
        review of, 695
        sponges, 667f, 670–71
In vitro culturing, angiosperm, 807, 814–15, 816
In vitro DNA amplification, 403–4
In vitro fertilization (IVF), **1018**
In vitro mutagenesis, **410**
Involution, 1028
Iodine, 32, 877–78t, 988
Ion channel proteins, 1053
Ion channels, **135**, **1048**
        in mechanoreceptors, 1088
        neuron membrane potentials and gated, 1050–53
        neuron resting potential and, 1048–50
        venom and, 850–51
Ionic bonds, 39–**40**
Ionic compounds, **40**
Ionotropic receptors, 1056, 1058
Ion pumps, 136–37, 1048–50
Ions, **40**, 910–11, 1048t
Iridium, 522
Iris, **1096**–97
Irish famine, 588–89
Iron
        human requirements for, 877–78t
        iron oxide and, 516
        ocean fertilization using, 1223–24
        plant deficiency in, 790
Irrigation, 787–88
Island biogeography, 1212–13
Island species, 466
Isolated systems, 144, 148f
Isoleucine, 79f, 160
Isomers, **62**–63

Isomorphic generations, **587**
Isoosmotic solutions, 954
Isopods, **691**
Isotonic solutions, **133**, 954
Isotopes, **34**–35f, 187, 1230
Italy, 1188–89
Iteroparity, **1180**
Ivanowsky, Dmitri, 382
Ivory, 1243

J
Jackrabbit, 852
Jackson, Rob, 1143f, 1201f
Jacob, François, 352, 529
Jacoby, G. C., 753f
Janzen, David, 1253
Japan, 1189, 1235f
Japanese snails, 503–4
Javan rhinoceros, 1240f
Jawfish, 1131f
Jawless vertebrates, 703–4
Jaws
        evolution of gnathostome and vertebrate, 704–5
        mammalian, 512–14
        snake, 482
Jejunum, 887
Jellies, 667f, 672, 898f
Jenner, Edward, 945
Joint Genome Institute, 10f
Joints, human, 1112f
Jost, Alfred, 992
Joule (J), **48**, 869
J-shaped exponential growth curve, 1177
Jukes, Thomas, 550
Jumping genes, 435. See also Transposable elements
Juncus gerardi, 1200
June solstice, 1147f
Juniper, 623f
Juvenile hormone, 980
Juxtaglomerular apparatus (JGA), **970**
Juxtamedullary nephrons, **962**f, 967

K
Kalahari Desert, 764, 778
Kanamycin, 736
Kangaroo rats, 956
Kangaroos, 722, 1113, 1133f
Kaposi's sarcoma herpesvirus, 949, 950
Kartagener's syndrome, 1042
Karyogamy, **639**
Karyotypes, **250**
        in fetal testing, 280, 281f
        genome sequencing and, 427
        of human chromosomes, 322f
Katydids, 690f
Kelps, 586
Keratin, 326, 715
Kestrels, 1180–81
Ketones, **64**f
Ketoses, 70
Keystone species, **1204**–5, 1249
Kidneys, **962**f
        adaptations of vertebrate, to diverse environments,
                967–68
        homeostatic regulation of, 971
        hormonal regulation of, 968–71, 984–85f
        human, 966f
        human cystic kidney disease, 1041
        mammalian, 962f–63f, 968–71
        nephron processing of blood filtrate to urine in,
                964–65
        osmoregulation by, in marine animals, 954–55
        solute osmolarity gradients and water conservation
                by, 965–67
        structure of, 962f–63f
        in vertebrate excretory systems, 962–63

Kilocalorie (kcal), **48**, 869
Kimura, Motoo, 550
Kinase cascades, 823–24
Kinases, 212f
Kinetic energy, **48**, **143**
Kinetochore microtubules, 232f, 234, 235f
Kinetochores, **231**, 232f
Kinetoplastids, **580**–81
Kinetoplasts, 580
King, Jack, 550
King, Mary-Claire, 377
King, Thomas, 413
Kingdoms (taxonomy), 13–14, **537**, 551–52
Kingsley, David, 528f
Kingsnake case study, 20–23
Kin selection, 1137–**38**
Kissimmee River restoration project, 1234f
Kiwi bird, 1235f
Klinefelter syndrome, 299–300
Knee-jerk reflex, 1064
KNOTTED-1 gene, 758
Koalas, 722, 890
Kodiak bears, 875
Kolbe, Hermann, 59
Kombu, 586
Korarchaeota, clade, 567
Kornberg, Roger, 85–86f
Krait, 850
Krebs, Hans, 170
Krebs cycle. See Citric acid cycle
Krill, 50f, 691
K-selection, **1181**
Kudzu, 1242–43
Kuru, 393
Kuzdzal-Fick, Jennie, 1186f
Kyoto Protocol, 1258

L
Labeling, GMO food, 818
Labia majora, **1003**
Labia minora, **1003**
Labor, **1014**
Labrador Current, 1148
Lacks, Henrietta, 242
Lac operon, 353–55
Lactate, 178, 1108
Lactation, **1015**
Lacteals, **888**
Lactic acid fermentation, **178**
Lactose, 70, 157, 353–55
lacZ gene, 399–400
Lagging strand, **315**–16
Lagomorpha, 725f
Lakes, 1157–58, 1159f, 1224, 1255
Lake Vesijärvi, 1206
Lake Victoria, 497, 500–501f
Lam, W. F., 743f
Lamarck, Jean-Baptiste de, 453f, 454–55
λ (lambda) phage, 386f
Lampreys (Petromyzontida), 703
Lamp shells, 667f, 677
Lancelets (Cephalochordata), **699**–701
Land. See also Terrestrial biomes
        colonization of, 518–19
        global human use of, 1190
        locomotion on, 1113
        osmoregulation in animals living on, 956
        subsidence of, 788
Land plants, 600–635. See also Plant(s);
                Vascular plants
        adaptive radiations of, 524
        derived traits of, 601–4
        evolutionary links between animals and, 632
        evolution of resource acquisition adaptations in,
                764–65
        gametophyte-sporophyte relationships in, 619f

morphological and molecular evidence for evolution of, from algae, 600–601
nonvascular bryophytes, 606–10
origin and diversification of, 604–6
phylogeny of, 605f
red and green algae and, 590
review of, 616
seedless vascular, 610–15
seed plants (*see* Seed plants)
ten phyla of extant, 605t
terrestrial adaptations of, 601, 641
Landscape ecology, **1145**f, 1249–54
biodiversity hot spots in, 1251–52
establishing protected areas in, 1251–53
landscape fragmentation and edges in, 1249–50
movement corridors in, 1250–51
philosophy of nature reserves in, 1252
zoned reserves in, 1252–53
Landscapes, **1145**f
Land snails, 678f, 680–81f
Language
brain function and, 1073–74
FOXP2 gene and, 443–44
Large intestine, **888**–90
Largemouth bass, 860f
Large-scale disturbances, 1208
Larva, **655**, 689
Larynx, 884, **918**–19
Latency, viral, 949
Lateral geniculate nuclei, **1099**
Lateral inhibition, **1099**
Lateralization, cerebral cortex, **1073**–74
Lateral line system, **705**, 707, **1094**
Lateral meristems, **746**. *See also* Secondary growth, plant
Lateral roots, **739**, 749
Latitude, sunlight intensity and, 1146f
Latitudinal gradients, 1211
Law of conservation of mass, **1219**
Law of independent assortment, 267–**69**, 286–87f
Law of segregation, 264, **265**–67, 286–87f
Laws of probability. *See* Probability
L-dopa, 1081
Leaching, 786
Leading strand, **315**–16
Leaf (leaves), **612**, **741**
abscisic acid in abscission of, 831–32
anatomy of, in C$_4$ plants, 200–201
auxin in pattern formation of, 828
brassinosteroids in abscission of, 831
effects of transpiration on wilting and temperature of, 778
ethylene in abscission of, 834
evolution of, in seedless vascular plants, 613f
evolution of, in vascular plants, 612
green color of, 190
leaf area index and arrangements of, 766
monocot vs. eudicot, 631f
photosynthesis in, 186–87
tissue organization of, 750–51f
Leaf area index, 766
Leaf-cutter ants, 648–49
Leaf primordia, **749**
Leafy liverworts, 608f
Learned behaviors, 1126–27
Learning, **1123**–28
associative, 1125–26
cognition, problem solving, and, 1126
cognitive maps and spatial, 1124–25
development of learned behaviors, 1126–27
imprinting in, 1123–24
sleep and, 1067
social, 1127–28
synapses and, 1077
Leaves. *See* Leaf (leaves)
Leber's hereditary neuropathy, 301

Leeches, 683, 1063f
Left atrium, 902f, 903f
Left ventricle, 902f, 903f
Legionnaires' disease, 568f
Legumes, 794–95
Lemaitre, Bruno, 931
Lemurs, 726
Length, carbon skeleton, 61
Lens, **1096**f
Lenski, Richard, 561f
Lenticels, **754**
Leopards, 537
Lepidoptera, 690f
Lepidosaurs, **715**, 716–17
Leprosy, 569f
Leptin, 893f, **894**
Lettuce seed germination, 836–37
Leucine, 79f
Leukemia, 300, 377, 418, 946, 1241
Leukocytes, 857f, 910f, **911**, 912–13
Lewis, Edward B., 371
Lewis dot structures, 38f
Leydig cells, **1004**, 1010–11
Lichens, 645, **649**–50, 1232–33
Life, 1–27
abiotic synthesis of organic molecules as origin of, 59
biology as scientific study of, 1–2 (*see also* Biology)
carbon in organic compounds as backbone of, 58–59, 66 (*see also* Organic compounds)
cells as fundamental units of, 8, 94, 228 (*see also* Cell(s))
chemical context of (*see* Chemistry)
classification of (*see* Taxonomy)
conditions on early Earth and origin of, 507–10
diversity of (*see* Biodiversity)
DNA in continuity of, 8–10 (*see also* DNA (deoxyribonucleic acid))
energy conversion for, 142 (*see also* Metabolism)
essential elements and trace elements for, 32
evolution of unity and diversity in, as core theme of biology, 1, 11–18 (*see also* Darwin, Charles; Evolution)
fossil record as documentation of history of, 510–14
heredity and hereditary variation in (*see* Genetics)
key events in history of, 514–19
levels of organization of, and themes of biology, 2–11
mass extinctions and diversity of, 521f
molecules of, 68 (*see also* Biological molecules)
origin of, and RNA, 247
photosynthesis as process that feeds all, 184–85 (*see also* Photosynthesis)
possible evolution of, on planets with water, 52
properties of, 2f
review of themes of, 25–26
rise and fall of groups of, 519–25f
scientific method and inquiry in study of, 18–25 (*see also* Science)
tree of, 16–17 (*see also* Phylogenetic trees)
viruses and characteristics of, 381, 390
water and (*see* Water)
Life cycles, **250**
of angiosperms, 627–28, 802f
of apicomplexan *Plasmodium*, 583f
of blood fluke *Schistosoma mansoni*, 675f
of brown algae *Laminaria*, 587f
of cellular slime mold *Dictyostelium*, 595f
of ciliate *Paramecium caudatum*, 584f
of fern as vascular plant, 611f
of fruit fly (*Drosophila*), 370–71
of fungi, 639f, 643f, 645f, 647f
of green algae chlorophyte *Chlamydomonas*, 592f
of human diseases and pathogens, 1214–15
of humans, 251–52
of hydrozoan *Obelia*, 673f
of moss, 607f

of pine trees, 624f, 625
of plasmodial slime mold, 594f
sexual (*see* Sexual life cycles)
of water mold, 588f
Life expectancy at birth, human, 1189–90, 1260
Life histories, **1179**–81
Life tables, **1173**
Ligaments, **857**f
Ligand binding, 210
Ligand-gated ion channels, **213**f, 1055f, **1056**, 1057–58
Ligands, **138**, **210**, 216
Light chains, **935**–36
Light-detecting organs, 1095
Light detector, euglenid, 581f
Light energy. *See also* Solar energy; Sunlight; Ultraviolet (UV) radiation
conversion of, to chemical energy (*see* Light reactions)
excitation of chlorophyll by, 192
plant responses to (*see* Light energy, plant responses to)
properties of, 189
sunlight as, 6–7, 143, 149, 163, 184
Light energy, plant responses to, 835–41
action spectrum of, 835–36
biological clocks and circadian rhythms in, 838–39
blue-light photoreceptors in, 836
de-etiolation (greening) responses, 822, 823f, 824
electromagnetic receptors and, 1089
photomorphogenesis and, 835–36
photoperiodism and seasonal responses in, 839–41
photosynthesis (*see* Photosynthesis)
phototropism and, 825–26
phytochromes as photoreceptors in, 836–37
plant shoot architecture and, 765–66
primary production in aquatic ecosystems and limitations of light, 1223
stomatal opening and closing as, 777–78
Light-harvesting complexes, **192**–93
Light microscope (LM), **95**
Light microscopy (LM), **96**f
Light reactions, **188**, 189–97f
chemiosmosis in chloroplasts vs. in mitochondria, 196–97f
cyclic electron flow in, 195
determination of absorption spectrum for, 190f
excitation of chlorophyll by light energy in, 192
linear electron flow in, 193–95
most effective wavelengths for, 191f
nature of sunlight and, 189
photosynthetic pigments as light receptors in, 190–92
photosystems of, 192–93
as stage of photosynthesis, 188–89
in thylakoids of chloroplasts, 189
Light responses, rod cell, 1099f
Lignin, **612**, 646
Likens, Eugene, 1231
Lilly, John, 1070
Lily, 630f
Limbic system, 1071–72
Limbs
genes for formation of, 526, 527f
homologous structures in, 463
tetrapod, 709, 711f
vertebrate formation of, 1040–41
Limiting nutrients, **1223**–25
Limnetic zone, **1159**f
Limp cells, 770
Limpets, 1165f
LINE-1 retrotransposons, 436
Lineage-based mechanisms, 758
Linear electron flow, **193**–95
Linkage groups, 296–97
Linkage maps, **296**–97, **427**–28

Linked genes, **292**–97
  genetic recombination and, 294–95
  inheritance of, 292–94
  mapping of, 296–97
  sex-linked genes vs., 292
Linker DNA, 320*f*
Linnaean classification, 12*f*, 537–38. *See also* Taxonomy
Linnaeus, Carolus, 453–54, 458, 537, 821
Linoleic acid, 876
Lionfish, 708*f*
Lipid bilayers, 99, 125–27, 131. *See also* Cellular membranes; Plasma membranes
Lipids, **74**–77
  in cellular membranes, 99, 102, 110, 125
  evolution of differences in cellular membrane composition of, 128
  fats as, 74–76
  phospholipids as, 76–77
  in protocells, 509
  smooth ER synthesis of, 105
  steroids as, 77
  Tay-Sachs disease and, 272
Lipid-soluble hormones, 976–77*f*, 978
Lipopolysaccharides, 557–58
Literacy rate, 1260
Lithops, 764
Litter decomposition, 1230*f*
Litter size, 1179
Little greenbul, 1250
Littoral zone, **1159***f*
Liver, **887**
  bile production by, 887
  blood flow through, 888
  in glucose homeostasis, 892–93*f*
  lowering plasma LDL levels by inactivating enzyme of, 914*f*
Livers, **887**
Liverworts (Hepatophyta), 602*f*–3*f*, **606**, 608*f*. *See also* Bryophytes
Living fossils, 615, 686*f*
Lizards, 536, 716*f*, 717, 863*f*, 868, 998, 999*f*, 1133, 1195*f*
Loam, **786**
Lobe-fins (Sarcopterygii), 707, **708**–9, 954–55, 968
Lobes, brain, 1072, 1073*f*
Lobopods, 684
Lobotomy, 1075
Lobsters, 659*f*, 685*f*, 691
Local biogeochemical cycles, 1227
Local cell signaling, 208
Local extinctions, 1240
Local inflammatory response, 934
Local regulators, **208**, **975**, 979, 1059–60
Localized determinants, 1036–38, 1043
Lock-and-key recognition, fertilization, 1022
Lock-and-key specificity, viral, 384
Locomotion, **1113**–15
  energy costs of, 1114–15
  flying, 1114
  interaction of muscles and skeletons in, 1110–11 (*see also* Motor systems; Skeletal systems)
  on land, 1113
  swimming, 1113–14
Locoweeds, 1198
Locus, gene, **249**, 265
Lodgepole pines, 1208
Logging, 1210
Logistic population growth model, **1177**–79
Long-day plants, **839**
Long-distance cell signaling, 208*f*–9
Long-night plants, 839–40
Long-term memory, **1077**
Long-term potentiation (LTP), **1077**–78
Looped domains, DNA, 321*f*, 322
Loop of Henle, **963***f*, 964*f*, 965, 966–67
Loose connective tissue, 857*f*

Lophophorates, 677
Lophophores, **664**, 674, 677
Lophotrochozoans (Lophotrochozoa), **663**–64, 667*f*–68*f*, 674–82
  annelids, 681–83
  flatworms, 674–76
  lophophorates, ectoprocts, and brachiopods, 677
  molluscs, 677–81*f*
  rotifers, 676–77
Lorenz, Konrad, 1119, 1123–24
Loricifera, 668*f*
Lorises, 726
Lou Gehrig's disease, 1106
Low-density lipoproteins (LDLs), 138, **913**, 914
LSD, 1058
Luciferase, 838
Lung cancer, 432
Lung cells, newt, 8*f*
Lungfishes, 709
Lungs, **918**–22
  breathing and ventilation of, 920–22
  vertebrate and mammalian respiratory systems and, 918–20
Lupines, 1233
Lupus, 247, 947
Luteal phase, **1009**
Luteinizing hormone (LH), 985*f*, 986*t*, **989**, 1008–11
Lycophytes (Lycophyta), **605**, 612, 613, 614*f*
Lyell, Charles, 453*f*, 454, 456
Lyme disease, 569*f*, 571–72, 1214*f*
Lymph, **909**, 933*f*
Lymphatic systems, **909**
  cellular innate immunity and, 933
  circulatory system fluid return by, 909
  human, 933*f*
  lacteals in, 888
Lymph nodes, **909**
Lymphocytes, 910*f*, 912*f*, **935**–40
Lymphoid stem cells, 912
Lymph vessels, 909
Lynx, 1185–86
Lyon, Mary, 291–92
Lysine, 79*f*
Lysis, 933
Lysogenic cycle, **386**–87
Lysosomal storage diseases, 107
Lysosomes, 100*f*, **106**–7
Lysozymes, 51*f*, 81*f*, 440–41, **930**, 932
Lysus, 946
Lytic cycle, **385**–86

M

Macaca mulatta (rhesus macaque), 426
MacArthur, Robert, 1212–13
MacLeod, Colin, 306
Macroclimate, **1147**
Macroevolution, **488**, **507**–33
  adaptive radiations and, 524–25*f*
  of development as major changes in body forms, 525–29
  early Earth conditions for origin of life and, 507–10
  fossil record as documentation of history of life and, 510–14
  key events in history of life and, 514–19
  mass extinctions and, 521–24
  novelties and trends in, 529–31*f*
  plate tectonics and, 519–21
  review of, 531–32
  rise and fall of groups of organisms and, 519–25*f*
  speciation and, 488, 504 (*see also* Speciation)
Macromolecules, **68**–69. *See also* Biological molecules; Carbohydrates; Nucleic acids; Proteins
  abiotic synthesis of, 509

digestion of, 106–7
florigen as, 841
transport of, in phloem, 782
Macronuclei, cilate, 584*f*–85
Macronutrients, **790**, 791*t*
Macrophages, 107, 122, **857***f*, 929, **932**, 934*f*
Macular degeneration, 411
Madagascar, 1241
Madagascar orchids, 806*f*
Mad cow disease, 85, 393
Madreporite, sea star, 693*f*
MADS-box genes, 447, 526, 760
Maggot flies, 496–97
Maggots, 881*f*
Magnesium, 32*t*, 790, 877–78*t*
Magnetic field, Earth's, 1089, 1120
Magnetite, 1089, 1120
Magnification, 95
Magnolia tree, 630*f*
Magnoliids, **630**
Maidenhair tree, 622*f*, 623*f*
Maize (corn), 633. *See also* Corn (*Zea mays*)
  action spectrum for, 835*f*
  artificial selection of, 815
  corn smut and, 650*f*
  cytokinin in, 829
  health of transgenic *Bt*, 818
  mineral deficiencies in, 791*f*
  precocious germination in, 832*f*
  proteins in, 876
  seed germination of, 809*f*
  seed structure of, 808*f*
  transgenic, 737
  transposable elements and, 435
Major depressive disorder, **1080**
Major histocompatibility complex (MHC) molecule, **937**, 946
Malaria, 278, 484*f*, 579*f*, 583–84, 596, 691
Male gametophytes, angiosperm, 803
Males
  competition between, for mates, 1132–33
  female mate choice and, 1131–32
  hormonal control of reproductive systems of, 1010–11
  parental care by, 1130–31
  reproductive anatomy of human, 1004–5
  sex determination of, 289–90
  sexual competition between, 482
  spermatogenesis in human, 1005–6*f*
Malignant tumors, **242**
Malnutrition, 816–17, 878, 988
Malpighian tubules, 688*f*, **961**–62
Malthus, Thomas, 453*f*, 459
Maltose, 70, 71*f*
Mammals (Mammalia), **720**–28
  adaptive radiation of, 524
  amniotic eggs of, 714*f*
  bats as, 16
  blood composition of, 910*f*
  brains of, 1046–47*f*
  breathing in, 921–22
  cellular respiration in hibernating, 177
  circadian clocks in hibernating, 871
  comparison of chromosome sequences among, 439*f*
  control of circadian rhythms in, 1070–71*f*
  convergent evolution of, 464–65, 723*f*
  derived characters of, 720
  digestive systems of (*see* Digestive systems)
  double circulation in, 901*f*
  early evolution of, 721
  embryonic development in placental, 1011–18
  endangered or threatened, 1239
  eutherians (placental mammals), 723–28
  evolution of melanocyte-stimulating hormone (MSH) in, 988–89

excretory system of, 962–71 (*see also* Excretory systems)
extraembryonic membranes in, 1031
fertilization in, 1024–25
gamete production and delivery in, 1002
genomic imprinting in, 300–301
hearts in circulatory systems of, 902–4
hominins and humans as, 728–33
homologous structures in, 463
hormonal regulation of reproduction in, 1008–11
inactivation of x-linked genes in female, 291–92
ion concentrations inside and outside of neurons of, 1048*t*
kidneys of, 962*f*–63*f*, 967
marsupials, 722–23*f*
mechanoreceptors for hearing and equilibrium in, 1090–94
modeling neurons of, 1049*f*
molecular clock for, 550*f*
monotremes, 721–22
nitrogenous wastes of, 958–59
organ systems of, 855*t*
origination of cetaceans as land animals, 465–66
origin of, 512–14
phylogeny of, 724*f*–25*f*
reproductive cloning of, 413–15
respiratory adaptations of diving, 925–26
respiratory systems of, 918–20
sex determination in, 290, 992
taste in, 1101–2
visual systems of (*see* Visual systems, vertebrate)
water balance in, 956
Mammary glands, 720, 981–82, 984–85*f*, **1004**
Manatee, 1198*f*
Mandibles, **687**, 688*f*
Mangold, Hilda, 1039
Manic-depressive disorder, 20, 1080
Mantids, 460*f*
Mantle, **677**, 678*f*
Mantle cavity, **677**, 678*f*
Mapping
    of brain activity, 1072*f*
    genetic, 296–97
Map units, **296**
Maquis, 1154*f*
Marchantia, 602*f*–3*f*, 608*f*
March equinox, 1147*f*
Margulis, Lynn, 534
Marine animals
    kidney adaptations in, 968
    mass extinctions and, 523–24
    osmoregulation in, 954–55
Marine benthic zones, **1162***f*
Marine biomes, 1157–58. *See also* Aquatic biomes
Marine birds, 957–58
Marine food chains, 1202*f*
Marine molluscs, 450–51
Marine reserves, 1253
Marine worm, 916*f*
Mark-recapture method, **1171**
Mars, 52
Marshall, Barry, 886
Marsh gas, 567
Marsupials (Marsupialia), 464–65, 521, **722**–23*f*, 725*f*
Marsupium, 722
Martindale, Mark, 659*f*
Martinez, Lucia, 1134*f*
Mass, 31*footnote*, 33
Mass, conservation of, 1219
Mass extinctions, **521**–24. *See also* Extinctions
    consequences of, 523–24
    of dinosaurs, 716
    diversity of life and, 521*f*
    first five, including Permian and Cretaceous, 521–22
    sixth, possible, 522–23, 634, 680

speciation tempo after, 503
Mass number, **33**
Mast cells, **934**, 947
Master regulatory genes, 526, 527*f*, 1134
Mate choice, 482–83, 497*f*, 1131–32. *See also* Mating
Mate-choice copying, **1132**
Mate recognition, 490*f*
Maternal age, Down syndrome and, 299
Maternal alleles, 358
Maternal chromosomes, 257
Maternal effect genes, **371**–73
Maternal inheritance, 300–301
Matheos, Dina, 221*f*
Mating. *See also* Animal reproduction; Mate choice; Mating behavior; Reproduction
    animal reproduction and, 996
    bioluminescence in, 142
    cell signaling in, 206–7, 219–20, 221*f*
    clumped dispersion and, 1172
    earthworm, 682
    fertilization and, 1000
    human, 277, 1011
    human sexual arousal and, 1059
    hybrid zones and, 498–501
    insect, 689
    interspecific, and hybrids, 489
    of pea plants, 263*f*–64
    prokaryotic mating bridges, 563
    random, 474, 475
    reproductive isolation and (*see* Reproductive barriers; Reproductive isolation)
Mating behavior, 1129–34. *See also* Mating
    applying game theory to, 1133
    mating systems and parental care in, 1130–31
    mating systems and sexual dimorphism in, 1129–30
    sexual selection and mate choice in, 1131–33
Mating systems, 1129–31
Matorral, 1154*f*
Matter, **31**–32
Maungatautari restoration project, 1235*f*
Maximum likelihood, **545**–47
Maximum parsimony, **544**–47
Mayer, Adolf, 381–82
Maze experiments, 1126
McCarty, Maclyn, 306
McClintock, Barbara, 435
McIntosh, Michael, 851
Meadowlarks, 489*f*
Mean annual precipitation, 1224
Measles virus, 384, 945
Meat eating, human, 1191, 1226
Mechanical isolation, 490*f*
Mechanical signaling, 120
Mechanical stimuli, plant responses to, 842–43
Mechanical stress, plant responses to, 833
Mechanical work, 149, 151
Mechanism vs. vitalism, 59
Mechanoreceptors, **1088**, 1090–94
Mediator proteins, 360
Medicine(s). *See also* Drugs; Pharmaceutical products
    antibodies as tools in, 945
    application of systems biology to, 431–32
    applications of DNA technology in, 417–20
    blocking HIV entry into cells as treatment, 130*f*
    careers in, 851
    fungal, 651
    induced pluripotent stem (iPS) cells and regenerative, 416–17*f*
    medical leeches, 683
    radioactive isotopes in, 34–35*f*
    from seed plants in, 633*t*
Mediterranean Sea, 1148
Medulla, 1069*f*
Medulla oblongata, 922, **1069***f*
Medusa, **671**

Megapascal (MPa), **769**
Megaphylls, **612**, 613*f*
Megasporangia, 619–20
Megaspores, **613**, 619–20, **803**
Megasporocytes, 803
Meiosis, **252**, 253–57
    in animal cells, 254*f*–55*f*
    errors in, 298–99
    genetic variation from gene alteration during, 472
    genome evolution and errors in, 439–41
    in gonads, 230
    human fertilization and, 251–52
    human gametogenesis and, 1005
    mitosis vs., 256*f*–57
    nondisjunction during, 297–98
    reduction of chromosome number by cell division of, 253*f*
    review of, 260–61
    stages of, 253–55*f*
    types of sexual life cycles and, 252–53 (*see also* Sexual life cycles)
Meiosis I, **253**, 254*f*, 257–58
Meiosis II, **253**, 255*f*, 257
Melanocyte-stimulating hormone (MSH), 985*f*, **988**–89
Melatonin, 862*f*, 986*t*, **993**, 1070
Membrane attack complex, 943
Membrane potentials, **136**–37, **1048**–51
Membrane proteins
    ATP work and, 151*f*
    cellular membrane fluidity and, 127–28
    rough ER and, 105
    types and functions of, 129–30
Membranes, amniotic egg extraembryonic, 713–14
Membranes, cellular. *See* Cellular membranes
Memory
    sleep and, 1067
    synapses and, 1077
Memory cells, **939**
Menaker, Michael, 1071*f*
Mendel, Gregor. *See also* Mendelian inheritance
    experimental, quantitative approach of, 262–64
    idea of genes as hereditary factors, 262, 286
    law of independent assortment of, 267–69
    law of segregation of, 264–67
    monohybrid and dihybrid crosses of, 267–69
    particulate model of inheritance of, 470
    testcross of, 267
Mendelian inheritance, 262–85. *See also* Genetics
    C. Darwin's theory and, 470
    environmental impacts on phenotypes and, 274–75
    evolution of gene concept from, 347
    exceptions to, 300–302
    extending, for multiple genes, 273–74
    extending, for single gene, 271–73
    human patterns of inheritance and, 275–81 (*see also* Human genetics)
    integrating, with emergent properties, 275
    law of independent assortment of, 267–69
    law of segregation of, 264–67
    laws of probability governing, 269–71
    G. Mendel's experimental quantitative approach, 262–64
    physical basis of, in behavior of chromosomes, 286–89 (*see also* Chromosomal basis of inheritance)
    review of, 282–83
Menopause, **1010**
Menstrual cycle, **1008**, 1009–10
Menstrual flow phase, **1010**
Menstruation, **1008**
Mercury pollution, 1256
Meristem identity genes, **760**, 841
Meristems, **746**–47, 828–29
Meroblastic cleavage, **1026**
Merozoites, 583*f*

Meselson, Matthew, 312
Mesenchyme cells, 1028, 1032–33
Mesoderm, **660**, **1027**
Mesoglea, 671f
Mesohyl, **670**–71
Mesonychoteuthis hamiltoni, 680
Mesophyll, **186**, 200–201, **750**
Mesozoic era, 514, 515t, 658
Messaging, cellular. *See* Cell signaling
Messenger molecules, 208
Messenger RNA (mRNA), **328**
    alteration of ends of, 334
    cell signaling and synthesis of, 219
    circadian rhythms in synthesis of, 838
    degradation of, 363
    effects of microRNAs and small interfering RNAs
        on, 365
    mutations affecting, 344–46
    protein synthesis and, 86–87
    ribosome model with, 339f
    in situ hybridization and, 410
    synthesis of, 102, 330–31
    transcription of, 331–32
    in translation, 246, 337 (*see also* Translation)
    viruses and, 387t, 388–90
Metabolic defects, 326–28
Metabolic pathways, **142**
    gene specification of enzymes functioning in, 327f
    regulation of, 352
    types of, 142–43
Metabolic rate, **869**–70
Metabolism, **142**–62. *See also* Cell(s)
    adjustment of, for heat production, 866–67
    bioenergetics and animal, 868–69
    cellular respiration and, 179–80 (*see also* Cellular
        respiration)
    corticosteroids and, 991–92
    coupling of exergonic and endergonic reactions in,
        by ATP, 149–51
    as energy conversion for life, 142
    enzymatic catalysis of reactions in, 152–57, 181
    equilibrium and, 148–49
    exergonic and endergonic reactions in, 147–48
    fermentation and (*see* Fermentation)
    forms of energy for, 143–44
    free-energy change, equilibrium, and, 146–49
    laws of thermodynamics and, 144–45
    melanocyte-stimulating hormone (MSH) in, 988–89
    metabolic pathways of, 142–43
    metabolic rate calculation, 869
    nitrogenous wastes and, 959
    osmoregulation and, 956–57
    photosynthesis and (*see* Photosynthesis)
    prokaryotic, 564–65
    protocell, 509
    radioactive tracers and research on, 34
    regulation of enzyme activity to control, 158–60
    review of, 161
    role of enzymes as catalysts in, 77
    secondary compounds of land plant, 604
    thyroid hormone and control of, 987–88
Metabotropic receptors, 1057–59
Metagenomics, **428**–29, 534–35, 566
Metamorphosis, **655**
    amphibian, 711–12
    insect, 689, 974, 980, 988
    lancelet, 699
    tunicate, 700
Metanephridia, 682f, **961**
Metaphase, **231**, 233f
Metaphase chromosomes, 321f, 322
Metaphase I, 254f, 257–58
Metaphase II, 255f
Metaphase plate, 233f, **234**, 257
Metapopulations, **1186**–87
Metastasis, **243**

Metazoans (Metazoa), 662
Meteorites, 508
Methane
    carbon and bonds in, 60f
    combustion of, as redox reaction, 165
    covalent bonding and, 38f–39
    molecular shape of, 41f–42
Methanogens, **567**
Methanosarcina barkeri, 433t
Methicillin, 462
Methicillin-resistant *S. aureus* (MRSA), 461–62
Methionine, 79f, 330
Methylated compounds, 65f
Methylation, 357, 358
Methyl group, **65**f
Methyljasmonic acid, 846
Methylsalicylic acid, 846–47
Mexico, 736–37, 1188
MHC (major histocompatibility complex) molecule, 946
Mice. *See* Mouse
Microarray chips, human genome, 432
Microbial diversity, 535, 1201f
Microclimate, **1147**, 1149
Microevolution, **469**–87, **488**
    gene flow as cause of, 479–80
    genetic drift as cause of, 477–79
    genetic variation and, 469–73, 483–84, 485f
    natural selection as cause of, 476
    natural selection as cause of adaptive evolution in,
        480–86
    review of, 486
    sexual selection in, 482–83
    speciation and, 488 (*see also* Speciation)
    using Hardy-Weinberg equation to test, 473–76
Microfibrils
    in plant cell walls, 118–19
    in structural polysaccharides, 72
Microfilaments, **116**
    animal cell, 100f
    in animal cytokinesis, 234
    cell motility and, 112–13
    cytoskeleton structure and function and, 113t
    in morphogenesis, 1034
    plant cell, 101f
    structure and function of, 116–18
Microglia, 1065f
Micronuclei, ciliate, 584f–85
Micronutrients, **790**, 791t
Microphylls, **612**, 613f
Micropyles, **628**, 803
MicroRNAs (miRNAs), 247, **365**, 366
Microscopy, 94–97
Microsporangia, 619, 803
Microspores, **613**, 619, **803**
Microsporidia, 641
Microsporocytes, 803
Microtubule-organizing center, 231. *See also*
    Centrosomes
Microtubules, **113**. *See also* Centrosomes
    animal cell, 100f
    centrosomes, centrioles, and, 114
    cilia, flagella, and, 114–16
    cytoskeleton structure and function and, 113t
    in mitotic spindle, 231–34, 235f
    phragmoplasts, 601
    plant cell, 101f
    plant cell walls and, 119
    structure and function of, 113–14
Microvilli, 99, 100f, 117, 887f, **888**
Midbrain, **1068**f
Middle ear, **1091**f
Middle lamella, **119**
Mifepristone (RU486), 1017
Migration, **1119**
    assisted, 1258
    electromagnetic receptors and, 1089

    as fixed action pattern, 1119–20
    genetic variation in patterns of, 1136
    global climate change and bird, 29
    movement corridors and, 1250–51
Milk release, mammalian, 981–82, 984–85f
Milkweed, 626f
Miller, Stanley, 59, 508
Millipedes, 687–88
Mimicry
    endorphin, 1059
    molecular, 42, 81
    predation defense adaptations of, 1197–98
    snake mimicry case study, 20–23
Mimimal medium, 326
Mimivirus, 390
Mimosa pudica, 842–43
Mineralized dental elements, 703–4
Mineralocorticoids, 986t, 991–**92**
Minerals, **877**
    deficiency of, in plants, 790–91
    as essential nutrients, 877–78t
    mineralocorticoids and metabolism of, 992
    mycorrhizae and plant deficiencies of, 797
    root architecture and acquisition of, 766–67
    smart plants and deficiencies of, 792
    transpiration of, from roots to shoots via xylem,
        772–76
    vascular plant transport of, 767–71
Miniaturization, gametophyte, 618–19
Minimum viable population (MVP), **1245**, 1252
Minke whales, 539f–40
Minorities, science and, 25
Minorsky, Peter, 737f
Miscarriages, 1017
Misfolding, protein, 85
Mismatch repairs, **317**
Missense mutations, **344**–45
Mistletoe, 798f
Mites, 686, 846
Mitochondria, **109**
    animal cell, 100f
    animal hibernation and, 177
    chemical energy conversion by, 110
    chemiosmosis in, 173–74, 196–97f
    electron transport chains in, 167, 172
    endosymbiontic origin of, 109–10, 516–17, 576
    enzymes in, 160
    fungal cell, 100f
    inheritance of genes of, 300–301
    plant cell, 101f
    protists and, 577
    pyruvate in, 170
    using cell fractionation to study, 97
Mitochondria DNA (mtDNA)
    analysis of Neanderthal, 732f
    evolutionary rate of, 548
    species identity in, 539f
Mitochondrial matrix, **110**
Mitochondrial myopathy, 301
Mitosis, **230**. *See also* Cell cycle
    in animal cells, 231–36
    in chromatin packing, 321f, 322
    evolution of, 237
    in human life cycle, 251f
    meiosis vs., 256f–57
    in plant cells, 236f
    term, 230
Mitosomes, 580
Mitotic (M) phase, **231**
Mitotic spindles, **231**–34, 235f
Mixotrophs, **576**, 581, 590
Mobile genetic elements, evolution of viruses and, 390
Model organisms, 24, **1022**. *See also Escherichia coli*
        (E. coli) bacteria
    Arabidopsis thaliana, 755–56
    Caenorhabditis elegans, 684

in developmental biology, **1022**
for DNA research, 305
for T. Morgan's experiments on chromosome theory
of inheritance, 288–89
Neurospora crassa, 646
scientific cooperation and, 24
Models
atomic, 33*f*
electron orbital, 37*f*
molecular-shape, 41*f*
Modified leaves, 742*f*
Modified roots, 740*f*
Modified stems, 741*f*
Molarity, 51–**52**
Molar mass, 52
Molds, **639**–40, 642*f*, 643–44
Mole (mol), **51**–52
Molecular basis of inheritance, 305–24. *See also* DNA
(deoxyribonucleic acid); Genetics
chromatin packing of DNA and proteins in eukary-
otic chromosomes, 320–22
discovery of double helix structure of DNA, 308–10
DNA as life's operating system, 305
DNA replication and repair, 311–19
evidence for DNA as genetic material, 305–8
evolution of gene concept from, 347
review of, 323
Molecular biology
Arabidopsis thaliana as model organism for, 755–56
B. L. Bassler's work in, 92–93
W. F. Doolittle's work in, 534–35
L. Herrera-Estrella's work in, 736–37
importance of viruses to, 381
measures of evolution in, 89
molecular systematics and, 548
of plant development, 755–61
of secondary growth, 754–55
Molecular clocks, **549**–51
application of, to origin of HIV, 550–51
calibration of, 549–50
difficulties with, 550
fungal lineages determined by, 640
for mammals, 550*f*
neutral theory and, 550
Molecular formulas, 38*f*, 60*f*
Molecular genetics, 246–47, 651, 1021, 1243. *See also*
Genetics
Molecular homologies, 463, 540–42
Molecular homoplasies, 542
Molecular identification tags, 106
Molecular mass, **51**–52
Molecular recognition, immune system, 929
Molecular systematics, 541–**42**
animal phylogeny and, 662–64
constructing phylogenetic trees from shared characters in, 542–48
future of animal, 664
gene and genome evolution in, 548–49
prokaryotic phylogenies and, 565–70
Molecular tags, 322*f*
Molecules, **38**. *See also* Compounds
carbon and small organic (*see* Organic compounds)
chemical bonds and formation of, 38–42
land plant secondary, 604
large biological (*see* Biological molecules)
as level of biological organization, 5*f*
origin of self-replicating, 507–10
shape and function of, 41–42
structure of DNA and RNA, 8–10, 88–89*f* (*see also*
DNA (deoxyribonucleic acid); Molecular basis
of inheritance; RNA (ribonucleic acid))
Moles, 540–41, 1085–86
Molluscs (Mollusca), 518, 668*f*, 677–81*f*, 1063*f*
bivalves, 679
body plan of, 678*f*
cephalopods, 680

chitons, 678
eye complexity in, 529*f*
gastropods, 678–79
protecting freshwater and terrestrial, from extinction,
680–81*f*
venomous, 850–51
G. J. Vermeij's work on evolution of, 450–51
Molting, 663–64, **683**
Monarch butterflies, 818, 1125
Monera, kingdom, 551
Monkey flower, 504
Monkeys, 726–27*f*
Monocilia, 1041–42
Monoclonal antibodies, **945**
Monocots, **630**, 631*f*, 748, 750, 808*f*
Monocytes, 910*f*, 912*f*
Monod, Jacques, 352
Monogamous mating, 1002, **1129**–31
Monoglycerides, 888*f*
Monohybrid crosses, **267**, 269–70
Monohybrids, **267**
Monomers, **68**–69
Monophyletic clades, 542*f*, 543
Monophyletic groups, **543**
Monosaccharides, **69**–70, 71*f*
Monosomic cells, **298**
Monosomy X, 300
Monotremes (Monotremata), **721**–22, 725*f*
Monozygotic twins, 1014, 1039
Monster flower, 632*f*
Montmorillonite, 509
Montreal Protocol, 1259
Moon jelly, 898*f*
Moose, 1184–85
Moray eel, 708*f*
Morels, 644*f*, 651
Morgan, Thomas Hunt, 288–89, 292–95*f*, 305
Mormon tea, 623*f*
"Morning-after" birth control pills, 1017
Morning sickness, 1014
Morphine, 42, 81
Morphogenesis, **367**, **755**, **1027**–35
adaptations of amniote, 1031
apoptosis in, 1034–35
cytoskeletons in, 1033–34
gastrulation in, 1027–31
hormonal regulation of, 989
mechanisms of, 1033–35
organogenesis in, 1031–33
plant development and, 755, 758
Morphogen gradients, 372–73, 1038
Morphogens, **372**–73
Morphological homologies, 540
Morphological isolation, 490*f*
Morphological species concept, **492**
Morphology
animal (*see* Animal form and function)
animal phylogeny and, 662–63
evolution of developmental genes and, 525–29
fungal, 637–38
plant (*see* Plant structure)
Mortality rates, 1181. *See also* Deaths
Mosaicism, 292
Mosquitoes, 480, 583–84, 690*f*, 881*f*
Mosquitofish, 493–94
Mosses (Bryophyta), 603*f*, **606**, 608*f*. *See also* Bryophytes
Mother-of-pearl plant, 1
Moths, 690*f*, 805*f*
Motile cilia, 1041–42
Motility. *See* Cell motility; Movement
Motion. *See* Locomotion
Motor, flagellum, 558–59
Motor cortex, 1074–75
Motor neurons, **1046**, 1047*f*, 1064*f*, 1106–7*f*, 1108
Motor proteins, 78*f*, **112**
ATP work and, 151*f*

cell motility and, 112–13
cilia, flagella, and, 116
in kinetochore microtubules, 234, 235*f*
Motor systems, **1066**, 1103–15
energy costs of locomotion in, 1114–15
interaction of muscles and skeletons in locomotion
in, 1110–11
nonskeletal muscle types in, 1109–10
review of, 1115–16
sensory systems and, 1085–86, 1103–4 (*see also*
Sensory systems)
skeletal muscle contraction in, 1104–9
skeletal systems in, 1111–13
types of locomotion in, 1113–14
Motor unit, **1108**
Motrypsin, 887
Mountains, 1148–49
Mount Kinabalu, 785
Mouse. *See also Mus musculus* (mouse)
appetite regulation genes in, 893–94
comparing human genome to genome of, 442–43
comparison of chromosome sequences of humans
and, 438, 439*f*
complete genome sequence for, 426
cross-fostering of, 1123
FOXP2 gene evolution in, 443–44
genome size of, 433*t*
genomic imprinting of insulin-like growth factor
gene of, 301
geographic variation of, 471
homeotic genes in, 446*f*
paw development of, 225
Movement. *See also* Locomotion
cell (*see* Cell motility)
mechanoreceptors for sensing, in humans, 1093–94
prokaryotic, 558–59
Movement corridors, **1250**–51
MPF (maturation-promoting factor), **239**–40
mRNA. *See* Messenger RNA (mRNA)
Mucous cells, 885*f*
Mucus, **884**, 885*f*, 932
Mucus escalator, 919
Mueller, Ken, 1102*f*
Mukhametov, Lev, 1070
Mule deer foraging behavior, 1129
Mules, 491*f*
Muller, Hermann, 346
Müllerian mimicry, **1197**–98
Multicellular asexual reproduction, 249
Multicellular organisms, 517–18
Multicellular slime mold adaptation, 1186
Multienzyme complexes, 160
Multifactorial characters, **275**
Multifactorial disorders, human, 279
Multigene families, **437**–38
Multiple fruits, **810**
Multiple sclerosis, 947
Multiplication rule, **269**–71
Multiprotein complexes, 172–73
Multiwell plates, 400*f*, 401, 402
Mummichog fish, 471
Murchison meteorite, 508
Muscle cells
animal, 655
determination and differentiation of, 368–69
Muscle contraction, 1104–9
nervous system regulation of graded, 1108–9*f*
regulation of, 1106–7*f*
sliding-filament model of, 1104–6
types of skeletal muscle fibers and, 1109
Muscles
interaction of skeletons, and, in locomotion, 1110–11
nonskeletal types of, 1109–10
skeletal, and contraction of, 1104–9
skeletal systems, locomotion, and, 1110–15 (*see also*
Locomotion; Skeletal systems)

Muscle tissue, 117, **858***f*, 883–84
Muscular dystrophy, 291
Mushrooms, 636, 642*f*, 644*f*, 646, 647*f*, 651. *See also* Fungi
Mus musculus (mouse). *See also* Mouse
    complete genome sequence for, 426
    genome size of, 433*t*
    geographic variation of, 471
    as model organism, 24
Mussels, 679
Mustard plant. *See Arabidopsis thaliana* (mustard plant)
Mutagens, **346**
Mutant phenotypes, 288–89
Mutations, **344**
    abnormal pattern formation, 371*f*
    alterations of chromosome structure, 438–39
    in aquaporins causing diabetes insipidus, 970*f*
    cancer-causing, 373–74, 432
    cellular slime mold, 595–96
    creating, in molecular biology, 756
    duplication and divergence of chromosomal regions, 439–41
    duplication of entire chromosome sets, 438
    effects of, during cell division, 375*f*
    embryonic lethals, 371
    as errors in proofreading, 317–18
    evolution of enzymes by, 157
    exon duplication and exon shuffling in, 441
    in flowering, 760
    gene variability and silent, 470–71
    genome evolution and, 438–42
    Hox genes and, 526
    of ion channel protein genes, 1053
    missense vs. nonsense, 344–45
    in mitochondrial DNA, 301
    mutagens as cause of, 346
    mutant phenotypes and, 288–89
    neutral theory on, 550
    nucleotide-pair insertions and deletions, 345–46
    nucleotide-pair substitutions, 344–45
    in prokaryotes, 561
    quorum sensing and, 92
    random, as source of alleles, 259, 297
    as sources of genetic variation, 471–72
    transposable elements and, 441–42
    types of small-scale, 344–46
Mutualism, **570**–71, **1199**
    bacterial, 571
    disruption of plant-fungi, 797*f*
    in flower pollination, 801, 806
    fungal, 637, 648–50
    fungus-animal, 648–49
    fungus-plant, 648
    as interspecific interaction, 1199
    mycorrhizae as plant-fungi, 767, 795–97
    nutrient limitations and, 1224
    plant-bacteria, 793–95
    in plant nutrition, 792–98*f*
    symbols for, 1194–95
    vertebrate digestive adaptations and, 890–91
Myasthenia gravis, 1106
Mycelium (mycelia), **637**, 639
Mycetozoans, 594–96
Mycobacterium tuberculosis, 572
Mycoplasms, 98, 569*f*
Mycorrhizae, **638**, **767**, **795**
    agricultural and ecological importance of, 797
    bioremediation using, 1233
    disruption of, by garlic mustard, 797*f*
    evolution of, 641
    as mutualism, 1199
    nutrient limitations and, 1224
    plant evolution and, 796
    plant nutrition and, 795–97
    as root-fungi mutualism, 638, 767
    strigolactones and, 832
    types of, 796–97

Mycosis, **650**
Myelin sheath, **1054**
Myeloid stem cells, 912
Myllokunmingia fengjiaoa, 697, 702
Myoblasts, 368–69
Myocardial infarctions, 913–14
MyoD protein, 359*f*, 369
Myofibrils, **1104**
Myoglobin, **926**, **1109**
Myosin, 78*f*, **117**, 234, 593, 858*f*
Myosin filaments, 1104–6
Myotonia, **1011**, 1053
Myriapods, **686**, 687–88
Myxini, 702
Myxobacteria, 207*f*, 568*f*

N

NAD$^+$ (nicotinamide adenine dinucleotide), **165**–67, 171–72, 177–79
NADH, 171–72, 177–79
NADP$^+$ (nicotinamide adenine dinucleotide phosphate), **188**–89
NADP$^+$ reductase, 195
NADPH, 188–89, 193–95
Naked mole rats, 1137–8
Nanoarchaeota, clade, 567
Nasal glands, marine bird, 957
Nash, John, 1133
National Cancer Institute, 432
National Center for Biotechnology Information (NCBI), 429, 430*f*
National Institutes of Health (NIH), 429, 432
National Library of Medicine, 429
National Medal of Science, 920
Natural family planning, **1016**
Natural killer (NK) cells, **933**
Natural plastics, 572
Natural range expansions, 1164–65
Natural selection, **15**, **456**, 480–86. *See also* Adaptations; Evolution
    as cause of microevolution and adaptive evolution, 476
    C. Darwin's theory of descent with modification by, 14–16, 456–60 (*see also* Descent with modification theory)
    density-dependent and density-independent, 1181
    directional, and molecular clocks, 550
    directional, disruptive, and stabilizing selection in, 480–81
    of ecological niches, 1195–96
    evolution of developmental genes and, 527
    in evolution of drug resistance, 461–62
    evolution of enzymes by, 157
    genetic variation for, from genetic recombination, 295
    insect evolution by, due to food source changes, 461
    key role of, in adaptive evolution, 482
    life histories and, 1179–80
    limitations of, in creating perfect organisms, 484–85
    molecular level, 509–10
    mutations and, 318
    neutral theory on fitness and, 550
    relative fitness and, 480
    sexual reproduction, genetic variation, and, 259–60
    species selection as, 530
Natural vs. supernatural explanations, 20
Nature reserves, philosophy of, 1252
Nature vs. nurture, 274–75, 1123
Navigation, migration and, 1119–20
Neanderthals, 731–32
Near vision, 1101*f*
Nectarine, 626*f*
Negative feedback, **10**, **861**, **982**
    in endocrine system feedback regulation, 982
    in feedback regulation, 10–11

    in homeostasis, 861
    in population regulation, 1182–84
Negative gene regulation, bacterial, 353–55
Negative gravitropism, 841
Negative pressure breathing, **921**
Nematocysts, **671**
Nematodes (Nematoda), 669*f*, 683–84, 1111–12
Nemertea, 668*f*
Neocortex, 1075
Neodenticula seminae, 1149
Neoproterozoic era, 656–57
Neornithes, 719–20
Nepenthes rajah, 785
Nephridium, 678*f*
Nephrons, **962***f*
    Bowman's capsule in, 963
    processing of blood filtrate to urine by, 963–65
    structure of mammalian kidneys and, 962*f*–63*f* (*see also* Kidneys)
Neritic zones, **1162***f*
Nerve cells, 94, 655
Nerve cell signaling, 125
Nerve cord, 688*f*, 699
Nerve gas, 1058
Nerve impulses, 859
Nerve nets, **1063**
Nerves, **1063**
Nervous systems, **974**, 1062–84
    brain research and, 1062
    cell signaling in, 859
    cellular membrane selective permeability and, 125
    central nervous systems and peripheral nervous systems in, 1063, 1064*f*
    cerebral cortex functions in, 1072–76
    cognitive maps in, 1124–25
    control of heart rhythm by, 904
    control of skeletal muscle tension in, 1108–9*f*
    coordination of endocrine systems and, 984–86*t*
    disorders of, 1079–82
    diversity of, 1063*f*
    embryonic development of, 1076
    glia in, 1065–66
    Huntington's disease and, 278–79
    long-distance cell signaling in, 209
    neuroendocrine signaling and, 975, 980
    neurons and nerves of, 1062–63
    peripheral nervous system structure and function, 1066–67
    regulation of digestion by, 891–92
    review of, 1082–83
    squid, 1046*f*
    synaptic connections in, and learning and memory, 1076–79
    venom and, 850–51
    vertebrate, 1063–67
    vertebrate brain in, 1067–76
Nervous tissue, **858***f*
Nests
    of birds and dinosaurs, 547–48
    red-cockaded woodpecker, 1248–49
Net ecosystem production (NEP), **1222**
Net primary production (NPP), **1221**–22
Neural crest, **701**, **1032**
Neural pathways, 1099–1100
Neural plasticity, **1076**–77
Neural plate, 1032
Neural stem cells, 1078–79
Neural tube birth defects, human, 879
Neural tubes, **1032**–33
Neuroendocrine signaling, 975, 980, 981
Neurofibrillary tangles, 1081
Neurohormones, **975**, 985*f*
Neuromuscular junctions, 1057–58
Neurons, 858*f*, **1045**–61
    action potentials of, as axon signals, 1050–55
    cell signaling in animal nervous systems and, 859

communication between cells and, at synapses, 1055–60
communication by, 1045
death of, and synapse elimination, 1076
exocytosis and, 138
in human brain, 1062
information processing and, 1046
ion concentrations inside and outside of mammalian, 1048t
ion pumps, ion channels, and resting potential of, 1048–50
nervous systems and, 1062–63 (see also Nervous systems)
neurotransmitters and, 975, 981
olfactory, 1102–3
review of, 1060–61
in sensory transmission, 1086–87
structure and function of, 1046–47f
Neuropeptides, 1058t, **1059**
Neurosecretory cells, 975, 980, 984–85f
Neurospora crassa (bread mold), 326, 327f, 645–46, 931f
Neurotransmitters, **975, 1046**
acetycholine, 1057–58
amino acids, 1058
biogenic amines, 1058–59
chemical synapses and, 1055–56
clearing of, from synaptic clefts, 1056
exocytosis and, 138
gases, 1059–60
major, 1058t
modulated signaling by, 1057
neuropeptides, 1059
Neurulation, 1032–34
Neutralization, 943
Neutral theory, **550**
Neutral variation, **483**
Neutrons, **33**, 34
Neutrophils, 910f, 912f, **932**, 934
Nevada, 1234f
Newborn screening, 280–81
Newton, Isaac, 23
Newts, 8f, 1039f
New World monkeys, 726–27f
New Zealand, 1235f
Niches. See Ecological niches
Nicolson, G., 126
Nicotine, 1058, 1198
Night length, flowering and, 839–40
Nirenberg, Marshall, 330
Nitrates, 1254
Nitric oxide, 214, 907, **979**, 1059–60
Nitrification, 793
Nitrogen
bryophyte reduction of leaching of, from soil, 609f
as essential element, 32, 58, 66
as limiting nutrient, 1223–25
nutrient enrichment and pollution by, 1254–55
plant deficiency in, 791f
recycling, 568f
soil fertilization and, 788
Nitrogen cycle, **793**, 1229f
Nitrogen fixation, **564, 794**
bacterial, 793–95
bioremediation using plants for, 1233
bryophyte, 608f, 609
cyanobacteria and, 569f
lichens and, 650
as mutualism, 1199
nitrogen cycle and, 1229f
prokaryotic, 564–65
Nitrogenous bases
as components of nucleic acids, 87–88
ratios of, in DNA, 308
Nitrogenous wastes, 958–59
ammonia as, 958
excretion of, 953

influence of evolution and environment on, 959
urea as, 958–59
uric acid as, 959
Nitrogen oxides, 55–56
Nobel Prizes
R. Axel and L. Buck, 1103
M. Capecchi, M. Evans, and O. Smithies, 410
A. Huxley and A. Hodgkin, 1051
F. Jacob, 529
R. Kornberg, 86f
B. Marshall and R. Warren, 886
B. McClintock, 435
C. Nüsslein-Volhard and E. Wieschaus, 371
S. Prusiner, 394
F. Sanger, 409
N. Tinbergen, K. von Frisch, and K. Lorenz, 1119
J. Watson, F. Crick, and M. Wilkins, 310
H. zur Hausen, 950f
Nociceptors, **1089**–90
Nocturnal animals, 1122
Nodes, **740**
Nodes of Ranvier, **1054**
Nodules, **794**–95
Nomarski microscopy, **96**f
Nonbreeding adults, 1184f
Noncoding DNA
gene density and, 434
simple sequence DNA and short-tandem repeats (STRs), 436–37
transposable elements, 434–36
Noncoding RNAs (ncRNAs), 364–66
Noncompetitive inhibitors, 156f, **157**
Nondisjunction, **297**–98, 299–300
Nonequilibrium model, community, **1207**
Nonheritable variation, 470f
Nonhomologous chromosomes, 286–87f
Nonidentical DNA sequences, 437–38
Nonkinetochore microtubules, 232f, 234
Non-native species, 1242–43
Nonparental types, 295
Nonpolar covalent bonds, **39**
Nonpolar side chains, 79f
Nonrenewable resources, 1191
Nonself recognition, immune system, 929
Nonsense mutations, **345**
Nonshivering thermogenesis, 866, 868
Nonsister chromatids, 251f, 258, 259f
Nonspontaneous processes, 145
Nonsteroidal anti-inflammatory drugs (NSAIDs), 991
Nonsteroid hormones, 362
Nontemplate strand, DNA, 330
Nontropic hormones, 985f
Nonvascular plants, 604–5. See also Bryophytes
Norepinephrine (noradrenaline), 986t, **990**–91, 1057, **1058**–59
Nori, 591
Norm of reaction, **274**–75
North Atlantic Subtropical Gyre, 1148f
Northern blotting, **409**
Northern coniferous forests, **1155**f
North Pacific Subtropical Gyre, 1148f
No-till agriculture, **789**
Notochords, 698–99, **1032**–33
Novelties, evolutionary, 529–30
N-terminus, 80, 320f, 340, 357
Nuclear envelopes, 100f, 101f, **102**, 103f, 322, 328
Nucleariids, 596, **640**
Nuclear lamina, **102**, 103f, 118, 322
Nuclear magnetic resonance (NMR) spectroscopy, 85
Nuclear matrix, 102, 316, 322
Nuclear responses, cell-signaling, 219–20
Nuclear transplantation, animal cloning and, 413–15
Nucleases, **318**
Nucleic acid hybridization, **401**–2, 406–7
Nucleic acid probes, **401**–2

Nucleic acids, **86**
components of, 87–88
digestion, 886f
genes, nucleotides, and, 86
as genetic material, 305
as macromolecules, 68
as nucleotide polymers, 88
roles and structures of DNA and RNA, 86–89f (see also DNA (deoxyribonucleic acid); RNA (ribonucleic acid))
separating, with gel electrophoresis, 405–6
viroids as, 393
viruses as molecules of, 382
Nucleoids, **98, 321, 560**
Nucleolus, 100f, 101f, **102**
Nucleomorphs, 576
Nucleosides, 87
Nucleoside triphosphates, 314
Nucleosomes, **320**f
Nucleotide excision repairs, **318**
Nucleotide-pair insertions and deletions, 345–46
Nucleotide-pair substitutions, **344**–45
Nucleotides, **87**. See also DNA sequences
amino acids specified by triplets of, 329–30
coding and noncoding, 334–35
as components of nucleic acids, 87–88
determining sequences of, in DNA, 407–9
evolutionary significance of altered DNA, 318
in genetic code, 9
mutations as base-pair insertions and deletions of, 345–46
mutations as base-pair substitutions of, 344–45
nucleic acids as polymers of, 86
variability of, 470–71
Nucleus, **102**
animal cell, 100f
atomic, 33
cell-signaling responses in, 219–20
ciliate types of, 584f–85
DNA in eukaryotic cell, 98
as eukaryotic cell information center, 102, 103f
fungal cell, 100f
gene expression and architecture of, 362
hormone receptors in, 977f
mitosis and genetic material in, 230
plant cell, 101f
reproductive cloning by transplantation of eukaryotic cell, 413–15
types of nuclear division, 237
Nucleus accumbens, 1072f, 1081
Nudibranchs, 996
Nursing, 981–82, 984–85f
Nurture vs. nature, 274–75, 1123
Nüsslein-Volhard, Christiane, 371, 372–73
Nutrient cycling
biogeochemical cycles and, 1227–32
as chemical cycling in ecosystems, 570
decomposition and, 1227
decomposition and rates of, 1230–31
energy flow and, in ecosystems, 1218
general model of, 1227f
Hubbard Brook Experimental Forest case study in, 1231
trophic levels and, 1219–20
Nutrient enrichment, global, 1254–55
Nutrient enrichment experiments, 1223
Nutrients
primary production in aquatic ecosystems and limitations of, 1223–24
primary production in terrestrial ecosystems and limitations of, 1224–25
prokaryotic recycling of, 570
Nutrition, **875**
animal, 654, 875 (see also Animal nutrition)

essential elements and trace elements for, 32
eukaryote kingdoms classified by modes of, 14
fungal, 636–37
of molluscs, 450
photosynthesis and modes of, 184–85
plant (*see* Plant nutrition)
prokaryotic, 564–65
protist, 576
transgenic plant crops, 421–22*f*
Nymphs, 689, 690*f*

O

Oak Ridge National Laboratory, bioremediation
    of, 1233
Oak trees, 596, 631*f*
Obelia, 673*f*
Obesity, 893–95
ob gene, 893–94
Obligate aerobes, **564**
Obligate anaerobes, **179**, **564**
Obligate mutualism, 1199
Observations
    of evolutionary change, 460–62
    scientific, 18–19
Occam's razor, 544
Occipital lobe, 1074*f*
Ocean acidification, 29, **55**–56
Ocean anoxia, 522
Ocean currents, climate and, 1147–48
Oceanic pelagic zone, **1161***f*
Oceans
    acidification of, 29, 55–56
    climate and currents of, 1147–48
    determining net ecosystem production for, 1222*f*
    iron fertilization of, 1223–24
    marine benthic zones of, 1162*f*
    as marine biome, 1157–58
    moderation of climate by, 49
    pelagic zones of, 1161*f*
Ocean trawling, 1210
Ocelli, 1095
Ocotillo, 779*f*
Octopuses, 677, 680
Odor, pheromones and communication by, 1122
Odorant receptors (ORs), 1103
Odorants, **1101**, 1103
Odum, Eugene, 1195
Offspring
    number of, 1179
    survival of, 1000, 1001*f*
    survival rates of, 1180
Oil. *See* Fossil fuels
Oil spills, 572*f*, 573
Okazaki fragments, **315**
Old World monkeys, 726–27*f*
Oleander, 779*f*
Olfaction, **1101**, 1102–3
Olfactory bulb, brain, 1102–3
Olfactory nerve, 1066
Olfactory receptor genes, human, 472, 548
Oligochaetes (Oligochaeta), 681–82
Oligodendrocytes, **1054**, 1065*f*
Oligotrophic lakes, **1159***f*
Olivera, Baldomero M., 850–51, 1045
Omasum, 891*f*
Omega-3 fatty acids, 76
Ommatidia, **1095**
Omnivores, **875**, 889*f*
Oncogenes, **373**–74, 376
One-child policy, China's, 1188
One gene–one enzyme hypothesis, 326, 646
One gene–one polypeptide hypothesis, 326
One gene–one protein hypothesis, 326
One-shot reproduction, 1180
On the Origin of Species by Means of Natural Selection
    (book), 14, 452, 457, 466–7, 469–70

Onychophorans (Onychophora), 669*f*, 685*f*
Onymacris unguicularis, 452
Oocytes, **1003**, 1007*f*
Oogenesis, **1005**, 1007*f*
Oogonia, 1006*f*, **1007***f*
Oomycetes, **587**–89
Oost, Bernard van, 970*f*
Oparin, A. I., 508
Oparin-Haldane hypothesis, 508
Open circulatory systems, **686**, **899**
Open-pit mine restoration, 1232
Open systems, 144, 148*f*, 149
Operant conditioning, 1125
Operators, **352**
Operculum, **707**
Operons, **352**
    basic concept of bacterial gene regulation and role
      of, 352–53
      positive gene regulation and, 355
      repressible and inducible, in negative gene
        regulation, 353–55
Ophiuroidea, 693
Opiates, 42, 81, 1059
Opisthokonts, **596**, **640**
Opossums, 722
Opposable thumb, **723**
Opposite phyllotaxy, 766
Opsin, **1097***f*
Opsonization, 943
Optic chiasm, **1099**
Optic disk, 1096*f*
Optic nerves, 1099
Optimal conditions, enzymatic catalysis, 155–56
Optimal foraging model, **1128**–29
Oral cavity, **883**–84
Orangutans, 726–27*f*, 731
Orbitals, **37**
Orbitals, hybrid, 41–42
Orcas, 1204–5
Orchids, 15*f*, 631*f*, 801, 806*f*
Order, as property of life, 2*f*, 145
Orders (taxonomy), **537**
Organelles, **95**
    endomembrane system of (*see* Endomembrane
      system)
    as enzyme locations, 160
    of eukaryotic cells, 98, 99
    inheritance of genes in, 301–2
    as level of biological organization, 5*f*
    lysosomal digestion of, 107
    plastids in plant cells, 111
    using electron microscopy to study, 95
Organic chemistry, **58**–59
Organic compounds, 58–67
    abiotic synthesis of, 59, 508
    ATP as, 66
    carbon atoms and bonds to other atoms to form,
      60–63
    carbon in, as backbone of life, 58, 66
    chemical functional groups and, 63–65*f*
    organic chemistry as study of, 58–59
    review of, 66–67
Organic fertilizers, 788, 959
Organic phosphates, **65***f*
Organ identity genes, **760**, 841
Organismal cloning, 412–17*f*
    of animals, 413–15
    animal stem cells and, 415–17*f*
    of plants, 412–13*f*
    problems with animal, 415
Organismal ecology, **1145***f*
Organisms. *See also* Animal(s); Plant(s)
    acidic and basic conditions affecting, 52–56
    Cambrian explosion in numbers of, 518
    cells as fundamental units of, 8, 94
    cloning of (*see* Organismal cloning)

differential gene expression and different cell types
    in multicellular, 366–73
DNA in development of, 8–10 (*see also* DNA
    (deoxyribonucleic acid))
environment of, 452
genomics and bioinformatics in study of genomes
    of, 10
importance of water for, 46
inherited DNA and development of, 8–10
interactions of, as theme in biology, 6
as level of biological organization, 4*f*
metabolism in (*see* Metabolism)
model (*see* Model organisms)
as open systems, 144
origin of mammalian, 512–14
origin of multicellular, 517–19
origin of single-celled, 514–17
populations of (*see* Population(s))
possible effects of transgenic crops on nontarget, 818
rise and fall of groups of, 519–25*f*
single-celled, 5*f*
in topsoil, 787
Organizer, Spemann's, 1039–40
Organ of Corti, **1091***f*
Organogenesis, **1014**, **1027**, 1031–33
Organs, **738**, **855**
    animal, 855
    embryonic germ layers and, 1027*f*
    endocrine system, 976
    excretory, 962*f*–63*f*
    eyes and light-detecting, 1095–97
    floral, 802
    formation of (*see* Organogenesis)
    human reproductive, 1002–8
    immune system rejection of transplanted, 946
    as level of biological organization, 5*f*
    of mammalian digestive system, 883–89
    plant, 738–42
    smooth muscle and vertebrate, 1110
Organ systems, 5*f*, **855**
Orgasm, **1011**
Orientation
    leaf, 766
    plant cell expansion, 757–58
Orienting, 1120*f*
Origin of Eukaryotic Cells (book), 534
Origin of Species, The (book), 14, 452, 457, 466, 467, 469–70
Origins of replication, **236**, 237*f*, **313**–14
Ornithine, 327*f*
Ornithischians, 715
Orthologous genes, **548**, 549*f*
Orthoptera, 690*f*
Oryza sativa (rice), 433*t*
Osculum, **670**
Osmoconformers, **954**
Osmolarity, 953–**54**, 965–67
Osmoreceptors, 1088
Osmoregulation, **134**, 953–58. See also Excretory systems
    in animals living in temporary waters, 955–56
    cell walls and, 134
    energetics of, 956–57
    in freshwater animals, 955
    kidneys and (*see* Kidneys)
    in land animals, 956
    in marine animals, 954–55
    osmosis and osmolarity in, 953–54
    osmotic challenges in, 954–56
    salinity and, 1166
    transport epithelia in, 957–58
Osmoregulators, **954**
Osmosis, **133**, **768**
    diffusion of water by, across plant plasma mem-
      branes, 768–71
    effects of, on water balance, 133–34
    osmolarity and, 953–54
    in thigmotropism, 842

Osmotic pressure, blood, 909
Osteichthyans (Osteichthyes), **707**–9
Osteoblasts, 857*f*
Osteons, 857*f*
Otoliths, 1093–94
Outer ear, **1091***f*
Outgroups, **543**
Oval window, **1091***f*
Ovarian cancer, 432
Ovarian cycle, **1008**–9
Ovaries, **626**, **802**
    angiosperm, 626, 628, 809
    flowers and, 802
    human, 251–52, 986*t*, 989, 1003
    seed plant, 606
Ovchinnikov, Igor, 732*f*
Overgrazing, 1210, 1240
Overharvesting, 680–81*f*, 708, 1243–44
Overnourishment, 893–94
Overproduction, offspring, 458–59
Oviducts, **1003**
Oviparous organisms, **707**
Oviraptor dinosaurs, 547–48
Ovoviviparous organisms, **707**
Ovulation, **998**, 1003
Ovules, 619–**20**, **802**
Oxidation, 111, **164**–65. *See also* Redox (oxidation-
    reduction) reactions
Oxidative muscle fibers, 1109
Oxidative phosphorylation, 167–**68**, 172–75*f*
Oxidizing agents, **164**–65
Oxygen
    atmospheric, and animal evolution, 657
    in capillaries, 908–9
    catabolic pathways and, 164
    in circulation and gas exchange, 923–24
    development of photosynthesis and
        atmospheric, 516
    electronegativity of, 39
    as essential element, 32, 58, 66
    gas exchange and, 915–16 (*see also* Gas exchange)
    in mammalian circulation, 902
    metabolic rate as consumption of, 869
    net ecosystem production in oceans and, 1222*f*
    ocean anoxia and low levels of, 522
    in plant composition, 789
    as product of photosynthesis, 185, 203
    role of, in prokaryotic metabolism, 564
    species distributions and availability of, 1166
    storage of, by diving mammals, 925–26
Oxygen molecules
    covalent bonding and, 38–39
    in photosynthesis, 43
Oxytocin, **981**–82, 984–85*f*, 986*t*, 1011, 1014–15*f*
Oyster drills, 523–24
Oysters, 677, 679
Ozone depletion, 28–29, 1258–59

P
p21 gene, 376
p53 gene, **374**–76
P680 chlorophyll *a*, 193
P700 chlorophyll *a*, 193
Pacemaker, heart, 904
Pacific diatom, 1150
Pacific Island land snails, 680–81*f*
Pacman mechanism, 234
Paedomorphosis, **526**, 711
Pain, 851, 1059
Paine, Robert, 1205*f*
Pain receptors, **1089**–90
Pair bonding, 1124, 1135
Paleoanthropology, 727, **728**
Paleobotanists, 604
Paleontology, 14–16, **454**, 510–14
Paleozoic era, 514, 515*t*, 657–58

Palisade mesophyll, 750
Pallium, 1075–76
Palumbi, S. R., 539*f*
Pampas, 1155*f*
Pancreas, **887**, **981**, 986*t*
    control of blood glucose by, 982–84
    exocytosis and, 138
    in glucose homeostasis, 892–93*f*
    rough ER and, 105
    secretions of, 887
    in simple endocrine pathway, 981
Pancreatic islets, 983
Pandemics, 391*f*, **392**–93, 1214
Pangaea, **466**, **520**
Panthera pardus (leopard), 537
Pan troglodytes (chimpanzee), 426
Papaya, 792, 816
Paper, 633, 652
Paper wasps, 690*f*
Papillae, 1102*f*
Papillomaviruses, 377
Parabasalids, **580**
Parabronchi, 920
Parachutes, seed and fruit, 811*f*
Paracrine signaling, 208, **975**, 979
Parakeets, 1114
Paralogous genes, **548**, 549*f*
Paramecium, 14*f*, 134*f*, 584*f*, 1179*f*, 1195
Paramyosin, 1110
Paraphyletic groups, 542*f*, **543**
Parapodia, 681, 682
Parar\eptiles, **715**
Parasites, 569*f*, **570**–71, **1198**
    antigenic variation in, 948–49
    apicomplexans as, 583–84
    cercozoans, 590
    entamoebas, 596
    flatworms, 675–76
    fungi as, 637, 643, 646, 650–51*f*
    lampreys as, 703
    microsporidia as fungal, 641
    nematodes, 684
    oomycetes as, 588
    plants as, 797, 798*f*
    protists as, 578*f*, 580, 596
    ticks and mites as, 686
Parasitism, **570**–71, **1198**
Parasympathetic division, peripheral nervous system,
        904, 1066–**67**
Parathyroid glands, 986*t*, **989**–90
Parathyroid hormone (PTH), 986*t*, **990**
Parenchyma cells, **744***f*, 748–49, 750
Parental alleles, genomic imprinting and, 300–301
Parental care, 1000, 1001*f*
    mating systems and, 1130–31
    survival costs of, 1180–81
Parental types, **294**
Parietal cells, 885
Parietal lobe, 1074*f*
Parkinson's disease, 85, 225, 416, 651, 1059,
        1081–82
Parmesan, Camille, 1142–43, 1149
Parsimony, maximum, 544–47
Parthenogenesis, **676**–77, **997**, 998, 999*f*
Parthion, 157
Partial pressure, **915**
Particulate hypothesis on heredity, 262. *See also*
        Mendelian inheritance
Particulate model of inheritance, 470
Passive immunity, **944**–45
Passive transport, **133**
    active transport vs., 136*f*
    diffusion as, 132–35
    of water across plant plasma membranes, 768–71
Paternal alleles, 358

Paternal chromosomes, 257
Paternity
    certainty of, 1130–31
    tests for, 420–21
Pathogenicity, 306
Pathogens, **570**, **1213**–15
    bacterial, 567–69*f*, 571–72
    B cells and antibodies as responses to extracellular,
        942–43
    community structure and, 1213–14
    cytotoxic T cell response to cells infected by, 941–42
    evasion of innate immunity by, 934–35
    evolutionary adaptations of, that evade immune
        systems, 948–50
    fungi as, 637, 645, 646, 650–51
    identifying hosts and vectors for, 1214*f*
    immune system recognition and response to,
        929–30 (*see also* Immune systems)
    plant defenses against, 846–47
    prokaryotic, 570–71
    viruses as, 390–94
    zoonotic, and emerging human diseases, 1214–15
Pattern
    evolution and, 452, 467, 535, 536
    taxonomy based on, 454
Pattern formation, **369**–73, **758**, 828–29, 841, 1039*f*,
        1040–41
Pattern pluralism, 535
Pattle, Richard, 920
Patzek, Tad, 817
Pauling, Linus, 308
Pavlov, Ivan, 1125
Pax-6 gene, 403
PCBs (polychlorinated biphenyls), 1255
PCSK9 enzyme, 914*f*
Peacocks, 482*f*
Pea fruit, 810*f*
Pearl mussels, 680–81*f*
Peas, G. Mendel's, 262–69
Peat, **610**, 615
Peatlands, 610, 1230
Pectin, 119
Pedigo, L. P., 743*f*
Pedigrees, **275**–76
Pedipalps, 686
Pelagic zone, **1157**, 1162*f*
Pellicle, 581*f*
Penguins, 719, 853*f*, 871, 876
Penicillin, 157, 462, 651
Penicillium, 639*f*
Penis, 1004*f*, **1005**, 1011, 1059
Pentoses, 70
PEP carboxylase, **200**–201
Pepsin, 156, **885**–86
Pepsinogen, **885**–86
Peptide bonds, **80**, 341*f*
Peptide hormones, 976–77*f*
Peptides
    antimicrobial, 930–31, 933
    in cone snail venom, 850–51
Peptidoglycan, **557**–58
Per capita birth rate, 1176
Per capita death rate, 1176
Per capita rate of increase, 1176
Perception, **1087**, 1099–1100
Perch, 955*f*
Perennials, 747
Pericycle, **749**
Periderm, **742**, 754, 846
Perilymph, 1092, 1093*f*
Periodic table of elements, 36*f*
Peripheral nervous system (PNS), 1046, 1058, 1060,
        1063, 1064*f*, 1066–67
Peripheral proteins, **129**
Peripheral vision, 1100–1101
Perissodactyla, 725*f*

Peristalsis, **883**–84, **1111**, 1113
Peristome, **609**
Peritubular capillaries, **963***f*
Periwinkles, 1241
Permafrost, 1156*f*
Permian mass extinction, 521–22
Peroxisome enzymes, 600–601
Peroxisomes, 100*f*, 101*f*, **111,**
Personalized medicine, 418
Pert, Candace, 1059
Pesticides
    DDT, 157, 1256
    transgenic, 816–17
Pest outbreaks, 1152
Pest resistance, DNA cloning and, 397*f*
Petals, **625, 802**
Petioles, **741**
Petrels, 894–95
Petroleum. *See* Fossil fuels
Petromyzontida, 703
PET scanners, 34–35*f*
Pévet, Paul, 871*f*
Pfennig, David and Karen, 21–23
Pfiesteria shumwayae, 596
P (parental) generations, **264**
P granules, 1036
pH, **54**
    acid precipitation and, 1244
    adjusting soil, 788
    buffers and, 54–55
    enzymatic catalysis and, 155–56
    and hemoglobin dissociation, 924*f*
    of human cerebrospinal fluid, 922
    pH scale and, 53–54
    prokaryotes and, 556
    protein denaturation and, 84–85
    soil, in ecological succession, 1209–10
    species distributions and soil, 1167
PHA (polyhydroxyalkanoate), 572
Phages, **306, 383**–84. *See also* Bacteriophages (phages)
    evidence for viral DNA in, 306–8
    replicative cycles of, 385–87
    temperate and prophages, 386–87
    transduction of, 562
    virulent, 385–86
Phagocytic cells, 932–33
Phagocytosis, **107, 139***f*, **930**
    cellular integration of, 122
    as endocytosis, 138–39*f*
    immune systems and, 932–33, 934*f*, 943
    lysosomes and, 107, 108
    protist, 581
Phanerochaete chrysosporium, 652
Phanerozoic eon, 514, 515*t*
Phantom limb syndrome, 1077
Pharmaceutical products. *See also* Drugs; Medicine(s)
    DNA technology and development of, 419–20
    enantiomers in, 63
    fungal, 651
    transgenic animals, 419–20
Pharyngeal clefts, **699**
Pharyngeal slits, **699**, 700*f*
Pharyngolepis, 704*f*
Pharynx, 675*f*, **884**
Phase changes, plant development, **759**–60
Phase-contrast microscopy, **96***f*
Phelloderm, 754
Phenobarbital, 105
Phenotypes, **266**
    dominance and, 272
    gene expression as link between genotypes and, 325
        (*see also* Gene expression)
    genes and, 347
    genetic mapping and, 297*f*
    genetic variation and, 470
    genotypes vs., 266–67, 275

    impact of environment on, 274–75
    mutant, 288–89, 318
    phages and, 386–87
    relative fitness and, 480
    transformation and, 306
Phenylalanine, 79*f*, 280, 330, 475–76
Phenylketonuria (PKU), 280, 475–76
Pheromones, **639**, 651, **976**, 1000, 1088–89*f*, 1101, **1122**
Philadelphia chromosome, 300
Philippine eagle, 1240*f*
Phloem, **612, 743**
    electrical signaling in, 782
    primary growth and, 748
    resource acquisition and, 765
    sugar-conducting cells of, 745*f*
    sugar transport from sources to sinks via, 779–81
    systemic communication through, 782
    vascular plant, 612
Phloem sap, **779**–81
Phoenix spacecraft, 52
Phosphate group, **65***f*, 88
Phosphates, algal blooms and, 1223–24
Phosphodiesterase, 223
Phosphofructokinase, 181
Phospholipid bilayers, 99, 125–27, 131. *See also* Cellular
    membranes; Plasma membranes
Phospholipids, **76**–77, 126
    in cellular membranes, 76–77, 99, 102, 110, 125
    Golgi apparatus and, 106
    movement of, in cellular membranes, 127–28
Phosphorus, 32, 58, 66, 307–8, 788, 791*f*, 797, 1223–25
Phosphorus cycle, 1229*f*
Phosphorylated intermediates, **151**
Phosphorylation
    amino acid, 823–24
    histone, 357
    in light reactions of photosynthesis, 188–89
    of proteins in signal transduction, 215–16
Photic zone, **1157**–58
Photoautotrophs, 184, 185*f*, 565*f*, 576
Photoheterotrophs, 565*f*
Photomorphogenesis, **835**–36
Photons, **189**, 192
Photoperiodism, **839**–41
Photophosphorylation, **188**
Photoprotection, 191–92, 195, 200
Photopsins, 1100
Photoreceptors, **1095**, 1096*f*–97*f*, 1098–99
Photorespiration, **200**
Photosynthates, 739
Photosynthesis, **184**–205. *See also* Cell(s)
    alternative mechanisms of carbon fixation in, 199–202
    biofuels and, 185*f*
    bryophyte, 609
    C_4 plants and C_4 pathway of, 200–201
    Calvin cycle of, 198–99
    CAM plants and crassulacean acid metabolism in,
        201–2
    cellular respiration, energy flow, and, 163
    cellular respiration vs., 188
    cercozoan, 590
    chloroplasts in, 5*f*, 109, 110–11, 186–87
    conversion of light energy to chemical energy by,
        186–89
    cyanobacteria and, 569*f*
    determining rate of, with satellites, 1221*f*
    development of, and atmospheric oxygen, 516
    in ecosystems, 1218, 1219
    energy flow and, 6–7
    evolution of adaptations for, 764–65
    formula for chemical reactions in, 43
    importance of, 203, 615
    lichens and, 649–50
    light reactions of, 189–97*f* (*see also* Light reactions)
    photorespiration in, 199–200
    Plantae, kingdom, and, 14

    as process that feeds all life, 184–85
    prokaryotic, 559*f*
    protist, 576, 579*f*, 597
    red and green algae, 590–92
    as redox process, 188
    review of, 203–4
    stramenopile, 585
    sunlight availability and, 1166
    tracking atoms through, 187–88
    two stages of, 188–89
    in vascular plants, 612
    zonation of aquatic biomes and, 1157
Photosystem I (PS I), **193**–95
Photosystem II (PS II), **193**–95
Photosystems, **192**–95
Phototrophs, 564
Phototropin, 836
Phototropism, **825**–26
Phragmoplasts, **601**
pH scale, 53–54
Phycoerythrin, 590–91
Phyla (taxonomy), **537**
    angiosperm, 625
    bryophyte, 608*f*
    gymnosperm, 622*f*–23*f*
    land plant, 605*t*
Phyllotaxy, **766**, 828
PhyloCode, **538**–39
Phylogenetic bracketing, 547–48
Phylogenetic species concept, **492**
Phylogenetic trees, **538**–40, 542–48. *See also* Evolutionary
        trees; Phylogenies
    amniotes, 713*f*
    animal molecular, 663*f*
    animal morphological and developmental, 662*f*
    applications of, 539–40
    chordates, 698*f*
    cladistics and, 542–43
    construction of, from shared and derived
        characters, 543
    eukaryotic, 593*f*
    homologies and, 464
    horizontal gene transfer and, 534–35
    as hypotheses, 547–48
    interpreting, 539
    linking taxonomy and, 538–39
    mammals, 724*f*
    maximum parsimony and maximum likelihood in,
        544–47
    primates, 726*f*
    of prokaryotes, 566*f*
    proportional branch lengths of, 544, 545*f*
    of protists, 578*f*
    tetrapods, 711*f*
    tree of life and, 16–17
Phylogenies, **536**–55. *See also* Phylogenetic trees
    angiosperm, 629*f*
    animal, 662–64
    documentation of, in genomes, 548–49
    of fungi, 641–48
    gymnosperm, 622*f*–23*f*
    inferring, from morphological and molecular data,
        540–42
    investigating tree of life with, 536, 551–53
    land plant, 605*t*
    of living chordates, 698*f*
    of mammals, 724*f*–25*f*
    molecular clocks and evolutionary time in, 549–51
    prokaryotic, 565–70
    of protists, 575, 576–79*f*
    review of, 554–55
    shared characters in, 542–48
    systematics and, 536
    taxonomy and evolutionary relationships in,
        537–40, 551–52 (*see also* Taxonomy)
    tetrapod, 709–10, 711*f*

Physical maps, genome, **427**–28
Physical reconstruction, 1232
Physiological thermostats, 867–68
Physiology, **852**
Phytoalexins, 846
Phytochemicals, 192
Phytochromes, **836**
    in circadian rhythms, 839
    in plant signal transduction pathways, 822–23
    in seed germination, 836–37
    in shade avoidance in plants, 837
    structure of, 837f
Phytophthora, 579f, 588–89, 596, 1214
Phytoplankton, **569**f
    blooms, 1224
    diatoms, 585
    dinoflagellate, 582–83
    forams, 589
    golden algae, 586
    green algae, 591–92
    inverted biomass pyramids of, 1226
    net ecosystem production by, in oceans, 1222f
    nitrogen limitation of production by, 1223f
    nitrogen pollution and blooms of, 1255
    ozone hole and, 28
    seasonality and, 1147
Phytoremediation, **789**
Picrophilus oshimae, 556
Pied flycatchers, 500
Pigeons, 1126
Pigmentation, 274, 301
Pigments
    as photosynthetic light receptors, 190–92
    in photosystems, 192–93
    red algae, 590–91
    respiratory, 923–25
    visual, 1100
Pili, **558**
Pill bugs, 691
Pilobolus, 644f
Pimentel, David, 817
Pineal gland, 984f, 986t, **993**
Pineapple fruit, 810f
Pine beetles, 29
Pine trees, 29, 623f, 624f, 625
Pin flower, 813f
Pinocytosis, 138–**39**f
Pinworms, 684
Pisaster ochraceus, 1205f
Pistils, **802**
Pitch, 1092
Pitcher plants, 785, 798f
Pitch pine canker, 650
Pith, **743**, 750f
Pituitary dwarfism, 989
Pituitary gland, 969, **984**–86t, 1008
Pit vipers, 716f, 717, 1089f
Pivot joints, 1112f
Piwi-associated RNAs (piRNAs), 366
Placenta, **722**, **1013**
Placental mammals. *See* Eutherians (placental mammals)
Placental transfer cells, **602**f
Placoderms, 511f, **705**
Placozoa, 667f
Plains, 1155f
Planarians, **674**–75, 898f, 960–61, 1063f
Planes, plant cell division, 756–57
Planets, possible evolution of life on other, 52
Plankton, 691
Plant(s)
    adaptations that reduce terrestrial nutrient
        limitations, 1224–25
    adaptations of, to toxic elements, 32
    adaptive radiations of, 524–25f
    alternation of generations in, 252
    biofuels from, 185f

bioremediation using, 1232–33
carbon in organic compounds and, 58
carnivorous, 797, 798f
cells of (*see* Plant cells)
cloning, 412–13f
community stability and diversity of, 1201–2
crop (*see* Crop plants)
in domain Eukarya and kingdom Plantae, 13–14
domestication, artificial selection, and genetic engi-
    neering of crop, 801
elements in composition of, 789
endangered or threatened, 1239
epiphytes, 797, 798f
essential elements and trace elements for, 32 (*see also*
    Plant nutrition)
as eukaryotes, 8
evolutionary links between animals and, 632
facilitation in, 1200
fungi as pathogens for, 645, 646, 650
gametophyte-sporophyte relationships in, 619f
genetic engineering and, 421–22f, 792
global climate change and, 1148–49
habitat loss and, 1242
herbivore defenses of, 743f
hormonal signaling in, 209 (*see also* Plant
    hormones)
importance of insects to, 691
inheritance of organelle genes in, 300–301
invasive exotic plants, 797
land colonization by, 518–19 (*see also* Land plants)
mutualism between fungi and, 648, 796
nematode parasites of, 684
parasitic, 797, 798f
as photoautotrophs, 184, 185f
photosynthesis by (*see* Photosynthesis)
polyploidy in, 298
predation defense adaptations of, 1198
protists as pathogens of, 596
red and green algae and land, 590
relationship to humans, 536f
reproduction of (*see* Plant reproduction)
resource acquisition for, 764–67
responses of (*see* Plant responses)
rising carbon dioxide levels and, 1256–57
seed plants (*see* Seed plants)
starch as storage polysaccharide for, 71–72
structure, growth, and development of (*see* Plant
    development; Plant growth; Plant structure)
sympatric speciation in, 495–96
transgenic, 572, 736–37
transport in (*see* Transport in vascular plants;
    Vascular plants)
tumors in, 568f
underground, 764
water balance of cells of, 134
water transport in, 47–48
Plantae, kingdom, 13–14, 551–52, 601. *See also* Eukarya,
    domain
Plant cells
    cell fate in pattern formation, 758
    cellulose as structural polysaccharide for, 72–74
    cell walls of, 118–19
    chloroplasts in, 110–11
    common types of, 743–45f
    cytokinesis in, 235f–36
    cytoplasmic streaming in, 117f–18
    as eukaryotic cells, 101f
    gene expression and control of cell differentiation
        in, 759
    local cell signaling in, 208
    orientation of cell expansion in, 757–58
    plane and symmetry of cell division in, 756–57
    plasmodesmata as cell junctions in, 120–21
Plant development, 755–61. *See also* Plant growth
    auxin in, 828–29
    comparing animal development and, 447

gene expression and control of cell differentiation
    in, 759
genetic control of flowering in, 760–61
growth, morphogenesis, and cell differentiation
    in, 755
morphogenesis and pattern formation in, 758
orientation of cell expansion in, 757–58
phase changes in, 759–60
plane and symmetry of cell division in, 756–57
using model organisms in molecular biology to
    study, 755–56
Plant growth, 746–61. *See also* Plant development
    cell division, cell expansion, and, 756–58
    determinate and indeterminate, 746
    meristem generation of cells for primary and
        secondary, 746–47
    plant development and, 755
    primary, 747–51f
    regulators of, 209, 825 (*see also* Plant hormones)
    secondary, 751–55
Plant-growth-promoting rhizobacteria, 793
Plant hormones, **824**–35
    abscisic acid, 827t, 831–32
    auxin, 827–29
    brassinosteroids, 827t, 831
    cytokinins, 827t, 829–30
    in de-etiolation (greening) responses, 824
    discovery of, 825–26
    ethylene, 827t, 832–34
    florigen, 840–41
    gibberellins, 827t, 830–31
    overview of, 827t
    as plant growth regulators, 824–25
    signal transduction pathways and, 826–27
    strigolactones, 827t
    systems biology and interactions of, 834–35
Plant nutrition, **785**–800
    essential elements required for, 789–92
    mutualistic relationships with other organisms and,
        792–97
    nonmutualistic relationships with other organisms
        and, 797–98f
    review of, 799
    soil properties and soil quality for, 785–89 (*see
        also* Soil)
    unusual adaptations in, 797, 798f
    vascular plant acquisition of water and minerals,
        766–67
    vascular plant transport of water and minerals, 767–71
Plant reproduction
    agriculture and breeding in, 815–16
    agriculture and vegetative propagation in, 814–15
    alternation of generations in land plants, 602f
    angiosperm asexual, 812–15
    angiosperm sexual, 801–11f
    biotechnology in, 815–19
    double fertilization in, 806–7
    flower structure and function in, 802–6
    fruit and seed dispersal in, 811f
    fruits in, 809–10, 811f
    pollination of flowers in, 804f–5f
    prevention of angiosperm self-fertilization in, 813
    seeds in, 807–9
Plant responses, 821–49
    to abiotic environmental stresses, 843–45
    to attacks by herbivores, 845–46
    to attacks by pathogens, 846–47
    to biotic stresses of pathogens and herbivores,
        845–47
    to cold stress, 844–45
    to drought, 843
    to environmental stimuli other than light, 841–45
    evolution of defensive, 845
    to flooding, 843–44
    to gravity, 841–42
    to heat stress, 844

to light, 835–41
to mechanical stimuli, 842–43
plant hormones and, 824–35
review of, 848–49
to salt stress, 844
signal transduction pathways linking signal
reception to, 821–24
Plant structure, 736–63
cells (*see also* Plant cells)
cells in, 743–45*f*
diversity in, 738
growth and (*see also* Plant growth)
L. Herrera-Estrella's work on, 736–37
hierarchy of organs, tissues, and cells in, 738–45*f*
meristem generation of cells for primary and secondary growth of, 746–47
organs in, 739–42
plant development and, 755–61
primary growth of roots and shoots of, 747–51*f*
review of, 762
secondary growth of stems and roots in woody
plants, 751–55
tissues in, 742–43
Plaque, 914
Plasma, **910**–11
Plasma cells, **942**
Plasma membranes, **98**. *See also* Cellular membranes
animal cell, 100*f*
apoplast, symplast, and transport across plant,
767–71
electron transport chains in prokaryotic, 167,
172–74
hormone receptors in, 977*f*
microfilaments in, 116–17
nuclear envelopes as, 102
plant cell, 101*f*
of prokaryotic and eukaryotic cells, 98–99
receptor proteins in, 210–14
Plasmids, **397**, **560**
eukaryotic gene cloning in bacterial, 398–402
evolution of viruses and, 390
F factor as, in conjugation, 563
gene cloning and, 397
libraries of, 400*f*
producing clones of cells carrying recombinant,
399–400
producing transgenic plants using Ti, 421–22*f*
prokaryotic, 559*f*, **560**
R, and antibiotic resistance in bacteria, 564
Plasmodesmata, **120**
as cell junctions in plants, 120–21
plant cell, 101*f*
plant cell walls and, 119
in plant local cell signaling, 208
symplastic communication and, 782
Plasmodial slime molds, **594**–95
Plasmodium (protist), 579*f*, 583–84, 596, 691
Plasmodium mass, **594**–95
Plasmogamy, **639**
Plasmolysis, **134**, **770**
Plastics, natural, 572
Plastids, **111**
chromalveolates and, 582
endosymbiotic origin of, 516–17
eukaryotic endosymbiosis and evolution of, 576, 577*f*
Plastocyanin, 194
Plastoquinone, 194
Platelet-derived growth factor (PDGF), 241
Platelets, 857*f*, 910*f*, **911**, 912–13
Plate tectonics, **519**–21
Platyhelminthes, 667*f*, 674–76, 960–61
Platypus, 1089
Pleasure, brain activity and, 1072*f*
Pleiotropy, **273**
Plesiosaur fossil, 511*f*
Pleurozium, 609

Plumule, 808
Pluripotent cells, **416**–17*f*
Pneumatophores, 740*f*
Pneumonia, 305–6, 562
Poaching, elephant, 1243
Podium, sea star, 693*f*
Poikilotherms, 863
Point mutations, **344**–46
cancer genes and, 373–74
mutagens as cause of, 346
sickle-cell disease and (*see* Sickle-cell disease)
as sources of genetic variation, 472
types of, 344–46
Poison dart frog, 1197*f*
Poisons. *See* Toxins
Polar bears, 46, 492*f*, 500
Polar covalent bonds, **39**, **46**–47
Polarity, **757**, 856*f*
Polar microtubules, 234
Polar molecules, **46**
Polar side chains, 79*f*
Polar transport, auxin, 827–28
Policy, science and, 29
Poliovirus, 391
Pollen cones, 625
Pollen grains, **620**, 627–28, 631*f*, **803**
Pollen tubes, **803**, 806
Pollination, **620**, **805**
angiosperm cross-pollination, 627–28
asexual reproduction vs., 812
coevolution of flowers and pollinators, 806
cross-pollination in breeding plants, 815–16
flowers and angiosperm, 625–26
flower shape and insect, 632
genetic engineering of flowers to force
self-pollination, 818
insects and, 691
mechanisms of flower, 804*f*–5*f*
G. Mendel's techniques of, 263–64
mutualistic relationships in, 801
seed plant, 620
Pollinators
coevolution of flowers and, 806
reproductive isolation and choice of, 504
Pollution
biomanipulation and, 1206
coral reefs and, 673
lichens and, 650
molluscs and water, 680–81*f*
nutrient, 1254–55
ocean acidification and acid precipitation, 55–56
prokaryotes and bioremediation of, 573
toxin, 1255–56
Polyadenylation signal sequence, 334
Polyandry, 1130–31
Poly-A tail, **334**, 401
Polychaetes (Polychaeta), 681
Polychaos dubia (amoeba), 433
Polyclonal antibodies, 945
Polydactyly, 272
Polygamous mating, **1129**–31
Polygenic inheritance, **274**, 279
Polygyny, 1130–31
Polymerase chain reaction (PCR), **403**
amplifying DNA *in vitro* using, 403–4
diagnosing diseases with, 417
extreme thermophile used in, 567, 1241
in forensic ecology, 1243*f*
in forensic science, 420
gene cloning vs., 404
genetic prospecting with, 566
RT-PCR analysis and, 409*f*
Polymerases, 384–85
Polymerization, 231
Polymers, **68**–69
Polymorphisms, 406, 417–18

Polynucleotides, **87**–88. *See also* Nucleic acids
Polypeptide hormones, 976–77*f*
Polypeptides, **77**
amino acid monomers of, 78–80 (*see also*
Amino acids)
as amino acid polymers, 80
mutations affecting structure and function of, 344–46
one gene-directed production of one, 326 (*see also*
Protein synthesis)
proteins as composed of, 77–80
targeting, to specific locations, 343
translation as synthesis of, 328
translation stages in synthesis of, 340–42
Polyphyletic groups, 542*f*, **543**, 575–76
Polyploidy, **298**, 438, **495**–96
Polyps, 376, **671**
Polyribosomes (polysomes), 341–**42**
Polysaccharides, **70**–74, 106
Polyspermy, 807, 1022–23
Polytomies, **539**
Polytrichum, 608*f*, 609*f*
Pongo, 726
Pons, **1069***f*
Poplar trees, 754–55, 817, 835
Poppy, 631*f*
Population(s), **473**, **1145***f*, **1170**. *See also* Population
conservation; Population ecology
boundaries and size of, 1170–71
carrying capacity and size of, 1177
C. Darwin on natural selection and, 15–16
decline of honeybee, 804*f*
density and dispersion of, 1171–73 (*see also* Density,
population; Dispersion, population)
determining size of, using mark-recapture
method, 1171*f*
diffusion of, of molecules, 132
dynamics of (*see* Population dynamics)
effective size for, 1245–46
evolution of genetic variation in, 259–60 (*see also*
Evolution; Microevolution; Population
genetics)
genetic diversity and, 1239
genetic variation between, and within, 470–71
growth of (*see* Population growth)
human (*see* Human population)
as level of biological organization, 4*f*
metapopulations, 1186–87
minimum viable size for, 1245
natural selection and evolution of, 457–60
regulation of (*see* Population regulation)
using Hardy-Weinberg equation to test evolution
in, 473–76
Population conservation
declining-population approach, 1247–49
small-population approach, 1245–47
weighing conflicting demands in, 1249
Population cycles, 1185–86
Population dynamics, **1184**–87
feedback regulation in, 1182–84
immigration, emigration, and metapopulations in,
1186–87
population cycles and, 1185–86
population density and, 1171*f*–72
stability and fluctuation in, 1184–85
Population ecology, **1145***f*, **1170**–93
density-dependent population regulation in,
1182–84
exponential population growth model in, 1175–77
human population growth in, 1187–91
life history traits produced by natural selection in,
1179–81
logistic population growth model in, 1177–79
population density, dispersion and demographics in,
1170–75
population dynamics in, 1171*f*–72, 1184–87
review of, 1191–92

Population genetics. *See also* Microevolution
  causes of microevolution in, 476–80
  genetic variation within and between populations
      in, 470–71
  sources of genetic variation in, 471–73
  using Hardy-Weinberg equation to test evolution in,
      473–76
Population growth
  density-dependent regulation of, 1182–84
  exponential model of, 1175–77
  human, 1187–91
  logistical model of, 1177–79
  population dynamics and, 1184–87
Population regulation, 1182–88
  mechanisms of density-dependent, 1182–84
  population density and, 1182
  population dynamics and, 1184–87
Pore complexes, 102, 103*f*
Pores, nuclear, 102, 103*f*
Porifera, 667*f*, 670–71
Porphyrin ring, 191*f*
Porpoises, 465–66
Positional information, **370**, **1040**
Position-based mechanisms, plant, 758
Positive feedback, **11**, **861**, **982**
  in endocrine system feedback regulation, 982
  in feedback regulation, 10–11
  in homeostasis, 861
  neuron action potentials and, 1051
  posterior pituitary hormones and, 985
Positive gene regulation in bacteria, 355
Positive gravitropism, 841
Positive pressure breathing, **920**
Positron-emission tomography (PET), 1072*f*
Possum, 722*f*
Posterior end, **658**
Posterior pituitary gland, **984**–85*f*, 986*t*
Postsynaptic cells, 1046–47*f*
Postsynaptic neurons, 1056
Postsynaptic potentials, 1056–57*f*
Post-transcriptional regulation, 356*f*, 362–64
Post-translational modifications, 342
Postzygotic barriers, **489**, 491*f*
Potassium
  cellular membranes and, 125
  as essential element, 32
  human requirements for, 877–78*t*
  plant deficiency in, 791*f*
  plant wilting and, 832
  soil fertilization and, 788
Potassium ions, 1048–53
Potato blight, 579*f*, 588–89
Potatoes, 633, 821–22
Potential, cell developmental, 1038–39
Potential energy, **35**, **143**
Potential evapotranspiration, 1211
Potential range, 1165
Prairie chickens, 478–79
Prairies, 1155*f*
Prairie voles, 1135
Precapillary sphincters, 908
Precipitation
  acid (*see* Acid precipitation)
  climographs of, 1151
  global patterns of, 1146*f*
  primary production and, 1224
  tropical rain forest deforestation and, 633*f*
  water vapor and, 49
Precocious germination, 832
Predation, **1197**
  density-dependent population regulation
      through, 1183*f*
  genetic variation in, 1135–36
  as interspecific interaction, 1197–98
  marine molluscs and, 450–51
  population cycles and, 1185–86

  as risk, 1129
  snake mimicry case study of, 20–23
  symbols for, 1194
  top-down model of trophic control and, 1206
Predators
  as biotic factors limiting species distribution,
      1165–66
  cephalopods as, 680
  evolution of, 657
  insects as, 691
  mass extinctions and, 523–24
  plant recruitment of, as herbivore defense, 845
Predictions
  of paleontology, 510
  scientific, 20
Pregnancy, **1012**–15
  conception and, 1012–13
  detecting disorders during, 1017
  detecting human, 945
  first trimester of, 1013–14
  human, 992–93
  prevention of human, 1015–17
  second and third trimesters of, 1014–15
Pre-mRNA, 328, 334–36, 358, 359*f*
Prenatally and Postnatally Diagnosed Conditions
      Awareness Act, 299
Preprophase band, 756
Prepuce, **1004**
Pressure
  receptors for, 1088, 1092
  root, 773–74
  water potential and, 769–70
Pressure-flow hypothesis, 780–81
Pressure potential, **769**
Presynaptic cells, 1046–47*f*
Presynaptic neurons, 1056
Prey
  defense adaptations of, 1197–98
  genetic variation in selection of, 1135–36
Prezygotic barriers, **489**–90*f*
Priapula, 668*f*
Primary cell walls, **118**–19
Primary cilium, 114
Primary consumers, **1220**
Primary electron acceptors, **193**
Primary growth, plant, **746**
  meristem generation of cells for, 746–47
  of roots, 747–49
  of woody stems, 752*f*
Primary immune response, **939**–40
Primary motor cortex, 1074*f*
Primary oocytes, **1007**f
Primary producers, **1219**–20
Primary production, **1220**–25
  in aquatic ecosystems, 1223–24
  determining, for oceans, 1222*f*
  determining, with satellites, 1221*f*
  ecosystem energy budgets and, 1221–22
  in terrestrial ecosystems, 1224–25
Primary somatosensory cortex, 1074*f*
Primary structure, protein, 82*f*
Primary succession, **1208**–10
Primary transcripts, **328**
Primary visual cortex, **1099**–1100
Primase, **314**
Primates, 723–28
  cloning of, 415
  derived characters of, 723
  HIV in, 550–51
  living, 726–28
  mammalian phylogeny and, 724*f*–25*f*
  phylogenetic tree of, 726*f*
Primer, **314**
Primitive streak, **1030**
Primordial germ cells, 1006*f*–7*f*
Principle of conservation of energy, 144

Printing press, 25
Prions, **393**–94
Probability
  laws of, 269–71
  principle of maximum likelihood and, 545–47
Probiotics, 93
Problem solving, **1126**
Proboscidea, 725*f*
Proboscis, 668*f*, 690*f*, 806
Process, evolutionary, 452, 467, 535, 536
Process pluralism, 535
Producers, **597**
  autotrophs as, 184
  energy flow and, 6–7
  protists as, 597
Production efficiency, **1225**
Products, **42**–43, 633
Progesterone, **992**, 1008
Progestins, 986*t*, **992**, 1016–17
Proglottids, 676
Programmed cell death. *See* Apoptosis
Progymnosperms, **621**
Prokaryotes, 556–74
  adaptive abilities of, 556
  archaea as, 566–67 (*see also* Archaea)
  bacteria and archaea as, 8
  bacteria as, 567–70 (*see also* Bacteria)
  beneficial and harmful impacts of, on humans,
      571–73
  bioremediation using, 1233
  cell signaling in ancient, 207
  cells of (*see* Prokaryotic cells)
  as detritivores, 1220
  ecological roles of, in biosphere, 570–71
  electron transport chains in, 172
  as endosymbionts, 516–17
  first, 514–16
  genetic diversity in, 561–64
  land colonization by, 518–19
  molecular systematics and phylogenies of, 565–70
  nutritional and metabolic adaptations of, 564–65
  photosynthesis in, 184
  review of, 573–74
  shapes of, 557*f*
  size of and number of genes in genomes of, 432–33
  structural and functional adaptations of, 556–61*f*
  taxonomy of, 551–52
Prokaryotic cells, **8**, **98**. *See also* Cell(s)
  DNA replication in, 312–16, 317*f*
  eukaryotic cells vs., 8, 98–99 (*see also* Eukaryotic
      cells)
  horizontal gene transfer in, 534–35
  structure of, 98*f*
Prolactin, **985**, 986*t*, 988, 1011
Prolactin-releasing hormone, 985
Proliferative phase, **1009**
Proline, 79*f*, 331
Prometaphase, **231**, 232*f*
Promiscuous mating, **1129**–31
Promoters, **332**, 333*f*, 792
Proofreading, DNA, 316–18
Propanal, 64*f*
Properties
  atomic structure and, of elements, 32
  electron distribution and chemical, 36
  emergent (*see* Emergent properties)
Prophages, 386–87
Prophase, **231**, 232*f*
Prophase I, 254*f*, 258, 259*f*
Prophase II, 255*f*
Prop roots, 740*f*
Prostaglandins, **979**, 1014–15*f*, 1090
Prostate glands, 980, **1005**
Prosthetic groups, 172–73
Proteases, **885**
Proteasomes, **363**–64

Protected areas, 1251–53
  biodiversity hotspots, 1251–52
  philosophy of nature reserves, 1252
  zoned reserves, 1252–53
Protein Data Bank, 429
Protein hormones, 976–77f
Protein interaction network, yeast, 431
Protein kinases, **215**–17
Protein phosphatases, **216**
Proteins, **77**
  amino acids of, 78–80
  antibiotics and prokaryotic synthesis of, 560
  in bacterial binary fission, 236
  in blood plasma, 910–11
  as built from amino acids, 69
  cell-signaling nuclear responses and, 219
  cell-signaling receptor, 210–14
  in cellular membranes, 126–27
  cellulose-synthesizing, 600–601f
  as composed of polypeptides, 77–80
  Conserved Domain Database (CDD) of structures
      of, 430f
  de-etiolation, in plants, 824
  denaturation and renaturation of, 84–85
  digestion of, 886f
  DNA and synthesis of, 9–10
  in DNA replication (see DNA replication)
  DNA vs., as genetic material, 305, 307f
  domains of, 336
  in electron transport chains, 167, 172–73
  as enzymes, 77, 152, 157 (see also Enzymes)
  essential amino acids, 876
  facilitated diffusion and, 134–35
  folding and post-translational modifications
      of, 342
  folding of, in cells, 85–86f
  four levels of structure of, 81–83f
  as fuel for catabolism, 180
  functions of types of, 78f
  heat-shock, 844
  human dietary deficiencies in, 878
  innate immune response and, 931, 933
  as macromolecules, 68, 77–86
  as measures of evolution, 89
  membrane (see Membrane proteins)
  messenger RNA role in synthesis of, 102
  nucleic acids and synthesis of, 86–87
  phosphorylation and dephosphorylation of, in
      signal transduction, 215–16
  in photosystems, 192–93
  polypeptides vs., 80
  post-translational modification of, in plant re-
      sponses, 823–24
  prions as infectious, 393–94
  production of, by "pharm" animals, 419–20
  production of, in cell cultures, 419
  in prokaryotic flagella, 558–59
  Protein Data Bank of structures of, 429
  proteomics as study of full sets of, 431
  regulation of gene expression by processing and
      degradation of, 363–64
  repressor, 353
  scaffolding, 222–23
  separating, with gel electrophoresis, 405–6
  structure and function of, 80–86f
  synthesis of (see Protein synthesis)
  systems biology approach to studying, 431–32
  transcription factors, 332
  transport, 768, 769f, 771
  in viruses, 383–84
  water-soluble, 51f
Protein synthesis, 325–50
  gene concept and, 347
  gene specification of, 325–31
  genetic code and, 328–31
  mutations affecting, 344–46

protein folding and post-translational
      modifications, 342
  review of, 349–50
  by ribosomes, 102–4
  RNA modification following transcription as phase
      of, 334–36
  summary of, 348f
  targeting polypeptides to specific locations
      following, 343
  transcription and RNA synthesis as phase of, 331–34
  transcription and translation in, 328
  translation and polypeptide synthesis as phase of,
      337–44
Proteobacteria, 568f
Proteoglycans, **119–20**
Proteomes, 431
Proteomics, **431**
Proterozoic eon, 514, 515t
Prothoracicotropic hormone (PITH), 980
Protista, kingdom, 551, 575
Protists, **575**–99
  Archaeplastida and red and green algae, 590–92
  cells of, 101f (see also Eukaryotic cells)
  chromalveolates, 582–89
  contractile vacuoles of, 108
  in domain Eukarya, 13f, 14 (see also Eukarya, domain)
  ecological roles of, 596–97
  endosymbiosis in evolution of, 576, 577f
  excavates, 580–81
  origin of fungi in, 640
  photosynthesis in, 184, 597
  phylogeny of, 576–79f
  review of, 598–99
  rhizarians, 589–90
  sexual life cycle of, 252
  as single-celled eukaryotes, 575–76
  structural and functional diversity of, 576
  symbiotic, 596
  unikonts, 593–96
Protocells, **508**, 509–10
Protonema (protonemata), **606**
Protonephridia, **674**, **960**–61
Proton gradients, 173–74
Proton-motive force, **174**, 176
Proton pumps, **137**, 768, 769f, 828
Protons, **33**
Proto-oncogenes, **373**–74, 376
Protoplast fusion, **814**–15
Protoplasts, **769**, 814–15
Protostome development, **660**–64
Protozoans, 551
Proviruses, **389**–90
Proximal control elements, 359–60
Proximal-distal axis, 1040
Proximal tubule, 963f, **964**
Proximate causation, 1119
Prozac, 1059, 1080
PR proteins, 846
Prusiner, Stanley, 394
Pseudocoelomates, **660**
Pseudogenes, **434**, 463
Pseudopodia, **118**, 139f, 579f, **589**
Pseudostratified columnar epithelium, 856f
Psilophyta, 613
Psilotum, 614f, 615
P site (peptidyl-tRNA binding site), 339f, **340**
Psychoactive drugs, 1058
Pteraspis, 704f
Pterophytes (Pterophyta), **605**, 611f, 613–15
Pterosaurs, **715**, 1114
Puberty, human, 1008
Puffballs, 646
Pufferfish, 850
Pulmocutaneous circuit, **900**–901
Pulmonary circuit, **900**–901
Pulp, fruit, 810

Pulse, **906**
Punctuated equilibria, **502**
Puncture vine, 811f
Punnett squares, **266**, 273–74
Pupil, **1096**–97
Pure elements, 39
Purines, 87f–**88**, 310, 959
Pus, 934
Puszta, 1155f
Pygmy date palm, 631f
Pyramid of net production, 1226
Pyramid of production, 1226
Pyrenean oak, 631f
Pyrimidines, 87f–**88**, 310
Pyrococcus furiosus, 567
Pyruvate
  in fermentation, 177–79
  oxidation of, as stage of cellular respiration, 167–68
  oxidation of, to acetyl CoA, 170
  oxidation of glucose to, by glycolysis, 168–69f
PYY hormone, 893f

Q
Qualitative data, 18
Quantitative approach, G. Mendel's, 262–64
Quantitative characters, **274**, 470
Quantitative data, 18–19
Quaternary structure, protein, **83**f
Quillworts (Lycophyta), 613, 614f
Quorum sensing, 92–93, 207

R
R17 virus, 246–47
Rabbits, 890
Radial canal, sea star, 693f
Radial cleavage, **661**
Radial glia, 1066
Radial symmetry, 632, **658**–59
Radiation, **864**f
  alterations of chromosome structure by, 298
  as cancer treatment, 243
  DNA damage from, 28
  mutagenic, 346
  prokaryotes and, 556
Radiations, adaptive. See Adaptive radiations
Radicle, **808**
Radioactive isotopes, **34**–35f, 307–8, 512, 1230
Radioactive tracers, 34–35f
Radiolarians, **589**
Radiometric dating, **512**
Radula, **677**, 678f
Rafflesia arnoldii, 632f
Rain. See Precipitation
Rain shadow, 1148–49
Random dispersion, 1172f, 1173
Random fertilization, 258–59
Random mating, 474, 475
Random mutations, 259, 297
Randomness, entropy and, 144–45
Range expansions, species, 1164–65
ras gene, **374**–76
Raspberry fruit, 810f
Ras protein, 374
Ratfish, 706f
Ratites (Struthioniformes), **719**
Rattlesnakes, 717, 1089f
Ray-finned fishes (Actinopterygii), 707, **708**, 954–55, 968
Rays, 705–7
Reabsorption, **960**
Reactants, **42**–43
Reaction-center complexes, **192**–93
Reading frame, **331**, 345f, 346
Realized niches, 1195, 1196f
Reasoning
  deductive, 19–20
  inductive, 19

Receptacles, **802**
Reception, **209**
    as cell-signaling stage, 209
    cell-surface transmembrane receptors in, 211*f*–13*f*
    intracellular receptors in, 214
    ligands, ligand binding, and receptor proteins in, 210
    in plant cell signaling, 822
    plasma membrane proteins as receptors in,
        210–13
    sensory, 1086
Receptive fields, 1099
Receptor-mediated endocytosis, 138–**39***f*
Receptor potential, **1086**
Receptor proteins, 78*f*
Receptors
    antigen (*see* Antigen receptors)
    cellular innate immunity and, 932–33
    dendrites as, 1046
    homeostatic, 861
    hormone, 975
    lipid-soluble hormone, 978
    opiate, 1059
    sensory (*see* Sensory receptors)
    somatosensory, 1074–75
    water-soluble hormone, 977–78
Receptor tyrosine kinases (RTKs), **212***f*
    cancer and, 213, 243*f*
    protein phosphorylation by, 215–16
Recessive alleles, **265**–66, 276–77, 483
Recessively inherited human disorders, 276–80
Recessive traits, 264, 265*t*, 277*f*, 290–92
Reciprocal altruism, **1138**–39
Recombinant bacteria, 397
Recombinant chromosomes, **258**, 259*f*
Recombinant DNA, **396**
    ethical issues on, 422–23
    gene cloning and, 397–98
    L. Herrera-Estrella's work with, 736–37
    hirudin from leeches and, 683
    stem cells and, 411
    studying plant development using, 756
    using restrictions enzymes to make, 398
Recombinant plasmids, 399–400
Recombinants (recombinant types), **294**. *See also* Genetic recombination
Recombination frequencies, 296–97
Reconstruction, physical, 1232
Recruitment, motor neuron, 1108
Recruitment of animal predators, plant, 845
Rectum, **889**
Red algae, 576, 577*f*, 579*f*, **590**–91
Red blood cells, 84, 910*f*, 911
Red-cockaded woodpecker, 1248–49
Red colobus monkey, 7*f*
Red deer, 1130*f*
Red kangaroos, 1163–64
Red light, plant responses to, 836–37, 840
Red mangrove, 832*f*
Redox (oxidation-reduction) reactions, **164**–67
    cellular respiration and oxidation of organic fuel
        molecules by, 165
    oxidation and reduction in, 164–65
    photosynthesis as, 188
    stepwise energy harvest via NAD$^+$ and electron
        transport chain in, 165–67
Red tide, 583
Reduced hybrid fertility, 491*f*
Reduced hybrid viability, 491*f*
Reducing agents, **164**–65. *See also* Redox
    (oxidation-reduction) reactions
Reduction, **164**–65, 199. *See also* Redox
    (oxidation-reduction) reactions
Reductional division, 257
Reductionism, 3
Redundancy, genetic code, 330, 344
Redwood trees, 249*f*, 623*f*

Reece, Jane, 29*f*, 93*f*, 247*f*, 451*f*, 535*f*, 737*f*, 851*f*, 1143*f*
Reef builders, ectoproct, 677
Reflexes, 884, **1064**
Refractory period, 1011, **1053**
Regeneration, 682, 692, 997
Regenerative medicine, 416–17*f*
Regional adaptive radiation, 524–25*f*
Regulation
    of afferent neurons in sensory transmission, 1086–87
    of animal digestion, energy storage, and appetite,
        891–95
    by animal endocrine and nervous systems, 859
    of biological clocks, 1070–71*f*
    biology's unifying theme of feedback, 1182
    of blood pressure, 906–7
    cell signaling and, 206
    of cellular respiration via feedback mechanisms, 181
    of cleavage, 1027
    density-dependent factors in population, 1182–84
    of enzymatic catalysis, 158–60
    extracellular matrix role of, 120
    feedback mechanisms of, as biological theme, 10–11
    of gene expression (*see* Gene expression, regulation of)
    homeostatic, 861
    hormonal, of animal sexual reproduction, 1008–11
    hormonal, of human sexual response, 1011
    of muscle contraction, 1106–7*f*
    as property of life, 2*f*
Regulator animals, **860**
Regulators, **860**
Regulatory genes, **353**
Regulatory proteins, 1106–7*f*
Reinforcement, 499–**500**
Rejection, immune, 945–46
Relatedness, altruism and, 1137–38
Relative abundance, **1200**–1201
Relative fitness, **480**
Release factors, 341, 342*f*
Release stage, phage lytic cycle, 385*f*
Releasing, 984–85*f*
Releasing hormones, 985
Renal cortex, **962***f*
Renal medulla, **962***f*
Renal pelvis, **962***f*
Renaturation, protein, 84–85
Renin-angiotensin-aldosterone system (RAAS), **970**–71
Repair, DNA, 316–18
Repetitive DNA, **434**–37
Replication, DNA. *See* DNA replication
Replication fork, **314**
Replicative cycles, viral, 384–90
    of animal viruses, 387–90
    general features of, 384–85
    of phages, 385–87
Repolarization, 1053
Repressible enzymes, 354–55
Repressible operons, 353–55
Repressors, **353**, 824
Reproduction
    alternation of generations in land plants, 602*f*
    animal (*see* Animal reproduction)
    bryophyte, 607–9
    as cell division function, 228*f*
    crustacean, 691
    C. Darwin on natural selection and, 15–16
    delayed, 1188
    of DNA (*see* DNA replication)
    effective population size and, 1246
    endocrine disruptors and human, 992–93
    evolution and differential success in, 259–60, 1002
    fungal, 638–40
    genetics and sexual vs. asexual, 249 (*see also* Asexual
        reproduction; Sexual life cycles; Sexual
        reproduction)
    heterochrony and differential reproductive
        development, 526

    insect, 689
    iteroparity vs. semelparity in, 1180
    life histories and, 1179–81
    natural selection and, 1179
    overreproduction of offspring and natural selection,
        458–59
    pheromones and, 1122
    plant (*see* Plant reproduction)
    as property of life, 2*f*
    prostaglandins and, 980
    protist, 576
    protocell, 509
    rapid, as source of genetic variation in viruses, 472
    rapid prokaryotic, and adaptive evolution, 560–61*f*
    rates of, 1174–75, 1183*f*
    sexual, as source of genetic variation, 472
Reproductive barriers
    reinforcement of, 499–500
    species fusion and weakening of, 500–501*f*
    stability of, and continued hybrid formation, 501
    types of, 490*f*–91*f*
Reproductive cells. *See* Eggs; Gametes; Spermatogonia
Reproductive cloning, 413–15
Reproductive cycles, animal, 998, 999*f*, 1008–10
Reproductive isolation, **489**–91*f*
    allopatric speciation and, 493–95
    hybrid zones and, 498–501
    pollinator choice and, 504
    sexual selection and, 497*f*
    types of reproductive barriers in, 490*f*–91*f*
Reproductive leaves, 742*f*
Reproductive organs, human, 1002–8
    female, 1002–4
    gametogenesis in, 1005–8
    male, 1004–5
Reproductive rates, 1174–75, 1183*f*
Reproductive success, 259–60, 1002
Reproductive tables, **1174**–75
Reptiles (Reptilia), **715**–20
    alligators and crocodiles, 717
    amniotic eggs of, 714*f*
    birds, 717–20
    double circulatory system of, 901*f*
    evolution of, 658
    extraembryonic membranes in, 1031
    hearing and equilibrium in, 1094
    kidney adaptations in, 967
    lepidosaurs, 716–17
    in Mesozoic era, 514
    nitrogenous wastes of, 958–59
    origin and evolutionary radiation of, 715–16
    thermoregulation in, 866
    turtles, 717
Research
    antibodies as tools in, 945
    G. Mendel's, 262–69
    prokaryotes in, 572–73
Research methods
    applying parsimony in molecular systematics, 546*f*
    cell fractionation, 97*f*
    cloning genes in bacterial plasmids, 399*f*
    constructing linkage maps, 296*f*
    crossing pea plants, 263*f*
    detecting specific DNA sequence using nucleic acid
        probe, 402*f*
    determining absorption spectrums using spec-
        trophotometers, 190*f*
    determining population size using mark-recapture
        method, 1171*f*
    determining primary production with satellites, 1221*f*
    dideoxy chain-termination method for DNA
        sequencing, 408*f*
    DNA microarray assay of gene expression
        levels, 411*f*
    freeze-fracture, 126*f*
    gel electrophoresis, 405*f*

hydroponic culture, 790*f*
intracellular recording, 1050*f*
molecular tools for determining microbial
    diversity, 1201*f*
polymerase chain reaction, 404*f*
preparing karyotypes, 250*f*
radioactive tracers, 34*f*
reproductive cloning of mammal by nuclear trans-
    plantation, 414*f*
reverse transcriptase-polymerase chain reaction
    analysis of single gene expression, 409*f*
Southern blotting of DNA fragments, 407*f*
testcrosses, 267*f*
using dendrochronology to study climate, 753*f*
using Ti plasmid to produce transgenic plants, 422*f*
Residual volume, **922**
Resistance genes, 564
Resolution, 95
Resource acquisition, vascular plant, 764–67
    evolution of, 764–65
    overview of, 765*f*
    review of, 783
    root architecture and acquisition of water and
        minerals, 766–67
    shoot architecture and light capture, 765–66
Resource competition, population regulation
        through, 1183*f*
Resource partitioning, **1195**–96
Respiration, cellular. *See* Cellular respiration
Respiratory diseases, human, 1184*f*
Respiratory distress syndrome (RDS), 920
Respiratory media, 915
Respiratory pigments, **923**–25
Respiratory surfaces, 915–16
Respiratory systems, 854*f*, 918–20. *See also* Gas exchange
Response pathways, hormone, 977–78
Responses, **210**, **861**
    cell signaling, 210
    cell-signaling specificity and coordination of, 220–22
    fine-tuning of, 220–23
    homeostatic, 861
    increasing signaling efficiency in, 222–23
    nuclear and cytoplasmic, 219–20
    plant (*see* Plant responses)
    signal amplification in, 220
    signal termination in, 223
Response stage, cell-signaling, 210
Response to environment, as property of life, 2*f*
Rest and digest responses, 1067
Resting potentials, neuron, **1048**–50
    formation of, 1048–49
    modeling of, 1049–50
Resting potential state, action potential, 1052
Restoration ecology, 1232–35
    biological augmentation in, 1233
    biomanipulation of trophic levels in, 1206
    bioremediation in, 1232–33
    worldwide restoration projects, 1233–35*f*
Restriction endonucleases, 398
Restriction enzymes, **385**–86, **398**
Restriction fragment analysis, 406
Restriction fragment length polymorphism (RFLP),
    406, 1201*f*
Restriction fragments, **398**
Restriction sites, **398**
Reticular fibers, 857*f*
Reticular formation, **1070**
Reticulum, 891*f*
Retina, **1096***f*
Retinal, **1097***f*, 1098
Retinitis pigmentosa, 477–78
Retrotransposons, **435**–36
Retroviral vector, gene therapy using, 418*f*
Retroviruses, **388**–90
Reverse transcriptase, **388**–90, 401

Reverse transcriptase-polymerase chain reaction (RT-
    PCR), **409**–10, 417
Reward system, brain, 1080–81
Reward vs. risk, foraging behavior and, 1129
R groups, amino acid, 78–80, 154
Rhabditophora, 674–76
Rhesus macaque (*Macaca mulatta*), 426
Rheumatoid arthritis, 947
Rhine River restoration project, 1235*f*
Rhinoceros, 1179*f*, 1240*f*
Rhizarians (Rhizaria), 579*f*, **589**–90
    cercozoans, 590
    forams, 589–90
    radiolarians, 589
Rhizobacteria, **793**
Rhizobium bacteria, 794–95
Rhizoids, **606**–7, 764. *See also* Roots
Rhizomes, 741*f*
Rhizosphere, **793**
Rhodopsin, **1097***f*, 1098
Rhythm method, **1016**
Ribbon model, 81*f*
Ribbon worms, 668*f*
Riboflavin, 171–72
Ribonucleic acid. *See* RNA (ribonucleic acid)
Ribose, **88**
    in ATP, 149
    as monosaccharide, 70*f*
    in nucleic acids, 87*f*-88
    in RNA, 87*f*-88
Ribosomal RNA (rRNA), **339**
    in eukaryotic cell nucleus, 102
    evolutionary rate of, 548
    gene family of, 437
    simple tree of life based on, 552–53
Ribosomes, **102**, **328**
    anatomy of functioning, 339*f*
    animal cell, 100*f*
    association of, and translation initiation, 340
    plant cell, 101*f*
    polyribosomes, 341–42
    of prokaryotic and eukaryotic cells, 98
    prokaryotic cell, 98*f*, 560
    protein synthesis and, 87
    rough ER and, 105
    in translation, 246
Ribozymes, 152, **336**, **509**–10
Ribulose, 70*f*
Rice, 433*t*, 491*f*, 633, 795, 830, 835, 1241
Rieseberg, Loren, 503*f*
Right atrium, 902*f*, 903*f*
Right-left axis, 1036–38
Right ventricle, 902*f*, 903*f*
Ring of life, 553
Ring spot virus, 816
Ring structures
    of carbon skeletons, 61
    of cellulose-synthesizing proteins, 600–601*f*
    of glucose, 71*f*
Ringworm, 650
Rising phase, action potential, 1052
Risk
    cardiovascular disease risk factors, 914–15
    foraging behavior and, 1129
    plant biotechnology and, 819
Rituals, courtship. *See* Courtship rituals
Riverine wetlands, 1159*f*
River otters, 860*f*
Rivers, 1160*f*
RNA (ribonucleic acid), **86**
    ATP in, 149
    in circadian clock genes during hibernation, 871*f*
    components of, 87–88
    development of self-replicating, 509–10
    in DNA replication, 314

elongation of strands of, 333
gene density in genomes and, 434
gene expression and, 9–10
as genetic material of viruses, 388–90
messenger (*see* Messenger RNA (mRNA))
as molecular homology, 463
noncoding, and regulation of gene expression, 364–66
post-transcription modification of, 334–36
in regulation of cleavage, 1027
replicative cycles of RNA viruses, 388*f*
ribosomal (*see* Ribosomal RNA)
ribosomal RNA gene family, 437
RNA-RNA base pairing, 247
roles of DNA vs., 86–87
sequencing, 246–47
J. A. Steitz's work on, 246–47
structure of, 88–89*f*
transcription and synthesis of, 328, 329*f*, 331–34
transfer (*see* Transfer RNA)
viruses, 382, 384–85, 387*t*, 393
RNA cataloging, 534
RNA enzymes, 152
RNA interference (RNAi), **365**, **411**
RNA polymerases, 85–86*f*, **331**–34
RNA processing, **334**–36, 348*f*, 359*f*, 362–63
RNA-RNA base pairing, 247
RNA splicing, 247, **334**–36, 362–63
Roadrunner, 967*f*
Rock python, 881*f*
Rocks
    dating of, 512
    species distributions and, 1167
Rodents (Rodentia), 725*f*, 890
Rods, 1096*f*, **1097***f*, 1098–99, 1100–1101
Rod-shaped prokaryotes, 557*f*
Romanesco, 738
Roosevelt elk, 58*f*
Root caps, **747**
Rooted phylogenetic trees, **539**
Root fungi, 519
Root hairs, **739**–40, 772
Root pressure, **773**–74
Roots, **612**, **739**–40
    absence of, 615
    apical meristems of, 603*f*
    architecture of, and acquisition of water and
        minerals, 766–67
    drought responses of, 843
    evolution of, in vascular plants, 612
    fungal mycorrhizae and, 767
    gravitropism in, 841–42
    monocot vs. eudicot, 631*f*
    mycorrhizal fungi and, 638
    nitrogen-fixing bacteria and legume, 794–95
    primary growth of, 747–49
    rhizoids vs., 606–7
    secondary growth of, 751–55
    soil texture and, 786
    transpiration of water and minerals from, to shoots
        via xylem, 772–76
Root systems, **739**
Rose, Mark, 221*f*
Rosy periwinkle, 1241
Rotifers (Rotifera), 667*f*, 676–77
Rough ER, 100*f*, 101*f*, 104*f*-5
Round dance, honeybee, 1121
Round window, **1092**
Roundworms, 669*f*, 683–84, 1036, 1111
Rous, Peyton, 377
Roux, Hans, 1038*f*
R plasmids, **564**
rRNA. *See* Ribosomal RNA
R-selection, **1181**
RU486 (mifepristone), 1017
Rubisco (RuBP carboxylase), **199**

Ruffed grouse, 1250
Rule of multiplication, 474
Rumen, 891*f*
Ruminants, **890**–91
Rusts, 646
Ryba, Nick, 1102*f*
Ryther, John, 1223*f*

S

Saccharomyces cerevisiae (yeast), 206–7, 431, 433, 640*f*, 651–52, 1183*f*
Saccule, **1093**–94
Sac fungi, 642*f*, 644–46
Safety issues
    DNA technology, 422–23
    transgenic crop, 817–19
Sahelanthropus tchadensis, 728
Salamanders, 491*f*, 494–95, 526, 710–12, 897, 1038*f*, 1063*f*
Salicylic acid, **847**
Salinity
    extreme halophiles and, 566, 567
    osmosis, water balance, and, 133–34
    prokaryotes and, 556
    soil salinization and, 788
    species distributions and, 1166
Saliva, 883–84
Salivary glands, **883**–84, 976
Salmon, 875, 955, 1166, 1180
Salmonella species, 572
Saltatory conduction, **1054**
Salt concentration, aquatic biome, 1157
Salt marshes, 1200
Salts, **40**. *See also* Sodium chloride
    in blood plasma, 910–11
    osmoregulation of, 953–58
Saltwater, 953, 954, 957–58
Salty taste, 1101–2
Sampling techniques, population, 1171
San Andreas fault, 520
Sand dollars, 228*f*, 694, 1023*f*
Sandhill cranes, 1124
Sanger, Frederick, 80, 246–47, 409
Sapwood, 754
Sarcomeres, **1104**
Sarcoplasmic reticulum (SR), **1106**–7*f*, 1109
Sarcopterygii, 707
Sargasso Sea nutrient enrichment experiment, 1223*t*
Sarin, 157, 1058
Satellites, determining primary production with, 1221*f*
Satiety center, 893, 894*f*
Saturated enzymes, 155
Saturated fats, 75–76, 128
Saturated fatty acids, **75**–76
Saurischians, 715–16
Savannas, 730, **1154***f*
Savory taste, 1101–2
Scaffolding proteins, **222**–23
Scala naturae (scale of nature), Aristotle's, 453
Scale-eating fish, 484, 485*f*
Scales
    fish, 707
    reptile, 715
Scallops, 679
Scanning electron microscope (SEM), **95**, **96***f*
Scarlet fever, 387
Schatten, Gerald, 1024*f*
Scheer, Justin, 159*f*
Schematic model, ribosome, 339*f*
Schemske, Douglas, 504
Schistosomiasis, 675
Schizophrenia, 20, **1079**–80
Schmidt-Nielsen, Knut, 957–58, 1114
Schwann cells, **1054**, 1065*f*

Science, **18**–25
    biology as scientific study of life, 1–2
    cooperation in social process of, 23–24
    flexibility of scientific method in, 20
    hypotheses, hypothesis testing, and deductive reasoning in, 19–20
    inquiry process of, 18 (*see also* Inquiry, scientific; Inquiry studies)
    G. Mendel's experimental quantitative approach, 262–64
    policy and, 29
    questions that can and cannot be addressed by, 20
    research methods (*see* Research methods)
    review of, 25–26
    technology, society, and, 24–25 (*see also* Biotechnology)
    theories in, 23
    types of data and inductive reasoning in, 18–19
    value of diverse viewpoints in, 25
Scientific method, 20. *See also* Science
Scion, **814**
Sclera, 1096*f*
Sclereids, **744***f*
Sclerenchyma cells, **744***f*
Scolex, 676
Scorpions, 669*f*, 686, 687*f*
Scrapie, 393
Scr gene, 526
Scrotum, **1004**
Scutellum, 808
Scyphozoans (Scyphozoa), 672
Sea anemones, 659*f*, 672*f*, 997*f*
Seabirds, 957–58
Sea cucumbers, 694
Sea daisies, 692–93*f*
Seagrasses, 600
Sea horse, 708*f*
Sea lampreys, 703
Sea lettuce, 591*f*
Sea lilies, 694
Seals, 853*f*, 925–26
Sea otters, 1204–5
Sea slugs, 678*f*, 996
Seasonality, 1147
Seasonal turnover, lake, 1157–58
Sea spiders, 686
Sea squirts, 700*f*
Sea stars (starfish), 692–93*f*, 916*f*, 1063*f*, 1204–5
Sea surface temperature (SST), 597*f*
Sea urchins, 145*f*, 491*f*, 669*f*, 694, 1022, 1023*f*, 1028, 1165–66, 1194
Sea wasps, 672
Seawater, 953, 954, 957–58
Seaweed, 579*f*, 586, 591, 1165–66
Secondary cell walls, **119**
Secondary compounds, 604
Secondary consumers, **1220**
Secondary endosymbiosis, **576**, 577*f*
Secondary growth, plant, **746**, 751–55
    cork cambium and periderm production in, 754
    evolution of, 754–55
    meristem generation of cells for, 746–47
    of stems and roots in woody plants, 751–55
    vascular cambium and secondary vascular tissue for, 751–54
    of woody stems, 752*f*
Secondary immune response, **939**–40
Secondary oocytes, **1007***f*
Secondary production, **1225**–27
    production efficiency in, 1225
    trophic efficiency and ecological pyramids in, 1225–26
Secondary structure, protein, **82***f*
Secondary succession, **1208**–10
Secondary vascular tissue, 751–54
Second law of thermodynamics, **145**, 1219

Second messengers, **216**, **822**
    calcium ions, inositol trisphosphate (IP_3), and diacylglycerol (DAG) as, 217–18
    cyclic AMP as, 216–17
    in hormone pathways, 978
    neurotransmitters and, 1057
    in plant signal transduction, 822–23
    sensory amplification and, 1087–88
Second trimester, 1014
Secretin, **892***f*, 981–82
Secretions, **960**
    cell signaling and, 975–76
    hormone (*see* Hormones)
    of liver, 887
    of pancreas, 887
    of small intestine, 887
    stomach gastric juice as, 885–86
Secretory phase, **1010**
Secretory proteins, 105
Secretory systems, prokaryotic, 559
Secretory tubules, marine bird, 957*f*
Seed coat, **808**
Seedless vascular plants, **605**, 610–15. *See also* Plant(s)
    gametophyte-sporophyte relationships in, 619*f*
    importance of, 615
    life cycle of fern, 611*f*
    origin and traits of, 610–13
    phylogeny of, 605*t*, 613–15
Seed plants, 605–6, 618–35. *See also* Plant(s)
    advantages of gametophyte reduction for, 618–19
    angiosperms, 619*f*, 625–32 (*see also* Angiosperms)
    domestication of, 618, 633
    evolutionary advantage of seeds for, 620–21
    gymnosperms, 619*f*, 620*f*, 621–25 (*see also* Gymnosperms)
    heterospory among, 619
    importance of, to human welfare, 618, 632–34
    ovules and production of eggs in, 619–20
    phylogeny of, 605*t*
    pollen and production of sperm in, 620
    products from, 633
    review of, 634–35
    terrestrial adaptations of, 618–21
    threats to biodiversity of, 633–34
Seeds, **605**, **618**. *See also* Fruits
    abscisic acid in dormancy of, 832
    dispersal of, 626*f*, 811*f*
    dormancy of, 808–9
    embryo development and, 807–8
    endosperm development and, 807
    evolutionary advantage of, 620–21
    fruits and angiosperm, 626
    germination of, and seedling development, 809
    gibberellins in germination of, 831
    glyoxysomes in, 111
    phytochromes and germination of, 836–37
    strigolactones in germination of, 832
    structure of mature, 808
    variation in size of crops of, 1181*f*
Seehausen, Ole, 497*f*
Segmental ganglia, earthworm, 682*f*
Segmented bodies, vertebrate and chordate, 1032–33
Segmented worms, 668*f*, 681–83
Segregation, law of, 264, **265**–67, 286–87*f*
Seizures, 1053
Selective breeding, 458–59*f*
Selective degradation, 363–64
Selective inhibition, enzyme, 157
Selective permeability, **125**, 131–32, 1048, 1049*f*
Selenium, 1198
Self-assembly, protocell, 509
Self-fertilization, mechanisms for preventing angiosperm, 813
Self-incompatibility, **813**
Selfing, 813

Self-pollination, 264f
Self-pruning, 766
Self-replicating molecules, 507–10
Self-thinning, 781
Self-tolerance, 938
Semelparity, **1180**
Semen, 980, **1005**, 1012
Semicircular canals, **1091**f, 1093f
Semiconservative model, DNA replication, **311**–12
Semilunar valves, **903**
Seminal vesicles, **1005**
Seminiferous tubules, **1004**, 1006f, 1010–11
Senescence, 833–**34**
Senile dementia, 85
Sensitive period, **1123**
Sensitive plants, 782, 842–43
Sensors, homeostatic, **861**
Sensory adaptation, **1088**
Sensory neurons, **1046**, 1047f, 1064f
Sensory pathways, 1086–88
    amplification and adaptation in, 1087–88
    perception in, 1087
    sensory reception and transduction in, 1086
    transmission in, 1086–87
Sensory reception, **1086**
Sensory receptors, **1086**, 1088–90
    chemoreceptors, 1088–89f
    electromagnetic receptors, 1089
    mechanoreceptors, 1088
    nociceptors (pain receptors), 1089–90
    thermoreceptors, 1089
Sensory systems, 1085–1117
    arthropod, 686
    mechanoreceptors for hearing and equilibrium in, 1090–94
    motor systems and, 1085–86, 1103–4 (see also Motor systems)
    muscle contraction and, 1103–10
    review of, 1115–16
    scientific data and, 18
    sensory pathways in, 1086–88
    sensory receptors in, 1088–90
    shark, 706
    skeletal systems, locomotion, and, 1110–15
    snake, 717
    taste and smell receptors in, 1101–3
    visual receptors in, 1095–1101
Sensory transduction, **1086**, 1092–93, 1098
Sepals, **625**, **802**
Separase, 234
Separate electron orbitals model, 37f
Septa, **637**
September equinox, 1147f
Septic shock, 934
Sequencing, DNA. See DNA sequencing; Genome sequencing
Sequencing by synthesis technique, 428–29
Sequoia trees, 623f, 754f
Serial endosymbiosis, **516**–17
Serial transfer, 561f
Serine, 79f, 215
Serotonin, **1058**–59
Serpentine plant communities, 32
Serpentine soil, 785
Sertoli cells, 1010
Serum, 910
Seta, sporophyte, **609**
Set point, homeostatic, **861**
Severe combined immunodeficiency (SCID), 418, 948
Sex
    cell signaling and, 206–7, 219–20, 221f
    chromosomal basis of, 289–90
    determination of, by mammalian sex hormones, 992
    genomic imprinting and, 300–301
    nitric oxide and, 979
    systems for determination of, 289–90

Sex chromosomes, **250**
    aneuploidy of human, 299–300
    as chromosomal basis of sex, 289–90
    human, 250–51, 289f
    inactivation of x-linked genes in female mammals, 291–92
    inheritance of x-linked genes, 290–91
    patterns of inheritance of, 289–92
Sex hormones, 992–93
    endocrine disruptors and, 992–93
    functional groups and, 63
    as intracellular chemical signals, 214
    regulation of mammalian reproduction by, 1008–11
    role of, in mammalian sex determination, 992f
    smooth ER synthesis of, 105
    as steroids, 77
Sex-linked genes, **290**
    inheritance and, 290–92
    linked genes vs., 292
Sex pili, 558, 562–63
Sex reversal, 999
Sexual dimorphism, **482**, 1130
Sexual intercourse, 1011, 1015–17, 1059. See also Contraception, human
Sexual life cycles, 248–61. See also Genetics; Heredity; Inheritance; Sexual reproduction
    alternation of fertilization and meiosis in, 250–53 (see also Fertilization, reproductive; Meiosis)
    angiosperm, 802f
    behavior of chromosomes in, as physical basis of Mendelian inheritance, 286–89
    evolution and genetic variation produced in, 257–60
    human chromosome sets in, 250–52
    inheritance of genes in, 248–49
    karyotypes of chromosomes and, 250f
    meiosis and three types of, 252–53
    protist, 576
    review of, 260–61
Sexually transmitted diseases (STDs), 569f, 580, 949–50, 1013, 1016. See also AIDS (acquired immunodeficiency syndrome); HIV (human immunodeficiency virus)
Sexual reproduction, **249**, **996**. See also Sexual life cycles
    angiosperm asexual reproduction vs., 812–13
    in angiosperms, 801–11f
    animal, 655 (see also Animal reproduction)
    asexual reproduction vs., 996–97
    bryophyte, 607–9
    embryonic development in, 1011–18 (see also Embryonic development)
    as evolutionary enigma, 997–98
    flowers and angiosperm, 625–26
    fungal, 639
    gamete production and delivery in, 1000–1002
    gametogenesis in, 1005–8
    hormonal regulation of animal, 1008–11
    human reproductive organs in, 1002–8
    inheritance and, 249 (see also Sexual life cycles)
    insect, 689
    microevolution due to, 482–83
    reproductive cycles in, 998, 999f
    as source of genetic variation, 472
    variations in patterns of, 998–99
Sexual response, human, 1011
Sexual selection, **482**–83, 1131–33
    female mate choice in, 1131–32
    male competition in, 1132–33
    reproductive isolation and, 497f
    sympatric speciation and, 497
S genes, 813
Shade avoidance, plant, 837
Shaffer, Mark, 1246–47
Shannon diversity, **1200**–1201
Shapes
    cell, 116–17, 118
    enzyme, 153–54, 158–59, 215–16

insect pollinators and flower, 632
    molecular, 41–42
    morphogenesis and cell, 1033–34
    prokaryotic, 557f
Shapiro, Michael, 528f
Shared ancestral characters, **543**
Shared derived characters, **543**
Sharks, 705–7, 954–55
Sheep, 1170, 1182, 1185
Shelf fungi, 646
Shell drilling adaptation, 523–24
Shells, electron, 35–37
Shells, marine mollusc, 450–51
Shigella bacteria, 564
Shivering thermogenesis, 866–67, 868
Shmoos (yeast cells), 221f
Shoots
    apical meristems of, 603f
    light capture and architecture of, 765–66
    primary growth of, 749–51f
    transpiration of water and minerals from roots to, via xylem, 772–76
Shoot systems, **739**, 828f
Short-day plants, **839**
Short tandem repeats (STRs), 420–21, **436**–37
Short-term memory, **1077**
Shrimp, 446f, 494, 691
Sibling species, 494
Sickle-cell disease, **84**, **277**–78, **911**
    malaria and heterozygote advantage in, 278, 484f
    pleiotropy and, 273
    point mutations and, 344, 472
    protein primary structure changes and, 84
    as recessively inherited, 277–78
    restriction fragment analysis and, 406
    as topic at different levels of biology, 24
Side-blotched lizards, 1133
Side chains, amino acid, 78–80
Sidedness, cellular membrane, 130–31f
Sieve plates, **745**f, 779
Sieve-tube elements, **745**f
Sieve tubes, 779, 781f
Signaling, cell. See Cell signaling
Signal peptides, **343**
Signal-recognition particles (SRPs), **343**
Signals, animal, **1120**–22
Signal transduction, **977**. See also Signal transduction pathways; Transduction
    in hormone pathways, 977–78
    membrane proteins and, 129f
Signal transduction pathways, **207**
    coordinate control of, 362
    evolution of, 207
    general model for, in plants, 822f
    induction in differential gene expression and, 367, 368f
    integration of, in apoptosis, 223–25
    linking signal reception to plant responses, 821–24
    neurotransmitters and, 1057
    second messengers in, 216–18
    sensory amplification in, 1087–88
    in transduction stage of cell signaling, 210, 214
    in visual sensory transduction, 1098
Sign stimulus, **1119**
Silencing
    gene expression, 410–11
    transcription, 360, 366
Silent mutations, **344**, 345f, 470–71
Silent Spring (book), 1256
Silk, 82f, 687
Silkworm moths, 976, 1088–89f
Silverfish, 690f
Silverman, Mike, 92
Silversword plants, 540
Silver-washed fritillaries, 1149
Similarity, species and, 489f

Simple columnar epithelium, 856f
Simple endocrine pathway, 981
Simple fruits, **810**
Simple leaves, 741f
Simple neuroendocrine pathway, 981
Simple sequence DNA, **436**–37
Simple squamous epithelium, 856f
Singer, S. J., 126
Singing, fruit fly, 1120f
Single bonds, **38**
Single-celled organisms
    eukaryotes and protists as, 575–76
    first, 514–17
Single circulation, **900**
Single-lens eyes, **1096**–97
Single nucleotide polymorphisms (SNPs), **411**–12,
    417–18, 445
Single-strand binding proteins, **314**
Single-stranded DNA (ssDNA) viruses, 387t
Single-stranded RNA (ssRNA) viruses, 387t, 388f
Sinoatrial (SA) nodes, **904**
Siphons, cone snail, 850
Sirenia, 725f
Sister cells, 228
Sister chromatid cohesion, 229, 253, 257
Sister chromatids, **229**–30, 251f, 255f, 257
Sister taxa, **538**–39
Sitis inversus, 1042
Size
    carrying capacity and population, 1177–79
    evolution of axon, 1054
    of genomes, 432–33
    of hormones, 209
    locomotion costs and, 1115
    metabolic rate and animal body, 870
    of offspring litter or clutch, 1179
    population, 1170–71
    prokaryote, 557–58
    of prokaryotic vs. eukaryotic cells, 8f, 98
    protist, 575
    of skeletons, 1112–13
    variation in seed crop, 1181f
Skeletal muscle, 858f, **1104**–9
    nervous system regulation of tension of,
        1108–9f
    regulation of contraction of, 1106–7f
    sliding-filament model of muscle contraction and,
        1104–6
    types of fibers in, 1109
Skeletal systems, 1110–13
    endoskeletons, 1112
    energy costs of locomotion in, 1114–15
    exoskeletons, 1111–12
    hydrostatic skeletons, 1111
    interaction of muscles and skeletons in locomotion
        in, 1110–11 (see also Locomotion)
    size and scale of skeletons in, 1112–13
    types of, 1111–13
Skeletons, carbon, 61–63
Skin
    cancer of, 28, 318, 1259
    color of, 988
    human, 1088f
    mammalian, 864
    pigmentation of human, 274
Skinner, B. F., 1125
Skulls, human vs. chimpanzee, 525–26, 541
Skunks, 490f
Slash-and-burn agriculture, 634
Sleep, brain functions and, 1067–70
Sleeping sickness, 580–81, 691, 948
Sleep movements, plant, 838
Sliding-filament model, **1104**–6
Slime, hagfish, 702
Slime bacteria, 207f
Slime layer, 558

Slime molds, 594–96, 1186
Slow block to polyspermy, **1023**
Slow-twitch fibers, **1109**
Slugs, 677
Small interfering RNAs (siRNAs), **365**, 366
Small intestine, **887**
    absorption in, 887–88
    digestion in, 886f, 887–88
    evolutionary adaptations of, 890
    secretions of, 887
Small nuclear ribonucleoproteins (snRNPs), 247, 335
Small nuclear RNA (snRNA), 335–36
Small-population approach, population conservation,
    1245–47
Smallpox, 391, 945
Small-scale mutations, 344–46
Smart plants, 792
Smithells, Richard, 879
Smithies, Oliver, 410
Smooth ER, 100f, 101f, 104f–**5**
Smooth muscle, **858**f, **1110**
Smuts, 646
Snails, 490f, 503–4, 677, 680–81f
Snakes, 20–23, 482f, 716f, 717, 871, 890, 945, 1089f,
    1135–36, 1242
Snapdragons, 271–72
Snapping shrimp, 494
Snook, Rhonda, 1002f
Snowball Earth hypothesis, 517–18
Snow geese, 1119f
Snow pea, 631f
Snowshoe hares, 1185–86
Snyder, Solomon, 1059
Soapberry bugs, 461
Soay sheep, 1170, 1182, 1185
Social behavior, 1139
Social learning, **1127**–28, 1132
Society
    plant biotechnology and, 819
    population age structure and, 1189
    science, technology, and, 24–25
    science as social process, 23–24
Sociobiology, **1139**
Sociobiology: The New Synthesis (book), 1139
Sockeye salmon, 955f
Sodium, 32t, 877–78t
Sodium chloride, 31, 39–40
    dissolving of, in water, 50–51f
    elimination of excess, by marine birds, 957–58
    human diets and, 877–78t
    kidney processing of, 965–67
    nephron processing of, 964–65
    plant responses to excessive, 844
    in treating diarrhea, 137–38
Sodium ions, 1048–53
Sodium-potassium pump, **136**
    as active transport, 136
    membrane proteins and, 137
    neuron resting potential and, 1048–53
Software, systems biology and, 430–32
Soil
    bacteria in, 568f, 570, 792–95
    bryophyte reduction of nitrogen leaching
        from, 609f
    determining diversity of bacteria in, 1201f
    phytoremediation of, 789
    plant resource acquisition from, 766–67
    plant response to excessive salt in, 844
    serpentine, 785
    species distributions and, 1167
    sustainable agriculture and conservation of, 787–89
    texture of, 786
    topsoil composition, 786–87
Soil conservation, 787–89
    adjusting soil pH in, 788
    controlling erosion in, 788–89

    fertilization in, 788
    irrigation in, 787–88
    phytoremediation in, 788–89
Soil horizons, **786**
Soil worm. See Caenorhabditis elegans (soil worm)
Solar energy. See also Energy; Sunlight
    global energy budget and, 1221
    in photosynthesis, 43, 184
    transfer and transformation of, as theme in biology,
        6–7
Solid water. See Ice
Solomon, Susan, 28–29, 50, 1258–59
Solute potential, **769**
Solutes, **50**
    animal osmoregulation of, 953–58
    concentrations of, in aqueous solutions, 51–52
    diffusion of, 132–33
    effects of, on water potential, 769–70
    short-distance transport of, across plant plasma
        membranes, 768, 769f
    two-solute model of kidney water conservation,
        965–67
Solutions, **50**
Solvents, **50**–52
Somatic cells, **229**–30, **249**
Somatosensory cortex, 1074–75
Somites, 700, **1032**–33
Songs
    courtship, 1134–35
    learning of, by birds, 1126–27
Sonic hedgehog growth factor, 1041
Soredia, **649**
Sori, **612**
Sound, 1088, 1090–94
Sour taste, 1101–2
South Africa, 1235f
South American vampire bats, 968–69
South Atlantic Subtropical Gyre, 1148f
Southern, Edwin, 406
Southern blotting, **406**–7
South Pacific Subtropical Gyre, 1148f
Soybeans, 794–95, 993
Space-filling models, 38f, 41f, 60f, 76f, 81f, 309f
Spacek, Sissy, 248
Spanish flu, 391f, 392
Spatial learning, **1124**–25
Spatial summation, **1056**–57f
Spawning, 999–1000
Speciation, **488**–506. See also Evolution
    allopatric, 493–95
    allopatric vs. sympatric, 493f, 497–98
    as conception bridge between microevolution and
        macroevolution, 488
    C. Darwin on, 457–60
    differential, and species selection, 530
    forest edges and, 1250
    genetics of, 503–4
    geographic separation and, 493–98
    hybrid zones, reproductive isolation, and, 498–501
    macroevolution and, 504
    morphological, ecological, and phylogenetic species
        concepts and, 492
    orthologous genes and, 548, 549f
    reproductive isolation and biological species concept,
        488–92
    review of, 505
    sympatric, 495–98
    time course of, 501–3
Species, **489**
    adaptive radiations of, and tree of life, 16–17 (see also
        Phylogenetic trees)
    biological concept of, 488–92
    classification of, 12–14, 453–54, 537–38 (see also
        Taxonomy)
    communities and, 4f (see also Communities;
        Community ecology)

comparing developmental processes of, 445–47
comparing genomes of, 442–45
with complete genome sequences available, 426, 432
cross-species gene expression and evolutionary
    ancestry of, 403
C. Darwin's theory of origin of, 14–16, 457–60 (*see
    also* Evolution; Natural selection)
determining number of genes in, 432, 433*t*
discovery of new, 1238
distributions of (*see* Species distributions)
diversity of (*see* Biodiversity; Species diversity)
dominant and keystone, 1204–5
edge, 1250
endangered or threatened, 1239–40, 1251
endemic, 466
extinction of mollusc, 680–81*f*
extinctions of (*see* Extinctions; Mass extinctions)
fusion of, 500–501*f*
geographic distribution of, 466
homologous genes in, 548, 549*f*
identifying, of whale meat, 539*f*–40
introduced, 1242–43
keystone, 1249
loss of amphibian, 712
loss of seed plant, 633–34
metagenomics and genome sequencing of groups of,
    428–29
morphological, ecological, and phylogenetic
    concepts of, 492
morphology and, 488
origin of (*see* Speciation)
vertebrate, 697
Species-area curve, **1211**–12
Species distributions, 1163–67
    abiotic factors in, 1166–67
    in aquatic biomes, 1158
    biotic and abiotic factors in, 1163–64
    biotic factors in, 1165–66
    dispersal factors in, 1164–65
    ecological time vs. evolutionary time in, 1163
    factors limiting, 1164*f*
    global climate change and, 1148–49
    habitat selection behavior and, 1165
    natural range expansions and adaptive radiations in,
        1164–65
    rocks and soil in, 1167
    salinity and, 1166
    species transplants in, 1165
    sunlight availability and, 1166–67
    temperature and, 1166
    water and oxygen availability and, 1166
Species diversity, **1200**. *See also* Biodiversity; Species
    richness
    benefits of, 1240–41
    biogeographical factors affecting, 1211–13
    community stability and, 1201–2
    crisis in, 1239–40
    ecological succession and, 1208–10
    human impacts on, 1210
    intermediate disturbances and, 1207–8
    species richness, relative abundance, and,
        1200–1201
    trophic structure and, 1202–6
Species richness, **1200**–1201
    island equilibrium model and, 1212–13
    latitudinal gradients of, 1211
    species-area curve of, 1211–12
Species selection, 530
Species transplants, 1165
Specific heat, **48**–49
Specificity
    cell-signaling, 220–22
    enzyme substrate, 153–54
    PCR, 404
    viral, 384

Specific transcription factors, 359–60, 824
Spectrophotometer, **190**
Speech
    brain function and, 1073–74
    FOXP2 gene and, 443–44
Spemann, Hans, 1038, 1039
Spemann's organizer, 1039–40
Sperm, **996**. *See also* Fertilization, reproductive
    acrosomal reaction in, 1022
    biased usage of, in female fruit flies, 1002*f*
    chromosomes in human, 229–30
    competition, 1002, 1130
    conception and, 1012
    flagellated, in land plants, 601
    as male gametes, 996, 1001–2
    mammalian sex determination and, 290
    pollen and production of, in seed plants, 620
    spermatogenesis and, 1005–6*f*
    sperm binding during fertilization, 1023, 1024
Spermathecae, 689, **1001**–2
Spermatids, 1006*f*
Spermatocytes, 1006*f*
Spermatogenesis, **1005**–6*f*
Spermatogonia, **1006***f*
Sphagnum moss, 603*f*, 610, 1209–10
S phase, **231**
Spheniciformes, 719
Sphenophyta, 613
Spherical prokaryotes, 557*f*
Sphincters, **883**–84
Sphygmomanometer, 907*f*
Spiders, 686–87
Spiegelman, Sol, 534, 535
Spike mosses (Lycophyta), 613, 614*f*
Spina bifida, 1033
Spinal cords, 1063–65
Spines, 693*f*, 742*f*
Spinnerets, 687
Spiny-headed worms, 668*f*
Spiny mouse, 1196
Spiral cleavage, **660**
Spiral phyllotaxy, 766
Spiral prokaryotes, 557*f*
Spiral valve, shark, 706
Spirituality, 1143
Spirochetes, 569*f*
Spliceosomes, 247, **335**
Split-brain effect, 1073–74
Sponges (Porifera), 518, 662, 667*f*, 670–71
Spongocoel, **670**
Spongy mesophyll, 750
Spontaneous abortions, 297, 1017
Spontaneous mutations, 346
Spontaneous processes, **145**–48
Sporangia, 603*f*, 609, 612–13, 625, 643–44
Spores, 602*f*, **638**
    brown algae, 587
    cell signaling and bacterial, 207*f*
    fungal, 638–40
    meiosis and, 263
    seeds vs., 620–21
    variations of, in vascular plants, 612–13
    walled, in land plants, 603*f*
Sporocytes, 603*f*
Sporophylls, **612**–13
Sporophytes, **602***f*
    of bryophytes, 609
    gametophyte relationships with, in plants, 619*f*
    of land plants, 602*f*
    pine trees as, 625
    in seedless vascular plants, 611–12
Sporopollenin, **601**, 603*f*
Sporozites, 583
Spotted ratfish, 706*f*
Spotted skunks, 490*f*

Squamous epithelium, 856*f*
Squids, 142, 677, 680, 1046*f*, 1051, 1063*f*
Squirrel monkeys, 1100
Squirrels, 493*f*
Srb, Adrian, 326, 327*f*
S-shaped logistical growth curve, 1178–79*f*
Stability
    community, 1201–2, 1207
    free energy and, 146–47*f*
    hybrid zone, 501
    population, 1184–85, 1188
Stabilizing selection, **481**
Stable isotopes, 34
Staghorn coral, 1214
Staghorn fern, 798*f*
Stahl, Franklin, 312
Stalk-eyed flies, 1131
Stamens, 263, **626**, **802**
Staminate flowers, 813
Standard metabolic rate (SMR), **870**
Standing crop, 1221, 1225*f*
Stanley, Steven, 530
Stanley, Wendell, 382
Staphylococcus aureus, 461–62
Star anise, 630*f*
Starches, **71**
    as fuel for catabolism, 180
    as product of photosynthesis, 203
    as storage polysaccharides, 71–72
Starfish (sea stars), 692–93*f*
Starling, 1243
Star-nosed moles, 1085–86
Start codons, 330
Start point, **332**
Statins, 914
Stationary cilia, 1041–42
Statocysts, **1090**
Statoliths, **841**–42, **1090**
STDs. *See* Sexually transmitted diseases
Stechmann, Alexandra, 593
Steinbeck, John, 787
Steinhardt, Rick, 1024*f*
Steitz, Joan A., 246–47, 335, 340
Stele, **743**, 748
Stem cells, 411, **415**–17*f*, 746, **912**–13, 1066, 1078–79
Stems, **740**–41
    ethylene in triple response of, to mechanical
        stress, 833
    gibberellins in elongation of plant, 830–31
    monocot vs. eudicot, 631*f*
    primary and secondary growth of, 746*f*
    primary and secondary growth of woody, 752*f*
    primary growth of, 749–51*f*
    secondary growth of, 751–55
Stenohaline animals, 954
Stents, 914
Steppes, 1155*f*
Sterility, 491*f*, 504, 818
Sterilization, human, 1017
Steroid hormones, **77**, 976–77*f*
    adrenal gland and, 991–92
    coordinate control by, 361–62
    functional groups and, 63
    as intracellular chemical signals, 214
    as lipids, 77
    receptors for, 976, 978
    smooth ER synthesis of, 105
Steward, F. C., 412
Stickleback fish, 465, 527–29, 1119
Sticky end, DNA, **398**
Stigma, **626**, **802**
Stimulus, **861**
    environmental, 1119–20
    homeostatic, 861
    strength of sensory, 1085, 1087

Stimulus-response chains, 1121
Stingrays, 705–7
Stink bugs, 690f
Stinson, Kristina, 797f
Stipes, **586**
Stock, **814**
Stolons, 741f
Stomach, **885**–86
　chemical digestion in, 885–86
　dynamics of, 886
　evolutionary adaptations of, 890
Stomach ulcers, 568f
Stomata, **186**, **609**, **750**
　of CAM plants, 201–2
　mechanisms of opening and closing of, 777
　as pathway for water loss, 776–77
　sporophyte, 609
　stimuli for opening and closing of, 777–78
　transpiration and, 199
Stone plants, 764, 778
Stop codons, 330, 341, 342f
Storage leaves, 742f
Storage polysaccharides, 71–72
Storage proteins, 78f
Storage roots, 740f
Storms, 1152, 1207
Stramenopiles, **585**–89
　alteration of generations in, 586–87
　brown algae, 586
　diatoms, 585
　golden algae, 586
　oomycetes, 587–89
Strands, DNA. *See* DNA strands
Strangling aerial roots, 740f
Strata, **454**, 510–11f, 1157–58
Stratified squamous epithelium, 856f
Streams, 1160f
Streptococcus pneumoniae, 306, 934–35
Stress
　adrenal gland response to, 990–92
　cellular response pathways and, 977–78
　ethylene in plant responses to, 832–34
　immune systems and, 947–48
Stretch receptors, 1088
Striated muscle, 858f, **1104**
Striga (witchweed), 832
Strigolactones, 827t, 830, **832**
Strobili, **612**
Strokes, **914**
Stroke volume, **903**
Stroma, **110**–11, **186**, 189, 196–97f
Stromatolites, 511f, **514**
Structural formulas, 60f, 76f
Structural isomers, **62**
Structural polysaccharides, 72–74
Structural proteins, 78f
Structure and function
　animal (*see* Animal form and function)
　bird wings and feathers, 718f
　of DNA, 8–10
　molecular, 41–42
　plant (*see* Plant structure)
　as theme in biology, 7
　of transfer RNA, 337–39
Structure formula model, 38f
Struthioniformes, 719
Strychnine, 1058, 1198
Sturtevant, Alfred H., 296
Styles, **626**, **802**
Subatomic particles, 33
Suberin, 754
Submergence 1A-1 gene, 792
Submergence responses, plant, 843–44
Submergence tolerance, plant, 792
Substance P, 1059

Substrate feeders, **881**f
Substrate-level phosphorylation, **168**
Substrates, **153**–54
Succulent Karoo restoration project, 1235f
Succulent plants, 201–2
Suckling, 1015
Sucrase, 153
Sucrose
　as disaccharide, 70, 71f
　molecular mass of, 51–52
　as product of photosynthesis, 203
　transport of, in vascular plants, 779–81
Sudden oak death (SOD), 596, 1214
Sugar gliders, 465
Sugar-phosphate backbone, DNA, 308, 309–10
Sugars. *See also* Carbohydrates
　as components of nucleic acids, 87–88
　conduction of, in plant cells, 745f
　monosaccharides and disaccharides, 69–70, 71f
　as products of photosynthesis, 189, 198–99, 203
　translocation of, from sources to sinks via phloem, 779–81
Sugar sinks, **780**
Sugar sources, **780**
Suicide genes, 376
Sulfhydryl group, **65**f
Sulfur, 32, 58, 66, 307–8
Sulfur bacteria, 568f
Sulfur dioxide, 1244
Sulfur oxides, 55–56
Sulston, John, 1036
Summation, muscle tension, 1108–9f
Summerbell, Dennis, 1041f
Sundews, 798f
Sunflowers, 502–3
Sunlight. *See also* Ultraviolet (UV) radiation
　aquatic biomes and, 1157
　cancer and, 377
　DNA damage from, 28, 318
　as energy for life, 6–7, 149, 163 (*see also* Light energy; Solar energy)
　latitudinal variation in intensity of, 1146f
　photosynthesis and, 184
　primary production in aquatic ecosystems and limitations of, 1223
　properties of, 189
　species distributions and availability of, 1166–67
Sunspot activity, 1185–86
Supercontinent, 519, 520
Supergroups, 576–79f
Superimposed electron orbitals model, 37f
Supernatural vs. natural explanations, 20
Super-resolution microscopy, **96**f, 97
Suprachiasmatic nucleus (SCN), 871f, 993, **1070**–71f
Surface area, leaf, 612
Surface area-volume relationships, 99
Surface tension, **48**
Surfactants, **920**
Survival
　adaptations, natural selection and, 458–60, 1179
　life histories and, 1179–81
　parental care and, 1180–81
Survivorship curves, **1173**–74
Suspension feeders, **670**, 699, 706, **881**f
Suspensor cells, 807
Sustainability, 1260
Sustainable agriculture, **787**–89
　adjusting soil pH in, 788
　controlling erosion in, 788–89
　in Costa Rica zoned reserves, 1253
　fertilization in, 788
　irrigation in, 787–88
　phytoremediation in, 788–89
Sustainable Biosphere Initiative, 1260

Sustainable development, **1260**–61
　in Costa Rica, 1260–61
　future of biosphere and, 1261
　Sustainable Biosphere Initiative and, 1260
Sutherland, Earl W., 209, 216–17
Sutton, Walter S., 286
Swallowing reflex, 884
Sweden, 1188
Sweet potatoes, 633
Sweet taste, 1101–2
Swim bladders, **707**, 1094
Swimming, 1113–15
Swine flu, 1214
Switchgrass, 817
Symbionts, **570**, 642f, 643
Symbiosis, **570**, **1198**–99
　commensalism as, 1199
　in flower pollination, 801
　fungus-animal, 648–49
　lichens as fungal, 649–50
　mutualism as, 1199
　parasitism as, 1198
　protists and, 596
Symmetry
　body, 658–59, 1036–38
　flower, 632
　plant cell division, 756–57
Sympathetic division, peripheral nervous system, 904, 1066–**67**
Sympatric populations, character displacement in, 1196
Sympatric speciation, **495**–98
　allopatric speciation vs., 493f, 497–98
　habitat differentiation and, 496–97
　polyploidy and, 495–96
　sexual selection and, 497
Symplast, **767**–68
Symplastic communication, 781–82
Symplastic domains, 782
Symplastic route, 768, 773f
Synapses, **1046**, 1055–60
　electrical and chemical, and neurotransmitters, 1055–56
　embryonic development of, 1076
　generation of postsynaptic potentials and, 1056
　long-term potentiation (LTP) and, 1077–78
　memory, learning, and, 1077
　modulated signaling at, 1057
　neural plasticity of, 1076–77
　neurotransmitters and, 1057–60
　regulation of muscle contraction and, 1106–7f
　summation of postsynaptic potentials and, 1056–57f
Synapsids, 513f, **721**
Synapsis, **254**f, 257
Synaptic cleft, 1058
Synaptic signaling, 208, 975
Synaptic terminals, 1046
Synaptic vesicles, 1057
Syndromes, 299
Synergids, 804
Syngamy, 587
Synthetases, 338–39
Syphilis, 569f
Systematics, **536**. *See also* Phylogenies; Taxonomy
　animal phylogeny and, 662–64
　constructing phylogenetic trees from shared characters in molecular, 542–48
　future of animal, 664
　molecular, 541–42
　molecular, and prokaryotic phylogenies, 565–70
Systemic acquired resistance, **846**–47
Systemic circuits, **901**
Systemic inflammatory response, 934
Systemic lupus erythematosus, 947
Systemic mycoses, 650

Systems
  systems biology and, 3–6
  thermodynamics and, 144
Systems biology, **3**
  applications of, to medicine, 432
  levels of biological organization and emergent properties in, 3–6
  plant hormone interactions in, 834–35
  in study of genomes, genes, and gene expression, 430–32 (*see also* Bioinformatics)
  study of protein interactions by, 431–32
Systole phase, **903**
Systolic pressure, **906**, 907*f*

T
T2 phage, 307
T4 phage, 381, 383*f*, 385*f*
Table salt. *See* Sodium chloride
Table sugar. *See* Sucrose
Tactile communication, 1121
Tadpoles, 711
Taiga, 1155*f*
Tail, muscular post-anal, 699
Tails, histone, 320*f*
Takahe bird, 1235*f*
Tannins, 1198
Tansley, A. G., 1207
Tapeworms, 667*f*, 676
Tapping, 1120*f*
Taproots, **739**, 767
Taq polymerase, 403, 1241
Tardigrades (Tardigrada), 669*f*, 956
Target cells, hormone, 975
Tarsiers, 726
Tar spot fungus, 650*f*
Tastants, **1101**–2
Taste
  mammalian, 1101–2
  pheromones and communication by, 1122
Taste buds, **1102**
TATA boxes, **332**, 333*f*
Tatum, Edward, 326, 327*f*
Tau protein, 1081
Taxis, **558**–59
Taxol, 243
Taxon, **537**, 539
Taxonomy, **537**–40. *See also* Systematics
  angiosperm, 625
  applying phylogenies in, 539–40
  binomial nomenclature in, 537
  early schemes of, 453–54
  grouping of species in, 12–13
  gymnosperm, 622*f*–23*f*
  hierarchical classification in, 537–38
  interpreting phylogenies in, 539
  linking phylogenies and, 538–39
  Linnaean system of, 12*f*
  mammalian, 725*f*
  possible plant kingdoms, 601
  protist, 575
  ten phyla of extant land plants, 605*t*
  three-domain system of, 13–14, 551–52
Taylor, Dick, 1114
Taylor Glacier, 1218
Tay-Sachs disease, **272**
  allele dominance and, 272
  fetal testing for, 280
  as lysosomal storage disease, 107
  uneven distribution of, 277
T cells, **935**
  antigen recognition by, 936–37
  cell-mediated immune response and, 940–41
  development of, 937–40
  diversity of, 937–38
  proliferation of, 939
Tea, 633

Technology, **24**. *See also* Biotechnology
  global human carrying capacity and, 1191
  prokaryotes in research and, 572–73
  science, society, and, 24–25
  systems biology and, 430–32
Teeth. *See also* Dentition
  conodont mineralized dental elements and, 703–4
  diet and adaptations of, 889–90
  mammalian, 512–14, 720
  origins of, 704
Telomerase, 319
Telomeres, **318**–19
Telomeric DNA, 437
Telophase, **231**, 233*f*
Telophase I, 254*f*
Telophase II, 255*f*
Temperate broadleaf forests, **1156***f*
Temperate grasslands, **1155***f*
Temperate phages, **386**
Temperature, **48**
  aquatic biomes and, 1157–58
  circadian rhythms in regulation of human body, 862
  climographs of, 1151
  clines of, 471
  effects of, on litter decomposition in ecosystems, 1230*f*
  effects of transpiration on leaf, 778
  enzymatic catalysis and, 155–56
  global, and extinction rates, 523
  heat vs., 48
  membrane proteins and, 128
  moderation of, by water, 48–49
  plant response to cold, 844–45
  plant response to heat, 844
  protein denaturation and, 84–85
  species distributions and, 1166
Temperature conformers, 860*f*
Temperature regulators, 860*f*
Templates, viral, 387*t*, 388–90
Template strands, DNA, 311–12, 314, 317*f*, **329**
Tempo, speciation, 501–3
Temporal fenestra, 513*f*, 721
Temporal isolation, 490*f*
Temporal lobe, 1074*f*
Temporal summation, **1056**–57*f*
Tendons, **857***f*
Tendrils, 742*f*
Tension, muscle, 1108–9*f*
Tentacles, 666, 671, 677, 680
Teosinte grass, 737
Termination codons, 330
Termination stage
  transcription, 332*f*
  translation, 341, 342*f*
Terminators, **332**
Termites, 596, 637
Terrestrial adaptations
  mycorrhizae as, 796
  seed plant, 618–21
Terrestrial biomes, 1150–56*f*
  adaptations to, 199–202
  animal osmoregulation in, 956
  chaparral, 1154*f*
  climate and, 1151
  deserts, 1153*f*
  disturbance and, 1152
  food chains in, 1202*f*
  general features of, 1151–52
  global distribution of, 1151*f*
  hot spots of, 1251
  locomotion in, 1113
  northern coniferous forests, 1155*f*
  primary production in, 1224–25
  savannas, 1154*f*
  temperate broadleaf forests, 1156*f*
  temperate grasslands, 1155*f*

  tropical forests, 1153*f*
  tundra, 1156*f*
Territoriality, **1172**, 1184*f*
Tertiary consumers, **1220**
Tertiary structure, protein, **83***f*
Testable hypotheses, 20
Testcrosses, **267**, 292–95*f*
Testes, 251–52, 986*t*, 989, **1004**, 1010–11
Testicles, 1004
Testing, genetic. *See* Genetic testing
Testing, hypothesis, 18, 19–20
Testosterone, 63, 214, **992**, 1008, 1011
Tests, **589**
Test-tube cloning, 814–15
Tetanus, **1108**–9
Tetraploids, 298, 495–96
Tetrapods, **709**–13
  amniotes as, 713
  amphibians, 710–12
  derived characters of, 709
  evolution of, 658
  homologous characteristics of, 464
  land colonization by, 519
  as lobe-fins, 709
  origin of, 512–14, 709–10, 711*f*
  phylogenetic tree of, 711*f*
Texture, soil, 786
Thalamus, **1069***f*, 1071, 1074
Thalloid liverworts, 608*f*
Thallus, **586**
Theobroma cacao, 648*f*
Theories, **23**, 467
Therapeutic cloning, 416
Therapsids, 513*f*
Thermal energy, 132, **143**
Thermocline, **1157**
Thermodynamics, **144**
  ecosystems and laws of, 1219
  first law of, 144
  second law of, 144–45
Thermogenesis, 866–67, 868
Thermoreceptors, **1089**
Thermoregulation, **863**–68
  acclimatization in, 867
  aquatic animal, 860*f*
  balancing heat loss and gain in environmental heat exchanges in, 864–67
  in endothermic and ectothermic animals, 863
  jackrabbit ears and, 852
  physiological thermostats and fever in, 867–68
  variation in body temperature and, 863–64
Thermostatic thermoregulation, 867–68
Thermus aquaticus, 403–4
Theropods, **716**, 718–19
Thick filaments, **1104**, 1110
Thigmomorphogenesis, **842**
Thigmotropism, **842**–43
Thin filaments, **1104**, 1110
Thiols, **65***f*
Thiomargarita namibiensis, 557
Third trimester, 1014–15
Thirst, 1088
Thompson seedless grapes, 831*f*
Thomson's gazelles, 206
Thoracic cavities, 921
Thorax, insect, 688*f*
Threatened species, **1239**–40, 1251
Threonine, 79*f*, 215
Threshold, **1051**
Thrombin, 911–12
Thrombus, **912**, 914
Thrum flower, 813*f*
Thucydides, 939
Thumbs, opposable, 723
Thylakoid membranes, 186–87, 193, 196–97*f*

Thylakoids, **110**, **186**
  in chloroplasts, 110–11
  light reactions in, 189
  as sites of photosynthesis in chloroplasts, 186–87
Thylakoid space, 186
Thymidylate synthase (TS), 593*f*
Thymine, 87*f*–88, 308
Thymine dimers, 318
Thymus, **935**
Thyroid gland, 986*t*, **987**–88, 990
Thyroid hormones, 214
Thyroid-stimulating hormone (TSH), 985*f*, 986*t*, 987
Thyrotropin-releasing hormone (TRH), 987
Thyroxine (T₄), 976–77*f*, 978, 986*t*, **988**
Thysanura, 690*f*
Ticks, 686, 1214*f*
Tidal rhythms, 1120
Tidal volume, **922**
Tight junctions, **121***f*, 1066
Tiktaalik, 510–11*f*, 709–10
Time
  hybrid zones over, 499–501
  phylogenetic tree branch lengths and, 544, 545*f*
  required for human cell division, 231
  in species distributions, 1163
Tinbergen, Niko, 1118–19, 1124, 1125*f*
Tinman gene, 1022
Ti (tumor-inducing) plasmids, **421**–22*f*, 736–37
Tissue culture methods, plant, 807, 814–15, 816, 829
Tissue plasminogen activator (TPA), 419, 441
Tissues, **655**, **738**, **855**
  animal, 655, 855–58*f*
  animal body plan and, 659–60
  animal connective, 857*f*, 858
  animal epithelial, 856*f*
  animal muscle, 858*f*
  animal nervous, 858
  culturing plant, 814–15
  endocrine system, 976
  immune system rejection of transplanted, 946
  as level of biological organization, 5*f*
  plant, 738 (*see also* Tissue systems, plant)
  proteins specific to, 368
  renewal of, as cell division function, 228*f*
  target, for insulin and glucagon, 983
Tissue systems, plant, **742**–43
  in leaves, 750–51*f*
  in primary growth of roots, 748–49
  in stems, 749–50
Tit-for-tat strategy, 1139
Tmesipteris, 614*f*, 615
Toadfish, 1109
Toads, 498–99, 501, 710–12, 1144, 1166
Tobacco, 792, 839
Tobacco mosaic virus (TMV), 381–82, 383*f*, 393
Tolerance. *See* Self-tolerance
Toll-like receptor (TLR), **932**
Tollund man, 610*f*
Tomatoes, 626*f*, 829
Tongues, 884, 1102*f*
Tonicity, **133**–34
Tools
  antibodies as, 945
  hominin use of, 730–31
Tooth cavities, 93, 207
Top-down model, trophic control, **1206**
Topoisomerases, **314**, 321*f*
Topsoil, **786**–87
Torpor, **871**–72
Torsion, **679**
Tortoiseshell cats, 292
Total biomass accumulation, 1222
Totipotent cells, **412**–13, **1038**–39
Touch, plant response to, 842–43
Touch receptors, 1088
Tourism, 1253

Toxicity
  Bt toxin and plant, 816–18
  soil, 789
  soil aluminum, 788, 792
  toxic elements, 32
Toxic waste
  bioremediation of toxic metals in, 1232–33
  density-dependent population regulation
    through, 1183*f*
  DNA cloning and cleanup of, 397*f*
Toxins. *See also* Detoxification
  detoxification and, 105
  dinoflagellate, 583
  environmental, 1255–56
  enzymatic catalysis and, 157
  neurotransmission and, 1058
  in prey defense adaptations, 1197
  in venoms, 850–51
Trace elements, **32**
Tracers, radioactive, 34–35*f*, 187
Trachea, 884, **918**–19
Tracheal systems, 686, **917**–18
Tracheal tubes, insect, 688*f*
Tracheids, **612**, **745***f*
Trade-offs, life history, 1180–81
Traits, **263**. *See also* Traits
  characters and, 263 (*see also* Characters)
  C. Darwin on natural selection and, 15–16
  dominant vs. recessive, 264
  inheritance of, 458–60
  inheritance of x-linked genes and recessive, 290–92
  land plant derived, 601–4
  recessive, 277*f*
  seedless vascular plant, 610–13
  transmission of (*see* Heredity; Inheritance)
Transacetylase, 354*f*
Transcription, **328**
  in bacterial cells, 347*f*
  cell-type specific, 361*f*
  effects of ncRNAs on, 366
  in eukaryotic and bacterial cells, 329*f*
  in eukaryotic cells, 333*f*, 334–36, 348*f*
  molecular components of, 331–32
  post-transcription modification of RNA, 334–36
  regulation of bacterial, 351–56
  regulation of gene expression following, 362–64
  regulation of gene expression in plant responses, 824
  regulation of initiation in eukaryotic, 358–62
  stages of, 332*f*
  synthesis of RNA transcript during, 332–34
  template strand for, 329
  termination of, 333–34
  translation and, 328
Transcription activators, 359–61
Transcription factories, 362
Transcription factors, **332**, 333*f*, 358–61
  in cell-signaling nuclear responses, 219
  control of gene activation and, 360–61
  enhancers and specific, 359–60
  general, 358–59
  genes for, 702
  testosterone as, 214
Transcription initiation complex, **332**, 333*f*, 358
Transcription units, **332**
Transduction (signal transduction pathway), **210**,
    214–19, **562**, 1086, 1092–93, 1098. *See also* Sig-
    nal transduction
  as cell-signaling stage, 210
  of cell signals, 207
  multistep pathways and signal amplification in, 214
  in plant cell signaling, 822–23
  protein phosphorylation and dephosphorylation in,
    215–16
  signal transduction pathways in, 215
  small molecules and ions as second messengers in,
    216–18

Transduction, viral, **562**
trans face, Golgi apparatus, 105–6
Trans fats, 62, **76**, 914–15
Transfer RNA (tRNA), **337**
  ribosomal binding sites for, 340
  ribosome model with, 339*f*
  structure and function of, in translation, 337–39
  structure of, 88–89*f*
Transformation, cancer, **242**
Transformation, DNA, **306**, 756
Transformation, energy, 143, 144–45. *See also* Metabolism
Transformation, prokaryotic, 561–**62**
Transfusions, blood, 946
Transgene escape issue, 818
Transgenes, 419, 816, 818
Transgenic crops. *See also* Genetically modified (GM)
    organisms; Transgenic organisms
  as biofuels to reduce fossil fuel dependency, 817
  biotechnology, genetic engineering, and, 816–19
  debate over, 817–19
  DNA technology and, 421–22*f*
  L. Herrera-Estrella's work with, 736–37
  prokaryotes in creating, 572
  reducing hunger and malnutrition with, 816–17
Transgenic organisms, **419**–22*f*, **814**. *See also* Genetically
    modified (GM) organisms; Transgenic crops
trans isomers, 62
Transitional ER, 105
Transition state, 152
Translation, **328**, 337–44
  in bacterial cells, 347*f*
  basic concept of, 337*f*
  building polypeptides in, 340–42
  completing and targeting functional proteins in, 343
  elongation cycles of, 341*f*
  in eukaryotic and bacterial cells, 329*f*
  in eukaryotic cells, 348*f*
  initiation of, 340*f*
  molecular components of, 337–40
  post-translational protein modification in plant
    responses, 823–24
  regulation of gene expression at initiation of, 363
  termination of, 341, 342*f*
  transcription and, 328
Translation initiation complex, 340
Translation initiation factors, 363
Translocation, cancer gene, 373–74
Translocation, chromosome, 298–99, 300
Translocation, plant transport, 341*f*, **779**–81
Transmembrane proteins, 129, 210–13
Transmembrane route, 768, 773*f*
Transmission, sensory, **1086**–87
Transmission electron microscope (TEM), **95**, **96***f*
Transmission rate, disease, 1184*f*
Transpiration, **772**–79*f*
  effects of, on plant wilting and leaf temperature, 778
  plant adaptations that reduce evaporative water loss
    by, 778–79*f*
  stomata opening and closing as control on, 776–78
  of water and minerals from roots to shoots via xylem
    and, 772–76
Transpirational pull, 774–75
Transplants
  immune system rejection of organ, 946
  species, 1165
Transport epithelia, **957**–58, 964*f*
Transport function, membrane protein, 129*f*
Transport in animals. *See* Circulatory systems
Transport in vascular plants, 612, 764–84. *See also* Plant
    nutrition
  apoplast and symplast in, 767–68
  long-distance transport by bulk flow in, 771
  overview of, 765*f*
  phloem as information superhighway in, 782
  regulation of transpiration rate by stomata in,
    776–79*f*

resource acquisition and, 764–67 (*see also* Resource acquisition, vascular plant)
review of, 783
short-distance and long-distance mechanisms of, 767–71
solute transport across plasma membranes by active transport in, 768, 769f
sugar-conducting cells in phloem, 745f
sugar transport from sources to sinks via phloem in, 779–81
symplastic communication and changes in, 781–82
three routes for, 767–68
transpiration of water and minerals from roots to shoots via xylem in, 772–76
water-conducting cells in xylem, 745f
water transport across plasma membranes by osmosis, 768–71
Transport proteins, **131**
in active transport, 135–36
aquaporins, 771
cellular membrane selective permeability and, 131–32
channel proteins (*see* Channel proteins)
as cotransporters, 137–38
facilitated diffusion and, 134–35
ion pumps and, 137
solute transport and, 768, 769f
water diffusion and role of, 771
Transport vesicles, **105**–6, 138–39f
Transport work, 149, 151
Transposable elements, **435**
DNA sequences related to, 436
genome evolution and role of, 441–42
transposition process and, 434–35
transposons, retroposons, and, 435–36
Transposition process, 435, 441–42
Transposons, 366, 390, **435**–36
Transthyretin protein, 82f–83f, 85
Transverse (T) tubules, **1106**–7f
Tree frogs, 483f
Tree of life, 16–17. *See also* Biodiversity; Phylogenetic trees
C. Darwin's evolutionary tree, 457–58
phylogenies and, 536, 551–53 (*see also* Phylogenies)
as ring, 553
simple, of all life, 552–53
three-domain taxonomy of, 551–52 (*see also* Taxonomy)
Tree rings, 753
Tree thinking, 464, 538–540, 547–548
Tree trunks, 754f
Trehalose, 956
Trematodes, 675–76
Trends, evolutionary, 530–31f
Triacylglycerols, **74**–76
Trial-and-error learning, 1125–26
Tricarboxylic acid cycle. *See* Citric acid cycle
Trichinosis, 684
Trichomes, 742–43, 779f
Trichomonas vaginalis, 580
Triglycerides, 74–76, 888f
Triiodothyronine (T$_3$), 986t, **988**
Trilobites, 684f
Trimesters, human pregnancy, **1013**–15
Trimethylamine oxide (TMAO), 955
Trioses, 70
Triple response, plant, **833**
Triplet code, **329**–30
Triploblastic animals, **660**
Triploidy, 298
Trisomic cells, **298**
Trisomy 21. *See* Down syndrome
Trisomy X (XXX), 300
Tristan da Cunha, 477–78
Triticale grain, 816
tRNA. *See* Transfer RNA (tRNA)
Trochophore larva, **664**, 674
Trophic cascade model, 1206

Trophic efficiency, **1225**–26
Trophic structure, **1202**–6
biomanipulation of, 1206
bottom-up and top-down controls of, 1206
dominant species in, 1204
ecosystem engineers in, 1205
in ecosystems, 1218, 1219–20
food chains and, 1202
food webs in, 1202–3
keystone species in, 1204–5
limits on food chain length in, 1203–4
trophic efficiency and ecological pyramids, 1225–26
Trophoblasts, **1013**, **1031**
Tropical dry forests, **1153**f
Tropical rain forests, **1153**f
deforestation of, as threat to seed plant biodiversity, 633–34
nutrient cycling in, 1230
primary production in, 1224
Tropic hormones, **984**, 985f, 989, 1008–11
Tropic of Cancer, 1146f
Tropic of Capricorn, 1146f
Tropics, **1146**f, 1211
Tropisms, **825**
Tropomyosin, **1106**–7f
Troponin complex, **1106**–7f
Troponin T, 362, 363f
Trout, 1183f
Trp operon, 352–53
TRP (transient receptor potential) proteins, 1089, 1102
Trp repressor, **353**
Truckee River restoration project, 1234f
True-breeding organisms, **264**
True bugs, 690f
Truffles, 644f, 651
Trypanosoma, 580–81, 691
Trypanosomiasis, 948
Trypsin, 156, 887
Tryptophan, 79f, 352, 353f, 1058
Tuataras, 715, 716–17
Tubal ligation, **1017**
Tubal pregnancies, 1013
Tube cells, 627, 803
Tube feet, **692**–93f
Tuberculosis, 569f, 571, 935, 1184f
Tubers, 741f
Tubeworms, 890–91
Tubules, kidneys as, 962
Tubulidentata, 725f
Tubulin, 113–14
Tucker, Vance, 1114
Tumbleweeds, 811f
Tumors, cancer, 242–43. *See also* Cancer
Tumor-suppressor genes, **374**–76
Tumor viruses, 377
Tuna, 708f, 853f
Tundra, **1156**f
Túngara frogs, 485f
Tunicates (Urochordata), **700**, 701, 1035f
Turgid cells, **134**, **770**
Turgor movements, plant, 842–43
Turgor pressure, 134, **769**
Turner syndrome, 300
Turnover, **1158**
Turnover time, **1226**
Turrids, 851
Turtles, 716f, 717
Tutu, Desmond, 445
Twins, 1014, 1039
Twin studies, **1123**
Tympanic membrane, 1090, **1091**f
Type 1 diabetes, 947, 983–84
Type 2 diabetes, 983–84
Typhoid fever, 572
Tyrannosaurus rex, 716
Tyrosine, 79f, 988, 1058

U
Ubiquinone (Q), 172–73
Ubiquitin, 363–64
Ubx gene, 526, 527, 685f
Ulcers, 886
Ultimate causation, 1119
Ultrasound fetal testing, 280
Ultraviolet (UV) radiation. *See also* Sunlight
atmospheric ozone hole and, 28–29
cancer and, 377
DNA damage from, 28, 318
elevation and, 1167
insect vision and, 1096
mutations and, 346
ozone depletion and, 1258–59
Ulva, 592
Umami taste, 1101–2
Uncoupling protein, 177
Underground plants, 764
Undernutrition, 879
Undershoot phase, action potential, 1052
Unger, Franz, 263
Ungulates, 465–66
Unicellular organisms, first, 514–17
Uniform dispersion, 1172
Uniformitarianism, **454**
Unikonta (unikonts), 579f, **593**–96
Unisexual flowers, 802
United States, 1188–89
Unity
in biodiversity, 14, 15f, 16
evolution and, 452, 457
universality of genetic code and, 331
Unlinked genes
mapping, 296
recombination of, 295
Unsaturated fats, 75–76, 128
Unsaturated fatty acids, **75**–76
Unselfish behavior, 1137–39
Untranslated regions (UTRs), 334, 363
Upright posture, hominin, 728–29
Uracil, 87f–88, 328
Uranium, bioremediation of, 1233
Uranium-238, 512
Urea, 58–59, 61, 955, **958**–59, 965–67
Ureter, **962**f
Urethra, **962**f, **1005**
Urey, Harold, 59, 508
Uric acid, **959**
Urinary bladder, **962**f
Urine
hyperosmotic, 967
nephron processing of blood filtrate to, 964–65
two-solute model of concentration of, 966–67
Urochordates (Urochordata), 698, 700, 701
Urodela, 710–12
Urry, Lisa, 93f, 247f
USA300 bacteria, 462
Use and disuse principle, Lamarck's, 454–55
U. S. Endangered Species Act (ESA), 1239
Uterine cycle, **1008**, 1009–10
Uterus, 723, **1003**
Utricle, **1093**–94

V
Vaccination, **945**, 950f
Vaccines, **391**
Vacuoles, 100f, 101f, **107**–8
Vagina, **1003**–4
Valence, **39**, 61f
Valence electrons, **36**, 38
Valence shells, **36**
Valine, 79f
Valium, 1058
Vampire bats, 968–69
van Alphen, Jacques, 497f

van der Waals interactions, 40–**41**, 83*f*
Van Helmont, Jan Baptista, 789
van Leeuwenhoek, Antoni, 94, 575, 1190
van Niel, C. B., 187
Variation, **248**. *See also* Genetic variation
Variegation, 301
Vasa recta, **963***f*, 966–67
Vascular bundles, 743, 750
Vascular cambium, **746**, 751–54, 828–29
Vascular cylinder, 743
Vascular plants, **604**–6
    origin and traits of, 610–13
    overview of resource acquisition and transport in, 765*f*
    phylogeny of, 605*t*
    resource acquisition for, 764–67
    seedless, 605, 610–15
    seed plants, 605–6 (*see also* Seed plants)
    transport in (*see* Transport in vascular plants)
Vascular rays, 753
Vascular tissue, **604**, 765. *See also* Phloem; Xylem
Vascular tissue system, plant, 742*f*, **743**, 745*f*
Vascular transport, 518–19, 612
Vas deferens, **1005**
Vasectomy, **1017**
Vasocongestion, **1011**
Vasoconstriction, 864, **907**
Vasodilation, 864, **907**, 979, 1005
Vasopressin, 969–70, 975, 985, 1135
Vectors, **1214**–15
Vegetal plate, 1028*f*
Vegetal pole, **1025**
Vegetarian diets, 876
Vegetation, terrestrial biomes and, 1150, 1151–52
Vegetative propagation
    agriculture and methods of, 814–15
    auxin in, 829
Vegetative reproduction, **812**
Veins, blood, **899**–900, 905, 907–8
Veins, leaf, 186, **741**, 750, 828
Veldts, 1155*f*
Velvet worms, 669*f*
Venomous snails, 850–51, 1045
Venomous snakes, 20–23, 717
Venter, Craig, 428–29
Ventilation, **916**–17
Ventral nerve cords
    earthworm, 682*f*
    planarian, 675*f*
Ventral sides, **658**
Ventral tegmental area (VTA), 1080–81
Ventricles, brain, **1065**
Ventricles, heart, **900**, 902–3
Venules, **899**–900, 905*f*
Venus flytrap, 782, 798*f*, 842
Vermeij, Geerat J., 450–51
Vernalization, **840**
Vertebrates, **697**–735
    action potential conduction speed in, 1054
    adaptive immunity in, 935–46
    amniotes and development of terrestrially adapted
        egg in, 713–20
    anatomical similarities in embryos of, 463
    brains of, 1067–76
    as chordates, 697–701
    circulatory systems of, 899–902
    coordination of endocrine and nervous systems in,
        984–86*t*
    as craniates, 701–4
    derived characters of, 703
    development in (*see* Animal development)
    evolutionary adaptations of digestive systems of,
        889–91
    evolution of, 657–58, 697
    evolution of brains of, 1075–76
    fossils of early, 703–4
    gamete production and delivery in, 1002

gnathostomes and development of jaws in, 704–9
hominins and humans, 728–33 (*see also* Humans)
innate immunity in, 932–34
kidneys of, 962–63, 967–68
limb formation in, 1040–41
mammals, 720–28 (*see also* Mammals (Mammalia))
mechanoreceptors for hearing and equilibrium in,
    1090–94
nervous systems of, 1063–67
organogenesis in, 1031–33
origins of bone and teeth in, 704
reproduction in (*see* Animal reproduction)
review of, 734–35
tetrapods and development of limbs in, 709–13
visual systems of, 1097–1101
Vertical layering, terrestrial biome, 1152
Vertical transmission, 393
Vervet monkeys, 1127
Vesicles, **104**. *See also* Vacuoles
    abiotically produced, as protocells, 509
    in endomembrane system, 104
    in exocytosis and endocytosis, 138–39*f*
    in plant cytokinesis, 236
    transport, 105–6
Vessel elements, **745***f*
Vessels, **745***f*
Vessels, circulatory, 898. *See also* Blood vessels
Vestibular glands, 1004
Vestigial structures, **463**
Viagra, 217, 979, 1059
Vibrio bacteria, 92–93
Viewpoints, science and diverse, 25
Villi, 887*f*, **888**
Vinegar, Allen, 867*f*
Viral envelopes, **383**, 387–88
Viral integration, 377
Viral movement proteins, 782
Virchow, Rudolf, 228
Viroids, **393**
Virtual plants, computer-generated, 756
Virulent pathogens, **846**
Virulent phages, **385**–86
Viruses, **307**, **381**–95. *See also* Genetics
    in bacteria (*see* Bacteriophages (phages))
    cancer-causing, 950
    capsids and envelopes of, 383–84
    cellular RNAi pathway and, 365
    classes of animal, 387*t*
    discovery of, 381–82
    emerging, 391–93
    evidence for viral DNA in bacteriophages, 306–8
    evolution of, 390
    general features of replicative cycles of, 384–85
    host range of, 384
    latency of, 949
    as pathogens, 381–82, 383*f*, 390–94
    rapid reproduction of, as source of genetic
        variation, 472
    replicative cycles of animal, 387–90
    replicative cycles of phages, 385–87
    review of, 394–95
    J. A. Steitz's work on, 246–47
    structure of, 382–84
    tumor viruses, viral integration, and cancer, 377
    viral movement proteins of plant, 782
Visceral mass, **677**, 678*f*
Visible light, **189**
Vision. *See* Visual systems
Visual communication, 1121
Visual cortex, 1074, 1099–1100
Visual pigments, 1097*f*, 1100
Visual systems, 1095–1101. *See also* Eyes
    compound eyes in, 1095–96
    evolution of, 1095–97
    gene therapy for vision and, 1100*f*
    light-detecting organs in, 1095

single-lens eyes in, 1096–97
structure of human eyes in, 1096*f*–97
vertebrate, 1097–1101
Visual systems, vertebrate
    color vision in, 1100
    fields of vision and focusing in, 1100–1101
    gene therapy for vision and, 1100*f*
    sensory transduction in, 1098
    visual information processing in brain in,
        1099–1100
    visual information processing in retina in, 1098–99
Vital capacity, **922**
Vitalism, 58–59
Vitamin A, 816, 817*f*, 878–79
Vitamin B$_9$, 879
Vitamin D, 978, 990
Vitamins, 156, **876**–77, 879, 978, 990
Vitelline layer, 1022–23
Vitellogenin, 978
Vitreous humor, 1096*f*
Viviparous organisms, **707**
Vocal cords, 919
Vocal folds, 919
Vocalization, *FOXP2* gene and, 443–44
Vogt, Walther, 1035
Volcanic springs, 567
Volcanoes, 59, 508, 522
Voles, 1135
Voltage, 1054
Voltage-gated ion channels, 213*f*, **1051**–54
Volume, 1092
Volume-surface area relationships, 99
Voluntary contraception, 1188
Voluntary population control, 1187
Volvox, 579*f*, 591
von Frisch, Karl, 1119, 1121
von Humboldt, Alexander, 1211–12
Vulva, **1003**–4

W
Waggle dance, honeybee, 1121–22
Wagler's pit viper, 716*f*
Waists, chromatid, 230
Walking, 1113–15
Wallace, Alfred Russel, 453*f*, 456–57, 1211
Walrus, 863*f*
Warming, global. *See* Global warming
Warning coloration case study, 20–23
Warren, Robin, 886
Wasps, 690*f*, 801, 845, 1124, 1125*f*
Wasser, Samuel, 1243*f*
Wasserman, Steve, 851*f*
Wastes, nitrogenous. *See* Nitrogenous wastes
Water, 46–57
    acidic and basic conditions of, and living organisms,
        52–56
    acidification as threat to quality of, 55–56
    albatross drinking of salt, 953
    balance (*see* Water balance)
    biomanipulation and quality of, 1206
    in blood plasma, 910
    cohesion of molecules of, and transport in plants,
        47–48
    conduction of, in plant cells, 745*f*
    covalent bonding and, 38*f*–39
    emergent properties of, 47–52
    evapotranspiration of, 1211
    evolution of life on planets with, 52
    floating of ice on liquid, 49–50
    forms of, 46
    fruit and seed dispersal by, 811*f*
    global human use of, 1190
    hydrogen bonds and, 41*f*
    ions in, 40
    irrigation with, 787–88
    kidney adaptations that conserve, 967–68

kidney role in conserving, 965–67
moderation of temperature by, 48–49
molecular shape of, 41
osmoregulation in animals living in, 954–56
plant adaptations that reduce evaporative loss of, 778–79f
in plant composition, 789
plant response to submergence in, 843–44
polar covalent bonds and hydrogen bonding in, 46–47
review of, 56
root architecture and acquisition of, 766–67
seed dispersal by, 626
seed germination and imbibition of, 809
as solvent of life, 50–52
species distributions and availability of, 1166
splitting of, in photosynthesis, 187
in thigmotropism, 842
threat of ocean acidification to coral reef ecosystems, 55f
transpiration and plant loss of, 776–79f
transpiration of, from roots to shoots via xylem, 772–76
transport of, across plant plasma membranes, 768–71
Water balance
of cells without walls, 133–34
of cells with walls, 134
hormonal regulation of, 968–71
in insects, 961–62
nitrogenous wastes and, 958
osmoregulation of, 953–58
Water bears (tardigrades), 669f, 956
Water bodies, climate and, 1147–48, 1149f
Water buffalo, 1199f
Water bugs, 1000f
Water conservation
kidney adaptations, 967–68
kidney role in, 965–67
Water cycle, 1228f
Water fleas, 998, 1179f
Water lily, 630f
Water molds, 587–89
Water pollution, 680–81f
Water potential, **768**–70, 771
Water-soluble hormones, 976–78
Water-soluble vitamins, 876–77t
Water spiders, 686
Water vapor, 46
Water vascular system, **692**
Watkinson, Andrew, 1182
Watson, James
discovery of DNA molecular structure by, 3, 24, 305, 308–10
model of DNA replication of, 311–12
J. A. Steitz's work with, 246
Wattled smoky honeyeaters, 1238
Wavelengths, **189**, 190–91
Weak acids, 53
Weather, population fluctuations and, 1184–85
Weddell seals, 925–26
Weeds, transgene escape and, 818
Weight, mass vs., 31footnote
Welch, Allison, 483f
Welwitschia, 622f
Went, Friz, 826
Wernicke, Karl, 1073–74
Wernicke's area, 1073–74

Westemeier, Ronald, 1246f
Western garter snakes, 1135–36
West Nile virus, 384, 391
Wetlands, **1159f**, 1240
Whales, 465–66, 539f–40, 691, 1243
Wheat, 496, 633, 1183f
Whisk ferns (Pterophyta), 613–15
White-band disease, 1214
White blood cells, 223f, 910f, 911
White-crowned sparrows, 1126–27
White matter, **1065**
White rhinoceros, 1179f
White rot fungi, 652
Whole-genome shotgun genome-sequencing approach, 428–29
Whooping cranes, 1124
Whorled phyllotaxy, 766
Widow's peak pedigree analysis case, 275–76
Wieschaus, Eric, 371
Wikramanayake, Athula, 659f
Wildfires, 1152
Wild types, **288**
Wilkins, Maurice, 308–10
Wilson, E. O., 1139, 1212–13, 1240, 1261
Wilson's phalaropes, 1130f
Wilting, **770**, 778, 832, 843
Wind
dispersal of mosses by, 609
flower pollination by, 804f
fruit and seed dispersal by, 811f
global patterns of, 1146f
seed dispersal by, 626
Winged fruits and seeds, 811f
Wings
bat vs. bird, 541
bird, 718
evolutionary adaptation of bat, 16
evolution of, 658
flight muscles and, 1114
form and function of bird, 7f
insect, 688–89, 690f
muscle contraction and, 1110
pterosaur, 715
seed, 626f
Wiskott-Aldrich syndrome (WAS), 223
Witchweed, 832
Wobble, **339**
Woese, Carl, 566
Wöhler, Friedrich, 58–59
Wollemi pine, 623f
Wolves, 1185, 1249
Women, science and, 25. *See also* Females
Wood, 633, 652
Work
ATP hydrolysis and, 150–51
types of cellular, 149
Worms, 1111

X
Xanthopan morganii praedicta, 806f
X chromosomes, 250, 289–92
Xenarthra, 725f
Xeroderma pigmentosum, 318
Xerophytes, **778**–79f
X-linked genes, **290**
inactivation of, in female mammals, 291–92
inheritance and, 290–91

X-O sex determination system, 290f
X-ray crystallography, **85**
in determining structure of G protein-coupled receptors, 213f
of DNA, 309
revelation of RNA polymerase structure using, 85–86f
X-rays, mutations and, 346
Xylem, **612**, **743**
primary growth and, 748
resource acquisition and, 765
transpiration of water and minerals from roots to shoots via, 772–76
vascular plant, 612
water-conducting cells of, 745f
Xylem sap, **772**–76
X-Y sex determination system, 290f

Y
Yangtze River dolphin, 1240f
Y chromosomes, 250, 289–90
Yeager, Justin, 1144
Yeast artificial chromosome (YAC), 427–28
Yeast cells, 100f
Yeast infections, 650
Yeasts
alcohol fermentation and, 178
cell division in, 237f
cell signaling in, 206–7, 219–20, 221f
fungi as, 637, 640, 651
Yellowfin tuna, 708f
Yellow jacket, 1197f
Yellowstone National Park, 567, 1208–9, 1246–47, 1249, 1252
Y-linked genes, 290
Yolk, **1025**–26
Yolk sac, 714f, 1031
Yucca, 805f

Z
Zambia, 1243
Zambryski, Patricia, 736
Zea mays (corn), 426, 433t, 633. *See also* Maize (corn)
Zeatin, 829
Zeaxanthin, 836
Zebra finches, 1131–32
Zebrafish. *See Danio rerio* (zebrafish)
Zebra mussels, 1242
Zero population growth (ZPG), **1176**, 1188
Zinc
plant deficiency in, 791
removal of, from soil, 789
Zona pellucida, **1024**–25
Zonation, aquatic, 1157–58
Zoned reserves, **1252**–53
Zone of cell division, 747f, 748
Zone of differentiation, 747f, 748
Zone of elongation, 747f, 748
Zone of polarizing activity (ZPA), **1040**–41
Zoonotic pathogens, **1214**–15
Zoospores, 587, **641**, 641f
Zucchini, 631f
Zuker, Charles, 1102f
zur Hausen, Harald, 950f
Z-W sex determination system, 290f
Zygomycetes (Zygomycota), 642f, **643**–44
Zygosporangium, **644**
Zygotes, **251**–52, **996**, 1012f